STANDARD CATALOG OF ®

Modern World Gold Coins

1801-Present

Platinum and Palladium issues included

Based on the original work of
Chester L. Krause and Clifford Mishler

Colin R. Bruce II
Senior Editor

Thomas Michael
Market Analyst

Harry Miller
U.S. Market Analyst

Merna Dudley
Coordinating Editor

Deborah McCue
Database Specialist

George Cuhaj
Editor

Fred J. Borgmann
New Issues Editor

Randy Thern
Numismatic Cataloging Supervisor

Sally Olson
Book Designer

Bullion Value (BV) Market Valuations

Valuations for all platinum, gold, palladium and silver coins of the more common,
basically bullion types, or those possessing only modest numismatic premiums are presented in this edition
based on the market ranges of:

$1,150 - $1,350 per ounce for **platinum**

$650 - $670 per ounce for **gold**

$330 - $350 per ounce for **palladium**

©2007 Krause Publications

Published by

700 East State Street • Iola, WI 54990-0001
715-445-2214 • 888-457-2873
www.krausebooks.com

Our toll-free number to place an order or obtain
a free catalog is (800) 258-0929.

All rights reserved. No portion of this publication may be reproduced or transmitted in any form or by any means, electronic or mechanical, including photocopy, recording, or any information storage and retrieval system, without permission in writing from the publisher, except by a reviewer who may quote brief passages in a critical article or review to be printed in a magazine or newspaper, or electronically transmitted on radio, television, or the Internet.

Library of Congress Control Number: 2007927491

ISBN-13: 978-0-89689-643-7
ISBN-10: 0-89689-643-9

Designed by: Sally Olson
Edited by: George Cuhaj

Printed in the United States of America

TABLE OF CONTENTS

Title Page	I
Copyright Page	II
Introduction	IV
Standard International Numeral Systems	VI
Country Index	VIII
Foreign Exchange	XIV
How To Use This Catalog	XVIII
Gold Coin Value Chart	XXVI
Platinum Coin Value Chart	XXX
Hejira	XXXV
Eastern Mint Names	XXXVI

ADVERTISING INDEX

Ponterio And Associates, Inc.	V
Steinberg's	VII
Stack's	IX
Knightbridge Coins	XI
William Youngerman	XIII
I.A.P.N.	XV
Jean Elsen	XVII
Numismatik Lanz	XVII
Massie Dustin	XVII
C.I.C.F.	XXV

INTRODUCTION

What an exciting time for the precious metals market! The investment community has taken gold to heart and collectors will find both amazing opportunities and great challenges ahead. To assist both the collector and investor in navigating the burgeoning growth of the gold market we offer this handy new tool, The Standard Catalog of Modern World Gold Coins, 1st edition.

This new volume in the Standard Catalog series is designed to meet the needs of all the gold bugs trying to work and play within a quickly changing precious metals market. We have focused this catalogs contents on the most heavily traded, as well as the most widely available gold coin issues. In addition you will find both platinum and palladium coins scattered throughout this catalog. Though not the recipients of worldwide attention to the extreme level of gold, they too are areas of potential opportunity for collectors and investors.

Weather you are looking for an inflation hedge, a long-term investment, a new guide to building a modern gold collection, or your curiosity has been piqued by recent news stories touting the explosion in precious metals values, this catalog will help in your quest. With coverage from 1801 to 2006 you have in your hands over 200 years of world gold, platinum and palladium coinage, accurately described and valued, for quick and easy reference. This catalog will empower you to trade with confidence!

Arranged in a basic alphabetic fashion by country and with groupings for political structure, coinage type and denomination to help better organize the data, this volume is as easy to use as the phone book. You will find photographs of many coins, information on metal content, descriptions of types and varieties, date listings and of course values presented in multiple grades. In short, just about all the information you could want on the most heavily collected modern gold, platinum and palladium coins issued over the last 200 + years.

Dive into the world of modern gold coins with confidence and please let us know if you have any comments or questions.

Best Wishes,

The Editorial Staff of the
Standard Catalog of World Coins.

BUYING WORLD RARITIES

Whether you have a single rare coin or an entire collection for sale, it will pay for you to contact us.

OF PARTICULAR INTEREST

American Coins
Mexican Coins
Spain and all Spanish Colonial Coins
South & Central American Coins
Germany, Austria & Switzerland
British & British Colonial
Japan, Korea & Philippines
Ancient Coins
Rare World Bank Notes
Rare U.S. & World Gold Coins

All transactions held in strict confidence.
  Other services: We also provide both public auctions and mail bid sales.
  If your collection warrants, we will travel anywhere in the world to inspect and purchase your coins.

Visit our Web site at: www.ponterio.com

... THE SCALES ARE TIPPED IN YOUR FAVOR

PONTERIO AND ASSOCIATES, INC.

*1818 Robinson Avenue
San Diego, CA 92103 U.S.A.*
(800) 854-2888 • (619) 299-0400
FAX: 619-299-6952
E-mail: coins@ponterio.com

STANDARD INTERNATIONAL NUMERAL SYSTEMS

Prepared especially for the *Standard Catalog of World Coins*© 2007 by Krause Publications

	0	½	1	2	3	4	5	6	7	8	9	10	50	100	500	1000
Western																
Roman			I	II	III	IV	V	VI	VII	VIII	IX	X	L	C	D	M
Arabic-Turkish																
Malay-Persian																
Eastern Arabic																
Hyderabad Arabic																
Indian (Sanskrit)																
Assamese																
Bengali																
Gujarati																
Kutch																
Devavnagri																
Nepalese																
Tibetan																
Mongolian																
Burmese																
Thai-Lao																
Lao-Laotian																
Javanese																
Ordinary Chinese Japanese-Korean	零	半	一	二	三	四	五	六	七	八	九	十	十五	百	百五	千
Official Chinese			壹	貳	參	肆	伍	陸	柒	捌	玖	拾	拾伍	佰	佰伍	仟
Commercial Chinese																
Korean		반	일	이	삼	사	오	육	칠	팔	구	십	오십	백	오백	천
Georgian																
Ethiopian	♦																
Hebrew			א	ב	ג	ד	ה	ו	ז	ח	ט	י	נ	ק	תק	
Greek			Α	Β	Γ	Δ	Ε	Ζ	Η	Θ	Ι	Ν	Ρ	Φ	Α	

THE LARGEST SELECTION OF CERTIFIED GOLD COINS OF THE WORLD

Send for our new current price list of PCGS/NGC third-party certified graded world gold or visit our Web site:

www.steinbergs.com

STEINBERG'S
Numismatic Gold Specialists Since 1950

P.O. Box 5665 Dept. GB, Cary, NC 27512-5665

Tel.: 919-363-5544 * **Fax:** 919-363-0555

E-mail: info@steinbergs.com

COUNTRY INDEX

A

Afghanistan	1
Ajman	6
Albania	6
Alderney	10
Algeria	11
Algiers	11
Alwar	346
American Samoa	12
Andorra	13
Anguilla	16
Anhalt-Bernburg	245
Anhalt-Dessau	245
Antigua & Barbuda	17
Argentina	17
Armenia	20
Aruba	21
Ascension Island	22
Asiago	445
Assam	340
Australia	22
Austria	41
Awadh	346
Azerbaijan	49

B

Baden	245
Bahamas	50
Bahawalpur	348
Bahrain	56
Bajranggarh	348
Bamberg	247
Banswara	348
Barbados	57
Baroda	349
Bavaria	247
Belarus	58
Belgium	58
Belize	61
Bengal Presidency	368
Benin	63
Bermuda	63
Bern	665
Bharatpur	349
Bhutan	65
Biafra	67
Biberach	250
Bikanir	349
Bolivia	67
Bombay Presidency	368
Bophuthatswana	70
Bosnia and Herzegovina	71
Botswana	73
Bouillon	238
Brandenburg-Ansbach-Bayreuth	250
Brazil	73

Bremen	250
British Columbia	77
British Virgin Islands	77
Brunei	81
Brunei	82
Brunswick-Luneburg-Calenberg-Hannover	250
Brunswick-wolfenbuttel	251
Bukhara	106
Bulgaria	82
Bundi	350
Burkina Faso	84
Burma	84
Burundi	85

C

California	731
Cambodia	86
Cameroon	87
Campilioni	670
Canada	88
Cape Verde	101
Catalonia	657
Catamarca	19
Cayman Islands	101
Central African Republic	104
Central American Republic	104
Central Asia	106
Ceylon	108
Chad	108
Chihli Province	116
Chile	109
China	114
China, People's Republic	120
China, Republic Of	119
Cocos (Keeling) Islands	147
Colombia	148
Colorado	739
Comoros	156
Congo Republic	156
Congo Democratic Republic	157
Cooch Behar	350
Cook Islands	158
Costa Rica	164
Croatia	167
Cuba	169
Curacao	175
Cyprus	175
Czech Republic	176
Czechoslovakia	178

D

Dahomey	181
Danish West Indies	181
Danzig	182
Datia	351
Denmark	182
Dhar	351

Djibouti	184
Dominica	185
Dominican Republic	185
Dungarpur	351
Durango	509

E

East Africa	187
East Caribbean States	188
Ecuador	189
Egypt	190
El Salvador	202
Emilia	432
Empire	116
Equatorial African States	204
Equatorial Guinea	204
Eritrea	206
Estonia	206
Ethiopia	207
Europa	210

F

Falkland Islands	211
Faridkot	351
Fiji	215
Finland	216
France	217
Frankfurt Am Main	253
French Guiana	238
French Polynesia	239
French Southern & Antarctic Territories	239
Fujairah	239

G

Gabon	240
Gambia	241
Garhwal	351
Geneva	665
Genoa	432
Georgia	242
German East Africa	242
German New Guinea	243
German States	244
German States-Wurzburg	274
German-Democratic Republic	284
Germany - Federal Republic	276
Germany, Weimar Republic	274
Germany-empire	274
Ghana	284
Gibraltar	285
Goa	363
Graubunden	665
Great Britain	303
Greece	315
Greenland	318
Grenada	319
Guadalajara	508

Stack's

THE SOURCE
for all your collecting needs

America's oldest and most prestigious rare coin dealer

WE HAVE BEEN BUILDING THE WORLD'S FINEST COIN COLLECTIONS FOR OVER SEVEN DECADES

HOW MAY WE BE OF SERVICE TO YOU?

No collection too large - No collector too small

123 West 57th St. • New York, NY 10019 • 800-566-2580 • www.stacks.com
P.O. Box 1804 • Wolfeboro, NH 03894 • 866-811-1804 • email: info@stacks.com
Auctions • Appraisals • Retail • Since 1935

Visit us at www.stacks.com for on-line catalogs, color images and interactive bidding

COUNTRY INDEX

Guadeloupe	319
Guam	320
Guatemala	320
Guernsey	322
Guerrero	509
Guinea	324
Gurk	49
Guyana	325
Gwalior	351

H

Haiti	326
Hamburg	253
Hannover	254
Hejaz	330
Hesse-Cassel	257
Hesse-Darmstadt	258
Hohenlohe-Neuenstein-Oehringen	259
Honduras	330
Hong Kong	331
Hungary	333
Hyderabad	352
Hyderabad Feudatories - Kalayani	354

I

Iceland	338
India - Independent Kingdoms	340
India - Mughal Empire	338
India - Princely States	345
India-British	364
India-French	363
India-Portuguese	364
India-republic	371
Indonesia	371
Indore	354
Iran	373
Iraq	387
Ireland	388
Ireland Republic	389
Isenburg	259
Isle Of Man	389
Israel	426
Italian Republic	432
Italian States	432
Italy	441
Ivory Coast	446

J

Jaipur	355
Jaisalmir	356
Jamaica	446
Janjira Island	356
Japan	448
Java	537
Jersey	452
Jodhpur	356
Jordan	454
Jubbal	357
Junagadh	358

K

Kaithal	358
Karauli	358
Kashmir	358
Katanga	456
Kazakhstan	456
Kenya	456
Khiva	106
Khoqand	107
Kingdom Of Napoleon	432
Kiribati	457
Kishangarh	359
Knyphausen	259
Korea	458
Korea-North	458
Korea-South	460
Kotah	359
Kurdistan	462
Kutch	340
Kuwait	462
Kwangtung Province	117
Kyrgyzstan	463

L

La Rioja	19
Laos	463
Latvia	464
Lebanon	465
Lesotho	465
Liberia	467
Libya	473
Liechtenstein	474
Lithuania	475
Lombardy-Venetia	433
Lubeck	259
Luxembourg	476
Luzern	665

M

Macao	477
Macedonia	480
Madagascar	481
Madeira Islands	481
Madras Presidency	369
Malawi	482
Malaysia	483
Malaysia	484
Maldive Islands	484
Maler Kotla	359
Mali	485
Malta, Order Of	487
Malta	485
Manipur	341
Manitoba	100
Maratha Confederacy	342
Marshall Islands	490
Martinique	490
Mauritania	491
Mauritius	492
Mayotte	492
Mecklenburg-Schwerin	260
Mecklenburg-Strelitz	260
Mewar	359
Mewar Feudatories - Shahpur	360
Mexico	493
Mexico-Revolutionary	509
Mombasa	510
Monaco	511
Mongolia	513
Montenegro	516
Morocco	517
Mozambique	519
Muscat & Oman	520
Myanmar	521
Mysore	360

N

Nabha	360
Nagorno-Karabakh	522
Namibia	522
Naples & Sicily	434
Nassau	261
Nauru	523
Nawanagar	360
Nepal	523
Netherlands	532
Netherlands Antilles	536
Netherlands East Indies	537
New Caledonia	538
New Hebrides	538
New Zealand	538
Nicaragua	539
Niger	540
Nigeria	541
Niue	542
North Carolina	740
North Peru	566
North Viet Nam	763
Northern Mariana Islands	543
Norway	544
Nurnberg	261

O

Oaxaca	510
Occussi - Ambeno	545
Oldenburg	261
Olmutz	49
Oman	545
Oregon	742

P

Pakistan	548
Palau	548
Palestine	550
Panama	550
Papal States	436
Papua New Guinea	553
Paraguay	555
Parma	438
Patiala	360
Peru	560

Knightsbridge Coins

WE ARE ALWAYS KEEN TO PURCHASE CHOICE COINS, ESPECIALLY:
British, USA, Australian

We will purchase single items or complete collections and can travel anywhere to view at short notice. If you have coins, medallions or banknotes you wish to sell, please contact us at the address below.

Knightsbridge Coins (S. Fenton)
43 Duke Street, St James's, London SW1Y 6DD, UK
Telephone: 020 7930 7597/8215/7888 Fax: 020 7930 8214

The only coin dealer with membership of all four Numismatic Organisations

St James's Auctions

Our sixth auction has been successfully completed and we are now planning Auction 7 and 8.

Consignments for these auctions are now being accepted.

Knightsbridge Coins / S. Fenton
43 Duke Street, St James's
London SW1Y 6DD
Tel: 020 7930 7597 / 7888 / 8215
Fax: 020 7930 8214

M. Louis Teller
16055 Ventura Blvd., Suite 635, Encino, CA 91436
Tel: 818-783-8454   Fax: 818-783-9083

XII COUNTRY INDEX

Philippines 567
Piedmont Republic 438
Pitcairn Islands 569
Poland 570
Portugal 576
Prussia 262

Q

Qatar 584

R

Radhanpur 361
Rajkot 361
Ras Al-khaimah 584
Reunion 585
Reuss-Obergreiz 264
Reuss-Schleiz 265
Rewa 361
Rhenish Confederation 265
Rhodesia 586
Romania 586
Russia 591
Russia (Kaliningrad) 607
Rwanda 607

S

Saarland 608
Saharawi Arab Democratic
 Republic 608
Saint Barthelemy 608
Saint Helena 609
Saint Helena & Ascension 609
Saint Kitts & Nevis 610
Saint Lucia 610
Saint Thomas & Prince Island 610
Saint Vincent 611
Salzburg 49
Samoa 612
San Marino 613
Sardinia 438
Saudi Arabia 619
Saxe-Altenburg 265
Saxe-Coburg-Gotha 265
Saxe-Meiningen 265
Saxe-Weimar-Eisenach 266
Saxony 266
Schaumburg-Lippe 269
Schleswig-Holstein 270
Schwarzburg-Rudolstadt 270
Schwarzburg-Sondershausen 270
Schwyz 666
Senegal 620
Serbia 621
Seychelles 621
Shah Dynasty 524
Shantung Province 117
Sharjah 623
Sierra Leone 623
Sikh Empire 342
Singapore 627

Sinkiang Province 117
Slovakia 636
Slovenia 637
Socialist Republic 763
Solomon Islands 638
Solothurn 666
Somalia 640
South Africa 642
South Australia 39
South Georgia And The South Sandwich Islands 647
South Peru 566
Southern Rhodesia 647
Spain 648
Sri Lanka 657
Stolberg-Wernigerode 270
Straits Settlements 657
Sudan 658
Suriname 659
Swaziland 660
Sweden 661
Swiss Cantons 665
Switzerland 666
Syria 670

T

Taiwan 120
Tanzania 671
Thailand 672
Tibet 676
Tierra Del Fuego 19
Togo 677
Tokelau 678
Tonga 678
Tonk 362
Travancore 362
Trinidad & Tobago 681
Tripoli 473
Tripura 343
Tristan Da Cunha 682
Tunis 685
Tunisia 683
Turkey 687
Turks & Caicos Islands 702
Tuscany 440
Tuvalu 704

U

Uganda 705
Ukraine 706
Umm Al Qaiwain 708
United Arab Emirates 708
United Kingdom 709
United Kingdoms 619
United States 710
Uruguay 742
Us Territorial Gold 731
Utah 742
Utopia - A World United 745
Uzbekistan 745

V

Valencia 657
Vanuatu 745
Vatican City 746
Venezuela 748
Victoria 40
Vietnam 753

W

Waldeck-pyrmont 270
Wales 314
Wallenstein 180
Wallmoden-Gimborn 271
West African States 764
Westphalia 271
Wurttemberg 272
Wurzburg 273

Y

Yemen Arab Republic 765
Yemen Eastern Aden
 Protectorate 767
Yemen Mutawakkilite 764
Yemen, Democratic Republic
 Of 767
Yugoslavia 767
Yunnan Province 118

Z

Zaire 770
Zambia 771
Zanzibar 772
Zurich 666

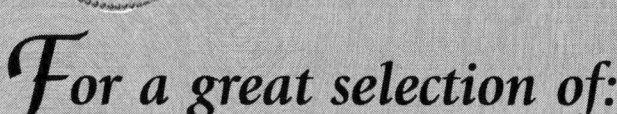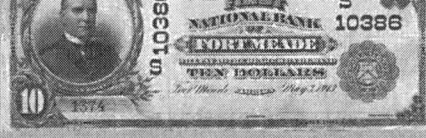

FOREIGN EXCHANGE TABLE

The latest foreign exchange rates below apply to trade with banks in the country of origin. The left column shows the number of units per U.S. dollar at the official rate. The right column shows the number of units per dollar at the free market rate.

Country	Official #/$	Market #/$
Afghanistan (New Afghani)	49.6	–
Albania (Lek)	93	–
Algeria (Dinar)	69	–
Andorra uses Euro	.757	–
Angola (Readjust Kwanza)	80	–
Anguilla uses E.C. Dollar	2.7	–
Antigua uses E.C. Dollar	2.7	–
Argentina (Peso)	3.06	–
Armenia (Dram)	365	–
Aruba (Florin)	1.79	–
Australia (Dollar)	1.273	–
Austria (Euro)	.757	–
Azerbaijan (Manat)	4,600	–
Bahamas (Dollar)	1.0	–
Bahrain Is. (Dinar)	.377	–
Bangladesh (Taka)	70	–
Barbados (Dollar)	2.0	–
Belarus (Ruble)	2,140	–
Belgium (Euro)	.757	–
Belize (Dollar)	1.97	–
Benin uses CFA Franc West	490	–
Bermuda (Dollar)	1.0	–
Bhutan (Ngultrum)	45	–
Bolivia (Boliviano)	7.99	–
Bosnia-Herzegovina (Conv. marka)	1.47	–
Botswana (Pula)	6.05	–
British Virgin Islands uses U.S. Dollar	1.00	–
Brazil (Real)	2.14	–
Brunei (Dollar)	1.54	–
Bulgaria (Lev)	1.47	–
Burkina Faso uses CFA Fr.West	490	–
Burma (Kyat)	6.42	1,250
Burundi (Franc)	1,040	–
Cambodia (Riel)	4,050	–
Cameroon uses CFA Franc Central	490	–
Canada (Dollar)	1.149	–
Cape Verde (Escudo)	83.1	–
Cayman Is.(Dollar)	0.82	–
Central African Rep.	490	–
CFA Franc Central	490	–
CFA Franc West	490	–
CFP Franc	90	–
Chad uses CFA Franc Central	490	–
Chile (Peso)	525	–
China, P.R. (Renminbi Yuan)	7.825	–
Colombia (Peso)	2,280	–
Comoros (Franc)	370	–
Congo uses CFA Franc Central	490	–
Congo-Dem.Rep. (Congolese Franc)	490	–
Cook Islands (Dollar)	1.73	–
Costa Rica (Colon)	517	–
Croatia (Kuna)	5.74	–
Cuba (Peso)	1.00	27.00
Cyprus (Pound)	.43	–
Czech Republic (Koruna)	21.1	–
Denmark (Danish Krone)	5.65	–
Djibouti (Franc)	178	–
Dominica uses E.C. Dollar	2.7	–
Dominican Republic (Peso)	32.8	–
East Caribbean (Dollar)	2.7	–
Ecuador uses U.S. Dollar		
Egypt (Pound)	5.72	–
El Salvador (U.S. Dollar)	1.00	–
England (Sterling Pound)	.512	–
Equatorial Guinea uses CFA Franc Central	490	–
Eritrea (Nafka)	15	–
Estonia (Kroon)	11.9	–
Ethiopia (Birr)	8.75	–
Euro	.757	–
Falkland Is. (Pound)	.512	–
Faroe Islands (Krona)	5.65	–

Country	Official #/$	Market #/$
Fiji Islands (Dollar)	1.67	–
Finland (Euro)	.757	–
France (Euro)	.757	–
French Polynesia uses CFP Franc	90	–
Gabon (CFA Franc)	490	–
Gambia (Dalasi)	28	–
Georgia (Lari)	1.73	–
Germany (Euro)	.757	–
Ghana (Cedi)	9,200	–
Gibraltar (Pound)	.512	–
Greece (Euro)	.757	–
Greenland uses Danish Krone	5.65	–
Grenada uses E.C. Dollar	2.7	–
Guatemala (Quetzal)	7.63	–
Guernsey uses Sterling Pound	.512	–
Guinea Bissau (CFA Franc)	490	–
Guinea Conakry (Franc)	5,550	–
Guyana (Dollar)	200	–
Haiti (Gourde)	38.9	–
Honduras (Lempira)	18.9	–
Hong Kong (Dollar)	7.773	–
Hungary (Forint)	195	–
Iceland (Krona)	69.5	–
India (Rupee)	44.7	–
Indonesia (Rupiah)	9,075	–
Iran (Rial)	9,230	–
Iraq (Dinar)	1,425	–
Ireland (Euro)	.757	–
Isle of Man uses Sterling Pound	.512	–
Israel (New Sheqalim)	4.19	–
Italy (Euro)	.757	–
Ivory Coast uses CFA Franc West	490	–
Jamaica (Dollar)	67	–
Japan (Yen)	116.3	–
Jersey uses Sterling Pound	.512	–
Jordan (Dinar)	.71	–
Kazakhstan (Tenge)	130	–
Kenya (Shilling)	70	–
Kiribati uses Australian Dollar	1.273	–
Korea-PDR (Won)	2.2	500
Korea-Rep. (Won)	920	–
Kuwait (Dinar)	.289	–
Kyrgyzstan (Som)	39	–
Laos (Kip)	9720	–
Latvia (Lats)	.53	–
Lebanon (Pound)	1,510	–
Lesotho (Maloti)	7.09	–
Liberia (Dollar)	53.3	–
Libya (Dinar)	1.27	–
Liechtenstein uses Swiss Franc	1.205	–
Lithuania (Litas)	2.62	–
Luxembourg (Euro)	.757	–
Macao (Pataca)	8.0	–
Macedonia (New Denar)	46	–
Madagascar (Franc)	2,040	–
Malawi (Kwacha)	140	–
Malaysia (Ringgit)	3.55	–
Maldives (Rufiya)	12.8	–
Mali uses CFA Franc West	490	–
Malta (Lira)	3.1	–
Marshall Islands uses U.S.Dollar		
Mauritania (Ouguiya)	270	–
Mauritius (Rupee)	32.5	–
Mexico (Peso)	10.82	–
Moldova (Leu)	13.1	–
Monaco uses Euro	.757	–
Mongolia (Tugrik)	1,165	–
Montenegro uses Euro	.757	–
Montserrat uses E.C. Dollar	2.7	–
Morocco (Dirham)	8.44	–
Mozambique (New Metical)	26.3	–
Myanmar (Burma) (Kyat)	6.42	1,250
Namibia (Rand)	7.09	–
Nauru uses Australian Dollar	1.456	–
Nepal (Rupee)	71.6	–
Netherlands (Euro)	.757	–

Country	Official #/$	Market #/$
Netherlands Antilles (Gulden)	1.79	–
New Caledonia uses CFP Franc	90	–
New Zealand (Dollar)	1.493	–
Nicaragua (Cordoba Oro)	17.9	–
Niger uses CFA Franc West	490	–
Nigeria (Naira)	128	–
Northern Ireland uses Sterling Pound	.512	–
Norway (Krone)	6.16	–
Oman (Rial)	.385	–
Pakistan (Rupee)	60.9	–
Palau uses U.S.Dollar		
Panama (Balboa) uses U.S.Dollar		
Papua New Guinea (Kina)	3.02	–
Paraguay (Guarani)	5,400	–
Peru (Nuevo Sol)	3.21	–
Philippines (Peso)	50	–
Poland (Zloty)	2.9	–
Portugal (Euro)	.757	–
Qatar (Riyal)	3.64	–
Romania (New Leu)	2.6	–
Russia (New Ruble)	26.3	–
Rwanda (Franc)	550	–
St. Helena (Pound)	.512	–
St. Kitts uses E.C. Dollar	2.7	–
St. Lucia uses E.C. Dollar	2.7	–
St. Vincent uses E.C. Dollar	2.7	–
San Marino uses Euro	.757	–
Sao Tome e Principe (Dobra)	6,780	–
Saudi Arabia (Riyal)	3.75	–
Scotland uses Sterling Pound	.512	–
Senegal uses CFA Franc West	490	–
Serbia (Dinar)	59.9	–
Seychelles (Rupee)	5.59	6.40
Sierra Leone (Leone)	2,990	–
Singapore (Dollar)	1.55	–
Slovakia (Sk. Koruna)	26.8	–
Slovenia (Tolar)	180	–
Solomon Is.(Dollar)	7.63	–
Somalia (Shilling)	1,370	–
Somaliland (Somali Shilling)	1,800	4,000
South Africa (Rand)	7.09	–
Spain (Euro)	.757	–
Sri Lanka (Rupee)	110	–
Sudan (Dinar)	200	300
Surinam (Dollar)	2.75	–
Swaziland (Lilangeni)	7.09	–
Sweden (Krona)	6.87	–
Switzerland (Franc)	1.205	–
Syria (Pound)	52.2	–
Taiwan (NT Dollar)	32.4	–
Tajikistan (Somoni)	3.40	–
Tanzania (Shilling)	1,280	–
Thailand (Baht)	35.5	–
Togo uses CFA Franc West	490	–
Tonga (Pa'anga)	1.99	–
Transdniestra (Ruble)	6.51	–
Trinidad & Tobago (Dollar)	6.28	–
Tunisia (Dinar)	1.3	–
Turkey (New Lira)	1.43	–
Turkmenistan (Manat)	5,200	–
Turks & Caicos uses U.S. Dollar		
Tuvalu uses Australian Dollar	1.273	–
Uganda (Shilling)	1,800	–
Ukraine (Hryvnia)	5.03	–
United Arab Emirates (Dirham)	3.673	–
Uruguay (Peso Uruguayo)	24.3	–
Uzbekistan (Sum)	1,235	–
Vanuatu (Vatu)	106	–
Vatican City uses Euro	.757	–
Venezuela (Bolivar)	2,150	2,300
Vietnam (Dong)	16,050	–
Western Samoa (Tala)	2.66	–
Yemen (Rial)	198	–
Zambia (Kwacha)	4,050	–
Zimbabwe (revalued Dollar)	250	–

"The I.A.P.N. dealer, your guide to the world of numismatics"

More than one hundred of the world's most respected coin dealers are members of the I.A.P.N. (International Association of Professional Numismatists). I.A.P.N. members offer the collector an exceptional selection of quality material, expert cataloguing, outstanding service and realistic pricing.

The I.A.P.N. also maintains the International Bureau for the Suppression of Counterfeit Coins (I.B.S.C.C.) which for a fee can provide expert opinions on the authenticity of coins submitted to it.

A booklet listing the names, addresses and specialties of all I.A.P.N. members is available without charge by writing to the I.A.P.N. General Secretary, Jean-Luc Van der Schueren, 14 rue de la Bourse, B-1000 BRUXELLES, Belgium. Tel: +32-2-513 3400; Fax: +32-2-512 2528; E-mail: iapnsecret@compuserve.com; Web site: http://www.iapn.ch.

ARGENTINA
DERMAN, Alberto José
Avenida Corrientes 368
1043 BUENOS AIRES

AUSTRALIA
NOBLE NUMISMATICS Pty Ltd
169 Macquarie Street
SYDNEY, NSW 2000

AUSTRIA
HERINEK, Gerhard
Josefstädterstrasse 27
1080 WIEN
MOZELT Numismatik
Postfach 19
1043 WIEN

BELGIUM
FRANCESCHI & FILS, B.
Rue de la Croix-de-Fer 10
1000 BRUXELLES
JEAN ELSEN & ses Fils s.a.
Avenue de Tervueren 65
1040 BRUXELLES
VAN DER SCHUEREN, Jean-Luc
Rue de la Bourse 14
1000 BRUXELLES

CANADA
WEIR NUMISMATICS Ltd
P.O. Box 64577
UNIONVILLE, ONT. L3R 0M9

EGYPT
BAJOCCHI JEWELLERS
Abdel Khalek Sarwat Street 45
CAIRO 11511

FRANCE
BOURGEY, Sabine
Rue Drouot 7
75009 PARIS
BURGAN, Claude - Maison FLORANGE
Rue du 4 Septembre 8
75002 PARIS
MAISON PLATT S.A.
B.P. 2612
75026 PARIS Cedex 01
NUMISMATIQUE & CHANGE DE PARIS
Rue de la Bourse 3
75002 PARIS
O.G.N.
Rue de Richelieu 64
75002 PARIS
POINSIGNON-NUMISMATIQUE (A.)
Rue des Francs Bourgeois 4
67000 STRASBOURG
SILBERSTEIN, Claude - COMPTOIR de NUMISMATIQUE
Rue Vivienne 39
75002 PARIS
SPES NUMISMATIQUE
Rue de Richelieu 54
75001 PARIS
VINCHON - NUMISMATIQUE
Rue de Richelieu 77
75002 PARIS

GERMANY
DILLER, Johannes
Postfach 70 04 29
81304 MÜNCHEN
GORNY & MOSCH - GIESSENER MÜNZHANDLUNG GmbH
Maximiliansplatz 20
D - 80333 MÜNCHEN
HIRSCH NACHF., Gerhard
Promenadeplatz 10/II
80333 MÜNCHEN
JACQUIER, Paul-Francis
Honsellstrasse 8
77694 KEHL am RHEIN
KAISER MÜNZFACHGESCHÄFT
Mittelweg 54
60318 FRANKFURT
KRICHELDORF NACHF.
Günterstalstrasse 16
79102 FREIBURG i. Br.
KÜNKER MÜNZHANDLUNG
Gutenbergstrasse 23
49076 OSNABRÜCK
KURPFÄLZISCHE MÜNZHANDLUNG
Augusta-Anlage 52
68165 MANNHEIM
LEIPZIGER MÜNZHANDLUNG
Nicolaistr. 25
04109 LEIPZIG
MEISTER, Michael
Moltkestrasse 6
D-71634 LUDWIGSBURG
MÜNZEN- UND MEDAILLENHANDLUNG STUTTGART
Charlottenstrasse 4
70182 STUTTGART
NEUMANN GmbH
Wätteplatz 6
89312 GÜNZBURG
NUMISMATIK LANZ
Luitpoldblock - Maximiliansplatz 10
80333 MÜNCHEN
OLDING, Manfred
Goldbreede 14
49078 OSNABRÜCK
PEUS NACHF.
Bornwiesenweg 34
60322 FRANKFURT / M
RITTER MÜNZHANDLUNG GmbH
Postfach 24 01 26
40090 DÜSSELDORF
TIETJEN + Co
Spitalerstrasse 30
20095 HAMBURG
WESTFÄLISCHE AUKTIONSGESELLSCHAFT
Nordring 22
59821 ARNSBERG

HUNGARY
NUMISMATICA EREMBOLT
Vörösmarty Tér 6
1051 BUDAPEST

ISRAEL
QEDAR, Shraga
P.O. Box 520
91004 JERUSALEM 93399

ITALY
BARANOWSKY S.A.S.
Via del Corso 184
00187 ROMA
CRIPPA NUMISMATICA S.A.S.
Via Cavalieri del S. Sepolcro 10
20121 MILANO
DE FALCO, Alberto
Corso Umberto 24
80138 NAPOLI
FALLANI, Carlo-Maria
Via del Babuino 58a
00187 ROMA
GIULIO BERNARDI S.R.L.
Casella Postale 560
34121 TRIESTE
MARCHESI GINO & FIGLIO
Viale Pietramellara 35
40121 BOLOGNA
PAOLUCCI, Raffaele
Via San Francesco 154
35121 PADOVA
RINALDI, Marco
Via Cappello 23 (Casa di Giulietta)
37121 VERONA
VARESI NUMISMATICA S.A.S.
Via Robolini 1
27100 PAVIA

JAPAN
DARUMA INTERNATIONAL GALLERIES
2-16-32-701, Takanawa, Minato-ku
TOKYO 108-0074
WORLD COINS JAPAN
1-15-5, Hamamatsu-cho, Minato-ku
TOKYO 105-0013

MONACO
EDITIONS VICTOR GADOURY
57 rue Grimaldi "Le Panorama"
98000 MONACO

NETHERLANDS
MEVIUS NUMISBOOKS INTERNATIONAL BV
Oosteinde 97
7671 AT VRIEZENVEEN
SCHULMAN BV, Laurens
Brinklaan 84a
1404 GM BUSSUM
VERSCHOOR, Munthandel
Binnensingel 3
3291 TB STRIJEN
WESTERHOF, Jille Binne
Trekpad 38-40
8742 KP BURGWERD

NORWAY
OSLO MYNTHANDEL AS
Postboks 355 Sentrum
0101 OSLO

PORTUGAL
NUMISPORTO LDA
Av. Combatentes Grande Guerra 610 Lj6
4200-186 PORTO

SINGAPORE
TAISEI STAMPS & COINS
116 Middle Road #09-02
IBC Enterpr. house
188972 SINGAPORE

SPAIN
CALICO, X. & F.
Plaza del Angel 2
08002 BARCELONA
CAYON - JANO S.L.
Alcala 35
28014 MADRID
SEGARRA, Fernando P.
Plaza Mayor 26
28012 MADRID
VICO S.A., Jesús
Jorge Juan n 83 Duplicado
28009 MADRID

SWEDEN
NORDLINDS MYNTHANDEL AB
P.O. Box 5132
102 43 STOCKHOLM

SWITZERLAND
HESS AG, Adolph
Postfach 7070
8023 ZÜRICH
HESS-DIVO AG
Postfach 7070
8023 ZÜRICH
NUMISMATICA GENEVENSIS S.A.
1 Rond-Point de Plainpalais
1205 GENEVE
LHS NUMISMATICS LTD.
P.O. Box 2553 8022 ZÜRICH
STERNBERG AG, Frank
Schanzengasse 10
8001 ZÜRICH

UNITED KINGDOM
BALDWIN & SONS Ltd
Adelphi Terrace 11
LONDON, WC2N 6BJ
DAVIES, Paul, Ltd.
P.O. Box 17
ILKLEY, W.Yorkshire LS29 8TZ
DIX NOONAN WEBB
16 Bolton Street, Piccadilly
LONDON W1J 8BQ
EIMER, Christopher
P.O. Box 352
LONDON NW11 7RF
FORMAT OF BIRMINGHAM Ltd
Burlington Court 18 Lower Temple Street
BIRMINGHAM B2 4JD
KNIGHTSBRIDGE COINS
Duke Street 43 St. James's
LONDON SW1Y 6DD
LUBBOCK & SON Ltd
P.O. Box 35732
LONDON E14 7WB
NUMISMATICA ARS CLASSICA AG
3rd Floor Genavco House
17 Waterloo Place
LONDON SW1 4AR
RASMUSSEN, MARK
P.O. Box 42
BETCHWORTH RH3 7YR
RUDD, Chris
P. O. Box 222
AYLSHAM, Norfolk NR11 6TY
SPINK & SON, Ltd
69 Southampton Row Bloomsbury
LONDON WC1B 4ET

USA
BASOK, Alexander
1954 First Street #186
HIGHLAND PARK, IL 60035
BERK, Ltd., Harlan J.
North Clark Street, 31
CHICAGO, IL 60602
BULLOWA, C.E. - COINHUNTER
1616 Walnut Street, Suite 2112
PHILADELPHIA, PA 19103
CLASSICAL NUMISMATIC GROUP
P.O. Box 479
LANCASTER, PA 17608-0479
COIN AND CURRENCY INSTITUTE, Inc.
P.O. Box 1057
CLIFTON, NJ 07014
COIN GALLERIES
123 West 57th Street
NEW YORK, NY 10019
CRAIG, Freeman
P.O. Box 4176
SAN RAFAEL, CA 94913
DAVISSON'S, LTD.
COLD SPRING, MN 56320-1050
DUNIGAN, Mike
5332 Birchman
FORT WORTH, TX 76107
FREEMAN & SEAR
P.O. Box 641352
LOS ANGELES, CA 90064-6352
FROSETH, INC.
P.O. Box 23116
MINNEAPOLIS, MN 55423
GEORGE FREDERICK KOLBE - FINE NUMISMATIC BOOKS
P.O. Drawer 3100
CRESTLINE, CA 92325-3100
GILLIO, INC.
8 West Figueroa Street
SANTA BARBARA, CA 93101
HARVEY, Stephen
P.O. Box 3778
BEVERLY HILLS, CA 90212
KERN, Jonathan K.
441 South Ashland Avenue
LEXINGTON, KY 40502-2114
KOVACS, Frank L.
P.O. Box 151790
SAN RAFAEL, CA 94915-1790
KREINDLER, B. & H.
236 Altessa Blvd.
MELVILLE, NY 11747
MALTER GALLERIES, Inc.
17003 Ventura Boulevard, Suite 205
ENCINO, CA 91316
MARGOLIS, Richard
P.O. Box 2054
TEANECK, NJ 07666
MARKOV, Dmitry
P.O. Box 950
NEW YORK, NY 10272
MILCAREK, Dr. Ron
P.O. Box 1028
GREENFIELD, MA 01302
PEGASI NUMISMATICS
P.O. Box 131040
ANN ARBOR, MI 48113
PONTERIO & ASSOCIATES, INC.
1818 Robinson Avenue
SAN DIEGO, CA 92103
RARCOA, INC.
6262 South Route 83, Suite 200
WILLOWBROOK, IL 60527-2998
RARE COIN GALLERIES
P.O. Box 569
GLENDALE, CA 91209
ROSENBLUM, William M.
P.O. Box 355
EVERGREEN, CO 80437-0355
RYNEARSON, Dr. Paul
P.O. Box 4009
MALIBU, CA 90264
STACK'S
123 West 57th Street
NEW YORK, NY 10019
STEPHENS, INC., Karl
P.O. Box 3038
FALLBROOK, CA 92088
SUBAK, INC.
22 West Monroe Street, Room 1506
CHICAGO, IL 60603
TELLER NUMISMATIC ENTERPRISES
16055 Ventura Boulevard, Suite 635
ENCINO, CA 91436
WADDELL, Edward J., Ltd.
P.O. Box 3759
FREDERICK, MD 21705-3759
WORLD-WIDE COINS OF CALIFORNIA
P.O. Box 3684
SANTA ROSA, CA 95402

VENEZUELA
NUMISMATICA GLOBUS
Apartado de Correos 50418
CARACAS 1050

NUMISMATIK LANZ MÜNCHEN

Jean ELSEN & ses Fils s.a.

QUARTERLY AUCTIONS
FIXED PRICE LISTS

WWW.ELSEN.EU

Avenue de Tervueren, 65
B-1040 Brussels

AUCTIONS   **RETAIL**

 Dr. Hubert Lanz
Maximiliansplatz 10
80333 Munich
Germany
Tel.+49-89-299070 Fax. +49-89-220762
www.Lanz.com   info@Lanz.com
www.taxfreegold.de

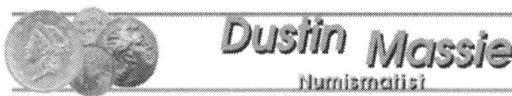

P.O. Box 234 - Madison, IL 62060
Phone: (618) 444-2442 - Fax: (618) 452-7095

REASONS TO TRY US FOR SELLING YOUR COINS OR BUYING FOR YOUR COLLECTION

* **STRONG BUYERS OF WORLD GOLD COINS**

** **COMPETITIVE SELL PRICES**

*** **SEE US AT LONG BEACH, BALTIMORE, SANTA CLARA, THE ANA & MOST MAJOR SHOWS**

**** **CHECK OUR WEB SITE WWW.DUSTINEM.COM FOR OTHER SCHEDULED SHOWS**

***** **PROFESSIONAL NUMISMATIST GUILD MEMBER DEALER #643**

Five day return. Checks must clear. All coins guaranteed genuine.
Postage & Handling on all purchases: $11.00

Sending Scanned Images by Email

We have been receiving an ever-increasing number of new images for the Standard Catalog series and we are grateful to everyone for your efforts. We continue to encourage readers to assess the quality of our images and to send scans of better examples. Unfortunately, many submissions cannot be used due to the scanning method. We want to avoid this in the future as your time and ours is valuable. Here are a few simple instructions to assist you in producing these scans:

• Scan all images with a resolution of 300 dpi

• Size setting should always be 100%

• Scan as a 4-color image

• Save each image as a 'jpeg' or 'tiff'

• Clearly name each image, indicating the country and using 'f' for obverse and 'b' for reverse. Indicate the KM number if known

• Please email images with a request for a confirmation of receipt

• Please send all images to:
Randy.Thern@Fwpubs.com

• When possible, please email or call before sending images to avoid duplication

Thanks again for your interest in improving the image quality in the Standard Catalog of World Coins.

HOW TO USE THIS CATALOG

This catalog series is designed to serve the needs of both the novice and advanced collectors. It provides a comprehensive guide to over 200 years of world coinage. It is generally arranged so that persons with no more than a basic knowledge of world history and a casual acquaintance with coin collecting can consult it with confidence and ease. The following explanations summarize the general practices used in preparing this catalog's listings. However, because of specialized requirements, which may vary by country and era, these must not be considered ironclad. Where these standards have been set aside, appropriate notations of the variations are incorporated in that particular listing.

ARRANGEMENT

Countries are arranged alphabetically. Political changes within a country are arranged chronologically. In countries where Rulers are the single most significant political entity a chronological arrangement by Ruler has been employed. Distinctive sub-geographic regions are listed alphabetically following the country's main listings. A few exceptions to these rules may exist. Refer to the Country Index.

Diverse coinage types relating to fabrication methods, revaluations, denomination systems, non-circulating cCountries are arranged alphabetically. Political changes within a country are arranged chronologically. In countries where Rulers are the single most significant political entity a chronological arrangement by Ruler has been employed. Distinctive sub-geographic regions are listed alphabetically following the country's main listings. A few exceptions to these rules may exist. Refer to the Country Index.

Diverse coinage types relating to fabrication methods, revaluations, denomination systems, non-circulating categories and such have been identified, separated and arranged in logical fashion. Chronological arrangement is employed for most circulating coinage, i.e., Hammered coinage will normally precede Milled coinage, monetary reforms will flow in order of their institution. Non-circulating types such as Essais, Piéforts, Patterns, Trial Strikes, Mint and Proof sets will follow the main listings, as will Medallic coinage and Token coinage.

Within a coinage type coins will be listed by denomination, from smallest to largest. Numbered types within a denomination will be ordered by their first date of issue. Generally speaking, denomination types such as fractions and multiples of Escudos, Ducats, Ashrafis, Mohurs, etc. are grouped together.rmally precede Milled coinage, monetary reforms will flow in order of their institution. Non-circulating types such as Essais, Piéforts, Patterns, Trial Strikes, Mint and Proof sets will follow the main listings, as will Medallic coinage and Token coinage.

Within a coinage type coins will be listed by denomination, from smallest to largest. Numbered types within a denomination will be ordered by their first date of issue. Generally speaking, denomination types such as fractions and multiples of Escudos, Ducats, Ashrafis, Mohurs, etc. are grouped together.

IDENTIFICATION

The most important step in the identification of a coin is the determination of the nation of origin. This is generally easily accomplished where English-speaking lands are concerned, however, use of the country index is sometimes required. The coins of Great Britain provide an interesting challenge. For hundreds of years the only indication of the country of origin was in the abbreviated Latin legends. In recent times there have been occasions when there has been no indication of origin. Only through the familiarity of the monarchical portraits, symbols and legends or indication of currency system are they identifiable.

The coins of many countries beyond the English-language realm, such as those of French, Italian or Spanish heritage, are also quite easy to identify through reference to their legends, which appear in the national languages based on Western alphabets. In many instances the name is spelled exactly the same in English as in the national language, such as France; while in other cases it varies only slightly, like Italia for Italy, Belgique or Belgie for Belgium, Brasil for Brazil and Danmark for Denmark.

This is not always the case, however, as in Norge for Norway, Espana for Spain, Sverige for Sweden and Helvetia for Switzerland. Some other examples include:

DEUTSCHES REICH - Germany 1873-1945
BUNDESREPUBLIC DEUTSCHLAND - Federal Republic of Germany.
DEUTSCHE DEMOKRATISCHE REPUBLIK - German Democratic Republic.
EMPIRE CHERIFIEN MAROC - Morocco.
ESTADOS UNIDOS MEXICANOS - United Mexican States (Mexico).
ETAT DU GRAND LIBAN - State of Great Lebanon (Lebanon).

Thus it can be seen there are instances in which a little schooling in the rudiments of foreign languages can be most helpful. In general, colonial possessions of countries using the Western alphabet are similarly identifiable as they often carry portraits of their current rulers, the familiar lettering, sometimes in combination with a companion designation in the local language.

Collectors have the greatest difficulty with coins that do not bear legends or dates in the Western systems. These include coins bearing Cyrillic lettering, attributable to Bulgaria, Russia, the Slavic states and Mongolia, the Greek script peculiar to Greece, Crete and the Ionian Islands; The Amharic characters of Ethiopia, or Hebrew in the case of Israel. Dragons and sunbursts along with the distinctive word characters attribute a coin to the Oriental countries of China, Japan, Korea, Tibet, Viet Nam and their component parts.

The most difficult coins to identify are those bearing only Persian or Arabic script and its derivatives, found on the issues of nations stretching in a wide swath across North Africa and East Asia, from Morocco to Indonesia, and the Indian subcontinent coinages which surely are more confusing in their vast array of Nagari, Sanskrit, Ahom, Assamese and other local dialects found on the local issues of the Indian Princely States. Although the task of identification on the more modern issues of these lands is often eased by the added presence of Western alphabet legends, a feature sometimes adopted as early as the late 19th Century, for the earlier pieces it is often necessary for the uninitiated to laboriously seek and find.

HOW TO USE THIS CATALOG

Except for the cruder issues, however, it will be found that certain characteristics and symbols featured in addition to the predominant legends are typical on coins from a given country or group of countries. The toughra monogram, for instance, occurs on some of the coins of Afghanistan, Egypt, the Sudan, Pakistan, Turkey and other areas of the late Ottoman Empire. A predominant design feature on the coins of Nepal is the trident; while neighboring Tibet features a lotus blossom or lion on many of their issues.

To assist in identification of the more difficult coins, we have assembled the Instant Identifier and Monogram sections presented on the following pages. They are designed to provide a point of beginning for collectors by allowing them to compare unidentified coins with photographic details from typical issues.

We also suggest reference to the Index of Coin Denominations presented here and also the comprehensive Country Index, where the inscription will be found listed just as it appears on the coin for nations using the Western alphabet.

DATING

Coin dating is the final basic attribution consideration. Here, the problem can be more difficult because the reading of a coin date is subject not only to the vagaries of numeric styling, but to calendar variations caused by the observance of various religious eras or regal periods from country to country, or even within a country. Here again with the exception of the sphere from North Africa through the Orient, it will be found that most countries rely on Western date numerals and Christian (AD) era reckoning, although in a few instances, coin dating has been tied to the year of a reign or government. The Vatican, for example dates its coinage according to the year of reign of the current pope, in addition to the Christian- era date.

Countries in the Arabic sphere generally date their coins to the Muslim era (AH), which commenced on July 16, 622 AD (Julian calendar), when the prophet Mohammed fled from Mecca to Medina. As their calendar is reckoned by the lunar year of 354 days, which is about three percent (precisely 2.98%) shorter than the Christian year, a formula is required to convert AH dating to its Western equivalent. To convert an AH date to the approximate AD date, subtract three percent of the AH date (round to the closest whole number) from the AH date and add 622. A chart converting all AH years from 1010 (July 2, 1601) to 1421 (May 25, 2028) is presented as the Heijra Chart on page 10.

The Muslim calendar is not always based on the lunar year (AH), however, causing some confusion, particularly in Afghanistan and Iran, where a calendar based on the solar year (SH) was introduced around 1920. These dates can be converted to AD by simply adding 621. In 1976 the government of Iran implemented a new solar calendar based on the foundation of the Iranian monarchy in 559 BC. The first year observed on the new calendar was 2535 (MS), which commenced March 20, 1976. A reversion to the traditional SH dating standard occurred a few years later.

Several different eras of reckoning, including Christian and Muslim (AH), have been used to date coins of the Indian subcontinent. The two basic systems are the Vikrama Samvat (VS), which dates from Oct. 18, 58 BC, and the Saka era, the origin of which is reckoned from March 3, 78 AD. Dating according to both eras appears on various coins of the area.

Coins of Thailand (Siam) are found dated by three different eras. The most predominant is the Buddhist era (BE), which originated in 543 BC. Next is the Bangkok or Ratanakosindsok (RS) era, dating from 1781 AD; followed by the Chula-Sakarat (CS) era, dating from 638 AD. The latter era originated in Burma and is used on that country's coins.

Other calendars include that of the Ethiopian era (EE), which commenced seven years, eight months after AD dating; and that of the Jewish people, which commenced on Oct. 7, 3761 BC. Korea claims a legendary dating from 2333 BC, which is acknowledged in some of its coin dating. Some coin issues of the Indonesian area carry dates determined by the Javanese Aji Saka era (AS), a calendar of 354 days (100 Javanese years equal 97 Christian or Gregorian calendar years), which can be matched to AD dating by comparing it to AH dating.

The following table indicates the year dating for the various eras, which correspond to 2007 in Christian calendar reckoning, but it must be remembered that there are overlaps between the eras in some instances.

Christian era (AD)	2007
Muslim era (AH)	AH1429
Solar year (SH)	SH1385
Monarchic Solar era (MS)	MS2566
Vikrama Samvat (VS)	S2064
Saka era (SE)	SE1929
Buddhist era (BE)	BE2550
Bangkok era (RS)	RS226
Chula-Sakarat era (CS)	CS1369
Ethiopian era (EE	EE2001
Korean era	4340
Javanese Aji Saka era (AS)	AS1940
Fasli era (FE)	FE1417
Jewish era (JE)	JE5767

Coins of Asian origin - principally Japan, Korea, China, Turkestan and Tibet and some modern gold issues of Turkey - are generally dated to the year of the government, dynasty, reign or cyclic eras, with the dates indicated in Asian characters which usually read from right to left. In recent years, however, some dating has been according to the Christian calendar and in Western numerals. In Japan, Asian character dating was reversed to read from left to right in Showa year 23 (1948 AD).

More detailed guides to less prevalent coin dating systems, which are strictly local in nature, are presented with the appropriate listings.

Some coins carry dates according to both locally observed and Christian eras. This is particularly true in the Arabic world, where the Hejira date may be indicated in Arabic numerals and the Christian date in Western numerals, or both dates in either form.

The date actually carried on a given coin is generally cataloged here in the first column (Date) to the right of the catalog number. If this date is by a non-Christian dating system, such as 'AH'(Muslim), the Christian equivalent date will appear in parentheses(), for example AH1336(1917). Dates listed alone in the date column which do not actually appear on a given coin, or dates which are known, but do not appear on the coin, are generally enclosed by parentheses with 'ND' at the left, for example ND(1926).

Timing differentials between some era of reckoning, particularly the 354-day Mohammedan and 365-day Christian years, cause situations whereby coins which carry dates for both eras exist bearing two year dates from one calendar combined with a single date from another.

Countermarked Coinage is presented with both 'Countermark Date' and 'Host Coin' date for each type. Actual date representation follows the rules outlined above.

NUMBERING SYSTEM

Some catalog numbers assigned in this volume are based on established references. This practice has been observed for two reasons: First, when world coins are listed chronologically they are basically self-cataloging; second, there was no need to confuse collectors with totally new numeric designations where appropriate systems already existed. As time progressed we found many of these established systems incomplete and inadequate and have now replaced many with new KM numbers. When numbers change appropriate cross-referencing has been provided.

Some of the coins listed in this catalog are identified or cross-referenced by numbers assigned by R.S. Yeoman (Y#), or slight adaptations thereof, in his Modern World Coins, and Current Coins of the World. For the pre-Yeoman dated issues, the numbers assigned by William D. Craig (C#) in his Coins of the World (1750-1850 period), 3rd edition, have generally been applied.

In some countries, listings are cross-referenced to Robert Friedberg's (FR#) Gold Coins of the World or Coins of the British World. Major Fred Pridmore's (P#) studies of British colonial coinage are also referenced, as are W.H. Valentine's (V#) references on the Modern Copper Coins of the Muhammadan States. Coins issued under the Chinese sphere of influence are assigned numbers from E. Kann's (K#) Illustrated Catalog of Chinese Coins and T.K. Hsu's (Su) work of similar title. In most cases, these cross-reference numbers are presented in the descriptive text for each type.

DENOMINATIONS

The second basic consideration to be met in the attribution of a coin is the determination of denomination. Since denominations are usually expressed in numeric, rather than word form on a coin, this is usually quite easily accomplished on coins from nations, which use Western numerals, except in those instances where issues are devoid of any mention of face value, and denomination must be attributed by size, metallic composition or weight. Coins listed in this volume are generally illustrated in actual size. Where size is critical to proper attribution, the coin's millimeter size is indicated.

The sphere of countries stretching from North Africa through the Orient, on which numeric symbols generally unfamiliar to Westerners are employed, often provide the collector with a much greater challenge. This is particularly true on nearly all pre-20th Century issues. On some of the more modern issues and increasingly so as the years progress, Western-style numerals usually presented in combination with the local numeric system are becoming more commonplace on these coins.

Determination of a coin's currency system can also be valuable in attributing the issue to its country of origin. A comprehensive alphabetical index of currency names, applicable to the countries as cataloged in this volume, with all individual nations of use for each, is presented in this section.

The included table of Standard International Numeral Systems presents charts of the basic numeric designations found on coins of non-Western origin. Although denomination numerals are generally prominently displayed on coins, it must be remembered that these are general representations of characters, which individual coin engravers may have rendered in widely varying styles. Where numeric or script denominations designation forms peculiar to a given coin or country apply, such as the script used on some Persian (Iranian) issues. They are so indicated or illustrated in conjunction with the appropriate listings.

MINTAGES

Quantities minted of each date are indicated where that information is available. On quantities of a few thousand or less, actual mintages are generally indicated. For combined mintage figures the abbreviation "Inc. Above" means Included Above, while "Inc. Below" means Included Below. "Est." beside a mintage figure indicates the number given is an estimate or mintage limit.

MINT AND PRIVY MARKS

The presence of distinctive, but frequently inconspicuously placed, mintmarks indicates the mint of issue for many of the coins listed in this catalog. An appropriate designation in the date listings notes the presence, if any, of a mint mark on a particular coin type by incorporating the letter or letters of the mint mark adjoining the date, i.e., 1950D or 1927R.

The presence of mint and/or mintmaster's privy marks on a coin in non-letter form is indicated by incorporating the mint letter in lower case within parentheses adjoining the date; i.e. 1927(a). The corresponding mark is illustrated or identified in the introduction of the country.

In countries such as France and Mexico, where many mints may be producing like coinage in the same denomination during the same time period, divisions by mint have been employed. In these cases the mint mark may appear next to the individual date listings and/or the mint name or mint mark may be listed in the Note field of the type description.

Where listings incorporate mintmaster initials, they are always presented in capital letters separated from the date by one character space; i.e., 1850 MF. The different mintmark and mintmaster letters found on the coins of any country, state or city of issue are always shown at the beginning of listings.

METALS

Each numbered type listing will contain a description of the coins metallic content. The traditional coinage metals and their symbolic chemical abbreviations sometimes used in this catalog are:

Gold - (Au)   Platinum - (Pt)   Palladium – (Pd)

During the 18th and 19th centuries, most of the world's coins were struck of copper or bronze, silver and gold. Commencing in the early years of the 20th century, however, numerous new coinage metals, primarily non-precious metal alloys, were introduced. Gold has not been widely used for circulation coinages since World War I, although silver remained a popular coinage metal in most parts of the world until after World War II. With the disappearance of silver for circulation coinage, numerous additional compositions were introduced to coinage applications.

Most recent is the development of clad or plated planchets in order to maintain circulation life and extend the life of a set of production dies as used in the production of the copper-nickel clad copper 50 centesimos of Panama or in the latter case to reduce production costs of the planchets and yet provide a coin quite similar in appearance to its predecessor as in the case of the copper plated zinc core United States 1983 cent.

Modern commemorative coins have employed still more unusual methods such as bimetallic coins, color applications and precious metal or gem inlays.

OFF-METAL STRIKES

Off-metal strikes previously designated by "(OMS)" which also included the wide range of error coinage struck in other than their officially authorized compositions have been incorporated into Pattern listings along with special issues, which were struck for presentation or other reasons.

Collectors of Germanic coinage may be familiar with the term "Abschlag" which quickly identifies similar types of coinage.

PRECIOUS METAL WEIGHTS

Listings of weight, fineness and actual gold (AGW), platinum or palladium (APW) content of most machine-struck gold, platinum and palladium coins are provided in this edition. This information will be found incorporated in each separate type listing, along with other data related to the coin.

The ASW, AGW and APW figures were determined by multiplying the gross weight of a given coin by its known or tested fineness and converting the resulting gram or grain weight to troy ounces, rounded to the nearest ten-thousandth of an ounce. A gold coin with a 24.25-gram weight and .875 fineness for example, would have a fine weight of approximately 21.2188 grams, or a .6822 AGW, a factor that can be used to accurately determine the intrinsic value for multiple examples.

The AGW or APW figure can be multiplied by the spot price of each precious metal to determine the current intrinsic value of any coin accompanied by these designations.

Coin weights are indicated in grams (abbreviated "g") along with fineness where the information is of value in differentiating between types. These weights are based on 31.103 grams per troy (scientific) ounce, as opposed to the avoirdupois (commercial) standard of 28.35 grams. Actual coin weights are generally shown in hundredths or thousands of a gram; i.e., 0.910 GOLD 5.589g.

WEIGHTS AND FINENESSES

As the silver and gold bullion markets have advanced and declined sharply in recent years, the fineness and total precious metal content of coins has become especially significant where bullion coins - issues which trade on the basis of their intrinsic metallic content rather than numismatic value - are concerned. In many instances, such issues have become worth more in bullion form than their nominal collector values or denominations indicate.

Establishing the weight of a coin can also be valuable for determining its denomination. Actual weight is also necessary to ascertain the specific gravity of the coin's metallic content, an important factor in determining authenticity.

TROY WEIGHT STANDARDS

24 Grains = 1 Pennyweight
480 Grains = 1 Ounce
31.103 Grams = 1 Ounce

UNIFORM WEIGHTS

15.432 Grains = 1 Gram
0.0648 Gram = 1 Grain

AVOIRDUPOIS STANDARDS

27-11/32 Grains = 11 Dram
437-1/2 Grains = 1 Ounce
28.350 Grams = 1 Ounce

BULLION VALUE CHARTS

Universal gold and platinum bullion value charts are provided for use in combination with the AGW and APW factors to determine approximate intrinsic values of listed coins. By adding the component weights as shown in troy ounces on each chart, the approximate intrinsic value of any gold and platinum coin's precious metal content can be determined.

Again referring to the examples presented in the above section, the intrinsic value of a gold coin with a .6822 AGW would be indicated as $286.44 + based on the application of the gold bullion chart. This result is obtained by moving across the top to the $650.00 column, then moving down to the line indicated .680 in the far left hand corner which reveals a bullion value of $442.00. To determine the value of the remaining .0022 of AGW, return up the same column to the .002 line, the closest factor available, where a $ 1.30 value is indicted. The two factors total $443.30, which would be slightly less than actual value.

The gold bullion chart is arranged in $10 increments from $500 to $900. The platinum bullion chart is arranged in $10 increments from $1000 to $1400. Though a similar chart for Palladium is not present, a similar formula can be applied.

Valuations for most of the gold, platinum and palladium coins listed in this edition are based on assumed market value ranges of $650-$670 per troy ounce for gold, $1150-$1350 for platinum, and $330-$350 for palladium. To arrive at accurate current market indications for these issues, increase or decrease the valuations appropriately based on any variations in these indicated levels.

HOMELAND TYPES

Homeland types are coins which colonial powers used in a colony, but do not bear that location's name. In some cases they were legal tender in the homeland, in others not. They are listed under the homeland and cross-referenced at the colony listing.

COUNTERMARKS/COUNTERSTAMPS

There is some confusion among collectors over the terms "countermark" and "counterstamp" when applied to a coin bearing an additional mark or change of design and/or denomination.

To clarify, a countermark might be considered similar to

the "hall mark" applied to a piece of silverware, by which a silversmith assured the quality of the piece. In the same way, a countermark assures the quality of the coin on which it is placed, as, for example, when the royal crown of England was countermarked (punched into) on segmented Spanish reales, allowing them to circulate in commerce in the British West Indies. An additional countermark indicating the new denomination may also be encountered on these coins.

Countermarks are generally applied singularly and in most cases indiscriminately on either side of the "host" coin.

Counterstamped coins are more extensively altered. The counterstamping is done with a set of dies, rather than a hand punch. The coin being counterstamped is placed between the new dies and struck as if it were a blank planchet as found with the Manila 8 reales issue of the Philippines. A more unusual application where the counterstamp dies were smaller than the host coin in the revalidated 50 centimos and 1 colon of Costa Rica issued in 1923.

PHOTOGRAPHS

To assist the reader in coin identification, every effort has been made to present actual size photographs of every coinage type listed. Obverse and reverse are illustrated, except when a change in design is restricted to one side, and the coin has a diameter of 39mm or larger, in which case only the side required for identification of the type is generally illustrated. All coins up to 60mm are illustrated actual size, to the nearest 1/2mm up to 25mm, and to the nearest 1mm thereafter. Coins larger than 60mm diameter are illustrated in reduced size, with the actual size noted in the descriptive text block. Where slight change in size is important to coin type identification, actual millimeter measurements are stated.

TRADE COINS

From approximately 1750-1940, a number of nations, particularly European colonial powers and commercial traders, minted trade coins to facilitate commerce with the local populace of Africa, the Arab countries, the Indian subcontinental, Southeast Asia and the Far East. Such coins generally circulated at a value based on the weight and fineness of their silver or gold content, rather than their stated denomination. Examples include the sovereigns of Great Britain and the gold ducat issues of Austria, Hungary and the Netherlands. Trade coinage will sometimes be found listed at the end of the domestic issues.

VALUATIONS

Values quoted in this catalog represent the current market and are compiled from recommendations provided and verified through various source documents and specialized consultants. It should be stressed, however, that this book is intended to serve only as an aid for evaluating coins, actual market conditions are constantly changing and additional influences, such as particularly strong local demand for certain coin series, fluctuation of international exchange rates and worldwide collection patterns must also be considered. Publication of this catalog is not intended as a solicitation by the publisher, editors or contributors to buy or sell the coins listed at the prices indicated.

All valuations are stated in U.S. dollars, based on careful assessment of the varied international collector market. Valuations for coins priced below $100.00 are generally stated in full amounts - i.e. 37.50 or 95.00 - while valuations at or above that figure are rounded off in even dollars - i.e. $125.00 is expressed 125. A comma is added to indicate thousands of dollars in value.

For the convenience of overseas collectors and for U.S. collectors doing business with overseas dealers, the base exchange rate for the national currencies of approximately 180 countries are presented in the Foreign Exchange Table.

It should be noted that when particularly select uncirculated or proof-like examples of uncirculated coins become available they can be expected to command proportionately high premiums. Such examples in reference to choice Germanic Thalers are referred to as "erst schlage" or first strikes.

TOKEN COINAGE

At times local economic conditions have forced regular coinage from circulation or found mints unable to cope with the demand for coinage, giving rise to privately issued token coinage substitutes. British tokens of the early 1880s and the German and French and French Colonial emergency emissions of the World War I era are examples of such tokens being freely accepted in monetary transactions over wide areas. Tokens were likewise introduced to satisfy specific restricted needs, such as the leper colony issues of Brazil, Colombia and the Philippines.

This catalog includes introductory or detailed listings with "Tn" prefixes of many token coinage issues, particularly those which enjoyed wide circulation and where the series was limited in diversity. More complex series, and those more restricted in scope of circulation are generally not listed, although a representative sample may be illustrated and a specialty reference provided.

MEDALLIC ISSUES

Medallic issues are segregated following the regular issue listings. Grouped there are coin-type issues, which can generally be identified as commemoratives produced to the country's established coinage standards but without the usual indicator of denomination. These pieces may or may not feature designs adapted from the country's regular issue or commemorative coinage, and may or may not have been issued in conjunction with related coinage issues.

RESTRIKES, COUNTERFEITS

Deceptive restrike and counterfeit (both contemporary and modern) examples exist of some coin issues. Where possible, the existence of restrikes is noted. Warnings are also incorporated in instances where particularly deceptive counterfeits are known to exist. Collectors who are uncertain about the authenticity of a coin held in their collection, or being offered for sale, should take the precaution of having it authenticated by the American Numismatic Association Authentication Bureau, 818 N. Cascade, Colorado Springs, CO 80903. Their reasonably priced certification tests are widely accepted by collectors and dealers alike.

NON-CIRCULATING LEGAL TENDER COINS

Coins of non-circulating legal tender (NCLT) origin are individually listed and integrated by denomination into the regular listings for each country. These coins fall outside the customary definitions of coin-of-the- realm issues, but where created and sold by, or under authorization of, agencies of sovereign governments expressly for collectors. These are primarily individual coins and sets of a commemorative nature, marketed at prices substantially in excess of face value, and usually do not have counterparts released for circulation.

EDGE VARIETIES

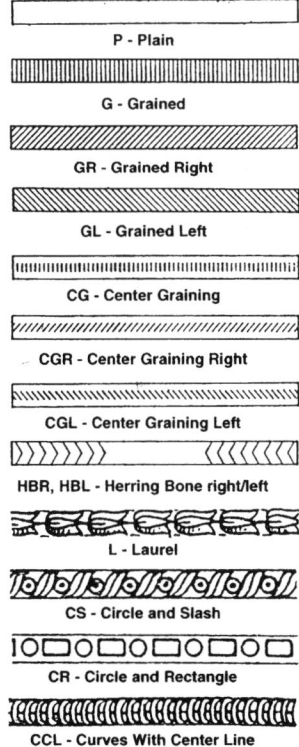

NEW ISSUES

All newly released coins that have been physically observed by our staff and those that have been confirmed by press time have been incorporated in this edition. Exceptions exist in some countries where current date coin production lags far behind and other countries whose fiscal year actually begins in the latter half of the current year.

Collectors and dealers alike are kept up to date with worldwide new issues having newly assigned catalog reference numbers in the monthly feature "World Coin Roundup" in World Coin News. A free sample copy will be sent upon request. Overseas requests should include 1 international postal reply coupon for surface mail or 2 international postal reply coupons for air mail dispatch: Write to World Coin News, 700 East State St., Iola, WI 54990 USA.

SETS

Listings in this catalog for specimen, proof and mint sets are for official, government-produced sets. In many instances privately packaged sets also exist.

Mint Sets/Fleur de Coin Sets: Specially prepared by worldwide mints to provide banks, collectors and government dignitaries with examples of current coinage. Usually subjected to rigorous inspection to insure that top quality specimens of selected business strikes are provided. One of the most popular mint set is that given out by the monarch of Great Britain each year on Maunday Thursday. This set contains four special coins in denominations of 1, 2, 3 and 4 pence, struck in silver and contained in a little pouch. They have been given away in a special ceremony for the poor for more than two centuries.

The Paris Mint introduced polyvinyl plastic cases packed within a cardboard box for homeland and colonial Fleur de Coin sets of the 1960s. British colonial sets were issued in velvet-lined metal cases similar to those used for proof sets. For its client nations, the Franklin Mint introduced a sealed composition of cardboard and specially molded hard clear plastic protective container inserted in a soft plastic wallet. Recent discovery that soft polyvinyl packaging has proved hazardous to coins has resulted in a change to the use of hard, inert plastics for virtually all mint sets.

Some of the highest quality mint sets ever produced were those struck by the Franklin Mint during 1972-74. In many cases matte finish dies were used to strike a polished proof planchet. Later on, from 1975, sets contained highly polished, glassy-looking coins (similar to those struck by the Bombay Mint) for collectors over a period of 12 years.

Specimen Sets: Forerunners of today's proof sets. In most cases the coins were specially struck, perhaps even double struck, to produce a very soft or matte finish on the effigies and fields, along with high, sharp, "wire" rims. The finish is rather dull to the naked eye.

The original purpose of these sets was to provide VIPs, monarchs and mintmasters around the world with samples of the highest quality workmanship of a particular mint. These were usually housed in elaborate velvet-lined leather and metal cases.

Proof-like Sets are relatively new to the field of numismatics. During the mid 1950s the Royal Canadian Mint furnished the hobby with specially selected early business strike coins that exhibited some qualities similar to proof coinage. However, the "proof-like" fields are generally flawed and the edges are rounded. These pieces are not double struck. These are commonly encountered in cardboard holders, later in soft plastic or pliofilm packaging. Of late, the Royal Canadian Mint packages such sets in rigid plastic cases.

Many worldwide officially issued proof sets would in reality fall into this category upon careful examination of the quality of the coin's finish.

Another term encountered in this category is "Special Select," used to describe the crowns of the Union of South

Africa and 100-schilling coins produced for collectors in the late 1970s by the Austrian Mint.

Proof Sets: This is undoubtedly among the most misused terms in the hobby, not only by collectors and dealers, but also by many of the world mints.

A true proof set must be at least double-struck on specially prepared polished planchets and struck using dies (often themselves polished) of the highest quality.

Modern-day proof quality consists of frosted effigies surrounded by absolute mirror-like fields.

Listings for proof sets in this catalog are for officially issued proof sets so designated by the issuing authority, and may or may not possess what are considered modern proof quality standards.

It is necessary for collectors to acquire the knowledge to allow them to differentiate true proof sets from would-be proof sets and proof-like sets which may be encountered.

CONDITIONS/GRADING

Wherever possible, coin valuations are given in four or five grades of preservation. For modern commemoratives, which do not circulate, only uncirculated values are usually sufficient. Proof issues are indicated by the word "Proof" next to the date, with valuation proceeded by the word "value" following the mintage. For very recent circulating coins and coins of limited value, one, two or three grade values are presented.

There are almost no grading guides for world coins. What follows is an attempt to help bridge that gap until a detailed, illustrated guide becomes available.

In grading world coins, there are two elements to look for: 1) Overall wear, and 2) loss of design details, such as strands of hair, feathers on eagles, designs on coats of arms, etc.

The age, rarity or type of a coin should not be a consideration in grading.

Grade each coin by the weaker of the two sides. This method appears to give results most nearly consistent with conservative American Numismatic Association standards for U.S. coins. Split grades, i.e., F/VF for obverse and reverse, respectively, are normally no more than one grade apart. If the two sides are more than one grade apart, the series of coins probably wears differently on each side and should then be graded by the weaker side alone.

Grade by the amount of overall wear and loss of design detail evident on each side of the coin. On coins with a moderately small design element, which is prone to early wear, grade by that design alone. For example, the 5-ore (KM#554) of Sweden has a crown above the monogram on which the beads on the arches show wear most clearly. So, grade by the crown alone.

For **Brilliant Uncirculated** (BU) grades there will be no visible signs of wear or handling, even under a 30-power microscope. Full mint luster will be present. Ideally no bags marks will be evident.

For **Uncirculated** (Unc.) grades there will be no visible signs of wear or handling, even under a 30-power microscope. Bag marks may be present.

For **Almost Uncirculated** (AU), all detail will be visible. There will be wear only on the highest point of the coin. There will often be half or more of the original mint luster present.

On the **Extremely Fine** (XF or EF) coin, there will be about 95% of the original detail visible. Or, on a coin with a design with no inner detail to wear down, there will be a light wear over nearly all the coin. If a small design is used as the grading area, about 90% of the original detail will be visible. This latter rule stems from the logic that a smaller amount of detail needs to be present because a small area is being used to grade the whole coin.

The **Very Fine** (VF) coin will have about 75% of the original detail visible. Or, on a coin with no inner detail, there will be moderate wear over the entire coin. Corners of letters and numbers may be weak. A small grading area will have about 66% of the original detail.

For **Fine** (F), there will be about 50% of the original detail visible. Or, on a coin with no inner detail, there will be fairly heavy wear over all of the coin. Sides of letters will be weak. A typically uncleaned coin will often appear as dirty or dull. A small grading area will have just under 50% of the original detail.

On the **Very Good** (VG) coin, there will be about 25% of the original detail visible. There will be heavy wear on all of the coin.

The **Good** (G) coin's design will be clearly outlined but with substantial wear. Some of the larger detail may be visible. The rim may have a few weak spots of wear.

On the **About Good** (AG) coin, there will typically be only a silhouette of a large design. The rim will be worn down into the letters if any.

Strong or weak strikes, partially weak strikes, damage, corrosion, attractive or unattractive toning, dipping or cleaning should be described along with the above grades. These factors affect the quality of the coin just as do wear and loss of detail, but are easier to describe.

In the case of countermarked/counterstamped coins, the condition of the host coin will have a bearing on the end valuation. The important factor in determining the grade is the condition, clarity and completeness of the countermark itself. This is in reference to countermarks/counterstamps having raised design while being struck in a depression.

Incuse countermarks cannot be graded for wear. They are graded by the clarity and completeness including the condition of the host coin which will also have more bearing on the final grade/valuation determined.

The World is Coming to the ......
33rd Annual
Chicago International Coin Fair

Thursday-Friday-Saturday-Sunday
April 24-27, 2008

(Professional Preview
Thursday, April 24 • 2 p.m.-6 p.m.)

Crowne Plaza Chicago O'Hare
5440 North River Road, Rosemont, Illinois

Hotel Reservations:
Call the Crowne Plaza Chicago O'Hare at (847) 671-6350 and ask for the $112 Chicago International Coin Fair rate. Book early. Space is limited.

- **90 Dealer Bourse Area**
- **Society Meetings**
- **Ponterio and Associates Auction**
- **Educational Programs**
- **Complimentary Airport Shuttle**

For more information
on this show,
go to our Web site:
www.cicfshow.com

Show Hours:
Thursday, April 24   2 pm-6 pm   Saturday, April 26   10 am-6 pm
(Professional Preview — $50)   Sunday, April 27   10 am-1 pm
Friday, April 25   10 am-6 pm

**A Two-Day Pass Valid Friday and Saturday is $5.00.
Free admission Sunday only.
Children 16 and younger are free.**

Bourse Information:
Kevin Foley – CICF Chairman
P.O. Box 573 – Milwaukee, WI 53201
(414) 421-3484 – FAX: (414) 423-0343
E-mail: kfoley2@wi.rr.com

The Chicago International Coin Fair is sponsored by **F+W**, the world's largest publisher of hobby-related publications, including *World Coin News* and the *Standard Catalog of World Coins*.

GOLD BULLION VALUE CHART

Oz.	500.00	510.00	520.00	530.00	540.00	550.00	560.00	570.00	580.00	590.00	600.00	610.00	620.00	630.00	640.00	650.00	660.00	670.00	680.00	690.00
0.001	0.50	0.51	0.52	0.53	0.54	0.55	0.56	0.57	0.58	0.59	0.60	0.61	0.62	0.63	0.64	0.65	0.66	0.67	0.68	0.69
0.002	1.00	1.02	1.04	1.06	1.08	1.10	1.12	1.14	1.16	1.18	1.20	1.22	1.24	1.26	1.28	1.30	1.32	1.34	1.36	1.38
0.003	1.50	1.53	1.56	1.59	1.62	1.65	1.68	1.71	1.74	1.77	1.80	1.83	1.86	1.89	1.92	1.95	1.98	2.01	2.04	2.07
0.004	2.00	2.04	2.08	2.12	2.16	2.20	2.24	2.28	2.32	2.36	2.40	2.44	2.48	2.52	2.56	2.60	2.64	2.68	2.72	2.76
0.005	2.50	2.55	2.60	2.65	2.70	2.75	2.80	2.85	2.90	2.95	3.00	3.05	3.10	3.15	3.20	3.25	3.30	3.35	3.40	3.45
0.006	3.00	3.06	3.12	3.18	3.24	3.30	3.36	3.42	3.48	3.54	3.60	3.66	3.72	3.78	3.84	3.90	3.96	4.02	4.08	4.14
0.007	3.50	3.57	3.64	3.71	3.78	3.85	3.92	3.99	4.06	4.13	4.20	4.27	4.34	4.41	4.48	4.55	4.62	4.69	4.76	4.83
0.008	4.00	4.08	4.16	4.24	4.32	4.40	4.48	4.56	4.64	4.72	4.80	4.88	4.96	5.04	5.12	5.20	5.28	5.36	5.44	5.52
0.009	4.50	4.59	4.68	4.77	4.86	4.95	5.04	5.13	5.22	5.31	5.40	5.49	5.58	5.67	5.76	5.85	5.94	6.03	6.12	6.21
0.010	5.00	5.10	5.20	5.30	5.40	5.50	5.60	5.70	5.80	5.90	6.00	6.10	6.20	6.30	6.40	6.50	6.60	6.70	6.80	6.90
0.020	10.00	10.20	10.40	10.60	10.80	11.00	11.20	11.40	11.60	11.80	12.00	12.20	12.40	12.60	12.80	13.00	13.20	13.40	13.60	13.80
0.030	15.00	15.30	15.60	15.90	16.20	16.50	16.80	17.10	17.40	17.70	18.00	18.30	18.60	18.90	19.20	19.50	19.80	20.10	20.40	20.70
0.040	20.00	20.40	20.80	21.20	21.60	22.00	22.40	22.80	23.20	23.60	24.00	24.40	24.80	25.20	25.60	26.00	26.40	26.80	27.20	27.60
0.050	25.00	25.50	26.00	26.50	27.00	27.50	28.00	28.50	29.00	29.50	30.00	30.50	31.00	31.50	32.00	32.50	33.00	33.50	34.00	34.50
0.060	30.00	30.60	31.20	31.80	32.40	33.00	33.60	34.20	34.80	35.40	36.00	36.60	37.20	37.80	38.40	39.00	39.60	40.20	40.80	41.40
0.070	35.00	35.70	36.40	37.10	37.80	38.50	39.20	39.90	40.60	41.30	42.00	42.70	43.40	44.10	44.80	45.50	46.20	46.90	47.60	48.30
0.080	40.00	40.80	41.60	42.40	43.20	44.00	44.80	45.60	46.40	47.20	48.00	48.80	49.60	50.40	51.20	52.00	52.80	53.60	54.40	55.20
0.090	45.00	45.90	46.80	47.70	48.60	49.50	50.40	51.30	52.20	53.10	54.00	54.90	55.80	56.70	57.60	58.50	59.40	60.30	61.20	62.10
0.100	50.00	51.00	52.00	53.00	54.00	55.00	56.00	57.00	58.00	59.00	60.00	61.00	62.00	63.00	64.00	65.00	66.00	67.00	68.00	69.00
0.110	55.00	56.10	57.20	58.30	59.40	60.50	61.60	62.70	63.80	64.90	66.00	67.10	68.20	69.30	70.40	71.50	72.60	73.70	74.80	75.90
0.120	60.00	61.20	62.40	63.60	64.80	66.00	67.20	68.40	69.60	70.80	72.00	73.20	74.40	75.60	76.80	78.00	79.20	80.40	81.60	82.80
0.130	65.00	66.30	67.60	68.90	70.20	71.50	72.80	74.10	75.40	76.70	78.00	79.30	80.60	81.90	83.20	84.50	85.80	87.10	88.40	89.70
0.140	70.00	71.40	72.80	74.20	75.60	77.00	78.40	79.80	81.20	82.60	84.00	85.40	86.80	88.20	89.60	91.00	92.40	93.80	95.20	96.60
0.150	75.00	76.50	78.00	79.50	81.00	82.50	84.00	85.50	87.00	88.50	90.00	91.50	93.00	94.50	96.00	97.50	99.00	100.50	102.00	103.50
0.160	80.00	81.60	83.20	84.80	86.40	88.00	89.60	91.20	92.80	94.40	96.00	97.60	99.20	100.80	102.40	104.00	105.60	107.20	108.80	110.40
0.170	85.00	86.70	88.40	90.10	91.80	93.50	95.20	96.90	98.60	100.30	102.00	103.70	105.40	107.10	108.80	110.50	112.20	113.90	115.60	117.30
0.180	90.00	91.80	93.60	95.40	97.20	99.00	100.80	102.60	104.40	106.20	108.00	109.80	111.60	113.40	115.20	117.00	118.80	120.60	122.40	124.20
0.190	95.00	96.90	98.80	100.70	102.60	104.50	106.40	108.30	110.20	112.10	114.00	115.90	117.80	119.70	121.60	123.50	125.40	127.30	129.20	131.10
0.200	100.00	102.00	104.00	106.00	108.00	110.00	112.00	114.00	116.00	118.00	120.00	122.00	124.00	126.00	128.00	130.00	132.00	134.00	136.00	138.00
0.210	105.00	107.10	109.20	111.30	113.40	115.50	117.60	119.70	121.80	123.90	126.00	128.10	130.20	132.30	134.40	136.50	138.60	140.70	142.80	144.90
0.220	110.00	112.20	114.40	116.60	118.80	121.00	123.20	125.40	127.60	129.80	132.00	134.20	136.40	138.60	140.80	143.00	145.20	147.40	149.60	151.80
0.230	115.00	117.30	119.60	121.90	124.20	126.50	128.80	131.10	133.40	135.70	138.00	140.30	142.60	144.90	147.20	149.50	151.80	154.10	156.40	158.70
0.240	120.00	122.40	124.80	127.20	129.60	132.00	134.40	136.80	139.20	141.60	144.00	146.40	148.80	151.20	153.60	156.00	158.40	160.80	163.20	165.60
0.250	125.00	127.50	130.00	132.50	135.00	137.50	140.00	142.50	145.00	147.50	150.00	152.50	155.00	157.50	160.00	162.50	165.00	167.50	170.00	172.50
0.260	130.00	132.60	135.20	137.80	140.40	143.00	145.60	148.20	150.80	153.40	156.00	158.60	161.20	163.80	166.40	169.00	171.60	174.20	176.80	179.40
0.270	135.00	137.70	140.40	143.10	145.80	148.50	151.20	153.90	156.60	159.30	162.00	164.70	167.40	170.10	172.80	175.50	178.20	180.90	183.60	186.30
0.280	140.00	142.80	145.60	148.40	151.20	154.00	156.80	159.60	162.40	165.20	168.00	170.80	173.60	176.40	179.20	182.00	184.80	187.60	190.40	193.20
0.290	145.00	147.90	150.80	153.70	156.60	159.50	162.40	165.30	168.20	171.10	174.00	176.90	179.80	182.70	185.60	188.50	191.40	194.30	197.20	200.10
0.300	150.00	153.00	156.00	159.00	162.00	165.00	168.00	171.00	174.00	177.00	180.00	183.00	186.00	189.00	192.00	195.00	198.00	201.00	204.00	207.00
0.310	155.00	158.10	161.20	164.30	167.40	170.50	173.60	176.70	179.80	182.90	186.00	189.10	192.20	195.30	198.40	201.50	204.60	207.70	210.80	213.90
0.320	160.00	163.20	166.40	169.60	172.80	176.00	179.20	182.40	185.60	188.80	192.00	195.20	198.40	201.60	204.80	208.00	211.20	214.40	217.60	220.80
0.330	165.00	168.30	171.60	174.90	178.20	181.50	184.80	188.10	191.40	194.70	198.00	201.30	204.60	207.90	211.20	214.50	217.80	221.10	224.40	227.70
0.340	170.00	173.40	176.80	180.20	183.60	187.00	190.40	193.80	197.20	200.60	204.00	207.40	210.80	214.20	217.60	221.00	224.40	227.80	231.20	234.60
0.350	175.00	178.50	182.00	185.50	189.00	192.50	196.00	199.50	203.00	206.50	210.00	213.50	217.00	220.50	224.00	227.50	231.00	234.50	238.00	241.50
0.360	180.00	183.60	187.20	190.80	194.40	198.00	201.60	205.20	208.80	212.40	216.00	219.60	223.20	226.80	230.40	234.00	237.60	241.20	244.80	248.40
0.370	185.00	188.70	192.40	196.10	199.80	203.50	207.20	210.90	214.60	218.30	222.00	225.70	229.40	233.10	236.80	240.50	244.20	247.90	251.60	255.30
0.380	190.00	193.80	197.60	201.40	205.20	209.00	212.80	216.60	220.40	224.20	228.00	231.80	235.60	239.40	243.20	247.00	250.80	254.60	258.40	262.20
0.390	195.00	198.90	202.80	206.70	210.60	214.50	218.40	222.30	226.20	230.10	234.00	237.90	241.80	245.70	249.60	253.50	257.40	261.30	265.20	269.10
0.400	200.00	204.00	208.00	212.00	216.00	220.00	224.00	228.00	232.00	236.00	240.00	244.00	248.00	252.00	256.00	260.00	264.00	268.00	272.00	276.00
0.410	205.00	209.10	213.20	217.30	221.40	225.50	229.60	233.70	237.80	241.90	246.00	250.10	254.20	258.30	262.40	266.50	270.60	274.70	278.80	282.90
0.420	210.00	214.20	218.40	222.60	226.80	231.00	235.20	239.40	243.60	247.80	252.00	256.20	260.40	264.60	268.80	273.00	277.20	281.40	285.60	289.80
0.430	215.00	219.30	223.60	227.90	232.20	236.50	240.80	245.10	249.40	253.70	258.00	262.30	266.60	270.90	275.20	279.50	283.80	288.10	292.40	296.70
0.440	220.00	224.40	228.80	233.20	237.60	242.00	246.40	250.80	255.20	259.60	264.00	268.40	272.80	277.20	281.60	286.00	290.40	294.80	299.20	303.60
0.450	225.00	229.50	234.00	238.50	243.00	247.50	252.00	256.50	261.00	265.50	270.00	274.50	279.00	283.50	288.00	292.50	297.00	301.50	306.00	310.50
0.460	230.00	234.60	239.20	243.80	248.40	253.00	257.60	262.20	266.80	271.40	276.00	280.60	285.20	289.80	294.40	299.00	303.60	308.20	312.80	317.40

GOLD BULLION VALUE CHART

Oz.	500.00	510.00	520.00	530.00	540.00	550.00	560.00	570.00	580.00	590.00	600.00	610.00	620.00	630.00	640.00	650.00	660.00	670.00	680.00	690.00
0.470	235.00	239.70	244.40	249.10	253.80	258.50	263.20	267.90	272.60	277.30	282.00	286.70	291.40	296.10	300.80	305.50	310.20	314.90	319.60	324.30
0.480	240.00	244.80	249.60	254.40	259.20	264.00	268.80	273.60	278.40	283.20	288.00	292.80	297.60	302.40	307.20	312.00	316.80	321.60	326.40	331.20
0.490	245.00	249.90	254.80	259.70	264.60	269.50	274.40	279.30	284.20	289.10	294.00	298.90	303.80	308.70	313.60	318.50	323.40	328.30	333.20	338.10
0.500	250.00	255.00	260.00	265.00	270.00	275.00	280.00	285.00	290.00	295.00	300.00	305.00	310.00	315.00	320.00	325.00	330.00	335.00	340.00	345.00
0.510	255.00	260.10	265.20	270.30	275.40	280.50	285.60	290.70	295.80	300.90	306.00	311.10	316.20	321.30	326.40	331.50	336.60	341.70	346.80	351.90
0.520	260.00	265.20	270.40	275.60	280.80	286.00	291.20	296.40	301.60	306.80	312.00	317.20	322.40	327.60	332.80	338.00	343.20	348.40	353.60	358.80
0.530	265.00	270.30	275.60	280.90	286.20	291.50	296.80	302.10	307.40	312.70	318.00	323.30	328.60	333.90	339.20	344.50	349.80	355.10	360.40	365.70
0.540	270.00	275.40	280.80	286.20	291.60	297.00	302.40	307.80	313.20	318.60	324.00	329.40	334.80	340.20	345.60	351.00	356.40	361.80	367.20	372.60
0.550	275.00	280.50	286.00	291.50	297.00	302.50	308.00	313.50	319.00	324.50	330.00	335.50	341.00	346.50	352.00	357.50	363.00	368.50	374.00	379.50
0.560	280.00	285.60	291.20	296.80	302.40	308.00	313.60	319.20	324.80	330.40	336.00	341.60	347.20	352.80	358.40	364.00	369.60	375.20	380.80	386.40
0.570	285.00	290.70	296.40	302.10	307.80	313.50	319.20	324.90	330.60	336.30	342.00	347.70	353.40	359.10	364.80	370.50	376.20	381.90	387.60	393.30
0.580	290.00	295.80	301.60	307.40	313.20	319.00	324.80	330.60	336.40	342.20	348.00	353.80	359.60	365.40	371.20	377.00	382.80	388.60	394.40	400.20
0.590	295.00	300.90	306.80	312.70	318.60	324.50	330.40	336.30	342.20	348.10	354.00	359.90	365.80	371.70	377.60	383.50	389.40	395.30	401.20	407.10
0.600	300.00	306.00	312.00	318.00	324.00	330.00	336.00	342.00	348.00	354.00	360.00	366.00	372.00	378.00	384.00	390.00	396.00	402.00	408.00	414.00
0.610	305.00	311.10	317.20	323.30	329.40	335.50	341.60	347.70	353.80	359.90	366.00	372.10	378.20	384.30	390.40	396.50	402.60	408.70	414.80	420.90
0.620	310.00	316.20	322.40	328.60	334.80	341.00	347.20	353.40	359.60	365.80	372.00	378.20	384.40	390.60	396.80	403.00	409.20	415.40	421.60	427.80
0.630	315.00	321.30	327.60	333.90	340.20	346.50	352.80	359.10	365.40	371.70	378.00	384.30	390.60	396.90	403.20	409.50	415.80	422.10	428.40	434.70
0.640	320.00	326.40	332.80	339.20	345.60	352.00	358.40	364.80	371.20	377.60	384.00	390.40	396.80	403.20	409.60	416.00	422.40	428.80	435.20	441.60
0.650	325.00	331.50	338.00	344.50	351.00	357.50	364.00	370.50	377.00	383.50	390.00	396.50	403.00	409.50	416.00	422.50	429.00	435.50	442.00	448.50
0.660	330.00	336.60	343.20	349.80	356.40	363.00	369.60	376.20	382.80	389.40	396.00	402.60	409.20	415.80	422.40	429.00	435.60	442.20	448.80	455.40
0.670	335.00	341.70	348.40	355.10	361.80	368.50	375.20	381.90	388.60	395.30	402.00	408.70	415.40	422.10	428.80	435.50	442.20	448.90	455.60	462.30
0.680	340.00	346.80	353.60	360.40	367.20	374.00	380.80	387.60	394.40	401.20	408.00	414.80	421.60	428.40	435.20	442.00	448.80	455.60	462.40	469.20
0.690	345.00	351.90	358.80	365.70	372.60	379.50	386.40	393.30	400.20	407.10	414.00	420.90	427.80	434.70	441.60	448.50	455.40	462.30	469.20	476.10
0.700	350.00	357.00	364.00	371.00	378.00	385.00	392.00	399.00	406.00	413.00	420.00	427.00	434.00	441.00	448.00	455.00	462.00	469.00	476.00	483.00
0.710	355.00	362.10	369.20	376.30	383.40	390.50	397.60	404.70	411.80	418.90	426.00	433.10	440.20	447.30	454.40	461.50	468.60	475.70	482.80	489.90
0.720	360.00	367.20	374.40	381.60	388.80	396.00	403.20	410.40	417.60	424.80	432.00	439.20	446.40	453.60	460.80	468.00	475.20	482.40	489.60	496.80
0.730	365.00	372.30	379.60	386.90	394.20	401.50	408.80	416.10	423.40	430.70	438.00	445.30	452.60	459.90	467.20	474.50	481.80	489.10	496.40	503.70
0.740	370.00	377.40	384.80	392.20	399.60	407.00	414.40	421.80	429.20	436.60	444.00	451.40	458.80	466.20	473.60	481.00	488.40	495.80	503.20	510.60
0.750	375.00	382.50	390.00	397.50	405.00	412.50	420.00	427.50	435.00	442.50	450.00	457.50	465.00	472.50	480.00	487.50	495.00	502.50	510.00	517.50
0.760	380.00	387.60	395.20	402.80	410.40	418.00	425.60	433.20	440.80	448.40	456.00	463.60	471.20	478.80	486.40	494.00	501.60	509.20	516.80	524.40
0.770	385.00	392.70	400.40	408.10	415.80	423.50	431.20	438.90	446.60	454.30	462.00	469.70	477.40	485.10	492.80	500.50	508.20	515.90	523.60	531.30
0.780	390.00	397.80	405.60	413.40	421.20	429.00	436.80	444.60	452.40	460.20	468.00	475.80	483.60	491.40	499.20	507.00	514.80	522.60	530.40	538.20
0.790	395.00	402.90	410.80	418.70	426.60	434.50	442.40	450.30	458.20	466.10	474.00	481.90	489.80	497.70	505.60	513.50	521.40	529.30	537.20	545.10
0.800	400.00	408.00	416.00	424.00	432.00	440.00	448.00	456.00	464.00	472.00	480.00	488.00	496.00	504.00	512.00	520.00	528.00	536.00	544.00	552.00
0.810	405.00	413.10	421.20	429.30	437.40	445.50	453.60	461.70	469.80	477.90	486.00	494.10	502.20	510.30	518.40	526.50	534.60	542.70	550.80	558.90
0.820	410.00	418.20	426.40	434.60	442.80	451.00	459.20	467.40	475.60	483.80	492.00	500.20	508.40	516.60	524.80	533.00	541.20	549.40	557.60	565.80
0.830	415.00	423.30	431.60	439.90	448.20	456.50	464.80	473.10	481.40	489.70	498.00	506.30	514.60	522.90	531.20	539.50	547.80	556.10	564.40	572.70
0.840	420.00	428.40	436.80	445.20	453.60	462.00	470.40	478.80	487.20	495.60	504.00	512.40	520.80	529.20	537.60	546.00	554.40	562.80	571.20	579.60
0.850	425.00	433.50	442.00	450.50	459.00	467.50	476.00	484.50	493.00	501.50	510.00	518.50	527.00	535.50	544.00	552.50	561.00	569.50	578.00	586.50
0.860	430.00	438.60	447.20	455.80	464.40	473.00	481.60	490.20	498.80	507.40	516.00	524.60	533.20	541.80	550.40	559.00	567.60	576.20	584.80	593.40
0.870	435.00	443.70	452.40	461.10	469.80	478.50	487.20	495.90	504.60	513.30	522.00	530.70	539.40	548.10	556.80	565.50	574.20	582.90	591.60	600.30
0.880	440.00	448.80	457.60	466.40	475.20	484.00	492.80	501.60	510.40	519.20	528.00	536.80	545.60	554.40	563.20	572.00	580.80	589.60	598.40	607.20
0.890	445.00	453.90	462.80	471.70	480.60	489.50	498.40	507.30	516.20	525.10	534.00	542.90	551.80	560.70	569.60	578.50	587.40	596.30	605.20	614.10
0.900	450.00	459.00	468.00	477.00	486.00	495.00	504.00	513.00	522.00	531.00	540.00	549.00	558.00	567.00	576.00	585.00	594.00	603.00	612.00	621.00
0.910	455.00	464.10	473.20	482.30	491.40	500.50	509.60	518.70	527.80	536.90	546.00	555.10	564.20	573.30	582.40	591.50	600.60	609.70	618.80	627.90
0.920	460.00	469.20	478.40	487.60	496.80	506.00	515.20	524.40	533.60	542.80	552.00	561.20	570.40	579.60	588.80	598.00	607.20	616.40	625.60	634.80
0.930	465.00	474.30	483.60	492.90	502.20	511.50	520.80	530.10	539.40	548.70	558.00	567.30	576.60	585.90	595.20	604.50	613.80	623.10	632.40	641.70
0.940	470.00	479.40	488.80	498.20	507.60	517.00	526.40	535.80	545.20	554.60	564.00	573.40	582.80	592.20	601.60	611.00	620.40	629.80	639.20	648.60
0.950	475.00	484.50	494.00	503.50	513.00	522.50	532.00	541.50	551.00	560.50	570.00	579.50	589.00	598.50	608.00	617.50	627.00	636.50	646.00	655.50
0.960	480.00	489.60	499.20	508.80	518.40	528.00	537.60	547.20	556.80	566.40	576.00	585.60	595.20	604.80	614.40	624.00	633.60	643.20	652.80	662.40
0.970	485.00	494.70	504.40	514.10	523.80	533.50	543.20	552.90	562.60	572.30	582.00	591.70	601.40	611.10	620.80	630.50	640.20	649.90	659.60	669.30
0.980	490.00	499.80	509.60	519.40	529.20	539.00	548.80	558.60	568.40	578.20	588.00	597.80	607.60	617.40	627.20	637.00	646.80	656.60	666.40	676.20
0.990	495.00	504.90	514.80	524.70	534.60	544.50	554.40	564.30	574.20	584.10	594.00	603.90	613.80	623.70	633.60	643.50	653.40	663.30	673.20	683.10
1.000	500.00	510.00	520.00	530.00	540.00	550.00	560.00	570.00	580.00	590.00	600.00	610.00	620.00	630.00	640.00	650.00	660.00	670.00	680.00	690.00

GOLD BULLION VALUE CHART

Oz.	700.00	710.00	720.00	730.00	740.00	750.00	760.00	770.00	780.00	790.00	800.00	810.00	820.00	830.00	840.00	850.00	860.00	870.00	880.00	890.00	900.00
0.001	0.70	0.71	0.72	0.73	0.74	0.75	0.76	0.77	0.78	0.79	0.80	0.81	0.82	0.83	0.84	0.85	0.86	0.87	0.88	0.89	0.90
0.002	1.40	1.42	1.44	1.46	1.48	1.50	1.52	1.54	1.56	1.58	1.60	1.62	1.64	1.66	1.68	1.70	1.72	1.74	1.76	1.78	1.80
0.003	2.10	2.13	2.16	2.19	2.22	2.25	2.28	2.31	2.34	2.37	2.40	2.43	2.46	2.49	2.52	2.55	2.58	2.61	2.64	2.67	2.70
0.004	2.80	2.84	2.88	2.92	2.96	3.00	3.04	3.08	3.12	3.16	3.20	3.24	3.28	3.32	3.36	3.40	3.44	3.48	3.52	3.56	3.60
0.005	3.50	3.55	3.60	3.65	3.70	3.75	3.80	3.85	3.90	3.95	4.00	4.05	4.10	4.15	4.20	4.25	4.30	4.35	4.40	4.45	4.50
0.006	4.20	4.26	4.32	4.38	4.44	4.50	4.56	4.62	4.68	4.74	4.80	4.86	4.92	4.98	5.04	5.10	5.16	5.22	5.28	5.34	5.40
0.007	4.90	4.97	5.04	5.11	5.18	5.25	5.32	5.39	5.46	5.53	5.60	5.67	5.74	5.81	5.88	5.95	6.02	6.09	6.16	6.23	6.30
0.008	5.60	5.68	5.76	5.84	5.92	6.00	6.08	6.16	6.24	6.32	6.40	6.48	6.56	6.64	6.72	6.80	6.88	6.96	7.04	7.12	7.20
0.009	6.30	6.39	6.48	6.57	6.66	6.75	6.84	6.93	7.02	7.11	7.20	7.29	7.38	7.47	7.56	7.65	7.74	7.83	7.92	8.01	8.10
0.010	7.00	7.10	7.20	7.30	7.40	7.50	7.60	7.70	7.80	7.90	8.00	8.10	8.20	8.30	8.40	8.50	8.60	8.70	8.80	8.90	9.00
0.020	14.00	14.20	14.40	14.60	14.80	15.00	15.20	15.40	15.60	15.80	16.00	16.20	16.40	16.60	16.80	17.00	17.20	17.40	17.60	17.80	18.00
0.030	21.00	21.30	21.60	21.90	22.20	22.50	22.80	23.10	23.40	23.70	24.00	24.30	24.60	24.90	25.20	25.50	25.80	26.10	26.40	26.70	27.00
0.040	28.00	28.40	28.80	29.20	29.60	30.00	30.40	30.80	31.20	31.60	32.00	32.40	32.80	33.20	33.60	34.00	34.40	34.80	35.20	35.60	36.00
0.050	35.00	35.50	36.00	36.50	37.00	37.50	38.00	38.50	39.00	39.50	40.00	40.50	41.00	41.50	42.00	42.50	43.00	43.50	44.00	44.50	45.00
0.060	42.00	42.60	43.20	43.80	44.40	45.00	45.60	46.20	46.80	47.40	48.00	48.60	49.20	49.80	50.40	51.00	51.60	52.20	52.80	53.40	54.00
0.070	49.00	49.70	50.40	51.10	51.80	52.50	53.20	53.90	54.60	55.30	56.00	56.70	57.40	58.10	58.80	59.50	60.20	60.90	61.60	62.30	63.00
0.080	56.00	56.80	57.60	58.40	59.20	60.00	60.80	61.60	62.40	63.20	64.00	64.80	65.60	66.40	67.20	68.00	68.80	69.60	70.40	71.20	72.00
0.090	63.00	63.90	64.80	65.70	66.60	67.50	68.40	69.30	70.20	71.10	72.00	72.90	73.80	74.70	75.60	76.50	77.40	78.30	79.20	80.10	81.00
0.100	70.00	71.00	72.00	73.00	74.00	75.00	76.00	77.00	78.00	79.00	80.00	81.00	82.00	83.00	84.00	85.00	86.00	87.00	88.00	89.00	90.00
0.110	77.00	78.10	79.20	80.30	81.40	82.50	83.60	84.70	85.80	86.90	88.00	89.10	90.20	91.30	92.40	93.50	94.60	95.70	96.80	97.90	99.00
0.120	84.00	85.20	86.40	87.60	88.80	90.00	91.20	92.40	93.60	94.80	96.00	97.20	98.40	99.60	100.80	102.00	103.20	104.40	105.60	106.80	108.00
0.130	91.00	92.30	93.60	94.90	96.20	97.50	98.80	100.10	101.40	102.70	104.00	105.30	106.60	107.90	109.20	110.50	111.80	113.10	114.40	115.70	117.00
0.140	98.00	99.40	100.80	102.20	103.60	105.00	106.40	107.80	109.20	110.60	112.00	113.40	114.80	116.20	117.60	119.00	120.40	121.80	123.20	124.60	126.00
0.150	105.00	106.50	108.00	109.50	111.00	112.50	114.00	115.50	117.00	118.50	120.00	121.50	123.00	124.50	126.00	127.50	129.00	130.50	132.00	133.50	135.00
0.160	112.00	113.60	115.20	116.80	118.40	120.00	121.60	123.20	124.80	126.40	128.00	129.60	131.20	132.80	134.40	136.00	137.60	139.20	140.80	142.40	144.00
0.170	119.00	120.70	122.40	124.10	125.80	127.50	129.20	130.90	132.60	134.30	136.00	137.70	139.40	141.10	142.80	144.50	146.20	147.90	149.60	151.30	153.00
0.180	126.00	127.80	129.60	131.40	133.20	135.00	136.80	138.60	140.40	142.20	144.00	145.80	147.60	149.40	151.20	153.00	154.80	156.60	158.40	160.20	162.00
0.190	133.00	134.90	136.80	138.70	140.60	142.50	144.40	146.30	148.20	150.10	152.00	153.90	155.80	157.70	159.60	161.50	163.40	165.30	167.20	169.10	171.00
0.200	140.00	142.00	144.00	146.00	148.00	150.00	152.00	154.00	156.00	158.00	160.00	162.00	164.00	166.00	168.00	170.00	172.00	174.00	176.00	178.00	180.00
0.210	147.00	149.10	151.20	153.30	155.40	157.50	159.60	161.70	163.80	165.90	168.00	170.10	172.20	174.30	176.40	178.50	180.60	182.70	184.80	186.90	189.00
0.220	154.00	156.20	158.40	160.60	162.80	165.00	167.20	169.40	171.60	173.80	176.00	178.20	180.40	182.60	184.80	187.00	189.20	191.40	193.60	195.80	198.00
0.230	161.00	163.30	165.60	167.90	170.20	172.50	174.80	177.10	179.40	181.70	184.00	186.30	188.60	190.90	193.20	195.50	197.80	200.10	202.40	204.70	207.00
0.240	168.00	170.40	172.80	175.20	177.60	180.00	182.40	184.80	187.20	189.60	192.00	194.40	196.80	199.20	201.60	204.00	206.40	208.80	211.20	213.60	216.00
0.250	175.00	177.50	180.00	182.50	185.00	187.50	190.00	192.50	195.00	197.50	200.00	202.50	205.00	207.50	210.00	212.50	215.00	217.50	220.00	222.50	225.00
0.260	182.00	184.60	187.20	189.80	192.40	195.00	197.60	200.20	202.80	205.40	208.00	210.60	213.20	215.80	218.40	221.00	223.60	226.20	228.80	231.40	234.00
0.270	189.00	191.70	194.40	197.10	199.80	202.50	205.20	207.90	210.60	213.30	216.00	218.70	221.40	224.10	226.80	229.50	232.20	234.90	237.60	240.30	243.00
0.280	196.00	198.80	201.60	204.40	207.20	210.00	212.80	215.60	218.40	221.20	224.00	226.80	229.60	232.40	235.20	238.00	240.80	243.60	246.40	249.20	252.00
0.290	203.00	205.90	208.80	211.70	214.60	217.50	220.40	223.30	226.20	229.10	232.00	234.90	237.80	240.70	243.60	246.50	249.40	252.30	255.20	258.10	261.00
0.300	210.00	213.00	216.00	219.00	222.00	225.00	228.00	231.00	234.00	237.00	240.00	243.00	246.00	249.00	252.00	255.00	258.00	261.00	264.00	267.00	270.00
0.310	217.00	220.10	223.20	226.30	229.40	232.50	235.60	238.70	241.80	244.90	248.00	251.10	254.20	257.30	260.40	263.50	266.60	269.70	272.80	275.90	279.00
0.320	224.00	227.20	230.40	233.60	236.80	240.00	243.20	246.40	249.60	252.80	256.00	259.20	262.40	265.60	268.80	272.00	275.20	278.40	281.60	284.80	288.00
0.330	231.00	234.30	237.60	240.90	244.20	247.50	250.80	254.10	257.40	260.70	264.00	267.30	270.60	273.90	277.20	280.50	283.80	287.10	290.40	293.70	297.00
0.340	238.00	241.40	244.80	248.20	251.60	255.00	258.40	261.80	265.20	268.60	272.00	275.40	278.80	282.20	285.60	289.00	292.40	295.80	299.20	302.60	306.00
0.350	245.00	248.50	252.00	255.50	259.00	262.50	266.00	269.50	273.00	276.50	280.00	283.50	287.00	290.50	294.00	297.50	301.00	304.50	308.00	311.50	315.00
0.360	252.00	255.60	259.20	262.80	266.40	270.00	273.60	277.20	280.80	284.40	288.00	291.60	295.20	298.80	302.40	306.00	309.60	313.20	316.80	320.40	324.00
0.370	259.00	262.70	266.40	270.10	273.80	277.50	281.20	284.90	288.60	292.30	296.00	299.70	303.40	307.10	310.80	314.50	318.20	321.90	325.60	329.30	333.00
0.380	266.00	269.80	273.60	277.40	281.20	285.00	288.80	292.60	296.40	300.20	304.00	307.80	311.60	315.40	319.20	323.00	326.80	330.60	334.40	338.20	342.00
0.390	273.00	276.90	280.80	284.70	288.60	292.50	296.40	300.30	304.20	308.10	312.00	315.90	319.80	323.70	327.60	331.50	335.40	339.30	343.20	347.10	351.00
0.400	280.00	284.00	288.00	292.00	296.00	300.00	304.00	308.00	312.00	316.00	320.00	324.00	328.00	332.00	336.00	340.00	344.00	348.00	352.00	356.00	360.00
0.410	287.00	291.10	295.20	299.30	303.40	307.50	311.60	315.70	319.80	323.90	328.00	332.10	336.20	340.30	344.40	348.50	352.60	356.70	360.80	364.90	369.00
0.420	294.00	298.20	302.40	306.60	310.80	315.00	319.20	323.40	327.60	331.80	336.00	340.20	344.40	348.60	352.80	357.00	361.20	365.40	369.60	373.80	378.00
0.430	301.00	305.30	309.60	313.90	318.20	322.50	326.80	331.10	335.40	339.70	344.00	348.30	352.60	356.90	361.20	365.50	369.80	374.10	378.40	382.70	387.00
0.440	308.00	312.40	316.80	321.20	325.60	330.00	334.40	338.80	343.20	347.60	352.00	356.40	360.80	365.20	369.60	374.00	378.40	382.80	387.20	391.60	396.00
0.450	315.00	319.50	324.00	328.50	333.00	337.50	342.00	346.50	351.00	355.50	360.00	364.50	369.00	373.50	378.00	382.50	387.00	391.50	396.00	400.50	405.00
0.460	322.00	326.60	331.20	335.80	340.40	345.00	349.60	354.20	358.80	363.40	368.00	372.60	377.20	381.80	386.40	391.00	395.60	400.20	404.80	409.40	414.00

GOLD BULLION VALUE CHART

Oz.	700.00	710.00	720.00	730.00	740.00	750.00	760.00	770.00	780.00	790.00	800.00	810.00	820.00	830.00	840.00	850.00	860.00	870.00	880.00	890.00	900.00
0.470	329.00	333.70	338.40	343.10	347.80	352.50	357.20	361.90	366.60	371.30	376.00	380.70	385.40	390.10	394.80	399.50	404.20	408.90	413.60	418.30	423.00
0.480	336.00	340.80	345.60	350.40	355.20	360.00	364.80	369.60	374.40	379.20	384.00	388.80	393.60	398.40	403.20	408.00	412.80	417.60	422.40	427.20	432.00
0.490	343.00	347.90	352.80	357.70	362.60	367.50	372.40	377.30	382.20	387.10	392.00	396.90	401.80	406.70	411.60	416.50	421.40	426.30	431.20	436.10	441.00
0.500	350.00	355.00	360.00	365.00	370.00	375.00	380.00	385.00	390.00	395.00	400.00	405.00	410.00	415.00	420.00	425.00	430.00	435.00	440.00	445.00	450.00
0.510	357.00	362.10	367.20	372.30	377.40	382.50	387.60	392.70	397.80	402.90	408.00	413.10	418.20	423.30	428.40	433.50	438.60	443.70	448.80	453.90	459.00
0.520	364.00	369.20	374.40	379.60	384.80	390.00	395.20	400.40	405.60	410.80	416.00	421.20	426.40	431.60	436.80	442.00	447.20	452.40	457.60	462.80	468.00
0.530	371.00	376.30	381.60	386.90	392.20	397.50	402.80	408.10	413.40	418.70	424.00	429.30	434.60	439.90	445.20	450.50	455.80	461.10	466.40	471.70	477.00
0.540	378.00	383.40	388.80	394.20	399.60	405.00	410.40	415.80	421.20	426.60	432.00	437.40	442.80	448.20	453.60	459.00	464.40	469.80	475.20	480.60	486.00
0.550	385.00	390.50	396.00	401.50	407.00	412.50	418.00	423.50	429.00	434.50	440.00	445.50	451.00	456.50	462.00	467.50	473.00	478.50	484.00	489.50	495.00
0.560	392.00	397.60	403.20	408.80	414.40	420.00	425.60	431.20	436.80	442.40	448.00	453.60	459.20	464.80	470.40	476.00	481.60	487.20	492.80	498.40	504.00
0.570	399.00	404.70	410.40	416.10	421.80	427.50	433.20	438.90	444.60	450.30	456.00	461.70	467.40	473.10	478.80	484.50	490.20	495.90	501.60	507.30	513.00
0.580	406.00	411.80	417.60	423.40	429.20	435.00	440.80	446.60	452.40	458.20	464.00	469.80	475.60	481.40	487.20	493.00	498.80	504.60	510.40	516.20	522.00
0.590	413.00	418.90	424.80	430.70	436.60	442.50	448.40	454.30	460.20	466.10	472.00	477.90	483.80	489.70	495.60	501.50	507.40	513.30	519.20	525.10	531.00
0.600	420.00	426.00	432.00	438.00	444.00	450.00	456.00	462.00	468.00	474.00	480.00	486.00	492.00	498.00	504.00	510.00	516.00	522.00	528.00	534.00	540.00
0.610	427.00	433.10	439.20	445.30	451.40	457.50	463.60	469.70	475.80	481.90	488.00	494.10	500.20	506.30	512.40	518.50	524.60	530.70	536.80	542.90	549.00
0.620	434.00	440.20	446.40	452.60	458.80	465.00	471.20	477.40	483.60	489.80	496.00	502.20	508.40	514.60	520.80	527.00	533.20	539.40	545.60	551.80	558.00
0.630	441.00	447.30	453.60	459.90	466.20	472.50	478.80	485.10	491.40	497.70	504.00	510.30	516.60	522.90	529.20	535.50	541.80	548.10	554.40	560.70	567.00
0.640	448.00	454.40	460.80	467.20	473.60	480.00	486.40	492.80	499.20	505.60	512.00	518.40	524.80	531.20	537.60	544.00	550.40	556.80	563.20	569.60	576.00
0.650	455.00	461.50	468.00	474.50	481.00	487.50	494.00	500.50	507.00	513.50	520.00	526.50	533.00	539.50	546.00	552.50	559.00	565.50	572.00	578.50	585.00
0.660	462.00	468.60	475.20	481.80	488.40	495.00	501.60	508.20	514.80	521.40	528.00	534.60	541.20	547.80	554.40	561.00	567.60	574.20	580.80	587.40	594.00
0.670	469.00	475.70	482.40	489.10	495.80	502.50	509.20	515.90	522.60	529.30	536.00	542.70	549.40	556.10	562.80	569.50	576.20	582.90	589.60	596.30	603.00
0.680	476.00	482.80	489.60	496.40	503.20	510.00	516.80	523.60	530.40	537.20	544.00	550.80	557.60	564.40	571.20	578.00	584.80	591.60	598.40	605.20	612.00
0.690	483.00	489.90	496.80	503.70	510.60	517.50	524.40	531.30	538.20	545.10	552.00	558.90	565.80	572.70	579.60	586.50	593.40	600.30	607.20	614.10	621.00
0.700	490.00	497.00	504.00	511.00	518.00	525.00	532.00	539.00	546.00	553.00	560.00	567.00	574.00	581.00	588.00	595.00	602.00	609.00	616.00	623.00	630.00
0.710	497.00	504.10	511.20	518.30	525.40	532.50	539.60	546.70	553.80	560.90	568.00	575.10	582.20	589.30	596.40	603.50	610.60	617.70	624.80	631.90	639.00
0.720	504.00	511.20	518.40	525.60	532.80	540.00	547.20	554.40	561.60	568.80	576.00	583.20	590.40	597.60	604.80	612.00	619.20	626.40	633.60	640.80	648.00
0.730	511.00	518.30	525.60	532.90	540.20	547.50	554.80	562.10	569.40	576.70	584.00	591.30	598.60	605.90	613.20	620.50	627.80	635.10	642.40	649.70	657.00
0.740	518.00	525.40	532.80	540.20	547.60	555.00	562.40	569.80	577.20	584.60	592.00	599.40	606.80	614.20	621.60	629.00	636.40	643.80	651.20	658.60	666.00
0.750	525.00	532.50	540.00	547.50	555.00	562.50	570.00	577.50	585.00	592.50	600.00	607.50	615.00	622.50	630.00	637.50	645.00	652.50	660.00	667.50	675.00
0.760	532.00	539.60	547.20	554.80	562.40	570.00	577.60	585.20	592.80	600.40	608.00	615.60	623.20	630.80	638.40	646.00	653.60	661.20	668.80	676.40	684.00
0.770	539.00	546.70	554.40	562.10	569.80	577.50	585.20	592.90	600.60	608.30	616.00	623.70	631.40	639.10	646.80	654.50	662.20	669.90	677.60	685.30	693.00
0.780	546.00	553.80	561.60	569.40	577.20	585.00	592.80	600.60	608.40	616.20	624.00	631.80	639.60	647.40	655.20	663.00	670.80	678.60	686.40	694.20	702.00
0.790	553.00	560.90	568.80	576.70	584.60	592.50	600.40	608.30	616.20	624.10	632.00	639.90	647.80	655.70	663.60	671.50	679.40	687.30	695.20	703.10	711.00
0.800	560.00	568.00	576.00	584.00	592.00	600.00	608.00	616.00	624.00	632.00	640.00	648.00	656.00	664.00	672.00	680.00	688.00	696.00	704.00	712.00	720.00
0.810	567.00	575.10	583.20	591.30	599.40	607.50	615.60	623.70	631.80	639.90	648.00	656.10	664.20	672.30	680.40	688.50	696.60	704.70	712.80	720.90	729.00
0.820	574.00	582.20	590.40	598.60	606.80	615.00	623.20	631.40	639.60	647.80	656.00	664.20	672.40	680.60	688.80	697.00	705.20	713.40	721.60	729.80	738.00
0.830	581.00	589.30	597.60	605.90	614.20	622.50	630.80	639.10	647.40	655.70	664.00	672.30	680.60	688.90	697.20	705.50	713.80	722.10	730.40	738.70	747.00
0.840	588.00	596.40	604.80	613.20	621.60	630.00	638.40	646.80	655.20	663.60	672.00	680.40	688.80	697.20	705.60	714.00	722.40	730.80	739.20	747.60	756.00
0.850	595.00	603.50	612.00	620.50	629.00	637.50	646.00	654.50	663.00	671.50	680.00	688.50	697.00	705.50	714.00	722.50	731.00	739.50	748.00	756.50	765.00
0.860	602.00	610.60	619.20	627.80	636.40	645.00	653.60	662.20	670.80	679.40	688.00	696.60	705.20	713.80	722.40	731.00	739.60	748.20	756.80	765.40	774.00
0.870	609.00	617.70	626.40	635.10	643.80	652.50	661.20	669.90	678.60	687.30	696.00	704.70	713.40	722.10	730.80	739.50	748.20	756.90	765.60	774.30	783.00
0.880	616.00	624.80	633.60	642.40	651.20	660.00	668.80	677.60	686.40	695.20	704.00	712.80	721.60	730.40	739.20	748.00	756.80	765.60	774.40	783.20	792.00
0.890	623.00	631.90	640.80	649.70	658.60	667.50	676.40	685.30	694.20	703.10	712.00	720.90	729.80	738.70	747.60	756.50	765.40	774.30	783.20	792.10	801.00
0.900	630.00	639.00	648.00	657.00	666.00	675.00	684.00	693.00	702.00	711.00	720.00	729.00	738.00	747.00	756.00	765.00	774.00	783.00	792.00	801.00	810.00
0.910	637.00	646.10	655.20	664.30	673.40	682.50	691.60	700.70	709.80	718.90	728.00	737.10	746.20	755.30	764.40	773.50	782.60	791.70	800.80	809.90	819.00
0.920	644.00	653.20	662.40	671.60	680.80	690.00	699.20	708.40	717.60	726.80	736.00	745.20	754.40	763.60	772.80	782.00	791.20	800.40	809.60	818.80	828.00
0.930	651.00	660.30	669.60	678.90	688.20	697.50	706.80	716.10	725.40	734.70	744.00	753.30	762.60	771.90	781.20	790.50	799.80	809.10	818.40	827.70	837.00
0.940	658.00	667.40	676.80	686.20	695.60	705.00	714.40	723.80	733.20	742.60	752.00	761.40	770.80	780.20	789.60	799.00	808.40	817.80	827.20	836.60	846.00
0.950	665.00	674.50	684.00	693.50	703.00	712.50	722.00	731.50	741.00	750.50	760.00	769.50	779.00	788.50	798.00	807.50	817.00	826.50	836.00	845.50	855.00
0.960	672.00	681.60	691.20	700.80	710.40	720.00	729.60	739.20	748.80	758.40	768.00	777.60	787.20	796.80	806.40	816.00	825.60	835.20	844.80	854.40	864.00
0.970	679.00	688.70	698.40	708.10	717.80	727.50	737.20	746.90	756.60	766.30	776.00	785.70	795.40	805.10	814.80	824.50	834.20	843.90	853.60	863.30	873.00
0.980	686.00	695.80	705.60	715.40	725.20	735.00	744.80	754.60	764.40	774.20	784.00	793.80	803.60	813.40	823.20	833.00	842.80	852.60	862.40	872.20	882.00
0.990	693.00	702.90	712.80	722.70	732.60	742.50	752.40	762.30	772.20	782.10	792.00	801.90	811.80	821.70	831.60	841.50	851.40	861.30	871.20	881.10	891.00
1.000	700.00	710.00	720.00	730.00	740.00	750.00	760.00	770.00	780.00	790.00	800.00	810.00	820.00	830.00	840.00	850.00	860.00	870.00	880.00	890.00	900.00

XXX PLATINUM BULLION VALUE CHART

PLATINUM BULLION VALUE CHART

Oz.	1000.00	1010.00	1020.00	1030.00	1040.00	1050.00	1060.00	1070.00	1080.00	1090.00	1100.00	1110.00	1120.00	1130.00	1140.00	1150.00	1160.00	1170.00	1180.00	1190.00
0.001	1.00	1.01	1.02	1.03	1.04	1.05	1.06	1.07	1.08	1.09	1.10	1.11	1.12	1.13	1.14	1.15	1.16	1.17	1.18	1.19
0.002	2.00	2.02	2.04	2.06	2.08	2.10	2.12	2.14	2.16	2.18	2.20	2.22	2.24	2.26	2.28	2.30	2.32	2.34	2.36	2.38
0.003	3.00	3.03	3.06	3.09	3.12	3.15	3.18	3.21	3.24	3.27	3.30	3.33	3.36	3.39	3.42	3.45	3.48	3.51	3.54	3.57
0.004	4.00	4.04	4.08	4.12	4.16	4.20	4.24	4.28	4.32	4.36	4.40	4.44	4.48	4.52	4.56	4.60	4.64	4.68	4.72	4.76
0.005	5.00	5.05	5.10	5.15	5.20	5.25	5.30	5.35	5.40	5.45	5.50	5.55	5.60	5.65	5.70	5.75	5.80	5.85	5.90	5.95
0.006	6.00	6.06	6.12	6.18	6.24	6.30	6.36	6.42	6.48	6.54	6.60	6.66	6.72	6.78	6.84	6.90	6.96	7.02	7.08	7.14
0.007	7.00	7.07	7.14	7.21	7.28	7.35	7.42	7.49	7.56	7.63	7.70	7.77	7.84	7.91	7.98	8.05	8.12	8.19	8.26	8.33
0.008	8.00	8.08	8.16	8.24	8.32	8.40	8.48	8.56	8.64	8.72	8.80	8.88	8.96	9.04	9.12	9.20	9.28	9.36	9.44	9.52
0.009	9.00	9.09	9.18	9.27	9.36	9.45	9.54	9.63	9.72	9.81	9.90	9.99	10.08	10.17	10.26	10.35	10.44	10.53	10.62	10.71
0.010	10.00	10.10	10.20	10.30	10.40	10.50	10.60	10.70	10.80	10.90	11.00	11.10	11.20	11.30	11.40	11.50	11.60	11.70	11.80	11.90
0.020	20.00	20.20	20.40	20.60	20.80	21.00	21.20	21.40	21.60	21.80	22.00	22.20	22.40	22.60	22.80	23.00	23.20	23.40	23.60	23.80
0.030	30.00	30.30	30.60	30.90	31.20	31.50	31.80	32.10	32.40	32.70	33.00	33.30	33.60	33.90	34.20	34.50	34.80	35.10	35.40	35.70
0.040	40.00	40.40	40.80	41.20	41.60	42.00	42.40	42.80	43.20	43.60	44.00	44.40	44.80	45.20	45.60	46.00	46.40	46.80	47.20	47.60
0.050	50.00	50.50	51.00	51.50	52.00	52.50	53.00	53.50	54.00	54.50	55.00	55.50	56.00	56.50	57.00	57.50	58.00	58.50	59.00	59.50
0.060	60.00	60.60	61.20	61.80	62.40	63.00	63.60	64.20	64.80	65.40	66.00	66.60	67.20	67.80	68.40	69.00	69.60	70.20	70.80	71.40
0.070	70.00	70.70	71.40	72.10	72.80	73.50	74.20	74.90	75.60	76.30	77.00	77.70	78.40	79.10	79.80	80.50	81.20	81.90	82.60	83.30
0.080	80.00	80.80	81.60	82.40	83.20	84.00	84.80	85.60	86.40	87.20	88.00	88.80	89.60	90.40	91.20	92.00	92.80	93.60	94.40	95.20
0.090	90.00	90.90	91.80	92.70	93.60	94.50	95.40	96.30	97.20	98.10	99.00	99.90	100.80	101.70	102.60	103.50	104.40	105.30	106.20	107.10
0.100	100.00	101.00	102.00	103.00	104.00	105.00	106.00	107.00	108.00	109.00	110.00	111.00	112.00	113.00	114.00	115.00	116.00	117.00	118.00	119.00
0.110	110.00	111.10	112.20	113.30	114.40	115.50	116.60	117.70	118.80	119.90	121.00	122.10	123.20	124.30	125.40	126.50	127.60	128.70	129.80	130.90
0.120	120.00	121.20	122.40	123.60	124.80	126.00	127.20	128.40	129.60	130.80	132.00	133.20	134.40	135.60	136.80	138.00	139.20	140.40	141.60	142.80
0.130	130.00	131.30	132.60	133.90	135.20	136.50	137.80	139.10	140.40	141.70	143.00	144.30	145.60	146.90	148.20	149.50	150.80	152.10	153.40	154.70
0.140	140.00	141.40	142.80	144.20	145.60	147.00	148.40	149.80	151.20	152.60	154.00	155.40	156.80	158.20	159.60	161.00	162.40	163.80	165.20	166.60
0.150	150.00	151.50	153.00	154.50	156.00	157.50	159.00	160.50	162.00	163.50	165.00	166.50	168.00	169.50	171.00	172.50	174.00	175.50	177.00	178.50
0.160	160.00	161.60	163.20	164.80	166.40	168.00	169.60	171.20	172.80	174.40	176.00	177.60	179.20	180.80	182.40	184.00	185.60	187.20	188.80	190.40
0.170	170.00	171.70	173.40	175.10	176.80	178.50	180.20	181.90	183.60	185.30	187.00	188.70	190.40	192.10	193.80	195.50	197.20	198.90	200.60	202.30
0.180	180.00	181.80	183.60	185.40	187.20	189.00	190.80	192.60	194.40	196.20	198.00	199.80	201.60	203.40	205.20	207.00	208.80	210.60	212.40	214.20
0.190	190.00	191.90	193.80	195.70	197.60	199.50	201.40	203.30	205.20	207.10	209.00	210.90	212.80	214.70	216.60	218.50	220.40	222.30	224.20	226.10
0.200	200.00	202.00	204.00	206.00	208.00	210.00	212.00	214.00	216.00	218.00	220.00	222.00	224.00	226.00	228.00	230.00	232.00	234.00	236.00	238.00
0.210	210.00	212.10	214.20	216.30	218.40	220.50	222.60	224.70	226.80	228.90	231.00	233.10	235.20	237.30	239.40	241.50	243.60	245.70	247.80	249.90
0.220	220.00	222.20	224.40	226.60	228.80	231.00	233.20	235.40	237.60	239.80	242.00	244.20	246.40	248.60	250.80	253.00	255.20	257.40	259.60	261.80
0.230	230.00	232.30	234.60	236.90	239.20	241.50	243.80	246.10	248.40	250.70	253.00	255.30	257.60	259.90	262.20	264.50	266.80	269.10	271.40	273.70
0.240	240.00	242.40	244.80	247.20	249.60	252.00	254.40	256.80	259.20	261.60	264.00	266.40	268.80	271.20	273.60	276.00	278.40	280.80	283.20	285.60
0.250	250.00	252.50	255.00	257.50	260.00	262.50	265.00	267.50	270.00	272.50	275.00	277.50	280.00	282.50	285.00	287.50	290.00	292.50	295.00	297.50
0.260	260.00	262.60	265.20	267.80	270.40	273.00	275.60	278.20	280.80	283.40	286.00	288.60	291.20	293.80	296.40	299.00	301.60	304.20	306.80	309.40
0.270	270.00	272.70	275.40	278.10	280.80	283.50	286.20	288.90	291.60	294.30	297.00	299.70	302.40	305.10	307.80	310.50	313.20	315.90	318.60	321.30
0.280	280.00	282.80	285.60	288.40	291.20	294.00	296.80	299.60	302.40	305.20	308.00	310.80	313.60	316.40	319.20	322.00	324.80	327.60	330.40	333.20
0.290	290.00	292.90	295.80	298.70	301.60	304.50	307.40	310.30	313.20	316.10	319.00	321.90	324.80	327.70	330.60	333.50	336.40	339.30	342.20	345.10
0.300	300.00	303.00	306.00	309.00	312.00	315.00	318.00	321.00	324.00	327.00	330.00	333.00	336.00	339.00	342.00	345.00	348.00	351.00	354.00	357.00
0.310	310.00	313.10	316.20	319.30	322.40	325.50	328.60	331.70	334.80	337.90	341.00	344.10	347.20	350.30	353.40	356.50	359.60	362.70	365.80	368.90
0.320	320.00	323.20	326.40	329.60	332.80	336.00	339.20	342.40	345.60	348.80	352.00	355.20	358.40	361.60	364.80	368.00	371.20	374.40	377.60	380.80
0.330	330.00	333.30	336.60	339.90	343.20	346.50	349.80	353.10	356.40	359.70	363.00	366.30	369.60	372.90	376.20	379.50	382.80	386.10	389.40	392.70
0.340	340.00	343.40	346.80	350.20	353.60	357.00	360.40	363.80	367.20	370.60	374.00	377.40	380.80	384.20	387.60	391.00	394.40	397.80	401.20	404.60
0.350	350.00	353.50	357.00	360.50	364.00	367.50	371.00	374.50	378.00	381.50	385.00	388.50	392.00	395.50	399.00	402.50	406.00	409.50	413.00	416.50
0.360	360.00	363.60	367.20	370.80	374.40	378.00	381.60	385.20	388.80	392.40	396.00	399.60	403.20	406.80	410.40	414.00	417.60	421.20	424.80	428.40
0.370	370.00	373.70	377.40	381.10	384.80	388.50	392.20	395.90	399.60	403.30	407.00	410.70	414.40	418.10	421.80	425.50	429.20	432.90	436.60	440.30
0.380	380.00	383.80	387.60	391.40	395.20	399.00	402.80	406.60	410.40	414.20	418.00	421.80	425.60	429.40	433.20	437.00	440.80	444.60	448.40	452.20
0.390	390.00	393.90	397.80	401.70	405.60	409.50	413.40	417.30	421.20	425.10	429.00	432.90	436.80	440.70	444.60	448.50	452.40	456.30	460.20	464.10
0.400	400.00	404.00	408.00	412.00	416.00	420.00	424.00	428.00	432.00	436.00	440.00	444.00	448.00	452.00	456.00	460.00	464.00	468.00	472.00	476.00
0.410	410.00	414.10	418.20	422.30	426.40	430.50	434.60	438.70	442.80	446.90	451.00	455.10	459.20	463.30	467.40	471.50	475.60	479.70	483.80	487.90
0.420	420.00	424.20	428.40	432.60	436.80	441.00	445.20	449.40	453.60	457.80	462.00	466.20	470.40	474.60	478.80	483.00	487.20	491.40	495.60	499.80
0.430	430.00	434.30	438.60	442.90	447.20	451.50	455.80	460.10	464.40	468.70	473.00	477.30	481.60	485.90	490.20	494.50	498.80	503.10	507.40	511.70
0.440	440.00	444.40	448.80	453.20	457.60	462.00	466.40	470.80	475.20	479.60	484.00	488.40	492.80	497.20	501.60	506.00	510.40	514.80	519.20	523.60
0.450	450.00	454.50	459.00	463.50	468.00	472.50	477.00	481.50	486.00	490.50	495.00	499.50	504.00	508.50	513.00	517.50	522.00	526.50	531.00	535.50
0.460	460.00	464.60	469.20	473.80	478.40	483.00	487.60	492.20	496.80	501.40	506.00	510.60	515.20	519.80	524.40	529.00	533.60	538.20	542.80	547.40

PLATINUM BULLION VALUE CHART

Oz.	1000.00	1010.00	1020.00	1030.00	1040.00	1050.00	1060.00	1070.00	1080.00	1090.00	1100.00	1110.00	1120.00	1130.00	1140.00	1150.00	1160.00	1170.00	1180.00	1190.00
0.470	470.00	474.70	479.40	484.10	488.80	493.50	498.20	502.90	507.60	512.30	517.00	521.70	526.40	531.10	535.80	540.50	545.20	549.90	554.60	559.30
0.480	480.00	484.80	489.60	494.40	499.20	504.00	508.80	513.60	518.40	523.20	528.00	532.80	537.60	542.40	547.20	552.00	556.80	561.60	566.40	571.20
0.490	490.00	494.90	499.80	504.70	509.60	514.50	519.40	524.30	529.20	534.10	539.00	543.90	548.80	553.70	558.60	563.50	568.40	573.30	578.20	583.10
0.500	500.00	505.00	510.00	515.00	520.00	525.00	530.00	535.00	540.00	545.00	550.00	555.00	560.00	565.00	570.00	575.00	580.00	585.00	590.00	595.00
0.510	510.00	515.10	520.20	525.30	530.40	535.50	540.60	545.70	550.80	555.90	561.00	566.10	571.20	576.30	581.40	586.50	591.60	596.70	601.80	606.90
0.520	520.00	525.20	530.40	535.60	540.80	546.00	551.20	556.40	561.60	566.80	572.00	577.20	582.40	587.60	592.80	598.00	603.20	608.40	613.60	618.80
0.530	530.00	535.30	540.60	545.90	551.20	556.50	561.80	567.10	572.40	577.70	583.00	588.30	593.60	598.90	604.20	609.50	614.80	620.10	625.40	630.70
0.540	540.00	545.40	550.80	556.20	561.60	567.00	572.40	577.80	583.20	588.60	594.00	599.40	604.80	610.20	615.60	621.00	626.40	631.80	637.20	642.60
0.550	550.00	555.50	561.00	566.50	572.00	577.50	583.00	588.50	594.00	599.50	605.00	610.50	616.00	621.50	627.00	632.50	638.00	643.50	649.00	654.50
0.560	560.00	565.60	571.20	576.80	582.40	588.00	593.60	599.20	604.80	610.40	616.00	621.60	627.20	632.80	638.40	644.00	649.60	655.20	660.80	666.40
0.570	570.00	575.70	581.40	587.10	592.80	598.50	604.20	609.90	615.60	621.30	627.00	632.70	638.40	644.10	649.80	655.50	661.20	666.90	672.60	678.30
0.580	580.00	585.80	591.60	597.40	603.20	609.00	614.80	620.60	626.40	632.20	638.00	643.80	649.60	655.40	661.20	667.00	672.80	678.60	684.40	690.20
0.590	590.00	595.90	601.80	607.70	613.60	619.50	625.40	631.30	637.20	643.10	649.00	654.90	660.80	666.70	672.60	678.50	684.40	690.30	696.20	702.10
0.600	600.00	606.00	612.00	618.00	624.00	630.00	636.00	642.00	648.00	654.00	660.00	666.00	672.00	678.00	684.00	690.00	696.00	702.00	708.00	714.00
0.610	610.00	616.10	622.20	628.30	634.40	640.50	646.60	652.70	658.80	664.90	671.00	677.10	683.20	689.30	695.40	701.50	707.60	713.70	719.80	725.90
0.620	620.00	626.20	632.40	638.60	644.80	651.00	657.20	663.40	669.60	675.80	682.00	688.20	694.40	700.60	706.80	713.00	719.20	725.40	731.60	737.80
0.630	630.00	636.30	642.60	648.90	655.20	661.50	667.80	674.10	680.40	686.70	693.00	699.30	705.60	711.90	718.20	724.50	730.80	737.10	743.40	749.70
0.640	640.00	646.40	652.80	659.20	665.60	672.00	678.40	684.80	691.20	697.60	704.00	710.40	716.80	723.20	729.60	736.00	742.40	748.80	755.20	761.60
0.650	650.00	656.50	663.00	669.50	676.00	682.50	689.00	695.50	702.00	708.50	715.00	721.50	728.00	734.50	741.00	747.50	754.00	760.50	767.00	773.50
0.660	660.00	666.60	673.20	679.80	686.40	693.00	699.60	706.20	712.80	719.40	726.00	732.60	739.20	745.80	752.40	759.00	765.60	772.20	778.80	785.40
0.670	670.00	676.70	683.40	690.10	696.80	703.50	710.20	716.90	723.60	730.30	737.00	743.70	750.40	757.10	763.80	770.50	777.20	783.90	790.60	797.30
0.680	680.00	686.80	693.60	700.40	707.20	714.00	720.80	727.60	734.40	741.20	748.00	754.80	761.60	768.40	775.20	782.00	788.80	795.60	802.40	809.20
0.690	690.00	696.90	703.80	710.70	717.60	724.50	731.40	738.30	745.20	752.10	759.00	765.90	772.80	779.70	786.60	793.50	800.40	807.30	814.20	821.10
0.700	700.00	707.00	714.00	721.00	728.00	735.00	742.00	749.00	756.00	763.00	770.00	777.00	784.00	791.00	798.00	805.00	812.00	819.00	826.00	833.00
0.710	710.00	717.10	724.20	731.30	738.40	745.50	752.60	759.70	766.80	773.90	781.00	788.10	795.20	802.30	809.40	816.50	823.60	830.70	837.80	844.90
0.720	720.00	727.20	734.40	741.60	748.80	756.00	763.20	770.40	777.60	784.80	792.00	799.20	806.40	813.60	820.80	828.00	835.20	842.40	849.60	856.80
0.730	730.00	737.30	744.60	751.90	759.20	766.50	773.80	781.10	788.40	795.70	803.00	810.30	817.60	824.90	832.20	839.50	846.80	854.10	861.40	868.70
0.740	740.00	747.40	754.80	762.20	769.60	777.00	784.40	791.80	799.20	806.60	814.00	821.40	828.80	836.20	843.60	851.00	858.40	865.80	873.20	880.60
0.750	750.00	757.50	765.00	772.50	780.00	787.50	795.00	802.50	810.00	817.50	825.00	832.50	840.00	847.50	855.00	862.50	870.00	877.50	885.00	892.50
0.760	760.00	767.60	775.20	782.80	790.40	798.00	805.60	813.20	820.80	828.40	836.00	843.60	851.20	858.80	866.40	874.00	881.60	889.20	896.80	904.40
0.770	770.00	777.70	785.40	793.10	800.80	808.50	816.20	823.90	831.60	839.30	847.00	854.70	862.40	870.10	877.80	885.50	893.20	900.90	908.60	916.30
0.780	780.00	787.80	795.60	803.40	811.20	819.00	826.80	834.60	842.40	850.20	858.00	865.80	873.60	881.40	889.20	897.00	904.80	912.60	920.40	928.20
0.790	790.00	797.90	805.80	813.70	821.60	829.50	837.40	845.30	853.20	861.10	869.00	876.90	884.80	892.70	900.60	908.50	916.40	924.30	932.20	940.10
0.800	800.00	808.00	816.00	824.00	832.00	840.00	848.00	856.00	864.00	872.00	880.00	888.00	896.00	904.00	912.00	920.00	928.00	936.00	944.00	952.00
0.810	810.00	818.10	826.20	834.30	842.40	850.50	858.60	866.70	874.80	882.90	891.00	899.10	907.20	915.30	923.40	931.50	939.60	947.70	955.80	963.90
0.820	820.00	828.20	836.40	844.60	852.80	861.00	869.20	877.40	885.60	893.80	902.00	910.20	918.40	926.60	934.80	943.00	951.20	959.40	967.60	975.80
0.830	830.00	838.30	846.60	854.90	863.20	871.50	879.80	888.10	896.40	904.70	913.00	921.30	929.60	937.90	946.20	954.50	962.80	971.10	979.40	987.70
0.840	840.00	848.40	856.80	865.20	873.60	882.00	890.40	898.80	907.20	915.60	924.00	932.40	940.80	949.20	957.60	966.00	974.40	982.80	991.20	999.60
0.850	850.00	858.50	867.00	875.50	884.00	892.50	901.00	909.50	918.00	926.50	935.00	943.50	952.00	960.50	969.00	977.50	986.00	994.50	1003.00	1011.50
0.860	860.00	868.60	877.20	885.80	894.40	903.00	911.60	920.20	928.80	937.40	946.00	954.60	963.20	971.80	980.40	989.00	997.60	1006.20	1014.80	1023.40
0.870	870.00	878.70	887.40	896.10	904.80	913.50	922.20	930.90	939.60	948.30	957.00	965.70	974.40	983.10	991.80	1000.50	1009.20	1017.90	1026.60	1035.30
0.880	880.00	888.80	897.60	906.40	915.20	924.00	932.80	941.60	950.40	959.20	968.00	976.80	985.60	994.40	1003.20	1012.00	1020.80	1029.60	1038.40	1047.20
0.890	890.00	898.90	907.80	916.70	925.60	934.50	943.40	952.30	961.20	970.10	979.00	987.90	996.80	1005.70	1014.60	1023.50	1032.40	1041.30	1050.20	1059.10
0.900	900.00	909.00	918.00	927.00	936.00	945.00	954.00	963.00	972.00	981.00	990.00	999.00	1008.00	1017.00	1026.00	1035.00	1044.00	1053.00	1062.00	1071.00
0.910	910.00	919.10	928.20	937.30	946.40	955.50	964.60	973.70	982.80	991.90	1001.00	1010.10	1019.20	1028.30	1037.40	1046.50	1055.60	1064.70	1073.80	1082.90
0.920	920.00	929.20	938.40	947.60	956.80	966.00	975.20	984.40	993.60	1002.80	1012.00	1021.20	1030.40	1039.60	1048.80	1058.00	1067.20	1076.40	1085.60	1094.80
0.930	930.00	939.30	948.60	957.90	967.20	976.50	985.80	995.10	1004.40	1013.70	1023.00	1032.30	1041.60	1050.90	1060.20	1069.50	1078.80	1088.10	1097.40	1106.70
0.940	940.00	949.40	958.80	968.20	977.60	987.00	996.40	1005.80	1015.20	1024.60	1034.00	1043.40	1052.80	1062.20	1071.60	1081.00	1090.40	1099.80	1109.20	1118.60
0.950	950.00	959.50	969.00	978.50	988.00	997.50	1007.00	1016.50	1026.00	1035.50	1045.00	1054.50	1064.00	1073.50	1083.00	1092.50	1102.00	1111.50	1121.00	1130.50
0.960	960.00	969.60	979.20	988.80	998.40	1008.00	1017.60	1027.20	1036.80	1046.40	1056.00	1065.60	1075.20	1084.80	1094.40	1104.00	1113.60	1123.20	1132.80	1142.40
0.970	970.00	979.70	989.40	999.10	1008.80	1018.50	1028.20	1037.90	1047.60	1057.30	1067.00	1076.70	1086.40	1096.10	1105.80	1115.50	1125.20	1134.90	1144.60	1154.30
0.980	980.00	989.80	999.60	1009.40	1019.20	1029.00	1038.80	1048.60	1058.40	1068.20	1078.00	1087.80	1097.60	1107.40	1117.20	1127.00	1136.80	1146.60	1156.40	1166.20
0.990	990.00	999.90	1009.80	1019.70	1029.60	1039.50	1049.40	1059.30	1069.20	1079.10	1089.00	1098.90	1108.80	1118.70	1128.60	1138.50	1148.40	1158.30	1168.20	1178.10
1.000	1000.00	1010.00	1020.00	1030.00	1040.00	1050.00	1060.00	1070.00	1080.00	1090.00	1100.00	1110.00	1120.00	1130.00	1140.00	1150.00	1160.00	1170.00	1180.00	1190.00

PLATINUM BULLION VALUE CHART

Oz.	1200.00	1210.00	1220.00	1230.00	1240.00	1250.00	1260.00	1270.00	1280.00	1290.00	1300.00	1310.00	1320.00	1330.00	1340.00	1350.00	1360.00	1370.00	1380.00	1390.00	1400.00
0.001	1.20	1.21	1.22	1.23	1.24	1.25	1.26	1.27	1.28	1.29	1.30	1.31	1.32	1.33	1.34	1.35	1.36	1.37	1.38	1.39	1.40
0.002	2.40	2.42	2.44	2.46	2.48	2.50	2.52	2.54	2.56	2.58	2.60	2.62	2.64	2.66	2.68	2.70	2.72	2.74	2.76	2.78	2.80
0.003	3.60	3.63	3.66	3.69	3.72	3.75	3.78	3.81	3.84	3.87	3.90	3.93	3.96	3.99	4.02	4.05	4.08	4.11	4.14	4.17	4.20
0.004	4.80	4.84	4.88	4.92	4.96	5.00	5.04	5.08	5.12	5.16	5.20	5.24	5.28	5.32	5.36	5.40	5.44	5.48	5.52	5.56	5.60
0.005	6.00	6.05	6.10	6.15	6.20	6.25	6.30	6.35	6.40	6.45	6.50	6.55	6.60	6.65	6.70	6.75	6.80	6.85	6.90	6.95	7.00
0.006	7.20	7.26	7.32	7.38	7.44	7.50	7.56	7.62	7.68	7.74	7.80	7.86	7.92	7.98	8.04	8.10	8.16	8.22	8.28	8.34	8.40
0.007	8.40	8.47	8.54	8.61	8.68	8.75	8.82	8.89	8.96	9.03	9.10	9.17	9.24	9.31	9.38	9.45	9.52	9.59	9.66	9.73	9.80
0.008	9.60	9.68	9.76	9.84	9.92	10.00	10.08	10.16	10.24	10.32	10.40	10.48	10.56	10.64	10.72	10.80	10.88	10.96	11.04	11.12	11.20
0.009	10.80	10.89	10.98	11.07	11.16	11.25	11.34	11.43	11.52	11.61	11.70	11.79	11.88	11.97	12.06	12.15	12.24	12.33	12.42	12.51	12.60
0.010	12.00	12.10	12.20	12.30	12.40	12.50	12.60	12.70	12.80	12.90	13.00	13.10	13.20	13.30	13.40	13.50	13.60	13.70	13.80	13.90	14.00
0.020	24.00	24.20	24.40	24.60	24.80	25.00	25.20	25.40	25.60	25.80	26.00	26.20	26.40	26.60	26.80	27.00	27.20	27.40	27.60	27.80	28.00
0.030	36.00	36.30	36.60	36.90	37.20	37.50	37.80	38.10	38.40	38.70	39.00	39.30	39.60	39.90	40.20	40.50	40.80	41.10	41.40	41.70	42.00
0.040	48.00	48.40	48.80	49.20	49.60	50.00	50.40	50.80	51.20	51.60	52.00	52.40	52.80	53.20	53.60	54.00	54.40	54.80	55.20	55.60	56.00
0.050	60.00	60.50	61.00	61.50	62.00	62.50	63.00	63.50	64.00	64.50	65.00	65.50	66.00	66.50	67.00	67.50	68.00	68.50	69.00	69.50	70.00
0.060	72.00	72.60	73.20	73.80	74.40	75.00	75.60	76.20	76.80	77.40	78.00	78.60	79.20	79.80	80.40	81.00	81.60	82.20	82.80	83.40	84.00
0.070	84.00	84.70	85.40	86.10	86.80	87.50	88.20	88.90	89.60	90.30	91.00	91.70	92.40	93.10	93.80	94.50	95.20	95.90	96.60	97.30	98.00
0.080	96.00	96.80	97.60	98.40	99.20	100.00	100.80	101.60	102.40	103.20	104.00	104.80	105.60	106.40	107.20	108.00	108.80	109.60	110.40	111.20	112.00
0.090	108.00	108.90	109.80	110.70	111.60	112.50	113.40	114.30	115.20	116.10	117.00	117.90	118.80	119.70	120.60	121.50	122.40	123.30	124.20	125.10	126.00
0.100	120.00	121.00	122.00	123.00	124.00	125.00	126.00	127.00	128.00	129.00	130.00	131.00	132.00	133.00	134.00	135.00	136.00	137.00	138.00	139.00	140.00
0.110	132.00	133.10	134.20	135.30	136.40	137.50	138.60	139.70	140.80	141.90	143.00	144.10	145.20	146.30	147.40	148.50	149.60	150.70	151.80	152.90	154.00
0.120	144.00	145.20	146.40	147.60	148.80	150.00	151.20	152.40	153.60	154.80	156.00	157.20	158.40	159.60	160.80	162.00	163.20	164.40	165.60	166.80	168.00
0.130	156.00	157.30	158.60	159.90	161.20	162.50	163.80	165.10	166.40	167.70	169.00	170.30	171.60	172.90	174.20	175.50	176.80	178.10	179.40	180.70	182.00
0.140	168.00	169.40	170.80	172.20	173.60	175.00	176.40	177.80	179.20	180.60	182.00	183.40	184.80	186.20	187.60	189.00	190.40	191.80	193.20	194.60	196.00
0.150	180.00	181.50	183.00	184.50	186.00	187.50	189.00	190.50	192.00	193.50	195.00	196.50	198.00	199.50	201.00	202.50	204.00	205.50	207.00	208.50	210.00
0.160	192.00	193.60	195.20	196.80	198.40	200.00	201.60	203.20	204.80	206.40	208.00	209.60	211.20	212.80	214.40	216.00	217.60	219.20	220.80	222.40	224.00
0.170	204.00	205.70	207.40	209.10	210.80	212.50	214.20	215.90	217.60	219.30	221.00	222.70	224.40	226.10	227.80	229.50	231.20	232.90	234.60	236.30	238.00
0.180	216.00	217.80	219.60	221.40	223.20	225.00	226.80	228.60	230.40	232.20	234.00	235.80	237.60	239.40	241.20	243.00	244.80	246.60	248.40	250.20	252.00
0.190	228.00	229.90	231.80	233.70	235.60	237.50	239.40	241.30	243.20	245.10	247.00	248.90	250.80	252.70	254.60	256.50	258.40	260.30	262.20	264.10	266.00
0.200	240.00	242.00	244.00	246.00	248.00	250.00	252.00	254.00	256.00	258.00	260.00	262.00	264.00	266.00	268.00	270.00	272.00	274.00	276.00	278.00	280.00
0.210	252.00	254.10	256.20	258.30	260.40	262.50	264.60	266.70	268.80	270.90	273.00	275.10	277.20	279.30	281.40	283.50	285.60	287.70	289.80	291.90	294.00
0.220	264.00	266.20	268.40	270.60	272.80	275.00	277.20	279.40	281.60	283.80	286.00	288.20	290.40	292.60	294.80	297.00	299.20	301.40	303.60	305.80	308.00
0.230	276.00	278.30	280.60	282.90	285.20	287.50	289.80	292.10	294.40	296.70	299.00	301.30	303.60	305.90	308.20	310.50	312.80	315.10	317.40	319.70	322.00
0.240	288.00	290.40	292.80	295.20	297.60	300.00	302.40	304.80	307.20	309.60	312.00	314.40	316.80	319.20	321.60	324.00	326.40	328.80	331.20	333.60	336.00
0.250	300.00	302.50	305.00	307.50	310.00	312.50	315.00	317.50	320.00	322.50	325.00	327.50	330.00	332.50	335.00	337.50	340.00	342.50	345.00	347.50	350.00
0.260	312.00	314.60	317.20	319.80	322.40	325.00	327.60	330.20	332.80	335.40	338.00	340.60	343.20	345.80	348.40	351.00	353.60	356.20	358.80	361.40	364.00
0.270	324.00	326.70	329.40	332.10	334.80	337.50	340.20	342.90	345.60	348.30	351.00	353.70	356.40	359.10	361.80	364.50	367.20	369.90	372.60	375.30	378.00
0.280	336.00	338.80	341.60	344.40	347.20	350.00	352.80	355.60	358.40	361.20	364.00	366.80	369.60	372.40	375.20	378.00	380.80	383.60	386.40	389.20	392.00
0.290	348.00	350.90	353.80	356.70	359.60	362.50	365.40	368.30	371.20	374.10	377.00	379.90	382.80	385.70	388.60	391.50	394.40	397.30	400.20	403.10	406.00
0.300	360.00	363.00	366.00	369.00	372.00	375.00	378.00	381.00	384.00	387.00	390.00	393.00	396.00	399.00	402.00	405.00	408.00	411.00	414.00	417.00	420.00
0.310	372.00	375.10	378.20	381.30	384.40	387.50	390.60	393.70	396.80	399.90	403.00	406.10	409.20	412.30	415.40	418.50	421.60	424.70	427.80	430.90	434.00
0.320	384.00	387.20	390.40	393.60	396.80	400.00	403.20	406.40	409.60	412.80	416.00	419.20	422.40	425.60	428.80	432.00	435.20	438.40	441.60	444.80	448.00
0.330	396.00	399.30	402.60	405.90	409.20	412.50	415.80	419.10	422.40	425.70	429.00	432.30	435.60	438.90	442.20	445.50	448.80	452.10	455.40	458.70	462.00
0.340	408.00	411.40	414.80	418.20	421.60	425.00	428.40	431.80	435.20	438.60	442.00	445.40	448.80	452.20	455.60	459.00	462.40	465.80	469.20	472.60	476.00
0.350	420.00	423.50	427.00	430.50	434.00	437.50	441.00	444.50	448.00	451.50	455.00	458.50	462.00	465.50	469.00	472.50	476.00	479.50	483.00	486.50	490.00
0.360	432.00	435.60	439.20	442.80	446.40	450.00	453.60	457.20	460.80	464.40	468.00	471.60	475.20	478.80	482.40	486.00	489.60	493.20	496.80	500.40	504.00
0.370	444.00	447.70	451.40	455.10	458.80	462.50	466.20	469.90	473.60	477.30	481.00	484.70	488.40	492.10	495.80	499.50	503.20	506.90	510.60	514.30	518.00
0.380	456.00	459.80	463.60	467.40	471.20	475.00	478.80	482.60	486.40	490.20	494.00	497.80	501.60	505.40	509.20	513.00	516.80	520.60	524.40	528.20	532.00
0.390	468.00	471.90	475.80	479.70	483.60	487.50	491.40	495.30	499.20	503.10	507.00	510.90	514.80	518.70	522.60	526.50	530.40	534.30	538.20	542.10	546.00
0.400	480.00	484.00	488.00	492.00	496.00	500.00	504.00	508.00	512.00	516.00	520.00	524.00	528.00	532.00	536.00	540.00	544.00	548.00	552.00	556.00	560.00
0.410	492.00	496.10	500.20	504.30	508.40	512.50	516.60	520.70	524.80	528.90	533.00	537.10	541.20	545.30	549.40	553.50	557.60	561.70	565.80	569.90	574.00
0.420	504.00	508.20	512.40	516.60	520.80	525.00	529.20	533.40	537.60	541.80	546.00	550.20	554.40	558.60	562.80	567.00	571.20	575.40	579.60	583.80	588.00
0.430	516.00	520.30	524.60	528.90	533.20	537.50	541.80	546.10	550.40	554.70	559.00	563.30	567.60	571.90	576.20	580.50	584.80	589.10	593.40	597.70	602.00
0.440	528.00	532.40	536.80	541.20	545.60	550.00	554.40	558.80	563.20	567.60	572.00	576.40	580.80	585.20	589.60	594.00	598.40	602.80	607.20	611.60	616.00
0.450	540.00	544.50	549.00	553.50	558.00	562.50	567.00	571.50	576.00	580.50	585.00	589.50	594.00	598.50	603.00	607.50	612.00	616.50	621.00	625.50	630.00
0.460	552.00	556.60	561.20	565.80	570.40	575.00	579.60	584.20	588.80	593.40	598.00	602.60	607.20	611.80	616.40	621.00	625.60	630.20	634.80	639.40	644.00

PLATINUM BULLION VALUE CHART

Oz.	1200.00	1210.00	1220.00	1230.00	1240.00	1250.00	1260.00	1270.00	1280.00	1290.00	1300.00	1310.00	1320.00	1330.00	1340.00	1350.00	1360.00	1370.00	1380.00	1390.00	1400.00
0.470	564.00	568.70	573.40	578.10	582.80	587.50	592.20	596.90	601.60	606.30	611.00	615.70	620.40	625.10	629.80	634.50	639.20	643.90	648.60	653.30	658.00
0.480	576.00	580.80	585.60	590.40	595.20	600.00	604.80	609.60	614.40	619.20	624.00	628.80	633.60	638.40	643.20	648.00	652.80	657.60	662.40	667.20	672.00
0.490	588.00	592.90	597.80	602.70	607.60	612.50	617.40	622.30	627.20	632.10	637.00	641.90	646.80	651.70	656.60	661.50	666.40	671.30	676.20	681.10	686.00
0.500	600.00	605.00	610.00	615.00	620.00	625.00	630.00	635.00	640.00	645.00	650.00	655.00	660.00	665.00	670.00	675.00	680.00	685.00	690.00	695.00	700.00
0.510	612.00	617.10	622.20	627.30	632.40	637.50	642.60	647.70	652.80	657.90	663.00	668.10	673.20	678.30	683.40	688.50	693.60	698.70	703.80	708.90	714.00
0.520	624.00	629.20	634.40	639.60	644.80	650.00	655.20	660.40	665.60	670.80	676.00	681.20	686.40	691.60	696.80	702.00	707.20	712.40	717.60	722.80	728.00
0.530	636.00	641.30	646.60	651.90	657.20	662.50	667.80	673.10	678.40	683.70	689.00	694.30	699.60	704.90	710.20	715.50	720.80	726.10	731.40	736.70	742.00
0.540	648.00	653.40	658.80	664.20	669.60	675.00	680.40	685.80	691.20	696.60	702.00	707.40	712.80	718.20	723.60	729.00	734.40	739.80	745.20	750.60	756.00
0.550	660.00	665.50	671.00	676.50	682.00	687.50	693.00	698.50	704.00	709.50	715.00	720.50	726.00	731.50	737.00	742.50	748.00	753.50	759.00	764.50	770.00
0.560	672.00	677.60	683.20	688.80	694.40	700.00	705.60	711.20	716.80	722.40	728.00	733.60	739.20	744.80	750.40	756.00	761.60	767.20	772.80	778.40	784.00
0.570	684.00	689.70	695.40	701.10	706.80	712.50	718.20	723.90	729.60	735.30	741.00	746.70	752.40	758.10	763.80	769.50	775.20	780.90	786.60	792.30	798.00
0.580	696.00	701.80	707.60	713.40	719.20	725.00	730.80	736.60	742.40	748.20	754.00	759.80	765.60	771.40	777.20	783.00	788.80	794.60	800.40	806.20	812.00
0.590	708.00	713.90	719.80	725.70	731.60	737.50	743.40	749.30	755.20	761.10	767.00	772.90	778.80	784.70	790.60	796.50	802.40	808.30	814.20	820.10	826.00
0.600	720.00	726.00	732.00	738.00	744.00	750.00	756.00	762.00	768.00	774.00	780.00	786.00	792.00	798.00	804.00	810.00	816.00	822.00	828.00	834.00	840.00
0.610	732.00	738.10	744.20	750.30	756.40	762.50	768.60	774.70	780.80	786.90	793.00	799.10	805.20	811.30	817.40	823.50	829.60	835.70	841.80	847.90	854.00
0.620	744.00	750.20	756.40	762.60	768.80	775.00	781.20	787.40	793.60	799.80	806.00	812.20	818.40	824.60	830.80	837.00	843.20	849.40	855.60	861.80	868.00
0.630	756.00	762.30	768.60	774.90	781.20	787.50	793.80	800.10	806.40	812.70	819.00	825.30	831.60	837.90	844.20	850.50	856.80	863.10	869.40	875.70	882.00
0.640	768.00	774.40	780.80	787.20	793.60	800.00	806.40	812.80	819.20	825.60	832.00	838.40	844.80	851.20	857.60	864.00	870.40	876.80	883.20	889.60	896.00
0.650	780.00	786.50	793.00	799.50	806.00	812.50	819.00	825.50	832.00	838.50	845.00	851.50	858.00	864.50	871.00	877.50	884.00	890.50	897.00	903.50	910.00
0.660	792.00	798.60	805.20	811.80	818.40	825.00	831.60	838.20	844.80	851.40	858.00	864.60	871.20	877.80	884.40	891.00	897.60	904.20	910.80	917.40	924.00
0.670	804.00	810.70	817.40	824.10	830.80	837.50	844.20	850.90	857.60	864.30	871.00	877.70	884.40	891.10	897.80	904.50	911.20	917.90	924.60	931.30	938.00
0.680	816.00	822.80	829.60	836.40	843.20	850.00	856.80	863.60	870.40	877.20	884.00	890.80	897.60	904.40	911.20	918.00	924.80	931.60	938.40	945.20	952.00
0.690	828.00	834.90	841.80	848.70	855.60	862.50	869.40	876.30	883.20	890.10	897.00	903.90	910.80	917.70	924.60	931.50	938.40	945.30	952.20	959.10	966.00
0.700	840.00	847.00	854.00	861.00	868.00	875.00	882.00	889.00	896.00	903.00	910.00	917.00	924.00	931.00	938.00	945.00	952.00	959.00	966.00	973.00	980.00
0.710	852.00	859.10	866.20	873.30	880.40	887.50	894.60	901.70	908.80	915.90	923.00	930.10	937.20	944.30	951.40	958.50	965.60	972.70	979.80	986.90	994.00
0.720	864.00	871.20	878.40	885.60	892.80	900.00	907.20	914.40	921.60	928.80	936.00	943.20	950.40	957.60	964.80	972.00	979.20	986.40	993.60	1000.80	1008.00
0.730	876.00	883.30	890.60	897.90	905.20	912.50	919.80	927.10	934.40	941.70	949.00	956.30	963.60	970.90	978.20	985.50	992.80	1000.10	1007.40	1014.70	1022.00
0.740	888.00	895.40	902.80	910.20	917.60	925.00	932.40	939.80	947.20	954.60	962.00	969.40	976.80	984.20	991.60	999.00	1006.40	1013.80	1021.20	1028.60	1036.00
0.750	900.00	907.50	915.00	922.50	930.00	937.50	945.00	952.50	960.00	967.50	975.00	982.50	990.00	997.50	1005.00	1012.50	1020.00	1027.50	1035.00	1042.50	1050.00
0.760	912.00	919.60	927.20	934.80	942.40	950.00	957.60	965.20	972.80	980.40	988.00	995.60	1003.20	1010.80	1018.40	1026.00	1033.60	1041.20	1048.80	1056.40	1064.00
0.770	924.00	931.70	939.40	947.10	954.80	962.50	970.20	977.90	985.60	993.30	1001.00	1008.70	1016.40	1024.10	1031.80	1039.50	1047.20	1054.90	1062.60	1070.30	1078.00
0.780	936.00	943.80	951.60	959.40	967.20	975.00	982.80	990.60	998.40	1006.20	1014.00	1021.80	1029.60	1037.40	1045.20	1053.00	1060.80	1068.60	1076.40	1084.20	1092.00
0.790	948.00	955.90	963.80	971.70	979.60	987.50	995.40	1003.30	1011.20	1019.10	1027.00	1034.90	1042.80	1050.70	1058.60	1066.50	1074.40	1082.30	1090.20	1098.10	1106.00
0.800	960.00	968.00	976.00	984.00	992.00	1000.00	1008.00	1016.00	1024.00	1032.00	1040.00	1048.00	1056.00	1064.00	1072.00	1080.00	1088.00	1096.00	1104.00	1112.00	1120.00
0.810	972.00	980.10	988.20	996.30	1004.40	1012.50	1020.60	1028.70	1036.80	1044.90	1053.00	1061.10	1069.20	1077.30	1085.40	1093.50	1101.60	1109.70	1117.80	1125.90	1134.00
0.820	984.00	992.20	1000.40	1008.60	1016.80	1025.00	1033.20	1041.40	1049.60	1057.80	1066.00	1074.20	1082.40	1090.60	1098.80	1107.00	1115.20	1123.40	1131.60	1139.80	1148.00
0.830	996.00	1004.30	1012.60	1020.90	1029.20	1037.50	1045.80	1054.10	1062.40	1070.70	1079.00	1087.30	1095.60	1103.90	1112.20	1120.50	1128.80	1137.10	1145.40	1153.70	1162.00
0.840	1008.00	1016.40	1024.80	1033.20	1041.60	1050.00	1058.40	1066.80	1075.20	1083.60	1092.00	1100.40	1108.80	1117.20	1125.60	1134.00	1142.40	1150.80	1159.20	1167.60	1176.00
0.850	1020.00	1028.50	1037.00	1045.50	1054.00	1062.50	1071.00	1079.50	1088.00	1096.50	1105.00	1113.50	1122.00	1130.50	1139.00	1147.50	1156.00	1164.50	1173.00	1181.50	1190.00
0.860	1032.00	1040.60	1049.20	1057.80	1066.40	1075.00	1083.60	1092.20	1100.80	1109.40	1118.00	1126.60	1135.20	1143.80	1152.40	1161.00	1169.60	1178.20	1186.80	1195.40	1204.00
0.870	1044.00	1052.70	1061.40	1070.10	1078.80	1087.50	1096.20	1104.90	1113.60	1122.30	1131.00	1139.70	1148.40	1157.10	1165.80	1174.50	1183.20	1191.90	1200.60	1209.30	1218.00
0.880	1056.00	1064.80	1073.60	1082.40	1091.20	1100.00	1108.80	1117.60	1126.40	1135.20	1144.00	1152.80	1161.60	1170.40	1179.20	1188.00	1196.80	1205.60	1214.40	1223.20	1232.00
0.890	1068.00	1076.90	1085.80	1094.70	1103.60	1112.50	1121.40	1130.30	1139.20	1148.10	1157.00	1165.90	1174.80	1183.70	1192.60	1201.50	1210.40	1219.30	1228.20	1237.10	1246.00
0.900	1080.00	1089.00	1098.00	1107.00	1116.00	1125.00	1134.00	1143.00	1152.00	1161.00	1170.00	1179.00	1188.00	1197.00	1206.00	1215.00	1224.00	1233.00	1242.00	1251.00	1260.00
0.910	1092.00	1101.10	1110.20	1119.30	1128.40	1137.50	1146.60	1155.70	1164.80	1173.90	1183.00	1192.10	1201.20	1210.30	1219.40	1228.50	1237.60	1246.70	1255.80	1264.90	1274.00
0.920	1104.00	1113.20	1122.40	1131.60	1140.80	1150.00	1159.20	1168.40	1177.60	1186.80	1196.00	1205.20	1214.40	1223.60	1232.80	1242.00	1251.20	1260.40	1269.60	1278.80	1288.00
0.930	1116.00	1125.30	1134.60	1143.90	1153.20	1162.50	1171.80	1181.10	1190.40	1199.70	1209.00	1218.30	1227.60	1236.90	1246.20	1255.50	1264.80	1274.10	1283.40	1292.70	1302.00
0.940	1128.00	1137.40	1146.80	1156.20	1165.60	1175.00	1184.40	1193.80	1203.20	1212.60	1222.00	1231.40	1240.80	1250.20	1259.60	1269.00	1278.40	1287.80	1297.20	1306.60	1316.00
0.950	1140.00	1149.50	1159.00	1168.50	1178.00	1187.50	1197.00	1206.50	1216.00	1225.50	1235.00	1244.50	1254.00	1263.50	1273.00	1282.50	1292.00	1301.50	1311.00	1320.50	1330.00
0.960	1152.00	1161.60	1171.20	1180.80	1190.40	1200.00	1209.60	1219.20	1228.80	1238.40	1248.00	1257.60	1267.20	1276.80	1286.40	1296.00	1305.60	1315.20	1324.80	1334.40	1344.00
0.970	1164.00	1173.70	1183.40	1193.10	1202.80	1212.50	1222.20	1231.90	1241.60	1251.30	1261.00	1270.70	1280.40	1290.10	1299.80	1309.50	1319.20	1328.90	1338.60	1348.30	1358.00
0.980	1176.00	1185.80	1195.60	1205.40	1215.20	1225.00	1234.80	1244.60	1254.40	1264.20	1274.00	1283.80	1293.60	1303.40	1313.20	1323.00	1332.80	1342.60	1352.40	1362.20	1372.00
0.990	1188.00	1197.90	1207.80	1217.70	1227.60	1237.50	1247.40	1257.30	1267.20	1277.10	1287.00	1296.90	1306.80	1316.70	1326.60	1336.50	1346.40	1356.30	1366.20	1376.10	1386.00
1.000	1200.00	1210.00	1220.00	1230.00	1240.00	1250.00	1260.00	1270.00	1280.00	1290.00	1300.00	1310.00	1320.00	1330.00	1340.00	1350.00	1360.00	1370.00	1380.00	1390.00	1400.00

More Must-Have Coin Guides

Standard Catalog of® World Coins, 1801-1900
5th Edition
by Colin R. Bruce II, Senior Editor; Thomas Michael, Market Analyst

Keep pace with today's world coins market, with current collector values, mintage figures, historical notes and the essential reference sections in this collector's must-have.
Softcover • 8-1/4 x 10-7/8
1,200 pages • 27,500 b&w photos
Item# SCN05 • $65.00

Ancient Coin Collecting III
The Roman World - Politics and Propaganda
2nd Edition
by Wayne G. Sayles

Approach early Roman coinage with the expertise and enthusiasm of an art-inspired ancient coin collector using this expanded new edition
Hardcover • 6 x 9 • 304 pages
300 b&w photos
Item# Z0742 • $29.99

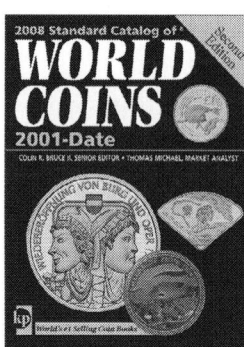

2008 Standard Catalog of® World Coins 2001 to Date
2nd Edition
by Colin R. Bruce, Senior Editor; Thomas Michael, Market Analyst

Increase the efficiency of your modern world coin collecting by accessing the up-to-date pricing and extensive listings in this Standard Catalog of® World Coins guide.
Softcover • 8-1/4 x 10-7/8
384 pages • 5,250 b&w photos
Item# Z0772 • $30.00

Strike It Rich with Pocket Change!
by Ken Potter and Brian Allen

Identify and easily determine the value of countless errors and varieties of coins with this one-of-a-kind guide, complete with 1,500+ large illustrations and grading scale.
Softcover • 6 x 9 • 272 pages
1,500+ b&w photos
Item# Z0497 • $16.99

Coins of Northern Europe & Russia
by George S. Cuhaj, Editor; Thomas Michael Senior Analyst

Easily identify coins from more than 25 countries of the region, issued between the late 1800s through 2000, using the 2,500 detailed photos and current pricing featured in this book.
Softcover • 6 x 9 • 600 pages
5,000 b&w photos and illus.
Item# Z0354 • $24.99

Order directly from the publisher
by calling **800-258-0929** M-F 8 am - 5 pm,
Online at
www.krausebooks.com
or from booksellers and other retailers nationwide.

 **Krause Publications**
700 E. State Street
Iola, WI 54990
www.krausebooks.com

Please reference offer **NUB7** with all direct-to-publisher orders.

HEJIRA DATE CONVERSION CHART

JEHIRA DATE CHART

HEJIRA (Hijira, Hegira), the name of the Muslim era (A.H. = Anno Hegirae) dates back to the Christian year 622 when Mohammed "fled" from Mecca, escaping to Medina to avoid persecution from the Koreish tribemen. Based on a lunar year the Muslim year is 11 days shorter.

*=Leap Year (Christian Calendar)

AH Hejira	AD Christian Date
1010	1601, July 2
1011	1602, June 21
1012	1603, June 11
1013	1604, May 30
1014	1605, May 19
1015	1606, May 19
1016	1607, May 9
1017	1608, April 28
1018	1609, April 6
1017	1608, April 28
1018	1609, April 6
1019	1610, March 26
1020	1611, March 16
1021	1612, March 4
1022	1613, February 21
1023	1614, February 11
1024	1615, January 31
1025	1616, January 20
1026	1617, January 9
1027	1617, December 29
1028	1618, December 19
1029	1619, December 8
1030	1620, November 26
1031	1621, November 16
1032	1622, November 5
1033	1623, October 25
1034	1624, October 14
1035	1625, October 3
1036	1626, September 22
1037	1627, Septembe 12
1038	1628, August 31
1039	1629, August 21
1040	1630, July 10
1041	1631, July 30
1042	1632, July 19
1043	1633, July 8
1044	1634, June 27
1045	1635, June 17
1046	1636, June 5
1047	1637, May 26
1048	1638, May 15
1049	1639, May 4
1050	1640, April 23
1051	1641, April 12
1052	1642, April 1
1053	1643, March 22
1054	1644, March 10
1055	1645, February 27
1056	1646, February 17
1057	1647, February 6
1058	1648, January 27
1059	1649, January 15
1060	1650, January 4
1061	1650, December 25
1062	1651, December 14
1063	1652, December 2
1064	1653, November 22
1065	1654, November 11
1066	1655, October 31
1067	1656, October 20
1068	1657, October 9
1069	1658, September 29
1070	1659, September 18
1071	1660, September 6
1072	1661, August 27
1073	1662, August 16
1074	1663, August 5
1075	1664, July 25
1076	1665, July 14
1077	1666, July 4
1078	1667, June 23
1079	1668, June 11
1080	1669, June 1
1081	1670, May 21
1082	1671, may 10
1083	1672, April 29
1084	1673, April 18
1085	1674, April 7

AH Hejira	AD Christian Date
1086	1675, March 28
1087	1676, March 16*
1088	1677, March 6
1089	1678, February 23
1090	1679, February 12
1091	1680, February 2*
1092	1681, January 21
1093	1682, January 10
1094	1682, December 31
1095	1683, December 20
1096	1684, December 8*
1097	1685, November 28
1098	1686, November 17
1099	1687, November 7
1100	1688, October 26*
1101	1689, October 15
1102	1690, October 5
1103	1691, September 24
1104	1692, September 12*
1105	1693, September 2
1106	1694, August 22
1107	1695, August 12
1108	1696, July 31*
1109	1697, July 20
1110	1698, July 10
1111	1699, June 29
1112	1700, June 18
1113	1701, June 8
1114	1702, May 28
1115	1703, May 17
1116	1704, May 6*
1117	1705, April 25
1118	1706, April 15
1119	1707, April 4
1120	1708, March 23*
1121	1709, March 13
1122	1710, March 2
1123	1711, February 19
1124	1712, Feburary 9*
1125	1713, January 28
1126	1714, January 17
1127	1715, January 7
1128	1715, December 27
1129	1716, December 16*
1130	1717, December 5
1131	1718, November 24
1132	1719, November 14
1133	1720, November 2*
1134	1721, October 22
1135	1722, October 12
1136	1723, October 1
1137	1724, September 19
1138	1725, September 9
1139	1726, August 29
1140	1727, August 19
1141	1728, August 7*
1142	1729, July 27
1143	1730, July 17
1144	1731, July 6
1145	1732, June 24*
1146	1733, June 14
1147	1734, June 3
1148	1735, May 24
1149	1736, May 12*
1150	1737, May 1
1151	1738, April 21
1152	1739, April 10
1153	1740, March 29*
1154	1741, March 19
1155	1742, March 8
1156	1743, Febuary 25
1157	1744, February 15*
1158	1745, February 3
1159	1746, January 24
1160	1747, January 13
1161	1748, January 2
1162	1748, December 22*
1163	1749, December 11
1164	1750, November 30
1165	1751, November 20
1166	1752, November 8*
1167	1753, October 29
1168	1754, October 18
1169	1755, October 7
1170	1756, September 26*
1171	1757, September 15
1172	1758, September 4
1173	1759, August 25
1174	1760, August 13*
1175	1761, August 2
1176	1762, July 23

AH Hejira	AD Christian Date
1177	1763, July 12
1178	1764, July 1*
1179	1765, June 20
1180	1766, June 9
1181	1767, May 30
1182	1768, May 18*
1183	1769, May 7
1184	1770, April 27
1185	1771, April 16
1186	1772, April 4*
1187	1773, March 25
1188	1774, March 14
1189	1775, March 4
1190	1776, February 21*
1191	1777, February 91
1192	1778, January 30
1193	1779, January 19
1194	1780, January 8*
1195	1780, December 28*
1196	1781, December 17
1197	1782, December 7
1198	1783, November 26
1199	1784, November 14*
1200	1785, November 4
1201	1786, October 24
1202	1787, October 13
1203	1788, October 2*
1204	1789, September 21
1205	1790, September 10
1206	1791, August 31
1207	1792, August 19*
1208	1793, August 9
1209	1794, July 29
1210	1795, July 18
1211	1796, July 7*
1212	1797, June 26
1213	1798, June 15
1214	1799, June 5
1215	1800, May 25
1216	1801, May 14
1217	1802, May 4
1218	1803, April 23
1219	1804, April 12*
1220	1805, April 1
1221	1806, March 21
1222	1807, March 11
1223	1808, February 28*
1224	1809, February 16
1225	1810, Febauary 6
1226	1811, January 26
1227	1812, January 16*
1228	1813, Janaury 26
1229	1813, December 24
1230	1814, December 14
1231	1815, December 3
1232	1816, November 21*
1233	1817, November 11
1234	1818, October 31
1235	1819, October 20
1236	1820, October 9*
1237	1821, September 28
1238	1822, September 18
1239	1823, September 18
1240	1824, August 26*
1241	1825, August 16
1242	1826, August 5
1243	1827, July 25
1244	1828, July 14*
1245	1829, July 3
1246	1830, June 22
1247	1831, June 12
1248	1832, May 31*
1249	1833, May 21
1250	1834, May 10
1251	1835, April 29
1252	1836, April 18*
1253	1837, April 7
1254	1838, March 27
1255	1839, March 17
1256	1840, March 5*
1257	1841, February 23
1258	1842, February 12
1259	1843, February 1
1260	1844, January 22*
1261	1845, January 10
1262	1845, December 30
1263	1846, December 20
1264	1847, December 9
1265	1848, November 27*
1266	1849, November 17
1267	1850, November 6

AH Hejira	AD Christian Date
1268	1851, October 27
1269	1852, October 15*
1270	1853, October 4
1271	1854, September 24
1272	1855, September 13
1273	1856, September 1*
1274	1857, August 22
1275	1858, August 11
1276	1859, July 31
1277	1860, July 20*
1278	1861, July 9
1279	1862, June 29
1280	1863, June 18
1281	1864, June 6*
1282	1865, May 27
1283	1866, May 16
1284	1867, May 5
1285	1868, April 24*
1286	1869, April 13
1287	1870, April 3
1288	1871, March 23
1289	1872, March 11*
1290	1873, March 1
1291	1874, February 18
1292	1875, Febuary 7
1293	1876, January 28*
1294	1877, January 16
1295	1878, January 5
1296	1878, December 26
1297	1879, December 15
1298	1880, December 4*
1299	1881, November 23
1300	1882, November 12
1301	1883, November 2
1302	1884, October 21*
1303	1885, October 10
1304	1886, September 30
1305	1887, September 19
1306	1888, September 7*
1307	1889, August 28
1308	1890, August 17
1309	1891, August 7
1310	1892, July 26*
1311	1893, July 15
1312	1894, July 5
1313	1895, June 24
1314	1896, June 12*
1315	1897, June 2
1316	1898, May 22
1317	1899, May 12
1318	1900, May 1
1319	1901, April 20
1320	1902, april 10
1321	1903, March 30
1322	1904, March 18*
1323	1905, March 8
1324	1906, February 25
1325	1907, February 14
1326	1908, February 4*
1327	1909, January 23
1328	1910, January 13
1329	1911, January 2
1330	1911, December 22
1332	1913, November 30
1333	1914, November 19
1334	1915, November 9
1335	1916, October 28*
1336	1917, October 17
1337	1918, October 7
1338	1919, September 26
1339	1920, September 15*
1340	1921, September 4
1341	1922, August 24
1342	1923, August 14
1343	1924, August 2*
1344	1925, July 22
1345	1926, July 12
1346	1927, July 1
1347	1928, June 20*
1348	1929, June 9
1349	1930, May 29
1350	1931, May 19
1351	1932, May 7*
1352	1933, April 26
1353	1934, April 16
1354	1935, April 5
1355	1936, March 24*
1356	1937, March 14
1357	1938, March 3
1358	1939, February 21
1359	1940, February 10*

AH Hejira	AD Christian Date
1360	1941, January 29
1361	1942, January 19
1362	1943, January 8
1363	1943, December 28
1364	1944, December 17*
1365	1945, December 6
1366	1946, November 25
1367	1947, November 15
1368	1948, November 3*
1369	1949, October 24
1370	1950, October 13
1371	1951, October 2
1372	1952, September 21*
1373	1953, September 10
1374	1954, August 30
1375	1955, August 20
1376	1956, August 8*
1377	1957, July 29
1378	1958, July 18
1379	1959, July 7
1380	1960, June 25*
1381	1961, June 14
1382	1962, June 4
1383	1963, May 25
1384	1964, May 13*
1385	1965, May 2
1386	1966, April 22
1387	1967, April 11
1388	1968, March 31*
1389	1969, march 20
1390	1970, March 9
1391	1971, February 27
1392	1972, February 16*
1393	1973, February 4
1394	1974, January 25
1395	1975, January 14
1396	1976, January 3*
1397	1976, December 23*
1398	1977, December 12
1399	1978, December 2
1400	1979, November 21
1401	1980, November 9*
1402	1981, October 30
1403	1982, October 19
1404	1984, October 8
1405	1984, September 27*
1406	1985, September 16
1407	1986, September 6
1409	1987, August 26
1409	1988, August 14*
1410	1989, August 3
1411	1990, July 24
1412	1991, July 13
1413	1992, July 2*
1414	1993, June 21
1415	1994, June 10
1416	1995, May 31
1417	1996, May 19*
1418	1997, May 9
1419	1998, April 28
1420	1999, April 17
1421	2000, April 6*
1422	2001, March 26
1423	2002, March 15
1424	2003, March 5
1425	2004, February 22*
1426	2005, February 10
1427	2006, January 31
1428	2007, January 20
1429	2008, January 10*
1430	2008, December 29
1431	2009, December 18
1432	2010, December 8
1433	2011, November 27*
1434	2012, November 15
1435	2013, November 5
1436	2014, October 25
1437	2015, October 15*
1438	2016, October 3
1439	2017, September 22
1440	2018, September 12
1441	2019, September 11*
1442	2020, August 20
1443	2021, August 10
1444	2022, July 30
1445	2023, July 19*
1446	2024, July 8
1447	2025, June 27
1448	2026, June 17
1449	2027, June 6*
1450	2028, May25

ILLUSTRATED GUIDE TO EASTERN MINT NAMES
Compiled by Dr. N. Douglas Nicol, 2006

Abarquh (Iran)	ابرقوه
'Abdullahnagar (Pihani)	عبدالله نگر
Abu Arish (the Yemen)	ابو عریش
Abushahr (Bushire - Iran)	ابو سهر
'Adan (Aden - the Yemen)	عدن
Adoni (Imtiyazgarh - Mughal)	ادوني
Adrana (see Edirne)	
Advani (Adoni - Mughal)	ادواني
Afghanistan	افغانستان
Agra (Mughal)	اگره
Ahmadabad (Gujarat Sultanate, Mughal, Maratha, Bombay Presidency, Baroda)	احمداباد
Ahmadnagar (Ahmadnagar Sultanate, Mughal)	احمدنگر
Ahmadnagar Farrukhabad (state, Afghanistan)	احمدنگر فرخ اباد
Ahmadpur (Bahawalpur, Afghanistan)	احمدپور
Ahmadshahi (Qandahar - Afghanistan)	احمدشاهي
Ahsanabad (Kulbarga - Mughal)	احسن اباد
Ajman (United Arab Emirates)	عجمان
Ajmer (Salimabad - Mughal, Maratha, Gwalior, Jodhpur)	اجمیر
Ajmer Salimabad (Mughal)	اجمیر سلیم اباد
Akalpurakh (Kashmir, Sikh)	اکال پورخ
Akbarabad (Agra - Mughal, Maratha, Bharatpur)	اکبراباد
Akbarnagar (Rajmahal - Mughal)	اکبرنگر
Akbarpur (Tanda - Mughal)	اکبرپور
Akbarpur Tanda (Mughal)	اکبرپور تانده
Akhtarnagar (Awadh - Mughal)	اخترنگر
'Akka (Ottoman Turkey)	عکّا عکّة
Aksu (China - Sinkiang)	اقسو اقسو
al-Aliya	العالية
'Alamgirnagar (Mughal, Koch)	عالمگیرنگر
'Alamgirpur (Bhilsa, Vidisha - Mughal, Gwalior)	عالم گیرپور
Amul (Iran)	آمل
al-'Arabiya as-Sa'udiya (Saudi Arabia)	العربية السعودية
al-'Ara'ish (Larache - Morocco)	العرائش
Algeria (al-Jaza'ir)	الجزائر
'Alinagar (Calcutta - Mughal)	علي نگر
'Alinagar Kalkatah (Calcutta - Bengal Pres.)	علي نگر کلکته
Allahabad (Mughal, Awadh)	الله اباد
Almora (Gurkha)	سهارنپور
Alwar (Mughal)	الوار
Amaravati (Hyderabad)	امراوتي
Amasya (Amasia - Turkey)	اماسية
Amid (Turkey)	آمد
Amritsar (Ambratsar - Sikh)	امبرت سر امرت سر
Amirkot (Umarkot - Mughal)	امیرکوت
Anandgharh (Anandpur - Mughal)	انندگهره
Andijan (Andigan - Central Asia)	اندجان اندگان
Anhirwala Pattan (Mughal)	انحیروالا پتن
Ankaland (Bi-Ankaland - in England, Birmingham and London mints for Morocco)	انکلند بانکلند
Ankara (Anguriya, Engüriye - Turkey)	انگورية انقرية انقرة
Anupnagar Shahabad (Mughal)	انوپنگر شاه باد
Anwala (Anola - Mughal, Rohilkhand, Afghanistan)	انوله
Aqsara (Aqsaray, Aksara - the Yemen)	اقصرا اقصراي اکصرا
Ardabil (Iran)	اردبیل
Ardanuç (Turkey)	اردنوچ اردانیچ
Ardanush (Iran)	اردنوش
Arjish (Iran)	ارجیش
Arkat (Arcot - Mughal, French India, Madras Presidency)	ارکات
Asafabad (Bareli - Mughal, Awadh)	اصف اباد
Asafabad Bareli (Mughal, Awadh)	اصفاباد
Asafnagar (Aklooj - Mughal, Rohilkhand, Awadh)	اصف نگر اصفنگر
Asfarayin (Central Asia, Iran)	اسفراین
Asfi (Safi - Morocco)	اسفي
Asir (Asirgarh - Mughal)	اسیر
Astarabad (Central Asia, Iran)	استراباد
Atak (Attock - Mughal, Afghanistan)	اتك
Atak Banaras (Mughal)	اتك بنارس
Atcheh (Sultanate, Netherlands East Indies)	اچه
Athani (Maratha)	اثاني
Aurangabad (Khujista Bunyad - Mughal, Hyderabad)	اورنگ اباد
Aurangnagar (Mughal, Maratha)	اورنگ نگر
Ausa (Mughal)	اوسا
Awadh (Oudh, Khitta - Awadh state)	اوده
Awbah (Central Asia)	اوبه
Ayasluk (Ayasoluq, Ephesus - Turkey)	ایاسلق ایاثلق
Aydaj (Iran)	ایدج
Azak (Azow - Turkey)	آزاق آزق
A'zamnagar (Gokak - Mughal)	اعظم نگر
A'zamnagar Bankapur (Mughal)	اعظم نگر بنکاپور
A'zamnagar Gokak (Belgaum - Mughal, Kolhapur)	اعظم نگر گوکاك
'Azimabad (Patna - Mughal, Bengal Presidency)	عظیم اباد
Badakhshan (Mughal, Central Asia, Afghanistan)	بدخشان
Bagalkot (Maratha)	بگلکوت
Bagchih Serai (Krim)	باغچه سراي
Baghdad (Bagdad - Iraq)	بغداد
Bahadurgarh (Mughal)	بهادرگره
Bahawalpur (Bahawalpur state, Afghanistan)	بهاولپور
Bahraich (Mughal)	بهرایچ بهریچ

Bahrain (al-Bahrayn)	البحرين
Bairata (Mughal)	بيراتة
Bakhar (Bakkar, Bakhar, Bhakhar, Bhakkar - Mughal, Sind, Afghanistan)	بهگّر بهکهر
Baku (Bakuya - Iran)	باکو باکویه
Balanagor Gadha (Mandla - Maratha)	بالانگر گڈہا
Balapur (two places - one in Kandesh, one in Sira - Mughal)	بالاپور
Balhari (Bellary - Mysore)	بلهاري
Balikesir (Turkey)	بالکسیر
Balkh (Mughal, Central Asia, Afghanistan)	بلخ
Balwantnagar (Jhansi-Mughal, Maratha, Gwalior)	بلونت نگر
Banaras (Benares, Varanasi - Mughal, Bengal Presidency, Awadh)	بنارس
Banda Malwari (Maratha)	بنده ملواري
Bandar (Iran)	بندر
Bandar Abbas (Iran)	بندر عباس
Bandar Abu Shahr (Iran)	بندر ابو شهر
Bandar Shahi (Mughal)	بندرشاهي
Bandhu (Qila - Mughal)	بندحو
Bangala (Mughal)	بنگالة
Banjarmasin (Netherlands East Indies)	بنجرمسن
Bankapur (Mughal)	بنکپ بنکاپور
Baramati (Sultanate, Mughal)	بارامتي برامتي
Bareli (Bareilly - Mughal, Rohilkhand, Awadh, Afghanistan)	بريلي
Bariz (Paris, in Paris - Morocco)	باریز بباریز
Baroda (Vadodara - Baroda state)	بروده
Basoda (Gwalior)	بسوده
al-Basra (Basra - Iraq)	البصرة
Batan (Baltistan? - Ladakh)	بتان
Bela (Las Bela state)	بیله
Belgrad (Turkey)	بنگالور
Bengalur (Bangalor - Mysore)	بنگالور
Berar (Mughal)	برار
Berlin (for Morocco)	برلین
Bhakkar, Bhakar (See Bakkar)	
Bharatpur (Braj Indrapur)	بهرت پور
Bhaunagar (Mughal)	بهاونگر
Bhelah (See Bela)	بهله
Bhilsa (Alamgirpur - Mughal)	بهيلسة
Bhilwara (Mewar)	بهيلوارا
Bhopal (Bhopal state)	بهوپال
Bhuj (Kutch)	بهوج
Bhujnagar (Bhuj - Kutch)	بهوج نگر
Bidlis (Bitlis - Turkey)	بدلیس بتلیس
Bidrur (Mughal)	بدرور
Bihbihan (Behbehan - Iran)	بهبهان
Bijapur (Bijapur Sultanate, Mughal)	بیجاپور
Bikanir (Mughal, Bikanir state)	بیکانیر
Bindraban (Vrindavan - Mughal, Bindraban state)	بندربن
Bisauli (Rohilkhand)	بسولے بسولي
Biyar (Iran)	بیار
Borujerd (Iran)	بروجرد
Bosna (Sarajevo - Turkey)	بوسنه
Bosna Saray (Sarajevo - Turkey)	بوسنة سراي
Braj Indrapur (Bharatpur)	برج اندرپور
Broach (Baroch, Bharoch - Mughal, Broach state, Gwalior)	بروني
Brunei (Malaya)	بروني
Bukhara (Central Asia)	بخارا
Bukhara-yi Sharif (Central Asia)	بخاراي شریف
Bundi (Bundi state)	بوندي
Burhanabad (Mughal)	برهان اباد
Burhanpur (Mughal, Maratha, Gwalior)	برهانپور
Bursa (Brusa - Turkey)	برسه بروسه
Bushanj (Iran)	بوشنج
Bushire (see Abushahr)	
Çaniçe (Chanicha - Turkey)	چانیچه چاینیچه
Chakan (Maratha)	چاکن
Champanir (Gujarat Sultanate)	چانپانیر
Chanda (Maratha)	چانده
Chanderi (Gwalior)	چندیري
Chandor (Maratha, Indore)	چاندور
Chhachrauli (Kalsia)	چچروليي
Chhatarpur (Chhatarpur state)	چترپور
Chikodi (Maratha)	چکودي
Chinapattan (Madras - Mughal)	چیناپتن
Chinchwar (Maratha)	چنچور
Chitor (Akbarpur - Mughal)	چیتور
Chunar (Mughal)	چنار
Cuttack (see Katak)	
Dadiyan (Iran)	دادیان
Dalipnagar (Datia)	دلیپ نگر
Damarvar (Mysore)	دماروار
al-Damigh (the Yemen)	الدامغ
Damla (Mughal)	داملا
Darband (Derbent - Azerbaijan, Iran)	دربند
Darfur (see al-Fashir)	
Darur (Mughal)	درور دارر
Daulatabad (Deogir - Mughal, Hyderabad)	دولت اباد دولتاباد
Daulat Anjazanchiya (see Comoros)	دولة انجزنچية
Daulatgarh (Rahatgarh - Bharatpur, Gwalior)	دولت گرہ
Daulat Qatar (State of Qatar - Qatar)	دولة قطر
Dawar (Iran)	داور
al-Dawla al-Mughribiya (Empire of Morocco)	الدولة المغربية
Dawlatabad (Iran)	دولتاباد
Dawraq (Iran)	دورق
Dehdasht (Iran)	دهدشت

ILLUSTRATED GUIDE TO EASTERN MINT NAMES — XXXVII

ILLUSTRATED GUIDE TO EASTERN MINT NAMES

Dehli دهلي
(Shahjahanabad - Mughal, Afghanistan)

Deli دلي
(Netherlands East Indies)

Deogarh ديوگره
(Partabgarh)

Deogir ديوگير
(Daulatabad - Mughal)

Dera ديره
(Derah - Mughal, Sikh, Afghanistan)

Derajat ديره جات
(Mughal, Sikh, Afghanistan)

Dewal Bandar ديول بندر
(Mughal)

Dezful دزفول
(Iran)

Dhamar ذمار
(the Yemen)

Dharwar دهاروار
(Mysore)

Dholapur دهولپور
(Dholapur state)

Dicholi ديچولي
(Mughal, Maratha)

Dilshadabad دلشاداباد
(Mughal, Narayanpett)

Dimashq دمشق
(Damascus - Syria)

Diyar Bakr جيبوتي
(Turkey)

Djibouti جيبوتي
(Jaibuti - French Somaliland)

Dogam دوگام
(Dogaon - Mughal)

Dogaon دوگاون
(Mughal)

Edirne ادرنه
(Adrianople - Turkey)

Elichpur ايلچپور
(Mughal, Hyderabad)

Erzurum ارزروم
(Theodosiopolis - Turkey)

Faiz Hisar فعز حصار
(Gooty - Mysore)

Farahabad فرح اباد
(Iran)

Farkhanda Bunyad فرخنده بنياد
(Hyderabad - Mughal)

Farrukhabad فرخ اباد
(Ahmadnagar - Mughal, Bengal Presidency)

Farrukhi فرخي
(Feroke - Mysore)

Farrukhnagar فرخ نگر
(Mughal)

Farrukhyab Hisar فرخياب حصار
(Chitradurga - Mysore)

Fas فاس
(Fez - Morocco)

Fas al-Jadid فاش الجديد
(see al-Madina al-Bayda' - Morocco)

al-Fashir الفشير
(Darfur, Sudan)

Fathabad Dharur فتح اباد دهرور
(Mughal)

Fathnagar فتحنگر
(Aurangabad - Mughal)

Fathpur فتحپور
(Nusratabad, Sikri - Mughal)

Fedala فضالة
(Fadalat al-Muhammadiya - Morocco)

Fergana فرغانة
(Central Asia)

Filastin فاسطين
(Palestine)

Filibe فيليپ فلبه
(Philipopolis, Plovdiv - Turkey)

Firozgarh فيروزگره
(Yadgir - Mughal)

Firoznagar فيروزنگر
(Mughal, Hyderabad)

al-Fujaira الفجيرة
(United Arab Emirates)

Fuman فومان
(Iran)

Gadraula گدرولة
(Mughal)

Gadwal گدوال
(Hyderabad)

Gajjikota گجيكوتا
(Mughal)

Ganja گنجه
(Ganjah, Genje - Elizabethpol, Kirovabad in Azerbaijan, Iran, Turkey)

Ganjikot گنجيكوت
(Genjikot - Mughal)

Gargaon گرگاو
(Assam)

Garha گارحة
(Mughal)

Gelibolu گليبولي
(Gallipoli - Turkey)

Ghazni غزني
(Afghanistan)

al-Ghurfa الغرفة
(Hadhramaut)

Gilan گنلان
(Iran)

Gobindpur گوبندپور
(Mughal)

Gohad گوهد
(Mughal, Dholapur)

Gokak گوكاك
(Belgaum, 'Azamnagar - Mughal)

Gokul گوكل
(Bindraban)

Gokulgarh گوكل گره
(Mughal)

Gorakpur گوركپور
(Muazzamabad - Mughal)

Gözlü گوزلو
(see Shahr-Gözlü - Krim)

Gulbarga گلبرگة
(Kulbarga, Ahsanabad - Mughal)

Gulkanda گلكندة
(Golkona - Sultanate, Mughal)

Gulshanabad گلشن اباد
(Nasik - Mughal, Maratha)

Gümüsh-hane گمشخانه
(Turkey)

Guti گوتي
(Gooty - Mughal, Mysore)

Guzelhisar گوزلحصر
(Turkey)

Gwaliar گواليار
(Mughal, Gwalior state, Gwalior Fort)

Hafizabad هافظاباد
(Mughal)

Haidarabad حيدراباد
(Hyderabad, Haidrabad, Farkhanda Bunyad - Golkanda Sultanate, Mughal, Hyderabad state, Sind, Afghanistan)

Haidarnagar حيدرنگر
(Bednur, Nagar - Mysore)

Hajipur حجيپور
(Mughal)

Halab بلب
(Aleppo - Syria)

Hamadan همدان
(Iran)

Hansi هانسي
(Qanauj - Mughal, Awadh)

al-Haramayn ash-Sharifayn الشريفين الحرمين
(Mecca and Medina in Arabia - Ottoman Turkey)

al-Harar الهرر
(Ethiopia)

Hardwar هاردوار
(Haridwar, Tirath - Mughal, Saharanpur)

Harput, Harburt
(see Khartapirt)

Harran حران
(Turkey)

Hasanabad حسن اباد
(Mughal)

Hathras هاتهرس
(Mughal, Awadh)

Hathrasa هاتهرسا
(Hathras)

Hawran حوران
(Horan - Syria)

Hawta حوطة
(the Yemen)

Hawz حوز
(Morocco)

al-Hejaz الحجاز
(Saudi Arabia)

Herat هراة هرات
(Afghanistan, Central Asia, Iran)

al-Hilla الحلة
(Hille - Iraq)

Hinganhat حنگنهات
(Maratha)

Hisar حصار
(Mughal)

Hisar حصر
(Central Asia)

Hisar Firoza حصار فيروزة
(Mughal)

ILLUSTRATED GUIDE TO EASTERN MINT NAMES XXXIX

al-Hisn (el-Hisin - Turkey) الحصن	**Jalalnagar** (Mughal) جلال نگر	**al-Jumhuriya as-Suriiya** (The Republic of Syria) الجمهورية السورية
Hizan (Khizan - Turkey) هزان خيزان	**Jalalpur** (Mughal) جلالپور	**al-Jumhuriya at-Tunisiya** (The Republic of Tunisia) الجمهورية التونسية
Hukeri (Mughal, Maratha) هوكري	**Jalaun** (Jalon - Maratha) جلون	**al-Jumhuriya al-Yaman al-Dimuqratia al-Shu'ubiya** (The Peoples' Democratic Republic of the Yemen) الجمهورية اليمن الديمقراطية الشعبية
Husaingarh (Mughal) حسين گره	**Jalesar** (Mughal) جليسار	**Jumhuriyeti Turkiye** (The Republic of Turkey) جمهوريتى توركيه
Huwayza (Iran) حويزة	**Jallandar** (Jullundur - Mughal) جالندر جلّندر	**Junagarh** (Junagadh - Mughal) جونة گره
Ibb (the Yemen) ايب	**Jalnapur** (Jalna - Mughal) جالنة پور	**al-Junub al-Arabi** (South Arabia) الجنوب العربي
Ilahabad (Allahabad) اله اباد	**Jambusar** (Baroda) جمبوسر	**Kabul** (Mughal, Afghanistan) كابل
Ilahabas (Mughal) اله اباس	**Jammu** (Jamun - Kashmir) جمون	**Kaffa** (Krim) كفّة
Ili (China - Sinkiang) الي	**Jaora** (Jaora state) جاوره	**Kalanur** (Mughal) كالانور
al-Imarat al-'Arabiya al-Muttahida (United Arab Emirates) امتيازگره	**Jaunpur** (Mughal) جونپور	**Kalat** (Kalat state) قلات كلات
Imtiyazgarh (Adoni - Mughal) امتيازگره	**Java** (Netherlands East Indies) جاو جاوا	**Kalian** (Kalayani - Hyderabad) كليان
Indore (Indore state) اندور	**Jaytapur** (Jaiyatpur - Mughal) جيت پور	**Kalikut** (Calicut, Kozhikode - Mysore) كليكوت
Inebolu (Turkey) اينه بولي	**Jaza'ir** (Algiers) جزائر	**Kalkatah** (Calcutta, Alinagar - Mughal, Bengal Presidency) كلكته
Inegöl (Turkey) اينه كول	**Jaza'ir Gharb** (Algiers) جزائر غرب	**Kalpi** (Mughal, Maratha) كلپي
Iran ايران	**al-Jaza'ir-i Gharb** (Algiers) الجزائر غرب	**Kanauj** (Qanauj - Mughal, Awadh) قنوج
al-Iraq	**Jelu** (Jelou - Iran) جلو	**Kanauj urf Shahgarh** (Qanauj - Mughal, Awadh) قنوج عرف شاه گره
Iravan (Eravan, Erewan, Revan - Iran, Yeravan – Armenia) ايروان	**Jerba** (Cerbe, Gabes - Tunis) جربة	**Kanbyat** (Kambayat, Kanbat, Khambayat - Mughal, Cambay state) كمبايت كهنبايت كنبات كنبايت
'Isagarh (Gwalior) عيسى گره	**Jering** (Jaring, Jerin - Thailand) جريج جرين	**Kandahar** (see Qandahar)
Isfahan (Iran) اصفهان	**Jhalawar** (Jhalawar state) جهالاوار	**Kangun** (Hosakote - Mughal) كنگون
Islamabad (Mathura – Mughal, Bindraban) اسلام اباد	**Jinji** (Nusratgarh - Mughal) جنجي	**Kanji** (Conjeeveram - Mughal) كنجي
Islam Bandar (Rajapur – Mughal) اسلام بندر	**Jind** (Jind state) جيند	**Kankurti** (Mughal, Maratha) كانكرتي
Islambul (Istanbul – Turkey) اسلامبول	**Jodhpur** (Mughal, Jodhpur state) جودهپور	**Kara Amid** (Turkey) قره آمد
Islamnagar (Navanagar – Mughal) اسلام نگر	**Jordan** (al-Urdunn) الاردن	**Karahisar** (Qara-Hisar - Turkey) قراحصار قره حصار
Ismailgarh (Mughal) اسمعيل گره	**al-Jumhuriya al-'Arabiya al-Muttahida** (The United Arab Republic - Egypt, Syria and the Yemen) الجمهورية العربية المتحدة	**Kararabad** (Karad - Mughal) كرارآباد
Italian Somaliland (Somalia) الصومال الايطالianية	**al-Jumhuriya al-'Arabiya al-Suriya** (The Arab Republic of Syria) الجمهورية العربية السورية	**Karatova** (Kratova - Turkey) قراطوه قراطوه
Itawa (Mughal, Maratha, Rohilkhand, Awadh) اتاوه اتاوا	**al-Jumhuriya al-'Arabiya al-Yamaniya** (The Arab Republic of the Yemen) الجمهورية العربية اليمنية	**Karauli** (Karauli state) كرولي
Izmir (Turkey) ازمير ازمر	**al-Jumhuriya al-'Iraqiya** (The Republic of Iraq) الجمهورية العراقية	**Karimabad** (Mughal) كريم اباد
Jabbalpur جبالپور	**al-Jumhuriya al-Libiya** (The Republic of Libya) الجمهورية الليبية	**Karnatak** (Carnatic - Mughal) كرناتك
Ja'farabad urf Chandor (Indore) جعفراباد عرف چاندور	**al-Jumhuriya al-Lubnaniya** (The Republic of Lebanon) الجمهورية اللبنانية	**Karpa** (Kurpa - Mughal) كرپا
Jahangirnagar (Dacca - Mughal, Bengal Presidency) جهانگيرنگر	**al-Jumhuriya as-Somal** (The Republic of Somalia) الجمهورية الصومال	**Kars** (Qars - Turkey) قارص قارس
Jaipur (Sawai - Mughal) جي پور	**al-Jumhuriya as-Sudan** (The Republic of the Sudan) الجمهورية السودان	**Kashan** (Iran) كاشان
Jaisalmir (Jaisalmir state) جيسلمير	**al-Jumhuriya as-Sudan al-Dimuqratiya** (The Democratic Republic of the Sudan) الجمهورية السودان الديمقراطية	

XL ILLUSTRATED GUIDE TO EASTERN MINT NAMES

Kashgar (China - Sinkiang) كاشغر كشغر كشقر

Kashmir (Srinagar - Kashmir Sultanate, Mughal, Sikh, Afghanistan) كشمير

Kastamonu (Turkey) قسطمونى

Katak (Cuttack - Mughal, Maratha) كتك

Katak Banaras (Mughal) كتك بنارس

Kawkaban (the Yemen) كوكبان

Kayeri (Turkey) قيصري قيسري

Kedah (Straits Settlements, Malaya) كداه

Kelantan (Straits Settlements, Malaya) كلنتن

Kemasin (Straits Settlements, Malaya) كماسن

Khairabad (Mughal) خيراباد

Khairnagar (Mughal) خيرنگر

Khairpur (Mughal, Sind) خيرپور

Khaliqabad (Dindigal - Mysore) خالق اباد

Khambayat (Kanbayat - Mughal) كمبايت

Khanabad (Afghanistan) خان اباد

Khanja (Canca, Hanca - Turkey) خانجة خانجا

Khanpur (Bahawalpur) خانپور

Khartapirt (Harput, Harburt - Turkey) خرتبرت خربت خربرت

Khizan (Turkey) خيزان

Khoqand (Central Asia) خوقند

Khotan (Khutan, China - Sinkiang) خوتن ختن

Khoy (Khoi, Khui - Iran) خوي

Khujista Bunyad (Aurangabad - Mughal, Hyderabad) خجسته بنياد

al-Khurfa (the Yemen) الخرفاة

Khurshid Sawad (Mysore) خورشيد سواد

Khwarizm (Central Asia) خوارزم

Kighi (Turkey) كيغي

Kirman (Kerman - Iran) كرمان

Kirmanshahan (Kermanshah - Iran) كرمانساهان

Kishangar (Kishangar state) كشنگره

Kishtwar (Mughal) كشتوار

Koçaniye (Kochana - Turkey) قوچانية

Koilkunda (Mughal) كويلكونده

Kolapur (Mughal, Kolhapur) كولاپور كلاپور

Konya (Turkey) قونية

Kora (Mughal, Maratha, Awadh) كورا

Kosantina (see Qusantinia)

Kosova (Kosovo - Turkey) قوصوه قوسوه

Kostantaniye (see Qustantaniya)

Kotah (Kotah state) كوته

Kotah urf Nandgaon كوته عرف نندگانو

Kubrus (Cyprus - Turkey) قبرص

Kuch Hijri (Kunch) كوچ حجري

Kuchaman (Mughal) كچامن

Kuche (China - Sinkiang) كوچا

Kufan (Kufin - Central Asia) كوفن كوفين

Kulbarga (see Gulbarga)

Kumber (Kumbar - see Maha Indrapur)

Kunar (Maratha) كنار

Kunch (Maratha) كونچ

Kurdasht (Azerbaijan) كرداشت كردشت

Kuwait (al-Kuwayt) الكويت

Ladakh (Ladakah - Kashmir, Afghanistan) لداكه لداخ

Lahej (the Yemen) لحج

Lahijan (Iran) لاهيجان

Lahore (Lahur - Mughal, Sikh, Afghanistan) لاهور

Lahri Bandar (Mughal) لهري بندر

Lar (Iran) لار

Larenda (Turkey) لارندة

Lashkar (Gwalior) لاشكار

Lebanon (Lubnan) لبنان

Legeh (Thailand) لغكه

Libya ليبيا

Lucknow (Lakhnau - Mughal, Awadh) لكهنو

Machhli Bandar (Masulipatam) مچهلي بندر

Machhlipatan (Masulipatam - Mughal, French India, Madras Pres.) مچهلي پتن

Madankot (Mughal) مدنكوت

al-Madina al-Bayda' (see Fas al-Jadid - Morocco) المدينة البيضاء

Madrid (for Morocco) مدريد

al-Maghrib (Morocco) المغرب

Maha Indrapur (Dig, Kumbar - Mughal, Bharatpur) مه اندرپور

Mahle (Male - Maldive Islands) محلي

Mahmud Bandar (Porto Novo - Mughal) محمودبندر

Mahoba (Maratha) مهوبة

Mailapur (Madras - Mughal) ميلاپور

Makhsusabad (Murshidabad - Mughal) مخصوص اباد

Malharnagar (Indore, also for Maheshwar) ملهارنگر

Malher (Malhar, Mulher - Mughal) ملهر

Maliknagar (Mughal) ملك نگر

Malnapur (Mughal) مالناپور

Malpur (Mughal) مالپور

Maluka (Netherlands East Indies) ملوكة

al-Mamlaka al-'Arabiya as-Sa'udiya (The Kingdom of Saudi Arabia) المملكة العربية السعودية

al-Mamlaka al-Libiya (The Kingdom of Libya) المملكة الليبية

al-Mamlaka al-Maghribiya (The Kingdom of Morocco) المملكة المغربية

al-Mamlaka al-Misriya (The Kingdom of Egypt) المملكة المصرية

al-Mamlaka al-Mutawakkiliya al-Yamaniya (The Mutawakkilite Kingdom of the Yemen) المملكة المتوكلية اليمنية

al-Mamlaka al-Tunisiya (The Kingdom of Tunisia) المملكة التونسية

al-Mamlaka al-Urdunniya al-Hashimiya (The Hashimite Kingdom of Jordan) الاردنية الهاشمية

Manastir (Turkey) مناستر

Mandasor (Gwalior) منديسور

Mandla (Maratha) مندلا

Mandu (Mughal) مندو

Mangarh (Mughal) مانگره

Manghir (Monghyr - Bihar) مانگهير

ILLUSTRATED GUIDE TO EASTERN MINT NAMES

Manikpur (Mughal)	مانکپور
Maragha (Azerbaijan, Iran)	مراغة
Marakesh (Marrakech - Morocco)	مراکش
Mar'ash (Turkey)	مرعش
Mardin (Turkey)	ماردین
Marv (Central Asia, Iran)	ماروار
Marwar (Jodhpur, Nagor, Pali, Sojat)	ماروار
al-Mu'askar (Mascara - Algeria)	المعسکر
Mashhad (Iran)	مشهد
Mashhad Imam Rida (Iran)	مشهد امام رضی
Mathura (Islamabad - Mughal, Bindraban)	متهره
Mazandaran (Iran)	مازندران
Mecca (Makkah - al-Hejaz)	مکّة
Medea (Algeria)	مدية
Meknes (Miknas - Morocco)	مکناس
Menangkabau (Netherlands East Indies)	منڠکابو
Merta (Mirath - Mughal, Jodhpur)	میرتا میرتة
Misr (Egypt, Turkey)	مصر
Modava (Moldava - Turkey)	موداوه مداوه
Mombasa (Kenya)	موداوه مداوه
Mosul (al-Mawsil - Iraq)	موصل الموصل
Muazzamabad (Gorakpur - Mughal, Awadh)	معظم اباد
Muhammadabad (Udaipur - Mughal)	محمداباد
Muhammadabad Banaras (Mughal, Awadh, Bengal Presidency, fictitious for Lucknow)	محمداباد بنارس
Muhammadabad urf Kalpi (Kalpi)	محمداباد عرف کلپي
al-Muhammadiya (al-Masila - Morocco)	المحمدية
al-Muhammadiya ash-Sharifa (Morocco)	المحمدية الشريفة
Muhammadnagar Tandah (Awadh)	محمدنگر تانده
Muhiabad Poona (Maratha)	محیی اباد پونه
Mujahidabad (Mughal)	مجاهداباد
Mujibalanagar (Rohilkhand)	مجی بالانگر
al-Mukala (the Yemen)	المکلا
Mukha (Mocca - the Yemen)	مخا
Mukhtara (the Yemen)	مختارة
Müküs (Turkey)	مکس
Multan (Mughal, Sikh, Afghanistan)	ملتان
Muminabad (Bindraban)	مؤمن اباد
Munbai (Mumbai, Bombay - Mughal, Bombay Presidency)	منبي
Mungir (Mughal)	مهنگیر
Muradabad (Mughal, Rohilkhand, Awadh, Afghanistan)	مراداباد
Murshidabad (Makhsusabad - Mughal, French India, Bengal Pres.)	مرشداباد
Murtazabad (Mughal)	مرتضاباد
Muscat (Oman)	مسقط
Mustafabad (Rampur - Rohilkhand)	مصطفاباد
Muzaffargarh (Jhajjar - Mughal)	مظفرگره
Mysore (Mahisur - Mysore state)	مهیسور مهي سور
Nabha (Sirkar - Nabha state)	سرکار نابهه
Nagar (Ahmadnagar, Bednur - Maratha, Mysore)	نگر
Nagar Ijri (Srinagar in Bundelkand)	نگر یجری
Nagor (Mughal, Jodhpur)	ناگور
Nagpur (Maratha)	ناگپور
Nahan (Sirmur)	ناهن
Nahtarnagar (Trichinopoly - Arcot)	نهتر نگر
Najafgarh (Mughal, Rohilkhand)	نجف گره
Najibabad (Mughal, Sikh, Rohilkhand, Awadh, Afghanistan)	نجیب اباد نجیباباد
Nakhjuvan (Iran, Azerbaijan)	نخجوان
Nandgaon (Nandgano - Kotah)	نندگانو
Nandgaon urf Kotah	نندگانو عرف کوته
Narnol (Mughal)	نارنول
Narwar (Sipri - Mughal, Gwalior, Narwar state)	نرور
Nasirabad (Sagar, Wanparti - Hyderabad)	نصر اباد
Nasirabad (Dharwar - Mughal)	نصیراباد
Nasiri (Iran)	ناصري
Nasrullahnagar (Rohilkhand)	نصرالله نگر
Nazarbar (Mysore)	نظربار
Nejd (Saudi Arabia)	نجد
Nigbolu (Turkey)	نگبولو
Nihavand (Iran)	نهاوند
Nimak (Sikh)	نمک
Nimruz (Central Asia, Iran)	نمرز نیمروز
Nipani (Maratha)	نپني
Nisa (Iran)	نسا
Nishapur (Naysabur - Iran)	نیشاپور
Novabirda (Novoberda - Turkey)	نوابرده
Novar (Turkey)	نوار
Nukhwi (Iran, Azerbaijan)	نخوي
Nusratabad (Dharwar, Nasratabad, Fathpur - Mughal)	نصرت اباد
Nusratgarh (Jinji - Mughal)	نصرت گره
Ohri (Okhri, Ochrida - Turkey)	اوخری
Oman ('Uman)	عمان
Omdurman (Umm Durman - the Sudan)	ام درمان
Orchha (Orchha state)	اورچهه
Ordu-Bagh (Iran)	اوردوباغ
Ordu-yi Humayun (Turkey)	اردو همایون
Orissa (Mughal)	اوریسة
Pahang (Straits Settlements)	فاخغ
Pakistan	پاکستان
Palembang (Netherlands East Indies)	فلمبغ
Palestine (see Filastin)	
Pali (Jodhpur)	پالي
Panahabad (Iran, Karabagh)	پناه اباد
Panipat (Mughal)	پاني پت
Parenda (Purenda - Mughal)	پرینده پرنده
Parnala (Qila) (Mughal)	پرنالا (قلع)
Patan (Seringapatan - Mysore)	پتن

XLII ILLUSTRATED GUIDE TO EASTERN MINT NAMES

al-Patani (Patani - Thailand)	الفطاني
Pathankot	پٹھنکوٹ
Patna (Azimabad - Mughal, Bengal Presidency)	پتنہ
Pattan (Anhirwala - Mughal)	پتن
Pattan Deo (Somnath – Mughal)	پتن دیو
Perak (Straits Settlements, Malaya)	فيرق
Peshawar (Mughal, Sikh, Afghanistan, Iran)	پشاور
Petlad (Baroda)	پتلاد
Phonda (Mughal)	پھونده
Pondichery (Pholcheri - French India)	پرچري
Pondichery (Porcheri - French India)	پرچري
Poona (Punah, Pune, Muhiabad - Mughal, Maratha)	پونہ
Pulu Malayu (Island of the Malays - Sumatra, Netherlands East Indies)	فولو ملايو
Pulu Penang (Penang, Prince of Wales Island - Straits Settlements, Malaya)	فولو فنينغ
Pulu Percha (Island of Sumatra - Netherlands East Indies)	فولو فرج
Punamali (Mughal)	پوناماليّ
Punch (Mughal)	پونچ
Purbandar (Porbandar - Mughal)	پوربندر
Qafsa (Capsa - Tunis, Tunisia)	قفصة
al-Qahira (Cairo - Egypt)	القاهرة
Qaiti (the Yemen)	القعياطي
Qamarnagar (Karnul - Mughal)	قمرنگر
Qanauj (see Kanauj)	
Qandahar (Ahmadshahi - Mughal, Afghanistan, Iran)	قندھار
Qarshi (Central Asia)	قرشي
Qasbah Panipat (Rohilkhand)	قصبة پاني پت
Qatar wa Dubai (Qatar and Dubai - Qatar)	قطر و دبي
Qazvin (Iran)	قزوين
Qubba (Azerbaijan)	قبة
Qumm (Qomm - Iran)	قم
Qunduz (Central Asia)	قندوز
Qusantinia (Qustantina, Qusantina - Constantine, Algiers)	قسنطينية قسنطينة قسنطينة
Qustantaniya (Constantinople - Turkey)	قسطنطنية
Rabat (Morocco)	رباط
Rabat al-Fath (Rabat - Morocco)	رباط الفتح
Rada' (the Yemen)	رادا ء
Radhanpur (Radhanpur state)	رادهنپور
Rajapur (Islam Bandar - Mughal)	راجاپور
Rajgarh (Alwar)	راج گڑھ
Ramhurmuz (Iran)	رامهرمز
Ra'nash (Ramhurmuz - Iran)	رعنش
Rangpur (Assam)	رنگپور
Ranthor (Ranthambhor - Mughal)	رنتھور
Ras al-Khaima (United Arab Emirates)	رأس الخيمة
Rasht (Resht - Iran)	رشت
Ratlam (Ratlam state)	رتلام
Ravishnagar Sagar (Garhakota - Gwalior)	روش نگر ساگر
Rehman (Reman - Thailand)	رحمن
Revan (Iravan - Armenia)	روان
Rewan (Rewa)	ريوان
Reza'iyeh (Urumi - Iran)	رضائية
Rikab (Rekab - Afghanistan, Iran)	ركاب
Rohtas (Rohtak - Mughal)	رحتاس رهتاس
Rudana (Taroudant - Morocco)	ردانة
Ruha (al-Ruha - Turkey)	الرها رها رهي
Sa'adnagar (Aklaj - Mughal)	سعدنگر
Sabzavar (Iran)	سبزوار
Sa'da (the Yemen)	صعدة
Sagar (Maratha, Bengal Pres.)	ساگر
Saharanpur (Mughal)	سهارنپور
Sahibabad Hansi (Hansi state)	صاحب اباد هنسي
Sahrind (Sarhind - Mughal, Cis-Sutlej Patiala, Afghanistan)	سرهند سرهند سهرند
Sailana (Sailana state)	سيلانہ
Saimur (Mughal)	سيمور
al-Saiwi (Sai, Saiburi, Teluban - Thailand)	السيوي
Sakiz (Saqyz, Scio - Turkey)	سكيز ساقز
Sakkhar (Mughal)	سكهر
Sala (Sale - Morocco)	سلا
Salamabad (Satyamangalam - Mysore)	سلام اباد
Salimabad (Ajmer - Mughal)	سليم اباد
Samandra (Turkey)	سمندرہ
Samarqand (Central Asia)	سمرقند
San'a (the Yemen)	صنعاء
Sanbal (Sambhal - Mughal)	سنبل
Sanbhar (Sambhar - Mughal)	سانبھر
Sangamner (Mughal)	سنگمنر
Sangli (Maratha)	سنگلي
al-Saniya (Turkey)	السنية
Sarakhs (Iran)	سرخس
Sarangpur (Mughal)	سارنگپور
Saray (Turkey)	سراي
Sari (Iran)	ساري
Sari Pol (Afghanistan)	سر پل
Sarhind (see Sahrind)	
Sashti (in Devanagari) (Maratha)	
Satara (Mughal)	ستارا
Saudi Arabia (see al-Hejaz, Nejd)	العربية السعودية
Sawai Jaipur (Jaipur, fictitious for Karauli)	سواي جيپور
Sawai Madhopur (Jaipur, fictitious for Sikar)	سواي مادهوپور
Sawuj Balaq (Iran)	ساوج بلاق
Selam (Selam state)	سيلم
Selanghur (Selangor - Straits Settlements, Malaya)	سلاغور
Selanik (Salonika - Turkey)	سلانيك
Selefke (Turkey)	سلفكه
Semnan (Simnan - Iran)	سمنان

ILLUSTRATED GUIDE TO EASTERN MINT NAMES

Serbernik (Turkey)	سربرنيك
Serez (see Siroz - Turkey)	سرز سريز
Seringapatan (Mysore)	
Shadiabad Urf Mandu (Mughal)	شاديآباد ارف مندو
Shadman (Central Asia)	شادمان
Shadora (Gwalior)	شادهوره
Shahabad (Awadh)	شاه آباد قنوج شاهآباد
Shahabad Qanauj (Mughal, Rohilkhand, Awadh)	شاه آباد قنوج
Shahgarh Qanauj (Mughal)	شاه گره قنوج
Shahjahanabad (Dehli - Mughal, Bhilwara, Bindraban, Chitor, Mathura, Shapura, Udaipur, also fictitious for Bagalkot, Jaisalmir, Satara-EIC)	شاه جهان اباد
Shahr-Gözlü (see Gözlü - Krim)	شهرگوزلو
Shakola (Mughal)	شكولا
Shamakhi (Shamakha, Shemakhi - Iran, Azerbaijan)	شماخي شماخه
Sharakat Almaniya (German East Africa Co.)	شراكة المانيا
ash-Sharja (Sharja - United Arab Emirates)	الشارجة
Shekki (Iran)	شكّي
Sheopur (Gwalior)	شيوپور
Shergarh (Shirgarh - Mughal)	شيرگره
Sherkot (Mughal)	شيركوت
Sherpur (Shirpur - Mughal)	شيرپور
Shikarpur (Sind)	شكارپور
Shiraz (Iran)	شيراز
Shirvan (Azerbaijan, Iran, Turkey)	شيروان شروان
Sholapur (Mughal)	شولاپور
Shustar (Iran)	شوستر
Siak (Netherlands East Indies)	سيك
Sidrekipsi (Turkey)	بسدره قپسی
Siirt (Sa'irt - Turkey)	سعرت
Sijilmasa (Sizilmassa - Morocco)	سجلماسة
Sikakul (Chicacole - Mughal)	سيكاكل
Sikandarah (Sikandra – Mughal)	سكندره
Sind (Mughal, Sind state, Afghanistan, Iran)	سند
Singgora (Thailand)	سڠورا
Sira (Mughal)	سيرة
Sironj (Mughal, Indore, Tonk)	سرونج
Siroz (see Serez - Turkey)	سيروز
Sistan (Iran)	سيستان
Sitamau (Sitamo)	سيتامو
Sitapur (Mughal)	سيتاپور
Sitpur (Sidhpur in Gujarat? - Mughal)	سيتپور
Sivas (Siwas - Turkey)	سيواس
Sofia (Turkey)	صوفية
Sojat (Jodhpur)	سوجت
al-Somal al-Italyaniya (Italian Somaliland, Somalia)	الصومال الايطاليانية
Srebernice (Serbernichna - Turkey)	سربرنيچه
Sri (Amritsar)	سري
Sri Akalpur (Malkarian)	سري اكلپور
Srinagar (Mughal, Garhwal, Kashmir)	سرينگر
Srinagar (in Bundelkhand - Maratha)	سرينگر
Sultanabad (Iran)	سلطاناباد
Sultanpur (Mughal)	سلطانپور
Sumenep (Netherlands East Indies)	سمنف
Surat (Mughal, French India, Bombay Presidency, fictitious for Chand)	سورت
Suriya (Syria)	سورية
al-Suwair/al-Suwaira (Essaouir, Essaouira - Mogador, Morocco)	السوير الصويرة
Tabaristan (Iran)	طبرستان
Tabriz (Iran, Turkey)	تبريز
Tadpatri (Mughal)	تدپتري
Ta'izz (the Yemen)	تعز
Tanah Malayu (Land of the Malays - Sumatra, Malacca, Straits Settlements)	تانة ملايو
Tana Ugi (Land of the Bugis - Netherlands East Indies)	تانة اغيسى
Tanda (Akbarpur - Bengal Sultanate, Mughal, Awadh)	تانده
Tanja (Tangier - Morocco)	طنجة
Tappal (Mughal)	تپّل
Taqidemt (Algiers)	تاقدمت
Tarablus (Tripoli in Lebanon)	طرابلس
Tarablus Gharb (Tripoli West - in Libya)	طرابلس غرب
Tarapatri (Mughal)	تراپتري
Tarim (the Yemen)	تريم
Tashkand (Tashkent - Central Asia)	تشكند
Tashqurghan (Afghanistan)	تاشقورغان
Tatta (Tattah - Mughal, Sind, Afghanistan)	تته
Tehran (Iran)	طهران
Tellicherry (French India, Bombay Presidency)	تلجري تالچري
Termez (Central Asia)	ترمذ
Tetuan (Tetouan, Titwan - Morocco)	تطوان
Tibet (Mughal, Ladakh)	تبت
Tiflis (Georgia, Iran)	تفليس
Tilimsan (Tlemcen, Aghadir - Algiers)	تلمسان
Tirat Hardwar (Hardwar)	تيرتهردوار
Tire (Turkey)	تيره
Tokat (Tuqat - Turkey)	توقاط توقات دوقات طوقات
Tonk (Tonk state)	تونك
Toragal (Mughal, Maratha)	تورگل توراگال
Trabzon (Trebizond - Turkey)	طرابزون طرابزن
Trengganu (Straits Settlements, Malaya)	ترغگانو
Tunis (Tunisia)	تونس
Tuyserkan (Iran)	توي سركان
Udaipur (Muhammadabad - Mughal)	اوديپور اديپور
Udgir (Mughal)	ادگير
Ujjain (Mughal, Gwalior)	اجين
Ujjain Dar al-Fath (Gwalior)	اجين دارالفتح
Ujjainpur (Mughal)	اجين پور
Umarkot (Mughal)	امركوت
Umm al-Qaiwain (United Arab Emirates)	ام القيوين

XLIV   ILLUSTRATED GUIDE TO EASTERN MINT NAMES

United Arab Emirates
(see al-Imarat al-'Arabiya al-Muttahida)

Urdu اردو
(Camp mint - Mughal, Central Asia, Iran)

Urdu Dar Rahi-i-Dakkin اردو دار راه دكين
(Mughal)

Urdu Zafar Qirin اردو ظفر قرين
(Mughal)

al-Urdunn الاردن
(Jordan)

Urumchi ارومچي
(China - Sinkiang)

Urumi ارومي ارومية ارمية
(Urumia, Urmia, Reza'iya - Iran)

Ushi اوش
(China - Sinkiang)

Usküp اسكوپ
(Uskub, Skopje, Kosovo - Turkey)

Van وان
(Wan - Turkey, Armenia)

Varne ورنه
(Turkey)

al-Yaman اليمن
(the Yemen)

Yarkand يارقند
(China - Sinkiang)

Yarkhissarmaran ياركسارمرن
(China - Sinkiang)

Yazd يزد
(Iran)

Yenishehr ينكى شهر
(Larissa - Turkey)

Za صا
(Taorirt - Morocco)

Zabid زبيد
(the Yemen)

Zafarabad ظفراباد
(Bidar - Mughal, Gurramkonda - Mysore)

Zafarnagar ظفرنگر
(Fathabad - Mughal)

Zafarpur ظفرپور
(Mughal)

Zain-ul-Bilad زين البلاد
(Ahmadabad - Mughal)

Zanjibar زنجبار زنجبارا
(Zanjibara - Zanzibar)

Zebabad زيب اباد
(Mughal, Sardhanah)

Zegam زگام
(Zigam - Iran)

Zinjan زنجان
(Zanjan - Iran)

al-Zuhra الزهرة
(the Yemen)

Geographical Terms:

Baldat بلدات
(City - Agra, Allahabad, Burhanpur, Bikanir, Patna, Sarhind, Ujjain)

Bandar بندر
(Port - Dewal, Hari, Surat, Machhlipatan)

Dakhil داخل
(Breach, Entrance - Chitor)

Dawla/Daula دولة
(State, State of)

Hazrat حضرة
(Royal Residence - Fas, Marakesh, Dehli)

Khitta خطة
(District - Awadh, Kalpi, Kashmir, Lakhnau)

Negri نكري
(State of - Straits Settlements, Malaya, Netherlands East Indies, Thailand)

Qasba قصبة
(Town - Panipat, Sherkot)

Qila قلعة قلع
(Fort - Agra, Alwar, Bandhu, Gwalior, Punch)

Qila Muqam قلعة مقام
(Fort Residence - Gwalior)

Qita قطة
(District - Bareli)

Sarkar سركار
(County - Lakhnau, Torgal)

Shahr شهر
(City - Anhirwala Pattan)

Suba سوبة
(Province - Awadh)

Tirtha ترتة
(Shrine - Hardwar)

Poetic Allusion:

Ashraf al-Bilad اشراف البلاد
(Most Noble of Cities - Qandahar/Ahmadshahi)

Baldat-i-Fakhira بلدات فخيرة
(Splendid City - Burhanpur)

Bandar-i-Mubarak بندر مبارك
(Blessed Port - Surat)

Dar-ul-Aman دار الامان
(Abode of Security - Agra, Jammu, Multan, Sarhind)

Dar-ul-Barakat دار البركات
(Abode of Blessings - Jodhpur, Nagor)

Dar-ul-Fath دار الفتح
(Seat of Conquest - Ujjain)

Dar-ul-Islam دار الاسلام
(Abode of Islam - Bahawalpur, Dogaon, Mandisor)

Dar-ul-Jihad دار الجهاد
(Seat of Holy War - Hyderabad)

Dar-ul-Khair دار الخير
(Abode of Beneficence - Ajmer)

Dar-ul-Khilafa دار الخلافة
(Abode of the Caliphate - Agra, Ahmadabad, Akbarabad, Akbarpur Tanda, Awadh, Bahraich, Daulatabad, Dogaon, Gorakpur, Gwalior, Jaunpur, Kanauj, Lahore, Lakhnau, Malpur, Shahgarh, Shahjahanabad, Tehran, the Yemen)

Dar-ul-Mansur دار المنصور
(Abode of the Victorious - Ajmer, Jodhpur)

Dar-ul-Mulk دار الملك
(Seat of Kingship - Dehli, Fathpur, Kabul)

Dar an-Nusrat دار النصرات
(Abode of Succor - Herat)

Dar-ur-Riyasa دار الرياسة
(Seat of the Chief of State - Jaisalmir)

Dar-us-Salam دار السلام
(Abode of Peace - Dogaon, Mandisor, Legeh)

Dar-us-Saltana دار السلطنة
(Seat of the Sultanate - Ahmadabad, Burhanpur, Fathpur, Herat, Kabul, Kora, Lahore)

Dar-ul-Surur دار السرور
(Abode of Happiness - Bahawalpur, Burhanpur, Saharanpur)

Dar-uz-Zafar دار الظفر
(Seat of Victory - Advani, Bijapur)

Dar-uz-Zarb دار الضرب
(Seat of the Mint - Jaunpur, Kalpi, Patna)

Farkhanda Bunyad فرخنده بنياد
(Of Auspicious Foundation - Hyderabad)

Hazrat حضرت
(Venerable - Dehli)

Khujista Bunyad خجستة بنياد
(Of Fortunate Foundation - Aurangabad)

Mustaqarr-ul-Khilafa مستقر الخلافة
(Residence of the Caliphate - Akbarabad, Ajmer)

Mustaqarr-ul-Mulk مستقر الملك
(Abode of Kingship - Akbarabad, Azimabad)

Sawai سواي
(One-fourth, i.e. "a notch better" - Jaipur)

Umm al-Bilad ام البلاد
(Mother of Cities - Balkh)

Zain-ul-Bilad زين البلاد
(The Most-Beautiful of Cities – Ahmadabad)

AFGHANISTAN

The Islamic State of Afghanistan, which occupies a mountainous region of Southwest Asia, has an area of 251,825 sq. mi. (652,090 sq. km.) and a population of 25.59 million. Presently, about a fifth of the total population lives in exile as refugees, (mostly in Pakistan). Capital: Kabul. It is bordered by Iran, Pakistan, Turkmenistan, Uzbekistan, Tajikistan, and China's Sinkiang Province. Agriculture and herding are the principal industries; textile mills and cement factories add to the industrial sector. Cotton, wool, fruits, nuts, oil, sheepskin coats and hand-woven carpets are normally exported but foreign trade has been interrupted since 1979.

Because of its strategic position astride the ancient land route to India, Afghanistan (formerly known as Aryana and Khorasan) was invaded by Darius I, Alexander the Great, various Scythian tribes, the White Huns, the Arabs, the Turks, Genghis Khan, Tamerlane, the Mughals, the Persians, and in more recent times by Great Britain. It was a powerful empire under the Kushans, Hephthalites, Ghaznavids and Ghorids. The name Afghanistan, "Land of the Afghans," came into use in the eighteenth and nineteenth centuries to describe the realm of the Afghan kings. For a short period, this mountainous region was the easternmost frontier of the Iranian world, with strong cultural influences from the Turks and Mongols to the north and India to the south.

Previous to 1747, Afghan Kings ruled not only in Afghanistan, but also in India, of which Sher Shah Suri was one. Ahmad Shah Abdali, founder of the Durrani dynasty, established his rule at Qandahar in 1747. His clan was known as Saddozai. He conquered large territories in India and eastern Iran, which were lost by his grandson Shah Zaman. A new family, the Barakzai, drove the Durrani king out of Kabul, the capital, in 1819, but the Durranis were not eliminated completely until 1858. Further conflicts among the Barakzai prevented full unity until the reign of Abdur Rahman beginning in 1880. In 1929, King Amanullah, grandson of Abdul Rahman, was driven out of the country by a commoner known as Baccha-i-Saqao, "Son of the Water-Carrier", who ruled as Habibullah for less than a year before he was defeated by Muhammad Nadir Shah, a relative of the Barakzai. The last king, Muhammad Zahir Shah, became a constitutional though still autocratic monarch in 1964. In 1973 a coup d'etat displaced him and created the Republic of Afghanistan. A subsequent military coup established the pro-Soviet Democratic Republic of Afghanistan in 1978. Mounting resistance in the countryside and violence within the government led to the Soviet invasion of late 1979 and the installation of Babrak Karmal as prime minister. A brutal civil war ensued, which continues to the present, even after Soviet forces withdrew in 1989 and Karmal's government was defeated. An unstable coalition of former *Mujahideen* (Freedom Fighters) factions attempted to govern for several years but have been gradually overcome by the Taleban, a Muslim fundamentalist force supported from Pakistan.

Afghanistan's traditional coinage was much like that of its neighbors Iran and India. There were four major mints: Kabul, Qandahar, Balkh and Herat. The early Durranis also controlled mints in Iran and India. On gold and silver coins, the inscriptions in Persian (called *Dari* in Afghanistan) included the name of the mint city and, normally, of the ruler recognized there, but some issues are anonymous. The arrangement of the inscriptions, and frequently the name of the ruler, was different at each mint. Copper coins were controlled locally and usually did not name any ruler. For these reasons the coinage of each mint is treated separately. The relative values of gold, silver, and copper coins were not fixed but were determined in the marketplace.

In 1891 Abdur Rahman had a modern mint set up in Kabul using British minting machinery and the help of British advisors. The other mints were closed down, except for the issue of local coppers. The new system had 60 paisa equal one rupee; intermediate denominations also had special names. In 1901 the name Afghanistan appeared on coins for the first time. A decimal system, 100 puls to the afghani, was introduced in 1925. The gold amani, rated at 20 afghanis, was a bullion coin.

The national symbol on most coins of the kingdom is a stylized mosque, within which is seen the *mihrab*, a niche indicating the direction of Mecca, and the *minbar*, the pulpit, with a flight of steps leading up to it. Inscriptions in Pashtu were first used under the rebel Habibullah, but did not become standard until 1950.

Until 1919, coins were dated by the lunar Islamic Hejira calendar (AH), often with the king's regnal year as a second date. The solar Hejira (SH) calendar was introduced in 1919 (1337 AH, 1298 SH). The rebel Habibullah reinstated lunar Hejira dating (AH 1347-50), but the solar calendar was used thereafter. The solar Hejira year begins on the first day of spring, about March 21. Adding 621 to the SH year yields the AD year in which it begins.

RULERS

Names of rulers are shown in Perso-Arabic script in the style usually found on their coins; they are not always in a straight line.

DURRANI OR SADDOZAI DYNASTY

شاه زمان
Shah Zaman, AH1207-1216/1793-1801AD

محمود شاه
Mahmud Shah Shuja al-Mulk, 1st reign, AH1216-1218/1801-1803AD

قیصر شاه
Qaisar Shah, AH1218/1803AD

شاه شجاع الملک
Shah Shuja al-Mulk, 2nd reign, AH1218-1224/1803-1808AD

Mahmud Shah, 2nd reign, AH1224-1233/1808-1817A

ایوب شاه
Ayyub Shah, Puppet of Dost Muhammad, AH1233-1245/1817-1829AD

شیردل خان
Sherdil Khan, AH1240-1242/1824-1826ADD

پردل خان
Purdil Khan, AH1242-1245/1826-1829AD

سلطان محمد
Sultan Muhammad, at Peshawar AH1247-1250/1831-1834AD

کهندل خان
Kohandil Khan, 1st reign, at Qandahar AH1245-1254/1829-1838AD

Shah Shuja al-Mulk, as nominee of British East India Co., 3rd reign, AH1255-1258/1839-1842AD

فتح جنگ
Fath Jang AH1258/1842AD

شاه پور شاه
Shahpur Shah AH1258/1842AD

کهندل خان
Kohandil Khan, 2nd reign AH1259-1272/1843-1855AD

رحامدل خان
Rahamdil Khan, AH1272/1855AD

Succession at Kashmir, AH1221-1234

قیصر شاه
Qaisar Shah, AH1221-1223/1806-1808AD

Azim Khan, coins in name of Mahmud Shah, AH1228-1234/1813-1818AD

Succession at Herat, AH1216-1298
Mahmud Shah, AH1216-1245/1801-1829AD

کامران شاه
Kamran Shah, AH1245-1258/1829-1842AD

یار محمد خان برکزای
Yar Muhammad Khan Barakzai, AH1258-1267/1842-1851AD

محمد یوسف خان سادوزای
Muhammad Yusuf Khan Sadozai, AH1267-1272/1851-1856AD,

Iranian Occupation of Herat (coins in name of Nasir al-Din Shah): AH1272-1280/1856-1863AD

محمد افضل شیر علی
Sher Ali, AH1280-1296/1863-1879AD

محمد یعقوب
Muhammad Yaqub AH1296-1298/1879-1881AD
thereafter, as in the rest of Afghanistan

BARAKZAI DYNASTY

عبد الرحمن
Abdur Rahman, AH1297-1319/1880-1901AD

Habibullah, AH1319-1337/1901-1919AD

Amanullah, AH1337, SH1298-1307/1919-1929AD

Habibullah (rebel, known as Baccha-i-Saqao), AH1347-1348/1929AD

Muhammed Nadir Shah, AH1348-1350, SH1310-1312/1929-1933AD

Muhammad Zahir Shah, SH1312-1352/1933-1973AD

Republic, SH1352-1358/1973-1979AD

Democratic Republic, SH1358-1373/1979-1994 AD

Islamic Republic, SH1373-1381/1994-2002AD

MINT NAMES

Coins were struck at numerous mints in Afghanistan and adjacent lands. These are listed below, together with their honorific titles, and shown in the style ordinarily found on the coins.

افغانستان
Afghanistan

احمدنگر فرخ اباد
Ahmadnagar-Farrukhabad

احمد شاهی
Ahmadshahi, see Qandahar

Until AH 1273, this mint was almost always given on the coins as *Ahmadshahi*, a name given it by Ahmad Shah in honor of himself in AH1171, often with the honorific *Ashraf as-Bilad* (meaning 'Most Noble of Cities'). On later issues, after AH1271, the traditional name *Qandahar* is generally used.

Although Qandahar was Ahmad Shah's capital throughout his reign, he did not issue coins from there until AH1171 (1758AD).

اشرف البلاد
'Ashraf al-Bilad', Most Noble of Cities

Anwala

Attock

AFGHANISTAN

بلخ

Balkh,
Located in northern Afghanistan, Balkh bore the honorary epithet of *Umm al-Bilad*, 'Mother of Cities', because of its great age. It was taken by Ahmad Shah from the Amir of Bukhara in AH1180 (1765AD) and lost by Taimur Shah to the Uzbeks in AH1206 (1792AD).

ام البلاد

'Umm al-Bilad',
Mother of Cities

بریلی

Bareli

بھکر

Bhakkar
The mint is found variously spelled, as *Bhakhar* (most common), *Bakhar*, and *Bakkar*.

دھلی

Dehli,
see Shahjahanabad

دیرہ

Dera,
Dera Ghazi Khan
The mint of Dera was located at Dera Ghazi Khan, taken by the Sikhs in AH1235 (1819AD), and now within Pakistan.

دیرہ جات

Derajat,
Dera Isma'il Khan
The mint of Derajat was located at Dera Ismail Khan, which fell to the Sikhs in AH1236 (1820-21AD). Issues in the name of Mahmud Shah dated AH1236 and later are actually Sikh issues. The Sikhs formally annexed Derajat in AH1281 (1835AD).

حیدرآباد سند

Haidarabad Sind

ھرات

Herat

دار السلطنۃ

'Dar as-Sultanat',
Abode of the Sultanate

جلال آباد

Jalalabad

کابل

Kabul,
'Dar as-Sultanat', see Herat

کشمیر

Kashmir

ਰਾਮ ਸੀਰ

Lahore

مشھد

Mashhad
Mashhad, entitled Muqaddas (holy), was the chief city of Iranian Khorasan. From AH1161/1748AD until AH1218/1803AD, it was the capital of the Afsharid principality which remained under nominal Durrani suzerainty from AH1163/1750AD onwards. Coins were struck in the name of Durrani rulers in AH1163, 1168-1186, 1198-1218.

دار الامان

Multan
Multan was annexed by Ahmad Shah in AH1165/1752AD, and held under Afghan rule until lost to the Sikhs in AH1233/1818AD, except for an interval of Maratha control in AH1173/1759AD and Sikh control from AH1185-1194/1771-1780AD.

مرادآباد

Muradabad

نجیب آباد

Najibabad

پشاور

Peshawar
Peshawar passed to Ahmad Shah after the death of Nadir Shah Afshar, who had seized it from the Mughals in AH1151/1738AD. It was lost to the Sikhs in AH1250/1834AD. Although the winter capital of the Durranis, it was never granted an honorific epithet.

قندھار

Qandahar,
see Ahmadshahi
Issues of this mint are listed together with those of Ahmadshahi, which was a name of Qandahar granted in honor of Ahmad Shah, founder of the Durrani Kingdom.

رکاب

Rikab,
'Mubarak',
Auspicious
The Camp mint brought *Mubarak* with the royal entourage while traveling.

سھرند

Sahrind,
(Sarhind)

شاہ جھان آباد

Shahjahanabad,
see Delhi
Shahjahanabad was the Mughal name for Delhi, which was twice seized by Ahmad Shah, once for a couple of months in AH1170/winter 1756-1757AD, a second time in AH1173-1174/1760-1761AD for thirteen months.

سند

Sind

تتہ

Tatta

NAMED HAMMERED COINAGE

Unlike the anonymous copper coinage, which was purely local, the silver and gold coins, as well as some of the early copper coins, bear the name or characteristic type of the ruler. Because the sequence of rulers often varied at different mint cities, each ruled by different princes, the coins are best organized according to mint. Each mint employed characteristic types and calligraphy, which continued from one ruler to the next. It is hoped that this system will facilitate identification of these coins.

The following listings include not only the mints situated in contiguous territories under Durrani and Barakzai rule for extended periods of time, but also mints in Kashmir or in other parts of India which the Afghans occupied for relatively brief intervals.

KINGDOM

Mahmud Shah
AH1216-1218 / 1801-1803AD First reign

HAMMERED COINAGE

Mint: Ahmadshahi
KM# 144 ASHRAFI
3.5000 g., Gold, 25 mm.

Date	Mintage	Good	VG	F	VF	XF
AH1218//3 Rare	—	—	—	—	—	—

Mint: Ahmadshahi
KM# 145 MOHUR
10.9000 g., Gold

Date	Mintage	Good	VG	F	VF	XF
AH1217	—	—	250	350	450	600
AH1218//2	—	—	250	350	450	600
AH1218//3	—	—	250	350	450	600

Mint: Bahawalpur
KM# 245 MOHUR
11.0000 g., Gold

Date	Mintage	Good	VG	F	VF	XF
AH1218//2	—	—	275	350	550	800

Mint: Kabul
KM# 450 MOHUR
Gold Note: Weight varies: 10.80-11.00 grams.

Date	Mintage	Good	VG	F	VF	XF
AH-//1	—	—	300	375	550	800
AH1218//3	—	—	300	375	550	800

Mint: Bahawalpur
KM# 246 2 MOHURS
Gold Note: Weight varies: 22.00-22.20 grams.

Date	Mintage	Good	VG	F	VF	XF
AH1217//1	—	—	700	1,150	1,750	2,500
AH1217//2	—	—	700	1,150	1,750	2,500
AH1218//2	—	—	700	1,150	1,750	2,500

Qaisar Shah
AH1218 / 1803AD

HAMMERED COINAGE

Mint: Ahmadshahi
KM# 149 MOHUR
10.9000 g., Gold Note: Rebel issue.

Date	Mintage	Good	VG	F	VF	XF
AH1218	—	—	600	1,000	1,500	1,750

Shah Shuja al-Mulk
AH1218-1224 / 1803-1808AD Second reign

HAMMERED COINAGE

Mint: Ahmadshahi
KM# 154 ASHRAFI
Gold Note: Weight varies: 3.00-3.50 grams.

Date	Mintage	Good	VG	F	VF	XF
AH1220/3 Rare	—	—	—	—	—	—
AH1222 Rare	—	—	—	—	—	—

AFGHANISTAN

Mint: Ahmadshahi
KM# 155 MOHUR
10.9000 g., Gold

Date	Mintage	Good	VG	F	VF	XF
AH-//2	—	—	275	400	600	850
AH1220//3	—	—	275	400	600	850
AH1222	—	—	275	400	600	850

Mint: Bahawalpur
KM# 255 MOHUR
Gold Note: Weight varies: 11.00-11.10 grams.

Date	Mintage	Good	VG	F	VF	XF
AH1218//1	—	—	250	350	550	850

Mint: Dera - Dera Ghazi Khan
KM# 345 MOHUR
Gold Note: Weight varies 10.9-11 grams.

Date	Mintage	Good	VG	F	VF	XF
AH1218//1 Rare	—	—	—	—	—	—

Mint: Herat - Dar as-Sultanat
KM# 399 MOHUR
10.9000 g., Gold

Date	Mintage	VG	F	VF	XF	Unc
AH1218	—	—	300	450	650	—
AH122x	—	—	300	450	650	—

Mint: Kabul
KM# 459 MOHUR
10.9500 g., Gold

Date	Mintage	Good	VG	F	VF	XF
AH1222//4	—	—	250	350	550	850
AH1223	—	—	250	350	550	850

Mint: Kabul
KM# 487 MOHUR
Gold Note: Weight varies: 10.70-10.80 grams.

Date	Mintage	Good	VG	F	VF	XF
AH1255	—	—	250	300	450	775
AH1258	—	—	250	300	450	775

Mint: Multan - Dar al-Aman
KM# 675 MOHUR
Gold Note: Weight varies: 10.90-11.00 grams.

Date	Mintage	Good	VG	F	VF	XF
AH1218//1 Rare	—	—	—	—	—	—
AH1224//8 Rare	—	—	—	—	—	—

Mint: Qandahar
KM# 749 MOHUR
Gold Note: Weight varies: 10.80-10.90 grams.

Date	Mintage	Good	VG	F	VF	XF
AH1219 Rare	—	—	—	—	—	—

Mint: Bahawalpur
KM# 256 2 MOHURS
22.0000 g., Gold

Date	Mintage	Good	VG	F	VF	XF
AH1218//1	—	—	700	1,150	1,750	2,500

Qaisar Shah
AH1221-1223 / 1806-1808AD
HAMMERED COINAGE

Mint: Kabul
KM# 455 MOHUR
11.0000 g., Gold Note: Rebel issue.

Date	Mintage	Good	VG	F	VF	XF
AH1222 Rare	—	—	—	—	—	—

Ata Muhammad - Bamizai Khan
AH1223-1228 / 1808-1813AD
HAMMERED COINAGE

Mint: Kashmir
KM# 607 2 MOHURS
Gold Obv. Inscription: "Shah Nur al-Din" Note: Weight varies: 21.60-21.80 grams.

Date	Mintage	Good	VG	F	VF	XF
AH1225//2	—	—	—	—	5,000	6,500

Mint: Kashmir
KM# 608 2 MOHURS
Gold Obv. Inscription: "Shah Nur al-Din" Note: Weight varies: 21.60-21.80 grams.

Date	Mintage	Good	VG	F	VF	XF
AH1225//3	—	—	2,000	3,250	5,000	6,500

Mahmud Shah
AH1224-1245 / 1808-1817AD Second reign
HAMMERED COINAGE

Mint: Ahmadshahi
KM# 159 ASHRAFI
2.4000 g., Gold, 28 mm.

Date	Mintage	Good	VG	F	VF	XF
AH1224 Rare	—	—	—	—	—	—
AH1226 Rare	—	—	—	—	—	—

Mint: Bahawalpur
KM# 265 MOHUR
11.0000 g., Gold, 21.5 mm.

Date	Mintage	Good	VG	F	VF	XF
AH1225//1 Rare	—	—	—	—	—	—

Mint: Kabul
KM# 465 MOHUR
Gold Note: Weight varies: 10.90-11.00 grams.

Date	Mintage	Good	VG	F	VF	XF
AH1224//2	—	—	275	425	650	1,000
AH122x//8	—	—	275	425	650	1,000

Ayyub Shah
AH1233-1245 / 1817-1829
HAMMERED COINAGE

Mint: Kabul
KM# 469 MOHUR
10.7900 g., Gold

Date	Mintage	Good	VG	F	VF	XF
AH1237	—	—	—	—	1,600	2,000

Mint: Peshawar
KM# 735 MOHUR
Gold, 21.5 mm. Note: Weight varies: 10.50-10.60 grams.

Date	Mintage	Good	VG	F	VF	XF
AH-//6	—	—	400	650	1,000	1,750
AH-//7	—	—	400	650	1,000	1,750

Dost Muhammad
AH1258-1280 / 1842-1863AD
HAMMERED COINAGE

Mint: Kabul
KM# 499 TILLA
Gold

Date	Mintage	Good	VG	F	VF	XF
AH1269 Rare	—	—	—	—	—	—

Muhammad Yusuf Khan Sadozai
AH1267-1272 / 1851-1856AD
HAMMERED COINAGE

Mint: Herat - Dar as-Sultanat
KM# 409 TILLA
Gold Obv: Kalimah

Date	Mintage	Good	VG	F	VF	XF
AH1272	—	—	—	300	450	650

Sher Ali
AH1280-1283 / 1863-1866AD First reign
HAMMERED COINAGE

Mint: Qandahar
KM# 194 TILLA
Gold

AFGHANISTAN

Date	Mintage	Good	VG	F	VF	XF
AH1283	—	—	275	450	700	1,000
AH1284	—	—	275	450	700	1,000
AH1285	—	—	275	450	700	1,000

Mint: Kabul
KM# 524 TOMAN
3.4500 g., Gold

Date	Mintage	Good	VG	F	VF	XF
AH1294	—	—	250	400	600	850
AH1295	—	—	250	400	600	850
AH1296	—	—	250	400	600	850

Sher Ali
AH1285-1296 / 1868-1879AD Second reign

HAMMERED COINAGE

Mint: Kabul
KM# 525 MOHUR
10.9000 g., Gold

Date	Mintage	Good	VG	F	VF	XF
AH1288	—	—	275	450	650	900

Wali Sher Ali
AH1297 / 1880AD

HAMMERED COINAGE

Mint: Qandahar
KM# 219 TILLA
Gold

Date	Mintage	Good	VG	F	VF	XF
AH1297	—	—	400	650	1,000	1,350

Abdur Rahman
AH1297-1319 / 1880-1901AD

HAMMERED COINAGE

Mint: Qandahar
KM# 226 TILLA
Gold

Date	Mintage	Good	VG	F	VF	XF
AH1298 Rare	—	—	—	—	—	—

MILLED COINAGE

10 Dinar = 1 Paisa; 5 Paise = 1 Shahi; 2 Shahi = 1 Sanar; 2 Sanar = 1 Abbasi; 1-1/2 Abbasi = 1 Qiran; 2 Qiran = 1 Kabuli Rupee; 1 Tilla = 10 Rupees

Mint: Without Mint Name
KM# 821 TILLA
4.6000 g., 0.9000 Gold .1331 oz. AGW **Rev:** Date below mosque

Date	Mintage	VG	F	VF	XF	Unc
AH1314	—	90.00	110	125	200	—
AH1316	—	100	120	145	225	—

Mint: Kabul
KM# 807 TILLA
4.6000 g., 0.9000 Gold .1331 oz. AGW, 22 mm. **Rev:** Legend above mosque **Rev. Legend:** "Allah Akbar"

Date	Mintage	Good	VG	F	VF	XF
AH1309	—	—	95.00	115	150	250

Mint: Kabul
KM# 815 TILLA
4.6000 g., 0.9000 Gold .1331 oz. AGW, 19 mm. **Rev:** Legend above **Rev. Legend:** "Allah Akbar"

Date	Mintage	Good	VG	F	VF	XF
AH1313	—	—	100	125	200	280

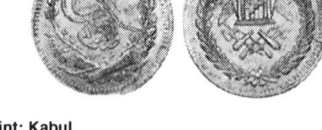

Mint: Kabul
KM# 822 TILLA
4.6000 g., 0.9000 Gold .1331 oz. AGW **Obv:** Date below toughra

Date	Mintage	Good	VG	F	VF	XF
AH1314	—	—	90.00	110	135	215
AH1316	—	—	90.00	110	135	215

Mint: Kabul
KM# 808 2 TILLAS
9.2000 g., 0.9000 Gold .2661 oz. AGW

Date	Mintage	Good	VG	F	VF	XF
AH1309	—	—	185	225	275	325

Habibullah
AH1319-1337 / 1901-1919AD

MILLED COINAGE

10 Dinar = 1 Paisa; 5 Paise = 1 Shahi; 2 Shahi = 1 Sanar; 2 Sanar = 1 Abbasi; 1-1/2 Abbasi = 1 Qiran; 2 Qiran = 1 Kabuli Rupee; 1 Tilla = 10 Rupees

Mint: Without Mint Name
KM# 853a RUPEE
10.0500 g., 0.9000 Gold 0.2908 oz. AGW, 26 mm. **Obv:** Name and titles within wreath **Rev:** Mosque within 8-pointed star, wreath surrounds

Date	Mintage	F	VF	XF	Unc
AH1334	—	—	—	1,625	—

Mint: Afghanistan
KM# 835 TILLA
4.6000 g., 0.9000 Gold .1331 oz. AGW, 21 mm. **Obv:** Star above toughra within wreath **Rev:** Flags flank mosque above weapons, wreath surrounds

Date	Mintage	VG	F	VF	XF	Unc
AH1319	—	90.00	115	170	240	—

Mint: Afghanistan
KM# 836.1 TILLA
4.6000 g., 0.9000 Gold .1331 oz. AGW, 21 mm. **Obv:** Legend divided by star above toughra, wreath surrounds **Obv. Legend:** "Afghanistan" **Rev:** Flags flank mosque above weapons, wreath surrounds

Date	Mintage	VG	F	VF	XF	Unc
AH1319	—	95.00	125	180	250	—

Mint: Afghanistan
KM# 836.2 TILLA
4.6000 g., 0.9000 Gold .1331 oz. AGW, 21 mm. **Obv:** Legend above toughra with star to right, wreath surrounds **Obv. Legend:** "Afghanistan" **Rev:** Flags flank mosque above weapons, wreath surrounds

Date	Mintage	VG	F	VF	XF	Unc
AH1320	—	95.00	125	180	250	—

Mint: Afghanistan
KM# A856 TILLA
4.6000 g., 0.9000 Gold .1331 oz. AGW **Obv:** Date divided

Date	Mintage	VG	F	VF	XF	Unc
AH1325	—	—	450	650	900	—

Mint: Afghanistan
KM# 856 TILLA
4.6000 g., 0.9000 Gold .1331 oz. AGW, 21 mm. **Obv. Legend:** Habibullah...

Date	Mintage	VG	F	VF	XF	Unc
AH1335	—	170	200	260	330	—
AH1336	—	100	120	175	240	—
AH1337	—	110	130	180	220	—

Mint: Afghanistan
KM# 879 2 TILLAS
9.2000 g., 0.9000 Gold .2661 oz. AGW, 22 mm. **Obv:** Text above date, wreath surrounds **Rev:** Mosque within 8-pointed star, denomination above, wreath surrounds

Date	Mintage	F	VF	XF	Unc
SH1298 (1919)	—	BV	185	250	400

Mint: Afghanistan
KM# 903 4 TILLAS
18.5300 g., 0.9000 Gold .1997 oz. AGW **Obv:** Text within wreath **Rev:** Mosque within 8-pointed star, spray below

Date	Mintage	VG	F	VF	XF	Unc
AH1337 Rare	—	—	—	—	—	—

Mint: Afghanistan
KM# 889 5 AMANI
23.0000 g., 0.9000 Gold .6656 oz. AGW, 34 mm. **Obv:** Tughra within wreath, Persian "5" above toughra; "Al Ghazi" at right **Rev:** Legend above mosque within 7-pointed star, wreath surrounds **Rev. Legend:** "Amaniya"

Date	Mintage	VG	F	VF	XF	Unc
SH1299 (1920)	—	BV	450	675	1,500	—

Mint: Afghanistan
KM# 890 5 AMANI
23.0000 g., 0.9000 Gold .6656 oz. AGW, 34 mm. **Obv:** Star above toughra within wreath **Rev:** Mosque within 7-pointed star, wreath surrounds, persian "5" above mosque

Date	Mintage	F	VF	XF	Unc
SH1299	—	BV	450	675	1,500	—

AFGHANISTAN

Amanullah
AH1337-1348 / 1919-1929AD
MILLED COINAGE

10 Dinar = 1 Paisa; 5 Paise = 1 Shahi; 2 Shahi = 1 Sanar; 2 Sanar = 1 Abbasi; 1-1/2 Abbasi = 1 Qiran; 2 Qiran = 1 Kabuli Rupee; 1 Tilla = 10 Rupees

Mint: Afghanistan
KM# 886 1/2 AMANI
2.3000 g., 0.9000 Gold .0665 oz. AGW, 16 mm. **Obv:** Tughra within wreath **Rev:** Mosque within 7-pointed star, wreath surrounds

Date	Mintage	VG	F	VF	XF	Unc
SH1299 (1920)	—	55.00	70.00	95.00	135	—

Mint: Afghanistan
KM# 911 1/2 AMANI
3.0000 g., 0.9000 Gold .0868 oz. AGW, 18 mm.

Date	Mintage	VG	F	VF	XF	Unc
SH1304/7 (1925)	—	—	65.00	90.00	115	160
SH1305/8 (1926)	—	—	65.00	90.00	115	160
SH1306/9 (1927)	—	—	65.00	90.00	115	160

Mint: Afghanistan
KM# 868.1 TILLA
4.6000 g., 0.9000 Gold .1331 oz. AGW, 21 mm. **Obv:** Text within wreath **Obv. Legend:** "Amanullah..." **Rev:** Mosque within 8-pointed star, crossed swords below mosque, wreath surrounds

Date	Mintage	VG	F	VF	XF	Unc
AH1337 (1918)	—	100	125	160	225	—

Mint: Afghanistan
KM# 868.2 TILLA
4.6000 g., 0.9000 Gold .1331 oz. AGW, 21 mm. **Obv:** Text within wreath **Rev:** Mosque within 8-pointed star, 6-pointed star below mosque, wreath surrounds

Date	Mintage	VG	F	VF	XF	Unc
AH1337 (1918)	—	100	135	175	250	—

Mint: Afghanistan
KM# 887 AMANI
4.6000 g., 0.9000 Gold .1331 oz. AGW, 22 mm. **Obv:** Tughra above date within wreath **Rev:** Mosque within 7-pointed star, wreath surrounds

Date	Mintage	VG	F	VF	XF	Unc
SH1299 (1920)	—	BV	100	130	175	—

Mint: Afghanistan
KM# 912 AMANI
6.0000 g., 0.9000 Gold .1736 oz. AGW, 23 mm.

Date	Mintage	F	VF	XF	Unc
SH1304/7 (1925)	—	BV	120	130	180
SH1305/8 (1926)	—	BV	120	150	220
SH1306/9 (1927)	—	BV	120	130	180

Mint: Afghanistan
KM# 888 2 AMANI
9.2000 g., 0.9000 Gold .2662 oz. AGW, 24 mm. **Obv:** Tughra above date within wreath **Rev:** Mosque within 7 pointed star, wreath surrounds

Date	Mintage	VG	F	VF	XF	Unc
SH1299 (1920)	—	BV	175	200	275	300
SH1300 (1921)	—	BV	175	200	275	300
SH1301 (1922)	—	BV	175	200	275	300
SH1302 (1923)	—	BV	175	200	275	300
SH1303 (1924)	—	BV	175	200	275	300

Mint: Afghanistan
KM# 914 2-1/2 AMANI
15.0000 g., 0.9000 Gold .4340 oz. AGW, 29 mm. **Obv:** Tughra above date within wreath **Rev:** Mosque within wreath

Date	Mintage	F	VF	XF	Unc
SH1306/9 (1927)	—	—	—	5,000	7,000

Mint: Without Mint Name
KM# 900 HABIBI
4.6000 g., 0.9000 Gold .1331 oz. AGW **Obv:** Small star replaces "30 Rupees" in legend

Date	Mintage	VG	F	VF	XF	Unc
AH1347	—	90.00	130	200	325	—

Muhammed Nadir Shah
AH1348-1350 / 1929-1933AD
MILLED COINAGE

10 Dinar = 1 Paisa; 5 Paise = 1 Shahi; 2 Shahi = 1 Sanar; 2 Sanar = 1 Abbasi; 1-1/2 Abbasi = 1 Qiran; 2 Qiran = 1 Kabuli Rupee; 1 Tilla = 10 Rupees

Mint: Afghanistan
KM# 899 HABIBI
4.6000 g., 0.9000 Gold .1331 oz. AGW, 21 mm. **Obv:** Text within wreath **Rev:** Mosque within 8-pointed star, wreath surrounds

Date	Mintage	VG	F	VF	XF	Unc
AH1347	—	90.00	130	200	325	—

DECIMAL COINAGE

100 Pul = 1 Afghani; 20 Afghani = 1 Amani

Mint: Afghanistan
KM# 925 20 AFGHANIS
6.0000 g., 0.9000 Gold .1736 oz. AGW, 22 mm.

Date	Mintage	F	VF	XF	Unc
AH1348	—	130	175	200	300
AH1349	—	BV	120	165	240
AH1350	—	BV	120	165	240

Muhammed Zahir Shah
SH1312-1352 / 1933-1973AD
DECIMAL COINAGE

100 Pul = 1 Afghani; 20 Afghani = 1 Amani

Mint: Afghanistan
KM# 935 4 GRAMS
4.0000 g., 0.9000 Gold .1157 oz. AGW, 19 mm.

Date	Mintage	F	VF	XF	Unc
SH1315 (1936)	—	BV	90.00	125	165
SH1317 (1938)	—	BV	90.00	125	165

Mint: Afghanistan
KM# 933 TILLA
6.0000 g., 0.9000 Gold .1736 oz. AGW, 22 mm.

Date	Mintage	F	VF	XF	Unc
SH1313 (1934)	—	125	150	185	275

Mint: Afghanistan
KM# 934 8 GRAMS
8.0000 g., 0.9000 Gold .2314 oz. AGW, 22 mm.

Date	Mintage	F	VF	XF	Unc
SH1314 (1935)	—	BV	155	175	250
SH1315 (1936)	—	BV	155	175	250
SH1317 (1938)	—	BV	155	175	250

Mint: Afghanistan
KM# 952 8 GRAMS
8.0000 g., 0.9000 Gold .2314 oz. AGW, 22 mm. **Obv:** Tughra **Rev:** Eagles divide date and flank figure above horse within cornucopias

Date	Mintage	F	VF	XF	Unc
SH1339 (1960)	200	—	—	325	800

Note: Struck for royal presentation purposes. Specimens struck with the same dies (including the "8 grams", the "8" having been effaced after striking), but on thin planchets weighing 3.9-4.0 grams, exist, they are regarded as "mint sports". Market value $250.00 in Unc

REPUBLIC
SH1352-1357 / 1973-1978AD
STANDARD COINAGE

KM# 982 10000 AFGHANIS
33.4370 g., 0.9000 Gold .9676 oz. AGW **Subject:** Conservation **Obv:** National arms **Rev:** Marco Polo Sheep

Date	Mintage	F	VF	XF	Unc
1978	694	—	—	—	650
1978 Proof	181	Value: 1,100			

DEMOCRATIC REPUBLIC
SH1358-1371 / 1979-1992AD
STANDARD COINAGE

KM# 1019 10000 AFGHANIS
33.6600 g., 0.9000 Gold .9739 oz. AGW **Subject:** Conservation **Obv:** National Arms **Rev:** Marco Polo Sheep

Date	Mintage	F	VF	XF	Unc
1978 4 known	—	—	—	—	2,000

AJMAN - U.A.E.

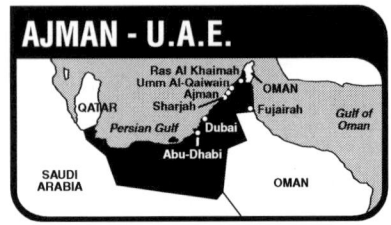

Ajman is the smallest and poorest of the emirates in the United Arab Emirates. It has an estimated area of 100 sq. mi. (250 sq. km.) and a population of 6,000. Ajman's first act as an autonomous entity was entering into a treaty with Great Britain in 1820. On December 2, 1971 Ajman became one of the 6 original members of the United Arab Emirates.

TITLES

عجمان

Ajman

RULERS
Abdul Aziz Bin Humaid al-Naimi, 1900-1908
Humaid Bin Abdul Aziz al-Naimi, 1908-1928
Rashid Bin Hamad al-Naimi, 1928-1981
Humaid Bin Rashid al-Naimi, 1981--

MONETARY SYSTEM
100 Dirhams = 1 Riyal

UNITED ARAB EMIRATE

NON-CIRCULATING LEGAL TENDER COINAGE

KM# 28 25 RIYALS
5.1750 g., 0.9000 Gold .1497 oz. AGW **Ruler:** Rashid Bin Hamad al-Naimi 1928-1981 **Obv:** State emblem, denomination above **Rev:** Head left, denomination below

Date	Mintage	F	VF	XF	Unc	BU
ND(1970) Proof	—				Value: 165	

KM# 29 25 RIYALS
5.1750 g., 0.9000 Gold .1497 oz. AGW **Ruler:** Rashid Bin Hamad al-Naimi 1928-1981 **Obv:** State emblem, denomination above **Rev:** Head left, denomination below

Date	Mintage	F	VF	XF	Unc	BU
ND(1970) Proof	—				Value: 165	

KM# 30 25 RIYALS
5.1750 g., 0.9000 Gold .1497 oz. AGW **Ruler:** Rashid Bin Hamad al-Naimi 1928-1981 **Obv:** State emblem, denomination above **Rev:** Head left, denomination below

Date	Mintage	F	VF	XF	Unc	BU
ND(1970) Proof	—				Value: 165	

KM# 31 25 RIYALS
5.1750 g., 0.9000 Gold .1497 oz. AGW **Ruler:** Rashid Bin Hamad al-Naimi 1928-1981 **Obv:** State emblem, denomination above **Rev:** Head left, denomination below

Date	Mintage	F	VF	XF	Unc	BU
ND(1970) Proof	—				Value: 165	

KM# 32 25 RIYALS
5.1750 g., 0.9000 Gold .1497 oz. AGW **Ruler:** Rashid Bin Hamad al-Naimi 1928-1981 **Obv:** State emblem, denomination above **Rev:** Head 3/4 left, denomination below

Date	Mintage	F	VF	XF	Unc	BU
ND(1970) Proof	—				Value: 165	

KM# 33 25 RIYALS
5.1750 g., 0.9000 Gold .1497 oz. AGW **Ruler:** Rashid Bin Hamad al-Naimi 1928-1981 **Obv:** State emblem, denomination above **Rev:** Head left, denomination below

Date	Mintage	F	VF	XF	Unc	BU
ND(1970) Proof	—				Value: 165	

KM# 34 25 RIYALS
5.1750 g., 0.9000 Gold .1497 oz. AGW **Ruler:** Rashid Bin Hamad al-Naimi 1928-1981 **Obv:** State emblem, denomination above **Rev:** Head 3/4 right, denomination below

Date	Mintage	F	VF	XF	Unc	BU
ND(1970) Proof	—				Value: 165	

KM# 35 25 RIYALS
5.1750 g., 0.9000 Gold .1497 oz. AGW **Ruler:** Rashid Bin Hamad al-Naimi 1928-1981 **Obv:** State emblem, denomination above **Rev:** Head 3/4 left, denomination below

Date	Mintage	F	VF	XF	Unc	BU
ND(1970) Proof	—				Value: 165	

KM# 15 25 RIYALS
5.1750 g., 0.9000 Gold .1497 oz. AGW **Ruler:** Rashid Bin Hamad al-Naimi 1928-1981 **Subject:** Death of Gamal Abdel Nassar **Obv:** State emblem divides denomination **Rev:** Head left divides dates **Note:** Some examples have a serial number on the obverse below the bust.

Date	Mintage	F	VF	XF	Unc	BU
AH1390 Proof	1,100				Value: 145	

KM# 36 25 RIYALS
5.1750 g., 0.9000 Gold .1497 oz. AGW **Ruler:** Rashid Bin Hamad al-Naimi 1928-1981 **Rev:** Two men ringing large bell **Rev. Legend:** Save Venice

Date	Mintage	F	VF	XF	Unc	BU
ND(1971) Proof	—				Value: 200	

KM# 16 50 RIYALS
10.3500 g., 0.9000 Gold .2995 oz. AGW **Ruler:** Rashid Bin Hamad al-Naimi 1928-1981 **Subject:** Death of Gamal Abdel Nassar **Obv:** State emblem divides denomination **Rev:** Head left divides dates **Note:** Some examples have a serial number below the bust on the obverse

Date	Mintage	F	VF	XF	Unc	BU
AH1390 Proof	700				Value: 250	

KM# 39 50 RIYALS
10.3500 g., 0.9000 Gold .2995 oz. AGW **Ruler:** Rashid Bin Hamad al-Naimi 1928-1981 **Subject:** Save Venice **Obv:** State emblem, denomination above, bust below **Rev:** Stallion divides denomination

Date	Mintage	F	VF	XF	Unc	BU
ND(1971) Proof	—				Value: 365	

KM# 41 75 RIYALS
15.5300 g., 0.9000 Gold .4494 oz. AGW **Ruler:** Rashid Bin Hamad al-Naimi 1928-1981 **Series:** F.A.O.

Date	Mintage	F	VF	XF	Unc	BU
AH1389-1969 Proof	—				Value: 425	

KM# 10 100 RIYALS
20.7000 g., 0.9000 Gold .5990 oz. AGW **Ruler:** Rashid Bin Hamad al-Naimi 1928-1981 **Obv:** State emblem, denomination above **Rev:** Head left, denomination at left

Date	Mintage	F	VF	XF	Unc	BU
ND(1970) Proof	1,000				Value: 475	

KM# 40 100 RIYALS
20.7000 g., 0.9000 Gold .5990 oz. AGW **Ruler:** Rashid Bin Hamad al-Naimi 1928-1981 **Subject:** Save Venice **Obv:** State emblem, denomination above, bust below **Rev:** Courthouse, denomination lower left

Date	Mintage	F	VF	XF	Unc	BU
ND(1971) Proof	—				Value: 500	

MINT SETS

KM#	Date	Mintage	Identification	Issue Price	Mkt Val
MS1	1969 (3)	—	KM#1.1-3.1	—	55.00
MS2	1970 (3)	4,350	KM#5-7	—	185

PROOF SETS

KM#	Date	Mintage	Identification	Issue Price	Mkt Val
PS1	1969 (3)	1,200	KM#1.1-3.1	11.22	160
PS2	1970 (8)	1,175	KM#17-24	—	600
PS3	1970 (8)	—	KM#28-35	—	1,320
PS4	1970 (4)	—	KM#12, 13, 15, 16	—	475
PS5	1970 (3)	100	KM#E4-6	—	190
PS6	1970 (3)	650	KM#5-7	19.50	275
PS7	1970 (3)	—	KM#E9, E7, 10	—	620
PS8	1970 (2)	800	KM#E7, 10	—	520
PS9	1970 (2)	5,000	KM#12, 13	9.50	80.00
PS10	1970 (3)	—	KM#12, 13, 15	—	225
PS11	1970 (3)	—	KM#9.1, 9.2, 10	—	700
PS12	1971 (4)	—	KM#27, 36, 39, 40	—	1,200

ALBANIA

The Republic of Albania, a Balkan republic bounded by Macedonia, Greece, Montenegro, and the Adriatic Sea, has an area of 11,100 sq. mi. (28,748 sq. km.) and a population of 3.49 million. Capital: Tirane. The country is predominantly agricultural, although recent progress has been made in the manufacturing and mining sectors. Petroleum, chrome, iron, copper, cotton textiles, tobacco and wood products are exported.

Since it had been part of the Greek and Roman empires little is known of the early history of Albania. After the disintegration of the Roman Empire Albania was overrun by Goths, Byzantines, Venetians and Turks. Skanderbeg, the national hero, resisted the Turks and established an independent Albania in 1443, but in 1468 the country again fell to the Turks and remained part of the Ottoman Empire for more than 400 years.

Independence was re-established by revolt in 1912, and the present borders established in 1913 by a conference of European powers, which, in 1914, placed Prince William of Wied on the throne; popular discontent forced his abdication within months. In 1920, following World War I occupancy by several nations, a republic was set up. Ahmed Zogu seized the presidency in 1925, and in 1928 he proclaimed himself king with the title of Zog I. King Zog fled when Italy occupied Albania in 1939 and enthroned King Victor Emanuel of Italy. Upon the surrender of Italy to the Allies in 1943, German troops occupied the country. They withdrew in 1944, and communist partisans seized power, naming Gen. Enver Hoxha provisional president. In 1946, following a victory by the communist front in the 1945 elections, a new constitution modeled on that of the USSR was adopted. In accordance with the constitution of Dec. 28, 1976, the official name of Albania was changed from the Peoples Republic of Albania to the Peoples Socialist Republic of Albania.

Albania's former communists were routed in elections. March 1992, amid economic collapse and social unrest, Sali Berisha was elected as the first non-communist president since World War II. Rexhep Mejdani, elected president in 1997, succeeds him.

RULERS
Ahmed Bey Zogu - King Zog I, 1928-1939
Vittorio Emanuele III, 1939-1943

MINT MARKS
L – London
R – Rome
V – Vienna

MONETARY SYSTEM
100 Qindar Leku = 1 Lek
100 Qindar Ari = 1 Frang Ar = 5 Lek

KINGDOM
STANDARD COINAGE

KM# 9 10 FRANGA ARI
3.2258 g., 0.9000 Gold .0933 oz. AGW **Ruler:** Ahmed Bey Zogu - King Zog I **Obv:** Head left **Rev:** Double imperial eagle divides denomination below **Designer:** Romagnoli

Date	Mintage	F	VF	XF	Unc	BU
1927R	6,000	120	150	250	360	—

KM# 10 20 FRANGA ARI
6.4516 g., 0.9000 Gold .1867 oz. AGW, 21 mm. **Ruler:** Ahmed Bey Zogu - King Zog I **Obv:** Head left **Rev:** Double imperial eagle divides denomination below **Designer:** Romagnoli

Date	Mintage	F	VF	XF	Unc	BU
1926R	—	BV	155	260	360	—
1927R	6,000	BV	150	250	375	—

ALBANIA

KM# 12 20 FRANGA ARI
6.4516 g., 0.9000 Gold .1867 oz. AGW, 21 mm. **Subject:** George Kastrioti "Skanderbeg" **Obv:** Lion of St. Mark right divides denomination, date below **Rev:** Bust right **Designer:** Romagnoli

Date	Mintage	F	VF	XF	Unc	BU
1926R	5,900	140	180	330	440	—
1926 Fasces	100	—	—	4,200	6,500	—

Note: 90 pieces were reported melted

| 1927V | 5,053 | 120 | 160 | 290 | 390 | — |

KM# 20 20 FRANGA ARI
6.4516 g., 0.9000 Gold .1867 oz. AGW, 21 mm. **Ruler:** Ahmed Bey Zogu - King Zog I **Subject:** 25th Anniversary of Independence **Obv:** Head right, date below **Rev:** Kings arms, denomination below

Date	Mintage	F	VF	XF	Unc	BU
1937R	2,500	—	200	300	450	—

KM# 22 20 FRANGA ARI
6.4516 g., 0.9000 Gold .1867 oz. AGW, 21 mm. **Ruler:** Ahmed Bey Zogu - King Zog I **Subject:** Marriage of King Zog to Countess Geraldine Apponyi, April 27, 1938 **Obv:** Head right, date below **Rev:** Kings arms, denomination below

Date	Mintage	F	VF	XF	Unc	BU
1938R	2,500	—	200	300	450	—

KM# 24 20 FRANGA ARI
6.4516 g., 0.9000 Gold .1867 oz. AGW, 21 mm. **Ruler:** Ahmed Bey Zogu - King Zog I **Subject:** 10th Anniversary - Reign of King Zog **Obv:** Head right, date below **Rev:** Kings arms, denomination below

Date	Mintage	F	VF	XF	Unc	BU
1938R	1,000	—	200	350	520	—

Note: Pieces struck in 1969 from new dies

KM# 25 50 FRANGA ARI
16.1290 g., 0.9000 Gold .4667 oz. AGW **Ruler:** Ahmed Bey Zogu - King Zog I **Subject:** 10th Anniversary - Reign of King Zog **Obv:** Head right, date below **Rev:** Kings Arms, denomination below

Date	Mintage	F	VF	XF	Unc	BU
1938R	600	—	550	850	1,600	—

Note: Pieces struck in 1969 from new dies

KM# 11.1 100 FRANGA ARI
32.2580 g., 0.9000 Gold .9335 oz. AGW, 35 mm. **Ruler:** Ahmed Bey Zogu - King Zog I **Obv:** Head left **Rev:** Biga right, denomination below **Designer:** Giuseppe Romagnoli

Date	Mintage	F	VF	XF	Unc	BU
1926R	6,614	—	650	900	1,500	—

Note: Mintage figures includes provas, Pr7-9

KM# 11.2 100 FRANGA ARI
32.2580 g., 0.9000 Gold .9335 oz. AGW, 35 mm. **Ruler:** Ahmed Bey Zogu - King Zog I **Obv:** Head left, star below **Rev:** Biga right, denomination below **Designer:** Giuseppe Romagnoli

Date	Mintage	F	VF	XF	Unc	BU
1926R	Inc. above	—	650	1,000	1,600	—

KM# 11.3 100 FRANGA ARI
32.2580 g., 0.9000 Gold .9335 oz. AGW, 35 mm. **Ruler:** Ahmed Bey Zogu - King Zog I **Obv:** Head left, two stars below **Rev:** Biga right, denomination below **Designer:** Romagnoli

Date	Mintage	F	VF	XF	Unc	BU
1926R	Inc. above	—	650	1,000	1,600	—

KM# 11a.1 100 FRANGA ARI
32.2580 g., 0.9000 Gold .9335 oz. AGW, 35 mm. **Ruler:** Ahmed Bey Zogu - King Zog I **Obv:** Head left **Rev:** Biga right, denomination below **Designer:** Romagnoli

Date	Mintage	F	VF	XF	Unc	BU
1927R	5,000	—	600	800	1,300	—

Note: Mintage figure includes provas, Pr17-19

KM# 11a.2 100 FRANGA ARI
32.2580 g., 0.9000 Gold .9335 oz. AGW, 35 mm. **Ruler:** Ahmed Bey Zogu - King Zog I **Obv:** Head left, star below **Rev:** Biga right, denomination below

Date	Mintage	F	VF	XF	Unc	BU
1927R	Inc. above	—	650	1,000	1,700	—

KM# 11a.3 100 FRANGA ARI
32.2580 g., 0.9000 Gold .9335 oz. AGW, 35 mm. **Ruler:** Ahmed Bey Zogu - King Zog I **Obv:** Head left, two stars below **Rev:** Biga right, denomination below

Date	Mintage	F	VF	XF	Unc	BU
1927R	Inc. above	—	650	1,000	1,700	—

KM# 21 100 FRANGA ARI
32.2580 g., 0.9000 Gold .9335 oz. AGW, 35 mm. **Ruler:** Ahmed Bey Zogu - King Zog I **Subject:** 25th Anniversary of Independence **Obv:** Head right, date below **Rev:** Kings arms divide denomination below

Date	Mintage	F	VF	XF	Unc	BU
1937R	500	—	900	1,500	2,200	—

KM# 23 100 FRANGA ARI
32.2580 g., 0.9000 Gold .9335 oz. AGW, 35 mm. **Ruler:** Ahmed Bey Zogu - King Zog I **Subject:** Marriage of King Zog to Countess Geraldine Apponyi, April 27, 1938 **Obv:** Head right, date below **Rev:** Kings Arms divide denomination below

Date	Mintage	F	VF	XF	Unc	BU
1938R	500	—	900	1,500	2,200	—

KM# 26 100 FRANGA ARI
32.2580 g., 0.9000 Gold .9335 oz. AGW, 35 mm. **Ruler:** Ahmed Bey Zogu - King Zog I **Subject:** 10th Anniversary - Reign of King Zog **Obv:** Head right, date below **Rev:** Kings Arms divide denomination below

Date	Mintage	F	VF	XF	Unc	BU
1938R	500	—	900	1,500	2,200	—

Note: Pieces restruck in 1969 from new dies

PEOPLE'S SOCIALIST REPUBLIC
1945 - 1990

ECU COINAGE

X# 2 100 ECU
31.1030 g., 0.7500 Gold 0.75 oz. AGW, 38 mm. **Obv:** Arms **Obv. Legend:** REPUBLIKA SHQIPËRISE **Rev:** Early sailing ship **Rev. Legend:** ALBANIA **Edge:** Reeded

Date	Mintage	F	VF	XF	Unc	BU
1993 Proof	1,000	Value: 750				

STANDARD COINAGE

KM# 57a 5 LEKE
50.0000 g., 0.9000 Gold 1.4470 oz. AGW **Subject:** Seaport of Durazzo **Obv:** National arms, date below **Rev:** Seaport left of sailing ship, denomination below

Date	Mintage	F	VF	XF	Unc	BU
1987 Proof	5	Value: 2,500				

KM# 51.1 20 LEKE
3.9500 g., 0.9000 Gold .1143 oz. AGW **Subject:** 500th Anniversary - Death of Prince Skanderbeg **Obv:** Skanderbeg helmet within wreath, scythe at left of helmet **Rev:** Arms, value below, oval fineness countermark punched in

Date	Mintage	F	VF	XF	Unc	BU
1968	2,920	Value: 95.00				

Note: Countermark for 1968 and 1969 coins were hand positioned, then punched. The result is a variety of countermark positions, to the left and right of LEKE

KM# 51.2 20 LEKE
3.9500 g., 0.9000 Gold .1143 oz. AGW **Obv:** Skanderbeg helmet within wreath, scythe at left of helmet **Rev:** Without fineness countermark (error)

Date	Mintage	F	VF	XF	Unc	BU
1968 Proof	Inc. above	Value: 95.00				

ALBANIA

KM# 51.3 20 LEKE
3.9500 g., 0.9000 Gold .1143 oz. AGW **Obv:** Skanderbeg helmet within wreath, scythe at left of helmet **Rev:** Cornucopia countermark at right of LEKE **Note:** Variety of countermark positions.

Date	Mintage	F	VF	XF	Unc	BU
1968 Paris	24	—	—	350	420	450

KM# 51.4 20 LEKE
3.9500 g., 0.9000 Gold .1143 oz. AGW **Obv:** Skanderbeg helmet within wreath, scythe at left **Rev:** Date added below arms **Note:** Variety of countermark positions.

Date	Mintage	F	VF	XF	Unc	BU
1969 Proof	650	Value: 140				

KM# 51.5 20 LEKE
3.9500 g., 0.9000 Gold .1143 oz. AGW **Obv:** Skanderbeg helmet within wreath, scythe to left of helmet **Rev:** Date below arms, oval fineness in relief, incorporated in dies

Date	Mintage	F	VF	XF	Unc	BU
1970 Proof	500	Value: 150				

KM# 51.6 20 LEKE
3.9500 g., 0.9000 Gold .1143 oz. AGW **Obv:** Skanderbeg helmet within wreath, scythe to left of helmet **Rev:** Sunken countermark 1 AR left of LEKE and raised oval fineness countermark on right incorporated into the dies

Date	Mintage	F	VF	XF	Unc	BU
1970 Proof	—	Value: 200				

KM# 53.1 50 LEKE
9.8700 g., 0.9000 Gold .2856 oz. AGW **Obv:** Argirocastrum Ruins, date below **Rev:** Oval fineness countermark

Date	Mintage	F	VF	XF	Unc	BU
1968 Proof	3,120	Value: 185				

KM# 53.2 50 LEKE
9.8700 g., 0.9000 Gold .2856 oz. AGW **Obv:** Argirocastrum ruins, date below **Rev:** Date below arms, oval fineness countermark, value below date

Date	Mintage	F	VF	XF	Unc	BU
1969 Proof	500	Value: 275				

KM# 53.3 50 LEKE
9.8700 g., 0.9000 Gold .2856 oz. AGW **Obv:** Ruins, without date **Rev:** Oval fineness countermark in relief

Date	Mintage	F	VF	XF	Unc	BU
1970 Proof	100	Value: 420				

Note: For the 1970 issue the fineness marking has been incorporated in the dies

KM# 58a 50 LEKE
155.5000 g., 0.9990 Gold 4.9950 oz. AGW **Subject:** Seaport of Durazzo **Obv:** National arms, date below **Rev:** Seaport left of sailing ship, denomination below

Date	Mintage	F	VF	XF	Unc	BU
1987 Proof	5	Value: 6,500				

KM# 54.1 100 LEKE
19.7500 g., 0.9000 Gold .5715 oz. AGW **Obv:** Peasant girl in national dress, date below **Rev:** Oval fineness countermark

Date	Mintage	F	VF	XF	Unc	BU
1968 Proof	3,470	Value: 385				

KM# 54.2 100 LEKE
19.7500 g., 0.9000 Gold .5715 oz. AGW **Obv:** Peasant girl in national dress, date below **Rev:** Date below arms, oval fineness countermark

Date	Mintage	F	VF	XF	Unc	BU
1969 Proof	450	Value: 480				

KM# 54.3 100 LEKE
19.7500 g., 0.9000 Gold .5715 oz. AGW **Obv:** Without date **Rev:** Oval fineness countermark in relief incorporated into the dies

Date	Mintage	F	VF	XF	Unc	BU
1970 Proof	Inc. above	Value: 500				

KM# 59 100 LEKE
6.4500 g., 0.9000 Gold .1866 oz. AGW **Subject:** Seaport of Durazzo **Obv:** National arms, date below **Rev:** Seaport left of sailing ship, denomination below

Date	Mintage	F	VF	XF	Unc	BU
1987 Proof	5,000	Value: 185				

KM# 63 100 LEKE
6.4500 g., 0.9000 Gold .1866 oz. AGW **Subject:** 42nd Anniversary - First Railroad **Obv:** Train engine emerging from tunnel **Rev:** Caboose entering tunnel **Note:** Without hole in coin

Date	Mintage	F	VF	XF	Unc	BU
1988 Proof	2,000	Value: 280				

KM# 55.1 200 LEKE
39.4900 g., 0.9000 Gold 1.1427 oz. AGW **Subject:** Buthrotum Ruins **Obv:** Head right, date at left, ruins in background **Rev:** Arms above denomination

Date	Mintage	F	VF	XF	Unc	BU
1968 Proof	2,170	Value: 750				

KM# 55.2 200 LEKE
39.4900 g., 0.9000 Gold 1.1427 oz. AGW **Obv:** Head right, date at left, ruins in background **Rev:** Date below arms, oval fineness countermark in a variety of positions

Date	Mintage	F	VF	XF	Unc	BU
1969 Proof	200	Value: 820				

KM# 55.3 200 LEKE
39.4900 g., 0.9000 Gold 1.1427 oz. AGW **Obv:** Head right, ruins in background, without date **Rev:** Oval fineness countermark in relief incorporated into the die

Date	Mintage	F	VF	XF	Unc	BU
1970 Proof	Inc. above	Value: 850				

KM# 56.1 500 LEKE
98.7400 g., 0.9000 Gold 2.8574 oz. AGW **Subject:** 500th Anniversary - Death of Prince Skanderbeg **Rev:** National arms above denomination

Date	Mintage	F	VF	XF	Unc	BU
1968 Proof	1,520	Value: 1,875				

KM# 56.2 500 LEKE
98.7400 g., 0.9000 Gold 2.8574 oz. AGW **Rev:** Date below arms, oval fineness countermark in a variety of positions

Date	Mintage	F	VF	XF	Unc	BU
1969 Proof	200	Value: 1,950				

KM# 56.3 500 LEKE
98.7400 g., 0.9000 Gold 2.8574 oz. AGW **Obv:** Without date **Rev:** Oval fineness countermark in relief incorporated into the die

Date	Mintage	F	VF	XF	Unc	BU
1970 Proof	Inc. above	Value: 2,000				

KM# 64 7500 LEKE
483.7500 g., 0.9000 Gold 13.9992 oz. AGW **Subject:** 42nd Anniversary - First Railroad **Obv:** Engine emerging from tunnel **Rev:** Caboose entering tunnel **Note:** Similar to 50 Leke, KM#62.

Date	Mintage	F	VF	XF	Unc	BU
1988 Proof	50	Value: 10,000				

REPUBLIC

STANDARD COINAGE

KM# 83 200 LEKE
7.6500 g., 0.9000 Gold 0.2214 oz. AGW, 25.45 mm. **Subject:** Michaelangelo's "David" **Obv:** City plaza **Rev:** Statue of "David" and denomination **Edge:** Reeded

Date	Mintage	F	VF	XF	Unc	BU
2001	500	—	—	—	190	230

TRIAL STRIKES

KM#	Date	Mintage	Identification	Issue Price	Mkt Val
TS1	1969	—	500 Leke. Goldine-Brass. 56.3200 g. 55 mm. Blank with MET countermark. Like KM56.2.	—	175

ESSAIS

KM#	Date	Mintage	Identification	Mkt Val
E12	1938	—	100 Franga Ari. Gold. Without signature. Prev. KM#Pn15.	—

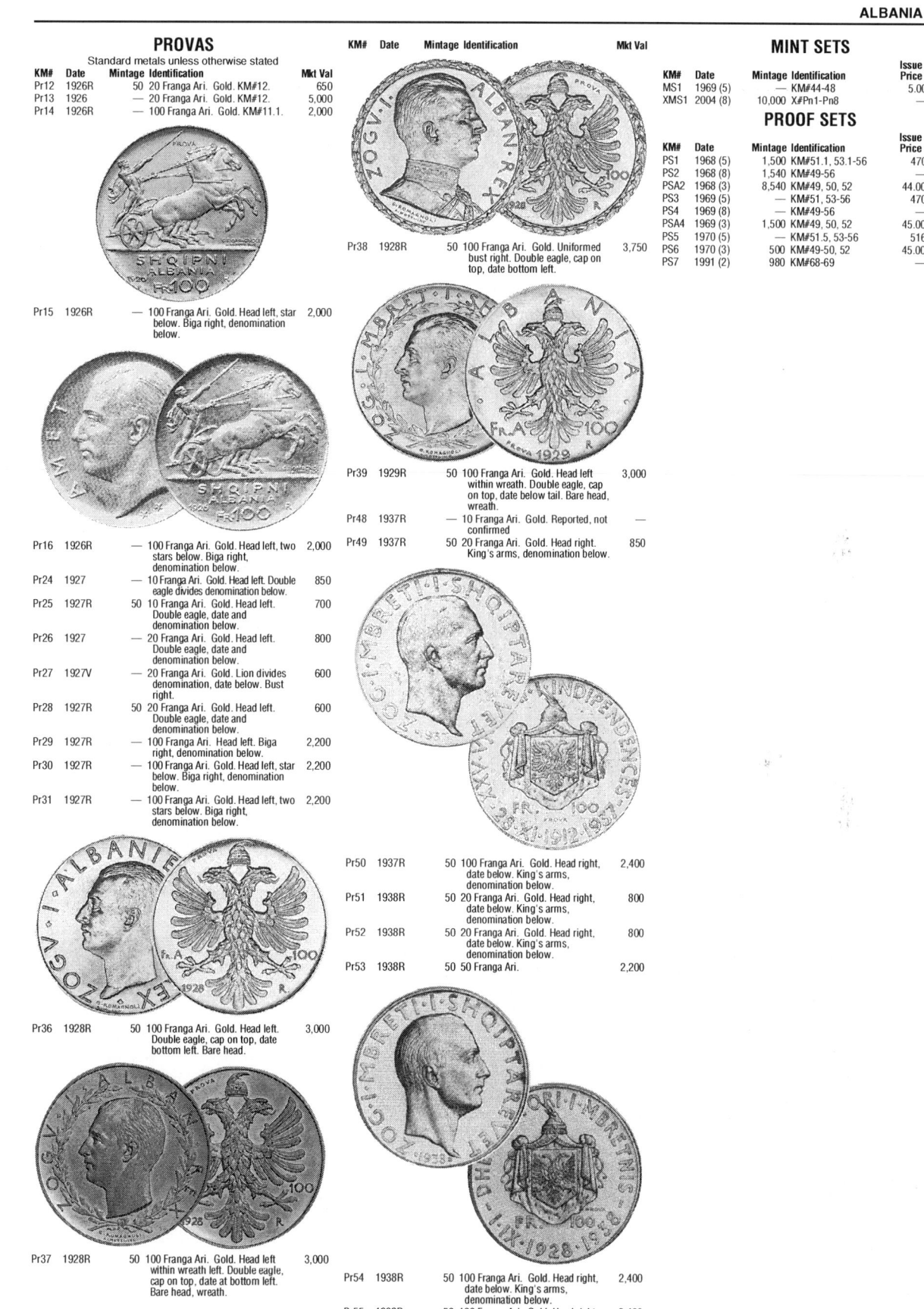

ALBANIA

PROVAS
Standard metals unless otherwise stated

KM#	Date	Mintage	Identification	Mkt Val
Pr12	1926R	50	20 Franga Ari. Gold. KM#12.	650
Pr13	1926	—	20 Franga Ari. Gold. KM#12.	5,000
Pr14	1926R	—	100 Franga Ari. Gold. KM#11.1.	2,000
Pr15	1926R	—	100 Franga Ari. Gold. Head left, star below. Biga right, denomination below.	2,000
Pr16	1926R	—	100 Franga Ari. Gold. Head left, two stars below. Biga right, denomination below.	2,000
Pr24	1927	—	10 Franga Ari. Gold. Head left. Double eagle divides denomination below.	850
Pr25	1927R	50	10 Franga Ari. Gold. Head left. Double eagle, date and denomination below.	700
Pr26	1927	—	20 Franga Ari. Gold. Head left. Double eagle, date and denomination below.	800
Pr27	1927V	—	20 Franga Ari. Gold. Lion divides denomination, date below. Bust right.	600
Pr28	1927R	50	20 Franga Ari. Gold. Head left. Double eagle, date and denomination below.	600
Pr29	1927R	—	100 Franga Ari. Head left. Biga right, denomination below.	2,200
Pr30	1927R	—	100 Franga Ari. Gold. Head left, star below. Biga right, denomination below.	2,200
Pr31	1927R	—	100 Franga Ari. Gold. Head left, two stars below. Biga right, denomination below.	2,200
Pr36	1928R	50	100 Franga Ari. Gold. Head left. Double eagle, cap on top, date bottom left. Bare head.	3,000
Pr37	1928R	50	100 Franga Ari. Gold. Head left within wreath left. Double eagle, cap on top, date at bottom left. Bare head, wreath.	3,000
Pr38	1928R	50	100 Franga Ari. Gold. Uniformed bust right. Double eagle, cap on top, date bottom left.	3,750
Pr39	1929R	50	100 Franga Ari. Gold. Head left within wreath. Double eagle, cap on top, date below tail. Bare head, wreath.	3,000
Pr48	1937R	—	10 Franga Ari. Gold. Reported, not confirmed	—
Pr49	1937R	50	20 Franga Ari. Gold. Head right. King's arms, denomination below.	850
Pr50	1937R	50	100 Franga Ari. Gold. Head right, date below. King's arms, denomination below.	2,400
Pr51	1938R	50	20 Franga Ari. Gold. Head right, date below. King's arms, denomination below.	800
Pr52	1938R	50	20 Franga Ari. Gold. Head right, date below. King's arms, denomination below.	800
Pr53	1938R	50	50 Franga Ari.	2,200
Pr54	1938R	50	100 Franga Ari. Gold. Head right, date below. King's arms, denomination below.	2,400
Pr55	1938R	50	100 Franga Ari. Gold. Head right, date below. King's arms, denomination below.	2,400

MINT SETS

KM#	Date	Mintage	Identification	Issue Price	Mkt Val
MS1	1969 (5)	—	KM#44-48	5.00	25.00
XMS1	2004 (8)	10,000	X#Pn1-Pn8	—	30.00

PROOF SETS

KM#	Date	Mintage	Identification	Issue Price	Mkt Val
PS1	1968 (5)	1,500	KM#51.1, 53.1-56	470	3,000
PS2	1968 (8)	1,540	KM#49-56	—	3,200
PSA2	1968 (3)	8,540	KM#49, 50, 52	44.00	110
PS3	1969 (5)	—	KM#51, 53-56	470	3,385
PS4	1969 (8)	—	KM#49-56	—	3,525
PSA4	1969 (3)	1,500	KM#49, 50, 52	45.00	135
PS5	1970 (5)	—	KM#51.5, 53-56	516	3,525
PS6	1970 (3)	500	KM#49-50, 52	45.00	170
PS7	1991 (2)	980	KM#68-69	—	400

ALDERNEY

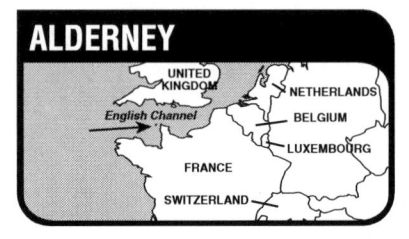

Alderney, the northernmost and third largest of the Channel Islands, separated from the coast of France by the dangerous 8-mile-wide tidal channel, has an area of 3 sq. mi. (8 km.) and a population of 1,686. It is a dependency of the British island of Guernsey, to the southwest. Capital: St. Anne. Principal industries are agriculture and raising cattle.

There is evidence of settlement in prehistoric times and Roman coins have been discovered on the island along with evidence of their buildings. Toward the close of the reign of Henry VIII, France began making plans to seize the Island of Sark. The English, realizing its strategic importance, began to build a defensive fort, which was abandoned some years later when Edward VI died. France constructed a large naval base at its northern tip, which incited the English into making Alderney the "Gibraltar of the Channel." Most of the Islanders were evacuated before the German occupation in 1940 but returned in 1945 when the Germans surrendered.

The Channel Islands have never been subject to the British Parliament and are self-governing units under the direct rule of the Crown acting through the Privy Council. Alderney is within the Bailiwick of Guernsey (q.v.). It is one of the nine Channel Islands, the only part of the Duchy of Normandy still belonging to the British Crown, and has been a British possession since the Norman Conquest of 1066. Legislation was only recently introduced for the issue of its own coinage, a right it now shares with Jersey and Guernsey.

RULERS
British

MONETARY SYSTEM
100 Pence = 1 Pound Sterling

DEPENDENCY

STANDARD COINAGE

KM# 12a POUND
15.8000 g., 0.9160 Gold .4653 oz. AGW, 22.5 mm. **Ruler:** Elizabeth II **Subject:** VE Day **Rev:** VE Monogram and dove
Date	Mintage	F	VF	XF	Unc	BU
ND(1995) Proof	500	Value: 345				

KM# 1b 2 POUNDS
47.5400 g., 0.9170 Gold 1.4011 oz. AGW **Ruler:** Elizabeth II **Subject:** Royal Visit
Date	Mintage	F	VF	XF	Unc	BU
1989 Proof	100	Value: 1,000				

KM# 2b 2 POUNDS
47.5400 g., 0.9170 Gold 1.4011 oz. AGW **Ruler:** Elizabeth II **Subject:** Queen Mother's 90th Birthday
Date	Mintage	F	VF	XF	Unc	BU
1990 Proof	90	Value: 1,100				

KM# 3b 2 POUNDS
47.5400 g., 0.9170 Gold 1.4011 oz. AGW **Ruler:** Elizabeth II **Subject:** 40th Anniversary - Queen's Reign
Date	Mintage	F	VF	XF	Unc	BU
1992 Proof	150	Value: 985				

KM# 13b 2 POUNDS
47.5400 g., 0.9160 Gold 1.4011 oz. AGW **Ruler:** Elizabeth II **Subject:** Islander's Return **Rev:** Steamship
Date	Mintage	F	VF	XF	Unc	BU
ND(1995) Proof	250	Value: 945				

KM# 18b 2 POUNDS
47.5400 g., 0.9170 Gold 1.4011 oz. AGW **Ruler:** Elizabeth II **Subject:** Total Eclipse of the Sun **Obv:** Queen's portrait **Rev:** 2 sea birds and church
Date	Mintage	F	VF	XF	Unc	BU
1999 Proof	Est. 100	Value: 1,300				

KM# 14b 5 POUNDS
47.5400 g., 0.9160 Gold 1.4011 oz. AGW **Ruler:** Elizabeth II **Subject:** Queen Mother - Children
Date	Mintage	F	VF	XF	Unc	BU
1995 Proof	150	Value: 965				

KM# 15b 5 POUNDS
47.5400 g., 0.9170 Gold 1.4012 oz. AGW **Ruler:** Elizabeth II **Subject:** Queen Elizabeth's 70th Birthday - Flowers
Date	Mintage	F	VF	XF	Unc	BU
1996 Proof	250	Value: 1,225				

KM# 20a 5 POUNDS
47.5400 g., 0.9166 Gold 1.4011 oz. AGW **Ruler:** Elizabeth II **Subject:** Winston Churchill **Obv:** Queen's portrait **Rev:** Winston Churchill wearing hat **Edge Lettering:** And our dear Channel Islands are also to be freed today
Date	Mintage	F	VF	XF	Unc	BU
1999 Proof	125	Value: 950				

KM# 27b 5 POUNDS
39.9400 g., 0.9167 Gold 1.1771 oz. AGW, 38.6 mm. **Ruler:** Elizabeth II **Subject:** Princess Diana **Obv:** Queens portrait **Rev:** Diana accepting flowers from girl **Edge:** Reeded
Date	Mintage	F	VF	XF	Unc	BU
2002 Proof	100	Value: 945				

KM# 29b 5 POUNDS
39.9400 g., 0.9167 Gold 1.1771 oz. AGW, 38.6 mm. **Ruler:** Elizabeth II **Subject:** The Duke of Wellington **Obv:** Queens portrait **Rev:** Coat of arms, castle and portrait **Rev. Designer:** Willem Vis **Edge:** Reeded
Date	Mintage	VG	F	VF	XF	Unc
2002 Proof	200	Value: 925				

KM# 45b 5 POUNDS
39.9400 g., 0.9167 Gold 1.1771 oz. AGW, 38.6 mm. **Ruler:** Elizabeth II **Obv:** Queens portrait **Rev:** Alfred the Great on ship **Rev. Designer:** Willem Vis **Edge:** Reeded
Date	Mintage	F	VF	XF	Unc	BU
2003 Proof	500	Value: 975				

KM# 31b 5 POUNDS
39.9400 g., 0.9166 Gold 1.177 oz. AGW, 38.6 mm. **Ruler:** Elizabeth II **Subject:** Prince William **Obv:** Queens portrait **Obv. Designer:** Raphael Maklouf **Rev:** Portrait with open shirt collar **Edge:** Reeded
Date	Mintage	F	VF	XF	Unc	BU
2003 Proof	200	Value: 950				

KM# 35b 5 POUNDS
39.9400 g., 0.9166 Gold 1.177 oz. AGW, 38.6 mm. **Ruler:** Elizabeth II **Obv:** Queens portrait **Rev:** Concorde in flight, October 24, 2003 **Rev. Designer:** Emma Noble **Edge:** Reeded
Date	Mintage	F	VF	XF	Unc	BU
2003 Proof	500	Value: 925				

KM# 38b 5 POUNDS
39.9400 g., 0.9167 Gold 1.1771 oz. AGW, 38.6 mm. **Ruler:** Elizabeth II **Obv:** Queens portrait **Rev:** Battleship and transports **Rev. Designer:** Mike Guilfoyle
Date	Mintage	F	VF	XF	Unc	BU
2004 Proof	500	Value: 975				

KM# 43b 5 POUNDS
39.9400 g., 0.9166 Gold 1.177 oz. AGW, 38.6 mm. **Ruler:** Elizabeth II **Obv:** Queens portrait **Rev:** Florence Nightingale head above Battle of Inkerman scene with one multicolor soldier **Edge:** Reeded
Date	Mintage	F	VF	XF	Unc	BU
2004 Proof	500	Value: 975				

KM# 47b 5 POUNDS
39.9400 g., 0.9167 Gold 1.1771 oz. AGW, 38.6 mm. **Ruler:** Elizabeth II **Obv:** Queens portrait **Rev:** Locomotive, The Rocket **Rev. Designer:** Robert Lowe **Edge:** Reeded
Date	Mintage	F	VF	XF	Unc	BU
2004 Proof	500	Value: 975				

KM# 53b 5 POUNDS
39.9400 g., 0.9167 Gold 1.1771 oz. AGW, 38.6 mm. **Ruler:** Elizabeth II **Subject:** End of WWII **Obv:** Elizabeth II by Maklouf **Rev:** Flag waving crowd **Edge:** Reeded
Date	Mintage	F	VF	XF	Unc	BU
2005 Proof	150	Value: 1,000				

KM# 54a 5 POUNDS
39.9400 g., 0.9167 Gold 1.1771 oz. AGW, 38.6 mm. **Ruler:** Elizabeth II **Subject:** WWII Liberation **Obv:** Elizabeth II by Maklouf **Rev:** Churchill flashing the "V" sign **Edge:** Reeded
Date	Mintage	F	VF	XF	Unc	BU
2005 Proof	150	Value: 1,000				

KM# 8 10 POUNDS
3.1300 g., 0.9990 Gold .1005 oz. AGW **Ruler:** Elizabeth II **Subject:** Normandy Invasion **Obv. Designer:** Raphael Maklouf **Rev:** Paratroopers and Transport Plane
Date	Mintage	F	VF	XF	Unc	BU
1994 Proof	Est. 1,000	Value: 95.00				

KM# 6 25 POUNDS
8.5130 g., 0.9170 Gold .2507 oz. AGW **Ruler:** Elizabeth II **Subject:** 40th Anniversary - Coronation **Obv. Designer:** Raphael Maklouf **Rev:** Royal carriage **Rev. Designer:** John Savage
Date	Mintage	F	VF	XF	Unc	BU
1993 Proof	Est. 1,000	Value: 210				

KM# 9 25 POUNDS
7.8100 g., 0.9990 Gold .2509 oz. AGW **Ruler:** Elizabeth II **Subject:** Normandy Invasion **Obv. Designer:** Raphael Maklouf **Rev:** Fighter planes and tank
Date	Mintage	F	VF	XF	Unc	BU
1994 Proof	Est. 1,000	Value: 210				

KM# 57 25 POUNDS
7.8100 g., 0.9990 Gold 0.2508 oz. AGW **Ruler:** Elizabeth II **Subject:** Normandy Invasion **Rev:** Fighter planes and tank
Date	Mintage	F	VF	XF	Unc	BU
1994 Proof	—	Value: 200				

KM# 23b 25 POUNDS
8.4300 g., 0.9160 Gold .2483 oz. AGW **Ruler:** Elizabeth II **Subject:** Golden Wedding Anniversary - Elizabeth and Philip **Obv:** Queen Elizabeth's head right **Rev:** Queen Elizabeth crowning Charles as Prince of Wales, date (1947-1997) in legend
Date	Mintage	F	VF	XF	Unc	BU
ND(1997) Proof	—	Value: 200				

KM# 22 25 POUNDS
7.8100 g., 0.9160 Gold .2302 oz. AGW **Ruler:** Elizabeth II **Subject:** 60th Anniversary - Battle of Britain **Obv:** Queen Elizabeth's head right **Rev:** Two spitfires in flight, pilot at bottom center **Edge:** Reeded
Date	Mintage	F	VF	XF	Unc	BU
2000	—	Value: 275				

KM# 61 25 POUNDS
7.9800 g., 0.9167 Gold 0.2352 oz. AGW, 22 mm. **Ruler:** Elizabeth II **Subject:** Queen's 75th Birthday **Obv:** Queens portrait right **Obv. Designer:** Raphael Maklouf **Rev:** Queen in casual dress surrounded by rose, thistle, daffodil and pimper nickel **Rev. Designer:** David Cornell
Date	Mintage	F	VF	XF	Unc	BU
2001 Proof	—	Value: 325				

KM# 28 25 POUNDS
7.9800 g., 0.9167 Gold 0.2352 oz. AGW, 22.05 mm. **Ruler:** Elizabeth II **Subject:** Princess Diana **Obv:** Queens portrait **Rev:** Diana's cameo portrait above denomination **Rev. Designer:** Avril Vaughan **Edge:** Reeded
Date	Mintage	VG	F	VF	XF	Unc
2002 Proof	2,500	Value: 275				

KM# 30 25 POUNDS
7.9800 g., 0.9166 Gold 0.2352 oz. AGW, 22 mm. **Ruler:** Elizabeth II **Subject:** The Duke of Wellington **Obv:** Queens portrait **Rev:** Coat of arms, castle and portrait **Rev. Designer:** Willem Vis **Edge:** Reeded
Date	Mintage	VG	F	VF	XF	Unc
2002 Proof	2,500	Value: 300				

KM# 58 25 POUNDS
7.9800 g., 0.9166 Gold 0.2352 oz. AGW, 22 mm. **Ruler:** Elizabeth II **Obv:** Queen's portrait right
Date	Mintage	F	VF	XF	Unc	BU
2002 Proof	2,500	Value: 300				

KM# 32 25 POUNDS
7.9800 g., 0.9166 Gold 0.2352 oz. AGW, 22 mm. **Ruler:** Elizabeth II **Subject:** Prince William **Obv:** Queens portrait **Rev:** Portrait with open shirt collar **Edge:** Reeded
Date	Mintage	F	VF	XF	Unc	BU
2003 Proof	1,500	Value: 325				

KM# 46 25 POUNDS
7.9800 g., 0.9167 Gold 0.2352 oz. AGW, 22 mm. **Ruler:** Elizabeth II **Obv:** Queens portrait **Rev:** HMS Mary Rose **Rev. Designer:** Willem Vis **Edge:** Reeded
Date	Mintage	F	VF	XF	Unc	BU
2003 Proof	2,500	Value: 365				

KM# 39 25 POUNDS
7.9800 g., 0.9167 Gold 0.2352 oz. AGW, 22 mm. **Ruler:** Elizabeth II **Subject:** D-Day **Obv:** Queens portrait **Rev:** Battleship and transports **Edge:** Reeded
Date	Mintage	F	VF	XF	Unc	BU
2004 Proof	500	Value: 325				

ALGERIA

KM# 50 25 POUNDS
7.9800 g., 0.9167 Gold 0.2352 oz. AGW, 22 mm. **Ruler:** Elizabeth II **Obv:** Queens portrait **Rev:** Locomotive, The Rocket **Rev. Designer:** Robert Lowe **Edge:** Reeded

Date	Mintage	F	VF	XF	Unc	BU
2004 Proof	2,500	Value: 365				

KM# 51 25 POUNDS
7.9800 g., 0.9167 Gold 0.2352 oz. AGW, 22 mm. **Ruler:** Elizabeth II **Obv:** Queens portrait **Rev:** Locomotive, The Merchant Navy 21C1 **Rev. Designer:** Robert Lowe **Edge:** Reeded

Date	Mintage	F	VF	XF	Unc	BU
2004 Proof	1,500	Value: 365				

KM# 67 25 POUNDS
7.9800 g., 0.9167 Gold 0.2352 oz. AGW, 22 mm. **Ruler:** Elizabeth II **Subject:** Viscount Samuel Hood on his flagship after the Battle of Saints Passage in 1782 **Obv:** Queens portrait **Rev. Designer:** Willem Vis

Date	Mintage	F	VF	XF	Unc	BU
2005 Proof	—	Value: 300				

KM# 69 25 POUNDS
7.9800 g., 0.9167 Gold 0.2352 oz. AGW, 22 mm. **Ruler:** Elizabeth II **Obv:** Queens portrait right **Rev:** HMS Revenge fighting at Azores, 1591 **Rev. Designer:** Willem Vis

Date	Mintage	F	VF	XF	Unc	BU
2005 Proof	—	Value: 365				

KM# 10 50 POUNDS
15.6000 g., 0.9990 Gold .5014 oz. AGW **Ruler:** Elizabeth II **Subject:** Normandy Invasion **Obv. Designer:** Raphael Maklouf **Rev:** British gliders

Date	Mintage	F	VF	XF	Unc	BU
1994	Est. 1,000	Value: 450				

Note: In Proof sets only

KM# 11 100 POUNDS
31.2100 g., 0.9990 Gold 1.0025 oz. AGW **Ruler:** Elizabeth II **Subject:** Normandy Invasion **Obv:** Crowned bust, right, date below **Obv. Designer:** Raphael Maklouf **Rev:** Normandy beach landing scene

Date	Mintage	F	VF	XF	Unc	BU
1994 Proof	Est. 500	Value: 825				

KM# 34 100 POUNDS
1000.0000 g., 0.9166 Gold 29.4694 oz. AGW, 100 mm. **Ruler:** Elizabeth II **Subject:** Prince William **Obv:** Queens portrait **Rev:** Portrait with open shirt collar **Edge:** Reeded

Date	Mintage	F	VF	XF	Unc	BU
2003 Proof	—	Value: 24,500				

KM# 37 1000 POUNDS
1090.8600 g., 0.9166 Gold 32.1469 oz. AGW, 100 mm. **Ruler:** Elizabeth II **Subject:** Last Flight of the Concorde **Obv:** Queens portrait **Rev:** Concorde in flight **Edge:** Reeded

Date	Mintage	F	VF	XF	Unc	BU
2003 Proof	34	Value: 25,000				

KM# 41 1000 POUNDS
1000.0000 g., 0.9167 Gold 29.4726 oz. AGW, 100 mm. **Ruler:** Elizabeth II **Subject:** D-Day **Obv:** Queens portrait **Rev:** US and British troops wading ashore **Rev. Designer:** Matthew Bonaccorsi **Edge:** Reeded

Date	Mintage	F	VF	XF	Unc	BU
2004 Proof	60	Value: 24,000				

MINT SETS

KM#	Date	Mintage	Identification	Issue Price	Mkt Val
XMS1	2004 (8)	10,000	X#Pn1-Pn8	—	30.00

PROOF SETS

KM#	Date	Mintage	Identification	Issue Price	Mkt Val
PS1	1994 (5)	500	KM#7a, 8-11	—	1,650
PS2	1994 (4)	I.A.	KM#8-11	—	1,600
PS3	1994 (4)	500	KM#7a, 8-10	—	800
PS4	1994 (3)	I.A.	KM#8-10	—	750
XPS1	2004 (9)	5,000	X#Pn1-Pn9	—	50.00

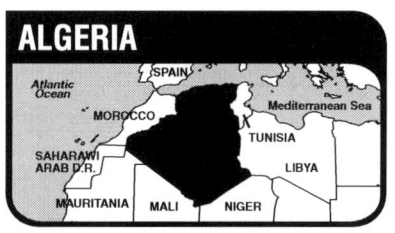

The Democratic and Popular Republic of Algeria, a North African country fronting on the Mediterranean Sea between Tunisia and Morocco, has an area of 919,595 sq. mi. (2,381,740 sq. km.) and a population of 31.6 million. Capital: Algiers (Alger). Most of the country's working population is engaged in agriculture although a recent industrial diversification, financed by oil revenues, is making steady progress. Wines, fruits, iron and zinc ores, phosphates, tobacco products, liquified natural gas, and petroleum are exported.

Algiers, the capital and chief seaport of Algeria, was the site of Phoenician and Roman settlements before the present Moslem city was founded about 950. Nominally part of the sultanate of Tilimsan, Algiers had a large measure of independence under the amirs of its own. In 1492 the Jews and Moors who had been expelled from Spain settled in Algiers and enjoyed an increasing influence until the imposition of Turkish control in 1518. For the following three centuries, Algiers was the headquarters of the notorious Barbary pirates as Turkish control became more and more nominal. The French took Algiers in 1830, and after a long and wearisome war completed the conquest of Algeria and annexed it to France, 1848. Following the armistice signed by France and Nazi Germany on June 22, 1940, Algeria fell under Vichy Government control until liberated by the Allied invasion forces under the command of Gen. D. D. Eisenhower on Nov. 8, 1942. The inability to obtain equal rights with Frenchmen led to an organized revolt which began on Nov. 1, 1954 and lasted until a ceasefire was signed on July I, 1962. Independence was proclaimed on July 5, 1962, following a self-determination referendum, and the Republic was declared on September 25, 1962.

RULERS
Ottoman, until 1830
Abd-el-Kader (rebel), AH1250-1264/1834-1847AD

ALGIERS

MINTNAMES

جزاير
Jaza'ir

المعسكر
al-Mascara
During revolt of Abd-el-Kader
AH1250-1264/1834-1847AD

مديه
Medea
AH1246/1830AD

قسنطينة
Qusantinah
Constantine
AH1245-1254/1830-1837AD

تاقدمت
Taqidemt
During revolt of Abd-el-Kader
AH1250-1264/1834-1847AD

تلمسان
Tilimsan
AH964-1026/1556-1617AD

NOTE: The dots above and below the letters are integral parts of the letters, but for stylistic reasons, are occasionally omitted.

MONETARY SYSTEM

(Until 1847)
14-1/2 Asper (Akche, Dirham Saghir) = 1 Kharub
2 Kharuba = 1 Muzuna
24 Muzuna = 3 Batlaka (Pataka) = 1 Budju

NOTE: Coin denominations are not expressed on the coins, and are best determined by size and weight. The silver Budju weighed about 13.5 g until AH1236/1821AD, when it was reduced to about 10.0 g. The fractional pieces varied in proportion to the Budju. They had secondary names, which are given in the text.

In 1829 three new silver coins were introduced and Budju became Tugrali-rial, Tugrali-batlaka = 1/3 Rial = 8 Muzuna and Tugralinessflik = 1/2 Batlaka = 4 Muzuna. The gold Sultani was officially valued at 108 Muzuna, but varied in accordance with the market price of gold expressed in silver. It weighed 3.20-3.40 g. The Zeri Mahbub was valued at 80 Muzuna & weighed 2.38-3.10 g.

OTTOMAN

Selim III
AH1203-1222/1789-1807AD

HAMMERED COINAGE

KM# 44 1/4 SULTANI
0.8500 g., Gold, 15-16 mm. **Obv:** Legend has 2 lines **Rev:** Mintname above date. **Note:** Size varies.

Date	Mintage	F	VF	XF	Unc
AH1217	—	65.00	100	200	250	—
AH1219	—	65.00	100	200	250	—
AH1222	—	65.00	100	200	250	—

KM# 49 1/4 SULTANI
0.8500 g., Gold **Rev:** Mint name within octagram

Date	Mintage	F	VF	XF	Unc
AH1221	—	150	225	300	375	—
AH1222	—	150	225	300	375	—

KM# 46 1/2 SULTANI
Gold, 18-19 mm. **Obv:** Inscription within beaded circle **Rev:** Inscription within beaded circle **Note:** Weight varies: 1.54-1.70g. Size varies

Date	Mintage	VG	F	VF	XF	Unc
AH1216	—	100	150	200	275	—
AH1217	—	100	150	200	275	—
AH1218	—	100	150	200	275	—
AH1219	—	100	150	200	275	—
AH1220	—	100	150	200	275	—

KM# 50 1/2 SULTANI
Gold **Rev:** Mint name within octagram

Date	Mintage	VG	F	VF	XF	Unc
AH1221	—	200	275	375	500	—
AH1222	—	200	275	375	500	—

KM# 41 SULTANI
Gold, 22-25 mm. **Obv:** Star of Solomon **Rev:** Inscription **Note:** Weight varies: 3.25-3.40g. Size varies.

Date	Mintage	VG	F	VF	XF	Unc
AH1216	—	200	275	375	500	—
AH1217	—	200	275	375	500	—
AH1218	—	200	275	375	500	—
AH1219	—	200	275	375	500	—
AH1220	—	200	275	375	500	—
AH1221	—	200	275	375	500	—
AH1222	—	200	275	375	500	—

KM# 51 SULTANI
3.1000 g., Gold **Rev:** Mint name with octagram

Date	Mintage	VG	F	VF	XF	Unc
AH1221 Rare	—	—	—	—	—	—
AH1222 Rare	—	—	—	—	—	—

Mustafa IV
AH1222-1223/1807-1808AD

HAMMERED COINAGE

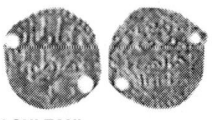

KM# 55 1/4 SULTANI
0.8000 g., Gold **Note:** Mint name in octagram.

ALGERIA / ALGIERS

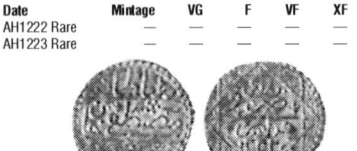

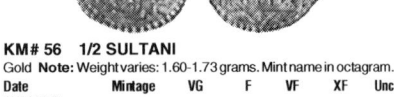

Date	Mintage	VG	F	VF	XF	Unc
AH1222 Rare	—	—	—	—	—	—
AH1223 Rare	—	—	—	—	—	—

KM# 56 1/2 SULTANI
Gold **Note:** Weight varies: 1.60-1.73 grams. Mint name in octagram.

Date	Mintage	VG	F	VF	XF	Unc
AH1222 Rare	—	—	—	—	—	—
AH1223 Rare	—	—	—	—	—	—

KM# 57 SULTANI
Gold **Note:** Weight varies: 3.15-3.40 grams. Mint name in octagram.

Date	Mintage	VG	F	VF	XF	Unc
AH1222 Rare	—	—	—	—	—	—
AH1223 Rare	—	—	—	—	—	—

Mahmud II
AH1223-1252/1808-1839AD
HAMMERED COINAGE

KM# 63 1/4 SULTANI
Gold **Obv. Legend:** Legend is Sultan Mahmud **Note:** Weight varies: 0.78-0.85 grams. Size varies: 14-15mm.

Date	Mintage	VG	F	VF	XF	Unc
AH1224 Rare	—	—	—	—	—	—
AH1228 Rare	—	—	—	—	—	—
AH1231	—	85.00	125	175	250	—
AH1232	—	85.00	125	175	250	—
AH1234 Rare	—	—	—	—	—	—
AH1238	—	85.00	125	175	250	—
AH1240	—	85.00	125	175	250	—
AH1243	—	85.00	125	175	250	—

KM# 64 1/4 SULTANI
0.7050 g., Gold

Date	Mintage	VG	F	VF	XF	Unc
AH1246 Rare	—	—	—	—	2,500	—

KM# 65 1/2 SULTANI
Gold **Note:** Weight varies: 1.15-1.60 grams. Varieties exist.

Date	Mintage	VG	F	VF	XF	Unc
AH1230	—	100	140	200	275	—
AH1231	—	100	140	200	275	—
AH1232	—	100	140	200	275	—
AH1234	—	100	140	200	275	—
AH1236	—	100	140	200	275	—
AH1237	—	100	140	200	275	—
AH1238	—	100	140	200	275	—
AH1239	—	100	140	200	275	—
AH1240	—	100	140	200	275	—

KM# 60 SULTANI
3.2000 g., Gold **Rev:** Year in fourth line **Note:** Size varies: 22-24mm.

Date	Mintage	VG	F	VF	XF	Unc
AH1223	—	250	350	450	575	—
AH1224	—	250	350	450	575	—
AH1225	—	250	350	450	575	—
AH1226	—	250	350	450	575	—
AH1228	—	250	350	450	575	—
AH1231	—	250	350	450	575	—
AH1232	—	250	350	450	575	—
AH1234	—	250	350	450	575	—

KM# 66 SULTANI
3.2000 g., Gold **Rev:** Year in third line

Date	Mintage	VG	F	VF	XF	Unc
AH1235	—	165	225	300	400	—
AH1236	—	165	225	300	400	—
AH1237	—	165	225	300	400	—
AH1238	—	165	225	300	400	—
AH1239	—	165	225	300	400	—
AH1240	—	165	225	300	400	—
AH1241	—	165	225	300	400	—
AH1243	—	165	225	300	400	—
AH3421 (Error)	—	165	225	300	400	—
AH1244	—	165	225	300	400	—
AH1245	—	275	400	550	750	—

KM# 69 SULTANI
2.3800 g., Gold **Obv:** Toughra **Rev:** 4-line legend with 20 above ibn

Date	Mintage	VG	F	VF	XF	Unc
AH1246	—	—	—	—	—	—

Note: The regnal year 20 is probably an error for 23

ALGERIA
REPUBLIC

MONETARY SYSTEM
100 Centimes = 1 Dinar

STANDARD COINAGE

KM# 120 DINAR
3.2200 g., 0.9200 Gold .0953 oz. AGW **Subject:** Historical Coin - 5 Aspers of Abd-el-Kader **Obv:** Old Islamic coin at center **Rev:** Old Islamic coin

Date	Mintage	F	VF	XF	Unc	BU
AH1411	—	—	—	—	125	150

KM# 121 2 DINARS
6.4500 g., 0.9200 Gold .1908 oz. AGW **Subject:** Historical Coin - Dinar of 762 A.D. Rostomiden Dynasty

Date	Mintage	F	VF	XF	Unc	BU
AH1411	—	—	—	—	250	300

KM# 133 2 DINARS
Gold **Subject:** Historical Coin - 2 Dinar of Abd Al-Qadir, AH1222-1300

Date	Mintage	F	VF	XF	Unc	BU
AH1417	—	—	—	—	275	325

KM# 122 5 DINARS
16.1200 g., 0.9200 Gold .4768 oz. AGW **Subject:** Historical Coin - Denar of Numidian King Massinissa, 238-148 B.C. **Obv:** Standing elephant left, within circle flanked by value **Rev:** King, left within beaded circle

Date	Mintage	F	VF	XF	Unc	BU
AH1411-1991	—	—	—	—	550	650

KM# 110b 10 DINARS
24.5000 g., 0.9000 Gold .7090 oz. AGW

Date	Mintage	F	VF	XF	Unc	BU
1979	100	—	—	—	1,000	1,250

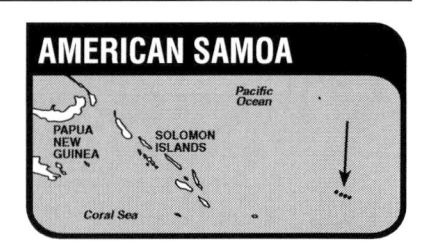

AMERICAN SAMOA

The Territory of American Samoa, with a population of 41,000, consists of seven major islands with a total land area of 76 sq. mi. (199 sq. km.) which are located about 2300 miles south-southwest of Hawaii. American Samoa was settled by the Polynesians around 600 BC. The capital is Pago Pago.

Samoa's long isolation from the western world ended in 1722 when the Dutch explorer, Jacob Roggeveen, came upon the islands. However, it wasn't until 1831 that European influence had any real impact. In that year, John Williams of the London Missionary Society arrived with eight Tahitian missionaries.

By 1900 the Samoan islands were being claimed by both Germany and the United States. Germany annexed several islands, which now comprise Western Samoa; the U.S. took Tutuila to use Pago Pago Bay as a coaling station for naval ships.

As Japan began emerging as an international power in the mid-1930's, the U.S. Naval station on Tutuila began to acquire new strategic importance; and in 1940 the Samoan Islands became a training and staging area for the U.S. Marine Corps.

A. P. Lutali, Governor of American Samoa, signed a historic proclamation on May 23, 1988 that authorized the minting of the first numismatic issue for this unincorporated territory administered by the United States Department of the Interior.

MONETARY SYSTEM
100 Cents = 1 Dollar

U.S. TERRITORY
MILLED COINAGE

KM# 4 50 DOLLARS
8.6397 g., 0.9000 Gold .2500 oz. AGW **Subject:** America's Cup **Obv:** Olympic symbols **Rev:** Americas Cup

Date	Mintage	F	VF	XF	Unc	BU
1988 Proof	100	Value: 300				

KM# 5 100 DOLLARS
31.1000 g., 0.9990 Gold 1.0000 oz. AGW **Subject:** America's Cup **Obv:** State seal **Rev:** USA's yacht passing New Zealand's yacht

Date	Mintage	F	VF	XF	Unc	BU
1988 Proof	50	Value: 975				

KM# 8 100 DOLLARS
31.1000 g., 0.9990 Gold 1.0000 oz. AGW **Subject:** XXIV Olympics **Obv:** State seal **Rev:** Olympic rings and Chamshil Stadium above denomination

Date	Mintage	F	VF	XF	Unc	BU
1988 Proof	50	Value: 1,250				

KM# 11 100 DOLLARS
31.1000 g., 0.9990 Gold 1.0000 oz. AGW **Obv:** USA's yacht passing New Zealand's yacht **Rev:** Olympic rings and Chamshil Stadium above denomination **Note:** Mule.

Date	Mintage	F	VF	XF	Unc	BU
1988 Proof	5	Value: 2,250				

PROOF SETS

KM#	Date	Mintage Identification	Issue Price	Mkt Val
PS1	1988 (3)	— KM#2-4	315	575

ANDORRA

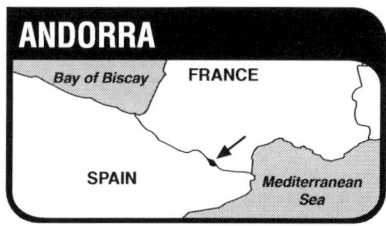

Principality of Andorra (Principat d'Andorra), situated on the southern slopes of the Pyrenees Mountains between France and Spain, has an area of 181 sq. mi. (453 sq. km.) and a population of 80,000. Capital: Andorra la Vella. Tourism is the chief source of income. Timber, cattle and derivatives, and furniture are exported.

According to tradition, the independence of Andorra derives from a charter Charlemagne granted the people of Andorra in 806 in recognition of their help in battling the Moors. An agreement between the Count of Foix (France) and the Bishop of Seo de Urgel (Spanish) in 1278 to recognize each other as Co-Princes of Andorra gave the state what has been its political form and territorial extent continuously to the present day. Over the years, the title on the French side passed to the Kings of Navarre, then to the Kings of France, and is now held by the President of France.

RULERS
Joan D.M. Bisbe D'Urgell I

MONETARY SYSTEM
100 Centims = 1 Diner
100 Pesetas = 1 Diner, 1983-85
125 Pesetas = 1 Diner, 1986-
NOTE: The Diners have been struck for collectors while the Euro is used in everyday commerce.

MINT MARKS
Crowned M = Madrid

PRINCIPALITY

DECIMAL COINAGE

KM# 134 50 CENTIMS
0.6221 g., 0.9990 Gold .0100 oz. AGW **Obv:** Fleury cross **Rev:** Portrait of Queen Isabella I **Note:** Similar to 20 Diners, KM#137.
Date	Mintage	F	VF	XF	Unc	BU
1997 Proof	Est. 50,000	Value: 35.00				

KM# 135 DINER
1.2441 g., 0.9990 Gold .0400 oz. AGW **Obv:** Fleury cross **Rev:** Portrait of Queen Isabella I **Note:** Similar to 20 Diners, KM#137.
Date	Mintage	F	VF	XF	Unc	BU
1997 Proof	Est. 10,000	Value: 55.00				

KM# 111 5 DINERS
1.2500 g., 0.9990 Gold .0401 oz. AGW **Subject:** Wildlife **Obv:** Crowned arms to left of five line inscription, value below, date at bottom **Rev:** Red squirrel, left
Date	Mintage	F	VF	XF	Unc	BU
1994 Proof	—	Value: 70.00				

KM# 112 5 DINERS
1.5552 g., 0.9990 Gold .0500 oz. AGW **Obv:** Defiant eagle **Rev:** Crowned denomination within wreath
Date	Mintage	F	VF	XF	Unc	BU
1995 Proof	—	Value: 60.00				

KM# 117 5 DINERS
1.2441 g., 0.9990 Gold .0400 oz. AGW **Subject:** Wildlife **Obv:** Crowned arms to left of five line inscription, value below, date at bottom **Rev:** Chamois, left
Date	Mintage	F	VF	XF	Unc	BU
1996 Proof	Est. 100,000	Value: 55.00				

KM# 118 5 DINERS
1.2441 g., 0.9990 Gold .0400 oz. AGW **Subject:** Wildlife **Rev:** Brown bear and cub
Date	Mintage	F	VF	XF	Unc	BU
1996 Proof	Est. 100,000	Value: 55.00				

KM# 141 5 DINERS
3.1103 g., 0.5850 Gold .0585 oz. AGW **Subject:** 1998 Winter Olympics **Obv:** Crowned arms to left of five line inscription, value below, date at bottom **Rev:** Downhill skier
Date	Mintage	F	VF	XF	Unc	BU
1997 (1998) Proof	5,000	Value: 65.00				

KM# 193 5 DINERS
1.2400 g., 0.9990 Gold .0398 oz. AGW, 13.92 mm. **Obv:** National arms **Rev:** The Escorial Palace in Madrid **Edge:** Reeded
Date	Mintage	F	VF	XF	Unc	BU
2004 Proof	3,000	Value: 65.00				

KM# 194 5 DINERS
1.2400 g., 0.9990 Gold .0398 oz. AGW, 13.92 mm. **Obv:** National arms **Rev:** Eiffel Tower **Edge:** Reeded
Date	Mintage	F	VF	XF	Unc	BU
2004 Proof	3,000	Value: 65.00				

KM# 195 5 DINERS
1.2400 g., 0.9990 Gold .0398 oz. AGW, 13.92 mm. **Obv:** National arms **Rev:** Atomic model monument **Edge:** Reeded
Date	Mintage	F	VF	XF	Unc	BU
2004 Proof	3,000	Value: 65.00				

KM# 196 5 DINERS
1.2400 g., 0.9990 Gold .0398 oz. AGW, 13.92 mm. **Subject:** Andorran membership in the United Nations **Obv:** National arms **Rev:** Seated woman, world globe and UN logo **Edge:** Reeded
Date	Mintage	F	VF	XF	Unc	BU
2004 Proof	3,000	Value: 75.00				

KM# 136 10 DINERS
3.1103 g., 0.9990 Gold .1000 oz. AGW **Obv:** Fleury cross **Rev:** Portrait of Isabella I **Note:** Similar to 20 Diners, KM#137
Date	Mintage	F	VF	XF	Unc	BU
1997 Proof	Est. 5,000	Value: 100				

KM# 217 10 DINERS
3.1100 g., 0.9999 Gold 0.1 oz. AGW, 20 mm. **Obv:** National arms **Rev:** Jesus carrying the cross **Edge:** Reeded
Date	Mintage	F	VF	XF	Unc	BU
2006 Proof	9,999	Value: 100				

KM# 137 20 DINERS
6.2207 g., 0.9990 Gold .2000 oz. AGW **Obv:** Fleury cross **Rev:** Portrait of Isabella I, right
Date	Mintage	F	VF	XF	Unc	BU
1997 Proof	Est. 3,500	Value: 185				

KM# 73 25 DINERS
7.7700 g., 0.5830 Gold .1456 oz. AGW, 25 mm. **Subject:** ECU Customs Union **Obv:** Arms with "ECU" below within circle of stars/beads **Rev:** St. Ermengol
Date	Mintage	F	VF	XF	Unc	BU
1992 Proof	3,000	Value: 115				

KM# 81 25 DINERS
7.7700 g., 0.5830 Gold .1456 oz. AGW **Subject:** 1994 Winter Olympic Games, Lillehammer **Obv:** Crowned arms to left of five line inscription, value below, date at bottom **Rev:** Downhill skier
Date	Mintage	F	VF	XF	Unc	BU
1993 Proof	6,000	Value: 125				

KM# 91 25 DINERS
7.7700 g., 0.5830 Gold .1456 oz. AGW **Subject:** ECU Customs Union **Obv:** Arms above "ECU" within circle of stars/beads **Rev:** Bishop riding a horse
Date	Mintage	F	VF	XF	Unc	BU
1993 Proof	5,000	Value: 115				

KM# 92 25 DINERS
7.7700 g., 0.5830 Gold .1456 oz. AGW **Subject:** 1994 World Cup Soccer **Obv:** Crowned arms to left of five line inscription, value below, date at bottom **Rev:** Soccer player on right, outline of bird on top left
Date	Mintage	F	VF	XF	Unc	BU
1993 Proof	5,000	Value: 125				

KM# 96 25 DINERS
7.7700 g., 0.5830 Gold .1456 oz. AGW **Subject:** 1994 Summer Olympic Games **Rev:** Tennis
Date	Mintage	F	VF	XF	Unc	BU
1994 Proof	5,000	Value: 125				

KM# 101 25 DINERS
7.7700 g., 0.5830 Gold .1456 oz. AGW **Subject:** ECU Customs Union **Obv:** Coat of arms **Rev:** Bishop Pere D'Urg standing
Date	Mintage	F	VF	XF	Unc	BU
1994 Proof	5,000	Value: 115				

KM# 107 25 DINERS
7.7700 g., 0.5830 Gold .1456 oz. AGW **Subject:** ECU Customs Union **Obv:** Coat of arms **Rev:** Bishop Pere D'Urg seated

14 ANDORRA

KM# 123 25 DINERS
7.7700 g., 0.5830 Gold .1456 oz. AGW **Obv:** Arms and "ECU" **Rev:** Seated Europa

Date	Mintage	F	VF	XF	Unc	BU
1995 Proof	5,000				Value: 115	
1996 Proof	Est. 5,000				Value: 115	

KM# 129 25 DINERS
7.7700 g., 0.5830 Gold .1456 oz. AGW **Subject:** Treaty of Rome **Obv:** Crowned arms **Rev:** Europa on knee, holding large "EURO" shield

Date	Mintage	F	VF	XF	Unc	BU
1997 Proof	5,000				Value: 115	

KM# 139 25 DINERS
Bi-Metallic Gold center in Platinum ring **Obv:** Fleury cross **Rev:** Swan in water

Date	Mintage	F	VF	XF	Unc	BU
1997 Proof	10,000				Value: 250	

KM# 145 25 DINERS
7.7700 g., 0.5850 Gold .1461 oz. AGW **Subject:** Human Rights **Obv:** Crowned arms **Rev:** Seated woman with quill

Date	Mintage	F	VF	XF	Unc	BU
1998 Proof	5,000				Value: 115	

KM# 174 25 DINERS
12.4414 g., 0.9990 Gold 0.3996 oz. AGW, 26 mm. **Subject:** Christmas **Obv:** National arms **Rev:** Nativity scene **Edge:** Reeded

Date	Mintage	F	VF	XF	Unc	BU
2001 Proof	3,000				Value: 320	

KM# 184 25 DINERS
10.0000 g., 0.9999 Gold 0.3215 oz. AGW, 26 mm. **Subject:** Christmas **Obv:** National arms **Rev:** Standing Christ child **Edge:** Reeded

Date	Mintage	F	VF	XF	Unc	BU
2002 Proof	2,000				Value: 280	

KM# 185 25 DINERS
7.7759 g., 0.9990 Gold 0.2498 oz. AGW, 26 mm. **Subject:** Christmas **Obv:** National arms **Rev:** Madonna-like mother and child **Edge:** Reeded

Date	Mintage	F	VF	XF	Unc	BU
2003 Proof	3,000				Value: 260	

KM# 197 25 DINERS
8.0000 g., 0.9990 Gold 0.2569 oz. AGW, 26 mm. **Subject:** Christmas **Obv:** National arms **Rev:** Nativity scene **Edge:** Reeded

Date	Mintage	F	VF	XF	Unc	BU
2004 Proof	5,000				Value: 230	

KM# 216 25 DINERS
6.0000 g., 0.9999 Gold 0.1929 oz. AGW, 26 mm. **Obv:** National arms **Rev:** St. Joseph holding infant Jesus **Edge:** Reeded

Date	Mintage	F	VF	XF	Unc	BU
2005 Proof	9,999				Value: 200	

KM# 63 50 DINERS
15.5500 g., 0.9990 Gold .5000 oz. AGW, 30 mm. **Obv:** Defiant eagle **Rev:** Arms within circle **Note:** There is a similar 1988 half-ounce without the denomination.

Date	Mintage	F	VF	XF	Unc	BU
1989	3,000	—	—	—	—	345
1989 Proof	—				Value: 375	

KM# 62 50 DINERS
17.0250 g., 0.9170 Gold .5000 oz. AGW, 29 mm. **Obv:** Arms within circle outlined with dots, value below **Rev:** Castle, Antoni Gaudi to left, two dates to right

Date	Mintage	F	VF	XF	Unc	BU
1990 Proof	3,000				Value: 350	

KM# 64 50 DINERS
15.5500 g., 0.9990 Gold .5000 oz. AGW, 27 mm. **Subject:** Wildlife **Rev:** Red squirrel

Date	Mintage	F	VF	XF	Unc	BU
1990 Proof	2,500				Value: 350	

KM# 68 50 DINERS
15.5500 g., 0.9990 Gold .5000 oz. AGW, 27 mm. **Subject:** Wildlife **Obv:** Crowned arms to left of five line inscription, value below, date below **Rev:** Chamois

Date	Mintage	F	VF	XF	Unc	BU
1991 Proof	Est. 2,500				Value: 350	

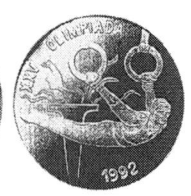

KM# 70 50 DINERS
13.3400 g., 0.5850 Gold .2509 oz. AGW, 27.5 mm. **Subject:** 1992 Summer Olympic Games **Obv:** Crowned arms to left of five line inscription, value below, date at bottom **Rev:** Gymnast on rings

Date	Mintage	F	VF	XF	Unc	BU
1991 Proof	3,000				Value: 225	

KM# 93 50 DINERS
13.3400 g., 0.5850 Gold .2509 oz. AGW **Obv:** Defiant eagle **Rev:** Crowned value within wreath

Date	Mintage	F	VF	XF	Unc	BU
1992	—	—	—	—	225	250

KM# 77 50 DINERS
15.5520 g., 0.9999 Gold .4995 oz. AGW, 27 mm. **Subject:** Wildlife **Obv:** Crowned arms to left of five line inscription, value below, date at bottom **Rev:** Bears

Date	Mintage	F	VF	XF	Unc	BU
1992 Proof	2,500				Value: 350	

KM# 82 50 DINERS
16.9650 g., 0.9160 Gold .4996 oz. AGW **Obv:** Crowned arms to left of five line inscription, value below, date at bottom **Rev:** Musician Pau Casals

Date	Mintage	F	VF	XF	Unc	BU
1993 Proof	5,000				Value: 345	

KM# 152 50 DINERS
15.5520 g., 0.9160 Gold .4583 oz. AGW **Subject:** 250th Anniversary - Synod Constitution **Obv:** Clerical arms **Rev:** Madonna and child

Date	Mintage	F	VF	XF	Unc	BU
1998 Proof	1,998				Value: 350	

ANDORRA

KM# 186 50 DINERS
159.5000 g., 0.9990 Bi-Metallic Gold And Silver .999 Silver 155.5g coin with .999 Gold 4g, 20x50mm insert 5.1229 oz., 65 mm. **Subject:** 10th Anniversary of Constitution **Obv:** National arms **Rev:** Seated allegorical woman holding scrolled constitution **Edge:** Reeded

Date	Mintage	F	VF	XF	Unc	BU
2003	3,000	—	—	—	275	325

KM# 41 100 DINERS
5.0000 g., 0.9990 Gold .1607 oz. AGW, 22 mm. **Obv:** Joan D.M. Bisbe D'Urgell I, left **Rev:** Value, date below, within crowned wreath

Date	Mintage	F	VF	XF	Unc	BU
1987	2,000	—	—	—	165	195

KM# 42 100 DINERS
5.0000 g., 0.9990 Gold .1607 oz. AGW **Obv:** Arms within circle **Rev:** Flying bird, mountains in background, date below

Date	Mintage	F	VF	XF	Unc	BU
1988	2,000	—	—	—	250	275

KM# 79 100 DINERS
31.1035 g., 0.9990 Gold 1 oz. AGW, 35 mm. **Obv:** Defiant eagle above value **Note:** There is a similar 1988 one-ounce without the denomination.

Date	Mintage	F	VF	XF	Unc	BU
1989	3,000	—	—	—	675	700

KM# 94 100 DINERS
31.1035 g., 0.9990 Gold 1 oz. AGW **Obv:** Defiant eagle, date below **Rev:** Value within crowned wreath

Date	Mintage	F	VF	XF	Unc	BU
1992	—	—	—	—	675	700

KM# 45 250 DINERS
12.0000 g., 0.9990 Gold .3858 oz. AGW, 28.1 mm. **Subject:** 700th Anniversary - Andorra's Governing Charter **Obv:** Fleury cross, value at bottom **Rev:** Grasped hands, right hand armored, left hand has mark on back

Date	Mintage	F	VF	XF	Unc	BU
ND(1988)	3,000	—	—	—	310	335

KM# 30 SOVEREIGN
8.0000 g., 0.9180 Gold .2361 oz. AGW **Obv:** Joan D.M. Bisbe D'Urgell I, left **Rev:** Divided arms, value at top **Note:** Latin legend.

Date	Mintage	F	VF	XF	Unc	BU
1982	1,500	—	—	—	185	210

KM# 31 SOVEREIGN
8.0000 g., 0.9180 Gold .2361 oz. AGW **Obv:** Joan D.M. Bisbe D'Urgell I, left **Rev:** Divided arms, value at top **Note:** Catalan legend.

Date	Mintage	F	VF	XF	Unc	BU
1982	1,500	—	—	—	185	210

KM# 32 SOVEREIGN
8.0000 g., 0.9180 Gold .2361 oz. AGW **Obv:** Joan D.M. Bisbe D'Urgell I, right **Rev:** Crowned arms flanked by cherubs, value below **Note:** Latin legends.

Date	Mintage	F	VF	XF	Unc	BU
1983	1,500	—	—	—	185	210

MEDALLIC COINAGE

Struck by the Bavarian State Mint, then of West Germany. Contracted for and distributed by Hans M.F. Schulman, New York, NY, U.S.A., with the approval of the Andorran Government

X# MA1a 25 DINERS
Gold   **Obv:** National arms **Rev:** Charlemagne

Date	Mintage	F	VF	XF	Unc	BU
1960 Proof	8	Value: 850				

X# MA1b 25 DINERS
Platinum APW **Obv:** National arms **Rev:** Charlemagne

Date	Mintage	F	VF	XF	Unc	BU
1960 Proof	3	Value: 900				

X# M2a 25 DINERS
Gold   **Obv:** National arms **Rev:** Bishop Benlloch of Urgel

Date	Mintage	F	VF	XF	Unc	BU
1963 Proof	8	Value: 600				

X# M2b 25 DINERS
Platinum APW **Obv:** National arms **Rev:** Bishop Benlloch of Urgel

Date	Mintage	F	VF	XF	Unc	BU
1963 Proof	3	Value: 900				

X# M4a 25 DINERS
Gold   **Obv:** Ornate arms **Rev:** Laureate head of Napoleon left **Rev. Legend:** NAPOLEO • I • EMP • D • FRANCA • Co • PR • D • L • V • D'ANDORRA • **Note:** Prev. KM#M5a.

Date	Mintage	F	VF	XF	Unc	BU
1964 Proof	8	Value: 600				

X# M4b 25 DINERS
Platinum APW **Obv:** Ornate arms **Rev:** Laureate head of Napoleon left **Rev. Legend:** NAPOLEO • I • EMP • D • FRANCA • Co • PR • D • L • V • D'ANDORRA • **Note:** Prev. KM#M5b.

Date	Mintage	F	VF	XF	Unc	BU
1964 Proof	3	Value: 850				

X# M6a 25 DINERS
Gold   **Obv:** National arms **Rev:** House of Council of Justice

Date	Mintage	F	VF	XF	Unc	BU
1965 Proof	8	Value: 600				

X# M6b 25 DINERS
Platinum APW **Obv:** National arms **Rev:** House of Council of Justice

Date	Mintage	F	VF	XF	Unc	BU
1965 Proof	3	Value: 900				

X# M1a 50 DINERS
Gold, 38 mm. **Obv:** National arms **Rev:** Charlemagne

Date	Mintage	F	VF	XF	Unc	BU
1960 Proof	8	Value: 1,400				

X# M1b 50 DINERS
Platinum APW, 38 mm. **Obv:** National arms **Rev:** Charlemagne

Date	Mintage	F	VF	XF	Unc	BU
1960 Proof	3	Value: 2,700				

X# M3a 50 DINERS
Gold, 38 mm. **Obv:** National arms **Rev:** Bishop Benlloch of Urgel

Date	Mintage	F	VF	XF	Unc	BU
1963 Proof	8	Value: 1,100				

X# M3b 50 DINERS
Platinum APW, 38 mm. **Obv:** National arms **Rev:** Bishop Benlloch of Urgel

Date	Mintage	F	VF	XF	Unc	BU
1963 Proof	3	Value: 2,600				

ANDORRA

X# M5a 50 DINERS
Gold, 38 mm. **Obv:** Ornate arms **Rev:** Laureate head of Napoleon left **Rev. Legend:** NAPOLEO • I • EMP • D • FRANCA • Co • PR • D • L • V • D'ANDORRA •

Date	Mintage	F	VF	XF	Unc	BU
1964 Proof	8	Value: 1,000				

X# M5b 50 DINERS
Platinum APW, 38 mm. **Obv:** Ornate arms **Rev:** Laureate head of Napoleon left **Rev. Legend:** NAPOLEO • I • EMP • D • FRANCA • Co • PR • D • L • V • D'ANDORRA •

Date	Mintage	F	VF	XF	Unc	BU
1964 Proof	3	Value: 2,250				

X# M7a 50 DINERS
Gold, 38 mm. **Obv:** National arms **Rev:** House of Council of Justice

Date	Mintage	F	VF	XF	Unc	BU
1965 Proof	8	Value: 950				

X# M7b 50 DINERS
Platinum APW, 38 mm. **Obv:** National arms **Rev:** House of Council of Justice

Date	Mintage	F	VF	XF	Unc	BU
1965 Proof	3	Value: 1,750				

PROOF SETS

KM#	Date	Mintage	Identification	Issue Price	Mkt Val
PS3	1964 (2)	4	X#M5a, M6a	—	1,700
PS5	1965 (2)	—	X#M7a, M8a	—	1,700

ANGUILLA

The British dependency of Anguilla, a self-governing British territory situated in the east Caribbean Sea about 60 miles (100 km.) northwest of St. Kitts, has an area of 35 sq. mi. (91 sq. km.) and an approximate population of 12,000. Capital: The Valley. In recent years, tourism has replaced the traditional fishing, stock raising and salt production as the main industry.

Anguilla was discovered by Columbus in 1493 and became a British colony in 1650. As the other British areas in the West Indies did, Anguilla officially adapted to sterling beginning in 1825. From 1950 to 1965, Anguilla was a member of the British Caribbean Territories (Eastern Group) Currency Board, whose coinage it used. In March 1967, Anguilla was joined politically with St. Christopher (St. Kitts), as it had been for much of its colonial history, and Nevis to form a British associated state.

On June 16, 1967, the Provisional Government of Anguilla unilaterally declared its independence and seceded from the Federation. Later, on July 11, 1967, a vote of confidence was taken and the results favored independence. Britain refused to accept the declaration (nor did any other country recognize it) and appointed a British administrator whom Anguilla accepted. However, in Feb. 1969 Anguilla ousted the British emissary, voted to sever all ties with Britain, and established the Republic of Anguilla. The following month Britain landed a force of paratroopers and policemen. This bloodless counteraction ended the self-proclaimed republic and resulted in the installation of a governing commissioner. The troops were withdrawn in Sept. 1969, and the Anguilla Act of July 1971 placed Anguilla directly under British control. A new constitution in 1976 established Anguilla as a self-governing British dependant territory. Britain retains power over defense, police and civil service, and foreign affairs. Since 1981, Anguilla has employed the coinage of the East Caribbean States.

NOTE: There is no evidence that the issues of the self-proclaimed Provisional Government ever actually circulated. The c/s series most likely served as souvenirs of the "revolution".

RULERS
British

PROVISIONAL GOVERNMENT
1967 and 1969

COUNTERMARKED COINAGE

Authorized by the Anguilla Island Council. Each Liberty Dollar was to have been redeemed for 10 U.S. dollars. The countermarking was privately done in San Francisco, California, U.S.A.

X# 14 100 LIBERTY DOLLARS
Gold **Countermark:** 100 LIBERTY DOLLARS **Note:** Prev. KM#14. Countermark on Mexico 50 Pesos, KM#481.

CM Date	Host Date	Good	VG	F	VF	XF
1967	ND(1921-47)	3,000	—	—	—	—

BRITISH COLONY

DECIMAL COINAGE

KM# 20 5 DOLLARS
2.4600 g., 0.9000 Gold .0711 oz. AGW **Obv:** Methodist Church of West End

Date	Mintage	F	VF	XF	Unc	BU
ND Proof	1,925	Value: 85.00				
1969 Proof	Inc. above	Value: 85.00				
1970 Proof	Inc. above	Value: 85.00				

KM# 21 10 DOLLARS
4.9300 g., 0.9000 Gold .1426 oz. AGW **Obv:** Dolphin, Caribbean Silver Lobster, Starfish

Date	Mintage	F	VF	XF	Unc	BU
ND Proof	1,615	Value: 125				
1969 Proof	Inc. above	Value: 125				
1970 Proof	Inc. above	Value: 125				

KM# 22 20 DOLLARS
9.8700 g., 0.9000 Gold .2856 oz. AGW **Obv:** Mermaids

Date	Mintage	F	VF	XF	Unc	BU
ND Proof	1,395	Value: 285				
1969 Proof	Inc. above	Value: 285				
1970 Proof	Inc. above	Value: 285				

KM# 23 100 DOLLARS
49.3700 g., 0.9000 Gold 1.4287 oz. AGW **Subject:** Demonstrating Population **Obv:** People of Anguilla within beaded circle, grain spray below circle

Date	Mintage	F	VF	XF	Unc	BU
ND Proof	710	Value: 1,000				
1969 Proof	—	Value: 1,000				
1970 Proof	Inc. above	Value: 1,000				

KM# 27 200 DOLLARS
38.0000 g., 0.9170 Gold 1.1203 oz. AGW **Subject:** 1st Year of Independence **Obv:** Three intertwined dolphins form circle **Rev:** President Ronald Webster bust left

Date	Mintage	F	VF	XF	Unc	BU
1968 Proof	—	Value: 800				

TRIAL STRIKES

KM#	Date	Mintage	Identification	Mkt Val
TS1	ND (1969)	—	5 Dollars. Goldine-Brass. 1.5100 g. 50 mm. Design of KM-20. Blank with MET countermark. Reeded edge. Uniface.	75.00

KM#	Date	Mintage	Identification	Mkt Val
TS2	1969	—	100 Dollars. Goldine. 50 mm.	—
TS3	ND (1969)	—	5 Dollars. Goldine-Brass. 29.2100 g. 14 mm. Design of KM-23. Blank with MET countermark. Reeded edge.	200

PROOF SETS

KM#	Date	Mintage	Identification	Issue Price	Mkt Val
PS1	1969 (8)	—	KM#15-18.1, 20-23	226	1,650
PS3	1969 (4)	—	KM#20-23	200	1,500
PS4	1970 (8)	—	KM#15-18.1, 20-23	226	1,650
PS6	1970 (4)	—	KM#20-23	200	1,500

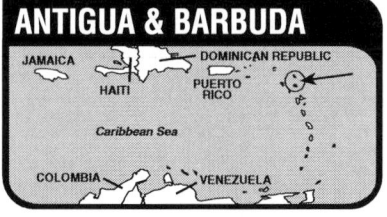

ANTIGUA & BARBUDA

Antigua and Barbuda are located on the eastern edge of the Leeward Islands in the Caribbean Sea, have an area of 170 sq. mi. (440 sq. km.) and an estimated population of 68,000. Capital: St. John's. Prior to 1967, Antigua and its dependencies Barbuda and Redonda, comprised a presidency of the Leeward Islands. The mountainous island produces sugar, molasses, rum, cotton and fruit. Tourism is making an increasingly valuable contribution to the economy.

Antigua was discovered by Columbus in 1493, settled by British colonists from St. Kitts in 1632, occupied by the French in 1666, and ceded to Britain in 1667. It became an associated state with internal self-government on February 27, 1967. On November 1, 1981 it became independent as Antigua and Barbuda. As a constitutional monarchy, Elizabeth II is Queen of Antigua and Barbuda and Head of State.

Spanish silver coinage and French colonial "Black Dogs" were used throughout the islands' early history; however, late in the seventeenth century the introduction of British tin farthings was attempted with complete lack of success. In 1822, British colonial Anchor Money was introduced.

From 1825 to 1955, Antigua was on the sterling standard and used British coins. Coins of the British Caribbean Territories (Eastern Group) and East Caribbean States circulated from 1955, and banknotes of East Caribbean Currency Authority are now used on the island. The early coinage was augmented by that of the East Caribbean States in 1981.

RULERS
British

BRITISH ADMINISTRATION
DECIMAL COINAGE

KM# 5 10 DOLLARS
Copper-Nickel, 38.8 mm. **Ruler:** Elizabeth II **Subject:** Royal Visit **Obv:** Crowned bust of Queen Elizabeth II right **Obv. Designer:** Raphael Maklouf **Rev:** Arms in circle with country name above, date in legend, value below

Date	Mintage	F	VF	XF	Unc	BU
1985	100,000	—	—	—	25.00	35.00

KM# 7 500 DOLLARS
47.5400 g., 0.9170 Gold 1.4013 oz. AGW **Ruler:** Elizabeth II

Date	Mintage	F	VF	XF	Unc	BU
1985 Proof	250	Value: 1,250				

ARGENTINA

The Argentine Republic, located in southern South America, has an area of 1,073,518 sq. mi. (3,761,274 sq. km.) and an estimated population of 37.03 million. Capital: Buenos Aires. Its varied topography ranges from the subtropical lowlands of the north to the towering Andean Mountains in the west and the wind-swept Patagonian steppe in the south. The rolling, fertile pampas of central Argentina are ideal for agriculture and grazing, and support most of the republic's population. Meat packing, flour milling, textiles, sugar refining and dairy products are the principal industries. Oil is found in Patagonia, but most mineral requirements must be imported.

Argentina was discovered in 1516 by the Spanish navigator Juan de Solis. A permanent Spanish colony was established at Buenos Aires in 1580, but the colony developed slowly. When Napoleon conquered Spain, the Argentines set up their own government on May 25, 1810. Independence was formally declared on July 9, 1816. A strong tendency toward local autonomy, fostered by difficult transportation, resulted in a federalized union with much authority left to the states or provinces, which resulted in the coinage of 1817-1867.

Internal conflict through the first half century of Argentine independence resulted in a provisional national coinage, chiefly of crown-sized silver. This was supplemented by provincial issues, mainly of minor denominations.

RULERS
Spanish until 1810

MINT MARKS
A = Korea
B = Great Britain
BA = Buenos Aires
CORDOBA, CORDOVA
C = France
PTS = Potosi monogram (Bolivia)
R, RA, RIOJA, RIOXA
SE = Santiago del Estero
T, TM = Tucuman
TIERRA DEL FUEGO

In the Colonial era, Potosi-struck coinage was used in Argentina (see Bolivia for these issues). During the War for Independence Potosi was held and used to strike coinage by both the Royalist and Independence forces. The mint was captured in 1813 by Independence forces who held it for eight months, using the facilities and some remaining workers to strike their new coinage until it was retaken in 1814 by Royalist forces. The Royalists set about recalling the Independence coinage and using the mint to strike coins of the old type with the King's portrait. Royalists abandoned the mint in April 1815 with the reappearance of Independence forces who again occupied and made use of the mint until it was retaken by the Spanish army in November 1815. The Royalists held the mint and used it to strike the King's coinage until 1824 when Independence was finally secured.

MONETARY SYSTEM
8 Reales = 8 Soles = 1/2 Escudo
16 Reales or Soles = 1 Escudo
10 Decimos = 1 Real
100 Centavos = 1 Peso
10 Pesos = 1 Argentino
    (Commencing 1970)
100 Old Pesos = 1 New Peso
    (Commencing June 1983)
10,000 New Pesos = 1 Peso Argentino
1,000 Pesos Argentino = 1 Austral
    (Commencing 1985)
1,000 Pesos Argentinos = 1 Austral
100 Centavos = 1 Austral
    (Commencing 1992)
10,000 Australs = 1 Peso

18 ARGENTINA

PROVINCIAS DEL RIO DE LA PLATA
REAL COINAGE

KM# 6 ESCUDO
3.3750 g., 0.8750 Gold .0949 oz. AGW **Obv:** Radiant sun with face **Rev:** Arms within wreath **Note:** Mint mark in monogram.

Date	Mintage	VG	F	VF	XF	Unc
1813PTS Rare	—	—	—	—	—	—

KM# 7 2 ESCUDOS
6.7500 g., 0.8750 Gold .1899 oz. AGW **Note:** Mint mark in monogram.

Date	Mintage	VG	F	VF	XF	Unc
1813PTS J Rare	—	—	—	—	—	—

KM# 19.1 2 ESCUDOS
6.7500 g., 0.8750 Gold .1899 oz. AGW **Obv:** Radiant sun with face **Rev:** Flagged arms within wreath crossed at top, cannons and drum below

Date	Mintage	VG	F	VF	XF	Unc
1824RA DS	—	200	350	600	1,100	—
1825RA CA DE B AS	—	200	350	600	1,100	—
1826RA P	—	200	300	500	1,000	—

KM# 19.2 2 ESCUDOS
6.7500 g., 0.8750 Gold .1899 oz. AGW **Obv:** Radiant sun with face **Rev:** Flagged arms within wreath, cannons and drum below **Rev. Legend:** P omitted from legend **Note:** Struck in medal and coin alignment.

Date	Mintage	VG	F	VF	XF	Unc
1826RA	—	200	300	500	1,000	2,250

KM# 8 4 ESCUDOS
13.5000 g., 0.8750 Gold .3798 oz. AGW **Note:** Mint mark in monogram.

Date	Mintage	VG	F	VF	XF	Unc
1813PTS J	—	—	—	—	—	—

Note: Reported, not confirmed

KM# 9 8 ESCUDOS
27.0000 g., 0.8750 Gold .7596 oz. AGW **Obv:** Radiant sun with face **Rev:** Flagged arms within wreath crossed at top, cannons and drum below **Note:** Mint mark in monogram.

Date	Mintage	VG	F	VF	XF	Unc
1813PTS J Rare	—	—	—	—	—	—

Note: American Numismatic Rarities Eilasberg sale 4-05, EF realized $55,200. Superior Casterline sale 5-89 choice VF realized $11,000

KM# 21 8 ESCUDOS
27.0000 g., 0.8750 Gold .7596 oz. AGW **Obv:** Radiant sun with face **Rev:** Flagged arms within wreath, cannons and drum below

Date	Mintage	VG	F	VF	XF	Unc
1826RA P	—	650	1,350	2,000	3,000	—
1826/6RA P	—	800	1,500	2,500	4,000	—
1828RA P	—	650	1,350	2,000	3,000	—
1829RA P Rare	—	—	—	—	—	—
1830RA P	—	1,650	3,500	5,500	8,000	—
1831/0RA	—	1,200	2,000	3,500	7,000	—
1831RA P	—	650	1,350	2,000	3,000	—
1832RA P	—	600	1,250	1,900	2,850	—
1833RA P	—	700	1,350	2,150	3,200	—
1834RA P	—	700	1,350	2,150	3,200	—
1835RA P	—	700	1,350	2,150	3,200	—

REPUBLIC
DECIMAL COINAGE

KM# 30 1/2 ARGENTINO
4.0322 g., 0.9000 Gold .1167 oz. AGW **Obv:** Flagged arms within wreath, 1/2 radiant sun above **Rev:** Capped liberty head right **Note:** Prev. KM#5.

Date	Mintage	F	VF	XF	Unc	BU
1881 Rare	9	—	—	—	—	—
1884	421	550	900	1,250	1,850	—

KM# 31 ARGENTINO
8.0645 g., 0.9000 Gold .2334 oz. AGW **Obv:** Flagged arms within wreath, 1/2 radiant sun above **Rev:** Capped liberty head right **Note:** Prev. KM#6.

Date	Mintage	F	VF	XF	Unc	BU
1881	37,000	125	145	185	285	—
1882	252,000	100	120	145	220	—
1883	906,000	100	120	145	220	—
1884	448,000	100	120	145	220	—
1885	204,000	100	120	145	220	—
1886	398,000	100	120	145	220	—
1887	1,835,000	100	115	135	200	285
1888	1,663,000	100	115	135	200	285
1889	404,000	175	275	375	550	—
1896	197,000	100	120	145	220	—

KM# 136 5 PESOS
8.0640 g., 0.9000 Gold 0.2333 oz. AGW **Subject:** 50th Anniversary O.N.U.

Date	Mintage	F	VF	XF	Unc	BU
1995 Proof	—	Value: 250				

REFORM COINAGE
1992; 10,000 Australes = 1 Peso

KM# 134 5 PESOS
8.0640 g., 0.9000 Gold 0.2333 oz. AGW, 22 mm. **Obv:** Writer Jorge Luis Borges, left, (1899-1986) **Rev:** Sundial within labyrinth **Edge:** Reeded

Date	Mintage	F	VF	XF	Unc	BU
1999 Proof	2,000	Value: 185				

KM# 137 5 PESOS
8.0640 g., 0.9000 Gold 0.2333 oz. AGW, 22 mm. **Obv:** San Martin **Rev:** Building and value **Edge:** Reeded

Date	Mintage	F	VF	XF	Unc	BU
2000 Proof	1,000	Value: 250				

KM# 133 5 PESOS
8.0640 g., 0.9000 Gold 0.2333 oz. AGW, 22 mm. **Subject:** Gral. Justo Jose de Urquiza **Obv:** Stylized portrait facing **Rev:** Church tower and denomination **Edge:** Reeded

Date	Mintage	F	VF	XF	Unc	BU
2001	1,000	—	—	—	190	210

KM# 116 25 PESOS
4.0320 g., 0.9000 Gold .1167 oz. AGW **Subject:** National Constitution Convention **Obv:** Argentine arms above two small arms **Rev:** Open book, ribbon across left page, five line inscription on right page **Note:** Prev. KM#91.

Date	Mintage	F	VF	XF	Unc	BU
ND(1994)	5,000	—	—	—	90.00	100
ND(1994) Proof	1,000	Value: 135				

KM# 117 50 PESOS
8.0640 g., 0.9000 Gold .2334 oz. AGW **Subject:** National Constitution Convention **Obv:** Argentine arms above two small arms **Rev:** Open book, ribbon across left page, five line inscription on right page **Note:** Prev. KM#92.

Date	Mintage	F	VF	XF	Unc	BU
ND (1994)	5,000	—	—	—	165	180
ND (1994) Proof	1,000	Value: 225				

BULLION COINAGE
Morro Velho Mines Issues

X# B1.1 3-1/4 OUNCE
101.1300 g., 0.9955 Gold 3.2368 oz. AGW **Obv. Inscription:** MMV / AZ **Shape:** 40mm x 23mm rectangular **Note:** Uniface. Prev. X#B1.

Date	Mintage	F	VF	XF	Unc	BU
ND(c.1880)	—	—	—	2,450	—	—

X# B1.2 3-1/4 OUNCE
102.0000 g., 0.9954 Gold 3.2643 oz. AGW **Obv. Inscription:** MMV / BC **Shape:** 42mm x 22mm rectangular **Note:** Uniface.

Date	Mintage	F	VF	XF	Unc	BU
ND(c.1880)	—	—	—	2,450	—	—

X# B2 7 OUNCES
218.0000 g., 0.9999 Gold 7.0083 oz. AGW **Obv. Inscription:** MMV - FF **Shape:** 63mm x 24mm rectangular **Note:** Uniface.

Date	Mintage	F	VF	XF	Unc	BU
ND(c.1880)	—	—	—	5,250	—	—

PATTERNS
Including off metal strikes

KM#	Date	Mintage	Identification	Mkt Val
Pn27	1881	9	1/2 Argentino. Gold.	—

PROOF SETS

KM#	Date	Mintage	Identification	Issue Price	Mkt Val
PS5	ND(1994) (2)	1,000	KM#116, 117	375	360

TIERRA DEL FUEGO ARGENTINA 19

CATAMARCA

A province located in northwest Argentina having an area of 38,540 sq. mi. and a population of 309,130. Capital: Catamarca. Agriculture and mining are the main industries.

PROVINCE

TOKEN COINAGE
Stabilization Currency Unit
KM# Tn2 4000000 AUSTRALES
20.0000 g., 0.7500 Gold .4823 oz. AGW **Subject:** Fray Mamerto Esquiu **Note:** Denomination determined upon release.

Date	Mintage	F	VF	XF	Unc	BU
1990	200	—	—	—	920	940

LA RIOJA

La Rioja (Rioxa), a city and province in northwest Argentina, directly to the south of Catamarca. More than one third of its population of 270,702 resides in the capital city of La Rioja. Total area of the province is 35,649 sq. mi. and the main industries are centered around agriculture and include olive trees, grapes and wine production.

PROVINCE

REAL COINAGE
KM# 7 ESCUDO
3.3750 g., 0.8750 Gold .0949 oz. AGW **Obv:** Sun above arms in branches **Rev:** Legend in wreath **Rev. Legend:** SUD AMERICA 1823 RIOXA

Date	Mintage	VG	F	VF	XF	Unc
1823 Rare	—	—	—	—	—	—

KM# 13 2 ESCUDOS
6.7500 g., 0.8750 Gold .1899 oz. AGW **Subject:** General Rosas **Obv:** Uniformed bust left **Rev:** Flagged arms within wreath, radiant sun with face above

Date	Mintage	VG	F	VF	XF	Unc
1842 R	—	250	450	800	1,500	—

KM# 17 2 ESCUDOS
6.7500 g., 0.8750 Gold .1899 oz. AGW **Obv:** Radiant sun with face above mountain, flags below **Rev:** Arms within wreath, flags and cannons surround

Date	Mintage	VG	F	VF	XF	Unc
1843 RB	—	200	325	550	950	—

KM# A9 8 ESCUDOS
27.0000 g., 0.8750 Gold .7596 oz. AGW **Subject:** General Rosas **Obv:** Uniformed bust left **Rev:** Flags and cannons below mountains

Date	Mintage	VG	F	VF	XF	Unc
1836 R Rare	—	—	—	—	—	—

Note: American Numismatic Rarities Eliasberg sale 4-05, EF-45 realized $149,500.

KM# 9 8 ESCUDOS
27.0000 g., 0.8750 Gold .7596 oz. AGW **Obv:** Flags and cannons below mountains **Rev:** Arms within wreath and flags, radiant sun with face above **Note:** General Rosas.

Date	Mintage	VG	F	VF	XF	Unc
1838 R	—	650	1,150	2,000	3,750	—
1840 R	—	750	1,250	2,250	4,500	—

KM# 11 8 ESCUDOS
27.0000 g., 0.8750 Gold .7596 oz. AGW **Obv. Legend:** REPUBLICA ARGENTINA

Date	Mintage	VG	F	VF	XF	Unc
1840 R	—	850	1,350	2,250	4,000	—

KM# 14 8 ESCUDOS
27.0000 g., 0.8750 Gold .7596 oz. AGW **Subject:** General Rosas **Obv:** Uniformed bust left **Rev:** Arms within wreath and flags, radiant sun with face above

Date	Mintage	VG	F	VF	XF	Unc
1842 R Rare	—	—	—	—	—	—

Note: American Numismatic Rarities Eliasberg sale, 4-05, EF realized $39,100. Superior Heifetz sale 12-89 VF realized $18,700.

KM# 19 8 ESCUDOS
27.0000 g., 0.8750 Gold .7596 oz. AGW **Obv:** Mountain with flag and sword below on pointed shield within wreath **Rev:** Arms within wreath and flags, radiant sun with face above

Date	Mintage	VG	F	VF	XF	Unc
1845 B	—	1,200	1,800	2,700	5,000	—

TOKEN COINAGE
Stabilization Currency Unit
KM# Tn2 4000000 AUSTRALES
20.0000 g., 0.7500 Gold .4823 oz. AGW **Subject:** 400th Anniversary - Foundation of La Rioja

Date	Mintage	F	VF	XF	Unc	BU
1991	1,000	—	—	—	900	920

TIERRA DEL FUEGO

The largest island in the archipelago south of the tip of South America. The western part is under Chilean rule, the eastern part is under Argentine rule. Julius Popper was a Romanian born Jewish engineer/adventurer who was given permission to mine gold and strike coins on the Argentine side of the island. Popper's company was named Lavaderos de Oro del Sud (Gold Washers of the South) and his first mine was named El Paramo. In 1889 Popper hand-engraved dies and struck 2 varieties each of 1 Gramo and 5 Gramo tokens. The results of this effort were unsatisfactory, so Popper later used a government connection to have at least 10kg of gold tokens struck at Casa de Moneda (the Buenos Aires mint). The first 1 Gramo dies from this effort broke after only 6 tokens were struck. Another variety of 1 Gramo token of unknown origin is known in both bronze and gold and may be a pattern or contemporary counterfeit. Popper died in Buenos Aires in 1893 under mysterious circumstances while under house arrest for suspicion of murdering island natives.

NOTE: In 1995 Museo del Fin del Mundo in USHUAIA borrowed the surviving pair of Casa de Moneda 1 Gramo dies and struck 100 tokens with an outer ring marked USHUAIA. Additional tokens have been struck by oversize copy dies, also with an outer ring marked USHUAIA. Caution is advised, as these could be cut down and passed as genuine. Although rare and collectible, these restrike tokens are not priced in this catalog. Please refer to the fourth edition of *Unusual World Coins* by Colin R. Bruce II for detailed listings of these types.

TERRITORY

TOKEN COINAGE
X# 9 GRAMO
Gold **Issuer:** Museo del Fin del Mundo **Obv:** Legend and date **Rev:** Legend, crossed mining tools and denomination **Note:** Series 1 with USHUAIA on outer ring, struck from surviving original Buenos Aires dies in 1995.

Date	Mintage	F	VF	XF	Unc	BU
1889	100	—	—	—	—	—

KM# Tn1 GRAMO
Gold **Issuer:** Julius Popper **Obv:** POPPER 1 divides shaded circle **Rev:** Pick axe and sledge hammer within shaded circle **Note:** Struck from hand engraved dies.

Date	Mintage	F	VF	XF	Unc	BU
ND(1889) Rare	—	—	—	—	—	—

KM# Tn2 GRAMO
Gold **Issuer:** Julius Popper **Obv:** Legend and date flanked by stars **Rev:** Legend and mining tools **Note:** Struck from hand engraved dies.

Date	Mintage	F	VF	XF	Unc	BU
1889 Rare	—	—	—	—	—	—

KM# Tn3 GRAMO
Gold **Issuer:** Julius Popper **Obv:** Legend and date flanked by dots **Rev. Designer:** Legend and mining tools **Note:** Struck from hand engraved dies.

Date	Mintage	F	VF	XF	Unc	BU
.1889. Rare	—	—	—	—	—	—

KM# Tn4 GRAMO
Gold **Issuer:** Julius Popper, Buenos Aires issue **Obv:** Date and legend, similar to Tn5 **Rev:** Mining tools and legend, similar to Tn5 **Note:** First Buenos Aires die with small letters on obverse and reverse.

Date	Mintage	F	VF	XF	Unc	BU
1889 Unique	—	—	—	—	—	—

KM# Tn5 GRAMO
Gold **Issuer:** Julius Popper, Buenos Aires issue **Obv:** POPPER divides shaded circle **Rev:** Pick axe and sledge hammer within shaded circle **Note:** Second Buenos Aires die with large letters on obverse and reverse.

Date	Mintage	F	VF	XF	Unc	BU
1889	—	—	—	650	1,000	—

X# 10 GRAMO
Gold **Issuer:** Museo del Fin del Mundo **Obv:** Legend and date

20 ARGENTINA — TIERRA DEL FUEGO

Rev: Legend and crossed mining tools **Note:** Series 2 with USHUAIA on outer ring, struck from copy dies on larger flan after 1995.

Date	Mintage	F	VF	XF	Unc	BU
1889	100	—	—	—	125	—

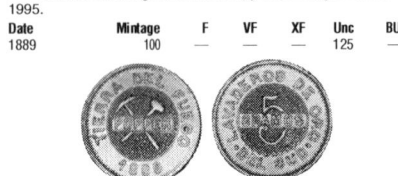

KM# Tn6 5 GRAMOS
Gold **Issuer:** Julius Popper **Obv:** POPPER above date flanked by stars **Rev:** Denomination and legend **Note:** Struck from hand engraved dies with large letters on obverse and reverse.

Date	Mintage	F	VF	XF	Unc	BU
1889 Rare	—	—	—	—	—	—

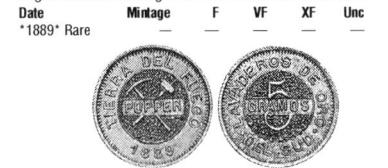

KM# Tn7 5 GRAMOS
Gold **Issuer:** Julius Popper **Obv:** POPPER over crossed mining tools above date flanked by stars **Rev:** Denomination and legend **Note:** Struck from hand engraved dies with small letters on obverse and reverse.

Date	Mintage	F	VF	XF	Unc	BU
1889 Rare	—	—	—	—	—	—

KM# Tn8 5 GRAMOS
Gold **Issuer:** Julius Popper, Buenos Aires issue **Obv:** POPPER atop mining tools within shaded circle **Rev:** Denomination within shaded circle

Date	Mintage	F	VF	XF	Unc	BU
1889	—	—	—	3,000	4,750	—

ARMENIA

The Republic of Armenia (formerly Armenian S.S.R.) is bounded in the north by Georgia, to the east by Azerbaijan and to the south and west by Turkey and Iran. It has an area of 11,506 sq. mi. (29,800 sq. km) and an estimated population of 3.66 million. Capital: Yerevan. Agriculture including cotton, vineyards and orchards, hydroelectricity, chemicals - primarily synthetic rubber and fertilizers, vast mineral deposits of copper, zinc and aluminum, and production of steel and paper are major industries.

Russia occupied Armenia in 1801 until the Russo-Turkish war of 1878. British intervention excluded either side from remaining although the Armenians remained more loyal to the Ottoman Turks, but in 1894 the Ottoman Turks sent in an expeditionary force of Kurds fearing a revolutionary movement. Large massacres were followed by retaliations, then amnesty was proclaimed which led right into WW I and once again occupation by Russian forces in 1916. After the Russian revolution the Georgians, Armenians and Azerbaijanis formed the short lived Transcaucasian Federal Republic on Sept. 20, 1917 which broke up into three independent republics on May 26, 1918. Communism developed and in Sept. 1920 the Turks attacked the Armenian Republic; the Russians soon followed suit from Azerbaijan routing the Turks. On Nov. 29, 1920 Armenia was proclaimed a Soviet Socialist Republic. On March 12, 1922, Armenia, Georgia and Azerbaijan were combined to form the Transcaucasian Soviet Federated Socialist Republic, which on Dec. 30, 1922, became a part of U.S.S.R. On Dec. 5, 1936, the Transcaucasian federation was dissolved and Armenia became a constituent Republic of the U.S.S.R. A new constitution was adopted in April 1978. Elections took place on May 20, 1990. The Supreme Soviet adopted a declaration of sovereignty in Aug. 1991, voting to unite Armenia with Nagorno - Karabakh. This newly constituted "Republic of Armenia" became fully independent by popular vote in Sept. 1991. It became a member of the CIS in Dec. 1991.

Fighting between Christians in Armenia and Muslim forces of Azerbaijan escalated in 1992 and continued through early 1994. Each country claimed the Nagorno-Karabakh, an Armenian ethnic enclave, in Azerbaijan. A temporary cease-fire was announced in May, 1994.

RULERS
Russian, 1801-1878

MINT NAMES
Revan, (Erevan, now Yerevan)

MONETARY SYSTEM
50 Luma = 1 Dram

REPUBLIC

STANDARD COINAGE

KM# 86a 100 DRAM
31.1000 g., 0.9990 Gold Plated Silver 0.997 oz. ASW AGW, 38 mm. **Obv:** National arms **Obv. Inscription:** Bust of General Garegin Nzhdeh facing at right **Edge:** Plain **Edge Lettering:** Serial number

Date	Mintage	F	VF	XF	Unc	BU
2001 Proof	30	Value: 500				

KM# 109 1000 DRAM
15.5500 g., 0.5850 Gold 0.2925 oz. AGW, 26 mm. **Obv:** National arms on ancient coin design **Rev:** Tigran the Great ancient coin portrait

Date	Mintage	F	VF	XF	Unc	BU
2003	500	—	—	—	785	800

KM# 90 10000 DRAMS
8.6400 g., 0.9000 Gold 0.25 oz. AGW, 22 mm. **Subject:** Christian Armenia - Ani **Obv:** National arms **Rev:** Church tower **Edge:** Plain with serial number

Date	Mintage	F	VF	XF	Unc	BU
1998 Proof	1,700	Value: 250				

KM# 91 10000 DRAMS
8.6400 g., 0.9000 Gold 0.25 oz. AGW, 22 mm. **Subject:** 1700th Anniversary of the adoption of Christianity in Armenia **Obv:** National arms **Rev:** Multi-towered church **Edge:** Plain with serial number

Date	Mintage	F	VF	XF	Unc	BU
1998 Proof	1,700	Value: 250				

KM# 107 10000 DRAMS
8.6000 g., 0.9990 Gold 0.2762 oz. AGW, 22 mm. **Obv:** Mesrop Mashtots, creater of the Armenian Alphabet **Rev:** Armenian Alphabet

Date	Mintage	F	VF	XF	Unc	BU
2002 Proof	1,000	Value: 300				

KM# 108 10000 DRAMS
8.6000 g., 0.9990 Gold 0.2762 oz. AGW, 22 mm. **Obv:** Building above value **Rev:** Aram Khachatryan left birth centennial

Date	Mintage	F	VF	XF	Unc	BU
2002 Proof	500	Value: 300				

KM# 114 10000 DRAMS
8.6000 g., 0.9990 Gold 0.2762 oz. AGW, 22 mm. **Subject:** Arshile Gorky birth April 15, 1904 **Obv:** Bust of Gorky **Rev:** Denomination

Date	Mintage	F	VF	XF	Unc	BU
2004 Proof	1,000	Value: 300				

KM# 116 10000 DRAMS
8.6000 g., 0.9990 Gold 0.2762 oz. AGW, 22 mm. **Subject:** Martiros Sarian 125th Anniversary of Birth **Obv:** Bust of Sarian **Rev:** Landscape, denomination

Date	Mintage	F	VF	XF	Unc	BU
2005 Proof	1,000	Value: 300				

KM# 75.1 25000 DRAM
4.3000 g., 0.9000 Gold .1244 oz. AGW, 18 mm. **Obv:** National arms **Rev:** Portrait of goddess Anahit **Edge:** Reeded

Date	Mintage	F	VF	XF	Unc	BU
1997 Proof	—	Value: 160				

KM# 75.2 25000 DRAM
4.3000 g., 0.9000 Gold .1244 oz. AGW, 18 mm. **Obv:** National arms **Rev:** Portrait of goddess Anahit left **Edge:** Plain

Date	Mintage	F	VF	XF	Unc	BU
1997 Proof	—	Value: 160				

KM# 92 50000 DRAMS
8.6400 g., 0.9000 Gold 0.25 oz. AGW, 22 mm. **Subject:** 1700th Anniversary of the Adoption of Christianity in Armenia **Obv:** National arms **Rev:** Holy Cross Church (915) Aghtamer Island in Lake Van **Edge:** Plain with serial number

Date	Mintage	F	VF	XF	Unc	BU
1999 Proof	1,700	Value: 250				

ARUBA

KM# 105 50000 DRAMS
8.6000 g., 0.9000 Gold 0.2488 oz. AGW, 22 mm. **Obv:** National arms on an ancient coin design **Rev:** Ancient Armenian King Tigran the Great 95-55 BC

Date	Mintage	F	VF	XF	Unc	BU
1999 Proof	500	Value: 265				

KM# 118 50000 DRAMS
8.6000 g., 0.9990 Gold 0.2762 oz. AGW, 22 mm. **Subject:** Armenian Armed Forces **Obv:** Order of the Combat Cross of the Second Degree and the Emblem of the Ministry of Defense of the Republic of Armenia **Obv. Designer:** H. Samuelian **Rev:** Arms, date and denomination

Date	Mintage	F	VF	XF	Unc	BU
2005 Proof	1,000	Value: 300				

KM# 102 100000 DRAMS
17.2000 g., 0.9000 Gold 0.4977 oz. AGW, 30 mm. **Obv:** National arms **Rev:** Noah's descent from Mt. Ararat

Date	Mintage	F	VF	XF	Unc	BU
1999 Proof	1,000	Value: 425				

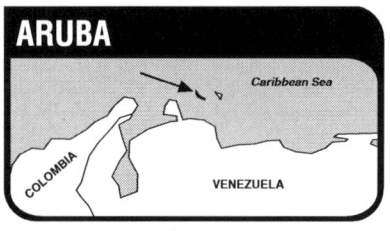

Aruba, formerly a part of the Netherlands Antilles, achieved on Jan. 1, 1986 a special status, "status aparte" as the third state under the Dutch crown, together with the Netherlands and the remaining five islands of the Netherlands Antilles. On Dec. 15, 1954 the Netherlands Antilles were given complete domestic autonomy and granted equality within the Kingdom of the Netherlands. The separate constitution put in place for Aruba in 1986 established it as an autonomous government within the Kingdom of the Netherlands. In 1990 Aruba opted to remain a part of the Kingdom without the promise of future independence.

The second largest island of the Netherlands Antilles, Aruba is situated near the Venezuelan coast. The island has an area of 74-1/2 sq. mi. (193 sq. km.) and a population of 65,974. Capital: Oranjestad, named after the Dutch royal family. Aruba was important in the processing and transportation of petroleum products in the first part of the twentieth century, but today the chief industry is tourism.

For earlier issues see Curacao and the Netherlands Antilles.

RULERS
Dutch

MINT MARKS
(u) Utrecht - Privy marks only
   Anvil, 1986-1988
   Bow and Arrow, 1989-1999
   Bow and Arrow w/star, 2000-

MONETARY SYSTEM
100 Cents = 1 Florin

DUTCH STATE
"Status Aparte"

REGULAR COINAGE

KM# 26 10 FLORIN
6.7200 g., 0.9000 Gold 0.1944 oz. AGW, 22.5 mm. **Subject:** 50th Anniversary of Autonomy **Obv:** Head left **Rev:** Royal seal **Edge:** Reeded **Designer:** E. Fingal

Date	Mintage	F	VF	XF	Unc	BU
2004 Proof	1,000	Value: 185				

KM# 33 10 FLORIN
1.2442 g., 0.9990 Gold 0.04 oz. AGW, 13.9 mm. **Subject:** Death of Juliana **Obv:** Head left **Obv. Designer:** E. Fingal **Rev:** Juliana in center **Edge:** Reeded

Date	Mintage	F	VF	XF	Unc	BU
ND (2004)(u) Proof	10,000	Value: 60.00				

KM# 35 10 FLORIN
6.7200 g., 0.9000 Gold 0.1944 oz. AGW, 22.5 mm. **Subject:** Queen's Silver Jubilee **Obv:** Head left **Rev:** Flag **Edge:** Reeded **Designer:** F.L. Croes

Date	Mintage	F	VF	XF	Unc	BU
2005(u) Proof	1,500	Value: 180				

KM# 9 50 FLORIN
6.7200 g., 0.9000 Gold .1945 oz. AGW, 22.5 mm. **Subject:** Independence **Obv:** Head of Queen Beatrix left **Rev:** Triangular portion of flag, treaty name and date **Edge:** Grained **Designer:** E. Fingal

Date	Mintage	F	VF	XF	Unc	BU
ND(1991)(u) Proof	2,600	Value: 200				

KM# 17 100 FLORIN
6.7200 g., 0.9000 Gold .1945 oz. AGW, 22.5 mm. **Subject:** 10th Anniversary of Autonomy **Obv:** Head of Queen Beatrix left **Rev:** Portions of national flag and anthem score **Edge:** Grained **Designer:** E. Fingal

Date	Mintage	F	VF	XF	Unc	BU
ND(1996)(u) Proof	535	Value: 250				

KM# 19 100 FLORIN
6.7200 g., 0.9000 Gold .1945 oz. AGW, 22.5 mm. **Subject:** Tradition With Vision - Discovery 1499 **Obv:** Portrait of Vespucci, sailing vessel, map **Rev:** Spanish fan and aboriginal design, dates **Rev. Designer:** E. Fingal **Edge:** Grained **Note:** Similar to 25 Florin, KM#18.

Date	Mintage	F	VF	XF	Unc	BU
ND(1999)(u) Proof	1,100	Value: 240				

KM# 23 100 FLORIN
6.7200 g., Gold, 22.5 mm. **Subject:** Independence **Obv:** Arms, treaty name, dates **Rev:** Head left **Edge:** Grained

Date	Mintage	F	VF	XF	Unc	BU
2001 Proof	1,000	Value: 265				

PROOF SETS

KM#	Date	Mintage	Identification	Issue Price	Mkt Val
PS1	1999 (5)	—	KM#18-19, with Netherlands Antilles KM#45-47 Tradition with Vision 1499-1999	580	850

ASCENSION ISLAND

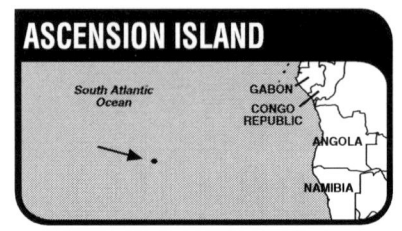

An island of volcanic origin, Ascension Island lies in the South Atlantic, 700 miles (1,100 km.) northwest of St. Helena. It has an area of 34 sq. mi. (88 sq. km.) on an island 9 miles (14 km.) long and 6 miles (10 km.) wide. Approximate population: 1,146. Although having little vegetation and scant rainfall, the island has a very healthy climate. The island is the nesting place for a large number of sea turtles and sooty terns. Phosphates and guano are the chief natural sources of income.

The island was discovered on Ascension Day, 1501, by Joao da Nova, a Portuguese navigator. It lay unoccupied until 1815, when occupied by the British. It was under Admiralty rule until 1922 when it was annexed as a dependency of St. Helena. During World War II an airfield was built that has been used as a fueling stop for Transatlantic flights to Southern Europe, North Africa and the Near-East.

RULERS
British

MINT MARK
PM - Pobjoy Mint

BRITISH ADMINISTRATION
STANDARD COINAGE

KM# 7b 50 PENCE
47.5400 g., 0.9160 Gold 1.4001 oz. AGW **Obv:** Crowned bust of Queen Elizabeth II right **Rev:** Queen Mother fishing with waders and hat

Date	Mintage	F	VF	XF	Unc	BU
1995 Proof	150	Value: 950				

KM# 12b 50 PENCE
47.5400 g., 0.9166 Gold 1.401 oz. AGW, 38.6 mm. **Subject:** Queen Mother's 100th Birthday **Obv:** Crowned bust of Queen Elizabeth II, right **Obv. Designer:** Raphael Maklouf **Rev:** Queen Mother above dates 1900-2000 **Edge:** Reeded

Date	Mintage	F	VF	XF	Unc	BU
ND(2000) Proof	100	Value: 1,150				

KM# 13b 50 PENCE
47.5400 g., 0.9166 Gold 1.401 oz. AGW, 38.6 mm. **Subject:** Queen Elizabeth II's 75th Birthday **Obv:** Crowned bust right, denomination below **Obv. Designer:** Raphael Maklouf **Rev:** Crowned monogram above roses within circle, date below **Edge:** Reeded

Date	Mintage	F	VF	XF	Unc	BU
2001 Proof	75	Value: 1,100				

KM# 14b 50 PENCE
47.5400 g., 0.9166 Gold 1.401 oz. AGW, 38.6 mm. **Subject:** Centennial of Queen Victoria's Death **Obv:** Crowned bust right, denomination below **Obv. Designer:** Raphael Maklouf **Rev:** Crowned bust left, three dates **Edge:** Reeded

Date	Mintage	F	VF	XF	Unc	BU
2001 Proof	100	Value: 1,100				

KM# 16b 50 PENCE
39.9400 g., 0.9166 Gold 1.177 oz. AGW, 38.6 mm. **Subject:** Queen Elizabeth II's - 50th Anniversary of Coronation **Obv:** Crowned bust right, denomination below **Obv. Designer:** Raphael Maklouf **Rev:** Crown, two sceptres and the ampula **Edge:** Reeded

Date	Mintage	F	VF	XF	Unc	BU
ND(2003) Proof	50	Value: 975				

KM# 17b 50 PENCE
39.9400 g., 0.9166 Gold 1.177 oz. AGW, 38.6 mm. **Subject:** Queen Elizabeth II's - 50th Anniversary of Coronation **Obv:** Crowned bust right, denomination below **Obv. Designer:** Raphael Maklouf **Rev:** Crowned monogram **Edge:** Reeded

Date	Mintage	F	VF	XF	Unc	BU
ND(2003) Proof	50	Value: 975				

KM# 5 2 POUNDS
15.9800 g., 0.9170 Gold .4712 oz. AGW **Series:** International Year of the Scout **Rev:** Boy Scout

Date	Mintage	F	VF	XF	Unc	BU
1983	2,000	—	—	—	450	475
1983 Proof	2,000	Value: 500				

AUSTRALIA

The Commonwealth of Australia, the smallest continent and largest island in the world, is located south of Indonesia between the Indian and Pacific oceans. It has an area of 2,967,893 sq. mi. (7,686,850 sq. km.) and an estimated population of 18.84 million. Capital: Canberra. Due to its early and sustained isolation, Australia is the habitat of such curious and unique fauna as the kangaroo, koala, platypus, wombat, echidna and frilled-necked lizard. The continent possesses extensive mineral deposits, the most important of which are iron ore, coal, gold, silver, nickel, uranium, lead and zinc. Livestock raising, mining and manufacturing are the principal industries. Chief exports are wool, meat, wheat, iron ore, coal and nonferrous metals.

The first caucasians to see Australia probably were Portuguese and Spanish navigators of the late 16th century. In 1770, Captain James Cook explored the east coast and annexed it for Great Britain. New South Wales was founded as a penal colony following the loss of British North America by Capt. Arthur Phillip on January 26, 1788, a date now celebrated as Australia Day. Dates of creation of the six colonies that now comprise the states of the Australian Commonwealth are: New South Wales, 1823; Tasmania, 1825; Western Australia, 1838; South Australia, 1842; Victoria, 1851; Queensland, 1859. A constitution providing for federation of the colonies was approved by the British Parliament in 1900; the Commonwealth of Australia came into being in 1901. Australia passed the Statute of Westminster Adoption Act on October 9, 1942, which officially established Australia's complete autonomy in external and internal affairs, thereby formalizing a situation that had existed for years. Australia is a member of the Commonwealth of Nations. Elizabeth II is Head of State as Queen of Australia.

Australia's currency system was changed from Pounds-Shillings-Pence to a decimal system of Dollars and Cents on Feb. 14, 1966.

RULERS
British

MINT MARKS

Abbr.	Mint	Mark
A	Adelaide	-
B	Brisbane	-
C	Canberra	-
M	Melbourne	M above date on the ground on gold coins w/St. George
P	Perth	P above date on the ground on gold coins w/St. George
P	Perth	Nuggets, 1986
S	Sydney	S above date on the ground on gold coins w/St. George
(sy)	Sydney	None, 1919-1926

Mint designations are shown in ( ). Ex. 1978(m).
Mint marks are shown after date. Ex. 1978M.

PRIVY MARKS

(ae) - American Eagle

(aa) - Adelaide Assay

(ba) - Basler Stab

(bg) - Brandenburg Gate

(d) – Ducat

AUSTRALIA

(dp) – Dump
(e) – Emu
(ev) – Edward V
(f) – Fok
(f1) – Rev. 1 Florin, KM#31
(f3) – Rev. 1 Florin, KM#33
(f7) – Rev. 1 Florin, KM#47
(ge) – Golden Eagle
(gv) – George V, small head
(gV) – George V, large head
(h) – Hague
(hd) – Holey Dollar
(j) – Johanna
(jw) – Japanese Royal Wedding
(l) – Luk
(lh) – Liberty Head
(p) – Prospector
(qv) – Queen Victoria
(rv) – Royal Visit Florin, Rev. 1 Florin, KM#55
(s) – Shu
(sg) – Spade Guinea
(sm) – Sydney Mint Sovereign
(so) – Sydney Opera House

(sp) – Star Pagoda
(sr) – Swan River/Rottnest Island Tercentenary
(ta) – Team Australia (Commonwealth Games)
(w) – Whales
(ww) – 50 Years Beyond WWII

MONETARY SYSTEM

(Until 1966)
12 Pence = 1 Shilling
2 Shillings = 1 Florin
5 Shillings = 1 Crown
20 Shillings = 1 Pound

Commencing 1966)
100 Cents = 1 Dollar

BRITISH COLONY

TRADE COINAGE

KM# 1 1/2 SOVEREIGN
3.9940 g., 0.9170 Gold .1177 oz. AGW **Ruler:** Victoria **Obv:** Fillet head left **Rev:** Crowned AUSTRALIA within wreath

Date	Mintage	F	VF	XF	Unc	BU
1855(sy)	21,000	8,500	16,500	45,000	95,000	—
1856(sy)	478,000	500	1,750	4,500	12,500	—

KM# 3 1/2 SOVEREIGN
3.9940 g., 0.9170 Gold .1177 oz. AGW **Ruler:** Victoria **Obv:** Head left, hair tied with banksia wreath **Rev:** AUSTRALIA within wreath

Date	Mintage	F	VF	XF	Unc	BU
1857(sy)	537,000	250	350	4,500	10,000	—
1857(sy) Proof	—	Value: 85,000				
1858(sy)	483,000	250	350	5,000	14,500	—
1858(sy) (Error)	—	—	—	—	—	—
1859(sy)	341,000	250	350	5,500	18,000	—
1860(sy)	156,000	450	1,750	12,000	30,000	—
1861(sy)	186,000	250	375	5,000	12,500	—
1862(sy)	210,000	250	375	5,500	15,000	—
1863(sy)	348,000	250	350	5,500	15,000	—
1864(sy)	141,000	250	650	7,000	20,000	—
1865(sy)	62,000	300	650	6,500	18,500	—
1866(sy)	154,000	275	600	5,500	17,500	—
1866(sy) Proof	—	Value: 60,000				

KM# 5 1/2 SOVEREIGN
3.9940 g., 0.9170 Gold .1177 oz. AGW **Ruler:** Victoria **Obv:** Young head left **Rev:** Crowned shield, mint mark below

Date	Mintage	F	VF	XF	Unc	BU
1871S	180,000	85.00	165	1,650	10,000	—
1871S Proof	—	Value: 50,000				
1872S	356,000	85.00	165	1,650	10,000	—
1873M	165,000	85.00	165	1,850	11,250	—
1875S	252,000	85.00	165	1,650	10,000	—
1877M	140,000	100	200	1,850	11,250	—
1879S	220,000	85.00	165	1,350	8,500	—
1880S	80,000	85.00	185	2,250	12,250	—
1880S Proof	—	Value: 45,000				
1881S	62,000	85.00	185	2,500	13,500	—
1881M	42,000	95.00	225	2,750	15,500	—
1881 Proof	—	Value: 45,000				
1882S	52,000	125	250	3,750	25,000	—
1882M	106,000	85.00	175	1,750	10,000	—
1883S	220,000	80.00	155	1,100	6,750	—
1883S Proof	—	Value: 45,000				
1884M	48,000	95.00	225	3,250	20,000	—
1884M Proof	—	Value: 45,000				
1885M	11,000	250	550	5,500	35,000	—
1886S	82,000	85.00	165	1,750	11,500	—
1886M	38,000	85.00	175	2,250	12,500	—
1886 Proof	—	Value: 45,000				
1887S	134,000	85.00	165	1,550	10,000	—
1887S Proof	—	Value: 45,000				
1887M	64,000	125	250	3,750	27,500	—

KM# 9 1/2 SOVEREIGN
3.9940 g., 0.9170 Gold .1177 oz. AGW **Ruler:** Victoria **Obv:** Jubilee head left **Rev:** Crowned shield, mint mark below

Date	Mintage	F	VF	XF	Unc	BU
1887S	Inc. above	80.00	120	375	3,500	—
1887S Proof	—	Value: 50,000				
1887M	Inc. above	90.00	130	450	4,750	—
1887M Proof	—	Value: 50,000				
1888M Proof	—	Value: 52,500				
1889S	64,000	90.00	130	675	6,750	—
1889M Proof	—	Value: 52,500				
1890M Proof	—	Value: 52,500				
1891S With J.E.B.	154,000	100	160	975	9,500	—
1891S Without J.E.B.	Inc. above	90.00	130	675	6,750	—
1891M Proof	—	Value: 52,500				
1892S Proof	—	Value: 52,500				
1892M Proof	—	Value: 52,500				
1893S Proof	—	Value: 52,500				
1893M	110,000	80.00	120	600	6,250	—
1893M Proof	—	Value: 45,000				

KM# 12 1/2 SOVEREIGN
3.9940 g., 0.9170 Gold .1177 oz. AGW **Ruler:** Victoria **Obv:** Veiled head left **Obv. Designer:** Thomas Brock **Rev:** St. George slaying dragon, mint mark above date

Date	Mintage	F	VF	XF	Unc	BU
1893S	250,000	75.00	100	500	2,750	—
1893S Proof	—	Value: 50,000				
1893M	—	10,000	—	—	—	—
1893M Proof	—	Value: 52,500				
1894M Proof	—	Value: 52,500				
1895M Proof	—	Value: 52,500				
1896M	218,000	80.00	130	600	3,250	—
1896M Proof	—	Value: 45,000				
1897S	230,000	75.00	100	500	3,000	—
1897M Proof	—	Value: 52,500				
1898M Proof	—	Value: 52,500				
1899M	90,000	80.00	130	800	3,250	—
1899M Proof	—	Value: 45,000				
1899P Proof	—	—				
1900S	260,000	75.00	100	500	3,000	—
1900M	113,000	80.00	130	800	3,250	—
1900M Proof	—	Value: 45,000				
1900P	119,000	80.00	130	800	3,250	—
1901M Proof	—	Value: 55,000				
1901P Proof	—	Value: 70,000				

Note: Imperfect proofs worth substantially less.

KM# 2 SOVEREIGN
7.9811 g., 0.9170 Gold 0.2353 oz. AGW **Ruler:** Victoria **Obv:** Fillet head

Date	Mintage	F	VF	XF	Unc	BU
1855(sy)	502,000	1,500	4,000	12,000	65,000	—
1856(sy)	981,000	1,500	4,000	12,000	65,000	—

AUSTRALIA

KM# 4 SOVEREIGN
7.9811 g., 0.9170 Gold 0.2353 oz. AGW **Ruler:** Victoria **Obv:** Hair tied with banksia wreath **Note:** 51,202,600 pieces reported in 1869 are dated 1868.

Date	Mintage	F	VF	XF	Unc	BU
1857(sy)	499,000	225	475	2,500	12,500	—
1857(sy) (Plain or milled edge); Proof	—	Value: 100,000				
1858(sy)	1,101,000	265	650	5,000	25,000	—
1859(sy)	1,050,000	235	550	1,750	11,500	—
1860(sy)	1,573,000	325	850	6,000	22,500	—
1861(sy)	1,626,000	175	350	1,750	7,000	—
1862(sy)	2,477,000	225	475	2,500	13,500	—
1863(sy)	1,255,000	175	400	1,650	7,500	—
1864(sy)	2,698,000	155	250	750	5,000	—
1865(sy)	2,130,000	165	300	1,750	6,500	—
1866(sy)	2,911,000	155	250	550	3,500	—
1866(sy) Proof	—	Value: 95,000				
1867/6(sy)	Inc. above	—	—	—	—	—
1867(sy)	2,370,000	155	250	550	3,500	—
1868(sy)	3,522,000	155	250	550	3,500	—
1870(sy)	1,220,000	155	225	450	2,500	—
1870(sy) Proof	—	Value: 125,000				

KM# 7 SOVEREIGN
7.9881 g., 0.9170 Gold .2354 oz. AGW **Ruler:** Victoria **Obv:** Young head left, mint mark below **Rev:** St. George slaying dragon **Note:** Mintage figures include St. George and shield types. No separate mintage figures are known.

Date	Mintage	F	VF	XF	Unc	BU
1871S	2,814,000	BV	200	1,250	5,000	—
1871S Proof	—	Value: 50,000				
1872S	1,815,000	—	BV	275	2,200	—
1872M	748,000	BV	325	1,750	6,000	—
1873S	1,478,000	—	BV	250	2,500	—
1873M	752,000	—	BV	225	2,000	—
1873M Proof	—	Value: 45,000				
1874S	1,899,000	—	BV	225	2,500	—
1874M	1,373,000	—	BV	200	2,000	—
1874M Proof	—	Value: 45,000				
1875S	2,122,000	—	BV	225	1,850	—
1875M	1,888,000	—	BV	225	1,500	—
1875M Proof	—	Value: 45,000				
1876S	1,613,000	—	BV	160	1,750	—
1876M	2,124,000	—	BV	160	1,250	—
1877S Rare	2	—	—	—	—	—
1877M	1,487,000	—	BV	160	1,150	—
1878M	2,171,000	—	BV	160	1,150	—
1879S	1,366,000	175	300	1,650	5,500	—
1879M	2,740,000	—	BV	160	1,000	—
1880S	1,459,000	—	BV	225	1,850	—
1880S Proof	—	Value: 45,000				
1880M	3,053,000	—	BV	160	1,150	—
1881S	1,360,000	—	BV	225	1,500	—
1881M	2,324,000	—	BV	160	1,150	—
1881M Proof	—	Value: 45,000				
1882S	1,298,000	—	BV	160	1,250	—
1882M	2,466,000	—	BV	160	1,250	—
1883S	1,108,000	BV	175	600	3,000	—
1883M	2,050,000	—	BV	160	1,000	—
1883M Proof	—	Value: 45,000				
1884S	1,595,000	—	BV	160	1,000	—
1884M	2,942,000	—	BV	160	950	—
1884M Proof	—	Value: 45,000				
1885S	1,486,000	—	BV	160	1,150	—
1885M	2,957,000	—	BV	160	1,000	—
1885M Proof	—	Value: 45,000				
1886S	1,677,000	—	BV	160	1,150	—
1886M	2,902,000	—	BV	160	950	—
1886M Proof	—	Value: 45,000				
1887S	1,000,000	—	BV	225	1,350	—
1887M	1,915,000	—	BV	225	1,350	—
1887M Proof	—	Value: 45,000				

KM# 6 SOVEREIGN
7.9881 g., 0.9170 Gold .2354 oz. AGW **Ruler:** Elizabeth II **Obv:** Young head left, date below **Rev:** Mint mark below crowned shield **Note:** Mintage figures include St. George and shield types. No separate mintage figures are known. Mint mark placement varies.

Date	Mintage	F	VF	XF	Unc	BU
1871S Incuse ww	2,814,000	—	BV	200	1,250	—
1871S Raised ww	Inc. above	—	BV	200	1,250	—
1871S Proof	—	Value: 50,000				
1872S	1,815,000	—	BV	200	1,500	—
1872/1M	748,000	225	475	1,250	2,250	—
1872M	Inc. above	—	BV	200	1,250	—
1873S	1,478,000	—	BV	200	1,250	—
1874M	1,373,000	—	BV	225	2,000	—
1875S	2,122,000	—	BV	200	1,000	—
1875S Proof	—	Value: 50,000				
1877S	1,590,000	—	BV	200	1,000	—
1878S	1,259,000	—	BV	200	1,000	—
1879S	1,366,000	—	BV	200	1,000	—
1880S	1,459,000	—	BV	200	1,000	—
1880S Proof	—	Value: 50,000				
1880M	3,053,000	700	1,850	4,250	9,500	—
1880M Proof	—	Value: 50,000				
1881S	1,360,000	—	BV	200	1,450	—
1881M	2,324,000	BV	175	325	1,500	—
1882S	1,298,000	—	BV	200	1,450	—
1882M	2,466,000	—	BV	200	1,450	—
1883S	1,108,000	—	BV	185	950	—
1883S Proof	—	Value: 50,000				
1883M	2,049,999	200	325	1,000	3,750	—
1883M Proof	—	Value: 50,000				
1884S	1,595,000	—	BV	185	1,000	—
1884M	2,942,000	—	BV	185	1,000	—
1884M Proof	—	Value: 50,000				
1885S	1,486,000	—	BV	185	950	—
1885M	2,957,000	—	BV	185	950	—
1885M Proof	—	Value: 50,000				
1886S	1,677,000	—	BV	185	1,000	—
1886S Proof	—	Value: 50,000				
1886M	2,902,000	3,750	7,500	11,500	30,000	—
1886M Proof	—	Value: 75,000				
1887S	1,000,000	—	BV	285	2,000	—
1887S Proof	—	Value: 50,000				
1887M	1,915,000	750	1,650	4,000	10,000	—
1887M Proof	—	Value: 50,000				

KM# 10 SOVEREIGN
7.9881 g., 0.9170 Gold .2354 oz. AGW **Ruler:** Victoria **Obv:** Jubilee head left **Rev:** St. George slaying dragon, mint mark above date **Note:** Designers initials on reverse omitted on some pieces 1880S-1882S and 1881M-1882M. Mint mark placement varies.

Date	Mintage	F	VF	XF	Unc	BU
1887S	1,002,000	BV	185	450	1,150	—
1887S Proof	—	Value: 40,000				
1887M	940,000	—	BV	165	275	—
1887M Proof	—	Value: 40,000				
1888S	2,187,000	—	BV	160	245	—
1888M	2,830,000	—	BV	160	245	—
1888M Proof	—	Value: 40,000				
1889S	3,262,000	—	BV	160	245	—
1889M	2,732,000	—	BV	160	245	—
1889M Proof	—	Value: 40,000				
1890S	2,808,000	—	BV	160	245	—
1890M	2,473,000	—	BV	160	245	—
1890M Proof	—	Value: 40,000				
1891S	2,596,000	—	BV	160	245	—
1891M	2,749,000	—	BV	160	245	—
1892S	2,837,000	—	BV	160	245	—
1892M	3,488,000	—	BV	160	245	—
1893S	1,498,000	—	BV	160	245	—
1893S Proof	—	Value: 40,000				
1893M	1,649,000	—	BV	160	245	—
1893M Proof	—	Value: 40,000				

KM# 13 SOVEREIGN
7.9881 g., 0.9170 Gold .2354 oz. AGW **Ruler:** Victoria **Obv:** Older veiled head left **Rev:** St. George slaying the dragon

Date	Mintage	F	VF	XF	Unc	BU
1893S	1,346,000	—	BV	155	225	—
1893S Proof	—	Value: 40,000				
1893M	1,914,000	—	BV	155	225	—
1893M Proof	—	Value: 40,000				
1894S	3,067,000	—	BV	155	200	—
1894S Proof	—	Value: 40,000				
1894M	4,166,000	—	BV	155	200	—
1894M Proof	—	Value: 40,000				
1895S	2,758,000	—	BV	155	200	—
1895M	4,165,000	—	BV	155	200	—
1895M Proof	—	Value: 40,000				
1896S	2,544,000	—	BV	155	200	—
1896M	4,456,000	—	BV	155	200	—
1896M Proof	—	Value: 40,000				
1897S	2,532,000	—	BV	155	225	—
1897M	5,130,000	—	BV	155	200	—
1897M Proof	—	Value: 40,000				
1898S	2,548,000	—	BV	155	225	—
1898M	5,509,000	—	BV	155	200	—
1898M Proof	—	Value: 40,000				
1899S	3,259,000	—	BV	155	185	—
1899M	5,579,000	—	BV	155	185	—
1899M Proof	—	Value: 40,000				
1899P	690,000	BV	250	900	2,250	—
1899P Proof	—	Value: 45,000				
1900S	3,586,000	—	BV	155	185	—
1900M	4,305,000	—	BV	155	185	—
1900M Proof	—	Value: 40,000				
1900P	1,886,000	—	BV	155	220	—
1901S	3,012,000	—	BV	155	220	—
1901M	3,987,000	—	BV	155	220	—
1901M Proof	—	Value: 45,000				
1901P	2,889,000	—	BV	155	220	—
1901P Proof	—	Value: 45,000				

KM# 8 2 POUNDS
15.9761 g., 0.9170 Gold .4707 oz. AGW **Ruler:** Victoria **Subject:** 50th Anniversary of Reign **Obv:** Jubilee head left **Rev:** St. George slaying the dragon

Date	Mintage	F	VF	XF	Unc	BU
1887S Proof	Est. 11	Value: 45,000				

Note: Spink Australia Sale #30 11-89 nearly FDC realized $16,940

KM# 11 5 POUNDS
39.9403 g., 0.9170 Gold 1.1771 oz. AGW **Ruler:** Victoria **Subject:** 50th Anniversary of Reign **Obv:** Jubilee head left **Rev:** St. George slaying the dragon

Date	Mintage	F	VF	XF	Unc	BU
1887 Proof; Rare	Est. 3	—	—	—	—	—

Note: Spink Australia Sale #30 11-89 nearly FDC realized $62,370. David Akers Numismatics Pittman sale 8-99 Choice Proof realized $103,500

COMMONWEALTH OF AUSTRALIA

MINT MARKS

M – Melbourne
P – Perth
S – Sydney
(sy) – Sydney

TRADE COINAGE

KM# 14 1/2 SOVEREIGN
3.9940 g., 0.9170 Gold .1177 oz. AGW **Ruler:** Edward VII **Obv:** Head right **Obv. Designer:** G.W. DeSaulles **Rev:** St. George slaying dragon

Date	Mintage	F	VF	XF	Unc	BU
1902S	84,000	BV	100	150	500	—
1902S Proof	—	Value: 60,000				
1902S Frosted, Proof	—	Value: 55,000				
1903S	231,000	BV	100	150	550	—
1904P	60,000	100	250	750	2,000	—
1906S	308,000	BV	100	125	400	—
1906M	82,000	100	175	400	1,500	—
1907M	400,000	BV	100	125	475	—
1908S	538,000	BV	100	125	450	—
1908M	—	BV	100	125	550	—
1908P	25,000	120	250	700	2,000	—
1909M	186,000	BV	100	125	375	—
1909P	44,000	100	225	425	1,500	—
1910S	474,000	BV	100	125	375	—

KM# 28 1/2 SOVEREIGN
3.9940 g., 0.9170 Gold .1177 oz. AGW **Ruler:** George V **Obv:** Head left **Rev:** St. George slaying dragon

Date	Mintage	F	VF	XF	Unc	BU
1911S	252,000	BV	90.00	100	160	—
1911S Matte Proof	—	Value: 47,500				
1911P	130,000	80.00	110	165	300	—
1912S	278,000	BV	90.00	100	150	—
1914S	322,000	BV	90.00	100	150	—
1915P	138,000	BV	90.00	125	250	—
1915S	892,000	BV	80.00	100	150	—
1915M	125,000	BV	90.00	100	160	—
1916S	448,000	BV	85.00	100	150	—
1918P	—	300	500	1,100	2,000	—

Note: Estimated 200-250 pieces minted

KM# 15 SOVEREIGN
7.9881 g., 0.9170 Gold .2354 oz. AGW **Ruler:** Edward VII **Obv:** Head right **Obv. Designer:** G.W. DeSaulles **Rev:** St. George on horseback with sword slaying the dragon

Date	Mintage	F	VF	XF	Unc	BU
1902S	2,813,000	—	—	BV	165	—
1902S Proof	—	Value: 50,000				
1902S Frosted proof	—	Value: 60,000				
1902M	4,267,000	—	—	BV	165	—
1902P	4,289,000	—	—	BV	170	—
1903S	2,806,000	—	—	BV	165	—
1903M	3,521,000	—	—	BV	165	—
1903P	4,674,000	—	—	BV	180	—
1904S	2,986,000	—	—	BV	165	—
1904M	3,743,000	—	—	BV	165	—
1904M Proof	—	Value: 50,000				
1904P	4,506,000	—	—	BV	180	—
1905S	2,778,000	—	—	BV	165	—
1905M	3,633,000	—	—	BV	165	—
1905P	4,876,000	—	—	BV	180	—
1906S	2,792,000	—	—	BV	165	—
1906M	3,657,000	—	—	BV	165	—
1906P	4,829,000	—	—	BV	180	—
1907S	2,539,000	—	—	BV	165	—
1907M	3,332,000	—	—	BV	165	—
1907P	4,972,000	—	—	BV	175	—
1908S	2,017,000	—	—	BV	165	—
1908M	3,080,000	—	—	BV	165	—
1908P	4,875,000	—	—	BV	165	—
1909S	2,057,000	—	—	BV	165	—
1909M	3,029,000	—	—	BV	165	—
1909P	4,524,000	—	—	BV	165	—
1910S	2,135,000	—	—	BV	165	—
1910M	3,054,000	—	—	BV	165	—
1910M Proof	—	Value: 50,000				
1910P	4,690,000	—	—	BV	165	—

KM# 29 SOVEREIGN
7.9881 g., 0.9170 Gold .2354 oz. AGW **Ruler:** George V **Obv:** Head left **Rev:** St. George on horseback with sword slaying the dragon

Date	Mintage	F	VF	XF	Unc	BU
1911S	2,519,000	—	—	BV	160	—
1911S Proof	—	Value: 50,000				
1911M	2,851,000	—	—	BV	160	—
1911M Proof	—	Value: 50,000				
1911P	4,373,000	—	—	BV	160	—
1912S	2,227,000	—	—	BV	160	—
1912M	2,467,000	—	—	BV	160	—
1912P	4,278,000	—	—	BV	160	—
1913S	2,249,000	—	—	BV	160	—
1913M	2,323,000	—	—	BV	160	—
1913P	4,635,000	—	—	BV	160	—
1914S	1,774,000	—	—	BV	160	—
1914S Proof	—	Value: 47,500				
1914M	2,012,000	—	—	BV	160	—
1914P	4,815,000	—	—	BV	160	—
1915S	1,346,000	—	—	BV	160	—
1915M	1,637,000	—	—	BV	160	—
1915P	4,373,000	—	—	BV	160	—
1916S	1,242,000	—	—	BV	160	—
1916M	1,277,000	—	—	BV	160	—
1916P	4,906,000	—	—	BV	160	—
1917S	1,666,000	—	—	BV	160	—
1917M	934,000	—	—	BV	160	—
1917P	4,110,000	—	—	BV	160	—
1918S	3,716,000	—	—	BV	160	—
1918M	4,969,000	—	—	BV	160	—
1918P	3,812,000	—	—	BV	160	—
1919S	1,835,000	—	—	BV	160	—
1919M	514,000	—	BV	160	200	—
1919P	2,995,000	—	—	BV	160	—
1920S	360,000	20,000	30,000	50,000	120,000	—
1920M	530,000	1,100	1,750	2,500	3,000	—
1920P	2,421,000	—	—	BV	160	—
1921S	839,000	400	850	1,300	2,000	—
1921M	240,000	2,000	4,500	6,000	8,500	—
1921P	2,314,000	—	—	BV	160	—
1922S	578,000	3,000	6,000	9,500	14,000	—
1922S Proof	—	Value: 55,000				
1922M	608,000	1,250	3,000	5,250	7,500	—
1922P	2,298,000	—	—	BV	160	—
1923S	416,000	1,500	3,500	5,500	9,500	—
1923S Proof	—	Value: 50,000				
1923M	510,000	—	—	BV	200	—
1923P	2,124,000	—	—	BV	160	—
1924S	394,000	275	625	900	1,600	—
1924M	278,000	—	BV	160	200	—
1924P	1,464,000	BV	155	175	250	—
1925S	5,632,000	—	—	BV	160	—
1925M	3,311,000	—	—	BV	160	—
1925P	1,837,000	—	BV	160	200	—
1926S	1,030,999	5,000	8,000	12,000	15,000	—
1926S Proof	—	Value: 60,000				
1926M	211,000	—	BV	155	200	—
1926P	1,131,000	400	1,100	1,500	2,000	—
1927M	310,000					

Note: None known.

1927P	1,383,000	BV	175	250	400	—
1928M	413,000	800	1,250	1,800	2,250	—
1928P	1,333,000	BV	160	175	225	—

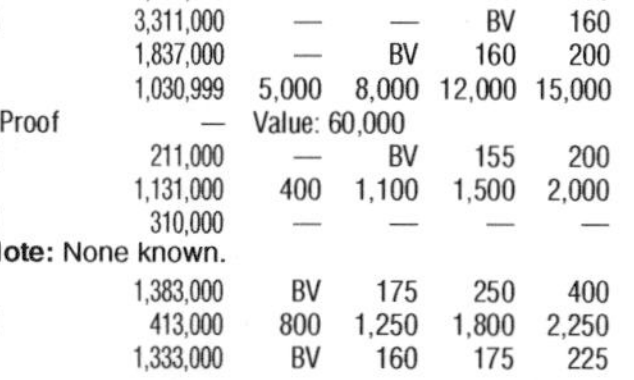

KM# 32 SOVEREIGN
7.9881 g., 0.9170 Gold .2354 oz. AGW **Ruler:** George V **Obv:** Head left **Rev:** St. George on horseback with sword slaying the dragon

Date	Mintage	F	VF	XF	Unc	BU
1929M	436,000	600	1,000	1,750	2,750	—
1929M Proof	—	Value: 40,000				
1929P	1,606,000	—	—	BV	185	—
1930M	77,000	BV	160	200	275	—
1930M Proof	—	Value: 40,000				
1930P	1,915,000	—	—	BV	185	—
1931M	57,000	185	250	350	500	—
1931M Proof	—	Value: 45,000				
1931P	1,173,000	—	—	BV	185	—

KM# 16 2 POUNDS
15.9761 g., 0.9170 Gold .4707 oz. AGW **Ruler:** Edward VII **Obv:** Head right **Obv. Designer:** G.W. DeSaulles **Rev:** St. George on horseback with sword slaying the dragon **Note:** Gilt lead electrotypes exist.

Date	Mintage	F	VF	XF	Unc	BU
1902S Matte Proof Rare	4	—	—	—	—	—

KM# 17 5 POUNDS
39.9403 g., 0.9170 Gold 1.1771 oz. AGW **Ruler:** Edward VII **Obv:** Head right **Obv. Designer:** G.W. DeSaulles **Rev:** St. George on horseback with sword slaying the dragon **Note:** Gilt lead electrotypes exist.

Date	Mintage	F	VF	XF	Unc	BU
1902S Proof; Rare	Est. 3	—	—	—	—	—
1902S Matte Proof; Rare	Inc. above	—	—	—	—	—

Note: Spink Australia Sale #30 11-89 nearly FDC realized $38,500

DECIMAL COINAGE

KM# 767b CENT
5.6100 g., 0.9990 Gold 0.1802 oz. AGW, 17.53 mm. **Ruler:** Elizabeth II **Obv:** Head with tiara right **Obv. Designer:** Ian Rank-Broadley **Rev:** Feather-tailed glider **Rev. Designer:** Stuart Devlin **Edge:** Plain

Date	Mintage	F	VF	XF	Unc	BU
2006 Proof	300	—	—	—	—	—

KM# 768b 2 CENTS
11.3100 g., 0.9990 Gold 0.3633 oz. AGW, 21.59 mm. **Ruler:** Elizabeth II **Obv:** Head with tiara right **Obv. Designer:** Ian Rank-Broadley **Rev:** Frilled-necked lizard **Rev. Designer:** Stuart Devlin **Edge:** Plain

Date	Mintage	F	VF	XF	Unc	BU
2006 Proof	—	—	—	—	—	—

KM# 401a 5 CENTS
6.0300 g., 0.9990 Gold, 19.41 mm. **Ruler:** Elizabeth II **Subject:** Federation Centennial **Obv:** Head with tiara right **Obv. Designer:** Ian Rank-Broadley **Rev:** Short-beaked Spiny Anteater **Rev. Designer:** Stuart Devlin

Date	Mintage	F	VF	XF	Unc	BU
2001 Proof	350	Value: 320				
2005 Proof	650	Value: 320				
2006 Proof	300	Value: 320				

KM# 402a 10 CENTS
12.1400 g., 0.9999 Gold 0.3951 oz. AGW, 23.6 mm. **Ruler:** Elizabeth II **Subject:** Federation Centennial **Obv:** Head with tiara right **Obv. Designer:** Ian Rank-Broadley **Rev:** Super Lyre-bird **Rev. Designer:** Stuart Devlin **Edge:** Reeded

Date	Mintage	F	VF	XF	Unc	BU
2001 Proof	350	Value: 640				
2005 Proof	650	Value: 640				
2006 Proof	300	—	—	—	—	—

KM# 819 20 CENTS
24.3600 g., 0.9990 Gold 0.7824 oz. AGW, 28.52 mm. **Ruler:** Elizabeth II **Obv:** Head with tiara right **Obv. Designer:** Ian Rank-Broadley **Rev:** Platypus with federation star **Rev. Designer:** Stuart Devlin **Edge:** Reeded

Date	Mintage	F	VF	XF	Unc	BU
2001 Proof	350	—	—	—	—	—

KM# 403a 20 CENTS
24.5600 g., 0.9999 Gold 0.7895 oz. AGW, 28.52 mm. **Ruler:** Elizabeth II **Subject:** Federation Centennial **Obv:** Elizabeth II **Rev:** Duckbill Platypus

Date	Mintage	F	VF	XF	Unc	BU
2001 Proof	650	Value: 1,280				

26 AUSTRALIA

KM# 745b   20 CENTS
24.3600 g., 0.9999 Gold 0.7831 oz. AGW, 28.52 mm. **Ruler:** Elizabeth II **Obv:** Head right **Rev:** Soldier with wife and child **Edge:** Reeded

Date	Mintage	F	VF	XF	Unc	BU
2005 Proof	650	Value: 625				

KM# 491.1a   50 CENTS
33.8800 g., 0.9999 Gold 1.0892 oz. AGW, 31.51 mm. **Ruler:** Elizabeth II **Subject:** Federation Centennial **Obv:** Elizabeth II **Rev:** Commonwealth arms above value

Date	Mintage	F	VF	XF	Unc	BU
2001 Proof	650	Value: 1,770				

KM# 746b   50 CENTS
33.6300 g., 0.9999 Gold 1.0811 oz. AGW, 31.51 mm. **Ruler:** Elizabeth II **Obv:** Head with tiara right **Rev:** Military cemetery scene **Edge:** Plain **Shape:** 12-sided

Date	Mintage	F	VF	XF	Unc	BU
2005 Proof	650	Value: 850				

KM# 534.1a   DOLLAR
21.7000 g., 0.9999 Gold 0.6976 oz. AGW, 25 mm. **Ruler:** Elizabeth II **Subject:** Federation Centennial **Obv:** Elizabeth II **Rev:** Federation logo

Date	Mintage	F	VF	XF	Unc	BU
2001 Proof	650	Value: 1,130				

KM# 747b   DOLLAR
21.5200 g., 0.9999 Gold 0.6918 oz. AGW, 25 mm. **Ruler:** Elizabeth II **Obv:** Queens head right **Rev:** Happy man **Edge:** Segmented reeding

Date	Mintage	F	VF	XF	Unc	BU
2005 Proof	650	Value: 550				

KM# 749a   DOLLAR
31.1035 g., 0.9990 Silver Partially Gold Plated 0.999 oz. ASW, 40 mm. **Ruler:** Elizabeth II **Obv:** Queens head right **Rev:** Kangaroo and stars **Edge:** Reeded

Date	Mintage	F	VF	XF	Unc	BU
2005 Proof	12,500	Value: 55.00				

KM# 406a   2 DOLLARS
16.0300 g., 0.9999 Gold 0.5153 oz. AGW, 20.5 mm. **Ruler:** Elizabeth II **Subject:** Federation Centennial **Obv:** Elizabeth II **Rev:** Aboriginal man and stars

Date	Mintage	F	VF	XF	Unc	BU
2001 Proof	650	Value: 835				
2005 Proof	—	Value: 835				

KM# 751   10 DOLLARS
60.5000 g., 0.9990 Silver Partially Gold Plated 1.9432 oz. ASW, 50 mm. **Ruler:** Elizabeth II **Subject:** 150th Anniversary - Sydney Mint **Obv:** 7-line center inscription between two coin designs **Rev:** Mint building **Edge:** Reeded

Date	Mintage	F	VF	XF	Unc	BU
ND(2005) Proof	10,000	Value: 70.00				

KM# 519   20 DOLLARS
Bi-Metallic Gold center in Silver ring, 32 mm. **Ruler:** Elizabeth II **Subject:** Millennium **Obv:** Head with tiara right within circle, denomination below **Obv. Designer:** Ian Rank-Broadley **Rev:** Earth view from space **Edge:** Reeded

Date	Mintage	F	VF	XF	Unc	BU
2000 Prooflike	Est. 7,500	—	—	—	—	550

KM# 595   20 DOLLARS
Bi-Metallic .999 4.5287 Silver center in .9999 9.499 Gold ring, 32.1 mm. **Ruler:** Elizabeth II **Subject:** Gregorian Millennium **Obv:** Head with tiara right, beaded circle surrounds, denomination below **Obv. Designer:** Ian Rank-Broadley **Rev:** Chronograph watch face with observatory in center and three depictions of the Earth's rotation **Edge:** Reeded **Note:** 14.03 grams total weight.

Date	Mintage	F	VF	XF	Unc	BU
2001 Prooflike	7,500	—	—	—	—	275

KM# 597   20 DOLLARS
Bi-Metallic .9999 8.8645 Gold center in .9999 10.7618 Silver ring, 32.1 mm. **Ruler:** Elizabeth II **Subject:** Centenary of Federation **Obv:** Head with tiara right within star design, denomination below **Obv. Designer:** Ian Rank-Broadley **Rev:** National arms on a flowery background **Edge:** Reeded **Note:** 19.63 grams total weight.

Date	Mintage	F	VF	XF	Unc	BU
ND(2001) Prooflike	7,500	—	—	—	—	250

KM# 760   20 DOLLARS
Bi-Metallic Gold center in Silver ring **Ruler:** Elizabeth II **Rev:** Sir Donald Bradman portrait

Date	Mintage	F	VF	XF	Unc	BU
2001 Proof	—	Value: 200				

KM# 634   20 DOLLARS
18.3510 g., Bi-Metallic .999 Silver, 4.6655g, breast star shaped center in a .9999 Gold ,13.6855g outer ring, 32.1 mm. **Ruler:** Elizabeth II **Subject:** Queen's Golden Jubilee **Obv:** Queens head right **Rev:** Queen before Buckingham Palace **Edge:** Reeded

Date	Mintage	F	VF	XF	Unc	BU
2002P Proof	7,500	Value: 225				

KM# 687   20 DOLLARS
13.4056 g., 0.9990 Bi-Metallic .999 Gold 8.3979g Center in a .999 Silver 5.0077g Ring 0.4306 oz., 32 mm. **Ruler:** Elizabeth II **Subject:** Golden Jubilee of Coronation **Obv:** Head with tiara right within circle, denomination below **Obv. Designer:** Ian Rank-Broadley **Rev:** Four different coinage portraits of Queen Elizabeth II **Rev. Designer:** Mary Gillick, Arnold Machin, Raphael Maklouf and Ian Rank-Broadley **Edge:** Reeded

Date	Mintage	F	VF	XF	Unc	BU
2003P Proof	7,500	Value: 450				

KM# 313   40 DOLLARS
31.1850 g., 0.9995 Palladium 1.0021 oz. **Ruler:** Elizabeth II **Obv:** Crowned head right, denomination below **Obv. Designer:** Raphael Maklouf **Rev:** The Australian emu, left, date below

Date	Mintage	F	VF	XF	Unc	BU
1995	—	—	—	—	500	—
1995 Proof	Est. 2,500	Value: 550				

KM# 343   40 DOLLARS
31.1850 g., 0.9995 Palladium 1.0021 oz. **Ruler:** Elizabeth II **Obv:** Crowned head right, denomination below **Rev:** Emu and chicks

Date	Mintage	F	VF	XF	Unc	BU
1996 Proof	Est. 2,500	Value: 550				

KM# 648   50 DOLLARS
36.5100 g., Tri-Metallic .9999 Gold 7.8g, 13.1 mm center in .999 Silver 13.39g, 26.85mm inner ring within a copper 15.32g, 3, 38.74 mm. **Ruler:** Elizabeth II **Subject:** Commonwealth Games **Obv:** Head with tiara right, denomination below **Obv. Designer:** Ian Rank-Broadley **Rev:** Victorious athletes within inscriptions and runners **Edge:** Reeded

Date	Mintage	F	VF	XF	Unc	BU
2002 Proof	5,000	Value: 300				

KM# 724   50 DOLLARS
36.5100 g., 0.9990 Tri-Metallic .999 Gold 7.8g center in .999 Silver 13.39g ring within .999 Copper 15.32g outer ring 1.1726 oz., 38.74 mm. **Ruler:** Elizabeth II **Subject:** Olympics **Obv:** Head with tiara right, denomination below **Rev:** Multicolor flag above Olympic rings on shield within wreath **Edge:** Reeded

Date	Mintage	F	VF	XF	Unc	BU
2004 Proof	2,500	Value: 375				

KM# 785   50 DOLLARS
Tri-Metallic Gold center within Silver ring within Copper outer ring **Ruler:** Elizabeth II **Subject:** Commonwealth Games **Obv:** Head with tiara right, denomination below **Rev:** Victory wreath at center of legend

Date	Mintage	F	VF	XF	Unc	BU
2006 Proof	5,000	Value: 300				

KM# 308   100 DOLLARS
10.3678 g., 0.9160 Gold .3053 oz. AGW **Ruler:** Elizabeth II **Obv:** Queens portrait **Rev:** The Waratah Flower, value below **Rev. Designer:** Horst Hahne

Date	Mintage	F	VF	XF	Unc	BU
1995	3,000	—	—	—	210	—

KM# 308a   100 DOLLARS
10.3678 g., 0.9999 Gold .3333 oz. AGW **Ruler:** Elizabeth II **Obv:** Queens portrait **Rev:** The Waratah flower **Rev. Designer:** Horst Hahne

Date	Mintage	F	VF	XF	Unc	BU
1995 Proof	2,500	Value: 300				

KM# 333   100 DOLLARS
10.3678 g., 0.9160 Gold .3053 oz. AGW **Ruler:** Elizabeth II **Subject:** Tasmanial Blue Gum Flower **Obv:** Queens portrait **Rev:** Flowering plant with long, droopy leaves

Date	Mintage	F	VF	XF	Unc	BU
1996	—	—	—	—	210	—

KM# 333a   100 DOLLARS
10.3678 g., 0.9999 Gold .3333 oz. AGW **Ruler:** Elizabeth II **Subject:** Tasmanial Blue Gum flower **Obv:** Queens portrait **Rev:** Flowering plant with long, droopy leaves

Date	Mintage	F	VF	XF	Unc	BU
1996 Proof	—	Value: 300				

KM# 384   100 DOLLARS
10.3678 g., 0.9167 Gold .3053 oz. AGW **Ruler:** Elizabeth II **Subject:** Mangles' Kangaroo Paw Flower, value below **Obv:** Queens portrait **Rev:** Flower

Date	Mintage	F	VF	XF	Unc	BU
1997	3,000	—	—	—	210	—

AUSTRALIA 27

KM# 373 100 DOLLARS
10.0210 g., 0.9999 Gold .3222 oz. AGW **Ruler:** Elizabeth II
Series: Sydney Olympics 2000 **Obv:** Crowned head right, denomination below **Obv. Designer:** Raphael Maklouf **Rev:** Runner training in rain, Olympic logo above right foot **Rev. Designer:** Stuart Devlin

Date	Mintage	F	VF	XF	Unc	BU
2000 (1998) Proof	—				Value: 265	

KM# 383 100 DOLLARS
10.0210 g., 0.9999 Gold .3222 oz. AGW **Ruler:** Elizabeth II
Series: Sydney Olympics 2000 **Obv:** Crowned head right, denomination below **Obv. Designer:** Raphael Maklouf **Rev:** Multicolor games logo within wreath **Rev. Designer:** Stuart Devlin

Date	Mintage	F	VF	XF	Unc	BU
2000 (1998) Proof	Est. 30,000				Value: 265	

KM# 480 100 DOLLARS
10.3678 g., 0.9160 Gold .3056 oz. AGW, 25 mm. **Ruler:** Elizabeth II **Subject:** Stuart's Desert Pea **Obv:** Queens portrait **Rev:** Plant with pods **Edge:** Reeded

Date	Mintage	F	VF	XF	Unc	BU
1998	3,000	—	—	—	210	—

KM# 480a 100 DOLLARS
10.3678 g., 0.9990 Gold .3333 oz. AGW, 25 mm. **Ruler:** Elizabeth II **Subject:** Stuart's Desert Pea **Obv:** Queens portrait **Rev:** Plant with pods **Edge:** Reeded

Date	Mintage	F	VF	XF	Unc	BU
1998 Proof	2,500				Value: 275	

KM# 487a 100 DOLLARS
10.3678 g., 0.9990 Gold .3333 oz. AGW, 25 mm. **Ruler:** Elizabeth II **Obv:** Queens portrait **Rev:** Common Heath flowers **Edge:** Reeded

Date	Mintage	F	VF	XF	Unc	BU
1999 Proof	2,500				Value: 275	

KM# 442 100 DOLLARS
10.0000 g., 0.9990 Gold .3215 oz. AGW **Ruler:** Elizabeth II
Series: Sydney Olympics 2000 **Obv:** Crowned head right **Rev:** 3 athletic workout scenes, Olympic logo at bottom **Rev. Designer:** Stuart Devlin **Edge:** Reeded

Date	Mintage	F	VF	XF	Unc	BU
2000 (1999) Proof	30,000				Value: 265	

KM# 443 100 DOLLARS
10.0000 g., 0.9990 Gold .3215 oz. AGW **Ruler:** Elizabeth II
Series: Sydney Olympics 2000 **Obv:** Crowned head right **Rev:** Shot putter teaching seated children, Olympic logo below **Rev. Designer:** Stuart Devlin **Edge:** Reeded

Date	Mintage	F	VF	XF	Unc	BU
2000 (1999) Proof	30,000				Value: 265	

KM# 444 100 DOLLARS
10.0000 g., 0.9990 Gold .3215 oz. AGW **Ruler:** Elizabeth II
Series: Sydney Olympics 2000 **Obv:** Crowned head right **Rev:** Sprinter being coached, Olympic logo at bottom **Rev. Designer:** Stuart Devlin **Edge:** Reeded

Date	Mintage	F	VF	XF	Unc	BU
2000 (1999) Proof	30,000				Value: 265	

KM# 474 100 DOLLARS
Bi-Metallic Gold center in Silver ring .2354 oz. **Ruler:** Elizabeth II **Subject:** Perth Mint Centennial Sovereign **Obv:** Head with tiara right within inner circle **Obv. Designer:** Ian Rank-Broadley **Rev:** St. George with sword on horseback slaying dragon, circle surrounds all, dates below **Rev. Designer:** Bernardo Pistrucci **Edge:** Reeded

Date	Mintage	F	VF	XF	Unc	BU
ND(1999) Proof	7,500				Value: 500	

KM# 512 100 DOLLARS
10.3678 g., 0.9160 Gold .3056 oz. AGW, 25 mm. **Ruler:** Elizabeth II **Subject:** Cooktown Orchid **Obv:** Queens portrait **Rev:** Orchid and denomination **Edge:** Reeded

Date	Mintage	F	VF	XF	Unc	BU
2000	3,000	—	—	—	210	—

KM# 512a 100 DOLLARS
10.3678 g., 0.9990 Gold .3333 oz. AGW, 25 mm. **Ruler:** Elizabeth II **Subject:** Cooktown Orchid **Obv:** Queens portrait **Rev:** Orchid and denomination **Edge:** Reeded

Date	Mintage	F	VF	XF	Unc	BU
2000 Proof	2,500				Value: 275	

KM# 521 100 DOLLARS
10.0000 g., 0.9990 Gold .3215 oz. AGW, 25 mm. **Ruler:** Elizabeth II **Series:** Olympics **Obv:** Head with tiara right, denomination below **Obv. Designer:** Ian Rank-Broadley **Rev:** Multicolor torch flames within circle of figures **Rev. Designer:** Stuart Devlin **Edge:** Reeded

Date	Mintage	F	VF	XF	Unc	BU
2000 Proof	20,000				Value: 385	

KM# 643 100 DOLLARS
10.3678 g., 0.9999 Gold 0.3333 oz. AGW, 25 mm. **Ruler:** Elizabeth II **Subject:** Golden Wattle Flower **Obv:** Queens head right **Rev:** Flower and denomination **Edge:** Reeded

Date	Mintage	F	VF	XF	Unc	BU
2001	3,000	—	—	—	275	285
2001 Proof	2,500				Value: 300	

KM# 635 100 DOLLARS
31.1035 g., 0.9999 Gold 0.9999 oz. AGW, 32.1 mm. **Ruler:** Elizabeth II **Subject:** Gold Panning **Obv:** Queens head right **Rev:** Two prospectors dry panning for gold with color highlighted pans and dust **Edge:** Reeded

Date	Mintage	F	VF	XF	Unc	BU
2002P Proof	1,500				Value: 775	

KM# 636 100 DOLLARS
31.1035 g., 0.9995 Platinum 0.9995 oz. APW, 32.1 mm. **Ruler:** Elizabeth II **Subject:** Multiculturalism **Obv:** Queens head right **Rev:** Six racially diverse portraits against a blue background **Edge:** Reeded

Date	Mintage	F	VF	XF	Unc	BU
2002P Proof	1,000				Value: 1,450	

KM# 646 100 DOLLARS
31.4000 g., 0.9999 Gold 1.0094 oz. AGW, 34.1 mm. **Ruler:** Elizabeth II **Subject:** Queen's 50th Anniversary of Accession **Obv:** Queens head right **Rev:** Silhouette of George VI, Queen's portrait and denomination **Rev. Designer:** Peter Soobik **Edge:** Reeded

Date	Mintage	F	VF	XF	Unc	BU
2002 Proof	2,002				Value: 800	

KM# 657 100 DOLLARS
10.3678 g., 0.9999 Gold 0.3333 oz. AGW, 25 mm. **Ruler:** Elizabeth II **Obv:** Queens head right **Rev:** Sturt's Desert Rose **Rev. Designer:** Horst Hahne **Edge:** Reeded

Date	Mintage	F	VF	XF	Unc	BU
2002	3,000	—	—	—	275	285
2002 Proof	2,500				Value: 300	

KM# 741 100 DOLLARS
31.1035 g., 0.9999 Gold 0.9999 oz. AGW, 32 mm. **Ruler:** Elizabeth II **Obv:** Head with tiara right, denomination below **Rev:** Eureka Stockade leader Peter Lalor and blue flag **Edge:** Reeded

Date	Mintage	F	VF	XF	Unc	BU
2004P Proof	1,500				Value: 1,000	

KM# 742 100 DOLLARS
31.1035 g., 0.9995 Platinum 0.9995 oz. APW, 32.1 mm. **Ruler:** Elizabeth II **Obv:** Head with tiara right, denomination below **Obv. Designer:** Ian Rank-Broadley **Rev:** Four different sport athletes and multicolor background **Edge:** Reeded

Date	Mintage	F	VF	XF	Unc	BU
2004P Proof	1,000				Value: 1,900	

KM# 797 100 DOLLARS
31.1070 g., 0.9990 Gold 0.9991 oz. AGW, 25.1 mm. **Ruler:** Elizabeth II **Obv:** Elizabeth II **Rev:** Latent news real photographic images of a dancing man celebrating the end of WWII

Date	Mintage	F	VF	XF	Unc	BU
2005 Proof	750				Value: 950	

28   AUSTRALIA

KM# 309 150 DOLLARS
15.5517 g., 0.9999 Gold .5000 oz. AGW **Ruler:** Elizabeth II
Obv: Queens portrait **Rev:** The Waratah Flower above value

Date	Mintage	F	VF	XF	Unc	BU
1995 Proof	1,500	Value: 600				

KM# 334 150 DOLLARS
15.5517 g., 0.9999 Gold .5000 oz. AGW **Ruler:** Elizabeth II
Subject: Tasmanian Blue Gum Flower **Obv:** Queens portrait
Rev: Tasmanian Blue Gum Flower above value **Rev. Designer:** Horst Hahne

Date	Mintage	F	VF	XF	Unc	BU
1996 Proof	—	Value: 500				

KM# 413 150 DOLLARS
15.5517 g., 0.9999 Gold .5000 oz. AGW **Ruler:** Elizabeth II
Obv: Queens portrait **Rev:** Stuart's desert pea

Date	Mintage	F	VF	XF	Unc	BU
1998 Proof	1,500	Value: 450				

KM# 475 150 DOLLARS
15.5517 g., 0.9999 Gold .5000 oz. AGW **Ruler:** Elizabeth II
Subject: Common Heath Flower **Obv:** Queens portrait **Rev:** Heath flowers above value **Rev. Designer:** Horst Hahne **Edge:** Reeded

Date	Mintage	F	VF	XF	Unc	BU
1999 Proof	1,500	Value: 450				

KM# 513 150 DOLLARS
15.5518 g., 0.9990 Gold .5000 oz. AGW, 30 mm. **Ruler:** Elizabeth II
Subject: Cooktown Orchid **Obv:** Queens portrait **Rev:** Orchid above value **Rev. Designer:** Horst Hahne **Edge:** Reeded

Date	Mintage	F	VF	XF	Unc	BU
2000 Proof	1,500	Value: 500				

KM# 644 150 DOLLARS
15.5517 g., 0.9999 Gold 0.4999 oz. AGW, 30 mm. **Ruler:** Elizabeth II **Obv:** Queens head right **Rev:** Golden Wattle Flower, value **Edge:** Reeded

Date	Mintage	F	VF	XF	Unc	BU
2001 Proof	1,500	Value: 400				

KM# 658 150 DOLLARS
15.5517 g., 0.9999 Gold 0.4999 oz. AGW, 30 mm. **Ruler:** Elizabeth II **Subject:** Sturt's Desert Rose Flower **Obv:** Queens head right **Rev:** Flowers **Rev. Designer:** Horst Hahne **Edge:** Reeded

Date	Mintage	F	VF	XF	Unc	BU
2002 Proof	1,500	Value: 400				

KM# 731 150 DOLLARS
10.3678 g., 0.9990 Gold 0.333 oz. AGW, 25 mm. **Ruler:** Elizabeth II **Obv:** Queens head right **Rev:** Cassowary bird **Edge:** Reeded

Date	Mintage	F	VF	XF	Unc	BU
2004 Proof	2,500	Value: 275				

KM# 752 150 DOLLARS
10.3678 g., 0.9999 Gold 0.3333 oz. AGW, 25 mm. **Ruler:** Elizabeth II **Obv:** Queens head right **Rev:** Malleefowl bird **Edge:** Reeded

Date	Mintage	F	VF	XF	Unc	BU
2005 Proof	2,500	Value: 335				

KM# 71 200 DOLLARS
10.0000 g., 0.9170 Gold .2948 oz. AGW **Ruler:** Elizabeth II
Obv: Young bust right **Obv. Designer:** Arnold Machin **Rev:** Koala in tree, value below **Rev. Designer:** Stuart Devlin

Date	Mintage	F	VF	XF	Unc	BU
1980	207,500	—	—	—	200	—
1980 Proof	50,077	Value: 220				
1983	88,000	—	—	—	200	—
1983 Proof	15,889	Value: 220				
1984	49,200	—	—	—	200	—
1984 Proof	12,559	Value: 220				

KM# 73 200 DOLLARS
10.0000 g., 0.9170 Gold .2948 oz. AGW **Ruler:** Elizabeth II
Subject: Wedding of Prince Charles and Lady Diana **Obv:** Young bust right **Obv. Designer:** Arnold Machin **Rev:** Conjoined heads of Prince Charles and Lady Diana left **Rev. Designer:** Stuart Devlin

Date	Mintage	F	VF	XF	Unc	BU
1981	77,890	—	—	—	200	—

KM# 76 200 DOLLARS
10.0000 g., 0.9170 Gold .2948 oz. AGW **Ruler:** Elizabeth II
Subject: XII Commonwealth Games - Brisbane **Obv:** Young bust right **Obv. Designer:** Arnold Machin **Rev:** Athlete running over hurdles, value below hurdler **Rev. Designer:** Margaret Priest

Date	Mintage	F	VF	XF	Unc	BU
1982	77,206	—	—	—	200	—
1982 Proof	30,032	Value: 220				

KM# 86 200 DOLLARS
10.0000 g., 0.9170 Gold .2948 oz. AGW **Ruler:** Elizabeth II
Obv: Crowned head right **Obv. Designer:** Raphael Maklouf **Rev:** Koala in tree, value below **Rev. Designer:** Stuart Devlin

Date	Mintage	F	VF	XF	Unc	BU
1985	29,186	—	—	—	200	—
1985 Proof	16,691	Value: 220				
1986	15,298	—	—	—	200	—
1986 Proof	16,654	Value: 220				

KM# 94 200 DOLLARS
10.0000 g., 0.9170 Gold .2948 oz. AGW **Ruler:** Elizabeth II
Obv: Crowned head right **Obv. Designer:** Raphael Maklouf **Rev:** 1/2-length bust right, value below, 1787 above right shoulder **Rev. Designer:** Horst Hahne

Date	Mintage	F	VF	XF	Unc	BU
1987	20,800	—	—	—	200	—
1987 Proof	20,000	Value: 220				

KM# 115 200 DOLLARS
10.0000 g., 0.9170 Gold .2948 oz. AGW **Ruler:** Elizabeth II
Subject: Bicentennial of Australia **Obv:** Crowned head right **Obv. Designer:** Raphael Maklouf **Rev:** Early colonist standing in front of water in Sydney Cove, ship in background at right, value below

Date	Mintage	F	VF	XF	Unc	BU
1988	11,000	—	—	—	200	—
1988 Proof	20,000	Value: 220				

KM# 116 200 DOLLARS
10.0000 g., 0.9170 Gold .2948 oz. AGW **Ruler:** Elizabeth II
Subject: Pride of Australia **Obv:** Crowned head right **Obv. Designer:** Raphael Maklouf **Rev:** Frilled-neck lizard, value below

Date	Mintage	F	VF	XF	Unc	BU
1989	10,020	—	—	—	200	—
1989 Proof	24,736	Value: 220				

KM# 135 200 DOLLARS
10.0000 g., 0.9170 Gold .2948 oz. AGW **Ruler:** Elizabeth II
Subject: Pride of Australia **Obv:** Crowned head right **Obv. Designer:** Raphael Maklouf **Rev:** Platypus above value **Rev. Designer:** Horst Hahne

Date	Mintage	F	VF	XF	Unc	BU
1990	8,340	—	—	—	200	—
1990 Proof	14,616	Value: 220				

AUSTRALIA

KM# 160 200 DOLLARS
10.0000 g., 0.9170 Gold .2948 oz. AGW **Ruler:** Elizabeth II **Subject:** Pride of Australia **Obv:** Crowned head right **Obv. Designer:** Raphael Maklouf **Rev:** Standing emu between tall grass, value below

Date	Mintage	F	VF	XF	Unc	BU
1991	6,879	—	—	—	200	—
1991 Proof	9,560	Value: 220				

KM# 259 200 DOLLARS
10.0000 g., 0.9170 Gold .2948 oz. AGW **Ruler:** Elizabeth II **Subject:** Pride of Australia **Obv:** Crowned head right **Obv. Designer:** Raphael Maklouf **Rev:** Echidna above value

Date	Mintage	F	VF	XF	Unc	BU
1992	3,935	—	—	—	210	—
1992 Proof	5,921	Value: 225				

KM# 220 200 DOLLARS
16.8200 g., 0.9170 Gold .4958 oz. AGW **Ruler:** Elizabeth II **Series:** Olympic Centenary - 1896-1996 **Obv:** Crowned head right **Obv. Designer:** Raphael Maklouf **Rev:** Gymnast in flight, Olympic logo top right **Edge Lettering:** CITIUS ALTIUS FORTIUS

Date	Mintage	F	VF	XF	Unc	BU
1993 Proof	60,000	Value: 350				

KM# 222 200 DOLLARS
10.0000 g., 0.9170 Gold .2948 oz. AGW **Ruler:** Elizabeth II **Subject:** Pride of Australia **Obv:** Crowned head right **Obv. Designer:** Raphael Maklouf **Rev:** Squirrel glider possum, value below

Date	Mintage	F	VF	XF	Unc	BU
1993	3,014	—	—	—	210	—
1993 Proof	5,000	Value: 225				

KM# 262 200 DOLLARS
10.0000 g., 0.9170 Gold .2948 oz. AGW **Ruler:** Elizabeth II **Subject:** Pride of Australia **Obv:** Crowned head right **Obv. Designer:** Raphael Maklouf **Rev:** Tasmanian devil, value below **Rev. Designer:** Horst Hahne

Date	Mintage	F	VF	XF	Unc	BU
1994	4,000	—	—	—	210	—
1994 Proof	5,000	Value: 225				

KM# 385 200 DOLLARS
15.5517 g., 0.9999 Gold .5000 oz. AGW **Ruler:** Elizabeth II **Subject:** Mangles' Kangaroo Paw Flower **Obv:** Queens portrait **Rev:** Flower

Date	Mintage	F	VF	XF	Unc	BU
1997 Proof	—	Value: 400				

KM# 732 200 DOLLARS
15.5518 g., 0.9990 Gold 0.4995 oz. AGW, 30 mm. **Ruler:** Elizabeth II **Obv:** Queens head right **Rev:** Cassowary bird **Edge:** Reeded

Date	Mintage	F	VF	XF	Unc	BU
2004 Proof	2,500	Value: 385				

KM# 753 200 DOLLARS
15.5518 g., 0.9999 Gold 0.5 oz. AGW, 30 mm. **Ruler:** Elizabeth II **Obv:** Queens head right **Rev:** Malleefowl bird **Edge:** Reeded

Date	Mintage	F	VF	XF	Unc	BU
2005 Proof	2,500	Value: 480				

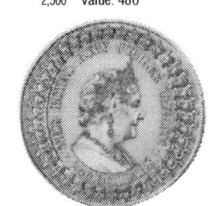

KM# 204 250 DOLLARS
16.9500 g., 0.9170 Gold .4995 oz. AGW **Ruler:** Elizabeth II **Subject:** 40th Anniversary - Reign of Queen Elizabeth II - Queen Mother **Obv:** Queens portrait **Rev:** Portrait of Queen Mother right, within circle of crowns **Rev. Designer:** Stuart Devlin

Date	Mintage	F	VF	XF	Unc	BU
1992 Proof	Est. 5,000	Value: 345				

KM# 205 250 DOLLARS
16.9500 g., 0.9170 Gold .4995 oz. AGW **Ruler:** Elizabeth II **Subject:** 40th Anniversary - Reign of Queen Elizabeth II - Princess Diana **Obv:** Queens portrait **Rev:** Portrait of Princess Diana right, within circle of crowns **Rev. Designer:** Stuart Devlin

Date	Mintage	F	VF	XF	Unc	BU
1992 Proof	Est. 5,000	Value: 350				

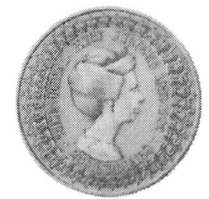

KM# 206 250 DOLLARS
16.9500 g., 0.9170 Gold .4995 oz. AGW **Ruler:** Elizabeth II **Subject:** 40th Anniversary - Reign of Queen Elizabeth II - Princess Anne **Obv:** Queens portrait **Rev:** Portrait of Princess Anne right, within circle of crowns **Rev. Designer:** Stuart Devlin

Date	Mintage	F	VF	XF	Unc	BU
1992 Proof	Est. 5,000	Value: 345				

KM# 207 250 DOLLARS
16.9500 g., 0.9170 Gold .4995 oz. AGW **Ruler:** Elizabeth II **Subject:** 40th Anniversary - Reign of Queen Elizabeth II - Princess Margaret **Obv:** Queens portrait **Rev:** Bust of Princess Margaret left, within circle of crowns **Rev. Designer:** Stuart Devlin

Date	Mintage	F	VF	XF	Unc	BU
1992 Proof	Est. 5,000	Value: 345				

MEDALLIC COINAGE
INA Retro Series

X# M11c.1 DOUBLE FLORIN
0.9167 Gold **Ruler:** Victoria **Obv:** Veiled bust left **Obv. Legend:** VICTORIA • DEI GRATIA • IND • IMP **Rev:** Arms **Edge:** reeded **Note:** Weight varies: 31.9-32.6 grams.

Date	Mintage	F	VF	XF	Unc	BU
1901 Matte Proof	1	—	—	—	—	—
Note: Medal alignment						
1901 Proof	1	—	—	—	—	—
Note: Coin alignment						

X# M11c.2 DOUBLE FLORIN
32.3000 g., 0.9167 Gold 0.952 oz. AGW **Ruler:** Victoria **Obv:** Veiled bust left **Obv. Legend:** VICTORIA • DEI GRATIA • IND • IMP **Rev:** Arms **Edge:** Plain

Date	Mintage	F	VF	XF	Unc	BU
1901 Matte Proof	1	—	—	—	—	—

X# M12 DOUBLE FLORIN
32.6000 g., 0.9167 Gold 0.9608 oz. AGW **Ruler:** Victoria **Obv:** Veiled bust left **Obv. Legend:** VICTORIA • DEI GRA • BRITT • REGINA •FID • DEF • IND • IMP **Rev:** Arms **Edge:** Reeded **Note:** Medal alignment.

Date	Mintage	F	VF	XF	Unc	BU
1901 Proof	1	—	—	—	—	—

X# M13c.1 DOUBLE FLORIN
33.3000 g., 0.9167 Gold 0.9814 oz. AGW **Ruler:** Edward VII **Obv:** Crowned bust right **Obv. Legend:** EDWARDVS VII D: G: BRITT: OMN: REX F: D: IND: IMP: **Rev:** Arms **Edge:** Reeded **Note:** Medal alignment.

Date	Mintage	F	VF	XF	Unc	BU
1901 Proof	1	—	—	—	—	—

X# M13c.2 DOUBLE FLORIN
0.9167 Gold **Ruler:** Edward VII **Obv:** Crowned bust right **Obv. Legend:** EDWARDVS VII D: G: BRITT: OMN: REX F: D: IND: IMP: **Rev:** Arms **Edge:** Plain

Date	Mintage	F	VF	XF	Unc	BU
1901 Proof	1	—	—	—	—	—
Note: Medal alignment						
1901 Proof	1	—	—	—	—	—
Note: Coin alignment						

X# M14 DOUBLE FLORIN
33.2000 g., 0.9167 Gold 0.9785 oz. AGW **Ruler:** Edward VII **Obv:** Head right within pellet circle **Obv. Legend:** EDWARDVS VII DEI GRATIA INDIAE IMPERATOR **Rev:** Arms **Edge:** Plain **Note:** Medal alignment.

Date	Mintage	F	VF	XF	Unc	BU
1901 Proof	1	—	—	—	—	—

X# 1c 5 SHILLINGS
32.2000 g., 0.9167 Gold 0.949 oz. AGW **Ruler:** George V **Obv:** Crowned bust left **Obv. Legend:** GEORGIVS V D. G. BRITT: OMN: REX **Rev:** Kookaburra in flight right below large 5 divides date **Edge:** Plain **Note:** 35 x 35mm.

Date	Mintage	F	VF	XF	Unc	BU
1920 Proof	1	—	—	—	650	—
Note: Coin alignment						
1920 Proof	1	—	—	—	650	—
Note: Medal alignment						

X# 2 5 SHILLINGS
31.8000 g., 0.9167 Gold 0.9372 oz. AGW **Ruler:** George V **Obv:** Head left **Obv. Legend:** GEORGIVS V D. G. BRITT: OMN: REX **Rev:** Kookaburra in flight right below large 5 divides date **Edge:** Plain **Shape:** Square **Note:** 35 x 35mm. Medal alignment.

Date	Mintage	F	VF	XF	Unc	BU
1920 Proof	1	—	—	—	—	—

AUSTRALIA

X# 3c 5 SHILLINGS
32.2000 g., 0.9167 Gold 0.949 oz. AGW **Ruler:** George V **Obv:** Head left **Obv. Legend:** GEORGIVS V D. G. BRITT: OMN: REX **Rev:** Kangaroo left in lower part of large 5 divides date **Edge:** Plain **Shape:** Square **Note:** 35 x 35mm.

Date	Mintage	F	VF	XF	Unc	BU
1921 Matte Proof	1	—	—	—	—	—

X# 4 5 SHILLINGS
32.2000 g., 0.9167 Gold 0.949 oz. AGW **Obv:** Crowned bust left **Obv. Legend:** GEORGIVS V D. G. BRITT: OMN: REX **Rev:** Kangaroo left in lower part of large 5 divides date **Edge:** Plain **Shape:** Square **Note:** 35 x 35mm.

Date	Mintage	F	VF	XF	Unc	BU
1921 Proof	1	—	—	—	—	—

X# M15c.1 CROWN
39.9000 g., 0.9167 Gold 1.176 oz. AGW **Ruler:** Edward VIII **Obv:** Head left **Obv. Legend:** EDWARDVS VIII D: G: BR: OMN: REX F: D: IND: IMP: **Rev:** Large crown **Edge:** Reeded **Note:** Medal alignment.

Date	Mintage	F	VF	XF	Unc	BU
1937 Proof	1	—	—	—	—	—

X# M15c.2 CROWN
40.0000 g., 0.9167 Gold 1.1789 oz. AGW **Ruler:** Edward VIII **Obv:** Head left **Obv. Legend:** EDWARDVS VIII D: G: BR: OMN: REX F: D: IND: IMP: **Rev:** Large crown **Edge:** Plain **Note:** Medal alignment.

Date	Mintage	F	VF	XF	Unc	BU
1937 Proof	1	—	—	—	—	—

X# M16c.1 CROWN
39.9000 g., 0.9167 Gold 1.176 oz. AGW, 37.90 mm. **Ruler:** Edward VIII **Obv:** Head left **Obv. Legend:** EDWARDVS VIII D: G: BR: OMN: REX **Rev:** Large crown **Edge:** Reeded

Date	Mintage	F	VF	XF	Unc	BU
1937 Proof	1	—	—	—	—	—
Note: Medal alignment.						
1937 Proof	1	—	—	—	—	—
Note: Coin alignment.						

X# M16c.2 CROWN
0.9167 Gold, 37.9 mm. **Ruler:** Edward VIII **Obv:** Head left **Obv. Legend:** EDWARDVS VIII D: G: BR: OMN: REX **Rev:** Large crown **Edge:** Plain

Date	Mintage	F	VF	XF	Unc	BU
1937 Proof	1	—	—	—	—	—

X# M17 CROWN
39.5000 g., 0.9167 Gold 1.1642 oz. AGW **Ruler:** Edward VIII **Obv:** Crowned bust left **Obv. Legend:** EDWARD VIII KING EMPEROR **Rev:** Large crown **Edge:** Plain

Date	Mintage	F	VF	XF	Unc	BU
1937 Proof	1	—	—	—	—	—

X# M18 CROWN
39.4000 g., 0.9167 Gold 1.1612 oz. AGW **Ruler:** Edward VIII **Obv:** Crowned bust left **Obv. Legend:** EDWARDVS VIII REX IMPERATOR **Rev:** Large crown **Edge:** Plain **Note:** Medal alignment.

Date	Mintage	F	VF	XF	Unc	BU
1937 Proof	1	—	—	—	—	—

MEDALLIC COINAGE
1954 Geoffrey Hearn Series

X# M1c CROWN
Gold **Obv:** Edward VIII **Note:** Restrikes known.

Date	Mintage	F	VF	XF	Unc	BU
1936 Proof	10	Value: 800				

X# M1d CROWN
Platinum APW **Obv:** Edward VIII

Date	Mintage	F	VF	XF	Unc	BU
1936 Proof	10	Value: 1,600				

MEDALLIC COINAGE
Richard Lobel Series

X# M4 SOVEREIGN
0.3750 Gold **Obv:** Edward VIII

Date	Mintage	F	VF	XF	Unc	BU
1936 Proof	250	Value: 125				

MEDALLIC COINAGE
1967 Andor Meszaros Series

X# M2a DOLLAR
56.0000 g., Gold **Edge:** Plain

Date	Mintage	F	VF	XF	Unc	BU
1967 Proof	10	Value: 1,450				

Note: 3 pieces remelted

BULLION - LUNAR YEAR

KM# 566 5 DOLLARS
1.5552 g., 0.9990 Gold 0.05 oz. AGW, 14.1 mm. **Ruler:** Elizabeth II **Subject:** Year of the Rat **Obv:** Crowned head right, denomination below **Rev:** Rat, right **Edge:** Reeded

Date	Mintage	F	VF	XF	Unc	BU
1996P	100,000	—	—	—	—	45.00

KM# 567 5 DOLLARS
1.5552 g., 0.9990 Gold 0.05 oz. AGW, 14.1 mm. **Ruler:** Elizabeth II **Subject:** Year of the Ox **Obv:** Crowned head right, denomination below **Rev:** Ox, left **Edge:** Reeded

Date	Mintage	F	VF	XF	Unc	BU
1997P	100,000	—	—	—	—	45.00

KM# 568 5 DOLLARS
1.5552 g., 0.9990 Gold 0.05 oz. AGW, 14.1 mm. **Ruler:** Elizabeth II **Subject:** Year of the Tiger **Obv:** Crowned head right, denomination below **Rev:** Tiger springing right **Edge:** Reeded

Date	Mintage	F	VF	XF	Unc	BU
1998P	100,000	—	—	—	—	45.00

KM# 425 5 DOLLARS
1.5710 g., 0.9999 Gold .0500 oz. AGW **Ruler:** Elizabeth II **Subject:** Year of the Rabbit **Obv:** Crowned head right, denomination below **Rev:** Rabbit **Note:** Similar to 100 Dollars, KM#428.

Date	Mintage	F	VF	XF	Unc	BU
1999	Est. 100,000	—	—	—	—	45.00

KM# 569 5 DOLLARS
1.5552 g., 0.9990 Gold 0.05 oz. AGW, 14.1 mm. **Ruler:** Elizabeth II **Subject:** Year of the Dragon **Obv:** Crowned head right, denomination below **Rev:** Dragon **Edge:** Reeded

Date	Mintage	F	VF	XF	Unc	BU
2000P	100,000	—	—	—	—	40.00

KM# 538 5 DOLLARS
1.5710 g., 0.9990 Gold .0500 oz. AGW, 14.1 mm. **Ruler:** Elizabeth II **Subject:** Year of the Snake **Obv:** Head with tiara right, denomination below **Rev:** Snake in tree **Edge:** Reeded

Date	Mintage	F	VF	XF	Unc	BU
2001	100,000	—	—	—	—	40.00
2001P Proof	100,000	Value: 50.00				

KM# 582 5 DOLLARS
1.5552 g., 0.9990 Gold 0.05 oz. AGW, 14.1 mm. **Ruler:** Elizabeth II **Subject:** Year of the Horse **Obv:** Head with tiara right, denomination below **Rev:** Horse galloping towards us **Edge:** Reeded

Date	Mintage	F	VF	XF	Unc	BU
2002P	100,000	—	—	—	—	50.00

KM# 668 5 DOLLARS
1.5710 g., 0.9999 Gold 0.0505 oz. AGW, 14.1 mm. **Ruler:** Elizabeth II **Subject:** Year of the Monkey **Obv:** Head with tiara right, denomination below **Obv. Designer:** Ian Rank-Broadley **Rev:** Monkey **Edge:** Reeded

Date	Mintage	F	VF	XF	Unc	BU
2004(2003)P Proof	100,000	Value: 50.00				

KM# 298 15 DOLLARS
3.1103 g., 0.9990 Gold .1000 oz. AGW **Ruler:** Elizabeth II **Subject:** Year of the Rat **Obv:** Crowned head right, denomination below **Rev:** Rat facing right

Date	Mintage	F	VF	XF	Unc	BU
1996	—	—	—	—	—	80.00
1996 Proof	—	Value: 75.00				

KM# 335 15 DOLLARS
3.1103 g., 0.9990 Gold .1000 oz. AGW **Ruler:** Elizabeth II **Subject:** Year of the Ox **Obv:** Crowned head right, denomination below **Rev:** Bull ox looking right

Date	Mintage	F	VF	XF	Unc	BU
1997	—	—	—	—	—	75.00
1997 Proof	—	Value: 95.00				

AUSTRALIA

KM# 506 15 DOLLARS
3.1103 g., 0.9990 Gold 0.0999 oz. AGW, 16.1 mm. **Ruler:** Elizabeth II **Subject:** Year of the Tiger **Obv:** Crowned head right, denomination below **Rev:** Tiger springing right **Edge:** Reeded

Date	Mintage	F	VF	XF	Unc	BU
1998	—	—	—	—	—	75.00
1998P	—	—	—	—	—	95.00

KM# 426 15 DOLLARS
3.1130 g., 0.9999 Gold .1000 oz. AGW **Ruler:** Elizabeth II **Subject:** Year of the Rabbit **Obv:** Crowned head right, denomination below **Rev:** Rabbit facing right **Note:** Similar to 100 Dollars, KM#428.

Date	Mintage	F	VF	XF	Unc	BU
1999	Est. 80,000	—	—	—	—	75.00
1999 Proof	—	Value: 95.00				

KM# 526 15 DOLLARS
3.1103 g., 0.9990 Gold .1000 oz. AGW, 16.1 mm. **Ruler:** Elizabeth II **Subject:** Year of the Dragon **Obv:** Crowned head right, denomination below **Rev:** Dragon **Edge:** Reeded

Date	Mintage	F	VF	XF	Unc	BU
2000	—	—	—	—	—	85.00
2000 Proof	—	Value: 100				

KM# 540 15 DOLLARS
3.1103 g., 0.9990 Gold .1000 oz. AGW, 16.1 mm. **Ruler:** Elizabeth II **Subject:** Year of the Snake **Obv:** Head with tiara right, denomination below **Rev:** Snake in tree **Edge:** Reeded

Date	Mintage	F	VF	XF	Unc	BU
2001	80,000	—	—	—	—	85.00
2001P Proof	7,000	Value: 100				

KM# 584 15 DOLLARS
3.1103 g., 0.9990 Gold 0.0999 oz. AGW, 16.1 mm. **Ruler:** Elizabeth II **Subject:** Year of the Horse **Obv:** Head with tiara right, denomination below **Rev:** Horse galloping left **Edge:** Reeded

Date	Mintage	F	VF	XF	Unc	BU
2002P	—	—	—	—	—	85.00
2002P Proof	7,000	Value: 100				

KM# 669 15 DOLLARS
3.1103 g., 0.9999 Gold 0.1 oz. AGW, 16.1 mm. **Ruler:** Elizabeth II **Subject:** Year of the Monkey **Obv:** Head with tiara right, denomination below **Rev:** Monkey **Edge:** Reeded

Date	Mintage	F	VF	XF	Unc	BU
2004P	—	—	—	—	—	85.00
2004(2003)P Proof	80,000	Value: 115				

KM# 711 15 DOLLARS
3.1100 g., 0.9999 Gold 0.1 oz. AGW **Ruler:** Elizabeth II **Subject:** Year of the Goat **Obv:** Head with tiara right, denomination below **Rev:** Goat

Date	Mintage	F	VF	XF	Unc	BU
2003	—	—	—	—	—	85.00
2003 Proof	—	Value: 100				

KM# 794 15 DOLLARS
3.1103 g., 0.9999 Gold 0.1 oz. AGW, 16.1 mm. **Ruler:** Elizabeth II **Subject:** Year of the Rooster **Obv:** Elizabeth II **Rev:** Standing Rooster right **Edge:** Reeded

Date	Mintage	F	VF	XF	Unc	BU
2005P Proof	7,000	Value: 75.00				

KM# 299 25 DOLLARS
7.7508 g., 0.9990 Gold .2500 oz. AGW **Ruler:** Elizabeth II **Subject:** Year of the Rat **Obv:** Crowned head right, denomination below **Rev:** Rat facing right

Date	Mintage	F	VF	XF	Unc	BU
1996	—	—	—	—	—	170
1996 Proof	—	Value: 225				

KM# 336 25 DOLLARS
7.7508 g., 0.9990 Gold .2500 oz. AGW **Ruler:** Elizabeth II **Subject:** Year of the Ox **Obv:** Crowned head right, denomination below **Rev:** Bull ox looking right

Date	Mintage	F	VF	XF	Unc	BU
1997	—	—	—	—	—	170
1997 Proof	8,888	Value: 225				

KM# 507 25 DOLLARS
7.7759 g., 0.9990 Gold .2498 oz. AGW, 20.1 mm. **Ruler:** Elizabeth II **Subject:** Year of the Tiger **Obv:** Crowned head right, denomination below **Rev:** Tiger springing right **Edge:** Reeded

Date	Mintage	F	VF	XF	Unc	BU
1998P	—	—	—	—	—	170
1998P Proof	—	Value: 225				

KM# 427 25 DOLLARS
7.8070 g., 0.9999 Gold .2510 oz. AGW **Ruler:** Elizabeth II **Subject:** Year of the Rabbit **Obv:** Crowned head right, denomination below **Rev:** Rabbit facing right **Edge:** Reeded

Date	Mintage	F	VF	XF	Unc	BU
1999	Est. 60,000	—	—	—	—	170
1999 Proof	—	Value: 200				

KM# 527 25 DOLLARS
7.7508 g., 0.9990 Gold .2500 oz. AGW, 20.1 mm. **Ruler:** Elizabeth II **Subject:** Year of the Dragon **Obv:** Crowned head right, denomination below **Rev:** Dragon **Edge:** Reeded

Date	Mintage	F	VF	XF	Unc	BU
2000	—	—	—	—	—	185
2000 Proof	—	Value: 225				

KM# 541 25 DOLLARS
7.7508 g., 0.9990 Gold .2500 oz. AGW, 20.1 mm. **Ruler:** Elizabeth II **Subject:** Year of the Snake **Obv:** Head with tiara right, denomination below **Rev:** Snake in tree **Edge:** Reeded

Date	Mintage	F	VF	XF	Unc	BU
2001	60,000	—	—	—	—	185
2001P Proof	7,000	Value: 225				

KM# 585 25 DOLLARS
7.7759 g., 0.9990 Gold 0.2498 oz. AGW, 20.1 mm. **Ruler:** Elizabeth II **Subject:** Year of the Horse **Obv:** Head with tiara right, denomination below **Rev:** Horse galloping half left **Edge:** Reeded

Date	Mintage	F	VF	XF	Unc	BU
2002P	—	—	—	—	—	185
2002P Proof	7,000	Value: 225				

KM# 670 25 DOLLARS
7.7508 g., 0.9999 Gold 0.2492 oz. AGW, 20.1 mm. **Ruler:** Elizabeth II **Subject:** Year of the Monkey **Obv:** Head with tiara right, denomination below **Rev:** Monkey **Edge:** Reeded

Date	Mintage	F	VF	XF	Unc	BU
2004P	—	—	—	—	—	190
2004(2003)P Proof	60,000	Value: 300				

KM# 712 25 DOLLARS
7.7500 g., 0.9999 Gold 0.2491 oz. AGW **Ruler:** Elizabeth II **Subject:** Year of the Goat **Obv:** Head with tiara right, denomination below **Rev:** Goat

Date	Mintage	F	VF	XF	Unc	BU
2003	—	—	—	—	—	185
2003 Proof	—	Value: 225				

KM# 795 25 DOLLARS
7.7759 g., 0.9999 Gold 0.25 oz. AGW, 20.1 mm. **Ruler:** Elizabeth II **Subject:** Year of the Rooster **Obv:** Elizabeth II **Rev:** Standing Rooster right **Edge:** Reeded

Date	Mintage	F	VF	XF	Unc	BU
2005P Proof	7,000	Value: 185				

KM# 671 50 DOLLARS
15.5940 g., 0.9999 Gold 0.5013 oz. AGW, 25.1 mm. **Ruler:** Elizabeth II **Subject:** Year of the Monkey **Obv:** Head with tiara right, denomination below **Rev:** Monkey **Edge:** Reeded

Date	Mintage	F	VF	XF	Unc	BU
2004(2003)P Proof	40,000	Value: 385				

KM# 300 100 DOLLARS
31.1035 g., 0.9990 Gold 1.0000 oz. AGW **Ruler:** Elizabeth II **Subject:** Year of the Rat **Obv:** Crowned head right, denomination below **Obv. Designer:** Raphael Maklouf **Rev:** Rat facing right, date at left

Date	Mintage	F	VF	XF	Unc	BU
1996	—	—	—	—	—	675
1996 Proof	—	Value: 725				

KM# 337 100 DOLLARS
31.1035 g., 0.9990 Gold 1.0000 oz. AGW **Ruler:** Elizabeth II **Subject:** Year of the Ox **Obv:** Crowned head right, denomination below **Obv. Designer:** Raphael Maklouf **Rev:** Ox left, looking right, date at left

Date	Mintage	F	VF	XF	Unc	BU
1997	—	—	—	—	—	675
1997 Proof	8,888	Value: 725				

KM# 508 100 DOLLARS
31.1035 g., 0.9990 Gold 0.999 oz. AGW, 32.1 mm. **Ruler:** Elizabeth II **Subject:** Year of the Tiger **Obv:** Crowned head right, denomination below **Rev:** Tiger springing right, date at left **Edge:** Reeded

Date	Mintage	F	VF	XF	Unc	BU
1998	—	—	—	—	—	675
1998P Proof	—	Value: 750				

KM# 428 100 DOLLARS
31.1620 g., 0.9999 Gold 1.0529 oz. AGW **Ruler:** Elizabeth II **Subject:** Year of the Rabbit **Obv:** Crowned head right, denomination below **Rev:** Seated rabbit left, date at left **Edge:** Reeded

Date	Mintage	F	VF	XF	Unc	BU
1999	Est. 30,000	—	—	—	—	675
1999 Proof	—	Value: 725				

KM# 528 100 DOLLARS
31.1035 g., 0.9990 Gold 1. oz. AGW, 32.1 mm. **Ruler:** Elizabeth II **Subject:** Year of the Dragon **Obv:** Crowned head right, denomination below **Rev:** Dragon **Edge:** Reeded

Date	Mintage	F	VF	XF	Unc	BU
2000	—	—	—	—	—	750
2000 Proof	—	Value: 800				

KM# 543 100 DOLLARS
31.1035 g., 0.9990 Gold 1. oz. AGW, 32.1 mm. **Ruler:** Elizabeth II **Subject:** Year of the Snake **Obv:** Head with tiara right, denomination below **Obv. Designer:** Ian Rank-Broadley **Rev:** Snake in tree **Edge:** Reeded

Date	Mintage	F	VF	XF	Unc	BU
2001	30,000	—	—	—	—	725
2001P Proof	—	Value: 825				

KM# 587 100 DOLLARS
31.1035 g., 0.9990 Gold 0.999 oz. AGW, 32.1 mm. **Ruler:** Elizabeth II **Subject:** Year of the Horse **Obv:** Head with tiara right, denomination below **Rev:** Horse running left **Edge:** Reeded

Date	Mintage	F	VF	XF	Unc	BU
2002	—	—	—	—	—	725
2002P Proof	—	Value: 800				

KM# 672 100 DOLLARS
31.1035 g., 0.9999 Gold 0.999 oz. AGW, 32.1 mm. **Ruler:** Elizabeth II **Subject:** Year of the Monkey **Obv:** Head with tiara right, denomination below **Rev:** Monkey **Edge:** Reeded

Date	Mintage	F	VF	XF	Unc	BU
2004	—	—	—	—	—	725
2004(2003)P Proof	30,000	Value: 800				

AUSTRALIA

KM# 713 100 DOLLARS
31.1035 g., 0.9999 Gold 0.9999 oz. AGW **Ruler:** Elizabeth II
Subject: Year of the Goat **Obv:** Head with tiara right, denomination below **Rev:** Goat

Date	Mintage	F	VF	XF	Unc	BU
2003	—	—	—	—	—	725
2003 Proof	—	Value: 800				

KM# 796 100 DOLLARS
31.1035 g., 0.9999 Gold 0.9999 oz. AGW, 32.1 mm. **Ruler:** Elizabeth II **Subject:** Year of the Rooster **Obv:** Elizabeth II **Rev:** Standing Rooster right **Edge:** Reeded

Date	Mintage	F	VF	XF	Unc	BU
2005P Proof	3,000	Value: 600				

KM# 667 200 DOLLARS
62.2140 g., 0.9990 Gold 1.9982 oz. AGW, 40.6 mm. **Ruler:** Elizabeth II **Subject:** Year of the Dragon **Obv:** Crowned head right, denomination below **Rev:** Dragon **Edge:** Reeded

Date	Mintage	F	VF	XF	Unc	BU
2000	—	—	—	—	—	1,350

KM# 704 200 DOLLARS
62.2140 g., 0.9990 Gold 2 oz. AGW **Ruler:** Elizabeth II **Subject:** Year of the Snake **Obv:** Head with tiara right, denomination below **Rev:** Snake

Date	Mintage	F	VF	XF	Unc	BU
2001 Proof	—	Value: 1,500				

KM# 707 200 DOLLARS
62.2140 g., 0.9990 Gold 2 oz. AGW **Ruler:** Elizabeth II **Subject:** Year of the Horse **Rev:** Horse

Date	Mintage	F	VF	XF	Unc	BU
2002 Proof	—	Value: 1,500				

KM# 714 200 DOLLARS
62.2140 g., 0.9990 Gold 2 oz. AGW **Ruler:** Elizabeth II **Subject:** Year of the Goat **Obv:** Head with tiara right, denomination below **Rev:** Goat

Date	Mintage	F	VF	XF	Unc	BU
2003 Proof	—	Value: 1,500				

KM# 717 200 DOLLARS
62.2100 g., 0.9990 Gold 1.9999 oz. AGW **Ruler:** Elizabeth II **Subject:** Year of the Monkey **Obv:** Head with tiara right, denomination below **Rev:** Monkey

Date	Mintage	F	VF	XF	Unc	BU
2004 Proof	—	Value: 1,500				

KM# 698 200 DOLLARS
62.2100 g., 0.9999 Gold 1.9999 oz. AGW **Ruler:** Elizabeth II **Subject:** Year of the Rooster **Obv:** Head with tiara right, denomination below **Rev:** Rooster

Date	Mintage	F	VF	XF	Unc	BU
2005 Proof	—	Value: 1,500				

KM# 702 1000 DOLLARS
311.0480 g., 0.9999 Gold 10.0000 oz. AGW **Ruler:** Elizabeth II **Subject:** Year of the Dragon **Obv:** Crowned head right, denomination below **Rev:** Dragon

Date	Mintage	F	VF	XF	Unc	BU
2000	—	—	—	—	—	7,500

KM# 705 1000 DOLLARS
311.0480 g., 0.9999 Gold 9.9994 oz. AGW **Ruler:** Elizabeth II **Subject:** Year of the Snake **Obv:** Head with tiara right, denomination below **Rev:** Snake

Date	Mintage	F	VF	XF	Unc	BU
2001	—	—	—	—	—	7,500

KM# 708 1000 DOLLARS
311.0480 g., 0.9999 Gold 9.9994 oz. AGW **Ruler:** Elizabeth II **Subject:** Year of the Horse **Obv:** Head with tiara right, denomination below **Rev:** Horse

Date	Mintage	F	VF	XF	Unc	BU
2002	—	—	—	—	—	7,500

KM# 715 1000 DOLLARS
311.0480 g., 0.9999 Gold 9.9994 oz. AGW **Ruler:** Elizabeth II **Subject:** Year of the Goat **Obv:** Head with tiara right, denomination below **Rev:** Goat

Date	Mintage	F	VF	XF	Unc	BU
2003	—	—	—	—	—	7,500

KM# 718 1000 DOLLARS
311.0480 g., 0.9999 Gold 9.9994 oz. AGW **Ruler:** Elizabeth II **Subject:** Year of the Monkey **Obv:** Head with tiara right, denomination below **Rev:** Monkey

Date	Mintage	F	VF	XF	Unc	BU
2004	—	—	—	—	—	7,500

KM# 699 1000 DOLLARS
311.0480 g., 0.9999 Gold 9.9994 oz. AGW **Ruler:** Elizabeth II **Subject:** Year of the Rooster **Obv:** Head with tiara right, denomination below **Rev:** Rooster

Date	Mintage	F	VF	XF	Unc	BU
2005	—	—	—	—	—	7,500

KM# 703 3000 DOLLARS
1000.0000 g., 0.9999 Gold 32.1475 oz. AGW **Ruler:** Elizabeth II **Subject:** Year of the Dragon **Obv:** Crowned head right, denomination below **Rev:** Dragon

Date	Mintage	F	VF	XF	Unc	BU
2000	—	—	—	—	—BV+10%	—

KM# 706 3000 DOLLARS
1000.0000 g., 0.9999 Gold 32.1475 oz. AGW **Ruler:** Elizabeth II **Subject:** Year of the Snake **Obv:** Head with tiara right, denomination below **Rev:** Snake

Date	Mintage	F	VF	XF	Unc	BU
2001	—	—	—	—	—BV+10%	—

KM# 709 3000 DOLLARS
1000.0000 g., 0.9999 Gold 32.1475 oz. AGW **Ruler:** Elizabeth II **Subject:** Year of the Horse **Obv:** Head with tiara right, denomination below **Rev:** Horse

Date	Mintage	F	VF	XF	Unc	BU
2002	—	—	—	—	—BV+10%	—

KM# 716 3000 DOLLARS
1000.0000 g., 0.9999 Gold 32.1475 oz. AGW **Ruler:** Elizabeth II **Subject:** Year of the Goat **Obv:** Head with tiara right, denomination below **Rev:** Goat

Date	Mintage	F	VF	XF	Unc	BU
2003	—	—	—	—	—BV+10%	—

KM# 719 3000 DOLLARS
1000.0000 g., 0.9999 Gold 32.1475 oz. AGW **Ruler:** Elizabeth II **Subject:** Year of the Monkey **Obv:** Head with tiara right, denomination below **Rev:** Monkey

Date	Mintage	F	VF	XF	Unc	BU
2004	—	—	—	—	—BV+10%	—

KM# 700 3000 DOLLARS
1000.0000 g., 0.9999 Gold 32.1475 oz. AGW **Ruler:** Elizabeth II **Subject:** Year of the Rooster **Obv:** Head with tiara right, denomination below **Rev:** Rooster

Date	Mintage	F	VF	XF	Unc	BU
2005	—	—	—	—	—BV+10%	—

GOLD BULLION - KANGAROO

KM# 117 5 DOLLARS
1.5710 g., 0.9990 Gold .0500 oz. AGW **Ruler:** Elizabeth II **Subject:** Red Kangaroo **Obv:** Crowned head right, denomination below **Rev:** Kangaroo leaping left, date below **Rev. Designer:** Stuart Devlin

Date	Mintage	F	VF	XF	Unc	BU
1989 Proof	2,200	Value: 50.00				
1990	Est. 200,000					

KM# 140 5 DOLLARS
1.5710 g., 0.9990 Gold .0500 oz. AGW **Ruler:** Elizabeth II **Obv:** Crowned head right, denomination below **Rev:** Gray Kangaroo right, date below **Rev. Designer:** Stuart Devlin

Date	Mintage	F	VF	XF	Unc	BU
1990 Proof	7,000	Value: 50.00				
1991	200,000	—	—	—	—BV+35%	—

KM# 389 5 DOLLARS
1.5710 g., 0.9990 Gold .0500 oz. AGW **Ruler:** Elizabeth II **Obv:** Crowned head right, denomination below **Rev:** Nail-tailed Wallaby

Date	Mintage	F	VF	XF	Unc	BU
1992 (ae) Proof	500	Value: 60.00				

KM# 165 5 DOLLARS
1.5710 g., 0.9990 Gold .0500 oz. AGW **Ruler:** Elizabeth II **Subject:** Common Wallaroo **Obv:** Crowned head right, denomination below **Rev:** Kangaroo bounding left, date below **Note:** 1992 (ae) previously listed here is now KM#389.

Date	Mintage	F	VF	XF	Unc	BU
1992	200,000	—	—	—	BV+35%	—

KM# 233 5 DOLLARS
1.5710 g., 0.9990 Gold .0500 oz. AGW **Ruler:** Elizabeth II **Obv:** Crowned head right, denomination below **Rev:** Whiptail Wallaby

Date	Mintage	F	VF	XF	Unc	BU
1993 Proof	—	Value: 55.00				
1994	—	—	—	—	BV+35%	—

KM# 241 5 DOLLARS
1.5710 g., 0.9990 Gold .0500 oz. AGW **Ruler:** Elizabeth II **Obv. Legend:** Crowned head right, denomination below **Rev:** Red Kangaroo facing front, date below **Rev. Designer:** Stuart Devlin

Date	Mintage	F	VF	XF	Unc	BU
1995	200,000	—	—	—	—BV+35%	—

KM# 272 5 DOLLARS
1.5710 g., 0.9990 Gold .0500 oz. AGW **Ruler:** Elizabeth II **Obv:** Crowned head right, denomination below **Rev:** Two kangaroos standing, date below **Rev. Designer:** Stuart Devlin

Date	Mintage	F	VF	XF	Unc	BU
1995 Proof	300	Value: 55.00				
1996	200,000	—	—	—	—BV+35%	—

KM# 320 5 DOLLARS
1.5710 g., 0.9990 Gold .0500 oz. AGW **Ruler:** Elizabeth II **Obv:** Crowned head right, denomination below **Rev:** Kangaroo bounding right

Date	Mintage	F	VF	XF	Unc	BU
1996P Proof	—	Value: 60.00				

Note: In proof sets only

KM# 338 5 DOLLARS
1.5710 g., 0.9990 Gold .0500 oz. AGW **Ruler:** Elizabeth II **Obv:** Crowned head right, denomination below **Rev:** Kangaroo bounding right

Date	Mintage	F	VF	XF	Unc	BU
1997	200,000	—	—	—	BV+35%	—
1997 Proof	—	Value: 50.00				

KM# 448 5 DOLLARS
1.5710 g., 0.9990 Gold .0505 oz. AGW **Ruler:** Elizabeth II **Obv:** Crowned head right, denomination below **Rev:** Kangaroo facing left **Edge:** Reeded

Date	Mintage	F	VF	XF	Unc	BU
1999	200,000	—	—	—	—	50.00

KM# 464 5 DOLLARS
1.5710 g., 0.9990 Gold .0505 oz. AGW **Ruler:** Elizabeth II **Obv:** Crowned head right, denomination below **Rev:** Two kangaroos bounding left

Date	Mintage	F	VF	XF	Unc	BU
2000	—	—	—	—	—	50.00

KM# 118 15 DOLLARS
3.1103 g., 0.9990 Gold .1000 oz. AGW **Ruler:** Elizabeth II **Obv:** Crowned head right, denomination below **Rev:** Red kangaroo leaping left, date below **Rev. Designer:** Stuart Devlin

Date	Mintage	F	VF	XF	Unc	BU
1989 Proof	2,200	Value: 80.00				
1990	200,000	—	—	—	—BV+12%	—

KM# 141 15 DOLLARS
3.1103 g., 0.9990 Gold .1000 oz. AGW **Ruler:** Elizabeth II **Obv:** Crowned head right, denomination below **Rev:** Gray kangaroo standing facing left, date below **Rev. Designer:** Stuart Devlin

Date	Mintage	F	VF	XF	Unc	BU
1990 Proof	7,000	Value: 80.00				
1991	150,000	—	—	—	—BV+12%	—

KM# 166 15 DOLLARS
3.1103 g., 0.9990 Gold .1000 oz. AGW **Ruler:** Elizabeth II **Subject:** Common Wallaroo **Obv:** Crowned head right, denomination below **Rev:** Radiant common walleroo facing right

Date	Mintage	F	VF	XF	Unc	BU
1991 Proof	1,975	Value: 80.00				
1992	150,000	—	—	—	—BV+12%	—

KM# 390 15 DOLLARS
3.1103 g., 0.9990 Gold .1000 oz. AGW **Ruler:** Elizabeth II **Obv:** Crowned head right, denomination below **Rev:** Nail-tailed wallaby

Date	Mintage	F	VF	XF	Unc	BU
1992 (ae) Proof	500	Value: 110				

KM# 234 15 DOLLARS
3.1103 g., 0.9990 Gold .1000 oz. AGW **Ruler:** Elizabeth II **Obv:** Crowned head right, denomination below **Rev:** Whiptail wallaby

Date	Mintage	F	VF	XF	Unc	BU
1993 Proof	—	Value: 85.00				
1994	—	—	—	—	—BV+12%	—

AUSTRALIA 33

KM# 242 15 DOLLARS
3.1103 g., 0.9990 Gold .1000 oz. AGW **Ruler:** Elizabeth II **Obv:** Crowned head right, denomination below **Rev:** Red kangaroo standing facing forward, date below **Rev. Designer:** Stuart Devlin

Date	Mintage	F	VF	XF	Unc	BU
1994 Proof	—	Value: 85.00				
1995	200,000	—	—	—	BV+12%	—

KM# 273 15 DOLLARS
3.1103 g., 0.9990 Gold .1000 oz. AGW **Ruler:** Elizabeth II **Obv:** Crowned head right, denomination below **Rev:** Two kangaroos, date below **Rev. Designer:** Stuart Devlin

Date	Mintage	F	VF	XF	Unc	BU
1995 Proof	900	Value: 85.00				
1996	200,000	—	—	—	BV+12%	—

KM# 321 15 DOLLARS
3.1103 g., 0.9990 Gold .1000 oz. AGW **Ruler:** Elizabeth II **Obv:** Crowned head right, denomination below **Rev:** Kangaroo bounding right

Date	Mintage	F	VF	XF	Unc	BU
1996P Proof	400	Value: 200				

Note: In Proof sets only

KM# 339 15 DOLLARS
3.1103 g., 0.9990 Gold .1000 oz. AGW **Ruler:** Elizabeth II **Obv:** Crowned head right, denomination below **Rev:** Kangaroo bounding right

Date	Mintage	F	VF	XF	Unc	BU
1997	200,000	—	—	—	70.00	—
1997 Proof	—	Value: 80.00				

KM# 449 15 DOLLARS
3.1330 g., 0.9990 Gold .1000 oz. AGW **Ruler:** Elizabeth II **Obv:** Crowned head right, denomination below **Rev:** Kangaroo facing left **Edge:** Reeded

Date	Mintage	F	VF	XF	Unc	BU
1999	200,000	—	—	—	70.00	—

KM# 465 15 DOLLARS
3.1330 g., 0.9990 Gold .1000 oz. AGW **Ruler:** Elizabeth II **Obv:** Crowned head right, denomination below **Rev:** Two kangaroos bounding left **Edge:** Reeded

Date	Mintage	F	VF	XF	Unc	BU
2000	—	—	—	—	70.00	—

KM# 119 25 DOLLARS
7.7508 g., 0.9990 Gold .2500 oz. AGW **Ruler:** Elizabeth II **Obv:** Crowned head right, denomination below **Rev:** Red kangaroo **Rev. Designer:** Stuart Devlin

Date	Mintage	F	VF	XF	Unc	BU
1989 Proof	2,200	Value: 185				
1990	Est. 200,000	—	—	—	BV+10%	—

KM# 142 25 DOLLARS
7.7508 g., 0.9990 Gold .2500 oz. AGW **Ruler:** Elizabeth II **Obv:** Crowned head right, denomination below **Rev:** Gray kangaroo standing right, date below **Rev. Designer:** Stuart Devlin

Date	Mintage	F	VF	XF	Unc	BU
1990 Proof	7,000	Value: 185				
1991	100,000	—	—	—	BV+10%	—

KM# 167 25 DOLLARS
7.7508 g., 0.9990 Gold .2500 oz. AGW **Ruler:** Elizabeth II **Subject:** Common Wallaroo **Obv:** Crowned head right, denomination below **Rev:** Radiant walleroo facing right

Date	Mintage	F	VF	XF	Unc	BU
1991 Proof	1,991	Value: 185				
1992	100,000	—	—	—	BV+10%	—

KM# 391 25 DOLLARS
7.7508 g., 0.9990 Gold .2500 oz. AGW **Ruler:** Elizabeth II **Obv:** Crowned head right, denomination below **Obv. Designer:** Raphael Maklouf **Rev:** Nail-tailed wallaby standing right, date below **Rev. Designer:** Stuart Devlin

Date	Mintage	F	VF	XF	Unc	BU
1992 (ae) Proof	500	Value: 225				

KM# 235 25 DOLLARS
7.7508 g., 0.9990 Gold .2500 oz. AGW **Ruler:** Elizabeth II **Obv:** Crowned head right, denomination below **Rev:** Whiptail wallaby

Date	Mintage	F	VF	XF	Unc	BU
1993 Proof	—	Value: 190				
1993 (f) Proof	200	—	—	—	—	—
1994	—	—	—	—	BV+10%	—

KM# 243 25 DOLLARS
7.7508 g., 0.9990 Gold .2500 oz. AGW **Ruler:** Elizabeth II **Obv:** Crowned head right, denomination below **Rev:** Red kangaroo standing facing, date below **Rev. Designer:** Stuart Devlin

Date	Mintage	F	VF	XF	Unc	BU
1994 Proof	—	Value: 190				
1995	150,000	—	—	—	BV+10%	—

KM# 274 25 DOLLARS
7.7508 g., 0.9990 Gold .2500 oz. AGW **Ruler:** Elizabeth II **Obv:** Crowned head right, denomination below **Rev:** Two kangaroos, date below **Rev. Designer:** Stuart Devlin

Date	Mintage	F	VF	XF	Unc	BU
1995 Proof	650	Value: 190				
1996	150,000	—	—	—	BV+10%	—

KM# 322 25 DOLLARS
7.7508 g., 0.9990 Gold .2500 oz. AGW **Ruler:** Elizabeth II **Obv:** Crowned head right, denomination below **Rev:** Kangaroo bounding right

Date	Mintage	F	VF	XF	Unc	BU
1996(p) Proof	400	Value: 350				

Note: In sets only

KM# 340 25 DOLLARS
7.7508 g., 0.9990 Gold .2500 oz. AGW **Ruler:** Elizabeth II **Obv:** Crowned head right, denomination below **Rev:** Kangaroo bounding right

Date	Mintage	F	VF	XF	Unc	BU
1997	200,000	—	—	—	BV+10%	—
1997 Proof	—	Value: 190				

KM# 450 25 DOLLARS
7.8070 g., 0.9990 Gold .2500 oz. AGW **Ruler:** Elizabeth II **Obv:** Crowned head right, denomination below **Rev:** Kangaroo facing left **Edge:** Reeded

Date	Mintage	F	VF	XF	Unc	BU
1999	150,000	—	—	—	BV+10%	—

KM# 466 25 DOLLARS
7.8070 g., 0.9990 Gold .2500 oz. AGW **Ruler:** Elizabeth II **Obv:** Crowned head right, denomination below **Rev:** Two kangaroos bounding left **Edge:** Reeded

Date	Mintage	F	VF	XF	Unc	BU
2000	—	—	—	—	BV+10%	—

KM# 120 50 DOLLARS
15.5017 g., 0.9990 Gold .5000 oz. AGW **Ruler:** Elizabeth II **Obv:** Crowned head right, denomination below **Rev:** Red kangaroo leaping left, date below **Rev. Designer:** Stuart Devlin

Date	Mintage	F	VF	XF	Unc	BU
1989 Proof	2,200	Value: 350				
1990	Est. 240,000	—	—	—	BV+7%	—

KM# 143 50 DOLLARS
15.5017 g., 0.9990 Gold .5000 oz. AGW **Ruler:** Elizabeth II **Obv:** Crowned head right, denomination below **Rev:** Gray kangaroo facing right looking left, date below **Rev. Designer:** Stuart Devlin

Date	Mintage	F	VF	XF	Unc	BU
1990 Proof	5,000	Value: 350				
1991	100,000	—	—	—	BV+7%	—

KM# 168 50 DOLLARS
15.5017 g., 0.9990 Gold .5000 oz. AGW **Ruler:** Elizabeth II **Subject:** Common wallaroo **Obv:** Crowned head right, denomination below **Rev:** Radiant common wallaroo facing right

Date	Mintage	F	VF	XF	Unc	BU
1991 Proof	1,096	Value: 365				
1992	100,000	—	—	—	BV+7%	—

KM# 392 50 DOLLARS
15.5017 g., 0.9990 Gold .5000 oz. AGW **Ruler:** Elizabeth II **Obv:** Crowned head right, denomination below **Rev:** Nail-tailed wallaby

Date	Mintage	F	VF	XF	Unc	BU
1992 (ae) Proof	500	Value: 500				

KM# 236 50 DOLLARS
15.5017 g., 0.9990 Gold .5000 oz. AGW **Ruler:** Elizabeth II **Obv:** Crowned head right, denomination below **Rev:** Whiptail wallaby

Date	Mintage	F	VF	XF	Unc	BU
1993 Proof	—	Value: 380				
1994	—	—	—	—	BV+7%	—

KM# 244 50 DOLLARS
15.5017 g., 0.9990 Gold .5000 oz. AGW **Ruler:** Elizabeth II **Obv:** Crowned head right, denomination below **Rev:** Red kangaroo standing facing front, date below **Rev. Designer:** Stuart Devlin

Date	Mintage	F	VF	XF	Unc	BU
1994 Proof	—	Value: 380				
1995	30,000	—	—	—	BV+10%	—
1995 (f) Proof	10,000	Value: 350				

KM# 275.1 50 DOLLARS
15.5017 g., 0.9990 Gold .5000 oz. AGW **Ruler:** Elizabeth II **Obv:** Crowned head right, denomination below **Rev:** Two kangaroos, date below **Rev. Designer:** Stuart Devlin

Date	Mintage	F	VF	XF	Unc	BU
1995 Proof	300	Value: 380				
1996	100,000	—	—	—	BV+7%	—
1996 (s) Proof	13,000	Value: 350				
1996 (I) Proof	3,000	Value: 350				

Note: In Proof sets only

| 1996 (f) Proof | 13,000 | Value: 350 | | | | |

KM# 275.2 50 DOLLARS
15.5017 g., 0.9990 Gold .5000 oz. AGW **Ruler:** Elizabeth II **Obv:** Crowned head right, denomination below **Rev:** Two kangaroos, date below **Edge:** Reeded and inscribed with date and serial number

Date	Mintage	F	VF	XF	Unc	BU
1996 Proof	500	Value: 360				

34 AUSTRALIA

KM# 341 50 DOLLARS
15.5017 g., 0.9990 Gold .5000 oz. AGW **Ruler:** Elizabeth II
Obv: Crowned head right, denomination below **Rev:** Kangaroo bounding right

Date	Mintage	F	VF	XF	Unc	BU
1996 (p) Proof	400	Value: 600				
Note: In Proof sets only						
1997	100,000	—	—	—	—	340
1997 Proof	—	Value: 350				
1997 (f) Proof	13,000	Value: 350				
1997 (I) Proof	10,000	Value: 350				
Note: In Proof sets only						
1997 (s) Proof	13,000	Value: 350				

KM# 451 50 DOLLARS
15.5940 g., 0.9990 Gold .5000 oz. AGW **Ruler:** Elizabeth II
Obv: Crowned head right, denomination below **Rev:** Kangaroo facing left **Edge:** Reeded

Date	Mintage	F	VF	XF	Unc	BU
1999	100,000	—	—	—	—	340

KM# 467 50 DOLLARS
15.5940 g., 0.9990 Gold .5000 oz. AGW **Obv:** Crowned head right, denomination below **Rev:** Two kangaroos bounding left **Edge:** Reeded

Date	Mintage	F	VF	XF	Unc	BU
2000	—	—	—	—	—	340

KM# 692 50 DOLLARS
15.5540 g., 0.9999 Gold 0.5 oz. AGW, 25.1 mm. **Ruler:** Elizabeth II **Obv:** Head with tiara right, denomination below **Obv. Designer:** Ian Rank-Broadley **Rev:** Two kangaroos on map above silver Liberty Bell insert **Edge:** Reeded

Date	Mintage	F	VF	XF	Unc	BU
2002	—	—	—	—	—	400

KM# 121 100 DOLLARS
31.1035 g., 0.9990 Gold 1.0000 oz. AGW **Ruler:** Elizabeth II
Obv: Crowned head right, denomination below **Rev:** Red kangaroo bounding left, date below **Rev. Designer:** Stuart Devlin

Date	Mintage	F	VF	XF	Unc	BU
1989 Proof	2,200	Value: 690				
1990	—	—	—	—	BV+4%	—

KM# 144 100 DOLLARS
31.1035 g., 0.9990 Gold 1.0000 oz. AGW **Ruler:** Elizabeth II **Obv. Designer:** Raphael Maklouf **Rev:** Gray kangaroo standing looking left, date below **Rev. Designer:** Stuart Devlin

Date	Mintage	F	VF	XF	Unc	BU
1990 Proof	8,000	Value: 690				
1991	250,000	—	—	—	BV+4%	—

KM# 169 100 DOLLARS
31.1035 g., 0.9990 Gold 1.0000 oz. AGW **Ruler:** Elizabeth II **Obv:** Crowned head right, denomination below **Rev:** Common wallaroo on all fours facing right, date below **Rev. Designer:** Stuart Devlin

Date	Mintage	F	VF	XF	Unc	BU
1991 Proof	3,000	Value: 690				
1992	250,000	—	—	—	BV+4%	—

KM# 393 100 DOLLARS
31.1035 g., 0.9990 Gold 1.0000 oz. AGW **Ruler:** Elizabeth II **Obv:** Crowned head right, denomination below **Rev:** Nail-tailed wallaby

Date	Mintage	F	VF	XF	Unc	BU
1992 Proof	784	Value: 690				
1993	—	—	—	—	BV+4%	—

KM# 237 100 DOLLARS
31.1035 g., 0.9990 Gold 1.0000 oz. AGW **Ruler:** Elizabeth II **Obv:** Crowned head right, denomination below **Rev:** Whiptail wallaby

Date	Mintage	F	VF	XF	Unc	BU
1993 Proof	—	Value: 700				
1993 (f) Proof	150	Value: 750				
1994	—	—	—	—	BV+4%	—

KM# 245 100 DOLLARS
31.1035 g., 0.9990 Gold 1.0000 oz. AGW **Ruler:** Elizabeth II **Obv:** Crowned head right, denomination below **Obv. Designer:** Raphael Maklouf **Rev:** Red kangaroo facing forward, date below **Rev. Designer:** Stuart Devlin

Date	Mintage	F	VF	XF	Unc	BU
1994 Proof	—	Value: 690				
1995	350,000	—	—	—	BV+4%	—

X# B5 100 DOLLARS
Gilt Copper **Issuer:** Monex Deposit Company **Rev:** Kangaroo left **Rev. Legend:** THE AUSTRALIAN NUGGET **Note:** Uniface. Salesman's sample.

Date	Mintage	F	VF	XF	Unc	BU
1994(L)	—	—	—	—	6.00	—

KM# 276 100 DOLLARS
31.1035 g., 0.9990 Gold 1.0000 oz. AGW **Ruler:** Elizabeth II **Obv:** Crowned head right, denomination below **Obv. Designer:** Raphael Maklouf **Rev:** Two kangaroos **Rev. Designer:** Stuart Devlin

Date	Mintage	F	VF	XF	Unc	BU
1995 Proof	300	Value: 725				
1995 (ww) Proof	600	Value: 700				
1996	350,000	—	—	—	BV+4%	—

KM# 342 100 DOLLARS
31.1035 g., 0.9990 Gold 1.0000 oz. AGW **Ruler:** Elizabeth II **Obv:** Crowned head right, denomination below **Rev:** Kangaroo bounding right

Date	Mintage	F	VF	XF	Unc	BU
1996 (p) Proof	—	Value: 695				
Note: In Proof sets only						
1997	350,000	—	—	—	BV+4%	—
1997 Proof	—	Value: 690				

KM# 452 100 DOLLARS
31.1620 g., 0.9990 Gold 1.0000 oz. AGW **Ruler:** Elizabeth II **Obv:** Crowned head right, denomination below **Rev:** Kangaroo facing left **Edge:** Reeded

Date	Mintage	F	VF	XF	Unc	BU
1999	350,000	—	—	—	BV+4%	—

KM# 468 100 DOLLARS
31.1620 g., 0.9990 Gold 1.0000 oz. AGW **Ruler:** Elizabeth II **Obv:** Crowned head right, denomination below **Rev:** Two kangaroos bounding left, date below **Edge:** Reeded

Date	Mintage	F	VF	XF	Unc	BU
2000	—	—	—	—	BV+4%	—

KM# 693 100 DOLLARS
31.1070 g., 0.9999 Gold 1 oz. AGW, 32.1 mm. **Ruler:** Elizabeth II **Obv:** Head with tiara right, denomination below **Obv. Designer:** Ian Rank-Broadley **Rev:** Two kangaroos on map above silver Liberty Bell insert **Edge:** Reeded

Date	Mintage	F	VF	XF	Unc	BU
2002	—	—	—	—	—	750

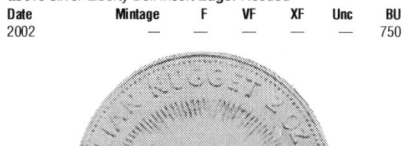

KM# 182 200 DOLLARS
62.2140 g., 0.9990 Gold 2.0000 oz. AGW **Ruler:** Elizabeth II **Obv:** Crowned head right, denomination below **Rev:** Red kangaroo leaping left, date below **Rev. Designer:** Stuart Devlin

Date	Mintage	F	VF	XF	Unc	BU
1992	—	—	—	—	BV+4%	—
1994 Prooflike	—	—	—	—	BV+4%	—
1995	—	—	—	—	BV+4%	—
1996	—	—	—	—	BV+4%	—
1997	—	—	—	—	BV+4%	—

KM# 394 200 DOLLARS
62.2140 g., 0.9990 Gold 2.0000 oz. AGW **Ruler:** Elizabeth II **Obv:** Crowned head right, denomination below **Rev:** Nail-tailed wallaby

Date	Mintage	F	VF	XF	Unc	BU
1992 Proof	152	Value: 1,450				

KM# 238 200 DOLLARS
62.2140 g., 0.9999 Gold 2.0000 oz. AGW **Ruler:** Elizabeth II **Obv:** Crowned head right, denomination below **Rev:** Whiptail wallaby

Date	Mintage	F	VF	XF	Unc	BU
1993 Proof	—	Value: 1,650				

KM# 246 200 DOLLARS
62.2140 g., 0.9999 Gold 2.0000 oz. AGW **Ruler:** Elizabeth II **Obv:** Crowned head right, denomination below **Rev:** Red kangaroo

Date	Mintage	F	VF	XF	Unc	BU
1994 Proof	325	Value: 1,700				

AUSTRALIA 35

KM# 277 200 DOLLARS
62.2140 g., 0.9999 Gold 2.0000 oz. AGW **Ruler:** Elizabeth II **Obv:** Crowned head right, denomination below **Rev:** Two kangaroos, date below **Rev. Designer:** Stuart Devlin

Date	Mintage	F	VF	XF	Unc	BU
1995 Proof	100	Value: 1,800				

KM# 150 500 DOLLARS
62.2140 g., 0.9990 Gold 2.0000 oz. AGW **Ruler:** Elizabeth II **Obv:** Crowned head right, denomination below **Rev:** Red kangaroo facing left

Date	Mintage	F	VF	XF	Unc	BU
1991	—	—	—	—	BV+4%	—
1991 Proof	491	Value: 1,650				

KM# 395 1000 DOLLARS
311.0670 g., 0.9990 Gold 10.0000 oz. AGW **Ruler:** Elizabeth II **Obv:** Crowned head right, denomination below **Rev:** Nail-tailed wallaby

Date	Mintage	F	VF	XF	Unc	BU
1992 Proof	40	Value: 8,000				

KM# 239 1000 DOLLARS
311.0670 g., 0.9999 Gold 10.0000 oz. AGW **Ruler:** Elizabeth II **Obv:** Crowned head right, denomination below **Rev:** Red kangaroo

Date	Mintage	F	VF	XF	Unc	BU
1993 Proof	—	Value: 7,500				

KM# 247 1000 DOLLARS
311.0670 g., 0.9999 Gold 10.0000 oz. AGW **Ruler:** Elizabeth II **Obv:** Crowned head right, denomination below **Rev:** Kangaroo in diamond shape

Date	Mintage	F	VF	XF	Unc	BU
1994 Proof	—	Value: 7,500				

KM# 183 1000 DOLLARS
311.0670 g., 0.9999 Gold 10.0000 oz. AGW **Ruler:** Elizabeth II **Obv:** Crowned head right, denomination below **Rev:** Red kangaroo

Date	Mintage	F	VF	XF	Unc	BU
1995	—	—	—	—	BV+3%	—
1996	—	—	—	—	BV+3%	—
1997	—	—	—	—	BV+3%	—

KM# 454 1000 DOLLARS
311.3170 g., 0.9990 Gold 10.0000 oz. AGW **Ruler:** Elizabeth II **Obv:** Crowned head right, denomination below **Rev:** Red kangaroo bounding left **Edge:** Reeded

Date	Mintage	F	VF	XF	Unc	BU
1999	—	—	—	—	7,000	—

KM# 151 2500 DOLLARS
311.0670 g., 0.9990 Gold 10.0000 oz. AGW **Ruler:** Elizabeth II **Obv:** Crowned head right, denomination below **Rev:** Red kangaroo

Date	Mintage	F	VF	XF	Unc	BU
1991	—	—	—	—	BV+3%	—
1991 Proof	124	Value: 7,500				

KM# 184 3000 DOLLARS
1000.1000 g., 0.9999 Gold 32.1575 oz. AGW **Ruler:** Elizabeth II **Obv:** Crowned head right, denomination below **Rev:** Red kangaroo

Date	Mintage	F	VF	XF	Unc	BU
1992	—	—	—	—	BV+3%	—
1992 Proof	25	Value: 24,500				
1995	—	—	—	—	BV+4%	—
1996	—	—	—	—	BV+3%	—
1997	—	—	—	—	BV+3%	—

KM# 396 3000 DOLLARS
1000.1000 g., 0.9999 Platinum 32.1575 oz. APW **Ruler:** Elizabeth II **Obv:** Crowned head right, denomination below **Rev:** Nail-tailed wallaby

Date	Mintage	F	VF	XF	Unc	BU
1992 Proof	25	Value: 42,500				

KM# 240 3000 DOLLARS
1000.1000 g., 0.9999 Gold 32.1575 oz. AGW **Ruler:** Elizabeth II **Obv:** Crowned head right, denomination below **Rev:** Whiptail wallaby **Rev. Designer:** Stuart Devlin

Date	Mintage	F	VF	XF	Unc	BU
1993 Proof	—	Value: 22,500				

KM# 248 3000 DOLLARS
1000.1000 g., 0.9999 Gold 32.1575 oz. AGW **Ruler:** Elizabeth II **Obv:** Crowned head right, denomination below **Rev:** Kangaroo in diamond shape **Rev. Designer:** Stuart Devlin

Date	Mintage	F	VF	XF	Unc	BU
1994 Proof	—	Value: 22,500				

KM# 455 3000 DOLLARS
1000.3500 g., 0.9990 Gold 32.1588 oz. AGW **Ruler:** Elizabeth II **Obv:** Crowned head right, denomination below **Rev:** Red kangaroo bounding left **Rev. Designer:** Stuart Devlin **Edge:** Reeded

Date	Mintage	F	VF	XF	Unc	BU
1999	—	—	—	—	21,500	—

KM# 152 10000 DOLLARS
1000.1000 g., 0.9990 Gold 32.1575 oz. AGW **Ruler:** Elizabeth II **Obv:** Crowned head right, denomination below **Obv. Designer:** Raphael Maklouf **Rev:** Red kangaroo leaping left, date below **Rev. Designer:** Stuart Devlin

Date	Mintage	F	VF	XF	Unc	BU
1991	—	—	—	—	BV+3%	—
1991 Proof	95	Value: 22,500				

GOLD BULLION - NUGGET

KM# 89 15 DOLLARS
3.1103 g., 0.9990 Gold .1000 oz. AGW **Ruler:** Elizabeth II **Obv:** Crowned head right, denomination below **Rev:** Little Hero, date below **Rev. Designer:** Stuart Devlin

Date	Mintage	F	VF	XF	Unc	BU
1986P Proof	15,000	Value: 85.00				
1987	266,000	—	—	—	BV+12%	—
1988	104,000	—	—	—	BV+12%	—
1989	—	—	—	—	BV+12%	—

KM# 95 15 DOLLARS
3.1103 g., 0.9990 Gold .1000 oz. AGW **Ruler:** Elizabeth II **Obv:** Crowned head right, denomination below **Rev:** Golden Aussie, date below **Rev. Designer:** Stuart Devlin

Date	Mintage	F	VF	XF	Unc	BU
1987P Proof	15,000	Value: 80.00				

KM# 104 15 DOLLARS
3.1103 g., 0.9990 Gold .1000 oz. AGW **Ruler:** Elizabeth II **Obv:** Crowned head right, denomination below **Rev:** Jubilee Nugget, date below **Rev. Designer:** Stuart Devlin

Date	Mintage	F	VF	XF	Unc	BU
1988P Proof	Est. 10,000	Value: 80.00				

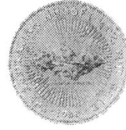

KM# 90 25 DOLLARS
7.7508 g., 0.9990 Gold .2500 oz. AGW **Ruler:** Elizabeth II **Obv:** Crowned head right, denomination below **Rev:** Golden Eagle, date below **Rev. Designer:** Stuart Devlin

Date	Mintage	F	VF	XF	Unc	BU
1986P Proof	15,000	Value: 180				
1987	233,000	—	—	—	BV+10%	—
1988	75,000	—	—	—	BV+10%	—
1989	—	—	—	—	BV+10%	—

KM# 96 25 DOLLARS
7.7508 g., 0.9990 Gold .2500 oz. AGW **Ruler:** Elizabeth II **Obv:** Crowned head right, denomination below **Rev:** Father's Day, date below **Rev. Designer:** Stuart Devlin

Date	Mintage	F	VF	XF	Unc	BU
1987P Proof	15,000	Value: 180				

KM# 105 25 DOLLARS
7.7508 g., 0.9990 Gold .2500 oz. AGW **Ruler:** Elizabeth II **Obv:** Crowned head right, denomination below **Rev:** Ruby Well Nugget, date below **Rev. Designer:** Stuart Devlin

Date	Mintage	F	VF	XF	Unc	BU
1988P Proof	15,000	Value: 180				

KM# 124 25 DOLLARS
7.7508 g., 0.9990 Gold .2500 oz. AGW **Ruler:** Elizabeth II **Obv:** Crowned head right, denomination below **Rev:** Koala bear with cub on its back sitting on branch

Date	Mintage	F	VF	XF	Unc	BU
1989 Proof	2,400	Value: 200				
1990 Proof	—	Value: 200				

KM# 91 50 DOLLARS
15.5017 g., 0.9990 Gold .5000 oz. AGW **Ruler:** Elizabeth II **Obv:** Crowned head right, denomination below **Rev:** Hand of Faith, date below **Rev. Designer:** Stuart Devlin

Date	Mintage	F	VF	XF	Unc	BU
1986P Proof	15,000	Value: 360				
1987	188,000	—	—	—	BV+7%	—
1988	75,000	—	—	—	BV+7%	—
1989	100,000	—	—	—	BV+7%	—

KM# 97 50 DOLLARS
15.5017 g., 0.9990 Gold .5000 oz. AGW **Ruler:** Elizabeth II **Obv:** Crowned head right, denomination below **Obv. Designer:** Raphael Maklouf **Rev:** Bobby Dazzler, date below **Rev. Designer:** Stuart Devlin

Date	Mintage	F	VF	XF	Unc	BU
1987P Proof	15,000	Value: 360				

KM# 106 50 DOLLARS
15.5017 g., 0.9990 Gold .5000 oz. AGW **Ruler:** Elizabeth II **Obv:** Crowned head right, denomination below **Rev:** Welcome nugget, date below **Rev. Designer:** Stuart Devlin

Date	Mintage	F	VF	XF	Unc	BU
1988P Proof	Est. 10,000	Value: 360				

AUSTRALIA

KM# 92 100 DOLLARS
31.1035 g., 0.9990 Gold 1.0000 oz. AGW **Ruler:** Elizabeth II **Obv:** Crowned head right, denomination below **Obv. Designer:** Raphael Maklouf **Rev:** Welcome Stranger, date below **Rev. Designer:** Stuart Devlin

Date	Mintage	F	VF	XF	Unc	BU
1986P Proof	15,000	Value: 690				
1987	259,000	—	—	—	BV+4%	—
1988	116,000	—	—	—	BV+4%	—
1989	—	—	—	—	BV+4%	—

KM# 98 100 DOLLARS
31.1035 g., 0.9990 Gold 1.0000 oz. AGW **Ruler:** Elizabeth II **Obv:** Crowned head right, denomination below **Rev:** Poseidon, date below **Rev. Designer:** Stuart Devlin

Date	Mintage	F	VF	XF	Unc	BU
1987P Proof	15,000	Value: 690				

KM# 107 100 DOLLARS
31.1035 g., 0.9990 Gold 1.0000 oz. AGW **Ruler:** Elizabeth II **Obv:** Crowned head right, denomination below **Obv. Designer:** Raphael Maklouf **Rev:** Pride of Australia nugget **Rev. Designer:** Stuart Devlin

Date	Mintage	F	VF	XF	Unc	BU
1988P Proof	Est. 10,000	Value: 690				

PLATINUM BULLION
Koala

KM# 122 5 DOLLARS
1.5710 g., 0.9990 Platinum .0500 oz. APW **Ruler:** Elizabeth II **Obv:** Crowned head right, denomination below **Rev:** Koala

Date	Mintage	F	VF	XF	Unc	BU
1989 Proof	2,400	Value: 85.00				
1990 Proof	—	Value: 85.00				

KM# 145 5 DOLLARS
1.5710 g., 0.9990 Platinum .0500 oz. APW **Ruler:** Elizabeth II **Obv:** Crowned head right, denomination below **Rev:** Koala on tree limb facing right, date below

Date	Mintage	F	VF	XF	Unc	BU
1990 Proof	2,500	Value: 90.00				
1991	20,000	—	—	—	BV+35%	—
1991 Proof	1,000	Value: 90.00				

KM# 170 5 DOLLARS
1.5710 g., 0.9990 Platinum .0500 oz. APW **Ruler:** Elizabeth II **Subject:** Koala **Obv:** Crowned head right, denomination below **Rev:** Koala sitting facing in crook of tree

Date	Mintage	F	VF	XF	Unc	BU
1992	20,000	—	—	—	BV+35%	—

KM# 191 5 DOLLARS
1.5710 g., 0.9990 Platinum .0500 oz. APW **Ruler:** Elizabeth II **Obv:** Crowned head right, denomination below **Rev:** Koala facing left, sitting on branch, date below

Date	Mintage	F	VF	XF	Unc	BU
1993	Est. 20,000	—	—	—	BV+35%	—

KM# 249 5 DOLLARS
1.5710 g., 0.9990 Platinum .0500 oz. APW **Ruler:** Elizabeth II **Obv:** Crowned head right, denomination below **Obv. Designer:** Raphael Maklouf **Rev:** Koala mother and baby on branch facing, date below

Date	Mintage	F	VF	XF	Unc	BU
1994	20,000	—	—	—	BV+35%	—

KM# 278 5 DOLLARS
1.5710 g., 0.9990 Platinum .0500 oz. APW **Ruler:** Elizabeth II **Obv:** Crowned head right, denomination below **Obv. Designer:** Raphael Maklouf **Rev:** Koala in fork of tree facing, date below

Date	Mintage	F	VF	XF	Unc	BU
1994 Proof	—	Value: 90.00				
1995	—	—	—	—	BV+35%	—

KM# 283 5 DOLLARS
1.5710 g., 0.9990 Platinum .0500 oz. APW **Ruler:** Elizabeth II **Obv:** Crowned head right, denomination below **Rev:** Baby koala on branch right, facing, date below

Date	Mintage	F	VF	XF	Unc	BU
1995 Proof	200	Value: 90.00				
1996	20,000	—	—	—	BV+35%	—

KM# 344 5 DOLLARS
1.5710 g., 0.9995 Platinum .0500 oz. APW **Ruler:** Elizabeth II **Subject:** Koala Bullion **Obv:** Crowned head right, denomination below **Rev:** Cuddling koalas

Date	Mintage	F	VF	XF	Unc	BU
1997	20,000	—	—	—	BV+35%	—
1997 Proof	—	Value: 90.00				

KM# 456 5 DOLLARS
1.5710 g., 0.9990 Platinum .0500 oz. APW **Ruler:** Elizabeth II **Obv:** Crowned head right, denomination below **Rev:** Koala on log

Date	Mintage	F	VF	XF	Unc	BU
1999	20,000	—	—	—	—	BV+4%

KM# 469 5 DOLLARS
1.5710 g., 0.9990 Platinum .0500 oz. APW **Ruler:** Elizabeth II **Obv:** Crowned head right, denomination below **Rev:** Seated koala

Date	Mintage	F	VF	XF	Unc	BU
2000	—	—	—	—	—	BV+4%

KM# 123 15 DOLLARS
3.1370 g., 0.9990 Platinum .1000 oz. APW **Ruler:** Elizabeth II **Obv:** Crowned head right, denomination below **Rev:** Koala on tree branch with cub on her back

Date	Mintage	F	VF	XF	Unc	BU
1989 Proof	2,400	Value: 150				
1990 Proof	—	Value: 150				

KM# 146 15 DOLLARS
3.1370 g., 0.9990 Platinum .1000 oz. APW **Ruler:** Elizabeth II **Subject:** Koala **Obv:** Crowned head right, denomination below **Rev:** Koala on branch facing left, looking right, date below

Date	Mintage	F	VF	XF	Unc	BU
1990 Proof	2,500	Value: 150				
1991	20,000	—	—	—	BV+15%	—
1991 Proof	1,000	Value: 150				

KM# 171 15 DOLLARS
3.1370 g., 0.9990 Platinum .1000 oz. APW **Ruler:** Elizabeth II **Subject:** Koala Bullion **Obv:** Crowned head right, denomination below **Rev:** Koala in crook of tree facing

Date	Mintage	F	VF	XF	Unc	BU
1992	20,000	—	—	—	BV+15%	—

KM# 192 15 DOLLARS
3.1370 g., 0.9990 Platinum .1000 oz. APW **Ruler:** Elizabeth II **Obv:** Crowned head right, denomination below **Rev:** Koala climbing tree

Date	Mintage	F	VF	XF	Unc	BU
1993	Est. 20,000	—	—	—	BV+15%	—

KM# 250 15 DOLLARS
3.1370 g., 0.9990 Platinum .1000 oz. APW **Ruler:** Elizabeth II **Obv:** Crowned head right, denomination below **Obv. Designer:** Raphael Maklouf **Rev:** Koala mother and baby facing forward, date below

Date	Mintage	F	VF	XF	Unc	BU
1994	20,000	—	—	—	BV+15%	—

KM# 279 15 DOLLARS
3.1370 g., 0.9990 Platinum .1000 oz. APW **Ruler:** Elizabeth II **Obv:** Crowned head right, denomination below **Rev:** Koala in fork of tree facing forward, date below

Date	Mintage	F	VF	XF	Unc	BU
1994 Proof	—	Value: 150				
1995	—	—	—	—	BV+15%	—

KM# 284 15 DOLLARS
3.1370 g., 0.9990 Platinum .1000 oz. APW **Ruler:** Elizabeth II **Obv:** Crowned head right, denomination below **Rev:** Baby koala on branch, right facing forward, date below

Date	Mintage	F	VF	XF	Unc	BU
1995 Proof	800	Value: 150				
1996	20,000	—	—	—	BV+15%	—

KM# 345 15 DOLLARS
3.1103 g., 0.9995 Platinum .1000 oz. APW **Ruler:** Elizabeth II **Subject:** Koalas **Obv:** Crowned head right, denomination below **Rev:** Cuddling koalas

Date	Mintage	F	VF	XF	Unc	BU
1997	20,000	—	—	—	BV+15%	—
1997 Proof	—	Value: 150				

KM# 457 15 DOLLARS
3.1370 g., 0.9990 Platinum .1000 oz. APW **Ruler:** Elizabeth II **Obv:** Crowned head right, denomination below **Rev:** Koala on log facing forward, date below **Edge:** Reeded

Date	Mintage	F	VF	XF	Unc	BU
1999	20,000	—	—	—	BV+15%	—

KM# 470 15 DOLLARS
3.1370 g., 0.9990 Platinum .1000 oz. APW **Ruler:** Elizabeth II **Obv:** Crowned head right, denomination below **Rev:** Seated koala **Edge:** Reeded

Date	Mintage	F	VF	XF	Unc	BU
2000	—	—	—	—	BV+15%	—

KM# 109 25 DOLLARS
7.8150 g., 0.9990 Platinum .2500 oz. APW **Ruler:** Elizabeth II **Obv:** Crowned head right, denomination below **Rev:** Seated koala facing

Date	Mintage	F	VF	XF	Unc	BU
1988	—	—	—	—	BV+10%	—
1989 Proof	—	Value: 360				

KM# 147 25 DOLLARS
7.8150 g., 0.9990 Platinum .2500 oz. APW **Ruler:** Elizabeth II **Obv:** Crowned head right, denomination below **Rev:** Koala on branch left facing right, date below

Date	Mintage	F	VF	XF	Unc	BU
1990 Proof	2,500	Value: 350				

AUSTRALIA

Date	Mintage	F	VF	XF	Unc	BU
1991	20,000	—	—	—	BV+10%	—
1991 Proof	1,000	Value: 350				

KM# 172 25 DOLLARS
7.8150 g., 0.9990 Platinum .2500 oz. APW **Ruler:** Elizabeth II **Subject:** Koala **Obv:** Crowned head right, denomination below **Rev:** Koala seated crook of tree

Date	Mintage	F	VF	XF	Unc	BU
1992	20,000	—	—	—	BV+10%	—

KM# 193 25 DOLLARS
7.8150 g., 0.9990 Platinum .2500 oz. APW **Ruler:** Elizabeth II **Obv:** Crowned head right, denomination below **Obv. Designer:** Raphael Maklouf **Rev:** Koala sitting in tree right facing left, date below

Date	Mintage	F	VF	XF	Unc	BU
1992 (ae) Proof	750	Value: 350				
1993	Est. 20,000	—	—	—	BV+10%	—

KM# 251 25 DOLLARS
7.8150 g., 0.9990 Platinum .2500 oz. APW **Ruler:** Elizabeth II **Obv:** Crowned head right, denomination below **Obv. Designer:** Raphael Maklouf **Rev:** Koala mother and baby on branch facing forward, date below

Date	Mintage	F	VF	XF	Unc	BU
1994	20,000	—	—	—	BV+10%	—

KM# 285 25 DOLLARS
7.8150 g., 0.9990 Platinum .2500 oz. APW **Ruler:** Elizabeth II **Obv:** Crowned head right, denomination below **Rev:** Baby koala on branch right facing forward, date below

Date	Mintage	F	VF	XF	Unc	BU
1995 Proof	200	Value: 360				
1996	20,000	—	—	—	BV+10%	—

KM# 346 25 DOLLARS
7.7508 g., 0.9995 Platinum .2500 oz. APW **Ruler:** Elizabeth II **Subject:** Koala Bullion **Obv:** Crowned head right, denomination below **Rev:** Cuddling koalas

Date	Mintage	F	VF	XF	Unc	BU
1997	20,000	—	—	—	BV+10%	—
1997 Proof	—	Value: 360				

KM# 458 25 DOLLARS
7.8150 g., 0.9990 Platinum .2500 oz. APW **Ruler:** Elizabeth II **Obv:** Crowned head right, denomination below **Rev:** Koala on log facing forward, date below **Edge:** Reeded

Date	Mintage	F	VF	XF	Unc	BU
1999	20,000	—	—	—	BV+10%	—

KM# 471 25 DOLLARS
7.8150 g., 0.9990 Platinum .2500 oz. APW **Ruler:** Elizabeth II **Obv:** Crowned head right, denomination below **Rev:** Seated koala **Edge:** Reeded

Date	Mintage	F	VF	XF	Unc	BU
2000	—	—	—	—	BV+10%	—

KM# 110 50 DOLLARS
15.6050 g., 0.9990 Platinum .5000 oz. APW **Ruler:** Elizabeth II **Obv:** Crowned head right, denomination below **Obv. Designer:** Raphael Maklouf **Rev:** Koala bear on log facing forward, date below **Rev. Designer:** Michael Tracey

Date	Mintage	F	VF	XF	Unc	BU
1988	—	—	—	—	BV+7%	—
1988 Proof	12,000	Value: 690				
1989 Proof	—	Value: 690				

KM# 125 50 DOLLARS
15.6050 g., 0.9990 Platinum .5000 oz. APW **Ruler:** Elizabeth II **Obv:** Crowned head right, denomination below **Rev:** Koala bear on tree branch with cub on back

Date	Mintage	F	VF	XF	Unc	BU
1989 Proof	2,400	Value: 690				
1990 Proof	8,000	Value: 690				

KM# 148 50 DOLLARS
15.6050 g., 0.9990 Platinum .5000 oz. APW **Ruler:** Elizabeth II **Obv:** Crowned head right, denomination below **Obv. Designer:** Raphael Maklouf **Rev:** Koala bear in tree left facing right, date below

Date	Mintage	F	VF	XF	Unc	BU
1990 Proof	5,500	Value: 690				
1991	20,000	—	—	—	BV+7%	—
1991 Proof	2,000	Value: 690				

KM# 173 50 DOLLARS
15.6050 g., 0.9990 Platinum .5000 oz. APW **Ruler:** Elizabeth II **Subject:** Koala **Obv:** Crowned head right, denomination below **Rev:** Koala in crook of tree facing

Date	Mintage	F	VF	XF	Unc	BU
1992	20,000	—	—	—	BV+7%	—

KM# 194 50 DOLLARS
15.6050 g., 0.9990 Platinum .5000 oz. APW **Ruler:** Elizabeth II **Obv:** Crowned head right, denomination below **Rev:** Koala sitting in tree right, facing left, date below

Date	Mintage	F	VF	XF	Unc	BU
1993	Est. 20,000	—	—	—	BV+7%	—

KM# 252 50 DOLLARS
15.6050 g., 0.9990 Platinum .5000 oz. APW **Ruler:** Elizabeth II **Obv:** Crowned head right, denomination below **Obv. Designer:** Raphael Maklouf **Rev:** Koala mother and baby in tree facing forward, date below

Date	Mintage	F	VF	XF	Unc	BU
1994	5,000	—	—	—	BV+7%	—

KM# 281 50 DOLLARS
15.6050 g., 0.9990 Platinum .5000 oz. APW **Ruler:** Elizabeth II **Obv:** Crowned head right, denomination below **Rev:** Koala in fork of tree left, facing forward

Date	Mintage	F	VF	XF	Unc	BU
1994 Proof	—	Value: 690				
1995	—	—	—	—	BV+7%	—

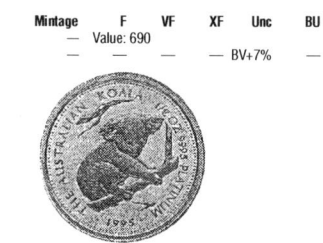

KM# 286 50 DOLLARS
15.6050 g., 0.9990 Platinum .5000 oz. APW **Ruler:** Elizabeth II **Obv:** Crowned head right, denomination below **Rev:** Baby koala on branch right, facing forward, date below

Date	Mintage	F	VF	XF	Unc	BU
1995 (ww) Proof	300	Value: 690				
Note: In Proof sets only						
1995 Proof	450	Value: 690				
1996	5,000	—	—	—	BV+7%	—

KM# 347 50 DOLLARS
15.5518 g., 0.9995 Platinum .5000 oz. APW **Ruler:** Elizabeth II **Subject:** Koala Bullion **Obv:** Crowned head right, denomination below **Rev:** Cuddling koalas

Date	Mintage	F	VF	XF	Unc	BU
1997	5,000	—	—	—	BV+7%	—
1997 Proof	—	Value: 690				

KM# 459 50 DOLLARS
15.6050 g., 0.9990 Platinum .5000 oz. APW **Ruler:** Elizabeth II **Obv:** Crowned head right, denomination below **Rev:** Koala on log left, facing forward **Edge:** Reeded

Date	Mintage	F	VF	XF	Unc	BU
1999	5,000	—	—	—	BV+7%	—

KM# 472 50 DOLLARS
15.6050 g., 0.9990 Platinum .5000 oz. APW **Ruler:** Elizabeth II **Obv:** Crowned head right, denomination below **Rev:** Seated koala **Edge:** Reeded

Date	Mintage	F	VF	XF	Unc	BU
2000	—	—	—	—	BV+7%	—

KM# 111 100 DOLLARS
31.1850 g., 0.9990 Platinum 1.0000 oz. APW **Ruler:** Elizabeth II **Obv:** Crowned head right, denomination below **Obv. Designer:** Raphael Maklouf **Rev:** Seated Koala facing forward, date below

Date	Mintage	F	VF	XF	Unc	BU
1988	—	—	—	—	BV+4%	—
1989 Proof	—	Value: 1,350				

KM# 126 100 DOLLARS
31.1850 g., 0.9990 Platinum 1.0000 oz. APW **Ruler:** Elizabeth II **Obv:** Crowned head right, denomination below **Obv. Designer:** Raphael Maklouf **Rev:** Koala with baby on branch left, facing right

AUSTRALIA

Date	Mintage	F	VF	XF	Unc	BU
1989 Proof	2,400	Value: 1,350				
1990 Proof	—	Value: 1,350				

KM# 149 100 DOLLARS
31.1850 g., 0.9990 Platinum 1.0000 oz. APW **Ruler:** Elizabeth II **Obv:** Crowned head right, denomination below **Rev:** Koala bear in tree left, facing right

Date	Mintage	F	VF	XF	Unc	BU
1990 Proof	3,500	Value: 1,350				
1991	75,000	—	—	—	BV+4%	—
1991 Proof	1,000	Value: 1,350				

KM# 174 100 DOLLARS
31.1850 g., 0.9990 Platinum 1.0000 oz. APW **Ruler:** Elizabeth II **Obv:** Crowned head right, denomination below **Rev:** Koala in fork of tree facing, date below

Date	Mintage	F	VF	XF	Unc	BU
1992	75,000	—	—	—	BV+4%	—

KM# 195 100 DOLLARS
31.1850 g., 0.9990 Platinum 1.0000 oz. APW **Ruler:** Elizabeth II **Obv:** Crowned head right, denomination below **Obv. Designer:** Raphael Maklouf **Rev:** Koala in fork of tree right, facing left, date below

Date	Mintage	F	VF	XF	Unc	BU
1993	Est. 80,000	—	—	—	BV+4%	—

KM# 253 100 DOLLARS
31.1850 g., 0.9990 Platinum 1.0000 oz. APW **Ruler:** Elizabeth II **Obv:** Crowned head right, denomination below **Obv. Designer:** Raphael Maklouf **Rev:** Koala mother and baby on branch facing forward. date below

Date	Mintage	F	VF	XF	Unc	BU
1994 Prooflike	100,000	—	—	—	BV+4%	—

KM# 282 100 DOLLARS
31.1850 g., 0.9990 Platinum 1.0000 oz. APW **Ruler:** Elizabeth II **Obv:** Crowned head of Queen Elizabeth II, right **Obv. Designer:** Raphael Maklouf **Rev:** Koala in fork of tree left, facing forward, date below

Date	Mintage	F	VF	XF	Unc	BU
1994 Proof	—	Value: 1,350				
1995	—	—	—	—	BV+4%	—

KM# 287 100 DOLLARS
31.1850 g., 0.9990 Platinum 1.0000 oz. APW **Ruler:** Elizabeth II **Obv:** Crowned head right, denomination below **Obv. Designer:** Raphael Maklouf **Rev:** Baby koala on branch right, date below

Date	Mintage	F	VF	XF	Unc	BU
1995 Proof	200	Value: 1,350				
1996	100,000	—	—	—	BV+4%	—

KM# 348 100 DOLLARS
31.1850 g., 0.9990 Platinum 1.0000 oz. APW **Ruler:** Elizabeth II **Subject:** Koala Bullion **Obv:** Crowned head right, denomination below **Rev:** Cuddling koalas

Date	Mintage	F	VF	XF	Unc	BU
1997	100,000	—	—	—	BV+4%	—
1997 Proof	—	Value: 1,350				

KM# 460 100 DOLLARS
31.1850 g., 0.9990 Platinum 1.0000 oz. APW **Ruler:** Elizabeth II **Obv:** Crowned head right, denomination below **Rev:** Koala on log left, date below **Edge:** Reeded

Date	Mintage	F	VF	XF	Unc	BU
1999	100,000	—	—	—	BV+4%	—

KM# 473 100 DOLLARS
31.1850 g., 0.9990 Platinum 1.0000 oz. APW **Ruler:** Elizabeth II **Obv:** Crowned head right, denomination below **Rev:** Seated koala with branches left, date below **Edge:** Reeded

Date	Mintage	F	VF	XF	Unc	BU
2000	—	—	—	—	BV+4%	—

KM# 185 200 DOLLARS
62.2140 g., 0.9995 Platinum 2.0000 oz. APW **Ruler:** Elizabeth II **Obv:** Crowned head right, denomination below **Rev:** Koala bear in tree left, looking right, date below

Date	Mintage	F	VF	XF	Unc	BU
1992	—	—	—	—	BV+4%	—
1992 Proof	—	Value: 2,650				
1996	—	—	—	—	BV+4%	—

KM# 196 200 DOLLARS
62.2140 g., 0.9995 Platinum 2.0000 oz. APW **Ruler:** Elizabeth II **Obv:** Crowned head right, denomination below **Rev:** Koala bear in tree left, looking right, date below

Date	Mintage	F	VF	XF	Unc	BU
1993	—	—	—	—	BV+4%	—
1994	—	—	—	—	BV+4%	—
1995	—	—	—	—	BV+4%	—
1997	—	—	—	—	BV+4%	—

KM# 254 200 DOLLARS
62.2140 g., 0.9995 Platinum 2.0000 oz. APW **Ruler:** Elizabeth II **Obv:** Crowned head right, denomination below **Rev:** Koala with cub

Date	Mintage	F	VF	XF	Unc	BU
1994 Proof	—	Value: 2,650				

KM# 288 200 DOLLARS
62.2140 g., 0.9995 Platinum 2.0000 oz. APW **Ruler:** Elizabeth II **Obv:** Crowned head right, denomination below **Rev:** Baby koala on branch right, date below

Date	Mintage	F	VF	XF	Unc	BU
1995 Proof	100	Value: 2,650				

KM# 461 200 DOLLARS
62.3130 g., 0.9990 Platinum 2.0000 oz. APW **Ruler:** Elizabeth II **Obv:** Crowned head right, denomination below **Rev:** Koala in tree left, looking right, date below **Edge:** Reeded

Date	Mintage	F	VF	XF	Unc	BU
1999	—	—	—	—	BV+4%	—

SOUTH AUSTRALIA — AUSTRALIA

KM# 157 500 DOLLARS
62.2140 g., 0.9990 Platinum 2.0000 oz. APW **Ruler:** Elizabeth II
Subject: Koala Bullion **Obv:** Crowned head right, denomination below **Rev:** Koala in tree

Date	Mintage	F	VF	XF	Unc	BU
1991	—	—	—	—	BV+4%	—
1991 Proof	250	Value: 2,650				

KM# 186 1000 DOLLARS
311.0670 g., 0.9995 Platinum 10.0000 oz. APW **Ruler:** Elizabeth II **Obv:** Crowned head right, denomination below **Rev:** Koala

Date	Mintage	F	VF	XF	Unc	BU
1992	—	—	—	—	BV+4%	—
1992 Proof	—	Value: 13,250				
1996	—	—	—	—	BV+4%	—

KM# 197 1000 DOLLARS
311.0670 g., 0.9995 Platinum 10.0000 oz. APW, 60.3 mm.
Ruler: Elizabeth II **Obv:** Crowned head right, denomination below **Rev:** Koala on branch left, looking right, date below **Note:** Illustration reduced.

Date	Mintage	F	VF	XF	Unc	BU
1993	—	—	—	—	BV+4%	—
1994	—	—	—	—	BV+4%	—
1995	—	—	—	—	BV+4%	—
1997	—	—	—	—	BV+4%	—

KM# 255 1000 DOLLARS
311.0670 g., 0.9995 Platinum 10.0000 oz. APW **Ruler:** Elizabeth II **Obv:** Crowned head right, denomination below **Rev:** Koala with cub

Date	Mintage	F	VF	XF	Unc	BU
1994	—	—	—	—	BV+4%	—

KM# 462 1000 DOLLARS
311.6910 g., 0.9990 Platinum 10.0000 oz. APW **Ruler:** Elizabeth II **Obv:** Crowned head right, denomination below **Rev:** Koala in tree **Edge:** Reeded **Note:** Photo reduced.

Date	Mintage	F	VF	XF	Unc	BU
1999	—	—	—	—	BV+4%	—

KM# 158 2500 DOLLARS
311.0670 g., 0.9990 Platinum 10.0000 oz. APW **Ruler:** Elizabeth II **Subject:** Koala Bullion **Obv:** Crowned head right, denomination below **Rev:** Koala in tree

Date	Mintage	F	VF	XF	Unc	BU
1991	—	—	—	—	BV+4%	—
1991 Proof	100	Value: 13,250				

KM# 187 3000 DOLLARS
1000.1000 g., 0.9999 Platinum 32.1575 oz. APW **Ruler:** Elizabeth II **Obv:** Crowned head right, denomination below **Rev:** Koala in tree, date below

Date	Mintage	F	VF	XF	Unc	BU
1992	—	—	—	—	BV+3.5%	—
1992 Proof	—	Value: 42,250				
1996	—	—	—	—	BV+3.5%	—

KM# 198 3000 DOLLARS
1000.1000 g., 0.9999 Platinum 32.1575 oz. APW, 75.3 mm.
Ruler: Elizabeth II **Obv:** Crowned head right, denomination below **Rev:** Koala on tree branch left, looking right, date below **Note:** Illustration reduced.

Date	Mintage	F	VF	XF	Unc	BU
1993	—	—	—	—	BV+3.5%	—
1994	—	—	—	—	BV+3.5%	—
1995	—	—	—	—	BV+3.5%	—
1997	—	—	—	—	BV+3.5%	—

KM# 256 3000 DOLLARS
1000.1000 g., 0.9995 Platinum 32.1575 oz. APW **Ruler:** Elizabeth II **Obv:** Crowned head right, denomination below **Rev:** Koala with cub

Date	Mintage	F	VF	XF	Unc	BU
1994	—	—	—	—	BV+3.5%	—

KM# 463 3000 DOLLARS
1001.0000 g., 0.9990 Platinum 32.1668 oz. APW **Ruler:** Elizabeth II **Obv:** Crowned head right, denomination below **Rev:** Koala in tree **Edge:** Reeded **Note:** Photo reduced.

Date	Mintage	F	VF	XF	Unc	BU
1999	—	—	—	—	BV+3.5%	—

KM# 159 10000 DOLLARS
1000.1000 g., 0.9990 Platinum 32.1575 oz. APW **Ruler:** Elizabeth II **Subject:** Koala Bullion **Obv:** Crowned head right, denomination below **Rev:** Koala

Date	Mintage	F	VF	XF	Unc	BU
1991	—	—	—	—	BV+3.5%	—
1991 Proof	50	Value: 42,250				

PATTERNS
Including off metal strikes

KM#	Date	Mintage	Identification	Mkt Val
Pn1	1853	—	1/2 Sovereign. Gold. T. 1.	60,000
Pn2	1853	—	Sovereign. Gold. Head left. Crowned AUSTRALIA within wreath. T. 1.	75,000
Pn3	1855	—	1/2 Sovereign. Gold. Head left. Crowned AUSTRALIA within wreath. Milled edge. T. 2.	49,500
Pn4	1855	—	Sovereign. Gold. Milled edge. T. 2.	55,000
Pn5	1856	—	1/2 Sovereign. Gold. Head left. Crowned AUSTRALIA within wreath. Plain edge. T. 2.	25,000
Pn6	1856	—	Sovereign. Gold. Head left. Crowned AUSTRALIA within wreath. Plain edge. T. 2.	55,000

PROOF SETS

KM#	Date	Mintage	Identification	Issue Price	Mkt Val
PSA1	1887 (4)	2	KM#8-11 Rare	—	—
PS1	1902S (4)	—	KM14-17 Rare	—	—
PS49	1986P (4)	12,000	KM89-92	1,445	1,350
PS50	1986P (2)	3,000	KM89,90	305	325
PS52	1987 (4)	12,000	KM95-98	1,440	1,300
PS53	1987 (2)	3,000	KM95, 96	305	350
PS57	1988	9,000	KM104-107	—	1,300
PS58	1988 (2)	1,000	KM104-105	—	235
PS62	1989 (5)	2,200	KM117-121	1,595	1,300
PS63	1989 (5)	2,400	KM122-126	1,995	1,300
PS68	1990 (5)	5,000	KM140-144	—	1,300
PS69	1990 (5)	2,500	KM145-149	—	1,300
PS70	1990 (3)	2,000	KM140-142	464	300
PS71	1990 (3)	1,000	KM138,144,149	1,900	1,800
PS74	1991 (3)	1,000	KM140-142	—	300
PS76	1991 (8)	1,000	KM78-82,84,101a,139	—	70.00
PS77	1991 (8)	23,000	KM78a-82a, 84a, 101a, 139a	—	140
PS78	1991 (5)	2,000	KM140-144	—	1,100
PS79	1991 (5)	1,000	PS145-149	—	2,750
PS81	1992 (4)	500	KM165-168	—	750
PS83	1992 (4)	5,000	KM204-207 plus medal	1,520	1,600
PSA84	1992 (3)	264	KM389-391	252	375
PSB84	1992 (3)	628	KM389-393	1,058	1,600
PSC84	1992 (4)	500	KM389-392 plus medal	759	1,000
PSD84	1992(ae) (3)	750	KM193, 209, 391	—	800
PS88	1994 (3)	20,000	KM182, 232 (2), 253	—	2,000
PS89	1994 (3)	25	KM241, 260, 278	304	350
PSA89	1994 (4)	—	KM#260, 261, 270, 271	—	850
PS90	1995 (5)	300	KM272-276	—	1,300
PS91	1995 (5)	200	KM283-287	—	1,300
PS92	1995 (4)	1,000	KM289-292	—	1,290
PSA92	1995 (3)	300	KM276, 286, 290	—	1,300
PSA98	1996 (3)	400	KM321-322, 341	1,500	1,350
PS95	1996 (3)	3,000	KM275, (f), (I), (s) privy marks	—	800
PS98	1997 (3)	3,888	KM335-337	914	975
PS99	1997 (3)	3,000	KM341 (f), (I), (s) privy marks	782	900
MSB36	1999 (5)	500	KM501-505	—	1,050
MSC36	1999 (3)	—	KM426-428	—	875
PS127	2005 (6)	650	KM#401a, 402a, 406a, 745b, 746b, 747b	—	5,850

SOUTH AUSTRALIA
BRITISH COLONY
STANDARD COINAGE

KM# 1 ADELAIDE POUND
8.7500 g., 0.9170 Gold .2579 oz. AGW **Obv:** Crown **Rev:** Denomination

Date	Mintage	F	VF	XF	Unc	BU
1852 20-50 pieces	—	—	47,500	85,000	125,000	—

Note: Noble Numismatics sale No. 82, 7-06, nearly XF realized $83,200. Noble Numismatics sale No. 61 (Part A), 8-99, XF realized $37,500

40 AUSTRALIA

KM# 2 ADELAIDE POUND
8.7500 g., 0.9170 Gold .2579 oz. AGW **Obv:** Crown **Rev:** Dentilated inner circle

Date	Mintage	F	VF	XF	Unc	BU
1852	25,000	5,500	11,000	26,500	40,000	—

Note: Noble Numismatics sale No. 82, 7-06, XF realized $26,475. Noble Numismatics sale No. 81, 3-06, nearly Unc realized $37,820. Noble Numismatic sale No. 75, 4-04, Good/VF with scratch realized approximately $18,700. Noble Numismatics sale No. 73, 7-03, Good/XF realized approximately $25,800 and nearly uncirculated realized approximately $36,500. David Akers Numismatics Pittman sale 8-99 AU realized $13,800.

PATTERNS
Including off metal strikes

KM#	Date	Mintage	Identification	Mkt Val
Pn1	1852	7	5 Pounds. 0.9170 Gold. Crown. Denomination. Restrike. The item was produced at the Melbourne branch of the Royal Mint in 1921.	—

VICTORIA
COLONY
PRIVATE PATTERNS
Hodgkin, Taylor and Tyndall Series

Port Phillip, Kangaroo Office

These extremely rare gold patterns originated from a commercial venture set up by Messrs. Hodgkin, Taylor and Tyndall of England. Their idea was to buy up gold dust and use it to strike their own gold of 1/4, 1/2, 1 and 2 ounces which they proposed to pass on as bullion currency from their store in Melbourne. The dies were cut by W. J. Taylor and the machinery provided. This equipment arrived at Hobson's Bay on October 23, 1853, but before it could be removed and set up at the store, known as the Kangaroo Office, the availability of the British sovereign pre-empted the venture.

X# Pn1 1/4 OUNCE
7.7900 g., Gold **Issuer:** Port Phillip, Kangaroo Office **Edge:** Milled **Note:** Prev. KM#Pn1. Uniface gilt copper electrotypes of both obverses and reverses of all denominations, with the exception of the 1/2 Ounce obverse, are known to exist for Pn1-Pn4e. Values range from $100 to $200. Bonded pairs have been noted.

Date	Mintage	F	VF	XF	Unc	BU
1853 Rare	—	—	—	—	—	—

Note: P.J. Downie Sale 5-87 AXF realized $23,100

X# Pn2 1/2 OUNCE
Gold **Issuer:** Port Phillip, Kangaroo Office **Edge:** Milled **Note:** Prev. KM#Pn2.

Date	Mintage	F	VF	XF	Unc	BU
1853 Rare	—	—	—	—	—	—

Note: Spink Australia Sale 10-77 XF realized $27,100

X# Pn3 OUNCE
Gold **Issuer:** Port Phillip, Kangaroo Office **Edge:** Milled **Note:** Prev. KM#Pn3.

Date	Mintage	F	VF	XF	Unc	BU
1853 Rare	—	—	—	—	—	—

X# Pn4 2 OUNCES
Gold **Issuer:** Port Phillip, Kangaroo Office **Note:** Prev. KM#Pn4.

Date	Mintage	F	VF	XF	Unc	BU
1853 Rare	—	—	—	—	—	—

X# Pn5a 4 PENCE
41.0000 g., Gold, 35 mm. **Issuer:** Port Phillip, Kangaroo Office

Date	Mintage	F	VF	XF	Unc	BU
ND(1855) 1 known	—	—	—	—	—	—

Note: Noble Numismatics sale No. 73, 7-03, as struck realized approximately $35,600.

PRIVATE PATTERNS
W. J. Taylor Issues

X# Pn6f 6 PENCE
Gold **Issuer:** Port Phillip, Kangaroo Office **Edge:** Milled

Date	Mintage	F	VF	XF	Unc	BU
ND(1855) Rare	—	—	—	—	—	—

X# Pn6g 6 PENCE
Gold **Issuer:** Port Phillip, Kangaroo Office **Edge:** Plain **Note:** Prev. KM#Pn6g.

Date	Mintage	F	VF	XF	Unc	BU
ND(1855)	—	—	—	—	—	—

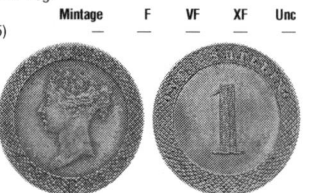

X# Pn7f SHILLING
Gold **Issuer:** Port Phillip, Kangaroo Office **Edge:** Reeded **Note:** Prev. KM#Pn7f.

Date	Mintage	F	VF	XF	Unc	BU
ND(1855)	—	—	—	—	—	—

PRIVATE PATTERNS
W. J. Taylor - Wiener Issues

X# Pn8d SHILLING
Gold **Issuer:** Port Phillip, Kangaroo Office **Obv:** Coronet bust **Obv. Legend:** DEI GRATIA **Edge:** Milled

Date	Mintage	F	VF	XF	Unc	BU
ND(1860) Reported, not confirmed	—	—	—	—	—	—

X# Pn8e SHILLING
Gold **Issuer:** Port Phillip, Kangaroo Office **Obv:** Coronet bust **Obv. Legend:** DEI GRATIA **Edge:** Plain

Date	Mintage	F	VF	XF	Unc	BU
ND(1860) Reported, not confirmed	—	—	—	—	—	—

X# Pn9d SHILLING
Gold **Issuer:** Port Phillip, Kangaroo Office **Obv:** Laureate bust **Obv. Legend:** DEI GRATIA

Date	Mintage	F	VF	XF	Unc	BU
ND(1860) Reported, not confirmed	—	—	—	—	—	—

AUSTRIA

Presently the Republic of Austria, a parliamentary democracy located in mountainous central Europe, has an area of 32,374 sq. mi. (83,850 sq. km.) and a population of 8.08 million. Capital: Wien (Vienna). Austria is primarily an industrial country. Machinery, iron, steel, textiles, yarns and timber are exported.

The territories later to be known as Austria were overrun in pre-Roman times by various tribes, including the Celts. Upon the fall of the Roman Empire, the country became a margravate of Charlemagne's Empire. Premysl II of Otaker, King of Bohemia, gained possession in 1252, only to lose the territory to Rudolf of Habsburg in 1276. Thereafter, until World War I, the story of Austria was conducted by the ruling Habsburgs.

During the 17th century, Austrian coinage reflected the geopolitical strife of three wars. From 1618-1648, the Thirty Years' War between northern Protestants and southern Catholics produced low quality, "kipperwhipper" strikes of 12, 24, 30, 60, 75 and 150 Kreuzer. Later, during the Austrian-Turkish War, 1660-1664, coinages used to maintain soldier's salaries also reported the steady division of Hungarian territories. Finally, between 1683 and 1699, during the second Austrian-Turkish conflict, new issues of 3, 6 and 15 Kreuzers were struck, being necessary to help defray mounting expenses of the war effort.

RULERS

Holy Roman Emperors and Archdukes
Franz (II, 1792-1806 (Holy Roman Empire ends);
  Franz I, 1806-1918 (Start of Austro-Hungarian
  Empire 1806-1918
Ferdinand I, 1835-48
Franz Josef, 1848-1916
Karl I, 1916-18
Republic, 1918 to date

MINT MARKS
A, W, WI - Vienna (Wien)
(a) - Vienna (Wien)
AI,AL-IV,C-A,E,GA - Karlsburg (Alba Iulia, Transylvania)
B,K,KB - Kremnica (Kremnitz, Hungary)
BE,BE/V,BEZ,B.T. - Bistrice (Romania)
CB,CI,CI-BI(NI),CW,H,HS - Hermannstadt (Sibiu)
  (Transylvania)
D - Salzburg
D,G,GR - Graz (Styria)
F, HA - Hall
G,H,P-R - Gunzburg
GM - Mantua (Mantova)
(h) Shield - Vienna (Wien)
M - Milan (Milano, Lombardy)
MB 1693-1697, 1702 - Breh (Brzeg)
NB - Nagybanya (Baia Mare, Hungary)
O - Olmutz (Olomouc)
O - Oravicza (Oravita, Hungary)
S - Schmollnitz (Smolnik, Hungary)
V - Venice (Venice, Venetia)
(v) Eagle - Hall
W - Breslau (Wroclaw, Vratislav, Poland)

MINT IDENTIFICATION

To aid in determining an Austrian (Habsburg) coin's mint it is necessary to first check the coat of arms. In some cases the coat of arms will dominate the reverse. The Hungarian Madonna and child is a prime example. On more traditional Austrian design types the provincial coat of arms will be the only one on the imperial eagle's breast. When a more complicated coat of arms is used the provincial arms will usually be found in the center or at the top center usually overlapping neighboring arms.

Legend endings frequently reflect the various provincial coats of arms. Sometimes mint marks appear on coins such as the letter W for Breslau. Mintmaster's and mint officials' initials or symbols also appear and can be used to confirm the mint identity.

The following pages will present the mint name, illustrate or describe the provincial coats of arms, legend endings, mint marks, and mint officials' initials or symbols with which the mint identity can be determined.

REFERENCES:
E = Erich Egg, *Die Münzen Kaiser Maximilians I.*, Innsbruck, 1977
H = Ludwig Herinek, *Österreichische Münzprägungen: Ferdinand II und Ferdinand III als Erzherzog und Kaiser von 1592-1657*, Vienna, 1984.
MLH = Viktor Miller zu Aichholz, A. Loehr, E. Holzmaair, *Österreichische Münzprägungen 1519-1938*, 2 vols., 2nd edition. Chicago, 1981
S = Hugo Frhr. Von Saurma-Jeltsch, *Die Saurmasche Münzsammlung Deutscher, schweizerischer und polnischer Gepräge von etwa dem Beginn der Groschenzeit bis zur Kipperperiode*, Berlin, 1892
Sch = Wolfgang Schulten, *Deutsche Münzen aus der Zeit Karls V.*, Frankfurt am Main, 1974
Sz = Alfred Szego, *The Coinage of Medieval Austria 1156-1521*, Oakdale NY, 1970

EMPIRE
UNIFORM COINAGE

KM# 2260 4 FLORIN 10 FRANCS
3.2258 g., 0.9000 Gold .0933 oz. AGW **Ruler:** Franz Joseph I **Obv:** Laureate head right, heavy whiskers **Rev:** Crowned imperial double eagle

Date	Mintage	F	VF	XF	Unc	BU
1870	7,440	70.00	100	160	250	—
1871	6,665	70.00	100	160	250	—
1872	4,960	65.00	90.00	140	225	—
1877	3,004	80.00	160	250	350	—
1878	6,820	65.00	90.00	140	225	—
1881	8,370	65.00	90.00	140	200	—
1883	3,720	75.00	120	180	325	—
1884	7,518	65.00	90.00	115	200	—
1885	38,000	65.00	80.00	110	165	—
1888	4,145	65.00	100	140	250	—
1889	5,707	65.00	90.00	135	225	—
1890	2,947	75.00	120	180	300	—
1891	11,000	65.00	70.00	90.00	175	—
1892 Restrike	—	—	—	BV	55.00	—

KM# 2269 8 FLORINS - 20 FRANCS
6.4516 g., 0.9000 Gold .1867 oz. AGW **Ruler:** Franz Joseph I **Obv:** Laureate head right, heavy whiskers **Rev:** Crowned imperial double eagle divides denominations

Date	Mintage	F	VF	XF	Unc	BU
1870	25,000	BV	130	175	250	—
1871	34,000	BV	125	150	200	—
1872	5,185	400	1,000	1,750	2,250	—
1873	23,000	BV	130	175	250	—
1874	42,000	BV	125	160	200	—
1875	86,000	BV	125	160	200	—
1876	146,000	BV	125	160	200	—
1877	125,000	BV	125	160	200	—
1878	125,000	BV	125	160	200	—
1879	43,000	BV	130	175	250	—
1880	62,000	BV	125	160	200	—
1881	62,000	BV	125	160	200	—
1882	115,000	BV	125	160	200	—
1883	31,000	BV	125	160	200	—
1884	91,000	BV	125	160	200	—
1885	178,000	BV	125	160	200	—
1886	140,000	BV	125	160	200	—
1887	174,000	BV	125	160	200	—
1888	114,000	BV	125	160	200	—
1889	208,000	BV	125	160	185	—
1890	43,000	BV	125	160	200	—
1891	19,000	125	160	225	325	—
1892 Restrike	—	—	—	BV	130	—

KM# 2251 1/2 KRONE
5.5555 g., 0.9000 Gold .1608 oz. AGW **Ruler:** Franz Joseph I **Obv:** Laureate head right **Rev:** Denomination and date within wreath

Date	Mintage	F	VF	XF	Unc	BU
1858A	20,000	350	750	1,500	2,250	—
1858E	25,000	300	550	1,000	1,750	—
1858V	947	1,500	2,000	2,750	3,750	—
1859A	402,000	275	525	1,000	1,750	—
1859B	4,376	350	725	1,400	2,200	—
1859E	17,000	350	725	1,400	2,200	—
1860A	201,000	175	350	800	1,500	—
1860B	43,000	325	700	1,300	2,000	—
1861A	2,868	525	875	1,600	2,450	—
1861B	18,000	375	750	1,450	2,250	—
1861E	55,000	275	525	1,000	1,750	—
1863A	40	2,500	5,000	10,000	14,000	—
1864A	980	1,100	1,650	2,150	3,500	—
1865A	2,690	750	1,250	1,750	2,500	—

KM# 2252 1/2 KRONE
5.5555 g., 0.9000 Gold .1608 oz. AGW **Ruler:** Franz Joseph I **Obv:** Laureate head right, heavy whiskers **Rev:** Denomination and date within wreath

Date	Mintage	F	VF	XF	Unc	BU
1866A	4,000	750	1,250	1,800	3,000	—

KM# 2253 KRONE
11.1111 g., 0.9000 Gold .3215 oz. AGW **Ruler:** Franz Joseph I **Obv:** Laureate head right **Rev:** Denomination and date within wreath

Date	Mintage	F	VF	XF	Unc	BU
1858A	47,000	500	1,000	1,500	2,750	—
1858E	31,000	350	600	1,000	1,850	—
1858V	600	1,150	1,850	2,750	4,500	—
1859A	10,000	450	800	1,500	2,750	—
1859M	3,974	750	1,500	3,000	5,000	—
1859V	1,885	1,000	2,000	4,000	6,000	—
1860A	557	1,250	2,500	3,250	5,500	—
1861A	2,010	650	1,100	1,850	2,850	—
1863A	1,000	750	1,350	2,150	3,500	—
1864A	1,530	650	1,150	1,950	3,000	—
1865A	2,800	650	1,150	1,950	3,000	—

KM# 2255 KRONE
11.1111 g., 0.9000 Gold .3215 oz. AGW **Ruler:** Franz Joseph I **Obv:** Laureate head right, full whiskers **Rev:** Denomination and date within wreath

Date	Mintage	F	VF	XF	Unc	BU
1866A	3,000	1,150	1,850	2,750	4,500	—

REFORM COINAGE
100 Heller = 1 Corona

KM# 2805 10 CORONA
3.3875 g., 0.9000 Gold .0980 oz. AGW, 19 mm. **Ruler:** Franz Joseph I **Obv:** Laureate, bearded head right **Rev:** Crowned imperial double eagle

Date	Mintage	F	VF	XF	Unc	BU
1892 - MDCCCXCII	—	1,000	1,500	2,500	3,500	—
1893 - MDCCCXCIII Rare	—	—	—	—	—	—
1896 - MDCCCXCVI	211,000	—	BV	70.00	90.00	—
1897 - MDCCCXCVII	1,803,000	—	BV	70.00	90.00	—
1905 - MDCCCCV	1,933,230	—	BV	70.00	90.00	—
1906 - MDCCCCVI	1,081,161	—	BV	70.00	90.00	—

KM# 2810 10 CORONA
3.3875 g., 0.9000 Gold .0980 oz. AGW, 19 mm. **Ruler:** Franz Joseph I **Subject:** 60th Anniversary of Reign **Obv:** Small plain head right **Rev:** Crowned double eagle, tail divides two dates, value at bottom **Designer:** R. Marshall & R. Neuberger

Date	Mintage	F	VF	XF	Unc	BU
ND(1908)	654,022	—	BV	70.00	100	—

42 AUSTRIA

KM# 2815 10 CORONA
3.3875 g., 0.9000 Gold .0980 oz. AGW, 19 mm. **Ruler:** Franz Joseph I **Obv:** Head right **Rev:** Crowned double eagle, date and value at bottom

Date	Mintage	F	VF	XF	Unc	BU
1909 - MDCCCCIX	2,319,872	—	BV	65.00	85.00	—

KM# 2816 10 CORONA
3.3875 g., 0.9000 Gold .0980 oz. AGW, 19 mm. **Ruler:** Franz Joseph I **Obv:** Large right **Rev:** Crowned double eagle, date and value at bottom

Date	Mintage	F	VF	XF	Unc	BU
1909 - MDCCCCIX	192,135	—	65.00	80.00	100	—
1910 - MDCCCCX	1,055,387	—	BV	65.00	80.00	—
1911 - MDCCCCXI	1,285,667	—	BV	65.00	80.00	—
1912 - MDCCCCXII Restrike	—	—	—	—	BV+ 10%	—

KM# 2806 20 CORONA
6.7751 g., 0.9000 Gold .1960 oz. AGW, 21 mm. **Ruler:** Franz Joseph I **Obv:** Laureate, bearded head right **Rev:** Crowned imperial double eagle

Date	Mintage	F	VF	XF	Unc	BU
1892 - MDCCCXCII	653,000	—	BV	130	160	—
1893 - MDCCCXCIII	7,872,000	—	—	BV	135	—
1894 - MDCCCXCIV	6,714,000	—	—	BV	135	—
1895 - MDCCCXCV	2,266,000	—	—	BV	135	—
1896 - MDCCCXCVI	6,868,000	—	—	BV	135	—
1897 - MDCCCXCVII	5,133,000	—	—	BV	135	—
1898 - MDCCCXCVIII	1,874,000	—	—	BV	135	—
1899 - MDCCCXCIX	98,000	—	BV	130	160	—
1900 - MDCCCC	27,000	200	400	600	800	—
1901 - MDCCCCI	48,677	200	400	600	800	—
1902 - MDCCCCII	440,751	—	BV	130	160	—
1903 - MDCCCCIII	322,679	—	BV	130	160	—
1904 - MDCCCCIV	494,356	—	BV	130	160	—
1905 - MDCCCCV	146,097	BV	130	150	170	—

KM# 2811 20 CORONA
6.7751 g., 0.9000 Gold .1960 oz. AGW, 21 mm. **Ruler:** Franz Joseph I **Subject:** 60th Anniversary of Reign **Obv:** Head right **Rev:** Crowned double eagle, crown divides two dates, value at bottom **Designer:** R. Marshall & R. Neuberger

Date	Mintage	F	VF	XF	Unc	BU
1908	188,000	BV	195	285	380	—

KM# 2817 20 CORONA
6.7751 g., 0.9000 Gold .1960 oz. AGW, 21 mm. **Ruler:** Franz Joseph I **Rev:** Crowned double eagle, value and date at bottom **Designer:** Rudolf Marschall

Date	Mintage	F	VF	XF	Unc	BU
1909 - MDCCCCIX	227,754	450	750	1,400	1,800	—

KM# 2818 20 CORONA
6.7751 g., 0.9000 Gold .1960 oz. AGW, 21 mm. **Ruler:** Franz Joseph I **Obv:** Head of Franz Joseph I, right

Date	Mintage	F	VF	XF	Unc	BU
MDCCCCIX (1909)	102,404	575	1,150	2,000	2,800	—
MDCCCCX (1910)	386,031	BV	150	250	350	—
MDCCCCXI (1911)	59,313	135	550	800	975	—
MDCCCCXII (1912)	4,460	250	550	1,350	2,000	—
MDCCCCXIII (1913)	28,058	350	900	1,800	3,000	—
MDCCCCXIV (1914)	82,104	135	550	800	1,000	—
MDCCCCXV (1915) Restrike	—	—	—	—	BV+ 5%	—
MDCCCCXVI (1916)	71,763	2,500	3,500	5,500	7,500	—

KM# 2827 20 CORONA
6.7751 g., 0.9000 Gold .1960 oz. AGW, 21 mm. **Ruler:** Franz Joseph I **Obv:** Head right **Rev:** Austrian shield on crowned double eagle, value and date at bottom

Date	Mintage	F	VF	XF	Unc	BU
1916 - MDCCCCXVI	Inc. above	450	750	900	1,200	—

KM# 2828 20 CORONA
6.7751 g., 0.9000 Gold .1960 oz. AGW, 21 mm. **Ruler:** Karl I **Obv:** Head right **Rev:** Crowned national arms, date below divides denomination **Note:** 2000 pieces struck, all but one specimen were remelted.

Date	Mintage	F	VF	XF	Unc	BU
1918 - MDCCCCXVIII Unique	Est. 2,000	—	—	—	—	—

KM# 2812 100 CORONA
33.8753 g., 0.9000 Gold .9803 oz. AGW, 37 mm. **Ruler:** Franz Joseph I **Subject:** 60th Anniversary of Reign **Obv:** Head right **Rev:** Resting figure of Fame **Designer:** Rudolf Marschall

Date	Mintage	F	VF	XF	Unc	BU
ND(1908)	16,000	BV	950	1,200	1,700	—
ND(1908) Proof	—	Value: 1,850				

KM# 2819 100 CORONA
33.8753 g., 0.9000 Gold .9803 oz. AGW, 37 mm. **Ruler:** Franz Joseph I **Obv:** Head right **Obv. Designer:** Stefan Schwartz **Rev:** Crowned double eagle, tail dividing value, date at bottom

Date	Mintage	F	VF	XF	Unc	BU
1909	3,203	BV	650	950	1,500	—
1910	3,074	BV	650	950	1,500	—
1911	11,165	BV	650	950	1,500	—
1912	3,591	640	850	1,150	2,000	—
1913	2,696	BV	800	1,200	1,700	—

Date	Mintage	F	VF	XF	Unc	BU
1914	1,195	BV	650	1,000	1,600	—
1915 Restrike	—	—	—	—	BV+ 2%	—
1915 Restrike, Proof	—	—	—	—	—	—

TRADE COINAGE

KM# 1886 DUCAT
3.4909 g., 0.9860 Gold .1106 oz. AGW **Ruler:** Franz II (I) **Obv:** Laureate head right **Obv. Legend:** FRANC. II. D. G. R... **Rev:** Crowned imperial double eagle **Note:** Prev. KM#2166.

Date	Mintage	F	VF	XF	Unc	BU
1801A	—	120	200	290	450	—
1802A	—	110	180	260	400	—
1802B	—	100	160	250	375	—
1802G	—	110	170	250	375	—
1803A	—	120	200	290	450	—
1804A	—	110	180	260	400	—
1804E	—	100	160	250	375	—

KM# 2167 DUCAT
3.4909 g., 0.9860 Gold .1106 oz. AGW **Ruler:** Franz II (I) **Obv:** Laureate head right **Obv. Legend:** FRANCISCVS II D. G. ROM... **Rev:** Crowned imperial double eagle **Rev. Legend:** ...D. LOTH. VEN. SAL.

Date	Mintage	F	VF	XF	Unc	BU
1804A	—	325	650	1,000	1,750	—
1805A	—	325	650	1,000	1,750	—
1806A	—	300	600	900	1,600	—
1806B	—	325	650	1,000	1,750	—
1806C	—	750	1,500	2,250	3,000	—
1806D	—	325	650	1,000	1,750	—

KM# 2168 DUCAT
3.4909 g., 0.9860 Gold .1106 oz. AGW **Ruler:** Franz II (I) **Obv:** Laureate head right **Rev:** Crowned imperial double eagle **Rev. Legend:** ... D. LO. SAL. WIRC.

Date	Mintage	F	VF	XF	Unc	BU
1806A	—	160	250	375	550	—
1806D	—	750	1,250	1,500	2,000	—
1807A	—	125	200	275	450	—
1807C	—	180	275	425	650	—
1808A	—	125	200	275	450	—
1808D Rare	—	—	—	—	—	—
1809A	—	125	200	275	450	—
1809B	—	160	250	375	575	—
1809D	—	500	700	950	1,200	—
1810A	—	125	200	275	450	—

KM# 2169 DUCAT
3.4909 g., 0.9860 Gold .1106 oz. AGW **Ruler:** Franz II (I) **Rev. Legend:** ...LO: WI: ET IN. FR: DVX.

Date	Mintage	F	VF	XF	Unc	BU
1811A	—	85.00	125	200	300	—
1811B	—	85.00	125	200	300	—
1812A	—	85.00	125	200	300	—
1812B	—	85.00	125	200	300	—
1812G Rare	—	—	—	—	—	—
1813A	—	100	140	225	325	—
1813B	—	85.00	125	200	300	—
1813E	—	100	140	225	325	—
1813G Rare	—	—	—	—	—	—
1814A	—	85.00	125	200	300	—
1814B	—	100	140	225	325	—
1814E	—	100	140	225	325	—
1814G Rare	—	—	—	—	—	—
1815A	—	85.00	125	200	300	—
1815B	—	85.00	125	200	300	—
1815E	—	85.00	125	200	300	—
1815G	—	100	150	250	350	—

KM# 2170 DUCAT
3.4909 g., 0.9860 Gold .1106 oz. AGW **Ruler:** Franz II (I) **Obv:** Laureate bust right **Rev:** Crowned imperial double eagle **Rev. Legend:** ...GAL. LOD. IL. REX. A. A.

Date	Mintage	F	VF	XF	Unc	BU
1816A	—	85.00	125	200	300	—
1817A	—	85.00	125	200	300	—

AUSTRIA 43

Date	Mintage	F	VF	XF	Unc	BU
1818A	—	85.00	125	200	300	—
1818B	—	85.00	125	200	300	—
1818E	—	85.00	125	200	300	—
1818G	—	100	140	225	325	—
1819A	—	85.00	125	200	300	—
1819B	—	100	140	225	325	—
1819E	—	85.00	125	200	300	—
1819G	—	100	140	225	325	—
1819V	—	350	525	700	1,050	—
1820A	—	85.00	125	200	300	—
1820B	—	85.00	125	200	300	—
1820E	—	85.00	125	200	300	—
1820G	—	85.00	125	200	300	—
1821A	—	85.00	125	200	300	—
1821B	—	85.00	125	200	300	—
1821E	—	85.00	125	200	300	—
1821G	—	85.00	125	200	300	—
1822A	—	85.00	125	200	300	—
1822B	—	85.00	125	200	300	—
1822E	—	85.00	125	200	300	—
1822G	—	85.00	125	200	300	—
1823A	—	85.00	125	200	300	—
1823B	—	85.00	125	200	300	—
1823E	—	85.00	125	200	300	—
1823G	—	85.00	125	200	300	—
1824A	—	85.00	125	200	300	—
1824B	—	85.00	125	200	300	—
1824E	—	85.00	125	200	300	—
1824G	—	100	140	225	325	—
1824V	—	350	525	700	1,050	—

KM# 2171 DUCAT
3.4909 g., 0.9860 Gold .1106 oz. AGW **Ruler:** Franz II (I) **Obv:** Ribbons on wreath forward across neck **Rev:** Crowned imperial double eagle

Date	Mintage	F	VF	XF	Unc	BU
1825A	—	85.00	125	200	300	—
1825B	—	100	135	225	325	—
1825E	—	110	160	250	375	—
1825G	—	—	—	—	—	—
1826A	—	85.00	125	200	300	—
1826B	—	110	160	250	375	—
1826E	—	90.00	130	200	300	—
1826G Rare	—	—	—	—	—	—
1827A	—	85.00	125	200	300	—
1827B	—	110	160	250	375	—
1827E	—	110	160	250	375	—
1828A	—	100	140	225	325	—
1828B	—	85.00	125	200	300	—
1828E	—	85.00	125	200	300	—
1829A	—	85.00	125	180	275	—
1829B	—	85.00	125	200	300	—
1829E	—	85.00	125	200	300	—
1830A	—	85.00	125	180	275	—
1830B	—	100	130	200	300	—
1830E	—	90.00	130	200	300	—
1831A	—	1,100	1,600	2,400	3,200	—

KM# 2172 DUCAT
3.4909 g., 0.9860 Gold .1106 oz. AGW **Ruler:** Franz II (I) **Obv:** Ribbons on wreath behind neck **Rev:** Crowned imperial double eagle

Date	Mintage	F	VF	XF	Unc	BU
1831A	—	110	160	250	375	—
1832A	—	100	120	200	300	—
1832B	—	100	120	200	300	—
1833A	—	100	120	200	300	—
1833B	—	100	120	200	300	—
1833E	—	110	160	250	375	—
1834A	—	100	120	200	300	—
1834B	—	100	120	200	300	—
1834E	—	110	160	250	375	—
1835A	—	100	120	200	300	—
1835B	—	100	120	200	300	—
1835E	—	110	160	250	375	—

KM# 2261 DUCAT
3.5000 g., 0.9860 Gold 0.111 oz. AGW **Ruler:** Ferdinand I **Obv:** Laureate bust right **Obv. Legend:** FERDINANDVS I. D.G. AVSTRIAE. IMPERATOR. **Rev:** Crowned imperial double eagle **Rev. Legend:** HVNG. BOH. LOMB. ET VEN. - GAL. LOD. IL. REX. A. A.

Date	Mintage	F	VF	XF	Unc	BU
1835 A	—	275	500	800	1,200	—
1835 E	—	275	500	800	1,200	—
1836 A	—	160	275	450	650	—
1836 E	—	200	325	525	800	—

KM# 2262 DUCAT
3.4909 g., 0.9860 Gold .1106 oz. AGW **Ruler:** Ferdinand I **Obv:** Laureate head right **Rev:** Crowned imperial double eagle

Date	Mintage	F	VF	XF	Unc	BU
1837A	—	BV	80.00	130	200	—
1837B	—	80.00	115	190	275	—
1837E	—	80.00	115	190	275	—
1838A	—	BV	80.00	180	275	—
1838B	—	80.00	115	190	275	—
1838E	—	80.00	115	190	275	—
1839A	—	BV	80.00	130	200	—
1839B	—	80.00	115	200	275	—
1839E	—	80.00	115	200	275	—
1840A	—	BV	80.00	130	200	—
1840B	—	BV	80.00	130	200	—
1840E	—	BV	80.00	140	225	—
1840V	—	475	650	975	1,275	—
1841A	—	BV	80.00	130	200	—
1841B	—	BV	80.00	110	180	—
1841E	—	BV	80.00	110	180	—
1841V	—	250	350	525	725	—
1842A	—	75.00	100	160	250	—
1842B	—	100	130	200	350	—
1842E	—	BV	80.00	110	180	—
1842V	—	200	275	700	1,000	—
1843A	—	BV	80.00	110	180	—
1843B	—	BV	80.00	130	200	—
1843E	—	BV	80.00	130	200	—
1843V	—	200	275	700	1,350	—
1844A	—	BV	80.00	110	180	—
1844B	—	BV	80.00	110	180	—
1844E	—	BV	80.00	110	180	—
1844V	—	200	275	700	1,350	—
1845A	—	BV	80.00	110	180	—
1845B	—	BV	80.00	110	180	—
1845E	—	BV	80.00	130	200	—
1845V	—	200	275	700	1,200	—
1846A	—	BV	80.00	130	200	—
1846B	—	BV	80.00	130	200	—
1846E	—	BV	80.00	130	200	—
1846V	—	200	275	700	1,000	—
1847A	—	BV	80.00	110	180	—
1847B	—	BV	80.00	110	180	—
1847E	—	80.00	100	180	250	—
1847V	—	250	350	550	775	—
1848A	—	BV	80.00	110	180	—
1848B	—	BV	80.00	110	180	—
1848E	—	BV	80.00	110	180	—
1848V	—	250	350	550	775	—

KM# 2268 DUCAT
3.4909 g., 0.9860 Gold .1106 oz. AGW **Ruler:** Franz Joseph I **Subject:** 50th Jubilee **Obv:** Laureate head left **Rev:** Second date below eagle

Date	Mintage	F	VF	XF	Unc	BU
1848/1898A	27,000	150	250	350	500	—
1849/1898A	2,292	500	1,000	1,300	1,800	—
1850/1898A	2,292	500	1,000	1,300	1,800	—
1851/1898A	2,292	500	1,000	1,300	1,800	—

KM# 2263 DUCAT
3.4909 g., 0.9860 Gold .1106 oz. AGW **Ruler:** Franz Joseph I **Obv:** Laureate head right **Rev:** Crowned imperial double eagle

Date	Mintage	F	VF	XF	Unc	BU
1852A	—	80.00	100	160	225	—
1853A	—	90.00	120	180	250	—
1853B	114,000	90.00	110	180	250	—
1853E	—	100	130	200	250	—
1854A	—	BV	80.00	120	180	—
1854B	87,000	110	135	225	350	—
1854E	—	100	130	200	250	—
1854V	—	350	600	1,000	1,750	—
1855A	—	BV	80.00	120	180	—
1855B	133,000	160	225	350	550	—
1855E	—	90.00	110	180	250	—
1855V	—	250	450	800	1,200	—
1856A	—	BV	80.00	140	200	—
1856B	121,000	80.00	110	180	250	—
1856E	—	BV	80.00	140	200	—
1856V	—	250	450	800	1,200	—
1857A	—	BV	80.00	130	180	—
1857B	86,000	BV	80.00	130	200	—
1857E	—	100	140	225	350	—
1857V	—	250	450	800	1,200	—
1858A	—	BV	80.00	110	160	—
1858B	71,000	100	130	200	250	—
1858E	—	90.00	110	180	250	—
1858M	—	300	1,000	2,000	2,750	—
1858V	—	250	450	800	1,200	—
1859A	—	BV	80.00	110	160	—
1859B	34,000	BV	80.00	140	200	—
1859E	—	BV	80.00	110	180	—
1859V	—	250	450	800	1,200	—

KM# 2264 DUCAT
3.4909 g., 0.9860 Gold .1106 oz. AGW **Ruler:** Franz Joseph I **Obv:** Laureate head right **Rev:** Crowned imperial double eagle

Date	Mintage	F	VF	XF	Unc	BU
1860A	—	75.00	100	140	225	—
1860B	56,000	85.00	120	180	275	—
1860E	—	100	140	200	325	—
1860V	—	250	400	800	1,200	—
1861A	—	BV	80.00	120	200	—
1861B	121,000	75.00	100	160	250	—
1861E	—	90.00	120	200	325	—
1861V	—	325	800	1,750	2,500	—
1862A	—	BV	80.00	120	225	—
1862B	68,000	BV	90.00	140	225	—
1862E	—	75.00	100	160	225	—
1862V	—	200	400	800	1,200	—
1863A	—	BV	80.00	120	225	—
1863B	58,000	BV	80.00	120	225	—
1863E	—	BV	80.00	120	225	—
1863V	—	175	375	600	1,000	—
1864A	—	75.00	100	160	250	—
1864B	99,000	80.00	120	180	275	—
1864E	—	75.00	100	160	250	—
1864V	—	275	800	1,750	2,500	—
1865A	—	75.00	100	160	250	—
1865B	81,000	75.00	100	160	250	—
1865E	—	75.00	100	160	250	—
1865V	—	250	475	800	1,200	—

KM# 2265 DUCAT
3.4909 g., 0.9860 Gold .1106 oz. AGW **Ruler:** Franz Joseph I **Obv:** Head right with heavier side whiskers **Rev:** Crowned imperial double eagle

Date	Mintage	F	VF	XF	Unc	BU
1866A	—	80.00	115	200	350	—
1866B	76,000	80.00	140	225	400	—
1866E	—	80.00	115	200	350	—
1866V	—	275	575	1,100	1,700	—

AUSTRIA

KM# 2266 DUCAT
3.4909 g., 0.9860 Gold .1106 oz. AGW **Ruler:** Franz Joseph I **Obv:** Laureate head right **Rev:** Crowned imperial double eagle

Date	Mintage	F	VF	XF	Unc	BU
1867A	—	BV	90.00	130	180	—
1867B	112,000	BV	100	140	200	—
1867E	—	75.00	110	160	225	—
1868A	—	BV	90.00	130	180	—
1869A	—	BV	90.00	130	180	—
1870A	—	BV	90.00	130	180	—
1871A	—	BV	90.00	130	180	—
1872A	—	BV	90.00	130	180	—

KM# 2267 DUCAT
3.4909 g., 0.9860 Gold .1106 oz. AGW **Ruler:** Franz Joseph I **Obv:** Laureate head right, heavy whiskers **Rev:** Crowned imperial double eagle **Note:** 996,721 pieces were struck from 1920-1936.

Date	Mintage	F	VF	XF	Unc	BU
1872	460,000	BV	100	125	175	—
1873	516,000	BV	100	125	175	—
1874	353,000	BV	100	125	175	—
1875	184,000	BV	100	125	175	—
1876	680,000	BV	80.00	125	150	—
1877	823,000	BV	80.00	125	175	—
1878	281,000	BV	80.00	125	175	—
1879	362,000	BV	80.00	125	175	—
1880	341,000	BV	100	150	225	—
1881	477,000	BV	80.00	125	175	—
1882	390,000	BV	100	125	175	—
1883	409,000	BV	100	125	175	—
1884	238,000	BV	80.00	125	175	—
1885	257,000	BV	80.00	125	150	—
1886	291,000	BV	80.00	125	150	—
1887	223,000	BV	80.00	100	150	—
1888	309,000	BV	80.00	100	150	—
1889	335,000	BV	80.00	100	150	—
1890	374,000	BV	80.00	100	150	—
1891	325,000	BV	80.00	100	150	—
1901	348,621	BV	100	125	175	—
1902	311,471	BV	100	125	175	—
1903	380,014	BV	100	125	175	—
1904	517,118	BV	100	125	175	—
1905	391,534	BV	125	150	200	—
1906	491,574	BV	125	150	200	—
1907	554,205	BV	125	175	250	—
1908	408,832	BV	80.00	125	175	—
1909	366,318	BV	80.00	100	150	—
1910	440,424	BV	80.00	100	150	—
1911	590,826	BV	80.00	100	125	—
1912	494,991	BV	80.00	100	125	—
1913	319,926	BV	80.00	100	125	—
1914	378,241	BV	80.00	100	125	—
1915 Restrike	—	—	—	—	BV+ 10%	—
1915 Restrike, Proof	—	BV+5%				
1951 Error for 1915	—	75.00	125	150	225	—

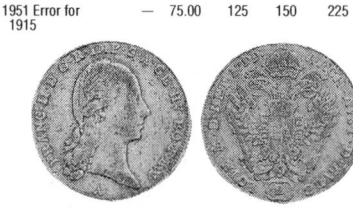

KM# 1888 2 DUCAT
7.0000 g., 0.9860 Gold .2219 oz. AGW **Ruler:** Franz II (I) **Obv:** Head right **Rev:** Crowned imperial double eagle **Note:** Prev. KM#2173.

Date	Mintage	VG	F	VF	XF	Unc
1803A Rare	—	—	—	—	—	—

KM# 2179 2 DUCAT
7.0000 g., 0.9860 Gold .2219 oz. AGW **Ruler:** Franz II (I) **Obv:** Laureate head right **Rev:** Crowned imperial double eagle

Date	Mintage	VG	F	VF	XF	Unc
1804A Rare	—	—	—	—	—	—

KM# 1887 4 DUCAT
14.0000 g., 0.9860 Gold .4438 oz. AGW **Ruler:** Franz II (I) **Obv:** **Legend:** FRANCISCVS II. D. G. R. IMP... **Rev. Legend:** ...LOTH. M. D. HET. **Note:** Prev. KM#2174.

Date	Mintage	F	VF	XF	Unc	BU
1801A	—	350	900	2,150	3,000	—
1802A	—	350	950	2,500	3,500	—
1803A	—	350	900	2,150	3,000	—
1804A	—	350	900	2,150	3,000	—

KM# 2175 4 DUCAT
14.0000 g., 0.9860 Gold .4438 oz. AGW **Ruler:** Franz II (I) **Obv:** Laureate bust right **Obv. Legend:** FRANCISCVS II. D. G. ROM. ET... **Rev:** Crowned imperial double eagle, heads in haloes **Rev. Legend:** ...D. LOTH. VEN. SAL.

Date	Mintage	F	VF	XF	Unc	BU
1804A	—	475	1,500	2,500	3,250	—
1805A	—	425	1,350	2,000	2,500	—
1806A	—	400	1,000	1,800	2,500	—

KM# 2176 4 DUCAT
14.0000 g., 0.9860 Gold .4438 oz. AGW **Ruler:** Franz II (I) **Obv. Legend:** ...AVSTRIAE IMPERATOR. **Rev. Legend:** ...D. LO. SAL. WIRC.

Date	Mintage	F	VF	XF	Unc	BU
1807A	—	425	1,200	3,000	4,250	—
1808A	—	400	1,100	2,800	3,750	—
1809A	—	350	950	2,700	3,250	—
1810A	—	425	1,200	3,000	4,250	—

KM# 2177 4 DUCAT
14.0000 g., 0.9860 Gold .4438 oz. AGW **Ruler:** Franz II (I) **Rev. Legend:** ...LO: WI: ET IN. FR: DVX.

Date	Mintage	F	VF	XF	Unc	BU
1811A	—	350	900	1,850	2,650	—
1812A	—	400	950	2,000	3,000	—
1813A	—	350	900	1,850	2,650	—
1814A	—	400	950	2,000	3,000	—
1815A	—	350	900	1,850	2,650	—

KM# 2178 4 DUCAT
14.0000 g., 0.9860 Gold .4438 oz. AGW **Ruler:** Franz II (I) **Obv:** Laureate bust right **Rev:** Crowned imperial double eagle **Rev. Legend:** ...GAL. LOD. IL. REX. A. A.

Date	Mintage	F	VF	XF	Unc	BU
1816A	—	350	650	1,800	3,000	—
1817A	—	350	650	1,800	3,000	—
1818A	—	400	800	2,000	3,250	—
1819A	—	350	650	1,800	3,000	—
1820A	—	350	650	1,800	3,000	—
1821A	—	350	650	1,800	3,000	—
1822A	—	350	650	1,800	3,000	—
1823A	—	350	650	1,800	3,000	—
1824A	—	350	650	1,800	3,000	—
1825A	—	300	600	1,500	2,500	—
1826A	—	350	650	1,800	3,000	—
1827A	—	350	650	1,800	3,000	—
1828A	—	300	600	1,500	2,500	—
1829A	—	300	600	1,500	2,500	—
1830A	—	300	600	1,500	2,500	—

KM# 2270 4 DUCAT
13.9636 g., 0.9860 Gold .4430 oz. AGW **Obv:** Laureate, armored bust right **Rev:** Crowned imperial double eagle

Date	Mintage	F	VF	XF	Unc	BU
1835A Rare						
1837A	—	285	500	1,200	2,500	—
1838A	—	285	500	1,200	2,500	—
1839A	—	285	500	1,200	2,500	—
1840A	—	285	500	1,200	2,500	—
1841A	—	285	500	1,200	2,500	—
1842A	—	285	500	1,200	2,500	—
1843A	—	285	500	1,200	2,500	—
1844A	—	285	500	1,200	2,500	—
1845A	—	285	500	1,200	2,500	—
1846A	—	285	500	1,200	2,500	—
1847A	—	285	500	1,200	2,500	—
1848A	4,411	285	500	1,200	2,500	—
1848E	—	300	600	1,500	3,000	—

KM# 2271.1 4 DUCAT
13.9636 g., 0.9860 Gold .4430 oz. AGW **Ruler:** Franz Joseph I **Obv:** Laureate, armored bust right **Rev:** Crowned imperial double eagle

Date	Mintage	F	VF	XF	Unc	BU
1852A	—	—	—	—	—	—
	Note: No specimens known					
1853A	—	—	—	—	—	—
	Note: No specimens known					
1854A	—	300	600	1,500	3,000	—
1855A	—	300	600	1,500	3,000	—
1856A	—	300	600	1,500	3,000	—
1857A	—	285	500	1,200	2,500	—
1858A	—	285	500	1,200	2,500	—
1859A	13,000	285	500	1,200	2,500	—

KM# 2271.2 4 DUCAT
13.9636 g., 0.9860 Gold .4430 oz. AGW **Ruler:** Franz Joseph I **Obv:** Laurel wreath without berries **Rev:** Crowned imperial double eagle

Date	Mintage	F	VF	XF	Unc	BU
1854A	—	400	900	2,000	3,250	—
1855A Rare						
1857V	—	950	1,950	3,500	4,750	—

AUSTRIA

KM# 2272 4 DUCAT
13.9636 g., 0.9860 Gold .4430 oz. AGW **Ruler:** Franz Joseph I
Obv: Laureate, armored bust right **Rev:** Crowned imperial double eagle

Date	Mintage	F	VF	XF	Unc	BU
1860A	6,303	300	650	1,850	3,250	—
1861A	7,664	300	650	1,850	3,250	—
1862A	8,944	300	600	1,500	2,750	—
1863A	22,000	285	500	1,200	2,500	—
1864A	45,000	285	500	1,200	2,500	—
1864V	4,463	700	1,450	2,850	4,250	—
1865A	13,000	285	500	1,200	2,500	—
1865V	10,000	700	1,450	2,850	4,250	—

KM# 2273 4 DUCAT
13.9636 g., 0.9860 Gold .4430 oz. AGW **Ruler:** Franz Joseph I
Obv: Laureate bust with heavier side whiskers **Rev:** Crowned imperial double eagle

Date	Mintage	F	VF	XF	Unc	BU
1866A	8,463	400	800	2,000	3,250	—

KM# 2274 4 DUCAT
13.9636 g., 0.9860 Gold .4430 oz. AGW **Ruler:** Franz Joseph I
Obv: Laureate, armored bust right **Rev:** Crowned imperial double eagle

Date	Mintage	F	VF	XF	Unc	BU
1867A	16,000	350	725	2,000	3,250	—
1868A	17,000	350	725	2,000	3,250	—
1869A	19,000	350	725	2,000	3,250	—
1870A	12,000	350	725	2,000	3,250	—
1871A	19,000	350	725	2,000	3,250	—
1872A	Est. 12,000	350	725	2,000	3,250	—

KM# 2276 4 DUCAT
13.9636 g., 0.9860 Gold .4430 oz. AGW **Ruler:** Franz Joseph I
Obv: Laureate, armored bust right **Rev:** Crowned imperial double eagle **Note:** without mint

Date	Mintage	F	VF	XF	Unc	BU
1872	Est. 12,000	300	625	975	1,650	—
1873	24,000	285	475	875	1,400	—
1874	15,000	285	475	875	1,400	—
1875	12,000	285	450	875	1,400	—
1876	5,243	300	550	1,000	1,750	—
1877	5,970	300	550	1,000	1,750	—
1878	23,000	285	460	850	1,200	—
1879	29,000	285	460	850	1,200	—
1880	23,000	285	460	850	1,200	—
1881	35,000	285	460	850	1,200	—
1882	29,000	285	460	850	1,200	—
1883	37,000	285	460	850	1,200	—
1884	35,000	285	460	850	1,200	—
1885	28,000	285	460	850	1,200	—
1886	18,000	285	450	825	1,200	—
1887	27,000	285	450	825	1,200	—
1888	36,000	285	450	825	1,200	—
1889	31,000	285	450	825	1,200	—
1890	47,000	285	450	825	1,200	—
1891	54,000	285	450	825	1,200	—
1892	58,000	285	450	825	1,200	—
1893	54,000	285	450	800	1,150	—
1894	35,000	285	450	800	1,150	—
1895	40,000	285	450	800	1,150	—
1896	49,000	285	450	800	1,150	—
1897	35,000	285	450	800	1,150	—
1898	54,000	285	450	800	1,150	—
1899	54,000	285	450	800	1,100	—
1900	47,000	285	450	800	1,100	—
1901	51,597	290	450	800	1,100	—
1902	69,380	290	450	800	1,100	—
1903	72,658	290	450	800	1,100	—
1904	80,086	290	450	800	1,100	—
1905	90,906	290	450	800	1,100	—
1906	123,443	290	350	500	800	—
1907	104,295	290	350	500	800	—
1908	80,428	290	350	550	870	—
1909	83,852	285	300	450	680	—
1910	101,000	285	300	350	580	—
1911	141,857	285	300	325	450	—
1912	150,691	285	300	325	450	—
1913	119,133	285	300	325	450	—
1914	102,712	285	300	325	450	—
1915 (- 1936) Restrike	—	—	—	—	BV+ 8%	—

Note: 496,501 pieces were struck from 1920-1936.

MEDALLIC COINAGE

X# M12 4 DUCAT
14.0000 g., 0.9860 Gold .4438 oz. AGW **Subject:** Vienna Shooting Festival

Date	Mintage	F	VF	XF	Unc	BU
1873	—	—	—	2,750	4,500	—
1873 Proof	—	Value: 7,500				

REPUBLIC

REFORM COINAGE
10,000 Kronen = 1 Schilling

KM# 2830 20 KRONEN
6.7751 g., 0.9000 Gold .1960 oz. AGW **Obv:** Imperial Eagle, date below **Rev:** Value within wreath **Designer:** Richard Placht

Date	Mintage	F	VF	XF	Unc	BU
1923	6,988	650	1,400	1,850	2,500	—
1924	10,337	650	1,400	1,850	2,500	—

KM# 2831 100 KRONEN
33.8753 g., 0.9000 Gold .9802 oz. AGW **Obv:** Imperial Eagle, date below **Rev:** Value within wreath **Designer:** Richard Placht

Date	Mintage	F	VF	XF	Unc	BU
1923	617	750	1,550	2,250	3,500	—
1923 Proof	—	Value: 4,000				
1924	2,851	750	1,550	2,250	3,500	—

PRE WWII DECIMAL COINAGE
100 Groschen = 1 Schilling

KM# 2841 25 SCHILLING
5.8810 g., 0.9000 Gold .1702 oz. AGW **Obv:** Imperial Eagle with Austrian shield on breast, holding hammer and sickle, **Rev:** Value at top flanked by edelweiss sprays, date divided by sprigs at bottom **Designer:** Arnold Hartig

Date	Mintage	F	VF	XF	Unc	BU
1926 Prooflike	276,705	—	—	—	125	—
1927 Prooflike	72,672	—	—	—	135	—
1928 Prooflike	134,041	—	—	—	125	—
1929 Prooflike	243,269	—	—	—	125	—
1930 Prooflike	129,535	—	—	—	135	—
1931 Prooflike	169,002	—	—	—	125	—
1933 Prooflike	4,944	—	—	—	1,850	—
1934 Prooflike	11,000	—	—	—	600	—

KM# 2856 25 SCHILLING
5.8810 g., 0.9000 Gold .1702 oz. AGW **Obv:** Haloed double eagle with Austrian shield on breast, value below **Obv. Designer:** Joseph Prinz **Rev:** Half figure of St. Leopold, facing 3/4 forward, date at bottom **Rev. Designer:** Edwin Grienauer

Date	Mintage	F	VF	XF	Unc	BU
1935 Prooflike	2,880	—	—	—	1,000	—
1936 Prooflike	7,260	—	—	—	850	—
1937 Prooflike	7,660	—	—	—	850	—
1938 Prooflike	1,360	—	—	—	25,000	—

KM# 2842 100 SCHILLING
23.5245 g., 0.9000 Gold .6806 oz. AGW **Obv:** Imperial Eagle with Austrian shield on breast holding hammer and sickle **Rev:** Value at top flanked by edelweiss sprays, date below, one star on either side **Designer:** Arnold Hartig

Date	Mintage	F	VF	XF	Unc	BU
1926 Prooflike	63,795	—	—	—	455	—
1927 Prooflike	68,746	—	—	—	455	—
1928 Prooflike	40,188	—	—	—	550	—
1929 Prooflike	74,849	—	—	—	455	—
1930 Prooflike	24,849	—	—	—	455	—
1931 Prooflike	101,935	—	—	—	455	—
1933 Prooflike	4,727	—	—	—	1,550	—
1934 Prooflike	9,383	—	—	—	600	—

KM# 2857 100 SCHILLING
23.5245 g., 0.9000 Gold .6806 oz. AGW **Obv:** Haloed eagle with Austrian shield on breast, value below **Rev:** Standing figure of Madonna of Mariazell, facing, date below

Date	Mintage	F	VF	XF	Unc	BU
1935 Prooflike	951	—	—	—	5,500	—
1936 Prooflike	12,000	—	—	—	1,650	—
1937 Prooflike	2,900	—	—	—	2,250	—
1938 Prooflike	1,400	—	—	—	25,000	—

AUSTRIA

POST WWII DECIMAL COINAGE
100 Groschen = 1 Schilling

KM# 2997 500 SCHILLING
8.1130 g., 0.9860 Gold .2578 oz. AGW **Obv:** Bust of Mozart, 3/4 right, value at lower right **Rev:** Half-length figure of Don Giovanni playing instrument, facing, looking right **Designer:** Herbert Wähner

Date	Mintage	F	VF	XF	Unc	BU
1991 Proof	50,000	Value: 245				

KM# 3006 500 SCHILLING
8.1130 g., 0.9860 Gold .2578 oz. AGW **Subject:** 150th Anniversary - Vienna Philharmonic **Obv:** Vienna Philharmonic Hall, date below, value at bottom **Rev:** Orchestra instruments, five violins facing

Date	Mintage	F	VF	XF	Unc	BU
1992 Proof	43,000	Value: 185				

KM# 3012 500 SCHILLING
8.1130 g., 0.9860 Gold .2578 oz. AGW **Obv:** City building, date at right, value at bottom **Rev:** Aligned heads of Emperors Rudolf II, Ferdinand II, and Archduke Leopold Wilhelm, right

Date	Mintage	F	VF	XF	Unc	BU
1993 Proof	50,000	Value: 650				

KM# 3015 500 SCHILLING
8.1130 g., 0.9860 Gold .2578 oz. AGW **Obv:** Congress of Vienna, value below **Rev:** Armored bust of Franz I, facing, looking left, small crown at left, two dates on right

Date	Mintage	F	VF	XF	Unc	BU
1994 Proof	50,000	Value: 225				

KM# 3032 500 SCHILLING
8.1130 g., 0.9860 Gold .2578 oz. AGW **Obv:** Men on horseback, value below, date at lower right **Rev:** Half-length figure of Heinrich II Jasomirgott, sword in right hand, 3/4 facing

Date	Mintage	F	VF	XF	Unc	BU
1996 Proof	Est. 50,000	Value: 255				

KM# 3040 500 SCHILLING
8.0400 g., 0.9950 Gold .2578 oz. AGW **Obv:** Franz Schubert at piano, S. M. Vogl in foreground, form a sepia sketch by Moritz von Schwind **Rev:** Bust of Franz Schubert, facing, two dates at left, line of musical score **Designer:** Leopold Kupel Wieser

Date	Mintage	F	VF	XF	Unc	BU
1997 Proof	Est. 50,000	Value: 240				

KM# 3047 500 SCHILLING
8.0400 g., 0.9950 Gold .2559 oz. AGW, 22 mm. **Obv:** New York and Kyoto views, value at bottom **Rev:** Vienna Boy's Choir **Designer:** Thomas Pesendorfer

Date	Mintage	F	VF	XF	Unc	BU
ND(1998) Proof	Est. 50,000	Value: 250				

KM# 3055 500 SCHILLING
8.0400 g., 0.9250 Gold .2559 oz. AGW, 22 mm. **Obv:** Waltzing couple and Strauss monument, value below **Obv. Designer:** Thomas Pesendorfer **Rev:** Busts of Johann Strauss and son, Johann, 3/4 left, dates to left and right of busts **Rev. Designer:** Herbert Wähner

Date	Mintage	F	VF	XF	Unc	BU
1999 Proof	Est. 50,000	Value: 250				

KM# 3065 500 SCHILLING
10.1400 g., 0.9860 Gold .3170 oz. AGW, 22 mm. **Subject:** 2000th Birthday of Jesus Christ **Obv:** Three wise men presenting gifts within circle, value below circle **Rev:** Portrait of Jesus, facing **Designer:** Thomas Pesendorfer

Date	Mintage	F	VF	XF	Unc	BU
2000 Proof	Est. 50,000	Value: 265				

KM# 3074 500 SCHILLING
10.1400 g., 0.9860 Gold .3170 oz. AGW, 22 mm. **Subject:** 2000 Years of Christianity - Bible **Obv:** Bible and symbols of the saints: Matthew, Luke, Mark, and John **Rev:** St. Paul reading from a scroll to two listeners **Edge:** Reeded **Designer:** Thomas Pesendorfer

Date	Mintage	F	VF	XF	Unc	BU
2001	50,000	—	—	—	—	235

KM# 2933 1000 SCHILLING
13.5000 g., 0.9000 Gold .3906 oz. AGW **Subject:** Babenberg Dynasty Millennium **Obv:** Imperial Eagle with Austrian shield on breast, holding hammer and sickle, value below **Rev:** Seal of Duke Friedrich II within circle, dates above circle **Note:** Exists in shades of red to yellow gold.

Date	Mintage	F	VF	XF	Unc	BU
ND(1976)	1,800,000	—	—	—	—	265

KM# 2999 1000 SCHILLING
16.2250 g., 0.9860 Gold .5155 oz. AGW **Obv:** Head of Mozart with high collar, left, date below collar, violin on right **Rev:** The Magic Flute Opera from a 1789 drawing by Dora Stode **Designer:** Alfred Zieger

Date	Mintage	F	VF	XF	Unc	BU
1991 Proof	30,000	Value: 485				

KM# 3008 1000 SCHILLING
16.2250 g., 0.9860 Gold .5155 oz. AGW **Obv:** City building, value below, date upper right **Rev:** 1/2-length figure of Johann Strauss playing violin looking forward

Date	Mintage	F	VF	XF	Unc	BU
1992 Proof	42,000	Value: 345				

KM# 3013 1000 SCHILLING
16.2250 g., 0.9860 Gold .5155 oz. AGW **Obv:** Buildings, date below, value at bottom **Rev:** 3/4 length torso of Maria Theresa holding scepter in right hand, half facing right

Date	Mintage	F	VF	XF	Unc	BU
1993 Proof	50,000	Value: 350				

KM# 3018 1000 SCHILLING
Bi-Metallic Gold center in Silver ring **Subject:** 800th Anniversary of the Vienna Mint **Obv:** Symbol at center of three circles, two dates above **Rev:** Crowned figure on horseback in center of three circles surrounded by circle of laborers **Designer:** Alfred Ziegler

Date	Mintage	F	VF	XF	Unc	BU
ND(1994) Proof	50,000	Value: 330				

AUSTRIA

KM# 3028 1000 SCHILLING
16.9700 g., 0.9170 Gold .5014 oz. AGW **Series:** Olympics **Obv:** Building, statue on right, date at base, shield on left, value above **Rev:** Head of Zeus on left, facing, Olympic logo, flame to the right **Edge Lettering:** CITIUS ALTIUS FORTIUS

Date	Mintage	F	VF	XF	Unc	BU
1995 Proof	Est. 60,000			Value: 335		

KM# 3030 1000 SCHILLING
16.2250 g., 0.9860 Gold .5155 oz. AGW **Subject:** 50th Anniversary - Second Republic **Obv:** Five men aligned behind railing, center man holding book, date below railing, value at bottom **Rev:** Stylized design

Date	Mintage	F	VF	XF	Unc	BU
1995 Proof	49,000			Value: 350		

KM# 3037 1000 SCHILLING
16.2250 g., 0.9860 Gold .5155 oz. AGW **Subject:** Millennium of the Name Osterreich **Obv:** Land grant within circle, dates at bottom, value below circle **Rev:** Seated, crowned figure of Otto III, facing

Date	Mintage	F	VF	XF	Unc	BU
ND(1996) Proof	50,000			Value: 340		

KM# 3043 1000 SCHILLING
16.0800 g., 0.9950 Gold .5118 oz. AGW **Subject:** Habsburg Tragedies - Marie Antoinette **Obv:** Half-length figure of Marie holding flowers, 3/4 right, value and date lower left **Rev:** Marie on trial

Date	Mintage	F	VF	XF	Unc	BU
1997 Proof	Est. 50,000			Value: 335		

KM# 3052 1000 SCHILLING
16.0800 g., 0.9950 Gold .5155 oz. AGW, 30 mm. **Subject:** 100th Anniversary of Queen Elisabeth's Assassination by Luigi Luccheni in Geneva **Obv:** Bust of Empress Elisabeth, Queen of Hungary, 3/4 right **Rev:** Scene of Elizabeth's final moment

Date	Mintage	F	VF	XF	Unc	BU
1998 Proof	Est. 50,000			Value: 340		

KM# 3062 1000 SCHILLING
16.0800 g., 0.9950 Gold .5118 oz. AGW, 30 mm. **Obv:** Emperor Karl I bust facing **Rev:** Interior view Habsburg crypt

Date	Mintage	F	VF	XF	Unc	BU
1999 Proof	Est. 50,000			Value: 335		

KM# 3072 1000 SCHILLING
16.2200 g., 0.9860 Gold .5027 oz. AGW **Obv:** Heidentor ancient gate and statue **Rev:** Constantius II portrait **Edge:** Reeded **Designer:** Herbert Wähner

Date	Mintage	F	VF	XF	Unc	BU
2000	30,000	—	—	—	—	330

KM# 3081 1000 SCHILLING
16.2200 g., 0.9860 Gold .5072 oz. AGW, 30 mm. **Subject:** Austrian National Library **Obv:** Archduke Maximilian as a student **Obv. Designer:** Thomas Pesendorfer **Rev:** Library interior view **Rev. Designer:** Herbert Wähner **Edge:** Reeded

Date	Mintage	F	VF	XF	Unc	BU
2001	30,000	—	—	—	—	375

BULLION COINAGE
Philharmonic Issues

KM# 3004 200 SCHILLING
3.1100 g., 0.9999 Gold .1000 oz. AGW **Series:** Vienna Philharmonic Orchestra **Obv:** The Golden Hall organ **Rev:** Instruments **Designer:** Thomas Pesendorfer

Date	Mintage	F	VF	XF	Unc	BU
1991	93,000	—	—	—BV+13%	—
1992	102,000	—	—	—BV+13%	—
1993	107,500	—	—	—BV+13%	—
1994	94,500	—	—	—BV+13%	—
1995	169,500	—	—	—BV+13%	—
1996	170,000	—	—	—BV+13%	—
1997	59,000	—	—	—BV+13%	—
1998	88,500	—	—	—BV+13%	—
1999	101,500	—	—	—BV+13%	—
2000	85,500	—	—	—BV+13%	—
2001	26,400	—	—	—BV+13%	—

KM# 2989 500 SCHILLING
7.7760 g., 0.9999 Gold .2505 oz. AGW **Series:** Vienna Philharmonic Orchestra **Obv:** The Golden Hall organ **Rev:** Orchestra instruments, five violins facing **Designer:** Thomas Pesendorfer

Date	Mintage	F	VF	XF	Unc	BU
1989	586,000	—	—	—BV+10%	—
1990	46,000	—	—	—BV+10%	—
1991	24,000	—	—	—BV+10%	—
1992	186,000	—	—	—BV+10%	—
1993	166,000	—	—	—BV+10%	—
1994	12,000	—	—	—BV+10%	—
1995	174,000	—	—	—BV+10%	—
1996	184,000	—	—	—BV+10%	—
1997	66,000	—	—	—BV+10%	—
1998	38,000	—	—	—BV+10%	—
1999	81,600	—	—	—BV+10%	—
2000	38,000	—	—	—BV+10%	—
2001	25,800	—	—	—BV+10%	—

KM# 3031 1000 SCHILLING
15.5500 g., 0.9999 Gold .5000 oz. AGW **Series:** Vienna Philharmonic Orchestra **Obv:** The Golden Hall organ **Rev:** Orchestra instruments, five violins facing **Designer:** Thomas Pesendorfer

Date	Mintage	F	VF	XF	Unc	BU
1994	79,000	—	—	—	BV+8%	—
1995	105,500	—	—	—	BV+8%	—
1996	82,500	—	—	—	BV+8%	—
1997	65,500	—	—	—	BV+8%	—
1998	34,000	—	—	—	BV+8%	—
1999	10,000	—	—	—	BV+8%	—
2000	38,500	—	—	—	BV+8%	—
2001	26,800	—	—	—	BV+8%	—

KM# 2990 2000 SCHILLING
31.1035 g., 0.9999 Gold 1.0002 oz. AGW **Series:** Vienna Philharmonic Orchestra **Obv:** The Golden Hall organ **Rev:** Orchestra instruments, five violins facing **Designer:** Thomas Pesendorfer

Date	Mintage	F	VF	XF	Unc	BU
1989	484,000	—	—	—	BV+4%	—
1990	406,500	—	—	—	BV+4%	—
1991	341,000	—	—	—	BV+4%	—
1992	444,500	—	—	—	BV+4%	—
1993	339,500	—	—	—	BV+4%	—
1994	68,000	—	—	—	BV+4%	—
1995	650,000	—	—	—	BV+4%	—
1996	400,500	—	—	—	BV+4%	—
1997	381,500	—	—	—	BV+4%	—
1998	294,000	—	—	—	BV+4%	—
1999	275,000	—	—	—	BV+4%	—
2000	125,500	—	—	—	BV+4%	—
2001	51,700	—	—	—	BV+4%	—

EURO COINAGE
European Economic Community Issues

KM# 3090 50 EURO
10.0000 g., 0.9860 Gold 0.317 oz. AGW, 22 mm. **Subject:** Saints Benedict and Scholastica **Obv:** St. Benedict and his sister St. Scholastica **Rev:** Monk copying a manuscript **Edge:** Reeded

Date	Mintage	F	VF	XF	Unc	BU
2002	50,000	—	—	—	—	235

KM# 3102 50 EURO
10.1420 g., 0.9860 Gold 0.3215 oz. AGW, 22 mm. **Subject:** Christian Charity **Obv:** Nursing Sister with hospital patient **Rev:** The Good Samaritan **Edge:** Reeded

Date	Mintage	F	VF	XF	Unc	BU
2003	50,000	—	—	—	—	245

48 AUSTRIA

KM# 3110 50 EURO
10.1420 g., 0.9860 Gold 0.3215 oz. AGW, 22 mm. **Subject:** Joseph Hayden (1732-1809) **Obv:** Esterhazy Palace **Rev:** Bust 3/4 right **Edge:** Reeded

Date	Mintage	F	VF	XF	Unc	BU
2004 Proof	50,000	Value: 245				

KM# 3118 50 EURO
10.1420 g., 0.9860 Gold 0.3215 oz. AGW, 22 mm. **Subject:** Ludwig Van Beethoven (1770-1827) **Obv:** Lobkowitz Palace above value and document **Rev:** Bust 3/4 facing, dates at left **Edge:** Reeded

Date	Mintage	F	VF	XF	Unc	BU
2005 Proof	50,000	Value: 245				

KM# 3130 50 EURO
10.1420 g., 0.9860 Gold 0.3215 oz. AGW, 22 mm. **Subject:** Mozart **Obv:** Mozart's birthplace, denomination below **Rev:** Leopold and Wolfgang Mozart **Edge:** Reeded

Date	Mintage	F	VF	XF	Unc	BU
2006 Proof	50,000	Value: 300				

KM# 3138 50 EURO
10.0000 g., 0.9860 Gold 0.317 oz. AGW, 22 mm. **Obv:** Gerard Van Swieten holding book and facing value **Rev:** Akademie der Wissenschaften building **Edge:** Reeded

Date	Mintage	F	VF	XF	Unc	BU
2007	50,000	Value: 360				

KM# 3100 100 EURO
16.2272 g., 0.9860 Gold 0.5072 oz. AGW, 30 mm. **Subject:** Raphael Donner **Obv:** Portrait in front of building **Rev:** Providentia Fountain **Edge:** Reeded

Date	Mintage	F	VF	XF	Unc	BU
2002	30,000	—	—	—	—	375

KM# 3108 100 EURO
16.2272 g., 0.9860 Gold 0.5072 oz. AGW, 30 mm. **Obv:** Gustav Klimt standing **Rev:** Klimt's painting "The Kiss" **Edge:** Reeded

Date	Mintage	F	VF	XF	Unc	BU
2003	30,000	—	—	—	—	400

KM# 3116 100 EURO
16.2272 g., 0.9860 Gold 0.5144 oz. AGW, 30 mm. **Obv:** Secession Exhibit Hall in Vienna **Rev:** Knight in armor, "strength" with two women, "ambition and sympathy" **Edge:** Reeded

Date	Mintage	F	VF	XF	Unc	BU
2004 Proof	30,000	Value: 400				

KM# 3128 100 EURO
16.2272 g., 0.9860 Gold 0.5144 oz. AGW, 30 mm. **Subject:** St. Leopold's Church at Steinhof **Obv:** Domed church building, denomination below **Rev:** Two angels flank stained glass portrait **Edge:** Reeded

Date	Mintage	F	VF	XF	Unc	BU
2005 Proof	30,000	Value: 450				

KM# 3136 100 EURO
16.2272 g., 0.9860 Gold 0.5144 oz. AGW, 30 mm. **Subject:** Vienna's River Gate Park **Obv:** Bridge over river scene **Rev:** One of two "sculpted ladies" flanking the park entrance **Edge:** Reeded

Date	Mintage	F	VF	XF	Unc	BU
2006 Proof	30,000	Value: 600				

EURO BULLION COINAGE
Philharmonic Orchestra

KM# 3092 10 EURO
3.1210 g., 0.9999 Gold 0.1003 oz. AGW, 16 mm. **Subject:** Vienna Philharmonic **Obv:** The Golden Hall organ **Rev:** Musical instruments **Edge:** Segmented reeding

Date	Mintage	F	VF	XF	Unc	BU
2002	75,800	—	—	—	—	BV+13%
2003	59,700	—	—	—	—	BV+13%
2004	68,100	—	—	—	—	BV+13%
2005	—	—	—	—	—	BV+13%
2006	—	—	—	—	—	BV+13%

KM# 3093 25 EURO
7.7760 g., 0.9999 Gold 0.25 oz. AGW, 22 mm. **Subject:** Vienna Philharmonic **Obv:** The Golden Hall organ **Rev:** Musical instruments **Edge:** Segmented reeding

Date	Mintage	F	VF	XF	Unc	BU
2002	40,800	—	—	—	—	BV+10%
2003	34,000	—	—	—	—	BV+10%
2004	26,600	—	—	—	—	BV+10%
2005	—	—	—	—	—	BV+10%
2006	—	—	—	—	—	BV+10%

KM# 3094 50 EURO
15.5520 g., 0.9999 Gold 0.5 oz. AGW, 28 mm. **Subject:** Vienna Philharmonic **Obv:** The Golden Hall organ **Rev:** Musical instruments **Edge:** Segmented reeding

Date	Mintage	F	VF	XF	Unc	BU
2002	40,900	—	—	—	—	BV+8%
2003	26,800	—	—	—	—	BV+8%
2004	21,800	—	—	—	—	BV+8%
2005	—	—	—	—	—	BV+8%
2006	—	—	—	—	—	BV+8%

KM# 3095 100 EURO
31.1035 g., 0.9999 Gold 0.9999 oz. AGW, 37 mm. **Subject:** Vienna Philharmonic **Obv:** The Golden Hall organ **Rev:** Musical instruments **Edge:** Segmented reeding

Date	Mintage	F	VF	XF	Unc	BU
2002	164,100	—	—	—	—	BV+4%
2003	179,900	—	—	—	—	BV+4%
2004	169,800	—	—	—	—	BV+4%
2005	—	—	—	—	—	BV+4%
2006	—	—	—	—	—	BV+4%

KM# 3123 100000 EURO
31103.5000 g., 0.9999 Gold 999.9 oz. AGW **Subject:** World's Largest Gold Bullion Coin **Obv:** The Golden Hall organ **Rev:** Musical instruments **Edge:** Reeded

Date	Mintage	F	VF	XF	Unc	BU
2004 Proof	—	BV+3%				

MEDALLIC BULLION COINAGE
X# MB2a 5 UNZEN (5 Ounces)
155.5150 g., 0.9990 Gold 4.9949 oz. AGW **Ruler:** Maria Theresa **Obv:** Bust right **Rev:** Arms

Date	Mintage	F	VF	XF	Unc	BU
1780A (1986) Proof FDC	26	Value: 3,350				

PATTERNS
Including off metal strikes

KM#	Date	Mintage	Identification	Mkt Val
Pn47	1855A	—	5 Gulden. Gold.	—
Pn48	1855A	—	10 Gulden. Gold.	—
Pn49	1855A	—	20 Gulden. Gold.	—
Pn50	1855M	—	Ducat. Gold. KM#2263	—
Pn58	1859B	—	Krone. Gold. KM#2253	32,000
Pn93	1918	—	20 Kronen. Gold.	—
Pn103	1931	—	5 Groschen. Gold. KM#2846.	1,200
Pn111	1935	—	25 Schilling. Gold. J. Prinz.	—
Pn112	1935	—	100 Schilling. Gold. J. Prinz.	—
Pn114	1938	—	5 Groschen. Gold. KM#2846.	1,200

AUSTRIAN STATES

GURK

A bishopric in the Austrian Alpine province of Carinthia. It was founded in 1071. In 1806 it was mediatized and assigned to Austria.

RULERS
Franz Xavier V, Count Salm-Reifferscheid,
(later Prince), 1783-1822

BISHROPRIC
TRADE COINAGE

KM# 3 DUCAT
3.5000 g., 0.9860 Gold .1109 oz. AGW **Ruler:** Franz Xavier V Count Salm-Reifferscheid (later Prince) **Obv:** Bust right **Rev:** Crowned and mantled arms

Date	Mintage	VG	F	VF	XF	Unc
1806	—	750	1,400	2,750	5,000	

OLMUTZ

In Moravia
Olmutz (Olomouc), a town in the eastern part of the Czech Republic which was, until 1640, the recognized capital of Moravia, obtained the right to mint coinage in 1144, but exercised it sparingly until the 17th century, when it became an archbishopric.

RULERS
Anton Theodor, Count von Colloredo, 1777-1811
Maria Thaddaus, Count von Trauttmansdorf, 1811-1819
Rudolph Johann, Archduke of Austria, 1819-1831

BISHOPRIC
TRADE COINAGE

KM# 198 DUCAT
3.5000 g., 0.9860 Gold .1109 oz. AGW, 21.5 mm. **Ruler:** Rudolph Johann **Obv:** Bust left **Rev:** Crowned and mantled arms

Date	Mintage	VG	F	VF	XF	Unc
1820	—	275	475	1,000	2,000	2,400

SALZBURG

A town on the Austro-Bavarian frontier which grew up around a monastery and bishopric that was founded circa 700. It was raised to the rank of archbishopric in 798. In 1803 Salzburg was secularized and given to an archduke of Austria. In 1803 it was annexed to Austria but years later passed to Bavaria, returning to Austria in 1813. It became a crownland in 1849, remaining so until becoming part of the Austrian Republic in 1918.

RULERS
Hieronymus, 1772-1803
Ferdinand, Elector, 1803-1805

ENGRAVERS' INITIALS

Initial	Date	Name
FM, M	1755-1805	Franz Xavier Matzenkopf, Jr.

MONETARY SYSTEM
4 Pfenning = 1 Kreutzer
120 Kreutzer = 1 Convention Thaler

REFERENCES:
P = Günther Probszt, **Die Münzen Salzburgs**, Basel/Graz, 1959.
Sch = Wolfgang Schulten, **Deutsche M.nzen aus der Zeit Karls V.** Frankfurt am Main, 1974.

ARCHBISHOPRIC
TRADE COINAGE

KM# 463 DUCAT
3.5000 g., 0.9860 Gold .1109 oz. AGW **Ruler:** Hieronymus **Obv:** Bust right **Rev:** Crowned and mantled arms

Date	Mintage	VG	F	VF	XF	Unc
1801 M	—	85.00	125	250	450	—
1802 M	—	85.00	125	250	450	—

KM# 487 DUCAT
3.5000 g., 0.9860 Gold .1109 oz. AGW **Ruler:** Ferdinand Elector **Obv:** Head right **Rev:** Crowned and mantled arms

Date	Mintage	VG	F	VF	XF	Unc
1803 M	—	100	250	800	1,300	—
1804 M	—	125	275	850	1,400	—

KM# 486 DUCAT
3.5000 g., 0.9860 Gold .1109 oz. AGW **Ruler:** Hieronymus **Obv:** Bust right **Rev:** Crowned and mantled arms **Note:** Varieties exist

Date	Mintage	VG	F	VF	XF	Unc
1803 M	—	350	750	2,250	4,000	—

KM# 498 DUCAT
3.5000 g., 0.9860 Gold .1109 oz. AGW **Ruler:** Ferdinand Elector **Obv:** Head right **Rev:** Crowned and mantled arms

Date	Mintage	VG	F	VF	XF	Unc
1805 M	—	100	250	750	1,250	—
1806 M	—	100	250	750	1,250	—

AZERBAIJAN

The Republic of Azerbaijan (formerly Azerbaijan S.S.R.) includes the Nakhichevan Autonomous Republic. Situated in the eastern area of Transcaucasia, it is bordered in the west by Armenia, in the north by Georgia and Dagestan, to the east by the Caspian Sea and to the south by Iran. It has an area of 33,430 sq. mi. (86,600 sq. km.) and a population of 7.8 million. Capital: Baku. The area is rich in mineral deposits of aluminum, copper, iron, lead, salt and zinc, with oil as its leading industry. Agriculture and livestock follow in importance.

In 1990 it adopted a declaration of republican sovereignty and in Aug. 1991 declared itself formally independent. This action was approved by a vote of referendum in Jan. 1992. It announced its intention of joining the CIS in Dec. 1991, but a parliamentary resolution of Oct. 1992 declined to confirm its involvement. On Sept. 20, 1993, Azerbaijan became a member of the CIS. Communist President Mutaibov was relieved of his office in May 1992. On June 7, in the first democratic election in the country's history, a National Council replaced Mutaibov with Abulfez Elchibey. Surat Huseynov led a military coup against Elchibey and seized power on June 30, 1993. Huseynov became prime minister with former communist Geidar Aliyev, president.

Fighting commenced between Muslim forces of Azerbaijan and Christian forces of Armenia in 1992 and continued through early 1994. Each faction claimed the Nagorno-Karabakh, an Armenian ethnic enclave, in Azerbaijan. A cease-fire was declared in May 1994.

MINT NAMES
Genge (Elisabethpol, Kirovabad)
Nackhchawan
Shamakhi
Shirvan

MONETARY SYSTEM
100 Qapik = 1 Manat

REPUBLIC
DECIMAL COINAGE

KM# 6 100 MANAT
7.9800 g., 0.9167 Gold .2354 oz. AGW **Subject:** 500th Anniversary Mehemmed Fuzuli **Obv:** Deer by man comforting fallen comrade **Rev:** Portrait of Fuzuli

Date	Mintage	F	VF	XF	Unc	BU
1996 Proof	500	Value: 325				

BAHAMAS

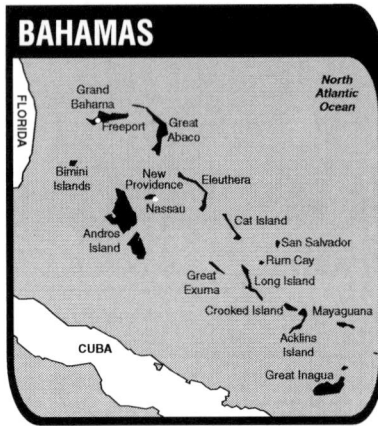

The Commonwealth of the Bahamas is an archipelago of about 3,000 islands, cays and rocks located in the Atlantic Ocean east of Florida and north of Cuba. The total land area of the 800 mile (1,287 km.) long chain of islands is 5,382 sq. mi. (13,935 sq. km.). They have a population of 302,000. Capital: Nassau. The Bahamas import most of their food and manufactured products and export cement, refined oil, pulpwood and lobsters. Tourism is the principal industry.

The Bahamas were discovered by Columbus October, 1492, upon his sighting of the island of San Salvador, but Spain made no attempt to settle them. British influence began in 1626 when Charles I granted them to the lord proprietors of Carolina, with settlements in 1629 at New Providence by colonists from the northern territory. Although the Bahamas were temporarily under Spanish control in 1641 and 1703, they continued under British proprietors until 1717, when, as the result of political and economic mismanagement, the civil and military governments were surrendered to the King and the islands designated a British Crown Colony. Full international agreement on British possession of the islands resulted from the Treaty of Versailles in 1783. The Bahamas obtained complete internal self-government under the constitution of Jan. 7, 1964. Full independence was achieved on July 10, 1973. The Bahamas is a member of the Caribbean community and the common market. Elizabeth II is Head of State, as Queen of the United Kingdom and is represented by a governor general.

The coinage of Great Britain was legal tender in the Bahamas from 1825 to the issuing of a definitive coinage in 1966.

RULERS
British

MINT MARKS
Through 1969 all decimal coinage of the Bahamas was executed at the Royal Mint in England. Since that time issues have been struck at both the Royal Mint and at the Franklin Mint (FM) in the U.S.A. While the mint mark of the latter appears on coins dated 1971 and subsequently, it is missing from the 1970 issues.
JP – John Pinches, London
None – Royal Mint
(t) – Tower of London
FM – Franklin Mint, U.S.A.

MONETARY SYSTEM
12 Pence = 1 Shilling

COMMONWEALTH

DECIMAL COINAGE
100 Cents = 1 Dollar

KM# 186 DOLLAR
1.2442 g., 0.9999 Gold .0400 oz. AGW **Ruler:** Elizabeth II **Rev:** Two flamingos **Note:** Similar to 5 Dollars, KM#188.

Date	Mintage	F	VF	XF	Unc	BU
1995 Proof	—	Value: 50.00				

KM# 187 2 DOLLARS
3.1103 g., 0.9999 Gold .1000 oz. AGW **Ruler:** Elizabeth II **Obv:** Crowned bust right, date below **Rev:** Two flamingos

Date	Mintage	F	VF	XF	Unc	BU
1995 Proof	—	Value: 85.00				

KM# 177 2 DOLLARS
3.1103 g., 0.9999 Gold .1000 oz. AGW **Ruler:** Elizabeth II **Subject:** Third Millennium - Year 2000 **Obv:** Queen's portrait **Rev:** Sea shell shaped map **Note:** Similar to 1 Dollar, KM#176.

Date	Mintage	F	VF	XF	Unc	BU
1996 Proof	10,000	Value: 80.00				

KM# 192 5 DOLLARS
1.5550 g., 0.5000 Gold .0250 oz. AGW **Ruler:** Elizabeth II **Obv:** Crowned bust of Queen Elizabeth II right, date below **Obv. Designer:** Raphael Maklouf **Rev:** Facing pair of flamingos, value above **Rev. Designer:** Arnold Machin

Date	Mintage	F	VF	XF	Unc	BU
1992 Proof	Est. 750	Value: 70.00				

KM# 201 5 DOLLARS
3.1103 g., 0.9990 Gold .1000 oz. AGW **Ruler:** Elizabeth II **Subject:** Golf - Hole in One **Obv:** National arms within 3/4 circle, legend around, date below **Obv. Legend:** COMMONWEALTH OF THE BAHAMAS **Rev:** Golf ball rolling towards cup, value lower right

Date	Mintage	F	VF	XF	Unc	BU
1994 Proof	250,000	Value: 120				

KM# 188 5 DOLLARS
6.2207 g., 0.9999 Gold .2000 oz. AGW **Ruler:** Elizabeth II **Obv:** Crowned bust of Queen Elizabeth II right, date below **Obv. Designer:** Raphael Maklouf **Rev:** Two flamingos facing, value below **Rev. Designer:** Arnold Machin

Date	Mintage	F	VF	XF	Unc	BU
1995 Proof	—	Value: 185				

KM# 178 5 DOLLARS
7.7758 g., 0.9999 Gold .2500 oz. AGW **Ruler:** Elizabeth II **Subject:** Third Millennium - Year 2000 **Obv:** Bust of Queen Elizabeth II right **Rev:** Seashell-shaped world map

Date	Mintage	F	VF	XF	Unc	BU
1996 Proof	5,000	Value: 180				

KM# 11 10 DOLLARS
3.9943 g., 0.9170 Gold .1177 oz. AGW **Ruler:** Elizabeth II **Subject:** Adoption of New Constitution **Obv:** Bust of Queen Elizabeth II right with tiara **Rev:** Fortress, date below, value above **Designer:** Arnold Machin

Date	Mintage	F	VF	XF	Unc	BU
1967	6,200	—	—	—	85.00	—
1967 Proof	850	Value: 100				

KM# 25 10 DOLLARS
3.9943 g., 0.9170 Gold .1177 oz. AGW **Ruler:** Elizabeth II **Obv:** Bust of Queen Elizabeth II right with tiara **Rev:** Fortress, date below, value above **Designer:** Arnold Machin

Date	Mintage	F	VF	XF	Unc	BU
1971	23,000	—	—	—	80.00	—
1971(t) Proof	1,250	Value: 90.00				

KM# 26.1 10 DOLLARS
3.9943 g., 0.9170 Gold .1177 oz. AGW **Ruler:** Elizabeth II **Obv:** Bust of Queen Elizabeth II right with tiara **Rev:** Fortress, date below, value above, hallmark and fineness stamped right of date **Designer:** Arnold Machin **Note:** Struck by the Gori and Zucchi Mint, Italy. Prev. KM#26.

Date	Mintage	F	VF	XF	Unc	BU
1971	—	—	—	—	80.00	—

KM# 26.2 10 DOLLARS
3.9943 g., 0.9170 Gold 0.1177 oz. AGW **Ruler:** Elizabeth II **Rev:** Hallmark and finess stamped left of date **Note:** Struck by the Gori and Zucchi Mint, Italy.

Date	Mintage	F	VF	XF	Unc	BU
1971	—	—	—	—	80.00	—

KM# 34 10 DOLLARS
3.1950 g., 0.9170 Gold .0940 oz. AGW **Ruler:** Elizabeth II **Obv:** Bust of Queen Elizabeth II right **Rev:** Fortress, date below, value above **Designer:** Arnold Machin

Date	Mintage	F	VF	XF	Unc	BU
1972	11,000	—	—	—	65.00	—
1972 Proof	1,250	Value: 75.00				

KM# 40.1 10 DOLLARS
1.4500 g., 0.7500 Gold .0349 oz. AGW, 15 mm. **Ruler:** Elizabeth II **Subject:** Independence Day - July 10 **Obv:** Bust of Queen Elizabeth II right with tiara, date below **Rev:** Tobacco Dove, value, without fineness and date **Designer:** Arnold Machin

Date	Mintage	F	VF	XF	Unc	BU
1973	—	—	—	—	30.00	—
1973 Proof	—	Value: 35.00				

KM# 40.2 10 DOLLARS
1.4500 g., 0.7500 Gold .0349 oz. AGW, 15 mm. **Ruler:** Elizabeth II **Obv:** Bust of Queen Elizabeth II right with tiara, date below **Rev:** Tobacco Dove divides value, date at right, date without fineness **Designer:** Arnold Machin

Date	Mintage	F	VF	XF	Unc	BU
1973	—	—	—	—	30.00	—

KM# 41 10 DOLLARS
1.4500 g., 0.5850 Gold .0272 oz. AGW, 15 mm. **Ruler:** Elizabeth II **Obv:** Bust of Queen Elizabeth II right with tiara, date below **Rev:** Tobacco Dove divides value, date at right, .585 fineness and date **Designer:** Arnold Machin

Date	Mintage	F	VF	XF	Unc	BU
1973	9,960	—	—	—	32.00	—
1973 Proof	1,260	Value: 35.00				

KM# 109a 10 DOLLARS
47.5400 g., 0.9170 Gold 1.4013 oz. AGW **Ruler:** Elizabeth II **Subject:** Royal Visit

Date	Mintage	F	VF	XF	Unc	BU
1985 Proof	Est. 250	Value: 925				

KM# 193 10 DOLLARS
3.1450 g., 0.5000 Gold .0505 oz. AGW **Ruler:** Elizabeth II **Obv:** Bust of Queen Elizabeth II right, date below **Obv. Designer:** Raphael Maklouf **Rev:** Two flamingos facing, value above

Date	Mintage	F	VF	XF	Unc	BU
1992 Proof	Est. 750	Value: 100				

KM# 156 10 DOLLARS
7.7759 g., 0.9990 Gold .2500 oz. AGW **Ruler:** Elizabeth II **Subject:** Golf - Hole-in-One **Obv:** National arms **Rev:** Golfer making hole-in-one

Date	Mintage	F	VF	XF	Unc	BU
1994 Proof	2,500	Value: 225				

KM# 168 10 DOLLARS
15.5518 g., 0.9990 Gold .5000 oz. AGW **Ruler:** Elizabeth II **Obv:** Queen's portrait **Rev:** Bahama Parrot

Date	Mintage	F	VF	XF	Unc	BU
1995 Proof	2,000	Value: 345				

KM# 189 10 DOLLARS
15.5517 g., 0.9999 Gold .5000 oz. AGW **Ruler:** Elizabeth II **Obv:** Queen's portrait **Rev:** Two flamingos facing

Date	Mintage	F	VF	XF	Unc	BU
1995 Proof	—	Value: 345				

KM# 179 10 DOLLARS
15.5517 g., 0.9999 Gold .5000 oz. AGW **Ruler:** Elizabeth II **Subject:** Third Millennium - Year 2000 **Obv:** Queen's portrait **Rev:** Seashell-shaped world map

Date	Mintage	F	VF	XF	Unc	BU
1996 Proof	5,000	Value: 345				

BAHAMAS 51

KM# 12 20 DOLLARS
7.9880 g., 0.9170 Gold .2355 oz. AGW **Ruler:** Elizabeth II **Subject:** Adoption of New Constitution **Obv:** Bust of Queen Elizabeth II right **Rev:** Lighthouse, date below **Rev. Designer:** Arnold Machin

Date	Mintage	F	VF	XF	Unc	BU
1967	6,200	—	—	—	160	—
1967 Proof	850	Value: 175				

KM# 27 20 DOLLARS
7.9880 g., 0.9170 Gold .2355 oz. AGW **Ruler:** Elizabeth II **Obv:** Bust of Queen Elizabeth II with tiara right **Rev:** Lighthouse, value at top, date at bottom **Designer:** Arnold Machin

Date	Mintage	F	VF	XF	Unc	BU
1971	22,000	—	—	—	160	—
1971(t) Proof	1,250	Value: 170				

KM# 28 20 DOLLARS
7.9880 g., 0.9170 Gold .2355 oz. AGW **Ruler:** Elizabeth II **Obv:** Bust of Queen Elizabeth II right with tiara **Rev:** Lighthouse above date, value at top, hallmark and fineness stamped at bottom **Designer:** Arnold Machin **Note:** Struck by the Gori and Zucchi Mint, Italy.

Date	Mintage	F	VF	XF	Unc	BU
1971 Proof	—	—	—	—	160	—

KM# 35 20 DOLLARS
6.4800 g., 0.9170 Gold .1880 oz. AGW **Ruler:** Elizabeth II **Obv:** Bust of Queen Elizabeth II right **Rev:** Lighthouse above date, value at top **Rev. Designer:** Arnold Machin

Date	Mintage	F	VF	XF	Unc	BU
1972	10,000	—	—	—	125	—
1972 Proof	1,250	Value: 135				

KM# 43.1 20 DOLLARS
2.9000 g., 0.7500 Gold .0699 oz. AGW, 19 mm. **Ruler:** Elizabeth II **Subject:** Independence Day - July 10 **Obv:** Bust of Queen Elizabeth II right with tiara, date below **Rev:** Flamingos, without fineness and date, value at bottom **Designer:** Arnold Machin

Date	Mintage	F	VF	XF	Unc	BU
1973	—	—	—	—	50.00	—
1973 Proof	—	Value: 60.00				

KM# 43.2 20 DOLLARS
2.9000 g., 0.7500 Gold .0699 oz. AGW, 19 mm. **Ruler:** Elizabeth II **Subject:** Independence Day - July 10 **Obv:** Bust of Queen Elizabeth II right with tiara **Rev:** Flamingos, without fineness, high date

Date	Mintage	F	VF	XF	Unc	BU
1973	—	—	—	—	50.00	—
1973 Proof	—	Value: 60.00				

KM# 44 20 DOLLARS
2.9000 g., 0.5850 Gold .0545 oz. AGW, 19 mm. **Ruler:** Elizabeth II **Obv:** Bust of Queen Elizabeth II right with tiara, date below **Rev:** Flamingos, .585 fineness, low date, value at bottom **Designer:** Arnold Machin

Date	Mintage	F	VF	XF	Unc	BU
1973	8,660	—	—	—	45.00	—
1973 Proof	1,260	Value: 50.00				

KM# 157 20 DOLLARS
15.5517 g., 0.9990 Gold .5000 oz. AGW **Ruler:** Elizabeth II **Obv:** Arms **Rev:** Golfer making hole-in-one

Date	Mintage	F	VF	XF	Unc	BU
1994 Proof	2,500	Value: 345				

KM# 194 25 DOLLARS
7.8300 g., 0.5000 Gold .1258 oz. AGW **Ruler:** Elizabeth II **Obv:** Bust of Queen Elizabeth II right, date below **Obv. Designer:** Raphael Maklouf **Rev:** Pair of flamingos, value above **Rev. Designer:** Arnold Machin

Date	Mintage	F	VF	XF	Unc	BU
1992 Proof	Est. 750	Value: 175				

KM# 202 25 DOLLARS
31.1035 g., 0.9999 Gold 1.0000 oz. AGW **Ruler:** Elizabeth II **Subject:** Golf - Hole-in-One **Obv:** National arms **Rev:** Golf ball rolling towards hole

Date	Mintage	F	VF	XF	Unc	BU
1994 Proof	—	Value: 675				

KM# 190 25 DOLLARS
31.1035 g., 0.9999 Gold 1.0000 oz. AGW **Ruler:** Elizabeth II **Obv:** Bust of Queen Elizabeth II right, date below **Obv. Designer:** Raphael Maklouf **Rev:** Two flamingos, value at bottom **Rev. Designer:** Arnold Machin

Date	Mintage	F	VF	XF	Unc	BU
1995 Proof	—	Value: 650				

KM# 180 25 DOLLARS
31.1035 g., 0.9999 Gold 1.0000 oz. AGW **Ruler:** Elizabeth II **Subject:** Third Millennium - Year 2000 **Obv:** Bust of Queen Elizabeth II right **Rev:** Seashell-shaped world map

Date	Mintage	F	VF	XF	Unc	BU
1996 Proof	5,000	Value: 650				

KM# 13 50 DOLLARS
19.9710 g., 0.9170 Gold .5888 oz. AGW **Ruler:** Elizabeth II **Subject:** Adoption of New Constitution **Obv:** Bust of Queen Elizabeth II right with tiara **Rev:** Santa Maria in full sail, value and date above

Date	Mintage	F	VF	XF	Unc	BU
1967	1,200	—	—	—	385	—
1967 Proof	850	Value: 400				

KM# 29 50 DOLLARS
19.9710 g., 0.9170 Gold .5888 oz. AGW **Ruler:** Elizabeth II **Obv:** Bust of Queen Elizabeth II right with tiara **Rev:** Santa Maria in full sail, value and date above **Designer:** Arnold Machin

Date	Mintage	F	VF	XF	Unc	BU
1971	6,800	—	—	—	385	—
1971(t) Proof	1,250	Value: 400				

KM# 30 50 DOLLARS
19.9710 g., 0.9170 Gold .5888 oz. AGW **Ruler:** Elizabeth II **Obv:** Bust of Queen Elizabeth II right with tiara **Rev:** Santa Maria in full sail, value and above, hallmark and fineness stamped at bottom **Designer:** Arnold Machin **Note:** Struck by the Gori and Zucchi Mint, Italy.

Date	Mintage	F	VF	XF	Unc	BU
1971	—	—	—	—	385	—

KM# 36 50 DOLLARS
15.9700 g., 0.9170 Gold .4708 oz. AGW **Ruler:** Elizabeth II **Obv:** Bust of Queen Elizabeth II right

Date	Mintage	F	VF	XF	Unc	BU
1972	2,250	—	—	—	325	—
1972 Proof	1,250	Value: 350				

KM# 45 50 DOLLARS
7.2700 g., 0.7500 Gold .1753 oz. AGW, 22 mm. **Ruler:** Elizabeth II **Subject:** Independence Day - July 10 **Obv:** Bust of Queen Elizabeth II right, date below **Rev:** Spiny lobster, date below, value at bottom; without fineness **Designer:** Arnold Machin

Date	Mintage	F	VF	XF	Unc	BU
1973	—	—	—	—	120	—
1973 Proof	—	Value: 130				

KM# 46 50 DOLLARS
7.2700 g., 0.5850 Gold .1367 oz. AGW, 22 mm. **Ruler:** Elizabeth II **Obv:** Bust of Queen Elizabeth II right with tiara, date below **Rev:** Spiny lobster, .585 fineness to left, date to right, value at bottom **Designer:** Arnold Machin

Date	Mintage	F	VF	XF	Unc	BU
1973	5,160	—	—	—	95.00	—
1973 Proof	1,260	Value: 110				

KM# 47 50 DOLLARS
7.3000 g., 0.7500 Gold .1760 oz. AGW, 22 mm. **Ruler:** Elizabeth II **Obv:** Bust of Queen Elizabeth II right with tiara, date below **Rev:** Spiny lobster, without date or fineness, value at bottom **Designer:** Arnold Machin

Date	Mintage	F	VF	XF	Unc	BU
1973	—	—	—	—	135	—

52 BAHAMAS

KM# 48 50 DOLLARS
15.6448 g., 0.5000 Gold .2515 oz. AGW, 29.2 mm. **Ruler:** Elizabeth II **Subject:** Independence Day - July 10 **Obv:** Bust of Queen Elizabeth II right with tiara **Rev:** Two flamingos, value below **Designer:** Arnold Machin

Date	Mintage	F	VF	XF	Unc	BU
1973JP	23,000	—	—	—	165	—
1973JP	18,000	Value: 175				

KM# 69 50 DOLLARS
2.7300 g., 0.9170 Gold .0804 oz. AGW, 17 mm. **Ruler:** Elizabeth II **Subject:** 1st Anniversary of Independence **Obv:** Bust of Queen Elizabeth II right with tiara, date below **Rev:** Tobacco Dove, value, date, without fineness **Designer:** Arnold Machin

Date	Mintage	F	VF	XF	Unc	BU
1974	34,000	—	—	—	55.00	—
1974 Proof	20,000	Value: 60.00				
1975	26,000	—	—	—	60.00	—
1975 Proof	15,000	Value: 65.00				
1976	2,207	—	—	—	70.00	—
1976 Proof	Inc. above	Value: 65.00				
1977	1,090	—	—	—	70.00	—
1977 Proof	—	Value: 85.00				

KM# 70 50 DOLLARS
2.7300 g., 0.9170 Gold .0804 oz. AGW **Ruler:** Elizabeth II **Obv:** Bust of Queen Elizabeth II right with tiara, date below **Rev:** Tobacco Dove, value date, .917 fineness **Designer:** Arnold Machin

Date	Mintage	F	VF	XF	Unc	BU
1974	—	—	—	—	60.00	—

KM# 86 50 DOLLARS
2.6800 g., 0.5000 Gold .0430 oz. AGW **Ruler:** Elizabeth II **Obv:** National arms **Rev:** Flamingos in flight

Date	Mintage	F	VF	XF	Unc	BU
1981FM Proof	2,050	Value: 65.00				

KM# 92 50 DOLLARS
2.6800 g., 0.5000 Gold .0430 oz. AGW **Ruler:** Elizabeth II **Obv:** National arms, date below **Rev:** Marlin (Swordfish), value above

Date	Mintage	F	VF	XF	Unc	BU
1982FM Proof	841	Value: 125				

KM# 98 50 DOLLARS
2.6800 g., 0.5000 Gold .0430 oz. AGW **Ruler:** Elizabeth II **Subject:** 10th Anniversary of Independence **Obv:** National arms, date below **Rev:** Flamingo, value above

Date	Mintage	F	VF	XF	Unc	BU
1983FM Proof	962	Value: 100				

KM# 103 50 DOLLARS
2.6800 g., 0.5000 Gold .0430 oz. AGW **Ruler:** Elizabeth II **Obv:** National arms, date below **Rev:** Golden Allamanda, value above

Date	Mintage	F	VF	XF	Unc	BU
1984FM Proof	3,716	Value: 50.00				

KM# 108 50 DOLLARS
2.6800 g., 0.5000 Gold .0430 oz. AGW **Ruler:** Elizabeth II **Obv:** National arms, date below **Rev:** Santa Maria, value above

Date	Mintage	F	VF	XF	Unc	BU
1985FM Proof	1,575	Value: 70.00				

KM# 199 50 DOLLARS
6.4800 g., 0.9167 Gold .1875 oz. AGW **Ruler:** Elizabeth II **Subject:** Junkanoo Festival **Obv:** Crowned bust of Queen Elizabeth II right, date below **Obv. Designer:** Raphael Maklouf **Rev:** Three costumed musicians, value below

Date	Mintage	F	VF	XF	Unc	BU
1994 Proof	—	Value: 150				

KM# 14 100 DOLLARS
39.9400 g., 0.9170 Gold 1.1776 oz. AGW **Ruler:** Elizabeth II **Subject:** Adoption of New Constitution **Obv:** Bust of Queen Elizabeth II right with tiara **Rev:** Columbus, date divides value at bottom **Designer:** Arnold Machin

Date	Mintage	F	VF	XF	Unc	BU
1967	1,200	—	—	—	775	—
1967 Proof	850	Value: 820				

KM# 31 100 DOLLARS
39.9400 g., 0.9170 Gold 1.1776 oz. AGW **Ruler:** Elizabeth II **Obv:** Bust of Queen Elizabeth II right with tiara **Obv. Designer:** Arnold Machin **Rev:** Shield with crown at top, sailing ship at bottom, ribbon below shield, garland above, value, date

Date	Mintage	F	VF	XF	Unc	BU
1971	6,800	—	—	—	775	—
1971(t) Proof	1,250	Value: 820				

KM# 32.1 100 DOLLARS
39.9400 g., 0.9170 Gold 1.1776 oz. AGW **Ruler:** Elizabeth II **Obv:** Bust of Queen Elizabeth II right with tiara **Obv. Designer:** Arnold Machin **Rev:** Shield with crown at top, sailing ship at bottom, ribbon below shield, garland above, value, date; hallmark and fineness at bottom right

Date	Mintage	F	VF	XF	Unc	BU
1971	—	—	—	—	775	—

KM# 32.2 100 DOLLARS
39.9400 g., 0.9170 Gold 1.1776 oz. AGW **Ruler:** Elizabeth II **Obv:** Bust of Queen Elizabeth II right with tiara **Obv. Designer:** Arnold Machin **Rev:** Shield with crown at top, sailing ship at bottom, ribbon below shield, garland on top, value, date; hallmark at bottom right, without fineness

Date	Mintage	F	VF	XF	Unc	BU
1971	—	—	—	—	775	—

KM# 32.3 100 DOLLARS
39.9400 g., 0.9170 Gold 1.1776 oz. AGW **Ruler:** Elizabeth II **Obv:** Bust of Queen Elizabeth II right with tiara **Obv. Designer:** Arnold Machin **Rev:** Shield with crown at top, sailing ship at bottom, ribbon below shield, garland above, value, date; fineness at bottom right without hallmark **Note:** Struck by the Gori and Zucchi Mint, Italy.

Date	Mintage	F	VF	XF	Unc	BU
1971	—	—	—	—	775	—

KM# 37 100 DOLLARS
31.9500 g., 0.9170 Gold .9420 oz. AGW **Ruler:** Elizabeth II **Obv:** Bust of Queen Elizabeth II right **Note:** The 1972 proof $100 is serially numbered on the edge.

Date	Mintage	F	VF	XF	Unc	BU
1972	2,250	—	—	—	620	—
1972 Proof	1,250	Value: 640				

KM# 49.1 100 DOLLARS
14.5400 g., 0.7500 Gold .3506 oz. AGW, 28 mm. **Ruler:** Elizabeth II **Subject:** Independence Day - July 10 **Obv:** Bust of Queen Elizabeth II right with tiara, date below **Rev:** National arms, value above, date below; without fineness **Designer:** Arnold Machin

Date	Mintage	F	VF	XF	Unc	BU
1973	—	—	—	—	235	—

BAHAMAS 53

KM# 49.2 100 DOLLARS
14.5400 g., 0.7500 Gold .3506 oz. AGW, 28 mm. **Ruler:** Elizabeth II **Subject:** Independence Day - July 10 **Obv:** Bust of Queen Elizabeth II right with tiara, date below **Rev:** National arms, value above; without date or fineness **Designer:** Arnold Machin

Date	Mintage	F	VF	XF	Unc	BU
1973 Proof	—	Value: 235				

KM# 50.1 100 DOLLARS
14.5400 g., 0.5850 Gold .2735 oz. AGW, 28 mm. **Ruler:** Elizabeth II **Obv:** Bust of Queen Elizabeth II right with tiara, date below **Rev:** National arms, value above, .585 fineness to left, date to right **Designer:** Arnold Machin

Date	Mintage	F	VF	XF	Unc	BU
1973	4,660	—	—	—	185	—
1973 Proof	1,260	Value: 200				

Note: Serial number on reverse

KM# 50.2 100 DOLLARS
14.5400 g., 0.5850 Gold .2735 oz. AGW, 28 mm. **Ruler:** Elizabeth II **Obv:** Bust of Queen Elizabeth II right, date below **Obv. Designer:** Arnold Machin **Rev:** National arms, value above, date and fineness at right, serial number at left

Date	Mintage	F	VF	XF	Unc	BU
1973	—	—	—	—	185	—

KM# 50.3 100 DOLLARS
14.5400 g., 0.5850 Gold .2735 oz. AGW, 28 mm. **Ruler:** Elizabeth II **Obv:** Bust of Queen Elizabeth II right with tiara, date below **Obv. Designer:** Arnold Machin **Rev:** National arms, value above, serial number at left, fineness below, date at right

Date	Mintage	F	VF	XF	Unc	BU
1973	—	—	—	—	185	—

KM# 71 100 DOLLARS
18.0145 g., 0.5000 Gold .2896 oz. AGW, 33 mm. **Ruler:** Elizabeth II **Subject:** 1st Anniversary of Independence **Obv:** National arms, date below **Rev:** Two flamingos, value at bottom, date at right **Designer:** Arnold Machin

Date	Mintage	F	VF	XF	Unc	BU
1974	4,486	—	—	—	190	—
1974 Proof	4,153	Value: 200				

KM# 72 100 DOLLARS
5.4600 g., 0.9170 Gold .1609 oz. AGW, 21 mm. **Ruler:** Elizabeth II **Obv:** Bust of Queen Elizabeth II right with tiara, date below **Rev:** Broken waves behind flamingos' legs, value at bottom **Designer:** Arnold Machin

Date	Mintage	F	VF	XF	Unc	BU
1974	29,000	—	—	—	110	—
1975	—	—	—	—	125	—

KM# 73 100 DOLLARS
5.4600 g., 0.9170 Gold .1609 oz. AGW, 21 mm. **Ruler:** Elizabeth II **Obv:** Bust of Queen Elizabeth II right with tiara, date below **Rev:** Unbroken waves behind flamingos' legs, value at bottom **Designer:** Arnold Machin

Date	Mintage	F	VF	XF	Unc	BU
1974 Proof	17,000	Value: 110				
1975 Proof	—	Value: 120				
1976	—	—	—	—	110	—
1976 Proof	—	Value: 120				
1977	—	—	—	—	120	—
1977 Proof	—	Value: 130				

KM# 74 100 DOLLARS
5.4600 g., 0.9170 Gold .1609 oz. AGW, 21 mm. **Ruler:** Elizabeth II **Obv:** Bust of Queen Elizabeth II right with tiara, date below **Rev:** Unbroken waves behind flamingos legs, date at right, value at bottom; .917 fineness in oval **Designer:** Arnold Machin

Date	Mintage	F	VF	XF	Unc	BU
1974	—	—	—	—	110	—

KM# 77 100 DOLLARS
18.0145 g., 0.5000 Gold .2896 oz. AGW **Ruler:** Elizabeth II **Subject:** 2nd Anniversary of Independence **Obv:** National arms, date below **Rev:** Bahama Amazon Parrot, value at bottom

Date	Mintage	F	VF	XF	Unc	BU
1975	3,694	—	—	—	190	—
1975 Proof	3,145	Value: 200				
1976 Proof	761	Value: 210				
1977 Proof	2,023	Value: 200				

KM# 80 100 DOLLARS
13.6000 g., 0.9630 Gold .4211 oz. AGW **Ruler:** Elizabeth II **Subject:** 5th Anniversary of Independence **Obv:** National arms, date below **Rev:** Bust of H.R.H Prince Charles, right, value below

Date	Mintage	F	VF	XF	Unc	BU
1978 Proof	3,275	Value: 285				

KM# 81 100 DOLLARS
13.6000 g., 0.9630 Gold .4211 oz. AGW **Ruler:** Elizabeth II **Subject:** 5th Anniversary of Independence **Obv:** National arms, date below **Rev:** Head of Sir Milo B. Butler, 1/2 left, value at bottom

Date	Mintage	F	VF	XF	Unc	BU
1978 Proof	25,000	Value: 285				

KM# 87 100 DOLLARS
6.4800 g., 0.9000 Gold .1875 oz. AGW **Ruler:** Elizabeth II **Subject:** Wedding of Prince Charles and Lady Diana **Obv:** Bust of Queen Elizabeth II right with tiara **Obv. Designer:** Arnold Machin **Rev:** Conjoined busts of royal couple left

Date	Mintage	F	VF	XF	Unc	BU
1981 Proof	10,000	Value: 180				

KM# 99 100 DOLLARS
6.4800 g., 0.9000 Gold .1875 oz. AGW **Ruler:** Elizabeth II **Subject:** 10th Anniversary of Independence **Obv:** National arms, date below **Rev:** Bust of soldier left within unfurled flag, value at bottom

Date	Mintage	F	VF	XF	Unc	BU
1983 Proof	400	Value: 200				

KM# 111 100 DOLLARS
6.4800 g., 0.9000 Gold .1875 oz. AGW **Ruler:** Elizabeth II **Subject:** Columbus' Discovery of America **Obv:** National arms **Rev:** Columbus with group of people, date at bottom, value at top

Date	Mintage	F	VF	XF	Unc	BU
1985 Proof	450	Value: 200				

KM# 119 100 DOLLARS
6.4800 g., 0.9000 Gold .1875 oz. AGW **Ruler:** Elizabeth II **Obv:** Crowned bust of Queen Elizabeth II right **Obv. Designer:** Raphael Maklouf **Rev:** Queen Isabella receiving Christopher Columbus, date below, value at top

Date	Mintage	F	VF	XF	Unc	BU
1987 Proof	849	Value: 185				

KM# 125 100 DOLLARS
6.4800 g., 0.9000 Gold .1875 oz. AGW **Ruler:** Elizabeth II **Subject:** Columbus Discovering America **Obv:** Bust of Queen Elizabeth II right **Rev:** Columbus sighting America

Date	Mintage	F	VF	XF	Unc	BU
1988 Proof	854	Value: 185				

KM# 130 100 DOLLARS
6.4800 g., 0.9000 Gold .1875 oz. AGW **Ruler:** Elizabeth II **Obv:** Queen Elizabeth **Rev:** Christopher Columbus, radiant sun and ocean in background within circle, date below, and at right of circle

Date	Mintage	F	VF	XF	Unc	BU
1989 Proof	Est. 5,000	Value: 180				

54 BAHAMAS

KM# 135 100 DOLLARS
6.4800 g., 0.9000 Gold .1875 oz. AGW **Ruler:** Elizabeth II
Subject: Discovery of New World **Obv:** Queen Elizabeth II, date below **Rev:** Bust of Columbus left, value below circle

Date	Mintage	F	VF	XF	Unc	BU
1990	500	—	—	—	250	—
1990 Proof	5,000	Value: 175				

KM# 151 100 DOLLARS
6.4800 g., 0.9000 Gold .1875 oz. AGW **Ruler:** Elizabeth II
Subject: Discovery of New World **Obv:** Crowned bust of Queen Elizabeth II right, date below **Obv. Designer:** Raphael Maklouf **Rev:** 5 men rowing boat, ships in background within inner circle, legend above, value below

Date	Mintage	F	VF	XF	Unc	BU
1991	500	—	—	—	250	—

KM# 152 100 DOLLARS
6.4800 g., 0.9000 Gold .1875 oz. AGW **Ruler:** Elizabeth II
Subject: Discovery of New World **Obv:** Crowned bust of Queen Elizabeth II right, date below **Obv. Designer:** Raphael Maklouf **Rev:** Columbus' ships within circle, value below circle

Date	Mintage	F	VF	XF	Unc	BU
1992 Proof	Est. 5,000,000	Value: 170				
1992 Matte	—	Value: 250				

KM# 51 150 DOLLARS
8.1900 g., 0.9170 Gold .2414 oz. AGW, 24 mm. **Ruler:** Elizabeth II **Subject:** Independence Day - July 10 **Obv:** Bust of Queen Elizabeth II right with tiara, date below **Rev:** Spiny Lobster, value, small date at right **Designer:** Arnold Machin

Date	Mintage	F	VF	XF	Unc	BU
1973	—	—	—	—	160	—
1973 Proof	—	Value: 170				
1974	7,128	—	—	—	165	—
1974 Proof	4,787	Value: 170				
1975	3,141	—	—	—	165	—
1975 Proof	2,770	Value: 180				
1976 Proof	168	Value: 300				
1977 Proof	327	Value: 240				

KM# 52 150 DOLLARS
8.1900 g., 0.9170 Gold .2414 oz. AGW **Ruler:** Elizabeth II **Obv:** Bust of Queen Elizabeth II right with tiara, date below **Rev:** Spiny Lobster, value, small date at right **Designer:** Arnold Machin

Date	Mintage	F	VF	XF	Unc	BU
1974 Proof	—	Value: 170				

KM# 53 150 DOLLARS
8.1900 g., 0.9170 Gold .2414 oz. AGW **Ruler:** Elizabeth II **Obv:** Bust of Queen Elizabeth II right with tiara, date below **Rev:** Spiny Lobster, value, small date at right; .917 fineness in oval **Designer:** Arnold Machin

Date	Mintage	F	VF	XF	Unc	BU
1974	—	—	—	—	170	—

KM# 54 200 DOLLARS
10.9200 g., 0.9170 Gold .3219 oz. AGW, 28 mm. **Ruler:** Elizabeth II **Subject:** Independence Day - July 10 **Obv:** Bust of Queen Elizabeth II right with tiara, date below **Obv. Designer:** Arnold Machin **Rev:** National arms, value above small date at right

Date	Mintage	F	VF	XF	Unc	BU
1973	—	—	—	—	210	—
1973 Proof	—	Value: 225				
1974	5,528	—	—	—	210	—
1974 Proof	3,587	Value: 225				
1975	1,545	—	—	—	215	—
1975 Proof	1,570	Value: 235				
1976 Proof	168	Value: 300				
1977 Proof	321	Value: 280				

KM# 56 200 DOLLARS
10.9200 g., 0.9170 Gold .3219 oz. AGW **Ruler:** Elizabeth II **Obv:** Bust of Queen Elizabeth II right with tiara, date below **Obv. Designer:** Arnold Machin **Rev:** National arms, value above, small date at right; .917 fineness in oval

Date	Mintage	F	VF	XF	Unc	BU
1974	—	—	—	—	210	—

KM# 57 200 DOLLARS
10.9200 g., 0.9170 Gold .3219 oz. AGW **Ruler:** Elizabeth II **Obv:** Bust of Queen Elizabeth II right **Rev:** .916 fineness at left, serial number stamped below arms

Date	Mintage	F	VF	XF	Unc	BU
1974	—	—	—	—	210	—

KM# 83 250 DOLLARS
10.5800 g., 0.9000 Gold .3061 oz. AGW **Ruler:** Elizabeth II **Subject:** 250th Anniversary of Parliament **Obv:** Princess Anne's bust 1/2 left in inner circle, value below **Rev:** National arms, date below

Date	Mintage	F	VF	XF	Unc	BU
1979 Proof	1,835	Value: 225				

KM# 117 250 DOLLARS
47.5400 g., 0.9170 Gold 1.4017 oz. AGW **Ruler:** Elizabeth II **Subject:** Commonwealth Games **Obv:** National arms **Rev:** Competitor running left, value at right, logo below

Date	Mintage	F	VF	XF	Unc	BU
1985 Proof	101	Value: 1,000				

KM# 137 250 DOLLARS
47.5400 g., 0.9170 Gold 1.4017 oz. AGW **Ruler:** Elizabeth II **Subject:** Royal Visit **Obv:** Crowned bust of Queen Elizabeth II, right **Obv. Designer:** Raphael Maklouf **Rev:** National arms, value below

Date	Mintage	F	VF	XF	Unc	BU
1985 Proof	100	Value: 1,000				

KM# 121 250 DOLLARS
47.5400 g., 0.9170 Gold 1.4017 oz. AGW **Ruler:** Elizabeth II **Obv:** Bust of Queen Elizabeth II right **Obv. Designer:** Raphael Maklouf **Rev:** Queen Isabella receiving Columbus, date at bottom, value at top

Date	Mintage	F	VF	XF	Unc	BU
1987 Proof	100	Value: 1,000				

KM# 126 250 DOLLARS
47.5400 g., 0.9170 Gold 1.4017 oz. AGW **Ruler:** Elizabeth II **Subject:** Columbus Discovers the New World **Obv:** Bust of Queen Elizabeth II right **Rev:** Columbus sighting land, date at bottom, value at top

Date	Mintage	F	VF	XF	Unc	BU
1988 Proof	53	Value: 1,100				

KM# 131 250 DOLLARS
47.5400 g., 0.9170 Gold 1.4017 oz. AGW **Ruler:** Elizabeth II **Obv:** Bust of Queen Elizabeth II right **Rev:** Christopher Columbus

Date	Mintage	F	VF	XF	Unc	BU
1989 Proof	Est. 250	Value: 950				

BAHAMAS 55

KM# 136 250 DOLLARS
47.5400 g., 0.9170 Gold 1.4017 oz. AGW **Ruler:** Elizabeth II **Subject:** Discovery of New World **Obv:** Bust of Queen Elizabeth II right **Rev:** Native American facing right, within circle, value at bottom
Date	Mintage	F	VF	XF	Unc	BU
1990 Proof	500	Value: 925				

KM# 175 250 DOLLARS
47.5400 g., 0.9170 Gold 1.4017 oz. AGW **Ruler:** Elizabeth II **Subject:** Discovery of the New World **Rev:** Columbus meeting native Americans, within circle, value below circle
Date	Mintage	F	VF	XF	Unc	BU
1992 Proof	Est. 500	Value: 925				

KM# 182 250 DOLLARS
47.5400 g., 0.9170 Gold 1.4017 oz. AGW **Ruler:** Elizabeth II **Subject:** Royal Visit **Note:** Similar to 2 Dollars, KM#158.
Date	Mintage	F	VF	XF	Unc	BU
1994 Proof	100	Value: 1,200				

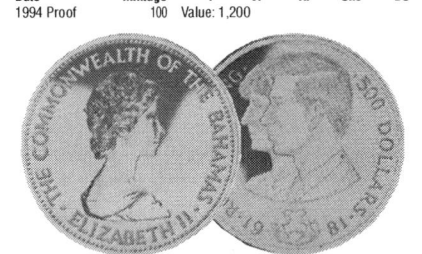

KM# 88 500 DOLLARS
25.9200 g., 0.9000 Gold .7500 oz. AGW **Ruler:** Elizabeth II **Subject:** Wedding of Prince Charles and Lady Diana **Obv:** Bust of Queen Elizabeth II right with tiara **Obv. Designer:** Arnold Machin **Rev:** Conjoined busts of royal couple left
Date	Mintage	F	VF	XF	Unc	BU
1981 Proof	5,000	Value: 520				

KM# 100 1000 DOLLARS
41.4700 g., 0.9000 Gold 1.2001 oz. AGW **Ruler:** Elizabeth II **Subject:** America's Cup Challenge **Obv:** Bust of Queen Elizabeth II right with tiara, date below **Obv. Designer:** Arnold Machin **Rev:** Sailboat, value at left
Date	Mintage	F	VF	XF	Unc	BU
1983 Proof	300	Value: 820				

KM# 75 2500 DOLLARS
407.2600 g., 0.9170 Gold 12.0082 oz. AGW, 72 mm. **Ruler:** Elizabeth II **Obv:** National arms **Rev:** Two flamingos, value above, date below **Note:** Illustration reduced.
Date	Mintage	F	VF	XF	Unc	BU
1974 Proof	204	Value: 8,000				
1977 Proof	168	Value: 9,000				

KM# 101 2500 DOLLARS
407.2600 g., 0.9170 Gold 12.0082 oz. AGW, 72 mm. **Ruler:** Elizabeth II **Subject:** 10th Anniversary of Independence **Obv:** Bust of young Queen Elizabeth II right **Rev:** National arms, value below
Date	Mintage	F	VF	XF	Unc	BU
1983 Proof	55	Value: 9,500				

KM# 112 2500 DOLLARS
407.2600 g., 0.9170 Gold 12.0082 oz. AGW, 72 mm. **Ruler:** Elizabeth II **Subject:** Columbus' Discovery of America **Obv:** Bust of Queen Elizabeth II right **Rev:** Columbus with crew claiming land for Spain, planting flag, date below
Date	Mintage	F	VF	XF	Unc	BU
1985 Proof	37	Value: 10,000				

KM# 116 2500 DOLLARS
407.2600 g., 0.9170 Gold 12.0082 oz. AGW, 72 mm. **Ruler:** Elizabeth II **Rev:** Kneeling Columbus and Queen Isabella, date at bottom **Rev. Designer:** Frank Gasparro
Date	Mintage	F	VF	XF	Unc	BU
1987 Proof	20	Value: 10,250				

BAHAMAS

KM# 122 2500 DOLLARS
407.2600 g., 0.9170 Gold 12.0082 oz. AGW **Ruler:** Elizabeth II
Obv: Bust of Queen Elizabeth II right **Rev:** Columbus sighting "New World"

Date	Mintage	F	VF	XF	Unc	BU
1988 Proof	32	Value: 10,000				

MINT SETS

KM#	Date	Mintage	Identification	Issue Price	Mkt Val
MS3	1967 (4)	1,200	KM#11-14	180	1,350
MS7	1971 (4)	6,800	KM#25, 27, 29, 31	185	1,100
MS9	1972 (4)	2,250	KM#34-37	185	900
MS11	1973 (4)	4,660	KM#40, 43, 47, 49.1	—	460
MS14	1974 (4)	5,528	KM#51, 54, 69, 72	—	575
MS15	1974 (2)	—	KM#68, 71	—	200
MS17	1975 (4)	1,545	KM#51, 54, 69, 72	—	650

PROOF SETS

KM#	Date	Mintage	Identification	Issue Price	Mkt Val
PS1	1967 (4)	850	KM#11-14	252	1,300
PS5A	1971 (4)	1,250	KM#25, 27, 29, 31	298	1,200
PS5B	1971 (4)	—	KM#26, 28, 30, 32.1	—	1,000
PS7	1972 (4)	1,250	KM#34-37	565	1,200
PS9	1973 (4)	1,260	KM#41, 44, 46, 50	402	500
PS11	1974 (4)	3,587	KM#51, 54, 69, 73	1,000	600
PS13	1975 (4)	1,570	KM#51, 54, 69, 73	1,000	650
PS15	1976 (4)	—	KM#51, 54, 69, 73	1,000	750
PS17	1977 (4)	—	KM#51, 54, 69, 73	—	700
PS20	1979 (2)	—	KM#82-83	445	375
PS29	1992 (3)	750	KM#192-194 + gold-plated silver ingot	—	400

BAHRAIN

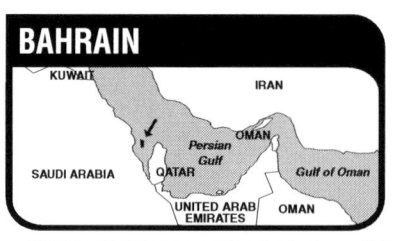

The State of Bahrain, a group of islands in the Persian Gulf off Saudi Arabia, has an area of 268 sq. mi. (622 sq. km.) and a population of 618,000. Capital: Manama. Prior to the depression of the 1930's, the economy was based on pearl fishing. Petroleum and aluminum industries and transit trade are the vital factors in the economy today.

The Portuguese occupied the islands in 1507 but were driven out in 1602 by Arab subjects of Persia. The Portuguese were ejected by Arabs of the Ataiba tribe from the Arabian mainland. They have maintained possession up to the present time. The ruling sheikh of Bahrain entered into relations with Great Britain in 1805 and concluded a binding treaty of protection in 1861. In 1968 Great Britain decided to terminate treaty relations with the Persian Gulf sheikhdoms. Unable to agree on terms of union with the other sheikhdoms, Bahrain decided to seek independence as a separate entity and became fully independent on August 14, 1971.

Bahrain took part in the Arab oil embargo against the U.S. and other nations. The government bought controlling interest in the oil industry in 1975.

The coinage of the State of Bahrain was struck at the Royal Mint, London, England.

RULERS

Al Khalifa Dynasty
Salman Bin Ahmad, 1796-1825
  with Abdullah Bin Ahmad, 1796-1843
  with Khalifa Bin Salman, 1825-1834
Muhammad Bin Khalifa
  with Muhammad Bin Abdullah, 1843-1868
Ali Bin Khalifa, 1868-1869
Muhammad Bin Abdullah
  with Muhammad Bin Khalifa, 1869
Isa Bin Ali, 1869-1932
Hamad Bin Isa, 1932-1942
Salman Bin Hamad, 1942-1961
Isa Bin Salman, 1961-

MINT MARKS

البحرين
Bahrain

البحرين
al-Bahrain = of the two seas

MONETARY SYSTEM
1000 Fils = 1 Dinar

KINGDOM OF BAHRAIN

STANDARD COINAGE

KM# 11 50 DINARS
15.9800 g., 0.9170 Gold .4712 oz. AGW **Ruler:** Isa Bin Salman
Subject: 50th Anniversary of Bahrain Monetary Agency

Date	Mintage	F	VF	XF	Unc	BU
AH1398-1978 Proof	5,000	Value: 350				

KM# 12 100 DINARS
31.9600 g., 0.9170 Gold .9424 oz. AGW **Ruler:** Isa Bin Salman
Subject: 50th Anniversary of Bahrain Monetary Agency **Obv:** Bust left **Rev:** Coat of arms divides dates

Date	Mintage	F	VF	XF	Unc	BU
AH1398-1978 Proof	5,000	Value: 675				

MEDALLIC COINAGE

X# 1 10 DINARS
16.0000 g., 0.9170 Gold .4717 oz. AGW **Rev:** Opening of Isa Town

Date	Mintage	F	VF	XF	Unc	BU
AH1388	3,000	—	—	—	400	—

X# 2 10 DINARS
16.0000 g., 0.9170 Gold .4717 oz. AGW **Rev:** Independence Commemorative

Date	Mintage	F	VF	XF	Unc	BU
AH1391	3,000	—	—	—	400	—

X# 3 10 DINARS
16.0000 g., 0.9170 Gold .4717 oz. AGW **Rev:** Opening of Hamad Town

Date	Mintage	F	VF	XF	Unc	BU
AH1404 Proof	—	Value: 400				

BARBADOS

Barbados, an independent state within the British Commonwealth, is located in the Windward Islands of the West Indies east of St. Vincent. The coral island has an area of 166 sq. mi. (430 sq. km.) and a population of 269,000. Capital: Bridgetown. The economy is based on sugar and tourism. Sugar, petroleum products, molasses, and rum are exported.

Barbados was named by the Portuguese who achieved the first landing on the island in 1563. British sailors landed at the site of present-day Holetown in 1624. Barbados was under uninterrupted British control from the time of the first British settlement in 1627 until it obtained independence on Nov. 30, 1966. It is a member of the Commonwealth of Nations. Elizabeth II is Head of State as Queen of Barbados.

Unmarked side cut pieces of Spanish and Spanish Colonial 1, 2 and 8 reales were the principal coinage medium of 18th-century Barbados. The "Neptune" tokens issued by Sir Phillip Gibbs, a local plantation owner, circulated freely but were never established as legal coinage. The coinage and banknotes of the British Caribbean Territories (Eastern Group) were employed prior to 1973 when Barbados issued a decimal coinage.

RULERS
British, until 1966

MINT MARKS
FM - Franklin Mint, U.S.A.*
None - Royal Mint
   *NOTE: From 1975-1985 the Franklin Mint produced coinage in up to 3 different qualities. Qualities of issue are designated in ( ) after each date and are defined as follows:
   (M) MATTE - Normal circulation strike or a dull finish produced by sandblasting special uncirculated (polish finish) or proof quality dies.
   (U) SPECIAL UNCIRCULATED - Polished or proof-like in appearance without any frosted features.
   (P) PROOF - The highest quality obtainable having mirror-like fields and frosted features.

MONETARY SYSTEM
100 Cents = 1 Dollar

INDEPENDENT SOVEREIGN STATE
within the British Commonwealth
DECIMAL COINAGE

KM# 60   10 DOLLARS
7.7800 g., 0.5830 Gold .1458 oz. AGW **Subject:** Queen Mother's Engagement **Obv:** National arms **Rev:** Bust right, spray below

Date	Mintage	F	VF	XF	Unc	BU
1995 Proof	Est. 5,000			Value: 150		

KM# 51   50 DOLLARS
15.9800 g., 0.9170 Gold .4709 oz. AGW **Subject:** International Cricket Belt Buckle **Obv:** National arms **Rev:** Belt buckle

Date	Mintage	F	VF	XF	Unc	BU
1991 Proof	500			Value: 530		

KM# 56   50 DOLLARS
15.9800 g., 0.9170 Gold .4709 oz. AGW **Subject:** UN Global SIDS Conference **Obv:** National arms **Rev:** Small house and tree within hand design **Designer:** Robert Elderton

Date	Mintage	F	VF	XF	Unc	BU
1994 Proof	100			Value: 550		

KM# 18   100 DOLLARS
6.2100 g., 0.5000 Gold .0998 oz. AGW **Subject:** 350th Anniversary - The English Ship **Obv:** National arms **Rev:** Olive Blossom with full sails

Date	Mintage	F	VF	XF	Unc	BU
ND(1975)FM (M)	50	—	—	—	250	—
ND(1975)FM (U)	16,000	—	—	—	75.00	—
ND(1975)FM (P)	23,000	Value: 85.00				

KM# 28   100 DOLLARS
4.0600 g., 0.9000 Gold .1174 oz. AGW **Subject:** Human Rights **Obv:** National arms **Rev:** Praying hands beneath rolled scroll

Date	Mintage	F	VF	XF	Unc	BU
1978	1,114	—	—	—	125	—

KM# 28a   100 DOLLARS
5.0500 g., 0.9000 Gold .1461 oz. AGW **Subject:** Human Rights **Obv:** National arms **Rev:** Praying hands beneath rolled scroll

Date	Mintage	F	VF	XF	Unc	BU
1978 Proof	Inc. above			Value: 150		

KM# 38   100 DOLLARS
6.2100 g., 0.5000 Gold .0998 oz. AGW **Subject:** Neptune, God of the Sea **Obv:** National arms **Rev:** Standing figure looking right

Date	Mintage	F	VF	XF	Unc	BU
1983FM (U)	3	—	—	—	—	—
1983FM (P)	484			Value: 225		

KM# 39   100 DOLLARS
6.2100 g., 0.5000 Gold .0998 oz. AGW **Subject:** Triton, Son of Neptune **Obv:** National arms **Rev:** Full figure left blowing horn

Date	Mintage	F	VF	XF	Unc	BU
1984FM (P)	1,103			Value: 170		

KM# 41   100 DOLLARS
6.2100 g., 0.5000 Gold .0998 oz. AGW **Subject:** Amphitrite, Wife of Neptune **Obv:** National arms **Rev:** Full figure facing looking left

Date	Mintage	F	VF	XF	Unc	BU
1985FM (P)	1,276			Value: 185		

KM# 48   100 DOLLARS
15.9760 g., 0.9170 Gold .4709 oz. AGW **Subject:** 350th Anniversary of Parliament **Obv:** Crowned bust right **Rev:** Parliament Building

Date	Mintage	F	VF	XF	Unc	BU
ND(1989)FM	Est. 500			Value: 350		

KM# 33   150 DOLLARS
7.1300 g., 0.5000 Gold .1146 oz. AGW **Subject:** National Flower - Poinciana **Obv:** National arms **Rev:** Flower and map

Date	Mintage	F	VF	XF	Unc	BU
1981FM (U)	7	—	—	—	—	—
1981FM (P)	1,140			Value: 125		

KM# 29   200 DOLLARS
8.1200 g., 0.9000 Gold .2349 oz. AGW **Subject:** Year of the Child **Obv:** National arms **Rev:** Shaded circle above large shaded letter "Y" depicts child figure

Date	Mintage	F	VF	XF	Unc	BU
1979	1,121	—	—	—	225	—

KM# 29a   200 DOLLARS
10.1000 g., 0.9000 Gold .2922 oz. AGW **Subject:** Year of the Child **Obv:** National arms **Rev:** Shaded circle above large shaded letter "Y" depicts child figure

Date	Mintage	F	VF	XF	Unc	BU
1979 Proof	Inc. above			Value: 275		

KM# 35   250 DOLLARS
6.6000 g., 0.9000 Gold .1910 oz. AGW **Subject:** 250th Anniversary of Birth of George Washington **Obv:** National arms **Rev:** Small head left below building

Date	Mintage	F	VF	XF	Unc	BU
1982FM (P)	802			Value: 185		

KM# 45   250 DOLLARS
47.5400 g., 0.9170 Gold 1.4017 oz. AGW **Subject:** Commonwealth Games **Obv:** National arms **Rev:** Discus thrower right

Date	Mintage	F	VF	XF	Unc	BU
1986 Proof	150			Value: 985		

KM# 71   500 DOLLARS
47.5400 g., 0.9170 Gold 1.4013 oz. AGW **Subject:** Royal Visit **Obv:** Crowned bust right **Rev:** National arms

Date	Mintage	F	VF	XF	Unc	BU
1985	Est. 250			Value: 965		

BELARUS

Belarus (Byelorussia, Belorussia, or White Russia- formerly the Belorussian S.S.R.) is situated along the western Dvina and Dnieper Rivers, bounded in the west by Poland, to the north by Latvia and Lithuania, to the east by Russia and the south by the Ukraine. It has an area of 80,154 sq. mi. (207,600 sq. km.) and a population of 4.8 million. Capital: Minsk. Chief products: peat, salt, and agricultural products including flax, fodder and grasses for cattle breeding and dairy products.

There never existed an independent state of Byelorussia. Until the partitions of Poland at the end of the 18th century, the history of Byelorussia is identical with that of Lithuania.

When Russia incorporated the whole of Byelorussia into its territories in 1795, it claimed to be recovering old Russian lands and denied that the Byelorussians were a separate nation. Significant efforts for independence did not occur until 1918 and were met by external antagonism from German, Polish, and Russian influences.

Soviet and anti-Communist sympathies continued to reflect the political and social unrest of the U.S.S.R. for Byelorussia. Finally, on August 25, 1991, following an unsuccessful coup, the Supreme Soviet adopted a declaration of independence, and the "Republic of Belarus" was proclaimed in September. In December, it became a founder member of the CIS.

MONETARY SYSTEM
100 Kapeek = 1 Rouble

REPUBLIC
STANDARD COINAGE

KM# 31 ROUBLE
7.9800 g., 0.9167 Gold .2532 oz. AGW, 22.85 mm. **Subject:** United Nations 50th Anniversary **Obv:** National arms, date at bottom **Rev:** Crane flying over map and U.N. logo **Designer:** A.I. Zimenko and D.G. Belitsky

Date	Mintage	F	VF	XF	Unc	BU
1996 Proof	5,000	Value: 1,500				

KM# 32 50 ROUBLES
7.7800 g., 0.9990 Gold .2499 oz. AGW, 22 mm. **Subject:** Olympics **Obv:** National arms and denomination **Rev:** Ribbon dancer **Designer:** A.I. Zimenko and D.G. Belitsky

Date	Mintage	F	VF	XF	Unc	BU
1996 Proof	500	Value: 600				

KM# 33 50 ROUBLES
7.7800 g., 0.9990 Gold .2499 oz. AGW, 22 mm. **Obv:** National arms and denomination **Rev:** Gymnast on rings **Designer:** A.I. Zimenko and D.G. Belitsky

Date	Mintage	F	VF	XF	Unc	BU
1996 Proof	500	Value: 600				

KM# 35 50 ROUBLES
7.7800 g., 0.9990 Gold .2499 oz. AGW, 22 mm. **Obv:** National arms and denomination **Obv. Designer:** A.I. Zimenko and D.G. Belitsky **Rev:** Biathalow skier with rifle **Rev. Designer:** T.S. Radivilko

Date	Mintage	F	VF	XF	Unc	BU
1997 Proof	500	Value: 550				

KM# 37 50 ROUBLES
7.7800 g., 0.9990 Gold .2499 oz. AGW, 22 mm. **Obv:** National arms and denomination **Obv. Designer:** A.I. Zimenko and D.G. Belitsky **Rev:** Two hockey players **Rev. Designer:** T.S. Radivilko

Date	Mintage	F	VF	XF	Unc	BU
1997 Proof	500	Value: 600				

KM# 38 50 ROUBLES
7.7800 g., 0.9990 Gold .2499 oz. AGW **Obv:** National arms and denomination **Obv. Designer:** A.I. Zimenko and D.G. Belitsky **Rev:** Two hurdlers

Date	Mintage	F	VF	XF	Unc	BU
1997 Proof	500	Value: 550				

KM# 103 200 ROUBLES
31.1000 g., 0.9990 Gold 0.9989 oz. AGW, 40 mm. **Obv:** National arms **Rev:** Belarussian ballerina

Date	Mintage	F	VF	XF	Unc	BU
2005 Proof	1,500	Value: 850				

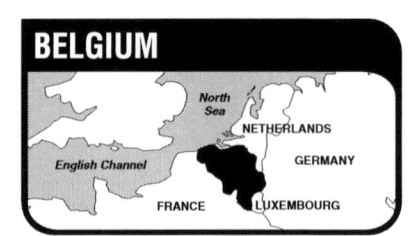

BELGIUM

The Kingdom of Belgium, a constitutional monarchy in northwest Europe, has an area of 11,780 sq. mi. (30,519 sq. km.) and a population of 10.1 million, chiefly Dutch-speaking Flemish and French-speaking Walloons. Capital: Brussels. Agriculture, dairy farming, and the processing of raw materials for re-export are the principal industries. Beurs voor Diamant in Antwerp is the world's largest diamond trading center. Iron and steel, machinery motor vehicles, chemicals, textile yarns and fabrics comprise the principal exports.

The Celtic tribe called Belgae', from which Belgium derived its name, was described by Caesar as the most courageous of all the tribes of Gaul. The Belgae eventually capitulated to Rome and the area remained for centuries as a part of the Roman Empire known as Belgica.

As Rome began its decline Frankish tribes migrated westward and established the Merovingian, and subsequently, the Carolingian empires. At the death of Charlemagne, Europe was divided among his three sons Karl, Lothar and Ludwig. The eastern part of today's Belgium lies in the Duchy of Lower Lorraine while much of the western parts eventually became the County of Flanders. After further divisions the area came under the control of the Duke of Burgundy from whence it passed under Hapsburg control when Marie of Burgundy married Maximilian of Austria. Philip I (the Fair), son of Maximilian and Marie then added Spain to the Hapsburg empire by marrying Johanna, daughter of Ferdinand and Isabella. Charles and Ferdinand, sons of Philip and Johanna, began the separate Spanish and Austrian lines of the Hapsburg family. The Burgundian lands, along with the northern provinces which make up present day Netherlands, became the Spanish Netherlands. The northern provinces successfully rebelled and broke away from Hapsburg rule in the late 16th century and early 17th century. The southern provinces along with the Duchy of Luxembourg remained under the influence of Spain until the year 1700 when Charles II, last of the Spanish Hapsburg line, died without leaving an heir and the Spanish crown went to the Bourbon family of France. The Spanish Netherlands then reverted to the control of the Austrian line of Hapsburgs and became the Austrian Netherlands. The Austrian Netherlands along with the Bishopric of Liege fell to the French Republic in 1794.

At the Congress of Vienna in 1815 the area was reunited with the Netherlands, but in 1830 independence was gained and the constitutional monarchy of Belgium was established. A large part of the Duchy of Luxembourg was incorporated into Belgium and the first king was Leopold I of Saxe-Coburg-Gotha. It was invaded by the German Army in August, 1914 and the German forces carried on a devastating occupation of most of the territory until the Armistice. Belgium joined the League of Nations. On May 10, 1940 it was invaded again by the German army. The Belgian and Allied forces were quickly overwhelmed and were evacuated through Dunkirk. Allied troops reached Belgium again in Sept. 1944. Prince Charles, Count of Flanders, assumed King Leopold's responsibilities until liberation by the U.S. Army in Austria on May 8, 1945. As of January 1, 1989, Belgium became a federal kingdom.

RULERS
Leopold I, 1831-1865
Leopold II, 1865-1909
Albert I, 1909-1934
Leopold III, 1934-1950
Baudouin I, 1951-1993
Albert II, 1993-

MINT MARKS
Angel head - Brussels

MINTMASTERS' INITIALS & PRIVY MARKS
(b) - bird - Vogeleer
Lamb head – Lambret
NOTE: Beginning in 1987, the letters "qp" appear on the coins - (quality proof)

MONETARY SYSTEM
100 Centimes = 1 Franc
1 Ecu - 1 Euro

LEGENDS
Belgian coins are usually inscribed either in Dutch, French or both. However some modern coins are being inscribed in Latin or German. The language used is best told by noting the spelling of the name of the country.
(Fr) French: BELGIQUE or BELGES
(Du) Dutch: BELGIE or BELGEN
(La) Latin: BELGICA
(Ge) German: BELGIEN

Many Belgian coins are collected by what is known as Position A and Position B edges. Some dates command a premium depending on the edge positions which are as follows:
Position A: Coins with portrait side down having upright edge lettering.
Position B: Coins with portrait side up having upright edge lettering.

BELGIUM

KINGDOM
DECIMAL COINAGE

KM# 18   10 FRANCS (10 Frank)
3.1662 g., 0.9000 Gold .0916 oz. AGW **Ruler:** Leopold I **Obv:** Head right **Obv. Legend:** LEOPOLD PREMIER ROI DES BELGES **Rev:** Crowned and mantled arms divide denomination **Rev. Legend:** L'UNION FAIT LA FORCE **Note:** 54,890 pieces dated 1849 and 1850 were withdrawn from circulation.

Date	Mintage	VG	F	VF	XF	Unc
1849	37,000	—	600	1,500	2,500	4,000
1850	63,000	—	500	1,200	2,000	3,000

KM# A33   10 FRANCS (10 Frank)
3.1662 g., 0.9000 Gold .0916 oz. AGW **Ruler:** Leopold II

Date	Mintage	VG	F	VF	XF	Unc
1865 Restrike						
1867	—	—	1,800	3,200	6,500	11,000

KM# A23.1   20 FRANCS (20 Frank)
6.4516 g., 0.9000 Gold .1867 oz. AGW **Ruler:** Leopold I **Obv:** Head right **Obv. Legend:** LEOPOLD PREMIER ROI DES BELGES **Rev:** Denomination within wreath **Edge:** Lettered

Date	Mintage	F	VF	XF	Unc	BU
1834	—	950	4,800	8,000	13,000	—
1835	—	1,200	6,000	10,000	15,000	—
1838 1 known						
1841	—	1,300	6,500	12,000	17,000	—

KM# A23.2   20 FRANCS (20 Frank)
6.4516 g., 0.9000 Gold .1867 oz. AGW **Ruler:** Leopold I **Obv:** Head right **Obv. Legend:** LEOPOLD PREMIER ROI DES BELGES **Rev:** Denomination within wreath **Edge:** Milled

Date	Mintage	F	VF	XF	Unc	BU
1834 Restrike	—	—	—	—	—	—
1835 Restrike	—	—	—	—	—	—
1838 Restrike	—	—	—	—	—	—
1841 Restrike	—	—	—	—	—	—

KM# A23.3   20 FRANCS (20 Frank)
6.4516 g., 0.9000 Gold .1867 oz. AGW **Ruler:** Leopold I **Obv:** Head right **Obv. Legend:** LEOPOLD PREMIER ROI DES BELGES **Rev:** Denomination within wreath **Edge:** Plain

Date	Mintage	F	VF	XF	Unc	BU
1834 Restrike	—	—	—	—	—	—
1835 Restrike	—	—	—	—	—	—
1838 Restrike	—	—	—	—	—	—
1841 Restrike	—	—	—	—	—	—

KM# 23   20 FRANCS (20 Frank)
6.4516 g., 0.9000 Gold .1867 oz. AGW **Ruler:** Leopold I **Obv:** Head right **Obv. Legend:** LEOPOLD PREMIER ROI DES BELGES **Rev:** Denomination and date within wreath **Note:** Approximately 1/3 of the 1865 mintage was struck in 1866. Each variety of name below the bust exists both in positon A and position B, with values being the same.

Date	Mintage	F	VF	XF	Unc	BU
1865 L. WIENER	1,548,000	—	BV	125	150	300
1865 L WIENER	Inc. above	—	BV	125	150	250
1865 L WINNER Error	Inc. above	150	400	600	1,200	2,000

KM# 32   20 FRANCS (20 Frank)
6.4516 g., 0.9000 Gold .1867 oz. AGW **Ruler:** Leopold II **Obv:** Head right, heavy coarser beard **Obv. Legend:** LEOPOLD II ROI DES BELGES **Rev:** Crowned and mantled arms **Rev. Legend:** L'UNION FAIT LA FORCE

Date	Mintage	F	VF	XF	Unc	BU
1867	1,341,000	—	—	BV	125	130
1868	1,382,000	—	—	BV	125	130
1869 Position A	1,234,000	—	—	BV	125	130
1869 Position B	Inc. above	BV	150	175	250	375
1870	3,191,000	—	—	BV	130	165

KM# 37   20 FRANCS (20 Frank)
6.4516 g., 0.9000 Gold .1867 oz. AGW **Ruler:** Leopold II **Obv:** Finer beard

Date	Mintage	F	VF	XF	Unc	BU
1870 Position A	Inc. above	—	—	BV	125	—
1870 Position B	Inc. above	BV	125	150	200	—
1871 Long beard	Inc. below	—	BV	125	135	—
1871 Position A	2,259,000	BV	125	140	160	—
1871 Position B	Inc. above	BV	160	180	220	—
1874 Position A	3,046,000	BV	125	140	160	—
1874 Position B	Inc. above	—	—	BV	125	—
1875	4,134,000	—	—	BV	125	—
1876 Position A	2,070,000	—	—	BV	125	—
1876 Position B	Inc. above	150	350	500	700	—
1877	5,906,000	—	—	BV	125	—
1878	2,505,000	—	—	BV	125	—
1882	522,000	—	BV	125	135	—

KM# 78   20 FRANCS (20 Frank)
6.4516 g., 0.9000 Gold .1867 oz. AGW **Obv:** Armored bust of Albert, left, legend in French **Obv. Legend:** DES BELGES **Rev:** Crowned arms divide denomination and date

Date	Mintage	F	VF	XF	Unc	BU
1914 Position A	125,000	—	—	BV	150	250
1914 Position B	Inc. above	300	600	800	1,000	—

KM# 79   20 FRANCS (20 Frank)
6.4516 g., 0.9000 Gold .1867 oz. AGW **Obv:** Armored bust of Albert, left, legend in Dutch **Obv. Legend:** DER BELGEN **Rev:** Crowned arms divide denomination and date

Date	Mintage	F	VF	XF	Unc	BU
1914 Position A	125,000	—	—	BV	125	160
1914 Position B	Inc. above	—	BV	125	140	185

KM# 13.1   25 FRANCS
7.9155 g., 0.9000 Gold .2291 oz. AGW **Ruler:** Leopold I **Obv:** Head right **Obv. Legend:** LEOPOLD PREMIER ROI DES BELGES **Rev:** Crowned and mantled arms **Rev. Legend:** L'UNION FAIT LA FORCE **Note:** 16.5% of the total mintage of KM13.1 and 13.2 was melted. Actual number melted per date is unavailable.

Date	Mintage	F	VF	XF	Unc	BU
1848	321,000	600	1,400	2,000	3,400	—
1849	150,000	1,000	2,500	3,500	7,000	—

KM# 13.2   25 FRANCS
7.9155 g., 0.9000 Gold .2291 oz. AGW **Ruler:** Leopold I **Obv:** Larger head **Obv. Legend:** LEOPOLD PREMIER ROI DES BELGES **Rev:** 900/M **Rev. Legend:** L'UNION FAIT LA FORCE

Date	Mintage	F	VF	XF	Unc	BU
1850	74,000	800	1,800	3,000	4,500	—

KM# 13.3   25 FRANCS
7.9155 g., 0.9000 Gold 0.2291 oz. AGW **Ruler:** Leopold I **Obv:** Larger head **Obv. Legend:** LEOPOLD PREMIER ROI DES BELGES **Rev:** 900 M **Rev. Legend:** L'UNION FAIT LA FORCE

Date	Mintage	F	VF	XF	Unc	BU
1850	Inc. above	900	2,000	3,300	5,000	—

KM# B23.1   40 FRANCS (40 Frank)
12.9032 g., 0.9000 Gold .3734 oz. AGW **Ruler:** Leopold I **Obv:** Laureate head right **Obv. Legend:** LEOPOLD PREMIER ROI DES BELGES **Rev:** Denomination within wreath **Edge:** Lettered

Date	Mintage	F	VF	XF	Unc	BU
1834	—	2,500	8,000	14,000	22,000	—
1835	—	2,500	8,000	14,000	22,000	—
1838	—	3,500	9,500	17,000	26,000	—
1841	—	2,500	9,000	15,000	23,000	—

KM# B23.2   40 FRANCS (40 Frank)
12.9032 g., 0.9000 Gold .3734 oz. AGW **Ruler:** Leopold I **Obv:** Laureate head right **Obv. Legend:** LEOPOLD PREMIER ROI DES BELGES **Rev:** Denomination within wreath **Note:** Medal alignment.

Date	Mintage	F	VF	XF	Unc	BU
1834	—	1,500	8,000	13,000	22,000	—

KM# 210   5000 FRANCS
15.5500 g., 0.9990 Gold .4994 oz. AGW **Subject:** Brussels - European Culture Capital **Obv:** Denomination and European map **Rev:** Portraits of Albert and Elizabeth in ruffled collars **Edge:** Plain

Date	Mintage	F	VF	XF	Unc	BU
ND(1999) (qp)	2,000	Value: 500				

KM# 220   5000 FRANCS
15.5500 g., 0.9990 Gold .4994 oz. AGW, 29 mm. **Subject:** Europe: Charles V **Obv:** Map and denomination **Rev:** Charles V of Spain with building **Edge:** Plain

Date	Mintage	F	VF	XF	Unc	BU
ND(2000) (qp)	2,000	Value: 500				

KM# 223   5000 FRANCS
15.5500 g., 0.9990 Gold .4994 oz. AGW, 29 mm. **Ruler:** Albert II **Subject:** Europa: Europa and the Bull **Obv:** Map and denomination **Rev:** Europa sitting on a bull **Edge:** Plain

Date	Mintage	F	VF	XF	Unc	BU
2001 (qp) Proof	2,000	Value: 550				

TRADE COINAGE
European Currency Units

KM# 172   10 ECU
3.1100 g., 0.9990 Gold .1000 oz. AGW **Rev:** Charles V bust right

Date	Mintage	F	VF	XF	Unc	BU
1989 (qp)	2,000	Value: 200				
1990 (qp)	5,000	Value: 140				

KM# 176   10 ECU
Bi-Metallic 5.30g .900 Gold center in 3.11g .833 Silver ring **Subject:** 60th Birthday of King Baudouin **Rev:** Denomination, date and stars within circle

Date	Mintage	F	VF	XF	Unc	BU
1990 (qp)	42,000	Value: 75.00				

BELGIUM

KM# 181 10 ECU
Bi-Metallic 5.30g .900 Gold center in 3.11g .833 Silver ring
Subject: 40th Year of Reign of King Baudouin **Obv:** Head of King Baudouin, left within circle, two dates below circle **Rev:** Denomination, date and stars within circle

Date	Mintage	F	VF	XF	Unc	BU
1991 (qp)	16,000	Value: 90.00				

KM# 177 20 ECU
Bi-Metallic 10.50g .900 Gold center in 6.22g .833 Silver ring
Subject: 60th Birthday of King Baudouin **Obv:** Head of King Baudouin, left, within circle, two dates below circle **Rev:** Denomination, date and stars within circle

Date	Mintage	F	VF	XF	Unc	BU
1990 (qp)	35,000	Value: 160				

KM# 182 20 ECU
Bi-Metallic Gold center in Silver ring **Subject:** 40th Year of Reign of King Baudouin

Date	Mintage	F	VF	XF	Unc	BU
1991 (qp)	13,000	Value: 185				

KM# 173 25 ECU
7.7750 g., 0.9990 Gold .2500 oz. AGW **Obv:** Denomination, date and stars within circle **Rev:** Laureate Diocletian bust, right

Date	Mintage	F	VF	XF	Unc	BU
1989	30,000	—	—	BV	170	—
1989 (qp)	2,000	Value: 225				
1990 (qp)	5,000	Value: 180				

KM# 167 50 ECU
17.2800 g., 0.9000 Gold .5000 oz. AGW **Subject:** 30th Anniversary - Treaties of Rome **Obv:** Denomination, date and stars within circle

Date	Mintage	F	VF	XF	Unc	BU
1987	1,502,000	—	—	BV	340	—
1987 (qp)	15,000	Value: 350				
1988 (qp)	15,000	Value: 350				

KM# 174 50 ECU
15.5550 g., 0.9990 Gold .5000 oz. AGW **Obv:** Denomination, date and stars within circle **Rev:** Charlemagne seated on dais, facing

Date	Mintage	F	VF	XF	Unc	BU
1989	60,000	—	—	BV	340	—
1989 (qp)	2,000	Value: 400				
1990 (qp)	5,000	Value: 350				

KM# 184 50 ECU
15.5550 g., 0.9990 Gold .5000 oz. AGW **Rev:** Charlemagne bust right

Date	Mintage	F	VF	XF	Unc	BU
1991 (qp)	4,000	Value: 450				

KM# 213 50 ECU
15.5550 g., 0.9990 Gold .5000 oz. AGW **Subject:** Belgian Presidency of the E.C.

Date	Mintage	F	VF	XF	Unc	BU
1993 (qp)	10,000	Value: 375				

KM# 201 50 ECU
15.5550 g., 0.9990 Gold .5000 oz. AGW **Subject:** 50th Anniversary - United Nations

Date	Mintage	F	VF	XF	Unc	BU
1995 (qp)	2,500	Value: 400				

KM# 204 50 ECU
15.5550 g., 0.9990 Gold .5000 oz. AGW **Subject:** 50th Anniversary - UNICEF **Obv:** Conjoined busts of Royal couple, left, denomination above date at right **Rev:** UNICEF logo

Date	Mintage	F	VF	XF	Unc	BU
1996 (qp)	2,500	Value: 450				

KM# 206 50 ECU
15.5550 g., 0.9990 Gold .5000 oz. AGW **Subject:** 40th Anniversary - Treaty of Rome **Obv:** Conjoined heads of Albert II and Baudouin, left, date below, denomination at right **Rev:** European Union map

Date	Mintage	F	VF	XF	Unc	BU
1997 (qp)	2,500	Value: 500				

KM# 211 50 ECU
15.5550 g., 0.9990 Gold .5000 oz. AGW **Subject:** 50th Anniversary - Human Rights Declaration

Date	Mintage	F	VF	XF	Unc	BU
1998 (qp)	2,500	Value: 500				

KM# 175 100 ECU
31.1030 g., 0.9990 Gold 1.0000 oz. AGW **Obv:** Denomination, date and stars within circle **Rev:** Bust of Maria Theresa, stateswoman, right

Date	Mintage	F	VF	XF	Unc	BU
1989	50,000	—	—	BV	675	—
1989 (qp)	2,000	Value: 800				
1990 (qp)	5,000	Value: 700				

EURO COINAGE
European Union Issues
KM# 237 100 EURO
15.5500 g., 0.9990 Gold 0.4994 oz. AGW, 29 mm. **Ruler:** Albert II **Subject:** Founding Fathers

Date	Mintage	F	VF	XF	Unc	BU
2002 Proof	5,000	Value: 550				

KM# 238 100 EURO
15.5500 g., 0.9990 Gold 0.4994 oz. AGW, 29 mm. **Ruler:** Albert II **Subject:** 10th Anniversary of Reign

Date	Mintage	F	VF	XF	Unc	BU
2003 Proof	5,000	Value: 475				

KM# 239 100 EURO
15.5500 g., 0.9990 Gold 0.4994 oz. AGW, 29 mm. **Ruler:** Albert II **Subject:** Franc Germinal

Date	Mintage	F	VF	XF	Unc	BU
2004 Proof	5,000	Value: 475				

MEDALLIC COINAGE
X# M8b 5 FRANCS
Gold **Note:** Prev. KM#M9b.

Date	Mintage	F	VF	XF	Unc	BU
1880 Rare	—	—	—	—	—	—

Note: Fewer than 10 pieces are known to exist

X# M9 40 FRANCS
12.9000 g., 0.9000 Gold .3733 oz. AGW **Subject:** 25th Anniversary of Independence **Rev:** French legend **Rev. Legend:** .... DE L'INAUGURATION **Note:** Prev. KM#M10.

Date	Mintage	F	VF	XF	Unc	BU
1856	449	—	4,000	9,000	12,000	—

X# M10 40 FRANCS
12.9000 g., 0.9000 Gold .3733 oz. AGW **Rev:** Flemish legend **Rev. Legend:** ... VAN S'KONINGS **Note:** Prev. KM#M12. Forgeries exist with weight: 16.8 grams.

Date	Mintage	F	VF	XF	Unc	BU
1856 Restrike	50	—	400	800	1,250	—

X# M3.1 100 FRANCS
31.6600 g., 0.9000 Gold .9161 oz. AGW **Subject:** Marriage of Duke and Dutchess of Brabant **Rev:** Date: 21-22 AOUT 1853 **Note:** Prev. KM#M11.1.

Date	Mintage	F	VF	XF	Unc	BU
1853	482	—	2,500	4,000	6,000	—

X# M3.2 100 FRANCS
31.6600 g., 0.9000 Gold .9161 oz. AGW **Rev:** Date: 21.22 AOUT 1853 **Note:** Prev. KM#M11.2. Examples without raised dot or - between 21 and 22 are restrikes.

Date	Mintage	F	VF	XF	Unc	BU
1853	Inc. above	—	2,500	4,000	6,000	—

X# M15 100 FRANCS
31.6600 g., 0.9000 Gold 0.9161 oz. AGW **Obv:** Queen Elizabeth

Date	Mintage	F	VF	XF	Unc	BU
1965 Proof	—	Value: 575				

X# M42 SOUVERAIN
5.5400 g., 0.9990 Gold 0.1779 oz. AGW, 25 mm. **Obv:** Crowned rampant lion left with sword and globe **Obv. Legend:** CAROL • II • D • G • HISP • ET • IND • REX **Rev:** Crowned arms in order chain **Rev. Legend:** ARCHID • AVST • DVX BVRG • BRABAN • Zc

Date	Mintage	F	VF	XF	Unc	BU
1996 Proof	1,000	Value: 230				
1997 Proof	1,000	Value: 215				
1998 Proof	1,000	Value: 200				

MEDALLIC ECU COINAGE

X# M32 ECU
6.4500 g., 0.7500 Gold 0.1555 oz. AGW, 25 mm. **Ruler:** Baudouin I **Obv:** Artistic outline of Europa and bull's head, Atomium shield below, 12 stars in circle at right, date within **Obv. Legend:** E • U • R • O • P • E • A • N • E • C • U **Rev:** Medieval copy of gold coin with King Johann III of Brabant facing, seated on throne **Rev. Legend:** BRABANCIE : DVC : MONA : 10HIS : DEI • GRA **Edge:** Reeded

Date	Mintage	F	VF	XF	Unc	BU
1993 Proof	2,500	Value: 225				

PATTERNS
Including off metal strikes

KM#	Date	Mintage Identification	Mkt Val
Pn45	1847	— 25 Francs. 0.9000 Gold.	—
Pn49	1854	— 100 Francs. Gold.	—
PnA64	1862	— 20 Francs. Gold. KM#23	20,000
PnB64	1864	— 20 Francs. Gold. KM#23	8,000
Pn71	1866	— 20 Francs. Gold. KM#32	7,000
Pn72	1867	— 10 Francs. Gold.	3,000
Pn75	1870	— 10 Francs. Gold.	3,000
Pn151	1910	— 5 Centimes. Gold. Not holed, KM#67	1,000
Pn165	1911	— 10 Centimes. Gold. KM#85.1.	1,600
Pn170	1911	— 10 Centimes. Gold. KM#86	—
Pn178	1911	— 2 Francs. Gold.	1,500
Pn179	1911	— 10 Francs. Gold. Dutch legend.	2,000
Pn180	1911	— 10 Francs. Gold. French legend.	2,000
Pn183	1911	— 20 Francs. Gold. Dutch legend.	2,250
Pn184	1911	— 20 Francs. Gold. French legend.	2,500
Pn190	1912	— 10 Francs. Gold. Dutch legend.	2,000
Pn191	1912	— 10 Francs. Gold. French legend.	2,000
Pn192	1912	— 10 Francs. Gold. Reeded edge.	—
Pn193	1912	3 100 Francs. Gold. Dutch legend.	16,000
Pn194	1912	6 100 Francs. Gold. French legend.	12,500
Pn206	1918	— 50 Centimes. Gold. KM#83.	1,500
Pn279	1926	— 5 Francs. Gold. Wreath, UN BELGA CINQ FRANCS.	1,750
Pn284	1926	— 5 Francs. Gold. Lion in shield, SF flanking.	1,750
Pn295	1929	— 10 Centimes. Gold. KM#85.1.	1,000
Pn300	1929	— 25 Centimes. Gold. ESSAI, KM#68.1.	1,200
Pn305	1929	— 25 Centimes. Gold. ESSAI, KM#69.	1,200
Pn349	1935	— 40 Francs. Gold. Reeded edge. Expo commemorative.	—
Pn356	1935	— 40 Francs. Gold. Expo commemorative, thin planchet	2,000
Pn368	1935	— 50 Francs. Gold. Reeded edge. KM#106.1.	—
Pn439	1949	— 1000 Francs. Gold. ESSAI	10,920

TRIAL STRIKES

KM#	Date	Mintage Identification	Mkt Val
TS10	1911	— 20 Francs. Gold. Error obverse.	1,250

PROOF SETS

KM#	Date	Mintage Identification	Issue Price	Mkt Val
PS1	1987 (2)	15,000 KM#166-167	395	350
PS2	1988 (2)	15,000 KM#166-167	395	350
PS3	1989 (4)	2,000 KM#172-175	1,300	1,650
PS4	1990 (4)	5,000 KM#172-175	1,300	900

BELIZE

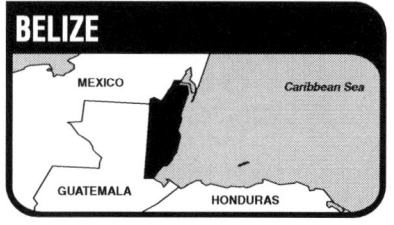

Belize, formerly British Honduras, but now an independent member of the Commonwealth of Nations, is situated in Central America south of Mexico and east and north of Guatemala, with an area of 8,867 sq. mi. (22,960 sq. km.) and a population of *242,000. Capital: Belmopan. Tourism now augments Belize's economy, in addition to sugar, citrus fruits, chicle and hardwoods which are exported.

The area, site of the ancient Mayan civilization, was sighted by Columbus in 1502, and settled by shipwrecked English seamen in 1638. British buccaneers settled the former capital of Belize in the 17th century. Britain claimed administrative right over the area after the emancipation of Central America from Spain. In 1825, Imperial coins were introduced into the colony and were rated against the Spanish dollar and Honduran currency. It was declared a colony subordinate to Jamaica in 1862 and was established as the separate Crown Colony of British Honduras in 1884. In May, 1885 an order in Council authorized coins for the colony, with the first shipment arriving in July. While the Guatemalan peso was originally the standard of value, in 1894 the colony changed to the gold standard, based on the U.S. gold dollar. The anti-British Peoples United Party, which attained power in 1954, won a constitution, effective in 1964 which established self-government under a British appointed governor. British Honduras became Belize on June 1, 1973, following the passage of a surprise bill by the Peoples United Party, but the constitutional relationship with Britain remained unchanged.

In Dec. 1975, the U.N. General Assembly adopted a resolution supporting the right of the people of Belize to self-determination, and asking Britain and Guatemala to renew their negotiations on the future of Belize. Independence was obtained on Sept. 21, 1981. Elizabeth II is Head of State as Queen of Belize.

RULERS
British, until 1981

MINT MARKS
H - Birmingham Mint
No mm - Royal Mint
*NOTE: From 1975-1985 the Franklin Mint produced coinage in up to 3 different qualities. Qualities of issue are designated in ( ) after each date and are defined as follows:
(M) MATTE - Normal circulation strike or a dull finish produced by sandblasting special uncirculated (polish finish) or proof quality dies.
(U) SPECIAL UNCIRCULATED - Polished or proof-like in appearance without any frosted features.
(P) PROOF - The highest quality obtainable having mirror-like fields and frosted features.

MONETARY SYSTEM
Circa 1765-1855
6 Shillings 8 Pence (Jamaican) = 8 Reales
1855-1864
1 Dollar = 8 Rials = 4 Shillings (Sterling)
Commencing 1864
100 Cents = 1 Dollar

BRITISH COLONIAL & CONSTITUTIONAL
DECIMAL COINAGE

KM# 110 25 DOLLARS
3.1300 g., 0.9990 Gold .1000 oz. AGW **Subject:** 50th Anniversary - Battle of El Alamein **Obv:** Bust of Queen Elizabeth II right **Rev:** 4 tanks, denomination at bottom **Rev. Designer:** Willem Vis

Date	Mintage	F	VF	XF	Unc	BU
1992 Proof	Est. 500	Value: 85.00				

KM# 66 50 DOLLARS
1.5000 g., 0.5000 Gold .0241 oz. AGW **Obv:** National arms, date below, 3/4 wreath surrounds **Rev:** White-necked Jacobin hummingbird, right, drinking from flower, date below

Date	Mintage	F	VF	XF	Unc	BU
1981FM (U)	200	—	—	—	65.00	70.00
1981FM (P)	2,873	Value: 50.00				

KM# 111 50 DOLLARS
7.8100 g., 0.9990 Gold .2511 oz. AGW **Subject:** 50th Anniversary - Battle of El Alamein **Obv:** Bust of Queen Elizabeth II right **Rev:** Field Marshall Rommel, right, in uniform, denomination lower right **Rev. Designer:** Willem Vis

Date	Mintage	F	VF	XF	Unc	BU
1992 Proof	Est. 500	Value: 225				

KM# 51 100 DOLLARS
6.2100 g., 0.5000 Gold .0998 oz. AGW **Subject:** 30th Anniversary of United Nations **Obv:** National arms above date within wreath **Rev:** Buildings, design above, denomination at top

Date	Mintage	F	VF	XF	Unc	BU
1975FM (M)	100	—	—	—	200	—
1975FM (U)	2,028	—	—	—	75.00	—
1975FM (P)	8,126	Value: 70.00				

KM# 52 100 DOLLARS
6.2100 g., 0.5000 Gold .0998 oz. AGW **Obv:** National arms above date, denomination below **Rev:** Ancient Mayan symbols representing numbers and days

Date	Mintage	F	VF	XF	Unc	BU
1976FM (M)	216	—	—	—	175	—
1976FM (P)	11,000	Value: 70.00				

KM# 53 100 DOLLARS
6.2100 g., 0.5000 Gold .0998 oz. AGW **Obv:** National arms above date, denomination at bottom **Rev:** Kinich Ahau, Mayan sun god

Date	Mintage	F	VF	XF	Unc	BU
1977FM (M)	200	—	—	—	135	—
1977FM (U)	51	—	—	—	350	—
1977FM (P)	7,859	Value: 70.00				

KM# 55 100 DOLLARS
6.2100 g., 0.5000 Gold .0998 oz. AGW **Obv:** National arms above date, denomination below **Rev:** Itzamna Lord of Heaven, Ruler of the Gods

Date	Mintage	F	VF	XF	Unc	BU
1978FM (U)	351	—	—	—	150	—
1978FM (P)	7,178	Value: 70.00				

62 BELIZE

KM# 58 100 DOLLARS
6.2100 g., 0.5000 Gold .0998 oz. AGW **Obv:** National arms, denomination below **Rev:** Queen angelfish, left, date below

Date	Mintage	F	VF	XF	Unc	BU
1979FM (U)	400	—	—	—	125	—
1979FM (P)	4,465	Value: 90.00				

KM# 59 100 DOLLARS
6.4700 g., 0.5000 Gold .1040 oz. AGW **Obv:** National arms, denomination below **Rev:** Star of Bethlehem, date below

Date	Mintage	F	VF	XF	Unc	BU
1979FM (U)	—	—	—	—	120	—
1979FM (P)	—	Value: 80.00				

KM# 62 100 DOLLARS
6.2100 g., 0.5000 Gold .0998 oz. AGW **Obv:** National arms, denomination below **Rev:** Moorish idol reef fish, date below

Date	Mintage	F	VF	XF	Unc	BU
1980FM (U)	400	—	—	—	150	—
1980FM (P)	3,993	Value: 100				

KM# 63 100 DOLLARS
6.2100 g., 0.5000 Gold .0998 oz. AGW **Obv:** National arms, denomination below **Rev:** Orchids, date below

Date	Mintage	F	VF	XF	Unc	BU
1980FM (U)	250	—	—	—	140	—
1980FM (P)	2,454	Value: 95.00				

KM# 67 100 DOLLARS
6.2100 g., 0.5000 Gold .0998 oz. AGW **Obv:** National arms above denomination within circle **Rev:** Yellow swallowtail butterfly within circle, date below **Shape:** Five-sided coin

Date	Mintage	F	VF	XF	Unc	BU
1981FM (U)	200	—	—	—	200	—
1981FM (P)	1,658	Value: 250				

KM# 68 100 DOLLARS
6.2100 g., 0.5000 Gold .0998 oz. AGW **Subject:** National independence **Rev:** Vertical date to left of map

Date	Mintage	F	VF	XF	Unc	BU
1981FM (U)	50	—	—	—	325	—
1981FM (P)	1,401	Value: 125				

KM# 70 100 DOLLARS
6.2100 g., 0.5000 Gold .0998 oz. AGW **Obv:** National arms within wreath, denomination below **Rev:** Kinkajou, left, date below

Date	Mintage	F	VF	XF	Unc	BU
1982FM (U)	10	—	—	—	500	—
1982FM (P)	586	Value: 200				

KM# 73 100 DOLLARS
6.2100 g., 0.5000 Gold .0998 oz. AGW **Obv:** National arms within wreath, denomination below **Rev:** Margay jungle cat, right, date below

Date	Mintage	F	VF	XF	Unc	BU
1983FM (U)	20	—	—	—	400	—
1983FM (P)	494	Value: 250				

KM# 74 100 DOLLARS
6.2100 g., 0.5000 Gold .0998 oz. AGW **Obv:** National arms within wreath, denomination below **Rev:** White-tailed deer, facing, date lower right

Date	Mintage	F	VF	XF	Unc	BU
1984FM (P)	965	Value: 150				

KM# 76 100 DOLLARS
6.2100 g., 0.5000 Gold .0998 oz. AGW **Obv:** national arms within wreath, denomination below **Rev:** Ocelot, facing, date below

Date	Mintage	F	VF	XF	Unc	BU
1985FM (P) Proof	899	Value: 250				

KM# 103 100 DOLLARS
15.9760 g., 0.9170 Gold .4708 oz. AGW **Subject:** 10th Anniversary of Independence **Note:** Similar to 10 Dollars, KM#102.

Date	Mintage	F	VF	XF	Unc	BU
1991 Proof	Est. 500	Value: 550				

KM# 112 100 DOLLARS
15.6000 g., 0.9990 Gold .5016 oz. AGW **Subject:** 50th Anniversary - Battle of El Alamein **Obv:** Bust of Queen Elizabeth II right **Rev:** Infantry advancing, denomination below **Rev. Designer:** Willem Vis

Date	Mintage	F	VF	XF	Unc	BU
1992 Proof	Est. 500	Value: 450				

KM# 129 100 DOLLARS
15.9700 g., 0.9170 Gold .4707 oz. AGW **Subject:** Battle of St. George's Caye **Note:** Similar to KM#128.

Date	Mintage	F	VF	XF	Unc	BU
ND(1998) Proof	—	Value: 675				

KM# 56 250 DOLLARS
8.8100 g., 0.9000 Gold .2549 oz. AGW **Obv:** National arms above date, denomination below **Rev:** Jaguar, date at right **Rev. Designer:** Gilroy Roberts

Date	Mintage	F	VF	XF	Unc	BU
1978FM (U)	200	—	—	—	210	225
1978FM (P)	Est. 3,399	Value: 220				

Note: 1,712 pieces were used in first-day covers

KM# 98 250 DOLLARS
15.9800 g., 0.9170 Gold .4708 oz. AGW **Subject:** 500th Anniversary of Columbus' Discovery of America

Date	Mintage	F	VF	XF	Unc	BU
1989 Proof	Est. 500	Value: 375				

KM# 105 250 DOLLARS
15.9800 g., 0.9170 Gold .4708 oz. AGW **Subject:** 10th Anniversary of Central Bank **Rev:** Jabiru stork **Note:** Similar to KM#104.

Date	Mintage	F	VF	XF	Unc	BU
1992	Est. 500	Value: 350				

KM# 113 250 DOLLARS
31.2100 g., 0.9990 Gold 1.0035 oz. AGW **Subject:** 50th Anniversary - Battle of El Alamein **Obv:** Bust of Queen Elizabeth II right **Rev:** Lt. Gen. Montgomery, denomination at bottom **Rev. Designer:** Willem Vis

Date	Mintage	F	VF	XF	Unc	BU
1992 Proof	Est. 500	Value: 700				

KM# 101 500 DOLLARS
47.5400 g., 0.9170 Gold 1.4018 oz. AGW **Subject:** Royal Visit **Note:** Similar to KM#78.

Date	Mintage	F	VF	XF	Unc	BU
1985 Proof	Est. 250	Value: 1,000				

KM# 120 500 DOLLARS
47.5400 g., 0.9170 Gold 1.4018 oz. AGW **Subject:** 40th Anniversary - Coronation of Queen Elizabeth II

Date	Mintage	F	VF	XF	Unc	BU
1993 Proof	Est. 100	Value: 1,150				

KM# 122 500 DOLLARS
47.5400 g., 0.9170 Gold 1.4018 oz. AGW **Subject:** Royal Visit **Rev:** Cameo portraits, flanked by roses, flowers above denomination

Date	Mintage	F	VF	XF	Unc	BU
1994 Proof	—	Value: 1,150				

PROOF SETS

KM#	Date	Mintage	Identification	Issue Price	Mkt Val
PS24	1992 (4)	500	KM110-113	1,600	1,450

BENIN

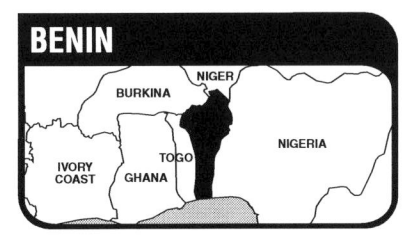

The Republic of Benin (formerly the Republic of Dahomey), located on the south side of the African bulge between Togo and Nigeria, has an area of 43,500 sq. mi. (112,620 sq. km.) and a population of 5.5 million. Capital: Porto-Novo. The principal industry of Benin, one of the poorest countries of West Africa, is the processing of palm oil products. Palm kernel oil, peanuts, cotton, and coffee are exported.

Porto-Novo, on the Bight of Benin, was founded as a trading post by the Portuguese in the 17th century. At that time, Benin was composed of an aggregation of mutually suspicious tribes, the majority of which were tributary to the powerful northern Kingdom of Abomey. In 1863, the King of Porto-Novo petitioned France for protection from Abomey. The French subjugated other militant tribes as well, and in 1892 organized the area as a protectorate of France; in 1904 it was incorporated into French West Africa as the Territory of Dahomey. After the establishment of the Fifth French Republic, the Territory at Dahomey became an autonomous state within the French community. On Aug. 1, 1960, it became the fully independent Republic of Dahomey. In 1974, the republic began a transition to a socialist society with Marxism-Leninism as its revolutionary philosophy under Col. Ahmed Kerekow. On Nov. 30, 1975, the name of the Republic of Dahomey was changed to the Peoples Republic of Benin. As a result of Benin's first free presidential election in 30 years, Nicephore Soglo defeated Colonel Kerekou.

MINT MARKS
1 AR - Uno-A-Erre, Arezzo, Italy

PEOPLES REPUBLIC

STANDARD COINAGE

KM# 45a 6000 CFA FRANCS - 4 AFRICA
11.0000 g., 0.9990 Bi-Metallic .999 Silver center in .999 Gold ring 0.3533 oz., 28.3 mm. **Obv:** Olympic athletic figures **Rev:** Elephant head on map **Edge:** Plain

Date	Mintage	F	VF	XF	Unc	BU
2005	10	—	—	—	400	—

KM# 46a 6000 CFA FRANCS - 4 AFRICA
11.0000 g., 0.9990 Bi-Metallic .999 Silver center in .999 Gold ring 0.3533 oz., 28.3 mm. **Obv:** Papal visit scene **Rev:** Elephant head on map **Edge:** Plain

Date	Mintage	F	VF	XF	Unc	BU
2005	10	—	—	—	400	—

KM# 29 30000 FRANCS
15.5500 g., 0.9990 Gold .4494 oz. AGW **Obv:** National arms **Rev:** Map in radiant sun **Edge:** Reeded

Date	Mintage	F	VF	XF	Unc	BU
ND(1992) Proof	Est. 100	Value: 600				

KM# 30 100000 FRANCS
31.1035 g., 0.9990 Gold 1.0000 oz. AGW **Obv:** National arms **Rev:** President **Edge:** Reeded

Date	Mintage	F	VF	XF	Unc	BU
1992 Rare	Est. 10	Value: 1,500				

KM# 42a 150000 CFA FRANCS - 100 AFRICA
0.9990 Gold Plated Silver **Obv:** Map left of President **Rev:** Elephant head on map

Date	Mintage	F	VF	XF	Unc	BU
2003	25	—	—	—	275	—

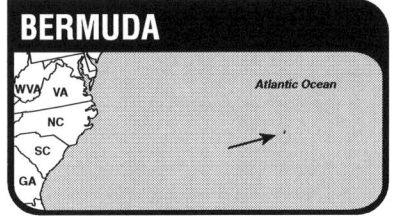

BERMUDA

The Parliamentary British Colony of Bermuda, situated in the western Atlantic Ocean 660 miles (1,062 km.) east of North Carolina, has an area of 20.6 sq. mi. (53 sq. km.) and a population of 61,600. Capital: Hamilton. Concentrated essences, beauty preparations, and cut flowers are exported. Most Bermudians derive their livelihood from tourism.

Bermuda was discovered by Juan de Bermudez, a Spanish navigator, in about 1503. British influence dates from 1609 when a group of Virginia-bound British colonists under the command of Sir George Somers was shipwrecked on the islands for 10 months. The islands were settled in 1612 by 60 British colonists from the Virginia Colony and became a crown colony in 1684. The earliest coins issued for the island were the "Hogge Money" series of 2, 3, 6 and 12 pence, the name derived from the pig in the obverse design, a recognition of the quantity of such animals then found there. The next issue for Bermuda was the Birmingham coppers of 1793; all locally circulating coinage was demonetized in 1842, when the currency of the United Kingdom became standard. Internal autonomy was obtained by the constitution of June 8, 1968.

In February, 1970, Bermuda converted from its former currency, which was sterling, to a decimal currency, the dollar unit which is equal to one U.S. dollar. On July 31, 1972, Bermuda severed its monetary link with the British pound sterling and pegged its dollar to be the same gold value as the U.S. dollar.

RULERS
British

MINT MARKS
CHI - Valcambi, Switzerland
FM - Franklin Mint, U.S.A.*
*NOTE: From 1975-1985 the Franklin Mint produced coinage in up to 3 different qualities. Qualities of issue are designated in ( ) after each date and are defined as follows:
(M) MATTE - Normal circulation strike or a dull finish produced by sandblasting special uncirculated (polish finish) or proof quality dies.
(U) SPECIAL UNCIRCUALTED - Polished or proof-like in appearance without any frosted features.
(P) PROOF - The highest quality obtainable having mirror-like fields and frosted features.

MONETARY SYSTEM
12 Pence = 1 Shilling
20 Shillings = 1 Pound

BRITISH ADMINISTRATION

DECIMAL COINAGE

100 Cents = 1 Dollar

KM# 44d CENT
6.2000 g., 0.9170 Gold .1827 oz. AGW, 19 mm. **Ruler:** Elizabeth II **Obv:** Crowned head right **Rev:** Wild boar left **Note:** In sets only.

Date	Mintage	F	VF	XF	Unc	BU
1995 Proof	500	Value: 145				

KM# 46b 10 CENTS
4.7500 g., 0.9170 Gold .1400 oz. AGW, 17.8 mm. **Ruler:** Elizabeth II **Obv:** Crowned head right **Rev:** Bermuda lily **Note:** In sets only.

Date	Mintage	F	VF	XF	Unc	BU
1995 Proof	500	Value: 140				

KM# 47b 25 CENTS
11.7000 g., 0.9170 Gold .3448 oz. AGW, 24 mm. **Ruler:** Elizabeth II **Subject:** Yellow-billed tropical bird right **Obv:** Crowned head right **Note:** In sets only.

Date	Mintage	F	VF	XF	Unc	BU
1995 Proof	500	Value: 250				

KM# 56b DOLLAR
15.5000 g., 0.9170 Gold .4568 oz. AGW **Ruler:** Elizabeth II **Obv:** Crowned head right **Rev:** Train

Date	Mintage	F	VF	XF	Unc	BU
1995 Proof	500	Value: 400				

Note: In sets only.

KM# 106a 3 DOLLARS
31.4890 g., 0.9990 Gold 1.0114 oz. AGW, 35 mm. **Ruler:** Elizabeth II **Obv:** Crowned head right **Rev:** Ship on map **Edge:** Plain **Shape:** Triangular

Date	Mintage	F	VF	XF	Unc	BU
1998	—	—	—	—	—	1,400

KM# 141 3 DOLLARS
1.5550 g., 0.9990 Gold 0.0499 oz. AGW, 15 mm. **Subject:** Shipwreck Series **Obv:** Elizabeth II **Rev:** The Mary Celestia **Edge:** Plain **Shape:** Triangular

Date	Mintage	F	VF	XF	Unc	BU
2006 Proof	15,000	Value: 100				

KM# 149 3 DOLLARS
1.5550 g., 0.9990 Gold 0.0499 oz. AGW, 15 mm. **Subject:** Shipwreck Series **Obv:** Elizabeth II **Rev:** The Constellation **Edge:** Plain **Shape:** Triangular

Date	Mintage	F	VF	XF	Unc	BU
2006 Proof	15,000	Value: 100				

KM# 57 10 DOLLARS
3.1340 g., 0.9990 Gold .1007 oz. AGW **Ruler:** Elizabeth II **Subject:** Hogge money **Obv:** Crowned head right **Rev:** Wild pig

Date	Mintage	F	VF	XF	Unc	BU
1989 Proof	500	Value: 100				

KM# 74 10 DOLLARS
3.1340 g., 0.9990 Gold .1007 oz. AGW **Ruler:** Elizabeth II **Subject:** Hogge money **Obv:** Crowned head right **Obv. Designer:** Raphael Maklouf **Rev:** Ship circle

Date	Mintage	F	VF	XF	Unc	BU
1990 Proof	500	Value: 100				

KM# 66 10 DOLLARS
3.1340 g., 0.9990 Gold .1007 oz. AGW **Ruler:** Elizabeth II **Subject:** Wildlife **Obv:** Crowned head right **Rev:** Tree frog

Date	Mintage	F	VF	XF	Unc	BU
1990 Proof	500	Value: 85.00				

KM# 70 10 DOLLARS
3.1340 g., 0.9990 Gold .1007 oz. AGW **Ruler:** Elizabeth II **Obv:** Crowned head right **Rev:** Yellow-crowned night heron

Date	Mintage	F	VF	XF	Unc	BU
1991	2,500	—	—	—	80.00	

KM# 73 10 DOLLARS
3.1340 g., 0.9990 Gold .1007 oz. AGW **Ruler:** Elizabeth II **Obv:** Crowned head right **Rev:** Bluebird feeding nestling

Date	Mintage	F	VF	XF	Unc	BU
1992	2,500	—	—	—	80.00	

KM# 132 10 DOLLARS
3.1340 g., 0.9990 Gold 0.1007 oz. AGW, 17 mm. **Ruler:** Elizabeth II **Obv:** Crowned head right **Rev:** White-tailed Tropic Bird **Edge:** Reeded

Date	Mintage	F	VF	XF	Unc	BU
1993	1,501	—	—	—	80.00	

KM# 133 10 DOLLARS
3.1340 g., 0.9990 Gold 0.1007 oz. AGW, 17 mm. **Ruler:** Elizabeth II **Obv:** Crowned head right **Rev:** Sea Horse **Edge:** Reeded

Date	Mintage	F	VF	XF	Unc	BU
1994	1,000	—	—	—	80.00	

KM# 138 10 DOLLARS
7.7760 g., 0.5830 Gold Alloyed with .417 Silver 0.1458 oz. AGW, 25 mm. **Ruler:** Elizabeth II **Obv:** Crowned head right **Rev:** 1937 Coronation portrait **Edge:** Reeded

Date	Mintage	F	VF	XF	Unc	BU
1996 Proof	5,000	Value: 175				

KM# 118 15 DOLLARS
15.9700 g., 0.9990 Gold .5129 oz. AGW, 28.4 mm. **Ruler:** Elizabeth II **Subject:** Tall Ships **Obv:** Head with tiara right **Obv. Designer:** Ian Rank-Broadley **Rev:** Three-masted sailing ship **Edge:** Reeded

Date	Mintage	F	VF	XF	Unc	BU
2000 Proof	1,500	Value: 385				

64 BERMUDA

KM# 21 20 DOLLARS
7.9881 g., 0.9170 Gold .2355 oz. AGW **Ruler:** Elizabeth II **Obv:** Young bust right **Obv. Designer:** Arnold Machin **Rev:** Cahow in flight left **Rev. Designer:** Michael Rizzello

Date	Mintage	F	VF	XF	Unc	BU
1970 Proof	1,000				Value: 250	

KM# 53 25 DOLLARS
31.1000 g., 0.9990 Palladium 1 oz. **Ruler:** Elizabeth II **Subject:** Sea Venture **Obv:** Crowned head right **Obv. Designer:** Raphael Maklouf **Rev:** Ship

Date	Mintage	F	VF	XF	Unc	BU
1987 Proof	15,800				Value: 400	

KM# 63 25 DOLLARS
31.1000 g., 0.9990 Palladium 1 oz. **Ruler:** Elizabeth II **Subject:** Shipwreck of San Antonio **Obv:** Crowned head right **Rev:** Capsizing ship

Date	Mintage	F	VF	XF	Unc	BU
1988 Proof	2,000				Value: 425	

KM# 58 25 DOLLARS
7.8140 g., 0.9990 Gold .2512 oz. AGW **Ruler:** Elizabeth II **Subject:** Hogge Money **Obv:** Crowned head right **Obv. Designer:** Raphael Maklouf **Rev:** Ship

Date	Mintage	F	VF	XF	Unc	BU
1989 Proof	500				Value: 225	

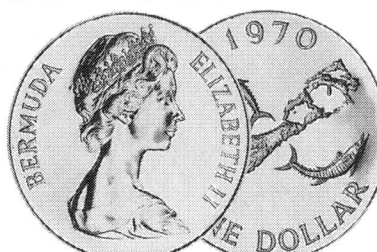

KM# 75 25 DOLLARS
7.8140 g., 0.9990 Gold .2512 oz. AGW **Ruler:** Elizabeth II **Subject:** Hogge Money **Obv:** Crowned head right **Obv. Designer:** Raphael Maklouf **Rev:** Wild pig

Date	Mintage	F	VF	XF	Unc	BU
1990 Proof	500				Value: 225	

KM# 97 30 DOLLARS
15.5518 g., 0.9990 Gold .5 oz. AGW **Ruler:** Elizabeth II **Subject:** Bermuda Triangle **Obv:** Crowned head right **Rev:** Map, compass, capsizing ship

Date	Mintage	F	VF	XF	Unc	BU
1996 Proof	Est. 1,500				Value: 385	

KM# 101 30 DOLLARS
15.5518 g., 0.9990 Gold .5 oz. AGW **Ruler:** Elizabeth II **Subject:** Wreck of the Sea Venture **Obv:** Crowned head right **Rev:** Shipwreck scene

Date	Mintage	F	VF	XF	Unc	BU
1997 Proof	1,500				Value: 385	

KM# 113 30 DOLLARS
15.5500 g., 0.9990 Gold .4994 oz. AGW **Ruler:** Elizabeth II **Obv:** Crowned head right **Rev:** Sailing ship Deliverance and map **Rev. Designer:** John Warwick

Date	Mintage	F	VF	XF	Unc	BU
1998 Proof	1,500				Value: 385	

KM# 143 30 DOLLARS
31.4890 g., 0.9990 Gold 1.0114 oz. AGW, 35 mm. **Subject:** Shipwreck Series **Obv:** Elizabeth II **Rev:** The Mary Celestia **Edge:** Plain **Shape:** Triangular

Date	Mintage	F	VF	XF	Unc	BU
2006 Proof	750				Value: 800	

KM# 151 30 DOLLARS
31.4890 g., 0.9990 Gold 1.0114 oz. AGW, 35 mm. **Subject:** Shipwreck Series **Obv:** Elizabeth II **Rev:** The Constellation **Edge:** Plain **Shape:** Triangular

Date	Mintage	F	VF	XF	Unc	BU
2006 Proof	750				Value: 800	

KM# 26 50 DOLLARS
4.0500 g., 0.9000 Gold .1172 oz. AGW **Ruler:** Elizabeth II **Subject:** Queen's Silver Jubilee **Obv:** Young bust right **Obv. Designer:** Arnold Machin **Rev:** Sailboat

Date	Mintage	F	VF	XF	Unc	BU
1977Chi	3,950	—	—	—	90.00	—
1977Chi Proof	4,070				Value: 110	
1977	Est. 520	—	—	—	235	—

Note: Struck at the Royal Canadian Mint

| 1977 Proof | Est. 580 | | | | Value: 240 | |

Note: Struck at the Royal Canadian Mint

KM# 59 50 DOLLARS
15.6080 g., 0.9990 Gold .5018 oz. AGW **Ruler:** Elizabeth II **Subject:** Hogge Money **Obv:** Crowned head right **Rev:** Wild pig **Rev. Designer:** Raphael Maklouf

Date	Mintage	F	VF	XF	Unc	BU
1989 Proof	500				Value: 350	

KM# 76 50 DOLLARS
15.6080 g., 0.9990 Gold .5018 oz. AGW **Ruler:** Elizabeth II **Subject:** Hogge Money **Obv:** Crowned head right **Rev:** Ship **Rev. Designer:** Raphael Maklouf

Date	Mintage	F	VF	XF	Unc	BU
1990 Proof	500				Value: 350	

KM# 93 60 DOLLARS
31.4890 g., 0.9990 Gold 1.0124 oz. AGW **Ruler:** Elizabeth II **Subject:** Bermuda Triangle **Obv:** Crowned head right **Obv. Designer:** Raphael Maklouf **Rev:** Map, compass and capsizing ship **Shape:** Triangular

Date	Mintage	F	VF	XF	Unc	BU
1996 Proof	1,500				Value: 785	

KM# 102 60 DOLLARS
31.4890 g., 0.9990 Gold 1.0124 oz. AGW **Ruler:** Elizabeth II **Subject:** Wreck of the Sea Venture **Obv:** Crowned head right **Obv. Designer:** Raphael Maklouf **Rev:** Shipwreck scene **Shape:** Triangular

Date	Mintage	F	VF	XF	Unc	BU
1997 Proof	1,500				Value: 785	

KM# 114 60 DOLLARS
31.4800 g., 0.9990 Gold 1.0111 oz. AGW **Ruler:** Elizabeth II **Obv:** Crowned head right **Obv. Designer:** Raphael Maklouf **Rev:** Sailing ship Deliverance and map **Rev. Designer:** John Warwick **Shape:** Triangular

Date	Mintage	F	VF	XF	Unc	BU
1998 Proof	1,500				Value: 785	

KM# 145 90 DOLLARS
155.5200 g., 0.9990 Gold 4.9951 oz. AGW, 65 mm. **Subject:** Shipwreck Series **Obv:** Elizabeth II **Rev:** The Mary Celestia **Edge:** Plain **Shape:** Triangular

Date	Mintage	F	VF	XF	Unc	BU
2006 Proof	90				Value: 3,500	

KM# 153 90 DOLLARS
155.5200 g., 0.9990 Gold 4.9951 oz. AGW, 65 mm. **Subject:** Shipwreck Series **Obv:** Elizabeth II **Rev:** The Constellation **Edge:** Plain **Shape:** Triangular

Date	Mintage	F	VF	XF	Unc	BU
2006 Proof	90				Value: 3,500	

KM# 24 100 DOLLARS
7.0300 g., 0.9000 Gold .2034 oz. AGW **Ruler:** Elizabeth II **Subject:** Royal Visit **Obv:** Young bust right **Obv. Designer:** Arnold Machin **Rev:** Sceptre divides royal emblems

Date	Mintage	F	VF	XF	Unc	BU
1975FM (M) Trial pieces	25	—	—	—	350	—
1975FM (M)	18,852	—	—	—	140	—
1975FM (M) Proof	27,270				Value: 145	

KM# 27 100 DOLLARS
8.1000 g., 0.9000 Gold .2344 oz. AGW **Ruler:** Elizabeth II **Subject:** Queen's Silver Jubilee **Obv:** Young bust right **Obv. Designer:** Arnold Machin **Rev:** Sailing ship Deliverance

Date	Mintage	F	VF	XF	Unc	BU
1977Chi	6,225	—	—	—	160	—
1977Chi Proof	5,613				Value: 175	
1977	Est. 2,312	—	—	—	225	—

BHUTAN 65

Note: Struck at the Royal Canadian Mint

Date	Mintage	F	VF	XF	Unc	BU
1977 Proof	Est. 1,887				Value: 265	

Note: Struck at the Royal Canadian Mint

KM# 60 100 DOLLARS
31.2100 g., 0.9990 Gold 1.0035 oz. AGW **Ruler:** Elizabeth II
Subject: Hogge Money **Obv:** Crowned head right **Obv.**
Designer: Raphael Maklouf **Rev:** Ship

Date	Mintage	F	VF	XF	Unc	BU
1989 Proof	500				Value: 675	

KM# 77 100 DOLLARS
31.2100 g., 0.9990 Gold 1.0035 oz. AGW **Ruler:** Elizabeth II
Subject: Hogge Money **Obv:** Crowned head right **Obv.**
Designer: Raphael Maklouf **Rev:** Wild pig

Date	Mintage	F	VF	XF	Unc	BU
1990 Proof	500				Value: 675	

KM# 80 100 DOLLARS
47.5400 g., 0.9170 Gold 1.4017 oz. AGW **Ruler:** Elizabeth II
Series: Olympics **Subject:** Crowned head right **Rev:** Olympic rings

Date	Mintage	F	VF	XF	Unc	BU
1992 Proof	Est. 250				Value: 950	

KM# 134 100 DOLLARS
47.5400 g., 0.9170 Gold 1.4016 oz. AGW, 38.6 mm. **Ruler:** Elizabeth II **Subject:** Royal Visit **Obv:** Crowned head right **Rev:** Royal couple above map **Edge:** Reeded

Date	Mintage	F	VF	XF	Unc	BU
1994 Proof	250				Value: 950	

KM# 98 180 DOLLARS
155.5175 g., 0.9990 Gold 5 oz. AGW **Ruler:** Elizabeth II
Subject: Bermuda Triangle **Obv:** Crowned head right **Rev:** Map, compass, capsizing ship

Date	Mintage	F	VF	XF	Unc	BU
1996 Proof	Est. 1,500				Value: 3,350	

KM# 103 180 DOLLARS
155.5175 g., 0.9990 Gold 5 oz. AGW **Ruler:** Elizabeth II
Subject: Wreck of the Sea Venture **Obv:** Crowned head right **Rev:** Shipwreck scene

Date	Mintage	F	VF	XF	Unc	BU
1997 Proof	99				Value: 4,000	

KM# 115 180 DOLLARS
155.5200 g., 0.9990 Gold 4.9951 oz. AGW **Ruler:** Elizabeth II
Obv: Crowned head right **Rev:** Sailing ship Deliverance and map
Shape: Triangular

Date	Mintage	F	VF	XF	Unc	BU
1998 Proof	99				Value: 4,000	

KM# 82 200 DOLLARS
28.5000 g., 0.9990 Gold .9154 oz. AGW **Ruler:** Elizabeth II
Subject: 200 Years - Bermudan Coinage **Obv:** Crowned head right **Obv. Designer:** Raphael Maklouf **Rev:** Sailing ship

Date	Mintage	F	VF	XF	Unc	BU
1993 Proof	200				Value: 625	

KM# 29 250 DOLLARS
15.9760 g., 0.9170 Gold .471 oz. AGW **Ruler:** Elizabeth II
Subject: Wedding of Prince Charles and Lady Diana **Obv:** Crowned head right **Rev:** Jugate heads of the royal couple right

Date	Mintage	F	VF	XF	Unc	BU
1981	217	—	—	—	475	525
1981 Proof	790				Value: 375	

KM# 154 300 DOLLARS
155.5200 g., 0.9995 Platinum 4.9976 oz. APW, 65 mm.
Subject: Shipwreck Series **Obv:** Elizabeth II **Rev:** The Constellation **Edge:** Plain **Shape:** Triangular

Date	Mintage	F	VF	XF	Unc	BU
2006 Proof	60				Value: 6,500	

KM# 147 600 DOLLARS
1096.0000 g., 0.9180 Gold 32.3477 oz. AGW, 100 mm.
Subject: Shipwreck Series **Obv:** Elizabeth II **Rev:** The Mary Celestia **Edge:** Plain **Shape:** Triangular

Date	Mintage	F	VF	XF	Unc	BU
2007 Proof	300				Value: 21,000	

KM# 155 600 DOLLARS
1096.0000 g., 0.9180 Gold 32.3477 oz. AGW, 100 mm.
Subject: Shipwreck Series **Obv:** Elizabeth II **Rev:** The Constellation **Edge:** Plain **Shape:** Triangular

Date	Mintage	F	VF	XF	Unc	BU
2007 Proof	300				Value: 21,000	

MEDALLIC COINAGE
1954 Geoffrey Hearn Series

X# 1c CROWN
Gold **Obv:** Edward VIII

Date	Mintage	F	VF	XF	Unc	BU
1936 Proof	10				Value: 800	

Note: Restrikes known

PIEFORTS

KM#	Date	Mintage	Identification		Mkt Val
P1	1981	690	250 Dollars. 31.9520 g. KM29.		650

MINT SETS

KM#	Date	Mintage	Identification	Issue Price	Mkt Val
MS2	1977Chi (3)	—	KM25-27	175	250
MS3	1977Chi (2)	—	KM26-27	150	225
MSA2	1977 (3)	—	KM25-27	—	750

PROOF SETS

KM#	Date	Mintage	Identification	Issue Price	Mkt Val
PS2	1970 (7)	1,000	KM15-21	216	280
PSA3	1977 (3)	—	KM25-27	—	800
PS3	1977Chi (3)	—	KM25-27	245	350
PS4	1977Chi (2)	—	KM26-27	210	265
PS5	1981 (3)	500	KM28a, 29, (P1), numbered set	1,500	1,350
PS10	1989 (4)	500	KM57-60	1,495	1,250
PS11	1990 (4)	500	KM74-77	—	1,250
PS12	1992 (3)	250	KM78-80	1,075	1,050
PS14	1995 (5)	500	KM44d, 45b-47b, 56b	1,100	1,350
PS15	1996 (2)	1,000	KM96-97	—	600

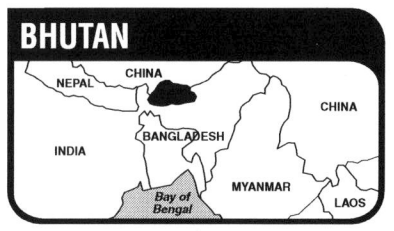

BHUTAN

The Kingdom of Bhutan, a landlocked Himalayan country bordered by Tibet and India, has an area of 18,150 sq. mi. (47,000 sq. km.) and a population of *2.03 million. Capital: Thimphu. Virtually the entire population is engaged in agricultural and pastoral activities. Rice, wheat, barley, and yak butter are produced in sufficient quantity to make the country self-sufficient in food. The economy of Bhutan is primitive and many transactions are conducted on a barter basis.

Bhutan's early history is obscure, but is thought to have resembled that of rural medieval Europe. The country was conquered by Tibet in the 9th century, and a dual temporal and spiritual rule developed which operated until the mid-19th century, when the southern part of the country was occupied by the British and annexed to British India. Bhutan was established as a hereditary monarchy in 1907, and in 1910 agreed to British control of its external affairs. In 1949, India and Bhutan concluded a treaty whereby India assumed Britain's role in subsidizing Bhutan and guiding its foreign affairs. In 1971 Bhutan became a full member of the United Nations.

RULERS
Ugyen Wangchuk, 1907-1926
Jigme Wangchuk, 1926-1952
Jigme Dorji Wangchuk, 1952-1972
Jigme Singye Wangchuk, 1972-

MONETARY SYSTEM
100 Naye Paisa = 1 Rupee
100 Rupees = 1 Sertum

KINGDOM
DECIMAL COINAGE

KM# 33 SERTUM
7.9800 g., 0.9170 Gold .2352 oz. AGW **Subject:** 40th Anniversary - Accession of Jigme Wangchuk **Obv:** Crowned bust left, dates below **Rev:** Emblem divides date, denomination below

Date	Mintage	F	VF	XF	Unc	BU
1966	2,300	—	—	—	170	—
1966 Proof	598				Value: 200	

KM# 33a SERTUM
9.8400 g., 0.9500 Platinum .3005 oz. APW **Subject:** 40th Anniversary - Accession of Jigme Wangchuk

Date	Mintage	F	VF	XF	Unc	BU
1966 Proof	72				Value: 425	

KM# 36 SERTUM
7.9800 g., 0.9170 Gold .2352 oz. AGW **Obv:** Bust, right, date below

Date	Mintage	F	VF	XF	Unc	BU
1970	3,111	—	—	—	165	180

KM# 34 2 SERTUMS
15.9800 g., 0.9170 Gold .4711 oz. AGW **Subject:** 40th Anniversary - Accession of Jigme Wangchuk **Obv:** Crowned bust, left, dates below **Rev:** Emblem divides date, denomination below

Date	Mintage	F	VF	XF	Unc	BU
1966	800	—	—	—	335	—
1966 Proof	598				Value: 385	

BHUTAN

KM# 34a 2 SERTUMS
19.6700 g., 0.9500 Platinum .6008 oz. APW **Subject:** 40th Anniversary - Accession of Jigme Wangchuk

Date	Mintage	F	VF	XF	Unc	BU
1966 Proof	72	Value: 825				

KM# 35 5 SERTUMS
39.9400 g., 0.9170 Gold 1.1776 oz. AGW **Subject:** 40th Anniversary - Accession of Jigme Wangchuk **Obv:** Crowned bust, left, dates below **Rev:** Emblem divides date, denomination below

Date	Mintage	F	VF	XF	Unc	BU
1966	800	—	—	—	825	—
1966 Proof	598	Value: 875				

KM# 35a 5 SERTUMS
49.1800 g., 0.9500 Platinum 1.5022 oz. APW **Subject:** 40th Anniversary - Accession of Jigme Wangchuk **Obv:** Crowned bust, left, dates below **Rev:** Emblem divides date, denomination below

Date	Mintage	F	VF	XF	Unc	BU
1966 Proof	72	Value: 1,950				

REFORM COINAGE

Commencing 1974; 100 Chetrums (Paisa) = 1 Ngultrum (Rupee); 100 Ngultrums = 1 Sertum

KM# 102 300 NGULTRUMS
1.2441 g., 0.9990 Gold .04 oz. AGW **Obv:** National emblem within circle divides dates **Rev:** Mask, facing, denomination at lower right

Date	Mintage	F	VF	XF	Unc	BU
1997 Proof	—	Value: 45.00				

KM# 51 SERTUM
7.9800 g., 0.9170 Gold .2352 oz. AGW **Obv:** Crowned bust, left, dates below **Rev:** Two dragons around inner circle

Date	Mintage	F	VF	XF	Unc	BU
1979	1,000	—	—	—	165	—
1979 Proof	1,000	Value: 185				

KM# 51a SERTUM
9.8500 g., 0.9500 Platinum .3008 oz. APW **Obv:** Crowned bust, left, dates below **Rev:** Two dragons around inner circle

Date	Mintage	F	VF	XF	Unc	BU
1979 Proof	—	Value: 400				

KM# 56 SERTUM
7.9900 g., 0.9170 Gold .2356 oz. AGW **Subject:** 75th Anniversary of Monarchy

Date	Mintage	F	VF	XF	Unc	BU
1982(1983)	1,000	—	—	—	165	—
1982(1983) Proof	1,000	Value: 185				

KM# 85 SERTUM
1.2442 g., 0.9999 Gold .04 oz. AGW **Subject:** 40th Anniversary - Queen Elizabeth II's Coronation **Obv:** National emblem within circle divides dates **Rev:** Royal Guard, palace in background, denomination and dates below

Date	Mintage	F	VF	XF	Unc	BU
1995	Est. 250,000	—	—	—	50.00	—

KM# 52 2 SERTUMS
15.9800 g., 0.9170 Gold .4711 oz. AGW **Obv:** Crowned bust, left, dates below **Rev:** Two dragons around inner circle

Date	Mintage	F	VF	XF	Unc	BU
1979	1,000	—	—	—	325	—
1979 Proof	1,000	Value: 350				

KM# 52a 2 SERTUMS
19.7000 g., 0.9500 Platinum .6017 oz. APW **Obv:** Crowned bust, left, dates below **Rev:** Two dragons around inner circle

Date	Mintage	F	VF	XF	Unc	BU
1979 Proof	—	Value: 775				

KM# 60 2 SERTUMS
15.9800 g., 0.9170 Gold .4711 oz. AGW **Series:** International Year of Disabled Persons **Obv:** Dragon, date below, denomination at right **Rev:** Typist

Date	Mintage	F	VF	XF	Unc	BU
1981	—	—	—	—	700	—
1981 Proof	—	Value: 900				

KM# 53 5 SERTUMS
39.9400 g., 0.9170 Gold 1.1776 oz. AGW **Obv:** Crowned bust, left, dates below **Rev:** Two dragons around inner circle

Date	Mintage	F	VF	XF	Unc	BU
1979	1,000	—	—	—	825	—
1979 Proof	1,000	Value: 850				

KM# 53a 5 SERTUMS
49.2000 g., 0.9500 Platinum 1.5022 oz. APW **Obv:** Crowned bust, left, dates below **Rev:** Two dragons around inner circle

Date	Mintage	F	VF	XF	Unc	BU
1979 Proof	—	Value: 1,950				

KM# 64 5 SERTRUMS
7.7760 g., 0.5833 Gold .1458 oz. AGW **Series:** Endangered Wildlife **Obv:** National emblem within circle divides dates **Rev:** Black-necked crane, denomination below

Date	Mintage	F	VF	XF	Unc	BU
1992 Proof	2,000	Value: 145				

KM# 70 5 SERTRUMS
7.7760 g., 0.5833 Gold .1458 oz. AGW **Series:** 1992 Olympics **Obv:** National emblem within circle divides dates **Rev:** Archer, denomination below

Date	Mintage	F	VF	XF	Unc	BU
1993 Proof	Est. 3,000	Value: 165				

KM# 71 5 SERTRUMS
7.7760 g., 0.5833 Gold .1458 oz. AGW **Subject:** World Cup '94 Soccer **Obv:** National emblem within circle divides dates **Rev:** Soccer players, denomination below

Date	Mintage	F	VF	XF	Unc	BU
1993 Proof	Est. 2,000	Value: 165				

KM# 82 5 SERTRUMS
7.7760 g., 0.5833 Gold .1458 oz. AGW **Series:** Olympics **Subject:** Tae kwon do **Obv:** National emblem within circle divides dates **Rev:** Karate practitioner, denomination below

Date	Mintage	F	VF	XF	Unc	BU
1994 Proof	Est. 3,000	Value: 165				

PIEFORTS

KM#	Date	Mintage	Identification	Mkt Val
P1	1981	—	2 Sertums. Gold. KM60.	1,500

MINT SETS

KM#	Date	Mintage	Identification	Issue Price	Mkt Val
MS1	1966 (3)	300	KM33-35	175	900
MS4	1979 (3)	1,000	KM51-53	1,575	900

PROOF SETS

KM#	Date	Mintage	Identification	Issue Price	Mkt Val
PS2	1966 (3)	598	KM33-35	300	1,250
PS3	1966 (3)	72	KM33a-35a	685	2,250
PS7	1979 (3)	1,000	KM51-53	2,100	1,125
PS8	1979 (3)	—	KM51a-53a	2,400	2,250

BIAFRA

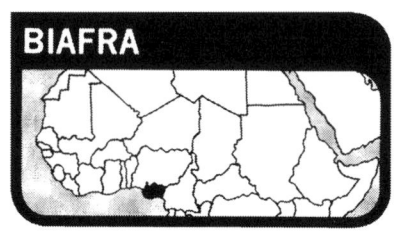

On May 30, 1967, the Eastern Region of the Republic of Nigeria, an area occupied principally by the proud and resourceful Ibo tribe, seceded from Nigeria and proclaimed itself the independent Republic of Biafra with Odumegwu Ojukwu as Chief of State. Civil war erupted and raged for 31 months. Casualties, including civilian, were about two million, the majority succumbing to malnutrition and disease. Biafra surrendered to the federal government on January 15, 1970.

MONETARY SYSTEM
12 Pence = 1 Shilling
20 Shillings = 1 Pound

INDEPENDENT REPUBLIC OF BIAFRA

STANDARD COINAGE

KM# 7 POUND
3.9940 g., 0.9170 Gold .1177 oz. AGW **Subject:** 2nd Anniversary of Independence **Obv:** Similar to 25 Pounds, KM#11, (national arms) **Rev:** Defiant eagle with scroll, wreathed shield at back, denomination below

Date	Mintage	F	VF	XF	Unc	BU
1969 Proof	3,000	Value: 175				

KM# 8 2 POUNDS
7.9881 g., 0.9170 Gold .2354 oz. AGW **Subject:** 2nd Anniversary of Independence **Obv:** Similar to 25 Pounds, KM#11, (national arms) **Rev:** Defiant eagle with scroll, wreathed shield at back, denomination below

Date	Mintage	F	VF	XF	Unc	BU
1969 Proof	3,000	Value: 250				

KM# 9 5 POUNDS
15.9761 g., 0.9170 Gold .4710 oz. AGW **Subject:** 2nd Anniversary of Independence **Obv:** Similar to 25 Pounds, KM#11, (national arms) **Rev:** Defiant eagle with scroll, wreathed shield at back, denomination below

Date	Mintage	F	VF	XF	Unc	BU
1969 Proof	3,000	Value: 500				

KM# 10 10 POUNDS
39.9403 g., 0.9170 Gold 1.1776 oz. AGW **Subject:** 2nd Anniversary of Independence **Obv:** Similar to 25 Pounds, KM#11, (national arms) **Rev:** Defiant eagle with scroll, wreathed shield at back, denomination below

Date	Mintage	F	VF	XF	Unc	BU
1969 Proof	3,000	Value: 845				

KM# 11 25 POUNDS
79.8805 g., 0.9170 Gold 2.3553 oz. AGW **Subject:** 2nd Anniversary of Independence **Obv:** National arms **Rev:** Defiant eagle with scroll, wreathed shield at back, denomination below

Date	Mintage	F	VF	XF	Unc	BU
1969 Proof	3,000	Value: 1,600				

PROOF SETS

KM#	Date	Mintage	Identification	Issue Price	Mkt Val
PS1	1969 (5)	3,000	KM7-11	464	3,375

BOLIVIA

The Republic of Bolivia, a landlocked country in west central South America, has an area of 424,165 sq. mi. (1,098,580 sq. km.) and a population of *8.33 million. Its capitals are: La Paz (administrative) and Sucre (constitutional). Principal exports are tin, zinc, antimony, tungsten, petroleum, natural gas, cotton and coffee.

Much of present day Bolivia was first dominated by the Tiahuanaco Culture ca.400 BC. It had in turn been incorporated into the Inca Empire by 1440AD prior to the arrival of the Spanish, in 1535, who reduced the Indian population to virtual slavery. When Joseph Napoleon was placed upon the throne of occupied Spain in 1809, a fervor of revolutionary activity quickened throughout Alto Peru - culminating in the 1809 Proclamation of Liberty. Sixteen bloody years of struggle ensued before the republic, named for the famed liberator Simon Bolivar, was established on August 6, 1825. Since then Bolivia has survived more than 16 constitutions, 78 Presidents, 3 military juntas and over 160 revolutions.

The Imperial City of Potosi, founded by Villarroel in 1546, was established in the midst of what is estimated to have been the world's richest silver mines (having produced in excess of 2 billion dollars worth of silver).

The first mint, early in 1574, used equipment brought over from Lima. Before that it had been used at La Plata where the operation failed. The oldest type was a cob with the Hapsburg arms on the obverse and cross with quartered castles and lions on the reverse. To the heraldic right of the shield (at the left as one faces it) is a "p" and, under it, the assayer's initial, although in some early examples the "P" and assayer can appear to the right of the shield. While production at the "Casa de Moneda" was enormous, the quality of the coinage was at times so poor that some 50 were condemned to death by their superiors.

Therefore, by royal decree of February 17, 1651, the design was changed to the quartered castles and lions for the obverse and two crowned pillars of Hercules floating above the waves of the sea for the reverse. A new transitional series was introduced in 1651-1652 followed by a new standard design in 1652 and as the last cob type continued on for several years along with the milled pillars and bust pieces from 1767 through 1773. In the final years under Charles III the planchet is compact and dumpy, very irregular and of poor style, contrasting sharply with their counterpart denominations of the pillar and bust types.

Rarely, and at very high prices, we may be offered almost perfectly round cobs, with the dies well-centered, showing the legend and date completely. These have gained importance in the last decades and are known as "royal" or "presentation" pieces. Every year a few of these specimens were coined, using dies in excellent condition and a specially prepared round planchet, to prove the quality of the minting to the Viceroy or even to the King. Another very unusual and rare variety is specially struck specimens on heart-shaped flans. While many heart-shaped examples are encountered in today's market, a careful examination will reveal that most are underweight and were created after striking for jewelry and souvenir purposes. Most surviving specimens are holed, plugged or countermarked as found in Guatemala listings. The rest of the production was of primitive quality due to the shortage of equipment, skilled laborers and the volume to be struck.

Most pre-decimal coinage of independent Bolivia carries the assayers' initials on the reverse near the rim to the left of the date, in 4 to 5 o'clock position. The mint mark or name appears in the 7 to 8 o'clock area.

RULERS
Spanish until 1825

MINT MARKS
A - Paris
(a) - Paris, privy marks only
CHI - Valcambia
H - Heaton
KN - Kings' Norton
PTA monogram - La Plata (Sucre)
OR monogram – Oruro
PAZ - La Paz
P or PTS monogram - Potosi
So - Santiago

ASSAYERS' INITIALS
There is little information available to establish the chronology of the assayers during the reign of Phillip II, 1555-1598, so the assayers initials are listed in alphabetical order. Calbeto in *Compendio de las Piezas de Ocho Reales* describes a piece with A overstruck over B, indicating A was later.

Initial	Date	Name
F	1815	Francisco Jose de Matos
F	1830, 1848-67	Fortunato Equivar
FE	1867-90	Fortunato Equivar
J	1803-12, 1814-32	Juan Palomo y Sierra
J	1813	Jose Antonio de Sierra
J	1853-62	Joaquin Zemborain
L	1825-26	Leandro Osio

BOLIVIA

L	1825, 1830-43	Luis de Aquilar
M	1826-29, 1833-39	Digo Miguel Lopez
M	1848-55	Manuel Berrios
P	1776-1802	Pedro de Mazondo
P	1795-1824	Pedro Martin de Albizu
R	1839-47	Rafael Mariano Bustillo
R	1848	Manuel Telesforo Ramires

MONETARY SYSTEM
16 Reales = 1 Escudo

COLONIAL
MILLED COINAGE

KM# 78 ESCUDO
3.3834 g., 0.8750 Gold .0952 oz. AGW **Ruler:** Charles IIII **Obv:** Armored bust right **Obv. Legend:** CAROL • IIII • D • G • HISP • ET IND • R • **Rev:** Crowned arms within order chain **Note:** Mint mark in monogram.

Date	Mintage	VG	F	VF	XF	Unc
1801PTS PP	1,363	150	200	275	475	—
1802PTS PP	376	150	200	275	475	—
1803PTS PJ	410	150	200	275	600	—
1804PTS PJ	476	150	200	275	600	—
1805PTS PJ	613	150	200	275	600	—
1806PTS PJ	204	150	200	275	600	—
1807PTS PJ	1,123	150	200	275	600	—
1808PTS PJ	884	150	200	275	600	—

KM# 92 ESCUDO
3.3834 g., 0.8750 Gold .0952 oz. AGW **Ruler:** Ferdinand VII **Obv:** Laureate head right **Obv. Legend:** FERDIN • VII • D • G • HISP • ET IND • R • **Rev:** Crowned arms within order chain **Note:** Mint mark in monogram.

Date	Mintage	VG	F	VF	XF	Unc
1822PTS PJ	—	200	300	450	1,250	—
1823PTS PJ	—	250	400	650	1,500	—
1824PTS PJ	—	300	500	850	1,800	—

KM# 79 2 ESCUDOS
6.7668 g., 0.8750 Gold .1904 oz. AGW **Ruler:** Charles IIII **Obv:** Uniformed bust right **Obv. Legend:** CAROLUS • IIII • D • G • HISP • ET IND • R • **Rev:** Crowned arms within order chain **Note:** Mint mark in monogram.

Date	Mintage	VG	F	VF	XF	Unc
1801PTS PP	545	250	400	525	1,000	—
1802PTS PP	273	400	550	700	1,300	—
1803PTS PJ	273	400	550	700	1,300	—
1804PTS PJ	204	250	400	550	1,100	—
1805PTS PJ	306	325	475	700	1,300	—
1806PTS PJ	476	400	550	800	1,300	—
1807PTS PJ	748	250	350	525	850	—
1808PTS PJ	647	325	475	700	1,100	—

KM# 80 4 ESCUDOS
13.5337 g., 0.8750 Gold .3807 oz. AGW **Ruler:** Charles IIII **Obv:** Armored bust right **Obv. Legend:** CAROL • IIII • D • G • HISP • ET IND • R • **Rev:** Crowned arms within order chain **Note:** Mint mark in monogram.

Date	Mintage	VG	F	VF	XF	Unc
1801PTS PP	13,000	400	550	950	2,450	—
1802PTS PP	698	475	600	1,100	2,500	—
1803PTS PJ	408	800	1,100	1,600	3,550	—
1804PTS PJ	187	950	1,300	1,750	3,750	—
1805PTS PJ	255	500	700	1,100	2,500	—
1806PTS PJ	221	500	700	1,100	2,500	—
1807PTS PJ	527	475	600	950	2,450	—
1808PTS PJ	323	475	600	950	2,450	—

KM# 81 8 ESCUDOS
27.0674 g., 0.8750 Gold .7615 oz. AGW **Ruler:** Charles IIII **Obv:** Armored bust right **Obv. Legend:** CAROL • IIII • D • G • HISP • ET IND • R • **Rev:** Crowned arms within order chain **Note:** Mint mark in monogram.

Date	Mintage	VG	F	VF	XF	Unc
1801PTS PP	29,000	375	425	650	950	—
1802PTS PP	20,000	375	425	650	950	—
1803PTS PJ	17,000	375	425	650	950	—
1804PTS PJ	22,000	375	425	650	950	—
1805PTS PJ	49,000	375	425	650	950	—
1806PTS PJ	38,000	375	425	650	950	—
1807PTS PJ	39,000	375	425	650	950	—
1808PTS PJ	35,000	375	425	650	950	—

KM# 86 8 ESCUDOS
27.0674 g., 0.8750 Gold .7615 oz. AGW **Ruler:** Ferdinand VII **Obv:** Uniformed bust of Ferdinand VII **Obv. Legend:** FERDIN • VII • D • G • HISP • ET IND • R • **Note:** Mint mark in monogram.

Date	Mintage	VG	F	VF	XF	Unc
1809PTS PJ	—	—	—	—	—	—

KM# 91 8 ESCUDOS
27.0730 g., 0.8750 Gold .7616 oz. AGW **Ruler:** Ferdinand VII **Obv:** Laureate head right **Obv. Legend:** FERDIN. VII... **Rev:** Crowned arms within order chain **Note:** Mint mark in monogram. This type is most often encountered with a weak strike, fully struck coins with good bust detail command a strong premium.

Date	Mintage	VG	F	VF	XF	Unc
1822PTS PJ	—	375	450	850	1,450	—
1823PTS PJ	—	400	550	1,000	2,500	—
1824PTS PJ	—	400	500	900	2,000	—

REPUBLIC
SOL / SCUDO COINAGE

KM# 100 1/2 SCUDO
1.7000 g., 0.8750 Gold .0478 oz. AGW **Obv:** Mountain with llama at left, sheaf at right, sun above and stars below **Rev:** Uniformed bust right **Note:** Mint mark in monogram.

Date	Mintage	VG	F	VF	XF	Unc
1834PTS LM Rare	—	—	—	—	—	—
1838PTS LM	—	80.00	140	210	400	—
1839PTS LM	—	80.00	130	200	375	—
1840PTS LR	—	80.00	140	210	400	—

KM# 104 1/2 SCUDO
1.7000 g., 0.8750 Gold .0478 oz. AGW **Obv:** Mountain with llama at left, sheaf at right, sun above and stars below **Rev:** Laureate head right **Note:** Mint mark in monogram.

Date	Mintage	VG	F	VF	XF	Unc
1841PTS LR/PL	—	55.00	75.00	100	165	—
1841PTS LR	—	55.00	75.00	100	165	—
1842PTS LR	—	55.00	75.00	100	165	—
1842PTS LR	—	55.00	75.00	100	165	—
Note: Error "BOLIAR" below bust						
1843PTS LR	—	55.00	75.00	100	165	—
1844PTS R	—	55.00	75.00	100	165	—
1845PTS R	—	55.00	75.00	100	165	—
1846PTS R	—	55.00	75.00	100	165	—
1847PTS R	—	55.00	75.00	100	165	—

KM# 113 1/2 SCUDO
1.7000 g., 0.8750 Gold .0478 oz. AGW **Obv:** Mountain with llama at left, sheaf at right, sun above and stars below **Rev:** Laureate head right **Note:** Mint mark in monogram.

Date	Mintage	F	VF	XF	Unc	BU
1852/1PTS FP	—	85.00	150	200	400	—
1852PTS MJ	—	70.00	125	175	325	—
1852PTS FP	—	65.00	120	170	300	—
1853PTS FP	—	65.00	120	170	300	—
1854PTS FP	—	70.00	125	175	325	—
1855PTS MF/FJ	—	65.00	120	170	300	—
1855PTS FP	—	65.00	120	170	300	—
1855PTS M	—	65.00	120	170	300	—
1855PTS NJ	—	65.00	120	170	300	—
1855PTS FS	—	65.00	120	170	300	—
1856PTS FJ	—	65.00	120	170	300	—
1856PTS FS	—	65.00	120	170	300	—

KM# 140 1/2 SCUDO
1.2500 g., 0.9000 Gold .0361 oz. AGW **Obv:** Crossed flags and weapons behind condor topped oval arms **Rev:** Denomination within wreath

Date	Mintage	F	VF	XF	Unc	BU
1868 FE	—	300	550	650	1,000	—

KM# 98 SCUDO
3.4000 g., 0.8750 Gold .0956 oz. AGW **Obv:** Mountain with llama at left, sheaf at right, sun above and stars below **Rev:** Armored bust right **Note:** Mint mark in monogram.

Date	Mintage	VG	F	VF	XF	Unc
1831PTS JL	—	85.00	120	220	325	—
1832/1PTS JL	—	100	150	275	400	—
1832PTS JL	—	85.00	120	220	300	—
1833PTS JL	—	85.00	120	220	325	—
1833PTS LM	—	85.00	120	220	325	—
1834PTS JL	—	70.00	100	200	300	—
1834PTS LM	—	85.00	120	220	325	—
1835PTS LM	—	85.00	120	220	325	—
1836PTS LM	—	85.00	120	220	325	—
1837PTS LM	—	85.00	120	220	325	—
1838PTS LM	—	85.00	120	220	325	—
1839PTS LM	—	85.00	120	220	325	—
1840PTS LR	—	120	165	300	485	—

KM# 105 SCUDO
3.4000 g., 0.8750 Gold .0956 oz. AGW **Obv:** Mountain with llama at left, sheaf at right, sun above and stars below **Rev:** Laureate head right **Note:** Mint mark in monogram.

Date	Mintage	VG	F	VF	XF	Unc
1841PTS LR	—	85.00	120	220	325	—
1842PTS LR	—	85.00	120	220	325	—
1846PTS R	—	85.00	120	220	325	—

KM# 114 SCUDO
3.4000 g., 0.8750 Gold .0956 oz. AGW **Obv:** Mountain with llama at left, sheaf at right, sun above and stars below **Rev:** Laureate bust right **Note:** Mint mark in monogram.

Date	Mintage	F	VF	XF	Unc	BU
1852PTS FP	—	80.00	120	200	350	—
1853PTS FP	—	80.00	120	200	350	—
1855PTS LM/J	—	80.00	120	200	350	—
1856PTS FJ	—	80.00	120	220	350	—

BOLIVIA 69

KM# 141 SCUDO
2.5000 g., 0.9000 Gold .0723 oz. AGW **Obv:** Crossed flags and weapons behind condor topped oval arms **Rev:** Denomination within wreath

Date	Mintage	F	VF	XF	Unc	BU
1868 FE	—	200	300	450	800	—

KM# 101 2 SCUDOS
6.8000 g., 0.8750 Gold .1913 oz. AGW **Obv:** Mountain with llama at left, sheaf at right, sun above and stars below **Rev:** Uniformed bust right **Note:** Mint mark in monogram.

Date	Mintage	VG	F	VF	XF	Unc
1834PTS LM	—	225	350	575	900	—
1835PTS LM	—	200	300	500	800	—

KM# 106 2 SCUDOS
6.8000 g., 0.8750 Gold .1913 oz. AGW **Obv:** Mountains with llama at left, sheaf at right, sun above and stars below **Rev:** Laureate head right **Note:** Mint mark in monogram.

Date	Mintage	VG	F	VF	XF	Unc
1841PTS LR	—	400	550	850	1,500	—

KM# 102 4 SCUDOS
13.5000 g., 0.8750 Gold .3798 oz. AGW **Obv:** Mountain with llama at left, sheaf at right, sun above and stars below **Rev:** Uniformed bust right **Note:** Mint mark in monogram.

Date	Mintage	VG	F	VF	XF	Unc
1834PTS JL	—	650	1,000	1,750	3,500	—
1834PTS LM Rare	—	—	—	—	—	—

KM# 107 4 SCUDOS
13.5000 g., 0.8750 Gold .3798 oz. AGW **Obv:** Mountain with llama at left, sheaf at right, sun above and stars below **Rev:** Laureate head right **Note:** Mint mark in monogram.

Date	Mintage	VG	F	VF	XF	Unc
1841PTS LR	—	900	1,500	2,500	4,000	—

KM# 99 8 SCUDOS
27.0000 g., 0.8750 Gold .7596 oz. AGW **Obv:** Mountains with llama at left, sheaf at right, sun above and stars below **Rev:** Uniformed bust right **Note:** Mint mark in monogram.

Date	Mintage	VG	F	VF	XF	Unc
1831PTS JL	—	550	675	950	1,650	—
1832PTS JL	—	550	675	950	1,650	—
1833PTS JL	—	550	675	950	1,650	—
1833PTS LM	—	550	675	950	1,650	—
1834PTS JL	—	550	675	950	1,650	—
1834PTS JM	—	650	775	1,000	1,750	—
1834PTS LM	—	550	675	950	1,650	—
1835PTS JM	—	550	675	950	1,650	—
1835PTS LM	—	550	675	950	1,650	—
1836PTS LM	—	650	775	1,000	1,750	—
1837PTS LM	—	520	625	900	1,500	—
1838PTS LM	—	600	675	950	1,650	—
1839PTS LM	—	520	625	900	1,500	—
1840PTS LR	—	520	625	900	1,500	—

KM# 108.1 8 SCUDOS
27.0000 g., 0.8750 Gold .7596 oz. AGW **Obv:** Mountains with llama at left, sheaf at right, sun above and stars below **Rev:** Laureate head right **Note:** Large bust, mint mark in monogram.

Date	Mintage	VG	F	VF	XF	Unc
1841PTS LR	—	600	700	950	1,650	—

KM# 108.2 8 SCUDOS
27.0000 g., 0.8750 Gold .7596 oz. AGW **Obv:** Mountains with llama at left, sheaf at right, sun above and stars below **Rev:** Laureate head right **Note:** Mint mark in monogram.

Date	Mintage	VG	F	VF	XF	Unc
1841PTS LR	—	BV	550	650	1,000	—
1842PTS LR	—	BV	550	650	1,000	—
1843PTS LR	—	BV	550	650	1,000	—
1844PTS LR	—	BV	550	650	1,000	—
1844PTS R	—	625	750	1,000	1,750	—
1845PTS R	—	625	750	1,000	1,750	—
1846PTS R	—	625	750	1,000	1,750	—
1847PTS R	—	625	750	1,000	1,750	—

KM# 110 8 SCUDOS
27.0000 g., 0.8750 Gold .7596 oz. AGW **Obv:** Sun with dense rays **Rev:** Head left **Note:** Mint mark in monogram.

Date	Mintage	VG	F	VF	XF	Unc
1851PTS MF	—	900	1,500	2,750	4,500	—

KM# 115 8 SCUDOS
27.0000 g., 0.8750 Gold .7596 oz. AGW **Obv:** Sun with dense rays **Rev:** Laureate head left **Note:** Mint mark in monogram.

Date	Mintage	F	VF	XF	Unc	BU
1852PTS FP	—	3,500	6,000	8,500	12,500	—

KM# 116 8 SCUDOS
27.0000 g., 0.8750 Gold .7596 oz. AGW **Obv:** Sun with dense rays **Rev:** Laureate head right **Note:** Mint mark in monogram.

Date	Mintage	F	VF	XF	Unc	BU
1852PTS FP	—	500	650	1,000	1,850	—
1853/2PTS	—	500	650	1,000	1,850	—
1853PTS FP	—	500	650	1,000	1,850	—
1854PTS M	—	500	650	1,000	1,750	—
1854PTS MJ	—	500	650	1,000	1,750	—
1855PTS LM	—	500	650	1,000	1,750	—
1855PTS MJ	—	500	650	1,000	1,750	—
1856PTS FJ/MJ	—	500	650	1,000	1,750	—
1856PTS FJ	—	500	650	1,000	1,750	—
1857/6PTS FJ	—	500	650	1,000	1,750	—
1857PTS FJ	—	500	650	1,000	1,750	—

DECIMAL COINAGE
100 Centecimos = 1 Boliviano

KM# 142 ONZA
32.4000 g., 0.9000 Gold .9375 oz. AGW **Obv:** Crossed flags and weapons behind condor topped oval arms, stars below **Rev:** Denomination within wreath **Note:** Mint mark in monogram.

Date	Mintage	F	VF	XF	Unc	BU
1868PTS FE Rare	—	—	—	—	—	—

Note: Stack's Hammel sale 9-82 AU realized $13,000., Pacific Coast Auction Galleries, Long Beach sale 6-86 AU realized $15,500., Superior Parker/Casterline sale 12-89 AU realized $15,400

| 1868PTS FP Rare | — | — | — | — | — | — |

MEDALLIC COINAGE

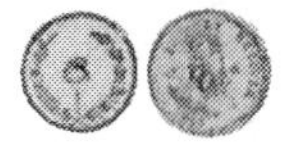

X# M1 1/2 GRAMO
0.5800 g., Gold **Rev. Legend:** POTOSI BOLIVIA

Date	Mintage	F	VF	XF	Unc	BU
1860	—	—	15.00	20.00	35.00	—

X# M3 GRAMO
1.3000 g., Gold, 13 mm. **Obv:** Nine stars surround moutain peak **Rev:** Llama standing right

Date	Mintage	F	VF	XF	Unc	BU
1852	—	—	—	30.00	45.00	—

BOLIVIA

X# M2 GRAMO
1.1500 g., Gold **Rev:** Llama

Date	Mintage	F	VF	XF	Unc	BU
1879	—	—	25.00	35.00	55.00	—

X# M4 1-1/2 GRAMOS
1.7000 g., Gold, 14.5 mm. **Obv:** Arms **Obv. Legend:** REPUBLICA DE BOLIVIA **Rev:** Llama standing right **Rev. Legend:** POTOSI

Date	Mintage	F	VF	XF	Unc	BU
1846	—	—	—	30.00	45.00	—

REFORM COINAGE
1965-1979; 100 Centavos = 1 Peso Boliviano

KM# 199 4000 PESOS BOLIVIANOS
17.1700 g., 0.9000 Gold .4968 oz. AGW **Subject:** International Year of the Child **Obv:** State emblem within circle, eagle at top, stars below **Rev:** Child playing flute divides symbols, date below, denomination above

Date	Mintage	F	VF	XF	Unc	BU
1979 Proof	6,315	Value: 345				

MEDALLIC COINAGE
1952 - Gold Bullion

X# 15 3-1/2 GRAMOS (5 Bolivianos)
3.8900 g., 0.9000 Gold .1125 oz. AGW **Subject:** 1952 Revolution Commemorative **Note:** Prev. KM#MB1.

Date	Mintage	F	VF	XF	Unc	BU
1952(a)	29,000	—	—	—	BV+20%	—

X# 11 7 GRAMOS (10 Bolivianos)
7.7800 g., 0.9000 Gold .2251 oz. AGW **Subject:** 1952 Revolution Commemorative **Note:** Prev. KM#MB2.

Date	Mintage	F	VF	XF	Unc	BU
1952(a)	79,000	—	—	—	BV+15%	—

X# 12 14 GRAMOS (20 Bolivianos)
15.5600 g., 0.9000 Gold .4502 oz. AGW **Subject:** 1952 Revolution Commemorative **Note:** Prev. KM#MB3.

Date	Mintage	F	VF	XF	Unc	BU
1952(a)	7,142	—	—	—	BV+10%	—

X# 13 35 GRAMOS (50 Bolivianos)
38.9000 g., 0.9000 Gold 1.1257 oz. AGW **Subject:** 1952 Revolution Commemorative **Note:** Prev. KM#MB4.

Date	Mintage	F	VF	XF	Unc	BU
1952(a)	2,857	—	—	—	BV+10%	—

PATTERNS
Including off metal strikes

KM#	Date	Mintage	Identification	Mkt Val
Pn7	1865 FP	—	Onza. Gold. Struck at Potosi.	25,000
Pn11	1868 CT	—	Boliviano. Gold. Reeded edge. Struck at Potosi.	20,900
Pn16	1868 CT	—	5 Centavos. Gold. Struck at La Paz.	2,500
Pn18	1868 CT	—	10 Centavos. Gold. Struck at La Paz.	3,500
Pn47	1887 F.E.	—	Escudo. Gold. Struck at La Paz.	2,500
Pn48	1887 F.E.	—	1/2 Bolivar. 0.9000 Gold.	—
Pn49	1887 F.E.	—	Bolivar. Gold. Struck at La Paz.	—
Pn53	1900 So	—	50 Centavos. 0.9000 Gold. Struck at La Paz. KM#175.2	4,000

PIEFORTS

KM#	Date	Mintage	Identification	Issue Price	Mkt Val
P10	1979	47	4000 Pesos. Gold. KM#199.	—	1,000

MINT SETS

KM#	Date	Mintage	Identification	Issue Price	Mkt Val
XMS1	1952 (4)	—	X#MB1-MB4; Market Value is BV+10%	—	—

BOPHUTHATSWANA

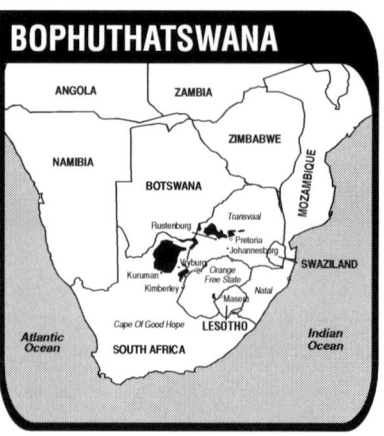

Bophuthatswana is a group of non-contiguous black enclaves located partially in Bechuanaland, Botswana and in the northwestern area of South Africa. Established in 1977, it ceased to exist with the end of apartheid in 1994. Population: 1,382,637. Capital: Mmabatho. The exportation of platinum is their main source of income.

The Botswana people have occupied their general area from the beginnings of their history. In 1871 the British recognized their sovereignty. In 1895 their land, known as British Bechuanaland, was claimed by the British and the Boers. The people were scattered across the sub-continent.

SOVEREIGN ENCLAVE
GOLD BULLION MEDALLIC COINAGE

X# 1 NKWE
16.9660 g., 0.9170 Gold .5 oz. AGW **Subject:** 10th Anniversary of Independence **Note:** Prev. KM#M1. Similar to Lowe, KM#2.

Date	Mintage	F	VF	XF	Unc	BU
1987 Proof	—	Value: 300				

PLATINUM BULLION MEDALLIC COINAGE

X# 2 LOWE
31.2100 g., 0.9995 Platinum 1 oz. APW **Subject:** 10th Anniversary of Independence **Note:** Prev. KM#M2.

Date	Mintage	F	VF	XF	Unc	BU
1987 Proof	3,000	Value: 1,100				

BOSNIA AND HERZEGOVINA

The Republic of Bosnia and Herzegovina borders Croatia to the north and west, Serbia to the east and Montenegro in the southeast with only 12.4 mi. of coastline. The total land area is 19,735 sq. mi. (51,129 sq. km.). They have a population of *4.34 million. Capital: Sarajevo. Electricity, mining and agriculture are leading industries.

Under Roman rule, Bosnia formed part of Illyria. Bosnia's first ruler of importance was the Ban Kulin, 1180-1204. Stephen Kotromanic was invested with Bosnia, held loyally to Hungary and extended his rule to the principality of Hum or Zahumlje, the future Herzegovina, which until then led a rather independent existence since the 10th century. His daughter Elisabeth married Louis the Great and he died in the same year. His nephew Tvrtko succeeded and during the weakening of Serbian power he assumed the title "Stephen Tvrtko, in Christ God King of the Serbs and Bosnia and the Coastland. Later he assumed the title of "King of Dalmatia and Croatia", but died before he could consolidate power. Successors also asserted their right to the Serbian throne. His brother surrendered Croatia and Dalmatia to Sigismund of Hungary. Interior conflicts led to the invasion of the Turks. In 1459 the Turks invaded Serbia and the King of Bosnia was blamed by Hungary and the pope as being responsible for the disaster. Bosnia was then invaded in 1463 and Herzegovina in 1483. During Turkish rule they had an isolated world from Europe and Constantinople. Islam replaced Catholicism. During the 16th to 17th centuries Bosnia was an important Turkish outpost in continuing warfare with the Hapsburgs and Venice. When Hungary was freed of the Turkish yoke, the Imperialists penetrated into Bosnia, and in 1697 Prince Eugene captured Sarajevo. Later, by the Treaty of Karlowitz in 1699, the northern boundary of Bosnia became the northernmost limit of the Turkish Empire while the eastern area was ceded to Austria, but later restored to Turkey in 1739 lasting until 1878 following revolts of 1821, 1828, 1831 and 1862. On June 30, 1871 Serbia and Montenegro declared war on Turkey and were quickly defeated. The Turkish war with Russia led to the occupation by Austria-Hungary. Insurgents attempted armed resistance and Austria-Hungary invaded in mass quelling the uprising in 1878. The Austrian Occupation provided a period of prosperity while at the same time prevented relations with Serbia and Croatia. Strengthening political and religious movements from within forced the annexation by Austria on Oct. 7, 1908. Hungary's establishment of a dictatorship in Croatia and following the victories of Serbian forces in the Balkan War roused the whole Yugoslav population of Austria-Hungary to feverish excitement. The Bosnian group, mainly students, devoted their efforts to revolutionary ideas. Jealousy developed between the provincial Government in Sarajevo and the finance ministry of Vienna. In 1913 the Bosnian Diet was closed and various Serbian societies were dissolved. During military maneuvers in Bosnia in June 1914 the assassination of the visiting Archduke Francis Ferdinand and his consort, the Duchess of Hohenberg triggered WWI. After Austria's Balkan front collapsed in Oct. 1918, the union with Yugoslavia developed and on Dec. 1, 1918 the former Kingdom of the Serbs, Croats, and Slovenes was proclaimed later to become the Kingdom of Yugoslavia on Oct. 3, 1929.

After the defeat of Germany in WWII, during which Bosnia was under the control of Pavelic of Croatia, a new Socialist Republic was formed under Marshall Tito having six constituent republics, all subservient, quite similar to the constitution of the U.S.S.R. Military and civil loyalty was with Tito, not with Moscow. In Jan. 1990, the Yugoslav Government announced a rewriting of the Constitution, abolishing the Communist Party's monopoly of power. Opposition parties were legalized in July 1990. On Oct. 15, 1991 the National Assembly adopted a "Memorandum on Sovereignty", the envisaged Bosnian autonomy within a Yugoslav federation. In March 1992, an agreement was reached under EC auspices by Moslems, Serbs and Croats to set up 3 autonomous ethnic communities under a central Bosnian authority. Independence was declared on April 5, 1992. The 2 Serbian members of government resigned and fighting broke out between all 3 ethnic communities. The Dayton (Ohio) Peace Accord was signed in 1995, which recognized the Federation of Bosnia and Herzegovina and the Srpska (Serbian) Republic. Both governments maintain separate military forces, school systems, etc. The United Nations is currently providing humanitarian aid while a recent peace treaty allowed NATO "Peace Keeping" forces to be deployed in Dec. 1995 replacing the United Nations troops previously acting in a similar role.

MINT MARKS

PM - Pobjoy Mint

MONETARY SYSTEM

1 Dinara = 100 Para, 1992-1998

1 Convertible Marka = 100 Convertible Feniga =

1 Deutschemark 1998-

NOTE: German Euros circulate freely.

REPUBLIC

DINARA COINAGE

KM# 3 10000 DINARA

6.2200 g., 0.9990 Gold .1998 oz. AGW **Series:** Preserve Planet Earth **Obv:** National arms above bridge, date below **Rev:** Brontosaurus, facing back, looking left, denomination below

Date	Mintage	F	VF	XF	Unc	BU
1993 Proof	Est. 5,000	Value: 185				

KM# 6 10000 DINARA

6.2200 g., 0.9990 Gold .1998 oz. AGW **Series:** Preserve Planet Earth **Obv:** National arms above bridge, date below **Rev:** Tyrannosaurus Rex, facing right, looking left, denomination below

Date	Mintage	F	VF	XF	Unc	BU
1993 Proof	Est. 5,000	Value: 185				

KM# 8 10000 DINARA

6.2200 g., 0.9990 Gold .1998 oz. AGW **Series:** Olympics **Obv:** National arms above bridge, date below **Rev:** Two bobsledders starting race

Date	Mintage	F	VF	XF	Unc	BU
1993 Proof	Est. 5,000	Value: 190				

KM# 10 10000 DINARA

6.2200 g., 0.9990 Gold .1998 oz. AGW **Series:** Olympics **Obv:** National arms above bridge, date below **Rev:** Downhill skier

Date	Mintage	F	VF	XF	Unc	BU
1993	Est. 5,000	Value: 190				

KM# 12 10000 DINARA

6.2200 g., 0.9990 Gold .1998 oz. AGW **Series:** Olympics **Obv:** National arms above bridge, date below **Rev:** Cross-country skier

Date	Mintage	F	VF	XF	Unc	BU
1993 Proof	Est. 5,000	Value: 190				

KM# 14 10000 DINARA

6.2200 g., 0.9990 Gold .1998 oz. AGW **Series:** Olympics **Obv:** National arms above bridge, date below **Rev:** Pair skating

Date	Mintage	F	VF	XF	Unc	BU
1993 Proof	Est. 5,000	Value: 190				

KM# 22 10000 DINARA

6.2200 g., 0.9990 Gold .1998 oz. AGW **Series:** Preserve Planet Earth **Obv:** National arms above bridge, date below **Rev:** Eohippu, right, denomination below

Date	Mintage	F	VF	XF	Unc	BU
1994 Proof	Est. 5,000	Value: 185				

KM# 29 10000 DINARA

6.2200 g., 0.9990 Gold .1998 oz. AGW **Series:** Preserve Planet Earth **Obv:** National arms above bridge, date below **Rev:** Wolf walking right

Date	Mintage	F	VF	XF	Unc	BU
1994 Proof	5,000	Value: 185				

KM# 30 10000 DINARA

6.2200 g., 0.9990 Gold .1998 oz. AGW **Series:** Preserve Planet Earth **Obv:** National arms above bridge, date below **Rev:** Black bear and cub walking right

Date	Mintage	F	VF	XF	Unc	BU
1994 Proof	5,000	Value: 185				

KM# 31 10000 DINARA

6.2200 g., 0.9990 Gold .1998 oz. AGW **Series:** Preserve Planet Earth **Obv:** National arms above bridge, date below **Rev:** Kingfisher left with fish in bill

Date	Mintage	F	VF	XF	Unc	BU
1994 Proof	5,000	Value: 185				

KM# 41 10000 DINARA

6.2200 g., 0.9990 Gold .1998 oz. AGW **Series:** Preserve Planet Earth **Obv:** National arms above bridge, date below **Rev:** Przewalskii horses

Date	Mintage	F	VF	XF	Unc	BU
1995 Proof	Est. 5,000	Value: 185				

KM# 44 10000 DINARA

6.2200 g., 0.9990 Gold .1998 oz. AGW **Series:** Preserve Planet Earth **Obv:** National arms above bridge, date below **Rev:** Hedgehogs

Date	Mintage	F	VF	XF	Unc	BU
1995 Proof	Est. 5,000	Value: 185				

KM# 60 10000 DINARA

6.2200 g., 0.9990 Gold .1998 oz. AGW **Series:** Olympics **Obv:** National arms above bridge, date below **Rev:** Long jumper

Date	Mintage	F	VF	XF	Unc	BU
1996 Proof	Est. 5,000	Value: 200				

KM# 61 10000 DINARA

6.2200 g., 0.9990 Gold .1998 oz. AGW **Series:** Olympics **Obv:** National arms above bridge, date below **Rev:** Sprinter

Date	Mintage	F	VF	XF	Unc	BU
1996 Proof	Est. 5,000	Value: 200				

KM# 62 10000 DINARA

6.2200 g., 0.9990 Gold .1998 oz. AGW **Series:** Olympics **Obv:** National arms above bridge, date below **Rev:** Wrestlers

Date	Mintage	F	VF	XF	Unc	BU
1996 Proof	Est. 5,000	Value: 200				

KM# 63 10000 DINARA

6.2200 g., 0.9990 Gold .1998 oz. AGW **Series:** Olympics **Obv:** National arms above bridge, date below **Rev:** Fencers

Date	Mintage	F	VF	XF	Unc	BU
1996 Proof	Est. 5,000	Value: 200				

KM# 78 10000 DINARA

6.2200 g., 0.9990 Gold .1998 oz. AGW **Series:** Preserve Planet Earth **Obv:** National arms above bridge, date below **Rev:** Hoopoe birds

Date	Mintage	F	VF	XF	Unc	BU
1996 Proof	Est. 5,000	Value: 185				

KM# 81 10000 DINARA

6.2200 g., 0.9990 Gold .1998 oz. AGW **Series:** Preserve Planet Earth **Obv:** National arms above bridge, date below **Rev:** Goosander birds

Date	Mintage	F	VF	XF	Unc	BU
1996 Proof	Est. 5,000	Value: 185				

KM# 97 10000 DINARA

6.2200 g., 0.9990 Gold .1998 oz. AGW **Subject:** Jurassic Park **Obv:** National arms above bridge, date below **Rev:** Tyrannosaurus Rex, left, Jurassic Park logo above, denomination below

Date	Mintage	F	VF	XF	Unc	BU
1997 Proof	Est. 2,500	Value: 185				

MARKA / MARAKA COINAGE

KM# 100 20 MARKA

1.2441 g., 0.9999 Gold .0400 oz. AGW **Subject:** Princess Diana **Obv:** National arms above bridge, date below **Rev:** Portrait and map

Date	Mintage	F	VF	XF	Unc	BU
1998 Proof	Est. 10,000	Value: 55.00				

KM# 101 50 MARKA

3.1103 g., 0.9999 Gold .1000 oz. AGW **Subject:** Princess Diana **Obv:** National arms above bridge, date below **Rev:** Portrait and map

Date	Mintage	F	VF	XF	Unc	BU
1998 Proof	Est. 7,500	Value: 110				

KM# 102 100 MARKA

6.2206 g., 0.9999 Gold .2000 oz. AGW **Subject:** Princess Diana **Obv:** National arms above bridge, date below **Rev:** Portrait and map

Date	Mintage	F	VF	XF	Unc	BU
1998 Proof	Est. 5,000	Value: 185				

KM# 113 100 MARKA

6.2206 g., 0.9999 Gold .2000 oz. AGW **Subject:** Sydney 2000 - 27th Summer Olympics **Obv:** National arms above bridge, date below **Rev:** Javelin thrower

Date	Mintage	F	VF	XF	Unc	BU
1998 Proof	Est. 5,000	Value: 185				

KM# 103 250 MARKA

15.5517 g., 0.9999 Gold .5000 oz. AGW **Subject:** Princess Diana **Obv:** National arms above bridge, date below **Rev:** Portrait and map

Date	Mintage	F	VF	XF	Unc	BU
1998 Proof	Est. 3,000	Value: 385				

TRADE COINAGE

KM# 15 1/25 DUKAT

1.2440 g., 0.9999 Gold .0400 oz. AGW **Subject:** Hajj - Kaaba in Mecca **Obv:** National arms above bridge, date below **Rev:** Building and denomination within circle

Date	Mintage	F	VF	XF	Unc	BU
1993 Proof	Est. 25,000	Value: 50.00				

KM# 16 1/10 DUKAT

3.1103 g., 0.9999 Gold .1000 oz. AGW **Subject:** Hajj - Kaaba in Mecca **Obv:** National arms above bridge, date below **Rev:** Building and denomination within circle

Date	Mintage	F	VF	XF	Unc	BU
1993 Proof	Est. 20,000	Value: 95.00				

KM# 17 1/5 DUKAT

6.2200 g., 0.9999 Gold .2000 oz. AGW **Subject:** Hajj - Kaaba in Mecca **Obv:** National arms above bridge, date below **Rev:** Building and denomination within circle

Date	Mintage	F	VF	XF	Unc	BU
1993 Proof	Est. 5,000	Value: 185				

KM# 18 1/2 DUKAT

15.5510 g., 0.9999 Gold .5000 oz. AGW **Subject:** Hajj - Kaaba in Mecca **Obv:** National arms above bridge, date below **Rev:** Building and denomination within circle

Date	Mintage	F	VF	XF	Unc	BU
1993 Proof	Est. 5,000	Value: 375				

BOSNIA-HERZEGOVINA

KM# 19 DUKAT
31.1030 g., 0.9999 Gold 1.0000 oz. AGW **Subject:** Hajj - Kaaba in Mecca **Obv:** National arms above bridge, date below **Rev:** Building and denomination within circle

Date	Mintage	F	VF	XF	Unc	BU
1993 Proof	Est. 5,000	Value: 675				
1994 Proof	—	Value: 675				

KM# 32 1/25 SUVERENA
1.2441 g., 0.9999 Gold .0400 oz. AGW **Subject:** Lipizzaner Stallion **Obv:** National arms above bridge, date below **Rev:** Horse rearing right, denomination below

Date	Mintage	F	VF	XF	Unc	BU
1994 Proof	—	Value: 52.00				

KM# 45 1/25 SUVERENA
1.2441 g., 0.9999 Gold .0400 oz. AGW **Subject:** English Hack **Obv:** National arms above bridge, date below **Rev:** Horse running left, denomination below

Date	Mintage	F	VF	XF	Unc	BU
1995 Proof	Est. 15,000	Value: 52.00				

KM# 70 1/25 SUVERENA
1.2441 g., 0.9999 Gold .0400 oz. AGW **Subject:** Hanoverian Stallion **Obv:** National arms above bridge, date below **Rev:** Horse left, denomination below

Date	Mintage	F	VF	XF	Unc	BU
1996 Proof	Est. 15,000	Value: 52.00				

KM# 89 1/25 SUVERENA
1.2441 g., 0.9999 Gold .0400 oz. AGW **Subject:** The Arab **Obv:** National arms above bridge, date below **Rev:** Horse right, denomination below

Date	Mintage	F	VF	XF	Unc	BU
1997 Proof	Est. 15,000	Value: 52.00				

KM# 104 1/25 SUVERENA
1.2441 g., 0.9999 Gold .0400 oz. AGW **Subject:** Chinese Horse **Obv:** National arms above bridge, date below **Rev:** Horse, denomination below

Date	Mintage	F	VF	XF	Unc	BU
1998 Proof	Est. 15,000	Value: 52.00				

KM# 33 1/10 SUVERENA
3.1103 g., 0.9999 Gold .1000 oz. AGW **Subject:** Lipizzaner Stallion **Obv:** National arms above bridge, date below **Rev:** Horse rearing right, denomination below

Date	Mintage	F	VF	XF	Unc	BU
1994 Proof	—	Value: 100				

KM# 46 1/10 SUVERENA
3.1103 g., 0.9999 Gold .1000 oz. AGW **Subject:** English Hack **Obv:** National arms above bridge, date below **Rev:** Horse running left, denomination below

Date	Mintage	F	VF	XF	Unc	BU
1995 Proof	Est. 10,000	Value: 100				

KM# 71 1/10 SUVERENA
3.1103 g., 0.9999 Gold .1000 oz. AGW **Subject:** Hanoverian Stallion **Obv:** National arms above bridge, date below **Rev:** Horse left, denomination below

Date	Mintage	F	VF	XF	Unc	BU
1996 Proof	Est. 10,000	Value: 100				

KM# 90 1/10 SUVERENA
3.1103 g., 0.9999 Gold .1000 oz. AGW **Subject:** The Arab **Obv:** National arms above bridge, date below **Rev:** Horse right, denomination below

Date	Mintage	F	VF	XF	Unc	BU
1997 Proof	Est. 10,000	Value: 100				

KM# 105 1/10 SUVERENA
3.1103 g., 0.9999 Gold .1000 oz. AGW **Subject:** Chinese Horse **Obv:** National arms above bridge, date below **Rev:** Horse left, denomination below

Date	Mintage	F	VF	XF	Unc	BU
1998 Proof	Est. 10,000	Value: 100				

KM# 34 1/5 SUVERENA
6.2207 g., 0.9999 Gold .2000 oz. AGW **Subject:** Lipizzaner Stallion **Obv:** National arms above bridge, date below **Rev:** Horse rearing right, denomination below

Date	Mintage	F	VF	XF	Unc	BU
1994 Proof	—	Value: 185				

KM# 47 1/5 SUVERENA
6.2207 g., 0.9999 Gold .2000 oz. AGW **Subject:** English Hack **Obv:** National arms above bridge, date below **Rev:** Horse running left, denomination below

Date	Mintage	F	VF	XF	Unc	BU
1995 Proof	Est. 5,000	Value: 185				

KM# 72 1/5 SUVERENA
6.2207 g., 0.9999 Gold .2000 oz. AGW **Subject:** Hanoverian Stallion **Obv:** National arms above bridge, date below **Rev:** Horse left, denomination below

Date	Mintage	F	VF	XF	Unc	BU
1996 Proof	Est. 5,000	Value: 185				

KM# 91 1/5 SUVERENA
6.2207 g., 0.9999 Gold .2000 oz. AGW **Subject:** The Arab **Obv:** National arms above bridge, date below **Rev:** Horse right, denomination below

Date	Mintage	F	VF	XF	Unc	BU
1997 Proof	Est. 5,000	Value: 185				

KM# 106 1/5 SUVERENA
6.2207 g., 0.9999 Gold .2000 oz. AGW **Subject:** Chinese Horse **Obv:** National arms above bridge, date below **Rev:** Horse left, denomination below

Date	Mintage	F	VF	XF	Unc	BU
1998 Proof	Est. 5,000	Value: 185				

KM# 35 1/2 SUVERENA
15.5517 g., 0.9999 Gold .5000 oz. AGW **Subject:** Lipizzaner Stallion **Obv:** National arms above bridge, date below **Rev:** Horse rearing right, denomination below

Date	Mintage	F	VF	XF	Unc	BU
1994 Proof	—	Value: 375				

KM# 48 1/2 SUVERENA
15.5517 g., 0.9999 Gold .5000 oz. AGW **Subject:** English Hack **Obv:** National arms above bridge, date below **Rev:** Horse running left, denomination below

Date	Mintage	F	VF	XF	Unc	BU
1995 Proof	Est. 2,500	Value: 375				

KM# 73 1/2 SUVERENA
15.5517 g., 0.9999 Gold .5000 oz. AGW **Subject:** Hanoverian Stallion **Obv:** National arms above bridge, date below **Rev:** Horse left, denomination below

Date	Mintage	F	VF	XF	Unc	BU
1996 Proof	Est. 2,500	Value: 375				

KM# 92 1/2 SUVERENA
15.5517 g., 0.9999 Gold .5000 oz. AGW **Subject:** The Arab **Obv:** National arms above bridge, date below **Rev:** Horse right, denomination below

Date	Mintage	F	VF	XF	Unc	BU
1997 Proof	Est. 2,500	Value: 375				

KM# 107 1/2 SUVERENA
15.5517 g., 0.9999 Gold .5000 oz. AGW **Subject:** Chinese Horse **Obv:** National arms above bridge, date below **Rev:** Horse left, denomination below

Date	Mintage	F	VF	XF	Unc	BU
1998 Proof	Est. 2,500	Value: 375				

KM# 37a SUVERENA
31.1035 g., 0.9999 Gold 1.0000 oz. AGW **Subject:** Lipizzaner Stallion **Obv:** National arms above bridge, date below **Rev:** Horse rearing right, denomination below

Date	Mintage	F	VF	XF	Unc	BU
1994 Proof	—	Value: 700				

KM# 51 SUVERENA
31.1035 g., 0.9999 Gold 1.0000 oz. AGW **Subject:** English Hack **Obv:** National arms above bridge, date below **Rev:** Horse running left, denomination below

Date	Mintage	F	VF	XF	Unc	BU
1995 Proof	Est. 850	Value: 700				

KM# A76 SUVERENA
31.1035 g., 0.9999 Gold 1.0000 oz. AGW **Subject:** Hanoverian Horse **Obv:** National arms above bridge, date below **Rev:** Horse left, denomination below

Date	Mintage	F	VF	XF	Unc	BU
1996 Proof	850	Value: 700				

KM# 93b SUVERENA
31.1035 g., 0.9999 Gold 1.0000 oz. AGW **Subject:** The Arab **Obv:** National arms above bridge, date below **Rev:** Horse right, denomination below

Date	Mintage	F	VF	XF	Unc	BU
1997 Proof	850	Value: 700				

KM# 109 SUVERENA
31.1035 g., 0.9999 Gold 1.0000 oz. AGW **Subject:** Chinese Horse **Obv:** National arms above bridge, date below **Rev:** Horse left, denomination below

Date	Mintage	F	VF	XF	Unc	BU
1998 Proof	—	Value: 700				

KM# 87 70 ECUS + 10
6.2200 g., 0.9990 Gold .2000 oz. AGW **Subject:** War Relief Funding - Sarajevo Mosque **Obv:** National arms above bridge, date below **Rev:** Dove of Peace above Sarajevo Mosque

Date	Mintage	F	VF	XF	Unc	BU
1993 Proof	Est. 5,000	Value: 185				

PROOF SETS

KM#	Date	Mintage	Identification	Issue Price	Mkt Val
PS1	1996 (5)	500	KM#70-73, 76	—	1,400

BRAZIL 73

BOTSWANA

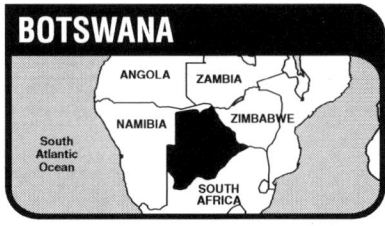

The Republic of Botswana (formerly Bechuanaland), located in south central Africa between Namibia and Zimbabwe, has an area of 224,607 sq. mi. (600,370 sq. km.) and a population of *1.62 million. Capital: Gaborone. Botswana is a member of a Customs Union with South Africa, Lesotho, and Swaziland. The economy is primarily pastoral with a rapidly developing mining industry, of which diamonds, copper and nickel are the chief elements. Meat products and diamonds comprise 85 percent of the exports.

Little is known of the origin of the peoples of Botswana. The early inhabitants, the Bushmen, did not develop a recorded history and are now dying out. The ancestors of the present Botswana residents probably arrived about 1600AD in Bantu migrations from the north and east. Bechuanaland was first united early in the 19th century under Chief Khama III to more effectively resist incursions by the Boer trekkers from Transvaal and by the neighboring Matabeles. As the Boer threat intensified, appeals for protection were made to the British Government, which proclaimed the whole of Bechuanaland a British protectorate in 1885. In 1895, the southern part of the protectorate was annexed to Cape Province. The northern part, known as the Bechuanaland Protectorate, remained under British administration until it became the independent Republic of Botswana on Sept. 30, 1966. Botswana is a member of the Commonwealth of Nations. The president is Chief of State and Head of government.

MINT MARKS
B - Berne

MONETARY SYSTEM
100 Cents = 1 Thebe

REPUBLIC
STANDARD COINAGE

KM# 2 10 THEBE
11.2900 g., 0.9000 Gold .3270 oz. AGW **Subject:** Independence Commemorative **Obv:** National arms with supporters, denomination below **Rev:** Sir Seretse Khama left **Designer:** J. H. Waser

Date	Mintage	F	VF	XF	Unc	BU
ND(1966)B	5,100	—	—	—	235	—

REFORM COINAGE
100 Thebe = 1 Pula

KM# 19 5 PULA
15.9800 g., 0.9170 Gold .4711 oz. AGW **Subject:** Wildlife **Obv:** National arms with supporters, date below **Rev:** Red Lechwes (kobus leche leche) right, denomination above left

Date	Mintage	F	VF	XF	Unc	BU
1986 Proof	Est. 5,000	Value: 325				

KM# 23 5 PULA
10.0000 g., 0.9170 Gold .2948 oz. AGW **Subject:** Save the Children Fund **Obv:** National arms with supporters, date below **Rev:** Woman with child left, denomination on left

Date	Mintage	F	VF	XF	Unc	BU
1989 Proof	Est. 3,000	Value: 350				

KM# 10 150 PULA
15.9800 g., 0.9170 Gold .4711 oz. AGW **Subject:** 10th Anniversary of Independence **Obv:** National arms with supporters, denomination above **Rev:** Bust left

Date	Mintage	F	VF	XF	Unc	BU
ND(1976)	2,520	—	—	—	320	340
ND(1976) Proof	2,000	Value: 365				

KM# 13 150 PULA
33.4370 g., 0.9000 Gold .9676 oz. AGW **Subject:** Wildlife **Obv:** National arms with supporters, date below **Rev:** Brown Hyena facing, denomination above left

Date	Mintage	F	VF	XF	Unc	BU
1978	664	—	—	—	675	750
1978 Proof	219	Value: 950				

KM# 16 150 PULA
15.9800 g., 0.9170 Gold .4711 oz. AGW **Subject:** International Year of Disabled Persons **Obv:** National arms with supporters, date below **Rev:** Figures with box, denomination lower right

Date	Mintage	F	VF	XF	Unc	BU
1981	4,158	—	—	—	320	340
1981 Proof	4,155	Value: 365				

PIEFORTS

KM#	Date	Mintage	Identification	Issue Price	Mkt Val
P2	1981	510	150 Pula. Gold. KM#16.	—	925

BRAZIL

The Federative Republic of Brazil, which comprises half the continent of South America and is the only Latin American country deriving its culture and language from Portugal, has an area of 3,286,488 sq. mi. (8,511,965 sq. km.) and a population of *169.2 million. Capital: Brasilia. The economy of Brazil is as varied and complex as any in the developing world. Agriculture is a mainstay of the economy, while only 4 percent of the area is under cultivation. Known mineral resources are almost unlimited in variety and size of reserves. A large, relatively sophisticated industry ranges from basic steel and chemical production to finished consumer goods. Coffee, cotton, iron ore and cocoa are the chief exports.

Brazil was discovered and claimed for Portugal by Admiral Pedro Alvares Cabral in 1500. Portugal established a settlement in 1532 and proclaimed the area a royal colony in 1549. During the Napoleonic Wars, Dom Joao VI established the seat of Portuguese government in Rio de Janeiro. When he returned to Portugal, his son Dom Pedro I declared Brazil's independence on Sept. 7, 1822, and became emperor of Brazil. The Empire of Brazil was maintained until 1889 when the federal republic was established. The Federative Republic was established in 1946 by terms of a constitution drawn up by a constituent assembly. Following a coup in 1964 the armed forces retained overall control under a dictatorship until civilian government was restored on March 15, 1985. The current constitution was adopted in 1988.

RULERS

Portuguese
Maria I, 1786-1816
Joao, Prince Regent, 1799-1818
Joao VI, 1818-1822

Brazilean
Pedro I, 1822-1831
Pedro II, 1831-1889

MINT MARKS
(a) - Paris, privy marks only
A - Berlin 1913
B - Bahia
C - Cuiaba (Mato Grosso) 1823-1833
G - Goias 1823-1833
M - Minas Gerais 1823-1828
P - Pernambuco
R - Rio de Janeiro
SP - Sao Paulo 1825-1832
W/o mint mark - Lisbon 1715-1805

MONETARY SYSTEM
(Until 1833)
120 Reis = 1 Real
6400 Reis 1 Peca (Dobra = Johannes (Joe) = 4 Escudos
(1833-1942)
1000 Reis = 1 Mil Reis
(1942-1967)
100 Centavos = 1 Cruzeiro

PORTUGUESE COLONY
MILLED COINAGE

KM# 225.2 4000 REIS
8.0683 g., 0.9170 Gold .2378 oz. AGW **Obv:** Crowned arms, denomination **Obv. Legend:** MARIA I. D. G.. **Rev:** Cross at center of ornamented ribbon and lined circle **Note:** Struck at Bahia without mint mark.

74 BRAZIL

Date	Mintage	F	VF	XF	Unc	BU
1801	3,705	175	275	450	750	—
1802	7,738	175	275	450	750	—
1803	7,807	175	275	450	750	—
1804/2	Inc. above	175	275	450	750	—
1805/2	Inc. below	175	275	450	750	—

KM# 235.1 4000 REIS
8.0683 g., 0.9170 Gold .2378 oz. AGW **Obv:** Large crown above arms **Obv. Legend:** JOANNES. D. G.. **Rev:** Dots on either side of date **Note:** Struck at Bahia without mint mark.

Date	Mintage	F	VF	XF	Unc	BU
1805	10,000	160	245	375	500	—
1806	12,000	160	245	375	500	—
1807	7,725	160	245	375	500	—
1808	37,000	160	245	375	500	950
1809/8	19,000	160	245	375	500	950
1809	Inc. above	160	245	375	500	950
1810	Inc. above	16.00	245	375	500	950
1811	19,000	160	245	375	500	950
1813	11,000	160	245	375	500	—
1814	9,494	160	245	375	500	—
1815	—	160	245	375	500	—
1816	7,522	160	245	375	500	—

KM# 235.2 4000 REIS
8.0683 g., 0.9170 Gold .2378 oz. AGW **Obv:** Small crown above arms **Rev:** Flower on either side of date **Note:** Struck at Rio de Janiero without mint mark.

Date	Mintage	F	VF	XF	Unc	BU
1808	128,000	160	245	375	500	—
1809/8	94,000	160	245	375	500	—
1809	Inc. above	160	245	375	500	—
1810/09	66,000	160	245	400	500	—
1810	Inc. above	160	245	400	500	—
1811/10	87,000	160	245	400	500	—
1811	Inc. above	160	245	400	500	—
1812/11	124,000	200	325	450	800	—
1812	Inc. above	160	245	400	500	850
181.2	Inc. above	165	275	450	550	—
1812 Error: PROT	Inc. above	175	300	500	750	—
1813/2	148,000	160	245	400	500	850
1813	Inc. above	160	245	400	500	1,500
1814/3	102,000	160	245	400	500	850
1814	Inc. above	160	245	400	500	850
1815/4	83,000	160	245	400	500	850
1815	Inc. above	160	245	400	500	850
1816	91,000	160	245	400	500	850
1817	71,000	160	245	400	500	850

KM# 235.3 4000 REIS
8.0683 g., 0.9170 Gold .2378 oz. AGW **Obv:** Crowned arms **Obv. Legend:** PORT. ET. BRAS (error) **Rev:** Cross at center on ornamented ribbon and lined circle **Note:** Struck at Rio de Janiero without mint mark.

Date	Mintage	F	VF	XF	Unc	BU
1812	Inc. above	175	275	450	600	—

KM# 312 4000 REIS
8.0683 g., 0.9170 Gold .2378 oz. AGW **Obv:** Crowned arms **Obv. Legend:** PORT. BRAS. ET. ALG **Rev:** Cross at center of ornamented ribbon and lined circle **Rev. Legend:** PRINCEPS. REGENS.. **Note:** Struck at Rio de Janiero without mint mark.

Date	Mintage	F	VF	XF	Unc	BU
1816	Inc. above	250	650	1,200	2,000	3,000

KM# 327.1 4000 REIS
8.0683 g., 0.9170 Gold .2378 oz. AGW **Obv:** 6-petal flower on either side of date **Rev:** Crowned arms within wreath **Note:** Struck at Rio de Janiero without mint mark.

Date	Mintage	F	VF	XF	Unc	BU
1818	64,000	175	300	500	750	1,000
1819	49,000	200	300	500	750	1,000
1820	87,000	175	300	500	750	1,000
1821/0	35,000	175	300	500	750	1,000
1821	Inc. above	175	300	500	750	1,000
1822/0	54,000	185	320	520	775	1,100
1822/1	Inc. above	185	320	520	775	1,100
1822	Inc. above	185	320	520	775	1,100

KM# 327.2 4000 REIS
8.0683 g., 0.9170 Gold .2378 oz. AGW **Obv:** 4-petal flower on either side of date **Rev:** Crowned arms within wreath **Note:** Struck at Rio de Janiero without mint mark.

Date	Mintage	F	VF	XF	Unc	BU
1819	Inc. above	180	300	500	750	1,000

KM# 327.3 4000 REIS
8.0683 g., 0.9170 Gold .2378 oz. AGW **Obv:** Date between crosses **Rev:** Crowned arms within wreath **Note:** Struck at Bahia without mint mark.

Date	Mintage	F	VF	XF	Unc	BU
1819	1,864	600	1,200	2,000	3,000	—
1820	4,374	850	1,500	2,500	3,500	—

KM# 226.1 6400 REIS
14.3436 g., 0.9170 Gold .4229 oz. AGW **Obv:** Bust right with bejeweled headdress **Rev:** Crowned ornate arms

Date	Mintage	F	VF	XF	Unc	BU
1801R	185,000	285	345	450	750	1,250
1802R	168,000	285	345	450	750	1,250
1803R	176,000	285	345	450	750	1,250
1804R	128,000	285	345	450	750	1,250
1805R	109,000	285	345	450	750	1,250

KM# 226.2 6400 REIS
14.3436 g., 0.9170 Gold .4229 oz. AGW **Obv:** Bust right with jeweled headdress **Rev:** Crowned ornate arms

Date	Mintage	F	VF	XF	Unc	BU
1801B	12,000	295	375	550	850	1,850
1802B	3,324	295	375	550	850	1,850
1803B	3,743	295	375	550	850	1,850
1804B	3,539	295	375	550	850	1,850

KM# 236.1 6400 REIS
14.3436 g., 0.9170 Gold .4229 oz. AGW **Obv:** Laureate bust right **Obv. Legend:** JOANNES. D. G. PORT. ET. ALG. P. REGENS **Rev:** Crowned ornate arms

Date	Mintage	F	VF	XF	Unc	BU
1805R	Inc. above	285	375	525	900	1,450
1806R	96,000	285	375	525	900	1,450
1807R	59,000	285	375	525	900	1,450
1808/7R	133,000	285	375	525	900	1,450
1808R	Inc. above	285	375	525	900	1,450
1809/8R	188,000	285	375	525	900	1,450
1809R	Inc. above	300	375	525	900	1,450
1810/09R	159,000	300	375	525	900	1,450
1810R	Inc. above	300	425	600	1,150	1,750
1811/10R	82,000	325	425	600	1,150	1,750
1811R	Inc. above	350	425	600	1,150	1,750
1812R	64,000	350	450	600	1,150	1,850
1813R	53,000	350	450	600	1,150	1,850
1814/3R	42,000	360	475	750	1,150	1,850
1814R	Inc. above	360	475	750	1,250	—
1815R	40,000	400	450	750	1,250	—
1816R	39,000	420	600	1,200	6,500	—
1817R	32,000	450	600	1,200	7,500	—

KM# 236.2 6400 REIS
14.3436 g., 0.9170 Gold .4229 oz. AGW **Obv:** Laureate bust right **Obv. Legend:** PORT. BRAS. ET. ALG. P. REG **Rev:** Crowned ornat arms

Date	Mintage	F	VF	XF	Unc	BU
1816R	Inc. above	3,500	4,500	6,000	9,000	—

KM# 328 6400 REIS
14.3436 g., 0.9170 Gold .4229 oz. AGW **Obv:** Laureate bust right **Obv. Legend:** JOANNES. VI. D. G. PORT. BRAS. ET. ALG. REX **Rev:** Crowned ornate arms

Date	Mintage	F	VF	XF	Unc	BU
1818R	14,000	1,000	2,000	3,000	4,500	6,500
1819R	9,227	2,000	3,000	4,000	5,500	—
1820R	3,286	2,700	4,000	5,500	6,500	—
1821R Unique	2,122					
1822R Rare	599	—	—	—	—	—

GOLD BARS
Cuiaba
KM# GB1 NON-DENOMINATED
Gold **Counterstamp:** CUYABA below crown in branches **Note:** Known dates: 1821, 1822. Actual bar size: 89x18mm.

Date	Mintage	Good	VG	F	VF	XF
(1821-22)	—		—	—	—	—

GOLD BARS
Serro Frio
KM# Gb6 NON-DENOMINATED
Gold, 80x17 mm. **Counterstamp:** "S.-F." above or "SERRO FRIO" below crowned arms and AAB monogram in beaded circle **Note:** Known dates: 1809-14, 1816, 1818, 1820, 1829, 1830-32.

Date	Mintage	Good	VG	F	VF	XF
(1809-1832)						

EMPIRE
GOLD COINAGE
National Standard

KM# 369.1 4000 REIS
8.2000 g., 0.9170 Gold .2417 oz. AGW **Ruler:** Pedro I **Obv:** Uniformed bust left **Rev:** Crowned arms within wreath

BRAZIL

Date	Mintage	F	VF	XF	Unc	BU
1823R	21,000	250	450	650	1,200	—
1824R	38,000	250	450	650	1,200	—
1825R	20,000	250	450	650	1,400	1,850
1826R	9,142	350	650	1,450	2,000	—
1827/6R	7,771	3,500	6,500	12,500	—	—
1827R	Inc. above	3,500	6,500	12,500	—	—

KM# 369.2 4000 REIS
8.2000 g., 0.9170 Gold .2417 oz. AGW **Ruler:** Pedro I **Obv:** Uniformed bust left **Rev:** Crowned arms within wreath

Date	Mintage	F	VF	XF	Unc	BU
1825B	—	1,200	2,500	6,000	13,000	—
1826B	—	1,500	3,000	7,000	15,000	—
1828B	—	3,000	5,000	—	—	—

KM# 386.1 4000 REIS
8.2000 g., 0.9170 Gold .2417 oz. AGW **Ruler:** Pedro II **Obv:** Boys head right **Rev:** Crowned arms within wreath

Date	Mintage	F	VF	XF	Unc	BU
1832R Rare	64	—	—	—	—	—

Note: American Numismatic Rarites Eliasberg sale, 4-05, MS-62 realized $17,250. Spink America Norweb sale 3-97 Unc realized $14,300.

| 1833/2R | 257 | 4,500 | 7,500 | 12,500 | — | — |

KM# 386.2 4000 REIS
8.2000 g., 0.9170 Gold .2417 oz. AGW **Ruler:** Pedro II **Obv:** AZEVEDO below bust **Rev:** Crowned arms within wreath

Date	Mintage	F	VF	XF	Unc	BU
1832 Rare, 5 known	—	—	—	—	—	—

KM# 361 6400 REIS
14.3400 g., 0.9170 Gold .4228 oz. AGW **Ruler:** Pedro I **Subject:** Pedro I Coronation **Obv:** Laureate head left **Rev:** Crowned arms within wreath

Date	Mintage	F	VF	XF	Unc	BU
1822 Rare	64	—	—	—	—	—

Note: Spink London sale No. 52, 6-86 near XF realized $87,000. Spink America Norweb sale 3-97 choice VF realized $82,500. American Numismatic Rarites Eliasberg sale, 4-05, VF realized $69,000.

KM# 370.1 6400 REIS
14.3400 g., 0.9170 Gold .4228 oz. AGW **Ruler:** Pedro I **Obv:** Uniformed bust left **Rev:** Crowned arms within wreath

Date	Mintage	F	VF	XF	Unc	BU
1823R	931	1,200	4,500	6,000	9,000	—
1824R	235	2,000	5,000	8,000	12,500	—
1825R	776	1,500	4,500	6,500	11,500	—
1827R	637	1,500	4,500	6,500	11,500	—
1828/7	650	1,500	4,500	6,500	11,500	—
1828R	Inc. above	1,500	4,500	6,500	11,500	—
1830R Unique	—	—	—	—	—	—

KM# 370.2 6400 REIS
14.3400 g., 0.9170 Gold .4228 oz. AGW **Ruler:** Pedro I **Obv:** Uniformed bust left **Rev:** Crowned arms within wreath

Date	Mintage	F	VF	XF	Unc	BU
1825B	—	3,000	5,500	9,000	14,500	—
1826B	—	3,000	5,500	9,000	14,500	—
1828B	423	3,000	5,500	9,000	14,500	—

KM# 387.1 6400 REIS
14.3400 g., 0.9170 Gold .4228 oz. AGW **Ruler:** Pedro II **Obv:** Boys head right **Rev:** Crowned arms within wreath

Date	Mintage	F	VF	XF	Unc	BU
1832R	30,000	450	850	1,650	2,500	—
1833R	11,000	450	850	1,650	2,500	—

KM# 387.2 6400 REIS
14.3400 g., 0.9170 Gold .4228 oz. AGW **Ruler:** Pedro II **Obv:** AZEVEDO below bust **Rev:** Crowned arms within wreath

Date	Mintage	F	VF	XF	Unc	BU
1832R	4,101	600	1,500	3,000	5,500	—

REFORM COINAGE
1834-1889

KM# 470 5000 REIS
4.4824 g., 0.9170 Gold .1321 oz. AGW **Ruler:** Pedro II **Obv:** Head left **Rev:** Crowned arms within wreath

Date	Mintage	F	VF	XF	Unc	BU
1854	21,000	95.00	110	135	200	250
1855	47,000	110	130	160	250	300
1856	27,000	95.00	110	135	200	250
1857	4,631	800	1,200	2,000	2,500	—
1858	1,146	2,000	4,000	7,000	12,000	—
1859	493	3,000	5,000	8,000	—	—

KM# 451 10000 REIS
14.3400 g., 0.9170 Gold .4228 oz. AGW **Ruler:** Pedro II **Obv:** Boys head right **Rev:** Crowned arms within wreath

Date	Mintage	F	VF	XF	Unc	BU
1833	7,304	300	500	700	1,150	—
1834	5,617	300	500	700	1,150	—
1835	13,000	300	500	700	1,150	—
1836	11,000	350	550	750	1,250	—
1838	482	650	1,250	2,500	4,000	—
1839	567	650	1,250	2,500	4,000	—
1840	4,462	350	700	1,450	2,200	—

KM# 457 10000 REIS
14.3400 g., 0.9170 Gold .4228 oz. AGW **Ruler:** Pedro II **Obv:** Uniformed bust left **Rev:** Crowned arms within wreath

Date	Mintage	F	VF	XF	Unc	BU
1841	3,454	700	1,500	3,500	7,000	—
1842	1,146	700	1,500	3,500	7,000	—
1843	544	2,000	3,500	6,500	10,000	—
1844	1,989	700	1,500	3,500	7,000	—
1845	3,834	650	1,250	2,750	7,000	—
1847	26,000	450	900	2,000	5,000	—
1848	4,567	500	1,000	2,500	6,000	—

KM# 460 10000 REIS
8.9648 g., 0.9170 Gold .2643 oz. AGW **Ruler:** Pedro II **Obv:** Bust with high ruffled collar left **Rev:** Crowned arms within wreath
Note: Reduced size, 26 millimeters.

Date	Mintage	F	VF	XF	Unc	BU
1849	1,678	350	850	1,250	2,200	—
1850	7,359	185	275	375	750	1,150
1851	11,000	185	275	375	750	1,150

KM# 467 10000 REIS
8.9648 g., 0.9170 Gold .2643 oz. AGW **Ruler:** Pedro II **Obv:** Head left **Rev:** Crowned arms within wreath

Date	Mintage	F	VF	XF	Unc	BU
1853	40,000	—	175	200	300	400
1854	163,000	—	175	200	300	400
1855	41,000	—	175	200	300	400
1856	208,000	—	175	200	300	400
1857	98,000	—	175	200	300	400
1858	55,000	—	175	200	300	400
1859	16,000	400	1,000	2,000	3,000	—
1861	—	—	175	200	300	400
1863	—	400	1,000	2,000	3,000	—
1865	—	—	175	200	300	400
1866	—	—	175	200	300	400
1867	—	—	175	200	300	400
1871	—	—	195	300	400	500
1872	—	—	195	300	400	500
1873	—	—	195	300	400	500
1874	—	—	195	300	400	500
1875	—	—	195	300	400	500
1876	20,000	—	195	300	400	500
1877	3,441	—	220	320	420	550
1878	10,000	—	185	320	420	550
1879	6,431	—	185	320	420	550
1880	9,806	—	220	350	500	600
1882	4,671	—	225	350	500	600
1883	10,000	—	240	350	500	600
1884	11,000	—	240	350	500	600
1885	7,955	—	300	400	600	700
1886	3,782	—	300	400	600	700
1887	1,180	200	450	700	1,200	1,400
1888	5,359	—	350	500	800	900
1889	—	185	400	600	900	1,000

76 BRAZIL

KM# 461 20000 REIS
17.9296 g., 0.9170 Gold .5286 oz. AGW **Ruler:** Pedro II **Obv:** Bust with high collar left **Rev:** Crowned arms within wreath

Date	Mintage	F	VF	XF	Unc	BU
1849	6,464	350	500	700	950	—
1850	42,000	325	375	475	675	—
1851	303,000	325	375	475	675	—

KM# 463 20000 REIS
17.9296 g., 0.9170 Gold .5286 oz. AGW **Ruler:** Pedro II **Obv:** Head left **Rev:** Crowned arms within wreath

Date	Mintage	F	VF	XF	Unc	BU
1851	Inc. above	—	345	385	700	1,000
1852	186,000	—	345	385	700	1,000

KM# 468 20000 REIS
17.9296 g., 0.9170 Gold .5286 oz. AGW **Ruler:** Pedro II **Obv:** Larger head left **Rev:** Crowned arms within wreath

Date	Mintage	F	VF	XF	Unc	BU
1853	246,000	—	—	350	550	—
1854	26,000	—	350	450	650	—
1855	48,000	—	—	350	550	—
1856	262,000	—	—	350	550	—
1857/6	315,000	—	—	350	550	—
1857	Inc. above	—	—	350	550	—
1858	32,000	—	—	350	550	—
1859	47,000	—	—	350	550	—
1860	—	—	345	400	750	—
1861	—	—	345	400	750	—
1862 Rare						

Note: Spink America Norweb sale 3-97 VF realized $11,000

1863	—	425	500	700	1,000	—
1864	—	350	500	700	1,000	—
1865	—	—	345	400	700	—
1867	—	—	345	400	700	—
1889	—	—	345	400	700	—

REPUBLIC
FIRST COINAGE - REIS
1889-1942

KM# 496 10000 REIS
8.9645 g., 0.9170 Gold .2643 oz. AGW **Obv:** Liberty head left within circle **Rev:** Star with wreath in background

Date	Mintage	F	VF	XF	Unc	BU
1889	7,302	185	250	600	1,000	1,850
1892 Rare	2,289	—	—	—	—	—
1893	—	185	250	600	1,000	—
1895	306	185	250	700	1,150	—
1896 Rare	383	—	—	—	—	—
1897	421	185	250	650	1,100	—
1898	216	250	500	1,500	2,000	—
1899	238	185	250	700	1,150	3,000
1901	111	185	250	700	1,150	—
1902 Unique	—	—	—	—	—	—
1903	391	185	250	700	1,150	—
1904	541	185	250	700	1,150	—
1906	572	185	250	700	1,150	—
1907	878	185	250	600	1,100	—
1908	689	185	250	600	1,100	1,500
1909	1,069	185	250	600	1,100	1,750
1911	137	220	350	800	1,350	—
1914	969	250	500	1,500	2,400	—
1915	4,314	250	500	1,400	2,000	—
1916	4,720	185	250	700	1,150	—
1919	526	185	250	700	1,150	—
1921	2,435	185	250	600	1,000	—
1922 Rare	6	—	—	—	—	—

KM# 497 20000 REIS
17.9290 g., 0.9170 Gold .5286 oz. AGW **Obv:** Liberty head left **Rev:** Stars at center surrounded by circle of stars

Date	Mintage	F	VF	XF	Unc	BU
1889	91,000	BV	350	550	1,100	—
1892 Rare	7,738	—	—	—	—	—
1893	4,303	BV	350	550	1,100	—
1894	4,267	BV	350	550	1,100	—
1895	4,811	BV	350	550	1,100	1,500
1896	7,043	BV	350	550	1,100	—
1897	11,000	BV	350	550	1,100	1,500
1898	14,000	BV	350	550	1,100	—
1899	9,558	BV	350	550	1,100	—
1900	7,551	BV	350	550	1,100	—
1901	784	BV	375	700	1,350	1,850
1902	884	BV	375	700	1,350	—
1903	675	BV	375	700	1,350	—
1904	444	BV	375	700	1,350	—
1906	396	BV	500	900	1,600	—
1907	3,310	BV	360	550	1,100	—
1908	6,001,000	BV	360	550	1,100	—
1909	4,427	BV	360	550	1,100	—
1910	5,119	BV	360	550	1,100	1,350
1911	8,467	BV	360	550	1,100	—
1912	4,878	BV	360	550	1,100	—
1913	5,182	BV	360	600	1,200	—
1914	1,980	BV	375	700	1,400	—
1917	2,269	BV	400	800	1,550	—
1918	1,216	BV	400	800	1,550	—
1921	5,924	BV	360	600	1,200	—
1922	2,681	BV	400	800	1,550	—

REFORM COINAGE
1967-1985

1000 Old Cruzeiros = 1 Cruzeiro Novo (New); 100 Centavos = 1 (New) Cruzeiro

KM# 584 300 CRUZEIROS
16.6500 g., 0.9200 Gold .4925 oz. AGW **Subject:** 150th Anniversary of Independence **Obv:** Pedro I and general Emilio Garrastazu Medici heads left, date below **Rev:** Denomination below map **Edge Lettering:** SESQUICENTENARIO DA INDEPENDENCIA

Date	Mintage	F	VF	XF	Unc	BU
1972(a)	30,000	—	—	—	335	350

REFORM COINAGE
1994-present

2750 Cruzeiros Reais = 1 Real; 100 Centavos = 1 Real

KM# 639 20 REAIS
8.0000 g., 0.9000 Gold .2315 oz. AGW **Subject:** World Cup Soccer **Obv:** Hand held trophy **Rev:** Denomination in net

Date	Mintage	F	VF	XF	Unc	BU
1994 Proof	Est. 2,000	Value: 245				

KM# 644 20 REAIS
8.0000 g., 0.9000 Gold .2315 oz. AGW **Subject:** Ayrton Senna - Race Driver

Date	Mintage	F	VF	XF	Unc	BU
1995 Proof	5,000	Value: 245				

KM# 655 20 REAIS
8.0000 g., 0.9000 Gold .2315 oz. AGW, 22 mm. **Subject:** 500 Years - Discovery of Brazil **Obv:** Partial compass face and feathers at right, anniversary dates at left **Rev:** Ornamented map, denomination at left **Edge:** Reeded

Date	Mintage	F	VF	XF	Unc	BU
ND(2000) Proof	—	Value: 245				

KM# 659 20 REAIS
8.0000 g., 0.9000 Gold 0.2315 oz. AGW, 22 mm. **Obv:** Juscelino Kubitschek de Oliveira's portrait **Rev:** Value **Edge:** Reeded

Date	Mintage	F	VF	XF	Unc	BU
2002 Proof	2,500	Value: 235				

KM# 660 20 REAIS
8.0000 g., 0.9000 Gold 0.2315 oz. AGW, 22 mm. **Obv:** Carlos Drummond de Andrade portrait and value **Rev:** Andrade caricature, name and dates **Edge:** Reeded

Date	Mintage	F	VF	XF	Unc	BU
ND(2002) Proof	2,500	Value: 235				

KM# 662 20 REAIS
8.0000 g., 0.9000 Gold 0.2315 oz. AGW, 22 mm. **Obv:** Soccer player **Rev:** Value, inscription and shooting stars **Edge:** Reeded

Date	Mintage	F	VF	XF	Unc	BU
2002	2,500	Value: 235				

KM# 664 20 REAIS
8.0000 g., 0.9000 Gold 0.2315 oz. AGW, 22 mm. **Subject:** Centennial - Ary Barroso **Obv:** Piano keyboard and music above value **Rev:** Caricature of Ary Barroso **Edge:** Reeded

Date	Mintage	F	VF	XF	Unc	BU
ND(2003) Proof	2,500	Value: 235				

FEDERAL REPUBLIC
MEDALLIC BULLION COINAGE

X# MB5 2 OUNCES
62.2600 g., 0.9999 Gold 2.0015 oz. AGW, 38.9 mm. **Subject:** 500th Anniversary Discovery of Brazil **Obv:** Liberty head between two dish antennas, jet fighter below **Obv. Legend:** REPUBLICA FEDERATIVA DO BRASIL **Rev:** Weight in wreath **Rev. Legend:** ★5°. CENTENARIO DO DESCOBRIMENTO DO BRASIL **Edge:** Reeded

Date	Mintage	F	VF	XF	Unc	BU
ND(2000) Proof	30	—	—	—	—	—

X# MB6 2 OUNCES
62.2600 g., 0.9999 Gold 2.0015 oz. AGW, 38.9 mm. **Subject:** 500th Anniversary Discovery of Brazil **Obv:** Medieval sailing ship **Obv. Legend:** REPUBLICA FEDERATIVA DO BRASIL **Rev:** Weight in wreath **Rev. Legend:** ★ 5°. CENTENARIO DO DESCOBRIMENTO DO BRASIL **Edge:** Reeded

Date	Mintage	F	VF	XF	Unc	BU
ND(2000) Proof	30	—	—	—	—	—

X# MB7 2 OUNCES
62.2600 g., 0.9999 Gold 2.0015 oz. AGW, 38.9 mm. **Subject:** 500th Anniversary Discovery of Brazil **Obv:** Portuguese and Brazilian arms **Obv. Legend:** REPUBLICA FEDERATIVA DO BRASIL **Rev:** Pedro Alvarres Cabral standing facing with flag **Rev. Legend:** 5 °. CENTENARIO DO DESCOBRIMENTO DO BRASIL **Edge:** Reeded

Date	Mintage	F	VF	XF	Unc	BU
ND(2000) Proof	25	—	—	—	—	—

X# MB8 2 OUNCES
62.2600 g., 0.9999 Gold 2.0015 oz. AGW, 38.9 mm. **Subject:** 500th Anniversary Discovery of Brazil **Obv:** Portuguese cross **Obv. Legend:** REPUBLICA FEDERATIVA DO BRASIL **Rev:** Weight in wreath **Rev. Legend:** ★ 5°. CENTENARIO DO DESCOBRIMENTO DO BRASIL **Edge:** Reeded

Date	Mintage	F	VF	XF	Unc	BU
ND(2000) Proof	25	—	—	—	—	—

PATTERNS
Including off metal strikes

KM#	Date	Mintage	Identification	Mkt Val
Pn60	1840	—	10000 Reis. Gold. Monogram on reverse.	—
Pn63	1840	—	10000 Reis. Gold. Arms.	—
Pn86	1855	—	20000 Reis. Gold.	2,500
Pn104	1863	—	10 Reis. Palladium.	550
Pn183	1901	—	100 Reis. Gold.	1,200
Pn188	1901	—	200 Reis. Gold.	1,950
Pn193	1901	—	400 Reis. Gold.	2,850
Pn229	1921	—	10000 Reis. Gold.	1,100
Pn230	1921	—	20000 Reis. Gold.	1,100
Pn260	1927	—	Cruzeiro. Gold.	285
Pn261	1927	—	2 Cruzeiros. Gold.	300
Pn361	1950	—	Cruzeiro. Gold.	—

PROVAS

KM#	Date	Mintage	Identification	Mkt Val
Pr8	1972	—	300 Cruzeiros. Gold. KM#584.	400

BRITISH COLUMBIA (CANADA)
PATTERNS

KM#	Date	Mintage	Identification	Mkt Val
Pn2	1862	—	10 Dollars. Gold.	—
Pn4	1862	—	20 Dollars. Gold. Crown. Denomination and date within wreath. 5 pieces.	—

Note: Bowers and Merena Norweb Sale 11-96, Specimen 61 realized $143,000; David Akers Pittman sale 8-99, AU realized $149,500

BRITISH VIRGIN ISLANDS

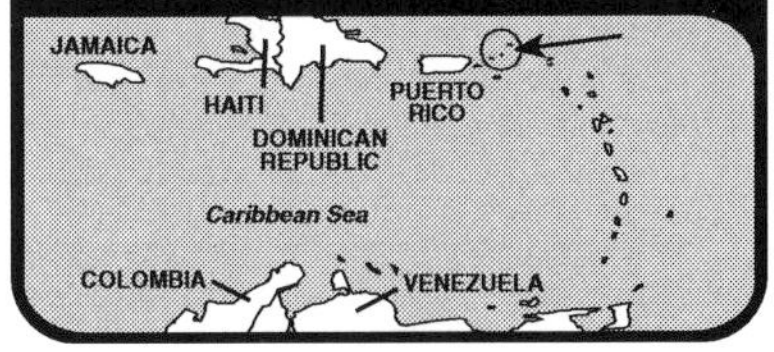

The Colony of the Virgin Islands, a British colony situated in the Caribbean Sea northeast of Puerto Rico and west of the Leeward Islands, has an area of 59 sq. mi. (155 sq. km.) and a population of 13,000. Capital: Road Town. The principal islands of the 36-island group are Tortola, Virgin Gorda, Anegada, and Jost Van Dyke. The chief industries are fishing and stock raising. Fish, livestock and bananas are exported.

The Virgin Islands were discovered by Columbus in 1493, and named by him, Las Virgienes, in honor of St. Ursula and her companions. The British Virgin Islands were formerly part of the administration of the Leeward Islands but received a separate administration as a Crown Colony in 1950. A new constitution promulgated in 1967 provided for a ministerial form of government headed by the Governor.

The Government of the British Virgin Islands issued the first official coinage in its history on June 30, 1973, in honor of 300 years of constitutional government in the islands. U.S. coins and currency continue to be the primary medium of exchange, though the coinage of the British Virgin Islands is legal tender.

*NOTE: From 1975-1985 the Franklin Mint produced coinage in up to 3 different qualities. Qualities of issue are designated in ( ) after each date and are defined as follows:

(M) MATTE - Normal circulation strike or a dull finish produced by sandblasting special uncirculated (polish finish) or proof quality dies.

(U) SPECIAL UNCIRCULATED - Polished or proof-like in appearance without any frosted features.

(P) PROOF - The highest quality obtainable having mirror-like fields and frosted features.

BRITISH COLONY
STANDARD COINAGE

KM# 311 10 DOLLARS
28.3000 g., 0.9250 Gold Clad Silver 0.8416 oz., 38.6 mm. **Subject:** Queen Elizabeth's Golden Coronation Jubilee **Obv:** Elizabeth II **Rev:** Cameo portrait above ship "Gothic" **Edge:** Reeded

Date	Mintage	F	VF	XF	Unc	BU
2003 Proof	—	Value: 50.00				

KM# 274 10 DOLLARS
1.2440 g., 0.9999 Gold 0.04 oz. AGW, 14 mm. **Obv:** Queens portrait right **Obv. Designer:** Ian Rank-Broadley **Rev:** Hernando Pizarro **Edge:** Reeded

Date	Mintage	F	VF	XF	Unc	BU
2004 Proof	350	Value: 75.00				

KM# 288 10 DOLLARS
1.2440 g., 0.9999 Gold 0.04 oz. AGW, 14 mm. **Obv:** Queens portrait right **Obv. Designer:** Ian Rank-Broadley **Rev:** Dolphin **Edge:** Reeded

Date	Mintage	F	VF	XF	Unc	BU
2004 Proof	10,000	Value: 55.00				

KM# 314 10 DOLLARS
1.2440 g., 0.9999 Gold 0.04 oz. AGW, 13.92 mm. **Obv:** Bust of Queen Elizabeth II right **Rev:** Mother and baby dolphins **Edge:** Reeded

Date	Mintage	F	VF	XF	Unc	BU
2005 Proof	10,000	Value: 50.00				

KM# 201 20 DOLLARS
1.2441 g., 0.9999 Gold 0.04 oz. AGW, 13.92 mm. **Subject:** Teddy Bear Centennial **Obv:** Queens portrait right **Obv. Designer:** Ian Rank-Broadley **Rev:** Teddy bear **Edge:** Reeded

Date	Mintage	F	VF	XF	Unc	BU
2002 Proof	10,000	Value: 45.00				

KM# 227 20 DOLLARS
1.2440 g., 0.9999 Gold 0.0399 oz. AGW, 13.92 mm. **Subject:** Kennedy Assasination **Obv:** Queens portrait right **Obv. Designer:** Ian Rank-Broadley **Rev:** President Kennedy's portrait **Edge:** Reeded

Date	Mintage	F	VF	XF	Unc	BU
2003 Proof	10,000	Value: 45.00				

KM# 271 20 DOLLARS
1.2440 g., 0.9999 Gold 0.04 oz. AGW, 14 mm. **Obv:** Queens portrait right **Obv. Designer:** Ian Rank-Broadley **Rev:** Peter Rabbit **Edge:** Reeded

Date	Mintage	F	VF	XF	Unc	BU
2004 Proof	5,000	Value: 50.00				

BRITISH VIRGIN ISLANDS

KM# 27 25 DOLLARS
1.5000 g., 0.5000 Gold .0241 oz. AGW **Ruler:** Elizabeth II **Obv:** Young bust right **Obv. Designer:** Arnold Machin **Rev:** Diving Osprey left **Rev. Designer:** Gilroy Roberts

Date	Mintage	F	VF	XF	Unc	BU
1980FM (P)	11,000				Value: 40.00	

KM# 31.1 25 DOLLARS
1.5000 g., 0.5000 Gold .0241 oz. AGW **Ruler:** Elizabeth II **Obv:** Young bust right **Obv. Designer:** Arnold Machin **Rev:** Caribbean Sparrow Hawk right **Rev. Designer:** Gilroy Roberts

Date	Mintage	F	VF	XF	Unc	BU
1981FM (P)	2,513				Value: 50.00	

KM# 31.2 25 DOLLARS
1.5000 g., 0.5000 Gold .0241 oz. AGW **Ruler:** Elizabeth II **Obv:** Young bust right, error, without FM mint mark **Rev:** Caribbean Sparrow Hawk right

Date	Mintage	F	VF	XF	Unc	BU
1981 (P)	—				Value: 60.00	

KM# 41 25 DOLLARS
1.5000 g., 0.5000 Gold .0241 oz. AGW **Ruler:** Elizabeth II **Obv:** Young bust right **Obv. Designer:** Arnold Machin **Rev:** Hawk in flight

Date	Mintage	F	VF	XF	Unc	BU
1982FM (P)	3,819				Value: 55.00	

KM# 37 25 DOLLARS
1.5000 g., 0.5000 Gold .0241 oz. AGW **Ruler:** Elizabeth II **Obv:** Young bust right **Obv. Designer:** Arnold Machin **Rev:** Merlin Hawk left **Rev. Designer:** Gilroy Roberts

Date	Mintage	F	VF	XF	Unc	BU
1983FM (P)	5,949				Value: 50.00	

KM# 40 25 DOLLARS
1.5000 g., 0.5000 Gold .0241 oz. AGW **Ruler:** Elizabeth II **Obv:** Young bust right **Obv. Designer:** Arnold Machin **Rev:** Peregrine Falcon

Date	Mintage	F	VF	XF	Unc	BU
1984FM (P)	97				Value: 115	

KM# 73 25 DOLLARS
1.5000 g., 0.5000 Gold .0241 oz. AGW **Ruler:** Elizabeth II **Obv:** Crowned head right **Obv. Designer:** Raphael Maklouf **Rev:** Marsh Hawk

Date	Mintage	F	VF	XF	Unc	BU
1985FM (P)	1,294				Value: 80.00	

KM# 275 25 DOLLARS
3.1100 g., 0.9999 Gold 0.1 oz. AGW, 18 mm. **Obv:** Queens portrait right **Obv. Designer:** Ian Rank-Broadley **Rev:** Hernando Pizarro portrait and life events pictorial **Edge:** Reeded

Date	Mintage	F	VF	XF	Unc	BU
2004 Proof	350				Value: 125	

KM# 289 25 DOLLARS
3.1100 g., 0.9999 Gold 0.1 oz. AGW, 18 mm. **Obv:** Queens portrait right **Obv. Designer:** Ian Rank-Broadley **Rev:** Dolphin **Edge:** Reeded

Date	Mintage	F	VF	XF	Unc	BU
2004 Proof	6,000				Value: 115	

KM# 315 25 DOLLARS
3.1100 g., 0.9999 Gold 0.1 oz. AGW, 18 mm. **Obv:** Bust of Queen Elizabeth II right **Rev:** Mother and baby dolphins **Edge:** Reeded

Date	Mintage	F	VF	XF	Unc	BU
2005 Proof	6,000				Value: 125	

KM# 28 50 DOLLARS
2.6800 g., 0.5000 Gold .0430 oz. AGW **Ruler:** Elizabeth II **Obv:** Young bust right **Rev:** Golden Dove of Christmas

Date	Mintage	F	VF	XF	Unc	BU
1980 Proof	6,379				Value: 60.00	

KM# 75 50 DOLLARS
2.0687 g., 0.5000 Gold .0332 oz. AGW **Ruler:** Elizabeth II **Obv:** Crowned head right **Rev:** Flute player

Date	Mintage	F	VF	XF	Unc	BU
1988 Proof	—				Value: 55.00	

KM# 76 50 DOLLARS
2.0687 g., 0.5000 Gold .0332 oz. AGW **Ruler:** Elizabeth II **Obv:** Crowned head right **Rev:** Bird's-head staff

Date	Mintage	F	VF	XF	Unc	BU
1988 Proof	—				Value: 55.00	

KM# 77 50 DOLLARS
2.0687 g., 0.5000 Gold .0332 oz. AGW **Ruler:** Elizabeth II **Obv:** Crowned head right **Rev:** Double-spouted vessel

Date	Mintage	F	VF	XF	Unc	BU
1988 Proof	—				Value: 55.00	

KM# 78 50 DOLLARS
2.0687 g., 0.5000 Gold .0332 oz. AGW **Ruler:** Elizabeth II **Obv:** Crowned head right **Rev:** Deer-top bell

Date	Mintage	F	VF	XF	Unc	BU
1988 Proof	—				Value: 55.00	

KM# 79 50 DOLLARS
2.0687 g., 0.5000 Gold .0332 oz. AGW **Ruler:** Elizabeth II **Obv:** Crowned head right **Rev:** Two-headed animal

Date	Mintage	F	VF	XF	Unc	BU
1988 Proof	—				Value: 55.00	

KM# 80 50 DOLLARS
2.0687 g., 0.5000 Gold .0332 oz. AGW **Ruler:** Elizabeth II **Obv:** Crowned head right **Rev:** Turtle

Date	Mintage	F	VF	XF	Unc	BU
1988 Proof	—				Value: 55.00	

KM# 81 50 DOLLARS
2.0687 g., 0.5000 Gold .0332 oz. AGW **Ruler:** Elizabeth II **Obv:** Crowned head right **Rev:** Frog

Date	Mintage	F	VF	XF	Unc	BU
1988 Proof	—				Value: 55.00	

KM# 82 50 DOLLARS
2.0687 g., 0.5000 Gold .0332 oz. AGW **Ruler:** Elizabeth II **Obv:** Crowned head right **Rev:** Mixtec mask

Date	Mintage	F	VF	XF	Unc	BU
1988 Proof	—				Value: 55.00	

KM# 83 50 DOLLARS
2.0687 g., 0.5000 Gold .0332 oz. AGW **Ruler:** Elizabeth II **Obv:** Crowned head right **Rev:** Chimu gold beaker

Date	Mintage	F	VF	XF	Unc	BU
1988 Proof	—				Value: 55.00	

KM# 84 50 DOLLARS
2.0687 g., 0.5000 Gold .0332 oz. AGW **Ruler:** Elizabeth II **Obv:** Crowned head right **Rev:** Bird vessel

Date	Mintage	F	VF	XF	Unc	BU
1988 Proof	—				Value: 55.00	

KM# 85 50 DOLLARS
2.0687 g., 0.5000 Gold .0332 oz. AGW **Ruler:** Elizabeth II **Obv:** Crowned head right **Rev:** Ceremonial headdress

Date	Mintage	F	VF	XF	Unc	BU
1988 Proof	—				Value: 55.00	

KM# 86 50 DOLLARS
2.0687 g., 0.5000 Gold .0332 oz. AGW **Ruler:** Elizabeth II **Obv:** Crowned head right **Rev:** Sacrificial knife

Date	Mintage	F	VF	XF	Unc	BU
1988 Proof	—				Value: 55.00	

KM# 87 50 DOLLARS
2.0687 g., 0.5000 Gold .0332 oz. AGW **Ruler:** Elizabeth II **Obv:** Crowned head right **Rev:** Ceremonial dancer

Date	Mintage	F	VF	XF	Unc	BU
1988 Proof	—				Value: 55.00	

KM# 88 50 DOLLARS
2.0687 g., 0.5000 Gold .0332 oz. AGW **Ruler:** Elizabeth II **Obv:** Crowned head right **Rev:** Spanish Colonial gold coin

Date	Mintage	F	VF	XF	Unc	BU
1988 Proof	—				Value: 55.00	

KM# 89 50 DOLLARS
2.0687 g., 0.5000 Gold .0332 oz. AGW **Ruler:** Elizabeth II **Obv:** Crowned head right **Rev:** Crossed hands

Date	Mintage	F	VF	XF	Unc	BU
1988 Proof	—				Value: 55.00	

BRITISH VIRGIN ISLANDS

KM# 202 50 DOLLARS
3.1104 g., 0.9999 Gold 0.1 oz. AGW, 17.95 mm. **Subject:** Teddy Bear Centennial **Obv:** Queens portrait right **Obv. Designer:** Ian Rank-Broadley **Rev:** Teddy bear **Edge:** Reeded

Date	Mintage	F	VF	XF	Unc	BU
2002 Proof	7,000			Value: 85.00		

KM# 272 50 DOLLARS
3.1100 g., 0.9999 Gold 0.1 oz. AGW, 18 mm. **Obv:** Queens portrait right **Obv. Designer:** Ian Rank-Broadley **Rev:** Peter Rabbit **Edge:** Reeded

Date	Mintage	F	VF	XF	Unc	BU
2004 Proof	3,000			Value: 100		

KM# 276 50 DOLLARS
6.2200 g., 0.9999 Gold 0.2 oz. AGW, 22 mm. **Obv:** Queens portrait right **Obv. Designer:** Ian Rank-Broadley **Rev:** Treasure ship with blue color sail **Edge:** Reeded

Date	Mintage	F	VF	XF	Unc	BU
2004 Proof	350			Value: 225		

KM# 290 50 DOLLARS
6.2200 g., 0.9999 Gold 0.2 oz. AGW, 22 mm. **Obv:** Queens portrait right **Obv. Designer:** Ian Rank-Broadley **Rev:** Dolphin **Edge:** Reeded

Date	Mintage	F	VF	XF	Unc	BU
2004 Proof	3,500			Value: 215		

KM# 316 50 DOLLARS
6.2200 g., 0.9999 Gold 0.2 oz. AGW, 22 mm. **Obv:** Bust of Queen Elizabeth II right **Rev:** Mother and baby dolphins **Edge:** Reeded

Date	Mintage	F	VF	XF	Unc	BU
2005	3,500			Value: 250		

KM# 7 100 DOLLARS
7.1000 g., 0.9000 Gold .2054 oz. AGW **Ruler:** Elizabeth II **Obv:** Young bust right **Obv. Designer:** Arnold Machin **Rev:** Royal Tern **Rev. Designer:** Gilroy Roberts

Date	Mintage	F	VF	XF	Unc	BU
1975FM (M) Rare	10	—	—	—	—	—
1975FM (U)	13,000	—	—	—	145	—
1975FM (P)	Est. 23,000			Value: 150		

Note: Includes 8,754 in First Day Covers

KM# 8 100 DOLLARS
7.1000 g., 0.9000 Gold .2054 oz. AGW **Ruler:** Elizabeth II **Subject:** 50th Birthday of Queen Elizabeth II **Obv:** Young bust right **Rev:** Crowned monogram above shield with woman and twelve lamps, VIGILATE on banner below

Date	Mintage	F	VF	XF	Unc	BU
1976FM (M) Rare	10	—	—	—	—	—
1976FM (U)	1,752	—	—	—	145	—
1976FM (P)	12,000			Value: 150		

KM# 15 100 DOLLARS
7.1000 g., 0.9000 Gold .2054 oz. AGW **Ruler:** Elizabeth II **Subject:** Queen's Silver Jubilee **Obv:** Young bust right **Rev:** Imperial crown above two dates

Date	Mintage	F	VF	XF	Unc	BU
1977FM (U) Rare	10	—	—	—	—	—
1977FM (P)	6,715			Value: 155		

KM# 23 100 DOLLARS
7.1000 g., 0.9000 Gold .2054 oz. AGW **Ruler:** Elizabeth II **Subject:** Coronation Jubilee **Obv:** Young bust right **Rev:** Crossed sceptres with royal orb at center **Shape:** 25-sided

Date	Mintage	F	VF	XF	Unc	BU
1978FM (P)	5,772			Value: 160		

KM# 25 100 DOLLARS
7.1000 g., 0.9000 Gold .2054 oz. AGW **Ruler:** Elizabeth II **Obv:** Young bust right **Rev:** Bust of Sir Francis Drake with ruffed collar right

Date	Mintage	F	VF	XF	Unc	BU
1979FM (P)	3,216			Value: 170		

KM# 29 100 DOLLARS
7.1000 g., 0.9000 Gold .2054 oz. AGW **Ruler:** Elizabeth II **Subject:** 400th Anniversary of Drake's Voyage **Obv:** Young bust right **Rev:** The Golden Hind

Date	Mintage	F	VF	XF	Unc	BU
1980 Proof	5,412			Value: 165		

KM# 32 100 DOLLARS
7.1000 g., 0.9000 Gold .2054 oz. AGW **Ruler:** Elizabeth II **Subject:** Knighting of Sir Francis Drake **Obv:** Young bust right **Rev:** Queen with kneeling figure

Date	Mintage	F	VF	XF	Unc	BU
1981FM (P)	1,321			Value: 185		

KM# 34 100 DOLLARS
7.1000 g., 0.9000 Gold .2054 oz. AGW **Ruler:** Elizabeth II **Subject:** 30th Anniversary - Reign of Queen Elizabeth II **Obv:** Young bust right **Rev:** Crowned monogram **Shape:** 6-sided

Date	Mintage	F	VF	XF	Unc	BU
1982FM (P)	620			Value: 230		

KM# 38 100 DOLLARS
7.1000 g., 0.9000 Gold .2054 oz. AGW **Ruler:** Elizabeth II **Subject:** 30th Anniversary - Coronation of Queen Elizabeth II **Obv:** Young bust right **Rev:** Sceptres divide royal symbols and dates **Shape:** 6-sided

Date	Mintage	F	VF	XF	Unc	BU
1983FM (P)	624			Value: 230		

KM# 39 100 DOLLARS
7.1000 g., 0.9000 Gold .2054 oz. AGW **Ruler:** Elizabeth II **Subject:** Flora - Ginger Thomas **Obv:** Young bust right **Rev:** Flower

Date	Mintage	F	VF	XF	Unc	BU
1984FM (P)	25			Value: 475		

KM# 74 100 DOLLARS
7.1000 g., 0.9000 Gold .2054 oz. AGW **Ruler:** Elizabeth II **Subject:** Sir Francis Drake's West Indian Voyage **Obv:** Crowned head right **Rev:** Ship **Shape:** 6-sided

Date	Mintage	F	VF	XF	Unc	BU
1985FM (P)	772			Value: 220		

KM# 119 100 DOLLARS
4.1180 g., 0.5000 Gold .0662 oz. AGW **Subject:** Discovery of America - King Ferdinand of Spain **Obv:** Crowned head right **Rev:** Bust facing

Date	Mintage	F	VF	XF	Unc	BU
ND(1991)FM (P)	—			Value: 100		

KM# 162 100 DOLLARS
4.1180 g., 0.5000 Gold .0662 oz. AGW **Ruler:** Elizabeth II **Obv:** Crowned head right **Rev:** The Pinta

Date	Mintage	F	VF	XF	Unc	BU
ND(1994) Proof	—			Value: 100		

KM# 256 100 DOLLARS
4.3100 g., 0.5000 Gold 0.0662 oz. AGW, 20.75 mm. **Ruler:** Elizabeth II **Obv:** Crowned head right **Rev:** Columbus' landing scene **Edge:** Reeded

Date	Mintage	F	VF	XF	Unc	BU
ND(1996?)FM Proof	—			Value: 100		

KM# 174.1 100 DOLLARS
6.2200 g., 0.9990 Gold 0.2000 oz. AGW **Ruler:** Elizabeth II **Subject:** Queen Mother's 100th Birthday **Obv:** Crowned head right **Rev:** Bust facing divides dates **Edge:** Reeded

Date	Mintage	F	VF	XF	Unc	BU
2000 Proof	5,000			Value: 165		

KM# 174.2 100 DOLLARS
6.2200 g., 0.9999 Gold 0.2 oz. AGW, 22 mm. **Ruler:** Elizabeth II **Subject:** Queen Mother's 100th Birthday **Obv:** Crowned head right **Rev:** Bust facing, tiny black sapphire mounted on her broach **Edge:** Reeded

Date	Mintage	F	VF	XF	Unc	BU
2000 Proof	1,000			Value: 195		

KM# 177 100 DOLLARS
6.2200 g., 0.9990 Gold 0.2000 oz. AGW **Ruler:** Elizabeth II **Subject:** 1st Anniversary - Earl and Countess of Wessex **Obv:** Crowned head right **Rev:** 1/2 figures facing, anniversary dates below **Edge:** Reeded

Date	Mintage	F	VF	XF	Unc	BU
2000 Proof	5,000			Value: 175		

80 BRITISH VIRGIN ISLANDS

KM# 182 100 DOLLARS
6.2200 g., 0.9990 Gold 0.1998 oz. AGW, 22 mm. **Subject:** Sir Francis Drake **Obv:** Queens portrait right **Obv. Designer:** Ian Rank-Broadley **Rev:** Ship, portrait and map **Edge:** Reeded

Date	Mintage	F	VF	XF	Unc	BU
2002 Proof	5,000	Value: 185				

KM# 185 100 DOLLARS
6.2200 g., 0.9990 Gold 0.1998 oz. AGW, 22 mm. **Subject:** Sir Walter Raleigh **Obv:** Queens portrait right **Obv. Designer:** Ian Rank-Broadley **Rev:** Ship, portrait and map **Edge:** Reeded

Date	Mintage	F	VF	XF	Unc	BU
2002 Proof	5,000	Value: 185				

KM# 189 100 DOLLARS
6.2208 g., 0.9999 Gold 0.2 oz. AGW, 22 mm. **Subject:** Queen's Golden Jubilee **Obv:** Queens portrait right **Obv. Designer:** Ian Rank-Broadley **Rev:** Queen on horse **Edge:** Reeded

Date	Mintage	F	VF	XF	Unc	BU
2002 Proof	2,002	Value: 185				

KM# 192 100 DOLLARS
6.2208 g., 0.9999 Gold 0.2 oz. AGW, 22 mm. **Subject:** Queen's Golden Jubilee **Obv:** Queens portrait right **Obv. Designer:** Ian Rank-Broadley **Rev:** Queen on throne **Edge:** Reeded

Date	Mintage	F	VF	XF	Unc	BU
2002 Proof	2,002	Value: 185				

KM# 195 100 DOLLARS
6.2208 g., 0.9999 Gold 0.2 oz. AGW, 22 mm. **Subject:** Queen's Golden Jubilee **Obv:** Queens portrait right **Obv. Designer:** Ian Rank-Broadley **Rev:** Queen with President Ronald Reagan and Mrs. Nancy Reagan **Edge:** Reeded

Date	Mintage	F	VF	XF	Unc	BU
2002 Proof	2,002	Value: 185				

KM# 198 100 DOLLARS
6.2208 g., 0.9999 Gold 0.2 oz. AGW, 22 mm. **Subject:** Queen's Golden Jubilee **Obv:** Queens portrait right **Obv. Designer:** Ian Rank-Broadley **Rev:** Carnival dancers **Edge:** Reeded

Date	Mintage	F	VF	XF	Unc	BU
2002 Proof	2,002	Value: 185				

KM# 203 100 DOLLARS
6.2200 g., 0.9999 Gold 0.2 oz. AGW, 22 mm. **Subject:** Teddy Bear Centennial **Obv:** Queens portrait right **Obv. Designer:** Ian Rank-Broadley **Rev:** Teddy bear **Edge:** Reeded

Date	Mintage	F	VF	XF	Unc	BU
2002 Proof	5,000	Value: 185				

KM# 206 100 DOLLARS
6.2200 g., 0.9999 Gold 0.2 oz. AGW, 22 mm. **Subject:** Princess Diana **Obv:** Queens portrait right **Obv. Designer:** Ian Rank-Broadley **Rev:** Diana's portrait **Edge:** Reeded

Date	Mintage	F	VF	XF	Unc	BU
2002 Proof	5,000	Value: 185				

KM# 209.1 100 DOLLARS
6.2200 g., 0.9999 Gold 0.2 oz. AGW, 22 mm. **Subject:** September 11, 2001 **Obv:** Queens portrait right **Obv. Designer:** Ian Rank-Broadley **Rev:** World Trade Center twin towers **Edge:** Reeded

Date	Mintage	F	VF	XF	Unc	BU
2002 Proof	5,000	Value: 185				

KM# 209.2 100 DOLLARS
6.2200 g., 0.9999 Gold 0.2 oz. AGW, 22 mm. **Subject:** September 11, 2001 **Obv:** Queens portrait right **Obv. Designer:** Ian Rank-Broadley **Rev:** Holographic multicolor World Trade Center twin towers **Edge:** Reeded

Date	Mintage	F	VF	XF	Unc	BU
2002 Proof	5,000	Value: 185				

KM# 212 100 DOLLARS
6.2200 g., 0.9999 Gold 0.2 oz. AGW, 22 mm. **Subject:** September 11, 2001 **Obv:** Queens portrait right **Obv. Designer:** Ian Rank-Broadley **Rev:** Statue of Liberty **Edge:** Reeded

Date	Mintage	F	VF	XF	Unc	BU
2002 Proof	5,000	Value: 185				

KM# 215 100 DOLLARS
6.2200 g., 0.9999 Gold 0.2 oz. AGW, 22 mm. **Subject:** Queen Mother Series **Obv:** Queens portrait right **Obv. Designer:** Ian Rank-Broadley **Rev:** Queen Mother with young Prince Charles **Edge:** Reeded

Date	Mintage	F	VF	XF	Unc	BU
2002 Proof	5,000	Value: 185				

KM# 218 100 DOLLARS
6.2200 g., 0.9999 Gold 0.2 oz. AGW, 22 mm. **Subject:** Queen Mother Series **Obv:** Queens portrait right **Obv. Designer:** Ian Rank-Broadley **Rev:** Queen Mother with four grandchildren **Edge:** Reeded

Date	Mintage	F	VF	XF	Unc	BU
2002 Proof	5,000	Value: 185				

KM# 221 100 DOLLARS
6.2200 g., 0.9999 Gold 0.2 oz. AGW, 22 mm. **Subject:** Queen Mother Series **Obv:** Queens portrait right **Obv. Designer:** Ian Rank-Broadley **Rev:** Queen Mother with uniformed Prince Charles **Edge:** Reeded

Date	Mintage	F	VF	XF	Unc	BU
2002 Proof	5,000	Value: 185				

KM# 224 100 DOLLARS
6.2200 g., 0.9999 Gold 0.2 oz. AGW, 22 mm. **Subject:** Queen Mother Series **Obv:** Queens portrait right **Obv. Designer:** Ian Rank-Broadley **Rev:** Queen Mother's coffin **Edge:** Reeded

Date	Mintage	F	VF	XF	Unc	BU
2002 Proof	5,000	Value: 185				

KM# 228 100 DOLLARS
6.2200 g., 0.9999 Gold 0.2 oz. AGW, 22 mm. **Subject:** Kennedy Assasination **Obv:** Queens portrait right **Obv. Designer:** Ian Rank-Broadley **Rev:** President Kennedy's portrait **Edge:** Reeded

Date	Mintage	F	VF	XF	Unc	BU
2003 Proof	5,000	Value: 185				

KM# 231 100 DOLLARS
15.5500 g., 0.9999 Gold 0.4999 oz. AGW, 30 mm. **Subject:** Powered Flight Centennial **Obv:** Queens portrait right **Obv. Designer:** Ian Rank-Broadley **Rev:** Three historic airplanes and rocket **Edge:** Reeded

Date	Mintage	F	VF	XF	Unc	BU
2003 Proof	—	Value: 375				

KM# 234 100 DOLLARS
6.2200 g., 0.9999 Gold 0.2 oz. AGW, 22 mm. **Obv:** Queens portrait right **Obv. Designer:** Ian Rank-Broadley **Rev:** Henry VIII and Elizabeth I **Edge:** Reeded

Date	Mintage	F	VF	XF	Unc	BU
2003 Proof	5,000	Value: 185				

KM# 237 100 DOLLARS
6.2200 g., 0.9999 Gold 0.2 oz. AGW, 22 mm. **Obv:** Queens portrait right **Obv. Designer:** Ian Rank-Broadley **Rev:** Matthew Parker, Archbishop of Canterbury **Edge:** Reeded

Date	Mintage	F	VF	XF	Unc	BU
2003 Proof	5,000	Value: 185				

KM# 240 100 DOLLARS
6.2200 g., 0.9999 Gold 0.2 oz. AGW, 22 mm. **Obv:** Queens portrait right **Obv. Designer:** Ian Rank-Broadley **Rev:** Sir Francis Drake and ships **Edge:** Reeded

Date	Mintage	F	VF	XF	Unc	BU
2003 Proof	5,000	Value: 185				

KM# 243 100 DOLLARS
6.2200 g., 0.9999 Gold 0.2 oz. AGW, 22 mm. **Obv:** Queens portrait right **Obv. Designer:** Ian Rank-Broadley **Rev:** Sir Walter Raleigh **Edge:** Reeded

Date	Mintage	F	VF	XF	Unc	BU
2003 Proof	5,000	Value: 185				

KM# 246 100 DOLLARS
6.2200 g., 0.9999 Gold 0.2 oz. AGW, 22 mm. **Obv:** Queens portrait right **Obv. Designer:** Ian Rank-Broadley **Rev:** Sir William Shakespeare **Edge:** Reeded

Date	Mintage	F	VF	XF	Unc	BU
2003 Proof	5,000	Value: 185				

KM# 249 100 DOLLARS
6.2200 g., 0.9999 Gold 0.2 oz. AGW, 22 mm. **Obv:** Queens portrait right **Obv. Designer:** Ian Rank-Broadley **Rev:** Elizabeth I above her funeral procession **Edge:** Reeded

Date	Mintage	F	VF	XF	Unc	BU
2003 Proof	5,000	Value: 185				

KM# 252 100 DOLLARS
6.2200 g., 0.9999 Gold 0.2 oz. AGW, 22 mm. **Subject:** Olympics **Obv:** Queens portrait right **Obv. Designer:** Ian Rank-Broadley **Rev:** Ancient bust, runners and coin **Edge:** Reeded

Date	Mintage	F	VF	XF	Unc	BU
2003 Proof	5,000	Value: 185				

KM# 255 100 DOLLARS
6.2200 g., 0.9999 Gold 0.2 oz. AGW, 22 mm. **Subject:** Olympics **Obv:** Queens portrait right **Obv. Designer:** Ian Rank-Broadley **Rev:** Ancient bust, charioteer and coin **Edge:** Reeded

Date	Mintage	F	VF	XF	Unc	BU
2003 Proof	5,000	Value: 185				

KM# 273.1 100 DOLLARS
6.2200 g., 0.9999 Gold 0.2 oz. AGW, 22 mm. **Obv:** Queens portrait right **Obv. Designer:** Ian Rank-Broadley **Rev:** Peter Rabbit **Edge:** Reeded

Date	Mintage	F	VF	XF	Unc	BU
2004 Proof	2,000	Value: 185				

KM# 273.2 100 DOLLARS
6.2200 g., 0.9999 Gold 0.2 oz. AGW, 22 mm. **Obv:** Queens portrait right **Obv. Designer:** Ian Rank-Broadley **Rev:** Multicolor Peter Rabbit **Edge:** Reeded

Date	Mintage	F	VF	XF	Unc	BU
2004 Proof	—	Value: 240				

KM# 283 100 DOLLARS
6.2200 g., 0.9999 Gold 0.2 oz. AGW, 22 mm. **Obv:** Queens portrait right **Obv. Designer:** Ian Rank-Broadley **Rev:** Sailor above two D-Day landing craft **Edge:** Reeded

Date	Mintage	F	VF	XF	Unc	BU
2004 Proof	5,000	Value: 185				

KM# 299 100 DOLLARS
6.2200 g., 0.9999 Gold 0.2 oz. AGW, 22 mm. **Obv:** Queens portrait right **Obv. Designer:** Ian Rank-Broadley **Rev:** Soldier above tank and jeeps **Edge:** Reeded

Date	Mintage	F	VF	XF	Unc	BU
2004 Proof	5,000	Value: 185				

KM# 302 100 DOLLARS
6.2200 g., 0.9999 Gold 0.2 oz. AGW, 22 mm. **Obv:** Queens portrait right **Obv. Designer:** Ian Rank-Broadley **Rev:** Pilot and planes above D-Day landing **Edge:** Reeded

Date	Mintage	F	VF	XF	Unc	BU
2004 Proof	5,000	Value: 185				

KM# 305 100 DOLLARS
6.2200 g., 0.9999 Gold 0.2 oz. AGW, 22 mm. **Obv:** Queens portrait right **Obv. Designer:** Ian Rank-Broadley **Rev:** Ancient Olympic bust, runners and owl coin **Edge:** Reeded

Date	Mintage	F	VF	XF	Unc	BU
2004 Proof	5,000	Value: 185				

KM# 308 100 DOLLARS
6.2200 g., 0.9999 Gold 0.2 oz. AGW, 22 mm. **Obv:** Queens portrait right **Obv. Designer:** Ian Rank-Broadley **Rev:** Ancient Olympic bust, charioteer and Zeus coin **Edge:** Reeded

Date	Mintage	F	VF	XF	Unc	BU
2004 Proof	5,000	Value: 185				

KM# 317 125 DOLLARS
15.5510 g., 0.9999 Gold 0.4999 oz. AGW, 30 mm. **Obv:** Bust of Queen Elizabeth II right **Rev:** Mother and baby dolphins **Edge:** Reeded

Date	Mintage	F	VF	XF	Unc	BU
2005	1,500	Value: 400				

KM# 120 250 DOLLARS
8.0494 g., 0.5000 Gold .1294 oz. AGW **Ruler:** Elizabeth II **Subject:** Quincentennial - Discovery of America **Obv:** Crowned head right **Rev:** Bust of young Queen Isabella 3/4 left

Date	Mintage	F	VF	XF	Unc	BU
ND(1991)FM (P)	—	Value: 290				

KM# 163 250 DOLLARS
8.0494 g., 0.5000 Gold .1294 oz. AGW **Ruler:** Elizabeth II **Subject:** The Nina **Obv:** Crowned head right **Rev:** Ship

Date	Mintage	F	VF	XF	Unc	BU
ND(1994) Proof	—	Value: 290				

KM# 257 250 DOLLARS
8.1700 g., 0.5000 Gold 0.1294 oz. AGW, 26 mm. **Ruler:** Elizabeth II **Obv:** Crowned head right **Rev:** Columbus' personal coat of arms **Edge:** Reeded

Date	Mintage	F	VF	XF	Unc	BU
ND(1996?)FM Proof	—	Value: 250				

KM# 309 250 DOLLARS
15.5517 g., 0.9990 Gold 0.4995 oz. AGW, 30 mm. **Obv:** Queens portrait right **Obv. Designer:** Ian Rank-Broadley **Rev:** Statue of Liberty and the date "11 Sept. 2001" **Edge:** Reeded

Date	Mintage	F	VF	XF	Unc	BU
2002	250	Value: 375				

KM# 280 250 DOLLARS
58.0000 g., 0.5000 Gold 0.9324 oz. AGW, 50 mm. **Obv:** Queens portrait right **Obv. Designer:** Ian Rank-Broadley **Rev:** 1896 Olympic medal design **Edge:** Reeded

Date	Mintage	F	VF	XF	Unc	BU
2004 Proof	1,000	Value: 700				

KM# 318 250 DOLLARS
31.1030 g., 0.9999 Gold 0.9999 oz. AGW, 32.7 mm. **Obv:** Bust of Queen Elizabeth II right **Rev:** Mother and baby dolphins **Edge:** Reeded

Date	Mintage	F	VF	XF	Unc	BU
2005 Proof	750	Value: 950				

BRUNEI 81

KM# 121 500 DOLLARS
19.8126 g., 0.5000 Gold .3185 oz. AGW **Ruler:** Elizabeth II
Subject: Discovery of America **Obv:** Crowned head right **Rev:** Christopher Columbus 3/4 facing

Date	Mintage	F	VF	XF	Unc	BU
ND(1991)FM (P)	—	Value: 500				

KM# 164 500 DOLLARS
19.8126 g., 0.5000 Gold .3185 oz. AGW **Ruler:** Elizabeth II
Subject: The Santa Maria **Obv:** Crowned head right **Rev:** Ship sailing left, no gulls

Date	Mintage	F	VF	XF	Unc	BU
ND(1994) Proof	—	Value: 500				

KM# 258 500 DOLLARS
20.2200 g., 0.5000 Gold 0.3185 oz. AGW, 35.75 mm. **Ruler:** Elizabeth II **Obv:** Crowned head right **Rev:** Columbus' three ships crossing the Atlantic to America **Edge:** Reeded

Date	Mintage	F	VF	XF	Unc	BU
ND(1996?)FM Proof	—	Value: 550				

KM# 156 1000 DOLLARS
14.8000 g., 0.9990 Platinum .4758 oz. APW **Ruler:** Elizabeth II **Subject:** Discovery of America **Obv:** Crowned head right **Rev:** Three ships sailing

Date	Mintage	F	VF	XF	Unc	BU
ND(1992) Proof	—	Value: 1,150				

PROOF SETS

KM#	Date	Mintage	Identification	Issue Price	Mkt Val
PS17	ND (1991) (3)	—	KM#119-121	975	1,050
PS18	ND (1994) (3)	—	KM#162-164	975	1,075
PS19	ND (1996) (3)	—	KM#256, 257, 258	—	1,025

BRUNEI

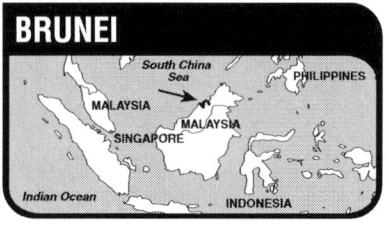

Negara Brunei Darussalam (State of Brunei), an independent sultanate on the northwest coast of the island of Borneo, has an area of 2,226 sq. mi. (5,765 sq. km.) and a population of *326,000. Capital: Bandar Seri Begawan. Crude oil and rubber are exported.

Magellan was the first European to visit Brunei in 1521. It was a powerful state, ruling over northern Borneo and adjacent islands from the 16th to the 19th century. Brunei became a British protectorate in 1888 and a British dependency in 1905. The Constitution of 1959 restored control over internal affairs to the sultan, while delegating responsibility for defense and foreign affairs to Britain. On January 1, 1984 it became independent.

TITLES
Negri Brunei

RULERS
Sultan Muhammad Tajuddin, 1795-1804
Sultan Muhammad Jamalul Alam I, 1804
Sultan Muhammad Tajuddin, 1804-1807
Sultan Muhammad Kanzul Alam, 1807-1826
Sultan Muhammad Alam, 1826-1828
Sultan Omar Ali Saifuddin II, 1828-1852
Sultan Abdul Mumin, 1852-1885
Sultan Hashim Jalal, 1885-1906
British 1906-1950
Sultan Sir Omar Ali Saifuddin III, 1950-1967
Sultan Hassanal Bolkiah I, 1967-

MONETARY SYSTEM
100 Cents = 1 Straits Dollar
100 Sen = 1 Dollar

SULTANATE
DECIMAL COINAGE
100 Sen = 1 Dollar (Ringgit)

KM# 47a DOLLAR
0.9170 Gold **Ruler:** Sultan Hassanal Bolkiah I **Subject:** 25th Anniversary of Brunei Currency Board **Obv:** Sultan Hassanal Bolkiah **Rev:** Mosque

Date	Mintage	F	VF	XF	Unc	BU
1992 Proof	1,000	Value: 350				

KM# 48 5 DOLLARS
0.9170 Gold **Ruler:** Sultan Hassanal Bolkiah I **Subject:** 25th Anniversary of Brunei Currency Board **Obv:** Sultan Hassanal Bolkiah **Rev:** Mosque

Date	Mintage	F	VF	XF	Unc	BU
1992 Proof	1,000	Value: 365				

KM# 49 10 DOLLARS
0.9170 Gold **Ruler:** Sultan Hassanal Bolkiah I **Subject:** 25th Anniversary of Brunei Currency Board **Obv:** Bust right **Rev:** Mosque

Date	Mintage	F	VF	XF	Unc	BU
1992 Proof	1,000	Value: 465				

KM# 50a 25 DOLLARS
Gold **Ruler:** Sultan Hassanal Bolkiah I **Subject:** 25th Anniversary of Brunei Currency Board **Obv:** Sultan Hassanal Bolkiah. **Rev:** Mosque.

Date	Mintage	F	VF	XF	Unc	BU
1992 Proof	1,000	—	—	—	—	—

KM# 39a 25 DOLLARS
0.9170 Gold **Subject:** 25th Anniversary of Accession

Date	Mintage	F	VF	XF	Unc	BU
ND(1992) Proof	—	Value: 585				

KM# 70 30 DOLLARS
31.1000 g., 0.9170 Gold .9169 oz. AGW **Subject:** 30 Years - ASEAN **Obv:** Sultan Hassanal Bolkiah **Rev:** ASEAN logo

Date	Mintage	F	VF	XF	Unc	BU
1997 Proof	300	Value: 665				

KM# 40a 50 DOLLARS
0.9170 Gold **Ruler:** Sultan Hassanal Bolkiah I **Subject:** 25th Anniversary of Accession **Obv:** Sultan Hassanal Bolkiah **Rev:** Royal procession

Date	Mintage	F	VF	XF	Unc	BU
ND(1992)	—	—	—	—	—	—

KM# 51 50 DOLLARS
0.9170 Gold **Ruler:** Sultan Hassanal Bolkiah I **Subject:** 25th Anniversary of Brunei Currency Board **Obv:** Sultan Hassanal Bolkiah **Rev:** Mosque

Date	Mintage	F	VF	XF	Unc	BU
1992 Proof	1,000	Value: 485				

KM# 67 50 DOLLARS
31.1035 g., 0.9170 Gold 1.0000 oz. AGW **Ruler:** Sultan Hassanal Bolkiah I **Subject:** 50th Birthday **Obv:** Sultan Hassanal Bolkiah **Rev:** Mosque

Date	Mintage	F	VF	XF	Unc	BU
ND(1996) Proof	500	Value: 685				

KM# 33 100 DOLLARS
13.5000 g., 0.9170 Gold .3976 oz. AGW **Ruler:** Sultan Hassanal Bolkiah I **Subject:** 20th Anniversary of Brunei Currency Board **Obv:** Uniformed bust 3/4 right **Rev:** Mosque above denomination

Date	Mintage	F	VF	XF	Unc	BU
1987 Proof	1,000	Value: 500				

KM# 52 100 DOLLARS
0.9170 Gold **Ruler:** Sultan Hassanal Bolkiah I **Subject:** 25th Anniversary of Brunei Currency Board **Obv:** Sultan Hassanal Bolkiah **Rev:** Mosque

Date	Mintage	F	VF	XF	Unc	BU
1992 Proof	1,000	Value: 585				

KM# 62 100 DOLLARS
0.9170 White Gold **Ruler:** Sultan Hassanal Bolkiah I **Subject:** 10th Year of Independence **Obv:** Sultan Hassanal Bolkiah I **Rev:** National arms

Date	Mintage	F	VF	XF	Unc	BU
ND(1994)	1,480	—	—	—	525	545
ND(1994) Proof	1,500	Value: 565				

KM# 73 200 DOLLARS
31.1000 g., 0.9170 Gold .9169 oz. AGW **Ruler:** Sultan Hassanal Bolkiah I **Subject:** 20th SEA Games **Obv:** Sultan Hassanal Bolkiah I **Rev:** Multicolor logo above stadium

Date	Mintage	F	VF	XF	Unc	BU
1999 Proof	100	Value: 685				

KM# 53 250 DOLLARS
0.9170 Gold **Ruler:** Sultan Hassanal Bolkiah I **Subject:** 25th Anniversary of Brunei Currency Board **Obv:** Sultan Hassanal Bolkiah I **Rev:** Mosque

Date	Mintage	F	VF	XF	Unc	BU
1992 Proof	1,000	Value: 735				

KM# 41 500 DOLLARS
50.0000 g., 0.9170 Gold 1.4727 oz. AGW **Ruler:** Sultan Hassanal Bolkiah I **Subject:** 25th Anniversary of Accession **Obv:** Sultan's portrait **Rev:** Other portrait

Date	Mintage	F	VF	XF	Unc	BU
MS(1992) Proof	1,500	Value: 1,350				

KM# 25 750 DOLLARS
15.9800 g., 0.9170 Gold .4711 oz. AGW **Ruler:** Sultan Hassanal Bolkiah I **Subject:** Year of Hejira 1400 **Obv:** Head right **Rev:** Design above denomination

Date	Mintage	F	VF	XF	Unc	BU
AH1400 (1980) Proof	1,000	Value: 650				

KM# 22 1000 DOLLARS
50.0000 g., 0.9170 Gold 1.4742 oz. AGW **Ruler:** Sultan Hassanal Bolkiah I **Subject:** 10th Anniversary of Sultan's Coronation **Obv:** Head right **Rev:** Coronation design above denomination, date at right

Date	Mintage	F	VF	XF	Unc	BU
ND(1978) Proof	1,000	Value: 1,450				

82   BRUNEI

KM# 28 1000 DOLLARS
50.0000 g., 0.9170 Gold 1.4742 oz. AGW **Ruler:** Sultan Hassanal Bolkiah I **Subject:** Independence Day **Obv:** Bust half right **Rev:** Off-shore oil rig, denomination below

Date	Mintage	F	VF	XF	Unc	BU
1984	4,000	—	—	—	1,050	1,150
1984 Proof	1,000	Value: 1,300				

KM# 31 1000 DOLLARS
50.0000 g., 0.9170 Gold 1.4742 oz. AGW **Ruler:** Sultan Hassanal Bolkiah I **Subject:** 20th Anniversary of Coronation **Obv:** Uniformed bust 3/4 right **Rev:** Arms within wreath divide dates at top, denomination below

Date	Mintage	F	VF	XF	Unc	BU
ND(1988) Proof	1,000	Value: 1,150				

KM# 63 1000 DOLLARS
0.9990 Gold **Ruler:** Sultan Hassanal Bolkiah I **Subject:** 10 Years of Independence **Obv:** Sultan Hassanal Bolkiah I **Rev:** National arms

Date	Mintage	F	VF	XF	Unc	BU
ND(1994)	500	—	—	—	1,275	1,350
ND(1994) Proof	480	Value: 1,450				

PROOF SETS

KM#	Date	Mintage	Identification	Issue Price	Mkt Val
PS3	1984 (3)	500	KM26-28	—	1,500
PS13	1992 (7)	1,000	KM47a, 48-53	—	3,000
PS16	1996 (4)	500	KM64-67	—	1,075
PS17	1997 (3)	500	KM68-70	—	740
PS18	1999 (3)	350	KM71-73	—	765

SPECIMEN SETS (SS)

KM#	Date	Mintage	Identification	Issue Price	Mkt Val
MS3	1984 (3)	500	KM26-28	—	1,250

BULGARIA

The Republic of Bulgaria, formerly the Peoples Republic of Bulgaria, a Balkan country on the Black Sea in southeastern Europe, has an area of 42,855 sq. mi. (110,910 sq. km.) and a population of *8.31 million. Capital: Sofia. Agriculture remains a key component of the economy but industrialization, particularly heavy industry, has been emphasized since the late 1940s. Machinery, tobacco and cigarettes, wines and spirits, clothing and metals are the chief exports.

The area now occupied by Bulgaria was conquered by the Bulgars, an Asiatic tribe, in the 7th century. Bulgarian kingdoms continued to exist on the Bulgarian peninsula until it came under Turkish rule in 1395. In 1878, after nearly 500 years of Turkish rule, Bulgaria was made a principality under Turkish suzerainty. Union seven years later with Eastern Rumelia created a Balkan state with borders approximating those of present-day Bulgaria. A Bulgarian kingdom, fully independent of Turkey, was proclaimed Sept. 22, 1908. During WWI Bulgaria had been aligned with Germany. After the Armistice certain land concessions were given to Greece and Romania. In 1934 King Boris III suspended all political parties and established a dictatorial monarchy. In 1938 the military began rearming through the aide of the Anglo-French loan. As WW II developed, Bulgaria again supported the Germans but protected their Jewish community. Boris died mysteriously in 1943 and Simeon II became King at the age of six. The country was then ruled by a pro-Nazi regency until it was liberated by Soviet forces in 1944.

The monarchy was abolished and Simeon was ousted by plebiscite in 1946 and Bulgaria became a Peoples Republic on the Soviet pattern. After democratic reforms in 1989 the name was changed to the Republic of Bulgaria.

Coinage of the Peoples Republic features a number of politically oriented commemoratives.

RULERS
Alexander I, as Prince, 1879-1886
Ferdinand I, as Prince, 1887-1908
  As King, 1908-1918
Boris III, 1918-1943

MINT MARKS
A - Berlin
(a) Cornucopia & torch - Paris
BP - Budapest
H - Heaton Mint, Birmingham
KB - Kormoczbanya
(p) Poissy - Thunderbolt

MONETARY SYSTEM
100 Stotinki = 1 Lev

PRINCIPALITY
Under Turkish Suzerainty
STANDARD COINAGE

KM# 19 10 LEVA
3.2258 g., 0.9000 Gold .0933 oz. AGW **Ruler:** Ferdinand I as Prince **Obv:** Head left **Rev:** Crowned ornate arms

Date	Mintage	F	VF	XF	Unc	BU
1894KB	75,000	65.00	140	180	480	—
1894KB Proof	—	Value: 3,000				

KM# 20 20 LEVA
6.4516 g., 0.9000 Gold .1867 oz. AGW **Ruler:** Ferdinand I as Prince **Obv:** Head left **Rev:** Crowned ornate arms

Date	Mintage	F	VF	XF	Unc	BU
1894KB	100,000	125	145	245	550	—
1894KB Proof	—	Value: 6,000				

KM# 21 100 LEVA
32.2580 g., 0.9000 Gold .9334 oz. AGW **Ruler:** Ferdinand I as Prince **Obv:** Head left **Rev:** Crowned ornate arms

Date	Mintage	F	VF	XF	Unc	BU
1894KB	2,500	625	750	1,350	3,500	—
1894KB Proof	—	Value: 8,000				

KINGDOM
STANDARD COINAGE

KM# 33 20 LEVA
6.4516 g., 0.9000 Gold .1867 oz. AGW, 21 mm. **Subject:** Declaration of Independence **Obv:** Head left **Rev:** Crowned arms, denomination and date below

Date	Mintage	F	VF	XF	Unc	BU
1912	75,000	BV	175	275	460	—
1912 Proof	Inc. above	Value: 3,000				
1912 Proof; restrike	2,950	Value: 275				

Note: Official restrikes of this type were produced at the Bulgarian Mint in Sophia from 1967-68 and released prior to 2002; These pieces can be distinguished by their thicker more widely spaced edge legends

KM# 34 100 LEVA
32.2580 g., 0.9000 Gold .9334 oz. AGW, 35 mm. **Subject:** Declaration of Independence **Obv:** Head left **Rev:** Crowned arms divide denomination, date below

Date	Mintage	F	VF	XF	Unc	BU
1912	5,000	640	950	1,850	3,200	—
1912 Proof	Inc. above	Value: 6,000				
1912 Proof; restrike	1,000	Value: 1,000				

Note: Official restrikes of this type were produced at the Bulgarian Mint in Sophia from 1967-68 and released prior to 2002; These pieces can be distinguished by their thicker more widely spaced edge legends

MEDALLIC COINAGE

Originally produced as a jewelry item. A similar piece with Russian legends also exists.

KM# M1 4 DUKAT
13.9600 g., 0.9860 Gold .4425 oz. AGW **Countermark:** Crown and government mark

Date	Mintage	F	VF	XF	Unc	BU
1910	—	BV	325	375	525	—
1911	—	BV	350	400	550	—

BULGARIA

Date	Mintage	F	VF	XF	Unc	BU
1912	—	BV	325	375	525	—
1914	—	BV	400	500	900	—
1917	—	BV	400	500	900	—
1918	—	BV	350	400	550	—
1919	—	300	400	500	900	—

Note: Values above are for holed or holed and plugged specimens; unholed specimens command 5 times the values indicated

KM# M2 4 DUKAT
13.9600 g., 0.9860 Gold .4425 oz. AGW **Countermark:** Crown and government mark

Date	Mintage	F	VF	XF	Unc	BU
ND1921	—	375	475	800	2,000	—
1926	—	375	475	800	2,000	—

Note: Values above are for holed or holed and plugged specimens; unholed specimens command 5 times the values indicated

PEOPLES REPUBLIC
STANDARD COINAGE

KM# 67 10 LEVA
8.4444 g., 0.9000 Gold .2443 oz. AGW **Subject:** 1100th Anniversary - Slavic Alphabet **Obv:** Denomination above shield **Rev:** Two figures above dates

Date	Mintage	F	VF	XF	Unc	BU
ND(1963) Proof	7,000	Value: 185				

KM# 71 10 LEVA
8.4444 g., 0.9000 Gold .2443 oz. AGW **Subject:** 20th Anniversary - Peoples Republic **Obv:** Flag above denomination, two dates below **Rev:** Head of Georgi Dimitrov, left, two dates below

Date	Mintage	F	VF	XF	Unc	BU
ND(1964) Proof	10,000	Value: 165				

KM# 68 20 LEVA
16.8889 g., 0.9000 Gold .4887 oz. AGW **Subject:** 100th Anniversary - Slavic Alphabet **Obv:** Denomination above shield **Rev:** Two figures above dates

Date	Mintage	F	VF	XF	Unc	BU
ND(1963) Proof	3,000	Value: 360				

KM# 72 20 LEVA
16.8889 g., 0.9000 Gold .4887 oz. AGW **Subject:** 20th Anniversary - Peoples Republic **Obv:** Flag above denomination, dates at bottom **Rev:** Head of Georgi Dimitrov, left, two dates below

Date	Mintage	F	VF	XF	Unc	BU
ND(1964) Proof	5,000	Value: 335				

KM# 150 100 LEVA
8.4444 g., 0.9000 Gold .2443 oz. AGW **Subject:** International Womens Decade **Obv:** National arms within wreath, date and denomination below **Rev:** Woman with child divides dates **Note:** .076 Silver, .024 Copper

Date	Mintage	F	VF	XF	Unc	BU
1984 Proof	500	Value: 350				

KM# 150a 100 LEVA
8.4444 g., 0.9000 Gold .2443 oz. AGW **Subject:** International Womens Decade **Obv:** National arms within wreath, date and denomination below **Rev:** Woman with child divides date **Note:** .100 Copper

Date	Mintage	F	VF	XF	Unc	BU
1984	2,032	Value: 250				

KM# 139 1000 LEVA
16.8800 g., 0.9000 Gold .4885 oz. AGW **Subject:** 1300th Anniversary of Nationhood **Obv:** National arms above denomination and date **Rev:** Mother and child in front of radiant sun

Date	Mintage	F	VF	XF	Unc	BU
1981 Proof	2,000	Value: 385				

REPUBLIC
ECU COINAGE

X# 2 250 ECU
31.1030 g., 0.7500 Gold 0.75 oz. AGW, 38 mm. **Issuer:** Numex S.A., Madrid **Obv:** Arms **Obv. Legend:** РЕПУБЛИКА БЪЛГАРИЯ **Rev:** Ancient galley, value above **Edge:** Reeded

Date	Mintage	F	VF	XF	Unc	BU
1993 Proof	500	Value: 700				

STANDARD COINAGE

KM# 207 5000 LEVA
8.6400 g., 0.9000 Gold .2500 oz. AGW **Subject:** European Community - Slavonic Alphabet **Obv:** ECU monogram and date within circle of stars **Rev:** Denomination to left of design

Date	Mintage	F	VF	XF	Unc	BU
1993 Proof	Est. 2,500	Value: 200				

KM# 208 10000 LEVA
15.5670 g., 0.9990 Platinum .4999 oz. APW **Rev:** Bust of Sevastokratoritza Desislava 1/2 right, founder of Boyana church, denomination at right

Date	Mintage	F	VF	XF	Unc	BU
1993 Proof	Est. 2,500	Value: 650				

KM# 218 10000 LEVA
8.6400 g., 0.9000 Gold .2500 oz. AGW **Obv:** Denomination above date within wreath **Rev:** St. Alexander Nevski Cathedral

Date	Mintage	F	VF	XF	Unc	BU
1994 Proof	30,000	Value: 200				

KM# 236 20000 LEVA
1.5552 g., 0.9990 Gold .0500 oz. AGW **Subject:** Czar Ivan Alexander **Obv:** Stylized lion, left, date and denomination below **Rev:** Four human figure sculptures

Date	Mintage	F	VF	XF	Unc	BU
1998 Proof	—	Value: 75.00				

REFORM COINAGE

KM# 257 LEV
15.5500 g., 0.9990 Gold .4994 oz. AGW **Obv:** St. Ivan of Rila **Rev:** Large number one **Edge:** Plain

Date	Mintage	F	VF	XF	Unc	BU
2002 Proof	2,000	Value: 450				

KM# 258 5 LEVA
1.2400 g., 0.9990 Gold 0.0398 oz. AGW **Obv:** Denomination **Rev:** Olympic archer **Edge:** Plain

Date	Mintage	F	VF	XF	Unc	BU
2002 Proof	12,000	Value: 47.50				

KM# 259 5 LEVA
1.2400 g., 0.9990 Gold 0.0398 oz. AGW **Obv:** Denomination **Rev:** Olympic cyclist **Edge:** Plain

Date	Mintage	F	VF	XF	Unc	BU
2002 Proof	12,000	Value: 47.50				

KM# 260 5 LEVA
1.2400 g., 0.9990 Gold 0.0398 oz. AGW **Obv:** Denomination **Rev:** Olympic fencing **Edge:** Plain

Date	Mintage	F	VF	XF	Unc	BU
2002 Proof	12,000	Value: 47.50				

KM# 261 5 LEVA
1.2400 g., 0.9990 Gold 0.0398 oz. AGW **Obv:** Denomination **Rev:** Olympic wrestling **Edge:** Plain

Date	Mintage	F	VF	XF	Unc	BU
2002 Proof	12,000	Value: 47.50				

KM# 262 5 LEVA
1.2400 g., 0.9990 Gold 0.0398 oz. AGW, 14 mm. **Obv:** Denomination **Rev:** Olympic gymnastics **Edge:** Plain

Date	Mintage	F	VF	XF	Unc	BU
2002 Proof	12,000	Value: 47.50				

KM# 263 5 LEVA
1.2400 g., 0.9990 Gold 0.0398 oz. AGW, 14 mm. **Obv:** Denomination **Rev:** Olympics founder Pierre du Coubertin **Edge:** Plain

Date	Mintage	F	VF	XF	Unc	BU
2002 Proof	17,000	Value: 47.50				

BULGARIA

KM# 264 5 LEVA
1.2400 g., 0.9990 Gold 0.0398 oz. AGW, 14 mm. **Obv:** Denomination **Rev:** Olympic running **Edge:** Plain

Date	Mintage	F	VF	XF	Unc	BU
2002 Proof	12,000	Value: 47.50				

KM# 265 5 LEVA
1.2400 g., 0.9990 Gold 0.0398 oz. AGW, 14 mm. **Obv:** Denomination **Rev:** Olympic swimming **Edge:** Plain

Date	Mintage	F	VF	XF	Unc	BU
2002 Proof	12,000	Value: 47.50				

KM# 266 5 LEVA
1.2400 g., 0.9990 Gold 0.0398 oz. AGW, 14 mm. **Obv:** Denomination **Rev:** Olympic tennis **Edge:** Plain

Date	Mintage	F	VF	XF	Unc	BU
2002 Proof	12,000	Value: 47.50				

KM# 267 5 LEVA
1.2400 g., 0.9990 Gold 0.0398 oz. AGW, 14 mm. **Obv:** Denomination **Rev:** Olympic weight lifting **Edge:** Plain

Date	Mintage	F	VF	XF	Unc	BU
2002 Proof	12,000	Value: 47.50				

KM# 269 20 LEVA
1.5500 g., 0.9990 Gold 0.0498 oz. AGW, 16 mm. **Obv:** Denomination **Rev:** Mother of God **Edge:** Plain

Date	Mintage	F	VF	XF	Unc	BU
2003 Proof	20,000	Value: 55.00				

KM# 255 100 LEVA
16.0000 g., 0.9000 Gold 0.4758 oz. AGW, 30 mm. **Subject:** Todor Burmov **Obv:** Bust 3/4 facing, date and denomination below **Rev:** "EURO" and map **Edge:** Plain

Date	Mintage	F	VF	XF	Unc	BU
1999 Proof	5,000	Value: 450				

KM# 271 125 LEVA
7.7800 g., 0.9990 Gold 0.2499 oz. AGW, 21 mm. **Subject:** Bulgarian National Bank 125th Anniversary

Date	Mintage	F	VF	XF	Unc	BU
2004 Proof	3,000	Value: 250				

KM# 256 20000 LEVA
1.5500 g., 0.9990 Gold 0.0498 oz. AGW **Obv:** National arms **Rev:** National Bank building, date and denomination below **Edge:** Plain

Date	Mintage	F	VF	XF	Unc	BU
1999 Proof	30,000	Value: 45.00				

PROOF SETS

KM#	Date	Mintage	Identification	Issue Price	Mkt Val
PS1	1912 (2)	—	KM#33-34. Official restrikes of these types were made in the 1960's.	—	7,500

BURKINA FASO

Burkina Faso is a republic in western Africa bordered on the north and west by Mali, to the south by Ivory Coast, Ghana, Togo and Benin and the east by Niger. It consists of 105,869 sq. mi. (274,201 sq. km.); population 9,780,000. Chief products from agriculture are sorghum, corn, rice, cotton, peanuts and millet. They also raise livestock. The land is on a plateau, savanna, grassy in north and partly forested in the south. Its history is mainly tied into French colonization, skirmishes with Mali to the north, Niger to the east. The country went through several coups in the 80's, military rule ended and a new constitution was adopted in 1991.

DEMOCRATIC REPUBLIC

INSTITUT MONETAIRE

KM# 1b 6000 CFA FRANCS - 4 AFRICA
11.0000 g., 0.9990 Bi-Metallic .999 Silver center in Gold ring 0.3533 oz., 28.3 mm. **Obv:** Bird and Rhinoceros **Rev:** Elephant head on map **Edge:** Plain

Date	Mintage	F	VF	XF	Unc	BU
2003	5	—	—	—	450	—

REPUBLIC

INSTITUT MONETAIRE

KM# 2a 6000 CFA FRANCS - 4 AFRICA
11.0000 g., 0.9990 Bi-Metallic .999 Silver center in .999 Gold plated .999 Silver ring 0.3533 oz., 28.4 mm. **Obv:** Rhincerous and bird **Rev:** Elephant head on full African map within Presidential legend **Edge:** Plain

Date	Mintage	F	VF	XF	Unc	BU
2003	5	—	—	—	480	—

MEDALLIC BULLION COINAGE

X# 1a OUNCE
31.1000 g., 0.9990 Gold 0.9989 oz. AGW, 38.5 mm. **Issuer:** Burkina Faso Numismatic Agency **Obv:** Arms **Obv. Inscription:** LA PATRE OU LA MORT... **Rev:** Eagle's head left and right **Edge:** Reeded

Date	Mintage	F	VF	XF	Unc	BU
1990 Proof	30	Value: 900				

BURMA

Burma, a country of Southeast Asia fronting on the Bay of Bengal and the Andaman Sea, had an area of 261,218 sq. mi. (678,500 sq. km.).

The first European to reach Burma, in about 1435, was Nicolo Di Conti, a Venetian merchant. During the beginning of the reign of Bodawpaya (1781-1819AD) the kingdom comprised most of the same area as it does today including Arakan which was taken over in 1784-85. The British East India Company, while unsuccessful in its 1612 effort to establish posts along the Bay of Bengal, was enabled by the Anglo-Burmese Wars of 1824-86 to expand to the whole of Burma and to secure its annexation to British India.

The coins issued by kings Mindon and Thibaw between 1852 and 1885 circulated in Upper Burma. Indian coins were current in Lower Burma, which was annexed in 1852. Burmese coins are frequently known by the equivalent Indian denominations, although their values are inscribed in Burmese units. Upper Burma was annexed in 1885 and the Burmese coinage remained in circulation until 1889, when Indian coins became current throughout Burma. Coins were again issued in the old Burmese denominations after independence in 1948, but these were replaced by decimal issues in 1952. The Chula-Sakarat (CS) dating is sometimes referred to as BE-Burmese Era and began in 638AD.

NOTE: For later coinage, see Myanmar.

RULERS
Bodawpaya, CS1143-1181/1782-1819AD
Bagyidaw, CS1181-1198/1819-1837AD
Tharawaddy, CS1198-1207/1837-46AD
Pagan, CS1207-1214/1846-53AD
Mindon, CS1214-1240/1853-78AD
Thibaw, CS1240-1248/1880-85AD
British, 1886-1948

MONETARY SYSTEM
(Until 1952)
4 Pyas = 1 Pe
2 Pe = 1 Mu
2 Mu = 1 Mat
5 Mat = 1 Kyat
NOTE: Originally 10 light Mu = 1 Kyat, eventually 8 heavy Mu = 1 Kyat.

Indian Equivalents
1 Silver Kyat = 1 Rupee = 16 Annas
1 Gold Kyat = 1 Mohur = 16 Rupees

UNION

MEDALLIC COINAGE
Patriotic Liberation Army Issues

X# 3 MU
2.0000 g., 1.0000 Gold 0.0643 oz. AGW **Obv:** Legend around peacock **Obv. Legend:** UNION OF BURMA GOVERNMENT 1970-1971 **Rev. Legend:** U NU in star with SHWE MUZI below **Note:** Prev. KM#43.

Date	Mintage	F	VF	XF	Unc	BU
1970-71	—	—	—	—	125	160

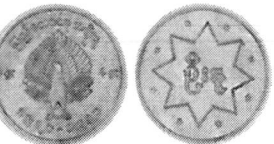

X# 4 2 MU
4.0000 g., 1.0000 Gold 0.1286 oz. AGW **Note:** Prev. KM#44.

Date	Mintage	F	VF	XF	Unc	BU
1970-71	—	—	—	—	245	280

BURUNDI 85

X# 5 4 MU
8.0000 g., 1.0000 Gold 0.2572 oz. AGW. **Note:** Prev. KM#45.

Date	Mintage	F	VF	XF	Unc	BU
1970-71	—	—	—	—	475	500

SHAN STATES
REBEL COINAGE

Issued by guerilla rebels about 1981

X# 1 1/8 TICAL
1.9000 g., Gold **Obv:** Crude outline map of Rebel held territories

Date	Mintage	F	VF	XF	Unc	BU
ND(c.1981)	—	—	—	100	150	—

X# 2 1/4 TICAL
3.8000 g., Gold **Obv:** Crude outline map of Rebel held territories

Date	Mintage	F	VF	XF	Unc	BU
ND(c.1981)	—	—	—	125	175	—

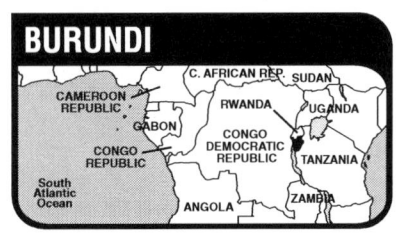

BURUNDI

The Republic of Burundi, a landlocked country in central Africa, was a kingdom with a feudalistic society, caste system and Mwami (king) for more than 400 years before independence. It has an area of 10,740 sq. mi. (27,830 sq. km.) and a population of 6.3 million. Capital: Bujumbura. Plagued by poor soil, irregular rainfall and a single-crop economy, coffee, Burundi is barely able to feed itself. Coffee and tea are exported.

Although the area was visited by European explorers and missionaries in the latter half of the 19th century, it wasn't until the 1890s that it, together with Rwanda, fell under European domination as part of German East Africa. Following World War I, the territory was mandated to Belgium by the League of Nations and administered with the Belgian Congo. After World War II it became a U.N. Trust Territory. Limited self-government was established by U.N.-supervised elections in 1961. Burundi gained independence as a kingdom under Mwami Mwambutsa IV on July 1, 1962. The republic was established by military coup in 1966.

NOTE: For earlier coinage see Belgian Congo, and Rwanda and Burundi. For previously listed coinage dated 1966, coins of Mwambutsa IV and Ntare V, refer to *UNUSUAL WORLD COINS*, 3rd edition, Krause Publications, 1992.

RULERS
Mwambutsa IV, 1962-1966
Ntare V, 1966

MINT MARKS
PM - Pobjoy Mint
(b) - Privy Marks, Brussels

MONETARY SYSTEM
100 Centimes = 1 Franc

KINGDOM
STANDARD COINAGE

KM# 2 10 FRANCS
3.2000 g., 0.9000 Gold .0926 oz. AGW **Ruler:** Mwambutsa IV **Subject:** Burundi Independence **Obv:** Uniformed bust left, beaded rim **Rev:** Arms, date and denomination below, beaded rim

Date	Mintage	F	VF	XF	Unc	BU
1962 Proof	7,500	Value: 75.00				

KM# 7 10 FRANCS
3.0000 g., 0.9000 Gold .0868 oz. AGW **Ruler:** Mwambutsa IV **Subject:** 50th Anniversary - Reign of Mwambutsa IV **Obv:** Uniformed bust 3/4 facing divides dates, beaded rim **Rev:** Arms, denomination below, beaded rim

Date	Mintage	F	VF	XF	Unc	BU
ND(1965)	—	—	—	—	60.00	—
ND(1965) Proof	5,000	Value: 75.00				

KM# 3 25 FRANCS
8.0000 g., 0.9000 Gold .2315 oz. AGW **Ruler:** Mwambutsa IV **Subject:** Burundi Independence **Obv:** Uniformed bust left, beaded rim **Rev:** Arms, denomination and date below, beaded rim

Date	Mintage	F	VF	XF	Unc	BU
1962 Proof	15,000	Value: 160				

KM# 8 25 FRANCS
7.5000 g., 0.9000 Gold .217 oz. AGW **Ruler:** Mwambutsa IV **Subject:** 50th Anniversary - Reign of Mwambutsa IV **Obv:** Uniformed bust 3/4 facing divides dates, beaded rim **Rev:** Arms, denomination below, beaded rim

Date	Mintage	F	VF	XF	Unc	BU
ND(1965)	—	—	—	—	155	—
ND(1965) Proof	5,000	Value: 170				

KM# 4 50 FRANCS
16.0000 g., 0.9000 Gold .4630 oz. AGW **Ruler:** Mwambutsa IV **Subject:** Burundi Independence **Obv:** Uniformed bust left, beaded rim **Rev:** Arms, denomination and date below, beaded rim

Date	Mintage	F	VF	XF	Unc	BU
1962 Proof	3,500	Value: 335				

KM# 9 50 FRANCS
15.0000 g., 0.9000 Gold .4340 oz. AGW **Ruler:** Mwambutsa IV **Subject:** 50th Anniversary - Reign of Mwambutsa IV **Obv:** Uniformed bust 3/4 facing divides dates, beaded rim **Rev:** Arms, denomination below, beaded rim

Date	Mintage	F	VF	XF	Unc	BU
ND(1965)	—	—	—	—	300	—
ND(1965) Proof	5,000	Value: 350				

KM# 5 100 FRANCS
32.0000 g., 0.9000 Gold .9260 oz. AGW **Ruler:** Mwambutsa IV **Subject:** Burundi Independence **Obv:** Uniformed bust left, beaded rim **Rev:** Arms, denomination and date below, beaded rim

Date	Mintage	F	VF	XF	Unc	BU
1962 Proof	2,500	Value: 685				

KM# 10 100 FRANCS
30.0000 g., 0.9000 Gold .8681 oz. AGW **Ruler:** Mwambutsa IV **Subject:** 50th Anniversary - Reign of Mwambutsa IV **Obv:** Uniformed bust 3/4 facing divides dates, beaded rim **Rev:** Arms, denomination below, beaded rim

Date	Mintage	F	VF	XF	Unc	BU
ND(1965)	—	—	—	—	600	—
ND(1965) Proof	5,000	Value: 650				

BURUNDI

REPUBLIC
1966-
STANDARD COINAGE

KM# 11 10 FRANCS
3.2000 g., 0.9000 Gold .0926 oz. AGW **Subject:** First Anniversary of Republic

Date	Mintage	F	VF	XF	Unc	BU
1967 Proof	—	Value: 85.00				

KM# 12 20 FRANCS
6.4000 g., 0.9000 Gold .1852 oz. AGW **Subject:** First Anniversary of Republic

Date	Mintage	F	VF	XF	Unc	BU
ND(1967) Proof	—	Value: 135				

KM# 13 25 FRANCS
8.0000 g., 0.9000 Gold .2315 oz. AGW **Subject:** First Anniversary of Republic

Date	Mintage	F	VF	XF	Unc	BU
ND(1967) Proof	—	Value: 165				

KM# 14 50 FRANCS
16.0000 g., 0.9000 Gold .4630 oz. AGW **Subject:** First Anniversary of Republic **Obv:** Bust, facing **Rev:** Arms above denomination

Date	Mintage	F	VF	XF	Unc	BU
ND(1967) Proof	—	Value: 335				

KM# 15 100 FRANCS
32.0000 g., 0.9000 Gold .9261 oz. AGW **Subject:** First Anniversary of Republic

Date	Mintage	F	VF	XF	Unc	BU
ND(1967) Proof	—	Value: 665				

PROOF SETS

KM#	Date	Mintage	Identification	Issue Price	Mkt Val
PS1	1962 (4)	2,500	KM2-5	—	1,255
PS2	1965 (4)	5,000	KM7-10	—	1,245
PS3	1967 (5)	—	KM11-15	—	1,385

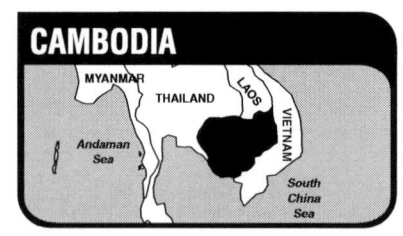

CAMBODIA

The State of Cambodia, formerly Democratic Kampuchea and the Khmer Republic, a land of paddy fields and forest-clad hills located on the Indo-Chinese peninsula, fronting on the Gulf of Thailand, has an area of 70,238 sq. mi. (181,040 sq. km.) and a population of *11.21 million. Capital: Phnom Penh. Agriculture is the basis of the economy, with rice the chief crop. Native industries include cattle breeding, weaving and rice milling. Rubber, cattle, corn, and timber are exported.

The region was the nucleus of the Khmer empire which flourished from the 5th to the 12th century and attained an excellence in art and architecture still evident in the magnificent ruins at Angkor. The Khmer empire once ruled over much of Southeast Asia, but began to decline in the 13th century as the Thai and Vietnamese invaded the region and attached its territories. At the request of the Cambodian king, a French protectorate attached to Cochin-China was established over the country in 1863, saving it from dissolution, and in 1885, Cambodia was included in the French Union of Indo-China.

France established a constitutional monarchy for Cambodia within the French Union in 1949. The 1954 Geneva Convention resulted in full independence for the Kingdom of Cambodia. King Sihanouk abdicated to his father and won the office of Prime Minister.

Prince Sihanouk was toppled by a bloodless coup led by Lon Nol in March of 1970. Sihanouk moved to Peking to head a government-in-exile. On Oct. 9, 1970, Cambodia became the Khmer Republic, and Lon Nol its President. The government of Lon Nol was in turn toppled, April 17, 1975, by the Khmer Rouge insurgents who took control of the government and renamed the country Democratic Kampuchea.

The Khmer Rouge completely eliminated the economy and created a state without money, exchange or barter while exterminating about 2 million Cambodians. These atrocities were finally halted at the beginning of 1979 when the Vietnamese regulars and Cambodian rebels launched an offensive that drove the Khmer Rouge out of Phnom Penh and the country acquired another new title - The Peoples Republic of Kampuchea.

In 1993 Prince Norodom Sihanouk returned to Kampuchea to lead the Supreme National Council.

RULERS
Kings of Cambodia
Norodom I, 1835-1904
Sisowath, 1904-1927
Sisowath Monivong, 1927-1941
Norodom Sihanouk, 1941-1955
Norodom Suramarit, 1955-1960
Heng Samrin, 1979-1985
Hun Sen, 1985-1991
Norodom Sihanouk, 1991-1993
    Chairman, Supreme National Council
    King, 1993-

MINT MARKS
(a) - Paris, privy marks only
(k) - Key, Havana, Cuba

MONETARY SYSTEM
(Until 1860)
2 Att = 1 Pe (Pey)
4 Pe = 1 Fuang (Fuong)
8 Fuang = 1 Tical
4 Salong = 1 Tical
(Commencing 1860)
100 Centimes = 1 Franc

KINGDOM
MEDALLIC COINAGE

X# 2b 5 CENTIMES
Gold **Note:** Prev. KM#Pn3.

Date	Mintage	F	VF	XF	Unc	BU
1860	—	—	—	—	—	—

X# 3b 10 CENTIMES
Gold **Note:** Prev. KM#Pn5.

Date	Mintage	F	VF	XF	Unc	BU
1860	—	—	—	—	—	—

X# 4b 25 CENTIMES
Gold **Note:** Prev. KM#Pn6.

Date	Mintage	F	VF	XF	Unc	BU
1860	—	—	—	—	—	—

X# 5b 50 CENTIMES
Gold **Note:** Prev. KM#Pn7.

Date	Mintage	F	VF	XF	Unc	BU
1860	—	—	—	—	—	—

X# 6b FRANC
Gold **Note:** Prev. KM#Pn8.

Date	Mintage	F	VF	XF	Unc	BU
1860	—	—	—	—	—	—

X# 7b 2 FRANCS
Gold **Note:** Prev. KM#Pn9.

Date	Mintage	F	VF	XF	Unc	BU
1860	—	—	—	—	—	—

X# 8b 4 FRANCS
Gold **Note:** Prev. KM#Pn10.

Date	Mintage	F	VF	XF	Unc	BU
1860	—	—	—	—	2,250	—

X# 9b PIASTRE
Gold **Note:** Prev. KM#Pn11.

Date	Mintage	F	VF	XF	Unc	BU
1860	—	—	—	—	—	—

KHMER REPUBLIC
1970 - 1975
DECIMAL COINAGE

KM# 64 50000 RIELS
6.7100 g., 0.9000 Gold .1941 oz. AGW **Obv:** Cambodian dancers **Rev:** Royal emblem above denomination

Date	Mintage	F	VF	XF	Unc	BU
1974	3,250	—	—	—	150	180
1974 Proof	2,300	Value: 225				

KM# 65 50000 RIELS
6.7100 g., 0.9000 Gold .1941 oz. AGW **Obv:** Celestial dancer **Rev:** Royal emblem above denomination

Date	Mintage	F	VF	XF	Unc	BU
1974	450	—	—	—	250	275
1974 Proof	300	Value: 375				

KM# 66 100000 RIELS
19.1700 g., 0.9000 Gold .5547 oz. AGW **Obv:** Bust of President Lon Nol left **Rev:** Royal emblem above denomination

Date	Mintage	F	VF	XF	Unc	BU
1974	250	—	—	—	450	475
1974 Proof	100	Value: 725				

PEOPLE'S REPUBLIC OF KAMPUCHEA
1979 - 1990
DECIMAL COINAGE

KM# 77 40 RIELS
3.1500 g., 0.9990 Gold .1012 oz. AGW **Obv:** Royal emblem above denomination **Rev:** Angkor Wat Temples

Date	Mintage	F	VF	XF	Unc	BU
1989	500	—	—	—	145	—

KM# 82 40 RIELS
3.1500 g., 0.9990 Gold .1012 oz. AGW **Obv:** Royal emblem above denomination **Rev:** Folklore dance, date lower left

Date	Mintage	F	VF	XF	Unc	BU
1990	500			Value: 175		

KINGDOM OF CAMBODIA
1993 -
DECIMAL COINAGE
KM# 99 3000 RIELS
1.2441 g., 0.9999 Gold 0.04 oz. AGW, 13.92 mm. **Subject:** Angkor Wat **Obv:** Armless statue of Jayavarman VII **Rev:** View of Angkor Wat in center **Edge:** Reeded

Date	Mintage	F	VF	XF	Unc	BU
2001	28,000	—	—	—	45.00	55.00

KM# 104 3000 RIELS
1.2440 g., 0.9990 Gold 0.04 oz. AGW, 13.92 mm. **Obv:** King Jayavarman VII (1162-1201) **Rev:** Sphinx and pyramid **Edge:** Reeded

Date	Mintage	F	VF	XF	Unc	BU
2004 Proof	27,900			Value: 45.00		

KM# 102 10000 RIELS
31.1035 g., 0.9990 Silver .9990 oz. ASW **Center Weight:** 3.5000 g. **Center Composition:** 0.9999 Gold 0.1125 oz. AGW , 40.7 mm. **Subject:** Angkor Wat **Obv:** Armless statue of Jayavarman **Rev:** Multicolor holographic view of Angkor Wat in center **Edge:** Reeded

Date	Mintage	F	VF	XF	Unc	BU
2001 Proof	3,000			Value: 95.00		

PATTERNS
Including off metal strikes

KM#	Date	Mintage	Identification	Mkt Val
PnA3	ND	—	2 Pe. Gold. 2.9800 g. KM#26.	1,250

MINT SETS

KM#	Date	Mintage	Identification	Issue Price	Mkt Val
MS2	1974 (7)	250	KM60-66	—	1,250
MS3	1974 (4)	500	KM60-63	—	400

PROOF SETS

KM#	Date	Mintage	Identification	Issue Price	Mkt Val
PS1	1974 (7)	100	KM60-66	—	1,750
PS2	1974 (4)	800	KM60-63	—	425

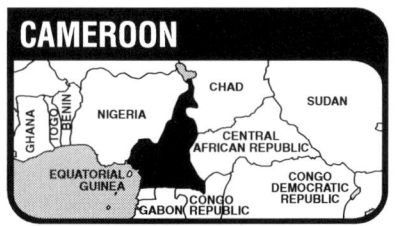

CAMEROON

The Republic of Cameroon, located in west-central Africa on the Gulf of Guinea, has an area of 183,569 sq. mi. (475,445 sq. km.) and a population of *15.13 million. Capital: Yaounde. About 90 percent of the labor force is employed on the land; cash crops account for 80 percent of the country's export revenue. Cocoa, coffee, aluminum, cotton, rubber, and timber are exported.

European contact with what is now the United Republic of Cameroon began in the 16th century with the voyage of Portuguese navigator Fernando Po. The following three centuries saw continuous activity by Spanish, Dutch, and British traders and missionaries. The land was spared colonial rule until 1884, when treaties with tribal chiefs brought German domination. In 1919, the League of Nations divided the Cameroons between Great Britain and France, with the larger eastern area going to France. The French and British mandates were converted into United Nations trusteeships in 1946. French Cameroon became the independent Cameroon Republic on Jan. 1, 1960. The federation of East (French) and West (British) Cameroon was established in 1961 when the southern part of British Cameroon voted for reunification with the Cameroon Republic, and the northern part for union with Nigeria Cameroon joined the Commonwealth of Nations in November 1995.

Coins of French Equatorial Africa and of the monetary unions identified as the Equatorial African States and Central African States are also current in Cameroon.

MINT MARKS
(a) - Paris, privy marks only
SA - Pretoria, 1943

MONETARY SYSTEM
100 Centimes = 1 Franc

REPUBLIC
INSTITUT MONETAIRE
KM# 24a 4500 CFA FRANCS - 3 AFRICA
Bi-Metallic .999 Silver center in .999 Gold plated .999 Silver ring, 26 mm. **Obv:** Pope Benedict XVI **Rev:** Elephant head on Central Africa map

Date	Mintage	F	VF	XF	Unc	BU
2005	25	—	—	—	550	—

STANDARD COINAGE

KM# 18 1000 FRANCS
3.5000 g., 0.9000 Gold .1012 oz. AGW **Subject:** 10th Anniversary of Independence **Obv:** Head of President El Hajj Ahmadou Ahidjo left **Rev:** Design at center, denomination below, arms above

Date	Mintage	F	VF	XF	Unc	BU
1970 Proof	4,000			Value: 95.00		

KM# 19 3000 FRANCS
10.5000 g., 0.9000 Gold .3038 oz. AGW **Subject:** 10th Anniversary of Independence **Obv:** Head of President El Hajj Ahmadou Ahidjo left **Rev:** Design at center, denomination below, arms above

Date	Mintage	F	VF	XF	Unc	BU
1970 Proof	4,000			Value: 220		

Note: With or without cornucopia mint mark on reverse

KM# 20 5000 FRANCS
17.5000 g., 0.9000 Gold .5064 oz. AGW **Subject:** 10th Anniversary of Independence **Obv:** Head of President El Hajj Ahmadou Ahidjo **Rev:** Head, left, within center circle, denomination below, arms above

Date	Mintage	F	VF	XF	Unc	BU
1970 Proof	4,000			Value: 350		

KM# 21 10000 FRANCS
35.0000 g., 0.9000 Gold 1.0128 oz. AGW **Subject:** 10th Anniversary of Independence **Obv:** President El Hajj Ahmadou Ahidjo left **Rev:** Elands facing center, denomination below, arms above

Date	Mintage	F	VF	XF	Unc	BU
1970 Proof	4,000			Value: 700		

KM# 22 20000 FRANCS
70.0000 g., 0.9000 Gold 2.0257 oz. AGW **Subject:** 10th Anniversary of Independence **Obv:** Head of President El Hajj Ahmadou Ahidjo left **Rev:** Arms, denomination below

Date	Mintage	F	VF	XF	Unc	BU
1970 Proof	4,000			Value: 1,375		

ESSAIS
Standard metals unless otherwise noted

KM#	Date	Mintage	Identification	Issue Price	Mkt Val
E14	1971	6	100 Francs. Gold. KM15.	—	1,300

PROOF SETS

KM#	Date	Mintage	Identification	Issue Price	Mkt Val
PS1	1970 (5)	4,000	KM18-22	—	2,750

CANADA

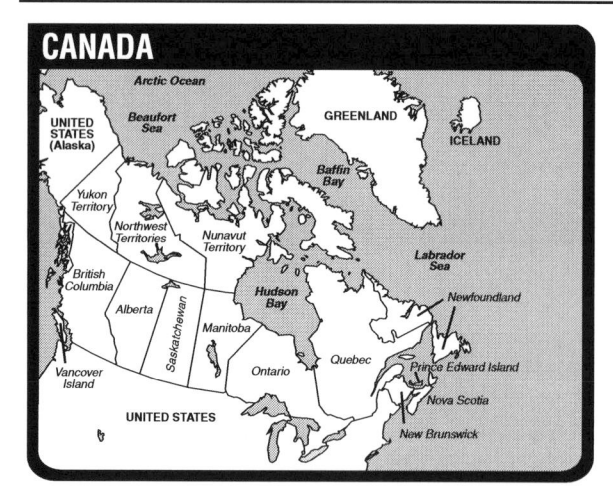

Canada is located to the north of the United States, and spans the full breadth of the northern portion of North America from Atlantic to Pacific oceans, except for the State of Alaska. It has a total area of 3,850,000 sq. mi. (9,971,550 sq. km.) and a population of 30.29 million. Capital: Ottawa.

Jacques Cartier, a French explorer, took possession of Canada for France in 1534, and for more than a century the history of Canada was that of a French colony. Samuel de Champlain helped to establish the first permanent colony in North America, in 1604 at Port Royal, Acadia – now Annapolis Royal, Nova Scotia. Four years later he founded the settlement in Quebec.

The British settled along the coast to the south while the French, motivated by a grand design, pushed into the interior. France's plan for a great American empire was to occupy the Mississippi heartland of the country, and from there to press in upon the narrow strip of English coastal settlements from the west. Inevitably, armed conflict erupted between the French and the British; consequently, Britain acquired Hudson Bay, Newfoundland and Nova Scotia from the French in 1713. British control of the rest of New France was secured in 1763, largely because of James Wolfe's great victory over Montcalm near Quebec in 1759.

During the American Revolution, Canada became a refuge for great numbers of American Royalists, most of whom settled in Ontario, thereby creating an English majority west of the Ottawa River. The ethnic imbalance contravened the effectiveness of the prevailing French type of government, and in 1791 the Constitutional act was passed by the British parliament, dividing Canada at the Ottawa River into two parts, each with its own government: Upper Canada, chiefly English and consisting of the southern section of what is now Ontario; and Lower Canada, chiefly French and consisting principally of the southern section of Quebec. Subsequent revolt by dissidents in both sections caused the British government to pass the Union Act, July 23, 1840, which united Lower and Upper Canada (as Canada East and Canada West) to form the Province of Canada, with one council and one assembly in which the two sections had equal numbers.

The union of the two provinces did not encourage political stability; the equal strength of the French and British made the task of government all but impossible. A further change was made with the passage of the British North American Act, which took effect on July 1, 1867, and established Canada as the first federal union in the British Empire. Four provinces entered the union at first: Upper Canada as Ontario, Lower Canada as Quebec, Nova Scotia and New Brunswick. The Hudson Bay Company's territories were acquired in 1869 out of which were formed the provinces of Manitoba, Saskatchewan and Alberta. British Columbia joined in 1871 and Prince Edward Island in 1873. Canada took over the Arctic Archipelago in 1895. In 1949 Newfoundland came into the confederation.

In the early years, Canada's coins were struck in England at the Royal Mint in London or at the Heaton Mint in Birmingham. Issues struck at the Royal Mint do not bear a mint mark, but those produced by Heaton carry an "H". All Canadian coins have been struck since January 2, 1908, at the Royal Canadian Mints at Ottawa and Winnipeg except for some 1968 pure nickel dimes struck at the U.S. Mint in Philadelphia, and do not bear mint marks. Ottawa's mint mark (C) does not appear on some 20th Century Newfoundland issues, however, as it does on English type sovereigns struck there from 1908 through 1918.

Canada is a member of the Commonwealth of Nations. Elizabeth II is Head of State as Queen of Canada.

RULER
British 1763-

MONETARY SYSTEM
1 Dollar = 100 Cents

CONFEDERATION

CIRCULATION COINAGE

KM# 14 SOVEREIGN Weight: 7.9881 g. Composition: 0.9170 Gold .2354 oz. AGW
Ruler: Edward VII Reverse: St. George slaying dragon, mint mark below horse's rear hooves

Date	Mintage	F-12	VF-20	XF-40	AU-50	MS-60	MS-63
1908C	636	1,250	1,850	2,350	2,600	2,850	4,000
1909C	16,273	160	200	245	285	500	1,600
1910C	28,012	BV	185	225	265	500	2,000

KM# 20 SOVEREIGN Weight: 7.9881 g. Composition: 0.9170 Gold 0.2354 oz. AGW
Ruler: George V Reverse: St. George slaying dragon, mint mark below horse's rear hooves

Date	Mintage	F-12	VF-20	XF-40	AU-50	MS-60	MS-63
1911C	256,946	—	—	BV	155	160	180
1913C	3,715	550	700	950	1,200	1,500	3,000
1914C	14,871	175	225	350	450	600	950
1916C About 20 known	—	8,000	12,500	15,750	17,750	20,000	27,500

Note: Stacks' A.G. Carter Jr. Sale 12-89 Gem BU realized $82,500

Date	Mintage	F-12	VF-20	XF-40	AU-50	MS-60	MS-63
1917C	58,845	—	—	BV	160	175	500
1918C	106,514	—	—	BV	160	175	750
1919C	135,889	—	—	BV	160	175	650

KM# 357b 2 DOLLARS Composition: Gold Ruler: Elizabeth II Subject: Nunavut
Obverse: Crowned head right Reverse: Drum dancer

Date	Mintage	MS-63	P/L	Proof
1999 Proof	10,000	—	—	175

KM# 399b 2 DOLLARS Weight: 6.3100 g. Composition: 0.9160 Gold Ruler: Elizabeth II Subject: Knowledge Obverse: Crowned head right within circle, denomination below Reverse: Polar bear and two cubs right within circle, date above

Date	Mintage	MS-63	P/L	Proof
2000 Proof	—	—	—	175

KM# 496a 2 DOLLARS Weight: 10.8414 g. Composition: 0.9250 Bi-Metallic Gold And Silver 0.3224 oz. Ruler: Elizabeth II Obverse: Head right Obv. Designer: Suanne Blunt Reverse: Polar Bear Edge: Segmented reeding Size: 28 mm.

Date	Mintage	MS-63	Proof
2004 Proof	—	—	25.00

KM# 584 2 DOLLARS Composition: Bi-Metallic Ruler: Elizabeth II Subject: 10th Anniversary of Polar Bear $2.00 Obverse: Crowned head right Reverse: Polar bear

Date	Mintage	MS-63	Proof
2006 Proof	3,000	—	385

KM# 26 5 DOLLARS Weight: 8.3592 g. Composition: 0.9000 Gold 0.2419 oz. AGW
Ruler: George V Obverse: Crowned bust left Obv. Designer: E. B. MacKennal Reverse: Arms within wreath, date and denomination below Rev. Designer: W. H. J. Blakemore

Date	Mintage	F-12	VF-20	XF-40	AU-50	MS-60	MS-63
1912	165,680	BV	160	175	200	250	550
1913	98,832	BV	160	175	200	250	600
1914	31,122	175	275	350	425	650	2,000

KM# 519 5 DOLLARS Weight: 8.3600 g. Composition: 0.9000 Gold 0.2419 oz. AGW
Ruler: Elizabeth II Obverse: Crowned head right Reverse: National arms Edge: Reeded Size: 21.6 mm.

Date	Mintage	MS-63	Proof
ND (2002) Proof	2,002	—	230

KM# 27 10 DOLLARS Weight: 16.7185 g. Composition: 0.9000 Gold 0.4838 oz. AGW
Ruler: George V Obverse: Crowned bust left Obv. Designer: E. B. MacKennal Reverse: Arms within wreath, date and denomination below Rev. Designer: W. H. J. Blakemore

Date	Mintage	F-12	VF-20	XF-40	AU-50	MS-60	MS-63
1912	74,759	BV	320	360	400	550	2,000
1913	149,232	BV	325	375	400	600	2,600
1914	140,068	BV	330	400	450	700	2,750

CANADA

KM# 520 10 DOLLARS **Weight:** 16.7200 g. **Composition:** 0.9000 Gold 0.4838 oz. AGW **Ruler:** Elizabeth II **Obverse:** Crowned head right **Reverse:** National arms **Edge:** Reeded **Size:** 26.92 mm.

Date	Mintage	MS-63	Proof
ND (2002) Proof	2,002	—	465

KM# 71 20 DOLLARS **Weight:** 18.2733 g. **Composition:** 0.9000 Gold 0.5288 oz. AGW **Ruler:** Elizabeth II **Subject:** Centennial **Obverse:** Crowned head right **Reverse:** Crowned and supported arms **Edge:** Reeded **Size:** 27.05 mm.

Date	Mintage	MS-63	Proof
1967 Proof	337,688	—	350

KM# 566 50 DOLLARS **Composition:** Gold **Ruler:** Elizabeth II **Subject:** WWII **Obverse:** Head right **Reverse:** Large V and three portraits

Date	Mintage	MS-63	Proof
2005 Proof	—	—	275

KM# 567 75 DOLLARS **Composition:** 0.9999 Gold **Ruler:** Elizabeth II **Subject:** Pope John Paul II **Obverse:** Head right

Date	Mintage	MS-63	Proof
2005 Proof	—	—	400

KM# 115 100 DOLLARS **Weight:** 13.3375 g. **Composition:** 0.5830 Gold 0.2500 oz. AGW **Ruler:** Elizabeth II **Subject:** 1976 Montreal Olympics **Obverse:** Young bust right, maple leaf below, date at right, beaded borders **Reverse:** Past and present Olympic figures, denomination at right **Rev. Designer:** Dora dePedery-Hunt **Size:** 27 mm.

Date	Mintage	MS-63	Proof
1976	650,000	175	—

KM# 116 100 DOLLARS **Weight:** 16.9655 g. **Composition:** 0.9170 Gold 0.5000 oz. AGW **Ruler:** Elizabeth II **Subject:** 1976 Montreal Olympics **Obverse:** Young bust right, maple leaf below, date at right, plain borders **Reverse:** Past and present Olympic figures, denomination at right **Rev. Designer:** Dora dePedery-Hunt **Size:** 25 mm.

Date	Mintage	MS-63	Proof
1976 Proof	337,342	—	340

KM# 119 100 DOLLARS **Weight:** 16.9655 g. **Composition:** 0.9170 Gold 0.5000 oz. AGW **Ruler:** Elizabeth II **Subject:** Queen's silver jubilee **Obverse:** Young bust right **Reverse:** Bouquet of provincial flowers, denomination below **Rev. Designer:** Raymond Lee

Date	Mintage	MS-63	Proof
ND(1977) Proof	180,396	—	340

KM# 122 100 DOLLARS **Weight:** 16.9655 g. **Composition:** 0.9170 Gold 0.5000 oz. AGW **Ruler:** Elizabeth II **Subject:** Canadian unification **Obverse:** Young bust right, denomination at left, date upper right **Reverse:** Geese (representing the provinces) in flight formation **Rev. Designer:** Roger Savage

Date	Mintage	MS-63	Proof
1978 Proof	200,000	—	345

KM# 126 100 DOLLARS **Weight:** 16.9655 g. **Composition:** 0.9170 Gold 0.5000 oz. AGW **Ruler:** Elizabeth II **Subject:** International Year of the Child **Obverse:** Young bust right **Reverse:** Children with hands joined divide denomination and date **Rev. Designer:** Carola Tietz

Date	Mintage	MS-63	Proof
1979 Proof	250,000	—	340

KM# 129 100 DOLLARS **Weight:** 16.9655 g. **Composition:** 0.9170 Gold 0.5000 oz. AGW **Ruler:** Elizabeth II **Subject:** Arctic Territories **Obverse:** Young bust right, denomination at left, date above right **Reverse:** Kayaker **Rev. Designer:** Arnaldo Marchetti

Date	Mintage	MS-63	Proof
1980 Proof	300,000	—	340

KM# 131 100 DOLLARS **Weight:** 16.9655 g. **Composition:** 0.9170 Gold 0.5000 oz. AGW **Ruler:** Elizabeth II **Subject:** National anthem **Obverse:** Young bust right, denomination at left, date above right **Reverse:** Music score on map **Rev. Designer:** Roger Savage

Date	Mintage	MS-63	Proof
1981 Proof	102,000	—	340

KM# 137 100 DOLLARS **Weight:** 16.9655 g. **Composition:** 0.9170 Gold 0.5000 oz. AGW **Ruler:** Elizabeth II **Subject:** New Constitution **Obverse:** Young bust right, denomination at left **Reverse:** Open book, maple leaf on right page, date below **Rev. Designer:** Friedrich Peter

Date	Mintage	MS-63	Proof
1982 Proof	121,708	—	340

KM# 139 100 DOLLARS **Weight:** 16.9655 g. **Composition:** 0.9170 Gold 0.5000 oz. AGW **Ruler:** Elizabeth II **Subject:** 400th Anniversary of St. John's, Newfoundland **Obverse:** Young bust right **Reverse:** Anchor divides building and ship, denomination below, dates above **Rev. Designer:** John Jaciw

90 CANADA

Date	Mintage	MS-63	Proof
ND(1983) Proof	83,128	—	340

KM# 142 100 DOLLARS Weight: 16.9655 g. Composition: 0.9170 Gold 0.5000 oz. AGW Ruler: Elizabeth II Subject: Jacques Cartier Obverse: Young bust right Reverse: Cartier head on right facing left, ship on left, date lower right, denomination above Rev. Designer: Carola Tietz

Date	Mintage	MS-63	Proof
ND(1984) Proof	67,662	—	340

KM# 144 100 DOLLARS Weight: 16.9655 g. Composition: 0.9170 Gold 0.5000 oz. AGW Ruler: Elizabeth II Subject: National Parks Obverse: Young bust right Reverse: Bighorn sheep, denomination divides dates below Rev. Designer: Hector Greville

Date	Mintage	MS-63	Proof
ND(1985) Proof	61,332	—	340

KM# 152 100 DOLLARS Weight: 16.9655 g. Composition: 0.9170 Gold 0.5000 oz. AGW Ruler: Elizabeth II Subject: Peace Obverse: Young bust right Reverse: Maple leaves and letters intertwined, date at right, denomination below Rev. Designer: Dora dePedery-Hunt

Date	Mintage	MS-63	Proof
1986 Proof	76,409	—	340

KM# 158 100 DOLLARS Weight: 13.3375 g. Composition: 0.5830 Gold 0.2500 oz. AGW Ruler: Elizabeth II Subject: 1988 Calgary Olympics Obverse: Young bust right, maple leaf below, date at right Reverse: Torch and logo, denomination below Rev. Designer: Friedrich Peter Edge: Lettered in English and French

Date	Mintage	MS-63	Proof
1987 Proof	142,750	—	175
Note: lettered edge			
1987 Proof	Inc. above	—	350
Note: plain edge			

KM# 162 100 DOLLARS Weight: 13.3375 g. Composition: 0.5830 Gold 0.2500 oz. AGW Ruler: Elizabeth II Subject: Bowhead Whales, balaera mysticetus Reverse: Whales left, date below, within circle, denomination below Rev. Designer: Robert R. Carmichael

Date	Mintage	MS-63	Proof
1988 Proof	52,594	—	180

KM# 169 100 DOLLARS Weight: 13.3375 g. Composition: 0.5830 Gold 0.2500 oz. AGW Ruler: Elizabeth II Subject: Sainte-Marie Obverse: Young bust right Reverse: Huron Indian, Missionary and Mission building, denomination below, dates above Rev. Designer: D. J. Craig

Date	Mintage	MS-63	Proof
ND(1989) Proof	59,657	—	175

KM# 171 100 DOLLARS Weight: 13.3375 g. Composition: 0.5830 Gold 0.2500 oz. AGW Ruler: Elizabeth II Subject: International Literacy Year Obverse: Crowned head right, date below Reverse: Woman with children, denomination below Rev. Designer: John Mardon

Date	Mintage	MS-63	Proof
1990 Proof	49,940	—	175

KM# 180 100 DOLLARS Weight: 13.3375 g. Composition: 0.5830 Gold 0.2500 oz. AGW Ruler: Elizabeth II Subject: S.S. Empress of India Obverse: Crowned head right, date below Reverse: Ship,"SS Empress", denomination below Rev. Designer: Karsten Smith

Date	Mintage	MS-63	Proof
1991 Proof	33,966	—	175

KM# 211 100 DOLLARS Weight: 13.3375 g. Composition: 0.5830 Gold 0.2500 oz. AGW Ruler: Elizabeth II Subject: Montreal Obverse: Crowned head right, date below Reverse: Half figure in foreground with paper, buildings in back, denomination below Rev. Designer: Stewart Sherwood

Date	Mintage	MS-63	Proof
1992 Proof	28,162	—	175

KM# 245 100 DOLLARS Weight: 13.3375 g. Composition: 0.5830 Gold 0.2500 oz. AGW Ruler: Elizabeth II Subject: Antique Automobiles Obverse: Crowned head right, date below Reverse: German Bene Victoria; Simmonds Steam Carriage; French Panhard-Levassor's Daimler; American Duryea; Canadian Featherston Haugh in center, denomination below Rev. Designer: John Mardon

Date	Mintage	MS-63	Proof
1993 Proof	25,971	—	180

KM# 249 100 DOLLARS Weight: 13.3375 g. Composition: 0.5830 Gold 0.2500 oz. AGW Ruler: Elizabeth II Subject: World War II Home Front Obverse: Crowned head right, date below Reverse: Kneeling figure working on plane, denomination below Rev. Designer: Paraskeva Clark

Date	Mintage	MS-63	Proof
1994 Proof	16,201	—	170

CANADA

KM# 260 100 DOLLARS Weight: 13.3375 g. Composition: 0.5830 Gold 0.2500 oz.
AGW **Ruler:** Elizabeth II **Subject:** Louisbourg **Obverse:** Crowned head right, date below
Reverse: Ship and buildings, dates and denomination above **Rev. Designer:** Lewis Parker

Date	Mintage	MS-63	Proof
1995 Proof	16,916	—	180

KM# 273 100 DOLLARS Weight: 13.3375 g. Composition: 0.5830 Gold 0.2500 oz.
AGW **Ruler:** Elizabeth II **Subject:** Klondike Gold Rush Centennial **Obverse:** Crowned head right, date below **Reverse:** Scene of Kate Carmack panning for gold, dates above, denomination lower left **Rev. Designer:** John Mantha

Date	Mintage	MS-63	Proof
ND(1996) Proof	17,973	—	180

KM# 287 100 DOLLARS Weight: 13.3375 g. Composition: 0.5830 Gold 0.2500 oz.
AGW **Ruler:** Elizabeth II **Subject:** Alexander Graham Bell **Obverse:** Crowned head right, date below **Reverse:** A. G. Bell head right, globe and telephone, denomination upper right **Rev. Designer:** Donald H. Carley

Date	Mintage	MS-63	Proof
1997 Proof	14,775	—	180

KM# 307 100 DOLLARS Weight: 13.3375 g. Composition: 0.5830 Gold 0.2500 oz.
AGW **Ruler:** Elizabeth II **Subject:** Discovery of Insulin **Obverse:** Crowned head right, date below
Reverse: Nobel prize award figurine, dates at left, denomination at right **Rev. Designer:** Robert R. Carmichael

Date	Mintage	MS-63	Proof
1998 Proof	11,220	—	180

KM# 341 100 DOLLARS Weight: 13.3375 g. Composition: 0.5830 Gold 0.2500 oz.
AGW **Ruler:** Elizabeth II **Subject:** 50th Anniversary Newfoundland Unity With Canada **Obverse:** Crowned head right, date below **Reverse:** Two designs at front, mountains in back, denomination below **Rev. Designer:** Jackie Gale-Vaillancourt

Date	Mintage	MS-63	Proof
1999 Proof	10,242	—	190

KM# 402 100 DOLLARS Weight: 13.3375 g. Composition: 0.5830 Gold 0.2500 oz.
AGW **Ruler:** Elizabeth II **Subject:** McClure's Arctic expedition **Obverse:** Crowned head right, date below **Reverse:** Six men pulling supply sled to an icebound ship, denomination below
Rev. Designer: John Mardon **Edge:** Reeded **Size:** 27 mm.

Date	Mintage	MS-63	Proof
2000 Proof	9,767	—	190

KM# 416 100 DOLLARS Weight: 13.3375 g. Composition: 0.5830 Gold 0.2500 oz.
AGW **Ruler:** Elizabeth II **Subject:** Library of Parliament **Obverse:** Crowned head right
Obv. Designer: Dora dePedery-Hunt **Reverse:** Statue in domed building **Rev. Designer:** Robert R. Carmichael **Edge:** Reeded **Size:** 27 mm.

Date	Mintage	MS-63	Proof
2001 Proof	8,080	—	175

KM# 452 100 DOLLARS Weight: 13.3375 g. Composition: 0.5830 Gold 0.2500 oz.
AGW **Ruler:** Elizabeth II **Subject:** Discovery of Oil in Alberta **Obverse:** Crowned head right
Reverse: Oil well with black oil spill on ground **Rev. Designer:** John Marden **Edge:** Reeded
Size: 27 mm.

Date	Mintage	MS-63	Proof
2002 Proof	9,992	—	250

KM# 486 100 DOLLARS Weight: 13.3375 g. Composition: 0.5830 Gold .2500 oz.
AGW **Ruler:** Elizabeth II **Subject:** 100th Anniversary of the Discovery of Marquis Wheat
Obverse: Head right

Date	Mintage	MS-63	Proof
2003 Proof	10,000	—	200

KM# 528 100 DOLLARS Weight: 12.0000 g. Composition: 0.5830 Gold **Ruler:**
Elizabeth II **Subject:** St. Lawrence Seaway, 50th Anniversary **Obverse:** Head right

Date	Mintage	MS-63	Proof
2004 Proof	—	—	200

KM# 616 100 DOLLARS Weight: 12.0000 g. Composition: 0.5833 Gold **Ruler:**
Elizabeth II **Subject:** Supreme Court **Obverse:** Head right **Reverse:** Draped figure with sword

Date	Mintage	MS-63	Proof
2005 Proof	—	—	225

KM# 591 100 DOLLARS Weight: 12.0000 g. Composition: 0.5833 Gold **Ruler:**
Elizabeth II **Subject:** 75th Anniversary, Hockey Classic between Royal Military College and U.S. Military Academy **Obverse:** Head right

Date	Mintage	MS-63	Proof
2006 Proof	—	—	225

KM# 388 150 DOLLARS Weight: 13.6100 g. Composition: 0.7500 Gold .3282 oz.
AGW **Ruler:** Elizabeth II **Subject:** Year of the Dragon **Obverse:** Crowned head right
Rev. Designer: Harvey Chan

Date	Mintage	MS-63	Proof
2000 Proof	8,851	—	650

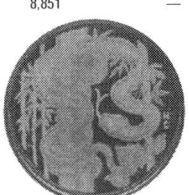

KM# 417 150 DOLLARS Weight: 13.6100 g. Composition: 0.7500 Gold .3282 oz.
AGW **Ruler:** Elizabeth II **Subject:** Year of the Snake **Obverse:** Crowned head right
Obv. Designer: Dora dePedery-Hunt **Reverse:** Multicolor snake hologram **Edge:** Reeded **Size:** 28 mm.

Date	Mintage	MS-63	Proof
2001 Proof	6,571	—	285

KM# 604 150 DOLLARS Weight: 13.6100 g. Composition: 0.7500 Gold .3282 oz.
AGW **Ruler:** Elizabeth II **Obverse:** Head right **Reverse:** Year of the Horse, hologram

Date	Mintage	MS-63	Proof
2002 Proof	6,843	—	320

KM# 487 150 DOLLARS Weight: 13.6100 g. Composition: 0.7500 Gold .3282 oz.
AGW **Ruler:** Elizabeth II **Subject:** Year of the Ram **Obverse:** Crowned head right **Reverse:** Stylized ram left **Rev. Designer:** Harvey Chan

Date	Mintage	MS-63	Proof
2003 Proof	6,888	—	325

KM# 614 150 DOLLARS Weight: 13.6100 g. Composition: 0.7500 Gold .3282 oz.
AGW **Ruler:** Elizabeth II **Obverse:** Head right **Reverse:** Year of the Monkey, hologram

Date	Mintage	MS-63	Proof
2004 Proof	—	—	345

KM# 568 150 DOLLARS Weight: 13.6100 g. Composition: 0.7500 Gold .3282 oz.
AGW **Ruler:** Elizabeth II **Subject:** Year of the Rooster **Obverse:** Head right **Reverse:** Rooster left

Date	Mintage	MS-63	Proof
2005 Proof	—	—	350

KM# 592 150 DOLLARS Weight: 13.6100 g. Composition: 0.7500 Gold .3282 oz.
AGW **Ruler:** Elizabeth II **Subject:** Year of the Dog, hologram **Obverse:** Head right **Reverse:** Stylized dog left

Date	Mintage	MS-63	Proof
2006 Proof	4,888	—	350

92 CANADA

KM# 217 175 DOLLARS Weight: 16.9700 g. Composition: 0.9170 Gold 0.5000 oz. AGW Ruler: Elizabeth II Subject: 1992 Olympics Obverse: Crowned head right, date at left, denomination below Reverse: Passing the torch Rev. Designer: Stewart Sherwood Edge: Lettered

Date	Mintage	MS-63	Proof
1992 Proof	22,092	—	340

KM# 178 200 DOLLARS Weight: 17.1350 g. Composition: 0.9170 Gold 0.5115 oz. AGW Ruler: Elizabeth II Subject: Canadian flag silver jubilee Obverse: Crowned head right, date below Reverse: People with flag, denomination above Rev. Designer: Stewart Sherwood Size: 29 mm.

Date	Mintage	MS-63	Proof
1990 Proof	20,980	—	350

KM# 202 200 DOLLARS Weight: 17.1350 g. Composition: 0.9170 Gold 0.5115 oz. AGW Ruler: Elizabeth II Subject: Hockey Obverse: Crowned head right Reverse: Hockey players, denomination above Rev. Designer: Stewart Sherwood Size: 29 mm.

Date	Mintage	MS-63	Proof
1991 Proof	10,215	—	350

KM# 230 200 DOLLARS Weight: 17.1350 g. Composition: 0.9170 Gold 0.5115 oz. AGW Ruler: Elizabeth II Subject: Niagara Falls Obverse: Crowned head right Reverse: Niagara Falls, denomination above Rev. Designer: John Mardon Size: 29 mm.

Date	Mintage	MS-63	Proof
1992 Proof	9,465	—	350

KM# 244 200 DOLLARS Weight: 17.1350 g. Composition: 0.9170 Gold 0.5115 oz. AGW Ruler: Elizabeth II Subject: Mounted police Obverse: Crowned head right, date below Reverse: Mountie with children, denomination above Rev. Designer: Stewart Sherwood Size: 29 mm.

Date	Mintage	MS-63	Proof
1993 Proof	10,807	—	350

KM# 250 200 DOLLARS Weight: 17.1350 g. Composition: 0.9170 Gold 0.5115 oz. AGW Ruler: Elizabeth II Subject: Interpretation of 1908 novel by Lucy Maud Montgomery, 1874-1942, Anne of Green Gables Obverse: Crowned head right Reverse: Figure sitting in window, denomination above Rev. Designer: Phoebe Gilman Size: 29 mm.

Date	Mintage	MS-63	Proof
1994 Proof	10,655	—	350

KM# 265 200 DOLLARS Weight: 17.1350 g. Composition: 0.9170 Gold 0.5115 oz. AGW Ruler: Elizabeth II Subject: Maple-syrup production Obverse: Crowned head right, date below Reverse: Maple syrup making, denomination at right Rev. Designer: J. D. Mantha Size: 29 mm.

Date	Mintage	MS-63	Proof
1995 Proof	6,579	—	350

KM# 275 200 DOLLARS Weight: 17.1350 g. Composition: 0.9170 Gold 0.5115 oz. AGW Ruler: Elizabeth II Subject: Transcontinental Canadian Railway Obverse: Crowned head right, date below Reverse: Train going through mountains, denomination below Rev. Designer: Suzanne Duranceau Size: 29 mm.

Date	Mintage	MS-63	Proof
1996 Proof	8,047	—	350

KM# 288 200 DOLLARS Weight: 17.1350 g. Composition: 0.9170 Gold 0.5115 oz. AGW Ruler: Elizabeth II Subject: Haida mask Obverse: Crowned head right, date below Reverse: Haida mask Rev. Designer: Robert Davidson Size: 29 mm.

Date	Mintage	MS-63	Proof
1997 Proof	11,610	—	450

KM# 317 200 DOLLARS Weight: 17.1350 g. Composition: 0.9170 Gold 0.5115 oz. AGW Ruler: Elizabeth II Subject: Legendary white buffalo Obverse: Crowned head right, date below Reverse: Buffalo Rev. Designer: Alex Janvier Size: 29 mm.

Date	Mintage	MS-63	Proof
1998 Proof	7,149	—	350

CANADA 93

KM# 358 200 DOLLARS Weight: 17.1350 g. Composition: 0.9170 Gold 0.5115 oz. AGW Ruler: Elizabeth II Subject: Mikmaq butterfly Obverse: Crowned head right Reverse: Butterfly within design Rev. Designer: Alan Syliboy Size: 29 mm.

Date	Mintage	MS-63	Proof
1999 Proof	6,510	—	350

KM# 403 200 DOLLARS Weight: 17.1350 g. Composition: 0.9170 Gold 0.5115 oz. AGW Ruler: Elizabeth II Subject: Motherhood Obverse: Crowned head right, date above, denomination at right Reverse: Inuit mother with infant Rev. Designer: Germaine Arnaktauyak Edge: Reeded Size: 29 mm.

Date	Mintage	MS-63	Proof
2000 Proof	6,284	—	350

KM# 418 200 DOLLARS Weight: 17.1350 g. Composition: 0.9170 Gold 0.5115 oz. AGW Ruler: Elizabeth II Subject: Cornelius D. Krieghoff's "The Habitant farm" Obverse: Queens head right Edge: Reeded Size: 29 mm.

Date	Mintage	MS-63	Proof
2001 Proof	5,406	—	350

KM# 466 200 DOLLARS Weight: 17.1350 g. Composition: 0.9170 Gold .5115 oz. AGW Ruler: Elizabeth II Subject: Thomas Thompson "The Jack Pine" (1916-17) Obverse: Crowned head right Size: 29 mm.

Date	Mintage	MS-63	Proof
2002 Proof	5,264	—	350

KM# 488 200 DOLLARS Weight: 17.1350 g. Composition: 0.9170 Gold .5115 oz. AGW Ruler: Elizabeth II Subject: Fitzgerald's "Houses" (1929) Obverse: Crowned head right Reverse: House with trees

Date	Mintage	MS-63	Proof
2003 Proof	10,000	—	350

KM# 516 200 DOLLARS Weight: 16.0000 g. Composition: 0.9170 Gold 0.4716 oz. AGW Ruler: Elizabeth II Subject: "Fragments" Obverse: Crowned head right Reverse: Fragmented face Edge: Reeded Size: 29 mm.

Date	Mintage	MS-63	Proof
2004 Proof	—	—	350

KM# 569 200 DOLLARS Weight: 16.0000 g. Composition: 0.9170 Gold Ruler: Elizabeth II Subject: Fur traders Obverse: Head right Reverse: Men in canoe riding wave

Date	Mintage	MS-63	Proof
2005 Proof	—	—	400

KM# 593 200 DOLLARS Weight: 16.0000 g. Composition: 0.9170 Gold Ruler: Elizabeth II Subject: 130th Anniversary, Supreme Court Obverse: Head right

Date	Mintage	MS-63	Proof
2006 Proof	—	—	420

KM# 594 200 DOLLARS Weight: 16.0000 g. Composition: 0.9170 Gold Ruler: Elizabeth II Subject: Timber trade Obverse: Head right Reverse: Lumberjacks felling tree

Date	Mintage	MS-63	Proof
2006 Proof	—	—	400

KM# 501 300 DOLLARS Weight: 60.0000 g. Composition: Bi-Metallic Gold And Silver Ruler: Elizabeth II Obverse: Triple cameo portraits of Queen Elizabeth II by Gillick, Machin and de Pedery-Hunt, each in 14K gold, rose in center Reverse: Dates "1952-2002" and denomination in legend, rose in center Size: 50 mm. Note: Housed in anodized gold-colored aluminum box with cherrywood stained siding

Date	Mintage	MS-63	Proof
ND(2002) Proof	993	—	1,000

KM# 517 300 DOLLARS Weight: 60.0000 g. Composition: 0.5833 Gold 1.1252 oz. AGW Ruler: Elizabeth II Obverse: Four coinage portraits of Elizabeth II Reverse: Canadian arms above value Edge: Plain Size: 50 mm.

Date	Mintage	MS-63	Proof
2004 Proof	1,000	—	1,050

KM# 570 300 DOLLARS Weight: 60.0000 g. Composition: 0.5833 Gold 1.1252 oz. AGW Ruler: Elizabeth II Subject: Standard Time Obverse: Head right Reverse: Roman numeral clock with world inside

Date	Mintage	MS-63	Proof
2005 Proof	—	—	900

KM# 596 300 DOLLARS Weight: 60.0000 g. Composition: 0.5833 Gold 1.1252 oz. AGW Ruler: Elizabeth II Subject: Shinplaster Obverse: Head right Reverse: Britannia bust, spear over shoulder

Date	Mintage	MS-63	Proof
2005 Proof	—	—	1,050

KM# 600 300 DOLLARS Weight: 60.0000 g. Composition: 0.5833 Gold 1.1252 oz. AGW Ruler: Elizabeth II Subject: Welcome Figure Totem Pole Obverse: Head right Reverse: Men with totem pole

Date	Mintage	MS-63	Proof
2005 Proof	—	—	900

KM# 595 300 DOLLARS Weight: 60.0000 g. Composition: 0.5833 Gold 1.1252 oz. AGW Ruler: Elizabeth II Subject: The Shinplaster Obverse: Head right Reverse: Seated Britannia with shield

Date	Mintage	MS-63	Proof
2006 Proof	—	—	1,050

KM# 308 350 DOLLARS Weight: 38.0500 g. Composition: 0.9999 Gold 1.2233 oz. AGW Ruler: Elizabeth II Subject: Flowers of Canada's Coat of Arms Obverse: Crowned head right, date behind, denomination at bottom Reverse: Flowers Rev. Designer: Pierre Leduc

Date	Mintage	MS-63	Proof
1998 Proof	664	—	875

KM# 370 350 DOLLARS Weight: 38.0500 g. Composition: 0.9999 Gold 1.2233 oz. AGW Ruler: Elizabeth II Reverse: Lady's slipper Rev. Designer: Henry Purdy

Date	Mintage	MS-63	Proof
1999 Proof	1,990	—	845

KM# 404 350 DOLLARS Weight: 38.0500 g. Composition: 0.9999 Gold 1.2233 oz. AGW Ruler: Elizabeth II Obverse: Crowned head right Reverse: Three Pacific Dogwood flowers Rev. Designer: Caren Heine Edge: Reeded Size: 34 mm.

Date	Mintage	MS-63	Proof
2000 Proof	1,506	—	845

KM# 433 350 DOLLARS Weight: 38.0500 g. Composition: 0.9999 Gold 1.2233 oz. AGW Ruler: Elizabeth II Subject: The Mayflower Flower Obverse: Crowned head right Reverse: Two flowers Rev. Designer: Bonnie Ross Edge: Reeded Size: 34 mm.

Date	Mintage	MS-63	Proof
2001 Proof	—	—	850

KM# 502 350 DOLLARS Weight: 38.0500 g. Composition: 0.9999 Gold 1.2233 oz. AGW Ruler: Elizabeth II Subject: The Wild Rose Obverse: Crowned head right Obv. Designer: Dora de Pedery-Hunt Reverse: Wild rose plant Rev. Designer: Dr. Andreas Kare Hellum Size: 34 mm.

Date	Mintage	MS-63	Proof
2002 Proof	1,803	—	900

KM# 504 350 DOLLARS Weight: 38.0500 g. Composition: 0.9999 Gold 1.2233 oz. AGW Ruler: Elizabeth II Subject: The White Trillium Obverse: Crowned head right Obv. Designer: Dora de Pedery-Hunt Reverse: White Trillium Size: 34 mm.

Date	Mintage	MS-63	Proof
2003 Proof	3,003	—	900

KM# 601 350 DOLLARS Weight: 38.0500 g. Composition: 0.9999 Gold 1.2233 oz. AGW Ruler: Elizabeth II Subject: Western Red Lilly Obverse: Head right Reverse: Western Red Lilies

Date	Mintage	MS-63	Proof
2005 Proof	—	—	900

94 CANADA

KM# 626 350 DOLLARS Weight: 38.0500 g. **Composition:** 0.9999 Gold 1.2232 oz. AGW **Ruler:** Elizabeth II **Subject:** Iris Vericolor **Obverse:** Crowned head right **Reverse:** Iris **Size:** 34 mm.

Date	Mintage	MS-63	Proof
2006 Proof	—	—	950

GOLD BULLION COINAGE

KM# 542 50 CENTS Composition: 0.9999 Gold .0425 oz. AGW **Ruler:** Elizabeth II **Subject:** Voyageurs **Obverse:** Head right

Date	Mintage	MS-63	Proof
2005 Proof	—	—	65.00

KM# 238 DOLLAR Weight: 1.5551 g. **Composition:** 0.9999 Gold 0.05 oz. AGW **Ruler:** Elizabeth II **Obverse:** Crowned head right, denomination and date below **Reverse:** Maple leaf flanked by 9999

Date	Mintage	MS-63	Proof
1993	37,080	BV+37%	—
1994	78,860	BV+37%	—
1995	85,920	BV+37%	—
1996	56,520	BV+37%	—
1997	59,720	BV+37%	—
1998	44,260	BV+37%	—
1999	—	BV+46%	—

Note: Maple leaf with oval

KM# 365 DOLLAR Weight: 1.5551 g. **Composition:** 0.9999 Gold 0.05 oz. AGW **Ruler:** Elizabeth II **Obverse:** Crowned head right **Reverse:** Maple leaf hologram

Date	Mintage	MS-63	Proof
1999	500	90.00	—

KM# 438 DOLLAR Weight: 1.5810 g. **Composition:** 0.9990 Gold 0.0508 oz. AGW **Ruler:** Elizabeth II **Subject:** Holographic Maple Leaves **Obverse:** Crowned head right **Reverse:** Three maple leaves multicolor hologram **Edge:** Reeded. **Size:** 14.1 mm.

Date	Mintage	MS-63	Proof
2001 in sets only	600	75.00	—

KM# 256 2 DOLLARS Weight: 2.0735 g. **Composition:** 0.9999 Gold 0.0666 oz. AGW **Ruler:** Elizabeth II **Obverse:** Crowned head right, denomination and date below **Reverse:** Maple leaf flanked by 9999

Date	Mintage	MS-63	Proof
1994	5,493	85.00	—

KM# 135 5 DOLLARS Weight: 3.1200 g. **Composition:** 0.9999 Gold .1000 oz. AGW **Ruler:** Elizabeth II **Obverse:** Young bust right, date and denomination below **Obv. Designer:** Arnold Machin **Reverse:** Maple leaf flanked by 9999

Date	Mintage	MS-63	Proof
1982	246,000	BV+14%	—
1983	304,000	BV+14%	—
1984	262,000	BV+14%	—
1985	398,000	BV+14%	—
1986	529,516	BV+14%	—
1987	459,000	BV+14%	—
1988	506,500	BV+14%	—
1989	539,000	BV+14%	—
1989 Proof	16,992	—	80.00

KM# 188 5 DOLLARS Weight: 3.1200 g. **Composition:** 0.9999 Gold 0.1000 oz. AGW **Ruler:** Elizabeth II **Obverse:** Elizabeth II effigy **Obv. Designer:** Dora dePedery-Hunt **Reverse:** Maple leaf

Date	Mintage	MS-63	Proof
1990	476,000	BV+14%	—
1991	322,000	BV+14%	—
1992	384,000	BV+14%	—
1993	248,630	BV+14%	—
1994	313,150	BV+14%	—
1995	294,890	BV+14%	—
1996	179,220	BV+14%	—
1997	188,540	BV+14%	—
1998	301,940	BV+14%	—
1999	—	BV+19%	—

Note: Maple leaf with oval "20 Years ANS" privy mark

KM# 366 5 DOLLARS Weight: 3.1200 g. **Composition:** 0.9999 Gold 0.1000 oz. AGW **Ruler:** Elizabeth II **Reverse:** Maple leaf hologram

Date	Mintage	MS-63	Proof
1999	500	160	—

KM# 439 5 DOLLARS Weight: 3.1310 g. **Composition:** 0.9999 Gold 0.1007 oz. AGW **Ruler:** Elizabeth II **Subject:** Holographic Maple Leaves **Obverse:** Crowned head right **Reverse:** Three maple leaves multicolor hologram **Edge:** Reeded **Size:** 16 mm.

Date	Mintage	MS-63	Proof
2001 in sets only	600	150	—

KM# 136 10 DOLLARS Weight: 7.7850 g. **Composition:** 0.9999 Gold 0.2500 oz. AGW **Ruler:** Elizabeth II **Obverse:** Young bust right, date and denomination below **Obv. Designer:** Arnold Machin **Reverse:** Maple leaf flanked by 9999

Date	Mintage	MS-63	Proof
1982	184,000	BV+10%	—
1983	308,800	BV+10%	—
1984	242,400	BV+10%	—
1985	620,000	BV+10%	—
1986	915,200	BV+10%	—
1987	376,000	BV+10%	—
1988	436,000	BV+10%	—
1989	328,800	BV+10%	—
1989 Proof	6,998	—	185

KM# 189 10 DOLLARS Weight: 7.7850 g. **Composition:** 0.9999 Gold 0.2500 oz. AGW **Ruler:** Elizabeth II **Obverse:** Crowned head right, date and denomination below **Obv. Designer:** Dora dePedery-Hunt **Reverse:** Maple leaf flanked by 9999

Date	Mintage	MS-63	Proof
1990	253,600	BV+10%	—
1991	166,400	BV+10%	—
1992	179,600	BV+10%	—
1993	158,452	BV+10%	—
1994	148,792	BV+10%	—
1995	127,596	BV+10%	—
1996	89,148	BV+10%	—
1997	98,104	BV+10%	—
1998	85,472	BV+10%	—
1999	—	BV+15%	—

Note: Maple leaf with oval "20 Years ANS" privy mark

KM# 367 10 DOLLARS Weight: 7.7850 g. **Composition:** 0.9999 Gold 0.2500 oz. AGW **Ruler:** Elizabeth II **Reverse:** Maple leaf hologram

Date	Mintage	MS-63	Proof
1999	—	210	—

KM# 440 10 DOLLARS Weight: 7.7970 g. **Composition:** 0.9999 Gold 0.2507 oz. AGW **Ruler:** Elizabeth II **Subject:** Holographic Maples Leaves **Obverse:** Crowned head right **Reverse:** Three maple leaves multicolor hologram **Edge:** Reeded **Size:** 20 mm.

Date	Mintage	MS-63	Proof
2001	15,000	180	—

KM# 153 20 DOLLARS Weight: 15.5515 g. **Composition:** 0.9999 Gold 0.5000 oz. AGW **Ruler:** Elizabeth II **Obverse:** Young bust right, date and denomination below **Obv. Designer:** Arnold Machin **Reverse:** Maple leaf flanked by 9999 **Size:** 32 mm.

Date	Mintage	MS-63	Proof
1986	529,200	BV+7%	—
1987	332,800	BV+7%	—
1988	538,400	BV+7%	—
1989	259,200	BV+7%	—
1989 Proof	6,998	—	360

KM# 190 20 DOLLARS Weight: 15.5515 g. **Composition:** 0.9999 Gold 0.5000 oz. AGW **Ruler:** Elizabeth II **Obverse:** Crowned head right, date and denomination below **Obv. Designer:** Dora dePedery-Hunt **Reverse:** Maple leaf flanked by 9999

Date	Mintage	MS-63	Proof
1990	174,400	BV+7%	—
1991	96,200	BV+7%	—

CANADA

Date	Mintage	MS-63	Proof
1992	108,000	BV+7%	—
1993	99,492	BV+7%	—
1994	104,766	BV+7%	—
1995	103,162	BV+7%	—
1996	66,246	BV+7%	—
1997	63,354	BV+7%	—
1998	65,366	BV+7%	—
1999	—	BV+12%	—

Note: Maple leaf with oval "20 Years ANS" privy mark

KM# 368 20 DOLLARS **Weight:** 15.5515 g. **Composition:** 0.9999 Gold 0.5000 oz. AGW **Ruler:** Elizabeth II **Reverse:** Maple leaf hologram

Date	Mintage	MS-63	Proof
1999	500	700	—

KM# 441 20 DOLLARS **Weight:** 15.5840 g. **Composition:** 0.9999 Gold 0.501 oz. AGW **Ruler:** Elizabeth II **Subject:** Holographic Maples Leaves **Obverse:** Crowned head right **Reverse:** Three maple leaves multicolor hologram **Edge:** Reeded **Size:** 25 mm.

Date	Mintage	MS-63	Proof
2001 in sets only	600	675	—

KM# 125.1 50 DOLLARS **Weight:** 31.1030 g. **Composition:** 0.9990 Gold 1.0000 oz. AGW **Ruler:** Elizabeth II **Obverse:** Young bust right, denomination and date below **Reverse:** Maple leaf flanked by .999

Date	Mintage	MS-63	Proof
1979	1,000,000	BV+4%	—
1980	1,251,500	BV+4%	—
1981	863,000	BV+4%	—
1982	883,000	BV+4%	—

KM# 125.2 50 DOLLARS **Weight:** 31.1030 g. **Composition:** 0.9999 Gold 1.0000 oz. AGW **Ruler:** Elizabeth II **Obverse:** Young bust right, date and denomination below **Reverse:** Maple leaf flanked by .9999

Date	Mintage	MS-63	Proof
1983	843,000	BV+4%	—
1984	1,067,500	BV+4%	—
1985	1,908,000	BV+4%	—
1986	779,115	BV+4%	—
1987	978,000	BV+4%	—
1988	826,500	BV+4%	—
1989	856,000	BV+4%	—
1989 Proof	17,781	—	685

KM# 191 50 DOLLARS **Weight:** 31.1030 g. **Composition:** 0.9999 Gold 1.000 oz. AGW **Ruler:** Elizabeth II **Obverse:** Crowned head right, date and denomination below **Obv. Designer:** Dora dePedery-Hunt **Reverse:** Maple leaf flanked by .9999

Date	Mintage	MS-63	Proof
1990	815,000	BV+4%	—
1991	290,000	BV+4%	—
1992	368,900	BV+4%	—
1993	321,413	BV+4%	—
1994	180,357	BV+4%	—
1995	208,729	BV+4%	—
1996	143,682	BV+4%	—
1997	478,211	BV+4%	—
1998	593,704	BV+4%	—
1999	—	BV+7%	—

Note: Maple leaf with oval "20 Years ANS" privy mark

KM# 305 50 DOLLARS **Weight:** 31.1030 g. **Composition:** 0.9999 Gold 1 oz. AGW **Ruler:** Elizabeth II **Obverse:** Crowned head denomination below, within circle, dates below **Reverse:** Mountie at gallop right, within circle **Rev. Designer:** Ago Aarand **Shape:** 10-sided

Date	Mintage	MS-63	Proof
1997	12,913	685	—

KM# 369 50 DOLLARS **Weight:** 31.1030 g. **Composition:** 0.9999 Gold 1.0000 oz. AGW **Obverse:** Crowned head right, denomination and date below **Reverse:** Maple leaf hologram flanked by 9999, with fireworks privy mark

Date	Mintage	MS-63	Proof
2000	500	1,400	—

KM# 364 50 DOLLARS **Weight:** 31.1030 g. **Composition:** 0.9999 Gold 1.0000 oz. AGW **Ruler:** Elizabeth II **Obverse:** Crowned head right, denomination and date below **Reverse:** Maple leaf flanked by 9999, with fireworks privy mark

Date	Mintage	MS-63	Proof
2000	—	785	—

KM# 442 50 DOLLARS **Weight:** 31.1500 g. **Composition:** 0.9999 Gold 1.0014 oz. AGW **Ruler:** Elizabeth II **Subject:** Holographic Maples Leaves **Obverse:** Crowned head right **Reverse:** Three maple leaves multicolor hologram **Edge:** Reeded **Size:** 30 mm.

Date	Mintage	MS-63	Proof
2001 in sets only	600	1,350	—

PLATINUM BULLION COINAGE

KM# 239 DOLLAR **Weight:** 1.5552 g. **Composition:** 0.9995 Platinum 0.0500 oz. APW **Ruler:** Elizabeth II **Obverse:** Crowned head right, date and denomination below **Reverse:** Maple leaf flanked by 9995

Date	Mintage	MS-63	Proof
1993	2,120	BV+35%	—
1994	4,260	BV+35%	—
1995	460	135	—
1996	1,640	BV+35%	—
1997	1,340	BV+35%	—
1998	2,000	BV+35%	—
1999	2,000	BV+35%	—

KM# 257 2 DOLLARS **Weight:** 2.0735 g. **Composition:** 0.9995 Platinum 0.0666 oz. APW **Ruler:** Elizabeth II **Obverse:** Crowned head right, date and denomination below **Reverse:** Maple leaf flanked by 9995

Date	Mintage	MS-63	Proof
1994	1,470	235	—

KM# 164 5 DOLLARS **Weight:** 3.1203 g. **Composition:** 0.9995 Platinum 0.1000 oz. APW **Ruler:** Elizabeth II **Obverse:** Young bust right, date and denomination below **Obv. Designer:** Arnold Machin **Reverse:** Maple leaf flanked by 9995

Date	Mintage	MS-63	Proof
1988	74,000	BV+18%	—

96 CANADA

Date	Mintage	MS-63	Proof
1989	18,000	BV+18%	—
1989 Proof	11,999	—	150

KM# 192 5 DOLLARS Weight: 3.1203 g. Composition: 0.9995 Platinum 0.1000 oz. APW Ruler: Elizabeth II Obv. Designer: dePedery-Hunt Reverse: Maple leaf

Date	Mintage	MS-63	Proof
1990	9,000	BV+18%	—
1991	13,000	BV+18%	—
1992	16,000	BV+18%	—
1993	14,020	BV+18%	—
1994	19,190	BV+18%	—
1995	8,940	BV+18%	—
1996	8,820	BV+18%	—
1997	7,050	BV+18%	—
1998	5,710	BV+18%	—
1999	2,000	BV+18%	—

KM# 165 10 DOLLARS Weight: 7.7857 g. Composition: 0.9995 Platinum 0.2500 oz. APW Ruler: Elizabeth II Obverse: Young bust right, date and denomination below Obv. Designer: Machin Reverse: Maple leaf flanked by 9995

Date	Mintage	MS-63	Proof
1988	93,600	BV+13%	—
1989	3,200	BV+13%	—
1989 Proof	1,999	—	360

KM# 193 10 DOLLARS Weight: 7.7857 g. Composition: 0.9995 Platinum 0.2500 oz. APW Ruler: Elizabeth II Obv. Designer: dePedery-Hunt Reverse: Maple leaf

Date	Mintage	MS-63	Proof
1990	1,600	BV+13%	—
1991	7,200	BV+13%	—
1992	11,600	BV+13%	—
1993	8,048	BV+13%	—
1994	9,456	BV+13%	—
1995	6,524	BV+13%	—
1996	6,160	BV+13%	—
1997	4,552	BV+13%	—
1998	3,816	BV+13%	—
1999	2,000	BV+13%	—

KM# 166 20 DOLLARS Weight: 15.5519 g. Composition: 0.9995 Platinum 0.5000 oz. APW Ruler: Elizabeth II Obverse: Young bust right, denomination and date below Obv. Designer: Machin Reverse: Maple leaf flanked by 9995

Date	Mintage	MS-63	Proof
1988	23,600	BV+9%	—
1989	4,800	BV+9%	—
1989 Proof	1,999	—	700

KM# 194 20 DOLLARS Weight: 15.5519 g. Composition: 0.9995 Platinum 0.5000 oz. APW Ruler: Elizabeth II Obv. Designer: dePedery-Hunt Reverse: Maple leaf

Date	Mintage	MS-63	Proof
1990	2,600	BV+9%	—
1991	5,600	BV+9%	—
1992	12,800	BV+9%	—
1993	6,022	BV+9%	—
1994	6,710	BV+9%	—
1995	6,308	BV+9%	—
1996	5,490	BV+9%	—
1997	3,990	BV+9%	—
1998	5,486	BV+9%	—
1999	500	BV+15%	—

KM# 174 30 DOLLARS Weight: 3.1100 g. Composition: 0.9990 Platinum 0.1000 oz. APW Ruler: Elizabeth II Obverse: Crowned head right Reverse: Polar bear swimming, denomination below Rev. Designer: Robert Bateman

Date	Mintage	MS-63	Proof
1990 Proof	2,629	—	145

KM# 198 30 DOLLARS Weight: 3.1100 g. Composition: 0.9990 Platinum 0.1000 oz. APW Ruler: Elizabeth II Obverse: Crowned head right Reverse: Snowy owl, denomination below Rev. Designer: Glen Loates

Date	Mintage	MS-63	Proof
1991 Proof	3,500	—	145

KM# 226 30 DOLLARS Weight: 3.1100 g. Composition: 0.9990 Platinum 0.1000 oz. APW Ruler: Elizabeth II Obverse: Crowned head right Reverse: Cougar head and shoulders, denomination below Rev. Designer: George McLean

Date	Mintage	MS-63	Proof
1992 Proof	3,500	—	145

KM# 240 30 DOLLARS Weight: 3.1100 g. Composition: 0.9990 Platinum 0.1000 oz. APW Ruler: Elizabeth II Obverse: Crowned head right Reverse: Arctic fox, denomination below Rev. Designer: Claude D'Angelo

Date	Mintage	MS-63	Proof
1993 Proof	3,500	—	150

KM# 252 30 DOLLARS Weight: 3.1100 g. Composition: 0.9990 Platinum 0.1000 oz. APW Ruler: Elizabeth II Obverse: Crowned head right, date below Reverse: Sea otter, denomination below Rev. Designer: Ron S. Parker

Date	Mintage	MS-63	Proof
1994 Proof	1,500	—	150

KM# 266 30 DOLLARS Weight: 3.1100 g. Composition: 0.9990 Platinum 0.1000 oz. APW Ruler: Elizabeth II Obverse: Crowned head right, date below Reverse: Canadian lynx, denomination below Rev. Designer: Michael Dumas

Date	Mintage	MS-63	Proof
1995 Proof	620	—	150

KM# 278 30 DOLLARS Weight: 3.1100 g. Composition: 0.9990 Platinum 0.1000 oz. APW Ruler: Elizabeth II Obverse: Crowned head right, date below Reverse: Falcon portrait, denomination below Rev. Designer: Dwayne Harty

Date	Mintage	MS-63	Proof
1996 Proof	489	—	150

KM# 300 30 DOLLARS Weight: 3.1100 g. Composition: 0.9995 Platinum 0.1000 oz. APW Ruler: Elizabeth II Obverse: Crowned head right, date below Reverse: Bison head, denomination below Rev. Designer: Chris Bacon

Date	Mintage	MS-63	Proof
1997 Proof	5,000	—	135

KM# 322 30 DOLLARS Weight: 3.1100 g. Composition: 0.9990 Platinum 0.1000 oz. APW Ruler: Elizabeth II Obverse: Crowned head right, date below Reverse: Grey wolf Rev. Designer: Kerr Burnett

Date	Mintage	MS-63	Proof
ND(1998) Proof	2,000	—	150

KM# 359 30 DOLLARS Weight: 3.1100 g. Composition: 0.9995 Platinum 0.1000 oz. APW Ruler: Elizabeth II Obverse: Crowned head right, date below Reverse: Musk ox Rev. Designer: Mark Hobson

Date	Mintage	MS-63	Proof
1999 Proof	1,500	—	150

KM# 405 30 DOLLARS Weight: 3.1100 g. Composition: 0.9995 Platinum .1000 oz. APW Ruler: Elizabeth II Obverse: Crowned head right, date below Reverse: Pronghorn antelope head, denomination below Rev. Designer: Mark Hobson Edge: Reeded Size: 16 mm.

Date	Mintage	MS-63	Proof
2000 Proof	600	—	150

CANADA

KM# 167 50 DOLLARS Weight: 31.1030 g. Composition: 0.9995 Platinum 1.0000 oz. APW Ruler: Elizabeth II Obverse: Young bust right, denomination and date below Obv. Designer: Machin Reverse: Maple leaf flanked by 9995

Date	Mintage	MS-63	Proof
1988	37,500	BV+4%	—
1989	10,000	BV+4%	—
1989 Proof	5,965	—	1,325

KM# 195 50 DOLLARS Weight: 31.1030 g. Composition: 0.9995 Platinum 1.0000 oz. APW Ruler: Elizabeth II Obv. Designer: dePedery-Hunt Reverse: Maple leaf

Date	Mintage	MS-63	Proof
1990	15,100	BV+4%	—
1991	31,900	BV+4%	—
1992	40,500	BV+4%	—
1993	17,666	BV+4%	—
1994	36,245	BV+4%	—
1995	25,829	BV+4%	—
1996	62,273	BV+4%	—
1997	25,480	BV+4%	—
1998	10,403	BV+4%	—
1999	1,300	BV+10%	—

KM# 175 75 DOLLARS Weight: 7.7760 g. Composition: 0.9990 Platinum 0.2500 oz. APW Ruler: Elizabeth II Obverse: Crowned head right Reverse: Polar bear resting, denomination below Rev. Designer: Robert Bateman

Date	Mintage	MS-63	Proof
1990 Proof	2,629	—	325

KM# 199 75 DOLLARS Weight: 7.7760 g. Composition: 0.9990 Platinum 0.2500 oz. APW Ruler: Elizabeth II Obverse: Crowned head right Reverse: Snowy owls perched on branch, denomination below Rev. Designer: Glen Loates

Date	Mintage	MS-63	Proof
1991 Proof	3,500	—	325

KM# 227 75 DOLLARS Weight: 7.7760 g. Composition: 0.9990 Platinum 0.2500 oz. APW Ruler: Elizabeth II Obverse: Crowned head right Reverse: Cougar prowling, denomination below Rev. Designer: George McLean

Date	Mintage	MS-63	Proof
1992 Proof	3,500	—	340

KM# 241 75 DOLLARS Weight: 7.7760 g. Composition: 0.9990 Platinum 0.2500 oz. APW Ruler: Elizabeth II Obverse: Crowned head right Reverse: Two Arctic foxes, denomination below Rev. Designer: Claude D'Angelo

Date	Mintage	MS-63	Proof
1993 Proof	3,500	—	340

KM# 253 75 DOLLARS Weight: 7.7760 g. Composition: 0.9990 Platinum 0.2500 oz. APW Ruler: Elizabeth II Obverse: Crowned head right, date below Reverse: Sea otter eating urchin, denomination below Rev. Designer: Ron S. Parker

Date	Mintage	MS-63	Proof
1994 Proof	1,500	—	340

KM# 267 75 DOLLARS Weight: 7.7760 g. Composition: 0.9990 Platinum 0.2500 oz. APW Ruler: Elizabeth II Obverse: Crowned head right, date below Reverse: Two lynx kittens, denomination below Rev. Designer: Michael Dumas

Date	Mintage	MS-63	Proof
1995 Proof	1,500	—	340

KM# 279 75 DOLLARS Weight: 7.7760 g. Composition: 0.9990 Platinum 0.2500 oz. APW Ruler: Elizabeth II Obverse: Crowned head right, date below Reverse: Peregrine falcon, denomination below Rev. Designer: Dwayne Harty

Date	Mintage	MS-63	Proof
1996 Proof	1,500	—	340

KM# 301 75 DOLLARS Weight: 7.7760 g. Composition: 0.9990 Platinum 0.2500 oz. APW Ruler: Elizabeth II Obverse: Crowned head right, date below Reverse: Two bison calves, denomination below Rev. Designer: Chris Bacon

Date	Mintage	MS-63	Proof
1997 Proof	1,500	—	340

KM# 323 75 DOLLARS Weight: 7.7760 g. Composition: 0.9990 Platinum 0.2500 oz. APW Ruler: Elizabeth II Obverse: Crowned head right, date below Reverse: Gray wolf Rev. Designer: Kerr Burnett

Date	Mintage	MS-63	Proof
1998 Proof	1,000	—	340

KM# 360 75 DOLLARS Weight: 7.7760 g. Composition: 0.9990 Platinum 0.2500 oz. APW Ruler: Elizabeth II Obverse: Crowned head right, date below Reverse: Musk ox Rev. Designer: Mark Hobson

Date	Mintage	MS-63	Proof
1999 Proof	500	—	345

KM# 406 75 DOLLARS Weight: 7.7760 g. Composition: 0.9990 Platinum .2500 oz. APW Ruler: Elizabeth II Obverse: Crowned head right Reverse: Standing pronghorn antelope, denomination below Rev. Designer: Mark Hobson Edge: Reeded Size: 20 mm.

Date	Mintage	MS-63	Proof
2000 Proof	600	—	345

KM# 430 75 DOLLARS Weight: 7.7760 g. Composition: 0.9995 Platinum .2500 oz. APW Ruler: Elizabeth II Obverse: Crowned head right Reverse: Harlequin duck in flight Rev. Designer: Cosme Saffioti and Susan Taylor Edge: Reeded Size: 20 mm.

Date	Mintage	MS-63	Proof
2001 Proof	448	—	375

KM# 176 150 DOLLARS Weight: 15.5520 g. Composition: 0.9990 Platinum 0.5000 oz. APW Ruler: Elizabeth II Obverse: Crowned head right Reverse: Polar bear walking, denomination below Rev. Designer: Robert Bateman

Date	Mintage	MS-63	Proof
1990 Proof	2,629	—	675

98 CANADA

KM# 200 150 DOLLARS **Weight:** 15.5520 g. **Composition:** 0.9990 Platinum 0.5000 oz. APW **Ruler:** Elizabeth II **Obverse:** Crowned head right **Reverse:** Snowy owl flying, denomination below **Rev. Designer:** Glen Loates

Date	Mintage	MS-63	Proof
1991 Proof	3,500	—	675

KM# 228 150 DOLLARS **Weight:** 15.5520 g. **Composition:** 0.9990 Platinum 0.5000 oz. APW **Ruler:** Elizabeth II **Obverse:** Crowned head right **Reverse:** Cougar mother and cub, denomination below **Rev. Designer:** George McLean

Date	Mintage	MS-63	Proof
1992 Proof	3,500	—	685

KM# 242 150 DOLLARS **Weight:** 15.5520 g. **Composition:** 0.9990 Platinum 0.5000 oz. APW **Ruler:** Elizabeth II **Obverse:** Crowned head right **Reverse:** Arctic fox by lake, denomination below **Rev. Designer:** Claude D'Angelo

Date	Mintage	MS-63	Proof
1993 Proof	3,500	—	685

KM# 254 150 DOLLARS **Weight:** 15.5520 g. **Composition:** 0.9990 Platinum 0.5000 oz. APW **Ruler:** Elizabeth II **Obverse:** Crowned head right, date below **Reverse:** Sea otter mother carrying pup, denomination below **Rev. Designer:** Ron S. Parker

Date	Mintage	MS-63	Proof
1994 Proof	—	—	700

KM# 268 150 DOLLARS **Weight:** 15.5520 g. **Composition:** 0.9990 Platinum 0.5000 oz. APW **Ruler:** Elizabeth II **Obverse:** Crowned head right, date below **Reverse:** Prowling lynx, denomination below **Rev. Designer:** Michael Dumas

Date	Mintage	MS-63	Proof
1995 Proof	226	—	685

KM# 280 150 DOLLARS **Weight:** 15.5520 g. **Composition:** 0.9990 Platinum 0.5000 oz. APW **Ruler:** Elizabeth II **Obverse:** Crowned head right, date below **Reverse:** Peregrine falcon on branch, denomination below **Rev. Designer:** Dwayne Harty

Date	Mintage	MS-63	Proof
1996 Proof	100	—	685

KM# 302 150 DOLLARS **Weight:** 15.5520 g. **Composition:** 0.9990 Platinum 0.5000 oz. APW **Ruler:** Elizabeth II **Obverse:** Crowned head right, date below **Reverse:** Bison bull, denomination below **Rev. Designer:** Chris Bacon

Date	Mintage	MS-63	Proof
1997 Proof	4,000	—	685

KM# 324 150 DOLLARS **Weight:** 15.5520 g. **Composition:** 0.9990 Platinum 0.5000 oz. APW **Ruler:** Elizabeth II **Obverse:** Crowned head right, date below **Reverse:** Two gray wolf cubs, denomination below **Rev. Designer:** Kerr Burnett

Date	Mintage	MS-63	Proof
1998 Proof	2,000	—	685

KM# 361 150 DOLLARS **Weight:** 15.5520 g. **Composition:** 0.9990 Platinum 0.5000 oz. APW **Ruler:** Elizabeth II **Obverse:** Crowned head right **Reverse:** Musk ox, denomination below **Rev. Designer:** Mark Hobson

Date	Mintage	MS-63	Proof
1999 Proof	500	—	700

KM# 407 150 DOLLARS **Weight:** 15.5500 g. **Composition:** 0.9990 Platinum .5000 oz. APW **Ruler:** Elizabeth II **Obverse:** Crowned head right **Reverse:** Two pronghorn antelope, denomination below **Rev. Designer:** Mark Hobson **Edge:** Reeded **Size:** 25 mm.

Date	Mintage	MS-63	Proof
2000 Proof	600	—	700

KM# 431 150 DOLLARS **Weight:** 15.5500 g. **Composition:** 0.9995 Platinum .5000 oz. APW **Ruler:** Elizabeth II **Obverse:** Crowned head right **Reverse:** Two harlequin ducks **Rev. Designer:** Cosme Saffioti and Susan Taylor **Edge:** Reeded **Size:** 25 mm.

Date	Mintage	MS-63	Proof
2001 Proof	448	—	700

KM# 177 300 DOLLARS **Weight:** 31.1035 g. **Composition:** 0.9990 Platinum 1.0000 oz. APW **Ruler:** Elizabeth II **Obverse:** Crowned head right **Reverse:** Polar bear mother and cub, denomination below **Rev. Designer:** Robert Bateman

Date	Mintage	MS-63	Proof
1990 Proof	2,629	—	1,325

CANADA 99

KM# 201 300 DOLLARS **Weight:** 31.1035 g. **Composition:** 0.9990 Platinum 1.0000 oz. APW **Ruler:** Elizabeth II **Obverse:** Crowned head right **Reverse:** Snowy owl with chicks, denomination below **Rev. Designer:** Glen Loates

Date	Mintage	MS-63	Proof
1991 Proof	3,500	—	1,325

KM# 229 300 DOLLARS **Weight:** 31.1035 g. **Composition:** 0.9990 Platinum 1.0000 oz. APW **Ruler:** Elizabeth II **Obverse:** Crowned head right **Reverse:** Cougar resting in tree, denomination below **Rev. Designer:** George McLean

Date	Mintage	MS-63	Proof
1992 Proof	3,500	—	1,325

KM# 243 300 DOLLARS **Weight:** 31.1035 g. **Composition:** 0.9990 Platinum 1.0000 oz. APW **Ruler:** Elizabeth II **Obverse:** Crowned head right **Reverse:** Mother fox and three kits, denomination below **Rev. Designer:** Claude D'Angelo

Date	Mintage	MS-63	Proof
1993 Proof	3,500	—	1,325

KM# 255 300 DOLLARS **Weight:** 31.1035 g. **Composition:** 0.9990 Platinum 1.0000 oz. APW **Ruler:** Elizabeth II **Obverse:** Crowned head right, date below **Reverse:** Two otters swimming, denomination below **Rev. Designer:** Ron S. Parker

Date	Mintage	MS-63	Proof
1994 Proof	—	—	1,325

KM# 269 300 DOLLARS **Weight:** 31.1035 g. **Composition:** 0.9990 Platinum 1.0000 oz. APW **Ruler:** Elizabeth II **Obverse:** Crowned head right, date below **Reverse:** Female lynx and three kittens, denomination below **Rev. Designer:** Michael Dumas

Date	Mintage	MS-63	Proof
1995 Proof	1,500	—	1,325

KM# 281 300 DOLLARS **Weight:** 31.1035 g. **Composition:** 0.9990 Platinum 1.0000 oz. APW **Ruler:** Elizabeth II **Obverse:** Crowned head right, date below **Reverse:** Peregrine falcon feeding nestlings, denomination below **Rev. Designer:** Dwayne Harty

Date	Mintage	MS-63	Proof
1996 Proof	1,500	—	1,325

KM# 303 300 DOLLARS **Weight:** 31.1035 g. **Composition:** 0.9990 Platinum 1.0000 oz. APW **Ruler:** Elizabeth II **Obverse:** Crowned head right, date below **Reverse:** Bison family, denomination below **Rev. Designer:** Chris Bacon

Date	Mintage	MS-63	Proof
1997 Proof	1,500	—	1,325

KM# 325 300 DOLLARS **Weight:** 31.1035 g. **Composition:** 0.9990 Platinum 1.0000 oz. APW **Ruler:** Elizabeth II **Obverse:** Crowned head right, date below **Reverse:** Gray wolf and two cubs, denomination below **Rev. Designer:** Kerr Burnett

Date	Mintage	MS-63	Proof
1998 Proof	—	—	1,325

KM# 362 300 DOLLARS **Weight:** 31.1035 g. **Composition:** 0.9990 Platinum 1.0000 oz. APW **Ruler:** Elizabeth II **Obverse:** Crowned head right, date below **Reverse:** Musk ox **Rev. Designer:** Mark Hobson

Date	Mintage	MS-63	Proof
1999 Proof	500	—	1,325

KM# 408 300 DOLLARS **Weight:** 31.1035 g. **Composition:** 0.9990 Platinum 1.0000 oz. APW **Ruler:** Elizabeth II **Obverse:** Crowned head right, date below **Reverse:** Four pronghorn antelope, denomination below **Rev. Designer:** Mark Hobson **Edge:** Reeded **Size:** 30 mm.

Date	Mintage	MS-63	Proof
2000 Proof	600	—	1,325

KM# 432 300 DOLLARS **Weight:** 31.1035 g. **Composition:** 0.9995 Platinum 1.0000 oz. APW **Ruler:** Elizabeth II **Obverse:** Crowned head right **Reverse:** Two standing harlequin ducks **Rev. Designer:** Cosme Saffioti and Susan Taylor **Edge:** Reeded **Size:** 30 mm.

Date	Mintage	MS-63	Proof
2001 Proof	448	—	1,300

PATTERNS

Including off metal strikes

KM	Date	Mintage	Identification	Mkt Val
Pn17	1911	—	5 Dollars. Gold.	—
Pn18	1911	—	10 Dollars. Gold.	—

CANADA

MINT SETS

KM	Date	Mintage	Identification	Issue Price	Mkt Val
MS8	2001	600	KM438-442	1,996	2,450

PROOF SETS

KM	Date	Mintage	Identification	Issue Price	Mkt Val
PS10	1989	6,823	KM125.2, 135-136, 153	1,190	1,100
PS11	1989	1,995	KM164-167	1,700	2,100
PS12	1989	2,550	KM125.2, 163, 167	1,530	1,775
PS13	1989	9,979	KM135, 163-164	165	225
PS15	1990	2,629	KM174-177	1,720	2,475
PS17	1991	873	KM198-201	1,760	2,475
PS20	1992	3,500	KM226-229	1,680	2,500
PS22	1993	3,500	KM240-243	1,329	2,500
PS25	1994	1,500	KM252-255	915	2,520
PS29	1995	682	KM266-269	1,555	2,500
PS32	1996	423	KM278-281	1,555	2,500
PS35	1997	I.A.	KM182a, 183a, 184a, 209, 270c, 282, 289.	60.00	30.00
PS37	1997	I.A.	KM300-303	1,530	2,485
PS38	1998	I.A.	KM182a, 183a, 184a, 186, 270b, 289, 290a, 306	59.45	50.00
PS42	1998	1,000	KM322-325	1,552	2,500
PS47	1999	I.A.	KM359-362	1,425	2,520
PS50	2000	600	KM405-408	1,416	2,520
PS51	2001	—	KM429, 430, 431, 432	—	2,300
PS54	2002	—	KM#519, 520	750	725

PROOF-LIKE SETS (PL)

KM	Date	Mintage	Identification	Issue Price	Mkt Val
PL18B	1967	337,688	KM65-71 (black box)	40.00	250

SPECIMEN SETS (SS)

KM	Date	Mintage	Identification	Issue Price	Mkt Val
SS17	1911/12	5	KM15-20, 26-27	—	52,250

BRITISH COLUMBIA

PATTERNS

KM	Date	Mintage	Identification	Mkt Val
Pn1	1862	—	10 Dollars. Silver. Crown. Denomination and date within wreath. 5-10 pieces.	32,500

Note: Bowers and Merena Norweb Sale 11-96, Specimen 58 realized $18,700; David Akers Pittman Sale 8-99, Choice AU realized $32,200

KM	Date	Mintage	Identification	Mkt Val
Pn2	1862	—	10 Dollars. Gold.	—
Pn3	1862	—	20 Dollars. Silver. . 5-10 pieces.	38,500

Note: Bowers and Merena Norweb Sale 11-96, Specimen 61 realized $25,300

KM	Date	Mintage	Identification	Mkt Val
Pn4	1862	—	20 Dollars. Gold. Crown. Denomination and date within wreath. 5 pieces.	—

Note: Bowers and Merena Norweb Sale 11-96, Specimen 61 realized $143,000; David Akers Pittman sale 8-99, AU realized $149,500

MANITOBA

CONFEDERATION

MEDALLIC COINAGE

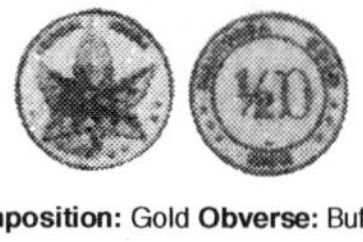

X#11 1/2 DOLLAR Composition: Gold **Obverse:** Buffalo on large maple leaf

Date	Mintage	XF	UNC
1898	—	175	275

X#12 DOLLAR Composition: Gold **Obverse:** Buffalo on large maple leaf

Date	Mintage	XF	UNC
1898	—	300	500

NEWFOUNDLAND

Island which along with Labrador became a province of Canada. Prehistoric inhabitants left evidence of an early presence on the island. Norsemen briefly settled on the island but officially discovered in 1497 by Italian explorer John Cabot. English settlements were sporadic and disputed by France. The English settled along the east coast and the French along the west coast of the island. With the treaty of Utrecht in 1713, it officially became English, but the fishing rights went to France. Controversies continued through the 19th century. Boundaries were set in 1927, colonial government reestablished 1934, became a province of Canada 1949.

PROVINCE

CIRCULATION COINAGE

KM# 5 2 DOLLARS Weight: 3.3284 g. **Composition:** 0.9170 Gold .0981 oz. AGW
Obverse: Laureate head left **Obv. Legend:** VICTORIA D: G: REG:
NEWFOUNDLAND **Reverse:** Denomination and date within circle

Date	Mintage	F-12	VF-20	XF-40	AU-50	MS-60	MS-63
1865	10,000	150	175	300	375	1,100	5,000
1865 plain edge, Specimen-63, $15,000.	Est. 10	—	—	—	—	—	—
1870	10,000	150	175	300	375	1,100	5,850
1870 reeded edge, Specimen-63 $20,000.	Est. 5	—	—	—	—	—	—
1872	6,050	175	300	375	700	2,200	8,800
1872 Specimen-63 $12,500.	Est. 10	—	—	—	—	—	—
1880	2,500	800	1,000	1,200	2,300	4,650	14,250
1880/70							

Note: Specimen. Bowers and Merena Norweb sale 11-96, specimen 64 realized $70,400.

Date	Mintage	F-12	VF-20	XF-40	AU-50	MS-60	MS-63
1881	10,000	130	150	200	325	1,200	5,400
1881 Specimen; Rare							
1882H	25,000	130	150	200	225	425	1,600
1882H Specimen $4,250.							
1885	10,000	130	150	200	225	700	2,700
1885 Specimen							

Note: Bowers and Merena Norweb sale 11-96, specimen 66 realized $44,000

Date	Mintage	F-12	VF-20	XF-40	AU-50	MS-60	MS-63
1888	25,000	115	140	170	200	365	1,550
1888 Specimen; Rare							

PATTERNS

KM	Date	Mintage	Identification	Mkt Val
Pn14	1865	—	2 Dollars. Gold.	—
Pn15	1865	—	2 Dollars. Gold.	—

Note: Bowers and Merena Norweb Sale 11-96, Specimen 63 realized $39,600

CAPE VERDE

The Republic of Cape Verde, Africa's smallest republic, is located in the Atlantic Ocean, about 370 miles (595 km.) west of Dakar, Senegal, off the coast of Africa. The 14-island republic has an area of 1,557 sq. mi. (4,033 sq. km.) and a population of 435,983. Capital: Praia. The refueling of ships and aircraft is the chief economic function of the country. Fishing is important and agriculture is widely practiced, but the Cape Verdes are not self-sufficient in food. Fish products, salt, bananas, and shellfish are exported.

The date of discovery of the islands is uncertain. Possibly they were visited by Venetian captain Alvise Cadamosto in 1456. Portuguese navigator Diogo Gomes claimed them for Portugal in May of 1460. Settlement began two years later. The early importance and wealth of the islands, which caused them to be attacked by Sir Francis Drake and the Dutch, resulted from the monopoly of the Guinea slave trade granted the inhabitants in 1466. Poverty and famine occasioned by frequent periods of severe drought have marked the history of the country since abolition of the slave trade in 1876.

After 500 years of Portuguese rule, the Cape Verdes became independent on July 5, 1975. At the first general election, all seats of the new national assembly were won by the Party for the Independence of Guinea-Bissau and Cape Verde (PAIGC). The PAIGC linked the two former colonies into one state. Antonio Mascarenhas Monteiro won the first free presidential election in 1991.

RULER
Portuguese, until 1975

MONETARY SYSTEM
100 Centavos = 1 Escudo

REPUBLIC

DECIMAL COINAGE

KM# 23b ESCUDO
6.0000 g., 0.7500 Gold .1447 oz. AGW **Subject:** 10th Anniversary of Independence **Obv:** Emblem within wreath below denomination and date **Rev:** Inscription below building

Date	Mintage	F	VF	XF	Unc	BU
1985 Proof	50	Value: 250				

KM# 24b 10 ESCUDOS
9.0000 g., 0.7500 Gold .2170 oz. AGW **Subject:** 10th Anniversary of Independence **Obv:** Emblem within wreath below denomination and date **Rev:** Letter design at center, star above

Date	Mintage	F	VF	XF	Unc	BU
1985 Proof	50	Value: 400				

KM# 22b 50 ESCUDOS
27.0000 g., 0.9170 Gold .7958 oz. AGW **Series:** F.A.O. **Subject:** World Fisheries Conference **Rev:** White sea bream fish left, two dates below

Date	Mintage	F	VF	XF	Unc	BU
1984 Proof	Est. 100,000	Value: 1,500				

KM# 47 50 ESCUDOS
1.5550 g., 0.9990 Gold 0.0499 oz. AGW, 16 mm. **Obv:** Value above national arms **Rev:** Jesus **Edge:** Plain

Date	Mintage	F	VF	XF	Unc	BU
2006 Proof	—	Value: 65.00				

KM# 25b 100 ESCUDOS
33.4000 g., 0.9000 Gold .9666 oz. AGW **Subject:** Papal Visit **Obv:** Emblem within wreath above denomination and date **Rev:** Half figure of Pope

Date	Mintage	F	VF	XF	Unc	BU
1990 Proof	—	—				

KM# 14 2500 ESCUDOS
8.0000 g., 0.9000 Gold .2315 oz. AGW **Subject:** 1st Anniversary of Independence **Obv:** Emblem within wreath above denomination **Rev:** Head left, date below

Date	Mintage	F	VF	XF	Unc	BU
1976 Proof	3,409	Value: 245				

PROOF SETS

KM#	Date	Mintage	Identification	Issue Price	Mkt Val
PS1	1976-77 (4)	—	KM13-14 1976, KM17-18 1977	—	300

CAYMAN ISLANDS

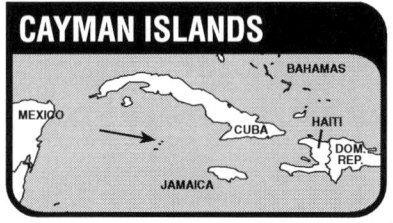

The Cayman Islands is a dependent territory of the United Kingdom with the British monarch as head of state. It is situated about 180 miles (290 km.) northwest of Jamaica, consists of three islands: Grand Cayman, Little Cayman, and Cayman Brac. The islands have an area of 102 sq. mi. (259 sq. km.) and a population of 33,200. Capital: George Town. Seafaring, commerce, banking, and tourism are the principal industries. Rope, turtle shells, and sharkskins are exported.

The islands were discovered by Columbus in 1503, and named by him Tortugas (Spanish for 'turtles') because of the great number of turtles in the nearby waters. Ceded to Britain in 1670, they were colonized from Jamaica by the British and remained dependencies of Jamaica until 1959, when they became a unit territory within the Federation of the West Indies. They became a separate colony when the Federation was dissolved in 1962. Since 1972 a form of self-government has existed, with the Governor responsible for defense and certain other affairs.

While the islands used Jamaican currency for much of their history, the Caymans issued its first national coinage in 1972. The $25 gold and silver commemorative coins issued in 1972 to celebrate the silver wedding anniversary of Queen Elizabeth II and Prince Philip are the first coins in 300 years of Commonwealth coinage to portray a member of the British royal family other than the reigning monarch.

RULER
British

MINT MARKS
CHI - Valcambi
FM - Franklin Mint, U.S.A.*

MONETARY SYSTEM
100 Cents = 1 Dollar

BRITISH COLONY

DECIMAL COINAGE

KM# 9a 25 DOLLARS
15.7500 g., 0.5000 Gold .2531 oz. AGW, 27 mm. **Ruler:** Elizabeth II **Subject:** Queen Elizabeth II and Philip's 25th Wedding Anniversary **Obv:** Young bust right **Rev:** Jugate heads right

Date	Mintage	F	VF	XF	Unc	BU
1972	7,706	—	—	—	—	175
1972 Proof	21,000	Value: 170				

KM# 104 25 DOLLARS
3.1340 g., 0.9990 Gold .1006 oz. AGW **Ruler:** Elizabeth II **Subject:** Winston Churchill **Obv:** Young bust right **Rev:** Evacuation of Dunkirk **Rev. Designer:** Robert Elderton

Date	Mintage	F	VF	XF	Unc	BU
1990 Proof	Est. 500	Value: 95.00				

KM# 21 50 DOLLARS
11.3400 g., 0.5000 Gold .1823 oz. AGW **Ruler:** Elizabeth II **Subject:** Queen Mary I, 1553-1558 **Obv:** Young bust right **Rev:** Bust 3/4 facing **Rev. Designer:** Michael Rizzello

Date	Mintage	F	VF	XF	Unc	BU
1977 Proof	1,999	Value: 135				

KM# 22 50 DOLLARS
11.3400 g., 0.5000 Gold .1823 oz. AGW **Ruler:** Elizabeth II **Subject:** Queen Elizabeth I, 1558-1603 **Obv:** Young bust right **Rev:** Bust with high ruffled collar 3/4 right **Rev. Designer:** Michael Rizzello

Date	Mintage	F	VF	XF	Unc	BU
1977 Proof	1,969	Value: 135				

KM# 23 50 DOLLARS
11.3400 g., 0.5000 Gold .1823 oz. AGW **Ruler:** Elizabeth II **Subject:** Queen Mary II, 1688-1694 **Obv:** Young bust right **Rev:** Bust 3/4 right **Rev. Designer:** Michael Rizzello

Date	Mintage	F	VF	XF	Unc	BU
1977 Proof	1,961	Value: 135				

KM# 24 50 DOLLARS
11.3400 g., 0.5000 Gold .1823 oz. AGW **Ruler:** Elizabeth II **Subject:** Queen Anne, 1702-1714 **Obv:** Young bust right **Rev:** Bust 3/4 left **Rev. Designer:** Michael Rizzello

Date	Mintage	F	VF	XF	Unc	BU
1977 Proof	1,938	Value: 135				

KM# 25 50 DOLLARS
11.3400 g., 0.5000 Gold .1823 oz. AGW **Ruler:** Elizabeth II **Subject:** Queen Victoria, 1837-1901 **Obv:** Young bust right **Rev:** Crowned bust left **Rev. Designer:** Michael Rizzello

Date	Mintage	F	VF	XF	Unc	BU
1977 Proof	1,932	Value: 135				

KM# 42 50 DOLLARS
11.3400 g., 0.5000 Gold .1823 oz. AGW **Ruler:** Elizabeth II **Subject:** 25th Anniversary of Coronation **Obv:** Young bust right **Rev:** The Ampulla

Date	Mintage	F	VF	XF	Unc	BU
1978 Proof	771	Value: 145				

KM# 43 50 DOLLARS
11.3400 g., 0.5000 Gold .1823 oz. AGW **Ruler:** Elizabeth II **Subject:** 25th Anniversary of Coronation **Obv:** Young bust right **Rev:** Royal orb

Date	Mintage	F	VF	XF	Unc	BU
1978 Proof	771	Value: 145				

102 CAYMAN ISLANDS

KM# 44 50 DOLLARS
11.3400 g., 0.5000 Gold .1823 oz. AGW **Ruler:** Elizabeth II
Subject: 25th Anniversary of Coronation **Obv:** Young bust right
Rev: St. Edward's Crown

Date	Mintage	F	VF	XF	Unc	BU
1978 Proof	771	Value: 145				

KM# 45 50 DOLLARS
11.3400 g., 0.5000 Gold .1823 oz. AGW **Ruler:** Elizabeth II
Subject: 25th Anniversary of Coronation **Obv:** Young bust right
Rev: Coronation chair

Date	Mintage	F	VF	XF	Unc	BU
1978 Proof	771	Value: 145				

KM# 46 50 DOLLARS
11.3400 g., 0.5000 Gold .1823 oz. AGW **Ruler:** Elizabeth II
Subject: 25th Anniversary of Coronation **Obv:** Young bust right
Rev: Scepter

Date	Mintage	F	VF	XF	Unc	BU
1978 Proof	771	Value: 145				

KM# 47 50 DOLLARS
11.3400 g., 0.5000 Gold .1823 oz. AGW **Ruler:** Elizabeth II
Subject: 25th Anniversary of Coronation **Obv:** Young bust right
Rev: Spoon

Date	Mintage	F	VF	XF	Unc	BU
1978 Proof	771	Value: 145				

KM# 58 50 DOLLARS
11.3400 g., 0.5000 Gold .1823 oz. AGW **Ruler:** Elizabeth II
Obv: Young bust right **Rev:** Saxon Kings **Rev. Designer:** Michael Rizzello

Date	Mintage	F	VF	XF	Unc	BU
1980 Proof	10,000	Value: 145				

KM# 59 50 DOLLARS
11.3400 g., 0.5000 Gold .1823 oz. AGW **Ruler:** Elizabeth II
Obv: Young bust right **Rev:** Norman Kings **Rev. Designer:** Michael Rizzello

Date	Mintage	F	VF	XF	Unc	BU
1980 Proof	10,000	Value: 145				

KM# 60 50 DOLLARS
11.3400 g., 0.5000 Gold .1823 oz. AGW **Ruler:** Elizabeth II
Obv: Young bust right **Rev:** House of Plantagenet - I **Rev. Designer:** Michael Rizzello

Date	Mintage	F	VF	XF	Unc	BU
1980 Proof	11,000	Value: 145				

KM# 61 50 DOLLARS
11.3400 g., 0.5000 Gold .1823 oz. AGW **Ruler:** Elizabeth II
Obv: Young bust right **Rev:** House of Plantagenet - II **Rev. Designer:** Michael Rizzello

Date	Mintage	F	VF	XF	Unc	BU
1980 Proof	11,000	Value: 145				

KM# 62 50 DOLLARS
11.3400 g., 0.5000 Gold .1823 oz. AGW **Ruler:** Elizabeth II
Obv: Young bust right **Rev:** House of Lancaster **Rev. Designer:** Michael Rizzello

Date	Mintage	F	VF	XF	Unc	BU
1980 Proof	11,000	Value: 145				

KM# 63 50 DOLLARS
11.3400 g., 0.5000 Gold .1823 oz. AGW **Ruler:** Elizabeth II
Obv: Young bust right **Rev:** House of York **Rev. Designer:** Michael Rizzello

Date	Mintage	F	VF	XF	Unc	BU
1980 Proof	11,000	Value: 145				

KM# 64 50 DOLLARS
11.3400 g., 0.5000 Gold .1823 oz. AGW **Ruler:** Elizabeth II
Obv: Young bust right **Rev:** House of Tudor **Rev. Designer:** Michael Rizzello

Date	Mintage	F	VF	XF	Unc	BU
1980 Proof	11,000	Value: 145				

KM# 65 50 DOLLARS
11.3400 g., 0.5000 Gold .1823 oz. AGW **Ruler:** Elizabeth II
Obv: Young bust right **Rev:** House of Stuart and Orange **Rev. Designer:** Michael Rizzello

Date	Mintage	F	VF	XF	Unc	BU
1980 Proof	11,000	Value: 145				

KM# 66 50 DOLLARS
11.3400 g., 0.5000 Gold .1823 oz. AGW **Ruler:** Elizabeth II
Obv: Young bust right **Rev:** House of Hanover **Rev. Designer:** Michael Rizzello

Date	Mintage	F	VF	XF	Unc	BU
1980 Proof	11,000	Value: 145				

KM# 67 50 DOLLARS
11.3400 g., 0.5000 Gold .1823 oz. AGW **Ruler:** Elizabeth II
Obv: Young bust right **Rev:** House of Saxe-Coburg and Windsor **Rev. Designer:** Michael Rizzello

Date	Mintage	F	VF	XF	Unc	BU
1980 Proof	11,000	Value: 145				

KM# 71 50 DOLLARS
5.0000 g., 0.9000 Gold .1447 oz. AGW **Ruler:** Elizabeth II
Subject: 150th Anniversary of Parliamentary Government **Obv:** Young bust right **Rev:** Island arms

Date	Mintage	F	VF	XF	Unc	BU
1982 Proof	585	Value: 135				

KM# 79 50 DOLLARS
5.1900 g., 0.9170 Gold .1530 oz. AGW **Ruler:** Elizabeth II
Subject: Royal Visit **Obv:** Young bust right **Rev:** Royal couple facing each other above small arms

CAYMAN ISLANDS

Date	Mintage	F	VF	XF	Unc	BU
1983	5,000	—	—	—	125	—

KM# 105 50 DOLLARS
7.8140 g., 0.9990 Gold .2509 oz. AGW **Ruler:** Elizabeth II **Obv:** Crowned bust right **Rev:** Cameo Winston Churchill above Spitfires over Dover **Rev. Designer:** Robert Elderton

Date	Mintage	F	VF	XF	Unc	BU
1990 Proof	Est. 500	Value: 190				

KM# 115 50 DOLLARS
15.9800 g., 0.9170 Gold .4708 oz. AGW **Ruler:** Elizabeth II **Obv:** Crowned bust right **Rev:** Wreck of the "Ten Sails" **Rev. Designer:** John Savage

Date	Mintage	F	VF	XF	Unc	BU
1994 Proof	Est. 200	Value: 500				

KM# 11 100 DOLLARS
22.6801 g., 0.5000 Gold .3646 oz. AGW **Ruler:** Elizabeth II **Subject:** Winston Churchill Centenary **Obv:** Island arms **Rev:** Bust facing **Rev. Designer:** Michael Rizzello

Date	Mintage	F	VF	XF	Unc	BU
1974	1,400	—	—	—	250	—
1974 Proof	6,300	Value: 245				

KM# 13 100 DOLLARS
22.6801 g., 0.5000 Gold .3646 oz. AGW **Ruler:** Elizabeth II **Obv:** Young bust right **Rev:** Sovereign Queens of England in circle **Rev. Designer:** Michael Rizzello

Date	Mintage	F	VF	XF	Unc	BU
1975	8,053	—	—	—	245	—
1975 Proof	4,950	Value: 250				
1976	2,028	—	—	—	245	—
1976 Proof	3,560	Value: 250				
1977	—	—	—	—	245	—
1977 Proof	2,845	Value: 250				

KM# 15 100 DOLLARS
22.6801 g., 0.5000 Gold .3646 oz. AGW **Ruler:** Elizabeth II **Subject:** Queen's Silver Jubilee **Obv:** Young bust right **Rev:** Crowned arms with supporters

Date	Mintage	F	VF	XF	Unc	BU
1977	562	—	—	—	245	—
1977 Proof	4,386	Value: 250				

KM# 35 100 DOLLARS
22.6801 g., 0.5000 Gold .3646 oz. AGW **Ruler:** Elizabeth II **Obv:** Young bust right **Rev:** Sovereign Queens of England in circle

Date	Mintage	F	VF	XF	Unc	BU
1978 Proof	1,973	Value: 260				

KM# 69 100 DOLLARS
8.0352 g., 0.9170 Gold .2369 oz. AGW **Ruler:** Elizabeth II **Subject:** Wedding of Prince Charles and Lady Diana **Obv:** Young bust right **Rev:** Busts facing, small island arms above

Date	Mintage	F	VF	XF	Unc	BU
1981 Proof	11,000	Value: 165				

KM# 97 100 DOLLARS
15.9800 g., 0.9170 Gold .4708 oz. AGW **Ruler:** Elizabeth II **Subject:** 500th Anniversary of Columbus' Discovery of America **Rev. Designer:** Robert Elderton

Date	Mintage	F	VF	XF	Unc	BU
1988 Proof	380	Value: 375				

KM# 101 100 DOLLARS
15.9800 g., 0.9170 Gold .4708 oz. AGW **Ruler:** Elizabeth II **Subject:** 100 Years of Postal Service **Obv:** Crowned bust right **Rev:** Ship with small shield above

Date	Mintage	F	VF	XF	Unc	BU
1989 Proof	93	Value: 475				

KM# 106 100 DOLLARS
15.6080 g., 0.9990 Gold .5013 oz. AGW **Ruler:** Elizabeth II **Subject:** Winston Churchill **Obv:** Crowned bust right **Rev:** Evacuation of Dunkirk **Rev. Designer:** Robert Elderton

Date	Mintage	F	VF	XF	Unc	BU
1990 Proof	500	Value: 360				

KM# 117 100 DOLLARS
30.5000 g., 0.9170 Gold .8974 oz. AGW **Ruler:** Elizabeth II **Obv:** Crowned bust right **Rev:** Cayman Ironwood Tree

Date	Mintage	F	VF	XF	Unc	BU
1994 Proof	Est. 15,000	Value: 635				

KM# 123 100 DOLLARS
15.9800 g., 0.9170 Gold .4708 oz. AGW **Ruler:** Elizabeth II **Obv:** Crowned bust right **Rev:** Amazona Leucocephala Caymanesis - Parrot

Date	Mintage	F	VF	XF	Unc	BU
1996 Proof	Est. 150	Value: 450				

KM# 82 250 DOLLARS
47.5400 g., 0.9170 Gold 1.4001 oz. AGW, 38.61 mm. **Ruler:** Elizabeth II **Subject:** 250th Anniversary of Royal Land Grant **Obv:** Crowned bust right **Rev:** Map of islands

Date	Mintage	F	VF	XF	Unc	BU
1985 Proof	Est. 250	Value: 950				

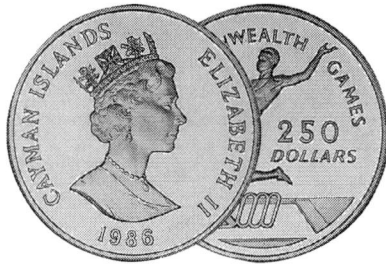

KM# 84 250 DOLLARS
47.5400 g., 0.9170 Gold 1.4001 oz. AGW **Ruler:** Elizabeth II **Subject:** Commonwealth Games **Obv:** Crowned bust right **Rev:** Long jumper

Date	Mintage	F	VF	XF	Unc	BU
1986 Proof	64	Value: 1,100				

KM# 86 250 DOLLARS
47.5400 g., 0.9170 Gold 1.4001 oz. AGW **Ruler:** Elizabeth II **Subject:** Queen Elizabeth II and Philip's 40th Wedding Anniversary **Obv:** Crowned bust right **Rev:** E & P monogram **Rev. Designer:** Norman Sillman

Date	Mintage	F	VF	XF	Unc	BU
ND Proof	75	Value: 1,100				

KM# 99 250 DOLLARS
47.5400 g., 0.9170 Gold 1.4001 oz. AGW **Ruler:** Elizabeth II **Subject:** Visit of Princess Alexandra **Obv:** Crowned bust right **Rev:** Royal Arms of Princess Alexandra

Date	Mintage	F	VF	XF	Unc	BU
1988 Proof	86	Value: 1,100				

KM# 107 250 DOLLARS
31.2100 g., 0.9990 Gold 1.0014 oz. AGW **Ruler:** Elizabeth II **Obv:** Crowned bust right **Rev:** Cameo Winston Churchill above Spitfires over Dover **Rev. Designer:** Robert Ederton

Date	Mintage	F	VF	XF	Unc	BU
1990 Proof	Est. 500	Value: 775				

KM# 113 250 DOLLARS
47.5400 g., 0.9170 Gold 1.4013 oz. AGW **Ruler:** Elizabeth II **Subject:** 40th Anniversary - Coronation of Queen Elizabeth II

Date	Mintage	F	VF	XF	Unc	BU
1993 Proof	Est. 100	Value: 1,100				

KM# 119 250 DOLLARS
47.5400 g., 0.9170 Gold 1.4013 oz. AGW **Ruler:** Elizabeth II **Subject:** Royal Visit **Obv:** Crowned bust right **Rev:** Royal couple above yacht "Britannia"

Date	Mintage	F	VF	XF	Unc	BU
1994 Proof	200	Value: 1,100				

PROOF SETS

KM#	Date	Mintage	Identification	Issue Price	Mkt Val
PS4	1974 (2)	2,400	KM10-11	245	255
PS7	1975 (2)	3,650	KM12-13	293	295
PS9	1976 (2)	1,531	KM12-13	293	295
PS13	1977 (6)	1,932	KM13, 21-25	651	775
PS14	1977 (2)	223	KM14-15	290	275
PS17	1978 (6)	771	KM42-47	600	850
PS28	1990 (4)	500	KM104-107	1,650	1,400

CENTRAL AFRICAN REPUBLIC

The Central African Republic, a landlocked country in Central Africa, bounded by Chad on the north, Cameroon on the west, Congo (Brazzaville) and Congo Democratic Republic, (formerly Zaire) on the south and the Sudan on the east, has an area of 240,324 sq. mi. (622,984 sq. km.) and a population of 3.2 million. Capital: Bangui. Deposits of uranium, iron ore, manganese and copper remain to be developed. Diamonds, cotton, timber and coffee are exported.

The area that is now the Central African Republic was constituted as the French territory of Ubangi-Shari in 1894. It was united with Chad in 1905 and joined with Middle Congo and Gabon in 1910, becoming one of the four territories of French Equatorial Africa. Upon dissolution of the federation on Dec. 1, 1958, the constituent territories became fully autonomous members of the French Community. Ubangi-Shari proclaimed its complete independence as the Central African Republic on Aug. 13, 1960.

On Jan. 1, 1966, Col. Jean-Bedel Bokassa, Chief of Staff of the Armed Forces, overthrew the government of President David Dacko and assumed power as president of the republic. President Bokassa abolished the constitution of 1959 and dissolved the National Assembly. In 1975 the Congress of the sole political party appointed Bokassa president for life. The republic became a constitutional monarchy on Dec. 4, 1976; President Bokassa was named Emperor Bokassa I. Bokassa was ousted as Central African emperor in a bloodless takeover of the government led by former president David Dacko on Sept. 20, 1979, and the African nation proclaimed once again a republic.

NOTE: For earlier coinage see French Equatorial Africa and Equatorial African States including later coinage as listed in Central African States.

RULERS
French, until 1960
Marshal Jean-Bedel Bokassa, 1976-1979

MINT MARKS
(a) - Paris, privy marks only

MONETARY SYSTEM
100 Centimes = 1 Franc

FIRST REPUBLIC
DECIMAL COINAGE

KM# 1 1000 FRANCS
3.5000 g., 0.9000 Gold .1012 oz. AGW **Subject:** 10th Anniversary of Independence **Obv:** Bust of President Jean Bedel Bokassa facing **Rev:** Three joined shields, radiant sun above center shield, denomination below

Date	Mintage	F	VF	XF	Unc	BU
1970 Proof	4,000	Value: 100				

KM# 2 3000 FRANCS
10.5000 g., 0.9000 Gold .3038 oz. AGW **Subject:** 10th Anniversary of Independence **Rev:** Bust with mortarboard facing, denomination below

Date	Mintage	F	VF	XF	Unc	BU
1970 Proof	4,000	Value: 225				

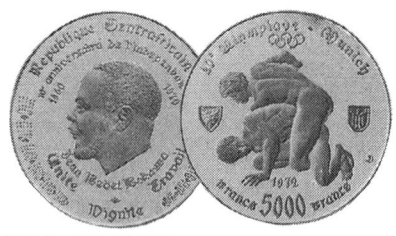

KM# 3 5000 FRANCS
17.5000 g., 0.9000 Gold .5064 oz. AGW **Subject:** 10th Anniversary of Independence; 1972 Munich Olympics **Obv:** Head left divides dates **Rev:** Wrestlers, date and denomination below

Date	Mintage	F	VF	XF	Unc	BU
1970 Proof	4,000	Value: 375				

KM# 4 10000 FRANCS
35.0000 g., 0.9000 Gold 1.0128 oz. AGW **Subject:** 10th Anniversary of Independence; ONU 24th Anniversary **Obv:** Head left divides dates **Rev:** Map at center, heads above, denomination below

Date	Mintage	F	VF	XF	Unc	BU
1970 Proof	4,000	Value: 745				

KM# 5 20000 FRANCS
70.0000 g., 0.9000 Gold 2.025728 oz. AGW **Subject:** 10th Anniversary of Independence; Operation Bokassa **Obv:** Head of Bokassa left, divides dates **Rev:** Symbols of independence, denomination below

Date	Mintage	F	VF	XF	Unc	BU
1970 Proof	4,000	Value: 1,550				

ESSAIS

KM#	Date	Mintage	Identification	Issue Price	Mkt Val
E3	1971	4	100 Francs. Gold. KM6.	—	1,400

PROOF SETS

KM#	Date	Mintage	Identification	Issue Price	Mkt Val
PS1	1970 (5)	40,000	KM1-5	375	3,000

CENTRAL AMERICAN REP.

The Central American Republic (Provincias Unidas del Centro de America, Republic of the United States of Central America, Central American Confederation) was an 1823-39 confederation of the former provinces of the Captaincy General of Guatemala - Guatemala, Honduras, El Salvador, Nicaragua and Costa Rica - formed from the southernmost provinces of the short-lived Mexican empire of Augustin de Iturbide. The confederation, which included all Central America between Mexico and Panama, had a population of fewer than 1.5 million.

On Sept. 15, 1821, the leaders of the Captaincy General that governed the five provinces of Central America for Spain, declared Central America independent. The following year, Iturbide crowned himself Augustin I of Mexico and invited the Central Americans to join his empire. Guatemala, Honduras, Nicaragua and Costa Rica did so. El Salvador, which desired to become a part of the United States, refused and was invaded and conquered for Mexico by Vicente Filisola, the military governor Iturbide had sent to Guatemala. But almost before El Salvador had been forced into the Mexican empire, Iturbide was ousted. Filisola then reconvened the National Constituent Assembly that had been established by the Central American declaration of independence of 1821. On July 1, 1823, the Assembly issued a second declaration of independence, from Mexico as well as Spain, and established the Central American Republic.

Historically the confederation, which lasted 15 years, was an anomaly for a government: It had neither permanent capital, army nor treasury and was all but powerless to raise funds. Its written constitution, was as unsatisfactory as the first constitution of the United States, the Articles of Confederation.

Divided by geography as well as religious and class animosity the citizens of the Republic had no sense of nationhood. By 1827 the entire Republic was embroiled in civil war. By 1839 every state but El Salvador had seceded from the union; interestingly, Costa Rica, Guatemala and Honduras continued to strike coins in the confederation style - until 1850, 1851 and 1861, respectively. Costa Rica then countermarked many coins of this series for continued circulation within its boundaries.

MINT MARKS
CR - San Jose, Costa Rica
G, NG - Guatemala
T - Tegucigalpa, Honduras

MONETARY SYSTEM
16 Reales = 1 Escudo

REPUBLIC
STANDARD COINAGE

KM# 5 1/2 ESCUDO
1.6875 g., 0.8750 Gold .0474 oz. AGW **Obv:** Radiant sun with face above three mountains **Rev:** Tree

Date	Mintage	VG	F	VF	XF	Unc
1824NG M	—	50.00	85.00	150	300	—
1825/4NG M	—	60.00	90.00	175	275	—
1825NG M	—	45.00	65.00	125	225	1,250
1826NG M	—	60.00	90.00	175	275	—
1843NG M	—	100	175	325	500	—

KM# 11 1/2 ESCUDO
1.6875 g., 0.8750 Gold .0474 oz. AGW **Note:** Provisional issue. At least 4 examples are known.

Date	Mintage	VG	F	VF	XF	Unc
1825CR MU Rare	—	—	—	—	—	—

CENTRAL AMERICAN REPUBLIC

KM# 13.1 1/2 ESCUDO
1.6875 g., 0.8750 Gold .0474 oz. AGW **Obv:** Sun above mountains **Rev:** Tree divides denomination

Date	Mintage	VG	F	VF	XF	Unc
1828CR F	4,435	75.00	125	225	350	1,275
1843CR M	593	200	300	500	900	—
1846CR JB	13,000	65.00	100	150	200	—
1847CR JB	23,000	75.00	125	225	350	1,000
1848CR JB	14,000	85.00	145	245	550	—
1849CR JB	Inc. above	150	250	450	750	—

KM# 13.2 1/2 ESCUDO
1.6875 g., 0.8750 Gold .0474 oz. AGW **Obv:** Sun above mountains **Rev:** Tree divides denomination **Note:** Inverted "C" in mint mark.

Date	Mintage	VG	F	VF	XF	Unc
1847CR JB	Inc. above	85.00	150	250	575	—
1848CR JB	Inc. above	85.00	150	250	575	—

KM# 6 ESCUDO
3.3750 g., 0.8750 Gold .0949 oz. AGW **Obv:** Sun left of five mountains

Date	Mintage	VG	F	VF	XF	Unc
1824NG M	—	120	300	750	1,200	—
1825NG M	—	95.00	175	375	800	—

KM# 14 ESCUDO
3.3750 g., 0.8750 Gold .0949 oz. AGW **Obv:** Sun above five mountains **Rev:** Tree divides denomination

Date	Mintage	VG	F	VF	XF	Unc
1828CR F Rare, 4 known	—	—	—	—	—	—

Note: American Numismatic Rarities Eliasberg sale 4-05, VF realized $6325.

Date	Mintage	VG	F	VF	XF	Unc
1833CR E	10,000	85.00	150	350	850	—
1844CR M	6,353	85.00	150	350	850	—
1845CR JB	8,672	90.00	170	400	900	—
1846CR JB	2,722	90.00	175	450	1,000	—
1847CR JB	3,510	85.00	125	225	550	—
1848CR JB	10,000	80.00	120	200	500	3,000
1849CR JB	13,000	80.00	120	200	500	—

KM# 12 2 ESCUDOS
6.7500 g., 0.8750 Gold .1899 oz. AGW **Obv:** Sun above five mountains **Rev:** Tree divides denomination

Date	Mintage	VG	F	VF	XF	Unc
1825NG M	—	135	185	320	600	4,250
1826NG M	—	135	185	320	600	—
1827NG M	—	135	185	320	600	4,250
1828NG M	—	135	185	320	600	—
1830/29NG M Rare	—	—	—	—	—	—

Note: American Numismatic Rarities Eliasberg sale 4-05, MS-65 PL realized $16,100.

Date	Mintage	VG	F	VF	XF	Unc
1830NG M	—	135	250	400	700	—
1834NG M	—	175	375	750	1,200	—
1835NG M	—	135	185	320	600	—
1836NG M	—	145	200	400	650	—
1837NG BA	—	145	200	425	850	—
1840NG MA Rare, three known	—	—	—	—	—	—

Note: American Numismatic Rarities Eliasberg sale 4-05, MS-62 realized $16,100.

Date	Mintage	VG	F	VF	XF	Unc
1842NG MA	—	145	200	400	800	—
1844NG B	—	145	200	425	850	—
1846NG A	—	145	200	400	650	4,500
1847NG A	—	145	200	400	700	—

KM# 15 2 ESCUDOS
6.7500 g., 0.8750 Gold .1899 oz. AGW

Date	Mintage	VG	F	VF	XF	Unc
1828CR F	2,750	150	225	375	800	5,500
1835CR F	5,452	145	200	350	600	2,500
1843CR M	4,482	150	225	375	900	—

Note: American Numismatic rarities Eliasberg sale 4-05, AU-58 realized $10,925.

Date	Mintage	VG	F	VF	XF	Unc
1850CR JB	7,432	BV	150	250	500	—

KM# 7 4 ESCUDOS
13.5000 g., 0.8750 Gold .3798 oz. AGW **Obv:** Sun with large face above five mountains **Rev:** Tree divides denomination

Date	Mintage	VG	F	VF	XF	Unc
1824NG M	—	750	1,450	2,750	4,500	—
1825NG M	—	1,000	1,800	3,250	5,500	—

KM# 16 4 ESCUDOS
13.5000 g., 0.8750 Gold .3798 oz. AGW **Obv:** Radiant sun with large face above five mountains **Rev:** Tree divides denomination

Date	Mintage	VG	F	VF	XF	Unc
1828CR F	3,048	450	650	1,250	4,500	—
1835CR F	697	350	550	1,100	4,000	—
1837CR E	11,000	350	600	1,200	4,250	7,000
1837CR F Rare	Inc. above	—	—	—	—	—
1849CR JB	441	2,000	3,500	7,500	15,000	—

Note: American Numismatic Rarities Eliasberg sale 4-05, EF realized $14,950.

KM# 8 8 ESCUDOS
27.0000 g., 0.8750 Gold .7596 oz. AGW **Obv:** Radiant sun with large face above five mountains **Rev:** Tree divides denomination

Date	Mintage	VG	F	VF	XF	Unc
1824NG M	—	1,200	2,500	4,500	8,500	—

Note: Stack's Hammel sale 9-82 Unc 1824 M realized $27,000

Date	Mintage	VG	F	VF	XF	Unc
1825NG M	—	1,800	3,500	7,500	15,000	—

KM# 17 8 ESCUDOS
27.0000 g., 0.8750 Gold .7596 oz. AGW **Obv:** Radiant sun with face above five mountains **Rev:** Tree divides denomination

Date	Mintage	VG	F	VF	XF	Unc
1828CR F	5,302	600	1,000	2,000	3,500	—

Note: American Numismatic Rarities Eliasberg sale 4-05, MS-62 realized $29,900. Stack's Hammel sale 9-82 AU 1828 F realized $9,500

Date	Mintage	VG	F	VF	XF	Unc
1833CR F	4,459	600	1,000	2,000	3,500	—
1837CR E	2,028	950	1,550	3,250	6,000	—
1837CR F	Inc. above	1,200	2,200	4,500	7,500	—

CENTRAL ASIA

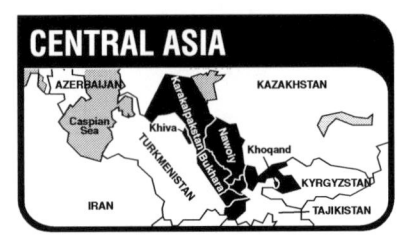

In the several centuries prior to 1500 which witnessed the breakup of the Mongol Empire and the subsequent rise of smaller successor states, no single power or dynasty was able to control the vast expanses of Western and Central Asia. The region known previously as Transoxiana, the land beyond the Oxus River (modern Amu Darya), became the domain of the Shaybanids, then the Janids. The territory ruled by these dynasties had no set borders, which rather expanded and contracted as the fortunes of the rulers ebbed and flowed. At their greatest extent, the khanate took in parts of what are now northern Iran and Afghanistan, as well as part or all of modern Turkmenistan, Uzbekistan, Kazakhstan, Tadzhikistan and Kyrgyzstan. Coins are known to have been struck by virtually every ruler, but some are quite scarce owing to short reigns or the ever-changing political and economic situation.

MINTS
Asfarayin
Astarabad
Awbah
Badakhshan
Balkh
Bukhara
Heart
Hisar
Marw
Mashhad
Nimruz
Qarshi (copper only)
Qunduz
Samarqand
Tashkent (Tashkand)
Termez
Urdu (camp mint)

BUKHARA

Bukhara, a city and former emirate in southern Russian Turkestan, formed part (Sogdiana) of the Seleucid Empire after the conquest of Alexander the Great and incessantly remained an important region throughout the middle ages, often serving as the capital center for a succession of ruling dynasties of Iranian and Turkish origin until the 19th century. It became virtually a Russian vassal in 1868 as a consequence of the Czarist invasion of 1866, following which it gradually became a part of Russian Turkestan and then part of Uzbekistan S.S.R., now Uzbekistan.

RULERS
Russian Vassal,
  (since AH1284/1868AD)
Emir Abd al-Ahad,
  AH1303-1328 / 1886-1910AD
Emir Sayyid Alim Khan,
  AH1329-1339 / 1911-1920AD

MINT NAME

بخاراي شريف   بخارا

Bukhara   Bukhara-yi Sharif

MONETARY SYSTEM
Until AH1322/1905AD: 45 to 64 Pul (Fulus) = 4 Miri = 1 silver Tenga
19 to 21 Tenga = 1 Tilla (gold 4.55 g.)
Until AH1336-1338/1918-1920AD: copper Tenga or Tenga-fulus
Within the protectorate period, Russian currency of Roubles and Kopeks were officially in circulation: 1 silver Tenga = 20 Kopeks

Note: All copper, bronze and brass issues of Bukhara in the 20th century are anonymous. Some silver and gold issues traditionally bear the names of Emirs long since deceased.

Note: Denominations of 1/32 Tenga & Tilla are of very similar design under various rulers, but can be distinguished by date.

Note: Tilla coins are known with a date appearing as "134-", which is actually 1316 with the "1" and "6" stuck close together, appearing as a Persian "4".

Note: Most copper, bronze and brass AH1336-1338 dated coins of 2, 3, 10 and especially 20 Tenga exhibit considerable flat spots, die shifts and other defects. Well-struck specimens with fully struck design demand a considerable premium.

Note: The numerals "0" and "5" have variant forms in Bukhara, including an open "J" – type symbol for "5" instead of a closed symbol:

o   O   and   ◆

5   ࡐ   or   ࡐ   instead of   ࡏ   ࡏ

KHANATE
HAMMERED COINAGE

KM# 27 TILLA
Gold **Ruler:** Haidar Tora AH1215-1242/1800-1826 AD **Obv:** Teardrop **Rev:** Circle

Date	Mintage	Good	VG	F	VF	XF
AH1217//1216	—	—	95.00	120	175	250
AH1218	—	—	85.00	110	160	220
AH1219//1218	—	95.00	120	175	250	—
AH1219	—	—	85.00	110	160	220
AH1220//1216	—	—	95.00	120	175	250

KM# 30 TILLA
Gold **Ruler:** Haidar Tora AH1215-1242/1800-1826 AD **Rev:** Octagon

Date	Mintage	VG	F	VF	XF	Unc
AH1221	—	100	150	225	325	—
AH1222	—	100	150	225	325	—
AH1225	—	100	150	225	325	—
AH1226	—	100	150	225	325	—
AH1227	—	100	150	225	325	—
AH1229	—	100	150	225	325	—

KM# 32 TILLA
Gold **Ruler:** Haidar Tora AH1215-1242/1800-1826 AD **Obv:** Teardrop **Rev:** Circle

Date	Mintage	VG	F	VF	XF	Unc
AH1225	—	75.00	100	150	200	—

KM# 34 TILLA
Gold **Ruler:** Haidar Tora AH1215-1242/1800-1826 AD **Obv:** Teardrop border **Obv. Inscription:** "Ma'sum Ibn Daniyal"

Date	Mintage	VG	F	VF	XF	Unc
AH1229	—	85.00	110	160	220	—
AH1230//1229	—	95.00	120	175	250	—
AH1230	—	85.00	110	160	220	—
AH1231	—	85.00	110	160	220	—
AH1233//1033 (sic)	—	95.00	120	175	250	—
AH1233//1232	—	95.00	120	175	250	—
AH1234	—	85.00	110	160	220	—

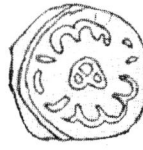

KM# 43 TILLA
Gold **Ruler:** Haidar Tora AH1215-1242/1800-1826 AD **Obv:** Circular border **Obv. Inscription:** "Ma'sum Ibn Daniyal" **Rev:** Circular border

Date	Mintage	VG	F	VF	XF	Unc
AH1232//1233	—	75.00	100	150	200	—
AH1233	—	75.00	100	150	200	—
AH1234	—	75.00	100	150	200	—
AH1235	—	75.00	100	150	200	—

KM# 52 TILLA
Gold **Ruler:** Haidar Tora AH1215-1242/1800-1826 AD **Obv. Inscription:** "Ma'sum Ibn Daniyal"

Date	Mintage	VG	F	VF	XF	Unc
AH1235	—	75.00	100	150	200	—
AH1236//1235	—	75.00	100	150	200	—
AH1236	—	75.00	100	150	200	—
AH1239//1240	—	85.00	110	175	250	—
AH1241	—	75.00	100	150	200	—

KM# 65 TILLA
4.5500 g., Gold **Ruler:** Emir Abd Al-Ahad AH1303-1328/1886-1910AD **Note:** Struck in the name of late Ma'sum Ghazi (Emir Shah Murad). Die varieties exist with and without date on reverse. Prev. #Y3.

Date	Mintage	Good	VG	F	VF	XF
AH1243//1242	—	—	95.00	115	165	225
AH1243	—	—	90.00	110	150	200
AH1244//1245	—	—	95.00	115	165	225
AH1244	—	—	85.00	110	150	200
AH1246	—	—	80.00	115	150	200
AH1247//1244	—	—	95.00	115	165	225
AH1247/6//1246	—	—	95.00	115	165	225
AH1248	—	—	85.00	110	150	200
AH1254	—	—	85.00	110	150	200
AH1255//1254	—	—	95.00	115	165	225
AH1255	—	—	85.00	110	150	200
AH1256//1254	—	—	95.00	115	165	225
AH1256//1255	—	—	95.00	115	165	225
AH1256	—	—	85.00	110	150	200
AH1257//1258	—	—	95.00	115	165	225
AH1857//1261	—	—	85.00	110	150	200
AH1264	—	—	85.00	110	150	200
AH1265//1266	—	—	95.00	115	165	225
AH1272//1275	—	—	95.00	115	165	225
AH1273//1243(sic)	—	—	95.00	115	165	225
AH1273//1274	—	—	85.00	110	150	200
AH1273//1275	—	—	85.00	110	150	200
AH1278	—	—	85.00	100	120	175
AH1279	—	—	85.00	100	120	175

Note: Date combination of AH1279 obverse and AH1285 reverse is reported

AH1283	—	—	85.00	100	120	175
AH1284	—	—	85.00	100	120	175
AH1285	—	—	85.00	100	120	175
AH1289	—	—	85.00	100	120	175
AH1291	—	—	85.00	100	120	175
AH1294	—	—	85.00	100	120	175
AH1296//1300	—	—	85.00	110	150	200
AH1296	—	—	85.00	100	120	175
AH1297	—	—	85.00	100	120	175
AH1298//1298	—	—	85.00	110	150	200
AH1299	—	—	85.00	100	120	175
AH1303	—	—	85.00	110	135	185
AH1306	—	—	85.00	110	135	185
AH1309	—	—	85.00	110	135	185
AH1315	—	—	85.00	110	135	185
AH1316	—	—	85.00	110	135	185
AH1319	—	—	95.00	110	135	185
AH1321	—	—	125	165	250	350
AH1322//1322	—	—	95.00	110	135	185
AH1324/1324	—	—	95.00	110	135	185
AH1324//1316	—	—	125	165	250	350
AH1324//1321	—	—	125	165	250	350
AH1325//1325	—	—	95.00	110	135	185
AH1325//1325	—	—	115	155	225	320

Note: Reverse date recut from 1324

AH1327	—	—	100	135	200	300
AH1328	—	—	100	135	200	300
AH1328//1292	—	—	175	250	350	500
AH1328//1304	—	—	125	165	250	350
AH1328//1321	—	—	175	250	350	500

KHIVA

Khwarezm (Khiva), a historical region, once a great kingdom under the names of Chorasmia, Khwarezm and Gurganj (Urgench), is located in the lower stream and the delta of the Amu Darya River, east of the Caspian Sea and south of the Aral Sea. Russia established relations with Khwarezm (Khiva Khanate) in the 17th century, occupied it in 1873, and annexed it in 1875. Revolution concentrated Russia's preoccupation elsewhere during 1917 and Khiva seized this opportunity to declare its independence. It was able to sustain this status for a scant two years. By 1919 the Soviet regime had reestablished control over the region and extinguished the independent state. In AH1338/1920AD it was proclaimed Khorezm People's Soviet Republic and later became part of the Uzbekistan S.S.R. (Qaraqalpak Autonomous Republic), now Uzbekistan.

RULERS
Russian Vassals
  (since AH1290 / 1873AD)
Sayyid Muhammad Rahim
  AH1282-1328 / 1865-910AD
Isfandiyar
  AH1328-1336 / 1910-1918AD
Sayyid Abdullah
  Normally in AH1337-1338 / 1919-1920AD
  Actual ruler – Muhammad Qurban Sardar (Junaid Khan)
  AH1334-1338 / 1916-1920AD

KHOQAND

MINT NAMES

خوارزم

Khwarezm

دار الاسلام خوارزم

Dar al-Islam Khwarezm

Note: All copper, bronze and brass issues of Khiva (Khorezm, Khwarezm) in the 20th century are anonymous, except the silver Tenga Y#8, which bears the name of a Khan, long since deceased.

MONETARY SYSTEM
24 to 32 Pul (Fulus) = 4 Shahi = 1 silver Tenga
about 20 Tenga = 1 Tilla (gold 4.55 g.)

AH1337-1338 / 1918-1920AD: copper Tenga or Tenga-fulus

Within the protectorate period, Russian currency of Rubles and Kopeks were officially in circulation : 1 silver Tenga was equivalent to 20 Kopeks.

Note: Denomination of Pul are of similar design under various rulers, but can be distinguished by date.
2 ½ & 5 Tenga: Ornamentation, size and design of borders and die rotation vary considerably. Crudely engraved dies with mostly simplified design are known struck on cast flans. Cast specimens exist.

Note: 50, 200 & 1000 Roubles coins with crude inscriptions are modern fantasies.

KHANATE

HAMMERED COINAGE

C# 65 1/2 TILLA
Gold Ruler: Muhammad Amin AH1261-1271 / 1845-1855 AD

Date	Mintage	VG	F	VF	XF	Unc
AH1261	—	200	350	550	800	—
AH1265	—	200	350	550	800	—

C# 65a 1/2 TILLA
Gold Ruler: Muhammad Amin AH1261-1271 / 1845-1855 AD

Date	Mintage	VG	F	VF	XF	Unc
AH1270	—	200	350	550	800	—
AH1271	—	200	350	550	800	—

Y# A1 1/2 TILLA
Gold Ruler: Qutlugh Muhammad AH1271-1272 / 1855-1856 AD

Date	Mintage	VG	F	VF	XF	Unc
AH1271	—	250	450	750	1,100	—
AH1272	—	250	450	750	1,100	—

Y# A3 TILLA
Gold Ruler: Sayyid Muhammad Khan AH1272-1282 / 1856-1864 AD

Date	Mintage	VG	F	VF	XF	Unc
AH1276	—	275	450	700	1,000	—
AH1277	—	275	450	700	1,000	—

KHOQAND

Khoqand, a town and former khanate in eastern Turkestan, was a powerful state in the 18th century. Russian superiority in the area was recognized following the holy war of 1875 and was annexed in 1875. It regained its independence briefly during 1918-1920 and became a Soviet Peoples Republic briefly between 1920-1924, and finally was absorbed into Uzbekistan S.S.R., now Uzbekistan.

RULERS
Muhammad Ali Khan,
    AH1238-1256/1822-1840AD
Sher Ali,
    AH1258-1261/1842-1845AD
Muhammad Khudayar Khan, 1st reign,
    AH1261-1275/1845-1858AD
Malla Khan,
    AH1275-1278/1858-1862AD
Shah Murad,
    AH1278-1279/1862AD
Muhammad Khudayar Khan, 2nd reign,
    AH1279-1280/1862-1863AD
Sayyid Sultan,
    AH1280-1282/1863-1865AD
Muhammad Khudayer Khan, 3rd reign,
    AH1282-1292/1865-1875AD
Independent until AH1283/1866AD
Russian Vassal AH1283-1293/ 1866-1876AD
Nasir al-Din,
    AH1292-1293/1875-1876AD
Annexed To Russia, 1875-1876AD
Muhammad Fulad, Rebel,
    AH1292-1293/1875-1876AD

MINT NAMES
Until AH1257, the coinage of Khoqand was struck at two mints.

فرغانة

Fe - Fergana(t)

خوقند

Kd – Khoqand

KHANATE

STANDARD COINAGE

C# 67 TILLA
Gold Ruler: Muhammad Ali Khan AH1238-56/1822-40AD

Date	Mintage	VG	F	VF	XF	Unc
AH1247 Fa Rare	—	—	—	—	—	—

C# 68 TILLA
Gold Ruler: Muhammad Ali Khan AH1238-56/1822-40AD

Date	Mintage	VG	F	VF	XF	Unc
AH1252	—	75.00	100	175	265	—
AH1254	—	75.00	100	175	265	—
AH1255	—	75.00	100	175	265	—
AH1256	—	75.00	100	175	265	—
AH1257	—	75.00	100	175	265	—

Note: AH1257 dated strikes are posthumous issues

C# 78 TILLA
Gold Ruler: Sher Ali AH1258-61/1842-45AD

Date	Mintage	VG	F	VF	XF	Unc
AH1259//1258	—	100	125	225	300	—
AH1259	—	80.00	100	225	300	—
AH1260	—	80.00	100	225	300	—

C# 100 TILLA
Gold Ruler: Muhammad Khudayar Khan, 1st reign AH1261-75/1845-58AD

Date	Mintage	VG	F	VF	XF	Unc
AH1260	—	100	140	170	225	—
AH1261//1264	—	125	175	200	250	—
AH1261	—	100	140	170	225	—
AH1262//1261	—	125	175	200	250	—
AH1263	—	100	140	170	225	—
AH1264	—	100	140	170	225	—
AH1265	—	100	140	170	225	—
AH1266	—	100	140	170	225	—
AH1270	—	100	140	170	225	—
AH1272	—	100	140	170	225	—
AH1273	—	100	140	170	225	—
AH1274	—	100	140	170	225	—
AH1275	—	100	140	170	225	—

C# 100.5 TILLA
Gold Ruler: Muhammad Khudayar Khan, 1st reign AH1261-75/1845-58AD **Obv:** New title

Date	Mintage	VG	F	VF	XF	Unc
AH1261//1262	—	125	275	425	600	—
AH1265	—	125	275	425	600	—

C# 118 TILLA
Gold Ruler: Muhammad Malla Khan AH1275-78/1858-62AD

Date	Mintage	VG	F	VF	XF	Unc
AH1275	—	100	140	170	225	—
AH1276	—	100	140	170	225	—
AH1277	—	100	140	170	225	—
AH1278	—	100	140	170	225	—

C# 128 TILLA
Gold Ruler: Shah Murad AH1278-79/1862AD

Date	Mintage	VG	F	VF	XF	Unc
AH1278	—	100	150	250	350	—

C# 135 TILLA
Gold Ruler: Muhammad Khudayar Khan, 2nd reign AH1279-80/1862-63AD

Date	Mintage	VG	F	VF	XF	Unc
ND	—	—	—	—	—	—

Note: Reported, not confirmed

C# 145 TILLA
Gold Ruler: Sayyid Sultan AH1280-82/1863-65AD

Date	Mintage	VG	F	VF	XF	Unc
AH1280	—	100	140	170	225	—
AH1281	—	100	140	170	225	—

C# 155 TILLA
Gold Ruler: Muhammad Khudayer Khan, 3rd reign AH1282-92/1865-75AD **Obv. Inscription:** "Muhammad Malla Khan"

Date	Mintage	VG	F	VF	XF	Unc
AH1282	—	90.00	120	160	190	—
AH1283	—	90.00	120	160	190	—
AH1285	—	90.00	120	160	190	—
AH1288	—	90.00	120	160	190	—
AH1289	—	90.00	120	160	190	—

C# 165 TILLA
Gold Ruler: Nasir al-Din AH1292-93/1875-76AD

Date	Mintage	VG	F	VF	XF	Unc
AH1292	—	—	—	—	—	—

Note: Reported, not confirmed

CEYLON

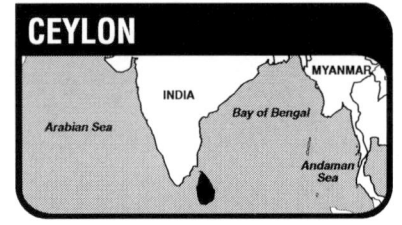

The earliest known inhabitants of Ceylon, the Veddahs, were subjugated by the Sinhalese from northern India in the 6th century B.C. Sinhalese rule was maintained until 1408, after which the island was controlled by China for 30 years. The Portuguese came to Ceylon in 1505 and maintained control of the coastal area for 150 years. The Dutch supplanted them in 1658, which were in turn supplanted by the British who seized the Dutch colonies in 1796, and made them a Crown Colony in 1802. In 1815, the British conquered the independent Kingdom of Kandy in the central part of the island. Constitutional changes in 1931 and 1946 granted the Ceylonese a measure of autonomy and a parliamentary form of government. Britain granted Ceylon independence as a self-governing state within the British Commonwealth on Feb. 4, 1948. On May 22, 1972, the Ceylonese adopted a new Constitution, which declared Ceylon to be the Republic of Sri Lanka –"Resplendent Island"

RULERS
Portuguese, until 1655
Dutch until 1796
British, 1796-1948

MINT MARKS
H – Heaton, Birmingham
B – Bombay

BRITISH COLONIAL
DECIMAL COINAGE
100 Cents = 1 Rupee

KM# 90b 1/4 CENT
Gold **Ruler:** Victoria **Obv:** Head left within circle **Obv. Legend:** QUEEN VICTORIA **Rev:** Tree within circle

Date	Mintage	F	VF	XF	Unc	BU
1870 Proof	—	Value: 1,250				
1891 Proof	—	Value: 1,250				

KM# 100a 1/4 CENT
Gold **Ruler:** Edward VII **Obv:** Crowned bust right **Rev:** Tree within circle, date below, denomination above

Date	Mintage	F	VF	XF	Unc	BU
1904	—	Value: 1,000				

KM# 91b 1/2 CENT
Gold **Ruler:** Victoria **Obv:** Head left within circle **Obv. Legend:** QUEEN VICTORIA **Rev:** Tree within circle

Date	Mintage	F	VF	XF	Unc	BU
1870 Proof	—	Value: 1,250				
1891 Proof	—	Value: 1,250				
1895 Proof	—	Value: 1,250				

KM# 92b CENT
Gold **Ruler:** Victoria **Obv:** Head left within circle **Obv. Legend:** QUEEN VICTORIA **Rev:** Tree within circle

Date	Mintage	F	VF	XF	Unc	BU
1870 Proof	—	Value: 1,350				
1891 Proof	—	Value: 1,350				

KM# 93b 5 CENTS
Gold **Ruler:** Victoria **Obv:** Head left within circle **Obv. Legend:** QUEEN VICTORIA **Rev:** Tree within circle

Date	Mintage	F	VF	XF	Unc	BU
1870 Proof	—	Value: 1,500				
1891 Proof	—	Value: 1,500				

CHAD

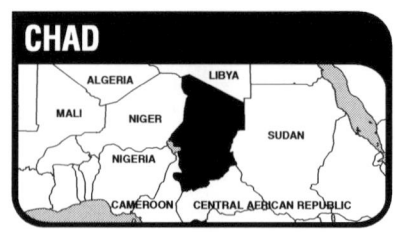

The Republic of Chad, a landlocked country of central Africa, is the largest country of former French Equatorial Africa. It has an area of 495,755 sq. mi. (1,284,000 sq. km.) and a population of *7.27 million. Capital: N'Djamena. An expanding livestock industry produces camels, cattle and sheep. Cotton (the chief product), ivory and palm oil are important exports.

Although supposedly known to Ptolemy, the Chad area was first visited by white men in 1823. Exaggerated estimates of its economic importance led to a race for its possession (1890-93), which resulted in the territory being divided by treaty between Great Britain, France and Germany. As a consequence of World War I, the German area was mandated to France in 1919. Chad was absorbed into the colony of French Equatorial Africa, as part of Ubangi-Shari, in 1910 and became a separate colony in 1920. Upon dissolution of French Equatorial Africa in 1959, the component states became autonomous members of the French Union. Chad became an independent republic on Aug. 11, 1960.

NOTE: For earlier and related coinage see French Equatorial Africa and the Equatorial African States. For later coinage see Central African States.

MINT MARKS
(a) - Paris, privy marks only
(b) = Brussels
NI - Numismatic Italiana, Arezzo, Italy

REPUBLIC
DECIMAL COINAGE

KM# 8 1000 FRANCS
3.5000 g., 0.9000 Gold .1012 oz. AGW **Subject:** 10th Anniversary of Independence **Obv:** Nude half figure of woman right, shield of arms above, denomination at right **Rev:** Commandant Lamy 3/4 facing, date below

Date	Mintage	F	VF	XF	Unc	BU
ND(1970)(a)NI Proof	4,000	Value: 185				
ND(1970)NI Proof	Inc. above	Value: 185				

KM# 9 3000 FRANCS
10.5000 g., 0.9000 Gold .3038 oz. AGW **Subject:** 10th Anniversary of Independence **Obv:** Shield of arms above map, denomination below, right **Rev:** Governor Eboue 3/4 left, date below

Date	Mintage	F	VF	XF	Unc	BU
ND(1970)(a)NI	4,000	Value: 240				
ND(1970)NI	Inc. above	Value: 240				

KM# 10 5000 FRANCS
17.5000 g., 0.9000 Gold .5064 oz. AGW **Subject:** 10th Anniversary of Independence **Obv:** Trees divide arch and arms, denomination below **Rev:** General Leclerc 3/4 facing, date below

Date	Mintage	F	VF	XF	Unc	BU
ND(1970)(a)NI Proof	4,000	Value: 350				
ND(1970)NI Proof	Inc. above	Value: 350				

CHILE 109

KM# 11 10000 FRANCS
36.0000 g., 0.9000 Gold 1.0128 oz. AGW **Subject:** 10th Anniversary of Independence **Obv:** Arms above double cross, denomination below **Rev:** General Charles de Gaulle right, date below **Rev. Designer:** G. Simon

Date	Mintage	F	VF	XF	Unc	BU
ND(1970)(a)NI Proof	4,000	Value: 750				
ND (1970)NI Proof	Inc. above	Value: 750				

KM# 12 20000 FRANCS
70.0000 g., 0.9000 Gold 2.0257 oz. AGW **Subject:** 10th Anniversary of Independence **Obv:** Francois Tombalbaye, left, date lower right **Rev. Designer:** G. Simon

Date	Mintage	F	VF	XF	Unc	BU
ND (1970)(a)NI Proof	Est. 4,000	Value: 1,600				
ND (1970)NI Proof	Inc. above	Value: 1,600				

ESSAIS
Standard metals unless otherwise noted

KM#	Date	Mintage	Identification	Issue Price	Mkt Val
E4	1971	4	100 Francs. Gold. KM#2.	—	1,500

PROOF SETS

KM#	Date	Mintage	Identification	Issue Price	Mkt Val
PS1	1970 (5)	4,000	KM8-12	413	3,125

KM# 14 10000 FRANCS
36.0000 g., 0.9000 Gold 1.0128 oz. AGW **Subject:** 10th Anniversary of Independence **Obv:** Map of African continent, denomination at left **Rev:** Egypt's President Nasser facing

Date	Mintage	F	VF	XF	Unc	BU
1970(b) Proof	205	Value: 1,175				

KM# 15 10000 FRANCS
36.0000 g., 0.9000 Gold 1.0128 oz. AGW **Subject:** 10th Anniversary of Independence **Obv:** Map of Africa **Rev:** Charles de Gaulle facing

Date	Mintage	F	VF	XF	Unc	BU
1970 Proof	90	Value: 1,350				

CHILE

The Republic of Chile, a ribbon-like country on the Pacific coast of southern South America, has an area of 292,135 sq. mi. (756,950 sq. km.) and a population of *15.21 million. Capital: Santiago. Historically, the economic base of Chile has been the rich mineral deposits of its northern provinces. Copper has accounted for more than 75 percent of Chile's export earnings in recent years. Other important mineral exports are iron ore, iodine and nitrate of soda. Fresh fruits and vegetables, as well as wine are increasingly significant in inter-hemispheric trade.

Diego de Almargo was the first Spaniard to attempt to wrest Chile from the Incas and Araucanian tribes in 1536. He failed, and was followed by Pedro de Valdivia, a favorite of Pizarro, who founded Santiago in 1541. When the Napoleonic Wars involved Spain, leaving the constituent parts of the Spanish Empire to their own devices, Chilean patriots formed a national government and proclaimed the country's independence, Sept. 18, 1810. Independence however, was not secured until Feb. 12, 1818, after a bitter struggle led by Bernardo O'Higgins and San Martin. Despite a long steady history of monetary devaluation, reflected in declining weight and fineness in its currency, Chile developed a strong democracy. This was displaced when rampant inflation characterized chaotic and subsequently repressive governments in the mid to late 20th century.

RULER
Spanish until 1818

MINT MARK
So - Santiago

MINT OFFICIALS' INITIALS

A	1768-1801	Agustin de Infante y Prado
AJ	1800-01	Agustin de Infante y Prado and Jose Maria de Bobadilla
D	1773-99	Domingo Eizaguirre
DA	1772-99	Domingo Eizaguirre and Agustin de Infante y Prado
F	1803-17	Francisco Rodriguez Brochero
FJ, JF	1803-17	Francisco Rodriguez Brochero and Jose Maria de Bobadilla
J	1749-67	Jose Larrañeta
J	1800-17	Jose Maria de Bobadilla

MONETARY SYSTEM
16 Reales = 1 Escudo

COLONIAL
MILLED COINAGE

KM# 61 ESCUDO
3.3834 g., 0.8750 Gold .0952 oz. AGW, 19 mm. **Ruler:** Carlos IV **Obv:** Laureate bust right **Obv. Legend:** CAROL IIII... **Rev:** Crowned arms in order chain **Note:** Mint mark So.

Date	Mintage	VG	F	VF	XF	Unc
1801 AJ	1,088	175	300	450	1,000	—
1802 JJ	748	225	350	425	950	—
1803 FJ/JJ	1,156	275	500	850	1,650	—
1803 FJ	Inc. above	200	285	300	650	—
1804 FJ	1,428	200	285	300	650	—
1805 FJ/JJ	816	250	450	700	1,350	—
1805 FJ	Inc. above	200	285	300	650	—
1806 FJ	544	200	300	375	825	—
1807 FJ	544	200	300	375	825	—
1808 FJ	2,448	200	300	285	650	—

KM# 69 ESCUDO
3.3841 g., 0.9040 Gold 0.0984 oz. AGW **Obv:** Imaginary military bust right **Obv. Legend:** FERDIN. VII... **Rev:** Crowned arms

Date	Mintage	VG	F	VF	XF	Unc
1808 Rare	3,986	—	—	—	—	—
1809 Rare	5,026	—	—	—	—	—

110 CHILE

KM# 76 ESCUDO
3.3841 g., 0.8750 Gold .0952 oz. AGW, 19 mm. **Obv:** Laureate bust right **Obv. Legend:** FERDIN. VII. D. G.... **Rev:** Crowned arms in order chain **Note:** Mint mark So. An additional 17,860 pieces were struck between 1818-1823; the actual date on the coin is unknown.

Date	Mintage	VG	F	VF	XF	Unc
1808 FJ	3,986,000	200	325	550	1,100	—
1809 FJ	5,026,000	175	250	375	850	—
1810 FJ	816	175	250	400	875	—
1811 FJ	680	175	250	400	875	—
1812/1 FJ	952	175	275	425	925	—
1812 FJ	Inc. above	175	250	375	850	—
1813 FJ	4,556	150	225	350	800	—
1814 FJ	1,152	175	250	400	875	—
1815 FJ	816	175	250	400	875	—
1816 FJ	408	225	375	750	1,350	—
1817 FJ	22,000	150	225	350	800	—
1817 JF MM to right	Inc. above	475	800	1,200	1,850	—

KM# 53 2 ESCUDOS
6.7668 g., 0.8750 Gold .1904 oz. AGW, 23 mm. **Ruler:** Carlos IV **Obv:** Laureate bust right **Obv. Legend:** CAROL. IIII... **Rev:** Crowned arms **Note:** Mint mark So.

Date	Mintage	VG	F	VF	XF	Unc
1801 AJ	680	450	700	975	1,600	—
1802 JJ	374	425	650	975	1,500	—
1803 FJ	578	450	700	975	1,600	—
1804 FJ	544	425	650	900	1,500	—
1805 FJ	646	425	650	900	1,500	—
1806 FJ	306	450	700	1,000	1,850	—
1807 FJ	340	450	700	1,000	1,850	—
1808/7 FJ	1,020	400	600	800	1,250	—
1808 FJ	Inc. above	275	400	550	950	—

KM# 70 2 ESCUDOS
6.7668 g., 0.8750 Gold .1904 oz. AGW, 23 mm. **Obv:** Laureate bust right **Obv. Legend:** FERDIN. VII... **Rev:** Crowned arms in order chain **Note:** Mint mark So.

Date	Mintage	VG	F	VF	XF	Unc
1810 FJ	Inc. above	425	650	900	1,500	—
1811 FJ	Inc. above	600	1,000	1,400	2,250	—

KM# 81 2 ESCUDOS
6.7668 g., 0.8750 Gold .1904 oz. AGW, 22.5 mm. **Obv:** Laureate bust right **Obv. Legend:** FERDIN. VII... **Rev:** Crowned arms in order chain **Note:** Mint mark So. An additional 19,876 pieces were struck between 1818-1823; the actual dates of these coins are unknown.

Date	Mintage	VG	F	VF	XF	Unc
1813 FJ	Inc. below	700	1,150	1,500	2,500	—
1814 FJ	682	425	650	900	1,500	—
1815 FJ	408	425	650	900	1,500	—
1816 FJ	608	500	900	1,250	2,000	—
1817 FJ	168	400	600	800	1,250	—

KM# 62 4 ESCUDOS
13.5337 g., 0.8750 Gold .3807 oz. AGW, 30.5 mm. **Ruler:** Carlos IV **Obv:** Laureate bust right **Obv. Legend:** CAROL. IIII... **Rev:** Crowned arms in order chain **Note:** Mint mark So.

Date	Mintage	VG	F	VF	XF	Unc
1801 AJ	340	550	800	1,200	2,000	—
1802 JJ	374	550	800	1,200	2,000	—
1803 FJ	476	550	800	1,200	2,000	—
1804 FJ	255	750	1,200	1,600	3,000	—
1805 FJ	323	550	800	1,200	2,000	—
1806 FJ	204	550	800	1,200	2,000	—
1807 FJ	187	850	1,350	1,750	3,250	—
1808/7 FJ	1,207	600	850	1,250	2,250	—
1808 FJ	Inc. above	550	800	1,200	2,000	—

KM# 77 4 ESCUDOS
13.5337 g., 0.8750 Gold .3807 oz. AGW, 30.5 mm. **Obv:** Laureate bust right **Obv. Legend:** FERDIN VII... **Rev:** Crowned arms in order chain **Note:** Mint mark So. An additional 6,560 pieces were struck between 1818-1823; the actual date on the coin is unknown.

Date	Mintage	VG	F	VF	XF	Unc
1810 FJ	272	475	750	1,350	2,250	—
1811 FJ	170	525	800	1,400	2,350	—
1812 FJ	254	425	700	1,250	2,150	—
1813 FJ	1,462	425	700	1,250	2,150	—
1816 FJ	100	700	1,100	1,600	2,750	—
1817 FJ	68	475	750	1,350	2,250	—

KM# 54 8 ESCUDOS
27.0674 g., 0.8750 Gold .7615 oz. AGW, 37.5 mm. **Ruler:** Carlos IV **Obv:** Laureate bust right **Obv. Legend:** CAROL. IIII... **Rev:** Crowned arms in order chain **Rev. Legend:** IN UTROQ FELIX AUSPICE DEO **Note:** Mint mark So.

Date	Mintage	VG	F	VF	XF	Unc
1801 AJ	46,000	525	625	750	1,000	—
1802 JJ	49,000	525	625	750	1,000	—
1803/2 FJ/JJ	44,000	525	725	850	1,200	—
1803 FJ	Inc. above	525	625	750	1,000	—
1804 FJ	40,000	525	625	750	1,000	—
1805 FJ	44,000	525	625	750	1,000	—
1806/5 FJ	40,000	525	625	750	1,000	—
1806 FJ	Inc. above	525	625	750	1,000	—
1806 JF	Inc. above	750	1,150	1,650	2,650	—
1807 FJ	39,000	525	625	750	1,000	—
1807 JF	Inc. above	525	625	750	1,000	—
1808 FJ	39,000	525	625	750	1,000	—

KM# 72 8 ESCUDOS
27.0674 g., 0.8750 Gold .7615 oz. AGW, 38 mm. **Obv:** Imaginary military bust right **Obv. Legend:** FERDIN. VII... **Rev:** Crowned arms in order chain **Note:** Struck for exclusive use in Chile, mint mark So.

Date	Mintage	VG	F	VF	XF	Unc
1808 FJ	Inc. below	750	1,250	1,600	2,250	—
1809 FJ	41,000	550	700	1,000	1,600	—
1810 FJ	55,000	550	700	1,000	1,600	—
1810 FJ Inverted mint mark	Inc. above	600	900	1,250	1,850	—
1811 FJ	44,000	550	700	1,000	1,600	—

KM# 78 8 ESCUDOS
27.0730 g., 0.8750 Gold .7616 oz. AGW, 38 mm. **Obv:** Laureate military bust right **Obv. Legend:** FERDIN VII... **Rev:** Crowned arms in order chain **Note:** For exclusive use in Chile, mint mark So.

Date	Mintage	VG	F	VF	XF	Unc
1811 FJ	—	1,500	3,000	4,500	7,500	—
1812 FJ	48,000	525	650	750	950	—
1813/2 FT	37,000	525	650	750	950	—
1813 FJ	Inc. above	525	650	750	950	—
1814 FJ	29,000	525	650	750	950	—
1815 FN	39,000	525	650	750	950	—
1816 FJ	30,000	525	650	750	950	—
1817/6 FJ	11,000	525	650	750	950	—
1817/8 FJ	Inc. above	550	675	800	1,000	—
1817 FJ	Inc. above	525	650	750	950	—

REPUBLIC

COUNTERMARKED COINAGE
1833 — Serena

KM# A109 8 ESCUDOS
Gold **Countermark:** Mountains/SER **Note:** Countermark on Argentina 8 Escudos, KM#9.

CM Date	Host Date	Good	VG	F	VF	XF
ND(1833)	1813 Rare	—	—	—	—	—

REAL/ESCUDO COINAGE

KM# 85 ESCUDO
3.3000 g., 0.8750 Gold .0928 oz. AGW, 19 mm. **Obv:** Sun between volcanic mountains within wreath **Rev:** Crossed flags behind pillar within wreath

Date	Mintage	VG	F	VF	XF	Unc
1824 I	3,400	95.00	135	185	450	2,250
1825 I	2,920	95.00	135	185	450	2,250
1826 I	4,280	95.00	135	185	450	—
1827 I	408	165	245	350	600	—
1828 I	4,488	95.00	135	185	450	—
1830 I	3,328	95.00	135	185	450	—
1832 I	2,338	95.00	135	185	450	—
1833/0 I	2,620	150	225	325	550	—
1833 I	Inc. above	145	200	300	500	—
1834 I	10,614	145	200	300	500	—

KM# 99 ESCUDO
3.3000 g., 0.8750 Gold .0928 oz. AGW, 18.5 mm. **Obv:** Plumed and supported arms **Rev:** Hand on book below sun rays **Note:** Issued by law 1117 of October 24, 1834.

Date	Mintage	VG	F	VF	XF	Unc
1838 IJ	6,122	125	185	225	400	—

KM# 101.1 ESCUDO
3.3000 g., 0.8750 Gold .0928 oz. AGW, 18.5 mm. **Obv:** Plumed and supported arms **Rev:** Liberty standing, column at left, fasces and cornucopia at right **Note:** Decree of January 17, 1839 authorized the change of coin type.

Date	Mintage	VG	F	VF	XF	Unc
1839 IJ	4,946	100	135	175	325	—
1840 IJ	4,312	100	135	175	325	—
1841 IJ	3,992	100	135	175	325	—
1842 IJ	5,076	100	135	175	325	—
1843 IJ	4,632	100	135	175	325	—

CHILE

Date	Mintage	VG	F	VF	XF	Unc
1844 IJ	—	100	135	175	325	—
1845 IJ	—	100	135	175	325	—

KM# 101.2 ESCUDO
3.3000 g., 0.8750 Gold .0928 oz. AGW, 18.5 mm. **Obv:** Plumed and supported arms **Rev:** Liberty standing scene rendered on smaller scale

Date	Mintage	VG	F	VF	XF	Unc
1846 IJ	—	150	200	350	550	—
1847 IJ	—	125	175	225	400	—
1848 JM	—	100	135	185	350	—
1849 ML	—	100	135	185	350	—
1850 LA	—	100	135	185	350	—
1851 LA	—	125	175	225	400	—

KM# 86 2 ESCUDOS
6.7000 g., 0.8750 Gold .1885 oz. AGW, 22 mm. **Obv:** Sun between volcanic mountains within wreath **Rev:** Crossed flags behind pillar

Date	Mintage	VG	F	VF	XF	Unc
1824 I	1,700	165	200	350	500	2,250
1825 I	1,460	165	200	350	500	—
1826 I	1,936	165	200	350	500	—
1827 I	204	200	300	400	650	—
1832 I	493	200	300	400	650	—
1833 I	224	165	200	350	550	—
1834 IJ	4,648	150	185	225	450	—

KM# 97 2 ESCUDOS
6.7000 g., 0.8750 Gold .1885 oz. AGW, 22.5 mm. **Obv:** Plumed and supported arms **Rev:** Hand on book, sun rays above **Note:** Authorized by law 1117 October 24, 1834.

Date	Mintage	VG	F	VF	XF	Unc
1837 IJ	331	250	300	500	800	—
1838 IJ	3,449	150	200	300	550	3,250

KM# 102.1 2 ESCUDOS
6.7000 g., 0.8750 Gold .1885 oz. AGW, 23 mm. **Obv:** Plumed and supported arms **Rev:** Liberty standing, column at left, fasces and cornucopia at right

Date	Mintage	VG	F	VF	XF	Unc
1839 IJ	3,064	160	200	325	500	—
1840 IJ	2,396	160	200	325	500	—
1841 IJ	2,552	145	175	300	485	—
1842 IJ	2,986	145	175	300	485	—
1843 IJ	2,464	145	175	300	485	—
1844 IJ	—	145	175	300	485	—
1845 IJ	—	145	175	300	485	—

KM# 102.2 2 ESCUDOS
6.7000 g., 0.8750 Gold .1885 oz. AGW, 22.5 mm. **Obv:** Plumed and supported arms **Rev:** Liberty standing scene rendered on smaller scale

Date	Mintage	VG	F	VF	XF	Unc
1846 IJ	—	145	175	300	485	—
1847 IJ	—	145	175	300	485	—
1848 JM	—	145	175	300	485	—
1849 ML	—	145	175	300	485	—
1850 LA	—	145	175	300	485	—
1851 LA	—	145	175	300	485	—

KM# 87 4 ESCUDOS
13.5000 g., 0.8750 Gold .3798 oz. AGW, 30 mm. **Obv:** Sun between volcanic mountains within wreath **Rev:** Crossed flags behind pillar

Date	Mintage	VG	F	VF	XF	Unc
1824 FD	1,530	325	450	750	1,350	—
1825 I	986	350	550	900	1,600	—
1826 I	1,326	325	450	700	1,350	—
1833 I	321	375	600	950	1,750	—
1834 IJ	2,564	325	450	700	1,350	—

KM# 95 4 ESCUDOS
13.5000 g., 0.8750 Gold .3798 oz. AGW, 29 mm. **Obv:** Plumed and supported arms **Rev:** Hand on book, sun rays above

Date	Mintage	VG	F	VF	XF	Unc
1836 IJ	1,389	300	450	650	1,250	—
1837 IJ	321	400	650	1,000	2,000	7,500

KM# 103 4 ESCUDOS
13.5000 g., 0.8750 Gold .3798 oz. AGW, 29 mm. **Obv:** Plumed and supported arms **Rev:** Liberty standing, column at left, fasces and cornucopia at right

Date	Mintage	VG	F	VF	XF	Unc
1839 IJ	—	1,750	2,750	4,500	—	—
1840 IJ Rare	108	—	—	—	—	—
1841 IJ Rare	100	—	—	—	—	—

KM# 84 8 ESCUDOS
27.0000 g., 0.8750 Gold .7596 oz. AGW, 37 mm. **Obv:** Sun between volcanic mountains within wreath **Rev:** Crossed flags behind pillar **Note:** Published June 9, 1817, legalized February 6, 1824.

Date	Mintage	VG	F	VF	XF	Unc
1818 FD Constit	29,000	—	BV	550	850	3,500
1818 FD Constitu	Inc. above	—	BV	650	950	3,750
1819 FD	37,000	—	BV	550	850	—
1820 FD	35,000	—	BV	550	850	—
1821 FD	16,000	—	BV	550	850	—
1822 FI	31,000	—	BV	550	850	2,250
1823 FI	19,000	—	BV	550	850	—
1824 I	10,000	—	BV	550	850	2,250
1825 I	8,483	—	BV	550	800	—
1826 I	7,607	—	BV	550	800	—
1827 I	2,176	—	BV	550	800	—
1828/7 I	4,250	550	800	1,250	2,500	—
1828 I	Inc. above	—	BV	550	850	—
1829 I	—	—	BV	550	800	—
1830 I	3,068	—	BV	550	800	—
1831 I	1,745	—	BV	650	900	—
1832/1 I	11,000	—	BV	550	800	—
1832 I	Inc. above	—	BV	550	800	—
1833/2 I	25,000	BV	550	850	1,400	—
1833 I	Inc. above	—	BV	550	800	—
1834 IJ	31,000	—	BV	550	750	—

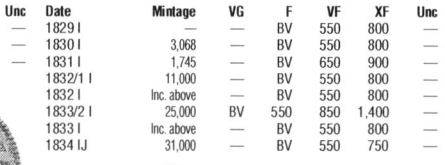

KM# 93 8 ESCUDOS
27.0000 g., 0.8750 Gold .7596 oz. AGW, 37.5 mm. **Obv:** Plumed and supported arms **Rev:** Hand on book, sun rays above **Note:** Issued by law 1117 of October 24, 1834. KM#93 has been rarely encountered struck over KM#84.

Date	Mintage	VG	F	VF	XF	Unc
1835 IJ	28,000	—	BV	550	900	—
1836 IJ	27,000	—	BV	550	900	2,100
1837 IJ	17,000	—	BV	550	900	—
1838 IJ	33,000	—	BV	550	900	2,300

KM# 104.1 8 ESCUDOS
27.0000 g., 0.8750 Gold .7596 oz. AGW, 36 mm. **Obv:** Plumed and supported arms **Rev:** Liberty standing, column at left, fasces and cornucopia at right **Edge:** Reeded

Date	Mintage	VG	F	VF	XF	Unc
1839 IJ	27,000	—	BV	525	700	2,000
1840 IJ	25,000	—	BV	525	700	2,200
1841 IJ	25,000	—	BV	525	700	2,000
1842 IJ	27,000	—	BV	525	700	—
1843/2 IJ	27,000	—	BV	550	800	—
1843 IJ	Inc. above	—	BV	525	700	—

KM# 104.2 8 ESCUDOS
27.0000 g., 0.8750 Gold .7596 oz. AGW, 35.5 mm. **Obv:** Plumed and supported arms **Rev:** Liberty standing, column at left, fasces and cornucopia at right **Edge:** Lettered **Note:** Edge lettering includes month of issue.

Date	Mintage	VG	F	VF	XF	Unc
1843 IJ	—	—	BV	550	850	—
1844 IJ	—	—	BV	550	850	—
1845 IJ	—	—	BV	550	850	—

112 CHILE

KM# 105 8 ESCUDOS
27.0000 g., 0.8750 Gold .7596 oz. AGW, 35.5 mm. **Obv:** Plumed and supported arms **Rev:** Liberty standing scene rendered on smaller scale **Note:** Edge lettering includes month of issue.

Date	Mintage	VG	F	VF	XF	Unc
1846 IJ	—	—	BV	525	700	—
1847 IJ	—	—	BV	525	700	—
1848/7 JM	—	—	BV	525	700	—
1848 JM	—	—	BV	525	700	—
1849 ML	—	—	BV	525	700	—
1850 LA	—	—	BV	525	700	—
1851 LA	—	—	BV	525	700	—

DECIMAL COINAGE

KM# 133 PESO
1.5235 g., 0.9000 Gold .0441 oz. AGW, 14 mm. **Obv:** Standing liberty **Rev:** Denomination within wreath **Note:** Crude style. Struck under law of July 28, 1860 and decree of August 20, 1860.

Date	Mintage	F	VF	XF	Unc	BU
1860	156,000	32.00	45.00	75.00	125	—
1861	176,000	32.00	45.00	75.00	125	—
1862	11,000	40.00	60.00	80.00	135	—
1863	55,000	32.00	45.00	75.00	125	—
1864	29,000	40.00	60.00	80.00	135	—

KM# 140 PESO
1.5235 g., 0.9000 Gold .0441 oz. AGW, 14 mm. **Note:** Fine style. Struck under law of July 28, 1860 and decree of August 20, 1860.

Date	Mintage	F	VF	XF	Unc	BU
1867	949	75.00	100	250	425	—
1873	16,000	40.00	60.00	80.00	130	—

KM# 132 2 PESOS
3.0506 g., 0.9000 Gold .0882 oz. AGW, 17 mm. **Obv:** Plumed arms with supporters **Rev:** Standing liberty **Note:** Fine style, bold letters. Struck by law of January 9, 1851.

Date	Mintage	F	VF	XF	Unc	BU
1856	—	120	250	350	—	—
1857	207,000	BV	65.00	90.00	175	—
1858/7	56,000	BV	70.00	100	150	—
1858	Inc. above	BV	60.00	80.00	165	—
1859	97,000	BV	60.00	80.00	165	—
1860	78,000	BV	60.00	80.00	165	—
1862	10,000	BV	65.00	90.00	175	—
1865	—	BV	250	350	—	—

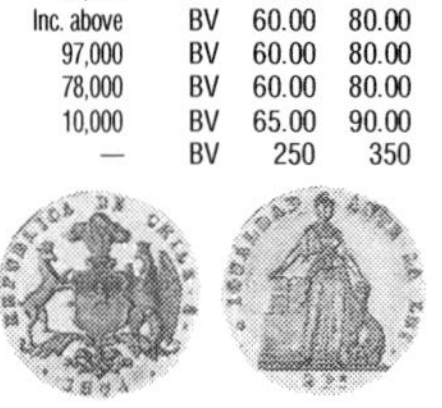

KM# 143 2 PESOS
3.0506 g., 0.9000 Gold .0882 oz. AGW **Obv:** Plumed arms with supporters **Rev:** Standing liberty **Note:** Modified arms. Fine letters.

Date	Mintage	F	VF	XF	Unc	BU
1867	841	175	350	600	950	—
1873	54,000	BV	60.00	75.00	145	—
1874	61,000	BV	60.00	75.00	145	—
1875	37,000	BV	65.00	85.00	170	—

KM# 122 5 PESOS
7.6265 g., 0.9000 Gold .2207 oz. AGW, 22.5 mm. **Obv:** Plumed arms with supporters **Rev:** Standing liberty **Note:** Crude style, bold letters. Struck by law of January 9, 1851.

Date	Mintage	F	VF	XF	Unc	BU
1851	3,735	BV	145	165	275	—
1852	20,000	—	BV	155	250	—
1853	5,987	BV	145	165	275	—

KM# 130 5 PESOS
7.6265 g., 0.9000 Gold .2207 oz. AGW **Obv:** Plumed arms with supporters **Rev:** Standing liberty **Note:** Fine style, fine letters. Struck by law of January 9, 1851.

Date	Mintage	F	VF	XF	Unc	BU
1854 Rare	953	—	—	—	—	—
1855	7,609	BV	145	165	265	—
1856/5	4,753	150	225	300	450	—
1856	Inc. above	BV	145	165	275	—
1857/6	25,000	BV	155	200	320	—
1857	Inc. above	—	BV	155	235	—
1858	11,000	—	BV	155	235	—
1859/8	66,000	—	BV	155	235	—
1859	Inc. above	—	BV	155	235	—
1862	6,738	BV	145	165	265	—
1865	5,110	BV	145	165	265	—
1866/5	6,249	BV	145	165	265	—
1866	Inc. above	BV	155	200	320	—
1867	10,000	—	BV	155	235	—

KM# 144 5 PESOS
7.6265 g., 0.9000 Gold .2207 oz. AGW **Obv:** Plumed arms with supporters **Rev:** Standing liberty **Note:** Modified arms. Struck by law of January 9, 1851.

Date	Mintage	F	VF	XF	Unc	BU
1867 Rare	Inc. above	—	—	—	—	—
1868	4,065	BV	150	165	265	—
1869	5,913	BV	150	165	265	—
1870	13,000	—	BV	155	235	—
1872	23,000	—	BV	155	235	—
1873	50,000	—	BV	155	225	—

KM# 153 5 PESOS
2.9955 g., 0.9170 Gold .0883 oz. AGW, 16.5 mm. **Obv:** Head left **Rev:** Plumed arms with supporters **Note:** Issued under law 277 of June 22, 1891.

Date	Mintage	F	VF	XF	Unc	BU
1895	3,002,000	BV	60.00	70.00	85.00	100
1896	24,000	BV	85.00	125	200	—

KM# 159 5 PESOS
2.9955 g., 0.9170 Gold .0883 oz. AGW, 16.5 mm. **Obv:** Head left **Rev:** Plumed arms with supporters

Date	Mintage	F	VF	XF	Unc	BU
1897 Rare	—	—	—	—	—	—
1898	426,000	BV	60.00	75.00	100	—
1900	1,265,000	65.00	90.00	120	150	—
1911	1,399	—	—	200	350	—

KM# 123 10 PESOS
15.2530 g., 0.9000 Gold .4414 oz. AGW **Obv:** Plumed arms with supporters **Rev:** Standing liberty **Note:** Crude style. Issued under law of February 9, 1851.

Date	Mintage	F	VF	XF	Unc	BU
1851	50,000	BV	285	300	375	—
1852	135,000	BV	285	300	375	—
1853	206,000	BV	285	300	325	—

KM# 131 10 PESOS
15.2530 g., 0.9000 Gold .4414 oz. AGW **Obv:** Plumed arms with supporters **Rev:** Standing liberty **Note:** Fine style. Issued under law of February 9, 1851.

Date	Mintage	F	VF	XF	Unc	BU
1854	195,000	BV	285	300	375	—
1855	61,000	BV	285	300	375	—
1856	66,000	BV	285	300	375	—
1857	20,000	BV	285	300	375	—
1858/7	52,000	BV	285	300	375	—
1858	Inc. above	BV	285	300	375	—
1859	281,000	BV	285	300	375	—
1860	31,000	BV	285	300	375	—
1861	15,000	BV	285	300	375	—
1862	21,000	BV	285	300	375	—
1863/2	25,000	BV	285	300	375	—
1863	Inc. above	BV	285	300	375	—
1864	26,000	BV	285	300	375	—
1865	45,000	BV	285	300	375	—
1866	66,000	BV	285	300	375	—
1867/6	121,000	BV	285	300	375	—
1867	Inc. above	BV	285	300	375	—

KM# 145 10 PESOS
15.2530 g., 0.9000 Gold .4414 oz. AGW **Obv:** Modified arms **Rev:** Standing liberty **Note:** Issued under law of February 9, 1851.

Date	Mintage	F	VF	XF	Unc	BU
1867	Inc. above	—	BV	285	365	—
1868	54,000	—	BV	285	365	—
1869	36,000	—	BV	285	365	—
1870	76,000	—	BV	285	365	—
1871	41,000	—	BV	285	365	—
1872	235,000	—	BV	285	365	—
1873	112,000	—	BV	285	365	—
1874	1,277	—	BV	300	400	—
1876	2,106	—	BV	300	400	—
1877	8,208	—	BV	300	385	—
1877 Proof	—	Value: 2,500				
1878	7,983	—	BV	300	385	—
1879	9,805	—	BV	300	385	—
1880	11,000	—	BV	285	365	—
1881	13,000	—	BV	285	365	—
1882	14,000	—	BV	285	365	—
1883	8,381	—	BV	300	385	—
1884	9,888	—	BV	300	385	—
1885	7,758	—	BV	300	385	—
1886	3,721	—	BV	300	385	—
1887	5,236	—	BV	300	385	—
1888	4,217	—	BV	300	385	—
1889	4,650	—	BV	300	385	—
1890	2,344	—	BV	300	400	—
1892	1,192	—	BV	300	400	—

CHILE

KM# 154 10 PESOS
5.9910 g., 0.9170 Gold .1766 oz. AGW **Obv:** Head left **Rev:** Plumed arms with supporters

Date	Mintage	F	VF	XF	Unc	BU
1895	808,000	—	BV	125	175	275

KM# 157 10 PESOS
5.9910 g., 0.9170 Gold .1766 oz. AGW, 21 mm. **Obv:** Head left **Rev:** Plumed arms with supporters

Date	Mintage	F	VF	XF	Unc	BU
1896	1,163,000	—	—	BV	135	175
1898	276,000	—	—	BV	155	200
1901	1,651,000	—	BV	130	200	—

KM# 158 20 PESOS
11.9821 g., 0.9170 Gold .3532 oz. AGW, 27 mm. **Obv:** Head left **Rev:** Plumed arms with supporters

Date	Mintage	F	VF	XF	Unc	BU
1896	149,000	—	BV	245	275	—
1906	41,000	—	BV	245	285	—
1907	12,000	—	BV	245	285	—
1908	26,000	—	BV	245	285	—
1910	28,000	—	BV	245	285	300
1911	17,000	—	BV	245	285	300
1913/11	18,000	—	BV	245	285	300
1913	Inc. above	—	BV	245	285	300
1914	22,000	—	BV	245	285	300
1915	65,000	—	BV	245	285	300
1916	36,000	—	BV	245	285	300
1917	717,000	—	BV	245	285	300

KM# 168 20 PESOS
4.0679 g., 0.9000 Gold .1177 oz. AGW **Obv:** Head left, date below **Rev:** Arms with supporters, denomination above

Date	Mintage	F	VF	XF	Unc	BU
1926	85,000	—	BV	80.00	100	—
1958	500	BV	80.00	140	220	—
1959	25,000	—	—	BV	85.00	—
1961	20,000	—	—	BV	85.00	—
1964	—	—	—	BV	85.00	—
1976	99,000	—	—	BV	85.00	—
1977	38,000	—	—	BV	85.00	—
1979	30,000	—	—	BV	85.00	—
1980	30,000	—	—	BV	85.00	—

KM# 188 20 PESOS
4.0679 g., 0.9000 Gold .1177 oz. AGW **Obv:** Head left, date below **Rev:** Coat of arms on ornamental vines, denomination above

Date	Mintage	F	VF	XF	Unc	BU
1976	Inc. above	—	BV	80.00	100	—

KM# 169 50 PESOS
10.1698 g., 0.9000 Gold .2943 oz. AGW **Obv:** Head left, date below **Rev:** Coat of arms, denomination above

Date	Mintage	F	VF	XF	Unc	BU
1926	126,000	—	—	BV	195	220
1958	10,000	—	—	BV	195	220
1961	20,000	—	—	BV	195	220
1962	30,000	—	—	BV	195	220
1965	—	—	—	BV	195	220
1966	—	—	—	BV	195	220
1967	—	—	—	BV	195	220
1968	—	—	—	BV	195	220
1969	—	—	—	BV	195	220
1970	—	—	—	—	650	—
1974	—	—	—	BV	195	220

KM# 184 50 PESOS
10.1698 g., 0.9000 Gold .2943 oz. AGW **Subject:** 150th Anniversary of Military Academy **Obv:** Coat of arms above denomination **Rev:** Armored bust right of Bernardo O'Higgins, two dates below

Date	Mintage	F	VF	XF	Unc	BU
1968 Proof	2,515	Value: 225				

KM# 170 100 PESOS
20.3397 g., 0.9000 Gold .5886 oz. AGW **Obv:** Head left, date below **Rev:** Coat of arms, denomination above

Date	Mintage	F	VF	XF	Unc	BU
1926	678,000	—	—	BV	385	420

KM# 175 100 PESOS
20.3397 g., 0.9000 Gold .5886 oz. AGW **Obv:** Head left, date below, revised bust and legend style **Rev:** Coat of arms, denomination above, revised legend style

Date	Mintage	F	VF	XF	Unc	BU
1932	9,315	—	BV	390	450	—
1946	260,000	—	—	BV	385	410
1947	540,000	—	—	BV	385	410
1948	420,000	—	—	BV	385	410
1949	310,000	—	—	BV	385	410
1950	20,000	—	—	BV	385	410
1951	145,000	—	—	BV	385	410
1952	245,000	—	—	BV	385	410
1953	175,000	—	—	BV	385	410
1954	190,000	—	—	BV	385	410
1955	150,000	—	—	BV	385	410
1956	60,000	—	—	BV	385	410
1957	40,000	—	—	BV	385	410
1958	157,000	—	—	BV	385	410
1959	90,000	—	—	BV	385	410
1960	200,000	—	—	BV	385	410
1961	295,000	—	—	BV	385	410
1962	260,000	—	—	BV	385	410
1963	210,000	—	—	BV	385	410
1964	—	—	—	BV	385	410
1968	—	—	—	BV	385	410
1969	—	—	—	BV	385	410
1970	—	—	—	BV	385	410
1971	—	—	—	BV	385	410
1972	—	—	—	BV	385	410
1973	—	—	—	BV	385	410
1974	—	—	—	BV	385	410
1976	172,000	—	—	BV	385	410
1977	25,000	—	—	BV	385	410
1979	100,000	—	—	BV	385	410
1980	50,000	—	—	BV	385	410

KM# 185 100 PESOS
20.3397 g., 0.9000 Gold .5886 oz. AGW **Subject:** 150th Anniversary of National Coinage **Obv:** Coat of arms, date at left, denomination below **Rev:** Coinage press, liberty bust left

Date	Mintage	F	VF	XF	Unc	BU
1968 Proof	1,815	Value: 445				

KM# 186 200 PESOS
40.6794 g., 0.9000 Gold 1.1771 oz. AGW **Subject:** 150th Anniversary of San Martin's passage through Andes Mountains, from a painting by Vila Prades **Obv:** Coat of arms, date at left, denomination below **Rev:** Riders passing through mountains, two dates below

Date	Mintage	F	VF	XF	Unc	BU
1968 Proof	965	Value: 800				

KM# 187 500 PESOS
101.6985 g., 0.9000 Gold 2.9427 oz. AGW **Subject:** 150th Anniversary of National Flag **Rev:** Liberty bust left, waving flag in background, two dates below

Date	Mintage	F	VF	XF	Unc	BU
1968 Proof	—	Value: 2,000				

114 CHILE

REFORM COINAGE
100 Centavos = 1 Peso; 1000 Old Escudos = 1 Peso

KM# 212 50 PESOS
10.1500 g., 0.9000 Gold .2937 oz. AGW **Subject:** 3rd Anniversary of New Government **Obv:** Coat of arms above denomination **Rev:** Winged figure with arms upraised, two dates above

Date	Mintage	F	VF	XF	Unc	BU
ND(1976)	1,900	—	—	—	220	275
ND(1976) Proof	Inc. above	Value: 325				

KM# 213 100 PESOS
20.3000 g., 0.9000 Gold .5874 oz. AGW **Subject:** 3rd Anniversary of New Government **Obv:** Coat of arms above date and denomination **Rev:** Winged figure with upraised arms, two dates above

Date	Mintage	F	VF	XF	Unc	BU
1976	2,900	—	—	—	420	450
1976 Proof	100	Value: 775				

KM# 214 500 PESOS
102.2700 g., 0.9000 Gold 2.9595 oz. AGW **Subject:** 3rd Anniversary of New Government **Obv:** Coat of arms, denomination below **Rev:** Winged figure with upraised arms, two dates above **Note:** Similar to 100 Pesos, KM#213.

Date	Mintage	F	VF	XF	Unc	BU
1976	500	—	—	—	2,000	2,150
1976 Proof	700	Value: 2,200				

GOLD BULLION COINAGE

X# 6 1/4 ONZA
8.6400 g., 0.9000 Gold .2500 oz. AGW **Subject:** 10th Anniversary of National Liberation **Note:** Prev. KM#220. Similar to KM#223.

Date	Mintage	F	VF	XF	Unc	BU
ND(1983)So	1,000	—	—	—	175	—

X# 7 1/2 ONZA
17.2800 g., 0.9000 Gold .5000 oz. AGW **Subject:** 10th Anniversary of National Liberation **Note:** Prev. KM#221. Similar to KM#224.

Date	Mintage	F	VF	XF	Unc	BU
ND(1983)So	1,000	—	—	—	350	—

X# 1 ONZA
31.1030 g., 1.0000 Gold 1 oz. AGW

Date	Mintage	F	VF	XF	Unc	BU
1948So	1,950	—	—	—	850	—

X# 2 ONZA
31.1000 g., 0.9990 Gold 1.0000 oz. AGW **Obv:** Crowned arms **Rev:** Crowned pillars and hemispheres **Note:** Prev. KM#215.

Date	Mintage	F	VF	XF	Unc	BU
1978So	—	—	—	—	750	—
1979So	1,580	—	—	—	600	—
1980So	1,730	—	—	—	600	—
1981So	200	—	—	—	700	—
1983So	999	—	—	—	650	—
1983So Proof	1	—	—	—	—	—

X# 8 ONZA
34.5590 g., 0.9000 Gold 1.0000 oz. AGW **Subject:** 10th Anniversary of National Liberation **Note:** Prev. KM#222. Similar to KM#225.

Date	Mintage	F	VF	XF	Unc	BU
1983	1,000	—	—	—	675	—

PATTERNS
Including off metal strikes

KM#	Date	Mintage	Identification	Mkt Val
Pn19	1868	—	2 Pesos. Gold-Plated Copper. KM#143.	350
Pn21	1868	—	5 Pesos. Gold-Plated Copper. KM#145.	400
Pn23	1868	—	10 Pesos. Gold-Plated Copper. KM#145.	475

PROOF SETS

KM#	Date	Mintage	Identification	Issue Price	Mkt Val
PS1	1968 (6)	—	KM#182-187. Total of 12,000 coins struck for each denomination including those available singly.	560	3,350
PS2	1968 (4)	—	KM#184-187. Total of 12,000 coins struck for each denomination including those available singly.	528	3,250

CHINA

Before 1912, China was ruled by an imperial government. The republican administration which replaced it was itself supplanted on the Chinese mainland by a communist government in 1949, but it has remained in control of Taiwan and other offshore islands in the China Sea with a land area of approximately 14,000 square miles and a population of more than 14 million. The People's Republic of China administers some 3.7 million square miles and an estimated 1.19 billion people. This communist government, officially established on October 1, 1949, was admitted to the United Nations, replacing its nationalist predecessor, the Republic of China, in 1971.

Cast coins in base metals were used in China many centuries before the Christian era, but locally struck coinages of the western type in gold, silver, copper and other metals did not appear until 1888. In spite of the relatively short time that modern coins have been in use, the number of varieties is exceptionally large.

Both Nationalist and Communist China, as well as the pre-revolutionary Imperial government and numerous provincial or other agencies, including some foreign-administered agencies and governments, have issued coins in China. Most of these have been in dollar (yüan) or dollar-fraction denominations, based on the internationally used dollar system, but coins in tael denominations were issued in the 1920's and earlier. The striking of coins nearly ceased in the late 1930's through the 1940's due to the war effort and a period of uncontrollable inflation while vast amounts of paper currency were issued by the Nationalist, Communist and Japanese occupation institutions.

同 治

T'ung-chih, (Mu-tsung), 2nd reign
1862-1875

Type A-2

同 治 通 寳

T'ung-chih T'ung-pao

Type B-2

同 治 重 寳

T'ung-chih Chung-pao

T'ung-chih - Born on April 27, 1856, T'ung-chih ascended the throne at the age of six with the reign-title Ch'i-hsiang and very few coins were struck with this title. He ruled under the regency of a triumvirate headed by his mother, the Empress Dowager Tz'u-hsi (1835-1908), in whose reign the Taiping rebels were suppressed and the government began attempts to understand and deal with the West. He assumed personal control of the government in 1873 when he was 17. T'ung-chih was a weak ruler whose affairs were constantly scrutinized by the Empress Dowager. He died January 12, 1875, in Peking.

CHINA

光緒
Kuang-hsü (Te-tsung)
1875-1908

Type A

光緒通寶
Kuang-hsü T'ung-pao

Type B

光緒重寶
Kuang-hsü Chung-pao

Kuang-hsü - When the previous emperor died, his mother, the Empress Dowager Tz'u-hsi, chose her four-year-old nephew, born August 14, 1871, as emperor. She adopted the boy so that she could act as regent and on February 25, 1875, the young prince ascended the throne, taking the reign title of Kuang-hsü. In 1898 he tried to assert himself and collected a group of progressive officials around him. He issued a series of edicts for revamping of the military, abolition of civil service examinations, improvement of agriculture and restructuring of administrative procedures. During Kuang-hsü's reign (1875-1908) the Empress Dowager totally dominated the government. She confined the emperor to his palace and spread rumors that he was deathly ill. Foreign powers let it be known they would not take kindly to the Emperor's death. This saved his life but thereafter he had no power over the government. On November 15, 1908, Tz'u-hsi died under highly suspicious circumstances and the usually healthy emperor was announced as having died the previous day.

宣統
HSÜAN-T'UNG 1908-1911

Type A

宣統
Hsüan-t'ung T'ung-pao (Xuantong)

Hsuan-t'ung - The last emperor of the Ch'ing dynasty in China and Japan's puppet emperor, under the assumed name of K'ang-te, in Manchoukuo from 1934 to 1945, was born on February 7, 1906. He succeeded to the throne at the age of three on November 14, 1908. He reigned under a regency for three years but on February 12, 1912, was forced to abdicate the throne. He was permitted to continue living in the palace in Peking until he left secretly in 1924. On March 9, 1932, he was installed as president, and from 1934 to 1945 was emperor of Manchoukuo under the reign title of K'ang-te. He was taken prisoner by the Russians in August of 1945 and returned to China as a war criminal in 1950. He was pardoned in 1959 and went to live in Peking where he worked in the repair shop of a botanical garden. He died peacefully in Peking in 1967.

Although Hsüan-t'ung became Emperor in 1908, all the coins of his reign are based on an Accession year of 1909.

憲洪
HUNG-HSIEN

宣統通
(Yuan Shih-k'ai)
Dec. 15, 1915 - March 21, 1916

憲洪通寶
Hung-hsien T'ung-pao

Hung-hsien (more popularly known as Yuan Shih-K'ai). Born in 1859 in Honan Province, he was the first Han Chinese to hold a viceroyalty and become a grand councillor without any academic qualifications. In 1885 he was made Chinese commissioner at Seoul. During the Boxer Rebellion of 1900, the division under his command was the only remnant of China's army to survive. He enjoyed the trust and support of the dowager empress, Tz'u-hsi, and at her death he was stripped of all his offices. However, when the tide of the revolution threatened to engulf the Manchus Yuan appeared as the only man who could lead the country to peace and unity. Both the Emperor and the provisional president recommended that Yuan be the first president of China. He contrived to make himself president for life and boldly tried to create a new imperial dynasty in 1915-1916. He died of uremia on June 6, 1916.

PROVINCIAL MINTNAMES
(and other source indicators)

Provincial names throughout the catalog are based on the Wade-Giles transliteration of the Chinese word. Current spellings, known as the "Pinyin" form, are widely adopted by the printed media. Example: Sinkiang = Xinjiang.

The column at left illustrates the full name as used on most provincial coinage while the column at right illustrates the abbreviated name that appears in the center of the obverse of the Tai-Ch'ing-Ti-Kuo copper coinage.

Full Name   Single Character (1)
Right to Left reading

隸直   直
CHIHLI   Chih
Also Hopei (after 1928) now Hebei

林吉   吉
KIRIN   Chi
Also Chi-lin, now Jilin

東廣   粵
KWANGTUNG   Yüeh
Also Kwang-tung, now Guangdong

東山   東
SHANTUNG   Tung
Also Shang-tung, Shan-tung, now Shandong (Lu)

疆新   新
SINKIANG   Hsin
(Chinese Turkestan)
Also Sin-kiang, Hsin-kiang Sungarei, now Xinjiang

南雲   雲   滇
YÜNNAN   Yün   (Alternate) (Tien)
Also Yun-nan, now Yunnan

NUMERALS

NUMBER	CONVENTIONAL	FORMAL	COMMERCIAL
1	一 元	壹 弌	1
2	二	弍 貳	11
3	三	叁 弎	111
4	四	肆	ㄨ
5	五	伍	8
6	六	陸	ㅗ
7	七	柒	土
8	八	捌	圭
9	九	玖	夂
10	十	拾 什	十
20	十二 or 廿	拾貳	11十
25	五十二 or 五廿	伍拾貳	11十々
30	十三 or 卅	拾叁	111十
100	百 一	佰壹	1百
1,000	千 一	仟壹	1千
10,000	萬 一	萬壹	1万
100,000	萬十 億一	萬拾 億壹	十万
1,000,000	萬百一	萬佰壹	1百万

NOTE: This table has been adapted from *Chinese Bank Notes* by Ward Smith and Brian Matravers.

MONETARY UNITS

Dollar Amounts

DOLLAR (Yuan)	元 or 員	圓 or 圜
HALF DOLLAR (Pan Yuan)	圓半	元中
50¢ (Chiao/Hao)	角伍	毫伍
10¢ (Chiao/Hao)	角壹	毫壹
1¢ (Fen/Hsien)	分壹	仙壹

Copper and Cash Coin Amounts

| COPPER (Mei) | 枚 | CASH (Wen) | 文 |

Tael Amounts

1 TAEL (Liang)	兩
HALF TAEL (Pan Liang)	兩半
5 MACE (Wu Ch'ien)	錢伍
1 MACE (I Ch'ien)	錢壹
1 CANDEREEN (I Fen)	分壹

Common Prefixes

| COPPER (T'ung) | 銅 | GOLD (Chin) | 金 |
| SILVER (Yin) | 銀 | Ku Ping (Tael)* | 平庫 |

NOTE: This table has been adapted from Chinese Bank Notes by Ward Smith and Brian Matravers.

116 CHINA EMPIRE

DATING

Most struck Chinese coins are dated by year within a given period, such as the regnal eras or the republican periods. A 1907 issue, for example, would be dated in the 33rd year of the Kuang Hsu era (1875 + 33 - 1 = 1907) or a 1926 issue is dated in the 15th year of the Republic (1912 + 15 - 1 = 1926). The mathematical discrepancy in both instances is accounted for by the fact that the first year is included in the elapsed time. Modern Chinese Communist coins are dated in western numerals using the western calendar, but earlier issues use conventional Chinese numerals. The coins of the Republic of China (Taiwan) are also dated in the year of the Republic, which is added to equal the calendar year. Still another method is a 60-year, repeating cycle, outlined in the table below. The date is shown by the combination of two characters, the first from the top row and the second from the column at left. In this catalog, when a cyclical date is used, the abbreviation CD appears before the AD date.

Dates not in parentheses are those which appear on the coins. For undated coins, dates appearing in parentheses are the years in which the coin was actually minted. Undated coins for which the year of minting is unknown are listed with ND (No Date) in the date or year column.

MONETARY SYSTEM

Dollar System
10 Cash (Wen, Ch'ien) = 1 Cent (Fen, Hsien)
10 Cents = 1 Chiao (Hao)
100 Cents = 1 Dollar (Yuan)
1 Dollar = 0.72 Tael

Tael System
10 Li = 1 Fen (Candareen)
10 Fen (Candareen) = 1 Ch'ien (Mace)
10 Ch'ien (Mace) = 1 Liang (Tael)

CHIHLI PROVINCE
Hebei, Hopei

A province located in northeastern China which contains the eastern end of the Great Wall. An important producer of coal and some iron ore. In 1928 the provincial name was changed from Chihli to Hopei. The Paoting mint was established in 1745 and only produced cast cash coins.

A mint for struck cash was established in 1888 and the mint for the Peiyang silver coinage was added in 1896. This was destroyed during the Boxer Rebellion. A replacement mint was built in 1902 for the provincial coinage and merged with the Tientsin (Tianjin) Central mint in 1910.

PATTERNS
Including off metal strikes

KM#	Date	Mintage	Identification	Mkt Val
Pn7	33(1907)	—	Tael. Gold. Y74.	—

EMPIRE

CH'ING DYNASTY
Manchu, 1644 - 1911

MEDALLIC COINAGE
Emperor Kuang Hsu Issues

X# M131 DOLLAR
Gold Ruler: Kuang-hsü Rev: 4 Chinese characters, "Made in Kwangtung Province," in center

Date	Mintage	F	VF	XF	Unc	BU
ND	—	—	—	2,500	3,500	—

X# M116 DOLLAR
Gold Ruler: Kuang-hsü Obv: 6 Chinese characters, "Made in 1885 Kuang Hsu." Rev: Border of Chinese character "Shou" (long life) Note: Kann#B13.

Date	Mintage	F	VF	XF	Unc	BU
CD1885	—	—	—	3,500	5,000	—

X# M155 5 DOLLARS
Gold Ruler: Kuang-hsü Rev: Facing dragons Note: Kann#B92.

Date	Mintage	F	VF	XF	Unc	BU
ND	—	—	—	550	750	—

X# M160 5 DOLLARS
Gold Ruler: Kuang-hsü Rev: 5 bats Note: Kann#B90.

Date	Mintage	F	VF	XF	Unc	BU
ND	—	—	—	450	650	—

X# M165 10 DOLLARS
Gold Ruler: Kuang-hsü Rev: Facing dragons

Date	Mintage	F	VF	XF	Unc	BU
ND	—	—	—	650	900	—

Tibet T'ung Chih Tael Issues

X# M455 5 TAELS
Gold Subject: 50th Anniversary Note: Kann#B102. Believed to have been struck in Shanghai ca.1919.

Date	Mintage	F	VF	XF	Unc	BU
CD1869 Proof	—	Value: 6,000				

X# M465 5//25 TAELS
94.9000 g., Gold Obv: 5 Chinese characters, "Value Five Taels Gold," at bottom

Date	Mintage	F	VF	XF	Unc	BU
ND(1871)/10 Proof	—	Value: 7,000				

X# M470 5//25 TAELS
94.9000 g., Gold

Date	Mintage	F	VF	XF	Unc	BU
ND(1871)/10 Proof	—	Value: 7,000				

KWANGTUNG PROVINCE

CHINA 117

X# M467 5//25 TAELS
94.9000 g., Gold Rev: Like XM465

Date	Mintage	F	VF	XF	Unc	BU
ND(1871)/10 Proof	—	Value: 7,000				

X# M475 50 TAELS
189.3000 g., Gold Obv: 5 Chinese characters, "Value Fifty Taels Gold," at bottom

Date	Mintage	F	VF	XF	Unc	BU
ND(1871)/10 Proof	—	Value: 10,000				

T'AI-P'ING REBELLION

CAST COINAGE
T'ai-p'ing Society

KM# 4 5 TAELS
Gold Obv. Inscription: T'ien-kuo Rev: Inscription reads top - bottom Rev. Inscription: Sheng-pao

Date	Mintage	Good	VG	F	VF	XF
ND(1853-64) 1 known	—	—	—	—	—	—

PATTERNS
Peking Tael Series

KM#	Date	Mintage	Identification	Mkt Val
Pn293	29(1903)	—	2 Ch'ien. Gold. K929v.	30,000
Pn296	29(1903)	—	Liang. Gold. K927v.	80,000

KM#	Date	Mintage	Identification	Mkt Val
Pn301	CD1906	—	Liang. Gold. K1540. Tientsin Mint. 39.5mm, 37g. Large clouds, plain edge.	50,000
PnA302	CD1906	—	Liang. Gold. Tientsin Mint. 39.5mm, 37g. Small clouds, reeded edge. Rare.	—
PnA303	CD1907	—	Liang. Gold. K1541a. Tientsin Mint. 39.5mm, 37g. Large clouds, plain edge. Rare.	—
Pn302	CD1907	—	Liang. Gold. K1541. Tientsin Mint. 39.5mm, 37g. Small clouds, reeded edge.	50,000

KWANGTUNG PROVINCE
Guangdong

A province located on the southeast coast of China. Kwangtung (Guangdong) lies mostly in the tropics and has both mountains and plains. Its coastline is nearly 800 miles long and provides many good harbors. Because of the location of Guangzhou (Canton) in the province, Kwangtung (Guangdong) was the first to be visited by seaborne foreign traders. Hong Kong was ceded to Great Britain after the First Opium War in 1841. Kowloon was later ceded to Britain in 1860 and the New Territories (100 year lease) in 1898 and Macao to Portugal in 1887, Kwangchowwan was leased to France in 1898 (a property was restored in 1946). A modern mint opened in Guangzhou (Canton) in 1889 with Edward Wyon as superintendent. The mint was a large issuer of coins until it closed in 1931. The Nationalists reopened the mint briefly in 1949, striking a few silver dollars, before abandoning the mainland for their retreat to Taiwan.

The large island of Hainan was split off from Kwangtung (Guangdong) Province in 1988 and established as a separate province.

Hong Kong was returned to China by Britain on July 1, 1997 and established as a special administrative region, retaining its own coinage.

PATTERNS
Including off metal strikes

KM#	Date	Mintage	Identification	Mkt Val
Pn23	13(1924)	—	20 Cents. Gold. Y424.	—
Pn26	ND(ca. 1929)	—	20 Cents. Gold. Y426.	850

SHANTUNG PROVINCE
Shandong

A province located on the northeastern coast of China. Confucius was born in this province. Parts of the province were leased to Great Britain and to Germany. Farming, fishing and mining are the chief occupations. A mint was opened at Tsinan in 1647 and was an intermittent producer for the empire. A modern mint was opened at Tsinan in 1905, but closed in 1906. Patterns were prepared between 1926-1933 in anticipation of a new coinage, but none were struck for circulation.

PATTERNS
Including off metal strikes

KM#	Date	Mintage	Identification	Mkt Val
Pn7	15(1926)	—	10 Dollars. Gold. K1536.	2,500
Pn9	15(1926)	—	20 Dollars. Gold. K1535.	3,000

SINKIANG PROVINCE
Hsinkiang, Xinjiang
"New Dominion"

An autonomous region in western China, often referred to as Chinese Turkestan. High mountains surround 2000 ft. tableland on three sides with a large desert in center of this province. Many salt lakes, mining and some farming and oil. Inhabited by early man and was referred to as the "Silk Route" to the West. Sinkiang (Xinjiang) has been historically under the control of many factions, including Genghis Khan. It became a province in 1884. China has made claim to Sinkiang (Xinjiang) for many, many years. This rule has been more nominal than actual. Sinkiang (Xinjiang) had eight imperial mints, only three of which were in operation toward the end of the reign of Kuang Hsu. Only two mints operated during the early years of the republic. In 1949, due to a drastic coin shortage and lack of confidence in the inflated paper money, it was planned to mint some dollars in Sinkiang (Xinjiang). These did not see much circulation, however, due to the defeat of the nationalists, though they have recently appeared in considerable numbers in today's market.

MONETARY SYSTEM
25 Cash = 10 Fen = 1 Miscal = 1 Ch'ien, Mace, Tanga
10 Miscals (Mace) = 1 Liang (Tael or Sar)
20 Miscals (Tangas) = 1 Tilla

LOCAL MINT NAMES AND MARKS

Mint	Chinese	Turki	Manchu
Kashgar, now Kashi	什喀	كشقر	 (Manchu script)

EMPIRE

REBEL COINAGE
Yakub Beg
AH1281-1294/1864-1877AD

Most of these coins were struck at Kashgar (Kashi) in the name of the Ottoman Sultan Abdul Aziz by the rebel Yakub Beg, who controlled much of Sinkiang (Xinjiang) between 1864 and 1877.

C# 37-2.1 TILLA
4.5000 g., Gold Rev. Inscription: Zarb Mahrusa Kashgar

Date	Mintage	VG	F	VF	XF	Unc
AH1290	—	120	225	400	650	—

C# 37-2.2 TILLA
4.5000 g., Gold Obv. Inscription: Abdul Aziz
Rev. Inscription: Zarb Dar us-Sultanat Kashgar

Date	Mintage	VG	F	VF	XF	Unc
AH1291//1290	—	135	245	450	750	—
AH1291	—	100	210	350	550	—

C# 37-2.3 TILLA
4.5000 g., Gold Obv: Inscription within dotted border within circles Obv. Inscription: Abdul Aziz Rev: Inscription within circle

Date	Mintage	VG	F	VF	XF	Unc
AH1291	—	100	210	350	550	—

C# 37-2.4 TILLA
4.5000 g., Gold Rev: Inscription within segmented circles

CHINA

YUNNAN PROVINCE

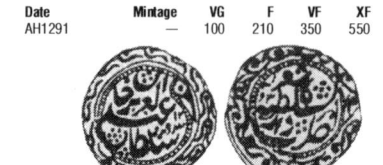

Date	Mintage	VG	F	VF	XF	Unc
AH1291	—	100	210	350	550	—

C# 37-2.6 TILLA
4.5000 g., Gold **Obv:** Inscription within segmented circles with loop **Obv. Inscription:** Abdul Aziz **Rev:** Inscription within segmented circles

Date	Mintage	VG	F	VF	XF	Unc
AH1292	—	90.00	180	300	500	—
AH1293	—	120	225	400	650	—
AH1294	—	120	225	400	650	—
AH1295	—	120	225	400	650	—

C# 37-2.5 TILLA
4.5000 g., Gold **Obv:** Inscription within dotted border within circles with loop **Obv. Inscription:** Abdul Aziz **Rev:** Inscription within dotted border within circles

Date	Mintage	VG	F	VF	XF	Unc
AH1292	—	120	225	400	650	—

C# 37-3 TILLA
4.5000 g., Gold **Obv. Inscription:** Abdulhamid II

Date	Mintage	VG	F	VF	XF	Unc
AH12xx	—	—	—	—	—	—

MILLED COINAGE

Y# 8 GOLD MISCAL (Mace)
3.9000 g., Gold **Ruler:** Kuang-hsü **Rev:** Turki legend around uncircled dragon

Date	Mintage	VG	F	VF	XF	Unc
ND(ca.1907)	—	145	400	650	950	1,350

Y# 8.1 GOLD MISCAL (Mace)
3.9000 g., Gold **Ruler:** Kuang-hsü **Rev:** Without Turki legend around uncircled dragon

Date	Mintage	VG	F	VF	XF	Unc
ND(ca.1907)	—	250	750	1,250	1,850	2,650

Y# 8.2 GOLD MISCAL (Mace)
3.9000 g., Gold **Ruler:** Kuang-hsü **Rev:** Turki legend at left differs

Date	Mintage	VG	F	VF	XF	Unc
ND(ca.1907)	—	160	450	750	1,150	1,650

Y# 8.3 GOLD MISCAL (Mace)
3.9000 g., Gold **Ruler:** Kuang-hsü **Rev:** Turki legend in outer circle

Date	Mintage	VG	F	VF	XF	Unc
ND(ca.1907)	—	185	550	950	1,350	2,000

Y# 9 GOLD 2 MISCALS
7.8000 g., Gold **Ruler:** Kuang-hsü **Obv:** Narrow-spaced Chinese "2" **Rev:** Turki legend around uncircled dragon

Date	Mintage	VG	F	VF	XF	Unc
ND(ca.1906)	—	250	750	1,350	2,000	2,800

Y# 9.1 GOLD 2 MISCALS
7.8000 g., Gold **Ruler:** Kuang-hsü **Obv:** Wide-spaced Chinese "2" **Rev:** Redesigned dragon

Date	Mintage	VG	F	VF	XF	Unc
ND(ca.1906)	—	250	750	1,350	2,000	2,800

YUNNAN PROVINCE

A province located in south China bordering Burma, Laos and Vietnam. It is very mountainous with many lakes. Yunnan was the home of various active imperial mints. A modern mint was established at Kunming in 1905 and the first struck copper coins were issued in 1906 and the first struck silver coins in 1908. General Tang Chi-yao issued coins in gold, silver and copper with his portrait in 1919. The last Republican coins were struck here in 1949.

REPUBLIC

STANDARD COINAGE

K# 1521 5 DOLLARS
Gold **Obv. Inscription:** "Equal to 5 (silver) Dollars"
Note: Uniface; Similar to 10 Dollars, K#1520.

Date	Mintage	VG	F	VF	XF	Unc
ND(1917) Rare	—	—	—	—	—	—

Y# 481.1 5 DOLLARS
4.5000 g., 0.7500 Gold, 18 mm. **Obv:** Bust of General T'ang Chi-yao facing **Rev:** Without numeral 2 below flag tassels

Date	Mintage	F	VF	XF	Unc	BU
ND(1919)	Inc. above					

Note: Reported, not confirmed

Y# 481 5 DOLLARS
4.5000 g., 0.7500 Gold .1085 oz. AGW, 18 mm. **Obv:** Bust of General T'ang Chi-yao facing **Rev:** With numeral 2 below flag tassels

Date	Mintage	VG	F	VF	XF	Unc
ND(1919)	Est. 60,000	75.00	220	500	800	1,250

K# 1529 5 DOLLARS
4.5000 g., 0.7500 Gold .1085 oz. AGW **Obv. Inscription:** Wu(5)-Yüan Chin-pi **Rev:** Tien in wheat sprays **Edge:** Plain

Date	Mintage	VG	F	VF	XF	Unc
ND(1925)	—	—	1,500	2,200	3,000	

K# 1520 10 DOLLARS
Gold **Obv. Inscription:** "Equal to 10 Silver Dollars" **Note:** Uniface.

Date	Mintage	VG	F	VF	XF	Unc
ND Rare	—	—	—	—	—	—

Y# 482 10 DOLLARS
8.5000 g., 0.7500 Gold .2050 oz. AGW, 23 mm. **Obv:** Bust of General T'ang Chi-yao facing **Rev:** With numeral 1 below flag tassels

Date	Mintage	VG	F	VF	XF	Unc
ND(1919)	900,000	135	275	650	1,000	1,400

Y# 482.1 10 DOLLARS
8.5000 g., 0.7500 Gold .2050 oz. AGW, 23 mm. **Obv:** Bust of General T'ang Chi-yao facing **Rev:** Without numeral 1 below flag tassels

Date	Mintage	VG	F	VF	XF	Unc
ND(1919)	Inc. above	135	275	900	1,200	1,800

K# 1528 10 DOLLARS
8.5000 g., 0.7500 Gold .2050 oz. AGW **Obv. Inscription:** Shih(10)-yüan Chin-pi **Rev:** Tien in wheat sprays **Edge:** Plain

Date	Mintage	VG	F	VF	XF	Unc
ND(1925)	—	—	1,500	2,200	3,000	

CHINA, REPUBLIC OF

REPUBLIC OF CHINA

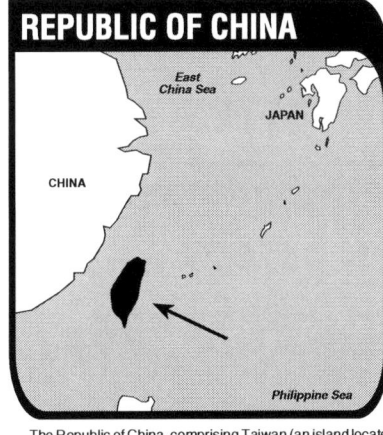

The Republic of China, comprising Taiwan (an island located 90 miles (145 km.) off the southeastern coast of mainland China), the offshore islands of Quemoy and Matsu and nearby islets of the Pescadores chain, has an area of 14,000 sq. mi. (35,980 sq. km.) and a population of 20.2 million. Capital: Taipei. During the past decade, manufacturing has replaced agriculture in importance. Fruits, vegetables, plywood, textile yarns and fabrics and clothing are exported.

Chinese migration to Taiwan began as early as the 6th century. The Dutch established a base on the island in 1624 and held it until 1661, when they were driven out by supporters of the Ming dynasty who used it as a base for their unsuccessful attempt to displace the ruling Manchu dynasty of mainland China. After being occupied by Manchu forces in 1683, Taiwan remained under the suzerainty of China until its cession to Japan in 1895. It was returned to China following World War II. On Dec. 8, 1949, Taiwan became the last remnant of Sun Yat-sen's vast Republic of China. Chiang Kai-Shek had quickly moved his government and nearly exhausted army from the mainland leaving the Communist forces under Mao Tse-tung victorious.

The coins of Nationalist China do not carry A.D. dating, but are dated according to the year of the republic, which was established in 1911. However, republican years are added to 1911 to find the western year. Thus republican year 38 plus 1911 equals Gregorian calendar year 1949AD.

MONETARY SYSTEM
10 Cents = 1 Chiao
10 Chiao = 1 Yuan (Dollar)

REPUBLIC

STANDARD COINAGE

Y# 333 10 DOLLARS
7.0500 g., Red Gold **Ruler:** Hung-hsien **Obv:** Bust of Hung-hsien left **Rev:** Winged dragon left **Note:** K#1515.

Date	Mintage	VG	F	VF	XF	Unc
1 (1916)	—	—	—	2,500	4,000	5,500

Y# 333a 10 DOLLARS
7.0500 g., Yellow Gold **Ruler:** Hung-hsien

Date	Mintage	VG	F	VF	XF	Unc
1 (1916)	—	—	—	2,500	4,000	5,500

Y# 330 10 DOLLARS
8.1500 g., 0.8500 Gold .2227 oz. AGW **Ruler:** Hung-hsien **Note:** K#1531.

Date	Mintage	VG	F	VF	XF	Unc
8 (1919)	—	—	—	2,000	2,850	4,000

Y# 331 20 DOLLARS
16.3000 g., 0.8500 Gold .4456 oz. AGW **Ruler:** Hung-hsien **Note:** K#1530.

Date	Mintage	VG	F	VF	XF	Unc
8 (1919)	—	—	—	—	5,500	8,500

MEDALLIC COINAGE
Flag Issues

X# M700 5 DOLLARS
0.9170 Gold

Date	Mintage	F	VF	XF	Unc	BU
1912	—	—	—	—	350	—

X# M660 2000 YUAN
29.9300 g., Gold **Subject:** 100th Anniversary of Birth **Obv:** Bust of Chiang Kai-shek facing **Rev:** Ornate patterns, rayed outlined map of Taiwan at center

Date	Mintage	F	VF	XF	Unc	BU
ND(1986)/75 Proof	—	Value: 550				

MEDALLIC COINAGE
Ni Szu-chung Issues

X# M990 50 CENTS
Gold **Rev:** 3 six-pointed stars below center

Date	Mintage	F	VF	XF	Unc	BU
ND(1920)/9	—	—	—	600	800	—

MEDALLIC COINAGE
Shung Feng Issue

X# M1010 DOLLAR
Gold **Subject:** 35th Anniversary **Obv:** Dragon around 2 Chinese characters "Shun Feng" **Rev:** 2 Chinese characters, "Mei Kung" in wreath with dates "1886-1921" below

Date	Mintage	F	VF	XF	Unc	BU
1921	—	—	—	600	800	—

MEDALLIC COINAGE
Sinkiang Issues

X# M1030 GOLD MACE
Gold **Obv:** Similar to XM1035 **Rev:** 4 Chinese characters, "One Mace Ration Gold," in center

Date	Mintage	F	VF	XF	Unc	BU
ND(1912)/1	—	—	250	350	500	—

X# M1031 GOLD MACE
Silver **Obv:** Similar to XM1035 **Rev:** 4 Chinese characters, "One Mace Ration Gold," in center

Date	Mintage	F	VF	XF	Unc	BU
ND(1912)/1 Reported, not confirmed	—	—	—	—	—	—

X# M1035 2 GOLD MACE
Gold **Rev:** 4 Chinese characters, "Two Mace Ration Gold," in center

Date	Mintage	F	VF	XF	Unc	BU
ND(1912)/1	—	—	325	450	700	—

X# M1036 2 GOLD MACE
Silver **Rev:** 4 Chinese characters, "Two Mace Ration Gold," in center

Date	Mintage	F	VF	XF	Unc	BU
ND(1912)/1 Reported, not confirmed	—	—	—	—	—	—

MEDALLIC COINAGE
Yüan Shih-kai Series

X# M1305 5 DOLLARS
4.4000 g., Gold, 18 mm. **Obv:** Bust of Yüan Shih-kai left **Rev:** Dragon **Note:** Kann#1517.

Date	Mintage	F	VF	XF	Unc	BU
Yr. 3 (1914)	—	—	—	2,750	4,000	—

X# M1290 100 DOLLARS
0.9000 Gold **Subject:** 2nd Anniversary of the Republic **Obv:** Crossed flags **Rev:** Bust of Yüan Shih-kai left

Date	Mintage	F	VF	XF	Unc	BU
Yr. 2 (1913)	—	—	—	17,500	25,000	—

MEDALLIC COINAGE
Yüan Shih-kai as Hung Hsien Series

X# M1331 10 CENTS
Gold **Obv:** Bust of Hung Hsien in ceremonial robe facing slightly left **Rev:** Dragon; 4 Chinese characters, "Commemorative of 1916"

Date	Mintage	F	VF	XF	Unc	BU
(1916)	—	—	—	1,250	2,250	—

X# M1336 20 CENTS
Gold **Obv:** Bust of Hung Hsien in ceremonial robe facing slightly left **Rev:** Dragon; 4 Chinese characters, "Commemorative of 1916"

Date	Mintage	F	VF	XF	Unc	BU
(1916) Reported, not confirmed	—	—	—	—	—	—

X# M1341 1/2 DOLLAR
Gold **Rev:** Dragon **Note:** Kann#B104.

Date	Mintage	F	VF	XF	Unc	BU
(1916)	—	—	—	2,000	3,500	—

X# M1361 1/2 DOLLAR
Gold **Rev:** Flying dragon

Date	Mintage	F	VF	XF	Unc	BU
Yr. 1 (1916)	—	—	—	2,000	3,500	—

X# M1381 DOLLAR
Gold **Note:** Kann#B103.

Date	Mintage	F	VF	XF	Unc	BU
Yr. 1 (1916)	—	—	—	—	—	—

X# M1370 5 DOLLARS
3.9900 g., Gold **Obv:** Facing dragon **Rev:** Bust of Hung Hsien in ceremonial robe facing slightly left

CHINA, REPUBLIC OF

Date	Mintage	F	VF	XF	Unc	BU
Yr. 1 (1916)	—	—	—	—	600	800

X# M1372 5 DOLLARS
3.9900 g., Gold **Note:** Kann#B99. Mule. **Obv:** XM1370. **Rev:** XM1331.

Date	Mintage	F	VF	XF	Unc	BU
Yr. 1 (1916)	—	—	—	—	—	—

X# M1375 10 DOLLARS
Gold, 23 mm. **Note:** Similar to 5 Dollars, XM1370.

Date	Mintage	F	VF	XF	Unc	BU
Yr. 1 (1916)	—	—	—	—	900	1,200

PATTERNS
Including off metal strikes

KM#	Date	Mintage	Identification	Mkt Val
Pn6	ND(1912)	—	10 Cash. Gold.	—
Pn7	ND(1912)	—	20 Cents. Gold. Y#317	3,500
Pn8	ND(1912)	—	Dollar. Gold. Y#318	—
Pn9	ND(1912)	—	Dollar. Gold. Y#318 - K#1550	20,000
Pn29	ND(1914)	—	Dollar. Gold. With L. GIORGI, Yuan Shih-kai; K#1558	25,000
Pn44	ND(1916)	—	Dollar. Gold. Y#332. It has been verified that the San Francisco Mint actually struck 2 pieces in gold in 1928.	14,000
Pn50	1(1916)	—	10 Dollars. Gold. with L. G. Hung-hsien, near shoulder; K#1515a	—
Pn53	ND(1916)	—	Dollar. Gold. With L. GIORGI; K#1560	50,000
Pn62	10(1921)	—	Dollar. Gold. K#1570	24,000
Pn65	10(1921)	—	Dollar. Gold. Reeded edge. K#1570	25,000
Pn66	10(1921)	—	Dollar. Gold. Plain edge. K#1570a	25,000
Pn67	ND(1923)	—	Dollar. Gold. K#1572	17,500
Pn70	12(1923)	—	Dollar. Gold. Y#336	25,000
Pn72	12(1923)	—	Dollar. Gold. Y#336.1	—
Pn73	ND(1924)	—	Dollar. Gold. K#1577	20,000
Pn81	16(1927)	—	10 Cents. Gold. Y#339	—
Pn82	ND(1927)	—	Dollar. Gold. Y#318	—
PnA92	17(1928)	—	Dollar. Gold. K#688z	—

TAIWAN

Chinese migration to Taiwan began as early as the sixth century. The Dutch established a base on the island in 1624 and held it until 1661, when they were driven out by supporters of the Ming dynasty who used it as a base for their unsuccessful attempt to displace the ruling Manchu dynasty of mainland China. After being occupied by Manchu forces in 1683, Taiwan remained under the suzerainty of China until its cession to Japan in 1895. The island was part of the province of Fukien (Fujian) until established as a separate province in the period 1885-1895. (It took 10 years to complete the conversion to a full-fledged province.)

REPUBLIC
STANDARD COINAGE

Y# 541 1000 YUAN
15.0000 g., 0.9000 Gold .4340 oz. AGW **Obv:** Bust of Sun Yat-sen left

Date	Mintage	F	VF	XF	Unc	BU
54(1965)	—	—	—	—	325	400

Y# 563 1000 YUAN
15.5540 g., 0.9990 Gold .5000 oz. AGW, 25 mm. **Subject:** Late President - Chiang Ching-kuo **Obv:** Bust of Ching-kuo facing **Rev:** Mausoleum **Edge:** Reeded

Date	Mintage	F	VF	XF	Unc	BU
87(1998)	30,000	—	—	—	325	375

Y# 542 2000 YUAN
30.0000 g., 0.9000 Gold .8681 oz. AGW **Obv:** Bust of Sun Yat-sen left **Rev:** Chinese symbols at center, budding branch wrappd around

Date	Mintage	F	VF	XF	Unc	BU
54(1965)	—	—	—	—	675	775

Y# 544 2000 YUAN
31.0600 g., 0.9000 Gold .8988 oz. AGW **Subject:** 80th Birthday of Chiang Kai-shek **Rev:** Two cranes standing on rock

Date	Mintage	F	VF	XF	Unc	BU
55(1966)	—	—	—	—	700	800

PATTERNS
Yuan System; Including off metal strikes

KG numbers in reference to Coinage of the Chinese Emigre Government 1949-1957 by E. Kann and D. Graham.

KM#	Date	Mintage	Identification	Mkt Val
Pn65	62(1973)	—	5 Yuan. Gold. Y#548	1,350
Pn66	64(1975)	—	Yuan. Gold. Y#536	950

CHINA / Peoples Republic

The Peoples Republic of China, located in eastern Asia, has an area of 3,696,100 sq. mi. (9,596,960 sq. km.) (including Manchuria and Tibet) and a population of *1.20 billion. Capital: Peking (Beijing). The economy is based on agriculture, mining, and manufacturing. Textiles, clothing, metal ores, tea and rice are exported.

China's ancient civilization began in east-central Henan's Huayang county, 2800-2300 B.C. The warring feudal states comprising early China were first united under Emperor Ch'in Shih (246-210 B.C.) who gave China its name and first central government. Subsequent dynasties alternated brilliant cultural achievements with internal disorder until the Empire was brought down by the revolution of 1911, and the Republic of China installed in its place. Chinese culture attained a pre-eminence in art, literature and philosophy, but a traditional backwardness in industry and administration ill prepared China for the demands of 19th century Western expansionism which exposed it to military and political humiliations, and mandated a drastic revision of political practice in order to secure an accommodation with the modern world.

The Republic of 1911 barely survived the stress of World War I, and was subsequently all but shattered by the rise of nationalism and the emergence of the Chinese Communist movement. Moscow, which practiced a policy of cooperation between Communists and other parties in movements for national liberation, sought to establish an entente between the Chinese Communist Party and the Kuomintang ('National Peoples Party') of Sun Yat-sen. The ensuing cooperation was based on little more than the hope each had of using the other.

An increasingly uneasy association between the Kuomintang and the Chinese Communist Party developed and continued until April 12, 1927, when Chiang Kai-shek, Sun Yat-sen's political heir, instituted a bloody purge to stamp out the Communists within the Kuomintang and the government and virtually paralyzed their ranks throughout China. Some time after the mid-1927 purges, the Chinese Communist Party turned to armed force to resist Chiang Kai-shek and during the period of 1930-34 acquired control over large parts of Kiangsi (Jiangxi), Fukien (Fujian), Hunan and Hupeh (Hubei). The Nationalist Nanking government responded with a series of campaigns against the soviet power bases and, by October of 1934, succeeded in driving the remnants of the Communist army to a refuge in Shensi (Shaanxi) Province. There the Communists reorganized under the leadership of Mao Tse-tung, defeated the Nationalist forces, and on Sept. 21, 1949, established the Peoples Republic of China. Thereafter relations between Russia and Communist China steadily deteriorated until 1958, when China emerged as an independent center of Communist power.

MONETARY SYSTEM
After 1949
10 Fen (Cents) = 1 Jiao
10 Jiao = 1 Renminbi Yuan

MINT MARKS
(b) - Beijing (Peking)
(s) - Shanghai
(y) - Shenyang (Mukden)

PEOPLES REPUBLIC
STANDARD COINAGE

Y# 187 5 YUAN
1.5552 g., 0.9990 Gold .0500 oz. AGW **Series:** Olympics **Note:** Similar to 100 Yuan, Y#191.

Date	Mintage	F	VF	XF	Unc	BU
1989	Est. 334,000	—	—	—	—	45.00
1989 Proof	8,000	Value: 55.00				

Y# 498 5 YUAN
1.5552 g., 0.9990 Gold .0500 oz. AGW **Subject:** Goddess of Mercy **Obv:** Great Wall, date below **Rev:** Goddess left, denomination at right

CHINA, PEOPLE'S REPUBLIC

Date	Mintage	F	VF	XF	Unc	BU
1993 Prooflike	40,000	—	—	—	—	45.00

Y# 500 5 YUAN
1.5552 g., 0.9990 Gold .0500 oz. AGW **Rev:** Goddess Kuan Yin - Seated in Flowers

Date	Mintage	F	VF	XF	Unc	BU
1993 Proof	1,000	Value: 65.00				

Y# 773 5 YUAN
1.5552 g., 0.9990 Gold .0500 oz. AGW **Subject:** Homeland Scenery **Obv:** Great Wall **Rev:** Temple at Mount Song

Date	Mintage	F	VF	XF	Unc	BU
1993 Proof	8,888	Value: 45.00				

Y# 419 5 YUAN
1.5552 g., 0.9990 Gold .0500 oz. AGW **Obv:** Crowned figure on horseback, date lower right **Rev:** Unicorn, denomination at left

Date	Mintage	F	VF	XF	Unc	BU
1994 Proof	31,000	Value: 65.00				

Y# 736 5 YUAN
1.5552 g., 0.9990 Gold .0500 oz. AGW **Obv:** Eastern unicorn rearing, left, date below **Rev:** Western unicorn with offspring, denomination at left

Date	Mintage	F	VF	XF	Unc	BU
1995 Proof	20,000	Value: 95.00				

Y# 740 5 YUAN
1.5552 g., 0.9990 Gold .0500 oz. AGW **Obv:** Eastern unicorn, date below **Rev:** Head of western unicorn, right, denomination at right

Date	Mintage	F	VF	XF	Unc	BU
1996	—	—	—	—	—	50.00
1996 Proof	5,000	Value: 130				

Y# 885 5 YUAN
1.5552 g., 0.9990 Gold .0500 oz. AGW **Subject:** Goddess Guanyin **Obv:** Temple, date below **Rev:** Goddess holding flower, denomination at left

Date	Mintage	F	VF	XF	Unc	BU
1996 Proof	5,000	Value: 45.00				

Y# 1197 5 YUAN
1.5550 g., 0.9990 Gold 0.0499 oz. AGW, 14 mm. **Subject:** Goddess Guanyin **Obv:** Temple **Rev:** Goddess holding vase and twig **Edge:** Reeded

Date	Mintage	F	VF	XF	Unc	BU
1996 Proof	35,000	Value: 42.50				

Y# 1198 5 YUAN
1.5550 g., 0.9990 Gold 0.0499 oz. AGW, 14 mm. **Obv:** Ornamental column **Rev:** Child holding a carp **Edge:** Reeded

Date	Mintage	F	VF	XF	Unc	BU
1997	100,000	—	—	—	—	42.50

Y# 982 5 YUAN
1.5552 g., 0.9990 Gold .0500 oz. AGW **Subject:** Pu Tuo Mountain

Date	Mintage	F	VF	XF	Unc	BU
1997	35,000	—	—	—	—	42.50

Y# 55 10 YUAN
1.2000 g., 0.9000 Gold .0347 oz. AGW **Obv:** Building, denomination at right **Rev:** Marco Polo bust, left, dates below

Date	Mintage	F	VF	XF	Unc	BU
1983 Proof	50,000	Value: 55.00				

Y# 206 10 YUAN
1.0000 g., 0.9990 Gold .0322 oz. AGW **Obv:** Great Wall, date below **Rev:** Phoenix and dragon, denomination at left

Date	Mintage	F	VF	XF	Unc	BU
1990 Proof	34,000	Value: 40.00				

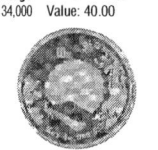

Y# 474 10 YUAN
3.1103 g., 0.9990 Gold .1000 oz. AGW **Obv:** Temple of Harmony **Rev:** 2 peacocks, denomination above **Rev. Designer:** Lanf Shih Ning

Date	Mintage	F	VF	XF	Unc	BU
1993 Prooflike	—	—	—	—	—	100

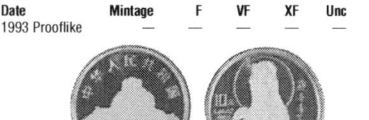

Y# 499 10 YUAN
3.1103 g., 0.9990 Gold .1000 oz. AGW **Obv:** Building above date **Rev:** Goddess of Mercy holding flower, denomination at left

Date	Mintage	F	VF	XF	Unc	BU
1993 Prooflike	20,000	—	—	—	—	75.00

Y# 501 10 YUAN
3.1103 g., 0.9990 Gold .1000 oz. AGW **Rev:** Goddess Guanyin seated in flowers, denomination at left

Date	Mintage	F	VF	XF	Unc	BU
1993 Proof	1,000	Value: 90.00				

Y# 774 10 YUAN
3.1030 g., 0.9990 Gold .1000 oz. AGW, 18 mm. **Subject:** Homeland Scenery **Obv:** Great Wall **Rev:** Cliffside building

Date	Mintage	F	VF	XF	Unc	BU
1993 Proof	8,888	Value: 75.00				

Y# 421 10 YUAN
3.1103 g., 0.9990 Gold .1000 oz. AGW **Rev:** Unicorn looking back towards right

Date	Mintage	F	VF	XF	Unc	BU
1994 Proof	5,100	Value: 110				

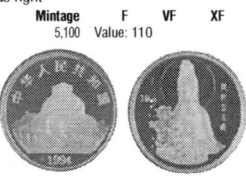

Y# 510 10 YUAN
3.1103 g., 0.9990 Gold .1000 oz. AGW **Obv:** Great Wall above date **Rev:** Guanyin-Goddess of Mercy, holding child, facing, denomination at left

Date	Mintage	F	VF	XF	Unc	BU
1994 Prooflike	8,000	—	—	—	—	75.00

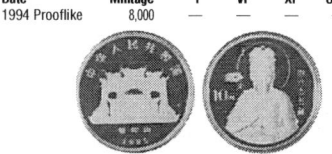

Y# 520 10 YUAN
3.1103 g., 0.9990 Gold .1000 oz. AGW **Obv:** Building, date below **Rev:** Guanyin - Goddess of Mercy with lotus flower, facing, denomination at left

Date	Mintage	F	VF	XF	Unc	BU
1995 Proof	3,000	Value: 115				

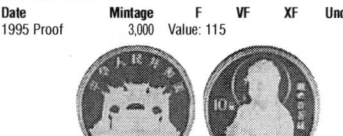

Y# 521 10 YUAN
3.1103 g., 0.9990 Gold .1000 oz. AGW **Obv:** Building, date below **Rev:** Guanyin, Goddess of Mercy with wheel, denomination at left

Date	Mintage	F	VF	XF	Unc	BU
1995 Proof	3,000	Value: 115				

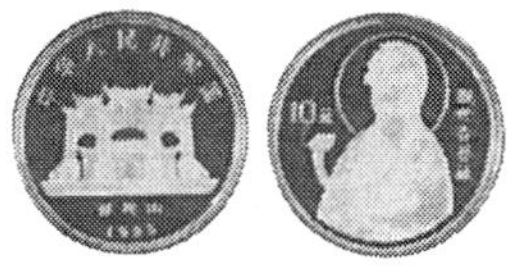

Y# 522 10 YUAN
3.1103 g., 0.9990 Gold .1000 oz. AGW **Obv:** Building, date below **Rev:** Guanyin - Goddess of Mercy with sceptre, denomination at left

Date	Mintage	F	VF	XF	Unc	BU
1995 Proof	3,000	Value: 115				

Y# 523 10 YUAN
3.1103 g., 0.9990 Gold .1000 oz. AGW **Obv:** Building, date below **Rev:** Guanyin, Goddess of Mercy with bowl, denomination at left

Date	Mintage	F	VF	XF	Unc	BU
1995 Proof	3,000	Value: 115				

Y# 737 10 YUAN
3.1100 g., 0.9990 Gold .0999 oz. AGW **Obv:** Eastern unicorn, date below **Rev:** Western unicorn with offspring, denomination at left

Date	Mintage	F	VF	XF	Unc	BU
1995 Proof	5,000	Value: 110				

Y# 799 10 YUAN
3.1103 g., 0.9990 Gold .1000 oz. AGW **Subject:** Chinese Culture Series **Obv:** Great Wall seen through arch, date below **Rev:** Pagoda of six harmonies, denomination at left

Date	Mintage	F	VF	XF	Unc	BU
1995 Proof	25,000	Value: 75.00				

Y# 800 10 YUAN
3.1103 g., 0.9990 Gold .1000 oz. AGW **Subject:** Chinese Culture Series **Obv:** Great Wall seen through arch **Rev:** Mencius seated at table, denomination below

Date	Mintage	F	VF	XF	Unc	BU
1995 Proof	25,000	Value: 75.00				

Y# 801 10 YUAN
3.1103 g., 0.9990 Gold .1000 oz. AGW **Subject:** Chinese Culture Series **Obv:** Great Wall seen through arch **Rev:** Tang Taizong seated, denomination at left

Date	Mintage	F	VF	XF	Unc	BU
1995 Proof	25,000	Value: 75.00				

Y# 802 10 YUAN
3.1103 g., 0.9990 Gold .1000 oz. AGW **Subject:** Chinese Culture Series **Obv:** Great Wall seen through arch **Rev:** Lion dance, denomination lower left

Date	Mintage	F	VF	XF	Unc	BU
1995 Proof	25,000	Value: 75.00				

122 CHINA, PEOPLE'S REPUBLIC

Y# 803 10 YUAN
3.1103 g., 0.9990 Gold .1000 oz. AGW **Subject:** Chinese Culture Series **Obv:** Great Wall seen through arch **Rev:** Female opera role

Date	Mintage	F	VF	XF	Unc	BU
1995 Proof	25,000	Value: 75.00				

Y# 742 10 YUAN
3.1100 g., 0.9990 Gold .0999 oz. AGW **Obv:** Eastern unicorn, date below **Rev:** Western unicorn in wreath, denomination lower left

Date	Mintage	F	VF	XF	Unc	BU
1996 Proof	5,000	Value: 110				

Y# 887 10 YUAN
3.1101 g., 0.9990 Gold .1000 oz. AGW **Subject:** Goddess Guanyin **Obv:** Temple **Rev:** Goddess holding flower

Date	Mintage	F	VF	XF	Unc	BU
1996 Proof	10,000	Value: 75.00				

Y# 912a 10 YUAN
3.1100 g., 0.9990 Gold .0999 oz. AGW **Obv:** Eastern unicorn **Rev:** Western unicorn

Date	Mintage	F	VF	XF	Unc	BU
1997 Proof	5,000	Value: 120				

Y# 913 10 YUAN
3.1100 g., 0.9990 Gold .1000 oz. AGW **Subject:** Goddess Guanyin **Obv:** Putuo Hill Temple **Rev:** Goddess holding jug of dew

Date	Mintage	F	VF	XF	Unc	BU
1997 Proof	10,000	Value: 75.00				

Y# 983 10 YUAN
3.1103 g., 0.9990 Gold .1000 oz. AGW **Subject:** Celebrating Spring **Obv:** Lantern **Rev:** Children setting off firecrackers

Date	Mintage	F	VF	XF	Unc	BU
1997	100,000	—	—	—	—	70.00

Y# 984 10 YUAN
3.1103 g., 0.9990 Gold .1000 oz. AGW **Obv:** Forbidden city, date below **Rev:** Bronze chinze, denomination upper right

Date	Mintage	F	VF	XF	Unc	BU
1997 Proof	11,000	Value: 75.00				

Y# 1191 10 YUAN
3.1100 g., 0.9990 Gold 0.0999 oz. AGW, 18 mm. **Obv:** Great Wall, date below **Rev:** Man with flag, denomination at left **Edge:** Reeded

Date	Mintage	F	VF	XF	Unc	BU
1997(y)	16,000	—	—	—	90.00	—

Y# 1192 10 YUAN
3.1100 g., 0.9990 Gold 0.0999 oz. AGW, 18 mm. **Obv:** Great Wall, date below **Rev:** Man with extended open hand, denomination at right **Edge:** Reeded

Date	Mintage	F	VF	XF	Unc	BU
1997(y)	16,000	—	—	—	90.00	—

Y# 1193 10 YUAN
3.1100 g., 0.9990 Gold 0.0999 oz. AGW, 18 mm. **Obv:** Great Wall, date below **Rev:** Astronomer, denomination upper left **Edge:** Reeded

Date	Mintage	F	VF	XF	Unc	BU
1997(y)	16,000	—	—	—	90.00	—

Y# 1194 10 YUAN
3.1100 g., 0.9990 Gold 0.0999 oz. AGW, 18 mm. **Obv:** Great Wall, date below **Rev:** Gymnast, denomination at right **Edge:** Reeded

Date	Mintage	F	VF	XF	Unc	BU
1997(y)	16,000	—	—	—	90.00	—

Y# 1195 10 YUAN
3.1100 g., 0.9990 Gold 0.0999 oz. AGW, 18 mm. **Obv:** Great Wall, date below **Rev:** Building, denomination below **Edge:** Reeded

Date	Mintage	F	VF	XF	Unc	BU
1997(y)	16,000	—	—	—	90.00	—

Y# 1199.1 10 YUAN
3.1100 g., 0.9990 Gold 0.0999 oz. AGW, 18 mm. **Obv:** Ornamental column **Rev:** Child holding a carp **Edge:** Reeded

Date	Mintage	F	VF	XF	Unc	BU
1997	100,000	—	—	—	75.00	—

Y# 1199.2 10 YUAN
3.1100 g., 0.9990 Gold 0.0999 oz. AGW, 18 mm. **Obv:** Ornamental column **Rev:** Multicolor child holding a carp **Edge:** Reeded

Date	Mintage	F	VF	XF	Unc	BU
1997 Proof	20,000	Value: 90.00				

Y# 987 10 YUAN
3.1103 g., 0.9990 Gold .1000 oz. AGW **Subject:** Culture of Dragons

Date	Mintage	F	VF	XF	Unc	BU
1998 Proof	6,000	Value: 75.00				

Y# 1065 10 YUAN
3.1100 g., 0.9990 Gold 0.0999 oz. AGW, 18 mm. **Subject:** Vault Protector **Obv:** Denomination, inscription and ornamental design **Rev:** Old cash coin characters **Edge:** Reeded **Note:** Square holed cash coin design.

Date	Mintage	F	VF	XF	Unc	BU
1998 Proof	6,000	Value: 120				

Y# 994 10 YUAN
3.1103 g., 0.9990 Gold .1000 oz. AGW **Subject:** Y2K

Date	Mintage	F	VF	XF	Unc	BU
2000	50,000	—	—	—	—	75.00

Y# 995 10 YUAN
3.1103 g., 0.9990 Gold .1000 oz. AGW **Subject:** Chinese Grotto Art

Date	Mintage	F	VF	XF	Unc	BU
2000	50,000	—	—	—	70.00	—

Y# 996 10 YUAN
3.1103 g., 0.9990 Gold .1000 oz. AGW, 18 mm. **Subject:** Goddess Kuan Yin **Obv:** Putuo Mountain Gate **Rev:** Standing Kuan Yin with holographic background **Edge:** Reeded

Date	Mintage	F	VF	XF	Unc	BU
2000	33,000	—	—	—	—	135

Y# 555 25 YUAN
8.4800 g., 0.9170 Gold .2500 oz. AGW **Subject:** Bronze Age Sculptures **Obv:** National emblem **Rev:** Ram

Date	Mintage	F	VF	XF	Unc	BU
1992 Proof	500	Value: 385				

Y# 556 25 YUAN
8.4800 g., 0.9170 Gold .2500 oz. AGW **Subject:** Bronze Age Sculptures **Rev:** Panther

Date	Mintage	F	VF	XF	Unc	BU
1992 Proof	500	Value: 385				

Y# 889 25 YUAN
7.7759 g., 0.9990 Gold .2500 oz. AGW **Obv:** Great Wall **Rev:** Horse and dragon

Date	Mintage	F	VF	XF	Unc	BU
1992 Proof	5,000	Value: 195				

Note: Issued in 1996

Y# 404 25 YUAN
7.7759 g., 0.9990 Gold .2500 oz. AGW **Rev:** Chinese Gods: Fu, Lu, and Shu

Date	Mintage	F	VF	XF	Unc	BU
1993	Est. 3,000	—	—	—	—	195

Y# 408 25 YUAN
8.4900 g., 0.9170 Gold .2500 oz. AGW **Subject:** Bronze Age Sculptures **Obv:** National emblem, date below **Rev:** Unicorn, right, denomination lower right

Date	Mintage	F	VF	XF	Unc	BU
1993 Proof	350	Value: 550				

Y# 475 25 YUAN
7.7758 g., 0.9990 Gold .2500 oz. AGW **Obv:** Temple of Heaven **Rev:** Two peacocks, denomination above

Date	Mintage	F	VF	XF	Unc	BU
1993 Prooflike	—	—	—	—	—	185

Y# 502 25 YUAN
7.7758 g., 0.9990 Gold .2500 oz. AGW **Rev:** Goddess Kuan Yin seated in flower, denomination at left

Date	Mintage	F	VF	XF	Unc	BU
1993 Proof	1,000	Value: 195				

Y# 775 25 YUAN
7.7758 g., 0.9990 Gold .2500 oz. AGW **Subject:** Homeland Scenery **Obv:** Great Wall **Rev:** Large temple at Mount Heng

Date	Mintage	F	VF	XF	Unc	BU
1993 Proof	8,888	Value: 220				

Y# 409 25 YUAN
8.4900 g., 0.9170 Gold .2500 oz. AGW **Subject:** Bronze Age Sculptures **Obv:** National emblem, date below **Rev:** Pig, left, denomination below

Date	Mintage	F	VF	XF	Unc	BU
1993 Proof	350	Value: 550				

Y# 422 25 YUAN
7.7758 g., Bi-Metallic Gold center in Silver ring .2500 oz. **Obv:** Building within circle, date below **Rev:** Unicorn, denomination at left, within circle **Note:** Similar to 10 Yuan, Y#420.

Date	Mintage	F	VF	XF	Unc	BU
1994 Proof	1,100	Value: 220				

Y# 1181 25 YUAN
7.7759 g., 0.9999 Platinum 0.25 oz. APW **Subject:** Chinese Inventions **Rev:** First tuned bells

Date	Mintage	F	VF	XF	Unc	BU
1994	100	Value: 1,050				

CHINA, PEOPLE'S REPUBLIC

Y# 1182 25 YUAN
7.7759 g., 0.9999 Platinum 0.25 oz. APW **Subject:** Chinese inventions **Rev:** First silk fabrics

Date	Mintage	F	VF	XF	Unc	BU
1994	100	Value: 1,050				

Y# 1183 25 YUAN
7.7759 g., 0.9999 Platinum 0.25 oz. APW **Subject:** Chinese inventions **Rev:** First recording of comets

Date	Mintage	F	VF	XF	Unc	BU
1994	100	Value: 1,150				

Y# 1184 25 YUAN
7.7759 g., 0.9999 Platinum 0.25 oz. APW **Subject:** Chinese inventions **Rev:** First masts for sailing

Date	Mintage	F	VF	XF	Unc	BU
1994	100	Value: 1,050				

Y# 1185 25 YUAN
7.7759 g., 0.9999 Platinum 0.25 oz. APW **Subject:** Chinese inventions **Rev:** First chain pumps used to draw water

Date	Mintage	F	VF	XF	Unc	BU
1994	100	Value: 1,050				

Y# 423 25 YUAN
7.7758 g., 0.9990 Gold .2500 oz. AGW **Obv:** Figure on Eastern unicorn, date below **Rev:** Unicorn, denomination at left, rose sprays below

Date	Mintage	F	VF	XF	Unc	BU
1994 Proof	5,100	Value: 220				

Y# 511 25 YUAN
3.1103 g., 0.9990 Gold .1000 oz. AGW **Obv:** Great Wall, date below **Rev:** Goddess Kuan Yin holding child, facing, denomination at left

Date	Mintage	F	VF	XF	Unc	BU
1994 Proof	1,000	Value: 220				

Y# 512 25 YUAN
3.1103 g., 0.9990 Gold .1000 oz. AGW **Obv:** Great Wall, date below **Rev:** Goddess Kuan Yin with bottle, 3/4 left, denomination at right

Date	Mintage	F	VF	XF	Unc	BU
1994 Proof	1,000	Value: 220				

Y# 513 25 YUAN
3.1103 g., 0.9990 Gold .1000 oz. AGW **Obv:** Great Wall, date below **Rev:** Goddess Kuan Yin standing, denomination at right

Date	Mintage	F	VF	XF	Unc	BU
1994 Proof	1,000	Value: 220				

Y# 514 25 YUAN
3.1103 g., 0.9990 Gold .1000 oz. AGW **Obv:** Great Wall, date below **Rev:** Goddess Kuan Yin seated, denomination at right

Date	Mintage	F	VF	XF	Unc	BU
1994 Proof	1,000	Value: 220				

Y# 524 25 YUAN
7.7758 g., 0.9990 Gold .2500 oz. AGW **Obv:** Pu-Tow temple **Rev:** Goddess of Mercy - with Lotus flower

Date	Mintage	F	VF	XF	Unc	BU
1995 Proof	1,000	Value: 220				

Y# 525 25 YUAN
7.7758 g., 0.9990 Gold .2500 oz. AGW **Rev:** Goddess of Mercy with wheel

Date	Mintage	F	VF	XF	Unc	BU
1995 Proof	1,000	Value: 220				

Y# 526 25 YUAN
7.7758 g., 0.9990 Gold .2500 oz. AGW **Rev:** Goddess of Mercy with sceptre

Date	Mintage	F	VF	XF	Unc	BU
1995 Proof	1,000	Value: 220				

Y# 527 25 YUAN
7.7758 g., 0.9990 Gold .2500 oz. AGW **Rev:** Goddess of Mercy with bowl

Date	Mintage	F	VF	XF	Unc	BU
1995 Proof	1,000	Value: 220				

Y# 687 25 YUAN
7.7758 g., Bi-Metallic Gold center in Silver ring .2500 oz. **Obv:** Building within circle, date below **Rev:** Unicorn with offspring, denomination at left, circle surrounds

Date	Mintage	F	VF	XF	Unc	BU
1995 Proof	2,000	Value: 220				

Y# 738 25 YUAN
7.8300 g., 0.9990 Gold .2515 oz. AGW **Obv:** Eastern unicorn rearing, date below **Rev:** Western unicorn with offspring, denomination at left

Date	Mintage	F	VF	XF	Unc	BU
1995 Proof	5,000	Value: 220				

Y# 835 25 YUAN
7.8300 g., 0.9990 Gold .2515 oz. AGW **Subject:** Sea Goddess Mazhu **Obv:** Mazhu Temple **Rev:** Mazhu's portrayal

Date	Mintage	F	VF	XF	Unc	BU
1995 Proof	3,000	Value: 220				

Y# 1061 25 YUAN
Bi-Metallic 0.999 Gold center in 0.999 Silver ring, 30 mm. **Obv:** Eastern unicorn **Rev:** Western unicorn with offspring **Edge:** Reeded

Date	Mintage	F	VF	XF	Unc	BU
1995 Proof	—	Value: 220				

Y# 867 25 YUAN
7.7759 g., 0.9990 Gold .2500 oz. AGW **Subject:** Centennial of Chinese Post Office **Obv:** Modern postal stamp, date below **Rev:** Imperial postal stamp, denomination at right

Date	Mintage	F	VF	XF	Unc	BU
1996 Proof	3,000	Value: 195				

Y# 743 25 YUAN
7.7759 g., 0.9990 Gold .2500 oz. AGW **Obv:** Eastern unicorn, date below **Rev:** Western unicorn and maiden, denomination at left

Date	Mintage	F	VF	XF	Unc	BU
1996 Proof	3,000	Value: 300				

Y# 743a 25 YUAN
7.7759 g., 0.9990 Platinum .2500 oz. APW

Date	Mintage	F	VF	XF	Unc	BU
1996 Proof	500	Value: 345				

Y# 915 25 YUAN
7.7759 g., 0.9990 Gold .2500 oz. AGW **Subject:** Celebrating Spring **Obv:** Radiant lantern, date below **Rev:** Children setting off firecrackers, denomination above

Date	Mintage	F	VF	XF	Unc	BU
1997 Proof	10,000	Value: 185				

Y# 997 25 YUAN
7.7759 g., 0.9990 Gold .2500 oz. AGW **Subject:** China Palace Museum **Obv:** Forbidden City **Rev:** Imperial Gardens

Date	Mintage	F	VF	XF	Unc	BU
1997 Proof	4,000	Value: 195				

Y# 998 25 YUAN
7.7759 g., 0.9990 Gold .2500 oz. AGW **Subject:** China Palace Museum **Obv:** Forbidden City **Rev:** Jin Shui

Date	Mintage	F	VF	XF	Unc	BU
1997 Proof	4,000	Value: 195				

Y# 999 25 YUAN
7.7759 g., 0.9990 Gold .2500 oz. AGW **Subject:** China Palace Museum **Obv:** Forbidden City **Rev:** Quan Quin Palace

Date	Mintage	F	VF	XF	Unc	BU
1997 Proof	4,000	Value: 195				

Y# 1000 25 YUAN
7.7759 g., 0.9990 Gold .2500 oz. AGW **Subject:** China Palace Museum **Obv:** Forbidden City **Rev:** Inner view of palace

Date	Mintage	F	VF	XF	Unc	BU
1997 Proof	4,000	Value: 195				

Y# 1135 25 YUAN
7.7758 g., 0.9999 Gold 0.25 oz. AGW **Subject:** Greeting Spring

Date	Mintage	F	VF	XF	Unc	BU
1998	10,000	—	—	—	—	190

Y# 1136 25 YUAN
7.7758 g., 0.9999 Gold 0.25 oz. AGW **Subject:** Bird **Note:** Multicolored.

Date	Mintage	F	VF	XF	Unc	BU
2000	8,800	—	—	—	—	330

Y# 704 50 YUAN
15.5517 g., 0.9990 Gold .5000 oz. AGW **Subject:** Taiwan Scenery Series **Obv:** Great Wall **Rev:** Pagoda

Date	Mintage	F	VF	XF	Unc	BU
1990 Proof	4,000	Value: 360				

Y# 705 50 YUAN
15.5517 g., 0.9990 Gold .5000 oz. AGW **Subject:** Taiwan Scenery Series **Obv:** Great Wall **Rev:** Pondside building

Date	Mintage	F	VF	XF	Unc	BU
1990 Proof	4,000	Value: 360				

Y# 706 50 YUAN
15.5517 g., 0.9990 Gold .5000 oz. AGW **Subject:** Taiwan Scenery Series **Obv:** Great Wall **Rev:** Hillside building

Date	Mintage	F	VF	XF	Unc	BU
1990 Proof	4,000	Value: 360				

Y# 707 50 YUAN
15.5517 g., 0.9990 Gold .5000 oz. AGW **Subject:** Taiwan Scenery Series **Obv:** Great Wall **Rev:** Three buildings joined by docks and bridge

Date	Mintage	F	VF	XF	Unc	BU
1990 Proof	4,000	Value: 360				

Y# 557 50 YUAN
16.9600 g., 0.9170 Gold .5000 oz. AGW **Subject:** Bronze Age Sculptures **Obv:** National emblem, date below **Rev:** Kneeling figure, denomination below

Date	Mintage	F	VF	XF	Unc	BU
1992 Proof	500	Value: 775				

Y# 378 50 YUAN
15.5517 g., 0.9990 Gold .5000 oz. AGW **Subject:** Chinese Inventions and Discoveries **Obv:** Great Wall, denomination below **Rev:** Chin with Yin Yang, denomination below

Date	Mintage	F	VF	XF	Unc	BU
1993 Proof	1,200	Value: 380				

124 CHINA, PEOPLE'S REPUBLIC

Y# 401 50 YUAN
15.5517 g., 0.9990 Gold .5000 oz. AGW **Subject:** Chinese Inventions and Discoveries **Obv:** Great Wall, date below **Rev:** Invention of the Umbrella, denomination at right

Date	Mintage	F	VF	XF	Unc	BU
1993 Proof	1,200	Value: 380				

Y# 410 50 YUAN
16.9800 g., 0.9170 Gold .5000 oz. AGW **Subject:** Bronze Age Sculptures **Obv:** National emblem, date below **Rev:** Kneeling man lantern, denomination at right

Date	Mintage	F	VF	XF	Unc	BU
1993 Proof	350	Value: 850				

Y# 414 50 YUAN
15.5517 g., 0.9990 Gold .5000 oz. AGW **Subject:** Chairman Mao **Rev:** Bust, 3/4 left, denomination at left

Date	Mintage	F	VF	XF	Unc	BU
1993 Proof	5,000	Value: 425				
1993(s) Proof	2,500	Value: 545				

Y# 445 50 YUAN
15.5517 g., 0.9990 Gold .5000 oz. AGW **Subject:** Taiwan Temples **Obv:** Great Wall, date below **Rev:** Buddha statue, denomination below

Date	Mintage	F	VF	XF	Unc	BU
1993 Proof	1,000	Value: 370				

Y# 446 50 YUAN
15.5517 g., 0.9990 Gold .5000 oz. AGW **Subject:** Taiwan Temples **Obv:** Great Wall, date below **Rev:** Large temple, denomination below

Date	Mintage	F	VF	XF	Unc	BU
1993 Proof	1,000	Value: 370				

Y# 447 50 YUAN
15.5517 g., 0.9990 Gold .5000 oz. AGW **Subject:** Taiwan Temples **Obv:** Great Wall, date below **Rev:** Small temple, denomination below

Date	Mintage	F	VF	XF	Unc	BU
1993 Proof	1,000	Value: 370				

Y# 448 50 YUAN
15.5517 g., 0.9990 Gold .5000 oz. AGW **Subject:** Taiwan Temples **Obv:** Great Wall, date below **Rev:** Tower temple, denomination below

Date	Mintage	F	VF	XF	Unc	BU
1993 Proof	—	Value: 370				

Y# 503 50 YUAN
15.5517 g., 0.9990 Gold .5000 oz. AGW **Obv:** Great Wall, date below **Rev:** Goddess Kuan Yin - seated in flower, denomination at left

Date	Mintage	F	VF	XF	Unc	BU
1993 Proof	1,000	Value: 380				

Y# 765 50 YUAN
15.5517 g., 0.9990 Gold .5000 oz. AGW **Subject:** Chinese Inventions and Discoveries **Obv:** Great Wall **Rev:** Stirrup

Date	Mintage	F	VF	XF	Unc	BU
1993 Proof	1,200	Value: 380				

Y# 766 50 YUAN
15.5517 g., 0.9990 Gold .5000 oz. AGW **Subject:** Chinese Inventions and Discoveries **Obv:** Great Wall **Rev:** Excavation of the Terra-cotta Army

Date	Mintage	F	VF	XF	Unc	BU
1993 Proof	1,200	Value: 380				

Y# 767 50 YUAN
15.5517 g., 0.9990 Gold .5000 oz. AGW **Subject:** Chinese Inventions and Discoveries **Obv:** Great Wall **Rev:** Discovery of mathematical zero

Date	Mintage	F	VF	XF	Unc	BU
1993 Proof	1,200	Value: 380				

Y# 425 50 YUAN
15.5517 g., 0.9990 Gold .5000 oz. AGW **Obv:** Figure on Eastern unicorn, date below **Rev:** Unicorn looking right, rose sprays below, denomination at left

Date	Mintage	F	VF	XF	Unc	BU
1994 Proof	1,100	Value: 400				

Y# 459 50 YUAN
15.5517 g., 0.9990 Gold .5000 oz. AGW **Subject:** Children At Play **Rev:** Two children with cat, denomination below

Date	Mintage	F	VF	XF	Unc	BU
1994 Proof	1,888	Value: 365				

Y# 460 50 YUAN
15.5517 g., 0.9990 Gold .5000 oz. AGW **Subject:** Children At Play **Obv:** Temple of Heaven **Rev:** Three children with toy boat, denomination below

Date	Mintage	F	VF	XF	Unc	BU
1994 Proof	1,888	Value: 365				

Y# 621 50 YUAN
15.5517 g., 0.9990 Gold .5000 oz. AGW **Subject:** Oriental Inventions **Obv:** Great Wall **Rev:** First tuned bells

Date	Mintage	F	VF	XF	Unc	BU
1994 Proof	1,200	Value: 380				

Y# 623 50 YUAN
15.5517 g., 0.9990 Gold .5000 oz. AGW **Subject:** Oriental Inventions - Astronomy **Obv:** Great Wall **Rev:** First records of comets

Date	Mintage	F	VF	XF	Unc	BU
1994 Proof	1,200	Value: 380				

Y# 624 50 YUAN
15.5517 g., 0.9990 Gold .5000 oz. AGW **Subject:** Oriental Inventions **Obv:** Great Wall **Rev:** First masts for sailing

Date	Mintage	F	VF	XF	Unc	BU
1994 Proof	1,200	Value: 380				

Y# 625 50 YUAN
15.5517 g., 0.9990 Gold .5000 oz. AGW **Subject:** Oriental Inventions **Obv:** Great Wall **Rev:** First chain pumps used to draw water

Date	Mintage	F	VF	XF	Unc	BU
1994 Proof	1,200	Value: 380				

Y# 622 50 YUAN
15.5517 g., 0.9990 Gold 0.4995 oz. AGW **Subject:** Oriental Inventions **Obv:** Great Wall **Rev:** First silken fabric

Date	Mintage	F	VF	XF	Unc	BU
1994 Proof	1,200	Value: 380				

Y# 634 50 YUAN
15.5517 g., 0.9990 Gold 0.4995 oz. AGW **Subject:** Oriental Inventions **Obv:** Great Wall **Rev:** Potter

Date	Mintage	F	VF	XF	Unc	BU
1995 Proof	1,200	Value: 380				

Y# 635 50 YUAN
15.5517 g., 0.9990 Gold 0.4995 oz. AGW **Subject:** Oriental Inventions **Obv:** Great Wall **Rev:** Chess players

Date	Mintage	F	VF	XF	Unc	BU
1995 Proof	1,200	Value: 380				

Y# 608 50 YUAN
11.3180 g., 0.9160 Gold .3333 oz. AGW **Subject:** Silk Road **Obv:** National emblem, date below **Rev:** Man riding camel, denomination at right

Date	Mintage	F	VF	XF	Unc	BU
1995 Proof	10,000	Value: 245				

Y# 471 50 YUAN
15.5517 g., 0.9990 Gold .5000 oz. AGW **Subject:** Dinosaur **Obv:** Tall building, date below **Rev:** Brontosaurus, denomination at left

Date	Mintage	F	VF	XF	Unc	BU
1995 Proof	2,000	Value: 365				

Y# 488 50 YUAN
15.5517 g., 0.9990 Gold .5000 oz. AGW **Series:** 50th Anniversary - United Nations **Obv:** United Nations logo, date below **Rev:** United Nations building, denomination upper left, dates at right

Date	Mintage	F	VF	XF	Unc	BU
1995 Proof	17,500	Value: 350				

Y# 532 50 YUAN
15.5517 g., 0.9990 Gold .5000 oz. AGW **Subject:** Return of Hong Kong to China - Series I **Obv:** Tiananmen building and monument **Rev:** Deng Xiaoping's portrait above Hong Kong skyline

Date	Mintage	F	VF	XF	Unc	BU
1995 Proof	11,800	Value: 365				

Y# 593 50 YUAN
15.5517 g., 0.9990 Gold .5000 oz. AGW **Subject:** Yellow River culture **Rev:** Nu Wa Rising, denomination below

Date	Mintage	F	VF	XF	Unc	BU
1995 Proof	2,500	Value: 400				

CHINA, PEOPLE'S REPUBLIC

Y# 632 50 YUAN
15.5517 g., 0.9990 Gold .5000 oz. AGW **Subject:** Oriental Inventions **Obv:** Great Wall, date below **Rev:** Soldiers with cannon and gunpowder, denomination lower left
Date	Mintage	F	VF	XF	Unc	BU
1995 Proof	1,200	Value: 380				

Y# 633 50 YUAN
15.5517 g., 0.9990 Gold .5000 oz. AGW **Subject:** Oriental Inventions **Obv:** Great Wall, date below **Rev:** Individual block printing, denomination at right
Date	Mintage	F	VF	XF	Unc	BU
1995 Proof	1,200	Value: 380				

Y# 636 50 YUAN
15.5517 g., 0.9990 Gold .5000 oz. AGW **Subject:** Oriental Inventions **Obv:** Great Wall, date below **Rev:** Teacher with anatomy chart of human body, denomination at left
Date	Mintage	F	VF	XF	Unc	BU
1995 Proof	1,200	Value: 380				

Y# 648 50 YUAN
15.5517 g., 0.9990 Gold .5000 oz. AGW **Rev:** Sailing ship
Date	Mintage	F	VF	XF	Unc	BU
1995 Proof	1,000	Value: 425				

Y# 651 50 YUAN
15.5517 g., 0.9990 Gold .5000 oz. AGW **Rev:** Junk
Date	Mintage	F	VF	XF	Unc	BU
1995 Proof	1,000	Value: 425				

Y# 690 50 YUAN
15.5517 g., 0.9990 Gold .5000 oz. AGW **Subject:** 50th Anniversary - Anti-Japanese War **Obv:** National emblem, date below **Rev:** Zhou and Mao above soldiers, denomination below
Date	Mintage	F	VF	XF	Unc	BU
1995 Proof	2,500	Value: 365				

Y# 691 50 YUAN
10.3600 g., Bi-Metallic Gold center in Silver ring .3335 oz. **Ring Weight:** 5.1800 g. **Ring Composition:** 0.9990 Silver .1667 oz. ASW **Subject:** World Women's Conference **Obv:** Logo above building **Rev:** Three women, denomination above within circle
Date	Mintage	F	VF	XF	Unc	BU
1995 Proof	3,000	Value: 275				

Y# 739 50 YUAN
15.5517 g., 0.9990 Gold .5000 oz. AGW **Obv:** Eastern unicorn, rearing, date below **Rev:** Western unicorn with offspring, denomination at left
Date	Mintage	F	VF	XF	Unc	BU
1995 Proof	2,000	Value: 380				

Y# 739a 50 YUAN
15.5517 g., 0.9995 Platinum .5000 oz. APW, 26.8 mm. **Subject:** Unicorn **Obv:** Eastern unicorn, rearing, date below **Rev:** Western unicorn with offspring, denomination at left **Edge:** Reeded
Date	Mintage	F	VF	XF	Unc	BU
1995 Proof	1,015	Value: 700				

Y# 814 50 YUAN
15.5517 g., 0.9990 Gold .5000 oz. AGW **Subject:** 50th Anniversary - For the return of Taiwan to China **Obv:** Great Wall **Rev:** Taiwan and China maps
Date	Mintage	F	VF	XF	Unc	BU
1995 Proof	3,000	Value: 365				

Y# 815 50 YUAN
15.5517 g., 0.9990 Gold .5000 oz. AGW **Subject:** 50th Anniversary - For the return of Taiwan to China **Obv:** Great Wall **Rev:** Zhongshan Hall
Date	Mintage	F	VF	XF	Unc	BU
1995 Proof	3,000	Value: 365				

Y# 821 50 YUAN
7.9020 g., 0.9160 Gold .2327 oz. AGW **Obv:** Bust of painter Xu Beihong, facing, date below **Rev:** Lion, denomination lower right
Date	Mintage	F	VF	XF	Unc	BU
1995 Proof	3,000	Value: 195				

Y# 829a 50 YUAN
155.5517 g., 0.9990 Gold .5000 oz. AGW **Subject:** Romance of Three Kingdoms **Obv:** Luo Guanzhong **Rev:** Three figures
Date	Mintage	F	VF	XF	Unc	BU
1995 Proof	2,000	Value: 365				

Y# 838 50 YUAN
10.3678 g., 0.9990 Gold .3333 oz. AGW **Subject:** Table Tennis **Obv:** Tianjing Stadium **Rev:** Table tennis player
Date	Mintage	F	VF	XF	Unc	BU
1995 Proof	2,000	Value: 245				

Y# 599 50 YUAN
15.5517 g., 0.9990 Gold .5000 oz. AGW **Obv:** Yangtze River scene, denomination lower left corner **Rev:** Large dam **Shape:** Rectangular
Date	Mintage	F	VF	XF	Unc	BU
1996 Proof	6,000	Value: 445				

Y# 609 50 YUAN
11.3180 g., 0.9160 Gold .3333 oz. AGW **Subject:** Silk Road **Obv:** National emblem, date below **Rev:** Water vendor, denomination lower right
Date	Mintage	F	VF	XF	Unc	BU
1996 Proof	10,000	Value: 245				

Y# 859 50 YUAN
155.5517 g., 0.9990 Gold .5000 oz. AGW **Obv:** Building, date below **Rev:** Sun Yat-sen bust facing, denomination below, fan sprays 3/4 around
Date	Mintage	F	VF	XF	Unc	BU
1996 Proof	3,000	Value: 365				

Y# 870 50 YUAN
155.5517 g., 0.9990 Gold .5000 oz. AGW **Subject:** 60th Anniversary - Long March **Obv:** Flag above building, date below **Rev:** Chairman Mao portrait, denomination at right
Date	Mintage	F	VF	XF	Unc	BU
1996 Proof	6,000	Value: 365				

Y# 881 50 YUAN
15.5517 g., 0.9990 Gold .5000 oz. AGW **Subject:** Romance of the Three Kingdoms Series **Obv:** Luo Guanzhong portrait **Rev:** Guand Du on horseback, leading his troops
Date	Mintage	F	VF	XF	Unc	BU
1996 Proof	2,000	Value: 365				

Y# 658 50 YUAN
15.5517 g., 0.9990 Gold .5000 oz. AGW **Subject:** Return of Hong Kong to China Series II **Obv:** Hong Kong Harbor
Date	Mintage	F	VF	XF	Unc	BU
1996 Proof	11,800	Value: 350				

Y# 1039 50 YUAN
15.5517 g., 0.9990 Gold .5000 oz. AGW, 27 mm. **Subject:** Unicorn **Obv:** Eastern unicorn, full body **Rev:** Western unicorn in wreath **Edge:** Reeded
Date	Mintage	F	VF	XF	Unc	BU
1996 Proof	1,000	Value: 425				

Y# 1091 50 YUAN
15.5518 g., 0.9990 Gold 0.4995 oz. AGW, 27 mm. **Subject:** Unicorns **Obv:** Eastern unicorn **Rev:** Western unicorn **Edge:** Reeded
Date	Mintage	F	VF	XF	Unc	BU
1996 Proof	1,000	Value: 400				

Y# 903 50 YUAN
15.5517 g., 0.9990 Gold .5000 oz. AGW **Subject:** Return of Hong Kong to China - Series III **Obv:** Tiananmen Square - Forbidden City **Rev:** Flag and fireworks above Hong Kong, denomination below
Date	Mintage	F	VF	XF	Unc	BU
1997 Proof	11,800	Value: 345				

Y# 1004 50 YUAN
15.5517 g., 0.9990 Gold .5000 oz. AGW **Subject:** Huang (Yellow) River Culture **Obv:** Archer **Rev:** Dragon
Date	Mintage	F	VF	XF	Unc	BU
1997 Proof	3,000	Value: 365				

Y# 906a 50 YUAN
155.5517 g., 0.9990 Gold .5000 oz. AGW **Subject:** Return of Macao to China **Obv:** Tiananmen Square - Forbidden City **Rev:** Deng Xiaoping viewing Macao
Date	Mintage	F	VF	XF	Unc	BU
1997 Proof	11,800	Value: 345				

Y# 910 50 YUAN
155.5517 g., 0.9990 Gold .5000 oz. AGW **Subject:** People's Liberation Army **Obv:** Radiant star above Great Wall **Rev:** Youthful Chairman Mao standing
Date	Mintage	F	VF	XF	Unc	BU
1997 Proof	12,000	Value: 345				

CHINA, PEOPLE'S REPUBLIC

Y# 921 50 YUAN
15.5517 g., 0.9990 Gold .50000 oz. AGW **Subject:** Chinese Wildlife **Obv:** National emblem, date below **Rev:** Two white dolphins, denomination at right

Date	Mintage	F	VF	XF	Unc	BU
1997 Proof	30,000	Value: 345				

Y# 1005 50 YUAN
15.5517 g., 0.9990 Gold .50000 oz. AGW **Obv:** Portrait of Qi Bashi **Rev:** Squirrels eating grapes **Shape:** Rectangular

Date	Mintage	F	VF	XF	Unc	BU
1997 Proof	5,000	Value: 400				

Y# 1179 50 YUAN
15.5517 g., 0.9999 Gold 0.4999 oz. AGW **Subject:** Romance of the Three Kingdoms **Rev:** Soldiers on a boat

Date	Mintage	F	VF	XF	Unc	BU
1997 Proof	3,000	Value: 365				

Y# 1180 50 YUAN
15.5517 g., 0.9999 Gold 0.4999 oz. AGW **Subject:** Liu Shao Qi **Obv:** Portrait **Rev:** Temple

Date	Mintage	F	VF	XF	Unc	BU
1998 Proof	8,000	Value: 360				

Y# 1007 50 YUAN
15.5517 g., 0.9990 Gold .5000 oz. AGW **Subject:** Zhou Enlai

Date	Mintage	F	VF	XF	Unc	BU
1998 Proof	8,000	Value: 345				

Y# 1008 50 YUAN
15.5517 g., 0.9990 Gold .5000 oz. AGW **Subject:** 50th Anniversary of People's Republic

Date	Mintage	F	VF	XF	Unc	BU
1999 Proof	15,700	Value: 400				

Y# 1137 50 YUAN
Bi-Metallic Gold center in Silver ring **Subject:** Y-2-K

Date	Mintage	F	VF	XF	Unc	BU
2000	20,000	Value: 385				

Y# 1050 50 YUAN
15.5518 g., 0.9990 Gold .5000 oz. AGW **Rev:** Dragons **Shape:** Fan

Date	Mintage	F	VF	XF	Unc	BU
2000	6,600	—	—	—	375	—

Y# 1236 50 YUAN
17.0000 g., 0.9990 Gold, 27 mm. **Subject:** Y2K **Obv:** Monument **Rev:** World Globe as an eye above value within silver plated outer ring **Edge:** Reeded

Date	Mintage	F	VF	XF	Unc	BU
2000 Proof	20,000	Value: 370				

Y# 1084 50 YUAN
3.1104 g., 0.9990 Gold 0.0999 oz. AGW **Subject:** Mogao Grottoes **Obv:** Eight story building **Rev:** Buddha-like statue **Edge:** Reeded.

Date	Mintage	F	VF	XF	Unc	BU
2001 Proof	50,000	Value: 90.00				

Y# 1139 50 YUAN
15.5500 g., 0.9990 Gold 0.4994 oz. AGW **Subject:** Bird **Note:** Multicolored

Date	Mintage	F	VF	XF	Unc	BU
2001	8,800	—	—	—	—	875

Y# 1140 50 YUAN
15.5500 g., 0.9990 Gold 0.4994 oz. AGW **Subject:** Caveman art **Note:** Multicolored

Date	Mintage	F	VF	XF	Unc	BU
2001	8,800	—	—	—	—	675

Y# 1237 50 YUAN
3.1100 g., 0.9990 Gold .0999 oz. AGW, 18 mm. **Obv:** Putuo Mountain Pilgrimage Gate **Rev:** Kuanyin and value **Edge:** Reeded

Date	Mintage	F	VF	XF	Unc	BU
2004 Proof	33,000	Value: 90.00				

Y# 1222 50 YUAN
3.1103 g., 0.9990 Gold 0.0999 oz. AGW, 18 mm. **Obv:** Dog-shaped belt-hook, an ancient Chinese bronze ware, decorative disign of dog tail-shaped plant leaves **Rev:** 2 dogs at play

Date	Mintage	F	VF	XF	Unc	BU
2006 Proof	30,000	Value: 90.00				

Y# 56 100 YUAN
11.0000 g., 0.9000 Gold .3183 oz. AGW **Obv:** Building, date at right **Rev:** Marco Polo bust, top right, ship below, denomination at bottom

Date	Mintage	F	VF	XF	Unc	BU
1983 Proof	1,030	Value: 550				

Y# 72 100 YUAN
11.3180 g., 0.9170 Gold .3337 oz. AGW **Obv:** National emblem, date below **Rev:** Emperor Huang Di, denomination below

Date	Mintage	F	VF	XF	Unc	BU
1984 Proof	10,000	Value: 250				

Y# 94 100 YUAN
11.3180 g., 0.9170 Gold .3337 oz. AGW, 23 mm. **Subject:** Founders of Chinese Culture **Rev:** Confucius, denomination at right

Date	Mintage	F	VF	XF	Unc	BU
1985 Proof	7,000	Value: 250				

Y# 107 100 YUAN
11.3180 g., 0.9170 Gold .3337 oz. AGW **Subject:** Wildlife **Obv:** National emblem, date below **Rev:** Wild Yak, left, denomination at left

Date	Mintage	F	VF	XF	Unc	BU
1986 Proof	3,000	Value: 275				

Y# 117 100 YUAN
11.3180 g., 0.9170 Gold .3337 oz. AGW, 23 mm. **Subject:** Chinese Culture **Obv:** National emblem, date below **Rev:** Revolutionary Soldier, Liu Bang on horseback, denomination at left

Date	Mintage	F	VF	XF	Unc	BU
1986 Proof	7,000	Value: 250				

Y# 120 100 YUAN
11.3180 g., 0.9170 Gold .3337 oz. AGW **Subject:** Year of Peace **Rev:** Statue of seated female **Note:** Similar to 5 Yuan, Y#119.

Date	Mintage	F	VF	XF	Unc	BU
1986 Proof	1,000	Value: 660				

Y# 139 100 YUAN
11.3180 g., 0.9170 Gold .3337 oz. AGW **Obv:** National emblem, date below **Rev:** Emperor Li Shih on horseback, denomination at right

Date	Mintage	F	VF	XF	Unc	BU
1987 Proof	7,000	Value: 275				

Y# 164 100 YUAN
11.3180 g., 0.9170 Gold .3337 oz. AGW **Rev:** Emperor Zhao Kuangyin, denomination at right

Date	Mintage	F	VF	XF	Unc	BU
1988 Proof	Est. 7,000	Value: 275				

Y# 167 100 YUAN
8.0000 g., 0.9170 Gold .2359 oz. AGW **Subject:** Rare Animal Protection **Obv:** National emblem, date below **Rev:** Golden monkey, denomination at left

Date	Mintage	F	VF	XF	Unc	BU
1988 Proof	29,000	Value: 195				

Y# 173 100 YUAN
15.5500 g., 0.9990 Gold .5000 oz. AGW **Series:** Seoul 1988 - 24th Summer Olympic Games **Obv:** National emblem, date below **Rev:** Rhythmic gymnast, denomination at right

Date	Mintage	F	VF	XF	Unc	BU
1988 Proof	5,500	Value: 380				

Y# 203 100 YUAN
8.0000 g., 0.9170 Gold .2359 oz. AGW **Subject:** 11th Asian Games - Beijing 1990 **Obv:** Stadium **Rev:** Ribbon dancer, denomination below

Date	Mintage	F	VF	XF	Unc	BU
1989 Proof	Est. 7,000	Value: 185				

Y# 217 100 YUAN
11.3180 g., 0.9170 Gold .3337 oz. AGW **Obv:** National emblem, date below **Rev:** Genghis Khan on horseback, denomination at left

Date	Mintage	F	VF	XF	Unc	BU
1989 Proof	Est. 7,000	Value: 300				

Y# 231 100 YUAN
11.3180 g., 0.9170 Gold .3337 oz. AGW **Series:** Save the Children Fund **Obv:** National emblem, date below **Rev:** Child running flying kites, denomination lower right

Date	Mintage	F	VF	XF	Unc	BU
1989 Proof	5,000	Value: 245				

CHINA, PEOPLE'S REPUBLIC

Y# 250 100 YUAN
8.0000 g., 0.9170 Gold .2359 oz. AGW **Series:** Endangered Animals **Obv:** National emblem, date below **Rev:** Chinese tiger, denomination at left

Date	Mintage	F	VF	XF	Unc	BU
1989 Proof	14,000			Value: 195		

Y# 299 100 YUAN
7.7750 g., 0.9990 Gold .2500 oz. AGW **Subject:** 40th Anniversary of People's Republic **Obv:** National emblem, date at right **Rev:** Pair of flying cranes, denomination at left

Date	Mintage	F	VF	XF	Unc	BU
1989 Proof	1,000			Value: 275		

Y# 256 100 YUAN
8.0000 g., 0.9170 Gold .2359 oz. AGW **Subject:** XI Asian Games - Beijing 1990 **Obv:** Roman numeral above stadium, date below **Rev:** Swimmer, denomination lower left

Date	Mintage	F	VF	XF	Unc	BU
1990 Proof	10,000			Value: 175		

Y# 287 100 YUAN
10.3700 g., 0.9170 Gold .3054 oz. AGW **Obv:** National emblem, date below **Rev:** First emperor, Huang Di standing, denomination at right

Date	Mintage	F	VF	XF	Unc	BU
1990 Proof	20,000			Value: 275		

Y# 306 100 YUAN
11.3180 g., 0.9170 Gold .3333 oz. AGW **Obv:** National emblem, date below **Rev:** Emperor Zhu Yuanzhang seated, denomination upper left

Date	Mintage	F	VF	XF	Unc	BU
1990	Est. 7,000	—	—	—	—	300

Y# 327 100 YUAN
11.3180 g., 0.9170 Gold .3333 oz. AGW **Series:** Barcelona 1992 - 25th Summer Olympic Games **Obv:** National emblem, date below **Rev:** 2 women playing basketball, denomination at right

Date	Mintage	F	VF	XF	Unc	BU
1990	10,000	—	—	—	—	245

Y# 320 100 YUAN
8.0000 g., 0.9160 Gold .2357 oz. AGW **Subject:** Women's 1st World Football Cup **Obv:** Stadium, date below **Rev:** Woman kicking ball, denomination at right

Date	Mintage	F	VF	XF	Unc	BU
1991 Proof	1,400			Value: 175		

Y# 326 100 YUAN
8.0000 g., 0.9160 Gold .2357 oz. AGW **Subject:** Emperor Kang Xi, denomination at left **Obv:** National emblem, date below

Date	Mintage	F	VF	XF	Unc	BU
1991 Proof	Est. 7,000			Value: 300		

Y# 473 100 YUAN
11.3180 g., 0.9170 Gold .3334 oz. AGW **Series:** Albertville 1992 - 16th Winter Olympic Games **Obv:** National emblem, date below **Rev:** Pairs figure skating, denomination lower right

Date	Mintage	F	VF	XF	Unc	BU
1991 Proof	10,000			Value: 245		

Y# 478 100 YUAN
8.6000 g., 0.9170 Gold .2533 oz. AGW **Subject:** 80th Anniversary - 1911 Revolution **Obv:** Building **Rev:** Sun Yat-sen writing, denomination at right

Date	Mintage	F	VF	XF	Unc	BU
1991 Proof	2,500			Value: 315		

Y# 545 100 YUAN
11.3180 g., 0.9170 Gold .3337 oz. AGW **Rev:** Emperor Yan Di, denomination upper right

Date	Mintage	F	VF	XF	Unc	BU
1991 Proof	10,000			Value: 275		

Y# 479 100 YUAN
31.1035 g., 0.9990 Gold 1.0000 oz. AGW **Obv:** Building, two dates below **Rev:** Sun Yat-sen in uniform, facing, denomination at left **Note:** Photo reduced.

Date	Mintage	F	VF	XF	Unc	BU
ND(1991) Proof	1,000			Value: 1,000		

Y# 754 100 YUAN
33.9600 g., 0.9160 Gold 1.000 oz. AGW **Subject:** Archeological Finds **Obv:** National emblem **Rev:** Resting deer with long antlers

Date	Mintage	F	VF	XF	Unc	BU
1992 Proof	500			Value: 1,325		

Y# 336 100 YUAN
31.1035 g., 0.9990 Gold 1.0000 oz. AGW **Subject:** Chinese Inventions **Obv:** Great Wall, date below **Rev:** Ancient ships and shipbuilding, denomination lower left

Date	Mintage	F	VF	XF	Unc	BU
1992 Proof	1,000			Value: 700		

Y# 337 100 YUAN
31.1035 g., 0.9990 Gold 1.0000 oz. AGW **Subject:** Chinese Inventions **Rev:** First compass, denomination below

Date	Mintage	F	VF	XF	Unc	BU
1992 Proof	1,000			Value: 700		

Y# 338 100 YUAN
31.1035 g., 0.9990 Gold 1.0000 oz. AGW **Subject:** Chinese Inventions **Rev:** First seismograph, denomination below

Date	Mintage	F	VF	XF	Unc	BU
1992 Proof	1,000			Value: 700		

Y# 339 100 YUAN
31.1035 g., 0.9990 Gold 1.0000 oz. AGW **Subject:** Chinese Inventions **Obv:** Great Wall **Rev:** First kite, denomination below

Date	Mintage	F	VF	XF	Unc	BU
1992 Proof	1,000			Value: 700		

Y# 340 100 YUAN
31.1035 g., 0.9990 Gold 1.0000 oz. AGW **Obv:** Great Wall, date below **Rev:** Bronze Age Metal Working, large urn, denomination below

Date	Mintage	F	VF	XF	Unc	BU
1992 Proof	1,000			Value: 700		

128 CHINA, PEOPLE'S REPUBLIC

Y# 546 100 YUAN
10.3700 g., 0.9170 Gold .3054 oz. AGW **Obv:** National emblem, date below **Rev:** Emperor Da Yu, denomination at right

Date	Mintage	F	VF	XF	Unc	BU
1992 Proof	10,000	Value: 325				

Y# 554 100 YUAN
11.3180 g., 0.9170 Gold .3334 oz. AGW **Obv:** National emblem, date below **Rev:** Wu Zetian "The Iron Lady" 603-705AD, Stateswoman, denomination at right

Date	Mintage	F	VF	XF	Unc	BU
1992 Proof	25,000	Value: 245				

Y# 692 100 YUAN
11.3180 g., 0.9170 Gold .3334 oz. AGW **Series:** 1994 Olympics **Obv:** Temple of Heaven **Rev:** Male figure skater, denomination below

Date	Mintage	F	VF	XF	Unc	BU
1992 Proof	10,000	Value: 235				

Y# 693 100 YUAN
8.0000 g., 0.9170 Gold .2356 oz. AGW **Series:** Endangered Wildlife **Rev:** Mountain sheep, denomination below

Date	Mintage	F	VF	XF	Unc	BU
1992 Proof	5,000	Value: 250				

Y# 354 100 YUAN
31.1320 g., 0.9990 Gold 1.0000 oz. AGW **Obv:** Temple, date below **Rev:** Two peacocks, denomination above
Rev. Designer: Lang Shih Ning

Date	Mintage	F	VF	XF	Unc	BU
1993 Proof	1,200	Value: 725				

Y# 406 100 YUAN
31.1035 g., 0.9990 Gold 1.0000 oz. AGW **Obv:** Building and Great Wall **Rev:** Chinese Gods: Fu, Lu, and Shu

Date	Mintage	F	VF	XF	Unc	BU
1993 Proof	888	Value: 875				

Y# 411 100 YUAN
33.9500 g., 0.9170 Gold 1.0000 oz. AGW **Subject:** Bronze Age Sculptures **Obv:** National emblem, date below **Rev:** Bull lantern, denomination at left

Date	Mintage	F	VF	XF	Unc	BU
1993 Proof	350	Value: 1,650				

Y# 491 100 YUAN
10.3600 g., 0.9170 Gold .3053 oz. AGW **Subject:** World Cup Soccer **Obv:** National emblem, date below **Rev:** Player kicking ball, denomination at left

Date	Mintage	F	VF	XF	Unc	BU
1993 Proof	5,000	Value: 220				

Y# 504 100 YUAN
31.1035 g., 0.9990 Gold 1.0000 oz. AGW **Obv:** Great Wall, date below **Rev:** Guanyin, Goddess of Mercy, seated in flower, denomination at left

Date	Mintage	F	VF	XF	Unc	BU
1993 Proof	1,000	Value: 725				

Y# 538 100 YUAN
11.3180 g., 0.9170 Gold .3337 oz. AGW **Obv:** National emblem, date below **Rev:** Bust of Chairman Mao Zedong, right, denomination at left

Date	Mintage	F	VF	XF	Unc	BU
1993 Proof	Est. 7,000	Value: 330				

Y# 760 100 YUAN
8.0000 g., 0.9160 Gold .2356 oz. AGW **Obv:** National emblem, date below **Rev:** Bust of Soong Ching-ling half left, 1892-1981, Revolutionary Stateswoman, denomination at right

Date	Mintage	F	VF	XF	Unc	BU
1993 Proof	2,000	Value: 225				

Y# 763 100 YUAN
31.1035 g., 0.9990 Gold 1.0000 oz. AGW **Obv:** Home of Sun Yat-sen **Rev:** Bust of Sun Yat-sen, facing, denomination at right

Date	Mintage	F	VF	XF	Unc	BU
1993 Proof	8,888	Value: 675				

Y# 777 100 YUAN
31.1035 g., 0.9990 Gold 1.0000 oz. AGW **Subject:** Mount Tai **Obv:** Great Wall **Rev:** Temple

Date	Mintage	F	VF	XF	Unc	BU
1993 Proof	8,888	Value: 675				

Y# 427 100 YUAN
31.1035 g., 0.9990 Gold 1.0000 oz. AGW **Obv:** Child riding Eastern Unicorn, date below **Rev:** Unicorn, denomination at left, rose sprays below

Date	Mintage	F	VF	XF	Unc	BU
1994 Proof	1,100	Value: 675				

Y# 440 100 YUAN
8.0000 g., 0.9170 Gold .2356 oz. AGW **Subject:** 12th Asian Games **Obv:** National emblem, row of athletic figures below, date at bottom **Rev:** Gymnast on bars, denomination at right

Date	Mintage	F	VF	XF	Unc	BU
1994 Proof	3,000	Value: 175				

Y# 497 100 YUAN
10.3600 g., 0.9170 Gold .3053 oz. AGW **Series:** Atlanta 1994 - 26th Summer Olympic Games **Rev:** Female torch runner, denomination lower left

Date	Mintage	F	VF	XF	Unc	BU
1994 Proof	5,000	Value: 220				

Y# 543 100 YUAN
10.3600 g., 0.9170 Gold .3053 oz. AGW **Obv:** National emblem **Rev:** Emperor Zhou Wenwang, denomination at left

Date	Mintage	F	VF	XF	Unc	BU
1994 Proof	10,000	Value: 375				

CHINA, PEOPLE'S REPUBLIC

Y# 695 100 YUAN
15.5500 g., 0.9160 Gold .4579 oz. AGW **Obv:** Building, date below **Rev:** Black-billed magpie on branch, denomination below **Shape:** 12-sided

Date	Mintage	F	VF	XF	Unc	BU
1994 Proof	1,300	Value: 500				

Y# 1012 100 YUAN
31.1030 g., 0.9990 Gold 1.0000 oz. AGW **Rev:** Unicorn

Date	Mintage	F	VF	XF	Unc	BU
1995 Proof	1,500	Value: 675				

Y# 696 100 YUAN
31.1035 g., 0.9990 Gold 1.0000 oz. AGW **Subject:** 50th Anniversary - Anti-Japanese War **Rev:** People at wall, denomination below

Date	Mintage	F	VF	XF	Unc	BU
1995 Proof	1,400	Value: 680				

Y# 697 100 YUAN
31.1035 g., 0.9990 Gold 1.0000 oz. AGW **Rev:** Soldiers above bridge guarded by chinze, denomination at right

Date	Mintage	F	VF	XF	Unc	BU
1995 Proof	1,400	Value: 680				

Y# 804 100 YUAN
31.0103 g., 0.9990 Gold 1.0000 oz. AGW **Subject:** Chinese Culture Series **Obv:** Great Wall seen through arch **Rev:** Pagoda of Six Harmonies

Date	Mintage	F	VF	XF	Unc	BU
1995 Proof	1,000	Value: 665				

Y# 805 100 YUAN
31.0103 g., 0.9990 Gold 1.0000 oz. AGW **Subject:** Chinese Culture Series **Obv:** Great Wall seen through arch **Rev:** Mencius seated at table

Date	Mintage	F	VF	XF	Unc	BU
1995 Proof	1,000	Value: 665				

Y# 806 100 YUAN
31.0103 g., 0.9990 Gold 1.0000 oz. AGW **Subject:** Chinese Culture Series **Obv:** Great Wall seen through arch **Rev:** Tang Taizong seated

Date	Mintage	F	VF	XF	Unc	BU
1995 Proof	1,000	Value: 665				

Y# 807 100 YUAN
31.0103 g., 0.9990 Gold 1.0000 oz. AGW **Subject:** Chinese Culture Series **Obv:** Great Wall seen through arch **Rev:** Lion dance

Date	Mintage	F	VF	XF	Unc	BU
1995 Proof	1,000	Value: 665				

Y# 808 100 YUAN
31.0103 g., 0.9990 Gold 1.0000 oz. AGW **Subject:** Chinese Culture Series **Obv:** Great Wall seen through arch **Rev:** Female opera role

Date	Mintage	F	VF	XF	Unc	BU
1995 Proof	1,000	Value: 665				

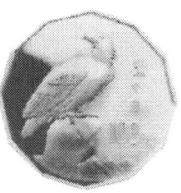

Y# 810 100 YUAN
16.9779 g., 0.9160 Gold .5000 oz. AGW **Obv:** Great Wall, date below **Rev:** Perched eagle, denomination lower right **Shape:** 12-sided

Date	Mintage	F	VF	XF	Unc	BU
1995 Proof	1,300	Value: 350				

Y# 830 100 YUAN
31.1035 g., 0.9990 Gold 1.0000 oz. AGW **Subject:** Romance of the Three Kingdoms **Obv:** Luo Guanzhong **Rev:** Standing Liu Bei with flags

Date	Mintage	F	VF	XF	Unc	BU
1995 Proof	1,500	Value: 665				

Y# 831 100 YUAN
31.1035 g., 0.9990 Gold 1.0000 oz. AGW **Subject:** Romance of the Three Kingdoms **Obv:** Luo Guanzhong **Rev:** Seated Guan Yu reading

Date	Mintage	F	VF	XF	Unc	BU
1995 Proof	1,500	Value: 665				

Y# 832 100 YUAN
31.1035 g., 0.9990 Gold 1.0000 oz. AGW **Subject:** Romance of the Three Kingdoms **Obv:** Luo Guanzhong **Rev:** Zhang Fei on horseback

Date	Mintage	F	VF	XF	Unc	BU
1995 Proof	1,500	Value: 665				

Y# 833 100 YUAN
31.1035 g., 0.9990 Gold 1.0000 oz. AGW **Subject:** Romance of the Three Kingdoms **Obv:** Luo Guanzhong **Rev:** Zhuge Liang seated on throne

Date	Mintage	F	VF	XF	Unc	BU
1995 Proof	1,500	Value: 665				

Y# 843 100 YUAN
10.3678 g., 0.9990 Gold .3330 oz. AGW **Series:** 1996 Olympics **Obv:** National emblem, date below **Rev:** High diver, denomination below

Date	Mintage	F	VF	XF	Unc	BU
1995 Proof	10,000	Value: 240				

Y# 844 100 YUAN
10.3678 g., 0.9990 Gold .3330 oz. AGW **Series:** Olympics **Obv:** National emblem, date below **Rev:** Ribbon dancer, denomination at right

Date	Mintage	F	VF	XF	Unc	BU
1995 Proof	10,000	Value: 240				

Y# 1062 100 YUAN
31.1035 g., 0.9990 Gold 1.0000 oz. AGW, 32 mm. **Subject:** Unicorn **Obv:** Eastern unicorn **Rev:** Western unicorn with offspring **Edge:** Reeded

Date	Mintage	F	VF	XF	Unc	BU
1995 Proof	—	Value: 675				

Y# 1014 100 YUAN
31.1035 g., 0.9990 Gold 1.0000 oz. AGW, 32.1 mm. **Subject:** Unicorn **Obv:** Eastern unicorn, full body **Rev:** Western unicorn **Edge:** Reeded

Date	Mintage	F	VF	XF	Unc	BU
1996 Proof	1,250	Value: 665				

Y# 956 100 YUAN
31.1035 g., 0.9990 Gold 1.0000 oz. AGW, 32 mm. **Obv:** Eastern unicorn **Rev:** Western unicorn in wreath **Edge:** Reeded

Date	Mintage	F	VF	XF	Unc	BU
1996 Proof	1,250	Value: 675				

Y# 1211 100 YUAN
15.5500 g., 0.9990 Palladium 0.4994 oz., 27 mm. **Obv:** Temple of Heaven **Rev:** Panda mother and cub, "kissing pandas" **Edge:** Reeded

Date	Mintage	F	VF	XF	Unc	BU
2004 Proof	8,000	Value: 375				

Y# 1238 100 YUAN
3.1100 g., 0.9995 Platinum .0999 oz. APW, 18 mm. **Obv:** Putuo Mountain Pilgrimage Gate **Rev:** Kuanyin and value **Edge:** Reeded

Date	Mintage	F	VF	XF	Unc	BU
2004 Proof	33,000	Value: 160				

Y# 28 200 YUAN
8.4700 g., 0.9170 Gold .2497 oz. AGW **Subject:** Chinese Bronze Age Finds **Obv:** National emblem **Rev:** Leopard, denomination below

Date	Mintage	F	VF	XF	Unc	BU
1981 Proof	1,000	Value: 400				

Y# 29 200 YUAN
8.4700 g., 0.9170 Gold .2497 oz. AGW **Subject:** Chinese Bronze Age Finds **Obv:** National emblem **Rev:** Winged creature, denomination below

Date	Mintage	F	VF	XF	Unc	BU
1981 Proof	1,000	Value: 625				

Y# 37 200 YUAN
8.4700 g., 0.9170 Gold .2497 oz. AGW **Subject:** World Cup Soccer **Obv:** National emblem, date below **Rev:** Player kicking, denomination below

Date	Mintage	F	VF	XF	Unc	BU
1982 Proof	1,261	Value: 425				

Y# 209 200 YUAN
62.2060 g., 0.9990 Gold 2.0000 oz. AGW **Obv:** Great Wall, date below **Rev:** Denomination between Phoenix and dragon

Date	Mintage	F	VF	XF	Unc	BU
1990 Proof	2,538	Value: 925				
1990 Proof	2,538	Value: 1,350				
1990 Proof	2,538	Value: 1,450				

Y# 1085 200 YUAN
15.5518 g., 0.9990 Gold 0.4995 oz. AGW, 27 mm. **Subject:** Mogao Grottoes **Obv:** Eight story building **Rev:** Dancing drummer **Edge:** Reeded.

Date	Mintage	F	VF	XF	Unc	BU
2001 Proof	8,800	Value: 400				

130 CHINA, PEOPLE'S REPUBLIC

Y# 1087 200 YUAN
15.5518 g., 0.9990 Gold 0.4995 oz. AGW, 27 mm.
Subject: 50th Anniversary Chinese Occupation of Tibet
Obv: Five stars **Rev:** Denomination in flower **Edge:** Reeded

Date	Mintage	F	VF	XF	Unc	BU
2001 Proof	15,000	Value: 380				

Y# 1142 200 YUAN
15.5517 g., 0.9999 Gold 0.4999 oz. AGW, 27 mm.
Subject: Awarding of 2008 Olympics to Bjing

Date	Mintage	F	VF	XF	Unc	BU
2001	15,000	—	—	—	—	370

Y# 1145 200 YUAN
15.5500 g., 0.9990 Gold 0.4994 oz. AGW, 27 mm. **Subject:** Budda

Date	Mintage	F	VF	XF	Unc	BU
2002	8,800	—	—	—	—	400

Y# 1146 200 YUAN
15.5000 g., 0.9990 Gold 0.4978 oz. AGW **Subject:** Peking Opera

Date	Mintage	F	VF	XF	Unc	BU
2002	8,000	—	—	—	—	825

Y# 1147 200 YUAN
15.5000 g., 0.9990 Gold 0.4978 oz. AGW **Subject:** Dream of the Red Mansion **Shape:** Octagon

Date	Mintage	F	VF	XF	Unc	BU
2002 Proof	8,000	Value: 550				

Y# 1149 200 YUAN
15.5000 g., 0.9990 Gold 0.4978 oz. AGW **Subject:** Ceremonial Mask

Date	Mintage	F	VF	XF	Unc	BU
2002	5,000	—	—	—	—	420

Y# 1148 200 YUAN
15.5000 g., 0.9990 Gold 0.4978 oz. AGW **Subject:** Cave man art **Note:** Multicolor

Date	Mintage	F	VF	XF	Unc	BU
2002 Proof	8,800	Value: 525				

Y# 1159 200 YUAN
15.5519 g., 0.9999 Gold 0.5 oz. AGW **Subject:** Pilgrimage to the West

Date	Mintage	F	VF	XF	Unc	BU
2003	—	—	—	—	—	400

Y# 1160 200 YUAN
15.5519 g., 0.9999 Gold 0.5 oz. AGW **Subject:** Chinese Mythical Folk Tales

Date	Mintage	F	VF	XF	Unc	BU
2003	—	—	—	—	—	400

Y# 1213 200 YUAN
15.5500 g., 0.9990 Gold 0.4994 oz. AGW, 27 mm.
Obv: National arms above People's Congress Hall and ornamental column **Rev:** Multicolor hologram depicting the hall's overhead lighting **Edge:** Reeded

Date	Mintage	F	VF	XF	Unc	BU
2004 Proof	5,000	Value: 550				

Y# 1217 200 YUAN
15.5500 g., 0.9990 Gold 0.4994 oz. AGW, 27 mm. **Obv:** Monkey King leading the Master over bridge **Rev:** Multicolor Monkey King on one knee meeting the Master **Edge:** Reeded

Date	Mintage	F	VF	XF	Unc	BU
2004 Proof	11,800	Value: 475				

Y# 1241 200 YUAN
15.5518 g., 0.9990 Gold 0.4995 oz. AGW, 27 mm. **Obv:** Guangan Exposition Hall **Rev:** Deng Xiaoping and value **Edge:** Reeded

Date	Mintage	F	VF	XF	Unc	BU
2004 Proof	10,000	Value: 500				

Y# 1220 200 YUAN
15.6300 g., Gold **Obv:** Qing Yuan Gate of the China Great Wall **Rev:** 2 dogs at play **Shape:** 30° Fan

Date	Mintage	F	VF	XF	Unc	BU
2006 Proof	6,600	Value: 485				

Y# 1224 200 YUAN
15.6300 g., Gold, 27 mm. **Obv:** Dog-shaped belt-hook from ancient Chinese bronze ware, decorative design of dog tail-shaped plant leaves **Rev:** 2 smart dogs **Shape:** Scalloped

Date	Mintage	F	VF	XF	Unc	BU
2006 Proof	8,000	Value: 485				

Y# 22 250 YUAN
8.0000 g., 0.9170 Gold .2358 oz. AGW **Subject:** 1980 Winter Olympics **Obv:** State seal **Rev:** Alpine skiing

Date	Mintage	F	VF	XF	Unc	BU
1980 Proof	10,000	Value: 170				

Y# 23 300 YUAN
10.0000 g., 0.9170 Gold .2948 oz. AGW **Series:** 1980 Olympics **Subject:** Archery **Obv:** National emblem, denomination below **Rev:** Two archers, date below

Date	Mintage	F	VF	XF	Unc	BU
1980 Proof	15,000	Value: 225				

Y# 515 300 YUAN
103.1250 g., 0.9990 Gold 3.3155 oz. AGW **Obv:** Great Wall, date below **Rev:** Guanyin, Goddess of Mercy, holding child, facing, denomination at left

Date	Mintage	F	VF	XF	Unc	BU
1994 Proof	128	Value: 3,150				

Y# 4 400 YUAN
16.9500 g., 0.9170 Gold .4997 oz. AGW **Obv:** National emblem, two dates below **Rev:** 30th Anniversary of People's Republic - Tiananmen, denomination below

Date	Mintage	F	VF	XF	Unc	BU
ND(1979) Proof	Est. 23,000	Value: 345				

Y# 5 400 YUAN
16.9500 g., 0.9170 Gold .4997 oz. AGW **Subject:** 30th Anniversary of People's Republic **Obv:** National emblem, two dates below **Rev:** People's Heroes Monument, denomination below

Date	Mintage	F	VF	XF	Unc	BU
ND(1979) Proof	Est. 23,000	Value: 345				

Y# 6 400 YUAN
16.9500 g., 0.9170 Gold .4997 oz. AGW **Subject:** 30th Anniversary of People's Republic **Obv:** National emblem, two dates below **Rev:** Chairman Mao Memorial Hall, denomination below

Date	Mintage	F	VF	XF	Unc	BU
ND(1979) Proof	Est. 23,000	Value: 345				

Y# 7 400 YUAN
16.9500 g., 0.9170 Gold .4997 oz. AGW **Subject:** 30th Anniversary of People's Republic **Obv:** National emblem **Rev:** Great Hall of the People

Date	Mintage	F	VF	XF	Unc	BU
ND(1979) Proof	Est. 23,000	Value: 345				

Y# 30 400 YUAN
16.9500 g., 0.9170 Gold .4997 oz. AGW **Subject:** Chinese Bronze Age Finds **Obv:** State seal **Rev:** Rhinoceros, left, denomination below

Date	Mintage	F	VF	XF	Unc	BU
1981 Proof	1,000	Value: 675				

Y# 47 400 YUAN
13.3600 g., 0.9170 Gold .3939 oz. AGW **Subject:** 70th Anniversary of 1911 Revolution **Obv:** Bust of Sun-Yat-sen, facing, two dates below **Rev:** Nationalist troops attacking, denomination and date below

Date	Mintage	F	VF	XF	Unc	BU
1981 Proof	1,338	Value: 1,100				

Y# 9 450 YUAN
17.1700 g., 0.9000 Gold .4968 oz. AGW **Series:** International Year of the Child **Obv:** State seal above floral sprays **Rev:** Two children planting flower

Date	Mintage	F	VF	XF	Unc	BU
1979 Proof	Est. 12,000	Value: 340				

Y# 1178 500 YUAN
15.5517 g., 0.9999 Gold 0.4999 oz. AGW **Subject:** Domestic Scene

Date	Mintage	F	VF	XF	Unc	BU
1993	8,888	Value: 340				

Y# 356 500 YUAN
155.5150 g., 0.9990 Gold 5.0000 oz. AGW **Obv:** Temple of Harmony **Rev:** Two peacocks **Rev. Designer:** Lang Shih Ning

Date	Mintage	F	VF	XF	Unc	BU
1993 Proof	99	Value: 4,250				

Y# 764 500 YUAN
155.5150 g., 0.9990 Gold 5.0000 oz. AGW **Subject:** Sun Yat-sen **Obv:** Home of Sun Yat-sen, date below **Rev:** Bust of Sun Yat-sen, facing, denomination at right

Date	Mintage	F	VF	XF	Unc	BU
1993 Proof	99	Value: 5,000				

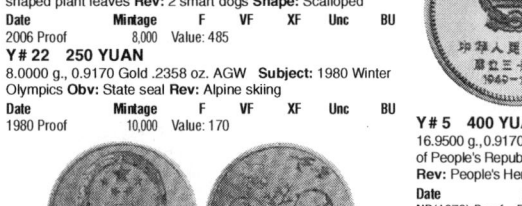

CHINA, PEOPLE'S REPUBLIC 131

Y# 778 500 YUAN
155.5150 g., 0.9990 Gold 5.0000 oz. AGW **Subject:** Tomb of Emperor Huang **Obv:** Great Wall, date below **Rev:** Tomb, denomination below

Date	Mintage	F	VF	XF	Unc	BU
1993 Proof	99	Value: 3,850				

Y# 395 500 YUAN
155.5150 g., 0.9990 Gold 5.0000 oz. AGW, 60 mm. **Subject:** Marco Polo bust on left, looking right, buildings at right, denomination below **Note:** Photo reduced.

Date	Mintage	F	VF	XF	Unc	BU
1993 Proof	100	Value: 3,450				

Y# 407 500 YUAN
155.5150 g., 0.9990 Gold 5.0000 oz. AGW, 60 mm. **Subject:** Chinese Gods: Fu, Lu and Shu, denomination below **Obv:** Building and Great Wall, date below **Rev:** Three gods with symbol on panel and child **Note:** Photo reduced.

Date	Mintage	F	VF	XF	Unc	BU
1993 Proof	99	Value: 3,450				

Y# 415 500 YUAN
155.5150 g., 0.9990 Gold 5.0000 oz. AGW, 60 mm. **Subject:** Chairman Mao **Obv:** Tall building, date at right **Rev:** 3/4 figure of Mao looking left, denomination at right **Note:** Photo reduced.

Date	Mintage	F	VF	XF	Unc	BU
1993 Proof	100	Value: 5,000				

Y# 417 500 YUAN
155.5150 g., 0.9990 Gold 5.0000 oz. AGW, 60 mm. **Subject:** Yandi, Semi-mythical First Emperor **Obv:** National emblem **Rev:** 3/4 figure looking left, denomination over right shoulder **Note:** Photo reduced.

Date	Mintage	F	VF	XF	Unc	BU
1993 Proof	99	Value: 3,450				

Y# 449 500 YUAN
155.5150 g., 0.9990 Gold 5.0000 oz. AGW, 60 mm. **Obv:** Taiwan Temple, date below **Rev:** Buddha statue, denomination below **Note:** Photo reduced.

Date	Mintage	F	VF	XF	Unc	BU
1994 Proof	76	Value: 4,000				

Y# 462 500 YUAN
155.5150 g., 0.9990 Gold 5.0000 oz. AGW, 60 mm. **Subject:** Children At Play **Rev:** Two children with cat, denomination below **Note:** Photo reduced.

Date	Mintage	F	VF	XF	Unc	BU
1994 Proof	99	Value: 3,550				

Y# 701 500 YUAN
155.5150 g., 0.9990 Gold 5.0000 oz. AGW **Subject:** Sino-Singapore Friendship **Obv:** Great Wall, date below **Rev:** Singapore Harbor, denomination below **Note:** Photo reduced.

Date	Mintage	F	VF	XF	Unc	BU
1994 Proof	91	Value: 3,550				

CHINA, PEOPLE'S REPUBLIC

Y# 429 500 YUAN
155.5150 g., 0.9990 Gold 5.0000 oz. AGW **Obv:** Eastern unicorn with rider, date below **Rev:** Unicorn above sprays of roses, denomination at left

Date	Mintage	F	VF	XF	Unc	BU
1994 Proof	99	Value: 3,850				

Y# 533 500 YUAN
155.5150 g., 0.9990 Gold 5.0000 oz. AGW **Subject:** Return of Hong Kong to China - Series I **Obv:** Tiananmen Square, date below **Rev:** Bust of Deng Xiaoping over Hong Kong city view

Date	Mintage	F	VF	XF	Unc	BU
1995 Proof	228	Value: 3,750				

Y# 656 500 YUAN
155.5150 g., 0.9990 Gold 5.0000 oz. AGW, 60 mm.
Subject: Unicorn **Obv:** Eastern unicorn **Rev:** Unicorn mother and baby **Edge:** Reeded

Date	Mintage	F	VF	XF	Unc	BU
1995 Proof	99	Value: 3,550				

Y# 824 500 YUAN
155.5175 g., 0.9999 Gold 5.0000 oz. AGW **Subject:** Zheng Chenggong **Obv:** Chiqian Building **Rev:** Standing figure with flag, war ships in background, two dates upper right, denomination lower right

Date	Mintage	F	VF	XF	Unc	BU
1995 Proof	99	Value: 3,450				

Y# 834 500 YUAN
155.5175 g., 0.9999 Gold 5.0000 oz. AGW **Subject:** Romance of the Three Kingdoms Series **Obv:** Bust of Luo Guanzhong, looking right **Rev:** Three heroes of Shu Han, denomination above

Date	Mintage	F	VF	XF	Unc	BU
1995 Proof	99	Value: 3,450				

Y# 594 500 YUAN
155.5150 g., 0.9990 Gold 5.0000 oz. AGW, 60 mm.
Subject: Yellow River culture **Rev:** Nu Wa Rising, denomination below **Note:** Photo reduced.

Date	Mintage	F	VF	XF	Unc	BU
1995 Proof	99	Value: 3,550				

Y# 649 500 YUAN
155.5150 g., 0.9990 Gold 5.0000 oz. AGW, 60 mm.
Rev: Dragon boat, denomination below **Note:** Photo reduced.

Date	Mintage	F	VF	XF	Unc	BU
1995 Proof	99	Value: 4,350				

Y# 817 500 YUAN
155.5175 g., 0.9999 Gold 5.0000 oz. AGW **Subject:** 50th Anniversary - Taiwan's Return to China **Obv:** Great Wall, date below **Rev:** Taiwan and China maps, date at right, denomination lower left **Note:** Photo reduced.

Date	Mintage	F	VF	XF	Unc	BU
1995 Proof	99	Value: 4,350				

Y# 882 500 YUAN
155.5175 g., 0.9999 Gold 5.0000 oz. AGW **Subject:** Romance of the Three Kingdoms Series **Obv:** Bust of Luo Guanzhong **Rev:** Guan Du on horseback leading troops, denomination at left **Note:** Photo reduced.

Date	Mintage	F	VF	XF	Unc	BU
1996 Proof	99	Value: 3,450				

Y# 657 500 YUAN
155.5175 g., 0.9999 Gold 5.0000 oz. AGW **Obv:** Western unicorn on hind legs, surrounded by roses **Rev:** Eastern unicorn standing

Date	Mintage	F	VF	XF	Unc	BU
1996 Proof	108	Value: 3,350				

Y# 659 500 YUAN
155.5175 g., 0.9999 Gold 5.0000 oz. AGW **Subject:** Return of Hong Kong to China - Series II

Date	Mintage	F	VF	XF	Unc	BU
1996 Proof	228	Value: 3,500				

Y# 904 500 YUAN
155.5175 g., 0.9990 Gold 5.0000 oz. AGW **Subject:** Return of Hong Kong to China - Series III **Obv:** Tiananmen Square **Rev:** Bust of Deng Xiaoping above city, denomination at left

CHINA, PEOPLE'S REPUBLIC 133

Date	Mintage	F	VF	XF	Unc	BU
1997 Proof	228	Value: 3,500				

Y# 907 500 YUAN
155.5175 g., 0.9990 Gold 5.0000 oz. AGW **Subject:** Return of Macao to China **Obv:** Tiananmen Square **Rev:** Deng Xiaoping standing viewing Macao, denomination at right

Date	Mintage	F	VF	XF	Unc	BU
1997 Proof	228	Value: 3,500				

Y# 1022 500 YUAN
155.5175 g., 0.9990 Gold 5.0000 oz. AGW **Subject:** Greeting Spring **Obv:** Lantern **Rev:** Children lighting firecrackers

Date	Mintage	F	VF	XF	Unc	BU
1997 Proof	108	Value: 3,350				

Y# 1029 500 YUAN
155.5175 g., 0.9990 Gold 5.0000 oz. AGW **Obv:** Bust of Qi Bashi **Rev:** Squirrels eating grapes

Date	Mintage	F	VF	XF	Unc	BU
1997 Proof	99	Value: 3,850				

Y# 1023 500 YUAN
155.5175 g., 0.9990 Gold 5.0000 oz. AGW **Subject:** Greeting Spring **Obv:** Lantern **Rev:** Children making kites

Date	Mintage	F	VF	XF	Unc	BU
1998 Proof	128	Value: 3,250				

Y# 1026 500 YUAN
155.5175 g., 0.9990 Gold 5.0000 oz. AGW **Subject:** 50th Anniversary of People's Republic Founding Ceremony **Shape:** Rectangular

Date	Mintage	F	VF	XF	Unc	BU
1999 Proof	990	Value: 3,750				

Y# 1028 500 YUAN
155.5175 g., 0.9990 Gold 5.0000 oz. AGW **Subject:** Y2K

Date	Mintage	F	VF	XF	Unc	BU
2000 Proof	1,000	Value: 3,500				

Y# 31 800 YUAN
33.2000 g., 0.9170 Gold .9789 oz. AGW **Subject:** Chinese Bronze Age Finds **Obv:** National emblem, date below **Rev:** Elephant statue, left, denomination below

Date	Mintage	F	VF	XF	Unc	BU
1981 Proof	1,000	Value: 1,150				

Y# 210 1500 YUAN
622.6000 g., 0.9990 Gold 20.0000 oz. AGW **Obv:** Great Wall **Rev:** Denomination divides Phoenix and dragon

Date	Mintage	F	VF	XF	Unc	BU
1989 Proof	250	Value: 14,000				

Y# 232 1500 YUAN
622.6000 g., 0.9990 Gold 20.0000 oz. AGW, 90 mm. **Subject:** Anniversary of People's Republic **Obv:** National emblem above city view with fireworks in sky **Rev:** Man giving speech, people in background, denomination below **Note:** Photo reduced.

Date	Mintage	F	VF	XF	Unc	BU
1989 Proof	100	Value: 31,000				

Y# 505 1500 YUAN
562.5068 g., 0.9990 Gold 18.0850 oz. AGW, 85 mm. **Rev:** Guanyin, Goddess of Mercy, seated in flower, denomination at left **Note:** Photo reduced.

Date	Mintage	F	VF	XF	Unc	BU
1993 Proof	88	Value: 15,500				

Y# 357 1500 YUAN
622.6000 g., 0.9990 Gold 20.0000 oz. AGW **Obv:** Temple of Harmony **Rev:** Two peacocks **Rev. Designer:** Land Shih Ning

Date	Mintage	F	VF	XF	Unc	BU
1993 Proof	66	Value: 16,500				

Y# 749 2000 YUAN
1000.0000 g., 0.9990 Gold 32.1500 oz. AGW **Subject:** Chinese Inventions and Discoveries **Obv:** Great Wall **Rev:** Seismograph

Date	Mintage	F	VF	XF	Unc	BU
1992 Proof	Est. 4	Value: 31,500				

Y# 402 2000 YUAN
1000.0000 g., 0.9990 Gold 32.1500 oz. AGW, 100 mm. **Subject:** Chinese inventions **Rev:** First compass, denomination below **Note:** Photo reduced.

Date	Mintage	F	VF	XF	Unc	BU
1992 Proof	10	Value: 27,000				

Y# 703 2000 YUAN
1000.0000 g., 0.9990 Gold 32.1500 oz. AGW, 112 mm. **Subject:** Sino-Singapore Friendship **Obv:** Great Wall, date below **Rev:** Singapore Harbor, denomination below **Note:** Photo reduced.

Date	Mintage	F	VF	XF	Unc	BU
1994	15	—	—	—	—	22,500

Y# 430 2000 YUAN
1000.0000 g., 0.9990 Gold 32.1500 oz. AGW **Obv:** Figure on Eastern unicorn, date below **Rev:** Unicorn, denomination below, rose sprays below

Date	Mintage	F	VF	XF	Unc	BU
1994 Proof	20	Value: 22,000				

Y# 818 2000 YUAN
1000.0000 g., 0.9990 Gold 32.1500 oz. AGW **Subject:** 50th Anniversary - Taiwan's Return to China **Obv:** Great Wall **Rev:** Taiwan and China maps

Date	Mintage	F	VF	XF	Unc	BU
1995 Proof	25	Value: 23,500				

Y# 957 2000 YUAN
1000.0000 g., 0.9990 Gold 32.1500 oz. AGW **Obv:** Eastern unicorn **Rev:** Western unicorn with maiden

Date	Mintage	F	VF	XF	Unc	BU
1996 Proof	18	Value: 22,000				

Y# 1086 2000 YUAN
155.5175 g., 0.9990 Gold 4.995 oz. AGW, 60 mm. **Subject:** Mogao Grottoes **Obv:** Eight story building **Rev:** Two dancers **Edge:** Reeded

Date	Mintage	F	VF	XF	Unc	BU
2001 Proof	288	Value: 3,650				

Y# 1151 2000 YUAN
155.5175 g., 0.9990 Gold 4.995 oz. AGW, 60 mm. **Subject:** Buddest Ceremony

Date	Mintage	F	VF	XF	Unc	BU
2002	288	—	—	—	—	4,250

134 CHINA, PEOPLE'S REPUBLIC

Y# 1206 2000 YUAN
155.5175 g., 0.9990 Gold 4.995 oz. AGW, 60 mm.
Subject: Maijishan Grottos **Obv:** Grotto view **Rev:** Buddha portrait within halo of flying devatas **Edge:** Reeded

Date	Mintage	F	VF	XF	Unc	BU
2004(y) Proof	288	Value: 3,650				

Y# 1218 2000 YUAN
155.5175 g., 0.9990 Gold 4.995 oz. AGW, 64x40 mm. **Obv:** Monkey King leading Master over bridge **Rev:** Multicolor Monkey King fighting the Pig "Demon of Bones" **Edge:** Plain **Shape:** Ingot

Date	Mintage	F	VF	XF	Unc	BU
2004 Proof	500	Value: 5,300				

Y# 1243 2000 YUAN
155.5175 g., 0.9990 Gold 4.995 oz. AGW, 60 mm. **Obv:** Guangan Exposition Hall **Rev:** Deng Xiaoping and value **Edge:** Reeded

Date	Mintage	F	VF	XF	Unc	BU
2004 Proof	600	Value: 5,000				

Y# 1070 30000 YUAN
10000.0000 g., 0.9999 Gold 321.50 oz. AGW, 180 mm.
Subject: Third Millennium **Obv:** China Centenary Altar **Rev:** Denominations **Edge:** Plain

Date	Mintage	F	VF	XF	Unc	BU
2000	20	—	—	—	—	210,000

GOLD BULLION COINAGE
Panda Series

Y# 307 3 YUAN
1.0000 g., 0.9990 Gold 0.0321 oz. AGW **Obv:** Temple of Heaven **Rev:** Seated panda left, denomination at left

Date	Mintage	F	VF	XF	Unc	BU
1991 Proof	110,000	Value: 37.50				

Y# 48 5 YUAN
1.5552 g., 0.9990 Gold .0500 oz. AGW **Obv:** Temple of Heaven, date below **Rev:** Panda on all fours right, within circle

Date	Mintage	F	VF	XF	Unc	BU
1983 Proof	Est. 58,000	Value: 70.00				

Y# 73 5 YUAN
1.5552 g., 0.9990 Gold .0500 oz. AGW **Obv:** Temple of Heaven, date below **Rev:** Panda holding bamboo branch, reclined, denomination at right

Date	Mintage	F	VF	XF	Unc	BU
1984 Proof	Est. 86,000	Value: 47.50				

Y# 80 5 YUAN
1.5552 g., 0.9990 Gold .0500 oz. AGW **Obv:** Temple of Heaven, date below **Rev:** Panda hanging from branch, denomination upper left

Date	Mintage	F	VF	XF	Unc	BU
1985 Proof	Est. 217,000	Value: 47.50				

Y# 101 5 YUAN
1.5552 g., 0.9990 Gold .0500 oz. AGW **Obv:** Temple of Heaven, date below **Rev:** Panda, denomination below

Date	Mintage	F	VF	XF	Unc	BU
1986	Est. 87,500	—	—	—	—	40.00
1986 P Proof	10,000	Value: 45.00				

Y# 124 5 YUAN
1.5552 g., 0.9990 Gold .0500 oz. AGW **Obv:** Temple of Heaven, date below **Rev:** Panda left, denomination below

Date	Mintage	F	VF	XF	Unc	BU
1987(s)	Est. 103,000	—	—	—	—	40.00
1987(y)	Est. 39,000	—	—	—	—	40.00
1987 P Proof	10,000	Value: 45.00				

Y# 152 5 YUAN
1.5552 g., 0.9990 Gold .0500 oz. AGW **Obv:** Temple of Heaven, date below **Rev:** Panda pawing bamboo

Date	Mintage	F	VF	XF	Unc	BU
1988	Est. 482,000	—	—	—	—	40.00
1988 Proof	10,000	Value: 45.00				

Y# 238 5 YUAN
1.5552 g., 0.9990 Gold .0500 oz. AGW **Obv:** Temple of Heaven, date below **Rev:** Panda climbing rock, denomination below

Date	Mintage	F	VF	XF	Unc	BU
1990	Est. 337,000	—	—	—	—	40.00
1990 Proof	5,000	Value: 47.50				

Y# 309 5 YUAN
1.5552 g., 0.9990 Gold .0500 oz. AGW **Obv:** Temple of Heaven **Rev:** Panda with hind feet in water eating bamboo

Date	Mintage	F	VF	XF	Unc	BU
1991	—	—	—	—	—	50.00
1991 Proof	3,500	Value: 60.00				

Y# 610 5 YUAN
1.5552 g., 0.9990 Gold .0500 oz. AGW **Obv:** Temple of Heaven, date below **Rev:** Panda pawing bamboo

Date	Mintage	F	VF	XF	Unc	BU
1993	—	—	—	—	—	45.00
1993 Proof	2,500	Value: 55.00				

Y# 1203 5 YUAN
1.5550 g., 0.9990 Gold 0.0499 oz. AGW, 14 mm. **Obv:** Temple of Heaven **Rev:** Panda seated on flat rock **Edge:** Reeded

Date	Mintage	F	VF	XF	Unc	BU
1993(y)	—	—	—	—	—	45.00
1993P(y) Proof	2,500	Value: 65.00				

Y# 431 5 YUAN
1.5552 g., 0.9990 Gold .0500 oz. AGW **Obv:** Temple of Heaven, date below **Rev:** Panda sitting, denomination below

Date	Mintage	F	VF	XF	Unc	BU
1994	—	—	—	—	—	45.00
1994 Proof	—	Value: 55.00				

Y# 640 5 YUAN
1.5552 g., 0.9990 Gold .0500 oz. AGW **Obv:** Temple of Heaven, date below **Rev:** Panda holding bamboo stick, denomination at left

Date	Mintage	F	VF	XF	Unc	BU
1995	—	—	—	—	—	45.00

Y# 716 5 YUAN
1.5552 g., 0.9990 Gold .0500 oz. AGW **Obv:** Temple of Heaven **Rev:** Panda on branch **Note:** Large and small date varieties exist.

Date	Mintage	F	VF	XF	Unc	BU
1997	—	—	—	—	—	45.00

Note: Exists in large and small date varieties

Y# 990 5 YUAN
1.5600 g., 0.9990 Gold .0500 oz. AGW **Obv:** Temple of Heaven **Rev:** Panda seated on rock

Date	Mintage	F	VF	XF	Unc	BU
1998	—	—	—	—	—	40.00

Y# 981 5 YUAN
1.5600 g., 0.9990 Gold .0500 oz. AGW **Obv:** Temple of Heaven **Rev:** Panda on ledge

Date	Mintage	F	VF	XF	Unc	BU
1999	—	—	—	—	—	40.00

Note: Exists in Large and Small date varieties.

Y# 945 5 YUAN
1.5600 g., 0.9990 Gold .0500 oz. AGW **Obv:** Temple of Heaven **Rev:** Panda seated on leaves **Note:** Large and small date varieties exist.

Date	Mintage	F	VF	XF	Unc	BU
2000	—	—	—	—	—	40.00

Note: Domestic Chinese examples struck with mirror fields, overseas examples struck with frosted fields

Y# 49 10 YUAN
3.1103 g., 0.9990 Gold .1000 oz. AGW **Obv:** Temple of Heaven, date below **Rev:** Panda right

Date	Mintage	F	VF	XF	Unc	BU
1983	Est. 74,000	—	—	—	—	85.00

Y# 74 10 YUAN
3.1103 g., 0.9990 Gold .1000 oz. AGW **Obv:** Temple of Heaven **Rev:** Panda holding bamboo branch, reclined, denomination at right

Date	Mintage	F	VF	XF	Unc	BU
1984	10,000	—	—	—	—	185

Y# 81 10 YUAN
3.1103 g., 0.9990 Gold .1000 oz. AGW **Obv:** Temple of Heaven, date below **Rev:** Panda hanging from branch, denomination upper left

Date	Mintage	F	VF	XF	Unc	BU
1985	Est. 150,000	—	—	—	—	85.00

Y# 102 10 YUAN
3.1103 g., 0.9990 Gold .1000 oz. AGW **Obv:** Temple of Heaven **Rev:** Panda, denomination below

Date	Mintage	F	VF	XF	Unc	BU
1986	Est. 45,000	—	—	—	—	75.00
1986 P Proof	10,000	Value: 80.00				

Y# 125 10 YUAN
3.1103 g., 0.9990 Gold .1000 oz. AGW **Obv:** Temple of Heaven, date below **Rev:** Panda, denomination below

Date	Mintage	F	VF	XF	Unc	BU
1987(s)	Est. 108,000	—	—	—	—	75.00
1987(y)	Est. 37,000	—	—	—	—	75.00
1987 P Proof	10,000	Value: 80.00				

CHINA, PEOPLE'S REPUBLIC

Y# 153 10 YUAN
3.1103 g., 0.9990 Gold .1000 oz. AGW **Obv:** Temple of Heaven, date below **Rev:** Panda pawing bamboo, denomination below

Date	Mintage	F	VF	XF	Unc	BU
1988	Est. 290,000	—	—	—	—	70.00
1988 Proof	10,000	Value: 75.00				

Y# 188 10 YUAN
3.1103 g., 0.9990 Gold .1000 oz. AGW **Obv:** Temple of Heaven, date below **Rev:** Panda reclining, grid behind, denomination below

Date	Mintage	F	VF	XF	Unc	BU
1989	Est. 128,000	—	—	—	—	70.00
1989 Proof	8,000	Value: 75.00				

Y# 239 10 YUAN
3.1100 g., 0.9990 Gold .0322 oz. AGW **Obv:** Temple of Heaven, date below **Rev:** Panda, denomination below

Date	Mintage	F	VF	XF	Unc	BU
1990	Est. 214,000	—	—	—	—	75.00
1990 Proof	5,000	Value: 80.00				

Y# 310 10 YUAN
3.1100 g., 0.9990 Gold .10000 oz. AGW **Obv:** Temple of Heaven **Rev:** Panda with hind feet in water eating bamboo **Note:** Similar to 100 Yuan, KM#313.

Date	Mintage	F	VF	XF	Unc	BU
1991	—	—	—	—	—	75.00
1991 Proof	3,500	Value: 90.00				

Y# 342 10 YUAN
3.1103 g., 0.9990 Gold .1000 oz. AGW **Obv:** Temple of Heaven, date below **Rev:** Panda climbing right on eucalyptus branch

Date	Mintage	F	VF	XF	Unc	BU
1992	—	—	—	—	—	75.00
1992 Proof	2,000	Value: 95.00				

Y# 484 10 YUAN
3.1103 g., 0.9990 Gold .1000 oz. AGW **Obv:** Temple of Heaven **Rev:** Panda on flat rock

Date	Mintage	F	VF	XF	Unc	BU
1993	—	—	—	—	—	75.00
1993 Proof	2,500	Value: 95.00				

Y# 432 10 YUAN
3.1103 g., 0.9990 Gold .1000 oz. AGW **Obv:** Temple of Heaven, date below **Rev:** Seated panda eating, denomination below

Date	Mintage	F	VF	XF	Unc	BU
1994	—	—	—	—	—	75.00
1994 Proof	2,500	Value: 95.00				

Y# 641 10 YUAN
3.1103 g., 0.9990 Gold .1000 oz. AGW **Obv:** Temple of Heaven **Rev:** Panda eating bamboo, denomination at left

Date	Mintage	F	VF	XF	Unc	BU
1995	—	—	—	—	—	75.00

Y# 581 10 YUAN
1.5552 g., 0.9990 Gold .0500 oz. AGW **Obv:** Temple of Heaven, date below **Rev:** Panda in tree looking down, denomination lower left **Note:** Large and small date varieties exist.

Date	Mintage	F	VF	XF	Unc	BU
1996	—	—	—	—	—	55.00

Y# 575 10 YUAN
3.1103 g., 0.9990 Gold .1000 oz. AGW **Obv:** Temple of Heaven, date below **Rev:** Panda in tree **Note:** Large and small date varieties exist.

Date	Mintage	F	VF	XF	Unc	BU
1996	—	—	—	—	—	75.00

Y# 848 10 YUAN
3.1103 g., 0.9990 Gold .1000 oz. AGW **Subject:** 15th Anniversary - Gold Panda Coins **Obv:** Temple of Heaven with additional legend **Rev:** Panda in tree **Note:** Large and small date varieties exist.

Date	Mintage	F	VF	XF	Unc	BU
1996 Proof	20,000	Value: 80.00				

Y# 717 10 YUAN
3.1103 g., 0.9990 Gold .1000 oz. AGW **Obv:** Temple of Heaven **Rev:** Panda on branch **Note:** Large and small date varieties exist.

Date	Mintage	F	VF	XF	Unc	BU
1997	—	—	—	—	—	70.00

Note: Exists in large and small date varieties

Y# 988 10 YUAN
3.1103 g., 0.9990 Gold .1000 oz. AGW **Obv:** Temple of Heaven **Rev:** Panda seated on rock **Note:** Large and small date varieties exist.

Date	Mintage	F	VF	XF	Unc	BU
1998	—	—	—	—	—	70.00

Y# 989 10 YUAN
3.1103 g., 0.9990 Gold .1000 oz. AGW **Obv:** Temple of Heaven **Rev:** Panda on ledge

Date	Mintage	F	VF	XF	Unc	BU
1999	—	—	—	—	—	70.00

Note: Exists in Large and Small date varieties.

Y# 946 10 YUAN
3.1103 g., 0.9990 Gold .1000 oz. AGW **Obv:** Temple of Heaven **Rev:** Panda seated on leaves **Note:** Large and small date varieties exist.

Date	Mintage	F	VF	XF	Unc	BU
2000 Proof	—	Value: 75.00				

Y# 1112 20 YUAN
1.5600 g., 0.9990 Gold 0.0501 oz. AGW, 14 mm. **Obv:** Temple of Heaven **Rev:** Panda walking left through bamboo **Edge:** Reeded **Note:** Large and small date varieties exist.

Date	Mintage	F	VF	XF	Unc	BU
2001	100,000	—	—	—	—	40.00
2001 D	200,000	—	—	—	—	40.00

Y# 1154 20 YUAN
3.1103 g., 0.9990 Gold 0.1 oz. AGW **Subject:** Panda **Note:** Large and small date varieties exist.

Date	Mintage	F	VF	XF	Unc	BU
2003	—	—	—	—	—	75.00

Y# 1172 20 YUAN
1.5552 g., 0.9999 Gold 0.05 oz. AGW **Subject:** Panda **Note:** Large and small date varieties exist.

Date	Mintage	F	VF	XF	Unc	BU
2004	—	—	—	—	—	40.00

Y# 50 25 YUAN
7.7758 g., 0.9990 Gold .2500 oz. AGW **Obv:** Temple of Heaven, date below **Rev:** Panda walking right, in inner circle, denomination below

Date	Mintage	F	VF	XF	Unc	BU
1983	Est. 39,000	—	—	—	—	180

Y# 75 25 YUAN
7.7758 g., 0.9990 Gold .2500 oz. AGW **Obv:** Temple of Heaven, date below **Rev:** Lounging Panda with bamboo

Date	Mintage	F	VF	XF	Unc	BU
1984	Est. 38,000	—	—	—	—	180

Y# 82 25 YUAN
7.7758 g., 0.9990 Gold .2500 oz. AGW **Obv:** Temple of Heaven, date below **Rev:** Panda hanging on bamboo branch, denomination upper left

Date	Mintage	F	VF	XF	Unc	BU
1985	Est. 95,000	—	—	—	—	200

Y# 103 25 YUAN
7.7758 g., 0.9990 Gold .2500 oz. AGW **Obv:** Temple of Heaven **Rev:** Facing panda standing, denomination below

Date	Mintage	F	VF	XF	Unc	BU
1986	Est. 33,000	—	—	—	—	170
1986 P Proof	10,000	Value: 175				

Y# 126 25 YUAN
7.7758 g., 0.9990 Gold .2500 oz. AGW **Obv:** Temple of Heaven, date below **Rev:** Panda drinking, denomination below

Date	Mintage	F	VF	XF	Unc	BU
1987(s)	Est. 81,000	—	—	—	—	170
1987(y)	Est. 31,000	—	—	—	—	170
1987 P Proof	10,000	Value: 175				

Y# 154 25 YUAN
7.7758 g., 0.9990 Gold .2500 oz. AGW **Obv:** Temple of Heaven **Rev:** Panda pawing bamboo

Date	Mintage	F	VF	XF	Unc	BU
1988	Est. 122,000	—	—	—	—	170
1988 Proof	10,000	Value: 175				

Y# 189 25 YUAN
7.7758 g., 0.9990 Gold .2500 oz. AGW **Obv:** Temple of Heaven, date below **Rev:** Panda reclining, grid behind, denomination below

Date	Mintage	F	VF	XF	Unc	BU
1989	Est. 71,000	—	—	—	—	170
1989 Proof	8,000	Value: 175				

Y# 240 25 YUAN
7.7758 g., 0.9990 Gold .2500 oz. AGW **Obv:** Temple of Heaven, date below **Rev:** Panda, denomination lower right

Date	Mintage	F	VF	XF	Unc	BU
1990	—	—	—	—	—	175
1990 Proof	5,000	Value: 180				

Y# 311 25 YUAN
7.7758 g., 0.9990 Gold .2500 oz. AGW, 22 mm. **Obv:** Temple of Heaven, date below **Edge:** Reeded

Date	Mintage	F	VF	XF	Unc	BU
1991	—	—	—	—	—	180
1991 Proof	—	Value: 200				

Y# 343 25 YUAN
7.7758 g., 0.9990 Gold .2500 oz. AGW **Obv:** Temple of Heaven, date below **Rev:** Panda on limb

Date	Mintage	F	VF	XF	Unc	BU
1992	—	—	—	—	—	175
1992 Proof	—	Value: 195				

Y# 612 25 YUAN
7.7758 g., 0.9990 Gold .2500 oz. AGW **Obv:** Temple of Heaven, date below **Rev:** Panda tugging on bamboo sprig, denomination below, within circle, date below

Date	Mintage	F	VF	XF	Unc	BU
1993	—	—	—	—	—	185
1993 Proof	—	Value: 200				

Y# 1204 25 YUAN
7.7758 g., 0.9990 Gold 0.2497 oz. AGW, 22 mm. **Obv:** Temple of Heaven **Rev:** Panda seated on flat rock **Edge:** Reeded

Date	Mintage	F	VF	XF	Unc	BU
1993P(y) Proof	2,500	Value: 175				
1993(y)	—	—	—	—	—	170

Y# 433 25 YUAN
7.7758 g., 0.9990 Gold .2500 oz. AGW **Obv:** Temple of Heaven **Rev:** Panda tugging on bamboo sprig

Date	Mintage	F	VF	XF	Unc	BU
1994	35,000	—	—	—	—	195
1994 Proof	—	Value: 220				

Y# 642 25 YUAN
7.7600 g., 0.9990 Gold .2500 oz. AGW **Obv:** Temple of Heaven, date below **Rev:** Panda

Date	Mintage	F	VF	XF	Unc	BU
1995	—	—	—	—	—	195

Y# 576 25 YUAN
7.8300 g., 0.9990 Gold .2515 oz. AGW **Obv:** Temple of Heaven, date below **Rev:** Panda **Note:** Large and small date varieties exist.

Date	Mintage	F	VF	XF	Unc	BU
1996	—	—	—	—	—	195

Y# 849 25 YUAN
7.7759 g., 0.9990 Gold .2500 oz. AGW **Subject:** 15th Anniversary - Gold Panda Coinage **Obv:** Temple of Heaven with additional legend **Rev:** Panda in tree **Note:** Large and small date varieties exist.

Date	Mintage	F	VF	XF	Unc	BU
1996 Proof	8,000	Value: 220				

CHINA, PEOPLE'S REPUBLIC

Y# 718 25 YUAN
7.7759 g., 0.9990 Gold .2500 oz. AGW **Obv:** Temple of Heaven
Rev: Panda on branch

Date	Mintage	F	VF	XF	Unc	BU
1997	—	—	—	—	—	170

Note: Exists in Large and Small date varieties.

Y# 1002 25 YUAN
7.7758 g., 0.9990 Gold .2500 oz. AGW **Obv:** Temple of Heaven
Rev: Panda seated on rock **Note:** Large and small date varieties exist.

Date	Mintage	F	VF	XF	Unc	BU
1998	—	—	—	—	—	170

Note: Exists in both large and small date varieties

Y# 1003 25 YUAN
7.7758 g., 0.9990 Gold .2500 oz. AGW **Obv:** Temple of Heaven
Rev: Panda on ledge **Note:** Large and small date varieties exist.

Date	Mintage	F	VF	XF	Unc	BU
1999	—	—	—	—	—	170

Y# 947 25 YUAN
7.7758 g., 0.9990 Gold .2500 oz. AGW **Obv:** Temple of Heaven
Rev: Panda seated on leaves **Note:** Large and small date varieties exist.

Date	Mintage	F	VF	XF	Unc	BU
2000	—	—	—	—	—	170

Note: Domestic Chinese examples struck with mirror fields, overseas examples struck with frosted fields

Y# 51 50 YUAN
15.5517 g., 0.9990 Gold .5000 oz. AGW **Obv:** Temple of Heaven, date below **Rev:** Panda walking right, in inner circle, date below

Date	Mintage	F	VF	XF	Unc	BU
1983 Proof	Est. 23,000	Value: 360

Y# 76 50 YUAN
15.5517 g., 0.9990 Gold .5000 oz. AGW **Obv:** Temple of Heaven, date below **Rev:** Lounging panda with bamboo sprig, denomination at right

Date	Mintage	F	VF	XF	Unc	BU
1984 Proof	Est. 17,000	Value: 375

Y# 83 50 YUAN
15.5517 g., 0.9990 Gold .5000 oz. AGW **Obv:** Temple of Heaven, date below **Rev:** Panda hanging from bamboo branch, denomination upper left

Date	Mintage	F	VF	XF	Unc	BU
1985	Est. 76,000	—	—	—	—	360

Y# 104 50 YUAN
15.5517 g., 0.9990 Gold .5000 oz. AGW **Obv:** Temple of Heaven, date below **Rev:** Facing panda standing, denomination below

Date	Mintage	F	VF	XF	Unc	BU
1986	Est. 60,000	—	—	—	—	360
1986 P Proof	10,000	Value: 375

Y# 127 50 YUAN
15.5517 g., 0.9990 Gold .5000 oz. AGW **Obv:** Temple of Heaven, date below **Rev:** Panda drinking water, denomination below

Date	Mintage	F	VF	XF	Unc	BU
1987(s)	Est. 91,000	—	—	—	—	360
1987(y)	Est. 17,000	—	—	—	—	360
1987 P Proof	10,000	Value: 375

Y# 155 50 YUAN
15.5517 g., 0.9990 Gold .5000 oz. AGW **Obv:** Temple of Heaven, date below **Rev:** Panda pawing bamboo within circle, denomination below

Date	Mintage	F	VF	XF	Unc	BU
1988	Est. 104,000	—	—	—	—	360
1988 Proof	10,000	Value: 375

Y# 190 50 YUAN
15.5517 g., 0.9990 Gold .5000 oz. AGW **Obv:** Temple of Heaven
Rev: Grid behind panda

Date	Mintage	F	VF	XF	Unc	BU
1989	Est. 46,000	—	—	—	—	360
1989 Proof	8,000	Value: 375

Y# 220 50 YUAN
31.1030 g., 0.9990 Palladium 1.0000 oz. **Obv:** Building, date below **Rev:** Panda on grid background, denomination lower right

Date	Mintage	F	VF	XF	Unc	BU
1989	3,000	—	—	—	—	440

Y# 241 50 YUAN
15.5517 g., 0.9990 Gold .5000 oz. AGW **Obv:** Temple of Heaven, date below **Rev:** Panda

Date	Mintage	F	VF	XF	Unc	BU
1990	Est. 35,000	—	—	—	—	375
1990 Proof	5,000	Value: 400

Y# 312 50 YUAN
15.5517 g., 0.9990 Gold .5000 oz. AGW **Obv:** Temple of Heaven, date below **Rev:** Panda tugging on bamboo sprig, denomination below, within circle, date below

Date	Mintage	F	VF	XF	Unc	BU
1991	—	—	—	—	—	395
1991 Proof	3,500	Value: 425

Y# 315 50 YUAN
31.1035 g., 0.9990 Gold 1.0000 oz. AGW **Subject:** 10th Anniversary of Panda Coinage **Obv:** Temple of Heaven, date below **Rev:** Panda climbing bamboo branch **Note:** Double thickness.

Date	Mintage	F	VF	XF	Unc	BU
1991 Proof	2,500	Value: 725

Y# 344 50 YUAN
15.5660 g., 0.9990 Gold .5000 oz. AGW **Obv:** Temple of Heaven, date below **Rev:** Panda on tree branch

Date	Mintage	F	VF	XF	Unc	BU
1992	—	—	—	—	—	395
1992 Proof	2,000	Value: 450

Y# 613 50 YUAN
15.5517 g., 0.9990 Gold .5000 oz. AGW **Obv:** Temple of Heaven **Rev:** Pandas

Date	Mintage	F	VF	XF	Unc	BU
1993	—	—	—	—	—	395
1993 Proof	2,500	Value: 450

Y# 1205 50 YUAN
15.5500 g., 0.9990 Gold 0.4994 oz. AGW, 27 mm. **Obv:** Temple of Heaven **Rev:** Panda seated on flat rock **Edge:** Reeded

Date	Mintage	F	VF	XF	Unc	BU
1993(y)	—	—	—	—	—	395
1993P(y) Proof	2,500	Value: 450

Y# 434 50 YUAN
15.5517 g., 0.9990 Gold .5000 oz. AGW **Obv:** Temple of Heaven
Rev: Panda seated, eating bamboo shoots, denomination below

Date	Mintage	F	VF	XF	Unc	BU
1994	—	—	—	—	—	395
1994 Proof	2,500	Value: 450

Y# 643 50 YUAN
15.5517 g., 0.9990 Gold .5000 oz. AGW **Obv:** Temple of Heaven
Rev: Panda eating bamboo, denomination at left

Date	Mintage	F	VF	XF	Unc	BU
1995	—	—	—	—	—	395

Y# 577 50 YUAN
15.5517 g., 0.9990 Gold .5000 oz. AGW **Obv:** Temple of Heaven, date below **Rev:** Panda in tree **Note:** Large and small date varieties exist.

Date	Mintage	F	VF	XF	Unc	BU
1996	—	—	—	—	—	395

Y# 719 50 YUAN
15.5517 g., 0.9990 Gold .5000 oz. AGW **Obv:** Temple of Heaven within circle, date below **Rev:** Panda on large tree branch, denomination below

Date	Mintage	F	VF	XF	Unc	BU
1997	—	—	—	—	—	360

Note: Exists in Large and Small date varieties

Y# 1010 50 YUAN
15.5517 g., 0.9990 Gold .5000 oz. AGW **Obv:** Temple of Heaven
Rev: Panda seated on rock

Date	Mintage	F	VF	XF	Unc	BU
1998	—	—	—	—	—	360

Note: Exists in Large and Small date varieties

Y# 1011 50 YUAN
15.5517 g., 0.9990 Gold .5000 oz. AGW **Obv:** Temple of Heaven
Rev: Panda on ledge

Date	Mintage	F	VF	XF	Unc	BU
1999	—	—	—	—	—	360

Note: Exists in Large and Small date varieties

Y# 948 50 YUAN
15.5518 g., 0.9990 Gold .5000 oz. AGW **Obv:** Temple of Heaven
Rev: Panda seated on leaves **Note:** Large and small date varieties exist.

Date	Mintage	F	VF	XF	Unc	BU
2000 Proof	—	Value: 365

Note: Domestic Chinese examples struck with mirror fields, overseas examples struck with frosted fields

Y# 1113 50 YUAN
3.1103 g., 0.9990 Gold 0.0999 oz. AGW, 18 mm. **Obv:** Temple of Heaven **Rev:** Panda walking left through bamboo
Edge: Reeded **Note:** Large and small date varieties exist.

Date	Mintage	F	VF	XF	Unc	BU
2001	50,000	—	—	—	—	75.00
2001 D	150,000	—	—	—	—	75.00

Y# 1157 50 YUAN
3.1103 g., 0.9999 Gold 0.1 oz. AGW **Subject:** Panda
Note: Large and small date varieties exist.

Date	Mintage	F	VF	XF	Unc	BU
2003	—	—	—	—	—	75.00

Y# 1173 50 YUAN
3.1103 g., 0.9999 Gold 0.1 oz. AGW **Subject:** Panda
Note: Large and small date varieties exist.

Date	Mintage	F	VF	XF	Unc	BU
2004	—	—	—	—	—	75.00

CHINA, PEOPLE'S REPUBLIC

Y# 52 100 YUAN
31.1320 g., 0.9990 Gold 1.0000 oz. AGW **Obv:** Temple of Heaven, date below **Rev:** Panda right within circle, date below

Date	Mintage	F	VF	XF	Unc	BU
1983	22,000	—	—	—	—	BV+10%

Y# 77 100 YUAN
31.1320 g., 0.9990 Gold 1.0000 oz. AGW **Obv:** Temple of Heaven, date below **Rev:** Lounging panda with bamboo sprigs, denomination at right

Date	Mintage	F	VF	XF	Unc	BU
1984	23,000	—	—	—	—	BV+10%

Y# 84 100 YUAN
31.1320 g., 0.9990 Gold 1.0000 oz. AGW **Obv:** Temple of Heaven, date below **Rev:** Panda hanging from branch, denomination upper left

Date	Mintage	F	VF	XF	Unc	BU
1985	164,000	—	—	—	—	BV+10%

Y# 105 100 YUAN
31.1320 g., 0.9990 Gold 1.0000 oz. AGW **Obv:** Temple of Heaven, date below **Rev:** Panda amongst bamboo plants

Date	Mintage	F	VF	XF	Unc	BU
1986	97,000	—	—	—	—	BV+10%
1986 P Proof	10,000	—	—	—	—	BV+15%

Y# 128 100 YUAN
31.1320 g., 0.9990 Gold 1.0000 oz. AGW **Obv:** Temple of Heaven, date below **Rev:** Panda drinking at stream, denomination below

Date	Mintage	F	VF	XF	Unc	BU
1987(s)	84,000	—	—	—	—	BV+10%
1987(y)	47,000	—	—	—	—	BV+10%
1987 P Proof	10,000	—	—	—	—	BV+15%

Y# 156 100 YUAN
31.1320 g., 0.9990 Gold 1.0000 oz. AGW **Obv:** Temple of Heaven, date below **Rev:** Panda pawing bamboo within circle, denomination below

Date	Mintage	F	VF	XF	Unc	BU
1988	167,000	—	—	—	—	BV+10%
1988 Proof	10,000	—	—	—	—	BV+15%

Y# 191 100 YUAN
31.1320 g., 0.9990 Gold 1.0000 oz. AGW **Obv:** Temple of Heaven, date below **Rev:** Panda reclining, grid behind, denomination below

Date	Mintage	F	VF	XF	Unc	BU
1989	—	—	—	—	—	BV+10%
1989 Proof	8,000	—	—	—	—	BV+15%

Y# 242 100 YUAN
31.1320 g., 0.9990 Gold 1.0000 oz. AGW **Obv:** Temple of Heaven, date below **Rev:** Panda climbing rock, denomination below

Date	Mintage	F	VF	XF	Unc	BU
1990	—	—	—	—	—	BV+10%
1990 Proof	5,000	BV+15%				

Y# 313 100 YUAN
31.1320 g., 0.9990 Gold 1.0000 oz. AGW **Obv:** Temple of Heaven, date below **Rev:** Seated panda with hind feet in water, eating bamboo, denomination at left

Date	Mintage	F	VF	XF	Unc	BU
1991	—	—	—	—	—	BV+10%
1991 Proof	3,500	BV+15%				

Y# 345 100 YUAN
31.1035 g., 0.9990 Gold 1.0000 oz. AGW **Obv:** Temple of Heaven within circle, date below **Rev:** Panda on branch, denomination above

Date	Mintage	F	VF	XF	Unc	BU
1992	—	—	—	—	—	BV+10%
1992 Proof	2,000	BV+15%				

Y# 614 100 YUAN
31.1035 g., 0.9990 Gold 1.0000 oz. AGW **Obv:** Temple of Heaven **Rev:** Panda seated on rock

Date	Mintage	F	VF	XF	Unc	BU
1993	—	—	—	—	—	BV+10%

Y# 435 100 YUAN
31.1035 g., 0.9990 Gold 1.0000 oz. AGW **Obv:** Temple of Heaven, date below **Rev:** Panda seated, eating bamboo shoots, denomination below

Date	Mintage	F	VF	XF	Unc	BU
1994	—	—	—	—	—	BV+10%

Y# 694 100 YUAN
8.0000 g., 0.9160 Gold .2361 oz. AGW **Obv:** National emblem, date below **Rev:** Panda climbing tree, denomination at right

Date	Mintage	F	VF	XF	Unc	BU
1994 Proof	5,000	Value: 225				

Y# 644 100 YUAN
31.1030 g., 0.9990 Gold 1.0000 oz. AGW **Obv:** Temple of Heaven **Rev:** Panda eating bamboo

Date	Mintage	F	VF	XF	Unc	BU
1995	—	—	—	—	—	BV+10%

Y# 790 100 YUAN
31.0103 g., 0.9990 Gold 1.0000 oz. AGW **Obv:** Temple of Heaven within circle, date below **Rev:** Panda approaching water from right, denomination below

Date	Mintage	F	VF	XF	Unc	BU
1995 Proof	2,000	BV+15%				

Y# 578 100 YUAN
31.1035 g., 0.9990 Gold 1.0000 oz. AGW **Obv:** Temple of Heaven within circle, date below **Rev:** Panda in tree, denomination at left **Note:** Large and small date varieties exist.

Date	Mintage	F	VF	XF	Unc	BU
1996	—	—	—	—	—	BV+10%

Y# 1013 100 YUAN
31.1035 g., 0.9990 Gold 1.0000 oz. AGW **Obv:** Temple of Heaven **Rev:** Panda sitting on rock **Note:** Large and small date varieties exist.

Date	Mintage	F	VF	XF	Unc	BU
1996 Proof	1,500	BV+15%				

Y# 850 100 YUAN
31.1035 g., 0.9990 Gold 1.0000 oz. AGW **Subject:** 15th Anniversary - Gold Panda Coins **Obv:** Temple of Heaven with additional legend **Rev:** Panda in tree **Note:** Large and small date varieties exist.

Date	Mintage	F	VF	XF	Unc	BU
1996 Proof	1,500	BV+15%				

138 CHINA, PEOPLE'S REPUBLIC

Y# 720 100 YUAN
31.1035 g., 0.9990 Gold 1.0000 oz. AGW **Obv:** Temple of Heaven **Rev:** Panda on large branch, denomination below **Note:** Large and small date varieties exist.

Date	Mintage	F	VF	XF	Unc	BU
1997	—	—	—	—	—	BV+10%

Note: Exists in large and small date varieties

Y# 1016 100 YUAN
31.1320 g., 0.9990 Gold 1.0000 oz. AGW **Obv:** Temple of Heaven **Rev:** Panda seated on rock **Note:** Large and small date varieties exist.

Date	Mintage	F	VF	XF	Unc	BU
1998	—	—	—	—	—	BV+10%

Y# 1017 100 YUAN
31.1320 g., 0.9990 Gold 1.0000 oz. AGW **Obv:** Temple of Heaven **Rev:** Panda on ledge **Note:** Large and small date varieties exist.

Date	Mintage	F	VF	XF	Unc	BU
1999	—	—	—	—	—	BV+10%

Y# 949 100 YUAN
31.1036 g., 0.9990 Gold 1.0000 oz. AGW **Obv:** Temple of Heaven **Rev:** Panda seated on leaves **Note:** Large and small date varieties exist.

Date	Mintage	F	VF	XF	Unc	BU
2000	—	—	—	—	—	BV+10%

Note: Domestic Chinese examples struck with mirror fields, overseas examples struck with frosted fields

Y# 1114 100 YUAN
7.7759 g., 0.9990 Gold 0.2498 oz. AGW, 22 mm. **Obv:** Temple of Heaven **Rev:** Panda walking left through bamboo **Edge:** Reeded **Note:** Large and small date varieties exist.

Date	Mintage	F	VF	XF	Unc	BU
2001	30,000	—	—	—	—	185
2001 D	100,000	—	—	—	—	185

Y# 1158 100 YUAN
7.7759 g., 0.9999 Gold 0.25 oz. AGW **Subject:** Panda **Note:** Large and small date varieties exist.

Date	Mintage	F	VF	XF	Unc	BU
2003	—	—	—	—	—	185

Y# 1174 100 YUAN
7.7759 g., 0.9999 Gold 0.25 oz. AGW **Subject:** Panda **Note:** Large and small date varieties exist.

Date	Mintage	F	VF	XF	Unc	BU
2004	—	—	—	—	—	185

Y# 1105 200 YUAN
15.5518 g., 0.9990 Gold 0.4995 oz. AGW, 27 mm. **Obv:** Temple of Heaven **Rev:** Panda in bamboo forest **Edge:** Slanted reeding **Note:** Photo reduced. Large and small date varieties exist.

Date	Mintage	F	VF	XF	Unc	BU
2001	—	—	—	—	—	370
2001 D	100,000	—	—	—	—	370

Y# 1162 200 YUAN
15.5519 g., 0.9999 Gold 0.5 oz. AGW **Subject:** Panda **Note:** Large and small date varieties exist.

Date	Mintage	F	VF	XF	Unc	BU
2003	—	—	—	—	—	370

Y# 1175 200 YUAN
15.5519 g., 0.9990 Gold 0.4995 oz. AGW **Subject:** Panda **Note:** Large and small date varieties exist.

Date	Mintage	F	VF	XF	Unc	BU
2004	—	—	—	—	—	370

Y# 147 500 YUAN
155.5150 g., 0.9990 Gold 5.0000 oz. AGW, 60 mm. **Obv:** Temple of Heaven **Rev:** Panda with cub, denomination below **Note:** Photo reduced.

Date	Mintage	F	VF	XF	Unc	BU
1987 Proof	3,000	BV+15%				

Y# 233 500 YUAN
155.5150 g., 0.9990 Gold 5.0000 oz. AGW **Obv:** Temple of Heaven **Rev:** Two pandas in tree, denomination upper left

Date	Mintage	F	VF	XF	Unc	BU
1988 Proof	3,000	BV+15%				

Y# 369 500 YUAN
155.5150 g., 0.9990 Gold 5.0000 oz. AGW **Obv:** Temple of Heaven, date below **Rev:** Pandas

Date	Mintage	F	VF	XF	Unc	BU
1992 Proof	99	BV+25%				

Y# 761 500 YUAN
155.5150 g., 0.9990 Gold 5.0000 oz. AGW **Obv:** Temple of Heaven **Rev:** Two pandas climbing tree stumps

Date	Mintage	F	VF	XF	Unc	BU
1993 Proof	99	BV+25%				

Y# 639 500 YUAN
155.5150 g., 0.9990 Gold 5.0000 oz. AGW **Obv:** Temple of Heaven **Rev:** Two pandas, one in tree, denomination above

Date	Mintage	F	VF	XF	Unc	BU
1994 Proof	99	BV+25%				

Y# 1164 500 YUAN
31.1320 g., 0.9999 Gold 1.0008 oz. AGW **Subject:** Panda **Note:** Large and small date varieties exist.

Date	Mintage	F	VF	XF	Unc	BU
2003	—	—	—	—	—	750

Y# 1176 500 YUAN
31.1035 g., 0.9999 Gold 0.9999 oz. AGW **Subject:** Panda **Note:** Large and small date varieties exist.

Date	Mintage	F	VF	XF	Unc	BU
2004	—	—	—	—	—	750

Y# 66 1000 YUAN
373.2360 g., 0.9990 Gold 12.0000 oz. AGW, 70 mm. **Obv:** Temple of Heaven **Rev:** Panda seated left, denomination belo0w **Note:** Photo reduced.

Date	Mintage	F	VF	XF	Unc	BU
1984 Proof	250	BV+25%				

Note: A typical sealed proof exhibits some scuffing and is valued as above, while perfect examples can bring up to a 50% premium

Y# 118.1 1000 YUAN
373.2360 g., 0.9990 Gold 12.0000 oz. AGW, 70 mm. **Obv:** Temple of Heaven **Rev:** Panda eating bamboo shoot with cub, denomination at right **Note:** Photo reduced.

Date	Mintage	F	VF	XF	Unc	BU
1986 Proof	2,550	BV+15%				

Y# 118.2 1000 YUAN
373.2360 g., 0.9990 Gold 12.0000 oz. AGW **Obv:** Temple of Heaven **Rev:** Panda eating bamboo shoot with cub **Edge:** Plain

Date	Mintage	F	VF	XF	Unc	BU
1986 Proof	—					

Note: 2 known; Last traded privately at $45,000

CHINA, PEOPLE'S REPUBLIC

Y# 157 1000 YUAN
373.2360 g., 0.9990 Gold 12.0000 oz. AGW **Obv:** Temple of Heaven **Rev:** Panda with cub, denomination below **Shape:** 70 **Note:** Photo reduced.

Date	Mintage	F	VF	XF	Unc	BU
1987 Proof	2,445	BV+15%				

Y# 234 1000 YUAN
373.2360 g., 0.9990 Gold 12.0000 oz. AGW **Obv:** Temple of Heaven **Rev:** Pandas in tree **Note:** Similar to 500 Yuan, KM#233.

Date	Mintage	F	VF	XF	Unc	BU
1988 Proof	1,650	BV+15%				

Y# 282 1000 YUAN
373.2360 g., 0.9990 Gold 12.0000 oz. AGW, 70 mm. **Obv:** Temple of Heaven **Rev:** Three pandas, denomination upper right

Date	Mintage	F	VF	XF	Unc	BU
1990 Proof	500	BV+20%				

Y# 371 1000 YUAN
373.2360 g., 0.9990 Gold 12.0000 oz. AGW **Obv:** Temple of Heaven, date below **Rev:** Pandas

Date	Mintage	F	VF	XF	Unc	BU
1991 Proof	400	BV+20%				

Y# 372 1000 YUAN
373.2360 g., 0.9990 Gold 12.0000 oz. AGW **Obv:** Temple of Heaven **Rev:** Pandas

Date	Mintage	F	VF	XF	Unc	BU
1992 Proof	99	BV+30%				

Y# 762 1000 YUAN
373.2360 g., 0.9990 Gold 12.0000 oz. AGW **Obv:** Temple of Heaven **Rev:** Panda family of three

Date	Mintage	F	VF	XF	Unc	BU
1993 Proof	99	BV+30%				

Y# 1089 1000 YUAN
373.2420 g., 0.9990 Gold 11.988 oz. AGW, 70 mm. **Obv:** Temple of Heaven **Rev:** Panda and two cubs at water's edge **Edge:** Reeded

Date	Mintage	F	VF	XF	Unc	BU
1994 Proof	99	BV+30%				

Y# 1090 1000 YUAN
373.2420 g., 0.9990 Gold 11.988 oz. AGW, 70 mm. **Obv:** Temple of Heaven **Rev:** Two adult pandas with cub **Edge:** Reeded **Note:** Photo reduced.

Date	Mintage	F	VF	XF	Unc	BU
1995 Proof	99	BV+30%				

Y# 961 2000 YUAN
1000.0000 g., 0.9990 Gold 32.1500 oz. AGW **Obv:** Temple of Heaven **Rev:** Panda **Note:** Large and small date varieties exist.

Date	Mintage	F	VF	XF	Unc	BU
1997 Proof	58	BV+30%				

Y# 1036 2000 YUAN
1000.0000 g., 0.9990 Gold 32.1500 oz. AGW **Obv:** Temple of Heaven **Rev:** Panda **Note:** Large and small date varieties exist.

Date	Mintage	F	VF	XF	Unc	BU
1998 Proof	58	BV+20%				

Y# 972 2000 YUAN
1000.2108 g., 0.9990 Gold 32.1253 oz. AGW **Obv:** Temple of Heaven **Rev:** Panda on rock **Note:** Large and small date varieties exist.

Date	Mintage	F	VF	XF	Unc	BU
1999 Proof	68	BV+30%				

Y# 358 10000 YUAN
4851.6001 g., 0.9990 Gold 156.000 oz. AGW **Subject:** 10th Anniversary of Gold Panda Issue **Obv:** Temple of Heaven **Rev:** Panda on branch, denomination at right, in center of 10 panda coin designs

Date	Mintage	F	VF	XF	Unc	BU
1991 Proof, Rare	10	—	—	—	—	—

Y# 1138 10000 YUAN
321.5000 g., 0.9999 Gold 10.3354 oz. AGW **Subject:** Panda **Note:** Large and small date varieties exist.

Date	Mintage	F	VF	XF	Unc	BU
2001	68	—	—	—	—	17,000

Y# 1165 10000 YUAN
1000.0000 g., 0.9999 Gold 32.1475 oz. AGW **Subject:** Panda **Note:** Large and small date varieties exist.

Date	Mintage	F	VF	XF	Unc	BU
2003	—	—	—	—	—BV+25%	

Y# 1177 10000 YUAN
1000.0000 g., 0.9999 Gold 32.1475 oz. AGW **Subject:** Panda **Note:** Large and small date varieties exist.

Date	Mintage	F	VF	XF	Unc	BU
2004	68	—	—	—	—BV+25%	

GOLD BULLION COINAGE
Lunar Series

Y# 901 10 YUAN
3.1103 g., 0.9990 Gold .1000 oz. AGW **Subject:** Year of the Ox **Obv:** Mingyuan Pavilion **Rev:** Calf

Date	Mintage	F	VF	XF	Unc	BU
1997 Proof	48,000	Value: 95.00				

Y# 924 10 YUAN
3.1103 g., 0.9990 Gold .1000 oz. AGW **Subject:** Year of the Tiger **Obv:** Badaling building, date below **Rev:** Tiger cub, denomination at right

Date	Mintage	F	VF	XF	Unc	BU
1998 Proof	48,000	Value: 100				

Y# 925 10 YUAN
3.1103 g., 0.9990 Gold .1000 oz. AGW **Subject:** Year of the Tiger **Obv:** Badaling building, date below **Rev:** Multicolor tiger head, facing, denomination at right

Date	Mintage	F	VF	XF	Unc	BU
1998 Proof	30,000	Value: 265				

Y# 991 10 YUAN
3.1103 g., 0.9990 Gold .1000 oz. AGW **Rev:** Multicolor rabbit

Date	Mintage	F	VF	XF	Unc	BU
1999 Proof	30,000	Value: 225				

Y# 980 10 YUAN
3.1103 g., 0.9990 Gold .1000 oz. AGW **Subject:** Year of the Rabbit

Date	Mintage	F	VF	XF	Unc	BU
1999 Proof	48,000	Value: 95.00				

Y# 992 10 YUAN
3.1103 g., 0.9990 Gold .1000 oz. AGW **Subject:** Year of the Dragon

Date	Mintage	F	VF	XF	Unc	BU
2000 Proof	48,000	Value: 165				

Y# 1006 50 YUAN
15.5518 g., 0.9990 Gold .5000 oz. AGW **Subject:** Year of the Dragon **Shape:** Fan

Date	Mintage	F	VF	XF	Unc	BU
2000	6,600	—	—	—	—	575

Y# 1141.2 50 YUAN
3.1105 g., 0.9999 Gold 0.1 oz. AGW **Subject:** Year of the Snake **Note:** Multicolor

Date	Mintage	F	VF	XF	Unc	BU
2001	30,000	—	—	—	—	145

Y# 1043 50 YUAN
3.1104 g., 0.9990 Gold .1000 oz. AGW **Subject:** Year of the Snake

Date	Mintage	F	VF	XF	Unc	BU
2001	48,000	—	—	—	—	95.00

Y# 1141.1 50 YUAN
3.1103 g., 0.9990 Gold 0.0999 oz. AGW **Subject:** Year of the Snake

Date	Mintage	F	VF	XF	Unc	BU
2001	48,000	—	—	—	—	110

Y# 1143.1 50 YUAN
3.1050 g., 0.9999 Gold 0.0998 oz. AGW **Subject:** Year of the Horse

Date	Mintage	F	VF	XF	Unc	BU
2002	48,000	—	—	—	—	140

Y# 1144 50 YUAN
15.5500 g., 0.9999 Gold 0.4994 oz. AGW **Subject:** Year of the Horse **Shape:** Fan

Date	Mintage	F	VF	XF	Unc	BU
2002	6,600	—	—	—	—	650

Y# 1143.2 50 YUAN
3.1050 g., 0.9999 Gold 0.0998 oz. AGW **Subject:** Year of the Horse **Note:** Multicolor

Date	Mintage	F	VF	XF	Unc	BU
2002	30,000	—	—	—	—	275

Y# 1155.2 50 YUAN
3.1105 g., 0.9999 Gold 0.1 oz. AGW **Subject:** Year of the Goat **Note:** Multicolor

Date	Mintage	F	VF	XF	Unc	BU
2003	30,000	—	—	—	—	200

Y# 1155.1 50 YUAN
3.1103 g., 0.9999 Gold 0.1 oz. AGW **Subject:** Year of the Goat

Date	Mintage	F	VF	XF	Unc	BU
2003	48,000	—	—	—	—	110

Y# 1156 50 YUAN
15.5517 g., 0.9999 Gold 0.4999 oz. AGW **Subject:** Year of the Goat

Date	Mintage	F	VF	XF	Unc	BU
2003	6,600	—	—	—	—	485

Y# 1167.1 50 YUAN
3.1103 g., 0.9999 Gold 0.1 oz. AGW **Subject:** Year of the Monkey

Date	Mintage	F	VF	XF	Unc	BU
2004	48,000	—	—	—	—	140

Y# 1167.2 50 YUAN
3.1103 g., 0.9999 Gold 0.1 oz. AGW **Subject:** Year of the Monkey **Note:** Multicolor.

Date	Mintage	F	VF	XF	Unc	BU
2004	30,000	—	—	—	—	275

Y# 1226 50 YUAN
3.1103 g., 0.9999 Gold 0.0999 oz. AGW, 18 mm. **Obv:** Dog-shaped belt-hook from ancient Chinese bronze ware, decorative design of dog tail-shaped plant leaves **Rev:** 2 smart dogs

Date	Mintage	F	VF	XF	Unc	BU
2006	60,000	—	—	—	—	110

Y# 175 100 YUAN
31.1320 g., 0.9990 Gold 1.0000 oz. AGW **Subject:** Year of the Dragon **Obv:** Temple of Heaven **Rev:** 2 floating dragons

Date	Mintage	F	VF	XF	Unc	BU
1988 Proof	10,000	BV+10%				

Y# 184 100 YUAN
31.1320 g., 0.9990 Gold 1.0000 oz. AGW **Subject:** Year of the Snake **Obv:** National emblem **Rev:** Snake left, denomination below

Date	Mintage	F	VF	XF	Unc	BU
1989 Proof	3,000	BV+10%				

140 CHINA, PEOPLE'S REPUBLIC

Y# 225 100 YUAN
31.1320 g., 0.9990 Gold 1.0000 oz. AGW **Subject:** Year of the Horse **Obv:** National emblem, date below **Rev:** Prancing horse left, denomination lower right

Date	Mintage	F	VF	XF	Unc	BU
1990 Proof	6,000	BV+10%				

Y# 274 100 YUAN
31.1320 g., 0.9990 Gold 1.0000 oz. AGW **Subject:** Year of the Goat **Obv:** National emblem **Rev:** Two goats butting heads, denomination below

Date	Mintage	F	VF	XF	Unc	BU
1991 Proof	1,800	BV+15%				

Y# 295 100 YUAN
31.1035 g., 0.9990 Gold 1.0000 oz. AGW **Subject:** Year of the Monkey **Rev:** Monkey seated on branch, denomination at left

Date	Mintage	F	VF	XF	Unc	BU
1992 Proof	1,800	BV+15%				

Y# 568 100 YUAN
15.5517 g., 0.9170 Gold .5000 oz. AGW **Subject:** Year of the Rooster **Obv:** City gate, date below **Rev:** Rooster with sunflowers, denomination at left **Shape:** Scalloped

Date	Mintage	F	VF	XF	Unc	BU
1993 Proof	2,300	BV+15%				

Y# 570 100 YUAN
31.1035 g., 0.9990 Gold 1.0000 oz. AGW **Subject:** Year of the Rooster **Obv:** National emblem **Rev:** Rooster and hen, denomination at left

Date	Mintage	F	VF	XF	Unc	BU
1993 Proof	1,900	BV+15%				

Y# 397 100 YUAN
31.1320 g., 0.9990 Gold 1.0000 oz. AGW **Subject:** Year of the Dog **Rev:** Two dogs, denomination lower left

Date	Mintage	F	VF	XF	Unc	BU
1994 Proof	1,800	BV+15%				

Y# 780 100 YUAN
16.3980 g., 0.9160 Gold .5000 oz. AGW **Subject:** Year of the Dog **Obv:** Phoenix Pavilion, date below **Rev:** Lap dog, denomination at left **Shape:** Scalloped

Date	Mintage	F	VF	XF	Unc	BU
1994 Proof	2,300	BV+20%				

Y# 451 100 YUAN
31.1030 g., 0.9990 Gold 1.0000 oz. AGW **Subject:** Year of the Pig **Obv:** National emblem, date below **Rev:** Pig, denomination at right

Date	Mintage	F	VF	XF	Unc	BU
1995 Proof	1,800	BV+15%				

Y# 453 100 YUAN
15.5557 g., 0.9990 Gold .5000 oz. AGW **Subject:** Year of the Pig **Obv:** Building, date below **Rev:** Two pigs, denomination at lower left **Shape:** Scalloped

Date	Mintage	F	VF	XF	Unc	BU
1995 Proof	2,300	BV+20%				

Y# 586 100 YUAN
31.1035 g., 0.9990 Gold 1.0000 oz. AGW **Subject:** Year of the Rat **Rev:** Rat by oil lamp, denomination below

Date	Mintage	F	VF	XF	Unc	BU
1996 Proof	1,800	BV+20%				

Y# 856 100 YUAN
16.9779 g., 0.9160 Gold .5000 oz. AGW **Subject:** Year of the Rat **Obv:** Dengdu Pavilion, date below **Rev:** Rat on corn cob, denomination upper left **Shape:** Scalloped

Date	Mintage	F	VF	XF	Unc	BU
1996 Proof	2,300	BV+25%				

Y# 670 100 YUAN
15.5557 g., 0.9990 Gold .5000 oz. AGW **Subject:** Year of the Ox **Shape:** Scalloped

Date	Mintage	F	VF	XF	Unc	BU
1997 Proof	2,300	BV+20%				

Y# 900 100 YUAN
31.1035 g., 0.9990 Gold 1.0000 oz. AGW **Subject:** Year of the Ox **Obv:** National emblem, date below **Rev:** Ox, denomination below

Date	Mintage	F	VF	XF	Unc	BU
1997 Proof	1,600	BV+15%				

Y# 929 100 YUAN
31.1035 g., 0.9990 Gold 1.0000 oz. AGW **Subject:** Year of the Tiger **Obv:** State seal **Rev:** Tiger

Date	Mintage	F	VF	XF	Unc	BU
1998 Proof	1,600	BV+15%				

Y# 1015 100 YUAN
15.5557 g., 0.9990 Gold .5000 oz. AGW **Subject:** Year of the Tiger **Shape:** Scalloped

Date	Mintage	F	VF	XF	Unc	BU
1998 Proof	2,300	BV+20%				

Y# 1018 100 YUAN
31.1035 g., 0.9990 Gold 1.0000 oz. AGW **Subject:** Year of the Rabbit

Date	Mintage	F	VF	XF	Unc	BU
1999 Proof	—	BV+25%				

Y# 1019 100 YUAN
15.5551 g., 0.9990 Gold .5000 oz. AGW **Subject:** Year of the Rabbit **Shape:** Scalloped

Date	Mintage	F	VF	XF	Unc	BU
1999 Prof	—	BV+20%				

Y# 1051 100 YUAN
15.5518 g., 0.9160 Gold .4580 oz. AGW **Rev:** Dragons **Shape:** Scalloped

Date	Mintage	F	VF	XF	Unc	BU
2000 Proof	2,300	Value: 750				

Y# 45 150 YUAN
8.0000 g., 0.9170 Gold .2359 oz. AGW **Subject:** Year of the Pig **Obv:** Hillside pagoda, waterfront, date lower right **Rev:** Two pigs, denomination below

Date	Mintage	F	VF	XF	Unc	BU
1983 Proof	2,035	Value: 900				

Y# 60 150 YUAN
8.0000 g., 0.9170 Gold .2359 oz. AGW **Subject:** Year of the Rat **Obv:** Fortress, date lower right **Rev:** Rat with squash, denomination below. **Rev. Designer:** Qi Baishi

Date	Mintage	F	VF	XF	Unc	BU
1984 Proof	2,248	Value: 2,400				

CHINA, PEOPLE'S REPUBLIC 141

Y# 79 150 YUAN
8.0000 g., 0.9170 Gold .2359 oz. AGW **Subject:** Year of the Ox
Obv: Houseboat in harbor **Rev:** Ox left, denomination below
Date	Mintage	F	VF	XF	Unc	BU
1985 Proof	Est. 16,000	Value: 190				

Note: 5,000 pieces were struck and issued in boxes with certificates and are valued at $275

Y# 99 150 YUAN
8.0000 g., 0.9170 Gold .2359 oz. AGW **Subject:** Year of the Tiger **Obv:** Qing Dynasty Palace, date below **Rev:** Tiger advancing left, after a painting by He Ziang Ning, denomination above
Date	Mintage	F	VF	XF	Unc	BU
1986 Proof	5,480	Value: 400				

Y# 123 150 YUAN
8.0000 g., 0.9170 Gold .2359 oz. AGW **Subject:** Year of the Rabbit **Obv:** Pagoda, date below **Rev:** Two rabbits, denomination below **Rev. Designer:** Lin Ji Yon
Date	Mintage	F	VF	XF	Unc	BU
1987 Proof	4,780	Value: 285				

Y# 144 150 YUAN
8.0000 g., 0.9170 Gold .2359 oz. AGW **Subject:** Year of the Dragon **Obv:** Great Wall of China, date below **Rev:** Dragon attacking, denomination below
Date	Mintage	F	VF	XF	Unc	BU
1988 Proof	7,600	Value: 285				

Y# 180 150 YUAN
8.0000 g., 0.9170 Gold .2359 oz. AGW **Subject:** Year of the Snake **Obv:** Shanhaiguan Pass Gate, date below **Rev:** Snake left, denomination below
Date	Mintage	F	VF	XF	Unc	BU
1989 Proof	7,500	Value: 210				

Y# 227 150 YUAN
8.0000 g., 0.9170 Gold .2359 oz. AGW **Subject:** Year of the Horse **Obv:** Temple of Confucius, date below **Rev:** Horse galloping, denomination at left
Date	Mintage	F	VF	XF	Unc	BU
1990 Proof	7,500	Value: 260				

Y# 276 150 YUAN
8.0000 g., 0.9170 Gold .2359 oz. AGW **Subject:** Year of the Goat **Obv:** Chinese building and legend **Rev:** Goat reclining, denomination below
Date	Mintage	F	VF	XF	Unc	BU
1991 Proof	7,500	Value: 210				

Y# 291 150 YUAN
8.0000 g., 0.9170 Gold .2359 oz. AGW **Subject:** Year of the Monkey **Obv:** Pavilion of Emperor Teng **Rev:** Monkey sitting, denomination at right
Date	Mintage	F	VF	XF	Unc	BU
1992 Proof	5,000	Value: 285				

Y# 39 200 YUAN
8.4700 g., 0.9170 Gold .2497 oz. AGW **Subject:** Year of the Dog **Obv:** Temple of Heaven, date below **Rev:** Dog, denomination below
Date	Mintage	F	VF	XF	Unc	BU
1982 Proof	2,500	Value: 525				

Y# 1044 200 YUAN
15.5518 g., 0.9990 Gold .5000 oz. AGW **Subject:** Year of the Snake **Rev:** Fan
Date	Mintage	F	VF	XF	Unc	BU
2001	6,600	—	—	—	—	450

Y# 1045 200 YUAN
15.5518 g., 0.9990 Gold .5000 oz. AGW **Subject:** Year of the Snake **Shape:** Scalloped
Date	Mintage	F	VF	XF	Unc	BU
2001 Proof	2,300	Value: 400				

Y# 1150 200 YUAN
15.5000 g., 0.9990 Gold 0.4978 oz. AGW **Subject:** Year of the Horse
Date	Mintage	F	VF	XF	Unc	BU
2002	2,300	—	—	—	—	700

Y# 1161 200 YUAN
15.5519 g., 0.9999 Gold 0.5 oz. AGW **Subject:** Year of the Goat
Date	Mintage	F	VF	XF	Unc	BU
2003	2,300	—	—	—	—	525

Y# 1169 200 YUAN
15.5519 g., 0.9999 Gold 0.5 oz. AGW **Subject:** Year of the Monkey
Date	Mintage	F	VF	XF	Unc	BU
2004	2,300	—	—	—	—	800

Y# 33 250 YUAN
8.0000 g., 0.9170 Gold .2358 oz. AGW **Subject:** Year of the Rooster **Obv:** Monument, date lower left **Rev:** Rooster left, denomination at left
Date	Mintage	F	VF	XF	Unc	BU
1981 Proof	5,015	Value: 475				

Y# 145 500 YUAN
155.5150 g., 0.9990 Gold 5.0000 oz. AGW, 60 mm.
Subject: Year of the Dragon **Obv:** Great Wall **Rev:** Inner circle holds three dragons, four dragons surround, denomination below
Note: Photo reduced.
Date	Mintage	F	VF	XF	Unc	BU
1988 Proof	3,000	Value: 3,750				

Y# 181 500 YUAN
155.5150 g., 0.9990 Gold 5.0000 oz. AGW, 60 mm.
Subject: Year of the Snake **Obv:** National emblem **Rev:** Snake left, denomination below, within beaded circle **Note:** Photo reduced.
Date	Mintage	F	VF	XF	Unc	BU
1989 Proof	500	Value: 3,500				

Y# 228 500 YUAN
155.5150 g., 0.9990 Gold 5.0000 oz. AGW, 60 mm.
Obv: Temple of Confucius **Rev:** Two horses drinking water, denomination below **Note:** Photo reduced.
Date	Mintage	F	VF	XF	Unc	BU
1990 Proof	500	Value: 3,750				

CHINA, PEOPLE'S REPUBLIC

Y# 277 500 YUAN
155.5150 g., 0.9990 Gold 5.0000 oz. AGW, 60 mm.
Subject: Year of the Goat **Obv:** Two goats, one nursing offspring, denomination above **Note:** Photo reduced.

Date	Mintage	F	VF	XF	Unc	BU
1991 Proof	250	Value: 4,000				

Y# 292 500 YUAN
155.5150 g., 0.9990 Gold 5.0000 oz. AGW, 60 mm.
Subject: Year of the Monkey **Obv:** Chinese building **Rev:** Monkey seated, denomination at right **Note:** Photo reduced.

Date	Mintage	F	VF	XF	Unc	BU
1992 Proof	99	Value: 6,000				

Y# 384 500 YUAN
155.5150 g., 0.9990 Gold 5.0000 oz. AGW **Subject:** Year of the Rooster

Date	Mintage	F	VF	XF	Unc	BU
1993 Proof	99	Value: 5,000				

Y# 389 500 YUAN
155.5150 g., 0.9990 Gold 5.0000 oz. AGW **Subject:** Year of the Dog

Date	Mintage	F	VF	XF	Unc	BU
1994 Proof	99	Value: 5,000				

Y# 467 500 YUAN
155.5150 g., 0.9990 Gold 5.0000 oz. AGW **Subject:** Year of the Pig

Date	Mintage	F	VF	XF	Unc	BU
1995 Proof	99	Value: 5,000				

Y# 663 500 YUAN
155.5175 g., 0.9999 Gold 5.0000 oz. AGW **Subject:** Year of the Rat **Rev:** Rat eating grapes, denomination above

Date	Mintage	F	VF	XF	Unc	BU
1996 Proof	99	Value: 5,000				

Y# 672 500 YUAN
155.5175 g., 0.9990 Gold 5.0000 oz. AGW **Subject:** Year of the Ox

Date	Mintage	F	VF	XF	Unc	BU
1997 Proof	99	Value: 4,500				

Y# 1024 500 YUAN
155.5175 g., 0.9990 Gold 5.0000 oz. AGW **Subject:** Year of the Tiger

Date	Mintage	F	VF	XF	Unc	BU
1998 Proof	99	Value: 5,000				

Y# 1025 500 YUAN
155.5175 g., 0.9990 Gold 5.0000 oz. AGW **Subject:** Year of the Rabbit

Date	Mintage	F	VF	XF	Unc	BU
1999 Proof	99	Value: 4,500				

Y# 1027 500 YUAN
155.5175 g., 0.9990 Gold 5.0000 oz. AGW **Subject:** Year of the Dragon **Shape:** Rectangular

Date	Mintage	F	VF	XF	Unc	BU
2000 Proof	108	Value: 5,000				

Y# 1088 500 YUAN
31.1035 g., 0.9990 Gold 0.999 oz. AGW, 32 mm. **Obv:** Temple of Heaven **Rev:** Panda walking through bamboo **Edge:** Reeded

Date	Mintage	F	VF	XF	Unc	BU
2001	—	—	—	—	—BV+15%	
2001 D	150,000	—	—	—	—BV+15%	

Y# 1168 500 YUAN
15.5519 g., 0.9999 Gold 0.5 oz. AGW **Subject:** Year of the Monkey **Shape:** Fan

Date	Mintage	F	VF	XF	Unc	BU
2004	6,600	—	—	—	—	550

Y# 146 1000 YUAN
373.2360 g., 0.9990 Gold 12.0000 oz. AGW, 70 mm.
Subject: Year of the Dragon **Obv:** Great Wall **Rev:** Two facing dragons, denomination below **Note:** Photo reduced.

Date	Mintage	F	VF	XF	Unc	BU
1988 Proof	518	Value: 8,750				

Y# 182 1000 YUAN
373.2360 g., 0.9990 Gold 12.0000 oz. AGW, 70 mm.
Subject: Year of the Snake **Obv:** National emblem **Rev:** Snake left within beaded circle, denomination below **Note:** Photo reduced.

Date	Mintage	F	VF	XF	Unc	BU
1989 Proof	200	Value: 8,500				

Y# 229 1000 YUAN
373.2360 g., 0.9990 Gold 12.0000 oz. AGW, 70 mm.
Subject: Year of the Horse **Obv:** Temple of Confucius **Rev:** Two horses running, denomination below **Note:** Photo reduced.

Date	Mintage	F	VF	XF	Unc	BU
1990 Proof	500	Value: 8,250				

Y# 278 1000 YUAN
373.2360 g., 0.9990 Gold 12.0000 oz. AGW **Subject:** Year of the Goat **Obv:** Chinese building and legend **Rev:** Three goats, denomination at left **Note:** Photo reduced.

Date	Mintage	F	VF	XF	Unc	BU
1991 Proof	200	Value: 8,250				

Y# 293 1000 YUAN
373.2360 g., 0.9990 Gold 12.0000 oz. AGW **Subject:** Year of the Monkey **Obv:** Chinese building **Rev:** Five monkeys, denomination at left **Note:** Photo reduced.

Date	Mintage	F	VF	XF	Unc	BU
1992 Proof	99	Value: 9,000				

Y# 385 1000 YUAN
373.2360 g., 0.9990 Gold 12.0000 oz. AGW **Subject:** Year of the Rooster

Date	Mintage	F	VF	XF	Unc	BU
1993 Proof	99	Value: 8,750				

Y# 390 1000 YUAN
373.2360 g., 0.9990 Gold 12.0000 oz. AGW **Subject:** Year of the Dog

Date	Mintage	F	VF	XF	Unc	BU
1994 Proof	99	Value: 8,750				

Y# 468 1000 YUAN
373.2360 g., 0.9990 Gold 12.0000 oz. AGW **Subject:** Year of the Pig

Date	Mintage	F	VF	XF	Unc	BU
1995 Proof	99	Value: 9,000				

Y# 664 1000 YUAN
373.2360 g., 0.9990 Gold 12.0000 oz. AGW **Subject:** Year of the Rat

Date	Mintage	F	VF	XF	Unc	BU
1996 Proof	99	Value: 8,750				

CHINA, PEOPLE'S REPUBLIC 143

Y# 673 1000 YUAN
373.2360 g., 0.9990 Gold 12.0000 oz. AGW **Subject:** Year of the Ox

Date	Mintage	F	VF	XF	Unc	BU
1997 Proof	99	Value: 8,750				

Y# 1030 1000 YUAN
373.2360 g., 0.9990 Gold 12.0000 oz. AGW **Subject:** Year of the Tiger

Date	Mintage	F	VF	XF	Unc	BU
1998 Proof	99	Value: 8,750				

Y# 1031 1000 YUAN
373.2360 g., 0.9990 Gold 12.0000 oz. AGW **Subject:** Year of the Rabbit

Date	Mintage	F	VF	XF	Unc	BU
1999 Proof	99	Value: 8,750				

Y# 702 2000 YUAN
1000.0000 g., 0.9990 Gold 32.1500 oz. AGW, 100 mm. **Subject:** Completion of 150 Yuan Lunar Animal Coin Series **Obv:** Monument divides date and denomination within circle **Rev:** Ying/Yang symbol within octagon, twelve animal coins surround **Note:** Photo reduced.

Date	Mintage	F	VF	XF	Unc	BU
1992 Proof	21	Value: 35,000				

Y# 660 2000 YUAN
1000.0000 g., 0.9990 Gold 32.1500 oz. AGW **Subject:** Year of the Pig **Edge:** Scalloped

Date	Mintage	F	VF	XF	Unc	BU
1995 Proof	15	Value: 28,500				

Y# 665 2000 YUAN
1000.0000 g., 0.9990 Gold 32.1500 oz. AGW **Subject:** Year of the Rat **Shape:** Scalloped

Date	Mintage	F	VF	XF	Unc	BU
1996 Proof	15	Value: 28,500				

Y# 674 2000 YUAN
1000.0000 g., 0.9990 Gold 32.1500 oz. AGW **Subject:** Year of the Ox

Date	Mintage	F	VF	XF	Unc	BU
1997 Proof	15	Value: 28,500				

Y# 967 2000 YUAN
1000.0000 g., 0.9990 Gold 32.1500 oz. AGW **Subject:** Year of the Tiger **Shape:** Scalloped

Date	Mintage	F	VF	XF	Unc	BU
1998 Proof	15	Value: 28,500				

Y# 975 2000 YUAN
1000.0000 g., 0.9990 Gold 32.1500 oz. AGW **Subject:** Year of the Rabbit **Shape:** Scalloped

Date	Mintage	F	VF	XF	Unc	BU
1999 Proof	15	Value: 28,500				

Y# 977 2000 YUAN
1000.2108 g., 0.9990 Gold 32.1253 oz. AGW, Scalloped mm. **Subject:** Year of the Dragon

Date	Mintage	F	VF	XF	Unc	BU
2000 Proof	15	Value: 32,000				

Y# 1046 2000 YUAN
155.5175 g., 0.9990 Gold 5.0000 oz. AGW **Subject:** Year of the Snake **Shape:** Rectangle

Date	Mintage	F	VF	XF	Unc	BU
2001 Proof	118	Value: 3,750				

Y# 1152 2000 YUAN
155.5175 g., 0.9999 Gold 4.9995 oz. AGW **Subject:** Year of the Horse

Date	Mintage	F	VF	XF	Unc	BU
2002	—	—	—	—	—	5,000

Y# 1163 2000 YUAN
155.5190 g., 0.9999 Gold 4.9995 oz. AGW **Subject:** Year of the Goat

Date	Mintage	F	VF	XF	Unc	BU
2003	—	—	—	—	—	4,500

Y# 1170 2000 YUAN
155.1750 g., 0.9999 Gold 4.9885 oz. AGW **Subject:** Year of the Monkey

Date	Mintage	F	VF	XF	Unc	BU
2004	—	—	—	—	—	5,000

Y# 1052 10000 YUAN
1000.2108 g., 0.9990 Gold 32.1575 oz. AGW **Subject:** Year of the Snake **Rev:** Dragons **Shape:** Scalloped

Date	Mintage	F	VF	XF	Unc	BU
2000 Proof	15	Value: 30,000				

Y# 1047 10000 YUAN
1000.2108 g., 0.9990 Gold 32.1575 oz. AGW **Subject:** Year of the Snake **Shape:** Scalloped

Date	Mintage	F	VF	XF	Unc	BU
2001 Proof	15	Value: 28,500				

Y# 1153 10000 YUAN
1000.0000 g., 0.9999 Gold 32.1475 oz. AGW **Subject:** Year of the Horse **Shape:** Scalloped

Date	Mintage	F	VF	XF	Unc	BU
2002	15	—	—	—	—	35,000

Y# 1166 10000 YUAN
1000.0000 g., 0.9999 Gold 32.1475 oz. AGW **Subject:** Year of the Goat

Date	Mintage	F	VF	XF	Unc	BU
2003	15	—	—	—	—	35,000

Y# 1171 10000 YUAN
1000.0000 g., 0.9999 Gold 32.1475 oz. AGW **Subject:** Year of the Monkey

Date	Mintage	F	VF	XF	Unc	BU
2004	15	—	—	—	—	35,000

PLATINUM BULLION COINAGE
Lunar Series

Y# 176 100 YUAN
31.1030 g., 0.9995 Platinum 1.0000 oz. APW **Subject:** Year of the Dragon **Obv:** Temple of Heaven **Rev:** 2 floating dragons

Date	Mintage	F	VF	XF	Unc	BU
1988 Proof	2,000	BV+20%				

Y# 185 100 YUAN
31.1030 g., 0.9995 Platinum 1.0000 oz. APW **Subject:** Year of the Snake **Obv:** National emblem **Rev:** Snake, left, denomination below

Date	Mintage	F	VF	XF	Unc	BU
1989 Proof	1,000	BV+20%				

Y# 274a 100 YUAN
31.1030 g., 0.9995 Platinum 1.0000 oz. APW **Subject:** Year of the Goat **Obv:** National emblem **Rev:** Two goats butting heads, denomination below

Date	Mintage	F	VF	XF	Unc	BU
1991 Proof	500	BV+30%				

Y# 295a 100 YUAN
31.1030 g., 0.9995 Platinum 1.0000 oz. APW **Subject:** Year of the Monkey **Rev:** Monkey seated on branch, denomination at left

Date	Mintage	F	VF	XF	Unc	BU
1992 Proof	300	BV+35%				

Y# 382 100 YUAN
31.1030 g., 0.9995 Platinum 1.0000 oz. APW **Subject:** Year of the Rooster

Date	Mintage	F	VF	XF	Unc	BU
1993 Proof	300	BV+35%				

Y# 397a 100 YUAN
31.1030 g., 0.9995 Platinum 1.0000 oz. APW **Subject:** Year of the Dog

Date	Mintage	F	VF	XF	Unc	BU
1994 Proof	300	BV+35%				

Y# 465 100 YUAN
31.1030 g., 0.9995 Platinum 1.0000 oz. APW **Subject:** Year of the Pig

Date	Mintage	F	VF	XF	Unc	BU
1995 Proof	300	BV+35%				

Y# 900a 100 YUAN
31.1035 g., 0.9995 Platinum 1.0000 oz. APW **Subject:** Year of the Ox **Obv:** National emblem **Rev:** Ox, denomination below

Date	Mintage	F	VF	XF	Unc	BU
1997 Proof	300	BV+35%				

Y# 929a 100 YUAN
31.1035 g., 0.9990 Platinum 1.0000 oz. APW **Subject:** Year of the Tiger **Obv:** National emblem **Rev:** Tiger

Date	Mintage	F	VF	XF	Unc	BU
1998 Proof	300	BV+35%				

Y# 1018a 100 YUAN
31.1035 g., 0.9990 Platinum 1.0000 oz. APW **Subject:** Year of the Rabbit

Date	Mintage	F	VF	XF	Unc	BU
1999 Proof	—	BV+35%				

PLATINUM BULLION COINAGE
Panda Series

Y# 483 5 YUAN
1.5552 g., 0.9995 Platinum .0500 oz. APW **Obv:** Temple of Heaven within circle, date below **Rev:** Panda seated on rock, denomination upper left

Date	Mintage	F	VF	XF	Unc	BU
1993 Proof	2,500	Value: 75.00				

Y# 716a 5 YUAN
1.5552 g., 0.9990 Platinum 0.05 oz. APW **Obv:** Temple of Heaven **Rev:** Panda on branch

Date	Mintage	F	VF	XF	Unc	BU
1997 Prooflike	5,000	—	—	—	—	115

Y# 267 10 YUAN
3.1100 g., 0.9995 Platinum .1000 oz. APW **Obv:** Temple of Heaven, date below **Rev:** Panda with branch, denomination below

Date	Mintage	F	VF	XF	Unc	BU
1990 Proof	4,500	Value: 165				

Y# 484a 10 YUAN
3.1100 g., 0.9995 Platinum .1000 oz. APW **Obv:** Temple of Heaven within circle, date below **Rev:** Panda seated on rock, denomination upper left

Date	Mintage	F	VF	XF	Unc	BU
1993 Proof	2,500	—	—	—	—	165

Y# 432a 10 YUAN
3.1103 g., 0.9995 Platinum .1000 oz. APW **Obv:** Temple of Heaven, date below **Rev:** Seated panda eating, denomination below

Date	Mintage	F	VF	XF	Unc	BU
1994 Prooflike	2,500	—	—	—	—	235

Y# 641a 10 YUAN
3.1103 g., 0.9990 Platinum .1000 oz. APW **Obv:** Temple of Heaven, date below **Rev:** Panda eating bamboo, denomination at left

Date	Mintage	F	VF	XF	Unc	BU
1995 Prooflike	5,000	—	—	—	—	185

Y# 575a 10 YUAN
3.1103 g., 0.9990 Platinum .1000 oz. APW **Obv:** Temple of Heaven, date below **Rev:** Panda in tree

Date	Mintage	F	VF	XF	Unc	BU
1996 Prooflike	2,500	—	—	—	—	235

Y# 717a 10 YUAN
3.1100 g., 0.9990 Platinum .1000 oz. APW **Obv:** Temple of Heaven **Rev:** Panda on branch

Date	Mintage	F	VF	XF	Unc	BU
1997 Prooflike	2,500	—	—	—	—	165

144 CHINA, PEOPLE'S REPUBLIC

Y# 894a 10 YUAN
3.1100 g., 0.9995 Platinum .1000 oz. APW **Obv:** Temple of Heaven, date below **Rev:** Panda on branch

Date	Mintage	F	VF	XF	Unc	BU
1997 Proof	2,500	Value: 140				

Y# 268 25 YUAN
7.7758 g., 0.9995 Platinum .2500 oz. APW **Obv:** Temple of Heaven, date below **Rev:** Panda climbing tree, denomination at right

Date	Mintage	F	VF	XF	Unc	BU
1990 Proof	3,500	Value: 345				

Y# 269 50 YUAN
15.5517 g., 0.9995 Platinum .5000 oz. APW **Obv:** Temple of Heaven, date below **Rev:** Panda eating bamboo on rock, denomination below

Date	Mintage	F	VF	XF	Unc	BU
1990 Proof	2,500	Value: 685				

Y# 159 100 YUAN
31.1030 g., 0.9995 Platinum 1.0000 oz. APW **Obv:** Temple of Heaven, date below **Rev:** Panda grasping bamboo shoot, within circle, denomination below

Date	Mintage	F	VF	XF	Unc	BU
1988 Proof	2,000	BV+20%				

Y# 191a 100 YUAN
31.1030 g., 0.9995 Platinum 1.0000 oz. APW **Obv:** Temple of Heaven, date below **Rev:** Panda reclining, grid behind, denomination lower right

Date	Mintage	F	VF	XF	Unc	BU
1989 Proof	3,000	—	—	—	—	BV+ 20%

Y# 735 100 YUAN
31.1400 g., 0.9995 Platinum 1.0077 oz. APW **Obv:** Temple of Heaven, date below **Rev:** Panda on rock, denomination below

Date	Mintage	F	VF	XF	Unc	BU
1990 Proof	1,300	—	—	—	—	BV+ 30%

Y# 1115 100 YUAN
3.1103 g., 0.9995 Platinum 0.0999 oz. APW, 18 mm. **Subject:** Panda Coinage 20th Anniversary **Obv:** Seated panda design of 1982 **Rev:** Walking panda design of 2002 **Edge:** Reeded

Date	Mintage	F	VF	XF	Unc	BU
2002 Proof	20,000	Value: 200				

BI-METALLIC MEDALLIC BULLION COINAGE
Silver / Gold

Y# 391 10 YUAN
3.1103 g., Bi-Metallic Gold center in Silver ring .1000 oz. **Obv:** Temple of Heaven within circle, date below **Rev:** Panda on branch, denomination above, within circle

Date	Mintage	F	VF	XF	Unc	BU
1992 Proof	2,000	Value: 150				

Y# 463 10 YUAN
3.1103 g., Bi-Metallic Gold center in Silver ring .1000 oz. **Rev:** Phoenix and dragon

Date	Mintage	F	VF	XF	Unc	BU
1994	2,500	—	—	—	—	150

Y# 680 10 YUAN
3.1103 g., Bi-Metallic Gold center in Silver ring .1000 oz. **Obv:** Temple of Heaven within circle, date below **Rev:** Panda tugging bamboo sprig, denomination below, within circle

Date	Mintage	F	VF	XF	Unc	BU
1994 Proof	3,000	Value: 150				

Y# 571 10 YUAN
3.1103 g., Bi-Metallic Gold center in Silver ring .1000 oz. **Obv:** Temple of Heaven, date below **Rev:** Panda at stream, denomination below

Date	Mintage	F	VF	XF	Unc	BU
1995 Proof set	2,000	Value: 150				

Y# 851 10 YUAN
3.1103 g., Bi-Metallic Gold center in Silver ring .1000 oz. **Obv:** Temple of Heaven **Rev:** Panda seated in rock

Date	Mintage	F	VF	XF	Unc	BU
1996 Proof	2,500	Value: 150				

Y# 986 10 YUAN
3.1103 g., Bi-Metallic Gold center in Silver ring .1000 oz. **Obv:** Temple of Heaven, date below **Rev:** Panda climbing tree

Date	Mintage	F	VF	XF	Unc	BU
1997 Proof	2,800	Value: 135				

Y# 301 25 YUAN
7.7758 g., Bi-Metallic Gold center in Silver ring .2500 oz. **Obv:** Temple of Heaven, date below **Rev:** Seated panda, denomination at left, date below

Date	Mintage	F	VF	XF	Unc	BU
1991 Proof	2,000	Value: 285				

Y# 930 25 YUAN
7.7758 g., Bi-Metallic Gold center in Silver ring .2500 oz. **Obv:** Temple of Heaven, date below **Rev:** Panda on rock

Date	Mintage	F	VF	XF	Unc	BU
1993 Proof	2,500	Value: 285				

Y# 544 25 YUAN
7.7758 g., Bi-Metallic Gold center in Silver ring .2500 oz. **Obv:** Temple of Heaven within circle, date below **Rev:** Panda tugging on bamboo sprig, denomination below, within circle, date below

Date	Mintage	F	VF	XF	Unc	BU
1994 Proof	2,500	Value: 255				

Y# 572 25 YUAN
7.7758 g., Bi-Metallic Gold center in Silver ring .2500 oz. **Obv:** Temple of Heaven, date below **Rev:** Panda at stream, denomination below, within circle

Date	Mintage	F	VF	XF	Unc	BU
1995 Proof	2,000	Value: 260				

Y# 852 25 YUAN
7.7759 g., Bi-Metallic Gold center in Silver ring .2500 oz. **Obv:** Temple of Heaven **Rev:** Panda seated on rock

Date	Mintage	F	VF	XF	Unc	BU
1996 Proof	2,500	Value: 255				

Y# 1001 25 YUAN
7.7758 g., 0.9990 Bi-Metallic Gold center in Silver ring .2500 oz. **Obv:** Temple of Heaven, date below **Rev:** Panda climbing tree

Date	Mintage	F	VF	XF	Unc	BU
1997 Proof	2,800	Value: 260				

Y# 266 50 YUAN
15.5517 g., 0.9990 Bi-Metallic Gold center in Silver ring .5000 oz. **Obv:** Temple of Heaven, date below, within circle **Rev:** Panda walking, denomination below, within circle, date below

Date	Mintage	F	VF	XF	Unc	BU
1990 Proof	2,000	Value: 385				

CHINA, PEOPLE'S REPUBLIC

Y# 573 50 YUAN
21.7724 g., 0.9990 Bi-Metallic Gold center in Silver ring .5000 oz. **Obv:** Temple of Heaven within circle, date below **Rev:** Panda at stream, denomination below, within circle

Date	Mintage	F	VF	XF	Unc	BU
1995 Proof	2,000	Value: 395				

Y# 789 50 YUAN
15.5517 g., 9990.0000 Bi-Metallic Gold center in Silver ring .5000 oz. **Obv:** Temple of Heaven **Rev:** Panda approaching water from right

Date	Mintage	F	VF	XF	Unc	BU
1995 Proof	—	—	—	—	320	—

Y# 853 50 YUAN
15.5517 g., 0.9990 Bi-Metallic Gold center in Silver ring .5000 oz. **Obv:** Temple of Heaven **Rev:** Panda seated on rock

Date	Mintage	F	VF	XF	Unc	BU
1996 Proof	2,500	Value: 385				

Y# 1009 50 YUAN
15.5517 g., 0.9990 Bi-Metallic Gold center in Silver ring .5000 oz. **Obv:** Temple of Heaven, date below **Rev:** Panda climbing tree

Date	Mintage	F	VF	XF	Unc	BU
1997 Proof	2,800	Value: 385				

Y# 793 500 YUAN
155.5175 g., 0.9999 Bi-Metallic Gold center in Silver ring 5.0000 oz. **Obv:** Temple of Heaven **Rev:** Two pandas sitting on rock, denomination above, within circle

Date	Mintage	F	VF	XF	Unc	BU
1995 Proof	199	Value: 3,200				

Y# 1020 500 YUAN
155.5175 g., 0.9990 Bi-Metallic Gold center in Silver ring 5.0000 oz. **Obv:** Temple of Heaven, date below **Rev:** Panda

Date	Mintage	F	VF	XF	Unc	BU
1996 Proof	199	Value: 3,250				

Y# 1021 500 YUAN
155.5175 g., 0.9990 Bi-Metallic Gold center in Silver ring 5.0000 oz. **Obv:** Temple of Heaven **Rev:** Two pandas resting near stream

Date	Mintage	F	VF	XF	Unc	BU
1997 Proof	199	Value: 3,250				

MEDALLIC BULLION COINAGE
Gold

X# MB12 1.5 GRAMS
1.5000 g., 0.9999 Gold 0.0482 oz. AGW **Rev:** Yin-yang **Note:** Struck by the Singapore Mint.

Date	Mintage	F	VF	XF	Unc	BU
1984SM Proof	1,500	Value: 40.00				

X# MB32 1/20 OUNCE
1.5551 g., 0.9990 Gold 0.0499 oz. AGW **Subject:** Tokyo International Coin Show - "Tong-Tong"

Date	Mintage	F	VF	XF	Unc	BU
1987 Proof	25,025	Value: 35.00				

X# MB8 1/10 OUNCE
3.1103 g., 0.9990 Gold .1000 oz. AGW **Obv:** Temple of Heaven **Rev:** Panda with bamboo shoot **Note:** Prev. Y#40.

Date	Mintage	F	VF	XF	Unc	BU
1982	75,000	—	—	—	—	90.00

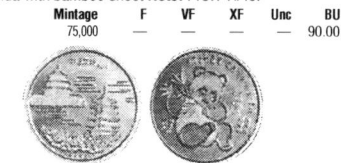

X# MB41 1/10 OUNCE
3.1103 g., 0.9990 Gold 0.0999 oz. AGW **Subject:** Tokyo International Coin Show

Date	Mintage	F	VF	XF	Unc	BU
1989 Proof	30,000	Value: 85.00				

X# MB9 1/4 OUNCE
7.7758 g., 0.9990 Gold 0.2497 oz. AGW **Obv:** Similar to 1 Ounce, Y#43 **Note:** Prev. Y#41.

Date	Mintage	F	VF	XF	Unc	BU
1982	40,000	—	—	—	—	185

Y# 41 (prevY41) 1/4 OUNCE
7.7758 g., 0.9990 Gold .2500 oz. AGW **Obv:** Temple of Heaven **Rev:** Panda with bamboo shoot

Date	Mintage	F	VF	XF	Unc	BU
1982	40,000	—	—	—	175	—
1982	40,000	—	—	—	175	—

X# MB36 1/4 OUNCE
7.7758 g., 0.9990 Gold .2500 oz. AGW **Subject:** Mazu

Date	Mintage	F	VF	XF	Unc	BU
1987	5,000	—	—	—	175	—
1987 Proof	2,000	Value: 190				

X# MB37 1/4 OUNCE
7.7758 g., 0.9990 Gold 0.2497 oz. AGW **Subject:** Sakyamnni Buddha

Date	Mintage	F	VF	XF	Unc	BU
1988	5,000	—	—	—	175	—
1988 Proof	2,000	Value: 190				

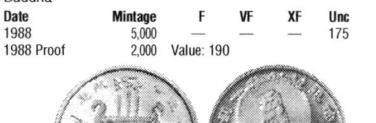

X# MB38 1/4 OUNCE
7.7758 g., 0.9990 Gold 0.2497 oz. AGW **Subject:** Badhisattva Avalokitesvara

Date	Mintage	F	VF	XF	Unc	BU
1988	5,000	—	—	—	175	—
1988 Proof	2,000	Value: 190				

X# MB47 1/4 OUNCE
7.7758 g., 0.9990 Gold 0.2497 oz. AGW **Subject:** Maitreya Buddha

Date	Mintage	F	VF	XF	Unc	BU
1989	5,000	—	—	—	175	—
1989 Proof	2,000	Value: 190				

X# MB49 1/4 OUNCE
7.7758 g., 0.9990 Gold 0.2497 oz. AGW **Subject:** General Guan Yu

Date	Mintage	F	VF	XF	Unc	BU
1989	5,000	—	—	—	175	—
1989 Proof	2,000	Value: 190				

X# MBA10 1/2 OUNCE
15.5517 g., 0.9990 Gold .5000 oz. AGW **Obv:** Temple of Heaven **Rev:** Panda with bamboo shoot

Date	Mintage	F	VF	XF	Unc	BU
1982	13,000	—	—	—	—	385

X# MB43 1/2 OUNCE
15.5517 g., 0.9990 Gold 0.4995 oz. AGW **Subject:** 2nd Hong Kong Coin Exposition - Great Wall

Date	Mintage	F	VF	XF	Unc	BU
1989 Proof	1,300	Value: 375				

X# MB44 1/2 OUNCE
15.5517 g., 0.9990 Gold 0.4995 oz. AGW **Subject:** Munich International Coin Exposition

Date	Mintage	F	VF	XF	Unc	BU
1989 Proof	1,500	Value: 375				

X# MB54 1/2 OUNCE
15.5517 g., 0.9990 Gold 0.4995 oz. AGW **Subject:** 18th New York International Numismatic Convention - Tang Horse

Date	Mintage	F	VF	XF	Unc	BU
1989 Proof	5,000	Value: 365				

146 CHINA, PEOPLE'S REPUBLIC

X# MB60 1/2 OUNCE
15.5517 g., 0.9990 Gold 0.4995 oz. AGW **Subject:** Munich International Coin Exposition

Date	Mintage	F	VF	XF	Unc	BU
1990 Proof	1,500		Value: 375			

X# MBA11 OUNCE
31.1035 g., 0.9990 Gold 1.0000 oz. AGW **Obv:** Temple of Heaven **Rev:** Panda with bamboo shoot

Date	Mintage	F	VF	XF	Unc	BU
1982	16,000	—	—	—	—	850

X# MB7 OUNCE
31.1035 g., 0.9990 Gold 0.999 oz. AGW **Subject:** 1st San Francisco International Coin Expo

Date	Mintage	F	VF	XF	Unc	BU
1987 Proof	3,000		Value: 750			

X# MB14 OUNCE
31.1035 g., 0.9990 Gold 0.999 oz. AGW **Subject:** 96th American Numismtic Association Convention - New Orleans

Date	Mintage	F	VF	XF	Unc	BU
1987 Proof	3,000		Value: 735			

X# MB16 OUNCE
31.1035 g., 0.9990 Gold 0.999 oz. AGW **Subject:** Tokyo International Coin Show - "Tong-Tong"

Date	Mintage	F	VF	XF	Unc	BU
1987 Proof	5,000		Value: 725			

X# MB18 OUNCE
31.1035 g., 0.9990 Gold 0.999 oz. AGW **Subject:** 16th New York International Numismatic Convention

Date	Mintage	F	VF	XF	Unc	BU
1987 Proof	2,000		Value: 735			

X# MB20 OUNCE
31.1035 g., 0.9990 Gold 0.999 oz. AGW **Subject:** Basel International Coin Week

Date	Mintage	F	VF	XF	Unc	BU
1988 Proof	450		Value: 900			

X# MB21 OUNCE
31.1035 g., 0.9990 Gold 0.999 oz. AGW **Note:** Error with "Pt." (platinum die)

Date	Mintage	F	VF	XF	Unc	BU
1988 Proof	550		Value: 850			

X# MB23 OUNCE
31.1035 g., 0.9990 Gold 0.999 oz. AGW **Subject:** 2nd San Francisco International Coin Expo

Date	Mintage	F	VF	XF	Unc	BU
1988 Proof	1,500		Value: 735			

X# MB25 OUNCE
31.1035 g., 0.9990 Gold 0.999 oz. AGW **Subject:** Munich Coin Bourse

Date	Mintage	F	VF	XF	Unc	BU
1988 Proof	2,000		Value: 725			

X# MB27 OUNCE
31.1035 g., 0.9990 Gold 0.999 oz. AGW **Subject:** 1st Hong Kong Coin Exposition - China

Date	Mintage	F	VF	XF	Unc	BU
1988 Proof	800		Value: 750			

X# MB29 OUNCE
31.1035 g., 0.9990 Gold 0.999 oz. AGW **Subject:** 97th American Numismatic Association Convention - Cincinnati

Date	Mintage	F	VF	XF	Unc	BU
1988 Proof	1,000		Value: 750			

X# MB31 OUNCE
31.1035 g., 0.9990 Gold 0.999 oz. AGW **Subject:** American Numismatic Association Convention - New Orleans

Date	Mintage	F	VF	XF	Unc	BU
1988 Proof	3,000		Value: 725			

X# MB51 OUNCE
31.1035 g., 0.9990 Gold 0.999 oz. AGW **Subject:** 3rd San Francisco International Coin Expo

Date	Mintage	F	VF	XF	Unc	BU
1989 Proof	1,500		Value: 725			

X# MB33 5 OUNCES
155.5150 g., 0.9990 Gold 4.9949 oz. AGW, 69 mm. **Subject:** Tokyo International Coin Show - "Tong-Tong" **Note:** Photo reduced.

Date	Mintage	F	VF	XF	Unc	BU
1987 Proof	1,500		Value: 3,500			

X# MB46 5 OUNCES
155.5150 g., 0.9990 Gold 4.9949 oz. AGW **Subject:** Bodhisattva Avalokitesvara

Date	Mintage	F	VF	XF	Unc	BU
1989 Proof	500		Value: 3,600			

X# MB50 5 OUNCES
155.5150 g., 0.9990 Gold 4.9949 oz. AGW **Subject:** General Guan Yu

Date	Mintage	F	VF	XF	Unc	BU
1989 Proof	500		Value: 3,600			

COCOS (KEELING) ISLANDS   147

X# MB34 12 OUNCES (Troy Pound)
375.2360 g., 0.9990 Gold 12.052 oz. AGW, 79 mm.
Rev: Longevity **Note:** Photo reduced.

Date	Mintage	F	VF	XF	Unc	BU
ND(1988) Proof	200	Value: 8,500				

MEDALLIC BULLION COINAGE
Palladium

X# MB30 OUNCE
31.1030 g., 0.9990 Palladium 0.999 oz. **Subject:** 17th New York International Numismatic Convention

Date	Mintage	F	VF	XF	Unc	BU
1988 Proof	1,000	Value: 385				

MEDALLIC BULLION COINAGE
Platinum

Y# 225a 100 YUAN
31.1030 g., 0.9995 Platinum 1.0000 oz. APW **Subject:** Year of the Horse **Obv:** National emblem **Rev:** Prancing horse

Date	Mintage	F	VF	XF	Unc	BU
1990 Proof	2,000	—	—	—	—	BV+20%

X# MB19 OUNCE
31.1030 g., 1.0000 Platinum 1 oz. APW **Subject:** 16th New York International Numismatic Convention

Date	Mintage	F	VF	XF	Unc	BU
1987 Proof	1,000	Value: 1,350				

PATTERNS
Including off metal strikes

KM#	Date	Mintage	Identification	Issue Price	Mkt Val
Pn2	1983	—	100 Yuan. Gilt Bronze.	—	600
Pn3	1985	—	200 Yuan. Gold. Decade for Women, KM#89.	—	—
Pn9	1991	—	10000 Yuan. Gold. Y#358.	—	—

PIEFORTS

KM#	Date	Mintage	Identification	Issue Price	Mkt Val
P2	1979	500	450 Yuan. 0.9000 Gold. Y#9.	—	2,350
P19	1980	360	250 Yuan. 0.9170 Gold. Alpine skiing, Y#22.	1,750	900
P20	1980	500	300 Yuan. 0.9170 Gold. Archery, Y#23.	—	1,300

MINT SETS

KM#	Date	Mintage	Identification	Issue Price	Mkt Val
MS3	1982 (4)	—	Y#40-43	750	3,400

PROOF SETS

KM#	Date	Mintage	Identification	Issue Price	Mkt Val
PS1	1979 (4)	70,000	Y#4-7	1,695	800
PS2	1980 (14)	1,000	Y#10-23	1,750	425
PS8	1981 (4)	1,000	Y#28-31	2,950	2,550
PS20	1986 (5)	10,000	Y#101-105	—	800
PS22	1987 (5)	10,000	Y#124-128	—	800
PS26	1988 (5)	10,000	Y#152-156	—	900
PS27	1989 (5)	8,000	Y#187-191	—	850
PS29	1990 (5)	5,000	Y#238-242	—	1,000
PS30	1990 (3)	2,500	Y#267-269	1,095	750
PS31	1990 (2)	2,000	Y#266 and medal	995	500
PSA32	1990 (5)	10,000	Y251-254, 256	—	265
PS33	1991 (2)	2,000	Y#301 and medal	575	350
PS34	1991 (5)	350	Y#309-313	—	1,000
PS37	1992 (5)	1,000	Y#336-340	—	4,500
PS38	1992 (5)	—	Y#341-345	—	1,000
PS40	1993 (4)	1,000	Y#445-448	1,600	1,350
PS41	1993 (3)	—	Y#352-354	—	925
PS42	1993 (5)	—	Y#610-614	—	600
PS44	1993 (5)	100	Y#1072-1076	1,875	2,000
PSA44	1993 (5)	2,500	Y484, 930, 1203-1205	—	850
PS45	1994 (12)	50	Y#419, 420 Unc/Proof, 421-429	—	6,000
PS46	1994 (11)	50	Y#419, 420 Unc/Proof, 421-428	—	4,500
PS47	1994 (5)	1,000	Y#419, 421-423, 425	—	1,385
PS48	1994 (4)	2,500	Y#419-421, 423	645	655
PS49	1994 (3)	1,000	Y#420-424, 426	—	845
PS51	1994 (5)	—	Y#431-434, 544	—	600
PS53	1995 (3)	2,000	Y#469-471	485	500
PS54	1995 (3)	2,000	Y#571-573	—	710
PS59	1995 (5)	1,000	Y#687, 736-739	—	1,385
PS63	1996 (4)	750	Y#740-743 Plus bottle	—	625

COCOS (KEELING) ISLANDS

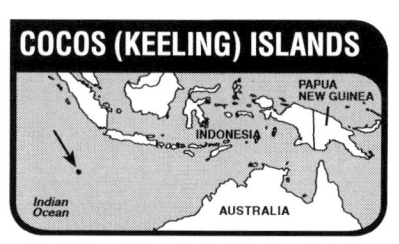

The Territory of Cocos (Keeling) Islands, an Australian territory, comprises a group of 27 coral islands located (see arrow on map of Australia) in the Indian Ocean 1,300 miles northwest of Australia. Only Direction and Home Islands are regularly inhabited. The group has an area of 5.4 sq. mi. and a population of about 569. Calcium, phosphate and coconut products are exported.

The islands were discovered by Capt. William Keeling of the British East India Co. in 1609. Alexander Hare, an English adventurer, established a settlement on one of the southern islands in 1823, but it lasted less than a year. A permanent settlement was established on Direction Island in 1827 by Hare and Capt. John Clunies Ross, a Scot, for the purpose of storing East Indian spices for reshipment to Europe during periods of shortage. When the experiment in spice futures did not develop satisfactorily, Hare left the islands (1829 or 1830), leaving Ross as sole owner. The coral group became a British protectorate in 1856; was attached to the colony of Ceylon in 1878; and was placed under the administration of the Straits Settlements in 1882. In 1903 the group was annexed to the Straits Settlements and incorporated into the colony of Singapore until November of 1955, when it was placed under the administration of Australia.

RULER
British

MONETARY SYSTEM
100 Cents = 1 Rupee

AUSTRALIAN TERRITORY
DECIMAL COINAGE

X# 21 100 DOLLARS
16.4300 g., 0.9166 Gold 0.4842 oz. AGW, 27.2 mm. **Obv:** Palm tree with additional Malay legend **Rev:** HMS Beagle (Darwin's ship) **Edge:** Reeded

Date	Mintage	F	VF	XF	Unc	BU
2003 Proof						

X# 10 150 RUPEES
0.7500 Gold **Subject:** 150th Anniversary - Keeling-Cocos Islands **Obv:** Palm tree and value **Rev:** Bust of John Clunies Ross left **Note:** The entire issue of X#10 was stolen with only 290 pieces being recovered. Previous KM#10.

Date	Mintage	F	VF	XF	Unc	BU
ND(1977)	2,000	—	—	—	—	—
ND(1977) Proof	2,000	—	—	—	—	—

X# 10a 150 RUPEES
8.4800 g., 0.9160 Gold .2497 oz. AGW **Obv:** Palm tree and value **Rev:** Bust of John Clunies Ross left **Note:** Prev. KM#10a.

Date	Mintage	F	VF	XF	Unc	BU
ND(1977)	2,000	—	—	—	300	—
ND(1977) Proof	2,000	Value: 400				

MINT SETS

KM#	Date	Mintage	Identification	Issue Price	Mkt Val
MS1	1977 (7)	—	X#1-7	—	325
MS2	1977 (2)	6,000	X#8-9	—	200

PROOF SETS

KM#	Date	Mintage	Identification	Issue Price	Mkt Val
PS1	1977 (2)	4,000	X#8-9	28.00	275

COLOMBIA

The Republic of Colombia, in the northwestern corner of South America, has an area of 440,831 sq. mi. (1,138,910 sq. km.) and a population of *42.3 million. Capital: Bogota. The economy is primarily agricultural with a mild, rich coffee being the chief crop. Colombia has the world's largest platinum deposits and important reserves of coal, iron ore, petroleum and limestone; other precious metals and emeralds are also mined. Coffee, crude oil, bananas, sugar and emeralds are exported.

The northern coast of present Colombia was one of the first parts of the American continent to be visited by Spanish navigators. At Darien in Panama is the site of the first permanent European settlement on the American mainland in 1510. New Granada, as Colombia was known until 1861, stemmed from the settlement of Santa Marta in 1525. New Granada was established as a Spanish colony in 1549. Independence was declared in 1810, and secured in 1819 when Simon Bolivar united Colombia, Venezuela, Panama and Ecuador as the Republic of Gran Colombia. Venezuela withdrew from the Republic in 1829; Ecuador in 1830; and Panama in 1903.

RULER
Spanish, until 1819

MINT MARKS
AM – Bogota
C, NER, NR, NRE, R, RN, S - Cartagena
B, BA, BOGOTA – Santa Fe de Bogota
B, F, FS, N, NR, S, SF – Nuevo Reino (Bogota)
A, M - Medellin (capital), Antioquia (state)
B - Bogota
(D) Denver, USA
H – Birmingham (Heaton & Sons)
M, (m) – Medellin, w/o mint mark
(Mo) - Mexico City
NI - Numismatica Italiana, Arezzo, Italy mint marks stylized in wreath
P, PN, Pn POPAYAN - Popayan
(P) - Philadelphia
(S) - San Francisco, USA.
SM – Santa Marta
(W) – Waterbury, CT (USA, Scoville mint)
caduceus - Bogota
floral spray - Popayan

ASSAYERS' INITIALS
Bogota and Popayan Mints

F	1800-22	Francisco Rodriguez
J	1780-1803, 1810-22	Juan Jose Truxillo y Mutienx
J	1803-22	Josef Antonio Rodriguez y Uzguiano

MONETARY SYSTEM
16 Reales = 1 Escudo

COLONIAL
MILLED COINAGE

KM# 56.1 ESCUDO
3.3834 g., 0.8750 Gold .0952 oz. AGW **Ruler:** Charles IV
Obv: Uniformed bust right **Rev:** Crowned arms within Order chain

Date	Mintage	VG	F	VF	XF	Unc
1802/1NR JJ	—	75.00	135	195	285	—
1802NR JJ	—	65.00	110	160	230	—
1803NR JJ	—	65.00	110	160	230	—
1804/3NR JJ	—	80.00	135	210	285	—
1804NR JJ	—	65.00	110	160	230	—
1805NR JJ	—	65.00	110	160	230	—
1806NR JJ	—	75.00	135	195	285	—
1807NR JJ	—	100	165	235	345	—

KM# 56.2 ESCUDO
3.3834 g., 0.8750 Gold .0952 oz. AGW **Ruler:** Charles IV
Obv: Uniformed bust right **Rev:** Crowned arms within Order chain

Date	Mintage	VG	F	VF	XF	Unc
1801P JF	—	75.00	110	160	245	—
1802P JF	—	75.00	110	160	245	—
1803P JF	—	75.00	110	160	245	—
1804P JF	—	75.00	110	160	245	—
1804P JT	—	100	150	225	350	—
1805P JF	—	75.00	110	160	245	—
1805P JF	—	100	150	225	350	—
1806P JT	—	75.00	110	160	245	—
1806P JF	—	75.00	110	160	245	—
1807P JF	—	75.00	110	160	245	—
1808/7P JF	—	75.00	110	160	245	—

KM# 64.1 ESCUDO
3.3834 g., 0.8750 Gold .0952 oz. AGW **Obv:** Uniformed bust of Charles IV **Obv. Legend:** FERDND VII.. **Rev:** Crowned arms within Order chain

Date	Mintage	VG	F	VF	XF	Unc
1808NR JF	—	70.00	100	150	245	—
1809NR JF	—	70.00	100	150	245	—
1810NR JF	—	65.00	95.00	145	245	—
1811NR JJ	—	70.00	100	150	245	—
1811NR JF	—	70.00	100	150	245	—
1812/1NR JJ	—	70.00	100	150	245	—
1812NR JF	—	65.00	95.00	145	225	—
1813NR JF	—	65.00	95.00	145	225	—
1814NR JF	—	65.00	95.00	145	225	—
1815NR JF	—	65.00	95.00	145	225	—
1816NR JF	—	65.00	95.00	145	225	—
1817NR JF	—	65.00	95.00	145	225	—
1818NR JF	—	65.00	95.00	145	225	500
1819NR JF	—	65.00	95.00	145	225	500
1820NR JF	—	70.00	100	150	245	500

KM# 64.2 ESCUDO
3.3834 g., 0.8750 Gold .0952 oz. AGW **Obv:** Uniformed bust of Charles IV right **Obv. Legend:** FERDND VII.. **Rev:** Crowned arms within Order chain

Date	Mintage	VG	F	VF	XF	Unc
1808P JF	—	65.00	95.00	145	225	650
1809P JF	—	65.00	95.00	145	225	—
1810P JF	—	65.00	95.00	145	225	—
1812P JF	—	65.00	95.00	145	225	—
1813/2P JF	—	65.00	95.00	145	225	—
1813P JF	—	65.00	95.00	145	225	—
1814/3P JF	—	65.00	95.00	145	225	350
1814P JF	—	65.00	95.00	145	225	—
1816P JF	—	70.00	100	160	245	—
1816P FM	—	65.00	95.00	145	225	—
1816P F	—	65.00	95.00	145	225	—
1817P FM	—	65.00	95.00	145	225	475
1818P FM	—	65.00	95.00	145	225	—
1819P FM	—	65.00	95.00	145	225	—

KM# 64.3 ESCUDO
3.3834 g., 0.8750 Gold .0952 oz. AGW **Obv:** Uniformed bust of Charles IV right **Obv. Legend:** FERDND VII.. **Rev:** Crowned arms within Order chain

Date	Mintage	VG	F	VF	XF	Unc
1815PN FR	—	80.00	150	250	300	—
1816PN FR	—	65.00	100	150	235	—

KM# 60.1 2 ESCUDOS
6.7668 g., 0.8750 Gold .1904 oz. AGW **Ruler:** Charles IV
Obv: Uniformed bust right **Rev:** Crowned arms within Order chain

Date	Mintage	VG	F	VF	XF	Unc
1801NR JJ	—	150	200	300	375	—
1803NR JJ	—	185	225	325	400	—
1804NR JJ	—	200	275	350	450	—
1805NR JJ	—	150	175	250	325	—
1806/5NR JJ	—	325	400	500	750	—
1806/5NR JJ	—	275	350	450	700	—
1806NR JJ	—	150	175	250	325	—

KM# 60.2 2 ESCUDOS
6.7668 g., 0.8750 Gold .1904 oz. AGW **Ruler:** Charles IV
Obv: Uniformed bust right **Rev:** Crowned arms within Order chain

Date	Mintage	VG	F	VF	XF	Unc
1802P JF	—	145	185	250	375	—
1804P JF	—	150	250	400	750	—

KM# 65.1 2 ESCUDOS
6.7668 g., 0.8750 Gold .1904 oz. AGW **Obv:** Uniformed bust of Charles IV **Obv. Legend:** FERDND VII.. **Rev:** Crowned arms within Order chain

Date	Mintage	VG	F	VF	XF	Unc
1808NR JF	—	200	275	350	525	—
1809NR JJ	—	145	200	275	450	—
1811NR JF	—	200	275	350	550	—
1811NR JF/J	—	200	275	350	550	—

KM# 65.2 2 ESCUDOS
6.7668 g., 0.8750 Gold .1904 oz. AGW **Obv:** Uniformed bust of Charles IV right **Obv. Legend:** FERDND VII.. **Rev:** Crowned arms within Order chain

Date	Mintage	VG	F	VF	XF	Unc
1817P FM	—	225	300	500	850	—
1818P FM	—	225	300	500	850	—
1819P FM	—	225	300	500	850	—

KM# 61.1 4 ESCUDOS
13.5337 g., 0.8750 Gold .3807 oz. AGW **Ruler:** Charles IV
Obv: Uniformed bust right **Obv. Legend:** CAROL IIII..
Rev: Crowned arms within Order chain

Date	Mintage	VG	F	VF	XF	Unc
1801NR JJ	—	275	450	600	1,200	—
1803NR JJ	—	275	450	600	1,200	—
1804/3NR JJ	—	275	450	700	1,350	—
1805NR JJ	—	275	450	650	1,250	—
1806NR JJ	—	275	450	650	1,250	—
1807NR JJ	—	350	650	1,000	1,650	—

KM# 61.2 4 ESCUDOS
13.5337 g., 0.8750 Gold .3807 oz. AGW **Ruler:** Charles IV
Obv: Uniformed bust right **Obv. Legend:** CAROL IIII..
Rev: Crowned arms within Order chain

Date	Mintage	VG	F	VF	XF	Unc
1801P JF	—	325	550	750	1,500	—

KM# 72 4 ESCUDOS
13.5337 g., 0.8750 Gold .3807 oz. AGW **Obv:** Uniformed bust of Charles IV right **Obv. Legend:** FERDND VII.. **Rev:** Crowned arms within Order chain

Date	Mintage	VG	F	VF	XF	Unc
1818NR JF	—	450	850	1,500	2,850	—
1819NR JF	—	450	850	1,500	2,850	—

COLOMBIA

KM# 62.1 8 ESCUDOS
27.0674 g., 0.8750 Gold .7615 oz. AGW **Ruler:** Charles IV
Obv: Uniformed bust right **Obv. Legend:** CAROL IIII..
Rev: Crowned arms within Order chain

Date	Mintage	VG	F	VF	XF	Unc
1801/0NR JJ	—	550	750	900	1,500	—
1801NR JJ	—	550	750	900	1,500	—
1802/1NR JJ	—	550	750	900	1,500	4,000
1802NR JJ	—	550	750	900	1,500	—
1803/2NR JJ	—	550	750	900	1,500	—
1803NR JJ	—	550	750	900	1,500	—
1804/3NR JJ	—	550	750	900	1,500	—
1804NR JJ	—	550	750	900	1,500	—
1805/4NR JJ	—	550	750	900	1,500	—
1805NR JJ	—	550	750	900	1,500	3,250
1806NR JJ	—	550	750	900	1,500	—
1807NR JJ	—	550	750	900	1,500	—
1808NR JJ	—	550	750	900	1,500	—
1808NR JJ D:G	—	550	750	900	1,500	—

KM# 62.2 8 ESCUDOS
27.0674 g., 0.8750 Gold .7615 oz. AGW **Ruler:** Charles IV
Obv: Uniformed bust right **Obv. Legend:** CAROL IIII..
Rev: Crowned arms within Order chain

Date	Mintage	VG	F	VF	XF	Unc
1801P JF	—	550	750	900	1,500	—
1802P JF	—	550	750	900	1,500	—
1803P JF	—	550	750	900	1,500	2,250
1804P JT	—	1,500	2,500	3,500	4,500	9,000
1804P JF	—	550	750	900	1,500	—
1805P JF	—	750	1,500	2,000	3,000	—
1805/4P JT	—	550	750	900	1,500	—
1805P JT	—	550	750	900	1,500	—
1806/5P JF	—	550	750	900	1,500	—
1806P JF	—	550	750	900	1,500	—
1807/6P JF	—	550	750	900	1,500	—
1807P JF	—	550	750	900	1,500	—
1808P JF	—	550	750	900	1,500	—

KM# 66.1 8 ESCUDOS
27.0674 g., 0.8750 Gold .7615 oz. AGW **Obv:** Uniformed bust of Charles IV right **Obv. Legend:** FERDND. VII.. **Rev:** Crowned arms within Order chain

Date	Mintage	VG	F	VF	XF	Unc
1808NR JJ	—	600	800	1,250	1,850	—
1808NR JF/JJ	—	600	750	950	1,500	—
1809/8NR JF/JJ	—	600	750	1,000	1,650	—
1809NR JF/JJ	—	550	700	850	1,250	—
1809NR JF	—	550	700	800	1,200	—
1810/9NR JF	—	550	700	850	1,250	—
1810NR JF	—	550	700	850	1,250	—
1811/0NR JF	—	550	700	850	1,250	—
1811NR JF	—	550	700	850	1,250	—
1812/1/0NR JF	—	550	700	850	1,250	—
1812/1NR JF	—	550	700	850	1,250	—
1812NR JF	—	550	700	850	1,250	—
1813/2NR JF	—	550	700	850	1,250	—
1813NR JF	—	550	700	850	1,250	—
1814/3NR JF	—	550	700	850	1,250	—
1814NR JF	—	550	700	850	1,250	—
1815/4NR JF	—	550	700	850	1,250	—
1815NR JF	—	550	700	850	1,250	—
1816/4NR JF	—	550	700	850	1,250	—
1816/5NR JF	—	550	700	850	1,250	—
1816NR JF	—	550	700	850	1,250	—
1817/6NR	—	550	700	850	1,250	—
1817NR JF	—	550	700	850	1,250	—
1818NR JF	—	550	700	850	1,250	—
1819NR JF	—	550	700	850	1,250	—
1819/29NR JF	—	550	700	850	1,250	—
1820NR JF	—	550	700	850	1,250	—

KM# 66.2 8 ESCUDOS
27.0674 g., 0.8750 Gold .7615 oz. AGW **Obv:** Uniformed bust of Charles IV right **Obv. Legend:** FERDND. VII.. **Rev:** Crowned arms within Order chain

Date	Mintage	VG	F	VF	XF	Unc
1808P JF	—	550	700	850	1,250	—
1809/8P JF	—	550	700	850	1,250	—
1809P JF	—	550	700	850	1,250	—
1810/09P JF	—	550	700	850	1,250	—
1810P JF	—	550	700	850	1,250	4,500
1811/0P JF	—	550	700	850	1,250	—
1811P JF	—	550	700	850	1,250	—
1812/11P JF	—	550	700	850	1,250	—
1812P JF	—	550	700	850	1,250	—
1813P JF	—	550	700	850	1,250	—
1814P JF	—	550	700	850	1,250	—
1815P JF	—	550	700	850	1,250	—
1816P JF	—	900	1,500	2,000	3,250	—
1816P F	—	650	1,000	1,350	2,000	—
1816P FM	—	600	800	1,100	1,650	—
1817P FM	—	550	700	850	1,150	—
1818P FM	—	550	700	850	1,150	—
1819P FM	—	550	700	850	1,150	—
1820P FM	—	550	700	850	1,150	—

KM# 66.3 8 ESCUDOS
27.0674 g., 0.8750 Gold .7615 oz. AGW **Obv:** Uniformed bust of Charles IV right **Obv. Legend:** FERDND. VII.. **Rev:** Crowned arms within Order chain

Date	Mintage	VG	F	VF	XF	Unc
1814Pn FR	—	650	950	1,500	2,500	—
1815Pn FR	—	1,500	2,500	4,000	6,000	—
1816Pn FR	—	600	800	1,150	1,750	2,750
1820Pn FM	—	600	800	1,150	1,750	—

REPUBLIC OF COLOMBIA
MILLED COINAGE

KM# 80 PESO
1.6875 g., 0.8750 Gold .0474 oz. AGW **Obv:** Head left
Rev: Fasces between cornucopias

Date	Mintage	Good	VG	F	VF	XF
1821 JF	—	100	200	350	500	—

Note: Authenticity currently under study

KM# 84 PESO
1.6875 g., 0.8750 Gold .0474 oz. AGW **Obv:** Head left
Rev: Fasces between cornucopias

Date	Mintage	VG	F	VF	XF	Unc
1825 JF	—	55.00	60.00	85.00	175	—
1826 JF	—	55.00	60.00	85.00	175	450
1826/5 JF	—	55.00	60.00	85.00	175	—
1826 JR	—	55.00	60.00	85.00	175	—

Note: Raised or lowered 6 in date

1826 PJ	—	55.00	60.00	85.00	175	—
1827 JF	—	55.00	60.00	85.00	175	—
1827 RR	—	55.00	60.00	85.00	175	—
1829/7 PJ	—	55.00	60.00	85.00	175	—
1829 JF	—	55.00	60.00	85.00	175	—
1829 RS	—	55.00	60.00	85.00	175	—
1830 RS	—	55.00	60.00	85.00	175	—
1834 RS	—	55.00	60.00	85.00	175	575
1835 RS	—	55.00	60.00	85.00	175	—
1836 RS	—	55.00	60.00	85.00	175	—

KM# 81.1 ESCUDO
3.3841 g., 0.8750 Gold .0952 oz. AGW **Obv:** Head left
Rev: Fasces between cornucopias **Note:** An 1821 dated piece is known and considered to be a contemporary counterfeit. Struck at the Bogota Mint.

Date	Mintage	VG	F	VF	XF	Unc
1823 JF	—	100	125	225	350	550
1825 JF	—	125	150	275	400	—

KM# 81.2 ESCUDO
3.3841 g., 0.8750 Gold .0952 oz. AGW **Obv:** Head left
Rev: Fasces between cornucopias

Date	Mintage	VG	F	VF	XF	Unc
1823 FM	—	65.00	75.00	125	185	—
1824 FM	—	65.00	75.00	115	175	—

Note: Narrow and wides dates with at least five varieties of numeral and letter placements known

| 1825 FM | — | 65.00 | 75.00 | 115 | 175 | — |

Note: Narrow and wide dates with E close to or far from cornucopias

| 1826 FM | — | 65.00 | 75.00 | 115 | 175 | — |

Note: Narrow or wide date

| 1827 FM | — | 65.00 | 75.00 | 115 | 175 | — |
| 1827 RU | — | 65.00 | 75.00 | 125 | 185 | — |

Note: Narrow or wide date

1828 RU	—	65.00	75.00	125	185	—
1829 RU	—	65.00	75.00	115	175	—
1830 RU	—	65.00	75.00	115	175	—
1831/21 RM	—	75.00	85.00	145	225	—
1831 RU	—	75.00	85.00	145	225	—
1832 RU	—	65.00	75.00	115	175	—
1833/2 RU	—	65.00	75.00	125	185	—
1834 RU	—	65.00	75.00	125	185	—
1836/4 RU	—	65.00	75.00	125	185	—
1836 RU	—	65.00	75.00	125	185	—

KM# 83 2 ESCUDOS
6.7682 g., 0.8750 Gold .1904 oz. AGW **Obv:** Head left
Rev: Fasces between cornucopias

Date	Mintage	VG	F	VF	XF	Unc
1823 JF	—	160	250	400	650	—
1824 JF	—	145	235	375	600	3,000
1825 JF	—	145	235	375	600	—
1826 JF	—	145	235	375	600	—
1829 JF	—	160	250	400	650	—
1829 PJ	—	160	250	400	650	—
1829 RS	—	135	225	350	550	—
1836 RS	—	135	225	350	550	—

COLOMBIA

KM# 86 4 ESCUDOS
13.5365 g., 0.8750 Gold .3808 oz. AGW **Obv:** Head left
Rev: Fasces between cornucopias

Date	Mintage	VG	F	VF	XF	Unc
1826 JF	—	2,000	3,000	5,000	—	—

Note: American Numismatic Rarities Eliasberg sale 4-05, MS-64 realized $42,550

KM# 82.1 8 ESCUDOS
27.0730 g., 0.8750 Gold .7616 oz. AGW **Obv:** Head left
Rev: Fasces between cornucopias

Date	Mintage	VG	F	VF	XF	Unc
1822 JF	—	550	650	1,000	1,500	—
1823 JF	—	500	550	750	1,000	—
1824/3 JF	—	500	550	750	1,000	—
1824 JF	—	500	550	750	1,000	1,950
1825 JF	—	500	550	750	1,000	1,500
1826 JF	—	500	550	750	1,000	1,950
1827 JF	—	500	550	750	1,000	—
1827 RR	—	550	650	950	1,350	—
1828 RR	—	550	650	950	1,350	—
1828 RS	—	500	550	750	1,000	—
1829 RS	—	500	550	750	1,000	—

Note: Narrow or wide date

1830 RS	—	500	550	750	1,000	—
1831 RS	—	500	550	750	1,000	—
1832 RS	—	500	550	750	1,000	—
1833 RS	—	500	550	750	1,000	—
1834 RS	—	500	550	750	1,000	—
1835 RS	—	500	550	750	1,000	4,000
1836 RS	—	500	550	750	1,000	—

KM# 82.2 8 ESCUDOS
27.0730 g., 0.8750 Gold .7616 oz. AGW **Obv:** Head left with earring **Rev:** Fasces between cornucopias

Date	Mintage	VG	F	VF	XF	Unc
1822 FM	—	550	650	850	1,350	—
1823 FM	—	500	550	750	1,000	—
1824 FM	—	500	550	750	1,000	—
1825 FM	—	500	550	750	1,000	3,000

Note: Varieties known with normal date and dropped 5 in date

| 1826 FM | — | 500 | 550 | 750 | 1,000 | — |
| 1827 FM | — | 500 | 550 | 750 | 1,000 | — |

Note: Narrow or wide date

1827 UR	—	550	650	800	1,250	—
1828 UR	—	500	550	750	1,000	—
1829 FM	—	550	650	800	1,250	—
1829 UR	—	500	550	750	1,000	—
1830 FW M inverted	—	550	650	1,000	1,500	—
1830 FM	—	550	650	1,000	1,500	—
1830 UR	—	500	550	750	1,000	3,000
1831 UR	—	550	650	1,000	1,500	—
1832/1 UR	—	500	550	750	1,000	—
1832 UR	—	500	550	750	1,000	—
1833/22 UR	—	550	750	1,250	2,000	—
1833 UR	—	500	550	750	1,000	—
1834/3 UR	—	600	900	1,650	2,500	—
1834 UR	—	550	750	1,250	2,000	—

Date	Mintage	VG	F	VF	XF	Unc
1835 UR	—	500	550	750	1,000	4,000
1836 UR	—	500	550	750	1,000	—
1838 UR Rare	—	—	—	—	—	—

REPUBLIC OF NUEVA GRANADA
MILLED COINAGE

KM# 93 PESO
1.6875 g., 0.8750 Gold .0474 oz. AGW **Obv:** Head left
Rev: Condor with banner above shielded arms

Date	Mintage	VG	F	VF	XF	Unc
1837 RS	—	40.00	60.00	90.00	145	175
1838 RS	—	60.00	90.00	135	225	450
1839 RS	—	60.00	90.00	135	225	—
1840/39 RS	—	50.00	80.00	120	200	—
1840 RS	—	45.00	70.00	100	175	—
1842 RS	—	40.00	60.00	90.00	150	350
1844 RS	—	45.00	70.00	100	175	225
1846 RS	—	40.00	60.00	90.00	145	175

KM# 95 2 PESOS
3.3750 g., 0.9000 Gold .0976 oz. AGW **Obv:** Head left
Rev: Condor with banner above shielded arms

Date	Mintage	VG	F	VF	XF	Unc
1838 RU	—	65.00	80.00	120	200	—
1842 VU	—	65.00	80.00	160	275	—
1843 UM	—	65.00	80.00	120	200	—
1843 VU	—	65.00	80.00	160	275	—
1844 UM	—	65.00	80.00	130	225	—
1845 UM	—	65.00	80.00	120	200	—
1845 UE	—	65.00	80.00	160	275	—
1846 UE	—	65.00	80.00	120	200	—
1846 UM	—	65.00	80.00	120	200	—

KM# 99 2 PESOS
3.2258 g., 0.9000 Gold .0933 oz. AGW **Obv:** Head left
Rev: Denomination within wreath

Date	Mintage	VG	F	VF	XF	Unc
1849	—	400	650	950	1,550	—
1851	—	600	1,200	1,800	2,700	—

KM# 94.1 16 PESOS (Diez I Seis)
27.0000 g., 0.8750 Gold .7596 oz. AGW **Obv:** Head left
Rev: Condor with banner above shielded arms

Date	Mintage	VG	F	VF	XF	Unc
1837 RS	—	BV	500	550	675	—
1838/7 RS	—	BV	500	550	700	—
1838 RS	—	BV	500	550	675	—
1839/8 RS	—	BV	500	550	700	—
1839 RS	—	BV	500	550	675	—
1840 RS	—	BV	500	550	675	1,275
1841 RS	—	BV	500	550	675	—
1842 RS	—	BV	500	550	675	—
1843 RS	—	BV	500	550	675	1,100
1844 RS	—	BV	500	550	675	—
1845 RS	—	BV	500	550	675	—
1846 RS	—	BV	500	550	675	—
1847 RS	—	BV	500	550	675	—
1848 RS	—	BV	550	650	950	—
1849 RS	—	BV	650	950	1,350	—

KM# 94.2 16 PESOS (Diez I Seis)
27.0000 g., 0.8750 Gold .7596 oz. AGW **Obv:** Head left
Rev: Condor with banner above shielded arms

Date	Mintage	VG	F	VF	XF	Unc
1837 RU	—	BV	500	550	675	1,250
1838 RU	—	BV	500	550	675	—
1839 RU	—	BV	500	550	675	—
1840 RU	—	BV	500	550	675	—
1841/0 RU	—	600	—	—	—	—
1841 RU	—	550	750	—	—	—
1841 VU	—	BV	500	550	675	—
1842 VU	—	BV	500	550	675	—
1843 UM	—	BV	500	550	675	—
1844 UM	—	BV	500	550	675	—
1845 UM	—	BV	500	550	675	—
1846 UM	—	BV	500	550	675	—
1846 UE	—	550	750	1,000	—	—
1846 UR	—	BV	500	550	675	—

KM# 100 16 PESOS (Diez I Seis)
25.8064 g., 0.9000 Gold .7468 oz. AGW **Obv:** Head left
Rev: Condor with spread wings above mantled arms

Date	Mintage	VG	F	VF	XF	Unc
1848	—	500	800	1,500	2,800	—
1849	—	500	800	1,500	2,800	5,000
1850	—	500	800	1,500	2,800	—
1851	—	600	1,200	2,000	4,000	—
1852	—	500	800	1,500	2,800	—
1853	—	500	800	1,500	2,800	—

DECIMAL COINAGE
10 Decimos de Real = 1 Real (1847-53)

KM# 119 PESO
1.6875 g., 0.8750 Gold .0474 oz. AGW **Obv:** Head left
Rev: Denomination within wreath

Date	Mintage	VG	F	VF	XF	Unc
1856	—	65.00	150	300	500	—
1858	—	65.00	150	300	500	—

KM# 121 2 PESOS
3.2258 g., 0.9000 Gold .0933 oz. AGW **Obv:** Head left
Rev: Denomination within wreath

Date	Mintage	VG	F	VF	XF	Unc
1857P	—	65.00	100	175	300	550
1858/48P	—	75.00	120	200	350	—
1858P	—	65.00	100	175	300	—

KM# 120.1 5 PESOS
8.0648 g., 0.9000 Gold .2333 oz. AGW **Obv:** Head left
Rev: Denomination within wreath

Date	Mintage	VG	F	VF	XF	Unc
1849B Unique	—	—	—	—	—	—
1857B	—	185	400	850	1,350	—

COLOMBIA

KM# 120.2 5 PESOS
8.0648 g., 0.9000 Gold .2333 oz. AGW **Obv:** Head left
Rev: PESOS in small letters

Date	Mintage	VG	F	VF	XF	Unc
1858	—	200	500	1,000	1,750	—

KM# 116.1 10 PESOS
16.4000 g., 0.9000 Gold .4745 oz. AGW **Obv:** Head left
Rev: Condor with spread wings above flagged arms

Date	Mintage	VG	F	VF	XF	Unc
1853	—	450	800	1,450	1,850	—
1854	—	350	650	1,250	1,500	—
1855	—	350	650	1,250	1,500	1,850
1856	—	350	650	1,250	1,500	—
1857	—	350	650	1,250	1,500	—

KM# 116.2 10 PESOS
16.4000 g., 0.9000 Gold .4745 oz. AGW **Obv:** Head left
Rev: Condor with spread wings above flagged arms

Date	Mintage	VG	F	VF	XF	Unc
1853	—	325	425	650	1,000	1,750
1856	—	450	800	1,450	1,850	—
1857	—	—	—	800	1,250	—

KM# 122.1 10 PESOS
16.1290 g., 0.9000 Gold .4667 oz. AGW **Obv:** Head left
Rev: Condor with spread wings above flagged arms
Rev. Legend: DIEZ PESOS

Date	Mintage	VG	F	VF	XF	Unc
1857	—	325	500	850	1,250	—
1858/7	—	350	550	900	1,350	—
1858	—	350	550	900	1,350	—

KM# 122.2 10 PESOS
16.1290 g., 0.9000 Gold .4667 oz. AGW **Obv:** Head left
Rev: Condor with spread wings above flagged arms
Rev. Legend: DIEZ PESOS

Date	Mintage	VG	F	VF	XF	Unc
1857	—	325	375	550	950	—
1858	—	325	375	550	950	—

GRANADINE CONFEDERATION
DECIMAL COINAGE
10 Decimos = 1 Peso (1853-72)

KM# 135 PESO
1.6129 g., 0.9000 Gold .0466 oz. AGW **Obv:** Head left
Rev: Denomination within wreath

Date	Mintage	VG	F	VF	XF	Unc
1862M Rare; 2 known						

KM# 127 2 PESOS
3.2258 g., 0.9000 Gold .0933 oz. AGW **Obv:** Head left
Rev: Denomination within wreath

Date	Mintage	VG	F	VF	XF	Unc
1859P	—	75.00	150	300	550	—
1860P	—	125	250	550	1,000	—

KM# 128 5 PESOS
8.0645 g., 0.9000 Gold .2333 oz. AGW **Obv:** Head left
Rev: Denomination within wreath

Date	Mintage	VG	F	VF	XF	Unc
1859P	—	—	—	—	5,000	—

KM# 136 5 PESOS
8.0645 g., 0.9000 Gold .2333 oz. AGW **Obv:** Head left
Rev: Denomination within wreath

Date	Mintage	VG	F	VF	XF	Unc
1862M	—	—	—	—	6,000	—

KM# 129.1 10 PESOS
16.1290 g., 0.9000 Gold .4667 oz. AGW **Obv:** Head left
Rev: Condor with spread wings above flagged arms

Date	Mintage	VG	F	VF	XF	Unc
1859	3,481	350	450	650	1,000	—
1860	9,687	325	400	550	900	—
1861	834	375	475	750	1,200	—

KM# 129.2 10 PESOS
16.1290 g., 0.9000 Gold .4667 oz. AGW **Obv:** Head left
Rev: Condor with spread wings above flagged arms

Date	Mintage	VG	F	VF	XF	Unc
1858	—	325	400	550	900	—
1859/58	—	350	450	650	1,000	—
1859	—	325	400	550	900	—
1860	—	350	450	650	1,000	—
1861	—	375	500	750	1,100	—
1862	—	350	450	650	1,000	—

KM# 130 20 PESOS
32.2580 g., 0.9000 Gold .9335 oz. AGW **Obv:** Head left
Rev: Condor with spread wings above flagged arms

Date	Mintage	VG	F	VF	XF	Unc
1859	2,002	1,000	2,000	3,500	6,000	—

ESTADOS UNIDOS DE COLOMBIA
DECIMAL COINAGE
10 Decimos = 1 Peso

KM# 146.1 PESO
1.6129 g., 0.9000 Gold .0466 oz. AGW **Obv:** Head left
Obv. Legend: ESTADOS UNIDOS DE COLOMBIA
Rev: Denomination within wreath

Date	Mintage	VG	F	VF	XF	Unc
1863	11,000	90.00	175	275	500	—

KM# 146.2 PESO
1.6129 g., 0.9000 Gold .0466 oz. AGW **Obv:** Head left
Obv. Legend: COLOMBIA **Rev:** Denomination within wreath

Date	Mintage	VG	F	VF	XF	Unc
1864	1,072	600	900	1,450	2,000	4,250

KM# 157.1 PESO
1.6129 g., 0.9000 Gold .0466 oz. AGW **Obv:** Head left
Rev: Condor with spread wings

Date	Mintage	VG	F	VF	XF	Unc
1872	Inc. above	35.00	50.00	75.00	120	—
1873/2	—	50.00	90.00	150	250	—
1873	—	50.00	90.00	150	250	—

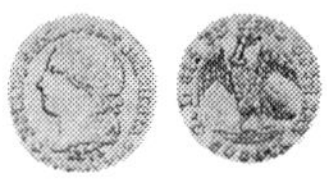

KM# 157.2 PESO
1.6129 g., 0.9000 Gold .0466 oz. AGW **Obv:** Head left
Rev: Condor with spread wings

Date	Mintage	VG	F	VF	XF	Unc
1871	—	60.00	120	200	400	—

Note: The 1871 date is more commonly encountered as a counterfeit than an authentic striking

Date	Mintage	VG	F	VF	XF	Unc
1872	—	35.00	50.00	75.00	120	—
1873	3,374	35.00	50.00	75.00	120	—
1874	14,000	35.00	50.00	80.00	125	—
1875	7,002	35.00	50.00	80.00	125	—
1878	—	75.00	150	250	350	—

KM# 156 PESO
1.6129 g., 0.9000 Gold .0466 oz. AGW **Obv:** Head left
Rev: Condor with spread wings above flagged arms

Date	Mintage	VG	F	VF	XF	Unc
1872/1	62,000	45.00	75.00	115	175	—
1872	Inc. above	35.00	60.00	90.00	135	—
1873	18,000	45.00	75.00	115	175	—

COLOMBIA

KM# 147 2 PESOS
3.2258 g., 0.9000 Gold .0933 oz. AGW **Obv:** Head left
Rev: Denomination within wreath

Date	Mintage	VG	F	VF	XF	Unc
1863	2,996	175	300	500	850	2,000

KM# A154 2 PESOS
3.2258 g., 0.9000 Gold .0933 oz. AGW **Obv:** Head left
Rev: Condor with spread wings above flagged arms

Date	Mintage	VG	F	VF	XF	Unc
1871	66,000	60.00	70.00	85.00	130	—
1872	30,000	65.00	80.00	120	175	—
1876	—	80.00	100	140	200	—

KM# A154a 2 PESOS
3.2258 g., 0.6660 Gold .0690 oz. AGW **Obv:** Head left
Rev: Condor with spread wings above flagged arms

Date	Mintage	VG	F	VF	XF	Unc
1885/74 Rare	—	—	—	—	—	—

KM# 140 5 PESOS
8.0645 g., 0.9000 Gold .2333 oz. AGW **Obv:** Head left
Obv. Legend: ESTADOS UNIDOS DE COLOMBIA
Rev: Denomination within wreath

Date	Mintage	VG	F	VF	XF	Unc
1863	29,000	1,500	2,500	4,000	5,750	—

KM# 148 5 PESOS
8.0645 g., 0.9000 Gold .2333 oz. AGW **Obv:** Head left
Obv. Legend: COLOMBIA above **Rev:** Denomination within wreath

Date	Mintage	VG	F	VF	XF	Unc
1864 Rare	8,035	—	—	—	—	—

Note: American Numismatic Rarities Eliasberg sale 4-05, EF-45 realized $12,650

KM# A148 5 PESOS
8.0645 g., 0.9000 Gold .2333 oz. AGW **Obv:** Head left
Rev: Denomination within wreath **Note:** Mule

Date	Mintage	VG	F	VF	XF	Unc
1864 Unique	—	—	—	—	—	—

KM# 163 5 PESOS
8.0645 g., 0.6660 Gold .1728 oz. AGW **Obv:** Head left
Rev: Condor with spread wings above flagged arms

Date	Mintage	VG	F	VF	XF	Unc
1885 Inverted 5	—	800	1,350	1,750	2,850	—
1885/74	—	800	1,350	1,750	2,850	—

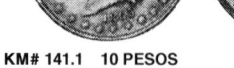

KM# 141.1 10 PESOS
16.1290 g., 0.9000 Gold .4667 oz. AGW **Obv:** Head left
Rev: Condor with spread wings above flagged arms

Date	Mintage	VG	F	VF	XF	Unc
1862	11,000	325	475	775	1,200	—
1863	17,000	325	475	750	1,150	—
1864	—	600	1,000	2,000	3,000	—
1866	—	1,000	2,000	3,500	5,000	—

KM# 141.2 10 PESOS
16.1290 g., 0.9000 Gold .4667 oz. AGW **Obv:** Head left
Rev: Condor with spread wings above flagged arms
Note: Varieties exist

Date	Mintage	VG	F	VF	XF	Unc
1864	—	350	475	775	1,250	—
1867	14,000	325	425	600	900	—
1868	18,000	325	400	525	800	1,000
1869	18,000	325	400	525	800	—
1870	7,786	325	425	600	900	—
1871	6,018	325	425	600	900	1,275

KM# 141.2a 10 PESOS
16.1290 g., 0.6660 Gold .3453 oz. AGW **Obv:** Small Phrygian cap **Rev:** Small date, inverted LEI 0.900

Date	Mintage	VG	F	VF	XF	Unc
1886/74 Rare	—	—	—	—	—	—

KM# 141.3 10 PESOS
16.1290 g., 0.9000 Gold .4667 oz. AGW **Obv:** Small Phrygian cap **Rev:** Small date, inverted LEI 0.900

Date	Mintage	VG	F	VF	XF	Unc
1863	—	325	450	650	900	—
1864	10,000	325	400	500	800	—
1865	8,727	325	450	650	900	—
1866	13,000	325	400	500	800	—
1867	—	350	475	700	1,000	—
1869	—	350	475	700	1,000	—
1870	—	600	1,000	2,000	3,000	—

KM# 141.4 10 PESOS
16.1290 g., 0.9000 Gold .4667 oz. AGW **Obv:** Small Phrygian cap **Rev:** Small date, inverted LEI 0.900 **Note:** Varieties exist.

Date	Mintage	VG	F	VF	XF	Unc
1873	8,623	345	450	650	1,000	—
1874	—	345	425	625	950	—
1875	—	325	400	550	850	—
1876/5	—	325	400	550	850	—
1876	—	325	400	550	850	—

KM# 142.1 20 PESOS
32.2580 g., 0.9000 Gold .9335 oz. AGW **Obv:** Head left
Rev: Condor with spread wings above flagged arms

Date	Mintage	VG	F	VF	XF	Unc
1862	—	625	675	1,000	1,850	—
1863	—	625	675	1,000	1,850	3,250
1867	—	700	1,200	2,000	3,250	—
1868	—	650	700	1,250	2,150	—
1869	—	650	700	1,250	2,150	—
1870	17,000	650	700	1,250	2,150	—
1871	1,641	675	800	1,600	2,750	—
1872	1,471	650	700	1,250	2,150	—
1873	2,731	650	700	1,250	2,150	—
1874	1,656	650	700	1,250	2,150	—
1875	1,696	650	700	1,250	2,150	—
1876	2,299	700	1,200	2,000	3,250	—
1877	—	1,250	2,000	3,500	6,000	10,000

KM# 142.2 20 PESOS
32.2580 g., 0.9000 Gold .9335 oz. AGW **Obv:** Head left
Rev: Condor with spread wings above flagged arms **Note:** On 1868, arrows in shield on reverse point between zeros in 0.900. On 1869, arrows point at zeros in 0.900

Date	Mintage	VG	F	VF	XF	Unc
1867	—	2,000	3,500	6,000	9,500	—
1868	7,984	625	675	1,000	1,500	—
1869/8	7,313	625	675	1,000	1,500	—
1869	Inc. above	625	675	1,000	1,500	—
1871	5,996	700	1,100	2,250	3,800	—
1872	17,000	625	675	1,000	1,600	—

KM# 142.3 20 PESOS
32.2580 g., 0.9000 Gold .9335 oz. AGW **Obv:** Head left
Rev: Condor with spread wings above flagged arms

Date	Mintage	VG	F	VF	XF	Unc
1863	—	625	675	1,100	1,700	—
1868	—	625	675	1,100	1,700	—
1869	—	625	675	1,100	1,700	2,250
1870	8,247	625	675	1,000	1,600	2,250
1871	5,885	625	675	1,100	1,700	—
1872	—	625	675	1,100	1,700	—
1873	—	625	675	1,100	1,700	—
1874/3	5,352	625	675	1,100	1,700	—
1874	Inc. above	625	675	1,100	1,700	—
1875	5,240	625	675	1,100	1,700	—
1877	1,219	900	1,500	2,750	5,000	—
1878	2,873	650	750	1,400	2,250	—

COLOMBIA

KM# 158 20 PESOS
32.2580 g., 0.9000 Gold .9335 oz. AGW **Obv:** Head left **Rev:** Condor with spread wings above flagged arms **Note:** Modified design

Date	Mintage	VG	F	VF	XF	Unc
1873	—	1,250	2,500	4,500	7,000	—

REPUBLIC
DECIMAL COINAGE
100 Centavos = 1 Peso

KM# 194 2-1/2 PESOS
3.9940 g., 0.9170 Gold .1177 oz. AGW **Obv:** Native, date below **Rev:** Arms and denomination

Date	Mintage	F	VF	XF	Unc	BU
1913	18,000	—	BV	85.00	125	—

KM# 200 2-1/2 PESOS
3.9940 g., 0.9170 Gold .1177 oz. AGW **Obv:** Simon Bolivar large head right, date below **Rev:** Arms and denomination

Date	Mintage	F	VF	XF	Unc	BU
1919A	—	—	BV	80.00	110	—

Note: Two varieties, with large or small first 1 in date

1919B	—	—	—	—	—	—
1919	34,000	—	BV	80.00	110	—
1920/19A	—	—	BV	80.00	110	—
1920A	—	—	BV	80.00	110	—
1920	34,000	—	BV	90.00	150	—

KM# 203 2-1/2 PESOS
3.9940 g., 0.9170 Gold .1177 oz. AGW **Obv:** Simon Bolivar small head, MEDELLIN below, date at bottom **Rev:** Arms and denomination

Date	Mintage	F	VF	XF	Unc	BU
1924	—	—	BV	80.00	110	—
1925 Rare	—	—	—	—	—	—
1927	—	—	BV	85.00	125	—
1928	14,000	—	BV	100	175	—
1929 Rare	—	—	—	—	—	—

KM# 195.1 5 PESOS
7.9881 g., 0.9170 Gold .2355 oz. AGW **Obv:** Native, date below **Rev:** Arms and denomination **Note:** Various rotations of dies exist.

Date	Mintage	F	VF	XF	Unc	BU
1913	17,000	—	—	150	220	—
1918/3	423,000	—	—	BV	180	—
1918	Inc. above	—	—	BV	180	—
1919	2,181,000	—	—	BV	150	165
1919 Long-tail 9	Inc. above	—	—	BV	150	165
1919 Dot over 9	Inc. above	—	—	—	180	—

KM# 195.2 5 PESOS
7.9881 g., 0.9170 Gold .2355 oz. AGW **Obv:** Native, date below **Rev:** Arms and denomination **Note:** Medallic die rotation.

Date	Mintage	F	VF	XF	Unc	BU
1913	Inc. above	—	—	BV	165	175
1917	43,000	—	—	BV	165	175
1918	Inc. above	—	—	BV	165	175
1919	Inc. above	—	—	BV	165	175

KM# 201.1 5 PESOS
7.9881 g., 0.9170 Gold .2355 oz. AGW **Obv:** Simon Bolivar, large head right **Rev:** Arms and denomination **Note:** 1920A dated coins come with mint mark centered or on right side of coat of arms; 1923B dated coins come with B on the left or right of coat of arms. The 1923B mint mark to right carries a 25% premium in value. Various rotations of dies exist.

Date	Mintage	F	VF	XF	Unc	BU
1919	Inc. above	—	—	BV	150	160

Note: Narrow or wide dates, with multiple varieties of numeral alignment

| 1919A | Inc. above | — | — | BV | 150 | 160 |

Note: Narrow or wide date

1919B	—	—	—	BV	155	165
1920	870,000	—	—	BV	150	160
1920A	—	—	—	BV	150	160

Note: Placement of A below coat of arms varies

| 1920B | 108,000 | — | — | BV | 155 | 165 |

Note: Placement of B varies

| 1921A | — | — | — | — | — | — |
| 1922B | 29,000 | — | — | BV | 150 | 160 |

Note: Two varieties known, with B touching or separated from coat of arms

| 1923B | 74,000 | — | — | BV | 150 | 160 |
| 1924B | 705,000 | — | — | BV | 150 | 160 |

Note: Placement of B varies

KM# 201.2 5 PESOS
7.9881 g., 0.9170 Gold .2355 oz. AGW **Obv:** Simon Bolivar, large head **Rev:** Arms and denomination **Note:** Medallic die rotation.

Date	Mintage	F	VF	XF	Unc	BU
1920	Inc. above	—	—	BV	150	160

KM# 204 5 PESOS
7.9881 g., 0.9170 Gold .2355 oz. AGW **Obv:** Simon Bolivar, small head, MEDELLIN below, date at bottom **Rev:** Arms and denomination **Note:** 1924 dated coins have several varieties in size of 2 and 4. 1925 dated coins exist with an Arabic and a Spanish style 5. 1930 dated coins have three varieties in size and placement of 3.

Date	Mintage	F	VF	XF	Unc	BU
1924 Large 2	120,000	—	—	BV	155	165
1924 Large 4	Inc. above	—	—	BV	150	160
1924 Small 4	Inc. above	—	—	BV	155	165
1924 MFDELLIN	Inc. above	—	—	BV	165	175
1925/4	668,000	—	—	BV	150	160
1925 MFDELLIN	Inc. above	—	—	BV	150	160

Note: Wide or narrow date

| 1925 MFDFLLIN | Inc. above | — | — | BV | 150 | 160 |

Note: Wide or narrow date

1926	383,000	—	—	BV	150	160
1926 MFDFLLIN	Inc. above	—	—	BV	150	160
1926 MFDFLLIN	Inc. above	—	—	BV	150	160

Note: With large 6 in date

| 1927 MFDFLLIN | 365,000 | — | — | BV | 150 | 160 |

Note: Wide or narrow date

| 1928 MFDFLLIN | 314,000 | — | — | BV | 150 | 160 |

Note: Narrow or wide date with large or normal 2

| 1929 MFDFLLIN | 321,000 | — | — | BV | 155 | 165 |

Note: Narrow or wide date

| 1930 MFDFLLIN | 502,000 | — | — | BV | 150 | 160 |

Note: Varieties known with aligned date or dropped 3 in date

KM# 202 10 PESOS
15.9761 g., 0.9170 Gold .4710 oz. AGW **Obv:** Head of Simon Bolivar right, date below **Rev:** Arms and denomination

Date	Mintage	F	VF	XF	Unc	BU
1919	101,000	—	BV	315	365	—
1924B	55,000	—	BV	315	365	—

Note: Varieties with aligned date and dropped 4 in date

KM# 231 100 PESOS
4.3000 g., 0.9000 Gold .1244 oz. AGW **Subject:** International Eucharistic Congress **Obv:** Arms divide denomination **Rev:** Bust of Pope Paul VI left and Bogota's Cathedral at left, date below

Date	Mintage	F	VF	XF	Unc	BU
1968	108,000	—	—	—	85.00	—
1968 Proof	8,000	Value: 95.00

KM# 238 100 PESOS
4.3000 g., 0.9000 Gold .1244 oz. AGW **Subject:** Battle of Boyaca - Joachim Paris **Obv:** Bust of Bolivar 3/4 facing **Rev:** Bust of Paris 3/4 facing, dates above, denomination below

Date	Mintage	F	VF	XF	Unc	BU
1969B Proof	6,000	Value: 100
1969NI Proof	Inc. above	Value: 100

KM# 248 100 PESOS
4.3000 g., 0.9000 Gold .1244 oz. AGW **Subject:** 6th Pan-American Games **Obv:** Games logo, date below **Rev:** Javelin thrower within circle, denomination below, 3/4 circle of athletes surround

Date	Mintage	F	VF	XF	Unc	BU
1971 Proof	6,000	Value: 110

KM# 232 200 PESOS
8.6000 g., 0.9000 Gold .2488 oz. AGW **Subject:** International Eucharistic Congress **Obv:** Bust of Pope Paul VI left and Bogota's Cathedral at left, date below **Rev:** Arms divide denomination

Date	Mintage	F	VF	XF	Unc	BU
1968	108,000	—	—	—	165	—
1968 Proof	8,000	Value: 175

KM# 239 200 PESOS
8.6000 g., 0.9000 Gold .2488 oz. AGW **Subject:** Battle of Boyaca - Carlos Soublette **Obv:** Bust of Bolivar 3/4 facing **Rev:** Bust of Soublette 3/4 facing, dates above, denomination below

Date	Mintage	F	VF	XF	Unc	BU
1969B Proof	6,000	Value: 180
1969NI Proof	Inc. above	Value: 180

KM# 249 200 PESOS
8.6000 g., 0.9000 Gold .2488 oz. AGW **Subject:** 6th Pan-American Games in Cali **Obv:** Games logo, date below **Rev:** Runner within circle, denomination below, 3/4 circle of athletes surround

Date	Mintage	F	VF	XF	Unc	BU
1971 Proof	6,000	Value: 190

COLOMBIA

KM# 233 300 PESOS
12.9000 g., 0.9000 Gold .3733 oz. AGW **Subject:** International Eucharistic Congress **Obv:** Bust of Pope Paul VI 3/4 left and Bogota's Cathedral at left, date below **Rev:** Arms above denomination

Date	Mintage	F	VF	XF	Unc	BU
1968	62,000	—	—	—	245	—
1968 Proof	8,000	Value: 260				

KM# 240 300 PESOS
12.9000 g., 0.9000 Gold .3733 oz. AGW **Subject:** Battle of Boyaca - Jose Anzoategui **Obv:** Bust of Bolivar 3/4 facing **Rev:** Bust of Anzoategui 3/4 facing, dates above, denomination below

Date	Mintage	F	VF	XF	Unc	BU
1969B Proof	6,000	Value: 265				
1969NI Proof	Inc. above	Value: 265				

KM# 250 300 PESOS
12.9000 g., 0.9000 Gold .3733 oz. AGW **Subject:** 6th Pan-American Games **Obv:** Games logo, date below **Rev:** Two figures within circle, denomination below, 3/4 circle of athletes surround

Date	Mintage	F	VF	XF	Unc	BU
1971 Proof	6,000	Value: 275				

KM# 234 500 PESOS
21.5000 g., 0.9000 Gold .6221 oz. AGW **Subject:** International Eucharistic Congress **Obv:** Bust of Pope Paul VI 3/4 left and Bogota's Cathedral left, date below **Rev:** Arms above denomination

Date	Mintage	F	VF	XF	Unc	BU
1968	14,000	—	—	—	415	—
1968 Proof	8,000	Value: 435				

KM# 241 500 PESOS
21.5000 g., 0.9000 Gold .6221 oz. AGW **Subject:** Battle of Boyaca **Obv:** Bust of Simon Bolivar 3/4 facing **Rev:** Bust of Juan Jose Rondon 3/4 facing, dates above, denomination below

Date	Mintage	F	VF	XF	Unc	BU
ND(1969)B Proof	6,000	Value: 435				
ND(1969)NI Proof	Inc. above	Value: 435				

KM# 251 500 PESOS
21.5000 g., 0.9000 Gold .6221 oz. AGW **Subject:** 6th Pan-American Games in Cali **Obv:** Games logo, date below **Rev:** Two figures within circle, denomination below, 3/4 circle of athletes surround

Date	Mintage	F	VF	XF	Unc	BU
1971 Proof	6,000	Value: 475				

KM# 254 1000 PESOS
4.3000 g., 0.9000 Gold .1244 oz. AGW **Subject:** 100th Anniversary - Birth of Guillermo Valencia **Obv:** Shield above denomination **Rev:** Head right

Date	Mintage	F	VF	XF	Unc	BU
1973 Proof	10,003	Value: 85.00				

KM# 259 1000 PESOS
4.3000 g., 0.9000 Gold .1244 oz. AGW **Subject:** 450th Anniversary - City of Santa Marta **Obv:** Bust 3/4 right, denomination below **Rev:** Symbol at center, dates below

Date	Mintage	F	VF	XF	Unc	BU
ND(1975) Proof	2,500	Value: 95.00				

KM# 260 1000 PESOS
4.3000 g., 0.9000 Gold .1244 oz. AGW **Subject:** Tricentennial - City of Medellin **Obv:** City gate on shield, sprays flank, dates below **Rev:** Symbol at center, denomination below **Shape:** Square

Date	Mintage	F	VF	XF	Unc	BU
ND(1975) Proof	4,000	Value: 90.00				

KM# 235 1500 PESOS
64.5000 g., 0.9000 Gold 1.8664 oz. AGW **Subject:** International Eucharistic Congress **Obv:** Pope's bust 3/4 left, cathedral at left **Rev:** Arms above denomination

Date	Mintage	F	VF	XF	Unc	BU
1968	5,722	—	—	—	1,250	—
1968 Proof	8,000	Value: 1,300				

KM# 242 1500 PESOS
64.5000 g., 0.9000 Gold 1.8664 oz. AGW **Subject:** Battle of Boyaca **Obv:** Armored bust of Bolivar 3/4 facing **Rev:** Head of Santander right, arms divide dates above, denomination below

Date	Mintage	F	VF	XF	Unc	BU
ND(1969)B Proof	6,000	Value: 1,350				
ND(1969)NI Proof	Inc. above	Value: 1,350				

KM# 252 1500 PESOS
64.5000 g., 0.9000 Gold 1.8664 oz. AGW **Subject:** 6th Pan-American Games **Obv:** Games logo, date below **Rev:** Symbols on raft within circle, denomination below, 3/4 circle of athletes surrounds

Date	Mintage	F	VF	XF	Unc	BU
1971 Proof	6,000	Value: 1,450				

COLOMBIA

KM# 255   1500 PESOS
19.1000 g., 0.9000 Gold .5527 oz. AGW **Subject:** 50th Anniversary - Gold Museum of Central Bank of Bogota **Rev:** Pre-Columbian urn made by Chibcha Indians

Date	Mintage	F	VF	XF	Unc	BU
ND(1973) Proof	4,911	Value: 375				

KM# 257   2000 PESOS
12.9000 g., 0.9000 Gold .3733 oz. AGW **Subject:** 100th Anniversary - Birth of Guillermo Valencia **Obv:** Shield above denomination, date below **Rev:** Bust right, two dates below

Date	Mintage	F	VF	XF	Unc	BU
1973 Proof	5,003	Value: 265				

KM# 261   2000 PESOS
8.6000 g., 0.9000 Gold .2488 oz. AGW **Subject:** 450th Anniversary - City of Santa Marta **Obv:** Bust 3/4 right, denomination below **Rev:** Symbol, dates below

Date	Mintage	F	VF	XF	Unc	BU
ND(1975) Proof	2,500	Value: 175				

KM# 262   2000 PESOS
8.6000 g., 0.9000 Gold .2488 oz. AGW **Subject:** Tricentennial - City of Medellin **Obv:** City gate on shield, sprays flank, two dates below **Rev:** Symbol at center, denomination below **Shape:** Square

Date	Mintage	F	VF	XF	Unc	BU
ND(1975) Proof	4,000	Value: 170				

KM# 266   15000 PESOS
33.4370 g., 0.9000 Gold .9676 oz. AGW **Subject:** Conservation **Obv:** Armored bust left **Rev:** Ocelot left, denomination below

Date	Mintage	F	VF	XF	Unc	BU
1978	490	—	—	—	700	—
1978 Proof	148	Value: 2,000				

KM# 276   15000 PESOS
17.2900 g., 0.9000 Gold .5000 oz. AGW **Subject:** 150th Anniversary - Death of Antonio Jose De Sucre **Obv:** Armored bust 3/4 left divides dates **Rev:** Cornucopias enclose symbol at center, denomination below

Date	Mintage	F	VF	XF	Unc	BU
1980 Proof	250	Value: 375				

KM# 278   15000 PESOS
17.2900 g., 0.9000 Gold .5000 oz. AGW **Subject:** 150th Anniversary - Death of Jose Maria Cordova **Obv:** Bust 3/4 facing, divides dates **Rev:** Cornucopias enclose symbol at center, denomination below

Date	Mintage	F	VF	XF	Unc	BU
1980 Proof	250	Value: 375				

KM# 289   20000 PESOS
8.6400 g., 0.9000 Gold .2500 oz. AGW **Subject:** Birth Centennial **Obv:** Bust of Alfonso Lopez-Pumarejo facing divides dates **Rev:** Building, denomination below

Date	Mintage	F	VF	XF	Unc	BU
ND(1986) Proof	1,351	Value: 210				

KM# 269   30000 PESOS
34.5800 g., 0.9000 Gold 1.0007 oz. AGW **Subject:** Death of Bolivar **Obv:** Funeral scene, dates below **Rev:** Cornucopias flank symbol at center, denomination below

Date	Mintage	F	VF	XF	Unc	BU
1980 Proof	500	Value: 725				

KM# 273   35000 PESOS
8.6400 g., 0.9000 Gold .2500 oz. AGW **Subject:** 100th Anniversary - Birth of President Santos **Obv:** Bust facing divides dates **Rev:** Inscription within wreath

Date	Mintage	F	VF	XF	Unc	BU
ND(1988) Proof	900	Value: 210				

KM# 292   40000 PESOS
17.2800 g., 0.9000 Gold .5000 oz. AGW **Subject:** Centennial - Birthday of Alfonso Lopez-Pumarejo **Obv:** Bust facing divides dates **Rev:** Building, denomination below

Date	Mintage	F	VF	XF	Unc	BU
ND(1986) Proof	1,351	Value: 410				

KM# 290   50000 PESOS
8.6400 g., 0.9000 Gold .2500 oz. AGW **Subject:** Centennial - Birthday of Mariano Ospina P **Obv:** Portrait facing divides dates **Rev:** Inscription within wreath

Date	Mintage	F	VF	XF	Unc	BU
ND(1991) Proof	900	Value: 210				

KM# 277   70000 PESOS
17.2800 g., 0.9000 Gold .5000 oz. AGW **Subject:** 100th Anniversary - Birth of President Santos **Obv:** Bust 3/4 facing divides dates **Rev:** Inscription within wreath

Date	Mintage	F	VF	XF	Unc	BU
ND(1988) Proof	600	Value: 380				

KM# 291   100000 PESOS
17.2800 g., 0.9000 Gold .5000 oz. AGW **Subject:** Centennial - Birthday of Mariano Ospina P **Obv:** Head facing divides dates **Rev:** Inscription within wreath

Date	Mintage	F	VF	XF	Unc	BU
ND(1991) Proof	600	Value: 410				

PATTERNS
Including off metal strikes

KM#	Date	Mintage Identification	Mkt Val
Pn15	1848	— 2 Pesos. 0.9000 Gold. Head left. Denomination within wreath.	4,500
Pn16	1848	— 4 Pesos. 0.9000 Gold. Head left. Denomination within wreath.	7,750
Pn17	1848	— 8 Pesos. 0.9000 Gold. Head left. Condor above flagged arms.	19,800
Pn18	1848	— 16 Pesos. 0.9000 Gold. Head left. Condor above flagged arms.	25,300
Pn34	1872	— 20 Pesos. Gold. Head left. ESSAI.	12,500
Pn48	1873	— 10 Pesos. Gold. Head left. Condor above flagged arms. ESSAI on both sides.	10,000

COLOMBIA

KM#	Date	Mintage	Identification	Mkt Val
Pn49	1873	—	20 Pesos. Gold. Head left. Condor above flagged arms. ESSAI on both sides.	12,500
Pn47	1873	—	10 Pesos. Gold. Head left. Condor above flagged arms.	—
Pn87	1913	—	2-1/2 Pesos. Gold. ENSAYO; KM#194.	—
Pn88	1913	—	5 Pesos. Gold. ENSAYO; KM#195.	—
Pn89	1915	—	2-1/2 Pesos. Gold. ENSAYO; KM#194.	—
Pn92	1923	—	2-1/2 Pesos. Gold. ENSAYO; KM#203.	2,450
Pn94	1923	—	5 Pesos. Gold. ENSAYO, KM#204.	—
Pn106	1956	—	Peso. Gold.	—

TRIAL STRIKES

KM#	Date	Mintage	Identification	Mkt Val
TS9	1873	—	10 Pesos. Gold Plated Bronze.	400
TS10	ND	—	10 Pesos. Gold Plated Bronze.	400
TS11	1873	—	20 Pesos. Gold Plated Bronze.	450
TS12	ND	—	20 Pesos. Gold Plated Bronze.	450

PROOF SETS

KM#	Date	Mintage	Identification	Issue Price	Mkt Val
PS1	1968 (5)	8,000	KM#231-235	340	2,150
PS2	1969 (5)	6,000	KM#238-242	—	2,150
PS3	1971 (5)	6,000	KM#248-252	—	2,450
PS4	1973 (3)	—	KM#254, 256, 257	—	475
PS5	1975 (2)	2,500	KM#260, 262	195	245
PS6	1975 (2)	4,000	KM#259, 261	195	265

COMOROS

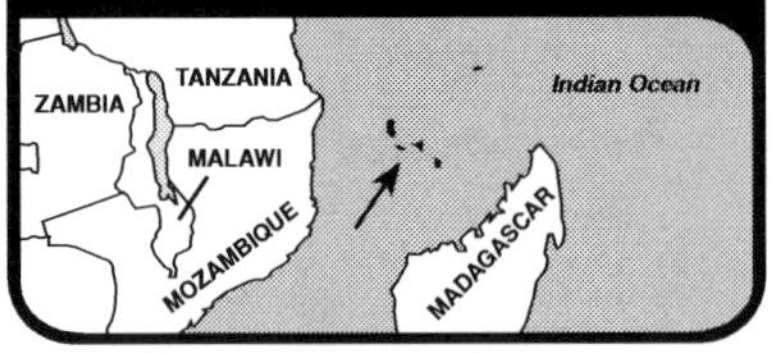

The Federal Islamic Republic of the Comoros, a volcanic archipelago located in the Mozambique Channel of the Indian Ocean 300 miles (483 km.) northwest of Madagascar, has an area of 719 sq. mi. (2,171 sq. km.) and a population of *714,000. Capital: Moroni. The economy of the islands is based on agriculture. There are practically no mineral resources. Vanilla, essence for perfumes, copra, and sisal are exported.

Ancient Phoenician traders were probably the first visitors to the Comoro Islands, but the first detailed knowledge of the area was gathered by Arab sailors. Arab dominion and culture were firmly established when the Portuguese, Dutch, and French arrived in the 16th century. In 1843 a Malagasy ruler ceded the island of Mayotte to France; the other three principal islands of the archipelago-Anjouan, Moheli, and Grand Comore came under French protection in 1886. The islands were joined administratively with Madagascar in 1912. The Comoros became partially autonomous, with the status of a French overseas territory, in 1946, and achieved complete internal autonomy in 1961. On Dec. 31, 1975, after 133 years of French association, the Comoro Islands became the independent Republic of the Comoros.

Mayotte retained the option of determining its future ties and in 1976 voted to remain French. Its present status is that of a French Territorial Collectivity. French currency now circulates there.

TITLES
Daulat Anjazanchiyah

RULERS
Said Ali ibn Said Amr, regnant, 1890
French, 1886-1975

MINT MARKS
(a) - Paris, privy marks only
A - Paris

MONETARY SYSTEM
100 Centimes = 1 Franc

FEDERAL ISLAMIC REPUBLIC

STANDARD COINAGE

KM# 11 10000 FRANCS
3.0700 g., 0.9000 Gold .0888 oz. AGW **Issuer:** Etat Comorien **Obv:** Anjouan sunbird, denomination below **Rev:** Bust of Said Mohamed Cheikh facing divides dates

Date	Mintage	F	VF	XF	Unc	BU
1976	500	—	—	—	100	120
1976 Proof	500	Value: 140				

KM# 12 20000 FRANCS
6.1400 g., 0.9000 Gold .1776 oz. AGW **Issuer:** Etat Comorien **Obv:** Coelacanth fish right, denomination below **Rev:** Bust of Said Mohamed Cheikh facing divides dates

Date	Mintage	F	VF	XF	Unc	BU
1976	500	—	—	—	250	275
1976 Proof	500	Value: 300				

MINT SETS

KM#	Date	Mintage	Identification	Issue Price	Mkt Val
MS1	1976 (3)	500	KM10-12	—	450

PROOF SETS

KM#	Date	Mintage	Identification	Issue Price	Mkt Val
PS1	1976 (3)	500	KM10-12	229	600

CONGO REPUBLIC

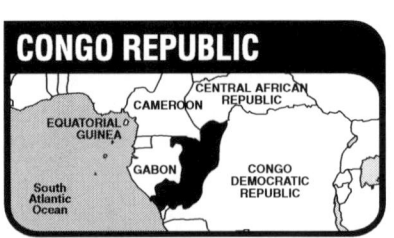

The Republic of the Congo (formerly the Peoples Republic of the Congo), located on the equator in west-central Africa, has an area of 132,047 sq. mi. (342,000 sq. km.) and a population of *2.98 million. Capital: Brazzaville. Agriculture forestry, mining, and food processing are the principal industries. Timber, industrial diamonds, potash, peanuts, and cocoa beans are exported.

The Portuguese were the first Europeans to explore the Congo (Brazzaville) area, 14th century. They conducted a slave trade with the tribal kingdoms of Teke, Loango, and Kongo without attempting developmental colonization. French influence was established in 1883 when the king of Teke signed a treaty with Savorgnan de Brazza, thereby placing his kingdom under the protection of France. While a French protectorate, the area was known as Middle Congo. In 1910 Middle Congo became a part of French Equatorial Africa, which also included Gabon, Ubangi-Shari (now the Central African Republic), and Chad. Following World War II, during which it was an important center of Free French activities, the Middle Congo was given a large measure of internal autonomy, and its inhabitants were made French citizens. Upon approval of the constitution of the Fifth French Republic, 1958, it became a member of the new French Community. On Aug. 15, 1960, Middle Congo became the independent Republic of the Congo-Brazzaville. In Jan. 1970 the country's name was changed to Peoples Republic of the Congo. A new constitution which asserts the government's advocacy of socialism was adopted in 1973.

In June and July of 1992, a new 125-member National Assembly was elected. Later that year a new president, Pascal Lissouba, was elected. In November, President Lissouba dismissed the previous government and dissolved the National Assembly. A new 23-member government, including members of the opposition, was formed in December, 1992, and the name was changed to Republique du Congo.

NOTE: For earlier and related coinage see French Equatorial Africa and the Equatorial African States. For later coinage see Central African States.

RULER
French until 1960

MINT MARK
(a) - Paris, privy marks only

MONETARY SYSTEM
100 Centimes = 1 Franc

ESSAIS
Standard metals unless otherwise noted

KM#	Date	Mintage	Identification	Mkt Val
E2	1971(a)	4	100 Francs. Gold.	1,350

CONGO, DEMOCRATIC REPUBLIC

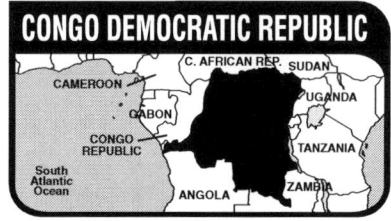

The Democratic Republic of the Congo (formerly the Republic of Zaire, and earlier the Belgian Congo), located in the south-central part of Africa, has an area of 905,568 sq. mi. (2,345,410 sq. km.) and a population of *47.4 million. Capital: Kinshasa. The mineral-rich country produces copper, tin, diamonds, gold, zinc, cobalt and uranium.

In ancient times the territory comprising former Zaire was occupied by Negrito peoples (Pygmies) pushed into the mountains by Bantu and Nilotic invaders. The interior was first explored by the American correspondent Henry Stanley, who was subsequently commissioned by King Leopold II of Belgium to conclude development treaties with the local chiefs. The Berlin conference of 1885 awarded the area to Leopold, who administered and exploited it as his private property until it was annexed to Belgium in 1908. Belgium received the mandate for the German territory of Ruanda-Urundi as a result of the international treaties after WWI. During World War II, Belgian Congolese troops fought on the side of the Allies, notably in Ethiopia. Following the eruption of bloody independence riots in 1959, Belgium granted the Belgian Congo independence as the Republic of the Congo on June 30, 1960. The nation officially changed its name to Zaire on Oct. 27, 1971, and following a Civil War in 1997 changed its name to the "Democratic Republic of the Congo."

REPUBLIC
1960 - 1971
DECIMAL COINAGE

KM# 2 10 FRANCS
3.2260 g., 0.9000 Gold .0934 oz. AGW **Subject:** 5th Anniversary of Independence **Obv:** President Joseph Kasa-Vubu **Rev:** Crossed palm trees, denomination below **Note:** Approximately 70 percent melted.

Date	Mintage	F	VF	XF	Unc	BU
1965 Proof	Est. 3,000	Value: 75.00				

KM# 3 20 FRANCS
6.4520 g., 0.9000 Gold .1867 oz. AGW **Subject:** 5th Anniversary of Independence **Obv:** Uniformed bust of President Joseph Kasa-Vubu 3/4 right **Rev:** Crossed palm trees, denomination below **Note:** Approximately 70 percent melted.

Date	Mintage	F	VF	XF	Unc	BU
1965 Proof	Est. 3,000	Value: 145				

KM# 4 25 FRANCS
8.0640 g., 0.9000 Gold .2334 oz. AGW **Subject:** 5th Anniversary of Independence **Rev:** Elephant left **Note:** Approximately 70 percent melted.

Date	Mintage	F	VF	XF	Unc	BU
1965 Proof	Est. 3,000	Value: 180				

KM# 5 50 FRANCS
16.1290 g., 0.9000 Gold .4668 oz. AGW **Subject:** 5th Anniversary of Independence **Obv:** Uniformed President's bust 3/4 right **Rev:** Elephant left, denomination and date below **Note:** Approximately 70 percent melted.

Date	Mintage	F	VF	XF	Unc	BU
1965 Proof	Est. 3,000	Value: 360				

KM# 6 100 FRANCS
32.2580 g., 0.9000 Gold .9335 oz. AGW **Subject:** 5th Anniversary of Independence **Obv:** Uniformed bust of President Joseph Kasa-Vubu 3/4 right **Rev:** Elephant left **Note:** Approximately 70 percent melted.

Date	Mintage	F	VF	XF	Unc	BU
1965 Proof	Est. 3,000	Value: 675				

REFORM COINAGE
100 Sengis = 1 Likuta; 100 Makuta (plural of Likuta) = 1 Zaire

KM# 10 10 SENGIS
3.2000 g., 0.9000 Gold .0926 oz. AGW **Subject:** 5th Year of Mobutu Presidency **Obv:** Arms above denomination **Rev:** Military bust of President Joseph Desire Mobutu 3/4 facing, date below

Date	Mintage	F	VF	XF	Unc	BU
1970	1,000	—	—	—	70.00	—
1970 Proof	1,000	Value: 95.00				

KM# 11a 25 MAKUTAS
8.0000 g., 0.9000 Gold .2315 oz. AGW **Subject:** 5th Year of Mobutu Presidency **Obv:** Arms above denomination **Rev:** President's bust facing

Date	Mintage	F	VF	XF	Unc	BU
1970	1,000	—	—	—	165	—
1970 Proof	1,000	Value: 185				

KM# 12a 50 MAKUTAS
16.0000 g., 0.9000 Gold .4630 oz. AGW **Subject:** 5th Year of Mobutu Presidency **Obv:** Arms above denomination **Rev:** President's bust 3/4 facing, date below

Date	Mintage	F	VF	XF	Unc	BU
1970	1,000	—	—	—	325	—
1970 Proof	1,000	Value: 345				

KM# 13a ZAIRE
32.0000 g., 0.9000 Gold .9261 oz. AGW **Subject:** 5th Year of Mobutu Presidency **Obv:** Arms above denomination **Rev:** President's bust, 3/4 facing, date below

Date	Mintage	F	VF	XF	Unc	BU
1970	1,000	—	—	—	665	—
1970 Proof	1,000	Value: 700				

DEMOCRATIC REPUBLIC
1998 -
REFORM COINAGE
Congo Francs replace Zaire; July 1998

KM# 29 20 FRANCS
1.5300 g., 0.9990 Gold .0492 oz. AGW **Subject:** 25th Anniversary - Visit of Pope John Paul II **Obv:** Standing lion facing, denomination below **Rev:** Bust right of Pope John Paul II **Note:** Prev. KM#52.

Date	Mintage	F	VF	XF	Unc	BU
2000 Proof	—	Value: 45.00				

KM# 136 20 FRANCS
1.2440 g., 0.9999 Gold 0.04 oz. AGW, 13.92 mm. **Obv:** Lion left **Rev:** Pope John Paul II with staff and mitre, waving **Edge:** Plain

Date	Mintage	F	VF	XF	Unc	BU
2003 Proof	—	Value: 55.00				

KM# 137 20 FRANCS
1.2440 g., 0.9999 Gold 0.04 oz. AGW, 13.92 mm. **Obv:** Lion left **Rev:** Skunk **Edge:** Plain

Date	Mintage	F	VF	XF	Unc	BU
2003 Proof	25,000	Value: 55.00				

KM# 138 20 FRANCS
1.2440 g., 0.9999 Gold 0.04 oz. AGW, 13.92 mm. **Obv:** Lion left **Rev:** Giant anteater right **Edge:** Plain

Date	Mintage	F	VF	XF	Unc	BU
2003 Proof	25,000	Value: 55.00				

KM# 139 20 FRANCS
1.2440 g., 0.9999 Gold 0.04 oz. AGW, 13.92 mm. **Obv:** Lion left **Rev:** Porcupine right **Edge:** Plain

Date	Mintage	F	VF	XF	Unc	BU
2003 Proof	25,000	Value: 55.00				

KM# 140 20 FRANCS
1.2440 g., 0.9999 Gold 0.04 oz. AGW, 13.92 mm. **Obv:** Lion left **Rev:** Chameleon **Edge:** Plain

Date	Mintage	F	VF	XF	Unc	BU
2003 Proof	25,000	Value: 55.00				

KM# 144 20 FRANCS
1.2440 g., 0.9999 Gold 0.04 oz. AGW, 13.92 mm. **Obv:** Lion left **Rev:** Ferrari coat of arms **Edge:** Plain

Date	Mintage	F	VF	XF	Unc	BU
2004 Proof	5,000	Value: 55.00				

KM# 177 100 FRANCS
39.2000 g., Gold **Obv:** Roaring lion **Rev:** Dr. Livingstone and river boat **Edge:** Reeded

Date	Mintage	F	VF	XF	Unc	BU
1999 Proof	—	—	—	—	—	—

KM# 42 100 FRANCS
31.5400 g., 0.9999 Gold 1.0139 oz. AGW, 37.3 mm. **Subject:** Wild Life Protection **Obv:** Standing lion facing, denomination below **Rev:** Multicolor holographic parrot with folded wings right **Edge:** Reeded **Note:** Prev. KM#65.

Date	Mintage	F	VF	XF	Unc	BU
2000 Proof	25	Value: 1,200				

CONGO DEMOCRATIC REPUBLIC

KM# 43   100 FRANCS
31.5400 g., 0.9999 Gold 1.0139 oz. AGW, 37.3 mm.
Subject: Wild Life Protection **Obv:** Standing lion facing, denomination below **Rev:** Multicolor holographic parrot with open wings left **Edge:** Reeded **Note:** Prev. KM#66.

Date	Mintage	F	VF	XF	Unc	BU
2000 Proof	25	Value: 1,200				

KM# 129   100 FRANCS
31.1000 g., 0.9999 Gold 0.9998 oz. AGW, 40 mm. **Obv:** Lion left **Rev:** Reflective multicolor swallowtail butterfly **Edge:** Reeded

Date	Mintage	F	VF	XF	Unc	BU
2002 Proof	50	Value: 1,000				

KM# 130   100 FRANCS
31.1000 g., 0.9999 Gold 0.9998 oz. AGW, 40 mm. **Obv:** Lion left **Rev:** Reflective multicolor dark greenish butterfly **Edge:** Reeded

Date	Mintage	F	VF	XF	Unc	BU
2002 Proof	50	Value: 1,000				

KM# 131   100 FRANCS
31.1000 g., 0.9999 Gold 0.9998 oz. AGW, 40 mm. **Obv:** Lion left **Rev:** Reflective multicolor red and black butterfly **Edge:** Reeded

Date	Mintage	F	VF	XF	Unc	BU
2002 Proof	50	Value: 1,000				

KM# 152   100 FRANCS
31.1035 g., 0.9999 Gold 0.9999 oz. AGW, 38.6 mm. **Obv:** Lion left **Rev:** Multicolor Quetzal bird **Edge:** Reeded

Date	Mintage	F	VF	XF	Unc	BU
2004 Proof	25	Value: 1,200				

KM# 153   100 FRANCS
31.1035 g., 0.9999 Gold 0.9999 oz. AGW, 38.6 mm. **Obv:** Lion left **Rev:** Multicolor Bird of Paradise left **Edge:** Reeded

Date	Mintage	F	VF	XF	Unc	BU
2004 Proof	25	Value: 1,200				

KM# 154   100 FRANCS
31.1035 g., 0.9999 Gold 0.9999 oz. AGW, 38.6 mm. **Obv:** Lion left **Rev:** Multicolor Kingfisher bird **Edge:** Reeded

Date	Mintage	F	VF	XF	Unc	BU
2004 Proof	25	Value: 1,200				

ESSAIS

KM#	Date	Mintage	Identification	Mkt Val
E6	1970	10	Zaire. Gold. ESSAI.	1,000

MINT SETS

KM#	Date	Mintage	Identification	Issue Price	Mkt Val
MS1	1970 (4)	1,000	KM10-13	1,300	1,000

PROOF SETS

KM#	Date	Mintage	Identification	Issue Price	Mkt Val
PS1	1965 (5)	3,000	KM2-6. Approximately 70 percent melted.	490	1,300
PS2	1970 (4)	1,000	KM10-13	—	1,100

COOK ISLANDS

Cook Islands, a self-governing dependency of New Zealand consisting of 15 islands, is located in the South Pacific Ocean about 2,000 miles (3,218 km.) northeast of New Zealand. It has an area of 93 sq. mi. (234 sq. km.) and a population of 17,185. Capital: Avarua. The United States claims the islands of Danger, Manahiki, Penrhyn, and Rakahanga atolls. Citrus and canned fruits and juices, copra, clothing, jewelry, and mother-of-pearl shell are exported.

Spanish navigator Alvaro de Mendada first sighted the islands in 1595. Portuguese navigator Pedro Fernandes de Quieros landed on Rakahanga in 1606. English navigator Capt. James Cook sailed to the islands on three occasions: 1773, 1774 and 1777. He named them Hervey Islands, in honor of Augustus John Hervey, a lord of the Admiralty. The islands were declared a British protectorate in 1888, and were annexed to New Zealand in 1901. They were granted internal self-government in 1965. New Zealand provides an annual subsidy and retains responsibility for defense and foreign affairs.

RULER
British

MINT MARKS
(b) - British Royal Mint
FM - Franklin Mint, U.S.A. *
PM - Pobjoy Mint
  *NOTE: From 1975-1985 the Franklin Mint produced coinage in up to three different qualities. Qualities of issue are designated in () after each date and are defined as follows:
  (M) MATTE - Normal circulation strike or a dull finish produced by sandblasting special uncirculated (polish finish) or proof quality dies.
  (U) SPECIAL UNCIRCULATED - Polished or proof-like in appearance without any frosted features.
  (P) PROOF - The highest quality obtainable having mirror-like fields and frosted features.

MONETARY SYSTEM
                    (Until 1967)
12 Pence = 1 Shilling
20 Shillings = 1 Pound
             (Commencing 1967)
100 Cents = 1 Dollar

DEPENDENCY OF NEW ZEALAND
DECIMAL COINAGE

KM# 30b   DOLLAR
39.8000 g., 0.9170 Gold 1.1735 oz. AGW, 38.5 mm.
Ruler: Elizabeth II **Subject:** 16th Forum, 2nd P.I.C. and Mini Games **Obv:** Young bust right, date below **Rev:** Tangaroa, Polynesian God of Creation

Date	Mintage	F	VF	XF	Unc	BU
1985 Proof	Est. 25	Value: 1,750				

COOK ISLANDS 159

KM# 31b DOLLAR
44.0000 g., 0.9170 Gold 1.2969 oz. AGW, 38.5 mm.
Ruler: Elizabeth II **Subject:** 60th Birthday of Queen Elizabeth II
Obv: Crowned bust right, date below **Rev:** Busts of Andrew and Sarah facing each other within wreath

Date	Mintage	F	VF	XF	Unc	BU
1986 Proof	Est. 60	Value: 950				

KM# 32b DOLLAR
44.0000 g., 0.9170 Gold 1.2969 oz. AGW, 38.5 mm.
Ruler: Elizabeth II **Subject:** Prince Andrews Wedding
Obv: Crowned bust right, date below **Rev:** Busts of Andrew and Sarah facing each other within wreath

Date	Mintage	F	VF	XF	Unc	BU
1986 Proof	Est. 75	Value: 950				

KM# 455a DOLLAR
25.2700 g., Gold Plated Copper-Nickel, 38.3 mm.
Ruler: Elizabeth II **Obv:** Elizabeth II **Rev:** Playboy magazine's 50th Anniversary logo **Edge:** Reeded

Date	Mintage	F	VF	XF	Unc	BU
2003 Proof	50,000	Value: 20.00				

KM# 455c DOLLAR
25.2700 g., 0.9990 Gold Plated Silver 0.8116 oz. ASW AGW, 38.3 mm. **Ruler:** Elizabeth II **Obv:** Elizabeth II **Rev:** Playboy magazine's 50th Anniversary logo **Edge:** Reeded

Date	Mintage	F	VF	XF	Unc	BU
2003 Proof	—	Value: 50.00				

KM# 424a DOLLAR
8.5000 g., 0.9990 Gold Plated Silver 0.273 oz. ASW AGW, 25.1 mm.
Ruler: Elizabeth II **Obv:** Crowned head above ornamental center
Rev: Encapslated emeralds above Crab (cancer)

Date	Mintage	F	VF	XF	Unc	BU
ND(2003) Proof	10,000	Value: 30.00				

KM# 425a DOLLAR
8.5000 g., 0.9990 Gold Plated Silver 0.273 oz. ASW AGW, 25.1 mm.
Ruler: Elizabeth II **Obv:** Crowned head above ornamental center
Rev: Encapsulated garnets with Aquarious in background

Date	Mintage	F	VF	XF	Unc	BU
ND(2003) Proof	10,000	Value: 30.00				

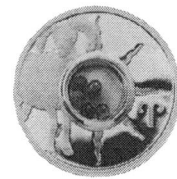

KM# 426a DOLLAR
8.5000 g., 0.9990 Gold Plated Silver 0.273 oz. ASW AGW, 25.1 mm.
Ruler: Elizabeth II **Obv:** Crowned head above ornamental center
Rev: Encapsulated Bloodstones in center with ram at left

Date	Mintage	F	VF	XF	Unc	BU
ND(2003) Proof	10,000	Value: 30.00				

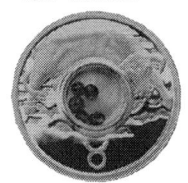

KM# 427a DOLLAR
8.5000 g., 0.9990 Gold Plated Silver 0.273 oz. ASW AGW, 25.1 mm. **Ruler:** Elizabeth II **Subject:** Zodiac Gemstones - Taurus **Obv:** Crowned head above ornamental center **Rev:** Encapsulated Sapphires with bull in background **Edge:** Reeded

Date	Mintage	F	VF	XF	Unc	BU
ND(2003) Proof	10,000	Value: 30.00				

KM# 428a DOLLAR
8.5000 g., 0.9990 Gold Plated Silver 0.273 oz. ASW AGW, 25.1 mm. **Ruler:** Elizabeth II **Obv:** Crowned head above ornamental center **Rev:** Encapsulated Agates between twins **Edge:** Reeded

Date	Mintage	F	VF	XF	Unc	BU
ND(2003) Proof	10,000	Value: 30.00				

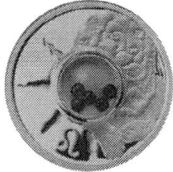

KM# 429a DOLLAR
8.5000 g., 0.9990 Gold Plated Silver 0.273 oz. ASW AGW, 25.1 mm. **Ruler:** Elizabeth II **Obv:** Crowned head above ornamental center **Rev:** Encapsulated Onyx stones with lion at right **Edge:** Reeded

Date	Mintage	F	VF	XF	Unc	BU
ND(2003) Proof	10,000	Value: 30.00				

KM# 430a DOLLAR
8.5000 g., 0.9990 Gold Plated Silver 0.273 oz. ASW AGW, 25.1 mm. **Ruler:** Elizabeth II **Subject:** Zodiac Gemstones - Virgo **Obv:** Crowned head above ornamental center **Rev:** Encapsulated Carnelian stones with Virgo at right **Edge:** Reeded

Date	Mintage	F	VF	XF	Unc	BU
ND(2003) Proof	10,000	Value: 30.00				

KM# 431a DOLLAR
8.5000 g., 0.9990 Gold Plated Silver 0.273 oz. ASW AGW, 25.1 mm. **Ruler:** Elizabeth II **Subject:** Zodiac Gemstones - Libra **Obv:** Crowned head above ornamental center **Rev:** Encapsulated Peridot stones with balance scale **Edge:** Reeded

Date	Mintage	F	VF	XF	Unc	BU
ND(2003) Proof	10,000	Value: 30.00				

KM# 432a DOLLAR
8.5000 g., 0.9990 Gold Plated Silver 0.273 oz. ASW AGW, 25.1 mm. **Ruler:** Elizabeth II **Subject:** Zodiac Gemstones - Scorpio **Obv:** Crowned head above ornamental center **Rev:** Encapsulated Aquamarine stones with scorpion at lower right **Edge:** Reeded

Date	Mintage	F	VF	XF	Unc	BU
ND(2003) Proof	10,000	Value: 30.00				

KM# 433a DOLLAR
8.5000 g., 0.9990 Gold Plated Silver 0.273 oz. ASW AGW, 25.1 mm. **Ruler:** Elizabeth II **Subject:** Zodiac Gemstones - Sagittarius **Obv:** Crowned head above ornamental center **Rev:** Encapsulated Topaz stones with centaur at right **Edge:** Reeded

Date	Mintage	F	VF	XF	Unc	BU
ND(2003) Proof	10,000	Value: 30.00				

KM# 434a DOLLAR
8.5000 g., 0.9990 Gold Plated Silver 0.273 oz. ASW AGW, 25.1 mm. **Ruler:** Elizabeth II **Subject:** Zodiac Gemstones - Capricorn **Obv:** Crowned head above ornamental center **Rev:** Encapsulated Rubies with goat at right **Edge:** Reeded

Date	Mintage	F	VF	XF	Unc	BU
ND(2003) Proof	10,000	Value: 30.00				

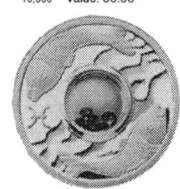

KM# 435a DOLLAR
8.5000 g., 0.9990 Gold Plated Silver 0.273 oz. ASW AGW, 25.1 mm. **Ruler:** Elizabeth II **Subject:** Zodiac Gemstones - Pices **Obv:** Crowned head above ornamental center **Rev:** Encapsulated Amethyst stones and 2 fish **Edge:** Reeded

Date	Mintage	F	VF	XF	Unc	BU
ND(2003) Proof	10,000	Value: 30.00				

KM# 457 5 DOLLARS
1.2000 g., 0.9995 Platinum 0.0386 oz. APW **Ruler:** Elizabeth II
Subject: Love Angels

Date	Mintage	F	VF	XF	Unc	BU
1997 Proof	250	Value: 45.00				

COOK ISLANDS

KM# 312 5 DOLLARS
1.2441 g., 0.9999 Gold .04 oz. AGW **Ruler:** Elizabeth II
Obv: Crowned head right, date below **Rev:** Portrait of Princess Diana, dates, denomination below
Date	Mintage	F	VF	XF	Unc	BU
1997 Proof	—	Value: 30.00				

KM# 285 10 DOLLARS
1.2441 g., 0.9990 Gold .0399 oz. AGW **Ruler:** Elizabeth II
Subject: Olympic National Park **Obv:** Crowned head right, date below **Rev:** Eagle's head right, denomination below
Rev. Designer: Alex Shagin
Date	Mintage	F	VF	XF	Unc	BU
1996 Proof	—	Value: 30.00				

KM# 286 10 DOLLARS
1.2441 g., 0.9990 Gold .0399 oz. AGW **Ruler:** Elizabeth II
Subject: Yellowstone National Park **Obv:** Crowned head right, date below **Rev. Designer:** Alex Shagin
Date	Mintage	F	VF	XF	Unc	BU
1996 Proof	—	Value: 30.00				

KM# 458 10 DOLLARS
2.5000 g., 0.9995 Platinum 0.0803 oz. APW **Ruler:** Elizabeth II
Subject: Love Angels
Date	Mintage	F	VF	XF	Unc	BU
1997 Proof	250	Value: 90.00				

KM# 236 20 DOLLARS
1.2441 g., 0.9990 Gold .04 oz. AGW **Ruler:** Elizabeth II
Subject: 500 Years of America **Obv:** Crowned head right, date below **Rev:** Columbus claims the New World, denomination below
Date	Mintage	F	VF	XF	Unc	BU
1995	Est. 25,000	—	—	—	30.00	—

KM# 237 20 DOLLARS
1.2441 g., 0.9990 Gilt Silver .04 oz. **Ruler:** Elizabeth II
Subject: 500 Years of America **Obv:** Crowned head right, date below **Rev:** Washington crossing the Delaware, denomination below
Date	Mintage	F	VF	XF	Unc	BU
1995	Est. 25,000	—	—	—	30.00	—

KM# 257 20 DOLLARS
1.2441 g., 0.9999 Gold .0400 oz. AGW **Ruler:** Elizabeth II
Subject: 500 Years of America **Obv:** Crowned head right, date below **Rev:** Statue of Liberty, denomination below
Date	Mintage	F	VF	XF	Unc	BU
1995	Est. 25,000	—	—	—	30.00	—

KM# 258 20 DOLLARS
1.2441 g., 0.9999 Gold .0400 oz. AGW **Ruler:** Elizabeth II
Subject: 500 Years of America **Obv:** Crowned head right, date below **Rev:** Capt. James Cook bust right, denomination below
Date	Mintage	F	VF	XF	Unc	BU
1995 Proof	Est. 25,000	Value: 30.00				

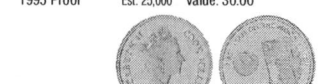

KM# 270 20 DOLLARS
1.2441 g., 0.9999 Gold .0400 oz. AGW **Ruler:** Elizabeth II
Subject: 500 Years of America **Obv:** Crowned head right, date below **Rev:** Astronaut on moon, denomination below
Date	Mintage	F	VF	XF	Unc	BU
Z1995 Proof	Est. 25,000	Value: 30.00				

KM# 298 20 DOLLARS
3.0000 g., 0.9999 Gold .0964 oz. AGW **Ruler:** Elizabeth II
Subject: Year of the Mouse **Obv:** Crowned head right, date below **Rev:** Multicolor Mickey Mouse portrait facing, denomination below
Date	Mintage	F	VF	XF	Unc	BU
1996 Proof	—	Value: 65.00				

KM# 83 25 DOLLARS
1.2144 g., 0.9990 Gold .0400 oz. AGW **Ruler:** Elizabeth II
Subject: Endangered Wildlife **Obv:** Crowned head right, date below **Rev:** Bison head left, denomination below
Date	Mintage	F	VF	XF	Unc	BU
1990 Proof	100,000	Value: 32.50				

KM# 84 25 DOLLARS
1.2144 g., 0.9990 Gold .0400 oz. AGW **Ruler:** Elizabeth II
Subject: Endangered Wildlife **Obv:** Crowned head right, date below **Rev:** Longhorn sheep head facing, denomination below
Date	Mintage	F	VF	XF	Unc	BU
1990 Proof	Est. 100,000	Value: 32.50				

KM# 85 25 DOLLARS
1.2144 g., 0.9990 Gold .0400 oz. AGW **Ruler:** Elizabeth II
Subject: Endangered Wildlife **Obv:** Crowned head right, date below **Rev:** Tiger head, denomination below
Date	Mintage	F	VF	XF	Unc	BU
1990 Proof	—	Value: 32.50				

KM# 86 25 DOLLARS
1.2144 g., 0.9990 Gold .0400 oz. AGW **Ruler:** Elizabeth II
Subject: Endangered Wildlife **Obv:** Crowned head right, date below **Rev:** Eagle
Date	Mintage	F	VF	XF	Unc	BU
1990 Proof	Est. 100,000	Value: 32.50				

KM# 87 25 DOLLARS
1.2144 g., 0.9990 Gold .0400 oz. AGW **Ruler:** Elizabeth II
Subject: Endangered Wildlife **Obv:** Crowned head right, date below **Rev:** Elephant head left, denomination below
Date	Mintage	F	VF	XF	Unc	BU
1990 Proof	Est. 100,000	Value: 32.50				

KM# 88 25 DOLLARS
1.2144 g., 0.9990 Gold .0400 oz. AGW **Ruler:** Elizabeth II
Subject: Endangered Wildlife **Obv:** Crowned head right, date below **Rev:** Lynx head left, denomination below
Date	Mintage	F	VF	XF	Unc	BU
1990 Proof	Est. 100,000	Value: 32.50				

KM# 239 25 DOLLARS
1.2144 g., 0.9990 Gold .0400 oz. AGW **Ruler:** Elizabeth II
Subject: Endangered Wildlife **Obv:** Crowned head right, date below **Rev:** Bee hummingbird right, denomination below
Date	Mintage	F	VF	XF	Unc	BU
1990 Proof	Est. 100,000	Value: 32.50				

KM# 240 25 DOLLARS
1.2144 g., 0.9990 Gold .0400 oz. AGW **Ruler:** Elizabeth II
Subject: Endangered Wildlife **Obv:** Crowned head right, date below **Rev:** Koala bear, denomination below
Date	Mintage	F	VF	XF	Unc	BU
1991 Proof	Est. 100,000	Value: 32.50				

KM# 241 25 DOLLARS
1.2144 g., 0.9990 Gold .0400 oz. AGW **Ruler:** Elizabeth II
Subject: Endangered Wildlife **Obv:** Crowned head right, date below **Rev:** Panda bear, denomination below
Date	Mintage	F	VF	XF	Unc	BU
1991 Proof	Est. 100,000	Value: 32.50				
1997PM Proof	—	Value: 37.50				

KM# 138 25 DOLLARS
1.2144 g., 0.9990 Gold .0400 oz. AGW **Ruler:** Elizabeth II
Subject: Endangered Wildlife **Obv:** Crowned head right, date below **Rev:** Przewalski's horse galloping right, denomination below
Date	Mintage	F	VF	XF	Unc	BU
1992 Prooflike	—	—	—	—	32.50	—

KM# 242 25 DOLLARS
1.2144 g., 0.9990 Gold .0400 oz. AGW **Ruler:** Elizabeth II
Subject: Endangered Wildlife **Obv:** Crowned head right, date below **Rev:** African lion, denomination below
Date	Mintage	F	VF	XF	Unc	BU
1992 Proof	Est. 100,000	Value: 32.50				

KM# 243 25 DOLLARS
1.2144 g., 0.9990 Gold .0400 oz. AGW **Ruler:** Elizabeth II
Subject: Endangered Wildlife **Obv:** Crowned head right, date below **Rev:** Butterfly, denomination below
Date	Mintage	F	VF	XF	Unc	BU
1992 Proof	Est. 100,000	Value: 32.50				

KM# 238 25 DOLLARS
6.2200 g., 0.5830 Gold .1166 oz. AGW **Ruler:** Elizabeth II
Subject: 1996 Olympics **Obv:** Crowned head right, date below **Rev:** Ancient archer within circle, denomination below
Date	Mintage	F	VF	XF	Unc	BU
1995 Proof	Est. 5,000	Value: 80.00				

KM# 291 25 DOLLARS
3.1103 g., 0.9990 Gold .1000 oz. AGW **Ruler:** Elizabeth II
Subject: Olympic National Park **Obv:** Crowned head right, date below **Rev:** Bald eagle head right, denomination below
Date	Mintage	F	VF	XF	Unc	BU
1996 Proof	—	Value: 70.00				

KM# 292 25 DOLLARS
3.1103 g., 0.9990 Gold .1000 oz. AGW **Ruler:** Elizabeth II
Subject: Yellowstone National Park **Obv:** Crowned head right, date below **Rev:** Grizzly bear
Date	Mintage	F	VF	XF	Unc	BU
1996 Proof	—	Value: 70.00				

COOK ISLANDS

KM# 439 30 DOLLARS
10.0000 g., 0.9999 Gold 0.3215 oz. AGW, 16.1 mm.
Ruler: Elizabeth II **Obv:** Crowned head right, date below
Rev: Multicolor Peony flower and denomination **Edge:** Reeded

Date	Mintage	F	VF	XF	Unc	BU
2004	10,000	—	—	—	—	225

KM# 440 35 DOLLARS
10.0000 g., 0.9999 Gold 0.3215 oz. AGW, 16.1 mm. **Ruler:** Elizabeth II **Obv:** Crowned head right, date below **Rev:** Multicolor Chinese man beating a tiger and denomination **Edge:** Reeded

Date	Mintage	F	VF	XF	Unc	BU
2004	6,000	—	—	—	—	225

KM# 441 35 DOLLARS
10.0000 g., 0.9999 Gold 0.3215 oz. AGW, 16.1 mm. **Ruler:** Elizabeth II **Obv:** Crowned head right, date below **Rev:** Multicolor Chinese man riding a horse and denomination **Edge:** Reeded

Date	Mintage	F	VF	XF	Unc	BU
2004	10,000	—	—	—	—	225

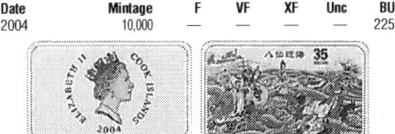

KM# 442 35 DOLLARS
10.0000 g., 0.9999 Gold 0.3215 oz. AGW, 25 x 15 mm.
Ruler: Elizabeth II **Obv:** Crowned head right, date below
Rev: Multicolor "Eight immortals crossing the sea" and denomination **Edge:** Plain **Shape:** Ingot

Date	Mintage	F	VF	XF	Unc	BU
2004	3,000	—	—	—	—	225

KM# 203 50 DOLLARS
3.9450 g., 0.5000 Gold 0.0634 oz. AGW **Ruler:** Elizabeth II
Obv: Young bust right, date below **Rev:** Denomination above plant

Date	Mintage	F	VF	XF	Unc	BU
1980 Proof	—	Value: 47.50				

KM# 27 50 DOLLARS
3.9450 g., 0.5000 Gold 0.0634 oz. AGW **Ruler:** Elizabeth II
Subject: Wedding of Prince Charles and Lady Diana **Obv:** Young bust right, date below **Rev:** Denomination below symbol

Date	Mintage	F	VF	XF	Unc	BU
1981	220	—	—	—	47.50	—
1981 Proof	1,309	Value: 52.50				

KM# 145 50 DOLLARS
7.7750 g., 0.5833 Gold .1458 oz. AGW **Ruler:** Elizabeth II
Subject: 500 Years of America **Obv:** Crowned head right, date below **Rev:** Columbus kneeling with flag, denomination below

Date	Mintage	F	VF	XF	Unc	BU
1991 Proof	Est. 60,000	Value: 95.00				

KM# 129 50 DOLLARS
7.7760 g., 0.5830 Gold .1458 oz. AGW **Ruler:** Elizabeth II
Subject: Endangered Wildlife **Obv:** Crowned head right, date below **Rev:** Eagles head

Date	Mintage	F	VF	XF	Unc	BU
1992 Proof	—	Value: 95.00				

KM# 131 50 DOLLARS
7.7760 g., 0.5830 Gold .1458 oz. AGW **Ruler:** Elizabeth II
Subject: Endangered Wildlife **Obv:** Crowned head right, date below **Rev:** Elephant head

Date	Mintage	F	VF	XF	Unc	BU
1992 Proof	—	Value: 95.00				

KM# 132 50 DOLLARS
7.7760 g., 0.5830 Gold .1458 oz. AGW **Ruler:** Elizabeth II
Subject: Endangered Wildlife **Obv:** Crowned head right, date below **Rev:** Tiger head

Date	Mintage	F	VF	XF	Unc	BU
1992 Proof	—	Value: 95.00				

KM# 176 50 DOLLARS
7.7760 g., 0.5833 Gold .1458 oz. AGW **Ruler:** Elizabeth II
Subject: 500 Years of America **Obv:** Crowned head right, date below **Rev:** Robert de La Salle

Date	Mintage	F	VF	XF	Unc	BU
1992 Proof	—	Value: 95.00				

KM# 204 50 DOLLARS
7.7760 g., 0.5833 Gold .1458 oz. AGW **Ruler:** Elizabeth II **Subject:** 500 Years of America **Obv:** Crowned head right, date below **Rev:** Bust of John Cabot at left, ship at right, denomination below

Date	Mintage	F	VF	XF	Unc	BU
1992 Proof	5,000	Value: 95.00				

KM# 249 50 DOLLARS
7.7760 g., 0.5830 Gold .1458 oz. AGW **Ruler:** Elizabeth II
Subject: 500 Years of America **Obv:** Crowned head right, date below **Rev:** Busts of Ferdinand and Isabella half right, denomination below

Date	Mintage	F	VF	XF	Unc	BU
1992 Proof	Est. 5,000	Value: 95.00				

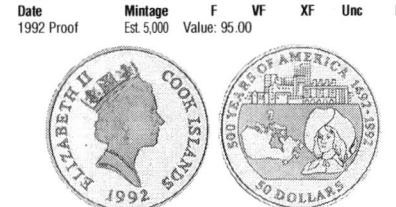

KM# 259 50 DOLLARS
7.7760 g., 0.5830 Gold .1458 oz. AGW **Ruler:** Elizabeth II
Subject: 500 Years of America **Obv:** Crowned head right, date below **Rev:** Paul de Maisonneuve, map and city view, denomination below

Date	Mintage	F	VF	XF	Unc	BU
1992 Proof	Est. 5,000	Value: 95.00				

KM# 260 50 DOLLARS
7.7760 g., 0.5830 Gold .1458 oz. AGW **Ruler:** Elizabeth II
Subject: 500 Years of America **Obv:** Crowned head right, date below **Rev:** Jakob le Maire, ship and map, denomination below

Date	Mintage	F	VF	XF	Unc	BU
1992 Proof	Est. 5,000	Value: 95.00				

KM# 153 50 DOLLARS
7.7760 g., 0.5833 Gold .1453 oz. AGW **Ruler:** Elizabeth II
Subject: Endangered Wildlife **Obv:** Crowned head right, date below **Rev:** Ibex

Date	Mintage	F	VF	XF	Unc	BU
1993 Proof	—	Value: 97.50				

KM# 154 50 DOLLARS
7.7760 g., 0.5833 Gold .1453 oz. AGW **Ruler:** Elizabeth II
Subject: Endangered Wildlife **Obv:** Crowned head right, date below **Rev:** Owl and parrot

Date	Mintage	F	VF	XF	Unc	BU
1993 Proof	—	Value: 97.50				

KM# 173 50 DOLLARS
7.7760 g., 0.5833 Gold .1458 oz. AGW **Ruler:** Elizabeth II
Subject: 500 Years of America **Obv:** Crowned head right, date below **Rev:** George Washington

Date	Mintage	F	VF	XF	Unc	BU
1993 Proof	—	Value: 95.00				

KM# 174 50 DOLLARS
7.7760 g., 0.5833 Gold .1458 oz. AGW **Ruler:** Elizabeth II
Subject: 500 Years of America **Obv:** Crowned head right, date below **Rev:** Alonso de Hojeda

Date	Mintage	F	VF	XF	Unc	BU
1993 Proof	—	Value: 95.00				

KM# 175 50 DOLLARS
7.7760 g., 0.5833 Gold .1458 oz. AGW **Ruler:** Elizabeth II
Subject: 500 Years of America **Obv:** Crowned head right, date below **Rev:** Thomas Jefferson

Date	Mintage	F	VF	XF	Unc	BU
1993 Proof	—	Value: 95.00				

KM# 177 50 DOLLARS
7.7760 g., 0.5833 Gold .1458 oz. AGW **Ruler:** Elizabeth II
Subject: 500 Years of America **Obv:** Crowned head right, date below **Rev:** Captain James Cook

Date	Mintage	F	VF	XF	Unc	BU
1993 Proof	—	Value: 95.00				

KM# 178 50 DOLLARS
7.7760 g., 0.5833 Gold .1458 oz. AGW **Ruler:** Elizabeth II
Subject: 500 Years of America **Obv:** Crowned head right, date below **Rev:** Christopher Columbus

Date	Mintage	F	VF	XF	Unc	BU
1993 Proof	—	Value: 95.00				

KM# 179 50 DOLLARS
7.7760 g., 0.5833 Gold .1458 oz. AGW **Ruler:** Elizabeth II
Subject: 500 Years of America **Obv:** Crowned head right, date below **Rev:** Statue of Liberty

Date	Mintage	F	VF	XF	Unc	BU
1993 Proof	—	Value: 95.00				

KM# 180 50 DOLLARS
7.7760 g., 0.5833 Gold .1458 oz. AGW **Ruler:** Elizabeth II
Subject: 1996 Olympics **Obv:** Crowned head right, date below **Rev:** Ribbon dancer, denomination below **Rev. Designer:** Doris Waschk-Balz

Date	Mintage	F	VF	XF	Unc	BU
1993 Proof	Est. 5,000	Value: 95.00				

KM# 245 50 DOLLARS
7.7760 g., 0.5833 Gold .1458 oz. AGW **Ruler:** Elizabeth II
Subject: Endangered Wildlife **Obv:** Crowned head right, date below **Rev:** African lion, denomination below

Date	Mintage	F	VF	XF	Unc	BU
1993 Proof	Est. 10,000	Value: 97.50				

162 COOK ISLANDS

KM# 246 50 DOLLARS
7.7760 g., 0.5830 Gold .1458 oz. AGW **Ruler:** Elizabeth II
Subject: Endangered Wildlife **Obv:** Crowned head right, date below **Rev:** Sea otter head, denomination below

Date	Mintage	F	VF	XF	Unc	BU
1994 Proof	Est. 10,000	Value: 97.50				

KM# 247 50 DOLLARS
7.7760 g., 0.5830 Gold .1458 oz. AGW **Ruler:** Elizabeth II
Subject: Endangered Wildlife **Obv:** Crowned head right, date below **Rev:** Przewalski's horse

Date	Mintage	F	VF	XF	Unc	BU
1994 Proof	Est. 10,000	Value: 97.50				

KM# 275 50 DOLLARS
7.7760 g., 0.5830 Gold .1458 oz. AGW **Ruler:** Elizabeth II
Subject: Endangered Wildlife **Obv:** Crowned head right, date below **Rev:** Poplar Admiral butterflies

Date	Mintage	F	VF	XF	Unc	BU
1994 Proof	Est. 10,000	Value: 97.50				

KM# 276 50 DOLLARS
7.7760 g., 0.5830 Gold .1458 oz. AGW **Ruler:** Elizabeth II **Obv:** Crowned head right, date below **Rev:** Queen Mother and daughters

Date	Mintage	F	VF	XF	Unc	BU
1995 Proof	Est. 5,000	Value: 97.50				

KM# 299 50 DOLLARS
8.0000 g., 0.9999 Gold .2572 oz. AGW **Ruler:** Elizabeth II
Subject: Year of the Mouse **Obv:** Crowned head right, date below **Rev:** Mickey and Minnie Mouse portrait, denomination below

Date	Mintage	F	VF	XF	Unc	BU
1996 Proof	—	Value: 165				

KM# 306 50 DOLLARS
Bi-Metallic Platinum center in Gold ring **Ruler:** Elizabeth II
Obv: Crowned head right within circle, date below **Rev:** Mother seal with pup within circle, date below

Date	Mintage	F	VF	XF	Unc	BU
1997 Proof	—	Value: 185				

KM# 381 50 DOLLARS
4.6000 g., 0.5833 Gold 0.0863 oz. AGW, 20.9 mm.
Ruler: Elizabeth II **Subject:** Explorers **Obv:** Crowned head right, date below **Rev:** Leif Ericson with battle axe facing, denomination at right **Edge:** Reeded

Date	Mintage	F	VF	XF	Unc	BU
1997 Proof	—	Value: 50.00				
1997FM Proof	—	Value: 65.00				

KM# 382 50 DOLLARS
4.6000 g., 0.5833 Gold 0.0863 oz. AGW, 20.9 mm.
Ruler: Elizabeth II **Subject:** Explorers **Obv:** Crowned head right, date below **Rev:** Marco Polo on camel **Edge:** Reeded

Date	Mintage	F	VF	XF	Unc	BU
1997FM Proof	—	Value: 60.00				

KM# 383 50 DOLLARS
4.6000 g., 0.5833 Gold 0.0863 oz. AGW, 20.9 mm.
Ruler: Elizabeth II **Subject:** Explorers **Obv:** Crowned head right, date below **Rev:** Vasco da Gama **Edge:** Reeded

Date	Mintage	F	VF	XF	Unc	BU
1997FM Proof	—	Value: 60.00				

KM# 384 50 DOLLARS
4.6000 g., 0.5833 Gold 0.0863 oz. AGW **Ruler:** Elizabeth II
Subject: Explorers **Obv:** Crowned head right, date below **Rev:** Vasco de Nuñez Balboa **Edge:** Reeded

Date	Mintage	F	VF	XF	Unc	BU
1997FM Proof	—	Value: 60.00				

KM# 385 50 DOLLARS
4.6000 g., 0.5833 Gold 0.0863 oz. AGW, 20.9 mm.
Ruler: Elizabeth II **Subject:** Explorers **Obv:** Crowned head right, date below **Rev:** Hernando Cortes **Edge:** Reeded

Date	Mintage	F	VF	XF	Unc	BU
1997FM Proof	—	Value: 60.00				

KM# 386 50 DOLLARS
4.6000 g., 0.5833 Gold 0.0863 oz. AGW, 20.9 mm. **Ruler:** Elizabeth II **Subject:** Explorers **Obv:** Crowned head right, date below **Rev:** Magellan's ships: Vittoria and Trinidad **Edge:** Reeded

Date	Mintage	F	VF	XF	Unc	BU
1997FM Proof	—	Value: 60.00				

KM# 390 50 DOLLARS
4.6000 g., 0.5833 Gold 0.0863 oz. AGW, 20.9 mm.
Ruler: Elizabeth II **Subject:** Explorers **Obv:** Crowned head right, date below **Rev:** Alexander the Great with sword on horseback, denomination above **Edge:** Reeded

Date	Mintage	F	VF	XF	Unc	BU
1997FM Proof	—	Value: 60.00				

KM# 391 50 DOLLARS
4.6000 g., 0.5833 Gold 0.0863 oz. AGW, 20.9 mm.
Ruler: Elizabeth II **Subject:** Explorers **Obv:** Crowned head right, date below **Rev:** Christopher Columbus **Edge:** Reeded

Date	Mintage	F	VF	XF	Unc	BU
1997FM Proof	—	Value: 60.00				

KM# 392 50 DOLLARS
4.6000 g., 0.5833 Gold 0.0863 oz. AGW, 20.9 mm.
Ruler: Elizabeth II **Subject:** Explorers **Obv:** Crowned head right, date below **Rev:** Sir Francis Drake **Edge:** Reeded

Date	Mintage	F	VF	XF	Unc	BU
1997FM Proof	—	Value: 60.00				

KM# 393 50 DOLLARS
4.6000 g., 0.5833 Gold 0.0863 oz. AGW, 20.9 mm.
Ruler: Elizabeth II **Subject:** Explorers **Obv:** Crowned head right, date below **Rev:** Abel Janszoon Tasman **Edge:** Reeded

Date	Mintage	F	VF	XF	Unc	BU
1997FM Proof	—	Value: 60.00				

KM# 394 50 DOLLARS
4.6000 g., 0.5833 Gold 0.0863 oz. AGW, 20.9 mm.
Ruler: Elizabeth II **Subject:** Explorers **Obv:** Crowned head right, date below **Rev:** Capt. James Cook **Edge:** Reeded

Date	Mintage	F	VF	XF	Unc	BU
1997FM Proof	—	Value: 60.00				

KM# 395 50 DOLLARS
4.6000 g., 0.5833 Gold 0.0863 oz. AGW, 20.9 mm.
Ruler: Elizabeth II **Subject:** Explorers **Obv:** Crowned head right, date below **Rev:** Richard E. Byrd **Edge:** Reeded

Date	Mintage	F	VF	XF	Unc	BU
1997FM Proof	—	Value: 60.00				

COOK ISLANDS 163

KM# 395.1 50 DOLLARS
6.3700 g., 0.5833 Gold 0.1195 oz. AGW, 21 mm.
Ruler: Elizabeth II **Obv:** Crowned head right, date below
Rev: Admiral Richard C. Byrd **Edge:** Reeded

Date	Mintage	F	VF	XF	Unc	BU
1997FM Proof	8	Value: 400				

Note: Struck on thicker than normal planchet resulting in a 38.5% heavier weight. 8 Pieces known.

KM# 460 50 DOLLARS
10.0000 g., 0.9995 Platinum 0.3213 oz. APW **Ruler:** Elizabeth II
Subject: Love Angels

Date	Mintage	F	VF	XF	Unc	BU
1997 Proof	250	Value: 350				

KM# 12 100 DOLLARS
16.7185 g., 0.9170 Gold .4929 oz. AGW, 27 mm. **Ruler:** Elizabeth II
Subject: Winston Churchill Centenary **Obv:** Young bust right, date below **Rev:** Churchill head at right looking left, Big Ben and flag at left, denomination below **Rev. Designer:** James Berry

Date	Mintage	F	VF	XF	Unc	BU
1974	368	—	—	—	325	—
1974 Proof	1,453	Value: 325				

KM# 13 100 DOLLARS
9.6000 g., 0.9000 Gold .2778 oz. AGW, 26 mm.
Ruler: Elizabeth II **Subject:** Bicentennial - Return of Captain James Cook from Second Pacific Voyage **Obv:** Young bust right, date below **Rev:** Ship divides portraits in cameos, denomination below **Rev. Designer:** James Berry

Date	Mintage	F	VF	XF	Unc	BU
1975FM (M)	100	—	—	—	210	—
1975FM (U)	7,447	—	—	—	180	—
1975FM Proof	17,000	Value: 185				

KM# 16 100 DOLLARS
9.6000 g., 0.9000 Gold .2778 oz. AGW, 26 mm.
Ruler: Elizabeth II **Subject:** U.S. Bicentennial **Obv:** Young bust right, date below **Rev:** Conjoined heads of Benjamin Franklin and James Cook left, denomination below

Date	Mintage	F	VF	XF	Unc	BU
1976FM (M)	50	—	—	—	285	—
1976FM (U)	852	—	—	—	180	—
1976FM Proof	9,373	Value: 185				

KM# 19 100 DOLLARS
9.6000 g., 0.9000 Gold .2778 oz. AGW, 26 mm.
Ruler: Elizabeth II **Subject:** Queen's Silver Jubilee **Obv:** Young bust right, date below **Rev:** Crowned EIIR monogram
Rev. Designer: James Berry

Date	Mintage	F	VF	XF	Unc	BU
1977FM (M)	50	—	—	—	285	—
1977FM (P)	562	—	—	—	185	—
1977FM Proof	9,364	Value: 180				

KM# 25 100 DOLLARS
9.6000 g., 0.9000 Gold .2778 oz. AGW, 26 mm.
Ruler: Elizabeth II **Subject:** Membership in Commonwealth of Nations **Obv:** Young bust right, date below **Rev:** Tangaroa head left, divides denomination, circle surrounds

Date	Mintage	F	VF	XF	Unc	BU
1979FM (U)	400	—	—	—	185	—
1979FM Proof	3,367	Value: 180				

KM# 74 100 DOLLARS
1.2441 g., 0.9990 Gold .0400 oz. AGW **Ruler:** Elizabeth II **Subject:** Endangered World Wildlife **Obv:** Crowned head right, date below **Rev:** American bald eagle head left, beak open, denomination below

Date	Mintage	F	VF	XF	Unc	BU
1990 Prooflike	1,320	—	—	—	30.00	—

KM# 75 100 DOLLARS
1.2441 g., 0.9990 Gold .0400 oz. AGW, 14 mm.
Ruler: Elizabeth II **Subject:** Endangered World Wildlife **Obv:** Crowned head right, date below **Rev:** Bison

Date	Mintage	F	VF	XF	Unc	BU
1990 Prooflike	320	—	—	—	32.50	—

KM# 76 100 DOLLARS
1.2441 g., 0.9990 Gold .0400 oz. AGW, 14 mm.
Ruler: Elizabeth II **Subject:** Endangered World Wildlife **Obv:** Crowned head right, date below **Rev:** Elephant

Date	Mintage	F	VF	XF	Unc	BU
1990 Prooflike	720	—	—	—	32.00	—

KM# 77 100 DOLLARS
1.2441 g., 0.9990 Gold .0400 oz. AGW, 14 mm.
Ruler: Elizabeth II **Subject:** Endangered World Wildlife **Obv:** Crowned head right, date below **Rev:** Tiger

Date	Mintage	F	VF	XF	Unc	BU
1990 Prooflike	420	—	—	—	65.00	—

KM# 78 100 DOLLARS
1.2441 g., 0.9990 Gold .0400 oz. AGW, 14 mm.
Ruler: Elizabeth II **Subject:** Endangered World Wildlife **Obv:** Crowned head right, date below **Rev:** European Mouflon

Date	Mintage	F	VF	XF	Unc	BU
1990 Prooflike	320	—	—	—	32.50	—

KM# 92 100 DOLLARS
3.4550 g., 0.9000 Gold .09999 oz. AGW, 18 mm. **Ruler:** Elizabeth II **Subject:** 1992 Summer Olympics **Obv:** Crowned head right, date below **Rev:** Bicyclists, denomination below

Date	Mintage	F	VF	XF	Unc	BU
1990 Proof	Est. 5,000	Value: 125				

KM# 250 100 DOLLARS
7.7761 g., 0.9990 Platinum .1458 oz. APW **Ruler:** Elizabeth II
Obv: Crowned head right, date below **Rev:** Javelin throwing

Date	Mintage	F	VF	XF	Unc	BU
1995 Proof	Est. 1,000	Value: 185				

KM# 293 100 DOLLARS
7.7800 g., 0.9990 Gold .2501 oz. AGW **Ruler:** Elizabeth II
Subject: Olympic National Park **Obv:** Crowned head right, date below **Rev:** Eagles head right, denomination below
Rev. Designer: Alex Shagin

Date	Mintage	F	VF	XF	Unc	BU
1996 Proof	—	Value: 165				

KM# 294 100 DOLLARS
7.7800 g., 0.9990 Gold .2501 oz. AGW **Ruler:** Elizabeth II
Subject: Yellowstone National Park **Obv:** Crowned head right, date below **Rev:** Grizzly Bear, denomination below
Rev. Designer: Alex Shagin

Date	Mintage	F	VF	XF	Unc	BU
1996 Proof	—	Value: 165				

KM# 300 100 DOLLARS
15.0000 g., 0.9999 Gold .4822 oz. AGW **Ruler:** Elizabeth II
Subject: Year of the Mouse **Obv:** Crowned head right, date below **Rev:** Mickey Mouse sailboarding, denomination below

Date	Mintage	F	VF	XF	Unc	BU
1996 Proof	—	Value: 320				

KM# 388 100 DOLLARS
7.7800 g., 0.9990 Gold 0.2499 oz. AGW, 22 mm.
Ruler: Elizabeth II **Subject:** Yellowstone National Park
Obv: Crowned head right, date below **Rev:** Bear on tree branch
Rev. Designer: Alex Shagin **Edge:** Reeded

Date	Mintage	F	VF	XF	Unc	BU
1996 Proof	—	Value: 165				

KM# 397 100 DOLLARS
23.3276 g., 0.9999 Gold Acrylic capsule center containing tiny diamonds, rubies and sapphires 0.7499 oz. AGW, 32.1 mm.
Ruler: Elizabeth II **Subject:** Crown Jewels **Obv:** Head with tiara right and legend **Rev:** Crowns and royal regalia **Edge:** Reeded

Date	Mintage	F	VF	XF	Unc	BU
2002 Proof	5,000	Value: 500				

KM# 22 200 DOLLARS
16.6000 g., 0.9000 Gold .4803 oz. AGW **Ruler:** Elizabeth II
Subject: Bicentennial - Discovery of Hawaii by Capt. James Cook
Obv: Young bust right, date below **Rev:** Capt. James Cook with crew, denomination below

Date	Mintage	F	VF	XF	Unc	BU
1978FM (M)	26	—	—	—	425	—
1978FM (U)	621	—	—	—	325	—
1978FM Proof	3,216	Value: 320				

COOK ISLANDS

KM# 26 200 DOLLARS
16.6000 g., 0.9000 Gold .4803 oz. AGW **Ruler:** Elizabeth II
Subject: Legacy of Capt. James Cook **Obv:** Young bust right, date below **Rev:** Bird flying right above banner, denomination below

Date	Mintage	F	VF	XF	Unc	BU
1979FM (U)	271	—	—	—	325	—
1979FM Proof	1,939	Value: 320				

KM# 29 200 DOLLARS
15.9800 g., 0.9170 Gold .4712 oz. AGW **Ruler:** Elizabeth II
Subject: International Year of the Scout **Obv:** Young bust right, date below **Rev:** Circle of stars around symbol at center, dates at lower left, denomination at lower right

Date	Mintage	F	VF	XF	Unc	BU
1983 Proof	—	Value: 310				

KM# 251 200 DOLLARS
15.5520 g., 0.9990 Platinum .2916 oz. APW **Ruler:** Elizabeth II
Obv: Crowned head right, date below **Rev:** Wrestling

Date	Mintage	F	VF	XF	Unc	BU
1995 Proof	1,000	Value: 365				

KM# 23 250 DOLLARS
17.9000 g., 0.9000 Gold .5180 oz. AGW **Ruler:** Elizabeth II
Subject: 250th Anniversary - Birth of James Cook **Obv:** Young bust right, date below **Rev:** Head left, denomination below

Date	Mintage	F	VF	XF	Unc	BU
1978FM (M)	25	—	—	—	425	—
1978FM (U)	200	—	—	—	335	—
1978FM Proof	1,757	Value: 350				

KM# 50 250 DOLLARS
7.7750 g., 0.9990 Gold .2500 oz. AGW **Ruler:** Elizabeth II
Subject: 500 Years of America **Obv:** Crowned head right, date below **Rev:** Cameos of Cook and Franklin flank sailing ship, denomination below

Date	Mintage	F	VF	XF	Unc	BU
1989 Proof	3,000	Value: 185				
1990 Proof	3,000	Value: 185				

KM# 51 250 DOLLARS
7.7750 g., 0.9990 Gold .2500 oz. AGW **Ruler:** Elizabeth II
Subject: 500 Years of America **Obv:** Crowned head right, date below **Rev:** Amerigo Vespucci bust at right looking left, ship at left

Date	Mintage	F	VF	XF	Unc	BU
1990 Proof	Est. 3,000	Value: 185				

KM# 82 250 DOLLARS
9.6000 g., 0.9000 Gold .2778 oz. AGW **Ruler:** Elizabeth II
Subject: Save the Children **Obv:** Crowned head right, date below **Rev:** Child behind large shell, denomination below

Date	Mintage	F	VF	XF	Unc	BU
1990 Proof	3,000	Value: 200				

KM# 71 250 DOLLARS
7.7750 g., 0.9990 Gold .2500 oz. AGW **Ruler:** Elizabeth II
Subject: 1992 Olympics **Obv:** Crowned head right, date below **Rev:** Torch, denomination below

Date	Mintage	F	VF	XF	Unc	BU
1991 Proof	Est. 5,000	Value: 185				

KM# 295 250 DOLLARS
31.1035 g., 0.9990 Gold 1.0000 oz. AGW **Ruler:** Elizabeth II
Subject: Olympic National Park **Obv:** Crowned head right, date below **Rev:** Multicolor bald eagle in flight

Date	Mintage	F	VF	XF	Unc	BU
1996 Proof	1,000	Value: 675				

KM# 296 250 DOLLARS
31.1035 g., 0.9990 Gold 1.0000 oz. AGW **Ruler:** Elizabeth II
Subject: Yellowstone National Park **Obv:** Crowned head right, date below **Rev:** Multicolored grizzly bear and cub

Date	Mintage	F	VF	XF	Unc	BU
1996 Proof	1,000	Value: 675				

KM# 415 500 DOLLARS
14.7400 g., 0.9990 Platinum 0.4734 oz. APW, 25.8 mm.
Ruler: Elizabeth II **Obv:** Crowned head right, date below **Rev:** Two of Ferdinand Magellan's ships **Edge:** Reeded

Date	Mintage	F	VF	XF	Unc	BU
1995FM Proof	1,000	Value: 625				

KM# 313 500 DOLLARS
14.7400 g., 0.9990 Platinum .4734 oz. APW **Ruler:** Elizabeth II
Obv: Crowned head right, date below **Rev:** Marco Polo, oriental building in background, denomination below

Date	Mintage	F	VF	XF	Unc	BU
1995 Proof	Est. 2,000	Value: 625				

PROOF SETS

KM#	Date	Mintage	Identification	Issue Price	Mkt Val
PS20	1996 (3)	—	KM298-300	—	500
PS21	1996 (6)	—	KM284, 286, 288, 292, 294, 296	—	935

PROOF-LIKE SETS (PL)

KM#	Date	Mintage	Identification	Issue Price	Mkt Val
PLS1	1990 (5)	—	KM74-78	325	250
PLS2	1997 (5)	250	KM#457-461	—	1,200

COSTA RICA

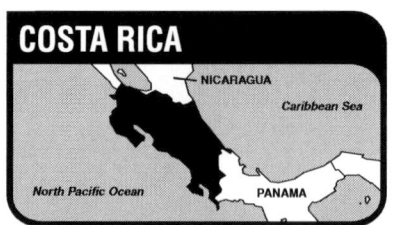

The Republic of Costa Rica, located in southern Central America between Nicaragua and Panama, has an area of 19,730 sq. mi. (51,100 sq. km.) and a population of 3.4 million. Capital: San Jose. Agriculture predominates; tourism and coffee, bananas, beef and sugar contribute heavily to the country's export earnings.

Costa Rica was discovered by Christopher Columbus in 1502, during his last voyage to the New World, and was a colony of Spain from 1522 until independence in 1821. Columbus named the territory Nueva Cartago; the name Costa Rica wasn't generally applied until 1540. Bartholomew Columbus attempted the first settlement but was driven off by Indian attacks and the country wasn't subdued until 1530. After centuries, as part of the Spanish Captaincy-General of Guatemala, Costa Rica was absorbed into the Mexican Empire of Augustin de Iturbide from 1821-1823. From 1823 to 1848, it was a constituent state of the Central American Republic (q.v.). Established as a republic in 1848, Costa Rica adopted democratic reforms in the 1870's and 80's. Today, Costa Rica remains a model of orderly democracy in Latin America, although, like most of the hemisphere - its economy is in stress.

NOTE: Also see Central American Republic.

MINT MARKS
CR - San Jose 1825-1947
HEATON - Heaton, Birmingham, England, 1889-93
BIRMm - Heaton, Birmingham, England, 1889-93
(P) – Philadelphia, 1905-1961
(L) – London, 1937, 1948

ISSUING BANK INITIALS - MINTS
BCCR - Philadelphia 1951-1958,1961
BICR - Philadelphia 1935
BNCR - London 1937,1948
BNCR - San Jose 1942-1947
GCR - Philadelphia 1905-1908,1929
GCR - San Jose 1917-1941

ASSAYERS' INITIALS
MM – Miguel Mora, 1842
JB – Juan Barth, 1847-1864
GW – Guillermo Witting, 1854-1890
CB – Carlos Blanco, 1889
CY – Carlos Yglesias, 1902
JCV – Jesus Cubrero Vargas, 1903
GCR – Gobierno de Costa Rica

MONETARY SYSTEM
8 Reales = 1 Peso
16 Pesos = 8 Escudos = 1 Onza

REPUBLIC
REAL/ESCUDO COINAGE

KM# 97 1/2 ESCUDO
1.6000 g., 0.8750 Gold .0450 oz. AGW **Obv:** Ornate arms
Rev: Indian woman leaning against column

Date	Mintage	VG	F	VF	XF	Unc
1850 JB	3,388	38.50	65.00	100	150	—
1851 JB	6,565	38.50	65.00	100	150	—
1853 JB	8,491	38.50	65.00	100	150	—
1854 JB	4,663	38.50	65.00	100	150	—
1855 JB	8,822	38.50	65.00	100	150	—
1855 GW	Inc. above	38.50	65.00	100	150	—
1864 JB	9,018	38.50	65.00	100	150	—

KM# 33.1 ESCUDO
3.0000 g., 0.8750 Gold .0844 oz. AGW **Obv:** Radiant star within circle, lopsided spray below **Rev:** Tree divides denomination within circle

Date	Mintage	VG	F	VF	XF	Unc
1842 MM	10,000	300	600	1,200	2,000	—

COSTA RICA 165

KM# 33.2 ESCUDO
3.1000 g., 0.8750 Gold .872 oz. AGW **Obv:** Radiant star within circle, fuller spray below **Rev:** Tree divides denomination within circle

Date	Mintage	VG	F	VF	XF	Unc
1842 MM	Inc. above	350	800	1,500	2,250	—

KM# 98 ESCUDO
3.1000 g., 0.8750 Gold .872 oz. AGW **Obv:** Ornate arms within sprays **Rev:** Indian woman leaning against column

Date	Mintage	VG	F	VF	XF	Unc
1850 JB	6,167	55.00	100	150	265	—
1851 JB	4,388	55.00	100	150	265	—
1853 JB	2,979	65.00	150	250	500	—
1855 JB	4,095	60.00	125	200	350	—

KM# 99 2 ESCUDOS
6.3000 g., 0.8750 Gold .1772 oz. AGW **Obv:** Ornate arms in sprays **Rev:** Indian woman leaning against column

Date	Mintage	VG	F	VF	XF	Unc
1850 JB	3,641	100	150	200	400	—
1854 JB	Inc. above	100	150	200	400	—
1854 GW	Inc. above	100	150	200	400	—
1855 JB	60,000	100	125	175	400	—
1855 GW	Inc. above	100	150	200	400	—
1858 GW	17,000	100	125	175	400	—
1862 GW	5,896	110	200	325	550	—
1863 GW	5,632	110	200	325	550	—

KM# 100 1/2 ONZA (4 Escudos)
12.6000 g., 0.8750 Gold .3545 oz. AGW **Obv:** Ornate arms in sprays **Rev:** Indian woman leaning against column

Date	Mintage	VG	F	VF	XF	Unc
1850 JB	18,000	200	300	400	800	—
1850 JB Proof	—	Value: 4,200				

COUNTERMARKED COINAGE
Type II • 1841-1842

Countermark: Radiant 6-pointed star in 4mm circle.

KM# 28 2 ESCUDOS
Gold **Countermark:** Type II **Note:** Countermark on Central American Republic 2 Escudos, KM#15.

CM Date	Host Date	Good	VG	F	VF	XF
ND(1841-42)	1825-37 Rare	—	—	—	—	—

KM# 29 4 ESCUDOS
Gold **Countermark:** Type II **Note:** Countermark on Central American Republic 4 Escudos, KM#16.

CM Date	Host Date	Good	VG	F	VF	XF
ND(1841-42)	1828-37 Rare	—	—	—	—	—

COUNTERMARKED COINAGE
Type VI • 1849-1857

Countermark: HABILITADA PO EL GOBIERNO around lion in 5mm circle.

KM# 80 1/2 ESCUDO
Gold **Countermark:** Type VI **Note:** Countermark on Central American Republic 1/2 Escudo, KM#13.

CM Date	Host Date	Good	VG	F	VF	XF
ND(1849-57)	1828CR F	—	55.00	100	150	225
ND(1849-57)	1843CR M	—	55.00	100	150	225
ND(1849-57)	1846CR JB	—	45.00	85.00	125	200
ND(1849-57)	1847CR JB	—	45.00	85.00	125	200
ND(1849-57)	1848CR JB	—	45.00	85.00	125	200
ND(1849-57)	1849CR JB	—	55.00	100	150	225

KM# 81 1/2 ESCUDO
Gold **Countermark:** Type VI **Note:** Countermark on Central American Republic 1/2 Escudo, KM#5.

CM Date	Host Date	Good	VG	F	VF	XF
ND(1849-57)	1825NG M	—	—	—	—	—

KM# 84 ESCUDO
Gold **Countermark:** Type VI **Note:** Countermark on Central American Republic 1 Escudo, KM#14.

CM Date	Host Date	Good	VG	F	VF	XF
ND(1849-57)	1833CR E	—	90.00	175	275	375
ND(1849-57)	1833CR F	—	90.00	175	275	375
ND(1849-57)	1844CR M	—	65.00	125	225	325
ND(1849-57)	1845CR JB	—	90.00	175	275	375
ND(1849-57)	1846CR JB	—	70.00	125	225	325
ND(1849-57)	1847CR JB	—	70.00	125	225	325
ND(1849-57)	1848CR JB	—	70.00	125	225	325
ND(1849-57)	1849CR JB	—	70.00	125	225	325

DECIMAL COINAGE
100 Centavos = 1 Peso

KM# 107.1 PESO
1.5253 g., 0.8750 Gold .0429 oz. AGW **Obv:** Arms above sprays **Rev:** Denomination within wreath

Date	Mintage	VG	F	VF	XF	Unc
1864 GW	6,383	35.00	70.00	110	175	—
1866 GW	35,000	30.00	55.00	95.00	150	—
1868 GW	—	45.00	85.00	125	200	—

KM# 107.2 PESO
1.5253 g., 0.8750 Gold .0429 oz. AGW **Obv:** Arms above sprays **Rev:** Large UN in center of wreath

Date	Mintage	VG	F	VF	XF	Unc
1866 GW	Inc. above	30.00	55.00	95.00	150	—

KM# 107.3 PESO
1.5253 g., 0.8750 Gold .0429 oz. AGW **Obv:** Arms above sprays **Rev:** Small UN, fineness omitted

Date	Mintage	VG	F	VF	XF	Unc
1866 GW	Inc. above	30.00	55.00	95.00	150	550

KM# 116 PESO
1.5253 g., 0.8750 Gold .0429 oz. AGW **Obv:** Arms above sprays **Rev:** Denomination within wreath **Note:** Design modified.

Date	Mintage	VG	F	VF	XF	Unc
1871 GW	11,000	30.00	55.00	90.00	150	—
1872 GW	37,000	30.00	55.00	90.00	150	—

KM# 113 2 PESOS (Dos)
2.9355 g., 0.8750 Gold .0825 oz. AGW **Obv:** Arms above sprays **Rev:** Denomination within wreath

Date	Mintage	VG	F	VF	XF	Unc
1866 GW	13,000	60.00	90.00	135	225	—
1867 GW	—	70.00	120	175	275	—
1868 GW	—	60.00	90.00	135	225	—

KM# 122 2 PESOS (Dos)
2.9355 g., 0.8750 Gold .0825 oz. AGW **Obv:** Arms above sprays **Rev:** Denomination within wreath **Note:** Design modified (19mm).

Date	Mintage	VG	F	VF	XF	Unc
1876 GW Rare	2,161	—	—	—	—	—

KM# 114 5 PESOS (Cinco)
7.3387 g., 0.8750 Gold .2064 oz. AGW **Obv:** Arms above sprays **Rev:** Denomination within wreath

Date	Mintage	VG	F	VF	XF	Unc
1867 GW	39,000	150	200	300	450	—
1868 GW	6,752	150	200	300	450	—
1869 GW	11,000	150	200	300	450	—
1870 GW	15,000	150	200	300	450	—

KM# 117 5 PESOS (Cinco)
7.3387 g., 0.8750 Gold .2064 oz. AGW **Obv:** Arms above sprays **Rev:** Denomination within wreath

Date	Mintage	VG	F	VF	XF	Unc
1873 GW	5,167	175	300	650	1,000	—
1875 GW	Inc. above	175	300	650	1,000	—

KM# 118 5 PESOS (Cinco)
8.0645 g., 0.9000 Gold .2333 oz. AGW **Obv:** Arms above sprays **Rev:** Denomination within wreath

Date	Mintage	VG	F	VF	XF	Unc
1873 GW	Inc. above	1,250	1,850	2,250	2,750	3,500

KM# 115 10 PESOS
14.6774 g., 0.8750 Gold .4129 oz. AGW **Obv:** Arms above sprays **Rev:** Denomination within wreath

Date	Mintage	VG	F	VF	XF	Unc
1870 GW	20,000	300	375	500	650	—
1871 GW	30,000	325	400	525	700	—
1872 GW	4,555	375	450	550	850	—

COSTA RICA

KM# 123 10 PESOS
14.6774 g., 0.8750 Gold .4129 oz. AGW **Obv:** Arms above sprays **Rev:** Denomination within wreath **Note:** Design modified.

Date	Mintage	VG	F	VF	XF	Unc
1876 GW	3,389	500	1,000	1,600	2,250	3,750

KM# 119 20 PESOS
32.2580 g., 0.9000 Gold .9334 oz. AGW **Obv:** Arms above sprays **Rev:** Denomination within wreath

Date	Mintage	F	VF	XF	Unc	BU
1873 Rare						

Note: American Numismatic Rarities Eliasberg sale 4-05, AU-50 realized $39,100. Superior Galleries Casterline sale 5-89 XF realized $16,500. Pacific Coast Auction Galleries, Long Beach sale 6-86 AU realized $17,000. Stack's Hammel sale 9-82 AU realized $16,000.

REFORM COINAGE
1897, 100 Centimos = 1 Colon

KM# 139 2 COLONES
1.5560 g., 0.9000 Gold .0456 oz. AGW **Obv:** National arms **Rev:** Bust of Colombus right

Date	Mintage	F	VF	XF	Unc	BU
1897 Proof	500	Value: 1,500				
1900	45,000	35.00	40.00	50.00	75.00	165
1915(P)	5,000	35.00	50.00	75.00	125	—
1916(P)	5,000	37.50	55.00	75.00	150	—
1921(P)	3,000	40.00	65.00	100	200	—
1922(P)	13,000	35.00	45.00	60.00	100	—
1926(P)	15,000	35.00	45.00	60.00	85.00	—
1928(P)	25,000	35.00	45.00	55.00	80.00	—

KM# 142 5 COLONES
3.8900 g., 0.9000 Gold .1125 oz. AGW **Obv:** National arms **Rev:** Bust of Colombus right

Date	Mintage	F	VF	XF	Unc	BU
1899	100,000	—	BV	80.00	135	245
1900	100,000	—	BV	80.00	135	245

KM# 140 10 COLONES
7.7800 g., 0.9000 Gold .2251 oz. AGW **Obv:** National arms **Rev:** Bust of Colombus right

Date	Mintage	F	VF	XF	Unc	BU
1897	60,000	—	BV	150	200	—
1899	50,000	—	BV	150	200	—
1900	140,000	—	BV	150	200	—

KM# 141 20 COLONES
15.5600 g., 0.9000 Gold .4502 oz. AGW **Obv:** National arms **Rev:** Bust of Colombus right

Date	Mintage	F	VF	XF	Unc	BU
1897	20,000	—	BV	300	475	—
1899	25,000	—	BV	300	475	—
1900	5,000	—	BV	400	700	—

REFORM COINAGE
1920, 100 Centimos = 1 Colon

KM# 195.1 50 COLONES
7.4500 g., 0.9000 Gold .2155 oz. AGW **Subject:** Inter-American Human Rights Convention **Obv:** National arms, date below **Rev:** Nude on globe background, denomination below

Date	Mintage	F	VF	XF	Unc	BU
1970 Proof	3,507	Value: 150				

KM# 195.2 50 COLONES
7.4500 g., 0.9000 Gold .2155 oz. AGW **Obv:** National arms, date below **Rev:** "1 AR" countermark above fineness statement

Date	Mintage	F	VF	XF	Unc	BU
1970 Proof	Inc. above	Value: 165				

KM# 196 100 COLONES
14.9000 g., 0.9000 Gold .4311 oz. AGW **Obv:** National arms **Rev:** Gold Vulture pendant in the style of the Chibcha Indians, denomination below

Date	Mintage	F	VF	XF	Unc	BU
1970 Proof	3,507	Value: 295				

KM# 197 200 COLONES
29.8000 g., 0.9000 Gold .8623 oz. AGW **Obv:** National arms **Rev:** Juan Santamaria and cannon

Date	Mintage	F	VF	XF	Unc	BU
1970 Proof	3,507	Value: 585				

KM# 198 500 COLONES
74.5200 g., 0.9000 Gold 2.1565 oz. AGW **Subject:** 100th Anniversary of Public Education **Obv:** National arms **Rev:** Jesus Jimenez and students at desks

Date	Mintage	F	VF	XF	Unc	BU
1970 Proof	3,507	Value: 1,450				

KM# 199 1000 COLONES
149.0400 g., 0.9000 Gold 4.3126 oz. AGW **Subject:** 150th Anniversary of Central American Independence **Obv:** National arms **Rev:** Face on radiant sun above mountains, water and map, denomination below **Note:** Illustration reduced.

Date	Mintage	F	VF	XF	Unc	BU
1970 Proof	3,507	Value: 3,150				

KM# 202 1500 COLONES
33.4370 g., 0.9000 Gold .9676 oz. AGW **Subject:** Conservation **Obv:** National arms, date below divides B.C. from C.R. **Rev:** Giant anteater, denomination below

Date	Mintage	F	VF	XF	Unc	BU
1974	2,418	—	—	—	650	—
1974 Proof	726	Value: 725				

KM# 213 1500 COLONES
6.9800 g., 0.5000 Gold .1122 oz. AGW **Rev:** Busts of Francisco Coronado and Christopher Columbus, denomination above **Note:** Although considered legal tender, these coins were never officially authorized for circulation.

Date	Mintage	F	VF	XF	Unc	BU
1982FM (P)	724	Value: 125				

CROATIA 167

KM# 218 1500 COLONES
6.9800 g., 0.5000 Gold .1122 oz. AGW **Obv:** National arms, date below **Rev:** Native figurine, denomination above, spray below

Date	Mintage	F	VF	XF	Unc	BU
1983FM (P)	272	Value: 275				

KM# 208 5000 COLONES
15.0000 g., 0.9000 Gold .4341 oz. AGW **Subject:** 125th Anniversary - Death of Juan Santamaria **Obv:** National arms, denomination below **Rev:** Figure standing with torch and rifle divides dates

Date	Mintage	F	VF	XF	Unc	BU
1981	—	—	—	—	295	—
1981 Proof	2,000	Value: 320				

KM# 232 5000 COLONES
15.0000 g., 0.9000 Gold .4341 oz. AGW **Subject:** Founding of Alajuela **Obv:** National arms **Rev:** Portrait of Ramirez

Date	Mintage	F	VF	XF	Unc	BU
1981 Proof	2,000	Value: 325				

KM# 226 25000 COLONES
15.0000 g., 0.9000 Gold .4341 oz. AGW **Obv:** National arms, denomination below **Rev:** Bust of President Dr. Oscar Arias S., divides dates

Date	Mintage	F	VF	XF	Unc	BU
1987 Proof	5,000	Value: 320				

KM# 238 100000 COLONES
15.5500 g., 0.9000 Gold .4499 oz. AGW **Subject:** 50 Years - Central Bank **Obv:** National arms **Rev:** Three standing citizens, denomination at right

Date	Mintage	F	VF	XF	Unc	BU
2000 Proof	2,500	Value: 350				

PATTERNS
Including off metal strikes

KM#	Date	Mintage	Identification	Mkt Val
Pn4	1850	—	Onza. Gold. Prev.# KMPn2.	—

PROOF SETS

KM#	Date	Mintage	Identification	Issue Price	Mkt Val
PS3	1970 (10)	570	KM#190-199	—	5,500
PS5	1970 (5)	3,000	KM#195-199	832	5,225

CROATIA

The Republic of Croatia, (Hrvatska) bordered on the west by the Adriatic Sea and the northeast by Hungary, has an area of 21,829 sq. mi. (56,538 sq. km.) and a population of 4.7 million. Capital: Zagreb.

The country was attached to the Kingdom of Hungary until Dec. 1, 1918, when it joined with the Serbs and Slovenes to form the Kingdom of the Serbs, Croats and Slovenes, which changed its name to the Kingdom of Yugoslavia on Oct. 3, 1929. On April 6, 1941, Hitler, angered by the coup d'etat that overthrew the pro-Nazi regime of regent Prince Paul, sent the Nazi armies crashing across the Yugoslav borders from Germany, Hungary, Romania and Bulgaria. Within a week the army of the Balkan Kingdom was prostrate and broken. Yugoslavia was dismembered to reward Hitler's Balkan allies. Croatia, reconstituted as a nominal kingdom, was given to the administration of an Italian princeling, who wisely decided to remain in Italy. By 1947 it was again totally part of the 6 Yugoslav Socialist Republics.

Croatia proclaimed their independence from Yugoslavia on Oct. 8, 1991.

Local Serbian forces, supported by the Yugoslav Federal Army, had developed a military stronghold and proclaimed an independent "SRPSKEKRAJINA" State in the area around Knin, located in southern Croatia having an estimated population of 350,000 Croat Serbs. In September 1995, Croat forces overwhelmed Croat Serb forces ending the short life of their proclaimed Serbian Republic.

NOTE: Coin dates starting with 1994 are followed with a period. Example: 1994.

MONETARY SYSTEM
100 Banica = 1 Kuna

The word kunas', related to the Russian Kunitsa, which means marten, reflects the use of furs for money in medieval Eastern Europe.

KINGDOM
DECIMAL COINAGE

KM# A3 500 KUNA
9.9500 g., 0.9000 Gold .2821 oz. AGW **Obv:** Ante Pavelió, date below **Rev:** Denomination above arms within braided circle **Designer:** Ivan Kerdic

Date	Mintage	F	VF	XF	Unc	BU
1941	170	—	1,750	2,250	3,000	—

KM# B3 500 KUNA
9.9500 g., 0.9000 Gold .2821 oz. AGW **Obv:** Kneeling figure with sheaf of grain, date below **Rev:** Denomination above arms within braided circle

Date	Mintage	F	VF	XF	Unc	BU
1941	—	—	—	—	3,400	—

REPUBLIC
REFORM COINAGE
May 30, 1994 - 1000 Dinara = 1 Kuna; 100 Lipa = 1 Kuna

For the circulating minor coins, the reverse legend (name of item) is in Croatian for odd dated years and Latin for even dated years.

KM# 3b LIPA
Gold, 17 mm. **Obv:** Denomination above arms **Rev:** Ears of corn

Date	Mintage	F	VF	XF	Unc	BU
1993 Proof, Rare	5	—	—	—	—	—

KM# 4b 2 LIPE
Gold, 19 mm. **Obv:** Denomination above crowned arms on half braid **Rev:** Grapevine

Date	Mintage	F	VF	XF	Unc	BU
1993 Proof, Rare	5	—	—	—	—	—

KM# 5b 5 LIPA
Gold, 18 mm. **Obv:** Denomination above crowned arms **Rev:** Oak leaves, date below **Designer:** Kuzma Kovacic

Date	Mintage	F	VF	XF	Unc	BU
1993 Proof, Rare	5	—	—	—	—	—

KM# 6b 10 LIPA
Gold, 20 mm. **Obv:** Denomination above crowned arms on half braid **Rev:** Oak leaves, date below **Designer:** Kuzma Kovacic

Date	Mintage	F	VF	XF	Unc	BU
1993 Proof, Rare	5	—	—	—	—	—

KM# 7b 20 LIPA
Gold, 18.5 mm. **Obv:** Denomination above crowned arms on half braid **Rev:** Olive branch, date below **Designer:** Kuzma Kovacic

Date	Mintage	F	VF	XF	Unc	BU
1993 Proof, Rare	5	—	—	—	—	—

KM# 8b 50 LIPA
Gold, 20.5 mm. **Obv:** Denomination above crowned arms on half braid **Rev:** Flowers, date below **Designer:** Kuzma Kovacic

Date	Mintage	F	VF	XF	Unc	BU
1993 Proof, Rare	5	—	—	—	—	—

KM# 9b KUNA
Gold **Obv:** Marten back of numeral, arms divide branches below **Rev:** Nightingale left

Date	Mintage	F	VF	XF	Unc	BU
1993 Proof, rare	—	—	—	—	—	—

KM# 9.1b KUNA
Gold, 22.5 mm. **Obv:** Marten back of numeral, arms divide branches below **Rev:** Nightingale left **Designer:** Kuzma Kovacic

Date	Mintage	F	VF	XF	Unc	BU
1993 Proof, Rare	5	—	—	—	—	—

KM# 10b 2 KUNE
Gold, 24.5 mm. **Obv:** Marten back of numeral, arms divide branches below **Rev:** Tuna right, date below **Designer:** Kuzma Kovacic

Date	Mintage	F	VF	XF	Unc	BU
1993 Proof, Rare	5	—	—	—	—	—

168 CROATIA

KM# 11b 5 KUNA
Gold, 26.7 mm. **Obv:** Marten back of numeral, arms divide branches below **Rev:** Brown bear left, date below

Date	Mintage	F	VF	XF	Unc	BU
1993 Proof, Rare	5	—	—	—	—	—

KM# 24b 5 KUNA
12.0000 g., 0.9000 Gold, 26.7 mm. **Subject:** 500th Anniversary - Senj **Obv:** Denomination on square divides arms above from shield below, circle surrounds **Rev:** Anniversary dates on symbols within circle

Date	Mintage	F	VF	XF	Unc	BU
1994	200	—	—	—	450	—

KM# 31.1 500 KUNA
3.5000 g., 0.9860 Gold .1109 oz. AGW **Obv:** Izborna Cathedral, denomination below **Rev:** Arms at top and bottom, cherubs flank

Date	Mintage	F	VF	XF	Unc	BU
1994. Proof	1,000	Value: 200				

KM# 31.2 500 KUNA
3.5000 g., 0.9860 Gold .1109 oz. AGW **Obv:** Izborna Cathedral, Series II added **Rev:** Arms at top and bottom, cherubs flank

Date	Mintage	F	VF	XF	Unc	BU
1994. Proof	1,000	Value: 185				

KM# 32 500 KUNA
3.5000 g., 0.9860 Gold .1109 oz. AGW **Subject:** 5th Anniversary of Independence

Date	Mintage	F	VF	XF	Unc	BU
1995. Proof	4,000	Value: 175				

KM# 52 500 KUNA
3.5000 g., 0.9860 Gold .1109 oz. AGW **Subject:** City of Split **Obv:** Towered building, denomination at left **Rev:** Ancient depiction of king on throne, dates at left

Date	Mintage	F	VF	XF	Unc	BU
ND(1995) Proof	3,950	Value: 150				

KM# 55 500 KUNA
3.5000 g., 0.9860 Gold .1109 oz. AGW **Subject:** University of Zadar **Obv:** Circle of arches, denomination at top, arms below **Rev:** Saint reading within circle, dates below

Date	Mintage	F	VF	XF	Unc	BU
ND(1996) Proof	1,000	Value: 185				

KM# 58 500 KUNA
3.5000 g., 0.9860 Gold .1109 oz. AGW **Subject:** 800th Anniversary - City of Osijek **Obv:** Crowned arms, denomination below **Rev:** City view

Date	Mintage	F	VF	XF	Unc	BU
ND(1996) Proof	1,000	Value: 185				

KM# 68 500 KUNA
3.5000 g., 0.9860 Gold 0.111 oz. AGW, 18 mm.
Subject: Vukovar **Obv:** Ceramic container, denomination at upper right **Rev:** Courtyard, date at right **Edge:** Plain

Date	Mintage	F	VF	XF	Unc	BU
1997. Proof	2,000	Value: 115				

KM# 70 500 KUNA
3.5000 g., 0.9860 Gold 0.111 oz. AGW, 18 mm. **Obv:** Wild flowers, denomination at right, arms above **Rev:** Eagle on branch **Edge:** Plain

Date	Mintage	F	VF	XF	Unc	BU
1997. Proof	1,000	Value: 125				

KM# 74 500 KUNA
3.5000 g., 0.9860 Gold 0.111 oz. AGW, 18 mm. **Obv:** Small national arms above religious arms and value, date divided **Rev:** Bust of Cardinal Stepinac (1898-1960) right **Edge:** Plain

Date	Mintage	F	VF	XF	Unc	BU
1998. Proof	2,000	Value: 115				

KM# 82 500 KUNA
3.5000 g., 0.9860 Gold 0.111 oz. AGW **Subject:** 10th Anniversary of Parliament **Obv:** View of session **Rev:** Parliament building

Date	Mintage	F	VF	XF	Unc	BU
ND (2000) Proof	500	Value: 125				

KM# 33 1000 KUNA
7.0000 g., 0.9860 Gold .2218 oz. AGW **Obv:** Crowned arms divides date above denomination **Rev:** Half-length portrait of Pope John Paul II, looking left

Date	Mintage	F	VF	XF	Unc	BU
1994. Proof	4,000	Value: 285				

KM# 34 1000 KUNA
7.0000 g., 0.9860 Gold .2218 oz. AGW **Subject:** 5th Anniversary of Independence **Obv:** Arms divide sprays below denomination, dotted background **Rev:** Map, inscription, and dates, dotted background

Date	Mintage	F	VF	XF	Unc	BU
ND(1995) Proof	4,000	Value: 285				

KM# 53 1000 KUNA
7.0000 g., 0.9860 Gold .2218 oz. AGW **Subject:** Spalatum **Obv:** Diocletian's palace, denomination and arms above **Rev:** Sarcophagus, dates above

Date	Mintage	F	VF	XF	Unc	BU
ND(1995) Proof	1,950	Value: 285				

KM# 72 1000 KUNA
7.0000 g., 0.9860 Gold 0.2219 oz. AGW, 22 mm. **Obv:** Wild flowers, arms above, denomination at right **Rev:** Three Black Storks **Edge:** Plain

Date	Mintage	F	VF	XF	Unc	BU
1997. Proof	1,000	Value: 275				

KM# 61 1000 KUNA
7.0000 g., 0.9860 Gold 0.2219 oz. AGW, 22 mm. **Obv:** National arms **Rev:** Dr. Tudman **Edge:** Plain **Note:** Death of Dr. Tudman

Date	Mintage	F	VF	XF	Unc	BU
1997. Proof	3,000	Value: 245				

TRADE COINAGE

KM# 35 DUCAT
3.5000 g., 0.9860 Gold .1109 oz. AGW, 20 mm. **Obv:** Crowned arms with supporters, denomination below **Rev:** Ruder Boskovic bust at left facing, dates at left **Designer:** Kuzma Kovacic

Date	Mintage	F	VF	XF	Unc	BU
1994 Proof	5,000	Value: 160				

KM# 62 DUCAT
3.5000 g., 0.9860 Gold .1109 oz. AGW **Subject:** Liberation of Knin **Obv:** Crowned arms, denomination below **Rev:** Regional view within circle

Date	Mintage	F	VF	XF	Unc	BU
ND(1995)	3,000	—	—	—	160	—

MEDALLIC COINAGE

X# M5 250 KUNA
5.0000 g., 0.9000 Gold 0.1447 oz. AGW **Subject:** 10th Anniversary of Death of Dr. Ante Pavelic **Note:** Struck by Descher Sohn, Munich, Germany for Croation Liberation Movement "Ustasa".

Date	Mintage	F	VF	XF	Unc	BU
1969 Proof	—	Value: 250				

X# M1 500 KUNA
9.7500 g., 0.9000 Gold 0.2821 oz. AGW **Subject:** Dr. Ante Pavelic **Note:** Prev. KM#M1.1.

Date	Mintage	F	VF	XF	Unc	BU
1941	170	—	1,750	2,250	3,000	—

CUBA

X# M1a 500 KUNA
0.9000 Gold, 27 mm. **Subject:** Dr. Ante Pavelic **Note:** Prev. KM#M1.2.

Date	Mintage	F	VF	XF	Unc	BU
1941	—	—	—	—	—	—

X# M1b 500 KUNA
Nickel, 22 mm. **Subject:** Dr. Ante Pavelic **Note:** Prev. KM#1.1a.

Date	Mintage	F	VF	XF	Unc	BU
1941	—	—	—	—	—	—

X# M3 500 KUNA
Aluminum, 22 mm. **Note:** Struck unofficially by order of Dr. Ante Pavelic.

Date	Mintage	F	VF	XF	Unc	BU
1941	—	—	—	400	600	—

PATTERNS
Including off metal strikes

KM#	Date	Mintage	Identification	Mkt Val
Pn12	1941	—	25 Banica. Gold. 16 or 17 mm.	3,500
Pn16	1941	—	50 Banica. Gold.	4,500
Pn22	1941	—	Kuna. Gold.	3,500
Pn27	1941	—	2 Kune. Gold.	4,500
Pn37	1941	—	500 Kuna. Gold. 27 mm. Chain. KMA3.	—

PROOF SETS

KM#	Date	Mintage	Identification	Issue Price	Mkt Val
PS3	1993 (9)	5	KM3b-11b, rare	—	—
PS7	1994 (2)	1,000	KM26, 33	240	360
PS8	ND (1994) (3)	250	KM25.1, 29.1, 31.1	154	325
PS9	ND (1994) (3)	500	KM25.2, 29.2, 31.2	154	350
PS6	1994 (3)	250	KM21, 23, 24b	—	475
PS14	1995 (5)	—	KM27, 28, 30, 32, 34	—	625
PS20	ND (1995) (5)	1,000	KM 27, 28, 30, 32, 34	406	620
PS21	ND (1995) (3)	2,000	KM 27, 30, 34	270	400
PS22	1995 (2)	2,000	KM28, 32	135	225
PS15	ND (1995) (4)	1,000	KM#69, 70	375	525
PS16	ND (1995) (2)	1,000	KM50, 51	62.50	75.00
PS17	ND (1995) (2)	1,000	KM50, 52	125	190
PS18	ND (1995) (2)	1,000	KM51, 53	250	345
PS19	ND (1995) (2)	1,000	KM52, 53	312	445
PS25	ND (1996)	500	KM54-55	146	250
PS26	ND (1996) (3)	300	KM56-58	177	285
PS27	1997 (3)	300	KM59-61	281	370
PS28	1997 (2)	300	KM#69, 70	141	170
PS29	1997 (2)	300	KM#71, 72	260	325
PS30	1997 (4)	300	KM#69, 70, 71, 72	401	500
PS31	1998 (2)	500	KM#73, 74	141	150

CUBA

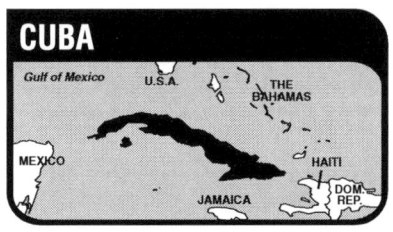

The Republic of Cuba, situated at the northern edge of the Caribbean Sea about 90 miles (145 km.) south of Florida, has an area of 42,804 sq. mi. (110,860 sq. km.) and a population of *11.2 million. Capital: Havana. The Cuban economy is based on the cultivation and refining of sugar, which provides 80 percent of export earnings.

Discovered by Columbus in 1492 and settled by Diego Velasquez in the early 1500s, Cuba remained a Spanish possession until 1898, except for a brief British occupancy of Havana in 1762-63. Cuban attempts to gain freedom were crushed, even while Spain was granting independence to its other American possessions. Ten years of warfare, 1868-78, between Spanish troops and Cuban rebels exacted guarantees of rights which were never implemented. The final revolt, begun in 1895, evoked American sympathy, and with the aid of U.S. troops independence was proclaimed on May 20, 1902. Fulgencio Batista seized the government in 1952 and established a dictatorship. Opposition to Batista, led by Fidel Castro, drove him into exile on Jan. 1, 1959. A communist-type, 25-member collective leadership headed by Castro was inaugurated in March, 1962.

RULER
Spanish, until 1898

MINT MARK
Key - Havana, 1977-

MONETARY SYSTEM
100 Centavos = 1 Peso

FIRST REPUBLIC
1902 - 1962
DECIMAL COINAGE

KM# 16 PESO
1.6718 g., 0.9000 Gold .0483 oz. AGW **Obv:** National arms within wreath, denomination below **Rev:** Head of Jose Marti right, date below

Date	Mintage	F	VF	XF	Unc	BU
1915	6,850	50.00	100	150	275	600
1915 Proof	140	Value: 1,750				
1916	11,000	50.00	100	150	300	700
1916 Proof	100	Value: 2,500				

KM# 17 2 PESOS
3.3436 g., 0.9000 Gold .0967 oz. AGW **Obv:** National arms within wreath, denomination below **Rev:** Head right, date below

Date	Mintage	F	VF	XF	Unc	BU
1915	10,000	70.00	90.00	175	500	1,000
1915 Proof	100	Value: 3,000				
1916	150,000	65.00	75.00	90.00	200	450
1916 Proof; Rare	8	—	—	—	—	—

KM# 18 4 PESOS
6.6872 g., 0.9000 Gold .1935 oz. AGW **Obv:** National arms within wreath, denomination below **Rev:** Head right, date below

Date	Mintage	F	VF	XF	Unc	BU
1915	6,300	135	175	375	1,100	1,600
1915 Proof	100	Value: 3,000				
1916	129,000	125	135	160	500	750
1916 Proof	90	Value: 4,500				

KM# 19 5 PESOS
8.3592 g., 0.9000 Gold .2419 oz. AGW **Obv:** National arms within wreath, denomination below **Rev:** Head right, date below

Date	Mintage	F	VF	XF	Unc	BU
1915	696,000	—	BV	165	210	475
1915 Proof	—	Value: 3,200				
1916	1,132,000	—	BV	160	200	450
1916 Proof	—	Value: 6,500				

Note: American Numismatic Rarities Eliasberg sale 4-05, Proof 65 realized $13,800.

KM# 20 10 PESOS
16.7185 g., 0.9000 Gold .4838 oz. AGW **Obv:** National arms within wreath, denomination below **Rev:** Head right, date below

Date	Mintage	F	VF	XF	Unc	BU
1915	95,000	—	BV	330	550	800
1915 Proof	—	Value: 7,500				
1916	1,169,000	—	BV	320	400	750
1916 Proof, Rare						

Note: David Akers John Jay Pittman sale 8-99 very choice Proof realized $19,550, choice Proof realized $14,950. American Numismatic Rarities Eliasberg sale 4-05, Proof 62 realized $29,900.

KM# 21 20 PESOS
33.4370 g., 0.9000 Gold .9676 oz. AGW **Subject:** Jose Marti **Obv:** National arms within wreath, denomination below **Rev:** Head right, date below

Date	Mintage	F	VF	XF	Unc	BU
1915	57,000	BV	675	800	1,500	3,000
1915 Proof; Rare	—	—	—	—	—	—

Note: David Akers John Jay Pittman sale 8-99 very choice proof 1915 realized $11,500.

| 1916 Proof; Rare | 10 | — | — | — | — | — |

Note: David Akers John Jay Pittman sale 8-99 nearly choice Proof 1916 realized $43,125.

SECOND REPUBLIC
1962 - Present
DECIMAL COINAGE

KM# 739 5 PESOS
1.2400 g., Gold, 14 mm. **Subject:** Wonders of the Ancient World **Obv:** Cuban arms **Rev:** Ancient lighthouse of Alexandria

Date	Mintage	F	VF	XF	Unc	BU
2005 Proof	5,000	Value: 40.00				

KM# 740 5 PESOS
1.2400 g., Gold, 14 mm. **Subject:** Wonders of the Ancient World **Obv:** Cuban arms **Rev:** Colossus of Rhodes

Date	Mintage	F	VF	XF	Unc	BU
2005 Proof	5,000	Value: 40.00				

170 CUBA

KM# 741 5 PESOS
1.2400 g., Gold, 14 mm. **Subject:** Wonders of the Ancient World **Obv:** Cuban arms **Rev:** Hanging Gardens of Babylon

Date	Mintage	F	VF	XF	Unc	BU
2005 Proof	5,000		Value: 40.00			

KM# 742 5 PESOS
1.2400 g., Gold, 14 mm. **Subject:** Wonders of the Ancient World **Obv:** Cuban arms **Rev:** Egyptian Pyramids

Date	Mintage	F	VF	XF	Unc	BU
2005	5,000		Value: 40.00			

KM# 743 5 PESOS
1.2400 g., Gold, 14 mm. **Subject:** Wonders of the Ancient World **Obv:** Cuban arms **Rev:** Temple of Artemis

Date	Mintage	F	VF	XF	Unc	BU
2005 Proof	5,000		Value: 40.00			

KM# 744 5 PESOS
1.2400 g., Gold, 14 mm. **Subject:** Wonders of the Ancient World **Obv:** Cuban arms **Rev:** Statue of Jupiter

Date	Mintage	F	VF	XF	Unc	BU
2005	5,000		Value: 40.00			

KM# 745 5 PESOS
1.2400 g., Gold, 14 mm. **Subject:** Wonders of the Ancient World **Obv:** Cuban arms **Rev:** Mausoleum of Halicarnas

Date	Mintage	F	VF	XF	Unc	BU
2005 Proof	5,000		Value: 40.00			

KM# 746 5 PESOS
1.2400 g., Gold, 14 mm. **Obv:** Cuban arms **Rev:** Cortes, Montezuma and Aztec Pyramid

Date	Mintage	F	VF	XF	Unc	BU
2005 Proof	15,000		Value: 40.00			

KM# 211 10 PESOS
3.1100 g., 0.9990 Gold .1000 oz. AGW **Obv:** National arms within wreath, denomination below **Rev:** Jose Marti

Date	Mintage	F	VF	XF	Unc	BU
1988	50	—	—	—	125	250
1988 Proof	10	Value: 250				
1989	50	—	—	—	125	250
1989 Proof	15	Value: 250				
1990	15	—	—	—	125	250
1990 Proof	12	Value: 250				

KM# 383 10 PESOS
3.1100 g., 0.9990 Gold .1000 oz. AGW **Obv:** National arms within wreath, denomination below **Rev:** Alexander von Humboldt

Date	Mintage	F	VF	XF	Unc	BU
1989	500	—	—	—	—	125
1989 Proof	—	Value: 100				

KM# 342 10 PESOS
3.1100 g., 0.9990 Gold .1000 oz. AGW **Series:** Olympics **Obv:** National arms within wreath, denomination below **Rev:** Basketball hoop, ball and hands, small date between arms below

Date	Mintage	F	VF	XF	Unc	BU
1990 Proof	Est. 5,000	Value: 100				

KM# 747 10 PESOS
3.1100 g., Gold, 16 mm. **Obv:** National arms and inscription **Rev:** Che Guevara standing

Date	Mintage	F	VF	XF	Unc	BU
1997 Proof	500	Value: 195				

KM# 748 10 PESOS
3.1100 g., Gold, 16 mm. **Obv:** National arms within wreath, denomination **Rev:** Bust of Che Guevara

Date	Mintage	F	VF	XF	Unc	BU
1997 Proof	500	Value: 195				

KM# 749 10 PESOS
3.1100 g., Gold, 18 mm. **Obv:** National arms within wreath, denomination **Rev:** Hummingbird in flight

Date	Mintage	F	VF	XF	Unc	BU
1999 Proof	1,000	Value: 100				

KM# 725 10 PESOS
3.1100 g., 0.9990 Gold .1000 oz. AGW, 18 mm. **Subject:** Zunzuncito **Obv:** National arms **Rev:** Hummingbird **Edge:** Reeded

Date	Mintage	F	VF	XF	Unc	BU
1999 Proof	1,000	Value: 100				

KM# 212 15 PESOS
3.8800 g., 0.9990 Gold .1250 oz. AGW **Obv:** National arms within wreath, denomination below **Rev:** Jose Marti head right, date below

Date	Mintage	F	VF	XF	Unc	BU
1988	50	—	—	—	200	—
1988 Proof	15	Value: 250				
1989	50	—	—	—	200	—
1989 Proof	15	Value: 250				
1990	15	—	—	—	250	—
1990 Proof	12	Value: 250				

KM# 213 25 PESOS
7.7700 g., 0.9990 Gold .2500 oz. AGW **Subject:** Jose Marti **Obv:** National arms within wreath, denomination below **Rev:** Head right

Date	Mintage	F	VF	XF	Unc	BU
1988	50	—	—	—	300	—
1988 Proof	15	Value: 400				
1989	50	—	—	—	300	—
1989 Proof	15	Value: 400				
1990	12	—	—	—	350	—
1990 Proof	12	Value: 400				

KM# 692 25 PESOS
7.7759 g., 0.9990 Gold .2500 oz. AGW, 20 mm. **Subject:** Zunzuncito **Obv:** National arms **Rev:** Hummingbird **Edge:** Reeded

Date	Mintage	F	VF	XF	Unc	BU
1999 Proof	1,000	Value: 185				

KM# 208 50 PESOS
15.5500 g., 0.9990 Gold .5000 oz. AGW **Subject:** 30th Anniversary - The March to Victory **Obv:** Arms on star background above half wreath **Rev:** Soldiers on the march, date above

Date	Mintage	F	VF	XF	Unc	BU
1988 Proof	150	Value: 360				

KM# 209 50 PESOS
15.5500 g., 0.9990 Gold .5000 oz. AGW **Subject:** 60th Anniversary - Birth of Ernesto Che Guevara **Obv:** Arms on star background above half wreath **Rev:** Bust right, date at left

Date	Mintage	F	VF	XF	Unc	BU
1988 Proof	150	Value: 360				

KM# 210 50 PESOS
15.5500 g., 0.9990 Gold .5000 oz. AGW **Subject:** Triumph of the Revolutionary **Obv:** Arms on star background above half wreath **Rev:** Castro with revolutionaries, divide dates

Date	Mintage	F	VF	XF	Unc	BU
1988 Proof	150	Value: 360				

KM# 214 50 PESOS
15.5500 g., 0.9990 Gold .5000 oz. AGW **Subject:** Jose Marti **Obv:** National arms within wreath, denomination **Rev:** Head right

Date	Mintage	F	VF	XF	Unc	BU
1988	12	—	—	—	450	—
1988 Proof	15	Value: 600				
1989	150	—	—	—	375	—
1989 Proof	15	Value: 600				
1990	15	—	—	—	450	—
1990 Proof	12	Value: 600				

KM# 313 50 PESOS
15.5500 g., 0.9990 Gold .5000 oz. AGW **Subject:** 160th Anniversary - First Train in England **Rev:** Train, Liverpool - Manchester

Date	Mintage	F	VF	XF	Unc	BU
1989 Proof	150	Value: 375				

KM# 314 50 PESOS
15.5500 g., 0.9990 Gold .5000 oz. AGW **Subject:** 150th Anniversary - First Train in Spanish America **Rev:** Train **Rev. Legend:** HABANA-BEJUCAL

Date	Mintage	F	VF	XF	Unc	BU
1989 Proof	150	Value: 375				

KM# 315 50 PESOS
15.5500 g., 0.9990 Gold .5000 oz. AGW **Subject:** 140th Anniversary - First Train in Spain **Rev:** Train **Rev. Legend:** BARCELONA-MATARD

Date	Mintage	F	VF	XF	Unc	BU
1989 Proof	150	Value: 375				

KM# 330 50 PESOS
15.5500 g., 0.9990 Gold .5000 oz. AGW **Subject:** Tania La Guerrillera **Rev:** Portrait of female guerilla fighter

Date	Mintage	F	VF	XF	Unc	BU
1989 Proof	150	Value: 375				

CUBA

KM# 331 50 PESOS
15.5500 g., 0.9990 oz. .5000 oz. AGW **Subject:** Camilo Cienfuegos Gornaran **Rev:** Portrait of Camilo Cienfuegos
Date	Mintage	F	VF	XF	Unc	BU
1989 Proof	150	Value: 375				

KM# 332 50 PESOS
15.5500 g., 0.9990 Gold .5000 oz. AGW **Subject:** Assault of the Moncada Garrison **Rev:** Battle scene
Date	Mintage	F	VF	XF	Unc	BU
1989 Proof	150	Value: 375				

KM# 281 50 PESOS
15.5500 g., 0.9990 Gold .5000 oz. AGW **Subject:** Simon Bolivar **Rev:** Portrait of Simon Bolivar
Date	Mintage	F	VF	XF	Unc	BU
1990 Proof	50	Value: 375				

KM# 298 50 PESOS
15.5500 g., 0.9990 Gold .5000 oz. AGW **Subject:** 500th Anniversary - Discovery of America **Obv:** National arms within wreath **Rev:** Portrait of Christopher Columbus
Date	Mintage	F	VF	XF	Unc	BU
1990 Proof	250	Value: 375				

KM# 299 50 PESOS
15.5500 g., 0.9990 Gold .5000 oz. AGW **Subject:** 500th Anniversary - Discovery of America **Obv:** National arms within wreath **Rev:** Portrait of King Ferdinand V
Date	Mintage	F	VF	XF	Unc	BU
1990 Proof	250	Value: 375				

KM# 300 50 PESOS
15.5500 g., 0.9990 Gold .5000 oz. AGW **Subject:** 500th Anniversary - Discovery of America **Obv:** National arms within wreath **Rev:** Portrait of Queen Isabella of Spain
Date	Mintage	F	VF	XF	Unc	BU
1990 Proof	250	Value: 375				

KM# 301 50 PESOS
15.5500 g., 0.9990 Gold .5000 oz. AGW **Subject:** 500th Anniversary - Discovery of America **Obv:** National arms within wreath **Rev:** Portrait of Juan de la Cosa
Date	Mintage	F	VF	XF	Unc	BU
1990 Proof	250	Value: 375				

KM# 321 50 PESOS
15.5500 g., 0.9990 Gold .5000 oz. AGW **Subject:** Pan American Games - Baseball **Obv:** National arms within wreath, denomination **Rev:** Baseball players
Date	Mintage	F	VF	XF	Unc	BU
1990 Proof	15	Value: 400				

KM# 322 50 PESOS
15.5500 g., 0.9990 Gold .5000 oz. AGW **Subject:** Pan American Games - High Jump **Obv:** National arms within wreath, denomination **Rev:** High jumper clearing pole
Date	Mintage	F	VF	XF	Unc	BU
1990 Proof	15	Value: 400				

KM# 323 50 PESOS
15.5500 g., 0.9990 Gold .5000 oz. AGW **Subject:** Pan American Games - Volleyball **Obv:** National arms within wreath, denomination **Rev:** Volleyball players
Date	Mintage	F	VF	XF	Unc	BU
1990 Proof	15	Value: 400				

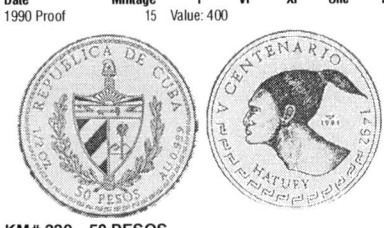

KM# 339 50 PESOS
15.5500 g., 0.9990 Gold .5000 oz. AGW **Rev:** Hatuey tribesman
Date	Mintage	F	VF	XF	Unc	BU
1991 Proof	200	Value: 375				

KM# 444 50 PESOS
15.5500 g., 0.9990 Gold .5000 oz. AGW **Subject:** Queen Joanna
Date	Mintage	F	VF	XF	Unc	BU
1991 Proof	200	Value: 375				

KM# 445 50 PESOS
15.5500 g., 0.9990 Gold .5000 oz. AGW **Subject:** Diego Valezquez
Date	Mintage	F	VF	XF	Unc	BU
1991 Proof	200	Value: 375				

KM# 446 50 PESOS
15.5500 g., 0.9990 Gold .5000 oz. AGW **Subject:** Pinzon Brothers
Date	Mintage	F	VF	XF	Unc	BU
1991 Proof	200	Value: 375				

KM# 490 50 PESOS
13.0000 g., 0.9170 Gold .3829 oz. AGW **Series:** Pirates of the Caribbean **Subject:** Blackbeard **Obv:** National arms within wreath, denomination below **Rev:** Bust 3/4 facing within circle, date below
Date	Mintage	F	VF	XF	Unc	BU
1995 Proof	Est. 1,000	Value: 300				

KM# 491 50 PESOS
13.0000 g., 0.9170 Gold .3829 oz. AGW **Series:** Pirates of the Caribbean **Subject:** Sir Henry Morgan **Obv:** National arms within wreath, denomination below **Rev:** Bust 3/4 right
Date	Mintage	F	VF	XF	Unc	BU
1995 Proof	Est. 1,000	Value: 300				

KM# 492 50 PESOS
13.0000 g., 0.9170 Gold .3829 oz. AGW **Series:** Pirates of the Caribbean **Subject:** Anne Bonny **Obv:** National arms within wreath, denomination below **Rev:** Bust with bare breast looking left
Date	Mintage	F	VF	XF	Unc	BU
1995 Proof	Est. 1,000	Value: 300				

KM# 493 50 PESOS
13.0000 g., 0.9170 Gold .3829 oz. AGW **Series:** Pirates of the Caribbean **Subject:** Mary Read **Obv:** National arms within wreath, denomination below **Rev:** Bust with bare breasts 3/4 right
Date	Mintage	F	VF	XF	Unc	BU
1995 Proof	Est. 1,000	Value: 300				

KM# 494 50 PESOS
13.0000 g., 0.9170 Gold .3829 oz. AGW **Series:** Pirates of the Caribbean **Subject:** Captain Kidd **Obv:** National arms within wreath, denomination below **Rev:** Bust left looking right
Date	Mintage	F	VF	XF	Unc	BU
1995 Proof	Est. 1,000	Value: 300				

KM# 495 50 PESOS
13.0000 g., 0.9170 Gold .3829 oz. AGW **Series:** Pirates of the Caribbean **Subject:** Piet Heyn **Obv:** National arms within wreath, denomination below **Rev:** Bust facing
Date	Mintage	F	VF	XF	Unc	BU
1995 Proof	Est. 1,000	Value: 300				

KM# 654 50 PESOS
15.5500 g., 0.9990 Gold .4999 oz. AGW **Subject:** Expo 2000 **Obv:** National arms within wreath **Rev:** Twipsy cartoon logo
Date	Mintage	F	VF	XF	Unc	BU
1998 Proof	3,125	Value: 360				

KM# 638 50 PESOS
15.5500 g., 0.9990 Gold .4999 oz. AGW, 30 mm. **Subject:** AIDS **Obv:** National arms within wreath **Rev:** AIDS ribbon on silhouette before world map
Date	Mintage	F	VF	XF	Unc	BU
1998 Proof	2,000	Value: 360				

KM# 704 50 PESOS
15.5518 g., 0.9990 Gold .5000 oz. AGW, 32.5 mm. **Obv:** National arms **Rev:** Hummingbird **Edge:** Reeded
Date	Mintage	F	VF	XF	Unc	BU
1999 Proof	1,000	Value: 375				

KM# 42 100 PESOS
12.0000 g., 0.9170 Gold .3538 oz. AGW **Subject:** 60th Anniversary of Socialist Revolution - Lenin **Obv:** National arms within wreath, denomination below **Rev:** Bust left divides dates
Date	Mintage	F	VF	XF	Unc	BU
ND(1977) Proof	10	Value: 10,000				

KM# 43 100 PESOS
12.0000 g., 0.9170 Gold .3538 oz. AGW **Obv:** Liberty cap above flagged arms, denomination **Rev:** Carlos Manuel de Cespedes
Date	Mintage	F	VF	XF	Unc	BU
ND(1977) Proof	25,000	Value: 260				

KM# 45 100 PESOS
12.0000 g., 0.9170 Gold .3538 oz. AGW **Subject:** Nonaligned Nations Conference **Obv:** National arms within wreath **Rev:** Number six within design
Date	Mintage	F	VF	XF	Unc	BU
1979	2,000	—	—	—	350	—
1979 Proof	20,000	Value: 275				

KM# 52 100 PESOS
12.0000 g., 0.9170 Gold .3538 oz. AGW **Subject:** First Soviet-Cuban space flight **Obv:** Arms **Rev:** Shuttle orbiting planet, date below
Date	Mintage	F	VF	XF	Unc	BU
1980	1,000	—	—	—	350	—

172 CUBA

KM# 85 100 PESOS
12.0000 g., 0.9170 Gold .3538 oz. AGW **Obv:** National arms within wreath, denomination below **Rev:** Columbus' ship - Niña

Date	Mintage	F	VF	XF	Unc	BU
1981	2,000	—	—	—	325	—

KM# 86 100 PESOS
12.0000 g., 0.9170 Gold .3538 oz. AGW **Obv:** National arms within wreath, denomination below **Rev:** Columbus' ship - Pinta

Date	Mintage	F	VF	XF	Unc	BU
1981	2,000	—	—	—	325	—

KM# 87 100 PESOS
12.0000 g., 0.9170 Gold .3538 oz. AGW **Obv:** National arms within wreath, denomination below **Rev:** Columbus' ship - Santa Maria

Date	Mintage	F	VF	XF	Unc	BU
1981	2,000	—	—	—	325	—

KM# 202 100 PESOS
31.1030 g., 0.9990 Gold 1.0000 oz. AGW **Subject:** 30th Anniversary of March to Victory **Obv:** Arms on star background above half wreath **Rev:** Soldiers on the march

Date	Mintage	F	VF	XF	Unc	BU
1988 Proof	100	Value: 720				

KM# 203 100 PESOS
31.1030 g., 0.9990 Gold 1.0000 oz. AGW **Subject:** 60th Anniversary - Birth of Ernesto Che Guevara **Obv:** Arms on star background above half wreath **Rev:** Bust right, dates at left

Date	Mintage	F	VF	XF	Unc	BU
1988 Proof	100	Value: 720				

KM# 204 100 PESOS
31.1030 g., 0.9990 Gold 1.0000 oz. AGW **Subject:** 30th Anniversary - Triumph of the Revolution **Obv:** Arms on star background above half wreath **Rev:** Scene of triumph, dates

Date	Mintage	F	VF	XF	Unc	BU
1988 Proof	100	Value: 720				

KM# 215 100 PESOS
31.1030 g., 0.9990 Gold 1.0000 oz. AGW **Subject:** Jose Marti **Obv:** National arms within wreath, denomination below **Rev:** Head right, date below

Date	Mintage	F	VF	XF	Unc	BU
1988	50	—	—	—	800	—
1988 Proof	15	Value: 1,200				
1989	150	—	—	—	700	—
1989 Proof	15	Value: 1,200				
1990	15	—	—	—	1,000	—
1990 Proof	12	Value: 1,250				

KM# 316 100 PESOS
31.1030 g., 0.9990 Gold 1.0000 oz. AGW **Subject:** 160th Anniversary - First train in England **Rev:** Train **Rev. Legend:** LIVERPOOL-MANCHESTER

Date	Mintage	F	VF	XF	Unc	BU
1989 Proof	150	Value: 720				

KM# 317 100 PESOS
31.1030 g., 0.9990 Gold 1.0000 oz. AGW **Subject:** 150th Anniversary - First train in Spanish America **Rev:** Train **Rev. Legend:** HABANA-BEJUCAL

Date	Mintage	F	VF	XF	Unc	BU
1989 Proof	150	Value: 720				

KM# 318 100 PESOS
31.1030 g., 0.9990 Gold 1.0000 oz. AGW **Subject:** 140th Anniversary - First train in Spain **Rev:** Train **Rev. Legend:** BARCELONA-MATARO

Date	Mintage	F	VF	XF	Unc	BU
1989 Proof	150	Value: 720				

KM# 319 100 PESOS
31.1030 g., 0.9990 Gold 1.0000 oz. AGW **Subject:** 200th Anniversary of French Revolution - Lady Justice **Rev:** Female revolutionary raising flag

Date	Mintage	F	VF	XF	Unc	BU
1989 Proof	150	Value: 800				

KM# 320 100 PESOS
31.1030 g., 0.9990 Gold 1.0000 oz. AGW **Subject:** 200th Anniversary of French Revolution - Bastille **Rev:** Bastille, soldiers in foreground

Date	Mintage	F	VF	XF	Unc	BU
1989	150	—	—	—	800	—

KM# 333 100 PESOS
31.1030 g., 0.9990 Gold 1.0000 oz. AGW **Subject:** Tania La Guerrillera **Rev:** Portrait of female guerilla fighter

Date	Mintage	F	VF	XF	Unc	BU
1989 Proof	150	Value: 800				

KM# 334 100 PESOS
31.1030 g., 0.9990 Gold 1.0000 oz. AGW **Subject:** Camilo Cienfuegos Gornaran **Rev:** Portrait of Camilo Cienfuegos

Date	Mintage	F	VF	XF	Unc	BU
1989 Proof	150	Value: 800				

KM# 335 100 PESOS
31.1030 g., 0.9990 Gold 1.0000 oz. AGW **Subject:** 35th Anniversary - Assault of the Moncada Garrison **Rev:** Battle scene

Date	Mintage	F	VF	XF	Unc	BU
1989 Proof	150	Value: 800				

KM# 447 100 PESOS
31.1030 g., 0.9990 Gold 1.0000 oz. AGW **Subject:** 30th Anniversary of Revolution **Obv:** National arms within wreath, denomination **Rev:** Armed, uniformed figure standing right

Date	Mintage	F	VF	XF	Unc	BU
1989 Proof	250	Value: 715				

KM# 448 100 PESOS
31.1030 g., 0.9990 Gold 1.0000 oz. AGW **Subject:** 30th Anniversary of Revolution **Obv:** National arms within wreath, denomination **Rev:** Armed, uniformed figure standing right

Date	Mintage	F	VF	XF	Unc	BU
1989 Proof	250	Value: 715				

KM# 449 100 PESOS
31.1030 g., 0.9990 Gold 1.0000 oz. AGW **Subject:** 30th Anniversary of Revolution **Obv:** National arms within wreath, denomination **Rev:** Armed, uniformed figure standing right

Date	Mintage	F	VF	XF	Unc	BU
1989 Proof	250	Value: 715				

KM# 302 100 PESOS
31.1030 g., 0.9990 Gold 1.0000 oz. AGW **Subject:** 500th Anniversary - Discovery of America **Rev:** Portrait of Columbus

Date	Mintage	F	VF	XF	Unc	BU
1990 Proof	250	Value: 825				

KM# 303 100 PESOS
31.1030 g., 0.9990 Gold 1.0000 oz. AGW **Subject:** 500th Anniversary - Discovery of America **Rev:** Portrait of King Ferdinand V

Date	Mintage	F	VF	XF	Unc	BU
1990 Proof	250	Value: 825				

KM# 304 100 PESOS
31.1030 g., 0.9990 Gold 1.0000 oz. AGW **Subject:** 500th Anniversary - Discovery of America **Rev:** Portrait of Queen Isabella

Date	Mintage	F	VF	XF	Unc	BU
1990 Proof	250	Value: 825				

KM# 305 100 PESOS
31.1030 g., 0.9990 Gold 1.0000 oz. AGW **Subject:** 500th Anniversary - Discovery of America **Rev:** Portrait of Juan de la Cosa

Date	Mintage	F	VF	XF	Unc	BU
1990 Proof	250	Value: 825				

KM# 450 100 PESOS
31.1030 g., 0.9990 Gold 1.0000 oz. AGW **Subject:** Pinzon brothers **Obv:** National arms within wreath

Date	Mintage	F	VF	XF	Unc	BU
1991 Proof	200	Value: 750				

KM# 451 100 PESOS
31.1030 g., 0.9990 Gold 1.0000 oz. AGW **Subject:** 500th Anniversary of the New World **Rev:** Head of Queen Joanna half right, 1479-1555, daughter of Queen Isabella I

Date	Mintage	F	VF	XF	Unc	BU
1991 Proof	200	Value: 750				

KM# 452 100 PESOS
31.1030 g., 0.9990 Gold 1.0000 oz. AGW **Subject:** 500th Anniversary **Obv:** National arms within wreath **Rev:** Diego Velazquez

Date	Mintage	F	VF	XF	Unc	BU
1991 Proof	200	Value: 750				

KM# 534 100 PESOS
31.1030 g., 0.9990 Gold 1.0000 oz. AGW **Series:** Olympics **Rev:** Stadium

Date	Mintage	F	VF	XF	Unc	BU
1991 Proof	225	Value: 800				

KM# 535 100 PESOS
31.1030 g., 0.9990 Gold 1.0000 oz. AGW **Subject:** Madrid - Alcala Gate **Rev:** Building with arches

CUBA 173

Date	Mintage	F	VF	XF	Unc	BU
1991 Proof	225				Value: 800	

KM# 569 100 PESOS
31.1030 g., 0.9990 Gold 1.0000 oz. AGW **Subject:** Hatuey People

Date	Mintage	F	VF	XF	Unc	BU
1991 Proof	—				Value: 800	

KM# 384 100 PESOS
31.1030 g., 0.9990 Gold 1.0000 oz. AGW **Subject:** Seville - Tower of Gold **Rev:** Tower of Gold in Seville

Date	Mintage	F	VF	XF	Unc	BU
1992 Proof	225				Value: 825	

KM# 385 100 PESOS
31.1030 g., 0.9990 Gold 1.0000 oz. AGW **Subject:** El Escorial **Rev:** El Escorial palace

Date	Mintage	F	VF	XF	Unc	BU
1992 Proof	225				Value: 825	

KM# 453 100 PESOS
31.1030 g., 0.9990 Gold 1.0000 oz. AGW **Subject:** 500th Anniversary **Obv:** National arms within wreath **Rev:** Bartolome de las Casas

Date	Mintage	F	VF	XF	Unc	BU
1992 Proof	100				Value: 750	

KM# 454 100 PESOS
31.1030 g., 0.9990 Gold 1.0000 oz. AGW **Subject:** 500th Anniversary **Obv:** National arms within wreath **Rev:** Guama Tribesman

Date	Mintage	F	VF	XF	Unc	BU
1992 Proof	100				Value: 750	

KM# 455 100 PESOS
31.1030 g., 0.9990 Gold 1.0000 oz. AGW **Subject:** 500th Anniversary **Obv:** National arms within wreath **Rev:** King Philipp

Date	Mintage	F	VF	XF	Unc	BU
1992 Proof	100				Value: 750	

KM# 456 100 PESOS
31.1030 g., 0.9990 Gold 1.0000 oz. AGW **Subject:** 500th Anniversary **Obv:** National arms within wreath **Rev:** Spanish kings and queens

Date	Mintage	F	VF	XF	Unc	BU
1992 Proof	100				Value: 750	

KM# 536 100 PESOS
31.1030 g., 0.9990 Gold 1.0000 oz. AGW **Subject:** San Jorge Palace

Date	Mintage	F	VF	XF	Unc	BU
1992 Proof	225				Value: 800	

KM# 570 100 PESOS
31.1030 g., 0.9990 Gold 1.0000 oz. AGW **Subject:** Ernesto Che Guevara **Obv:** National arms within wreath

Date	Mintage	F	VF	XF	Unc	BU
1992 Proof	—				Value: 715	

KM# 537 100 PESOS
31.1030 g., 0.9990 Gold 1.0000 oz. AGW **Subject:** 40th Anniversary of Moncada **Rev:** Fidel Castro

Date	Mintage	F	VF	XF	Unc	BU
1993 Proof	100				Value: 775	

KM# 538 100 PESOS
31.1030 g., 0.9990 Gold 1.0000 oz. AGW **Obv:** Two sets of arms and denomination **Rev:** St. Jacobi

Date	Mintage	F	VF	XF	Unc	BU
1993 Proof	100				Value: 775	

KM# 539 100 PESOS
31.1030 g., 0.9990 Gold 1.0000 oz. AGW **Rev:** Federico Garcia Lorca

Date	Mintage	F	VF	XF	Unc	BU
1993 Proof	100				Value: 775	

KM# 571 100 PESOS
31.1030 g., 0.9990 Gold 1.0000 oz. AGW **Obv:** National arms within wreath **Rev:** Jose Marti

Date	Mintage	F	VF	XF	Unc	BU
1994 Proof	—				Value: 715	

KM# 572 100 PESOS
31.1030 g., 0.9990 Gold 1.0000 oz. AGW **Subject:** Centennial of the Necessary War

Date	Mintage	F	VF	XF	Unc	BU
1995 Proof	—				Value: 715	

KM# 719 100 PESOS
31.1035 g., 0.9990 Gold 1.0000 oz. AGW, 38 mm. **Obv:** National arms **Rev:** Hummingbird **Edge:** Reeded

Date	Mintage	F	VF	XF	Unc	BU
1999 Proof	1,000				Value: 715	

KM# 542 200 PESOS
31.1000 g., Gold **Obv:** National arms within wreath **Rev:** Bolivar and Marti

Date	Mintage	F	VF	XF	Unc	BU
1993	100	—	—	—	750	—
1993 Proof	100				Value: 800	

KM# 543 200 PESOS
31.1000 g., Gold **Series:** Prehistoric Animals **Obv:** National arms within wreath **Rev:** Apatosaurus

Date	Mintage	F	VF	XF	Unc	BU
1993 Proof	100				Value: 800	

KM# 544 200 PESOS
31.1000 g., Gold **Series:** Prehistoric Animals **Rev:** Chalicotherium

Date	Mintage	F	VF	XF	Unc	BU
1993 Proof	100				Value: 900	

KM# 545 200 PESOS
31.1000 g., Gold **Subject:** Montecristi Manifesto **Rev:** Two seated figures facing each other, date lower left

Date	Mintage	F	VF	XF	Unc	BU
1994 Proof	100				Value: 800	

KM# 457 500 PESOS
155.5500 g., 0.9990 Gold 5.000 oz. AGW **Rev:** Christopher Columbus

Date	Mintage	F	VF	XF	Unc	BU
1990 Proof	15				Value: 5,500	

KM# 386 500 PESOS
155.5500 g., 0.9990 Gold 5.000 oz. AGW **Subject:** 500th Anniversary **Obv:** National arms within wreath **Rev:** Spanish Kings and Queens

Date	Mintage	F	VF	XF	Unc	BU
ND(1992) Proof	15				Value: 5,500	

KM# 605 500 PESOS
155.5500 g., 0.9990 Platinum 5.000 oz. APW **Subject:** Castro **Rev:** Fidel Castro

Date	Mintage	F	VF	XF	Unc	BU
1993 Proof	—				Value: 7,500	

MEDALLIC COINAGE

X# M31 PESO
41.0000 g., 0.9990 Gold 1.3169 oz. AGW, 40 mm.
Issuer: Central de Numismática y Medallística de Mexico
Obv: Arms **Obv. Legend:** REPUBLICA **Rev:** Bust of Ernesto Che Cuevara **Rev. Legend:** PATRIA O MUERTE - HASTA LA VICTORIA I SIEMPRE

Date	Mintage	F	VF	XF	Unc	BU
1970	—	—	—	—	—	—

MEDALLIC COINAGE
Richard Lobel Issues

X# M9 SOUVENIR PESO
0.5830 Gold **Subject:** 20th Anniversary Cubans in Exile
Obv: Arms **Obv. Legend:** CUBANOS EN EXILIO **Rev:** Short neck Type I, Liberty head right **Rev. Legend:** * PATRIA Y LIBERTAD * SOUVENIR

Date	Mintage	F	VF	XF	Unc	BU
1985 Proof	5				Value: 700	

174 CUBA

X# M13 SOUVENIR PESO
0.5830 Gold **Subject:** 20th Anniversary Cubans in Exile **Obv:** Arms **Obv. Legend:** CUBANOS EN EXILIO **Rev:** Long neck Type II, Liberty head right **Rev. Legend:** * PATRIA Y LIBERTAD * SOUVENIR

Date	Mintage	F	VF	XF	Unc	BU
1985 Proof	5 Value: 700					

MEDALLIC COINAGE
1969 Patriotic Issues

X# M17 PESO
30.0000 g., Gold **Obv:** Arms **Obv. Legend:** REPUBLICA DE CUBA EN ARMAS **Rev:** Bust 3/4 left **Rev. Legend:** GENERAL ANTONIO MACEO

Date	Mintage	F	VF	XF	Unc	BU
1969	—	—	—	—	700	—

X# M18 2 PESOS
Gold **Obv:** Arms **Obv. Legend:** CUBA EN EL EXILIO **Rev:** Bust of Jose Marti right

Date	Mintage	F	VF	XF	Unc	BU
1969	—	—	—	—	120	—

X# M19 4 PESOS
Gold **Obv:** Arms **Obv. Legend:** CUBA EN EL EXILIO **Rev:** Bust of Jose Marti right

Date	Mintage	F	VF	XF	Unc	BU
1969	—	—	—	—	175	—

X# M20 5 PESOS
Gold **Obv:** Arms **Obv. Legend:** CUBA EN EL EXILIO **Rev:** Bust of Jose Marti right

Date	Mintage	F	VF	XF	Unc	BU
1969	—	—	—	—	250	—

X# M21 10 PESOS
Gold **Obv:** Arms **Obv. Legend:** CUBA EN EL EXILIO **Rev:** Bust of Jose Marti right

Date	Mintage	F	VF	XF	Unc	BU
1969	—	—	—	—	375	—

X# M22 SOUVENIR 5 PESOS
Gold **Obv:** Arms **Obv. Legend:** REPUBLICA DE CUBA **Rev:** Bust of Jose Marti right **Rev. Legend:** PATRIA Y LIBERTAD

Date	Mintage	F	VF	XF	Unc	BU
1966	—	—	—	—	—	—

TRIAL STRIKES

KM#	Date	Mintage	Identification	Mkt Val
TS6	1994	10	100 Pesos. Gold. Reverse of KM467, uniface. Prev. KM#TS2.	2,000

PATTERNS
Including off metal strikes

KM#	Date	Mintage	Identification	Mkt Val
PnE11	1986	—	5 Pesos. 0.0500 Gold. KM326.	—
Pn11	1987	3	5 Pesos. 0.9990 Gold. KM159.	6,500
PnA13	1988	6	100 Pesos. 0.9990 Gold.	5,500
PnB13	1988	—	100 Pesos. 0.9990 Gold.	5,500
Pn13	1988	6	100 Pesos. Gold.	—
Pn108	1999	—	100 Pesos. Gold. KM710.	1,500
Pn129	2000	—	100 Pesos. Gold. KM712.	1,500
Pn130	2000	—	100 Pesos. Gold. KM711.	1,500
Pn131	2000	—	100 Pesos. Gold. KM713.	1,500
Pn132	2000	—	100 Pesos. Gold. KM718.	1,500
Pn133	2000	—	100 Pesos. Gold. KM717.	1,250
Pn134	2000	—	100 Pesos. Gold. KM714.	1,500
Pn135	2000	—	100 Pesos. Gold. KM715.	1,500
Pn136	2000	—	100 Pesos. Gold. KM716.	1,500

PIEFORTS

KM#	Date	Mintage	Identification	Mkt Val
P4	1988	30	10 Pesos. Gold. KM211.	1,200
P5	1988	30	10 Pesos. Gold. KM211.	1,200
P6	1988	15	15 Pesos. Gold. KM212.	1,200
P7	1988	15	15 Pesos. Gold. KM212.	1,200
P8	1988	10	25 Pesos. Gold. KM213.	1,600
P9	1988	10	25 Pesos. Gold. KM213.	1,600
P10	1988	10	50 Pesos. Gold. KM214.	1,600
P11	1988	10	50 Pesos. Gold. KM214.	1,600
P12	1988	10	100 Pesos. Gold. KM215.	2,200
P13	1988	10	100 Pesos. Gold. KM215.	2,200
P14	1989	30	10 Pesos. Gold. KM211.	1,200
P15	1989	30	10 Pesos. Gold. KM211.	1,200
P18	1989	15	15 Pesos. Gold. KM212.	1,200
P19	1989	15	15 Pesos. Gold. KM212.	1,200
P20	1989	10	25 Pesos. Gold. KM213.	1,600
P21	1989	15	25 Pesos. Gold. KM213.	1,600
P22	1989	10	50 Pesos. Gold. KM214.	2,200
P23	1989	15	50 Pesos. Gold. KM214.	2,200
P24	1989	12	50 Pesos. Gold. KM313.	1,800
P25	1989	12	50 Pesos. Gold. KM314.	1,800
P26	1989	12	50 Pesos. Gold. KM315.	1,800
P28	1989	10	100 Pesos. Gold. KM215.	2,200
P29	1989	15	100 Pesos. Gold. KM215.	2,200
P30	1989	12	100 Pesos. Gold. KM316.	1,800
P31	1989	12	100 Pesos. Gold. KM317.	1,800
P32	1989	12	100 Pesos. Gold. KM318.	1,800
P33	1989	12	100 Pesos. Gold. KM319.	2,200
P34	1989	12	100 Pesos. Gold. KM320.	2,200
P40	1990	12	10 Pesos. Gold. KM211.	1,200
P41	1990	12	10 Pesos. Gold. KM211.	1,200
P42	1990	12	15 Pesos. Gold. KM212.	1,200
P43	1990	12	15 Pesos. Gold. KM212.	1,200
P44	1990	12	25 Pesos. Gold. 15.5400 g. KM213.	—
P45	1990	12	25 Pesos. Gold. 15.5400 g. KM213.	—
P46	1990	12	50 Pesos. Gold. KM214.	2,200
P47	1990	12	50 Pesos. Gold. KM214.	2,200
P48	1990	12	50 Pesos. Gold. KM321.	2,200
P49	1990	12	50 Pesos. Gold. KM322.	2,200
P50	1990	12	50 Pesos. Gold. KM323.	2,200
P51	1990	12	100 Pesos. Gold. KM215.	2,200
P52	1990	15	100 Pesos. Gold. KM215.	2,200
P56	1993	15	200 Pesos. Gold. KM542.	2,200
P58	1993	—	100 Pesos. Gold. Similar to 200 Pesos; KM542.	—
P57	1994	10	100 Pesos. Gold. KM545.	1,750

PROOF SETS

KM#	Date	Mintage	Identification	Issue Price	Mkt Val
PS2	1915 (6)	24	KM#16-21; Rare	—	—
PS4	1916 (6)	—	KM#16-21; Rare	—	—
PS7	1977 (4)	—	KM#38-40, 43	290	335
PS8	1979 (2)	—	KM#44, 45	240	260
PS9	1988 (5)	15	KM#211-215	—	1,650
PS11	1999 (5)	—	KM#671, 673, 692, 704, 719	—	1,250

CURACAO

The island of Curacao, the largest of the Netherlands Antilles, which is an autonomous part of the Kingdom of the Netherlands located in the Caribbean Sea 40 miles off the coast of Venezuela, has an area of 173 sq. mi. (472 sq. km.) and a population of 127,900. Capital: Willemstad. The chief industries are banking and tourism. Salt, phosphates and cattle are exported.

Curacao was discovered by Spanish navigator Alonsode Ojeda in 1499 and was settled by Spain in 1527. The Dutch West India Company took the island from Spain in 1634 and administered it until 1787, when it was surrendered to the United Netherlands. The Dutch held it thereafter except for two periods during the Napoleonic Wars, 1800-1803 and 1807-16, when it was occupied by the British. During World War II, Curacao refined 60 percent of the oil used by the Allies; the refineries were protected by U.S. troops after Germany invaded the Netherlands in 1940.

During the second occupation of the Napoleonic period, the British created an emergency coinage for Curacao by cutting the Spanish dollar into 5 equal segments and countermarking each piece with a rosette indent.

MINT MARKS
D - Denver
P - Philadelphia
(u) - Utrecht

BRITISH OCCUPATION
COUNTERMARKED COINAGE

KM# 19   6 PESOS
Gold **Countermark:** W **Obv:** Countermark: GI, L, MH and B at edges, GH in center on false Brazil 6400 Reis type of KM#172.2. **Rev:** Countermark

CM Date	Host Date	Good	VG	F	VF	XF
ND(1815)	ND(1776) Unique					

KM# 20   6 PESOS
Gold **Countermark:** W **Obv:** Countermark: GI, L, MH and B at edges, GH in center on false Brazil 6400 Reis type of KM#199.1 **Rev:** Countermark

CM Date	Host Date	Good	VG	F	VF	XF
ND	ND(1815) Unique					

Note: American Numismatic Rarities Eliasberg sale 4-05, EF realized $97,750.

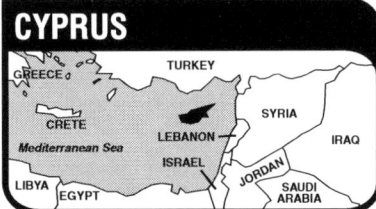

CYPRUS

The island of Cyprus lies in the eastern Mediterranean Sea 44 miles (71 km.) south of Turkey and 60 miles (97 km.) off the Syrian coast. It is the third largest island in the Mediterranean Sea, having an area of 3,572 sq. mi. (9,251 sq. km.) and a population of 736,636. Capital: Nicosia. Agriculture, light manufacturing and tourism are the chief industries. Citrus fruit, potatoes, footwear and clothing are exported

The importance of Cyprus dates from the Bronze Age when it was desired as a principal source of copper (from which the island derived its name) and as a strategic trading center. It was during this period that large numbers of Greeks settled on the island and gave it the predominantly Greek character. Its role as an international marketplace made it a prime disseminator of the then prevalent cultures, a role that still influences the civilization of Western man. Because of its fortuitous position and influential role, Cyprus was conquered by a succession of empires: the Assyrian, Egyptian, Persian, Macedonian, Ptolemaic, Roman and Byzantine. It was taken from Isaac Comnenus by Richard the Lion-Heart in 1191, sold to the Templar Knights and for the following 7 centuries was ruled by the Franks, the Venetians and the Ottomans. During the Ottoman period Cyprus acquired its Turkish community (18 percent of its population). In 1878 the island fell into British hands and was made a crown colony of Britain in 1925. Finally, on Aug. 16, 1960, it became an independent republic.

In 1964, the ethnic Turks withdrew from active participation in the government. Turkish forces invaded Cyprus in 1974, gained control of 40 percent of the island and forcibly separated the Greek and Turkish communities. In 1983, Turkish Cypriots proclaimed their own state in northern Cyprus, which remains without international recognition.

Cyprus is a member of the Commonwealth of Nations. The president is Chief of State and Head of Government.

RULER
British, until 1960

MINT MARKS
no mint mark - Royal Mint, London, England
H - Birmingham, England

MONETARY SYSTEM
9 Piastres = 1 Shilling
20 Shillings = 1 Pound

BRITISH COLONY

MEDALLIC COINAGE
INA Retro Issues

X# M11c.1   36 PIASTRES
Gold **Obv:** Veiled bust left **Obv. Legend:** VICTORIA • DEI GRATIA • IND • IMP **Rev:** Crowned shield with lion rampant left, divides date **Edge:** Reeded **Note:** Medal alignment.

Date	Mintage	F	VF	XF	Unc	BU
1901 Proof	1	—	—	—	—	—

X# M11c.2   36 PIASTRES
32.2000 g., 0.9167 Gold 0.949 oz. AGW **Obv:** Veiled bust left **Obv. Legend:** VICTORIA • DEI GRATIA • IND • IMP **Rev:** Crowned shield with lion rampant left, divides date **Edge:** Plain

Date	Mintage	F	VF	XF	Unc	BU
1901 Proof	1	—	—	—	—	—
Note: Coin alignment						
1901 Proof	1	—	—	—	—	—
Note: Medal alignment						

X# M12.1   36 PIASTRES
32.3000 g., 0.9167 Gold 0.952 oz. AGW **Obv:** Veiled bust left **Obv. Legend:** VICTORIA • DEI • GRA BRITT • REGINA • FID • DEF • IND • IMP **Rev:** Crowned shield with lion rampant left, divides date **Edge:** Reeded **Note:** Medal alignment.

Date	Mintage	F	VF	XF	Unc	BU
1901 Proof	1	—	—	—	—	—

X# M12.2   36 PIASTRES
31.7000 g., 0.9167 Gold 0.9343 oz. AGW **Obv:** Veiled bust left **Obv. Legend:** VICTORIA • DEI • GRA BRITT • REGINA • FID • DEF • IND • IMP **Rev:** Crowned shield with lion rampant left, divides date **Edge:** Plain **Note:** Medal alignment.

Date	Mintage	F	VF	XF	Unc	BU
1901 Proof	1	—	—	—	—	—

X# M13c.1   36 PIASTRES
32.7000 g., 0.9167 Gold 0.9638 oz. AGW **Obv:** Crowned bust right **Obv. Legend:** EDWARDVS VII D: G: BRITT: OMN: REX F: D: IND: IMP. **Rev:** Crowned shield with lion rampant left, divides date **Edge:** Reeded **Note:** Medal alignment.

Date	Mintage	F	VF	XF	Unc	BU
1901 Proof	1	—	—	—	—	—

X# M13c.2   36 PIASTRES
0.9167 Gold **Obv:** Crowned bust right **Obv. Legend:** EDWARDVS VII D: G: BRITT: OMN: REX F: D: IND: IMP. **Rev:** Crowned shield with lion rampant left, divides date **Edge:** Plain **Note:** Weight varies: 32-32.4 grams.

Date	Mintage	F	VF	XF	Unc	BU
1901 Proof	1	—	—	—	—	—
Note: Medal alignment						
1901 Proof	1	—	—	—	—	—
Note: Coin alignment						

X# M14c.1   36 PIASTRES
32.2000 g., 0.9167 Gold 0.949 oz. AGW **Obv:** Head right within beaded circle **Obv. Legend:** EDWARDVS VII DEI GRATIA INDIAE IMPERATOR **Rev:** Crowned shield with lion rampant left divides date **Edge:** Reeded **Note:** Medal alignment.

Date	Mintage	F	VF	XF	Unc	BU
1901 Proof	1	—	—	—	—	—

X# M14c.2   36 PIASTRES
32.5000 g., 0.9167 Gold 0.9579 oz. AGW **Obv:** Head right within beaded circle **Obv. Legend:** EDWARDVS VII DEI GRATIA INDIAE IMPERATOR **Rev:** Crowned shield with lion rampant left divides date **Edge:** Plain **Note:** Medal alignment.

Date	Mintage	F	VF	XF	Unc	BU
1901 Proof	1	—	—	—	—	—

X# M15c.1   45 PIASTRES
39.9000 g., 0.9167 Gold 1.176 oz. AGW **Obv:** Head left **Obv. Legend:** EDWARDVS VIII DEI GRATIA INDIAE IMPERATOR **Rev:** Two lions left, heads facing **Edge:** Reeded

Date	Mintage	F	VF	XF	Unc	BU
1937 Proof, medal alignment	1	—	—	—	—	—
1937 Proof, coin alignment	1	—	—	—	—	—

X# M15c.2   45 PIASTRES
40.0000 g., 0.9167 Gold 1.1789 oz. AGW **Obv:** Head left **Obv. Legend:** EDWARDVS VIII DEI GRATIA INDIAE IMPERATOR **Rev:** Two lions left, heads facing **Edge:** Plain **Note:** Medal alignment.

Date	Mintage	F	VF	XF	Unc	BU
1937 Proof						

X# M16   45 PIASTRES
0.9167 Gold **Obv:** Crowned bust left **Obv. Legend:** EDWARD VIII KING EMPEROR **Rev:** Two lions left, heads facing **Edge:** Plain **Note:** Weight varies: 39.4-39.8 grams.

Date	Mintage	F	VF	XF	Unc	BU
1937 Proof	1	—	—	—	—	—
Note: Medal alignment						
1937 Proof	1	—	—	—	—	—
Note: Coin alignment						

MEDALLIC COINAGE
Richard Lobel Issues

X# M2   SOVEREIGN
0.3750 Gold **Subject:** Edward VIII

Date	Mintage	F	VF	XF	Unc	BU
1936 Proof	200	Value: 125				

CYPRUS

REPUBLIC

DECIMAL COINAGE
50 Mils = 1 Shilling; 20 Shillings = 1 Pound; 1000 Mils = 1 Pound

KM# 47 50 POUNDS
15.9800 g., 0.9170 Gold .4711 oz. AGW **Obv:** Archbishop Makarios right, two dates **Rev:** Ship above map, dolphins, date and denomination below

Date	Mintage	F	VF	XF	Unc	BU
1977	39,000	—	—	—	345	—
1977 Proof	51,000	Value: 350				

REFORM COINAGE
100 Cents = 1 Pound

KM# 65 20 POUNDS
7.9881 g., 0.9170 Gold .2354 oz. AGW, 22 mm. **Subject:** 30th Anniversary of the Republic **Obv:** Shielded arms within wreath, date below **Rev:** Denomination within circle on stylized bird **Rev. Designer:** Antis Ionnides

Date	Mintage	F	VF	XF	Unc	BU
1990 Proof	5,000	Value: 250				

KM# 68 20 POUNDS
7.9881 g., 0.9170 Gold .2354 oz. AGW **Subject:** Museum Building Fund **Obv:** Shielded arms within wreath, date below **Rev:** Winged statue, left, denomination below

Date	Mintage	F	VF	XF	Unc	BU
1992 Proof	5,000	Value: 225				

KM# 74 100 POUNDS
Gold **Subject:** Millennium **Obv:** National arms and denomination at right **Rev:** Three line inscription **Shape:** Ox-hide shape of ancient ingot

Date	Mintage	F	VF	XF	Unc	BU
2000	750	—	—	—	1,000	—

MEDALLIC COINAGE
Archbishop Makarios Fund Issues

Struck at the Paris Mint, France.

X# M3 1/2 SOVEREIGN
3.9940 g., 0.9167 Gold 0.1177 oz. AGW **Obv:** Bust of Archbishop Makarios III left **Note:** Prev. KM#M1.

Date	Mintage	F	VF	XF	Unc	BU
1966 Proof	25,000	Value: 125				

X# M4 SOVEREIGN
7.9881 g., 0.9167 Gold 0.2354 oz. AGW **Obv:** Bust of Archbishop Makarios III left **Note:** Prev. KM#M2.

Date	Mintage	F	VF	XF	Unc	BU
1966 Proof	50,000	Value: 200				

X# M5.1 5 POUNDS
40.0000 g., 0.9170 Gold 1.1793 oz. AGW **Obv:** Bust of Archbishop Makarios III left **Note:** Prev. KM#M3.

Date	Mintage	F	VF	XF	Unc	BU
1966	1,500	—	—	1,200	1,750	—

X# M5.2 5 POUNDS
40.0000 g., 0.9170 Gold **Obv:** Bust of Archbishop Makarios III left **Edge:** Plain **Note:** Serial number added. Prev. KM#M4.

Date	Mintage	F	VF	XF	Unc	BU
1966	200	—	—	2,500	3,500	—

TRIAL STRIKES

KM#	Date	Mintage	Identification	Mkt Val
TS2	ND	—	45 Piastres. 0.9170 Gold. 40.0000 g. Uniface.	3,000

Note: 1 known

CZECH REPUBLIC

The Czech Republic was formerly united with Slovakia as Czechoslovakia. It is bordered in the west by Germany, to the north by Poland, to the east by Slovakia and to the south by Austria. It consists of 3 major regions: Bohemia, Moravia and Silesia and has an area of 30,450 sq. mi. (78,864 sq. km.) and a population of 10.4 million. Capital: Prague (Praha). Agriculture and livestock are chief occupations while coal deposits are the main mineral resources.

The Czech lands were united with the Slovaks to form the Czechoslovak State, which came into existence on Oct. 28, 1918 upon the dissolution of the Austrian-Hungarian Empire. In 1938, this territory was broken up for the benefit of Germany, Poland, and Hungary by the Munich (Munchen) Agreement. In March 1939 the German influenced Slovak government proclaimed Slovakia independent. Germany incorporated the Czech lands into the Third Reich as the "Protectorate of Bohemia and Moravia." A Czech government-in-exile was set up in London in July 1940. The Soviets and USA forces liberated the area by May 1945. Communist influence increased steadily while pressure for liberalization culminated in the overthrow of the Stalinist leader Antonin Novotny and his associates in 1968. The Communist Party then introduced far reaching reforms which resulted in warnings from Moscow (Moskva), followed by occupation and stationing of Soviet forces. Mass demonstrations for reform began again in Nov. 1989 and the Federal Assembly abolished the Communist Party's sole right to govern. The new government formed was the Czech and Slovak Federal Republic. A movement for Democratic Slovakia was apparent in the June 1992 elections and on December 31, 1992, the CSFR was dissolved and the two new republics came into being on Jan. 1, 1993.

NOTE: For earlier issues see Czechoslovakia, Bohemia and Moravia or Slovakia listings.

MINT MARKS
(c) - castle = Hamburg
(cr) - cross = British Royal Mint
(l) - leaf = Royal Canadian
(m) - crowned *b* or *CM* = Jablonec nad Nisou
(mk) - *MK* in circle = Kremnica
(o) - broken circle = Vienna (Wien)

MONETARY SYSTEM
1 Czechoslovak Koruna (Kcs) = 1 Czech Koruna (Kc)
1 Koruna = 100 Haleru

REPUBLIC

GOLD BULLION COINAGE

KM# 18 1000 KORUN
3.1103 g., 0.9999 Gold .1000 oz. AGW, 16 mm. **Subject:** Historic Coins - Tolar of Silesian Estates 12-1/2 tolar 1620. **Obv:** Imperial eagle, denomination below **Rev:** Tablet with four line inscription within circle **Designer:** Vladimir Oppl

Date	Mintage	F	VF	XF	Unc	BU
1995	1,997	—	—	—	—	100
1996	3,252	—	—	—	—	100
1996 Proof	741	Value: 145				
1997 Proof	2,247	Value: 120				

KM# 38 1000 KORUN
3.1103 g., 0.9999 Gold .1000 oz. AGW, 16 mm. **Obv:** Three shielded arms, dates below **Rev:** Old coin design at right, Quartered design in center **Designer:** J. Harcuba **Note:** Karlstejn Castle.

Date	Mintage	F	VF	XF	Unc	BU
1998	2,097	—	—	—	—	85.00
Note: Milled edge						
1998 Proof	2,206	Value: 100				
Note: Plain edge						
1999 Proof	1,997	Value: 100				

CZECH REPUBLIC

KM# 44 2000 KORUN
34.2140 g., 0.9990 Bi-Metallic Gold And Silver .9990 oz., 40 mm.
Subject: Millennium **Obv:** National arms hologram on gold inlay
Rev: Stylized 2000 **Edge Lettering:** *CNB* Ag 0.999* 31.103 g
CNB AU 999.9 *3.111 g* **Designer:** O. Dusek **Note:** With a 3.1110 gram, .999 gold, .0999 ounce actual gold weight gold inlay.

Date	Mintage	F	VF	XF	Unc	BU
ND(1999)(m)	11,358	—	—	—	85.00	100
ND(1999)(m) Proof	2,999	Value: 165				

KM# 65 2000 KORUN
6.2200 g., 0.9999 Gold 0.2 oz. AGW, 20 mm. **Subject:** Znojmo Rotunda **Obv:** Three heraldic animals **Rev:** Farmer and round building

Date	Mintage	F	VF	XF	Unc	BU
ND(2001)	2,197	—	—	—	—	145
Note: Reeded edge						
ND(2001) Proof	2,997	Value: 165				
Note: Plain edge						

KM# 66 2000 KORUN
6.2200 g., 0.9999 Gold 0.2 oz. AGW, 20 mm. **Subject:** Vyssi Brod Monastery **Obv:** Three heraldic animals above Gothic design **Rev:** Man holding church building model

Date	Mintage	F	VF	XF	Unc	BU
2001	2,197	—	—	—	—	145
Note: Reeded edge						
2001 Proof	2,997	Value: 165				
Note: Plain edge						

KM# 67 2000 KORUN
6.2200 g., 0.9999 Gold 0.2 oz. AGW, 20 mm. **Subject:** Kutna Hora Fountain **Obv:** Three heraldic animals **Rev:** Fountain enclosure

Date	Mintage	F	VF	XF	Unc	BU
2002	2,197	—	—	—	—	145
Note: Reeded edge						
2002	2,997	Value: 165				
Note: Plain edge						

KM# 61 2000 KORUN
6.2200 g., 0.9999 Gold 0.2 oz. AGW, 20 mm. **Subject:** Litomysl Castle **Obv:** Three heraldic animals above mermaid **Rev:** Aerial castle view and mythical creature

Date	Mintage	F	VF	XF	Unc	BU
2002	2,097	—	—	—	—	150
Note: Reeded edge						
2002 Proof	3,097	Value: 175				
Note: Plain edge						

KM# 68 2000 KORUN
6.2200 g., 0.9999 Gold 0.2 oz. AGW, 20 mm.
Subject: Slavonice House Gables **Obv:** Three heraldic animals above city view **Rev:** City arms

Date	Mintage	F	VF	XF	Unc	BU
2003	1,997	—	—	—	—	145
Note: Reeded edge						
2003 Proof	2,997	Value: 165				
Note: Plain edge						

KM# 69 2000 KORUN
6.2200 g., 0.9999 Gold 0.2 oz. AGW, 20 mm.
Subject: Buchlovice Palace **Obv:** Three heraldic animals above palace **Rev:** Palace view

Date	Mintage	F	VF	XF	Unc	BU
2003	1,997	—	—	—	—	145
Note: Reeded						
2003 Proof	3,197	Value: 165				
Note: Plain edge						

KM# 75.1 2000 KORUN
6.2200 g., 0.9999 Gold 0.2 oz. AGW, 20 mm. **Obv:** Ornamental porch below three heraldic animals **Rev:** Hluboka Castle with coat of arms in foreground

Date	Mintage	F	VF	XF	Unc	BU
2004	2,500	—	—	—	—	145
Note: Reeded edge						
2004 Proof	3,500	Value: 165				
Note: Plain edge						

KM# 19 2500 KORUN
7.7759 g., 0.9999 Gold .2500 oz. AGW, 22 mm.
Subject: Historic Coins - 1620 Tolar of Moravian Estates
Obv: Imperial eagle within circle, denomination below **Rev:** Vine climbing tower within circle **Designer:** Vladimir Oppl

Date	Mintage	F	VF	XF	Unc	BU
1995	1,997	—	—	—	—	250
1996	1,253	—	—	—	—	250
1996 Proof	741	Value: 300				
1997 Proof	1,697	Value: 265				

KM# 39 2500 KORUN
7.7759 g., 0.9999 Gold .2500 oz. AGW, 22 mm. **Rev:** Seal of Karel IV with legal document **Designer:** Jarmila Truhlikova-Spevakova

Date	Mintage	F	VF	XF	Unc	BU
1998	1,122	—	—	—	—	175
Note: Milled edge						
1998 Proof	1,855	Value: 200				
Note: Plain edge						
1999 Proof	1,497	Value: 185				

KM# 76 2500 KORUN
31.1040 g., 0.9990 Bi-Metallic Gold And Silver .9999 Gold 7.776g center in .999 Silver 23.328g ring 0.999 oz., 40 mm. **Subject:** Czech entry into the European Union **Obv:** Value within circle of shields **Rev:** "1.5.2004" within circle of dates and text **Edge:** Lettered **Edge Lettering:** " CNB * Ag 0.999 * 23,328 g * Au 999.9 * 7,776g * "

Date	Mintage	F	VF	XF	Unc	BU
ND (2004) Proof	10,000	Value: 265				

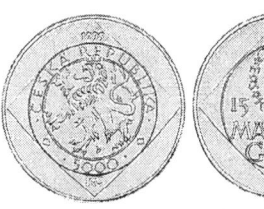

KM# 20 5000 KORUN
15.5517 g., 0.9999 Gold .5000 oz. AGW, 28 mm. **Subject:** Historic Coins **Obv:** Czech lion left within circle, denomination below **Rev:** Bohemian Maley Gros of 1587 **Designer:** Vladimir Oppl

Date	Mintage	F	VF	XF	Unc	BU
1995	997	—	—	—	—	560
1996	1,253	—	—	—	—	560
1996 Proof	741	Value: 625				
1997 Proof	1,496	Value: 575				

KM# 40 5000 KORUN
15.5530 g., 0.9999 Gold .5000 oz. AGW, 28 mm. **Obv:** Three shielded arms, date above, denomination below **Rev:** Karel IV, Charles University founder **Designer:** M. Vitanovsky

Date	Mintage	F	VF	XF	Unc	BU
1998	1,045	—	—	—	—	350
Note: Milled edge						
1998 Proof	1,854	Value: 375				
Note: Edge: CESKA NARODNI BANKA 18.553 g.						
1999 Proof	1,497	Value: 350				
Note: Edge: CESKA NARODNI BANKA 18.553 g.						

KM# 21 10000 KORUN
31.1035 g., 0.9999 Gold 1.0000 oz. AGW, 34 mm.
Subject: Historic Coins **Obv:** Elongated, stylized, unbordered arms, date and denomination below **Rev:** Lion holding Prague Groschen **Designer:** Jiri Harcuba

Date	Mintage	F	VF	XF	Unc	BU
1995	997	—	—	—	—	975
1996	1,251	—	—	—	—	975
1996 Proof	740	Value: 1,100				
1997 Proof	1,497	Value: 1,000				

KM# 41 10000 KORUN
31.1070 g., 0.9999 Gold 1.0000 oz. AGW, 34 mm. **Rev:** Karel IV and seals of Nove Mesto **Designer:** Vladimir Oppl

Date	Mintage	F	VF	XF	Unc	BU
1998	1,111	—	—	—	—	700
Note: Milled edge						
1998 Proof	1,996	Value: 725				
Note: Edge: CESKA NARODNI BANKA 31.107 g.						
1999 Proof	1,297	Value: 700				
Note: Edge: CESKA NARODNI BANKA 31.107 g.						

KM# 45 10000 KORUN
31.1070 g., 0.9999 Gold 1.0000 oz. AGW **Subject:** Karl IV **Obv:** 3 coats of arms **Rev:** Karl IV with 3 coin designs **Edge Lettering:** *CESKA NARODNI BANKA8 31.107 g*

Date	Mintage	F	VF	XF	Unc	BU
1999(m) Proof	6,000	Value: 675				

178 CZECHOSLOVAKIA

MEDALLIC COINAGE

X# 1 DUCAT
3.5000 g., 0.9860 Gold .1109 oz. AGW, 20 mm. **Subject:** Architectural Montage of Czech & Moravian Cities **Obv:** Crowned Bohemian lion rampant left **Edge:** Plain **Note:** Prev. KM#M1.

Date	Mintage	F	VF	XF	Unc	BU
1993(m) Proof	1,000	Value: 135				

X# 1a DUCAT
2.9600 g., 0.9990 Silver .0954 oz. ASW, 20 mm. **Obv:** Crowned Bohemian lion rampant lion **Edge:** Plain **Note:** Prev. KM#M1a.

Date	Mintage	F	VF	XF	Unc	BU
1993 Proof	1,000	Value: 17.50				

X# 3 DUCAT
3.5000 g., 0.9860 Gold .1109 oz. AGW, 20 mm. **Obv:** Crowned Bohemian lion rampant left **Rev:** Cathedral **Edge:** Plain **Note:** Prev. KM#M3. Similar to 5 Ducat, X#4.

Date	Mintage	F	VF	XF	Unc	BU
1994 Proof	620	Value: 200				

X# 5 DUCAT
3.5000 g., 0.9860 Gold .1109 oz. AGW, 20 mm. **Obv:** Crowned Bohemian lion rampant left **Rev:** Plzen city view **Edge:** Plain **Note:** Prev. KM#M5. Similar to 5 Ducats, X#M6a.

Date	Mintage	F	VF	XF	Unc	BU
1995 Proof	—	Value: 200				

X# 7 DUCAT
3.5000 g., 0.9860 Gold .1109 oz. AGW, 20 mm. **Obv:** Crowned Bohemian lion rampant left **Rev:** Karlstein Castle **Edge:** Plain **Note:** Prev. KM#M7. Similar to 5 Ducats, X#M8.

Date	Mintage	F	VF	XF	Unc	BU
1996 Proof	—	Value: 200				

X# 9 DUCAT
3.5000 g., 0.9860 Gold .1109 oz. AGW, 20 mm. **Obv:** Crowned Bohemian lion rampant left **Edge:** Plain **Note:** Prev. KM#M9. Similar to 5 Ducats, X#M10.

Date	Mintage	F	VF	XF	Unc	BU
1997 Proof	—	Value: 200				

X# 11 DUCAT
3.5000 g., 0.9850 Gold .1109 oz. AGW, 20 mm. **Obv:** Crowned Bohemian lion rampant left **Rev:** Haloed king **Edge:** Plain **Note:** Prev. KM#M11. Similar to 5 Ducats, X#M13.

Date	Mintage	F	VF	XF	Unc	BU
1998 Proof	Est. 1,500	Value: 150				

X# 17a DUCAT
14.9000 g., 0.9990 Silver .4786 oz. ASW, 20 mm. **Obv:** Crowned Bohemian lion rampant left **Edge:** Plain **Note:** Prev. KM#M17a.

Date	Mintage	F	VF	XF	Unc	BU
1999 Proof	Est. 5,000	Value: 20.00				

X# 15 DUCAT
3.5000 g., 0.9850 Gold .1109 oz. AGW, 20 mm. **Obv:** Crowned Bohemian lion rampant left **Rev:** St. Barbara's Cathedral **Edge:** Plain **Note:** Prev. KM#M15.

Date	Mintage	F	VF	XF	Unc	BU
1999 Proof	Est. 1,500	Value: 150				

X# 12 2 DUCAT
7.0000 g., 0.9860 Gold .2218 oz. AGW, 35.3 mm. **Subject:** St. Wenceslav **Obv:** Crowned Bohemian lion rampant left **Rev:** Haloed King **Edge:** Reeded **Note:** Prev. KM#M12. Similar to 5 Ducats, X#M13.

Date	Mintage	F	VF	XF	Unc	BU
1998 Proof	Est. 1,500	Value: 200				

X# 16 2 DUCAT
7.0000 g., 0.9860 Gold .2218 oz. AGW, 35.30 mm. **Obv:** Crowned Bohemian lion rampant left **Rev:** St. Barbara's Cathedral **Edge:** Reeded **Note:** Prev. KM#M16.

Date	Mintage	F	VF	XF	Unc	BU
1999 Proof	Est. 1,500	Value: 200				

X# 2 5 DUCAT
17.5000 g., 0.9860 Gold .5548 oz. AGW, 35.3 mm. **Subject:** Architectural Montage of Czech & Moravian Cities **Obv:** Crowned Bohemian lion rampant left **Edge:** Reeded **Note:** Prev. KM#M2.

Date	Mintage	F	VF	XF	Unc	BU
1993 Proof	128	Value: 675				

X# 4 5 DUCAT
17.5000 g., 0.9860 Gold .5548 oz. AGW, 35.3 mm. **Obv:** Crowned Bohemian lion rampant left **Rev:** Cathedral **Edge:** Reeded **Note:** Prev. KM#M4.

Date	Mintage	F	VF	XF	Unc	BU
1994 Proof	40	Value: 830				

X# 4a 5 DUCAT
14.8400 g., 0.9990 Silver .4771 oz. ASW, 35.3 mm. **Obv:** Crowned Bohemian lion rampant left **Edge:** Reeded **Note:** Prev. KM#M4a.

Date	Mintage	F	VF	XF	Unc	BU
1994 Proof	5,000	Value: 25.00				

X# 6 5 DUCAT
17.5000 g., 0.9860 Gold .5548 oz. AGW, 35.3 mm. **Obv:** Crowned Bohemian lion rampant left **Rev:** Plzen city view **Edge:** Reeded **Note:** Prev. KM#M6. Similar to KM#M6a.

Date	Mintage	F	VF	XF	Unc	BU
1995 Proof	—	Value: 830				

X# 6a 5 DUCAT
14.8400 g., 0.9990 Silver .4771 oz. ASW, 35.3 mm. **Obv:** Crowned Bohemian lion rampant left **Edge:** Reeded **Note:** Prev. KM#M6a.

Date	Mintage	F	VF	XF	Unc	BU
1995 Proof	5,000	Value: 25.00				

X# 8 5 DUCAT
17.5000 g., 0.9860 Gold .5548 oz. AGW, 35.3 mm. **Obv:** Crowned Bohemian lion rampant left **Rev:** Karlstein Castle **Edge:** Reeded **Note:** Prev. KM#M8.

Date	Mintage	F	VF	XF	Unc	BU
1996 Proof	—	Value: 830				

X# 8a 5 DUCAT
14.8400 g., 0.9990 Silver .4771 oz. ASW, 35.3 mm. **Obv:** Crowned Bohemian lion rampant left **Rev:** Karlstein Castle **Edge:** Reeded **Note:** Prev. KM#M8a.

Date	Mintage	F	VF	XF	Unc	BU
1996 Proof	—	Value: 25.00				

X# 10 5 DUCAT
17.5000 g., 0.9860 Gold .5548 oz. AGW, 35.3 mm. **Obv:** Crowned Bohemian lion rampant left **Rev:** Arch above Rudolph II monogram **Edge:** Reeded **Note:** Prev. KM#M10.

Date	Mintage	F	VF	XF	Unc	BU
1997 Proof	—	Value: 830				

X# 10a 5 DUCAT
14.8400 g., 0.9990 Silver .4771 oz. ASW, 35.3 mm. **Obv:** Crowned Bohemian lion rampant left **Edge:** Reeded **Note:** Prev. KM#M10a.

Date	Mintage	F	VF	XF	Unc	BU
1997 Proof	—	Value: 20.00				

X# 13a 5 DUCAT
14.8400 g., 0.9990 Silver .4771 oz. ASW, 35.3 mm. **Obv:** Crowned Bohemian lion rampant left **Edge:** Reeded **Note:** Prev. KM#M13a.

Date	Mintage	F	VF	XF	Unc	BU
1998 Proof	Est. 5,000	Value: 20.00				

X# 13 5 DUCAT
17.5000 g., 0.9860 Gold .5548 oz. AGW, 35.3 mm. **Subject:** St. Wenceslav **Obv:** Crowned Bohemian lion rampant left **Rev:** Haloed king **Edge:** Reeded **Note:** Prev. KM#M13.

Date	Mintage	F	VF	XF	Unc	BU
1998 Proof	Est. 1,500	Value: 800				

X# 17 5 DUCAT
17.5000 g., 0.9860 Gold .5548 oz. AGW, 35.3 mm. **Obv:** Crowned Bohemian lion rampant left **Rev:** St. Barbara's Cathedral **Edge:** Reeded **Note:** Prev. KM#M17.

Date	Mintage	F	VF	XF	Unc	BU
1999 Proof	Est. 1,500	Value: 800				

X# 14 10 DUCAT
35.0000 g., 0.9999 Silver .4771 oz. ASW, 35.3 mm. **Subject:** St. Wenceslav **Obv:** Crowned Bohemian lion rampant left **Rev:** Haloed king **Edge:** Reeded **Note:** Prev. KM#M14. Similar to 5 Ducats, KM#M13.

Date	Mintage	F	VF	XF	Unc	BU
1998 Proof	Est. 1,500	Value: 1,000				

X# 18 10 DUCAT
35.0000 g., 0.9999 Silver .4771 oz. ASW, 35.3 mm. **Obv:** Crowned Bohemian lion rampant left **Rev:** St. Barbar's Cathedral **Edge:** Reeded **Note:** Prev. KM#M18.

Date	Mintage	F	VF	XF	Unc	BU
1999 Proof	Est. 1,500	Value: 1,000				

CZECHOSLOVAKIA

The Republic of Czechoslovakia, founded at the end of World War I, was part of the old Austrian-Hungarian Empire. It had an area of 49,371 sq. mi. (127,870 sq. km.) and a population of 15.6 million. Capital: Prague (Praha).

Czechoslovakia proclaimed itself a republic on Oct. 28, 1918, with Tomas G. Masaryk as President. Hitler's rise to power in Germany provoked Czechoslovakia's German minority in the Sudetenland to agitate for autonomy. At Munich (Munchen) in Sept. of 1938, France and Britain, seeking to avoid World War II, forced the cession of the Sudetenland to Germany. In March, 1939, Germany invaded Czechoslovakia and established the "protectorate of Bohemia and Moravia". Bohemia is a historic province in northwest Czechoslovakia that includes the city of Prague, one of the oldest continually occupied sites in Europe. Moravia is an area of considerable mineral wealth in central Czechoslovakia. Slovakia, a province in southeastern Czechoslovakia under Nazi influence was constituted as a republic. The end of World War II saw the re-established independence of Czechoslovakia, while bringing it within the Russian sphere of influence. On Feb. 23-25, 1948, the Communists seized control of the government in a coup d'etat, and adopted a constitution making the country a 'people's republic'. A new constitution adopted June 11, 1960, converted the country into a 'socialist republic', which lasted until 1989. On Nov. 11, 1989, demonstrations against the communist government began and in Dec. of that same year, communism was overthrown, and the Czech and Slovak Federal Republic was formed. In 1993 the CSFR split into the Czech Republic and The Republic of Slovakia.

NOTE: For additional listings see Bohemia and Moravia, Czech Republic and Slovakia.

MINT MARKS
(k) - Kremnica
(l) - Leningrad

MONETARY SYSTEM
100 Haleru = 1 Koruna

REPUBLIC

TRADE COINAGE

KM# 7 DUKAT
3.4900 g., 0.9860 Gold .1106 oz. AGW **Subject:** 5th Anniversary of the Republic **Obv:** Shield with Czech lion and Slovak shield **Obv. Designer:** J. Benda **Rev:** Duke Wenceslas (Vaclav) half-length figure facing **Rev. Designer:** O. Spaniel **Edge:** Milled **Note:** Serially numbered below the duke. The number is in the die.

Date	Mintage	F	VF	XF	Unc	BU
1923	1,000	—	1,000	2,500	5,000	—

KM# 8 DUKAT
3.4900 g., 0.9860 Gold .1106 oz. AGW **Obv:** Czech lion with Slovak shield, date below **Obv. Designer:** J. Benda **Rev:** Duke Wenceslas (Vaclav) half-length figure facing **Rev. Designer:** O. Spaniel **Edge:** Milled **Note:** Similar to KM#7 but without serial numbers.

Date	Mintage	F	VF	XF	Unc	BU
1923	61,861	—	BV	80.00	125	—
1924	32,814	—	BV	80.00	125	—
1925	66,279	—	BV	80.00	125	—
1926	58,669	—	BV	80.00	125	—
1927	25,774	—	BV	80.00	125	—
1928	18,983	—	BV	80.00	135	—
1929	10,253	—	BV	85.00	165	—
1930	11,338	—	BV	85.00	165	—
1931	43,482	—	BV	80.00	125	—
1932	26,617	—	BV	80.00	125	—
1933	57,597	—	BV	80.00	125	—
1934	9,729	—	80.00	100	175	—
1935	13,178	—	BV	80.00	135	—
1936	14,566	—	BV	80.00	135	—
1937	324	—	275	650	1,000	—
1938	56	—	800	1,750	3,500	—

CZECHOSLOVAKIA

Date	Mintage	F	VF	XF	Unc	BU
1939	276					
Note: Czech reports show mintage of 20 for Czechoslovakia and 256 for state of Slovakia						
1951	500	—	325	725	1,500	—

KM# 9 2 DUKATY
6.9800 g., 0.9860 Gold .2212 oz. AGW, 25 mm. **Obv:** Czech lion with Slovak shield, denomination divides date below **Obv. Designer:** J. Benda **Rev:** Duke Wenceslas (Vaclav) half-length figure facing. **Rev. Designer:** O. Spaniel **Edge:** Milled

Date	Mintage	F	VF	XF	Unc	BU
1923	4,000	—	160	300	400	—
1929	3,262	—	160	300	400	—
1930	Inc. above	—	165	375	500	—
1931	2,994	—	160	300	400	—
1932	5,496	—	160	300	400	—
1933	4,671	—	160	300	400	—
1934	2,403	—	165	325	450	—
1935	2,577	—	160	300	450	—
1936	819	—	300	600	900	—
1937	8	—	3,000	7,500	10,000	—
1938	186	—	700	2,500	3,500	—
Note: Czech reports show mintage of 14 for Czechoslovakia and 172 for state of Slovakia						
1951	200	—	600	2,500	3,500	—

KM# 13 5 DUKATU
17.4500 g., 0.9860 Gold .5532 oz. AGW, 34 mm. **Obv:** Czech lion with Slovak shield, denomination and date below **Obv. Designer:** J. Benda **Rev:** Duke Wenceslas (Vaclav) on horseback right **Rev. Designer:** O. Spaniel **Edge:** Milled

Date	Mintage	F	VF	XF	Unc	BU
1929	1,827	—	375	650	975	—
1930	543	—	500	1,000	1,500	—
1931	1,528	—	375	650	975	—
1932	1,827	—	375	650	975	—
1933	1,752	—	375	650	975	—
1934	1,101	—	375	650	975	—
1935	1,037	—	375	650	975	—
1936	728	—	600	1,200	1,950	—
1937 Rare	4					
1938	56	—	2,500	4,500	6,500	—
Note: Czech reports show mintage of 12 for Czechoslovakia and 44 for state of Slovakia						
1951	100	—	2,000	4,000	5,500	—

KM# 14 10 DUKATU
34.9000 g., 0.9860 Gold 1.1064 oz. AGW, 42 mm. **Obv:** Czech lion with Slovak shield, denomination and date below **Obv. Designer:** J. Benda **Rev:** Duke Wenceslas (Vaclav) on horseback right **Rev. Designer:** O. Spaniel

Date	Mintage	F	VF	XF	Unc	BU
1929	1,564	—	750	1,700	2,250	—
1930	394	—	1,000	3,000	4,000	—
1931	1,239	—	750	1,700	2,250	—
1932	1,035	—	750	1,700	2,250	—
1933	1,780	—	750	1,700	2,250	—
1934	1,298	—	750	1,900	2,500	—
1935	600	—	800	2,000	3,000	—
1936	633	—	850	2,500	3,500	—
1937 Rare	34					
1938	192	—	2,500	7,500	10,000	—
1951	100	—	3,000	7,500	10,000	—
Note: Czech reports show mintage of 20 for Czechoslovakia and 172 for state of Slovakia						

GOLD MEDALLIC COINAGE

X# 7 DUKAT
4.0000 g., 0.9860 Gold .1268 oz. AGW **Subject:** 1000th Anniversary - Christianity in Bohemia **Note:** Prev. KM#M5.

Date	Mintage	F	VF	XF	Unc	BU
ND(1929)	1,631	—	—	400	550	—

X# 12 DUKAT
3.4900 g., 0.9860 Gold .1106 oz. AGW **Subject:** Tyrs - Sokol Movement **Note:** Prev. KM#M10.

Date	Mintage	F	VF	XF	Unc	BU
1932	1,742	—	—	300	450	—

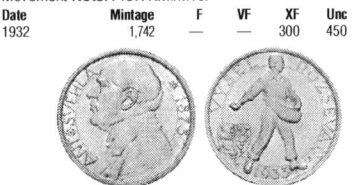

X# 15 DUKAT
3.4900 g., 0.9860 Gold .1106 oz. AGW **Obv:** Dr. Antonin Svehla **Note:** Prev. KM#M12.1.

Date	Mintage	F	VF	XF	Unc	BU
1933	1,000	—	—	300	450	—

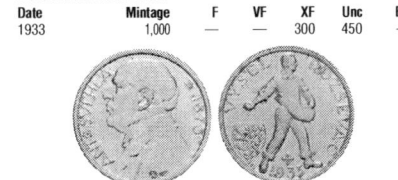

X# 16 DUKAT
3.4900 g., 0.9860 Gold .1106 oz. AGW **Obv:** Dr. Antonin Svehla **Rev:** Cross above date **Note:** Prev. KM#M12.2.

Date	Mintage	F	VF	XF	Unc	BU
1933	Inc. above	—	—	350	550	—

X# 14.1 DUKAT
3.4900 g., 0.9860 Gold .1106 oz. AGW **Subject:** Reopening of Kremnica Mines **Note:** Prev. KM#M14.1

Date	Mintage	F	VF	XF	Unc	BU
1934	288	—	—	700	950	—
Note: See X#14.2 for the 1971 dated restrike.						

X# 3 2 DUKATEN
6.9800 g., 0.9860 Gold .2212 oz. AGW **Subject:** 10th Anniversary of Republic **Note:** Prev. KM#M2.

Date	Mintage	F	VF	XF	Unc	BU
ND(1928)	—	—	—	250	350	—
ND(1928)	—	—	—	—	300	—
Restrike (1973)						

X# 19 2 DUKATEN
6.9800 g., 0.9860 Gold .2212 oz. AGW **Subject:** Reopening of Kremnica Mines **Note:** Prev. KM#M15.

Date	Mintage	F	VF	XF	Unc	BU
1934	159	—	—	1,250	1,650	—

X# 10 3 DUKATEN
10.0000 g., 0.9860 Gold .3170 oz. AGW **Subject:** 1000th Anniversary - Death of St. Wenzel **Note:** Prev. KM#M21.

Date	Mintage	F	VF	XF	Unc	BU
ND(1929)	750	—	—	1,000	1,400	—

X# 8 3 DUKATEN
12.0000 g., 0.9860 Gold .3804 oz. AGW **Subject:** 1000th Anniversary - Christianity in Bohemia **Note:** Prev. KM#M6.

Date	Mintage	F	VF	XF	Unc	BU
ND(1929)	1,058	—	—	750	1,000	—

X# 4 4 DUKATEN
13.9600 g., 0.9860 Gold .4425 oz. AGW **Subject:** 10th Anniversary of Republic **Note:** Prev. KM#M3.

Date	Mintage	F	VF	XF	Unc	BU
ND(1928)	—	—	—	350	500	—
ND(1928)	—	—	—	—	400	—
Note: Restrike (1973)						

X# 9 5 DUKATEN
20.0000 g., 0.9860 Gold .6340 oz. AGW **Subject:** 1000th Anniversary - Christianity in Bohemia **Note:** Prev. KM#M7.

Date	Mintage	F	VF	XF	Unc	BU
ND(1929)	787	—	—	1,400	1,750	—

180 CZECHOSLOVAKIA

X# 20 5 DUKATEN
17.4500 g., 0.9860 Gold .5532 oz. AGW **Subject:** Reopening of Kremnica Mine **Note:** Prev. KM#M16.

Date	Mintage	F	VF	XF	Unc	BU
1934	70	—	—	4,000	5,500	—

X# 21 10 DUKATEN
34.9000 g., 0.9860 Gold 1.1064 oz. AGW **Subject:** Reopening of Kremnica Mine **Note:** Prev. KM#M17.

Date	Mintage	F	VF	XF	Unc	BU
1934	68	—	—	6,500	8,500	—

SOCIALIST REPUBLIC
GOLD MEDALLIC COINAGE

X# 14.2 DUKAT
3.4900 g., 0.9860 Gold .1106 oz. AGW **Subject:** Reopening of Kremnica Mines **Note:** Prev. KM#M14.2.

Date	Mintage	F	VF	XF	Unc	BU
1971	—	—	—	—	90.00	—

X# 28 DUKAT
3.4900 g., 0.9860 Gold 0.1106 oz. AGW **Subject:** 600th Anniversary Death of Charles IV **Note:** Prev. KM#94.

Date	Mintage	F	VF	XF	Unc	BU
1978	20,000	—	—	90.00	125	—
1979	10,000	—	—	145	—	—
1980	10,000	—	—	145	—	—
1981	10,000	—	—	145	—	—
1982	10,000	—	—	145	—	—

X# 29 2 DUKATEN
6.9800 g., 0.9860 Gold 0.2213 oz. AGW **Subject:** 600th Anniversary Death of Charles IV **Note:** Prev. KM#95.

Date	Mintage	F	VF	XF	Unc	BU
1978	10,000	—	—	180	250	—

X# 30 5 DUKATEN
17.4500 g., 0.9860 Gold 0.5532 oz. AGW **Subject:** 600th Anniversary Death of Charles IV **Note:** Prev. KM#96.

Date	Mintage	F	VF	XF	Unc	BU
1978	10,000	—	—	425	600	—

X# 31 10 DUKATEN
34.9000 g., 0.9860 Gold 1.1064 oz. AGW **Subject:** 600th Anniversary Death of Charles IV

Date	Mintage	F	VF	XF	Unc	BU
1978	10,000	—	—	850	1,200	—

WALLENSTEIN
REPUBLIC
MEDALLIC ISSUES

X# 1 5 DUCATS
17.5000 g., 0.9860 Gold 0.5548 oz. AGW **Subject:** 300th Anniversary of Assassination of Albrecht von Wallenstein

Date	Mintage	F	VF	XF	Unc	BU
ND(1972) Proof; Restrike	—	Value: 1,000				

X# 3 10 DUCATS
35.0000 g., 0.9860 Gold 1.1095 oz. AGW **Subject:** 300th Anniversary of Assassination of Albrecht von Wallenstein

Date	Mintage	F	VF	XF	Unc	BU
ND(1972) Proof; Restrike	—	Value: 2,200				

# DAHOMEY

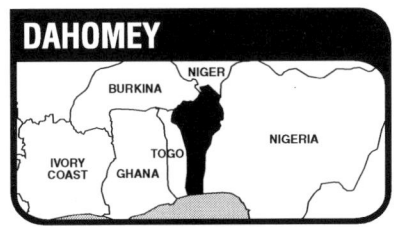

Porto-Novo, on the Bight of Benin, was founded as a trading post by the Portuguese in the 17th century. At that time, Dahomey (Benin) was composed of an aggregation of mutually suspicious tribes, the majority of which were tributary to the powerful northern Kingdom of Abomey. In 1863, the King of Porto-Novo petitioned France for protection from Abomey. The French subjugated other militant tribes as well, and in 1892 organized the area as a protectorate of France; in 1904 it was incorporated into French West Africa as the Territory of Dahomey. After the establishment of the Fifth French Republic, the Territory at Dahomey became an autonomous state within the French community. On Aug. 1, 1960, it became the fully independent Republic of Dahomey. In 1974, the republic began a transition to a socialist society with Marxism-Leninism as its revolutionary philosophy under Col. Ahmed Kerekow. On Nov. 30, 1975, the name of the Republic of Dahomey was changed to the Peoples Republic of Benin. As a result of Benin's first free presidential election in 30 years, Nicephore Soglo defeated Colonel Kerekou.

MINT MARK
1 AR — Uno-A-Erre, Arezzo, Italy

REPUBLIC
STANDARD COINAGE

KM# 6 2500 FRANCS
8.8800 g., 0.9000 Gold .2569 oz. AGW **Subject:** 10th Anniversary of Independence **Rev:** Dancers

Date	Mintage	F	VF	XF	Unc	BU
1971 Proof	960	Value: 275				

KM# 7 5000 FRANCS
17.7700 g., 0.9000 Gold .5142 oz. AGW **Subject:** 10th Anniversary of Independence **Obv:** Similar to 2500 Francs, KM#6 **Rev:** Water buffalos (suncerus caffer-bovidae)

Date	Mintage	F	VF	XF	Unc	BU
1971 Proof	610	Value: 550				

KM# 8 10000 FRANCS
35.5500 g., 0.9000 Gold 1.0287 oz. AGW **Subject:** 10th Anniversary of Independence **Obv:** Facing cornucopias top supported arms, date above, denomination below **Rev:** Acanthopholis

Date	Mintage	F	VF	XF	Unc	BU
1971 Proof	470	Value: 1,000				

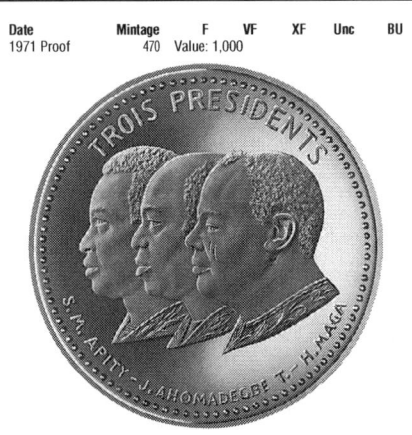

KM# 9 25000 FRANCS
88.8800 g., 0.9000 Gold 2.5720 oz. AGW **Subject:** 10th Anniversary of Independence **Obv:** Facing cornucopias top supported arms, date above, denomination below **Rev:** Aligned Presidents busts, left

Date	Mintage	F	VF	XF	Unc	BU
1971 Proof	380	Value: 2,000				

PROOF SETS

KM#	Date	Mintage	Identification	Issue Price	Mkt Val
PS1	1971 (8)	380	KM#1.1-4.1, 6-9	—	4,175

DANISH WEST INDIES

The Danish West Indies (now the U.S. organized unincorporated territory of the Virgin Islands of the United States) consisted of the islands of St. Thomas, St. John, St. Croix, and 62 islets in the Caribbean Sea roughly 40 miles (64 km.) east of Puerto Rico. The islands have a combined area of 133 sq. mi. (352 sq. km.) and a population of *106,000. Capital: Charlotte Amalie. Tourism is the principal industry. Watch movements, costume jewelry, pharmaceuticals, and rum are exported.

The Virgin Islands were discovered by Columbus in 1493, during his second voyage to America. During the 17th century, individual islands, actually the peaks of a submerged mountain range, were held by Spain, Holland, England, France and Denmark. These islands were also the favorite resorts of the buccaneers operating in the Caribbean and the coastal waters of eastern North America. Control of most of the 100-island group finally passed to Denmark, with England securing the easterly remainder. The Danish islands had their own coinage from the early 18th century, based on but unequal to, Denmark's homeland system. In the late 18th and early 19th centuries, Danish minor copper and silver coinage augmented the islands currency. The Danish islands were purchased by the United States in 1917 for $25 million, mainly to forestall their acquisition by Germany and because they command the Anegada Passage into the Caribbean Sea, a strategic point on the defense perimeter of the Panama Canal.

RULER
Danish, until 1917

MINT MARKS
Three mints were used for coinage of the eighteenth century.
(a) - Altona - tall, widely spaced crown
(c) - Copenhagen - symetrical crown
(h) - Copenhagen - heart
(k) - Kongsberg - boxy crown
(o) - Altona – orb

MINTMASTERS' INITIALS
See Denmark

MONEYERS' INITIALS

Initial	Date	Name
GJ	1901-33	Knud Gunnar Jensen
AH	1908-24	Andreas Frederik Vilhelm Hansen

MONETARY SYSTEM
(From 1904)
5 Bit = 1 Cent
5 Francs = 1 Daler

DANISH COLONY

The following listings are all believed to be spurious countermarks on a variety of host coins. The few genuine countermarked pieces are currently listed in the Standard Catalog of World Coins, 1801-1900.

DECIMAL COINAGE
20 Cents = 1 Franc

KM# 72 4 DALER (20 Francs)
6.4516 g., 0.9000 Gold .1867 oz. AGW **Ruler:** Christian IX **Obv:** Head left **Rev:** Seated liberty figure divides denominations **Note:** Mintmaster's initial: P. Moneyer's initials: GJ.

Date	Mintage	F	VF	XF	Unc	BU
1904(h)	121,000	150	250	400	650	—
1905(h)	Inc. above	150	275	425	775	—

KM# 73 10 DALER (50 Francs)
16.1290 g., 0.9000 Gold .4667 oz. AGW **Ruler:** Christian IX **Obv:** Head left **Rev:** Seated liberty figure divides denominations, date below **Note:** Mintmaster's initial: P. Moneyer's initials: GJ.

Date	Mintage	F	VF	XF	Unc	BU
1904(h)	2,005	1,250	2,000	4,275	6,900	—

DANZIG

Danzig is an important seaport on the northern coast of Poland with access to the Baltic Sea. It has at different times belonged to the Teutonic Knights, Pomerania, Russia, and Prussia. It was part of the Polish Kingdom from 1587-1772.

Danzig (Gdansk) was a free city from 1919 to 1939 during which most of its modern coinage was made.

RULERS
Friedrich Wilhelm III (of Prussia), 1797-1840
Marshal Lefebvre (as Duke), 1807-1814

MINT MARKS
A - Berlin

MONETARY SYSTEM
3 Schilling (Szelag) = 1 Groschen (Grosz)

FREE CITY
STANDARD COINAGE

KM# 148 25 GULDEN
7.9881 g., 0.9170 Gold .2354 oz. AGW **Obv:** Arms between columns with supporters, date below **Rev:** Statue from the Nepture fountain, denomination at left and divided below **Note:** Presented to senate members.

Date	Mintage	F	VF	XF	Unc	BU
1923	800	—	1,650	2,000	3,000	—
1923 Proof	200	Value: 4,000				

KM# 150 25 GULDEN
7.9881 g., 0.9170 Gold .2354 oz. AGW **Obv:** Shielded arms with supporters, date below **Rev:** Statue from the Nepture fountain, denomination at left and divided below **Note:** Not released for circulation. A few were distributed on Sept. 1, 1939, in VIP presentation cases.

Date	Mintage	F	VF	XF	Unc	BU
1930	Est. 4,000	—	—	7,000	10,000	—

PATTERNS
Including off metal strikes

KM#	Date	Mintage	Identification	Mkt Val
Pn36	1808	—	Schilling. Gold. KM#136.	3,500
Pn42	1812 M	—	Groschen. Gold. KM#137.	4,500
Pn47	1923	10	Gulden. Gold. KM145.	7,500

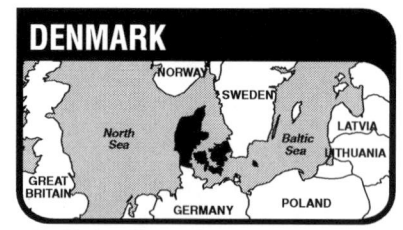

DENMARK

The Kingdom of Denmark (Danmark), a constitutional monarchy located at the mouth of the Baltic Sea, has an area of 16,639 sq. mi. (43,070 sq. km.) and a population of 5.2 million. Capital: Copenhagen. Most of the country is arable. Agriculture is conducted by large farms served by cooperatives. The largest industries are food processing, iron and metal, and fishing. Machinery, meats (chiefly bacon), dairy products and chemicals are exported.

(Danmark), is located at the mouth of the Baltic Sea. Denmark, a great power during the Viking period of the 9th-11th centuries, conducted raids on western Europe and England, and in the 11th century united England, Denmark and Norway under the rule of King Canute. Despite a struggle between the crown and the nobility (13th-14th centuries) which forced the King to grant a written constitution, Queen Margaret (Margrethe) (1387-1412) succeeded in uniting Denmark, Norway, Sweden, Finland and Greenland under the Danish crown, placing all of Scandinavia under the rule of Denmark. An unwise alliance with Napoleon contributed to the dismembering of the empire and fostered a liberal movement which succeeded in making Denmark a constitutional monarchy in 1849.

RULERS
Christian VII, 1766-1808
Frederik VI, 1808-1839
Christian VIII, 1839-1848
Frederik VII, 1848-1863
Christian IX, 1863-1906
Frederik VIII, 1906-1912
Christian X, 1912-1947
Frederik IX, 1947-1972
Margrethe II, 1972—

MINT OFFICIALS' INITIALS

Altona

Initial	Date	Name
MF	1786-1816	Michael Flor
CB	1817-19	Cajus Branth
FF, IFF	1819-56	Johan Friedrich Freund
TA	1848-51	Theodor Andersen
FA	1856-63	Hans Frederik Alsing

Copenhagen

Initial	Date	Name
HIAB	1797-1810	Hans Jacob Arnold Branth
None	1810-21	Ole Varberg
CFG	1821-31	Conrad Frederik Gerlach
VS, WS	1835-61	Georg Wilhelm Svendsen
RH	1861-69	Rasmus Hinnerup
CS	1869-93	Diderik Christian Andreas Svendsen
*P, VBP	1893-1918	Vilhelm Buchard Poulsen
HCN	1919-27	Hans Christian Nielsen
N	1927-55	Niels Peter Nielsen
C	1956-71	Alfred Frederik Christiansen
S	1971-78	Vagn Sorensen
B	1978-1981	Peter M. Bjarno
R, NR	1982-89	N. Norregaard Rasmussen
LG	1989-2001	Laust Grove

NOTE: The letter P was only used on Danish West Indies coins and Denmark, KM#802.

MONEYERS' INITIALS

Altona

Initial	Date	Name
FA	1825-55	Hans Frederik Alsing
FK	1841-63	Frederik Christopher Krohn
HL	1848-51	Carl Heinrich Lorenz
PP	1852-63	Peter Petersen

Copenhagen

Initial	Date	Name
PG	1798-1807	Peter Leonard Gianelli
D I ADLERFE	1808	Daniel Jensen Adzer
IC, ICF	1810-13, 1823-41	Johannes Conradsen
M	1813	Christian Andreas Muller
CC	1836	Christen Christensen
FK	1841-73	Frederik Christopher Krohn
HC	1873-1901	Harald Conradsen
GJ, GJ	1901-33	Knud Gunnar Jensen
AH	1908-24	Andreas Frederik Vilhelm Hansen
HS, S	1933-68	Harald Salomon
B	1968-83	Frode Bahnsen
A	1986-	Johan Alkjaer
HV	1986-	Hanne Varming
JP, JPA	1989-	Jan Petersen

MONETARY SYSTEM
(Until 1813)
16 Skillings = 1 Mark
64 Skilling Danske = 4 Mark = 1 Krone
96 Skilling Danske = 6 Mark = 1 Daler Specie
12 Mark = 1 Ducat
10 Ducat = 1 Portugaloser

KINGDOM
STANDARD COINAGE
Through 1813

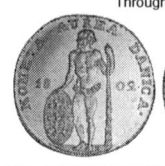

KM# 650 DUCAT SPECIE
3.4900 g., 0.9790 Gold .1098 oz. AGW **Ruler:** Christian VII **Obv:** Standing wildman with shield and staff divides date **Rev:** Five-line legend in square tablet

Date	Mintage	F	VF	XF	Unc	BU
1802	—	400	850	1,600	1,900	—

GOLD COINAGE
1840-1874

KM# 698 FR(EDERIKS) D'OR
6.6420 g., 0.8960 Gold .1913 oz. AGW **Ruler:** Frederik VI **Obv:** Head left **Obv. Legend:** FREDERICUS VI REX DANIÆ **Rev:** Denomination and date

Date	Mintage	VG	F	VF	XF	Unc
1827 IC//IFF	—	600	1,200	2,500	3,900	—

KM# 699 FR(EDERIKS) D'OR
6.6420 g., 0.8960 Gold .1913 oz. AGW **Ruler:** Frederik VI **Obv:** Head left **Obv. Legend:** FREDERICUS VI REX DANIÆ **Rev:** Crowned arms

Date	Mintage	VG	F	VF	XF	Unc
1828 IC//FF	21,000	450	900	1,800	3,200	—

KM# 701 FR(EDERIKS) D'OR
6.6420 g., 0.8960 Gold .1913 oz. AGW **Ruler:** Frederik VI **Obv:** Modified head left **Rev:** Crowned arms

Date	Mintage	VG	F	VF	XF	Unc
1829 FA//FF	7,625	300	550	1,300	2,450	—
1830 FA//FF	12,000	500	950	—	—	—
1831 FA//FF	—	300	550	1,300	2,200	—
1833 FA//FF	—	300	575	1,500	2,200	—
1834 FA//FF	—	400	900	2,500	4,100	—
1835 FA//FF	—	300	500	1,200	2,000	—
1837 FA//FF	—	300	500	1,200	2,000	—
1838 FA//FF	—	300	550	1,400	2,200	—

KM# 757 FR(EDERIKS) D'OR
6.6420 g., 0.8960 Gold .1913 oz. AGW **Ruler:** Frederik VII **Obv:** Head right **Obv. Legend:** FREDERICUS VII D G DANIÆ V G REX **Rev:** Crowned arms with supporters

DENMARK

Date	Mintage	VG	F	VF	XF	Unc
1853 FK//FF	678	400	775	2,450	3,800	—

KM# 730 CHR(ISTIANS) D'OR
6.6420 g., 0.8960 Gold .1913 oz. AGW **Ruler:** Christian VIII
Obv: Head right **Obv. Legend:** CHRISTIANVS VIII D G DANIÆ V G REX **Rev:** Crowned arms with supporters

Date	Mintage	VG	F	VF	XF	Unc
1843(o) FK//FF	38,000	235	475	1,200	2,250	—
1844(o) FK//FF	Inc. above	300	750	1,500	2,500	—
1845(o) FK//FF	Inc. above	250	550	1,200	2,500	—
1847(o) FK//FF	Inc. above	350	875	1,700	3,250	—

KM# 778 CHR(ISTIANS) D'OR
6.6420 g., 0.8960 Gold .1913 oz. AGW **Ruler:** Christian IX
Obv: Head right **Obv. Legend:** CHRISTIANVS IX D G DANIÆ V G REX **Rev:** Crowned arms with supporters

Date	Mintage	VG	F	VF	XF	Unc
1869 HC//CS	539	800	1,500	3,250	6,000	—

KM# 697 2 FR(EDERIKS) D'OR
13.2840 g., 0.8960 Gold .3827 oz. AGW **Ruler:** Frederik VI
Obv: Head left **Obv. Legend:** FREDERICUS IV REX DANIÆ **Rev:** Denomination and date

Date	Mintage	VG	F	VF	XF	Unc
1826 IC//IFF Unique	—	—	—	—	—	—
1827 IC//IFF	—	750	1,550	3,600	5,000	6,500

KM# 700 2 FR(EDERIKS) D'OR
13.2840 g., 0.8960 Gold .3827 oz. AGW **Ruler:** Frederik VI
Obv: Head left **Obv. Legend:** FREDERICUS VI REX DANIÆ **Rev:** Crowned arms

Date	Mintage	VG	F	VF	XF	Unc
1828 IC//FF	168,000	375	550	1,500	2,600	—
1829 IC//FF	96,000	400	600	1,750	3,000	—
1830 IC//FF	105,000	300	475	1,150	2,100	—
1833 IC//FF	—	375	550	1,500	2,800	—
1834 IC//FF	—	375	550	1,500	2,750	—
1835 IC//FF	—	350	525	1,400	2,500	—
1836 IC//FF Rare	—	—	—	—	—	—

KM# 713.1 2 FR(EDERIKS) D'OR
13.2840 g., 0.8960 Gold .3827 oz. AGW **Ruler:** Frederik VI
Obv: Head right **Obv. Legend:** FREDERICUS VI REX DANIÆ **Rev:** Crowned and mantled arms with supporters

Date	Mintage	VG	F	VF	XF	Unc
1836 CC//FF	—	350	700	1,500	2,700	—
1837 CC//FF	—	300	625	1,400	2,500	—
1838 CC//FF	—	300	625	1,400	2,500	—
1839 CC//FF	—	325	650	1,500	3,000	—

KM# 713.2 2 FR(EDERIKS) D'OR
13.2840 g., 0.8960 Gold .3827 oz. AGW **Ruler:** Frederik VI
Obv: Head right **Obv. Inscription:** FREDERUCUS VI REX DANIÆ **Rev:** Crowned and mantled arms with supporters

Date	Mintage	VG	F	VF	XF	Unc
1838 CC//WS	—	400	800	1,950	3,000	—

KM# 750.1 2 FR(EDERIKS) D'OR
13.2840 g., 0.8960 Gold .3827 oz. AGW **Ruler:** Frederik VII
Obv: Head right **Obv. Legend:** FREDERICUS VII D G DANIÆ V G REX **Rev:** Crowned and mantled arms with supporters
Note: Total mintage 1850VS and 1863RH 31,000.

Date	Mintage	VG	F	VF	XF	Unc
1850 FK//VS	—	275	600	2,000	3,000	—

KM# 750.2 2 FR(EDERIKS) D'OR
13.2840 g., 0.8960 Gold .3827 oz. AGW **Ruler:** Frederik VII
Obv: Head right **Obv. Legend:** FREDERICUS VII D G DANIÆ V G REX **Rev:** Crowned and mantled arms with supporters

Date	Mintage	VG	F	VF	XF	Unc
1851 FK//FF	1,205,000	325	700	2,000	3,100	—
1852 FK//FF	Inc. above	325	700	2,000	3,100	—
1853 FK//FF	Inc. above	300	600	1,650	2,700	—
1854 FK//FF	Inc. above	325	650	1,800	3,000	—
1855 FK//FF	Inc. above	325	650	1,800	3,000	—

KM# 750.3 2 FR(EDERIKS) D'OR
13.2840 g., 0.8960 Gold .3827 oz. AGW **Ruler:** Frederik VII
Obv: Head right **Obv. Legend:** FREDERICUS VII D G DANIÆ V G REX **Rev:** Crowned and mantled arms with supporters

Date	Mintage	VG	F	VF	XF	Unc
1856 FK//FA	Inc. above	325	650	1,800	3,000	—
1857 FK//FA	Inc. above	300	600	1,650	2,700	—
1859 FK//FA	Inc. above	300	650	1,800	3,000	—

KM# 750.4 2 FR(EDERIKS) D'OR
13.2840 g., 0.8960 Gold .3827 oz. AGW **Ruler:** Frederik VII
Obv: Head right **Rev:** Crowned and mantled arms with supporters
Note: Total mintage 1850VS and 1863RH 31,000.

Date	Mintage	VG	F	VF	XF	Unc
1863(c) FK//RH	—	350	700	2,000	3,000	—

KM# 722.1 2 CHR(ISTIANS) D'OR
13.2840 g., 0.8960 Gold .3827 oz. AGW **Ruler:** Christian VIII
Obv: Head right **Obv. Legend:** CHRISTIANVS VIII D G DANIÆ V G REX **Rev:** Crowned and mantled arms with supporters

Date	Mintage	VG	F	VF	XF	Unc
1841 CC	—	350	700	1,200	2,500	—
Note: Total mintage 1841(h) and 1844(c) 9,222

KM# 722.2 2 CHR(ISTIANS) D'OR
13.2840 g., 0.8960 Gold .3827 oz. AGW **Ruler:** Christian VIII
Obv: Head right **Rev:** Crowned and mantled arms with supporters

Date	Mintage	VG	F	VF	XF	Unc
1842(o) CC//FF	551,000	350	750	1,500	2,500	—
1844(o) CC//FF	Inc. above	300	525	1,400	2,350	—
1845(o) CC//FF	Inc. above	300	750	1,500	2,750	—
1847(o) CC//FF	Inc. above	300	550	1,350	2,350	—

KM# 722.3 2 CHR(ISTIANS) D'OR
13.2840 g., 0.8960 Gold .3827 oz. AGW **Ruler:** Christian VIII
Obv: Head right **Rev:** Crowned and mantled arms with supporters

Date	Mintage	VG	F	VF	XF	Unc
1844(c) CC//VS	—	300	600	1,400	2,400	3,600
Note: Total mintage 1841(h) and 1844(c) 9,222

KM# 773.1 2 CHR(ISTIANS) D'OR
13.2840 g., 0.8960 Gold .3827 oz. AGW **Ruler:** Christian IX
Obv: Head right **Obv. Legend:** CHRISTIANVS IX D G DANIÆ V G REX **Rev:** Crowned and mantled arms with supporters

Date	Mintage	VG	F	VF	XF	Unc
1866(c) HC//RH	42,000	400	800	2,400	4,500	—
1867(c) HC//RH Rare	Inc. above	—	—	—	—	—

KM# 773.2 2 CHR(ISTIANS) D'OR
13.2840 g., 0.8960 Gold .3827 oz. AGW **Ruler:** Christian IX
Obv: Head right **Obv. Legend:** CHRISTIANVS IX D G DANIÆ V G REX **Rev:** Crowned and mantled arms with supporters

Date	Mintage	VG	F	VF	XF	Unc
1869(c) HC//CS	Inc. above	400	800	2,250	4,400	—
1870(c) HC//CS Rare	Inc. above	—	—	—	—	—

DECIMAL COINAGE
100 Øre = 1 Krone; 1874-present

KM# 790.1 10 KRONER
4.4803 g., 0.9000 Gold .1296 oz. AGW **Ruler:** Christian IX
Obv: Head right **Rev:** Seated figure left with shield and porpoise

Date	Mintage	F	VF	XF	Unc	BU
1873(h) HC/CS	369,000	BV	90.00	155	275	—
1874(h) HC/CS	Inc. above	BV	95.00	165	300	—
1877(h) HC/CS	98,000	BV	125	180	375	—
1890(h) HC/CS	151,000	BV	90.00	155	250	—

KM# 790.2 10 KRONER
4.4803 g., 0.9000 Gold .1296 oz. AGW **Ruler:** Christian IX
Obv: Head right **Rev:** Seated figure left with shield and porpoise

Date	Mintage	F	VF	XF	Unc	BU
1898(h) HC/VBP	100,000	BV	95.00	165	270	—
1900(h) HC/VBP	204,000	BV	85.00	110	200	—

KM# 809 10 KRONER
4.4803 g., 0.9000 Gold .1296 oz. AGW **Ruler:** Frederik VIII
Obv: Head left with titles **Rev:** Draped crowned national arms above date, value, mint mark and initials VBP

Date	Mintage	F	VF	XF	Unc	BU
1908(h) VBP; GJ	308,000	—	100	120	140	—
1909(h) VBP; GJ	153,000	—	100	120	140	—

184 DENMARK

KM# 816 10 KRONER
4.4803 g., 0.9000 Gold .1296 oz. AGW **Ruler:** Christian X
Obv: Head right with title, date, mint mark, initials VBP. Initials AH at neck **Rev:** Draped crowned national arms above date, value, mint mark and initials VBP

Date	Mintage	F	VF	XF	Unc	BU
1913(h) AH/ GJ	312,000	—	100	120	135	—
1917(h) AH/ GJ	132,000	—	100	130	145	—

KM# 907 10 KRONER
8.6500 g., 0.9000 Gold 0.2503 oz. AGW, 22 mm.
Ruler: Margrethe II **Subject:** Hans Christian Andersen's The Ugly Duckling **Obv:** Queen **Rev:** Swan and reflection on water
Rev. Designer: Hans Pauli Olsen

Date	Mintage	F	VF	XF	Unc	BU
2005	7,000	—	—	—	—	400

KM# 911 (KM900b) 10 KRONER
8.6500 g., 0.9000 Gold 0.2214 oz. AGW, 22 mm.
Ruler: Margrethe II **Subject:** Hans Christian Andersen's Little Mermaid **Obv:** Queen **Rev:** Little Mermaid **Rev. Designer:** Tina Maria Nielsen

Date	Mintage	F	VF	XF	Unc	BU
2005	6,000	—	—	—	—	400
2005	6,000	—	—	—	—	400

KM# 915 10 KRONER
8.6500 g., 0.9000 Gold 0.2503 oz. AGW, 22 mm.
Ruler: Margrethe II **Subject:** The Snow Queen **Obv:** Queen
Obv. Designer: Hans Christian Andersen **Rev:** Icc pieces
Rev. Designer: Øivind Nygaard

Date	Mintage	F	VF	XF	Unc	BU
2006	4,000	—	—	—	—	400

KM# 791.1 20 KRONER
8.9606 g., 0.9000 Gold .2592 oz. AGW **Ruler:** Christian IX
Obv: Head right **Rev:** Seated figure left with shield and porpoise

Date	Mintage	F	VF	XF	Unc	BU
1873(h) HC/CS	1,153,000	—	BV	180	230	—
1874(h) HC/CS	Inc. above	800	1,500	2,250	3,500	—
1876(h) HC/CS	351,000	—	BV	190	280	—
1877(h) HC/CS	Inc. above	—	BV	285	380	—
1890(h) HC/CS	102,000	—	BV	285	380	—

KM# 791.2 20 KRONER
8.9606 g., 0.9000 Gold .2592 oz. AGW **Ruler:** Christian IX
Obv: Head right **Rev:** Seated figure left with shield and porpoise

Date	Mintage	F	VF	XF	Unc	BU
1900(h) CS/VBP	100,000	—	BV	230	340	—

KM# 810 20 KRONER
8.9606 g., 0.9000 Gold .2592 oz. AGW **Ruler:** Frederik VIII
Obv: Head left, with titles **Rev:** Crowned and mantled arms above date, value, mint mark and initials VBP

Date	Mintage	F	VF	XF	Unc	BU
1908(h) VBP; GJ	243,000	—	175	210	250	—
1909(h) VBP; GJ	365,000	—	180	220	260	—
1910(h) VBP; GJ	200,000	—	200	225	275	—
1911(h) VBP; GJ	183,000	—	180	220	260	—
1912(h) VBP; GJ	184,000	—	180	220	260	—

KM# 817.1 20 KRONER
8.9606 g., 0.9000 Gold .2592 oz. AGW **Ruler:** Christian X
Obv: Head right with title, date, mint mark, initials VBP, initials AH at neck **Rev:** Crowned and mantled arms above date, value, mint mark and initials VBP

Date	Mintage	F	VF	XF	Unc	BU
1913(h) AH/GJ	815,000	—	175	210	250	—
1914(h) AH/GJ	920,000	—	175	210	250	—
1915(h) AH/GJ	532,000	—	180	215	255	—
1916(h) AH/GJ	1,401,000	—	180	220	265	—
1917(h) AH/GJ	Inc. above	—	180	220	260	—

KM# 817.2 20 KRONER
8.9606 g., 0.9000 Gold .2592 oz. AGW **Ruler:** Christian X
Obv: Head right with title, date, mint mark, and initials HCN, initials AH at neck **Rev:** Crowned and mantled arms above date, value, mint mark, and initials HCN **Note:** 1926-1927 dated 20 Kroners were not released for circulation.

Date	Mintage	F	VF	XF	Unc	BU
1926(h) HCN	358,000	—	—	3,000	6,000	—
1927(h) HCN	Inc. above	—	—	3,000	6,000	—

KM# 817.3 20 KRONER
8.9606 g., 0.9000 Gold .2592 oz. AGW **Ruler:** Christian X
Obv: Head right with title, date, mint mark, and initials HCN. Initials AH at neck **Rev:** Crowned and mantled arms above date, value, mint mark and initials HCN **Note:** The 1930-1931 dated 20 Kroners were not released for circulation.

Date	Mintage	F	VF	XF	Unc	BU
1930(h) N	1,285,000	—	—	3,000	6,000	—
1931(h) N	Inc. above	—	—	3,000	6,000	—

MEDALLIC COINAGE

The Medallic Issues are similar to circulation coinage except they are without a denomination.

X# A1 2 KRONER
Gold **Subject:** Golden Wedding Anniversary

Date	Mintage	F	VF	XF	Unc	BU
1892	2	—	—	—	13,500	—

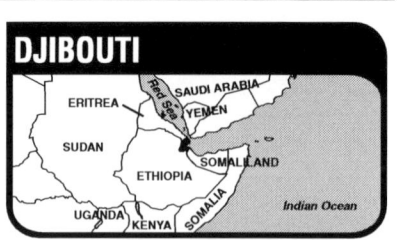

DJIBOUTI

The Republic of Djibouti (formerly French Somaliland and the French Overseas Territory of Afars and Issas), located in northeast Africa at the Bab el Mandeb Strait connecting the Suez Canal and the Red Sea with the Gulf of Aden and the Indian Ocean, has an area of 8,950 sq. mi. (22,000 sq. km.) and a population of 421,320. Capital: Djibouti. The tiny nation has less than one sq. mi. of arable land, and no natural resources except salt, sand, and camels. The commercial activities of the transshipment port of Djibouti and the Addis Abada-Djibouti railroad are the basis of the economy. Salt, fish and hides are exported.

French interest in former French Somaliland began in 1839 with concessions obtained by a French naval lieutenant from the provincial sultans. French Somaliland was made a protectorate in 1884 and its boundaries were delimited by the Franco-British and Ethiopian accords of 1887 and 1897. It became a colony in 1896 and a territory within the French Union in 1946. In 1958 it voted to join the new French Community as an overseas territory, and reaffirmed that choice by a referendum in March, 1967. Its name was changed from French Somaliland to the French Territory of Afars and Issas on July 5, 1967.

The French Tricolor, which had flown over the strategically important territory for 115 years, was lowered for the last time on June 27, 1977, when French Afars and Issas became Africa's 49th independent state, under the name of the Republic of Djibouti.

Djibouti, a seaport and capital city of the Republic of Djibouti (and formerly of French Somaliland and French Afars and Issas) is located on the east coast of Africa at the southernmost entrance to the Red Sea. The capital was moved from Obok to Djibouti in 1892 and established as the transshipment point for Ethiopia's foreign trade via the Franco-Ethiopian railway linking Djibouti and Addis Ababa.

RULER
French, until 1977

REPUBLIC

STANDARD COINAGE

KM# 36 250 FRANCS
1.2440 g., 0.9990 Gold, 13.95 mm. **Obv:** National arms within wreath, date below **Rev:** Old Portuguese Ship

Date	Mintage	F	VF	XF	Unc	BU
1996 Proof	—	Value: 75.00				

DOMINICA

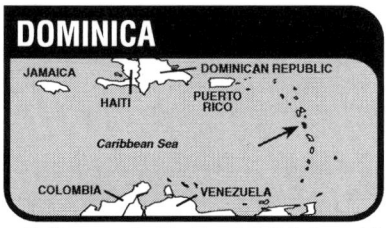

The Commonwealth of Dominica, situated in the Lesser Antilles midway between Guadeloupe to the north and Martinique to the south, has an area of 290 sq. mi. (750 sq. km.) and a population of 82,608. Capital: Roseau. Agriculture is the chief economic activity of the mountainous island. Bananas are the chief export.

Columbus discovered and named the island on Nov. 3, 1493. Spain neglected it and it was finally colonized by the French in 1632. The British drove the French from the island in 1756. Thereafter it changed hands between the French and British a dozen or more times before becoming permanently British in 1805. Around 1761, pierced or mutilated silver from Martinique was used on the island. A council in 1798 acknowledged and established value for these mutilated coins and ordered other cut and countermarked to be made in Dominica. These remained in use until 1862, when they were demonetized and sterling became the standard. Throughout the greater part of its British history, Dominica was a presidency of the Leeward Islands. In 1940 its administration was transferred to the Windward Islands and it was established as a separate colony with considerable local autonomy. From 1955, Dominica was a member of the currency board of the British Caribbean Territories (Eastern Group), which issued its own coins until 1965. Dominica became a West Indies associated state with a built in option for independence in 1967. Full independence was attained on Nov. 3, 1978. Dominica, which has a republican form of government, is a member of the Commonwealth of Nations.

RULER
British, until 1978

MINT MARKS

Mark	Mint
CHI in circle	Valcambi, Chiasso, Italy
(ml) – maple leaf	Canadian Royal Mint

MONETARY SYSTEM

(Until 1798)
10 Bits = 7 Shillings 6 Pence = 1 Dollar
(From 1798 until 1813)
11 Bits = 8 Shillings 3 Pence = 1 Dollar
(Commencing 1813)
100 Cents = 10 Shillings = 1 Dollar (Dominican)

COMMONWEALTH

MODERN COINAGE

KM# 14.1 150 DOLLARS
9.6000 g., 0.9000 Gold .2778 oz. AGW **Subject:** Independence - Imperial Parrot **Obv:** Young bust right **Obv. Designer:** Arnold Machin **Rev:** Map of Dominica and parrot, without fineness, denomination at left

Date	Mintage	F	VF	XF	Unc	BU
ND(1978)	300	—	—	—	225	—
ND(1978) Proof	400	Value: 250				

KM# 14.2 150 DOLLARS
9.6000 g., 0.9000 Gold .2778 oz. AGW **Subject:** Independence - Imperial Parrot **Obv:** Young bust right **Obv. Designer:** Arnold Machin **Rev:** Parrot and map, denomination at left, Canadian mint mark and .900 fineness added

Date	Mintage	F	VF	XF	Unc	BU
ND(1978)(ml)	18	—	—	—	—	—
ND(1978)(ml) Proof	116	Value: 300				

KM# 18 150 DOLLARS
9.6000 g., 0.9000 Gold .2778 oz. AGW **Subject:** Israel and Egypt Peace Treaty **Obv:** Young bust right **Obv. Designer:** Arnold Machin **Rev:** Heads of Carter, Sadat, and Begin with flags, denomination below

Date	Mintage	F	VF	XF	Unc	BU
ND(1979)CHI	100	—	—	—	500	—
ND(1979)CHI Proof	100	Value: 550				

KM# 15.1 300 DOLLARS
19.2000 g., 0.9000 Gold .5556 oz. AGW
Subject: Independence - Arms **Obv:** Young bust right **Obv. Designer:** Arnold Machin **Rev:** Lion tops arms with parrots, denomination below, without fineness

Date	Mintage	F	VF	XF	Unc	BU
ND(1978)	500	—	—	—	400	—
ND(1978) Proof	800	Value: 450				

KM# 15.2 300 DOLLARS
19.2000 g., 0.9000 Gold .5556 oz. AGW
Subject: Independence - Arms **Obv:** Young bust right **Obv. Designer:** Arnold Machin **Rev:** National arms, Canadian mint mark and .900 fineness added

Date	Mintage	F	VF	XF	Unc	BU
ND(1978)(ml)	18	—	—	—	—	—
ND(1978)(ml) Proof	82	Value: 500				

KM# 19 300 DOLLARS
19.2000 g., 0.9000 Gold .5556 oz. AGW **Subject:** Visit of Pope John Paul II **Obv:** Young bust right **Obv. Designer:** Arnold Machin **Rev:** Head with beanie left, denomination below

Date	Mintage	F	VF	XF	Unc	BU
ND(1979)CHI	5,000	—	—	—	375	—
ND(1979)CHI	300	—	—	—	550	—

KM# 22 500 DOLLARS
47.5400 g., 0.9170 Gold 1.4013 oz. AGW **Subject:** Royal Visit **Obv:** Crowned bust right **Rev:** Lion tops arms with parrots, circle surrounds

Date	Mintage	F	VF	XF	Unc	BU
1985 Proof	Est. 250	Value: 975				

PROOF SETS

KM#	Date	Mintage	Identification	Issue Price	Mkt Val
PS2	1978 (4)	—	KM#12.3, 13.2, 14.2, 15.2	—	1,000

DOMINICAN REPUBLIC

The Dominican Republic, which occupies the eastern two-thirds of the island of Hispaniola, has an area of 18,704 sq. mi. (48,734 sq. km.) and a population of 7.9 million. Capital: Santo Domingo. The largely agricultural economy produces sugar, coffee, tobacco and cocoa. Tourism and casino gaming are also a rising source of revenue.

Columbus discovered Hispaniola in 1492, and named it La Isla Espanola - 'the Spanish Island'. Santo Domingo, the oldest white settlement in the Western Hemisphere, was the base from which Spain conducted its exploration of the New World. Later, French buccaneers settled the western third of Hispaniola, naming the colony St. Dominique, which in 1697, was ceded to France by Spain. In 1804, following a bloody revolt by former slaves, the French colony became the Republic of Haiti - mountainous country'. The Spanish called their part of Hispaniola Santo Domingo. In 1822, the Haitians conquered the entire island and held it until 1844, when Juan Pablo Duarte, the national hero of the Dominican Republic, drove them out of Santo Domingo and established an independent Dominican Republic. The republic returned voluntarily to Spanish dominion from 1861 to 1865, after being rejected by France, Britain and the United States. Independence was reclaimed in 1866.

RULERS
Spanish, until 1822, 1861-1865
Haiti, 1822-1844

MINT MARKS
A - Paris
(a) - Berlin
(c) - Stylized maple leaf, Royal Canadian Mint
H - Heaton, Birmingham, England
Mo - Mexico
(o) - CHI in oval - Valcambi, Chiasso, Italy
(t) - Tower, Tower Mint, London

MONETARY SYSTEM
100 Centavos = 1 Peso Oro

REPUBLIC

REFORM COINAGE
1937

100 Centavos = 1 Peso Oro

KM# 66b PESO
31.1035 g., 0.9990 Gold 1 oz. AGW **Subject:** 500th Anniversary - Discovery and Evangelization **Obv:** Denomination, national arms **Rev:** 3 ships at sea

Date	Mintage	F	VF	XF	Unc	BU
1988 Proof	—	Value: 1,250				

KM# 74b PESO
31.1035 g., 0.9990 Gold 1 oz. AGW **Subject:** 500th Anniversary - Discovery and Evangelization **Obv:** Denomination, national arms **Rev:** Sailship landing

Date	Mintage	F	VF	XF	Unc	BU
1989(c) Proof	30	Value: 1,250				

KM# 77b PESO
31.1035 g., 0.9990 Gold 1 oz. AGW **Subject:** 500th Anniversary - Discovery and Evangelization **Obv:** National arms **Rev:** Two standing figures

Date	Mintage	F	VF	XF	Unc	BU
1990 Proof	50	—	—	—	1,000	—

DOMINICAN REPUBLIC

KM# 81b PESO
31.1035 g., 0.9990 Gold 1 oz. AGW **Subject:** Pinzon brothers on ship at sea **Obv:** Denomination, national arms **Rev:** Conjoined busts left on ship at sea

Date	Mintage	F	VF	XF	Unc	BU
1991 Proof	35	Value: 1,150				

KM# 82b PESO
31.1035 g., 0.9990 Gold 1 oz. AGW **Subject:** Christopher Columbus **Obv:** Denomination, national arms **Rev:** Bust 3/4 left

Date	Mintage	F	VF	XF	Unc	BU
1992(c) Proof	35	Value: 1,150				

KM# 24 30 PESOS
29.6220 g., 0.9000 Gold .8572 oz. AGW, 32 mm. **Subject:** 25th Anniversary of Trujillo regime **Obv:** National arms, denomination below **Rev:** Head left, date below

Date	Mintage	F	VF	XF	Unc	BU
1955	33,000	—	—	BV	575	600

KM# 36 30 PESOS
11.7000 g., 0.9000 Gold .3385 oz. AGW **Subject:** 12th Central American and Caribbean Games **Obv:** National arms **Rev:** Games symbol, denomination and date below

Date	Mintage	F	VF	XF	Unc	BU
1974	25,000	—	—	—	225	245
1974 Proof	5,000	Value: 265				

KM# 39 100 PESOS
10.0000 g., 0.9000 Gold .2893 oz. AGW **Subject:** Taino Art **Obv:** National arms, date below **Rev:** Native art divides denomination, date below

Date	Mintage	F	VF	XF	Unc	BU
1975	18,000	—	—	—	200	210
1975 Proof	2,000	Value: 225				

KM# 55 100 PESOS
12.0000 g., 0.9000 Gold .3472 oz. AGW **Subject:** Pope John Paul II's Visit **Obv:** National arms, denomination below **Rev:** Bust left, Vatican City and date at left

Date	Mintage	F	VF	XF	Unc	BU
ND(1979)	1,000	—	—	—	235	245
ND(1979) Proof	3,000	Value: 260				

KM# 75a 100 PESOS
155.5000 g., 0.9990 Gold 5 oz. AGW **Subject:** 500th Anniversary of Discovery and Evangelization of America **Obv:** Arms **Rev:** Columbus and crew

Date	Mintage	F	VF	XF	Unc	BU
1989 Proof	30	Value: 3,600				

KM# 78a 100 PESOS
155.5300 g., 0.9990 Gold 5 oz. AGW, 65 mm. **Subject:** 500th Anniversary of Discovery and Evangelization of America **Obv:** National arms **Rev:** Building a stockade **Note:** Illustration reduced.

Date	Mintage	F	VF	XF	Unc	BU
1990 Proof	50	Value: 3,350				

KM# 83a 100 PESOS
155.5300 g., 0.9990 Gold 5 oz. AGW, 65 mm. **Subject:** 500th Anniversary of Discovery and Evangelization of America **Obv:** National arms **Rev:** Columbus Presenting Native American to Court **Note:** Illustration reduced.

Date	Mintage	F	VF	XF	Unc	BU
1991 Proof	35	Value: 3,500				

KM# 84a 100 PESOS
155.5300 g., 0.9990 Gold 5 oz. AGW, 65 mm. **Subject:** 500th Anniversary - Discovery and Evangelization of America **Obv:** National arms **Rev:** Bust left and anchored ship

Date	Mintage	F	VF	XF	Unc	BU
1992 Proof	35	Value: 3,500				

KM# 47 200 PESOS
31.0000 g., 0.8000 Gold .7974 oz. AGW **Subject:** Centennial - Death of Juan Pablo Duarte **Obv:** National arms, date below **Rev:** Head facing divides denomination, two dates below **Note:** Large quantities of both varieties were melted for bullion.

Date	Mintage	F	VF	XF	Unc	BU
1977	1,000	—	—	—	525	545
1977 Proof	2,000	Value: 575				

KM# 58 200 PESOS
17.1700 g., 0.9000 Gold .4969 oz. AGW **Subject:** International Year of the Child **Obv:** National arms, date below **Rev:** Children dancing, denomination below

Date	Mintage	F	VF	XF	Unc	BU
1982 Proof	4,303	Value: 345				

KM# 105 200 PESOS
12.0000 g., 0.9000 Gold 0.3472 oz. AGW, 25 mm. **Subject:** 50th Anniversary - Central Bank **Obv:** National arms **Rev:** Seated woman holding up coin **Edge:** Reeded

Date	Mintage	F	VF	XF	Unc	BU
ND (1997)	500	—	—	—	—	375
ND (1997) Proof	2,000	Value: 450				

KM# 56 250 PESOS
31.1000 g., 0.9000 Gold .9000 oz. AGW **Subject:** Visit of Pope John Paul II

Date	Mintage	F	VF	XF	Unc	BU
1979	1,000	—	—	—	600	625
1979 Proof	3,000	Value: 650				

KM# 68 500 PESOS
31.1000 g., 0.9990 Gold .9989 oz. AGW **Subject:** Discovery of America - Columbus

Date	Mintage	F	VF	XF	Unc	BU
1988 Proof	2,600	Value: 720				

KM# 76 500 PESOS
31.1000 g., 0.9990 Gold .9989 oz. AGW **Subject:** 500th Anniversary - Discovery and Evangelization of America **Obv:** National arms, denomination below **Rev:** Portraits of Ferdinand and Isabella, date below

Date	Mintage	F	VF	XF	Unc	BU
1989 Proof	600	Value: 845				

KM# 76a 500 PESOS
31.1000 g., 0.9990 Platinum .9989 oz. APW **Subject:** 500th Anniversary - Discovery and Evangelization of America **Obv:** National arms **Rev:** Portraits of Ferdinand and Isabella

Date	Mintage	F	VF	XF	Unc	BU
1989 Proof	—	Value: 1,350				

KM# 79 500 PESOS
16.9600 g., 0.9170 Gold .5 oz. AGW **Subject:** 500th Anniversary - Discovery and Evangelization of America **Obv:** National arms, denomination below **Rev:** Santa Maria and landing crew, date below

Date	Mintage	F	VF	XF	Unc	BU
1990 Proof	1,500	Value: 375				

KM# 79a 500 PESOS
15.5500 g., 0.9990 Platinum .5 oz. APW **Subject:** 500th Anniversary - Discovery and Evangelization of America **Obv:** National arms **Rev:** Santa Maria and landing crew

Date	Mintage	F	VF	XF	Unc	BU
1990 Proof	50	Value: 700				

KM# 85 500 PESOS
16.9600 g., 0.9170 Gold .5 oz. AGW **Subject:** 500th Anniversary - Discovery and Evangelization of America **Obv:** National arms, denomination below **Rev:** American fruits, date below

Date	Mintage	F	VF	XF	Unc	BU
1991 Proof	1,500	Value: 375				

KM# 85a 500 PESOS
15.5500 g., 0.9990 Platinum .5 oz. APW **Subject:** 500th Anniversary - Discovery and Evangelization of America **Obv:** National arms **Rev:** American fruits

Date	Mintage	F	VF	XF	Unc	BU
1991 Proof	35	Value: 745				

KM# 86 500 PESOS
16.9600 g., 0.9170 Gold .5 oz. AGW **Subject:** 500th Anniversary - Discovery and Evangelization of America **Obv:** National arms, denomination below **Rev:** Enshrined tomb of Christopher Columbus, date below

Date	Mintage	F	VF	XF	Unc	BU
1992 Proof	2,000	Value: 360				

KM# 86a 500 PESOS
15.5000 g., 0.9990 Platinum .5 oz. APW **Subject:** 500th Anniversary - Discovery and Evangelization of America **Obv:** National arms **Rev:** Enshrined tomb of Christopher Columbus

Date	Mintage	F	VF	XF	Unc	BU
1992 Proof	35	Value: 745				

MEDALLIC COINAGE

X# 3 100 PESOS (Troy Onza)
31.1000 g., 0.9990 Gold 1 oz. AGW **Subject:** Enriquillo **Note:** Prev. KM#M3.

Date	Mintage	F	VF	XF	Unc	BU
1980 Proof	Est. 15	Value: 1,500				

X# 4a 100 PESOS (Troy Onza)
0.9000 Gold **Subject:** Human Rights

Date	Mintage	F	VF	XF	Unc	BU
1983 Proof	—	—	—	—	—	—

X# 1 500 PESOS
Gold, 40.1 mm. **Subject:** Visit of Juan Carlos and Sofia of Spain **Obv:** Arms **Obv. Legend:** REPUBLICA DOMINICANA **Note:** Prev. KM#M1a.

Date	Mintage	F	VF	XF	Unc	BU
1976 Proof	Est. 10	Value: 750				

X# 1d 500 PESOS
Platinum APW, 40.1 mm. **Subject:** Visit of Juan Carlos and Sofia of Spain **Obv:** Arms **Obv. Legend:** REPUBLICA DOMINICANA **Note:** Prev. KM#M1b.

Date	Mintage	F	VF	XF	Unc	BU
1976 Proof	—	—	—	—	—	—

X# 7 500 PESOS
0.9000 Gold **Subject:** 500th Anniversary - Discovery of America **Obv:** Arms **Rev:** Bust of Columbus right **Note:** Similar to KM#M6.

Date	Mintage	F	VF	XF	Unc	BU
1984 Proof	Est. 10	Value: 800				

PATTERNS
Including off metal strikes

KM#	Date	Mintage	Identification	Mkt Val
Pn17	1975	11	10 Pesos. 0.5000 Gold.	—
Pn18	1975	1	10 Pesos. 0.2940 Gold.	—
Pn19	1975	1	10 Pesos. 0.4000 Gold.	—
Pn20	1975	1	10 Pesos. 0.8000 Gold.	—
Pn21	1975	1	100 Pesos. 0.9000 Gold. without matte details.	—
Pn22	1975	1	100 Pesos. 0.8000 Gold. alloyed with .050 Silver and .150 Copper.	—
Pn23	1975	5	100 Pesos. 0.8000 Gold. alloyed with .150 Silver.	—
Pn24	1975	5	100 Pesos. 0.8000 Gold. alloyed with .150 Silver and .050 Copper, Proof.	—
Pn26	1977	5	30 Pesos. Gold. Proof.	—

PIEFORTS

KM#	Date	Mintage	Identification	Mkt Val
P1	1977	5	30 Pesos. Gold. Piefort.	—
P3	1982	42	200 Pesos.	2,250

PROOF SETS

KM#	Date	Mintage	Identification	Issue Price	Mkt Val
PS5	1974 (2)	500	KM#35-36	120	190
PS6	1975 (2)	500	KM#38-39	200	165

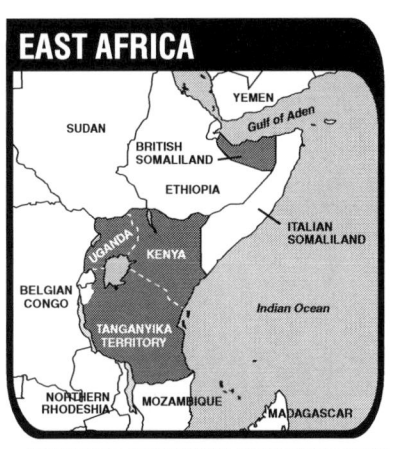

EAST AFRICA

East Africa was an administrative grouping of five separate British territories: Kenya, Uganda, the Sultanate of Zanzibar and British Somaliland.

The common interest of Kenya, Tanganyika and Uganda invited cooperation in economic matters and consideration of political union. The territorial governors, organized as the East Africa High Commission, met periodically to administer such common activities as taxation, industrial development and education. The authority of the Commission did not infringe upon the constitution and internal autonomy of the individual colonies. A common coinage and banknotes, which were also legal tender in Aden, were provided for use of the member colonies by the East Africa Currency Board. The coinage through 1919 had the legend "East Africa and Uganda Protectorate".

NOTE: For later coinage see Kenya, Tanzania and Uganda.

RULER
British

MINT MARK
no mint mark – British Royal Mint, London

PATTERNS
Including off metal strikes

KM#	Date	Mintage	Identification	Mkt Val
Pn2	1897	—	Pice. Gold. KM#1.	2,500
Pn5	1899	—	Pice. Gold. KM#1.	2,500

EAST CARIBBEAN STATES

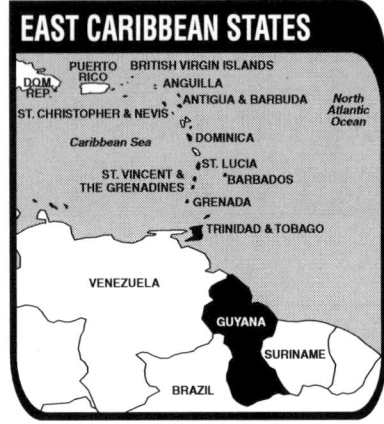

The East Caribbean States, formerly the British Caribbean Territories (Eastern group), formed a currency board in 1950 to provide the constituent territories of Trinidad & Tobago, Barbados, British Guiana (now Guyana), British Virgin Islands, Anguilla, St. Kitts, Nevis, Antigua, Dominica, St. Lucia, St. Vincent and Grenada with a common currency, thereby permitting withdrawal of the regular British Pound currency. This was dissolved in 1965 and after the breakup, the East Caribbean Territories, a grouping including Barbados, the Leeward and Windward Islands, came into being. Coinage of the dissolved 'Eastern Group' continues to circulate. Paper currency of the East Caribbean Authority was first issued in 1965 and although Barbados withdrew from the group they continued using them prior to 1973 when Barbados issued a decimal coinage.

A series of 4-dollar coins tied to the FAO coinage program were released in 1970 under the name of the Caribbean Development Bank by eight loosely federated island groupings in the eastern Caribbean. These issues are listed individually in this volume under Antigua, Barbados, Dominica, Grenada, Montserrat, St. Kitts, St. Lucia and St. Vincent.

RULER
British

EAST CARIBBEAN STATES
British Administration
STANDARD COINAGE
100 Cents = 1 Dollar

KM# 40 DOLLAR
28.2800 g., Gold Plated Copper-Nickel, 38.6 mm.
Ruler: Elizabeth II **Subject:** Golden Jubilee Monarchs
Obv: Head with tiara right **Obv. Designer:** Ian Rank-Broadley
Rev: Henry III (1216-1277) **Edge:** Reeded

Date	Mintage	F	VF	XF	Unc	BU
2002	5,000	—	—	—	22.50	25.00

KM# 42 DOLLAR
28.2800 g., Gold Plated Copper-Nickel, 38.6 mm.
Ruler: Elizabeth II **Subject:** Golden Jubilee Monarchs
Obv: Head with tiara right **Obv. Designer:** Ian Rank-Broadley
Rev: Edward III (1327-1377) **Edge:** Reeded

Date	Mintage	F	VF	XF	Unc	BU
2002	5,000	—	—	—	22.50	25.00

KM# 44 DOLLAR
28.2800 g., Gold Plated Copper-Nickel, 38.6 mm.
Ruler: Elizabeth II **Subject:** Golden Jubilee Monarchs
Obv: Head with tiara right **Obv. Designer:** Ian Rank-Broadley
Rev: George III (1760-1820) **Edge:** Reeded

Date	Mintage	F	VF	XF	Unc	BU
2002	5,000	—	—	—	22.50	25.00

KM# 46 DOLLAR
28.2800 g., Gold Plated Copper-Nickel, 38.6 mm.
Ruler: Elizabeth II **Subject:** Golden Jubilee Monarchs
Obv: Head with tiara right **Obv. Designer:** Ian Rank-Broadley
Rev: Queen Victoria (1837-1901) **Edge:** Reeded

Date	Mintage	F	VF	XF	Unc	BU
2002	5,000	—	—	—	22.50	25.00

KM# 48 DOLLAR
28.2800 g., Gold Plated Copper-Nickel, 38.6 mm.
Ruler: Elizabeth II **Subject:** Golden Jubilee Monarchs
Obv: Head with tiara right **Obv. Designer:** Ian Rank-Broadley
Rev: Queen Elizabeth II (1952-) **Edge:** Reeded

Date	Mintage	F	VF	XF	Unc	BU
2002	5,000	—	—	—	22.50	25.00

KM# 51 2 DOLLARS
56.5600 g., Gold Plated Copper-Nickel, 38.6 mm.
Ruler: Elizabeth II **Subject:** British Military Leaders **Obv:** Head with tiara right **Obv. Designer:** Ian Rank-Broadley
Rev: Wellington's portrait and battle scene **Edge:** Reeded

Date	Mintage	F	VF	XF	Unc	BU
2002 Proof	10,000	Value: 45.00				

KM# 54 2 DOLLARS
56.5600 g., Gold Plated Copper-Nickel, 38.6 mm.
Ruler: Elizabeth II **Subject:** British Military Leaders **Obv:** Head with tiara right **Obv. Designer:** Ian Rank-Broadley **Rev:** Admiral Nelson's portrait and naval battle scene **Edge:** Reeded

Date	Mintage	F	VF	XF	Unc	BU
2003 Proof	10,000	Value: 45.00				

KM# 57 2 DOLLARS
56.5600 g., Gold Plated Copper-Nickel, 38.6 mm.
Ruler: Elizabeth II **Subject:** British Military Leaders **Obv:** Head with tiara right **Obv. Designer:** Ian Rank-Broadley
Rev: Churchill's portrait and air battle scene **Edge:** Reeded

Date	Mintage	F	VF	XF	Unc	BU
2003 Proof	10,000	Value: 45.00				

KM# 41a 10 DOLLARS
39.9400 g., 0.9166 Gold 1.177 oz. AGW, 38.6 mm.
Ruler: Elizabeth II **Subject:** Golden Jubilee Monarchs
Obv: Head with tiara right **Obv. Designer:** Ian Rank-Broadley
Rev: Henry III (1216-1272) **Edge:** Reeded

Date	Mintage	F	VF	XF	Unc	BU
2002 Proof	100	Value: 1,100				

KM# 43a 10 DOLLARS
39.9400 g., 0.9166 Gold 1.177 oz. AGW, 38.6 mm.
Ruler: Elizabeth II **Subject:** Golden Jubilee Monarchs
Obv: Head with tiara right **Obv. Designer:** Ian Rank-Broadley
Rev: Edward III (1327-1377) **Edge:** Reeded

Date	Mintage	F	VF	XF	Unc	BU
2002 Proof	100	Value: 1,100				

KM# 45a 10 DOLLARS
39.9400 g., 0.9166 Gold 1.177 oz. AGW, 38.6 mm.
Ruler: Elizabeth II **Subject:** Golden Jubilee Monarchs
Obv: Head with tiara right **Obv. Designer:** Ian Rank-Broadley
Rev: George III (1760-1820) **Edge:** Reeded

Date	Mintage	F	VF	XF	Unc	BU
2002 Proof	100	Value: 1,100				

KM# 47 10 DOLLARS
28.2800 g., 0.9250 Silver With Partial Gold Plating 0.841 oz., 38.6 mm. **Ruler:** Elizabeth II **Subject:** Golden Jubilee Monarchs **Obv:** Head with tiara right **Obv. Designer:** Ian Rank-Broadley
Rev: Queen Victoria (1837-1901) **Edge:** Reeded

Date	Mintage	F	VF	XF	Unc	BU
2002 Proof	10,000	Value: 65.00				

KM# 47a 10 DOLLARS
39.9400 g., 0.9166 Gold 1.177 oz. AGW, 38.6 mm.
Ruler: Elizabeth II **Subject:** Golden Jubilee Monarchs
Obv: Head with tiara right **Obv. Designer:** Ian Rank-Broadley
Rev: Queen Victoria (1837-1901) **Edge:** Reeded

Date	Mintage	F	VF	XF	Unc	BU
2002 Proof	100	Value: 1,100				

KM# 49a 10 DOLLARS
39.9400 g., 0.9166 Gold 1.177 oz. AGW, 38.6 mm.
Ruler: Elizabeth II **Subject:** Golden Jubilee Monarchs
Obv: Head with tiara right **Obv. Designer:** Ian Rank-Broadley
Rev: Queen Elizabeth II (1952-) **Edge:** Reeded

Date	Mintage	F	VF	XF	Unc	BU
2002 Proof	100	Value: 1,100				

KM# 31 2000 CENTS (20 Dollars)
7.9800 g., 0.9170 Gold .2353 oz. AGW **Ruler:** Elizabeth II
Series: Millennium **Subject:** British Royal Mint **Obv:** Young bust right **Rev:** Ship, palm trees and radiant sun within circle divided by words "millennium", denomination below **Edge:** Reeded
Note: Prev. KM#22.

Date	Mintage	F	VF	XF	Unc	BU
2000	—	—	—	—	165	185

KM# 26 100 DOLLARS
15.9760 g., 0.9170 Gold .4708 oz. AGW **Ruler:** Elizabeth II
Subject: 10th Anniversary of Central Bank **Obv:** Bank building, dates below **Rev:** Bust facing, denomination below **Note:** Prev. KM#17.

Date	Mintage	F	VF	XF	Unc	BU
1993 Proof	150	Value: 525				

KM# 29 100 DOLLARS
15.9760 g., 0.9170 Gold .4708 oz. AGW **Ruler:** Elizabeth II
Subject: 50th Anniversary - University of West Indies **Obv:** Bust facing, denomination below **Rev:** University arms, pelican above, dates below **Note:** Prev. KM#20.

Date	Mintage	F	VF	XF	Unc	BU
ND(1999) Proof	300	Value: 535				

KM# 21 500 DOLLARS
15.9800 g., 0.9170 Gold .4712 oz. AGW **Ruler:** Elizabeth II
Series: International Year of Disabled Persons **Obv:** Young bust right **Rev:** Two figures raising center figure, denomination above, date at right **Note:** Prev. KM#12.

Date	Mintage	F	VF	XF	Unc	BU
1981	—	—	—	—	500	525
1981 Proof	—	Value: 750				

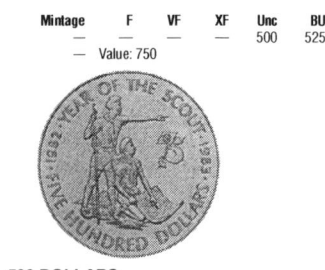

KM# 18 500 DOLLARS
15.9800 g., 0.9170 Gold .4712 oz. AGW **Ruler:** Elizabeth II
Series: International Year of the Scout **Obv:** Queens portrait
Rev: One scout standing, pointing; one scout kneeling with map, denomination below, date at right **Note:** Prev. KM#9.

Date	Mintage	F	VF	XF	Unc	BU
ND(1983)	2,000	—	—	—	375	425
ND(1983) Proof	2,000	Value: 550				

PIEFORTS

KM#	Date	Mintage	Identification	Mkt Val
P2	1981	—	500 Dollars. Gold. KM#21.	1,600

ECUADOR

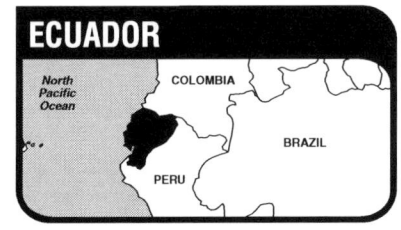

The Republic of Ecuador, located astride the equator on the Pacific Coast of South America, has an area of 105,037 sq. mi. (283,560 sq. km.) and a population of 10.9 million. Capital: Quito. Agriculture is the mainstay of the economy but there are appreciable deposits of minerals and petroleum. It is one of the world's largest exporters of bananas and balsa wood. Coffee, cacao, sugar and petroleum are also valuable exports.

Ecuador was first sighted in 1526 by Francisco Pizarro. Conquest was undertaken by Sebastian de Benalcazar, who founded Quito in 1534. Ecuador was part of the Viceroyalty of New Granada through the 16th and 17th centuries. After previous attempts to attain independence were crushed, Antonio Sucre, the able lieutenant of Bolivar, secured Ecuador's freedom in the Battle of Pinchincha, May 24, 1822. It then joined Venezuela and Colombia in a confederation known as Gran Colombia, and became an independent republic when it left the confederacy in 1830.

MINT MARKS
BIRMm - Birmingham, Heaton
Birmingham - Birmingham
QUITO – Quito

ASSAYERS' INITIALS

Initial	Name
FP	Feliciano Paredes
GJ	Guillermo Jameson
MV	Miguel Vergara
ST	Santiago Taylor

MONETARY SYSTEM
16 Reales = 1 Escudo

REPUBLIC
GENERAL COINAGE

KM# 15 ESCUDO
3.3000 g., 0.8750 Gold .0928 oz. AGW **Obv:** Head left **Rev:** Sun with face above volcanic mountains

Date	Mintage	VG	F	VF	XF	Unc
1828	—					

Note: 1828-dated coins are considered contemporary counterfeits

1833 GJ	—	200	425	850	1,650	—
1834 GJ	—	125	285	400	750	—
1835 GJ	—	220	450	900	1,850	—
1845 GJ	—	—	—	—	—	—

Note: 1845-dated coins are suspicious

KM# 16 2 ESCUDOS (Double)
6.7666 g., 0.8750 Gold .1903 oz. AGW **Obv:** Head left **Rev:** Sun with face above volcanic mountains divides denomination

Date	Mintage	VG	F	VF	XF	Unc
1833 GJ Rare	—	—	—	—	—	—
1834 GJ	—	550	950	1,650	—	—
1835 GJ	—	265	450	750	1,600	—
1835 FP 3 known	—	—	—	—	—	—

KM# 19 4 ESCUDOS
13.5000 g., 0.8750 Gold .3798 oz. AGW **Obv:** Sun face on banner above volcanic mountains **Rev:** Head left
Note: Engraver's initial A in front drape of bust.

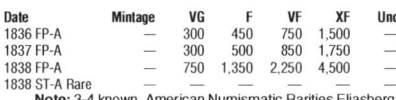

Date	Mintage	VG	F	VF	XF	Unc
1836 FP-A	—	300	450	750	1,500	—
1837 FP-A	—	300	500	850	1,750	—
1838 FP-A	—	750	1,350	2,250	4,500	—
1838 ST-A Rare						

Note: 3-4 known. American Numismatic Rarities Eliasberg sale 4-05, AU-55 realized $63,250.

| 1838 MV-A | — | 500 | 1,000 | 1,500 | 3,000 | — |
| 1839 MV-A | — | 375 | 750 | 1,150 | 2,500 | — |

Note: American Numismatic Rarities Eliasberg sale 4-05, MS-64 realized $9775

| 1841 MV-A | — | — | — | 7,000 | — | — |

Note: 2 known

KM# 23.1 8 ESCUDOS
27.0640 g., 0.8750 Gold .7614 oz. AGW **Obv:** Sun face on banner above volcanic mountains **Rev:** Head left
Note: Engraver's initial A in front drape of bust.

Date	Mintage	VG	F	VF	XF	Unc
1838 ST-A	—	900	1,750	3,750	8,000	—

Note: American Numismatic Rarities Eliasberg sale 4-05, AU-55 realized $39,100

| 1838 MV-A | — | 1,250 | 2,750 | 5,500 | — | — |

Note: American Numismatic Rarities Eliasberg sale 4-05, EF-40 realized $27,600

| 1839 MV-A | — | 800 | 1,500 | 3,500 | 7,500 | — |

Note: American Numismatic Rarities Eliasberg sale 4-05, MS-62 realized $27,600

| 1840 MV-A | — | 700 | 1,200 | 3,000 | 7,000 | — |

Note: American Numismatic Rarities Eliasberg sale 4-06, AU-55 realized $14,950

| 1841 MV-A | — | 650 | 1,100 | 2,500 | 6,500 | — |

KM# 23.2 8 ESCUDOS
0.8750 Gold **Obv:** Sun face on banner above volcanic mountains **Rev:** Head left **Note:** Reduced size. Engraver's initial S sideways in back drape of bust.

Date	Mintage	VG	F	VF	XF	Unc
1841 MV-S	—	1,000	2,250	4,000	9,500	—
1842 MV-S	—	700	1,250	3,000	7,000	—
1843 MV-S	—	700	1,250	3,250	7,500	—

Note: Heritage Whittier sale 6-06, MS-62 realized $16,100. American Numismatic Rarities Eliasberg sale 4-05, MS-62 realized $9200

KM# 28 8 ESCUDOS
0.8750 Gold **Obv:** Flag-draped arms with cannons **Rev:** Head right

Date	Mintage	VG	F	VF	XF	Unc
1844 MV Rare						

Note: Stack's Hammel sale 9-82 VF/G 1844 MV realized # $32,000

| 1845 MV Rare | — | — | — | — | — | — |

KM# 30 8 ESCUDOS
0.8750 Gold **Obv:** Flag-draped arms with cannons, flagpoles extend below arms **Rev:** Head left

Date	Mintage	VG	F	VF	XF	Unc
1845 MV	—	5,000	7,000	10,000	20,000	—

Note: American Numismatic Rarities Eliasberg sale 4-05, AU-53 realized $74,750

KM# 31 8 ESCUDOS
0.8750 Gold **Obv:** Flag-draped arms with cannons **Rev:** Head left

Date	Mintage	VG	F	VF	XF	Unc
1845 MV	—	5,000	7,000	10,000	20,000	—

KM# 34.1 8 ESCUDOS
0.8750 Gold **Obv:** Flag-draped arms **Rev:** Larger bust left

Date	Mintage	VG	F	VF	XF	Unc
1847 GJ Rare	—	—	—	—	—	—

Note: American Numismatic Rarities Eliasberg sale 4-06, EF-45 realized $32,200

| 1848 GJ Rare | | | | | | |

Note: American Numismatic Rarities Eliasberg sale 4-06, EF-45 realized $25,300

| 1849/7 GJ Rare | | | | | | |

Note: American Numismatic Rarities Eliasberg sale 4-06, AU-53 realized $52,900. Smith & Daughter sale No. 2 9-96 choice AU 1849/7 GJ realized $23,000

1850 GJ Rare	—	—	—	—	—	—
1852/0 GJ	—	—	1,250	2,000	3,500	—
1854 GJ	—	—	1,500	2,500	4,500	—
1855/2 GJ	—	—	1,250	2,000	3,500	—
1855 GJ	—	—	1,500	2,500	4,500	—

190 ECUADOR

KM# 34.2 8 ESCUDOS
0.8750 Gold **Obv:** Flag-draped arms **Rev:** Larger bust left with revised hairstyle

Date	Mintage	VG	F	VF	XF	Unc
1856 GJ Rare	—	—	—	—	—	—

Note: American Numismatic Rarities Eliasberg sale 4-06, AU-55 realized $17,250

DECIMAL COINAGE
10 Centavos = 1 Decimo; 10 Decimos = 1 Sucre; 25 Sucres = 1 Condor

KM# 111 SUCRE (Un)
31.1000 g., 0.9000 Gold 0.8999 oz. AGW, 40 mm. **Subject:** Central Bank's 70th Anniversary **Obv:** Partial view of bank building **Rev:** Coin designs of 1 escudo KM-15 **Edge:** Reeded

Date	Mintage	F	VF	XF	Unc	BU
ND (1997) Proof	2,000	Value: 665				

KM# 56 10 SUCRES (Diez)
8.1360 g., 0.9000 Gold .2354 oz. AGW **Obv:** Head of Sucre left **Rev:** Flag-draped arms **Note:** Most KM#56 mintages are held in reserve in the Banco Central del Ecuador vaults.

Date	Mintage	VG	F	VF	XF	Unc
1899Birmingham JM	50,000	—	—	BV	175	350
1900Birmingham JM	50,000	—	—	BV	175	350

KM# 74 CONDOR (Un)
8.3592 g., 0.9000 Gold .2419 oz. AGW **Obv:** Head of Bolivar left, date below **Rev:** Flag draped arms, denomination above **Note:** 5,000 were released into circulation; the remainder are held as the Central Bank gold reserve.

Date	Mintage	F	VF	XF	Unc	BU
1928Birmingham	20,000	BV	170	200	350	425

PATTERNS
Including off metal strikes

KM#	Date	Mintage	Identification	Mkt Val
Pn10	1862 GJ	—	50 Francos. 0.9000 Gold. Flag-draped arms. Head right.	—

EGYPT

The Arab Republic of Egypt, located on the northeastern corner of Africa, has an area of 385,229 sq. mi. (1,1001,450 sq. km.) and a population of 62.4 million. Capital: Cairo. Although Egypt is an almost rainless expanse of desert, its economy is predominantly agricultural. Cotton, rice and petroleum are exported. Other main sources of income are revenues from the Suez Canal, remittances of Egyptian workers abroad and tourism.

Egyptian history dates back to about 3000 B.C. when the empire was established by uniting the upper and lower kingdoms. Following its 'Golden Age' (16th to 13th centuries B.C.), Egypt was conquered by Persia (525 B.C.) and Alexander the Great (332 B.C.). The Ptolemies, descended from one of Alexander's generals, ruled until the suicide of Cleopatra (30 B.C.) when Egypt became the private domain of the Roman emperor, and subsequently part of the Byzantine world. Various Muslim dynasties ruled Egypt from 641 on, including Ayyubid Sultans to 1250 and Mamluks to 1517, when it was conquered by the Ottoman Turks, interrupted by the occupation of Napoleon (1798-1801). A semi-independent dynasty was founded by Muhammad Ali in 1805 which lasted until 1952. Turkish rule became increasingly casual, permitting Great Britain to inject its influence by purchasing shares in the Suez Canal. British troops occupied Egypt in 1882, becoming the de facto rulers. On Dec. 14, 1914, Egypt was made a protectorate of Britain. British occupation ended on Feb. 28, 1922, when Egypt became a sovereign, independent kingdom. The monarchy was abolished and a republic proclaimed on June 18, 1953.

On Feb. 1, 1958, Egypt and Syria formed the United Arab Republic. Yemen joined on March 8 in an association known as the United Arab States. Syria withdrew from the United Arab Republic on Sept. 29, 1961, and on Dec. 26 Egypt dissolved its ties with Yemen in the United Arab States. On Sept. 2, 1971, Egypt finally shed the name United Arab Republic in favor of the Arab Republic of Egypt.

RULERS
British, 1882-1922
Kingdom, 1922-1953
  Ahmed Fuad I, 1922-1936
  Farouk, 1936-1952
  Fuad II, 1952-1953
Republic, 1953-

MONETARY SYSTEM
(1885-1916)
10 Ushr-al-Qirsh = 1 Piastre
(Commencing 1916)
10 Milliemes = 1 Piastre (Qirsh)
100 Piastres = 1 Pound (Gunayh)

MINT MARKS
Egyptian coins issued prior to the advent of the British Protectorate series of Sultan Hussein Kamil introduced in 1916 were very similar to Turkish coins of the same period. They can best be distinguished by the presence of the Arabic word *Misr* Egypt) on the reverse, which generally appears immediately above the Muslim accession date of the ruler, which is presented in Arabic numerals. Each coin is individually dated according to the regnal years.
BP - Budapest, Hungary
H - Birmingham, England
KN - King's Norton, England

ENGRAVER
W - Emil Weigand, Berlin

INITIAL LETTERS
Letters, symbols and numerals were placed on coins during the reigns of Mustafa II (1695) until Selim III (1789). They have been observed in various positions but the most common position being over *bin* in the third row of the obverse. In Egypt these letters and others used on the Paras (Medins) above the word *duribe* on the reverse during this period.

REGNAL YEAR IDENTIFICATION

4
Duriba fi

Misr   Accession Date

DENOMINATIONS

Para   Qirsh

NOTE: The unit of value on coins of this period is generally presented on the obverse immediately below the toughra, as shown in the illustrations above.

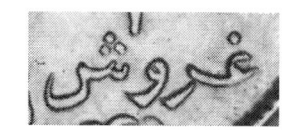

Milliemes   *Piastres* 1916-1933

Piastres 1934 –

TITLES

al-Mamlaka   al-Misriya
(The Kingdom of Egypt)

U.A.R. EGYPT

The legend illustrated is *Jumhuriyat Misr al-Arabiyya* which translates to 'The Arab Republic of Egypt'. Similar legends are found on the modern issues of Syria.

OTTOMAN EMPIRE
1595 - 1914AD

Selim III
Second Reign AH1216-1222/1801-1807AD

HAMMERED COINAGE

KM# 140 1/2 ZERI MAHBUB
Gold **Obv:** Toughra **Rev:** Legend **Note:** Weight varies: .95-1.30 grams.

EGYPT

Date	Mintage	VG	F	VF	XF	Unc
AH1203//20	—	50.00	100	200	400	—
AH1203//21	—	50.00	100	200	400	—

KM# 141 ZERI MAHBUB
Gold **Obv:** Toughra **Rev:** Legend **Note:** Weight varies: 2.50-2.60 grams.

Date	Mintage	VG	F	VF	XF	Unc
AH1203//15	—	70.00	120	200	275	—
AH1203//16	—	70.00	120	200	275	—

FRENCH OCCUPATION
AH1212-1216 / 1798-1801AD

OCCUPATION COINAGE

KM# 150 1/4 ZERI MAHBUB
0.6480 g., 0.6850 Gold .0143 oz. AGW, 17 mm. **Obv:** Toughra **Rev:** Legend **Note:** Initial letter was for Bonaparte

Date	Mintage	VG	F	VF	XF	Unc
AH1203//14						

KM# 151 1/2 ZERI MAHBUB
1.2960 g., 0.6850 Gold .0285 oz. AGW, 19 mm. **Obv:** Toughra **Rev:** Legend **Note:** Initial letter was for Bonaparte

Date	Mintage	VG	F	VF	XF	Unc
AH1203//14	—	800	1,000	1,200	1,500	—

KM# 152 ZERI MAHBUB
2.5920 g., 0.6850 Gold .0570 oz. AGW **Obv:** Toughra **Rev:** Legend **Note:** Initial letter was for Bonaparte

Date	Mintage	VG	F	VF	XF	Unc
AH1203//14	—	200	300	450	600	—
AH1203//15	—	200	300	450	600	—

KM# 153 2 ZERI MAHBUB
Gold, 35 mm. **Note:** Weight varies: 4.76-5.00 grams.

Date	Mintage	VG	F	VF	XF	Unc
AH1203//14	—	200	300	500	900	—

KM# 154 3 ZERI MAHBUB
7.7000 g., Gold, 35 mm.

Date	Mintage	VG	F	VF	XF	Unc
AH1203//14	—	350	500	1,000	1,500	—

OTTOMAN EMPIRE
Resumed

Mustafa IV
AH1222-1223/1807-1808AD

HAMMERED COINAGE

KM# 158 1/2 ZERI MAHBUB
1.6500 g., Gold, 20 mm. **Obv:** Tughra **Rev:** Legend

Date	Mintage	VG	F	VF	XF	Unc
AH1222//1 (1807)	—	350	500	800	1,350	—

KM# 159 ZERI MAHBUB
2.3000 g., Gold **Obv:** Tughra **Rev:** Legend

Date	Mintage	VG	F	VF	XF	Unc
AH1222//1 (1807)	—	275	400	700	1,100	—

KM# 160 2 ZERI MAHBUB
4.7000 g., Gold, 32 mm. **Obv:** Tughra **Rev:** Legend

Date	Mintage	VG	F	VF	XF	Unc
AH1222//1 (1807)	—	400	600	900	1,550	—

Mahmud II
AH1223-1255/1808-1839AD

PRE-REFORM COINAGE
Prior to AH1251 (1834AD)

The basic unit was the 'Mahbub' or 'Zer Mahbub' (Zer = Gold), which weighed approximately 2.35 g from AH1223 until 1247 (Yr. 15), when it was reduced to about 1.6 g. Fractional denominations were Halves (Nisfiya) and Quarters (Rubiya). The value of the Mahbub in terms of silver Piastres fluctuated according to the relative value of gold and silver, and the price of debased Egyptian silver coin.

KM# 194 1/2 ZERI MAHBUB (Nisfiya)
0.8750 Gold **Obv:** Tughra, text **Rev:** Legend **Note:** Weight varies: 1.15-1.20 grams. Size varies: 19-20 millimeters.

Date	Mintage	VG	F	VF	XF	Unc
AH1223//1 (1808)	—	75.00	135	350	650	—
AH1223//5 (1812)	—	75.00	135	350	650	—
AH1223//8 (1814)	—	75.00	135	350	650	—

KM# 195 1/2 ZERI MAHBUB (Khayriya)
0.8750 Gold, 16 mm. **Obv:** Tughra within center circle **Rev:** Text within center circle **Note:** Weight varies: 0.70-0.80 grams.

Date	Mintage	VG	F	VF	XF	Unc
AH1223//21 (1827)	—	25.00	35.00	75.00	150	—
AH1223//22 (1828)	—	25.00	35.00	65.00	125	—
AH1223//23 (1829)	—	25.00	35.00	65.00	125	—
AH1223//24 (1830)	—	25.00	35.00	65.00	125	—
AH1223//25 (1831)	—	25.00	35.00	65.00	125	—
AH1223//26 (1832)	—	25.00	35.00	75.00	150	—
AH1223//27 (1833)	—	30.00	40.00	100	200	—
AH1223//28 (1834)	—	40.00	50.00	125	250	—

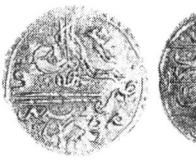

KM# 197 ZERI MAHBUB (Altin)
0.8750 Gold **Obv:** Tughra, text **Rev:** Legend **Note:** Crude flan. Weight varies: 2.19-2.38 grams. Size varies: 23-26 millimeters.

Date	Mintage	VG	F	VF	XF	Unc
AH1223//1 (1808)	—	90.00	175	350	600	—
AH1223//1 (1808)	—	—	—	—	—	—
Note: Dot right of toughra						
AH1223//2 (1809)	—	100	200	400	750	—
AH1223//3 (1810)	—	90.00	175	350	600	—
AH1223//5 (1812)	—	90.00	175	350	600	—
AH1223//7 (1813)	—	150	250	425	800	—
AH1223//8 (1814)	—	150	250	425	800	—
AH1223//10 (1816)	—	150	250	425	800	—
Note: Dot next to toughra						
AH1223//10 (1816)	—	180	300	425	800	—

Date	Mintage	VG	F	VF	XF	Unc
Note: Rose branch next to toughra						
AH1223//11 (1817)	—	90.00	175	350	600	—
AH1223//12 (1818)	—	—	—	—	—	—
Note: Rose branch right of toughra						
AH1223//13 (1819)	—	150	250	350	600	—
AH1223//14 (1820)	—	90.00	175	350	600	—

KM# 199 ZERI MAHBUB (Altin)
0.8750 Gold **Note:** Without "Azza Nashruhu".

Date	Mintage	VG	F	VF	XF	Unc
AH1223//5 (1812)	—	100	200	375	700	—

KM# 198 ZERI MAHBUB (Altin)
2.3500 g., 0.8750 Gold, 23 mm. **Note:** Thicker and well-shaped flan.

Date	Mintage	VG	F	VF	XF	Unc
AH1223//15 (1821)	—	120	220	425	1,000	—

KM# 189 1/4 MAHBUB (Rubiya)
0.8750 Gold **Obv:** Tughra **Rev:** Legend. Legend: "Azze Nashruhu Duribe Fi..." **Note:** Plain borders of dots. Weight varies: 0.35-0.60 grams. Size varies: 13-14mm.

Date	Mintage	VG	F	VF	XF	Unc
AH1223 (1808)	—	150	225	300	450	—

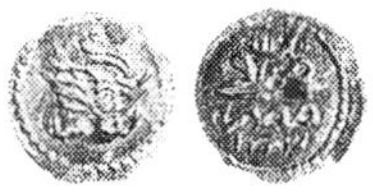

KM# 190 1/4 MAHBUB (Rubiya)
0.8750 Gold **Obv:** Tughra **Rev:** Legend

Date	Mintage	VG	F	VF	XF	Unc
AH1223//7 (1813)	—	35.00	55.00	85.00	110	—
AH1223//8 (1814)	—	35.00	55.00	85.00	110	—
AH1223//9 (1815)	—	35.00	55.00	85.00	110	—
AH1223//10 (1816)	—	35.00	55.00	85.00	110	—
AH1223//11 (1817)	—	35.00	55.00	85.00	110	—
AH1223//12 (1818)	—	35.00	55.00	85.00	110	—
AH1223//13 (1819)	—	35.00	55.00	85.00	110	—
AH1223//14 (1820)	—	35.00	55.00	85.00	110	—

KM# 191 1/4 MAHBUB (Rubiya)
0.8750 Gold **Obv:** Tughra **Rev:** Legend **Note:** Plain border of dots. Weight varies: 0.35-0.40 grams. Size varies: 12-13 millimeters.

Date	Mintage	VG	F	VF	XF	Unc
AH1223//15 (1821)	—	25.00	40.00	60.00	85.00	—
AH1223//16 (1822)	—	17.50	27.50	45.00	65.00	—
AH1223//17 (1823)	—	25.00	40.00	60.00	85.00	—
AH1223//18 (1824)	—	17.50	27.50	45.00	65.00	—
AH1223//19 (1825)	—	20.00	35.00	55.00	80.00	—
AH1223//20 (1826)	—	20.00	35.00	55.00	80.00	—
AH1223//21 (1827)	—	20.00	35.00	55.00	80.00	—

KM# 192 1/4 MAHBUB (Saadiya)
0.8750 Gold **Note:** Ornamental borders.

Date	Mintage	VG	F	VF	XF	Unc
AH1223//19 (1825)	—	30.00	50.00	65.00	75.00	—
AH1223//22 (1828)	—	40.00	65.00	90.00	115	—
AH1223//21 (1827)	—	60.00	90.00	115	140	—

KM# 201 1/4 MAHBUB (Coyrek Rumi)
0.8750 Gold **Note:** Different design and without year.

Date	Mintage	VG	F	VF	XF	Unc
AH1223 (1808)	—	—	—	—	—	—

KM# 193 1/4 MAHBUB (Coyrek Rumi)
0.8750 Gold **Obv:** Tughra within center circle, design surrounds **Rev:** Legend within center circle, design surrounds **Note:** Vine-like borders.

Date	Mintage	VG	F	VF	XF	Unc
AH1223//21 (1827)	—	25.00	35.00	50.00	100	—
AH1223//22 (1828)	—	25.00	35.00	50.00	100	—
AH1223//23 (1829)	—	25.00	35.00	50.00	100	—
AH1223//24 (1830)	—	25.00	35.00	50.00	100	—
AH1223//25 (1831)	—	25.00	35.00	50.00	100	—
AH1223//26 (1832)	—	20.00	30.00	40.00	90.00	—
AH1223//27 (1833)	—	30.00	40.00	70.00	150	—
AH1223//28 (1834)	—	100	175	275	375	—

192 EGYPT

KM# 200 2 ZERI MAHBUB
0.8750 Gold, 28 mm. **Obv:** Tughra at center of multiple beaded circles **Rev:** Legend at center of multiple beaded circles **Note:** Weight varies: 3.25-3.60 grams.

Date	Mintage	VG	F	VF	XF	Unc
AH1223//5 (1812)	—	300	500	850	1,750	—

Note: The above piece may be a medal, token or jewelry piece

KM# 202 TEK RUMI
2.3500 g., 0.8750 Gold, 23 mm. **Obv:** Tughra within center circle, design surrounds **Rev:** Legend within center circle, design surrounds

Date	Mintage	VG	F	VF	XF	Unc
AH1223//11 (1817) Rare	—	—	—	—	—	—

KM# 203 CHIFTE RUMI
3.6000 g., 0.8750 Gold, 28 mm. **Obv:** Tughra within center circle, design surrounds **Rev:** Legend within center circle, design surrounds

Date	Mintage	VG	F	VF	XF	Unc
AH1223//5 (1812) Rare	—	—	—	—	—	—

REFORM COINAGE

KM# 210 5 QIRSH
0.8750 Gold **Obv:** Tughra **Rev:** Legend **Note:** Weight varies: 0.30-0.35 grams.

Date	Mintage	VG	F	VF	XF	Unc
AH1223//28 (1834)	—	80.00	135	210	320	—
AH1223//29 (1835)	—	60.00	90.00	135	225	—

KM# 211 5 QIRSH
0.4200 g., 0.8750 Gold **Obv:** Without value below toughra **Rev:** Legend

Date	Mintage	VG	F	VF	XF	Unc
AH1223//29 (1835)	—	50.00	90.00	135	225	—

KM# 212 5 QIRSH
0.4200 g., 0.8750 Gold **Obv:** Denomination added below toughra **Rev:** Legend

Date	Mintage	VG	F	VF	XF	Unc
AH1223//29 (1835)	—	50.00	90.00	135	185	—
AH1223//30 (1836)	—	50.00	90.00	135	185	—
AH1223//31 (1837)	—	50.00	90.00	135	185	—
AH1223//32 (1838)	—	50.00	90.00	135	185	—

KM# 213 10 QIRSH
0.8750 Gold **Obv:** Tughra within wreath **Rev:** Legend within wreath **Note:** Weight varies: 0.70-0.75 grams.

Date	Mintage	VG	F	VF	XF	Unc
AH1223//28 (1834)	—	35.00	60.00	125	200	—
AH1223//29 (1835)	—	35.00	60.00	125	200	—

KM# 214 10 QIRSH
0.8500 g., 0.8750 Gold, 15 mm. **Obv:** Denomination beneath toughra **Rev:** Legend

Date	Mintage	VG	F	VF	XF	Unc
AH1223//29 (1835)	—	50.00	90.00	180	325	—
AH1223//30 (1836)	—	50.00	90.00	180	325	—
AH1223//32 (1838)	—	50.00	90.00	180	325	—

KM# 215 20 QIRSH
1.7000 g., 0.8750 Gold, 18 mm. **Obv:** Tughra **Rev:** Legend

Date	Mintage	VG	F	VF	XF	Unc
AH1223//29 (1835)	—	50.00	90.00	135	285	—
AH1223//30 (1836)	—	50.00	90.00	135	285	—
AH1223//31 (1837)	—	50.00	90.00	135	285	—
AH1223//32 (1838)	—	50.00	90.00	135	285	—

KM# 216 20 QIRSH
1.7000 g., 0.8750 Gold **Obv:** Four roses around edge **Rev:** Four roses around edge

Date	Mintage	VG	F	VF	XF	Unc
AH1223//32 (1838)	—	70.00	120	185	375	—

KM# 217 100 QIRSH (Pound)
8.4000 g., 0.8750 Gold, 22 mm.

Date	Mintage	VG	F	VF	XF	Unc
AH1223//30 (1836)	—	750	1,000	2,000	3,000	—
AH1223//31 (1837)	—	750	1,000	2,000	3,000	—

Abdul Mejid
AH1255-1277/1839-1861AD
REFORM COINAGE

KM# 230 5 QIRSH
0.4270 g., 0.8750 Gold **Obv:** Tughra, rose at right **Rev:** Legend

Date	Mintage	VG	F	VF	XF	Unc
AH1255//1 (1839)	—	16.50	28.00	40.00	75.00	—
AH1255//2 (1840)	—	16.50	28.00	40.00	75.00	—
AH1255//3 (1841)	—	16.50	28.00	40.00	75.00	—
AH1255//4 (1842)	—	16.50	28.00	40.00	75.00	—
AH1255//5 (1843)	—	16.50	28.00	40.00	75.00	—
AH1255//6 (1844)	—	16.50	28.00	40.00	75.00	—
AH1255//7 (1845)	—	16.50	28.00	40.00	75.00	—
AH1255//8 (1845)	—	16.50	28.00	40.00	75.00	—
AH1255//9 (1846)	—	16.50	28.00	40.00	75.00	—
AH1255//10 (1847)	—	16.50	28.00	40.00	75.00	—
AH1255//11 (1848)	—	16.50	28.00	40.00	75.00	—
AH1255//12 (1849)	—	16.50	28.00	40.00	75.00	—
AH1255//13 (1850)	—	20.00	35.00	55.00	120	—
AH1255//14 (1851)	—	16.50	28.00	40.00	75.00	—
AH1255//15 (1852)	—	16.50	28.00	40.00	75.00	—
AH1255//16 (1853)	—	16.50	28.00	40.00	75.00	—
AH1255//18 (1855)	—	16.50	28.00	40.00	75.00	—
AH1255//19 (1856)	—	16.50	28.00	40.00	75.00	—
AH1255//20 (1857)	—	16.50	28.00	40.00	75.00	—
AH1255//22 (1859)	—	16.50	28.00	40.00	75.00	—
AH1255//23 (1860)	—	16.50	28.00	40.00	75.00	—

KM# 231a 10 QIRSH
0.8400 g., 0.8750 Gold .0236 oz. AGW, 15 mm.

Date	Mintage	VG	F	VF	XF	Unc
AH1255//1 (1839)	—	—	—	—	—	—

KM# 233 20 QIRSH
1.7100 g., 0.8750 Gold .0481 oz. AGW **Obv:** Tughra, rose at right **Rev:** Legend

Date	Mintage	VG	F	VF	XF	Unc
AH1255//1 (1839)	—	400	650	1,250	1,800	—

KM# 234.1 50 QIRSH (1/2 Pound)
4.2720 g., 0.8750 Gold .1202 oz. AGW **Obv:** Tughra, rose at right **Rev:** Legend **Note:** Beaded border.

Date	Mintage	VG	F	VF	XF	Unc
AH1255//1 (1839)	550	185	285	550	750	—
AH1255//2 (1840)	—	95.00	145	300	475	—
AH1255//3 (1841)	—	90.00	125	250	385	—
AH1255//4 (1842)	—	85.00	110	200	300	—
AH1255//5 (1843)	—	85.00	110	200	300	—

KM# 234.2 50 QIRSH (1/2 Pound)
4.2720 g., 0.8750 Gold .1202 oz. AGW **Obv:** Tughra, rose at right **Rev:** Legend **Note:** Toothed border.

Date	Mintage	VG	F	VF	XF	Unc
AH1255//6 (1844)	—	85.00	125	225	375	—
AH1255//7 (1845)	—	85.00	135	275	450	—
AH1255//8 (1845)	—	85.00	135	275	450	—
AH1255//9 (1846)	—	85.00	135	275	450	—
AH1255//11 (1848)	—	85.00	135	275	450	—
AH1255//15 (1852)	—	BV	85.00	145	250	—
AH1255//16 (1853)	—	85.00	110	180	275	—

KM# 235.1 100 QIRSH (Pound)
8.5440 g., 0.8750 Gold .2404 oz. AGW **Obv:** Tughra, rose at right **Rev:** Legend **Note:** Beaded border.

Date	Mintage	VG	F	VF	XF	Unc
AH1255//1 (1839)	—	BV	175	265	450	—
AH1255//2 (1840)	—	BV	155	225	425	—

Note: For crude copy of regnal year 2 see Sudan KM#3

AH1255//3 (1841)	—	—	BV	200	400	—
AH1255//4 (1842)	—	—	BV	185	375	—
AH1255//5 (1843)	—	—	BV	185	375	—

KM# 235.2 100 QIRSH (Pound)
8.5440 g., 0.8750 Gold .2404 oz. AGW **Obv:** Tughra, rose at right **Rev:** Legend **Note:** Toothed border.

Date	Mintage	VG	F	VF	XF	Unc
AH1255//6 (1844)	—	—	—	BV	250	—
AH1255//7 (1845)	—	—	BV	160	320	—
AH1255//8 (1845)	—	—	BV	160	320	—
AH1255//9 (1846)	—	155	185	265	450	—
AH1255//10 (1847)	—	155	185	265	450	—
AH1255//11 (1848)	—	—	BV	160	320	—
AH1255//12 (1849)	—	—	BV	160	320	—
AH1255//13 (1850)	—	—	BV	160	320	—
AH1255//14 (1851)	—	—	BV	160	320	—
AH1255//15 (1852)	—	—	BV	155	225	—
AH1255//16 (1853)	—	—	BV	155	250	—
AH1255//17 (1854)	—	—	BV	160	320	—

Abdul Aziz
AH1277-1293/1861-1876AD
REFORM COINAGE

KM# 255 5 QIRSH
0.4272 g., 0.8750 Gold .0120 oz. AGW **Obv:** Tughra **Rev:** Legend

Date	Mintage	VG	F	VF	XF	Unc
AH1277//3 (1862)	—	18.00	28.00	35.00	60.00	—
AH1277//4 (1863)	—	18.00	28.00	35.00	60.00	—
AH1277//5 (1864)	—	18.00	28.00	35.00	60.00	—
AH1277//6 (1865)	—	18.00	28.00	35.00	60.00	—
AH1277//7 (1866)	—	18.00	28.00	35.00	60.00	—
AH1277//8 (1867)	—	18.00	28.00	35.00	60.00	—
AH1277//9 (1868)	—	18.00	28.00	35.00	60.00	—
AH1277//10 (1869)	—	18.00	28.00	35.00	60.00	—
AH1277//11 (1870)	—	18.00	28.00	35.00	60.00	—
AH1277//12 (1871)	—	18.00	28.00	35.00	60.00	—
AH1277//13 (1872)	—	18.00	28.00	35.00	60.00	—
AH1277//14 (1873)	—	18.00	28.00	35.00	60.00	—
AH1277//15 (1874)	—	18.00	28.00	35.00	60.00	—

EGYPT

KM# 259 10 QIRSH
0.8554 g., 0.8750 Gold .0240 oz. AGW **Obv:** Tughra, rose at right **Rev:** Legend

Date	Mintage	VG	F	VF	XF	Unc
AH1277//10 (1869)	—	45.00	65.00	80.00	110	—
AH1277//11 (1870)	—	45.00	65.00	80.00	110	—
AH1277//12 (1871)	—	45.00	65.00	80.00	110	—
AH1277//14 (1873)	—	45.00	65.00	80.00	110	—

KM# 261 25 QIRSH
2.1360 g., 0.8750 Gold .0601 oz. AGW **Obv:** Tughra, rose at right **Rev:** Legend

Date	Mintage	VG	F	VF	XF	Unc
AH1277//8 (1867)	—	40.00	50.00	80.00	150	—
AH1277//9 (1868)	—	40.00	50.00	80.00	150	—
AH1277//10 (1869)	—	40.00	50.00	80.00	150	—
AH1277//11 (1870)	—	40.00	50.00	80.00	150	—
AH1277//12 (1871)	—	40.00	50.00	80.00	150	—
AH1277//13 (1872)	—	50.00	70.00	120	200	—
AH1277//14 (1873)	—	50.00	70.00	120	200	—
AH1277//15 (1874)	—	50.00	70.00	120	200	—

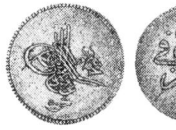

KM# 262 50 QIRSH (1/2 Pound)
4.2740 g., 0.8750 Gold .1202 oz. AGW **Obv:** Tughra **Rev:** Legend

Date	Mintage	VG	F	VF	XF	Unc
AH1277//11 (1870)	—	95.00	150	320	450	—
AH1277//12 (1871)	—	85.00	120	200	300	—
AH1277//13 (1872)	—	95.00	145	285	400	—
AH1277//14 (1873)	—	85.00	120	200	300	—
AH1277//15 (1874)	—	85.00	120	200	300	—
AH1277//16 (1875)	—	85.00	120	200	300	—

KM# 263 100 QIRSH (Pound)
8.5440 g., 0.8750 Gold .2404 oz. AGW **Obv:** Tughra, rose at right **Rev:** Legend

Date	Mintage	VG	F	VF	XF	Unc
AH1277//2 (1861)	—	BV	165	225	300	—
AH1277//4 (1863)	—	—	BV	165	220	—
AH1277//5 (1864)	—	—	BV	165	225	—
AH1277//6 (1865)	—	—	BV	165	225	—
AH1277//7 (1866)	—	—	BV	165	225	—
AH1277//8 (1867)	—	—	BV	165	225	—
AH1277//9 (1868)	—	—	BV	165	225	—
AH1277//10 (1869)	—	—	BV	165	225	—
AH1277//11 (1870)	—	—	BV	165	225	—
AH1277//12 (1871)	—	—	BV	165	225	—
AH1277//13 (1872)	—	—	BV	165	225	—
AH1277//14 (1873)	—	BV	185	265	350	—
AH1277//15 (1874)	—	BV	BV	165	225	—
AH1277//16 (1875)	—	BV	185	265	350	—

KM# 264 100 QIRSH (Pound)
8.5440 g., 0.8750 Gold .2404 oz. AGW **Obv:** Tughra **Rev:** Legend

Date	Mintage	VG	F	VF	XF	Unc
AH1277//4 (1863)	20,000	175	325	650	1,150	—

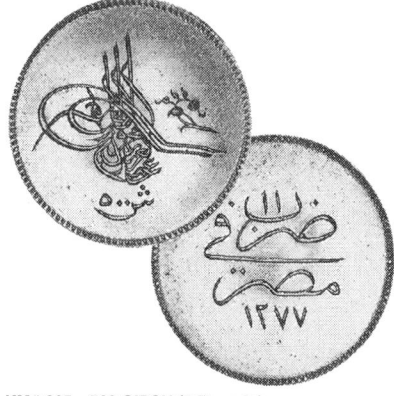

KM# 265 500 QIRSH (5 Pounds)
42.7200 g., 0.8750 Gold 1.2018 oz. AGW **Obv:** Tughra **Rev:** Legend

Date	Mintage	F	VF	XF	Unc
AH1277//8 (1867)	118	3,500	7,500	12,500	17,500
AH1277//9 (1868)	Inc. above	3,000	6,000	10,000	15,000
AH1277//11 (1870)	200	3,000	6,000	10,000	15,000

Note: Spink Zurich Auction 31 6-89 AU realized $13,400

| AH1277//15 (1874) | 56 | 3,000 | 6,000 | 10,000 | 15,000 |

Murad V
AH1293/1876AD
REFORM COINAGE

KM# 271 50 QIRSH (1/2 Pound)
4.2740 g., 0.8750 Gold .1202 oz. AGW **Obv:** Toughra of Murad V **Rev:** Legend

Date	Mintage	VG	F	VF	XF	Unc
AH1293//1 (1876)	—	375	650	1,000	1,500	—

KM# 272 100 QIRSH (Pound)
8.5440 g., 0.8750 Gold .2402 oz. AGW **Obv:** Toughra of Murad V **Rev:** Legend

Date	Mintage	VG	F	VF	XF	Unc
AH1293//1 (1876)	—	400	750	1,250	1,750	—

Abdul Hamid II
AH1293-1327/1876-1909AD
REFORM COINAGE

KM# 280 5 QIRSH
0.4200 g., 0.8750 Gold .0118 oz. AGW **Obv:** Flower at right of toughra **Rev:** Legend

Date	Mintage	VG	F	VF	XF	Unc
AH1293//2 (1877)	—	90.00	180	375	750	—
AH1293//3 (1878)	—	35.00	60.00	75.00	100	—
AH1293//5 (1879)	—	90.00	135	185	250	—
AH1293//6 (1880)	—	135	225	350	650	—
AH1293//7 (1881)	—	35.00	60.00	75.00	100	—
AH1293//22 (1896)	—	90.00	135	185	285	—

KM# A299 5 QIRSH
0.4200 g., 0.8750 Gold .0118 oz. AGW **Obv:** Tughra **Rev:** Legend in wreath

Date	Mintage	VG	F	VF	XF	Unc
AH1293//15 (1889)	—	100	200	350	600	—

KM# 298 5 QIRSH
0.4200 g., 0.8750 Gold .0118 oz. AGW **Obv:** "Al-Ghazi" at right of tughra **Rev:** Denomination

Date	Mintage	F	VF	XF	Unc
AH1293//15 (1889)	—	35.00	60.00	90.00	120
AH1293//16 (1890)	—	35.00	60.00	90.00	120
AH1293//18 (1892)	—	35.00	60.00	90.00	120
AH1293//24 (1898)	—	35.00	60.00	90.00	120
AH1293//26 (1900)	—	35.00	60.00	90.00	120
AH1293//34 (1908)	8,000	35.00	60.00	90.00	120

KM# A282 10 QIRSH
0.8544 g., 0.8750 Gold .0240 oz. AGW **Obv:** Tughra, rose at right **Rev:** Legend

Date	Mintage	VG	F	VF	XF	Unc
AH1293//4 (1878)	300	500	900	1,500	—	—

KM# 282 10 QIRSH
0.8544 g., 0.8750 Gold .0240 oz. AGW **Obv:** Al-Ghazi at right of tughra **Rev:** Denomination

Date	Mintage	F	VF	XF	Unc
AH1293//17 (1891)	—	40.00	65.00	115	—
AH1293//18 (1892)	—	50.00	75.00	120	—
AH1293//23 (1897)	—	55.00	85.00	135	—
AH1293//34 (1908)	5,000	45.00	90.00	150	—

KM# A284 25 QIRSH
2.1360 g., 0.8750 Gold .0601 oz. AGW **Obv:** Flower at right of toughra

Date	Mintage	F	VF	XF	Unc
AH1293//2 (1877)	—	—	—	—	—

Note: Reported, not confirmed

| AH1293//6 (1880) | 2 | — | — | — | 8,500 |

KM# 284 50 QIRSH (1/2 Pound)
4.2720 g., 0.8750 Gold .1202 oz. AGW **Obv:** Tughra, rose at right **Rev:** Legend

Date	Mintage	VG	F	VF	XF	Unc
AH1293//6 (1880)	2	—	—	—	9,000	—

KM# 285 100 QIRSH (Pound)
8.5440 g., 0.8750 Gold .2404 oz. AGW **Obv:** Tughra of Abdul Hamid II **Rev:** Legend

Date	Mintage	F	VF	XF	Unc
AH1293//1 (1876)	—	400	800	1,350	2,250
AH1293//4 (1878)	—	400	800	1,350	2,250
AH1293//6 (1880)	4	—	—	—	9,500
AH1293//8 (1882) Rare	—	—	—	—	—

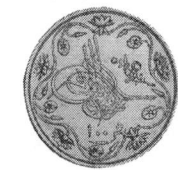

KM# 297 100 QIRSH (Pound)
8.5000 g., 0.8750 Gold .2391 oz. AGW **Obv:** Tughra within floral design **Rev:** Legend within floral design **Note:** Floral border.

Date	Mintage	F	VF	XF	Unc
AH1293//12 (1886)	52,000	175	200	250	325

194 EGYPT

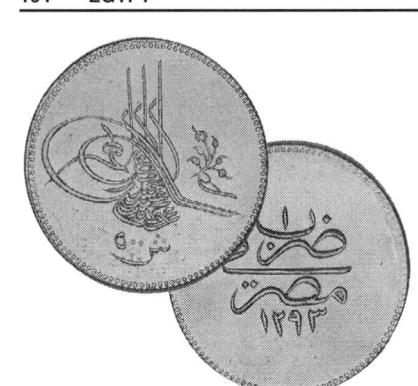

KM# 286 500 QIRSH (5 Pounds)
42.7400 g., 0.8750 Gold 1.2024 oz. AGW **Obv:** Tughra
Rev: Legend

Date	Mintage	F	VF	XF	Unc
AH1293//1 (1876)	—	1,500	3,500	5,500	9,000
AH1293//6 (1880)	5	3,500	6,500	11,500	16,500

Note: Spinks & Son Zurich Auction 18 2-86 super Unc. realized $14,520; Although the mint report documents only five pieces, perhaps ten pieces are thought to exist

BRITISH OCCUPATION
AH1333-1341 / 1914-1922AD

Hussein Kamil
As Sultan, AH1333-1336/1914-1917AD

OCCUPATION COINAGE
French

KM# 324 100 PIASTRES
8.5000 g., 0.8750 Gold .2391 oz. AGW **Obv:** Text above date within wreath **Rev:** Denomination within wreath, dates below

Date	Mintage	F	VF	XF	Unc
AH1335-1916	10,000	—	BV	180	275
AH1335-1916 Proof	—	Value: 1,500			

Note: Restrikes may exist

KINGDOM
AH1341-1372 / 1922-1952AD

Fuad I
As King, AH1341-1355/1922-1936AD

DECIMAL COINAGE

KM# 339 20 PIASTRES
1.7000 g., 0.8750 Gold .0478 oz. AGW **Obv:** Bust right
Rev: Denomination above center inscription, dates flank below

Date	Mintage	F	VF	XF	Unc
AH1341-1923	65,000	40.00	75.00	125	325

KM# 351 20 PIASTRES
1.7000 g., 0.8750 Gold .0478 oz. AGW **Obv:** Bust left

Date	Mintage	F	VF	XF	Unc
AH1348 Proof	—	—	—	—	—
AH1348-1929	—	37.50	55.00	70.00	120
AH1349-1930	—	37.50	55.00	70.00	120
AH1349-1930 Proof	—	—	—	—	—

KM# 340 50 PIASTRES
4.2500 g., 0.8750 Gold .1195 oz. AGW **Obv:** Bust right
Rev: Denomination above inscription, dates flank

Date	Mintage	F	VF	XF	Unc
AH1341-1923	18,000	BV	85.00	100	160

KM# 353 50 PIASTRES
4.2500 g., 0.8750 Gold .1195 oz. AGW **Obv:** Bust left
Rev: Denomination above inscription, dates flank below

Date	Mintage	F	VF	XF	Unc
AH1348-1929	—	BV	90.00	110	175
AH1348-1929 Proof	—	—	—	—	—
AH1349-1930	—	BV	80.00	95.00	150
AH1349-1930 Proof	—	—	—	—	—

KM# 341 100 PIASTRES
8.5000 g., 0.8750 Gold .2391 oz. AGW **Obv:** Bust right
Rev: Denomination above center circle, dates flank below

Date	Mintage	F	VF	XF	Unc
AH1340-1922	25,000	BV	160	175	250

KM# 354 100 PIASTRES
8.5000 g., 0.8750 Gold .2391 oz. AGW **Obv:** Bust left

Date	Mintage	F	VF	XF	Unc
AH1348-1929	—	BV	165	185	265
AH1349-1930	—	BV	160	175	250
AH1349-1930 Proof	—	—	—	—	—

KM# 342 500 PIASTRES
42.5000 g., 0.8750 Gold 1.1957 oz. AGW **Obv:** Bust right
Rev: Denomination above center circle, dates flank below

Date	Mintage	F	VF	XF	Unc
AH1340-1922	1,800	—	—	875	1,350
AH1340-1922 Proof	—	Value: 1,500			

Note: Circulation coins were struck in both red and yellow gold

KM# 355 500 PIASTRES
42.5000 g., 0.8750 Gold 1.1957 oz. AGW **Obv:** Uniformed bust left **Rev:** Denomination above center circle, dates flank below

Date	Mintage	F	VF	XF	Unc
AH1348-1929	—	—	—	850	1,250
AH1349-1930	—	—	—	850	1,250
AH1351-1932	—	—	—	850	1,250
AH1351-1932 Proof	—	Value: 1,500			

Farouk
AH1355-1372/1936-1952AD

DECIMAL COINAGE

KM# 370 20 PIASTRES
1.7000 g., 0.8750 Gold .0478 oz. AGW **Subject:** Royal Wedding
Obv: Uniformed bust looking left **Rev:** Dates within circle, denomination above, decorative vine surrounds

Date	Mintage	F	VF	XF	Unc
AH1357-1938	20,000	BV	65.00	90.00	125

KM# 371 50 PIASTRES
4.2500 g., 0.8750 Gold .1195 oz. AGW **Subject:** Royal Wedding
Obv: Uniformed bust looking left **Rev:** Dates within circle, denomination above, decorative vine surrounds

Date	Mintage	F	VF	XF	Unc
AH1357-1938	10,000	BV	95.00	140	240

KM# 372 100 PIASTRES
8.5000 g., 0.8750 Gold .2391 oz. AGW **Subject:** Royal Wedding
Obv: Uniformed bust looking left **Rev:** Dates within circle, denomination above, decorative vine surrounds

Date	Mintage	F	VF	XF	Unc
AH1357-1938	5,000	BV	165	195	300

Note: Circulation coins were struck in both red and yellow gold

KM# 373 500 PIASTRES
42.5000 g., 0.8750 Gold 1.1957 oz. AGW **Subject:** Royal Wedding **Obv:** Uniformed bust looking left **Rev:** Dates within circle, denomination above, decorative vine surrounds

Date	Mintage	F	VF	XF	Unc
AH1357-1938	—	—	—	1,250	1,850
AH1357-1938 Proof	—	Value: 2,200			

EGYPT

FIRST REPUBLIC
AH1373-1378 / 1953-1958AD

DECIMAL COINAGE

KM# 387 POUND
8.5000 g., 0.8750 Gold .2391 oz. AGW **Subject:** 3rd and 5th Anniversaries of Revolution **Obv:** Denomination and dates above wings **Rev:** Pharoah Ramses II in a war chariot

Date	Mintage	F	VF	XF	Unc
AH1374-1955	16,000	—	—	160	220
AH1377-1957	10,000	—	—	165	230

Note: Struck in red and yellow gold

KM# 388 5 POUNDS
42.5000 g., 0.8750 Gold 1.1957 oz. AGW **Subject:** 3rd and 5th Anniversaries of Revolution **Obv:** Denomination and dates above wings **Rev:** Horse, chariot, and archer

Date	Mintage	F	VF	XF	Unc
AH1374-1955	—	—	—	825	1,250
AH1377-1957	—	—	—	850	1,300

Note: Struck in red and yellow gold

UNITED ARAB REPUBLIC
AH1378-1391 / 1958-1971AD

DECIMAL COINAGE

KM# 391 1/2 POUND
4.2500 g., 0.8750 Gold .1195 oz. AGW, 20 mm. **Subject:** U.A.R. Founding **Obv:** Denomination and dates above wings **Rev:** Pharoah Ramses II in a war chariot

Date	Mintage	F	VF	XF	Unc
AH1377-1958	30,000	—	—	—	185

KM# 401 POUND
8.5000 g., 0.8750 Gold .2391 oz. AGW **Rev:** Aswan Dam

Date	Mintage	F	VF	XF	Unc
AH1379-1960	252,000	—	—	—	170

KM# 426 POUND
8.0000 g., 0.8750 Gold .2251 oz. AGW **Subject:** President Nasser **Obv:** Head of President Nasser right **Rev:** Denomination divides dates, legend above

Date	Mintage	F	VF	XF	Unc
AH1390-1970	10,000	—	—	—	160

KM# 402 5 POUNDS
42.5000 g., 0.8750 Gold 1.1957 oz. AGW **Obv:** Denomination and dates above wings **Rev:** Aswan Dam

Date	Mintage	F	VF	XF	Unc
AH1379-1960	5,000	—	—	—	800

KM# 408 5 POUNDS
26.0000 g., 0.8750 Gold .7315 oz. AGW **Subject:** Diversion of the Nile **Obv:** Denomination divides dates, legend above **Rev:** Nile River basin scene

Date	Mintage	F	VF	XF	Unc
AH1384-1964	—	—	—	—	520

KM# 416 5 POUNDS
26.0000 g., 0.8750 Gold .7315 oz. AGW **Subject:** 1400th Anniversary of the Koran **Obv:** Denomination and dates within center circle **Rev:** Open Koran book above globe with radiant sun in back

Date	Mintage	F	VF	XF	Unc
AH1388-1968	10,000	—	—	—	500

KM# 427 5 POUNDS
26.0000 g., 0.8750 Gold .7315 oz. AGW **Subject:** 1000th Anniversary - Al Azhar Mosque **Rev:** Al Azhar Mosque

Date	Mintage	F	VF	XF	Unc
AH1390-1970	—	—	—	—	510

KM# 428 5 POUNDS
26.0000 g., 0.8750 Gold .7315 oz. AGW **Subject:** President Nasser **Obv:** Head of President Nasser right

Date	Mintage	F	VF	XF	Unc
AH1390-1970	3,000	—	—	—	510

KM# 409 10 POUNDS
52.0000 g., 0.8750 Gold 1.4630 oz. AGW **Subject:** Diversion of the Nile **Obv:** Denomination divides dates **Rev:** Nile River basin scene

Date	Mintage	F	VF	XF	Unc
AH1384-1964	2,000	—	—	—	1,000

ARAB REPUBLIC
AH1391- / 1971- AD

DECIMAL COINAGE

KM# 834 1/2 POUND
4.0000 g., 0.8750 Gold .1125 oz. AGW **Subject:** El Akkad **Obv:** Legend and vase **Rev:** Portrait

Date	Mintage	F	VF	XF	Unc
AH1413-1992	600	—	—	—	250

KM# 809 1/2 POUND
4.0000 g., 0.8750 Gold .1125 oz. AGW **Subject:** 20th Anniversary - October War **Obv:** Smoking chimney text **Rev:** Soldier with flag

Date	Mintage	F	VF	XF	Unc
AH1414-1993	Est. 5,000	—	—	—	250

KM# 760 1/2 POUND
4.0000 g., 0.8750 Gold .1125 oz. AGW **Subject:** Salah El Din El-Ayubi **Obv:** Denomination **Rev:** Portrait

Date	Mintage	F	VF	XF	Unc
AH1414-1994	500	—	—	—	250

KM# 903 1/2 POUND
4.0000 g., 0.8750 Gold 0.1125 oz. AGW, 18 mm. **Subject:** Egyptian Museum Centennial **Obv:** Value **Rev:** Building **Edge:** Reeded

Date	Mintage	F	VF	XF	Unc
AH1423-2002	—	—	—	—	250

KM# 440 POUND
8.0000 g., 0.8750 Gold .2250 oz. AGW **Subject:** 75th Anniversary - National Bank of Egypt **Obv:** Denomination divides dates **Rev:** National Bank of Egypt building, globe at back, divides dates

Date	Mintage	F	VF	XF	Unc
AH1393-1973	7,000	—	—	—	160

KM# 456 POUND
8.0000 g., 0.8750 Gold .2250 oz. AGW **Rev:** Om Kalsoum right

Date	Mintage	F	VF	XF	Unc
AH1396-1976	5,000	—	—	—	170

KM# 458 POUND
8.0000 g., 0.8750 Gold .2250 oz. AGW **Obv:** Denomination divides dates **Rev:** Bust of King Faisal half right

Date	Mintage	F	VF	XF	Unc
AH1396-1976	8,000	—	—	—	165

EGYPT

KM# 475 POUND
8.0000 g., 0.8750 Gold .2250 oz. AGW **Subject:** 20th Anniversary - Economic Union

Date	Mintage	F	VF	XF	Unc
AH1397-1977	5,000	—	—	—	170

KM# 492 POUND
8.0000 g., 0.8750 Gold .2250 oz. AGW **Subject:** 100th Anniversary - Bank of Land Reform

Date	Mintage	F	VF	XF	Unc
AH1399-1979	4,200	—	—	—	165
AH1399-1979 Proof	800	Value: 225			

KM# 494 POUND
8.0000 g., 0.8750 Gold .2250 oz. AGW **Subject:** 1400th Anniversary - Mohammed's Flight

Date	Mintage	F	VF	XF	Unc
AH1400-1979	2,000	—	—	—	170
AH1400-1979 Proof	2,000	Value: 225			

KM# 509 POUND
8.0000 g., 0.8750 Gold .2250 oz. AGW **Subject:** Egyptian-Israeli Peace Treaty **Obv:** Denomination divides dates **Rev:** Head of Anwar Sadat left, with dove of peace at left

Date	Mintage	F	VF	XF	Unc
AH1400-1980	9,500	—	—	—	160
AH1400-1980 Proof	500	Value: 200			

KM# 512 POUND
8.0000 g., 0.8750 Gold .2250 oz. AGW **Subject:** Doctor's Day **Rev:** Seated healer with staff facing left

Date	Mintage	F	VF	XF	Unc
AH1400-1980 Proof	5,000	Value: 185			

KM# 516 POUND
8.0000 g., 0.8750 Gold .2250 oz. AGW **Obv:** Denomination divides dates **Rev:** Cairo University Law facility

Date	Mintage	F	VF	XF	Unc
AH1400-1980	2,000	—	—	—	170
AH1400-1980 Proof	—	Value: 225			

KM# 525 POUND
8.0000 g., 0.8750 Gold .2250 oz. AGW **Subject:** 3rd Anniversary - Suez Canal Reopening

Date	Mintage	F	VF	XF	Unc
AH1401-1981 Proof	150	Value: 250			

KM# 529 POUND
8.0000 g., 0.8750 Gold .2250 oz. AGW **Subject:** 25th Anniversary - Nationalization of Suez Canal **Obv:** Denomination divides dates **Rev:** Central design divides dates, grain spray below

Date	Mintage	F	VF	XF	Unc
AH1401-1981	3,000	—	—	—	180

KM# 531 POUND
8.0000 g., 0.8750 Gold .2250 oz. AGW **Subject:** 100th Anniversary - Revolt by Arabi Pasha **Rev:** Pasha mounted on horse in front of his followers

Date	Mintage	F	VF	XF	Unc
AH1402-1981	3,000	—	—	—	180

KM# 541 POUND
8.0000 g., 0.8750 Gold .2250 oz. AGW **Subject:** 1000th Anniversary - Al Azhar Mosque **Rev:** Mosque

Date	Mintage	F	VF	XF	Unc
AH1402-1982 Proof	2,000	Value: 190			

KM# 543 POUND
8.0000 g., 0.8750 Gold .2250 oz. AGW **Subject:** 50th Anniversary of Air Force **Rev:** Air Force insignia within wreath

Date	Mintage	F	VF	XF	Unc
AH1403-1982 Proof	2,000	Value: 190			

KM# 583 POUND
8.0000 g., 0.8750 Gold .2250 oz. AGW **Subject:** 50th Anniversary - Egyptian Radio Broadcasting

Date	Mintage	F	VF	XF	Unc
AH1404-1984	2,000	—	—	—	190

KM# 571 POUND
8.0000 g., 0.8750 Gold .2250 oz. AGW **Subject:** 25th Anniversary - National Planning Institute

Date	Mintage	F	VF	XF	Unc
AH1405-1985	200	—	—	—	275

KM# 574 POUND
8.0000 g., 0.8750 Gold .2250 oz. AGW **Subject:** 60th Anniversary - Egyptian Parliament **Rev:** Parliament building

Date	Mintage	F	VF	XF	Unc
AH1405-1985	1,000	—	—	—	210

KM# 577 POUND
8.0000 g., 0.8750 Gold .2250 oz. AGW **Subject:** 25th Anniversary - Cairo Stadium **Rev:** Stadium

Date	Mintage	F	VF	XF	Unc
AH1405-1985	300	—	—	—	250

KM# 580 POUND
8.0000 g., 0.8750 Gold .2250 oz. AGW **Subject:** 25th Anniversary - Egyptian Television

Date	Mintage	F	VF	XF	Unc
AH1405-1985	150	—	—	—	275

KM# 604 POUND
8.0000 g., 0.8750 Gold .2250 oz. AGW **Subject:** Commerce Day **Rev:** Stylized depictions of commercial activity

Date	Mintage	F	VF	XF	Unc
AH1405-1985 Proof	2,000	Value: 190			

KM# 605 POUND
8.0000 g., 0.8750 Gold .2250 oz. AGW **Subject:** Faculty of Economics and Political Science **Obv:** Arabic legends, seals, and date **Rev:** Graph within wreath, partial gear wheel

Date	Mintage	F	VF	XF	Unc
AH1405-1985 Proof	250	Value: 250			

KM# 635 POUND
8.0000 g., 0.8750 Gold .2250 oz. AGW **Subject:** 25th Anniversary - Cairo International Airport **Obv:** Stylized legend above dates, dividing two seals **Rev:** Two circling vultures within Arabic and English legends

Date	Mintage	F	VF	XF	Unc
AH1405-1985	200	—	—	—	250

KM# 632 POUND
8.0000 g., 0.8750 Gold .2250 oz. AGW **Subject:** Prophet's Mosque **Obv:** Minaret, globe, denomination, legends **Rev:** Crescent, mosque, minaret below legend arch

Date	Mintage	F	VF	XF	Unc
AH1406-1985	800	—	—	—	215

KM# 636 POUND
8.0000 g., 0.8750 Gold .2250 oz. AGW **Subject:** Cairo University Faculty of Commerce **Obv:** Stylized legend above dates, dividing two seals **Rev:** Ancient Egyptian commerce related scenes

Date	Mintage	F	VF	XF	Unc
AH1406-1986	200	—	—	—	250

KM# 637 POUND
8.0000 g., 0.8750 Gold .2250 oz. AGW **Subject:** 25th Anniversary - Egyptian Central Bank **Obv:** Stylized flowers, gear wheel and cotton within legend **Rev:** Ancient Egyptian sculptures, legends above and below within ornamental border

Date	Mintage	F	VF	XF	Unc
AH1406-1986	200	—	—	—	275

KM# 638 POUND
8.0000 g., 0.8750 Gold .2250 oz. AGW **Subject:** 100th Anniversary - Petroleum Industry **Obv:** Stylized legend above dates, dividing two seals **Rev:** Oil well and landscape within ornamental circle

Date	Mintage	F	VF	XF	Unc
AH1406-1986	800	—	—	—	215

KM# 640 POUND
8.0000 g., 0.8750 Gold .2250 oz. AGW **Subject:** 50th Anniversary - National Theater **Obv:** Stylized stage curtain, legend within **Rev:** Large building, two masks in foreground, legend above

Date	Mintage	F	VF	XF	Unc
AH1406-1986	250	—	—	—	235

KM# 644 POUND
8.0000 g., 0.8750 Gold .2250 oz. AGW **Subject:** Restoration of Parliament Building **Obv:** Arabic legends **Rev:** Dome and tower with scaffolding

Date	Mintage	F	VF	XF	Unc
AH1406-1986	400	—	—	—	220

KM# 639 POUND
8.0000 g., 0.8750 Gold .2250 oz. AGW **Subject:** Census **Obv:** Arabic legends, seals, date **Rev:** City view with paper doll cutout human figures

Date	Mintage	F	VF	XF	Unc
AH1407-1986	200	—	—	—	235

KM# 643 POUND
8.0000 g., 0.8750 Gold .2250 oz. AGW **Subject:** 40th Anniversary - Engineer's Syndicate **Obv:** Arabic legends, seals, dates **Rev:** Three triangles, legend, ornamentation

Date	Mintage	F	VF	XF	Unc
AH1407-1986	400	—	—	—	220

KM# 645 POUND
8.0000 g., 0.8750 Gold .2250 oz. AGW **Subject:** Parliament Museum **Obv:** Arabic legends, seals, dates **Rev:** Documents, quill, carriage, building with national emblem

Date	Mintage	F	VF	XF	Unc
AH1407-1987	400	—	—	—	220

KM# 653 POUND
8.0000 g., 0.8750 Gold .2250 oz. AGW **Subject:** Investment Bank **Obv:** Toughra, legends above and below, dates **Rev:** Symbol within stylized circle, legend around

Date	Mintage	F	VF	XF	Unc
AH1407-1987	600	—	—	—	215

KM# 673 POUND
8.0000 g., 0.8750 Gold .2250 oz. AGW **Subject:** First African Subway **Obv:** Stylized legends and denomination **Rev:** Subway emerging from tunnel with legend around rim

Date	Mintage	F	VF	XF	Unc
AH1408-1987 Proof	500	Value: 230			

KM# 647 POUND
8.0000 g., 0.8750 Gold .2250 oz. AGW **Subject:** Police Day **Obv:** Arabic and English legends, seals, dates **Rev:** Police emblem - eagle in wreath, legends

Date	Mintage	F	VF	XF	Unc
AH1408-1988	500	—	—	—	215

KM# 654 POUND
8.0000 g., 0.8750 Gold .2250 oz. AGW **Subject:** Dedication of Cairo Opera House **Obv:** Arabic legends, seals, dates **Rev:** Opera house, legends above and below

Date	Mintage	F	VF	XF	Unc
AH1409-1988	1,500	—	—	—	225

KM# 661 POUND
8.0000 g., 0.8750 Gold .2250 oz. AGW **Subject:** Naguib Mahfouz, Nobel Laureate **Obv:** Stylized quill ink and paper design with legend above **Rev:** Head of Mahfouz left

Date	Mintage	F	VF	XF	Unc
AH1409-1988 Proof	1,000	Value: 190			

KM# 664 POUND
8.0000 g., 0.8750 Gold .2250 oz. AGW **Subject:** United Parliamentary Union **Obv:** Kufic legend above denomination and dates **Rev:** Anniversary dates, map in wreath above domed building, and legend

Date	Mintage	F	VF	XF	Unc
AH1409-1989 Proof	200	Value: 275			

KM# 666 POUND
8.0000 g., 0.8750 Gold .2250 oz. AGW **Subject:** First Arab Olympics **Obv:** Kufic legend above denomination and dates **Rev:** 5 Olympic rings and map as part of torch held by hand within wreath and legend

Date	Mintage	F	VF	XF	Unc
AH1409-1989 Proof	300	Value: 250			

KM# 668 POUND
8.0000 g., 0.8750 Gold .2250 oz. AGW **Subject:** National Research Center **Obv:** Kufic legend above denomination and dates **Rev:** Stylized ancient and modern research elements

Date	Mintage	F	VF	XF	Unc
AH1409-1989 Proof	250	Value: 250			

KM# 677 POUND
8.0000 g., 0.8750 Gold .2250 oz. AGW **Subject:** University of Cairo, School of Agriculture **Obv:** Denomination between wheat ears above legend **Rev:** Ancient farming scene and coat of arms, building in background

Date	Mintage	F	VF	XF	Unc
AH1410-1989 Proof	200	Value: 275			

KM# 695 POUND
8.0000 g., 0.8750 Gold .2250 oz. AGW **Subject:** Export Trade Show **Obv:** Toughra, inscription above **Rev:** Display of symbols

Date	Mintage	F	VF	XF	Unc
AH1410-1989 Proof	200	Value: 275			

KM# 696 POUND
8.0000 g., 0.8750 Gold .2250 oz. AGW **Subject:** Union of African Parliament **Obv:** Toughra, denomination, date within circle and legend **Rev:** Map of Africa, laurel branch and Parliament building

Date	Mintage	F	VF	XF	Unc
AH1410-1990 Proof	200	Value: 275			

KM# 699 POUND
8.0000 g., 0.8750 Gold .2250 oz. AGW **Subject:** 5th African Games - Cairo **Obv:** Torch with legend and inscription **Rev:** Logo above rings within legend

Date	Mintage	F	VF	XF	Unc
AH1411-1991 Proof	200	Value: 275			

EGYPT

KM# 832 POUND
8.0000 g., 0.8750 Gold .2250 oz. AGW **Subject:** Library of Alexandria **Obv:** Legend and inscription **Rev:** Waterfront building with tower

Date	Mintage	F	VF	XF	Unc
AH1411-1991	300	—	—	—	400

KM# 726 POUND
8.0000 g., 0.8750 Gold .2250 oz. AGW **Subject:** Mohamed Abdel Wahab **Rev:** Bust of Mohamed Abdel Wahab left with music sheet in background

Date	Mintage	F	VF	XF	Unc
AH1412-1991	1,000	—	—	—	200

KM# 836 POUND
8.0000 g., 0.8750 Gold .2250 oz. AGW **Subject:** Rifa'a El Tahtaoui **Obv:** Legend and vase **Rev:** Portrait

Date	Mintage	F	VF	XF	Unc
AH1413-1992	800	—	—	—	400

KM# 811 POUND
8.0000 g., 0.8750 Gold .2250 oz. AGW **Subject:** 20th Anniversary - October War **Obv:** Smoking chimney, text **Rev:** Soldier with flag

Date	Mintage	F	VF	XF	Unc
AH1414-1993	Est. 3,000	—	—	—	400

KM# 762 POUND
8.0000 g., 0.8750 Gold .2250 oz. AGW **Subject:** Salah El Din El-Ayubi **Obv:** Denomination **Rev:** Portrait

Date	Mintage	F	VF	XF	Unc
AH1414-1994	300	—	—	—	400

KM# 767 POUND
8.0000 g., 0.8750 Gold .2250 oz. AGW **Subject:** 75 Years - Bank of Misr

Date	Mintage	F	VF	XF	Unc
AH1415-1995	1,000	—	—	—	275

KM# 771 POUND
8.0000 g., 0.8750 Gold .2250 oz. AGW **Subject:** Pediatrics International Conference **Obv:** Tughra divides dates and denomination **Rev:** Children and pyramids on globe, dates divided below

Date	Mintage	F	VF	XF	Unc
AH1416-1995	300	—	—	—	400

KM# 840 POUND
8.0000 g., 0.8750 Gold .2250 oz. AGW **Obv:** Denomination **Rev:** Abd Al Halem Hafez

Date	Mintage	F	VF	XF	Unc
AH1416-1995	500	—	—	—	400

KM# 905 POUND
8.0000 g., 0.8750 Gold 0.2250 oz. AGW, 24 mm. **Subject:** Egyptian Museum Centennial **Obv:** Value **Rev:** Building, centennial numerals in background **Edge:** Reeded

Date	Mintage	F	VF	XF	Unc
AH1423-2002	—	—	—	—	400

KM# 936 POUND
8.0000 g., 0.8750 Gold 0.2251 oz. AGW, 24 mm. **Subject:** 50th Anniversary of Egyptian Revolution **Obv:** Value **Rev:** Soldier with flag, pyramids and radiant sun **Edge:** Reeded

Date	Mintage	F	VF	XF	Unc
AH1423-2002	—	—	—	—	—

KM# 937 POUND
8.0000 g., 0.8750 Gold 0.2251 oz. AGW, 24 mm. **Subject:** 100th Anniversary of National Bank **Obv:** Value **Rev:** Flower through number 100 **Edge:** Reeded

Date	Mintage	F	VF	XF	Unc
AH1423-2002	—	—	—	—	—

KM# 938 POUND
8.0000 g., 0.8750 Gold 0.2251 oz. AGW, 24 mm. **Subject:** Alexandria Library **Obv:** Cufic text in center **Rev:** Arched inscription above slanted library roof **Edge:** Reeded

Date	Mintage	F	VF	XF	Unc
AH1423-2002	—	—	—	—	—

KM# 441 5 POUNDS
26.0000 g., 0.8750 Gold .7315 oz. AGW **Subject:** 75th Anniveresary - National Bank of Egypt **Obv:** Denomination and dates **Rev:** World globe back of bank building divides dates

Date	Mintage	F	VF	XF	Unc
AH1393-1973	1,000	—	—	—	525
AH1393-1973 Proof	—	Value: 650			

KM# 444 5 POUNDS
26.0000 g., 0.8750 Gold .7315 oz. AGW **Subject:** 1973 October War **Obv:** Denomination, dates, and legend **Rev:** Half-figure of soldier, 3/4 wreath surrounds above

Date	Mintage	F	VF	XF	Unc
AH1394-1974	1,000	—	—	—	550

KM# 459 5 POUNDS
26.0000 g., 0.8750 Gold .7315 oz. AGW **Subject:** King Faisal of Saudi Arabia **Obv:** Denomination divides dates **Rev:** Head 3/4 right

Date	Mintage	F	VF	XF	Unc
AH1396-1976	2,500	—	—	—	575

KM# 460 5 POUNDS
26.0000 g., 0.8750 Gold .7315 oz. AGW **Subject:** Reopening of Suez Canal

Date	Mintage	F	VF	XF	Unc
AH1396-1976	2,000	—	—	—	525

KM# 461 5 POUNDS
26.0000 g., 0.8750 Gold .7315 oz. AGW **Subject:** Om Kalsoum **Obv:** Denomination divides dates **Rev:** Head right, music symbol in hair

Date	Mintage	F	VF	XF	Unc
AH1396-1976	1,000	—	—	—	800

KM# 495 5 POUNDS
26.0000 g., 0.8750 Gold .7315 oz. AGW **Subject:** 100th Anniversary - Bank of Land Reform **Rev:** Seated man, farmer tilling soil with three oxen behind, mural showing workers cutting grain sheaves

Date	Mintage	F	VF	XF	Unc
AH1399-1979	1,750	—	—	—	500
AH1399-1979 Proof	250	Value: 625			

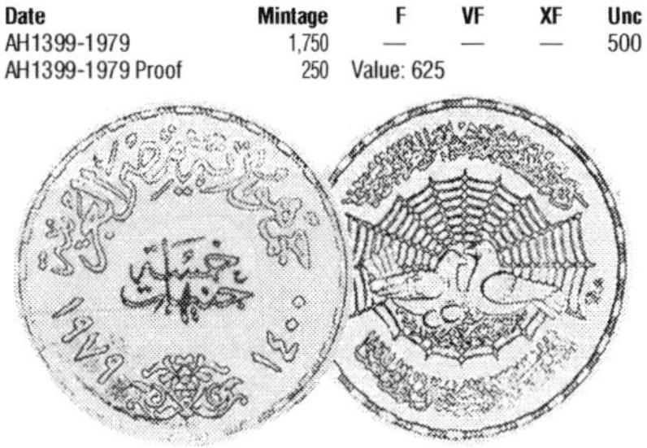

KM# 496 5 POUNDS
26.0000 g., 0.8750 Gold .7315 oz. AGW **Subject:** 1400th Anniversary - Mohammed's Flight **Obv:** Denomination divides dates, legend above **Rev:** Two doves with eggs in front of spider web

Date	Mintage	F	VF	XF	Unc
AH1400-1979	2,000	—	—	—	500

198 EGYPT

KM# 517 5 POUNDS
26.0000 g., 0.8750 Gold .7315 oz. AGW **Subject:** Egyptian-Israeli Peace Treaty **Obv:** Denomination divides dates, legend above **Rev:** Head of Anwar Sadat at right facing left, dove of peace at left behind

Date	Mintage	F	VF	XF	Unc
AH1400-1980	2,375	—	—	—	500
AH1400-1980 Proof	125	Value: 650			

KM# 518 5 POUNDS
26.0000 g., 0.8750 Gold .7315 oz. AGW **Subject:** Doctors' Day

Date	Mintage	F	VF	XF	Unc
AH1400-1980	1,000	—	—	—	585

KM# 534 5 POUNDS
26.0000 g., 0.8750 Gold .7315 oz. AGW **Subject:** 3rd Anniversary - Suez Canal Reopening

Date	Mintage	F	VF	XF	Unc
AH1401-1981 Proof	75	Value: 675			
AH1401-1981	925	—	—	—	525

KM# 535 5 POUNDS
26.0000 g., 0.8750 Gold .7315 oz. AGW **Subject:** 25th Anniversary - Ministry of Industry

Date	Mintage	F	VF	XF	Unc
AH1402-1981 Proof	1,500	Value: 500			

KM# 536 5 POUNDS
26.0000 g., 0.8750 Gold .7315 oz. AGW **Subject:** 100th Anniversary - Revolt by Arabi Pasha **Rev:** Pasha mounted on horse in front of his followers

Date	Mintage	F	VF	XF	Unc
AH1402-1981	1,000	—	—	—	520

KM# 537 5 POUNDS
26.0000 g., 0.8750 Gold .7315 oz. AGW **Subject:** 25th Anniversary - Nationalization of Suez Canal **Obv:** Denomination divides dates, legend above **Rev:** Design at center, grain spray below

Date	Mintage	F	VF	XF	Unc
AH1401-1981	1,000	—	—	—	520

KM# 546 5 POUNDS
26.0000 g., 0.8750 Gold .7315 oz. AGW **Subject:** 1000th Anniversary - Al Azhar Mosque **Rev:** Mosque

Date	Mintage	F	VF	XF	Unc
AH1402-1982	1,500	—	—	—	500

KM# 547 5 POUNDS
26.0000 g., 0.8750 Gold .7315 oz. AGW **Subject:** 50th Anniversary - Air Force **Rev:** Air Force insignia within wreath

Date	Mintage	F	VF	XF	Unc
AH1403-1982	1,000	—	—	—	520

KM# 671 5 POUNDS
26.0000 g., 0.8750 Gold .7315 oz. AGW **Subject:** 50th Anniversary - Egyptian Radio **Obv:** Arabic legends **Rev:** Tall buildings with transmitter

Date	Mintage	F	VF	XF	Unc
AH1404-1984 Proof	500	Value: 525			

KM# 564 5 POUNDS
40.0000 g., 0.8750 Gold 1.1253 oz. AGW **Subject:** 100th Anniversary - Moharram Printing Press Co.

Date	Mintage	F	VF	XF	Unc
AH1405-1985	200	—	—	—	1,850

KM# 576 5 POUNDS
26.0000 g., 0.8750 Gold .7315 oz. AGW **Subject:** 60th Anniversary - Egyptian Parliament **Rev:** Parliament building

Date	Mintage	F	VF	XF	Unc
AH1405-1985	500	—	—	—	1,750

KM# 633 5 POUNDS
26.0000 g., 0.8750 Gold .7315 oz. AGW **Subject:** Prophet's Mosque **Obv:** Minaret, globe, denomination, legends **Rev:** Crescent, mosque, minaret below legend arch

Date	Mintage	F	VF	XF	Unc
AH1406-1985	400	—	—	—	525

KM# 579 5 POUNDS
26.0000 g., 0.8750 Gold .7315 oz. AGW **Subject:** 25th Anniversary - Cairo Stadium **Rev:** Stadium

Date	Mintage	F	VF	XF	Unc
AH1405-1985	200	—	—	—	1,850

KM# 582 5 POUNDS
26.0000 g., 0.8750 Gold .7315 oz. AGW **Subject:** 25th Anniversary - Egyptian Television **Obv:** Arabic legends, dates below **Rev:** Television tower emitting signal divides dates

Date	Mintage	F	VF	XF	Unc
AH1405-1985	100	—	—	—	1,150

KM# 609a 5 POUNDS
26.0000 g., 0.8750 Gold .7315 oz. AGW **Subject:** Mecca **Obv:** Denomination and dates **Rev:** Building within circle

Date	Mintage	F	VF	XF	Unc
AH1406-1986 Proof	1,400	Value: 500			

KM# 614a 5 POUNDS
26.0000 g., 0.8750 Gold .7315 oz. AGW **Subject:** Restoration of Parliament Building **Obv:** Arabic legends **Rev:** Dome and tower with scaffolding

Date	Mintage	F	VF	XF	Unc
AH1406-1986	300	—	—	—	525

KM# 617a 5 POUNDS
26.0000 g., 0.8750 Gold .7315 oz. AGW **Subject:** Parliament Museum **Obv:** Arabic legends, seals and dates **Rev:** Documents, quill, carriage, building with national emblem

Date	Mintage	F	VF	XF	Unc
AH1407-1987	300	—	—	—	525

KM# 674 5 POUNDS
26.0000 g., 0.8750 Gold .7315 oz. AGW **Subject:** First African Subway **Obv:** Stylized legends and denomination **Rev:** Subway emerging from tunnel with legend around rim

Date	Mintage	F	VF	XF	Unc
AH1408-1987 Proof	200	Value: 575			

KM# 670 5 POUNDS
26.0000 g., 0.8750 Gold .7315 oz. AGW **Subject:** National Research Center **Obv:** Kufic legend above denomination and date **Rev:** Stylized ancient and modern research elements

Date	Mintage	F	VF	XF	Unc
AH1408-1988 Proof	—	Value: 575			
AH1409-1989 Proof	200	Value: 575			

KM# 655 5 POUNDS
26.0000 g., 0.8750 Gold .7315 oz. AGW **Subject:** Dedication of Cairo Opera House **Obv:** Arabic legends, seals, dates **Rev:** Opera house, legends above and below

Date	Mintage	F	VF	XF	Unc
AH1409-1988	200	—	—	—	560

KM# 728 5 POUNDS
26.0000 g., 0.8750 Gold .7314 oz. AGW **Subject:** Muhamed Abdel Wahab **Obv:** Arabic legends and inscriptions **Rev:** Bust left with music sheet in background

Date	Mintage	F	VF	XF	Unc
AH1412-1991 Proof	400	—	—	—	540

KM# 805a 5 POUNDS
26.0000 g., 0.8750 Gold .7314 oz. AGW **Subject:** Library of Alexandria **Obv:** Arabic inscription **Rev:** Library building complex **Edge:** Reeded **Note:** Struck at Cairo.

Date	Mintage	F	VF	XF	Unc
AH1411-1991 Proof	200	—	—	—	550

KM# 833 5 POUNDS
26.0000 g., 0.8750 Gold .7315 oz. AGW **Subject:** Library of Alexandria **Obv:** Legend and inscription **Rev:** Waterfront building with tower

Date	Mintage	F	VF	XF	Unc
AH1411-1991	200	—	—	—	550

KM# 879 5 POUNDS
26.0000 g., 0.8750 Gold .7315 oz. AGW **Subject:** Symbol of Unification **Obv:** Vulture, denomination above and dates below **Rev:** Two females representing the upper and lower Nile

Date	Mintage	F	VF	XF	Unc
AH1414-1993 Proof	3,000	—	—	—	500

KM# 874 5 POUNDS
26.0000 g., 0.8750 Gold .7315 oz. AGW **Rev:** Sphinx and pyramids

Date	Mintage	F	VF	XF	Unc
AH1415-1994 Proof	5,000	—	—	—	500

KM# 876 5 POUNDS
26.0000 g., 0.8750 Gold .7315 oz. AGW **Rev:** 3/4-length standing Sheikh El Balad

Date	Mintage	F	VF	XF	Unc
AH1415-1994 Proof	3,000	Value: 500			

KM# 878 5 POUNDS
26.0000 g., 0.8750 Gold .7315 oz. AGW **Obv:** Vulture, denomination above and dates below **Rev:** Dwarf Seneb and family

Date	Mintage	F	VF	XF	Unc
AH1415-1994 Proof	3,000	—	—	—	500

KM# 880 5 POUNDS
26.0000 g., 0.8750 Gold .7315 oz. AGW **Rev:** Kneeling King Pepi I facing

Date	Mintage	F	VF	XF	Unc
AH1415-1994 Proof	3,000	—	—	—	500

KM# 881 5 POUNDS
26.0000 g., 0.8750 Gold .7315 oz. AGW **Rev:** Statue of King Amenemhat III

Date	Mintage	F	VF	XF	Unc
AH1415-1994 Proof	3,000	—	—	—	500

KM# 774 5 POUNDS
26.0000 g., 0.8750 Gold .7315 oz. AGW **Subject:** 75 Years - Architects Association **Obv:** Tughra **Rev:** Head left

Date	Mintage	F	VF	XF	Unc
AH1416-1995	300	—	—	—	550

KM# 842 5 POUNDS
26.0000 g., 0.8750 Gold .7315 oz. AGW **Rev:** Abd Al Halem Hafez

Date	Mintage	F	VF	XF	Unc
AH1416-1995	500	—	—	—	550

KM# 907 5 POUNDS
26.0000 g., 0.8750 Gold 0.7314 oz. AGW, 33 mm. **Subject:** Egyptian Museum Centennial **Obv:** Value **Rev:** Building, centennial numerals in background **Edge:** Reeded

Date	Mintage	F	VF	XF	Unc
AH1423-2002	—	—	—	—	520

EGYPT

KM# 519 10 POUNDS
40.0000 g., 0.8750 Gold 1.1254 oz. AGW **Subject:** Egyptian-Israeli Peace Treaty **Obv:** Denomination divides dates **Rev:** Head at right facing left, dove with olive branch at left

Date	Mintage	F	VF	XF	Unc
AH1400-1980	950	—	—	—	875
AH1400-1980 Proof	50	Value: 1,200			

KM# 538 10 POUNDS
40.0000 g., 0.8750 Gold 1.1254 oz. AGW **Subject:** 25th Anniversary - Ministry of Industry **Obv:** Text, denomination and dates **Rev:** Factory building, cogwheel at right

Date	Mintage	F	VF	XF	Unc
AH1402-1981	18	—	—	—	1,500
AH1402-1981 Proof	1,000	Value: 800			

KM# 548 10 POUNDS
40.0000 g., 0.8750 Gold 1.1254 oz. AGW **Subject:** 1000th Anniversary - Al Azhar Mosque **Obv:** Text within circle divides dates **Rev:** Mosque

Date	Mintage	F	VF	XF	Unc
AH1402-1982 Proof	1,322	Value: 800			

KM# 634 10 POUNDS
40.0000 g., 0.8750 Gold 1.1254 oz. AGW **Subject:** Prophet's Mosque **Obv:** Minaret, globe, denomination, legends **Rev:** Crescent, mosque, minaret below legend arch

Date	Mintage	F	VF	XF	Unc
AH1406-1985 Proof	300	Value: 800			

KM# 908 10 POUNDS
40.0000 g., 0.8750 Gold 1.1253 oz. AGW, 37 mm.
Subject: Egyptian Museum Centennial **Obv:** Denomination **Rev:** Building, centennial numerals in background **Edge:** Reeded

Date	Mintage	F	VF	XF	Unc
AH1423-2002	—	—	—	—	750

KM# 672 50 POUNDS
8.5000 g., 0.9000 Gold .2460 oz. AGW **Series:** World Soccer Championships **Obv:** Stylized flowers, denomination, date and legends **Rev:** Soccer ball on road between Mexican and Egyptian pyramids

Date	Mintage	F	VF	XF	Unc
AH1406-1986	250	—	—	—	275
AH1406-1986 Proof	250	Value: 325			

KM# 641 50 POUNDS
8.5000 g., 0.9000 Gold .2460 oz. AGW **Subject:** Mecca **Obv:** Arabic legend, ornamentation **Rev:** Interior view of the Kaaba

Date	Mintage	F	VF	XF	Unc
AH1406-1986	14,000	—	—	—	200

KM# 612 50 POUNDS
8.5000 g., 0.9000 Gold .2460 oz. AGW **Subject:** Aida Opera **Obv:** Radiant sun, pillars and inscriptions **Rev:** Ancient figures among ruins

Date	Mintage	F	VF	XF	Unc
AH1407-1987	40,000	—	—	—	225

KM# 625 50 POUNDS
8.5000 g., 0.9000 Gold .2460 oz. AGW **Series:** Summer Olympics **Obv:** Arabic legend and ornamentation within English legend **Rev:** Pharoah and athletes

Date	Mintage	F	VF	XF	Unc
AH1408-1988	150	—	—	—	325
AH1408-1988 Proof	50	Value: 375			

KM# 627 50 POUNDS
8.5000 g., 0.9000 Gold .2460 oz. AGW **Series:** Summer Olympics **Rev:** Athletes and mythological figures

Date	Mintage	F	VF	XF	Unc
AH1408-1988	750	—	—	—	275
AH1408-1988 Proof	250	Value: 325			

KM# 629 50 POUNDS
8.5000 g., 0.9000 Gold .2460 oz. AGW **Series:** Winter Olympics **Obv:** Winged design, English legend, Arabic inscription **Rev:** Ski jumper and figure skater within Arabic legend

Date	Mintage	F	VF	XF	Unc
AH1408-1988	150	—	—	—	325
AH1408-1988 Proof	50	Value: 375			

KM# 680 50 POUNDS
8.5000 g., 0.9000 Gold .2460 oz. AGW **Subject:** Soccer World Championship - Italy **Obv:** Text within circle at center of wings, denomination and dates above **Rev:** Ancient gods

Date	Mintage	F	VF	XF	Unc
AH1410-1990 Proof	225	Value: 450			

KM# 683 50 POUNDS
8.5000 g., 0.9000 Gold .2460 oz. AGW **Subject:** Soccer World Championship **Rev:** Player chasing ball

Date	Mintage	F	VF	XF	Unc
AH1410-1990 Proof	75	Value: 525			

KM# 709 50 POUNDS
8.5000 g., 0.9000 Gold .2460 oz. AGW **Series:** Summer Olympics **Obv:** Text within circle at center of wings, denomination and dates above **Rev:** Fencing

Date	Mintage	F	VF	XF	Unc
AH1412-1992	49	—	—	—	475
AH1412-1992 Proof	99	Value: 475			

KM# 710 50 POUNDS
8.5000 g., 0.9000 Gold .2460 oz. AGW **Series:** Summer Olympics **Obv:** Text within circle at center of wings, denomination and dates above **Rev:** Wrestling, half globe below

Date	Mintage	F	VF	XF	Unc
AH1412-1992	49	—	—	—	475
AH1412-1992 Proof	99	Value: 475			

KM# 711 50 POUNDS
8.5000 g., 0.9000 Gold .2460 oz. AGW **Series:** Summer Olympics **Obv:** Text within circle at center of wings, denomination and dates above **Rev:** Archery

Date	Mintage	F	VF	XF	Unc
AH1412-1992	49	—	—	—	475
AH1412-1992 Proof	99	Value: 475			

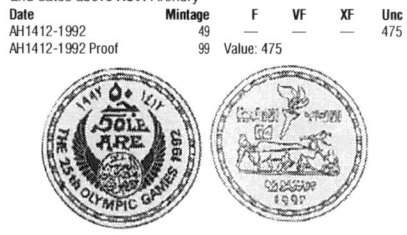

KM# 712 50 POUNDS
8.5000 g., 0.9000 Gold .2460 oz. AGW **Series:** Summer Olympics **Obv:** Text within circle at center of wings, denomination and dates above **Rev:** Many men wrestling an ox

Date	Mintage	F	VF	XF	Unc
AH1412-1992	49	—	—	—	475
AH1412-1992 Proof	99	Value: 475			

KM# 713 50 POUNDS
8.5000 g., 0.9000 Gold .2460 oz. AGW **Series:** Summer Olympics **Obv:** Text within circle at center of wings, denomination and dates above **Rev:** Swimmer stalking a duck

Date	Mintage	F	VF	XF	Unc
AH1412-1992	49	—	—	—	475
AH1412-1992 Proof	99	Value: 475			

KM# 714 50 POUNDS
8.5000 g., 0.9000 Gold .2460 oz. AGW **Series:** Summer Olympics **Obv:** Text within circle at center of wings, denomination and dates above **Rev:** Handball player

Date	Mintage	F	VF	XF	Unc
AH1412-1992	49	—	—	—	475
AH1412-1992 Proof	99	Value: 475			

KM# 715 50 POUNDS
8.5000 g., 0.9000 Gold .2460 oz. AGW **Series:** Summer Olympics **Obv:** Text within circle at center of wings, denomination and dates above **Rev:** Field hockey player

Date	Mintage	F	VF	XF	Unc
AH1412-1992	49	—	—	—	475
AH1412-1992 Proof	99	Value: 475			

KM# 716 50 POUNDS
8.5000 g., 0.9000 Gold .2460 oz. AGW **Series:** Summer Olympics **Obv:** Text within circle at center of wings, denomination and dates above **Rev:** Soccer player kicking ball

EGYPT

Date	Mintage	F	VF	XF	Unc
AH1412-1992	49	—	—	—	475
AH1412-1992 Proof	115	Value: 475			

KM# 755 50 POUNDS
8.5000 g., 0.9000 Gold .2460 oz. AGW **Obv:** Vulture, denomination above and dates below **Rev:** King Tutankhamen's burial mask

Date	Mintage	F	VF	XF	Unc
AH1414-1993 Proof	—	Value: 275			

KM# 756 50 POUNDS
8.5000 g., 0.9000 Gold .2460 oz. AGW **Subject:** Cleopatra **Obv:** Vulture, denomination above and dates below **Rev:** Bust left

Date	Mintage	F	VF	XF	Unc
AH1414-1993 Proof	—	Value: 250			

KM# 776 50 POUNDS
8.5000 g., 0.9000 Gold .2460 oz. AGW **Obv:** Vulture, denomination above and dates below **Rev:** Sphinx head

Date	Mintage	F	VF	XF	Unc
AH1414-1993 Proof	—	Value: 225			

KM# 777 50 POUNDS
8.5000 g., 0.9000 Gold .2460 oz. AGW **Obv:** Vulture, denomination above and dates below **Rev:** Standing Ramses II

Date	Mintage	F	VF	XF	Unc
AH1414-1993 Proof	—	Value: 225			

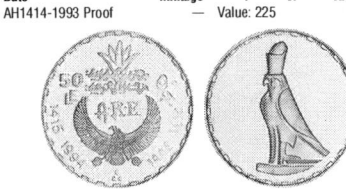

KM# 778 50 POUNDS
8.5000 g., 0.9000 Gold .2460 oz. AGW **Obv:** Vulture, denomination above and dates below **Rev:** Crowned falcon left

Date	Mintage	F	VF	XF	Unc
AH1414-1993 Proof	—	Value: 240			

KM# 868 50 POUNDS
8.5000 g., 0.9000 Gold .2460 oz. AGW **Subject:** King Narmer Palette **Obv:** Vulture, denomination above and dates below **Rev:** King killing a wounded foe

Date	Mintage	F	VF	XF	Unc
AH1414-1993 Proof	3,000	Value: 265			

KM# 870 50 POUNDS
8.5000 g., 0.9000 Gold .2460 oz. AGW **Subject:** King Kna-Sekhem **Obv:** Vulture, denomination above and dates below **Rev:** Seated king

Date	Mintage	F	VF	XF	Unc
AH1414-1993 Proof	3,000	Value: 265			

KM# 873 50 POUNDS
8.5000 g., 0.9000 Gold .2460 oz. AGW **Subject:** Menkaure Triad **Obv:** Vulture, denomination above and dates below **Rev:** Three carved figurines

Date	Mintage	F	VF	XF	Unc
AH1414-1993 Proof	3,000	Value: 265			

KM# 885 50 POUNDS
8.5000 g., 0.9000 Gold .2460 oz. AGW **Subject:** Thoutmosis III **Obv:** Vulture, denomination above and dates below **Rev:** Kneeling figure holding jar

Date	Mintage	F	VF	XF	Unc
AH1414-1993 Proof	3,000	Value: 265			

KM# 775 50 POUNDS
8.5000 g., 0.9000 Gold .2460 oz. AGW **Obv:** Vulture, denomination above and dates below **Rev:** Three pyramids

Date	Mintage	F	VF	XF	Unc
AH1414-1993 Proof	—	Value: 225			

KM# 737 50 POUNDS
8.5000 g., 0.9000 Gold .2460 oz. AGW **Series:** World Cup Soccer **Obv:** Text within circle at center of wings, oval shield above divides dates **Rev:** Two players, pyramid and Statue of Liberty

Date	Mintage	F	VF	XF	Unc
AH1415-1994	99	—	—	—	325
AH1415-1994 Proof	99	Value: 325			

KM# 739 50 POUNDS
8.5000 g., 0.9000 Gold .2460 oz. AGW **Series:** World Cup Soccer **Obv:** Text within circle at center of wings, oval shield above divides dates **Rev:** Stylized player

Date	Mintage	F	VF	XF	Unc
AH1415-1994	99	—	—	—	325
AH1415-1994 Proof	99	Value: 325			

KM# 779 50 POUNDS
8.5000 g., 0.9000 Gold .2460 oz. AGW **Subject:** Queen Nefertiti **Obv:** Vulture, denomination above and dates below **Rev:** Bust right

Date	Mintage	F	VF	XF	Unc
AH1415-1994 Proof	—	Value: 230			

KM# 780 50 POUNDS
8.5000 g., 0.9000 Gold .2460 oz. AGW **Obv:** Vulture, denomination above and dates below **Rev:** Seated cat right

Date	Mintage	F	VF	XF	Unc
AH1415-1994 Proof	—	Value: 230			

KM# 781 50 POUNDS
8.5000 g., 0.9000 Gold .2460 oz. AGW **Obv:** Vulture, denomination above and dates below **Rev:** Archer in chariot

Date	Mintage	F	VF	XF	Unc
AH1415-1994 Proof	—	Value: 245			

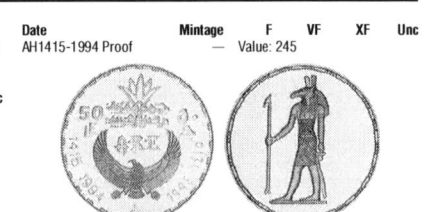

KM# 782 50 POUNDS
8.5000 g., 0.9000 Gold .2460 oz. AGW **Obv:** Vulture, denomination above and dates below **Rev:** Standing God Seth left

Date	Mintage	F	VF	XF	Unc
AH1415-1994 Proof	—	Value: 215			

KM# 814 50 POUNDS
8.5000 g., 0.9000 Gold .2460 oz. AGW **Obv:** Vulture, denomination above and dates below **Rev:** Hippopotamus

Date	Mintage	F	VF	XF	Unc
AH1415-1994 Proof	—	Value: 215			

KM# 815 50 POUNDS
8.5000 g., 0.9000 Gold .2460 oz. AGW **Obv:** Vulture, denomination above and dates below **Rev:** Egyptian gazelle

Date	Mintage	F	VF	XF	Unc
AH1415-1994 Proof	—	Value: 215			

KM# 816 50 POUNDS
8.5000 g., 0.9000 Gold .2460 oz. AGW **Obv:** Vulture, denomination above and dates below **Rev:** Phoenix birds

Date	Mintage	F	VF	XF	Unc
AH1415-1994 Proof	—	Value: 215			

KM# 817 50 POUNDS
8.5000 g., 0.9000 Gold .2460 oz. AGW **Obv:** Vulture, denomination above and dates below **Rev:** Egyptian geese

Date	Mintage	F	VF	XF	Unc
AH1415-1994 Proof	—	Value: 215			

KM# 818 50 POUNDS
8.5000 g., 0.9000 Gold .2460 oz. AGW **Obv:** Vulture, denomination above and dates below **Rev:** King Taharqa

Date	Mintage	F	VF	XF	Unc
AH1415-1994 Proof	—	Value: 215			

KM# 819 50 POUNDS
8.5000 g., 0.9000 Gold .2460 oz. AGW **Obv:** Vulture, denomination above and dates below **Rev:** Amenhotep Temple

Date	Mintage	F	VF	XF	Unc
AH1415-1994 Proof	—	Value: 215			

KM# 820 50 POUNDS
8.5000 g., 0.9000 Gold .2460 oz. AGW **Obv:** Vulture, denomination above and dates below **Rev:** Karnak Temple

Date	Mintage	F	VF	XF	Unc
AH1415-1994 Proof	—	Value: 215			

KM# 821 50 POUNDS
8.5000 g., 0.9000 Gold .2460 oz. AGW **Obv:** Vulture, denomination above and dates below **Rev:** Philae Temple

Date	Mintage	F	VF	XF	Unc
AH1415-1994 Proof	—	Value: 215			

KM# 822 50 POUNDS
8.5000 g., 0.9000 Gold .2460 oz. AGW **Obv:** Vulture, denomination above and dates below **Rev:** Khonsu Temple

Date	Mintage	F	VF	XF	Unc
AH1415-1994 Proof	—	Value: 215			

KM# 871 50 POUNDS
8.5000 g., 0.9000 Gold .2460 oz. AGW **Obv:** Vulture, denomination above and dates below **Rev:** King Djoser wearing the Red Crown

Date	Mintage	F	VF	XF	Unc
AH1415-1994 Proof	3,000	Value: 260			

KM# 872 50 POUNDS
8.5000 g., 0.9000 Gold .2460 oz. AGW **Obv:** Vulture, denomination above and dates below **Rev:** Seated King Khufu with flat-top hat

Date	Mintage	F	VF	XF	Unc
AH1415-1994 Proof	3,000	Value: 260			

KM# 882 50 POUNDS
8.5000 g., 0.9000 Gold .2460 oz. AGW **Subject:** King Sesostris I **Obv:** Vulture, denomination above and dates below **Rev:** RE (sun god) presenting the ANKH (symbol of life) to the king wearing the Double Crown

Date	Mintage	F	VF	XF	Unc
AH1415-1994 Proof	3,000	Value: 275			

KM# 884 50 POUNDS
8.5000 g., 0.9000 Gold .2460 oz. AGW **Subject:** King Horemheb **Obv:** Vulture, denomination above and dates below **Rev:** Seated King Horemheb

Date	Mintage	F	VF	XF	Unc
AH1415-1994 Proof	3,000	Value: 275			

KM# 886 50 POUNDS
8.5000 g., 0.9000 Gold .2460 oz. AGW **Subject:** King Khonsu **Obv:** Vulture, denomination above and dates below **Rev:** 1/2-length King Khonsu

Date	Mintage	F	VF	XF	Unc
AH1415-1994 Proof	3,000	Value: 275			

KM# 887 50 POUNDS
8.5000 g., 0.9000 Gold .2460 oz. AGW **Subject:** Tutankhamen's Throne **Obv:** Vulture, denomination above and dates below **Rev:** King Tut seated on throne with servant

Date	Mintage	F	VF	XF	Unc
AH1415-1994 Proof	3,000	Value: 300			

EGYPT

KM# 888 50 POUNDS
8.5000 g., 0.9000 Gold .2460 oz. AGW **Subject:** Queen Hatshepsut **Obv:** Vulture, denomination above and dates below **Rev:** Queen's facial sculpture

Date	Mintage	F	VF	XF	Unc
AH1415-1994 Proof	3,000	Value: 275			

KM# 890 50 POUNDS
8.5000 g., 0.9000 Gold .2460 oz. AGW **Subject:** Akhnaton and Family **Obv:** Vulture, denomination above and dates below **Rev:** Family scene

Date	Mintage	F	VF	XF	Unc
AH1415-1994 Proof	3,000	Value: 275			

KM# 891 50 POUNDS
8.5000 g., 0.9000 Gold .2460 oz. AGW **Obv:** Vulture, denomination above and dates below **Rev:** Akhnaton

Date	Mintage	F	VF	XF	Unc
AH1415-1994 Proof	3,000	Value: 275			

KM# 892 50 POUNDS
8.5000 g., 0.9000 Gold .2460 oz. AGW **Subject:** Queen Nefertari **Obv:** Vulture, denomination above and dates below **Rev:** Kneeling Queen Nefertari

Date	Mintage	F	VF	XF	Unc
AH1415-1994 Proof	5,000	Value: 275			

KM# 893 50 POUNDS
8.5000 g., 0.9000 Gold .2460 oz. AGW **Subject:** Ramses III **Obv:** Vulture, denomination above and dates below **Rev:** 3/4-length Ramses III

Date	Mintage	F	VF	XF	Unc
AH1415-1994 Proof	3,000	Value: 300			

KM# 895 50 POUNDS
8.5000 g., 0.9000 Gold .2460 oz. AGW **Obv:** Vulture, denomination above and dates below **Rev:** Amulet of Hathor

Date	Mintage	F	VF	XF	Unc
AH1415-1994 Proof	3,000	Value: 275			

KM# 877 50 POUNDS
26.0000 g., 0.8750 Gold .7315 oz. AGW **Obv:** Vulture, denomination above and dates below **Rev:** Seated scribe

Date	Mintage	F	VF	XF	Unc
AH1415-1994 Proof	3,000	Value: 500			

KM# 921 50 POUNDS
11.8000 g., 0.9000 Gold 0.341 oz. AGW, 26 mm. **Obv:** Value and inscription **Rev:** Statue of Ramses II seated **Edge:** Reeded

Date	Mintage	F	VF	XF	Unc
AH1420-1999 Proof	—	Value: 275			

KM# 550 100 POUNDS
17.1500 g., 0.9000 Gold .4963 oz. AGW **Obv:** Denomination, dates and text **Rev:** Bust of Queen Nefertiti right Rev. Designer: Dominic Angelini

Date	Mintage	F	VF	XF	Unc
AH1404-1983 Proof	16,000	Value: 725			

KM# 562 100 POUNDS
17.1500 g., 0.9000 Gold .4963 oz. AGW **Obv:** Denomination, dates and text **Rev:** Bust of Cleopatra VII in formal headdress left 69-30BC, Queen and statesperson

Date	Mintage	F	VF	XF	Unc
AH1404-1984 Proof	2,121	Value: 800			

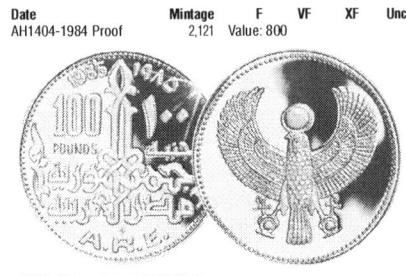

KM# 569 100 POUNDS
17.1500 g., 0.9000 Gold .4963 oz. AGW **Obv:** Denomination, dates and text **Rev:** The golden falcon, from an ancient breastplate found in King Tutankhamen's tomb

Date	Mintage	F	VF	XF	Unc
AH1405-1985 Proof	1,800	Value: 500			

KM# 591 100 POUNDS
17.1500 g., 0.9000 Gold .4963 oz. AGW **Rev:** Tutankhamen

Date	Mintage	F	VF	XF	Unc
AH1406-1986 Proof	7,500	Value: 775			

KM# 642 100 POUNDS
17.0000 g., 0.9000 Gold .4918 oz. AGW **Subject:** Mecca **Obv:** Arabic legend, ornamentation **Rev:** Interior view of the Kaaba

Date	Mintage	F	VF	XF	Unc
AH1406-1986	700	—	—	—	425

KM# 613 100 POUNDS
17.0000 g., 0.9000 Gold .4918 oz. AGW **Obv:** Denomination, dates and text **Rev:** The golden ram

Date	Mintage	F	VF	XF	Unc
AH1407-1987 Proof	7,500	Value: 475			

KM# 648 100 POUNDS
17.0000 g., 0.9000 Gold .4918 oz. AGW **Obv:** Denomination, dates and text **Rev:** The golden warrior

Date	Mintage	F	VF	XF	Unc
AH1408-1988 Proof	5,500	Value: 500			

KM# 656 100 POUNDS
17.1500 g., 0.9000 Gold .4963 oz. AGW **Obv:** Denomination, dates and text **Rev:** The golden cat

Date	Mintage	F	VF	XF	Unc
AH1409-1989 FM Proof	Est. 7,500	Value: 475			

KM# 681 100 POUNDS
17.0000 g., 0.9000 Gold .4918 oz. AGW **Series:** World Soccer Championship - Italy **Rev:** Ancient gods

Date	Mintage	F	VF	XF	Unc
AH1410-1990 Proof	125	Value: 800			

KM# 684 100 POUNDS
17.0000 g., 0.9000 Gold .4918 oz. AGW **Series:** World Soccer Championship - Italy **Rev:** Player chasing ball

Date	Mintage	F	VF	XF	Unc
AH1410-1990 Proof	75	Value: 825			

KM# 693 100 POUNDS
17.0000 g., 0.9000 Gold .4918 oz. AGW **Series:** Ancient Egyptian Culture **Obv:** Denomination, dates and text **Rev:** Sphinx

Date	Mintage	F	VF	XF	Unc
AH1410-1990 FM Proof	Est. 5,000	Value: 575			

KM# 729 100 POUNDS
17.0000 g., 0.9000 Gold .4918 oz. AGW **Series:** Ancient Egyptian Culture **Obv:** Denomination, dates and text **Rev:** Pyramids of Giza

Date	Mintage	F	VF	XF	Unc
AH1411-1991 Proof	Est. 5,000	Value: 575			

KM# 717 100 POUNDS
17.0000 g., 0.9000 Gold .4918 oz. AGW **Series:** Summer Olympics **Rev:** Fencing

Date	Mintage	F	VF	XF	Unc
AH1412-1992	49	—	—	—	845
AH1412-1992 Proof	99	Value: 845			

202 EGYPT

KM# 718 100 POUNDS
17.0000 g., 0.9000 Gold .4918 oz. AGW **Series:** Summer Olympics **Obv:** Text within circle at center of wings, denomination and dates above **Rev:** Wrestling matches

Date	Mintage	F	VF	XF	Unc
AH1412-1992	49	—	—	—	845
AH1412-1992 Proof	99	Value: 845			

KM# 720 100 POUNDS
17.0000 g., 0.9000 Gold .4918 oz. AGW **Series:** Summer Olympics **Obv:** Text within circle at center of wings, denomination and dates above **Rev:** Many men wrestling an ox

Date	Mintage	F	VF	XF	Unc
AH1412-1992	49	—	—	—	845
AH1412-1992 Proof	99	Value: 845			

KM# 721 100 POUNDS
17.0000 g., 0.9000 Gold .4918 oz. AGW **Series:** Summer Olympics **Rev:** Swimmer stalking a duck

Date	Mintage	F	VF	XF	Unc
AH1412-1992	49	—	—	—	845
AH1412-1992 Proof	99	Value: 845			

KM# 722 100 POUNDS
17.0000 g., 0.9000 Gold .4918 oz. AGW **Series:** Summer Olympics **Rev:** Handball player

Date	Mintage	F	VF	XF	Unc
AH1412-1992	49	—	—	—	845
AH1412-1992 Proof	99	Value: 845			

KM# 723 100 POUNDS
17.0000 g., 0.9000 Gold .4918 oz. AGW **Series:** Summer Olympics **Rev:** Field hockey player

Date	Mintage	F	VF	XF	Unc
AH1412-1992	49	—	—	—	845
AH1412-1992 Proof	99	Value: 845			

KM# 724 100 POUNDS
17.0000 g., 0.9000 Gold .4918 oz. AGW **Series:** Summer Olympics **Rev:** Soccer player

Date	Mintage	F	VF	XF	Unc
AH1412-1992	49	—	—	—	845
AH1412-1992 Proof	115	Value: 845			

KM# 730 100 POUNDS
17.1500 g., 0.9000 Gold .4963 oz. AGW **Subject:** The Golden Guardians **Obv:** Denomination, dates and text **Rev:** Two statues of Ramses II

Date	Mintage	F	VF	XF	Unc
1992 Proof	Est. 5,000	Value: 525			

KM# 719 100 POUNDS
17.0000 g., 0.9000 Gold .4918 oz. AGW **Series:** Summer Olympics **Obv:** Text within circle at center of wings, denomination and dates above **Rev:** Archery demonstration

Date	Mintage	F	VF	XF	Unc
AH1412-1992	49	—	—	—	845
AH1412-1992 Proof	99	Value: 845			

PATTERNS
Including off metal strikes

KM#	Date	Mintage	Identification	Mkt Val
Pn4	AH1277//4	—	25 Qirsh. 0.8750 Gold. Plain edge. Without flower.	
Pn5	AH1277//4	—	50 Qirsh. 0.8750 Gold. Plain edge. Without flower.	
Pn6	AH1277//4	—	100 Qirsh. 0.8750 Gold. Plain edge. Without flower.	
Pn7	AH1277//4	—	200 Qirsh. 0.8750 Gold. Plain edge. Without flower.	
Pn8	AH1277//4	—	400 Qirsh. 0.8750 Gold. Plain edge. Without flower.	
Pn24	AH1293//15	—	5 Qirsh. Gold.	750
Pn27	AH1942	—	2 Piastres. Platinum. KM#365	—

PROOF SETS

KM#	Date	Mintage	Identification	Issue Price	Mkt Val
PS1	1938 (4)	—	KM#370, 371, 372, 373	4,200	4,500
PS4	1980 (4)	—	KM#508, 509, 517, 519	—	2,000
PS5	1980 (3)	—	KM#509, 517, 519	—	1,975

SPECIMEN SETS (SS)

KM#	Date	Mintage	Identification	Issue Price	Mkt Val
SS1	1916/7 (10)	—	KM#312-316, 317.1, 318.1, 319, 321, 324	—	1,700

EL SALVADOR

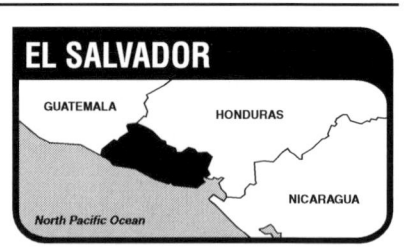

The Republic of El Salvador, a Central American country bordered by Guatemala, Honduras and the Pacific Ocean, has an area of 8,124 sq. mi. (21,040 sq. km.) and a population of 6.0 million. Capital: San Salvador. This most intensely cultivated of Latin American countries produces coffee (the major crop), sugar and balsam for export. Gold, silver and other metals are largely unexploited.

The first Spanish attempt to subjugate the area was undertaken in 1523 by Pedro de Alvarado, Cortes' lieutenant. He was forced to retreat by Indian forces, but returned in 1525 and succeeded in bringing the region under control of the Captaincy General of Guatemala. In 1821, El Salvador and the other Central American provinces jointly declared independence from Spain. In 1823, the Republic of Central America was formed by the five Central American states; this federation dissolved in 1839. El Salvador then became an independent republic in 1841.

Since 1960, El Salvador has been a part of the Central American Common Market. During the 1980's El Salvador went through a 12 year Civil War that ended in 1992 with the signing of a United Nations-sponsored Peace Accord. Free elections, with full participation of all political parties, were held in 1994, 1997 and 1999. Armando Calderon-Sol was elected president in 1994 for a 5-year term and Francisco Flores was elected in 1999 for a 5-year term as well.

MINT MARK
C.A.M. - Central American Mint, San Salvador

MONETARY SYSTEM
100 Centavos = 1 Peso

REPUBLIC OF EL SALVADOR

DECIMAL COINAGE
100 Centavos = 1 Peso

KM# 116 2-1/2 PESOS
4.0323 g., 0.9000 Gold .1167 oz. AGW **Obv:** Arms **Obv. Legend:** REPUBLICA DEL SALVADOR **Rev:** Laureate head left

Date	Mintage	F	VF	XF	Unc	BU
1892C.A.M.	597	250	475	750	1,650	—
1892C.A.M. Proof	—	Value: 2,000				

KM# 117 5 PESOS
8.0645 g., 0.9000 Gold .2334 oz. AGW **Obv:** Arms **Obv. Legend:** REPUBLICA DEL SALVADOR **Rev:** Laureate head left

Date	Mintage	F	VF	XF	Unc	BU
1892C.A.M.	558	350	650	1,000	2,250	—
1892C.A.M. Proof	—	Value: 3,500				

KM# 118 10 PESOS
16.1290 g., 0.9000 Gold .4667 oz. AGW **Obv:** Arms **Obv. Legend:** REPUBLICA DEL SALVADOR **Rev:** Laureate head left

Date	Mintage	F	VF	XF	Unc	BU
1892C.A.M.	321	600	1,000	2,500	4,500	—
1892C.A.M. Proof	—	Value: 6,000				

EL SALVADOR 203

KM# 119 20 PESOS
32.2580 g., 0.9000 Gold .9334 oz. AGW **Obv:** Arms **Obv.**
Legend: REPUBLICA DEL SALVADOR **Rev:** Laureate head left

Date	Mintage	F	VF	XF	Unc	BU
1892C.A.M.	300	1,000	1,650	2,750	6,500	—
1892C.A.M. Proof	—	Value: 8,000				

REFORM COINAGE
100 Centavos = 1 Colon

KM# 132 20 COLONES
15.5600 g., 0.9000 Gold .4502 oz. AGW, 27 mm. **Subject:** 400th Anniversary - San Salvador **Obv:** Flags flank triangular arms within wreath, denomination below **Obv. Designer:** Ignacio Cortes **Rev:** Alvarado and Quinonez busts left, dates above **Rev. Designer:** Jose C. Tovar

Date	Mintage	F	VF	XF	Unc	BU
ND(1925)Mo	200	—	800	1,600	2,500	—

KM# 143 25 COLONES
2.9400 g., 0.9000 Gold .0850 oz. AGW **Subject:** 150th Anniversary of Independence **Obv:** Flags flank triangular arms within wreath **Rev:** Salvador Dali image, "La Fecundida" within circle, denomination below

Date	Mintage	F	VF	XF	Unc	BU
1971 Proof	7,650	Value: 85.00				

KM# 144 50 COLONES
5.9000 g., 0.9000 Gold .1707 oz. AGW **Subject:** 150th Anniversary of Independence **Obv:** Flags flank triangular arms within wreath **Rev:** Liberty statue, Cañas bust at right, dates at left, denomination below

Date	Mintage	F	VF	XF	Unc	BU
1971 Proof	3,530	Value: 145				

KM# 145 100 COLONES
11.8000 g., 0.9000 Gold .3414 oz. AGW **Subject:** 150th Anniversary of Independence **Obv:** Flags flank triangular arms within wreath **Rev:** Map of El Salvador, denomination below

Date	Mintage	F	VF	XF	Unc	BU
1971 Proof	2,750	Value: 250				

KM# 146 200 COLONES
23.6000 g., 0.9000 Gold .6829 oz. AGW **Subject:** 150th Anniversary of Independence **Obv:** Flags flank triangular arms within wreath, bust at right, date below **Rev:** Panchimalco Church, denomination below

Date	Mintage	F	VF	XF	Unc	BU
1971 Proof	2,245	Value: 485				

KM# 152 250 COLONES
16.0000 g., 0.9170 Gold .4717 oz. AGW **Subject:** 18th Annual Governors' Assembly **Obv:** Flags flank triangular arms within wreath, denomination below **Rev:** First coin of C.A. Federation 1824, dates below

Date	Mintage	F	VF	XF	Unc	BU
1977	4,000	—	—	—	325	350
1977 Proof	400	Value: 385				

KM# 159 2500 COLONES
16.0000 g., 0.9170 Gold .4715 oz. AGW **Subject:** Union for Peace **Obv:** Four clasped hands, date below **Rev:** Denomination within wreath

Date	Mintage	F	VF	XF	Unc	BU
1992	—	—	—	—	375	—

KM# 161 2500 COLONES
16.0000 g., 0.9170 Gold .4715 oz. AGW **Subject:** Discovery of America **Obv:** Columbus' ships and world map, date below **Rev:** Denomination within wreath

Date	Mintage	F	VF	XF	Unc	BU
1992	—	—	—	—	375	—

MEDALLIC COINAGE
General Barrios Series

Originals were struck in Bronze and silver in 1861. These restrikes were produced about 1971.

X# 5d PESO
Gold **Subject:** General Barrios

Date	Mintage	F	VF	XF	Unc	BU
1861 Proof; Rare	—	—	—	—	—	—

PATTERNS
Including off metal strikes

KM#	Date	Mintage	Identification	Mkt Val
Pn21	1892C.A.M.	—	2-1/2 Pesos. 0.9000 Gold. KM#116. Prev. KM#Pn7.	—
Pn22	1892	—	2-1/2 Pesos. Bronze Gilt. Reeded edge.	—
Pn24	1892	—	2-1/2 Pesos. Copper Gilt.	—
Pn25	1892C.A.M.	—	5 Pesos. Copper. KM#117. Prev. KM#Pn8.	600
Pn26	1892	—	5 Pesos. Bronze Gilt. Reeded edge.	—
Pn27	1892	—	5 Pesos. Copper Gilt.	—
Pn28	1892C.A.M.	—	10 Pesos. Copper. KM#118. Prev. KM#Pn9.	850
Pn29	1892C.A.M.	—	20 Pesos. Gilt Bronze. KM#119. Prev. KM#Pn10.	1,200
Pn30	1892	—	10 Pesos. Copper Gilt.	—
Pn31	1892	—	20 Pesos. Copper.	—
Pn32	1892	—	20 Pesos. Bronze Gilt. Reeded edge.	—
Pn33	1892	—	20 Pesos. Copper Gilt.	—

PROOF SETS

KM#	Date	Mintage	Identification	Issue Price	Mkt Val
PS2	1892 (10)	—	KM#108-112, 114, 116-119	—	16,000
PS4	1971 (6)	—	KM#141-146	—	900
PS5	1971 (4)	—	KM#143-146	250	885

EQUATORIAL AFRICAN STATES

For historical background, see the introduction to Central African States.

ESSAIS
Standard metals unless otherwise noted

KM#	Date	Mintage	Identification	Issue Price	Mkt Val
E4	1961(a)	—	50 Francs. Gold. KM#4.	—	1,250

PIEFORTS

KM#	Date	Mintage	Identification	Issue Price	Mkt Val
P1	1965(a)	—	100 Francs. Gold. 23.4800 g. Three Giant Eland, left. Denomination, date above. KM#5. With ESSAI.	—	1,000

EQUATORIAL GUINEA

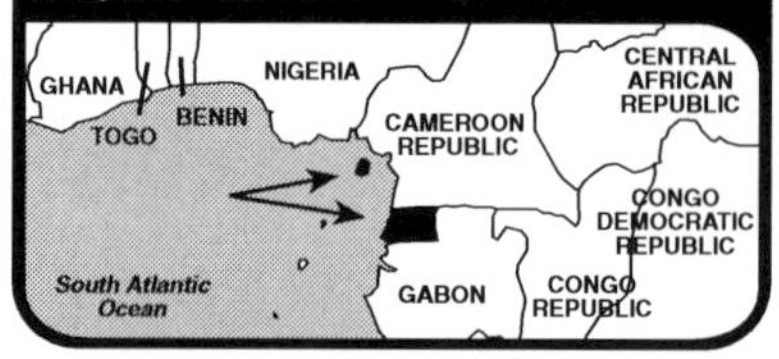

The Republic of Equatorial Guinea (formerly Spanish Guinea) consists of Rio Muni, located on the coast of West-Central Africa between Cameroon and Gabon, and the off-shore islands of Fernando Po, Annobon, Corisco, Elobey Grande and Elobey Chico. The equatorial country has an area of 10,831 sq. mi. (28,050 sq. km.) and a population of 420,293. Capital: Malabo. The economy is based on agriculture and forestry. Cacao, wood and coffee are exported.

Fernando Po was discovered between 1474 and 1496 by Portuguese navigators charting a route to the spice islands of the Far East. Portugal retained control of it and the adjacent islands until 1778 when they, together with trading rights to the African coast between the Ogooue and Niger Rivers, were ceded to Spain. Fernando Po was administered, with Spanish consent, by the British from 1827 to 1844 when it was reclaimed by Spain. Mainland Rio Muni was granted to Spain by the Berlin Conference of 1885. The name of the colony was changed from Spanish Guinea to Equatorial Guinea in Dec. of 1963. Independence was attained on Oct. 12, 1968.

Equatorial Guinea converted to the CFA currency system as issued for the Central African States issuing its first 100 Franc denomination in 1985.

NOTE: The 1969 coinage carries the actual minting date in the stars at the sides of the large date.

MINT MARK
(a) - Paris, privy marks only

REPUBLIC

PESETA COINAGE

KM# 20.1 250 PESETAS
3.5200 g., 0.9000 Gold .1018 oz. AGW **Obv:** Crossed tusks divide arms above and denomination below, fineness countermark at 8 o'clock by tusk base **Rev:** Goya's Naked Maja **Note:** Prev. KM#20.
Date	Mintage	F	VF	XF	Unc	BU
1970 Proof	3,500	Value: 100				

KM# 20.2 250 PESETAS
3.5200 g., 0.9000 Gold 0.1019 oz. AGW **Obv:** Crossed tusks divide arms above and denomination below, fineness countermark at 4o'clock by tusk base **Rev:** Goya's Naked Maja
Date	Mintage	F	VF	XF	Unc	BU
1970 Proof	—	Value: 100				

KM# 21 250 PESETAS
3.5200 g., 0.9000 Gold .1018 oz. AGW **Obv:** Crossed tusks divide arms above and denomination below **Rev:** Durer's Praying Hands
Date	Mintage	F	VF	XF	Unc	BU
1970 Proof	2,000	Value: 85.00				

KM# 22 500 PESETAS
7.0500 g., 0.9000 Gold .2040 oz. AGW **Obv:** Crossed tusks divide arms above and denomination below **Rev:** Bust of Pope John XXIII
Date	Mintage	F	VF	XF	Unc	BU
1970 Proof	1,680	Value: 165				

KM# 23 500 PESETAS
7.0500 g., 0.9000 Gold .2040 oz. AGW **Subject:** Vladimer Illyich Lenin **Obv:** Crossed tusks divide arms above and denomination below **Rev:** Head left divides dates
Date	Mintage	F	VF	XF	Unc	BU
1970 Proof	1,680	Value: 170				

KM# 24 500 PESETAS
7.0500 g., 0.9000 Gold .2040 oz. AGW **Obv:** Crossed tusks divide arms above and denomination below **Rev:** President Abraham Lincoln
Date	Mintage	F	VF	XF	Unc	BU
1970 Proof	1,700	Value: 160				

KM# 25 500 PESETAS
7.0500 g., 0.9000 Gold .2040 oz. AGW **Subject:** Centennial - Birth of Mahatma Gandhi **Obv:** Crossed tusks divide arms above and denomination below **Rev:** Portrait of Gandhi
Date	Mintage	F	VF	XF	Unc	BU
1970 Proof	1,680	Value: 170				

KM# 26 750 PESETAS
10.5700 g., 0.9000 Gold .3058 oz. AGW **Subject:** Centennial of the Capital Rome **Obv:** Crossed tusks divide arms above and denomination below **Rev:** Symbols of Rome
Date	Mintage	F	VF	XF	Unc	BU
1970 Proof	1,650	Value: 240				

KM# 27 750 PESETAS
10.5700 g., 0.9000 Gold .3058 oz. AGW **Subject:** Centennial of the Capital Rome **Obv:** Crossed tusks divide arms above and denomination below **Rev:** Colisseum
Date	Mintage	F	VF	XF	Unc	BU
1970 Proof	1,550	Value: 250				

KM# 28 750 PESETAS
10.5700 g., 0.9000 Gold .3058 oz. AGW **Subject:** Centennial of the Capital Rome **Obv:** Crossed tusks divide arms above and denomination below **Rev:** Athena divides dates and buildings
Date	Mintage	F	VF	XF	Unc	BU
1970 Proof	1,550	Value: 245				

KM# 29 750 PESETAS
10.5700 g., 0.9000 Gold .3058 oz. AGW **Subject:** Centennial of the Capital Rome **Obv:** Crossed tusks divide arms above and denomination below **Rev:** Head of Mercury left
Date	Mintage	F	VF	XF	Unc	BU
1970 Proof	1,550	Value: 245				

KM# 30 1000 PESETAS
14.1000 g., 0.9000 Gold .4080 oz. AGW **Subject:** World Soccer Championship in Mexico **Obv:** Crossed tusks divide arms above and denomination below **Rev:** Statue flanked by countries with dates, four on each side
Date	Mintage	F	VF	XF	Unc	BU
1970 Proof	1,190	Value: 320				

KM# 31 5000 PESETAS
70.5200 g., 0.9000 Gold 2.0407 oz. AGW **Subject:** First President - Francisco Macias **Obv:** Crossed tusks divide arms above and denomination below **Rev:** Head 3/4 right
Date	Mintage	F	VF	XF	Unc	BU
1970 Proof	330	Value: 1,600				

REFORM COINAGE
1975-1980

KM# 39 5000 EKUELE
6.9600 g., 0.9170 Gold .2052 oz. AGW **Obv:** Bank building, denomination below **Rev:** Head right, date below
Date	Mintage	F	VF	XF	Unc	BU
1978 Proof	31,000	Value: 165				

KM# 40 10000 EKUELE
13.9200 g., 0.9170 Gold .4104 oz. AGW **Obv:** Assorted tools, denomination below, rooster above **Rev:** Head right, date below
Date	Mintage	F	VF	XF	Unc	BU
1978 Proof	31,000	Value: 325				

KM# 41 10000 EKUELE
13.9200 g., 0.9170 Gold .4104 oz. AGW **Subject:** Soccer Games - Argentina 1978 **Obv:** Assorted tools, denomination below, rooster above **Rev:** Country name and map at center, soccer players flank, shields above and below
Date	Mintage	F	VF	XF	Unc	BU
ND(1979) Proof	121	Value: 550				

REFORM COINAGE
1980-1982

KM# 54 EKUELE
62.2900 g., 0.9990 Gold 2.0009 oz. AGW **Obv:** Coat of arms **Rev:** Pope John Paul II
Date	Mintage	F	VF	XF	Unc	BU
1982	—	—	—	—	1,650	—

EQUATORIAL GUINEA

REFORM COINAGE
1985-
KM# 105 7000 FRANCOS
7.7700 g., 0.9000 Gold .2248 oz. AGW **Subject:** Endangered Wildlife **Obv:** Arms above denomination **Rev:** Lions

Date	Mintage	F	VF	XF	Unc	BU
1992 Proof	450	Value: 200				

KM# 72 15000 FRANCOS
7.0000 g., 0.9170 Gold .2063 oz. AGW **Subject:** Discovery of America - Columbus **Obv:** Arms above denomination

Date	Mintage	F	VF	XF	Unc	BU
1991 Proof	1,500	Value: 165				

KM# 73 15000 FRANCOS
7.0000 g., 0.9170 Gold .2063 oz. AGW **Subject:** Expo Seville **Obv:** Arms above denomination **Rev:** Ship and Space Shuttle, dates below

Date	Mintage	F	VF	XF	Unc	BU
1991 Proof	1,500	Value: 165				

KM# 74 15000 FRANCOS
7.0000 g., 0.9170 Gold .2063 oz. AGW **Series:** Barcelona Olympics **Obv:** Arms above denomination **Rev:** Equestrian jumping

Date	Mintage	F	VF	XF	Unc	BU
1991 Proof	1,500	Value: 170				

KM# 106 15000 FRANCOS
15.5500 g., 0.9000 Gold .4499 oz. AGW **Subject:** Endangered Wildlife **Obv:** Topical map of Africa **Rev:** Elephant

Date	Mintage	F	VF	XF	Unc	BU
1992 Proof	450	Value: 350				

KM# 107 30000 FRANCOS
33.9300 g., 0.9170 Gold 1.0003 oz. AGW, 32.8 mm. **Subject:** Elephant Protection **Obv:** Arms above denomination **Rev:** Elephant **Edge:** Reeded

Date	Mintage	F	VF	XF	Unc	BU
1993 Proof	700	Value: 750				

Note: 400 pieces remelted at mint

MEDALLIC COINAGE
Banco Central Issues

X# M3 5000 BIPKWELE
4.0000 g., 0.9170 Gold 0.1179 oz. AGW, 20 mm. **Subject:** 1979 Spanish Royalty Visit **Obv:** Arms **Rev:** Jugate busts of Juan Carlos and Sofia left **Rev. Legend:** S.S.M.LOS REYES DE ESPAÑA VISITAN GUINEA **Note:** Previous KM#M5.

Date	Mintage	F	VF	XF	Unc	BU
(19)80	4,250	—	—	—	95.00	—
(19)80 Proof	2,000	Value: 120				

X# M7 5000 BIPKWELE
4.0000 g., 0.9170 Gold 0.1179 oz. AGW, 20 mm. **Subject:** 1979 Spanish Royalty Visit **Obv:** Arms **Rev:** Bust of Juan Carlos left **Obv. Legend:** REPUBLICA DE GUINEA ECUATORIAL **Note:** Previous KM#M6.

Date	Mintage	F	VF	XF	Unc	BU
(19)80	4,250	—	—	—	75.00	—
(19)80 Proof	2,000	Value: 100				

X# M4 10000 BIPKWELE
8.0000 g., 0.9170 Gold 0.2359 oz. AGW, 24 mm. **Subject:** 1979 Spanish Royalty Visit **Obv:** Arms **Obv. Legend:** REPUBLICA DE GUINEA ECUATORIAL **Rev:** Jugate busts of Juan Carlos and Sofia left **Rev. Legend:** S.S.M.M.LOS REYES DE ESPAÑA VISITAN GUINEA **Note:** Prev. KM#M7.

Date	Mintage	F	VF	XF	Unc	BU
(19)80	4,250	—	—	—	185	—
(19)80 Proof	2,000	Value: 220				

X# M8 10000 BIPKWELE
8.0000 g., 0.9170 Gold 0.2359 oz. AGW, 24 mm. **Subject:** 1979 Spanish Royalty Visit **Obv:** Arms **Obv. Legend:** REPUBLICA DE GUINEA ECUATORIAL **Rev:** Bust of Juan Carlos left **Rev. Legend:** S.M. DON JUAN CARLOS I VISITA GUINEA **Note:** Prev. KM#M8.

Date	Mintage	F	VF	XF	Unc	BU
(19)80	4,250	—	—	—	185	—
(19)80 Proof	2,000	Value: 220				

ESSAIS

KM#	Date	Mintage	Identification	Issue Price	Mkt Val
E5	1978	—	5000 Ekuele. Aluminum. KM#39.	—	35.00
E6	1978	—	5000 Ekuele. Copper. KM#39.	—	40.00
E7	1978	—	10000 Ekuele. Aluminum. KM#40.	—	45.00
E8	1978	—	10000 Ekuele. Copper. KM#40.	—	50.00
E11	ND(1979)	—	10000 Ekuele. Aluminum. KM#41.	—	25.00
E12	ND(1979)	—	10000 Ekuele. Copper. KM#41.	—	60.00
E13	1980	—	Bipkwele. Copper. KM#5.	—	20.00

PATTERNS
Including off metal strikes

Pn#	Date	Mintage	Identification	Mkt Val
Pn31	1992	—	15000 Francos. 0.9990 Gold Plated Silver. 12.6700 g.	—

PIEFORTS

KM#	Date	Mintage	Identification	Issue Price	Mkt Val
P4	1978	—	5000 Ekuele. Copper. 2.6 mm. Milled edge. KM#39.	—	175
P5	1978	—	5000 Ekuele. Copper. 4.1 mm. Plain edge.	—	150
P6	1978	—	10000 Ekuele. Copper. 3.4 mm. Milled edge. KM#41.	—	110
P10	ND(1979)	—	10000 Ekuele. Copper. KM#41.	—	225
P11	ND(1979)	—	10000 Ekuele. Gold. KM#41.	—	1,200
P12	ND(1979)	—	10000 Ekuele. Gilt Copper. KM#41.	—	200

TRIAL STRIKES

KM#	Date	Mintage	Identification	Issue Price	Mkt Val
TS3	1978	—	5000 Ekuele. Copper. 2.8 mm. KM39. PRUEBA.	—	75.00
TS4	1978	—	5000 Ekuele. Copper. 2.8 mm. KM39. PRUEBA.	—	75.00
TS5	1978	—	10000 Ekuele. Copper. 3.6 mm. KM40. PRUEBA.	—	75.00
TS6	1978	—	10000 Ekuele. Copper. PRUEBA. KM#40.	—	75.00

PROOF SETS

KM#	Date	Mintage	Identification	Issue Price	Mkt Val
PS1	1970 (27)	330	KM#5-31	—	3,500
PS3	1970 (12)	330	KM#20-31	—	3,150

ERITREA

The State of Eritrea, a former Ethiopian province fronting on the Red Sea, has an area of 45,300 sq. mi. (117,600 sq. km.) and a population of 3.6 million. It was an Italian colony from 1889 until its incorporation into Italian East Africa in 1936. It was under the British Military Administration from 1941 to Sept. 15, 1952, when the United Nations designated it an autonomous unit within the federation of Ethiopia and Eritrea. On Nov. 14, 1962, it was annexed with Ethiopia. In 1991 the Eritrean Peoples Liberation Front extended its control over the entire territory of Eritrea. Following 2 years of provisional government, Eritrea held a referendum on independence in May 1993. Overwhelming popular approval led to the proclamation of an independent Republic of Eritrea on May 24.

RULERS
Umberto I, 1889-1900
Vittorio Emanuele III, 1900-1945

MINT MARKS
M - Milan
PM - Pobjoy
R – Rome

MONETARY SYSTEM
100 Centesimi = 1 Lira
5 Lire = 1 Tallero
100 Cents = 1 Nakfa (from 1997)

REPUBLIC
DECIMAL COINAGE

100 Cents = 1 Dollar

KM# 8 50 DOLLARS
3.1100 g., 0.9990 Gold .1000 oz. AGW **Subject:** Independence Day **Obv:** Dhow, camel and tree within circle, denomination below **Rev:** Tree within laurel wreath, dates below, circle surrounds, denomination below

Date	Mintage	F	VF	XF	Unc	BU
1993 Proof	Est. 20,000	Value: 100				

KM# 9 100 DOLLARS
6.2200 g., 0.9990 Gold .2000 oz. AGW **Subject:** Independence Day **Obv:** Dhow, camel and palm tree, date below, all within circle **Rev:** Tree within laurel wreath, dates below, circle surrounds, denomination below

Date	Mintage	F	VF	XF	Unc	BU
1993 Proof	Est. 5,000	Value: 200				

KM# 12 100 DOLLARS
6.2200 g., 0.9990 Gold .2000 oz. AGW **Subject:** Preserve Planet Earth **Obv:** Dhow, camel and tree within circle, denomination below **Rev:** Triceratops, denomination below

Date	Mintage	F	VF	XF	Unc	BU
1993 Proof	Est. 5,000	Value: 175				

KM# 26 100 DOLLARS
6.2200 g., 0.9990 Gold .2000 oz. AGW **Subject:** Preserve Planet Earth **Obv:** Dhow, camel and palm tree, date below, all within circle **Rev:** Ankylosaurus

Date	Mintage	F	VF	XF	Unc	BU
1993 Proof	Est. 5,000	Value: 175				

KM# 27 100 DOLLARS
6.2200 g., 0.9990 Gold .2000 oz. AGW **Subject:** Preserve Planet Earth **Obv:** Dhow, camel and palm tree, date below, all within circle **Rev:** Pteranodon

Date	Mintage	F	VF	XF	Unc	BU
1993 Proof	Est. 5,000	Value: 175				

KM# 21 100 DOLLARS
6.2200 g., 0.9990 Gold .2000 oz. AGW **Subject:** Preserve Planet Earth **Obv:** Dhow, camel and palm tree, date below, all within circle **Rev:** Mother and baby cheetah

Date	Mintage	F	VF	XF	Unc	BU
1994 Proof	5,000	Value: 175				

KM# 22 100 DOLLARS
6.2200 g., 0.9990 Gold .2000 oz. AGW **Subject:** Preserve Planet Earth **Obv:** Dhow, camel and palm tree, date below, all within circle **Rev:** Rhinoceros head right

Date	Mintage	F	VF	XF	Unc	BU
1994 Proof	5,000	Value: 175				

KM# 23 100 DOLLARS
6.2200 g., 0.9990 Gold .2000 oz. AGW **Subject:** Preserve Planet Earth **Obv:** Dhow, camel and palm tree, date below, all within circle **Rev:** Colobus monkey

Date	Mintage	F	VF	XF	Unc	BU
1994 Proof	5,000	Value: 175				

KM# 30 100 DOLLARS
6.2200 g., 0.9990 Gold .2000 oz. AGW **Subject:** Preserve Planet Earth **Obv:** Dhow, camel and palm tree, date below, all within circle **Rev:** Female lion and cub

Date	Mintage	F	VF	XF	Unc	BU
1995 Proof	Est. 5,000	Value: 185				

KM# 33 100 DOLLARS
6.2200 g., 0.9990 Gold .2000 oz. AGW **Subject:** Preserve Planet Earth **Obv:** Dhow, camel and palm tree, date below, all within circle **Rev:** Cape eagle owl

Date	Mintage	F	VF	XF	Unc	BU
1995 Proof	Est. 5,000	Value: 175				

KM# 36 100 DOLLARS
6.2200 g., 0.9990 Gold .2000 oz. AGW **Subject:** Preserve Planet Earth **Obv:** Dhow, camel and palm tree, date below, all within circle **Rev:** Wattled cranes

Date	Mintage	F	VF	XF	Unc	BU
1996 Proof	Est. 5,000	Value: 175				

KM# 39 100 DOLLARS
6.2200 g., 0.9990 Gold .2000 oz. AGW **Subject:** Preserve Planet Earth **Obv:** Dhow, camel and palm tree, date below, all within circle **Rev:** Laner falcon

Date	Mintage	F	VF	XF	Unc	BU
1996 Proof	Est. 5,000	Value: 175				

KM# 42 100 DOLLARS
6.2200 g., 0.9990 Gold .2000 oz. AGW **Subject:** Jurassic Park **Obv:** Dhow, camel and tree within circle, denomination below **Rev:** Triceratops, Jurassic Park logo

Date	Mintage	F	VF	XF	Unc	BU
1997 Proof	Est. 2,500	Value: 185				

ESTONIA

The Republic of Estonia (formerly the Estonian Soviet Socialist Republic of the U.S.S.R.) is the northernmost of the three Baltic States in Eastern Europe. It has an area of 17,462 sq. mi. (45,100 sq. km.) and a population of 1.6 million. Capital: Tallinn. Agriculture and dairy farming are the principal industries. Butter, eggs, bacon, timber and petroleum are exported.

This small and ancient Baltic state had enjoyed but two decades of independence since the 13th century until the present time. After having been conquered by the Danes, the Livonian Knights, the Teutonic Knights of Germany (who reduced the people to serfdom), the Swedes, the Poles and Russia, Estonia declared itself an independent republic on Feb. 24, 1918 but was not freed until Feb. 1919. The peace treaty was signed Feb. 2, 1920. Shortly after the start of World War II, it was again occupied by Russia and incorporated as the 16th state of the U.S.S.R. Germany occupied the tiny state from 1941 to 1944, after which it was retaken by Russia. Most of the nations of the world, including the United States and Great Britain, did not recognize Estonia's incorporation into the Soviet Union.

The coinage, issued during the country's brief independence, is obsolete.

On August 20, 1991, the Parliament of the Estonian Soviet Socialist Republic voted to reassert the republic's independence.

MODERN REPUBLIC
1991 - present
STANDARD COINAGE

KM# 37 15.65 KROONI
1.7300 g., 0.9000 Gold .0501 oz. AGW **Subject:** Estonia's Euro Equivalent **Obv:** Three Czech lions within shield, wreath surrounds, date below **Rev:** Cross and stars design, denomination below

Date	Mintage	F	VF	XF	Unc	BU
1999 Proof	Est. 5,000	Value: 40.00				

KM# 39 100 KROONI
7.7760 g., 0.9999 Gold 0.25 oz. AGW **Subject:** Monetary Reform **Obv:** National arms **Rev:** Cross design **Edge:** Reeded

Date	Mintage	F	VF	XF	Unc	BU
2002	2,000	—	—	—	—	150

KM# 41 100 KROONI
7.7760 g., 0.9999 Gold 0.25 oz. AGW, 21.9 mm. **Subject:** Olympic Games **Obv:** National arms **Rev:** Olympic flame above rings in center **Edge:** Reeded

Date	Mintage	F	VF	XF	Unc	BU
2004	5,000	—	—	—	—	—

KM# 34 500 KROONI
8.6400 g., 0.9000 Gold .2500 oz. AGW **Subject:** 80th Anniversary of Nation **Obv:** Framed dates **Rev:** Male figure on horse, denomination above

Date	Mintage	F	VF	XF	Unc	BU
ND(1998) Proof	Est. 3,000	Value: 195				

GOVERNMENT IN EXILE
FANTASY COINAGE

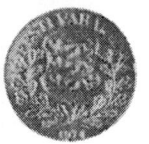

X# 2 DUCAT
3.5000 g., 0.9000 Gold 0.1013 oz. AGW **Subject:** Konstantine Paets

Date	Mintage	F	VF	XF	Unc	BU
1974	950	—	—	—	165	—

X# 3 DUCAT
3.5000 g., 0.9000 Gold 0.1013 oz. AGW **Subject:** Joan Tonisson

Date	Mintage	F	VF	XF	Unc	BU
1974	950	—	—	—	165	—

ETHIOPIA

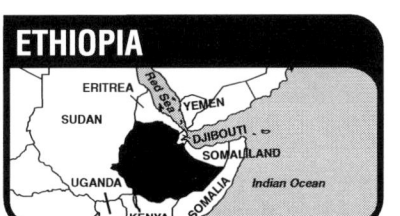

The People's Federal Republic of Ethiopia (formerly the Peoples Democratic Republic and the Empire of Ethiopia), Africa's oldest independent nation, faces the Red Sea in East-Central Africa. The country has an area of 424,214 sq. mi. (1,004,390 sq. km.) and a population of 56 million people who are divided among 40 tribes that speak some 270 languages and dialects. Capital: Addis Ababa. The economy is predominantly agricultural and pastoral. Gold and platinum are mined and petroleum fields are being developed. Coffee, oilseeds, hides and cereals are exported.

Legend claims that Menelik I, the son born to Solomon, King of Israel, by the Queen of Sheba, settled in Axum in North Ethiopia to establish the dynasty, which reigned with only brief interruptions until 1974. Modern Ethiopian history began with the reign of Emperor Menelik II (1889-1913) under whose guidance the country emerged from medieval isolation. Progress continued throughout the reigns of Menelik's daughter, Empress Zauditu, and her successor Emperor Haile Selassie I who was coronated in 1930. Ethiopia was invaded by Italy in 1935, and together with Italian Somaliland and Eritrea became part of Italian East Africa. Victor Emmanuel III, as declared by Mussolini, would be Ethiopia's emperor as well as a king of Italy. Liberated by British and Ethiopian troops in 1941, Ethiopia reinstated Haile Selassie I to the throne. The 225th consecutive Solomonic ruler was deposed by a military committee on Sept 12, 1974. In July 1976 Ethiopia's military provisional government referred to the country as Socialist Ethiopia. After establishing a new regime in 1991, Ethiopia became a federated state and is now the Federal Republic of Ethiopia. Following 2 years of provisional government, the province of Eritrea held a referendum on independence in May 1993 leading to the proclamation of its independence on May 24.

No coins, patterns or presentation pieces are known bearing Emperor Lij Yasu's likeness or titles. Coins of Menelik II were struck during this period with dates frozen.

RULERS
Menelik II, 1889-1913
Lij Yasu, 1913-1916
Zauditu, Empress, 1916-1930
Haile Selassie I
  1930-36, 1941-1974
Victor Emmanuel III, of Italy
  1936-1941

MINT MARKS
A - Paris
  (a) - Paris, privy marks only
  (b)
   Coinage of Menelik II, 1889-1913
  NOTE: The first national issue coinage, dated 1887 and 1888 E.E., carried a cornucopia, A, and fasces on the reverse. Subsequent dates have a torch substituted for the fasces, the A being dropped. All issues bearing these marks were struck at the Paris Mint. Coins without mint marks were struck in Addis Ababa.

MONETARY SYSTEM
(Until about 1903)
40 Besa = 20 Gersh = 1 Birr
(After 1903)
32 Besa = 16 Gersh = 1 Birr

DATING
Ethiopian coinage is dated by the Ethiopian Era calendar (E.E.), which commenced 7 years and 8 months after the advent of A.D. dating.

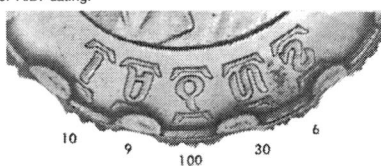

EXAMPLE
1900 (10 and 9 = 19 x 100)
  36 (Add 30 and 6)
1936 E.E.
   8 (Add)
1943/4 AD

EMPIRE OF ETHIOPIA
REFORM COINAGE

KM# 16 1/4 WERK
1.7500 g., 0.9000 Gold .0506 oz. AGW **Ruler:** Manelik II
EE1882-1906 / 1889-1913AD **Obv:** Crowned bust right
Rev: Crowned lion left, right foreleg raised holding ribboned cross

Date	Mintage	F	VF	XF	Unc	BU
EE1889	—	60.00	135	210	400	—

KM# 17 1/2 WERK
3.5000 g., 0.9000 Gold .1012 oz. AGW **Ruler:** Manelik II
EE1882-1906 / 1889-1913AD **Obv:** Crowned bust right, spray below **Rev:** Crowned lion left, right foreleg raised holding ribboned cross

Date	Mintage	F	VF	XF	Unc	BU
EE1889	—	100	165	245	450	—

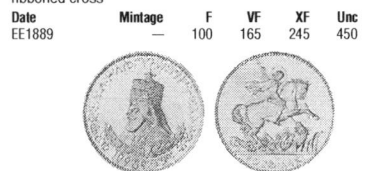

KM# 20 1/2 WERK
3.5000 g., 0.9000 Gold .1012 oz. AGW, 18 mm.
Ruler: Empress Zauditu (Waizero) EE1909-1923 / 1916-1930AD **Obv:** Crowned bust left, laurels below **Rev:** Haloed figure on horseback, right

Date	Mintage	F	VF	XF	Unc	BU
EE1923	—	250	500	900	1,500	—

KM# 18 WERK
7.0000 g., 0.9000 Gold .2025 oz. AGW **Ruler:** Manelik II
EE1882-1906 / 1889-1913AD **Obv:** Crowned bust right, spray below **Rev:** Crowned lion left, right foreleg raised holding ribboned cross

Date	Mintage	F	VF	XF	Unc	BU
EE1889	—	120	185	265	600	—

Note: KM#16-18 vary considerably in weight due to disparities in planchet thicknesses

KM# 21 WERK
7.0000 g., 0.9000 Gold .2025 oz. AGW, 21 mm.
Ruler: Empress Zauditu (Waizero) EE1909-1923 / 1916-1930AD **Obv:** Crowned bust left, laurels below **Rev:** Haloed figure on horseback, right

Date	Mintage	F	VF	XF	Unc	BU
EE1923	—	500	750	1,500	2,500	—

DECIMAL COINAGE

100 Santeems (Cents) = 1 Birr (Dollar)

100 Matonas = 100 Santeems

KM# 38 10 DOLLARS
4.0000 g., 0.9000 Gold .1157 oz. AGW **Ruler:** Haile Selassie Second Reign **Subject:** 75th Anniverary of Birth and 50th Jubilee of Reign of Emperor Haile Selassie I **Obv:** Bust 3/4 left divides crown and shield **Rev:** Crowned lion right, right foreleg raised holding ribboned cross

Date	Mintage	F	VF	XF	Unc	BU
EE1958 (1966) NI Proof	28,000	Value: 100				

KM# 39 20 DOLLARS
8.0000 g., 0.9000 Gold .2315 oz. AGW **Ruler:** Haile Selassie Second Reign **Subject:** 75th Anniversary of Birth and 50th Jubilee of Reign of Emperor Haile Selassie I **Obv:** Bust 3/4 left divides crown and shield **Rev:** Crowned lion right, right foreleg raised holding ribboned cross

Date	Mintage	F	VF	XF	Unc	BU
EE1958 (1966) NI Proof	25,000	Value: 185				

KM# 40 50 DOLLARS
20.0000 g., 0.9000 Gold .5787 oz. AGW **Ruler:** Haile Selassie Second Reign **Subject:** 75th Anniversary of Birth and 50th Jubilee of Reign of Emperor Haile Selassie I **Obv:** Bust 3/4 left divides crown and shield **Rev:** Crowned lion right, right foreleg raised holding ribboned cross

Date	Mintage	F	VF	XF	Unc	BU
EE1958 (1966) NI Proof	15,000	Value: 385				

KM# 55 50 DOLLARS
20.0000 g., 0.9000 Gold .5787 oz. AGW **Ruler:** Haile Selassie Second Reign **Obv:** Bust of Theodros II **Rev:** Lion

Date	Mintage	F	VF	XF	Unc	BU
EE1964 (1972) NI Proof	12,000	Value: 400				

KM# 56 50 DOLLARS
20.0000 g., 0.9000 Gold .5787 oz. AGW **Ruler:** Haile Selassie Second Reign **Obv:** Bust of Yohannes IV

Date	Mintage	F	VF	XF	Unc	BU
EE1964 (1972) NI Proof	12,000	Value: 400				

KM# 57 50 DOLLARS
20.0000 g., 0.9000 Gold .5787 oz. AGW **Ruler:** Haile Selassie Second Reign **Obv:** Bust of Menelik II

Date	Mintage	F	VF	XF	Unc	BU
EE1964 (1972) NI Proof	20,000	Value: 400				

KM# 58 50 DOLLARS
20.0000 g., 0.9000 Gold .5787 oz. AGW **Ruler:** Haile Selassie Second Reign **Obv:** Bust of Empress Zauditu

Date	Mintage	F	VF	XF	Unc	BU
EE1964 (1972) NI Proof	16,000	Value: 400				

KM# 41 100 DOLLARS
40.0000 g., 0.9000 Gold 1.1575 oz. AGW **Ruler:** Haile Selassie Second Reign **Subject:** 75th Anniversary of Birth and 50th Jubilee of Reign of Emperor Haile Selassie I **Rev:** Crowned lion right, right foreleg raised holding ribboned cross

Date	Mintage	F	VF	XF	Unc	BU
EE1958 (1966) NI Proof	11,000	Value: 800				

208 ETHIOPIA

KM# 59 100 DOLLARS
40.0000 g., 0.9000 Gold 1.1575 oz. AGW **Ruler:** Haile Selassie Second Reign **Obv:** Uniformed bust 3/4 facing **Rev:** Crowned lion right, right foreleg raised holding ribboned cross

Date	Mintage	F	VF	XF	Unc	BU
EE1964 (1972) NI Proof	10,000		Value: 800			

KM# 42 200 DOLLARS
80.0000 g., 0.9000 Gold 2.3151 oz. AGW **Ruler:** Haile Selassie Second Reign **Subject:** 75th Anniversary of Birth and 50th Jubilee of Reign of Emperor Haile Selassie I **Rev:** Crowned lion right, right foreleg raised holding ribboned cross

Date	Mintage	F	VF	XF	Unc	BU
EE1958 (1966) NI Proof	8,823		Value: 1,600			

MEDALLIC COINAGE
Birr / Talari Series

X# 3.1 1/8 BIRR
Gold **Obv:** Empress Zauditu **Rev:** Denomination obliterated

Date	Mintage	F	VF	XF	Unc	BU
EE1917 (1925)	—		500	900	1,800	—

X# 3.2 1/8 BIRR
Gold **Rev:** Denomination clear

Date	Mintage	F	VF	XF	Unc	BU
EE1917 (1925)	—		—	1,250	—	—

X# 4.1 1/4 BIRR
Gold **Obv:** Empress Zauditu **Rev:** Denomination obliterated

Date	Mintage	F	VF	XF	Unc	BU
EE1917 (1924)	—		750	1,500	2,500	—

X# 4.2 1/4 BIRR
Gold **Rev:** Denomination clear

Date	Mintage	F	VF	XF	Unc	BU
EE1917 (1925)	—		—	1,750	2,800	—

X# 5 1/2 BIRR
Gold **Obv:** Empress Zauditu **Rev:** Denomination obliterated
Note: Prev. KM#M3 (Y#24).

Date	Mintage	F	VF	XF	Unc	BU
EE1916 (1924)	—		2,500	3,500	5,500	—

X# 5a.2 1/2 BIRR
Silver **Rev:** Denomination clear

Date	Mintage	F	VF	XF	Unc	BU
EE1917 (1925)	—		2,000	2,800	3,900	—

X# 6 BIRR
Gold **Obv:** Empress Zauditu **Rev:** Denomination obliterated
Note: Prev. KM#M4.

Date	Mintage	F	VF	XF	Unc	BU
EE1916 (1924) Rare	2		—	—	—	—

Note: Bowers and Merena GUIA sale 3-88 AU realized $15,400

X# 11 1/4 TALARI
6.2900 g., Gold, 25 mm. **Subject:** Coronation of Haile Selassie I **Note:** Similar to Talari, XM12.

Date	Mintage	F	VF	XF	Unc	BU
EE1923 (1931) Prooflike	—		—	—	275	—

X# 18 1/2 TALARI
6.2900 g., Gold **Subject:** Coronation of Haile Selassie I
Note: Weight varies: 16.7-20.6 grams.

Date	Mintage	F	VF	XF	Unc	BU
EE1923 Prooflike	—		—	—	550	—

X# 19 1/2 TALARI
19.8000 g., Gold **Subject:** Coronation of Haile Selassie I

Date	Mintage	F	VF	XF	Unc	BU
EE1923 (1931)	—		—	600	850	1,250

X# 20 1/2 TALARI
13.8000 g., Gold **Subject:** 25th Anniversary of Reign

Date	Mintage	F	VF	XF	Unc	BU
EE1948 (1956)	—		—	—	375	575	—

X# 1 TALARI
40.2000 g., Gold **Subject:** Menelik II

Date	Mintage	F	VF	XF	Unc	BU
EE1889 (1897) Proof	—		Value: 800			

X# 2 TALARI
Silver **Subject:** Menelik II

Date	Mintage	F	VF	XF	Unc	BU
EE1889 (1897) Proof	—		Value: 65.00			

X# 17 TALARI
23.3000 g., Gold **Subject:** Ras Tafari

Date	Mintage	F	VF	XF	Unc	BU
EE1911 (1919)	—		—	550	750	1,100	—

X# 7 TALARI
Gold **Subject:** Haile Selassie I **Note:** Weight varies: 38.19-39.95 grams. Mintage figure per Kreisberg/Schulman sale Jan. 1963. Struck for Geoffrey Hearn by John Pinches, London, England.

ETHIOPIA

Date	Mintage	F	VF	XF	Unc	BU
EE1923 (1931) Proof	10	Value: 1,000				

X# 10 TALARI
Silver **Subject:** Coronation of Haile Selassie I

Date	Mintage	F	VF	XF	Unc	BU
EE1923 (1931)	—	—	100	175	275	

X# 8 TALARI
Silver **Subject:** Haile Selassie I

Date	Mintage	F	VF	XF	Unc	BU
EE1923 (1931) Proof	—	Value: 200				

X# 9 TALARI
Gold **Subject:** Coronation of Haile Selassie I

Date	Mintage	F	VF	XF	Unc	BU
EE1923 (1931)	—	—	1,500	2,500	4,500	—

X# 12 TALARI
29.4000 g., Gold **Subject:** Coronation of Haile Selassie I

Date	Mintage	F	VF	XF	Unc	BU
EE1923 (1931) Prooflike	—	—	—	—	850	—

X# 12a TALARI
Gold **Subject:** Coronation of Haile Selassie I **Note:** Weight varies: 43.20-47.60 grams.

Date	Mintage	F	VF	XF	Unc	BU
EE1923 (1931) Prooflike	—	—	—	—	1,000	—

MEDALLIC COINAGE
Crown Series
Struck by the Franklin Mint, Pennsylvania, U.S.A. Sold at the Ethiopian Pavilion at EXPO 1967.

X# 16 CROWN
0.7500 Gold **Note:** Struck by the Franklin Mint, Pennsylvania, U.S.A. Sold at the Ethiopian Pavilion at EXPO 1967.

Date	Mintage	F	VF	XF	Unc	BU
1967 Proof; Unique	—	—	—	—	—	—

MINT VISIT MEDALS
X# 22 BIRR
Gold **Ruler:** Empress Zauditu (Waizero) EE1909-1923 / 1916-1930AD **Obv:** Legend similar to rev. legend of KM#16 **Rev:** Crowned lion right, right foreleg raised holding ribboned cross

Date	Mintage	F	VF	XF	Unc	BU
1924 Unique						

PEOPLES DEMOCRATIC REPUBLIC
We have two varieties for KM#43.1 to KM#46.1. One was minted at the British Royal Mint, the other at the Berlin Mint. The main difference is where the lion's chin whiskers end above the date (easiest to see on the 2nd, 3rd and 4th characters).

British Royal Mint

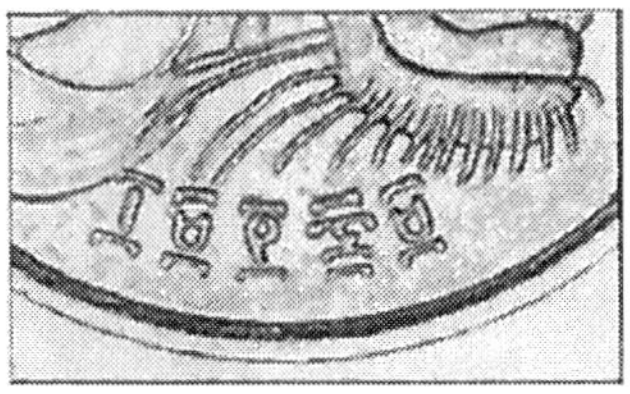

Berlin Mint

DECIMAL COINAGE
100 Santeems (Cents) = 1 Birr (Dollar)

100 Matonas = 100 Santeems

KM# 67 200 BIRR
7.1300 g., 0.9000 Gold .2063 oz. AGW **Subject:** World Soccer Games 1982 **Obv:** Lion head right **Rev:** Soccer players in front of two joined globes, denomination above

Date	Mintage	F	VF	XF	Unc	BU
1982 Proof	1,310	Value: 200				

KM# 72 200 BIRR
7.1300 g., 0.9000 Gold .2063 oz. AGW **Subject:** Decade for Women **Obv:** Small lion head right, denomination below **Rev:** Woman with child, writing

Date	Mintage	F	VF	XF	Unc	BU
1984 Proof	298	Value: 340				

KM# 60 400 BIRR
17.1700 g., 0.9000 Gold .4968 oz. AGW **Ruler:** Haile Selassie Second Reign **Subject:** International Year of the Child **Obv:** Silhouette of child, laurels flanking, logo above **Rev:** Children playing, denomination below, logo above

Date	Mintage	F	VF	XF	Unc	BU
EE1972 Proof	3,387	Value: 330				

KM# 68 500 BIRR
15.9800 g., 0.9170 Gold .5006 oz. AGW **Ruler:** Haile Selassie Second Reign **Subject:** International Year of the Disabled Persons **Obv:** Symbol within wreath **Rev:** Flanking figures on steps holding arms of central figure, denomination below

Date	Mintage	F	VF	XF	Unc	BU
EE1974	2,007	—	—	—	330	—
EE1974 Proof	2,042	Value: 345				

KM# 63 600 BIRR
33.4370 g., 0.9000 Gold .9676 oz. AGW **Ruler:** Haile Selassie Second Reign **Subject:** Conservation **Obv:** Lion within circle divides wreath surrounding symbols at center **Rev:** Walia Ibex right

Date	Mintage	F	VF	XF	Unc	BU
EE1970	547	—	—	—	800	—
EE1970 Proof	160	Value: 1,000				

PATTERNS
Including off metal strikes

KM#	Date	Mintage	Identification	Mkt Val
Pn1	EE1889	—	Gersh. Gold. 16 mm. KM13.	2,400
Pn2	EE1889	—	1/4 Birr. Gold. 6.7500 g. Reeded edge. KM14.	2,500
Pn3	EE1889	—	1/4 Birr. Gold. 14.5000 g. Plain edge. KM14.	3,500
Pn4	EE1889	—	1/2 Birr. Gold. KM15.	2,200

ETHIOPIA

KM#	Date	Mintage	Identification	Mkt Val
Pn5	EE1889	—	Birr. Gold. Crowned head right. Lion with staff left.	6,000
Pn7	EE1921	—	1/2 Werk. Gold. Similar to KM20 (proof)	—
Pn8	EE1921	—	Werk. Gold. Similar to KM21 (proof)	—

TRIAL STRIKES

KM#	Date	Mintage	Identification	Mkt Val
TS1	EE1887	—	Birr. Copper. KM5.	90.00
TS2	ND	—	Birr. Copper. KM5.	—
TS3	EE1889	—	1/4 Werk. Gold. KM16. Plain edge.	—
TS4	ND	—	1/4 Werk. Gold. KM16. Plain edge.	—
TS5	EE1889	—	1/2 Werk. Gold. KM17. Reeded edge.	—
TS6	ND	—	1/2 Werk. Gold. KM17. Reeded edge.	—
TS7	EE1889	—	Werk. Gold. KM18. Reeded edge.	—
TS8	ND	—	Werk. Gold. KM18. Plain edge.	—
TS9	EE1917	—	1/2 Birr. Pewter. KM M3. (thin)	300
TS10	EE1917	—	Birr. Pewter. KM M4. (thin)	500
TS11	1966	—	10 Dollars. Gilt Bronze. KM38	50.00
TS12	1966	—	20 Dollars. Gilt Bronze. KM39	80.00
TS13	1966	—	50 Dollars. Gilt Bronze. KM40	130
TS14	1966	—	100 Dollars. Gilt Bronze. KM41	240
TS15	1966	—	200 Dollars. Gilt Bronze. KM42	450

Note: Issued in cased set of five pieces

PIEFORTS

KM#	Date	Mintage	Identification	Issue Price	Mkt Val
P2	1980	8	400 Birr. Gold. KM60	—	775
P4	1982	520	500 Birr. Gold. KM68	—	650

PROOF SETS

KM#	Date	Mintage	Identification	Issue Price	Mkt Val
PS2	1966 (5)	8,823	KM38-42	—	2,450
PS3	1972 (10)	—	KM48-51, 53, 55-59	—	2,600
PS5	1972 (5)	10,000	KM55-59	—	2,300

EUROPA

INTERNATIONAL FEDERATION

EUROPA COINAGE

X# 6 FLORIN
5.8300 g., Gold Note: Prev. KY#14.

Date	Mintage	F	VF	XF	Unc	BU
ND(1934)	—	—	—	225	300	—

FEDERATED STATES

EUROPINO COINAGE

X# 13 2 1/2 EUROPINOS
Gold Note: Prev. KY#19c.

Date	Mintage	F	VF	XF	Unc	BU
1952HM	Unique					

X# 18 5 EUROPINOS
Gold Edge: Reeded Note: Prev. KY#18b.

Date	Mintage	F	VF	XF	Unc	BU
1952HM Proof	—	Value: 2,000				

X# 21 5 EUROPINOS
Gold Edge: Plain Note: Prev. KY#18c. Piefort.

Date	Mintage	F	VF	XF	Unc	BU
1952HM Proof						

EUROPEAN ECONOMIC COMMUNITY

ECU COINAGE

X# 32 ECU
50.0000 g., 0.9200 Gold 1.4789 oz. AGW

Date	Mintage	F	VF	XF	Unc	BU
1979(a) Prooflike	1,460	—	—	—	1,750	—

X# 35 ECU
50.0000 g., 0.9200 Gold 1.4789 oz. AGW Subject: 1st Anniversary of Ecu

Date	Mintage	F	VF	XF	Unc	BU
1980(a) Prooflike	1,900	—	—	—	1,200	—

X# 38 ECU
50.0000 g., 0.9200 Gold 1.4789 oz. AGW Subject: Greece Enters European Economic Community

Date	Mintage	F	VF	XF	Unc	BU
1981(a) Prooflike	2,000	—	—	—	1,200	—

X# 41 ECU
50.0000 g., 0.9200 Gold 1.4789 oz. AGW Subject: 25th Anniversary European Economic Community

Date	Mintage	F	VF	XF	Unc	BU
1982(a) Prooflike	2,000	—	—	—	1,200	—

X# 44 ECU
50.0000 g., 0.9200 Gold 1.4789 oz. AGW

Date	Mintage	F	VF	XF	Unc	BU
1983(a) Prooflike	2,000	—	—	—	1,200	—

X# 47 ECU
50.0000 g., 0.9200 Gold 1.4789 oz. AGW

Date	Mintage	F	VF	XF	Unc	BU
1984(a) Prooflike	2,000	—	—	—	1,200	—

X# 50 ECU
50.0000 g., 0.9200 Gold 1.4789 oz. AGW

Date	Mintage	F	VF	XF	Unc	BU
1985(a) Prooflike	2,000	—	—	—	1,200	—

X# 53 ECU
50.0000 g., 0.9200 Gold 1.4789 oz. AGW

Date	Mintage	F	VF	XF	Unc	BU
1986(a) Prooflike	2,000	—	—	—	1,200	—
1987(a) Prooflike	2,000	—	—	—	1,200	—
1988(a) Prooflike	2,000	—	—	—	1,400	—

X# 55a ECU
12.5000 g., 0.9200 Gold 0.3697 oz. AGW, 23 mm. Obv: Laureate bust of Europa left in sprays Obv. Inscription: EUROPA Rev: Letters ECU forming cross, date in angles Edge: Reeded

Date	Mintage	F	VF	XF	Unc	BU
1987(a) Prooflike	5,000	—	—	—	425	—

X# 55b ECU
13.7500 g., 0.9990 Platinum 0.4416 oz. APW, 23 mm. Obv: Laureate bust of Europa left in sprays Obv. Inscription: EUROPA Rev: Letters ECU forming cross, date in angles Edge: Reeded

Date	Mintage	F	VF	XF	Unc	BU
1987(a) Prooflike	1,000	—	—	—	750	—

X# 62 ECU
50.0000 g., 0.9200 Gold 1.4789 oz. AGW

Date	Mintage	F	VF	XF	Unc	BU
1989(a) Prooflike	—	—	—	—	1,500	—

X# 65 ECU
50.0000 g., 0.9200 Gold 1.4789 oz. AGW

Date	Mintage	F	VF	XF	Unc	BU
1990(a) Prooflike	1,450	—	—	—	1,750	—
1991(a) Prooflike	1,450	—	—	—	1,750	—

X# 69 ECU
50.0000 g., 0.9200 Gold 1.4789 oz. AGW, 41 mm. Obv: Laureate bust of Europa left in sprays Obv. Inscription: EUROPA Rev: Twelve coin like designs representing members in outer circle, date and value in center Edge: Reeded

Date	Mintage	F	VF	XF	Unc	BU
1992(a) Prooflike	—	—	—	—	1,650	—

X# 73 ECU
50.0000 g., 0.9200 Gold 1.4789 oz. AGW, 41 mm. Obv: Laureate bust of Europa left in sprays Obv. Inscription: EUROPA Rev: Twelve coin like designs representing members in outer circle, date and value in center Edge: Reeded

Date	Mintage	F	VF	XF	Unc	BU
1993(a) Prooflike	1,450	—	—	—	1,750	—

PANEUROPEAN UNION
Confederatio Europea - Bruxelles

ECU COINAGE

X# 173 10 ECU
3.0000 g., 0.9000 Gold .0868 oz. AGW, 18 mm. Subject: Richard de Condenhove-Kalergi Note: Prev. X#43.

Date	Mintage	F	VF	XF	Unc	BU
1972 Prooflike	10,000	—	—	—	120	—

X# 174 20 ECU
6.0000 g., 0.9000 Gold .1736 oz. AGW Subject: Jean Monnet and Paul Henri Spaak Note: Prev. X#44.

Date	Mintage	F	VF	XF	Unc	BU
1972	10,000	—	—	—	200	—

X# 175 50 ECU
15.0000 g., 0.9000 Gold .4340 oz. AGW, 30 mm. Subject: Winston Churchill and Edward Heath Note: Prev. X#45.

Date	Mintage	F	VF	XF	Unc	BU
1972 Prooflike	10,000	—	—	—	325	—

X# 89 50 ECU
5.5000 g., 0.9000 Gold 0.1591 oz. AGW, 22. mm.

Date	Mintage	F	VF	XF	Unc	BU
1979 Prooflike	10,000	—	—	—	225	—

X# 148 50 ECU
5.0000 g., 0.9000 Gold 0.1447 oz. AGW Note: Prev. X#118.

Date	Mintage	F	VF	XF	Unc	BU
1984 IPZS Proof	2,000	Value: 250				

X# 124 50 ECU
5.5000 g., 0.9000 Gold 0.1591 oz. AGW, 20 mm. Subject: Europe's Year of Music Obv: Bust of Johann Sebastion Bach facing 3/4 right Obv. Legend: CONFEDERATIO • EUROPA Rev: Greek temple, value below in sprays Edge: Plain

Date	Mintage	F	VF	XF	Unc	BU
1985 Proof	3,000	Value: 175				

X# 125 50 ECU
5.5000 g., 0.9000 Gold 0.1591 oz. AGW, 20 mm. Subject: Europe's Year of Music Obv: Bust of Georg Friedrich Händel facing 3/4 right Obv. Legend: CONFEDERATIO • EUROPA Rev: Greek temple, value below in sprays Edge: Plain

Date	Mintage	F	VF	XF	Unc	BU
1985 Proof	3,000	Value: 175				

FALKLAND ISLANDS

X# 126 50 ECU
5.5000 g., 0.9000 Gold 0.1591 oz. AGW, 20 mm.
Subject: Europe's Year of Music **Obv:** Bust of Domenico Scarlatti facing slightly right **Obv. Legend:** CONFEDERATIO • EUROPA **Rev:** Greek temple, value below in sprays **Edge:** Plain

Date	Mintage	F	VF	XF	Unc	BU
1985 Proof	3,000	Value: 175				

X# 134 50 ECU
7.0000 g., 0.9000 Gold 0.2025 oz. AGW, 24 mm. **Subject:** 40th Anniversary Europa **Obv:** Large "40" above 12 stars in flat circle **Obv. Legend:** CONFEDERATIO EUROPA **Rev:** Solidarity symbol **Rev. Legend:** SOLIDARITE / SOLIDARITY **Edge:** Reeded

Date	Mintage	F	VF	XF	Unc	BU
1989 Proof	—	Value: 350				

X# 176 100 ECU
30.0000 g., 0.9000 Gold .8680 oz. AGW **Subject:** K. Andenauer, A. De Gasperi and R. Schuman **Note:** Prev. X#46.

Date	Mintage	F	VF	XF	Unc	BU
1972 Prooflike	10,000	—	—	—	675	—

X# 90 100 ECU
11.0000 g., 0.9000 Gold 0.3183 oz. AGW, 28 mm.

Date	Mintage	F	VF	XF	Unc	BU
1979 Prooflike	5,000	—	—	—	375	—

X# 93 100 ECU
11.1100 g., 0.9000 Gold 0.3215 oz. AGW, 27 mm. **Subject:** 60th Anniversary Paneuropa Movement **Obv:** Paneuropa emblem above value **Obv. Legend:** CONFEDERATIO EUROPA **Rev:** Head of R. Coudenhove-Kalergi right **Rev. Legend:** RICHARD COUDENHOVE-KALERGI **Edge:** Reeded

Date	Mintage	F	VF	XF	Unc	BU
1982 Proof	700	Value: 500				

X# 94 100 ECU
11.1100 g., 0.9000 Gold 0.3215 oz. AGW, 27 mm. **Subject:** 60th Anniversary Paneuropa Movement **Obv:** Paneuropa emblem above value **Obv. Legend:** CONFEDERATIO EUROPA **Rev:** Head of Sir W. Churchill facing slightly left **Rev. Legend:** WINSTON CHURCHILL • LET EUROPE ARISE **Edge:** Reeded

Date	Mintage	F	VF	XF	Unc	BU
1982 Proof	700	Value: 500				

X# 149 100 ECU
9.0000 g., 0.9000 Gold 0.2604 oz. AGW **Note:** Prev. X#119.

Date	Mintage	F	VF	XF	Unc	BU
1984 IPZS Proof	1,000	Value: 475				

X# 127 100 ECU
11.0000 g., 0.9000 Gold 0.3183 oz. AGW, 26 mm.
Subject: Europe's Year of Music **Obv:** Head of Ludwig van Beethoven left **Obv. Legend:** CONFEDERATIO • EUROPA **Rev:** Europa standing before bars of music, value below **Rev. Legend:** AN DIE FREUDE **Edge:** Plain

Date	Mintage	F	VF	XF	Unc	BU
1985 Proof	—	Value: 500				

X# 135 100 ECU
14.0000 g., 0.9000 Gold 0.4051 oz. AGW, 28 mm.
Subject: 40th Anniversary Europa **Obv:** Large "40" above 12 stars in flat circle **Obv. Legend:** CONFEDERATIO EUROPA **Rev:** Human rights symbol **Rev. Legend:** DROITS DE L'HOMME / HUMAN RIGHTS **Rev. Designer:** D. Grieco **Edge:** Reeded

Date	Mintage	F	VF	XF	Unc	BU
1989 Proof	—	Value: 650				

PROOF SETS

KM#	Date	Mintage	Identification	Issue Price	Mkt Val
XPS1	1979 (5)	5,000	X86-X90	—	725
XPS3	1982 (4)	200	X91-X94	—	1,100
XPS7	1985 (5)	500	X121-X127	—	1,150
XPS8	1985 (4)	2,500	X121-X123, X127	—	600
XPS10	1985 (3)	1,000	X124-X126	—	525
XPS11	1989 (5)	—	X131-X135	—	1,300

FALKLAND ISLANDS

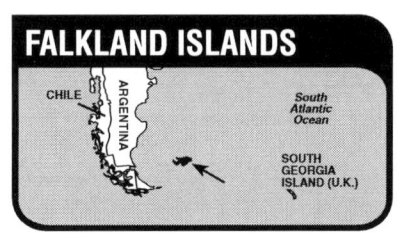

The Colony of the Falkland Islands and Dependencies, a British colony located in the South Atlantic about 500 miles northeast of Cape Horn, has an area of 4,700 sq. mi. (12,170 sq. km.) and a population of 2,121. East Falkland, West Falkland, South Georgia, and South Sandwich are the largest of the 200 islands. Capital: Stanley. Sheep grazing is the main industry. Wool, whale oil, and seal oil are exported.

The Falklands were discovered by British navigator John Davis (Davys) in 1592, and named by Capt. John Strong - for Viscount Falkland, treasurer of the British navy - in 1690. French navigator Louis De Bougainville established the first settlement, at Port Louis, in 1764. The following year Capt. John Byron claimed the islands for Britain and left a small party at Saunders Island. Spain later forced the French and British to abandon their settlements but did not implement its claim to the islands. In 1829 the Republic of Buenos Aires, which claimed to have inherited the Spanish rights, sent Louis Vernet to develop a colony on the islands. In 1831 he seized three American sealing vessels, whereupon the men of the corvette, the U.S.S. Lexington, destroyed his settlement and proclaimed the Falklands to be 'free of all governance'. Britain, which had never renounced its claim, then re-established its settlement in 1833.

RULER
British

MONETARY SYSTEM
100 Pence = 1 Pound

BRITISH COLONY
DECIMAL COINAGE

KM# 18b 50 PENCE
47.5000 g., 0.9170 Gold 1.4005 oz. AGW, 38.5 mm.
Ruler: Elizabeth II **Subject:** Liberation From Argentina Forces **Obv:** Young bust right, denomination below **Rev:** Flag design in background, state shield at left, date below

Date	Mintage	F	VF	XF	Unc	BU
ND(1982) Proof	25	Value: 5,500				

KM# 19b 50 PENCE
47.5400 g., 0.9170 Gold 1.4017 oz. AGW, 38.5 mm.
Ruler: Elizabeth II **Subject:** 150th Anniversary of British Rule **Obv:** Young bust right **Rev:** Ship divides dates

Date	Mintage	F	VF	XF	Unc	BU
ND(1983) Proof	150	Value: 1,250				

KM# 34b 50 PENCE
47.5400 g., 0.9170 Gold 1.4011 oz. AGW, 38.5 mm.
Ruler: Elizabeth II **Subject:** 40th Aniversary - Reign of Queen Elizabeth **Obv:** Crowned bust right **Rev:** Three figures, one at left is silhouette, dates below

Date	Mintage	F	VF	XF	Unc	BU
ND(1992) Proof	150	Value: 985				

KM# 45b 50 PENCE
47.5400 g., 0.9170 Gold 1.4011 oz. AGW, 38.5 mm. **Ruler:** Elizabeth II **Subject:** V.E. Day - 50th Anniversary **Obv:** Crowned bust right **Rev:** Denomination and dove divide flags, date below

Date	Mintage	F	VF	XF	Unc	BU
1995 Proof	Est. 100	Value: 985				

KM# 71b 50 PENCE
47.5400 g., 0.9160 Gold 1.4001 oz. AGW **Ruler:** Elizabeth II **Subject:** Queen Elizabeth's 75th Birthday **Obv:** Crowned bust right, denomination below **Rev:** Bust of Queen Elizabeth II left

Date	Mintage	F	VF	XF	Unc	BU
2001 Proof	Est. 100	Value: 975				

KM# 70b 50 PENCE
47.5400 g., 0.9166 Gold 1.401 oz. AGW, 38.6 mm.
Ruler: Elizabeth II **Subject:** Centennial of Queen Victoria's Death **Obv:** Crowned bust right, denomination below **Rev:** Crowned head left, three dates **Edge:** Reeded

Date	Mintage	F	VF	XF	Unc	BU
2001 Proof	100	Value: 950				

KM# 73b.1 50 PENCE
39.9400 g., 0.9166 Gold 1.177 oz. AGW, 38.6 mm.
Ruler: Elizabeth II **Obv:** Crowned bust right, denomination below **Rev:** Crowned queen with scepter and orb below multicolor bunting **Edge:** Reeded

Date	Mintage	F	VF	XF	Unc	BU
2002 Proof	150	Value: 925				

KM# 74b.1 50 PENCE
39.9400 g., 0.9166 Gold 1.177 oz. AGW, 38.6 mm.
Ruler: Elizabeth II **Subject:** Queen's Golden Jubilee **Obv:** Crowned bust right, denomination below **Rev:** Queen on horseback below multicolored bunting **Edge:** Reeded

Date	Mintage	F	VF	XF	Unc	BU
2002 Proof	150	Value: 925				

KM# 74b.2 50 PENCE
Gold **Ruler:** Elizabeth II **Obv:** Crowned bust right, denomination below **Rev:** With plain bunting

Date	Mintage	F	VF	XF	Unc	BU
2002 Proof	—	Value: 925				

KM# 75b.1 50 PENCE
39.9400 g., 0.9166 Gold 1.177 oz. AGW, 38.6 mm. **Ruler:** Elizabeth II **Subject:** Queen's Golden Jubilee **Obv:** Crowned bust right, denomination below **Rev:** Elizabeth speaking into a radio microphone below multicolored bunting **Edge:** Reeded

Date	Mintage	F	VF	XF	Unc	BU
2002 Proof	50	Value: 925				

212 FALKLAND ISLANDS

KM# 75b.2 50 PENCE
Gold **Ruler:** Elizabeth II **Subject:** Queen's Golden Jubilee **Obv:** Crowned bust right, denomination below **Rev:** With plain bunting

Date	Mintage	F	VF	XF	Unc	BU
2002 Proof	—				Value: 925	

KM# 76b.1 50 PENCE
39.9400 g., 0.9166 Gold 1.177 oz. AGW, 38.6 mm. **Ruler:** Elizabeth II **Subject:** Queen's Golden Jubilee **Obv:** Crowned bust right, denomination below **Rev:** Queen standing before a crowd below multicolored bunting **Edge:** Reeded

Date	Mintage	F	VF	XF	Unc	BU
2002 Proof	50				Value: 925	

KM# 76b.2 50 PENCE
Gold **Ruler:** Elizabeth II **Subject:** Queen's Golden Jubilee **Obv:** Crowned bust right, denomination below **Rev:** With plain bunting

Date	Mintage	F	VF	XF	Unc	BU
2002 Plain	—				Value: 925	

KM# 77b.1 50 PENCE
39.9400 g., 0.9166 Gold 1.177 oz. AGW, 38.6 mm. **Ruler:** Elizabeth II **Subject:** Queen's Golden Jubilee **Obv:** Crowned bust right, denomination below **Rev:** Elizabeth II, Prince Charles and his son William below multicolored bunting **Edge:** Reeded

Date	Mintage	F	VF	XF	Unc	BU
2002 Proof	50				Value: 925	

KM# 77b.2 50 PENCE
Gold **Ruler:** Elizabeth II **Obv:** Crowned bust right, denomination below **Rev:** With plain bunting

Date	Mintage	F	VF	XF	Unc	BU
2002 Proof	—				Value: 925	

KM# 78b.1 50 PENCE
39.9400 g., 0.9166 Gold 1.177 oz. AGW, 38.6 mm. **Ruler:** Elizabeth II **Subject:** Queen's Golden Jubilee **Obv:** Crowned bust right, denomination below **Rev:** Coronation coach below multicolor bunting **Edge:** Reeded

Date	Mintage	F	VF	XF	Unc	BU
2002 Proof	150				Value: 925	

KM# 78b.2 50 PENCE
Gold **Ruler:** Elizabeth II **Subject:** Queen's Golden Jubilee **Obv:** Crowned bust right, denomination below **Rev:** With plain bunting

Date	Mintage	F	VF	XF	Unc	BU
2002 Proof	—				Value: 925	

KM# 79b.1 50 PENCE
39.9400 g., 0.9166 Gold 1.177 oz. AGW, 38.6 mm. **Ruler:** Elizabeth II **Subject:** Queen's Golden Jubilee **Obv:** Crowned bust right, denomination below **Rev:** Orb and scepter below multicolor bunting **Edge:** Reeded

Date	Mintage	F	VF	XF	Unc	BU
2002 Proof	150				Value: 925	

KM# 79b.2 50 PENCE
Gold **Ruler:** Elizabeth II **Subject:** Queen's Golden Jubilee **Obv:** Crowned bust right, denomination below **Rev:** With plain bunting

Date	Mintage	F	VF	XF	Unc	BU
2002 Proof	—				Value: 925	

KM# 80b.2 50 PENCE
Gold **Ruler:** Elizabeth II **Subject:** Queen's Golden Jubilee **Obv:** Crowned bust right, denomination below **Rev:** With plain bunting

Date	Mintage	F	VF	XF	Unc	BU
2002 Proof	—				Value: 925	

KM# 81b.1 50 PENCE
39.9400 g., 0.9166 Gold 1.177 oz. AGW, 38.6 mm. **Ruler:** Elizabeth II **Subject:** Queen's Golden Jubilee **Obv:** Crowned bust right, denomination below **Rev:** Coronation Throne below multicolored bunting **Edge:** Reeded

Date	Mintage	F	VF	XF	Unc	BU
2002 Proof	150				Value: 925	

KM# 81b.2 50 PENCE
Gold **Ruler:** Elizabeth II **Obv:** Crowned bust right, denomination below **Rev:** With plain bunting

Date	Mintage	F	VF	XF	Unc	BU
2002 Proof	—				Value: 925	

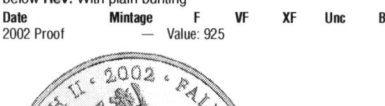

KM# 82b.1 50 PENCE
39.9400 g., 0.9166 Gold 1.177 oz. AGW, 38.6 mm. **Ruler:** Elizabeth II **Subject:** Queen's Golden Jubilee **Obv:** Crowned bust right, denomination below **Rev:** Queen seated on throne below multicolor bunting **Edge:** Reeded

Date	Mintage	F	VF	XF	Unc	BU
2002 Proof	50				Value: 925	

KM# 82b.2 50 PENCE
Gold **Ruler:** Elizabeth II **Subject:** Queen's Golden Jubilee **Obv:** Crowned bust right, denomination below **Rev:** With plain bunting

Date	Mintage	F	VF	XF	Unc	BU
2002 Proof	—				Value: 925	

KM# 83b.1 50 PENCE
39.9400 g., 0.9166 Gold 1.177 oz. AGW, 38.6 mm. **Ruler:** Elizabeth II **Subject:** Queen's Golden Jubilee **Obv:** Crowned bust right, denomination below **Rev:** Royal Family below multicolor bunting **Edge:** Reeded

Date	Mintage	F	VF	XF	Unc	BU
2002 Proof	50				Value: 925	

KM# 83b.2 50 PENCE
Gold **Ruler:** Elizabeth II **Subject:** Queen's Golden Jubilee **Obv:** Crowned bust right, denomination below **Rev:** With plain bunting

Date	Mintage	F	VF	XF	Unc	BU
2002 Proof	—				Value: 925	

KM# 84b.1 50 PENCE
39.9400 g., 0.9166 Gold 1.177 oz. AGW, 38.6 mm. **Ruler:** Elizabeth II **Subject:** Queen's Golden Jubilee **Obv:** Crowned bust right, denomination below **Rev:** Queen and tree house below multicolor bunting **Edge:** Reeded

Date	Mintage	F	VF	XF	Unc	BU
2002 Proof	50				Value: 925	

KM# 84b.2 50 PENCE
Gold **Ruler:** Elizabeth II **Subject:** Queen's Golden Jubilee **Obv:** Crowned bust right, denomination below **Rev:** With plain bunting

Date	Mintage	F	VF	XF	Unc	BU
2002 Proof	—				Value: 925	

KM# 90b.1 50 PENCE
39.9400 g., 0.9160 Gold 1.1762 oz. AGW, 38.6 mm. **Ruler:** Elizabeth II **Obv:** Crowned bust right, denomination below **Rev:** Elizabeth and Philip below multicolor bunting **Edge:** Reeded

Date	Mintage	F	VF	XF	Unc	BU
2002 Proof	50				Value: 925	

KM# 90b.2 50 PENCE
39.9400 g., 0.9160 Gold 1.1762 oz. AGW, 38.6 mm. **Ruler:** Elizabeth II **Obv:** Crowned bust right, denomination below **Rev:** With plain bunting **Edge:** Reeded

Date	Mintage	F	VF	XF	Unc	BU
2002 Proof	—				Value: 925	

KM# 91b.1 50 PENCE
28.2800 g., 0.9160 Gold 0.8328 oz. AGW, 38.6 mm. **Ruler:** Elizabeth II **Obv:** Crowned bust right, denomination below **Rev:** Queen and Aborigine dancers below multicolor bunting **Edge:** Reeded

Date	Mintage	F	VF	XF	Unc	BU
2002 Proof	50				Value: 925	

KM# 91b.2 50 PENCE
39.9400 g., 0.9160 Gold 1.1762 oz. AGW, 38.6 mm. **Ruler:** Elizabeth II **Obv:** Crowned bust right, denomination below **Rev:** With plain bunting **Edge:** Reeded

Date	Mintage	F	VF	XF	Unc	BU
2002 Proof	—	Value: 925				

KM# 92b.1 50 PENCE
39.9400 g., 0.9160 Gold 1.1762 oz. AGW, 38.6 mm.
Ruler: Elizabeth II **Obv:** Crowned bust right, denomination below **Rev:** Queen and St. Paul's Cathedral dome below multicolor bunting **Edge:** Reeded

Date	Mintage	F	VF	XF	Unc	BU
2002 Proof	50	Value: 925				

KM# 92b.2 50 PENCE
39.9400 g., 0.9160 Gold 1.1762 oz. AGW, 38.6 mm.
Ruler: Elizabeth II **Obv:** Crowned bust right, denomination below **Rev:** With plain bunting **Edge:** Reeded

Date	Mintage	F	VF	XF	Unc	BU
2002 Proof	—	Value: 925				

KM# 93b.1 50 PENCE
39.9400 g., 0.9160 Gold 1.1762 oz. AGW, 38.6 mm.
Ruler: Elizabeth II **Obv:** Crowned bust right, denomination below **Rev:** Elizabeth and Philip in coronation coach below multicolor bunting **Edge:** Reeded

Date	Mintage	F	VF	XF	Unc	BU
2002 Proof	50	Value: 925				

KM# 93b.2 50 PENCE
39.9400 g., 0.9160 Gold 1.1762 oz. AGW, 38.6 mm.
Ruler: Elizabeth II **Obv:** Crowned bust right, denomination below **Rev:** With plain bunting **Edge:** Reeded

Date	Mintage	F	VF	XF	Unc	BU
2002 Proof	—	Value: 925				

KM# 94b.1 50 PENCE
39.9400 g., 0.9160 Gold 1.1762 oz. AGW, 38.6 mm.
Ruler: Elizabeth II **Obv:** Crowned bust right, denomination below **Rev:** Queen and Prince Charles at flower show below multicolor bunting **Edge:** Reeded

Date	Mintage	F	VF	XF	Unc	BU
2002 Proof	50	Value: 925				

KM# 94b.2 50 PENCE
39.9400 g., 0.9160 Gold 1.1762 oz. AGW, 38.6 mm.
Ruler: Elizabeth II **Obv:** Crowned bust right, denomination below **Rev:** With plain bunting **Edge:** Reeded

Date	Mintage	F	VF	XF	Unc	BU
2002 Proof	—	Value: 925				

KM# 95b.1 50 PENCE
39.9400 g., 0.9160 Gold 1.1762 oz. AGW, 38.6 mm.
Ruler: Elizabeth II **Obv:** Crowned bust right, denomination below **Rev:** Elizabeth and Philip on balcony below multicolor bunting **Edge:** Reeded

Date	Mintage	F	VF	XF	Unc	BU
2002 Proof	50	Value: 925				

KM# 95b.2 50 PENCE
39.9400 g., 0.9160 Gold 1.1762 oz. AGW, 38.6 mm.
Ruler: Elizabeth II **Obv:** Crowned bust right, denomination below **Rev:** With plain bunting **Edge:** Reeded

Date	Mintage	F	VF	XF	Unc	BU
2002 Proof	—	Value: 925				

KM# 96b.1 50 PENCE
39.9400 g., 0.9160 Gold 1.1762 oz. AGW, 38.6 mm.
Ruler: Elizabeth II **Obv:** Crowned bust right, denomination below **Rev:** Multicolor jets below multicolor bunting **Edge:** Reeded

Date	Mintage	F	VF	XF	Unc	BU
2002 Proof	50	Value: 925				

KM# 96b.2 50 PENCE
39.9400 g., 0.9160 Gold 1.1762 oz. AGW, 38.6 mm.
Ruler: Elizabeth II **Obv:** Crowned bust right, denomination below **Rev:** With plain bunting **Edge:** Reeded

Date	Mintage	F	VF	XF	Unc	BU
2002 Proof	—	Value: 925				

KM# 97b.1 50 PENCE
39.9400 g., 0.9160 Gold 1.1762 oz. AGW, 38.6 mm. **Ruler:** Elizabeth II **Obv:** Crowned bust right, denomination below **Rev:** Queen and fireworks below multicolor bunting **Edge:** Reeded

Date	Mintage	F	VF	XF	Unc	BU
2002 Proof	50	Value: 925				

KM# 97b.2 50 PENCE
39.9400 g., 0.9160 Gold 1.1762 oz. AGW, 38.6 mm.
Ruler: Elizabeth II **Obv:** Crowned bust right, denomination below **Rev:** With plain bunting **Edge:** Reeded

Date	Mintage	F	VF	XF	Unc	BU
2002 Proof	—	Value: 925				

KM# 98b.1 50 PENCE
39.9400 g., 0.9160 Gold 1.1762 oz. AGW, 38.6 mm. **Ruler:** Elizabeth II **Obv:** Crowned bust right, denomination below **Rev:** UK map and four flags below multicolor bunting **Edge:** Reeded

Date	Mintage	F	VF	XF	Unc	BU
2002 Proof	50	Value: 925				

KM# 98b.2 50 PENCE
39.9400 g., 0.9160 Gold 1.1762 oz. AGW, 38.6 mm.
Ruler: Elizabeth II **Obv:** Crowned bust right, denomination below **Rev:** With plain bunting **Edge:** Reeded

Date	Mintage	F	VF	XF	Unc	BU
2002 Proof	—	Value: 925				

KM# 99b.1 50 PENCE
39.9400 g., 0.9160 Gold 1.1762 oz. AGW, 38.6 mm.
Ruler: Elizabeth II **Obv:** Crowned bust right, denomination below **Rev:** Queen and two Commonwealth Games athletes below multicolor bunting **Edge:** Reeded

Date	Mintage	F	VF	XF	Unc	BU
2002 Proof	50	Value: 925				

KM# 99b.2 50 PENCE
39.9400 g., 0.9160 Gold 1.1762 oz. AGW, 38.6 mm.
Ruler: Elizabeth II **Obv:** Crowned bust right, denomination below **Rev:** With plain bunting **Edge:** Reeded

Date	Mintage	F	VF	XF	Unc	BU
2002 Proof	—	Value: 925				

KM# 100b.1 50 PENCE
39.9400 g., 0.9160 Gold 1.1762 oz. AGW, 38.6 mm. **Ruler:** Elizabeth II **Obv:** Crowned bust right, denomination below **Rev:** Royal Ascot Carriage scene below multicolor bunting **Edge:** Reeded

Date	Mintage	F	VF	XF	Unc	BU
2002 Proof	50	Value: 925				

KM# 100b.2 50 PENCE
39.9400 g., 0.9160 Gold 1.1762 oz. AGW, 38.6 mm.
Ruler: Elizabeth II **Obv:** Crowned bust right, denomination below **Rev:** With plain bunting **Edge:** Reeded

Date	Mintage	F	VF	XF	Unc	BU
2002 Proof	—	Value: 925				

KM# 101b.1 50 PENCE
39.9400 g., 0.9160 Gold 1.1762 oz. AGW, 38.6 mm.
Ruler: Elizabeth II **Obv:** Crowned bust right, denomination below **Rev:** Queen and two hockey players below multicolor bunting **Edge:** Reeded

Date	Mintage	F	VF	XF	Unc	BU
2002 Proof	50	Value: 925				

KM# 101b.2 50 PENCE
39.9400 g., 0.9160 Gold 1.1762 oz. AGW, 38.6 mm.
Ruler: Elizabeth II **Obv:** Crowned bust right, denomination below **Rev:** With plain bunting **Edge:** Reeded

Date	Mintage	F	VF	XF	Unc	BU
2002 Proof	—	Value: 925				

1974
FALKLAND ISLANDS

KM# 6 1/2 POUND
3.9900 g., 0.9170 Gold .1176 oz. AGW **Ruler:** Elizabeth II **Obv:** Young bust right **Rev:** Romney marsh sheep left, date above **Rev. Designer:** William Gardner

Date	Mintage	F	VF	XF	Unc	BU
1974 Proof	2,673	Value: 165				

QUEEN ELIZABETH THE SECOND
1974
FALKLAND ISLANDS

KM# 7 POUND
7.9900 g., 0.9170 Gold .2356 oz. AGW **Ruler:** Elizabeth II **Obv:** Young bust right **Rev:** Romney marsh sheep left, date above **Rev. Designer:** William Gardner

Date	Mintage	F	VF	XF	Unc	BU
1974 Proof	2,675	Value: 265				

KM# 24b POUND
19.6500 g., 0.9170 Gold .5791 oz. AGW, 22.5 mm.
Ruler: Elizabeth II **Obv:** Crowned bust right **Rev:** State shield, date and denomination

Date	Mintage	F	VF	XF	Unc	BU
1987 Proof	Est. 200	Value: 625				

1974
FALKLAND ISLANDS

KM# 8 2 POUNDS
15.9800 g., 0.9170 Gold .4712 oz. AGW **Ruler:** Elizabeth II **Obv:** Young bust right **Rev:** Romney marsh sheep left, date above **Rev. Designer:** William Gardner

Date	Mintage	F	VF	XF	Unc	BU
1974 Proof	2,158	Value: 520				

KM# 104 2 POUNDS
1.2428 g., 0.9990 Gold 0.0399 oz. AGW, 14 mm.
Ruler: Elizabeth II **Obv:** Crowned bust right **Rev:** Egbert of Wessex 802-839 **Edge:** Reeded

Date	Mintage	F	VF	XF	Unc	BU
1997 Proof	—	Value: 45.00				

KM# 105 2 POUNDS
1.2428 g., 0.9990 Gold 0.0399 oz. AGW, 14 mm.
Ruler: Elizabeth II **Obv:** Crowned bust right **Rev:** Alfred the Great 871-899 **Edge:** Reeded

Date	Mintage	F	VF	XF	Unc	BU
1997 Proof	—	Value: 45.00				

KM# 106 2 POUNDS
1.2428 g., 0.9990 Gold 0.0399 oz. AGW, 14 mm.
Ruler: Elizabeth II **Obv:** Crowned bust right **Rev:** Edward the Confessor **Edge:** Reeded

Date	Mintage	F	VF	XF	Unc	BU
1997 Proof	—	Value: 45.00				

KM# 107 2 POUNDS
1.2428 g., 0.9990 Gold 0.0399 oz. AGW, 14 mm.
Ruler: Elizabeth II **Obv:** Crowned bust right **Rev:** William I the Conqueror 1066-87 **Edge:** Reeded

Date	Mintage	F	VF	XF	Unc	BU
1997 Proof	—	Value: 45.00				

KM# 108 2 POUNDS
1.2428 g., 0.9990 Gold 0.0399 oz. AGW, 14 mm.
Ruler: Elizabeth II **Obv:** Crowned bust right **Rev:** Henry II 1154-89 **Edge:** Reeded

Date	Mintage	F	VF	XF	Unc	BU
1997 Proof	—	Value: 45.00				

KM# 109 2 POUNDS
1.2428 g., 0.9990 Gold 0.0399 oz. AGW, 14 mm.
Ruler: Elizabeth II **Obv:** Crowned bust right **Rev:** Richard I the Lion Hearted, 1189-99 **Edge:** Reeded

Date	Mintage	F	VF	XF	Unc	BU
1997 Proof	—	Value: 45.00				

KM# 110 2 POUNDS
1.2428 g., 0.9990 Gold 0.0399 oz. AGW, 14 mm.
Ruler: Elizabeth II **Obv:** Crowned bust right **Rev:** Henry IV 1399-1413 **Edge:** Reeded

Date	Mintage	F	VF	XF	Unc	BU
1997 Proof	—	Value: 45.00				

KM# 111 2 POUNDS
1.2428 g., 0.9990 Gold 0.0399 oz. AGW, 14 mm.
Ruler: Elizabeth II **Obv:** Crowned bust right **Rev:** Edward IV 1461-83 **Edge:** Reeded

Date	Mintage	F	VF	XF	Unc	BU
1997 Proof	—	Value: 45.00				

KM# 112 2 POUNDS
1.2428 g., 0.9990 Gold 0.0399 oz. AGW, 14 mm.
Ruler: Elizabeth II **Obv:** Crowned bust right **Rev:** Henry VIII 1509-47 **Edge:** Reeded

Date	Mintage	F	VF	XF	Unc	BU
1997 Proof	—	Value: 45.00				

KM# 113 2 POUNDS
1.2428 g., 0.9990 Gold 0.0399 oz. AGW, 14 mm.
Ruler: Elizabeth II **Obv:** Crowned bust right **Rev:** Elizabeth I 1558-1603 **Edge:** Reeded

Date	Mintage	F	VF	XF	Unc	BU
1997 Proof	—	Value: 45.00				

KM# 114 2 POUNDS
1.2428 g., 0.9990 Gold 0.0399 oz. AGW, 14 mm.
Ruler: Elizabeth II **Obv:** Crowned bust right **Rev:** Charles I 1625-49 **Edge:** Reeded

Date	Mintage	F	VF	XF	Unc	BU
1997 Proof	—	Value: 45.00				

KM# 115 2 POUNDS
1.2428 g., 0.9990 Gold 0.0399 oz. AGW, 14 mm.
Ruler: Elizabeth II **Obv:** Crowned bust right **Rev:** Victoria 1837-1901 **Edge:** Reeded

Date	Mintage	F	VF	XF	Unc	BU
1998 Proof	—	Value: 45.00				

KM# 116 2 POUNDS
7.8000 g., 0.5830 Gold 0.2505 oz. AGW, 24.9 mm.
Ruler: Elizabeth II **Subject:** Royal Heritage - Egbert of Wessex 802-839 **Obv:** Crowned bust right **Rev:** Egbert in archway, dates divided **Edge:** Reeded

Date	Mintage	F	VF	XF	Unc	BU
1997 Proof	—	Value: 175				

KM# 117 2 POUNDS
7.8000 g., 0.5830 Gold 0.2505 oz. AGW, 24.9 mm.
Ruler: Elizabeth II **Obv:** Crowned bust right **Rev:** Alfred the Great 871-899 **Edge:** Reeded

Date	Mintage	F	VF	XF	Unc	BU
1997 Proof	—	Value: 175				

KM# 118 2 POUNDS
7.8000 g., 0.5830 Gold 0.2505 oz. AGW, 24.9 mm.
Ruler: Elizabeth II **Obv:** Crowned bust right **Rev:** Edward the Confessor 1042-66 **Edge:** Reeded

Date	Mintage	F	VF	XF	Unc	BU
1997 Proof	—	Value: 175				

KM# 119 2 POUNDS
7.8000 g., 0.5830 Gold 0.2505 oz. AGW, 24.9 mm.
Ruler: Elizabeth II **Obv:** Crowned bust right **Rev:** William I the Conqueror 1066-87 **Edge:** Reeded

Date	Mintage	F	VF	XF	Unc	BU
1997 Proof	—	Value: 175				

KM# 120 2 POUNDS
7.8000 g., 0.5830 Gold 0.2505 oz. AGW, 24.9 mm.
Ruler: Elizabeth II **Obv:** Crowned bust right **Rev:** Henry II 1154-89 **Edge:** Reeded

Date	Mintage	F	VF	XF	Unc	BU
1997 Proof	—	Value: 175				

KM# 121 2 POUNDS
7.8000 g., 0.5830 Gold 0.2505 oz. AGW, 24.9 mm.
Ruler: Elizabeth II **Obv:** Crowned bust right **Rev:** Richard I the Lion Hearted 1189-99 **Edge:** Reeded

Date	Mintage	F	VF	XF	Unc	BU
1997 Proof	—	Value: 175				

FALKLAND ISLANDS

KM# 122 2 POUNDS
7.8000 g., 0.5830 Gold 0.2505 oz. AGW, 24.9 mm.
Ruler: Elizabeth II **Obv:** Crowned bust right **Rev:** Henry IV 1399-1413 **Edge:** Reeded

Date	Mintage	F	VF	XF	Unc	BU
1997 Proof	—	Value: 175				

KM# 123 2 POUNDS
7.8000 g., 0.5830 Gold 0.2505 oz. AGW, 24.9 mm.
Ruler: Elizabeth II **Obv:** Crowned bust right **Rev:** Edward IV 1461-83 **Edge:** Reeded

Date	Mintage	F	VF	XF	Unc	BU
1997 Proof	—	Value: 175				

KM# 124 2 POUNDS
7.8700 g., 0.5830 Gold 0.2505 oz. AGW, 24.9 mm.
Ruler: Elizabeth II **Obv:** Crowned bust right **Rev:** Henry VIII 1509-47, shield at right, dates at left **Edge:** Reeded

Date	Mintage	F	VF	XF	Unc	BU
1997 Proof	—	Value: 175				

KM# 125 2 POUNDS
7.8000 g., 0.5830 Gold 0.2505 oz. AGW, 24.9 mm.
Ruler: Elizabeth II **Subject:** Royal Heritage - Elizabeth I 1558-1603 **Obv:** Crowned bust right **Rev:** Bust with high ruffled collar 3/4 facing, dates below **Edge:** Reeded

Date	Mintage	F	VF	XF	Unc	BU
1998 Proof	—	Value: 175				

KM# 126 2 POUNDS
7.8000 g., 0.5830 Gold 0.2505 oz. AGW, 24.9 mm.
Ruler: Elizabeth II **Obv:** Crowned bust right **Rev:** Charles I 1625-49 **Edge:** Reeded

Date	Mintage	F	VF	XF	Unc	BU
1998 Proof	—	Value: 175				

KM# 127 2 POUNDS
7.8000 g., 0.5830 Gold 0.2505 oz. AGW, 24.9 mm.
Ruler: Elizabeth II **Obv:** Crowned bust right **Rev:** Victoria 1837-1901 **Edge:** Reeded

Date	Mintage	F	VF	XF	Unc	BU
1998 Proof	—	Value: 175				

KM# 128 2 POUNDS
7.6700 g., 0.5830 Gold 0.1438 oz. AGW, 24.9 mm.
Ruler: Elizabeth II **Obv:** Crowned bust right, date below **Rev:** Queen Mother holding the baby within circle, denomination below **Edge:** Reeded

Date	Mintage	F	VF	XF	Unc	BU
1998 Proof	—	Value: 150				

KM# 69a 2 POUNDS
28.1500 g., 0.9250 Bi-Metallic Silver center in Gold-plated Silver ring 0.8372 oz., 38.61 mm. **Ruler:** Elizabeth II **Obv:** Crowned bust right within circle, dates below **Rev:** Islands map, radiant sun, and denomination within circle of local wildlife **Rev. Designer:** Matthew Bonaccorsi **Edge:** Reeded

Date	Mintage	F	VF	XF	Unc	BU
1999-2000 Proof	—	Value: 55.00				

KM# 9 5 POUNDS
39.9400 g., 0.9170 Gold 1.1773 oz. AGW **Ruler:** Elizabeth II **Obv:** Young bust right **Rev:** Romney marsh sheep left, date above **Rev. Designer:** William Gardner

Date	Mintage	F	VF	XF	Unc	BU
1974 Proof	2,158	Value: 1,150				

KM# 33 5 POUNDS
39.9400 g., 0.9170 Gold 1.1773 oz. AGW **Ruler:** Elizabeth II **Subject:** 10th Wedding Anniversary - Prince Charles and Lady Diana **Obv:** Crowned bust right **Rev:** Facing cameo portraits of Prince Charles and Princess Diana

Date	Mintage	F	VF	XF	Unc	BU
1991 Proof	Est. 200	Value: 900				

KM# 36b 5 POUNDS
39.9400 g., 0.9170 Gold 1.1773 oz. AGW **Ruler:** Elizabeth II **Subject:** 10th Anniversary of Liberation **Obv:** Crowned bust right **Rev:** Statue at center, inscription at right

Date	Mintage	F	VF	XF	Unc	BU
1992 Proof	100	Value: 1,100				

KM# 28 10 POUNDS
3.1300 g., 0.9990 Gold .1000 oz. AGW **Ruler:** Elizabeth II **Subject:** 90th Birthday of Queen Mother **Obv:** Crowned bust right **Rev:** Crowned arms with supporters, dates below

Date	Mintage	F	VF	XF	Unc	BU
ND(1990) Proof	Est. 750	Value: 85.00				

KM# 38 10 POUNDS
3.1300 g., 0.9990 Gold .1000 oz. AGW **Ruler:** Elizabeth II **Subject:** 400th Anniversary of Discovery - Ship "Desire" **Obv:** Crowned bust right **Rev:** Map above ship "Desire" at sea, dates at right

Date	Mintage	F	VF	XF	Unc	BU
ND(1992) Proof	Est. 400	Value: 75.00				

KM# 62 20 POUNDS
6.2200 g., 0.9990 Gold .2000 oz. AGW **Ruler:** Elizabeth II **Subject:** Flying Doctor Service **Obv:** Crowned bust right **Rev:** Two airplanes in flight

Date	Mintage	F	VF	XF	Unc	BU
1998 Proof	Est. 1,000	Value: 180				

KM# 65 20 POUNDS
6.2200 g., 0.9990 Gold .2000 oz. AGW **Ruler:** Elizabeth II **Subject:** Sir Ernest H. Shackleton **Obv:** Crowned bust right **Rev:** Cameo portrait and icebound ship

Date	Mintage	F	VF	XF	Unc	BU
1999 Proof	Est. 1,000	Value: 180				

KM# 68 20 POUNDS
6.2200 g., 0.9990 Gold .2000 oz. AGW **Ruler:** Elizabeth II **Subject:** The Gold Rush **Obv:** Crowned bust right **Rev:** "Vicar of Bray" in harbor **Edge:** Reeded

Date	Mintage	F	VF	XF	Unc	BU
2000 Proof	1,000	Value: 180				

KM# 29 25 POUNDS
7.8100 g., 0.9990 Gold .2500 oz. AGW **Ruler:** Elizabeth II **Subject:** 90th Birthday of Queen Mother **Obv:** Crowned bust right **Rev:** Queen Mother head left, within wreath and flowers, dates below

Date	Mintage	F	VF	XF	Unc	BU
ND(1990) Proof	Est. 750	Value: 220				

KM# 40 25 POUNDS
7.8100 g., 0.9990 Gold .2500 oz. AGW **Ruler:** Elizabeth II **Subject:** 100th Anniversary of Christchurch Cathedral **Obv:** Crowned bust right, denomination below **Rev:** Cathedral, cross, scepter, and mitre, dates at left

Date	Mintage	F	VF	XF	Unc	BU
1992 Proof	Est. 400	Value: 185				

KM# 103 25 POUNDS
7.8100 g., 0.9999 Gold 0.2511 oz. AGW, 22 mm. **Ruler:** Elizabeth II **Obv:** Crowned bust right, denomination below **Obv. Designer:** Raphael Maklouf **Rev:** Queen Mother as a young lady and as an elderly lady **Rev. Designer:** Willem Vis **Edge:** Reeded

Date	Mintage	F	VF	XF	Unc	BU
ND(2002) Proof	1,000	Value: 185				

KM# 30 50 POUNDS
15.6100 g., 0.9990 Gold .5000 oz. AGW **Ruler:** Elizabeth II **Subject:** 90th Birthday of Queen Mother **Obv:** Crowned bust right

Date	Mintage	F	VF	XF	Unc	BU
ND(1990) Proof	Est. 750	Value: 360				

KM# 41 50 POUNDS
15.6100 g., 0.9990 Gold .5000 oz. AGW **Ruler:** Elizabeth II **Subject:** 100th Anniversary of Defense **Obv:** Crowned bust right **Rev:** Soldier with shield, dates at right

Date	Mintage	F	VF	XF	Unc	BU
ND(1992) Proof	Est. 400	Value: 345				

KM# 44 50 POUNDS
47.5400 g., 0.9170 Gold 1.4013 oz. AGW **Ruler:** Elizabeth II **Subject:** 40th Anniversary - Coronation of Queen Elizabeth II

Date	Mintage	F	VF	XF	Unc	BU
ND(1993) Proof	Est. 100	Value: 1,150				

KM# 31 100 POUNDS
31.2100 g., 0.9990 Gold 1.0000 oz. AGW **Ruler:** Elizabeth II **Subject:** 90th Birthday of Queen Mother **Obv:** Crowned bust right **Rev:** Queen Mother's head left, within wreath and flowers, dates below

Date	Mintage	F	VF	XF	Unc	BU
ND(1990) Proof	Est. 750	Value: 725				

KM# 42 100 POUNDS
31.2100 g., 0.9990 Gold 1.0000 oz. AGW **Ruler:** Elizabeth II **Subject:** 400th Anniversary of Discovery - Ship "Desire' **Obv:** Crowned bust right **Rev:** Map above ship "Desire" at sea, dates at right

Date	Mintage	F	VF	XF	Unc	BU
ND(1992) Proof	Est. 400	Value: 710				

KM# 13 150 POUNDS
33.4370 g., 0.9000 Gold .9676 oz. AGW **Ruler:** Elizabeth II **Subject:** Conservation **Obv:** Young bust right **Rev:** Falkland Fur Seal, denomination below, date at right

Date	Mintage	F	VF	XF	Unc	BU
1979	488	—	—	—	765	—
1979 Proof	164	Value: 1,600				

MEDALLIC COINAGE
Richard Lobel Issue

X# 4 SOVEREIGN
0.3750 Gold **Ruler:** Elizabeth II **Subject:** Edward VIII

Date	Mintage	F	VF	XF	Unc	BU
1936 Proof	200	Value: 125				

PROOF SETS

KM#	Date	Mintage	Identification	Issue Price	Mkt Val
PS2	1974 (4)	2,000	KM6-9	1,100	2,000
PS8	1990 (4)	750	KM28-31	1,595	1,150
PS10	1992 (4)	400	KM38, 40-42	1,595	1,075

FIJI ISLANDS

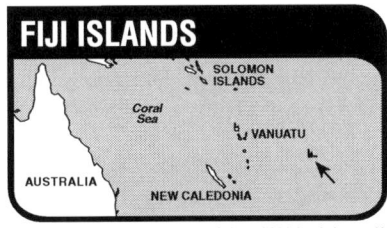

The Republic of Fiji, consists of about 320 islands located in the southwestern Pacific 1,100 miles (1,770 km.) north of New Zealand. The islands have a combined area of 7,056 sq. mi. (18,274 sq. km.) and a population of 772,891. Capital: Suva. Fiji's economy is based on agriculture and mining. Sugar, coconut products, manganese, and gold are exported.

The first European to sight Fiji was the Dutch navigator Abel Tasman in 1643 and the islands were visited by British naval captain James Cook in 1774. The first complete survey of the island was conducted by the United States in 1840. Settlement by mercenaries from Tonga, and traders attracted by the sandalwood trade, began in 1801. Following a lengthy period of intertribal warfare, the islands were unconditionally ceded to Great Britain in 1874 by King Cakobau. Fiji became a sovereign and independent nation on Oct. 10, 1970, the 96th anniversary of the cession of the islands to Queen Victoria.

Fiji was declared a Republic in 1987 following two military coups. It left the British Commonwealth and Queen Elizabeth ceased to be the Head of State. A new constitution was introduced in 1991. The country returned to the Commonwealth in 1997 with a revised constitution.

RULER
British until 1970

MINT MARKS
(c) – Australian Mint, Canberra
(H) – The Mint, Birmingham
(I) – Royal Mint, Llantrisant
(o) – Royal Canadian Mint, Ottawa
S – San Francisco, U.S.A.

MONETARY SYSTEM
12 Pence = 1 Shilling
2 Shillings = 1 Florin
20 Shillings = 1 Pound

REPUBLIC
British Administration until 1970
DECIMAL COINAGE
100 Cents = 1 Dollar

KM# 93 5 DOLLARS
1.5550 g., 0.9999 Gold 0.05 oz. AGW **Ruler:** Elizabeth II **Obv:** Crowned head right, date at right **Rev:** Arms

Date	Mintage	F	VF	XF	Unc	BU
2002	3,000	Value: 35.00				

KM# 97 10 DOLLARS
1.2500 g., 0.9990 Gold 0.0401 oz. AGW **Ruler:** Elizabeth II **Subject:** Discovery of Gold in Fiji - 1932 **Obv:** Crowned head right **Rev:** Gold panning

Date	Mintage	F	VF	XF	Unc	BU
1998 Proof	—	Value: 28.50				

KM# 94 10 DOLLARS
3.1100 g., 0.9999 Gold 0.1 oz. AGW **Ruler:** Elizabeth II **Obv:** Crowned head right, date at right **Rev:** Arms **Edge:** Reeded

Date	Mintage	F	VF	XF	Unc	BU
2002 Proof	2,000	Value: 75.00				

KM# 57 25 DOLLARS
7.7750 g., 0.7500 Gold .1875 oz. AGW **Ruler:** Elizabeth II **Obv:** Denomination at center of designs **Rev:** Balikula mint mark of Pacific Sovereign Mint, Fijian thatched temple **Designer:** David Holland

Date	Mintage	F	VF	XF	Unc	BU
ND(1990)	443	—	—	—	130	—
Note: Boar tusks						
ND(1991)	512	—	—	—	130	—
Note: War fan						
ND(1992)	50	—	—	—	150	—

KM# 58 50 DOLLARS
15.5500 g., 0.7500 Gold .3750 oz. AGW **Ruler:** Elizabeth II **Obv:** Denomination at center of patterns **Rev:** Balikula mint mark of Pacific Sovereign Mint, Fijian warrior **Designer:** David Holland

Date	Mintage	F	VF	XF	Unc	BU
ND(1990)	168	—	—	—	265	—
Note: Boar tusks						
ND(1991)	141	—	—	—	265	—
Note: War fan						
ND(1992)	43	—	—	—	300	—

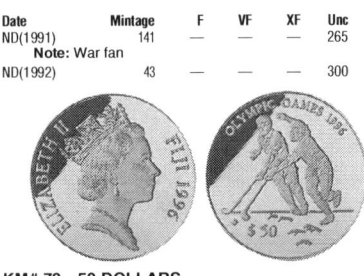

KM# 72 50 DOLLARS
7.7760 g., 0.5833 Gold .1458 oz. AGW **Ruler:** Elizabeth II **Subject:** Olympics **Obv:** Crowned head right, date at right **Rev:** Two field hockey players, denomination below

Date	Mintage	F	VF	XF	Unc	BU
1996	Est. 3,000	—	—	—	100	—

KM# 35 100 DOLLARS
31.3600 g., 0.5000 Gold .5042 oz. AGW **Ruler:** Elizabeth II **Subject:** 100th Anniversary - Cession to Great Britain **Obv:** Young bust right **Rev:** Bust of King Cakobau facing, denomination below

Date	Mintage	F	VF	XF	Unc	BU
1974	1,109	—	—	—	345	—
1974 Proof	2,321	Value: 365				

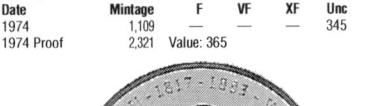

KM# 38 100 DOLLARS
31.3000 g., 0.5000 Gold .5032 oz. AGW **Ruler:** Elizabeth II **Obv:** Young bust right **Rev:** King Cakobau, facing denomination below

Date	Mintage	F	VF	XF	Unc	BU
1975	593	—	—	—	365	—
1975 Proof	3,197	Value: 350				

KM# 59 100 DOLLARS
31.1000 g., 0.7500 Gold .7500 oz. AGW **Ruler:** Elizabeth II **Obv:** Denomination within center, diamonds on pattern at top, bottom, right and left **Rev:** Balikula mint mark of Pacific Sovereign Mint **Designer:** David Holland **Note:** Dates are privy marks; 1990 - Boar Tusks; 1991 - War Fan; 1992 - ?.

Date	Mintage	F	VF	XF	Unc	BU
ND(1990)	161	—	—	—	530	—
ND(1991)	131	—	—	—	530	—
ND(1992)	41	—	—	—	575	—

KM# 65 100 DOLLARS
7.5000 g., 0.9170 Gold .2209 oz. AGW **Ruler:** Elizabeth II **Subject:** Discovery of Fiji **Obv:** Crowned head right, date at right **Rev:** James Cook in cameo right of sailing ship, denomination below

Date	Mintage	F	VF	XF	Unc	BU
1993 Proof	3,000	Value: 155				

KM# 98 100 DOLLARS
0.9990 Gold **Ruler:** Elizabeth II **Subject:** Silver Jubilee of Independence **Obv:** Crowned head right **Rev:** Arms

Date	Mintage	F	VF	XF	Unc	BU
1995 Proof	—	Value: 160				

KM# 99 100 DOLLARS
7.7800 g., 0.5850 Gold 0.1463 oz. AGW **Ruler:** Elizabeth II **Subject:** 2006 FIFA World Cup - Germany **Obv:** Crowned head right, date at right **Rev:** World Cup **Edge:** Reeded

Date	Mintage	F	VF	XF	Unc	BU
2003 Proof	25,000	Value: 110				

KM# 47 200 DOLLARS
15.9800 g., 0.9170 Gold .4712 oz. AGW **Ruler:** Elizabeth II **Subject:** 10th Anniversary of Independence **Obv:** Arms with supporters, date below **Rev:** Bust 3/4 facing, denomination below **Rev. Designer:** Michael Rizzello

Date	Mintage	F	VF	XF	Unc	BU
1980	500	—	—	—	325	—
1980 Proof	1,166	Value: 315				

KM# 56 200 DOLLARS
15.9800 g., 0.9170 Gold .4712 oz. AGW **Ruler:** Elizabeth II **Subject:** 25th Anniversary - World Wildlife Fund **Obv:** Young bust right **Rev:** Ogmodon

Date	Mintage	F	VF	XF	Unc	BU
1986 Proof	5,000	Value: 310				

KM# 61 200 DOLLARS
10.0000 g., 0.9170 Gold .2948 oz. AGW **Ruler:** Elizabeth II **Subject:** Save the Children Fund **Obv:** King Cakobau facing divides date **Rev:** Child with toy boat, figure in background with spear, denomination below

Date	Mintage	F	VF	XF	Unc	BU
1991 Proof	32,000	Value: 195				

KM# 43 250 DOLLARS
33.4370 g., 0.9000 Gold .9676 oz. AGW **Ruler:** Elizabeth II **Subject:** Conservation **Obv:** Young bust right **Rev:** Banded iguana, denomination at right

Date	Mintage	F	VF	XF	Unc	BU
1978	810	—	—	—	675	—
1978 Proof	252	Value: 825				

TRIAL STRIKES

KM#	Date	Mintage	Identification	Mkt Val
TS1	1974	—	100 Dollars. Bronze. KM35.	950

MINT SETS

KM#	Date	Mintage	Identification	Issue Price	Mkt Val
MS4	1978 (3)	—	KM41-43	444	750
MS9	1990 (3)	—	KM57-59	905	875

PROOF SETS

KM#	Date	Mintage	Identification	Issue Price	Mkt Val
PS5	1978 (3)	—	KM#41a, 42a, 43	726	865
PS9	1993 (3)	—	KM#63-65	370	225

216   FINLAND

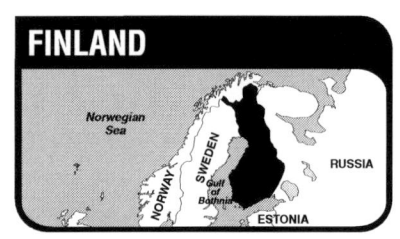

FINLAND

The Republic of Finland, the third most northerly state of the European continent, has an area of 130,559 sq. mi. (338,127 sq. km.) and a population of 5.1 million. Capital: Helsinki. Lumbering, shipbuilding, metal and woodworking are the leading industries. Paper, timber, woodpulp, plywood and metal products are exported.

The Finns, who probably originated in the Volga region of Russia, took Finland from the Lapps late in the 7th century. They were conquered in the 12th century by Eric IX of Sweden, and brought into contact with Western Christendom. In 1809, Sweden was conquered by Alexander I of Russia, and the peace terms gave Finland to Russia which became a grand duchy within the Russian Empire until Dec. 6, 1917, when, shortly after the Bolshevik revolution it declared its independence. After a brief but bitter civil war between the Russian sympathizers and Finnish nationalists in which the Whites (nationalists) were victorious, a new constitution was adopted, and on Dec. 6, 1917 Finland was established as a republic. In 1939 Soviet troops invaded Finland over disputed territorial concessions which were later granted in the peace treaty of 1940. When the Germans invaded Russia, Finland became involved and in the Armistice of 1944 lost the Petsamo area to the Soviets.

RULERS
Nicholas II, 1894-1917

MONETARY SYSTEM
100 Pennia = 1 Markka

Commencing 1963
100 Old Markka = 1 New Markka

MINT MARKS
H - Birmingham 1921
Heart (h) - Copenhagen 1922
No mm – Helsinki

MINT OFFICIALS' INITIALS

Letter	Date	Name
H	1948-1958	Peippo Uolevi Helle
H-M	1990`	Raimo Heino & Raimo Makkonen
K	1976-1983	Timo Koivuranta
K-H	1977, 1979	Timo Koivuranta & Heikki Haivaoja (Designer)
K-M	1983	Timo Koivuranta & Pertti Makinen
K-N	1978	Timo Koivuranta & Antti Neuvonen
K-T	1982	Timo Koivuranta & Erja Tielinen
L	1885-1912	Johan Conrad Lihr
L	1948	Vesa Uolevi Liuhto
L-M	1991	Arto Lappalainen & Raimo Makkonen
L-M	2000	Maija Lavonen & Raimo Makkonen
M	1987	Raimo Makkonen
M-G	1998	Raimo Makkonen & Henrik Gummerus
M-L	1997	Raimo Makkonen & Tero Lounas
M-L-L	1995	Raimo Makkonen & Arto Lappalainen & Marita Lappalainen
M-L-M	1989	Marjo Lahtinen & Raimo Makkonen
M-O	1998	Raimo Makkonen & Harri Ojala
M-S	1992, 1997	Raimo Makkonen & Erkki Salmela
N	1983-1987	Tapio Nevalainen
P-M	1989-1991, 1994-1995, 1997, 2000	Reijo Paavilainen & Raimo Makkonen
P-N	1985	Reijo Paavilainen & Tapio Nevalainen
P-V-M	1999	Juhani Pallasmaa, Jukka Veistola & Raimo Makkonen
R-M	1999	Jarkko Roth & Raimo Makkonen
S	1864-85	Aug. F. Soldan
S	1912-1947	Isak Gustaf Sundell
S	1958-1975	Allan Alarik Soiniemi
S-H	1967-1971	Allan Alarik Soiniemi & Heikki Haivaoja (Designer)
S-J	1960	Allan Alarik Soiniemi & Toivo Jaatinen
S-M	1995	Terho Sakki & Raimo Makkonen
T-M	1996, 2000	Erja Tielinen & Raimo Makkonen

GRAND DUCHY
DECIMAL COINAGE

KM# 8.1 10 MARKKAA
3.2258 g., 0.9000 Gold .0933 oz. AGW **Ruler:** Alexander II
Obv: Narrow eagle **Rev:** Denomination and date within circle
Note: Regal issues

Date	Mintage	F	VF	XF	Unc	BU
1878 S	254,000	100	150	175	200	—

KM# 8.2 10 MARKKAA
3.2258 g., 0.9000 Gold .0933 oz. AGW, 18.9 mm.
Ruler: Nicholas II **Obv:** Crowned imperial double eagle holding orb and scepter **Rev:** Denomination and date within circle, fineness around **Note:** Regal issues

Date	Mintage	F	VF	XF	Unc	BU
1879/0 S	—	1,500	3,000	5,000	—	—
	Note: Only a few pieces known					
1879 S	200,000	100	150	175	200	—
1881 S	100,000	120	160	200	240	—
1882 S	386,000	100	150	175	200	—
1904 L	102,000	250	350	400	500	—
1905 L	43,000	1,500	2,000	2,800	3,000	—
1913 L	396,000	100	150	175	200	—

KM# 9.1 20 MARKKAA
6.4516 g., 0.9000 Gold .1867 oz. AGW **Ruler:** Alexander II
Obv: Narrow eagle **Rev:** Denomination and date within circle
Note: Regal issues

Date	Mintage	F	VF	XF	Unc	BU
1878 S	Est. 235,000	150	180	220	270	—

Note: Some specimens may appear as prooflike; Proofs were never made officially by the mint

KM# 9.2 20 MARKKAA
6.4516 g., 0.9000 Gold .1867 oz. AGW, 21.3 mm.
Ruler: Nicholas II **Obv:** Crowned imperial double eagle holding orb and scepter **Rev:** Denomination and date within circle, fineness around **Note:** Regal issues.

Date	Mintage	F	VF	XF	Unc	BU
1879 S	300,000	150	180	200	220	—
1880 S	90,000	350	500	600	750	—
1891 L	91,000	170	200	220	250	—
1903 L	112,000	150	180	210	230	—
1904 L	188,000	150	180	200	220	—
1910 L	201,000	150	180	200	220	—
1911 L	161,000	150	180	200	220	—
1912 L	881,000	2,500	4,500	6,000	7,000	—
1912 S	Inc. above	150	180	200	220	—
1913 S	214,000	150	180	200	220	—

REPUBLIC
DECIMAL COINAGE

KM# 28 100 MARKKAA
4.2105 g., 0.9000 Gold .1218 oz. AGW, 18.5 mm.
Obv: Rampant lion left divides date **Rev:** Denomination flanked by sprigs **Designer:** Isak Sundell

Date	Mintage	F	VF	XF	Unc	BU
1926 S	50,000	—	950	1,150	1,300	—

KM# 29 200 MARKKAA
8.4210 g., 0.9000 Gold .2436 oz. AGW, 22.5 mm.
Obv: Rampant lion left divides date **Rev:** Denomination flanked by sprigs **Designer:** Isak Sundell

Date	Mintage	F	VF	XF	Unc	BU
1926 S	50,000	—	1,300	1,800	2,000	—

REFORM COINAGE
100 Old Markka = 1 New Markka 1963

KM# 95 MARKKA
8.6400 g., 0.7500 Gold .2083 oz. AGW, 22 mm. **Subject:** Last Markka Coin **Obv:** Rampant lion with sword left **Rev:** Stylized tree with roots **Edge:** Reeded **Designer:** Reijo Paavilainen

Date	Mintage	F	VF	XF	Unc	BU
2001 P-M Proof	55,000	Value: 200				

KM# 82a 10 MARKKAA
Bi-Metallic Gold center in Silver ring, 27.25 mm.
Subject: European Unity **Obv:** Swan in flight left within circle **Rev:** Denomination and branches **Designer:** Pertti Makinen and Antti Neuvonen **Note:** Total weight 12.200 grams.

Date	Mintage	F	VF	XF	Unc	BU
1995 M Proof	2,000	Value: 2,500				

KM# 72 1000 MARKKAA
9.0000 g., 0.9000 Gold .2604 oz. AGW, 22.1 mm. **Subject:** 75th Anniversary of Independence **Obv:** Dates above design **Rev:** Denomination below design **Designer:** Erkki Salmela

Date	Mintage	F	VF	XF	Unc	BU
1992 M-S	35,000	—	—	—	200	250

KM# 86 1000 MARKKAA
8.6400 g., 0.9000 Gold .2500 oz. AGW **Subject:** 80th Anniversary of Independence **Obv:** New shoot growing from tree stump, denomination above **Rev:** Symbolic design separating dates **Designer:** Reijo Paavilainen

Date	Mintage	F	VF	XF	Unc	BU
ND (1997) M-P Proof	20,000	Value: 330				

KM# 90 1000 MARKKAA
8.6400 g., 0.9000 Gold .2500 oz. AGW **Subject:** Jean Sibelius - Composer **Obv:** Head left **Rev:** Finlandia musical score, denomination above, date below **Designer:** Juhani Pallasmaa and Jukka Veistola

Date	Mintage	F	VF	XF	Unc	BU
1999 P-V-M Proof	25,000	Value: 350				

KM# 79 2000 MARKKAA
16.9700 g., 0.9000 Gold .4910 oz. AGW, 28 mm. **Subject:** 50 Years of Peace **Obv:** Design at center, date below **Rev:** Design above denomination **Designer:** Arto Lappalainen and Marita Lappalainen

Date	Mintage	F	VF	XF	Unc	BU
1995 M-L-L Proof	6,900	Value: 700				

EURO COINAGE
European Economic Community Issues

KM# 121 20 EURO
1.7300 g., 0.9000 Gold 0.0501 oz. AGW, 13.9 mm. **Subject:** 10th Anniversary - IAAF World Championships in Athletics **Obv:** Helsinki Stadium **Rev:** Two faces **Designer:** Pertti Mäkinen

Date	Mintage	F	VF	XF	Unc	BU
2005 M-M Proof	30,000			Value: 100		

KM# 113 50 EURO
13.2000 g., Bi-Metallic Gold And Silver **Ring Composition:** 0.9250 Silver **Center Composition:** 0.7500 Gold, 27.25 mm. **Subject:** Finnish art and design **Obv:** Snowflake design within box, beaded circle surrounds **Rev:** Snowflake design within beaded circle **Designer:** Matti Peltokangas

Date	Mintage	F	VF	XF	Unc	BU
2003 P-M Proof	10,600			Value: 300		

KM# 133 50 EURO
12.8000 g., Tri-Metallic 0.750 Gold 0.125 Silver 0.125 Copper center in 0.925 Silver and 0.075 Copper ring, 27.25 mm. **Subject:** Finland Presidency of European Union **Obv:** Letter decorations with 2006 and SUOMI-FINLAND **Rev:** 50 EURO below letter decoration **Rev. Designer:** Reijo Paavilainen

Date	Mintage	F	VF	XF	Unc	BU
2006 P-M Proof	8,000	—	—	—	—	—

KM# 109 100 EURO
8.6400 g., 0.9000 Gold 0.25 oz. AGW, 22 mm. **Subject:** Lapland **Obv:** Small tree and mountain stream **Rev:** Lake landscape beneath the midnight sun **Edge:** Plain with serial number **Designer:** Toivo Jaatinen

Date	Mintage	F	VF	XF	Unc	BU
2002 J-M Proof	25,000			Value: 225		

KM# 117 100 EURO
8.6400 g., 0.9000 Gold 0.25 oz. AGW, 22 mm. **Subject:** 150th Birthday of Albert Edelfelt **Obv:** Flower **Rev:** Head of Edelfelt **Designer:** Pertti Mäkinen

Date	Mintage	F	VF	XF	Unc	BU
2004 M-M Proof	8,500			Value: 280		

MEDALLIC COINAGE
Ecu Series

X# 3 150 ECU
6.7200 g., 0.7500 Gold .1620 oz. AGW, 23 mm. **Issuer:** Coin Invest Trust **Subject:** CSCE/KFZE Conference 20th Anniversary **Obv:** Artwork, head of Jean Sibelius **Rev:** Landscape, modern buildings **Edge:** Reeded **Note:** Similar to 5 Ecu, KM#M1.

Date	Mintage	F	VF	XF	Unc	BU
1992 Proof	Est. 1,000			Value: 200		

X# 16 150 ECU
6.7200 g., 0.7500 Gold 0.162 oz. AGW, 23 mm. **Obv:** Lapplander with reindeer **Rev:** Rovaniemi shield above bridge scene **Rev. Legend:** LAPIN PÄÄKAUPUNKI • ROVANIEMI - HAUPTSTADT LAPPLANDS **Edge:** Reeded

Date	Mintage	F	VF	XF	Unc	BU
1994 Proof	250			Value: 300		

MEDALLIC COINAGE
Euro Series

X# 12 50 EURO
8.6400 g., 0.9000 Gold .2500 oz. AGW **Subject:** Nagano Games **Rev:** Cross country skiing

Date	Mintage	F	VF	XF	Unc	BU
1998 Proof	5,000			Value: 200		

PATTERNS
Including off metal strikes

KM#	Date	Mintage	Identification	Mkt Val
Pn7	1867	—	10 Pennia. Gold.	—
Pn18	1926	—	200 Markkaa. Copper.	—

TRIAL STRIKES

KM#	Date	Mintage	Identification	Mkt Val
TSA4	1867	—	10 Pennia. Gold.	—
TS7	1960	—	(1000 Markkaa). Brass.	—
TS8	1960	—	(1000 Markkaa). Brass.	—

PROOF SETS

KM#	Date	Mintage	Identification	Issue Price	Mkt Val
PS2	1995 (2)	500	KM#80, 82a	802	1,350

FRANCE

a map of the **FRENCH MINTS**

The French Republic, largest of the West European nations, has an area of 210,026 sq. mi. (547,030 sq. km.) and a population of 58.1 million. Capital: Paris. Agriculture, manufacturing, tourist industry and financial services are the most important elements of France's diversified economy. Textiles and clothing, steel products, machinery and transportation equipment, chemicals, pharmaceuticals, nuclear electricity, agricultural products and wine are exported.

France, the Gaul of ancient times, emerged from the Renaissance as a modern centralized national state which reached its zenith during the reign of Louis XIV (1643-1715) when it became an absolute monarchy and the foremost power in Europe. Although his reign marks the golden age of French culture, the domestic abuses and extravagance of Louis XIV plunged France into a series of costly wars. This, along with a system of special privileges granted the nobility and other favored groups, weakened the monarchy and brought France to bankruptcy. This laid the way for the French Revolution of 1789-99 that shook Europe and affected the whole world.

The monarchy was abolished and the First Republic formed in 1793. The new government fell in 1799 to a coup led by Napoleon Bonaparte who, after declaring himself First Consul for life, in 1804 had himself proclaimed Emperor of France and King of Italy.

Napoleon's military victories made him master of much of Europe, but his disastrous Russian campaign of 1812 initiated a series of defeats that led to his abdication in 1814 and exile to the island of Elba. The monarchy was briefly restored under Louis XVIII. Napoleon returned to France in March 1815, but his efforts to uphold his power were totally crushed at the battle of Waterloo. He was exiled to the island of St. Helena where he died in 1821.

The monarchy under Louis XVIII was again restored in 1815, but the ultra reactionary regime of Charles X (1824-30) was overthrown by a liberal revolution and Louis Philippe of Orleans replaced him as monarch. The monarchy was ousted by the Revolution of 1848 and the Second Republic proclaimed. Louis Napoleon Bonaparte (nephew of Napoleon I) was elected president of the Second Republic. He was proclaimed emperor in 1852. As Napoleon III, he gave France two decades of prosperity under a stable, autocratic regime, but led it to defeat in the Franco-Prussian War of 1870, after which the Third Republic was established.

The Third Republic endured until 1940 and the capitulation of France to the swiftly maneuvering German forces. Marshal Philippe Petain formed a puppet government that sued for peace and ruled unoccupied France until 1942 from Vichy. Meanwhile, General Charles de Gaulle escaped to London where he formed a wartime government in exile and the Free French army. De Gaulle's provisional exile government was officially recognized by the Allies after the liberation of Paris in 1944, and De Gaulle, who had been serving as head of the provisional government, tacitly maintained that position. In October 1945, the people overwhelmingly rejected a return to the prewar government, thus paving the way for the formation the Fourth Republic in 1947 just after the dismissal of De Gaulle, at grips with a coalition of rival parties, the Communists especially.

In actual operation, the Fourth Republic was remarkably like the Third, with the National Assembly the focus of power causing a constant governmental instability. The later years of the Fourth Republic were marked by a burst of industrial expansion unmatched in modern French history. The growth rate, however, was marred by a two colonial wars, nagging inflationary trend that weakened the franc and undermined the betterment of the people's buying power. This and the Algerian conflict led to the recall of De Gaulle to power, the adoption of a new constitution vesting strong powers in the executive, and the establishment in 1959 of the current Fifth Republic.

RULERS
Consulate, 1799-1803, L'an 8-11
Napoleon as First Consul, 1799-1804
Napoleon I as Emperor, L'AN 12 1804-1814
(first restoration)
Louis XVIII, 1814-1815
Napoleon I, March-June 1815
(second restoration)
Louis XVIII, 1815-1824
Charles X, 1824-1830
Louis Philippe, 1830-1848
Second Republic, 1848-1852
Napoleon III, 1852-1870
Government of National Defense, 1870-1871
Third Republic, 1871-1940
Vichy State, 1940-1944
De Gaulle's Provisional Govt., 1944-1946
Fourth Republic, 1947-1958
Fifth Republic, 1959—

MINT MARKS AND PRIVY MARKS
In addition to the date and mint mark which are customary on western civilization coinage, most coins manufactured by the French Mints contain two or three small 'Marks or Differents' as the French call them. These privy marks represent the men responsible for the dies which struck the coins. One privy mark is sometimes for the Engraver General (since 1880 the title is Chief Engraver). The other privy mark is the signature of the Mint Director of each mint; another one is the different' of the local engraver. Three other marks appeared at the end of Louis XIV's reign: one for the Director General of Mints, one for the General Engineer of Mechanical edge-marking, one identifying over struck coins in 1690-1705 and in 1715-1723. Equally amazing and unique is that sometimes the local assayer's or Judge-custody's 'different' or 'secret pellet' appears.

Since 1880 this privy mark has represented the office rather than the personage of both the Administration of Coins & Medals and the Mint Director, and a standard privy mark has been used (cornucopia).

For most dates these privy marks are important though minor features for advanced collectors or local researchers. During some issue dates, however, the marks changed. To be even more accurate sometimes the marks changed when the date didn't, even though it should have. These coins can be attributed

FRANCE

to the proper mintage report only by considering the privy marks. Previous references (before G. Sobin and F. Droulers) have by and large ignored these privy marks. It is entirely possible that unattributed varieties may exist for any privy mark transition. All transition years which may have two or three varieties or combinations of privy marks have the known attribution indicated after the date (if it has been confirmed).

MONETARY SYSTEM
1726-1794
- 6 Livres = 1 Ecu
- 1 Louis d'or = 24 Livres
- 4 Ecus = 1 Louis d'or

Permanent Equivalence Table
- 1 Livre = 20 Sols
- 1 Sol = 12 Deniers
- 1 Liard = 3 Deniers

ENGRAVER GENERALS' PRIVY MARKS

Mark	Desc.	Date	Name
	Bow shooting Artemise	1795-1803	Augustus Dupre
	Cursive initial	1803-75	Pierre-Joseph Tiolier
	Horse's head	1815-16	Pierre-Joseph Tiolier
	Horse's head	1816-17	Nicolaus-Pierre Tiolier
	Cursive initial (pointed)	1818-29	Nicolaus-Pierre Tiolier
	Cursive initial (simple)	1825-30	Nicolaus-Pierre Tiolier
	Star	1830-42	Nicolaus-Pierre Tiolier
	Dog's head (d)	1843-55	Jean-Jacques Barre
	Anchor (a)	1855-79	Albert-Désiré Barre
	Anchor w/bar	1878-79	Auguste Barre
	Fasces	1880-96	
	Torch	1896-1926	Henri Patey
	Wing	1931-Oct. 1958	Lucien Bazor
	Owl	1958-74	Raymond Joly
	Dolphin	1974-94	Rousseau
	Bee	1994-	Pierre Rodier

LOCAL ENGRAVERS' PRIVY MARKS

Engraver Generals' and local engravers' privy marks may appear on coins of mints which are dated as follows:

MINT DIRECTORS' PRIVY MARKS

A – Paris, Central Mint

Some modern coins struck from dies produced at the Paris Mint have the A mint mark. In the absence of a mint mark, the cornucopia privy mark serves to attribute a coin to Paris design.

Mark	Desc.	Date	Name
	Cock	L'AN 6-1821	
	Anchor	1822-42	
	Prow of ship (p)	1843-45	
	Hand (ha)	1845-60	
	Bee (b)	1860-79	
	(Commune), Trident (tr)	1871	
	Cornucopia	1880	

B – Beaumont – Le Roger

Mark	Desc.	Date	Name
	Cornucopia	1943-58	

(b) - Brussels

B - Dieppe

B - Rouen

Mark	Desc	Date	Name
	Lamb with flag	1786-L'AN 2	Joseph Lambert
	Vase	L'AN 5-7	
	Sheep	L'AN 12 – 1844	
	Hand	1845-46	
	Pick & Shovel	1853-57	

BB - Strasbourg

Mark	Desc.	Date	Name
	Heart	1792-L'AN 2	
	Sheaf	L'AN 5 – 1825	
	Beaver (ba)	1826-34	
	Bee (be)	1834-60	
	Cross (c)	1860-70	

BD - Pau

C - Castelsarrasin

Mark	Desc.	Date	Name
C	Cornucopia	1914, 1943-46	

CH - Chalons

CL - Genoa

Mark	Desc.	Date	Name
	Prow w/banner	1813-14	Podesta
	Prow of ship	1805, 1813-14	

D - Lyon

Mark	Desc.	Date	Name
	Sheaf	L'AN 2	Jean-Francois Poret
	Dog	L'AN 4-7	
	Monogram	L'AN 8-XI	
	Bee (b)	L'AN XI – 1823	
	Ark (a)	1823-39	
	Tower (to)	1839-42	
	Lion	1848-57	

G - Geneve

Mark	Desc.	Date	Name
	Lion	L'AN 7-12	
	Fish left	L'AN 12	

H – La Rochelle

Mark	Desc.	Date	Name
	Anchor	1785-L'AN 2	Francois Seguy
	Monogram T.G.F.S.	L'AN 12-1817	Jean-Gualbert-Francois Seguy
	Lyre	1817-25	Denis Bernard
	Trident	1825-35	Eugene Morel

I - Limoges

Mark	Desc.	Date	Name
	Fasces of 3 arrows	1791-L'AN 2	Francois Allnaud
	Sunflower	L'AN 4-10	Francois Allnaud
	Horizontal clasped hands	L'AN 12 – 1822	Martial Parent
	Vertical clasped hands	1823-35	Jean Perant

K - Bordeaux

Mark	Desc.	Date	Name
	Caduceus	1788-L'AN 2	Laurent Bruno Lhoste
	Antique oil lamp	L'AN 5-12	Laurent Bruno Lhoste, (AN5-AN12; Guillaume Duthol, (AN 12 – AN13)
	Fish	L'AN 13 – 1809	Etienne Froidevaux
	Vine Leaf	1809-57	Hubert Vignes (1809-26); Alexander Vignes (1827-57)
	Pick & Hammer	1861-67	Ernest Dumas
	Slanted M in star	1870-71	Joseph Marchant Dupleny
	Trefoiled cross	1870-78	Henri Delbeque

L - Bayonne

Mark	Desc.	Date	Name
	Lion's head	L'AN 4-AN XI	Antoine Laa
	Lion's head	L'AN 6-AN XI	Antoine Laa
	Tulip	L'AN XI – 1829	Pierre-Romain d'Arripe (AN XI – 1810); Pierre-Boniface d'Arripe (1810-29)

M - Toulouse

Mark	Desc.	Date	Name
	Cow's head	1792-L'AN 2	
	Hammer	L'AN 14 – 1812	Daumy
	Cursive monogram CT	1812-36	Carayon – Talpayrac, Sr. (1812-18); Carayon – Talpayrac, Jr. (1823-26)

N - Montpellier

Mark	Desc.	Date	Name
	Rook	1791-94 L'AN 2	Paul-David Bazille, (1791-93);
	Rook	1793-AN II	Marc-David Bazille

O - Clermont

P - Semur

Q - Perpignan

Mark	Desc.	Date	Name
	Grapes	L'AN 5-1795-96, 1837	Joseph Dastros
		AN 5 – 1829	Jean-Marie de Sainte-Croix
		(1829-35)	Abel de Lorme

Crowned R – (R) Rome

Mark	Desc.	Date	Name
	She-wolf suckling rombus	1812-13	

R - London

Mark	Desc.	Date	Name
	Fleur-de-lis	1815	Wellesley

R - Orleáns

Mark	Desc.	Date	Name
	Dividers	1792-L'AN II	Charles-Pierre Delespine
	Cock	L'AN 5	Charles-Pierre Delespine

T - Nantes

Mark	Desc.	Date	Name
	Greyhound seated	1782-L'AN 2	Marie-Joseph Francois
	Anchor	L'AN 5-1818	Pierre Athenas
	Key	1818-20	Alexandre Lepot
	Olive branch	1826-35	G. Laurent Olivier d'Assenoy

U - Turin

Mark	Desc.	Date	Name
	Heart	L'AN 12 – 1813	Vittorio Modesto Paroletti

W - Lille

Mark	Desc.	Date	Name
	Level	1793-L'AN 2	Pierre-Claude Chesnel
	Caduceus	L'AN 6-1817	Louis Theophile Francois Lepage
	Caduceus	L'AN 5 – 1840 (L'AN 6 – 1817)	Louis-Theophile – Francois Lepage; Alexandre Beausier (1817-40)

FRANCE

	Retort	1840-46	Charles-Louis Dierickx
	Ancient lamp	1853-57	Charles-Frideric Kuhlmann

M (MA) Monogram - Marseille

Mark	Desc.	Date	Name
	Star	L'AN 9 – 1809	Cyprian Gaillard
	Monogram VR	1809-23	Victor Regis
	Lean palm tree	1824-30	Joseph-Augusta Ricard
	Large palm tree	1830-39	Jacques-Henri Ricard
🐚	Scallop	1853-57	Alexandre-Joseph Beaussier

Flag on mast w/banner - Utrecht

Mark	Desc.	Date	Name
	Fish	1812-13	Gideon Jan Langerak, Dumarchic Servaas

Star (s) - Madrid

Mark	Desc.	Date	Name
		1916	

Thunderbolt (tb) - Poissy

Mark	Desc.	Date	Name
	Cornucopia	1922-24	

CONSULSHIP
Napoleon as First Consul
DECIMAL COINAGE

KM# 652 40 FRANCS
12.9039 g., 0.9000 Gold .3734 oz. AGW **Obv:** Head left **Obv. Legend:** BONAPARTE PRIMIER CONSUL. **Rev:** Denomination within wreath **Rev. Legend:** REPUBLIQUE FRANCAISE.

Date	Mintage	F	VF	XF	Unc	BU
ANXIA	226,000	BV	275	325	2,250	—
AN12A	253,000	BV	275	325	1,850	—

MEDALLIC COINAGE

KM# M9b 5 FRANCS
Gold, 36.5 mm. **Subject:** Napoleon as First Consul Visit to Paris Mint

Date	Mintage	F	VF	XF	Unc	BU
1803(ANXI) Unique	—	—	—	—	—	—
1803(ANXI) Restrike	—	—	—	—	—	—

FIRST EMPIRE
Napoleon as Emperor
DECIMAL COINAGE

KM# 651 20 FRANCS
6.4516 g., 0.9000 Gold .1867 oz. AGW **Obv:** Head left **Obv. Legend:** BONAPARTE PREMIER CONSUL • **Rev:** Denomination within wreath **Rev. Legend:** REPUBLIQUE FRANCAISE

Date	Mintage	F	VF	XF	Unc	BU
ANXIA	58,000	150	225	450	1,400	—
AN12A	988,000	125	150	375	1,000	—
AN12A Proof	—	Value: 5,500				

KM# 661 20 FRANCS
6.4516 g., 0.9000 Gold .1867 oz. AGW
Obv. Legend: NAPOLEON EMPEREUR

Date	Mintage	F	VF	XF	Unc	BU
AN12A	428,000	125	150	350	1,500	—

KM# 663.1 20 FRANCS
6.4516 g., 0.9000 Gold .1867 oz. AGW **Obv:** Redesigned head **Obv. Legend:** NAPOLEON EMPEREUR **Rev:** Denomination within wreath **Rev. Legend:** REPUBLIQUE FRANCAISE

Date	Mintage	F	VF	XF	Unc	BU
AN13A	519,000	100	125	275	950	—
AN14A	148,000	125	150	350	1,000	—

KM# 663.2 20 FRANCS
6.4516 g., 0.9000 Gold .1867 oz. AGW **Obv:** Redesigned head **Rev:** Denomination within wreath

Date	Mintage	F	VF	XF	Unc	BU
AN13I	—	—	—	—	—	—
AN14I	1,646	750	1,250	2,500	4,750	—

KM# 663.3 20 FRANCS
6.4516 g., 0.9000 Gold .1867 oz. AGW **Obv:** Redesigned head **Rev:** Denomination within wreath

Date	Mintage	F	VF	XF	Unc	BU
AN13Q	522	1,000	1,500	3,000	—	—
AN14Q	2,710	375	625	1,250	2,250	—

KM# 663.4 20 FRANCS
6.4516 g., 0.9000 Gold .1867 oz. AGW **Obv:** Redesigned head **Rev:** Denomination within wreath

Date	Mintage	F	VF	XF	Unc	BU
AN13T	918	875	1,400	2,750	—	—

KM# 663.5 20 FRANCS
6.4516 g., 0.9000 Gold .1867 oz. AGW **Obv:** Redesigned head **Rev:** Denomination within wreath

Date	Mintage	F	VF	XF	Unc	BU
AN14U	1,755	500	800	1,500	—	—

KM# 663.6 20 FRANCS
6.4516 g., 0.9000 Gold .1867 oz. AGW **Obv:** Redesigned head **Rev:** Denomination within wreath

Date	Mintage	F	VF	XF	Unc	BU
AN14W	—	—	—	—	—	—

KM# 674.1 20 FRANCS
6.4516 g., 0.9000 Gold .1867 oz. AGW **Obv:** Head left **Obv. Legend:** NAPOLEON EMPEREUR **Rev:** Denomination within wreath **Rev. Legend:** REPUBLIQUE FRANCAISE

Date	Mintage	F	VF	XF	Unc	BU
1806A	964,000	100	125	225	1,000	—

KM# 674.2 20 FRANCS
6.4516 g., 0.9000 Gold .1867 oz. AGW **Obv:** Head left **Rev:** Denomination within wreath

Date	Mintage	F	VF	XF	Unc	BU
1806I	8,143	200	400	800	1,500	—

KM# 674.4 20 FRANCS
6.4516 g., 0.9000 Gold .1867 oz. AGW **Obv:** Head left **Rev:** Denomination within wreath

Date	Mintage	F	VF	XF	Unc	BU
1806Q	3,973	300	600	1,000	—	—

KM# 674.5 20 FRANCS
6.4516 g., 0.9000 Gold .1867 oz. AGW **Obv:** Head left **Rev:** Denomination within wreath

Date	Mintage	F	VF	XF	Unc	BU
1806U	17,000	150	300	600	1,250	—

KM# 674.6 20 FRANCS
6.4516 g., 0.9000 Gold .1867 oz. AGW **Obv:** Head left **Rev:** Denomination within wreath

Date	Mintage	F	VF	XF	Unc	BU
1806W	4,242	200	400	800	1,500	—

KM# A687.1 20 FRANCS
6.4516 g., 0.9000 Gold .1867 oz. AGW **Obv:** Laureate head left **Rev:** Denomination within wreath

Date	Mintage	F	VF	XF	Unc	BU
1807A	826,000	100	150	275	1,250	—

KM# A687.2 20 FRANCS
6.4516 g., 0.9000 Gold .1867 oz. AGW **Obv:** Laureate head left **Rev:** Denomination within wreath

Date	Mintage	F	VF	XF	Unc	BU
1807M	5,296	225	450	850	1,500	—

KM# A687.3 20 FRANCS
6.4516 g., 0.9000 Gold .1867 oz. AGW **Obv:** Laureate head left **Rev:** Denomination within wreath

Date	Mintage	F	VF	XF	Unc	BU
1807U	2,557	400	800	1,250	2,000	—

KM# A687.4 20 FRANCS
6.4516 g., 0.9000 Gold .1867 oz. AGW **Obv:** Laureate head left **Rev:** Denomination within wreath

Date	Mintage	F	VF	XF	Unc	BU
1807W	5,181	200	400	850	1,500	—

KM# 687.1 20 FRANCS
6.4516 g., 0.9000 Gold .1867 oz. AGW **Obv:** Laureate head left **Rev:** Denomination within wreath

Date	Mintage	F	VF	XF	Unc	BU
1807A	Inc. above	100	150	225	950	—
1808A	1,450,000	100	150	225	950	—

KM# 687.2 20 FRANCS
6.4516 g., 0.9000 Gold .1867 oz. AGW **Obv:** Laureate head left **Rev:** Denomination within wreath

Date	Mintage	F	VF	XF	Unc	BU
1808K Rare	281	—	—	—	—	—

KM# 687.3 20 FRANCS
6.4516 g., 0.9000 Gold .1867 oz. AGW **Obv:** Laureate head left **Rev:** Denomination within wreath

Date	Mintage	F	VF	XF	Unc	BU
1808M	22,000	150	250	500	1,000	—

KM# 687.4 20 FRANCS
6.4516 g., 0.9000 Gold .1867 oz. AGW **Obv:** Laureate head left **Rev:** Denomination within wreath

Date	Mintage	F	VF	XF	Unc	BU
1808Q Rare	646	—	—	—	—	—

KM# 687.5 20 FRANCS
6.4516 g., 0.9000 Gold .1867 oz. AGW **Obv:** Laureate head left **Rev:** Denomination within wreath

Date	Mintage	F	VF	XF	Unc	BU
1808U	1,505	375	625	1,250	1,750	—

KM# 687.6 20 FRANCS
6.4516 g., 0.9000 Gold .1867 oz. AGW **Obv:** Laureate head left **Rev:** Denomination within wreath

Date	Mintage	F	VF	XF	Unc	BU
1808W	8,489	200	350	750	1,250	—

KM# 695.1 20 FRANCS
6.4516 g., 0.9000 Gold .1867 oz. AGW **Obv:** Laureate head left **Obv. Legend:** NAPOLEON EMPEREUR **Rev:** Denomination within wreath **Rev. Legend:** EMPIRE FRANCAIS

Date	Mintage	F	VF	XF	Unc	BU
1809A	688,000	100	125	200	700	—
1810A	1,936,000	100	125	150	600	—
1811A	3,705,000	100	125	150	600	—
1812A	3,072,000	100	125	150	600	—
1813A	2,798,000	100	125	150	600	—
1814A	328,000	100	150	225	750	—

KM# 695.3 20 FRANCS
6.4516 g., 0.9000 Gold .1867 oz. AGW **Obv:** Laureate head left **Rev:** Denomination within wreath

Date	Mintage	F	VF	XF	Unc	BU
1809H	501	750	1,500	3,000	—	—
1810H	2,454	500	1,000	2,000	—	—
1811H	1,278	625	1,250	2,500	—	—

220 FRANCE

KM# 695.4 20 FRANCS
6.4516 g., 0.9000 Gold .1867 oz. AGW **Obv:** Laureate head left
Obv. Legend: NAPOLEON EMPEREUR **Rev:** Denomination within wreath **Rev. Legend:** EMPIRE FRANCAIS

Date	Mintage	F	VF	XF	Unc	BU
1809K	3,614	250	500	1,000	1,800	—
1810K	15,000	225	450	900	1,750	—
1811K	11,000	225	450	900	1,750	—
1812K	2,650	375	750	1,500	—	—
1813K	869	600	1,200	2,250	—	—

KM# 695.5 20 FRANCS
6.4516 g., 0.9000 Gold .1867 oz. AGW **Obv:** Laureate head left **Rev:** Denomination within wreath

Date	Mintage	F	VF	XF	Unc	BU
1809L	2,383	325	650	1,250	3,000	—
1812L	18,000	125	175	300	800	—
1813L	19,000	125	175	300	800	—

KM# 695.6 20 FRANCS
6.4516 g., 0.9000 Gold .1867 oz. AGW **Obv:** Laureate head left **Rev:** Denomination within wreath

Date	Mintage	F	VF	XF	Unc	BU
1809M	5,007	225	450	900	1,750	—
1810M	1,983	300	600	1,200	2,400	—
1811M	4,971	250	400	850	1,750	—
1812M	6,498	175	300	650	1,400	—

KM# 695.9 20 FRANCS
6.4516 g., 0.9000 Gold .1867 oz. AGW **Obv:** Laureate head left **Rev:** Denomination within wreath

Date	Mintage	F	VF	XF	Unc	BU
1809U	3,400	375	750	1,500	—	—
1810U	5,891	225	450	900	2,000	—
1811U	20,000	150	250	450	1,100	—
1812U	7,339	175	300	550	1,500	—
1813U	925	750	1,500	3,000	—	—

KM# 695.10 20 FRANCS
6.4516 g., 0.9000 Gold .1867 oz. AGW **Obv:** Laureate head left **Rev:** Denomination within wreath

Date	Mintage	F	VF	XF	Unc	BU
1809W	17,000	125	200	400	1,000	—
1810W	223,000	100	125	175	625	—
1811W	328,000	100	125	175	625	—
1812W	346,000	100	125	175	625	—
1813W	104,000	100	125	175	625	—
1814W	16,000	125	200	350	900	—

KM# 695.7 20 FRANCS
6.4516 g., 0.9000 Gold .1867 oz. AGW **Obv:** Laureate head left **Rev:** Denomination within wreath

Date	Mintage	F	VF	XF	Unc	BU
1810Q	2,343	450	875	1,750	—	—
1812Q	5,470	250	500	1,000	2,000	—
1813Q	13,000	175	350	700	1,400	—
1814Q	3,289	300	600	1,200	—	—

KM# 695.8 20 FRANCS
6.4516 g., 0.9000 Gold .1867 oz. AGW **Obv:** Laureate head left **Rev:** Denomination within wreath

Date	Mintage	F	VF	XF	Unc	BU
1812R (c)	14,000	250	500	750	2,000	—
1813R	5,532	300	600	1,000	—	—

KM# 695.11 20 FRANCS
6.4516 g., 0.9000 Gold .1867 oz. AGW **Obv:** Laureate head left **Rev:** Denomination within wreath **Note:** Mint mark: Flag.

Date	Mintage	F	VF	XF	Unc	BU
1813	90,000	150	250	350	1,100	—

KM# 695.2 20 FRANCS
6.4516 g., 0.9000 Gold .1867 oz. AGW **Obv:** Laureate head left **Rev:** Denomination within wreath

Date	Mintage	F	VF	XF	Unc	BU
1813CL	4,380	500	1,000	2,000	—	—
1814CL	887	750	1,500	3,000	—	—

KM# 664.1 40 FRANCS
12.9039 g., 0.9000 Gold .3734 oz. AGW **Obv:** Head left
Obv. Legend: NAPOLEON EMPEREUR **Rev:** Denomination within wreath **Rev. Legend:** REPUBLIQUE FRANCAISE

Date	Mintage	F	VF	XF	Unc	BU
AN13A	252,000	BV	250	400	1,750	—
AN13A Proof	—	Value: 10,000				
AN14A	121,000	BV	250	350	1,600	—

KM# 664.2 40 FRANCS
12.9039 g., 0.9000 Gold .3734 oz. AGW **Obv:** Head left **Rev:** Denomination within wreath

Date	Mintage	F	VF	XF	Unc	BU
AN14U Rare	—	—	—	—	—	—

KM# 664.3 40 FRANCS
12.9039 g., 0.9000 Gold .3734 oz. AGW **Obv:** Head left **Rev:** Denomination within wreath

Date	Mintage	F	VF	XF	Unc	BU
AN14W Rare	—	—	—	—	—	—

KM# 675.1 40 FRANCS
12.9039 g., 0.9000 Gold .3734 oz. AGW **Obv:** Head left
Obv. Legend: NAPOLEOON EMPEREUR **Rev:** Denomination within wreath **Rev. Legend:** REPUBLIQUE FRANCAISE

Date	Mintage	F	VF	XF	Unc	BU
1806A	196,000	BV	250	400	1,500	—

KM# 675.2 40 FRANCS
12.9039 g., 0.9000 Gold .3734 oz. AGW **Obv:** Head left **Rev:** Denomination within wreath

Date	Mintage	F	VF	XF	Unc	BU
1806CL Rare	—	—	—	—	—	—

KM# 675.3 40 FRANCS
12.9039 g., 0.9000 Gold .3734 oz. AGW **Obv:** Head left **Rev:** Denomination within wreath

Date	Mintage	F	VF	XF	Unc	BU
1806I	7,103	250	500	1,250	2,500	—

KM# 675.4 40 FRANCS
12.9039 g., 0.9000 Gold .3734 oz. AGW **Obv:** Head left **Rev:** Denomination within wreath

Date	Mintage	F	VF	XF	Unc	BU
1806M	—	—	—	—	—	—

KM# 675.5 40 FRANCS
12.9039 g., 0.9000 Gold .3734 oz. AGW **Obv:** Head left **Rev:** Denomination within wreath

Date	Mintage	F	VF	XF	Unc	BU
1806U	59,000	BV	275	500	2,000	—

KM# 675.6 40 FRANCS
12.9039 g., 0.9000 Gold .3734 oz. AGW **Obv:** Head left **Rev:** Denomination within wreath

Date	Mintage	F	VF	XF	Unc	BU
1806W	4,336	300	650	1,450	—	—

KM# A688.1 40 FRANCS
12.9039 g., 0.9000 Gold .3734 oz. AGW **Obv:** Large plain bust **Rev:** Denomination within wreath

Date	Mintage	F	VF	XF	Unc	BU
1807A	12,000	BV	450	900	2,000	—

KM# A688.2 40 FRANCS
12.9039 g., 0.9000 Gold .3734 oz. AGW **Obv:** Large plain bust **Rev:** Denomination within wreath

Date	Mintage	F	VF	XF	Unc	BU
1807I	1,859	350	750	2,000	—	—

KM# A688.3 40 FRANCS
12.9039 g., 0.9000 Gold .3734 oz. AGW **Obv:** Large plain bust **Rev:** Denomination within wreath

Date	Mintage	F	VF	XF	Unc	BU
1807M	4,994	300	650	1,450	2,600	—

KM# A688.4 40 FRANCS
12.9039 g., 0.9000 Gold .3734 oz. AGW **Obv:** Large plain bust **Rev:** Denomination within wreath

Date	Mintage	F	VF	XF	Unc	BU
1807U	619	1,000	2,000	3,750	—	—

KM# A688.5 40 FRANCS
12.9039 g., 0.9000 Gold .3734 oz. AGW **Obv:** Large plain bust **Rev:** Denomination within wreath

Date	Mintage	F	VF	XF	Unc	BU
1807W	6,043	300	650	1,450	—	—

KM# 688.1 40 FRANCS
12.9039 g., 0.9000 Gold .3734 oz. AGW **Obv:** Large laureate head left **Obv. Legend:** NAPOLEON EMPEREUR **Rev:** Denomination within wreath **Rev. Legend:** REPUBLIQUE FRANCAISE

Date	Mintage	F	VF	XF	Unc	BU
1807A	Est. 253,000	BV	450	750	2,000	—
1808A	44,000	BV	245	350	1,350	—

KM# 688.2 40 FRANCS
12.9039 g., 0.9000 Gold .3734 oz. AGW **Obv:** Large laureate head left **Rev:** Denomination within wreath

Date	Mintage	F	VF	XF	Unc	BU
1808H	12,000	225	450	900	2,250	—

KM# 688.3 40 FRANCS
12.9039 g., 0.9000 Gold .3734 oz. AGW **Obv:** Large laureate head left **Rev:** Denomination within wreath

Date	Mintage	F	VF	XF	Unc	BU
1808M	4,226	300	500	1,000	—	—

KM# 688.4 40 FRANCS
12.9039 g., 0.9000 Gold .3734 oz. AGW **Obv:** Large laureate head left **Rev:** Denomination within wreath

Date	Mintage	F	VF	XF	Unc	BU
1808U Rare	346	—	—	—	—	—

KM# 688.5 40 FRANCS
12.9039 g., 0.9000 Gold .3734 oz. AGW **Obv:** Large laureate head left **Rev:** Denomination within wreath

Date	Mintage	F	VF	XF	Unc	BU
1808W	6,356	225	450	950	2,400	—

KM# 696.1 40 FRANCS
12.9039 g., 0.9000 Gold .3734 oz. AGW **Obv:** Laureate head right **Obv. Legend:** NAPOLEON EMPEREUR **Rev:** Denomination within wreath **Rev. Legend:** EMPIRE FRANCAIS

Date	Mintage	F	VF	XF	Unc	BU
1809A	13,000	245	375	700	1,800	—
1809A Proof	—	Value: 10,000				
1811A	1,262,000	BV	245	250	850	—
1812A	693,000	BV	245	325	1,100	—
1813A	45,000	BV	245	600	1,500	—

KM# 696.4 40 FRANCS
12.9039 g., 0.9000 Gold .3734 oz. AGW **Obv:** Laureate head left **Rev:** Denomination within wreath

Date	Mintage	F	VF	XF	Unc	BU
1809M	1,402	500	1,000	1,750	—	—

KM# 696.5 40 FRANCS
12.9039 g., 0.9000 Gold .3734 oz. AGW **Obv:** Laureate head left **Rev:** Denomination within wreath

Date	Mintage	F	VF	XF	Unc	BU
1809U Rare	—	—	—	—	—	—

KM# 696.6 40 FRANCS
12.9039 g., 0.9000 Gold .3734 oz. AGW **Obv:** Laureate head left **Rev:** Denomination within wreath

Date	Mintage	F	VF	XF	Unc	BU
1809W	5,925	300	600	1,200	—	—
1810W	57,000	BV	250	450	1,500	—
1812W	14,000	BV	275	550	1,700	—

KM# 696.3 40 FRANCS
12.9039 g., 0.9000 Gold .3734 oz. AGW **Obv:** Laureate head left **Rev:** Denomination within wreath

Date	Mintage	F	VF	XF	Unc	BU
1810K	886	650	1,250	2,500	—	—
1811K	6,333	300	625	1,250	2,500	—

KM# 696.2 40 FRANCS
12.9039 g., 0.9000 Gold .3734 oz. AGW **Obv:** Laureate head left **Rev:** Denomination within wreath

Date	Mintage	F	VF	XF	Unc	BU
1813CL	3,070	500	1,000	2,000	—	—

MEDALLIC COINAGE

KM# M3b 2 FRANCS
Gold **Subject:** King of Saxony Visit to Paris Mint

Date	Mintage	F	VF	XF	Unc	BU
1809	—	—	750	1,500	2,400	—

FRANCE

KM# M4b 2 FRANCS
Gold **Subject:** King of Württemberg Visit to Paris Mint

Date	Mintage	F	VF	XF	Unc	BU
1809	—	—	750	1,600	2,800	—

KM# M6b 2 FRANCS
Gold **Subject:** King and Queen of Bavaria Visit to Paris Mint

Date	Mintage	F	VF	XF	Unc	BU
1810	—	—	1,000	1,750	3,500	—

SECOND KINGDOM

DECIMAL COINAGE

KM# 712.1 20 FRANCS
6.4516 g., 0.9000 Gold .1867 oz. AGW **Ruler:** Louis XVIII
Obv: Head right **Obv. Legend:** LOUIS XVIII ROI DE FRANCE
Rev: Crowned arms divide denomination within wreath

Date	Mintage	F	VF	XF	Unc	BU
1816A	522,000	BV	125	150	375	—
1817A	2,135,000	BV	125	150	375	—
1818A	2,681,000	BV	125	150	375	—
1819A	2,350,000	BV	125	150	375	—
1820A	1,317,000	BV	125	150	375	—
1821A	12,000	140	200	300	650	—
1822A	213,000	BV	125	150	375	—
1823A	12,000	125	200	300	600	—
1824A	1,510,000	BV	125	150	375	—

KM# 712.2 20 FRANCS
6.4516 g., 0.9000 Gold .1867 oz. AGW **Ruler:** Louis XVIII
Obv: Head right **Rev:** Denomination within wreath

Date	Mintage	F	VF	XF	Unc	BU
1816B	22,000	—	—	—	—	—

KM# 712.4 20 FRANCS
6.4516 g., 0.9000 Gold .1867 oz. AGW **Ruler:** Louis XVIII
Obv: Head right **Rev:** Denomination within wreath

Date	Mintage	F	VF	XF	Unc	BU
1816K	4,947	—	—	—	—	—
1817K	4,803	175	275	475	900	—

KM# 712.5 20 FRANCS
6.4516 g., 0.9000 Gold .1867 oz. AGW **Ruler:** Louis XVIII
Obv: Head right **Rev:** Denomination within wreath

Date	Mintage	F	VF	XF	Unc	BU
1816L	22,000	—	—	—	—	—
1817L	36,000	125	200	300	650	—
1818L	5,394	150	225	350	850	—

KM# 712.9 20 FRANCS
6.4516 g., 0.9000 Gold .1867 oz. AGW **Ruler:** Louis XVIII
Obv: Head right **Rev:** Denomination within wreath

Date	Mintage	F	VF	XF	Unc	BU
1816W	54,000	BV	130	200	600	—
1817W	156,000	BV	130	150	500	—
1818W	1,315,000	BV	130	150	450	—
1819W	219,000	BV	130	150	450	—
1820W	44,000	BV	130	200	600	—
1821W	8,446	BV	150	250	650	—
1822W	20,000	BV	130	200	600	—
1823W	7,655	BV	150	250	650	—
1824W	253,000	BV	130	150	425	—

KM# 712.7 20 FRANCS
6.4516 g., 0.9000 Gold .1867 oz. AGW **Ruler:** Louis XVIII
Obv: Head right **Rev:** Denomination within wreath

Date	Mintage	F	VF	XF	Unc	BU
1816Q	16,000	BV	150	225	550	—
1817Q	97,000	BV	130	200	500	—
1818Q	25,000	BV	150	200	500	—
1819Q	34,000	BV	130	225	550	—
1820Q	60,000	BV	130	225	550	—
1824Q	12,000	BV	150	275	650	—

KM# 712.8 20 FRANCS
6.4516 g., 0.9000 Gold .1867 oz. AGW **Ruler:** Louis XVIII
Obv: Head right **Rev:** Denomination within wreath

Date	Mintage	F	VF	XF	Unc	BU
1818T	16,000	BV	130	200	550	—
1819T	8,734	BV	150	250	600	—
1820T	5,749	BV	150	250	600	—

KM# 712.3 20 FRANCS
6.4516 g., 0.9000 Gold .1867 oz. AGW **Ruler:** Louis XVIII
Obv: Head right **Rev:** Denomination within wreath

Date	Mintage	F	VF	XF	Unc	BU
1822H	1,253	500	850	1,100	2,400	—

KM# 712.6 20 FRANCS
6.4516 g., 0.9000 Gold .1867 oz. AGW **Ruler:** Louis XVIII
Obv: Head right **Rev:** Denomination within wreath

Date	Mintage	F	VF	XF	Unc	BU
1824MA	2,001	625	1,250	1,500	3,000	—

KM# 726.1 20 FRANCS
6.4516 g., 0.9000 Gold .1867 oz. AGW **Obv:** Head right
Obv. Legend: CHARLES X ROI DE FRANCE **Rev:** Crowned arms divide denomination within wreath

Date	Mintage	F	VF	XF	Unc	BU
1825A	664,000	125	140	200	900	—
1826A	35,000	150	225	375	1,100	—
1827A	154,000	130	150	250	950	—
1828A	279,000	130	150	250	900	—
1829A	7,783	150	250	425	1,500	—
1830A	431,000	130	150	250	950	—

KM# 726.4 20 FRANCS
6.4516 g., 0.9000 Gold .1867 oz. AGW **Obv:** Head right
Rev: Crowned arms divide denomination within wreath

Date	Mintage	F	VF	XF	Unc	BU
1825W	62,000	130	200	300	950	—
1826W	6,436	200	275	450	1,400	—
1827W	3,431	225	350	550	1,600	—
1828W	15,000	150	250	350	1,200	—
1829W	5,946	200	275	450	1,400	—
1830W	15,000	150	250	350	1,200	—

KM# 726.2 20 FRANCS
6.4516 g., 0.9000 Gold .1867 oz. AGW **Obv:** Head right
Rev: Crowned arms divide denomination within wreath

Date	Mintage	F	VF	XF	Unc	BU
1826Q	4,574	500	1,000	1,250	2,400	—

KM# 726.3 20 FRANCS
6.4516 g., 0.9000 Gold .1867 oz. AGW **Obv:** Head right
Rev: Crowned arms divide denomination within wreath

Date	Mintage	F	VF	XF	Unc	BU
1828T	3,175	500	1,000	1,250	2,400	—

KM# A726 20 FRANCS
6.4516 g., 0.9000 Gold .1867 oz. AGW **Obv:** Head right **Rev:** Crowned arms divide denomination within wreath **Edge:** Reeded

Date	Mintage	F	VF	XF	Unc	BU
1830A	1,797	500	1,000	1,500	2,500	—

KM# 739.1 20 FRANCS
6.4516 g., 0.9000 Gold .1867 oz. AGW **Obv:** Head left
Obv. Legend: LOUIS PHILIPPE I ROI DES FRANCAIS
Rev: Denomination within wreath **Edge:** Incuse lettering

Date	Mintage	F	VF	XF	Unc	BU
1830A	18,000	130	200	300	1,000	—
1831A	2,162,000	BV	130	150	900	—

KM# 746.1 20 FRANCS
6.4516 g., 0.9000 Gold .1867 oz. AGW **Obv:** Head left
Obv. Legend: LOUIS PHILIPPE I ROI DES FRANCAIS
Rev: Denomination within wreath **Edge:** Raised lettering

Date	Mintage	F	VF	XF	Unc	BU
1830A	Inc. above	175	240	450	800	—
1831A	Inc. above	BV	150	200	800	—

KM# 746.2 20 FRANCS
6.4516 g., 0.9000 Gold .1867 oz. AGW **Obv:** Head left
Rev: Denomination within wreath

Date	Mintage	F	VF	XF	Unc	BU
1831B	—	135	175	250	950	—

KM# 746.3 20 FRANCS
6.4516 g., 0.9000 Gold .1867 oz. AGW **Obv:** Head left
Rev: Denomination within wreath

Date	Mintage	F	VF	XF	Unc	BU
1831T	—	500	800	1,250	—	—

KM# 746.4 20 FRANCS
6.4516 g., 0.9000 Gold .1867 oz. AGW **Obv:** Head left
Rev: Denomination within wreath

Date	Mintage	F	VF	XF	Unc	BU
1831W	Inc. above	BV	150	250	1,000	—

KM# 739.3 20 FRANCS
6.4516 g., 0.9000 Gold .1867 oz. AGW

Date	Mintage	F	VF	XF	Unc	BU
1831W	107,000	110	BV	200	1,200	—

KM# 739.2 20 FRANCS
6.4516 g., 0.9000 Gold .1867 oz. AGW

Date	Mintage	F	VF	XF	Unc	BU
1831B	88,000	150	300	550	1,500	—

KM# 750.1 20 FRANCS
6.4516 g., 0.9000 Gold .1867 oz. AGW **Obv:** Laureate head left
Obv. Legend: LOUIS PHILIPPE I ROI DES FRANCAIS
Rev: Denomination within wreath

Date	Mintage	F	VF	XF	Unc	BU
1832A	6,360	175	325	550	1,275	—
1832A Proof	—	Value: 4,500				
1833A	207,000	BV	125	150	775	—
1834A	744,000	BV	125	150	500	—
1835A	97,000	BV	125	150	725	—
1836A	139,000	BV	125	150	725	—
1837A	34,000	BV	130	175	775	—
1838A	173,000	BV	130	150	725	—
1839A	1,012,000	BV	125	140	500	—
1840A	2,045,000	BV	125	140	500	—
1841A	610,000	BV	130	150	500	—
1842A	71,000	BV	130	175	775	—
1843A	106,000	BV	125	150	775	—
1844A	103,000	BV	125	150	775	—
1845A	939	625	1,250	1,800	2,200	—
1846A	103,000	BV	125	150	775	—
1847A	385,000	BV	125	150	500	—
1848A	442,000	BV	125	140	500	—

KM# 750.2 20 FRANCS
6.4516 g., 0.9000 Gold .1867 oz. AGW **Obv:** Laureate head left
Rev: Denomination within wreath

Date	Mintage	F	VF	XF	Unc	BU
1832B	15,000	BV	125	175	775	—
1833B	155,000	BV	125	150	775	—
1834B	77,000	BV	125	150	775	—
1835B	26,000	BV	125	185	775	—

KM# 750.4 20 FRANCS
6.4516 g., 0.9000 Gold .1867 oz. AGW **Obv:** Laureate head left
Rev: Denomination within wreath

Date	Mintage	F	VF	XF	Unc	BU
1832T	868	750	1,500	2,250	—	—

KM# 750.5 20 FRANCS
6.4516 g., 0.9000 Gold .1867 oz. AGW

Date	Mintage	F	VF	XF	Unc	BU
1832W	27,000	BV	125	175	725	—
1833W	32,000	BV	125	175	725	—
1834W	41,000	BV	125	175	725	—
1835W	30,000	BV	125	175	725	—
1836W	10,000	BV	125	185	725	—
1837W	11,000	BV	125	185	725	—
1838W	12,000	BV	125	185	725	—
1839W	22,000	BV	125	175	850	—
1840W	4,550	150	250	350	1,150	—
1841W	8,524	125	225	325	1,000	—
1842W	22,000	BV	125	175	725	—
1843W	35,000	BV	125	175	725	—
1844W	34,000	BV	125	175	725	—
1845W	5,018	125	225	325	1,000	—
1846W	1,408	375	750	1,250	—	—

KM# 750.3 20 FRANCS
6.4516 g., 0.9000 Gold .1867 oz. AGW **Obv:** Laureate head left

Date	Mintage	F	VF	XF	Unc	BU
1834L	21,000	BV	130	175	775	—
1835L	856	625	1,250	2,000	—	—

KM# 713.4 40 FRANCS
12.9039 g., 0.9000 Gold .3734 oz. AGW **Ruler:** Louis XVIII **Obv:** Head right **Rev:** Crowned arms divide denomination within wreath

222 FRANCE

Date	Mintage	F	VF	XF	Unc	BU
1816L	2,923	375	675	1,200	3,000	—
1817L Rare	377	—	—	—	—	—

KM# 713.5 40 FRANCS
12.9039 g., 0.9000 Gold .3734 oz. AGW **Ruler:** Louis XVIII **Obv:** Head right **Rev:** Crowned arms divide denomination within wreath

Date	Mintage	F	VF	XF	Unc	BU
1816Q	11,000	BV	300	500	1,400	—

KM# 713.6 40 FRANCS
12.9039 g., 0.9000 Gold .3734 oz. AGW **Ruler:** Louis XVIII **Obv:** Head right **Rev:** Crowned arms divide denomination within wreath

Date	Mintage	F	VF	XF	Unc	BU
1816W	3,210	BV	300	600	1,500	—
1818W	353,000	BV	245	300	900	—
1819W	4,610	BV	300	600	1,500	—

KM# 713.1 40 FRANCS
12.9039 g., 0.9000 Gold .3734 oz. AGW **Ruler:** Louis XVIII **Obv:** Head right **Obv. Legend:** LOUIS XVIII ROI DE FRANCE **Rev:** Crowned arms divide denomination within wreath

Date	Mintage	F	VF	XF	Unc	BU
1816A	41,000	BV	300	600	1,000	—
1817A	90,000	BV	300	500	950	—
1818A	11,000	BV	350	750	1,250	—
1820A	5,480	250	500	1,000	2,250	—
1822A Rare	373	—	—	—	—	—
1823A Rare	161	—	—	—	—	—
1824A	15,000	BV	275	450	1,000	—

KM# 713.2 40 FRANCS
12.9039 g., 0.9000 Gold .3734 oz. AGW **Ruler:** Louis XVIII **Obv:** Head right **Rev:** Crowned arms divide denomination within wreath

Date	Mintage	F	VF	XF	Unc	BU
1816B	767	1,000	2,000	3,500	—	—

KM# 713.3 40 FRANCS
12.9039 g., 0.9000 Gold .3734 oz. AGW **Ruler:** Louis XVIII **Obv:** Head right **Rev:** Crowned arms divide denomination within wreath

Date	Mintage	F	VF	XF	Unc	BU
1822H	611	1,000	2,000	3,500	—	—

KM# 721.1 40 FRANCS
12.9039 g., 0.9000 Gold .3734 oz. AGW **Obv:** Head right **Rev:** Crowned arms divide denomination within wreath

Date	Mintage	F	VF	XF	Unc	BU
1824A	50,000	BV	275	450	1,400	—
1826A Rare	62	—	—	—	—	—
1827A Rare	106	—	—	—	—	—
1828A	52,000	BV	275	450	1,350	—
1829A	21,000	BV	300	500	1,500	—
1830A	354,000	BV	250	300	1,250	—
1830A	1,324	750	1,250	2,000	3,500	—

Note: Raised edge letters

KM# 721.2 40 FRANCS
12.9039 g., 0.9000 Gold .3734 oz. AGW **Obv:** Head right **Rev:** Crowned arms divide denomination within wreath

Date	Mintage	F	VF	XF	Unc	BU
1830MA	1,026	750	1,500	2,500	—	—

KM# 747.1 40 FRANCS
12.9039 g., 0.9000 Gold .3734 oz. AGW **Obv:** Laureate head left **Obv. Legend:** LOUIS PHILIPPE I ROI DES FRANCAIS **Rev:** Denomination within wreath

Date	Mintage	F	VF	XF	Unc	BU
1831A	63,000	BV	250	500	1,200	—
1832A	22,000	BV	275	500	1,200	—
1832A Proof	—	Value: 9,000				
1833A	221,000	BV	250	400	1,200	—
1834A	303,000	BV	225	400	1,200	—
1835A	36,000	BV	275	500	1,200	—
1836A	53,000	BV	275	500	1,200	—
1837A	28,000	BV	275	500	1,200	—
1838A	31,000	BV	275	500	1,250	—
1839A Rare	23	—	—	—	—	—

KM# 747.2 40 FRANCS
12.9039 g., 0.9000 Gold .3734 oz. AGW **Obv:** Laureate head left **Obv. Legend:** LOUIS PHILIPPE I ROI DES FRANCAIS **Rev:** Denomination within wreath

Date	Mintage	F	VF	XF	Unc	BU
1832B	3,947	300	450	900	2,200	—
1833B	1,392	450	900	1,750	—	—

KM# 747.3 40 FRANCS
12.9039 g., 0.9000 Gold .3734 oz. AGW **Obv:** Laureate head left **Rev:** Denomination within wreath

Date	Mintage	F	VF	XF	Unc	BU
1834L	12,000	250	325	600	1,800	—
1835L	856	600	1,200	2,000	—	—

MEDALLIC COINAGE

KM# M11b 5 FRANCS
Gold **Subject:** Comte D'Artois Visit to Marseille Mint **Obv:** Uniformed bust of Louis XVIII **Rev:** Six-line inscription

Date	Mintage	F	VF	XF	Unc	BU
1814 Unique	1	—	—	—	—	—

KM# M12d 5 FRANCS
Gold **Subject:** Duchess D'Angouleme Visit to Paris Mint

Date	Mintage	F	VF	XF	Unc	BU
1817	—	—	—	—	12,500	—

Note: Three known

KM# M15c 5 FRANCS
Gold **Subject:** Charles Philippe (later Charles X) Visit to Paris Mint

Date	Mintage	F	VF	XF	Unc	BU
1818	—	—	—	—	10,000	—

KM# M17b 5 FRANCS
Gold **Subject:** Visit of the King to Lille Mint **Obv:** Head of Charles X left **Rev:** Seven-line inscription

Date	Mintage	F	VF	XF	Unc	BU
1827 Unique	—	—	—	—	—	—

KM# M19c 5 FRANCS
Gold **Subject:** King and Queen of the Two Sicilies to Paris Mint **Obv:** Crowned shields of arms in branches **Rev:** 7-line inscription

Date	Mintage	F	VF	XF	Unc	BU
1830	13	—	—	—	7,500	—

KM# M20c 5 FRANCS
Gold **Subject:** Visit of King Louis Philippe I to Rouen mint

Date	Mintage	F	VF	XF	Unc	BU
1831	—	—	—	—	—	—

KM# M21 5 FRANCS
Gold **Subject:** Prince of Salerno Visit to Paris Mint **Obv:** Laureate head of Louis Philippe I right **Rev:** Seven-line inscription

Date	Mintage	F	VF	XF	Unc	BU
1846	50	—	—	650	950	—

PRETENDER COINAGE

X# 28.1a FRANC
Gold **Ruler:** Henry V **Note:** Prev. KM#PTP28.1a. Piefort.

Date	Mintage	F	VF	XF	Unc	BU
1832	—	—	750	1,250	2,000	—

X# 31.3a 2 FRANCS
19.1200 g., Gold **Ruler:** Henry V **Edge:** Lettered **Note:** Prev. KM#PTP31.3a.

Date	Mintage	F	VF	XF	Unc	BU
1832	—	—	—	2,000	4,250	—

X# 35g 5 FRANCS
71.9900 g., Gold Piefort **Ruler:** Henry V **Obv:** Bust left **Rev:** Denomination flanks arms, date below **Edge:** Plain **Note:** Only a few specimens known

Date	Mintage	F	VF	XF	Unc	BU
1832	—	—	—	—	16,000	—

X# 35a 5 FRANCS
27.4000 g., Gold **Ruler:** Henry V **Edge:** Plain **Note:** Prev. KM#PT35a.

Date	Mintage	F	VF	XF	Unc	BU
1832	—	—	—	—	12,000	—

X# 36b 5 FRANCS
Gold **Ruler:** Henry V **Note:** Prev. KM#PT36b.

Date	Mintage	F	VF	XF	Unc	BU
1843	—	—	—	4,250	6,500	—

PRETENDER COINAGE WITH ESSAI

X# E14b 5 FRANCS
Gold **Ruler:** Napoleon II **Note:** Prev. KM#PTE14b. Unofficial pieces (patterns?) struck during the reign of Napoleon III, possibly to give continuity to the dynasty.

Date	Mintage	F	VF	XF	Unc	BU
1816 Rare	—	—	—	—	—	—

FIRST RESTORATION
1814-1815

DECIMAL COINAGE

KM# 706.3 20 FRANCS
6.4516 g., 0.9000 Gold .1867 oz. AGW **Ruler:** Louis XVIII **Obv:** Uniformed bust right **Rev:** Crowned arms within wreath

Date	Mintage	F	VF	XF	Unc	BU
1814K	63,000	BV	150	200	600	—
1815K	30,000	BV	150	200	600	—

KM# 706.4 20 FRANCS
6.4516 g., 0.9000 Gold .1867 oz. AGW **Ruler:** Louis XVIII **Obv:** Uniformed bust right **Rev:** Crowned arms within wreath

Date	Mintage	F	VF	XF	Unc	BU
1814L	45,000	BV	150	200	600	—
1815L	34,000	BV	150	200	600	—

KM# 706.5 20 FRANCS
6.4516 g., 0.9000 Gold .1867 oz. AGW **Ruler:** Louis XVIII **Obv:** Uniformed bust right **Rev:** Crowned arms within wreath

Date	Mintage	F	VF	XF	Unc	BU
1814Q	29,000	130	175	250	650	—
1815Q	39,000	BV	150	200	600	—

KM# 706.6 20 FRANCS
6.4516 g., 0.9000 Gold .1867 oz. AGW **Ruler:** Louis XVIII **Obv:** Uniformed bust right **Rev:** Crowned arms within wreath

Date	Mintage	F	VF	XF	Unc	BU
1814W	60,000	BV	150	200	600	—
1815W	88,000	BV	150	200	600	—

FRANCE 223

KM# 706.1 20 FRANCS
6.4516 g., 0.9000 Gold .1867 oz. AGW **Ruler:** Louis XVIII
Obv: Uniformed bust right **Obv. Legend:** LOUIS XVIII ROI DE FRANCE **Rev:** Crowned arms within wreath **Note:** Engraver: Tiolier.

Date	Mintage	F	VF	XF	Unc	BU
1814A	2,684,000	BV	130	150	425	—
1815A	2,113,000	BV	130	150	425	—

KM# 706.2 20 FRANCS
6.4516 g., 0.9000 Gold .1867 oz. AGW **Ruler:** Louis XVIII
Obv: Uniformed bust right **Rev:** Crowned arms within wreath

Date	Mintage	F	VF	XF	Unc	BU
1815B	1,539	300	600	1,200	1,500	—

THE HUNDRED DAYS
Napoleon, 1815
DECIMAL COINAGE

KM# 705.2 20 FRANCS
6.4516 g., 0.9000 Gold .1867 oz. AGW

Date	Mintage	F	VF	XF	Unc	BU
1815L	18,000	165	200	400	1,100	—

KM# 705.3 20 FRANCS
6.4516 g., 0.9000 Gold .1867 oz. AGW

Date	Mintage	F	VF	XF	Unc	BU
1815W	9,369	200	350	700	1,500	—

KM# 705.1 20 FRANCS
6.4516 g., 0.9000 Gold .1867 oz. AGW **Note:** The Hundred Days.

Date	Mintage	F	VF	XF	Unc	BU
1815A	436,000	135	200	300	900	—

SECOND REPUBLIC
DECIMAL COINAGE

KM# 770 10 FRANCS
3.2258 g., 0.9000 Gold .0933 oz. AGW **Obv:** Liberty head with grain wreath right **Rev:** Denomination within wreath

Date	Mintage	F	VF	XF	Unc	BU
1850A	592,000	70.00	100	200	675	—
1850A Proof	—	Value: 4,000				
1851A	3,115,000	BV	75.00	150	575	—
1851A Proof	—	Value: 4,000				

KM# 757 20 FRANCS
6.4516 g., 0.9000 Gold .1867 oz. AGW **Obv:** Standing Genius writing the Constitution **Rev:** Denomination within oak leaf wreath

Date	Mintage	F	VF	XF	Unc	BU
1848A	1,543,000	125	150	175	500	—
1848A Proof	—	Value: 4,000				
1849A	1,303,000	125	150	175	500	—

KM# 762 20 FRANCS
6.4516 g., 0.9000 Gold .1867 oz. AGW **Obv:** Liberty head with oak leaf wreath right **Rev:** Denomination within wreath

Date	Mintage	F	VF	XF	Unc	BU
1849A	53,000	125	150	200	750	—
1850A	3,964,000	BV	150	175	400	—

Date	Mintage	F	VF	XF	Unc	BU
1850A Proof	—	Value: 3,750				
1851A	12,704,000	BV	125	150	350	—

SECOND EMPIRE
Napoleon III as Emperor
DECIMAL COINAGE

KM# 783 5 FRANCS
1.6290 g., 0.9000 Gold .0467 oz. AGW, 14.4 mm.
Ruler: Napoleon III **Obv:** Head right **Obv. Legend:** NAPOLEOON III EMPEROR **Rev:** Denomination within wreath **Rev. Legend:** EMPIRE FRANCAIS

Date	Mintage	F	VF	XF	Unc	BU
1854A	691,000	50.00	100	150	300	—
Note: Plain edge						
1854A Proof	—	Value: 1,250				
Note: Plain edge						
1854A	2,870,000	35.00	65.00	100	275	—
1855A	938,000	65.00	110	200	400	—

KM# 787.1 5 FRANCS
1.6290 g., 0.9000 Gold .0467 oz. AGW, 16.7 mm. **Ruler:** Napoleon III **Obv:** Head right **Rev:** Denomination within wreath

Date	Mintage	F	VF	XF	Unc	BU
1856	2,960,000	BV	40.00	65.00	225	—
1857	3,479,000	BV	40.00	65.00	225	—
1858	2,983,000	BV	40.00	65.00	225	—
1859	5,660,000	BV	40.00	65.00	225	—
1860	4,798,000	BV	40.00	65.00	225	—

KM# 787.2 5 FRANCS
1.6290 g., 0.9000 Gold .0467 oz. AGW **Ruler:** Napoleon III **Obv:** Head right **Obv. Legend:** NAPOLEON III EMPEREUR **Rev. Legend:** EMPIRE FRANCAIS

Date	Mintage	F	VF	XF	Unc	BU
1858BB	—	65.00	125	200	450	—
1859BB	2,279,000	30.00	40.00	65.00	225	—
1860BB	2,022,000	30.00	40.00	65.00	225	—

KM# 803.1 5 FRANCS
1.6129 g., 0.9000 Gold .0467 oz. AGW **Ruler:** Napoleon III **Obv:** Laureate head right **Obv. Legend:** NAPOLEON III EMPEREUR **Rev:** Denomination within wreath **Rev. Legend:** EMPIRE FRANCAIS

Date	Mintage	F	VF	XF	Unc	BU
1862A	1,101,000	35.00	45.00	65.00	200	—
1863A	1,591,000	35.00	45.00	65.00	200	—
1864A	2,240,000	35.00	45.00	65.00	200	—
1865A	824,000	35.00	45.00	65.00	200	—
1866A	1,949,000	35.00	45.00	65.00	200	—
1867A	1,006,000	BV	40.00	65.00	200	—
1868A	1,864,000	BV	40.00	65.00	200	—

KM# 803.2 5 FRANCS
1.6129 g., 0.9000 Gold .0467 oz. AGW **Ruler:** Napoleon III **Obv:** Laureate head right **Obv. Legend:** NAPOLEON III EMPEREUR **Rev:** Denomination within wreath **Rev. Legend:** EMPIRE FRANCAIS

Date	Mintage	F	VF	XF	Unc	BU
1862BB	882,000	BV	40.00	65.00	200	—
1863BB	1,104,000	BV	40.00	65.00	200	—
1864BB	1,000,000	BV	40.00	65.00	200	—
1865BB	828,000	BV	40.00	65.00	200	—
1866BB	1,388,000	BV	40.00	65.00	200	—
1867BB	1,504,000	BV	40.00	65.00	200	—
1868BB	439,000	BV	40.00	70.00	225	—
1869BB	288,000	BV	40.00	75.00	250	—

KM# 784.1 10 FRANCS
3.2258 g., 0.9000 Gold .0933 oz. AGW, 17.2 mm.
Ruler: Napoleon III **Obv:** Head right **Obv. Legend:** NAPOLEON III EMPEREUR **Rev:** Denomination within wreath **Rev. Legend:** EMPIRE FRANCAIS

Date	Mintage	F	VF	XF	Unc	BU
1854A	3,900,000	BV	75.00	200	800	—
1855A	6,117,000	BV	70.00	150	750	—

KM# 784.2 10 FRANCS
3.2258 g., 0.9000 Gold .0933 oz. AGW **Ruler:** Napoleon III **Obv:** Head right **Rev:** Denomination within wreath **Edge:** Plain

Date	Mintage	F	VF	XF	Unc	BU
1854A	Inc. above	75.00	125	300	900	—
1854A Proof	—	Value: 1,750				

KM# 784.3 10 FRANCS
3.2258 g., 0.9000 Gold .0933 oz. AGW **Ruler:** Napoleon III **Obv:** Head right **Rev:** Denomination within wreath

Date	Mintage	F	VF	XF	Unc	BU
1855A	6,117,000	—	BV	75.00	275	—
1856A	10,778,000	—	BV	75.00	275	—
1857A	14,498,000	—	BV	75.00	275	—
1858A	7,534,000	—	BV	75.00	275	—
1859A	10,111,000	—	BV	75.00	275	—
1860A	6,000,000	—	BV	75.00	275	—

KM# 784.4 10 FRANCS
3.2258 g., 0.9000 Gold .0933 oz. AGW **Ruler:** Napoleon III **Obv:** Head right **Rev:** Denomination within wreath

Date	Mintage	F	VF	XF	Unc	BU
1855BB	32,188	BV	100	150	500	—
1858BB	677,000	—	BV	85.00	275	—
1859BB	2,279	—	BV	85.00	275	—
1860BB	3,104,000	—	BV	85.00	275	—

KM# 800.1 10 FRANCS
3.2258 g., 0.9000 Gold .0933 oz. AGW **Ruler:** Napoleon III **Obv:** Laureate head right **Obv. Legend:** NAPOLEON III EMPEREUR **Rev:** Denomination within wreath **Rev. Legend:** EMPIRE FRANCAIS

Date	Mintage	F	VF	XF	Unc	BU
1861A	363,000	BV	—	125	300	—
1862A	2,844,000	—	BV	75.00	250	—
1863A	2,346,000	—	BV	75.00	250	—
1864A	3,339,000	—	BV	75.00	250	—
1865A	1,673,000	—	BV	75.00	250	—
1866A	3,720,000	—	BV	75.00	250	—
1867A	1,205,000	—	BV	75.00	250	—
aA	3,416,000	—	BV	75.00	250	—

KM# 800.2 10 FRANCS
3.2258 g., 0.9000 Gold .0933 oz. AGW **Ruler:** Napoleon III **Obv:** Laureate head right **Rev:** Denomination within wreath

Date	Mintage	F	VF	XF	Unc	BU
1861BB	44,000	75.00	100	150	300	—
1862BB	1,462,000	—	BV	75.00	250	—
1863BB	1,905,000	—	BV	75.00	250	—
1864BB	1,449,000	—	BV	75.00	250	—
1865BB	1,576,000	—	BV	75.00	250	—
1866BB	2,776,000	—	BV	75.00	250	—
1867BB	2,346,000	—	BV	75.00	250	—
1868BB	1,117,000	—	BV	75.00	250	—
1869BB	109,000	—	75.00	125	250	—

KM# 774 20 FRANCS
6.4516 g., 0.9000 Gold .1867 oz. AGW **Ruler:** Napoleon III **Obv:** Head right **Obv. Legend:** LOUIS-NAPOLEON BONAPARTE **Rev:** Denomination within wreath **Rev. Legend:** EMPIRE FRANCAIS

Date	Mintage	F	VF	XF	Unc	BU
1852A	10,494,000	—	BV	125	475	—
1852A Proof	—	Value: 3,250				

KM# 781.1 20 FRANCS
6.4516 g., 0.9000 Gold .1867 oz. AGW **Ruler:** Napoleon III **Obv:** Head right **Obv. Legend:** NAPOLEON III EMPEREUR **Rev:** Denomination within wreath **Rev. Legend:** EMPIRE FRANCAIS

Date	Mintage	F	VF	XF	Unc	BU
1853A	5,729,000	—	BV	BV	170	—
1853A Proof	—	Value: 2,850				
1854A	23,486,000	—	BV	BV	135	—
1854A Proof	—	Value: 2,600				
1855A (d)	16,595,000	—	—	BV	135	170	—

FRANCE

Date	Mintage	F	VF	XF	Unc	BU
1855A (a)	Inc. above	—	BV	135	170	—
1856A	17,303,000	—	BV	135	170	—
1857A	19,193,000	—	BV	135	170	—
1858A	16,861,000	—	BV	135	170	—
1859A	20,295,000	—	BV	135	170	—
1860A	10,220,000	—	BV	135	170	—

KM# 781.2 20 FRANCS
6.4516 g., 0.9000 Gold .1867 oz. AGW **Ruler:** Napoleon III
Obv: Head right **Rev:** Denomination within wreath

Date	Mintage	F	VF	XF	Unc	BU
1855BB	1,760,000	—	BV	130	175	—
1856BB	1,125,000	—	BV	130	175	—
1858BB	2,017,000	—	BV	130	175	—
1859BB	5,871,000	—	BV	BV	150	—
1860BB	5,727,000	—	BV	BV	150	—

KM# 781.3 20 FRANCS
6.4516 g., 0.9000 Gold .1867 oz. AGW **Ruler:** Napoleon III
Obv: Head right **Rev:** Denomination within wreath

Date	Mintage	F	VF	XF	Unc	BU
1855D	45,000	BV	125	150	400	—

KM# 801.1 20 FRANCS
6.4516 g., 0.9000 Gold .1867 oz. AGW **Ruler:** Napoleon III
Obv: Laureate head right **Obv. Legend:** NAPOLEON III EMPEREUR **Rev:** Crowned and mantled arms divide denomination **Rev. Legend:** EMPIRE FRANCAIS

Date	Mintage	F	VF	XF	Unc	BU
1861A	2,607,000	—	—	BV	130	150	—
1861A Proof	—	Value: 3,000				
1862A	4,826,000	—	—	BV	130	150	—
1863A	3,920,000	—	—	BV	130	150	—
1864A	7,059,000	—	—	BV	130	150	—
1865A	2,951,000	—	—	BV	130	150	—
1866A	6,992,000	—	—	BV	130	150	—
1867A	2,923,000	—	—	BV	130	150	—
1868A	9,281,000	—	—	BV	130	150	—
1869A	4,046,000	—	—	BV	130	150	—
1870A	865,000	—	—	BV	130	150	—

KM# 801.2 20 FRANCS
6.4516 g., 0.9000 Gold .1867 oz. AGW **Ruler:** Napoleon III
Obv: Laureate head right **Rev:** Crowned and mantled arms divide denomination

Date	Mintage	F	VF	XF	Unc	BU
1861BB	1,423,000	—	—	BV	130	150	—
1862BB	2,907,000	—	—	BV	130	150	—
1863BB	4,753,000	—	—	BV	130	150	—
1864BB	3,323,000	—	—	BV	130	150	—
1865BB	3,088,000	—	—	BV	130	150	—
1866BB	6,979,000	—	—	BV	130	150	—
1867BB	4,516,000	—	—	BV	130	150	—
1868BB	4,829,000	—	—	BV	130	150	—
1869BB	7,317,000	—	—	BV	130	150	—
1870BB	1,853,000	—	—	BV	130	150	—

KM# 785.1 50 FRANCS
16.1290 g., 0.9000 Gold .4667 oz. AGW **Ruler:** Napoleon III
Obv: Bare head right **Obv. Legend:** NAPOLEON III EMPEREUR **Rev:** Crowned and mantled arms divide denomination **Rev. Legend:** EMPIRE FRANCAIS

Date	Mintage	F	VF	XF	Unc	BU
1855A	152,000	350	375	400	500	—
1856A	97,000	350	375	450	550	—
1857A	320,000	350	375	450	500	—
1858A	85,000	350	375	425	500	—
1859A	34,000	350	375	425	500	—

KM# 785.2 50 FRANCS
16.1290 g., 0.9000 Gold .4667 oz. AGW **Ruler:** Napoleon III
Obv: Bare head right **Obv. Legend:** NAPOLEON III EMPEREUR **Rev:** Crowned and mantled arms divide denomination **Rev. Legend:** EMPIRE FRANCAIS

Date	Mintage	F	VF	XF	Unc	BU
1855BB	3,051	350	375	600	1,100	—
1856BB	3,803	350	375	600	1,100	—
1858BB	9,135	350	375	550	1,000	—
1859BB	32,000	350	375	425	600	—
1860BB	29,000	—	—	—	—	—

KM# 804.1 50 FRANCS
16.1290 g., 0.9000 Gold .4667 oz. AGW **Ruler:** Napoleon III
Obv: Laureate head right **Obv. Legend:** NAPOLEON III EMPEREUR **Rev:** Crowned and mantled arms divide denomination **Rev. Legend:** EMPIRE FRANCAIS

Date	Mintage	F	VF	XF	Unc	BU
1862A	24,000	350	375	425	700	—
1862A Proof	—	Value: 7,500				
1864A	29,000	350	375	425	700	—
1865A	3,740	350	375	550	950	—
1866A	39,000	350	375	425	700	—
1867A	2,000	350	375	550	950	—
1868A	16,000	350	375	425	750	—

KM# 804.2 50 FRANCS
16.1290 g., 0.9000 Gold .4667 oz. AGW **Ruler:** Napoleon III
Obv: Laureate head right **Obv. Legend:** NAPOLEON III EMPEREUR **Rev:** Crowned and mantled arms divide denomination **Rev. Legend:** EMPIRE FRANCAIS

Date	Mintage	F	VF	XF	Unc	BU
1862BB	7,310	350	375	425	850	—
1863BB	8,251	350	375	425	850	—
1866BB	17,000	350	375	425	700	—
1867BB	20,000	350	375	425	700	—
1868BB	1,795	350	375	600	1,250	—

KM# 786.1 100 FRANCS
32.2581 g., 0.9000 Gold .9335 oz. AGW **Ruler:** Napoleon III
Obv: Head right **Obv. Legend:** NAPOLEON III EMPEREUR **Rev:** Crowned and mantled arms divide denomination **Rev. Legend:** EMPIRE FRANCAIS

Date	Mintage	F	VF	XF	Unc	BU
1855A	51,000	650	700	750	900	—
1856A	57,000	650	700	750	900	—
1857A	103,000	650	700	750	900	—
1858A	92,000	650	700	750	900	—
1859A	22,000	650	700	750	900	—

KM# 786.2 100 FRANCS
32.2581 g., 0.9000 Gold .9335 oz. AGW **Ruler:** Napoleon III
Obv: Head right **Obv. Legend:** NAPOLEON III EMPEREUR **Rev. Legend:** EMPIRE FRANCAIS

Date	Mintage	F	VF	XF	Unc	BU
1855BB	4,173	650	700	800	1,150	—
1856BB	876	800	1,100	1,500	3,000	—
1858BB	1,928	650	700	800	1,300	—
1859BB	9,305	650	700	750	1,100	—
1860BB	5,405	650	700	800	1,150	—

KM# 802.1 100 FRANCS
32.2581 g., 0.9000 Gold .9335 oz. AGW **Ruler:** Napoleon III
Obv: Laureate head right **Obv. Legend:** NAPOLEON III EMPEREUR **Rev:** Crowned and mantled arms divide denomination **Rev. Legend:** EMPIRE FRANCAIS

Date	Mintage	F	VF	XF	Unc	BU
1861A Proof	—	Value: 10,000				
1862A	6,650	650	700	850	1,200	—
1864A	5,536	650	700	850	1,200	—
1865A	1,517	650	775	1,000	1,800	—
1866A	9,041	650	700	750	1,100	—
1867A	4,309	650	700	850	1,200	—
1868A	2,315	650	700	1,000	1,800	—
1869A	29,000	650	700	800	1,100	—
1870A	10,000	3,000	6,000	12,000	20,000	—

KM# 802.2 100 FRANCS
32.2581 g., 0.9000 Gold .9335 oz. AGW **Ruler:** Napoleon III
Obv: Laureate head right **Rev:** Crowned and mantled arms divide denomination

Date	Mintage	F	VF	XF	Unc	BU
1862BB	3,078	650	700	800	1,400	—
1863BB	3,745	650	700	800	1,400	—
1864BB	1,333	650	700	850	1,800	—
1866BB	3,075	650	700	850	1,600	—
1867BB	2,807	650	700	850	1,600	—
1868BB	789	750	850	1,200	2,000	—
1869BB	14,000	650	700	750	1,100	—

MEDALLIC COINAGE

KM# M23b 5 CENTIMES
Gold **Subject:** Emperor and Empress visit to the Bourse

Date	Mintage	F	VF	XF	Unc	BU
1853 (w)	—	350	500	900	1,800	—

KM# M24b 10 CENTIMES
Gold **Subject:** Emperor and Empress visit to the Bourse

FRANCE 225

Date	Mintage	F	VF	XF	Unc	BU
1853 (w) Rare	2	—	—	—	—	—

KM# M25b 10 CENTIMES
Gold **Subject:** Monument of Napoleon I erected

Date	Mintage	F	VF	XF	Unc	BU
1854 (w)	—	400	800	1,250	2,150	—

KM# M26b 10 CENTIMES
Gold **Subject:** Napoleon III to the mint

Date	Mintage	F	VF	XF	Unc	BU
1854 (a)	—	400	700	1,200	2,000	—

MODERN REPUBLICS
1870-
DECIMAL COINAGE

KM# 829 5 FRANCS
1.6929 g., 0.9000 Gold .0467 oz. AGW **Obv:** Laureate head right **Rev:** Denomination within wreath **Edge Lettering:** DIEU PROTEGE LA FRANCE

Date	Mintage	F	VF	XF	Unc	BU
1878A Proof	30	Value: 6,500				
1889A Proof	40	Value: 5,250				

KM# 830 10 FRANCS
3.2258 g., 0.9000 Gold .0933 oz. AGW **Obv:** Laureate head right **Rev:** Denomination within wreath

Date	Mintage	F	VF	XF	Unc	BU
1878A Proof	30	Value: 5,250				
1889A Proof	100	Value: 4,750				
1895A	214,000	—	BV	75.00	200	—
1896A	585,000	—	BV	75.00	150	—
1899A	1,600,000	—	BV	75.00	150	—

KM# 846 10 FRANCS
3.2258 g., 0.9000 Gold .0933 oz. AGW

Date	Mintage	F	VF	XF	Unc	BU
1899	699,000	—	BV	75.00	120	—
1899 Matte Proof	—	Value: 900				
1900	1,570,000	—	BV	75.00	95.00	115
1900 Proof	—	Value: 800				
1901	2,100,000	—	BV	65.00	85.00	125
1901	2,100,000	—	BV	65.00	85.00	125
1905	1,426,000	—	BV	65.00	85.00	125
1905	1,426,000	—	BV	65.00	85.00	125
1906	3,665,000	—	BV	65.00	85.00	125
1907	3,364,000	—	BV	65.00	85.00	125
1908	1,650,000	—	BV	65.00	85.00	125
1909	599,000	—	BV	70.00	120	255
1910	2,110,000	—	BV	65.00	85.00	125
1911	1,881,000	—	BV	65.00	85.00	125
1912	1,756,000	—	BV	65.00	85.00	125
1914	3,041,000	—	BV	65.00	85.00	125

KM# 825 20 FRANCS
6.4516 g., 0.9000 Gold .1867 oz. AGW **Obv:** Standing Genius writing the Constitution, rooster at right, fasces at left **Rev:** Denomination above date within circular wreath

Date	Mintage	F	VF	XF	Unc	BU
1871A	2,508,000	—	BV	125	140	—
1874A	1,216,000	—	BV	125	140	—
1875A	11,746,000	—	BV	125	140	—
1876A	8,825,000	—	BV	125	140	—
1877A	12,759,000	—	BV	125	140	—
1878A	9,189,000	—	BV	125	140	—
1878A Proof	30	Value: 5,000				
1879A	1,038,000	—	BV	125	140	—
1886A	985,000	—	BV	125	140	—
1887A	1,231,000	—	BV	125	140	—
1887A Proof	—	Value: 5,250				
1888A	28,000	—	BV	150	275	—
1889A	873,000	—	BV	125	140	—
1889A Proof	100	Value: 4,250				
1890A	1,030,000	—	BV	125	140	—
1891A	871,000	—	BV	125	140	—
1892A	226,000	—	BV	125	140	—
1893A	2,517,000	—	BV	125	140	—
1894A	491,000	—	BV	125	140	—
1895A	5,293,000	—	BV	125	140	—
1896A	5,330,000	—	BV	125	140	—
1897A	11,069,000	—	BV	125	140	—
1898A	8,866,000	—	BV	125	140	—

KM# 847 20 FRANCS
6.4516 g., 0.9000 Gold .1867 oz. AGW **Edge Lettering:** DIEU PROTEGE LA FRANCE

Date	Mintage	F	VF	XF	Unc	BU
1899A	1,500,000	—	—	BV	140	170
1899A Proof	—	Value: 1,250				
1900A	615,000	—	—	BV	140	165
1900A Proof	Inc. above	Value: 1,000				
1901A	2,643,000	—	—	BV	140	185
1901A	2,643,000	—	—	BV	140	185
1902A	2,394,000	—	—	BV	140	185
1902A	2,394,000	—	—	BV	140	185
1903A	4,405,000	—	—	BV	140	185
1904A	7,706,000	—	—	BV	140	185
1905A	9,158,000	—	—	BV	140	185
1906A	14,613,000	—	—	BV	140	185

KM# 857 20 FRANCS
6.4516 g., 0.9000 Gold .1867 oz. AGW **Obv:** Oak leaf wreath encircles liberty head right **Rev:** Rooster divides denomination, date below **Edge Lettering:** LIBERTE EGALITE FRATERNITE **Note:** All dates from 1907-1914 have been officially restruck.

Date	Mintage	F	VF	XF	Unc	BU
1906	—	—	—	BV	130	165
1907	17,716,000	—	—	BV	130	165
1908	6,721,000	—	—	BV	130	165
1909	9,637,000	—	—	BV	130	165
1910	5,779,000	—	—	BV	130	165
1911	5,346,000	—	—	BV	130	165
1912	10,332,000	—	—	BV	130	165
1913	12,163,000	—	—	BV	130	165
1914	6,518,000	—	—	BV	130	165

KM# 831 50 FRANCS
16.1290 g., 0.9000 Gold .4467 oz. AGW **Obv:** Standing Genius writing the Constitution, rooster at right, fasces at left **Rev:** Denomination above date within circular wreath

Date	Mintage	F	VF	XF	Unc	BU
1878A	5,294	400	700	1,350	2,000	—
1887A	301	550	1,250	2,250	3,700	—
1889A Proof	100	Value: 7,000				
1896A	800	500	900	1,800	2,800	—
1900A	200	650	1,500	2,500	4,500	—

Date	Mintage	F	VF	XF	Unc	BU
1900A Proof	—	Value: 8,000				
1904A	20,000	325	550	900	1,650	—

KM# 832 100 FRANCS
32.2581 g., 0.9000 Gold .9335 oz. AGW **Obv:** Standing Genius writing the Constitution, rooster on right, fasces on left **Rev:** Denomination above date within circular wreath **Edge Lettering:** DIEU PROTEGE LA FRANCE

Date	Mintage	F	VF	XF	Unc	BU
1878A	13,000	—	BV	650	700	1,000
1878A Proof	30	Value: 14,000				
1879A	39,000	—	BV	650	700	1,000
1881A	22,000	—	BV	650	700	1,000
1882A	37,000	—	BV	650	700	1,000
1885A	2,894	—	675	850	1,150	—
1886A	39,000	—	BV	650	800	1,000
1887A	234	850	1,750	3,500	6,500	—
1889A Proof	100	Value: 12,000				
1894A	143	1,250	2,750	2,750	10,000	—
1896A	400	750	1,100	650	5,500	—
1899A	10,000	750	BV	525	800	1,000
1900A	20,000	450	475	525	675	1,000
1900A Proof	—	Value: 5,000				
1901A	10,000	—	BV	625	800	1,200
1901A	10,000	—	BV	625	800	1,200
1902A	10,000	—	BV	625	800	1,200
1902A	10,000	—	BV	625	800	1,200
1903A	10,000	—	BV	625	800	1,200
1904A	20,000	—	BV	625	800	1,200
1905A	10,000	—	BV	625	800	1,200
1906A	30,000	—	BV	626	800	1,200

KM# 858 100 FRANCS
32.2581 g., 0.9000 Gold .9335 oz. AGW **Obv:** Standing Genius writing the constitution, rooster on right, column on the left **Rev:** Denomination and date within wreath **Edge Lettering:** LIBERTE EGALITE FRATERNITE

Date	Mintage	F	VF	XF	Unc	BU
1907A	20,000	—	—	BV	645	900
1908A	23,000	—	—	BV	645	900
1909A	20,000	—	—	BV	645	900
1910A	20,000	—	—	BV	645	900
1911A	30,000	—	—	BV	645	900
1912A	20,000	—	—	BV	645	900
1913A	30,000	—	—	BV	645	900
1914A Rare	1,281	—	—	—	—	—

KM# 880 100 FRANCS
6.5500 g., 0.9000 Gold .1895 oz. AGW **Obv:** Winged head left **Rev:** Denomination above grain sprig, date below, laurel and oak branches flank **Note:** Without mint mark.

Date	Mintage	F	VF	XF	Unc	BU
1929	50	—	—	2,500	4,000	—
1932	Est. 50	—	—	3,250	4,750	—
1933	Est. 300	—	—	1,650	2,500	—
1934 Rare	—	—	—	—	—	—
1935	6,102,000	—	—	—	500	800
1936	7,689,000	—	—	—	500	800

REFORM COINAGE

(Commencing 1960)

1 Old Franc = 1 New Centime; 100 New Centimes = 1 New Franc

KM# 979 FRANC

9.0000 g., 0.9200 Gold .2662 oz. AGW, 24 mm. **Subject:** 30th Anniversary of Fifth Republic

Date	Mintage	F	VF	XF	Unc	BU
1998 Proof	20,000	Value: 200				

KM# 1004.1a FRANC

9.0000 g., 0.9200 Gold .2662 oz. AGW, 24 mm. **Subject:** 200th Anniversary of the French Republic **Obv:** Liberty bust left **Rev:** Denomination within wreath

Date	Mintage	F	VF	XF	Unc	BU
1992 Proof	5,000	Value: 200				

KM# 1015 FRANC

17.0000 g., 0.9250 Gold .5028 oz. AGW **Subject:** Normandy Invasion **Obv:** American soldiers storming Omaha beach **Rev:** Head of Liberty Statue, flags, denomination and date

Date	Mintage	F	VF	XF	Unc	BU
1993 Proof	Est. 20,000	Value: 360				

KM# 925.1a FRANC

8.0000 g., 0.7500 Gold .1929 oz. AGW, 24 mm. **Obv:** The seed sower **Rev:** Laurel divides date and denomination **Edge:** Reeded **Designer:** Louis Oscar Roty **Note:** Medallic alignment.

Date	Mintage	F	VF	XF	Unc	BU
2000	5,000	—	—	—	140	160
2001	Est. 9,941	—	—	—	145	165

KM# 1290a FRANC

26.1000 g., 0.7500 Gold .6294 oz. AGW **Subject:** The Last Franc **Obv:** Legend on polished field **Obv. Legend:** UN ULTIME FRANC **Rev:** Number "1" on polished field **Edge Lettering:** REPUBLIQUE FRANCAISE. STARCK. LIBERTE. EGALITE. FRATERNITE (cornucopia) 2001 **Note:** This coin has an intentionally warped surface and the edge inscription is very weak.

Date	Mintage	F	VF	XF	Unc	BU
2001 Matte	4,963	—	—	—	450	475

KM# 968b 5 FRANCS

14.0000 g., 0.9250 Gold .4141 oz. AGW, 29 mm. **Subject:** Centennial - Erection of Eiffel Tower **Obv:** Denomination above tower base **Rev:** Tower view from bottom

Date	Mintage	F	VF	XF	Unc	BU
1989 Proof	30,000	Value: 300				

KM# 1006b 5 FRANCS

14.0000 g., 0.9200 Gold .4141 oz. AGW, 29 mm. **Obv:** Denomination within design **Rev:** Bust of Pierre Mendes France facing

Date	Mintage	F	VF	XF	Unc	BU
1992 Proof	1,000	Value: 300				

KM# 1118a 5 FRANCS

14.0000 g., 0.9200 Gold .4141 oz. AGW, 29 mm. **Obv:** Dove and branch left of denomination **Rev:** UN logo and dates

Date	Mintage	F	VF	XF	Unc	BU
1995 Proof	125,000	Value: 300				

KM# 958c 10 FRANCS

7.0000 g., 0.9200 Gold .2071 oz. AGW **Subject:** 100th Anniversary - Birth of Robert Schuman **Obv:** Rooster at left, denomination right **Rev:** Half head right

Date	Mintage	F	VF	XF	Unc	BU
1986 Proof	5,000	Value: 160				

KM# 961c 10 FRANCS

14.0000 g., 0.9990 Platinum .4497 oz. APW **Subject:** Millennium of King Capet and France **Obv:** Denomination and date within circle **Rev:** Crowned figure standing at center, rosettes in background

Date	Mintage	F	VF	XF	Unc	BU
1987 Proof	1,000	Value: 600				

KM# 961b 10 FRANCS

12.0000 g., 0.9200 Gold .3549 oz. AGW **Subject:** Millennium of King Capet and France **Obv:** Denomination and date within circle **Rev:** Crowned figure standing at center, rosettes in background

Date	Mintage	F	VF	XF	Unc	BU
1987 Proof	6,000	Value: 275				

KM# 965c 10 FRANCS

12.0000 g., 0.9200 Gold .3550 oz. AGW, 26 mm. **Subject:** 100th Anniversary - Birth of Roland Garros **Obv:** Wings above denomination **Rev:** Airplane above head right

Date	Mintage	F	VF	XF	Unc	BU
1988 Proof	3,000	Value: 275				

KM# 969a 10 FRANCS

Bi-Metallic Gold, Palladium and Silver alloy center in .920 Gold ring, 23 mm. **Subject:** 300th Anniversary - Birth of Montesquieu **Obv:** Bust right **Rev:** Patterned denomination above date

Date	Mintage	F	VF	XF	Unc	BU
1989 Proof	5,000	Value: 345				

KM# 1008.2a 20 FRANCS

12.6600 g., Tri-Metallic .720 Gold center plug, .950 Silver inner ring, .750 Gold outer ring., 27 mm. **Obv:** Mont St. Michel; 5 bands of stripes in outer ring **Rev:** Patterned denomination above date

Date	Mintage	F	VF	XF	Unc	BU
1992 Proof	15,000	Value: 210				

KM# 1008.2b 20 FRANCS

16.4600 g., Tri-Metallic .920 Gold center plug, .750 Gold inner ring, .920 Gold outer ring, 27 mm. **Obv:** Mont St. Michel **Rev:** Patterned denomination above date

Date	Mintage	F	VF	XF	Unc	BU
1992 Proof	5,000	Value: 375				

KM# 1145 50 FRANCS

8.4521 g., 0.9200 Gold .2500 oz. AGW **Subject:** World Class Soccer **Obv:** Soccer ball, denomination and date below **Rev:** Stylized dove, soccer ball

Date	Mintage	F	VF	XF	Unc	BU
1996 Proof	Est. 10,000	Value: 200				

KM# 1208 50 FRANCS

8.4521 g., 0.9200 Gold .2500 oz. AGW **Subject:** Treasures of the Nile **Obv:** Portrait above 'RF', obelisk at right **Rev:** Sphinx and pyramids, date at left, denomination below

Date	Mintage	F	VF	XF	Unc	BU
1998 Proof	3,000	Value: 275				

KM# 1236 50 FRANCS

8.4521 g., 0.9200 Gold .2500 oz. AGW **Subject:** Yves St. Laurent **Obv:** RF monogram, denomination **Rev:** Fashion show scene **Edge:** Plain

Date	Mintage	F	VF	XF	Unc	BU
2000 Proof	2,000	Value: 275				

KM# 1256 65.5997 FRANCS

8.4500 g., 0.9250 Gold .2499 oz. AGW **Series:** Euro Conversion Series **Obv:** Country names with euro currency equivalents around "RF", denomination and French coin designs **Rev:** Europa allegorical portrait **Edge:** Plain

Date	Mintage	F	VF	XF	Unc	BU
1999 Proof	10,000	Value: 275				

KM# 1260 65.5997 FRANCS

8.4500 g., 0.9250 Gold .2499 oz. AGW **Obv:** Country names with euro-currency equivalents around "RF", denomination and French euro coin designs

Date	Mintage	F	VF	XF	Unc	BU
2000 Proof	3,000	Value: 275				

KM# 1266 65.5997 FRANCS

8.4500 g., 0.9200 Gold .2499 oz. AGW **Subject:** Last Year of the French Franc **Obv:** French and other European euro currency equivalents **Rev:** Europa allegorical portrait, date below, "last year of the franc" logo after the date **Edge:** Reeded

Date	Mintage	F	VF	XF	Unc	BU
2001 Proof	3,000	Value: 200				

KM# 955b 100 FRANCS

17.0000 g., 0.9200 Gold .5028 oz. AGW **Subject:** 50th Anniversary - Death of Marie Curie **Obv:** Leafy branches divide date and denomination **Rev:** Head right, two dates

Date	Mintage	F	VF	XF	Unc	BU
1984 Proof	5,000	Value: 400				

KM# 957b 100 FRANCS

17.0000 g., 0.9200 Gold .5028 oz. AGW **Subject:** Centennial of Emile Zola's Novel **Rev:** Head right

Date	Mintage	F	VF	XF	Unc	BU
1985 Proof	5,000	Value: 375				

KM# 960b 100 FRANCS

17.0000 g., 0.9200 Gold .5028 oz. AGW **Subject:** Centennial - Statue of Liberty **Obv:** Top of statue facing **Rev:** Liberty cap over inscription above denomination, date below

Date	Mintage	F	VF	XF	Unc	BU
1986	13,000	—	—	—	340	360
1986 Proof	17,000	Value: 375				

KM# 960c 100 FRANCS

20.0000 g., 0.9990 Platinum .6430 oz. APW **Subject:** Centennial - Statue of Liberty **Obv:** Top of statue facing **Rev:** Liberty cap over inscription above denomination, date below

Date	Mintage	F	VF	XF	Unc	BU
1986 Proof	9,500	Value: 875				

KM# 960d 100 FRANCS

17.0000 g., 0.9000 Palladium .4920 oz. **Subject:** Centennial - Statue of Liberty **Obv:** Top of statue facing **Rev:** Liberty cap over inscription above denomination, date below

Date	Mintage	F	VF	XF	Unc	BU
1986 Proof	1,250	Value: 425				

KM# 962b 100 FRANCS

17.0000 g., 0.9200 Gold .5028 oz. AGW **Subject:** 230th Anniversary - Birth of General Lafayette **Obv:** Bust left **Rev:** Liberty cap over inscription above denomination, date below

Date	Mintage	F	VF	XF	Unc	BU
1987	10,000	—	—	—	340	360
1987 Proof	20,000	Value: 375				

KM# 962c 100 FRANCS

20.0000 g., 0.9990 Platinum .6430 oz. APW **Subject:** 230th Anniversary - Birth of General Lafayette **Obv:** Bust left **Rev:** Liberty cap over inscription above denomination, date below

Date	Mintage	F	VF	XF	Unc	BU
1987 Proof	8,500	Value: 875				

KM# 962d 100 FRANCS

17.0000 g., 0.9000 Palladium .4920 oz. **Subject:** 230th Anniversary - Birth of General Lafayette **Obv:** Bust left **Rev:** Liberty cap over inscription above denomination, date below

Date	Mintage	F	VF	XF	Unc	BU
1987 Proof	7,000	Value: 300				

KM# 966b 100 FRANCS

17.0000 g., 0.9200 Gold .5028 oz. AGW **Subject:** Fraternity **Obv:** Radiant head left with crown of cherubs **Rev:** Liberty cap over inscription above denomination, date below

Date	Mintage	F	VF	XF	Unc	BU
1988	3,000	—	—	—	450	475
1988 Proof	12,000	Value: 375				

KM# 966c 100 FRANCS

20.0000 g., 0.9990 Platinum .6430 oz. APW **Subject:** Fraternity **Obv:** Radiant head left with crown of cherubs **Rev:** Liberty cap over inscription above denomination, date below

Date	Mintage	F	VF	XF	Unc	BU
1988 Proof	5,000	Value: 875				

KM# 966d 100 FRANCS

17.0000 g., 0.9000 Palladium .4920 oz. **Subject:** Fraternity **Obv:** Radiant head left with crown of cherubs **Rev:** Liberty cap over inscription above denomination, date below

Date	Mintage	F	VF	XF	Unc	BU
1988 Proof	7,000	Value: 300				

KM# 970b 100 FRANCS

17.0000 g., 0.9200 Gold .5028 oz. AGW **Subject:** Human Rights **Obv:** Standing Genius writing the constitution **Rev:** Liberty cap over inscription above denomination, date below

Date	Mintage	F	VF	XF	Unc	BU
1989	1,000	—	—	—	600	650
1989 Proof	20,000	Value: 365				

KM# 970c 100 FRANCS

20.0000 g., 0.9990 Platinum .6430 oz. APW **Subject:** Human Rights **Obv:** Standing Genius writing the constitution **Rev:** Liberty cap over inscription above denomination, date below

Date	Mintage	F	VF	XF	Unc	BU
1989 Proof	1,000	Value: 900				

KM# 970d 100 FRANCS

17.0000 g., 0.9000 Palladium .4920 oz. **Subject:** Human Rights **Obv:** Standing Genius writing the constitution **Rev:** Liberty cap over inscription above denomination, date below

Date	Mintage	F	VF	XF	Unc	BU
1989 Proof	1,250	Value: 400				

KM# 1018.2a 100 FRANCS

17.0000 g., 0.9200 Gold .5028 oz. AGW **Series:** Bicentennial of the Louvre **Obv:** Liberty **Rev:** Patterned pyramids front museum, date and denomination below

Date	Mintage	F	VF	XF	Unc	BU
1993	—	—	—	—	—	—
1993 Proof	5,000	Value: 400				

KM# 1019a 100 FRANCS

17.0000 g., 0.9200 Gold .5028 oz. AGW **Series:** Bicentennial of the Louvre **Obv:** Victory **Rev:** Patterned pyramids front museum, date and denomination below

Date	Mintage	F	VF	XF	Unc	BU
1993	—	—	—	—	—	—
1993 Proof	5,000	Value: 400				

KM# 1021a 100 FRANCS

17.0000 g., 0.9200 Gold .5028 oz. AGW **Series:** Bicentennial of the Louvre **Obv:** Marie-Marguerite **Rev:** Patterned pyramids front museum, date and denomination below

Date	Mintage	F	VF	XF	Unc	BU
1993	—	—	—	—	—	—
1993 Proof	5,000	Value: 400				

KM# 1022a 100 FRANCS

17.0000 g., 0.9200 Gold .5028 oz. AGW **Series:** Bicentennial of the Louvre **Obv:** Napoleon crowning Josephine **Rev:** Patterned pyramids front museum, date and denomination below

Date	Mintage	F	VF	XF	Unc	BU
1993	—	—	—	—	—	—
1993 Proof	5,000	Value: 400				

KM# 1073 100 FRANCS

17.0000 g., 0.9200 Gold .5028 oz. AGW **Series:** Centennial of Cinema **Subject:** Lumiere Brothers **Obv:** Antique movie camera **Rev:** Conjoined busts right

Date	Mintage	F	VF	XF	Unc	BU
1994 Proof	5,000	Value: 400				

KM# 1077 100 FRANCS

17.0000 g., 0.9200 Gold .5028 oz. AGW **Series:** Centennial of Cinema **Subject:** Charlie Chaplan **Obv:** Antique movie camera **Rev:** Head facing

Date	Mintage	F	VF	XF	Unc	BU
1994 Proof	5,000	Value: 400				

FRANCE 227

KM# 1081 100 FRANCS
17.0000 g., 0.9200 Gold .5028 oz. AGW **Series:** Centennial of Cinema **Subject:** Leon Gaumont **Obv:** Antique movie camera **Rev:** Head facing

Date	Mintage	F	VF	XF	Unc	BU
1995 Proof	5,000	Value: 400				

KM# 1085 100 FRANCS
17.0000 g., 0.9200 Gold .5028 oz. AGW **Series:** Centennial of Cinema **Subject:** Jean Renoir **Obv:** Antique movie camera **Rev:** Head right

Date	Mintage	F	VF	XF	Unc	BU
1995 Proof	5,000	Value: 400				

KM# 1089 100 FRANCS
17.0000 g., 0.9200 Gold .5028 oz. AGW **Series:** Centennial of Cinema **Subject:** Alfred Hitchcock **Obv:** Antique movie camera **Rev:** Head 1/4 left

Date	Mintage	F	VF	XF	Unc	BU
1995 Proof	5,000	Value: 425				

KM# 1093 100 FRANCS
17.0000 g., 0.9200 Gold .5028 oz. AGW **Series:** Centennial of Cinema **Subject:** Greta Garbo 1905-1990, actress in "Camille & Ninotchka" **Obv:** Antique movie camera **Rev:** Head right

Date	Mintage	F	VF	XF	Unc	BU
1995 Proof	5,000	Value: 450				

KM# 1097 100 FRANCS
17.0000 g., 0.9200 Gold .5028 oz. AGW **Series:** Centennial of Cinema **Subject:** Audrey Hepburn **Obv:** Antique movie camera **Rev:** Head 3/4 left

Date	Mintage	F	VF	XF	Unc	BU
1994 Proof	5,000	Value: 425				

KM# 1101 100 FRANCS
17.0000 g., 0.9200 Gold .5028 oz. AGW **Series:** Centennial of Cinema **Subject:** Federico Fellini **Obv:** Antique movie camera **Rev:** Bust 3/4 right

Date	Mintage	F	VF	XF	Unc	BU
1995 Proof	5,000	Value: 425				

KM# 1105 100 FRANCS
17.0000 g., 0.9200 Gold .5028 oz. AGW **Series:** Centennial of Cinema **Subject:** Yves Montand **Obv:** Antique movie camera **Rev:** Bust 3/4 facing

Date	Mintage	F	VF	XF	Unc	BU
1994 Proof	5,000	Value: 400				

KM# 1109 100 FRANCS
17.0000 g., 0.9200 Gold .5028 oz. AGW **Series:** Centennial of Cinema **Subject:** Romy Schneider **Obv:** Antique movie camera **Rev:** Bust 3/4 left

Date	Mintage	F	VF	XF	Unc	BU
1995 Proof	5,000	Value: 400				

KM# 1172 100 FRANCS
17.0000 g., 0.9200 Gold .5028 oz. AGW **Subject:** Coupe du Monde 1998 - France **Obv:** World Cup 1998 logo above denomination and date **Rev:** Segment of Eiffel tower, soccer player

Date	Mintage	F	VF	XF	Unc	BU
1996 Proof	25,000	Value: 385				

KM# 1168 100 FRANCS
17.0000 g., 0.9200 Gold .5028 oz. AGW **Subject:** Coupe du Monde 1998 - Africa **Obv:** World Cup 1998 logo above denomination and date **Rev:** Soccer player and map of Africa, date below **Designer:** Joaquin Jimenez

Date	Mintage	F	VF	XF	Unc	BU
1997 Proof	25,000	Value: 400				

KM# 1169 100 FRANCS
17.0000 g., 0.9200 Gold .5028 oz. AGW **Subject:** Coupe du Monde 1998 - America **Obv:** World Cup 1998 logo above denomination and date below **Rev:** Soccer player and map of North & South America **Designer:** Joaquin Jimenez

Date	Mintage	F	VF	XF	Unc	BU
1997 Proof	25,000	Value: 400				

KM# 1170 100 FRANCS
17.0000 g., 0.9200 Gold .5028 oz. AGW **Subject:** Coupe du Monde 1998 - Asia **Rev:** Soccer player and map of Asia, date below **Designer:** Joaquin Jimenez

Date	Mintage	F	VF	XF	Unc	BU
1997 Proof	25,000	Value: 400				

KM# 1173 100 FRANCS
17.0000 g., 0.9200 Gold .5028 oz. AGW **Subject:** Coupe du Monde 1998 - Oceania **Rev:** Soccer player and map of the Pacific, with Australia highlighted in a box, date below **Designer:** Joaquin Jimenez

Date	Mintage	F	VF	XF	Unc	BU
1997 Proof	25,000	Value: 400				

KM# 1195 100 FRANCS
8.4500 g., 0.9200 Gold .2499 oz. AGW **Obv:** Pantheon, date below **Rev:** Denomination and tree design

Date	Mintage	F	VF	XF	Unc	BU
1997 Proof	500	Value: 350				

KM# 1171 100 FRANCS
17.0000 g., 0.9200 Gold .5028 oz. AGW **Subject:** Coupe du Monte 1998 - Europe **Obv:** World Cup 1998 logo, denomination and date below **Rev:** Soccer player and map of Europe, date below **Designer:** Joaquin Jimenez

Date	Mintage	F	VF	XF	Unc	BU
1998 Proof	25,000	Value: 400				

KM# 1209 100 FRANCS
17.0000 g., 0.9200 Gold .5028 oz. AGW **Subject:** Treasures of the Nile - King Tutankhamon **Obv:** Burial mask and dog **Rev:** Sphinx and pyramids

Date	Mintage	F	VF	XF	Unc	BU
1998 Proof	2,000	Value: 475				

KM# 1210 100 FRANCS
17.0000 g., 0.9200 Gold .5028 oz. AGW **Subject:** Treasures of the Nile - The Scribe Accroupi **Obv:** Seated scribe **Rev:** Pyramids, Sphinx, date at left, denomination below

Date	Mintage	F	VF	XF	Unc	BU
1998 Proof	2,000	Value: 475				

KM# 1232 100 FRANCS
17.0000 g., 0.9200 Gold .5028 oz. AGW **Subject:** 2000 Years - French Coinage **Obv:** Denomination **Rev:** 1st century B.C. Celtic Parisii Stater coin design **Edge:** Plain

Date	Mintage	F	VF	XF	Unc	BU
2000 Proof	1,000	Value: 450				

KM# 1233 100 FRANCS
17.0000 g., 0.9200 Gold .5028 oz. AGW **Subject:** 2000 Years - French Coinage **Rev:** Charlemagne Denar coin design

Date	Mintage	F	VF	XF	Unc	BU
2000 Proof	1,000	Value: 450				

KM# 1234 100 FRANCS
17.0000 g., 0.9200 Gold .5028 oz. AGW **Subject:** 2000 Years - French Coinage **Rev:** Louis IX gold Ecu coin design

Date	Mintage	F	VF	XF	Unc	BU
2000 Proof	1,000	Value: 450				

KM# 1238 100 FRANCS
17.0000 g., 0.9200 Gold .5028 oz. AGW **Series:** XXth Century **Subject:** Biology and Medicine **Obv:** Double X design **Rev:** Parents, fetus, hands

Date	Mintage	F	VF	XF	Unc	BU
2000 Proof	1,000	Value: 450				

KM# 1239 100 FRANCS
17.0000 g., 0.9200 Gold .5028 oz. AGW **Series:** XXth Century **Subject:** Physics **Rev:** Einstein's portrait, atom and formula

Date	Mintage	F	VF	XF	Unc	BU
2000 Proof	1,000	Value: 450				

KM# 1240 100 FRANCS
17.0000 g., 0.9200 Gold .5028 oz. AGW **Series:** XXth Century **Subject:** Communications **Rev:** World, satellites, keyboard

Date	Mintage	F	VF	XF	Unc	BU
2000 Proof	1,000	Value: 450				

KM# 1241 100 FRANCS
17.0000 g., 0.9200 Gold .5028 oz. AGW **Series:** XXth Century **Subject:** Automobile **Rev:** Race cars above horse

Date	Mintage	F	VF	XF	Unc	BU
2000 Proof	1,000	Value: 450				

228 FRANCE

KM# 1242 100 FRANCS
17.0000 g., 0.9200 Gold .5028 oz. AGW **Series:** XXth Century
Subject: Flight **Rev:** Icarus in flight above Bleriot monoplane

Date	Mintage	F	VF	XF	Unc	BU
2000 Proof	1,000	Value: 450				

KM# 1243 100 FRANCS
17.0000 g., 0.9200 Gold .5028 oz. AGW **Series:** XXth Century
Subject: Space Travel **Rev:** Astronaut, footprint on moon, planets

Date	Mintage	F	VF	XF	Unc	BU
2000 Proof	1,000	Value: 450				

KM# 1264 100 FRANCS
17.0000 g., 0.9200 Gold .5028 oz. AGW **Subject:** Antoine de St. Exupery **Obv:** Portrait, bi-plane **Rev:** The "Little Prince" standing on a small planet

Date	Mintage	F	VF	XF	Unc	BU
2000 Proof	1,000	Value: 450				

KM# 1269 100 FRANCS
17.0000 g., 0.9200 Gold .5028 oz. AGW **Subject:** Palace of Versailles **Obv:** Stylized French map **Rev:** Louis XIV with internal and external palace views **Edge:** Plain

Date	Mintage	F	VF	XF	Unc	BU
2001 Proof	105	Value: 350				

KM# 1271 100 FRANCS
17.0000 g., 0.9200 Gold .5028 oz. AGW **Obv:** Champs-Elysees **Rev:** Arch of Triumph partial close up and aerial views

Date	Mintage	F	VF	XF	Unc	BU
2001 Proof	115	Value: 365				

KM# 1273 100 FRANCS
17.0000 g., 0.9200 Gold .5028 oz. AGW **Obv:** Notre-Dame Cathedral **Rev:** Gargoyle and cathedral views

Date	Mintage	F	VF	XF	Unc	BU
2001 Proof	116	Value: 375				

KM# 1275 100 FRANCS
17.0000 g., 0.9200 Gold .5028 oz. AGW **Obv:** Eiffel Tower **Rev:** Two tower views

Date	Mintage	F	VF	XF	Unc	BU
2001 Proof	170	Value: 375				

KM# 974 500 FRANCS
17.0000 g., 0.9200 Gold .5029 oz. AGW **Series:** 1992 Olympics
Obv: Ice skating couple **Obv. Designer:** Georges Yoldjoglou **Rev:** Cross on flame divides date and denomination, Olympic logo below

Date	Mintage	F	VF	XF	Unc	BU
1989 Proof	Est. 17,000	Value: 360				

KM# 973 500 FRANCS
17.0000 g., 0.9200 Gold .5029 oz. AGW **Series:** 1992 Olympics
Obv: Alpine skiing **Obv. Designer:** Guy Brun **Rev:** Cross on flame, date and denomination, Olympic logo below **Note:** Without mint mark.

Date	Mintage	F	VF	XF	Unc	BU
1989 Proof	19,000	Value: 350				

KM# 985 500 FRANCS
17.0000 g., 0.9200 Gold .5029 oz. AGW **Series:** 1992 Olympics
Obv: Speed skating **Rev:** Crossed flame, date and denomination, logo below

Date	Mintage	F	VF	XF	Unc	BU
1990 Proof	13,000	Value: 355				

KM# 986 500 FRANCS
17.0000 g., 0.9200 Gold .5029 oz. AGW **Series:** 1992 Olympics
Obv: Bobsledding **Rev:** Games logo, value and legend

Date	Mintage	F	VF	XF	Unc	BU
1990 Proof	13,000	Value: 355				

KM# 987 500 FRANCS
17.0000 g., 0.9200 Gold .5029 oz. AGW **Series:** 1992 Olympics
Subject: Pierre de Coubertin **Obv:** Free-style skier watched by chamois **Rev:** Head facing

Date	Mintage	F	VF	XF	Unc	BU
1990 Proof	8,000	Value: 360				

KM# 988 500 FRANCS
17.0000 g., 0.9200 Gold .5029 oz. AGW **Series:** 1992 Olympics
Obv: Modern and old style slalom skiers

Date	Mintage	F	VF	XF	Unc	BU
1990 Proof	8,000	Value: 360				

KM# 977 500 FRANCS
17.0000 g., 0.9200 Gold .5029 oz. AGW **Subject:** 100th Anniversary of Basketball **Obv:** Player jumping for lay-up shot, hoop behind **Rev:** Star, ring, and globe, denomination and date below

Date	Mintage	F	VF	XF	Unc	BU
1991 Proof	5,000	Value: 365				

KM# 997 500 FRANCS
17.0000 g., 0.9200 Gold .5029 oz. AGW **Series:** 1992 Olympics
Obv: 2 hockey players and large ibex ram

Date	Mintage	F	VF	XF	Unc	BU
1991 Proof	8,000	Value: 350				

KM# 998 500 FRANCS
17.0000 g., 0.9200 Gold .5029 oz. AGW

Date	Mintage	F	VF	XF	Unc	BU
1991 Proof	8,000	Value: 350				

KM# 999 500 FRANCS
17.0000 g., 0.9200 Gold .5029 oz. AGW **Series:** 1992 Olympics
Obv: Old style and modern ski jumpers

Date	Mintage	F	VF	XF	Unc	BU
1991 Proof	8,000	Value: 360				

KM# 1000 500 FRANCS
17.0000 g., 0.9200 Gold .5029 oz. AGW **Series:** 1992 Olympics
Subject: Pierre de Coubertin **Obv:** Head facing **Rev:** Cross on flame divides date and denomination, Olympic logo below

Date	Mintage	F	VF	XF	Unc	BU
1991 Proof	28,000	Value: 350				

KM# 1001 500 FRANCS
17.0000 g., 0.9200 Gold .5029 oz. AGW **Obv:** Building, denomination and date below **Rev:** Mozart in Paris at piano

Date	Mintage	F	VF	XF	Unc	BU
1991 Proof	Est. 5,000	Value: 365				

KM# 1024 500 FRANCS
31.1040 g., 0.9990 Gold 1.0000 oz. AGW **Series:** Bicentennial of the Louvre **Obv:** Mona Lisa **Obv. Designer:** Emile Rousseau **Rev:** Pyramids front building, date and denomination below

Date	Mintage	F	VF	XF	Unc	BU
1993	—	—	—	—	—	—
1993 Proof	5,000	Value: 750				
1994 Proof	5,000	Value: 800				

KM# 1025.1 500 FRANCS
31.1040 g., 0.9990 Gold 1.0000 oz. AGW **Series:** Bicentennial of the Louvre **Obv:** Venus de Milo

Date	Mintage	F	VF	XF	Unc	BU
1993	—	—	—	—	—	—
1993 Proof	5,000	Value: 750				

KM# 1026 500 FRANCS
155.5175 g., 0.9990 Gold 5.0000 oz. AGW **Series:** Bicentennial of the Louvre **Obv:** Liberty **Rev:** Pyramids front building, date and denomination below

Date	Mintage	F	VF	XF	Unc	BU
1993 Proof	99	Value: 3,500				
1994 Proof	99	Value: 3,750				

KM# 1027 500 FRANCS
155.5175 g., 0.9990 Gold 5.0000 oz. AGW **Series:** Bicentennial of the Louvre **Obv:** Mona Lisa **Rev:** Patterned pyramids front building

Date	Mintage	F	VF	XF	Unc	BU
1993 Proof	99	Value: 3,750				
1994 Proof	99	Value: 3,800				

KM# 1028 500 FRANCS
17.0000 g., 0.9200 Gold .5028 oz. AGW **Subject:** Jean Moulin
Obv: Head facing
Date	Mintage	F	VF	XF	Unc	BU
1993 Proof	5,000	Value: 375				

KM# 1183 500 FRANCS
155.5175 g., 0.9990 Gold 5.0000 oz. AGW **Series:** Bicentennial of the Louvre **Obv:** Victory
Date	Mintage	F	VF	XF	Unc	BU
1993 Proof	99	Value: 4,150				
1994 Proof	99	Value: 4,250				

KM# 1184 500 FRANCS
155.5175 g., 0.9990 Gold 5.0000 oz. AGW **Series:** Bicentennial of the Louvre **Obv:** Napoleon and Josephine
Date	Mintage	F	VF	XF	Unc	BU
1993 Proof	99	Value: 3,750				
1994 Proof	99	Value: 3,800				

KM# 1185 500 FRANCS
155.5175 g., 0.9990 Gold 5.0000 oz. AGW **Series:** Bicentennial of the Louvre **Obv:** Marie Marguerite
Date	Mintage	F	VF	XF	Unc	BU
1993 Proof	99	Value: 3,750				
1994 Proof	99	Value: 3,800				

KM# 1025.2 500 FRANCS
155.5000 g., 0.9990 Gold 4.9944 oz. AGW, 50 mm. **Obv:** Venus de Milo **Rev:** The Louvre Building entrance above value
Date	Mintage	F	VF	XF	Unc	BU
1993 Proof	99	Value: 3,500				

KM# 1399 500 FRANCS
155.5175 g., 0.9990 Gold 4.995 oz. AGW, 50 mm.
Subject: Venus De Milo **Edge:** Plain
Date	Mintage	F	VF	XF	Unc	BU
1993A Proof	99	Value: 3,750				

KM# 1049 500 FRANCS
17.0000 g., 0.9200 Gold .5028 oz. AGW **Subject:** Winston Churchill **Obv:** Bust right, denomination and date **Rev:** Eleven line inscription on flag design, rampant lion at right
Date	Mintage	F	VF	XF	Unc	BU
1994 Proof	Est. 2,000	Value: 375				

KM# 1051 500 FRANCS
17.0000 g., 0.9200 Gold .5028 oz. AGW **Subject:** General Leclerc **Obv:** Bust facing
Date	Mintage	F	VF	XF	Unc	BU
1994 Proof	Est. 2,000	Value: 375				

KM# 1050 500 FRANCS
17.0000 g., 0.9200 Gold .5028 oz. AGW **Subject:** General de Gaulle **Obv:** 3/4 bust of General de Gaulle in front of microphone
Date	Mintage	F	VF	XF	Unc	BU
1994 Proof	Est. 5,000	Value: 375				

KM# 1052 500 FRANCS
17.0000 g., 0.9200 Gold .5028 oz. AGW **Subject:** General Marie Pierre Koenig **Obv:** Bust looking left
Date	Mintage	F	VF	XF	Unc	BU
1994 Proof	Est. 2,000	Value: 375				

KM# 1053 500 FRANCS
17.0000 g., 0.9200 Gold .5028 oz. AGW **Subject:** General Juin **Obv:** Bust right, map of Italy at right
Date	Mintage	F	VF	XF	Unc	BU
1994 Proof	Est. 2,000	Value: 375				

KM# 1054 500 FRANCS
17.0000 g., 0.9200 Gold .5028 oz. AGW **Subject:** Dwight David Eisenhower **Obv:** Uniformed bust left
Date	Mintage	F	VF	XF	Unc	BU
1994 Proof	Est. 2,000	Value: 375				

KM# 1055 500 FRANCS
17.0000 g., 0.9200 Gold .5028 oz. AGW **Rev:** Church of Sainte - Mere - Eglise, parachute behind
Date	Mintage	F	VF	XF	Unc	BU
1994 Proof	Est. 2,000	Value: 375				

KM# 1056 500 FRANCS
17.0000 g., 0.9200 Gold .5028 oz. AGW **Subject:** General de Lattre de Tassigny **Obv:** Head right
Date	Mintage	F	VF	XF	Unc	BU
1994 Proof	Est. 2,000	Value: 375				

KM# 1057 500 FRANCS
17.0000 g., 0.9200 Gold .5028 oz. AGW **Subject:** Liberation of Paris **Obv:** Triumphant troops marching down Champs Elysees
Date	Mintage	F	VF	XF	Unc	BU
1994 Proof	Est. 5,000	Value: 375				

KM# 1058 500 FRANCS
17.0000 g., 0.9200 Gold .5028 oz. AGW **Obv:** Heads of de Gaulle and Adenauer facing the center, date below
Date	Mintage	F	VF	XF	Unc	BU
1994 Proof	Est. 2,000	Value: 365				

KM# 1059 500 FRANCS
16.9700 g., 0.9170 Gold .5000 oz. AGW **Subject:** 1996 Olympics **Obv:** Head facing, date and denomination **Rev:** Archer in front of Eiffel Tower **Rev. Designer:** Joaquin Jimenez
Edge Lettering: CITIUS ALTIUS FORTTUS
Date	Mintage	F	VF	XF	Unc	BU
1994 Proof	60,000	Value: 350				

KM# 1074 500 FRANCS
31.0350 g., 0.9990 Gold 1.0000 oz. AGW **Series:** Centennial of Cinema **Subject:** Lumiere Brothers **Obv:** Antique camera **Rev:** Conjoined busts right
Date	Mintage	F	VF	XF	Unc	BU
1994 Proof	3,000	Value: 900				

KM# 1078 500 FRANCS
31.0350 g., 0.9990 Gold 1.0000 oz. AGW **Series:** Centennial of Cinema **Subject:** Charlie Chaplan **Obv:** Antique movie camera **Rev:** Head facing
Date	Mintage	F	VF	XF	Unc	BU
1994 Proof	3,000	Value: 900				

KM# 1079 500 FRANCS
155.5175 g., 0.9990 Gold 5.0000 oz. AGW **Series:** Centennial of Cinema **Subject:** Charlie Chaplan **Obv:** Antique movie camera **Rev:** Head facing
Date	Mintage	F	VF	XF	Unc	BU
1994 Proof	99	Value: 3,750				

KM# 1186 500 FRANCS
17.0000 g., 0.9200 Gold .5028 oz. AGW **Series:** Centennial of Cinema **Rev:** Voltaire
Date	Mintage	F	VF	XF	Unc	BU
1994 Proof	350	Value: 385				

230 FRANCE

KM# 1082 500 FRANCS
31.0350 g., 0.9990 Gold 1.0000 oz. AGW **Series:** Centennial of Cinema **Subject:** Leon Gaumont **Obv:** Antique movie camera **Rev:** Head facing

Date	Mintage	F	VF	XF	Unc	BU
1995 Proof	3,000	Value: 900				

KM# 1083 500 FRANCS
155.5175 g., 0.9990 Gold 5.0000 oz. AGW **Series:** Centennial of Cinema **Subject:** Leon Gaumont **Obv:** Antique movie camera **Rev:** Head facing

Date	Mintage	F	VF	XF	Unc	BU
1995 Proof	99	Value: 3,500				

KM# 1086 500 FRANCS
31.0350 g., 0.9990 Gold 1.0000 oz. AGW **Series:** Centennial of Cinema **Subject:** Jean Renoir **Obv:** Antique movie camera **Rev:** Head 3/4 right

Date	Mintage	F	VF	XF	Unc	BU
1995 Proof	3,000	Value: 900				

KM# 1087 500 FRANCS
155.5175 g., 0.9990 Gold 5.0000 oz. AGW **Series:** Centennial of Cinema **Subject:** Jean Renoir **Obv:** Antique movie camera **Rev:** Head 3/4 right

Date	Mintage	F	VF	XF	Unc	BU
1995 Proof	99	Value: 3,750				

KM# 1090 500 FRANCS
31.0350 g., 0.9990 Gold 1.0000 oz. AGW **Series:** Centennial of Cinema **Subject:** Alfred Hitchcock **Obv:** Antique movie camera **Rev:** Bust 3/4 facing

Date	Mintage	F	VF	XF	Unc	BU
1995 Proof	3,000	Value: 900				

KM# 1091 500 FRANCS
155.5175 g., 0.9990 Gold 5.0000 oz. AGW **Series:** Centennial of Cinema **Subject:** Alfred Hitchcock **Obv:** Antique movie camera **Rev:** Bust 3/4 facing

Date	Mintage	F	VF	XF	Unc	BU
1995 Proof	99	Value: 3,500				

KM# 1094 500 FRANCS
31.0350 g., 0.9990 Gold 1.0000 oz. AGW **Series:** Centennial of Cinema **Subject:** Greta Garbo 1905-1990; actress in "Camille & Ninotchka" **Obv:** Antique movie camera **Rev:** Head with high collar right

Date	Mintage	F	VF	XF	Unc	BU
1995 Proof	3,000	Value: 900				

KM# 1095 500 FRANCS
155.5175 g., 0.9990 Gold 5.0000 oz. AGW **Series:** Centennial of Cinema **Subject:** Greta Garbo 1905-1990; actress in "Camille & Ninotchka" **Obv:** Antique movie camera **Rev:** Head with high collar right

Date	Mintage	F	VF	XF	Unc	BU
1995 Proof	99	Value: 3,750				

KM# 1098 500 FRANCS
31.0350 g., 0.9990 Gold 1.0000 oz. AGW **Series:** Centennial of Cinema **Subject:** Audrey Hepburn **Obv:** Antique movie camera **Rev:** Head 3/4 left

Date	Mintage	F	VF	XF	Unc	BU
1994 Proof	3,000	Value: 900				

KM# 1099 500 FRANCS
155.5175 g., 0.9990 Gold 5.0000 oz. AGW **Series:** Centennial of Cinema **Subject:** Audrey Hepburn **Obv:** Antique movie camera **Rev:** Head 3/4 left

Date	Mintage	F	VF	XF	Unc	BU
1994 Proof	99	Value: 3,500				

KM# 1102 500 FRANCS
31.0350 g., 0.9990 Gold 1.0000 oz. AGW **Series:** Centennial of Cinema **Subject:** Federico Fellini **Obv:** Antique movie camera **Rev:** Bust 3/4 right

Date	Mintage	F	VF	XF	Unc	BU
1995 Proof	3,000	Value: 900				

KM# 1103 500 FRANCS
155.5175 g., 0.9990 Gold 5.0000 oz. AGW **Series:** Centennial of Cinema **Subject:** Federico Fellini **Obv:** Antique movie camera **Rev:** Bust 3/4 right

Date	Mintage	F	VF	XF	Unc	BU
1995 Proof	99	Value: 3,500				

KM# 1106 500 FRANCS
31.0350 g., 0.9990 Gold 1.0000 oz. AGW **Series:** Centennial of Cinema **Subject:** Yves Montand **Obv:** Antique movie camera **Rev:** Bust 3/4 facing

Date	Mintage	F	VF	XF	Unc	BU
1994 Proof	3,000	Value: 900				

KM# 1107 500 FRANCS
155.5175 g., 0.9990 Gold 5.0000 oz. AGW **Series:** Centennial of Cinema **Subject:** Yves Montand **Obv:** Antique movie camera **Rev:** Bust 3/4 facing

Date	Mintage	F	VF	XF	Unc	BU
1994 Proof	99	Value: 3,500				

KM# 1110 500 FRANCS
31.0350 g., 0.9990 Gold 1.0000 oz. AGW **Series:** Centennial of Cinema **Subject:** Romy Schneider **Obv:** Antique movie camera **Rev:** Bust 3/4 left

Date	Mintage	F	VF	XF	Unc	BU
1995 Proof	3,000	Value: 900				

KM# 1111 500 FRANCS
155.5175 g., 0.9990 Gold 5.0000 oz. AGW **Series:** Centennial of Cinema **Subject:** Romy Schneider **Obv:** Antique movie camera **Rev:** Bust 3/4 left

Date	Mintage	F	VF	XF	Unc	BU
1995 Proof	99	Value: 3,450				

KM# 1117 500 FRANCS
17.0000 g., 0.9200 Gold .5028 oz. AGW **Subject:** V.E. Day **Obv:** Victory in Europe date May 8, 1945, denomination **Rev:** Birds in flight above banners, PAX below

Date	Mintage	F	VF	XF	Unc	BU
1995 Proof	5,000	Value: 375				

KM# 1135 500 FRANCS
17.0000 g., 0.9200 Gold .5028 oz. AGW **Obv:** Louis Pasteur

Date	Mintage	F	VF	XF	Unc	BU
1995 Proof	1,000	Value: 385				

KM# 1137 500 FRANCS
17.0000 g., 0.9200 Gold .5028 oz. AGW **Obv:** Jean de la Fountain

Date	Mintage	F	VF	XF	Unc	BU
1995 Proof	1,000	Value: 385				

KM# 1311 500 FRANCS
155.5000 g., 0.9990 Gold 4.9944 oz. AGW, 50 mm. **Series:** Centennial of Cinema **Subject:** Gerard Philipe **Obv:** Antique movie camera **Rev:** Bust 3/4 facing

Date	Mintage	F	VF	XF	Unc	BU
1995 Proof	99	Value: 3,500				

KM# 1312 500 FRANCS
155.5000 g., 0.9990 Gold 4.9944 oz. AGW, 50 mm. **Series:** Centennial of Cinema **Subject:** George Melies **Obv:** Antique movie camera **Rev:** Head facing

Date	Mintage	F	VF	XF	Unc	BU
1995 Proof	99	Value: 3,500				

KM# 1313 500 FRANCS
155.5000 g., 0.9990 Gold 4.9944 oz. AGW, 50 mm. **Series:** Centennial of Cinema **Subject:** Arletty **Obv:** Antique movie camera **Rev:** Head left

Date	Mintage	F	VF	XF	Unc	BU
1995 Proof	99	Value: 3,500				

KM# 1314 500 FRANCS
155.5000 g., 0.9990 Gold 4.9944 oz. AGW, 50 mm. **Series:** Centennial of Cinema **Subject:** Marcel Pagnol **Obv:** Antique movie camera **Rev:** Head 3/4 left

Date	Mintage	F	VF	XF	Unc	BU
1995 Proof	—	Value: 3,500				

KM# 1139 500 FRANCS
17.0000 g., 0.9200 Gold .5028 oz. AGW **Subject:** 300th Anniversary - Death of Marie de Sevigne; letter writer, 1626-1696 **Obv:** Bust 1/2 left

Date	Mintage	F	VF	XF	Unc	BU
1996 Proof	500	Value: 675				

KM# 1181 500 FRANCS
17.0000 g., 0.9200 Gold .5028 oz. AGW **Subject:** King Clovis I **Obv:** Bust facing

Date	Mintage	F	VF	XF	Unc	BU
1996 Proof	250	Value: 700				

FRANCE 231

KM# 1197 500 FRANCS
17.0000 g., 0.9200 Gold .5028 oz. AGW **Subject:** Georges Guynemer **Obv:** Bust 3/4 facing **Rev:** Stork emblem and denomination

Date	Mintage	F	VF	XF	Unc	BU
1997 Proof	300	Value: 600				

KM# 1199 500 FRANCS
17.0000 g., 0.9200 Gold .5028 oz. AGW **Subject:** Pierre and Marie Curie 1867-1934, physicist - chemist **Obv:** Conjoined busts left **Rev:** Denomination

Date	Mintage	F	VF	XF	Unc	BU
1997 Proof	300	Value: 600				

KM# 1200 500 FRANCS
17.0000 g., 0.9200 Gold .5028 oz. AGW **Subject:** Andre Malraux **Obv:** Head facing **Rev:** Cats flanking denomination

Date	Mintage	F	VF	XF	Unc	BU
1997 Proof	300	Value: 600				

KM# 1202 500 FRANCS
17.0000 g., 0.9200 Gold .5028 oz. AGW **Subject:** Marquis de Condorcet **Obv:** Head right **Rev:** Denomination

Date	Mintage	F	VF	XF	Unc	BU
1998 Proof	300	Value: 600				

KM# 1204 500 FRANCS
17.0000 g., 0.9200 Gold .5028 oz. AGW **Subject:** Gaspard Monge **Obv:** Head 1/2 right **Rev:** Denomination

Date	Mintage	F	VF	XF	Unc	BU
1998 Proof	300	Value: 600				

KM# 1315 500 FRANCS - 75 EURO
155.5000 g., 0.9990 Gold 4.9944 oz. AGW, 50 mm.
Subject: "The Thinker" by Auguste Rodin **Obv:** Seated statue left **Rev:** Denominations-(francs and euros)

Date	Mintage	F	VF	XF	Unc	BU
1996 Proof	99	Value: 3,500				

KM# 1316 500 FRANCS - 75 EURO
155.5000 g., 0.9990 Gold 4.9944 oz. AGW, 50 mm.
Subject: Chinese Horseman **Obv:** Equestrian statue **Rev:** Denominations-(francs and euros)

Date	Mintage	F	VF	XF	Unc	BU
1996 Proof	99	Value: 3,500				

KM# 1317 500 FRANCS - 75 EURO
155.5000 g., 0.9990 Gold 4.9944 oz. AGW, 50 mm.
Subject: Klimt's "The Kiss" **Obv:** Two figures embraced **Rev:** Denominations-(francs and euros)

Date	Mintage	F	VF	XF	Unc	BU
1997 Proof	—	Value: 3,500				

KM# 1318 500 FRANCS - 75 EURO
155.5000 g., 0.9990 Gold 4.9944 oz. AGW, 50 mm.
Subject: Durer's Self Portrait **Obv:** Bust facing **Rev:** Denominations-(francs and euros)

Date	Mintage	F	VF	XF	Unc	BU
1997 Proof	99	Value: 3,500				

232 FRANCE

KM# 1319 500 FRANCS - 75 EURO
155.5000 g., 0.9990 Gold 4.9944 oz. AGW, 50 mm.
Obv: Japanese woman carrying a case **Rev:** Denominations-(francs and euros)
Date	Mintage	F	VF	XF	Unc	BU
1997 Proof	99	Value: 3,500				

KM# 1320 500 FRANCS - 75 EURO
155.5000 g., 0.9990 Gold 4.9944 oz. AGW, 50 mm.
Subject: "The Little Dancer" by Degas **Obv:** Figure in tutu left **Rev:** Denominations-(francs and euros)
Date	Mintage	F	VF	XF	Unc	BU
1997 Proof	99	Value: 3,500				

KM# 1257 655.957 FRANCS
31.1040 g., 0.9990 Gold .9990 oz. AGW **Series:** Euro conversion **Obv:** Country names with euro-currency equivalents around "RF", denomination and French coin designs **Rev:** Europa allegorical portrait **Edge:** Plain
Date	Mintage	F	VF	XF	Unc	BU
1999 Proof	2,000	Value: 775				

KM# 1261 655.957 FRANCS
31.1040 g., 0.9990 Gold .9990 oz. AGW **Obv:** Country names with euro-currency equivalents around "RF", denomination and French euro coin design
Date	Mintage	F	VF	XF	Unc	BU
2000 Proof	2,000	Value: 775				

KM# 1247 655.957 FRANCS
15.5520 g., 0.9990 Gold .4995 oz. AGW **Series:** European Art Styles - Renaissance **Obv:** Europe allegorical portrait **Rev:** Greek and Roman style buildings
Date	Mintage	F	VF	XF	Unc	BU
2000 Proof	2,000	Value: 485				

KM# 1248 655.957 FRANCS
15.5520 g., 0.9990 Gold .4995 oz. AGW **Series:** European Art Styles - Roman **Rev:** Roman sculpture and ancient buildings
Date	Mintage	F	VF	XF	Unc	BU
2000 Proof	2,000	Value: 485				

KM# 1249 655.957 FRANCS
15.5520 g., 0.9990 Gold .4995 oz. AGW **Series:** European Art Styles - Gothic **Rev:** Gothic sculpture and buildings
Date	Mintage	F	VF	XF	Unc	BU
2000 Proof	2,000	Value: 485				

KM# 1250 655.957 FRANCS
15.5520 g., 0.9990 Gold .4995 oz. AGW **Series:** European Art Styles - Renaissance **Rev:** Renaissance buildings
Date	Mintage	F	VF	XF	Unc	BU
2000 Proof	2,000	Value: 485				

KM# 1251 655.957 FRANCS
15.5520 g., 0.9990 Gold .4995 oz. AGW **Series:** European Art Styles - Classic and Baroque **Rev:** Classic and Baroque art
Date	Mintage	F	VF	XF	Unc	BU
2000 Proof	2,000	Value: 485				

KM# 1252 655.957 FRANCS
15.5520 g., 0.9990 Gold .4995 oz. AGW **Series:** European Art Styles - Art Nouveau **Rev:** Arches and scrollwork
Date	Mintage	F	VF	XF	Unc	BU
2000 Proof	2,000	Value: 485				

KM# 1253 655.957 FRANCS
15.5520 g., 0.9990 Gold .4995 oz. AGW **Series:** European Art Styles - Modern **Rev:** Modern artistic designs
Date	Mintage	F	VF	XF	Unc	BU
2000 Proof	2,000	Value: 485				

KM# 1267 655.957 FRANCS
31.1035 g., 0.9990 Gold 1.0000 oz. AGW **Subject:** Last Year of the French Franc **Obv:** French and other European euro currency equivalents **Rev:** Europa allegorical portrait, date below, "last year of the franc" logo after the date **Edge:** Plain
Date	Mintage	F	VF	XF	Unc	BU
2001 Proof	2,000	Value: 675				

KM# 1267.1 655.957 FRANCS
155.5175 g., 0.9990 Gold 5.0000 oz. AGW **Obv:** French and other European euro currency equivalents **Rev:** Europa allegorical portrait, date below, "last year of the franc" after the date **Edge:** Plain
Date	Mintage	F	VF	XF	Unc	BU
2001 Proof	99	Value: 4,000				

KM# 1279 655.957 FRANCS
17.0000 g., 0.9200 Gold .5028 oz. AGW **Subject:** Motto Series **Obv:** Denomination **Rev:** FRATERNITE **Edge:** Reeded
Date	Mintage	F	VF	XF	Unc	BU
2001 Proof	62	Value: 375				

KM# 1280 655.957 FRANCS
17.0000 g., 0.9200 Gold .5028 oz. AGW **Subject:** Motto Series **Obv:** Denomination **Rev:** EGALITE
Date	Mintage	F	VF	XF	Unc	BU
2001 Proof	64	Value: 375				

KM# 1281 655.957 FRANCS
17.0000 g., 0.9200 Gold .5028 oz. AGW **Subject:** Motto Series **Obv:** Denomination **Rev:** LIBERTE
Date	Mintage	F	VF	XF	Unc	BU
2001 Proof	63	Value: 375				

FRANCE 233

ECU / FRANCS COINAGE
European Currency Units

KM# 990 500 FRANCS - 70 ECUS
17.0000 g., 0.9200 Gold .5029 oz. AGW **Obv:** Center monogram divides date and denomination, laurel spray below **Rev:** Stylized head facing above denomination

Date	Mintage	F	VF	XF	Unc	BU
1990 Proof	5,000	Value: 385				

KM# 990a 500 FRANCS - 70 ECUS
20.0000 g., 0.9990 Platinum .6431 oz. APW **Obv:** Monogram divides denomination and date, spray below **Rev:** Stylized head facing, denomintion below

Date	Mintage	F	VF	XF	Unc	BU
1990 Proof	2,000	Value: 825				

KM# 1003a 500 FRANCS - 70 ECUS
20.0000 g., 0.9990 Platinum .6431 oz. APW **Subject:** Descartes **Obv:** Finger pointing to page with stars, denomination **Rev:** Head 3/4 facing

Date	Mintage	F	VF	XF	Unc	BU
1991 Proof	1,000	Value: 825				

KM# 1003 500 FRANCS - 70 ECUS
17.0000 g., 0.9200 Gold .5029 oz. AGW **Subject:** Descartes **Obv:** Finger pointing to page with stars **Rev:** Head 3/4 facing

Date	Mintage	F	VF	XF	Unc	BU
1991 Proof	3,000	Value: 425				

KM# 1013 500 FRANCS - 70 ECUS
17.0000 g., 0.9200 Gold .5029 oz. AGW **Subject:** Jean Monet **Obv:** Denomination and date within legend at center, chain surrounds, RF below **Rev:** Head left, denomination at right

Date	Mintage	F	VF	XF	Unc	BU
1992 Proof	5,000	Value: 400				

KM# 1013a 500 FRANCS - 70 ECUS
20.0000 g., 0.9990 Platinum .6431 oz. APW **Subject:** Jean Monet **Obv:** Denomination and date within legend at center, chain surrounds, RF below **Rev:** Head 3/4 left

Date	Mintage	F	VF	XF	Unc	BU
1992 Proof	2,000	Value: 825				

KM# 1033 500 FRANCS - 70 ECUS
17.0000 g., 0.9200 Gold .5029 oz. AGW **Subject:** Mediterranean Games **Obv:** Head left, denomination below **Rev:** Statue divides denomination above, rings divide date below

Date	Mintage	F	VF	XF	Unc	BU
1993 Proof	3,000	Value: 425				

KM# 1034 500 FRANCS - 70 ECUS
17.0000 g., 0.9200 Gold .5029 oz. AGW **Obv:** Denominations-(francs/ecus) **Rev:** Arc de Triumph, date below

Date	Mintage	F	VF	XF	Unc	BU
1993 Proof	5,000	Value: 385				

KM# 1034a 500 FRANCS - 70 ECUS
19.8000 g., 0.9900 Platinum .6303 oz. APW **Obv:** Denominations-(francs/ecus) **Rev:** Arc de Triumph

Date	Mintage	F	VF	XF	Unc	BU
1993 Proof	2,000	Value: 800				

KM# 1035 500 FRANCS - 70 ECUS
17.0000 g., 0.9200 Gold .5029 oz. AGW **Obv:** Denominations-(francs/ecus) **Rev:** Brandenburg Gate, date above

Date	Mintage	F	VF	XF	Unc	BU
1993 Proof	5,000	Value: 385				

KM# 1035a 500 FRANCS - 70 ECUS
19.8000 g., 0.9900 Platinum .6303 oz. APW **Obv:** Denominations-(francs/ecus) **Rev:** Brandenburg Gate

Date	Mintage	F	VF	XF	Unc	BU
1993 Proof	2,000	Value: 800				

KM# 1061 500 FRANCS - 70 ECUS
17.0000 g., 0.9200 Gold .5029 oz. AGW **Obv:** Stars surround denominations, (francs/euros) **Rev:** Channel Tunnel

Date	Mintage	F	VF	XF	Unc	BU
1994 Proof	5,000	Value: 375				

KM# 1069 500 FRANCS - 70 ECUS
17.0000 g., 0.9200 Gold .5028 oz. AGW **Obv:** Stars surround denominations, (francs/euros) **Rev:** St. Mark's Cathedral, Venice, date below

Date	Mintage	F	VF	XF	Unc	BU
1994 Proof	5,000	Value: 385				

KM# 1069a 500 FRANCS - 70 ECUS
20.0000 g., 0.9990 Platinum .6431 oz. APW **Obv:** Stars surround denominations, (francs/euros) **Rev:** St. Mark's Cathedral, Venice

Date	Mintage	F	VF	XF	Unc	BU
1994 Proof	2,000	Value: 825				

KM# 1071 500 FRANCS - 70 ECUS
17.0000 g., 0.9200 Gold .5028 oz. AGW **Obv:** Stars surround denominations, (francs/euros) **Rev:** Big Ben, London, date below

Date	Mintage	F	VF	XF	Unc	BU
1994 Proof	5,000	Value: 385				

KM# 1071a 500 FRANCS - 70 ECUS
20.0000 g., 0.9990 Platinum .6431 oz. APW **Obv:** Stars surround denominations, (francs/euros) **Rev:** Big Ben, London

Date	Mintage	F	VF	XF	Unc	BU
1994 Proof	2,000	Value: 825				

KM# 1113 500 FRANCS - 70 ECUS
17.0000 g., 0.9200 Gold .5028 oz. AGW **Obv:** Stars surround denominations, (francs/euros) **Rev:** The Alhambra, Granada

Date	Mintage	F	VF	XF	Unc	BU
1995 Proof	5,000	Value: 385				

KM# 1113a 500 FRANCS - 70 ECUS
20.0000 g., 0.9990 Platinum .6431 oz. APW **Obv:** Stars surround denominations, (francs/euros) **Rev:** The Alhambra, Granada

Date	Mintage	F	VF	XF	Unc	BU
1995 Proof	2,000	Value: 825				

KM# 1115 500 FRANCS - 70 ECUS
17.0000 g., 0.9200 Gold .5028 oz. AGW **Obv:** Stars surround denominations, (francs/euros) **Rev:** The Parthenon, Athens

Date	Mintage	F	VF	XF	Unc	BU
1995 Proof	5,000	Value: 385				

KM# 1115a 500 FRANCS - 70 ECUS
20.0000 g., 0.9990 Platinum .6431 oz. APW **Obv:** Stars surround denominations, (francs/euros) **Rev:** The Parthenon, Athens

Date	Mintage	F	VF	XF	Unc	BU
1995 Proof	2,000	Value: 825				

MEDALLIC COINAGE

KM# M27a 20 FRANCS
Gold **Subject:** President of Rene Coty Visit **Obv:** Head of Republic **Rev:** Coin press

Date	Mintage	F	VF	XF	Unc	BU
1955	—	—	300	350	550	—

KM# M28a 20 FRANCS
Gold **Subject:** Visit by President of Rene Coty **Obv:** Head of Republic **Rev:** Coin press

Date	Mintage	F	VF	XF	Unc	BU
1955	—	—	300	350	550	—

PRETENDER COINAGE

X# 37.2b 5 FRANCS
Gold **Ruler:** Henry V **Edge:** Reeded **Note:** Prev. KM#PTE37.2b.

Date	Mintage	F	VF	XF	Unc	BU
1871	—	—	—	4,500	7,000	—

EURO / FRANCS COINAGE

KM# 1125 100 FRANCS - 15 EURO
17.0000 g., 0.9200 Gold .5028 oz. AGW **Series:** Museum Treasures **Subject:** La Source by Raphael Jean A.D. Ingres **Obv:** Standing nude facing **Rev:** Denominations, (francs/euros), on lined field, stars surround

Date	Mintage	F	VF	XF	Unc	BU
1996 Proof	5,000	Value: 395				

KM# 1126 100 FRANCS - 15 EURO
17.0000 g., 0.9200 Gold .5028 oz. AGW **Series:** Museum Treasures **Subject:** Fife Player by Edouard Manet **Obv:** Standing figure facing **Rev:** Denominations, (francs/euros), on lined field, stars surround

Date	Mintage	F	VF	XF	Unc	BU
1996 Proof	5,000	Value: 385				

KM# 1127 100 FRANCS - 15 EURO
17.0000 g., 0.9200 Gold .5028 oz. AGW **Series:** Museum Treasures **Subject:** Shang Dynasty Elephant **Obv:** Elephant left **Rev:** Denominations, (francs/euros), on lined field, stars surround

Date	Mintage	F	VF	XF	Unc	BU
1996 Proof	5,000	Value: 385				

KM# 1149 100 FRANCS - 15 EURO
17.0000 g., 0.9200 Gold .5028 oz. AGW **Series:** Museum Treasures **Subject:** Van Gogh, Self Portrait **Obv:** Bust 3/4 left **Rev:** Denominations, (francs/euros), on lined field, stars surround

Date	Mintage	F	VF	XF	Unc	BU
1996 Proof	5,000	Value: 385				

KM# 1150 100 FRANCS - 15 EURO
17.0000 g., 0.9200 Gold .5028 oz. AGW **Series:** Museum Treasures **Subject:** Clothed Maya by Goya **Obv:** Reclined figure **Rev:** Stars surround denominations, (francs/euros), on lined field

Date	Mintage	F	VF	XF	Unc	BU
1996 Proof	5,000	Value: 385				

KM# 1159 100 FRANCS - 15 EURO
17.0000 g., 0.9200 Gold .5028 oz. AGW **Series:** Museum Treasures **Subject:** Chinese Horseman **Obv:** Equestrian statue **Rev:** Stars surround denominations, (francs/euros), on lined field

Date	Mintage	F	VF	XF	Unc	BU
1996 Proof	5,000	Value: 385				

KM# 1141a 500 FRANCS - 75 EURO
20.0000 g., 0.9990 Platinum .6431 oz. APW **Subject:** St. Stephen's Cathedral, Vienna **Obv:** Denominations-(francs/ecus) **Rev:** Cathedral

Date	Mintage	F	VF	XF	Unc	BU
1996 Prof	2,000	Value: 825				

KM# 1143a 500 FRANCS - 75 EURO
20.0000 g., 0.9990 Platinum .6431 oz. APW **Subject:** Grand Place, Bruxelles **Obv:** Denominations-(francs/ecus) **Rev:** Buildings with tower

Date	Mintage	F	VF	XF	Unc	BU
1996 Proof	2,000	Value: 825				

KM# 1157a 500 FRANCS - 75 EURO
20.0000 g., 0.9990 Platinum .6431 oz. APW **Subject:** Amsterdam Magere Brug

Date	Mintage	F	VF	XF	Unc	BU
1996 Proof	2,000	Value: 825				

KM# 1128 500 FRANCS - 75 EURO
31.1035 g., 0.9990 Gold 1.0000 oz. AGW **Series:** Museum Treasures **Subject:** "The Thinker", by Auguste Rodin **Obv:** Seated statue left **Rev:** Stars surround denominations, (francs/euros), on lined field

234 FRANCE

Date	Mintage	F	VF	XF	Unc	BU
1996 Proof	5,000			Value: 725		

KM# 1129 500 FRANCS - 75 EURO
155.5175 g., 0.9990 Gold 5.0000 oz. AGW **Series:** Museum Treasures **Subject:** La Source by Raphael Jean A.D. Ingres **Obv:** Standing nude facing **Rev:** Stars surround denominations, (francs/euros), on lined field

Date	Mintage	F	VF	XF	Unc	BU
1996 Proof	99			Value: 3,500		

KM# 1130 500 FRANCS - 75 EURO
155.5175 g., 0.9990 Gold 5.0000 oz. AGW **Series:** Museum Treasures **Subject:** Fife Player by Edouard Manet **Obv:** Standing figure facing **Rev:** Stars surround denominations, (francs/euros), on lined field

Date	Mintage	F	VF	XF	Unc	BU
1996 Proof	99			Value: 3,500		

KM# 1131 500 FRANCS - 75 EURO
155.5175 g., 0.9990 Gold 5.0000 oz. AGW **Series:** Museum Treasures **Subject:** Shang Dynasty Elephant **Obv:** Elephant left **Rev:** Stars surround denominations, (francs/euros), on lined field

Date	Mintage	F	VF	XF	Unc	BU
1996 Proof	99			Value: 3,500		

KM# 1141 500 FRANCS - 75 EURO
17.0000 g., 0.9200 Gold .5028 oz. AGW **Subject:** St. Stephen's Cathedral, Vienna **Obv:** Denominations, (francs/euro), on field of stars **Rev:** Cathedral, date at right

Date	Mintage	F	VF	XF	Unc	BU
1996 Proof	5,000			Value: 385		

KM# 1143 500 FRANCS - 75 EURO
17.0000 g., 0.9200 Gold .5028 oz. AGW **Subject:** Grand Place, Bruxelles **Obv:** Denominations-(francs/ecus) **Rev:** Buildings with tower, date below

Date	Mintage	F	VF	XF	Unc	BU
1996 Proof	5,000			Value: 385		

KM# 1151 500 FRANCS - 75 EURO
31.1035 g., 0.9990 Gold 1.0000 oz. AGW **Series:** Museum Treasures **Subject:** David by Michaelangelo **Obv:** Standing nude **Rev:** Denominations, (francs/euros), on lined field, stars surround

Date	Mintage	F	VF	XF	Unc	BU
1996 Proof	5,000			Value: 725		

KM# 1152 500 FRANCS - 75 EURO
155.5175 g., 0.9990 Gold 5.0000 oz. AGW **Series:** Museum Treasures **Subject:** David by Michaelangelo **Obv:** Standing nude **Rev:** Denominations-(francs/ecus), on lined field, stars surround

Date	Mintage	F	VF	XF	Unc	BU
1996 Proof	99			Value: 3,500		

KM# 1153 500 FRANCS - 75 EURO
155.5175 g., 0.9990 Gold 5.0000 oz. AGW **Series:** Museum Treasures **Subject:** Vincent Van Gogh, Self Portrait **Obv:** Bust 3/4 left, RF and date at left **Rev:** Denominations-(francs/ecus), on lined field, stars surround

Date	Mintage	F	VF	XF	Unc	BU
1996 Proof	99			Value: 3,500		

KM# 1154 500 FRANCS - 75 EURO
155.5175 g., 0.9990 Gold 5.0000 oz. AGW **Series:** Museum Treasures **Subject:** Clothed Maya by Goya **Obv:** Reclined figure, RF and date at left **Rev:** Denominations-(francs/ecus), on lined field, stars surround

Date	Mintage	F	VF	XF	Unc	BU
1996 Proof	99			Value: 3,500		

KM# 1157 500 FRANCS - 75 EURO
17.0000 g., 0.9200 Gold .5028 oz. AGW **Subject:** Amsterdam Magere Brug

Date	Mintage	F	VF	XF	Unc	BU
1996 Proof	5,000			Value: 385		

KM# 1175 500 FRANCS - 75 EURO
17.0000 g., 0.9200 Gold .5028 oz. AGW **Subject:** Lisbon **Obv:** Denominations **Rev:** Castle-like building Tour de Belem, date below

Date	Mintage	F	VF	XF	Unc	BU
1997 Proof	5,000			Value: 395		

KM# 1175a 500 FRANCS - 75 EURO
20.0000 g., 0.9990 Platinum .6431 oz. APW **Subject:** Lisbon **Obv:** Denominations **Rev:** Castle-like building Tour de Belem

Date	Mintage	F	VF	XF	Unc	BU
1997 Proof	2,000			Value: 825		

KM# 1179a 500 FRANCS - 75 EURO
20.0000 g., 0.9990 Platinum .6431 oz. APW **Subject:** Copenhagen **Obv:** Denominations **Rev:** Statue of Copenhagen's Little Mermaid, Petite Siren

Date	Mintage	F	VF	XF	Unc	BU
1997 Proof	2,000			Value: 845		

KM# 1190a 500 FRANCS - 75 EURO
20.0000 g., 0.9990 Platinum .6431 oz. APW **Subject:** Ireland - Rock of Cashel **Obv:** Denomination **Rev:** Celtic cross and castle

Date	Mintage	F	VF	XF	Unc	BU
1997 Proof	2,000			Value: 825		

KM# 1192a 500 FRANCS - 75 EURO
20.0000 g., 0.9990 Platinum .6431 oz. APW **Subject:** Luxembourg-Wenceslas Wall **Obv:** Denomination **Rev:** Walled palace

Date	Mintage	F	VF	XF	Unc	BU
1997 Proof	2,000			Value: 825		

KM# 1179 500 FRANCS - 75 EURO
17.0000 g., 0.9200 Gold .5028 oz. AGW **Subject:** Copenhagen **Obv:** Denominations, (francs/euros), on field of stars **Rev:** Statue of Copenhagen's Little Mermaid, Petite Siren, date at right

Date	Mintage	F	VF	XF	Unc	BU
1997 Proof	5,000			Value: 500		

KM# 1190 500 FRANCS - 75 EURO
17.0000 g., 0.9200 Gold .5028 oz. AGW **Subject:** Ireland - Rock of Cashel **Obv:** Denomination **Rev:** Celtic cross and castle

Date	Mintage	F	VF	XF	Unc	BU
1997 Proof	5,000			Value: 450		

KM# 1192 500 FRANCS - 75 EURO
17.0000 g., 0.9200 Gold .5028 oz. AGW **Subject:** Luxembourg - Wenceslas Wall **Obv:** Denomination **Rev:** Walled palace

Date	Mintage	F	VF	XF	Unc	BU
1997 Proof	5,000			Value: 450		

KM# 1194 500 FRANCS - 75 EURO
17.0000 g., 0.9200 Gold .5028 oz. AGW **Subject:** Stockholm - Hotel de Ville **Obv:** Denomination **Rev:** Tower and building

Date	Mintage	F	VF	XF	Unc	BU
1997 Proof	5,000			Value: 450		

KM# 1177 500 FRANCS - 75 EURO
17.0000 g., 0.9200 Gold .5028 oz. AGW **Subject:** Helsinki **Obv:** Denominations **Rev:** Cathedrale Saint Nicholas, date below

Date	Mintage	F	VF	XF	Unc	BU
1997 Proof	5,000			Value: 400		

KM# 1194a 500 FRANCS - 75 EURO
20.0000 g., 0.9990 Platinum .5028 oz. APW **Subject:** Stockholm - Hotel de Ville **Obv:** Denomination **Rev:** Tower and building

Date	Mintage	F	VF	XF	Unc	BU
1997 Proof	2,000			Value: 700		

KM# 1177a 500 FRANCS - 75 EURO
20.0000 g., 0.9990 Platinum .6431 oz. APW **Subject:** Helsinki **Obv:** Denominations **Rev:** Cathedral, Cathedrale Saint Nicholas

Date	Mintage	F	VF	XF	Unc	BU
1997 Proof	2,000			Value: 825		

EURO COINAGE
European Union Issues

KM# 1331 1/4 EURO
3.1100 g., 0.9990 Gold 0.0999 oz. AGW, 15 mm. **Subject:** Children's Design **Obv:** Euro globe with children **Rev:** Denomination **Edge:** Plain

Date	Mintage	F	VF	XF	Unc	BU
2002 Proof	5,000			Value: 135		

FRANCE

KM# 1350 1/4 EURO
3.1100 g., 0.9999 Gold 0.1 oz. AGW, 15 mm. **Obv:** Obverse design of first one franc coin **Rev:** Reverse design of first one franc coin **Edge:** Plain

Date	Mintage	F	VF	XF	Unc	BU
2003 Proof	5,000	Value: 125				

KM# 1379 1-1/2 EURO
17.0000 g., 0.9200 Gold 0.5028 oz. AGW, 31 mm. **Obv:** Compass rose **Rev:** Ocean liner **Edge:** Plain

Date	Mintage	F	VF	XF	Unc	BU
2004 Proof	1,000	Value: 550				

KM# 1347 5 EURO
24.9000 g., 0.9000 Bi-Metallic Gold And Silver .900 Silver 22.2g planchet with .750 Gold 2.7 insert 0.7205 oz., 37 mm. **Obv:** The seed sower on gold insert **Rev:** Denomination and map **Edge:** Plain

Date	Mintage	F	VF	XF	Unc	BU
2003 Proof	10,000	Value: 475				

KM# 1371 5 EURO
24.9000 g., Bi-Metallic Gold And Silver .750 Gold 2.7 g insert on .900 Silver 22.2g planchet, 37 mm. **Obv:** The seed sower on gold insert **Rev:** French face map and denomination **Edge:** Plain

Date	Mintage	F	VF	XF	Unc	BU
2004 Proof	3,000	Value: 475				

KM# 1302 10 EURO
8.4500 g., 0.9990 Gold 0.2714 oz. AGW, 22 mm. **Subject:** Europa **Obv:** Eight French euro coin designs **Rev:** Portrait and flags design of 6.55957 francs KM-1265 **Edge:** Reeded

Date	Mintage	F	VF	XF	Unc	BU
2002 Proof	3,000	Value: 285				

KM# 1326 10 EURO
8.4500 g., 0.9200 Gold 0.2499 oz. AGW, 22 mm. **Obv:** Tour de France logo **Rev:** Cyclist going left **Edge:** Reeded

Date	Mintage	F	VF	XF	Unc	BU
2003A Proof	5,000	Value: 200				

KM# 1327 10 EURO
8.4500 g., 0.9200 Gold 0.2499 oz. AGW, 22 mm. **Obv:** Tour de France logo **Rev:** Group of cyclists and Arch de Triumph **Edge:** Reeded

Date	Mintage	F	VF	XF	Unc	BU
2003A Proof	5,000	Value: 200				

KM# 1328 10 EURO
8.4500 g., 0.9200 Gold 0.2499 oz. AGW, 22 mm. **Obv:** Tour de France logo **Rev:** Two cyclists and spectators **Edge:** Reeded

Date	Mintage	F	VF	XF	Unc	BU
2003A Proof	5,000	Value: 200				

KM# 1329 10 EURO
8.4500 g., 0.9200 Gold 0.2499 oz. AGW, 22 mm. **Obv:** Tour de France logo **Rev:** Two groups of cyclists **Edge:** Reeded

Date	Mintage	F	VF	XF	Unc	BU
2003A Proof	5,000	Value: 200				

KM# 1330 10 EURO
8.4500 g., 0.9200 Gold 0.2499 oz. AGW, 22 mm. **Obv:** Tour de France logo **Rev:** Cyclist, stop watch and gears **Edge:** Reeded

Date	Mintage	F	VF	XF	Unc	BU
2003A Proof	5,000	Value: 200				

KM# 1348 10 EURO
8.4500 g., 0.9200 Gold 0.2499 oz. AGW, 22 mm. **Obv:** The seed sower **Rev:** Denomination and map **Edge:** Plain

Date	Mintage	F	VF	XF	Unc	BU
2003 Proof	15,000	Value: 265				

KM# 1352 10 EURO
8.4500 g., 0.9200 Gold 0.2499 oz. AGW, 22 mm. **Obv:** Obverse design of first one franc coin **Rev:** Reverse design of first one franc coin **Edge:** Plain

Date	Mintage	F	VF	XF	Unc	BU
2003 Proof	10,000	Value: 265				

KM# 1362 10 EURO
8.4500 g., 0.9200 Gold 0.2499 oz. AGW, 22 mm. **Obv:** Pierre de Coubertin **Rev:** Olympic runners **Edge:** Plain

Date	Mintage	F	VF	XF	Unc	BU
2003 Proof	15,000	Value: 285				

KM# 1367 10 EURO
6.4100 g., 0.9000 Gold 0.1855 oz. AGW, 22 mm. **Obv:** Book, denomination and eagle **Rev:** Napoleon and coronation scene **Edge:** Plain

Date	Mintage	F	VF	XF	Unc	BU
2004 Proof	5,000	Value: 300				

KM# 1375 10 EURO
8.4500 g., 0.9200 Gold 0.2499 oz. AGW, 22 mm. **Obv:** Half soccer ball and denomination **Rev:** Eiffel tower and soccer balls **Edge:** Plain

Date	Mintage	F	VF	XF	Unc	BU
2004 Proof	10,000	Value: 300				

KM# 1392 10 EURO
8.4500 g., 0.9200 Gold 0.2499 oz. AGW, 22 mm. **Subject:** European Union Expansion **Obv:** Partial face and flags **Rev:** Puzzle map **Edge:** Reeded

Date	Mintage	F	VF	XF	Unc	BU
2004 Proof	5,000	Value: 245				

KM# 1403 10 EURO
8.4500 g., 0.9200 Gold 0.2499 oz. AGW, 22 mm. **Subject:** Jules Verne **Obv:** Various scenes from Verne's novel "Around The World in 80 Days" **Rev:** Jules Verne's portrait left of value and date

Date	Mintage	F	VF	XF	Unc	BU
2005 Proof	2,000	Value: 300				

KM# 1416 10 EURO
8.4500 g., 0.9200 Gold 0.2499 oz. AGW, 22 mm. **Obv:** Jean de la Fontaine, value, Chinese astrological animals, date, Paris mint privy marks but without national identification **Rev:** Dog in wreath **Edge:** Reeded **Note:** Anonymous issue

Date	Mintage	F	VF	XF	Unc	BU
2006 Proof	500	Value: 350				

KM# 1418 10 EURO
8.4500 g., 0.9200 Gold 0.2499 oz. AGW, 22 mm. **Obv:** Jean de la Fontaine, value, Chinese astrological animals, date, Paris mint privy marks but without national identification **Rev:** Pig in wreath **Edge:** Reeded **Note:** anonymous issue

Date	Mintage	F	VF	XF	Unc	BU
2007 Proof	500	Value: 350				

KM# 1306 20 EURO
17.0000 g., 0.9200 Gold 0.5028 oz. AGW, 31 mm. **Subject:** French Landmarks **Obv:** French map **Rev:** Le Mont St. Michel **Edge:** Plain

Date	Mintage	F	VF	XF	Unc	BU
2002 Proof	1,000	Value: 550				

KM# 1308 20 EURO
17.0000 g., 0.9200 Gold 0.5028 oz. AGW, 31 mm. **Subject:** French Landmarks **Obv:** French map **Rev:** La Butte Montmartre **Edge:** Plain

Date	Mintage	F	VF	XF	Unc	BU
2002 Proof	1,000	Value: 550				

KM# 1333 20 EURO
17.0000 g., 0.9200 Gold 0.5028 oz. AGW, 31 mm. **Obv:** Victor Hugo, denomination and map **Rev:** "Gavroche" **Edge:** Plain

Date	Mintage	F	VF	XF	Unc	BU
2002 Proof	2,000	Value: 475				

KM# 1334 20 EURO
17.0000 g., 0.9200 Gold 0.5028 oz. AGW, 31 mm. **Obv:** Tour de France logo **Rev:** Cyclist going left **Edge:** Plain

Date	Mintage	F	VF	XF	Unc	BU
2003 Proof	5,000	Value: 475				

KM# 1337 20 EURO
17.0000 g., 0.9200 Gold 0.5028 oz. AGW, 31 mm. **Obv:** Jefferson and Napoleon with Louisiana Purchase map **Rev:** Jazz musician, mansion and river boat **Edge:** Plain

Date	Mintage	F	VF	XF	Unc	BU
2003 Proof	1,000	Value: 525				

KM# 1339 20 EURO
17.0000 g., 0.9200 Gold 0.5028 oz. AGW, 31 mm. **Obv:** Curved cross design with multiple values **Rev:** Goddess Europa and flags **Edge:** Plain

Date	Mintage	F	VF	XF	Unc	BU
2003 Proof	3,000	Value: 525				

KM# 1342 20 EURO
17.0000 g., 0.9200 Gold 0.5028 oz. AGW, 31 mm. **Obv:** Denomination and compass face **Rev:** SS Normandie and New York City skyline **Edge:** Plain

Date	Mintage	F	VF	XF	Unc	BU
2003 Proof	1,000	Value: 525				

KM# 1344 20 EURO
17.0000 g., 0.9200 Gold 0.5028 oz. AGW, 31 mm. **Obv:** Denomination and compass face **Rev:** Airplane and Tokyo Geisha **Edge:** Plain

Date	Mintage	F	VF	XF	Unc	BU
2003 Proof	1,000	Value: 525				

KM# 1346 20 EURO
17.0000 g., 0.9200 Gold 0.5028 oz. AGW, 31 mm. **Obv:** Paul Gauguin **Rev:** Native woman **Edge:** Plain

Date	Mintage	F	VF	XF	Unc	BU
2003 Proof	2,000	Value: 545				

KM# 1349 20 EURO
17.0000 g., 0.9200 Gold 0.5028 oz. AGW, 31 mm. **Obv:** The seed sower **Rev:** Denomination and map **Edge:** Plain

Date	Mintage	F	VF	XF	Unc	BU
2003 Proof	5,000	Value: 575				

KM# 1354 20 EURO
17.0000 g., 0.9200 Gold 0.5028 oz. AGW, 31 mm. **Obv:** Mona Lisa **Rev:** Leonardo da Vinci and denomination **Edge:** Plain

Date	Mintage	F	VF	XF	Unc	BU
2003 Proof	1,000	Value: 545				

KM# 1356 20 EURO
17.0000 g., 0.9200 Gold 0.5028 oz. AGW, 31 mm. **Obv:** Map and denomination **Rev:** Chateau Chambord **Edge:** Plain

Date	Mintage	F	VF	XF	Unc	BU
2003 Proof	1,000	Value: 525				

KM# 1358 20 EURO
17.0000 g., 0.9200 Gold 0.5028 oz. AGW, 31 mm. **Obv:** Denomination in swirling design **Rev:** Hansel and Gretel, witch and house **Edge:** Plain

Date	Mintage	F	VF	XF	Unc	BU
2003 Proof	1,000	Value: 545				

KM# 1360 20 EURO
17.0000 g., 0.9200 Gold 0.5028 oz. AGW, 31 mm. **Obv:** Denomination in swirling design **Rev:** Alice in Wonderland **Edge:** Plain

Date	Mintage	F	VF	XF	Unc	BU
2003 Proof	1,000	Value: 545				

KM# 1363 20 EURO
17.0000 g., 0.9200 Gold 0.5028 oz. AGW, 31 mm. **Obv:** Pierre de Coubertin **Rev:** Olympic runners **Edge:** Plain

Date	Mintage	F	VF	XF	Unc	BU
2003 Proof	3,000	Value: 525				

KM# 1365 20 EURO
17.0000 g., 0.9200 Gold 0.5028 oz. AGW, 31 mm. **Obv:** Map with denomination **Rev:** Avignon Popes Palace **Edge:** Plain

Date	Mintage	F	VF	XF	Unc	BU
2004 Proof	1,000	Value: 600				

KM# 1370 20 EURO
17.0000 g., 0.9200 Gold 0.5028 oz. AGW, 31 mm. **Obv:** Soldiers and Normandy invasion scene **Rev:** "D-DAY" above denomination **Edge:** Plain

Date	Mintage	F	VF	XF	Unc	BU
2004 Proof	2,000	Value: 600				

KM# 1376 20 EURO
17.0000 g., 0.9200 Gold 0.5028 oz. AGW, 31 mm. **Obv:** The seed sower **Rev:** Denomination and French map face design **Edge:** Plain

Date	Mintage	F	VF	XF	Unc	BU
2004 Proof	3,000	Value: 575				

236 FRANCE

KM# 1381 20 EURO
17.0000 g., 0.9200 Gold 0.5028 oz. AGW, 31 mm.
Obv: Compass rose **Rev:** Trans-Siberian Railroad **Edge:** Plain

Date	Mintage	F	VF	XF	Unc	BU
2004 Proof	1,000	Value: 535				

KM# 1383 20 EURO
17.0000 g., 0.9200 Gold 0.5028 oz. AGW, 31 mm.
Obv: Compass rose **Rev:** Half-track vehicle **Edge:** Plain

Date	Mintage	F	VF	XF	Unc	BU
2004 Proof	1,000	Value: 535				

KM# 1385 20 EURO
17.0000 g., 0.9200 Gold 0.5028 oz. AGW, 31 mm.
Obv: Compass rose **Rev:** Biplane airliner **Edge:** Plain

Date	Mintage	F	VF	XF	Unc	BU
2004 Proof	1,000	Value: 535				

KM# 1388 20 EURO
17.0000 g., 0.9200 Gold 0.5028 oz. AGW, 31 mm. **Obv:** Statue of Liberty **Rev:** F. A. Bartholdi **Edge:** Plain

Date	Mintage	F	VF	XF	Unc	BU
2004 Proof	2,000	Value: 550				

KM# 1393 20 EURO
17.0000 g., 0.9200 Gold 0.5028 oz. AGW, 31 mm.
Subject: European Union Expansion **Obv:** Partial face and flags **Rev:** Puzzle map **Edge:** Plain

Date	Mintage	F	VF	XF	Unc	BU
2004 Proof	3,000	Value: 550				

KM# 1303 50 EURO
31.0000 g., 0.9990 Gold 0.9957 oz. AGW, 37 mm.
Subject: Europa **Obv:** Eight French euro coin designs **Rev:** Portrait and flags design of 6.55957 francs KM-1265 **Edge:** Plain

Date	Mintage	F	VF	XF	Unc	BU
2002 Proof	2,000	Value: 925				

KM# 1335 50 EURO
31.1000 g., 0.9990 Gold 0.9989 oz. AGW, 37 mm. **Obv:** Tour de France logo **Rev:** Cyclist going left **Edge:** Plain

Date	Mintage	F	VF	XF	Unc	BU
2003 Proof	5,000	Value: 875				

KM# 1368 50 EURO
31.1000 g., 0.9990 Gold 0.9989 oz. AGW, 37 mm. **Obv:** Book, denomination and eagle **Rev:** Napoleon and coronation scene **Edge:** Plain

Date	Mintage	F	VF	XF	Unc	BU
2004 Proof	2,000	Value: 990				

KM# 1394 50 EURO
31.1040 g., 0.9990 Gold 0.999 oz. AGW, 37 mm.
Subject: European Union Expansion **Obv:** Partial face and flags **Rev:** Puzzle map **Edge:** Plain

Date	Mintage	F	VF	XF	Unc	BU
2004 Proof	2,000	Value: 950				

KM# 1304 100 EURO
155.5175 g., 0.9990 Gold 4.995 oz. AGW, 50 mm.
Subject: Europa **Obv:** Eight French euro coin designs **Rev:** Portrait and flags design of 6.55957 francs KM-1265 **Edge:** Plain

Date	Mintage	F	VF	XF	Unc	BU
2002 Proof	99	Value: 5,750				

KM# 1377 100 EURO
155.5175 g., 0.9990 Gold 4.995 oz. AGW, 50 mm. **Subject:** D-Day 60th Anniversary **Obv:** Soldiers and Normandy invasion scene **Rev:** "D-Day" inscription above denomination **Edge:** Plain

Date	Mintage	F	VF	XF	Unc	BU
2004 Proof	299	Value: 4,000				

KM# 1389 100 EURO
155.5000 g., 0.9990 Gold 4.9944 oz. AGW, 50 mm. **Obv:** Statue of Liberty **Rev:** F. A. Bartholdi **Edge:** Plain

Date	Mintage	F	VF	XF	Unc	BU
2004 Proof	99	Value: 4,000				

KM# 1395 100 EURO
155.5000 g., 0.9990 Gold 4.996 oz. AGW, 50 mm.
Subject: European Union Expansion **Obv:** Partial face and flags **Rev:** Puzzle map **Edge:** Plain

Date	Mintage	F	VF	XF	Unc	BU
2004 Proof	99	Value: 4,000				

KM# 1396 500 EURO
1000.0000 g., 0.9990 Gold 32.1186 oz. AGW, 85 mm.
Subject: European Union Expansion **Obv:** Partial face and flags **Rev:** Puzzle map **Edge:** Plain **NOTE:** Illustration reduced.

Date	Mintage	F	VF	XF	Unc	BU
2004 Proof, Rare	20	—	—	—	—	—

SATIRICAL COINAGE
Mac-Mahon I 1874

X# E50a 5 FRANCS
Gold Obv: Head left, NAPOLEON F. below **Obv. Legend:** MAC-MAHON I — SEPTENNAT **Rev:** Hatted and crowned arms with Order of the Golden Fleece below, ESSAI at lower right **Rev. Legend:** REPUBLIQUE FRANÇAISE **Edge:** Plain
Note: Prev. KY#98b.

Date	Mintage	F	VF	XF	Unc	BU
1874 Proof	—	Value: 2,750				

ESSAIS
Standard metals unless otherwise noted

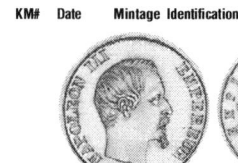

KM#	Date	Mintage	Identification	Mkt Val
E13	1848	—	20 Francs. Gold. Armored head right. Denomination within wreath.	—
E14	1848A	—	20 Francs. Gold. Laureate head right. Crossed branched above denomination.	4,000
E-A21	1855	—	10 Francs. Gold. Bare head, date below. Denomination in wreath.	1,250
E25	1861	—	20 Francs. Gold. Laureate head right. Crowned and mantled arms.	—
E29	1867	—	5 Dollars/25 Francs. Gold. Laureate head left. Denomination.	7,000
E30	1867	—	10 Florins/25 Francs. Gold.	5,000
E34	1878 (a)	—	100 Francs. Gold. KM#832.	13,000
E51	1929 (a)	15	100 Francs. Gold. Winged head left. Leafy branches flank grain sprig, denomination above, date below.	3,850
E52	1929	15	100 Francs. Gold. Globe with sprays flanking, denomination below.	3,850
E53	1929 (a)	15	100 Francs. Gold. Laureate head left. Grain sprig left and branch right divide denomination and date.	3,850
E54	1929 (a)	15	100 Francs. Gold. Laureate bust left. Ribboned branches and torch divide RF above denomination and date.	3,850
E55	1929 (a)	15	100 Francs. Gold. Braided head left. Caduceus divides denomination, cornucopias, and date below.	3,850

FRANCE

KM#	Date	Mintage	Identification	Mkt Val
E56	1929 (a)	15	100 Francs. Gold. Laureate head left. Denomination and date within wreath.	3,850
E57	1929 (a)	15	100 Francs. Gold. Laureate head left. Denomination and date within wreath.	3,850
E58	1929 (a)	15	100 Francs. Gold. Laureate head left. Five grain sprigs divide denomination and date below.	3,850
E59	1929 (a)	15	100 Francs. Gold. Head left. Oak tree divides denomination.	3,850
E60	1929 (a)	15	100 Francs. Gold. Head left, hair in bun. Three grain sprigs divide date and denomination.	3,850
E62	1929 (a)	15	100 Francs. Gold. With Essai, KM#880.	3,900
E116	1974	9	10 Francs. Gold. KM#940.	2,750
E118	1974	5	50 Francs. Gold. KM#941.	3,250
E121	1978	12	2 Francs. Gold. KM#942.	1,350
E125	1983	9	10 Francs. Gold. Baloon, KM#952.	1,850
E127	1983	9	10 Francs. Gold. Standhal, KM#953.	1,850
E133	1986	9	10 Francs. Gold. KM#959.	1,850

PATTERNS
Including off metal strikes

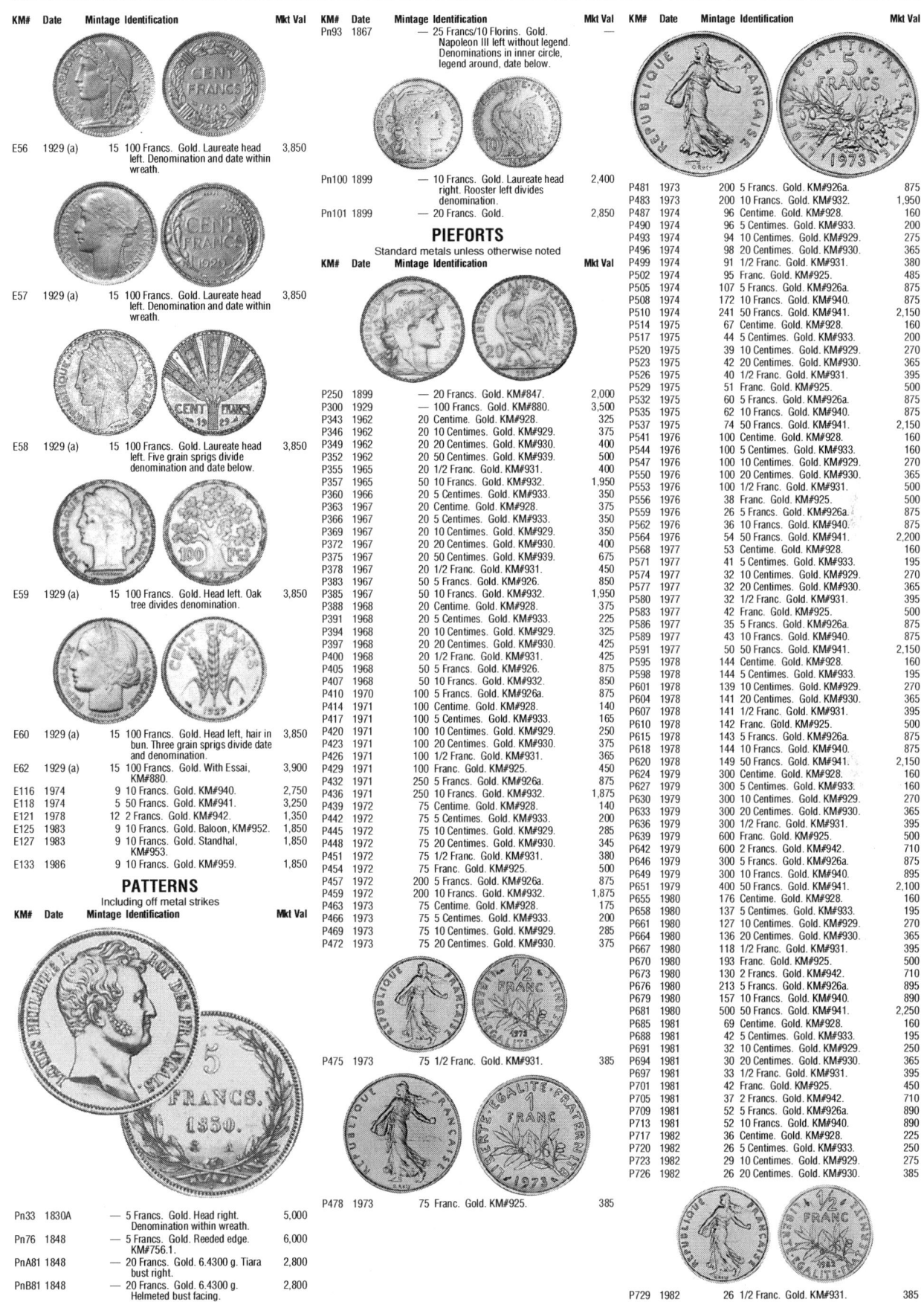

KM#	Date	Mintage	Identification	Mkt Val
Pn33	1830A	—	5 Francs. Gold. Head right. Denomination within wreath.	5,000
Pn76	1848	—	5 Francs. Gold. Reeded edge. KM#756.1.	6,000
PnA81	1848	—	20 Francs. Gold. 6.4300 g. Tiara bust right.	2,800
PnB81	1848	—	20 Francs. Gold. 6.4300 g. Helmeted bust facing.	2,800
Pn93	1867	—	25 Francs/10 Florins. Gold. Napoleon III left without legend. Denominations in inner circle, legend around, date below.	—
Pn100	1899	—	10 Francs. Gold. Laureate head right. Rooster left divides denomination.	2,400
Pn101	1899	—	20 Francs. Gold.	2,850

PIEFORTS
Standard metals unless otherwise noted

KM#	Date	Mintage	Identification	Mkt Val
P250	1899	—	20 Francs. Gold. KM#847.	2,000
P300	1929	—	100 Francs. Gold. KM#880.	3,500
P343	1962	20	Centime. Gold. KM#928.	325
P346	1962	20	10 Centimes. Gold. KM#929.	375
P349	1962	20	20 Centimes. Gold. KM#930.	400
P352	1962	20	50 Centimes. Gold. KM#939.	500
P355	1965	20	1/2 Franc. Gold. KM#931.	400
P357	1965	50	10 Francs. Gold. KM#932.	1,950
P360	1966	20	5 Centimes. Gold. KM#933.	350
P363	1967	20	Centime. Gold. KM#928.	375
P366	1967	20	5 Centimes. Gold. KM#933.	350
P369	1967	20	10 Centimes. Gold. KM#929.	350
P372	1967	20	20 Centimes. Gold. KM#930.	400
P375	1967	20	50 Centimes. Gold. KM#939.	675
P378	1967	20	1/2 Franc. Gold. KM#931.	450
P383	1967	50	5 Francs. Gold. KM#926.	850
P385	1967	50	10 Francs. Gold. KM#932.	1,950
P388	1968	20	Centime. Gold. KM#928.	375
P391	1968	20	5 Centimes. Gold. KM#933.	225
P394	1968	20	10 Centimes. Gold. KM#929.	325
P397	1968	20	20 Centimes. Gold. KM#930.	425
P400	1968	20	1/2 Franc. Gold. KM#931.	425
P405	1968	50	5 Francs. Gold. KM#926.	875
P407	1968	50	10 Francs. Gold. KM#932.	850
P410	1970	100	5 Francs. Gold. KM#926a.	875
P414	1971	100	Centime. Gold. KM#928.	140
P417	1971	100	5 Centimes. Gold. KM#933.	165
P420	1971	100	10 Centimes. Gold. KM#929.	250
P423	1971	100	20 Centimes. Gold. KM#930.	375
P426	1971	100	1/2 Franc. Gold. KM#931.	365
P429	1971	100	Franc. Gold. KM#925.	450
P432	1971	250	5 Francs. Gold. KM#926a.	875
P436	1971	250	10 Francs. Gold. KM#932.	1,875
P439	1972	75	Centime. Gold. KM#928.	140
P442	1972	75	5 Centimes. Gold. KM#933.	200
P445	1972	75	10 Centimes. Gold. KM#929.	285
P448	1972	75	20 Centimes. Gold. KM#930.	345
P451	1972	75	1/2 Franc. Gold. KM#931.	380
P454	1972	75	Franc. Gold. KM#925.	500
P457	1972	200	5 Francs. Gold. KM#926a.	875
P459	1972	200	10 Francs. Gold. KM#932.	1,875
P463	1973	75	Centime. Gold. KM#928.	175
P466	1973	75	5 Centimes. Gold. KM#933.	200
P469	1973	75	10 Centimes. Gold. KM#929.	285
P472	1973	75	20 Centimes. Gold. KM#930.	375
P475	1973	75	1/2 Franc. Gold. KM#931.	385
P478	1973	75	Franc. Gold. KM#925.	385
P481	1973	200	5 Francs. Gold. KM#926a.	875
P483	1973	200	10 Francs. Gold. KM#932.	1,950
P487	1974	96	Centime. Gold. KM#928.	160
P490	1974	96	5 Centimes. Gold. KM#933.	200
P493	1974	94	10 Centimes. Gold. KM#929.	275
P496	1974	98	20 Centimes. Gold. KM#930.	365
P499	1974	91	1/2 Franc. Gold. KM#931.	380
P502	1974	95	Franc. Gold. KM#925.	485
P505	1974	107	5 Francs. Gold. KM#926a.	875
P508	1974	172	10 Francs. Gold. KM#940.	875
P510	1974	241	50 Francs. Gold. KM#941.	2,150
P514	1975	67	Centime. Gold. KM#928.	160
P517	1975	44	5 Centimes. Gold. KM#933.	200
P520	1975	39	10 Centimes. Gold. KM#929.	270
P523	1975	42	20 Centimes. Gold. KM#930.	365
P526	1975	40	1/2 Franc. Gold. KM#931.	395
P529	1975	51	Franc. Gold. KM#925.	500
P532	1975	60	5 Francs. Gold. KM#926a.	875
P535	1975	62	10 Francs. Gold. KM#940.	875
P537	1975	74	50 Francs. Gold. KM#941.	2,150
P541	1976	100	Centime. Gold. KM#928.	160
P544	1976	100	5 Centimes. Gold. KM#933.	160
P547	1976	100	10 Centimes. Gold. KM#929.	270
P550	1976	100	20 Centimes. Gold. KM#930.	365
P553	1976	100	1/2 Franc. Gold. KM#931.	500
P556	1976	38	Franc. Gold. KM#925.	500
P559	1976	26	5 Francs. Gold. KM#926a.	875
P562	1976	36	10 Francs. Gold. KM#940.	875
P564	1976	54	50 Francs. Gold. KM#941.	2,200
P568	1977	53	Centime. Gold. KM#928.	160
P571	1977	41	5 Centimes. Gold. KM#933.	195
P574	1977	32	10 Centimes. Gold. KM#929.	270
P577	1977	32	20 Centimes. Gold. KM#930.	365
P580	1977	32	1/2 Franc. Gold. KM#931.	395
P583	1977	42	Franc. Gold. KM#925.	500
P586	1977	35	5 Francs. Gold. KM#926a.	875
P589	1977	43	10 Francs. Gold. KM#940.	875
P591	1977	50	50 Francs. Gold. KM#941.	2,150
P595	1978	144	Centime. Gold. KM#928.	160
P598	1978	144	5 Centimes. Gold. KM#933.	195
P601	1978	139	10 Centimes. Gold. KM#929.	270
P604	1978	141	20 Centimes. Gold. KM#930.	365
P607	1978	141	1/2 Franc. Gold. KM#931.	395
P610	1978	142	Franc. Gold. KM#925.	500
P615	1978	143	5 Francs. Gold. KM#926a.	875
P618	1978	144	10 Francs. Gold. KM#940.	875
P620	1978	149	50 Francs. Gold. KM#941.	2,150
P624	1979	300	Centime. Gold. KM#928.	160
P627	1979	300	5 Centimes. Gold. KM#933.	160
P630	1979	300	10 Centimes. Gold. KM#929.	270
P633	1979	300	20 Centimes. Gold. KM#930.	365
P636	1979	300	1/2 Franc. Gold. KM#931.	395
P639	1979	600	Franc. Gold. KM#925.	500
P642	1979	600	2 Francs. Gold. KM#942.	710
P646	1979	300	5 Francs. Gold. KM#926a.	875
P649	1979	300	10 Francs. Gold. KM#940.	895
P651	1979	400	50 Francs. Gold. KM#941.	2,100
P655	1980	176	Centime. Gold. KM#928.	160
P658	1980	137	5 Centimes. Gold. KM#933.	195
P661	1980	127	10 Centimes. Gold. KM#929.	270
P664	1980	136	20 Centimes. Gold. KM#930.	365
P667	1980	118	1/2 Franc. Gold. KM#931.	395
P670	1980	193	Franc. Gold. KM#925.	500
P673	1980	130	2 Francs. Gold. KM#942.	710
P676	1980	213	5 Francs. Gold. KM#926a.	895
P679	1980	157	10 Francs. Gold. KM#940.	890
P681	1980	500	50 Francs. Gold. KM#941.	2,250
P685	1981	69	Centime. Gold. KM#928.	160
P688	1981	42	5 Centimes. Gold. KM#933.	195
P691	1981	32	10 Centimes. Gold. KM#929.	250
P694	1981	30	20 Centimes. Gold. KM#930.	365
P697	1981	33	1/2 Franc. Gold. KM#931.	395
P701	1981	42	Franc. Gold. KM#925.	450
P705	1981	37	2 Francs. Gold. KM#942.	710
P709	1981	52	5 Francs. Gold. KM#926a.	890
P713	1981	52	10 Francs. Gold. KM#940.	890
P717	1982	36	Centime. Gold. KM#928.	225
P720	1982	26	5 Centimes. Gold. KM#933.	250
P723	1982	29	10 Centimes. Gold. KM#929.	275
P726	1982	26	20 Centimes. Gold. KM#930.	385
P729	1982	26	1/2 Franc. Gold. KM#931.	385

238 FRANCE

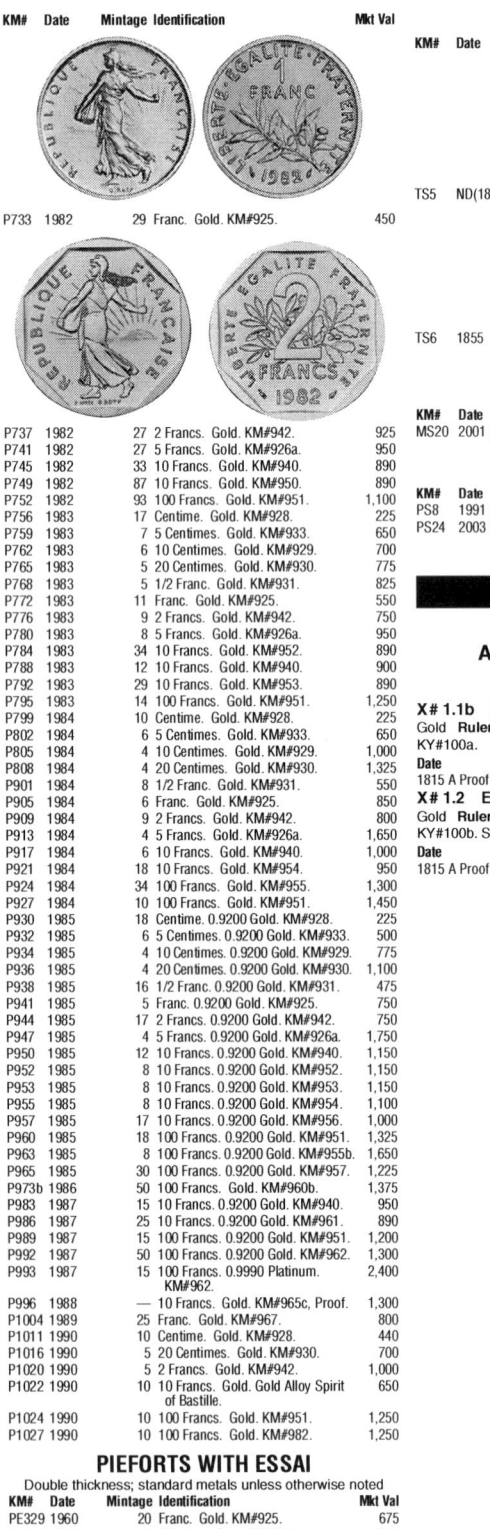

KM#	Date	Mintage	Identification	Mkt Val
P733	1982	29	Franc. Gold. KM#925.	450
P737	1982	27	2 Francs. Gold. KM#942.	925
P741	1982	27	5 Francs. Gold. KM#926a.	950
P745	1982	33	10 Francs. Gold. KM#940.	890
P749	1982	87	10 Francs. Gold. KM#950.	890
P752	1982	93	100 Francs. Gold. KM#951.	1,100
P756	1983	17	Centime. Gold. KM#928.	225
P759	1983	7	5 Centimes. Gold. KM#933.	650
P762	1983	6	10 Centimes. Gold. KM#929.	700
P765	1983	5	20 Centimes. Gold. KM#930.	775
P768	1983	5	1/2 Franc. Gold. KM#931.	825
P772	1983	11	Franc. Gold. KM#925.	550
P776	1983	9	2 Francs. Gold. KM#942.	750
P780	1983	8	5 Francs. Gold. KM#926a.	950
P784	1983	34	10 Francs. Gold. KM#952.	890
P788	1983	12	10 Francs. Gold. KM#940.	900
P792	1983	29	10 Francs. Gold. KM#953.	890
P795	1983	14	100 Francs. Gold. KM#951.	1,250
P799	1984	10	Centime. Gold. KM#928.	225
P802	1984	6	5 Centimes. Gold. KM#933.	650
P805	1984	4	10 Francs. Gold. KM#929.	1,000
P808	1984	4	20 Centimes. Gold. KM#930.	1,325
P901	1984	8	1/2 Franc. Gold. KM#931.	550
P905	1984	6	Franc. Gold. KM#925.	850
P909	1984	9	2 Francs. Gold. KM#942.	800
P913	1984	4	5 Francs. Gold. KM#926a.	1,650
P917	1984	6	10 Francs. Gold. KM#940.	1,000
P921	1984	18	10 Francs. Gold. KM#954.	950
P924	1984	34	100 Francs. Gold. KM#955.	1,300
P927	1984	10	100 Francs. Gold. KM#951.	1,450
P930	1985	18	Centime. 0.9200 Gold. KM#928.	225
P932	1985	6	5 Centimes. 0.9200 Gold. KM#933.	500
P934	1985	4	10 Centimes. 0.9200 Gold. KM#929.	775
P936	1985	4	20 Centimes. 0.9200 Gold. KM#930.	1,100
P938	1985	16	1/2 Franc. 0.9200 Gold. KM#931.	475
P941	1985	5	Franc. 0.9200 Gold. KM#925.	750
P944	1985	17	2 Francs. 0.9200 Gold. KM#942.	750
P947	1985	4	5 Francs. 0.9200 Gold. KM#926a.	1,750
P950	1985	12	10 Francs. 0.9200 Gold. KM#940.	1,150
P952	1985	8	10 Francs. 0.9200 Gold. KM#952.	1,150
P953	1985	8	10 Francs. 0.9200 Gold. KM#953.	1,150
P955	1985	8	10 Francs. 0.9200 Gold. KM#954.	1,100
P957	1985	17	10 Francs. 0.9200 Gold. KM#956.	1,000
P960	1985	18	100 Francs. 0.9200 Gold. KM#951.	1,325
P963	1985	8	100 Francs. 0.9200 Gold. KM#955b.	1,650
P965	1985	30	100 Francs. 0.9200 Gold. KM#957.	1,225
P973b	1986	50	100 Francs. Gold. KM#960b.	1,375
P983	1987	15	10 Francs. 0.9200 Gold. KM#940.	950
P986	1987	25	10 Francs. 0.9200 Gold. KM#961.	890
P989	1987	15	100 Francs. 0.9200 Gold. KM#951.	1,200
P992	1987	50	100 Francs. 0.9200 Gold. KM#962.	1,300
P993	1987	15	100 Francs. 0.9990 Platinum. KM#962.	2,400
P996	1988	—	10 Francs. Gold. KM#965c, Proof.	1,300
P1004	1989	25	Franc. Gold. KM#967.	800
P1011	1990	10	Centime. Gold. KM#928.	440
P1016	1990	5	20 Centimes. Gold. KM#930.	700
P1020	1990	5	2 Francs. Gold. KM#942.	1,000
P1022	1990	10	10 Francs. Gold. Gold Alloy Spirit of Bastille.	650
P1024	1990	10	100 Francs. Gold. KM#951.	1,250
P1027	1990	10	100 Francs. Gold. KM#982.	1,250

PIEFORTS WITH ESSAI
Double thickness; standard metals unless otherwise noted

KM#	Date	Mintage	Identification	Mkt Val
PE329	1960	20	Franc. Gold. KM#925.	675
PE332	1960	50	5 Francs. Gold. KM#926.	900
PE337	1961	20	5 Centimes. Gold. KM#927.	590
PE434	1971	100	5 Francs. Platinum. KM#926a.	1,500

TRIAL STRIKES

KM#	Date	Mintage	Identification	Mkt Val
TS5	ND(1855)	—	5 Francs. Gold. Napoleon III right.	—
TS6	1855	—	5 Francs. Gold. Denomination and date in wreath.	—

MINT SETS

KM#	Date	Mintage Identification	Issue Price	Mkt Val
MS20	2001 (2)	10,000 KM#925.1a, 928a	—	190

PROOF SETS

KM#	Date	Mintage Identification	Issue Price	Mkt Val
PS8	1991 (3)	15,000 KM#977, 991-992	—	500
PS24	2003 (5)	5,000 KM#1326, 1327, 1328, 1329, 1330	—	875

BOUILLON
DUCHY
Admiral Philip of Auvergne
ECU COINAGE

X# 1.1b ECU
Gold **Ruler:** Phillippe d' Auvergne **Edge:** Plain **Note:** Prev. KY#100a.

Date	Mintage	F	VF	XF	Unc	BU
1815 A Proof	—	—	—	—	—	—

X# 1.2 ECU
Gold **Ruler:** Phillippe d' Auvergne **Edge:** Lettered **Note:** Prev. KY#100b. Struck ca. 1870-1880.

Date	Mintage	F	VF	XF	Unc	BU
1815 A Proof	—	—	—	—	—	—

FRENCH GUIANA

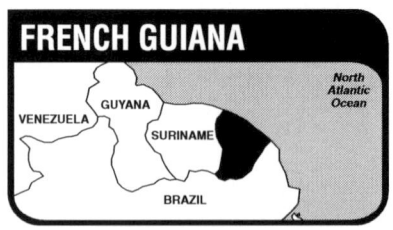

The French Overseas Department of Guiana, located on the northeast coast of South America, bordered by Surinam and Brazil, has an area of 33,399 sq. mi. (91,000 sq. km.). Capital: Cayenne. Placer gold mining and shrimp processing are the chief industries. Shrimp, lumber, gold, cocoa, and bananas are exported.

The coast of Guiana was sighted by Columbus in 1498 and explored by Amerigo Vespucci in 1499. The French established the first successful trading stations and settlements, and placed the area under direct control of the French Crown in 1674. Portuguese and British forces occupied French Guiana for five years during the Napoleonic Wars. Devil's Island, the notorious penal colony in French Guiana where Capt. Alfred Dreyfus was imprisoned, was established in 1852 and finally closed in 1947. When France adopted a new constitution in 1946, French Guiana voted to remain within the French Union as an Overseas Department. It now hosts some of the French and Common Market space and satellite stations.

In the late 18th century, a series of 2 sous coins was struck for the colony. It is probable that contemporary imitations of these issues, many emanating from Birmingham, England, outnumber the originals. These, both genuine and bogus, host coins for many West Indies counterstamps. As an Overseas Department, Guiana now uses the coins of metropolitan France, however, the franc used in the former colony was always distinct in value from that of the homeland as well as that used in the islands of the French West Indies.

RULER
French

MINT MARK
A – Paris

MONETARY SYSTEM
(Commencing 1794)
100 Centimes = 10 Decimes = 1 Franc

FRENCH COLONY
ESSAIS

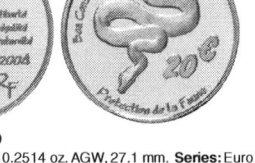

X# E15   20 EURO
8.5300 g., 0.9167 Gold 0.2514 oz. AGW, 27.1 mm. **Series:** Euro **Obv:** Arms **Obv. Legend:** GUYANE FRANÇAISE **Rev:** Boa constrictor **Rev. Legend:** Protection de la Faune **Edge:** Plain

Date	Mintage	F	VF	XF	Unc	BU
2004 Proof	300	Value: 295				

FRENCH POLYNESIA

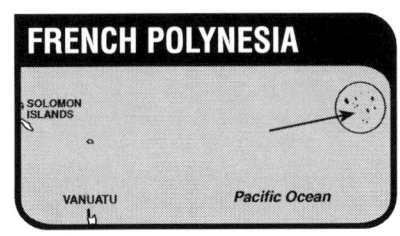

The Territory of French Polynesia (formerly French Oceania) has an area of 1,544 sq. mi. (3,941 sq. km.) and a population of 220,000. It is comprised of the same five archipelagoes that were grouped administratively to form French Oceania.

The colony of French Oceania became the Territory of French Polynesia by act of the French National Assembly in March, 1957. In Sept. of 1958 it voted in favor of the new constitution of the Fifth Republic, thereby electing to remain within the new French Community.

Picturesque, mountainous Tahiti, the setting of many tales of adventure and romance, is one of the most inspiringly beautiful islands in the world. Robert Louis Stevenson called it 'God's sweetest works'. It was there that Paul Gaugin, one of the pioneers of the Impressionist movement, painted the brilliant, exotic pictures that later made him famous. The arid coral atolls of Tuamotu comprise the most economically valuable area of French Polynesia. Pearl oysters thrive in the warm, limpid lagoons, and extensive portions of the atolls are valuable phosphate rock.

RULER
French

MINT MARKS
(a) - Paris, privy marks only
(b)

MONETARY SYSTEM
100 Centimes = 1 Franc

PIEFORTS

KM#	Date	Mintage	Identification	Issue Price	Mkt Val
P3	1967(a)	20	10 Francs. 0.9200 Gold. KM5.	—	950
P6	1967(a)	20	20 Francs. 0.9200 Gold. KM6.	—	1,250
P9	1967(a)	20	50 Francs. 0.9200 Gold. KM7.	—	1,450
P12	1979(a)	93	50 Centimes. 0.9200 Gold. KM11.	—	450
P15	1979(a)	94	2 Francs. 0.9200 Gold. KM10.	—	650
P18	1979(a)	95	5 Francs. 0.9200 Gold. KM12.	—	900
P21	1979(a)	94	10 Francs. 0.9200 Gold. KM8.	—	700
P24	1979(a)	93	20 Francs. 0.9200 Gold. KM9.	—	850
P27	1979(a)	94	50 Francs. 0.9200 Gold. KM13.	—	1,200
P30	1979(a)	98	100 Francs. 0.9200 Gold. KM14.	—	1,250

FRENCH SOUTHERN & ANTARCTIC TERRITORIES

FRENCH TERRITORY

ESSAIS

X# E15 20 EURO
8.5300 g., 0.9167 Gold 0.2514 oz. AGW, 27.1 mm. **Obv:** Arms **Rev:** Emperor Penguin with chick **Edge:** Plain

Date	Mintage	F	VF	XF	Unc	BU
2004 Proof	300	Value: 250				

AL FUJAIRAH

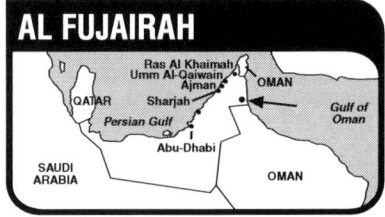

An original member of the United Arab Emirates, al-Fujairah is the only emirate that does not have territory on the Persian Gulf. It is on the eastern side of the "horn" of Oman. It has an estimated area of 450 sq. mi. (1200 sq. km.) and a population of 27,000. Al-Fujairah has been, historically a frequent rival of Sharjah. As recently as 1952 Great Britain recognized al-Fujairah as an autonomous state.

TITLES

الفجيرة

al Fujaira(t)

RULERS
Muhammad bin Hamad al-Sharqi, 1952-74
Hamad bin Muhammad al-Sharqi, 1974--

EMIRATE

NON-CIRCULATING LEGAL TENDER COINAGE

KM# 7 25 RIYALS
5.1800 g., 0.9000 Gold .1499 oz. AGW **Ruler:** Muhammad bin Hamad al-Sharqi **Subject:** U.S. President Richard Nixon **Obv:** Arms-flags above rifles on pointed shield **Rev:** Head 3/4 right

Date	Mintage	F	VF	XF	Unc	BU
AH1388-1969 Proof	3,280	Value: 150				

Note: Fineness incuse

AH1389-1970 Proof Inc. above Value: 150
Note: Fineness both raised and incuse

KM# 8 50 RIYALS
10.3600 g., 0.9000 Gold .2998 oz. AGW **Ruler:** Muhammad bin Hamad al-Sharqi **Series:** 1972 Munich Olympics **Obv:** Arms-flags above rifles on pointed shield **Rev:** Olympic logo and symbols with date

Date	Mintage	F	VF	XF	Unc	BU
AH1388-1969 Proof	1,230	Value: 260				
AH1389-1970 Proof	400	Value: 275				

KM# 9 100 RIYALS
20.7300 g., 0.9000 Gold .5999 oz. AGW **Ruler:** Muhammad bin Hamad al-Sharqi **Subject:** Apollo X **Obv:** Arms-flags above rifles on pointed shield **Rev:** Three astronauts and moon

Date	Mintage	F	VF	XF	Unc	BU
AH1388-1969 Proof	2,140	Value: 450				

FUJAIRAH

KM# 10 100 RIYALS
20.7300 g., 0.9000 Gold .5999 oz. AGW **Ruler:** Muhammad bin Hamad al-Sharqi **Subject:** Apollo XII **Obv:** Arms-flags above rifles on pointed shield **Rev:** Four shields on moon surface at left, three astronauts on shield at right

Date	Mintage	F	VF	XF	Unc	BU
AH1388-1969 Proof	3,040	Value: 435				
AH1389-1970 Proof	—	Value: 435				

KM# 23 100 RIYALS
20.7300 g., 0.9000 Gold .5999 oz. AGW **Ruler:** Muhammad bin Hamad al-Sharqi **Subject:** Apollo XIII **Obv:** Arms-flags above rifles on pointed shield **Rev:** Five shields at left, Arab riders and sun at right

Date	Mintage	F	VF	XF	Unc	BU
AH1389-1970 Proof	600	Value: 475				

KM# 24 100 RIYALS
20.7300 g., 0.9000 Gold .5999 oz. AGW **Ruler:** Muhammad bin Hamad al-Sharqi **Subject:** Visit of Pope Paul VI to Philippines **Obv:** Arms-flags above rifles on pointed shield **Rev:** Buildings, Pope's profile at right

Date	Mintage	F	VF	XF	Unc	BU
AH1389-1970 Proof	290	Value: 550				

KM# 26 100 RIYALS
20.7300 g., 0.9000 Gold .5999 oz. AGW **Ruler:** Muhammad bin Hamad al-Sharqi **Subject:** Visit of Pope Paul VI to Australia **Obv:** Arms-flags above rifles on pointed shield **Rev:** Pope's profile at left, crown with keys and kangaroo on map at right

Date	Mintage	F	VF	XF	Unc	BU
AH1389-1970 Proof	250	Value: 550				

KM# 25 100 RIYALS
20.7300 g., 0.9000 Gold .5999 oz. AGW **Ruler:** Muhammad bin Hamad al-Sharqi **Subject:** Apollo XIV **Obv:** Arms-flags above rifles on pointed shield **Rev:** Moon above shooting star within ring, planet lower left

Date	Mintage	F	VF	XF	Unc	BU
AH1389-1971 Proof	550	Value: 435				

KM# 11 200 RIYALS
41.4600 g., 0.9000 Gold 1.1998 oz. AGW **Ruler:** Muhammad bin Hamad al-Sharqi **Subject:** Mohamad bin Hamad al-Sharqi **Obv:** Arms-flags above rifles on pointed shield **Rev:** Bust left

Date	Mintage	F	VF	XF	Unc	BU
AH1388-1969 Proof	680	Value: 850				

Note: Serially numbered on the obverse

PROOF SETS

KM#	Date	Mintage	Identification	Issue Price	Mkt Val
PS3	1969-71 (8)	—	KM#4.2, 5, 19, 22, 9, 10, 23, 25	—	2,000
PS4	1969 (8)	—	KM#1-4.2, 7-9, 11	—	1,875
PS6	1969 (5)	5,000	KM#7-11	280	2,150

GABON

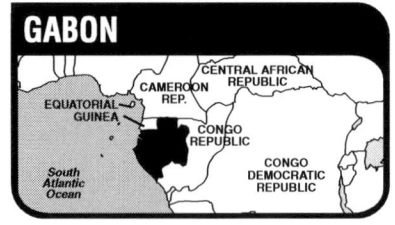

The Gabonese Republic, a member of the French Community, straddles the equator on the west coast of Africa. The hot and humid rain forest country has an area of 103,347 sq. mi. (267,670 sq. km.) and a population of 1.2 million, almost all of Bantu origin. Capital: Libreville. Extravagantly rich in resources, Gabon exports crude oil, manganese ore, gold and timbers.

Gabon was first visited by Portuguese navigator Diego Cam in the 15th century. Dutch, French and British traders, lured by the rich stands of hard woods and oil palms, quickly followed. The French founded their first settlement on the left bank of the Gabon River in 1839 and established their presence by signing treaties with the tribal chiefs. After gradually extending their influence into the interior during the last half of the 19th century, France occupied Gabon in 1885 and, in 1910, organized it as one of the four territories of French Equatorial Africa. It became an autonomous republic within the French Union in 1946, and on Aug. 17, 1960, became a completely independent republic within the new French Community.

For earlier coinage see French Equatorial Africa, Central African States and the Equatorial African States.

MINT MARKS
(a) - Paris, privy marks only
(t) - Poissy, privy marks only, thunderbolt

REPUBLIC

INSTITUT MONETAIRE

KM# 15a 4500 CFA FRANCS - 3 AFRICA
Bi-Metallic .999 Silver center in .999Gold plated .999 Silver ring, 26 mm. **Obv:** Oil drop on map **Rev:** Elephant head on full African map

Date	Mintage	F	VF	XF	Unc	BU
2005	25	—	—	—	400	—

DECIMAL COINAGE

KM# 1 10 FRANCS
4.2000 g., 0.9000 Gold .1215 oz. AGW **Subject:** Independence **Obv:** Head of Mba right, date below **Rev:** Arms with supporters, denomination below

Date	Mintage	F	VF	XF	Unc	BU
1960 Proof	500	Value: 110				

KM# 2 25 FRANCS
8.0000 g., 0.9000 Gold .2315 oz. AGW **Subject:** Independence **Obv:** Head of Mba right, date below **Rev:** Arms with supporters, denomination below

Date	Mintage	F	VF	XF	Unc	BU
1960	10,000	—	—	—	165	—
1960 Proof	500	Value: 185				

KM# 3 50 FRANCS
16.0000 g., 0.9000 Gold .4630 oz. AGW **Subject:** Independence **Obv:** Head of Mba right, date below **Rev:** Arms with supporters, denomination below

Date	Mintage	F	VF	XF	Unc	BU
1960 Proof	500	Value: 325				

KM# 4 100 FRANCS
32.0000 g., 0.9000 Gold .9260 oz. AGW **Subject:** Independence **Obv:** Head of Mba right, date below **Rev:** Arms with supporters, denomination below

Date	Mintage	F	VF	XF	Unc	BU
1960 Proof	500	Value: 650				

KM# 6 1000 FRANCS
3.5000 g., 0.9000 Gold .1012 oz. AGW **Obv:** Head of Bongo left **Rev:** Stump of okume tree, denomination below, arms above

Date	Mintage	F	VF	XF	Unc	BU
1969 Proof	4,000	Value: 100				

KM# 7 3000 FRANCS
10.5000 g., 0.9000 Gold .3038 oz. AGW **Obv:** Head of Bongo left **Rev:** Arms with supporters, denomination below

Date	Mintage	F	VF	XF	Unc	BU
1969 Proof	4,000	Value: 215				

KM# 8 5000 FRANCS
17.5000 g., 0.9000 Gold .5064 oz. AGW **Obv:** Head of Bongo left **Rev:** Reliquary figure of Bakota, denomination below, arms above

Date	Mintage	F	VF	XF	Unc	BU
1969 Proof	4,000	Value: 345				

KM# 11 5000 FRANCS
17.5000 g., 0.9000 Gold .5064 oz. AGW **Subject:** Visit of French President Georges Pompidou **Rev:** Head left

Date	Mintage	F	VF	XF	Unc	BU
1971 Proof	—	Value: 525				

GAMBIA

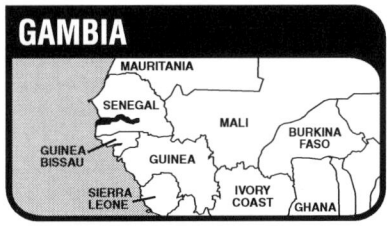

The Republic of The Gambia, occupies a strip of land 7 miles (11 km.) to 20 miles (32 km.) wide and 200 miles (322 km.) long encompassing both sides of West Africa's Gambia River, and completely surrounded by Senegal. The republic, one of Africa's smallest countries, has an area of 4,127 sq. mi. (11,300 sq. km.) and a population of 989,273. Capital: Banjul. Agriculture and tourism are the principal industries. Peanuts constitute 95 per cent of export earnings.

The Gambia was once part of the great empires of Ghana and Songhay. When Portuguese gold seekers and slave traders visited The Gambia in the 15th century, it was part of the Kingdom of Mali. In 1588 the territory became, through purchase, the first British colony in Africa. English slavers established Fort James, the first settlement, on a small island a dozen miles up the Gambia River in 1664. After alternate periods of union with Sierra Leone and existence as a separate colony The Gambia became a British colony in 1888. On Feb. 18, 1965, The Gambia achieved independence as a constitutional monarchy within the Commonwealth of Nations, with Elizabeth II as Head of State as Queen of The Gambia. It became a republic on April 24, 1970, remaining a member of the Commonwealth, but with the president as Chief of State and Head of Government.

Together with Senegal, The Gambia formed a confederation on February 1, 1982. This confederation was officially dissolved on September 21, 1989. In July, 1994 a military junta took control of The Gambia and disbanded its elected government.

For earlier coinage see British West Africa.

RULER
British until 1970

MONETARY SYSTEM
12 Pence = 1 Shilling
20 Shillings = 1 Pound

KM# 9 10000 FRANCS
35.0000 g., 0.9000 Gold 1.0128 oz. AGW **Subject:** 1st Moon landing **Obv:** Head of Bongo left **Rev:** Lunar module, denomination below

Date	Mintage	F	VF	XF	Unc	BU
1969 Proof	4,000	Value: 700				

KM# 10 20000 FRANCS
70.0000 g., 0.9000 Gold 2.0257 oz. AGW **Subject:** 1st Moon landing - Cape Kennedy **Obv:** Head of Bongo left **Rev:** Apollo XI at launching pad, denomination below

Date	Mintage	F	VF	XF	Unc	BU
1969 Proof	4,000	Value: 1,375				

ESSAIS
Standard metals unless otherwise noted

KM#	Date	Mintage	Identification	Issue Price	Mkt Val
E1	1960	10	25 Francs. Gold. KM2.	—	750
E2	1960	—	25 Francs. Silver. KM2.	—	250
E4	1971(a)	4	100 Francs. Gold. KM12.	—	1,800
E5	1971(a)	—	5000 Francs. Copper-Aluminum-Nickel. KM11.	—	200

PROOF SETS

KM#	Date	Mintage	Identification	Issue Price	Mkt Val
PS1	1960 (4)	500	KM1-4	—	1,275
PS2	1969 (5)	4,000	KM6-10	—	2,740

REPUBLIC
DECIMAL COINAGE
100 Bututs = 1 Dalasi

KM# 42 20 DALASIS
7.7760 g., 0.5833 Gold .1458 oz. AGW **Subject:** Endangered Wildlife **Obv:** National arms, date below **Rev:** Black rhinoceros, denomination below

Date	Mintage	F	VF	XF	Unc	BU
1995	Est. 2,000	—	—	—	120	135

KM# 43 20 DALASIS
7.7760 g., 0.5833 Gold .1458 oz. AGW **Subject:** Endangered Wildlife **Obv:** National arms, date below **Rev:** African elephant, denomination below

Date	Mintage	F	VF	XF	Unc	BU
1995	Est. 2,000	—	—	—	120	135

KM# 52 50 DALASIS
1.2441 g., 0.9990 Gold .0400 oz. AGW **Subject:** Kankan Manga Musa **Obv:** National arms, date below **Rev:** Seated king and supplicant, denomination below

Date	Mintage	F	VF	XF	Unc	BU
1997 Proof	—	Value: 45.00				

KM# 53 100 DALASIS
3.1100 g., 0.5833 Gold .0583 oz. AGW **Series:** Olympic Games 2000 **Obv:** National arms, date below **Rev:** Silhouette of three runners, denomination below

Date	Mintage	F	VF	XF	Unc	BU
1997 Proof	5,000	Value: 60.00				

KM# 61 150 DALASIS
7.7760 g., 0.5830 Gold .1458 oz. AGW **Subject:** British Year of 3 Kings and Queen Mother **Obv:** National arms, date below **Rev:** Busts of Edward VIII, George V and George VI facing within circles

Date	Mintage	F	VF	XF	Unc	BU
1996 Proof	—	Value: 175				

KM# 48 200 DALASIS
31.1035 g., 0.9990 Gold 1 oz. AGW **Subject:** Endangered Wildlife **Rev:** Lion right, denomination below

Date	Mintage	F	VF	XF	Unc	BU
1996 Proof	1,000	Value: 725				

KM# 22 250 DALASIS
15.9800 g., 0.9170 Gold .4712 oz. AGW **Subject:** Year of the Scout **Obv:** President's bust in beret left **Rev:** Scout emblem above motto, denomination below

Date	Mintage	F	VF	XF	Unc	BU
1983	2,000	—	—	—	335	
1983 Proof	2,000	Value: 360				

KM# 31 250 DALASIS
47.5400 g., 0.9170 Gold 1.4011 oz. AGW **Subject:** Papal Visit **Obv:** National arms **Rev:** Pope John Paul II giving a blessing

Date	Mintage	F	VF	XF	Unc	BU
1992 Proof	100	Value: 1,250				

KM# 19 500 DALASIS
33.4370 g., 0.9000 Gold .9676 oz. AGW **Subject:** Conservation **Obv:** President's bust left **Obv. Designer:** Michael Rizzello **Rev:** Sitatunga divides denomination

Date	Mintage	F	VF	XF	Unc	BU
1977	699	—	—	—	675	
1977 Proof	285	Value: 820				

GAMBIA

KM# 25 1000 DALASIS
10.0000 g., 0.9170 Gold .2948 oz. AGW **Subject:** World Wildlife Fund **Obv:** President's bust left **Obv. Designer:** Michael Rizzello **Rev:** Gambian puffback bird divides denomination

Date	Mintage	F	VF	XF	Unc	BU
1987 Proof	Est. 5,000	Value: 215				

KM# 27 1000 DALASIS
10.0000 g., 0.9170 Gold .2948 oz. AGW **Subject:** Save the Children Fund **Obv:** President's bust left **Obv. Designer:** Michael Rizzello

Date	Mintage	F	VF	XF	Unc	BU
1989 Proof	Est. 3,000	Value: 235				

GEORGIA

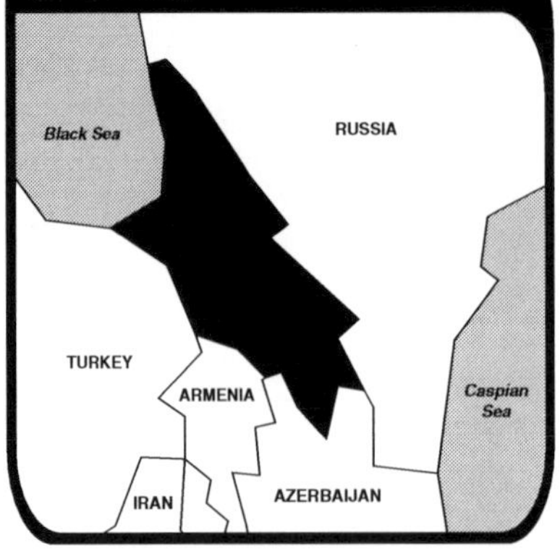

Georgia (formerly the Georgian Social Democratic Republic under the U.S.S.R.), is bounded by the Black Sea to the west and by Turkey, Armenia and Azerbaijan. It occupies the western part of Transcaucasia covering an area of 26,900 sq. mi. (69,700 sq. km.) and a population of 5.7 million. Capitol: Tbilisi. Hydro-electricity, minerals, forestry and agriculture are the chief industries.

On May 20, 1920, Soviet Russia concluded a peace treaty, recognizing its independence, but later invaded on Feb. 11, 1921 and a soviet republic was proclaimed. On March 12, 1922 Stalin included Georgia in a newly formed Transcaucasian Soviet Federated Socialist Republic. On Dec. 5, 1936 the T.S.F.S.R. was dissolved and Georgia became a direct member of the U.S.S.R. The collapse of the U.S.S.R. allowed full transition to independence and on April 9, 1991 a unanimous vote declared the republic an independent state based on its original treaty of independence of May 1918.

RULERS
David, Regent
  AH1215-1216/1801AD

MONETARY SYSTEM
5 Dinar = 1 Puli (Kazbegi)
4 Puli = 1 Bisti
2-1/2 Bisti = 1 Shahi
1/4 Abazi (Abassi) = 4 Para
1/2 Abazi = 8 Para
8 Para = 1 Beslik
4 Shahi = 1 Abazi
1 Abazi = 16 Para
16 Para = 1 Onluk
5 Abazi = 1 Rouble

MINT
Tiflis

INDEPENDENT STATE (C.I.S.)

STANDARD COINAGE
100 Thetri = 1 Lari

KM# 82 500 LARI
17.0000 g., 0.9170 Gold .5010 oz. AGW **Subject:** 50th Anniversary - Defeat of Fascism **Obv:** Stylized candelabra divides date above denomination **Rev:** Profiles of Stalin, Roosevelt, Churchill and de Gaulle left, date below

Date	Mintage	F	VF	XF	Unc	BU
1995 Proof	2,000	Value: 500				

GERMAN EAST AFRICA

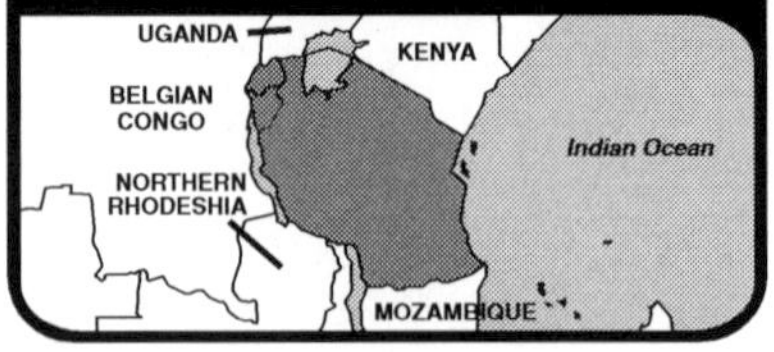

German East Africa (Tanganyika), located on the coast of east-central Africa between British East Africa (now Kenya) and Portuguese East Africa (now Mozambique), had an area of 362,284 sq. mi. (938,216 sq. km.) and a population of about 6 million. Capital: Dar es Salaam. Chief products prior to German control were ivory and slaves; after German control, sisal, coffee, and rubber. Germany acquired control of the area by treaties with coastal chiefs in 1884, established it as a protectorate in 1891, and proclaimed it the Colony of German East Africa in 1897. After World War I, Tanganyika was entrusted to Great Britain as a League of Nations mandate, and after World War II as a United Nations trust territory. Tanganyika became an independent nation within the British Commonwealth on Dec. 9, 1961. Coins dated up until 1902 were issued by the German East Africa Company. From 1904 onwards, the government issued coins.

NOTE: For later coinage see East Africa.

RULER
Wilhelm II, 1888-1918

MINT MARKS
A - Berlin
J - Hamburg
T - Tabora

MONETARY SYSTEM
Until 1904
64 Pesa = 1 Rupie
Commencing 1904
100 Heller = 1 Rupie

COLONIAL

STANDARD COINAGE
64 Pesa = 1 Rupee until 1904; 100 Heller = 1 Rupie commencing 1904

KM# 16.1 15 RUPIEN
7.1680 g., 0.7500 Gold .1728 oz. AGW **Ruler:** Wihelm II **Obv:** Crowned imperial eagle, right arabesque ends below "T" of "OSTAFRIKA" **Rev:** Elephant roaring right above date **Note:** Tabora Emergency Issue.

Date	Mintage	F	VF	XF	Unc	BU
1916T	9,803	650	950	1,400	2,250	2,750

KM# 16.2 15 RUPIEN
7.1680 g., 0.7500 Gold .1728 oz. AGW **Ruler:** Wihelm II **Obv:** Crowned imperial eagle above denomination, right arabesque ends below first "A" of "OSTAFRIKA" **Rev:** Elephant roaring right above date **Note:** Tabora Emergency Issue.

Date	Mintage	F	VF	XF	Unc	BU
1916T	6,395	650	1,000	1,500	2,250	2,750

GERMAN NEW GUINEA

In 1884 Germany annexed the area known as German New Guinea (also Neu Guinea or Kaiser Wilhelmsland) comprising the northern section of eastern New Guinea, and granted its administration and development to the Neu-Guinea Compagnie. Administration reverted to Germany in 1899 following the failure of the company to exercise adequate administration. While a German protectorate, German New Guinea had an area of 92,159 sq. mi. (238,692 sq. km.) and a population of about 250,000. Capital: Herbertshohe, 1 of 4 capitals of German New Guinea. The seat of government was transferred to Rabaul in 1910. Copra was the chief crop.

Australian troops occupied German New Guinea in Aug. 1914, shortly after Great Britain declared war on Germany. It was mandated to Australia by the League of Nations in 1920, known as the Territory of New Guinea. The territory was invaded and most of it was occupied by Japan in 1942. Following the Japanese surrender, it came under U.N. trusteeship, Dec. 13, 1946, with Australia as the administration power.

RULER
German, 1884-1914

MINT MARK
A - Berlin

MONETARY SYSTEM
100 Pfennig = 1 Mark

GERMAN PROTECTORATE
STANDARD COINAGE

KM# 8   10 MARK
3.9820 g., 0.9000 Gold 0.1152 oz. AGW **Obv:** Denomination and date in palm wreath **Rev:** Bird of Paradise

Date	Mintage	F	VF	XF	Unc	BU
1895A	2,000	—	4,000	8,250	12,000	—
1895A Proof		—	Value: 15,500			

KM# 9   20 MARK
7.9650 g., 0.9000 Gold 0.2305 oz. AGW **Obv:** Denomination and date in palm wreath **Rev:** Bird of Paradise

Date	Mintage	F	VF	XF	Unc	BU
1895A	1,500	—	4,250	8,750	12,500	—
1895A Proof		—	Value: 16,500			

Put your **money** where your **mouse** is.

Identifying and valuing your coins has never been easier! Visit www.numismaster.com to enjoy:

- Free access to coin information
- All-new "Find My Coin" search
- Collecting tools, including Portfolio and Want List
- My NumisMaster page
  (upload your photo today!)
- Expanded coverage of collecting news and events

**50+ years of data …
just clicks away!**

NUMISMASTER.com
POWERED BY KRAUSE PUBLICATIONS

GERMAN STATES

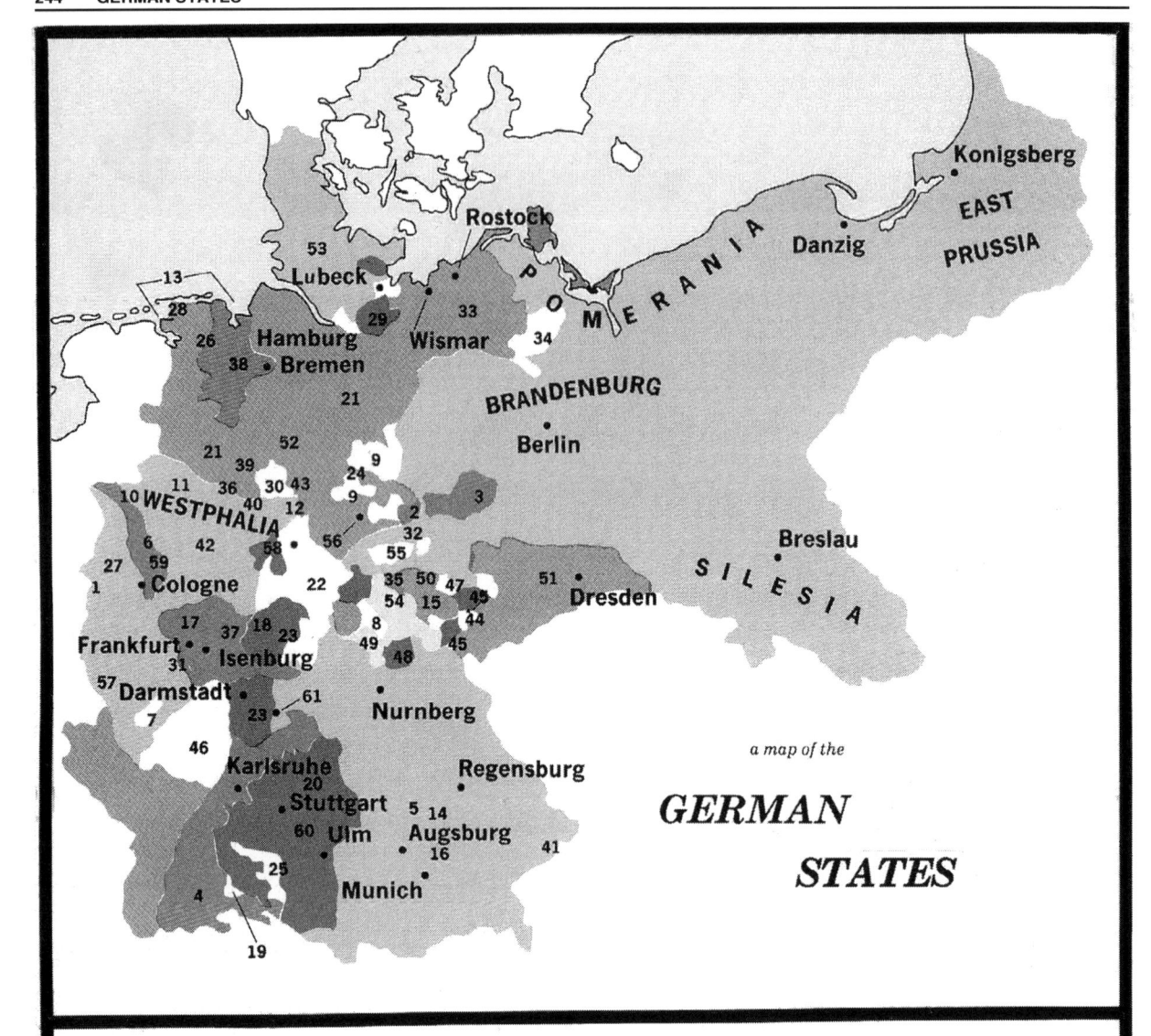

a map of the

GERMAN STATES

1 Aachen	21 Hannover	43 Pyrmont
2 Anhalt-Bernburg	22 Hesse-Cassel	44 Reuss-Greiz
3 Anhalt-Dessau	23 Hesse-Darmstadt	45 Reuss-Schleiz
4 Baden	24 Hildesheim	46 Rhein-Pfalz
5 Bavaria	25 Hohenzollern	47 Saxe-Altenburg
6 Berg	26 Jever	48 Saxe-Coburg-Gotha
7 Birkenfeld	27 Julich	49 Saxe-Meiningen
8 Brandenburg-Ansbach Bayreuth	28 Knyphausen	50 Saxe-Weimar-Eisenach
9 Brunswick-Luneburg & Wolfenbuttel	29 Lauenburg	51 Saxony
	30 Lippe-Detmold	52 Schaumberg-Hessen & Lippe
	31 Mainz	
10 Cleve	32 Mansfeld	53 Schleswig-Holstein
11 Coesfeld	33 Mecklenburg-Schwerin	54 Schwarzburg-Rudolstadt
12 Corvey	34 Mecklenburg-Strelitz	55 Schwarzburg Sonderhausen
13 East Friesland	35 Muhlhausen	
14 Eichstadt	36 Munster	56 Stolberg-Wernigerode
15 Erfurt	37 Nassau	57 Trier
16 Freising	38 Oldenburg	58 Wallmoden-Pyrmont
17 Friedberg	39 Osnabruck	59 Wallmoden-Gimborn
18 Fulda	40 Paderborn	60 Wurttemberg
19 Furstenberg	41 Passau	61 Wurzburg
20 Halle	42 Prussia	

GERMAN STATES

Although the origin of the German Empire can be traced to the Treaty of Verdun that ceded Charlemagne's lands east of the Rhine to German Prince Louis, it was for centuries little more than a geographic expression, consisting of hundreds of effectively autonomous big and little states. Nominally the states owed their allegiance to the Holy Roman Emperor, who was also a German king, but as the Emperors exhibited less and less concern for Germany the actual power devolved on the lords of the individual states. The fragmentation of the empire climaxed with the tragic denouement of the Thirty Years War, 1618-48, which devastated much of Germany, destroyed its agriculture and medieval commercial eminence and ended the attempt of the Hapsburgs to unify Germany. Deprived of administrative capacity by a lack of resources, the imperial authority became utterly powerless. At this time Germany contained an estimated 1,800 individual states, some with a population of as little as 300. The German Empire of recent history (the creation of Bismarck) was formed on April 14, 1871, when the king of Prussia became German Emperor William I. The new empire comprised 4 kingdoms, 6 grand duchies, 12 duchies and principalities, 3 free cities and the non-autonomous province of Alsace-Lorraine. The states had the right to issue gold and silver coins of higher value than 1 Mark; coins of 1 Mark and under were general issues of the empire.

MINT MARKS
A - Berlin, 1750-date
A - Clausthal (Hannover), 1833-1849
B - Bayreuth, Franconia (Prussia), 1796-1804
B - Breslau (Prussia, Silesia), 1750-1826
B - Brunswick (Brunswick), 1850-1860
B - Brunswick (Westphalia), 1809-1813
B - Dresden (Saxony), 1861-1872
B - Hannover (Brunswick), 1860-1871
B - Hannover (East Friesland), 1823-1825
B - Hannover (Germany), 1872-1878
B - Hannover (Hannover) 1821-1866
B - Hannover (Prussia) 1866-1873
B - Regensburg (Regensburg) 1809
B.H. Frankfurt (Free City of Frankfurt), 1808
B (rosette) H - Regensburg (Rhenish Confederation) 1802-1812
C - Cassel (Westphalia), 1810-1813
C - Clausthal (Brunswick)
C - Clausthal (Hannover), 1813-1834
C - Clausthal (Westphalia), 1810-1811
C - Dresden (Saxony), 1779-1804
C - Frankfurt (Germany), 1866-1879
D - Aurich (East Friesland under Prussia), 1750-1806
D - Dusseldorf, Rhineland (Prussia), 1816-1848
D - Munich (Germany), 1872-date
E - Dresden (Germany), 1872-1887
E - Muldenhutten (Germany), 1887-1953
F - Dresden (Saxony), 1845-1858
F - Magdeburg (Prussia), 1750-1806
F - Cassel (Hesse-Cassel), 1803-1807
F - Stuttgart (Germany) 1872-date
G - Dresden (Saxony), 1833-1844, 1850-1854
G - Glatz (Prussian Silesia) 1807-1809
G - Karlsruhe (Germany) 1872-date
G - Stettin In Pomerania (Prussia), 1750-1806
GN-BW - Bamberg (Bamberg)
H - Darmstadt (Germany) 1872-1882
H - Dresden (Saxony) 1804-1812
H.K. - Rostock (Rostock) 1862-1864
I - Hamburg (Germany)
J - Hamburg (Germany) 1873-date
J - Paris (Westphalia) 1808-1809
M.C. - Brunswick (Brunswick), 1813-14, 1820
P.R. - Dusseldorf (Julich-Berg), 1783-1804
S - Dresden (Saxony) 1813-1832
S - Hannover (Hannover) 1839-1844

MONETARY SYSTEM
Until 1871 the Mark (Marck) was a measure of weight.

North German States until 1837
2 Heller = 1 Pfennig
8 Pfennige = 1 Mariengroschen
12 Pfennige = 1 Groschen
24 Groschen = 1 Thaler
2 Gulden = 1-1/3 Reichsthaler
  1 Speciesthaler (before 1753)
  1 Convention Thaler (after 1753)

North German States after 1837
12 Pfennige = 1 Groschen
30 Groschen = 1 Thaler
1 Vereinsthaler (after 1857)

South German States until 1837
8 Heller = 4 Pfennige = 1 Kreuzer
24 Kreuzer Landmunze = 20 Kreuzer Convention Munze
120 Convention Kreuzer = 2 Convention Gulden = 1 Convention Thaler

South German States after 1837
8 Heller = 1 Pfennig = 1 Kreuzer

German States 1857-1871
As a result of the Monetary Convention of 1857, all the German States adopted a Vereinsthaler of uniform weight being 1/30 fine pound silver. They did continue to use their regional minor coin units to divide the Vereinsthaler for small change purposes.

After the German unification in 1871 when the old Thaler system was abandoned in favor of the Mark system (100 Pfennig = 1 Mark) the Vereinsthaler continued to circulate as a legal tender 3 Mark coin, and the double Thaler as a 6 Mark coin until 1908. In 1908 the Vereinsthalers were officially demonetized and the Thaler coinage was replaced by the new 3 Mark coin which had the same specifications as the old Vereinsthaler. The double Thaler coinage was not replaced as there was no great demand for a 6 Mark coin. Until the 1930's the German public continued to refer to the 3 Mark piece as a "Thaler".<

Commencing 1871
100 Pfennig = 1 Mark

VERRECHNUNGS & GUTSCHRIFTS TOKENS
These were metallic indebtedness receipts used for commercial and banking purposes due to the lack of available subsidiary coinage. These tokens could be redeemed in sufficient quantities.

ANHALT-BERNBURG

Located in north-central Germany. Appeared as part of the patrimony of Albrecht the Bear of Brandenburg in 1170. Bracteates were first made in the 12th century. It was originally in the inheritance of Heinrich the Fat in 1252 and became extinct in 1468. The division of 1603, among the sons of Joachim Ernst, revitalized Anhalt-Bernburg. Bernburg passed to Dessau after the death of Alexander Carl in 1863.

RULERS
Alexius Friedrich Christian, 1796-1834
Alexander Carl, 1834-1863

MINT OFFICIALS' INITIALS

Initials	Date	Name
HS	1795-1821	Hans Schluter
IGS	1753-67	Johann Gottfried Siegel
Z	1821-48	Johann Carl Ludwig Zincken

DUCHY
TRADE COINAGE

KM# 80 DUCAT
3.5000 g., 0.9860 Gold .1109 oz. AGW **Ruler:** Alexius Friedrich Christian **Obv:** Denomination, date **Obv. Legend:** ALEXIUS FRIED CHRIST... **Rev:** Crowned bear walking left on wall **Rev. Legend:** EX AURO ANHALTINO

Date	Mintage	F	VF	XF	Unc	BU
1825 Z	116	850	1,400	2,400	3,750	—

ANHALT-DESSAU

Dessau was part of the 1252 division that included Zerbst and Cothen. In 1396 Zerbst divided into Zerbst and Dessau. In 1508 Zerbst was absorbed into Dessau. Dessau was given to the eldest son of Joachim Ernst in the division of 1603. As other lines became extinct, they fell to Dessau, which united all branches in 1863.

RULERS
Leopold Friedrich Franz, 1751-1817
Leopold Friedrich, 1817-1871
Friedrich I, 1871-1904
Friedrich II, 1904-1918

DUCHY
REFORM COINAGE

KM# 25 10 MARK
3.9820 g., 0.9000 Gold .1152 oz. AGW **Ruler:** Friedrich I **Obv:** Head right **Obv. Legend:** FRIEDRICH HERZOG VON ANHALT **Rev:** Crowned imperial German eagle **Rev. Legend:** DEUTSCHES REICH date 10 MARK

Date	Mintage	F	VF	XF	Unc	BU
1896A	20,000	600	1,000	1,600	2,250	3,000
1896A Proof	200	Value: 2,700				
1901A	20,000	750	1,200	1,700	2,700	3,500
1901A Proof	200	Value: 4,250				

KM# 21 20 MARK
7.9650 g., 0.9000 Gold .2304 oz. AGW **Ruler:** Friedrich I **Obv:** Large head right **Obv. Legend:** FRIEDRICH HERZOG V.ANHALT **Rev:** Crowned imperial German eagle **Rev. Legend:** DEUTSCHES REICH date 20 MARK

Date	Mintage	F	VF	XF	Unc	BU
1875A	25,000	500	900	1,350	2,500	3,500
1875A Proof	—	Value: 3,750				

KM# 26 20 MARK
7.9650 g., 0.9000 Gold .2304 oz. AGW **Ruler:** Friedrich I **Obv:** Small head right **Obv. Legend:** FRIEDRICH HERZOG VON ANHALT **Rev:** Crowned imperial German eagle **Rev. Legend:** DEUTSCHES REICH date ZWEI MARK

Date	Mintage	F	VF	XF	Unc	BU
1896A	15,000	600	900	1,600	2,000	3,000
1896A Proof	200	Value: 3,250				
1901A	15,000	750	1,200	1,700	2,700	3,500
1901A Proof	200	Value: 4,250				

KM# 28 20 MARK
7.9650 g., 0.9000 Gold .2304 oz. AGW **Ruler:** Friedrich II **Obv:** Head left **Rev:** Crowned imperial German eagle, shield on breast

Date	Mintage	F	VF	XF	Unc	BU
1904A	25,000	600	1,000	1,400	2,500	3,500
1904A Proof	200	Value: 3,750				

BADEN

The earliest rulers of Baden, in the southwestern part of Germany along the Rhine, descended from the dukes of Zähringen in the late 11th century. The first division of the territory occurred in 1190, when separate lines of margraves were established in Baden and in Hachberg. Immediately prior to its extinction in 1418, Hachberg was sold back to Baden, which underwent several minor divisions itself during the next century. Baden acquired most of the Countship of Sponheim from Electoral Pfalz near the end of the 15th century. In 1515, the most significant division of the patrimony took place, in which the Baden-Baden and Baden-(Pforzheim) Durlach lines were established.

UNITED BADEN LINE
REGULAR COINAGE

KM# 176.2 5 GULDEN
3.4390 g., 0.9030 Gold .0998 oz. AGW **Ruler:** Ludwig I **Obv:** Without engraver's initials below head **Obv. Legend:** LUDWIG GROSHERZOG VON BADEN **Rev:** Crowned shield divides denomination within wreath

Date	Mintage	F	VF	XF	Unc	BU
1819	695	650	1,000	1,500	2,200	—
1821	465	1,125	1,750	2,500		—
1822	1,718	525	875	1,500	2,200	—
1823	1,854	525	875	1,500	2,200	—
1824	2,763	450	750	1,350	1,850	—
1825	1,508	525	875	1,500	2,200	—
1826	887	600	1,000	1,650	2,450	—

KM# 176.1 5 GULDEN
3.4390 g., 0.9030 Gold .0998 oz. AGW **Ruler:** Ludwig I **Obv:** Head right **Rev:** Crowned shield divides denomination within wreath

Date	Mintage	F	VF	XF	Unc	BU
1819 PH	3,000	500	1,000	1,500	2,200	—

246 GERMAN STATES — BADEN

KM# 190 5 GULDEN
3.4390 g., 0.9030 Gold .0998 oz. AGW **Ruler:** Ludwig I **Obv:** Head with curly hair right **Obv. Legend:** LUDWIG GROSHERZOG VON BADEN **Rev:** Crowned shield divides denomination within wreath

Date	Mintage	F	VF	XF	Unc	BU
1827	2,877	450	850	2,250	3,250	—
1828	2,317	450	850	2,250	3,250	—

KM# 177.1 10 GULDEN
6.8780 g., 0.9030 Gold .1997 oz. AGW **Ruler:** Ludwig I **Obv:** Head right **Rev:** Crowned shield divides denomination within wreath

Date	Mintage	F	VF	XF	Unc	BU
1819 PH	4,332	950	1,500	2,350	3,500	—

KM# 177.2 10 GULDEN
6.8780 g., 0.9030 Gold .1997 oz. AGW **Ruler:** Ludwig I **Obv:** Without engraver's initials below head **Obv. Legend:** LUDWIG GROSHERZOG VON BADEN. **Rev:** Crowned shield divides denomination within wreath

Date	Mintage	F	VF	XF	Unc	BU
1821	812	1,150	1,800	2,500	4,000	—
1823	373	1,250	2,000	2,750	4,250	—
1824	328	1,400	2,200	3,000	4,500	—
1825	Inc. above	1,400	2,200	3,000	4,500	—

KM# 196 5 THALER (500 Kreuzer)
5.7320 g., 0.9030 Gold .1664 oz. AGW **Ruler:** Ludwig I **Obv:** Head right **Obv. Legend:** LUDWIG GROSHERZOG VON BADEN **Rev:** Crown above shield within chain, wreath surrounds

Date	Mintage	F	VF	XF	Unc	BU
1830	1,788	800	1,250	2,000	3,000	—

TRADE COINAGE

KM# 143 DUCAT
3.6600 g., 0.9380 Gold .1103 oz. AGW **Ruler:** Karl Friedrich as Grand Duke **Obv:** Head right

Date	Mintage	F	VF	XF	Unc	BU
1807	1,022	—	1,500	2,500	4,500	—

KM# 201 DUCAT
3.6600 g., 0.9380 Gold .1103 oz. AGW **Ruler:** Leopold I **Obv:** Head right **Obv. Legend:** LEOPOLD GROSHERZOG VON BADEN **Rev:** Crowned shield within wreath **Rev. Legend:** EIN DUCAT AUS RHEINGOLD ZU...

Date	Mintage	F	VF	XF	Unc	BU
1832	6,631	—	1,000	1,500	2,250	—
1833	2,496	—	1,100	1,600	2,350	—
1834	1,992	—	1,150	1,650	2,450	—
1835	2,470	—	1,100	1,600	2,350	—
1836	1,777	—	1,150	1,650	2,450	—

KM# 208 DUCAT
3.6600 g., 0.9380 Gold .1103 oz. AGW **Ruler:** Leopold I **Obv:** Without designer's initial or star below head **Obv. Legend:** LEOPOLD GROSHERZOG VON BADEN **Rev:** Crowned shield within wreath **Rev. Legend:** EIN DUCAT AUS RHINGOLD ZU...

Date	Mintage	F	VF	XF	Unc	BU
1837	1,467	—	1,125	1,650	2,450	—
1838	2,095	—	1,125	1,650	2,450	—
1839	2,448	—	1,100	1,600	2,350	—
1840	2,044	—	1,125	1,650	2,450	—
1841	2,145	—	1,125	1,650	2,450	—
1842	2,130	—	1,125	1,650	2,450	—

KM# 215 DUCAT
3.6600 g., 0.9380 Gold .1103 oz. AGW

Date	Mintage	F	VF	XF	Unc	BU
1843	1,350	—	1,300	1,700	2,500	—
1844	850	—	1,500	2,000	2,750	—
1845	2,097	—	1,200	1,600	2,350	—
1846	1,950	—	1,200	1,600	2,350	—

KM# 223.1 DUCAT
3.6600 g., 0.9380 Gold .1103 oz. AGW **Ruler:** Leopold I **Obv:** Larger head right **Obv. Legend:** LEOPOLD GROSHERZOG VON BADEN **Rev:** Crowned shield within wreath **Rev. Legend:** EIN DUCAT AUS RHEINGOLD ZU...

Date	Mintage	F	VF	XF	Unc	BU
1847	1,870	—	1,200	1,600	2,350	—
1848	1,590	—	1,200	1,600	2,350	—
1849	1,420	—	1,200	1,600	2,350	—
1850	1,390	—	1,200	1,600	2,350	—
1851	1,280	—	1,200	1,600	2,350	—
1852	1,450	—	1,350	1,750	2,550	—

KM# 223.2 DUCAT
3.6600 g., 0.9380 Gold .1103 oz. AGW **Ruler:** Leopold I **Obv:** Star below head **Rev:** Crowned shield within wreath **Note:** Posthumous issue.

Date	Mintage	F	VF	XF	Unc	BU
1852	Inc. above	—	1,350	1,750	2,550	—

KM# 227 DUCAT
3.6600 g., 0.9380 Gold .1103 oz. AGW **Ruler:** Friedrich I as Prince Regent **Obv:** Head right

Date	Mintage	F	VF	XF	Unc	BU
1854	1,820	—	1,500	3,000	4,750	—

REFORM COINAGE

KM# 266 5 MARK
1.9910 g., 0.9000 Gold .0576 oz. AGW **Ruler:** Friedrich I as Grand Duke **Obv:** Head left **Obv. Legend:** FRIEDRICH GROSHERZOG VON BADEN **Rev:** Crowned imperial German eagle **Rev. Legend:** DEUTSCHES REICH date 5 MARK

Date	Mintage	F	VF	XF	Unc	BU
1877G	345,000	200	300	450	800	1,200
1877G Proof	—	Value: 1,500				

KM# 260 10 MARK
3.9820 g., 0.9000 Gold .1152 oz. AGW **Ruler:** Friedrich I as Grand Duke **Obv:** Head left **Rev:** Type I

Date	Mintage	F	VF	XF	Unc	BU
1872G	273,000	85.00	200	300	600	1,000
1873G	466,000	85.00	200	300	600	1,000
1873G Proof	—	Value: 1,750				

KM# 264 10 MARK
3.9820 g., 0.9000 Gold .1152 oz. AGW **Ruler:** Friedrich I as Grand Duke **Obv:** Head left **Obv. Legend:** FRIEDRICH GROSHERZOG VON BADEN **Rev:** Type II **Rev. Legend:** DEUTSCHES REICH date 10 MARK

Date	Mintage	F	VF	XF	Unc	BU
1875	339,000	80.00	160	225	400	800
1876G	1,396,000	80.00	125	225	500	750
1877G	159,000	80.00	160	275	600	1,000
1878G	236,000	80.00	160	225	500	900
1879G	98,000	100	200	350	800	1,200
1880G	1,169	7,500	15,000	20,000	30,000	50,000
1881G	196,000	80.00	175	300	700	1,000
1888G	122,000	80.00	160	300	700	1,000
(1876-88)G Proof; common date	—	Value: 1,300				

KM# 267 10 MARK
3.9820 g., 0.9000 Gold .1152 oz. AGW **Ruler:** Friedrich I as Grand Duke **Obv:** Head left **Obv. Legend:** FRIEDRICH GROSHERZOG VON BADEN **Rev:** Crowned imperial German eagle **Rev. Legend:** DEUTSCHES REICH date 10 MARK

Date	Mintage	F	VF	XF	Unc	BU
1890G	73,000	125	225	325	550	650
1891G	110,000	125	200	275	400	600
1893G	183,000	125	175	250	400	575
1896G	52,000	125	225	325	500	700
1897G	70,000	125	250	300	450	600
1898G	256,000	115	180	250	400	500
1900G	31,000	150	350	500	800	1,000
1900G Proof	—	Value: 5,000				
1901G	91,000	125	250	350	500	600
1901G Proof	—	Value: 1,700				

KM# 275 10 MARK
3.9820 g., 0.9000 Gold .1152 oz. AGW **Ruler:** Friedrich I as Grand Duke **Obv:** Head right **Rev:** Crowned imperial German eagle, shield on breast

Date	Mintage	F	VF	XF	Unc	BU
1902G	30,000	175	300	450	750	1,250
1903G	110,000	125	200	265	450	700
1904G	150,000	110	200	245	400	700
1905G	96,000	125	200	265	500	700
1906G	120,000	125	200	245	400	700
1907G	120,000	110	200	245	400	700
(1902-1907)G Proof	—	Value: 2,000				

KM# 282 10 MARK
3.9820 g., 0.9000 Gold .1152 oz. AGW **Ruler:** Friedrich II **Obv:** Head right **Rev:** Crowned imperial German eagle, shield on breast

Date	Mintage	F	VF	XF	Unc	BU
1909G	86,000	225	500	650	950	1,300
1910G	61,000	225	500	650	950	1,300
1911G	29,000	2,000	4,000	5,000	6,750	8,000
1912G	26,000	700	1,000	1,600	2,000	3,000
1913G	42,000	500	700	850	1,250	2,000
(1909-1913)G Proof	—	Value: 2,000				

KM# 261 20 MARK
7.9650 g., 0.9000 Gold .2304 oz. AGW **Ruler:** Friedrich I as Grand Duke **Obv:** Head left **Obv. Legend:** FRIEDRICH GROSHERZOG VON BADEN **Rev:** Type I **Rev. Legend:** DEUTSCHES REICH 20 date M.

Date	Mintage	F	VF	XF	Unc	BU
1872G	398,000	125	150	250	500	800
1873G	517,000	125	160	250	500	800
(1872-73) Proof; common date	—	Value: 2,250				

KM# 262 20 MARK
7.9650 g., 0.9000 Gold .2304 oz. AGW **Ruler:** Friedrich I as Grand Duke **Rev:** Type II

Date	Mintage	F	VF	XF	Unc	BU
1874G	155,000	225	375	600	1,250	1,600
1874G Proof	—	Value: 3,000				

BAVARIA

KM# 270 20 MARK
7.9650 g., 0.9000 Gold .2304 oz. AGW **Ruler:** Friedrich I as Grand Duke **Obv:** Head left **Obv. Legend:** FRIEDRICH GROSHERZOG VON BADEN **Rev:** Type III **Rev. Legend:** DEUTSCHES REICH date 20 MARK

Date	Mintage	F	VF	XF	Unc	BU
1894G Small 4	400,000	135	160	250	400	500
1894G Large 4	400,000	135	160	250	400	500
1895G	100,000	135	225	325	500	700
(1894-95) Proof; common date	—	Value: 1,300				

KM# 284 20 MARK
7.9650 g., 0.9000 Gold .2304 oz. AGW **Ruler:** Friedrich II **Obv:** Head left **Rev:** Crowned imperial German eagle, shield on breast

Date	Mintage	F	VF	XF	Unc	BU
1911G	190,000	BV	175	225	320	425
1912G	310,000	BV	175	220	300	425
1913G	85,000	BV	175	225	350	425
1914G	280,000	BV	175	220	320	425
(1911-1914)G Proof	—	Value: 1,750				

PATTERNS
Including off metal strikes

KM#	Date	Mintage	Identification	Mkt Val
Pn21	ND(1805)	—	Ducat. Silver. KM#143.	—
Pn22	ND(1805)	—	Ducat. Copper. KM#143.	—
Pn25	1842	—	Kreuzer. Gold. KM#203.	—
Pn27	1844	—	Kreuzer. Gold. KM#203.	—
Pn31	1875G	—	10 Mark. Copper. KM#264.	—

BAMBERG

BISHOPRIC

The bishopric was founded in 1007 by Emperor Heinrich II (1002-24) in the town of Bamberg, 32 miles (53 kilometers) northwest of Nürnberg. The bishops began issuing their own coinage almost from the beginning and were given the rank of Prince of the Empire by the emperor about 1250. The bishopric was secularized in 1801 and was incorporated into Bavaria the following year.

RULERS
Christoph Franz, Freiherr von Buseck, 1795-1801 (d. 1807)
Georg Karl, von Fechenbach, 1802-1803

ARMS Lion rampant left over which superimposed a diagonal band from upper left to lower right.

MINT MARKS
B - Bamberg Mint
F - Fürth Mint

TRADE COINAGE

KM# 154 DUCAT
3.5000 g., 0.9860 Gold .1109 oz. AGW **Subject:** Union of Bamberg with Bavaria **Obv:** Standing figures with shields flank tree **Rev:** Inscription within wreath **Rev. Inscription:** SENATUS POPULUSQUE BAMBERGENSIS INREUNIONEM FRANCONIAECUM BAVARIA

Date	Mintage	F	VF	XF	Unc	BU
1802	—	350	750	1,350	2,000	—

PATTERNS
Including off metal strikes

KM#	Date	Mintage	Identification	Mkt Val
Pn11	1802	—	Ducat. Silver. KM#154	—

BAVARIA
(Bayern)

One of the largest states in Germany, Bavaria was a duchy from earliest times, ruled by the Agilholfingen dynasty from 553 until it was suppressed by Charlemagne in 788. Bavaria remained a territory of the Carolingian Empire from that time until 911, when the son of the Count of Scheyern was made duke and began a new line of rulers there. A number of dukes during the next century and a half were elected emperor, but when the mail line became extinct, Empress Agnes gave Bavaria to the Counts of Nordheim in 1061. His descendant, Heinrich XII the Lion, fell out of favor with the emperor and was deposed. The duchy was then entrusted to Otto VI von Wittelsbach, Count of Scheyern and descendant of the counts who had ruled from the early 10th century. Duke Otto I, as he was known from 1180 on, was the ancestor of the dynasty which ruled in Bavaria until 1918 and, from the late 13th century, in the Rhine Palatinate as well (see Electoral Pfalz). The first of several divisions took place in 1255 when lines in Upper and Lower Bavaria were established. The line in Lower Bavaria became extinct in 1340 and the territory reverted to Upper Bavaria. Meanwhile, the division of Upper Bavaria and the Palatinate took place and was confirmed by treaty in 1329, although the electoral vote residing with the Wittelsbachs was to be held jointly by the two branches. In 1347, Bavaria and all other holdings of the family in Brandenburg, the Tyrol and Holland were divided among six brothers. Munich had become the chief city of the duchy by this time. In 1475, Duke Stephen I, who had reunited most of the family's holdings in Bavaria, died and left three sons who promptly divided their patrimony once again. The lines of Ingolstadt, Landshut and Munich were founded, but as the other lines died out, the one seated in Munich regained control of all of Bavaria. Duke Albrecht IV instituted primogeniture in 1506 and from that time on, Bavaria remained united. When Elector Friedrich V of the Palatinate (Pfalz) was elected King of Bohemia in 1618, an event which helped precipitate the Thirty Years' War, Duke Maximilian I of Bavaria sided with the emperor against his kinsman. The electoral dignity had been given to the Pfalz branch of the Wittelsbachs by the Golden Bull of 1356, a fact which was a source of contention with the Bavarian branch of the family. With the ouster of Friedrich V, Maximilian I obtained the electoral right and control of the Palatinate in 1623, then also ruled over the Upper Palatinate (Oberpfalz) from 1628 until the conclusion of the war and the Peace of Westphalia. The Bavarian Wittelsbachs became extinct in 1777 and the line in Electoral Pfalz acquired Bavaria, thus uniting the two main territories of the dynasty under a single ruler for the first time since the early 14th century. When Napoleon abolished the Holy Roman Empire in 1806, bringing an end to the electoral system, the ruler of Bavaria was raised to the rank of king. The 19th century saw tragedy upon tragedy visit the royal family. Because of his opposition to the parliamentary reform movement, Ludwig I was forced to abdicate in 1848. His grandson, Ludwig II, inspired by his upbringing to spend his fortune building the fairy tale castle of Neuschwanstein, was forcibly removed by court nobles and died under mysterious circumstances in 1886. His younger brother, Otto, was declared insane and the kingdom was ruled by his uncle, the beloved Prince Luitpold, as prince regent. Ludwig II, the last King of Bavaria, was forced to abdicate at the end of World War I.

RULERS
Maximilian I, 1598-1651
Ferdinand Maria, 1651-1679
Maximilian II, Emanuel, 1679-1726

ARMS
Wittelsbach and Bavaria – field of lozenges (diamond shapes); Pfalz – rampant lion, usually to the left

MINT MARKS
M - Munich

DUCHY

TRADE COINAGE

KM# 314.2 DUCAT
3.4900 g., 0.9370 Gold .1051 oz. AGW **Ruler:** Maximilian IV, Josef as Elector **Obv:** Head right **Obv. Legend:** D • G • MAXIM • IOSEPH • C • P • R • V • B • D • S • R • I • A • & • EL • **Rev:** Crowned three-fold arms within branches **Rev. Legend:** PRO DEO ET POPULO

Date	Mintage	F	VF	XF	Unc	BU
1801	—	1,000	1,500	2,500	3,000	—
1802	—	1,000	1,500	2,500	3,000	—
1803	—	1,100	1,600	2,650	3,500	—

KM# 314.1 DUCAT
3.4900 g., 0.9370 Gold .1051 oz. AGW **Ruler:** Maximilian IV, Josef as Elector **Obv:** Head right **Obv. Legend:** D • G • MAX • IOS • C • P • R • V • B • D • S • R • I • A • & • EL • D • I • C • & • M • **Rev:** Crowned three-fold arms within branches **Rev. Legend:** PRO DEO ET POPULO **Note:** Fr. #262.

Date	Mintage	F	VF	XF	Unc	BU
1801	—	750	1,250	2,250	2,850	—
1802	—	1,000	1,500	2,500	3,200	—

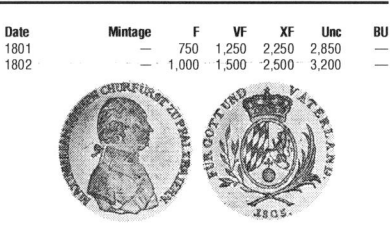

KM# 335 DUCAT
3.4900 g., 0.9370 Gold .1051 oz. AGW **Ruler:** Maximilian IV, Josef as Elector **Obv:** Uniformed bust right **Obv. Legend:** MAXIMILIAN IOSEPH CHURFURST ZU PFALZBAIERN **Rev:** Crowned three-fold arms within branches **Rev. Legend:** FUR GOTT UND VATERLAND **Note:** Fr. #263.

Date	Mintage	F	VF	XF	Unc	BU
1804	—	1,500	2,000	3,000	4,000	—
1805	—	1,250	1,500	2,500	3,250	—

KINGDOM

REGULAR COINAGE

KM# 469 1/2 KRONE
5.5550 g., 0.9000 Gold .1607 oz. AGW **Ruler:** Maximilian II **Obv:** Head right **Obv. Legend:** MAXIMILIAN II KOENIG V. BAYERN **Rev:** Denomination above date within wreath **Rev. Legend:** * VEREINSMUNZE * 100 EIN PFUND FEIN

Date	Mintage	F	VF	XF	Unc	BU
1857	1,749	—	2,500	4,000	7,000	—
1858	1,020	—	3,000	4,500	7,500	—
1859	1,200	—	3,000	4,500	7,500	—
1860	—	—	—	8,000	12,000	—
1861	32	—	—	8,000	12,000	—
1863	—	—	—	8,000	12,000	—
1863 Proof	—	—	—	—	—	—

Note: Stack's Hammel sale 9/82 Proof realized $13,000

| 1864 | — | — | — | 8,000 | 12,000 | — |

KM# 482 1/2 KRONE
5.0000 g., 0.9000 Gold .1446 oz. AGW **Ruler:** Ludwig II **Obv:** Head right **Obv. Legend:** LUDWIG II KOENIG V. BAYERN **Rev:** Denomination above date within wreath **Rev. Legend:** * VEREINSMUNZE * 100 EIN PFUND FEIN

Date	Mintage	F	VF	XF	Unc	BU
1864 Rare	—	—	—	—	—	—
1865 Rare	—	—	—	—	—	—
1866 Rare	—	—	—	—	—	—
1867 Rare	12	—	—	—	—	—
1868 Rare	—	—	—	—	—	—
1869 Rare	—	—	—	—	—	—
1869 Proof	—	—	—	—	—	—

Note: Stack's Hammel sale 9/82 Proof realized $17,000

KM# 470 KRONE
11.1110 g., 0.9000 Gold .3215 oz. AGW **Ruler:** Maximilian II **Obv:** Head right **Obv. Legend:** MAXIMILIAN II KOENIG V.BAYERN **Rev:** Denomination above date within wreath **Rev. Legend:** * VEREINSMUNZE * 50 EIN PFUND FEIN

Date	Mintage	F	VF	XF	Unc	BU
1857	771	—	5,000	8,000	12,000	—
1858	753	—	5,000	8,000	12,000	—
1859	200	—	6,000	10,000	15,000	—
1860	45	—	—	12,000	18,000	—
1861	65	—	—	12,000	18,000	—
1863	—	—	—	12,000	18,000	—
1864	—	—	—	12,000	18,000	—

248 GERMAN STATES   BAVARIA

KM# 483 KRONE
10.0000 g., 0.9000 Gold .2892 oz. AGW **Ruler:** Ludwig II **Obv:** Head right **Obv. Legend:** LUDWIG II KOENIG V.BAYERN **Rev:** Denomination above date within wreath **Rev. Legend:** * VEREINSMUNZE * 50 EIN PFUND FEIN

Date	Mintage	F	VF	XF	Unc	BU
1864	—	—	—	—	—	—
1865	—	—	—	—	—	—
1865 Proof	12	—	—	—	—	—
Note: Stack's Hammel sale 9/82 Proof realized $29,000
1866	—	—	—	—	—	—
1867	12	—	—	—	—	—
1868	—	—	—	—	—	—
1869	—	—	—	—	—	—

TRADE COINAGE

KM# 351 DUCAT
3.4900 g., 0.9370 Gold .1051 oz. AGW **Ruler:** Maximilian IV, as King Maximilian I, Josef **Obv:** Uniformed bust right **Obv. Legend:** MAXIMILIAN IOSEPH KONIG VON BAIERN. **Rev:** Crowned arms with supporters **Rev. Legend:** FUR GOTT UND VATERLAND **Note:** Fr. #264.

Date	Mintage	F	VF	XF	Unc	BU
1806	3,937	1,750	2,250	3,250	4,250	—

KM# 356 DUCAT
3.4900 g., 0.9370 Gold .1051 oz. AGW **Ruler:** Maximilian IV, as King Maximilian I, Josef **Obv:** Head right **Obv. Legend:** MAXIMILIAN IOSEPH KONIG VON BAIERN. **Rev:** Crowned arms with supporters **Rev. Legend:** FUR GOTT UND VATERLAND **Note:** Fr. #265.

Date	Mintage	F	VF	XF	Unc	BU
1807	2,260	650	1,125	1,750	2,500	—
1808	1,465	500	1,050	1,600	2,250	—
1809	3,263	750	1,250	2,000	2,750	—
1810	3,124	850	1,350	2,250	3,000	—
1811	—	600	1,100	1,750	2,500	—
1812	—	850	1,350	2,250	3,000	—
1813	—	600	1,100	1,750	2,500	—
1814	—	600	1,100	1,750	2,500	—
1815	—	750	1,250	2,000	2,750	—
1816	—	600	1,000	1,600	2,250	—
1817	—	600	1,100	1,750	2,500	—
1818	—	600	1,100	1,750	2,500	—
1819	—	750	1,250	2,000	2,750	—
1820	—	600	1,100	1,750	2,500	—
1821	—	500	1,050	1,600	2,250	—
1822	—	600	1,100	1,750	2,500	—

KM# 362 DUCAT
3.4900 g., 0.9370 Gold .1051 oz. AGW **Ruler:** Maximilian IV, as King Maximilian I, Josef **Obv:** Head right **Obv. Legend:** MAXIMILIAN IOSEPH KONIG VON BAIERN **Rev:** Crowned arms with supporters **Rev. Legend:** FUR GOTT UND VATERLAND **Note:** Fr. #265.

Date	Mintage	F	VF	XF	Unc	BU
1821	—	1,250	1,950	3,000	4,200	—
1822	—	750	1,250	1,850	2,650	—

KM# 363 DUCAT
3.4900 g., 0.9370 Gold .1051 oz. AGW **Ruler:** Maximilian IV, as King Maximilian I, Josef **Rev:** Legend above river god **Rev. Legend:** EX AURO DANUBIT **Note:** Fr. #266.

Date	Mintage	F	VF	XF	Unc	BU
1821	—	2,000	3,000	4,250	7,500	—

KM# 364 DUCAT
3.4900 g., 0.9370 Gold .1051 oz. AGW **Ruler:** Maximilian IV, as King Maximilian I, Josef **Rev:** Legend above river god **Rev. Legend:** EX AURO DENI **Note:** Fr. #267.

Date	Mintage	F	VF	XF	Unc	BU
1821	—	2,200	3,200	5,500	8,500	—

KM# 365 DUCAT
3.4900 g., 0.9370 Gold .1051 oz. AGW **Ruler:** Maximilian IV, as King Maximilian I, Josef **Subject:** Isar **Obv:** Head right **Obv. Legend:** MAXIMILIANUS IOSEPHUS BAVARIAE REX **Rev:** Legend above river god **Rev. Legend:** EX AURO ISARAE **Note:** Fr. #268.

Date	Mintage	F	VF	XF	Unc	BU
1821	—	1,500	2,850	5,000	7,750	—

KM# 366 DUCAT
3.4900 g., 0.9370 Gold .1051 oz. AGW **Ruler:** Maximilian IV, as King Maximilian I, Josef **Subject:** Rhine **Obv:** Head right **Obv. Legend:** MAXIMILIAS IOSEPH KONIG VON BAIERN **Rev:** Crowned arms with supporters **Rev. Legend:** FUR GOTT UND VATERLAND **Note:** Fr. #269.

Date	Mintage	F	VF	XF	Unc	BU
1821	—	1,000	1,750	3,250	4,750	—

KM# 368 DUCAT
3.4900 g., 0.9370 Gold .1051 oz. AGW **Ruler:** Maximilian IV, as King Maximilian I, Josef **Obv:** Older head right **Obv. Legend:** MAXIMILIAS IOSEPH KONIG VON BAIERN **Rev:** Crowned arms with supporters **Rev. Legend:** FUR GOTT UND VATERLAND

Date	Mintage	F	VF	XF	Unc	BU
1823	4,400	600	1,000	1,600	2,250	—
1824	19,000	750	1,250	2,000	2,750	—
1825	3,000	600	1,100	1,650	2,300	—

KM# 375 DUCAT
3.4900 g., 0.9370 Gold .1051 oz. AGW **Ruler:** Ludwig I **Obv:** Head right **Obv. Legend:** LUDWIG KOENIG VON BAYERN **Rev:** Crowned arms with supporters **Rev. Legend:** GERECHT UND BEHARRLICH **Note:** Fr. #270.

Date	Mintage	F	VF	XF	Unc	BU
1826	696	1,250	1,850	2,375	2,850	—
1827	4,200	1,750	2,500	3,250	3,850	—
1828	3,090	1,750	2,000	2,500	3,000	—

KM# 388.1 DUCAT
3.4900 g., 0.9370 Gold .1051 oz. AGW **Ruler:** Ludwig I **Obv:** Head right **Obv. Legend:** LUDWIG I KOENIG VON BAYERN **Rev:** Crowned arms with supporters **Rev. Legend:** GERECHT UND BEHARRLICH **Note:** Fr. #270a.

Date	Mintage	F	VF	XF	Unc	BU
1828	1,351	800	1,300	1,800	2,350	—
1829	1,143	600	1,000	1,500	2,150	—
1830	1,731	600	1,000	1,500	2,150	—
1831	3,907	1,000	1,500	2,100	2,600	—
1832	1,884	600	1,000	1,500	2,150	—
1833	1,230	1,000	1,500	2,100	2,600	—
1834	1,711	1,200	1,800	2,600	3,250	—

KM# 395.1 DUCAT
3.4900 g., 0.9370 Gold .1051 oz. AGW **Ruler:** Ludwig I **Obv:** Head right **Obv. Legend:** LUDOVICUS I BAVARIAE REX **Rev:** Legend above river god **Rev. Legend:** EX AURO DANUBII **Note:** Fr. #272.

Date	Mintage	F	VF	XF	Unc	BU
1830	—	1,200	2,500	4,250	7,500	—

KM# 395.2 DUCAT
3.4900 g., 0.9370 Gold .1051 oz. AGW **Ruler:** Ludwig I **Obv:** Head right **Rev:** Inverted "C" in date

Date	Mintage	F	VF	XF	Unc	BU
1830	—	1,200	2,550	4,350	8,000	—

KM# 396 DUCAT
3.4900 g., 0.9370 Gold .1051 oz. AGW **Ruler:** Ludwig I **Obv. Legend:** LUDWIG I...

Date	Mintage	F	VF	XF	Unc	BU
1830	—	1,200	2,500	4,250	7,500	—

KM# 397 DUCAT
3.4900 g., 0.9370 Gold .1051 oz. AGW **Ruler:** Ludwig I **Subject:** Inn **Obv:** Head right **Obv. Legend:** LUDOVICUS I BAVARIAE REX **Rev:** Legend above river god **Rev. Legend:** EX AURO OENI **Note:** Fr. #273.

Date	Mintage	F	VF	XF	Unc	BU
1830	—	1,200	2,750	4,500	8,500	—

KM# 398 DUCAT
3.4900 g., 0.9370 Gold .1051 oz. AGW **Ruler:** Ludwig I **Subject:** Isar **Obv:** Head right **Rev:** Legend above river god **Rev. Legend:** EX AURO ISARAE **Note:** Fr. #274.

Date	Mintage	F	VF	XF	Unc	BU
1830	—	1,200	2,500	4,250	7,500	—

KM# 399 DUCAT
3.4900 g., 0.9370 Gold .1051 oz. AGW **Ruler:** Ludwig I **Subject:** Rhine **Obv:** Head right **Obv. Legend:** LUDOVICUS I BAVARIAE REX **Rev:** River scene **Rev. Legend:** AUGUSTA MENETUM... **Note:** Fr. #275.

Date	Mintage	F	VF	XF	Unc	BU
1830	—	1,000	2,250	4,000	7,000	—

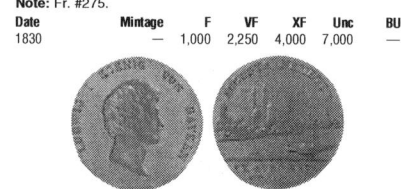

KM# 400 DUCAT
3.4900 g., 0.9370 Gold .1051 oz. AGW **Ruler:** Ludwig I **Obv:** Head right **Obv. Legend:** LUDWIG I KOENIG VON BAYERN **Rev:** River scene

Date	Mintage	F	VF	XF	Unc	BU
1830	—	1,000	2,250	4,000	7,000	—

BAVARIA

GERMAN STATES

KM# 388.2 DUCAT
3.4900 g., 0.9370 Gold .1051 oz. AGW **Ruler:** Ludwig I **Obv:** Head right **Obv. Legend:** LUDWIG I KOENIG VON BAYERN **Rev:** Crowned arms with supporters **Rev. Legend:** GERECHT UND BEHARRLICH **Note:** Struck in collared dies. Fr. #270b.

Date	Mintage	F	VF	XF	Unc	BU
1835	2,048	600	1,000	1,500	2,150	—

KM# 428 DUCAT
3.4900 g., 0.9370 Gold .1051 oz. AGW **Ruler:** Ludwig I **Obv:** Head right **Obv. Legend:** LUDWIG I KOENIG VON BAYERN **Rev:** Crowned arms with supporters **Rev. Legend:** GERECHT UND BEHARRLICH **Note:** Fr. #271.

Date	Mintage	F	VF	XF	Unc	BU
1840	5,000	600	1,000	1,500	2,150	—
1841	2,309	650	1,150	1,800	2,350	—
1842	810	650	1,150	1,800	2,350	—
1843	2,358	650	1,150	1,800	2,350	—
1844	4,259	850	1,500	2,350	3,150	—
1845	2,470	600	1,000	1,500	2,150	—
1846	3,642	650	1,150	1,800	2,350	—
1847	5,122	600	1,000	1,500	2,150	—
1848	1,470	600	1,000	1,500	2,150	—

KM# 433 DUCAT
3.4900 g., 0.9370 Gold .1051 oz. AGW **Ruler:** Ludwig I **Subject:** Rhine **Obv:** Head right **Obv. Legend:** LUDOVICUS I BAVARIAE REX **Rev:** River scene **Rev. Legend:** EX AURO RHENI **Note:** Fr. #276.

Date	Mintage	F	VF	XF	Unc	BU
1842	—	500	1,250	2,250	3,500	—
1846	—	400	1,000	2,000	3,250	—

KM# 457 DUCAT
3.4900 g., 0.9370 Gold .1051 oz. AGW **Ruler:** Maximilian II **Obv:** Head right **Obv. Legend:** MAXIMILIAN II KOENIG V BAYERN **Rev:** Crowned arms with supporters **Rev. Legend:** EIN DUCATEN **Note:** Fr. #277.

Date	Mintage	F	VF	XF	Unc	BU
1849	1,470	750	1,250	1,750	2,250	—
1850	1,519	500	1,000	1,250	1,750	—
1851	3,815	400	600	900	1,200	—
1852	4,396	400	600	900	1,200	—
1853	5,603	400	600	900	1,200	—
1854	5,707	400	600	900	1,200	—
1855	1,540	500	1,000	1,250	1,750	—
1856	3,782	400	600	900	1,200	—

KM# 462 DUCAT
3.4900 g., 0.9370 Gold .1051 oz. AGW **Ruler:** Maximilian II **Subject:** Rhine **Obv:** Head right **Obv. Legend:** MAXIMILIAN II BAVARIAE REX **Rev:** River scene **Note:** Fr. #278.

Date	Mintage	F	VF	XF	Unc	BU
MDCCCL (1850)	—	500	1,000	1,700	2,000	—
MDCCCLI (1851)	—	550	1,200	2,000	2,250	—
MDCCCLII (1852)	—	500	1,000	1,700	2,000	—
MDCCCLIII (1853)	—	500	1,000	1,700	2,000	—
MDCCCLIV (1854)	—	425	900	1,500	1,800	—
MDCCCLV (1855)	—	600	1,400	2,500	3,000	—
MDCCCLVI (1856)	—	425	900	1,500	1,800	—

KM# 461 DUCAT
3.4900 g., 0.9370 Gold .1051 oz. AGW **Ruler:** Maximilian II **Obv. Legend:** ...BAVARIAE REX

Date	Mintage	F	VF	XF	Unc	BU
1850	100	1,750	2,250	3,500	5,250	—

KM# 466 DUCAT
3.4900 g., 0.9370 Gold .1051 oz. AGW **Ruler:** Maximilian II **Rev. Legend:** ...BERGBAU BEI GOLDKRONACH **Note:** Fr. #279.

Date	Mintage	F	VF	XF	Unc	BU
1855	—	12,500	17,500	25,000	35,000	—

KM# 477 DUCAT
3.4900 g., 0.9370 Gold .1051 oz. AGW **Ruler:** Maximilian II **Note:** Reduced size. Fr. #278.

Date	Mintage	F	VF	XF	Unc	BU
1863	—	1,500	2,500	4,000	5,000	—

REFORM COINAGE

KM# 506 5 MARK
1.9910 g., 0.9000 Gold .0576 oz. AGW **Ruler:** Ludwig II **Obv:** Head right **Obv. Legend:** LUDWIG II KOENIG V. BAYERN **Rev:** Crowned imperial German eagle **Rev. Legend:** DEUTSCHES REICH, 5 MARK

Date	Mintage	F	VF	XF	Unc	BU
1877	635,000	200	350	450	700	1,000

KM# 500 10 MARK
3.9820 g., 0.9000 Gold .1152 oz. AGW **Ruler:** Ludwig II **Obv:** J. REIS below truncation **Obv. Legend:** LUDWIG II KOENIG V.BAYERN **Rev:** Type I **Rev. Legend:** DEUTSCHES REICH

Date	Mintage	F	VF	XF	Unc	BU
1872D	626,000	100	200	300	550	850
1872D Proof	—	Value: 1,600				
1873D	1,198,000	85.00	150	250	450	650
1873D Proof	—	Value: 1,600				

KM# 503 10 MARK
3.9820 g., 0.9000 Gold .1152 oz. AGW **Ruler:** Ludwig II **Obv:** Head right **Obv. Legend:** LUDWIG II KONIG V. BAYERN **Rev:** Type II **Rev. Legend:** DEUTSCHES REICH

Date	Mintage	F	VF	XF	Unc	BU
1874D	407,000	80.00	130	200	325	450
1874D Proof	—	Value: 1,350				
1875D	816,000	80.00	130	200	325	450
1876D	684,000	80.00	130	200	325	450
1877D	283,000	80.00	130	200	325	450
1878D	638,000	80.00	130	200	325	450
1879D	224,000	80.00	130	200	325	450
1880D	299,000	80.00	130	200	325	450
1881D	157,000	80.00	130	200	325	450
1881D Proof	—	Value: 1,350				

KM# 509 10 MARK
3.9820 g., 0.9000 Gold .1152 oz. AGW **Ruler:** Otto **Obv:** Head left **Obv. Legend:** OTTO KOENIG VON BAYERN **Rev:** Type II **Rev. Legend:** DEUTSCHES REICH

Date	Mintage	F	VF	XF	Unc	BU
1888D	281,000	150	275	375	550	800
1888D Proof	—	Value: 1,350				

KM# 510 10 MARK
3.9820 g., 0.9000 Gold .1152 oz. AGW **Ruler:** Otto **Obv:** Head left **Rev:** Type III

Date	Mintage	F	VF	XF	Unc	BU
1890D	420,000	85.00	150	200	250	350
1893D	422,000	85.00	150	200	250	350
1896D	281,000	85.00	150	200	250	350
1898D	589,000	85.00	150	200	250	350
1900D	141,000	100	160	250	350	500
1900D Proof	—	Value: 700				

KM# 514 10 MARK
3.9820 g., 0.9000 Gold .1152 oz. AGW **Ruler:** Otto **Obv:** Head left **Obv. Legend:** OTTO KOENIG V. BAYERN **Rev:** Crowned imperial German eagle **Rev. Legend:** DEUTSCHES REICH

Date	Mintage	F	VF	XF	Unc	BU
1900D	Inc. above	90.00	150	225	300	400
1900D Proof	—	Value: 900				
1901D	141,000	90.00	135	190	275	425
1902D	68,000	90.00	135	190	275	425
1903D	534,000	90.00	130	190	275	425
1904D	211,000	90.00	130	185	275	425
1905D	281,000	90.00	130	185	275	425
1906D	141,000	90.00	135	200	300	425
1907D	211,000	90.00	130	195	275	425
1909D	209,000	90.00	130	195	275	425
1910D	141,000	90.00	130	195	275	425
1911D	72,000	90.00	135	215	325	425
1912D	141,000	90.00	135	200	285	425
(1901-1912)D Proof	—	Value: 1,000				

KM# 501 20 MARK
7.9650 g., 0.9000 Gold .2304 oz. AGW **Ruler:** Ludwig II **Obv:** Head right **Obv. Legend:** LUDWIG II KOENIG V. BAYERN **Rev:** Type I **Rev. Legend:** DEUTSCHES REICH

Date	Mintage	F	VF	XF	Unc	BU
1872D	1,556,000	155	170	250	550	750
1872D Proof	—	Value: 1,600				
1873D	2,770,000	155	170	250	500	700
1873D Proof	—	Value: 1,700				

KM# 504 20 MARK
7.9650 g., 0.9000 Gold .2304 oz. AGW **Ruler:** Ludwig II **Obv:** Head right **Obv. Legend:** LUDWIG II KOENIG V. BAYERN **Rev:** Type II

Date	Mintage	F	VF	XF	Unc	BU
1874D	615,000	155	170	225	300	450
1875D	—	725	1,200	1,800	2,250	3,000
1875D Proof	—	Value: 1,500				
1876D	454,000	155	170	225	400	500
1878D	50,000	300	600	850	1,200	1,400
1878D Proof	—	Value: 1,600				

KM# 513 20 MARK
7.9650 g., 0.9000 Gold .2304 oz. AGW **Ruler:** Otto **Obv:** Head left **Obv. Legend:** OTTO KOENIG VON BAYERN **Rev:** Type III **Rev. Legend:** DEUTSCHES REICH

Date	Mintage	F	VF	XF	Unc	BU
1895D	501,000	BV	175	200	275	375
1895D Proof	—	Value: 800				
1900D	501,000	BV	160	200	275	325
1905D	501,000	BV	175	200	275	375
1905D Proof	—	Value: 1,600				
1913D	311,000	Value: 30,000				
1913D Proof	—	Value: 35,000				

GERMAN STATES

BAVARIA

KM# 522 20 MARK
7.9650 g., 0.9000 Gold .2304 oz. AGW **Ruler:** Ludwig III **Obv:** Head left **Rev:** Crowned imperial eagle, shield on breast **Note:** Never officially released.

Date	Mintage	F	VF	XF	Unc	BU
1914D	533,000	—	2,000	2,800	3,300	4,250
1914D Proof	—	—	—	Value: 4,500		

MEDALLIC COINAGE
Karl Goetz Series

X# 1d 2 MARK
Gold **Ruler:** Ludwig III **Obv:** Bust left **Rev:** Crowned eagle above shield

Date	Mintage	F	VF	XF	Unc	BU
1913 Proof	—	—	Value: 400			

X# 1e 2 MARK
Platinum APW **Ruler:** Ludwig III **Obv:** Bust left **Rev:** Crowned eagle above shield

Date	Mintage	F	VF	XF	Unc	BU
1913 Proof	—	—	Value: 1,500			

X# 2b 3 MARK
Gold **Ruler:** Ludwig III **Obv:** Head left **Rev:** Eagle, wing over crowned shield

Date	Mintage	F	VF	XF	Unc	BU
1913 Proof	—	—	Value: 550			

X# 3c 5 MARK
33.7500 g., Gold **Ruler:** Ludwig III **Obv:** Bust left **Rev:** Eagle with wings spread over crown at left, shield below

Date	Mintage	F	VF	XF	Unc	BU
1913 Prooflike	—	—	—	—	975	

X# 3d 5 MARK
56.2000 g., Platinum APW **Ruler:** Ludwig III **Obv:** Bust left **Rev:** Eagle with wings spread over crown at left, shield below

Date	Mintage	F	VF	XF	Unc	BU
1913 Prooflike	2	—	—	—	2,800	

X# 4 10 MARK
Gold **Ruler:** Ludwig III **Obv:** Bust left **Rev:** Crown, sceptre below

Date	Mintage	F	VF	XF	Unc	BU
1913 Proof	—	—	Value: 320			

X# 5 20 MARK
8.5000 g., Gold **Ruler:** Ludwig III **Obv:** Bust left **Rev:** Allegorical male supporting crown, eagle at his feet

Date	Mintage	F	VF	XF	Unc	BU
1913 Proof	—	—	Value: 320			

X# 5g 20 MARK
16.0000 g., Platinum APW **Ruler:** Ludwig III

Date	Mintage	F	VF	XF	Unc	BU
1913 Proof	—	—	Value: 950			

PATTERNS
Including off metal strikes

KM#	Date	Mintage	Identification	Mkt Val
Pn3	1818	—	Thaler. Gold.	—
Pn9	1871D	—	20 Mark. Tin. Like KM#501	—
Pn13	1877D	—	5 Mark. Silver. KM#506	—
Pn38	1914D	—	20 Mark. Gold. Lettered edge.	10,000
Pn39	1914D	—	20 Mark. Silver Gilt. Hallmarked, plain edge.	150
Pn40	1914D	—	20 Mark. Silver Gilt. Hallmarked, plain edge. KM522.	—
Pn41	1914D	—	20 Mark. Gold. Denticled rim. KM522. Plain edge.	9,000
Pn42	1914D	—	20 Mark. Silver Gilt. Denticled rim. KM522. Hallmarked, plain edge.	—
Pn43	1914D	—	20 Mark. Gold. 18-millimeter bust. KM522. Lettered edge.	8,000
Pn44	1914D	—	20 Mark. Silver Gilt. 18-millimeter bust. KM522. Hallmarked, plain edge.	—
Pn45	1914D	—	20 Mark. Gold. Plain rim. KM522. Plain edge.	9,000
Pn46	1914D	—	20 Mark. Gold. Plain rim. KM522. Lettered edge.	9,000
Pn47	1914D	—	20 Mark. Gold. Round "O" in KOENIG. Lettered edge.	9,000
Pn48	1914D	—	20 Mark. Silver Gilt. Round "O" in KOENIG. KM522. Hallmarked, plain edge.	—
Pn49	ND J	—	Gulden. Gold. Bust of Ludwig III in uniform. Main bridge of Wurzburger.	—

TRIAL STRIKES

KM#	Date	Mintage	Identification	Mkt Val
TS11	1855	—	Ducat. Gold.	—
TS14	ND(1865)	—	Thaler. Gold.	—

BIBERACH

Located in Württemberg 22 miles to the southwest of Ulm, Biberach became a free imperial city in 1312. The city came under the control of Baden in 1803 and then of Württemberg in 1806.

FREE CITY
TRADE COINAGE

KM# 20 DUCAT
3.5000 g., 0.9860 Gold .1109 oz. AGW **Subject:** Peace of Luneville **Obv:** City god kneeling at altar, eye of God with rays above **Rev:** Nine-line inscription with Roman numeral date

Date	Mintage	VG	F	VF	XF	Unc
1801 Rare	—	—	—	—	—	—

PATTERNS
Including off metal strikes

KM#	Date	Mintage	Identification	Mkt Val
Pn3	1801	—	Ducat. Copper. KM#20	120
Pn4	1801	—	Ducat. Silver. KM#20	150

BRANDENBURG-ANSBACH-BAYREUTH

Held by Prussia from 1791 to 1805 and then given to Bavaria.

RULERS
Friedrich Wilhelm II of Prussia, 1791-1797
Friedrich Wilhelm III of Prussia, 1797-1805

MARGRAVIATE
TRADE COINAGE

KM# 19 DUCAT
3.5000 g., 0.9860 Gold .1109 oz. AGW **Ruler:** Friedrich Wilhelm III of Prussia **Obv:** Crowned imperial eagle within oval, wreath surrounds **Rev:** Inscription above branches

Date	Mintage	F	VF	XF	Unc	BU
1803B Rare	—	—	—	—	—	—

BREMEN

Established at about the same time as the bishopric in 787, Bremen was under the control of the bishops and archbishops until joining the Hanseatic League in 1276. Archbishop Albrecht II granted the mint right to the city in 1369, but this was not formalized by imperial decree until 1541. In 1646, Bremen was raised to free imperial status and continued to strike its own coins into the early 20th century. The city lost its free imperial status in 1803 and was controlled by France from 1806 until 1813. Regaining it independence in 1815, Bremen joined the North German Confederation in 1867 and the German Empire in 1871.

MINT OFFICIALS' INITIALS

Initials	Date	Name
DB, RDDB	1780-1811	Eberhard Christian Poppe, warden
	1811-32	Matthias Poppe
	1805-42	Hans Schierven Knoph, mintmaster in Hamburg
	1837-57	Eberhard Christian Poppe, warden
	1840	Ernst Julius Strauch, warden
	1840-59	Martin Heinrich Wilkens, mintmaster
B	1844-68	Th. W. Bruel in Hannover

ARMS
Key, often in shield

FREE CITY
REGULAR COINAGE

KM# 253 10 MARK
3.9820 g., 0.9000 Gold .1152 oz. AGW **Obv:** Key on crowned shield with supporters **Rev:** Crowned imperial eagle, shield on breast, date at right, denomination below

Date	Mintage	F	VF	XF	Unc	BU
1907 J	20,000	425	850	1,250	1,700	2,500
1907 J Proof	—	—	Value: 2,800			

KM# 252 20 MARK
7.9650 g., 0.9000 Gold .2304 oz. AGW

Date	Mintage	F	VF	XF	Unc	BU
1906 J	20,000	425	850	1,150	1,750	2,500
1906 J Proof	—	—	Value: 2,800			

PATTERNS
Including off metal strikes

KM#	Date	Mintage	Identification	Mkt Val
Pn39	1840	—	Groten. Gold. KM#230	800

BRUNSWICK-LUNEBURG-CALENBERG-HANNOVER

Located in north-central Germany. The first duke began his rule in 1235. The first coinage appeared c. 1175. There was considerable shuffling of territory until 1692 when Ernst August became the elector of Hannover. George Ludwig became George I of England in 1714. There was separate coinage for Lüneburg until during the reign of George III. The name was changed to Hannover in 1814.

RULERS
George III, (King of Great Britain), 1760-1814
After 1814 see Kingdom of Hannover

MINT OFFICIALS' INITIALS
Clausthal Mint

Initials	Date	Name
A	1833-49	Vacant Mintmastership
C	1751-53, 1790-92, 1800-02	Commission
GM, GFM	1802-07	Georg Friedrich Michaelis
IWL	1807-19	Johann Wilhelm Lunde
WAJA	1821-38	Wilhelm August Julius Albert

Hannover Mint

Initials	Date	Name
Star, C, star	1800-06	Commission

NOTE: From 1715 on, the titles are changed on the coinage to reflect the ruler's elevation to "King of Great Britain, France and Ireland" as well as elector and duke of Brunswick and Lüneburg.

DUCHY
TRADE COINAGE

KM# 416 DUCAT
3.5000 g., 0.9860 Gold .1109 oz. AGW **Ruler:** George III **Obv:** Large modified arms **Rev:** Legend above horse **Rev. Legend:** EX AURO...

Date	Mintage	F	VF	XF	Unc	BU
1802 .C.	—	350	525	900	1,500	—
1802 GFM	—	400	600	1,000	1,650	—
1804 GFM	—	300	525	800	1,450	—

KM# 418 PISTOLE
6.6500 g., 0.9000 Gold .1924 oz. AGW **Ruler:** George III **Obv:** Rearing horse left **Rev:** Denomination, date

Date	Mintage	F	VF	XF	Unc	BU
1803 C	—	350	650	1,100	2,000	—

BRUNSWICK-WOLFENBUTTEL

(Braunschweig-Wolfenbüttel)
Located in north-central Germany. Wolfenbüttel was annexed to Brunswick in 1257. One of the five surviving sons of Albrecht II founded the first line in Wolfenbüttel in 1318. A further division in Wolfenbüttel and Lüneburg was undertaken in 1373. Another division occurred in 1495, but the Wolfenbüttel duchy survived in the younger line. Heinrich IX was forced out of his territory during the religious wars of the mid-sixteenth century by Duke Johann Friedrich I of Saxony and Landgrave Philipp of Hessen in 1542, but was restored to his possessions in 1547. Duke Friedrich Ulrich was forced to cede the Grubenhagen lands, which had been acquired by Wolfenbüttel in 1596, to Lüneburg in 1617. When the succession died out in 1634, the lands and titles fell to the cadet line in Dannenberg. The line became extinct once again and passed to Brunswick-Bevern in 1735 from which a new succession of Wolfenbüttel dukes descended. The ducal family was beset by continual personal and political tragedy during the nineteenth century. Two of the dukes were killed in battles with Napoleon, the territories were occupied by the French and became part of the Kingdom of Westphalia, another duke was forced out by a revolt in 1823. From 1884 until 1913, Brunswick-Wolfenbüttel was governed by Prussia and then turned over to a younger prince of Brunswick who married a daughter of Kaiser Wilhelm II. His reign was short, however, as he was forced to abdicate at the end of World War I.

RULERS
Karl Wilhelm Ferdinand, 1780-1806
Friedrich Wilhelm, 1806-1815
Karl II (under regency of George III of Great Britain), 1815-1820
Karl II (under regency of George IV of Great Britain), 1820-1823
Karl II, 1823-1830
Wilhelm, 1831-1884
Prussian rule, 1884-1913
Ernst August, 1913-1918

MINT OFFICIALS' INITIALS
Brunswick Mint

Initials	Date	Name
K	1766-1802	Christian Friedrich Krull, die-cutter
MC	1779-1806, 1820	Münz-Commission
B	1850-59	Johann W. Chr. Brumleu in Brunswick
CvC	1820-50	Cramer von Clausbruch in Brunswick
FR	1814-20	Friedrich Ritter in Brunswick
K	1776-1802	Christian Friedrich Krull, die-cutter in Brunswick
MC	1779-1806, 1820	Munz – Commission at Brunswick

Hannover Mint

Initial	Date	Name
B, LB	1844-66	Theodor Wilhelm Bruel in Hannover
RB	1673-1676	Rudolf Bornemann

DUCHY
REGULAR COINAGE

KM# 1032 2-1/2 THALER
3.3200 g., 0.9000 Gold .0961 oz. AGW **Ruler:** Karl Wilhelm Ferdinand **Obv:** Arms change **Rev:** Value and date

Date	Mintage	F	VF	XF	Unc	BU
1801 MC	—	375	750	1,350	2,000	—
1801 MC	—	375	750	1,350	2,000	—
1802 MC	—	300	625	1,150	1,750	—
1806 MC	—	300	625	1,150	2,000	—

KM# 1066 2-1/2 THALER
3.3200 g., 0.9000 Gold .0961 oz. AGW **Obv:** Crowned many quartered arms with garlands **Rev:** Denomination, F.R. below

Date	Mintage	F	VF	XF	Unc	BU
1815 FR	—	600	1,000	1,650	2,500	—

KM# 1072 2-1/2 THALER
3.3200 g., 0.9000 Gold .0961 oz. AGW **Ruler:** Karl II under regency of George III of Great Britain **Obv:** Crowned arms **Obv. Legend:** PRINC REGENS GEORGIVS D dot G dot **Rev:** Denomination, date **Rev. Legend:** BR. . .

Date	Mintage	F	VF	XF	Unc	BU
1816 FR	—	575	800	1,125	1,750	—
1818 FR	—	825	1,150	1,350	2,000	—
1819 FR	—	700	950	1,250	1,750	—

KM# 1095 2-1/2 THALER
3.3200 g., 0.9000 Gold .0961 oz. AGW **Ruler:** Karl II under regency of George IV of Great Britain **Obv:** Crowned arms **Obv. Legend:** REX BRITAIN GEORG dot IV.... **Rev:** Denomination, date

Date	Mintage	F	VF	XF	Unc	BU
1822 CvC	—	550	900	1,500	2,000	—

KM# 1113 2-1/2 THALER
3.3200 g., 0.9000 Gold .0961 oz. AGW **Ruler:** Karl II **Rev:** Without legend around border

Date	Mintage	F	VF	XF	Unc	BU
1825 CvC	—	350	500	875	1,500	—
1828 CvC	—	425	625	1,000	1,650	—

KM# 1117 2-1/2 THALER
3.3200 g., 0.9000 Gold .0961 oz. AGW **Ruler:** Karl II **Obv:** Uniformed bust left **Obv. Legend:** CARL SOUV. HERZOG V. BRAUNSCH. U. LUEN. **Rev:** Crowned, mantled and supported arms **Rev. Legend:** 2 1/2 THALER

Date	Mintage	F	VF	XF	Unc	BU
1829 CvC	—	400	600	900	1,500	—

KM# 1125 2-1/2 THALER
3.3200 g., 0.9000 Gold .0961 oz. AGW **Ruler:** Wilhelm **Obv:** Crowned arms with supporters **Obv. Legend:** WILHELM HERZOG, Z.BR.U.L. below **Rev:** Denomination

Date	Mintage	F	VF	XF	Unc	BU
1832 CvC	—	450	650	1,000	1,500	—

KM# 1145 2-1/2 THALER
3.3200 g., 0.9000 Gold .0961 oz. AGW **Ruler:** Wilhelm **Obv:** Head right **Obv. Legend:** WILHELM HERZOG Z. BRAUNSCHW. U. L. **Rev:** Denomination, date

Date	Mintage	F	VF	XF	Unc	BU
1851 B	4,138	350	500	750	1,100	—

KM# 1025 5 THALER
6.6500 g., 0.9000 Gold .1924 oz. AGW **Ruler:** Karl Wilhelm Ferdinand **Obv:** Crowned arms within Order chain **Obv. Legend:** FERDINANDVS CAROLVS GVILIELMVS **Rev:** Value, date

Date	Mintage	F	VF	XF	Unc	BU
1801 MC	—	475	875	1,250	2,000	—
1802 MC	—	325	625	1,000	1,800	—
1803 MC Rare	—	—	—	—	—	—
1804 MC	—	475	875	1,250	2,000	—
1805 MC	—	450	750	1,150	1,850	—
1806 MC	—	450	750	1,150	1,850	—

KM# 1081 5 THALER
6.6500 g., 0.9000 Gold .1924 oz. AGW **Ruler:** Fredrich Wilhelm **Obv:** Crowned arms **Obv. Legend:** FRIDERICVS GVILIELMVS **Rev:** Denomination, date

Date	Mintage	F	VF	XF	Unc	BU
1814 FR	—	—	—	—	—	—

KM# 1062 5 THALER
6.6500 g., 0.9000 Gold .1924 oz. AGW **Obv:** Crowned arms **Rev:** Denomination

Date	Mintage	F	VF	XF	Unc	BU
1814 FR	—	500	925	1,350	2,000	—
1815 FR	—	425	800	1,200	1,850	—

KM# 1073 5 THALER
6.6500 g., 0.9000 Gold .1924 oz. AGW **Ruler:** Karl II under regency of George III of Great Britain **Rev. Legend:** Ends:... BR. ET LVN

Date	Mintage	F	VF	XF	Unc	BU
1816 FR	—	575	1,000	1,650	2,250	—
1817 FR	—	475	875	1,500	2,150	—
1818 FR	—	575	1,000	1,650	2,250	—
1819 FR	—	575	1,000	1,650	2,250	—

KM# 1096 5 THALER
6.6500 g., 0.9000 Gold .1924 oz. AGW **Ruler:** Karl II under regency of George IV of Great Britain

Date	Mintage	F	VF	XF	Unc	BU
1822 CvC	—	575	1,000	1,650	2,250	—
1823 CvC	—	750	1,250	1,850	2,750	—

KM# 1110 5 THALER
6.6500 g., 0.9000 Gold .1924 oz. AGW **Ruler:** Karl II **Obv:** Crowned arms **Obv. Legend:** ZU BR. U. LUEN. CARL HERZOG **Rev:** Denomination, date

Date	Mintage	F	VF	XF	Unc	BU
1824 CvC	—	325	625	950	1,500	—
1825 CvC	—	345	675	1,000	1,650	—

GERMAN STATES — BRUNSWICK-WOLFENBUTTEL

Date	Mintage	F	VF	XF	Unc	BU
1828 CvC	—	345	675	1,000	1,650	—
1830 CvC	—	400	775	1,150	1,750	—

KM# 1126 5 THALER
6.6500 g., 0.9000 Gold .1924 oz. AGW **Ruler:** Wilhelm **Obv:** Crowned arms flanked by wildmen **Rev:** Denomination, date

Date	Mintage	F	VF	XF	Unc	BU
1832 CvC	—	425	800	1,250	1,850	—
1834 CvC	—	475	900	1,500	2,150	—

KM# 1041 10 THALER
13.3000 g., 0.9000 Gold .3848 oz. AGW **Ruler:** Karl Wilhelm Ferdinand **Obv:** Change in arms **Obv. Legend:** FERDINANDVS CAROLVS GVILIELMVS **Rev:** Value, date

Date	Mintage	F	VF	XF	Unc	BU
1801 MC	—	675	1,150	2,000	3,000	—
1804 MC	—	750	1,250	2,000	3,000	—
1805 MC	—	550	875	1,500	2,500	—
1806 MC	—	750	1,250	1,850	2,750	—

KM# 1054 10 THALER
13.3000 g., 0.9000 Gold .3848 oz. AGW **Ruler:** Fredrich Wilhelm **Obv:** Crowned arms **Obv. Legend:** FRIDERICVS GVILIELMVS **Rev:** Denomination, date

Date	Mintage	F	VF	XF	Unc	BU
1813 MC	—	750	1,250	1,850	2,750	—
1814 MC	—	675	1,150	1,750	2,350	—

KM# 1055 10 THALER
13.3000 g., 0.9000 Gold .3848 oz. AGW **Ruler:** Fredrich Wilhelm

Date	Mintage	F	VF	XF	Unc	BU
1814 FR	—	750	1,250	1,850	3,000	—

KM# 1074 10 THALER
13.3000 g., 0.9000 Gold .3848 oz. AGW **Ruler:** Karl II under regency of George III of Great Britain **Obv:** Crowned arms **Obv. Legend:** PRINC. REGENS GRORGIVS D dot G dot **Rev:** Denomination, date

Date	Mintage	F	VF	XF	Unc	BU
1817 FR	—	675	1,150	1,750	2,500	—
1818 FR	—	550	875	1,500	2,500	—
1819 FR	—	675	1,150	1,750	2,500	—

KM# 1097 10 THALER
13.3000 g., 0.9000 Gold .3848 oz. AGW **Ruler:** Karl II under regency of George IV of Great Britain

Date	Mintage	F	VF	XF	Unc	BU
1822 CvC	—	750	1,250	1,850	3,000	—

KM# 1111 10 THALER
13.3000 g., 0.9000 Gold .3848 oz. AGW **Ruler:** Karl II **Obv:** Crowned arms **Obv. Legend:** ZU BR. U. LUEN. CARL HERZOG **Rev:** Denomination, date

Date	Mintage	F	VF	XF	Unc	BU
1824 CvC	—	750	1,250	1,850	2,750	—
1825 CvC	—	600	1,000	1,650	2,500	—
1829 CvC	—	825	1,350	2,000	2,750	—
1830 CvC	—	750	1,250	1,850	2,500	—

KM# 1115 10 THALER
13.3000 g., 0.9000 Gold .3848 oz. AGW **Ruler:** Karl II **Obv:** Uniformed bust left **Obv. Legend:** CARL SOUV. HERZOG V. BRAUNSCH. U. LUENEB. **Rev:** Crowned and supported arms within crowned mantle

Date	Mintage	F	VF	XF	Unc	BU
1827 CvC	—	900	1,500	2,500	3,750	—
1828 CvC	—	900	1,500	2,500	3,750	—
1829 CvC	—	825	1,350	2,000	3,000	—
1829 CvC Proof	—	Value: 5,500				

KM# 1121 10 THALER
13.3000 g., 0.9000 Gold .3848 oz. AGW **Ruler:** Wilhelm **Obv:** Rearing horse left **Obv. Legend:** WILHELM HERZOG V. BR. U. LUEN. **Rev:** Denomination, date

Date	Mintage	F	VF	XF	Unc	BU
1831 CvC	—	750	1,250	1,850	2,500	—

KM# 1122 10 THALER
13.3000 g., 0.9000 Gold .3848 oz. AGW **Ruler:** Wilhelm **Obv:** Wildmen flanking crowned arms **Obv. Legend:** WILHELM HERZOG, Z.BR.U.L. below **Rev:** Denomination and date within wreath

Date	Mintage	F	VF	XF	Unc	BU
1831 CvC	—	525	875	1,350	2,250	—
1832 CvC	—	525	875	1,350	2,250	—
1833 CvC	—	600	1,000	1,500	2,250	—
1834 CvC	—	450	750	1,250	2,250	—

KM# 1141 10 THALER
13.3000 g., 0.9000 Gold .3848 oz. AGW **Ruler:** Wilhelm **Obv:** Head right **Obv. Legend:** WILHELM HERZOG Z. BRAUNSCHW.U.L. **Rev:** Crowned and mantled arms

Date	Mintage	F	VF	XF	Unc	BU
1850 B	9,763	975	1,650	2,150	2,750	—

KM# 1147 10 THALER
13.3000 g., 0.9000 Gold .3848 oz. AGW **Ruler:** Wilhelm **Obv:** Head right **Obv. Legend:** WILHELM HERZOG Z. BRAUNSCHW. U. LUN. **Rev:** Crowned and mantled arms **Rev. Legend:** ZWEI THALER E.M. 258 GR. E.

Date	Mintage	F	VF	XF	Unc	BU
1853 B	150,000	400	650	1,000	2,000	—
1854 B	163,000	400	650	1,000	2,000	—
1855 B	20,000	750	1,250	1,750	2,500	—
1856 B	57,000	400	650	1,000	2,000	—
1857 B	54,000	400	650	1,100	2,250	—

KM# 1153 KRONE
11.1110 g., 0.9000 Gold .3215 oz. AGW **Ruler:** Wilhelm **Obv:** Head right **Obv. Legend:** WILHELM HERZOG Z. BRAUN-SCHWEIG U. LUN. **Rev:** Denomination above date within wreath **Rev. Legend:** * VEREINSMUNZE *, 50 EIN PFUND FEIN below

Date	Mintage	F	VF	XF	Unc	BU
1858 B	32,000	500	950	1,450	2,500	—
1859 B	13,000	600	1,150	1,850	3,000	—

KM# 1160 20 MARK
7.9650 g., 0.9000 Gold .2304 oz. AGW **Ruler:** Wilhelm **Obv:** Head left **Obv. Legend:** WILHELM HERZOG Z. BRAUNSCHWEIG U. LUN. **Rev:** Type II **Rev. Legend:** DEUTSCHES REICH 1875, 20 MARK below

Date	Mintage	F	VF	XF	Unc	BU
1875A	100,000	350	700	1,000	1,750	2,500

TRADE COINAGE

KM# 1023 DUCAT
3.5000 g., 0.9860 Gold .1109 oz. AGW **Ruler:** Karl Wilhelm Ferdinand **Obv:** Crowned arms **Rev:** Value, date

Date	Mintage	F	VF	XF	Unc	BU
1801 MC	—	450	750	1,250	1,600	—

KM# 1063 DUCAT
3.5000 g., 0.9860 Gold .1109 oz. AGW **Ruler:** Fredrich Wilhelm **Obv:** Crowned many quartered arms with garlands **Rev:** Denomination, EX AVRO HERCINIA

Date	Mintage	F	VF	XF	Unc	BU
ND1814 HC	376	575	1,000	1,750	2,350	—

KM# 1067 DUCAT
3.5000 g., 0.9860 Gold .1109 oz. AGW **Ruler:** Fredrich Wilhelm **Obv:** Crowned arms **Rev:** Denomination, date

Date	Mintage	F	VF	XF	Unc	BU
ND1815 FR	220	725	1,250	2,000	2,750	—

KM# 1114 DUCAT
3.5000 g., 0.9860 Gold .1109 oz. AGW **Ruler:** Karl II

Date	Mintage	F	VF	XF	Unc	BU
ND1825 CvC	—	530	750	1,250	2,100	2,850

HAMBURG

GERMAN STATES 253

PATTERNS
Including off metal strikes

KM#	Date	Mintage	Identification	Mkt Val
Pn44	1813	—	5 Thaler. Crowned arms. Denomination, date.	—
Pn46	1827	—	10 Thaler. Copper. Uniformed bust left. Crowned arms with supporters within crowned mantle.	—
Pn47	1827	—	10 Thaler. Silver.	—
Pn48	1827	—	10 Thaler. Silver. Uniface.	—
Pn53	1857 B	—	Krone. 0.9000 Gold. KM#1153.	3,000

FRANKFURT AM MAIN

One of the largest cities of modern Germany, Frankfurt is located on the north bank of the Main River about 25 miles (42 kilometers) upstream from where it joins the Rhine at Mainz. It was the site of a Roman camp in the first century. Frankfurt was a commercial center from the early Middle Ages and became a favored location for imperial councils during the Carolingian period because of its central location. An imperial mint operated from early times and had a large production during the 12th to 14th centuries. Local issues were produced from at least the mid-14th century, but it was not until 1428 that the city was officially granted the right to coin its own money. In establishing the seven permanent electors of the Empire in 1356, the Golden Bull also made Frankfurt the site of those elections and increased the prestige of the city even further. Frankfurt remained a free city until 1806 and then was the capital of the Grand Duchy of Frankfurt from 1810 until 1814, only to regain its free status in 1815. The city chose the wrong side in the Austro-Prussian War of 1866 and thus was absorbed by victorious Prussia in the latter year.

RULER
Carl Theodor v. Dalberg, 1810-15

MINT MARKS
F - Frankfurt

MINT OFFICIALS' INITIALS

Frankfurt Mint

Initials	Date	Name
A. V. NORDHEIM	1857-66	An engraver
G.B., I.G.B.	1790-1825	Johann Georg Bunsen
GH	1798-1816	Georg Hille, warden
S.T.	1836-37	Samuel Tomschutz
Z	1843-56	Johann Philipp Zollman

Wiesbaden Mint

ZOLLMANN	1818-43	Johann Philipp, engraver

NOTE: In some instances old dies were used with initials beyond the date range of the man that held the position.

ARMS
Crowned eagle, usually in circle.

FREE CITY
TRADE COINAGE

KM# 302 DUCAT
3.5000 g., 0.9860 Gold 0.111 oz. AGW **Subject:** 300th Anniversary of the Reformation

Date	Mintage	VG	F	VF	XF	Unc
1817	—	—	80.00	140	250	400

KM# 352 DUCAT
3.5000 g., 0.9860 Gold .1109 oz. AGW **Obv:** Crowned eagle with wings open **Rev:** Inscription: Denomination and date within wreath

Date	Mintage	F	VF	XF	Unc	BU
1853	1,121	300	450	900	1,600	—
1856	665	325	700	1,200	1,800	—

MEDALLIC ISSUES

X# 1a DUCAT
Silver **Subject:** Reformation **Note:** Prev. Pn49. Similar to M1.

Date	Mintage	F	VF	XF	Unc	BU
1817	—	—	—	—	—	—

X# 1 DUCAT
3.5000 g., 0.9860 Gold .1109 oz. AGW **Subject:** 300th Anniversary of the Reformation **Note:** Prev. KM#302; KM#M1.

Date	Mintage	F	VF	XF	Unc	BU
1817	—	850	130	200	350	—

X# 2 2 DUCAT
7.0000 g., 0.9860 Gold .2219 oz. AGW **Subject:** 300th Anniversary of the Reformation **Note:** Prev. KM#303; KM#M2.

Date	Mintage	F	VF	XF	Unc	BU
1817	—	—	—	—	—	—

PATTERNS
Including off metal strikes

KM#	Date	Mintage	Identification	Mkt Val
Pn54	1839	—	Gulden. Silver. Proof	3,000
Pn55	1848	—	2 Gulden. Gold. KM#333.	—
Pn56	1849	—	2 Gulden. Gold. KM#341.1.	150

HAMBURG

The city of Hamburg is located on the Elbe River about 75 miles from the North Sea. It was founded by Charlemagne in the 9th century. In 1241 it joined Lübeck to form the Hanseatic League. The mint right was leased to the citizens in 1292. However, the first local halfpennies had been struck almost 50 years earlier. In 1510 Hamburg was formally made a Free City, though, in fact, it had been free for about 250 years. It was occupied by the French during the Napoleonic period. In 1866 it joined the North German Confederation and became a part of the German Empire in 1871. The Hamburg coinage is almost continuous up to the time of World War I.

MINT OFFICIALS' INITIALS

Initials	Date	Name
CAIG, CAJG	1813	C.A.J. Ginquembre, French director of mint
HSK	1805-42	Hans Schierven Knoph
OHK	1761-1805	Otto Heinrich Knorre
	1772-1806	Johann Joachim Struve, warden

CITY ARMS
A triple-turreted gate, often includes nettleleaf of Holstein.

FREE CITY
TRADE COINAGE

KM# 227.1 DUCAT
3.4900 g., 0.9790 Gold .1099 oz. AGW **Obv:** Titles of Franz II **Rev:** Legend within square, castle above, ornaments surround

Date	Mintage	F	VF	XF	Unc	BU
1801	7,236	375	625	1,000	1,500	—
1802	9,199	375	625	1,000	1,500	—
1803	6,365	375	625	1,000	1,500	—
1804	7,284	375	625	1,000	1,500	—
1805	9,466	375	625	1,000	1,500	—

KM# 227.2 DUCAT
3.4900 g., 0.9790 Gold .1099 oz. AGW **Obv:** Crowned orb at center of double eagle holding sword and sceptre **Rev:** Legend within square, castle above, ornaments surround

Date	Mintage	F	VF	XF	Unc	BU
1806	7,521	375	625	1,000	1,500	—

KM# 237 DUCAT
3.4900 g., 0.9790 Gold .1099 oz. AGW **Obv:** Standing figure with shield **Rev:** Legend within square, castle above, ornaments surround

Date	Mintage	F	VF	XF	Unc	BU
1807	6,000	375	625	1,100	1,650	—

KM# 239 DUCAT
3.4900 g., 0.9790 Gold .1099 oz. AGW **Obv:** Castle, date below **Rev:** Legend within square, castle above, ornaments surround

Date	Mintage	F	VF	XF	Unc	BU
1808	7,500	350	575	950	1,450	—
1809	7,500	300	500	875	1,400	—
1810	7,407	300	500	875	1,400	—

KM# 245 DUCAT
3.4900 g., 0.9790 Gold .1099 oz. AGW **Obv:** Knight with lance and raised shield **Rev:** Legend within square, castle above, ornaments surround

Date	Mintage	F	VF	XF	Unc	BU
1811	11,000	300	500	875	1,250	—
1815	9,965	300	500	875	1,250	—
1817	5,000	325	550	975	1,350	—
1818	7,000	325	550	975	1,350	—
1819	8,901	300	500	875	1,250	—
1820	7,000	300	500	875	1,250	—
1821	9,900	300	500	875	1,250	—
1822	13,000	300	500	875	1,250	—
1823	8,700	300	500	875	1,250	—
1824	6,970	300	500	875	1,250	—
1825	10,000	300	500	875	1,250	—
1826	12,000	300	500	875	1,250	—
1827	11,000	300	500	875	1,250	—
1828	8,601	300	500	875	1,250	—
1829	9,606	300	500	875	1,250	—
1830	12,000	300	500	875	1,250	—
1831	9,200	300	500	875	1,250	—
1832	9,500	300	500	875	1,250	—
1833	9,440	300	500	875	1,250	—
1834	10,000	250	400	750	1,000	—

KM# 256 DUCAT
3.4900 g., 0.9790 Gold .1099 oz. AGW **Obv:** Knight with lance **Rev:** Legend within square, castle above, ornaments surround

Date	Mintage	F	VF	XF	Unc	BU
1835	10,000	250	425	750	1,150	—
1836	8,067	250	425	750	1,150	—
1837	8,156	250	425	750	1,150	—
1838	9,000	250	425	750	1,150	—
1839	9,045	250	425	750	1,150	—
1840	9,882	250	425	750	1,150	—
1841	10,000	250	425	750	1,150	—
1842	12,000	225	375	625	1,000	—

KM# 263 DUCAT
3.4900 g., 0.9790 Gold .1099 oz. AGW **Obv:** Knight with lance left, shield down **Rev:** Legend within ornamental frame **Note:** Struck in a collar.

Date	Mintage	F	VF	XF	Unc	BU
1843	12,000	225	375	625	1,000	—
1844	9,768	250	425	750	1,150	—

GERMAN STATES

HAMBURG

Date	Mintage	F	VF	XF	Unc	BU
1845	12,000	200	325	550	875	—
1846	11,000	200	325	550	875	—
1847	10,000	200	325	550	875	—
1848	13,000	200	325	550	875	—
1849	10,000	200	325	550	875	—
1850	11,000	200	325	550	875	—

KM# 273 DUCAT
3.4900 g., 0.9790 Gold .1099 oz. AGW **Obv:** Knights' shield redesigned **Rev:** Legend within ornamental frame

Date	Mintage	F	VF	XF	Unc	BU
1851	8,497	225	375	750	1,000	—
1852	9,476	225	375	750	1,000	—
1853	10,000	225	375	750	1,000	—

KM# 274 DUCAT
3.4900 g., 0.9790 Gold .1099 oz. AGW **Obv:** Knight with pointed shield **Rev:** Legend within ornamental frame **Rev. Legend:** ...979 MILLES

Date	Mintage	F	VF	XF	Unc	BU
1854	12,000	175	250	400	750	—
1855	11,000	175	250	400	750	—
1856	11,000	175	250	400	750	—
1857	12,000	175	250	400	750	—
1858	10,000	175	250	400	750	—
1859	14,000	175	250	400	750	—
1860	15,000	175	250	400	750	—
1861	15,000	175	250	400	750	—
1862	17,000	150	200	350	700	—
1863	20,000	150	200	350	700	—
1864	24,000	150	200	350	700	—
1865	17,000	150	200	350	700	—
1866	24,000	150	200	350	700	—
1867	26,000	150	200	350	700	—

KM# 280 DUCAT
3.4900 g., 0.9790 Gold .1099 oz. AGW **Obv:** Knight with pointed shield **Rev:** Mint mark B below shell

Date	Mintage	F	VF	XF	Unc	BU
1868B	25,000	135	175	300	600	—
1869B	26,000	135	175	300	600	—
1870B	30,000	135	175	300	600	—
1871B	30,000	135	175	300	600	—
1872B	30,000	135	175	300	600	—

KM# 228.1 2 DUCAT
6.9800 g., 0.9790 Gold .2197 oz. AGW **Obv:** Crowned orb at center of double eagle with sword and sceptre **Obv. Legend:** FRANCISVS II D. G. ROM. IMP... **Rev:** Legend within square ornamental frame

Date	Mintage	F	VF	XF	Unc	BU
1801	1,273	650	1,250	1,750	2,450	—
1802	1,256	650	1,250	1,750	2,450	—
1803	837	650	1,350	2,350	3,000	—
1804	—	650	1,300	2,000	2,750	—
1805	—	650	1,250	1,750	2,450	—

Note: Mintage included in KM#227.1

KM# 228.2 2 DUCAT
6.9800 g., 0.9790 Gold .2197 oz. AGW **Obv:** Crowned orb at center of double eagle with sword and sceptre **Obv. Legend:** ...D. G. R. IMP... **Rev:** Legend within square ornamental frame

Date	Mintage	F	VF	XF	Unc	BU
1804	1,072	650	1,250	1,750	2,450	—
1806	1,201	650	1,250	1,750	2,450	—

KM# 240 2 DUCAT
6.9800 g., 0.9790 Gold .2197 oz. AGW

Date	Mintage	F	VF	XF	Unc	BU
1808	1,250	500	1,000	1,500	2,150	—
1809	1,250	500	1,000	1,500	2,150	—
1810	1,050	500	1,000	1,500	2,150	—

REFORM COINAGE

KM# 291 5 MARK
1.9910 g., 0.9000 Gold .0576 oz. AGW **Obv:** Helmeted arms with lion supporters **Obv. Legend:** FREIE UND HANSESTADT HAMBURG **Rev:** Crowned imperial eagle **Rev. Legend:** DEUTSCHES REICH 1977, 5 MARK below

Date	Mintage	F	VF	XF	Unc	BU
1877J	441,000	200	300	400	600	800
1877J Proof; Rare	—	—	—	—	—	—

KM# 285 10 MARK
3.9820 g., 0.9000 Gold .1152 oz. AGW **Obv:** Helmeted ornate arms **Obv. Legend:** FREIE UND HANSESTADT HAMBURG **Rev:** Type I **Rev. Legend:** DEUTSCHES REICH

Date	Mintage	F	VF	XF	Unc	BU
1873B	25,000	600	1,300	2,000	3,500	4,500
1873B Proof; Rare	—	—	—	—	—	—

KM# 286 10 MARK
3.9820 g., 0.9000 Gold .1152 oz. AGW **Obv:** Helmeted ornate arms **Obv. Legend:** FREIE UND HANSESTADT HAMBURG **Rev:** Type II **Rev. Legend:** DEUTSCHES REICH

Date	Mintage	F	VF	XF	Unc	BU
1874B	50,000	450	800	1,500	2,500	3,000

KM# 288 10 MARK
3.9820 g., 0.9000 Gold .1152 oz. AGW **Obv:** Helmeted arms with lion supporters **Obv. Legend:** FREIE UND HANSESTADT HAMBURG **Rev:** Crowned imperial eagle **Rev. Legend:** DEUTSCHES REICH

Date	Mintage	F	VF	XF	Unc	BU
1875J	608,000	85.00	125	250	400	500
1875J Proof	—	Value: 1,000				
1876J	6,321	550	850	1,350	1,750	2,000
1877J	221,000	85.00	125	200	350	450
1878J	316,000	85.00	125	200	350	450
1879J	255,000	85.00	125	225	400	500
1880J	139,000	85.00	125	200	350	450
1888J	163,000	85.00	125	200	350	450

KM# 292 10 MARK
3.9820 g., 0.9000 Gold .1152 oz. AGW **Obv:** Helmeted arms with lion supporters **Obv. Legend:** FREIE UND HANSESTADT HAMBURG **Rev:** Crowned imperial eagle, type II **Rev. Legend:** DEUTSCHES REICH

Date	Mintage	F	VF	XF	Unc	BU
1890J	245,000	90.00	150	225	350	400
1893J	246,000	90.00	150	225	350	400
1896J	164,000	90.00	150	225	350	400
1898J	344,000	90.00	150	225	350	400
1900J	82,000	90.00	150	225	350	450
1901J	82,000	90.00	150	175	385	500
1902J	41,000	120	225	350	650	1,000
1903J	310,000	90.00	150	175	350	500
1905J	164,000	90.00	150	175	350	500
1906J	164,000	90.00	150	175	350	500
1907J	111,000	90.00	150	175	350	500
1908J	32,000	150	300	450	800	1,300
1909J	122,000	90.00	150	175	350	500
1909J Proof	—	Value: 1,600				
1910J	41,000	120	225	300	600	1,000
1910J Proof	—	Value: 2,000				
1911J	75,000	95.00	175	250	300	800
1911J Proof	—	Value: 6,000				
1912J	48,000	145	245	350	500	1,000
1912J Proof	—	Value: 2,000				
1913J	41,000	145	245	300	400	1,000
1913J Proof	—	Value: 2,000				

KM# 289 20 MARK
7.9650 g., 0.9000 Gold .2304 oz. AGW **Obv:** Helmeted arms with lion supporters **Obv. Legend:** FREIE UND HANSESTADT HAMBURG **Rev:** Crowned imperial eagle, type II **Rev. Legend:** DEUTSCHES REICH

Date	Mintage	F	VF	XF	Unc	BU
1875J	313,000	—	160	190	285	350
1876J	1,723,000	—	BV	155	250	325
1877J	1,324,000	—	BV	160	250	325
1878J	2,008,000	—	BV	160	250	325
1879J	104,000	225	375	700	1,250	1,500
1880J	120,000	BV	165	275	400	500
1881J	500	10,000	15,000	20,000	30,000	35,000
1883J	125,000	—	BV	175	300	400
1884J	639,000	—	BV	175	300	400
1887J	251,000	—	BV	165	300	375
1889J	14,000	400	900	1,250	1,800	2,200

KM# 295 20 MARK
7.9650 g., 0.9000 Gold .2304 oz. AGW **Obv:** Helmeted arms with lion supporters **Obv. Legend:** FREIE UND HANSESTADT HAMBURG **Rev:** Crowned imperial eagle, type III **Rev. Legend:** DEUTSCHES REICH

Date	Mintage	F	VF	XF	Unc	BU
1893J	815,000	—	BV	180	225	300
1894J	501,000	—	BV	180	225	300
1895J	501,000	—	BV	180	225	300
1897J	500,000	—	BV	180	225	300
1899J	1,002,000	—	BV	160	200	275
1900J	501,000	—	BV	170	225	300
1908J Rare	14	—	—	—	75,000	—
1913J	491,000	—	BV	160	200	275
1913J Proof	—	Value: 1,000				

PATTERNS
Including off metal strikes

KM#	Date	Mintage	Identification	Mkt Val
Pn15	1826 HSK	—	Schilling. Gold. KM#251.1	400
Pn16	1836 HSK	—	Sechsling. Gold. KM#236	175
Pn17	1877J	—	10 Mark. Silver. Plain edge. KM#288	—
Pn18	1877J	—	10 Mark. Copper. KM#288	—
Pn19	1882J	—	20 Mark. Silver. Plain edge. KM#288	—

HANNOVER
KINGDOM

Located in North Central Germany, Hannover had its beginnings as early as the 12th century. The city obtained the mint right in 1331, but fell under the control of the dukes of Brunswick who later made it their residence. Hannover eventually became the capital of the Kingdom of the same name. The city coinage lasted until 1674.

RULERS
George III, 1760-1820
Georg IV, 1820-1830
Wilhelm IV, 1830-1837
Ernst August, 1837-1851
Georg V, 1851-1866

MINT MARKS
A - Clausthal, 1832-1849
B - Hannover, 1866-1878
C - Clausthal, 1814-1833

HANNOVER

GERMAN STATES

MINT OFFICIALS' INITIALS

Initial	Date	Name
B	1817-38	Ludwig August Bruel
B	1844-68	Theodor Wilhelm Bruel
CHH, H	1802-17	Christian Heinrich Haase
LAB, LB	1817-38	Ludwig August Bruel
S	1839-44	Carl Schulter

ARMS
3-petaled flower or complex arms consisting of twin-towered city gate, 3-petaled flower in portal and rampant lion left between towers.

REGULAR COINAGE

KM# 109 2-1/2 THALER
3.3400 g., 0.9030 Gold .0970 oz. AGW **Ruler:** George III **Obv:** Rearing horse left **Rev:** Denomination, date

Date	Mintage	F	VF	XF	Unc	BU
1814 CHH	—	325	500	750	1,150	—

KM# 130 2-1/2 THALER
3.3400 g., 0.9030 Gold .0970 oz. AGW **Ruler:** Georg IV **Obv:** Laureate head left **Rev:** Denomination, date

Date	Mintage	F	VF	XF	Unc	BU
1821B	—	225	450	675	1,100	—
1827B	—	225	450	675	1,100	—
1830B	—	225	450	675	1,100	—

KM# 152 2-1/2 THALER
3.3400 g., 0.9030 Gold .0970 oz. AGW **Ruler:** Wilhelm IV **Obv:** Head right **Rev:** Denomination, date

Date	Mintage	F	VF	XF	Unc	BU
1832B	—	200	400	600	1,000	—
1833B	—	200	400	600	1,000	—
1835B	—	200	400	600	1,000	—

KM# 152a 2-1/2 THALER
3.3200 g., 0.8960 Gold .0956 oz. AGW **Ruler:** Wilhelm IV **Obv:** Head right **Rev:** Denomination, date

Date	Mintage	F	VF	XF	Unc	BU
1836B	—	150	300	550	900	—
1837B	—	150	300	550	900	—

KM# 185.1 2-1/2 THALER
3.3200 g., 0.8960 Gold .0956 oz. AGW **Ruler:** Ernst August **Obv:** Head right **Obv. Legend:** ERNST AUGUST V.G.G. KOENIG V. HANNOVER **Rev:** Denomination, date

Date	Mintage	F	VF	XF	Unc	BU
1839 S	—	225	400	600	1,000	—
1840 S	—	225	400	600	1,000	—
1843 S	—	225	400	600	1,000	—

KM# 185.2 2-1/2 THALER
3.3200 g., 0.8960 Gold .0956 oz. AGW **Ruler:** Ernst August **Obv:** Head right **Rev:** Denomination, date

Date	Mintage	F	VF	XF	Unc	BU
1845B	—	225	400	600	1,000	—
1846B	—	225	400	600	1,000	—
1847B	—	225	400	600	1,000	—
1848B	—	225	400	600	1,000	—

KM# 215 2-1/2 THALER
3.3200 g., 0.8960 Gold .0956 oz. AGW **Ruler:** Ernst August **Obv:** Head right **Obv. Legend:** ERNST AUGUST KOENIG VON HANNOVER **Rev:** Crowned arms

Date	Mintage	F	VF	XF	Unc	BU
1850B	—	200	300	500	900	—

KM# 223 2-1/2 THALER
3.3200 g., 0.8960 Gold .0956 oz. AGW **Ruler:** Georg V **Obv:** BREHMER F. at truncation, B below **Obv. Legend:** GEORG V v. G. G. KOENIG v. HANNOVER **Rev:** Crowned arms

Date	Mintage	F	VF	XF	Unc	BU
1853B	—	250	500	1,000	1,500	—
1855B	—	175	350	700	1,000	—

KM# 101 5 THALER
6.6500 g., 0.8960 Gold .1916 oz. AGW **Ruler:** George III **Obv:** Crowned arms **Obv. Legend:** GEORGIVS III• D•G•BRITANNIARVM REX•F•D **Rev:** Denomination, date **Rev. Legend:** BRUNSVICENS ET LUNEBVRG DVX•S•R•I•A•T•ET•E **Edge:** Reeded **Note:** Fr#619.

Date	Mintage	F	VF	XF	Unc	BU
1813 TW	—	200	300	750	1,500	—
1814 TW	—	200	300	750	1,500	—
1815 TW	—	250	400	875	1,750	—

KM# 110 5 THALER
6.6800 g., 0.9030 Gold .1940 oz. AGW **Ruler:** George III **Obv:** Rearing horse left **Rev:** Denomination, date

Date	Mintage	F	VF	XF	Unc	BU
1814C	—	825	1,200	2,000	3,250	—
1815C Rare	—	—	—	—	—	—

KM# 131 5 THALER
6.6800 g., 0.9030 Gold .1940 oz. AGW **Ruler:** Georg IV **Obv:** Rearing horse left **Rev:** Denomination, date

Date	Mintage	F	VF	XF	Unc	BU
1821C	185	1,500	2,000	3,000	7,500	—

KM# 132 5 THALER
6.6800 g., 0.9030 Gold .1940 oz. AGW **Ruler:** Georg IV **Obv:** Laureate head left **Rev:** Denomination, date

Date	Mintage	F	VF	XF	Unc	BU
1821B	—	250	450	700	1,000	—
1825B	—	250	450	700	1,000	—
1828B	—	250	450	700	1,000	—
1829B	—	250	450	700	1,000	—
1830B	—	250	450	700	1,000	—

KM# 170 5 THALER
6.6500 g., 0.8960 Gold .1916 oz. AGW **Ruler:** Wilhelm IV **Obv:** Head right **Obv. Legend:** WILHELM IV KOENIG V.GR.BRIT.U.HANNOVER **Rev:** Crowned circled arms **Rev. Legend:** FUNF THAL.

Date	Mintage	F	VF	XF	Unc	BU
1835B	—	350	500	750	1,500	—

KM# 186 5 THALER
6.6500 g., 0.8960 Gold .1916 oz. AGW **Ruler:** Ernst August **Obv:** Head right **Obv. Legend:** ERNST AUGUST V.G.G.KOENIG V.HANNOVER **Rev:** Crowned circled arms **Rev. Legend:** FUNF THAL.

Date	Mintage	F	VF	XF	Unc	BU
1839 S	—	400	700	1,000	1,800	—

KM# 204 5 THALER
6.6500 g., 0.8960 Gold .1916 oz. AGW **Ruler:** Ernst August **Obv:** B below head right **Obv. Legend:** ERNST AUGUST KOENIG V. HANNOVER **Rev:** Crowned arms **Rev. Legend:** FUNF THAL.

Date	Mintage	F	VF	XF	Unc	BU
1845B	—	300	500	800	1,350	—
1846B	—	375	650	1,000	1,600	—
1848B	—	375	650	1,000	1,600	—

KM# 210 5 THALER
6.6500 g., 0.8960 Gold .1916 oz. AGW **Ruler:** Ernst August **Obv:** Head right **Obv. Legend:** ERNST AUGUST KOENIG V. HANNOVER **Rev:** Crowned arms **Rev. Legend:** FUNF THLR.

Date	Mintage	F	VF	XF	Unc	BU
1849B	—	300	500	750	1,350	—
1851B	—	300	500	750	1,350	—

KM# 211 5 THALER
6.6500 g., 0.8960 Gold .1916 oz. AGW **Ruler:** Ernst August **Rev:** HARZ GOLD added to legend

Date	Mintage	F	VF	XF	Unc	BU
1849B	—	350	550	800	1,400	—
1850B	—	300	500	750	1,300	—

KM# 224 5 THALER
6.6500 g., 0.8960 Gold .1916 oz. AGW **Ruler:** Georg V **Obv:** BREHMER F. at truncation, B below **Obv. Legend:** GEORG V.v.G.G.KOENIG v.HANNOVER **Rev:** Crowned arms **Rev. Legend:** FUNF THLR.

GERMAN STATES — HANNOVER

Date	Mintage	F	VF	XF	Unc	BU
1853B	—	300	500	750	1,200	—
1855B	—	300	500	750	1,200	—
1856B	—	400	800	1,000	2,000	—

KM# 225 5 THALER
6.6500 g., 0.8960 Gold .1916 oz. AGW **Ruler:** Georg V **Obv:** Head left **Rev:** HARZ GOLD added to legend

Date	Mintage	F	VF	XF	Unc	BU
1853B	—	500	875	1,200	2,250	—
1856B	—	550	1,150	1,500	2,650	—

KM# 102 10 THALER
13.3600 g., 0.9030 Gold .3879 oz. AGW **Ruler:** George III **Obv:** Rearing horse left **Rev:** Denomination, date

Date	Mintage	F	VF	XF	Unc	BU
1813 CHH	—	1,000	1,500	2,000	3,250	—
1814 CHH	—	750	1,100	1,500	2,500	—

KM# 133 10 THALER
13.3600 g., 0.9030 Gold .3879 oz. AGW **Ruler:** Georg IV **Obv:** Laureate head left **Rev:** Denomination, date

Date	Mintage	F	VF	XF	Unc	BU
1821B	—	600	1,000	1,500	2,200	—
1822B	—	475	800	1,300	1,800	—
1822B HAONV	—	—	—	—	—	—
1823B	—	475	800	1,300	1,800	—
1824B	—	475	800	1,300	1,800	—
1825B	—	325	550	1,100	1,600	—
1827B	—	325	550	1,100	1,600	—
1828B	—	325	550	1,100	1,600	—
1829B	—	325	550	1,100	1,600	—
1830B	—	325	550	1,100	1,600	—

KM# 153 10 THALER
13.3600 g., 0.9030 Gold .3879 oz. AGW **Ruler:** Wilhelm IV **Obv:** Head right **Rev:** Crowned circular arms

Date	Mintage	F	VF	XF	Unc	BU
1832	—	550	900	1,250	2,500	—

KM# 155 10 THALER
13.3600 g., 0.9030 Gold .3879 oz. AGW **Ruler:** Wilhelm IV **Obv:** Head right **Rev:** Crowned circled arms

Date	Mintage	F	VF	XF	Unc	BU
1833	—	550	900	1,250	2,500	—

KM# 171.1 10 THALER
13.3000 g., 0.8960 Gold .3832 oz. AGW **Ruler:** Wilhelm IV **Obv:** B below head right **Obv. Legend:** ... HANNOV **Rev:** Crowned circled arms

Date	Mintage	F	VF	XF	Unc	BU
1835B	—	675	1,150	1,900	2,650	—

KM# 171.2 10 THALER
13.3000 g., 0.8960 Gold .3832 oz. AGW **Ruler:** Wilhelm IV **Obv:** Head right **Obv. Legend:** ... HANNOVER **Rev:** Crowned circled arms

Date	Mintage	F	VF	XF	Unc	BU
1835B	—	675	1,150	1,900	2,650	—

KM# 171.3 10 THALER
13.3000 g., 0.8960 Gold .3832 oz. AGW **Ruler:** Wilhelm IV **Obv:** Head right **Rev:** Date at bottom

Date	Mintage	F	VF	XF	Unc	BU
1836B	—	650	1,125	1,875	2,600	—
1837B	—	550	1,000	1,500	2,250	—

KM# 171.4 10 THALER
13.3000 g., 0.8960 Gold .3832 oz. AGW **Ruler:** Wilhelm IV **Obv:** Head right **Obv. Legend:** KONIG **Rev:** Crowned circled arms

Date	Mintage	F	VF	XF	Unc	BU
1836B	—	650	1,125	1,875	2,600	—

KM# 175 10 THALER
13.3000 g., 0.8960 Gold .3832 oz. AGW **Ruler:** Ernst August **Obv:** Head right **Obv. Legend:** ERNST AUGUST V.G.G.KOENIG V.HANNOVER **Rev:** Crowned circled arms

Date	Mintage	F	VF	XF	Unc	BU
1837B	—	—	—	10,000	15,000	—
1838B	—	500	900	1,500	2,250	—

KM# 187 10 THALER
13.3000 g., 0.8960 Gold .3832 oz. AGW **Ruler:** Ernst August **Obv:** S below head **Obv. Legend:** ERNST AUGUST V.G.G.KOENIG V.HANNOVER **Rev:** Crowned circled arms

Date	Mintage	F	VF	XF	Unc	BU
1839 S	—	400	600	1,200	2,000	—

KM# 200.1 10 THALER
13.3000 g., 0.8960 Gold .3832 oz. AGW **Ruler:** Ernst August **Obv:** BRANDT F. on truncation **Obv. Legend:** ERNST AUGUST V.G.G.KOENIG V.HANNOVER **Rev:** Crowned arms

Date	Mintage	F	VF	XF	Unc	BU
1844 S	—	600	1,000	1,500	2,250	—

KM# 200.2 10 THALER
13.3000 g., 0.8960 Gold .3832 oz. AGW **Ruler:** Ernst August **Obv:** B below head **Obv. Legend:** ERNST AUGUST V.G.G.KOENIG V.HANNOVER **Rev:** Crowned arms

Date	Mintage	F	VF	XF	Unc	BU
1844B	—	600	1,000	1,500	2,500	—

KM# 200.3 10 THALER
13.3000 g., 0.8960 Gold .3832 oz. AGW **Ruler:** Ernst August **Obv:** Without markings on truncation **Obv. Legend:** ERNST AUGUST V.G.G.KOENIG V.HANNOVER **Rev:** Crowned arms

Date	Mintage	F	VF	XF	Unc	BU
1846B	—	400	800	1,200	2,000	—
1847B	—	400	800	1,200	2,000	—
1848B	—	300	600	900	1,500	—

KM# 212 10 THALER
13.3000 g., 0.8960 Gold .3832 oz. AGW **Ruler:** Ernst August **Obv:** Head right **Obv. Legend:** ERNST AUGUST KOENIG VON HANNOVER **Rev:** Crowned arms

Date	Mintage	F	VF	XF	Unc	BU
1849B	—	500	1,000	1,500	2,250	—
1850B	—	350	600	1,000	1,500	—
1851B	—	500	1,000	1,500	2,250	—

KM# 226 10 THALER
13.3000 g., 0.8960 Gold .3832 oz. AGW **Ruler:** Georg V **Obv:** Head left **Obv. Legend:** GEORG V v. G.G. KOENIG v. HANNOVER **Rev:** Crowned arms **Rev. Legend:** ZEHN THLR.

Date	Mintage	F	VF	XF	Unc	BU
1853B	—	450	750	1,250	1,750	—
1854B	—	300	500	900	1,250	—
1855B	—	450	750	1,250	1,750	—
1856B	—	500	900	1,500	2,150	—

HESSE-CASSEL

TRADE COINAGE

KM# 111 DUCAT
3.5000 g., 0.8960 Gold .1109 oz. AGW **Ruler:** George III **Obv:** Rearing horse left **Rev:** Denomination, date

Date	Mintage	F	VF	XF	Unc	BU
1815C	—	525	875	1,400	2,000	—
1818C	—	600	1,000	1,650	2,250	—

KM# 134 DUCAT
3.5000 g., 0.8960 Gold .1109 oz. AGW **Ruler:** Georg IV

Date	Mintage	F	VF	XF	Unc	BU
1821C	252	975	1,650	2,400	3,250	—
1824C	749	900	1,500	2,250	3,000	—
1827C	1,300	825	1,400	2,000	2,750	—

KM# 149 DUCAT
3.5000 g., 0.8960 Gold .1109 oz. AGW **Ruler:** Wilhelm IV **Obv:** Rearing horse left **Rev:** Denomination, date

Date	Mintage	F	VF	XF	Unc	BU
1831C	1,550	750	1,250	1,900	2,500	—

KM# 231 1/2 KRONE
5.5500 g., 0.9000 Gold .1606 oz. AGW **Ruler:** Georg V **Obv:** Head left **Obv. Legend:** GEORG V.v.G.G.KOENIG v.HANNOVER **Rev:** Denomination and date within wreath **Rev. Legend:** * VEREINSMUNZE * 100 EIN PFUND FEIN

Date	Mintage	F	VF	XF	Unc	BU
1857B	4,105	300	600	950	1,500	—
1858B	116	900	1,500	2,200	3,500	—
1859B	790	400	800	1,200	1,800	—
1862B	96	1,500	2,000	3,000	5,000	—
1864B	13,000	300	600	950	1,500	—
1866B	2,909	300	600	950	1,500	—

KM# 232 KRONE
11.1100 g., 0.9000 Gold .3215 oz. AGW **Ruler:** Georg V **Obv:** Head left **Obv. Legend:** GEORG V.v.G.G.KOENIG v.HANNOVER **Rev:** Denomination and date within wreath **Rev. Legend:** * VEREINSMUNZE * 50 EIN PFUND FEIN

Date	Mintage	F	VF	XF	Unc	BU
1857B	145,000	350	500	900	1,500	—
1858B	47,000	450	800	1,200	1,800	—
1859B	20,000	500	850	1,300	1,900	—
1860B	15,000	550	1,000	1,500	2,250	—
1861B	780	1,000	1,500	2,000	3,000	—
1862B	20,000	525	875	1,400	1,900	—
1863B	126,000	350	500	900	1,500	—
1864B	14,000	450	800	1,100	1,700	—
1866B	383,000	350	500	900	1,500	—

PATTERNS
Inlcuding off metal strikes

KM#	Date	Mintage	Identification	Mkt Val
Pn4	1813	—	5 Thaler. Gold. Plain edge. KM#101.	1,500

HESSE-CASSEL
(Hessen-Kassel)

The Hesse principalities were located for the most part north of the Main River, bounded by Westphalia on the west, the Brunswick duchies on the north, the Saxon-Thuringian duchies on the east and Rhine Palatinate and the bishoprics of Mainz and Fulda on the south. The rule of the landgraves of Hesse began in the second half of the 13th century, the dignity of Prince of the Empire being acquired in 1292. In 1567 the patrimony was divided by four surviving sons, only those of Cassel and Darmstadt surviving for more than a generation in Hesse-Cassel the landgrave was raised to the rank of elector in 1803. The electorate formed part of the Kingdom of Westphalia from 1806 to 1813. In 1866 Hesse-Cassel was annexed by Prussia and became the province of Hesse-Nassau.

RULERS
Wilhelm IX, 1785-1803

MINT MARKS
C – Cassel
C – Clausthal
(.L.) – Lippoldsberg

MINT OFFICIALS' INITIALS

Initials	Date	Name
CP	1820-61	Christoph Pfeuffer, die-cutter
D.F., F.	1774-1831	Dietrich Flalda
FH	1786-1821	Friedrich Heenwagen
H	1775-1820	Carl Ludwig Holzemer, die-cutter
K	1804-33	Wilhelm Korner

ARMS
Hessian lion rampant left.
Diez – 2 leopards passant to left, one above the other.
Katzenelnbogen – Crowned lion springing to left.
Nidda – 2-fold divided horizontally, two 8-pointed stars in upper half, lower half shaded.
Ziegenhain – 2-fold divided horizontally, 6-pointed star in upper half, lower half shaded.

PRINCIPALITY

REGULAR COINAGE

KM# 545 5 THALER (1 Pistole or Friedrich d'or)
6.6500 g., 0.9000 Gold .1924 oz. AGW **Ruler:** Wilhelm IX **Obv:** Head right **Rev:** Lion lying at front of crowned arms, flags at left, fasces and swords at right

Date	Mintage	F	VF	XF	Unc	BU
1801 F	—	900	1,800	2,600	3,600	—

KM# 557 5 THALER (1 Pistole or Friedrich d'or)
6.6500 g., 0.9000 Gold .1924 oz. AGW **Ruler:** Wilhelm I, as Elector **Obv:** Bust right **Obv. Legend:** WILHELMUS I.D.G.S.R.I.ELECTOR H.L. **Rev:** Lion lying at front of crowned arms, flags at left, fasces and swords at right

Date	Mintage	F	VF	XF	Unc	BU
1803 F	1,659	2,300	3,900	5,200	7,500	—
1805 F	1,941	2,300	3,400	5,200	7,500	—
1806 F Rare, 3 known	875					

KM# 563 5 THALER (1 Pistole or Friedrich d'or)
6.6500 g., 0.9000 Gold .1924 oz. AGW **Ruler:** Wilhelm I, as Elector **Obv:** Bust right **Obv. Legend:** WILHELMUS I.D.G.ELECT. LANDG.HASS. **Rev:** Crowned and mantled arms above sprays

Date	Mintage	F	VF	XF	Unc	BU
1815	2,226	1,600	2,600	3,800	4,800	—

KM# 566 5 THALER (1 Pistole or Friedrich d'or)
6.6500 g., 0.9000 Gold .1924 oz. AGW **Ruler:** Wilhelm I, as Elector **Obv:** Bust right **Obv. Legend:** WILHELMUS I. ELECT. HASS. LANDGR.M.D.FULD. **Rev:** Crowned and mantled arms

Date	Mintage	F	VF	XF	Unc	BU
1817	2,352	1,500	2,600	3,700	5,500	—
1819	1,548	1,700	2,800	4,100	6,000	—

KM# 570 5 THALER (1 Pistole or Friedrich d'or)
6.6500 g., 0.9000 Gold .1924 oz. AGW **Ruler:** Wilhelm I, as Elector **Obv. Legend:** WILHALM I KURF...

Date	Mintage	F	VF	XF	Unc	BU
1820	534	4,000	6,000	9,000	12,000	—

KM# 574.1 5 THALER (1 Pistole or Friedrich d'or)
6.6500 g., 0.9000 Gold .1924 oz. AGW **Ruler:** Wilhelm II **Obv:** Uniformed bust right **Obv. Legend:** WILHELM II KURF. S. L. Z. HESSEN GR. V. FULDA. **Rev:** Crowned and mantled arms

Date	Mintage	F	VF	XF	Unc	BU
1821	1,142	1,200	2,200	3,300	5,500	—
1823	1,140	1,200	2,200	3,300	5,500	—

KM# 574.2 5 THALER (1 Pistole or Friedrich d'or)
6.6500 g., 0.9000 Gold .1924 oz. AGW **Ruler:** Wilhelm II **Obv:** Uniformed bust right **Obv. Legend:** ...KURF. S. L. V. HESSEN... **Rev:** Crowned and mantled arms

Date	Mintage	F	VF	XF	Unc	BU
1823	518	1,800	3,500	5,000	8,000	—
1825	409	1,800	3,500	5,000	8,000	—
1828	952	1,800	3,500	5,000	8,000	—
1829	502	1,800	3,500	5,000	8,000	—

KM# 591 5 THALER (1 Pistole or Friedrich d'or)
6.6500 g., 0.9000 Gold .1924 oz. AGW **Ruler:** Wilhelm II and Friedrich Wilhelm **Obv:** Crowned arms within circle **Rev:** Denomination, date

Date	Mintage	F	VF	XF	Unc	BU
1834	1,025	450	750	1,600	2,400	—
1836	2,002	450	750	1,600	2,400	—
1837	256	650	1,200	2,000	3,000	—
1839	1,996	450	750	1,500	2,300	—
1840	17,000	425	700	1,350	2,100	—
1841	16,000	425	700	1,350	2,100	—
1842	6,909	450	750	1,500	2,300	—
1843	1,657	500	850	1,500	2,300	—
1844	1,495	500	850	1,500	2,300	—
1845	1,364	500	850	1,500	2,300	—

KM# 611 5 THALER (1 Pistole or Friedrich d'or)
6.6500 g., 0.9000 Gold .1924 oz. AGW **Ruler:** Wilhelm II and Friedrich Wilhelm **Obv:** Crowned arms within circle **Obv. Legend:** ...KURPR.-MITREG **Rev:** Denomination, date

Date	Mintage	F	VF	XF	Unc	BU
1847	1,438	1,000	1,600	2,800	4,800	—

KM# 619 5 THALER (1 Pistole or Friedrich d'or)
6.6500 g., 0.9000 Gold .1924 oz. AGW **Ruler:** Friedrich Wilhelm **Obv:** CP on truncation **Obv. Legend:** FRIEDR. WILHELM I. KURFURST V. HESSEN **Rev:** Crowned arms within oval necklance

Date	Mintage	F	VF	XF	Unc	BU
1851 CP	596	1,400	1,900	2,800	3,800	—

258 GERMAN STATES

HESSE-CASSEL

KM# 594 10 THALER (2 Pistolen or 2 Friedrich d'or)
13.3000 g., 0.9000 Gold .3848 oz. AGW **Ruler:** Wilhelm II and Friedrich Wilhelm **Obv:** Crowned arms within necklace **Rev:** Denomination, date **Note:** 1840 and 1841 mintage numbers included in KM#591.

Date	Mintage	F	VF	XF	Unc	BU
1838	126	1,600	2,500	3,800	6,500	—
1840	—	1,200	1,800	3,000	6,000	—
1841	—	1,200	1,800	3,000	6,000	—

PATTERNS
Including off metal strikes

KM#	Date	Mintage	Identification	Mkt Val
Pn34	1814	3	5 Thaler. 0.9000 Gold.	

HESSE-DARMSTADT

Founded by the youngest of Philipp I's four sons upon the death of their father in 1567, Hesse-Darmstadt was one of the two main branches of the family which survived past the beginning of the 17th century. The Countship of Hanau-Lichtenberg was through marriage when the male line failed in 1736. Ludwig X was forced to cede that territory to France in 1801. In 1803, Darmstadt acquired part of the Palatinate, the city of Friedberg, part of the city of Mainz, and the Duchy of Westphalia in a general settlement with France. The Landgrave was elevated to the status of Grand Duke in 1806 and reacquired Hesse-Homburg. In 1815 the Congress of Vienna awarded Hesse-Darmstadt the city of Worms and all of Mainz. These were relinquished, along with Hesse-Homburg, to Prussia in 1866 and Hesse-Darmstadt was called just Hesse from 1867 onwards. Hesse became part of the German Empire in 1871, but ceased to exist as a semi-sovereign state at the end of World War I.

RULERS
Ludwig X, 1790-1806
As Grand Duke Ludwig I, 1806-1830
Ludwig II, 1830-1848
Ludwig III, 1848-1877
Ludwig IV, 1877-1892
Ernst Ludwig, 1892-1918

MINT OFFICIALS' INITIALS

Initials	Date	Name
HR	1817-	Hector Roessler
RF	1772-1809	Remigius Fehr

GRAND DUCHY
REGULAR COINAGE
KM# 300 5 GULDEN
3.4250 g., 0.9040 Gold .0995 oz. AGW **Ruler:** Ludwig II **Obv:** Head left, C.V. below **Rev:** Crowned and mantled arms, value 5G **Rev. Legend:** AUS HESS. RHEINGOLD

Date	Mintage	F	VF	XF	Unc	BU
1835 CV-HR	60	2,500	5,000	11,000	25,000	—

KM# 301 5 GULDEN
3.4250 g., 0.9040 Gold .0995 oz. AGW **Ruler:** Ludwig II

Date	Mintage	F	VF	XF	Unc	BU
1835 CV-HR	22,000	900	1,800	2,500	3,800	—
1840 CV-HR	Inc. above	500	850	1,800	3,000	—
1841 CV-HR	Inc. above	500	850	1,800	3,000	—
1842 CV-HR	Inc. above	500	850	1,800	3,000	—

KM# 293 10 GULDEN
6.8500 g., 0.9040 Gold .1991 oz. AGW **Ruler:** Ludwig X As Grand Duke Ludwig I

Date	Mintage	F	VF	XF	Unc	BU
1826 HR	1,700	1,300	2,500	4,000	5,500	—
1827 HR	1,705	1,300	2,500	4,000	5,500	—

KM# 315 10 GULDEN
6.8500 g., 0.9040 Gold .1991 oz. AGW **Ruler:** Ludwig II **Obv:** Head left **Obv. Legend:** LUDWIG II GROSHERZOG VON HESSEN **Rev:** Crowned and mantled arms **Rev. Legend:** ZEHN GULDEN

Date	Mintage	F	VF	XF	Unc	BU
1840 CV-HR	17,000	750	1,500	2,500	4,200	—
1841 CV-HR	Inc. above	750	1,500	2,500	4,200	—
1842 CV-HR	Inc. above	750	1,500	2,500	4,200	—

REFORM COINAGE
Grossherzogtum within the German Empire

KM# 356 5 MARK
1.9910 g., 0.9000 Gold .0576 oz. AGW **Ruler:** Ludwig III **Obv:** Head right **Obv. Legend:** LUDWIG III GROSHERZOG VON HESSEN **Rev:** Crowned imperial eagle **Rev. Legend:** DEUTSCHES REICH date, 5 MARK below

Date	Mintage	F	VF	XF	Unc	BU
1877H	103,000	800	1,300	1,800	3,000	4,000
1877H Proof; Rare	—	—	—	—	—	—

KM# 357 5 MARK
1.9910 g., 0.9000 Gold .0576 oz. AGW **Ruler:** Ludwig IV **Obv:** Head right **Obv. Legend:** LUDWIG IV GROSHERZOG VON HESSEN **Rev:** Crowned imperial eagle, type II **Rev. Legend:** DEUTSCHES REICH date, 5 MARK below

Date	Mintage	F	VF	XF	Unc	BU
1877H	79,000	800	1,400	2,000	3,200	4,000
1877H Proof	—	Value: 3,500				

KM# 350 10 MARK
3.9820 g., 0.9000 Gold .1152 oz. AGW **Ruler:** Ludwig III **Obv:** Head right **Obv. Legend:** LUDWIG III GROSHERZOG VON HESSEN **Rev:** Crowned imperial eagle **Rev. Legend:** DEUTSCHES REICH

Date	Mintage	F	VF	XF	Unc	BU
1872H	30,000	180	360	4,000	1,500	2,000
1872H Proof	—	Value: 2,500				
1873H	432,000	200	300	450	1,300	2,000
1873H Proof	—	Value: 2,500				

KM# 354 10 MARK
3.9820 g., 0.9000 Gold .1152 oz. AGW **Ruler:** Ludwig III **Obv:** Head right **Obv. Legend:** LUDWIG III GROSHERZOG VON HESSEN **Rev:** Crowned imperial eagle, type II **Rev. Legend:** DEUTSCHES REICH date, 10 MARK below

Date	Mintage	F	VF	XF	Unc	BU
1875H	191,000	180	320	480	3,300	4,200
1876H	513,000	150	300	450	2,200	4,000
1877H	94,000	220	360	500	3,500	4,200

KM# 358 10 MARK
3.9820 g., 0.9000 Gold .1152 oz. AGW **Ruler:** Ludwig IV **Obv:** Head right **Obv. Legend:** LUDWIG IV GROSHERZOG VON HESSEN **Rev:** Crowned imperial eagle **Rev. Legend:** DEUTSCHES REICH date, 10 MARK below

Date	Mintage	F	VF	XF	Unc	BU
1878H	132,000	250	500	700	1,700	2,000
1878H Proof	—	Value: 2,800				
1879H	56,000	300	600	800	2,000	2,500
1879H Proof	—	Value: 2,800				
1880H	109,000	300	550	650	1,700	2,000
1880H Proof	—	Value: 2,800				

KM# 361 10 MARK
3.9820 g., 0.9000 Gold .1152 oz. AGW **Ruler:** Ludwig IV

Date	Mintage	F	VF	XF	Unc	BU
1888A	36,000	350	750	1,200	2,400	3,000
1888A Proof	500	Value: 4,000				

KM# 362 10 MARK
3.9820 g., 0.9000 Gold .1152 oz. AGW **Ruler:** Ludwig IV **Edge:** Vines and stars

Date	Mintage	F	VF	XF	Unc	BU
1890A	54,000	400	650	1,000	2,000	2,600

KM# 366 10 MARK
3.9820 g., 0.9000 Gold .1152 oz. AGW **Ruler:** Ernst Ludwig **Obv:** Head left **Obv. Legend:** ERNST LUDWIG GROSHERZOG VON HESSEN **Rev:** Crowned imperial eagle, type III **Rev. Legend:** DEUTSCHES REICH date, 10 MARK below

Date	Mintage	F	VF	XF	Unc	BU
1893A	54,000	550	1,000	1,500	3,000	3,500
1893A Proof	450	Value: 3,500				

KM# 370 10 MARK
3.9820 g., 0.9000 Gold .1152 oz. AGW **Ruler:** Ernst Ludwig **Obv:** Head left **Obv. Legend:** ERNST LUDWIG GROSHERZOG VON HESSEN **Rev:** Crowned imperial eagle **Rev. Legend:** DEUTSCHES REICH date, 10 MARK below

Date	Mintage	F	VF	XF	Unc	BU
1896A	36,000	280	600	1,000	2,000	2,500
1896A Proof	230	Value: 2,800				
1898A	75,000	240	500	900	1,800	2,400
1898A Proof	500	Value: 2,800				

KM# 351 20 MARK
7.9650 g., 0.9000 Gold .2304 oz. AGW **Ruler:** Ludwig III **Obv:** Head right **Obv. Legend:** LUDWIG III GROSHERZOG VON HESSEN **Rev:** Crowned imperial eagle, type I **Rev. Legend:** DEUTSCHES REICH

Date	Mintage	F	VF	XF	Unc	BU
1872H	183,000	150	300	600	1,700	2,000
1872H Proof	—	Value: 3,000				
1873H	521,000	130	280	550	1,500	2,000

KM# 352 20 MARK
7.9650 g., 0.9000 Gold .2304 oz. AGW **Ruler:** Ludwig III **Obv:** Head right **Obv. Legend:** LUDWIG III GROSHERZOG VON HESSEN **Rev:** Crowned imperial eagle, type II **Rev. Legend:** DEUTSCHES REICH date, 20 MARK below

Date	Mintage	F	VF	XF	Unc	BU
1874H	134,000	350	600	800	2,800	4,000

KM# 365 20 MARK
7.9650 g., 0.9000 Gold .2304 oz. AGW **Ruler:** Ludwig IV **Obv:** Head right **Obv. Legend:** ERNST LUDWIG GROSHERZOG VON HESSEN **Rev:** Crowned imperial eagle **Rev. Legend:** DEUTSCHES REICH date, 20 MARK below

Date	Mintage	F	VF	XF	Unc	BU
1892A	25,000	800	1,500	2,100	4,500	5,000
1892A Proof	—	Value: 6,000				

LUBECK

KM# 367 20 MARK
7.9650 g., 0.9000 Gold .2304 oz. AGW **Ruler:** Ernst Ludwig
Obv: Head left **Obv. Legend:** ERNST LUDWIG GROSHERZOG VON HESSEN **Rev:** Crowned imperial eagle, type III **Rev. Legend:** DEUTSCHES REICH date, 20 MARK below

Date	Mintage	F	VF	XF	Unc	BU
1893A	25,000	700	1,400	1,900	3,500	4,000
1893A Proof	—	Value: 4,000				

KM# 371 20 MARK
7.9650 g., 0.9000 Gold .2304 oz. AGW **Ruler:** Ernst Ludwig
Obv: Head left **Obv. Legend:** ERNST LUDWIG GROSHERZOG VON HESSEN **Rev:** Crowned imperial eagle **Rev. Legend:** DEUTSCHES REICH date, 20 MARK below

Date	Mintage	F	VF	XF	Unc	BU
1896A	15,000	450	900	1,500	2,500	3,000
1896A Proof	230	Value: 2,500				
1897A	45,000	200	350	600	1,600	2,000
1897A Proof	400	Value: 2,500				
1898A	70,000	200	350	650	1,250	2,000
1898A Proof	500	Value: 2,500				
1899A	40,000	220	400	700	1,400	2,000
1899A Proof	600	Value: 2,500				
1900A	40,000	220	400	700	1,400	2,000
1900A Proof	500	Value: 2,500				
1901A	80,000	220	400	700	1,400	2,000
1901A Proof	600	Value: 2,500				
1903A	40,000	220	400	700	1,400	2,000
1903A Proof	100	Value: 2,500				

KM# 374 20 MARK
7.9650 g., 0.9000 Gold .2304 oz. AGW **Ruler:** Ernst Ludwig
Obv: Head left **Rev:** Crowned imperial eagle, shield on breast

Date	Mintage	F	VF	XF	Unc	BU
1905A	45,000	350	450	1,000	1,200	1,250
1905A Proof	200	Value: 2,400				
1906A	85,000	155	310	400	900	1,250
1906A Proof	199	Value: 2,250				
1908A	40,000	165	350	400	1,000	1,250
1908A Proof	—	Value: 2,250				
1911A	150,000	165	310	400	900	1,250
1911A Proof	—	Value: 2,250				

HOHENLOHE-NEUENSTEIN-OEHRINGEN

This principality was located in southern Germany. The Neuenstein-Oehringen line was founded in 1610 and the first prince of the empire from this line was proclaimed in 1764. The line became extinct in 1805 and the lands passed to Ingelfingen.

RULERS
Ludwig Friedrich Karl, 1765-1805

PRINCIPALITY
TRADE COINAGE

KM# 71 DUCAT
3.5000 g., 0.9860 Gold .1109 oz. AGW **Ruler:** Ludwig Friedrich Karl **Subject:** 81st Birthday - L.F. Karl **Obv:** Uniformed bust right **Rev:** Crowned and mantled arms

Date	Mintage	F	VF	XF	Unc	BU
1804 D	—	1,000	2,000	4,000	7,000	—

KM# 72 2 DUCAT
7.0000 g., 0.9860 Gold .2219 oz. AGW **Ruler:** Ludwig Friedrich Karl **Subject:** 81st Birthday - L.F. Karl **Obv:** Bust right **Rev:** Crowned arms

Date	Mintage	F	VF	XF	Unc	BU
1804 D Rare	—	—	—	—	—	—

PATTERNS
Including off metal strikes

KM#	Date	Mintage	Identification	Mkt Val
Pn1	1804 D	—	Ducat. Silver. 81st Birthday.	300

ISENBURG

The lands of the counts of Isenburg lay on both sides of the Main River to the east of Frankfurt. The dynasty traces its lineage back to the 10th century and began issuing coins in the mid-13th century. The county underwent many divisions in the Middle Ages, but by the early 17th century only one dominant branch was producing coins. This was Isenburg-Birstein, divided once again into Isenburg-Offenbach-Birstein and Isenburg-Büdingen in 1635. The latter was further divided into four branches in 1673/1687 and two of the substrata became extinct in 1725 and 1780 respectively. Isenburg-Offenbach-Birstein was raised to the rank of prince in 1744 and all other branches had to relinquish their sovereignty to his descendant in 1806. The latter lost his sole leadership in 1813 because he sided with Napoleon and the lands of Isenburg-Offenbach-Birstein were mediatized to Hesse-Darmstadt in 1815. The subdivisions of Isenburg-Büdigen did not issue a regular coinage, but struck the series of the quasi-official snipe hellers during the 19th century.

RULERS
Wolfgang Ernst II, 1754-1803
Karl I, 1803-1820
Wolfgang Ernst III, 1820-1866
Karl II, 1866--
 Isenburg-Budingen
Ernst Kasimir II, 1775-1801
Ernst Kasimir III, 1801-1848
Adolf II (in Wachtersbach), 1805-1847
Ernst Kasimir IV, 1848-1861
Bruno, 1861-1906

COUNTY
TRADE COINAGE

KM# 49 DUCAT
3.5000 g., 0.9860 Gold .1109 oz. AGW **Ruler:** Karl I **Obv:** Head left **Obv. Legend:** CARL FURST ZU ISENBURG **Rev:** Crowned and mantled arms

Date	Mintage	F	VF	XF	Unc	BU
1811	—	—	—	—	—	—

KM# 50 2 DUCAT
7.0000 g., 0.9860 Gold .2218 oz. AGW **Ruler:** Karl I **Note:** Struck with 1 Ducat dies, KM#49.

Date	Mintage	F	VF	XF	Unc	BU
1811	—	2,000	3,000	6,000	9,000	—

PATTERNS
Including off metal strikes

KM#	Date	Mintage	Identification	Mkt Val
Pn5	1811	—	Ducat. Silver. KM#49.	250
Pn6	1811	—	2 Ducat. Silver. KM#50.	350

KNYPHAUSEN

The district of Knyphausen was located in northwestern Germany in East Friesland. Local nobility ruled from the 14th century until 1623 when it was sold to Olden-burg. It became autonomous in 1653 and was acquired through marriage to the Bentinck family in 1733. Coins were struck c. 1800. It was claimed by both Anhalt and Oldenburg, and the arms of Knyphausen appear on coins of both places.

RULER
Wilhelm Gustav Friedrich, 1774-1835

PATTERNS
Including off metal strikes

KM#	Date	Mintage	Identification	Mkt Val
Pn1	1806	—	2-1/2 Thaler. Gold.	—
Pn2	1806	—	5 Thaler. Gold.	—
Pn3	1806	—	10 Thaler. Gold.	—

LUBECK

Lübeck became a free city of the empire in 1188 and from c. 1190 into the 13th century an imperial mint existed in the town. It was granted the mint right in 1188, 1226 and 1340, but actually began its first civic coinage c.1350. Occupied by the French during the Napoleonic Wars, it was restored as a free city in 1813 and became part of the German Empire in 1871.

MINT OFFICIALS' INITIALS

Initials	Date	Name
HDF	1773-1801	Hermann David Friederichsen

REFERENCES
Heinrich Behrens, *Münzen und Medaillen der Stadt und des Bisthums Lübeck*, Berlin, 1905
Wolfgang Schulten, *Deutsche Münzen aus der Zeit Karls V.*, Frankfurt am Main, 1974.

FREE CITY
REFORM COINAGE

KM# 211 10 MARK
3.9820 g., 0.9000 Gold .1152 oz. AGW **Obv:** Double imperial eagle with divided shield on breast **Rev:** Crowned imperial eagle, shield on breast

Date	Mintage	F	VF	XF	Unc	BU
1901A	10,000	375	850	1,200	1,650	2,300
1901A Proof	200	Value: 2,700				
1904A	10,000	375	850	1,200	1,650	2,300
1904A Proof	130	Value: 2,700				

KM# 214 10 MARK
3.9820 g., 0.9000 Gold .1152 oz. AGW **Obv:** Double imperial eagle with divided shield on breast **Rev:** Crowned imperial eagle, shield on breast

Date	Mintage	F	VF	XF	Unc	BU
1905A	10,000	300	800	1,200	1,650	2,250
1905A Proof	247	Value: 2,750				
1906A	10,000	300	800	1,200	1,650	2,250
1906A Proof	216	Value: 3,000				
1909A	10,000	300	800	1,200	1,650	2,250
1909A Proof	—	Value: 2,750				
1910A	10,000	300	800	1,200	1,650	2,250
1910A Proof	—	Value: 3,000				

TRADE COINAGE

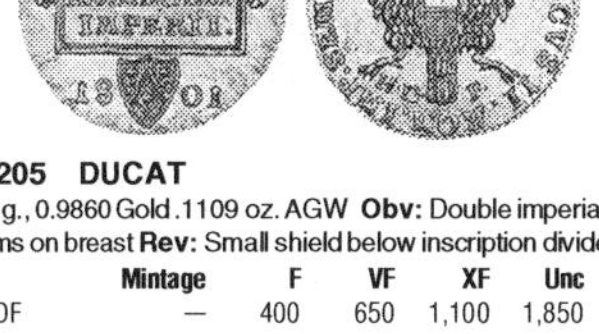

KM# 205 DUCAT
3.5000 g., 0.9860 Gold .1109 oz. AGW **Obv:** Double imperial eagle with arms on breast **Rev:** Small shield below inscription divides date

Date	Mintage	F	VF	XF	Unc	BU
1801 HDF	—	400	650	1,100	1,850	—

MECKLENBURG-SCHWERIN

The duchy of Mecklenburg was located along the Baltic coast between Holstein and Pomerania. Schwerin was annexed to Mecklenburg in 1357. During the Thirty Years' War, the dukes of Mecklenburg sided with the Protestant forces against the emperor. Albrecht von Wallenstein, the imperialist general, ousted the Mecklenburg dukes from their territories in 1628. They were restored to their lands in 1632. In 1658 the Mecklenburg dynasty was divided into two lines. No coinage was produced for Mecklenburg-Schwerin from 1708 until 1750. The 1815 Congress of Vienna elevated the duchy to the status of grand duchy and it became a part of the German Empire in 1871 until 1918 when the last grand duke abdicated.

RULERS
Friedrich Franz I, 1785-1837
Paul Friedrich, 1837-1842
Friedrich Franz II, 1842-1883
Friedrich Franz III, 1883-1897
Friedrich Franz IV, 1897-1918

MINT MARKS
A - Berlin
B - Hannover

GRAND DUCHY
REGULAR COINAGE

KM# 284   2-1/2 THALER
3.3300 g., 0.8960 Gold .0959 oz. AGW **Ruler:** Friedrich Franz I **Obv:** Head left **Rev:** Crowned arms

Date	Mintage	F	VF	XF	Unc	BU
1831	7,755	375	750	1,250	2,500	—
1833	124	600	1,000	1,750	2,750	—
1835	195	600	1,000	1,750	2,750	—

KM# 295   2-1/2 THALER
3.3300 g., 0.8960 Gold .0959 oz. AGW **Ruler:** Paul Friedrich **Obv:** Head right **Rev:** Crowned and mantled arms

Date	Mintage	F	VF	XF	Unc	BU
1840	2,910	300	500	750	1,100	—

KM# 271   5 THALER
6.6600 g., 0.8960 Gold .1919 oz. AGW **Ruler:** Friedrich Franz I **Obv:** Head left **Rev:** Crowned and mantled arms

Date	Mintage	F	VF	XF	Unc	BU
1828	1,753	600	1,200	1,800	3,000	—
1831	3,878	600	1,200	1,800	3,000	—
1832	3,334	600	1,200	1,800	3,000	—
1833	125	1,000	2,000	4,000	6,000	—
1835	100	1,000	2,000	4,000	6,000	—

KM# 296   5 THALER
6.6600 g., 0.8960 Gold .1919 oz. AGW **Ruler:** Paul Friedrich **Obv:** Head right **Rev:** Crowned and mantled arms

Date	Mintage	F	VF	XF	Unc	BU
1840	1,454	650	1,250	1,750	3,000	—

KM# 272   10 THALER
13.3200 g., 0.8960 Gold .3837 oz. AGW **Ruler:** Friedrich Franz I **Obv:** Head left **Rev:** Crowned arms with supporters within crowned mantle

Date	Mintage	F	VF	XF	Unc	BU
1828	876	1,250	2,500	3,750	5,000	—
1831	1,938	1,000	2,000	3,250	4,750	—
1832	1,667	1,000	2,000	3,250	4,750	—
1833	128	1,500	3,500	5,000	8,000	—

KM# 289   10 THALER
13.3200 g., 0.8960 Gold .3837 oz. AGW **Ruler:** Paul Friedrich **Obv:** Head right **Rev:** Crowned arms with supporters within crowned mantle

Date	Mintage	F	VF	XF	Unc	BU
1839	92,000	550	1,150	1,750	3,250	—

REFORM COINAGE

KM# 318   10 MARK
3.9820 g., 0.9000 Gold .1152 oz. AGW **Ruler:** Friedrich Franz II **Obv:** Head right **Rev:** Crowned imperial eagle, type I

Date	Mintage	F	VF	XF	Unc	BU
1872A	16,000	1,500	2,000	3,000	6,000	9,000
1872A Proof	100	Value: 9,500				

KM# 321   10 MARK
3.9820 g., 0.9000 Gold .1152 oz. AGW **Ruler:** Friedrich Franz II **Obv:** Head right **Rev:** Crowned imperial eagle, type II

Date	Mintage	F	VF	XF	Unc	BU
1878A	50,000	500	1,000	1,500	2,000	2,500
1878A Proof	—	Value: 3,000				

KM# 325   10 MARK
3.9820 g., 0.9000 Gold .1152 oz. AGW **Ruler:** Friedrich Franz III **Obv:** Head right **Rev:** Crowned imperial eagle

Date	Mintage	F	VF	XF	Unc	BU
1890A	100,000	250	600	900	1,400	1,800
1890A Proof	—	Value: 2,500				

KM# 331   10 MARK
3.9820 g., 0.9000 Gold .1152 oz. AGW **Ruler:** Friedrich Franz IV **Subject:** Grand Duke Coming of Age **Obv:** Head right **Rev:** Crowned imperial eagle, shield on breast, type III

Date	Mintage	F	VF	XF	Unc	BU
1901A	10,000	750	1,600	2,700	4,000	6,000
1901A Proof	200	Value: 7,000				

KM# 319   20 MARK
7.9650 g., 0.9000 Gold .2304 oz. AGW **Ruler:** Friedrich Franz II **Obv:** Head right **Rev:** Crowned imperial eagle, type I

Date	Mintage	F	VF	XF	Unc	BU
1872A	69,000	450	1,000	1,750	2,500	3,000
1872A Proof	200	Value: 5,000				

KM# 332   20 MARK
7.9650 g., 0.9000 Gold .2304 oz. AGW **Ruler:** Friedrich Franz IV **Subject:** Grand Duke Coming of Age **Obv:** Head right **Rev:** Crowned imperial eagle, shield on breast, type III

Date	Mintage	F	VF	XF	Unc	BU
1901A	5,000	1,000	2,700	4,200	5,750	8,000
1901A Proof	200	Value: 8,500				

PATTERNS
Including off metal strikes

KM#	Date	Mintage	Identification	Mkt Val
Pn24	1828	—	5 Thaler. Gold. KM#271.	10,000
Pn25	1830	—	2 Thaler. 0.8750 Gold.	6,000

MECKLENBURG-STRELITZ

The duchy of Mecklenburg was located along the Baltic Coast between Holstein and Pomerania. The Strelitz line was founded in 1658 when the Mecklenburg line was divided into two lines. The 1815 Congress of Vienna elevated the duchy to the status of grand duchy. It became a part of the German Empire in 1871 until 1918 when the last grand duke died.

RULERS
Karl II, 1794-1816
Georg, 1816-1860
Friedrich Wilhelm, 1860-1904
Adolf Friedrich V, 1904-1914
Adolf Friedrich VI, 1914-1918

MINT OFFICIALS' INITIALS

Initials	Date	Name
FN	1832-49	Franz Anton Nubell
IHL	1813	Johann Heinrich Lowe in Berlin

GRAND DUCHY
REFORM COINAGE

KM# 104   10 MARK
3.9820 g., 0.9000 Gold .1152 oz. AGW **Ruler:** Friedrich Wilhelm **Obv:** Head left **Obv. Legend:** FRIEDRICH WILH. V. G. G. GROSSH. V. MECKLENB. STRL. **Rev:** Crowned imperial eagle, type I **Rev. Legend:** DEUTSCHES REICH

Date	Mintage	F	VF	XF	Unc	BU
1873A	1,500	5,000	10,000	15,000	20,000	30,000
1873A Proof	—	Value: 28,500				

OLDENBURG   GERMAN STATES   261

KM# 106 10 MARK
3.9820 g., 0.9000 Gold .1152 oz. AGW **Ruler:** Friedrich Wilhelm
Obv: Head left **Obv. Legend:** FRIEDRICH WILH. V. G. G.
GROSSH. V. MECKLENB. STRL. **Rev:** Crowned imperial eagle
Rev. Legend: DEUTSCHES REICH date, 10 MARK below

Date	Mintage	F	VF	XF	Unc	BU
1874A	3,000	2,250	4,000	6,500	8,500	11,000
1880A	4,000	2,250	4,000	6,500	8,500	11,000

KM# 116 10 MARK
3.9820 g., 0.9000 Gold .1152 oz. AGW **Ruler:** Adolph Friedrich V
Obv: Head left **Rev:** Crowned imperial eagle, shield on breast

Date	Mintage	F	VF	XF	Unc	BU
1905A	1,000	1,750	3,000	5,000	6,500	8,000
1905A Proof	150	Value: 9,000				

KM# 105 20 MARK
7.9650 g., 0.9000 Gold .2304 oz. AGW **Ruler:** Friedrich Wilhelm
Obv: Head left **Obv. Legend:** FRIEDRICH WILH. V. G. G.
GROSSH. V. MECKLENB. STRL. **Rev:** Crowned imperial eagle
Rev. Legend: DEUTSCHES REICH

Date	Mintage	F	VF	XF	Unc	BU
1873A	6,750	1,750	3,500	6,000	8,000	10,000

KM# 107 20 MARK
7.9650 g., 0.9000 Gold .2304 oz. AGW **Ruler:** Friedrich Wilhelm
Obv: Head left **Obv. Legend:** FRIEDRICH WILH. V. G. G.
GROSSH. V. MECKLENB. STRL. **Rev:** Crowned imperial eagle, type II **Rev. Legend:** DEUTSCHES REICH date, 20 MARK below

Date	Mintage	F	VF	XF	Unc	BU
1874A	6,000	1,750	3,500	5,000	7,500	10,000

KM# 117 20 MARK
7.9650 g., 0.9000 Gold .2304 oz. AGW **Ruler:** Adolph
Friedrich V **Obv:** Head left **Rev:** Crowned imperial eagle, shield on breast, type III

Date	Mintage	F	VF	XF	Unc	BU
1905A	1,000	2,000	4,250	6,500	8,500	12,000
1905A Proof	160	Value: 13,000				

NASSAU

The Countship of Nassau had its origins in the area of the Lahn of the central Rhineland, with territory on both sides of that river. The first count who attained the title with recognition from the emperor was Walram in 1158. His grandsons, Walram I (1255-88) and Otto I (1255-90), divided their patrimony. Walram claimed the left bank of the Lahn and made Weisbaden his principal seat, whereas Otto took the right bank and ruled from Siegen. Thus, the division of 1255 established the two main lines over the ensuing centuries.

Several times, various branches of the family issued joint coinage, notably in the late 17th and again in the early 19th centuries. Eventually, through extinction of the various lines and the elevation of one ruler to the throne of the Netherlands, all Nassau was reunited under the house of Nassau-Weilburg.

ARMS
Nassau – lion rampant left on field of billets (small vertical rectangles)
Holzappel – griffin rampant left holding apple

NASSAU-WEILBURG AND NASSAU-USINGEN
Duchy

RULERS
Friedrich Wilhelm, 1788-1816
Friedrich August, 1803-1816

Initial	Date	Name
CT		Christian Teichmann

TRADE COINAGE
Separate coinage of Nassau-Weilburg

C# 8 DUCAT
3.5000 g., 0.9860 Gold .1109 oz. AGW **Obv:** Crowned arms

Date	Mintage	F	VF	XF	Unc	BU
1809	3,543	500	1,000	1,600	3,000	—

UNITED DUCHIES OF NASSAU
TRADE COINAGE
Separate coinage of Nassau-Weilburg

C# 50 DUCAT
3.5000 g., 0.9860 Gold .1109 oz. AGW **Obv:** Head right **Rev:** Crowned mantled arms

Date	Mintage	F	VF	XF	Unc	BU
1818 CT	501	650	1,250	2,200	4,000	—

NURNBERG

Nürnberg, (Nüremberg) in Franconia, was made a Free City in 1219. In that same year an Imperial mint was established there and continued throughout the rest of the century. The mint right was obtained in 1376 and again in 1422. City coins were struck from ca.1390 to 1806 when the city was made part of Bavaria. It was briefly occupied by Swedish forces until the death of Gustav II Adolfus in 1632.

MINT OFFICIALS' INITIALS

Initials	Date	Name
IER	1806-07	Johann Egydius Rosch

CITY ARMS
Divided vertically, eagle (or half eagle) on left, six diagonal bars downward to right on right side.

Paschal Lamb
The paschal lamb, Lamb of God or Agnes Dei was used in the gold Ducat series. It appears standing on a globe holding a banner with the word "PAX" (peace).

FREE CITY
TRADE COINAGE

KM# 416 DUCAT
3.5000 g., 0.9860 Gold .1109 oz. AGW **Obv:** City view **Rev:** Paschal lamb left

Date	Mintage	F	VF	XF	Unc	BU
1806 KR	—	350	600	1,250	2,200	

KM# 417 2 DUCAT
7.0000 g., 0.9860 Gold .2219 oz. AGW **Obv:** City view **Rev:** Paschal lamb

Date	Mintage	F	VF	XF	Unc	BU
1806 KR	—	650	1,250	2,750	5,000	

KM# 418 3 DUCAT
10.5000 g., 0.9860 Gold .3329 oz. AGW **Obv:** City view, date below **Rev:** Paschal lamb

Date	Mintage	F	VF	XF	Unc	BU
1806 KR	—	1,200	2,500	4,500	7,500	

MEDALLIC COINAGE

X# M4 3 DUCAT
3.5000 g., 0.9860 Gold .1109 oz. AGW **Obv:** Two figures before altar with crucifix **Rev:** Two figures standing beside Christ

Date	Mintage	F	VF	XF	Unc	BU
ND	—	275	525	1,000	1,600	—

OLDENBURG

The county of Oldenburg was situated on the North Seacoast, to the east of the principality of East Friesland. It was originally part of the old duchy of Saxony and the first recorded lord ruled from the beginning of the 11th century. The first count was named in 1091 and had already acquired the county of Delmenhorst prior to that time. The first identifiable Oldenburg coinage was struck in the first half of the 13th century. Oldenburg was divided into Oldenburg and Delmenhorst in 1270, but the two lines were reunited by marriage five generations later. Through another marriage to the heiress of the duchy of Schleswig and county of Holstein, the royal house of Denmark descended through the Oldenburg line beginning in 1448, while a junior branch continued as counts of Oldenburg. The lordship of Jever was added to the county's domains in 1575. In 1667, the last count died without a direct heir and Oldenburg reverted to Denmark until 1773. In the following year, Oldenburg was given to the bishop of Lübeck, of the Holstein-Gottorp line, and raised to the status of a duchy. Oldenburg was occupied several times during the Napoleonic Wars and became a grand duchy in 1829. In 1817, Oldenburg acquired the principality of Birkenfeld from Prussia and struck coins in denominations used there. World War I spelled the end of temporal power for the grand duke in 1918, but the title has continued up to the present time. Grand Duke Anton Gunther was born in 1923.

RULERS
Peter Friedrich Wilhelm, 1785-1823
Peter Friedrich Ludwig, as Administrator 1785-1823, as Duke, 1823-1829
Paul Friedrich August, 1829-1853
Nicolaus Friedrich Peter, 1853-1900
Friedrich August, 1900-1918

MINT OFFICIALS' INITIALS

Initial	Date	Name
B	1817-38	Ludwig August Bruel in Hannover
B	1844-68	Theodor Wilhelm Bruel in Hannover
S	1839-44	Karl Schluter in Hannover

ARMS
Oldenburg: Two bars on field.
Delmenhorst: Cross with pointed bottom bar.
Jever: Lion rampant to left.
NOTE: Coins struck for lordship of Jever are listed under the latter.

DUCHY
REFORM COINAGE

KM# 200 10 MARK
3.9820 g., 0.9000 Gold .1152 oz. AGW **Ruler:** Nicolaus Friedrich Peter **Obv:** Head left **Obv. Legend:** NICOLAUS FRIEDR. PETER GR.H. V. OLDENBURG **Rev:** Crowned imperial eagle with wreathed arms on breast **Rev. Legend:** DEUTSCHES REICH date, 10 MARK below

Date	Mintage	F	VF	XF	Unc	BU
1874 B	15,000	1,000	2,500	4,500	7,000	10,000
1874 B Proof	—	Value: 12,500				

PATTERNS
Including off metal strikes

KM#	Date	Mintage	Identification	Mkt Val
Pn1	1816	—	6 Grote. Gold. KM#157.	—
Pn2	1816	—	1/3 Thaler. Gold. KM#159.	—

GERMAN STATES

PRUSSIA

The Kingdom of Prussia, located in north central Germany came into being in 1701. The ruler received the title of King in Prussia in exchange for his support during the War of the Spanish Succession. During the Napoleonic Wars, Prussia allied itself with Saxony. When they were defeated in 1806 they were forced to cede a large portion of their territory. In 1813 the French were expelled and their territories were returned to them plus additional territories. After defeating Denmark and Austria, in 1864 and 1866 they acquired more territory. Prussia was the pivotal state of unification of Germany in 1871 and their King was proclaimed emperor of all Germany. World War I brought an end to the Empire and the Kingdom of Prussia in 1918.

RULERS
Friedrich Wilhelm III, 1797-1840
Friedrich Wilhelm IV, 1840-1861
Wilhelm I, 1861-1888
Friedrich III, March 1888-June 1888
Wilhelm II, 1888-1918

MINT MARKS
A - Berlin = Prussia, East Friesland, East Prussia, Posen
B - Bayreuth = Brandenburg-Ansbach-Bayreuth
B - Breslau = Silesia, Posen, South Prussia
C - Cleve
D - Aurich = East Friesland, Prussia
E - Konigsberg = East Prussia
F - Magdeburg
G - Stettin
G - Schwerin, Plon-Rethwisch Mint, 1763 only
S - Schwabach = Brandenburg-Ansbach-Bayreuth
Star - Dresden

KINGDOM

REGULAR COINAGE

A series of counterfeit Prussian 5, 10 and 20 Mark gold pieces all dated 1887A were being marketed in the early 1970's. They were created by a dentist in Bonn, West Germany and the previously unknown date listed above aroused the curiosity of the numismatic community and eventually exposed the scam.

KM# 475 1/2 KRONE
5.5550 g., 0.9000 Gold .1607 oz. AGW **Ruler:** Friedrich Wilhelm IV **Obv:** Head right **Obv. Legend:** FRIEDR. WILHELM IV KOENIG V. PREUSSEN **Rev:** Denomination within wreath **Rev. Legend:** VEREINSMUNZE, 100 EIN PFUND FEIN below

Date	Mintage	F	VF	XF	Unc	BU
1858A	2,036	800	1,500	2,000	3,250	—

KM# 493 1/2 KRONE
5.5550 g., 0.9000 Gold .1607 oz. AGW **Ruler:** Wilhelm I

Date	Mintage	F	VF	XF	Unc	BU
1862A	6,365	500	900	1,250	2,000	—
1863A	3,642	500	900	1,250	2,000	—
1864A	4,840	500	900	1,250	2,000	—
1866A	14,000	500	900	1,250	2,000	—
1867A	5,711	500	900	1,250	2,000	—
1868A	92,000	400	800	1,200	1,600	—
1868B	3,718	800	1,500	2,000	3,750	—
1869A	—	800	1,500	2,000	3,200	—

KM# 476 KRONE
11.1110 g., 0.9000 Gold .3272 oz. AGW **Ruler:** Wilhelm I

Date	Mintage	F	VF	XF	Unc	BU
1858A	6,320	600	1,400	1,800	3,000	—
1859A	34,000	500	1,200	1,600	2,600	—
1860A	16,000	650	1,500	2,000	3,250	—

KM# 492 KRONE
11.1110 g., 0.9160 Gold .3272 oz. AGW **Ruler:** Wilhelm I **Obv:** Head right **Obv. Legend:** WILHELM KOENIG VON PREUSSEN **Rev:** Denomination and date within wreath **Rev. Legend:** VEREINSMUNZE, 50 EIN PFUND FEIN below

Date	Mintage	F	VF	XF	Unc	BU
1861A	2,488	650	1,200	1,700	3,000	—
1862A	5,558	650	1,200	1,700	3,000	—
1863A	2,653	650	1,200	1,700	3,000	—
1864A	792	800	1,400	2,000	3,250	—
1866A	720	800	1,400	2,000	3,250	—
1867A	4,087	400	800	1,200	2,000	—
1867A Proof	—	Value: 2,500				
1867B	15,000	500	1,200	1,700	3,000	—
1868A	97,000	400	800	1,200	2,000	—
1868B	40,000	500	1,200	1,700	3,000	—
1869A	—	1,000	1,400	2,000	3,600	—
1870A	1,764	800	1,400	2,000	3,250	—

X# 20 5 MARK
3.9825 g., 0.9000 Gold 0.1152 oz. AGW

Date	Mintage	F	VF	XF	Unc	BU
1887A	—	—	—	—	BV	—

X# 21 10 MARK
7.9650 g., 0.9000 Gold 0.2305 oz. AGW

Date	Mintage	F	VF	XF	Unc	BU
1887A	—	—	—	—	BV	—

X# 22 20 MARK
15.9300 g., 0.9000 Gold 0.4609 oz. AGW

Date	Mintage	F	VF	XF	Unc	BU
1887A	—	—	—	—	BV	—

TRADE COINAGE

KM# 382 1/2 FREDERICK D'OR
3.3410 g., 0.9030 Gold .0970 oz. AGW **Ruler:** Friedrich Wilhelm III **Obv:** L at truncation **Obv. Legend:** FRIEDR. WILH. III KOENIG V. PREUSSEN **Rev:** Crowned eagle above fasces

Date	Mintage	F	VF	XF	Unc	BU
1802A	—	275	350	800	1,500	—
1803A	—	550	800	1,200	2,000	—
1804A	—	300	500	900	1,625	—
1806A	—	275	400	800	1,500	—
1814A	—	300	500	900	1,625	—
1816A	—	350	600	1,000	1,750	—

KM# 397 1/2 FREDERICK D'OR
3.3410 g., 0.9030 Gold .0970 oz. AGW **Ruler:** Friedrich Wilhelm III **Obv:** Uniformed bust left **Obv. Legend:** FRIEDR. WILH. III KOENIG V. PREUSSEN **Rev:** Crowned eagle above cannon

Date	Mintage	F	VF	XF	Unc	BU
1817A	—	300	500	700	1,250	—

KM# 414 1/2 FREDERICK D'OR
3.3410 g., 0.9030 Gold .0970 oz. AGW **Ruler:** Friedrich Wilhelm III **Obv:** Head right **Obv. Legend:** FRIEDR. WILH. III KOENIG V. PREUSSEN **Rev:** Crowned eagle perched on cannon

Date	Mintage	F	VF	XF	Unc	BU
1825A	—	300	500	750	1,000	—
1827A	—	375	650	875	1,125	—
1828A	—	600	1,000	1,250	1,500	—
1829A	—	500	875	1,125	1,375	—
1830A	—	350	625	875	1,125	—
1831A	—	350	625	875	1,125	—
1832A	—	350	625	875	1,125	—
1833A	—	350	625	875	1,125	—
1834A	—	350	625	875	1,125	—
1838A	—	350	625	875	1,125	—
1839A	—	400	750	1,000	1,250	—
1840A	—	500	875	1,125	1,375	—

KM# 441 1/2 FREDERICK D'OR
3.3410 g., 0.9030 Gold .0970 oz. AGW **Ruler:** Friedrich Wilhelm IV **Obv:** Head right **Obv. Legend:** FRIEDR. WILH. IV KOENIG V. PREUSSEN **Rev:** Crowned eagle perched on cannon

Date	Mintage	F	VF	XF	Unc	BU
1841A	—	300	500	750	1,000	—
1842A	—	300	500	750	1,000	—
1843A	—	400	750	1,000	1,250	—
1844A	—	400	750	1,000	1,250	—
1845A	—	400	750	1,000	1,250	—
1846A	—	400	750	1,000	1,250	—
1849A	—	400	750	1,000	1,250	—

KM# 468 1/2 FREDERICK D'OR
3.3410 g., 0.9030 Gold .0970 oz. AGW **Ruler:** Friedrich Wilhelm IV **Obv:** Head right **Obv. Legend:** FRIEDR. WILH. IV KOENIG V. PREUSSEN **Rev:** Crowned eagle perched on cannon

Date	Mintage	F	VF	XF	Unc	BU
1853A	—	500	900	1,250	1,600	—

KM# 371 FREDERICK D'OR
6.6820 g., 0.9030 Gold .1940 oz. AGW **Ruler:** Friedrich Wilhelm III **Obv:** Uniformed bust left **Obv. Legend:** FRIEDR. WILHELM III KOENIG VON PREUSSEN **Rev:** Crowned eagle above fasces

Date	Mintage	F	VF	XF	Unc	BU
1801A	—	450	600	950	1,600	—
1801A	—	400	600	950	1,600	—
1801B	—	450	600	950	1,600	—
1802A	—	450	600	950	1,600	—
1802B	—	450	600	950	1,600	—
1803A	—	400	475	800	1,400	—
1803B	—	550	800	1,200	2,000	—
1804A	—	450	600	950	1,600	—
1804B	—	550	800	1,200	2,000	—
1805A	—	350	525	950	1,400	—
1805B	—	550	800	1,200	2,000	—
1806A	—	350	525	950	1,500	—
1807A	—	350	525	950	1,500	—
1808A	—	550	800	1,200	1,850	—
1809A	—	350	475	950	1,400	—
1810A	—	450	600	950	1,600	—
1811A	—	450	600	950	1,600	—
1812A	—	350	475	800	1,400	—
1813A	—	400	525	875	1,450	—
1816A	—	450	600	950	1,600	—

KM# 398 FREDERICK D'OR
6.6820 g., 0.9030 Gold .1940 oz. AGW **Ruler:** Friedrich Wilhelm III **Obv:** Uniformed bust left **Rev:** Crowned eagle above fasces

Date	Mintage	F	VF	XF	Unc	BU
1817A	—	500	800	1,200	2,000	—
1818A	—	400	550	1,000	1,800	—
1819A	—	650	1,000	1,500	2,250	—
1822A	—	400	550	1,100	1,850	—

KM# 415 FREDERICK D'OR
6.6820 g., 0.9030 Gold .1940 oz. AGW **Ruler:** Friedrich Wilhelm III **Obv:** Head right **Obv. Legend:** FRIEDR. WILH. III KOENIG V. PREUSSEN **Rev:** Crowned eagle perched on cannon

Date	Mintage	F	VF	XF	Unc	BU
1825A	—	300	400	800	1,400	—
1827A	—	400	600	1,000	1,650	—
1828A	—	300	400	800	1,400	—
1829A	—	400	550	1,000	1,650	—
1830A	—	400	550	1,000	1,650	—
1831A	—	300	550	900	1,550	—
1832A	—	300	550	900	1,550	—
1833A	—	300	550	900	1,550	—
1834A	—	300	550	1,000	1,650	—
1836A	—	300	550	1,000	1,650	—
1837A	—	300	550	800	1,550	—

PRUSSIA

Date	Mintage	F	VF	XF	Unc	BU
1838A	—	300	550	800	1,650	—
1839A	—	300	550	800	1,550	—
1840A	—	300	550	800	1,400	—

KM# 442 FREDERICK D'OR
6.6820 g., 0.9030 Gold .1940 oz. AGW **Ruler:** Friedrich Wilhelm IV **Obv:** Head right **Obv. Legend:** FRIEDR. WILH. IV KOENIG V. PREUSSEN **Rev:** Crowned eagle perched on cannon

Date	Mintage	F	VF	XF	Unc	BU
1841A	—	300	550	800	1,400	—
1842A	—	300	550	800	1,400	—
1843A	—	300	550	800	1,550	—
1844A	—	300	550	800	1,400	—
1845A	—	300	550	800	1,400	—
1846A	—	300	550	800	1,400	—
1847A	—	300	550	800	1,550	—
1848A	—	300	550	800	1,400	—
1849A	—	300	550	800	1,400	—
1850A	—	300	550	800	1,550	—
1851A	—	300	550	800	1,650	—
1852A	—	300	550	800	1,550	—

KM# 469 FREDERICK D'OR
6.6820 g., 0.9030 Gold .1940 oz. AGW **Ruler:** Friedrich Wilhelm IV **Obv:** Head right **Obv. Legend:** FRIEDR. WILHELM IV KOENIG V. PREUSSEN **Rev:** Crowned eagle perched on cannon

Date	Mintage	F	VF	XF	Unc	BU
1853A	—	300	750	1,200	1,750	—
1854A	—	300	750	1,200	1,750	—
1855A	—	300	750	1,200	1,750	—

KM# 381 2 FREDERICK D'OR
13.3630 g., 0.9030 Gold .3880 oz. AGW **Ruler:** Friedrich Wilhelm III **Obv:** L at truncation **Obv. Legend:** FRIEDR. WILHELM III KOENIG VON PREUSSEN **Rev:** Crowned eagle above fasces

Date	Mintage	F	VF	XF	Unc	BU
1801A	—	700	975	1,800	2,600	—
1801A	—	700	975	1,800	2,600	—
1802A	—	800	1,250	2,200	3,000	—
1806A	—	800	1,250	2,200	3,000	—
1811A	—	700	975	1,800	2,600	—
1813A	—	725	1,000	2,000	2,800	—
1814A	—	800	1,250	2,200	3,000	—

KM# 416 2 FREDERICK D'OR
13.3630 g., 0.9030 Gold .3880 oz. AGW **Ruler:** Friedrich Wilhelm III **Obv:** Head right **Obv. Legend:** FRIEDR. WILH. III KOENIG V. PREUSSEN **Rev:** Crowned eagle above cannon

Date	Mintage	F	VF	XF	Unc	BU
1825A	—	800	1,200	1,600	2,000	—
1826A	—	700	1,100	1,500	1,800	—
1827A	—	600	1,000	1,400	1,600	—
1828A	—	600	1,000	1,400	1,600	—
1829A	—	700	1,100	1,500	1,800	—
1830A	—	550	900	1,300	1,500	—
1831A	—	550	900	1,300	1,500	—
1832A	—	700	1,100	1,500	1,800	—
1836A	—	800	1,200	1,600	2,000	—
1837A	—	550	900	1,300	1,500	—
1838A	—	600	1,000	1,400	1,600	—

Date	Mintage	F	VF	XF	Unc	BU
1839A	—	500	800	1,200	1,400	—
1840A	—	500	800	1,200	1,400	—

KM# 443 2 FREDERICK D'OR
13.3630 g., 0.9030 Gold .3880 oz. AGW **Ruler:** Friedrich Wilhelm IV **Obv:** Head right **Obv. Legend:** FRIEDR. WILH. IV KOENIG V. PREUSSEN **Rev:** Crowned eagle perched on cannon

Date	Mintage	F	VF	XF	Unc	BU
1841A	—	500	800	1,200	1,500	—
1842A	—	500	800	1,200	1,500	—
1843A	—	600	1,250	1,750	2,000	—
1844A	—	800	1,500	2,000	2,250	—
1845A	—	800	1,500	2,000	2,250	—
1846A	—	500	800	1,200	1,500	—
1848A	—	500	800	1,200	1,500	—
1849A	—	500	800	1,200	1,500	—
1852A	—	500	800	1,200	1,500	—

KM# 470 2 FREDERICK D'OR
13.3630 g., 0.9030 Gold .3880 oz. AGW **Ruler:** Friedrich Wilhelm IV **Obv:** Head right **Obv. Legend:** FRIEDR. WILHELM IV KOENIG V. PREUSSEN **Rev:** Crowned eagle perched on cannnon

Date	Mintage	F	VF	XF	Unc	BU
1853A	—	500	800	1,200	2,000	—
1854A	—	500	800	1,200	2,000	—
1855A	—	750	1,500	2,000	2,500	—

REFORM COINAGE

KM# 507 5 MARK
1.9910 g., 0.9000 Gold .0576 oz. AGW **Ruler:** Wilhelm I **Obv:** Head right **Obv. Legend:** WILHELM DEUTSCHER KAISER KONIG V. PREUSSEN **Rev:** Crowned imperial eagle **Rev. Legend:** DEUTSCHES REICH date, 5 MARK below

Date	Mintage	F	VF	XF	Unc	BU
1877A	1,217,000	125	200	300	500	650
1877A Proof	—	Value: 1,300				
1877B	517,000	125	200	300	500	650
1877B Proof	—	Value: 1,200				
1877C	688,000	125	200	300	500	650
1878A	502,000	125	200	300	500	650
1878A Proof	—	Value: 1,300				

KM# 502 10 MARK
3.9820 g., 0.9000 Gold .1152 oz. AGW **Ruler:** Wilhelm I **Obv:** Head right **Obv. Legend:** WILHELM DEUTSCHER KAISER KONIG V. PREUSSEN **Rev:** Crowned imperial eagle **Rev. Legend:** DEUTSCHES REICH

Date	Mintage	F	VF	XF	Unc	BU
1872A	3,123,000	BV	85.00	110	200	250
1872A Proof	—	Value: 1,600				
1872B	1,418,000	BV	95.00	120	225	275
1872C	1,747,000	BV	85.00	130	275	325
1873A	3,016,000	—	BV	90.00	200	250
1873A Proof	—	Value: 1,600				
1873B	2,273,000	BV	100	125	275	325
1873C	2,295,000	BV	95.00	120	275	325

KM# 504 10 MARK
3.9820 g., 0.9000 Gold .1152 oz. AGW **Ruler:** Wilhelm I **Obv:** Head right **Obv. Legend:** WILHELM DEUTSCHER KAISER KONIG V. PREUSSEN **Rev:** Type II **Rev. Legend:** DEUTSCHES REICH date, 10 MARK below

Date	Mintage	F	VF	XF	Unc	BU
1874A	833,000	BV	95.00	120	250	300
1874A Proof	—	Value: 1,100				
1874B	1,028,000	BV	95.00	120	250	300
1874C	321,000	BV	95.00	120	250	300
1874C Proof	—	Value: 1,300				
1875A	2,430,000	BV	95.00	120	250	300
1875B	456,000	BV	95.00	120	300	350
1875C	1,532,000	BV	95.00	120	250	300
1876B	2,800	1,000	1,600	2,200	3,000	3,500
1876B Proof	—	Value: 10,000				
1876C	27,000	500	1,200	1,600	2,500	3,000
1877A	851,000	BV	95.00	120	250	350
1877B	247,000	BV	105	120	350	450
1877C	328,000	BV	85.00	120	300	350
1878A	1,126,000	BV	85.00	110	250	300
1878B	15,000	45,000	60,000	85,000	100,000	120,000
1878C	516,000	BV	100	130	300	350
1879A	1,012,000	BV	95.00	120	225	275
1879A Proof	—	Value: 800				
1879C	282,000	BV	125	150	300	400
1880A	1,762,000	BV	85.00	120	250	325
1882A	8,382	1,500	3,200	4,500	6,500	8,500
1883A	13,000	1,200	1,800	2,400	3,000	4,500
1883A Proof	—	Value: 10,000				
1886A	14,000	1,500	2,000	3,200	5,000	6,000
1888A	189,000	BV	95.00	130	275	325
1888A Proof	—	Value: 1,300				

KM# 514 10 MARK
3.9820 g., 0.9000 Gold .1152 oz. AGW **Ruler:** Friedrich III March - June **Obv:** Head right **Obv. Legend:** FRIEDRICH DEUTSCHER KAISER KONIG V. PREUSSEN **Rev:** Crowned imperial eagle **Rev. Legend:** DEUTSCHES REICH date, 10 MARK below

Date	Mintage	F	VF	XF	Unc	BU
1888A	876,000	BV	95.00	120	175	225
1888A Proof	—	Value: 700				

KM# 517 10 MARK
3.9820 g., 0.9000 Gold .1152 oz. AGW **Ruler:** Wilhelm II **Obv:** Head right **Obv. Legend:** WILHELM II DEUTSCHER KAISER KONIG V. PREUSSEN **Rev:** Type II **Rev. Legend:** DEUTSCHES REICH date, 10 MARK below

Date	Mintage	F	VF	XF	Unc	BU
1889A	24,000	1,600	3,000	3,500	4,500	6,500
1889A Proof	—	Value: 6,500				

KM# 520 10 MARK
3.9820 g., 0.9000 Gold .1152 oz. AGW **Ruler:** Wilhelm II **Obv:** Head right **Obv. Legend:** WILHELM II DEUTSCHER KAISER KONIG V. PREUSSEN **Rev:** Crowned imperial eagle, type III **Rev. Legend:** DEUTSCHES REICH date, 10 MARK below

Date	Mintage	F	VF	XF	Unc	BU
1890A	1,512,000	BV	100	120	275	325
1890A Proof	—	Value: 1,000				
1892A	35,000	400	600	1,000	1,500	2,000
1893A	1,591,000	BV	100	120	275	325
1894A	18,000	550	1,100	1,450	2,000	2,500
1895A	29,000	400	700	1,200	1,900	2,250
1896A	1,081,000	BV	100	120	275	325
1897A	114,000	BV	120	200	300	400
1898A	2,280,000	BV	95.00	120	275	325
1899A	300,000	BV	110	165	275	325
1900A	742,000	BV	95.00	120	275	325
1900A Proof	—	Value: 900				

GERMAN STATES — PRUSSIA

Date	Mintage	F	VF	XF	Unc	BU
1901A	702,000	BV	95.00	120	250	400
1901A Proof	—	Value: 1,300				
1902A	271,000	BV	135	185	275	425
1902A Proof	—	Value: 1,300				
1903A	1,685,000	BV	95.00	125	250	400
1903A Proof	—	Value: 1,300				
1904A	1,178,000	BV	95.00	125	250	400
1905A	1,063,000	BV	95.00	125	250	400
1905A Proof	117	Value: 1,300				
1906A	542,000	BV	100	135	265	425
1906A Proof	150	Value: 1,300				
1907A	813,000	BV	95.00	125	250	400
1907A Proof	—	Value: 1,300				
1909A	532,000	BV	100	135	265	425
1909A Proof	—	Value: 1,300				
1910A	803,000	BV	95.00	125	250	400
1911A	271,000	BV	130	180	275	400
1911A Proof	—	Value: 1,300				
1912A	542,000	BV	95.00	125	250	400
1912A Proof	—	Value: 1,300				

KM# 501 20 MARK
7.9650 g., 0.9000 Gold .2304 oz. AGW **Ruler:** Wilhelm I **Obv:** Head right **Obv. Legend:** WILHELM DEUTSCHER KAISER KONIG V. PREUSSEN **Rev:** Crowned imperial eagle **Rev. Legend:** DEUTSCHES REICH

Date	Mintage	F	VF	XF	Unc	BU
1871A	502,000	125	200	275	500	750
1871A Proof	—	Value: 1,800				
1872A	7,717,000	—	BV	170	200	250
1872A Proof	2,491	Value: 1,800				
1872B	1,918,000	—	BV	180	225	275
1872C	3,056,000	—	BV	180	225	275
1873A	9,063,000	—	BV	180	225	275
1873A Proof	—	Value: 1,800				
1873B	3,441,000	—	BV	180	225	275
1873C	5,228,000	—	BV	180	225	275
1873C Proof	—	Value: 1,800				

KM# 505 20 MARK
7.9650 g., 0.9000 Gold .2304 oz. AGW **Ruler:** Wilhelm I **Obv:** Head right **Obv. Legend:** WILHELM DEUTSCHER KAISER KONIG V. PREUSSEN **Rev:** Type II **Rev. Legend:** DEUTSCHES REICH date, 20 MARK below

Date	Mintage	F	VF	XF	Unc	BU
1874A	762,000	—	BV	155	200	300
1874A Proof	—	Value: 1,300				
1874B	824,000	—	BV	160	225	300
1874C	88,000	—	BV	175	250	300
1875A	4,203,000	—	BV	155	200	300
1875B	Est. 1,500	180	350	600	1,200	1,600
1876A	2,673,000	—	BV	155	200	250
1876C	423,000	160	250	400	600	1,000
1877A	1,250,000	—	BV	155	200	250
1877B	501,000	—	BV	200	300	350
1877C	6,384	1,000	1,700	2,400	3,000	4,500
1878A	2,175,000	—	BV	155	200	250
1878C	82,000	160	250	400	600	900
1879A	1,022,999	—	BV	155	200	250
1881A	428,000	—	BV	155	200	250
1882A	655,000	—	BV	155	200	250
1882A Proof	—	Value: 1,500				
1883A	4,283,000	—	BV	155	200	250
1884A	224,000	—	BV	155	200	250
1885A	407,000	—	BV	155	200	250
1886A	176,000	—	BV	155	200	250
1887A	5,645,000	—	BV	155	200	250
1887A Proof	—	Value: 1,500				
1888A	534,000	—	BV	155	200	250
1888A Proof	—	Value: 1,500				

KM# 515 20 MARK
7.9650 g., 0.9000 Gold .2304 oz. AGW **Ruler:** Friedrich III March - June **Obv:** Head right **Obv. Legend:** FRIEDRICH DEUTSCHER KAISER KONIG V. PREUSSEN **Rev:** Crowned imperial eagle **Rev. Legend:** DEUTSCHES REICH date, 20 MARK below

Date	Mintage	F	VF	XF	Unc	BU
1888A	5,364,000	—	BV	155	225	300
1888A Proof	—	Value: 900				

KM# 516 20 MARK
7.9650 g., 0.9000 Gold .2304 oz. AGW **Ruler:** Wilhelm II **Obv:** Head right **Obv. Legend:** WILHELM II DEUTSCHES KAISER KONIG V. PREUSSEN **Rev:** Crowned imperial eagle **Rev. Legend:** DEUTSCHES REICH date, 20 MARK below

Date	Mintage	F	VF	XF	Unc	BU
1888A	756,000	—	BV	155	275	350
1888A Proof	—	Value: 1,250				
1889A	9,642,000	—	BV	155	200	275
1889A Proof	—	Value: 1,100				

KM# 521 20 MARK
7.9650 g., 0.9000 Gold .2304 oz. AGW **Ruler:** Wilhelm II **Obv:** Head right **Obv. Legend:** WILHELM II DEUTSCHER KAISER KONIG V. PREUSSEN **Rev:** Crowned imperial eagle, type III **Rev. Legend:** DEUTSCHES REICH date, 20 MARK below

Date	Mintage	F	VF	XF	Unc	BU
1890A	3,695,000	—	BV 160+10%	225	275	
1891A	2,752,000	—	BV 160+10%	225	275	
1891A Proof	—	Value: 1,000				
1892A	1,815,000	—	BV 160+10%	225	275	
1893A	3,172,000	—	BV 160+10%	225	275	
1894A	5,815,000	—	BV 160+10%	225	275	
1895A	4,135,000	—	BV 160+10%	225	275	
1896A	4,239,000	—	BV 160+10%	225	275	
1896A Proof	—	Value: 1,000				
1897A	5,394,000	—	BV 160+10%	225	275	
1898A	6,542,000	—	BV 160+10%	225	275	
1899A	5,873,000	—	BV 160+10%	225	275	
1899A Proof	—	Value: 1,000				
1900A	5,163,000	—	BV 160+10%	225	275	
1901A	5,188,000	—	BV 160+10%	225	400	
1901A Proof	—	Value: 1,400				
1902A	4,138,000	—	BV 160+10%	225	400	
1902A Proof	—	Value: 1,400				
1903A	2,870,000	—	BV 160+10%	225	400	
1903A Proof	—	Value: 1,400				
1904A	3,453,000	—	BV 160+10%	225	400	
1904A Proof	—	Value: 1,250				
1905A	4,176,000	—	BV 160+10%	225	400	
1905A Proof	287	Value: 1,250				
1905J	921,000	BV+5%	BV+10%	190	300	400
1906A	7,788,000	—	BV 160+10%	250	400	
1906A Proof	124	Value: 1,250				
1906J	82,000	BV+5%	290	380	600	400
1907A	2,576,000	—	BV 160+10%	225	400	
1907A Proof	—	Value: 1,250				
1908A	3,274,000	—	BV 160+10%	225	400	
1908A Proof	—	Value: 1,200				
1909A	5,213,000	—	BV 160+10%	225	400	
1909J	350,000	BV+5%	BV+10%	190	300	400
1909A Proof	—	Value: 1,200				
1909J Proof	—	Value: 1,750				
1910A	8,646,000	—	BV 160+10%	225	400	
1910J	753,000	—	BV 160+10%	225	400	
1911A	4,746,000	—	BV 160+10%	225	400	
1912A	5,569,000	—	BV 160+10%	225	400	
1912J	503,000	BV+3%	BV+5%	190	300	400
1913A	6,102,000	—	BV 160+10%	225	400	
1913A Proof	—	Value: 1,000				

KM# 537 20 MARK
7.9650 g., 0.9000 Gold .2304 oz. AGW **Ruler:** Wilhelm II **Obv:** Uniformed bust right **Rev:** Crowned imperial eagle with shield on breast

Date	Mintage	F	VF	XF	Unc	BU
1913A	—	BV	BV+5%	180	250	300
1913A Proof	—	Value: 1,500				
1914A	2,137,000	BV	BV+5%	180	250	300
1914A Proof	—	Value: 1,500				
1915A	1,271,000	—	1,100	1,400	2,000	2,500

PATTERNS
Karl Goetz Issues
Struck in Munich, Bavaria

X# 2c 2 MARK
24.4400 g., Platinum APW, 28.2 mm. **Subject:** Wilhelm II

Date	Mintage	F	VF	XF	Unc	BU
1913 Proof	—	Value: 950				

X# 4c 5 MARK
Gold **Subject:** Wilhelm II

Date	Mintage	F	VF	XF	Unc	BU
1913 Proof	—	—	—	—	—	—

X# 4d 5 MARK
56.5700 g., Platinum APW **Subject:** Wilhelm II

Date	Mintage	F	VF	XF	Unc	BU
1913 Proof	—	Value: 2,850				

X# 5 10 MARK
2.8000 g., Gold **Subject:** Wilhelm II

Date	Mintage	F	VF	XF	Unc	BU
1913 Proof	—	—	—	—	—	—

X# 6 20 MARK
4.2000 g., Gold **Subject:** Wilhelm II

Date	Mintage	F	VF	XF	Unc	BU
1913 Proof	—	—	—	—	—	—

PATTERNS
Including off metal strikes

KM#	Date	Mintage	Identification	Mkt Val
Pn23	1878	—	20 Mark. Silver Or Silvered. KM#505.	—
Pn26	1888A	—	10 Mark. Silver. Weak edge, KM#517.	—
PnA27	1890A	—	10 Mark. Copper. 2.0300 g.	—
Pn27	1900	—	20 Mark. Silver. KM#521.	300
PnA30	1901A	—	20 Mark. Silver. Plain edge.	350
PnA40	1907A	—	20 Mark. Copper. 4.1100 g.	—
Pn42	1908J	—	20 Mark. Gold. KM521.2. Extra rare.	—

REUSS-OBERGREIZ

The other branch of the division of 1635, Obergreiz went through a number of consolidations and further divisions. Upon the extinction of the Ruess-Untergreiz line in 1768, the latter passed to Reuss-Obergreiz and this line continued on into the 20th century, obtaining the rank of count back in 1673 and that of prince in 1778.

RULERS
Heinrich XI, 1723-1800
Heinrich XIII, 1800-1817
Heinrich XIX, 1817-1836
Heinrich XX, 1836-1859
Heinrich XXII, 1859-1902
Heinrich XXIV, 1902-1918

PRINCIPALITY
REFORM COINAGE

KM# 125 20 MARK
7.9650 g., 0.9000 Gold .2304 oz. AGW **Ruler:** Heinrich XXII **Obv:** Head right **Obv. Legend:** HEINRICH XXII v. G. G. ALT. L. SOUV. FRUST REUSS **Rev:** Type II **Rev. Legend:** DEUTSCHES REICH date, 20 MARK below

Date	Mintage	F	VF	XF	Unc	BU
1875B	1,510	6,500	12,000	16,000	22,500	30,000
1875B Proof	—	Value: 32,000				

REUSS-SCHLEIZ

Originally part of the holdings of Reuss-Gera, Schleiz was ruled separately on and off during the first half of the 16th century. When the Gera line died out in 1550, Schleiz passed to Obergreiz. Schleiz was reintegrated into a new line of Gera and a separate countship at Schleiz was founded in 1635, only to last one generation. At its extinction in 1666, Schleiz passed to Reuss-Saalburg which thereafter took the name of Reuss-Schleiz.

RULERS
Heinrich XLII, 1784-1818
Heinrich LXII, 1818-1854
Heinrich LXVII, 1854-1867
Heinrich XIV, 1867-1913
Heinrich XXVII, 1913-1918

PRINCIPALITY

REFORM COINAGE

KM# 81 10 MARK
3.9820 g., 0.9000 Gold .1152 oz. AGW **Ruler:** Heinrich XIV **Obv:** Head left **Obv. Legend:** HEINRICH XIV J. L. REG. FURST REUSS **Rev:** Crowned imperial eagle **Rev. Legend:** DEUTSCHES REICH date, 10 MARK below

Date	Mintage	F	VF	XF	Unc	BU
1882A	4,800	1,500	3,500	5,500	7,500	10,000
1882A Proof	200	Value: 11,500				

KM# 80 20 MARK
7.9650 g., 0.9000 Gold .2304 oz. AGW **Ruler:** Heinrich XIV **Obv:** Head left **Obv. Legend:** HEINRICH XIV J. L. REG. FURST REUSS **Rev:** Crowned imperial eagle **Rev. Legend:** DEUTSCHES REICH date, 20 MARK below

Date	Mintage	F	VF	XF	Unc	BU
1881	12,000	1,250	2,250	3,500	5,000	6,500
1881 Proof	500	Value: 7,000				

RHENISH CONFEDERATION

Issues for Carl von Dahlberg, 1804-1817

MINT OFFICIALS' INITIALS

Initial	Date	Name
B, CB	1773-1811	Christoph Busch, Regensburg
BH	1790-1825	Johann Georg Bunsen, mintmaster in Frankfurt
	1798-1816	Johann Georg Hille, mintwarden in Frankfurt

NAPOLEONIC PRINCIPALITY

TRADE COINAGE

C# 8 DUCAT
3.5000 g., 0.9860 Gold .1109 oz. AGW **Obv:** Uniformed bust right **Rev:** Crowned arms

Date	Mintage	F	VF	XF	Unc	BU
1809 BH	—	400	900	1,600	2,250	—

SAXE-ALTENBURG

(Sachsen-Gotha-Altenburg)

When the seven sons of Ernst the Pious of Saxe-New-Gotha divided the lands of their father in 1680, the eldest established the line of Saxe-Gotha-Altenburg. The line became extinct in 1825 and the following year witnessed the division of the territory which resulted in a general reorganization of the Thuringian duchies. Altenburg itself was inherited by the duke of Saxe-Hildburghausen, who transferred Hildburghausen to Saxe-Meiningen and became the founder of a new line of Saxe-Altenburg. Saxe-Meiningen also received Saalfeld from Saxe-Coburg, which in turn had acquired Gotha as part of the proceedings. The line of Saxe-Coburg-Gotha was established as a result. See under each of the foregoing regarding developments after the realignment of 1826. For a short period of time, from 1688 to 1692, the duke leased the abbey of Walkenried from Brunswick-Wolfenbüttel and struck a series of coins for that district.

RULERS
Ernst II Ludwig, 1772-1804

DUCHY

REFORM COINAGE

Y# 146 20 MARK
7.9650 g., 0.9000 Gold .2304 oz. AGW **Ruler:** Ernst I **Obv:** Head right **Obv. Legend:** ERNST HERZOG VON SACHSEN ALTENBURG **Rev:** Crowned imperial eagle **Rev. Legend:** DEUTSCHES REICH date, 20 MARK below

Date	Mintage	F	VF	XF	Unc	BU
1887A	15,000	900	1,600	2,250	3,500	4,500
1887A Proof	—	Value: 4,750				

SAXE-COBURG-GOTHA

Upon the extinction of the ducal line in Saxe-Gotha-Altenburg in 1826, Gotha was assigned to Saxe-Coburg-Saalfeld and Saxe-Meiningen received Saalfeld. The resulting duchy became called Saxe-Coburg-Gotha. Albert, the son of Ernst I and younger brother of Ernst II, married Queen Victoria of Great Britain and the British royal dynastic name was that of Saxe-Coburg-Gotha. Their son, Alfred was made the Duke of Edinburgh and succeeded his uncle, Ernst II, as Duke of Saxe-Coburg-Gotha. Alfred's older brother, Eduard Albert, followed their mother as King Edward VII (1901-1910). The last duke of Saxe-Coburg-Gotha was Alfred's son, Karl Eduard, forced to abdicate in 1918 as a result of World War I, which was fought in part against his cousin, King George V.

RULERS
Ernst I, 1826-1844
Ernst II, 1844-1893
Alfred, 1893-1900
Karl Eduard, 1900-1918

MINT OFFICIALS' INITIALS

Initial	Date	Name
B	1860-87	Gustav Julius Buschick
EK	1828-38	Ernst Kleinsteuber
F	1845-60	Gustav Theodor Fischer
G	1826-28	Graupner
G	1838-44	Johann Georg Grohmann
ST	1826-28	Strebel

DUCHY

TRADE COINAGE

C# 108 DUCAT
3.5000 g., 0.9860 Gold .1109 oz. AGW **Ruler:** Ernst I **Obv:** Head left **Obv. Legend:** ERNST HERZOG Z.S. COBURG U. GOTHA F.Z. LICHTENB. **Rev:** Crowned arms within branches **Rev. Legend:** EIN DUCATEN

Date	Mintage	F	VF	XF	Unc	BU
1831 E-K	600	1,000	2,500	3,500	5,000	—

C# 108a DUCAT
3.5000 g., 0.9860 Gold .1109 oz. AGW **Ruler:** Ernst I **Obv:** Head left **Obv. Legend:** ERNST HERZOG ZU SACHSEN COBURG-GOTHA **Rev:** Crowned arms within wreath **Rev. Legend:** EIN DUCATEN

Date	Mintage	F	VF	XF	Unc	BU
1836	1,600	750	1,250	2,500	3,750	—
1842	508	750	1,500	3,000	4,000	—

REFORM COINAGE

KM# 154 10 MARK
3.9820 g., 0.9000 Gold .1152 oz. AGW **Ruler:** Karl Eduard **Obv:** Head right **Rev:** Crowned imperial eagle with shield on breast

Date	Mintage	F	VF	XF	Unc	BU
1905A	9,511	650	1,200	1,800	2,250	3,250
1905A Proof	489	Value: 4,000				

Y# 148 20 MARK
1.9650 g., 0.9000 Gold .2304 oz. AGW **Ruler:** Ernst II **Obv:** Head left **Obv. Legend:** ERNST HERZOG V. SACH. COBURG U. GOTHA **Rev:** Type I **Rev. Legend:** DEUTSCHES REICH date, 20 MARK below

Date	Mintage	F	VF	XF	Unc	BU
1872E	1,000	15,000	25,000	35,000	50,000	70,000
1872E Proof, rare						

Y# 148a 20 MARK
1.9650 g., 0.9000 Gold .2304 oz. AGW **Ruler:** Ernst II **Obv:** Head left **Obv. Legend:** ERNST HERZOG V. SACHS. COBURG U. GOTHA **Rev:** Crowned imperial eagle **Rev. Legend:** DEUTSCHES REICH date, 20 MARK below

Date	Mintage	F	VF	XF	Unc	BU
1886A	20,000	1,000	2,000	3,000	5,000	6,000
1886A Proof	—	Value: 6,500				

Y# 151 20 MARK
1.9650 g., 0.9000 Gold .2304 oz. AGW **Ruler:** Alfred **Obv:** Head right **Obv. Legend:** ALFRED HERZOG VON SACHSEN COBURG U. GOTHA **Rev:** Crowned imperial eagle **Rev. Legend:** DEUTSCHES REICH date, 20 MARK below

Date	Mintage	F	VF	XF	Unc	BU
1895A	10,000	1,200	2,000	2,500	3,500	4,000
1895A Proof	—	Value: 4,500				

KM# 155 20 MARK
7.9650 g., 0.9000 Gold .2304 oz. AGW **Ruler:** Karl Eduard **Obv:** Head, right **Rev:** Crowned imperial eagle with shield on breast, type I

Date	Mintage	F	VF	XF	Unc	BU
1905A	10,000	700	1,350	2,000	2,800	3,500
1905A Proof	484	Value: 4,500				

SAXE-MEININGEN

(Sachsen-Meiningen)

The duchy of Saxe-Meiningen was located in Thuringia, sandwiched between Saxe-Weimar-Eisenach on the west and north and the enclave of Schmalkalden belonging to Hesse-Cassel on the east. It was founded upon the division of the Ernestine line in Saxe-Gotha in 1680. In 1735, due to an exchange of some territory, the duchy became known as Saxe-Coburg-Meiningen. In 1826, Saxe-Coburg-Gotha assigned Saalfeld to Saxe-Meiningen. The duchy came under the strong influence of Prussia from 1866, when Bernhard II was forced to abdicate because of his support of Austria. The monarchy ended with the defeat of Germany in 1918.

266 GERMAN STATES — SAXE-MEININGEN

RULERS
Georg I, 1782-1803
Bernhard Erich Freund, under Regency of
Louise Eleonore, 1803-1821
Bernhard II, 1821-1866
Georg II, 1866-1914
Bernhard III, 1914-1918

MINT OFFICIALS' INITIALS

Initial	Date	Name
F. HELFRICHT	d. 1892	Ferdinand Helfricht, die-cutter and chief medailleur
K	1835-37	Georg Krell, warden then mintmaster
L	1803-33	Georg Christoph Loewel

NOTE: Between 1691 and 1703, Saxe-Meiningen struck coins in various denominations for its part of Henneberg-Ilmenau.

DUCHY
REFORM COINAGE

KM# 190 10 MARK
3.9820 g., 0.9000 Gold .1152 oz. AGW **Ruler:** Georg II **Obv:** Head left **Obv. Legend:** GEORG HERZOG VON SACHSEN MEININGEN **Rev:** Crowned imperial eagle **Rev. Legend:** DEUTSCHES REICH date, 10 MARK below

Date	Mintage	F	VF	XF	Unc	BU
1890D	2,000	1,500	3,000	3,500	5,000	6,000
1890D Proof	—	Value: 7,000				
1898D	2,000	1,500	3,000	3,500	5,000	6,000
1898D Proof	—	Value: 7,000				

KM# 202 10 MARK
3.9820 g., 0.9000 Gold .1152 oz. AGW **Ruler:** Georg II **Obv:** Head left, long beard **Rev:** Crowned imperial eagle with shield on breast

Date	Mintage	F	VF	XF	Unc	BU
1902D	2,000	900	2,000	3,000	4,000	5,500
1902D Proof	—	Value: 6,000				
1909D	2,000	900	2,000	3,000	4,000	5,500
1909D Proof	—	Value: 6,000				
1914D	1,002	950	2,250	3,000	4,500	5,500
1914D Proof	—	Value: 6,750				

KM# 180 20 MARK
7.9650 g., 0.9000 Gold .2304 oz. AGW **Ruler:** Georg II **Obv:** Head right **Obv. Legend:** GEORG HERZOG ZU SACHSEN MEININGEN **Rev:** Type I **Rev. Legend:** DEUTSCHES REICH

Date	Mintage	F	VF	XF	Unc	BU
1872D	3,000	3,500	7,000	10,000	16,000	20,000
1872D Proof	—	Value: 18,500				

KM# 185 20 MARK
7.9650 g., 0.9000 Gold .2304 oz. AGW **Ruler:** Georg II **Obv:** Head right **Obv. Legend:** GEORG HERZOG ZU SACHSEN MEININGEN **Rev:** Type II **Rev. Legend:** DEUTSCHES REICH date, 20 MARK below

Date	Mintage	F	VF	XF	Unc	BU
1882D	3,061	2,500	5,000	6,000	12,000	16,000
1882D Proof	—	Value: 14,500				

KM# 186 20 MARK
7.9650 g., 0.9000 Gold .2304 oz. AGW **Ruler:** Georg II **Obv:** Head left **Obv. Legend:** GEORG HERZOG VON SACHSEN MEININGEN **Rev:** DEUTSCHES REICH date, 20 MARK below

Date	Mintage	F	VF	XF	Unc	BU
1889D	4,032	2,000	4,000	6,000	8,000	11,000
1889D Proof	—	Value: 11,000				

KM# 195 20 MARK
7.9650 g., 0.9000 Gold .2304 oz. AGW **Ruler:** Georg II **Obv:** Head left, short beard **Obv. Legend:** GEORG HERZOG VON SACHSEN MEININGEN **Rev:** Crowned imperial eagle, type III **Rev. Legend:** DEUTSCHES REICH date, 20 MARK below

Date	Mintage	F	VF	XF	Unc	BU
1900D	1,005	3,000	5,000	7,500	12,500	15,000
1900D Proof	—	Value: 12,500				
1905D	1,000	3,000	5,000	7,500	12,500	15,000
1905D Proof	—	Value: 15,000				

KM# 205 20 MARK
7.9650 g., 0.9000 Gold .2304 oz. AGW **Ruler:** Georg II **Obv:** Head left, long beard **Rev:** Crowned imperial eagle with shield on breast

Date	Mintage	F	VF	XF	Unc	BU
1910D	1,004	1,500	3,000	4,750	6,000	7,500
1910D Proof	—	Value: 8,500				
1914D	1,000	1,500	3,000	4,750	6,000	7,500
1914D Proof	—	Value: 8,500				

PATTERNS
Including off metal strikes

KM#	Date	Mintage	Identification	Mkt Val
Pn11	1881D	—	20 Mark. Gold. KM#185.	25,000

TRIAL STRIKES

KM#	Date	Mintage	Identification	Mkt Val
TS1	ND	—	20 Mark. Gold. Uniface.	—

SAXE-WEIMAR-EISENACH
(Sachsen-Weimar-Eisenach)

When the death of the duke of Saxe-Eisenach in 1741 heralded the extinction of that line, its possessions reverted to Saxe-Weimar, which henceforth was known as Saxe-Weimar-Eisenach. Because of the strong role played by the duke during the Napoleonic Wars, Saxe-Weimar-Eisenach was raised to the rank of a grand duchy in 1814 and granted the territory of Neustadt, taken from Saxony. The last grand duke abdicated at the end of World War I.

RULERS
Karl August, 1758-1828 under regency of his
  mother, Anna Amalia of Brunswick, 1758-1775
Karl Alexander, 1853-1901
Wilhelm Ernst, 1901-1918

MINT OFFICIALS' INITIALS

Initials	Date	Name
Lion or ILST, LS, LST, ST	1835-45	Georg Godecke, mintmaster in Saafeld

GRAND DUCHY
REFORM COINAGE

Y# 169 20 MARK
7.9650 g., 0.9000 Gold .2304 oz. AGW **Ruler:** Karl Alexander **Subject:** Golden Wedding of Carl Alexander **Obv:** Head left **Obv. Legend:** CARL ALEXANDER GROSSERZOG V. SACHSEN **Rev:** Crowned imperial eagle **Rev. Legend:** DEUTSCHES REICH date, 20 MARK below

Date	Mintage	F	VF	XF	Unc	BU
1892A	5,000	600	1,200	1,600	3,000	3,600
1892A Proof	—	Value: 5,000				
1896A	15,000	700	1,150	1,600	2,500	3,000
1896A Proof	380	Value: 5,000				

Y# 171 20 MARK
7.9650 g., 0.9000 Gold .2304 oz. AGW **Ruler:** Wilhelm Ernst **Subject:** Golden Wedding of Carl Alexander **Obv:** Head left **Rev:** Crowned imperial eagle with shield on breast

Date	Mintage	F	VF	XF	Unc	BU
1901A	5,000	1,000	2,100	2,800	4,000	5,000
1901A Proof	—	Value: 6,500				

SAXONY

Saxony, located in southeast Germany was founded in 850. The first coinage was struck c. 990. It was divided into two lines in 1464. The electoral right was obtained by the elder line in 1547. During the time of the Reformation, Saxony was one of the more powerful states in central Europe. It became a kingdom in 1806. At the Congress of Vienna in 1815, they were forced to cede half its territories to Prussia.

RULERS
Friedrich August III, 1763-1806
  as Friedrich August I, 1806-1827
Anton, 1827-1836
Friedrich August II, 1836-1854
Johann, 1854-1873
Albert, 1873-1902
Georg, 1902-1904
Friedrich August III, 1904-1918

MINT MARKS
L - Leipzig

MINT OFFICIALS' INITIALS
Dresden Mint

Initials	Date	Name
B	1860-87	Gustav Julius Buschick
C, IC, IEC	1779-1804	Johann Ernst Croll
F	1845-60	Gustav Theodor Fischer
G	1833-44	Johann Georg Grohmann
GS, IGS, S	1812-32	Johann Gotthelf Studer
H, SGH	1804-13	Samuel Gottlieb Helbig

Arms of Electoral Saxony
2-fold arms divided vertically, 2 crossed swords on left, opened crown curving diagonally from upper left to lower right on right side.

ROYAL DUCHY
Until 1806 when it became a Kingdom
REGULAR COINAGE

KM# 1028 5 THALER (August D'or)
6.6820 g., 0.9020 Gold .1940 oz. AGW **Obv:** Uniformed bust right **Obv. Legend:** FRID. AVG. D. G. DVX SAX. ELECTOR **Rev:** Crowned oval arms within branches

Date	Mintage	F	VF	XF	Unc	BU
1801 IEC	—	400	900	1,500	3,000	—
1802 IEC	—	400	900	1,500	3,000	—

SAXONY

GERMAN STATES

KM# 1047 5 THALER (August D'or)
6.6820 g., 0.9020 Gold .1940 oz. AGW **Ruler:** Friedrich August III **Obv:** Uniformed bust right **Obv. Legend:** FRID. AVG. D. G. DVX SAX. ELECTOR **Rev:** Crowned oval arms within branches

Date	Mintage	F	VF	XF	Unc	BU
1805 SGH	—	500	1,000	1,500	3,500	—
1806 SGH	—	500	1,000	1,500	3,500	—

KM# 1029 10 THALER (2 August D'or)
13.3640 g., 0.9020 Gold .3880 oz. AGW **Ruler:** Friedrich August III **Obv:** Uniformed bust right **Obv. Legend:** FRID. AVGVST. D. G. DVX SAX. ELECTOR **Rev:** Crowned oval arms within branches

Date	Mintage	F	VF	XF	Unc	BU
1801 IEC	—	800	2,000	3,000	5,000	—
1802 IEC	—	800	2,000	3,000	5,000	—
1803 IEC	—	800	2,000	3,000	5,000	—
1804 IEC	—	600	1,500	2,750	4,000	—
1804 IEC	—	500	1,100	2,250	4,000	—
1805 IEC	—	600	1,500	2,750	4,000	—
1806 IEC	—	500	1,100	2,250	4,000	—

TRADE COINAGE

KM# 1030 DUCAT
3.5000 g., 0.9860 Gold .1109 oz. AGW **Ruler:** Friedrich August III **Obv:** Uniformed bust right **Obv. Legend:** FRID. AVG. D. G. DVX SAX. ELECTOR **Rev:** Crowned oval arms within branches

Date	Mintage	F	VF	XF	Unc	BU
1801 IEC	—	300	600	1,250	3,000	—
1802 IEC	—	200	400	850	2,000	—
1803 IEC	—	300	600	1,250	3,000	—
1804 IEC	—	250	500	1,000	2,500	—

KM# 1046 DUCAT
3.5000 g., 0.9860 Gold .1109 oz. AGW **Ruler:** Friedrich August III **Obv:** Uniformed bust right **Obv. Legend:** FRID. AVG. D. G. DVX SAX. ELECTOR **Rev:** Crowned oval arms within branches

Date	Mintage	F	VF	XF	Unc	BU
1804 SGH	—	300	700	1,250	2,500	—
1805 SGH	—	350	800	1,500	3,000	—
1806 SGH	—	300	700	1,250	2,500	—

KINGDOM
REGULAR COINAGE

KM# 1164 2-1/2 THALER
3.3410 g., 0.9020 Gold .0970 oz. AGW **Ruler:** Friedrich August II **Obv:** Head right **Obv. Legend:** FRIEDR. AUG. V.G.G. KOENIG V. SACHSEN **Rev:** Arms within crowned mantle **Rev. Legend:** ZWEI UND EIN HALB. THALER

Date	Mintage	F	VF	XF	Unc	BU
1842 G	560	300	600	1,000	2,250	—
1845 F	420	300	600	1,200	2,500	—

Date	Mintage	F	VF	XF	Unc	BU
1848 F	2,445	250	500	1,000	2,000	—
1854 F	308	400	700	1,200	2,500	—

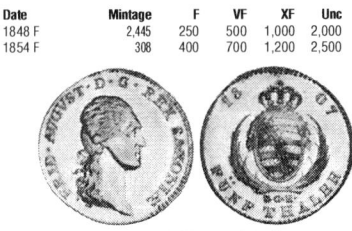

KM# 1054 5 THALER (August D'or)
6.6820 g., 0.9020 Gold .1940 oz. AGW **Ruler:** Friedrich August III as Friedrich August I **Obv. Legend:** FRID. AVGVST. D. G. REX SAXONIE **Rev:** Crowned oval arms within branches **Rev. Legend:** FUNF THALER

Date	Mintage	F	VF	XF	Unc	BU
1806 SGH	44,000	750	1,500	3,500	6,000	—
1807 SGH	152,000	400	900	1,500	3,000	—
1808 SGH	135,000	300	600	1,250	2,750	—
1809 SGH	54,000	300	600	1,250	2,750	—
1810 SGH	235,000	300	600	1,250	2,750	—
1812 SGH	98,000	300	600	1,250	2,750	—
1813 SGH	118,000	300	600	1,250	2,750	—
1815 IGS	20,000	250	500	1,250	2,500	—
1816 IGS	—	400	900	1,500	3,250	—
1817 IGS	—	250	500	1,250	2,500	—

KM# 1080 5 THALER (August D'or)
6.6820 g., 0.9020 Gold .1940 oz. AGW **Ruler:** Friedrich August III as Friedrich August I **Obv:** Uniformed and draped bust left **Rev:** Crowned arched arms

Date	Mintage	F	VF	XF	Unc	BU
1818 igs	—	800	2,000	3,500	7,500	—

KM# 1102 5 THALER (August D'or)
6.6820 g., 0.9020 Gold .1940 oz. AGW **Ruler:** Friedrich August III as Friedrich August I **Obv:** Uniformed bust left **Obv. Legend:** FRIEDR. AUG. KOENIG V. SACHSEN **Rev:** Crowned arms **Rev. Legend:** FUNF THALER

Date	Mintage	F	VF	XF	Unc	BU
1825 S	60,000	250	600	1,500	3,000	—
1826 S	2,590	400	1,000	2,000	4,000	—
1827 S	700	500	1,200	3,000	5,000	—

KM# 1113 5 THALER (August D'or)
6.6820 g., 0.9020 Gold .1940 oz. AGW **Ruler:** Anton **Obv:** Head right **Obv. Legend:** ANTON V. G. G. KOENIG VON SACHSEN **Rev:** Crowned arched arms within branches **Rev. Legend:** FUNF THALER

Date	Mintage	F	VF	XF	Unc	BU
1827 S	405	500	1,000	2,000	4,000	—
1828 S	855	500	1,000	2,000	4,000	—

KM# 1123 5 THALER (August D'or)
6.6820 g., 0.9020 Gold .1940 oz. AGW **Ruler:** Anton **Obv:** Older head right **Obv. Legend:** ANTON V. G. G. KOENIG VON SACHSEN **Rev:** Crowned arched arms within branches **Rev. Legend:** FUNF THALER

Date	Mintage	F	VF	XF	Unc	BU
1829 S	385	500	1,000	2,000	4,000	—
1830 S	2,800	550	1,100	2,000	4,250	—
1831 S	245	700	1,500	3,000	5,000	—
1832 S	175	700	1,250	3,000	6,000	—
1834 S	490	700	1,250	2,750	5,000	—
1835 S	380	700	1,250	3,000	6,000	—
1836 S	455	700	1,500	2,500	5,000	—

KM# 1146 5 THALER (August D'or)
6.6820 g., 0.9020 Gold .1940 oz. AGW **Ruler:** Friedrich August II **Obv:** Head right **Obv. Legend:** FRIEDRICH AUGUST V.G.G. KOENIG SACHSEN **Rev:** Crowned arched arms within branches **Rev. Legend:** FUNF THALER

Date	Mintage	F	VF	XF	Unc	BU
1837 G	490	400	750	2,000	3,250	—
1838 G	175	500	850	2,500	5,000	—
1839 G	210	500	850	2,150	4,000	—

KM# 1165 5 THALER (August D'or)
6.6820 g., 0.9020 Gold .1940 oz. AGW **Ruler:** Friedrich August II **Obv:** Head right **Obv. Legend:** FRIEDR. AUG. V. G. G. KOENIG V. SACHSEN **Rev:** Crowned arched arms within branches **Rev. Legend:** FUNF THLR.

Date	Mintage	F	VF	XF	Unc	BU
1842 G	4,455	250	400	1,000	2,000	—
1845 F	1,483	300	500	1,200	2,250	—
1848 F	1,964	300	500	1,200	2,250	—
1849 F	1,110	300	500	1,200	2,250	—
1853 F	511	450	800	2,000	3,000	—
1854 F	4,570	300	500	1,200	2,250	—

KM# 1055 10 THALER (2 August D'or)
13.3640 g., 0.9020 Gold .3880 oz. AGW **Ruler:** Friedrich August III as Friedrich August I **Obv:** Head right **Obv. Legend:** FRID. AVGVST. D. G. REX SAXONIE **Rev:** Crowned oval arms within branches **Rev. Legend:** ZEHN THALER

Date	Mintage	F	VF	XF	Unc	BU
1806 SGH	—	600	1,250	2,500	4,000	—
1807 SGH	—	600	1,250	2,500	4,000	—
1808 SGH	—	500	1,000	2,500	4,000	—
1809 SGH	—	600	1,250	2,500	4,000	—
1810 SGH	—	500	1,000	2,000	4,000	—
1811 SGH	—	500	1,000	2,000	3,500	—
1812 SGH	—	500	1,000	2,000	3,500	—
1813 SGH	—	450	850	1,750	2,500	—
1813 IGS	—	475	950	1,750	2,500	—
1815 IGS	—	450	850	1,750	3,000	—
1816 IGS	—	600	1,250	2,500	3,000	—
1817 IGS	—	450	850	1,750	2,500	—

KM# 1081 10 THALER (2 August D'or)
13.3640 g., 0.9020 Gold .3880 oz. AGW **Ruler:** Friedrich August III as Friedrich August I **Obv:** Uniformed bust left **Obv. Legend:** FRIEDRICH AUGUST KOENIG V. SACHSEN **Rev:** Crowned oval arms within branches **Rev. Legend:** ZEHN THALER

Date	Mintage	F	VF	XF	Unc	BU
1818 IGS	—	2,000	4,000	7,500	9,500	—

268 GERMAN STATES / SAXONY

KM# 1103 10 THALER (2 August D'or)
13.3640 g., 0.9020 Gold .3880 oz. AGW **Ruler:** Friedrich August III as Friedrich August I **Obv:** Uniformed and draped bust left **Obv. Legend:** FRIEDR. AUGUST KOENIG V. SACHSEN **Rev:** Crowned arched arms **Rev. Legend:** ZEHN THALER

Date	Mintage	F	VF	XF	Unc	BU
1825 S	—	800	2,000	4,000	5,500	—
1826 S	—	700	1,500	3,000	4,500	—
1827 S	9,250	700	1,500	3,000	4,500	—

KM# 1114 10 THALER (2 August D'or)
13.3640 g., 0.9020 Gold .3880 oz. AGW **Ruler:** Anton **Obv:** Head right **Rev:** Crowned arched arms within crossed branches

Date	Mintage	F	VF	XF	Unc	BU
1827 S	875	1,200	3,000	6,000	9,000	—
1828 S	5,530	800	2,500	5,000	6,500	—

KM# 1124 10 THALER (2 August D'or)
13.3640 g., 0.9020 Gold .3880 oz. AGW **Ruler:** Anton **Obv:** Older head right **Obv. Legend:** ANTON V. G. G. KOENIG VON SACHSEN **Rev:** Crowned arched arms within branches **Rev. Legend:** ZEHN THALER

Date	Mintage	F	VF	XF	Unc	BU
1829 S	3,010	800	2,000	4,000	5,500	—
1830 S	18,000	650	1,600	3,000	4,500	—
1831	3,255	1,250	2,500	5,000	7,000	—
1832 S	2,625	800	2,000	4,000	5,500	—
1833 S	—	1,250	2,500	5,000	7,000	—
1834 S	3,080	1,250	2,500	5,000	7,000	—
1835 S	2,715	1,250	2,500	5,000	7,000	—
1836 S	4,655	1,250	2,500	5,000	7,000	—

KM# 1144 10 THALER (2 August D'or)
13.3640 g., 0.9020 Gold .3880 oz. AGW **Ruler:** Friedrich August II **Obv:** Different head **Rev:** Crowned arms

Date	Mintage	F	VF	XF	Unc	BU
1836 G	1,110	600	1,250	2,500	3,500	—
1837 G	2,400	600	1,250	2,500	3,500	—
1838 G	1,750	700	1,500	3,000	4,000	—
1839 G	1,855	700	1,500	3,000	4,000	—

KM# 1150 10 THALER (2 August D'or)
13.3640 g., 0.9020 Gold .3880 oz. AGW **Ruler:** Friedrich August II **Obv:** Head right **Obv. Legend:** FRIEDR. AUG. V. G. G. KOENIG V. SACHSEN **Rev:** Arms within crowned mantle **Rev. Legend:** ZEHN THLR.

Date	Mintage	F	VF	XF	Unc	BU
1839 G	1,855	800	2,000	4,000	5,500	—
1845 F	2,100	600	1,250	2,500	3,500	—
1848 F	4,761	700	1,500	3,000	4,500	—
1849 F	1,928	700	1,500	3,000	4,500	—
1853 F	1,038	700	1,500	3,000	4,500	—
1854 F	1,620	800	2,000	4,000	5,500	—

KM# 1196 1/2 KRONE
5.5560 g., 0.9000 Gold .1608 oz. AGW **Ruler:** Johann **Obv:** Head left **Obv. Legend:** IOHANN V. G. G. KOENIG V. SACHSEN **Rev:** Denomination and date within oak wreath **Rev. Legend:** VEREINSMUNZE, 100 EIN PFUND FEIN below

Date	Mintage	F	VF	XF	Unc	BU
1857 F	4,831	475	1,000	2,000	3,000	—
1858 F	2,455	475	1,000	2,000	3,000	—

Date	Mintage	F	VF	XF	Unc	BU
1862 B	2,177	550	1,200	2,250	3,000	—
1866 B	1,559	550	1,200	2,250	3,200	—
1868 B	1,516	550	1,200	2,500	3,500	—
1870 B	1,740	550	1,200	2,500	3,500	—

KM# 1197 KRONE
11.1110 g., 0.9000 Gold .3215 oz. AGW **Ruler:** Johann **Obv:** Head left **Obv. Legend:** IOHANN V. G. G. KOENIG V. SACHSEN **Rev:** Denomination and date within oak wreath **Rev. Legend:** VEREINSMUNZE, 50 EIN PFUND FEIN below

Date	Mintage	F	VF	XF	Unc	BU
1857 F	3,580	525	1,350	2,500	3,200	—
1858 F	4,610	525	1,350	2,500	3,200	—
1859 F	9,040	525	1,350	2,500	3,200	—
1860 B	5,067	525	1,350	2,750	3,700	—
1861 B	3,908	525	1,350	2,500	3,200	—
1862 B	3,229	525	1,350	2,750	3,700	—
1863 B	3,538	525	1,350	2,750	3,700	—
1865 B	4,371	525	1,350	2,500	3,200	—
1867 B	2,155	525	1,350	2,750	3,700	—
1868 B	5,262	525	1,350	2,500	3,200	—
1870 B	2,700	525	1,350	2,500	3,200	—
1871 B	2,140	525	1,350	2,750	3,200	—

TRADE COINAGE

KM# 1056 DUCAT
3.5000 g., 0.9860 Gold .1109 oz. AGW **Ruler:** Friedrich August III as Friedrich August I **Obv:** Head right **Obv. Legend:** FRID. AVGVST. D. G. REX SAXONIE **Rev:** Crowned oval arms within branches

Date	Mintage	F	VF	XF	Unc	BU
1806 SGH	3,207	200	400	1,000	2,000	—
1807 SGH	2,660	300	800	1,500	2,500	—
1808 SGH	2,010	300	800	1,500	2,500	—
1809 SGH	1,608	300	800	1,500	2,500	—
1810 SGH	1,072	300	800	1,500	2,500	—
1811 SGH	268	500	1,000	2,000	3,500	—
1812 SGH	67	500	1,000	2,000	4,000	—
1813 SGH	—	300	600	1,500	2,500	—

KM# 1063 DUCAT
3.5000 g., 0.9860 Gold .1109 oz. AGW **Ruler:** Friedrich August III as Friedrich August I **Subject:** 400th Jubilee of Leipzig University **Obv:** Bust in coronet and cape **Rev. Legend:** SALVA SIT

Date	Mintage	F	VF	XF	Unc	BU
1809	—	300	600	1,200	2,000	—

KM# 1073 DUCAT
3.5000 g., 0.9860 Gold .1109 oz. AGW **Ruler:** Friedrich August III as Friedrich August I **Obv:** Head right **Obv. Legend:** FRID. AVGVST. D. G. REX SAXONIE **Rev:** Crowned oval arms within branches

Date	Mintage	F	VF	XF	Unc	BU
1813 IGS	—	300	600	1,500	2,500	—
1814 IGS	134	500	1,000	2,000	3,500	—
1815 IGS	804	350	800	1,750	3,000	—
1816 IGS	2,243	300	600	1,200	2,200	—
1817 IGS	1,812	300	600	1,200	2,200	—
1818 IGS	1,466	300	600	1,200	2,200	—
1819 IGS	1,466	300	600	1,200	2,200	—
1820 IGS	2,502	300	600	1,200	2,200	—
1821 IGS	1,948	300	600	1,200	2,200	—
1822 IGS	1,898	300	600	1,200	2,200	—

KM# 1099 DUCAT
3.5000 g., 0.9860 Gold .1109 oz. AGW **Ruler:** Friedrich August III as Friedrich August I **Obv:** Uniformed bust left **Obv. Legend:** FRIEDR. AUG. KOEN. V. SACHSEN **Rev:** Crowned arms divide date

Date	Mintage	F	VF	XF	Unc	BU
1824 IGS	2,847	300	600	1,000	1,500	—

KM# 1104 DUCAT
3.5000 g., 0.9860 Gold .1109 oz. AGW **Ruler:** Friedrich August III as Friedrich August I **Obv:** Uniformed bust left **Obv. Legend:** FRIEDR. AUG. KOEN. V. SACHSEN **Rev:** Crowned arms divide date

Date	Mintage	F	VF	XF	Unc	BU
1825 IGS	1,725	300	600	1,200	2,000	—
1826 IGS	2,415	300	600	1,200	2,000	—
1827 IGS	1,639	300	600	1,200	2,000	—

KM# 1115 DUCAT
3.5000 g., 0.9860 Gold .1109 oz. AGW **Ruler:** Anton **Obv:** Head right **Obv. Legend:** ANTON V. G. G. KOENIG VON SACHSEN **Rev:** Crowned arched arms within branches

Date	Mintage	F	VF	XF	Unc	BU
1827 S	587	400	900	1,500	2,500	—
1828 S	771	400	900	1,500	2,500	—

KM# 1125 DUCAT
3.5000 g., 0.9860 Gold .1109 oz. AGW **Ruler:** Anton **Obv:** Head right **Obv. Legend:** ANTON V. G. G. KOENIG VON SACHSEN **Rev:** Crowned arched arms within branches

Date	Mintage	F	VF	XF	Unc	BU
1829 S	2,070	300	600	1,200	2,000	—
1830 S	1,898	300	600	1,200	2,000	—
1831 S	862	400	900	1,500	2,500	—
1832 S	776	400	900	1,500	2,500	—
1833 S	2,156	400	900	1,500	2,500	—
1834 S	1,582	400	900	1,500	2,500	—
1835 S	119	600	1,300	2,500	4,000	—
1836 S	804	600	1,250	2,000	3,000	—

KM# 1145 DUCAT
3.5000 g., 0.9860 Gold .1109 oz. AGW **Ruler:** Friedrich August II **Obv:** Different head

Date	Mintage	F	VF	XF	Unc	BU
1836 G	100	600	1,250	2,250	3,250	—
1837 G	168	600	1,250	2,250	3,250	—
1838 G	637	400	1,100	2,250	3,250	—

REFORM COINAGE

KM# 1239 5 MARK
1.9910 g., 0.9000 Gold .0576 oz. AGW **Ruler:** Albert **Obv:** Head right **Obv. Legend:** ALBERT KOENIG VON SACHSEN **Rev:** Type I **Rev. Legend:** DEUTSCHES REICH date, 5 MARK below

Date	Mintage	F	VF	XF	Unc	BU
1877E	402,000	175	300	500	750	900
1877E Proof	—	Value: 1,000				

KM# 1232 10 MARK
3.9820 g., 0.9000 Gold .1152 oz. AGW **Ruler:** Johann **Obv:** Head left **Obv. Legend:** IOHANN V. G. G. KOENIG VON SACHSEN **Rev:** Crowned imperial eagle **Rev. Legend:** DEUTSCHES REICH

Date	Mintage	F	VF	XF	Unc	BU
1872E	339,000	95.00	200	350	600	1,200
1873E	822,000	95.00	200	350	600	1,200

SCHAUMBURG-LIPPE — GERMAN STATES

KM# 1235 10 MARK
3.9820 g., 0.9000 Gold .1152 oz. AGW **Ruler:** Albert **Obv:** Head left **Obv. Legend:** ALBERT KOENIG VON SACHSEN **Rev:** Type II **Rev. Legend:** DEUTSCHES REICH date, 10 MARK below

Date	Mintage	F	VF	XF	Unc	BU
1874E	48,000	450	750	1,200	2,500	3,000
1875E	528,000	80.00	120	200	400	600
1877E	201,000	80.00	120	200	500	750
1878E	225,000	80.00	120	200	500	750
1879E	182,000	80.00	120	200	500	750
1881E	240,000	80.00	120	200	500	750
1888E	149,000	80.00	120	200	600	900

KM# 1247 10 MARK
3.9820 g., 0.9000 Gold .1152 oz. AGW **Ruler:** Albert **Rev:** Crowned imperial eagle, type III

Date	Mintage	F	VF	XF	Unc	BU
1891 E	224,000	100	160	200	450	550
1893E	224,000	100	175	250	500	650
1896E	150,000	100	175	250	500	650
1898E	313,000	100	175	250	500	650
1900E	74,000	100	175	250	500	650
1900E Proof	—	Value: 1,500				
1901E	75,000	100	175	250	500	650
1902E	37,000	100	175	250	500	700
1902E Proof	—	Value: 2,000				

KM# 1259 10 MARK
3.9820 g., 0.9000 Gold .1152 oz. AGW **Ruler:** Georg **Obv:** Head right **Rev:** Crowned imperial eagle with shield on breast

Date	Mintage	F	VF	XF	Unc	BU
1903E	284,000	100	210	350	600	1,000
1903E Proof	100	Value: 2,250				
1904E	149,000	100	210	350	600	1,000
1904E Proof	—	Value: 2,000				

KM# 1264 10 MARK
3.9820 g., 0.9000 Gold .1152 oz. AGW **Ruler:** Friedrich August III **Obv:** Head right **Rev:** Crowned imperial eagle with shield on breast

Date	Mintage	F	VF	XF	Unc	BU
1905E	112,000	120	250	325	500	750
1905E Proof	100	Value: 2,000				
1906E	75,000	120	250	325	500	750
1906E Proof	—	Value: 2,000				
1907E Proof	—	Value: 2,000				
1907E	112,000	120	250	325	500	750
1909E	112,000	120	250	325	500	750
1910E	75,000	120	250	325	500	750
1910E Proof	—	Value: 2,000				
1911E	38,000	120	250	325	500	750
1912E	75,000	120	250	325	500	750
1912E Proof	—	Value: 2,250				

KM# 1233 20 MARK
7.9650 g., 0.9000 Gold .2304 oz. AGW **Ruler:** Johann **Obv:** Head left **Obv. Legend:** IOHANN V. G. G. KOENIG VON SACHSEN **Rev:** Crowned imperial eagle, type I **Rev. Legend:** DEUTSCHES REICH

Date	Mintage	F	VF	XF	Unc	BU
1872E	890,000	160	200	300	600	800
1872E Proof	—	Value: 3,000				

KM# 1234 20 MARK
7.9650 g., 0.9000 Gold .2304 oz. AGW **Ruler:** Johann **Obv:** Large letters in legend **Obv. Legend:** IOHANN V. G. G. KOENIG VON SACHSEN **Rev:** Crowned imperial eagle **Rev. Legend:** DEUTSCHES REICH

Date	Mintage	F	VF	XF	Unc	BU
1873E	203,000	160	200	300	600	800

KM# 1236 20 MARK
7.9650 g., 0.9000 Gold .2304 oz. AGW **Ruler:** Albert **Obv:** Head right **Obv. Legend:** ALBERT KOENIG VON SACHSEN **Rev:** Type II **Rev. Legend:** DEUTSCHES REICH date, 20 MARK below

Date	Mintage	F	VF	XF	Unc	BU
1874E	153,000	160	200	250	500	700
1876E	482,000	160	200	250	500	700
1876E Proof	—	Value: 1,800				
1877E	1,181	8,000	15,000	20,000	30,000	40,000
1878E	1,564	9,500	17,500	27,500	35,000	45,000

KM# 1248 20 MARK
7.9650 g., 0.9000 Gold .2304 oz. AGW **Ruler:** Albert **Obv:** Head right **Obv. Legend:** ALBERT KOENIG VON SACHSEN **Rev:** Type III **Rev. Legend:** DEUTSCHES REICH date, 20 MARK below

Date	Mintage	F	VF	XF	Unc	BU
1894E	639,000	BV	160	225	350	450
1895E	113,000	BV	175	250	425	525

KM# 1260 20 MARK
7.9650 g., 0.9000 Gold .2304 oz. AGW **Ruler:** Georg **Obv:** Head right **Rev:** Crowned imperial eagle with shield on breast, type III

Date	Mintage	F	VF	XF	Unc	BU
1903E	250,000	BV	200	300	450	550
1903E Proof	—	Value: 2,500				

KM# 1265 20 MARK
7.9650 g., 0.9000 Gold .2304 oz. AGW **Ruler:** Friedrich August III **Obv:** Head right **Rev:** Crowned imperial eagle with shield on breast

Date	Mintage	F	VF	XF	Unc	BU
1905E	500,000	BV	200	400	500	600
1905E Proof	86	Value: 1,500				
1913E	121,000	BV	200	500	600	750
1914E	325,000	BV	200	375	450	550
1914E Proof	—	Value: 1,750				

PATTERNS
Including off metal strikes

KM#	Date	Mintage	Identification	Mkt Val
Pn60	1804	—	Heller. Gold. KM1002.	1,200
Pn61	1804	—	Pfennig. Gold. KM1000.	—
Pn62	1805	—	Pfennig. Gold. KM1000.	—
Pn63	1808 H	—	Pfennig. Gold. KM1057.	—
Pn68	1814 IGS	134	Ducat. Gold.	6,000
Pn69	1816	—	1/24 Thaler. Gold. KM1075.	—
Pn74	1873 E	—	10 Mark. Copper. KM1235. KM1232. Plain edge.	—
Pn75	1873 E	—	20 Mark. Copper. KM1233. KM1236. Plain edge.	—
Pn77	1876 E	—	10 Mark. Silver. Plain edge, KM1235.	—
PnA78	1905E	—	20 Mark. Copper. 4.0600 g.	—
PnB78	1905E	—	20 Mark. Copper. 4.8900 g. Bust in uniform.	—

SCHAUMBURG-LIPPE

Located in northwest Germany, Schaumburg-Lippe was founded in 1640 when Schaumburg-Gehmen was divided between Hesse-Cassel and Lippe-Alverdissen. The two became known as Schaumburg-Hessen and Schaumburg-Lippe. They were elevated into a county independent of Lippe. Schaumburg-Lippe minted currency into the 20th century. The last prince died in 1911.

RULERS
Georg Wilhelm, 1787-1860
Adolph Georg, 1860-1893
Albrecht Georg, 1893-1911

PRINCIPALITY
REGULAR COINAGE

C# 50 10 THALER
13.2840 g., 0.9000 Gold .3826 oz. AGW **Ruler:** Georg Wilhelm **Obv:** Head left **Obv. Legend:** GEORG WILH. R. FURST Z SCH. LIPPE N.N. **Rev:** Arms within crowned mantle **Rev. Legend:** ZEHN THALER

Date	Mintage	F	VF	XF	Unc	BU
1829 FF	874	4,500	10,000	20,000	28,500	—
Note: Stack's Hammel sale 9/92 AU realized $20,000						
1829 w/o FF	179	5,500	12,500	25,000	35,000	—

REFORM COINAGE

Y# 202 20 MARK
7.9650 g., 0.9000 Gold .2304 oz. AGW **Ruler:** Adolph Georg **Obv:** Head left **Obv. Legend:** ADOLF GEORG FURST Z. SCHAUMBURG-LIPPE **Rev:** Crowned imperial eagle **Rev. Legend:** DEUTSCHES REICH date, 20 MARK below

Date	Mintage	F	VF	XF	Unc	BU
1874B	3,000	2,250	4,000	6,000	9,000	10,000
1874B Proof	—	Value: 15,000				

Y# 205 20 MARK
7.9650 g., 0.9000 Gold 0.2304 oz. AGW **Ruler:** Albrecht Georg **Subject:** Death of Prince Georg **Obv:** Head left **Obv. Legend:** GEORG FURST ZU SCHAUMBURG-LIPPE **Rev:** Crowned imperial eagle with shield on breast **Rev. Legend:** DEUTSCHES REICH date, 20 MARK below

Date	Mintage	F	VF	XF	Unc	BU
1898A	5,000	750	1,400	2,000	3,000	3,750
1898A Proof	250	Value: 4,700				
1904A	5,500	750	1,600	2,400	3,250	4,000
1904A Proof	132	Value: 5,000				

GERMAN STATES — SCHLESWIG-HOLSTEIN

SCHLESWIG-HOLSTEIN

Schleswig-Holstein is the border area between Denmark and Germany. The duchy of Schleswig was Danish while Holstein was German. Christian I, son of Count Dietrich of Oldenburg (1423-40), was elected King of Denmark in 1448. By virtue of his marriage to Hedwig, the last surviving heir of the countship of Holstein-Rendsburg (see Holstein), Christian I became Duke of Schleswig and Count of Holstein in 1459. His status over Holstein was raised to that of duke in 1474 and from that year onwards, the dual duchies of Schleswig-Holstein were ruled by the Danish royal house. In 1533, a separate line for one of Friedrich I's sons was established in Gottorp. Similarly, a son of Christian III was given Sonderburg as his domain in 1559. The Danish kings continued to have coins struck for their remaining portions of Schleswig-Holstein during the next several centuries. Upon the dissolution of the Holy Roman Empire by Napoleon in 1806, Holstein was made a part of Denmark. However, Holstein, without Schleswig, joined the German Confederation following the final defeat of Napoleon in 1815. After Denmark tried to annex Schleswig and Holstein in 1846, she fought a war with Prussia for three years over control of the duchies, but it was inconclusive. In 1863, Denmark declared that Schleswig was part of that country although it had a German majority in the population. A second war was fought between Denmark against Prussia and Austria and Schleswig-Holstein was occupied by the victorious Prussians. The administration of Holstein was given to Austria, while that of Schleswig was obtained by Prussia in 1865. However, Austria was forced to give up Holstein after losing a war with Prussia in 1866. Schleswig-Holstein was controlled by Prussia and became part of the German Empire in 1871. Following World War I, a plebiscite was held in Schleswig and the northern part, with its majority Danish population, was ceded to Denmark in 1920.

RULERS
Christian VII (of Denmark), 1784-1808
Friedrich VI (of Denmark), 1808-1839
Christian VIII (of Denmark), 1839-1848

ALTONA MINT OFFICIALS' INITIALS
CB - Calus Branth
IFF, FF - Johann Friedrich Freund
MF, M.F. - Michael Flor
TA - Theodor C.W. Andersen

COPENHAGEN MINT OFFICIALS
VS - Georg Vilhelm Svendsen

MONETARY SYSTEM
4 Dreiling = 2 Sechsling = 1 Schilling
60 Schilling = 1 Speciesdaler
N = Nypraeg = Restrike

PATTERNS
Inlcuding off metal strikes

KM#	Date	Mintage Identification	Mkt Val
Pn10	1801	— 2-1/2 Schilling. Gold. C#4.	—

SCHWARZBURG-RUDOLSTADT

The Countship of Schwarzburg-Rudolstadt came into being as the younger line upon the division of Schwarzburg-Blankenburg in 1552. Its territory of about 360 square miles (600 square kilometers) is located in the center of Thuringia (Thüringen), surrounded by several of the Saxon duchies and Reuss-Obergreiz. The count attained the rank of prince in 1711 and the small state was able to weather the political perils of the Napoleonic Wars (1792-1815). Schwarzburg-Rudolstadt joined the German Confederation at the end of hostilities and subsequently became a member of the North German Confederation in 1867, then the German Empire in 1871. The last prince obtained Schwarzburg-Sondershausen upon the latter's extinction in 1909, then was forced to abdicate in 1918.

RULERS
Ludwig Friedrich II, 1793-1807
Friedrich Gunther, 1807-1867
Albert, 1867-1869
Georg, 1869-1890
Günther Viktor, 1890-1918

PRINCIPALITY
TRADE COINAGE

C# 55 DUCAT
3.5000 g., 0.9860 Gold .1109 oz. AGW **Ruler:** Ludwig Friedrich II **Obv:** Legend, date **Obv. Legend:** FURSTL: SCHWARZB: RUDOLSTAD: DUCATEN 1803 **Rev:** Crowned double imperial eagle with orb and sceptre

Date	Mintage	F	VF	XF	Unc	BU
1803	311	400	1,000	2,000	4,000	—

REFORM COINAGE

Y# 208 10 MARK
3.9820 g., 0.9000 Gold .1152 oz. AGW **Ruler:** Gunther Viktor **Obv:** Head left **Obv. Legend:** GUNTHER FURST ZU SCHWARZBURG RUDOLSTADT **Rev:** Crowned imperial eagle **Rev. Legend:** DEUTSCHES REICH date 10 MARK

Date	Mintage	F	VF	XF	Unc	BU
1898A	10,000	700	1,500	2,000	3,000	4,000
1898A Proof	700	Value: 4,500				

PATTERNS
Including off metal strikes

KM#	Date	Mintage Identification	Mkt Val
Pn1	1803	— Ducat. Copper. C#55.	300
Pn2	1803	— Ducat. Silver. C#55.	500

SCHWARZBURG-SONDERSHAUSEN

The Countship of Schwarzburg-Sondershausen contains territory of about 330 square miles (550 square kilometers) and is located just north of Thuringia (Thüringen), surrounded by the Prussian province of Saxony, between the ducal enclaves of Gotha and Weimar. The count was raised to the rank of prince in 1697 and underwent several minor divisions during the 18th century. Schwarzburg-Sondershausen joined the German Confederation in 1815 and became a member of the North German Confederation in 1867, as well as the German Empire in 1871. When Karl Günther died without an heir in 1909, his lands and titles went to Schwarzburg-Rudolstadt (see).

RULERS
Gunther Friedrich Carl I, 1794-1835
Gunther Friedrich Carl II, 1835-1880
Karl Gunther, 1880-1909

PRINCIPALITY
REFORM COINAGE

Y# 210 20 MARK
7.9650 g., 0.9000 Gold .2304 oz. AGW **Ruler:** Karl Gunther **Obv:** Head right **Obv. Legend:** KARL GUNTHER FURST Z. SCHWARZB. SONDERSH. **Rev:** Crowned imperial eagle **Rev. Legend:** DEUTSCHES REICH date 20 MARK

Date	Mintage	F	VF	XF	Unc	BU
1896A	5,000	850	1,750	2,750	3,500	4,500
1896A Proof	—	Value: 5,500				

STOLBERG-WERNIGERODE

The castle of Wernigerode is situated across the Harz Mountains to the north of Stolberg castle, some 12 miles (20 km) west-southwest of Halberstadt. An early division of the old Stolberg line in 1538 resulted in a separate line in Wernigerode. A second division in 1572 established Stolberg-Ortenberg and Stolberg Schwarza (Wernigerode) and the latter was divided further into 1876 divided further into the senior branch of Stolberg-Wernigerode and the junior branch of Stolberg-Stolberg. Once again, Stolberg-Wernigerode was the foundation of three separate lines at Gedern, Schwarza and Wernigerode in 1710. The first two fell extinct within a century, but Stolberg-Wernigerode lasted into the 20th century.

RULERS
Christian Friedrich, 1778-1824
Heinrich XXIII, 1824-1854
Otto, 1854-1896
Christian Ernst II, 1896-

DUCHY
TRADE COINAGE

C# 25 DUCAT
3.5000 g., 0.9860 Gold .1109 oz. AGW **Ruler:** Christian Friedrich **Subject:** Golden Wedding Anniversary **Obv:** Stag left **Rev:** Denomination and date within wreath

Date	Mintage	F	VF	XF	Unc	BU
1818	308	500	1,000	2,000	3,500	—

C# 26 DUCAT
3.5000 g., 0.9860 Gold .1109 oz. AGW **Subject:** Henrich XII **Obv:** Uniformed bust left **Rev:** Stag left, denomination and date

Date	Mintage	F	VF	XF	Unc	BU
1824	—	400	800	1,750	3,000	—

PATTERNS
Including off metal strikes

KM#	Date	Mintage Identification	Mkt Val
Pn9	1818	— Ducat. Silver. C#25	250

WALDECK-PYRMONT

The Count of Waldeck-Eisenberg inherited the Countship of Pyrmont, located between Lippe and Hannover, in 1625, thus creating an entity which encompassed about 672 square miles (1120 square kilometers). Waldeck and Pyrmont were permanently united in 1668, thus continuing the Eisenberg line as Waldeck-Pyrmont from that date. The count was raised to the rank of prince in 1712 and the unification of the two territories was confirmed in 1812. Waldeck-Pyrmont joined the German Confederation in 1815 and the North German Confederation in 1867. The prince renounced his sovereignty on 1 October of that year and Waldeck-Pyrmont was incorporated into Prussia. However, coinage was struck into the early 20th century for Waldeck-Pyrmont as a member of the German Empire. The hereditary territorial titles were lost along with the war in 1918. Some coins were struck for issue in Pyrmont only in the 18th through 20th centuries and those are listed separately under that name.

RULERS
Friedrich, 1763-1812
Georg, 1812-1813
Georg Friedrich Heinrich, 1813-1845
Georg Viktor, 1845-1893
  Under regency of his mother, Emma von Anhalt-Bernburg 1845-1852
Friedrich, 1893-1918 (d.1946)

MINT OFFICIALS' INITIALS

Initial	Date	Name
PS	1765-1806	Philipp Steinmetz, mintmaster in Arolsen
L	1808-1811?	Johann Lindenschmidt, die-cutter in Weisbaden
FW/W	1807-1826	Friedrich Welle, mintmaster in Arolsen
AW	1827-1840	Albert Welle, mintmaster in Arolsen
A	1842-1903	Berlin mint
B	1867	Hannover mint,

PRINCIPALITY
REFORM COINAGE

Y# 214 20 MARK
7.9650 g., 0.9000 Gold .2304 oz. AGW **Ruler:** Friedrich **Obv:** Head left **Rev:** Crowned imperial eagle with shield on breast

Date	Mintage	F	VF	XF	Unc	BU
1903A	2,000	2,400	4,000	6,500	110,000	13,000
1903A Proof	150	Value: 14,000				

WESTPHALIA — GERMAN STATES

WALLMODEN-GIMBORN

The town of Gimborn, located in Westphalia, was purchased from Schwarzenberg in 1782. The following year it was raised to the rank of county. In 1806, Wallmoden-Gimborn was annexed to Berg. In 1815, the land went to Prussia.

RULER
Johann Ludwig, 1782-1806

TOWN

TRADE COINAGE

C# 3 DUCAT
3.5000 g., 0.9860 Gold .1109 oz. AGW **Ruler:** Johann Ludwig **Obv:** Crowned monogram **Rev:** Denomination and date

Date	Mintage	F	VF	XF	Unc	BU
1802	400	1,250	2,500	4,500	8,000	—

PATTERNS
Including off metal strikes

KM#	Date	Mintage	Identification	Mkt Val
Pn1	1802	—	Ducat. Silver. C#3.	650

WESTPHALIA

The Duchy of Westphalia was very early the western part of the old Duchy of Saxony. In 1180, most of Westphalia fell to the archbishops of Cologne who added "Duke of Westphalia" to their titles. When Cologne was secularized in 1801, the duchy was administered by Hesse-Darmstadt until 1814 when it was annexed by Prussia. Coins were struck by the archbishops at the beginning of the 17th century and during the early years of the Thirty Years' War specifically for use in the duchy. For the names of the dukes and archbishops, see Cologne.

MINT OFFICIALS' INITIALS and MARKS

Initial	Date	Name
F	1783-1831	Dietrich Heinrich Fulda in Cassel

19th Century

A kingdom, located in western Germany, created by Napoleon for his brother. It was comprised of parts of Hesse-Cassel, Brunswick, Hildesheim, Paderborn, Halberstadt, Osnabruck, Minden, etc. In 1813 and 1814, Westphalia was divided and returned to its former owners.

RULER
Jerome (Hieronymus) Napoleon, 1807-1813

MINT MARKS
B - Brunswick
C,C. - Cassel, mm on rev.
C,C. - Clausthal, mm on obv.
F - Cassel

MINTMASTERS' MARKS
C & eagle head - Cassel
J & horse head - Cassel
J & horse head - Paris

KINGDOM

GERMAN STANDARD COINAGE

C# 13 5 THALER
6.6500 g., 0.9000 Gold .1924 oz. AGW **Ruler:** Jerome (Hieronymus) Napoleon **Obv:** Crowned arms within order chain **Obv. Legend:** HIERONYMUS NAPOLEON **Rev:** Denomination and date

Date	Mintage	F	VF	XF	Unc	BU
1810B	—	1,100	2,250	3,500	6,500	—

C# 14 5 THALER
6.6500 g., 0.9000 Gold .1924 oz. AGW **Ruler:** Jerome (Hieronymus) Napoleon **Obv:** Head left without laurel wreath **Rev:** Denomination and date

Date	Mintage	F	VF	XF	Unc	BU
1811B Rare	—	—	—	—	—	—

C# 14a 5 THALER
6.6500 g., 0.9000 Gold .1924 oz. AGW **Ruler:** Jerome (Hieronymus) Napoleon **Obv:** Laureate head left **Obv. Legend:** HIERONYMUS NAPOLEON. **Rev:** Denomination and date **Rev. Legend:** KOENIG VON WESTPHALEN FR.PR., * V * THALER * date * B. in center

Date	Mintage	F	VF	XF	Unc	BU
1811B	—	900	1,750	3,250	5,000	—
1812B	—	750	1,600	3,000	4,500	—
1813B	—	900	1,750	3,250	5,000	—

C# 15 10 THALER
13.3000 g., 0.9000 Gold .3848 oz. AGW **Ruler:** Jerome (Hieronymus) Napoleon **Obv:** Crowned arms within order chain **Obv. Legend:** HIERONYMUS NAPOLEON. **Rev:** Denomination and date **Rev. Legend:** KOENIG VON WESTPHALEN FR.PR., * X * THALER * date * B. in center

Date	Mintage	F	VF	XF	Unc	BU
1810B	—	1,000	2,000	3,500	5,500	—

C# 16 10 THALER
13.3000 g., 0.9000 Gold .3848 oz. AGW **Obv:** Head left without laurel wreath **Rev:** Denomination and date

Date	Mintage	F	VF	XF	Unc	BU
1811B Rare	—	—	—	—	—	—

C# 16a 10 THALER
13.3000 g., 0.9000 Gold .3848 oz. AGW **Ruler:** Jerome (Hieronymus) Napoleon **Obv:** Laureate head left **Obv. Legend:** HIERONYMUS NAOPLEON. **Rev:** Denomination and date **Rev. Legend:** KOENIG VON WESTPHALEN FR.PR., * X * THALER * date * B. in center

Date	Mintage	F	VF	XF	Unc	BU
1811B	—	725	1,650	3,000	4,850	—
1812B	—	650	1,550	2,750	4,500	—
1813B	—	725	1,650	2,500	4,250	—

FRENCH STANDARD COINAGE

C# 31 5 FRANKEN
1.6200 g., 0.9000 Gold .0469 oz. AGW **Ruler:** Jerome (Hieronymus) Napoleon **Rev:** Denomination and date

Date	Mintage	F	VF	XF	Unc	BU
1813C	1,045	225	350	500	1,200	—

C# 32.1 10 FRANKEN
3.2300 g., 0.9000 Gold .0936 oz. AGW **Ruler:** Jerome (Hieronymus) Napoleon **Obv:** Laureate head left **Rev:** Denomination

Date	Mintage	F	VF	XF	Unc	BU
1813	1,000	350	600	900	1,500	—

C# 32.2 10 FRANKEN
3.2300 g., 0.9000 Gold .0936 oz. AGW **Obv:** Laureate head left **Obv. Legend:** HIERON. NAPOL. **Rev:** Legend, denomination **Rev. Legend:** KOEN. V. WESTPH. FR. PR. date, 10 FRANK., in center, eagle head and C above date **Note:** Medal alignment.

Date	Mintage	F	VF	XF	Unc	BU
1813C Proof, rare	—	—	—	—	—	—

C# 33a 20 FRANKEN
6.4500 g., 0.9000 Gold .1868 oz. AGW **Ruler:** Jerome (Hieronymus) Napoleon **Obv:** Laureate head left **Obv. Legend:** HIERONYMUS NAPOLEON **Rev:** Denomination within laurel wreath **Rev. Legend:** KOENIG V. WESTPH. FR. PR., eagle head, date, C below **Note:** Mintmaster's mark: Eagle head.

Date	Mintage	F	VF	XF	Unc	BU
1808C	13,000	225	300	600	1,500	—
1809C	9,104	225	300	600	1,500	—
1811C	19,000	225	300	600	1,500	—
1813C	—	500	1,000	1,500	3,000	—

C# 33 20 FRANKEN
6.4500 g., 0.9000 Gold .1868 oz. AGW **Ruler:** Jerome (Hieronymus) Napoleon **Obv:** Laureate head left **Obv. Legend:** HIERONYMUS NAPOLEON **Rev:** Denomination within laurel wreath **Rev. Legend:** KOENIG V. WESTPH. FR. PR., horse head, date, J below **Note:** Mintmaster's mark: Horse head.

Date	Mintage	F	VF	XF	Unc	BU
1808 J	—	250	400	700	1,600	—
1809 J	—	225	350	600	1,500	—

C# 33b 20 FRANKEN
6.4500 g., 0.9000 Gold .1868 oz. AGW **Ruler:** Jerome (Hieronymus) Napoleon **Obv:** Laureate head left **Rev:** Denomination within laurel wreath **Note:** Mintmaster's mark: Horse head.

Date	Mintage	F	VF	XF	Unc	BU
1809C	—	200	300	600	1,500	—

C# 33c 20 FRANKEN
6.4500 g., 0.9000 Gold .1868 oz. AGW **Ruler:** Jerome (Hieronymus) Napoleon **Obv:** Laureate head left **Rev:** Denomination within laurel wreath **Note:** Without edge inscription (restrikes ca.1867).

Date	Mintage	F	VF	XF	Unc	BU
1813C	—	—	—	—	4,000	—

C# 34 40 FRANKEN
12.9000 g., 0.9000 Gold .3733 oz. AGW **Ruler:** Jerome (Hieronymus) Napoleon **Obv:** Laureate head left **Obv. Legend:** HIERONYMUS NAPOLEON. **Rev:** Denomination within laurel wreath **Rev. Legend:** KOENIG V. WESTPHALEN FR. PR., eagle head, date, C below

Date	Mintage	F	VF	XF	Unc	BU
1813C	80	3,000	5,000	8,000	12,000	—

C# 34a 40 FRANKEN
12.9000 g., 0.9000 Gold .3733 oz. AGW **Ruler:** Jerome (Hieronymus) Napoleon **Obv:** Laureate head left **Rev:** Denomination within laurel wreath **Note:** Without edge inscription (restrikes ca.1867).

Date	Mintage	F	VF	XF	Unc	BU
1813C	5,465	—	—	2,500	5,000	—

PATTERNS
Including off metal strikes

KM#	Date	Mintage	Identification	Mkt Val
Pn5	1808S	—	20 Franken. Without edge inscription.	2,000
Pn6	1808C	—	20 Franken. Without edge inscription.	2,000

GERMAN STATES — WESTPHALIA

KM#	Date	Mintage	Identification	Mkt Val
Pn7	1809C	—	20 Franken. Without edge inscription.	2,000
Pn8	1811C	22	2/3 Thaler. Gold. C#8.	20,000
Pn11	1813	1	5 Franken. Gold. C#31. Without mint mark.	—
Pn12	1813C	—	5 Franken. Copper. C#31.	450

WURTTEMBERG

Located in South Germany, between Baden and Bavaria, Württemberg takes its name from the ancestral castle of the ruling dynasty. The early countship was located in the old duchy of Swabia, most of which was given to Count Ulrich II (1265-79) in 1268 by Conradin von Hohenstaufen. Ulrich's son, Eberhard II (1279-1325) moved the seat of his rule to Stuttgart. Württemberg obtained the mint right in 1374 and joined the Swabian monetary union two years later. The countship was divided into the lines of Württemberg-Urach and Württemberg-Stuttgart in 1441 and the elder Urach branch was raised to the rank of duke in 1495. It became extinct in the following year and the younger line in Württemberg-Stuttgart inherited the lands and ducal title. A cadet line of the family had been established in Mömpelgard in 1473 and, when the Württemberg-Stuttgart line fell extinct in 1593, the primacy of the dynasty fell to Württemberg-Mömpelgard. The latter took the Stuttgart title and spun off several cadet branches in Neustadt, Neuenburg and Weiltingen-Brenz. Meanwhile, the duke in Stuttgart succumbed to the French advances under Napoleon. Land west of the Rhine was exchanged with France for territories in and around Reutlingen, Heilbronn and seven other towns in 1802. More territories were added in Swabia at the expense of Austria in 1805. Napoleon elevated the duke to the status of elector in 1803 and then to king in 1806. Even more land was given to Württemberg that year, doubling the kingdom's size, and it joined the Confederation of the Rhine. At the close of the Napoleonic Wars (1792-1815), Württemberg joined the German Confederation, but sided with Austria in its war with Prussia in 1866. It sided with Prussia against France in 1870 and became a member of the German Empire in 1871. King Wilhelm II was forced to abdicate at the end of World War I in 1918.

MINT MARKS
C, CT - Christophstal Mint
F - Freudenstadt Mint
S - Stuttgart Mint
T - Tubingen Mint

MINT OFFICIALS' INITIALS

Stuttgart Mint

AD/D	1837-70	Gottlob August Dietelbach, die-cutter
CH, ICH	1783-1813	Johann Christian Heuglin
CS, C, Sch F	d. 1877	Christian Schnitzspahn, die-cutter
C VOIGT	1838-?	Carl Friedrich Voigt, die-cutter in Berling 1425
ILW, LW, W	1798-1837	Johann Ludwig Wagner, die-cutter
PB	d. 1850	Peter Bruckman, die-cutter in Heilbronn, Augsburg in Karlsruhe
	d. 1850	Albert Wagner, die-cutter

ARMS
Württemberg: 3 stag antlers arranged vertically.
Teck (duchy): Field of lozenges (diamond shapes).
Mompelgart (principality): 2 fish standing on tails.

DUCHY

TRADE COINAGE

KM# 482 DUCAT
3.5000 g., 0.9860 Gold .1109 oz. AGW **Ruler:** Friedrich as Duke Friedrich II **Subject:** Visit of Duke to Mint **Obv:** Bust right **Rev:** IN HOCHST... within wreath

Date	Mintage	F	VF	XF	Unc	BU
1803 ILW Rare	—	—	—	—	—	—

KM# 485 DUCAT
3.5000 g., 0.9860 Gold .1109 oz. AGW **Ruler:** Friedrich as Elector Friedrich I **Obv:** Bust right **Rev:** DEN 9. IAN 1804 added

Date	Mintage	F	VF	XF	Unc	BU
1804 ILW Rare	—	—	—	—	—	—

KM# 486 DUCAT
3.5000 g., 0.9860 Gold .1109 oz. AGW **Ruler:** Friedrich as Elector Friedrich I **Rev:** Crowned circular arms within branches

Date	Mintage	F	VF	XF	Unc	BU
1804 ILW Rare	—	—	—	—	—	—

MEDALLIC COINAGE

X# 1 4 DUCAT
14.0000 g., 0.9860 Gold .4438 oz. AGW **Subject:** 25th Anniversary of Reign

Date	Mintage	F	VF	XF	Unc	BU
1841	6,236	600	1,000	1,600	2,400	—

X# 3 4 DUCAT
14.0000 g., 0.9860 Gold .4438 oz. AGW **Subject:** Visit of King Wilhelm to Mint

Date	Mintage	F	VF	XF	Unc	BU
1844	17	—	—	12,000	20,000	—

KINGDOM

REGULAR COINAGE

KM# 562 5 GULDEN
3.4250 g., 0.9040 Gold .0997 oz. AGW **Ruler:** Wilhelm I

Date	Mintage	F	VF	XF	Unc	BU
1824 W	2,282	500	1,100	1,800	2,750	—
1835 W	1,443	600	1,400	2,750	4,500	—
1835 W	1,443	600	1,400	2,750	4,500	—

KM# 563 5 GULDEN
3.4250 g., 0.9040 Gold .0997 oz. AGW **Ruler:** Wilhelm I **Obv:** Head right **Obv. Legend:** WILHELM KOENIG V. WURTTEMB. **Rev:** Crowned spade arms within branches **Rev. Legend:** FUNF GULDEN

Date	Mintage	F	VF	XF	Unc	BU
1825 W	5,956	350	650	1,200	2,000	—

KM# 579 5 GULDEN
3.4250 g., 0.9040 Gold .0997 oz. AGW **Ruler:** Wilhelm I

Date	Mintage	F	VF	XF	Unc	BU
1839 W	822	800	1,600	3,000	5,000	—

KM# 555 10 GULDEN
6.8500 g., 0.9040 Gold .1990 oz. AGW **Ruler:** Wilhelm I **Obv:** Head right **Obv. Legend:** WILHELM KOENIG V. WURTTEMB. **Rev:** Crowned spade arms within branches **Rev. Legend:** ZEHN GULDEN

Date	Mintage	F	VF	XF	Unc	BU
1824 W	1,896	900	1,800	3,200	5,500	—
1825 W	1,240	1,000	2,000	4,000	7,500	—
1825 W	1,240	1,000	2,000	4,000	7,500	—

KM# 564 10 GULDEN
6.8500 g., 0.9040 Gold .1990 oz. AGW **Ruler:** Wilhelm I **Subject:** Visit of King to Mint **Obv:** Head right **Rev:** Legend

Date	Mintage	F	VF	XF	Unc	BU
1825 W	8	—	—	18,500	25,000	—

REFORM COINAGE

KM# 627 5 MARK
1.9910 g., 0.9000 Gold .0576 oz. AGW **Ruler:** Karl I **Obv:** Head right **Obv. Legend:** KARL KOENIG VON WUERTTEMBERG **Rev:** Crowned imperial eagle **Rev. Legend:** DEUTSCHES REICH date, 5 MARK below

Date	Mintage	F	VF	XF	Unc	BU
1877F	488,000	150	275	300	500	600
1877F Proof	—	Value: 1,500				
1877F Proof	—	Value: 1,500				
1878F	50,000	400	650	1,000	1,500	2,000

KM# 621 10 MARK
3.9820 g., 0.9000 Gold .1152 oz. AGW **Ruler:** Karl I **Rev:** Type I

Date	Mintage	F	VF	XF	Unc	BU
1872F	271,000	100	150	300	550	700
1872F Proof	—	Value: 1,500				
1872F Proof	—	Value: 1,500				
1873F	675,000	100	150	300	550	700
1873F Proof	—	Value: 1,500				

KM# 624 10 MARK
3.9820 g., 0.9000 Gold .1152 oz. AGW **Ruler:** Karl I **Obv:** Head right **Obv. Legend:** KARL KOENIG VON WUERTTEMBERG **Rev:** Type II **Rev. Legend:** DEUTSCHES REICH date, 10 MARK below

Date	Mintage	F	VF	XF	Unc	BU
1874F	205,000	75.00	130	180	350	450
1875F	532,000	75.00	130	160	350	400
1875F	532,000	75.00	130	160	350	450
1876F	933,000	75.00	130	170	350	450
1876F Proof	—	Value: 1,500				
1877F	271,000	75.00	130	180	350	450
1878F	337,000	75.00	130	170	350	450
1879F	211,000	75.00	130	170	400	600
1880F	245,000	90.00	140	170	400	650
1881F	79,000	100	160	225	600	800
1888F	200,000	75.00	130	170	300	350
1888F Proof	—	Value: 1,500				

KM# 630 10 MARK
3.9820 g., 0.9000 Gold .1152 oz. AGW **Ruler:** Karl I **Obv:** Head right **Rev:** Type III

Date	Mintage	F	VF	XF	Unc	BU
1890F	220,000	150	225	300	500	600
1891F	80,000	150	250	300	600	800

KM# 633 10 MARK
3.9820 g., 0.9000 Gold .1152 oz. AGW **Ruler:** Wilhelm II **Obv:** Head right **Obv. Legend:** WILHELM II KOENIG VON WUERTTEMBERG **Rev:** Crowned imperial eagle with shield on breast **Rev. Legend:** DEUTSCHES REICH

Date	Mintage	F	VF	XF	Unc	BU
1893F	300,000	100	145	190	300	350
1896F	200,000	100	145	190	300	350
1898F	420,000	100	145	190	300	350
1900F	90,000	110	160	200	300	350
1901F	110,000	80.00	135	175	300	550
1902F	50,000	125	150	200	400	700
1903F	180,000	80.00	120	175	300	550
1903F Proof	—	Value: 1,750				
1904F	350,000	80.00	125	175	300	550
1904F Proof	—	Value: 1,750				
1905F	200,000	80.00	125	175	300	500
1905F Proof	—	Value: 1,750				
1906F	100,000	80.00	125	175	300	550
1906F Proof	50	Value: 1,750				
1907F	150,000	80.00	125	175	300	500
1907F Proof	—	Value: 1,750				
1909F	100,000	80.00	125	175	300	500
1909F Proof	—	Value: 1,750				
1910F	150,000	80.00	125	175	300	500
1910F Proof	—	Value: 1,750				
1911F	50,000	140	275	350	600	800
1911F Proof	—	Value: 1,750				
1912F	49,000	140	275	335	600	800
1912F Proof	—	Value: 1,750				
1913F	50,000	140	275	375	600	800
1913F Proof	—	Value: 1,750				

WURZBURG

GERMAN STATES

KM# 622 20 MARK
7.9650 g., 0.9000 Gold .2304 oz. AGW **Ruler:** Karl I **Obv:** Head right **Obv. Legend:** KARL KOENIG VON WUERTTEMBERG **Rev:** Type I **Rev. Legend:** DEUTSCHES REICH

Date	Mintage	F	VF	XF	Unc	BU
1872F	662,000	BV	200	250	600	700
1872F Proof	—	Value: 1,900				
1872F Proof	—	Value: 1,900				
1873F	1,357,000	BV	200	250	550	650
1873F Proof	—	Value: 1,900				

KM# 625 20 MARK
7.9650 g., 0.9000 Gold .2304 oz. AGW **Ruler:** Karl I **Obv:** Head right **Obv. Legend:** KARL KOENIG VON WUERTTEMBERG **Rev:** Type II **Rev. Legend:** DEUTSCHES REICH date, 20 MARK below

Date	Mintage	F	VF	XF	Unc	BU
1874F	322,000	BV	160	200	450	550
1876F	359,000	BV	160	200	450	550

KM# 634 20 MARK
7.9650 g., 0.9000 Gold .2304 oz. AGW **Ruler:** Wilhelm II **Obv:** Head right **Obv. Legend:** WILHELM II KOENIG VON WUERTTEMBERG **Rev:** Crowned imperial eagle with shield on breast **Rev. Legend:** DEUTSCHES REICH date, 20 MARK below

Date	Mintage	F	VF	XF	Unc	BU
1894F	501,000	—	BV	170	250	300
1897F	400,000	—	BV	170	250	300
1897F Proof	—	Value: 1,200				
1898F	106,000	BV	200	225	275	400
1900F	500,000	—	BV	200	250	300
1900F Proof	—	Value: 1,200				
1905F	506,000	—	BV	200	250	350
1905F Proof	—	Value: 2,000				
1913F	43,000	5,000	12,500	25,000	40,000	55,000
1913F Proof	—	Value: 70,000				
1914F	558,000	1,750	2,750	3,750	5,000	6,000
1914F Proof	—	Value: 8,000				

TRADE COINAGE

KM# 503 DUCAT
3.5000 g., 0.9860 Gold .1109 oz. AGW **Ruler:** Friedrich as King Friedrich I **Obv:** Uniformed bust left **Obv. Legend:** FRIDERICUS D. G. REX WURTEMB. **Rev:** Crowned arms with stag and lion supporters

Date	Mintage	F	VF	XF	Unc	BU
1808 CH Rare	—	—	—	—	—	—

KM# 523 DUCAT
3.5000 g., 0.9860 Gold .1109 oz. AGW **Ruler:** Friedrich as King Friedrich I **Obv:** Head right **Obv. Legend:** FRIDERICUS WURTEMB. REX **Rev:** Crowned arms with stag and lion supporters

Date	Mintage	F	VF	XF	Unc	BU
1813 ILW	—	800	1,750	3,000	5,000	—

KM# 535 DUCAT
3.5000 g., 0.9860 Gold .1109 oz. AGW **Ruler:** Wilhelm I **Obv:** Head right **Obv. Legend:** WILHELM KOENIG VON WURTTEMB: **Rev:** Crowned arms with stag and lion supporters

Date	Mintage	F	VF	XF	Unc	BU
1818 W	—	1,000	2,000	3,500	6,000	—

KM# 587 DUCAT
3.5000 g., 0.9860 Gold .1109 oz. AGW **Ruler:** Wilhelm I **Obv:** Head left **Obv. Legend:** WILHELM KONIG V. WURTTEMBERG **Rev:** Helmeted arms with stag and lion supporters

Date	Mintage	F	VF	XF	Unc	BU
1840 AD	81,000	200	350	525	850	—
1841	232,000	—	—	—	—	—
1841/0 AD	Inc. above	200	300	425	750	—
1841 AD	Inc. above	200	300	425	750	—
1842 AD	25,000	200	350	525	850	—
1848 AD	62,000	200	350	525	850	—

KM# 516 FREDERICK D'OR (= 1 Karolin)
6.6500 g., 0.9000 Gold .1924 oz. AGW **Ruler:** Friedrich as King Friedrich I **Obv:** Head right **Obv. Legend:** FRIDERICUS WURTEMB: REX **Rev:** Crowned arms with stag and lion supporters

Date	Mintage	F	VF	XF	Unc	BU
1810 ILW	—	2,500	4,000	7,000	10,000	—

PATTERNS
Including off metal strikes

KM#	Date	Mintage	Identification	Mkt Val
Pn27	1804 ILW	—	Ducat. Silver. C#136a.	1,000
Pn28	1804 CH	—	Ducat. Silver. C#137.	1,000
Pn29	1808 CH	—	Ducat. Silver. C#155.	1,000
Pn33	1824	—	10 Gulden. Tin.	—
Pn34	1825	—	10 Gulden. Tin.	—
Pn35	1825 W	—	10 Gulden. Silver. C#200.	1,000
Pn38	1846	—	2 Thaler. Gold. Marriage of Crown Prince, C#195.	25,000

WURZBURG
BISHOPRIC

The Bishopric, located in Franconia, was established in 741. The mint right was obtained in the 11th century. The first coins were struck c. 1040. In 1441 the bishops were confirmed as dukes. In 1802 the area was secularized and granted to Bavaria. It was made a grand duchy in 1806 but the 1815 Congress of Vienna returned it to Bavaria.

RULERS
Georg Karl, Freiherr von Fechenbach, Bishop, 1795-1802
Ferdinand, Grand Duke, 1806-1814

MINT MARKS
F - Furth
N - Nurnberg
- Wurzburg

MONETARY SYSTEM
3 Drier (Kortling) = 1 Shillinger
7 Shillinger = 15 Kreuzer
28 Shillinger = 1 Guter Gulden
44-4/5 Shillinger = 1 Convention Thaler

TRADE COINAGE

KM# 467 GOLDGULDEN
3.2500 g., 0.7700 Gold .0805 oz. AGW **Ruler:** Ferdinand, Grand Duke **Obv:** Head right **Rev:** Palm tree, arms, denomination and date

Date	Mintage	F	VF	XF	Unc	BU
1807	—	—	—	—	—	—
1809	—	1,000	2,000	4,000	6,500	—

KM# 477 GOLDGULDEN
3.2500 g., 0.7700 Gold .0805 oz. AGW **Ruler:** Ferdinand, Grand Duke

Date	Mintage	F	VF	XF	Unc	BU
1812 R	—	1,000	1,800	2,800	4,500	—

KM# 478 GOLDGULDEN
3.2500 g., 0.7700 Gold .0805 oz. AGW **Ruler:** Ferdinand, Grand Duke **Rev:** Crowned battle flag, denomination and date

Date	Mintage	F	VF	XF	Unc	BU
1813 R	—	4,000	7,000	10,000	12,500	—

KM# 479 GOLDGULDEN
3.2500 g., 0.7700 Gold .0805 oz. AGW **Ruler:** Ferdinand, Grand Duke

Date	Mintage	F	VF	XF	Unc	BU
1814 R	—	3,000	5,000	8,000	10,000	—

MEDALLIC COINAGE

X# M7 GOLDGULDEN
3.2500 g., 0.7700 Gold .0805 oz. AGW **Obv:** Head of Maximilian Joseph right **Rev:** Palm above Wurzburg coat-of-arms, value and date, with full inscription **Note:** Prev. KM#M7.

Date	Mintage	VG	F	VF	XF	Unc
1803	—	—	2,250	3,500	5,000	—

X# M8 GOLDGULDEN
3.2500 g., 0.7700 Gold .0805 oz. AGW **Rev:** Palm above Wurzburg coat-of-arms and S. P. - Q. W., abbreviated inscription **Note:** Prev. KM#M8.

Date	Mintage	VG	F	VF	XF	Unc
1803	—	—	1,500	2,500	3,500	—

X# M9 GOLDGULDEN
3.2500 g., 0.7700 Gold .0805 oz. AGW **Obv:** Head of Maximilian Joseph left **Rev:** City view of Wurzburg **Note:** Prev. KM#M9.

Date	Mintage	VG	F	VF	XF	Unc
1815	—	—	1,250	2,000	3,000	—

X# M10 GOLDGULDEN
3.2500 g., 0.7700 Gold .0805 oz. AGW **Rev:** Coat-of-arms, value **Note:** Prev. KM#M10.

Date	Mintage	VG	F	VF	XF	Unc
1817	—	—	2,000	3,500	5,000	—

X# M11 GOLDGULDEN
3.2500 g., 0.7700 Gold .0805 oz. AGW **Note:** Prev. KM#M11.

Date	Mintage	VG	F	VF	XF	Unc
ND(1817)	—	—	1,250	2,000	3,000	—

X# M12 GOLDGULDEN
3.2500 g., 0.7700 Gold .0805 oz. AGW **Obv:** Head of Ludwig left **Rev:** 6-line inscription **Note:** Prev. KM#M12.

Date	Mintage	VG	F	VF	XF	Unc
1826 Rare	65	—	—	—	—	—

X# M13 GOLDGULDEN
3.2500 g., 0.7700 Gold .0805 oz. AGW **Rev:** View of Wurzburg, value and date **Note:** Prev. KM#M13.

Date	Mintage	VG	F	VF	XF	Unc
ND(1827)	—	—	1,750	3,000	4,500	—

X# M14 GOLDGULDEN
3.2500 g., 0.7700 Gold .0805 oz. AGW **Note:** Prev. KM#M14. Roman I follows king's name.

Date	Mintage	VG	F	VF	XF	Unc
ND(ca.1835)	—	—	1,250	2,000	3,000	—

X# M15 GOLDGULDEN
3.2500 g., 0.7700 Gold .0805 oz. AGW **Rev:** City view of Wurzburg **Note:** Prev. KM#M15.

Date	Mintage	VG	F	VF	XF	Unc
ND(ca.1843)	—	—	1,500	2,500	3,500	—

X# M16 GOLDGULDEN
3.2500 g., 0.7700 Gold .0805 oz. AGW **Rev:** Arms in sprays **Edge:** Slant reeded **Note:** Prev. KM#M16.

Date	Mintage	VG	F	VF	XF	Unc
ND(ca.1843)	—	—	1,500	2,500	3,500	—

X# M17 GOLDGULDEN
3.2500 g., 0.7700 Gold .0805 oz. AGW **Edge:** Straight reeded **Note:** Prev. KM#M17.

Date	Mintage	VG	F	VF	XF	Unc
ND(ca.1843)	—	—	2,000	3,500	5,000	—

X# M18 GOLDGULDEN
3.2500 g., 0.7700 Gold .0805 oz. AGW **Obv:** Head of Ludwig right **Rev:** City view of Wurzburg **Note:** Prev. KM#M18.

GERMAN STATES-WURZBURG

Date	Mintage	VG	F	VF	XF	Unc
ND	300	—	1,250	2,000	3,000	—

X# M19 GOLDGULDEN
3.2500 g., 0.7700 Gold .0805 oz. AGW **Rev:** Arms in sprays, value GOLD GULDEN **Note:** Prev. KM#M19.

Date	Mintage	VG	F	VF	XF	Unc
ND	Inc. above	—	1,250	2,000	3,000	—

X# M20 GOLDGULDEN
3.2500 g., 0.7700 Gold .0805 oz. AGW **Rev:** Value: GOLDGULDEN **Note:** Prev. KM#M20.

Date	Mintage	VG	F	VF	XF	Unc
ND	Inc. above	—	1,250	2,250	3,500	—

X# M21 GOLDGULDEN
3.2500 g., 0.7700 Gold .0805 oz. AGW **Obv:** Head of Maximilian right **Obv. Legend:** ....KOENIG **Note:** Prev. KM#M21.

Date	Mintage	VG	F	VF	XF	Unc
ND(1850)	215	—	1,250	2,000	3,000	—

X# M22 GOLDGULDEN
3.2500 g., 0.7700 Gold .0805 oz. AGW **Obv. Legend:** ... REX **Note:** Prev. KM#M22.

Date	Mintage	VG	F	VF	XF	Unc
ND(1850)	Inc. above	—	1,250	2,250	3,500	—

X# M23 GOLDGULDEN
3.2500 g., 0.7700 Gold .0805 oz. AGW **Obv. Legend:** ...KOENIG **Rev:** City view of Wurzburg **Note:** Prev. KM#M23.

Date	Mintage	VG	F	VF	XF	Unc
ND(1850)	Inc. above	—	1,250	2,000	3,000	—

X# M24 GOLDGULDEN
3.2500 g., 0.7700 Gold .0805 oz. AGW **Obv. Legend:** ...REX **Note:** Prev. KM#M24.

Date	Mintage	VG	F	VF	XF	Unc
ND(1850)	Inc. above	—	1,250	2,250	3,500	—

X# M25 GOLDGULDEN
3.2500 g., 0.7700 Gold .0805 oz. AGW **Obv:** Head of Ludwig II right **Edge:** Reeded **Note:** Prev. KM#M25.

Date	Mintage	VG	F	VF	XF	Unc
ND(1864)	350	—	1,250	2,000	3,000	—

X# M26 GOLDGULDEN
3.2500 g., 0.7700 Gold .0805 oz. AGW **Edge:** Plain **Note:** Prev. KM#M26.

Date	Mintage	VG	F	VF	XF	Unc
ND(1864)	Inc. above	—	1,250	2,250	3,500	—

X# M27 GOLDGULDEN
3.2500 g., 0.7700 Gold .0805 oz. AGW **Obv:** Head of Ludwig II right **Rev:** Wurzburg coat-of-arms **Edge:** Reeded **Note:** Prev. KM#M27.

Date	Mintage	VG	F	VF	XF	Unc
ND(1864)	350	—	1,250	2,100	3,250	—

X# M28 GOLDGULDEN
3.2500 g., 0.7700 Gold .0805 oz. AGW **Edge:** Plain **Note:** Prev. KM#M28.

Date	Mintage	VG	F	VF	XF	Unc
ND	Inc. above	—	1,350	2,500	3,750	—

X# M29 GOLDGULDEN
5.3000 g., 0.7700 Gold .1312 oz. AGW **Obv:** Ludwig III **Rev:** St. Kilian and value **Note:** Prev. KM#M29.

Date	Mintage	VG	F	VF	XF	Unc
ND(1916)	Unique	—	—	—	—	—

GERMANY-EMPIRE
1871-1918

Germany, a nation of north-central Europe which from 1871 to 1945 was, successively, an empire, a republic and a totalitarian state, attained its territorial peak as an empire when it comprised a 208,780 sq. mi. (540,740 sq. km.) homeland and an overseas colonial empire.

As the power of the Roman Empire waned, several war-like tribes residing in northern Germany moved south and west, invading France, Belgium, England, Italy and Spain. In 800 A.D. the Frankish king Charlemagne, who ruled most of France and Germany, was crowned Emperor of the Holy Roman Empire, a loose federation of an estimated 1,800 German States that lasted until 1806. Modern Germany was formed from the eastern part of Charlemagne's empire.

After 1812, the German States were reduced to a federation of 32, of which Prussia was the strongest. In 1871, Prussian chancellor Otto von Bismarck united the German States into an empire ruled by William I, the Prussian king. The empire initiated a colonial endeavor and after initial diplomatic and military triumphs, expanded his goals beyond Europe into Africa and USSR which led it into final disaster in World War II, ending on VE Day, May 7, 1945.

It was reestablished as the Weimar Republic. The humiliation of defeat, economic depression, poverty and discontent gave rise to Adolf Hitler, 1933, who reconstituted Germany as the Third Reich and after initial diplomatic and military triumphs, expanded his goals beyond Europe into Africa and USSR which led it into final disaster in World War II, ending on VE Day, May 7, 1945.

RULERS
Wilhelm II, 1888-1918

MINT MARKS
A - Berlin
D - Munich
E - Muldenhutten (1887-1953)
F - Stuttgart
G - Karlsruhe
J - Hamburg

MONETARY SYSTEM
(Until 1923)
100 Pfennig = 1 Mark

(Commencing 1945)
100 Pfennig = 1 Mark

EMPIRE

PATTERNS
Karl Goetz Issues

X# 1c 25 PFENNIG
12.2000 g., Platinum APW

Date	Mintage	F	VF	XF	Unc	BU
1908	2	—	—	—	—	675

X# 60 25 PFENNIG
6.9300 g., Gold

Date	Mintage	F	VF	XF	Unc	BU
1908D	—	—	—	—	—	285

X# 60a 25 PFENNIG
Platinum APW

Date	Mintage	F	VF	XF	Unc	BU
1908D	—	—	—	—	—	675

GERMANY, WEIMAR REPUBLIC
1919-1933

The Imperial German government disintegrated in a flurry of royal abdications as World War I ended. Desperate German parliamentarians, fearful of impending anarchy and civil war, hastily declared a German Republic. The new National Assembly, which was convened Feb. 6, 1919 in Weimar had to establish a legal government, draft a constitution, and then conclude a peace treaty with the Allies. Friedrich Ebert was elected as Reichs President. The harsh terms of the peace treaty imposed on Germany were economically and psychologically unacceptable to the German population regardless of political persuasion and the problem of German treaty compliance was to plague the Republic until the worldwide Great Depression of 1929. The new constitution paid less attention to fundamental individual rights and concentrated more power in the President and Central Government to insure a more stable social and economic order. The German bureaucracy survived the transition intact and had a stifling effect on the democratic process. The army started training large numbers of reservists in conjunction with the U.S.S.R. thereby circumventing treaty limitations on the size of the German military.

New anti-democratic ideologies were forming. Communism and Fascism were spreading. The National Socialist German Workers Party, under Hitler's leadership, incorporated the ever-present anti-Semitism into a new virulent Nazi Catechism.

In spite of the historic German inflation, the French occupation of the Rhineland, and the loss of vast territories and resources, the republic survived. By 1929 the German economy had been restored to its pre-war level. Much of the economic gains however were dependent on the extensive assistance provided by the U.S.A. and collapsed along with the world economy in 1929. Even during the good times, the Republic was never able to muster any loyal public support or patriotism. By 1930, Nationalists, Nazis, and Communists held nearly half of the Reichstag seats and the government was forced to rely more and more on presidential decrees as the only means to effectuate policy. In 1932, the Nazis won 230 Reichstag seats. As head of the largest party, Hitler claimed the right to form the next government. President Hindenburg's opposition forced a second election in which the Nazis lost 34 seats. Von Papen, however, convinced Hindenburg to name Hitler Chancellor by arguing that Hitler could be controlled! Hitler formed his cabinet and immediately began consolidating his power and laying the groundwork for the Third Reich.

MONETARY SYSTEM
(During 1923-1924)
100 Rentenpfennig = 1 Rentenmark
(Commencing 1924)
100 Reichspfennig = 1 Reichsmark

WEIMAR REPUBLIC

PATTERNS
Josef Wild Issues

X# 101 50 GOLD PFENNIG
0.1700 g., 1.0000 Gold 0.0055 oz. AGW, 6 mm. **Obv. Inscription:** 50 / GOLD / PF **Rev. Inscription:** "1000"

Date	Mintage	F	VF	XF	Unc	BU
ND(1923)	—	—	—	—	300	—

X# 108 GOLD MARK
0.3700 g., 1.0000 Gold 0.0119 oz. AGW **Obv:** Arms **Obv. Legend:** DUSSELDORF **Rev. Inscription:** 1 / GOLD / M

Date	Mintage	F	VF	XF	Unc	BU
ND(1923)	—	—	—	—	425	—

X# 111 GOLD MARK
0.3600 g., 1.0000 Gold 0.0116 oz. AGW, 9.5 mm. **Obv:** Arms **Obv. Legend:** HANNOVER **Rev. Inscription:** 1 / GOLD / M

Date	Mintage	F	VF	XF	Unc	BU
ND(1923)	—	—	—	—	450	—

X# 113 GOLD MARK
0.3600 g., 1.0000 Gold 0.0116 oz. AGW, 9.5 mm. **Obv:** Munich child standing facing **Obv. Legend:** MÜNICH **Rev. Inscription:** 1 / GOLD / M

Date	Mintage	F	VF	XF	Unc	BU
ND(1923)	—	—	—	—	425	—

GERMANY, WEIMAR REPUBLIC

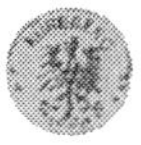

X# 114 GOLD MARK
0.3700 g., 1.0000 Gold 0.0119 oz. AGW, 9.5 mm. **Obv:** Eagle **Obv. Legend:** NÜRNBERG **Rev. Inscription:** 1 / GOLD / M

Date	Mintage	F	VF	XF	Unc	BU
ND(1923)	—	—	—	—	450	—

X# 115 GOLD MARK
0.3000 g., 1.0000 Gold 0.0096 oz. AGW, 9.5 mm. **Obv:** Arms **Obv. Legend:** REGENSBURG **Rev. Inscription:** 1 / GOLD / M

Date	Mintage	F	VF	XF	Unc	BU
ND(1924)	—	—	—	—	500	—

X# 116 GOLD MARK
0.3300 g., 1.0000 Gold 0.0106 oz. AGW, 9.5 mm. **Obv:** Arms **Obv. Legend:** ROTHENBURG **Rev. Inscription:** 1 / GOLD / M

Date	Mintage	F	VF	XF	Unc	BU
ND(1924)	—	—	—	—	450	—

X# 112 GOLD MARK
0.3400 g., 1.0000 Gold 0.0109 oz. AGW, 9.5 mm. **Obv:** Arms **Obv. Legend:** LÜBECK **Rev. Inscription:** 1 / GOLD / M

Date	Mintage	F	VF	XF	Unc	BU
ND(1924)	—	—	—	—	450	—

X# 107 GOLD MARK
0.3500 g., 1.0000 Gold 0.0113 oz. AGW, 9.5 mm. **Obv:** Arms **Obv. Legend:** BREMEN **Rev. Inscription:** 1 / GOLD / MARK

Date	Mintage	F	VF	XF	Unc	BU
ND(1924)	—	—	—	—	450	—

X# 110 GOLD MARK
0.3200 g., 1.0000 Gold 0.0103 oz. AGW, 9.5 mm. **Obv:** Arms **Obv. Legend:** HAMBURG **Rev. Inscription:** 1 / GOLD / M

Date	Mintage	F	VF	XF	Unc	BU
ND(1924)	—	—	—	—	425	—

X# 106 GOLD MARK
0.3600 g., 1.0000 Gold 0.0116 oz. AGW, 9 mm. **Obv:** Arms **Obv. Legend:** BAYREUTH **Rev. Inscription:** 1 / GOLD / M

Date	Mintage	F	VF	XF	Unc	BU
ND(1924)	—	—	—	—	425	—

X# 104 GOLD MARK
0.3700 g., 1.0000 Gold 0.0119 oz. AGW, 9 mm. **Obv:** Arms **Obv. Legend:** AUGSBURG **Rev. Inscription:** 1 / GOLD / M

Date	Mintage	F	VF	XF	Unc	BU
ND(1924)	—	—	—	—	500	—

X# 105 GOLD MARK
0.3700 g., 1.0000 Gold 0.0119 oz. AGW, 9.5 mm. **Obv:** Arms **Obv. Legend:** BAD KISSINGEN **Rev. Inscription:** 1 / GOLD / M

Date	Mintage	F	VF	XF	Unc	BU
ND(1925)	—	—	—	—	500	—

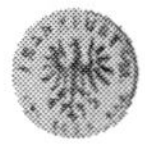

X# 109 GOLD MARK
0.3400 g., 1.0000 Gold 0.0109 oz. AGW, 9.5 mm. **Obv:** Arms **Obv. Legend:** FRANKFURT M. **Rev. Inscription:** 1 / GOLD / M

Date	Mintage	F	VF	XF	Unc	BU
ND(1925)	—	—	—	—	425	—

X# 117 GOLD MARK
0.3500 g., 1.0000 Gold 0.0113 oz. AGW, 9.5 mm. **Obv:** Horse left rearing **Obv. Legend:** STUTTGART **Rev. Inscription:** 1/GOLD/M

Date	Mintage	F	VF	XF	Unc	BU
ND(1925)	—	—	—	—	450	—

X# 118 3 GOLD MARK
1.0900 g., 1.0000 Gold 0.035 oz. AGW, 11.5 mm. **Obv:** Stylized eagle **Obv. Legend:** JOS. WILD NÜRNBERG **Rev. Inscription:** 3/GOLD/M

Date	Mintage	F	VF	XF	Unc	BU
1923	—	—	—	—	600	—

X# 119 5 GOLD MARK
1.8000 g., 1.0000 Gold 0.0579 oz. AGW, 14 mm. **Obv:** Stylized eagle **Obv. Legend:** JOS. WILD NÜRNBERG **Rev. Inscription:** 5/GOLD/M

Date	Mintage	F	VF	XF	Unc	BU
1923	—	—	—	—	650	—

X# 103 20 GOLD MARK
7.1400 g., 1.0000 Gold 0.2296 oz. AGW, 21.4 mm. **Obv:** Radiant sun **Obv. Legend:** KURSFÄHIGES GOLD **Rev. Inscription:** 20 / GOLDMARK

Date	Mintage	F	VF	XF	Unc	BU
ND(1923)	—	—	—	—	1,200	—

X# 122 20 GOLD MARK
7.1300 g., 1.0000 Gold 0.2292 oz. AGW, 21.5 mm. **Obv:** City view **Obv. Legend:** NÜRNBERG **Rev. Inscription:** 20 / GOLDMARK / 7.14 GRAMM / 1000-FEIN

Date	Mintage	F	VF	XF	Unc	BU
1927	—	—	—	—	1,000	—
1928	—	—	—	—	1,200	—

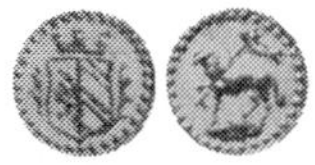

X# 120 1/32 DUCAT
0.1100 g., 1.0000 Gold 0.0035 oz. AGW, 5 mm. **Obv:** Crowned arms **Rev:** Paschal lamb left

Date	Mintage	F	VF	XF	Unc	BU
ND(1925)	—	—	—	—	450	—

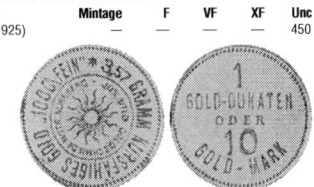

X# 102 DUCAT - 10 GOLD MARK
3.5700 g., 1.0000 Gold 0.1148 oz. AGW, 21.4 mm. **Obv:** Radiant sun **Obv. Legend:** KURSFÄHIGES GOLD **Rev. Inscription:** 1 / GOLD-DUKATEN / ODER / 10 / GOLD-MARK

Date	Mintage	F	VF	XF	Unc	BU
ND(1924)	—	—	—	—	1,000	—

X# 121 DUCAT
3.4300 g., 1.0000 Gold 0.1103 oz. AGW, 21.5 mm. **Subject:** Octoberfest **Obv:** Munich child standing facing **Rev:** Church of Our Lady

Date	Mintage	F	VF	XF	Unc	BU
1926	—	—	—	—	1,500	—

PATTERNS
Karl Goetz Issues
Struck in Munich, Bavaria

X# 18b 50 PFENNIG
6.9100 g., Gold

Date	Mintage	F	VF	XF	Unc	BU
1925D Proof	—	Value: 250				

X# 18c 50 PFENNIG
13.3900 g., Platinum APW

Date	Mintage	F	VF	XF	Unc	BU
1925D Proof	2					

X# 20b 50 PFENNIG
6.9100 g., Gold

Date	Mintage	F	VF	XF	Unc	BU
1925D Proof	—	Value: 450				

X# 20c 50 PFENNIG
Platinum APW

Date	Mintage	F	VF	XF	Unc	BU
1925D Proof	2	Value: 750				

X# 23a 2 MARK
17.6500 g., Platinum APW

Date	Mintage	F	VF	XF	Unc	BU
1926D Proof	—	Value: 800				

X# 24c 3 MARK
Platinum APW **Subject:** Bavaria

Date	Mintage	F	VF	XF	Unc	BU
1925 Proof	—	Value: 1,150				

X# 59 3 MARK
28.2300 g., Platinum APW

Date	Mintage	F	VF	XF	Unc	BU
1925 Proof	—	Value: 1,150				

X# 32a 3 MARK
17.4300 g., Gold

Date	Mintage	F	VF	XF	Unc	BU
1925D Proof	—	Value: 550				

X# 49a 3 MARK
Gold

Date	Mintage	F	VF	XF	Unc	BU
1926D Proof	—	Value: 800				

X# 50a 3 MARK
Gold

Date	Mintage	F	VF	XF	Unc	BU
1926D Proof	—	Value: 800				

X# 51a 3 MARK
Gold

Date	Mintage	F	VF	XF	Unc	BU
1926D Proof	—	Value: 800				

X# 52a 3 MARK
Gold

Date	Mintage	F	VF	XF	Unc	BU
1926D Proof	—	Value: 800				

X# 61 3 MARK
Gold

Date	Mintage	F	VF	XF	Unc	BU
1926D Proof	—	Value: 750				

GERMANY-WEIMAR REPUBLIC

X# 66b 5 MARK
28.6200 g., Gold

Date	Mintage	F	VF	XF	Unc	BU
1925D Proof	—			Value: 850		

X# 68b 5 MARK
40.6000 g., Platinum APW

Date	Mintage	F	VF	XF	Unc	BU
1925D Proof	2			Value: 1,750		

X# 70b 5 MARK
17.4300 g., Gold

Date	Mintage	F	VF	XF	Unc	BU
1925D Proof	—			Value: 850		

X# 79a 5 MARK
Platinum APW

Date	Mintage	F	VF	XF	Unc	BU
1925D Proof	2			Value: 1,800		

X# 83 5 MARK
34.8500 g., Gold

Date	Mintage	F	VF	XF	Unc	BU
1926D Proof	—			Value: 1,100		

X# 83a 5 MARK
40.6100 g., Platinum APW

Date	Mintage	F	VF	XF	Unc	BU
1926D Proof	3			Value: 2,000		

MEDALLIC COINAGE
Karl Goetz Issues

Struck in Munich, Bavaria

X# 1a 5 MARK
22.4700 g., Gold **Subject:** Von Hindenburg **Note:** Prev. KM#M1a.

Date	Mintage	F	VF	XF	Unc	BU
1927D	—	—	—	—	600	—

X# 1b 5 MARK
43.2600 g., Platinum APW **Note:** Prev. KM#M1b.

Date	Mintage	F	VF	XF	Unc	BU
1927D	—	—	—	—	1,650	—

X# 2 10 MARK
Gold **Subject:** Von Hindenburg **Note:** Prev. KM#M5.

Date	Mintage	F	VF	XF	Unc	BU
1928 Proof	—			Value: 300		

X# 3 20 MARK
6.4900 g., Gold **Subject:** Von Hindenburg **Note:** Prev. KM#M6.

Date	Mintage	F	VF	XF	Unc	BU
1928 Proof	—			Value: 325		

X# 7 25 MARK
6.9400 g., Gold **Note:** Prev. KM#M7.

Date	Mintage	F	VF	XF	Unc	BU
1932	—	—	—	—	325	—

X# 7a 25 MARK
10.1500 g., Platinum APW **Note:** Prev. KM#M7a.

Date	Mintage	F	VF	XF	Unc	BU
1932	5	—	—	—	950	—

MEDALLIC COINAGE
Bernhart Issues

X# 4a 5 MARK
23.0000 g., Gold **Subject:** Von Hindenburg **Note:** Prev. KM#M2a.

Date	Mintage	F	VF	XF	Unc	BU
1928 Proof	—			Value: 650		

X# M5 10 MARK
3.4200 g., 0.7500 Gold .0824 oz. AGW, 19.5 mm. **Subject:** Von Hindenburg **Obv:** Helmeted arms **Rev:** Head left **Note:** Prev. KM#M3.

Date	Mintage	F	VF	XF	Unc	BU
1928 Proof	—			Value: 200		

X# 6 20 MARK
6.3900 g., 0.7500 Gold .1541 oz. AGW, 22.5 mm. **Subject:** Von Hindenburg **Obv:** Helmeted arms **Rev:** Head left **Note:** Prev. KM#M4.

Date	Mintage	F	VF	XF	Unc	BU
1928 Proof	—			Value: 220		

PATTERNS
Including off metal strikes

KM#	Date	Mintage	Identification	Mkt Val
Pn283	1925E	—	20 Mark. Gold.	7,500
Pn284	1925E	—	20 Mark. Brass.	—

GERMANY-FEDERAL REP.

1949-1990

The Federal Republic of Germany, located in north-central Europe, has an area of 137,744 sq. mi. (356,910sq. km.) and a population of 81.1 million. Capital: Berlin. The economy centers about one of the world's foremost industrial establishments. Machinery, motor vehicles, iron, steel, yarns and fabrics are exported.

During the post-Normandy phase of World War II, Allied troops occupied the western German provinces of Schleswig-Holstein, Hamburg, Lower Saxony, Bremen, North Rhine-Westphalia, Hesse, Rhineland-Palatinate, Baden-Wurttemberg, Bavaria and Saarland. The conquered provinces were divided into American, British and French occupation zones. Five eastern German provinces were occupied and administered by the forces of the Soviet Union.

The post-World War II division of Germany was ended Oct. 3, 1990, when the German Democratic Republic (East Germany) ceased to exist and its five constituent provinces were formally admitted to the Federal Republic of Germany. An election Dec. 2, 1990, chose representatives to the united federal parliament (Bundestag), which then conducted its opening session in Berlin in the old Reichstag building. Berlin is again the capital of a United Germany.

MINT MARKS
A - Berlin
D - Munich
F - Stuttgart
G - Karlsruhe
J - Hamburg

MONETARY SYSTEM
100 Pfennig = 1 Deutsche Mark (DM)

FEDERAL REPUBLIC
STANDARD COINAGE

KM# 203 MARK
11.8500 g., 0.9990 Gold .3806 oz. AGW, 23.5 mm. **Subject:** Retirement of the Mark Currency **Obv:** Imperial eagle **Rev:** Denomination flanked by leaves, date below **Edge:** Lettered

Date	Mintage	F	VF	XF	Unc	BU
2001A Proof	200,000			Value: 335		
2001D Proof	200,000			Value: 335		
2001G Proof	200,000			Value: 335		
2001J Proof	200,000			Value: 335		
2001F Proof	200,000			Value: 335		

EURO COINAGE
European Economic Community Issues

KM# 220 100 EURO
15.5500 g., 0.9990 Gold 0.4994 oz. AGW, 28 mm. **Subject:** Introduction of the Euro Currency **Obv:** Stylized round eagle **Rev:** Euro symbol and arches **Edge:** Reeded

GERMANY - FEDERAL REPUBLIC

Date	Mintage	F	VF	XF	Unc	BU
2002A Proof	100,000	Value: 375				
2002D Proof	100,000	Value: 375				
2002F Proof	100,000	Value: 375				
2002G Proof	100,000	Value: 375				
2002J Proof	100,000	Value: 375				

KM# 228 100 EURO
15.5000 g., 0.9999 Gold 0.4983 oz. AGW, 28 mm. **Obv:** Stylized eagle, denomination below **Rev:** Quedlinburg Abbey in monogram **Edge:** Reeded

Date	Mintage	F	VF	XF	Unc	BU
2003A Proof	100,000	Value: 365				
2003D Proof	100,000	Value: 365				
2003F Proof	100,000	Value: 365				
2003G Proof	100,000	Value: 365				
2003J Proof	100,000	Value: 365				

KM# 235 100 EURO
15.5500 g., 0.9999 Gold 0.4999 oz. AGW, 28 mm. **Obv:** Stylized eagle, denomination below **Rev:** Bamberg city view **Edge:** Reeded

Date	Mintage	F	VF	XF	Unc	BU
2004A Proof	80,000	Value: 350				
2004D Proof	80,000	Value: 350				
2004F Proof	80,000	Value: 350				
2004G Proof	80,000	Value: 350				
2004J Proof	80,000	Value: 350				

KM# 236 100 EURO
15.5500 g., 0.9990 Gold 0.4994 oz. AGW **Subject:** UNESCO - Weimar **Obv:** Stylized eagle **Rev:** Historical City of Weimar buildings

Date	Mintage	F	VF	XF	Unc	BU
2006A	80,000	—	—	—	—	350
2006D	80,000	—	—	—	—	350
2006F	80,000	—	—	—	—	350
2006G	80,000	—	—	—	—	350
2006J	80,000	—	—	—	—	350

KM# 221 200 EURO
31.1000 g., 0.9990 Gold 0.9989 oz. AGW, 32.5 mm. **Subject:** Introduction of the Euro Currency **Obv:** Stylized round eagle **Rev:** Euro symbol and arches **Edge Lettering:** IM...ZEICHEN...DER...EINIGUNG...EUROPAS

Date	Mintage	F	VF	XF	Unc	BU
2002A Proof	20,000	Value: 1,250				
2002D Proof	20,000	Value: 1,250				
2002F Proof	20,000	Value: 1,250				
2002G Proof	20,000	Value: 1,250				
2002J Proof	20,000	Value: 1,250				

KM# 250 200 EURO
31.1000 g., 0.9990 Gold 0.9989 oz. AGW **Subject:** Quedlinburg Abbey

Date	Mintage	F	VF	XF	Unc	BU
2003A Proof	—	Value: 950				
2003D Proof	—	Value: 950				
2003F Proof	—	Value: 950				
2003G Proof	—	Value: 950				
2003J Proof	—	Value: 950				

KM# 251 200 EURO
31.1000 g., 0.9990 Gold 0.9989 oz. AGW **Subject:** City of Bamberg

Date	Mintage	F	VF	XF	Unc	BU
2004A Proof	—	Value: 850				
2004D Proof	—	Value: 850				
2004F Proof	—	Value: 850				
2004G Proof	—	Value: 850				
2004J Proof	—	Value: 850				

KM# 252 200 EURO
31.1000 g., 0.9990 Gold 0.9989 oz. AGW **Subject:** 2006 World Cup - Soccer

Date	Mintage	F	VF	XF	Unc	BU
2005A Proof	—	Value: 900				
2005D Proof	—	Value: 900				
2005F Proof	—	Value: 900				
2005G Proof	—	Value: 900				
2005J Proof	—	Value: 900				

MEDALLIC COINAGE
Aureus Magnus Issues

Private medals struck for Werner Graul (Aureus Magnus), West Germany by the Vienna, Austria and Hamburg, West Germany mints. These are currently struck for Dr. Jurgen Graul, his son

X# M211 1/2 DUCAT
1.7250 g., 0.9800 Gold 0.0544 oz. AGW, 15.5 mm. **Obv:** Value "S" in center of 6-pointed cross, lilies in angles **Obv. Legend:** PRO PROSPERITATE MUNDI **Rev:** Bust of Maria Theresia divides dates 1717-1780 **Rev. Legend:** MARIA • THERESIA IMPERATRIX • GER **Edge:** Plain

Date	Mintage	F	VF	XF	Unc	BU
1967 Proof	—	Value: 40.00				

X# M40 DUCAT
3.4500 g., 0.9800 Gold 0.1087 oz. AGW, 20 mm. **Obv:** Value "I" in center of 6-arm cross **Obv. Legend:** PRO PROSPERITATE MUNDI **Rev:** Bust of Pope Pius XII left **Rev. Legend:** PIUS XII.PONTIFEX MAXIMUS **Edge:** Plain

Date	Mintage	F	VF	XF	Unc	BU
1958 Proof	—	Value: 80.00				

X# M44 DUCAT
3.4500 g., 0.9800 Gold 0.1087 oz. AGW, 20 mm. **Subject:** Queen Nefertiti of Egypt **Obv:** Value "I" in center of 6-pointed cross, lilies in angles **Obv. Legend:** PRO PROSPERITATE MUNDI **Rev:** Head of Nefertiti left **Rev. Legend:** MATER OPERUM ATQUE ARTIFICIORUM • AEGYPTUS **Edge:** Plain

Date	Mintage	F	VF	XF	Unc	BU
1958 Proof	—	Value: 80.00				

X# M100 DUCAT
3.4500 g., 0.9800 Gold 0.1087 oz. AGW, 20 mm. **Subject:** Battle of Marathon **Obv:** Value "I" in center of 6-pointed cross, lilies in angles **Obv. Legend:** PRO PROSPERITATE MUNDI **Rev:** Athenian owl above helmeted head of Minerva left **Rev. Legend:** GRAECIA • ANNO A.CHR.N.CDXC. **Edge:** Plain

Date	Mintage	F	VF	XF	Unc	BU
ND(1960) Proof	—	Value: 80.00				

X# M81 DUCAT
3.4500 g., 0.9800 Gold 0.1087 oz. AGW, 20.1 mm. **Series:** Type II: Imperial currency **Subject:** Children of Earth **Obv:** Value "I" in center of 6-pointed cross, lilies in angles **Obv. Legend:** PRO PROSPERITATE MUNDI **Rev:** Radiant nude female standing facing, head 3/4 right **Rev. Legend:** OMNES EX EADEM TERRA NATI SUMUS • IMPERIUM MUNDI • **Edge:** Plain **Note:** Prev. X#M103.

Date	Mintage	F	VF	XF	Unc	BU
1960 Proof	—	Value: 80.00				

X# M86 DUCAT
3.4500 g., 0.9800 Gold 0.1087 oz. AGW, 20.1 mm. **Obv:** Value "I" in center of 6-pointed cross, lilies in angles **Obv. Legend:** PRO PROSPERITATE MUNDI **Rev:** Crowned Holy Mother Mary with Child **Rev. Legend:** + SANCTA MARIA MONACHII **Edge:** Plain **Note:** Prev. X#M85.

Date	Mintage	F	VF	XF	Unc	BU
1960 Proof	—	Value: 80.00				

X# M163 DUCAT
3.4500 g., 0.9800 Gold 0.1087 oz. AGW, 20.1 mm. **Subject:** JFK's Death **Obv:** Value "I" in center of 6-pointed cross, lilies in angles **Obv. Legend:** PRO PROSPERITATE MUNDI **Rev:** Bust of Kennedy left in sprays **Rev. Legend:** KENNEDY + 22 • X1 • 1963 **Edge:** Plain **Note:** Prev. X#M136.

Date	Mintage	F	VF	XF	Unc	BU
ND(1963) Proof	—	Value: 80.00				

X# M155 DUCAT
3.4500 g., 0.9800 Gold 0.1087 oz. AGW, 20.1 mm. **Subject:** Queen Cleopatra of Egypt **Obv:** Value "I" in center of 6-pointed cross, lilies in angles **Obv. Legend:** PRO PROSPERITATE MUNDI **Rev:** Bust of Cleopatra left **Rev. Legend:** AEGYPTUS **Edge:** Plain

Date	Mintage	F	VF	XF	Unc	BU
1963 Proof	—	Value: 80.00				

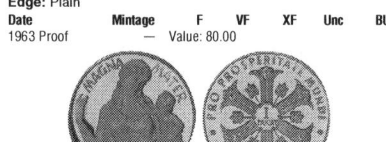

X# M244 DUCAT
3.3800 g., 0.9800 Gold 0.1065 oz. AGW, 20.15 mm. **Obv:** Value "I" in center of 6-pointed cross, lilies in angles **Obv. Legend:** PRO PROSPERITATE MUNDI **Rev:** Goddess of Motherhood with child **Rev. Legend:** MAGNA MATER **Edge:** Plain

Date	Mintage	F	VF	XF	Unc	BU
1964 Proof	—	Value: 80.00				

X# M207 DUCAT
3.4500 g., 0.9800 Gold 0.1087 oz. AGW, 21.7 mm. **Subject:** Canada's Centennial **Obv:** Value "I" in center of 6-pointed cross, lilies in angles **Obv. Legend:** PRO PROSPERITATE MUNDI **Rev:** Bust of Indian maiden right **Rev. Legend:** CANADA PATRIA NOSTRA **Edge:** Plain

278 GERMANY - FEDERAL REPUBLIC

Date	Mintage	F	VF	XF	Unc	BU
ND(1967) Proof	—	Value: 80.00				

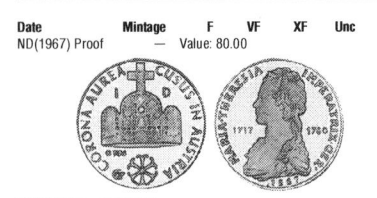

X# M212 DUCAT
3.4500 g., 0.9860 Gold 0.1094 oz. AGW, 19.7 mm. **Obv:** Crown above 6-pointed cross **Obv. Legend:** CORONA AUREA CUSUS IN AUSTRIA **Rev:** Bust of Maria Theresa left, divides dates 1717-1780 **Rev. Legend:** MARIA • THERESIA IMPERATRIX • GER • **Edge:** Plain **Note:** Prev. X#M209.

Date	Mintage	F	VF	XF	Unc	BU
1967 Proof	—	Value: 80.00				

X# M129 DUCAT
3.4500 g., 0.9800 Gold 0.1087 oz. AGW, 20.1 mm. **Subject:** 450th Anniversary Birth of Joan of Arc of France **Obv:** Value "I" in center of 6-arm cross **Obv. Legend:** PRO PROSPERITATE MUNDI **Rev:** Helmeted bust of Joan of Arc left **Rev. Legend:** IOHANNA ★ 1412 GALLIA **Edge:** Plain

Date	Mintage	F	VF	XF	Unc	BU
1992 Proof	—	Value: 80.00				

X# M78 2-1/2 DUCAT
8.6250 g., 0.9800 Gold 0.2718 oz. AGW, 26 mm. **Subject:** 1960 Rome Olympics **Obv:** Value "XXS" in center of 6-arm cross **Obv. Legend:** PRO PROSPERITATE MUNDI **Rev:** Head of Rome right **Rev. Legend:** OLYMPIA ROMA **Edge:** Plain

Date	Mintage	F	VF	XF	Unc	BU
1960 Proof	—	Value: 200				

X# M164 2-1/2 DUCAT
8.6250 g., 0.9800 Gold 0.2718 oz. AGW, 26 mm. **Subject:** JFK's Death **Obv:** Value "IIS" in center of 6-pointed cross, lilies in angles **Obv. Legend:** PRO PROSPERITATE MUNDI **Rev:** Bust of Kennedy left in sprays **Rev. Legend:** KENNEDY + 22 • X1 • 1963 **Edge:** Plain

Date	Mintage	F	VF	XF	Unc	BU
ND(1963) Proof	—	Value: 200				

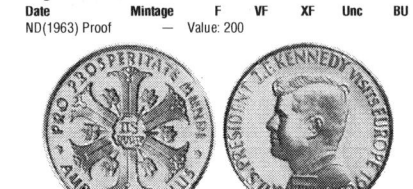

X# M137 2-1/2 DUCAT
8.6250 g., 0.9800 Gold 0.2718 oz. AGW, 26 mm. **Subject:** JFK Visits Europe **Obv:** Value "IIS" in center of 6-pointed cross, lilies in angles **Obv. Legend:** PRO PROSPERITATE MUNDI **Rev:** Bust of Kennedy left, shield below in sprays **Rev. Legend:** U.S. PRESIDENT J. F. KENNEDY VISITS EUROPE **Edge:** Plain

Date	Mintage	F	VF	XF	Unc	BU
1963 Proof	—	Value: 200				

X# M208 2-1/2 DUCAT
8.6250 g., 0.9800 Gold 0.2718 oz. AGW, 26 mm. **Subject:** Canada's Centennial **Obv:** Value "IIS" in center of 6-arm cross **Obv. Legend:** PRO PROSPERITATE MUNDI **Rev:** Bust of Indian maiden left **Rev. Legend:** CANADA PATRIA NOSTRA **Edge:** Plain

Date	Mintage	F	VF	XF	Unc	BU
ND(1967) Proof	—	Value: 200				

X# M5 5 DUCAT
17.5000 g., 0.9800 Gold 0.5514 oz. AGW, 35.20 mm. **Series:** Rome, Eternal City **Obv:** Value "V" in center of 6-pointed cross, lilies in angles **Obv. Legend:** PRO PROSPERITATE MUNDI **Rev:** Archways **Rev. Legend:** FAMA PERENIS ERIT - ROMA AETERNA **Edge:** Plain **Note:** Prev. X#M6.

Date	Mintage	F	VF	XF	Unc	BU
1947 Proof	—	Value: 400				

X# M13 5 DUCAT
17.2500 g., 0.9800 Gold 0.5435 oz. AGW, 35.2 mm. **Subject:** 800th Anniversary Coronation of Henry II of Austria **Obv:** Value "V" in center of 6-pointed cross, lilies in angles **Obv. Legend:** PRO PROSPERITATE MUNDI **Rev:** Crowned Henry II standing facing, head left, holding church and sword **Rev. Legend:** A • D • MCLVI AUSTRIA DUCATUS INSTAURATUS • HEINRICH JOSOMIR GOTT • **Edge:** Plain

Date	Mintage	F	VF	XF	Unc	BU
1956 Proof	—	Value: 400				

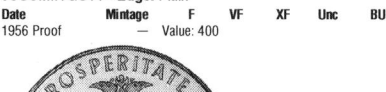

X# M9 5 DUCAT
17.2500 g., 0.9800 Gold 0.5435 oz. AGW **Subject:** 200th Anniversary Alcea Castle **Obv:** Value "V" in center of 6-pointed cross, lilies in angles **Obv. Legend:** PRO PROSPERITATE MUNDI **Rev:** Castle, shield at bottom **Rev. Legend:** CASTRUM ALCEA **Edge:** Plain

Date	Mintage	F	VF	XF	Unc	BU
ND(1957) Proof	—	Value: 400				

X# M36 5 DUCAT
17.2500 g., 0.9800 Gold 0.5435 oz. AGW, 35.2 mm. **Obv:** Value "V" in center of 6-pointed cross, lilies in angles **Obv. Legend:** PRO PROSPERITATE MUNDI **Rev:** Bust of Maria Theresa left divides dates 1717 - 1780 **Rev. Legend:** MARIA • THERESA **Edge:** Plain

Date	Mintage	F	VF	XF	Unc	BU
1957 Proof	—	Value: 400				

X# M71 5 DUCAT
17.2500 g., 0.9800 Gold 0.5435 oz. AGW, 35.2 mm. **Series:** Type I: Imperial Currency **Subject:** Children of Earth **Obv:** Value "V" in center of 6-pointed cross, lilies in angles **Obv. Legend:** PRO PROSPERITATE MUNDI **Rev:** Female nude standing facing, head 3/4 right **Rev. Legend:** OMNES EX EADEM TERRA NATI SUMUS • IMPERIUM MUNDI • **Edge:** Plain

Date	Mintage	F	VF	XF	Unc	BU
1959 Proof	—	Value: 400				

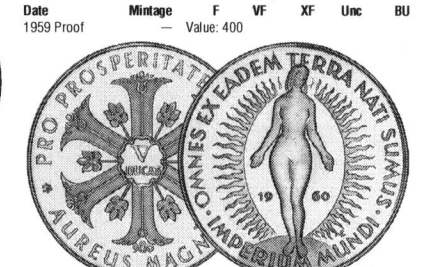

X# M82 5 DUCAT
17.2500 g., 0.9800 Gold 0.5435 oz. AGW **Series:** Type II: Imperial Currency **Subject:** Children of Earth **Obv:** Value "V" in center of 6-pointed cross, lilies in angles **Obv. Legend:** PRO PROSPERITATE MUNDI **Rev:** Radiant nude female standing facing, head 3/4 right **Rev. Legend:** OMNES EX EADEM TERRA NATI SUMUS • IMPERIUM MUNDI • **Edge:** Plain

Date	Mintage	F	VF	XF	Unc	BU
1960 Proof	—	Value: 400				

X# M102 5 DUCAT
17.2500 g., 0.9800 Gold 0.5435 oz. AGW, 35.2 mm. **Subject:** Battle of Marathon **Obv:** Value "V" in center of 6-arm cross **Obv. Legend:** PRO PROSPERITATE MUNDI **Rev:** Athentian owl above helmeted head of Minerva left **Rev. Legend:** GRACIA • ANNO A.CHR.N.CDXC...... **Edge:** Plain **Note:** Prev. X#M101.

Date	Mintage	F	VF	XF	Unc	BU
1960 Proof	—	Value: 400				

GERMANY - FEDERAL REPUBLIC

X# M91 5 DUCAT
17.2500 g., 0.9800 Gold 0.5435 oz. AGW, 35.2 mm. **Obv:** Value "V" in center of 6-pointed cross, lilies in angles **Obv. Legend:** PRO PROSPERITATE MUNDI **Rev:** Bust of Pope John XXIII left **Rev. Legend:** IOANNES XXIII PONTIFEX MAXIMUS **Edge:** Plain **Note:** Prev. X#M109.

Date	Mintage	F	VF	XF	Unc	BU
1960 Proof	—	Value: 400				

X# M165 5 DUCAT
17.2500 g., 0.9800 Gold 0.5435 oz. AGW, 35.2 mm. **Subject:** JFK's Death **Obv:** Value "V" in center of 6-arm cross **Obv. Legend:** PRO PROSPERITATE MUNDI **Rev:** Bust of Kennedy left in sprays **Rev. Legend:** KENNEDY + 22.X1.1963 **Edge:** Plain **Note:** Prev. X#M138.

Date	Mintage	F	VF	XF	Unc	BU
ND(1963) Proof	—	Value: 400				

X# M138 5 DUCAT
17.5000 g., 0.9800 Gold 0.5514 oz. AGW, 35.2 mm. **Subject:** JFK Visits Europe **Obv:** Value "V" in center of 6-pointed cross, lilies in angles **Obv. Legend:** PRO PROSPERITATE MUNDI **Rev:** Bust of Kennedy left, shield in sprays below **Rev. Legend:** U.S. PRESIDENT J. F. KENNEDY VISITS EUROPE **Edge:** Plain

Date	Mintage	F	VF	XF	Unc	BU
1963 Proof	—	Value: 400				

X# M11 10 DUCAT
34.5000 g., 0.9800 Gold 1.087 oz. AGW, 50 mm. **Obv:** Value "X" in center of 6-pointed cross, lilies in angles **Obv. Legend:** * AVORUM NON MORITURA VIRTUS * **Rev:** Prince Ludvig Wilhelm of Baden horseback left **Rev. Legend:** LUDOVICUS WILHELMUS PRINCEPS BADENSIS **Edge:** Plain

Date	Mintage	F	VF	XF	Unc	BU
1955 Proof	—	Value: 800				

X# M14 10 DUCAT
34.5000 g., 0.9800 Gold 1.0870 oz. AGW, 50 mm. **Subject:** 800th Anniversary Coronation of Henry II of Austria **Obv:** Value "X" in center of 6-pointed cross, lilies in angles **Obv. Legend:** PRO PROSPERITATE MUNDI **Rev:** Crowned Henry II standing facing, head left, holding church and sword **Rev. Legend:** A • D • MCLVI AUSTRIA DUCATUS INSTAURATUS • HEINRICH JOSOMIR GOTT **Edge:** Plain

Date	Mintage	F	VF	XF	Unc	BU
1956 Proof	—	Value: 800				

X# M6 10 DUCAT
39.9600 g., 0.9800 Gold 1.259 oz. AGW, 50 mm. **Obv:** Value "X" in center of 6-pointed cross, lilies in angles **Obv. Legend:** PRO PROSPERITATE MUNDI **Rev:** Archways **Rev. Legend:** FAMA PERENNIS ERIT - ROMA ÆTERNA **Edge:** Plain

Date	Mintage	F	VF	XF	Unc	BU
1947 Proof	—	Value: 925				

X# M7 10 DUCAT
35.3400 g., 0.9800 Gold 1.1135 oz. AGW, 51 mm. **Subject:** Liberation of West Germany **Obv:** Value "X" in center of 6-pointed cross, lilies in angles **Obv. Legend:** * SIGNATUS AD PRETIUM AURI CONSERVANDUM * **Rev:** Old sailing ship **Rev. Legend:** GERMANIA LIBERTATEM RECUPERAVIT **Edge:** Plain

Date	Mintage	F	VF	XF	Unc	BU
1955 Proof	—	Value: 825				

X# M16 10 DUCAT
35.3400 g., 0.9800 Gold 1.1135 oz. AGW, 51 mm. **Obv:** Value "X" in center of 6-pointed cross, lilies in angles **Obv. Legend:** SIGNATUS AD PRETIUM AURI CONSERVANDUM **Rev:** Old sailing ship **Rev. Legend:** GERMANIA PACEM ET LIBERTATEM AMAT **Edge:** Plain

Date	Mintage	F	VF	XF	Unc	BU
1956 Proof	—	Value: 825				

280 GERMANY - FEDERAL REPUBLIC

X# M19 10 DUCAT
34.5000 g., 0.9800 Gold 1.087 oz. AGW, 50 mm. **Subject:** 700th Anniversary Hessen **Obv:** Value "X" in center of 6-pointed cross, lilies in angles **Obv. Legend:** PRO PROSPERITATE MUNDI **Rev:** Knight standing left with sword and Hessen shield **Rev. Legend:** * IN HONOR • HASSIAE * **Edge:** Plain

Date	Mintage	F	VF	XF	Unc	BU
1956 Proof	—				Value: 800	

X# M37 10 DUCAT
34.5000 g., 0.9800 Gold 1.087 oz. AGW, 44.5 mm. **Obv:** Value "X" in center of 6-pointed cross, lilies in angles **Obv. Legend:** PRO PROSPERITATE MUNDI **Rev:** Bust of Maria Theresa left divides dates 1717-1780 **Rev. Legend:** MARIA • THERESIA IMPERATRIX • GER • **Edge:** Plain

Date	Mintage	F	VF	XF	Unc	BU
1957 Proof	—				Value: 800	

(X37) 10 DUCAT
34.5000 g., 0.9800 Gold 1.087 oz. AGW, 44.5 mm. **Obv:** Value "X" in center of 6-pointed cross, lilies in angles **Obv. Legend:** PRO PROSPERITATE MUNDI **Rev:** Bust of Maria Theresa left divides dates 1717 - 1780 **Rev. Legend:** MARIA • THERESIA IMPERATRIX • GER • **Edge:** Plain

Date	Mintage	F	VF	XF	Unc	BU
1957 Proof	—				Value: 650	

X# M22 10 DUCAT
34.5000 g., 0.9800 Gold 1.087 oz. AGW, 50 mm. **Subject:** Peace and Liberation of West Germany **Obv:** Value "X" in center of 6-pointed cross, lilies in angles **Obv. Legend:** * AVORUM NON MORITURA VIRTUS * **Rev:** Sailing ship, shield at left **Rev. Legend:** GERMANIA PACEM ET LIBERTATEM AMAT **Edge:** Plain

Date	Mintage	F	VF	XF	Unc	BU
1957 Proof	—				Value: 800	

X# M8 10 DUCAT
34.5000 g., 0.9800 Gold 1.087 oz. AGW, 50 mm. **Subject:** 400th Anniversary Hall in Swabia **Obv:** Value "X" in center of 6-pointed cross, lilies in angles **Obv. Legend:** * AVORUM NON MORITURA VIRTUS * **Rev:** City view, 2 shields above **Rev. Legend:** IN HONOREM HALAE SUEVICAE **Edge:** Plain

Date	Mintage	F	VF	XF	Unc	BU
ND(1956) Proof	—				Value: 800	

X# M21 10 DUCAT
34.5000 g., 0.9800 Gold 1.087 oz. AGW, 50 mm. **Subject:** Denmark **Obv:** Value "X" in center of 6-pointed cross, lilies in angles **Obv. Legend:** * AVORUM NON MORITURA VIRTUS * **Rev:** Sailing ship **Rev. Legend:** DANEBROG DANIAE DECUS **Edge:** Plain

Date	Mintage	F	VF	XF	Unc	BU
1957 Proof	—				Value: 800	

X# M24 10 DUCAT
34.8700 g., 0.9800 Gold 1.0987 oz. AGW, 50 mm. **Subject:** Return of Saarland to West Germany **Obv:** Eagle with shield on breast **Rev:** 11 shields around value **Rev. Legend:** • RÜCKKEHR DER SAAR • 1.JANUAR 1957

Date	Mintage	F	VF	XF	Unc	BU
1957 Proof	—				Value: 800	

GERMANY - FEDERAL REPUBLIC

X# M28 10 DUCAT
34.5000 g., 0.9800 Gold 1.087 oz. AGW, 50 mm. **Subject:** Security and Peace **Obv:** Germania seated left with shield and sprigs **Obv. Legend:** • KONRAD ADENAVER • SECVRITAS • ET • PAX. **Rev:** Head of Adenauer left **Edge:** Plain

Date	Mintage	F	VF	XF	Unc	BU
1957 Proof	—	Value: 800				

X# M32 10 DUCAT
34.5000 g., 0.9800 Gold 1.087 oz. AGW, 50 mm. **Subject:** Founding of Eltz Castle **Obv:** Value "X" in center of 6-pointed cross, lilies in angles **Rev:** Eltz castle **Edge:** Plain

Date	Mintage	F	VF	XF	Unc	BU
1957 Proof	—	Value: 800				

X# M46 10 DUCAT
34.5000 g., 0.9800 Gold 1.087 oz. AGW, 50 mm. **Subject:** Queen Nefertiti of Egypt **Obv:** Value "X" in center of 6-pointed cross, lilies in angles **Obv. Legend:** PRO PROSPERITATE MUNDI **Rev:** Head of Nefertiti left **Rev. Legend:** MATER OPERUM ATQUE ARTIFICIORUM • AEGYPTUS • **Edge:** Plain

Date	Mintage	F	VF	XF	Unc	BU
1958 Proof	—	Value: 800				

X# M48 10 DUCAT
34.5000 g., 0.9800 Gold 1.087 oz. AGW, 50 mm. **Subject:** 400th Anniversary Elizabeth I Coronation **Obv:** Value "X" in center of 6-pointed cross, lilies in angles **Obv. Legend:** * AVORUN NON MORITURA VIRTUS * **Rev:** The Fight for Freedom on the High Seas **Rev. Legend:** ELIZABETH I.1558 - 1603 • IN MEM.REGNI ANGLIAE REGINAE **Edge:** Plain

Date	Mintage	F	VF	XF	Unc	BU
1958 Proof	—	Value: 800				

X# M52 10 DUCAT
34.7200 g., 0.9800 Gold 1.0940 oz. AGW, 50 mm. **Subject:** 1000th Anniversary **Obv:** Value "X" in center of 6-pointed cross, lilies in angles **Obv. Legend:** * PRO PROSPERITATE MUNDI * **Rev:** Free Market, City of Trier **Rev. Legend:** FORUM CIVITATIS TREVERENSIS **Edge:** Plain

Date	Mintage	F	VF	XF	Unc	BU
1958 Proof	—	Value: 800				

X# M56 10 DUCAT
34.5000 g., 0.9800 Gold 1.087 oz. AGW, 50 mm. **Subject:** Free City of Hamburg, Germany **Obv:** Value "X" in center of 6-pointed cross, lilies in angles **Obv. Legend:** * AVORUM NON MORITURA VIRTUS * **Rev:** City view **Rev. Legend:** HAMBURGUM - CIV • HANSEAT • **Edge:** Plain

Date	Mintage	F	VF	XF	Unc	BU
1958 Proof	—	Value: 800				

X# M60 10 DUCAT
34.5000 g., 0.9800 Gold 1.087 oz. AGW, 50 mm. **Subject:** 800th Anniversary of Lubeck **Obv:** Value "X" in center of 6-pointed cross, lilies in angles **Obv. Legend:** * AVORUM NON MORITURA VIRTUS * **Rev:** Shield above castle **Rev. Legend:** IN HONOREM LUBECA **Rev. Inscription:** CONCORDIA DOMI/FORIS PAX **Edge:** Plain

Date	Mintage	F	VF	XF	Unc	BU
1958 Proof	—	Value: 800				

X# M64 10 DUCAT
34.8400 g., 0.9800 Gold 1.0987 oz. AGW **Subject:** Free City of Bremen, Member of Hanseatic League **Obv:** Value "X" in center of 6-pointed cross, lilies in angles **Obv. Legend:** * AVORUM NON MORITURA VIRTUS * **Rev:** Knight standing with sword and shield between buildings **Rev. Legend:** CIVITAS HANSEATICA - BREMA **Edge:** Plain

Date	Mintage	F	VF	XF	Unc	BU
1958 Proof	—	Value: 800				

282 GERMANY - FEDERAL REPUBLIC

X# M50 10 DUCAT
34.5000 g., 0.9800 Gold 1.087 oz. AGW, 50 mm. **Subject:** 1400th Anniversary City of Paris **Obv:** Value "X" in center of 6-pointed cross, lilies in angles **Obv. Legend:** * AVORUM NON MORITURA VIRTUS * **Rev:** City view, shield at bottom **Rev. Legend:** LUTETIA PARISIORUM CAPUT GALLIAE **Edge:** Plain

Date	Mintage	F	VF	XF	Unc	BU
1958 Proof	—	Value: 800				

X# M54 10 DUCAT
34.5000 g., 0.9800 Gold 1.087 oz. AGW, 50 mm. **Subject:** Augusburg **Obv:** Value "X" in center of 6-pointed cross, lilies in angles **Rev:** City view **Edge:** Plain

Date	Mintage	F	VF	XF	Unc	BU
1958 Proof	—	Value: 800				

X# M58 10 DUCAT
34.5000 g., 0.9800 Gold 1.087 oz. AGW, 50 mm. **Subject:** Luneberg **Obv:** Value "X" in center of 6-pointed cross, lilies in angles **Rev:** City view **Edge:** Plain

Date	Mintage	F	VF	XF	Unc	BU
1958 Proof	300	Value: 800				

X# M62 10 DUCAT
34.5000 g., 0.9800 Gold 1.087 oz. AGW, 50 mm. **Subject:** 800th Anniversary of Munich **Obv:** Value "X" in center of 6-pointed cross, lilies in angles **Obv. Legend:** * AVORUM NON MORITURA VIRTUS * **Rev:** City view, shield at bottom **Rev. Legend:** IN HONOREM CIVITATIS MONACENCIS **Edge:** Plain

Date	Mintage	F	VF	XF	Unc	BU
1958 Proof	—	Value: 800				

X# M68 10 DUCAT
34.5000 g., 0.9800 Gold 1.087 oz. AGW, 50 mm. **Subject:** 350th Anniversary Hudson in Manhattan **Obv:** Value "X" in center of 6-pointed cross, lilies in angles **Obv. Legend:** * AVORUM NON MORITURA VIRTUS * **Rev:** Hudson's ship **Rev. Legend:** A • D • MDCIX HENRICUS HUDSON INSULAM MANHATTAN APERUIT **Edge:** Plain

Date	Mintage	F	VF	XF	Unc	BU
1959 Proof	—	Value: 800				

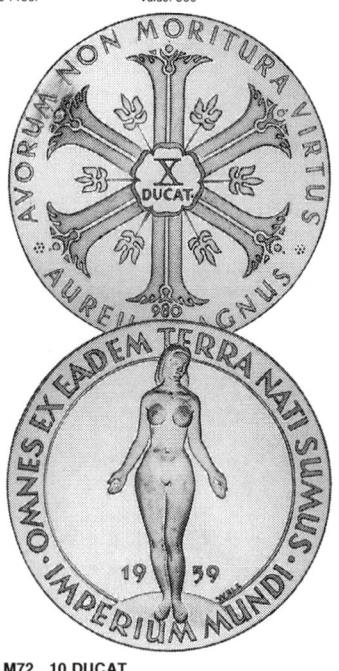

X# M72 10 DUCAT
34.5000 g., 0.9800 Gold 1.087 oz. AGW, 50 mm. **Series:** Type I: Imperial Currency **Subject:** Children of Earth **Obv:** Value "X" in center of 6-pointed cross, lilies in angles **Obv. Legend:** PRO PROSPERITATE MUNDI **Rev:** Female nude standing facing, head 3/4 right **Rev. Legend:** OMNES EX EADEM TERRA NATI SUMUS • IMPERIUM MUNDI • **Edge:** Plain

Date	Mintage	F	VF	XF	Unc	BU
1959 Proof	—	Value: 800				

X# M83 10 DUCAT
34.5000 g., 0.9800 Gold 1.087 oz. AGW, 50 mm. **Series:** Type II: Imperial Currency **Subject:** Children of Earth **Obv:** Value "X" in center of 6-pointed cross, lilies in angles **Obv. Legend:** PRO PROSPERITATE MUNDI **Rev:** Radiant nude female standing facing, head 3/4 right **Rev. Legend:** OMNES EX EADEM TERRA NATI SUMUS • IMPERIUM MUNDI • **Edge:** Plain

Date	Mintage	F	VF	XF	Unc	BU
1960 Proof	—	Value: 800				

X# M113 10 DUCAT
34.5000 g., 0.9800 Gold 1.087 oz. AGW, 44.50 mm. **Subject:** Germania (Germany) - Eternally **Obv:** Value "X" in center of 6-pointed cross, lilies in angles **Obv. Legend:** PRO PROSPERITATE MUNDI **Rev:** Crowned bust of Germania facing 3/4 left, divides date **Rev. Legend:** GERMANIA AETERNA **Edge:** Plain

Date	Mintage	F	VF	XF	Unc	BU
1961 Proof	—	Value: 800				

X# M123 10 DUCAT
34.5000 g., 0.9800 Gold 1.087 oz. AGW, 44.5 mm. **Subject:** Reunion, Life For Germany **Obv:** Value "X" in center of 6-pointed cross, lilies in angles **Obv. Legend:** PRO PROSPERITATE MUNDI **Rev:** Germania kneeling between two children **Rev. Legend:** CONCORDIA SALUS **Edge:** Plain

Date	Mintage	F	VF	XF	Unc	BU
1961 Proof	—	Value: 800				

GERMANY - FEDERAL REPUBLIC 283

X# M139 10 DUCAT
34.5000 g., 0.9800 Gold 1.087 oz. AGW, 50 mm. **Subject:** JFK Visits Europe **Obv:** Value "X" in center of 6-pointed cross, lilies in angles **Obv. Legend:** PRO PROSPERITATE MUNDI **Rev:** Bust of Kennedy left, shield in sprays below **Rev. Legend:** U.S. PRESIDENT J. F. KENNEDY VISITS EUROPE **Edge:** Plain

Date	Mintage	F	VF	XF	Unc	BU
1963 Proof	—	Value: 800				

X# M25 20 DUCAT
69.0000 g., 0.9800 Gold 2.1741 oz. AGW, 50 mm. **Subject:** Return of Saarland to West Germany **Obv:** Eagle with shield on breast **Rev:** 11 shields around value **Rev. Legend:** • RÜCKKEHR DER SAAR • 1.JANUAR 1957

Date	Mintage	F	VF	XF	Unc	BU
1957 Proof	—	Value: 1,550				

X# M69 20 DUCAT
69.0000 g., 0.9800 Gold 2.174 oz. AGW, 50 mm. **Subject:** 350th Anniversary Hudson in Manhattan **Obv:** Value "XX" in center of 6-pointed cross, lilies in angles **Obv. Legend:** * AVORUM NON MORITURA VIRTUS * **Rev:** Hudson's ship **Rev. Legend:** A • D • MDCIX HENRICUS HUDSON INSULAM MANHATTAN APERUIT **Edge:** Plain

Date	Mintage	F	VF	XF	Unc	BU
1959 Proof	—	Value: 1,550				

X# M167 20 DUCAT
69.0000 g., 0.9800 Gold 2.174 oz. AGW, 50 mm. **Subject:** JFK's Death **Obv:** Value "XX" in center of 6-pointed cross, lilies in angles **Obv. Legend:** PRO PROSPERITATE MUNDI **Rev:** Bust of Kennedy left in sprays **Rev. Legend:** KENNEDY + 22.X1.1963 **Edge:** Plain **Note:** Prev. KM#M35.

Date	Mintage	F	VF	XF	Unc	BU
ND(1963) Proof	—	Value: 1,550				

X# M70 30 DUCAT
103.5000 g., 0.9800 Gold 3.261 oz. AGW, 50 mm. **Subject:** 350th Anniversary Hudson in Manhattan **Obv:** Value XX in center of 6-pointed cross, lilies in angles **Obv. Legend:** ★ AVORUM NON MORITURA VIRTUS ★ **Rev:** Hudson's ship **Rev. Legend:** A • D • MDCIX HENRICUS HUDSON INSULAM MANHATTAN APERUIT **Edge:** Plain

Date	Mintage	F	VF	XF	Unc	BU
1959 Proof	—	Value: 2,350				

X# M29 20 DUCAT
69.0000 g., 0.9800 Gold 2.174 oz. AGW, 50 mm. **Subject:** Security and Peace **Obv:** Germania seated left with shield and sprigs **Obv. Legend:** • KONRAD ADENAVER • SECVRITAS • ET • PAX • **Rev:** Head of Adenauer left **Edge:** Plain

Date	Mintage	F	VF	XF	Unc	BU
1957 Proof	—	Value: 1,550				

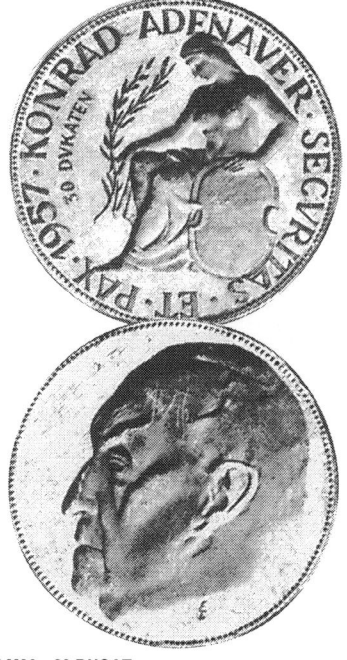

X# M30 30 DUCAT
103.5000 g., 0.9800 Gold 3.2611 oz. AGW, 50 mm. **Subject:** Security and Peace **Obv:** Germania seated left with shield and sprigs **Obv. Legend:** • KONRAD ADENAVER • SECVRITAS • ET • PAX. **Rev. Designer:** Head of Adenauer left **Edge:** Plain **Note:** Prev. Bruce #XM26.

Date	Mintage	F	VF	XF	Unc	BU
1957 Proof	—	Value: 2,350				

X# M168 30 DUCAT
103.5000 g., 0.9800 Gold 3.261 oz. AGW, 50 mm. **Subject:** JFK's Death **Obv:** Value "XXX" in center of 6-pointed cross, lilies in angles **Obv. Legend:** PRO PROSPERITATE MUNDI **Rev:** Bust of Kennedy left in sprays **Rev. Legend:** KENNEDY + 22.X1.1963 **Edge:** Plain **Note:** Prev. X#M141.

Date	Mintage	F	VF	XF	Unc	BU
ND(1963) Proof	—	Value: 2,350				

284 GERMAN-DEMOCRATIC REPUBLIC

MEDALLIC COINAGE
Hamburg Mint Issues

X# M352 5 REICHSMARK
373.6096 g., 0.9990 Gold 12.0000 oz. AGW, 71 mm. **Subject:** 160th Anniversary Bremerhaven Harbor Facility **Note:** Illustration reduced.

Date	Mintage	F	VF	XF	Unc	BU
1987	250	—	—	—	—	9,500

MEDALLIC COINAGE
Square Deal Productions Issues

X# M401a MARK
0.5800 Gold **Issuer:** Münsprägstatt München (Munich) **Obv:** Arms **Obv. Legend:** BUNDESREPUBLIK DEUTSCHLAND **Rev:** Large value between oak leaves **Edge:** Plain **Shape:** Square **Note:** 23.7x23.7mm.

Date	Mintage	F	VF	XF	Unc	BU
2001 Proof	2,500	Value: 350				

GERMANY-DEMOCRATIC REP.

1949-1990

The German Democratic Republic, formerly East Germany, was located on the great north European plain, had an area of 41,768 sq. mi. (108,330 sq. km.) and a population of 16.6 million. The figures included East Berlin, which had been incorporated into the G.D.R. Capital: East Berlin. The economy was highly industrialized. Machinery, transport equipment chemicals, and lignite were exported.

During the closing days of World War II in Europe, Soviet troops advancing into Germany from the east occupied the German provinces of Mecklenburg, Brandenburg, Lusatia, Saxony and Thuringia. These five provinces comprised the occupation zone administered by the Soviet Union after the cessation of hostilities. The other three zones were administered by the U.S., Great Britain and France. Under the Potsdam agreement, questions affecting Germany as a whole were to be settled by the commanders of the occupation zones acting jointly and by unanimous decision. When Soviet intransigence rendered the quadripartite commission inoperable, the three western zones were united to form the Federal Republic of Germany, May 23, 1949. Thereupon the Soviet Union dissolved its occupation zone and established it as the Democratic Republic of Germany, Oct. 7, 1949.

The post-WW II division of Germany was ended Oct. 3, 1990, when the German Democratic Republic (East Germany) ceased to exist and its five constituent provinces were formally admitted to the Federal Republic of Germany. An election Dec. 2, 1990, chose representatives to the united federal parliament (Bundestag), which then conducted its opening session in Berlin in the old Reichstag building.

MINT MARKS
A - Berlin
E - Muldenhutten

MONETARY SYSTEM
100 Pfennig = 1 Mark

PROBAS

KM#	Date	Mintage	Identification	Mkt Val
PR7	1968	—	20 Mark. 0.9990 Gold. KM#21.	—
PR37	1985A	266	10 Mark. 0.3330 Gold. Alloyed with silver, KM#16, Proof.	5,500

GHANA

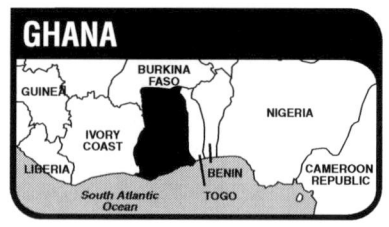

The Republic of Ghana, a member of the Commonwealth of Nations situated on the West Coast of Africa between Ivory Coast and Togo, has an area of 92,100 sq. mi. (238,540 sq. km.) and a population of 14 million, almost entirely African. Capital: Accra. Cocoa (the major crop), coconuts, palm kernels and coffee are exported. Mining, second in importance to agriculture, is concentrated on gold, manganese and industrial diamonds.

The state of Ghana, comprising the Gold Coast and British Togoland, obtained independence on March 6, 1957, becoming the first Negro African colony to do so. On July I, 1960, Ghana adopted a republican constitution, changing from a ministerial to a presidential form of government. The government was overthrown, the constitution suspended and the National Assembly dissolved by the Ghanaian army and police on Feb. 24, 1966. The government was returned to civilian authority in Oct. 1969, but was again seized by military officers in a bloodless coup on Jan. 13, 1972, but 3 further coups occurred in 1978, 1979 and 1981. The latter 2 coups were followed by suspension of the constitution and banning of political parties. A new constitution, which allowed multiparty politics, was approved in April 1992.

Ghana's monetary denomination of Cedi' is derived from the word 'sedie' meaning cowrie, a shell money commonly employed by coastal tribes.

MONETARY SYSTEM
12 Pence = 1 Shilling

REPUBLIC

DECIMAL COINAGE

KM# 21b 50 CEDIS
47.5400 g., 0.9170 Gold 1.4017 oz. AGW **Series:** F.A.O. **Subject:** World Fisheries Conference **Obv:** Bush drums **Rev:** People in boat on water, denomination

Date	Mintage	F	VF	XF	Unc	BU
ND(1984) Proof	105	Value: 2,000				

KM# 28 500 CEDIS
15.9800 g., 0.9170 Gold .4711 oz. AGW **Subject:** International Year of Disabled Persons **Obv:** Triangular symbol within wreath, date above **Rev:** Bust 3/4 left divides dates, denomination below

Date	Mintage	F	VF	XF	Unc	BU
1981	—	—	—	—	335	350
1981 Proof	—	Value: 400				

KM# 23 500 CEDIS
15.9800 g., 0.9170 Gold .4711 oz. AGW **Subject:** Year of the Scout **Obv:** Rampant lion at center of quartered shield, denomination below, rope encircles **Rev:** Scouting symbol within rope, dates below

Date	Mintage	F	VF	XF	Unc	BU
ND(1984)	2,000	—	—	—	315	335
ND(1984) Proof	2,000	Value: 375				

MEDALLIC COINAGE

X# 4 CROWN
28.2800 g., 0.9170 Gold .8338 oz. AGW **Note:** Prev. KM#M3.

Date	Mintage	F	VF	XF	Unc	BU
1965 Proof	50	Value: 750				

GIBRALTAR 285

X# 1 2 POUNDS
15.9800 g., 0.9170 Gold .4711 oz. AGW **Subject:** Republic Day
Note: Prev. KM#M5.
Date	Mintage	F	VF	XF	Unc	BU
ND(1960) Proof	15,000	Value: 350				

X# 5 2 POUNDS
15.9800 g., 0.9170 Gold .4711 oz. AGW **Subject:** OAU Summit Meeting **Note:** Prev. KM#M4.
Date	Mintage	F	VF	XF	Unc	BU
1965 Proof	2,020	Value: 375				

X# 6 2 POUNDS
15.9800 g., 0.9170 Gold .4711 oz. AGW **Subject:** Kotoka **Obv:** Arms with date below **Rev:** Bust of Kotoka 1/2 left **Note:** Prev. KM#M6.
Date	Mintage	F	VF	XF	Unc	BU
1968 Proof	2,000	Value: 375				

X# 7 2 POUNDS
15.9800 g., 0.9170 Gold .4711 oz. AGW **Subject:** Freedom in Unity **Note:** Prev. KM#M7.
Date	Mintage	F	VF	XF	Unc	BU
1973 Proof	2,000	Value: 375				

X# 8 2 POUNDS
15.9800 g., 0.9170 Gold .4711 oz. AGW **Subject:** Operation Feed Yourself **Obv:** Native planting crops **Rev:** Arms and date **Note:** Prev. KM#M8.
Date	Mintage	F	VF	XF	Unc	BU
1975 Proof	—	Value: 345				

X# 9 2 POUNDS
19.6700 g., 0.9170 Gold .5799 oz. AGW **Subject:** 20th Anniversary of Independence **Note:** Prev. KM#M9.
Date	Mintage	F	VF	XF	Unc	BU
ND(1977) Proof	4,397	Value: 450				

X# 10 4 POUNDS
39.5400 g., 0.9170 Gold 1.1658 oz. AGW **Subject:** 20th Anniversary of Independence **Note:** Prev. KM#M10.
Date	Mintage	F	VF	XF	Unc	BU
ND(1977) Proof	300	Value: 950				

PIEFORTS

KM#	Date	Mintage	Identification	Issue Price	Mkt Val
P2	1981	—	500 Cedis. Gold. KM28.	—	800

GIBRALTAR

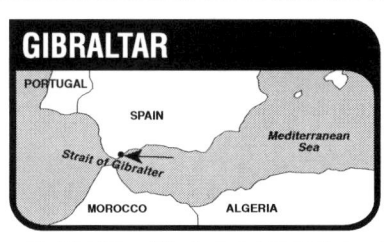

The British Colony of Gibraltar, located at the southernmost point of the Iberian Peninsula, has an area of 2.25 sq. mi. (6.5 sq. km.) and a population of 29,651. Capital (and only town): Gibraltar. Aside from its strategic importance as guardian of the western entrance to the Mediterranean Sea, Gibraltar is also a free port and a British naval base.

Gibraltar, rooted in Greek mythology as one of the Pillars of Hercules, has long been a coveted stronghold. Moslems took it from Spain and fortified it in 711. Spain retook it in 1309, lost it again to the Moors in 1333 and retook it in 1462. After 1540 Spain strengthened its defenses and held it until the War of the Spanish Succession when it was captured by a combined British and Dutch force in 1704. Britain held it against the Franco-Spanish attacks of 1704-05 and through the historic Great Siege of 1779-83. Recently Spain has attempted to discourage British occupancy by harassment and economic devices. In 1967, Gibraltar's inhabitants voted 12,138 to 44 to remain under British rule.

Gibraltar's celebrated Barbary Ape, the last monkey to be found in a wild state in Europe, is featured on the colony's first decimal crown, released in 1972.

RULERS
British

MINT MARKS
PM - Pobjoy Mint

MINT PRIVY MARKS
U - Unc finish

DECIMAL COINAGE
5 New Pence = 1 Shilling
25 New Pence = 1 Crown
1 Crown = 1 Royal
100 New Pence = 1 Pound Sterling

BRITISH COLONY
DECIMAL COINAGE

KM# 22c 5 PENCE
3.2500 g., 0.9170 Gold .0958 oz. AGW, 18 mm. **Ruler:** Elizabeth II **Obv:** Crowned head right **Rev:** Barbary ape left divides denomination
Date	Mintage	F	VF	XF	Unc	BU
1990 Proof	1,000	Value: 125				

KM# 112b 10 PENCE
6.5000 g., 0.9170 Gold .1916 oz. AGW **Ruler:** Elizabeth II **Obv:** Crowned head right **Rev:** Europort
Date	Mintage	F	VF	XF	Unc	BU
1992 Proof	3,500	Value: 165				

KM# 112c 10 PENCE
6.5000 g., 0.9500 Platinum .1985 oz. APW **Ruler:** Elizabeth II **Obv:** Crowned head right **Rev:** Europort
Date	Mintage	F	VF	XF	Unc	BU
1992 Proof	3,500	Value: 300				

KM# 19b 50 PENCE
26.0000 g., 0.9170 Gold .7665 oz. AGW, 30 mm. **Ruler:** Elizabeth II **Subject:** Christmas **Obv:** Crowned head right **Rev:** The Three Wise Men
Date	Mintage	F	VF	XF	Unc	BU
1988 Proof	250	Value: 550				

KM# 19c 50 PENCE
30.4000 g., 0.9950 Platinum .9725 oz. APW, 30 mm. **Ruler:** Elizabeth II **Subject:** Christmas **Obv:** Crowned head right **Rev:** The Three Wise Men
Date	Mintage	F	VF	XF	Unc	BU
1988 Proof	50	Value: 1,450				

KM# 31b 50 PENCE
26.0000 g., 0.9170 Gold .7665 oz. AGW, 30 mm. **Ruler:** Elizabeth II **Subject:** Christmas **Obv:** Crowned head right **Rev:** Choir boy

286 GIBRALTAR

KM# 31c 50 PENCE
30.4000 g., 0.9950 Platinum .9628 oz. APW, 30 mm. **Ruler:** Elizabeth II **Subject:** Christmas **Obv:** Crowned head right **Rev:** Choir boy

Date	Mintage	F	VF	XF	Unc	BU
1989 Proof	Est. 50				Value: 1,450	

KM# 39b 50 PENCE
26.0000 g., 0.9170 Gold .7665 oz. AGW, 30 mm. **Ruler:** Elizabeth II **Obv:** Crowned head right **Rev:** Dolphins

Date	Mintage	F	VF	XF	Unc	BU
1990 Proof	250				Value: 800	

KM# 47b 50 PENCE
26.0000 g., 0.9170 Gold .7665 oz. AGW, 30 mm. **Ruler:** Elizabeth II **Subject:** Christmas **Obv:** Crowned head right **Rev:** Mary and Joseph with child **Shape:** 7-sided

Date	Mintage	F	VF	XF	Unc	BU
1990 Proof	250				Value: 700	

KM# 47c 50 PENCE
30.4000 g., 0.9950 Platinum .9723 oz. APW, 30 mm. **Ruler:** Elizabeth II **Subject:** Christmas **Obv:** Crowned head right **Rev:** Mary and Joseph with child **Shape:** 7-sided

Date	Mintage	F	VF	XF	Unc	BU
1990 Proof	50				Value: 1,450	

KM# 83b 50 PENCE
26.0000 g., 0.9170 Gold .7665 oz. AGW, 30 mm. **Ruler:** Elizabeth II **Subject:** Christmas **Obv:** Crowned head right **Rev:** Family caroling **Shape:** 7-sided

Date	Mintage	F	VF	XF	Unc	BU
1991 Proof	250				Value: 685	

KM# 83c 50 PENCE
30.4000 g., 0.9500 Platinum .9286 oz. APW, 30 mm. **Ruler:** Elizabeth II **Subject:** Christmas **Obv:** Crowned head right **Rev:** Family caroling **Shape:** 7-sided

Date	Mintage	F	VF	XF	Unc	BU
1991 Proof	50				Value: 1,375	

KM# 108b 50 PENCE
26.0000 g., 0.9170 Gold .7665 oz. AGW, 30 mm. **Ruler:** Elizabeth II **Subject:** Christmas **Obv:** Crowned head right **Rev:** Bust of Santa facing **Shape:** 7-sided

Date	Mintage	F	VF	XF	Unc	BU
1992 Proof	250				Value: 685	

KM# 108c 50 PENCE
30.4000 g., 0.9950 Platinum .9725 oz. APW, 30 mm. **Ruler:** Elizabeth II **Subject:** Christmas **Obv:** Crowned head right **Rev:** Bust of Santa facing **Shape:** 7-sided

Date	Mintage	F	VF	XF	Unc	BU
1992 Proof	50				Value: 1,450	

KM# 190b 50 PENCE
26.0000 g., 0.9170 Gold .7665 oz. AGW, 30 mm. **Ruler:** Elizabeth II **Subject:** Christmas **Obv:** Crowned head right **Rev:** Santa in automobile **Shape:** 7-sided

Date	Mintage	F	VF	XF	Unc	BU
1993 Proof	Est. 250				Value: 685	

KM# 190c 50 PENCE
30.4000 g., 0.9500 Platinum .9286 oz. APW, 30 mm. **Ruler:** Elizabeth II **Subject:** Christmas **Obv:** Crowned head right **Rev:** Santa in automobile **Shape:** 7-sided

Date	Mintage	F	VF	XF	Unc	BU
1993 Proof	Est. 50				Value: 1,375	

KM# 294b 50 PENCE
26.0000 g., 0.9170 Gold .7665 oz. AGW, 30 mm. **Ruler:** Elizabeth II **Subject:** Christmas **Obv:** Crowned head right **Rev:** Santa with sack and hot air balloon **Shape:** 7-sided

Date	Mintage	F	VF	XF	Unc	BU
1994 Proof	Est. 250				Value: 700	

KM# 294c 50 PENCE
30.4000 g., 0.9500 Platinum .9286 oz. APW, 30 mm. **Ruler:** Elizabeth II **Subject:** Christmas **Obv:** Crowned head right **Rev:** Santa with sack and hot air balloon **Shape:** 7-sided

Date	Mintage	F	VF	XF	Unc	BU
1994 Proof	Est. 50				Value: 1,375	

KM# 336b 50 PENCE
26.0000 g., 0.9170 Gold .7665 oz. AGW, 30 mm. **Ruler:** Elizabeth II **Subject:** Christmas **Obv:** Crowned head right **Rev:** Penguins parading **Shape:** 7-sided

Date	Mintage	F	VF	XF	Unc	BU
1995 Proof	Est. 250				Value: 700	

KM# 336c 50 PENCE
30.4000 g., 0.9950 Platinum .9769 oz. APW, 30 mm. **Ruler:** Elizabeth II **Subject:** Christmas **Obv:** Crowned head right **Rev:** Penguins parading **Shape:** 7-sided

Date	Mintage	F	VF	XF	Unc	BU
1995 Proof	50				Value: 1,450	

KM# 453b 50 PENCE
26.0000 g., 0.9170 Gold .7665 oz. AGW, 30 mm. **Ruler:** Elizabeth II **Subject:** Christmas **Obv:** Crowned head right **Rev:** Santa Claus and biplane **Shape:** 7-sided

Date	Mintage	F	VF	XF	Unc	BU
1996 Proof	Est. 250				Value: 645	

KM# 606b 50 PENCE
8.0000 g., 0.9170 Gold .2359 oz. AGW, 27.3 mm. **Ruler:** Elizabeth II **Subject:** Christmas **Obv:** Crowned head right **Rev:** Santa in sleigh **Shape:** 7-sided

Date	Mintage	F	VF	XF	Unc	BU
1997 Proof	Est. 250				Value: 550	

KM# 39.1b 50 PENCE
8.0000 g., 0.9999 Gold .2569 oz. AGW, 27.3 mm. **Ruler:** Elizabeth II **Obv:** Crowned head right **Rev:** Dolphins surround denomination **Shape:** 7-sided

Date	Mintage	F	VF	XF	Unc	BU
1997 Proof	Est. 250				Value: 400	

KM# 769b 50 PENCE
8.0000 g., 0.9170 Gold .2359 oz. AGW, 27.3 mm. **Ruler:** Elizabeth II **Obv:** Head with tiara right **Rev:** Santa Claus in chimney **Shape:** 7-sided

Date	Mintage	F	VF	XF	Unc	BU
1998 Proof	Est. 250				Value: 550	

KM# 866b 50 PENCE
8.0000 g., 0.9170 Gold .2359 oz. AGW, 27.3 mm. **Ruler:** Elizabeth II **Obv:** Head with tiara right **Rev:** Santa with pair of monkeys **Shape:** 7-sided

Date	Mintage	F	VF	XF	Unc	BU
1999 Proof	Est. 250				Value: 550	

KM# 887b 50 PENCE
8.0000 g., 0.9160 Gold .2356 oz. AGW, 27.3 mm. **Ruler:** Elizabeth II **Subject:** Christmas **Obv:** Head with tiara right **Rev:** Madonna and child with angels **Shape:** 7-sided **Note:** KM#310-317 previously listed here do not exist and have been removed.

Date	Mintage	F	VF	XF	Unc	BU
2000 Proof	250				Value: 550	

KM# 310 1/25 CROWN
1.2440 g., 0.9990 Gold 0.04 oz. AGW, 13.9 mm. **Ruler:** Elizabeth II **Subject:** Barcelona Olympics **Obv:** Crowned bust right **Rev:** Ancient discus thrower within circle, denomination below **Edge:** Reeded

Date	Mintage	F	VF	XF	Unc	BU
1991 Proof	—				Value: 45.00	

KM# 311 1/25 CROWN
1.2440 g., 0.9990 Gold 0.04 oz. AGW, 13.9 mm. **Ruler:** Elizabeth II **Subject:** Barcelona Olympics **Obv:** Crowned bust right **Rev:** Ancient chariot racers within circle, denomination below **Edge:** Reeded

Date	Mintage	F	VF	XF	Unc	BU
1991 Proof	—				Value: 45.00	

KM# 312 1/25 CROWN
1.2440 g., 0.9990 Gold 0.04 oz. AGW, 13.9 mm. **Ruler:** Elizabeth II **Subject:** Barcelona Olympics **Obv:** Crowned bust right **Rev:** Ancient runners within circle, denomination below **Edge:** Reeded

Date	Mintage	F	VF	XF	Unc	BU
1991 Proof	—				Value: 45.00	

KM# 313 1/25 CROWN
1.2440 g., 0.9990 Gold 0.04 oz. AGW, 13.9 mm. **Ruler:** Elizabeth II **Subject:** Barcelona Olympics **Obv:** Crowned bust right **Rev:** Ancient javelin thrower within circle, denomination below **Edge:** Reeded

Date	Mintage	F	VF	XF	Unc	BU
1991 Proof	—				Value: 45.00	

KM# 314 1/25 CROWN
1.2440 g., 0.9990 Gold 0.04 oz. AGW, 13.9 mm. **Ruler:** Elizabeth II **Subject:** Barcelona Olympics **Obv:** Crowned bust right **Rev:** Ancient wrestlers, head at left looking right, circle surrounds **Edge:** Reeded

Date	Mintage	F	VF	XF	Unc	BU
1991 Proof	—				Value: 45.00	

KM# 315 1/25 CROWN
1.2440 g., 0.9990 Gold 0.04 oz. AGW, 13.9 mm. **Ruler:** Elizabeth II **Subject:** Barcelona Olympics **Obv:** Crowned bust right **Rev:** Ancient boxer within circle, denomination below **Edge:** Reeded

Date	Mintage	F	VF	XF	Unc	BU
1991 Proof	—				Value: 45.00	

KM# 316 1/25 CROWN
1.2440 g., 0.9990 Gold 0.04 oz. AGW, 13.9 mm. **Ruler:** Elizabeth II **Subject:** Barcelona Olympics **Obv:** Crowned bust right **Rev:** Long jumper within circle, denomination below **Edge:** Reeded

Date	Mintage	F	VF	XF	Unc	BU
1991 Proof	—				Value: 45.00	

KM# 317 1/25 CROWN
1.2440 g., 0.9990 Gold 0.04 oz. AGW, 13.9 mm. **Ruler:** Elizabeth II **Subject:** Barcelona Olympics **Obv:** Crowned bust right **Rev:** Ancient victor wearing laurels, denomination below **Edge:** Reeded

Date	Mintage	F	VF	XF	Unc	BU
1991 Proof	—				Value: 45.00	

KM# 124 1/25 CROWN
1.2440 g., 0.9990 Gold 0.04 oz. AGW, 13.9 mm. **Ruler:** Elizabeth II **Rev:** Japanese Royal Wedding

Date	Mintage	F	VF	XF	Unc	BU
1993 Proof	Est. 25,000				Value: 50.00	

KM# 183 1/25 CROWN
1.2440 g., 0.9990 Gold 0.04 oz. AGW, 13.9 mm. **Ruler:** Elizabeth II **Obv:** Crowned bust right **Rev:** Stylized panda **Edge:** Reeded

Date	Mintage	F	VF	XF	Unc	BU
1993 Proof	—				Value: 50.00	

KM# 187 1/25 CROWN
1.2440 g., 0.9990 Gold 0.04 oz. AGW, 13.9 mm. **Ruler:** Elizabeth II **Obv:** Crowned bust right **Rev:** Natural panda amongst bamboo shoots **Edge:** Reeded

Date	Mintage	F	VF	XF	Unc	BU
1993 Proof	—				Value: 50.00	

KM# 202 1/25 CROWN
1.2440 g., 0.9999 Gold .0400 oz. AGW, 13.9 mm. **Ruler:** Elizabeth II **Series:** Peter Rabbit Centennial **Subject:** The Tale of Peter Rabbit **Obv:** Crowned bust right **Rev:** Peter Rabbit eating carrots

Date	Mintage	F	VF	XF	Unc	BU
1993 Proof	Est. 25,000				Value: 40.00	

KM# 202a 1/25 CROWN
1.2440 g., 0.9950 Platinum .0400 oz. APW, 13.9 mm. **Ruler:** Elizabeth II **Series:** Peter Rabbit Centennial **Subject:** The Tale of Peter Rabbit **Obv:** Crowned bust right **Rev:** Peter Rabbit eating carrots

Date	Mintage	F	VF	XF	Unc	BU
1993 Proof	7,500				Value: 65.00	

KM# 206 1/25 CROWN
1.2440 g., 0.9999 Gold .0400 oz. AGW, 13.9 mm. **Ruler:** Elizabeth II **Series:** Peter Rabbit Centennial **Subject:** The Tale of Peter Rabbit **Obv:** Crowned bust right **Rev:** Mrs. Tiggy-Winkel ironing

Date	Mintage	F	VF	XF	Unc	BU
1993 Proof	Est. 25,000				Value: 40.00	

KM# 210 1/25 CROWN
1.2440 g., 0.9999 Gold .0400 oz. AGW, 13.9 mm. **Ruler:** Elizabeth II **Series:** Peter Rabbit Centennial **Subject:** The Tale of Peter Rabbit **Obv:** Crowned bust right **Rev:** Jeremy Fisher fishing

Date	Mintage	F	VF	XF	Unc	BU
1993 Proof	Est. 25,000				Value: 40.00	

KM# 214 1/25 CROWN

1.2440 g., 0.9999 Gold .0400 oz. AGW, 13.9 mm. **Ruler:** Elizabeth II **Series:** Peter Rabbit Centennial **Subject:** The Tale of Peter Rabbit **Obv:** Crowned bust right **Rev:** Tom Kitten with mother cat

Date	Mintage	F	VF	XF	Unc	BU
1993 Proof	Est. 25,000	Value: 40.00				

KM# 218 1/25 CROWN

1.2440 g., 0.9999 Gold .0400 oz. AGW, 13.9 mm. **Ruler:** Elizabeth II **Series:** Peter Rabbit Centennial **Subject:** The Tale of Peter Rabbit **Obv:** Crowned bust right **Rev:** Benjamin Bunny wearing hat and holding coat

Date	Mintage	F	VF	XF	Unc	BU
1993 Proof	Est. 25,000	Value: 40.00				

KM# 222 1/25 CROWN

1.2440 g., 0.9999 Gold .0400 oz. AGW, 13.9 mm. **Ruler:** Elizabeth II **Series:** Peter Rabbit Centennial **Subject:** The Tale of Peter Rabbit **Obv:** Crowned bust right **Rev:** Jemima Puddle Duck talking with fox

Date	Mintage	F	VF	XF	Unc	BU
1993 Proof	Est. 25,000	Value: 40.00				

KM# 437 1/25 CROWN

1.2440 g., 0.9999 Gold .0400 oz. AGW, 13.9 mm. **Ruler:** Elizabeth II **Series:** Peter Rabbit Centennial **Subject:** The Tale of Peter Rabbit **Obv:** Crowned bust right **Rev:** Mother and bunnies

Date	Mintage	F	VF	XF	Unc	BU
1994 Proof	25,000	Value: 45.00				

KM# 437a 1/25 CROWN

1.2440 g., 0.9950 Platinum .0400 oz. APW, 13.9 mm. **Ruler:** Elizabeth II **Series:** Peter Rabbit Centennial **Subject:** The Tale of Peter Rabbit **Obv:** Crowned bust right **Rev:** Mother and bunnies

Date	Mintage	F	VF	XF	Unc	BU
1994 Proof	Est. 7,500	Value: 65.00				

KM# 368 1/25 CROWN

1.2441 g., 0.9999 Gold .0400 oz. AGW, 13.9 mm. **Ruler:** Elizabeth II **Obv:** Crowned bust right **Rev:** Roses

Date	Mintage	F	VF	XF	Unc	BU
1996 Proof	Est. 25,000	Value: 45.00				

KM# 375 1/25 CROWN

1.2441 g., 0.9999 Gold .0400 oz. AGW, 13.9 mm. **Ruler:** Elizabeth II **Series:** Peter Rabbit Centennial **Subject:** The Tale of Peter Rabbit **Obv:** Crowned bust right **Rev:** Rabbit escaping the garden

Date	Mintage	F	VF	XF	Unc	BU
1996 Proof	Est. 25,000	Value: 45.00				

KM# 375a 1/25 CROWN

1.2500 g., 0.9950 Platinum .0400 oz. APW, 13.9 mm. **Ruler:** Elizabeth II **Series:** Peter Rabbit Centennial **Subject:** The Tale of Peter Rabbit **Obv:** Crowned bust right **Rev:** Rabbit escaping the garden

Date	Mintage	F	VF	XF	Unc	BU
1996 Proof	Est. 7,500	Value: 65.00				

KM# 390 1/25 CROWN

1.2441 g., 0.9999 Gold .0400 oz. AGW, 13.9 mm. **Ruler:** Elizabeth II **Series:** Centenary of the Cinema **Subject:** Grace Kelly - actress, 1929-82 **Obv:** Crowned bust right **Rev:** Bust 3/4 facing, denomination

Date	Mintage	F	VF	XF	Unc	BU
1996 Proof	Est. 25,000	Value: 45.00				

KM# 395 1/25 CROWN

1.2441 g., 0.9999 Gold .0400 oz. AGW, 13.9 mm. **Ruler:** Elizabeth II **Series:** Centenary of the Cinema **Subject:** James Dean **Obv:** Crowned bust right **Rev:** Standing central figure, dates at right

Date	Mintage	F	VF	XF	Unc	BU
1996 Proof	Est. 25,000	Value: 45.00				

KM# 400 1/25 CROWN

1.2441 g., 0.9999 Gold .0400 oz. AGW, 13.9 mm. **Ruler:** Elizabeth II **Series:** Centenary of the Cinema **Subject:** Marilyn Monroe - actress, 1926-62 **Obv:** Crowned bust right **Rev:** Bust looking back over shoulder

Date	Mintage	F	VF	XF	Unc	BU
1996 Proof	Est. 25,000	Value: 45.00				

KM# 405 1/25 CROWN

1.2441 g., 0.9999 Gold .0400 oz. AGW, 13.9 mm. **Ruler:** Elizabeth II **Series:** Centenary of the Cinema **Subject:** Audrey Hepburn - actress, 1929-93 **Obv:** Crowned bust right **Rev:** Head 3/4 facing

Date	Mintage	F	VF	XF	Unc	BU
1996 Proof	25,000	Value: 45.00				

KM# 405a 1/25 CROWN

1.2500 g., 0.9950 Platinum .0400 oz. APW, 13.9 mm. **Ruler:** Elizabeth II **Series:** Centenary of the Cinema **Subject:** Audrey Hepburn - actress, 1929-93 **Obv:** Crowned bust right **Rev:** Head 3/4 facing

Date	Mintage	F	VF	XF	Unc	BU
1996 Proof	Est. 1,000	Value: 75.00				

KM# 410 1/25 CROWN

1.2441 g., 0.9999 Gold .0400 oz. AGW, 13.9 mm. **Ruler:** Elizabeth II **Series:** Centenary of the Cinema **Subject:** Bruce Lee - actor, 1940-73 **Obv:** Crowned bust right **Rev:** Kickboxer and chinese dragon

Date	Mintage	F	VF	XF	Unc	BU
1996 Proof	Est. 25,000	Value: 55.00				

KM# 415 1/25 CROWN

1.2441 g., 0.9999 Gold .0400 oz. AGW, 13.9 mm. **Ruler:** Elizabeth II **Series:** Centenary of the Cinema **Subject:** Charlie Chaplan - actor, 1889-1977 **Obv:** Crowned bust right **Rev:** Standing central figure with cane, dates

Date	Mintage	F	VF	XF	Unc	BU
1996 Proof	Est. 25,000	Value: 55.00				

KM# 420 1/25 CROWN

1.2441 g., 0.9999 Gold .0400 oz. AGW, 13.9 mm. **Ruler:** Elizabeth II **Series:** Centenary of the Cinema **Subject:** Gone With The Wind **Obv:** Crowned bust right **Rev:** Rhett Butler and Scarlett O'Hara

Date	Mintage	F	VF	XF	Unc	BU
1996 Proof	Est. 25,000	Value: 55.00				

KM# 425 1/25 CROWN

1.2441 g., 0.9999 Gold .0400 oz. AGW, 13.9 mm. **Ruler:** Elizabeth II **Series:** Centenary of the Cinema **Obv:** Crowned bust right **Rev:** The Flintstones

Date	Mintage	F	VF	XF	Unc	BU
1996 Proof	Est. 25,000	Value: 55.00				

KM# 452 1/25 CROWN

1.2441 g., 0.9999 Gold .0400 oz. AGW, 13.9 mm. **Ruler:** Elizabeth II **Series:** Centenary of the Cinema **Subject:** James Dean - actor, 1931-55 **Obv:** Crowned bust right **Rev:** Standing central figure, dates

Date	Mintage	F	VF	XF	Unc	BU
1996 Proof	Est. 25,000	Value: 60.00				

KM# 454 1/25 CROWN

1.2441 g., 0.9999 Gold .0400 oz. AGW, 13.9 mm. **Ruler:** Elizabeth II **Series:** Centenary of the Cinema **Subject:** Wizard of Oz **Obv:** Crowned bust right **Rev:** Characters of Oz

Date	Mintage	F	VF	XF	Unc	BU
1996 Proof	Est. 25,000	Value: 45.00				

KM# 458 1/25 CROWN

1.2441 g., 0.9999 Gold .0400 oz. AGW, 13.9 mm. **Ruler:** Elizabeth II **Series:** Centenary of the Cinema **Subject:** The Marx Brothers - actors **Obv:** Crowned bust right **Rev:** Three busts 3/4 left

Date	Mintage	F	VF	XF	Unc	BU
1996 Proof	Est. 25,000	Value: 45.00				

KM# 462 1/25 CROWN

1.2441 g., 0.9999 Gold .0400 oz. AGW, 13.9 mm. **Ruler:** Elizabeth II **Series:** Centenary of the Cinema **Subject:** Elvis Presley - actor/entertainer, 1935-77 **Obv:** Crowned bust right **Rev:** Guitar beneath and behind bust 3/4 left

Date	Mintage	F	VF	XF	Unc	BU
1996 Proof	Est. 25,000	Value: 45.00				

KM# 466 1/25 CROWN

1.2441 g., 0.9999 Gold .0400 oz. AGW, 13.9 mm. **Ruler:** Elizabeth II **Series:** Centenary of the Cinema **Subject:** Casablanca **Obv:** Crowned bust right **Rev:** Bogart and Bergman

Date	Mintage	F	VF	XF	Unc	BU
1996 Proof	Est. 25,000	Value: 45.00				

KM# 470 1/25 CROWN

1.2441 g., 0.9999 Gold .0400 oz. AGW, 13.9 mm. **Ruler:** Elizabeth II **Series:** Centenary of the Cinema **Obv:** Crowned bust right **Rev:** E.T.

Date	Mintage	F	VF	XF	Unc	BU
1996 Proof	Est. 25,000	Value: 45.00				

KM# 474 1/25 CROWN

1.2441 g., 0.9999 Gold .0400 oz. AGW, 13.9 mm. **Ruler:** Elizabeth II **Series:** Centenary of the Cinema **Subject:** Alfred Hitchcock - Producer/Director, 1899-1980 **Obv:** Crowned bust right **Rev:** Bust facing looking at bird on left shoulder

Date	Mintage	F	VF	XF	Unc	BU
1996 Proof	Est. 25,000	Value: 45.00				

KM# 518 1/25 CROWN

1.2441 g., 0.9999 Gold .0400 oz. AGW, 13.9 mm. **Ruler:** Elizabeth II **Subject:** The Tale of Peter Rabbit **Obv:** Crowned bust right **Rev:** Standing rabbit

Date	Mintage	F	VF	XF	Unc	BU
1997 Proof	Est. 25,000	Value: 45.00				

KM# 518a 1/25 CROWN

1.2504 g., 0.9950 Platinum .0400 oz. APW, 13.9 mm. **Ruler:** Elizabeth II **Subject:** The Tale of Peter Rabbit **Obv:** Crowned bust right **Rev:** Standing rabbit

Date	Mintage	F	VF	XF	Unc	BU
1997 Proof	Est. 7,500	Value: 65.00				

KM# 537 1/25 CROWN

1.2440 g., 0.9999 Gold .0400 oz. AGW, 13.9 mm. **Ruler:** Elizabeth II **Obv:** Crowned bust right **Rev:** Peonies

Date	Mintage	F	VF	XF	Unc	BU
1997 Proof	Est. 25,000	Value: 45.00				

KM# 541 1/25 CROWN

1.2440 g., 0.9999 Gold .0400 oz. AGW, 13.9 mm. **Ruler:** Elizabeth II **Subject:** Nefertiti **Obv:** Crowned bust right **Rev:** Head right

Date	Mintage	F	VF	XF	Unc	BU
1997 Proof	Est. 10,000	Value: 45.00				

KM# 545 1/25 CROWN

1.2440 g., 0.9999 Gold .0400 oz. AGW, 13.9 mm. **Ruler:** Elizabeth II **Subject:** Cleopatra **Obv:** Crowned bust right **Rev:** Head facing

Date	Mintage	F	VF	XF	Unc	BU
1997 Proof	Est. 10,000	Value: 45.00				

KM# 549 1/25 CROWN

1.2440 g., 0.9999 Gold .0400 oz. AGW, 13.9 mm. **Ruler:** Elizabeth II **Subject:** Europa **Obv:** Crowned bust right **Rev:** Head 1/4 left

Date	Mintage	F	VF	XF	Unc	BU
1997 Proof	Est. 10,000	Value: 45.00				

KM# 553 1/25 CROWN

1.2440 g., 0.9999 Gold .0400 oz. AGW, 13.9 mm. **Ruler:** Elizabeth II **Subject:** Liberty **Obv:** Crowned bust right **Rev:** Laureate head right

Date	Mintage	F	VF	XF	Unc	BU
1997 Proof	Est. 10,000	Value: 45.00				

KM# 581 1/25 CROWN

1.2440 g., 0.9999 Gold .0400 oz. AGW, 13.9 mm. **Ruler:** Elizabeth II **Series:** Evolution of Mankind **Subject:** Egypt **Obv:** Crowned bust right **Rev:** Three ancient Egyptians, pyramids, hieroglyphics

Date	Mintage	F	VF	XF	Unc	BU
1997 Proof	Est. 15,000	Value: 40.00				

KM# 583 1/25 CROWN

1.2440 g., 0.9999 Gold .0400 oz. AGW, 13.9 mm. **Ruler:** Elizabeth II **Series:** Evolution of Mankind **Subject:** Israel **Obv:** Crowned bust right **Rev:** Star of David, Moses and Temple of Solomon

Date	Mintage	F	VF	XF	Unc	BU
1997 Proof	Est. 15,000	Value: 40.00				

KM# 585 1/25 CROWN

1.2440 g., 0.9999 Gold .0400 oz. AGW, 13.9 mm. **Ruler:** Elizabeth II **Series:** Evolution of Mankind **Subject:** China **Obv:** Crowned bust right **Rev:** Emperor and the Great Wall

Date	Mintage	F	VF	XF	Unc	BU
1997 Proof	Est. 15,000	Value: 40.00				

KM# 587 1/25 CROWN

1.2440 g., 0.9999 Gold .0400 oz. AGW, 13.9 mm. **Ruler:** Elizabeth II **Series:** Evolution of Mankind **Subject:** Greece **Obv:** Crowned bust right **Rev:** Aristotle, classic Greek building

Date	Mintage	F	VF	XF	Unc	BU
1997 Proof	Est. 15,000	Value: 40.00				

KM# 589 1/25 CROWN

1.2440 g., 0.9999 Gold .0400 oz. AGW, 13.9 mm. **Ruler:** Elizabeth II **Series:** Evolution of Mankind **Subject:** Rome **Obv:** Crowned bust right **Rev:** Julius Caesar and Stonehenge

Date	Mintage	F	VF	XF	Unc	BU
1997 Proof	Est. 15,000	Value: 40.00				

KM# 591 1/25 CROWN

1.2440 g., 0.9999 Gold .0400 oz. AGW, 13.9 mm. **Ruler:** Elizabeth II **Series:** Evolution of Mankind **Subject:** India **Obv:** Crowned bust right **Rev:** Krishna playing flute by a temple

Date	Mintage	F	VF	XF	Unc	BU
1997 Proof	Est. 15,000	Value: 40.00				

KM# 593 1/25 CROWN

1.2440 g., 0.9999 Gold .0400 oz. AGW, 13.9 mm. **Ruler:** Elizabeth II **Series:** Evolution of Mankind **Subject:** Holy Roman Empire **Obv:** Crowned bust right **Rev:** Charlemagne and soldiers on horseback

Date	Mintage	F	VF	XF	Unc	BU
1997 Proof	Est. 15,000	Value: 40.00				

KM# 595 1/25 CROWN

1.2440 g., 0.9999 Gold .0400 oz. AGW, 13.9 mm. **Ruler:** Elizabeth II **Series:** Evolution of Mankind **Subject:** Macedonia **Obv:** Crowned bust right **Rev:** Alexander the Great on horseback

Date	Mintage	F	VF	XF	Unc	BU
1997 Proof	Est. 15,000	Value: 40.00				

KM# 597 1/25 CROWN

1.2440 g., 0.9999 Gold .0400 oz. AGW, 13.9 mm. **Ruler:** Elizabeth II **Series:** Evolution of Mankind **Subject:** Native America **Obv:** Crowned bust right **Rev:** Native american on horseback, totem pole at left

Date	Mintage	F	VF	XF	Unc	BU
1997 Proof	Est. 15,000	Value: 40.00				

KM# 599 1/25 CROWN

1.2440 g., 0.9999 Gold .0400 oz. AGW, 13.9 mm. **Ruler:** Elizabeth II **Series:** Evolution of Mankind **Subject:** Asia **Obv:** Crowned bust right **Rev:** Buddha and temple

Date	Mintage	F	VF	XF	Unc	BU
1997 Proof	Est. 15,000	Value: 40.00				

KM# 601 1/25 CROWN

1.2440 g., 0.9999 Gold .0400 oz. AGW, 13.9 mm. **Ruler:** Elizabeth II **Series:** Evolution of Mankind **Subject:** Inca Empire **Obv:** Crowned bust right **Rev:** Incan Emperor and Machu Picchu

Date	Mintage	F	VF	XF	Unc	BU
1997 Proof	Est. 15,000	Value: 40.00				

KM# 603 1/25 CROWN

1.2440 g., 0.9999 Gold .0400 oz. AGW, 13.9 mm. **Ruler:** Elizabeth II **Series:** Evolution of Mankind **Subject:** Islamic Civilization **Obv:** Crowned bust right **Rev:** General Tariq Ibn Ziyad and building

Date	Mintage	F	VF	XF	Unc	BU
1997 Proof	Est. 15,000	Value: 40.00				

KM# 608 1/25 CROWN

1.2440 g., 0.9999 Gold .0400 oz. AGW, 13.9 mm. **Ruler:** Elizabeth II **Series:** Traders of the World **Subject:** Sir Francis Drake **Obv:** Crowned bust right **Rev:** Bust at right, ship and beach

Date	Mintage	F	VF	XF	Unc	BU
1997 Proof	Est. 15,000	Value: 45.00				

KM# 610 1/25 CROWN

1.2440 g., 0.9999 Gold .0400 oz. AGW, 13.9 mm. **Ruler:** Elizabeth II **Series:** Traders of the World **Subject:** Romans **Obv:** Crowned bust right **Rev:** Lion, lioness, ship, map

Date	Mintage	F	VF	XF	Unc	BU
1997 Proof	Est. 15,000	Value: 45.00				

KM# 612 1/25 CROWN
1.2440 g., 0.9999 Gold .0400 oz. AGW, 13.9 mm. **Ruler:** Elizabeth II **Series:** Traders of the World **Subject:** Venetians **Obv:** Crowned bust right **Rev:** Pair of oysters with pearls, Venetian canal scene

Date	Mintage	F	VF	XF	Unc	BU
1997 Proof	Est. 15,000	Value: 45.00				

KM# 614 1/25 CROWN
1.2440 g., 0.9999 Gold .0400 oz. AGW, 13.9 mm. **Ruler:** Elizabeth II **Series:** Traders of the World **Subject:** Portuguese **Obv:** Crowned bust right **Rev:** Gold ingots and Portuguese ship

Date	Mintage	F	VF	XF	Unc	BU
1997 Proof	Est. 15,000	Value: 45.00				

KM# 616 1/25 CROWN
1.2440 g., 0.9999 Gold .0400 oz. AGW, 13.9 mm. **Ruler:** Elizabeth II **Series:** Traders of the World **Subject:** Spanish **Obv:** Crowned bust right **Rev:** Tobacco leaves, ship, map and gems

Date	Mintage	F	VF	XF	Unc	BU
1997 Proof	Est. 15,000	Value: 45.00				

KM# 618 1/25 CROWN
1.2440 g., 0.9999 Gold .0400 oz. AGW, 13.9 mm. **Ruler:** Elizabeth II **Series:** Traders of the World **Subject:** English **Obv:** Crowned bust right **Rev:** Profile of Queen above fighting ships

Date	Mintage	F	VF	XF	Unc	BU
1997 Proof	Est. 15,000	Value: 45.00				

KM# 620 1/25 CROWN
1.2440 g., 0.9999 Gold .0400 oz. AGW, 13.9 mm. **Ruler:** Elizabeth II **Series:** Traders of the World **Subject:** Captain Bligh **Obv:** Crowned bust right **Rev:** Figure sitting on rock on beach, ship in background

Date	Mintage	F	VF	XF	Unc	BU
1997 Proof	Est. 15,000	Value: 45.00				

KM# 622 1/25 CROWN
1.2440 g., 0.9999 Gold .0400 oz. AGW **Series:** Traders of the World **Subject:** Captain Cook **Obv:** Crowned bust right **Rev:** Beaver on rock, ship, bust in background

Date	Mintage	F	VF	XF	Unc	BU
1997 Proof	Est. 15,000	Value: 45.00				

KM# 649 1/25 CROWN
1.2440 g., 0.9999 Gold .0400 oz. AGW, 13.9 mm. **Ruler:** Elizabeth II **Subject:** The Tale of Peter Rabbit **Obv:** Crowned bust right **Rev:** Standing rabbit facing

Date	Mintage	F	VF	XF	Unc	BU
1998 Proof	Est. 25,000	Value: 45.00				

KM# 649a 1/25 CROWN
1.2441 g., 0.9950 Platinum .0398 oz. APW, 13.9 mm. **Ruler:** Elizabeth II **Subject:** The Tale of Peter Rabbit **Obv:** Crowned bust right **Rev:** Standing rabbit facing

Date	Mintage	F	VF	XF	Unc	BU
1998 Proof	Est. 7,500	Value: 65.00				

KM# 657 1/25 CROWN
1.2441 g., 0.9999 Gold .0400 oz. AGW, 13.9 mm. **Ruler:** Elizabeth II **Subject:** Chrysanthemum **Obv:** Crowned bust right **Rev:** Three blossoms

Date	Mintage	F	VF	XF	Unc	BU
1998 Proof	Est. 25,000	Value: 45.00				

KM# 662 1/25 CROWN
1.2441 g., 0.9999 Gold .0400 oz. AGW, 13.9 mm. **Ruler:** Elizabeth II **Subject:** Britannia **Obv:** Crowned bust right **Rev:** Helmeted head right

Date	Mintage	F	VF	XF	Unc	BU
1998 Proof	Est. 10,000	Value: 45.00				

KM# 663 1/25 CROWN
1.2441 g., 0.9999 Gold .0400 oz. AGW, 13.9 mm. **Ruler:** Elizabeth II **Subject:** Juno **Obv:** Crowned bust right **Rev:** Head facing

Date	Mintage	F	VF	XF	Unc	BU
1998 Proof	Est. 10,000	Value: 45.00				

KM# 664 1/25 CROWN
1.2441 g., 0.9999 Gold .0400 oz. AGW, 13.9 mm. **Ruler:** Elizabeth II **Subject:** Athena **Obv:** Crowned bust right **Rev:** Helmeted head right

Date	Mintage	F	VF	XF	Unc	BU
1998 Proof	Est. 10,000	Value: 45.00				

KM# 665 1/25 CROWN
1.2441 g., 0.9999 Gold .0400 oz. AGW, 13.9 mm. **Subject:** Arethusa **Obv:** Crowned bust right **Rev:** Head left with dolphins

Date	Mintage	F	VF	XF	Unc	BU
1998 Proof	Est. 10,000	Value: 45.00				

KM# 678 1/25 CROWN
1.2441 g., 0.9999 Gold .0400 oz. AGW, 13.9 mm. **Ruler:** Elizabeth II **Obv:** Crowned bust right **Rev:** Paddington with suitcase

Date	Mintage	F	VF	XF	Unc	BU
1998 Proof	Est. 7,500	Value: 45.00				

KM# 678a 1/25 CROWN
1.2440 g., 0.9950 Platinum .0400 oz. APW, 13.9 mm. **Ruler:** Elizabeth II **Obv:** Crowned bust right **Rev:** Paddington with suitcase

Date	Mintage	F	VF	XF	Unc	BU
1998 Proof	Est. 5,000	Value: 65.00				

KM# 691 1/25 CROWN
1.2440 g., 0.9999 Gold .0400 oz. AGW, 13.9 mm. **Ruler:** Elizabeth II **Series:** Traders of the World **Subject:** Phoenecians, 200BC-600AD **Obv:** Crowned bust right **Rev:** Phoenician Galley, shells below

Date	Mintage	F	VF	XF	Unc	BU
1998 Proof	Est. 10,000	Value: 45.00				

KM# 693 1/25 CROWN
1.2440 g., 0.9999 Gold .0400 oz. AGW, 13.9 mm. **Ruler:** Elizabeth II **Series:** Traders of the World **Subject:** Vikings **Obv:** Crowned bust right **Rev:** Viking ship (900 AD), pair of fish

Date	Mintage	F	VF	XF	Unc	BU
1998 Proof	Est. 10,000	Value: 45.00				

KM# 695 1/25 CROWN
1.2440 g., 0.9999 Gold .0400 oz. AGW, 13.9 mm. **Ruler:** Elizabeth II **Series:** Traders of the World **Subject:** Marco Polo, 1254-1324 **Obv:** Crowned bust right **Rev:** Bust at right facing, ship at left

Date	Mintage	F	VF	XF	Unc	BU
1998 Proof	Est. 10,000	Value: 45.00				

KM# 697 1/25 CROWN
1.2440 g., 0.9999 Gold .0400 oz. AGW, 13.9 mm. **Ruler:** Elizabeth II **Series:** Traders of the World **Subject:** Hanseatic League Nations **Obv:** Crowned bust right **Rev:** Hanseatic Kogge (circa 1350), coins above ship

Date	Mintage	F	VF	XF	Unc	BU
1998 Proof	Est. 10,000	Value: 45.00				

KM# 699 1/25 CROWN
1.2440 g., 0.9999 Gold .0400 oz. AGW, 13.9 mm. **Ruler:** Elizabeth II **Series:** Traders of the World **Subject:** Chinese **Obv:** Crowned bust right **Rev:** Chinese Junk (1400s)

Date	Mintage	F	VF	XF	Unc	BU
1998 Proof	Est. 10,000	Value: 45.00				

KM# 701 1/25 CROWN
1.2440 g., 0.9999 Gold .0400 oz. AGW, 13.9 mm. **Ruler:** Elizabeth II **Series:** Traders of the World **Subject:** Christopher Columbus, 1451-1506 **Obv:** Crowned bust right **Rev:** Bust at left looking right and ship

Date	Mintage	F	VF	XF	Unc	BU
1998 Proof	Est. 10,000	Value: 45.00				

KM# 703 1/25 CROWN
1.2440 g., 0.9999 Gold .0400 oz. AGW, 13.9 mm. **Ruler:** Elizabeth II **Series:** Traders of the World **Subject:** Sir Walter Raleigh, 1552-1618 **Obv:** Crowned bust right **Rev:** Figure standing on beach, ship in background

Date	Mintage	F	VF	XF	Unc	BU
1998 Proof	Est. 10,000	Value: 45.00				

KM# 705 1/25 CROWN
1.2440 g., 0.9999 Gold .0400 oz. AGW, 13.9 mm. **Ruler:** Elizabeth II **Series:** Traders of the World **Obv:** Crowned bust right **Rev:** Sinking ships at the Boston Tea Party (1773), tea leaf

Date	Mintage	F	VF	XF	Unc	BU
1998 Proof	Est. 10,000	Value: 45.00				

KM# 707 1/25 CROWN
1.2440 g., 0.9999 Gold .0400 oz. AGW **Ruler:** Elizabeth II **Series:** Evolution of Mankind **Subject:** Australopithecus - Lucy **Obv:** Crowned head right **Rev:** Upright figure left, brain depiction at left

Date	Mintage	F	VF	XF	Unc	BU
1998 Proof	Est. 15,000	Value: 45.00				

KM# 709 1/25 CROWN
1.2440 g., 0.9999 Gold .0400 oz. AGW, 13.9 mm. **Ruler:** Elizabeth II **Series:** Traders of the World **Subject:** Homo Habilis **Obv:** Crowned head right **Rev:** Squatting figure using tools

Date	Mintage	F	VF	XF	Unc	BU
1998 Proof	Est. 15,000	Value: 45.00				

KM# 711 1/25 CROWN
1.2440 g., 0.9999 Gold .0400 oz. AGW, 13.9 mm. **Ruler:** Elizabeth II **Series:** Traders of the World **Subject:** Homo Erectus **Obv:** Crowned bust right **Rev:** Cave people using fire

Date	Mintage	F	VF	XF	Unc	BU
1998 Proof	Est. 15,000	Value: 45.00				

KM# 713 1/25 CROWN
1.2440 g., 0.9999 Gold .0400 oz. AGW, 13.9 mm. **Ruler:** Elizabeth II **Series:** Evolution of Mankind **Subject:** Gibraltar Skull **Obv:** Crowned bust right **Rev:** Caveman, skull and 'the rock'

Date	Mintage	F	VF	XF	Unc	BU
1998 Proof	Est. 15,000	Value: 45.00				

KM# 715 1/25 CROWN
1.2440 g., 0.9999 Gold .0400 oz. AGW, 13.9 mm. **Ruler:** Elizabeth II **Series:** Evolution of Mankind **Subject:** Neanderthal Man **Obv:** Crowned bust right **Rev:** Early man at burial scene, skull

Date	Mintage	F	VF	XF	Unc	BU
1998 Proof	Est. 15,000	Value: 45.00				

KM# 717 1/25 CROWN
1.2440 g., 0.9999 Gold .0400 oz. AGW, 13.9 mm. **Ruler:** Elizabeth II **Series:** Evolution of Mankind **Subject:** Homo Sapiens **Obv:** Crowned bust right **Rev:** Early man doing cave painting

Date	Mintage	F	VF	XF	Unc	BU
1998 Proof	Est. 15,000	Value: 45.00				

KM# 719 1/25 CROWN
1.2440 g., 0.9999 Gold .0400 oz. AGW, 13.9 mm. **Ruler:** Elizabeth II **Series:** Evolution of Mankind **Subject:** Homo Sapiens Hunting Mammoth **Obv:** Crowned bust right **Rev:** Figures spearing mammoth

Date	Mintage	F	VF	XF	Unc	BU
1998 Proof	Est. 15,000	Value: 45.00				

KM# 722 1/25 CROWN
1.2440 g., 0.9999 Gold .0400 oz. AGW, 13.9 mm. **Ruler:** Elizabeth II **Series:** Evolution of Mankind **Subject:** Theory of Evolution **Obv:** Crowned bust right **Rev:** Illustrated theory of evolution

Date	Mintage	F	VF	XF	Unc	BU
1998 Proof	Est. 15,000	Value: 45.00				

KM# 723 1/25 CROWN
1.2440 g., 0.9999 Gold .0400 oz. AGW, 13.9 mm. **Ruler:** Elizabeth II **Series:** Evolution of Mankind **Subject:** The Common Ancestry of Man and Ape **Obv:** Crowned bust right **Rev:** Human and primate mothers with young

Date	Mintage	F	VF	XF	Unc	BU
1998 Proof	Est. 15,000	Value: 45.00				

KM# 725 1/25 CROWN
1.2440 g., 0.9999 Gold .0400 oz. AGW, 13.9 mm. **Ruler:** Elizabeth II **Series:** Evolution of Mankind **Subject:** Charles Darwin **Obv:** Crowned bust right **Rev:** Bust facing, neanderthal and space shuttle

Date	Mintage	F	VF	XF	Unc	BU
1998 Proof	Est. 15,000	Value: 45.00				

KM# 727 1/25 CROWN
1.2440 g., 0.9999 Gold .0400 oz. AGW, 13.9 mm. **Ruler:** Elizabeth II **Series:** Evolution of Mankind **Subject:** Raymond Dart **Obv:** Crowned bust right **Rev:** Bust at left looking at skull on right

Date	Mintage	F	VF	XF	Unc	BU
1998 Proof	Est. 15,000	Value: 45.00				

KM# 729 1/25 CROWN
1.2440 g., 0.9999 Gold .0400 oz. AGW, 13.9 mm. **Ruler:** Elizabeth II **Series:** Evolution of Mankind **Subject:** 20th Century Homo Sapiens **Obv:** Crowned bust right **Rev:** Five depictions of evolution

Date	Mintage	F	VF	XF	Unc	BU
1998 Proof	Est. 15,000	Value: 45.00				

KM# 779.1 1/25 CROWN
1.2440 g., 0.9999 Gold .0400 oz. AGW, 13.9 mm. **Ruler:** Elizabeth II **Subject:** 1999 The Year of the Rabbit **Obv:** Crowned bust right **Rev:** Rabbit reading, sparrow and chinese characters

Date	Mintage	F	VF	XF	Unc	BU
1999 Proof	Est. 5,000	Value: 45.00				

KM# 779.1a 1/25 CROWN
1.2400 g., 0.9950 Platinum .0400 oz. APW, 13.9 mm. **Ruler:** Elizabeth II **Subject:** 1999 The Year of the Rabbit **Obv:** Crowned bust right **Rev:** Rabbit reading, sparrow and chinese characters

Date	Mintage	F	VF	XF	Unc	BU
1999 Proof	Est. 3,000	Value: 70.00				

KM# 779.2 1/25 CROWN
1.2440 g., 0.9999 Gold .0400 oz. AGW, 13.9 mm. **Ruler:** Elizabeth II **Subject:** The Year of the Rabbit **Obv:** Crowned bust right **Rev:** Rabbit reading, sparrow; without Chinese characters

Date	Mintage	F	VF	XF	Unc	BU
1999 Proof	Inc. above	Value: 45.00				

KM# 779.2a 1/25 CROWN
1.2400 g., 0.9950 Platinum .0400 oz. APW **Ruler:** Elizabeth II **Subject:** The Year of the Rabbit **Obv:** Crowned bust right **Rev:** Rabbit reading, sparrow; without Chinese characters

Date	Mintage	F	VF	XF	Unc	BU
1999 Proof	Inc. above	Value: 70.00				

KM# 988 1/25 CROWN
1.2240 g., 0.9990 Gold 0.0393 oz. AGW, 13.92 mm. **Ruler:** Elizabeth II **Subject:** Peter Rabbit Centennial **Obv:** Crowned bust right **Rev:** Peter Rabbit **Edge:** Reeded

Date	Mintage	F	VF	XF	Unc	BU
2002 Proof	5,000	Value: 50.00				

KM# 988a 1/25 CROWN
1.2240 g., 0.9990 Platinum 0.0393 oz. APW, 13.92 mm. **Ruler:** Elizabeth II **Subject:** Peter Rabbit Centennial **Obv:** Crowned bust right **Rev:** Peter Rabbit **Edge:** Reeded

Date	Mintage	F	VF	XF	Unc	BU
2002 Proof	3,000	Value: 65.00				

KM# 1016 1/25 CROWN
1.2441 g., 0.9999 Gold 0.04 oz. AGW, 13.92 mm. **Ruler:** Elizabeth II **Subject:** Peter Pan **Obv:** Crowned bust right **Rev:** Peter Pan and Tinkerbell flying above city **Edge:** Reeded

Date	Mintage	F	VF	XF	Unc	BU
2002 Proof	10,000	Value: 50.00				

KM# 50 1/10 CROWN
3.1100 g., 0.9999 Gold .1000 oz. AGW, 17.95 mm. **Ruler:** Elizabeth II **Series:** Barcelona Olympics **Obv:** Crowned bust right **Rev:** Discus thrower

Date	Mintage	F	VF	XF	Unc	BU
1991 Proof	Est. 20,000	Value: 80.00				
1992 Proof	Est. 20,000	Value: 90.00				

KM# 51 1/10 CROWN
3.1100 g., 0.9999 Gold .1000 oz. AGW, 17.95 mm. **Ruler:** Elizabeth II **Series:** Barcelona Olympics **Obv:** Crowned bust right **Rev:** Chariot racing

Date	Mintage	F	VF	XF	Unc	BU
1991 Proof	Est. 20,000	Value: 80.00				
1992 Proof	Est. 20,000	Value: 90.00				

KM# 52 1/10 CROWN
3.1100 g., 0.9999 Gold .1000 oz. AGW, 17.95 mm. **Ruler:** Elizabeth II **Series:** Barcelona Olympics **Obv:** Crowned bust right **Rev:** Runners

Date	Mintage	F	VF	XF	Unc	BU
1991 Proof	Est. 20,000	Value: 80.00				
1992 Proof	Est. 20,000	Value: 90.00				

KM# 53 1/10 CROWN
3.1100 g., 0.9999 Gold .1000 oz. AGW, 17.95 mm. **Ruler:** Elizabeth II **Series:** Barcelona Olympics **Obv:** Crowned bust right **Rev:** Javelin thrower

Date	Mintage	F	VF	XF	Unc	BU
1991 Proof	Est. 20,000	Value: 80.00				
1992 Proof	Est. 20,000	Value: 90.00				

KM# 54 1/10 CROWN
3.1100 g., 0.9999 Gold .1000 oz. AGW, 17.95 mm. **Ruler:** Elizabeth II **Series:** Barcelona Olympics **Obv:** Crowned bust right **Rev:** Wrestlers

GIBRALTAR 289

Date	Mintage	F	VF	XF	Unc	BU
1991 Proof	Est. 20,000	Value: 80.00				
1992 Proof	Est. 20,000	Value: 90.00				

KM# 55 1/10 CROWN

3.1100 g., 0.9999 Gold .1000 oz. AGW, 17.95 mm. **Ruler:** Elizabeth II **Series:** Barcelona Olympics **Obv:** Crowned bust right **Rev:** Boxers

Date	Mintage	F	VF	XF	Unc	BU
1991 Proof	Est. 20,000	Value: 80.00				
1992 Proof	Est. 20,000	Value: 90.00				

KM# 56 1/10 CROWN

3.1100 g., 0.9999 Gold .1000 oz. AGW, 17.95 mm. **Ruler:** Elizabeth II **Series:** Barcelona Olympics **Obv:** Crowned bust right **Rev:** Long jumper

Date	Mintage	F	VF	XF	Unc	BU
1991 Proof	Est. 20,000	Value: 80.00				
1992 Proof	Est. 20,000	Value: 90.00				

KM# 57 1/10 CROWN

3.1100 g., 0.9999 Gold .1000 oz. AGW, 17.95 mm. **Ruler:** Elizabeth II **Series:** Barcelona Olympics **Obv:** Crowned bust right **Rev:** Olympic victor

Date	Mintage	F	VF	XF	Unc	BU
1991 Proof	Est. 20,000	Value: 80.00				
1992 Proof	Est. 20,000	Value: 90.00				

KM# 125 1/10 CROWN

3.1100 g., 0.9999 Gold .1000 oz. AGW, 17.95 mm. **Ruler:** Elizabeth II **Subject:** Japanese Royal Wedding

Date	Mintage	F	VF	XF	Unc	BU
1993 Proof	Est. 10,000	Value: 95.00				

KM# 203 1/10 CROWN

3.1100 g., 0.9999 Gold .1000 oz. AGW, 17.95 mm. **Ruler:** Elizabeth II **Series:** Peter Rabbit Centennial **Subject:** The Tale of Peter Rabbit **Obv:** Crowned bust right **Rev:** Rabbit eating carrots, sparrow on handle

Date	Mintage	F	VF	XF	Unc	BU
1993 Proof	Est. 20,000	Value: 85.00				

KM# 203a 1/10 CROWN

3.1100 g., 0.9990 Platinum .1000 oz. APW **Ruler:** Elizabeth II **Series:** Peter Rabbit Centennial **Subject:** The Tale of Peter Rabbit **Obv:** Crowned bust right **Rev:** Rabbit eating carrots, sparrow on handle

Date	Mintage	F	VF	XF	Unc	BU
1993 Proof	Est. 5,000	Value: 145				

KM# 207 1/10 CROWN

3.1100 g., 0.9990 Platinum .1000 oz. APW **Ruler:** Elizabeth II **Series:** Peter Rabbit Centennial **Subject:** The Tale of Peter Rabbit **Obv:** Crowned bust right **Rev:** Mrs. Tiggy-Winkel ironing

Date	Mintage	F	VF	XF	Unc	BU
1993 Proof	Est. 20,000	Value: 145				

KM# 211 1/10 CROWN

3.1100 g., 0.9990 Platinum .1000 oz. APW **Ruler:** Elizabeth II **Series:** Peter Rabbit Centennial **Subject:** The Tale of Peter Rabbit **Obv:** Crowned bust right **Rev:** Jeremy Fisher fishing

Date	Mintage	F	VF	XF	Unc	BU
1993 Proof	Est. 20,000	Value: 145				

KM# 215 1/10 CROWN

3.1100 g., 0.9990 Platinum .1000 oz. APW **Ruler:** Elizabeth II **Series:** Peter Rabbit Centennial **Subject:** The Tale of Peter Rabbit **Obv:** Crowned bust right **Rev:** Tom Kitten with mother cat

Date	Mintage	F	VF	XF	Unc	BU
1993 Proof	Est. 20,000	Value: 145				

KM# 219 1/10 CROWN

3.1100 g., 0.9990 Platinum .1000 oz. APW **Ruler:** Elizabeth II **Series:** Peter Rabbit Centennial **Subject:** The Tale of Peter Rabbit **Obv:** Crowned bust right **Rev:** Benjamin Bunny wearing hat and holding coat

Date	Mintage	F	VF	XF	Unc	BU
1993 Proof	Est. 20,000	Value: 145				

KM# 223 1/10 CROWN

3.1100 g., 0.9990 Platinum .1000 oz. APW **Ruler:** Elizabeth II **Series:** Peter Rabbit Centennial **Subject:** The Tale of Peter Rabbit **Obv:** Crowned bust right **Rev:** Jemima Puddle Duck talking with fox

Date	Mintage	F	VF	XF	Unc	BU
1993 Proof	Est. 20,000	Value: 145				

KM# 439 1/10 CROWN

3.1100 g., 0.9990 Platinum .1000 oz. APW **Ruler:** Elizabeth II **Series:** Peter Rabbit Centennial **Subject:** The Tale of Peter Rabbit **Obv:** Crowned bust right **Rev:** Mother Rabbit and bunnies

Date	Mintage	F	VF	XF	Unc	BU
1994 Proof	Est. 20,000	Value: 145				

KM# 439a 1/10 CROWN

3.1103 g., 0.9950 Platinum .1000 oz. APW **Ruler:** Elizabeth II **Series:** Peter Rabbit Centennial **Obv:** Crowned bust right **Rev:** Mother Rabbit and bunnies

Date	Mintage	F	VF	XF	Unc	BU
1994 Proof	Est. 5,000	Value: 150				

KM# 369 1/10 CROWN

3.1103 g., 0.9999 Gold .1000 oz. AGW, 17.95 mm. **Ruler:** Elizabeth II **Subject:** Roses **Obv:** Crowned bust right

Date	Mintage	F	VF	XF	Unc	BU
1996 Proof	Est. 20,000	Value: 85.00				

KM# 377 1/10 CROWN

3.1103 g., 0.9999 Gold .1000 oz. AGW, 17.95 mm. **Ruler:** Elizabeth II **Series:** Peter Rabbit Centennial **Subject:** The Tale of Peter Rabbit **Obv:** Crowned bust right **Rev:** Rabbit escaping the garden

Date	Mintage	F	VF	XF	Unc	BU
1996 Proof	Est. 20,000	Value: 85.00				

KM# 377a 1/10 CROWN

3.1259 g., 0.9950 Platinum .1000 oz. APW **Ruler:** Elizabeth II **Series:** Peter Rabbit Centennial **Subject:** The Tale of Peter Rabbit **Obv:** Crowned bust right **Rev:** Rabbit escaping the garden

Date	Mintage	F	VF	XF	Unc	BU
1996 Proof	Est. 10,000	Value: 145				

KM# 391 1/10 CROWN

3.1103 g., 0.9999 Gold .1000 oz. AGW, 17.95 mm. **Ruler:** Elizabeth II **Series:** Centenary of the Cinema **Subject:** Grace Kelly - actress, 1929-82 **Obv:** Crowned bust right **Rev:** Bust 3/4 facing, dates

Date	Mintage	F	VF	XF	Unc	BU
1996 Proof	Est. 20,000	Value: 85.00				

KM# 396 1/10 CROWN

3.1103 g., 0.9999 Gold .1000 oz. AGW, 17.95 mm. **Ruler:** Elizabeth II **Series:** Centenary of the Cinema **Subject:** James Dean - actor, 1931-55 **Obv:** Crowned bust right **Rev:** Bust facing, dates

Date	Mintage	F	VF	XF	Unc	BU
1996 Proof	20,000	Value: 95.00				

KM# 401 1/10 CROWN

3.1103 g., 0.9999 Gold .1000 oz. AGW, 17.95 mm. **Ruler:** Elizabeth II **Series:** Centenary of the Cinema **Subject:** Marilyn Monroe - actress, 1926-62 **Obv:** Crowned bust right **Rev:** Bust looking back over shoulder, dates

Date	Mintage	F	VF	XF	Unc	BU
1996 Proof	Est. 20,000	Value: 85.00				

KM# 406 1/10 CROWN

3.1103 g., 0.9999 Gold .1000 oz. AGW, 17.95 mm. **Ruler:** Elizabeth II **Series:** Centenary of the Cinema **Subject:** Audrey Hepburn - actress, 1929-93 **Obv:** Crowned bust right **Rev:** Bust facing, dates

Date	Mintage	F	VF	XF	Unc	BU
1996 Proof	Est. 20,000	Value: 85.00				

KM# 406a 1/10 CROWN

3.1103 g., 0.9950 Platinum .1000 oz. APW **Ruler:** Elizabeth II **Series:** Centenary of the Cinema **Subject:** Audrey Hepburn - actress, 1929-93 **Obv:** Crowned bust right **Rev:** Bust facing, dates

Date	Mintage	F	VF	XF	Unc	BU
1996 Proof	Est. 1,000	Value: 155				

KM# 411 1/10 CROWN

3.1103 g., 0.9999 Gold .1000 oz. AGW, 17.95 mm. **Ruler:** Elizabeth II **Series:** Centenary of the Cinema **Subject:** Bruce Lee **Obv:** Crowned bust right **Rev:** Kickboxer and chinese dragon

Date	Mintage	F	VF	XF	Unc	BU
1996 Proof	Est. 20,000	Value: 85.00				

KM# 416 1/10 CROWN

3.1103 g., 0.9999 Gold .1000 oz. AGW, 17.95 mm. **Ruler:** Elizabeth II **Series:** Centenary of the Cinema **Subject:** Charlie Chaplan - actor, 1889-1977 **Obv:** Crowned bust right **Rev:** Standing central figure with cane, dates

Date	Mintage	F	VF	XF	Unc	BU
1996 Proof	Est. 20,000	Value: 80.00				

KM# 421 1/10 CROWN

3.1103 g., 0.9999 Gold .1000 oz. AGW, 17.95 mm. **Ruler:** Elizabeth II **Series:** Centenary of the Cinema **Subject:** Gone With The Wind **Obv:** Crowned bust right **Rev:** Rhett Butler and Scarlett O'Hara

Date	Mintage	F	VF	XF	Unc	BU
1996 Proof	Est. 20,000	Value: 85.00				

KM# 426 1/10 CROWN

3.1103 g., 0.9999 Gold .1000 oz. AGW, 17.95 mm. **Ruler:** Elizabeth II **Series:** Centenary of the Cinema **Obv:** Crowned bust right **Rev:** The Flintstones

Date	Mintage	F	VF	XF	Unc	BU
1996 Proof	Est. 20,000	Value: 85.00				

KM# 446 1/10 CROWN

3.1103 g., 0.9999 Gold .1000 oz. AGW, 17.95 mm. **Ruler:** Elizabeth II **Subject:** Lord Buddha **Rev:** Seated figure facing

Date	Mintage	F	VF	XF	Unc	BU
1996 Proof	Est. 10,000	Value: 95.00				

KM# 455 1/10 CROWN

3.1103 g., 0.9999 Gold .1000 oz. AGW, 17.95 mm. **Ruler:** Elizabeth II **Series:** Centenary of the Cinema **Subject:** Wizard of Oz **Obv:** Crowned bust right **Rev:** Wizard of Oz characters

Date	Mintage	F	VF	XF	Unc	BU
1996 Proof	Est. 20,000	Value: 85.00				

KM# 459 1/10 CROWN

3.1103 g., 0.9999 Gold .1000 oz. AGW, 17.95 mm. **Ruler:** Elizabeth II **Series:** Centenary of the Cinema **Subject:** Marx Brothers **Obv:** Crowned bust right **Rev:** Three busts left

Date	Mintage	F	VF	XF	Unc	BU
1996 Proof	Est. 20,000	Value: 85.00				

KM# 463 1/10 CROWN

3.1103 g., 0.9999 Gold .1000 oz. AGW, 17.95 mm. **Ruler:** Elizabeth II **Series:** Centenary of the Cinema **Subject:** Elvis Presley **Obv:** Crowned bust right **Rev:** Guitar beneath and behind bust 3/4 left

Date	Mintage	F	VF	XF	Unc	BU
1996 Proof	Est. 20,000	Value: 85.00				

KM# 467 1/10 CROWN

3.1103 g., 0.9999 Gold .1000 oz. AGW, 17.95 mm. **Ruler:** Elizabeth II **Series:** Centenary of the Cinema **Subject:** Casablanca **Obv:** Crowned bust right **Rev:** Bogart and Bergman

Date	Mintage	F	VF	XF	Unc	BU
1996 Proof	Est. 20,000	Value: 85.00				

KM# 471 1/10 CROWN

3.1103 g., 0.9999 Gold .1000 oz. AGW, 17.95 mm. **Ruler:** Elizabeth II **Series:** Centenary of the Cinema **Obv:** Crowned bust right **Rev:** E.T.

Date	Mintage	F	VF	XF	Unc	BU
1996 Proof	Est. 20,000	Value: 85.00				

KM# 475 1/10 CROWN

3.1103 g., 0.9999 Gold .1000 oz. AGW, 17.95 mm. **Ruler:** Elizabeth II **Series:** Centenary of the Cinema **Subject:** Alfred Hitchcock - Producer/Director, 1899-1980 **Obv:** Crowned bust right **Rev:** Bust facing looking at bird on left shoulder

Date	Mintage	F	VF	XF	Unc	BU
1996 Proof	Est. 20,000	Value: 85.00				

KM# 520 1/10 CROWN

3.1103 g., 0.9999 Gold .1000 oz. AGW, 17.95 mm. **Ruler:** Elizabeth II **Subject:** Tale of Peter Rabbit **Obv:** Crowned bust right **Rev:** Standing rabbit facing

Date	Mintage	F	VF	XF	Unc	BU
1997 Proof	Est. 20,000	Value: 85.00				

KM# 520a 1/10 CROWN

3.1259 g., 0.9950 Platinum .1000 oz. APW **Ruler:** Elizabeth II **Subject:** Tale of Peter Rabbit **Obv:** Crowned bust right **Rev:** Standing rabbit facing

Date	Mintage	F	VF	XF	Unc	BU
1997 Proof	Est. 5,000	Value: 155				

KM# 538 1/10 CROWN

3.1100 g., 0.9999 Gold .1000 oz. AGW, 17.95 mm. **Obv:** Crowned bust right **Rev:** Peonies

Date	Mintage	F	VF	XF	Unc	BU
1997 Proof	Est. 20,000	Value: 80.00				

KM# 542 1/10 CROWN

3.1100 g., 0.9999 Gold .1000 oz. AGW, 17.95 mm. **Ruler:** Elizabeth II **Subject:** Nefertiti **Obv:** Crowned bust right **Rev:** Head right

Date	Mintage	F	VF	XF	Unc	BU
1997 Proof	Est. 7,500	Value: 80.00				

KM# 546 1/10 CROWN

3.1100 g., 0.9999 Gold .1000 oz. AGW, 17.95 mm. **Ruler:** Elizabeth II **Subject:** Cleopatra **Obv:** Crowned bust right **Rev:** Head facing

Date	Mintage	F	VF	XF	Unc	BU
1997 Proof	Est. 7,500	Value: 80.00				

KM# 550 1/10 CROWN

3.1100 g., 0.9999 Gold .1000 oz. AGW, 17.95 mm. **Ruler:** Elizabeth II **Subject:** Europa **Obv:** Crowned bust right **Rev:** Head 3/4 left

Date	Mintage	F	VF	XF	Unc	BU
1997 Proof	Est. 7,500	Value: 80.00				

KM# 554 1/10 CROWN

3.1100 g., 0.9999 Gold .1000 oz. AGW, 17.95 mm. **Ruler:** Elizabeth II **Subject:** Liberty **Obv:** Crowned bust right **Rev:** Laureate head right

Date	Mintage	F	VF	XF	Unc	BU
1997 Proof	Est. 7,500	Value: 80.00				

KM# 651 1/10 CROWN

3.1100 g., 0.9999 Gold .1000 oz. AGW, 17.95 mm. **Ruler:** Elizabeth II **Subject:** Tale of Peter Rabbit **Obv:** Crowned bust right **Rev:** Standing rabbit facing, sparrow

Date	Mintage	F	VF	XF	Unc	BU
1998 Proof	Est. 20,000	Value: 90.00				

KM# 651a 1/10 CROWN

3.1103 g., 0.9950 Platinum .1000 oz. APW **Ruler:** Elizabeth II **Subject:** Tale of Peter Rabbit **Obv:** Crowned bust right **Rev:** Standing rabbit facing, sparrow

Date	Mintage	F	VF	XF	Unc	BU
1998 Proof	Est. 5,000	Value: 145				

KM# 658 1/10 CROWN

3.1100 g., 0.9999 Gold .1000 oz. AGW, 17.95 mm. **Ruler:** Elizabeth II **Subject:** Chrysanthemum **Obv:** Crowned bust right **Rev:** Three blossoms

Date	Mintage	F	VF	XF	Unc	BU
1998 Proof	Est. 20,000	Value: 90.00				

KM# 666 1/10 CROWN

3.1100 g., 0.9999 Gold .1000 oz. AGW, 17.95 mm. **Ruler:** Elizabeth II **Subject:** Brittania **Obv:** Crowned bust right **Rev:** Helmeted head right

Date	Mintage	F	VF	XF	Unc	BU
1998 Proof	Est. 7,500	Value: 90.00				

290 GIBRALTAR

KM# 667 1/10 CROWN
3.1100 g., 0.9999 Gold .1000 oz. AGW, 17.95 mm. **Ruler:** Elizabeth II **Subject:** Juno **Obv:** Crowned bust right **Rev:** Head 3/4 facing

Date	Mintage	F	VF	XF	Unc	BU
1998 Proof	Est. 7,500	Value: 90.00				

KM# 668 1/10 CROWN
3.1100 g., 0.9999 Gold .1000 oz. AGW, 17.95 mm. **Ruler:** Elizabeth II **Subject:** Athena **Obv:** Crowned bust right **Rev:** Helmeted head right

Date	Mintage	F	VF	XF	Unc	BU
1998 Proof	Est. 7,500	Value: 90.00				

KM# 669 1/10 CROWN
3.1100 g., 0.9999 Gold .1000 oz. AGW, 17.95 mm. **Ruler:** Elizabeth II **Subject:** Arethusa **Obv:** Crowned bust right **Rev:** Head left with dolphins

Date	Mintage	F	VF	XF	Unc	BU
1998 Proof	Est. 7,500	Value: 90.00				

KM# 679 1/10 CROWN
3.1100 g., 0.9999 Gold .1000 oz. AGW, 17.95 mm. **Ruler:** Elizabeth II **Subject:** Paddington Bear **Obv:** Crowned bust right **Rev:** Bear with suitcase

Date	Mintage	F	VF	XF	Unc	BU
1998 Proof	Est. 7,500	Value: 90.00				

KM# 679a 1/10 CROWN
3.1103 g., 0.9950 Platinum .1000 oz. APW **Ruler:** Elizabeth II **Subject:** Paddington Bear **Obv:** Crowned bust right **Rev:** Bear with suitcase

Date	Mintage	F	VF	XF	Unc	BU
1998 Proof	Est. 5,000	Value: 145				

KM# 989 1/10 CROWN
3.1100 g., 0.9990 Gold 0.0999 oz. AGW, 17.95 mm. **Ruler:** Elizabeth II **Subject:** Peter Rabbit Centennial **Obv:** Crowned bust right **Rev:** Peter Rabbit **Edge:** Reeded

Date	Mintage	F	VF	XF	Unc	BU
2002 Proof	5,000	Value: 95.00				

KM# 989a 1/10 CROWN
3.1100 g., 0.9990 Platinum 0.0999 oz. APW, 17395 mm. **Ruler:** Elizabeth II **Subject:** Peter Rabbit Centennial **Obv:** Crowned bust right **Rev:** Peter Rabbit **Edge:** Reeded

Date	Mintage	F	VF	XF	Unc	BU
2002 Proof	2,000	Value: 145				

KM# 1017 1/10 CROWN
3.1104 g., 0.9999 Gold 0.1 oz. AGW, 17.95 mm. **Ruler:** Elizabeth II **Subject:** Peter Pan **Obv:** Crowned bust right **Rev:** Peter Pan and Tinkerbell flying above city **Edge:** Reeded

Date	Mintage	F	VF	XF	Unc	BU
2002 Proof	7,500	Value: 95.00				

KM# 48 1/5 CROWN
6.2200 g., 0.9990 Gold .2000 oz. AGW, 22 mm. **Ruler:** Elizabeth II **Series:** 150th Anniversary of the First Adhesive Postage Stamp **Subject:** Penny Black Stamp **Obv:** Crowned bust right **Rev:** Heads flank stamp design

Date	Mintage	F	VF	XF	Unc	BU
1990 Proof	Est. 5,000	Value: 215				

KM# 76 1/5 CROWN
6.2200 g., 0.9990 Gold .2000 oz. AGW, 22 mm. **Ruler:** Elizabeth II **Series:** World Cup Soccer **Obv:** Crowned bust right **Rev:** Italian flag

Date	Mintage	F	VF	XF	Unc	BU
1990 Proof	Est. 5,000	Value: 215				

KM# 76a 1/5 CROWN
6.2200 g., 0.9950 Platinum .2000 oz. APW **Ruler:** Elizabeth II **Series:** World Cup Soccer **Obv:** Crowned bust right **Rev:** Italian flag

Date	Mintage	F	VF	XF	Unc	BU
1990 Proof	Est. 1,000	Value: 325				

KM# 77 1/5 CROWN
6.2200 g., 0.9999 Gold .2000 oz. AGW, 22 mm. **Ruler:** Elizabeth II **Series:** World Cup Soccer **Obv:** Crowned bust right **Rev:** Map of Italy

Date	Mintage	F	VF	XF	Unc	BU
1990 Proof	Est. 5,000	Value: 215				

KM# 77a 1/5 CROWN
6.2200 g., 0.9950 Platinum .2000 oz. APW, 22 mm. **Ruler:** Elizabeth II **Series:** World Cup Soccer **Obv:** Crowned bust right **Rev:** Map of Italy

Date	Mintage	F	VF	XF	Unc	BU
1990 Proof	Est. 1,000	Value: 325				

KM# 78 1/5 CROWN
6.2200 g., 0.9999 Gold .2000 oz. AGW, 22 mm. **Ruler:** Elizabeth II **Series:** World Cup Soccer **Obv:** Crowned bust right **Rev:** Goalie catching ball

Date	Mintage	F	VF	XF	Unc	BU
1990 Proof	Est. 5,000	Value: 215				

KM# 78a 1/5 CROWN
6.2200 g., 0.9950 Platinum .2000 oz. APW **Ruler:** Elizabeth II **Series:** World Cup Soccer **Obv:** Crowned bust right **Rev:** Goalie catching ball

Date	Mintage	F	VF	XF	Unc	BU
1990 Proof	Est. 1,000	Value: 325				

KM# 79 1/5 CROWN
6.2200 g., 0.9999 Gold .2000 oz. AGW, 22 mm. **Ruler:** Elizabeth II **Series:** World Cup Soccer **Obv:** Crowned bust right **Rev:** One player

Date	Mintage	F	VF	XF	Unc	BU
1990 Proof	Est. 5,000	Value: 215				

KM# 79a 1/5 CROWN
6.2200 g., 0.9950 Platinum .2000 oz. APW **Ruler:** Elizabeth II **Series:** World Cup Soccer **Obv:** Crowned bust right **Rev:** One player

Date	Mintage	F	VF	XF	Unc	BU
1990 Proof	Est. 1,000	Value: 325				

KM# 80 1/5 CROWN
6.2200 g., 0.9999 Gold .2000 oz. AGW, 22 mm. **Ruler:** Elizabeth II **Series:** World Cup Soccer **Obv:** Crowned bust right **Rev:** Two players

Date	Mintage	F	VF	XF	Unc	BU
1990 Proof	Est. 5,000	Value: 215				

KM# 80a 1/5 CROWN
6.2200 g., 0.9950 Platinum .2000 oz. APW **Ruler:** Elizabeth II **Series:** World Cup Soccer **Obv:** Crowned bust right **Rev:** Two players

Date	Mintage	F	VF	XF	Unc	BU
1990 Proof	Est. 1,000	Value: 325				

KM# 81 1/5 CROWN
6.2200 g., 0.9999 Gold .2000 oz. AGW, 22 mm. **Ruler:** Elizabeth II **Series:** World Cup Soccer **Obv:** Crowned bust right **Rev:** Three players

Date	Mintage	F	VF	XF	Unc	BU
1990 Proof	Est. 5,000	Value: 215				

KM# 81a 1/5 CROWN
6.2200 g., 0.9950 Platinum .2000 oz. APW **Ruler:** Elizabeth II **Series:** World Cup Soccer **Obv:** Crowned bust right **Rev:** Three players

Date	Mintage	F	VF	XF	Unc	BU
1990 Proof	Est. 1,000	Value: 325				

KM# 58 1/5 CROWN
6.2200 g., 0.9999 Gold .2000 oz. AGW, 22 mm. **Ruler:** Elizabeth II **Series:** Barcelona Olympics **Obv:** Crowned bust right **Rev:** Discus thrower

Date	Mintage	F	VF	XF	Unc	BU
1991 Proof	Est. 5,000	Value: 165				
1992 Proof	Est. 5,000	Value: 165				

KM# 58a 1/5 CROWN
6.2200 g., 0.9950 Platinum .2000 oz. APW **Ruler:** Elizabeth II **Series:** Barcelona Olympics **Obv:** Crowned bust right **Rev:** Discus thrower

Date	Mintage	F	VF	XF	Unc	BU
1991 Proof	Est. 1,000	Value: 300				

KM# 59 1/5 CROWN
6.2200 g., 0.9999 Gold .2000 oz. AGW, 22 mm. **Ruler:** Elizabeth II **Series:** Barcelona Olympics **Obv:** Crowned bust right **Rev:** Chariot racing

Date	Mintage	F	VF	XF	Unc	BU
1991 Proof	Est. 5,000	Value: 165				
1992 Proof	Est. 5,000	Value: 165				

KM# 59a 1/5 CROWN
6.2200 g., 0.9950 Platinum .2000 oz. APW **Ruler:** Elizabeth II **Series:** Barcelona Olympics **Obv:** Crowned bust right **Rev:** Chariot racing

Date	Mintage	F	VF	XF	Unc	BU
1991 Proof	Est. 1,000	Value: 300				

KM# 60 1/5 CROWN
6.2200 g., 0.9999 Gold .2000 oz. AGW, 22 mm. **Ruler:** Elizabeth II **Series:** Barcelona Olympics **Obv:** Crowned bust right **Rev:** Runners

Date	Mintage	F	VF	XF	Unc	BU
1991 Proof	Est. 5,000	Value: 165				
1992 Proof	Est. 5,000	Value: 165				

KM# 61 1/5 CROWN
6.2200 g., 0.9999 Gold .2000 oz. AGW, 22 mm. **Ruler:** Elizabeth II **Series:** Barcelona Olympics **Obv:** Crowned bust right **Rev:** Javelin thrower

Date	Mintage	F	VF	XF	Unc	BU
1991 Proof	Est. 5,000	Value: 165				
1992 Proof	Est. 5,000	Value: 165				

KM# 61a 1/5 CROWN
6.2200 g., 0.9950 Platinum .2000 oz. APW **Ruler:** Elizabeth II **Series:** Barcelona Olympics **Obv:** Crowned bust right **Rev:** Javelin thrower

Date	Mintage	F	VF	XF	Unc	BU
1991 Proof	Est. 1,000	Value: 300				

KM# 62 1/5 CROWN
6.2200 g., 0.9999 Gold .2000 oz. AGW, 22 mm. **Ruler:** Elizabeth II **Series:** Barcelona Olympics **Obv:** Crowned bust right **Rev:** Wrestlers

Date	Mintage	F	VF	XF	Unc	BU
1991 Proof	Est. 5,000	Value: 165				
1992 Proof	Est. 5,000	Value: 165				

KM# 62a 1/5 CROWN
6.2200 g., 0.9950 Platinum .2000 oz. APW **Ruler:** Elizabeth II **Series:** Barcelona Olympics **Obv:** Crowned bust right **Rev:** Wrestlers

Date	Mintage	F	VF	XF	Unc	BU
1991 Proof	Est. 1,000	Value: 300				

KM# 63 1/5 CROWN
6.2200 g., 0.9999 Gold .2000 oz. AGW, 22 mm. **Ruler:** Elizabeth II **Series:** Barcelona Olympics **Obv:** Crowned bust right **Rev:** Boxers

Date	Mintage	F	VF	XF	Unc	BU
1991 Proof	Est. 5,000	Value: 165				
1992 Proof	Est. 5,000	Value: 165				

KM# 63a 1/5 CROWN
6.2200 g., 0.9950 Platinum .2000 oz. APW **Ruler:** Elizabeth II **Series:** Barcelona Olympics **Obv:** Crowned bust right **Rev:** Boxers

Date	Mintage	F	VF	XF	Unc	BU
1991 Proof	Est. 1,000	Value: 300				

KM# 64 1/5 CROWN
6.2200 g., 0.9999 Gold .2000 oz. AGW, 22 mm. **Ruler:** Elizabeth II **Series:** Barcelona Olympics **Obv:** Crowned bust right **Rev:** Long jumper

Date	Mintage	F	VF	XF	Unc	BU
1991 Proof	Est. 5,000	Value: 165				
1992 Proof	Est. 5,000	Value: 165				

KM# 64a 1/5 CROWN
6.2200 g., 0.9950 Platinum .2000 oz. APW **Ruler:** Elizabeth II **Series:** Barcelona Olympics **Obv:** Crowned bust right **Rev:** Long jumper

Date	Mintage	F	VF	XF	Unc	BU
1991 Proof	Est. 1,000	Value: 300				

KM# 65 1/5 CROWN
6.2200 g., 0.9999 Gold .2000 oz. AGW, 22 mm. **Ruler:** Elizabeth II **Series:** Barcelona Olympics **Obv:** Crowned bust right **Rev:** Olympic victor

Date	Mintage	F	VF	XF	Unc	BU
1991 Proof	Est. 5,000	Value: 165				
1992 Proof	—	Value: 165				

KM# 65a 1/5 CROWN
6.2200 g., 0.9950 Platinum .2000 oz. APW **Ruler:** Elizabeth II **Series:** Barcelona Olympics **Obv:** Crowned bust right **Rev:** Olympic victor

Date	Mintage	F	VF	XF	Unc	BU
1991 Proof	Est. 1,000	Value: 300				

KM# 126 1/5 CROWN
6.2200 g., 0.9999 Gold .2000 oz. AGW, 22 mm. **Ruler:** Elizabeth II **Rev:** Japanese Royal Wedding **Note:** Similar to 1/2 Crown, KM#127.

Date	Mintage	F	VF	XF	Unc	BU
1993 Proof	Est. 10,000	Value: 145				

KM# 150 1/5 CROWN
6.2200 g., 0.9999 Gold .2000 oz. AGW **Ruler:** Elizabeth II **Series:** Preserve Planet Earth **Subject:** Cetiosaurus **Obv:** Crowned bust right **Rev:** Long-necked dinosaur

Date	Mintage	F	VF	XF	Unc	BU
1993 Proof	Est. 5,000	Value: 145				

KM# 152 1/5 CROWN
6.2200 g., 0.9999 Gold .2000 oz. AGW, 22 mm. **Ruler:** Elizabeth II **Series:** Preserve Planet Earth **Subject:** Stegosaurus **Obv:** Crowned bust right **Rev:** Dinosaur with pointed plates along spine

Date	Mintage	F	VF	XF	Unc	BU
1993 Proof	Est. 5,000	Value: 145				

KM# 153 1/5 CROWN
6.2200 g., 0.9999 Gold .2000 oz. AGW, 22 mm. **Ruler:** Elizabeth II **Series:** WWII Warships **Obv:** Crowned bust right **Rev:** USS Philadelphia

Date	Mintage	F	VF	XF	Unc	BU
1993 Proof	Est. 5,000	Value: 165				

GIBRALTAR

KM# 154 1/5 CROWN
6.2200 g., 0.9999 Gold .2000 oz. AGW, 22 mm. **Ruler:** Elizabeth II **Series:** WWII Warships **Obv:** Crowned bust right **Rev:** USS McLanahan

Date	Mintage	F	VF	XF	Unc	BU
1993 Proof	Est. 5,000			Value: 165		

KM# 155 1/5 CROWN
6.2200 g., 0.9999 Gold .2000 oz. AGW, 22 mm. **Ruler:** Elizabeth II **Series:** WWII Warships **Obv:** Crowned bust right **Rev:** HNLMS Isaac Sweers

Date	Mintage	F	VF	XF	Unc	BU
1993 Proof	Est. 5,000			Value: 165		

KM# 156 1/5 CROWN
6.2200 g., 0.9999 Gold .2000 oz. AGW, 22 mm. **Ruler:** Elizabeth II **Series:** WWII Warships **Obv:** Crowned bust right **Rev:** USS Weehawken

Date	Mintage	F	VF	XF	Unc	BU
1993 Proof	Est. 5,000			Value: 165		

KM# 157 1/5 CROWN
6.2200 g., 0.9999 Gold .2000 oz. AGW, 22 mm. **Ruler:** Elizabeth II **Series:** WWII Warships **Obv:** Crowned bust right **Rev:** HMS Warspite

Date	Mintage	F	VF	XF	Unc	BU
1993 Proof	Est. 5,000			Value: 165		

KM# 158 1/5 CROWN
6.2200 g., 0.9999 Gold .2000 oz. AGW, 22 mm. **Ruler:** Elizabeth II **Series:** WWII Warships **Obv:** Crowned bust right **Rev:** HMS Hood

Date	Mintage	F	VF	XF	Unc	BU
1993 Proof	Est. 5,000			Value: 165		

KM# 159 1/5 CROWN
6.2200 g., 0.9999 Gold .2000 oz. AGW, 22 mm. **Ruler:** Elizabeth II **Series:** WWII Warships **Obv:** Crowned bust right **Rev:** HMS Penelope

Date	Mintage	F	VF	XF	Unc	BU
1993 Proof	Est. 5,000			Value: 165		

KM# 160 1/5 CROWN
6.2200 g., 0.9999 Gold .2000 oz. AGW, 22 mm. **Ruler:** Elizabeth II **Series:** WWII Warships **Obv:** Crowned bust right **Rev:** HMCS Prescott

Date	Mintage	F	VF	XF	Unc	BU
1993 Proof	Est. 5,000			Value: 165		

KM# 161 1/5 CROWN
6.2200 g., 0.9999 Gold .2000 oz. AGW, 22 mm. **Ruler:** Elizabeth II **Series:** WWII Warships **Obv:** Crowned bust right **Rev:** HMS Ark Royal

Date	Mintage	F	VF	XF	Unc	BU
1993 Proof	Est. 5,000			Value: 165		

KM# 162 1/5 CROWN
6.2200 g., 0.9999 Gold .2000 oz. AGW, 22 mm. **Ruler:** Elizabeth II **Series:** WWII Warships **Obv:** Crowned bust right **Rev:** USS Gleaves

Date	Mintage	F	VF	XF	Unc	BU
1993 Proof	Est. 5,000			Value: 165		

KM# 163 1/5 CROWN
6.2200 g., 0.9999 Gold .2000 oz. AGW, 22 mm. **Ruler:** Elizabeth II **Series:** WWII Warships **Obv:** Crowned bust right **Rev:** HMAS Waterhen

Date	Mintage	F	VF	XF	Unc	BU
1993 Proof	Est. 5,000			Value: 165		

KM# 164 1/5 CROWN
6.2200 g., 0.9999 Gold .2000 oz. AGW, 22 mm. **Ruler:** Elizabeth II **Series:** WWII Warships **Obv:** Crowned bust right **Rev:** FSS Savorgnan de Brazza

Date	Mintage	F	VF	XF	Unc	BU
1993 Proof	Est. 5,000			Value: 165		

KM# 165 1/5 CROWN
6.2200 g., 0.9999 Gold .2000 oz. AGW, 22 mm. **Ruler:** Elizabeth II **Series:** House of - Stuart **Subject:** Queen Anne, 1702-1714 **Obv:** Young bust right **Rev:** Bust left

Date	Mintage	F	VF	XF	Unc	BU
1993 Proof	Est. 5,000			Value: 160		

KM# 166 1/5 CROWN
6.2200 g., 0.9999 Gold .2000 oz. AGW, 22 mm. **Ruler:** Elizabeth II **Series:** House of - Hanover **Subject:** King George I, 1714-1727 **Obv:** Young bust right **Rev:** Laureate bust right

Date	Mintage	F	VF	XF	Unc	BU
1993 Proof	Est. 5,000			Value: 160		

KM# 167 1/5 CROWN
6.2200 g., 0.9999 Gold .2000 oz. AGW, 22 mm. **Ruler:** Elizabeth II **Series:** House of - Hanover **Subject:** King George II, 1727-1760 **Obv:** Young bust right **Rev:** Bust left

Date	Mintage	F	VF	XF	Unc	BU
1993 Proof	Est. 5,000			Value: 160		

KM# 168 1/5 CROWN
6.2200 g., 0.9999 Gold .2000 oz. AGW, 22 mm. **Ruler:** Elizabeth II **Series:** House of - Hanover **Subject:** King George III, 1760-1820 **Obv:** Young bust right **Rev:** Bust right

Date	Mintage	F	VF	XF	Unc	BU
1993 Proof	Est. 5,000			Value: 160		

KM# 169 1/5 CROWN
6.2200 g., 0.9999 Gold .2000 oz. AGW, 22 mm. **Ruler:** Elizabeth II **Series:** House of - Hanover **Subject:** King George IV, 1820-1830 **Obv:** Young bust right **Rev:** Bust left

Date	Mintage	F	VF	XF	Unc	BU
1993 Proof	Est. 5,000			Value: 160		

KM# 170 1/5 CROWN
6.2200 g., 0.9999 Gold .2000 oz. AGW, 22 mm. **Ruler:** Elizabeth II **Series:** House of - Hanover **Subject:** King William IV, 1830-1837 **Obv:** Young bust right **Rev:** Bust right

Date	Mintage	F	VF	XF	Unc	BU
1993 Proof	Est. 5,000			Value: 160		

KM# 171 1/5 CROWN
6.2200 g., 0.9999 Gold .2000 oz. AGW, 22 mm. **Ruler:** Elizabeth II **Series:** House of - Hanover **Subject:** Queen Victoria, 1837-1901 **Obv:** Young bust right **Rev:** Bust left

Date	Mintage	F	VF	XF	Unc	BU
1993 Proof	Est. 5,000			Value: 160		

KM# 172 1/5 CROWN
6.2200 g., 0.9999 Gold .2000 oz. AGW, 22 mm. **Ruler:** Elizabeth II **Series:** House of - Saxe-Coburg **Subject:** King Edward VII, 1901-1910 **Obv:** Young bust right **Rev:** Uniformed bust right

Date	Mintage	F	VF	XF	Unc	BU
1993 Proof	Est. 5,000			Value: 160		

KM# 173 1/5 CROWN
6.2200 g., 0.9999 Gold .2000 oz. AGW, 22 mm. **Ruler:** Elizabeth II **Series:** House of - Windsor **Subject:** King George V, 1910-1936 **Obv:** Young bust right **Rev:** Uniformed bust left

Date	Mintage	F	VF	XF	Unc	BU
1993 Proof	Est. 5,000			Value: 160		

KM# 174 1/5 CROWN
6.2200 g., 0.9999 Gold .2000 oz. AGW, 22 mm. **Ruler:** Elizabeth II **Series:** House of - Windsor **Subject:** King Edward VIII, 1936 **Obv:** Young bust right **Rev:** Bust left

Date	Mintage	F	VF	XF	Unc	BU
1993 Proof	Est. 5,000			Value: 160		

KM# 175 1/5 CROWN
6.2200 g., 0.9999 Gold .2000 oz. AGW, 22 mm. **Ruler:** Elizabeth II **Series:** House of - Windsor **Subject:** King George VI, 1936-1952 **Obv:** Young bust right **Rev:** Bust left

Date	Mintage	F	VF	XF	Unc	BU
1993 Proof	Est. 5,000			Value: 160		

KM# 176 1/5 CROWN
6.2200 g., 0.9999 Gold .2000 oz. AGW, 22 mm. **Ruler:** Elizabeth II **Obv:** Crowned bust right **Rev:** Queen Elizabeth II bust left

Date	Mintage	F	VF	XF	Unc	BU
1993 Proof	Est. 5,000	Value: 160				

KM# 181 1/5 CROWN
6.2200 g., 0.9999 Gold .2000 oz. AGW, 22 mm. **Ruler:** Elizabeth II **Series:** International Friendship **Obv:** Crowned bust right **Rev:** Stylized panda

Date	Mintage	F	VF	XF	Unc	BU
1993 Proof	Est. 5,000	Value: 165				

KM# 185 1/5 CROWN
6.2200 g., 0.9999 Gold .2000 oz. AGW, 22 mm. **Ruler:** Elizabeth II **Series:** International Friendship **Obv:** Crowned bust right **Rev:** Natural panda

Date	Mintage	F	VF	XF	Unc	BU
1993 Proof	Est. 5,000	Value: 165				

KM# 189 1/5 CROWN
6.2200 g., 0.9999 Gold .2000 oz. AGW **Ruler:** Elizabeth II **Series:** International Friendship **Obv:** Crowned bust right **Rev:** General Sikarski portrait above B-24 bomber with Rock of Gibraltar in background

Date	Mintage	F	VF	XF	Unc	BU
1993 Proof	Est. 5,000	Value: 165				

KM# 199 1/5 CROWN
6.2143 g., 0.9999 Gold .1998 oz. AGW **Ruler:** Elizabeth II **Subject:** Dependent Territories Conference **Obv:** Crowned bust right **Rev:** 7 shields, 2 in center, 5 around with rope loops

Date	Mintage	F	VF	XF	Unc	BU
1993 Proof	Est. 5,000	Value: 160				

KM# 204 1/5 CROWN
6.2200 g., 0.9999 Gold .2000 oz. AGW, 22 mm. **Ruler:** Elizabeth II **Series:** Peter Rabbit Centennial **Subject:** The Tale of Peter Rabbit **Obv:** Crowned bust right **Rev:** Rabbit eating carrots, sparrow on handle

Date	Mintage	F	VF	XF	Unc	BU
1993 Proof	Est. 5,000	Value: 160				

KM# 204a 1/5 CROWN
6.2200 g., 0.9950 Platinum .2000 oz. APW **Ruler:** Elizabeth II **Series:** Peter Rabbit Centennial **Subject:** The Tale of Peter Rabbit **Obv:** Crowned bust right **Rev:** Rabbit eating carrots, sparrow on handle

Date	Mintage	F	VF	XF	Unc	BU
1993 Proof	Est. 5,000	Value: 300				

KM# 208 1/5 CROWN
6.2200 g., 0.9999 Gold .2000 oz. AGW, 22 mm. **Ruler:** Elizabeth II **Series:** Peter Rabbit Centennial **Subject:** The Tale of Peter Rabbit **Obv:** Crowned bust right **Rev:** Mrs. Tiggy-Winkel ironing

Date	Mintage	F	VF	XF	Unc	BU
1993 Proof	Est. 5,000	Value: 160				

KM# 212 1/5 CROWN
6.2200 g., 0.9999 Gold .2000 oz. AGW, 22 mm. **Ruler:** Elizabeth II **Series:** Peter Rabbit Centennial **Subject:** The Tale of Peter Rabbit **Obv:** Crowned bust right **Rev:** Jeremy Fisher fishing

Date	Mintage	F	VF	XF	Unc	BU
1993 Proof	Est. 5,000	Value: 160				

KM# 216 1/5 CROWN
6.2200 g., 0.9999 Gold .2000 oz. AGW, 22 mm. **Ruler:** Elizabeth II **Series:** Peter Rabbit Centennial **Subject:** The Tale of Peter Rabbit **Obv:** Crowned bust right **Rev:** Tom Kitten with mother cat

Date	Mintage	F	VF	XF	Unc	BU
1993 Proof	Est. 5,000	Value: 160				

KM# 220 1/5 CROWN
6.2200 g., 0.9999 Gold .2000 oz. AGW, 22 mm. **Ruler:** Elizabeth II **Series:** Peter Rabbit Centennial **Subject:** The Tale of Peter Rabbit **Obv:** Crowned bust right **Rev:** Benjamin Bunny wearing hat and holding coat

Date	Mintage	F	VF	XF	Unc	BU
1993 Proof	Est. 5,000	Value: 160				

KM# 224 1/5 CROWN
6.2200 g., 0.9999 Gold .2000 oz. AGW, 22 mm. **Ruler:** Elizabeth II **Series:** Peter Rabbit Centennial **Subject:** The Tale of Peter Rabbit **Obv:** Crowned bust right **Rev:** Jemima Puddle-Duck talking with fox

Date	Mintage	F	VF	XF	Unc	BU
1993 Proof	Est. 5,000	Value: 160				

KM# 643 1/5 CROWN
6.2200 g., 0.9999 Gold .2000 oz. AGW, 22 mm. **Series:** XVII Winter Olympics **Obv:** Crowned bust right **Rev:** Figure skaters

Date	Mintage	F	VF	XF	Unc	BU
1993 Proof	Est. 5,000	Value: 185				

KM# 644 1/5 CROWN
6.2200 g., 0.9999 Gold .2000 oz. AGW, 22 mm. **Ruler:** Elizabeth II **Series:** XVII Winter Olympics **Obv:** Crowned bust right **Rev:** Ice hockey

Date	Mintage	F	VF	XF	Unc	BU
1993 Proof	Est. 5,000	Value: 185				

KM# 645 1/5 CROWN
6.2200 g., 0.9999 Gold .2000 oz. AGW, 22 mm. **Ruler:** Elizabeth II **Series:** XVII Winter Olympics **Obv:** Crowned bust right **Rev:** Bobsledding

Date	Mintage	F	VF	XF	Unc	BU
1993 Proof	Est. 5,000	Value: 185				

KM# 646 1/5 CROWN
6.2200 g., 0.9999 Gold .2000 oz. AGW, 22 mm. **Ruler:** Elizabeth II **Series:** XVII Winter Olympics **Obv:** Crowned bust right **Rev:** Skiers

Date	Mintage	F	VF	XF	Unc	BU
1993 Proof	Est. 5,000	Value: 185				

KM# 226 1/5 CROWN
6.2200 g., 0.9999 Gold .2000 oz. AGW, 22 mm. **Ruler:** Elizabeth II **Series:** World Cup Soccer **Obv:** Crowned bust right **Rev:** 3 players kicking ball up field

Date	Mintage	F	VF	XF	Unc	BU
1994 Proof	Est. 5,000	Value: 160				

KM# 228 1/5 CROWN
6.2200 g., 0.9999 Gold .2000 oz. AGW, 22 mm. **Ruler:** Elizabeth II **Series:** World Cup Soccer **Obv:** Crowned bust right **Rev:** 2 players facing; 1 kicking and 1 defending

Date	Mintage	F	VF	XF	Unc	BU
1994 Proof	Est. 5,000	Value: 160				

KM# 230 1/5 CROWN
6.2200 g., 0.9999 Gold .2000 oz. AGW, 22 mm. **Ruler:** Elizabeth II **Series:** World Cup Soccer **Obv:** Crowned bust right **Rev:** 2 players; 1 goalie and 1 player trying to score

Date	Mintage	F	VF	XF	Unc	BU
1994 Proof	Est. 5,000	Value: 160				

KM# 232 1/5 CROWN
6.2200 g., 0.9999 Gold .2000 oz. AGW, 22 mm. **Ruler:** Elizabeth II **Series:** World Cup Soccer **Obv:** Crowned bust right **Rev:** 1 player looking up

Date	Mintage	F	VF	XF	Unc	BU
1994 Proof	Est. 5,000	Value: 160				

KM# 234 1/5 CROWN
6.2200 g., 0.9999 Gold .2000 oz. AGW, 22 mm. **Ruler:** Elizabeth II **Series:** World Cup Soccer **Obv:** Crowned bust right **Rev:** 1 player kicking, 1 player running forward

Date	Mintage	F	VF	XF	Unc	BU
1994 Proof	Est. 5,000	Value: 160				

KM# 236 1/5 CROWN
6.2200 g., 0.9999 Gold .2000 oz. AGW, 22 mm. **Ruler:** Elizabeth II **Series:** World Cup Soccer **Obv:** Crowned bust right **Rev:** Player in foreground heading ball to player

Date	Mintage	F	VF	XF	Unc	BU
1994 Proof	Est. 5,000	Value: 160				

KM# 238 1/5 CROWN
6.2200 g., 0.9999 Gold .2000 oz. AGW, 22 mm. **Ruler:** Elizabeth II **Series:** Preserve Planet Earth **Obv:** Crowned bust right **Rev:** Sabre Tooth Tiger

Date	Mintage	F	VF	XF	Unc	BU
1994 Proof	Est. 5,000	Value: 165				

KM# 240 1/5 CROWN
6.2200 g., 0.9999 Gold .2000 oz. AGW, 22 mm. **Ruler:** Elizabeth II **Series:** Preserve Planet Earth **Obv:** Crowned bust right **Rev:** Spanish Eagle flying above island

Date	Mintage	F	VF	XF	Unc	BU
1994 Proof	Est. 5,000	Value: 165				

KM# 242 1/5 CROWN
6.2200 g., 0.9999 Gold .2000 oz. AGW, 22 mm. **Ruler:** Elizabeth II **Series:** Preserve Planet Earth **Obv:** Crowned bust right **Rev:** Three Striped Dolphins

Date	Mintage	F	VF	XF	Unc	BU
1994 Proof	Est. 5,000	Value: 165				

KM# 244 1/5 CROWN
6.2200 g., 0.9999 Gold .2000 oz. AGW, 22 mm. **Ruler:** Elizabeth II **Series:** Preserve Planet Earth **Obv:** Crowned bust right **Rev:** Mother and baby elephants

Date	Mintage	F	VF	XF	Unc	BU
1994 Proof	Est. 5,000	Value: 165				

KM# 253 1/5 CROWN
6.2200 g., 0.9999 Gold .2000 oz. AGW, 22 mm. **Ruler:** Elizabeth II **Series:** World War II **Obv:** Crowned bust right **Rev:** Maltese convoy of ships

Date	Mintage	F	VF	XF	Unc	BU
1994 Proof	Est. 5,000	Value: 165				

KM# 254 1/5 CROWN
6.2200 g., 0.9999 Gold .2000 oz. AGW, 22 mm. **Ruler:** Elizabeth II **Series:** World War II **Obv:** Crowned bust right **Rev:** Squadron 202 flying, Rock of Gibraltar in background

Date	Mintage	F	VF	XF	Unc	BU
1994 Proof	Est. 5,000	Value: 165				

KM# 255 1/5 CROWN
6.2200 g., 0.9999 Gold .2000 oz. AGW, 22 mm. **Ruler:** Elizabeth II **Series:** World War II **Obv:** Crowned bust right **Rev:** Admiral Somerville, ship in background

Date	Mintage	F	VF	XF	Unc	BU
1994 Proof	Est. 5,000	Value: 165				

KM# 256 1/5 CROWN
6.2200 g., 0.9999 Gold .2000 oz. AGW, 22 mm. **Ruler:** Elizabeth II **Series:** World War II **Obv:** Crowned bust right **Rev:** Glen Miller and band

Date	Mintage	F	VF	XF	Unc	BU
1994 Proof	Est. 5,000	Value: 165				

KM# 257 1/5 CROWN
6.2200 g., 0.9999 Gold .2000 oz. AGW, 22 mm. **Ruler:** Elizabeth II **Series:** World War II **Obv:** Crowned bust right **Rev:** King George VI congratulating pilots

Date	Mintage	F	VF	XF	Unc	BU
1994 Proof	Est. 5,000	Value: 165				

KM# 258 1/5 CROWN
6.2200 g., 0.9999 Gold .2000 oz. AGW, 22 mm. **Ruler:** Elizabeth II **Series:** World War II **Obv:** Crowned bust right **Rev:** General Eisenhower, planes and ships in background

Date	Mintage	F	VF	XF	Unc	BU
1994 Proof	Est. 5,000	Value: 165				

KM# 265 1/5 CROWN
6.2200 g., 0.9999 Gold .2000 oz. AGW, 22 mm. **Ruler:** Elizabeth II **Series:** First Man on Moon **Obv:** Crowned bust right **Rev:** Dr. Wernher von Braun with replica of rocket

Date	Mintage	F	VF	XF	Unc	BU
1994 Proof	Est. 5,000	Value: 165				

KM# 266 1/5 CROWN
6.2200 g., 0.9999 Gold .2000 oz. AGW, 22 mm. **Ruler:** Elizabeth II **Series:** First Man on Moon **Obv:** Crowned bust right **Rev:** Rocket on pad before lift-off

Date	Mintage	F	VF	XF	Unc	BU
1994 Proof	Est. 5,000	Value: 165				

KM# 267 1/5 CROWN
6.2200 g., 0.9999 Gold .2000 oz. AGW, 22 mm. **Ruler:** Elizabeth II **Series:** First Man on Moon **Obv:** Crowned bust right **Rev:** Recovering space capsule after splashdown

Date	Mintage	F	VF	XF	Unc	BU
1994 Proof	Est. 5,000	Value: 165				

KM# 268 1/5 CROWN
6.2200 g., 0.9999 Gold .2000 oz. AGW, 22 mm. **Ruler:** Elizabeth II **Series:** First Man on Moon **Obv:** Crowned bust right **Rev:** Lunar Module landing on the moon

Date	Mintage	F	VF	XF	Unc	BU
1994 Proof	Est. 5,000	Value: 165				

KM# 269 1/5 CROWN
6.2200 g., 0.9999 Gold .2000 oz. AGW, 22 mm. **Ruler:** Elizabeth II **Series:** First Man on Moon **Obv:** Crowned bust right **Rev:** Astronaut stepping on the moon

Date	Mintage	F	VF	XF	Unc	BU
1994 Proof	Est. 5,000	Value: 165				

KM# 270 1/5 CROWN
6.2200 g., 0.9999 Gold .2000 oz. AGW, 22 mm. **Ruler:** Elizabeth II **Series:** First Man on Moon **Obv:** Crowned bust right **Rev:** Astronaut setting up flag on the moon

Date	Mintage	F	VF	XF	Unc	BU
1994 Proof	Est. 5,000	Value: 165				

KM# 277 1/5 CROWN
6.2200 g., 0.9999 Gold .2000 oz. AGW, 22 mm. **Ruler:** Elizabeth II **Series:** Sherlock Holmes **Obv:** Crowned bust right **Rev:** Holmes sitting with pipe in hand

Date	Mintage	F	VF	XF	Unc	BU
1994 Proof	Est. 5,000	Value: 165				

KM# 278 1/5 CROWN
6.2200 g., 0.9999 Gold .2000 oz. AGW, 22 mm. **Ruler:** Elizabeth II **Series:** Sherlock Holmes **Obv:** Crowned bust right **Rev:** Holmes playing violin, Dr. Watson watching

Date	Mintage	F	VF	XF	Unc	BU
1994 Proof	Est. 5,000	Value: 165				

KM# 279 1/5 CROWN
6.2200 g., 0.9999 Gold .2000 oz. AGW, 22 mm. **Ruler:** Elizabeth II **Series:** Sherlock Holmes **Obv:** Crowned bust right **Rev:** People talking before 221 B Baker St.

Date	Mintage	F	VF	XF	Unc	BU
1994 Proof	Est. 5,000	Value: 165				

KM# 280 1/5 CROWN
6.2200 g., 0.9999 Gold .2000 oz. AGW, 22 mm. **Ruler:** Elizabeth II **Series:** Sherlock Holmes **Obv:** Crowned bust right **Rev:** Scene from book "The Empty House"

Date	Mintage	F	VF	XF	Unc	BU
1994 Proof	Est. 5,000	Value: 165				

KM# 281 1/5 CROWN
6.2200 g., 0.9999 Gold .2000 oz. AGW, 22 mm. **Ruler:** Elizabeth II **Series:** Sherlock Holmes **Obv:** Crowned bust right **Rev:** Sailing ship "Mary Celeste"

Date	Mintage	F	VF	XF	Unc	BU
1994 Proof	Est. 5,000	Value: 175				

KM# 282 1/5 CROWN
6.2200 g., 0.9999 Gold .2000 oz. AGW, 22 mm. **Ruler:** Elizabeth II **Series:** Sherlock Holmes **Obv:** Crowned bust right **Rev:** Scene from the "Hound of the Baskervilles"

Date	Mintage	F	VF	XF	Unc	BU
1994 Proof	Est. 5,000	Value: 170				

KM# 283 1/5 CROWN
6.2200 g., 0.9999 Gold .2000 oz. AGW, 22 mm. **Ruler:** Elizabeth II **Series:** Sherlock Holmes **Obv:** Crowned bust right **Rev:** Scene from the "Three Garriders"

Date	Mintage	F	VF	XF	Unc	BU
1994 Proof	Est. 5,000	Value: 165				

KM# 284 1/5 CROWN
6.2200 g., 0.9999 Gold .2000 oz. AGW, 22 mm. **Ruler:** Elizabeth II **Series:** Sherlock Holmes **Obv:** Crowned bust right **Rev:** Scene from the "Final Problem"

Date	Mintage	F	VF	XF	Unc	BU
1994 Proof	Est. 5,000	Value: 165				

KM# 441 1/5 CROWN
6.2200 g., 0.9999 Gold .2000 oz. AGW, 22 mm. **Ruler:** Elizabeth II **Subject:** The Tale of Peter Rabbit **Obv:** Crowned bust right **Rev:** Peter rabbit with four little bunnies

Date	Mintage	F	VF	XF	Unc	BU
1994 Proof	Est. 10,000	Value: 185				

KM# 442 1/5 CROWN
6.2200 g., 0.9950 Platinum .2000 oz. APW, 22 mm. **Ruler:** Elizabeth II

Date	Mintage	F	VF	XF	Unc	BU
1994 Proof	Est. 2,500	Value: 295				

KM# 295 1/5 CROWN
6.2200 g., 0.9999 Gold .2000 oz. AGW, 22 mm. **Ruler:** Elizabeth II **Series:** Atlanta Olympics **Obv:** Crowned bust right **Rev:** Long jumpers

Date	Mintage	F	VF	XF	Unc	BU
1995 Proof	Est. 5,000	Value: 160				

KM# 296 1/5 CROWN
6.2200 g., 0.9999 Gold .2000 oz. AGW, 22 mm. **Ruler:** Elizabeth II **Series:** Atlanta Olympics **Obv:** Crowned bust right **Rev:** Discus throwers

Date	Mintage	F	VF	XF	Unc	BU
1995 Proof	Est. 5,000	Value: 160				

KM# 297 1/5 CROWN
6.2200 g., 0.9999 Gold .2000 oz. AGW, 22 mm. **Ruler:** Elizabeth II **Series:** Atlanta Olympics **Obv:** Crowned bust right **Rev:** Relay racers

Date	Mintage	F	VF	XF	Unc	BU
1995 Proof	Est. 5,000	Value: 160				

KM# 298 1/5 CROWN
6.2200 g., 0.9999 Gold .2000 oz. AGW, 22 mm. **Ruler:** Elizabeth II **Series:** Atlanta Olympics **Obv:** Crowned bust right **Rev:** Javelin throwers

Date	Mintage	F	VF	XF	Unc	BU
1995 Proof	Est. 5,000	Value: 160				

KM# 303 1/5 CROWN
6.2200 g., 0.9999 Gold .2000 oz. AGW, 22 mm. **Ruler:** Elizabeth II **Obv:** Crowned bust right **Rev:** Rock of Gibraltar and rising sun

Date	Mintage	F	VF	XF	Unc	BU
1995 Proof	Est. 5,000	Value: 165				

KM# 326 1/5 CROWN
6.2200 g., 0.9999 Gold .2000 oz. AGW, 22 mm. **Ruler:** Elizabeth II **Subject:** The Tale of Peter Rabbit **Obv:** Crowned bust right **Rev:** Peter Rabbit running right

Date	Mintage	F	VF	XF	Unc	BU
1995 Proof	Est. 5,000	Value: 165				

KM# 326a 1/5 CROWN
6.2200 g., 0.9950 Platinum .2000 oz. APW **Ruler:** Elizabeth II **Subject:** The Tale of Peter Rabbit **Obv:** Crowned bust right **Rev:** Peter rabbit running right

Date	Mintage	F	VF	XF	Unc	BU
1995 Proof	Est. 2,500	Value: 295				

KM# 328 1/5 CROWN
6.2200 g., 0.9999 Gold .2000 oz. AGW, 22 mm. **Ruler:** Elizabeth II **Series:** Island Games **Obv:** Crowned bust right **Rev:** Circle of athletes with shield at center

Date	Mintage	F	VF	XF	Unc	BU
1995 Proof	Est. 5,000	Value: 160				

KM# 330 1/5 CROWN
6.2200 g., 0.9999 Gold .2000 oz. AGW, 22 mm. **Ruler:** Elizabeth II **Series:** Island Games **Obv:** Crowned bust right **Rev:** Circle of athletes with shield at center

Date	Mintage	F	VF	XF	Unc	BU
1995 Proof	Est. 5,000	Value: 160				

KM# 342 1/5 CROWN
6.2200 g., 0.9999 Gold .2000 oz. AGW, 22 mm. **Ruler:** Elizabeth II **Series:** Olympics **Obv:** Crowned bust right **Rev:** Tennis player

Date	Mintage	F	VF	XF	Unc	BU
1996 Proof	Est. 5,000	Value: 165				

KM# 343 1/5 CROWN
6.2200 g., 0.9999 Gold .2000 oz. AGW, 22 mm. **Ruler:** Elizabeth II **Series:** Olympics **Obv:** Crowned bust right **Rev:** Wrestlers

Date	Mintage	F	VF	XF	Unc	BU
1996 Proof	Est. 5,000	Value: 165				

KM# 344 1/5 CROWN
6.2200 g., 0.9999 Gold .2000 oz. AGW, 22 mm. **Ruler:** Elizabeth II **Series:** Olympics **Obv:** Crowned bust right **Rev:** Baseball players

Date	Mintage	F	VF	XF	Unc	BU
1996 Proof	Est. 5,000	Value: 165				

KM# 345 1/5 CROWN
6.2200 g., 0.9999 Gold .2000 oz. AGW, 22 mm. **Ruler:** Elizabeth II **Series:** Olympics **Obv:** Crowned bust right **Rev:** Flame

Date	Mintage	F	VF	XF	Unc	BU
1996 Proof	Est. 5,000	Value: 165				

KM# 346 1/5 CROWN
6.2200 g., 0.9999 Gold .2000 oz. AGW, 22 mm. **Ruler:** Elizabeth II **Series:** Olympics **Obv:** Crowned bust right **Rev:** Volleyball game

Date	Mintage	F	VF	XF	Unc	BU
1996 Proof	Est. 5,000	Value: 165				

KM# 347 1/5 CROWN
6.2200 g., 0.9999 Gold .2000 oz. AGW, 22 mm. **Ruler:** Elizabeth II **Series:** Olympics **Obv:** Crowned bust right **Rev:** Basketball game

Date	Mintage	F	VF	XF	Unc	BU
1996 Proof	Est. 5,000	Value: 165				

KM# 357 1/5 CROWN
6.2200 g., 0.9999 Gold .2000 oz. AGW, 22 mm. **Ruler:** Elizabeth II **Subject:** Nefusat Yehuda Synagogue Renovation **Obv:** Crowned bust right **Rev:** Hebrew symbol, rock, arms and building

Date	Mintage	F	VF	XF	Unc	BU
1996 Proof	Est. 5,000	Value: 165				

KM# 360 1/5 CROWN
6.2200 g., 0.9999 Gold .2000 oz. AGW, 22 mm. **Ruler:** Elizabeth II **Series:** Euro 96 **Rev:** England

Date	Mintage	F	VF	XF	Unc	BU
1996 Proof	Est. 5,000	Value: 175				

KM# 370 1/5 CROWN
6.2200 g., 0.9999 Gold .2000 oz. AGW, 22 mm. **Ruler:** Elizabeth II **Obv:** Crowned bust right **Rev:** Roses

Date	Mintage	F	VF	XF	Unc	BU
1996 Proof	Est. 5,000	Value: 165				

KM# 370a 1/5 CROWN
6.2518 g., 0.9950 Platinum .2000 oz. APW **Ruler:** Elizabeth II **Obv:** Crowned bust right **Rev:** Roses

Date	Mintage	F	VF	XF	Unc	BU
1996 Proof	Est. 1,000	Value: 300				

KM# 379 1/5 CROWN
6.2207 g., 0.9999 Gold .2000 oz. AGW, 22 mm. **Ruler:** Elizabeth II **Series:** Peter Rabbit Centennial **Subject:** The Tale of Peter Rabbit **Obv:** Crowned bust right **Rev:** Peter Rabbit escaping garden

Date	Mintage	F	VF	XF	Unc	BU
1996 Proof	Est. 7,500	Value: 165				

KM# 379a 1/5 CROWN
6.2200 g., 0.9950 Platinum .2000 oz. APW **Ruler:** Elizabeth II **Series:** Peter Rabbit Centennial **Subject:** The Tale of Peter Rabbit **Obv:** Crowned bust right **Rev:** Peter Rabbit escaping garden

Date	Mintage	F	VF	XF	Unc	BU
1996 Proof	Est. 5,000	Value: 295				

KM# 384 1/5 CROWN
6.2207 g., 0.9999 Gold .2000 oz. AGW, 22 mm. **Ruler:** Elizabeth II **Series:** Preserve Planet Earth **Obv:** Crowned bust right **Rev:** Shag Birds

Date	Mintage	F	VF	XF	Unc	BU
1996 Proof	Est. 5,000	Value: 165				

KM# 385 1/5 CROWN
6.2207 g., 0.9999 Gold .2000 oz. AGW, 22 mm. **Ruler:** Elizabeth II **Series:** Preserve Planet Earth **Obv:** Crowned bust right **Rev:** Puffins

Date	Mintage	F	VF	XF	Unc	BU
1996 Proof	Est. 5,000	Value: 165				

KM# 392 1/5 CROWN
6.2207 g., 0.9999 Gold .2000 oz. AGW, 22 mm. **Ruler:** Elizabeth II **Series:** Cinema Centennial **Subject:** Grace Kelly - actress, 1929-82 **Obv:** Crowned bust right **Rev:** Bust 3/4 facing, dates

Date	Mintage	F	VF	XF	Unc	BU
1996 Proof	Est. 5,000	Value: 165				

KM# 392a 1/5 CROWN
6.2200 g., 0.9950 Platinum .2000 oz. APW **Ruler:** Elizabeth II **Series:** Cinema Centennial **Subject:** Grace Kelly - actress, 1929-82 **Obv:** Crowned bust right **Rev:** Bust 3/4 facing

Date	Mintage	F	VF	XF	Unc	BU
1996 Proof	Est. 1,000	Value: 300				

KM# 397 1/5 CROWN
6.2207 g., 0.9999 Gold .2000 oz. AGW, 22 mm. **Ruler:** Elizabeth II **Series:** Centenary of the Cinema **Subject:** James Dean - actor, 1931-55 **Obv:** Crowned bust right **Rev:** Standing central figure, dates

Date	Mintage	F	VF	XF	Unc	BU
1996 Proof	Est. 5,000	Value: 165				

KM# 397a 1/5 CROWN
6.2200 g., 0.9950 Platinum .2000 oz. APW **Ruler:** Elizabeth II **Series:** Centenary of the Cinema **Subject:** James Dean - actor, 1931-55 **Obv:** Crowned bust right **Rev:** Standing central figure, dates

Date	Mintage	F	VF	XF	Unc	BU
1996 Proof	Est. 1,000	Value: 300				

KM# 402 1/5 CROWN
6.2207 g., 0.9999 Gold .2000 oz. AGW, 22 mm. **Ruler:** Elizabeth II **Series:** Centenary of the Cinema **Subject:** Marilyn Monroe - actress, 1926-62 **Obv:** Crowned bust right **Rev:** Bust looking back over shoulder

Date	Mintage	F	VF	XF	Unc	BU
1996 Proof	Est. 5,000	Value: 165				

KM# 402a 1/5 CROWN
6.2200 g., 0.9950 Platinum .2000 oz. APW **Ruler:** Elizabeth II **Series:** Centenary of the Cinema **Subject:** Marilyn Monroe - actress, 1926-62 **Obv:** Crowned bust right **Rev:** Bust looking back over shoulder

Date	Mintage	F	VF	XF	Unc	BU
1996 Proof	Est. 1,000	Value: 300				

KM# 407 1/5 CROWN
6.2207 g., 0.9999 Gold .2000 oz. AGW, 22 mm. **Ruler:** Elizabeth II **Series:** Centenary of the Cinema **Subject:** Audrey Hepburn - actress, 1929-93 **Obv:** Crowned bust right **Rev:** Bust 3/4 facing, dates

Date	Mintage	F	VF	XF	Unc	BU
1996 Proof	Est. 5,000	Value: 165				

KM# 407a 1/5 CROWN
6.2200 g., 0.9950 Platinum .2000 oz. APW **Ruler:** Elizabeth II **Series:** Centenary of the Cinema **Subject:** Audrey Hepburn - actress, 1929-93 **Obv:** Crowned bust right **Rev:** Bust 3/4 facing, dates

Date	Mintage	F	VF	XF	Unc	BU
1996 Proof	Est. 1,000	Value: 300				

KM# 412 1/5 CROWN
6.2207 g., 0.9999 Gold .2000 oz. AGW, 22 mm. **Ruler:** Elizabeth II **Series:** Centenary of the Cinema **Subject:** Bruce Lee - actor, 1940-73 **Obv:** Crowned bust right **Rev:** Kickboxer and chinese dragon, dates

Date	Mintage	F	VF	XF	Unc	BU
1996 Proof	Est. 5,000	Value: 165				

KM# 417 1/5 CROWN
6.2207 g., 0.9999 Gold .2000 oz. AGW, 22 mm. **Ruler:** Elizabeth II **Series:** Centenary of the Cinema **Subject:** Charlie Chaplan - actor, 1889-1977 **Obv:** Crowned bust right **Rev:** Standing central figure with cane, dates

Date	Mintage	F	VF	XF	Unc	BU
1996 Proof	Est. 5,000	Value: 165				

KM# 422 1/5 CROWN
6.2207 g., 0.9999 Gold .2000 oz. AGW, 22 mm. **Ruler:** Elizabeth II **Series:** Centenary of the Cinema **Subject:** Gone With the Wind **Obv:** Crowned bust right **Rev:** Rhett Butler and Scarlett O'Hara

Date	Mintage	F	VF	XF	Unc	BU
1996 Proof	Est. 5,000	Value: 165				

KM# 427 1/5 CROWN
6.2207 g., 0.9999 Gold .2000 oz. AGW, 22 mm. **Ruler:** Elizabeth II **Series:** Centenary of the Cinema **Obv:** Crowned bust right **Rev:** The Flintstones

Date	Mintage	F	VF	XF	Unc	BU
1996 Proof	Est. 5,000	Value: 165				

KM# 431 1/5 CROWN
6.2207 g., 0.9999 Gold .2000 oz. AGW, 22 mm. **Ruler:** Elizabeth II **Series:** Duke of Edinburgh Awards Scheme **Obv:** Crowned bust right **Rev:** 7 Events surround central crowned arms

Date	Mintage	F	VF	XF	Unc	BU
1996 Proof	Est. 5,000	Value: 165				

KM# 434 1/5 CROWN

6.2207 g., 0.9999 Gold .2000 oz. AGW, 22 mm. **Ruler:** Elizabeth II **Series:** Duke of Edinburgh Awards Scheme **Obv:** Crowned bust right **Rev:** Cameo above team of horses pulling wagon

Date	Mintage	F	VF	XF	Unc	BU
1996 Proof	Est. 5,000	Value: 165				

KM# 447 1/5 CROWN

6.2207 g., 0.9999 Gold .2000 oz. AGW, 22 mm. **Ruler:** Elizabeth II **Subject:** Lord Buddha **Obv:** Crowned bust right **Rev:** Seated facing figure

Date	Mintage	F	VF	XF	Unc	BU
1996 Proof	Est. 8,000	Value: 185				

KM# 456 1/5 CROWN

6.2207 g., 0.9999 Gold .2000 oz. AGW, 22 mm. **Ruler:** Elizabeth II **Series:** Centenary of the Cinema **Subject:** Wizard of Oz **Obv:** Crowned bust right **Rev:** Wizard of Oz characters

Date	Mintage	F	VF	XF	Unc	BU
1996 Proof	Est. 5,000	Value: 165				

KM# 460 1/5 CROWN

6.2207 g., 0.9999 Gold .2000 oz. AGW, 22 mm. **Ruler:** Elizabeth II **Series:** Centenary of the Cinema **Subject:** Marx Brothers **Obv:** Crowned bust right **Rev:** Three busts 3/4 left

Date	Mintage	F	VF	XF	Unc	BU
1996 Proof	Est. 5,000	Value: 165				

KM# 464 1/5 CROWN

6.2207 g., 0.9999 Gold .2000 oz. AGW, 22 mm. **Ruler:** Elizabeth II **Series:** Centenary of the Cinema **Subject:** Elvis Presley - actor/entertainer, 1935-77 **Obv:** Crowned bust right **Rev:** Guitar below and behind bust 3/4 left, dates

Date	Mintage	F	VF	XF	Unc	BU
1996 Proof	Est. 5,000	Value: 165				

KM# 468 1/5 CROWN

6.2207 g., 0.9999 Gold .2000 oz. AGW, 22 mm. **Ruler:** Elizabeth II **Series:** Centenary of the Cinema **Subject:** Casablanca **Obv:** Crowned bust right **Rev:** Bogart and Bergman

Date	Mintage	F	VF	XF	Unc	BU
1996 Proof	Est. 5,000	Value: 165				

KM# 472 1/5 CROWN

6.2207 g., 0.9999 Gold .2000 oz. AGW, 22 mm. **Ruler:** Elizabeth II **Series:** Centenary of the Cinema **Obv:** Crowned bust right **Rev:** E.T.

Date	Mintage	F	VF	XF	Unc	BU
1996 Proof	Est. 5,000	Value: 165				

KM# 476 1/5 CROWN

6.2207 g., 0.9999 Gold .2000 oz. AGW, 22 mm. **Ruler:** Elizabeth II **Series:** Centenary of the Cinema **Subject:** Alfred Hitchcock - Producer/Director, 1899-1980 **Obv:** Crowned bust right **Rev:** Bust facing looking at bird on left shoulder

Date	Mintage	F	VF	XF	Unc	BU
1996 Proof	Est. 5,000	Value: 165				

KM# 513 1/5 CROWN

6.2207 g., 0.9999 Gold .2000 oz. AGW, 22 mm. **Ruler:** Elizabeth II **Obv:** Crowned bust right **Rev:** Peacocks, one with tail spread

Date	Mintage	F	VF	XF	Unc	BU
1997 Proof	Est. 5,000	Value: 185				

KM# 522 1/5 CROWN

6.2207 g., 0.9999 Gold .2000 oz. AGW, 22 mm. **Ruler:** Elizabeth II **Subject:** The Tale of Peter Rabbit **Obv:** Crowned bust right **Rev:** Standing rabbit 3/4 right

Date	Mintage	F	VF	XF	Unc	BU
1997 Proof	Est. 10,000	Value: 165				

KM# 522a 1/5 CROWN

6.2518 g., 0.9950 Platinum .2000 oz. APW **Ruler:** Elizabeth II **Subject:** The Tale of Peter Rabbit **Obv:** Crowned bust right **Rev:** Standing rabbit 3/4 right

Date	Mintage	F	VF	XF	Unc	BU
1997 Proof	Est. 2,500	Value: 295				

KM# 529 1/5 CROWN

6.2207 g., 0.9999 Gold .2000 oz. AGW, 22 mm. **Ruler:** Elizabeth II **Series:** Golden Wedding Anniversary **Subject:** Queen Elizabeth and Prince Philip **Obv:** Crowned bust right **Rev:** Engagement portrait

Date	Mintage	F	VF	XF	Unc	BU
1997 Proof	Est. 3,500	Value: 160				

KM# 531 1/5 CROWN

6.2207 g., 0.9999 Gold .2000 oz. AGW, 22 mm. **Ruler:** Elizabeth II **Series:** Golden Wedding Anniversary **Subject:** Queen Elizabeth and Prince Philip **Obv:** Crowned bust right **Rev:** Queen with her first born, Prince Charles

Date	Mintage	F	VF	XF	Unc	BU
1997 Proof	Est. 3,500	Value: 160				

KM# 533 1/5 CROWN

6.2207 g., 0.9999 Gold .2000 oz. AGW, 22 mm. **Ruler:** Elizabeth II **Series:** Golden Wedding Anniversary **Subject:** Queen Elizabeth and Prince Philip **Obv:** Crowned bust right **Rev:** the Queen, two children and a monkey

Date	Mintage	F	VF	XF	Unc	BU
1997 Proof	Est. 3,500	Value: 160				

KM# 535 1/5 CROWN

6.2207 g., 0.9999 Gold .2000 oz. AGW, 22 mm. **Ruler:** Elizabeth II **Series:** Golden Wedding Anniversary **Subject:** Queen Elizabeth and Prince Philip **Obv:** Crowned bust right **Rev:** Queen and adoring crowd

Date	Mintage	F	VF	XF	Unc	BU
1997 Proof	Est. 3,500	Value: 160				

KM# 539 1/5 CROWN

6.2207 g., 0.9999 Gold .2000 oz. AGW, 22 mm. **Ruler:** Elizabeth II **Obv:** Crowned bust right **Rev:** Peonies

Date	Mintage	F	VF	XF	Unc	BU
1997 Proof	Est. 5,000	Value: 160				

KM# 539a 1/5 CROWN

6.2200 g., 0.9950 Platinum .1990 oz. APW **Ruler:** Elizabeth II **Obv:** Crowned bust right **Rev:** Peonies

Date	Mintage	F	VF	XF	Unc	BU
1997 Proof	Est. 1,000	Value: 295				

KM# 543 1/5 CROWN

6.2200 g., 0.9999 Gold .2000 oz. AGW, 22 mm. **Ruler:** Elizabeth II **Subject:** Nefertiti **Obv:** Crowned bust right **Rev:** Head right

Date	Mintage	F	VF	XF	Unc	BU
1997 Proof	Est. 5,000	Value: 160				

KM# 543a 1/5 CROWN

6.2200 g., 0.9950 Platinum .1990 oz. APW **Ruler:** Elizabeth II **Subject:** Nefertiti **Obv:** Crowned bust right **Rev:** Head right

Date	Mintage	F	VF	XF	Unc	BU
1997 Proof	Est. 1,000	Value: 295				

KM# 547 1/5 CROWN

6.2200 g., 0.9999 Gold .2000 oz. AGW, 22 mm. **Ruler:** Elizabeth II **Subject:** Cleopatra **Obv:** Crowned bust right **Rev:** Head facing

Date	Mintage	F	VF	XF	Unc	BU
1997 Proof	Est. 5,000	Value: 160				

KM# 547a 1/5 CROWN

6.2200 g., 0.9950 Platinum .1990 oz. APW **Ruler:** Elizabeth II **Subject:** Cleopatra **Obv:** Crowned bust right **Rev:** Head facing

Date	Mintage	F	VF	XF	Unc	BU
1997 Proof	Est. 1,000	Value: 295				

KM# 551 1/5 CROWN

6.2200 g., 0.9999 Gold .2000 oz. AGW, 22 mm. **Ruler:** Elizabeth II **Subject:** Europa **Obv:** Crowned bust right **Rev:** Head 3/4 left

Date	Mintage	F	VF	XF	Unc	BU
1997 Proof	Est. 5,000	Value: 160				

KM# 551a 1/5 CROWN

6.2200 g., 0.9950 Platinum .1990 oz. APW **Ruler:** Elizabeth II **Subject:** Europa **Obv:** Crowned bust right **Rev:** Head 3/4 left

Date	Mintage	F	VF	XF	Unc	BU
1997 Proof	Est. 1,000	Value: 295				

KM# 555 1/5 CROWN

6.2200 g., 0.9999 Gold .2000 oz. AGW, 22 mm. **Ruler:** Elizabeth II **Subject:** Liberty **Obv:** Crowned bust right **Rev:** Laureate head right

Date	Mintage	F	VF	XF	Unc	BU
1997 Proof	Est. 5,000	Value: 160				

KM# 555a 1/5 CROWN

6.2200 g., 0.9950 Platinum .1990 oz. APW **Ruler:** Elizabeth II **Subject:** Liberty **Obv:** Crowned bust right **Rev:** Laureate head right

Date	Mintage	F	VF	XF	Unc	BU
1997 Proof	Est. 1,000	Value: 295				

KM# 562 1/5 CROWN

6.2200 g., 0.9999 Gold .2000 oz. AGW, 22 mm. **Ruler:** Elizabeth II **Series:** Queen's Birthday **Obv:** Crowned bust right **Rev:** Queen on horseback left

Date	Mintage	F	VF	XF	Unc	BU
1997 Proof	Est. 5,000	Value: 165				

KM# 563 1/5 CROWN

6.2200 g., 0.9999 Gold .2000 oz. AGW, 22 mm. **Ruler:** Elizabeth II **Series:** Queen's Birthday **Obv:** Crowned bust right **Rev:** Queen on horseback returning salute

Date	Mintage	F	VF	XF	Unc	BU
1997 Proof	Est. 5,000	Value: 165				

KM# 564 1/5 CROWN

6.2200 g., 0.9999 Gold .2000 oz. AGW, 22 mm. **Ruler:** Elizabeth II **Series:** Queen's Birthday **Obv:** Crowned bust right **Rev:** Trooping the Colors scene, cameo above

Date	Mintage	F	VF	XF	Unc	BU
1997 Proof	Est. 5,000	Value: 165				

KM# 565 1/5 CROWN

6.2200 g., 0.9999 Gold .2000 oz. AGW, 22 mm. **Ruler:** Elizabeth II **Series:** Queen's Birthday **Obv:** Crowned bust right **Rev:** Gurkha troops with dragons

Date	Mintage	F	VF	XF	Unc	BU
1997 Proof	Est. 5,000	Value: 165				

KM# 570 1/5 CROWN

6.2200 g., 0.9999 Gold .2000 oz. AGW, 22 mm. **Ruler:** Elizabeth II **Subject:** The New Mosque **Obv:** Crowned bust right **Rev:** Two cavalry riders with mosque in background

Date	Mintage	F	VF	XF	Unc	BU
1997 Proof	Est. 5,000	Value: 165				

KM# 635 1/5 CROWN

6.2200 g., 0.9999 Gold .2000 oz. AGW, 22 mm. **Ruler:** Elizabeth II **Subject:** Winter Olympics Japan **Obv:** Crowned bust right **Rev:** Speed skater and "Bullet Train"

Date	Mintage	F	VF	XF	Unc	BU
1998 Proof	Est. 5,000	Value: 165				

KM# 637 1/5 CROWN

6.2200 g., 0.9999 Gold .2000 oz. AGW, 22 mm. **Ruler:** Elizabeth II **Series:** Winter Olympics Japan **Obv:** Crowned bust right **Rev:** Ski jumper and Buddha

Date	Mintage	F	VF	XF	Unc	BU
1998 Proof	Est. 5,000	Value: 165				

KM# 639 1/5 CROWN

6.2200 g., 0.9999 Gold .2000 oz. AGW, 22 mm. **Ruler:** Elizabeth II **Series:** Winter Olympics Japan **Obv:** Crowned bust right **Rev:** Cross-country skiers

Date	Mintage	F	VF	XF	Unc	BU
1998 Proof	Est. 5,000	Value: 165				

KM# 641 1/5 CROWN

6.2200 g., 0.9999 Gold .2000 oz. AGW, 22 mm. **Ruler:** Elizabeth II **Series:** Winter Olympics Japan **Obv:** Crowned bust right **Rev:** Slalom skier and Zenkoji temple

Date	Mintage	F	VF	XF	Unc	BU
1998 Proof	Est. 5,000	Value: 165				

KM# 653 1/5 CROWN

6.2200 g., 0.9999 Gold .2000 oz. AGW, 22 mm. **Ruler:** Elizabeth II **Subject:** The Tale of Peter Rabbit **Obv:** Crowned bust right **Rev:** Standing rabbit facing with sparrow at left

Date	Mintage	F	VF	XF	Unc	BU
1998 Proof	Est. 10,000	Value: 165				

KM# 653a 1/5 CROWN

6.2200 g., 0.9950 Platinum .2000 oz. APW **Ruler:** Elizabeth II **Subject:** The Tale of Peter Rabbit **Obv:** Crowned bust right **Rev:** Standing rabbit facing with sparrow at left

Date	Mintage	F	VF	XF	Unc	BU
1998 Proof	Est. 2,500	Value: 295				

KM# 659 1/5 CROWN

6.2200 g., 0.9999 Gold .2000 oz. AGW, 22 mm. **Ruler:** Elizabeth II **Obv:** Crowned bust right **Rev:** Chrysanthemum

Date	Mintage	F	VF	XF	Unc	BU
1998 Proof	Est. 5,000	Value: 165				

KM# 659a 1/5 CROWN

6.2200 g., 0.9950 Platinum .2000 oz. APW **Ruler:** Elizabeth II **Obv:** Crowned bust right **Rev:** Chrysanthemum

Date	Mintage	F	VF	XF	Unc	BU
1998 Proof	Est. 1,000	Value: 295				

KM# 671 1/5 CROWN

6.2200 g., 0.9999 Gold .2000 oz. AGW, 22 mm. **Ruler:** Elizabeth II **Subject:** Juno **Obv:** Crowned bust right **Rev:** Head 3/4 facing

Date	Mintage	F	VF	XF	Unc	BU
1998 Proof	Est. 5,000	Value: 165				

KM# 671a 1/5 CROWN

6.2200 g., 0.9950 Platinum .2000 oz. APW **Ruler:** Elizabeth II **Subject:** Juno **Obv:** Crowned bust right **Rev:** Head 3/4 facing

Date	Mintage	F	VF	XF	Unc	BU
1998 Proof	Est. 1,000	Value: 295				

KM# 672 1/5 CROWN

6.2200 g., 0.9999 Gold .2000 oz. AGW, 22 mm. **Ruler:** Elizabeth II **Subject:** Athena **Obv:** Crowned bust right **Rev:** Helmeted head right

Date	Mintage	F	VF	XF	Unc	BU
1998 Proof	Est. 5,000	Value: 165				

KM# 672a 1/5 CROWN

6.2200 g., 0.9950 Platinum .2000 oz. APW **Subject:** Athena **Obv:** Crowned bust right **Rev:** Helmeted head right

Date	Mintage	F	VF	XF	Unc	BU
1998 Proof	Est. 1,000	Value: 295				

KM# 673 1/5 CROWN

6.2200 g., 0.9999 Gold .2000 oz. AGW, 22 mm. **Ruler:** Elizabeth II **Subject:** Arethusa **Obv:** Crowned bust right **Rev:** Head left with dolphins

Date	Mintage	F	VF	XF	Unc	BU
1998 Proof	Est. 5,000	Value: 165				

KM# 673a 1/5 CROWN

6.2200 g., 0.9950 Platinum .2000 oz. APW **Ruler:** Elizabeth II **Subject:** Arethusa **Obv:** Crowned bust right **Rev:** Head left with dolphins

Date	Mintage	F	VF	XF	Unc	BU
1998 Proof	Est. 1,000	Value: 295				

KM# 680 1/5 CROWN

6.2200 g., 0.9999 Gold .2000 oz. AGW, 22 mm. **Ruler:** Elizabeth II **Subject:** Paddington Bear **Obv:** Crowned bust right **Rev:** Bear with suitcase

Date	Mintage	F	VF	XF	Unc	BU
1998 Proof	Est. 5,000	Value: 165				

KM# 680a 1/5 CROWN

6.2200 g., 0.9950 Platinum .2000 oz. APW **Ruler:** Elizabeth II **Subject:** Paddington Bear **Obv:** Crowned bust right **Rev:** Bear with suitcase

Date	Mintage	F	VF	XF	Unc	BU
1998 Proof	Est. 2,000	Value: 295				

KM# 683 1/5 CROWN

6.2200 g., 0.9999 Gold .2000 oz. AGW, 22 mm. **Ruler:** Elizabeth II **Subject:** World Cup France 1998 **Obv:** Crowned bust right **Rev:** Goalie, map of Europe

Date	Mintage	F	VF	XF	Unc	BU
1998 Proof	Est. 5,000	Value: 165				

KM# 684 1/5 CROWN

6.2200 g., 0.9999 Gold .2000 oz. AGW, 22 mm. **Ruler:** Elizabeth II **Subject:** World Cup France 1998 **Obv:** Crowned bust right **Rev:** Player kicking to left

Date	Mintage	F	VF	XF	Unc	BU
1998 Proof	Est. 5,000	Value: 165				

KM# 685 1/5 CROWN

6.2200 g., 0.9999 Gold .2000 oz. AGW, 22 mm. **Ruler:** Elizabeth II **Subject:** World Cup France 1998 **Obv:** Crowned bust right **Rev:** Player dribbling ball

Date	Mintage	F	VF	XF	Unc	BU
1998 Proof	Est. 5,000	Value: 165				

GIBRALTAR

KM# 686 1/5 CROWN
6.2200 g., 0.9999 Gold .2000 oz. AGW, 22 mm. **Ruler:** Elizabeth II **Subject:** World Cup France 1998 **Obv:** Crowned bust right **Rev:** Two players, map of Europe

Date	Mintage	F	VF	XF	Unc	BU
1998 Proof	Est. 5,000	Value: 165				

KM# 731 1/5 CROWN
6.2200 g., 0.9999 Gold .2000 oz. AGW, 22 mm. **Ruler:** Elizabeth II **Obv:** Crowned bust right **Rev:** Cupid with hologram heart

Date	Mintage	F	VF	XF	Unc	BU
1998 Proof	Est. 5,000	Value: 165				

KM# 741 1/5 CROWN
6.2200 g., 0.9999 Gold .2000 oz. AGW, 22 mm. **Ruler:** Elizabeth II **Subject:** Year of the Ocean **Obv:** Crowned bust right **Rev:** Polar bear and walrus

Date	Mintage	F	VF	XF	Unc	BU
1998 Proof	Est. 5,000	Value: 170				

KM# 742 1/5 CROWN
6.2200 g., 0.9999 Gold .2000 oz. AGW, 22 mm. **Ruler:** Elizabeth II **Subject:** Year of the Ocean **Obv:** Crowned bust right **Rev:** Seals and penguins

Date	Mintage	F	VF	XF	Unc	BU
1998 Proof	Est. 5,000	Value: 170				

KM# 743 1/5 CROWN
6.2200 g., 0.9999 Gold .2000 oz. AGW, 22 mm. **Ruler:** Elizabeth II **Subject:** Year of the Ocean **Obv:** Crowned bust right **Rev:** Sea cow with calf

Date	Mintage	F	VF	XF	Unc	BU
1998 Proof	Est. 5,000	Value: 170				

KM# 744 1/5 CROWN
6.2200 g., 0.9999 Gold .2000 oz. AGW, 22 mm. **Ruler:** Elizabeth II **Subject:** Year of the Ocean **Obv:** Crowned bust right **Rev:** Surfer

Date	Mintage	F	VF	XF	Unc	BU
1998 Proof	Est. 5,000	Value: 165				

KM# 767 1/5 CROWN
6.2200 g., 0.9999 Gold .2000 oz. AGW, 22 mm. **Ruler:** Elizabeth II **Subject:** Gibraltar Regiment New Colours **Obv:** Crowned bust right **Rev:** Soldiers presenting keys

Date	Mintage	F	VF	XF	Unc	BU
1998 Proof	Est. 5,000	Value: 165				

KM# 798 1/5 CROWN
6.2200 g., 0.9999 Gold .2000 oz. AGW, 22 mm. **Ruler:** Elizabeth II **Series:** The World At War **Subject:** General D.D. Eisenhower **Obv:** Crowned bust right **Rev:** Bust facing and North African invasion scene

Date	Mintage	F	VF	XF	Unc	BU
1998 Proof	Est. 5,000	Value: 165				

KM# 781.1 1/5 CROWN
6.2200 g., 0.9999 Gold .2000 oz. AGW, 22 mm. **Ruler:** Elizabeth II **Subject:** 1999 Year of the Rabbit **Obv:** Crowned bust right **Rev:** Rabbit reading, sparrow, Chinese characters

Date	Mintage	F	VF	XF	Unc	BU
1999 Proof	Est. 3,500	Value: 165				

KM# 781.1a 1/5 CROWN
6.2200 g., 0.9950 Platinum .2000 oz. APW **Ruler:** Elizabeth II **Subject:** 1999 Year of the Rabbit **Obv:** Crowned bust right **Rev:** Rabbit reading, sparrow, Chinese characters

Date	Mintage	F	VF	XF	Unc	BU
1999 Proof	Est. 1,500	Value: 295				

KM# 781.2 1/5 CROWN
6.2200 g., 0.9999 Gold .2000 oz. AGW, 22 mm. **Ruler:** Elizabeth II **Obv:** Crowned bust right **Rev:** Rabbit reading, sparrow, without Chinese characters

Date	Mintage	F	VF	XF	Unc	BU
1999 Proof	Inc. above	Value: 165				

KM# 781.2a 1/5 CROWN
6.2200 g., 0.9950 Platinum .2000 oz. APW **Ruler:** Elizabeth II **Obv:** Crowned bust right **Rev:** Rabbit reading, sparrow; without Chinese characters

Date	Mintage	F	VF	XF	Unc	BU
1999 Proof	Inc. above	Value: 295				

KM# 784 1/5 CROWN
6.2200 g., 0.9999 Gold .2000 oz. AGW, 22 mm. **Ruler:** Elizabeth II **Series:** Summer Olympics - Sydney **Obv:** Crowned bust right **Rev:** Broad jumper with kangaroo

Date	Mintage	F	VF	XF	Unc	BU
1999 Proof	Est. 5,000	Value: 165				

KM# 786 1/5 CROWN
6.2200 g., 0.9999 Gold .2000 oz. AGW, 22 mm. **Ruler:** Elizabeth II **Series:** Summer Olympics - Sydney **Obv:** Crowned bust right **Rev:** Sailboats and platypus

Date	Mintage	F	VF	XF	Unc	BU
1999 Proof	Est. 5,000	Value: 165				

KM# 788 1/5 CROWN
6.2200 g., 0.9999 Gold .2000 oz. AGW, 22 mm. **Ruler:** Elizabeth II **Series:** Summer Olympics - Sydney **Obv:** Crowned bust right **Rev:** Swimmer and koala bear

Date	Mintage	F	VF	XF	Unc	BU
1999 Proof	Est. 5,000	Value: 165				

KM# 790 1/5 CROWN
6.2200 g., 0.9999 Gold .2000 oz. AGW, 22 mm. **Ruler:** Elizabeth II **Series:** Summer Olympics - Sydney **Obv:** Crowned bust right **Rev:** Two oarsmen and cockatoos

Date	Mintage	F	VF	XF	Unc	BU
1999 Proof	Est. 5,000	Value: 165				

KM# 792 1/5 CROWN
6.2200 g., 0.9999 Gold .2000 oz. AGW, 22 mm. **Ruler:** Elizabeth II **Series:** Summer Olympics - Sydney **Obv:** Crowned bust right **Rev:** Man with torch and dog

Date	Mintage	F	VF	XF	Unc	BU
1999 Proof	Est. 5,000	Value: 165				

KM# 794 1/5 CROWN
6.2200 g., 0.9999 Gold .2000 oz. AGW, 22 mm. **Ruler:** Elizabeth II **Series:** Summer Olympics - Sydney **Obv:** Crowned bust right **Rev:** Torch runner, portrait of Aborigini and Ayers Rock

Date	Mintage	F	VF	XF	Unc	BU
1999 Proof	Est. 5,000	Value: 165				

KM# 796 1/5 CROWN
6.2200 g., 0.9999 Gold .2000 oz. AGW, 22 mm. **Ruler:** Elizabeth II **Subject:** Millennium 2000 **Obv:** Head with tiara right **Rev:** Sundial, digital clock face, candle and traditional clock face

Date	Mintage	F	VF	XF	Unc	BU
1999 Proof	Est. 5,000	Value: 165				

KM# 800 1/5 CROWN
6.2200 g., 0.9999 Gold .2000 oz. AGW, 22 mm. **Ruler:** Elizabeth II **Subject:** King Alfred the Great, 871-899 **Obv:** Crowned bust right **Rev:** Crowned bust left

Date	Mintage	F	VF	XF	Unc	BU
1999 Proof	Est. 5,000	Value: 165				

KM# 802 1/5 CROWN
6.2200 g., 0.9999 Gold .2000 oz. AGW, 22 mm. **Ruler:** Elizabeth II **Subject:** King Canute, 1016-1035 **Obv:** Crowned bust right **Rev:** Crowned bust left

Date	Mintage	F	VF	XF	Unc	BU
1999 Proof	Est. 5,000	Value: 165				

KM# 804 1/5 CROWN
6.2200 g., 0.9999 Gold .2000 oz. AGW, 22 mm. **Ruler:** Elizabeth II **Subject:** King Edward the Confessor, 1042-1066 **Obv:** Crowned bust right **Rev:** Crowned bust left

Date	Mintage	F	VF	XF	Unc	BU
1999 Proof	Est. 5,000	Value: 165				

KM# 806 1/5 CROWN
6.2200 g., 0.9999 Gold .2000 oz. AGW, 22 mm. **Ruler:** Elizabeth II **Series:** House of - Normandy **Subject:** King William I, 1066-1087 **Obv:** Crowned bust right **Rev:** Crowned bust left

Date	Mintage	F	VF	XF	Unc	BU
1999 Proof	Est. 5,000	Value: 165				

KM# 808 1/5 CROWN
6.2200 g., 0.9999 Gold .2000 oz. AGW, 22 mm. **Ruler:** Elizabeth II **Series:** House of - Plantagenet **Subject:** King Richard I, 1189-1199 **Obv:** Crowned bust right **Rev:** Crowned bust right

Date	Mintage	F	VF	XF	Unc	BU
1999 Proof	Est. 5,000	Value: 165				

KM# 810 1/5 CROWN
6.2200 g., 0.9999 Gold .2000 oz. AGW, 22 mm. **Ruler:** Elizabeth II **Series:** House of - Plantagenet **Subject:** King John, 1199-1216 **Obv:** Crowned bust right **Rev:** Crowned bust left

Date	Mintage	F	VF	XF	Unc	BU
1999 Proof	Est. 5,000	Value: 165				

KM# 812 1/5 CROWN
6.2200 g., 0.9999 Gold .2000 oz. AGW, 22 mm. **Ruler:** Elizabeth II **Series:** House of - Lancaster **Subject:** King Henry V, 1413-1422 **Obv:** Crowned bust right **Rev:** Bust right

Date	Mintage	F	VF	XF	Unc	BU
1999 Proof	Est. 5,000	Value: 165				

KM# 814 1/5 CROWN
6.2200 g., 0.9999 Gold .2000 oz. AGW, 22 mm. **Ruler:** Elizabeth II **Series:** House of - York **Subject:** King Richard III, 1483-1485 **Obv:** Crowned bust right **Rev:** Bust with hat right

Date	Mintage	F	VF	XF	Unc	BU
1999 Proof	Est. 5,000	Value: 165				

KM# 816 1/5 CROWN
6.2200 g., 0.9999 Gold .2000 oz. AGW, 22 mm. **Ruler:** Elizabeth II **Series:** House of - Tudor **Subject:** King Henry VIII, 1509-1547 **Obv:** Crowned bust right **Rev:** Bust with hat right

Date	Mintage	F	VF	XF	Unc	BU
1999 Proof	Est. 5,000	Value: 165				

KM# 818 1/5 CROWN
6.2200 g., 0.9999 Gold .2000 oz. AGW, 22 mm. **Ruler:** Elizabeth II **Series:** House of - Tudor **Subject:** Queen Elizabeth, 1558-1603 **Obv:** Crowned bust right **Rev:** Crowned bust with high ruffled collar left

Date	Mintage	F	VF	XF	Unc	BU
1999 Proof	Est. 5,000	Value: 165				

KM# 820 1/5 CROWN
6.2200 g., 0.9999 Gold .2000 oz. AGW, 22 mm. **Ruler:** Elizabeth II **Series:** House of - Stuart **Subject:** King Charles I, 1625-1649 **Obv:** Crowned bust right **Rev:** Bust right

Date	Mintage	F	VF	XF	Unc	BU
1999 Proof	Est. 5,000	Value: 165				

KM# 822 1/5 CROWN
6.2200 g., 0.9999 Gold .2000 oz. AGW, 22 mm. **Ruler:** Elizabeth II **Series:** House of - Stuart **Subject:** King Charles II, 1660-1685 **Obv:** Crowned bust right **Rev:** Laureate bust right

Date	Mintage	F	VF	XF	Unc	BU
1999 Proof	Est. 5,000	Value: 165				

KM# 824 1/5 CROWN
6.2200 g., 0.9999 Gold .2000 oz. AGW, 22 mm. **Ruler:** Elizabeth II **Subject:** The Wedding of Prince Edward and Miss Sophie Rhys-Jones **Obv:** Crowned bust right **Rev:** Heads facing above banner and wedding bells

Date	Mintage	F	VF	XF	Unc	BU
1999 Proof	Est. 5,000	Value: 165				

KM# 826.1 1/5 CROWN
6.2200 g., 0.9999 Gold .2000 oz. AGW, 22 mm. **Ruler:** Elizabeth II **Subject:** The Wedding of Prince Edward and Miss Sophie Rhys-Jones **Obv:** Crowned bust right **Rev:** St. George's Chapel

Date	Mintage	F	VF	XF	Unc	BU
1999 Proof	Est. 5,000	Value: 165				

KM# 834 1/5 CROWN
6.2200 g., 0.9999 Gold .2000 oz. AGW, 22 mm. **Ruler:** Elizabeth II **Subject:** The Life of Queen Elizabeth **Obv:** Crowned bust right **Rev:** 1905 portrait of Queen Mother as a girl

Date	Mintage	F	VF	XF	Unc	BU
1999 Proof	Est. 5,000	Value: 165				

KM# 836 1/5 CROWN
6.2200 g., 0.9999 Gold .2000 oz. AGW, 22 mm. **Ruler:** Elizabeth II **Subject:** The Life of Queen Elizabeth **Obv:** Crowned bust right **Rev:** 1918 portrait of Queen Mother with wounded veteran

Date	Mintage	F	VF	XF	Unc	BU
1999 Proof	Est. 5,000	Value: 165				

KM# 838 1/5 CROWN
6.2200 g., 0.9999 Gold .2000 oz. AGW, 22 mm. **Ruler:** Elizabeth II **Subject:** The Life of Queen Elizabeth **Obv:** Crowned bust right **Rev:** 1923 wedding portrait

Date	Mintage	F	VF	XF	Unc	BU
1999 Proof	Est. 5,000	Value: 165				

296 GIBRALTAR

KM# 840 1/5 CROWN
6.2200 g., 0.9999 Gold .2000 oz. AGW, 22 mm. **Ruler:** Elizabeth II **Subject:** The Life of Queen Elizabeth **Obv:** Crowned bust right **Rev:** 1936 family portrait

Date	Mintage	F	VF	XF	Unc	BU
1999 Proof	Est. 5,000	Value: 165				

KM# 843 1/5 CROWN
6.2200 g., 0.9999 Gold .2000 oz. AGW, 22 mm. **Ruler:** Elizabeth II **Series:** The World At War **Subject:** Franklin D. Roosevelt **Obv:** Crowned bust right **Rev:** Bust writing at left, Zero fighter at right

Date	Mintage	F	VF	XF	Unc	BU
1999 Proof	—	Value: 165				

KM# 844 1/5 CROWN
6.2200 g., 0.9999 Gold .2000 oz. AGW, 22 mm. **Ruler:** Elizabeth II **Subject:** The World At War **Obv:** Crowned bust right **Rev:** Bomber dropping food packets

Date	Mintage	F	VF	XF	Unc	BU
1999 Proof	Est. 5,000	Value: 165				

KM# 847 1/5 CROWN
6.2200 g., 0.9999 Gold .2000 oz. AGW, 22 mm. **Ruler:** Elizabeth II **Subject:** The World At War **Obv:** Crowned bust right **Rev:** B-29, mushroom cloud and bust at right

Date	Mintage	F	VF	XF	Unc	BU
1999 Proof	Est. 5,000	Value: 165				

KM# 848 1/5 CROWN
6.2200 g., 0.9999 Gold .2000 oz. AGW, 22 mm. **Ruler:** Elizabeth II **Subject:** The World At War **Obv:** Crowned bust right **Rev:** Bust at left reading, bomber above dam

Date	Mintage	F	VF	XF	Unc	BU
1999 Proof	Est. 5,000	Value: 165				

KM# 850 1/5 CROWN
6.2200 g., 0.9999 Gold .2000 oz. AGW, 22 mm. **Ruler:** Elizabeth II **Subject:** The World At War **Obv:** Crowned bust right **Rev:** Bust at left facing, planes in combat

Date	Mintage	F	VF	XF	Unc	BU
1999 Proof	Est. 5,000	Value: 165				

KM# 852 1/5 CROWN
6.2200 g., 0.9999 Gold .2000 oz. AGW, 22 mm. **Ruler:** Elizabeth II **Subject:** Winston Churchill **Obv:** Crowned bust right **Rev:** Bust with hand showing 'V' sign, crowd in background

Date	Mintage	F	VF	XF	Unc	BU
1999 Proof	Est. 5,000	Value: 165				

KM# 854 1/5 CROWN
6.2200 g., 0.9999 Gold .2000 oz. AGW, 22 mm. **Ruler:** Elizabeth II **Subject:** Tirpitz **Obv:** Crowned bust right **Rev:** Battleship and sailor

Date	Mintage	F	VF	XF	Unc	BU
1999 Proof	Est. 5,000	Value: 165				

KM# 856 1/5 CROWN
6.2200 g., 0.9999 Gold .2000 oz. AGW, 22 mm. **Ruler:** Elizabeth II **Subject:** War Babies **Obv:** Crowned bust right **Rev:** Soldier kissing child

Date	Mintage	F	VF	XF	Unc	BU
1999 Proof	Est. 5,000	Value: 165				

KM# 858 1/5 CROWN
6.2200 g., 0.9999 Gold .2000 oz. AGW, 22 mm. **Ruler:** Elizabeth II **Subject:** The World At War **Obv:** Crowned bust right **Rev:** 2 firemen in action after air raid

Date	Mintage	F	VF	XF	Unc	BU
1999 Proof	Est. 5,000	Value: 165				

KM# 860 1/5 CROWN
6.2200 g., 0.9999 Gold .2000 oz. AGW, 22 mm. **Ruler:** Elizabeth II **Subject:** The World At War **Obv:** Crowned bust right **Rev:** Landing scene

Date	Mintage	F	VF	XF	Unc	BU
1999 Proof	Est. 5,000	Value: 165				

KM# 862 1/5 CROWN
6.2200 g., 0.9999 Gold .2000 oz. AGW, 22 mm. **Ruler:** Elizabeth II **Subject:** The World At War **Obv:** Crowned bust right **Rev:** Military skier

Date	Mintage	F	VF	XF	Unc	BU
1999 Proof	Est. 5,000	Value: 165				

KM# 864 1/5 CROWN
6.2200 g., 0.9999 Gold .2000 oz. AGW, 22 mm. **Ruler:** Elizabeth II **Subject:** The World At War **Obv:** Crowned bust right **Rev:** German tanks in Russia

Date	Mintage	F	VF	XF	Unc	BU
1999 Proof	Est. 5,000	Value: 165				

KM# 870 1/5 CROWN
6.2200 g., 0.9999 Gold .2000 oz. AGW, 22 mm. **Ruler:** Elizabeth II **Series:** Queen Mother **Obv:** Head with tiara right **Rev:** 1937 Coronation scene

Date	Mintage	F	VF	XF	Unc	BU
2000 Proof	5,000	Value: 175				

KM# 872 1/5 CROWN
6.2200 g., 0.9999 Gold .2000 oz. AGW, 22 mm. **Ruler:** Elizabeth II **Series:** Queen Mother **Obv:** Crowned bust right **Rev:** 1938 Visit to France

Date	Mintage	F	VF	XF	Unc	BU
2000 Proof	5,000	Value: 175				

KM# 874 1/5 CROWN
6.2200 g., 0.9999 Gold .2000 oz. AGW, 22 mm. **Ruler:** Elizabeth II **Series:** Queen Mother **Obv:** Crowned bust right **Rev:** 1940 Bomb damage

Date	Mintage	F	VF	XF	Unc	BU
2000 Proof	5,000	Value: 175				

KM# 876 1/5 CROWN
6.2200 g., 0.9999 Gold .2000 oz. AGW, 22 mm. **Ruler:** Elizabeth II **Series:** Queen Mother **Obv:** Crowned bust right

Date	Mintage	F	VF	XF	Unc	BU
2000 Proof	5,000	Value: 175				

KM# 879 1/5 CROWN
6.2200 g., 0.9999 Gold .2000 oz. AGW, 22 mm. **Ruler:** Elizabeth II **Subject:** 18th Birthday of Prince William **Obv:** Crowned bust right **Rev:** Bust facing **Edge:** Reeded

Date	Mintage	F	VF	XF	Unc	BU
2000 Proof	5,000	Value: 175				

KM# 881 1/5 CROWN
6.2200 g., 0.9999 Gold .2000 oz. AGW, 22 mm. **Ruler:** Elizabeth II **Series:** 100th Birthday of the Queen Mother **Obv:** Crowned bust right **Rev:** Bust facing **Note:** Queen Mother's portrait has a real diamond chip (.015) set in her crown.

Date	Mintage	F	VF	XF	Unc	BU
2000 Proof	2,000	Value: 175				

KM# 902 1/5 CROWN
6.2200 g., 0.9999 Gold .2000 oz. AGW, 22 mm. **Ruler:** Elizabeth II **Subject:** Queen Mother **Obv:** Bust with tiara right **Obv. Designer:** Ian Rank-Broadley **Rev:** 1953 Coronation scene **Edge:** Reeded

Date	Mintage	F	VF	XF	Unc	BU
2001 Proof	5,000	Value: 175				

KM# 903 1/5 CROWN
6.2200 g., 0.9999 Gold .2000 oz. AGW **Ruler:** Elizabeth II **Obv:** Bust with tiara right **Obv. Designer:** Ian Rank-Broadley **Rev:** Queen Mother and Prince Charles in 1954

Date	Mintage	F	VF	XF	Unc	BU
2001 Proof	5,000	Value: 175				

KM# 909 1/5 CROWN
6.2200 g., 0.9999 Gold .2000 oz. AGW, 22 mm. **Ruler:** Elizabeth II **Series:** Victorian Era - Victoria's Coronation 1838 **Obv:** Bust with tiara right **Obv. Designer:** Ian Rank-Broadley **Rev:** 1838 Coronation scene **Edge:** Reeded

Date	Mintage	F	VF	XF	Unc	BU
2001 Proof	5,000	Value: 175				

KM# 909.1 1/5 CROWN
6.2200 g., 0.9999 Gold .2000 oz. AGW, 22 mm. **Ruler:** Elizabeth II **Series:** Victorian Era **Obv:** Bust with tiara right **Obv. Designer:** Ian Rank-Broadley **Rev:** 1838 Coronation scene with a tiny emerald set in the field below the 1838 date **Edge:** Reeded

Date	Mintage	F	VF	XF	Unc	BU
2001 Proof	2,001	Value: 200				

KM# 911.1 1/5 CROWN
6.2200 g., 0.9999 Gold .2000 oz. AGW, 22 mm. **Ruler:** Elizabeth II **Series:** Victorian Era - Empress of India 1876 **Obv:** Bust with tiara right **Obv. Designer:** Ian Rank-Broadley **Rev:** Crowned portrait of Victoria and two elephants **Edge:** Reeded

Date	Mintage	F	VF	XF	Unc	BU
2001 Proof	5,000	Value: 175				

KM# 911.2 1/5 CROWN
6.2200 g., 0.9999 Gold .2000 oz. AGW, 22 mm. **Ruler:** Elizabeth II **Series:** Victorian Era - Empress of India 1876 **Obv:** Bust with tiara right **Obv. Designer:** Ian Rank-Broadley **Rev:** Tiny ruby set in the field behind Victoria's head **Edge:** Reeded

Date	Mintage	F	VF	XF	Unc	BU
2001 Proof	2,001	Value: 200				

KM# 913.1 1/5 CROWN
6.2200 g., 0.9999 Gold .2000 oz. AGW, 22 mm. **Ruler:** Elizabeth II **Series:** Victorian Era - Diamond Jubilee 1897 **Obv:** Bust with tiara right **Obv. Designer:** Ian Rank-Broadley **Rev:** Victoria's cameo portrait above naval ships **Edge:** Reeded

Date	Mintage	F	VF	XF	Unc	BU
2001 Proof	5,000	Value: 175				

KM# 913.2 1/5 CROWN
6.2200 g., 0.9999 Gold .2000 oz. AGW, 22 mm. **Ruler:** Elizabeth II **Series:** Victorian Era - Diamond Jubilee 1897 **Obv:** Bust with tiara right **Obv. Designer:** Ian Rank-Broadley **Rev:** Tiny diamond set at the top of the fourth mast **Edge:** Reeded

Date	Mintage	F	VF	XF	Unc	BU
2001 Proof	2,001	Value: 200				

KM# 915.1 1/5 CROWN
6.2200 g., 0.9999 Gold .2000 oz. AGW, 22 mm. **Ruler:** Elizabeth II **Series:** Victorian Era - Victoria's Death 1901 **Obv:** Bust with tiara right **Obv. Designer:** Ian Rank-Broadley **Rev:** Victoria's cameo portrait and Osborne Manor **Edge:** Reeded

Date	Mintage	F	VF	XF	Unc	BU
2001 Proof	5,000	Value: 175				

KM# 915.2 1/5 CROWN
6.2200 g., 0.9999 Gold .2000 oz. AGW, 22 mm. **Ruler:** Elizabeth II **Series:** Victorian Era - Victoria's Death 1901 **Obv:** Bust with tiara right **Obv. Designer:** Ian Rank-Broadley **Rev:** Tiny sapphire set in the field between the towers **Edge:** Reeded

Date	Mintage	F	VF	XF	Unc	BU
2001 Proof	2,001	Value: 200				

KM# 917 1/5 CROWN
6.2200 g., 0.9999 Gold .2000 oz. AGW, 22 mm. **Ruler:** Elizabeth II **Series:** Victorian Era - Prince Albert and the Great Exhibition 1851 **Obv:** Bust with tiara right **Obv. Designer:** Ian Rank-Broadley **Rev:** Albert's cameo portrait and the exhibit hall **Edge:** Reeded

Date	Mintage	F	VF	XF	Unc	BU
2001 Proof	5,000	Value: 175				

KM# 919 1/5 CROWN
6.2200 g., 0.9999 Gold .2000 oz. AGW, 22 mm. **Ruler:** Elizabeth II **Series:** Victorian Era - Isambard K. Brunel **Obv:** Bust with tiara right **Obv. Designer:** Ian Rank-Broadley **Rev:** Portrait in top hat and railroad bridge **Edge:** Reeded

Date	Mintage	F	VF	XF	Unc	BU
2001 Proof	5,000	Value: 175				

KM# 921 1/5 CROWN
6.2200 g., 0.9999 Gold .2000 oz. AGW, 22 mm. **Ruler:** Elizabeth II **Series:** Victorian Era - Charles Dickens **Obv:** Bust with tiara right **Obv. Designer:** Ian Rank-Broadley **Rev:** Portrait and scene from "Oliver Twist" **Edge:** Reeded

Date	Mintage	F	VF	XF	Unc	BU
2001 Proof	5,000	Value: 175				

KM# 923 1/5 CROWN
6.2200 g., 0.9999 Gold .2000 oz. AGW, 22 mm. **Ruler:** Elizabeth II **Series:** Victorian Era - Charles Darwin **Obv:** Bust with tiara right **Obv. Designer:** Ian Rank-Broadley **Rev:** Portrait, ship and a squatting aboriginal figure **Edge:** Reeded

Date	Mintage	F	VF	XF	Unc	BU
2001 Proof	5,000	Value: 175				

KM# 925 1/5 CROWN
6.2200 g., 0.9999 Gold .2000 oz. AGW, 22 mm. **Ruler:** Elizabeth II **Series:** Mythology of the Solar System **Obv:** Queens portrait **Rev:** Standing goddess with snake basket **Edge:** Reeded

Date	Mintage	F	VF	XF	Unc	BU
2001 Proof	5,000	Value: 175				

KM# 929.1 1/5 CROWN
6.2200 g., 0.9999 Gold .2000 oz. AGW, 22 mm. **Ruler:** Elizabeth II **Series:** Mythology of the Solar System - Sun **Obv:** Bust with tiara right **Obv. Designer:** Ian Rank-Broadley **Rev:** Helios in chariot and the sun **Edge:** Reeded

Date	Mintage	F	VF	XF	Unc	BU
2001 Proof	5,000	Value: 175				

KM# 929.2 1/5 CROWN
6.2200 g., 0.9999 Gold .2000 oz. AGW, 22 mm. **Ruler:** Elizabeth II **Series:** Mythology of the Solar System **Obv:** Bust with tiara right **Obv. Designer:** Ian Rank-Broadley **Rev:** Fiery hologram in the sun **Edge:** Reeded

Date	Mintage	F	VF	XF	Unc	BU
2001 In Proof sets only	999	Value: 350				

KM# 931.1 1/5 CROWN
6.2200 g., 0.9999 Gold .2000 oz. AGW, 22 mm. **Ruler:** Elizabeth II **Series:** Mythology of the Solar System - Moon **Obv:** Bust with tiara right **Obv. Designer:** Ian Rank-Broadley **Rev:** Goddess Diana and the moon **Edge:** Reeded

Date	Mintage	F	VF	XF	Unc	BU
2001 Proof	5,000	Value: 175				

KM# 931.2 1/5 CROWN
6.2200 g., 0.9999 Gold .2000 oz. AGW, 22 mm. **Ruler:** Elizabeth II **Series:** Mythology of the Solar System - Moon **Obv:** Bust with tiara right **Obv. Designer:** Ian Rank-Broadley **Rev:** Small pearl set in the moon **Edge:** Reeded

Date	Mintage	F	VF	XF	Unc	BU
2001 In Proof sets only	999	Value: 350				

KM# 933.1 1/5 CROWN
6.2200 g., 0.9999 Gold .2000 oz. AGW, 22 mm. **Ruler:** Elizabeth II **Series:** Mythology of the Solar System - Atlas **Obv:** Bust with tiara right **Obv. Designer:** Ian Rank-Broadley **Rev:** Atlas carrying the earth **Edge:** Reeded

Date	Mintage	F	VF	XF	Unc	BU
2001 Proof	5,000	Value: 175				

KM# 933.2 1/5 CROWN
6.2200 g., 0.9999 Gold .2000 oz. AGW, 22 mm. **Ruler:** Elizabeth II **Series:** Mythology of the Solar System - Atlas **Obv:** Bust with tiara right **Obv. Designer:** Ian Rank-Broadley **Rev:** Tiny diamond set in the earth **Edge:** Reeded

Date	Mintage	F	VF	XF	Unc	BU
2001 In Proof sets only	999	Value: 350				

KM# 935 1/5 CROWN
6.2200 g., 0.9999 Gold .2000 oz. AGW, 22 mm. **Ruler:** Elizabeth II **Series:** Mythology of the Solar System - Neptune **Obv:** Bust with tiara right **Obv. Designer:** Ian Rank-Broadley **Rev:** Seated god with trident and ringed planet **Edge:** Reeded

Date	Mintage	F	VF	XF	Unc	BU
2001 Proof	5,000	Value: 175				

KM# 937 1/5 CROWN
6.2200 g., 0.9999 Gold .2000 oz. AGW, 22 mm. **Ruler:** Elizabeth II **Series:** Mythology of the Solar System - Jupiter **Obv:** Bust with tiara right **Obv. Designer:** Ian Rank-Broadley **Rev:** Seated god with lightning bolts and a planet **Edge:** Reeded

Date	Mintage	F	VF	XF	Unc	BU
2001 Proof	5,000	Value: 175				

KM# 939 1/5 CROWN
6.2200 g., 0.9999 Gold .2000 oz. AGW, 22 mm. **Ruler:** Elizabeth II **Series:** Mythology of the Solar System - Mars **Obv:** Bust with tiara right **Obv. Designer:** Ian Rank-Broadley **Rev:** Standing Roman solider and a planet **Edge:** Reeded

Date	Mintage	F	VF	XF	Unc	BU
2001 Proof	5,000	Value: 175				

KM# 941 1/5 CROWN

6.2200 g., 0.9999 Gold .2000 oz. AGW, 22 mm. **Ruler:** Elizabeth II **Series:** Mythology of the Solar System - Mercury **Obv:** Bust with tiara right **Obv. Designer:** Ian Rank-Broadley **Rev:** Seated god with caduceus and a planet **Edge:** Reeded

Date	Mintage	F	VF	XF	Unc	BU
2001 Proof	5,000	Value: 175				

KM# 943 1/5 CROWN

6.2200 g., 0.9999 Gold .2000 oz. AGW, 22 mm. **Ruler:** Elizabeth II **Series:** Mythology of the Solar System - Uranus **Obv:** Bust with tiara right **Obv. Designer:** Ian Rank-Broadley **Rev:** Seated god with scepter **Edge:** Reeded

Date	Mintage	F	VF	XF	Unc	BU
2001 Proof	5,000	Value: 175				

KM# 945 1/5 CROWN

6.2200 g., 0.9999 Gold .2000 oz. AGW, 22 mm. **Ruler:** Elizabeth II **Series:** Mythology of the Solar System - Saturn **Obv:** Bust with tiara right **Obv. Designer:** Ian Rank-Broadley **Rev:** Seated god with long handled sickle and a ringed planet **Edge:** Reeded

Date	Mintage	F	VF	XF	Unc	BU
2001 Proof	5,000	Value: 175				

KM# 947 1/5 CROWN

6.2200 g., 0.9999 Gold .2000 oz. AGW, 22 mm. **Ruler:** Elizabeth II **Series:** Mythology of the Solar System - Pluto **Obv:** Bust with tiara right **Obv. Designer:** Ian Rank-Broadley **Rev:** Seated god with dogs and a planet **Edge:** Reeded

Date	Mintage	F	VF	XF	Unc	BU
2001 Proof	5,000	Value: 175				

KM# 949 1/5 CROWN

6.2200 g., 0.9999 Gold .2000 oz. AGW, 22 mm. **Ruler:** Elizabeth II **Series:** Mythology of the Solar System - Venus **Obv:** Bust with tiara right **Obv. Designer:** Ian Rank-Broadley **Rev:** Goddess seated on a half shell **Edge:** Reeded

Date	Mintage	F	VF	XF	Unc	BU
2001 Proof	5,000	Value: 175				

KM# 954 1/5 CROWN

6.2200 g., 0.9999 Gold .2000 oz. AGW, 22 mm. **Ruler:** Elizabeth II **Series:** Victorian Age Part II - Victoria's Accession to the Throne **Obv:** Bust with tiara right **Obv. Designer:** Ian Rank-Broadley **Rev:** Victoria learning of her accession **Edge:** Reeded

Date	Mintage	F	VF	XF	Unc	BU
2001 Proof	5,000	Value: 175				

KM# 956 1/5 CROWN

6.2200 g., 0.9999 Gold .2000 oz. AGW, 22 mm. **Ruler:** Elizabeth II **Series:** Victorian Age Part II - Royal Family **Rev:** Victoria and Albert seated with children **Edge:** Reeded

Date	Mintage	F	VF	XF	Unc	BU
2001 Proof	5,000	Value: 175				

KM# 958 1/5 CROWN

6.2200 g., 0.9999 Gold .2000 oz. AGW, 22 mm. **Ruler:** Elizabeth II **Series:** Victorian Age Part II - Victoria in Scotland **Obv:** Bust with tiara right **Obv. Designer:** Ian Rank-Broadley **Rev:** Victoria on horse and servant **Edge:** Reeded

Date	Mintage	F	VF	XF	Unc	BU
2001 Proof	5,000	Value: 175				

KM# 960 1/5 CROWN

6.2200 g., 0.9999 Gold .2000 oz. AGW, 22 mm. **Ruler:** Elizabeth II **Series:** Victorian Age Part II **Obv:** Bust with tiara right **Obv. Designer:** Ian Rank-Broadley **Rev:** Portraits of Gladstone and Disaraeli **Edge:** Reeded

Date	Mintage	F	VF	XF	Unc	BU
2001 Proof	5,000	Value: 175				

KM# 962 1/5 CROWN

6.2200 g., 0.9999 Gold .2000 oz. AGW, 22 mm. **Ruler:** Elizabeth II **Series:** Victorian Age Part II **Obv:** Bust with tiara right **Obv. Designer:** Ian Rank-Broadley **Rev:** Florence Nightingale holding lantern **Edge:** Reeded

Date	Mintage	F	VF	XF	Unc	BU
2001 Proof	5,000	Value: 175				

KM# 964 1/5 CROWN

6.2200 g., 0.9999 Gold .2000 oz. AGW, 22 mm. **Ruler:** Elizabeth II **Series:** Victorian Age Part II **Obv:** Bust with tiara right **Obv. Designer:** Ian Rank-Broadley **Rev:** Lord Tennyson with the Light Brigade in background **Edge:** Reeded

Date	Mintage	F	VF	XF	Unc	BU
2001 Proof	5,000	Value: 175				

KM# 966 1/5 CROWN

6.2200 g., 0.9999 Gold .2000 oz. AGW, 22 mm. **Ruler:** Elizabeth II **Series:** Victorian Age Part II **Obv:** Bust with tiara right **Obv. Designer:** Ian Rank-Broadley **Rev:** Stanley meeting Dr. Livingstone **Edge:** Reeded

Date	Mintage	F	VF	XF	Unc	BU
2001 Proof	5,000	Value: 175				

KM# 968 1/5 CROWN

6.2200 g., 0.9999 Gold .2000 oz. AGW, 22 mm. **Ruler:** Elizabeth II **Series:** Victorian Age Part II **Obv:** Bust with tiara right **Rev:** Bronte sisters **Edge:** Reeded

Date	Mintage	F	VF	XF	Unc	BU
2001 Proof	5,000	Value: 175				

KM# 978 1/5 CROWN

6.2200 g., 0.9990 Gold 0.1998 oz. AGW, 22 mm. **Ruler:** Elizabeth II **Subject:** Queen Mother's Life **Obv:** Bust right **Rev:** Prince William's christening scene **Edge:** Reeded

Date	Mintage	F	VF	XF	Unc	BU
2002 Proof	5,000	Value: 175				

KM# 980 1/5 CROWN

6.2200 g., 0.9999 Gold 0.2 oz. AGW, 22 mm. **Ruler:** Elizabeth II **Subject:** World Cup Soccer **Obv:** Bust right **Rev:** Two players about to collide **Edge:** Reeded

Date	Mintage	F	VF	XF	Unc	BU
2002 Proof	5,000	Value: 175				

KM# 982 1/5 CROWN

6.2200 g., 0.9999 Gold 0.2 oz. AGW, 22 mm. **Ruler:** Elizabeth II **Subject:** World Cup Soccer **Obv:** Bust right **Rev:** Two players facing viewer **Edge:** Reeded

Date	Mintage	F	VF	XF	Unc	BU
2002 Proof	5,000	Value: 175				

KM# 984 1/5 CROWN

6.2200 g., 0.9999 Gold 0.2 oz. AGW, 22 mm. **Ruler:** Elizabeth II **Subject:** World Cup Soccer **Obv:** Bust right **Rev:** Two horizontal players **Edge:** Reeded

Date	Mintage	F	VF	XF	Unc	BU
2002 Proof	5,000	Value: 175				

KM# 986 1/5 CROWN

6.2200 g., 0.9999 Gold 0.2 oz. AGW, 22 mm. **Ruler:** Elizabeth II **Subject:** World Cup Soccer **Obv:** Bust right **Rev:** Two players moving to the left **Edge:** Reeded

Date	Mintage	F	VF	XF	Unc	BU
2002 Proof	5,000	Value: 175				

KM# 990 1/5 CROWN

6.2200 g., 0.9990 Gold 0.1998 oz. AGW, 22 mm. **Ruler:** Elizabeth II **Subject:** Peter Rabbit Centennial **Obv:** Bust right **Rev:** Peter Rabbit **Edge:** Reeded

Date	Mintage	F	VF	XF	Unc	BU
2002 Proof	3,500	Value: 175				

KM# 990a 1/5 CROWN

6.2200 g., 0.9990 Platinum 0.1998 oz. APW, 22 mm. **Ruler:** Elizabeth II **Subject:** Peter Rabbit Centennial **Obv:** Bust right **Rev:** Peter Rabbit **Edge:** Reeded

Date	Mintage	F	VF	XF	Unc	BU
2002 Proof	1,500	Value: 275				

KM# 993 1/5 CROWN

6.2200 g., 0.3750 Gold 0.075 oz. AGW, 22 mm. **Ruler:** Elizabeth II **Subject:** Queen's Golden Jubilee **Obv:** Bust with tiara right **Obv. Designer:** Ian Rank-Broadley **Rev:** Royal couple and tree house **Edge:** Reeded

Date	Mintage	F	VF	XF	Unc	BU
2002 Proof	5,000	Value: 75.00				

KM# 993a 1/5 CROWN

6.2200 g., 0.9999 Gold 0.2 oz. AGW, 22 mm. **Ruler:** Elizabeth II **Subject:** Queen's Golden Jubilee **Obv:** Bust with tiara right **Obv. Designer:** Ian Rank-Broadley **Rev:** Royal couple and tree house **Edge:** Reeded

Date	Mintage	F	VF	XF	Unc	BU
2002 Proof	2,002	Value: 175				

KM# 995 1/5 CROWN

6.2200 g., 0.3750 Gold 0.075 oz. AGW, 22 mm. **Ruler:** Elizabeth II **Subject:** Queen's Golden Jubilee **Obv:** Bust with tiara right **Obv. Designer:** Ian Rank-Broadley **Rev:** Royal coach **Edge:** Reeded

Date	Mintage	F	VF	XF	Unc	BU
2002 Proof	5,000	Value: 75.00				

KM# 995a 1/5 CROWN

6.2200 g., 0.9999 Gold 0.2 oz. AGW, 22 mm. **Ruler:** Elizabeth II **Subject:** Queen's Golden Jubilee **Obv:** Bust with tiara right **Obv. Designer:** Ian Rank-Broadley **Rev:** Royal coach **Edge:** Reeded

Date	Mintage	F	VF	XF	Unc	BU
2002 Proof	2,002	Value: 175				

KM# 997 1/5 CROWN

6.2200 g., 0.3750 Gold 0.075 oz. AGW, 22 mm. **Ruler:** Elizabeth II **Subject:** Queen's Golden Jubilee **Obv:** Bust with tiara right **Obv. Designer:** Ian Rank-Broadley **Rev:** Queen holding baby **Edge:** Reeded

Date	Mintage	F	VF	XF	Unc	BU
2002 Proof	5,000	Value: 75.00				

KM# 997a 1/5 CROWN

6.2200 g., 0.9999 Gold 0.2 oz. AGW, 22 mm. **Ruler:** Elizabeth II **Subject:** Queen's Golden Jubilee **Obv:** Bust with tiara right **Obv. Designer:** Ian Rank-Broadley **Rev:** Queen holding baby **Edge:** Reeded

Date	Mintage	F	VF	XF	Unc	BU
2002 Proof	2,002	Value: 175				

KM# 999 1/5 CROWN

6.2200 g., 0.3750 Gold 0.075 oz. AGW, 22 mm. **Ruler:** Elizabeth II **Subject:** Queen's Golden Jubilee **Obv:** Bust with tiara right **Obv. Designer:** Ian Rank-Broadley **Rev:** Yacht under Tower bridge **Edge:** Reeded

Date	Mintage	F	VF	XF	Unc	BU
2002 Proof	5,000	Value: 75.00				

KM# 999a 1/5 CROWN

6.2200 g., 0.9999 Gold 0.2 oz. AGW, 22 mm. **Ruler:** Elizabeth II **Subject:** Queen's Golden Jubilee **Obv:** Bust with tiara right **Obv. Designer:** Ian Rank-Broadley **Rev:** Yacht under Tower bridge **Edge:** Reeded

Date	Mintage	F	VF	XF	Unc	BU
2002 Proof	2,002	Value: 175				

KM# 1001 1/5 CROWN

6.2200 g., 0.9999 Gold 0.2 oz. AGW, 22 mm. **Ruler:** Elizabeth II **Subject:** Queen's Golden Jubilee **Obv:** Bust with tiara right **Obv. Designer:** Ian Rank-Broadley **Rev:** Crown jewels inset with a tiny diamond, ruby, sapphire and emerald **Edge:** Reeded

Date	Mintage	F	VF	XF	Unc	BU
2002 Proof	2,002	Value: 175				

KM# 1003 1/5 CROWN

3.1100 g., 0.9990 Gold-Silver 0.0999 oz., 22 mm. **Ruler:** Elizabeth II **Series:** Electrum **Obv:** Bust with tiara right **Obv. Designer:** Ian Rank-Broadley **Rev:** Athena **Edge:** Reeded

Date	Mintage	F	VF	XF	Unc	BU
2002 Proof	3,500	Value: 95.00				

KM# 1005 1/5 CROWN

3.1100 g., 0.9990 Gold-Silver 0.0999 oz., 22 mm. **Ruler:** Elizabeth II **Series:** Electrum **Obv:** Bust with tiara right **Obv. Designer:** Ian Rank-Broadley **Rev:** Hercules **Edge:** Reeded

Date	Mintage	F	VF	XF	Unc	BU
2002 Proof	3,500	Value: 95.00				

KM# 1007 1/5 CROWN

3.1100 g., 0.9990 Gold-Silver 0.0999 oz., 22 mm. **Ruler:** Elizabeth II **Series:** Electrum **Obv:** Bust with tiara right **Obv. Designer:** Ian Rank-Broadley **Rev:** Pegasus **Edge:** Reeded

Date	Mintage	F	VF	XF	Unc	BU
2002 Proof	3,500	Value: 95.00				

KM# 1009 1/5 CROWN

3.1100 g., 0.9990 Gold-Silver 0.0999 oz., 22 mm. **Ruler:** Elizabeth II **Series:** Electrum **Obv:** Bust with tiara right **Obv. Designer:** Ian Rank-Broadley **Rev:** Lion and bull **Edge:** Reeded

Date	Mintage	F	VF	XF	Unc	BU
2002 Proof	3,500	Value: 95.00				

KM# 1012 1/5 CROWN

6.2200 g., 0.9999 Gold 0.2 oz. AGW, 22 mm. **Ruler:** Elizabeth II **Subject:** Queen Mother **Obv:** Bust with tiara right **Obv. Designer:** Ian Rank-Broadley **Rev:** Queen Mother trout fishing **Edge:** Reeded

Date	Mintage	F	VF	XF	Unc	BU
2002 Proof	5,000	Value: 175				

KM# 1014 1/5 CROWN

6.2200 g., 0.9999 Gold 0.2 oz. AGW, 22 mm. **Ruler:** Elizabeth II **Subject:** Princess Diana **Obv:** Bust right **Rev:** Diana's portrait **Edge:** Reeded

Date	Mintage	F	VF	XF	Unc	BU
2002 Proof	5,000	Value: 175				

KM# 1018 1/5 CROWN

6.2200 g., 0.9999 Gold 0.2 oz. AGW, 22 mm. **Ruler:** Elizabeth II **Subject:** Peter Pan **Obv:** Bust right **Rev:** Peter Pan and Tinkerbell flying above city **Edge:** Reeded

Date	Mintage	F	VF	XF	Unc	BU
2002 Proof	5,000	Value: 175				

KM# 1020 1/5 CROWN

6.2200 g., 0.9999 Gold 0.2 oz. AGW, 22 mm. **Ruler:** Elizabeth II **Subject:** Grand Masonic Lodge **Obv:** Bust right **Rev:** Masonic seal above Gibraltar **Edge:** Reeded

Date	Mintage	F	VF	XF	Unc	BU
2002 Proof	5,000	Value: 175				

KM# 886 1/2 CROWN

15.5500 g., 0.9999 Gold .5000 oz. AGW, 30 mm. **Ruler:** Elizabeth II **Subject:** Rotary Club of Gibraltar

Date	Mintage	F	VF	XF	Unc	BU
1991 Proof	5,000	Value: 500				

KM# 127 1/2 CROWN

15.5500 g., 0.9999 Gold .5000 oz. AGW, 30 mm. **Ruler:** Elizabeth II **Subject:** Japanese Royal Wedding **Obv:** Crowned bust right **Rev:** Peacocks

Date	Mintage	F	VF	XF	Unc	BU
1993 Proof	5,000	Value: 350				

KM# 443 1/2 CROWN

15.5500 g., 0.9999 Gold .5000 oz. AGW, 30 mm. **Ruler:** Elizabeth II **Series:** Peter Rabbit Centennial **Subject:** The Tale of Peter Rabbit **Obv:** Crowned bust right **Rev:** Mother and bunnies

Date	Mintage	F	VF	XF	Unc	BU
1994 Proof	Est. 5,000	Value: 375				

KM# 372 1/2 CROWN

15.5500 g., 0.9999 Gold .5000 oz. AGW, 30 mm. **Ruler:** Elizabeth II **Obv:** Crowned bust right **Rev:** Roses

Date	Mintage	F	VF	XF	Unc	BU
1996 Proof	Est. 3,000	Value: 365				

KM# 381 1/2 CROWN

15.5500 g., 0.9999 Gold .5000 oz. AGW, 30 mm. **Ruler:** Elizabeth II **Series:** Peter Rabbit Centennial **Subject:** The Tale of Peter Rabbit **Obv:** Crowned bust right **Rev:** Peter Rabbit escaping garden

Date	Mintage	F	VF	XF	Unc	BU
1996 Proof	Est. 5,000	Value: 375				

GIBRALTAR

KM# 448 1/2 CROWN
15.5500 g., 0.9999 Gold .5000 oz. AGW, 30 mm. **Ruler:** Elizabeth II **Subject:** Lord Buddha **Obv:** Crowned bust right **Rev:** Seated figure facing

Date	Mintage	F	VF	XF	Unc	BU
1996 Proof	Est. 5,000	Value: 365				

KM# 524 1/2 CROWN
15.5500 g., 0.9999 Gold .5000 oz. AGW, 30 mm. **Ruler:** Elizabeth II **Subject:** The Tale of Peter Rabbit **Obv:** Crowned bust right **Rev:** Standing rabbit 3/4 right

Date	Mintage	F	VF	XF	Unc	BU
1997 Proof	Est. 2,500	Value: 375				

KM# 647 1/2 CROWN
15.5500 g., 0.9999 Gold .5000 oz. AGW, 30 mm. **Ruler:** Elizabeth II **Obv:** Crowned bust right **Rev:** Cupid with hologram heart

Date	Mintage	F	VF	XF	Unc	BU
1998 Proof	Est. 3,500	Value: 350				

KM# 655 1/2 CROWN
15.5500 g., 0.9999 Gold .5000 oz. AGW, 30 mm. **Ruler:** Elizabeth II **Subject:** The Tale of Peter Rabbit **Obv:** Crowned bust right **Rev:** Standing rabbit facing, sparrow at left

Date	Mintage	F	VF	XF	Unc	BU
1998 Proof	Est. 2,500	Value: 375				

KM# 681 1/2 CROWN
15.5500 g., 0.9999 Gold .5000 oz. AGW, 30 mm. **Ruler:** Elizabeth II **Subject:** Paddington Bear **Obv:** Crowned bust right **Rev:** Bear with suitcase

Date	Mintage	F	VF	XF	Unc	BU
1998 Proof	Est. 2,500	Value: 365				

KM# 732 1/2 CROWN
15.5500 g., 0.9999 Gold .5000 oz. AGW, 30 mm. **Ruler:** Elizabeth II **Subject:** Peacocks **Obv:** Crowned bust right **Rev:** Pair of peacocks, one with full display in hologram, denomination below

Date	Mintage	F	VF	XF	Unc	BU
1998 Proof	Est. 3,500	Value: 385				

KM# 782.1 1/2 CROWN
15.5500 g., 0.9999 Gold .5000 oz. AGW, 30 mm. **Ruler:** Elizabeth II **Subject:** 1999 The Year of the Rabbit **Obv:** Crowned bust right **Rev:** Rabbit reading, sparrow, Chinese characters

Date	Mintage	F	VF	XF	Unc	BU
1999 Proof	Est. 1,000	Value: 350				

KM# 782.2 1/2 CROWN
15.5500 g., 0.9999 Gold .5000 oz. AGW, 30 mm. **Ruler:** Elizabeth II **Obv:** Crowned bust right **Rev:** Rabbit reading, sparrow; without Chinese characters

Date	Mintage	F	VF	XF	Unc	BU
1999	Inc. above	—	—	—	345	—

KM# 883 1/2 CROWN
Ring Weight: 9.0000 g. **Ring Composition:** 0.9990 Gold .2893 oz. AGW **Center Composition:** Titanium **Ruler:** Elizabeth II **Subject:** 160th Anniversary of the Uniform Penny Post **Obv:** Crowned bust right **Rev:** Postage stamp design **Edge:** Reeded

Date	Mintage	F	VF	XF	Unc	BU
2000 Proof	5,000	Value: 210				

KM# 894 1/2 CROWN
15.5517 g., 0.9990 Gold .5000 oz. AGW, 30 mm. **Ruler:** Elizabeth II **Obv:** Crowned bust right **Rev:** Postage stamp design **Edge:** Reeded

Date	Mintage	F	VF	XF	Unc	BU
2000 Proof	999	Value: 350				

KM# 991 1/2 CROWN
15.5500 g., 0.9990 Gold 0.4994 oz. AGW, 30 mm. **Ruler:** Elizabeth II **Subject:** Peter Rabbit Centennial **Obv:** Bust right **Rev:** Peter Rabbit **Edge:** Reeded

Date	Mintage	F	VF	XF	Unc	BU
2002 Proof	1,000	Value: 350				

KM# 1002 1/2 CROWN
15.5500 g., 0.9999 Gold 0.4999 oz. AGW, 30 mm. **Ruler:** Elizabeth II **Subject:** Queen's Golden Jubilee **Obv:** Bust with tiara right **Obv. Designer:** Ian Rank-Broadley **Rev:** Crown jewels inset with a tiny diamond, ruby, sapphire and emerald **Edge:** Reeded

Date	Mintage	F	VF	XF	Unc	BU
2002 Proof	999	Value: 350				

KM# 1004 1/2 CROWN
7.7750 g., 0.9990 Gold-Silver 0.2497 oz., 32.2 mm. **Ruler:** Elizabeth II **Series:** Electrum **Obv:** Bust with tiara right **Obv. Designer:** Ian Rank-Broadley **Rev:** Head of Athena left **Edge:** Reeded

Date	Mintage	F	VF	XF	Unc	BU
2002 Proof	2,000	Value: 220				

KM# 1006 1/2 CROWN
7.7750 g., 0.9990 Gold-Silver 0.2497 oz., 32.2 mm. **Ruler:** Elizabeth II **Series:** Electrum **Obv:** Bust with tiara right **Obv. Designer:** Ian Rank-Broadley **Rev:** Head of Hercules right **Edge:** Reeded

Date	Mintage	F	VF	XF	Unc	BU
2002 Proof	2,000	Value: 220				

KM# 1008 1/2 CROWN
7.7750 g., 0.9990 Gold-Silver 0.2497 oz., 32.2 mm. **Ruler:** Elizabeth II **Series:** Electrum **Obv:** Bust with tiara right **Obv. Designer:** Ian Rank-Broadley **Rev:** Pegasus **Edge:** Reeded

Date	Mintage	F	VF	XF	Unc	BU
2002 Proof	2,000	Value: 220				

KM# 1010 1/2 CROWN
7.7750 g., 0.9990 Gold-Silver 0.2497 oz., 32.2 mm. **Ruler:** Elizabeth II **Series:** Electrum **Obv:** Bust with tiara right **Obv. Designer:** Ian Rank-Broadley **Rev:** Lion and bull **Edge:** Reeded

Date	Mintage	F	VF	XF	Unc	BU
2002 Proof	2,000	Value: 220				

KM# 46b CROWN
6.2200 g., 0.9999 Gold .2000 oz. AGW **Ruler:** Elizabeth II **Obv:** Crowned bust right **Rev:** Head 3/4 left divides date

Date	Mintage	F	VF	XF	Unc	BU
1990 Proof	Est. 5,000	Value: 175				

KM# 46c CROWN
6.2200 g., 0.9950 Platinum .2000 oz. APW **Ruler:** Elizabeth II **Obv:** Crowned bust right **Rev:** Head 3/4 left divides dates

Date	Mintage	F	VF	XF	Unc	BU
1990 Proof	Est. 1,000	Value: 300				

KM# 49b CROWN
31.1000 g., 0.9999 Gold .9999 oz. AGW **Ruler:** Elizabeth II **Series:** 150th Anniversary of the First Adhesive Postage Stamp **Subject:** Penny Black Stamp **Obv:** Crowned bust right **Rev:** Heads flank stamp design

Date	Mintage	F	VF	XF	Unc	BU
1990 Proof	Est. 1,000	Value: 1,100				

KM# 49c CROWN
15.5500 g., 0.9999 Gold .4999 oz. AGW **Ruler:** Elizabeth II **Series:** 150th Anniversary of the First Adhesive Postage Stamp **Subject:** Penny Black Stamp **Obv:** Crowned bust right **Rev:** Heads flank stamp design

Date	Mintage	F	VF	XF	Unc	BU
1990 Proof	Est. 2,500	Value: 500				

KM# 74b CROWN
15.5500 g., 0.9990 Gold 0.4994 oz. AGW, 32.25 mm. **Ruler:** Elizabeth II **Subject:** Rotary Club of Gibraltar **Obv:** Crowned bust right **Rev:** Cogwheel design on globe

Date	Mintage	F	VF	XF	Unc	BU
1991 Proof	5,000	Value: 650				

KM# 84b CROWN
6.2200 g., 0.9999 Gold .2000 oz. AGW **Ruler:** Elizabeth II **Series:** 10th Wedding Anniversary **Subject:** Prince Charles **Rev:** Head 3/4 left

Date	Mintage	F	VF	XF	Unc	BU
1991 Proof	Est. 5,000	Value: 185				

KM# 85b CROWN
6.2200 g., 0.9999 Gold .2000 oz. AGW **Ruler:** Elizabeth II **Series:** 10th Wedding Anniversary **Subject:** Princess Diana **Rev:** Head 3/4 right

Date	Mintage	F	VF	XF	Unc	BU
1991 Proof	—	Value: 185				

KM# 86b CROWN
6.2200 g., 0.9999 Gold .2000 oz. AGW **Ruler:** Elizabeth II **Series:** 10th Wedding Anniversary **Subject:** Royal Yacht 'Britannia' **Rev:** Luxury liner at sea

Date	Mintage	F	VF	XF	Unc	BU
1991 Proof	Est. 5,000	Value: 185				

KM# 145b CROWN
6.2200 g., 0.9999 Gold .2000 oz. AGW **Ruler:** Elizabeth II **Series:** XVII Winter Olympics **Rev:** Skaters

Date	Mintage	F	VF	XF	Unc	BU
1993 Proof	Est. 5,000	Value: 200				

KM# 146b CROWN
6.2200 g., 0.9999 Gold .2000 oz. AGW **Ruler:** Elizabeth II **Series:** XVII Winter Olympics **Rev:** Ice hockey

Date	Mintage	F	VF	XF	Unc	BU
1993 Proof	Est. 5,000	Value: 200				

KM# 147b CROWN
6.2200 g., 0.9999 Gold .2000 oz. AGW **Ruler:** Elizabeth II **Series:** XVII Winter Olympics **Rev:** Bobsledding

Date	Mintage	F	VF	XF	Unc	BU
1993 Proof	Est. 5,000	Value: 200				

KM# 148b CROWN
6.2200 g., 0.9999 Gold .2000 oz. AGW **Ruler:** Elizabeth II **Rev:** XVII Winter Olympics

Date	Mintage	F	VF	XF	Unc	BU
1993 Proof	Est. 5,000	Value: 200				

KM# 796.1 CROWN
6.2200 g., 0.9999 Gold .2000 oz. AGW **Ruler:** Elizabeth II **Subject:** Millennium 2000 **Obv:** Head with tiara right **Obv. Designer:** Rank-Broadley **Rev:** Sundial, digital clock face, candle and traditional clock face

Date	Mintage	F	VF	XF	Unc	BU
1999 Proof	5,000	Value: 175				

KM# 884 CROWN
Bi-Metallic Titanium center in Gold ring, 38.8 mm. **Ruler:** Elizabeth II **Subject:** 160th Anniversary - Uniform Penny Post **Obv:** Queen's portrait **Rev:** Postage stamp design **Edge:** Reeded

Date	Mintage	F	VF	XF	Unc	BU
2000 Proof	999	Value: 625				

KM# 994b CROWN
28.2800 g., 0.9250 Gold Clad Silver 0.841 oz., 38.6 mm. **Ruler:** Elizabeth II **Subject:** Queen's Golden Jubilee **Obv:** Bust with tiara right **Obv. Designer:** Ian Rank-Broadley **Rev:** Royal couple and tree house **Edge:** Reeded

Date	Mintage	F	VF	XF	Unc	BU
2002 Proof	10,000	Value: 50.00				

KM# 998b CROWN
28.2800 g., 0.9250 Gold Clad Silver 0.841 oz., 38.6 mm. **Ruler:** Elizabeth II **Subject:** Queen's Golden Jubilee **Obv:** Bust with tiara right **Obv. Designer:** Ian Rank-Broadley **Rev:** Royal couple with baby **Edge:** Reeded

Date	Mintage	F	VF	XF	Unc	BU
2002 Proof	1,000	Value: 50.00				

KM# 1000b CROWN
28.2800 g., 0.9250 Gold Clad Silver 0.841 oz., 38.6 mm. **Ruler:** Elizabeth II **Subject:** Queen's Golden Jubilee **Obv:** Bust with tiara right **Obv. Designer:** Ian Rank-Broadley **Rev:** Royal yacht under Tower bridge **Edge:** Reeded

Date	Mintage	F	VF	XF	Unc	BU
2002 Proof	10,000	Value: 50.00				

KM# 1040a CROWN
31.1000 g., Tri-Metallic .9995 Platinum 5.2g center in .9999 Gold 14.2 g ring within .999 Silver 11.7 g outer ring, 38.6 mm. **Ruler:** Elizabeth II **Subject:** Centennial of Powered Flight **Obv:** Queens portrait **Rev:** Stealth bomber within circles of WWI and WWII planes **Edge:** Reeded

Date	Mintage	F	VF	XF	Unc	BU
2003PM Proof	999	Value: 600				

KM# 128a 2 CROWN
62.2070 g., 0.9999 Gold 2.0000 oz. AGW **Ruler:** Elizabeth II **Subject:** Japanese Royal Wedding **Obv:** Crowned bust right **Rev:** Pair of peacocks

Date	Mintage	F	VF	XF	Unc	BU
1993 Proof	Est. 2,500	Value: 1,450				

KM# 129a 2 CROWN
62.2070 g., 0.9999 Gold 2.0000 oz. AGW **Ruler:** Elizabeth II **Subject:** Japanese Royal Wedding **Obv:** Crowned bust right **Rev:** Two peacocks, one in full display

Date	Mintage	F	VF	XF	Unc	BU
1993 Proof	Est. 2,500	Value: 1,500				

KM# 1034a 2 CROWN
50.0000 g., Bi-Metallic .9999 Gold 20g star shaped center in Copper outer ring, 50 mm. **Ruler:** Elizabeth II **Subject:** 1st Anniversary - Euro **Obv:** Crowned bust right within star silhouette **Rev:** Europa riding the bull, stars and star silhouette in background **Edge:** Reeded

Date	Mintage	F	VF	XF	Unc	BU
2003PM Proof	2,003	Value: 775				

KM# 1034b 2 CROWN
56.3000 g., Bi-Metallic .9999 Gold 20.8g star shaped center in a .999 Silver 35.5g outer ring, 50 mm. **Ruler:** Elizabeth II **Subject:** 1st Anniversary - Euro **Obv:** Crowned bust right within star silhouette **Rev:** Europa riding the bull, stars and star silhouette in background **Edge:** Reeded

Date	Mintage	F	VF	XF	Unc	BU
2003PM Proof	2,003	Value: 800				

KM# 451 5 CROWN
155.5175 g., 0.9999 Gold 5.0000 oz. AGW **Ruler:** Elizabeth II **Subject:** Lord Buddha **Rev:** Seated figure facing

Date	Mintage	F	VF	XF	Unc	BU
1996 Proof	Est. 250	Value: 3,500				

KM# 18b POUND
9.5000 g., 0.9170 Gold .2801 oz. AGW, 22.5 mm. **Ruler:** Elizabeth II **Obv:** Crowned head right **Rev:** Gibraltar castle and key

Date	Mintage	F	VF	XF	Unc	BU
1988 Proof	—	Value: 350				

KM# 32b POUND
9.5000 g., 0.9170 Gold .2801 oz. AGW, 22.5 mm. **Ruler:** Elizabeth II **Subject:** 150th Anniversary of Gibraltar Coinage **Obv:** Crowned head right **Rev:** Gibraltar castle and key

Date	Mintage	F	VF	XF	Unc	BU
1989 Proof	150	Value: 350				

KM# 32c POUND
9.0000 g., 0.9500 Platinum .2749 oz. APW, 22.5 mm. **Ruler:** Elizabeth II **Obv:** Crowned head right **Rev:** Gibraltar castle and key

Date	Mintage	F	VF	XF	Unc	BU
1989 Proof	100	Value: 420				

KM# 191b POUND
9.5000 g., 0.9170 Gold .2801 oz. AGW, 22.5 mm. **Ruler:** Elizabeth II **Subject:** Referendum of 1967 **Obv:** Crowned head right **Rev:** Gibraltar arms above Rock of Gibraltar with Union Jack background

Date	Mintage	F	VF	XF	Unc	BU
1993 Proof	Est. 3,500	Value: 350				

KM# 98b 2 POUNDS
15.9400 g., 0.9170 Gold .4700 oz. AGW **Ruler:** Elizabeth II **Obv:** Crowned head right **Rev:** Columbus and ship

Date	Mintage	F	VF	XF	Unc	BU
1992 Proof	Est. 5,000	Value: 335				

KM# 98c 2 POUNDS
18.0000 g., 0.9500 Platinum .5498 oz. APW **Ruler:** Elizabeth II **Obv:** Crowned head right **Rev:** Columbus and ship

Date	Mintage	F	VF	XF	Unc	BU
1992 Proof	Est. 1,000	Value: 800				

KM# 309b 5 POUNDS
39.8300 g., 0.9170 Gold 1.1743 oz. AGW, 36 mm. **Ruler:** Elizabeth II **Obv:** Crowned bust right **Rev:** D-Day - Soldier, sailor and pilot above tank, plane, and ship

Date	Mintage	F	VF	XF	Unc	BU
1994 Proof	Est. 850	Value: 840				

KM# 332b 5 POUNDS
39.8300 g., 0.9170 Gold 1.1743 oz. AGW, 36 mm. **Ruler:** Elizabeth II **Obv:** Crowned head right **Rev:** 50th Anniversary - VE Day

Date	Mintage	F	VF	XF	Unc	BU
1995 Proof	Est. 850	Value: 850				

KM# 334b 5 POUNDS
39.8300 g., 0.9170 Gold 1.1743 oz. AGW, 36 mm. **Ruler:** Elizabeth II **Obv:** Crowned head right **Rev:** Queen Mother viewing bom- damaged Buckingham Palace

Date	Mintage	F	VF	XF	Unc	BU
1995 Proof	Est. 850	Value: 840				

KM# 335b 5 POUNDS
39.8300 g., 0.9170 Gold 1.1743 oz. AGW, 36 mm. **Ruler:** Elizabeth II **Obv:** Crowned head right **Rev:** VJ Day - Flag Raising

Date	Mintage	F	VF	XF	Unc	BU
1995 Proof	Est. 850	Value: 850				

KM# 341b 5 POUNDS
39.0830 g., 0.9170 Gold 1.1743 oz. AGW, 36 mm. **Ruler:** Elizabeth II **Subject:** 190th Anniversary - Death of Admiral Nelson **Obv:** Crowned head right **Rev:** Bust at right facing left, ship at left

Date	Mintage	F	VF	XF	Unc	BU
1995 Proof	Est. 850	Value: 900				

KM# 354b 5 POUNDS
39.8300 g., 0.9170 Gold 1.1743 oz. AGW, 36 mm. **Ruler:** Elizabeth II **Subject:** 70th Birthday of Queen Elizabeth II **Obv:** Crowned head right **Rev:** Monogram and castle within ribbon

Date	Mintage	F	VF	XF	Unc	BU
1996 Proof	Est. 850	Value: 835				

KM# 355b 5 POUNDS
39.8300 g., 0.9170 Gold 1.1743 oz. AGW, 36 mm. **Ruler:** Elizabeth II **Subject:** Centennial Olympics **Obv:** Crowned head right **Rev:** Zeus on Throne, various athletes flank

Date	Mintage	F	VF	XF	Unc	BU
1996 Proof	850	Value: 840				

KM# 527b 5 POUNDS
39.8300 g., 0.9170 Gold 1.1743 oz. AGW, 36 mm. **Ruler:** Elizabeth II **Subject:** Queen Elizabeth II's Golden Wedding Anniversary **Obv:** Crowned head right **Rev:** Two hands within wreath of ribbon

Date	Mintage	F	VF	XF	Unc	BU
1997 Proof	Est. 850	Value: 840				

KM# 605b 5 POUNDS
39.8300 g., 0.9170 Gold 1.1743 oz. AGW, 36 mm. **Ruler:** Elizabeth II **Subject:** Bicentennial - Arrival of Commodore Nelson **Obv:** Crowned head right **Rev:** Cameo left of full masted ship

Date	Mintage	F	VF	XF	Unc	BU
1997 Proof	Est. 850	Value: 850				

KM# 607b 5 POUNDS
39.8300 g., 0.9170 Gold 1.1743 oz. AGW, 36 mm. **Ruler:** Elizabeth II **Subject:** Last Voyage of Britannia **Obv:** Crowned head right **Rev:** Ship sailing past Gibraltar

Date	Mintage	F	VF	XF	Unc	BU
1997 Proof	Est. 850	Value: 850				

KM# 740b 5 POUNDS
39.8300 g., 0.9170 Gold 1.1743 oz. AGW, 36 mm. **Ruler:** Elizabeth II **Subject:** 40th Anniversary of Radio Gibraltar **Obv:** Head with tiara right **Rev:** Radio broadcaster, rock in background

Date	Mintage	F	VF	XF	Unc	BU
1998 Proof	Est. 850	Value: 850				

KM# 770b 5 POUNDS
39.8300 g., 0.9170 Gold 1.1743 oz. AGW, 36 mm. **Ruler:** Elizabeth II **Subject:** 80th Anniversary of the RAF **Obv:** Crowned head right **Rev:** Eurofighter over map

Date	Mintage	F	VF	XF	Unc	BU
1998 Proof	Est. 850	Value: 850				

KM# 771b 5 POUNDS
39.8300 g., 0.9170 Gold 1.1743 oz. AGW, 36 mm. **Ruler:** Elizabeth II **Obv:** Head with tiara right **Rev:** Millennium 2000

Date	Mintage	F	VF	XF	Unc	BU
1998 Proof	850	Value: 875				

KM# 772b 5 POUNDS
39.8300 g., 0.9170 Gold 1.1743 oz. AGW, 36 mm. **Ruler:** Elizabeth II **Subject:** 50th Birthday of Prince Charles **Obv:** Crowned head right **Rev:** Heads of Prince Charles and sons William and Harry

Date	Mintage	F	VF	XF	Unc	BU
1998 Proof	850	Value: 875				

KM# 867b 5 POUNDS
39.8300 g., 0.9170 Gold 1.1743 oz. AGW, 36 mm. **Ruler:** Elizabeth II **Subject:** Mediterranean Rowing Club **Obv:** Head with tiara right **Obv. Designer:** Rank-Broadley **Rev:** A one-man and a four-man row boat

Date	Mintage	F	VF	XF	Unc	BU
1999 Proof	Est. 850	Value: 885				

KM# 878b 5 POUNDS
39.8300 g., 0.9160 Gold 1.1738 oz. AGW, 36 mm. **Ruler:** Elizabeth II **Subject:** Battle of Britain **Obv:** Head with tiara right **Rev:** Spitfire in flight

Date	Mintage	F	VF	XF	Unc	BU
2000 Proof	Est. 850	Value: 885				

KM# 953b 5 POUNDS
39.8300 g., 0.9167 Gold 1.1739 oz. AGW, 36.1 mm. **Ruler:** Elizabeth II **Subject:** Gibraltar Chronicle 200 Years **Obv:** Head with tiara right **Obv. Designer:** Ian Rank-Broadley **Rev:** Naval battle scene with newspaper in background **Edge:** Reeded

Date	Mintage	F	VF	XF	Unc	BU
2001 Proof	850	Value: 885				

KM# 1011b 5 POUNDS
39.8300 g., 0.9166 Gold 1.1738 oz. AGW, 36.1 mm. **Ruler:** Elizabeth II **Subject:** Queen's Golden Jubilee **Obv:** Head with tiara right **Obv. Designer:** Ian Rank-Broadley **Rev:** Coronation scene **Edge:** Reeded

Date	Mintage	F	VF	XF	Unc	BU
2002 Proof	850	Value: 885				

KM# 7 25 POUNDS
7.7700 g., 0.9170 Gold .2291 oz. AGW **Ruler:** Elizabeth II **Subject:** 250th Anniversary - Introduction of British Sterling **Obv:** Young bust right **Obv. Designer:** Arnold Machin **Rev:** Lion and key **Rev. Designer:** Michael Rizzello

Date	Mintage	F	VF	XF	Unc	BU
1975	2,395	—	—	—	165	175
1975 Proof	750	Value: 200				

KM# 8 50 POUNDS
15.5500 g., 0.9170 Gold .4585 oz. AGW **Ruler:** Elizabeth II **Subject:** 250th Anniversary - Introduction of British Sterling **Obv:** Young bust right **Obv. Designer:** Arnold Machin **Rev:** Our Lady of Europa **Rev. Designer:** Michael Rizzello

Date	Mintage	F	VF	XF	Unc	BU
1975	1,625	—	—	—	325	335
1975 Proof	750	Value: 350				

KM# 13 50 POUNDS
15.9760 g., 0.9170 Gold .4711 oz. AGW **Ruler:** Elizabeth II **Subject:** 175th Anniversary - Death of Admiral Nelson **Obv:** Young bust right **Obv. Designer:** Arnold Machin **Rev:** Bust right of ship at left looking left

Date	Mintage	F	VF	XF	Unc	BU
1980	Est. 7,500	—	—	—	320	330
1980 Proof	Est. 5,000	Value: 340				

KM# 15 50 POUNDS
15.9760 g., 0.9170 Gold .4711 oz. AGW **Ruler:** Elizabeth II **Subject:** Wedding of Prince Charles and Lady Diana **Obv. Designer:** Arnold Machin **Rev:** The royal couple

Date	Mintage	F	VF	XF	Unc	BU
1981	—	—	—	—	320	330
1981 Proof	Est. 2,500	Value: 340				

KM# 9 100 POUNDS
31.1000 g., 0.9170 Gold .9170 oz. AGW **Ruler:** Elizabeth II **Subject:** 250th Anniversary - Introduction of British Sterling **Obv. Designer:** Arnold Machin **Rev:** Coat of arms **Rev. Designer:** Michael Rizzello

Date	Mintage	F	VF	XF	Unc	BU
1975	1,625	—	—	—	—	665
1975 Proof	750	Value: 685				

SOVEREIGN COINAGE

KM# 1037 1/5 SOVEREIGN
1.2200 g., 0.9999 Gold 0.0392 oz. AGW, 13.92 mm. **Ruler:** Elizabeth II **Subject:** Death of St. George **Obv:** Bust with tiara right **Obv. Designer:** Ian Rank-Broadley **Rev:** St. George and the dragon **Edge:** Reeded

Date	Mintage	F	VF	XF	Unc	BU
2003 Proof	10,000	Value: 50.00				

GIBRALTAR

KM# 26 1/4 SOVEREIGN
1.9900 g., 0.9170 Gold .0587 oz. AGW **Ruler:** Elizabeth II **Subject:** 150th Anniversary of Regal Coinage **Obv:** Crowned bust right **Obv. Designer:** Raphael Maklouf **Rev:** Queen and lion left

Date	Mintage	F	VF	XF	Unc	BU
1989 U	—	—	—	—	—	—
1989 Proof	Est. 1,989	Value: 70.00				

KM# 41 1/4 SOVEREIGN
1.9900 g., 0.9170 Gold .0587 oz. AGW **Ruler:** Elizabeth II **Subject:** 21st Anniversary - Constitution **Obv:** Crowned bust right **Obv. Designer:** Raphael Maklouf **Rev:** Standing figure with key and trident, shield lower right

Date	Mintage	F	VF	XF	Unc	BU
1990 Proof	Est. 1,000	Value: 65.00				

KM# 515 1/4 SOVEREIGN
1.2241 g., 0.9999 Gold .0400 oz. AGW **Ruler:** Elizabeth II **Obv:** Crowned bust right **Obv. Designer:** Raphael Maklouf **Rev:** Queen and lion left

Date	Mintage	F	VF	XF	Unc	BU
1997 Proof	—	Value: 50.00				

KM# 27 1/2 SOVEREIGN
3.9800 g., 0.9170 Gold .1173 oz. AGW **Ruler:** Elizabeth II **Subject:** 150th Anniversary of Regal Coinage **Obv:** Crowned bust right **Obv. Designer:** Raphael Maklouf **Rev:** Queen and lion left

Date	Mintage	F	VF	XF	Unc	BU
1989 U	—	—	—	—	—	—
1989 Proof	Est. 1,989	Value: 135				

KM# 42 1/2 SOVEREIGN
3.9800 g., 0.9170 Gold .1173 oz. AGW **Ruler:** Elizabeth II **Subject:** 21st Anniversary - Constitution **Obv:** Crowned bust right **Obv. Designer:** Raphael Maklouf **Rev:** Standing figure with key and trident, shield lower right

Date	Mintage	F	VF	XF	Unc	BU
1990 Proof	1,000	Value: 125				

KM# 516 1/2 SOVEREIGN
3.1103 g., 0.9999 Gold .10000 oz. AGW **Ruler:** Elizabeth II **Obv:** Crowned bust right **Obv. Designer:** Raphael Maklouf **Rev:** Queen and lion left

Date	Mintage	F	VF	XF	Unc	BU
1997 Proof	—	Value: 95.00				

KM# 28 SOVEREIGN
7.9600 g., 0.9170 Gold .2347 oz. AGW **Ruler:** Elizabeth II **Subject:** 150th Anniversary of Regal Coinage **Obv:** Crowned bust right **Obv. Designer:** Raphael Maklouf **Rev:** Queen and lion left

Date	Mintage	F	VF	XF	Unc	BU
1989 U	—	—	—	—	—	—
1989 Proof	Est. 1,989	Value: 265				

KM# 43 SOVEREIGN
7.9600 g., 0.9170 Gold .2347 oz. AGW **Ruler:** Elizabeth II **Subject:** 21st Anniversary - Constitution **Obv:** Crowned bust right **Obv. Designer:** Raphael Maklouf **Rev:** Standing figure with key and trident, shield at lower right

Date	Mintage	F	VF	XF	Unc	BU
1990 Proof	Est. 1,000	Value: 250				

KM# 517 SOVEREIGN
6.2207 g., 0.9999 Gold .2000 oz. AGW **Ruler:** Elizabeth II **Obv:** Crowned bust right **Obv. Designer:** Raphael Maklouf **Rev:** Queen and lion left

Date	Mintage	F	VF	XF	Unc	BU
1997 Proof	—	Value: 185				

KM# 1038 SOVEREIGN
6.2200 g., 0.9999 Gold 0.2 oz. AGW, 22 mm. **Ruler:** Elizabeth II **Subject:** Death of St. George **Obv:** Bust with tiara right **Obv. Designer:** Ian Rank-Broadley **Rev:** St. George and the dragon **Edge:** Reeded

Date	Mintage	F	VF	XF	Unc	BU
2003 Proof	5,000	Value: 185				

KM# 29 2 SOVEREIGNS
15.9400 g., 0.9170 Gold .4700 oz. AGW **Ruler:** Elizabeth II **Subject:** 150th Anniversary of Regal Coinage **Obv:** Crowned bust right **Obv. Designer:** Raphael Maklouf **Rev:** Queen and lion left

Date	Mintage	F	VF	XF	Unc	BU
1989 Proof	1,989	Value: 550				

KM# 44 2 SOVEREIGNS
15.9400 g., 0.9170 Gold .4700 oz. AGW **Ruler:** Elizabeth II **Subject:** 21st Anniversary - Constitution **Obv:** Crowned bust right **Obv. Designer:** Raphael Maklouf **Rev:** Standing figure with key and trident, shield lower right

Date	Mintage	F	VF	XF	Unc	BU
1990 Proof	1,000	Value: 525				

KM# 30 5 SOVEREIGNS
39.8300 g., 0.9170 Gold 1.1743 oz. AGW **Ruler:** Elizabeth II **Subject:** 150th Anniversary of Regal Coinage **Obv:** Crowned bust right **Obv. Designer:** Raphael Maklouf **Rev:** Queen and lion left

Date	Mintage	F	VF	XF	Unc	BU
1989 Proof	1,989	Value: 1,100				

KM# 45 5 SOVEREIGNS
39.8300 g., 0.9170 Gold 1.1743 oz. AGW **Ruler:** Elizabeth II **Subject:** 21st Anniversary - Constitution **Obv:** Crowned bust right **Obv. Designer:** Raphael Maklouf **Rev:** Standing figure with key and trident, shield lower right

Date	Mintage	F	VF	XF	Unc	BU
1990 Proof	Est. 1,000	Value: 975				

ROYAL COINAGE

KM# 91 1/25 ROYAL
1.2400 g., 0.9999 Gold .0400 oz. AGW **Ruler:** Elizabeth II **Subject:** Dogs **Obv:** Crowned bust right **Rev:** Corgi

Date	Mintage	F	VF	XF	Unc	BU
1991	—	—	—	—	75.00	—
1991 Proof	Est. 1,000	Value: 76.50				

KM# 99 1/25 ROYAL
1.2400 g., 0.9999 Gold .0400 oz. AGW **Ruler:** Elizabeth II **Subject:** Dogs **Obv:** Crowned bust right **Rev:** Cocker Spaniel

Date	Mintage	F	VF	XF	Unc	BU
1992	—	—	—	—	40.00	—
1992 Proof	Est. 1,000	Value: 42.50				

KM# 193 1/25 ROYAL
1.2400 g., 0.9999 Gold .0400 oz. AGW **Ruler:** Elizabeth II **Subject:** Dogs **Obv:** Crowned bust right **Rev:** Long-haired Dachshund

Date	Mintage	F	VF	XF	Unc	BU
1993	—	—	—	—	40.00	—
1993 Proof	Est. 1,000	Value: 42.50				

KM# 248 1/25 ROYAL
1.2400 g., 0.9999 Gold .0400 oz. AGW **Ruler:** Elizabeth II **Subject:** Dogs **Obv:** Crowned bust right **Rev:** Pekingese

Date	Mintage	F	VF	XF	Unc	BU
1994	—	—	—	—	40.00	—
1994 Proof	Est. 1,000	Value: 42.50				

KM# 319 1/25 ROYAL
1.2400 g., 0.9999 Gold .0400 oz. AGW **Ruler:** Elizabeth II **Subject:** Crowned bust right **Obv:** Crowned bust right **Rev:** Collie

Date	Mintage	F	VF	XF	Unc	BU
1995	—	—	—	—	40.00	—
1995 Proof	Est. 1,000	Value: 42.50				

KM# 361 1/25 ROYAL
1.2400 g., 0.9999 Gold .0400 oz. AGW **Ruler:** Elizabeth II **Subject:** Dogs **Obv:** Crowned bust right **Rev:** Bulldog

Date	Mintage	F	VF	XF	Unc	BU
1996	—	—	—	—	40.00	—
1996 Proof	Est. 1,000	Value: 42.50				

KM# 557 1/25 ROYAL
1.2400 g., 0.9999 Gold .0400 oz. AGW **Ruler:** Elizabeth II **Subject:** Dogs **Obv:** Crowned bust right **Rev:** Yorkshire Terrier

Date	Mintage	F	VF	XF	Unc	BU
1997	—	—	—	—	50.00	—
1997 Proof	Est. 1,000	Value: 52.00				

KM# 749 1/25 ROYAL
1.2400 g., 0.9999 Gold .0400 oz. AGW **Ruler:** Elizabeth II **Obv:** Crowned bust right **Obv. Designer:** Raphael Maklouf **Rev:** Kissing cherubs

Date	Mintage	F	VF	XF	Unc	BU
1998	—	—	—	—	50.00	—
1998 Proof	Est. 1,000	Value: 52.00				

KM# 749a 1/25 ROYAL
1.2400 g., 0.9950 Platinum .0400 oz. APW **Ruler:** Elizabeth II **Obv:** Crowned bust right **Rev:** Kissing cherubs

Date	Mintage	F	VF	XF	Unc	BU
1998 Proof	—	Value: 75.00				

KM# 828 1/25 ROYAL
1.2400 g., 0.9990 Gold .0400 oz. AGW **Ruler:** Elizabeth II **Obv:** Crowned bust right **Rev:** Cherub

Date	Mintage	F	VF	XF	Unc	BU
1999 U	—	—	—	—	35.00	—
1999 U Y2K	Est. 20,000	—	—	—	35.00	—
1999 Proof	Est. 1,000	Value: 40.00				

KM# 828a 1/25 ROYAL
1.2400 g., 0.9950 Platinum .0400 oz. APW **Ruler:** Elizabeth II **Obv:** Crowned bust right **Rev:** One cherub

Date	Mintage	F	VF	XF	Unc	BU
1999 Proof	Est. 1,000	Value: 75.00				

KM# 888 1/25 ROYAL
1.2441 g., 0.9990 Gold .0400 oz. AGW, 13.92 mm. **Ruler:** Elizabeth II **Subject:** Bullion **Obv:** Crowned bust right **Rev:** 2 cherubs **Edge:** Reeded

Date	Mintage	F	VF	XF	Unc	BU
2000	—	—	—	—	35.00	—
2000	1,000	Value: 40.00				

Note: In proof sets only

KM# 896 1/25 ROYAL
1.2441 g., 0.9999 Gold .0400 oz. AGW, 13.92 mm. **Ruler:** Elizabeth II **Subject:** Bullion **Obv:** Bust with tiara right **Obv. Designer:** Ian Rank-Broadley **Rev:** Two cherubs **Edge:** Reeded

Date	Mintage	F	VF	XF	Unc	BU
2001	—	—	—	—	35.00	—
2001 In Proof sets only	1,000	Value: 50.00				

KM# 972 1/25 ROYAL
1.2440 g., 0.9990 Gold 0.04 oz. AGW, 13.92 mm. **Ruler:** Elizabeth II **Subject:** Cherubs **Obv:** Bust with tiara right **Obv. Designer:** Ian Rank-Broadley **Rev:** Two cherubs shooting arrrows **Edge:** Reeded

Date	Mintage	F	VF	XF	Unc	BU
2002	—	—	—	—	35.00	—
2002 Proof	1,000	Value: 50.00				

KM# 1027 1/25 ROYAL
1.2440 g., 0.9999 Gold 0.04 oz. AGW, 13.92 mm. **Ruler:** Elizabeth II **Obv:** Bust with tiara right **Obv. Designer:** Ian Rank-Broadley **Rev:** Cherub with crossed arms **Edge:** Reeded

Date	Mintage	F	VF	XF	Unc	BU
2003PM	—	—	—	—	35.00	—
2003PM Proof	—	Value: 50.00				

KM# 92 1/10 ROYAL
3.1100 g., 0.9999 Gold .1000 oz. AGW **Ruler:** Elizabeth II **Subject:** Dogs **Obv:** Crowned bust right **Rev:** Corgi

Date	Mintage	F	VF	XF	Unc	BU
1991	—	—	—	—	77.50	—
1991 Proof	Est. 1,000	Value: 80.00				

KM# 100 1/10 ROYAL
3.1100 g., 0.9999 Gold .1000 oz. AGW **Ruler:** Elizabeth II **Subject:** Dogs **Obv:** Crowned bust right **Rev:** Cocker Spaniel

Date	Mintage	F	VF	XF	Unc	BU
1992	—	—	—	—	77.50	—
1992 Proof	Est. 1,000	Value: 80.00				

KM# 194 1/10 ROYAL
3.1100 g., 0.9999 Gold .1000 oz. AGW **Ruler:** Elizabeth II **Obv:** Crowned bust right **Rev:** Long-haired Dachshund

Date	Mintage	F	VF	XF	Unc	BU
1993	—	—	—	—	70.00	—
1993 Proof	Est. 1,000	Value: 72.50				

KM# 249 1/10 ROYAL
3.1100 g., 0.9999 Gold .1000 oz. AGW **Ruler:** Elizabeth II **Subject:** Dogs **Obv:** Crowned bust right **Rev:** Pekingese

Date	Mintage	F	VF	XF	Unc	BU
1994	—	—	—	—	70.00	—
1994 Proof	Est. 1,000	Value: 72.50				

GIBRALTAR

KM# 320 1/10 ROYAL
3.1100 g., 0.9999 Gold .1000 oz. AGW **Ruler:** Elizabeth II
Subject: Dogs **Obv:** Crowned bust right **Rev:** Collie

Date	Mintage	F	VF	XF	Unc	BU
1995	—	—	—	—	70.00	—
1995 Proof	Est. 1,000	Value: 72.50				

KM# 362 1/10 ROYAL
3.1100 g., 0.9999 Gold .1000 oz. AGW **Ruler:** Elizabeth II
Subject: Dogs **Obv:** Crowned bust right **Rev:** Bulldog

Date	Mintage	F	VF	XF	Unc	BU
1996	—	—	—	—	70.00	—
1996 Proof	Est. 1,000	Value: 72.50				

KM# 558 1/10 ROYAL
3.1100 g., 0.9999 Gold .1000 oz. AGW **Ruler:** Elizabeth II
Subject: Dogs **Obv:** Crowned bust right **Rev:** Yorkshire Terrier

Date	Mintage	F	VF	XF	Unc	BU
1997	—	—	—	—	75.00	—
1997 Proof	Est. 1,000	Value: 76.50				

KM# 750 1/10 ROYAL
3.1100 g., 0.9999 Gold .1000 oz. AGW **Ruler:** Elizabeth II **Obv:** Crowned bust right **Rev:** Kissing cherubs

Date	Mintage	F	VF	XF	Unc	BU
1998	—	—	—	—	75.00	—
1998 Proof	Est. 1,000	Value: 76.50				

KM# 829 1/10 ROYAL
3.1100 g., 0.9999 Gold .1000 oz. AGW **Ruler:** Elizabeth II **Obv:** Crowned bust right **Rev:** Cherub

Date	Mintage	F	VF	XF	Unc	BU
1999 U	—	—	—	—	68.00	—
1999 U Y2K	Est. 10,000	—	—	—	68.00	—
1999 Proof	—	Value: 70.00				

KM# 829a 1/10 ROYAL
3.1100 g., 0.9950 Platinum .0999 oz. APW **Ruler:** Elizabeth II **Obv:** Crowned bust right **Rev:** Cherub

Date	Mintage	F	VF	XF	Unc	BU
1999 Proof	Est. 1,000	Value: 145				

KM# 889 1/10 ROYAL
3.1100 g., 0.9990 Gold .1000 oz. AGW **Ruler:** Elizabeth II **Obv:** Crowned bust right **Rev:** Two cherubs **Edge:** Reeded

Date	Mintage	F	VF	XF	Unc	BU
2000	—	—	—	—	75.00	—
2000 Proof	1,000	Value: 76.50				

KM# 897 1/10 ROYAL
3.1100 g., 0.9999 Gold .1000 oz. AGW, 18 mm. **Ruler:** Elizabeth II **Subject:** Bullion **Obv:** Bust with tiara right **Obv. Designer:** Ian Rank-Broadley **Rev:** Two cherubs **Edge:** Reeded

Date	Mintage	F	VF	XF	Unc	BU
2001	—	—	—	—	75.00	—
2001 Proof	1,000	Value: 100				

KM# 973 1/10 ROYAL
3.1100 g., 0.9990 Gold 0.0999 oz. AGW, 17.95 mm. **Ruler:** Elizabeth II **Subject:** Cherubs **Obv:** Bust with tiara right **Obv. Designer:** Ian Rank-Broadley **Rev:** Two cherubs shooting arrows **Edge:** Reeded

Date	Mintage	F	VF	XF	Unc	BU
2002	—	—	—	—	75.00	—
2002 Proof	1,000	Value: 100				

KM# 93 1/5 ROYAL
6.2200 g., 0.9999 Gold .20000 oz. AGW **Ruler:** Elizabeth II
Subject: Dogs **Obv:** Crowned bust right **Rev:** Corgi

Date	Mintage	F	VF	XF	Unc	BU
1991	—	—	—	—	175	—
1991 Proof	Est. 1,000	Value: 177				

KM# 101 1/5 ROYAL
6.2200 g., 0.9999 Gold .20000 oz. AGW **Ruler:** Elizabeth II
Subject: Dogs **Obv:** Crowned bust right **Rev:** Cocker Spaniel

Date	Mintage	F	VF	XF	Unc	BU
1992	—	—	—	—	145	—
1992 Proof	Est. 1,000	Value: 150				

KM# 195 1/5 ROYAL
6.2200 g., 0.9999 Gold .20000 oz. AGW **Ruler:** Elizabeth II
Subject: Dogs **Obv:** Crowned bust right **Rev:** Long-haired Dachshund

Date	Mintage	F	VF	XF	Unc	BU
1993	—	—	—	—	145	—
1993 Proof	Est. 1,000	Value: 150				

KM# 250 1/5 ROYAL
6.2200 g., 0.9999 Gold .20000 oz. AGW **Ruler:** Elizabeth II
Subject: Dogs **Obv:** Crowned bust right **Rev:** Pekingese

Date	Mintage	F	VF	XF	Unc	BU
1994	—	—	—	—	145	—
1994 Proof	Est. 1,000	Value: 150				

KM# 321 1/5 ROYAL
6.2200 g., 0.9999 Gold .20000 oz. AGW **Ruler:** Elizabeth II
Subject: Dogs **Obv:** Crowned bust right **Rev:** Collie

Date	Mintage	F	VF	XF	Unc	BU
1995	—	—	—	—	145	—
1995 Proof	Est. 1,000	Value: 150				

KM# 363 1/5 ROYAL
6.2200 g., 0.9999 Gold .20000 oz. AGW **Ruler:** Elizabeth II
Subject: Dogs **Obv:** Crowned bust right **Rev:** Bulldog

Date	Mintage	F	VF	XF	Unc	BU
1996	—	—	—	—	145	—
1996 Proof	Est. 1,000	Value: 150				

KM# 559 1/5 ROYAL
6.2200 g., 0.9999 Gold .20000 oz. AGW **Ruler:** Elizabeth II
Subject: Dogs **Obv:** Crowned bust right **Rev:** Yorkshire Terrier

Date	Mintage	F	VF	XF	Unc	BU
1997	—	—	—	—	150	—
1997 Proof	Est. 1,000	Value: 152				

KM# 751 1/5 ROYAL
6.2200 g., 0.9999 Gold .20000 oz. AGW **Ruler:** Elizabeth II
Obv: Crowned bust right **Rev:** Kissing cherubs

Date	Mintage	F	VF	XF	Unc	BU
1998	—	—	—	—	145	—
1998 Proof	Est. 1,000	Value: 150				

KM# 830 1/5 ROYAL
6.2200 g., 0.9999 Gold .2000 oz. AGW **Ruler:** Elizabeth II **Obv:** Crowned bust right **Rev:** Four cherubs

Date	Mintage	F	VF	XF	Unc	BU
1999 U	—	—	—	—	140	—
1999 U Y2K	Est. 5,000	—	—	—	140	—
1999 Proof	—	Value: 145				

KM# 830a 1/5 ROYAL
6.2200 g., 0.9950 Platinum .2000 oz. APW **Ruler:** Elizabeth II
Obv: Crowned bust right **Rev:** Four cherubs

Date	Mintage	F	VF	XF	Unc	BU
1999 Proof	Est. 1,000	Value: 300				

KM# 890 1/5 ROYAL
6.2200 g., 0.9990 Gold .2000 oz. AGW **Ruler:** Elizabeth II **Obv:** Crowned bust right **Rev:** 2 cherubs **Edge:** Reeded

Date	Mintage	F	VF	XF	Unc	BU
2000	—	—	—	—	140	—
2000 Proof	1,000	Value: 185				

KM# 898 1/5 ROYAL
6.2200 g., 0.9990 Gold .2000 oz. AGW, 22 mm. **Ruler:** Elizabeth II **Subject:** Bullion **Obv:** Bust with tiara right **Obv. Designer:** Ian Rank-Broadley **Rev:** Two cherubs **Edge:** Reeded

Date	Mintage	F	VF	XF	Unc	BU
2001	—	—	—	—	145	—
2001 Proof	1,000	Value: 185				

KM# 1029 1/5 ROYAL
6.2200 g., 0.9999 Gold 0.2 oz. AGW, 22 mm. **Ruler:** Elizabeth II **Obv:** Bust with tiara right **Obv. Designer:** Ian Rank-Broadley **Rev:** Cherub with crossed arms **Edge:** Reeded

Date	Mintage	F	VF	XF	Unc	BU
2003PM	—	—	—	—	145	—
2003PM Proof	—	Value: 215				

KM# 94 1/2 ROYAL
15.5500 g., 0.9999 Gold .5000 oz. AGW **Ruler:** Elizabeth II
Subject: Dogs **Obv:** Crowned bust right **Rev:** Corgi

Date	Mintage	F	VF	XF	Unc	BU
1991	—	—	—	—	375	385
1991 Proof	Est. 1,000	Value: 390				

KM# 102 1/2 ROYAL
15.5500 g., 0.9999 Gold .5000 oz. AGW **Ruler:** Elizabeth II
Subject: Dogs **Obv:** Crowned bust right **Rev:** Cocker Spaniel

Date	Mintage	F	VF	XF	Unc	BU
1992	—	—	—	—	345	365
1992 Proof	Est. 1,000	Value: 375				

KM# 196 1/2 ROYAL
15.5500 g., 0.9999 Gold .5000 oz. AGW **Ruler:** Elizabeth II
Subject: Dogs **Obv:** Crowned bust right **Rev:** Long-haired Dachshund

Date	Mintage	F	VF	XF	Unc	BU
1993	—	—	—	—	345	365
1993 Proof	Est. 1,000	Value: 375				

KM# 251 1/2 ROYAL
15.5500 g., 0.9999 Gold .5000 oz. AGW **Ruler:** Elizabeth II
Subject: Dogs **Obv:** Crowned bust right **Rev:** Pekingese

Date	Mintage	F	VF	XF	Unc	BU
1994	—	—	—	—	345	365
1994 Proof	Est. 1,000	Value: 375				

KM# 322 1/2 ROYAL
15.5500 g., 0.9999 Gold .5000 oz. AGW **Ruler:** Elizabeth II
Subject: Dogs **Obv:** Crowned bust right **Rev:** Collie

Date	Mintage	F	VF	XF	Unc	BU
1995	—	—	—	—	345	365
1995 Proof	Est. 1,000	Value: 375				

KM# 364 1/2 ROYAL
15.5500 g., 0.9999 Gold .5000 oz. AGW **Ruler:** Elizabeth II
Subject: Dogs **Obv:** Crowned bust right **Rev:** Bulldog

Date	Mintage	F	VF	XF	Unc	BU
1996	—	—	—	—	345	365
1996 Proof	Est. 1,000	Value: 375				

KM# 560 1/2 ROYAL
15.5500 g., 0.9999 Gold .5000 oz. AGW **Ruler:** Elizabeth II
Subject: Dogs **Obv:** Crowned bust right **Rev:** Yorkshire Terrier

Date	Mintage	F	VF	XF	Unc	BU
1997	—	—	—	—	345	365
1997 Proof	Est. 1,000	Value: 375				

KM# 752 1/2 ROYAL
15.5500 g., 0.9999 Gold .5000 oz. AGW **Ruler:** Elizabeth II
Obv: Crowned bust right **Rev:** Kissing cherubs

Date	Mintage	F	VF	XF	Unc	BU
1998	—	—	—	—	340	350
1998 Proof	Est. 1,000	Value: 305				

KM# 831 1/2 ROYAL
15.5500 g., 0.9999 Gold .5000 oz. AGW **Ruler:** Elizabeth II
Obv: Crowned bust right **Rev:** Four cherubs

Date	Mintage	F	VF	XF	Unc	BU
1999	—	—	—	—	340	350
1999 Proof	—	Value: 360				

KM# 891 1/2 ROYAL
15.5500 g., 0.9999 Gold .5000 oz. AGW **Ruler:** Elizabeth II
Obv: Crowned bust right **Rev:** Two cherubs **Edge:** Reeded

Date	Mintage	F	VF	XF	Unc	BU
2000	—	—	—	—	340	350
2000 Proof	1,000	Value: 360				

KM# 899 1/2 ROYAL
15.5517 g., 0.9999 Gold .5000 oz. AGW, 30 mm. **Ruler:** Elizabeth II **Subject:** Bullion **Obv:** Bust with tiara right **Obv. Designer:** Ian Rank-Broadley **Rev:** Two cherubs **Edge:** Reeded

Date	Mintage	F	VF	XF	Unc	BU
2001	—	—	—	—	335	—
2001 Proof	1,000	Value: 375				

KM# 975 1/2 ROYAL
15.5510 g., 0.9990 Gold 0.4995 oz. AGW, 30 mm. **Ruler:** Elizabeth II **Obv:** Bust with tiara right **Obv. Designer:** Ian Rank-Broadley **Rev:** Two cherubs shooting arrows **Edge:** Reeded

Date	Mintage	F	VF	XF	Unc	BU
2002	—	—	—	—	335	—
2002 Proof	1,000	Value: 375				

KM# 1030 1/2 ROYAL
15.5510 g., 0.9999 Gold 0.4999 oz. AGW, 30 mm. **Ruler:** Elizabeth II **Obv:** Bust with tiara right **Obv. Designer:** Ian Rank-Broadley **Rev:** Cherub with crossed arms **Edge:** Reeded

Date	Mintage	F	VF	XF	Unc	BU
2003PM	—	—	—	—	335	—
2003PM Proof	—	Value: 400				

302 GIBRALTAR

KM# 97 ROYAL
31.1030 g., 0.9999 Gold 1.0000 oz. AGW **Ruler:** Elizabeth II
Obv: Crowned bust right **Rev:** Corgi

Date	Mintage	F	VF	XF	Unc	BU
1991	—	—	—	—	685	700
1991 Proof	Est. 1,000	Value: 675				

KM# 105 ROYAL
31.1030 g., 0.9999 Gold 1.0000 oz. AGW **Ruler:** Elizabeth II
Obv: Crowned bust right **Rev:** Cocker Spaniel

Date	Mintage	F	VF	XF	Unc	BU
1992	—	—	—	—	685	700
1992 Proof	Est. 1,000	Value: 675				

KM# 197 ROYAL
31.1030 g., 0.9999 Gold 1.0000 oz. AGW **Ruler:** Elizabeth II
Obv: Crowned bust right **Rev:** Long-haired Dachshund

Date	Mintage	F	VF	XF	Unc	BU
1993	—	—	—	—	685	700
1993 Proof	Est. 1,000	Value: 675				

KM# 252a ROYAL
31.1030 g., 0.9999 Gold 1.0000 oz. AGW **Ruler:** Elizabeth II
Subject: Dogs **Obv:** Crowned bust right **Rev:** Pekingese

Date	Mintage	F	VF	XF	Unc	BU
1994	—	—	—	—	665	685
1994 Proof	Est. 1,000	Value: 675				

KM# 318b ROYAL
31.1030 g., 0.9999 Gold 1.0000 oz. AGW **Ruler:** Elizabeth II
Subject: Dogs **Obv:** Crowned bust right **Rev:** Collie

Date	Mintage	F	VF	XF	Unc	BU
1995	—	—	—	—	665	685
1995 Proof	Est. 1,000	Value: 675				

KM# 365b ROYAL
31.1030 g., 0.9999 Gold 1.0000 oz. AGW **Ruler:** Elizabeth II
Subject: Dogs **Obv:** Crowned bust right **Rev:** Bulldog

Date	Mintage	F	VF	XF	Unc	BU
1996	—	—	—	—	665	685
1996 Proof	Est. 1,000	Value: 675				

KM# 561b ROYAL
31.1035 g., 0.9999 Gold 1.0000 oz. AGW **Ruler:** Elizabeth II
Subject: Dogs **Obv:** Crowned bust right **Rev:** Yorkshire terrier

Date	Mintage	F	VF	XF	Unc	BU
1997	—	—	—	—	665	685
1997 Proof	Est. 1,000	Value: 675				

KM# 754 ROYAL
31.1030 g., 0.9999 Gold 1.0000 oz. AGW **Ruler:** Elizabeth II
Obv: Crowned bust right **Rev:** Kissing cherubs

Date	Mintage	F	VF	XF	Unc	BU
1998	—	—	—	—	665	685
1998 Proof	Est. 1,000	Value: 675				

KM# 833 ROYAL
31.1030 g., 0.9999 Gold 1.0000 oz. AGW **Ruler:** Elizabeth II
Obv: Crowned bust right **Rev:** Four cherubs

Date	Mintage	F	VF	XF	Unc	BU
1999 U	—	—	—	—	665	685
1999 Proof	—	Value: 675				

KM# 893 ROYAL
31.1035 g., 0.9990 Gold 1.0000 oz. AGW **Ruler:** Elizabeth II
Obv: Crowned bust right **Rev:** Two cherubs **Edge:** Reeded

Date	Mintage	F	VF	XF	Unc	BU
2000	—	—	—	—	665	685
2000	1,000	Value: 675				

Note: In proof sets only

KM# 901 ROYAL
31.1035 g., 0.9999 Gold 1.0000 oz. AGW, 32.7 mm. **Ruler:** Elizabeth II **Subject:** Bullion **Obv:** Bust with tiara right **Obv. Designer:** Ian Rank-Broadley **Rev:** Two cherubs **Edge:** Reeded

Date	Mintage	F	VF	XF	Unc	BU
2001	—	—	—	—	650	675
2001 In Proof sets only	1,000	Value: 725				

KM# 977 ROYAL
31.1035 g., 0.9990 Gold 0.999 oz. AGW, 32.7 mm. **Ruler:** Elizabeth II **Obv:** Bust with tiara right **Obv. Designer:** Ian Rank-Broadley **Rev:** Two cherubs shooting arrows **Edge:** Reeded

Date	Mintage	F	VF	XF	Unc	BU
2002	—	—	—	—	650	675
2002 Proof	1,000	Value: 725				

KM# 1032 ROYAL
31.1035 g., 0.9999 Gold 0.9999 oz. AGW, 32.7 mm. **Ruler:** Elizabeth II **Obv:** Bust with tiara right **Obv. Designer:** Ian Rank-Broadley **Rev:** Cherub with crossed arms **Edge:** Reeded

Date	Mintage	F	VF	XF	Unc	BU
2003PM	—	—	—	—	650	675
2003PM Proof	—	Value: 725				

EUROPEAN CURRENCY UNITS
Dual Denomination Coinage

KM# 75 70 ECUS - 50 POUNDS
6.1200 g., 0.5000 Gold .1000 oz. AGW **Ruler:** Elizabeth II **Obv:** Crowned bust right **Rev:** Knight on horseback jumping left, stars encircle

Date	Mintage	F	VF	XF	Unc	BU
1991 Proof	Est. 5,000	Value: 200				
1991	—	—	—	—	85.00	90.00
1992	—	—	—	—	85.00	90.00
1992 Proof	Est. 2,000	Value: 225				
1994	—	—	—	—	250	270

KM# 111 70 ECUS - 50 POUNDS
6.1200 g., 0.5000 Gold .1000 oz. AGW **Ruler:** Elizabeth II **Obv:** Crowned bust right **Rev:** Knight on horseback jumping right, stars encircle

Date	Mintage	F	VF	XF	Unc	BU
1992 Proof	Est. 2,000	Value: 175				
1993 Proof	Est. 1,000	Value: 200				

KM# 339 70 ECUS - 50 POUNDS
6.1200 g., 0.5000 Gold .1000 oz. AGW **Ruler:** Elizabeth II **Obv:** Crowned bust right **Rev:** Knight on horseback jumping left, stars encircle

Date	Mintage	F	VF	XF	Unc	BU
1992 Proof	Est. 1,000	Value: 200				

KM# 626 70 ECUS - 50 POUNDS
6.1200 g., 0.5000 Gold .1000 oz. AGW **Ruler:** Elizabeth II **Obv:** Crowned bust right **Rev:** Knight on horseback jumping left, stars encircle

Date	Mintage	F	VF	XF	Unc	BU
1992 Proof	Est. 1,000	Value: 200				

KM# 629 70 ECUS - 50 POUNDS
6.1200 g., 0.5000 Gold .1000 oz. AGW **Ruler:** Elizabeth II **Obv:** Crowned bust right **Rev:** Knight on horseback jumping right, stars encircle

Date	Mintage	F	VF	XF	Unc	BU
1993 Proof	Est. 1,000	Value: 150				

STERLING ECU

KM# 497 15 ECUS
1.2400 g., 0.9999 Gold .0399 oz. AGW **Ruler:** Elizabeth II **Obv:** Crowned bust right **Rev:** Knight with shield and banner

Date	Mintage	F	VF	XF	Unc	BU
1995 Proof	15,000	Value: 32.50				

KM# 504 15 ECUS
1.2400 g., 0.9999 Gold .0399 oz. AGW **Ruler:** Elizabeth II **Obv:** Crowned bust right **Rev:** Sir Francis Drake's ship "Golden Hind"

Date	Mintage	F	VF	XF	Unc	BU
1996 Proof	Est. 1,500	Value: 40.00				

KM# 505 35 ECUS
3.1100 g., 0.9999 Gold .1000 oz. AGW **Ruler:** Elizabeth II **Obv:** Crowned bust right **Rev:** Ship "Hanseatic Kogge"

Date	Mintage	F	VF	XF	Unc	BU
1996 Proof	Est. 1,500	Value: 80.00				

KM# 634 70 ECUS
6.2200 g., 0.9999 Gold .2000 oz. AGW **Ruler:** Elizabeth II **Subject:** Ariane - European Space Programme **Obv:** Crowned bust right **Rev:** Rocket orbiting Earth, stars encircle

Date	Mintage	F	VF	XF	Unc	BU
1993 Proof	Est. 2,000	Value: 175				
1994 Proof	Est. 1,000	Value: 180				

KM# 488 70 ECUS
6.2200 g., 0.9999 Gold .2000 oz. AGW **Ruler:** Elizabeth II **Subject:** Euro Tunnel **Obv:** Crowned bust right **Rev:** Outreached hands above English Channel

Date	Mintage	F	VF	XF	Unc	BU
1994 Proof	Est. 2,000	Value: 150				

KM# 493 70 ECUS
6.2200 g., 0.9999 Gold .2000 oz. AGW **Ruler:** Elizabeth II **Subject:** Mythology **Obv:** Crowned bust right **Rev:** Europa sowing seeds

Date	Mintage	F	VF	XF	Unc	BU
1994 Proof	Est. 2,000	Value: 150				

KM# 502 70 ECUS
6.2200 g., 0.9999 Gold .2000 oz. AGW **Ruler:** Elizabeth II **Obv:** Crowned bust right **Rev:** Mercury above ship

Date	Mintage	F	VF	XF	Unc	BU
1995 Proof	Est. 2,000		Value: 170			

KM# 503 70 ECUS
6.2200 g., 0.9999 Gold .2000 oz. AGW **Ruler:** Elizabeth II **Obv:** Crowned bust right **Rev:** Richard the Lionheart

Date	Mintage	F	VF	XF	Unc	BU
1995 Proof	Est. 2,000		Value: 170			

KM# 506 70 ECUS
6.2200 g., 0.9999 Gold .2000 oz. AGW **Ruler:** Elizabeth II **Obv:** Crowned bust right **Rev:** HMS Victory

Date	Mintage	F	VF	XF	Unc	BU
1996 Proof	Est. 1,500		Value: 170			

KM# 512 70 ECUS
6.2200 g., 0.9999 Gold .2000 oz. AGW **Ruler:** Elizabeth II **Obv:** Crowned bust right **Rev:** Austrian Knight within circle of stars and shields

Date	Mintage	F	VF	XF	Unc	BU
1996 Proof	2,000		Value: 170			

KM# 528 75 ECUS
3.8880 g., 0.9995 Bi-Metallic Platinum center in Gold ring .1250 oz. **Ruler:** Elizabeth II **Subject:** Austrian Centennial **Obv:** Crowned bust right **Rev:** Standing allegorical figure with shield and trident

Date	Mintage	F	VF	XF	Unc	BU
1996 Proof	1,500		Value: 250			

KM# 507 140 ECUS
15.5500 g., 0.9999 Gold .4999 oz. AGW **Ruler:** Elizabeth II **Obv:** Crowned bust right **Rev:** Viking Longship

Date	Mintage	F	VF	XF	Unc	BU
1996	Est. 1,500	—	—	—	385	—

Note: In Proof sets only

MEDALLIC COINAGE
Richard Lobel Issues

X# 2 SOVEREIGN
0.3750 Gold **Subject:** Edward VIII

Date	Mintage	F	VF	XF	Unc	BU
1936 Proof	200		Value: 125			

PATTERNS
Including off metal strikes

KM#	Date	Mintage	Identification	Mkt Val
Pn4	1989	—	1/4 Sovereign. Gold. Similar to Pn8.	—
Pn5	1989	—	1/2 Sovereign. Gold. Similar to Pn8.	—
Pn6	1989	—	Sovereign. Gold. Similar to Pn8.	—
Pn7	1989	—	2 Sovereigns. Gold. Similar to Pn8.	—
Pn8	1989	—	5 Sovereigns. Gold. Una and the lion with the Rock of Gibraltar in background.	—

PIEFORTS

KM#	Date	Mintage	Identification	Mkt Val
P2	1990	1,000	5 Pence. 0.9160 Gold. 6.0000 g. KM#22c.	—

MINT SETS

KM#	Date	Mintage	Identification	Issue Price	Mkt Val
MS1	1975 (3)	1,625	KM#7-9	—	1,150

PROOF SETS

KM#	Date	Mintage	Identification	Issue Price	Mkt Val
PS1	1975 (3)	750	KM#7-9	875	1,150
PS2	1989 (5)	—	KM#26-30	—	2,250
PS3	1989 (2)	—	KM#29-30	—	1,700
PS4	1990 (6)	500	KM#76-81	—	1,500
PS5	1990 (6)	250	KM#76a-81a	—	2,100
PS6	1990 (5)	1,000	KM#41-45	1,800	1,975
PS7	1991 (8)	20,000	KM#50-57	—	650
PS8	1991 (8)	5,000	KM#58-65	—	1,350
PS9	1991 (8)	1,000	KM#58a-65a	—	2,300
PS11	1991 (5)	1,000	KM#91-94, 97	—	1,450
PS12	1992 (5)	1,000	KM#99-102, 105	—	1,250
PS13	1993 (5)	1,000	KM#193-197	—	1,200
PS14	1993 (5)	300	KM#124-128	—	675
PS15	1994 (5)	1,000	KM#248-251, 252a	—	1,200
PS19	1995 (5)	1,000	KM#319-323	—	1,200
PS21	1996 (5)	1,000	KM#361-364, 365b	—	1,200
PS22	1996 (4)	1,500	KM#504-507	—	650
PS23	1997 (5)	1,000	KM#557-560, 561b	—	1,200
PS24	1998 (5)	1,000	KM#749-752, 754	1,310	1,200
PS25	1999 (5)	1,000	KM#828-831, 833	1,310	1,200
PS26	2000 (5)	1,000	KM#888-891, 893	—	1,200
PS29	2001 (5)	1,000	KM#896-899, 901	—	1,350
PS30	2003 (5)	1,000	KM#1027-30, 1032	—	1,400
PS31	2003 (5)	1,000	KM#1161-1164, 1166	—	1,400

GREAT BRITAIN

The United Kingdom of Great Britain and Northern Ireland, located off the northwest coast of the European continent, has an area of 94,227 sq. mi. (244,820 sq. km.) and a population of 54 million. Capital: London. The economy is based on industrial activity and trading. Machinery, motor vehicles, chemicals, and textile yarns and fabrics are exported.

After the departure of the Romans, who brought Britain into a more active relationship with Europe, it fell prey to invaders from Scandinavia and the Low Countries who drove the original Britons into Scotland and Wales, and established a profusion of kingdoms that finally united in the 11th century under the Danish King Canute. Norman rule, following the conquest of 1066, stimulated the development of those institutions, which have since distinguished British life. Henry VIII (1509-47) turned Britain from continental adventuring and faced it to the sea - a decision that made Britain a world power during the reign of Elizabeth I (1558-1603). Strengthened by the Industrial Revolution and the defeat of Napoleon, 19th century Britain turned to the remote parts of the world and established a colonial empire of such extent and prosperity that the world has never seen its like. World Wars I and II sealed the fate of the Empire and relegated Britain to a lesser role in world affairs by draining her resources and inaugurating a worldwide movement toward national self-determination in her former colonies.

By the mid-20th century, most of the territories formerly comprising the British Empire had gained independence, and the empire had evolved into the Commonwealth of Nations, an association of equal and autonomous states, which enjoy special trade interests. The Commonwealth is presently composed of 54 member nations, including the United Kingdom. All recognize the British monarch as head of the Commonwealth. Sixteen continue to recognize the British monarch as Head of State. They are: United Kingdom, Antigua and Barbuda, Australia, Bahamas, Barbados, Belize, Canada, Grenada, Jamaica, New Zealand, Papua New Guinea, St. Christopher & Nevis, Saint Lucia, Saint Vincent and the Grenadines, Solomon Islands, and Tuvalu. Elizabeth II is personally, and separately, the Queen of the sovereign, independent countries just mentioned. There is no other British connection between the several individual, national sovereignties, except that High Commissioners represent them each instead of ambassadors in each others' countries.

RULERS
Victoria, 1837-1901
Edward VII, 1901-1910
George V, 1910-1936
Edward VIII, 1936
George VI, 1936-1952
Elizabeth II, 1952–

MINT MARKS
H - Heaton
KN - King's Norton

MONETARY SYSTEM
Colloquial Denomination Terms
Ha'penny = 1/2 Penny
Tanner = 6 Pence
Bob = 1 Shilling
Half a Crown (Half a Dollar) = 2 Shillings 6 Pence
Dollar = 5 Shillings
Half a quid = 10 Shillings
Quid = 1 Pound
Tenner = 10 Pounds
Pony = 20 Pounds

(Until 1970)
4 Farthings = 1 Penny
12 Pence = 1 Shilling
2 Shillings = 1 Florin
5 Shillings = 1 Crown
20 Shillings = 1 Pound (Sovereign)
21 Shillings = 1 Guinea
½ Sovereign = 10 Shillings (i.e. ½ Pound)
1 Sovereign = 1 Pound

NOTE: Proofs exist for many dates of British coins in the 19th and early 20th centuries and for virtually all coins between 1926 and 1964. Those not specifically listed here are extremely rare.
NOTE: Pound Coinage - Strictly red, original mint luster coins in the copper series command premiums.

KINGDOM
Resumed

POUND COINAGE
KM# 712a 6 PENCE
Palladium **Ruler:** William IV **Obv:** Head left **Rev:** Crown above denomination within wreath

Date	Mintage	F	VF	XF	Unc	BU
1831 Proof	—	—	—	—	—	—

304 GREAT BRITAIN

KM# 842b CROWN
47.8300 g., 0.9170 Gold 1.4096 oz. AGW, 38.5 mm. **Ruler:** George V **Subject:** Silver Jubilee **Obv:** Head left **Rev:** St. George slaying the dragon

Date	Mintage	F	VF	XF	Unc	BU
1935 Proof	28	Value: 14,500				

GUINEA COINAGE

KM# 648 1/3 GUINEA
2.7834 g., 0.9170 Gold .0820 oz. AGW **Ruler:** George III **Obv:** Laureate head right **Obv. Legend:** GEORGIVS III DEI GRATIA **Rev:** Crown above date **Rev. Legend:** BRITANNIARUM REX FIDEI DEFENSOR *

Date	Mintage	F	VF	XF	Unc	BU
1801	—	80.00	110	300	525	—
1802	—	80.00	110	300	525	—
1803	—	80.00	110	300	525	—

KM# 650 1/3 GUINEA
2.7834 g., 0.9170 Gold .0820 oz. AGW **Ruler:** George III **Obv:** Laureate head right **Obv. Legend:** GEORGIVS III DEI GRATIA **Rev:** Crown above date **Rev. Legend:** BRITANNIARUM REX FIDEI DEFENSOR *

Date	Mintage	F	VF	XF	Unc	BU
1804	—	80.00	110	350	550	—
1806	—	80.00	110	350	550	—
1808	—	80.00	110	350	550	—
1809	—	80.00	110	350	550	—
1810	—	80.00	110	350	550	—
1811	—	300	550	900	1,750	—
1813	—	175	375	825	1,550	—
1813 Proof	—	Value: 3,500				

KM# 649 1/2 GUINEA
4.1750 g., 0.9170 Gold .1230 oz. AGW **Ruler:** George III **Obv:** Laureate head right **Obv. Legend:** GEORGIVS III DEI GRATIA **Rev:** Crowned arms within circular legend **Rev. Legend:** BRITANNIARUM REX FIDEI DEFENSOR

Date	Mintage	F	VF	XF	Unc	BU
1801	—	125	150	400	850	—
1802	—	125	200	425	950	—
1803	—	125	200	425	950	—

KM# 651 1/2 GUINEA
4.1750 g., 0.9170 Gold .1230 oz. AGW **Ruler:** George III **Obv:** Laureate head right **Obv. Legend:** GEORGIVS III DEI GRATIA **Rev:** Crowned arms within circular legend **Rev. Legend:** BRITANNIARUM REX FIDEI DEFENSOR

Date	Mintage	F	VF	XF	Unc	BU
1804	—	125	150	400	850	—
1806	—	125	150	425	950	—
1808	—	125	150	425	950	—
1809	—	125	150	425	950	—
1810	—	125	150	425	950	—
1811	—	175	375	850	1,650	—
1813	—	125	325	600	1,250	—

KM# 664 GUINEA
8.3500 g., 0.9170 Gold .2461 oz. AGW **Ruler:** George III **Obv:** Laureate head right **Obv. Legend:** GEORGIVS III DEI GRATIA **Rev:** Crowned arms within circular legend **Rev. Legend:** BRITANNIARUM REX FIDEI DEFENSOR

Date	Mintage	F	VF	XF	Unc	BU
1813	—	450	1,000	2,000	4,000	—
1813 Proof	—	Value: 5,500				

SOVEREIGN COINAGE

KM# 673 1/2 SOVEREIGN
3.9940 g., 0.9170 Gold .1177 oz. AGW **Ruler:** George III **Obv:** Laureate head right **Obv. Legend:** GEORGIUS III DEI GRATIA **Rev:** Crowned arms **Rev. Legend:** BRITANNIARUM REX FID: DEF:

Date	Mintage	F	VF	XF	Unc	BU
1817	2,080,000	110	175	400	1,000	—
1817 Proof	—	Value: 6,300				
1818/7 Rare	1,030,000	—	—	—	—	—
1818	Inc. above	110	225	400	1,050	—
1818 Proof	—	Value: 5,000				
1820	35,000	100	175	400	1,050	—

KM# 681 1/2 SOVEREIGN
3.9940 g., 0.9170 Gold .1177 oz. AGW **Ruler:** George IV **Obv:** Laureate head left **Obv. Legend:** GEORGIUS IIII D:G: BRITANNIAR: REX F:D: **Rev:** Crowned arms within flower garland

Date	Mintage	F	VF	XF	Unc	BU
1821	231,000	450	1,100	2,600	4,500	—
1821 Proof	—	Value: 8,000				

KM# 689 1/2 SOVEREIGN
3.9940 g., 0.9170 Gold .1177 oz. AGW **Ruler:** George IV **Obv:** Laureate head left **Obv. Legend:** GEORGIUS IIII D:G: BRITANNIAR: REX F:D: **Rev:** Crowned arms

Date	Mintage	F	VF	XF	Unc	BU
1823	224,000	110	250	650	1,500	—
1823	—	Value: 7,500				
1824	592,000	100	225	600	1,500	—
1825	761,000	100	225	600	1,500	—
1825 Proof	—	Value: 4,500				

KM# 700 1/2 SOVEREIGN
3.9940 g., 0.9170 Gold .1177 oz. AGW **Ruler:** George IV **Obv:** Head left **Obv. Legend:** GEORGIUS IV DEI GRATIA **Rev:** Crowned arms within cartouche **Rev. Legend:** BRITANNIAR REX FID: DEF:

Date	Mintage	F	VF	XF	Unc	BU
1826	345,000	90.00	200	600	2,000	—
1826 Proof	—	Value: 3,750				
1827	492,000	100	225	600	1,600	—
1828	1,225,000	90.00	200	600	1,200	—

KM# 716 1/2 SOVEREIGN
3.9940 g., 0.9170 Gold .1177 oz. AGW **Ruler:** William IV

Date	Mintage	F	VF	XF	Unc	BU
1831 Proof	—	Value: 3,000				

KM# 720 1/2 SOVEREIGN
3.9940 g., 0.9170 Gold .1177 oz. AGW, 18 mm. **Ruler:** William IV **Obv:** Head right **Obv. Legend:** GULIELMUS IIII D:G: BRITANNIAR: REX F:D: **Rev:** Crowned arms within cartouche

Date	Mintage	F	VF	XF	Unc	BU
1834	134,000	125	275	850	1,800	—

KM# 722 1/2 SOVEREIGN
3.9940 g., 0.9170 Gold .1177 oz. AGW, 19 mm. **Ruler:** William IV **Obv:** Head right **Obv. Legend:** GULIELMUS IIII D:G: BRITANNIAR: REX F:D: **Rev:** Crowned arms within cartouche

Date	Mintage	F	VF	XF	Unc	BU
1835	773,000	150	225	800	1,600	—
1836	147,000	250	500	1,250	2,250	—
1837	160,000	150	250	800	1,600	—

KM# 735.1 1/2 SOVEREIGN
3.9940 g., 0.9170 Gold .1177 oz. AGW **Ruler:** Victoria **Obv:** Head left **Obv. Legend:** VICTORIA DEI GRATIA **Rev:** Without die number **Rev. Legend:** BRITANNIARUM REGINA FID: DEF:

Date	Mintage	F	VF	XF	Unc	BU
1838	273,000	100	175	500	1,400	—
1839 Proof	1,230	Value: 3,000				
1841	509,000	100	175	550	1,400	—
1842	2,223,000	90.00	100	300	800	—
1843	1,252,000	100	175	500	1,400	—
1844	1,127,000	100	140	450	1,100	—
1845	888,000	300	650	1,800	3,500	—
1846	1,064,000	95.00	140	450	1,100	—
1847	983,000	90.00	100	350	1,100	—
1848	411,000	100	200	400	1,250	—
1849	845,000	95.00	140	400	1,000	—
1850	180,000	275	450	1,600	2,800	—
1851	774,000	100	140	375	1,200	—
1852	1,378,000	100	135	350	1,000	—
1853	2,709,000	95.00	135	350	1,000	—
1853 Proof	—	Value: 5,500				
1854 Rare	1,125,000	—	—	—	—	—
1855	1,120,000	100	140	300	750	—
1856	2,392,000	90.00	130	300	700	—
1857	728,000	100	140	300	750	—
1858	856,000	90.00	100	300	700	—
1859	2,204,000	85.00	120	300	700	—
1860	1,132,000	90.00	130	325	750	—
1861	1,131,000	90.00	130	300	775	—
1862	—	750	1,800	4,500	11,000	—
1863	1,572,000	85.00	135	300	700	—
1880	1,008,999	80.00	100	300	600	—
1883	2,870,000	80.00	100	225	600	—
1884	1,114,000	80.00	100	225	600	—

Note: 1884 is much rarer than the mintage figure indicates

Date	Mintage	F	VF	XF	Unc	BU
1885/3	4,469,000	100	175	375	850	—
1885	Inc. above	80.00	110	225	550	—

KM# 735.2 1/2 SOVEREIGN
3.9940 g., 0.9170 Gold .1177 oz. AGW **Ruler:** Victoria **Obv:** Head left **Obv. Legend:** VICTORIA DEI GRATIA **Rev:** With die number **Rev. Legend:** BRITANNIARUM REGINA FID: DEF:

Date	Mintage	F	VF	XF	Unc	BU
1863	Inc. above	85.00	100	300	550	—
1864	1,758,000	85.00	100	225	600	—
1865	1,835,000	85.00	100	225	600	—
1866	2,059,000	85.00	100	225	600	—
1867	993,000	100	130	250	650	—
1869	1,862,000	90.00	130	250	650	—
1870	160,000	110	150	300	750	—
1871	2,063,000	90.00	150	260	600	—
1871 Proof	—	Value: 7,500				

Note: Plain edge

Date	Mintage	F	VF	XF	Unc	BU
1872	3,249,000	90.00	130	240	550	—
1873	1,927,000	100	130	260	650	—
1874	1,884,000	100	140	270	650	—
1875	516,000	100	150	280	650	—
1876	2,785,000	90.00	130	200	550	—
1877	2,197,000	90.00	130	200	550	—
1878	2,082,000	90.00	130	200	550	—
1879	35,000	125	200	400	900	—
1880	Inc. above	90.00	125	300	800	—

GREAT BRITAIN 305

KM# 766 1/2 SOVEREIGN
3.9940 g., 0.9170 Gold .1177 oz. AGW **Ruler:** Victoria **Obv:** Coroneted bust left **Obv. Legend:** VICTORIA DEI GRATIA **Rev:** Without die number **Rev. Legend:** BRITANNIARUM REGINA FID: DEF:

Date	Mintage	F	VF	XF	Unc	BU
1887	872,000	BV	85.00	120	240	—
1887 Proof	797	Value: 700				
1890	2,266,000	BV	85.00	120	250	—
1891	1,079,000	BV	85.00	120	250	—
1892	13,680,000	BV	85.00	120	250	—
1893	4,427,000	BV	85.00	120	250	—

KM# 784 1/2 SOVEREIGN
3.9940 g., 0.9170 Gold .1177 oz. AGW **Ruler:** Victoria **Obv:** Mature draped bust left **Obv. Legend:** VICTORIA. DEI. GRA. BRITT. REGINA. FID. DEF. IND. IMP. **Obv. Designer:** Thomas Brock **Rev:** St. George slaying the dragon right

Date	Mintage	F	VF	XF	Unc	BU
1893	Inc. above	BV	80.00	100	180	—
1893 Proof	773	Value: 700				
1894	3,795,000	BV	80.00	100	180	—
1895	2,869,000	BV	80.00	100	180	—
1896	2,947,000	BV	80.00	100	170	—
1897	3,568,000	BV	80.00	100	170	—
1898	2,869,000	BV	80.00	100	170	—
1899	3,362,000	BV	80.00	100	170	—
1900	4,307,000	BV	80.00	100	170	—
1901	2,037,999	—	BV	90.00	170	—

KM# 804 1/2 SOVEREIGN
3.9940 g., 0.9170 Gold .1177 oz. AGW **Ruler:** Edward VII **Obv:** Head right **Rev:** St. George slaying the dragon

Date	Mintage	F	VF	XF	Unc	BU
1902	4,244,000	—	80.00	90.00	120	—
1902 Proof	15,000	Value: 225				
1903	2,522,000	—	BV	90.00	120	—
1904	1,717,000	—	BV	90.00	120	—
1905	3,024,000	—	BV	90.00	120	—
1906	4,245,000	—	BV	90.00	120	—
1907	4,233,000	—	BV	90.00	120	—
1908	3,997,000	—	BV	90.00	120	—
1909	4,011,000	—	BV	90.00	120	—
1910	5,024,000	—	BV	90.00	120	—

KM# 819 1/2 SOVEREIGN
3.9940 g., 0.9170 Gold .1177 oz. AGW **Ruler:** George V **Obv:** Head left **Obv. Designer:** Bertram MacKennal **Rev:** St. George slaying the dragon

Date	Mintage	F	VF	XF	Unc	BU
1911	6,104,000	—	BV	90.00	120	—
1911 Proof	3,764	Value: 350				
1912	6,224,000	—	BV	90.00	120	—
1913	6,094,000	—	BV	90.00	120	—
1914	7,251,000	—	BV	90.00	120	—
1915	2,043,000	—	BV	90.00	120	—

KM# 858 1/2 SOVEREIGN
3.9940 g., 0.9170 Gold .1177 oz. AGW **Ruler:** George VI **Obv:** Head left **Obv. Designer:** T. H. Paget **Rev:** St. George slaying the dragon

Date	Mintage	F	VF	XF	Unc	BU
1937 Proof	5,500	Value: 400				
1937 Matte Proof; Unique	—					

KM# 922 1/2 SOVEREIGN
3.9900 g., 0.9170 Gold .1176 oz. AGW **Ruler:** Elizabeth II **Obv:** Young bust right **Obv. Designer:** Arnold Machin **Rev:** St. George slaying the dragon

Date	Mintage	F	VF	XF	Unc	BU
1980 Proof	10,000	Value: 110				
1982	2,500,000	—	—	—	90.00	—
1982 Proof	23,000	Value: 100				
1983 Proof	22,000	Value: 100				
1984 Proof	22,000	Value: 100				

KM# 942 1/2 SOVEREIGN
3.9900 g., 0.9170 Gold .1176 oz. AGW **Ruler:** Elizabeth II **Obv:** Crowned head right **Obv. Designer:** Raphael Maklouf **Rev:** St. George slaying the dragon

Date	Mintage	F	VF	XF	Unc	BU
1985 Proof	25,000	Value: 100				
1986 Proof	25,000	Value: 100				
1987 Proof	23,000	Value: 100				
1988 Proof	Est. 23,000	Value: 100				
1990 Proof	Est. 20,000	Value: 125				
1991 Proof	Est. 9,000	Value: 125				
1992 Proof	7,500	Value: 150				
1993 Proof	7,500	Value: 150				
1994 Proof	Est. 7,500	Value: 150				
1995 Proof	4,900	Value: 150				
1996 Proof	5,730	Value: 150				
1997 Proof	7,500	Value: 150				

KM# 955 1/2 SOVEREIGN
3.9900 g., 0.9170 Gold .1176 oz. AGW **Ruler:** Elizabeth II **Subject:** 500th Anniversary of the Gold Sovereign **Obv:** Elizabeth II seated on the Coronation throne **Rev:** Crowned and quartered shield on tudor rose **Designer:** Bernard R. Sindall

Date	Mintage	F	VF	XF	Unc	BU
ND(1989) Proof	Est. 25,000	Value: 200				

KM# 1001 1/2 SOVEREIGN
3.9900 g., 0.9170 Gold .1176 oz. AGW **Ruler:** Elizabeth II **Obv:** Head with tiara right **Obv. Designer:** Ian Rank-Broadley **Rev:** St. George slaying the dragon

Date	Mintage	F	VF	XF	Unc	BU
1998 Proof	6,144	Value: 150				
1999 Proof	7,500	Value: 175				
2000	146,542	—	—	—	90.00	—
2000 Proof	7,500	Value: 150				
2001	94,763	—	—	—	90.00	—
2001 Proof	10,000	Value: 145				
2002	61,347	—	—	—	90.00	—
2003	47,818	—	—	—	90.00	—
2003 Proof	14,750	Value: 145				
2004	34,924	—	—	—	90.00	—
2005	30,299	—	—	—	95.00	—
2006	—	—	—	—	100	—
2006 Proof	8,500	Value: 170				
2007	75,000	—	—	—	—	120

KM# 1025 1/2 SOVEREIGN
3.9900 g., 0.9167 Gold 0.1176 oz. AGW, 19.3 mm. **Ruler:** Elizabeth II **Subject:** Queen Elizabeth II's Golden Jubilee **Obv:** Head with tiara right **Obv. Designer:** Ian Rank-Broadley **Rev:** Crowned arms within wreath, date below **Edge:** Reeded

Date	Mintage	F	VF	XF	Unc	BU
2002 Proof	18,000	Value: 145				

KM# 1064 1/2 SOVEREIGN
3.9940 g., 0.9167 Gold 0.1177 oz. AGW, 19.3 mm. **Ruler:** Elizabeth II **Obv:** Head with tiara right **Obv. Designer:** Ian Rank-Broadley **Rev:** Knight fighting dragon with sword **Edge:** Reeded

Date	Mintage	F	VF	XF	Unc	BU
2005 Proof	12,500	Value: 175				

KM# 674 SOVEREIGN
7.9881 g., 0.9170 Gold .2354 oz. AGW **Ruler:** George III **Obv:** Laureate head right **Obv. Legend:** GEORGIUS III D.F. BRITANNIAR. REX F.D. **Rev:** St. George slaying the dragon right

Date	Mintage	F	VF	XF	Unc	BU
1817	3,235,000	225	375	900	1,600	—
1817 Proof	—	Value: 9,000				
1818	2,347,000	250	425	1,100	1,900	—
1818 Proof	—	Value: 12,000				
1819 Rare	3,574					
1820	932,000	250	400	1,000	1,600	—
1820 Proof	—	—	—	—	—	—

KM# 682 SOVEREIGN
7.9881 g., 0.9170 Gold .2354 oz. AGW **Ruler:** George IV **Obv:** Laureate head left **Obv. Legend:** GEORGIUS IIII D:G: BRITANNIAR: REX F:D: **Rev:** St. George slaying the dragon

Date	Mintage	F	VF	XF	Unc	BU
1821	9,405,000	225	375	1,000	1,500	—
1821 Proof	—	Value: 5,000				
1822	5,357,000	250	375	1,100	2,000	—
1823	617,000	375	1,200	3,500	8,000	—
1824	3,768,000	250	400	1,100	2,250	—
1825	4,200,000	350	1,000	2,800	6,250	—

KM# 696 SOVEREIGN
7.9881 g., 0.9170 Gold .2354 oz. AGW **Ruler:** George IV **Obv:** Head left **Obv. Legend:** GEORGIUS IV DEI GRATIA **Rev:** Crowned arms within cartouche **Rev. Legend:** BRITANNIARUM REX FID: DEF:

Date	Mintage	F	VF	XF	Unc	BU
1825	Inc. above	200	400	1,000	2,500	—
1825 Proof	—	Value: 5,500				
1825 Proof	—	Value: 6,500				
Note: Plain edge						
1826	5,724,000	200	350	1,000	1,600	—
1826 Proof	—	Value: 5,000				
1827	2,267,000	225	400	725	1,800	—
1828	386,000	1,800	3,500	12,000		—
Note: Only 6 or 7 known						
1829	2,445,000	250	425	1,000	2,000	—
1830	2,388,000	250	425	1,000	2,500	—
1830 Proof	—	—	—	—	—	—
1830 Proof	—	Value: 20,000				
Note: Plain edge						

GREAT BRITAIN

KM# 717 SOVEREIGN
7.9881 g., 0.9170 Gold .2354 oz. AGW **Ruler:** William IV **Obv:** Head right **Obv. Legend:** GULIELMUS IIII D:G: BRITANNIAR: REX F:D: **Rev:** Crowned arms within cartouche

Date	Mintage	F	VF	XF	Unc	BU
1831	599,000	250	450	1,200	2,000	—
1831 Proof	—	Value: 6,250				
1832	3,737,000	225	350	1,000	2,700	—
1833	1,225,000	250	400	1,100	2,800	—
1835	723,000	250	400	1,200	3,000	—
1836	1,714,000	250	400	1,100	2,800	—
1837	1,173,000	275	400	1,200	2,800	—
1837 Proof	—	Value: 12,500				

KM# 736.1 SOVEREIGN
7.9881 g., 0.9170 Gold .2354 oz. AGW **Ruler:** Victoria **Obv:** Head left **Obv. Legend:** VICTORIA DEI GRATIA **Rev:** Without die number **Rev. Legend:** BRITANNIARUM REGINA FID: DEF:

Date	Mintage	F	VF	XF	Unc	BU
1838	2,719,000	160	350	800	1,750	—
1838 Proof P.E.	—	Value: 12,500				
1838 Proof	—	Value: 8,000				
1839	504,000	250	700	1,400	3,000	—
1839 Proof	—	Value: 5,500				
1841	124,000	1,600	2,800	7,200	—	—
1842	4,865,000	BV	165	275	1,250	—
1843/2	5,982,000	600	—	—	—	—
1843	Inc. above	BV	175	275	1,100	—
1843 Narrow shield	Inc. above	4,500	7,000	—	—	—
1844	3,000,000	BV	175	275	1,100	—
1845	3,801,000	BV	175	275	1,200	—
1846	3,803,000	BV	175	275	1,700	—
1847	4,667,000	BV	175	275	1,200	—
1848	2,247,000	BV	BV	250	1,050	—
1849	1,755,000	BV	BV	275	1,100	—
1850	1,402,000	BV	175	300	1,350	—
1851	4,014,000	BV	BV	275	1,100	—
1852	8,053,000	BV	BV	250	1,050	—
1853 Proof	—	Value: 7,800				
1853 WW raised	10,598,000	BV	BV	250	900	—
1853 WW incuse	Inc. above	BV	BV	250	900	—
1854 WW raised	3,590,000	BV	180	355	1,250	—
1854 WW incuse	Inc. above	BV	BV	250	900	—
1855 WW raised	8,448,000	BV	200	275	950	—
1855	Inc. above	BV	BV	250	900	—
1856	4,806,000	BV	BV	200	900	—
1856 Small date	Inc. above	BV	BV	200	900	—
1857	4,496,000	BV	BV	200	900	—
1858	803,000	BV	BV	200	950	—
1859	1,548,000	BV	BV	200	900	—
1859 Small date	Inc. above	BV	BV	200	900	—
1860	2,556,000	BV	BV	250	1,100	—
1861	7,623,000	BV	BV	225	1,000	—
1862/1	—	—	—	—	—	—
1862	7,836,000	BV	BV	200	850	—
1863	5,922,000	BV	BV	200	850	—
1872	13,487,000	BV	BV	200	800	—

KM# 736.2 SOVEREIGN
7.9881 g., 0.9170 Gold .2354 oz. AGW **Ruler:** Victoria **Obv:** Head left **Obv. Legend:** VICTORIA DEI GRATIA **Rev:** Die number below wreath **Rev. Legend:** BRITANNIARUM REGINA FID: DEF:

Date	Mintage	F	VF	XF	Unc	BU
1863	Inc. above	BV	BV	185	750	—
1864	8,656,000	BV	BV	180	800	—
1865	1,450,000	BV	BV	200	800	—
1866	4,047,000	BV	BV	180	750	—
1868	1,653,000	BV	BV	185	750	—
1869	6,441,000	BV	BV	175	700	—
1869 Proof	—	Value: 6,500				
1870	2,190,000	BV	BV	180	700	—
1871	8,767,000	BV	BV	180	700	—
1872	Inc. above	BV	BV	180	700	—
1873	2,368,000	BV	BV	180	700	—
1874	521,000	1,500	2,500	6,500	—	—

KM# 736.3 SOVEREIGN
7.9881 g., 0.9170 Gold .2354 oz. AGW **Ruler:** Victoria **Obv:** Additional line on lower edge of ribbon **Rev:** Without die number **Note:** Ansell variety.

Date	Mintage	F	VF	XF	Unc	BU
1859	168,000	800	1,250	3,500	6,000	—

KM# 752 SOVEREIGN
7.9881 g., 0.9170 Gold .2354 oz. AGW **Ruler:** Victoria **Obv:** Head left **Obv. Legend:** VICTORIA D:G: BRITANNIAR: REG: F:D: **Rev:** St. George slaying the dragon

Date	Mintage	F	VF	XF	Unc	BU
1871	Inc. above	BV	BV	185	600	—
1871 Proof	—	Value: 8,500				
1872	Inc. above	BV	BV	185	600	—
1873	Inc. above	BV	BV	250	600	—
1874	Inc. above	BV	190	350	750	—
1876	3,319,000	BV	BV	225	650	—
1876 Proof	Inc. above	Value: 8,500				
1878	1,091,000	BV	BV	185	550	—
1879	20,000	200	800	1,700	5,000	—
1880	3,650,000	BV	BV	180	500	—
1880	—	BV	BV	180	500	—

Note: Without designer's initials on reverse

| 1884 | 1,770,000 | BV | 160 | 200 | 550 | — |
| 1885 | 718,000 | BV | 170 | 240 | 625 | — |

KM# 767 SOVEREIGN
7.9881 g., 0.9170 Gold .2354 oz. AGW **Ruler:** Victoria **Obv:** Coroneted bust left **Obv. Legend:** VICTORIA D:G: BRITT: REG: F:D: **Rev:** St. George slaying the dragon

Date	Mintage	F	VF	XF	Unc	BU
1887	1,111,000	—	BV	160	300	—
1887 Proof	797	Value: 950				
1888	2,777,000	—	BV	BV	300	—
1889	7,257,000	—	BV	BV	300	—
1890	6,530,000	—	BV	BV	300	—
1891	6,329,000	—	BV	BV	300	—
1892	7,105,000	—	BV	BV	300	—

KM# 785 SOVEREIGN
7.9881 g., 0.9170 Gold .2354 oz. AGW **Ruler:** Victoria **Obv:** Mature draped bust left **Obv. Legend:** VICTORIA. DEI. GRA. BRITT. REGINA. FID. DEF. IND. IMP. **Obv. Designer:** Thomas Brock **Rev:** St. George slaying the dragon

Date	Mintage	F	VF	XF	Unc	BU
1893	6,898,000	—	—	BV	235	—
1893 Proof	773	Value: 1,100				
1894	3,783,000	—	—	BV	270	—
1895	2,285,000	—	—	BV	235	—
1896	3,334,000	—	—	BV	235	—
1898	4,361,000	—	—	BV	235	—
1899	7,516,000	—	—	BV	235	—
1900	10,847,000	—	—	BV	235	—
1901	1,579,000	—	—	BV	235	—

KM# 805 SOVEREIGN
7.9881 g., 0.9170 Gold .2354 oz. AGW **Ruler:** Edward VII **Obv:** Head right **Rev:** St. George slaying the dragon

Date	Mintage	F	VF	XF	Unc	BU
1902	4,738,000	—	—	BV	170	—
1902 Proof	15,000	Value: 350				
1903	8,889,000	—	—	BV	170	—
1904	10,041,000	—	—	BV	170	—
1905	5,910,000	—	—	BV	170	—
1906	10,467,000	—	—	BV	170	—
1907	18,459,000	—	—	BV	170	—
1908	11,729,000	—	—	BV	170	—
1909	12,157,000	—	—	BV	170	—
1910	22,380,000	—	—	BV	170	—

KM# 820 SOVEREIGN
7.9881 g., 0.9170 Gold .2354 oz. AGW **Ruler:** George V **Obv:** Head left **Obv. Designer:** Bertram MacKennal **Rev:** St. George slaying the dragon

Date	Mintage	F	VF	XF	Unc	BU
1911	30,044,000	—	—	BV	170	—
1911 Proof	3,764	Value: 800				
1912	30,318,000	—	—	BV	170	—
1913	24,540,000	—	—	BV	170	—
1914	11,501,000	—	—	BV	170	—
1915	20,295,000	—	—	BV	170	—
1916	1,554,000	—	—	BV	185	—
1917	1,014,999	3,000	3,500	6,500	12,000	—
1925	4,406,000	—	—	BV	170	—

KM# 859 SOVEREIGN
7.9881 g., 0.9170 Gold .2354 oz. AGW **Ruler:** George VI **Obv:** Head left **Obv. Designer:** T. H. Paget **Rev:** St. George slaying the dragon

Date	Mintage	F	VF	XF	Unc	BU
1937 Proof	5,500	Value: 2,000				
1937 Matte Proof; Unique	—	—	—	—	—	—

KM# 908 SOVEREIGN
7.9881 g., 0.9170 Gold .2354 oz. AGW **Ruler:** Elizabeth II **Obv:** Laureate bust right **Obv. Designer:** Mary Gillick **Rev:** St. George slaying the dragon

Date	Mintage	F	VF	XF	Unc	BU
1957	2,072,000	—	—	BV	165	—
1957 Proof	—	—	—	—	—	—
1958	8,700,000	—	—	BV	165	—
1958 Proof	—	—	—	—	—	—
1959	1,358,000	—	—	BV	165	—
1959 Proof	—	—	—	—	—	—
1962	3,000,000	—	—	BV	165	—
1962 Proof	—	—	—	—	—	—
1963	7,400,000	—	—	BV	165	—
1963 Proof	—	—	—	—	—	—
1964	3,000,000	—	—	BV	165	—
1965	3,800,000	—	—	BV	165	—
1966	7,050,000	—	—	BV	165	—
1967	5,000,000	—	—	BV	165	—
1968	4,203,000	—	—	BV	165	—

GREAT BRITAIN

KM# 919 SOVEREIGN
7.9881 g., 0.9170 Gold .2354 oz. AGW **Ruler:** Elizabeth II **Obv:** Young bust right **Obv. Designer:** Arnold Machin **Rev:** St. George slaying the dragon

Date	Mintage	F	VF	XF	Unc	BU
1974	5,003,000	—	—	BV	165	—
1976	4,150,000	—	—	BV	165	—
1978	6,550,000	—	—	BV	165	—
1979	9,100,000	—	—	BV	165	—
1979 Proof	50,000	Value: 175				
1980	5,100,000	—	—	BV	165	—
1980 Proof	91,000	Value: 175				
1981	5,000,000	—	—	BV	165	—
1981 Proof	33,000	Value: 175				
1982	2,950,000	—	—	BV	165	—
1982 Proof	23,000	Value: 175				
1983 Proof	21,000	Value: 175				
1984 Proof	20,000	Value: 175				

KM# 943 SOVEREIGN
7.9881 g., 0.9170 Gold .2354 oz. AGW **Ruler:** Elizabeth II **Obv:** Crowned head right **Obv. Designer:** Raphael Maklouf **Rev:** St. George slaying the dragon

Date	Mintage	F	VF	XF	Unc	BU
1985 Proof	17,000	Value: 225				
1986 Proof	25,000	Value: 225				
1987 Proof	22,000	Value: 225				
1988 Proof	Est. 25,000	Value: 225				
1990 Proof	Est. 20,000	Value: 225				
1991 Proof	Est. 9,000	Value: 250				
1992 Proof	7,500	Value: 250				
1993 Proof	7,500	Value: 250				
1994 Proof	Est. 7,500	Value: 250				
1995 Proof	7,500	Value: 250				
1996 Proof	7,500	Value: 250				
1997 Proof	7,500	Value: 250				

KM# 956 SOVEREIGN
7.9881 g., 0.9170 Gold .2354 oz. AGW **Ruler:** Elizabeth II **Subject:** 500th Anniversary of the Gold Sovereign **Obv:** Elizabeth II seated on coronation throne **Rev:** Crowned and quartered shield on tudor rose **Designer:** Bernard R. Sindall

Date	Mintage	F	VF	XF	Unc	BU
ND(1989) Proof	Est. 28,000	Value: 300				

KM# 1002 SOVEREIGN
7.9881 g., 0.9170 Gold .2354 oz. AGW **Ruler:** Elizabeth II **Obv:** Head with tiara right **Obv. Designer:** Ian Rank-Broadley **Rev:** St. George slaying the dragon

Date	Mintage	F	VF	XF	Unc	BU
1998 Proof	10,000	Value: 250				
1999 Proof	10,000	Value: 350				
2000	129,069	—	—	—	200	—
2000 Proof	10,000	Value: 225				
2001	49,462	—	—	—	175	—
2001 Proof	15,000	Value: 225				
2002	75,264	—	—	—	175	—
2003	43,230	—	—	—	165	—
2003 Proof	19,750	Value: 225				
2004	30,688	—	—	—	175	—
2005	45,542	—	—	—	165	—
2006	—	—	—	—	195	—
2006 Proof	16,000	Value: 315				
2007	75,000	—	—	—	—	225

KM# 1026 SOVEREIGN
7.9800 g., 0.9167 Gold 0.2352 oz. AGW, 22 mm. **Ruler:** Elizabeth II **Subject:** Queen Elizabeth II's Golden Jubilee **Obv:** Head with tiara right **Obv. Designer:** Ian Rank-Broadley **Rev:** Crowned arms within wreath, date below **Edge:** Reeded

Date	Mintage	F	VF	XF	Unc	BU
2002 Proof	20,500	Value: 225				
2002	71,815	—	—	—	175	—

KM# 1065 SOVEREIGN
7.9880 g., 0.9176 Gold 0.2357 oz. AGW, 22.05 mm. **Ruler:** Elizabeth II **Obv:** Head with tiara right **Obv. Designer:** Ian Rank-Broadley **Rev:** Knight fighting dragon with sword **Edge:** Reeded

Date	Mintage	F	VF	XF	Unc	BU
2005	75,000	—	—	—	—	175
2005 Proof	17,500	Value: 275				

KM# 690 2 POUNDS
15.9761 g., 0.9170 Gold .4708 oz. AGW **Ruler:** George IV **Obv:** Head right **Obv. Legend:** GEORGIUS IIII D:G: BRITANNIAR: REX F:D: **Rev:** St. George slaying the dragon

Date	Mintage	F	VF	XF	Unc	BU
1823	—	450	700	1,000	3,200	—

KM# 701 2 POUNDS
15.9761 g., 0.9170 Gold .4708 oz. AGW **Ruler:** George IV **Obv:** Head left **Obv. Legend:** GEORGIUS IV DEI GRATIA **Rev:** Arms within crowned mantle **Rev. Legend:** BRITANNIARUM REX FID: DEF:

Date	Mintage	F	VF	XF	Unc	BU
1825 Proof	—	Value: 8,000				
1826 Proof	450	Value: 6,000				

KM# 718 2 POUNDS
15.9761 g., 0.9170 Gold .4708 oz. AGW **Ruler:** William IV **Obv:** Head right **Obv. Legend:** GULIELMUS IIII D:G: BRITANNIAR: REX F:D: **Rev:** Arms within crowned mantle

Date	Mintage	F	VF	XF	Unc	BU
1831 Proof	225	Value: 13,500				

KM# 768 2 POUNDS
15.9761 g., 0.9170 Gold .4708 oz. AGW **Ruler:** Victoria **Obv:** Coroneted bust left **Obv. Legend:** VICTORIA D:G: BRITT: REG: F:D: **Rev:** St. George slaying the dragon

Date	Mintage	F	VF	XF	Unc	BU
1887	91,000	320	350	550	1,250	—
1887 Proof	797	Value: 2,000				

Note: Proof issues with mint mark S below right rear hoof of horse were struck at Sydney, refer to Australia listings

KM# 786 2 POUNDS
15.9761 g., 0.9170 Gold .4708 oz. AGW **Ruler:** Victoria **Obv:** Mature draped bust left **Obv. Legend:** VICTORIA. DEI. GRA. BRITT. REGINA. FID. DEF. IND. IMP. **Rev:** St. George slaying the dragon

Date	Mintage	F	VF	XF	Unc	BU
1893	52,000	320	400	700	1,500	—
1893 Proof	773	Value: 2,250				

KM# 806 2 POUNDS
15.9761 g., 0.9170 Gold .4708 oz. AGW **Ruler:** Edward VII **Obv:** Head right **Rev:** St. George slaying the dragon

Date	Mintage	F	VF	XF	Unc	BU
1902	46,000	BV	325	400	700	—
1902 Proof	8,066	Value: 750				

Note: Proof issues with mint mark S below right rear hoof of horse were struck at Sydney, refer to Australia listings

KM# 821 2 POUNDS
15.9761 g., 0.9170 Gold .4708 oz. AGW **Ruler:** George V **Obv:** Head left **Obv. Designer:** Bertram MacKennal **Rev:** St. George slaying the dragon

Date	Mintage	F	VF	XF	Unc	BU
1911 Proof	2,812	Value: 1,100				

KM# 860 2 POUNDS
15.9761 g., 0.9170 Gold .4708 oz. AGW **Ruler:** George VI **Obv:** Head left **Obv. Designer:** T. H. Paget **Rev:** St. George slaying the dragon

Date	Mintage	F	VF	XF	Unc	BU
1937 Proof	5,500	Value: 1,100				
1937 Matte Proof; Unique	—	—	—	—	—	—

308 GREAT BRITAIN

KM# 923 2 POUNDS
15.9200 g., 0.9170 Gold .4694 oz. AGW **Ruler:** Elizabeth II **Obv:** Young bust right **Obv. Designer:** Arnold Machin

Date	Mintage	F	VF	XF	Unc	BU
1980 Proof	10,000	Value: 350				
1982 Proof	2,500	Value: 350				
1983 Proof	13,000	Value: 325				

KM# 944 2 POUNDS
15.9200 g., 0.9170 Gold .4694 oz. AGW **Ruler:** Elizabeth II **Obv:** Crowned head right **Obv. Designer:** Raphael Maklouf **Rev:** St. George slaying the dragon

Date	Mintage	F	VF	XF	Unc	BU
1985 Proof	5,849	Value: 350				
1987 Proof	14,000	Value: 350				
1988 Proof	15,000	Value: 350				
1990 Proof	Est. 12,000	Value: 375				
1991 Proof	Est. 5,000	Value: 375				
1992 Proof	3,000	Value: 375				
1993 Proof	3,000	Value: 375				
1999 Proof	—	Value: 500				

KM# 957 2 POUNDS
15.9800 g., 0.9170 Gold .4708 oz. AGW **Ruler:** Elizabeth II **Subject:** 500th Anniversary of the Gold Sovereign **Obv:** Elizabeth II seated on Coronation throne **Rev:** Crowned and quartered shield on tudor rose **Designer:** Bernard R. Sindall

Date	Mintage	F	VF	XF	Unc	BU
ND(1989) Proof	Est. 17,000	Value: 350				

KM# 1027 2 POUNDS
15.9700 g., 0.9167 Gold 0.4707 oz. AGW, 28.4 mm. **Ruler:** Elizabeth II **Subject:** Queen Elizabeth II's Golden Jubilee **Obv:** Head with tiara right **Obv. Designer:** Ian Rank-Broadley **Rev:** Crowned arms within wreath, date below **Edge:** Reeded **Note:** In proof sets only.

Date	Mintage	F	VF	XF	Unc	BU
2002	8,000	Value: 435				

KM# 702 5 POUNDS
39.9403 g., 0.9170 Gold 1.1773 oz. AGW **Ruler:** George IV **Obv:** Head left **Obv. Legend:** GEORGIUS IV DEI GRATIA **Rev:** Arms within crowned mantle **Rev. Legend:** BRITANNIARUM REX FID: DEF: **Edge:** Lettered

Date	Mintage	F	VF	XF	Unc	BU
1826 Proof	150	Value: 20,000				

Note: Includes lettered edge patterns KM#Pn96

KM# 742 5 POUNDS
39.9403 g., 0.9170 Gold 1.1773 oz. AGW **Ruler:** Victoria **Obv:** Head left **Rev:** Standing Queen with lion left

Date	Mintage	F	VF	XF	Unc	BU
1839 Proof	400	Value: 42,500				

KM# 769 5 POUNDS
39.9403 g., 0.9170 Gold 1.1773 oz. AGW **Ruler:** Victoria **Obv:** Coroneted bust left **Obv. Legend:** VICTORIA D:G: BRITT: REG: F:D: **Rev:** St. George slaying the dragon right

Date	Mintage	F	VF	XF	Unc	BU
1887	54,000	775	850	1,150	2,800	—
1887 Proof	797	Value: 4,500				

Note: Proof issues with mint mark S below right rear hoof of horse were struck at Sydney, refer to Australia listings

KM# 787 5 POUNDS
39.9403 g., 0.9170 Gold 1.1773 oz. AGW **Ruler:** Victoria **Obv:** Veiled bust left **Obv. Legend:** VICTORIA. DEI. GRA. BRITT. REGINA. FID. DEF. IND. IMP. **Rev:** St. George slaying the dragon right

Date	Mintage	F	VF	XF	Unc	BU
1893	20,000	775	850	1,400	3,000	—
1893 Proof	773	Value: 5,000				

KM# 807 5 POUNDS
39.9403 g., 0.9170 Gold 1.1773 oz. AGW **Ruler:** Edward VII **Obv:** Head right **Rev:** St. George slaying the dragon

Date	Mintage	F	VF	XF	Unc	BU
1902	Est. 35,000	—	BV	800	1,500	—

Note: 27,000 pieces were melted

Date	Mintage	F	VF	XF	Unc	BU
1902 Proof	8,066	Value: 1,400				

Note: Proof issues with mint mark S below right rear hoof of horse were struck at Sydney, refer to Australia listings

KM# 822 5 POUNDS
39.9403 g., 0.9170 Gold 1.1773 oz. AGW **Ruler:** George V **Obv:** Head left **Obv. Designer:** Bertram MacKennal **Rev:** St. George slaying the dragon

Date	Mintage	F	VF	XF	Unc	BU
1911 Proof	2,812	Value: 2,750				

KM# 861 5 POUNDS
39.9403 g., 0.9170 Gold 1.1773 oz. AGW **Ruler:** George V **Obv:** Head left **Obv. Designer:** T. H. Paget **Rev:** St. George slaying the dragon

Date	Mintage	F	VF	XF	Unc	BU
1937 Proof	5,500	Value: 1,500				

Note: Impaired and blemished proofs of the 1937 issue are common and trade at much lower values; The value listed here is for blemish-free examples

Date	Mintage	F	VF	XF	Unc	BU
1937 Matte Proof; Unique	—	—	—	—	—	—

KM# 924 5 POUNDS
39.9400 g., 0.9170 Gold 1.1775 oz. AGW **Ruler:** Elizabeth II **Obv:** Young bust right **Obv. Designer:** Arnold Machin **Rev:** St. George slaying the dragon

Date	Mintage	F	VF	XF	Unc	BU
1980 Proof	10,000	Value: 820				
1981 Proof	5,400	Value: 845				
1982 Proof	2,500	Value: 845				
1984	25,000	—	—	—	845	—
1984 Proof	8,000	Value: 850				

KM# 945 5 POUNDS
39.9400 g., 0.9170 Gold 1.1775 oz. AGW **Ruler:** Elizabeth II **Obv:** Crowned head right **Obv. Designer:** Raphael Maklouf **Rev:** St. George slaying the dragon

Date	Mintage	F	VF	XF	Unc	BU
1985	14,000	—	—	—	820	—
1985 Proof	13,000	Value: 845				
1986	7,723	—	—	—	820	—
1990	1,226	—	—	—	845	—

GREAT BRITAIN

Date	Mintage	F	VF	XF	Unc	BU
1990 Proof	Est. 2,500	Value: 845				
1991	976	—	—	—	845	—
1991 Proof	Est. 1,500	Value: 865				
1992 Proof	1,250	Value: 865				
1992	797	—	—	—	845	—
1993	906	—	—	—	845	—
1994 Proof	Est. 1,250	Value: 865				
1995 Proof	Est. 1,000	Value: 865				
1995 Proof	Est. 1,250	Value: 865				
1996	901	—	—	—	845	—
1997	802	—	—	—	845	—

KM# 949 5 POUNDS
39.9400 g., 0.9170 Gold 1.1775 oz. AGW **Ruler:** Elizabeth II **Obv:** Crowned head right **Obv. Designer:** Raphael Maklouf **Rev:** St. George slaying the dragon

Date	Mintage	F	VF	XF	Unc	BU
1987	10,000	—	—	—	820	—
1988	Est. 10,000	—	—	—	820	—

KM# 958 5 POUNDS
39.9400 g., 0.9170 Gold 1.1775 oz. AGW **Ruler:** Elizabeth II **Subject:** 500th Anniversary of the Gold Sovereign **Obv:** Elizabeth II seated on Coronation throne **Rev:** Crowned and quartered shield on tudor rose **Designer:** Bernard R. Sindall

Date	Mintage	F	VF	XF	Unc	BU
1989	10,000	—	—	—	820	—
1989 Proof	Est. 5,000	Value: 845				

KM# 1003 5 POUNDS
39.9400 g., 0.9170 Gold 1.1775 oz. AGW, 36 mm. **Ruler:** Elizabeth II **Obv:** Head with tiara right **Obv. Designer:** Ian Rank-Broadley **Rev:** St. George slaying dragon **Edge:** Reeded

Date	Mintage	F	VF	XF	Unc	BU
1999 Proof	—	Value: 975				
2000	10,000	—	—	—	865	—
2001 Proof	1,000	Value: 900				
2003 Proof	2,250	Value: 925				
2004	1,000	—	—	—	1,500	—
2006 Proof	1,750	Value: 1,160				
2006	1,000	—	—	—	1,425	—

KM# 1028 5 POUNDS
39.9400 g., 0.9167 Gold 1.1771 oz. AGW, 36 mm. **Ruler:** Elizabeth II **Subject:** Queen Elizabeth II's Golden Jubilee **Obv:** Head with tiara right **Obv. Designer:** Ian Rank-Broadley **Rev:** Crowned arms within wreath **Edge:** Reeded

Date	Mintage	F	VF	XF	Unc	BU
2002	3,000	Value: 875				

KM# 1067 5 POUNDS
39.9400 g., 0.9167 Gold 1.1771 oz. AGW, 36 mm. **Ruler:** Elizabeth II **Obv:** Head with tiara right **Obv. Designer:** Ian Rank-Broadley **Rev:** Knight fighting dragon with sword **Edge:** Reeded

Date	Mintage	F	VF	XF	Unc	BU
2005 Proof	2,500	Value: 950				

DECIMAL COINAGE

1971-1981, 100 New Pence = 1 Pound; 1982, 100 Pence = 1 Pound

KM# 963b 50 PENCE
26.3200 g., 0.9170 Gold .7757 oz. AGW, 30 mm. **Ruler:** Elizabeth II **Subject:** British Presidency of European Council of Ministers **Obv:** Crowned head right **Rev:** Stars on conference table

Date	Mintage	F	VF	XF	Unc	BU
ND(1992) Proof	Est. 2,500	Value: 550				

KM# 966b 50 PENCE
26.3200 g., 0.9170 Gold .7757 oz. AGW, 30 mm. **Ruler:** Elizabeth II **Obv:** Crowned head right **Rev:** Boats and planes

Date	Mintage	F	VF	XF	Unc	BU
1994 Proof	—	Value: 575				

KM# 996b 50 PENCE
15.5000 g., 0.9167 Gold .4568 oz. AGW, 27.3 mm. **Ruler:** Elizabeth II **Subject:** National Health Service **Obv:** Head with tiara right **Obv. Designer:** Rank-Broadley **Rev:** Radiant hands **Shape:** 7-sided

Date	Mintage	F	VF	XF	Unc	BU
1998 Proof	Est. 1,500	Value: 475				

KM# 1036b 50 PENCE
15.5000 g., 0.9166 Gold 0.4568 oz. AGW, 27.3 mm. **Ruler:** Elizabeth II **Obv:** Head with tiara right **Obv. Designer:** Ian Rank-Broadley **Rev:** Standing woman with banner **Edge:** Plain **Shape:** 7-sided

Date	Mintage	F	VF	XF	Unc	BU
2003 Proof	1,000	Value: 475				

KM# 1050b 50 PENCE
15.5000 g., 0.9167 Gold 0.4568 oz. AGW, 27.3 mm. **Ruler:** Elizabeth II **Subject:** 1st English Dictionary **Obv:** Head with tiara right **Obv. Designer:** Ian Rank-Broadley **Rev:** Sample page from Johnson's 1755 dictionary **Edge:** Plain **Shape:** 7-sided

Date	Mintage	F	VF	XF	Unc	BU
2005 Proof	1,000	Value: 550				

KM# 1073b 50 PENCE
15.5000 g., 0.9166 Gold 0.4568 oz. AGW, 27.3 mm. **Ruler:** Elizabeth II **Rev:** Fleur de Lis Scouting emblem **Edge:** Plain **Shape:** Seven sided **Note:** Scouting Centennial

Date	Mintage	F	VF	XF	Unc	BU
2007 Proof	1,250	—	—	—	—	—

KM# 1051b POUND
19.6190 g., 0.9167 Gold 0.5782 oz. AGW, 22.5 mm. **Ruler:** Elizabeth II **Obv:** Head with tiara right **Obv. Designer:** Ian Rank-Broadley **Rev:** Menai Bridge **Edge Lettering:** 'PLEIDOL WYF I'M GWLAD"

Date	Mintage	F	VF	XF	Unc	BU
2005 Proof	1,500	Value: 725				

KM# 1059b POUND
19.6190 g., 0.9167 Gold 0.5782 oz. AGW, 22.5 mm. **Ruler:** Elizabeth II **Obv:** Head with tiara right **Obv. Designer:** Ian Rank-Broadley **Rev:** Egyptian Arch Bridge **Edge Lettering:** "DECUS ET TUTAMEN"

Date	Mintage	F	VF	XF	Unc	BU
2006 Proof	—	Value: 725				

KM# 947c 2 POUNDS
15.9800 g., 0.9170 Gold .4710 oz. AGW, 28.4 mm. **Ruler:** Elizabeth II **Subject:** Commonwealth Games **Obv:** Crowned head right **Obv. Designer:** Raphael Maklouf **Rev:** Thistle on St. Andrew's Cross **Rev. Designer:** Norman Sillman

Date	Mintage	F	VF	XF	Unc	BU
1986 Proof	18,000	Value: 350				

KM# 968c 2 POUNDS
15.9800 g., 0.9170 Gold .4710 oz. AGW, 28.4 mm. **Ruler:** Elizabeth II **Subject:** 300th Anniversary - Bank of England **Obv:** Crowned head right **Obv. Designer:** Raphael Maklouf **Rev:** Britiannia seated within oval, Crowned WM monogram above

Date	Mintage	F	VF	XF	Unc	BU
ND(1994) Proof	Est. 3,500	Value: 470				

KM# 1012 2 POUNDS
15.9800 g., 0.9170 Gold .4710 oz. AGW, 28.4 mm. **Ruler:** Elizabeth II **Obv:** Crowned head right **Rev:** Britiannia seated within oval, crowned WM monogram above **Note:** Muled die error.

Date	Mintage	F	VF	XF	Unc	BU
ND(1994)	—	—	—	—	600	—

KM# 970c 2 POUNDS
15.9800 g., 0.9170 Gold .4710 oz. AGW, 28.4 mm. **Ruler:** Elizabeth II **Subject:** 50th Anniversary - End of World War II **Obv:** Crowned head right **Obv. Designer:** Raphael Maklouf **Rev:** Dove with laurel branch **Rev. Designer:** John Mills

Date	Mintage	F	VF	XF	Unc	BU
ND(1995) Proof	2,500	Value: 475				

KM# 971c 2 POUNDS
15.9760 g., 0.9170 Gold .4708 oz. AGW, 28.4 mm. **Ruler:**

310 GREAT BRITAIN

Elizabeth II **Subject:** 50th Anniversary - United Nations **Obv:** Crowned head right **Obv. Designer:** Raphael Maklouf **Rev:** Flags and UN Logo **Rev. Designer:** Michael Rizzello

Date	Mintage	F	VF	XF	Unc	BU
ND(1995) Proof	Est. 5,000 Value: 450					

KM# 976b 2 POUNDS
15.9800 g., 0.9170 Gold .4710 oz. AGW, 28.35 mm. **Ruler:** Elizabeth II **Obv:** Crowned head right **Obv. Designer:** Raphael Maklouf **Rev:** Celtic design within circle **Rev. Designer:** Bruce Rushin **Note:** Red gold ring, yellow gold center.

Date	Mintage	F	VF	XF	Unc	BU
1997 Proof	Est. 2,500 Value: 600					

KM# 999b 2 POUNDS
15.9800 g., 0.9170 Gold .4710 oz. AGW, 28.35 mm. **Ruler:** Elizabeth II **Subject:** Rugby World Cup **Obv:** Head with tiara right **Obv. Designer:** Ian Rank-Broadley **Rev:** 2-tone rugby design **Rev. Designer:** Ron Dutton

Date	Mintage	F	VF	XF	Unc	BU
1999 Proof	4,250 Value: 500					

KM# 1031b 2 POUNDS
15.9800 g., 0.9160 Gold Yellow gold center in Red Gold ring, 28.4 mm. **Ruler:** Elizabeth II **Subject:** Commonwealth Games - England **Obv:** Head with tiara right **Obv. Designer:** Ian Rank-Broadley **Rev:** Runner breaking ribbon at finish line **Rev. Designer:** Matthew Bonaccorsi **Edge:** Reeded and lettered

Date	Mintage	F	VF	XF	Unc	BU
2002 Proof	500 Value: 500					

KM# 1032b 2 POUNDS
15.9800 g., 0.9160 Gold Yellow gold center in Red Gold ring, 28.4 mm. **Ruler:** Elizabeth II **Subject:** Commonwealth Games - Scotland **Obv:** Head with tiara right **Obv. Designer:** Ian Rank-Broadley **Rev:** Runner breaking ribbon at finish line **Rev. Designer:** Matthew Bonaccorsi **Edge:** Reeded and lettered

Date	Mintage	F	VF	XF	Unc	BU
2002 Proof	500 Value: 500					

KM# 1033b 2 POUNDS
15.9800 g., 0.9160 Gold Gold center in Red Gold ring, 28.4 mm. **Ruler:** Elizabeth II **Subject:** Commonwealth Games - Wales **Obv:** Head with tiara right **Obv. Designer:** Ian Rank-Broadley **Rev:** Runner breaking ribbon at finish line **Rev. Designer:** Matthew Bonaccorsi **Edge:** Reeded and lettered

Date	Mintage	F	VF	XF	Unc	BU
2002 Proof	500 Value: 500					

KM# 1034b 2 POUNDS
15.9800 g., 0.9160 Gold Yellow Gold center in Red Gold ring, 28.4 mm. **Ruler:** Elizabeth II **Subject:** Commonwealth Games - Northern Ireland **Obv:** Head with tiara right **Obv. Designer:** Ian Rank-Broadley **Rev:** Runner breaking ribbon at finish line **Rev. Designer:** Matthew Bonaccorsi **Edge:** Reeded and lettered

Date	Mintage	F	VF	XF	Unc	BU
2002 Proof	500 Value: 500					

KM# 1037b 2 POUNDS
15.9800 g., 0.9167 Gold Yellow gold center in Red gold ring 0.471 oz. AGW, 28.4 mm. **Ruler:** Elizabeth II **Obv:** Head with tiara right **Obv. Designer:** Ian Rank-Broadley **Rev:** DNA Double Helix **Rev. Designer:** John Mills **Edge:** Reeded and lettered

Date	Mintage	F	VF	XF	Unc	BU
ND(2003) Proof	6,250 Value: 550					

KM# 1049b 2 POUNDS
15.9800 g., 0.9166 Bi-Metallic .9166 Yellow Gold center in .9166 Red Gold ring 0.4709 oz., 28.4 mm. **Ruler:** Elizabeth II **Obv:** Head with tiara right **Obv. Designer:** Ian Rank-Broadley **Rev:** First steam locomotive **Edge:** Reeded and lettered

Date	Mintage	F	VF	XF	Unc	BU
2004 Proof	1,500 Value: 450					

KM# 962b 5 POUNDS
39.9400 g., 0.9170 Gold 1.1775 oz. AGW, 38.61 mm. **Ruler:** Elizabeth II **Subject:** 90th Birthday of Queen Mother **Obv:** Crowned head right **Obv. Designer:** Raphael Maklouf **Rev:** Crowned monogram with rose and thistle flanking **Rev. Designer:** Robert Elderton

Date	Mintage	F	VF	XF	Unc	BU
ND(1990) Proof	Est. 2,500 Value: 845					

KM# 965b 5 POUNDS
39.9400 g., 0.9170 Gold 1.1775 oz. AGW, 38.61 mm. **Ruler:** Elizabeth II **Subject:** 40th Anniversary of Reign **Obv:** Laureate head right with circle of bugling horsemen **Obv. Designer:** Mary Gillick and Robert Elderton **Rev:** Crown within circle **Rev. Designer:** Robert Elderton

Date	Mintage	F	VF	XF	Unc	BU
ND(1993) Proof	Est. 2,500 Value: 900					

KM# 974b 5 POUNDS
39.9400 g., 0.9170 Gold 1.1775 oz. AGW, 38.61 mm. **Ruler:** Elizabeth II **Subject:** 70th Birthday of Queen Elizabeth II **Obv:** Crowned head right **Rev:** Five banners above Windsor Castle **Rev. Designer:** Avril Vaughan

Date	Mintage	F	VF	XF	Unc	BU
ND(1996) Proof	Est. 2,750 Value: 900					

KM# 977b 5 POUNDS
39.9400 g., 0.9170 Gold 1.1775 oz. AGW, 38.61 mm. **Ruler:** Elizabeth II **Subject:** Queen Elizabeth II and Prince Philip - Golden Wedding Anniversary **Obv:** Jugate busts right **Rev:** Crown above two shields, anchor below

Date	Mintage	F	VF	XF	Unc	BU
ND(1997) Proof	Est. 2,750 Value: 900					

KM# 995b 5 POUNDS
39.9400 g., 0.9167 Gold 1.1771 oz. AGW, 38.61 mm. **Ruler:** Elizabeth II **Subject:** 50th Birthday - Prince Charles **Obv:** Head with tiara right **Obv. Designer:** Ian Rank-Broadley **Rev:** Portrait of Prince Charles

Date	Mintage	F	VF	XF	Unc	BU
1998 Proof	773 Value: 900					

KM# 997b 5 POUNDS
39.9400 g., 0.9170 Gold 1.1775 oz. AGW, 38.61 mm. **Ruler:** Elizabeth II **Subject:** In Memory of Diana - Princess of Wales **Obv:** Head with tiara right **Obv. Designer:** Ian Rank-Broadley **Rev:** Head right, dates **Rev. Designer:** David Cornell

Date	Mintage	F	VF	XF	Unc	BU
1999 Proof	Est. 7,500 Value: 875					

KM# 1006b 5 POUNDS
39.9400 g., 0.9170 Gold 1.1771 oz. AGW, 38.61 mm. **Ruler:** Elizabeth II **Obv:** Head with tiara right **Rev:** Map with Greenwich Meridian **Rev. Designer:** Jeffrey Matthews

Date	Mintage	F	VF	XF	Unc	BU
1999 Proof	2,500 Value: 900					
2000 Proof	2,500 Value: 900					

KM# 1007b 5 POUNDS
39.9400 g., 0.9167 Gold 1.0003 oz. AGW, 38.61 mm. **Ruler:** Elizabeth II **Subject:** Queen Mother's Centennial **Obv:** Head with tiara right **Rev:** Head left with signature below **Designer:** Ian Rank-Broadley

Date	Mintage	F	VF	XF	Unc	BU
2000 Proof	3,000 Value: 900					

GREAT BRITAIN 311

KM# 1015b 5 POUNDS
39.9400 g., 0.9167 Gold 1.1771 oz. AGW **Ruler:** Elizabeth II
Subject: Centennial of Queen Victoria **Obv:** Head with tiara right
Obv. Designer: Ian Rank-Broadley **Rev:** Queen Victoria's portrait within "V" **Rev. Designer:** Mary Milner Dickens

Date	Mintage	F	VF	XF	Unc	BU
2001 Proof	1,000	Value: 1,000				

KM# 1024b 5 POUNDS
39.9400 g., 0.9167 Gold 1.0003 oz. AGW, 38.6 mm. **Ruler:** Elizabeth II **Subject:** Queen's Golden Jubilee of Reign **Obv:** Crowned bust in royal garb right **Rev:** Queen on horse **Edge:** Reeded

Date	Mintage	F	VF	XF	Unc	BU
2002 Proof	—	Value: 950				

KM# 1035b 5 POUNDS
39.9400 g., 0.9167 Gold 1.1771 oz. AGW, 38.6 mm. **Ruler:** Elizabeth II **Subject:** Queen Mother **Obv:** Head with tiara right **Obv. Designer:** Ian Rank-Broadley **Rev:** Queen Mother's portrait in wreath **Rev. Designer:** Avril Vaughan **Edge:** Reeded

Date	Mintage	F	VF	XF	Unc	BU
ND(2002) Proof	3,000	Value: 950				

KM# 1038b 5 POUNDS
39.9400 g., 0.9166 Gold 1.177 oz. AGW, 38.6 mm. **Ruler:** Elizabeth II **Subject:** Queen's Golden Jubilee **Obv:** Stylized Queens portrait **Rev:** Childlike lettering **Edge:** Reeded **Designer:** Tom Phillips

Date	Mintage	F	VF	XF	Unc	BU
2003 Proof	2,750	Value: 950				

KM# 1055b 5 POUNDS
39.9400 g., 0.9167 Gold 1.1771 oz. AGW, 38.6 mm. **Ruler:** Elizabeth II **Subject:** Entente Cordiale **Obv:** Head with tiara right **Obv. Designer:** Ian Rank-Broadley **Rev:** Britannia and Marianne **Edge:** Reeded

Date	Mintage	F	VF	XF	Unc	BU
2004 Proof	1,500	Value: 1,000				

KM# 1055c 5 POUNDS
94.2000 g., 0.9995 Platinum 3.0271 oz. APW, 38.6 mm. **Ruler:** Elizabeth II **Subject:** Entente Cordiale **Obv:** Head with tiara right **Obv. Designer:** Ian Rank-Broadley **Rev:** Britannia and Marianne **Edge:** Reeded

Date	Mintage	F	VF	XF	Unc	BU
2004 Proof	501	Value: 4,000				

KM# 1053b 5 POUNDS
39.9400 g., 0.9167 Gold 1.1771 oz. AGW, 38.6 mm. **Ruler:** Elizabeth II **Subject:** Battle of Trafalgar **Obv:** Head with tiara right **Obv. Designer:** Ian Rank-Broadley **Rev:** Ships HMS Victory and Temeraire at Trafalgar **Rev. Designer:** Clive Duncan **Edge:** Reeded

Date	Mintage	F	VF	XF	Unc	BU
2005 Proof	1,805	Value: 1,100				

BULLION COINAGE

Until 1990, .917 Gold was commonly alloyed with copper by the British Royal Mint.

All proof issues have designers name as P. Nathan. The uncirculated issues use only Nathan.

KM# 1066 2 POUNDS
15.9760 g., 0.9167 Gold 0.4709 oz. AGW, 28.4 mm. **Ruler:** Elizabeth II **Obv:** Head with tiara right **Obv. Designer:** Ian Rank-Broadley **Rev:** Knight fighting dragon with sword **Edge:** Reeded

Date	Mintage	F	VF	XF	Unc	BU
2005 Proof	5,000	Value: 450				

KM# 1018a 2 POUNDS
32.4500 g., 0.9580 Silver 0.9995 oz. ASW, 40 mm. **Ruler:** Elizabeth II **Subject:** Golden Silhouette Britannias **Obv:** Head with tiara right **Obv. Designer:** Ian Rank-Broadley **Rev:** Gold plated Britannia and Lion **Edge:** Reeded

Date	Mintage	F	VF	XF	Unc	BU
2006 Proof	3,000	Value: 100				

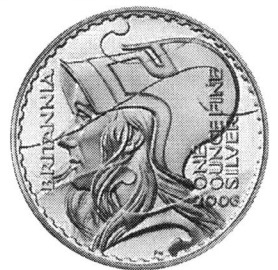

KM# 1039a 2 POUNDS
32.4500 g., 0.9580 Silver 0.9995 oz. ASW, 40 mm. **Ruler:** Elizabeth II **Subject:** Golden Silhouette Britannias **Obv:** Head with tiara right **Obv. Designer:** Ian Rank-Broadley **Rev:** Gold plated Britannia head **Edge:** Reeded

Date	Mintage	F	VF	XF	Unc	BU
2006 Proof	3,000	Value: 100				

KM# 1063a 2 POUNDS
32.4500 g., 0.9580 Gold 0.9995 oz. AGW, 40 mm. **Ruler:** Elizabeth II **Subject:** Golden Silhouette Britannias **Obv:** Head with tiara right **Obv. Designer:** Ian Rank-Broadley **Rev:** Gold plated Britannia seated **Edge:** Reeded

Date	Mintage	F	VF	XF	Unc	BU
2006 Proof	3,000	Value: 100				

KM# 1072 2 POUNDS
15.9700 g., 0.9167 Gold 0.4707 oz. AGW, 28.4 mm. **Ruler:** Elizabeth II **Obv:** Head with tiara right **Obv. Designer:** Ian Rank-Broadley **Rev:** St. George slaying the Dragon **Edge:** Reeded

Date	Mintage	F	VF	XF	Unc	BU
2006 Proof	3,500	Value: 450				

KM# 950 10 POUNDS (1/10 Ounce - Britannia)
3.4120 g., 0.9170 Gold .1000 oz. AGW **Ruler:** Elizabeth II **Obv:** Crowned head right **Rev:** Britannia standing **Note:** Copper alloy.

Date	Mintage	F	VF	XF	Unc	BU
1987	—				—BV+16%	
1987 Proof	3,500	Value: 80.00				
1988	—				—BV+16%	
1988 Proof	2,694	Value: 80.00				
1989	—				—BV+16%	
1989 Proof	1,609	Value: 80.00				

KM# 950a 10 POUNDS (1/10 Ounce - Britannia)
3.4120 g., 0.9170 Gold .1000 oz. AGW **Ruler:** Elizabeth II **Obv:** Crowned head right **Rev:** Britannia standing **Note:** Silver alloy.

Date	Mintage	F	VF	XF	Unc	BU
1990 Proof	1,571	Value: 80.00				
1991 Proof	954	Value: 125				
1992 Proof	1,000	Value: 125				
1993 Proof	997	Value: 125				
1994 Proof	994	Value: 110				
1995 Proof	1,500	Value: 110				
1996 Proof	2,379	Value: 110				
1999 Proof	Est. 5,750	Value: 100				

KM# 982 10 POUNDS (1/10 Ounce - Britannia)
3.4100 g., 0.9167 Gold .1005 oz. AGW **Ruler:** Elizabeth II **Obv:** Crowned head right **Rev:** Britannia in chariot

Date	Mintage	F	VF	XF	Unc	BU
1997 Proof	11,821	Value: 120				

KM# 1008 10 POUNDS (1/10 Ounce - Britannia)
3.4100 g., 0.9167 Gold .1005 oz. AGW **Ruler:** Elizabeth II **Obv:** Head with tiara right **Obv. Designer:** Ian Rank-Broadley **Rev:** Britannia standing **Rev. Designer:** Philip Nathan **Edge:** Reeded

Date	Mintage	F	VF	XF	Unc	BU
1999 Proof	1,058	Value: 115				
2000 Proof	659	Value: 100				
2002 Proof	1,500	Value: 115				
2004	—					
2004 Proof	—	Value: 200				

KM# 1020 10 POUNDS (1/10 Ounce - Britannia)
3.4100 g., 0.9167 Gold .1005 oz. AGW, 16.5 mm. **Ruler:** Elizabeth II **Subject:** Britannia Bullion **Obv:** Head with tiara right **Obv. Designer:** Ian Rank-Broadley **Rev:** Stylized "Britannia and the Lion" **Rev. Designer:** Philip Nathan **Edge:** Reeded

Date	Mintage	F	VF	XF	Unc	BU
2001	1,100	—	—		—BV+16%	—
2001 Proof	1,557	Value: 115				

KM# 1040 10 POUNDS (1/10 Ounce - Britannia)
3.4100 g., 0.9167 Gold 0.1005 oz. AGW, 16.5 mm. **Ruler:** Elizabeth II **Obv:** Head with tiara right **Obv. Designer:** Ian Rank-Broadley **Rev:** Britannia portrait behind wavy lines **Rev. Designer:** Philip Nathan **Edge:** Reeded

Date	Mintage	F	VF	XF	Unc	BU
2003	—	—	—		—BV+16%	—
2003 Proof	4,000	Value: 115				

KM# 1068 10 POUNDS (1/10 Ounce - Britannia)
3.4100 g., 0.9167 Gold 0.1005 oz. AGW, 16.5 mm. **Ruler:** Elizabeth II **Obv:** Head with tiara right **Obv. Designer:** Ian Rank-Broadley **Rev:** Seated Britannia **Rev. Designer:** Philip Nathan **Edge:** Reeded

Date	Mintage	F	VF	XF	Unc	BU
2005 Proof	3,500	Value: 150				

GREAT BRITAIN

KM# 951 25 POUNDS (1/4 Ounce - Britannia)
8.5130 g., 0.9170 Gold .2500 oz. AGW **Ruler:** Elizabeth II **Obv:** Crowned head right **Rev:** Britannia standing **Note:** Copper alloy.

Date	Mintage	F	VF	XF	Unc	BU
1987	—	—	—	—	—BV+10%	—
1987 Proof	3,500	Value: 185				
1988	—	—	—	—	—BV+10%	—
1988 Proof	Est. 14,000	Value: 185				
1989	—	—	—	—	—BV+10%	—
1989 Proof	Est. 4,000	Value: 185				

KM# 951a 25 POUNDS (1/4 Ounce - Britannia)
8.5130 g., 0.9170 Gold .2500 oz. AGW **Ruler:** Elizabeth II **Obv:** Crowned head right **Rev:** Britannia standing **Note:** Silver alloy.

Date	Mintage	F	VF	XF	Unc	BU
1990 Proof	Est. 2,500	Value: 195				
1991 Proof	750	Value: 225				
1992 Proof	500	Value: 225				
1993 Proof	Est. 500	Value: 225				
1994 Proof	500	Value: 215				
1995 Proof	500	Value: 215				
1996 Proof	2,500	Value: 215				
1999 Proof	1,750	Value: 215				

KM# 983 25 POUNDS (1/4 Ounce - Britannia)
8.5100 g., 0.9167 Gold .2508 oz. AGW **Ruler:** Elizabeth II **Obv:** Crowned head right **Rev:** Britannia in chariot

Date	Mintage	F	VF	XF	Unc	BU
1997 Proof	Est. 4,000	Value: 215				

KM# 1009 25 POUNDS (1/4 Ounce - Britannia)
8.5100 g., 0.9167 Gold .2508 oz. AGW **Ruler:** Elizabeth II **Obv:** Head with tiara right **Obv. Designer:** Ian Rank-Broadley **Rev:** Britannia standing **Rev. Designer:** Philip Nathan **Edge:** Reeded

Date	Mintage	F	VF	XF	Unc	BU
1999 Proof	1,000	Value: 220				
2000 Proof	Est. 500	Value: 200				
2002 Proof	750	Value: 225				
2004	—	—	—	—	—	—
2004 Proof	—	Value: 350				

KM# 1021 25 POUNDS (1/4 Ounce - Britannia)
8.5100 g., 0.9167 Gold .2508 oz. AGW, 22 mm. **Ruler:** Elizabeth II **Subject:** Britannia Bullion **Obv:** Head with tiara right **Obv. Designer:** Ian Rank-Broadley **Rev:** Stylized "Britannia and the Lion" **Rev. Designer:** Philip Nathan **Edge:** Reeded

Date	Mintage	F	VF	XF	Unc	BU
2001	1,100	—	—	—	—BV+35%	—
2001 Proof	1,500	Value: 225				

KM# 1041 25 POUNDS (1/4 Ounce - Britannia)
8.5100 g., 0.9167 Gold 0.2508 oz. AGW, 22 mm. **Ruler:** Elizabeth II **Obv:** Head with tiara right **Obv. Designer:** Ian Rank-Broadley **Rev:** Britannia portrait behind wavy lines **Rev. Designer:** Philip Nathan **Edge:** Reeded

Date	Mintage	F	VF	XF	Unc	BU
2003	604	—	—	—	—BV+35%	—
2003 Proof	3,250	Value: 225				

KM# 1069 25 POUNDS (1/4 Ounce - Britannia)
8.5100 g., 0.9167 Gold 0.2508 oz. AGW, 22 mm. **Ruler:** Elizabeth II **Obv:** Head with tiara right **Obv. Designer:** Ian Rank-Broadley **Rev:** Seated Britannia **Rev. Designer:** Philip Nathan **Edge:** Reeded

Date	Mintage	F	VF	XF	Unc	BU
2005 Proof	2,750	Value: 300				

KM# 952 50 POUNDS (1/2 Ounce - Britannia)
17.0250 g., 0.9170 Gold .5000 oz. AGW **Ruler:** Elizabeth II **Obv:** Crowned head right **Rev:** Britannia standing **Note:** Copper alloy.

Date	Mintage	F	VF	XF	Unc	BU
1987	—	—	—	—	—BV+10%	—
1987 Proof	2,486	Value: 375				
1988	—	—	—	—	—BV+10%	—
1988 Proof	626	Value: 375				
1989	—	—	—	—	—BV+10%	—
1989 Proof	338	Value: 375				

KM# 952a 50 POUNDS (1/2 Ounce - Britannia)
17.0250 g., 0.9170 Gold .5000 oz. AGW **Ruler:** Elizabeth II **Obv:** Crowned head right **Rev:** Britannia standing **Note:** Silver alloy.

Date	Mintage	F	VF	XF	Unc	BU
1990 Proof	527	Value: 375				
1991 Proof	509	Value: 400				
1992 Proof	500	Value: 425				
1993 Proof	462	—	—	—	—	—
1994 Proof	435	Value: 425				
1995 Proof	500	Value: 425				
1996 Proof	483	Value: 400				
1999 Proof	740	Value: 450				

KM# 984 50 POUNDS (1/2 Ounce - Britannia)
17.0300 g., 0.9167 Gold .5019 oz. AGW **Ruler:** Elizabeth II **Obv:** Crowned head right **Rev:** Britannia in chariot

Date	Mintage	F	VF	XF	Unc	BU
1997 Proof	Est. 1,500	Value: 400				

KM# 1010 50 POUNDS (1/2 Ounce - Britannia)
17.0300 g., 0.9167 Gold .5019 oz. AGW **Ruler:** Elizabeth II **Obv:** Head with tiara right **Obv. Designer:** Ian Rank-Broadley **Rev:** Britannia standing **Rev. Designer:** Philip Nathan **Edge:** Reeded

Date	Mintage	F	VF	XF	Unc	BU
1999 Proof	—	Value: 425				
2000 Proof	750	Value: 425				
2002 Proof	1,000	Value: 445				
2004	—	—	—	—	—	—
2004 Proof	—	Value: 500				

KM# 1022 50 POUNDS (1/2 Ounce - Britannia)
17.0200 g., 0.9167 Gold .5016 oz. AGW, 27 mm. **Ruler:** Elizabeth II **Subject:** Britannia Bullion **Obv:** Head with tiara right **Obv. Designer:** Ian Rank-Broadley **Rev:** Stylized "Britannia and the Lion" **Rev. Designer:** Philip Nathan **Edge:** Reeded

Date	Mintage	F	VF	XF	Unc	BU
2001	600	—	—	—	—BV+35%	—
2001 Proof	1,000	Value: 435				

KM# 1042 50 POUNDS (1/2 Ounce - Britannia)
17.0200 g., 0.9167 Gold 0.5016 oz. AGW, 27 mm. **Ruler:** Elizabeth II **Obv:** Head with tiara right **Obv. Designer:** Ian Rank-Broadley **Rev:** Britannia portrait behind wavy lines **Rev. Designer:** Philip Nathan **Edge:** Reeded

Date	Mintage	F	VF	XF	Unc	BU
2003	—	—	—	—	—BV+25%	—
2003 Proof	2,500	Value: 450				

KM# 1070 50 POUNDS (1/2 Ounce - Britannia)
17.0300 g., 0.9167 Gold 0.5019 oz. AGW, 27 mm. **Ruler:** Elizabeth II **Obv:** Head with tiara right **Obv. Designer:** Ian Rank-Broadley **Rev:** Seated Britannia **Rev. Designer:** Philip Nathan **Edge:** Reeded

Date	Mintage	F	VF	XF	Unc	BU
2005 Proof	2,000	Value: 450				

KM# 953 100 POUNDS (1 Ounce - Britannia)
34.0500 g., 0.9170 Gold 1.0000 oz. AGW **Ruler:** Elizabeth II **Obv:** Crowned head right **Rev:** Britannia standing **Note:** Copper alloy.

Date	Mintage	F	VF	XF	Unc	BU
1987	—	—	—	—	—BV+12%	—
1987 Proof	13,000	Value: 765				
1988	—	—	—	—	—BV+12%	—
1988 Proof	Est. 8,500	Value: 765				
1989	—	—	—	—	—BV+12%	—
1989 Proof	Est. 2,600	Value: 765				

KM# 953a 100 POUNDS (1 Ounce - Britannia)
34.0500 g., 0.9170 Gold 1.0000 oz. AGW **Ruler:** Elizabeth II **Obv:** Crowned head right **Rev:** Britannia standing **Note:** Silver alloy.

Date	Mintage	F	VF	XF	Unc	BU
1990 Proof	262	Value: 800				
1991 Proof	143	Value: 850				
1992 Proof	500	Value: 875				
1993 Proof	Est. 500	Value: 875				
1994 Proof	Est. 500	Value: 850				
1995 Proof	Est. 500	Value: 900				
1996 Proof	2,500	Value: 800				
1999 Proof	Est. 750	Value: 845				

KM# 985 100 POUNDS (1 Ounce - Britannia)
34.0500 g., 0.9167 Gold 1.0035 oz. AGW **Ruler:** Elizabeth II **Obv:** Crowned head right **Rev:** Britannia in chariot

Date	Mintage	F	VF	XF	Unc	BU
1997	—	—	—	—	—BV+15%	—
1997 Proof	164	Value: 865				

KM# 1011 100 POUNDS (1 Ounce - Britannia)
34.0500 g., 0.9167 Gold 1.0035 oz. AGW **Ruler:** Elizabeth II **Obv:** Head with tiara right **Obv. Designer:** Ian Rank-Broadley **Rev:** Britannia standing **Rev. Designer:** Philip Nathan **Edge:** Reeded

Date	Mintage	F	VF	XF	Unc	BU
1999 Proof	—	Value: 875				
2000 Proof	750	Value: 875				
2002 Proof	1,000	Value: 900				
2004	—	—	—	—	—	—
2004 Proof	—	Value: 875				

KM# 1023 100 POUNDS (1 Ounce - Britannia)
34.0500 g., 0.9167 Gold 1.0035 oz. AGW, 32.7 mm. **Ruler:** Elizabeth II **Subject:** Britannia Bullion **Obv:** Head with tiara right **Obv. Designer:** Ian Rank-Broadley **Rev:** Stylized "Britannia and the Lion" **Rev. Designer:** Philip Nathan **Edge:** Reeded

Date	Mintage	F	VF	XF	Unc	BU
2001	900	—	—	—	—BV+15%	—
2001 Proof	1,000	Value: 875				

KM# 1043 100 POUNDS (1 Ounce - Britannia)
34.0500 g., 0.9167 Gold 1.0035 oz. AGW, 32.7 mm. **Ruler:** Elizabeth II **Obv:** Head with tiara right **Obv. Designer:** Ian Rank-Broadley **Rev:** Britannia portrait behind wavy lines **Rev. Designer:** Philip Nathan **Edge:** Reeded

Date	Mintage	F	VF	XF	Unc	BU
2003	—	—	—	—	—BV+15%	—
2003 Proof	1,500	Value: 900				

KM# 1071 100 POUNDS (1 Ounce - Britannia)
34.0500 g., 0.9167 Gold 1.0035 oz. AGW, 32.7 mm. **Ruler:** Elizabeth II **Obv:** Head with tiara right **Obv. Designer:** Ian Rank-Broadley **Rev:** Seated Britannia **Edge:** Reeded

Date	Mintage	F	VF	XF	Unc	BU
2005 Proof	1,500	Value: 875				

TRADE COINAGE
Britannia Issues

Issued to facilitate British trade in the Orient, the reverse design incorporated the denomination in Chinese characters and Malay script.

This issue was struck at the Bombay (B) and Calcutta (C) Mints in India, except for 1925 and 1930 issues which were struck at London. Through error the mint marks did not appear on some early (1895-1900) issues as indicated.

KM# T5a DOLLAR
Gold **Obv:** Britannia standing **Rev:** Oriental design on cross **Designer:** G. W. de Saulies

Date	Mintage	F	VF	XF	Unc	BU
1895B Proof; restrike	—	Value: 7,500				
1895 Proof; restrike	—	Value: 7,500				
1896B Proof; restrike	—	Value: 7,500				
1897B Proof; restrike	—	Value: 7,500				
1897 Proof; restrike	—	Value: 7,500				
1898B Proof; restrike	—	Value: 7,500				
1899B Proof; restrike	—	Value: 7,500				
1900B Proof; restrike	—	Value: 7,500				
1901B Proof; restrike	—	Value: 7,500				
1902B Proof; restrike	—	Value: 7,500				

MEDALLIC COINAGE
Sterling Issues

X# 34d FARTHING
Gold **Ruler:** Victoria **Obv:** Young head left **Edge:** Milled **Note:** Prev. KM#PPn44.

Date	Mintage	F	VF	XF	Unc	BU
1860 Proof	—	Value: 2,200				

X# 35d FARTHING
Gold **Ruler:** Victoria **Rev:** Four crowned shields form cross **Edge:** Plain **Note:** Prev. KM#PPn49.

Date	Mintage	F	VF	XF	Unc	BU
1860 Proof	—	Value: 2,200				

X# 40d FARTHING
Gold **Ruler:** Victoria **Obv:** Crowned veiled bust left **Rev:** Four crowned shields form cross **Edge:** Milled **Note:** Prev. KM#PPn74.

Date	Mintage	F	VF	XF	Unc	BU
1887 Proof	—	Value: 2,000				

X# 41d FARTHING
Gold **Ruler:** Victoria **Edge:** Plain **Note:** Prev. KM#PPn79.

GREAT BRITAIN

X# 36d 1/2 PENNY
Gold **Ruler:** Victoria **Obv:** Young head left **Rev:** Four crowned shields form cross **Edge:** Milled **Note:** Prev. KM#PPn54.
Date	Mintage	F	VF	XF	Unc	BU
1887 Proof	—	Value: 2,000				

X# 37d 1/2 PENNY
Gold **Ruler:** Victoria **Obv:** Young head left **Rev:** Four crowned shields form cross **Edge:** Plain **Note:** Prev. KM#PPn59.
Date	Mintage	F	VF	XF	Unc	BU
1860 Proof	2,200	Value: 2,400				

X# 42d 1/2 PENNY
Gold **Ruler:** Victoria **Edge:** Plain **Note:** Prev. KM#PPn84.
Date	Mintage	F	VF	XF	Unc	BU
1860 Proof	—	Value: 2,400				

X# 43d 1/2 PENNY
Gold **Ruler:** Victoria **Obv:** Crowned bust left **Rev:** Four crowned shields form cross **Edge:** Milled **Note:** Prev. KM#PPn84.
Date	Mintage	F	VF	XF	Unc	BU
1887 Proof	—	Value: 3,200				

X# 43d 1/2 PENNY
Gold **Ruler:** Victoria **Edge:** Plain **Note:** Prev. KM#PPn89.
Date	Mintage	F	VF	XF	Unc	BU
1887 Proof	—	Value: 3,200				

X# 38d PENNY
Gold **Ruler:** Victoria **Obv:** Young head left **Rev:** Four crowned shields form cross **Edge:** Milled **Note:** Prev. KM#PPn64.
Date	Mintage	F	VF	XF	Unc	BU
1860 Proof	—	Value: 3,600				

X# 39d PENNY
Gold **Ruler:** Victoria **Edge:** Plain **Note:** Prev. KM#PPn69.
Date	Mintage	F	VF	XF	Unc	BU
1860 Proof	—	Value: 3,600				

X# 44d PENNY
Gold **Ruler:** Victoria **Obv:** Crowned veiled bust left **Rev:** Four crowned shields form cross **Edge:** Milled **Note:** Prev. KM#PPn94.
Date	Mintage	F	VF	XF	Unc	BU
1887 Proof	—	Value: 3,600				

X# 45d PENNY
Gold **Ruler:** Victoria **Edge:** Plain **Note:** Prev. KM#PPn99.
Date	Mintage	F	VF	XF	Unc	BU
1887 Proof	—	Value: 3,600				

PRIVATE PATTERNS

Smith on Decimal Currency Issues

X# 48d 2 CENTS
Gold **Ruler:** Victoria **Obv:** Young bust left **Note:** Prev. KM#PPn32.
Date	Mintage	F	VF	XF	Unc	BU
1846 Proof; Restrike	—	Value: 2,250				

Mills-Whiteaves Issues

X# 51a CROWN
Gold **Ruler:** George IV **Obv:** Large head left **Rev:** Supported helmed arms **Edge:** Plain **Note:** Prev. KM#PPn14.
Date	Mintage	F	VF	XF	Unc	BU
1820 Proof	—	Value: 35,000				

Bonomi-Thomas Issues

X# 53a CROWN
Gold **Ruler:** Victoria **Obv:** Young bust with tiara left **Obv. Legend:** VICTORIA REG DEL GRATIA **Rev:** Helmeted Minerva standing right with trident and shield releasing Nike **Rev. Inscription:** BRITT / MINERVA - VICTRIX / FID DEF **Edge:** Plain **Note:** Prev. KM#PPn17.
Date	Mintage	F	VF	XF	Unc	BU
1837 Proof	6	Value: 8,500				

Note: Numbered T1-T6 on edge

Spink & Sons Issues

X# 55a 6 PENCE
Gold **Ruler:** Victoria **Obv:** Crowned veiled bust left **Rev:** Crowned supported arms **Note:** Prev. KM#PPn101.
Date	Mintage	F	VF	XF	Unc	BU
1887 Proof	15	Value: 1,750				

X# 59a CROWN
Gold **Ruler:** Victoria **Obv:** Crowned veiled bust left **Rev:** Crowned supported arms **Edge:** Plain **Note:** Prev. KM#PPn109.
Date	Mintage	F	VF	XF	Unc	BU
1887 Proof	6	Value: 6,500				

X# 59g CROWN
Gold **Ruler:** Victoria **Obv:** Crowned veiled bust left **Rev:** Crowned supported arms **Edge:** Reeded **Note:** Prev. KM#PPn115.
Date	Mintage	F	VF	XF	Unc	BU
1887 Proof	6	Value: 6,500				

X# 61a CROWN
Gold **Ruler:** Edward VII **Obv:** King horseback left **Rev:** Oval arms **Edge:** Plain **Note:** Prev. KM#PPn120.
Date	Mintage	F	VF	XF	Unc	BU
1902 Proof	—	Value: 5,500				

A. G. Wyon Issues

X# 69b CROWN
Gold **Ruler:** George V **Obv:** Head left **Rev:** St. George horseback left slaying dragon **Edge:** Plain
Date	Mintage	F	VF	XF	Unc	BU
MDCDX (1910) Rare	—	—	—	—	—	—

X# 69c CROWN
Gold **Ruler:** George V **Obv:** Head left **Rev:** St. George horseback left slaying dragon **Edge:** Milled
Date	Mintage	F	VF	XF	Unc	BU
MDCDX (1910) Rare	—	—	—	—	—	—

X# 70c CROWN
Gold **Ruler:** George V **Obv:** Head left **Rev:** St. George horseback left slaying dragon **Edge:** Plain **Note:** Prev. KM#PPn120.
Date	Mintage	F	VF	XF	Unc	BU
1910 Rare	—	—	—	—	—	—

X# 70d CROWN
Gold **Ruler:** George V **Obv:** Head left **Rev:** St. George horseback left slaying dragon **Edge:** Milled
Date	Mintage	F	VF	XF	Unc	BU
1910 Rare	—	—	—	—	—	—

Reginald Huth Issues

X# 67a 8 PENCE
Gold **Ruler:** George V **Obv:** Draped bust left **Rev:** Four crowned shields form cross **Edge:** Reeded **Note:** Prev. KM#PPn132.
Date	Mintage	F	VF	XF	Unc	BU
1913 Proof	—	Value: 2,000				

X# 67b 8 PENCE
8.2000 g., Platinum APW **Ruler:** George V **Obv:** Draped bust left **Rev:** Four crowned shields form cross **Edge:** Reeded **Note:** Prev. KM#PPn133.
Date	Mintage	F	VF	XF	Unc	BU
1913 Proof	—	Value: 2,250				

X# 66a OCTORINO
Gold **Ruler:** George V **Obv:** Draped bust left **Rev:** Four crowned shields form cross **Edge:** Reeded **Note:** Prev. KM#PPn127.
Date	Mintage	F	VF	XF	Unc	BU
1913 Proof	—	Value: 2,000				

X# 66b OCTORINO
8.0000 g., Platinum APW **Ruler:** George V **Obv:** Draped bust left **Rev:** Four crowned shields form cross **Edge:** Reeded **Note:** Prev. KM#PPn128.
Date	Mintage	F	VF	XF	Unc	BU
1913 Proof	—	Value: 2,250				

X# 68b 12 GROATS
Platinum APW **Ruler:** George V **Obv:** Draped bust left **Rev:** Four crowned shields form cross
Date	Mintage	F	VF	XF	Unc	BU
1914 Proof	—	Value: 3,500				

X# 68c 12 GROATS
Gold **Ruler:** George V **Obv:** Draped bust left **Rev:** Four crowned shields form cross **Edge:** Reeded **Note:** Prev. KM#PPn139.
Date	Mintage	F	VF	XF	Unc	BU
1914 Proof	—	Value: 2,750				

MEDALLIC COINAGE

Richard Lobel Issues

X# M15c CROWN
Gold, 38.6 mm. **Ruler:** Edward VIII **Obv:** Head of Dutchess and bust of Duke facing **Obv. Legend:** DUKE & DUTCHESS OF WINDSOR **Rev:** St. George horseback left slaying dragon **Edge:** Plain
Date	Mintage	F	VF	XF	Unc	BU
1987 Proof	2	Value: 775				

X# M16 SOVEREIGN
Gold, 22 mm. **Ruler:** Edward VIII **Obv:** Head of Dutchess and bust of Duke facing **Obv. Legend:** DUKE & DUTCHESS OF WINDSOR **Rev:** St. George horseback left slaying dragon **Edge:** Plain
Date	Mintage	F	VF	XF	Unc	BU
1987 Proof	—	—	—	—	—	—

X# M14 SOVEREIGN
Gold, 22 mm. **Ruler:** Edward VIII **Obv:** Bust left, dates below **Obv. Legend:** EDWARD • VIII • KING • E • EMPEROR **Rev:** St. George horseback left, slaying dragon **Edge:** Plain
Date	Mintage	F	VF	XF	Unc	BU
1987 Proof	3	Value: 600				

MEDALLIC COINAGE

X# M9 SOVEREIGN
Gold, 22 mm. **Ruler:** Victoria **Obv:** Crowned bust left **Obv. Legend:** Victoria Dei Gratia - Britanniar • reg • f • d **Rev:** Four crowned shields forming a cross **Rev. Legend:** TVEATVR VNITA DEVS…
Date	Mintage	F	VF	XF	Unc	BU
MDCCCXLVII Proof	—	Value: 175				

PATTERNS

Including off metal strikes

KM#	Date	Mintage	Identification	Mkt Val
PnB68	1806	—	Farthing. Gold. KM#661.	
Pn68	1813	—	Guinea. Gold. Plain edge. George III	14,000
Pn69	1813	—	Guinea. Gold. Reeded edge. George III	14,000
Pn70	1813	—	Guinea. Gold. Arms in wreath. Plain edge. George III	—

GREAT BRITAIN

KM#	Date	Mintage	Identification	Mkt Val
Pn71	1813	—	Guinea. Gold. Arms in wreath. Reeded edge. George III.	14,000
Pn72	1813	—	Guinea. Gold. Banner. George III.	14,000
PnA73	1816	—	6 Pence. Gold. KM#665.	—
PnB73	1816	—	Shilling. Gold. KM#666.	—
Pn73	1816	—	Sovereign. Gold. George III.	17,500
Pn74	1816	—	Sovereign. Gold. George III.	19,500
Pn75	1816	—	1/2 Sovereign. Gold. George III.	5,250
Pn76	1816	—	1/2 Sovereign. Gold. Rose. George III.	3,150
PnC77	1817	—	Crown. Gold. George III.	255,000
Pn77	1817	—	Crown. 0.9160 Gold. George III.	125,000
Pn85	1820	12	1/2 Sovereign. Gold. George IV.	—
Pn80	1820	—	1/2 Sovereign. Gold. George III.	7,000
Pn81	1820	—	2 Pounds. Gold. Plain edge. George III.	31,500
Pn82	1820	60	2 Pounds. Gold. Lettered edge. George III.	12,200
Pn83	1820	—	5 Pounds. Gold. Plain edge. George III.	52,500
Pn84	1820	25	5 Pounds. Gold. Lettered edge. George III.	45,000
Pn86	1821	—	1/2 Sovereign. Gold. George IV.	—
Pn87	1824	—	Sovereign. Gold. George IV.	—
Pn88	1824	—	2 Pounds. Gold. Lettered edge. George IV.	25,000
Pn89	1825	—	1/2 Sovereign. Gold. George IV.	—
Pn91	1825	—	2 Pounds. Gold. Plain edge. George IV.	11,500
Pn92	1825	—	2 Pounds. Gold. Lettered edge. George IV.	11,500
Pn93	1826	—	2 Pounds. Gold. Plain edge. George IV.	—
Pn94	1826	—	2 Pounds. Gold. Lettered edge. George IV.	—
Pn95	1826	—	5 Pounds. Gold. Plain edge. George IV.	—
Pn96	1826	—	5 Pounds. Gold. Lettered edge. George IV.	17,000

Note: Mintage included with KM#702

| PnA97 | 1829 | — | 5 Pounds. Gold. Plain edge. George IV. | — |

Note: Stack's sale 12-92 BU realized $85,000.

Pn97	1830	—	Sovereign. Gold. Plain edge. William IV.	—
PnA98	1831	—	Crown. Gold. Plain edge. William IV.	125,000
Pn98	1831	—	2 Pounds. Gold. Plain edge. William IV.	—
Pn99	1831	—	5 Pounds. Gold. Plain edge. William IV.	—
PnC100	1836	—	4 Pence. Gold. KM#723.	6,500

KM#	Date	Mintage	Identification	Mkt Val
Pn102	1837	—	Sovereign. Gold. Victoria.	—
Pn103	1837	—	Sovereign. Gold. Victoria, large head.	—
Pn104	1837	—	Sovereign. Gold. Wide spaced letter. Victoria.	—
PnA105	1838	—	3 Pence. Gold. KM#730.	5,000
Pn105	1838	—	Sovereign. Gold. Victoria.	—
Pn106	1839	—	5 Pounds. Gold. Victoria. Plain mantle.	92,500
Pn107	1839	—	5 Pounds. Gold. Victoria. Garter star on mantle.	—
Pn108	1839	—	5 Pounds. Gold. Plain edge. Victoria.	—
Pn109	1839	—	5 Pounds. Silver. Lettered edge. Victoria.	—
Pn110	1839	—	5 Pounds. Copper. Victoria.	—
PnC111	1843	—	Sovereign. Gold. Victoria. KM#736.	10,000
PnD111	1847	—	Crown. Gold. Plain edge. KM#741.	—
PnA112	1848	—	Florin. Gold. KM#745.	15,000
Pn112	1853	—	5 Shilling. Gold. Victoria.	—
Pn113	1853	—	1/4 Sovereign. Gold. Victoria.	4,000
PnC114	1860	—	Penny. Gold. KM#749.2.	—
PnE114	1861	—	Farthing. Gold. KM#747.2.	—
PnJ114	1861	—	1/2 Penny. Gold. KM#748.2.	—
PnN114	1861	—	Penny. Gold. KM#749.2.	—
Pn114	1864	—	Sovereign. Gold. Victoria.	—
PnH115	1867	—	Ducat. Gold. Victoria.	4,500
PnS115	1868	—	Double Florin. Gold. Plain edge. Victoria.	4,000
Pn115	1868	—	Double Florin. Gold. Grained edge. Victoria.	4,000
Pn116	1870	—	Sovereign. Gold. Victoria.	—
PnA117	1874	—	1/2 Crown. 0.9170 Gold. KM#756.	—
PnA118	1880	—	1/2 Sovereign. Silver. Victoria.	6,500
PnB118	1880	—	Sovereign. Silver. Victoria.	8,500
PnA119	1887	—	Penny. Gold.	—
PnA121	1922	—	Florin. Gold. KM817a	15,000
PnD121	1924	1	3 Pence. Gold. KM813a	10,000
pnE121	1924	3	6 Pence. Gold. KM#815a.1	10,000
PnL122	1927	—	1/2 Crown. Gold. Modified Effigy. KM830	—
PnM122	1935	—	Crown. Gold. Similar to KM842.	18,000
Pn132	1937	6	Sovereign. 0.9160 Gold. Head left. St. George slaying the dragon. Edward VIII.	120,000
Pn135	1953	—	1/2 Sovereign. 0.9160 Gold.	—
Pn137	1953	—	2 Pounds. 0.9160 Gold.	—
Pn138	1953	—	5 Pounds. 0.9160 Gold.	—
Pn136	1953	—	Sovereign. 0.9160 Gold. Y#137.	40,000

PROOF SETS

KM#	Date	Mintage	Identification	Issue Price	Mkt Val
PS1	1821 (6)	5	KM#677-680, 681.1, 682	—	Rare
PS2	1826 (15)	150	KM#683-684, 685.2, 686, 691, 692a, 693a, 694-695, 697a, 699-702	—	40,000
PS3	1826 (11)	I.A.	KM#691, 692a, 693a, 694-696, 697a, 700-702	—	40,000
PS4	1831 (14)	225	KM#705, 706a, 707a, 709-713, 714.1, 716-718, 720, 835	—	35,000
PS5	1839 (15)	300	KM#725a-726a, 727, 729-730, 731.2, 732-736, 739a, 740-742	—	55,000
PS6	1839/48 (16)	I.A.	KM#725a-726a, 727, 729, 730,731.2, 732-736, 739a, 740-742, 745	—	55,000
PS7	1853 (17)	—	KM#725a-726a, 727, 729-730, 731.2, 732-736, 737a, 739a, 740a, 744, 746	—	40,000
PS8	1853 (16)	I.A.	KM#725a, 726a, 727, 729-730, 731.2, 732-736, 737a, 739a, 740a, 744, 746	—	40,000
PS9	1887 (11)	797	KM#758-759, 761-769	—	11,500
PS10	1887 (11)	I.A.	KM#758-762, 764-769	—	11,000
PS13	1893 (10)	773	KM#777, 779-787	—	12,000
PS15	1902 (13)	8,066	KM#795-797.1, 798-807	—	2,500
PS16	1902 (11)	7,057	KM#795-797.1, 798-805	—	900
PS17	1911 (12)	2,812	KM#811-818.1, 819-822	—	4,000
PS18	1911 (10)	952	KM#811-818.1, 819-820	—	1,150
PS37	1980 (4)	10,000	KM#919, 922-924	2,650	1,150
PS38	1981 (2)	2,500	KM#919, 925a	—	160
PS40	1981 (9)	5,000	KM#911-916, 919, 924, 925a	—	935
PS42	1982 (4)	2,500	KM#919, 922-924	—	1,350
PS44	1983 (3)	—	KM#919, 922-923	775	535
PS45	1984 (8)	125,000	KM#926-932, 934	29.95	23.50
PS46	1984 (3)	—	KM#919, 922, 924	1,275	910
PS48	1985 (4)	12,500	KM#942-945	1,395	1,175
PS50	1986 (3)	12,500	KM#942-943, 947c	675	535
PS52	1987 (4)	10,000	KM#950-953	1,595	1,000
PS53	1987 (3)	12,500	KM#942-944	675	535
PS54	1987 (2)	12,500	KM#950-951	325	190
PS56	1988 (4)	6,500	KM#950-953	1,595	1,000
PS57	1988 (3)	—	KM#942-944	775	510
PS58	1988 (2)	7,500	KM#950-951	340	190
PS60	1989 (4)	2,500	KM#950-953	1,595	1,000
PS61	1989 (4)	5,000	KM#955-958	1,595	1,600
PS62	1989 (3)	15,000	KM#955-957	775	675
PS63	1989 (2)	1,500	KM#950-951	340	200
PS68	1990 (4)	2,500	KM#942-944, 949	1,595	1,400
PS69	1990 (4)	2,500	KM#950a-953a	1,595	1,000
PS70	1990 (3)	7,500	KM#942-944	775	570
PS74	1991 (4)	1,500	KM#942-944, 949	1,750	1,500
PS75	1991 (4)	750	KM#950a-953a	1,750	1,500
PS76	1991 (3)	2,500	KM#942-944	895	665
PS79	1992 (4)	1,250	KM#942-945	1,750	1,450
PS81	1992 (3)	1,250	KM#942-944	895	710
PS85	1993 (4)	500	KM#950a-953a	1,755	1,600
PS86	1993 (4)	1,250	KM#942-945	1,560	1,530
PS87	1993 (3)	1,250	KM#942-944	800	670
PS90	1994 (4)	500	KM#950a-953a	1,499	1,500
PS91	1994 (4)	1,250	KM#942-943, 945, 968c	—	1,550
PS92	1994 (3)	1,250	KM#942-943, 968c	—	760
PS95	1995 (4)	1,250	KM#942-943, 945, 971c	—	1,675
PS96	1995 (4)	500	KM#950a-953a	1,500	1,500
PS97	1995 (3)	1,250	KM#942-943, 945	—	860
PS100	1996 (4)	2,500,000	KM#950a-953a	1,600	1,500
PS104	1997 (3)	1,500	KM#982-985	1,600	1,650
PS107	1999 (4)	1,000	KM#999a, 1001-1003	1,725	1,725
PS108	1999 (3)	1,250	KM#1001-1003	—	955
PS109	1999 (4)	750	KM#950a-953a	1,495	1,500
PS110	1999 (4)	—	KM#1008-1011	1,595	—
PS114	2000 (4)	750	KM#1008-1011	1,495	1,498
PSA115	2000 (3)	1,250	KM#994c, 1001, 1002	—	—
PS116	2001 (4)	1,500	KM#1001-1002, 1014a	795	—
PS117	2001 (4)	1,000	KM#1001-1003,1014a	1,645	—
PSA119	2001 (3)	1,500	KM#1001, 1002, 1014b	—	—
PSB119	2001 (4)	1,000	KM#1001, 1002, 1014b, 1015b	—	—
PS119	2001 (4)	1,000	KM#1020-1023	1,595	—
PS120	2002 (3)	5,000	KM#1025-1027	795	—
PS121	2002 (3)	3,000	KM#1025-1028	1,645	—
PS126	2002 (4)	1,000	KM#1008-1011	1,600	1,625
PS141	2005 (3)	2,000	KM#1068-1070	850	875
PS142	2005 (4)	1,500	KM#1068-1071	1,895	1,900
PS143	2005 (3)	2,500	KM#1064-1066	820	825
PS144	2005 (4)	2,500	KM#1064-1067	1,925	1,950
PS148	2006 (5)	3,000	KM#1000a, 1012a, 1018a, 1039, 1063a	475	500
PS149	2006 (3)	1,750	KM#1001, 1002, 1072	1,015	1,025
PS150	2006 (4)	1,750	KM#1001-1003, 1072	2,091	2,100

WALES

KINGDOM

ECU COINAGE

X# 2 ECU
3.0000 g., 0.7500 Gold 0.0723 oz. AGW, 22.5 mm. **Ruler:** Elizabeth II **Obv:** Neptune and Europa standing flanking circular outlined map of Europe **Obv. Legend:** • EUROPE ★ EUORPA • WALES **Obv. Designer:** R. D. Maklouf **Rev:** Helmeted bust of Edward the Black Prince facing

Date	Mintage	F	VF	XF	Unc	BU
1992 Proof	500	Value: 200				

X# 2a ECU
38.0000 g., 0.9167 Gold 1.12 oz. AGW, 38 mm. **Ruler:** Elizabeth II **Obv:** Neptune and Europa standing flanking circular outlined map of Europe **Obv. Legend:** • EUROPE ★ EUROPA • WALES **Obv. Designer:** R. D. Maklouf **Rev:** Helmeted bust of Edward the Black Prince facing

Date	Mintage	F	VF	XF	Unc	BU
1992 Proof	25	—	—	—	—	—

X# 4a 25 ECU
38.0000 g., 0.9167 Gold 1.12 oz. AGW, 38 mm. **Ruler:** Elizabeth II **Obv:** Neptune and Europa standing flanking circular outlined map of Europe **Obv. Legend:** • EUROPE ★ EUROPA • WALES **Obv. Designer:** R. D. Maklouf **Rev:** Helmeted bust of Edward the Black Prince facing

Date	Mintage	F	VF	XF	Unc	BU
1992 Proof	25	—	—	—	—	—

GREECE

The Hellenic (Greek) Republic is situated in southeastern Europe on the southern tip of the Balkan Peninsula. The republic includes many islands, the most important of which are Crete and the Ionian Islands.

Greece, the Mother of Western civilization, attained the peak of its culture in the 5th century B.C., when it contributed more to government, drama, art and architecture than any other people to this time. Greece fell under Roman domination in the 2nd and 1st centuries B.C., becoming part of the Byzantine Empire until Constantinople fell to the Crusaders in 1202. With the fall of Constantinople to the Turks in 1453, Greece became part of the Ottoman Empire. Independence from Turkey was won with the revolution of 1821-27. In 1833, Greece was established as a monarchy, with sovereignty guaranteed by Britain, France and Russia. After a lengthy power struggle between the monarchist forces and democratic factions, Greece was proclaimed a republic in 1925. The monarchy was restored in 1935 and reconfirmed by a plebiscite in 1946. The Italians invaded Greece via Albania on Oct. 28, 1940 but were driven back well within the Albanian border. Germany began their invasion in April 1941 and quickly overran the entire country and drove off a British Expeditionary force by the end of April. King George II and his new government went into exile. The German-Italian occupation of Greece lasted until Oct. 1944 after which only German troops remained until the end of the occupation. On April 21, 1967, a military junta took control of the government and suspended the constitution. King Constantine II made an unsuccessful attempt against the junta in the fall of 1968 and consequently fled to Italy. The monarchy was formally abolished by plebiscite, Dec. 8, 1974, and Greece was established as the Hellenic Republic, the third republic in Greek history.

RULERS
John Capodistrias, 1828-1831
Othon (Otto of Bavaria), 1832-1862
George I, 1863-1913
Constantine I, 1913-1917, 1920-1922
Alexander I, 1917-1920
George II, 1922-1923, 1935-1947
Paul I, 1947-1964
Constantine II, 1964-1973

MINT MARKS
(a) - Paris, privy marks only
A - Paris
B - Vienna
BB - Strassburg
(c) - Aegina (1828-1832), Chain and anchor
H - Heaton, Birmingham
K - Bordeaux
KN - King's Norton
(o) - Athens (1838-1855), Owl
(p) - Poissy - Thunderbolt

MONETARY SYSTEM
Until 1831
100 Lepta = 1 Phoenix
Commencing 1831
100 Lepta = 1 Drachma

KINGDOM

DECIMAL COINAGE

KM# 47 5 DRACHMAI
1.6129 g., 0.9000 Gold .0467 oz. AGW **Ruler:** George I **Obv:** Head right **Rev:** Denomination and date within wreath

Date	Mintage	F	VF	XF	Unc	BU
1876A	9,294	500	750	1,150	2,250	3,500

KM# 48 10 DRACHMAI
3.2258 g., 0.9000 Gold .0933 oz. AGW **Ruler:** George I **Obv:** Head right **Rev:** Denomination and date within wreath

Date	Mintage	F	VF	XF	Unc	BU
1876A	19,000	300	500	800	1,500	3,000

KM# 21 20 DRACHMAI
5.7760 g., 0.9000 Gold .1672 oz. AGW **Ruler:** Othon **Obv:** Head left **Rev:** Crowned arms within branches

Date	Mintage	F	VF	XF	Unc	BU
1833	18,000	450	750	1,250	5,750	6,000

KM# 49 20 DRACHMAI
6.4516 g., 0.9000 Gold .1867 oz. AGW **Ruler:** George I **Obv:** Head right **Rev:** Arms within crowned mantle

Date	Mintage	F	VF	XF	Unc	BU
1876A	37,000	250	400	750	2,200	3,500
1876A Proof	—	Value: 15,000				

Note: Hess-Divo Auction 284, 11-00, Proof FDC realized $6450. Spink Coin Auctions #10, 9-80, Brilliant FDC realized $12,000

KM# 56 20 DRACHMAI
6.4516 g., 0.9000 Gold .1867 oz. AGW **Ruler:** George I **Obv:** Head right **Rev:** Arms within crowned mantle

Date	Mintage	F	VF	XF	Unc	BU
1884A	550,000	100	150	200	400	600
1884A Proof	—	Value: 8,000				

KM# 50 50 DRACHMAI
16.1290 g., 0.9000 Gold .4667 oz. AGW **Ruler:** George I **Obv:** Head right **Rev:** Arms within crowned mantle

Date	Mintage	F	VF	XF	Unc	BU
1876A	182	3,500	5,500	8,500	17,500	—

KM# 51 100 DRACHMAI
32.2580 g., 0.9000 Gold .9335 oz. AGW **Ruler:** George I **Obv:** Head right **Rev:** Arms within crowned mantle

Date	Mintage	F	VF	XF	Unc	BU
1876A	76	6,000	10,000	20,000	40,000	—
1876A Proof	—	Value: 120,000				

MEDALLIC COINAGE

Private political issues created for use in suspension jewelry. These pieces are most often found holed, with jewelry mounts, or with traces of mounts having been removed. Values listed below are for original pieces with little or no detracting features. Holed pieces and examples with extensive damage from mounting maintain lower values.

316   GREECE

X# M5 2 DUCAT
Gold, 30.5 mm. **Subject:** Prime Minister Eleftherios Venizelos **Obv:** Double headed eagle with shield on breast, date in legend **Rev:** Bust 3/4 right

Date	Mintage	F	VF	XF	Unc	BU
1912	—	300	450	750	—	—

X# M1 2 DUCAT
5.2600 g., Gold **Subject:** Prime Minister Eleftherios Venizelos **Obv:** Crowned double headed eagle with shield on breast, anniversary date below **Rev:** Bust left

Date	Mintage	F	VF	XF	Unc	BU
ND(1919)	—	250	350	500	—	—
ND Restrike	—	—	—	—BV+20%	—	—

X# M3 4 DUCAT
11.0200 g., 0.9167 Gold 0.3248 oz. AGW, 39.5 mm. **Subject:** Prime Minister Eleftherios Venizelos **Obv:** Crowned double headed eagle with shield on breast, date below **Rev:** Bust right

Date	Mintage	F	VF	XF	Unc	BU
1919	—	450	750	1,250	—	—

X# M2 4 DUCAT
10.7900 g., Gold **Subject:** Prime Minister Eleftherios Venizelos **Obv:** Crowned double headed eagle with shield on breast, anniversary date below **Rev:** Bust left

Date	Mintage	F	VF	XF	Unc	BU
ND(1919)	—	400	700	1,200	—	—
ND Restrike	—	—	—	—BV+15%	—	—

X# M6 4 DUCAT
Gold, 40 mm. **Ruler:** Constantine I **Subject:** Constantine I **Obv:** Triple crowned double headed eagle with shield on breast, date below **Rev:** Bust left

Date	Mintage	F	VF	XF	Unc	BU
1920	—	600	1,000	1,750	—	—

KINGDOM
DECIMAL COINAGE

KM# 74 20 DRACHMAI
6.4516 g., 0.9000 Gold .1867 oz. AGW, 22 mm. **Ruler:** George II **Subject:** 5th Anniversary - Restoration of Monarchy **Obv:** Head left **Rev:** Denomination within crowned wreath

Date	Mintage	F	VF	XF	Unc	BU
ND(1940) Proof	200	Value: 15,000				

KM# 92 20 DRACHMAI
6.4516 g., 0.9000 Gold .1867 oz. AGW **Ruler:** Constantine II **Subject:** Commemorative of the April 21, 1967 revolution **Obv:** Crowned shield with supporters **Rev:** Soldier in front of Phoenix

Date	Mintage	F	VF	XF	Unc	BU
ND (1970)	20,000	—	—	—	350	450

X# M4 4 DUCAT
10.7900 g., Gold, 40 mm. **Subject:** Prime Minister Eleftherios Venizelos **Obv:** Crowned double headed eagle with shield on breast, date below **Rev:** Bust left

Date	Mintage	F	VF	XF	Unc	BU
1919	—	450	750	1,250	—	—

KM# 76 100 DRACHMAI
32.2580 g., 0.9000 Gold .9335 oz. AGW, 38 mm. **Ruler:** George II **Obv:** Head left **Rev:** Denomination within crowned wreath

Date	Mintage	F	VF	XF	Unc	BU
ND (1940) Proof	140	Value: 25,000				

KM# 95 100 DRACHMAI
32.2580 g., 0.9000 Gold .9335 oz. AGW **Ruler:** Constantine II **Subject:** April 21, 1967 Revolution **Obv:** Crowned arms with supporters **Rev:** Soldier in front of Phoenix

Date	Mintage	F	VF	XF	Unc	BU
ND (1970)	10,000	—	—	—	950	1,250
ND(1970)	10,000	—	—	—	950	1,250

REPUBLIC
DECIMAL COINAGE

KM# 189 DRACHMA
8.5000 g., 0.9167 Gold 0.2505 oz. AGW **Obv:** Sailing ship **Rev:** Bouboulina, heroine, bust left

Date	Mintage	F	VF	XF	Unc	BU
2000 Proof	—	Value: 400				

KM# 128 2500 DRACHMAI
6.4500 g., 0.9000 Gold .1866 oz. AGW **Series:** Pan-European Games **Subject:** Ancient Olympics, Agon **Obv:** Arms within wreath **Rev:** Winged figure holding rings

Date	Mintage	F	VF	XF	Unc	BU
1981 Proof	75,000	Value: 155				

KM# 141 2500 DRACHMAI
6.4500 g., 0.9000 Gold .1866 oz. AGW **Series:** Pan-European Games **Subject:** 1896 Olympics, Spiros **Obv:** Arms within wreath **Rev:** Half figure holding wreath

Date	Mintage	F	VF	XF	Unc	BU
1982 Proof	50,000	Value: 150				

KM# 142 2500 DRACHMAI
6.4500 g., 0.9000 Gold .1866 oz. AGW **Series:** Pan-European Games **Obv:** Arms within wreath **Rev:** Winged statue

Date	Mintage	F	VF	XF	Unc	BU
1982 Proof	50,000	Value: 155				

GREECE

KM# 129 5000 DRACHMAI
12.5000 g., 0.9000 Gold .3617 oz. AGW **Series:** Pan-European Games **Subject:** Ancient Olympics, Zeus **Obv:** Arms within wreath **Rev:** Laureate head left

Date	Mintage	F	VF	XF	Unc	BU
1981 Proof	75,000	Value: 265				

KM# 143 5000 DRACHMAI
12.5000 g., 0.9000 Gold .3617 oz. AGW **Series:** Pan-European Games **Subject:** 1896 Olympics, Pierre de Coubertin **Obv:** Arms within wreath **Rev:** Head 3/4 facing

Date	Mintage	F	VF	XF	Unc	BU
1982 Proof	50,000	Value: 265				

KM# 144 5000 DRACHMAI
12.5000 g., 0.9000 Gold .3617 oz. AGW **Series:** Pan-European Games **Obv:** Arms within wreath **Rev:** Birds flying

Date	Mintage	F	VF	XF	Unc	BU
1982 Proof	50,000	Value: 265				

KM# 146 5000 DRACHMES
8.0000 g., 0.9000 Gold .2315 oz. AGW **Subject:** Olympics **Obv:** Arms at left, torch at right **Rev:** Apollo

Date	Mintage	F	VF	XF	Unc	BU
1984 Proof	15,000	Value: 400				

KM# 123 10000 DRACHMES
20.0000 g., 0.9000 Gold .5787 oz. AGW **Subject:** Common Market Membership **Obv:** Inscription above denomination **Rev:** Seated figure left

Date	Mintage	F	VF	XF	Unc	BU
ND (1979) Proof	—	Value: 550				

KM# 149 10000 DRACHMES
7.1300 g., 0.9000 Gold .2063 oz. AGW **Subject:** Decade For Women **Obv:** Arms within wreath **Rev:** Standing figure

Date	Mintage	F	VF	XF	Unc	BU
1985 Proof	2,835	Value: 800				

KM# 158 10000 DRACHMES
8.0000 g., 0.9000 Gold .2315 oz. AGW **Subject:** XI Mediterranean Games **Obv:** Design, denomination **Rev:** Fish wearing hat, logo at right

Date	Mintage	F	VF	XF	Unc	BU
1991 Proof	2,000	Value: 400				

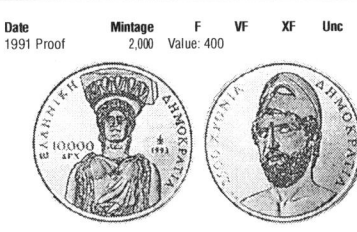

KM# 161 10000 DRACHMES
8.5000 g., 0.9170 Gold .2506 oz. AGW **Subject:** 2500th Anniversary of Democracy **Obv:** Statue **Rev:** Head left

Date	Mintage	F	VF	XF	Unc	BU
1993 Proof	Est. 10,000	Value: 450				

KM# 163 10000 DRACHMES
8.5000 g., 0.9170 Gold .2506 oz. AGW **Subject:** Volleyball Centennial **Obv:** Ancient coin divides date

Date	Mintage	F	VF	XF	Unc	BU
1994 Proof	669	Value: 1,500				

KM# 156 20000 DRACHMES
8.0000 g., 0.9000 Gold .2315 oz. AGW **Subject:** 50th Anniversary - Italian Invasion of Greece **Rev:** Soldiers and horse

Date	Mintage	F	VF	XF	Unc	BU
1990 Proof	1,000	Value: 2,000				

KM# 167 20000 DRACHMES
16.9700 g., 0.9170 Gold .5001 oz. AGW **Subject:** Olympics **Obv:** Track field **Rev:** Ancient javelin throwers **Edge Lettering:** CITIUS ALTIUS FORTIUS

Date	Mintage	F	VF	XF	Unc	BU
1996 Proof	60,000	Value: 500				

EURO COINAGE
European Economic Community Issues

KM# 192 100 EURO
0.9999 Gold, 25 mm. **Subject:** Olympics **Obv:** Olympic rings in wreath above value within circle of stars **Rev:** Knossos Palace **Edge:** Plain

Date	Mintage	F	VF	XF	Unc	BU
ND(2003) Proof	28,000	Value: 570				

KM# 195 100 EURO
10.0000 g., 0.9999 Gold 0.3215 oz. AGW, 25 mm. **Subject:** Olympics **Obv:** Olympic rings in wreath above value within circle of stars **Rev:** Krypte archway **Edge:** Plain

Date	Mintage	F	VF	XF	Unc	BU
ND(2003) Proof	28,000	Value: 570				

KM# 198 100 EURO
10.0000 g., 0.9999 Gold 0.3215 oz. AGW, 25 mm. **Subject:** Olympics **Obv:** Olympic rings in wreath above value within circle of stars **Rev:** Panathenean Stadium **Edge:** Plain

Date	Mintage	F	VF	XF	Unc	BU
ND(2003) Proof	28,000	Value: 570				

KM# 201 100 EURO
10.0000 g., 0.9999 Gold 0.3215 oz. AGW, 25 mm. **Subject:** Olympics **Obv:** Olympic rings in wreath above value within circle of stars **Rev:** Zappeion Mansion **Edge:** Plain

Date	Mintage	F	VF	XF	Unc	BU
ND(2003) Proof	28,000	Value: 570				

KM# 204 100 EURO
10.0000 g., 0.9999 Gold 0.3215 oz. AGW, 25 mm. **Subject:** Olympics **Obv:** Olympic rings in wreath above value within circle of stars **Rev:** Acropolis **Edge:** Plain

Date	Mintage	F	VF	XF	Unc	BU
ND(2004) Proof	28,000	Value: 570				

KM# 207 100 EURO
10.0000 g., 0.9999 Gold 0.3215 oz. AGW, 25 mm. **Subject:** Olympics **Obv:** Olympic rings in wreath above value within circle of stars **Rev:** Academy of Athens **Edge:** Plain

Date	Mintage	F	VF	XF	Unc	BU
ND(2004) Proof	28,000	Value: 570				

ECU COINAGE

X# 41 ECU
8.0000 g., Gold **Issuer:** Chelsea Coins, London **Obv:** Ancient galley above Greek flag within 12 stars **Rev:** Alexander the Great of Macedonia horseback right, 12 stars above **Edge:** Reeded

Date	Mintage	F	VF	XF	Unc	BU
1994 Proof	150	—	—	—	—	—

X# 33b 20 ECU
38.0000 g., 0.9167 Gold 1.12 oz. AGW, 38 mm. **Issuer:** Chelsea Coins, London **Obv:** Ancient galley above Greek flag within 12 stars **Rev:** Head of Alexander the Great of Macedonia right **Edge:** Plain

Date	Mintage	F	VF	XF	Unc	BU
1993 Proof	10	—	—	—	—	—

X# 23 150 ECU
6.7200 g., 0.7500 Gold 0.162 oz. AGW, 20 mm. **Obv:** Pegasus rearing left **Rev:** Cornucopia within 12 stars **Edge:** Reeded

Date	Mintage	F	VF	XF	Unc	BU
1991 Proof	250	—	—	—	—	—
1992 Proof	1,500	Value: 275				

X# 40 150 ECU
Bi-Metallic Silver/Gold **Issuer:** Chelsea Coins, London **Obv:** Ancient galley above Greek flag within 12 stars **Rev:** Alexander the Great of Macedonia horseback right, 12 stars above **Edge:** Reeded

Date	Mintage	F	VF	XF	Unc	BU
1994 Proof	400	—	—	—	—	—

X# 34 200 ECU
6.0000 g., 0.7500 Gold 0.1447 oz. AGW, 22.05 mm. **Issuer:** Chelsea Coins, London **Obv:** Ancient galley above Greek flag within 12 stars **Rev:** Head of Alexander the Great of Macedonia right **Edge:** Plain

Date	Mintage	F	VF	XF	Unc	BU
1993 Proof	100	Value: 300				

ESSAIS

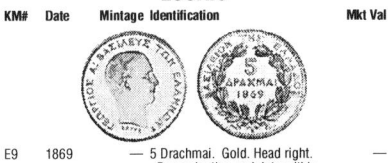

KM#	Date	Mintage	Identification	Mkt Val
E9	1869	—	5 Drachmai. Gold. Head right. Denomination and date within wreath. E (Essai)	—
E10	1869	—	10 Drachmai. Gold. Head right. Denomination and date within wreath. E (Essai)	—
E11	1869	—	20 Drachmai. Gold. Head right. Arms within crowned mantle. E (Essai)	—

318 GREECE

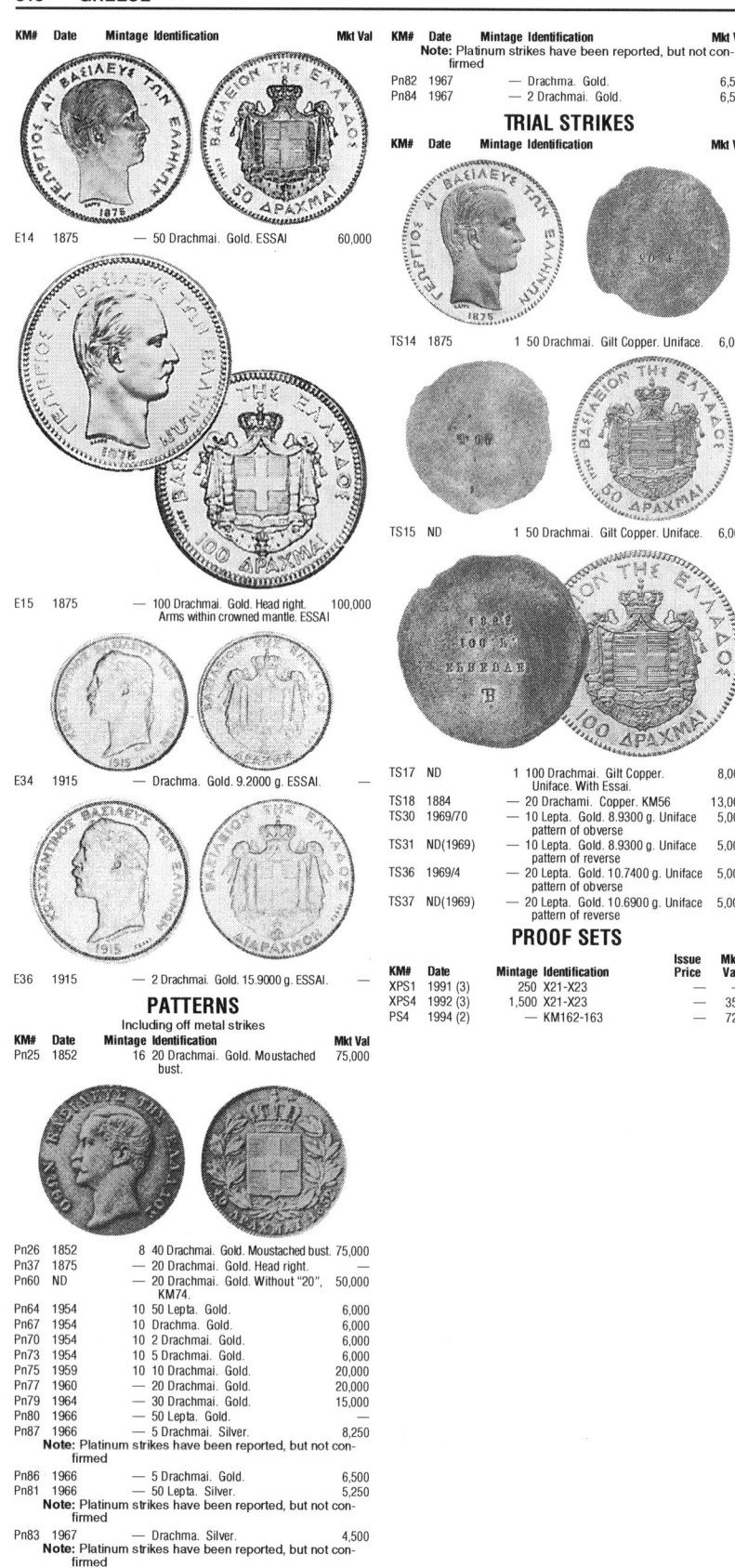

KM#	Date	Mintage Identification	Mkt Val
E14	1875	— 50 Drachmai. Gold. ESSAI	60,000
E15	1875	— 100 Drachmai. Gold. Head right. Arms within crowned mantle. ESSAI	100,000
E34	1915	— Drachma. Gold. 9.2000 g. ESSAI.	—
E36	1915	— 2 Drachmai. Gold. 15.9000 g. ESSAI.	—

PATTERNS
Including off metal strikes

KM#	Date	Mintage Identification	Mkt Val
Pn25	1852	16 20 Drachmai. Gold. Moustached bust.	75,000
Pn26	1852	8 40 Drachmai. Gold. Moustached bust.	75,000
Pn37	1875	— 20 Drachmai. Gold. Head right.	—
Pn60	ND	— 20 Drachmai. Gold. Without "20", KM74.	50,000
Pn64	1954	10 50 Lepta. Gold.	6,000
Pn67	1954	10 Drachma. Gold.	6,000
Pn70	1954	10 2 Drachmai. Gold.	6,000
Pn73	1954	10 5 Drachmai. Gold.	6,000
Pn75	1959	10 10 Drachmai. Gold.	20,000
Pn77	1960	— 20 Drachmai. Gold.	20,000
Pn79	1964	— 30 Drachmai. Gold.	15,000
Pn80	1966	— 50 Lepta. Gold.	—
Pn87	1966	— 5 Drachmai. Silver.	8,250

Note: Platinum strikes have been reported, but not confirmed

| Pn86 | 1966 | — 5 Drachmai. Gold. | 6,500 |
| Pn81 | 1966 | — 50 Lepta. Silver. | 5,250 |

Note: Platinum strikes have been reported, but not confirmed

| Pn83 | 1967 | — Drachma. Silver. | 4,500 |

Note: Platinum strikes have been reported, but not confirmed

| Pn85 | 1967 | — 2 Drachmai. Silver. | 5,250 |

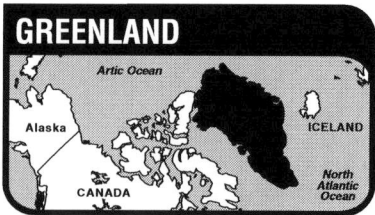

KM#	Date	Mintage Identification	Mkt Val

Note: Platinum strikes have been reported, but not confirmed

| Pn82 | 1967 | — Drachma. Gold. | 6,500 |
| Pn84 | 1967 | — 2 Drachmai. Gold. | 6,500 |

TRIAL STRIKES

KM#	Date	Mintage Identification	Mkt Val
TS14	1875	1 50 Drachmai. Gilt Copper. Uniface.	6,000
TS15	ND	1 50 Drachmai. Gilt Copper. Uniface.	6,000
TS17	ND	1 100 Drachmai. Gilt Copper. Uniface. With Essai.	8,000
TS18	1884	— 20 Drachami. Copper. KM56	13,000
TS30	1969/70	— 10 Lepta. Gold. 8.9300 g. Uniface pattern of obverse	5,000
TS31	ND(1969)	— 10 Lepta. Gold. 8.9300 g. Uniface pattern of reverse	5,000
TS36	1969/4	— 20 Lepta. Gold. 10.7400 g. Uniface pattern of obverse	5,000
TS37	ND(1969)	— 20 Lepta. Gold. 10.6900 g. Uniface pattern of reverse	5,000

PROOF SETS

KM#	Date	Mintage Identification	Issue Price	Mkt Val
XPS1	1991 (3)	250 X21-X23	—	—
XPS4	1992 (3)	1,500 X21-X23	—	350
PS4	1994 (2)	— KM162-163	—	725

GREENLAND

Greenland, an integral part of the Danish realm is situated between the North Atlantic Ocean and the Polar Sea, almost entirely within the Arctic Circle. An island nation, it has an area of 840,000 sq. mi. (2,175,600 sq. km.) and a population of 57,000. Capital: Nuuk (formerly Godthaab). Greenland is the world's only source of natural cryolite, a fluoride of sodium and aluminum important in making aluminum. Fish products and minerals are exported.

Eric the Red discovered Greenland in 982 and established the first settlement in 986. Greenland was a republic until 1261, when the sovereignty of Norway was extended to the island. The original colony was abandoned about 1400 when increasing cold interfered with the breeding of cattle. Successful recolonization was undertaken by Denmark in 1721. In 1921 Denmark extended its claim to include the entire island, and made it a colony of the crown in 1924. The island's colonial status was abolished by amendment to the Danish constitution on June 5, 1953, and Greenland became an integral part of the Kingdom of Denmark. The last Greenlandic coins were withdrawn on July 1, 1967, and since then, Danish coins have been used. Greenland has had home rule since May 1, 1979.

RULERS
Danish

MINT MARKS
Heart (h) Copenhagen (Kobenhavn)

MINTMASTERS' INITIALS
HCN - Hans Christian Nielsen, 1919-1927
C - Alfred Kristian Frederik Christiansen, 1956-1971
GJ - Knud Gunnar Jensen, 1901-1933
S - Harald Salomon, 1933-1968

MONETARY SYSTEM
100 Øre = 1 Krone

STATE

ECU COINAGE

X# 12 150 ECU
Gold, 38 mm. **Ruler:** Margrethe II **Issuer:** Numex S.A., Madrid **Obv:** Crowned Danish arms **Obv. Legend:** GRØNLANDS HJEMMESTYRE **Rev:** Polar bear with cub walking left **Edge:** Reeded

Date	Mintage	F	VF	XF	Unc	BU
1993 Proof	500	Value: 750				

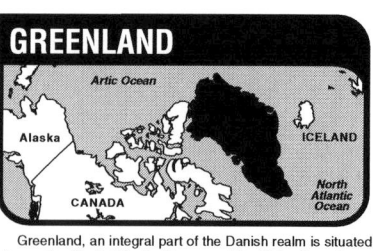

GRENADA

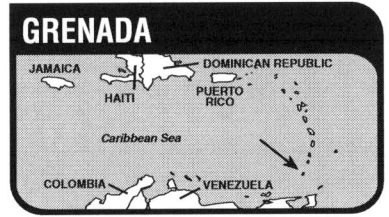

The State of Grenada, located in the Windward Islands of the Caribbean Sea 90 miles (145 km.) north of Trinidad, has (with Carriacou and Petit Martinique) an area of 133 sq. mi. (344 sq. km.) and a population of 94,000. Capital: St.George's. Grenada is the smallest independent nation in the Western Hemisphere. The economy is based on agriculture and tourism. Sugar, coconuts, nutmeg, cocoa and bananas are exported.

Columbus discovered Grenada in 1498 during his third voyage to the Americas. Spain failed to colonize the island, and in 1627 granted it to the British who sold it to the French who colonized it in 1650. Grenada was captured by the British in 1763, retaken by the French in 1779, and finally ceded to the British in 1783. In 1958 Grenada joined the Federation of the West Indies, which was dissolved in 1962. In 1967 it became an internally self-governing British associated state. Full independence was attained on Feb. 4, 1974. Grenada is a member of the Commonwealth of Nations. The prime minister is the Head of Government. Elizabeth II is Head of State as Queen of Grenada.

The early coinage of Grenada consists of cut and countermarked pieces of Spanish or Spanish Colonial Reales, which were valued at 11 Bits. In 1787 8 Reales coins were cut into 11 triangular pieces and countermarked with an incuse G. Later in 1814 large denomination cut pieces were issued being 1/2, 1/3 or 1/6 cuts and countermarked with a TR, incuse G and a number 6, 4,2, or 1 indicating the value in bitts.

RULERS
British

MONETARY SYSTEM
1789-1798
1 Bit = 9 Pence
11 Bits = 8 Shillings 3 Pence
= 1 Dollar
1798-1840
12 Bits = 9 Shillings = 1 Dollar

INDEPENDENT STATE
Commonwealth of Nations
MODERN COINAGE
KM# 16b 10 DOLLARS
47.5400 g., 0.9170 Gold 1.4013 oz. AGW **Subject:** Royal Visit **Obv:** Crowned bust right **Rev:** Arms with supporters within circle

Date	Mintage	F	VF	XF	Unc	BU
1985 Proof	Est. 250	Value: 1,350				

MEDALLIC COINAGE

X# M2 200 DOLLARS
37.9400 g., 0.9160 Gold 1.1174 oz. AGW **Subject:** Carifta Exposition - Premier Eric Gairy **Note:** Prev. KM#M2.

Date	Mintage	F	VF	XF	Unc	BU
1969 Proof	—	Value: 950				

GUADELOUPE

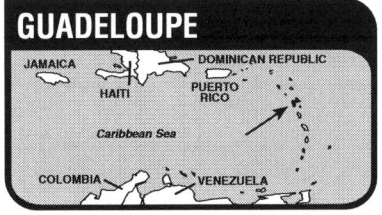

The French Overseas Department of Guadeloupe, located in the Leeward Islands of the West Indies about 300 miles (493 km.) southeast of Puerto Rico, has an area of 687 sq. mi. (1,780 sq. km.) and a population of 306,000. Actually it is two islands separated by a narrow salt water stream: volcanic Basse-Terre to the west and the flatter limestone formation of Grande-Terre to the east. Capital: Basse-Terre, on the island of that name. The principal industries are agriculture, the distillation of liquors, and tourism. Sugar, bananas, and rum are exported.

Guadeloupe was discovered by Columbus in 1493 and settled in 1635 by two Frenchmen, L'Olive and Duplessis, who took possession in the name of the French Company of the Islands of America. When repeated efforts by private companies to colonize the island failed, it was relinquished to the French crown in 1674, and established as a dependency of Martinique. The British occupied the island on two occasions, 1759-63 and 1810-16, before it passed permanently to France. A colony until 1946 Guadeloupe was then made an overseas territory of the French Union. In 1958 it voted to become an Overseas Department within the new French Community.

The well-known R.F. in garland oval countermark of the French Government is only legitimate if on a French Colonies 12 deniers dated 1767A, KM#6. Two other similar but incuse RF countermarks are on cut pieces in the values of 1 and 4 escalins. Contemporary and modern counterfeits are known of both these types.

RULERS
French, until 1759, 1763-1810, 1816-
British, 1759-1763, 1810-1816

MONETARY SYSTEM
3 Deniers = 1 Liard
4 Liards = 1 Sol (Sous)
20 Sols = 1 Livre
6 Livres = 1 Ecu
NOTE: During the British Occupation period the Spanish and Spanish Colonial 8 Reales equaled 10 Livres.

FRENCH OCCUPATION
COUNTERMARKED COINAGE

KM# 4.1 20 LIVRES
0.9170 Gold **Countermark:** 20 with small horse's head **Note:** Countermark on false Brazil 6400 Reis, type of KM#172.2.

CM Date	Host Date	Good	VG	F	VF	XF
ND(1803)	ND(1751-77)	—	—	5,000	7,000	—

KM# 4.2 20 LIVRES
0.9170 Gold **Countermark:** 20 with small horse's head **Note:** Countermark on false Brazil 6400 Reis, type of KM#199.2.

CM Date	Host Date	Good	VG	F	VF	XF
ND(1803)	ND(1777-86)	—	—	5,000	7,000	—

KM# 5 22 LIVRES
Gold **Countermark:** 22 with small bearded human face **Note:** Countermark on Brazil 6400 Reis, KM#199.2

CM Date	Host Date	Good	VG	F	VF	XF
ND(1803)	ND(1777-86)	—	—	7,000	9,500	—

BRITISH OCCUPATION
COUNTERMARKED COINAGE
KM# 27 82 LIVRES 10 SOLS
0.9170 Gold **Countermark:** Crowned G and 82.10 **Note:** Countermark on Brazil 6400 Reis, KM#172.

CM Date	Host Date	Good	VG	F	VF	XF
ND(1811)	ND(1751-77)	2,250	3,500	6,000	9,000	—

KM# 28 82 LIVRES 10 SOLS
0.9170 Gold **Countermark:** Crowned G and 82.10 **Note:** Countermark on Brazil 6400 Reis, KM#199.

CM Date	Host Date	Good	VG	F	VF	XF
ND(1811)	ND(1777-86)	1,500	2,500	4,000	6,000	—

KM# 29 82 LIVRES 10 SOLS
0.9170 Gold **Countermark:** Crowned G and 82.10 **Note:** Countermark on Brazil 6400 Reis, KM#226. Spurious countermarks on KM#27-29 lack the raised decimal point between 82 and 10.

CM Date	Host Date	Good	VG	F	VF	XF
ND(1811)	ND(1789-1805)	2,200	3,250	5,500	8,500	—

FRENCH COLONY
ESSAIS

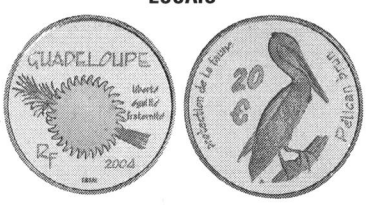

X# E15 20 EURO
8.5300 g., 0.9167 Gold 0.2514 oz. AGW, 27.1 mm. **Series:** Euro **Obv:** Arms **Obv. Inscription:** Liberté/égalité/fraternité **Rev:** Brown pelican **Rev. Legend:** Protection de la Faune **Edge:** Plain

Date	Mintage	F	VF	XF	Unc	BU
2004 Proof	300	Value: 285				

GUAM
TERRITORY
FANTASY BULLION COINAGE

X# 10 1/10 OUNCE
3.1106 g., 0.9999 Gold .1000 oz. AGW, 17.7 mm. **Ruler:** Guahan **Issuer:** Bernard von Nothaus **Obv:** Native male, bust right **Obv. Legend:** MAGA' LAHI MATA' PANG- GUAHAN **Rev:** Palm tree, island **Rev. Legend:** HALE'-TA TANO' TA **Rev. Inscription:** GUAM **Edge:** Reeded

Date	Mintage	F	VF	XF	Unc	BU
1994 Proof	—	Value: 75.00				

GUATEMALA

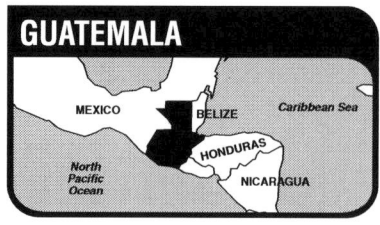

The Republic of Guatemala, the northernmost of the five Central American republics, has an area of 42,042 sq. mi. (108,890 sq. km.) and a population of 10.7 million. Capital: Guatemala City. The economy of Guatemala is heavily dependent on agriculture, however, the country is rich in nickel resources which are being developed. Coffee, cotton and bananas are exported.

Guatemala, once the site of an ancient Mayan civilization, was conquered by Pedro de Alvarado, the resourceful lieutenant of Cortes who undertook the conquest from Mexico. Cruel but strategically skillful, he progressed rapidly along the Pacific coastal lowlands to the highland plain of Quetzaltenango where the decisive battle for Guatemala was fought. After routing the Indian forces, he established the city of Guatemala in 1524. The Spanish Captaincy-General of Guatemala included all Central America but Panama. Guatemala declared its independence of Spain in 1821 and was absorbed into the Mexican empire of Augustin Iturbide (1822-23). From 1823 to 1839 Guatemala was a constituent state of the Central American Republic. Upon dissolution of that confederation, Guatemala proclaimed itself an independent republic. Like El Salvador, Guatemala suffered from internal strife between right-wing, US-backed military government and leftist indigenous peoples from ca. 1954 to ca. 1997.

RULER
Spanish until 1821

MINT MARKS
Antigua, the old capital city of Santiago de los Caballeros, including the mint, was destroyed by a volcanic eruption and earthquake in 1773. A new mint and capital city was established in Nueva Guatemala City. Coin production recommenced in late 1776 using the NG mint mark.
G or G-G - Guatemala until 1776, 1878-1889
H - Heaton, Birmingham
NG - Nueva Guatemala, 1777-1829, 1992

ASSAYERS' INITIALS
J, 1733-1759, Jose de Leon y Losa
P, 1759-1785, Pedro Sanchez de Guzman
M, 1785-1822, Manuel Eusebio Sanchez

SPANISH COLONY
COLONIAL MILLED COINAGE

KM# 55 ESCUDO
3.3834 g., 0.8750 Gold .0952 oz. AGW **Ruler:** Charles IV

Date	Mintage	VG	F	VF	XF	Unc
1801 NG M	—	225	500	850	1,250	—

KM# 74 ESCUDO
3.3834 g., 0.8750 Gold .0952 oz. AGW **Ruler:** Ferdinand VII **Obv:** Laureate head right **Rev:** Crowned arms within order chain

Date	Mintage	VG	F	VF	XF	Unc
1817 NG M	—	250	450	850	1,350	—

KM# 56 2 ESCUDOS
6.7668 g., 0.8750 Gold .1904 oz. AGW **Ruler:** Charles IV **Obv:** Bust of Charles IIII

Date	Mintage	VG	F	VF	XF	Unc
1801 NG M	—	500	1,000	1,750	3,250	—

KM# 70 2 ESCUDOS
6.7668 g., 0.8750 Gold .1904 oz. AGW **Ruler:** Ferdinand VII **Obv:** Laureate head right **Rev:** Crowned arms within order chain

Date	Mintage	VG	F	VF	XF	Unc
1808 NG M	—	750	1,500	2,750	5,500	—
1811 NG M Rare	—					
1817 NG M	—	400	750	1,400	2,500	—

Note: American Numismatic Rarities Eliasberg sale 4-05, MS-63 realized $8050

KM# 57 4 ESCUDOS
13.5337 g., 0.8750 Gold .3807 oz. AGW **Ruler:** Charles IV

Date	Mintage	VG	F	VF	XF	Unc
1801 NG M	—	1,000	2,000	3,750	7,000	—
1801 NG M	—	1,000	2,000	3,750	7,000	—

KM# 73 4 ESCUDOS
13.5337 g., 0.8750 Gold .3807 oz. AGW **Ruler:** Ferdinand VII **Obv:** Laureate head right **Rev:** Crowned arms within order chain

Date	Mintage	VG	F	VF	XF	Unc
1817 NG M	—	700	1,350	2,850	5,500	—

KM# 58 8 ESCUDOS
27.0674 g., 0.8750 Gold .7615 oz. AGW **Ruler:** Charles IV **Obv:** Uniformed bust right **Obv. Legend:** CAROL • IIII • D • G **Rev:** Crowned arms within order chain

Date	Mintage	VG	F	VF	XF	Unc
1801 NG M	—	—	2,000	5,500	9,500	—

KM# 71 8 ESCUDOS
27.0674 g., 0.8750 Gold .7615 oz. AGW **Ruler:** Ferdinand VII **Obv:** Laureate head right **Rev:** Crowned arms within order chain

Date	Mintage	VG	F	VF	XF	Unc
1808 NG M Rare	—	—	—	—	—	—

Note: American Numismatic Rarities Eliasberg sale 4-05, AU-50 realized $57,500

| 1811 NG M Rare | — | | | | | |

Note: American Numismatic Rarities Eliasberg sale 4-05, AU-53 realized $27,500

| 1817 NG M | — | — | 1,500 | 3,500 | 6,500 | — |

Note: American Numismatic Rarities Eliasberg sale 4-05, AU-55 realized $13,800

REPUBLIC
MEDALLIC COINAGE

X# M21 4/5 OUNCE
27.9500 g., 0.9000 Gold 0.8088 oz. AGW, 30.9 mm. **Series:** National Heroes **Obv:** Arms **Obv. Legend:** REPUBLICA DE GUATEMALA **Rev:** Bust of Tecun Uman wearing ornate headdress left **Edge:** Plain

Date	Mintage	F	VF	XF	Unc	BU
1965	—	—	—	600	700	—

STANDARD COINAGE
8 Reales = 1 Peso

KM# 135 4 REALES (Cuatro)
0.8459 g., 0.8750 Gold .0238 oz. AGW

GUATEMALA

Date	Mintage	F	VF	XF	Unc	BU
1860 R	—	20.00	35.00	50.00	90.00	—
1861 R	277,000	17.50	30.00	40.00	75.00	—
1864 R	—	25.00	55.00	85.00	150	—

DECIMAL COINAGE
100 Centavos (Centimos) = 1 Peso

KM# 179 PESO
1.6917 g., 0.8750 Gold .0476 oz. AGW **Obv:** Head right **Rev:** Denomination within wreath

Date	Mintage	VG	F	VF	XF	Unc
1859 R	—	35.00	50.00	75.00	150	—
1860 R	37,000	35.00	50.00	75.00	150	—

KM# 180 2 PESOS
3.3834 g., 0.8750 Gold .0952 oz. AGW **Obv:** Head right **Rev:** Shield divides denomination within wreath, sun above

Date	Mintage	VG	F	VF	XF	Unc
1859 R	—	70.00	85.00	145	225	—

KM# 181 4 PESOS
6.7669 g., 0.8750 Gold .1904 oz. AGW **Obv:** Head right **Rev:** Shield divides denomination within wreath, sun above

Date	Mintage	VG	F	VF	XF	Unc
1861 R	—	200	375	700	1,250	—
1862 R	—	200	375	700	1,250	3,750

KM# 187 4 PESOS
6.7669 g., 0.8750 Gold .1904 oz. AGW **Obv:** Head right **Rev:** Shield divides denomination within wreath, sun above

Date	Mintage	VG	F	VF	XF	Unc
1866 R Rare	561	850	1,500	2,750	4,500	—
1868 R	778	450	900	1,650	2,750	—
1869 R	20,000	150	200	300	500	—

KM# 191 5 PESOS
8.0645 g., 0.9000 Gold .2333 oz. AGW

Date	Mintage	VG	F	VF	XF	Unc
1869 R	49,000	165	200	275	375	700

KM# 198 5 PESOS
8.0645 g., 0.9000 Gold .2333 oz. AGW **Obv:** Laureate head left **Rev:** Quetzal with scroll and weapons within wreath

Date	Mintage	VG	F	VF	XF	Unc
1872 P	—	160	220	350	700	1,150
1873 P Rare	—	—	—	—	—	—
1874 P	—	160	220	350	600	850
1875 P Rare	—	—	—	—	—	—
1876 F Rare	—	—	—	—	—	—
1877 F	—	160	220	350	550	750
1878 D	—	160	220	350	550	750

KM# 184 8 PESOS
13.5337 g., 0.8750 Gold .3807 oz. AGW **Obv:** Head right **Rev:** Shield divides denomination within wreath, sun above

Date	Mintage	VG	F	VF	XF	Unc
1864 R	—	350	500	850	1,500	—

KM# 192 8 PESOS
13.5337 g., 0.8750 Gold .3807 oz. AGW **Obv:** Head right **Rev:** Shield divides denomination within wreath, sun above

Date	Mintage	VG	F	VF	XF	Unc
1869 R Rare	—	—	—	—	—	—

KM# 193 10 PESOS
16.1290 g., 0.9000 Gold .4667 oz. AGW **Obv:** Head right **Rev:** Shield divides denomination within wreath, sun above

Date	Mintage	VG	F	VF	XF	Unc
1869 R	20,000	350	450	550	750	1,150

KM# 183 16 PESOS
27.0296 g., 0.8750 Gold .7604 oz. AGW **Obv:** Head right **Rev:** Legend broken by rays at top

Date	Mintage	VG	F	VF	XF	Unc
1863 R	—	—	—	3,500	5,500	—

Note: A few AU-Unc specimens of the 1863R were found in a box shook loose from its hiding place during the 1977 Guatemala earthquake

| 1864 R Rare | — | — | — | — | — | — |
| 1865 R Rare | — | — | — | — | — | — |

KM# 185 16 PESOS
27.0296 g., 0.8750 Gold .7604 oz. AGW, 33.20 mm. **Obv:** Legend as KM#183 **Rev:** Legend unbroken at top, similar to KM#188 **Note:** Reduced size.

Date	Mintage	VG	F	VF	XF	Unc
1865 R Rare	190	—	—	—	—	—

Note: American Numismatic Rarities Eliasberg sale 4-05, MS-62 realized $20,700

KM# 188 16 PESOS
27.0296 g., 0.8750 Gold .7604 oz. AGW **Obv:** Head right **Rev:** Shield divides denomination within wreath, sun above

Date	Mintage	VG	F	VF	XF	Unc
1867 R	467	1,200	2,250	4,500	7,000	—
1869 R	3,465	550	700	1,200	2,500	—

KM# 194 20 PESOS
32.2580 g., 0.9000 Gold .9334 oz. AGW **Obv:** Head right **Rev:** Shield divides denomination within wreath, sun above

Date	Mintage	VG	F	VF	XF	Unc
1869 R	16,000	650	750	900	1,250	—

KM# 199 20 PESOS
32.2580 g., 0.9000 Gold .9334 oz. AGW **Obv:** Laureate head left **Rev:** Quetzal, scroll and weapons within wreath

Date	Mintage	VG	F	VF	XF	Unc
1877 F Rare	—	—	—	—	—	—

Note: American Numismatic Rarities Eliasberg sale 4-05, MS-62 realized $29,900

| 1878 F Rare | — | — | — | — | — | — |

REFORM COINAGE
100 Centavos = 1 Quetzal

KM# 238.1a 5 CENTAVOS
2.5000 g., 0.9000 Gold .0723 oz. AGW **Obv:** National arms **Rev:** Bird on pillar

Date	Mintage	F	VF	XF	Unc	BU
1925	8	—	—	750	950	—

KM# 257.1a 5 CENTAVOS
2.7300 g., 0.6200 Gold .0544 oz. AGW **Obv:** National arms **Rev:** Kapok tree **Note:** Distributed among delegates.

Date	Mintage	F	VF	XF	Unc	BU
1953	25	—	—	—	550	—

KM# 239.1a 10 CENTAVOS
5.0000 g., 0.9000 Gold .1446 oz. AGW **Obv:** National arms **Rev:** Long-tailed quetzal on pillar

Date	Mintage	F	VF	XF	Unc	BU
1925 Rare	8	—	—	—	—	—

KM# 240a 1/4 QUETZAL
0.9000 Gold **Obv:** National arms **Rev:** Quetzal on pillar

Date	Mintage	F	VF	XF	Unc	BU
1925 (P) Rare	8	—	—	—	—	—

KM# 244 5 QUETZALES
8.3592 g., 0.9000 Gold .2419 oz. AGW **Obv:** National arms **Rev:** Quetzal atop engraved pillar

Date	Mintage	F	VF	XF	Unc	BU
1926(P)	48,000	BV	210	275	350	—

KM# 245 10 QUETZALES
16.7185 g., 0.9000 Gold .4838 oz. AGW **Obv:** National arms **Rev:** Quetzal atop engraved pillar

Date	Mintage	F	VF	XF	Unc	BU
1926(P)	18,000	BV	345	450	750	—

GUATEMALA

KM# 246 20 QUETZALES
33.4370 g., 0.9000 Gold .9676 oz. AGW **Obv:** National arms
Rev: Quetzal atop engraved pillar

Date	Mintage	F	VF	XF	Unc	BU
1926(P)	49,000	650	675	750	1,000	—

PATTERNS
Including off metal strikes

KM#	Date	Mintage	Identification	Mkt Val
Pn10	1894(a)	10	5 Pesos. 0.9000 Gold. Small Liberty head left. With ESSAI.	14,500
Pn11	1894 CB	17	5 Pesos. 0.9000 Gold. Large Liberty head left.	10,000
Pn13	1894(a)	10	10 Pesos. 0.9000 Gold. Small Liberty head left. With ESSAI.	14,500
Pn14	1894 CB	17	10 Pesos. 0.9000 Gold. Large Liberty head left	11,500
Pn21	1923	—	5 Pesos. Gold. KM234	—

GUERNSEY

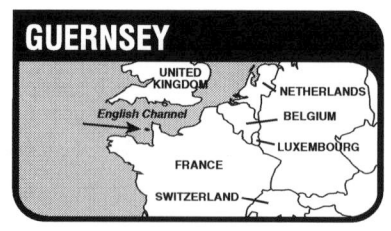

The Bailiwick of Guernsey, a British crown dependency located in the English Channel 30 miles (48 km.) west of Normandy, France, has an area of 30 sq. mi. (194 sq. km.)(including the isles of Alderney, Jethou, Herm, Brechou, and Sark), and a population of 54,000. Capital: St. Peter Port. Agriculture and cattle breeding are the main occupations.

Militant monks from the duchy of Normandy established the first permanent settlements on Guernsey prior to the Norman invasion of England, but the prevalence of prehistoric monuments suggests an earlier occupancy. The island, the only part of the duchy of Normandy belonging to the British crown, has been a possession of Britain since the Norman Conquest of 1066. During the Anglo-French wars, the harbors of Guernsey were employed in the building and out-fitting of ships for the English privateers preying on French shipping. Guernsey is administered by its own laws and customs. Unless the island is mentioned specifically, acts passed by the British Parliament are not applicable to Guernsey. During World War II, German troops occupied the island from June 30, 1940 till May 9,1945.

RULERS
British

MINT MARKS
H – Heaton, Birmingham

MONETARY SYSTEM
8 Doubles = 1 Penny
12 Pence = 1 Shilling
5 Shillings = 1 Crown
20 Shillings = 1 Pound

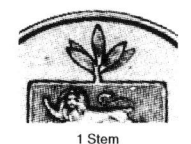

1 Stem    3 Stems

BRITISH DEPENDENCY

DECIMAL COINAGE
100 Pence = 1 Pound

KM# 105b 50 PENCE
15.5000 g., 0.9170 Gold .4570 oz. AGW, 27.3 mm. **Ruler:** Elizabeth II **Obv:** Head with tiara right **Rev:** Pilot and fighter plane **Edge:** Plain **Shape:** 7-sided

Date	Mintage	F	VF	XF	Unc	BU
2000 Proof	1,500	Value: 345				

KM# 37a POUND
8.0000 g., 0.9170 Gold .2358 oz. AGW, 22 mm. **Ruler:** Elizabeth II **Obv:** Arms **Rev:** Guernsey lily

Date	Mintage	F	VF	XF	Unc	BU
1981 Proof	4,500	Value: 170				

KM# 49b 2 POUNDS
47.5400 g., 0.9170 Gold 1.4012 oz. AGW, 38.5 mm. **Ruler:** Elizabeth II **Subject:** 900th Anniversary - Death of William the Conqueror **Obv:** Crowned head right, small arms at left **Rev:** Crowned bust left

Date	Mintage	F	VF	XF	Unc	BU
ND(1987) Proof	90	Value: 1,250				

KM# 67 5 POUNDS
7.8100 g., 0.9990 Gold .2508 oz. AGW **Ruler:** Elizabeth II **Obv:** Crowned head right **Rev:** Queen Mother

Date	Mintage	F	VF	XF	Unc	BU
1995 Proof	Est. 2,500	Value: 225				

KM# 94b 5 POUNDS
47.5400 g., 0.9166 Gold 1.4011 oz. AGW, 38.5 mm. **Ruler:** Elizabeth II **Subject:** Winston Churchill **Obv:** Head with tiara right **Obv. Designer:** Rank-Broadley **Rev:** Head right **Edge:** Reeded

Date	Mintage	F	VF	XF	Unc	BU
1999 Proof	125,000	Value: 975				

KM# 134 5 POUNDS
1.2440 g., 0.9990 Gold 0.04 oz. AGW, 13.9 mm. **Ruler:** Elizabeth II **Subject:** Queen Mother **Obv:** Head with tiara right **Rev:** Queen Mother's portrait **Edge:** Reeded

Date	Mintage	F	VF	XF	Unc	BU
1999	20,000	—	—	—	65.00	75.00

KM# 101 5 POUNDS
1.1300 g., 0.9170 Gold .0333 oz. AGW, 13.9 mm. **Ruler:** Elizabeth II **Subject:** Queen Mother's 100th Birthday **Obv:** Head with tiara right **Rev:** Queen Mother's portrait **Edge:** Reeded

Date	Mintage	F	VF	XF	Unc	BU
2000 Proof	20,000	Value: 65.00				

KM# 113 5 POUNDS
1.1300 g., 0.9170 Gold .0333 oz. AGW, 13.9 mm. **Ruler:** Elizabeth II **Subject:** 20th Century Monarchy **Obv:** Head with tiara right **Obv. Designer:** Rank-Broadley **Rev:** Portraits of past five sovereigns **Edge:** Reeded

Date	Mintage	F	VF	XF	Unc	BU
2000 Proof	—	Value: 65.00				

KM# 102b 5 POUNDS
39.9400 g., 0.9166 Gold 1.177 oz. AGW, 38.6 mm. **Ruler:** Elizabeth II **Subject:** Century of Monarchy **Obv:** Head with tiara right **Obv. Designer:** Rank-Broadley **Rev:** Portraits of past five sovereigns **Edge:** Reeded

Date	Mintage	F	VF	XF	Unc	BU
2000 Proof	200	Value: 925				

KM# 115 5 POUNDS
1.1300 g., 0.9170 Gold .0333 oz. AGW, 13.9 mm. **Ruler:** Elizabeth II **Subject:** 19th Century Monarchy **Obv:** Head with tiara right **Obv. Designer:** Ian Rank-Broadley **Rev:** Four portraits **Edge:** Reeded

Date	Mintage	F	VF	XF	Unc	BU
2001 Proof	—	Value: 65.00				

KM# 117 5 POUNDS
1.1300 g., 0.9170 Gold .0333 oz. AGW, 13.9 mm. **Ruler:** Elizabeth II **Subject:** Queen Victoria 1837-1901 **Obv:** Head with tiara right **Obv. Designer:** Ian Rank-Broadley **Rev:** Queen Victoria's portrait **Edge:** Reeded

Date	Mintage	F	VF	XF	Unc	BU
2001 Proof	300	Value: 65.00				

KM# 118 5 POUNDS
1.1300 g., 0.9170 Gold .0333 oz. AGW, 13.9 mm. **Ruler:** Elizabeth II **Subject:** Queen's 75th Birthday **Obv:** Head with tiara right **Obv. Designer:** Ian Rank-Broadley **Rev:** Queen's portrait in wreath **Edge:** Reeded

Date	Mintage	F	VF	XF	Unc	BU
2001 Proof	250	Value: 65.00				

KM# 114b 5 POUNDS
39.9400 g., 0.9166 Gold 1.177 oz. AGW, 38.6 mm. **Ruler:** Elizabeth II **Subject:** 19th Century Monarchy **Obv:** Head with tiara right **Obv. Designer:** Ian Rank-Broadley **Rev:** Four royal portraits **Edge:** Reeded

Date	Mintage	F	VF	XF	Unc	BU
2001 Proof	200	Value: 900				

KM# 119c 5 POUNDS
39.9400 g., 0.9166 Gold 1.177 oz. AGW, 38.6 mm. **Ruler:** Elizabeth II **Subject:** Golden Jubilee **Obv:** Head with tiara right **Obv. Designer:** Ian Rank-Broadley **Rev:** Queen in coach **Edge:** Reeded

Date	Mintage	F	VF	XF	Unc	BU
2002 Proof	250	Value: 875				

KM# 121b 5 POUNDS
39.9400 g., 0.9166 Gold 1.177 oz. AGW, 38.6 mm. **Ruler:** Elizabeth II **Subject:** Golden Jubilee **Obv:** Head with tiara right **Obv. Designer:** Ian Rank-Broadley **Rev:** Trooping the Colors scene **Edge:** Reeded

GUERNSEY

Date	Mintage	F	VF	XF	Unc	BU
2002 Proof	250				Value: 875	

KM# 122b 5 POUNDS
39.9400 g., 0.9167 Gold 1.1771 oz. AGW, 1.1771 mm. **Ruler:** Elizabeth II **Subject:** Princess Diana **Obv:** Head with tiara right **Obv. Designer:** Ian Rank-Broadley **Rev:** World and children behind Diana's cameo portrait **Edge:** Reeded

Date	Mintage	F	VF	XF	Unc	BU
2002 Proof	100				Value: 950	

KM# 124b 5 POUNDS
39.9400 g., 0.9166 Gold 1.177 oz. AGW, 38.6 mm. **Ruler:** Elizabeth II **Subject:** 18th Century British Monarchy **Obv:** Head with tiara right **Obv. Designer:** Ian Rank-Broadley **Rev:** Five royal portraits **Edge:** Reeded

Date	Mintage	F	VF	XF	Unc	BU
2002 Proof	200				Value: 900	

KM# 125 5 POUNDS
1.1300 g., 0.9166 Gold 0.0333 oz. AGW, 13.9 mm. **Ruler:** Elizabeth II **Subject:** 18th Century British Monarchy **Obv:** Head with tiara right **Obv. Designer:** Ian Rank-Broadley **Rev:** Five royal portraits **Edge:** Reeded **Note:** Prev. KM#124b.

Date	Mintage	F	VF	XF	Unc	BU
2002 Proof	55				Value: 70.00	

KM# 127b 5 POUNDS
39.9400 g., 0.9166 Gold 1.177 oz. AGW, 38.6 mm. **Ruler:** Elizabeth II **Subject:** Queen Mother **Obv:** Head with tiara right **Obv. Designer:** Ian Rank-Broadley **Rev:** Queen Mother's portrait **Edge:** Reeded

Date	Mintage	F	VF	XF	Unc	BU
2002 Proof	250				Value: 875	

KM# 128 5 POUNDS
1.1300 g., 0.9166 Gold 0.0333 oz. AGW, 13.9 mm. **Ruler:** Elizabeth II **Subject:** Queen Mother **Obv:** Head with tiara right **Obv. Designer:** Ian Rank-Broadley **Rev:** The late Queen Mother's portrait **Edge:** Reeded

Date	Mintage	F	VF	XF	Unc	BU
2002 Proof	—				Value: 65.00	

KM# 129b 5 POUNDS
39.9400 g., 0.9166 Gold 1.177 oz. AGW, 38.6 mm. **Ruler:** Elizabeth II **Subject:** Duke of Wellington **Obv:** Head with tiara right **Obv. Designer:** Ian Rank-Broadley **Rev:** Wellington's portrait with multicolor cavalry scene **Edge:** Reeded

Date	Mintage	F	VF	XF	Unc	BU
2002 Proof	200				Value: 900	

KM# 130 5 POUNDS
1.1300 g., 0.9166 Gold 0.0333 oz. AGW, 13.9 mm. **Ruler:** Elizabeth II **Subject:** The Duke of Wellington **Obv:** Head with tiara right **Obv. Designer:** Ian Rank-Broadley **Rev:** Portrait with mounted dragoons in background **Edge:** Reeded

Date	Mintage	F	VF	XF	Unc	BU
2002 Proof	—				Value: 65.00	

KM# 143b 5 POUNDS
39.9400 g., 0.9166 Gold 1.177 oz. AGW, 38.6 mm. **Ruler:** Elizabeth II **Obv:** Head with tiara right **Obv. Designer:** Ian Rank-Broadley **Rev:** Prince William wearing sweater **Edge:** Reeded

Date	Mintage	F	VF	XF	Unc	BU
2003 Proof	200				Value: 900	

KM# 154a 5 POUNDS
39.9400 g., 0.9167 Gold 1.1771 oz. AGW, 38.6 mm. **Ruler:** Elizabeth II **Subject:** D-Day **Obv:** Head with tiara right **Obv. Designer:** Ian Rank-Broadley **Rev:** British soldier advancing to left **Edge:** Reeded

Date	Mintage	F	VF	XF	Unc	BU
2004 Proof	500				Value: 1,000	

KM# 155b 5 POUNDS
39.9400 g., 0.9166 Gold 1.177 oz. AGW, 38.6 mm. **Ruler:** Elizabeth II **Obv:** Head with tiara right **Obv. Designer:** Ian Rank-Broadley **Rev:** Sgt. Luke O'Connor, first army Victoria Cross winner, above Battle of Alma scene with multicolor flag **Edge:** Reeded

Date	Mintage	F	VF	XF	Unc	BU
2004 Proof	500				Value: 1,000	

KM# 168b 5 POUNDS
39.9400 g., 0.9167 Gold 1.1771 oz. AGW, 38.6 mm. **Ruler:** Elizabeth II **Subject:** End of WWII **Obv:** Head with tiara right **Obv. Designer:** Ian Rank-Broadley **Rev:** Churchill and George VI **Edge:** Reeded

Date	Mintage	F	VF	XF	Unc	BU
2005 Proof	150				Value: 1,000	

KM# 169a 5 POUNDS
39.9400 g., 0.9167 Gold 1.1771 oz. AGW, 38.6 mm. **Ruler:** Elizabeth II **Subject:** WWII Liberation **Obv:** Head with tiara right **Obv. Designer:** Ian Rank-Broadley **Rev:** Soldiers and waving crowd **Edge:** Reeded

Date	Mintage	F	VF	XF	Unc	BU
2005 Proof	150				Value: 1,000	

KM# 57 10 POUNDS
3.1300 g., 0.9990 Gold .1005 oz. AGW **Ruler:** Elizabeth II **Subject:** 50th Anniversary - Normandy Invasion **Rev:** Soldiers and tank

Date	Mintage	F	VF	XF	Unc	BU
ND(1994)	Est. 500				Value: 85.00	

Note: Sold only in sets

KM# 62 10 POUNDS
3.1300 g., 0.9990 Gold .1005 oz. AGW **Ruler:** Elizabeth II **Subject:** 50th Anniversary of Liberation **Rev:** Uniformed figure giving speech

Date	Mintage	F	VF	XF	Unc	BU
ND(1995) Proof	Est. 500				Value: 85.00	

Note: Sold only in sets

KM# 138 10 POUNDS
13.6600 g., 0.9990 Gold 0.4387 oz. AGW, 19.35 mm. **Ruler:** Elizabeth II **Subject:** Millennium **Obv:** Head with tiara right **Rev:** Hands holding planet **Edge:** Reeded

Date	Mintage	F	VF	XF	Unc	BU
2000	7,500	—		—	550	—

KM# 58 25 POUNDS
7.8100 g., 0.9990 Gold .2509 oz. AGW **Ruler:** Elizabeth II **Subject:** 50th Anniversary - Normandy Invasion **Rev:** Uniformed figure standing at right, invasion scene in background

Date	Mintage	F	VF	XF	Unc	BU
ND(1994)	Est. 500	—	—	—	200	—
ND(1994) Proof	Est. 500				Value: 200	

Note: Sold only in sets

KM# 63 25 POUNDS
7.8100 g., 0.9990 Gold .2509 oz. AGW **Ruler:** Elizabeth II **Subject:** 50th Anniversary of Liberation **Obv:** Crowned head right, small arms at left **Rev:** Supply worker and ship

Date	Mintage	F	VF	XF	Unc	BU
ND(1995) In proof sets only	Est. 500				Value: 200	

KM# 69 25 POUNDS
7.8100 g., 0.9990 Gold .2509 oz. AGW **Ruler:** Elizabeth II **Subject:** European Football **Rev:** Soccer ball and European map

Date	Mintage	F	VF	XF	Unc	BU
1996 Proof	1,500				Value: 185	

KM# 72 25 POUNDS
7.8100 g., 0.9990 Gold .2509 oz. AGW **Ruler:** Elizabeth II **Subject:** Queen Elizabeth II's Golden Wedding Anniversary **Obv:** Crowned head right **Rev:** Queen Elizabeth II and Prince Philip, monogrammed shield and Westminster Abbey

Date	Mintage	F	VF	XF	Unc	BU
1997 Proof	Est. 5,000				Value: 275	

KM# 85 25 POUNDS
7.8100 g., 0.9990 Gold .2509 oz. AGW **Ruler:** Elizabeth II **Subject:** 80th Anniversary - Royal Air Force **Obv:** Head with tiara right **Rev:** Three Spitfires and RAF Benevolent Fund Crest

Date	Mintage	F	VF	XF	Unc	BU
1998 Proof	Est. 2,500				Value: 185	

KM# 132 25 POUNDS
7.8100 g., 0.9990 Gold 0.2508 oz. AGW, 22 mm. **Ruler:** Elizabeth II **Subject:** Winston Churchill **Obv:** Head with tiara right **Rev:** Head right **Edge:** Reeded

Date	Mintage	F	VF	XF	Unc	BU
1999 Proof	2,500				Value: 250	

KM# 135 25 POUNDS
7.8100 g., 0.9990 Gold 0.2508 oz. AGW, 22 mm. **Ruler:** Elizabeth II **Subject:** Queen Mother **Obv:** Head with tiara right **Rev:** Queen Mother's portrait **Edge:** Reeded

Date	Mintage	F	VF	XF	Unc	BU
1999 Proof	5,000				Value: 250	

KM# 137 25 POUNDS
7.8100 g., 0.9990 Gold 0.2508 oz. AGW, 22 mm. **Ruler:** Elizabeth II **Subject:** Prince Edward's Marriage **Obv:** Head with tiara right **Rev:** Jugate heads left of Edward and Sophie left **Edge:** Reeded

Date	Mintage	F	VF	XF	Unc	BU
1999 Proof	5,000				Value: 250	

KM# 103 25 POUNDS
7.8100 g., 0.9170 Gold .2303 oz. AGW, 22 mm. **Ruler:** Elizabeth II **Subject:** Queen Mother's 100th Birthday **Obv:** Head with tiara right **Rev:** Queen Mother's portrait **Edge:** Reeded

Date	Mintage	F	VF	XF	Unc	BU
2000 Proof	5,000				Value: 235	

KM# 107 25 POUNDS
7.8100 g., 0.9170 Gold .2303 oz. AGW, 22 mm. **Ruler:** Elizabeth II **Subject:** Queen Victoria Centennial **Obv:** Head with tiara right **Obv. Designer:** Ian Rank-Broadley **Rev:** Queen Victoria's portrait **Edge:** Reeded

Date	Mintage	F	VF	XF	Unc	BU
2001 Proof	2,500				Value: 270	

KM# 112 25 POUNDS
7.8100 g., 0.9170 Gold .2303 oz. AGW, 22 mm. **Ruler:** Elizabeth II **Subject:** Queen's 75th Birthday **Obv:** Head with tiara right **Obv. Designer:** Ian Rank-Broadley **Rev:** Queen's portrait in wreath **Edge:** Reeded

Date	Mintage	F	VF	XF	Unc	BU
2001 Proof	5,000				Value: 235	

KM# 139 25 POUNDS
7.9800 g., 0.9166 Gold 0.2352 oz. AGW, 22 mm. **Ruler:** Elizabeth II **Subject:** Golden Jubilee **Obv:** Head with tiara right **Obv. Designer:** Ian Rank-Broadley **Rev:** Queen in coach **Edge:** Reeded

Date	Mintage	F	VF	XF	Unc	BU
2002 Proof	5,000				Value: 300	

KM# 140 25 POUNDS
7.9800 g., 0.9166 Gold 0.2352 oz. AGW, 22 mm. **Ruler:** Elizabeth II **Subject:** Queen Mother **Obv:** Head with tiara right **Obv. Designer:** Ian Rank-Broadley **Rev:** Queen Mother's portrait **Edge:** Reeded

Date	Mintage	F	VF	XF	Unc	BU
2002 Proof	2,500				Value: 300	

KM# 123 25 POUNDS
7.9800 g., 0.9167 Gold 0.2352 oz. AGW, 22.05 mm. **Ruler:** Elizabeth II **Subject:** Princess Diana **Obv:** Head with tiara right **Obv. Designer:** Ian Rank-Broadley **Rev:** Diana's cameo portrait in wreath **Edge:** Reeded

Date	Mintage	F	VF	XF	Unc	BU
2002 Proof	2,500				Value: 285	

324 GUERNSEY

KM# 131 25 POUNDS
7.8100 g., 0.9166 Gold 0.2302 oz. AGW, 22 mm. **Ruler:** Elizabeth II **Subject:** The Duke of Wellington **Obv:** Head with tiara right **Obv. Designer:** Ian Rank-Broadley **Rev:** Portrait with mounted dragoons in the background **Edge:** Reeded

Date	Mintage	F	VF	XF	Unc	BU
2002 Proof	2,500	Value: 235				

KM# 141 25 POUNDS
7.9800 g., 0.9166 Gold 0.2352 oz. AGW, 22 mm. **Ruler:** Elizabeth II **Subject:** Golden Jubilee **Obv:** Head with tiara right **Obv. Designer:** Ian Rank-Broadley **Rev:** Trooping the Colors scene **Edge:** Reeded

Date	Mintage	F	VF	XF	Unc	BU
2003 Proof	5,000	Value: 300				

KM# 152 25 POUNDS
7.9800 g., 0.9167 Gold 0.2352 oz. AGW, 22 mm. **Ruler:** Elizabeth II **Subject:** D-Day **Obv:** Head with tiara right **Obv. Designer:** Ian Rank-Broadley **Rev:** Advancing British soldier **Edge:** Reeded

Date	Mintage	F	VF	XF	Unc	BU
2004 Proof	500	Value: 325				

KM# 59 50 POUNDS
15.6100 g., 0.9990 Gold .5014 oz. AGW **Ruler:** Elizabeth II **Subject:** 50th Anniversary - Normandy Invasion **Rev:** Parachuters

Date	Mintage	F	VF	XF	Unc	BU
ND(1994)	Est. 500	Value: 385				
Note: In sets only						

KM# 64 50 POUNDS
15.6100 g., 0.9990 Gold .5014 oz. AGW **Ruler:** Elizabeth II **Subject:** 50th Anniversary of Liberation **Rev:** Uniformed figure signing document, ship in background

Date	Mintage	F	VF	XF	Unc	BU
ND(1995)	Est. 500	Value: 385				
Note: In sets only						

KM# 136 50 POUNDS
15.5517 g., 0.9990 Gold 0.4995 oz. AGW, 27 mm. **Ruler:** Elizabeth II **Subject:** Queen Mother **Obv:** Head with tiara right **Rev:** Queen Mother's portrait **Edge:** Reeded

Date	Mintage	F	VF	XF	Unc	BU
1999 Proof	1,250	Value: 575				

KM# 60 100 POUNDS
31.2100 g., 0.9990 Gold 1.0025 oz. AGW **Ruler:** Elizabeth II **Subject:** 50th Anniversary - Normandy Invasion **Obv:** Crowned head right, small arms at left **Rev:** Cameo portrait above invasion scene

Date	Mintage	F	VF	XF	Unc	BU
ND(1994)	Est. 500	Value: 745				
Note: In sets only						

KM# 65 100 POUNDS
31.2100 g., 0.9990 Gold 1.0025 oz. AGW **Ruler:** Elizabeth II **Subject:** 50th Anniversary of Liberation **Rev:** Soldiers and ship

Date	Mintage	F	VF	XF	Unc	BU
ND(1995)	Est. 500	Value: 745				
Note: In sets only						

PIEFORTS

KM#	Date	Mintage	Identification	Mkt Val
P1	1981	500	Pound. 16.0000 g. KM#37a.	265
P3	2002	100	5 Pounds. 0.9166 Gold. 56.5600 g. 38.6 mm. Queen's portrait. Queen in coach. Reeded edge. Not a full weight piefort.	1,400

PROOF SETS

KM#	Date	Mintage	Identification	Issue Price	Mkt Val
PS17	1994 (4)	500	KM57-60	1,595	1,400
PS18	ND (1995) (4)	500	KM62-65	1,600	1,400
PS19	1996 (2)	1,500	KM68a, 69	—	275
PS20	1997 (3)	—	KM70, 71a, 72	—	420

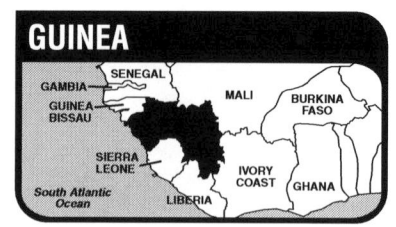

GUINEA

The Republic of Guinea, situated on the Atlantic Coast of Africa between Sierra Leone and Guinea-Bissau, has an area of 94,964 sq. mi. (245,860 sq. km.) and a population of 6.4 million. Capital: Conakry. Although Guinea contains one-third of the world's reserves of bauxite and significant deposits of iron ore, gold and diamonds, the economy is still dependent on agriculture, aluminum, bananas, copra and coffee are exported.

The coast of Guinea was known to Portuguese navigators of the 15th century but was seldom visited by European traders of the 16th-18th centuries because of its dangerous coastal waters. French penetration of the area began in the mid-19th century with the entering into of protectorate treaties with several of the coastal chiefs. After a long struggle with Guinea's native leader Samory Toure, France secured the area and until 1890 administered it as a part of Senegal. In 1895 the colony (Guinee Francais) became an autonomous part of the federation of French West Africa. The inhabitants were extended French citizenship in 1946 when the colony became an overseas territory of the French Union. Guinea became an independent republic on Oct. 2, 1958, when it declined to enter the new French Community.

MONETARY SYSTEM
100 Centimes = 1 Franc

REPUBLIC
DECIMAL COINAGE

KM# 17 1000 FRANCS
4.0000 g., 0.9000 Gold .1157 oz. AGW **Series:** 10th Anniversary of Independence **Subject:** John and Robert Kennedy **Obv:** Jugate heads right **Rev:** National arms

Date	Mintage	F	VF	XF	Unc	BU
1969 Proof	6,600	Value: 85.00				
1970 Proof	Inc. above	Value: 85.00				

KM# 18 2000 FRANCS
8.0000 g., 0.9000 Gold .2315 oz. AGW **Series:** 10th Anniversary of Independence **Subject:** Lunar Landing **Obv:** Planets bound together, space shuttle and astronaut **Rev:** National arms

Date	Mintage	F	VF	XF	Unc	BU
1969 Proof	15,000	Value: 165				

KM# 30 2000 FRANCS
8.0000 g., 0.9000 Gold .2315 oz. AGW **Series:** 10th Anniversary of Independence **Subject:** Apollo XIII **Obv:** Radiant planet back of three charging horses **Rev:** National arms

Date	Mintage	F	VF	XF	Unc	BU
1970 Proof	1,775	Value: 185				

KM# 31 2000 FRANCS
8.0000 g., 0.9000 Gold .2315 oz. AGW **Series:** 10th Anniversary of Independence **Subject:** Spacecraft Soyuz **Obv:** Spacecraft in flight **Rev:** National arms

Date	Mintage	F	VF	XF	Unc	BU
1970 Proof	2,840	Value: 170				

KM# 32 5000 FRANCS
20.0000 g., 0.9000 Gold .5787 oz. AGW **Series:** 10th Anniversary of Independence **Subject:** Munich Olympics **Obv:** Medals of the Olympics in Helsinki 1952; Melbourne 1956; Rome 1968; Tokyo 1964; Mexico City 1968 **Rev:** National arms

Date	Mintage	F	VF	XF	Unc	BU
1969 Proof	2,740	Value: 425				
1970 Proof	500	Value: 475				

KM# 19 5000 FRANCS
20.0000 g., 0.9000 Gold .5787 oz. AGW **Series:** 10th Anniversary of Independence **Subject:** Gamel Abdel Nasser **Obv:** Head right **Rev:** National arms

Date	Mintage	F	VF	XF	Unc	BU
1970 Proof	4,000	Value: 450				

KM# 33 5000 FRANCS
20.0000 g., 0.9000 Gold .5787 oz. AGW **Series:** 10th Anniversary of Independence **Subject:** Ikhnaton **Obv:** Head 3/4 facing **Rev:** National arms

Date	Mintage	F	VF	XF	Unc	BU
1970 Proof	685			Value: 500		

KM# 34 5000 FRANCS
20.0000 g., 0.9000 Gold .5787 oz. AGW **Series:** 10th Anniversary of Independence **Subject:** Chephren **Obv:** Head with parrot right **Rev:** National arms

Date	Mintage	F	VF	XF	Unc	BU
1970 Proof	675			Value: 500		

KM# 35 5000 FRANCS
20.0000 g., 0.9000 Gold .5787 oz. AGW **Series:** 10th Anniversary of Independence **Subject:** Cleopatra **Obv:** Head left **Rev:** National arms

Date	Mintage	F	VF	XF	Unc	BU
1970 Proof	789			Value: 500		

KM# 36 5000 FRANCS
20.0000 g., 0.9000 Gold .5787 oz. AGW **Series:** 10th Anniversary of Independence **Subject:** Queen Nefertiti, 1372-1350BC **Obv:** Head left **Rev:** National arms

Date	Mintage	F	VF	XF	Unc	BU
1970 Proof	774			Value: 500		

KM# 37 5000 FRANCS
20.0000 g., 0.9000 Gold .5787 oz. AGW **Series:** 10th Anniversary of Independence **Subject:** Ramses III **Obv:** Head right **Rev:** National arms

Date	Mintage	F	VF	XF	Unc	BU
1970 Proof	695			Value: 500		

KM# 38 5000 FRANCS
20.0000 g., 0.9000 Gold .5787 oz. AGW **Series:** 10th Anniversary of Independence **Subject:** Tutankhamen **Obv:** Bust facing **Rev:** National arms

Date	Mintage	F	VF	XF	Unc	BU
1970 Proof	675			Value: 500		

KM# 39 5000 FRANCS
20.0000 g., 0.9000 Gold .5787 oz. AGW **Series:** 10th Anniversary of Independence **Subject:** Queen Teyi, mother of Pharoah Amenophis IV (Ichnaton), reigned 1352-1336BC **Obv:** Head right **Rev:** National arms

Date	Mintage	F	VF	XF	Unc	BU
1970 Proof	685			Value: 500		

KM# 20 10000 FRANCS
40.0000 g., 0.9000 Gold 1.1575 oz. AGW **Series:** 10th Anniversary of Independence **Subject:** Ahmed Sekou Toure **Obv:** Head left **Rev:** National arms

Date	Mintage	F	VF	XF	Unc	BU
1969 Proof	2,300			Value: 800		
1970 Proof	—			Value: 975		

DECIMAL COINAGE
100 Cauris = 1 Syli

KM# 48 1000 SYLI
2.9300 g., 0.9000 Gold .0847 oz. AGW **Subject:** Miriam Makeba, South African singer in exile **Obv:** Bust right divides people at lower right and left **Rev:** National arms

Date	Mintage	F	VF	XF	Unc	BU
1977	300	—	—	—	90.00	100
1977 Proof	250			Value: 125		

KM# 49 1000 SYLI
2.9300 g., 0.9000 Gold .0847 oz. AGW **Subject:** Nkrumah **Obv:** Bust right **Rev:** National arms

Date	Mintage	F	VF	XF	Unc	BU
1977	150	—	—	—	110	125
1977 Proof	150			Value: 135		

KM# 50 2000 SYLI
5.8700 g., 0.9000 Gold .1698 oz. AGW **Subject:** Mao Tse Tung **Obv:** Bust facing **Rev:** National arms

Date	Mintage	F	VF	XF	Unc	BU
1977	200	—	—	—	200	225
1977 Proof	200			Value: 250		

KM# 51 2000 SYLI
5.8700 g., 0.9000 Gold .1698 oz. AGW **Subject:** Ahmen Sekou Toure **Obv:** Bust left **Rev:** National arms

Date	Mintage	F	VF	XF	Unc	BU
1977	100	—	—	—	225	250
1977 Proof	50			Value: 325		

REFORM COINAGE

KM# 62 10000 FRANCS
15.9760 g., 0.9170 Gold .4708 oz. AGW **Subject:** 30th Anniversary of Currency **Obv:** Arms with dates on each side **Rev:** Palm branches and denomination

Date	Mintage	F	VF	XF	Unc	BU
1990 Proof	Est. 200			Value: 500		

TRIAL STRIKES

KM#	Date	Mintage	Identification	Mkt Val
TS5	ND(1969)	—	1000 Francs. Goldine. Jugate heads right.	100

MINT SETS

KM#	Date	Mintage	Identification	Issue Price	Mkt Val
MS1	1977 (6)	—	KM46-51	—	830

PROOF SETS

KM#	Date	Mintage	Identification	Issue Price	Mkt Val
PS2	1969 (8)	—	KM9, 11, 13, 16-18, 20, 32	—	1,825
PS3	1969 (4)	—	KM#17-20	—	1,310
PS4	1969 (4)	4,000	KM#17, 18, 20, 32	223	1,235
PS5	1969-70 (17)	—	KM#9-21, 29-32	1,326	2,192
PS6	1969-70 (6)	—	KM#12, 14, 18, 21, 30-31	318	530
PS10	1970 (7)	—	KM#33-39	440	3,325
PS12	1970 (14)	—	KM#22-28, 33-39	1,650	3,570

GUYANA

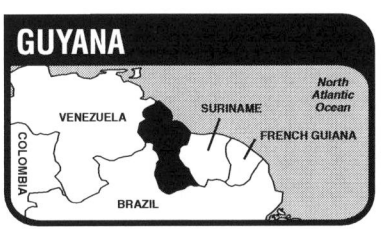

The Cooperative Republic of Guyana, is situated on the northeast coast of South America, has an area of 83,000 sq. mi. (214,970 sq. km.) and a population of 729,000. Capital: Georgetown. The economy is basically agrarian. Sugar, rice and bauxite are exported.

The original area of Essequibo and Demerary, which included present-day Suriname, French Guiana, and parts of Brazil and Venezuela was sighted by Columbus in 1498. The first European settlement was made late in the 16th century by the Dutch, however, the region was claimed for the British by Sir Walter Raleigh during the reign of Elizabeth I. For the next 150 years, possession alternated between the Dutch and the British, with a short interval of French control. The British exercised de facto control after 1796 over the Dutch colonies of Essequibo, Demerary and Berbice. They were not ceded to them by the Dutch until 1814. From 1803 to 1831, Essequibo and Demerary were administered separately from Berbice. The three colonies were united in the British Crown Colony of British Guiana in 1831. British Guiana won internal self-government in 1952 and full independence, under the traditional name of Guyana, on May 26, 1966. Guyana became a republic on Feb. 23, 1970. It is a member of the Commonwealth of Nations. The president is the Chief of State. The prime minister is the Head of Government. Guyana is a member of the Caribbean Community and Common Market (CARICOM).

RULER
British, until 1966

*NOTE: From 1975-1985 the Franklin Mint produced coinage in up to 3 different qualities. Qualities of issue are designated in ( ) after each date and are defined as follows:

(M) **MATTE** - Normal circulation strike or a dull finish produced by sandblasting special uncirculated (polish finish) or proof quality dies.

(U) **SPECIAL UNCIRCULATED** - Polished or proof-like in appearance without any frosted features.

(P) **PROOF** - The highest quality obtainable having mirror-like fields and frosted features.

REPUBLIC

DECIMAL COINAGE

KM# 46 100 DOLLARS
5.7400 g., 0.5000 Gold .0923 oz. AGW **Subject:** 10th Anniversary of Independence **Obv:** Helmeted and supported arms **Rev:** Arawak Indian

Date	Mintage	F	VF	XF	Unc	BU
1976FM (U)	100	—	—	—	95.00	110
1976FM (P)	21,000			Value: 75.00		

KM# 47 100 DOLLARS
5.5800 g., 0.5000 Gold .0897 oz. AGW **Obv:** Helmeted and supported arms **Rev:** Legendary Golden Man

Date	Mintage	F	VF	XF	Unc	BU
1977FM (U)	100	—	—	—	100	115
1977FM (P)	7,635			Value: 80.00		

326 GUYANA

KM# 49 500 DOLLARS
47.5400 g., 0.9170 Gold 1.4017 oz. AGW **Subject:** Royal Visit
Obv: Small portraits left of royals above people welcoming the royal ship

Date	Mintage	F	VF	XF	Unc	BU
1994 Proof	100	Value: 1,100				

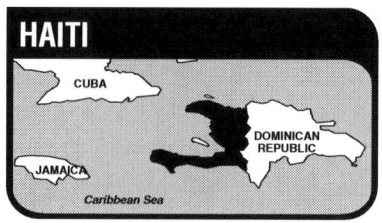

HAITI

Haiti, which occupies the western one-third of the island of Hispaniola in the Caribbean Sea between Puerto Rico and Cuba, has an area of 10,714 sq. mi. (27,750 sq. km.). Capital: Port-au-Prince.

Columbus discovered Hispaniola in 1492. Spain colonized the island, making Santo Domingo the base for exploration of the Western Hemisphere. The area that is now Haiti was ceded to France by Spain in 1697. Slaves brought from Africa to work the coffee and sugar cane plantations made it one of the richest colonies of the French Empire. A slave revolt erupted in the French section in 1791. The Spanish section was ceded to France in 1795. A British Occupation force was ousted in 1798 by Toussaint l'Ouverture, who remained in control of the island until his capture by the French in 1802. After the French evacuation in 1803, The establishment of the Republic of Haiti in 1804, making it the oldest Black republic in the world and the second oldest republic (after the United States) in the Western Hemisphere. Internal dissension and conflicting ambitions of revolutionary generals resulted in separate Haitian governments from 1807 to 1820 under the name of the State of Haiti. Northern Haiti had Henri Christophe as president (til March 1811) and king (1811-1820). The remainder of the old French colony called itself Republic of Haiti with President Petion followed by President Boyer in 1818. Reunited by 1820, President Boyer brought Spanish Santo Domingo under the Haitian flag from 1822-44. That year a Dominican Republic gained independence in the chaos following Gen. Boyer's death in 1843. Note also a 2nd regal government: The Empire of Haiti (1849-59) under ex-president of the republic, Faustin Soulugue, as Emperor Faustin I. This aberration endured until a revolt led by subsequent President N.F. Geffrard overturned it. Since 1859, Haiti has continued as an ostensible Republic under a succession of strong-men presidents.

The French language is used on Haitian coins although it is spoken by only about 10% of the populace. A form of Creole is the language of the Haitians.

Two dating systems are used on Haiti's 19th century coins. One is Christian, the other Revolutionary – beginning in 1803 when the French were permanently ousted by a native revolt. Thus, a date of AN30, (i.e., year 30) is equivalent to 1833 A.D. Some coins carry both date forms. In the listings which follow, coins dated only in the Revolutionary system are listed by AN years in the date column.

RULERS
French, until 1804
Jacques I (Dessalines), 1804-1807
Henri Christophe as President of North Haiti, 1807-1811
Alexandre Petition President Western Republic, 1807-1818
Henri I (Christophe) as King of North Haiti, 1811-1820
Jean Pierre Boyer, President Western Republic, 1818-1843
Louis Pierrot, President Western Republic, 1845-1846
Jean Baptiste Riche, President Western Republic, 1846-1847
Faustin Soulougne, President Western Republic, 1847-1849
Faustin I (Soulouque), 1849-1858
Nicholas F. Geffrard, President,, 1859-1867

MINT MARKS
A - Paris
(a) - Paris, privy marks only
HEATON - Birmingham
R - Rome
(w) = Waterbury (Connecticut, USA) (Scoville Mfg. Co.)

MONETARY SYSTEM
12 Deniers = 1 Sol
20 Sols = 1 Livre
100 Centimes = 1 Gourde

REPUBLIC
1863 -
DECIMAL COINAGE
100 Centimes = 1 Gourde

KM# 66 20 GOURDES
3.9500 g., 0.9000 Gold .1143 oz. AGW **Series:** 10th Anniversary of Revolution **Obv:** Native left with knife in left hand **Rev:** National arms **Note:** Mackandal

Date	Mintage	F	VF	XF	Unc	BU
1967 IC Proof	10,351	Value: 82.50				
1968 IC Proof	—	Value: 82.50				
1969 IC Proof	—	Value: 90.00				
1970 IC Proof	—	Value: 95.00				

KM# 72 30 GOURDES
9.1100 g., 0.8580 Gold .1713 oz. AGW **Series:** 10th Anniversary of Revolution **Obv:** Citadel of Saint Christopher **Rev:** National arms

Date	Mintage	F	VF	XF	Unc	BU
1969 IC Proof	1,185	Value: 135				
1970 IC Proof	Inc. above	Value: 165				

KM# 73 40 GOURDES
12.1500 g., 0.5850 Gold .2285 oz. AGW **Series:** 10th Anniversary of Revolution **Subject:** J.J. Dessalines **Obv:** Uniformed bust facing divides dates **Rev:** National arms

Date	Mintage	F	VF	XF	Unc	BU
1969 Proof	1,005	Value: 215				
1970 Proof	Inc. above	Value: 230				

KM# 68 50 GOURDES
9.8700 g., 0.9000 Gold .2856 oz. AGW **Series:** 10th Anniversary of Revolution **Obv:** Dancer **Rev:** National arms

Date	Mintage	F	VF	XF	Unc	BU
1967 IC Proof	8,681	Value: 210				
1968 IC Proof	—	Value: 220				
1969 IC Proof	—	Value: 230				
1970 IC Proof	—	Value: 250				

KM# 89 50 GOURDES
9.8700 g., 0.9000 Gold .2856 oz. AGW **Series:** 10th Anniversary of Revolution **Obv:** Soldiers **Rev:** National arms **Note:** Heros de Vertieres

Date	Mintage	F	VF	XF	Unc	BU
1971 IC Proof	485	Value: 300				

KM# 74 60 GOURDES
18.2200 g., 0.5850 Gold .3427 oz. AGW **Series:** 10th Anniversary of the Revolution **Obv:** Alexandre Petion **Rev:** National arms

Date	Mintage	F	VF	XF	Unc	BU
1969 IC Proof	935	Value: 245				
1970 IC Proof	Inc. above	Value: 385				

HAITI

KM# 69 100 GOURDES
19.7500 g., 0.9000 Gold .5715 oz. AGW **Series:** 10th Anniversary of the Revolution **Subject:** Marie Jeanne **Obv:** Half-figure left with knife in right hand **Rev:** National arms

Date	Mintage	F	VF	XF	Unc	BU
1967 IC Proof	Est. 8,682	Value: 400				
1968 IC Proof	—	Value: 420				
1969 IC Proof	—	Value: 420				
1970 IC Proof	—	Value: 450				

KM# 90 100 GOURDES
19.7500 g., 0.9000 Gold .5715 oz. AGW **Obv:** Seminole Tribal Chief - Osceola **Rev:** National arms

Date	Mintage	F	VF	XF	Unc	BU
1971 IC Proof	435	Value: 425				

KM# 91 100 GOURDES
19.7500 g., 0.9000 Gold .5715 oz. AGW **Obv:** Sioux Chief - Sitting Bull **Rev:** National arms

Date	Mintage	F	VF	XF	Unc	BU
1971 IC Proof	475	Value: 425				

KM# 92 100 GOURDES
19.7500 g., 0.9000 Gold .5715 oz. AGW **Obv:** Fox Chief - Playing Fox **Rev:** National arms

Date	Mintage	F	VF	XF	Unc	BU
1971 IC Proof	425	Value: 385				

KM# 93 100 GOURDES
19.7500 g., 0.9000 Gold .5715 oz. AGW **Obv:** Chiricahua Chief - Geronimo **Rev:** National arms

Date	Mintage	F	VF	XF	Unc	BU
1971 IC Proof	520	Value: 425				

KM# 94 100 GOURDES
19.7500 g., 0.9000 Gold .5715 oz. AGW **Obv:** Seminole Chief - Billy Bowlegs **Rev:** National arms

Date	Mintage	F	VF	XF	Unc	BU
1971 IC Proof	425	Value: 425				

KM# 95 100 GOURDES
19.7500 g., 0.9000 Gold .5715 oz. AGW **Obv:** Nez Perce Chief - Joseph **Rev:** National arms

Date	Mintage	F	VF	XF	Unc	BU
1971 IC Proof	455	Value: 425				

KM# 96 100 GOURDES
19.7500 g., 0.9000 Gold .5715 oz. AGW **Obv:** Yankton Sioux Chief - War Eagle **Rev:** National arms

Date	Mintage	F	VF	XF	Unc	BU
1971 IC Proof	455	Value: 425				

KM# 97 100 GOURDES
19.7500 g., 0.9000 Gold .5715 oz. AGW **Obv:** Oglala Sioux Chief - Red Cloud **Rev:** National arms

Date	Mintage	F	VF	XF	Unc	BU
1971 IC Proof	455	Value: 425				

KM# 98 100 GOURDES
19.7500 g., 0.9000 Gold .5715 oz. AGW **Obv:** Cherokee Chief - Stalking Turkey **Rev:** National arms

Date	Mintage	F	VF	XF	Unc	BU
1971 IC Proof	425	Value: 425				

KM# 107 100 GOURDES
1.4500 g., 0.9000 Gold .0419 oz. AGW **Subject:** Christopher Columbus **Obv:** Bust facing **Rev:** National arms

Date	Mintage	F	VF	XF	Unc	BU
1973	3,233	—	—	—	40.00	45.00
1973 Proof	915	Value: 55.00				

KM# 70 200 GOURDES
39.4900 g., 0.9000 Gold 1.1427 oz. AGW **Subject:** Revolt of Santo Domingo **Obv:** Native running with weapons **Rev:** National arms

Date	Mintage	F	VF	XF	Unc	BU
1967 IC Proof	Est. 4,199	Value: 800				
1968 IC Proof	—	Value: 825				
1969 IC Proof	—	Value: 825				
1970 IC Proof	—	Value: 850				

KM# 99 200 GOURDES
39.4900 g., 0.9000 Gold 1.1427 oz. AGW **Obv:** Revolutionist from Santo Domingo **Rev:** National arms

Date	Mintage	F	VF	XF	Unc	BU
1971 IC Proof	235	Value: 900				

KM# 108 200 GOURDES
2.9100 g., 0.9000 Gold .0842 oz. AGW **Series:** World Soccer Championship Games **Obv:** Games logo **Rev:** National arms

Date	Mintage	F	VF	XF	Unc	BU
1973	5,167	—	—	—	60.00	65.00
1973 Proof	915	Value: 85.00				

KM# 115 200 GOURDES
2.9100 g., 0.9000 Gold .0842 oz. AGW **Subject:** Holy Year **Obv:** Pope Paul and Praying hands above St. Peter's Square **Rev:** National arms, fineness stamped on hexagonal mound

Date	Mintage	F	VF	XF	Unc	BU
1974	4,965	—	—	—	65.00	70.00
1974 Proof	660	Value: 100				

328 HAITI

KM# 124 200 GOURDES
2.9100 g., 0.9000 Gold .0842 oz. AGW **Subject:** Holy Year **Obv:** Pope Paul and Praying hands above St. Peter's Square **Rev:** National arms, fineness stamped on oval mound

Date	Mintage	F	VF	XF	Unc	BU
1975 Proof	—	Value: 90.00				

KM# 125 200 GOURDES
2.9100 g., 0.9000 Gold .0842 oz. AGW **Series:** International Women's Year **Obv:** Two women with arms upraised **Rev:** National arms

Date	Mintage	F	VF	XF	Unc	BU
1975	2,260	—	—	—	65.00	70.00
1975 Proof	840	Value: 125				

KM# 75 250 GOURDES
75.9500 g., 0.5850 Gold 1.4286 oz. AGW **Series:** 10th Anniversary of Revolution **Obv:** King H. Christophe **Rev:** National arms

Date	Mintage	F	VF	XF	Unc	BU
1969 IC Proof	470	Value: 975				
1970 IC Proof	—	Value: 1,100				

KM# 136 250 GOURDES
4.2500 g., 0.9000 Gold .1229 oz. AGW **Subject:** Human Rights **Obv:** Kneeling figure with broken chains **Rev:** National arms

Date	Mintage	F	VF	XF	Unc	BU
1977	282	—	—	—	125	140
1977 Proof	288	Value: 145				

KM# 137 250 GOURDES
4.2500 g., 0.9000 Gold .1229 oz. AGW **Subject:** Presidents Sadat and Begin **Obv:** Profiles facing each other, Dove of Peace above **Rev:** National arms

Date	Mintage	F	VF	XF	Unc	BU
1977	270	—	—	—	110	120
1977 Proof	520	Value: 100				

KM# 138 250 GOURDES
4.2500 g., 0.9000 Gold .1229 oz. AGW **Subject:** 20th Anniversary of European Market **Obv:** Ships wheel and sailboat **Rev:** National arms

Date	Mintage	F	VF	XF	Unc	BU
1977	107	—	—	—	175	200
1977 Proof	107	Value: 210				

KM# 139 250 GOURDES
4.2500 g., 0.9000 Gold .1229 oz. AGW **Subject:** 50th Anniversary of Lindbergh's New York to Paris Flight **Obv:** Portrait of Lindbergh in flier's cap above "Spirit of St. Louis" **Rev:** National arms

Date	Mintage	F	VF	XF	Unc	BU
1977	107	—	—	—	225	245
1977 Proof	107	Value: 250				

KM# 76 500 GOURDES
151.9000 g., 0.5850 Gold 2.8572 oz. AGW, 68 mm. **Series:** 10th Anniversary of Revolution **Obv:** Haitian native art **Rev:** National arms **Note:** Illustration reduced.

Date	Mintage	F	VF	XF	Unc	BU
1969 IC Proof	435	Value: 2,000				
1970 IC Proof	—	Value: 2,500				

KM# 109 500 GOURDES
7.2800 g., 0.9000 Gold .2106 oz. AGW **Obv:** Woman with shell right **Rev:** National arms

Date	Mintage	F	VF	XF	Unc	BU
1973	2,380	—	—	—	155	165
1973 Proof	915	Value: 185				

KM# 110 500 GOURDES
7.2800 g., 0.9000 Gold .2106 oz. AGW **Obv:** Woman with child **Rev:** National arms

Date	Mintage	F	VF	XF	Unc	BU
1973	2,265	—	—	—	150	160
1973 Proof	915	Value: 175				

KM# 116 500 GOURDES
6.5000 g., 0.9000 Gold .1881 oz. AGW **Obv:** Battle scene **Rev:** National arms

Date	Mintage	F	VF	XF	Unc	BU
1974 Proof	—	Value: 165				

KM# 117 500 GOURDES
6.5000 g., 0.9000 Gold .1881 oz. AGW **Series:** 1976 Montreal Olympics **Obv:** Half-figure with torch above Olympic flame, athletes flank **Rev:** National arms, fineness stamped on hexagonal mound

Date	Mintage	F	VF	XF	Unc	BU
1974	3,489	—	—	—	135	150
1974 Proof	1,140	Value: 165				

KM# 126 500 GOURDES
6.5000 g., 0.9000 Gold .1881 oz. AGW **Series:** 1976 Montreal Olympics **Obv:** Half-figure with torch above Olympic flame, athletes flank **Rev:** National arms, fineness stamped on hexagonal mound

Date	Mintage	F	VF	XF	Unc	BU
1975	120	—	—	—	450	500

KM# 140 500 GOURDES
8.5000 g., 0.9000 Gold .2459 oz. AGW **Series:** World Soccer Championship Games **Obv:** Soccer ball with date in center **Rev:** National arms

Date	Mintage	F	VF	XF	Unc	BU
1977	450	—	—	—	185	200
1977 Proof	200	Value: 250				

KM# 141 500 GOURDES
8.5000 g., 0.9000 Gold .2459 oz. AGW **Series:** 1980 Moscow Olympics **Rev:** National arms

Date	Mintage	F	VF	XF	Unc	BU
1977	695	—	—	—	180	200
1977 Proof	504	Value: 210				
1978 Proof	Est. 350	Value: 350				

KM# 142 500 GOURDES
8.5000 g., 0.9000 Gold .2459 oz. AGW **Subject:** 20th Anniversary of European Common Market **Obv:** Map of Europe **Rev:** National arms

Date	Mintage	F	VF	XF	Unc	BU
1977	207	—	—	—	225	250
1977 Proof	257	Value: 265				
1978	—	—	—	—	275	300
1978 Proof	150	Value: 350				

KM# 143 500 GOURDES
8.5000 g., 0.9000 Gold .2459 oz. AGW **Subject:** Economic Connections **Rev:** National arms

Date	Mintage	F	VF	XF	Unc	BU
1977	107	—	—	—	235	260
1977 Proof	107	Value: 300				

KM# 144 500 GOURDES
8.5000 g., 0.9000 Gold .2459 oz. AGW **Obv:** Jean-Claude Duvalier **Rev:** National arms

Date	Mintage	F	VF	XF	Unc	BU
1977	107	—	—	—	235	250
1977 Proof	328	Value: 200				

HAITI

KM# 161 500 GOURDES
7.0000 g., 0.9000 Gold .2025 oz. AGW **Subject:** 10th Anniversary of the Presidency of Jean Claude Duvalier **Obv:** Head right without FAO **Rev:** Sun above farmer on tractor in field

Date	Mintage	F	VF	XF	Unc	BU
1981R Proof	—	Value: 650				

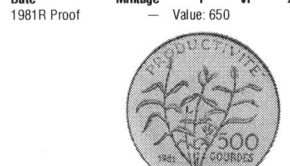

KM# 162 500 GOURDES
7.0000 g., 0.9000 Gold .2025 oz. AGW **Subject:** 10th Anniversary of the Presidency of Jean Claude Duvalier **Obv:** Head right without FAO **Rev:** Plants

Date	Mintage	F	VF	XF	Unc	BU
1981R Proof	—	Value: 650				

KM# 163 500 GOURDES
7.0000 g., 0.9000 Gold .2025 oz. AGW **Subject:** 10th Anniversary of the Presidency of Jean Claude Duvalier **Obv:** Head right without FAO **Rev:** Harvesters

Date	Mintage	F	VF	XF	Unc	BU
1981R Proof	—	Value: 650				

KM# 151 500 GOURDES
10.5000 g., 0.9000 Gold .3038 oz. AGW **Subject:** Papal Visit **Obv:** National arms **Rev:** Bust left above people

Date	Mintage	F	VF	XF	Unc	BU
1983R Proof	1,000	Value: 225				

KM# 71 1000 GOURDES
197.4800 g., 0.9000 Gold 5.7148 oz. AGW **Series:** 10th Anniversary of Revolution **Obv:** Dr. Francois Duvalier **Rev:** National arms

Date	Mintage	F	VF	XF	Unc	BU
1967 IC Proof	Est. 2,950	Value: 3,900				
1968 IC Proof	—	Value: 3,950				
1969 IC Proof	—	Value: 4,000				
1970 IC Proof	—	Value: 4,100				

KM# 111 1000 GOURDES
14.5600 g., 0.9000 Gold .4213 oz. AGW **Obv:** President Jean Claude Duvalier left **Rev:** National arms

Date	Mintage	F	VF	XF	Unc	BU
1973	—	—	—	—	300	320
1973 Proof	915	Value: 345				

KM# 118.1 1000 GOURDES
13.0000 g., 0.9000 Gold .3762 oz. AGW **Series:** United States Bicentennial **Obv:** Battle scene **Rev:** National arms

Date	Mintage	F	VF	XF	Unc	BU
1974	3,040	—	—	—	230	250
1974 Proof	480	Value: 325				
1975 Proof	—	Value: 600				

KM# 118.2 1000 GOURDES
13.0000 g., 0.9000 Gold .3762 oz. AGW **Obv:** Error; without country name at top **Rev:** National arms

Date	Mintage	F	VF	XF	Unc	BU
1974	—	—	—	—	650	700

KM# 164 1000 GOURDES
14.0000 g., 0.9000 Gold .4051 oz. AGW **Subject:** 10th Anniversary of the Presidency of Jean Claude Duvalier **Obv:** Head right without FAO **Rev:** Three nudes and flag

Date	Mintage	F	VF	XF	Unc	BU
1981R Proof	—	Value: 1,150				

PATTERNS
Including off metal strikes

KM#	Date	Mintage	Identification	Mkt Val
Pn22	1814	—	Crown. Base Metal. Crown. Crowned eagle.	650
Pn23	1814	—	Crown. Base Metal. Crown. Crowned eagle.	650
Pn67	1854	—	20 Gourdes. Gold.	20,000
Pn68	1854	—	20 Gourdes. Gold. Laureate, uniformed bust right. Crowned arms divides date. ESSAI.	20,000

TRIAL STRIKES

KM#	Date	Mintage	Identification	Mkt Val
TS1	ND(1971)	—	100 Gourdes. Gilt Bronze. Bust in headdress facing. Blank. KM#93	100

MINT SETS

KM#	Date	Mintage	Identification	Issue Price	Mkt Val
MS1	1973 (8)	8,000	KM#102, 104-105, 107-111,	490	600

PROOF SETS

KM#	Date	Mintage	Identification	Issue Price	Mkt Val
PSA1	1967 (8)	—	KM#64.1, 65-71	—	3,500
PS1	1967 (5)	2,525	KM#66, 68-71	722	3,900
PS3	1968 (5)	475	KM#66, 68-71	823	4,200
PS5	1969 (5)	435	KM#72-76	475	3,750
PS6	1969 (5)	140	KM#66, 68-71	823	4,650
PS8	1970 (5)	—	KM#66, 68-71	823	5,000
PS10	1971 (9)	—	KM#79-87	135	325
PS11	1971 (9)	—	KM#90-98	—	3,500
PSA11	1971 (18)	—	KM#79-87, 90-98	—	3,900
PS12	1973 (8)	1,250	KM#102-105, 107-109, 111	830	600
PS18	1978 (2)	350	KM#129, 141	—	475
PS19	1978 (2)	—	KM#130.2, 142	—	450
PS20	1981R (7)	10	KM#158-164	—	3,650

HEJAZ

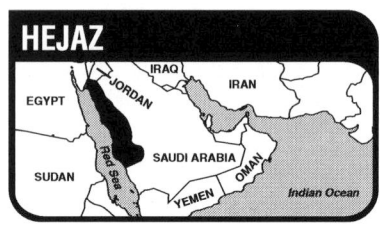

Hejaz, a province of Saudi Arabia and a former vilayet of the Ottoman Empire, occupies an 800-mile long (1,287km.) coastal strip between Nejd and the Red Sea. The province was a Turkish dependency until freed in World War I. Husain Ibn Ali, Amir of Mecca, opposed the Turkish control and, with the aid of Lawrence of Arabia, wrested much of Hejaz from the Turks and in 1916 assumed the title of King of Hejaz. Abd Al-Aziz Bin Sa'ud, of Nejd conquered Hejaz in 1925, and in 1926 combined it and Nejd into a single kingdom.

TITLES

الحجاز

Hal-Hejaz

RULERS
al Husain Ibn Ali, AH1334-42/1916-24AD
Abd Al-Aziz Bin Sa'ud, AH1343-1373/1925-1953AD

MONETARY SYSTEM
40 Para = 1 Piastre (Ghirsh)
20 Piastres = 1 Riyal
100 Piastres = 1 Dinar

KINGDOM
REGULAR COINAGE

All the regular coins of Hejaz bear the accessional date AH1334 of Al-Husain Ibn Ali, plus the regnal year. Many of the bronze coins occur with a light silver wash mostly on thicker specimens. A variety of planchet thicknesses exist.

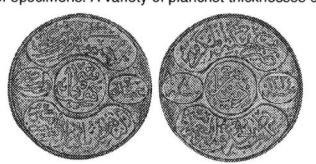

KM# 31 DINAR HASHIMI
Gold

Date	Mintage	VG	F	VF	XF	Unc
AH1334-8	—	—	250	400	600	1,000

HONDURAS

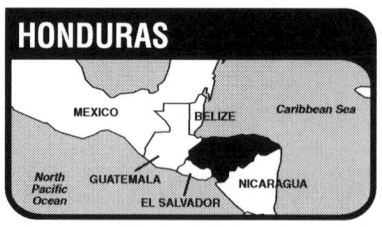

The Republic of Honduras, situated in Central America alongside El Salvador, between Nicaragua and Guatemala, has an area of 43,277sq. mi. (112,090 sq. km.) and a population of 5.6 million. Capital: Tegucigalpa. Agriculture, mining (gold and silver), and logging are the major economic activities, with increasing tourism and emerging petroleum resource discoveries. Precious metals, bananas, timber and coffee are exported.

The eastern part of Honduras was part of the ancient Mayan Empire; however, the largest Indian community in Honduras was the not too well known Lencas. Columbus claimed Honduras for Spain in 1502, during his last voyage to the Americas. Cristobal de Olid established the first settlement under orders from Hernando Cortes, then in Mexico. The area, regarded as one of the most promising sources of gold and silver in the New World, was a part of the Captaincy General of Guatemala throughout the colonial period. After declaring its independence from Spain on September 15, 1821, Honduras fell under the Mexican empire of Augustin de Iturbide, and then joined the Central American Republic (1823-39). Upon the effective dissolution of that federation (ca. 1840), Honduras reclaimed its independence as a self-standing republic. Honduras forces played a major part in permanently ending the threat of William Walker to establish a slave holding empire in Central America based on his self engineered elections to the Presidency of Nicaragua. Thrice expelled from Central America, Walker was shot by a Honduran firing squad in 1860. 1876 to 1933 saw a period of instability and for some months U.S. Marine Corp military occupation. From 1933 to 1940 General Tiburcio Carias Andino was dictator president of the Republic. Since 1990 democratic practices have become more consistent.

RULERS
Spanish, until 1821
Augustin Iturbide (Emperor of Mexico), 1822-1823

MINT MARKS
A - Paris, 1869-1871
P-Y - Provincia Yoro (?)
T - Tegucigalpa, 1825-1862
T.G. - Yoro
T.L. — Comayagua
NOTE: Extensive die varieties exist for coins struck in Honduras with almost endless date and overdate varieties. Federation style coinage continued to be struck until 1861. (See Central American Republic listings.)

MONETARY SYSTEM
16 Reales = 1 Escudo
100 Centavos = 1 Peso

REPUBLIC
DECIMAL COINAGE
100 Centavos = 1 Peso

KM# 39 PESO
1.6120 g., 0.9000 Gold .0467 oz. AGW Obv: Crowned, flagged arms Rev: Liberty head left Note: Mule.

Date	Mintage	F	VF	XF	Unc	BU
1871	—	250	500	1,000	2,000	—

KM# 38 PESO
1.6120 g., 0.9000 Gold .0467 oz. AGW Note: Similar to 5 Centavos, KM#34.

Date	Mintage	F	VF	XF	Unc	BU
1871 Rare	—	—	—	—	—	—

KM# 56 PESO
1.6120 g., 0.9000 Gold .0467 oz. AGW Obv: Arms within circle, bouquets flanking, banner and stars above Rev: Liberty head left

Date	Mintage	F	VF	XF	Unc	BU
1888	—	150	300	600	1,150	—
1889 5 Known	—	475	875	1,450	—	—
1895	43	150	300	600	1,150	—
1896	—	150	300	600	1,150	—
1899/1895 Rare	—	—	—	—	—	—

Note: American Numismatic Rarities Eliasberg sale 4-05, MS-63 realized $13,800.

Date	Mintage	F	VF	XF	Unc	BU
1901	—	150	300	600	1,150	—
1902	—	140	300	500	1,000	—
1907	—	140	250	450	900	—
1914/882	—	275	450	650	1,200	—
1914/03	—	275	450	600	1,150	—
1919	—	150	300	550	1,100	—
1920	—	150	300	550	1,100	—
1922	—	140	250	450	900	—
ND(ca.1922-25)	—	—	—	—	—	—

KM# 53 5 PESOS
8.0645 g., 0.9000 Gold .2333 oz. AGW Obv: Arms within inner circle, bouquets flank outer circle Rev: Liberty head left

Date	Mintage	F	VF	XF	Unc	BU
1883	—	450	650	1,000	2,500	—

Note: Heritage Whittier sale 6-06, MS-64 realized $9775. American Numismatic Rarities Eliasberg sale 4-05, MS-64 realized $10,925.

1888/3	—	450	650	1,000	2,250	—
1890	—	600	750	1,100	2,250	—
1895	20	600	900	1,650	3,000	—
1896	55	600	900	1,650	3,000	—
1897	—	450	650	1,000	2,500	—

Note: American Numismatic Rarities Eliasberg sale 4-05, MS-64 realized $14,950.

1900	—	450	650	1,000	2,500	—
1902	—	450	650	1,000	2,500	—
1908/888	—	450	650	1,000	2,500	—
1913	1,200	450	650	1,000	2,500	—

KM# 58 10 PESOS
16.1290 g., 0.9000 Gold .4667 oz. AGW Obv: Arms within inner circle, bouquets flank outer circle Rev: Liberty head left

Date	Mintage	F	VF	XF	Unc	BU
1883 Rare	—	—	—	—	—	—
1889 Rare	25	—	—	—	—	—

Note: American Numismatic Rarities Eliasberg sale 4-05, EF-45 realized $74,750.

KM# 57 20 PESOS
32.2580 g., 0.9000 Gold .9335 oz. AGW Obv: Arms within inner circle, bouquets flank outer circle Rev: Liberty head left

Date	Mintage	F	VF	XF	Unc	BU
1888 Rare	—	—	—	—	—	—

Note: American Numismatic Rarities Eliasberg sale 4-05, VF-20 realized $32,200.

1895/88 Rare	—	—	—	—	—	—
1895 Rare	—	—	—	—	—	—
1908/888 Rare	—	—	—	—	—	—
1908/897 Rare	—	—	—	—	—	—

Note: Stack's Hammel sale 9-82 VF 1908/897 realized $12,000. Ponterio & Associates NYINC. sale 12-86 choice XF realized $30,800. Superior Casterline sale 5-89 choice XF realized $28,600.

| 1908 Rare | — | — | — | — | — | — |

REFORM COINAGE

KM# 90 LEMPIRA
7.7750 g., 0.9990 Gold .2497 oz. AGW, 24 mm. **Subject:** Central Bank's 50th Anniversary **Obv:** National arms within beaded circle **Rev:** Bank building within beaded circle, wreath surrounds **Edge:** Reeded

Date	Mintage	F	VF	XF	Unc	BU
ND(2000) Proof	1,200	Value: 215				

KM# 86 200 LEMPIRAS
6.5000 g., 0.9000 Gold .1881 oz. AGW, 20 mm. **Subject:** Bicentenary of Birth - Gen. Francisco Morazan **Obv:** Emblem within legend **Rev:** Head left

Date	Mintage	F	VF	XF	Unc	BU
1992 Proof	1,500,000	Value: 175				

KM# 87 500 LEMPIRAS
12.5000 g., 0.9000 Gold .3617 oz. AGW, 26 mm. **Subject:** Bicentenary of Birth - Gen. Francisco Morazan

Date	Mintage	F	VF	XF	Unc	BU
1992	1,500,000	Value: 280				

PATTERNS
Including off metal strikes

Rosettes separate legends on Pn1-Pn5a.

KM#	Date	Mintage	Identification	Mkt Val
Pn21	1883	—	5 Pesos. Copper. KM#53.	450
Pn23	1919	—	Peso. Copper. KM#56.	100
	1995	—	10 Lempiras. 0.9167 Gold. 40.4000 g. Reeded edge. X1.1.	2,000
	1995	—	10 Lempiras. 0.9167 Gold. 40.1000 g. Plain edge. X1.2.	2,000
	1995	—	10 Lempiras. 0.9167 Gold. 40.3000 g. Reeded edge. X1.	2,000
	1995	—	10 Lempiras. 0.9167 Gold. 40.0000 g. Plain edge. X1.	2,000

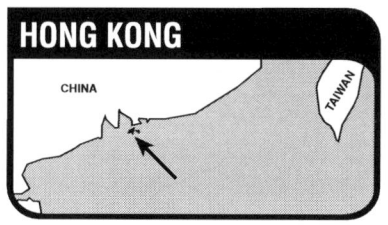

HONG KONG

Hong Kong, a former British colony, reverted to control of the People's Republic of China on July 1, 1997 as a Special Administrative Region. It is situated at the mouth of the Canton or Pearl River 90 miles (145 km.) southeast of Canton, has an area of 403 sq. mi. (1,040 sq. km.) and an estimated population of 6.3 million. Capital: Victoria. The free port of Hong Kong, the commercial center of the Far East, is a trans-shipment point for goods destined for China and the countries of the Pacific Rim. Light manufacturing and tourism are important components of the economy.

Long a haven for fishermen-pirates and opium smugglers, the island of Hong Kong was ceded to Britain at the conclusion of the first Opium War, 1839-1842. The acquisition of a 'barren rock' was ridiculed by London and English merchants operating in the Far East. The Kowloon Peninsula and Stonecutter's Island were ceded in 1860, and the so-called New Territories, comprising most of the mainland of the colony, were leased to Britain for 99 years in 1898.

The legends on Hong Kong coinage are bilingual: English and Chinese. The rare 1941 cent was dispatched to Hong Kong in several shipments. One fell into Japanese hands, while another was melted down by the British and a third was sunk during enemy action.

RULER
British 1842-1997

MINT MARKS
H - Heaton
KN - King's Norton

MONETARY SYSTEM
10 Mils (Wen, Ch'ien) = 1 Cent (Hsien)
10 Cents = 1 Chiao
100 Cents = 10 Chiao = 1 Dollar (Yuan)

BRITISH COLONY
DECIMAL COINAGE

KM# 38 1000 DOLLARS
15.9700 g., 0.9170 Gold .4708 oz. AGW **Ruler:** Elizabeth II **Subject:** Visit of Queen Elizabeth **Obv:** Young bust right **Rev:** Arms with supporters **Rev. Designer:** Leslie Durbin

Date	Mintage	F	VF	XF	Unc	BU
1975	15,000	—	—	—	300	350
1975 Proof	5,005	Value: 1,150				

KM# 40 1000 DOLLARS
15.9700 g., 0.9170 Gold .4708 oz. AGW **Ruler:** Elizabeth II **Subject:** Year of the Dragon **Obv:** Young bust right **Rev:** Dragon left **Rev. Designer:** Elizabeth Haddon-Care

Date	Mintage	F	VF	XF	Unc	BU
1976	20,000	—	—	—	465	500
1976 Proof	6,911	Value: 1,000				

KM# 42 1000 DOLLARS
15.9700 g., 0.9170 Gold .4708 oz. AGW **Ruler:** Elizabeth II **Subject:** Year of the Snake **Obv:** Young bust right **Rev:** Snake **Rev. Designer:** Elizabeth Haddon-Care

Date	Mintage	F	VF	XF	Unc	BU
1977	20,000	—	—	—	320	365
1977 Proof	10,000	Value: 475				

KM# 44 1000 DOLLARS
15.9700 g., 0.9170 Gold .4708 oz. AGW **Ruler:** Elizabeth II **Subject:** Year of the Horse **Obv:** Young bust right **Rev:** Horse left **Rev. Designer:** Elizabeth Haddon-Care

Date	Mintage	F	VF	XF	Unc	BU
1978	20,000	—	—	—	320	350
1978 Proof	10,000	Value: 450				

KM# 45 1000 DOLLARS
15.9700 g., 0.9170 Gold .4708 oz. AGW **Ruler:** Elizabeth II **Subject:** Year of the Goat **Obv:** Young bust right **Rev:** Goat left **Rev. Designer:** Elizabeth Haddon-Care

Date	Mintage	F	VF	XF	Unc	BU
1979	30,000	—	—	—	320	350
1979 Proof	15,000	Value: 350				

KM# 47 1000 DOLLARS
15.9700 g., 0.9170 Gold .4708 oz. AGW **Ruler:** Elizabeth II **Subject:** Year of the Monkey **Obv:** Young bust right **Rev:** Monkey seated right **Rev. Designer:** Elizabeth Haddon-Care

Date	Mintage	F	VF	XF	Unc	BU
1980	31,000	—	—	—	320	350
1980 Proof	18,000	Value: 375				

KM# 48 1000 DOLLARS
15.9700 g., 0.9170 Gold .4708 oz. AGW **Ruler:** Elizabeth II **Subject:** Year of the Cockerel **Obv:** Young bust right **Rev:** Rooster right **Rev. Designer:** Elizabeth Haddon-Care

Date	Mintage	F	VF	XF	Unc	BU
1981	33,000	—	—	—	320	350
1981 Proof	22,000	Value: 375				

332 HONG KONG

KM# 50 1000 DOLLARS
15.9700 g., 0.9170 Gold .4708 oz. AGW **Ruler:** Elizabeth II
Subject: Year of the Dog **Obv:** Young bust right **Rev:** Dog right
Rev. Designer: Elizabeth Haddon-Care

Date	Mintage	F	VF	XF	Unc	BU
1982	33,000	—	—	—	320	350
1982 Proof	22,000	Value: 375				

KM# 51 1000 DOLLARS
15.9700 g., 0.9170 Gold .4708 oz. AGW **Ruler:** Elizabeth II
Subject: Year of the Pig **Obv:** Young bust right **Rev:** Pig right
Rev. Designer: Elizabeth Haddon-Care

Date	Mintage	F	VF	XF	Unc	BU
1983	33,000	—	—	—	375	450
1983 Proof	22,000	Value: 650				

KM# 52 1000 DOLLARS
15.9700 g., 0.9170 Gold .4708 oz. AGW **Ruler:** Elizabeth II
Subject: Year of the Rat **Obv:** Young bust right **Rev:** Rat left
Rev. Designer: Elizabeth Haddon-Care

Date	Mintage	F	VF	XF	Unc	BU
1984	20,000	—	—	—	350	400
1984 Proof	10,000	Value: 525				

KM# 53 1000 DOLLARS
15.9700 g., 0.9170 Gold .4708 oz. AGW **Ruler:** Elizabeth II
Subject: Year of the Ox **Obv:** Young bust right **Rev:** Ox left **Rev. Designer:** Elizabeth Haddon-Care

Date	Mintage	F	VF	XF	Unc	BU
1985	30,000	—	—	—	325	375
1985 Proof	10,000	Value: 525				

KM# 54 1000 DOLLARS
15.9700 g., 0.9170 Gold .4708 oz. AGW **Ruler:** Elizabeth II
Subject: Year of the Tiger **Obv:** Young bust right **Rev:** Tiger **Rev. Designer:** Elizabeth Haddon-Care

Date	Mintage	F	VF	XF	Unc	BU
1986	20,000	—	—	—	320	345
1986 Proof	10,000	Value: 475				

KM# 57 1000 DOLLARS
15.9700 g., 0.9170 Gold .4708 oz. AGW **Ruler:** Elizabeth II
Subject: Royal visit of Queen Elizabeth II **Obv:** Crowned head right **Rev:** Arms with supporters **Rev. Designer:** Leslie Durbin

Date	Mintage	F	VF	XF	Unc	BU
1986	20,000	—	—	—	320	345
1986 Proof	12,000	Value: 375				

KM# 58 1000 DOLLARS
15.9700 g., 0.9170 Gold .4708 oz. AGW **Ruler:** Elizabeth II
Subject: Year of the Rabbit **Obv:** Young bust right **Rev:** Rabbit left **Rev. Designer:** Elizabeth Haddon-Care

Date	Mintage	F	VF	XF	Unc	BU
1987	20,000	—	—	—	325	345
1987 Proof	12,000	Value: 375				

BULLION COINAGE
Issuer Unknown

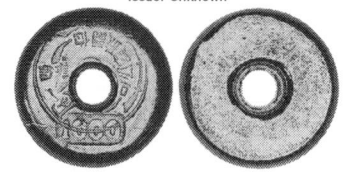

X# B19 TAEL
37.3236 g., 1.0000 Gold 1.2 oz. AGW, 22 mm. **Obv:** Chinese inscriptions, "1000" **Rev:** Uniface **Edge:** Plain

Date	Mintage	F	VF	XF	Unc	BU
ND(1930s)	—	BV	850	950	—	—

BULLION COINAGE
Fung Lai Chun, Gold dealer

X# B16 TAEL
37.4000 g., Gold, 26 mm. **Ruler:** George V **Obv:** Ancient "pu", tablet with inscriptions **Rev:** Lion **Rev. Legend:** FUNG LAI CHUN GOLD DEALER **Edge:** Plain

Date	Mintage	F	VF	XF	Unc	BU
ND(1930s)	—	BV	850	950	—	—

BULLION COINAGE
Chow Song Song Co. Ltd.

X# B17 TAEL
Gold, 24 mm. **Ruler:** George V **Obv:** Chinese legend and inscription **Rev. Legend:** CHOW SONG SONG CO. LTD. **Edge:** Plain

Date	Mintage	F	VF	XF	Unc	BU
ND(1930s)	—	BV	850	950	—	—

BULLION COINAGE
Nam Shing Co.

X# B18 TAEL
1.0000 Gold, 24 mm. **Ruler:** George V **Obv:** Chinese inscriptions, "1000" **Rev:** Uniface, small Chinese hallmark **Edge:** Plain

Date	Mintage	F	VF	XF	Unc	BU
ND(1930s)	—	BV	850	950	—	—

SPECIAL ADMINISTRATION REGION (S.A.R.)

DECIMAL COINAGE

KM# 80 50 DOLLARS
35.4300 g., 0.9250 Bi-Metallic Gold plated .925 Silver center in .925 Silver ring 1.0536 oz., 40 mm. **Subject:** "May your wishes come true" **Obv:** Bauhinia flower **Rev:** Jade Ju-I

Date	Mintage	F	VF	XF	Unc	BU
2002 Proof	60,000	Value: 60.00				

KM# 81 50 DOLLARS
35.4300 g., 0.9250 Bi-Metallic Gold plated .925 Silver center in .925 Silver ring 1.0536 oz., 40 mm. **Obv:** Bauhinia flower **Rev:** Fish

Date	Mintage	F	VF	XF	Unc	BU
2002 Proof	60,000	Value: 60.00				

HUNGARY 333

KM# 82 50 DOLLARS
35.2500 g., 0.9250 Bi-Metallic Gold plated .925 Silver center in .925 Silver ring 1.0483 oz., 40 mm. **Obv:** Bauhinia flower **Rev:** Horses

Date	Mintage	F	VF	XF	Unc	BU
2002 Proof	60,000	Value: 60.00				

KM# 83 50 DOLLARS
35.3400 g., 0.9250 Bi-Metallic Gold plated .925 Silver center in .925 Silver ring 1.0510 oz., 40 mm. **Obv:** Bauhinia flower **Rev:** Peony flower

Date	Mintage	F	VF	XF	Unc	BU
2002 Proof	60,000	Value: 60.00				

KM# 84 50 DOLLARS
35.1400 g., 0.9250 Bi-Metallic Gold plated .925 Silver center in .925 Silver ring 1.0450 oz., 40 mm. **Obv:** Bauhinia flower **Rev:** Windmills

Date	Mintage	F	VF	XF	Unc	BU
2002 Proof	60,000	Value: 60.00				

KM# 71 1000 DOLLARS
15.9700 g., 0.9170 Gold .4708 oz. AGW **Subject:** Return of Hong Kong to China **Obv:** Bauhinia flower **Rev:** Skyline view

Date	Mintage	F	VF	XF	Unc	BU
1997 Proof	97,000	Value: 330				

KM# 79 1000 DOLLARS
15.9700 g., 0.9170 Gold .4708 oz. AGW **Subject:** Hong Kong International Airport **Obv:** Bauhinia flower **Rev:** Stylized airplane lifting off from runway

Date	Mintage	F	VF	XF	Unc	BU
1998 Proof	15,000	Value: 450				

PROOF SETS

KM#	Date	Mintage	Identification	Issue Price	Mkt Val
PS7	2002 (6)	60,000	KM#80-84 plus gold medal	370	370

HUNGARY

The Republic of Hungary, located in central Europe, has an area of 35,929 sq. mi. (93,030 sq. km.) and a population of 10.7 million. Capital: Budapest. The economy is based on agriculture, bauxite and a rapidly expanding industrial sector. Machinery, chemicals, iron and steel, and fruits and vegetables are exported.

The ancient kingdom of Hungary, founded by the Magyars in the 9th century, achieved its greatest extension in the mid-14th century when its dominions touched the Baltic, Black and Mediterranean Seas. After suffering repeated Turkish invasions, Hungary accepted Habsburg rule to escape Turkish occupation, regaining independence in 1867 with the Emperor of Austria as king of a dual Austro-Hungarian monarchy.

After World War I, Hungary lost 2/3 of its territory and 1/2 of its population and underwent a period of drastic political revision. The short-lived republic of 1918 was followed by a chaotic interval of communist rule, 1919, and the restoration of the monarchy in 1920 with Admiral Horthy as regent of the kingdom. Although a German ally in World War II, Hungary was occupied by German troops who imposed a pro-Nazi dictatorship, 1944. Soviet armies drove out the Germans in 1945 and assisted the communist minority in seizing power. A revised constitution published on Aug. 20, 1949, established Hungary as a People's Republic' of the Soviet type. On October 23, 1989, Hungary was pro-claimed the Republic of Hungary.

RULERS
Habsburg Emperors of the
Holy Roman Empire of
The German Nation
Franz II, 1792-1835
Ferdinand V, 1835-1848
Franz Joseph I, 1848-1916
Karl I, 1916-1918

ARMS
Austria (Lower) – shaded horizontal bar
Bohemia – lion rampant left
Dalmatia – three leopard heads
Hungary – 8 horizontal bars, alternately shaded, often
 In combination with patriarchal cross having two cross
 bars; usually quartered with one or more arms of the
 domains of the royal house
Lausitz – steer
Moravia – eagle
Poland – eagle
Silesia – eagle with crescent on breast
Zápolya – wolf standing on hind legs to left
National patron saint – the Madonna and child usually
 Featured on one side

MINT MARKS
A, CA, WI - Vienna (Becs)
(a) =   C   +   = Kaschau
B, K, KB, KP - Kremnitz (Kormoczbanya)
BH - Buda
BP - Budapest
(b) =   Nagybanya
CB – Klausenburg
(cg) = 3-towered castle gate = Klausenburg
CH - Pressburg (Pozsony)
CM - Kaschau (Kassa)
CO-L – Vienna? (for Hungary)
(c) - castle - Pressburg
(d) - double trefoil - Pressburg
G, GN, NB - Nagybanya
(g) - GC script monogram - Pressburg
GYF – Karlsburg (Gyulafehervar)
HA – Hall
(ha) = h + =Hermannstadt
(hb) =   H   + = Hermannstadt
HN, HB, HP = Hermannstadt
HS - Kaschau
IK - Pressburg
LG – Budapest
LG – Kostainica
MS, SA, IT – Unidentified mintmarks, 1530-1531
N – Neusohl
NB, NP, NC, NI, SS – Nagybanya
NS - Neusohl
(L) - ICB monogram - Pressburg
(r) - rampant lion left - Pressburg
S - Schmollnitz (Szomolnok)
(z) = eagle's wing in shield = Nikolaus Zrínyi, private moneyer
 by royal license, 1530-1531

LEGEND VARIETIES
X: After 1750, during the reign of Maria Theresa, crossed staves which appear as an "X" were placed after the date denoting her reign over the Austrian Netherlands.

334 HUNGARY

MONETARY SYSTEM

Until 1857
2 Poltura = 3 Krajczar
60 Krajczar = 1 Forint (Gulden)
2 Forint = 1 Convention Thaler
1857-1891
100 Krajczar = 1 Forint
1892-1925
100 Filler = 1 Korona

NOTE: Many coins of Hungary through 1948, especially 1925-1945, have been restruck in recent times. These may be identified by a rosette in the vicinity of the mintmark. Restrike mintages for KM#440-449, 451-458, 468-469, 475-477, 480-483, 494, 496-498 are usually about 1000 pieces, later date mintages are not known.

REFERENCES: H = Lajos Huszár, *Münzkatalog Ungarn von 1000 bis Heute*, Munich, 1979.

R/P = Ladislaus Réthy and Günther Probszt, *Corpus Nummorum Hungariae*, Graz, 1958.

KINGDOM

REFORM COINAGE
100 Filler = 1 Korona

KM# 485 10 KORONA
3.3875 g., 0.9000 Gold .0980 oz. AGW **Ruler:** Franz Joseph I **Obv:** Emperor standing **Rev:** Crowned shield with angel supporters

Date	Mintage	F	VF	XF	Unc	BU
1892KB	1,087,000	—	BV	65.00	95.00	—
1892KB Restrike; proof	—	Value: 45.00				
1893KB	Inc. above	—	BV	65.00	95.00	—
1894KB	986,000	—	BV	65.00	95.00	—
1895KB	—	1,500	2,500	3,500	4,500	—
1895KB Restrike; proof	—	Value: 50.00				
1896KB	32,000	65.00	90.00	110	135	—
1897KB	259,000	—	BV	65.00	95.00	—
1898KB	218,000	—	BV	65.00	95.00	—
1899KB	231,000	—	BV	65.00	90.00	—
1900KB	228,000	—	BV	65.00	90.00	—
1901KB	230,000	—	BV	65.00	85.00	—
1902KB	243,000	—	BV	70.00	90.00	—
1903KB	228,000	—	BV	70.00	90.00	—
1904KB	1,531,000	—	BV	70.00	90.00	—
1905KB	869,000	—	BV	70.00	90.00	—
1906KB	748,000	—	BV	70.00	90.00	—
1907KB	752,000	—	BV	70.00	90.00	—
1908KB	509,000	—	BV	70.00	90.00	—
1909KB	574,000	—	BV	70.00	90.00	—
1910KB	1,362,000	—	BV	70.00	90.00	—
1911KB	1,828,000	—	BV	70.00	90.00	—
1912KB	739,000	BV	75.00	100	220	—
1913KB	137,000	BV	100	220	300	—
1914KB	115,000	BV	200	450	500	—
1915KB	54,000	1,000	2,000	3,000	4,000	—

KM# 486 20 KORONA
6.7750 g., 0.9000 Gold .1960 oz. AGW **Ruler:** Franz Joseph I **Obv:** Emperor standing **Rev:** Crowned shield with angel supporters

Date	Mintage	F	VF	XF	Unc	BU
1892KB	1,779,000	—	BV	130	150	—
1892KB Restrike; proof	—	Value: 135				
1893KB	5,089,000	—	BV	130	150	—
1894KB	2,526,000	—	BV	130	150	—
1895KB	1,935,000	—	BV	130	150	—
1895KB Restrike; proof	—	Value: 135				
1896KB	1,023,000	—	BV	130	150	—
1897KB	1,819,000	—	BV	130	150	—
1898KB	1,281,000	—	BV	130	150	—
1899KB	712,000	—	BV	130	150	—
1900KB	435,000	—	BV	130	150	—
1901KB	510,000	—	BV	130	135	—
1901KB	510,000	—	BV	95.00	150	—
1902KB	523,000	—	BV	135	150	—
1903KB	505,000	—	BV	135	150	—
1904KB	572,000	—	BV	135	150	—
1905KB	526,000	—	BV	135	150	—
1906KB	353,000	—	BV	135	150	—
1907KB	194,000	BV	150	175	200	—
1908KB	138,000	—	BV	135	150	—
1909KB	459,000	—	BV	135	150	—
1910KB	85,000	135	175	250	300	—
1911KB	63,000	—	BV	135	150	—
1912KB	211,000	—	BV	135	150	—
1913KB	320,000	BV	140	165	200	—
1914KB	176,000	—	BV	135	150	—
1915KB	690,000	BV	140	165	200	—

KM# 495 20 KORONA
6.7750 g., 0.9000 Gold .1960 oz. AGW **Ruler:** Franz Joseph I **Obv:** Emperor standing **Rev:** Crowned shield (Bosnian arms added) with angel supporters

Date	Mintage	F	VF	XF	Unc	BU
1914	—	—	BV	135	155	—
1915	—	—	—	—	—	—
1916	—	—	BV	175	275	400

KM# 500 20 KORONA
6.7750 g., 0.9000 Gold .1960 oz. AGW **Ruler:** Karl I **Obv. Legend:** KAROLY...

Date	Mintage	F	VF	XF	Unc	BU
1918 Rare	—	—	—	—	—	—

KM# 490 100 KORONA
33.8753 g., 0.9000 Gold .9802 oz. AGW, 36 mm. **Ruler:** Franz Joseph I **Subject:** 40th Anniversary - Coronation of Franz Josef **Obv:** Laureate head right **Rev:** Coronation scene **Edge Lettering:** BIZALMAM AZ ŐSI ERÉNYBEN **Designer:** Karoly Gerl

Date	Mintage	F	VF	XF	Unc	BU
1907KB	11,000	BV	675	950	1,350	—
1907KB U.P. Restrike	—	—	—	—	825	—

KM# 491 100 KORONA
33.8753 g., 0.9000 Gold .9802 oz. AGW **Ruler:** Franz Joseph I **Obv:** Emperor standing **Rev:** Crowned shield with angel supporters

Date	Mintage	F	VF	XF	Unc	BU
1907	1,088	BV	1,100	1,450	1,900	—
1907 U.P. Restrike	—	—	—	—	700	—
1908	4,038	BV	850	1,250	1,800	—
1908 U.P Restrike	—	—	—	—	700	—

TRADE COINAGE

KM# 419 DUCAT
3.4900 g., 0.9860 Gold .1106 oz. AGW **Ruler:** Franz II **Obv. Legend:** FRANC. I. D. G...

Date	Mintage	F	VF	XF	Unc	BU
1830	—	175	250	325	500	—
1832	—	200	300	400	550	—
1833	—	115	175	250	350	—
1834	—	115	175	250	350	—
1835	—	115	175	250	350	—

KM# 425 DUCAT
3.4900 g., 0.9860 Gold .1106 oz. AGW **Ruler:** Ferdinand V **Obv:** Emperor standing **Obv. Legend:** FERD. I. D. G... **Rev:** Madonna with child

Date	Mintage	F	VF	XF	Unc	BU
1837	—	175	250	400	600	—
1838	—	175	250	400	600	—
1839	—	110	150	250	375	—
1840	—	110	150	250	375	—
1841	—	110	150	250	375	—
1842	—	110	150	250	375	—
1843	—	175	250	400	600	—
1844	—	110	150	250	375	—
1845	—	175	250	400	600	—
1846	—	110	150	250	375	—
1847	—	110	150	250	375	—
1848	—	110	150	250	375	—

KM# 433 DUCAT
3.4900 g., 0.9860 Gold .1106 oz. AGW **Ruler:** Ferdinand V **Obv:** Emperor standing **Rev:** Madonna with child **Rev. Legend:** SZ. MARIA...

Date	Mintage	F	VF	XF	Unc	BU
1848	—	100	175	250	350	—

KM# 448.1 DUCAT
3.4900 g., 0.9860 Gold .1106 oz. AGW **Ruler:** Franz Joseph I **Obv:** Emperor standing **Rev:** Angels holding crown above shield within sprigs

Date	Mintage	F	VF	XF	Unc	BU
1868KB	127,531	100	200	275	400	—
1869KB	106,614	90.00	150	200	300	—

KM# 448.2 DUCAT
3.4900 g., 0.9860 Gold .1106 oz. AGW **Ruler:** Franz Joseph I **Obv:** Emperor standing **Rev:** Angels holding crown above shield within sprigs

Date	Mintage	F	VF	XF	Unc	BU
1868GYF	399,914	85.00	140	200	300	—
1869GYF	270,425	90.00	150	200	300	—

KM# 457 DUCAT
3.4900 g., 0.9860 Gold .1106 oz. AGW **Ruler:** Franz Joseph I **Obv:** Laureate head, right **Rev:** Crowned shield within circle, date below

Date	Mintage	F	VF	XF	Unc	BU
1870 Proof; restrike	—	Value: 100				
1877	452	800	1,250	1,500	2,500	—
1879	3,651	500	900	1,500	2,500	—
1880	5,075	600	1,000	1,500	2,000	—
1880 Proof; restrike	—	—	—	—	700	—
1881	Est. 43	1,250	2,000	2,500	4,000	—

KM# 454.1 4 FORINT 10 FRANCS
3.2258 g., 0.9000 Gold .0934 oz. AGW **Ruler:** Franz Joseph I **Obv:** Laureate head, right **Rev:** Crowned shield divides value within circle, date below

Date	Mintage	F	VF	XF	Unc	BU
1870GYF	48,672	60.00	70.00	90.00	125	—

HUNGARY

KM# 454.2 4 FORINT 10 FRANCS
3.2258 g., 0.9000 Gold .0934 oz. AGW **Ruler:** Franz Joseph I **Obv:** Laureate head, right **Rev:** Crowned shield divides value within circle, date below **Note:** Semi-official restrikes have the letters UP below the bust.

Date	Mintage	F	VF	XF	Unc	BU
1870KB	80,733	60.00	70.00	90.00	125	250
1870KB UP Restrike; proof	—	Value: 70.00				
1871KB	111,142	60.00	75.00	100	130	250
1872KB	53,108	60.00	70.00	90.00	125	250
1873KB	13,284	80.00	115	175	200	—
1874KB	8,229	80.00	115	175	210	—
1875KB	10,682	85.00	125	175	225	—
1876KB	24,284	60.00	75.00	100	130	250
1877KB	24,240	60.00	70.00	100	125	250
1878KB	14,838	60.00	75.00	100	130	250
1879KB	12,367	60.00	75.00	100	130	250

KM# 466 4 FORINT 10 FRANCS
3.2258 g., 0.9000 Gold .0934 oz. AGW **Ruler:** Franz Joseph I **Obv:** Laureate head, right **Rev:** Crowned shield divides value within circle, date below **Note:** Older head.

Date	Mintage	F	VF	XF	Unc	BU
1880	12,546	60.00	75.00	100	130	—
1881	11,737	60.00	75.00	100	130	—
1882	13,350	60.00	75.00	100	125	—
1883	11,865	60.00	75.00	100	125	—
1884	53,533	60.00	70.00	90.00	125	—
1885	64,277	60.00	70.00	95.00	125	—
1886	39,066	60.00	70.00	90.00	125	—
1887	38,842	60.00	70.00	90.00	125	—
1888	48,682	60.00	70.00	90.00	125	—
1889	19,204	100	150	225	300	—
1890	28,989	95.00	140	200	275	—

KM# 476.1 4 FORINT 10 FRANCS
3.2258 g., 0.9000 Gold .0934 oz. AGW **Ruler:** Franz Joseph I **Obv:** Laureate head, right **Rev:** Crowned shield divides value within circle, date below

Date	Mintage	F	VF	XF	Unc	BU
1890	Inc. above	200	300	375	500	—
1891	32,001	65.00	80.00	100	150	—

KM# 476.2 4 FORINT 10 FRANCS
3.2258 g., 0.9000 Gold .0934 oz. AGW **Ruler:** Franz Joseph I **Obv:** Laureate head, right **Rev:** Crowned shield divides value within circle, date below **Note:** Mint unknown.

Date	Mintage	F	VF	XF	Unc	BU
1892	—	800	1,100	1,800	3,000	—

KM# 455.1 8 FORINT 20 FRANCS
6.4516 g., 0.9000 Gold .1867 oz. AGW **Ruler:** Franz Joseph I **Obv:** Laureate head, right **Rev:** Crowned shield divides value within circle, date below

Date	Mintage	F	VF	XF	Unc	BU
1870	45,890	—	BV	125	180	—
1871	75,575	—	BV	125	165	—
1872	273,161	—	BV	125	165	—
1873	244,505	—	BV	125	165	—
1874	240,359	—	BV	125	165	—
1875	260,537	—	BV	125	165	—
1876	303,920	—	BV	125	165	—
1877	312,959	—	BV	125	165	—
1878	307,755	—	BV	125	165	—
1879	305,621	—	BV	125	165	—
1880	301,422	90.00	120	150	200	—

KM# 455.2 8 FORINT 20 FRANCS
6.4516 g., 0.9000 Gold .1867 oz. AGW **Ruler:** Franz Joseph I **Obv:** Laureate head, right **Rev:** Crowned shield divides value within circle, date below

Date	Mintage	F	VF	XF	Unc	BU
1870GYF	125,308	—	BV	125	180	—
1871GYF	177,047	—	BV	125	175	—

KM# 467 8 FORINT 20 FRANCS
6.4516 g., 0.9000 Gold .1867 oz. AGW **Ruler:** Franz Joseph I **Obv:** Laureate head, right **Rev:** Crowned shield divides value within circle, date below

Date	Mintage	F	VF	XF	Unc	BU
1880KB	Inc. above	—	BV	125	175	—
1881KB	308,789	—	BV	125	165	—
1882KB	304,152	—	BV	125	165	—
1883KB	300,429	—	BV	125	165	—
1884KB	284,185	—	BV	125	175	—
1885KB	266,928	—	BV	125	175	—
1886KB	312,611	—	BV	125	165	—
1887KB	294,112	—	BV	125	175	—
1888KB	296,147	—	BV	125	175	—
1889KB	351,370	—	BV	125	165	—
1890KB	329,221	—	BV	125	175	—

KM# 477 8 FORINT 20 FRANCS
6.4516 g., 0.9000 Gold .1867 oz. AGW **Ruler:** Franz Joseph I **Obv:** Laureate head, right **Rev:** Crowned shield divides value within circle, date below

Date	Mintage	F	VF	XF	Unc	BU
1890	Inc. above	—	BV	125	175	—
1891	378,201	—	BV	125	175	—
1892	232,194	—	BV	125	200	—

MEDALLIC COINAGE

X# M1c FORINT
Gold **Note:** Prev. KM#M1c.

Date	Mintage	F	VF	XF	Unc	BU
1878 Rare	3	—	—	—	—	—

SOUVENIR COINAGE
1000th Anniversary of the Kingdom of Hungary

Struck on demand using some earlier coin designs with new legends of Francis Joseph and dated 1896. In 1965 restrikes were produced of certain types.

X# 9 GOLDGULDEN
3.5600 g., Gold **Note:** Style of Karl Robert.

Date	Mintage	F	VF	XF	Unc	BU
1896	100	—	—	1,350	2,250	—

X# 13a THALER
30.0800 g., Gold **Rev:** Madonna and child above shield **Note:** Franz Joseph I.

Date	Mintage	F	VF	XF	Unc	BU
1896 KB	100	—	—	—	—	—

X# 8.1a 9 DUCAT
30.0800 g., Gold

Date	Mintage	F	VF	XF	Unc	BU
1896KB Prooflike	100	—	—	—	4,250	—

PATTERNS
1965 Commercial Series

Struck especially for a U.S. numismatic firm located in Ohio using pattern designs with additional U.P.(utanvert probaveret) letters.

X# Pn40 40 PENGO
11.6200 g., Gold, 27 mm. **Subject:** 200th Anniversary of Death of Rakoczi **Obv:** Crowned arms in order chain **Obv. Legend:** ★ MAGYAR KIRALYSAG ★ **Rev:** Franz Rakoczi horseback right **Rev. Legend:** RAKOCZI FERENC

Date	Mintage	F	VF	XF	Unc	BU
1935BP UP Restrike	—	—	—	—BV+10%	—

X# Pn41 100 PENGO
Gold **Note:** A modern fantasy according to leading authorities.

Date	Mintage	F	VF	XF	Unc	BU
1938BP Proof	—	—	—	—BV+10%	—

PEOPLES REPUBLIC
1949-1989
DECIMAL COINAGE

KM# 560 50 FORINT (Otven)
3.8380 g., 0.9860 Gold .1217 oz. AGW **Subject:** 150th Anniversary - Birth of Liszt, Musician **Obv:** Harp below denomination **Rev:** Head right

Date	Mintage	F	VF	XF	Unc	BU
1961 Proof	2,503	Value: 90.00				

KM# 562 50 FORINT (Otven)
3.8380 g., 0.9860 Gold .1217 oz. AGW **Subject:** 80th Anniversary - Birth of Bartok, Composer **Obv:** Small harp above denomination **Rev:** Head left

Date	Mintage	F	VF	XF	Unc	BU
1961 Proof	2,503	Value: 95.00				

KM# 583 50 FORINT (Otven)
4.2050 g., 0.9000 Gold .1217 oz. AGW **Subject:** 150th Anniversary - Birth of Semmelweis **Obv:** Head right **Rev:** Star above shield within wreath

Date	Mintage	F	VF	XF	Unc	BU
1968 Proof	25,000	Value: 85.00				

336 HUNGARY

KM# 563 100 FORINT (Szaz)
7.6760 g., 0.9860 Gold .2431 oz. AGW **Subject:** 150th Anniversary - Birth of Liszt, Musician **Obv:** Head right **Rev:** Harp below denomination

Date	Mintage	F	VF	XF	Unc	BU
1961BP Proof	2,500	Value: 175				

KM# 564 100 FORINT (Szaz)
7.6760 g., 0.9860 Gold .2431 oz. AGW **Subject:** 80th Anniversary - Birth of Bartok, Composer **Obv:** Head left **Rev:** Small harp above denomination

Date	Mintage	F	VF	XF	Unc	BU
1961 Proof	2,500	Value: 175				

KM# 569 100 FORINT (Szaz)
8.4100 g., 0.9000 Gold .2433 oz. AGW **Subject:** 400th Anniversary - Death of Zrinyi **Obv:** Monument **Rev:** Head 3/4 right

Date	Mintage	F	VF	XF	Unc	BU
1966 Proof	3,300	Value: 175				

KM# 585 100 FORINT (Szaz)
8.4100 g., 0.9000 Gold .2433 oz. AGW **Subject:** 150th Anniversary - Birth of Semmelweis **Obv:** Head right **Rev:** Star above shield within wreath

Date	Mintage	F	VF	XF	Unc	BU
1968 Proof	23,000	Value: 170				

KM# 586 200 FORINT (Ketszaz)
16.8210 g., 0.9000 Gold .4867 oz. AGW, 34 mm. **Subject:** 150th Anniversary - Birth of Ignac Semmelweis **Obv:** Head right **Rev:** Star above shield within wreath

Date	Mintage	F	VF	XF	Unc	BU
1968BP Proof	14,000	Value: 345				

KM# 565 500 FORINT (Otszaz)
38.3800 g., 0.9860 Gold 1.2168 oz. AGW, 40 mm. **Subject:** 150th Anniversary - Birth of Ferenc Liszt **Obv:** Harp below denomination **Rev:** Head right

Date	Mintage	F	VF	XF	Unc	BU
1961BP	2,503	Value: 875				

KM# 566 500 FORINT (Otszaz)
38.3800 g., 0.9860 Gold 1.2168 oz. AGW, 40 mm. **Subject:** 80th Anniversary - Birth of Bela Bartok, Composer **Obv:** Small harp above denomination **Rev:** Head left

Date	Mintage	F	VF	XF	Unc	BU
1961	2,503	Value: 875				

KM# 570 500 FORINT (Otszaz)
42.0522 g., 0.9000 Gold 1.2169 oz. AGW, 40 mm. **Subject:** 400th Anniversary - Death of Miklos Zrinyi **Obv:** Monument **Rev:** Head right

Date	Mintage	F	VF	XF	Unc	BU
1966 Proof	1,100	Value: 925				

KM# 580 500 FORINT (Otszaz)
42.0522 g., 0.9000 Gold 1.2169 oz. AGW, 40 mm. **Subject:** 85th Birthday of Zoltan Kodaly, Composer **Obv:** Peacock above denomination **Rev:** Bust 3/4 left

Date	Mintage	F	VF	XF	Unc	BU
1967	—	—	—	—	875	900
1967 Proof	1,000	Value: 950				

KM# 587 500 FORINT (Otszaz)
42.0522 g., 0.9000 Gold 1.2169 oz. AGW, 46 mm. **Subject:** 150th Anniversary - Birth of Ignacz Semmelweis **Obv:** Head right **Rev:** Star above shield within wreath

Date	Mintage	F	VF	XF	Unc	BU
1968 Proof	9,000	Value: 875				

KM# 571 1000 FORINT (Ezer)
84.1040 g., 0.9000 Gold 2.4339 oz. AGW **Subject:** 400th Anniversary - Death of Miklos Zrinyi **Obv:** Monument **Rev:** Head 3/4 right

Date	Mintage	F	VF	XF	Unc	BU
1966 Proof	330	Value: 1,900				

HUNGARY

KM# 581 1000 FORINT (Ezer)
84.1040 g., 0.9000 Gold 2.4339 oz. AGW **Subject:** 85th Birthday of Zoltan Kodaly, Composer **Obv:** Peacock above denomination **Rev:** Bust 3/4 left

Date	Mintage	F	VF	XF	Unc	BU
1967 Proof	500	Value: 1,800				

KM# 588 1000 FORINT (Ezer)
84.1040 g., 0.9000 Gold 2.4339 oz. AGW **Subject:** 150th Anniversary - Birth of Ignacz Semmelweis **Rev:** Star above shield within wreath

Date	Mintage	F	VF	XF	Unc	BU
1968	7,000	Value: 1,675				

MEDALLIC BULLION COINAGE

X# MB5 1/10 UNCIA
3.0700 g., Gold, 13 mm. **Obv:** Large crown **Obv. Legend:** MAGYARORSZAG **Rev:** Madonna and child **Rev. Legend:** S. MARIA MATER DEI PATRONA HUNGARIAE **Edge:** Reeded

Date	Mintage	F	VF	XF	Unc	BU
1987 Proof	—	BV+40%				

X# MB6 1/4 UNCIA
7.8200 g., Gold, 18 mm. **Obv:** Large crown **Obv. Legend:** MAGYARORSZAG **Rev:** Madonna and child **Rev. Legend:** S. MARIA MATER DEI PATRONA HUNGARIAE **Edge:** Reeded

Date	Mintage	F	VF	XF	Unc	BU
1987 Proof	—	BV+30%				

X# MB7 1/2 UNCIA
15.6100 g., Gold, 22.8 mm. **Obv:** Large crown **Obv. Legend:** MAGYARORSZAG **Rev:** Madonna and child **Rev. Legend:** S. MARIA MATER DEI PATRONA HUNGARIAE **Edge:** Reeded

Date	Mintage	F	VF	XF	Unc	BU
1987 Proof	—	BV+25%				

X# MB8 UNCIA
31.0400 g., Gold, 32.2 mm. **Obv:** Large crown **Obv. Legend:** MAGYARORSZAG **Rev:** Madonna and child **Rev. Legend:** S. MARIA MATER DEI PATRONA HUNGARIAE **Edge:** Reeded

Date	Mintage	F	VF	XF	Unc	BU
1987 Proof	—	BV+20%				

SECOND REPUBLIC
1989-present
DECIMAL COINAGE

KM# 681 5000 FORINT
6.9820 g., 0.9860 Gold .2213 oz. AGW **Subject:** 500th Anniversary - Death of Mathias I **Obv:** Hunyadi coat of arms **Rev:** Seated King Mathias with scepter and orb

Date	Mintage	F	VF	XF	Unc	BU
1990BP Proof	10,000	Value: 160				

KM# 711 5000 FORINT
7.7700 g., 0.5840 Gold .1459 oz. AGW **Obv:** Denomination and date **Rev:** Great Bustard Bird

Date	Mintage	F	VF	XF	Unc	BU
1994 Proof	5,000	Value: 120				

KM# 684 10000 FORINT (Tizezer)
6.9820 g., 0.9860 Gold .2213 oz. AGW **Subject:** Papal Visit **Obv:** Crowned shield within beaded circle **Rev:** Madonna and child

Date	Mintage	F	VF	XF	Unc	BU
1991BP Proof	10,000	Value: 170				

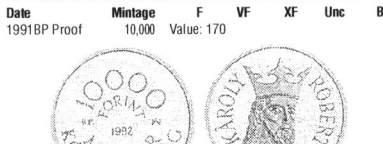

KM# 691 10000 FORINT (Tizezer)
6.9820 g., 0.9860 Gold .2213 oz. AGW **Subject:** 650th Anniversary - Death of King Karoly Robert **Obv:** Denomination **Rev:** Crowned head 3/4 right

Date	Mintage	F	VF	XF	Unc	BU
1992 Proof	10,000	Value: 165				

KM# 703 10000 FORINT (Tizezer)
6.9820 g., 0.9860 Gold .2213 oz. AGW **Subject:** Centennial - Death of Ferenc Erkel **Obv:** Denomination and date **Rev:** Bust 3/4 left

Date	Mintage	F	VF	XF	Unc	BU
1993 Proof	5,000	Value: 175				

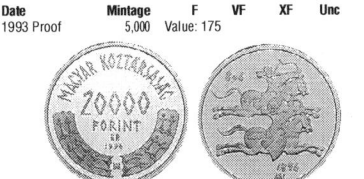

KM# 719 20000 FORINT
6.9820 g., 0.9860 Gold .2213 oz. AGW **Subject:** 1100th Anniversary of Hungarian Nationhood **Obv:** Denomination and date above designs at bottom **Rev:** Two equestrian archers right

Date	Mintage	F	VF	XF	Unc	BU
1996 Proof	5,000	Value: 225				

KM# 728 20000 FORINT
6.9820 g., 0.9860 Gold .2213 oz. AGW **Subject:** Revolution of 1848 **Obv:** Hungarian Order of Military Merit III Class **Rev:** Portrait of Lajos Batthyany

Date	Mintage	F	VF	XF	Unc	BU
1998 Proof	Est. 5,000	Value: 225				

KM# 742 20000 FORINT
6.9820 g., 0.9860 Gold .2213 oz. AGW **Subject:** Hungarian State Millennium **Obv:** Portrait of St. Michael the Archangel **Rev:** Crown of St. Stephen **Edge:** Plain

Date	Mintage	F	VF	XF	Unc	BU
1999 Proof	Est. 3,000	Value: 250				

KM# 753 20000 FORINT
6.9820 g., 0.9860 Gold .2213 oz. AGW, 22 mm. **Subject:** Hungarian Coinage Millennium **Obv:** Denomination **Rev:** Hammered coinage minting scene above old coin design **Edge:** Plain

Date	Mintage	F	VF	XF	Unc	BU
2001 Proof	3,000	Value: 220				

KM# 777 50000 FORINT
13.9640 g., 0.9860 Gold 0.4427 oz. AGW, 25 mm. **Obv:** Value and country name above Euro Union stars **Rev:** Mythical stag seen through ornate window **Edge:** Reeded

Date	Mintage	F	VF	XF	Unc	BU
2004BP Proof	7,000	Value: 450				

KM# 758 100000 FORINT
31.1040 g., 0.9860 Gold .9860 oz. AGW, 37 mm. **Subject:** Saint Stephen **Obv:** Angels crowning coat of arms **Rev:** King seated on throne **Edge:** Reeded

Date	Mintage	F	VF	XF	Unc	BU
2001 Proof	3,000	Value: 675				

PATTERNS
Including off metal strikes

KM#	Date	Mintage	Identification	Mkt Val
Pn104	1849	—	Ducat. Pewter.	—
Pn117	1878	—	Forint. Gold. KM#453.	—
Pn162	1927	—	10 Pengo. Gold.	—
Pn165	1927	—	20 Pengo. Gold. Denomination in grape-wheat ear wreath.	—
Pn166	1927	—	20 Pengo. Gold. Denomination in laurel wreath.	2,700
Pn167	1928BP	—	10 Pengo. Gold. Fr#100	2,700
Pn169	1928BP	—	20 Pengo. Gold. Fr#99.	2,700
Pn168	1928	—	20 Pengo. Brass. Smaller arms. Fr#99a.	—
Pn172	1929BP	—	20 Pengo. Gold. Fr#99a.	2,700

TRIAL STRIKES

KM#	Date	Mintage	Identification	Mkt Val
TS13	1849	—	Ducat. Lead. KM#425.	—
TS16	1868KB	—	4 Krajczar. Gold. KM#442.	—
TS21	1870KB	—	4 Forint 10 Francs. Copper. KM#454.	—
TS22	1870	—	4 Forint 10 Francs. Copper. KM#454.	—
TS23	1870KB	—	Ducat. Lead. KM#456.	—
TS24	1874KB	—	10 Krajczar. Gold. KM#451.	—
TS33	1891KB	—	4 Forint 10 Francs. Nickel. KM#476.	—
TS36	1892KB	—	8 Forint 20 Francs. Nickel. KM#477.	—

PROOF SETS

KM#	Date	Mintage	Identification	Issue Price	Mkt Val
PS1	1961 (6)	2,500	KM560, 562-566	—	2,200
PS4	1966 (3)	330	KM569-571	430	2,850
PS7	1967 (2)	500	KM580, 581	—	2,450
PS8	1968 (5)	7,000	KM583, 585-588	—	2,850
PS22	1998 (3)	5,000	KM726-728	268	275
PS24	1999 (2)	—	KM741, 742	240	310

ICELAND

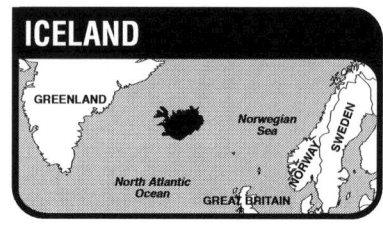

The Republic of Iceland, an island of recent volcanic origin in the North Atlantic east of Greenland and immediately south of the Arctic Circle, has an area of 39,768sq. mi. (103,000 sq. km.) and a population of 275,264. Capital: Reykjavik. Fishing is the chief industry and accounts for more than 70 percent of the exports.

Iceland came under Norwegian sovereignty in 1262, and passed to Denmark when Norway and Denmark were united under the Danish crown in 1380. In 1918 it was established as a virtually independent kingdom in union with Denmark. On June 17, 1944, while Denmark was still under occupation by troops of the Third Reich, Iceland was established by plebiscite as an independent republic.

RULER
Christian X, 1912-1944

MINT MARK
Heart (h) - Copenhagen

MINTMASTERS' INITIALS
HCN - Hans Christian Nielsen, 1919-1927
(for Iceland, 1922-1926)
N - Niels Peter Nielsen, 1927-1955
(for Iceland, 1929-1940)

MONEYERS' INITIALS
GJ - Knud Gunnar Jensen, 1901-1933

REPUBLIC
DECIMAL COINAGE

KM# 14   500 KRONUR
8.9604 g., 0.9000 Gold .2593 oz. AGW **Subject:** Jon Sigurdsson Sesquicentennial **Obv:** Arms with supporters **Rev:** Head right

Date	Mintage	F	VF	XF	Unc	BU
ND(1961)	10,000	—	—	—	200	—
ND(1961) Proof	—	Value: 825				

KM# 22   10000 KRONUR
15.5500 g., 0.9000 Gold .4485 oz. AGW **Subject:** 1100th Anniversary - 1st Settlement **Obv:** Quartered design of eagle, dragon, bull, giant **Rev:** Ingulfur Arnason getting ready to throw his home posts on the beach **Designer:** Throstur Magnusson

Date	Mintage	F	VF	XF	Unc	BU
ND(1974)	12,000	—	—	—	320	—
ND(1974) Proof	8,000	Value: 340				

REFORM COINAGE
100 Old Kronur = 1 New Krona

KM# 36   10000 KRONUR
8.6500 g., 0.9000 Gold .2503 oz. AGW **Subject:** 1000 Years of Christianity **Obv:** Arms with supporters **Rev:** Old crosier top

Date	Mintage	F	VF	XF	Unc	BU
ND(2000) Proof	3,000	Value: 285				

PROOF SETS

KM#	Date	Mintage	Identification	Issue Price	Mkt Val
PS1	1974 (3)	8,000	KM#20-22	272	350

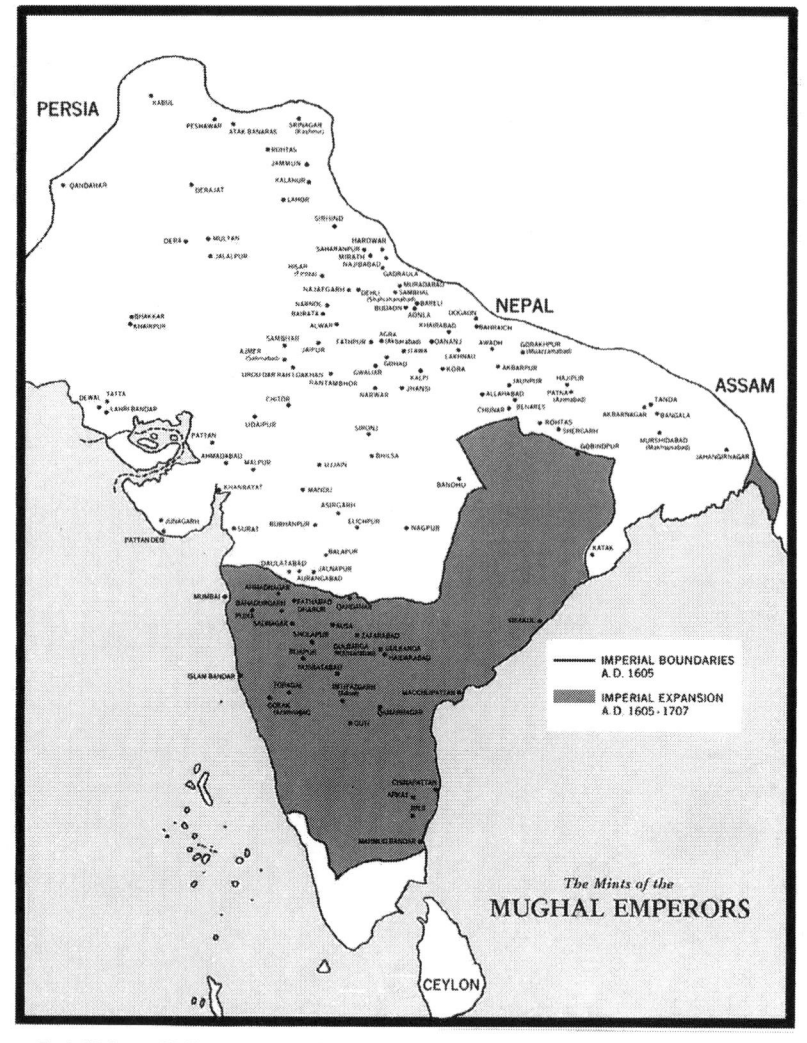

The Mints of the
MUGHAL EMPERORS

The Lodi Sultanate of Delhi was conquered by Zahir-ud-din Muhammad Babur, a Chagatai Turk descended from Tamerlane, in 1525AD. His son, Nasir-ud-din Muham-mad Humayun, lost the new empire in a series of battles with the Bihari Afghan Sher Shah, who founded the short-lived Suri dynasty. Humayun, with the assistance of the Emperor of Persia, recovered his kingdom from Sher Shah's successors in 1555AD. He did not long enjoy the fruits of victory for his fatal fall down his library steps brought his teenage son Jalal-ud-din Muhammad Akbar to the throne in the following year. During Akbar's long reign of a half century, the Mughal Empire was firmly established throughout much of North India. Under Akbar's son and grandson, the emperors Nur-ud-din Muhammad Jahangir and Shihab-ud-din Muhammad Shah Jahan, the state reached its apogee and art, culture and commerce flourished.

One of the major achievements of the Mughal government was the establishment of a universal silver currency, based on the rupee, a coin of 11.6 grams and as close to pure silver content as the metallurgy of the time was capable of attaining. Supplementary coins were the copper dam and gold mohur. The values of these coin denominations were nominally fixed at 40 dams to 1 rupee, and 8 rupees to 1 mohur; however, market forces determined actual exchange rates.

The maximum expansion of the geographical area under direct Mughal rule was achieved during the reign of Aurangzeb Alamgir. By his death in 1707AD, the whole peninsula, with minor exceptions, the whole subcontinent of India owed fealty to the Mughal emperor.

Aurangzeb's wars, lasting decades, upset the stability and prosperity of the kingdom. The internal dissension and rebellion which resulted brought the eclipse of the empire in succeeding reigns. The Mughal monetary system, especially the silver rupee, supplanted most local currencies throughout India. The number of Mughal mints rose sharply and direct central control declined, so that by the time of the emperor Shah Alam II, many nominally Mughal mints served independent states. The common element in all these coinage issues was the presence of the Mughal emperor's name and titles on the obverse. In the following listings no attempt has been made to solve the problem of separating Mughal from Princely State coins by historical criteria: all Mughal-style coins are considered products of the Mughal empire until the death of Muhammad Shah in 1784AD; thereafter all coins are considered Princely State issues unless there is evidence of the mint being under ever-diminishing Imperial control.

EMPERORS

شاه عالم

Shah Alam II, AH1174-1202/1759-1788AD and AH1203-1221/1789-1806AD

بیدار بخت

Bedar Bakht, Muhammad, in Delhi and Gujarat, AH1202-1203/1788AD

اکبر شاه

Akbar Shah AH1203/1788AD

محمد اکبر

Muhammad Akbar II AH1221-1253/1806-1837AD

سراج الدین محمد بہادر شاہ

Bahadur Shah II, Siraj-ud-din Muhammad AH1253-1273/1837-1858AD

MINT NAMES

احمداباد

Ahmadabad

اکبراباد

Akbarabad
(Agra)

الله اباد

Allahabad
(Ilahabad)

At the accession of Shah Alam II the city and fortress of Allahabad were in the possession of the Nawab-Vizier of Awadh. From 1765 to 1771 (AH1179-1185) the Mughal emperor was in residence in Allahabad; subsequently it was seized by the East India Company and sold to Awadh once more in 1773 (AH1187). For issues AH1173-1178/1759-1765AD and AH1187-1195/1773-1781AD see Indian Princely States, Awadh.

گوکل گڑھ

Gokulgarh

ہاردوار

Hardwar
(Tirath)

A mint of the Mughal governor of Saharanpur.

خجستہ بنیاد

Khujista Bunyad
(Aurangabad)

مظفرگڑھ

Muzaffargarh

NOTE: The placing of Muzaffargarh under Khetri has been discontinued as recent research has shown that no rupees had ever been struck there.

سارنگپور

Sarangpur

شاہ جہان اباد

Shahjahanabad
(Dehli)

NOTE: The size of the Shahjahanabad rupees of Shah Alam II was subject to a wide variance. The early issues tended to be normal size for the hammered coinage (about 22mm). As the power of the emperor waned, the flan size of the Shahjahanabad rupees waxed, reflecting the increasingly ceremonial role of the coinage. The later coins should not be confused with the Nazarana (presentation) coins, which always show a full border design around the legend.

سورت

Surat

The Nawab of Surat continued to issue coins in the name of his nominal Mughal suzerain Shah Alam II until the British took over Surat and its mint in 1800AD (AH1214/5), Shah Alam's 43rd regnal year. These coin types of the Nawab of Surat were replicated by the British East India Company in Surat using privy mark #1 and the frozen regnal year 46 of Shah Alam II, see Bombay Presidency types KM#209.1, 210.1, 211.1, 212.1 and 214.

EMPIRE

Shah Alam II
AH1174-1221 / 1759-1806AD
GOVERNORS' HAMMERED COINAGE

Mint: Zebabad
KM# 725 NAZARANA MOHUR
Gold **Note:** Weight varies 10.65-11.1 grams. Struck at Sardhanah in the year of the Lord Lake's victory of Dehli by Begum Somru, Zebu-n-nisa Begam.

Date	Mintage	VG	F	VF	XF	Unc
AHxxxx//45 Rare	—	—	—	—	—	—

HAMMERED COINAGE

Mint: Shahjahanabad
KM# 721 MOHUR
Gold **Obv:** Additional bush symbol, text, mint marks **Rev:** Text, beaded flowers

Date	Mintage	VG	F	VF	XF	Unc
AH1217//45	—	650	1,100	1,650	2,250	—
AH1218//46	—	650	1,100	1,650	2,250	—

Mint: Shahjahanabad
KM# 722 MOHUR
Gold **Obv:** Legend within wreath of roses, thistles and shamrocks **Rev:** Legend within wreath of roses, thistles and shamrocks

Date	Mintage	VG	F	VF	XF	Unc
AH1219//47	—	300	450	700	1,000	—
AH1220//48	—	300	450	700	1,000	—
AH1221//48	—	300	450	700	1,000	—

Muhammad Akbar II
AH1221-1253 / 1806-1837AD
HAMMERED COINAGE

Mint: Shahjahanabad
KM# 781 MOHUR
Gold **Obv:** Text, date, mint mark **Rev:** Text, beaded flowers
Note: Weight varies 10.70-11.40 grams.

Date	Mintage	VG	F	VF	XF	Unc
AH122x//2	—	220	350	500	700	—
AH1223//6 (sic)	—	220	350	500	700	—

Mint: Shahjahanabad
KM# 783 NAZARANA MOHUR
Gold **Obv:** Text, date, mint marks **Rev:** Text, beaded flowers
Note: Weight varies 10.70-11.40 grams.

Date	Mintage	VG	F	VF	XF	Unc
AH1221//1 Rare	—	—	—	—	—	—
AH1234//12 (sic) Rare	—	—	—	—	—	—
AH1237//17 Rare	—	—	—	—	—	—

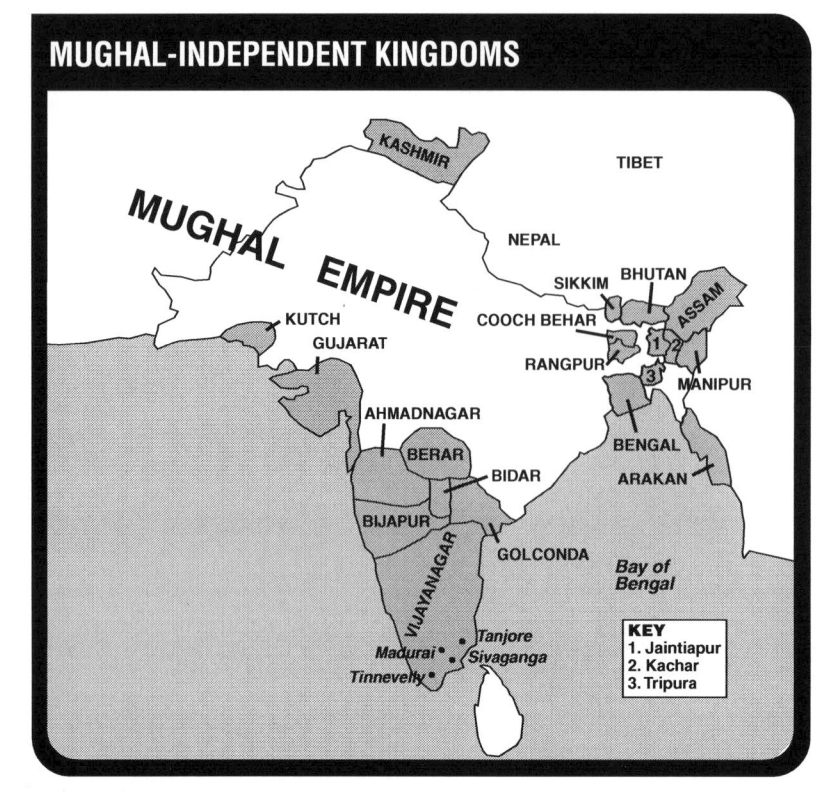

INDIA - INDEPENDENT KINGDOMS

MUGHAL-INDEPENDENT KINGDOMS

KEY
1. Jaintiapur
2. Kachar
3. Tripura

used for small change. Gold coins were struck throughout the period, often using the same dies as were used for the silver coins. A few copper coins were struck during the reign of Brajanatha Simha (1818-19), but these are very rare.

MINT NAME

دنگپور

Rangpur

Kamalesvara Simha
SE1718-1732 / 1796-1810AD

HAMMERED COINAGE
KM# 241 1/8 MOHUR
Gold **Note:** Octagonal. Weight varies: 1.34-1.42 grams.

Date	Mintage	Good	VG	F	VF	XF
ND(1796-1810)	—	—	50.00	90.00	175	275

KM# 244 MOHUR
Gold **Note:** Octagonal. Weight varies: 10.70-11.40 grams.

Date	Mintage	Good	VG	F	VF	XF
SE1720	—	—	225	425	700	1,200

Chandrakanta Simha (Sudingha)
SE1733-1740, 41- 43 / 1811-1818, 19 - 21AD

HAMMERED COINAGE
KM# 252 1/32 MOHUR
Gold **Note:** Weight varies: 0.34-0.36 grams.

Date	Mintage	Good	VG	F	VF	XF
ND(1811-18)	—	—	50.00	100	150	250

KM# 253 1/16 MOHUR
Gold **Note:** Weight varies: 0.67-0.72 grams.

Date	Mintage	Good	VG	F	VF	XF
ND(1811-18)	—	—	55.00	100	175	275

KM# 257 MOHUR
Gold **Note:** Weight varies: 10.70-11.40 grams.

Date	Mintage	Good	VG	F	VF	XF
SE1741 (1819)	—	—	325	600	1,000	1,750

Brajanatha Simha
SE1740-1741 / 1818-1819AD

HAMMERED COINAGE
KM# 266 1/32 MOHUR
Gold **Note:** Weight varies: 0.34-0.36 grams.

Date	Mintage	Good	VG	F	VF	XF
ND(1818-19)	—	—	50.00	100	150	250

KM# 268 1/8 MOHUR
Gold **Shape:** Octagonal **Note:** Weight varies: 1.34-1.42 grams.

Date	Mintage	Good	VG	F	VF	XF
ND(1818-19)	—	—	100	200	350	550

KM# 269 1/4 MOHUR
Gold **Shape:** Octagonal **Note:** Weight varies: 2.68-2.85 grams.

Date	Mintage	VG	F	VF	XF	Unc
SE1739 (1818) (1817)	—	175	300	500	800	—

KM# 271 MOHUR
Gold **Obverse:** Text, date, rulers' name **Reverse:** Text **Note:** Weight varies: 10.70-11.40 grams.

Date	Mintage	Good	VG	F	VF	XF
SE1739 (1818)	—	220	250	475	800	1,350
SE1740 (1819)	—	220	250	475	800	1,350

Jogesvara Simha
SE1743-1746 / 1821-1824 AD

HAMMERED COINAGE
KM# 281 1/2 MOHUR
Gold **Shape:** Octagonal **Note:** Weight varies: 2.68-2.85 grams.

Date	Mintage	Good	VG	F	VF	XF
SE1743 (1821)	—	220	250	450	750	1,250

KUTCH

State located in northwest India, consisting of a peninsula north of the Gulf of Kutch.

The rulers of Kutch were Jareja Rajputs who, coming from Tatta in Sind, conquered Kutch in the 14th or 15th centuries. The capital city of Bhuj is thought to date from the mid-16th century. In 1617, after Akbar's conquest of Gujerat and the fall of the Gujerat sultans, the Kutch ruler, Rao Bharmal I (1586-1632) vis-

ASSAM

AHOM KINGDOM

It was in the 13th century that a tribal leader called Sukapha, with about 9,000 followers, left their traditional home in the Shan States of Northern Burma, and carved out the Ahom Kingdom in upper Assam.

The Ahom Kingdom gradually increased in power and extent over the following centuries, particularly during the reign of King Suhungmung (1497-1539). This king also took on a Hindu title, Svarga Narayan, which shows the increasing influence of the Brahmins over the court. Although several of the other Hindu states in north-east India started a silver coinage during the 16th century, it was not until the mid-17th century that the Ahoms first struck coin.

From the time of Kusain Shah's invasion of Cooch Behar in 1494AD the Muslims had cast acquisitive eyes towards the valley of the Brahmaputra, but the Ahoms managed to preserve their independence. In 1661 Aurangzeb's governor in Bengal, Mir Jumla, made a determined effort to bring Assam under Mughal rule. Cooch Behar was annexed without difficulty, and in March 1662 Mir Jumla occupied Gargaon, the Ahom capital, without opposition. However, during the rainy season the Muslim forces suffered severely from disease, lack of food and from the occasional attacks from the Ahom forces, who had tactically withdrawn from the capital together with the king. After the end of the monsoon a supply line was opened with Bengal again, but morale in the Muslim army was low, so Mir Jumla was forced to agree to peach terms somewhat less onerous than the Mughals liked to impose on subjugated states. The Ahoms agreed to pay tribute, but the Ahom kingdom remained entirely independent of Mughal control, and never again did a Muslim army venture into upper Assam.

During the eighteenth century the kingdom became weakened with civil war, culminating in the expulsion of Gaurinatha Simha from his capital in 1787 by the Moamarias. The British helped Gaurinatha regain his kingdom in 1794, but otherwise took little interest in the affairs of Assam. The end of the Ahom Kingdom was not due to intervention from Bengal, but from Burma. After initial invasions commencing in 1816, the Burmese conquered the whole of Assam in 1821/2, and seemed bent on expanding their Kingdom even further. The British in Bengal were quick to retaliate and drove the Burmese from Assam in 1824, and from then on Assam became firmly under British control with no further independent coinage.

RULERS

Ruler's names, where present on the coins, usually appear on the obverse (dated) side, starting either at the end of the first line, after *Shri*, or in the second line. Most of the Ahom rulers after the adoption of Hinduism in about 1500AD had both an Ahom and a Hindu name.

HINDU NAME	AHOM NAME
Kamalesvara Simha	Suklingpha

কমলেশ্বৰসিংহ
SE1717-1733/1795-1811AD

Chandrakanta Simha	Sudingha

চন্দ্ৰকান্তসিংহ
SE1733-1740/1811-1818AD

Brajanatha Simha	

ব্ৰজনাথসিংহ
SE1740-1741/1818-1819AD

Chandrakanta Simha	Sudingpha

চন্দ্ৰকান্তসিংহ
SE1741-1743/1819-1821AD

Jogesvara Simha	

জোগেশ্বৰসিংহ
SE1743-1746/1821-1824AD

COINAGE

It is frequently stated that coins were first struck in Assam during the reign of King Suklenmung (1539-1552), but this is merely due to a misreading of the Ahom legend on the coins of King Supungmung (1663-70). The earliest Ahom coins known, therefore, were struck during the reign of King Jayadhvaja Simha (1648-1663).

Although the inscription and general design of these first coins of the Ahom Kingdom were copied from the coins of Cooch Behar, the octagonal shape was entirely Ahom, and according to tradition was chosen because of the belief that the Ahom country was eight sided. Apart from the unique shape, the coins were of similar fabric and weight standard to the Mughul rupee.

The earliest coins had inscriptions in Sanskrit using the Bengali script, but the retreat of the Moghul army under Mir Jumla in 1663 seems to have led to a revival of Ahom nationalism that may account for the fact that most of the coins struck between 1663 and 1696 had inscriptions in the old Ahom script, with invocations to Ahom deities.

Up to this time all the coins, following normal practice in Northeast India, were merely dated to the coronation year of the ruler, but Rudra Simha (1696-1714) instituted the practice of dating coins to the year of issue. This ruler was a fervent Hindu, and reinstated Sanskrit inscriptions on the coins. After this the Ahom script was used on a few rare ceremonial issues.

The majority of coins issued were of silver, with binary subdivisions down to a fraction of 1/32nd rupee. Cowrie shells were

ited Jahangir and established a relationship which was sufficiently warm as to leave Kutch virtually independent throughout the Mughal period. Early in the 19th century internal disorder and the existence of rival claimants to the throne resulted in British intrusion into the state's affairs. Rao Bharmalji II was deposed in favor of Rao Desalji II who proved much more amenable to the Government of India's wishes. He and his successors continued to rule in a manner considered by the British to be most enlightened and, as a result, Maharao Khengarji III was created a Knight Grand Commander of the Indian Empire. In view of its geographical isolation Kutch came under the direct control of the Central Government at India's independence.

First coinage was struck in 1617AD.

RULERS

Rayadhanji II, AH1192-1230/1778-1814AD

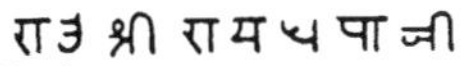

राउ श्री रायधनजी
Ra-o Sri Ra-y(a)-dh(a)-n-ji

Bharmalji II, AH1230-1235/1814-1819AD

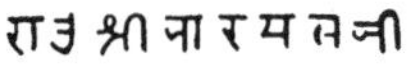

राउ श्री नारमनजी
Ra-o Sri Bha-r-m(a)-l-ji

Desalji II, AH1235-1277/VS1876-1917/1819-1860AD

राउ श्री देसलजी
Ra-o Sri De-sa-l-ji

Pragmalji II, VS1917-1932/1860-1875AD

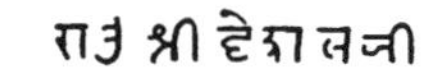

राउ श्री प्रगमलजी
Ra-o Sri Pra-g-m(a)-l-ji

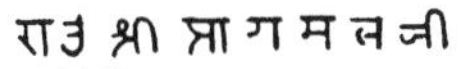

राउ श्री प्रागमलजी
M(a)-ha-ra-o Sri Pra-g-m(a)-l-ji

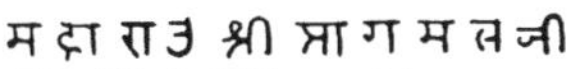

महाराउ श्री प्रागमलजी
Ma-ha-ra-ja Dhi-ra-j Mi-r-ja M(a)-ha-ra-o Sri

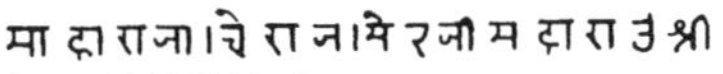

माहाराजाधिराजमिरजामहाराउश्री
Pra-g-m(a)-l-ji B(a)-ha-du-r

Khengarji III, VS1932-1999/1875-1942AD

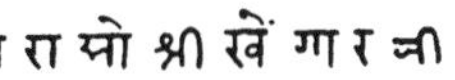

महाराओ श्री खेंगरजी
M(a)-ha-ra-o Sri Khen-ga-r-ji

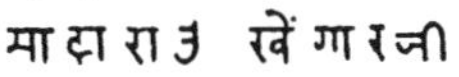

माहाराउ खेंगरजी
Ma-ha-ra-o Khen-ga-r-ji

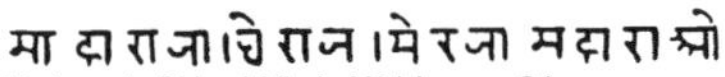

माहाराजाधिराज.मिरजा महाराओ श्री
Ma-ha-ra-ja Dhi-ra-j Mi-r-ja M(a)-ha-ra-o Sri

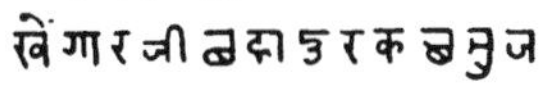

खेंगरजी बहादरक बहुज
Khen-ga-r-ji B(a)-ha-du-r K(a)-chh-bhu-j

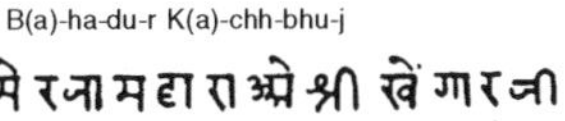

मिरजा महाराओ श्री खेंगरजी
Mi-r-jan M(a)-ha-ra-o Sri Khen-ga-r-ji

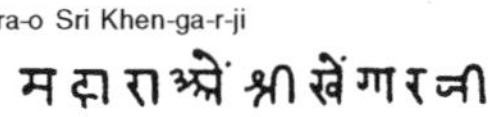

महाराओ श्री खेंगरजी
M(a)-ha-ra-o Sri Khen-ga-r-ji

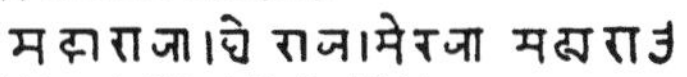

महाराजा धिराजमिरजा महाराउ
M(a)-ha-ra-ja Dhi-ra-j Mi-r-jan M(a)-ha-ra-o

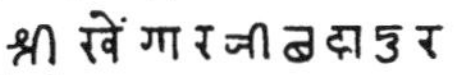

श्री खेंगरजी बहादर
Sri-Khen-ga-r-ji B(a)-ha-du-r

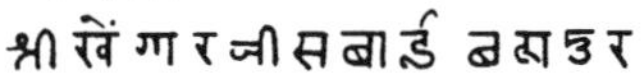

श्री खेंगरजी सवाई बहादर
Sri Khen-ga-r-ji Sa-va-i B(a)-ha-du-r

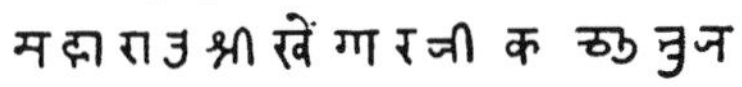

महाराउ श्री खेंगरजी क छ्बुज
M(a)-ha-ra-o Sri Khen-ga-r-ji K(a)-chchh-bhu-j

MINT

भुज or (Persian)
(Devanagari)
Bhuj

MONETARY SYSTEM
1/2 Trambiyo = 1 Babukiya
2 Tramiyo = 1 Dokda
3 Trambiyo = 1 Dhinglo
2 Dhinglo = 1 Dhabu
2 Dhabu = 1 Payalo
2 Payalo = 1 Adlinao
2 Adlina = 1 Kori

NOTE: All coins through Bharmalji II bear a common type, derived from the Gujarati coinage of Muzaffar III (late 16th century AD), and bear a stylized form of the date AH978 (1570AD). The silver issues of Bharmalji II also have the fictitious date AH1165. The rulers name appears in the Devanagri script on the obverse.

NOTE: Br#'s are in reference to *Coinage of Kutch* by Richard K. Bright.

Desalji II
AH1234-1277 / VS1875-1917 / 1818-1860AD

The coins of Desalji II may be divided into four basic series, which may be differentiated as follows:

FIRST SERIES: Similar to coins of Bharmalji, but w/Desalji's name in Devanagari on reverse.

SECOND SERIES: In the name of the Mughal Emperor Akbar II and of Desalji in Devanagari on obverse, mint and both dates in Persian leg. On reverse but actual SE date in Devangari numerals. AH date is frozen (12)34, SE dates 1875-1887.

THIRD SERIES: Obv: Persian legend, rev: in Devanagari script. Dates: AH1250-1266, VS1892-1904. Many sub-varieties of type, some w/only AH dates, some w/only SE dates, some w/both. In the name of Muhammad Akbar II.

FOURTH SERIES: Same as third series, but in the name of Bahadur II. VS1909-1916 on silver and gold issues and AH1267-1274 on copper.

NOTE: Although Muhammad Akbar II was succeeded by Bahadur II on the Mughal throne in AH1253, the change is not acknowledged on Kutch coinage until AH1263 and Bahadur Shah is honored until VS1916/1859AD, the year after he was deposed by the British following the mutiny.

HAMMERED COINAGE
Fourth Series

C# 67 25 KORI
4.6800 g., 0.9990 Gold Obv. Inscription: "Bahadur Shah II"

Date	Mintage	Good	VG	F	VF	XF
VS1911	—	—	100	120	135	185
VS1912	—	—	100	120	135	185
VS1913	—	—	100	120	135	185
VS1914	—	—	100	120	135	15.00
VS1915	—	—	100	120	135	185

Pragmalji II
VS1917-1932 / 1860-1875AD

Pragmalji II is the first ruler of Kutch to pay homage to Queen Victoria. He experimented with a joint formulation his first year, VS1917/1860AD, see the rare coin type Y#A14. In VS1919/1862AD he settled on standard type acknowledging "Queen Victoria, Mighty Queen" and himself as "Rao" or "Maharao", see types Y#13, 14 and 17.

MILLED COINAGE
Regal Series

Y# 17.1 25 KORI
4.6750 g., 0.9990 Gold .1501 oz. AGW Reverse: Closed crescent

Date	Mintage	VG	F	VF	XF	Unc
1862/VS1919	—	100	120	150	185	250
1863/VS1920	—	100	120	150	185	250

Y# 17.2 25 KORI
4.6750 g., 0.9990 Gold .1501 oz. AGW Reverse: Open crescent

Date	Mintage	VG	F	VF	XF	Unc
1863/VS1921	—	—	80.00	130	170	220

Y# 17a 25 KORI
4.6750 g., 0.9990 Gold .1501 oz. AGW

Date	Mintage	VG	F	VF	XF	Unc
1870/VS1926	—	100	120	150	185	250
1870/VS1926	—	100	120	150	185	250

Y# 18 50 KORI
9.3500 g., 0.9060 Gold .2723 oz. AGW

Date	Mintage	VG	F	VF	XF	Unc
1668/VS1923 (Sic, error for 1866)	—	200	250	300	500	675
1866/VS1923	—	200	235	300	425	575
1873/VS1930	—	200	235	300	425	575
1874/VS1930	—	200	235	300	425	575
1874/VS1931	—	200	235	300	425	575

Y# 19 100 KORI
18.7000 g., 0.9060 Gold .5446 oz. AGW

Date	Mintage	VG	F	VF	XF	Unc
1866/VS1922	—	200	255	350	550	775
1866/VS1923	—	200	255	350	550	775

Madanasinghji
VS2004-2005 / 1947-1948AD
MEDALLIC COINAGE

In the last years of its coinage history, Kutch struck some non-circulating coins which state denomination. At least one was a pattern which wasn't approved for circulation strikes and the others were probably presentation pieces.

X# M4a 10 KORI
Gold

Date	Mintage	Good	VG	F	VF	XF
VS1998/1941 Rare	—					

X# M6a 10 KORI
Gold Obverse: Small bust of Khengarji III left

Date	Mintage	VG	F	VF	XF	Unc
VS1998/1942 Rare	—					

X# M7 GOLD KORI
7.3600 g., Gold Subject: Coronation of Madanasinghji

Date	Mintage	VG	F	VF	XF	Unc
VS2004/1947	—	—	—	—	550	850

X# M8 MOHUR
18.7300 g., Gold Subject: Coronation of Maharani Pritidevi
Reverse: Turreted gateway

Date	Mintage	VG	F	VF	XF	Unc
VS2004/1947	30	—	—	—	3,500	5,000

Pragmalji III & Maharani Prittdevi
VS2048- / 1991AD-
MEDALLIC COINAGE

In the last years of its coinage history, Kutch struck some non-circulating coins which state denomination. At least one was a pattern which wasn't approved for circulation strikes and the others were probably presentation pieces.

X# M9 GOLD KORI
7.3600 g., Gold Subject: Coronation of Pragmalji III and Maharani Pritidevi

Date	Mintage	VG	F	VF	XF	Unc
VS2048/1991	—	—	—	—	550	850

MANIPUR

In 1798 Jai Singh abdicated and died the following year. The next 35 years were to see five of his eight sons on the throne, plotting against each other and enlisting Burmese support for their internecine rivalry. After 1812 the Manipuri King was little more than a puppet in the hands of the Burmese, and when the Kings tried to assert their independence they were ousted to become Kings of Kachar.

In 1824, after the 1st Burma war, the Burmese were finally driven out of Manipur and Gambhir Singh, one of the younger sons of Jai Singh, asked for British assistance to regain control of his kingdom. This was granted, and from 1825 until his death in 1834 Gambhir Singh ruled well and restored an element of prosperity to his kingdom. A British resident was stationed in Manipur, but the king ruled his country independently. The British stayed aloof from several palace intrigues and revolutions, and it was only in 1891, after several British Officials had been killed, that the administration was brought under the control of a British political agent.

RULERS
Labanya Chandra, SE1720-1723/1798-1801AD
Madhu Chandra, SE1723-1728/1801-1806AD

342 INDIA - INDEPENDENT KINGDOMS

Chaurajit Singh, SE1728-1734/1806-1812AD
Marjit Singh, under Burmese suzerainty, SE1734-1741/1812-1819AD
Huidromba Subol, SE1741-1742/1819-1820AD
Gambhir Singh, SE1742-1743/1820-1821AD
Jadu Singh, SE1743-1745/1821-1823AD
Raghab Singh, SE1745-1746/1823-1824AD
Bhadra Singh, SE1746-1747/1824-1825AD
Gambhir Singh, restored by the British, SE1747-1756/1825-1834AD
Chandra Kirti, SE1756-1765/1834-1843AD
Nar Singh, SE1765-1771/1843-1849AD
Chandra Kirti, SE1771-1808/1849-1886AD
Sura Chandra Singh, SE1808-1812/1886-1890AD
Kula Chandra Singh, SE1812-1813/1890-1891AD
Chura Chandra, SE1813-1862/1891-1941AD

COINAGE

The only coins struck in quantity for circulation in Manipur were small bell-metal (circa 74 percent copper, 23 percent tin, 3 percent zinc) coins called "sel". According to local tradition these coins were first struck in the 17th century, but this is doubtful, and it seems likely that the sels were first struck in the second half of the 18th century. Unfortunately few of the sels can be attributed to any particular ruler, as they merely bear a Nagari letter deemed auspicious for the particular reign, and it has not been recorded which letter was deemed auspicious for which ruler.

The value of the sel functioned relative to the rupees, which also circulated in Manipur for making large purchases, although Government accounts were kept in sel until 1891. Prior to 1838 the sel was valued at about 900 to the rupee, but after that date it rose in value to around 480 to the rupee, although there were occasional fluctuations. About 1878, speculative hoarding of sel forced the value up to 240 to the rupee, but large numbers of sel were struck at this time, and from then until 1891, when the sel were withdrawn from circulation, their value remained fairly stable at about 400 to the rupee.

During the years after 1714AD some square gold and silver coins were struck, but as few have survived, they were probably only struck in small quantities for ceremonial rather than monetary use.

Apart from the coins mentioned above, some larger bell-metal coins have been attributed to Manipur, but the attribution is still somewhat tentative. Also, several other gold coins, two with an image of Krishna playing the flute, have been discovered in Calcutta in recent years, but as their authenticity has been queried, they have not been included in the following listing.

DATING

Most of the silver and gold coins of Manipur are dated in the Saka era (Sake date + 78 = AD date), but at least one coin is dated in the Manipuri "Chandrabda" era, which may be converted to the AD year by adding 788 to the Chandrabda date.

MONETARY SYSTEM

(Until 1838AD)
880 to 960 Sel = 1 Rupee
(Commencing 1838AD)
420-480 Sel = 1 Rupee

Chaurajit Singh
SE1728-1734 / 1806-1812AD
HAMMERED COINAGE

C# 61 MOHUR
Gold Note: Weight varies: 11.20-12.50 grams.

Date	Mintage	VG	F	VF	XF	Unc
SE1731 (1809) Rare	—	—	—	—	—	—

Marjit Singh
SE1734-1741 / 1812-1819AD
HAMMERED COINAGE

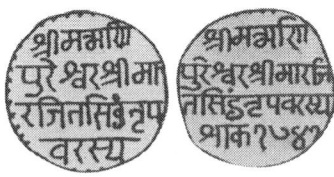

C# 75 MOHUR
Gold Obverse: Text, date Reverse: Text Note: Weight varies: 10.70-11.40 grams.

Date	Mintage	VG	F	VF	XF	Unc
SE1741 (1819) Rare	—	—	—	—	—	—

Gambhir Singh
SE1742-1743 / 1820-1821AD
HAMMERED COINAGE

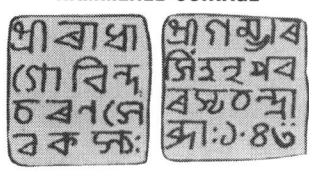

C# 85 MOHUR
Gold Obverse: Text, date Reverse: Text Note: Weight varies: 10.70-11.40 grams.

Date	Mintage	VG	F	VF	XF	Unc
CH1043 (1831) Rare	—	—	—	—	—	—

Note: Chandrabdah 1043 (a local dating system)

MARATHA CONFEDERACY

The origins of the Marathas are lost in the early history of the remote hill country of the Western Ghats in present-day Maharashtra.

PESHWAS

Shah Alam II
AH1173-1221 / 1759-1806AD
HAMMERED COINAGE

KM# 68 MOHUR
Gold Mint: Ajmer Note: Without mint mark. Weight varies: 10.70-11.40 grams.

Date	Mintage	VG	F	VF	XF	Unc
ND(1759-1806) Rare	—	—	—	—	—	—

Anonymous Ruler
HAMMERED COINAGE

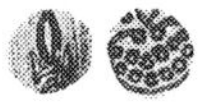

KM# 280 FANAM
0.4000 g., Gold Issuer: East India Company Mint: Tanjore

Date	Mintage	VG	F	VF	XF	Unc
ND(c.1820-30)	—	7.50	10.00	20.00	30.00	—

SIKH EMPIRE

The father of Sikhism, Guru Nanak (1469-1539), was distinguished from almost all others who founded states or empires in India by being a purely religious teacher. Deeply Indian in the basic premises, which underlay even those aspects of his theology which differed from the mainstream, he stressed the unity of God and the universal brotherhood of man. He was totally opposed to the divisions of the caste system and his teaching struggled to attain a practical balance between Hinduism and Islam. His message was a message of reconciliation, first with God, then with man. He exhibited no political ambition.

Guru Nanak was succeeded by nine other gurus of Sikhism. Together they laid the foundations of a religious community in the Punjab, which would, much later, transform itself into the Sikh Empire. Gradually this gentle religion of reconciliation became transformed into a formidable, aggressive military power. It was a metamorphosis, which was, at least partly, thrust upon the Sikh community by Mughal oppression. The fifth guru of Sikhism, Arjun, was executed in 1606 on the order of Jahangir. His successor, Hargobind, was to spend his years in constant struggle against the Mughals, first against Jahangir and later against Shah Jahan. The ninth guru, Tegh Bahadur, was executed by Aurangzeb for refusing to embrace Islam. The stage had been set for a full confrontation with Mughal authority. It was against such a background that Sikhism's tenth guru, Guru Govind Singh (1675-1708), set about organizing the Sikhs into a military power. He gave new discipline to Sikhism. Its adherents were forbidden wine and tobacco and they were required to conform to the 5 outward signs of allegiance - to keep their hair unshaven and to wear short drawers (kuchcha), a comb (kungha), an iron bangle (kara) and a dagger (kirpan).

With Govind Singh's death the Khalsa, the Sikh brotherhood, emerged as the controlling body of Sikhism and the Granth, the official compilation of Govind Singh's teaching, became the "Bible" of Sikhism. At this point the Sikhs took to the hills. It was here, constantly harassed by Mughal forces, that Sikh militarism was forged into an effective weapon and tempered by fire. Gradually the Sikhs emerged from their safe forts in the hills and made their presence felt in the plains of the Punjab. As Nadir Shah retired from Delhi laden with the prizes of war in 1739, the stragglers of his Persian army were cut down by the Sikhs. Similarly, Ahmad Shah Durrani's first intrusion into India (1747-1748) was made the more lively by Sikh sorties into his rear guard. Gradually the Sikhs became both more confident and more effective, and their quite frequent military reversals served only to strengthen their determination and to deepen their sense of identity. Their first notable success came about 1756 when the Sikhs temporarily occupied Lahore and used the Mughal mint to strike their own rupee bearing the inscription: *Coined by the grace of the Khalsa in the country of Ahmad, conquered by Jessa the Kalal.* But the Sikhs were, as yet, most effective as guerrilla bands operating out of the hill country. On Ahmad Shah's fifth expedition into India (1759-1761) the Sikhs reverted to their well-tried role of forming tight mobile units, which could choose both the time and the place of their attacks on the Durrani army. In spite of a serious reverse near Bernala in 1762 at the hands of Ahmad Shah, the Sikhs once again regrouped. In December 1763 they decisively defeated the Durrani governor of Sirhind and occupied the area.

The Sikhs now swept all before them, recapturing Lahore in 1765. The whole tract of land between the Jhelum and the Sutlej was now divided among the Sikh chieftains. At Lahore, and later at Amritsar, the Govind Shahi rupee proclaiming that Guru Govind Singh had received *Deg, Tegh and Fath* (Grace, Power and Victory) from Nanak was struck. The name of the Mughal emperor was pointedly omitted. The Sikhs now subdivided into twelve *misls* "equals", each responsible for its own fate and each conducting its own military adventures into surrounding areas. By 1792 the most prominent chief in the Punjab was Mahan Singh of the Sukerchakia *misl.* His death that same year left the boy destined to become Sikhism's best-known statesman, Ranjit Singh, as his successor. A year later Shah Zaman, King of Kabul, confirmed him as the possessor of Lahore.

For the next forty years Ranjit Singh dominated Sikh affairs. In 1802 he seized Amritsar and followed this by capturing Ludhiana (1806), Multan (1818), Kashmir (1819), Ladakh (1833) and Peshawar (1834). By the time of his death in June 1839 Ranjit was the only leader in India capable of offering a serious challenge to the East India Company.

By a treaty concluded in 1809 with the British, Ranjit had been confirmed as ruler of the tracts he had occupied south of the Sutlej, but the agreement had restricted him from seeking any further expansion to the north or west of the river. In spite of the terms of the treaty, the British remained suspicious of Ranjit's ultimate intentions. His steady policy of expansion frequently left apprehensions in the minds of the British - with whose interests Ranjit's own often clashed - that the Sikhs had secret ambitions against Company controlled territory. But it was to Ranjit's credit that he welded the Sikhs of the Punjab into an effective and unified fighting force, capable of resisting both the Afghans and the Marathas and able to stand up to British pressures. He inherited a loose alliance of fiercely independent chiefs, he left a disciplined and well equipped army of over fifty thousand men. He also left a well consolidated regional empire in the extreme northwest of India, roughly extending over the northern half of present-day Pakistan.

After the death of Ranjit the Sikh empire began to disintegrate as power passed from chief to chief in murderous rivalry. At the same time relationships with the British began to deteriorate. The treaty of 1809 no longer proved able to hold the peace, and the Sikh army attacked the British (1845-1846) only to be badly beaten in a series of confrontations. The Treaty of Lahore, which followed this first Anglo-Sikh war reduced the Sikh army to a maximum of twenty thousand men and twelve thousand cavalry. It obliged the Sikhs to cede the Jallandar Doab and Kashmir to the British, and required them to pay an indemnity of fifty thousand pounds and accept a British resident at their court. In 1848 the Sikhs again revolted, and were again crushed. In 1849 the Punjab was annexed and from that time onward they came under British rule.

RULERS
Ranjit Singh, VS1856-1896/1799-1839AD
Kharak Singh, VS1896-1897/1839-1840AD
Sher Singh, VS1897-1900/1840-1843AD
Dulip Singh, VS1900-1906/1843-1849AD

MINTS

Amritsar
(Ambratsar)

امرت سر

Lahore

لاهور

Multan

ملتان

NOTE: Most coins struck after the accession of Ranjit Singh bear a large leaf on one side, and have Persian or Gurmukhi (Punjabi) legends in the name of Gobind Singh, the tenth and last Guru of the Sikhs, 1675-1708AD. Earlier pieces are similar, but lack the leaf, except the Amritsar Mint where the leaf is present since VS1845.

There is a great variety of coppers, and only representative types are catalogued here; many crude pieces were struck at the official and at unofficial mints, and bear illegible or semi-literate inscriptions. None of the coins bear the name of the Sikh ruler.

HAMMERED COINAGE

TRIPURA — INDIA - INDEPENDENT KINGDOMS

KM# 87 GOLD RUPEE
0.5700 g., Gold **Obverse:** Text **Reverse:** Leaf **Mint:** Multan
Note: Varieties with plain and reeded edge exist.

Date	Mintage	VG	F	VF	XF	Unc
VS1905 (1848)	—	60.00	100	200	350	—

Note: Struck by Diwan Mulraj (April 1848 - Jan. 1849/VS1905)

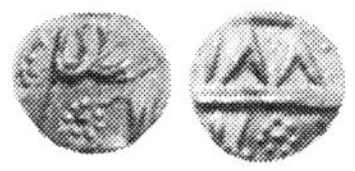

KM# A87 1/5 MOHUR
2.2100 g., Gold **Obverse:** Beaded flower **Reverse:** Beaded flower, date **Mint:** Lahore

Date	Mintage	VG	F	VF	XF	Unc
VS1885 (1828) Rare	—	—	—	—	—	—
VS1896/85 (1839) Rare	—	—	—	—	—	—

KM# 23 1/4 MOHUR
Gold **Mint:** Amritsar

Date	Mintage	VG	F	VF	XF	Unc
VS(18)95 (1838) Rare	—	—	—	—	—	—
VS(18)97 (1840) Rare	—	—	—	—	—	—

KM# 24 1/2 MOHUR
Gold **Obverse:** 5-petal flower **Reverse:** Leaf at far left **Mint:** Amritsar

Date	Mintage	VG	F	VF	XF	Unc
VS1877 (1820) Rare	—	—	—	—	—	—

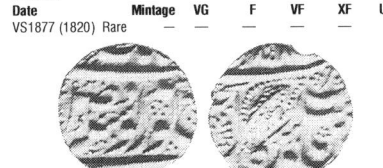

KM# 25.1 MOHUR
10.7600 g., Gold, 21 mm. **Obverse:** Beaded flower **Reverse:** Dotted leaf **Mint:** Amritsar

Date	Mintage	VG	F	VF	XF	Unc
VS1858 (1801)	—	1,000	2,000	4,000	5,000	—

KM# 25.2 MOHUR
10.7400 g., Gold **Obverse:** Fish at lower left **Reverse:** Leaf **Mint:** Amritsar

Date	Mintage	VG	F	VF	XF	Unc
VS1861 (1804) Rare	—	—	—	—	—	—

KM# 25.3 MOHUR
10.6900 g., Gold **Obverse:** Rosette of seven dots **Reverse:** Leaf **Mint:** Amritsar

Date	Mintage	VG	F	VF	XF	Unc
VS1863 (1806) Rare	—	—	—	—	—	—
VS1864 (1807) Rare	—	—	—	—	—	—
VS1882 (1825) Rare	—	—	—	—	—	—

KM# 26.1 MOHUR
Gold **Obverse:** Branches with berries **Mint:** Amritsar **Note:** "Mora" type. Similar to 1 Rupee, KM#20.

Date	Mintage	VG	F	VF	XF	Unc
VS1862 (1805) Rare	—	—	—	—	—	—

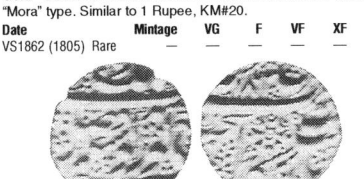

KM# 26.2 MOHUR
10.7500 g., Gold **Obverse:** Text, beaded flowers **Reverse:** Symbol said to be mirror **Mint:** Amritsar **Note:** The "Arisi" Mohur.

Date	Mintage	VG	F	VF	XF	Unc
VS1862 (1805) Rare	—	—	—	—	—	—
VS1863 (1806) Rare	—	—	—	—	—	—

KM# 87A MOHUR
10.8500 g., Gold **Mint:** Multan

Date	Mintage	VG	F	VF	XF	Unc
VS1876 (1815) Rare	—	—	—	—	—	—

KM# 69 MOHUR
10.8500 g., Gold **Mint:** Lahore

Date	Mintage	VG	F	VF	XF	Unc
VS1884 (1827) Rare	—	—	—	—	—	—
VS1892/84 (1835) Rare	—	—	—	—	—	—

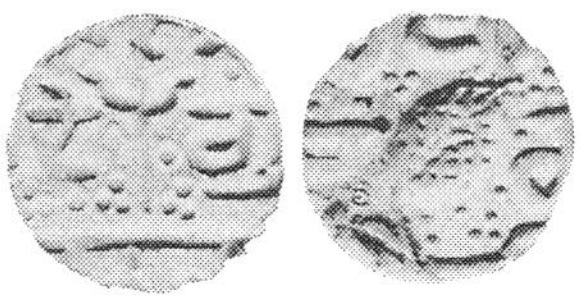

KM# 28A MOHUR
9.7200 g., Gold **Obverse:** Gurmakhi text, trident **Reverse:** Gurmakhi text, leaf **Mint:** Amritsar

Date	Mintage	VG	F	VF	XF	Unc
ND (1828) Rare	—	—	—	—	—	—

Note: Struck from the dies for the copper 1 Paisa KM7.5; Similar Double Paise shows date VS1885 (1828)

KM# 27 MOHUR
10.7300 g., Gold **Obverse:** Beaded flower **Reverse:** Without leaf symbol **Mint:** Amritsar

Date	Mintage	VG	F	VF	XF	Unc
VS(18)88 (1831) Rare	—	—	—	—	—	—
VS1901 (1844) Rare	—	—	—	—	—	—

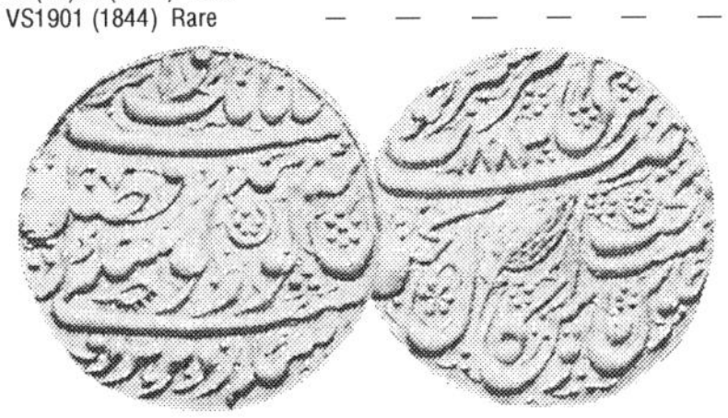

KM# 29A DOUBLE MOHUR
21.1600 g., Gold **Obverse:** Text, beaded flowers **Reverse:** Leaf, beaded flowers **Mint:** Amritsar

Date	Mintage	VG	F	VF	XF	Unc
VS1883 (1826) Rare	—	—	—	—	—	—

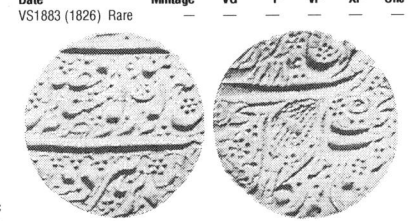

KM# 29B DOUBLE MOHUR
23.8900 g., Gold **Obverse:** Partial actual date, beaded flowers **Reverse:** Dated: VS1884, leaf, beaded flowers **Mint:** Amritsar

Date	Mintage	VG	F	VF	XF	Unc
VS(18)85 (1828) Rare	—	—	—	—	—	—

TOKEN COINAGE

KM# Tn1 MOHUR
Gold **Obverse:** Gurmukhi text **Reverse:** Gurmukhi text **Mint:** Uncertain Mint **Note:** Weight varies: 10.74-10.82 grams.

Date	Mintage	Good	VG	F	VF	XF
ND(1835-50) Rare	—	—	—	—	—	—

TRIPURA

Hill Tipperah

Tripura was a Hindu Kingdom consisting of a strip of the fertile plains east of Bengal, and a large tract of hill territory beyond, which had a reputation for providing wild elephants.

At times when Bengal was weak, Tripura rose to prominence and extended its rule into the plains, but when Bengal was strong the kingdom consisted purely of the hill area, which was virtually impregnable and not of enough economic worth to encourage the Muslims to conquer it. In this way Tripura was able to maintain its full independence until the 19th century.

The origins of the Kingdom are veiled in legend, but the first coins were struck during the reign of Ratna Manikya (1464-89) and copied the weight and fabric of the contemporary issues of the Sultans of Bengal. He also copied the lion design that had appeared on certain rare tangkas of Nasir-ud-din Mahmud Shah I dated AH849 (1445AD). In other respects the designs were purely Hindu, and the lion was retained on most of the later issues as a national emblem.

Tripura rose to a political zenith during the 16th century, while Muslim rule in Bengal was weak, and several coins were struck to commemorate successful military campaigns from Chittagong in the south to Sylhet in the north. These conquests were not sustained, and in the early 17th century the Mughal army was able to inflict severe defeats on Tripura, which was forced to pay tribute.

In about 1733AD all the territory in the plains was annexed by the Mughals, and the Raja merely managed his estate there as a zemindar, although he still retained control as independent King of his hill territory.

The situation remained unchanged when the British took over the administration of Bengal in 1765, and it was only in 1871 that the British appointed an agent in the hills, and began to assist the Maharaja in the administration of his hill territory, which became known as the State of Hill Tipperah.

After the middle of the 18th century, coins were not struck for monetary reasons, but merely for ceremonial use at coronations and other ceremonies, and to keep up the treasured right of coinage.

The coins of Tripura are unusual in that the majority have the name of the King together with that of his Queen, and is the only coinage in the world where this was done consistently.

In common with most other Hindu coinages of northeast India, the coins bear fixed dates. Usually the date used was that of the coronation ceremony, but during the 16th century, coins which were struck with a design commemorating a particular event, bore the date of that event, which can be useful as a historical source, where other written evidence is virtually non-existent.

All modern Tripura coins were presentation pieces, more medallic than monetary in nature. They were struck in very limited numbers and although not intended for local circulation as money, they are often encountered in worn condition.

RULERS

Rajadhara Manikya
SE1707-26/1785-1804AD

Rama Ganga Manikya

রাম গঙ্গা মানিক্য

SE1728-1731, 1735-1748/
1806-1809, 1813-1826AD
Queens of Rama Ganga Manikya
Queen Tara
Queen Chandra Tara

চন্দ্র তরা

Durga Manikya

দুর্গা মানিক্য

SE17311735/1809-1813AD
Queen of Durga Manikya
Queen Sumitra

সুমিত্রা

Kashi Chandra Manikya
SE1748-1752/1826-1830AD
Queens of Kashi Chandra Manikya
Queen Chandrarekha
Queen Kirti Lakshmi

Krishna Kishore Manikya SE1752-1772/1830-1850AD

কৃষ্ণ কিশোর মানিক্য

Queens of Krishna Kishore
Queen Akhilesvari
Queen Bidhukala
Queen Bidumukhi
Queen Ratna Mala

রত্ন মালা

Queen Purnakala
Queen Sudhakshina

Ishana Chandra Manikya
SE1772-1784/1850-1862AD
Queens of Ishana Chandra Manikya
Queen Chandresvari
Queen Muktabali
Queen Rajalakshmi

INDIA - INDEPENDENT KINGDOMS

TRIPURA

Vira Chandra Manikya

বীর চন্দ্র মানিক্য

SE1784-1818/TE1272-1306/1862-96AD
Queens of Vira Chandra Manikya
Queen Bhanumati

ভানুমতী

Queen Rajesvari

রাজেশ্বরী

Queen Manmohinia

Radha Kishore Manikya
TE1306-1319/1896-1909AD
Queens of Radha Kishore
Queen Ratnamanjari
Queen Tulsivati

DATING
While the early coinage is dated in the Saka Era (SE) the later issues are dated in the Tripurabda era (TE). To convert, TE date plus 590 = AD date. The dates appear to be accession years.

Durga Manikya
SE1731-1735 / 1809-1813AD
HAMMERED COINAGE

KM# 280 MOHUR
10.9400 g., Gold **Obverse:** Lion, trident within circle **Reverse:** Inscription

Date	Mintage	VG	F	VF	XF	Unc
SE1731 (1809)	—	700	1,000	1,500	2,000	—

Rama Ganga Manikya
SE1735-1748 / 1813-1826AD
HAMMERED COINAGE

KM# 295 MOHUR
Gold **Obverse:** Lion, trident within circle **Reverse:** Inscription

Date	Mintage	VG	F	VF	XF	Unc
SE1743 (1821)	—	700	1,000	1,500	2,000	—

Kashi Chandra Manikya
SE1748-1752 / 1826-1830AD
HAMMERED COINAGE

KM# 308 MOHUR
Gold **Obverse:** Lion, trident within circle **Reverse:** Inscription **Rev. Legend:** With *Queen Kirti Lakshmi*

Date	Mintage	VG	F	VF	XF	Unc
SE1748 (1826)	—	700	1,000	1,500	2,000	—

Krishna Kishora Manikya
SE1752-1772 / 1830-1850AD
HAMMERED COINAGE

KM# 323 MOHUR
11.5900 g., Gold **Obverse:** Lion, trident within circle **Reverse:** Inscription **Rev. Legend:** With *Queen Akhilesvari*

Date	Mintage	VG	F	VF	XF	Unc
SE1752 (1830)	—	700	1,000	1,500	2,000	—

KM# 324 MOHUR
11.5900 g., Gold **Obverse:** Lion, trident within circle **Reverse:** Inscription **Rev. Legend:** With *Sri Srimati Ratna Mala Maha Deva*

Date	Mintage	VG	F	VF	XF	Unc
SE1752 (1830)	—	500	700	1,300	1,800	—

KM# 325 MOHUR
11.5900 g., Gold **Obverse:** Lion, trident within circle **Reverse:** Inscription **Rev. Legend:** With *Queen Sudakshina* added

Date	Mintage	VG	F	VF	XF	Unc
SE1752 (1830)	—	700	1,000	1,500	2,000	—

Ishana Chandra Manikya
SE1772-1784 / 1850-1862AD
HAMMERED COINAGE

KM# 342 MOHUR
Gold **Obverse:** Lion, trident within circle **Reverse:** Inscription **Rev. Legend:** With *Queen Chandresvari*

Date	Mintage	VG	F	VF	XF	Unc
SE1771 (1849)	—	500	700	1,300	1,800	—

KM# 343 MOHUR
Gold **Rev. Legend:** With *Queen Muktavali*

Date	Mintage	VG	F	VF	XF	Unc
SE1771 (1849)	—	700	1,000	1,500	2,000	—

KM# 344 MOHUR
Gold **Rev. Legend:** With *Queen Raja Lakshmi*

Date	Mintage	VG	F	VF	XF	Unc
SE1771 (1849)	—	700	1,000	1,500	2,000	—

KM# 360 MOHUR
10.6400 g., Gold **Obverse:** Lion, trident within circle **Reverse:** Inscription **Note:** Similar to 1 Rupee, KM#354.

Date	Mintage	VG	F	VF	XF	Unc
SE1791 (1869)	—	500	700	1,300	1,800	—

KM# 363 MOHUR
Gold **Obverse:** Crossed flags above arms with supporters, within circle **Reverse:** Inscription **Edge:** Milled **Note:** Similar to 1 Rupee, KM#356.

Date	Mintage	Good	VG	F	VF	XF
TE1279 (1869)	—	—	500	700	1,300	1,800

KM# 364 MOHUR
Gold **Obverse:** Lion, trident within circle **Reverse:** Inscription **Rev. Legend:** With *Srimati Rajesvari Maha Devi* **Note:** Similar to 1 Rupee, KM#357.

Date	Mintage	VG	F	VF	XF	Unc
SE1791 (1869)	—	500	700	1,300	1,800	—

Radha Kishore Manikya
TE1306-1319 / 1896-1909AD
HAMMERED COINAGE

KM# 381 MOHUR
Gold **Reverse:** Inscription **Rev. Legend:** With *Queen Ratna Manjari* **Edge:** Milled

Date	Mintage	VG	F	VF	XF	Unc
TE1306 (1896)	—	700	1,000	1,500	2,000	—

Virendra Kishore Manikya
TE1319-1333 / 1909-1923AD
MEDALLIC COINAGE

X# 5 MOHUR
11.5000 g., Gold **Rev. Legend:** With "Queen Prabhavati" **Edge:** Milled **Note:** Prev. KM#396.

Date	Mintage	VG	F	VF	XF	Unc
TE1319(1909) Rare	—	—	—	1,000	1,250	1,500

X# 6 MOHUR
Gold **Rev. Legend:** With "Queen Jivankumari Devi" **Edge:** Milled **Note:** Prev. KM#397.

Date	Mintage	Good	VG	F	VF	XF
TE1319 (1909) Rare	—	—	—	—	1,000	1,250

Vira Vikrama Kishore Manikya
TE1333-1357 / 1923-1947AD
MEDALLIC COINAGE

X# 10 MOHUR
11.5000 g., Gold **Obverse:** Rampant lion left **Rev. Legend:** With "Sri Srimati Maharani Kanchan Prabha Maha Devi" **Edge:** Milled **Note:** Prev. KM#412.

Date	Mintage	VG	F	VF	XF	Unc
TE1341 (1934)	—	—	—	—	1,200	1,800

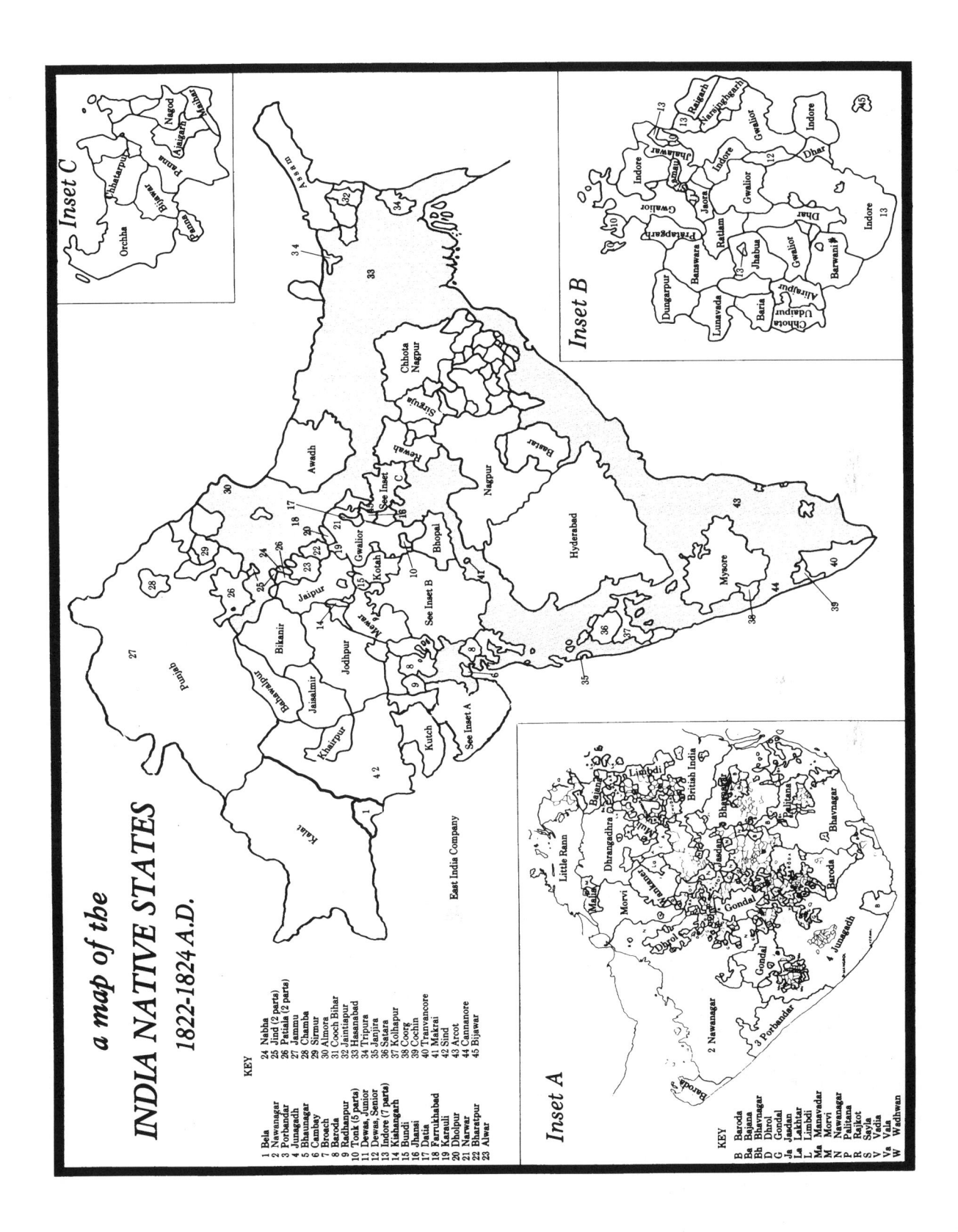

INDIA - PRINCELY STATES

a map of the INDIA NATIVE STATES 1822-1824 A.D.

KEY

1. Bela
2. Nawanagar
3. Porbandar
4. Junagedh
5. Bhaunagar
6. Cambay
7. Broach
8. Baroda
9. Radhanpur
10. Tonk (5 parts)
11. Dewas, Junior
12. Dewas, Senior
13. Indore (7 parts)
14. Kishangarh
15. Bundi
16. Jhansi
17. Datia
18. Farrukhabad
19. Karauli
20. Dholpur
21. Narwar
22. Bharatpur
23. Alwar
24. Nabha
25. Jind (2 parts)
26. Patiala (2 parts)
27. Jammu
28. Chamba
29. Sirmur
30. Almora
31. Cooch Bihar
32. Jaintiapur
33. Hasanabad
34. Tripura
35. Janjira
36. Satara
37. Kolhapur
38. Coorg
39. Cochin
40. Tranvancore
41. Makrai
42. Sind
43. Arcot
44. Cannanore
45. Bijawar

Inset A

KEY

- B — Baroda
- Ba — Bajana
- Bb — Bhavnagar
- D — Dhrol
- G — Gondal
- Ja — Jasdan
- L — Lakhtar
- Li — Limbdi
- Ma — Manavadar
- M — Morvi
- N — Nawanagar
- P — Palitana
- R — Rajkot
- S — Sayla
- V — Vala
- Va — Vadia
- W — Wadhwan

INDIA - PRINCELY STATES

MONETARY SYSTEMS

In each state, local rates of exchange prevailed. There was no fixed rate between copper, silver or gold coin, but the rates varied in accordance with the values of the metal and by the edict of the local authority.

Within the subcontinent, different regions used distinctive coinage standards. In North India and the Deccan, the silver rupee (11.6 g) and gold mohur (11.0 g) predominated. In Gujarat, the silver kori (4.7 g) and gold kori (6.4 g) were the main currency. In South India the silver fanam (0.7-1.0 g) and gold hun or Pagoda (3.4 g) were current. Copper coins in all parts of India were produced to a myriad of local metrologies with seemingly endless varieties.

NAZARANA ISSUES

Throughout the Indian Princely States listings are Nazarana designations for special full flan strikings of copper, silver and some gold coinage. The purpose of these issues was for presentation to the local monarch to gain favor. For example if one had an audience with one's ruler he would exchange goods, currency notes or the cruder struck circulating coinage for Nazarana pieces which he would present to the ruler as a gift. The borderline between true Nazarana pieces and well struck regular issues is often indistinct. The Nazaranas sometimes circulated alongside the cruder "dump" issues.

PRICING

As the demand for Indian Princely coinage develops, and more dealers handle the material, sale records and price lists enable a firmer basis for pricing most series. For scarcer types adequate sale records are often not available, and prices must be regarded as tentative. Inasmuch as date collectors of Princely States series are few, dates known to be scarce are usually worth little more than common ones. Coins of a dated type, which do not show the full date on their flans should be valued at about 70 per cent of the prices indicated.

DATING

Coins are dated in several eras. Arabic and Devanagari numerals are used in conjunction with the Hejira era (AH), the Vikrama Samvat (VS), Saka Samvat (Saka), Fasli era(FE) Mauludi era (AM), and Malabar era (ME), as well as the Christian era (AD).

GRADING

Copper coins are rarely found in high grade, as they were the workhorse of coinage circulation, and were everywhere used for day-to-day transactions. Moreover, they were carelessly struck and even when 'new', can often only be distinguished from VF coins with difficulty, if at all.

Silver coins were often hoarded and not infrequently, turn up in nearly as-struck condition. The silver coins of Hyderabad (dump coins) are common in high grades, and the rupees of some states are scarcer 'used' than 'new'. Great caution must be exercised in determining the value or scarcity of high grade dump coins.

Dump gold was rarely circulated, and usually occurs in high grades, or is found made into jewelry.

INDEX

ALWAR
Rajgarh
ARCOT
AWADH
Lucknow
Najibabad
BAHAWALPUR
Bahawalpur
BAJRANGGARH
See also Gwalior
BANSWARA
BARODA
Amreli
BHARATPUR
Bharatpur
Dig
BIKANIR
BUNDI
COOCH BEHAR
DATIA
Dalipnagar
DHAR
DUNGURPUR
Faridkot – Cis-Sutlej States
GARHWAL
GWALIOR
Bajranggarh
Burhanpur
Gwalior Fort
Lashkar
HYDERABAD
Hyderabad (Farkhanda Bunyad)
INDORE
Indore

JAISALMIR
JANJIRA ISLAND
JODHPUR (Marwar)
Jodhpur
JUNAGADH
KAITHAL
KARAULI
KASHMIR
Jammu
Srinagar
KISHANGARH
KOTAH
MALER kOTLA
MEWAR
Bhilwara
Chitarkot
Udaipur
MEWAR FEUDATORIES
Shahpura
MYSORE
Nabha – Cis-Sutlej States
NAWANAGAR
Patiala – Cis-Sutlej States
RADHANPUR
RAJKOT
REWA
TONK
Tonk
TRAVANCORE

ALWAR

State located in Rajputana in northwestern India.

Alwar was founded about 1722 by a Rajput chieftain of the Naruka clan, Rao Pratap Singh of Macheri (1740-1791), a descendant of the family, which had ruled Jaipur in the 14th century. Alwar was distinguished by being the first of the Princely States to use coins struck at the Calcutta Mint. These, first issued in 1877, were of the same weight and assay as the Imperial Rupee, and carried the bust of Queen Victoria, Empress of India. Alwar State, having allied itself with East India Company interests in their struggles against the Marathas early in the 19th century, continued to maintain a good relationship with the British right up to Indian Independence in 1947. In May 1949, Alwar was merged into Rajasthan.

LOCAL RULERS
Bakhtawar Singh, AH1206-1230/1791-1815AD
Bani Singh, AH1231-1273/1815-1857AD
Sheodan Singh, AH1274-1291/1857-1874AD
Mangal Singh, AH1291-1310/1874-1892

MINT

راج گڑہ

Rajgarh

ROYAL MARK

Parasol

MINT MARKS

Jhar

Fish

Mangal Singh
AH1291-1310 / 1874-1892AD
MILLED COINAGE

KM# 46a RUPEE
Gold **Obverse:** Crowned bust of left **Obv. Legend:** VICTORIA EMPRESS **Reverse:** Inscription, date within circle **Rev. Inscription:** "Maharaja Shri Sawai Mangal Singh" **Mint:** Rajgarh

Date	Mintage	Good	VG	F	VF	XF
1891	—	Value: 2,000				

AWADH

Oudh

Kingdom located in northeastern India. The Nawabs of Awadh traced their origins to Muhammed Amin, a Persian adventurer who had attached himself to the court of Muhammed Shah, the Mughal Emperor, early in the 18th century. In 1720 Muhammed Amin was appointed Mughal Subahdar of Awadh, in which capacity he soon exhibited a considerable measure of independence. Until 1819, after Ghazi-ud-din had been encouraged by the Governor-General, Lord Hastings, to accept the title of King, Muhammed Amim's successors were known simply as the Nawabs of Awadh. The British offer, and Ghazi-ud-din's acceptance of it provided a clear indication of just how far Mughal decline had proceeded. The Mughal Emperor was now little more than a pensioner of the East India Company. Yet the coinage of Ghazi-ud-din immediately after 1819 marks also the hesitation he felt in taking so dramatic, and in the eyes of some of the princes of India, so ungrateful a step.

In 1856 Awadh was annexed by the British on the grounds of internal misrule. The king makers were now also seen as the king breakers. In setting aside the royal house of Awadh, the Muslim princes of India were added to that growing list of those who had come to fear the outcome of British hegemony. And it was here, in Awadh, that the Great Revolt of 1857 found its most fertile soil.

In 1877, Awadh along with Agra was placed under one administrator. It was made part of the United Provinces in 1902.

RULERS
SSa'adat Ali, AH1213-1230/1798-1814AD
Ghazi-ud-Din Haidar,
 as Nawab, AH1230-1234/1814-1819AD
 as King, AH1234-1243/1819-1827AD
Nasir-ud-Din Haidar, AH1243-1253/1827-1837AD
Muhammad Ali Shah, AH1253-1258/1837-1842AD
Amjad Ali Shah, AH1258-1263/1842-1847AD
Wajid Ali Shah, AH1263-1272/1847-1856AD
Brijis Qadr, AH1273-1274/1857-1858AD

MINTS

اودہ

Awadh

بنارس

Banaras
 Under Awadh until AH1189/R.Y. 16/1775AD.
Mintname: Muhammadabad Banaras

لکھنو

Lucknow
 Mintname: Muhammadabad Banaras
The issues of the Nawab-Wazir in this mintname are distinguished from East India Company issues on the basis of distinctive fabric and fixed regnal year: 26 for Awadh, 17 for East India Company.

محمدآباد بنارس

Muhammadabad Banaras

AWADH

نجیب‌اباد

Najibabad

To Awadh in 1774AD (AH1188). For issues before AH1188/R.Y. 15, see Rohilkhand.

INDEPENDENT KINGS

Ghazi-Ud-Din Haidar

NOTE: Coins dated AH1234 have regnal year 5 for Haidar as Nawab; coins dated AH1235 and later have his regnal year as king AH1235/R.Y. 1.

NOTE: The mintname comes with 2 different epithets:
VARIETY I: AH1234-1235; *Dar ul-Amaret Lakhnau Suba Awadh*
VARIETY II: AH1236-1243 *Dar us-Sultanat Lakhnau Suba Awadh*

Nasir-Ud-Din Haidar

NOTE: This series comes in 2 major varieties, the difference being in the coat of arms and position of regnal years.
VARIETY I: Katar (knife) aabove and regnal year between fish
VARIETY II: Katar between fish and regnal year now in marginal inscription

Muhammad Ali Shah

NOTE: Mintname comes in 3 varieties.
VARIETY AIII. *Suba Awadh Dar-as-Sultanat Lakhnau* on coins dated AH1253/Yr. 3.
VARIETY IV. *Mulk Awadh Baitu-s-Sultanat Lakhnau* on all coins beginning with date AH1256/Yr. 3.

Wajid Ali Shah

NOTE: Wajid Alis coins come in 3 varieties, depending on form of mintname:
VARIETY IV: *Mulk Awadh Baitu-s-Sultanat Lakhnau*, AH1263-1267/Yr. 4.
VARIETY V: *Mulk Awadh Akhtarnagar*, AH1267/5 reported so far only for Rupees dated 1267/Yr. 5. The same date/year combination is also found in Var. VI.
VARIETY VI: *Baitus-s-Sultanat Lakhnau Mulk Awadh Akhtar-Nagar*, Variety IV/Yr. 5-1272.

Brijis Qadr

Nawab-Wazir during the Indian Mutiny

KINGDOM

HAMMERED COINAGE

Mughal Style

KM# B105 1/4 MOHUR
Gold **Obverse:** Inscription **Obv. Inscription:** "Shah Alam II"
Reverse: Inscription **Mint:** Lucknow **Note:** Weight varies: 2.67-2.85 grams.

Date	Mintage	VG	F	VF	XF	Unc
AH–//26	—	325	550	850	1,200	—

KM# A105 1/2 MOHUR
Gold **Obverse:** Inscription, date, star **Obv. Inscription:** "Shah Alam II" **Reverse:** Frozen regnal year **Mint:** Lucknow **Note:** Weight varies: 5.35-5.70 grams.

Date	Mintage	VG	F	VF	XF	Unc
AH1224//26	—	300	500	800	1,150	—

KM# 105 MOHUR
Gold **Obverse:** Inscription, star, date **Obv. Inscription:** "Shah Alam II" **Reverse:** Frozen regnal year **Mint:** Lucknow **Note:** Weight varies: 10.70-11.40 grams.

Date	Mintage	VG	F	VF	XF	Unc
AH1218//26	—	225	250	275	350	—
AH1222//26	—	225	250	275	350	—
AH1230//26	—	225	250	275	350	—
AH1231//26	—	225	250	275	350	—

Ghazi-ud-Din Haidar, as King
AH1234-1243 / 1819-1827AD
HAMMERED COINAGE

KM# 148 1/2 MOHUR
Gold **Obv. Inscription:** "Ghazi-ud-din Haidar" **Mint:** Lucknow **Note:** Weight varies: 5.35-5.70 grams.

Date	Mintage	VG	F	VF	XF	Unc
AH1234//26	—	200	300	500	700	—

KM# 150 MOHUR
Gold **Obverse:** Inscription, date **Obv. Inscription:** "Ghazi-ud-din Haidar" **Reverse:** Crown flanked by rampant lions holding flag, two upright fish below **Mint:** Lucknow **Note:** Weight varies: 10.70-11.40 grams.

Date	Mintage	VG	F	VF	XF	Unc
AH1234//26	—	225	250	295	375	—

KM# 168 1/4 ASHRAFI
Gold **Obv. Inscription:** "Ghazi-ud-din Haidar" **Mint:** Lucknow **Note:** Weight varies: 2.68-2.85 grams.

Date	Mintage	VG	F	VF	XF	Unc
AH1236//-	—	150	275	400	550	—
AH1243//-	—	150	275	400	550	—

KM# 170.1 ASHRAFI
Gold **Obverse:** Inscription, date **Obv. Inscription:** "Ghazi-ud-din Haidar" **Reverse:** Crown flanked by rampant lions holding flag, two upright fish below **Mint:** Lucknow **Note:** Epithet: Variety I. Weight varies: 10.70-11.40 grams.

Date	Mintage	VG	F	VF	XF	Unc
AH1234//5	—	250	285	325	425	—
AH1235//						

KM# 170.2 ASHRAFI
Gold **Obverse:** Inscription **Obv. Inscription:** "Ghazi-ud-din Haidar" **Reverse:** Crown flanked by rampant lions holding flag, two upright fish below **Mint:** Lucknow **Note:** Epithet: II. Weight varies: 10.70-11.40 grams.

Date	Mintage	VG	F	VF	XF	Unc
AH1235//(1) Ahad	—	250	285	325	425	—
AH1236//1	—	250	285	325	425	—
AH1236//2	—	250	285	325	425	—
AH1238//4	—	250	285	325	425	—
AH1239//5	—	250	285	325	425	—
AH1240//6	—	250	285	325	425	—
AH1241//7	—	250	285	325	425	—
AH1242//8	—	250	285	325	425	—

Nasir-ud-Din Haidar
AH1243-1253 / 1827-1837AD
HAMMERED COINAGE

KM# 189 1/2 ASHRAFI
Gold **Obv. Inscription:** Sulayman Jah **Mint:** Lucknow **Note:** Weight varies: 5.35 - 5.7 grams.

Date	Mintage	Good	VG	F	VF	XF
AH1243//1						

KM# 235 1/2 ASHRAFI
Gold **Obverse:** Inscription **Obv. Inscription:** Nasir-ud-Din Haidar **Reverse:** Crown flanked by rampant lions holding flag, two upright fish below **Mint:** Lucknow **Note:** Weight varies: 5.35-5.70 grams.

Date	Mintage	VG	F	VF	XF	Unc
AH1251//9	—	150	275	400	550	—

KM# 190 ASHRAFI
Gold **Obverse:** Inscription **Obv. Inscription:** Sulayman Jah **Reverse:** Crown flanked by rampant lions holding flag, two upright fish below **Mint:** Lucknow **Note:** Weight varies: 10.70-11.40 grams.

Date	Mintage	Good	VG	F	VF	XF
AH1243//1	—	—	225	235	325	450
AH1244//2	—	—	225	235	325	450

KM# 240 ASHRAFI
Gold, 25 mm. **Obverse:** Inscription **Obv. Inscription:** Nasir-ud-Din Haidar **Reverse:** Crown flanked by rampant lions holding flag, two upright fish below **Mint:** Lucknow **Note:** Weight varies: 10.70-11.40 grams. Mint mark: Variety I.

Date	Mintage	VG	F	VF	XF	Unc
AH1245//3	—	185	235	300	400	—
AH1246//3	—	185	235	300	400	—
AH1252//9	—	185	235	300	400	—

Muhammad Ali Shah
AH1253-1258 / 1837-1842AD
HAMMERED COINAGE

KM# 320 1/2 ASHRAFI
Gold **Obverse:** Inscription, date **Obv. Inscription:** Muhammad Ali Shah **Reverse:** Crown and fish flanked by people **Mint:** Lucknow **Note:** Weight varies: 5.35-5.70 grams.

Date	Mintage	VG	F	VF	XF	Unc
AH1253//1	—	175	285	400	550	—

KM# 322.1 ASHRAFI
Gold **Obverse:** Inscription **Obv. Inscription:** Muhammad Ali Shah **Reverse:** Crown and fish flanked by people **Mint:** Lucknow **Note:** Weight varies: 10.70-11.40 grams. Epithet: Variety III.

Date	Mintage	VG	F	VF	XF	Unc
AH1253//1	—	BV	BV	275	375	—
AH1255//3	—	BV	BV	275	375	—
AH1256//3	—	BV	BV	275	375	—

KM# 322.2 ASHRAFI
Gold **Obv. Inscription:** Muhammad Ali Shah **Mint:** Lucknow **Note:** Weight varies: 10.70-11.40 grams. Epithet: Variety IV.

Date	Mintage	VG	F	VF	XF	Unc
AH1258	—	135	225	275	375	—

Amjad Ali Shah
AH1258-1263 / 1842-1847AD
HAMMERED COINAGE

KM# 339 1/4 ASHRAFI
Gold **Obverse:** Inscription, date **Obv. Inscription:** Amjad Ali Shah **Reverse:** Parasol above crown and fish, flanked by curved swords **Mint:** Lucknow **Note:** Weight varies: 2.37-2.85 grams.

Date	Mintage	VG	F	VF	XF	Unc
AH1260	—	175	300	400	550	—

INDIA - PRINCELY STATES

AWADH

KM# 340 1/2 ASHRAFI
Gold **Obverse:** Inscription, date **Obv. Inscription:** Amjad Ali Shah **Reverse:** Parasol above crown and fish, flanked by curved swords **Mint:** Lucknow **Note:** Weight varies: 5.35-5.70 grams.

Date	Mintage	VG	F	VF	XF	Unc
AH1258	—	200	325	500	650	—
AH1259//2	—	200	325	500	650	—
AH1263	—	200	325	500	650	—

KM# 342 ASHRAFI
Gold **Obverse:** Inscription, date **Obv. Inscription:** Amjad Ali Shah **Reverse:** Parasol above crown and fish, flanked by curved swords **Mint:** Lucknow **Note:** Weight varies: 10.70-11.40 grams.

Date	Mintage	VG	F	VF	XF	Unc
AH1258	—	BV	BV	275	365	—
AH1259//2	—	BV	BV	275	365	—
AH1260//3	—	BV	BV	275	365	—
AH1260//3	—	BV	BV	275	365	—
AH1261//4	—	BV	BV	275	365	—
AH1262//5	—	BV	BV	275	365	—
AH1263	—	BV	BV	275	365	—

Wajid Ali Shah
AH1263-1272 / 1847-1856AD

HAMMERED COINAGE

KM# 370 1/16 ASHRAFI
Gold, 10 mm. **Obv. Inscription:** Wajid Ali Shah **Mint:** Lucknow **Note:** Weight varies: 0.67-0.71 grams.

Date	Mintage	VG	F	VF	XF	Unc
AH1270	—	100	175	250	350	—

KM# 372 1/8 ASHRAFI
Gold **Obv. Inscription:** Wajid Ali Shah **Mint:** Lucknow **Note:** Weight varies: 1.34-1.42 grams.

Date	Mintage	VG	F	VF	XF	Unc
AH1263-72	—	120	200	300	450	—

KM# 374 1/4 ASHRAFI
Gold **Obverse:** Inscription **Obv. Inscription:** Wajid Ali Shah **Reverse:** Parasol above crown, flanked by mermaids holding flag, crossed swords below **Mint:** Lucknow **Note:** Weight varies: 2.68-2.85 grams.

Date	Mintage	VG	F	VF	XF	Unc
AH1267//5	—	150	250	400	550	—
AH1268//5	—	150	250	400	550	—
AH1271	—	150	250	400	550	—

KM# 376 1/2 ASHRAFI
Gold **Obverse:** Inscription **Obv. Inscription:** Wajid Ali Shah **Reverse:** Parasol above crown, flanked by mermaids holding flag, crossed swords below **Mint:** Lucknow **Note:** Weight varies: 5.35-5.70 grams. Epithet: Variety IV.

Date	Mintage	VG	F	VF	XF	Unc
AH1263//1	—	165	275	400	550	—
AH1264//2	—	165	275	400	550	—
AH1265//3	—	165	275	400	550	—
AH1266//4	—	165	275	400	550	—
AH1267//4	—	165	275	400	550	—
AH1267//5	—	165	275	400	550	—
AH1271//-	—	—	—	—	—	—

KM# 378.1 ASHRAFI
Gold **Obverse:** Inscription **Obv. Inscription:** Wajid Ali Shah **Reverse:** Parasol above crown, flanked by mermaids holding flag, crossed swords below **Mint:** Lucknow **Note:** Size varies: 23-24mm. Weight varies: 10.70-11.40 grams. Epithet: Variety IV. Struck with rupee dies.

Date	Mintage	VG	F	VF	XF	Unc
AH1263//1	—	BV	BV	250	300	—
AH1263//2 (sic)	—	BV	BV	250	300	—
AH1264//2	—	BV	BV	250	300	—
AH1265//2	—	BV	BV	250	300	—
AH1265//3	—	BV	BV	250	300	—
AH1266//3	—	BV	BV	250	300	—
AH1266//4	—	BV	BV	250	300	—
AH1267//4	—	BV	BV	250	300	—
AH1268//5	—	BV	BV	250	300	—

KM# 378.2 ASHRAFI
Gold, 21.5 mm. **Obverse:** Inscription, date **Obv. Inscription:** Wajid Ali Shah **Reverse:** Parasol above crown, flanked by mermaids holding flag, crossed swords below **Mint:** Lucknow **Note:** Weight varies: 10.70-11.40 grams. Epithet: Variety IV. Struck with Asrafi dies.

Date	Mintage	VG	F	VF	XF	Unc
AH1264//2	—	BV	BV	250	300	—

KM# 378.3 ASHRAFI
Gold **Obverse:** Inscription **Obv. Inscription:** Wajid Ali Shah **Reverse:** Parasol above crown, flanked by mermaids holding flag, crossed swords below **Mint:** Lucknow **Note:** Size varies: 23-24mm. Weight varies: 10.70-11.40 grams. Epithet: Variety VI.

Date	Mintage	VG	F	VF	XF	Unc
AH1269//6	—	—	—	—	—	—
AH1272//9	—	165	200	250	300	—

Brijis Qadr
AH1273-1274 / 1857-1858AD

HAMMERED COINAGE
Nawab-Wazir during the Indian Mutiny

Fictitious dating in imitation of coinage before AH1234/1819. These are identifiable only by style and mint name, 'Awadh' appearing at top of reverse, and 'Subah' at the bottom, dated only AH1229/yr.26.

KM# 390 ASHRAFI
Gold **Obverse:** Inscription, date **Obv. Inscription:** "Shah Alam II" **Reverse:** Star, fish, flag **Mint:** Lucknow **Note:** Frozen date. Weight varies: 10.70-11.40 grams.

Date	Mintage	VG	F	VF	XF	Unc
AH1229//26	—	350	500	700	1,100	—

BAHAWALPUR

The Amirs of Bahawalpur established their independence from Afghan control towards the close of the 18th century. In the 1830's the state's independence under British suzerainty became guaranteed by treaty. With the creation of Pakistan in 1947 Bahawalpur, with an area of almost 17,500 square miles, became its premier Princely State. Bahawalpur State, named after its capital, stretched for almost three hundred miles along the left bank of the Sutlej, Panjnad and Indus rivers.

For earlier issues in the names of the Durrani rulers, see Afghanistan.

RULERS
Amirs
Sir Sadiq Muhammad Khan IV, AH1283-1317/1866-1899AD

MINTS

بهاولپور

Bahawalpur

MINT MARKS

تونك

Tonk
NOTE: All coins with both AH and AD dates clearly readable command about a 50 per cent premium.

Flower (on all)

Leaf (several forms)

Beginning with the reign of Muhammad Ibrahim Ali Khan, most coins have both AD and AH date. Coins with both dates fully legible are worth about 20% more than listed prices. Coins with one date fully legible are worth prices shown. Coins with both dates off are of little value.

There are many minor and major variations of type, varying with location of date, orientation of leaf, arrangement of legend. Although these fall into easily distinguished patterns, they are strictly for the specialist and are omitted here.

The Tonk rupee was known as the "Chanwarshahi".

Sir Sadiq Muhammad Khan V
AH1325-1365 / 1907-1947AD

MEDALLIC COINAGE

X# M10a ASHRAFI
10.0000 g., Gold **Obverse:** Bust of Muhammad Bahawal Khan V left **Reverse:** Ornate helmeted arms **Mint:** Bahawalpur **Note:** Fr. #1031. Design prepared for the nawab by Spink & Son Ltd., London. Prev. Y#11a.

Date	Mintage	VG	F	VF	XF	Unc
AH1343(1924-25) Proof	—	Value: 2,000				

BAJRANGGARH

Bajranggarh was a small state in the district of Gwalior. The mint epithet of Bajranggarh was Jainagar. All the coins, irrespective of when they were minted, were struck in the name of Maharaja Jai Singh and bore similar legends in the Devanagri script.

RULER
Jai Singh, 1797-1818AD

Jai Singh
AH1212-1234 / 1797-1818

HAMMERED COINAGE

KM# 13 MOHUR
Gold **Obverse:** Inscription within circle **Reverse:** Inscription within circle **Note:** Weight varies: 10.70-11.40 grams. Small lettering, without symbols.

Date	Mintage	VG	F	VF	XF	Unc
ND//16(1812)	—	250	450	750	1,500	—

BANSWARA

This state in southern Rajputana was founded in 1538 when the state of Dungarpur was divided between 2 sons of the Maharawal, the younger receiving the territory of Banswara with the title also of Maharawal. The rulers of Banswara were Sissodia Rajputs who claimed descent from the powerful Maharanas of Mewar-Udaipur.

During most of the 19th Century, Banswara used the "Salim Shahi" coinage of neighboring Pratapgarh State. But around 1870 Maharawal Lakshman Singh, defying a British prohibiting order of that year, introduced a series of crude coins in copper, silver and gold for use within the state. The legends on these coins are in a secret script, said to have been invented by Lakshman Singh himself. The central word in these legends has been tentatively identified as "Samsatraba" (for "Samba Satra", a designation for the Hindu deity Shiva) in the longer form, or "Samba" for the shorter form. All the gold and silver coins, and a few rare copper ones, carry the longer form. The copper coins were made for circulation, but the gold and silver were produced mainly for presentation.

RULERS
Lakshman Singh, 1844-1905AD

BIKANIR / INDIA - PRINCELY STATES

Shambhu Singh, 1906-1908AD
British Administration, 1908-1914AD
Pirthi singh II, 1914-1944AD
Chandravir Singh, 1944-1949AD

LEGENDS

Samsatraba
For Samba Satra

ANONYMOUS HAMMERED COINAGE
Samsatraba Series

KM# 25 NAZARANA MOHUR
12.0000 g., Gold **Obv. Legend:** "Samsatraba" **Rev. Legend:** "Samsatraba" **Note:** Broad, thin flan.

Date	Mintage	Good	VG	F	VF	XF
ND(1870)	—	250	375	500	700	—

KM# 18 NAZARANA MOHUR
12.0000 g., Gold **Obv. Legend:** "Samsatraba" **Rev. Legend:** "Samsatraba" **Note:** Thick flan.

Date	Mintage	Good	VG	F	VF	XF
ND(1870)	—	—	250	375	500	700

BARODA

Maratha state located in western India. The ruling line was descended from Damaji, a Maratha soldier, who received the title of "Distinguished Swordsman" in 1721 (hence the scimitar on most Baroda coins). The Baroda title "Gaikwara" comes from "gaikwar" or cow herd, Damaji's father's occupation.

The Maratha rulers of Baroda, the Gaekwar family rose to prominence in the mid-18th century by carving out for themselves a dominion from territories, which were previously under the control of the Poona Marathas, and to a lesser extent, of the Raja of Jodhpur. Chronic internal disputes regarding the succession to the masnad culminated in the intervention of British troops in support of one candidate, Anand Rao Gaekwar, in 1800. Then, in 1802, an agreement with the East India Company released the Baroda princes from their fear of domination by the Maratha Peshwa of Poona but subordinated them to Company interests. Nevertheless, for almost the next century and a half Baroda maintained a good relationship with the British and continued as a major Princely State right up to 1947, when it acceded to the Indian Union.

RULERS
Gaekwars
Anand Rao, AH1215-1235/1800-1819AD
Sayaji Rao II, AH1235-1264/1819-1847AD
Ganpat Rao, AH1264-1273/1847-1856AD
Khande Rao, AH1273-1287/1856-1870AD
Malhar Rao, AH1287-1292/1870-1875AD
Sayaji Rao III, AH1292-1357/VS1932-1995/1875-1938AD
Pratap Singh, VS1995-2008/1938-1951AD

MINTS
Baroda
Jambusar
Petlad

MINT MARKS
Nagari letters denoting Baroda ruler:

Kha Ga - Khande Rao, coins in own name, Baroda Mint.

Sa Ga - Sayaji Rao III, Baroda Mint.

NOTE: The first 2 marks are found only on the coins of Ahmadabad Mint, and serve to identify it. The remaining 16 marks are used to indicate the ruler under whom the coin was struck; when no mint name is given after the ruler's name in the above list, that shows that the symbol was used at all his mints. Note the various forms of 'G' and 'Ga' used above.

Khande Rao
AH 1273-1287 / 1856-1870AD

HAMMERED COINAGE

Y# B13 1/4 MOHUR
2.8000 g., Gold, 15 mm. **Obverse:** Inscription **Obv. Inscription:** "Commander of the Sovereign Band" **Reverse:** Nagari "Kha Ga" and scimitar **Mint:** Amreli **Note:** Obverse inscription refers to a title of the Gaekwar, ruler of Baroda.

Date	Mintage	Good	VG	F	VF	XF
AH127x Rare	—	—	—	—	—	—

Sayaji Rao III
AH1292-1357 / VS1932-95 / 1875-1938AD

MILLED COINAGE

Y# A37 1/6 MOHUR
Gold, 14.5 mm. **Obverse:** Crowned bust, right **Reverse:** Inscription, scimitar, date within wreath **Mint:** Baroda **Note:** Weight varies: 1.04-1.18 grams.

Date	Mintage	F	VF	XF	Unc
VS1953 (1896)	—	165	225	275	350

Y# 37 1/6 MOHUR
Gold, 14.5 mm. **Obverse:** Crowned bust, right **Reverse:** Inscription, scimitar, date within wreath **Mint:** Baroda **Note:** 1.04-1.18 grams.

Date	Mintage	VG	F	VF	XF	Unc
VS1951 (1894)	—	—	165	225	275	350
VS1951 (1894)	—	—	175	225	275	350
VS1953 (1896)	—	—	175	225	275	350
VS1959 (1902)	—	—	175	225	275	350

Y# A38 1/3 MOHUR
Gold, 16 mm. **Obverse:** Crowned bust, right **Reverse:** Inscription, scimitar, date within wreath **Mint:** Baroda **Note:** Weight varies: 2.07-2.39 grams.

Date	Mintage	F	VF	XF	Unc
VS1942 (1885)	—	185	250	325	400

Y# 38 1/3 MOHUR
Gold, 16 mm. **Obverse:** Bust of Sayaji Rao III right **Mint:** Baroda **Note:** Weight varies: 2.07-2.39 grams.

Date	Mintage	VG	F	VF	XF	Unc
VS1959 (1902)	—	—	225	275	350	450

Y# A39 MOHUR
Gold, 21 mm. **Obverse:** Crowned bust, right **Reverse:** Inscription, scimitar, date within wreath **Mint:** Baroda **Note:** Weight varies: 6.20-6.40 grams.

Date	Mintage	F	VF	XF	Unc
VS1942 (1885)	—	265	350	550	850

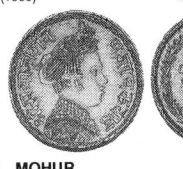

Y# 39 MOHUR
Gold, 21 mm. **Obverse:** Crowned bust, right **Reverse:** Inscription, scimitar, date within wreath **Mint:** Baroda **Note:** Weight varies: 6.20-6.40 grams.

Date	Mintage	VG	F	VF	XF	Unc
VS1945 (1888)	—	—	265	340	450	650
VS1952 (1895)	—	—	265	340	450	650
VS1953 (1896)	—	—	265	340	450	650
VS1959 (1902)	—	—	265	350	475	650

BHARATPUR

State located in Rajputana in northwest India.

Bharatpur was founded by Balchand, a Jat chieftain who took advantage of Mughal confusion and weakness after the death of Aurangzeb to seize the area. In 1756 the ruler at that time, Suraj Mal, received the title of Raja. Bharatpur became increasingly associated with Maratha ambitions and, in spite of treaty ties to the East India Company, assisted the Maratha Confederacy in their struggles against the British. This gained them few friends in British circles, but the early attempts by the British to force the submission of Bharatpur fortress proved abortive. In 1826 however, the British took the opportunity offered by a bitter internal feud concerning the succession finally to reduce the stronghold. The rival claimant was exiled to Allahabad and Balwant Singh, then a child of seven, was placed on the throne under the supervision of a British Political Agent. From that time onwards Bharatpur came under British control until it acceded to the Indian Union at Independence.

RULERS
Ranjit Singh, AH1190-1220/1776-1805AD
Randhir Singh, AH1220-1239/1805-1823AD
Baldeo Singh, AH1239-1241/1823-1824AD
Durjan Singh, AH1241-1242/1825-1826AD
Balwant Singh, AH1242-1269/1826-1853AD
Jaswant Singh, AH1269-1311/1853-1893AD/VS1909-1950
Ram Singh, 1893-1900AD
Kishan Singh, 1900-1929AD

MINTS
Akbarabad
Agra or Akbarabad was controlled by the Bharatpur Jats from AH1175-1186/1761-1773AD. For earlier or later issues see Mughal Empire: Akbarabad Mint.

Bharatpur
Mintname: Bharatpur or Braj Indrapur

Mint marks:

Dig
Mint name: Mahe Indrapur

Mintmarks:

HAMMERED COINAGE

KM# 110 MOHUR
Gold **Obverse:** Inscription **Obv. Inscription:** "Muhammad Akbar II" **Reverse:** Inscription, star **Mint:** Braj Indrapur **Note:** Weight varies: 10.70-11.40 grams.

Date	Mintage	VG	F	VF	XF	Unc
AH12xx//1	—	275	450	650	950	—
AH12xx//3	—	275	450	650	950	—
AH123x//11	—	275	450	650	950	—
AH12xx//14	—	275	450	650	950	—
AH12xx//15	—	275	450	650	950	—
AH1248//28	—	275	450	650	950	—

KM# 170 MOHUR
Gold **Obverse:** Head left **Obv. Inscription:** Queen Victoria **Reverse:** Inscription, katar, date, star **Note:** For similar coins with dagger at left and sword at right of Queen's bust, see Bindraban State. Struck at Bharatpur and Braj Indrapur. Weight varies: 10.70-11.40 grams.

Date	Mintage	VG	F	VF	XF	Unc
VS1915 - 1858	—	600	1,000	1,400	2,500	—
VS1916 - 1859	—	600	1,000	1,400	2,500	—
VS1918 - 1862	—	600	1,000	1,400	2,500	—
VS1919 - 1862	—	600	1,000	1,400	2,500	—

KM# 160 MOHUR
Gold **Obverse:** Head left **Obv. Inscription:** Queen Victoria **Reverse:** Katar at left of star and date **Rev. Inscription:** Jaswant Singh **Note:** Struck at Bharatpur and Braj Indrapur. Weight varies: 10.70-11.40 grams.

Date	Mintage	VG	F	VF	XF	Unc
VS1910 - 1858	—	600	1,000	1,400	2,500	—
VS1910 - 1858	—	600	1,000	1,400	2,500	—

BIKANIR

Bikanir, located in Rajputana was established as a state sometime between 1465 and 1504 by Jodhpur Rathor Rajput named Rao Bikaji. During the period of the Great Mughals Bikanir

350 INDIA - PRINCELY STATES

BIKANIR

was intimately linked to Delhi by ties of both loyalty and marriage. Both Akbar and Jahangir contracted marriages with princesses of the Bikanir Rajputs, and the Bikanir nobility rendered outstanding service in the Mughal armies. Bikanir came under British influence in 1817 and after 1947 was incorporated into Rajasthan.

RULERS
Ganga Singhji, VS1944-1999/1887-1942AD
Sadul Singh, VS1999-2004/1942-1947AD

MINT

بیکانیر

Bikanir

Ratan Singh
AH1244-1268 / 1828-1851AD

MUGHAL COINAGE

KM# 33   1/4 MOHUR
Gold **Obv. Inscription:** "Shah Alam II" **Note:** Weight varies: 2.67-2.90 grams.

Date	Mintage	VG	F	VF	XF	Unc
AHxxxx	—	1,500	2,200	3,000	—	—

Ganga Singh
VS1944-1999 / 1887-1942AD

MEDALLIC COINAGE

X# M1   NAZARANA RUPEE
Silver **Subject:** 50th Anniversary of Reign **Obverse:** Bust of Ganga Singh facing **Reverse:** Crowned monogram **Note:** Prev. KM#73.

Date	Mintage	F	VF	XF	Unc
VS1994 (1937)	—	—	20.00	30.00	45.00
VS1994 (1937) Restrike; Prooflike	—	—	—	—	20.00

X# M1a   NAZARANA RUPEE
Gold **Subject:** 50th Anniversary of Reign **Obverse:** Bust of Ganga Singh facing **Reverse:** Crowned monogram

Date	Mintage	VG	F	VF	XF	Unc
VS1994 Prooflike; Restrike; Rare						

X# M2   NAZARANA 1/2 MOHUR
Gold, 17 mm. **Subject:** 50th Anniversary of Reign **Obverse:** Bust of Ganga Singh facing **Reverse:** Crowned monogram **Note:** Prev. KM#74.

Date	Mintage	VG	F	VF	XF	Unc
VS1994 (1937)	—	—	—	175	225	300
VS1994 (1937) Restrike; Prooflike	—	—	—	—	—	225

X# M3   NAZARANA MOHUR
Gold **Subject:** 50th Anniversary of Reign **Obverse:** Bust of Ganga Singh facing **Reverse:** Crowned monogram **Note:** Prev. KM#75.

Date	Mintage	VG	F	VF	XF	Unc
VS1994 (1937)	—	—	—	250	325	450
VS1994 (1937) Restrike; Prooflike	—	—	—	—	—	325

MILLED COINAGE

KM# 70b   1/2 PICE
Gold **Obverse:** Crowned bust left **Reverse:** Value, date within beaded circle

Date	Mintage	VG	F	VF	XF	Unc
1894 Restrike; Proof	—	Value: 1,500				

KM# 71b   1/4 ANNA
Gold **Obverse:** Crowned bust left **Reverse:** Value, date within beaded circle

Date	Mintage	VG	F	VF	XF	Unc
VS1895 Restrike; Proof	—	Value: 2,500				

Sadul Singh
AH1361-1367 / 1942-1947AD

MEDALLIC COINAGE

X# M4   NAZARANA MOHUR
8.6800 g., Gold **Subject:** 50th Anniversary of Reign **Obverse:** Bust of Ganga Singh facing **Reverse:** Crowned monogram

Date	Mintage	VG	F	VF	XF	Unc
VS1999	—	—	—	—	1,000	2,000

State in Rajputana in northwest India.

BUNDI

Bundi was founded in 1342 by a Chauhan Rajput, Rao Dewa (Deoraj). Until the Maratha defeat early in the 19th century, Bundi was greatly harassed by the forces of Holkar and Sindhia. In 1818 it came under British protection and control and remained so until 1947. In 1948 the State was absorbed into Rajasthan.

RULERS
Ajit Singh, AH1185-1187/ VS1828-1830/1771-1773AD
Bishen Singh, AH1187-1236/ VS1830-1878/1773-1821AD

MINT

Perso-Arabic   Devanagari

Bundi

بندی بوندي

Mintname: Bundi

All of the coins of Bundi struck prior to the Mutiny (1857) are in the name of the Mughal emperor and bear the following 2 marks on the reverse, to the left and right of the regnal year, respectively:

On all Mughal issues: ॐ

Only on Muhammad Akbar and Muhammad Bahadur issues:
The same symbols appear on the coins of Kotah, but the difference is that the Kotah pieces have the mintname *Kotahurf Nandgaon* and later issues only have *Nandgaon*.

HAMMERED COINAGE
Mughal Series

C# 33   MOHUR
10.7000 g., Gold **Obverse:** Inscription **Reverse:** 19 divides flower and tree symbol

Date	Mintage	VG	F	VF	XF	Unc
AH-//15	—	225	325	500	700	—
AH-//17	—	225	325	500	700	—
AH-//19	—	225	325	500	700	—
AH-//33	—	225	325	500	700	—

COOCH BEHAR

Cooch Behar was relatively peaceful until there was a dispute over the succession in 1772. After a confusing period during which the Bhutanese installed their own nominated ruler and captured Dhairyendra Narandra, the Chief Minister appealed to the British for assistance. With an eye on the potentially lucrative Tibetan trade, which had increased somewhat in volume since Prithvi Narayan's rise to power in Nepal, the British agreed to support Darendra Narayan, so long as British suzerainty was acknowledged.

Over the following decades the British gradually increased their control over the state. After large numbers of debased silver half, or "Narainy" rupees had been struck, the British decided to close the mint, and after that a few coins only were struck at the coronation of each ruler, although it was only in 1866 that the local coins ceased to be legal tender.

RULERS
Nripendra Narayan, CB353-401/SE1785-1833/1863-1911AD
Raja Rajendra Narayan, CB401-403/SE1833-1835/1911-1913AD
Jitendra Narayan, CB403-412/SE1835-1844/1913-1922AD
Jagaddipendra Narayan, CB412-439/SE1844-1871/1922-1949AD

BRITISH PROTECTORATE

Shivendra Narayan
SE1761-1769 / 1839-1847AD

HAMMERED COINAGE
Presentation Issues

KM# 155   NAZARANA MOHUR
9.4000 g., Gold, 21 mm. **Obverse:** Inscription **Reverse:** Inscription **Note:** Similar to Nazarana 1/2 Rupee, KM#151.

Date	Mintage	VG	F	VF	XF	Unc
ND39 (1839-47) (1839)	—	500	750	1,500	2,500	—

Narendra Narayan
SE1769-1785 / 1847-1863AD

HAMMERED COINAGE
Presentation Issues

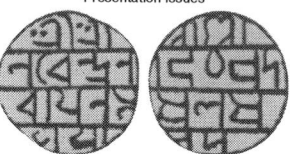

KM# 170   NAZARANA MOHUR
9.4000 g., Gold, 21 mm. **Obverse:** Inscription **Reverse:** Inscription **Note:** Similar to Nazarana 1/2 Rupee, KM#165.

Date	Mintage	Good	VG	F	VF	XF
ND(1847-63)	—	—	350	600	1,200	2,000

Nripendra Narayan
SE1785-1833 / 1863-1911AD

HAMMERED COINAGE
Presentation Issues

KM# 185   NAZARANA MOHUR
9.4000 g., Gold, 21 mm. **Obverse:** Inscription **Reverse:** Inscription within square

Date	Mintage	Good	VG	F	VF	XF
CB354 (1864)	—	—	—	300	500	1,200

Raja Rajendra Narayan
SE1833-1835 / 1911-1913AD

MEDALLIC COINAGE

X# M8   NAZARANA MOHUR
8.5000 g., Gold **Obverse:** Arms **Note:** Prev. KM#200.

Date	Mintage	F	VF	XF	Unc
CB402(1912)	100	—	—	1,200	1,800

Jitendra Narayan
SE1835-1844 / 1913-1922AD

MEDALLIC COINAGE

GWALIOR

X# M10 NAZARANA MOHUR
8.0000 g., Gold **Obverse:** Arms **Note:** Prev. KM#215.

Date	Mintage	F	VF	XF	Unc
CB404(1914)	100	—	—	1,200	1,800

Jagaddipendra Narayan
SE1844-1871 / 1922-1949AD

MEDALLIC COINAGE

X# M12 NAZARANA MOHUR
8.7000 g., Gold **Obverse:** Arms **Note:** Prev. KM#230.

Date	Mintage	F	VF	XF	Unc
CB413 (1923)	—	—	—	1,200	1,800

DATIA

State located in north-central India, governed by Maharajas. Datia was founded in 1735 by Bhagwan Das, son of Narsingh Dev of the Orchha royal house. In 1804 the State concluded its first treaty with the East India Company and thereafter came under British protection and control.

RULERS
Govind Singh, AH1325-1368/1907-1948AD

MINT

Dalipnagar: دلیپ نگر

BRITISH PROTECTORATE

Govind Singh
1907-1948AD

MEDALLIC COINAGE

X# 1 NAZARANA 1/2 MOHUR
Gold **Obverse:** Bust of Govind Singh 3/4 right **Reverse:** Arms **Note:** Prev. KM#M1. Weight varies: 5.35-5.78 grams.

Date	Mintage	F	VF	XF	Unc
ND(ca. 1940s)	—	—	750	1,500	2,500

DHAR

The territory in central India in which Dhar was located had been controlled by the Paramara clan of Rajputs from the 9th century to the 13th century, after which it passed into Muslim hands. The modern Princely State of Dhar originated in the first half of the 18th century when the Maratha Peshwa, Baji Rao, handed over the region as a fiefdom to Anand Rao Ponwar. He was of the same stock as the rulers of Dewas and a descendant of the original Paramara Rajputs. Sometimes in conflict with Holkar, sometimes with Sindhia, in 1819 Dhar came under British protection. No silver or gold coinage was ever struck at Dhar. In 1895 the British silver rupee was adopted.

LOCAL RULERS
Jaswant Rao, AH1250-1274/1834-1857AD
Anand Rao III, AH1276-1316/1860-1898AD
Anand Rao IV, AH1363-1368/1943-1948AD

BRITISH PROTECTORATE

MEDALLIC COINAGE

X# M10 MOHUR
6.4000 g., Gold, 20 mm. **Obverse:** Coat of Arms, English legend above, Persian legend below **Obv. Legend:** DHAR STATE...ZARB PIRAN DHAR **Note:** Previous KM#10.

Date	Mintage	VG	F	VF	XF	Unc
1943	—	1,000	1,300	1,600	2,000	—

Anand Rao III
AH1276-1316 / 1860-1898AD

MILLED COINAGE
Regal Style

KM# 12b 1/2 PICE
Gold **Obverse:** Crowned bust left **Reverse:** Value, date within beaded circle

Date	Mintage	Good	VG	F	VF	XF
1887 Proof, restrike	—	Value: 2,200				

KM# 11b 1/12 ANNA
Gold **Obverse:** Crowned bust left **Reverse:** Value, date within beaded circle

Date	Mintage	Good	VG	F	VF	XF
1887 Proof, restrike	—	Value: 1,500				

KM# 13b 1/4 ANNA
Gold **Obverse:** Crowned bust left **Reverse:** Value, date within beaded circle

Date	Mintage	Good	VG	F	VF	XF
1887 Proof, restrike	—	Value: 2,600				

Anand Rao IV
AH1363-1368 / 1943-1948AD

MEDALLIC COINAGE

X# 1 NAZARANA MOHUR
Gold **Note:** Prev. KM#M1.

Date	Mintage	F	VF	XF	Unc
1943	—	—	600	900	1,800

DUNGARPUR

A district in northwest India which became part of Rajasthan in 1948.

The maharawals of Dungarpur were descended from the Mewar chieftains of the 12th century. In 1527 the upper Mahi basin was bifurcated to form the Princely States of Dungarpur and Banswara. Thereafter Dungarpur came successively under Mughal and Maratha control until in 1818 it came under British protection.

RULERS
Udai Singh, VS1909-1955/1852-1898AD
Bijey Singh, VS1955-1975/1898-1918AD
Lakshman Singh, VS1975-2005/1918-1948AD

BRITISH PROTECTORATE

Udai Singh
VS1909-1955 / 1852-1898AD

HAMMERED COINAGE

KM# 6 MOHUR
11.0000 g., Gold **Obverse:** Sword and "jhar" to right **Rev. Inscription:** "Rajha Dungarpur" **Edge:** plain

Date	Mintage	Good	VG	F	VF	XF
VS1925 (1868)	—	—	—	—	—	850

KM# 5 NAZARANA MOHUR
11.0000 g., Gold **Obv. Inscription:** Sarkar/Dungarpur **Reverse:** Sword and "jhar" to right

Date	Mintage	Good	VG	F	VF	XF
VS1916 Rare						

Lakshman Singh
VS1975-2005 / 1918-1948AD

HAMMERED COINAGE

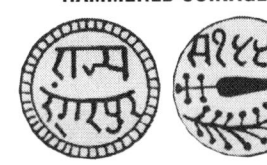

KM# 9 NAZARANA MOHUR
11.0000 g., Gold **Obverse:** Sword and "jhar" to right **Rev. Inscription:** Rajya/Dungarpur

Date	Mintage	Good	VG	F	VF	XF
VS1996 (1939)	—	—	1,000	1,500	2,000	3,500

FARIDKOT

State located in the Punjab.

RULER
Harindar Singh, 1918-1949AD

Harindar Singh

MEDALLIC COINAGE

X# M1 NAZARANA 1/2 RUPEE
Silver **Obverse:** Bust of Harinder Singh left **Reverse:** Arms **Note:** Prev. KM#M1.

Date	Mintage	F	VF	XF	Unc
1941	—	—	—	—	—

X# M2 NAZARANA RUPEE
Silver **Obverse:** Bust of Harinder Singh left **Reverse:** Arms **Note:** Prev. KM#M2.

Date	Mintage	F	VF	XF	Unc
1941 Rare					

X# M3 NAZARANA 1/3 MOHUR
Gold **Obverse:** Bust of Harinder Singh left **Reverse:** Arms **Note:** Prev. KM#M3. Weight varies: 3.57-3.80 grams.

Date	Mintage	F	VF	XF	Unc
1941	—	—	750	1,200	1,650

GARHWAL

Garhwal was a rugged tract embracing a number of peaks over twenty-three thousand feet in north India. The state dated from the 14th century when a number of local chieftains came under the sway of Ajai Pal. From that time onward his descendants ruled over this Himalayan kingdom until 1803, when the Gurkhas invaded both Garhwal and Kumaon. Shortly afterwards, in the Nepal War of 1814-1816, these States fell under British control and the State was then partially restored to its original ruler.

The Gurkhas captured Almora, the principal town of Kumaon, in 1790 and went on to seize Garhwal and Sirmur in 1803. From then until their definitive defeat at the hands of the East India Company, the Gurkhas issued coins from the Srinagar (Garhwal), Almora (Kumaon) and Nahan (Sirmur) mints.

MINT

Srinagar سرینگر

KINGDOM

Sudarshan Shah
VS1872-1906 / 1815-1859AD

HAMMERED COINAGE

KM# A1 1/2 MOHUR
5.3500 g., Gold **Obverse:** Inscription **Reverse:** Inscription

Date	Mintage	Good	VG	F	VF	XF
VS1872	—	—	—	—	900	1,800

KM# A2 MOHUR
10.7000 g., Gold **Obverse:** Inscription **Reverse:** Urdu, inscription

Date	Mintage	Good	VG	F	VF	XF
VS1872	—	—	—	—	1,350	2,500

GWALIOR

Sindhia

State located in central India. Capital originally was Ujjain (= Daru-I-fath), but was later transferred to Gwalior in 1810. The Gwalior ruling family, the Sindhias, were descendants of the Maratha chief Ranoji Sindhia (d.1750). His youngest son, Mahadji Sindhia (d.1794) was anxious to establish his independence from the overlordship of the Peshwas of Poona. Unable to achieve this alone, it was the Peshwa's crushing defeat by Ahmad Shah Durrani at Panipat in 1761, which helped realize his ambitions. Largely in the interests of sustaining this autonomy, but partly as

352 INDIA - PRINCELY STATES

GWALIOR

a result of a defeat at East India Company hands in 1781, Mahadji concluded an alliance with the British in 1782. In 1785, he reinstalled the fallen Mughal Emperor, Shah Alam, on the throne at Dehli. Very early in the 19th century, Gwalior's relationship with the British began to deteriorate, a situation which culminated in the Anglo-Maratha War of 1803. Gwalior's forces under Daulat Rao were defeated. In consequence, and by the terms of the peace treaty which followed, his territory was truncated. In 1818, Gwalior suffered a further loss of land at British hands. In the years that ensued, as the East India Company's possessions became transformed into empire and as the Pax Britannica swept across the subcontinent, the Sindhia family's relationship with their British overlords steadily improved.

RULERS
Daulat Rao, AH1209-1243/1794-1827AD
Baija Bai, Regent,
 (Widow of Daulat Rao) AH1243-1249/1827-1833AD
Jankoji Rao, AH1243-1259/1827-1843AD
Jayaji Rao, AH1259-1304/1843-1886AD

With initial Jl   Jayaji Rao

Madho Rao, VS1943-1982/1886-1925AD
Jivaji Rao, VS1982-2005/1925-1948AD

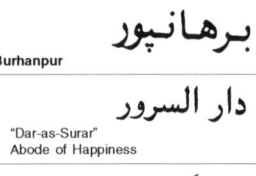

MINTS

برهانپور
Burhanpur

دار السرور
"Dar-as-Surar"
Abode of Happiness

گوالیار
Gwalior Fort

Lashkar

KINGDOM

Baija Bai - Regent
AH1243-1249 / 1827-1833AD

HAMMERED COINAGE
KM# 63   NAZARANA 1/3 MOHUR
Gold, 18 mm. **Obv. Inscription:** "Muhammad Shah" **Reverse:** Nagari "Shri" for Baija Rao **Mint:** Gwalior Fort **Note:** Weight varies 3.57-3.80 grams.
Date	Mintage	Good	VG	F	VF	XF
AH1130//2 Frozen	—	—	175	275	400	575

Note: Struck ca. 1827AD

KM# 126   MOHUR
Gold. **Obv. Inscription:** "Muhammad Shah" **Reverse:** Shri **Mint:** Lashkar **Note:** Weight varies 10.70-11.60 grams.
Date	Mintage	Good	VG	F	VF	XF
AH1130//2 Frozen	—	—	225	250	350	500

Jankoji Rao
AH1243-1259 / 1827-1843AD

HAMMERED COINAGE
KM# 66   NAZARANA 1/3 MOHUR
Gold **Obv. Inscription:** "Muhammad Shah" **Reverse:** Nagari "Ja" for Jankoji **Mint:** Gwalior Fort **Note:** Weight varies 3.57-3.80 grams.
Date	Mintage	Good	VG	F	VF	XF
AH1130//2 Frozen	—	—	175	275	400	575

Note: Struck ca.1834AD.

KM# 132   MOHUR
Gold. **Obv. Inscription:** "Muhammad Shah" **Reverse:** Bow and arrow points up, "Ja" **Mint:** Lashkar **Note:** Weight varies 10.70-11.40 grams.
Date	Mintage	Good	VG	F	VF	XF
AH1130//2 Frozen	—	—	225	250	350	500

KM# 133   MOHUR
Gold **Obv. Inscription:** "Muhammad Shah" **Reverse:** Bow and arrow points down, "Ja" **Mint:** Lashkar **Note:** Weight varies 10.70-11.40 grams.
Date	Mintage	Good	VG	F	VF	XF
AH1130//2 Frozen	—	—	225	250	350	500

Jayaji Rao
AH1259-1304 / 1843-1886AD

HAMMERED COINAGE
KM# A155   1/5 MOHUR
2.2100 g., Gold **Obv. Inscription:** "Shah Alam II" **Reverse:** "Ji" for Jayaji **Mint:** Lashkar
Date	Mintage	Good	VG	F	VF	XF
ND(1843-86) Rare						

KM# 74   NAZARANA 1/3 MOHUR
Gold **Obv. Inscription:** "Muhammad Shah" **Reverse:** Nagari "Ji" for Jayaji **Mint:** Gwalior Fort **Note:** Weight varies 3.57-3.80 grams.
Date	Mintage	Good	VG	F	VF	XF
AH1130//2 Frozen	—	—	175	275	400	575

Note: Struck ca.1843AD

KM# A75   MOHUR
Gold **Obv. Inscription:** "Muhammad Shah" **Reverse:** Nagari "Ji" for Jayaji **Mint:** Gwalior Fort
Date	Mintage	Good	VG	F	VF	XF
AH1130//2	—	—	400	475	550	700

KM# 155   MOHUR
Gold. **Obv. Inscription:** "Shah Alam II" **Reverse:** Bow and arrow points up, "Ji" for Jajaji **Mint:** Lashkar **Note:** Weight varies 10.70-11.40 grams.
Date	Mintage	Good	VG	F	VF	XF
AH1130//2 Frozen	—	—	250	325	500	800

Madho Rao
VS1943-1982 / 1886-1925AD

HAMMERED COINAGE

KM# A160   1/4 MOHUR
Gold **Mint:** Lashkar
Date	Mintage	Good	VG	F	VF	XF
ND(1886) Rare						

KM# 84   1/3 MOHUR
Gold, 21 mm. **Obv. Inscription:** "Muhammad Shah" **Reverse:** Nagari "Ma" for Madho Rao II **Mint:** Gwalior Fort **Note:** Weight varies 3.57-3.80 grams.
Date	Mintage	Good	VG	F	VF	XF
AH1130//2 Frozen	—	—	125	165	225	275

Note: Struck ca.1886AD.

KM# 160   MOHUR
Gold **Reverse:** Bow and arrow points up, "Ma" trisul **Mint:** Lashkar **Note:** Weight varies 10.70-11.40 grams.
Date	Mintage	Good	VG	F	VF	XF
AH1130//2 Frozen	—	—	250	325	400	500

HYDERABAD

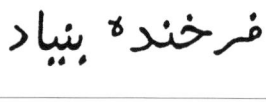

Haidarabad

Hyderabad State, the largest Indian State and the last remnant of Mughal suzerainty in South or Central India, traced its foundation to Nizam-ul Mulk, the Mughal viceroy in the Deccan. From about 1724 the first nizam, as the rulers of Hyderabad came to be called, took advantage of Mughal decline in the North to assert an all but ceremonial independence of the emperor. The East India Company defeated Hyderabad's natural enemies, the Muslim rulers of Mysore and the Marathas, with the help of troops furnished under alliances between them and the Nizam. This formed the beginning of a relationship, which persisted for a century and a half until India's Independence. Hyderabad City is located beside Golkonda, the citadel of the Qutb Shahi sultans until they were overthrown by Aurangzeb in 1687. A beautifully located city on the bank of the Musi river, the mint epithet was appropriately Farkhanda Bunyad, "of happy foundation".

Hyderabad exercised authority over a number of feudatories or samasthans. Some of these, such as Gadwal and Shorapur, paid tribute to both the Nizam and the Marathas. These feudatories were generally in the hands of local rajas whose ancestry predated the establishment of Hyderabad State. There were also many mints in the State, both private and government. There was little or no standardization of the purity of silver coinage until the 20th century. At least one banker, Pestonji Meherji by name, was distinguished by minting his own coins.

RULERS
Nizam Ali Khan, AH1175-1218/1761-1803AD
Sikandar Jah, AH1218-1244/1803-1829AD
Nasir-ad-Daula, AH1244-1273/1829-1857AD

ذ : ن ذ
Mint mark:

ن
Rev: Persian letter "N":

Afzal-ad-Daula, AH1273-1285/1857-1869AD

ج : ن ذ
Mint marks:
#2

Mir Mahbub Ali Khan II, AH1285-1329/1869-1911AD

م
Persian letter "M" for Mahbub above "k" of Mulk on obverse

Mir Usman Ali Khan, AH1329-1368/1911-1948AD

MINTS

فرخنده بنیاد
Haidarabad

ج : ن ذ
Mint mark:

س
Persian letter "S".

NIZAMATE

Sikandar Jah
AH1218-1244 / 1803-1829AD

HAMMERED COINAGE
C# 56   1/16 MOHUR
Gold **Obv. Inscription:** "Muhammad Akbar II" **Mint:** Haidarabad **Note:** Weight varies 0.67-0.70 grams.
Date	Mintage	Good	VG	F	VF	XF
AH123x	—	—	50.00	70.00	125	200

C# 57   1/8 MOHUR
Gold **Obv. Inscription:** "Muhammad Akbar II" **Mint:** Haidarabad **Note:** Weight varies 1.34-1.42 grams.
Date	Mintage	Good	VG	F	VF	XF
AH123x	—	—	60.00	85.00	150	225

C# 58   1/4 MOHUR
Gold **Obv. Inscription:** "Muhammad Akbar II" **Mint:** Haidarabad **Note:** Weight varies 2.68-2.85 grams.
Date	Mintage	Good	VG	F	VF	XF
AH1236//15	—	—	75.00	110	175	250

C# A58   NAZARANA 1/4 MOHUR
Gold **Mint:** Haidarabad **Note:** Weight varies 2.68-2.85 grams.
Date	Mintage	Good	VG	F	VF	XF
AH1236//15 Rare						

C# 59   1/2 MOHUR
Gold **Obv. Inscription:** "Muhammad Akbar II" **Mint:** Haidarabad **Note:** Weight varies 5.35-5.70 grams.
Date	Mintage	Good	VG	F	VF	XF
AH123x	—	—	120	150	250	350

HYDERABAD

INDIA - PRINCELY STATES

C# 60 MOHUR
Gold **Obv. Inscription:** "Muhammad Akbar II" **Mint:** Haidarabad **Note:** Weight varies 10.70-11.40 grams.

Date	Mintage	Good	VG	F	VF	XF
AH1226	—	—	225	250	285	400
AH1227	—	—	225	250	285	400
AH1228//7	—	—	225	250	285	400
AH1231	—	—	225	250	285	400
AH1234	—	—	225	250	285	400
AH1235	—	—	225	250	285	400
AH1236//15	—	—	225	250	285	400
AH1237//16	—	—	225	250	285	400
AH1238	—	—	225	250	285	400
AH1241	—	—	225	250	285	400
AH1242	—	—	225	250	285	400
AH1243//24 (sic)	—	—	225	250	285	400
AH1244	—	—	225	250	285	400

C# 60a NAZARANA MOHUR
Gold **Obv. Inscription:** "Muhammad Akbar II" **Mint:** Haidarabad **Note:** Weight varies 10.70-11.40 grams.

Date	Mintage	Good	VG	F	VF	XF
AH1236//15 Rare	—	—	—	—	—	—

Nasir-ad-Daula
AH1244-1273 / 1829-1857AD

HAMMERED COINAGE

C# 68 1/16 MOHUR
Gold **Obv. Inscription:** "Muhammad Akbar II" **Mint:** Haidarabad **Note:** Weight varies 0.67-.71 grams.

Date	Mintage	Good	VG	F	VF	XF
ND(1806-37)	—	—	25.00	35.00	60.00	100

C# 80 1/16 MOHUR
Gold **Obv. Inscription:** "Bahadur Shah" **Mint:** Haidarabad **Note:** Weight varies 0.67-0.71 grams.

Date	Mintage	Good	VG	F	VF	XF
ND(1837-58)	—	—	35.00	50.00	80.00	120

C# 69 1/8 MOHUR
Gold **Obv. Inscription:** "Muhammad Akbar II" **Mint:** Haidarabad **Note:** Weight varies 1.34-1.42 grams.

Date	Mintage	Good	VG	F	VF	XF
ND(1806-37)	—	—	35.00	50.00	90.00	125

C# 81 1/8 MOHUR
Gold **Obv. Inscription:** "Bahadur Shah" **Mint:** Haidarabad **Note:** Weight varies 1.34-1.42 grams.

Date	Mintage	Good	VG	F	VF	XF
ND(1837-58)	—	—	40.00	65.00	100	140

C# 70 1/4 MOHUR
Gold **Obv. Inscription:** "Muhammad Akbar II" **Mint:** Haidarabad **Note:** Weight varies 2.68-2.85 grams.

Date	Mintage	Good	VG	F	VF	XF
ND(1806-37)	—	—	50.00	85.00	130	175

C# 82 1/4 MOHUR
Gold **Obv. Inscription:** "Bahadur Shah" **Mint:** Haidarabad **Note:** Weight varies 2.68-2.85 grams.

Date	Mintage	Good	VG	F	VF	XF
ND(1837-58)	—	—	50.00	85.00	120	200

C# 71 1/2 MOHUR
Gold **Obv. Inscription:** "Muhammad Akbar II" **Mint:** Haidarabad **Note:** Weight varies 5.35-5.70 grams.

Date	Mintage	Good	VG	F	VF	XF
ND(1806-37)	—	—	120	150	200	275

C# 83 1/2 MOHUR
Gold **Obv. Inscription:** "Bahadur Shah" **Mint:** Haidarabad **Note:** Weight varies 5.35-5.70 grams.

Date	Mintage	Good	VG	F	VF	XF
ND(1837-58)	—	—	120	150	200	275

C# 72 MOHUR
Gold **Obv. Inscription:** "Muhammad Akbar II" **Mint:** Haidarabad **Note:** Size varies 22-23mm.

Date	Mintage	Good	VG	F	VF	XF
AH1244	—	—	225	250	300	375
AH1246	—	—	225	250	300	375
AH1248	—	—	225	250	300	375
AH1249	—	—	225	250	300	375
AH1251	—	—	225	250	300	375

C# 84 MOHUR
Gold, 22 mm. **Obv. Inscription:** "Bahadur Shah" **Mint:** Haidarabad **Note:** Weight varies 10.70-11.40 grams.

Date	Mintage	Good	VG	F	VF	XF
AH1258//6	—	—	225	250	275	325
AH1260	—	—	225	250	275	325
AH1261//8	—	—	225	250	275	325
AH1263//9 (sic)	—	—	225	250	275	325
AH1264	—	—	225	250	275	325
AH1265	—	—	225	250	275	325
AH1266//11 (sic)	—	—	225	250	275	325
AH1267//12 (sic)	—	—	225	250	275	325
AH1268	—	—	225	250	275	325
AH1269	—	—	225	250	275	325
AH1270//15 (sic)	—	—	225	250	275	325
AH1271	—	—	225	250	275	325
AH1273//17 (sic)	—	—	225	250	275	325
AH1273//18 (sic)	—	—	225	250	275	325

Afzal-ad-Daula
AH1273-1285 / 1857-1869AD

HAMMERED COINAGE

Y# 8 1/8 MOHUR
Gold, 11 mm. **Obv. Inscription:** "Asaf Jah, Nizam al-Mulk" **Mint:** Haidarabad **Note:** Weight varies 1.34-1.42 grams.

Date	Mintage	Good	VG	F	VF	XF
AH1279	—	—	40.00	55.00	90.00	125
AH1280	—	—	40.00	55.00	90.00	125
AH1281	—	—	40.00	55.00	90.00	125

Y# 9 1/4 MOHUR
Gold, 14 mm. **Obv. Inscription:** "Asaf Jah, Nizam al-Mulk" **Mint:** Haidarabad **Note:** Weight varies 2.68-2.85 grams.

Date	Mintage	Good	VG	F	VF	XF
AH1281	—	—	50.00	75.00	125	175

Y# 10 1/2 MOHUR
Gold, 16 mm. **Obv. Inscription:** "Asaf Jah, Nizam al-Mulk" **Mint:** Haidarabad **Note:** Weight varies 5.35-5.70 grams.

Date	Mintage	Good	VG	F	VF	XF
AH1281	—	—	120	140	175	250

C# 96 MOHUR
Gold, 23 mm. **Obv. Inscription:** "Bahadur Shah II" **Mint:** Haidarabad

Date	Mintage	Good	VG	F	VF	XF
AH1274	—	—	225	250	300	325
AH1275	—	—	225	250	300	325

Y# 11 MOHUR
Gold **Obv. Inscription:** "Asaf Jah, Nizam al-Mulk" **Mint:** Haidarabad **Note:** Weight varies 10.70-11.40 grams.

Date	Mintage	Good	VG	F	VF	XF
AH1275//2	—	—	225	250	270	290
AH1276	—	—	225	250	270	290
AH1277	—	—	225	250	270	290
AH1278	—	—	225	250	270	290
AH1279	—	—	225	250	270	290
AH1280	—	—	225	250	270	290
AH1281//8	—	—	225	250	270	290
AH1282	—	—	225	250	270	290
AH1283	—	—	225	250	270	290
AH1284	—	—	225	250	270	290
AH1285	—	—	225	250	270	290

Mir Mahbub Ali Khan II
AH1285-1329 / 1869-1911AD

HAMMERED COINAGE

Y# 18 1/16 ASHRAFI
0.6980 g., 0.9100 Gold **Obverse:** Persian letter "M" for Mahbub above "k" of "Mulk" **Obv. Inscription:** "Asaf Jah, Nizam al-Mulk" **Mint:** Haidarabad (Farkhanda Bunyad)

Date	Mintage	Good	VG	F	VF	XF
AH1305	—	15.00	22.00	32.00	40.00	60.00
AH1314	—	15.00	22.00	32.00	40.00	60.00
AH1315	—	15.00	22.00	32.00	40.00	60.00
AH1321//37	—	15.00	22.00	32.00	40.00	60.00

Y# 19 1/8 ASHRAFI
1.3970 g., 0.9100 Gold .0408 oz. AGW **Obverse:** Persian letter "M" for Mahbub above "k" of "Mulk" **Obv. Inscription:** "Asaf Jah, Nizam al-Mulk" **Mint:** Haidarabad (Farkhanda Bunyad)

Date	Mintage	Good	VG	F	VF	XF
AH1293	—	—	30.00	45.00	60.00	80.00
AH1302	—	—	30.00	45.00	60.00	80.00
AH1306	—	—	30.00	45.00	60.00	80.00
AH1309	—	—	30.00	45.00	60.00	80.00
AH1313	—	—	30.00	45.00	60.00	80.00
AH1316	—	—	30.00	45.00	60.00	80.00
AH1317//33	—	—	30.00	45.00	60.00	80.00
AH1318	—	—	30.00	45.00	60.00	80.00
AH1320	—	BV	30.00	45.00	60.00	80.00
AH1321	—	BV	30.00	45.00	60.00	80.00

Y# 20 1/4 ASHRAFI
2.7940 g., 0.9100 Gold .0817 oz. AGW **Obverse:** Persian letter "M" for Mahbub above "k" of "Mulk" **Obv. Inscription:** "Asaf Jah, Nizam al-Mulk" **Mint:** Haidarabad (Farkhanda Bunyad)

Date	Mintage	Good	VG	F	VF	XF
AH1301	—	—	BV	65.00	85.00	110
AH1304	—	—	BV	65.00	85.00	110
AH1306	—	—	BV	65.00	85.00	110
AH1309	—	—	BV	65.00	85.00	110
AH1314//30	—	—	BV	65.00	85.00	110
AH1315	—	—	BV	65.00	85.00	110
AH1316	—	—	BV	65.00	85.00	110
AH1318//35 (sic)	—	—	BV	65.00	85.00	110
AH1319//35	—	—	BV	65.00	85.00	110

Y# 21 1/2 ASHRAFI
5.5890 g., 0.9100 Gold .1635 oz. AGW **Obverse:** Persian letter "M" for Mahbub above "k" of "Mulk" **Obv. Inscription:** "Asaf Jah, Nizam al-Mulk" **Mint:** Haidarabad (Farkhanda Bunyad)

Date	Mintage	Good	VG	F	VF	XF
AH1301//17	—	—	BV	BV	125	150
AH1316	—	—	BV	BV	125	150
AH1317	—	—	BV	BV	125	150
AH1320	—	—	135	150	175	225
AH1321	—	—	135	150	175	225

Y# 22 ASHRAFI
11.1780 g., 0.9100 Gold .3270 oz. AGW **Obverse:** Persian letter "M" for Mahbub above "k" of "Mulk" **Obv. Inscription:** "Asaf Jah, Nizam al-Mulk" **Mint:** Haidarabad (Farkhanda Bunyad)

Date	Mintage	Good	VG	F	VF	XF
AH1286//1	—	—	BV	BV	BV	260
AH1287	—	—	BV	BV	BV	260
AH1288	—	—	BV	BV	BV	260
AH1289	—	—	BV	BV	BV	260
AH1290	—	—	BV	BV	BV	260
AH1292	—	—	BV	BV	BV	260
AH1293	—	—	BV	BV	BV	260
AH1294	—	—	BV	BV	BV	260
AH1295	—	—	BV	BV	BV	260
AH1296	—	—	BV	BV	BV	260
AH1297	—	—	BV	BV	BV	260
AH1298//14	—	—	BV	BV	BV	260
AH1299	—	—	BV	BV	BV	260
AH1300//16	—	—	BV	BV	BV	260
AH1301	—	—	BV	BV	BV	260
AH1302	—	—	BV	BV	BV	260
AH1303	—	—	BV	BV	BV	260
AH1304	—	—	BV	BV	BV	260
AH1305	—	—	BV	BV	BV	260
AH1306	—	—	BV	BV	BV	260
AH1307	—	—	BV	BV	BV	260
AH1308	—	—	BV	BV	BV	260
AH1309//25	—	—	BV	BV	BV	260
AH1310	—	—	BV	BV	BV	260
AH1311	—	—	BV	BV	BV	260
AH1312//28	—	—	BV	BV	BV	260
AH1313	—	—	BV	BV	BV	260
AH1314//30	—	—	BV	BV	BV	260
AH1314//31	—	—	BV	BV	BV	260
AH1315	—	—	BV	BV	BV	260

INDIA - PRINCELY STATES — HYDERABAD

Date	Mintage	Good	VG	F	VF	XF
AH1316	—	—	BV	BV	BV	260
AH1317	—	—	BV	BV	BV	260
AH1318	—	—	BV	BV	BV	260
AH1319	—	—	BV	235	250	300
AH1320	—	—	BV	235	250	300
AH1321	—	—	BV	235	250	300

MILLED COINAGE
Provisional Series

Y# 33 ASHRAFI
0.9100 Gold **Obverse:** Inscription and Persian letter "M" for Mahbub above "k" of "Mulk" **Obv. Inscription:** "Asaf Jah, Nizam al-Mulk" **Mint:** Haidarabad (Farkhanda Bunyad) **Note:** Weight varies 11.05-11.20 g.

Date	Mintage	VG	F	VF	XF	Unc
AH1311//27	—	450	650	800	1,000	

MILLED COINAGE
Standard Series

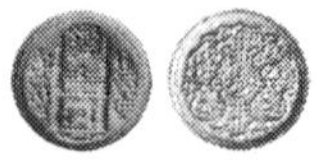

Y# 41.1 1/8 ASHRAFI
1.3940 g., 0.9100 Gold **Obverse:** Chahar Minar gateway, signature variety Type I between minarets **Mint:** Haidarabad (Farkhanda Bunyad)

Date	Mintage	VG	F	VF	XF	Unc
AH1325//41	—	30.00	38.00	55.00	75.00	100

Y# 41.2 1/8 ASHRAFI
1.3940 g., 0.9100 Gold **Obverse:** Chahar Minar gateway, signature variety Type II between minarets **Mint:** Haidarabad (Farkhanda Bunyad)

Date	Mintage	VG	F	VF	XF	Unc
AH1329//44	—	30.00	38.00	55.00	75.00	100

Y# 42.1 1/4 ASHRAFI
2.7940 g., 0.9100 Gold **Obverse:** Chahar Minar gateway, signature variety Type I between minarets **Mint:** Haidarabad (Farkhanda Bunyad)

Date	Mintage	VG	F	VF	XF	Unc
AH1325//41	—	60.00	70.00	85.00	110	150

Y# 42.2 1/4 ASHRAFI
2.7940 g., 0.9100 Gold **Obverse:** Chahar Minar gateway, signature variety Type II between minarets **Mint:** Haidarabad (Farkhanda Bunyad)

Date	Mintage	VG	F	VF	XF	Unc
AH1328//43	—	60.00	70.00	85.00	100	150
AH1329//44	—	60.00	70.00	85.00	100	150

Y# 43.1 1/2 ASHRAFI
5.5890 g., 0.9100 Gold **Obverse:** Chahar Minar gateway, signature variety Type I between minarets **Mint:** Haidarabad (Farkhanda Bunyad)

Date	Mintage	VG	F	VF	XF	Unc
AH1325//41	—	120	135	160	185	275
AH1326//41	—	120	135	160	185	275

Y# 43.2 1/2 ASHRAFI
5.5890 g., 0.9100 Gold **Obverse:** Chahar Minar gateway, signature variety Type II between minarets **Mint:** Haidarabad (Farkhanda Bunyad)

Date	Mintage	VG	F	VF	XF	Unc
AH1328//43	—	120	135	160	185	275
AH1329//44	—	120	135	160	185	275

Y# 44.1 ASHRAFI
11.1780 g., 0.9100 Gold **Obverse:** Chahar Minar gateway, signature variety Type I between minarets **Mint:** Haidarabad (Farkhanda Bunyad)

Date	Mintage	VG	F	VF	XF	Unc
AH1325//41	—	225	250	275	325	400

Y# 44.2 ASHRAFI
11.1780 g., 0.9100 Gold **Obverse:** Chahar Minar gateway, signature variety Type II between minarets **Mint:** Haidarabad (Farkhanda Bunyad)

Date	Mintage	VG	F	VF	XF	Unc
AH1328//43	—	225	250	275	325	400
AH1329//44	—	225	250	275	325	400

Mir Usman Ali Khan
AH1329-1367 / 1911-1948AD

MILLED COINAGE
First Series

Y# 54.1 1/8 ASHRAFI
1.3940 g., 0.9100 Gold .0408 oz. AGW **Obverse:** Chahar Minar gateway with short "Ain" in doorway **Mint:** Haidarabad (Farkhanda Bunyad)

Date	Mintage	VG	F	VF	XF	Unc
AH1329//1 Rare	—	—	—	—	—	—

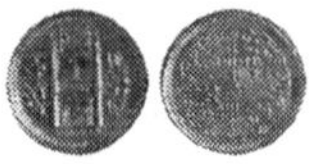

Y# 54.2 1/8 ASHRAFI
1.3940 g., 0.9100 Gold .0408 oz. AGW **Obverse:** Chahar Minar gateway with full "Ain" in doorway **Mint:** Haidarabad (Farkhanda Bunyad)

Date	Mintage	VG	F	VF	XF	Unc
AH1337//8	—	—	32.50	42.50	50.00	80.00
AH1340//11	—	—	32.50	42.50	50.00	80.00
AH1343	—	—	32.50	42.50	50.00	80.00
AH1344//15	—	—	32.50	42.50	50.00	80.00
AH1353	—	—	32.50	42.50	50.00	80.00
AH1354//25	—	—	32.50	42.50	50.00	80.00
AH1356//27	—	—	32.50	42.50	50.00	80.00
AH1360	—	—	32.50	42.50	50.00	80.00
AH1366//37	—	—	32.50	42.50	50.00	80.00
AH1368//39	—	—	32.50	42.50	50.00	80.00

Y# 55 1/4 ASHRAFI
2.7940 g., 0.9100 Gold .0817 oz. AGW **Obverse:** Chahar Minar gateway **Mint:** Haidarabad (Farkhanda Bunyad)

Date	Mintage	VG	F	VF	XF	Unc
AH1337//8	—	—	60.00	75.00	90.00	135
AH1342//13	—	—	60.00	75.00	90.00	135
AH1342//14	—	—	60.00	75.00	90.00	135
AH1349//20	—	—	60.00	75.00	90.00	135
AH1353//23 (sic)	—	—	60.00	75.00	90.00	135
AH1354//25	—	—	60.00	75.00	90.00	135
AH1357	—	—	60.00	75.00	90.00	135
AH1360//31	—	—	60.00	75.00	90.00	135
AH1367//38	—	—	60.00	75.00	90.00	135

Y# 56.1 1/2 ASHRAFI
5.5890 g., 0.9100 Gold .1635 oz. AGW **Obverse:** Chahar Minar gateway with short "Ain" in doorway **Mint:** Haidarabad (Farkhanda Bunyad)

Date	Mintage	VG	F	VF	XF	Unc
AH1329//1	—	—	100	135	185	300

Y# 56.2 1/2 ASHRAFI
5.5890 g., 0.9100 Gold .1635 oz. AGW **Obverse:** Chahar Minar gateway with full "Ain" in doorway **Mint:** Haidarabad (Farkhanda Bunyad)

Date	Mintage	VG	F	VF	XF	Unc
AH1337//8	—	—	120	150	175	250
AH1342//14	—	—	120	150	175	250
AH1343//14	—	—	120	150	175	250
AH1344//14 (sic)	—	—	120	150	175	250
AH1345//16	—	—	120	150	175	250
AH1349//20	—	—	120	150	175	250
AH1354//25	—	—	120	150	175	250
AH1357//29	—	—	120	150	175	250
AH1366//37	—	—	120	150	175	250
AH1367//38	—	—	120	150	175	250

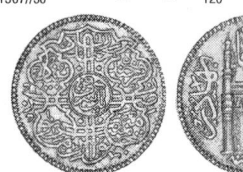

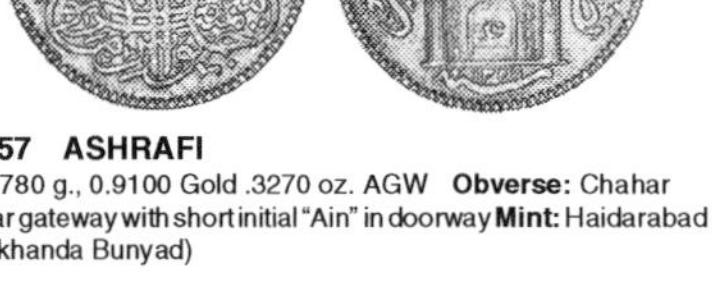

Y# 57 ASHRAFI
11.1780 g., 0.9100 Gold .3270 oz. AGW **Obverse:** Chahar Minar gateway with short initial "Ain" in doorway **Mint:** Haidarabad (Farkhanda Bunyad)

Date	Mintage	VG	F	VF	XF	Unc
AH1329//1	—	—	235	300	350	500
AH1330//1	—	—	235	300	350	500

Y# 57a ASHRAFI
11.1780 g., 0.9100 Gold .3270 oz. AGW **Obverse:** Chahar Minar gateway with full initial "Ain" in doorway **Mint:** Haidarabad (Farkhanda Bunyad)

Date	Mintage	VG	F	VF	XF	Unc
AH1331//3	—	—	225	285	325	450
AH1333//4	—	—	225	285	325	450
AH1337//8	—	—	225	285	325	450
AH1337//9	—	—	225	285	325	450
AH1338//9	—	—	225	285	325	450
AH1340//11	—	—	225	285	325	450
AH1342//14	—	—	225	285	325	450
AH1343//14	—	—	225	285	325	450
AH1344//15	—	—	225	285	325	450
AH1348//19	—	—	225	285	325	450
AH1349//20	—	—	225	285	325	450
AH1354//25	—	—	225	285	325	450
AH1358//30	—	—	225	285	325	450
AH1360//31	—	—	225	285	325	450
AH1362//34	—	—	225	285	325	450

MILLED COINAGE
Second Series

Y# 67 ASHRAFI
11.1780 g., 0.9100 Gold .3270 oz. AGW **Mint:** Haidarabad (Farkhanda Bunyad)

Date	Mintage	VG	F	VF	XF	Unc
AH1368//39	—	—	—	—	—	—

PATTERNS
Including off metal strikes

KM#	Date	Mintage	Identification	Mkt Val
Pn3	AH1311	—	Ashrafi. Gold. Y33a	—
Pn4	AH1311//27	—	Ashrafi. Copper. KM33.	—
Pn11	AH1324//40	—	1/2 Ashrafi. Silver. Y#43.	—
Pn12	AH1324//40	—	Ashrafi. Silver. Y#44.	—

HYDERABAD FEUDATORIES - KALAYANI

Kallian
A town located in north Mysore.

Nawab
Mohammad Shah Khair al-Din

Mint mark: كليان

TOWN
(Kallian)

Mohammad Shah Khair al-Din
Nawab

HAMMERED COINAGE

KM# 9 MOHUR
10.9400 g., Gold **Note:** Similar to 1 Rupee, KM#6.

Date	Mintage	Good	VG	F	VF	XF
AH12xx Rare	—	—	—	—	—	—

INDORE

The Holkars were one of the three dominant Maratha powers (with the Peshwas and Sindhias), with major landholdings in Central India.

Indore State originated in 1728 with a grant of land north of the Narbada river by the Maratha Peshwa of Poona to Malhar Rao Holkar, a cavalry commander in his service. After Holkar's death (ca.1765) his daughter-in-law, Ahalya Bai, assumed the position of Queen Regent. Together with Tukoji Rao she effectively ruled the State until her death thirty years later. But it was left to Tukoji's son, Jaswant Rao, to challenge the dominance of the Poona Marathas in the Maratha Confederacy, eventually defeating the Peshwa's army in 1802. But at this point the fortunes of the

Holkars suffered a serious reverse. Although Jaswant Rao had initially defeated a small British force under Col. William Monson, he was badly beaten by a contingent under Lord Lake. As a result Holkar was forced to cede a considerable portion of his territory and from this time until India's independence in 1947, the residual State of Indore was obliged to accept British protection.

For more detailed data on the Indore series, see *A Study of Holkar State Coinage*, by P.K. Sethi, S.K. Bhatt and R. Holkar (1976).

HOLKAR RULERS
Jaswant Rao, SE1719-1734/AH1213-1226/1798-1811AD
Mulhar Rao II, AH1226-1248/1811-1833AD
Martand Rao, AH1249/1834AD
Hari Rao, AH1250-1260/1834-1843AD
Khande Rao, AH1260-1261/1843-1844AD
Tukoji Rao II, VS1891-1943/SE1766-1808/AH1261-1304/1844-1886AD
Shivaji Rao, VS1943-1960/FE1296-1313/1886-1903AD

MINTS

Indore

BRITISH PROTECTORATE
Tukoji Rao II
VS1891-1943 / SE1766-1808 /
AH1261-1304 / 1844-1886AD
HAMMERED COINAGE

KM# 27   MOHUR
10.8300 g., Gold   **Mint:** Indore

Date	Mintage	Good	VG	F	VF	XF
VS1941 (1883) Rare	—	—	—	—	—	—

JAIPUR

Tradition has it that the region of Jaipur, located in northwest India, once belonged to an ancient Kachwaha Rajput dynasty which claimed descent from Kush, one of the sons of Rama, King of Ayodhya. But the Princely State of Jaipur originated in the 12th century. Comparatively small in size, the State remained largely unnoticed until after the 16th century when the Jaipur royal house became famous for its military skills and thereafter supplied the Mughals with some of their more distinguished generals. The city of Jaipur was founded about 1728 by Maharaja Jai Singh II who was well known for his knowledge of mathematics and astronomy. The late 18th and early 19th centuries were difficult times for Jaipur. They were marked by internal rivalry, exacerbated by Maratha or Pindari incursions. In 1818 this culminated with a treaty whereby Jaipur came under British protection and oversight.

RULERS
Pratap Singh, AH1192-1218/1778-1803AD
Jagat Singh II, AH1218-1234/1803-1818AD
Mohan Singh, AH1234-1235/1818-1819AD
Jai Singh III, AH1235-1251/1819-1835AD
Ram Singh, AH1251-1298/1835-1880AD
Madho Singh II, 1880-1922AD
Man Singh II, 1922-1949AD

All coins struck prior to AH1274/1857AD are in the name of the Mughal emperor. The corresponding AH date is listed in ( ) with each regnal year. Some overlapping of AH dates with regnal years will be found. Partial dates and recorded full dates are represented by partial ( ) or without ( ).

Beginning in 1857, coins were struck jointly in the names and corresponding AD dates of the British sovereign and the names and regnal years of the Maharajas of Jaipur.

The coins ordinarily bear both the AH date before 1857 or the AD date after 1857, as well as the regnal year, but as it is found only at the extreme right of the obverse die, it is almost never visible on the regular coinage but generally legible on the Nazarana coins which were struck utilizing the entire dies.

The listing of regnal years is very incomplete and many more years will turn up. In general, unlisted years are usually worth no more than years listed.

MINT NAMES
Coins were struck at two mints, which bear the following characteristic marks on the reverse:

Sawai Jaipur

Mint marks:

Jhar   Whisk   Leaf

Regal Issues
To distinguish coins between Ram Singh and his son/successor Madho Singh II, note that the coins of Ram Singh have a small slanting cross or dagger between the Ram and Singh symbols whereas the coins of Singh II do not.

In the names of Queen Victoria

and Ram Singh
Years 22-45/857-1880AD

In the names of Queen Victoria

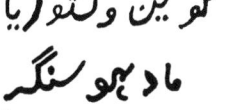

And Madho Singh II
Years 1-43/1880-1922AD
NOTE: Queen Victoria's name was retained on Madho Singh II's coinage until 1922AD. No coins were struck with Edward VII's name by Madho Singh II.

In the names of George V and

Manh Singh II
Years 1-14/1922-1935AD

In the names of George VI

And Man Singh II
Years 15-28/1936-1949AD
NOTE: Refer to George V and Man Singh II legends.

HAMMERED COINAGE

KM# 55   MOHUR
Gold   **Obv. Inscription:** "Shah Alam II"   **Mint:** Sawai Jaipur   **Note:** Weight varies 10.70-11.40 grams.

Date	Mintage	Good	VG	F	VF	XF
ND//43 (1802-03)	—	—	225	250	275	325
AH121x//44	—	—	225	250	275	325

HAMMERED COINAGE
Mughal Style

KM# 98   1/4 MOHUR
Gold   **Obv. Inscription:** "Bahadur Shah II"   **Mint:** Sawai Jaipur   **Note:** Weight varies 2.68-2.85 grams.

Date	Mintage	Good	VG	F	VF	XF
ND//12 (1847-48)	—	—	80.00	125	150	225

KM# 76   1/2 MOHUR
Gold   **Obv. Inscription:** "Muhammad Akbar II"   **Mint:** Sawai Jaipur   **Note:** Weight varies 5.35-5.80 grams.

Date	Mintage	Good	VG	F	VF	XF
AH124x//25	—	—	125	150	225	325

KM# 100   1/2 MOHUR
Gold   **Obv. Inscription:** "Bahadur Shah II"   **Mint:** Sawai Jaipur   **Note:** Weight varies 5.35-5.70 grams.

Date	Mintage	Good	VG	F	VF	XF
ND//12 (1847-48)	—	—	125	150	200	275

KM# 77   MOHUR
Gold   **Obv. Inscription:** "Muhammad Akbar II"   **Mint:** Sawai Jaipur   **Note:** Weight varies 10.70-11.60 grams.

Date	Mintage	Good	VG	F	VF	XF
AH122(x)//1	—	—	BV	BV	225	300
ND//2 (1807-08)	—	—	BV	BV	225	300
ND//5 (1810-11)	—	—	BV	BV	225	300
ND//7 (1812-13)	—	—	BV	BV	225	300
ND//8 (1813-14)	—	—	BV	BV	225	300
ND//9 (1814-15)	—	—	BV	BV	225	300
ND//11 (1816-17)	—	—	BV	BV	225	300
ND//12 (1817-18)	—	—	BV	BV	225	300
ND//16 (1821-22)	—	—	BV	BV	225	300
ND//19 (1824-25)	—	—	BV	BV	225	300
AH12(xx)//24	—	—	BV	BV	225	300
ND//29 (1834-35)	—	—	BV	BV	225	300
ND//30 (1835-36)	—	—	BV	BV	225	300

KM# 102   MOHUR
Gold   **Obv. Inscription:** "Bahadur Shah II"   **Mint:** Sawai Jaipur   **Note:** Weight varies 10.70-11.40 grams.

Date	Mintage	Good	VG	F	VF	XF
AH1253//1	—	—	BV	BV	250	325
AH12xx//17	—	—	BV	BV	250	325
ND//5 (1841-42)	—	—	BV	BV	250	325
AH12(xx)//7	—	—	BV	BV	250	325
AH1262//9	—	—	BV	BV	250	325
ND//10 (1845-46)	—	—	BV	BV	250	325
ND//11 (1846-47)	—	—	BV	BV	250	325
ND//12 (1847-48)	—	—	BV	BV	250	325
ND//13 (1848-49)	—	—	BV	BV	250	325
ND//14 (1849-50)	—	—	BV	BV	250	325
AH//15 (1850-51)	—	—	BV	BV	250	325
AH12xx//17	—	—	BV	BV	250	325
AH//17 (1852-53)	—	—	BV	BV	250	325
AH1272//18 (sic)	—	—	BV	BV	250	325
AH1272//19	—	—	BV	BV	250	325
ND//20 (1855-56)	—	—	BV	BV	250	325

HAMMERED COINAGE
Regal Style

To distinguish coins between Ram Singh and his son/successor Madho Singh II, note that the coins of Ram Singh have a small slanting cross or dagger between the Ram and Singh symbols, whereas the coins of Singh II do not.

KM# 125   MOHUR
Gold   **Obv. Inscription:** Victoria   **Rev. Inscription:** Ram Singh   **Mint:** Sawai Jaipur   **Note:** Weight varies 10.70-11.40 grams.

Date	Mintage	VG	F	VF	XF	Unc
ND//21 (1856)	—	BV	BV	BV	225	—
ND//22 (1857)	—	BV	BV	BV	225	—
ND//23 (1858)	—	BV	BV	BV	225	—
ND//24 (1859)	—	BV	BV	BV	225	—
ND//25 (1860)	—	BV	BV	BV	225	—
18(60)//25	—	BV	BV	BV	225	—
1861//26	—	BV	BV	BV	225	—
ND//27 (1862)	—	BV	BV	BV	225	—
ND//28 (1863)	—	BV	BV	BV	225	—
ND//29 (1864)	—	BV	BV	BV	225	—
ND//31 (1866)	—	BV	BV	BV	225	—
187(o)//35	—	BV	BV	BV	225	—
ND//36 (1871)	—	BV	BV	BV	225	—
ND//37 (1872)	—	BV	BV	BV	225	—
ND//41 (1876)	—	BV	BV	BV	225	—
ND//42 (1877)	—	BV	BV	BV	225	—
ND//43 (1878)	—	BV	BV	BV	225	—
ND//45 (1880)	—	BV	BV	BV	225	—

Madho Singh
1880-1922AD
HAMMERED COINAGE
Regal Style

To distinguish coins between Ram Singh and his son/successor Madho Singh II, note that the coins of Ram Singh have a small slanting cross or dagger between the Ram and Singh symbols, whereas the coins of Singh II do not.

KM# 150   MOHUR
Gold   **Obv. Inscription:** Victoria....   **Reverse:** Jhar   **Rev. Inscription:** "Madho Singh II"   **Mint:** Sawai Jaipur   **Note:** Weight varies 10.70-11.40 g.

Date	Mintage	Good	VG	F	VF	XF
ND//2 (1881)	—	—	BV	BV	BV	225
ND//5 (1884)	—	—	BV	BV	BV	225
18xx//10 (1889)	—	—	BV	BV	BV	225
ND//16 (1895)	—	—	BV	BV	BV	225
ND//17 (1896)	—	—	BV	BV	BV	225

INDIA - PRINCELY STATES

JAIPUR

Date	Mintage	Good	VG	F	VF	XF
189(8)//19	—	—	BV	BV	BV	225
ND//20 (1899)	—	—	BV	BV	BV	225
ND//24 (1904)	—	—	225	250	275	325
ND//37 (1916)	—	—	225	250	275	325
ND//37 (1916)	—	—	225	250	275	325
ND//40 (1919)	—	—	225	250	275	325
ND//41 (1920)	—	—	225	250	275	325

MILLED COINAGE

KM# 151 NAZARANA RUPEE
Gold **Obv. Inscription:** Victoria... **Reverse:** Jhar Rev. **Inscription:** "Madho Singh II" **Mint:** Sawai Jaipur **Note:** Size varies 29-36mm, weight varies 10.70-11.40 grams.

Date	Mintage	Good	VG	F	VF	XF
1880//1	—	—	425	700	2,000	3,500
1887//8	—	—	425	700	2,000	3,500
1888//9	—	—	425	700	2,000	3,500

Man Singh II
1922-1949AD

HAMMERED COINAGE
Regal Style

To distinguish coins between Ram Singh and his son/successor Madho Singh II, note that the coins of Ram Singh have a small slanting cross or dagger between the Ram and Singh symbols, whereas the coins of Singh II do not.

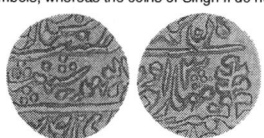

KM# 163 MOHUR
Gold **Obv. Inscription:** George V... **Reverse:** Jhar Rev. **Inscription:** Man Singh II... **Mint:** Sawai Jaipur **Note:** Weight varies 10.70-11.40 g.

Date	Mintage	Good	VG	F	VF	XF
ND//2 (1923)	—	—	235	265	300	425
1(924)//3	—	—	235	265	300	425
1925//4	—	—	235	265	300	425
19(28)//7	—	—	235	265	300	425

KM# 200 MOHUR
Gold **Obv. Inscription:** George (VI)... **Rev. Inscription:** Man Singh (II)... **Mint:** Sawai Jaipur **Note:** Weight varies 10.70-11.40 g.

Date	Mintage	Good	VG	F	VF	XF
ND//20 (1941)	—	—	225	250	275	325
ND//22 (1943)	—	—	225	250	275	325
ND//26 (1947)	—	—	225	250	275	325
ND//27 (1948)	—	—	225	250	275	325
1949//28	—	—	225	250	275	325

MILLED COINAGE

KM# 201 NAZARANA MOHUR
Gold **Obv. Inscription:** George (VI)... **Rev. Inscription:** Man Singh (II)... **Mint:** Sawai Jaipur

Date	Mintage	Good	VG	F	VF	XF
ND1949//28 Rare	—	—	—	—	—	—

JAISALMIR

Although the ruling Rajputs (or rawals) of this desert territory, located in northwest India traced their ancestry back to pre-Asokan times, the State of Jaisalmir was founded by Deoraj, the first rawal, only in the 10th century. Jaisalmir city was established by Rawal Jaisal, after whom both the city and the State were named. Like Jaipur, Jaisalmir reached its zenith in Mughal times, after being forced to acknowledge the supremacy of Delhi in the time of the Emperor Shah Jahan. With Mughal disintegration, Jaisalmir also fell upon hard times and most of its outlying provinces were lost. The state came under British protection in 1818, and on March 30th, 1949 it was merged into Rajasthan.

RULERS
BMulraj Singh, AH1176-1235/1762-1819AD

MINT
Jaisalmir

Regal Issues
In the name of Queen Victoria
Second Series:
Frozen regnal year 22 w/mint marks on reverse.

Bird   Umbrella

Ranjit Singh
AH1263-1281 / 1846-1864AD

HAMMERED COINAGE
Regal Style

KM# 28 NAZARANA 5 MOHURS
54.0000 g., Gold **Obv. Inscription:** "... Victoria farmen rawai Inglistan,,,", Gujarati "17" in "n" of "farmen" **Shape:** Hexagonal

Date	Mintage	Good	VG	F	VF	XF
ND//22 (1860) Rare	—	—	—	—	—	—

KM# 37 1/8 MOHUR
1.3500 g., Gold, 12 mm. **Obv. Inscription:** "... Victoria farmen rawai Inglistan...", Gujarati "17" in "n" of "farmen" **Note:** Mint mark: bird and umbrella on reverse.

Date	Mintage	Good	VG	F	VF	XF
ND//22 (1860) Rare	—	—	—	—	—	—

KM# 38 1/4 MOHUR
2.7000 g., Gold, 15 mm. **Obv. Inscription:** "... Victoria farmen rawai Inglistan...", Gujarati "17" in "n" of "farmen" **Note:** Mint mark: bird and umbrella on reverse.

Date	Mintage	Good	VG	F	VF	XF
ND//22 (1860) Rare	—	—	—	—	—	—

KM# 39 1/2 MOHUR
5.4000 g., Gold, 18 mm. **Obv. Inscription:** "... Victoria farmen rawai Inglistan...", Gujarati "17" in "n" of "farmen" **Note:** Mint mark: bird and umbrella on reverse.

Date	Mintage	Good	VG	F	VF	XF
ND//22 (1860) Rare	—	—	—	—	—	—

KM# 40 MOHUR
10.8000 g., Gold **Obv. Inscription:** "... Victoria farmen rawai Inglistan...", Gujarati "17" in "n" of "farmen" **Note:** Mint mark: bird and umbrella on reverse. Fr. #1202.

Date	Mintage	Good	VG	F	VF	XF
ND//22 (1860)	—	—	225	265	400	600

JANJIRA ISLAND

Island near Bombay. Dynasty of Nawabs dates from 1489AD.
The origin of the nawabs of Janjira is obscure. They were Sidi or Abyssinian Muslims whose ancestors, serving as admirals to the Muslim rulers of the Deccan, had been granted jagirs (revenue-producing land tenures) under the Adil Shahi sultans of Bijapur. In 1870, Janjira came under direct British rule. Until 1924 the nawabs of Janjira also exercised suzerainty over Jafarabad on the Kathiawar peninsular.

RULER
Sidi Ibrahim Khan III, AH1265-1297 / 1848-1879AD

Sidi Ibrahim Khan III
AH1265-1297 / 1848-1879AD

HAMMERED COINAGE
KM# 35 MOHUR
Gold, 23 mm.

Date	Mintage	Good	VG	F	VF	XF
AH1283	—	—	650	1,100	1,500	2,000

JODHPUR

Jodhpur, also known as Marwar, located in northwest India, was the largest Princely State in the Rajputana Agency. Its population in 1941 exceeded two and a half million. The "Maharajadhirajas" ("Great Kings of Kings") of Jodhpur were Rathor Rajputs who claimed an extremely ancient ancestry from Rama, king of Ayodhya. With the collapse of the Rathor rulers of Kanauj in 1194 the family entered Marwar where they laid the foundation of the new state. The city of Jodhpur was built by Rao Jodha in 1459, and the city and the state were named after him. In 1561 the Mughal Emperor Akbar invaded Jodhpur, forcing its submission. In 1679 Emperor Aurangzeb sacked the city, an experience which stimulated the Rajput royal house to forge a new unity among themselves in order to extricate themselves from Mughal hegemony. Internal dissension once again asserted itself and Rajput unity, which had both benefited from and accelerated Mughal decline, fell apart before the Marathas. In 1818 Jodhpur came under British protection and control and after Indian independence in 1947 the State was merged into Rajasthan. Jodhpur is best known for its particular style of riding breeches (jodpurs) which became very popular in the West in the late 19th century.

RULERS
The issues of the first four rulers before 1858AD bearing both the AH and VS dates as well as the regnal years, are rarely actual dates and years, but were "frozen" and used for many years without change, and were often quite indiscriminately applied. Mismatched regnal years and dates are frequently encountered, as well as blundered dates of all sorts. Dates lying outside the reigns of the rulers named on coins (after 1858AD) were often used. Thus the date or regnal year may not represent the actual dating of the coin.

Coinage of the first four rulers (until 1858AD) is not distinguished by reign, but by type of inscription, mint, and pseudo-date.
Bhim Singh, AH1207-1218/1792-1803AD
Man Singh, AH1218-1259/1803-1843AD
Takhat Singh, AH1259-1290/VS1900-1930/1843-1873AD
Jaswant Singh, AH1290-1313/VS1930-1952/1873-1895AD
Sardar Singh, VS1952-1968/1895-1911AD
Sumer Singh, VS1968-1975/1911-1918AD
Umaid Singh, VS1975-2004/1918-1947AD
Hanwant Singh, as Titular Ruler, VS2004-2009/1947-1949AD

MINTS
Jodhpur

Mint mark:

Jodhpur

KINGDOM

HAMMERED COINAGE
KM# 26 MOHUR
11.0000 g., Gold, 19 mm. **Obv. Inscription:** "Shah Alam II" **Mint:** Jodhpur

Date	Mintage	Good	VG	F	VF	XF
AH1218//45	—	—	200	300	425	600

KM# 40 MOHUR
11.0000 g., Gold, 20 mm. **Obverse:** Sword **Obv. Inscription:** "Muhammad Akbar II" **Mint:** Jodhpur

Date	Mintage	Good	VG	F	VF	XF
ND(1221)//22	—	—	200	300	425	600

Takhat Singh
AH1259-1290 / VS1900-1930 / 1843-1873AD
HAMMERED COINAGE

KM# 50 MOHUR
11.0000 g., Gold, 20 mm. Obv. Inscription: Victoria and Takhat Singh Mint: Jodhpur

Date	Mintage	Good	VG	F	VF	XF
ND//16 (1858-59)	—	—	175	250	350	500

KM# 70 MOHUR
10.9000 g., Gold Mint: Jodhpur Note: Struck with rupee dies.

Date	Mintage	Good	VG	F	VF	XF
VS1926 (1869)	—	—	—	—	—	—
Rare						

Jaswant Singh
AH1290-1313 / VS1930-1952 / 1873-1895AD
HAMMERED COINAGE

KM# 78 1/4 MOHUR
Gold Obv. Inscription: Victoria & Jaswant Singh Mint: Jodhpur

Date	Mintage	Good	VG	F	VF	XF
AH1293	—	—	—	—	—	—

KM# 79 1/2 MOHUR
5.5000 g., Gold Obv. Inscription: Victoria & Jaswant Singh Mint: Jodhpur

Date	Mintage	Good	VG	F	VF	XF
AH1293	—	—	—	—	—	—

KM# 80 MOHUR
10.1000 g., Gold Obv. Inscription: Victoria & Jaswant Singh Mint: Jodhpur

Date	Mintage	Good	VG	F	VF	XF
AH1293	—	—	—	—	—	—

KM# 81 MOHUR
11.0000 g., Gold, 20 mm. Obv. Inscription: Victoria & Jaswant Singh Mint: Jodhpur

Date	Mintage	Good	VG	F	VF	XF
VS1942 (1885)	—	—	225	250	350	550
VS1943 (1886)	—	—	225	250	350	550
VS1944 (1887)	—	—	225	250	350	550

Sardar Singh
VS1952-1968 / 1895-1911AD
HAMMERED COINAGE

KM# 88 1/4 MOHUR
2.7500 g., Gold, 15 mm. Obv. Inscription: Victoria and Sardar Singh Mint: Jodhpur

Date	Mintage	Good	VG	F	VF	XF
VS1952 (1895)	—	75.00	125	200	300	

KM# 98 1/4 MOHUR
2.8000 g., Gold Obv. Inscription: Edward (VII)... Rev. Inscription: Sardar Singh... Mint: Jodhpur Note: Y#23.

Date	Mintage	Good	VG	F	VF	XF
ND(1906)	—	—	65.00	85.00	110	165

KM# 89 1/2 MOHUR
5.5000 g., Gold, 18 mm. Obv. Inscription: Victoria and Sardar Singh Mint: Jodhpur

Date	Mintage	Good	VG	F	VF	XF
VS1952 (1895)	—	—	125	150	210	325

KM# 99 1/2 MOHUR
5.5000 g., Gold, 18 mm. Obv. Inscription: Edward (VII)... Rev. Inscription: Sardar Singh... Mint: Jodhpur Note: Y#24.

Date	Mintage	Good	VG	F	VF	XF
ND(1906)	—	—	125	165	225	300

KM# 90 MOHUR
11.0000 g., Gold, 21 mm. Obv. Inscription: Victoria and Sardar Singh Mint: Jodhpur

Date	Mintage	Good	VG	F	VF	XF
VS1952 (1895)	—	—	225	250	350	550

KM# 100.1 MOHUR
11.0000 g., Gold, 20 mm. Obverse: "Ma." Obv. Inscription: Edward (VII)... Rev. Inscription: Sardar Singh... Mint: Jodhpur Note: Y#25.

Date	Mintage	Good	VG	F	VF	XF
1906	—	—	225	285	375	550

KM# 100.2 MOHUR
11.0000 g., Gold, 20 mm. Obverse: "Sa." Obv. Inscription: Edward (VII)... Rev. Inscription: Sardar Singh... Mint: Jodhpur Note: Y#25.

Date	Mintage	Good	VG	F	VF	XF
1906	—	—	225	285	375	550

Sumar Singh
HAMMERED COINAGE

KM# 119 1/2 MOHUR
5.5000 g., Gold, 19 mm. Obv. Inscription: "Ha" Mint: Jodhpur Note: Y#26.

Date	Mintage	Good	VG	F	VF	XF
ND(1911-18)	—	—	120	150	190	250

KM# 120.1 MOHUR
11.0000 g., Gold, 18 mm. Obverse: "Ma." Mint: Jodhpur Note: Y#33.

Date	Mintage	Good	VG	F	VF	XF
ND(1911-18)	—	—	225	285	375	550

KM# 120.2 MOHUR
11.0000 g., Gold, 18 mm. Obv. Inscription: "Ha" Mint: Jodhpur Note: Y#33.

Date	Mintage	Good	VG	F	VF	XF
ND(1911-18)	—	—	225	300	400	600

Umaid Singh
HAMMERED COINAGE

KM# 127.1 1/4 MOHUR
2.7000 g., Gold, 16 mm. Obverse: "OM" Obv. Inscription: George (V)... Rev. Inscription: Umaid Singh... Mint: Jodhpur Note: Y#36.

Date	Mintage	Good	VG	F	VF	XF
ND(1918-35)	—	—	70.00	90.00	120	175

KM# 127.2 1/4 MOHUR
2.7000 g., Gold, 16 mm. Obverse: "Shri" Obv. Inscription: George (V)... Rev. Inscription: Umaid Singh... Mint: Jodhpur Note: Y#36.

Date	Mintage	Good	VG	F	VF	XF
ND(1918-35)	—	—	70.00	90.00	120	175

KM# 128 1/2 MOHUR
5.5000 g., Gold, 18 mm. Obv. Inscription: "George (V)..." Rev. Inscription: "Umaid Singh..." Mint: Jodhpur Note: Y#37.

Date	Mintage	Good	VG	F	VF	XF
ND(1918-35)	—	—	120	165	220	300

KM# 129 MOHUR
11.0000 g., Gold, 18-20 mm. Obverse: "Om" Obv. Inscription: "George (V)..." Rev. Inscription: "Umaid Singh..." Mint: Jodhpur Note: Y#38. Size varies.

Date	Mintage	Good	VG	F	VF	XF
19x8	—	—	225	285	375	550

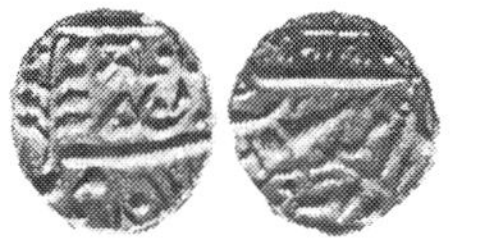

KM# 130 MOHUR
11.0000 g., Gold, 18-20 mm. Obverse: "Shri" Obv. Inscription: "George (V)..." Rev. Inscription: "Umaid Singh..." Mint: Jodhpur Note: Y#38. Size varies.

Date	Mintage	Good	VG	F	VF	XF
ND(1918-35)	—	—	225	265	325	450

KM# 140 MOHUR
11.0100 g., Gold Obv. Inscription: Edward VIII Mint: Jodhpur

Date	Mintage	Good	VG	F	VF	XF
1936	—	—	—	—	—	—

KM# 150 MOHUR
11.0000 g., Gold, 18 mm. Obverse: Large legend, Persian "6" after "George" Obv. Inscription: "George (VI)..." Reverse: Large legend, Persian "6" after "George" Rev. Inscription: "Umaid Singh..." Mint: Jodhpur Note: Y#42.

Date	Mintage	Good	VG	F	VF	XF
VS1997 (1940)	—	—	—	—	—	—
ND(1943)	—	—	250	325	450	650

KM# 151.1 MOHUR
11.0200 g., Gold Obverse: Small legend, without Persian "6" Obv. Inscription: "George (VI)..." Reverse: Small legend, without Persian "6" Rev. Inscription: "Umaid Singh..." Mint: Jodhpur

Date	Mintage	Good	VG	F	VF	XF
VS1999	—	—	250	325	450	650
ND(1942)	—	—	250	325	450	650
VS2000	—	—	250	325	450	650

Hanwant Singh
as Titular Ruler
HAMMERED COINAGE

KM# 158 1/4 MOHUR
2.7000 g., Gold Obv. Inscription: "George (VI)..." Rev. Inscription: "Hanwant Singh..." Mint: Jodhpur

Date	Mintage	Good	VG	F	VF	XF
VS(2004) Rare	—	—	—	—	—	—

KM# 160 MOHUR
11.0000 g., Gold Obv. Inscription: "George (VI)..." Rev. Inscription: "Hanwant Singh..." Mint: Jodhpur

Date	Mintage	Good	VG	F	VF	XF
VS(2004)	—	—	250	350	500	650

JUBBAL

Himalayan principality, 274 sq. mi., located 40 mi. from Simla between the states of Sirmoor and Bussahir; known as the "forest state." Bordered on the west by Balsan and Simla and on the east by Rawin, Tarooch and the district of Dehra Dun. Population: 26,021. Capital: Deorha.

The last Rana of Jubbal's ancestors were once the rulers of Sirmoor. They belong to the Rathor clan of Chandra Bansi Rajputs who descended from Bharata of Maha bharatta fame. The 3 sons of Ugar Chand, early ruler of Sirmoor, were the founders of Jubbal, Sairi, and Rawin. Jubbal came under British protection after the first Gurkha war, when in 1815 Puran Chand received a *sanad*. (In 1857, a *sanad* of adoption was granted.)

RULERS
Rana Padan Chandra, VS1934-1955/1877-1898AD
Raja Rana Shri Gyan Chandra, VS1956-1967/1899-1910AD
Raja Bhayat Chandra Bahadur, VS1967-2004, 1910-1947AD

358 INDIA - PRINCELY STATES

JUBBAL

Raja Bhayay Chandra Bahadur
VS1967-2004/1910-1947AD

MEDALLIC COINAGE

X# 1 1/2 MOHUR
5.5800 g., Gold Obverse: Supported arms Reverse: "Shri" in hexagram

Date	Mintage	VG	F	VF	XF	Unc
VS1988(1931)	—	—	—	—	950	1,250

X# 2 MOHUR
11.5900 g., Gold Obverse: Supported Arms Rev. Designer: "Shri" in hexagram

Date	Mintage	VG	F	VF	XF	Unc
VS1988(1931)	—	—	—	—	1,200	1,500

JUNAGADH

A state located in the Kathiawar peninsula of Western India was originally a petty Rajput kingdom until conquered by the Sultan of Ahmadabad in 1472. It became a Mughal dependency under the Emperor Akbar, administered by the Ahmadabad Subah. In 1735, when the empire began to disintegrate, a Mughal officer and military adventurer, Sher Khan Babi, expelled the Mughal governor and asserted his independence. From that time until Indian independence his descendents ruled the state as nawabs. In 1947 the Nawab of Junagadh tried to accede to the new nation of Pakistan but the Hindu majority in the state objected and Junagadh was absorbed by the Republic of India.

Junagadh first entered into treaty relations with the British in 1807 and maintained a close and friendly association with the Raj. In 1924 this relationship was formalized when Junagadh was placed under an Agent to the Governor General in the western India States. In 1935 the state comprised 3,337 square miles with a population of 545,152, four-fifths of whom were Hindus.

RULERS
Bahadur Khan,
  AH1226-1256/VS1868-1897/1811-1840AD
Hamid Khan II,
  AH1256-1268/VS1897-1908/1840-1851AD
Mahabat Khan II,
  AH1268-1300/VS1908-1939/1851-1882AD
Bahadur Khan III,
  AH1300-1309/VS1939-1948/1882-1891AD
Rasul Muhammad Khan,
  AH1309-1329/VS1948-1968/1891-1911AD

KINGDOM

Bahadur Khan III
AH1300-1309 / VS1939-1948 / 1882-1891AD

MILLED COINAGE

KM# 39 1/2 GOLD KORI
Gold

Date	Mintage	Good	VG	F	VF	XF
AH1309//VS1947	—	—	—	150	300	500

KM# 41 GOLD KORI
4.6100 g., Gold

Date	Mintage	Good	VG	F	VF	XF
AH1309//VS1947	—	—	—	225	450	750

Rasul Muhammad Khan
AH1309-1329 / VS1948-1968 / 1891-1911AD

MILLED COINAGE

KM# 56 GOLD KORI
Gold Obverse: Perso-Arabic inscription Obv. Inscription: "Nawab Bahadur Muhammad Khanji" Reverse: Date, mint name Mint: Junagadh Note: Weight varies 4.02-4.77 grams.

Date	Mintage	VG	F	VF	XF	Unc
AH1309//VS1948	—	—	—	550	900	1,300

KM# 57 GOLD KORI
Gold Obverse: Perso-Arabic inscription Obv. Inscription: "Nawab Bahadur Muhammad Khanji" Reverse: Date, mint name Mint: Junagadh Note: Weight varies 4.02-4.77 grams.

Date	Mintage	VG	F	VF	XF	Unc
AH1318//VS956	—	—	—	650	1,100	1,600

KM# 58 GOLD KORI
Gold Obverse: Perso-Arabic inscription Obv. Inscription: "Nawab Bahadur Muhammad Khanji" Reverse: Date, mint name Mint: Junagadh Note: Weight varies: 4.02-4.77 grams.

Date	Mintage	VG	F	VF	XF	Unc
AH1325/VS1963 (1908)	—	—	—	500	850	1,250

KM# 60 MOHUR
11.5400 g., Gold Obverse: Perso-Arabic inscription Obv. Inscription: "Nawab Bahadur Muhammad Khanji" Reverse: Date, mint name Mint: Junagadh

Date	Mintage	VG	F	VF	XF	Unc
AH1325/VS1963 (1908)	—	—	—	—	2,000	2,800

KM# 61 MOHUR
11.5400 g., Gold Obverse: "Shri Divan" in Devanagari below Mint: Junagadh

Date	Mintage	Good	VG	F	VF	XF
AH1325(1907) Rare	—	—	—	—	—	—

Mahabat Khan III
AH1329-1368 / VS1968-2005 / 1911-1948AD

MILLED COINAGE

KM# 34 GOLD KORI
Gold Note: Size varies 15-16mm.

Date	Mintage	Good	VG	F	VF	XF
AH1292//VS1932	—	—	—	225	450	750

KAITHAL

HAMMERED COINAGE

KM# 11 MOHUR
10.7000 g., Gold, 14 mm. Obv. Inscription: Shah Alam (II)

Date	Mintage	VG	F	VF	XF
ND(1767-1819)	—	—	600	900	1,400	2,000

KARAULI

State located in Rajputana, northwest India.
Karauli was established in the 11th century by Jadon Rajputs, of the same stock as the royal house of Jaisalmir. They are thought to have migrated to Rajasthan from the Mathura region some years earlier. The state passed successively under Mughal and Maratha suzerainty before coming under British authority in 1817.

The Maharajas of Karauli first struck coins in the reign of Manak Pal.

RULERS
Manak Pal, AH1186-1233/1772-1817AD
Harbaksh Pal, AH1233-1254/1817-1838AD
Pratap Pal, AH1255-1264/1838-1848AD
Nar Singh Pal, AH1264-1268/1848-1852AD
Bharat Pal, AH1268-1270/1852-1854AD
Madan Pal, AH1270-1286/1854-1869AD
Jai Singh Pal, 1869-1875AD
Arjun Pal, 1876-1886AD
Bhanwar Pal, 1886-1927

MINT
Karauli كرولي

KINGDOM, BRITISH PROTECTORATE

HAMMERED COINAGE
Regal Style

KM# 57 MOHUR
Gold Obv. Inscription: The exalted Queen, the Emperor for Queen Victoria Note: Similar to 1 Rupee, KM#56.

Date	Mintage	Good	VG	F	VF	XF
ND//3 (1878)	—	—	225	350	500	700

MEDALLIC COINAGE

X# 2 MOHUR
10.9500 g., Gold

Date	Mintage	Good	VG	F	VF	XF
ND//2 (1886) Rare	—	—	—	—	—	—

X# 1 1/2 MOHUR
5.4800 g., Gold

Date	Mintage	Good	VG	F	VF	XF
ND//2 (1886) Rare	—	—	—	—	—	—

KASHMIR

State located in extreme northern India. Part of Afghanistan, Durrani Empire 1752-1819AD, under Sikhs of Punjab 1819-1846AD, locally ruled by Dogra Rajas thereafter. For earlier coinage refer to Afghanistan and Sikh Empire.

RULERS
Dogra Rajas
Gulab Singh,
  VS1903-1913/1846-1856AD
Ranbir Singh,
  VS1914-1942/1857-1885AD
Pertab Singh,
  VS1942-1979/1885-1925AD

MINTS
Jammu جمون
Srinagar سرينگر

KINGDOM

Ranbir Singh
VS1914-1942 / 1857-1885AD

HAMMERED COINAGE

KM# 3 1/3 MOHUR
Gold Mint: Jammu Note: Weight varies 3.57-3.80 grams.

Date	Mintage	Good	VG	F	VF	XF
VS1921 (1864)	—	185	300	1,000	2,000	—

Y# 22 NAZARANA 1/4 MOHUR
2.3000 g., Gold Series: Fourth Silver (Chilki) Mint: Srinagar Note: Size varies 14-15mm.

Date	Mintage	Good	VG	F	VF	XF
VS193x (1873)	—	—	300	500	900	1,500

KISHANGARH

The maharajas of Kishangarh, a small state in northwest India, in the vicinity of Ajmer, belonged to the Rathor Rajputs. The town of Kishangarh, which gave its name to the state, was founded in 1611 and was itself named after Kishen Singh, the first ruler. The maharajas succeeded in reaching terms with Akbar in the late 16th century, and again in 1818 with the British. In 1949 the state was merged into Rajasthan.

RULERS
Kalyan Singh, VS1854-1889/1797-1832AD
Mokham Singh, VS1889-1898/1832-1841AD
Prithvi Singh, VS1898-1936/1841-1879AD
Sardul Singh, VS1936-1957/1879-1900AD
Madan Singh, VS1957-1983/1900-1926AD
Yaghyanarayan Singh, VS1983-1995/1926-1938AD
Sumer Singh, VS1995-2000/1938-1949AD

MINT

Kishangarh
Mint mark:

Symbol on reverse: Jhar

KINGDOM
HAMMERED COINAGE
Regal Style
1858-1879

Y# A1 MOHUR
10.9000 g., Gold Obv. Inscription: "Victoria Inglistan..." Rev. Inscription: "Prithvi Singh" Mint: Kishangarh

Date	Mintage	Good	VG	F	VF	XF
1858//24	—	—	—	—	—	—

HAMMERED COINAGE
Regal Style
1900-1926

Y# D3 MOHUR
10.9000 g., Gold Obv. Inscription: Empress Victoria... Reverse: Jhar Rev. Inscription: Madan Singh...

Date	Mintage	Good	VG	F	VF	XF
ND(1900-01)	—	225	250	300	550	900

HAMMERED COINAGE
1926-1938

Y# 7 1/2 MOHUR
Gold, 18 mm. Obv. Inscription: George (V)... Reverse: Jhar Rev. Inscription: Yaghyanarayan... Note: Approximately 5.50 grams.

Date	Mintage	Good	VG	F	VF	XF
ND//24 (sic) (1926-38)	—	—	145	225	550	850

Y# 8 MOHUR
Gold, 19 mm. Obv. Inscription: George (V)... Reverse: Jhar Rev. Inscription: Yaghyanarayan... Note: Approximately 11.00 grams.

Date	Mintage	Good	VG	F	VF	XF
ND//24 (sic) (1926-38)	—	—	225	300	500	800

KOTAH

Kotah State, located in northwest India was subdivided out of Bundi early in the 17th century when it was given to a younger son of the Bundi raja by the Mughal emperor. The ruler, or maharao, was a Chauhan Rajput. During the years of Maratha ascendancy Kotah fell on hard times, especially from the depredations of Holkar. In 1817 the State came under treaty with the British.

RULERS
Ram Singh II, VS1885-1923/1828-1866AD
Chattar Singh, VS1923-1946/1866-1889AD
Umed Singh II, VS1946-1992/1889-1935AD

MINT

Mintname: Nandgaon

Kotah urf Nandgaon
or Nandgaon urf Kotah on earliest issues.

MINT MARKS

1. ⊠   4.
2. ✤
3. ✿   5.

Mint mark #1 appears beneath #4 on most Kotah coins, and serves to distinguish coins of Kotah from similar issues of Bundi in the pre-Victoria period.

C#28 has mint mark #2 on obv., #1, 3 and 4 on rev. All later issues have #1 on obv., #1, 5 and 4 on rev.

BRITISH PROTECTORATE
HAMMERED COINAGE
Mughal Style

C# 30e MOHUR
10.7000 g., Gold Obv: Without mint mark #1 Obv. Inscription: "Muhammad Akbar II"

Date	Mintage	Good	VG	F	VF	XF
ND//2 (1807-08)	—	—	225	350	500	700

C# 30f MOHUR
10.7000 g., Gold Obv: Without mint mark #1 Obv. Inscription: "Muhammad Akbar II"

Date	Mintage	Good	VG	F	VF	XF
ND//19 (1824-25)	—	—	225	350	500	700

C# 33 MOHUR
11.2000 g., Gold, 19 mm. Obv. Inscription: "Muhammad Akbar II" Note: Weight varies 10.70-11.40 grams.

Date	Mintage	Good	VG	F	VF	XF
ND//1 (1837-38)	—	—	225	300	550	850
ND//19 (1855-56)	—	—	225	300	550	850
ND//20 (1856-57)	—	—	225	300	550	850
ND//21 (1857)	—	—	225	300	550	850

HAMMERED COINAGE
Regal Style

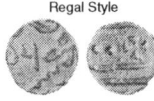

Y# A8a 1/8 MOHUR
1.3400 g., Gold Subject: 10th Anniversary of Reign of Umed Singh II and 80th Birthday of Queen Victoria Obv. Inscription: "Badshah Zaman Inglistan... (Victoria)"

Date	Mintage	Good	VG	F	VF	XF
VS(19)56	—	—	185	300	500	800

Y# C8 1/2 MOHUR
5.3500 g., Gold Obv. Inscription: "Badshah Zaman Inglistan... (Victoria)"

Date	Mintage	Good	VG	F	VF	XF
ND//42 (1899)	—	—	150	275	400	650

Y# 8 MOHUR
10.7000 g., Gold, 18 mm. Obv. Inscription: "Badshah Zaman Inglistan... (Victoria)"

Date	Mintage	Good	VG	F	VF	XF
ND//1 (1858)	—	—	225	275	400	600
ND//6 (1863)	—	—	225	275	400	600
ND//8 (1865)	—	—	225	275	400	600
ND//9 (1866)	—	—	225	275	400	600
ND//15 (1872)	—	—	225	275	400	600
ND//31 (1888)	—	—	225	275	400	600
ND//32 (1889)	—	—	225	275	400	600
ND//44 (1901)	—	—	250	300	400	600

MALER KOTLA

State located in the Punjab in northwest India, founded by the Maler Kotla family who were Sherwani Afghans who had travelled to India from Kabul in 1467 as officials of the Delhi emperors.

Coins are rupees of Ahmad Shah Durrani, and except for the last ruler, contain the chief's initial on the reverse. The chiefs were called Ra'is until 1821, Nawabs thereafter.

For similar issues see Jind, Nabha and Patiala.

RULERS
Ibrahim Ali Khan, AH1288-1326/1871-1908AD
Ahmad ali Khan, AH1326/1908AD

Ahmad Ali Khan
AH1326- / 1908- AD
HAMMERED COINAGE

Y# 11 1/2 MOHUR
5.9400 g., Gold Obverse: Persian inscription Obv. Inscription: Ahmad Ali Khan ...

Date	Mintage	F	VF	XF	Unc
AH1326 (1908-09)	—	—	—	—	—

MEWAR

State located in Rajputana, northwest India. Capital: Udaipur.

The rulers of Mewar were universally regarded as the highest ranking Rajput house in India. The maharana of Mewar was looked upon as the representative of Rama, the ancient king of Ayodhya - and the family who were Sesodia Rajputs of the Gehlot clan, traced its descent through Rama to Kanak Sen who ruled in the 2nd century. The clan is believed to have migrated to Chitor from Gujarat sometime in the 8th century.

After the sacking of Chitor the rana, Udai Singh, retired to the Aravali hills where he founded Udaipur, the capital after 1570. Udai Singh's son, Partab, refused to submit to the Mughal and recovered most of the territory lost in 1568. In the early 19th century Mewar suffered much at the hands of Marathas - Holkar, Sindhia and the Pindaris - until, in 1818, the State came under British supervision. In April 1948 Mewar was merged into Rajasthan and the maharana became governor Maharaj pramukh of the new province.

RULERS
Sirdar Singh, AH1254-1258/1838-1842AD
Swarup Singh, AH1258-1278/1842-1861AD
Shambhu Singh, AH1278-1291/1861-1874AD
Sajjan Singh, AH1291-1302/1874-1884AD
Fatteh Singh, VS1941-1986/1884-1929AD
Bhupal Singh, VS1987-2005/1930-1948AD

MINTS
NOTE: All Mewar coinage is struck without ruler's name, and is largely undated. Certain types were generally struck over several reigns.

Bhilwara

Chitarkot

Udaipur

New Chandori Series
Struck at the Udaipur mint between ca. 1780 to the middle of the 19th century with fictitious mint epithet: Dar al-Khilafat Shahjahanabad.

Mint mark:

and ✱ on obverse

Swarupshahi Series
Leg: Dosti Landhan "Friendship with London".

Struck at the Udaipur Mint between ca. 1858-1920AD. Many die varieties exist.

INDIA - PRINCELY STATES

MEWAR

BRITISH PROTECTORATE
HAMMERED COINAGE

Y# B12   1/8 MOHUR
1.3500 g., Gold **Series:** Swarupshahi **Obv. Inscription:** Chitarkot/Udaipur **Mint:** Udaipur

Date	Mintage	VG	F	VF	XF	Unc
ND(1858-1920)	—	—	150	225	400	600

Y# A12   1/4 MOHUR
Gold **Series:** Swarupshahi **Obv. Inscription:** Chitarkot/Udaipur **Mint:** Udaipur **Note:** Weight varies: 2.70-2.75 grams.

Date	Mintage	VG	F	VF	XF	Unc
ND(1858-1920)	—	—	150	300	500	750

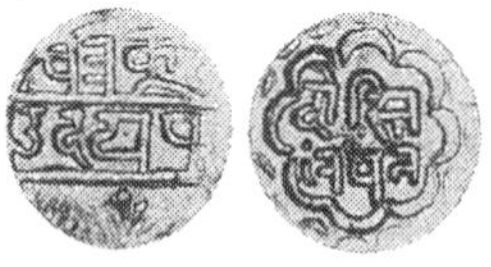

Y# C12   1/2 MOHUR
5.4000 g., Gold **Series:** Swarupshahi **Obv. Inscription:** Chitarkot/Udaipur **Mint:** Udaipur

Date	Mintage	VG	F	VF	XF	Unc
ND(1858-1920)	—	—	150	300	500	750

Y# 6   2/3 MOHUR
7.5200 g., Gold **Mint:** Udaipur **Note:** Weight varies 10.80-10.90 grams.

Date	Mintage	VG	F	VF	XF	Unc
ND(1842-90)	—	175	225	400	500	—

Y# 12   MOHUR
10.9500 g., Gold, 23-24 mm. **Series:** Swarupshahi **Obv. Inscription:** Chitarkot/Udaipur **Mint:** Udaipur **Note:** Size varies.

Date	Mintage	VG	F	VF	XF	Unc
ND(1858-1920)	—	—	BV	250	350	525

Fatteh Singh
VS1941-1986 / 1884-1929AD
MILLED COINAGE

VS1985 ie. 1928AD, but actually struck at the Alipore Mint in Calcutta between 1931-1932AD, the Y#22 rupee in 1931, the rest in 1932

Y# 21a   1/2 RUPEE
Gold, 24 mm. **Obv. Inscription:** "Chitarkot/Udaipur" **Rev. Inscription:** "Dosti Lundhun (Friendship with London)" **Note:** Weight varies: 5.35-5.70 grams.

Date	Mintage	VG	F	VF	XF	Unc
VS1985(1928) Proof	—	Value: 1,500				

Y# 22a   RUPEE
Gold, 30 mm. **Obv. Inscription:** Chitarkot/Udaipur **Rev. Inscription:** Dosti Lundhun (Friendship with London)

Date	Mintage	VG	F	VF	XF	Unc
VS1985(1928) Proof	—	Value: 2,500				

PATTERNS
Including off metal strikes

KM#	Date	Mintage	Identification	Mkt Val
Pn2	VS1985 (1928)	—	1/16 Rupee. Gold.	—
Pn4	VS1985 (1928)	—	1/8 Rupee. Gold.	—
Pn6	VS1985 (1928)	—	1/4 Rupee. Gold. KM20.	750
Pn8	VS1985 (1928)	—	1/2 Rupee. Gold.	—
Pn10	VS1985 (1928)	—	Rupee. Gold.	—

MEWAR FEUDATORIES - SHAHPUR

RULERS
Jagat Singh, AH1261-1270/1845-53AD
Lachman Singh, AH1270-1287/1853-70AD
Nahat Singh, AH1287-1351/1870-1932AD

HAMMERED COINAGE

C# 29   MOHUR
Gold, 18 mm. **Note:** Weight varies 10.30-10.50 grams.

Date	Mintage	Good	VG	F	VF	XF
AHxxx8//12	—	—	225	275	400	600

MYSORE

Large state in Southern India. Governed until 1761AD by various Hindu dynasties, then by Haider Ali and Tipu Sultan.

In 1831, Krishnaraja being deposed for mal-administration and pensioned off, the administration of Mysore State then came directly under the British. The coinage of Mysore ceased in 1843. After the Great Revolt of 1857, the policy of eliminating Indian princes was discontinued and as a result, Mysore was returned in 1881 to the control of an adopted son of Krishnaraja Wodeyar. The Wodeyars continued to hold the state until 1947 although they did not issue coins. In November 1956 modern Mysore was inaugurated as a linguistic state within the Indian Union.

NOTE: For earlier issues see Mysore, Independent Kingdoms during British rule.

RULERS
Dewan Purnaiya, regent AH1214-1225/1799-1810AD
Krishna Raja Wodeyar, AH1225-1285/1810-1868AD

MINTS

مهيسور   مهي سور

Mysore

BRITISH PROTECTORATE
ANONYMOUS HAMMERED COINAGE

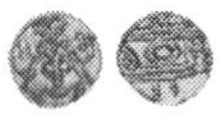

C# 212   FANAM
Gold **Subject:** Narasimha **Obv. Inscription:** "Shah Alam II" **Mint:** Mysore **Note:** Weight varies: 0.33-0.40 grams.

Date	Mintage	Good	VG	F	VF	XF
ND(1799-1810)	—	—	7.50	10.00	20.00	30.00

C# 215   1/4 MOHUR
Gold **Obv. Inscription:** "Shah Alam II" **Mint:** Mysore **Note:** Weight varies 2.68-2.85 grams.

Date	Mintage	Good	VG	F	VF	XF
ND//45 (1803-04) Rare	—	—	—	—	—	—

NABHA

Cis-Sutlej state located in the Punjab in northwest India and founded in the 18th century.

The ancestry of these rulers was identical to that of Jind. Until 1845 Nabha's history closely paralleled that of Patiala. At this point, however, the raja sided with the Sikhs. It was left to his son to make amends to the British in 1847 after the first Sikh war (1845-46). Their independence became somewhat circumscribed and in 1849 the Punjab was annexed and the states were merged into the new province of British India.

RULERS
Bharpur Singh, VS1903-1920/1846-1863AD
Identifying Marks:

On reverse

Hira Singh, VS1928-1968/1871-1911AD
Identifying Marks:

On reverse

MINTS

سركار نابه

Sarkar Nabha

Bharpur Singh
VS1903-1920 / 1846-1863AD
HAMMERED COINAGE

Y# A2   MOHUR
Gold **Obv. Inscription:** Guru Govind Singh **Note:** 9.50-9.60 grams.

Date	Mintage	Good	VG	F	VF	XF
VS1907 (1850)	—	—	275	400	600	800
VS1911 (1854)	—	—	275	400	600	800

Hira Singh
VS1928-1968 / 1871-1911AD
HAMMERED COINAGE

Y# 3   MOHUR
10.1500 g., Gold **Obverse:** Date **Obv. Inscription:** Guru Govind Singh **Reverse:** Branch and katar to left of stylized "4", date

Date	Mintage	Good	VG	F	VF	XF
VS192x (1873)	—	—	250	400	650	800

NAWANAGAR

(Navanagar)

State located on the Kathiawar peninsula, west-central India.

The rulers, or jams, of Kutch were Jareja Rajputs who had entered the Kathiawar peninsular from Kutch and dispossessed the ancient family of Jathwas. Nawanagar was founded about 1535 by Jam Raval, who was possibly the elder brother of the Jam of Kutch. The great fort of Nawanagar was built by Jam Jasaji (d. 1814). The state became tributary to the Gaekwar family and, in the 19th century, also to the British. In 1948 the state was merged into Saurashtra.

RULERS
Vibhaji, VS1909-1951/1852-1894AD
Jaswant Singh, VS1951-1964/1894-1907AD

MONETARY SYSTEM
8 Dokda = 1 Kori

Early Types: Stylized imitations of the coins of Muzaffar III of Gujarat (156-173AD), dated AH978 (= 1570AD), were struck from the end of the 16th century until the early part of the reign of Vibhaji. These show a steady degradation of style over the nearly 300 years of issue, but no types can be dated to specific rulers. The former attribution of these coins to Ranmalji II (1820-1852AD) is incorrect. All are inscribed Sri Jamji, title of all rulers of Nawanagar.

Varieties in this series are the rule, not the exception. These include legend style, small marks in the field such as a crescent, Katar (dagger), etc., and weight ranges.

BRITISH PROTECTORATE

Vibhaji
VS1909-1951 / 1852-1894AD
HAMMERED COINAGE

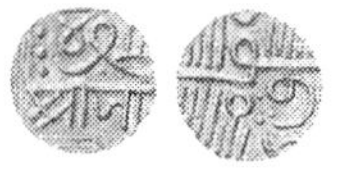

KM# 11   1/2 GOLD KORI
Gold **Note:** Weight varies: 3.20-3.30 grams.

Date	Mintage	VG	F	VF	XF	Unc
AH978 Frozen	—	135	225	350	500	—

KM# 12   GOLD KORI
Gold **Note:** Weight varies: 6.40-6.60 grams.

Date	Mintage	VG	F	VF	XF	Unc
AH(9)78 Frozen	—	135	225	350	500	—

PATIALA

State located in the Punjab in northwest India. In the mid-18th century the Raja was given his title and mint right by Ahmad Shah Durrani of Afghanistan, whose coin he copied.

The rulers became Maharajas in 1810AD. The maharaja of Patiala was also recognized as the leader of the Phulkean tribe. Unlike others, Patiala's Sikh rulers had never hesitated to seek British assistance at those times when they felt threatened by their co-religionist neighbors. In 1857, Patiala's forces were immediately made available on the side of the British.

INDIA - PRINCELY STATES

RULERS:
Karm Singh, AH1229-1261/1813-1845AD
Identifying marks:

On reverse

Narindar Singh, VS1902-1919/1845-1862AD
Identifying marks:

On reverse

Rajindar Singh, VS1933-1957/1876-1900AD
Identifying marks:

On reverse

Bhupindar Singh, VS1958-1994/1900-1937AD
Yadvindar Singh, VS1994-2005/1937-1948AD

MINT

سهرند

Sirhind (Sahrind)

Karm Singh
AH1229-1261 / 1813-1845AD
HAMMERED COINAGE

C# 35 MOHUR
10.5000 g., Gold **Reverse:** 3-pointed leaf to right

Date	Mintage	Good	VG	F	VF	XF
ND(1813-45)	—	—	BV	250	300	375
VS(18)96 (1896)	—	—	—	—	—	—

Narindar Singh
VS1902-1919 / 1845-1862AD
HAMMERED COINAGE

Y# 2 MOHUR
10.5000 g., Gold **Obv. Inscription:** Guru Govind Singh **Note:** 17-18mm.

Date	Mintage	Good	VG	F	VF	XF
VS190(6) (1849)	—	—	BV	250	300	375

Mahindar Singh
VS1919-1933 / 1862-1876AD
HAMMERED COINAGE

Y# 9 MOHUR
10.5000 g., Gold, 18 mm. **Reverse:** Katar at left

Date	Mintage	Good	VG	F	VF	XF
ND(1876-1900)	—	—	BV	250	300	375
VS(19)48 (1891)	—	—	BV	250	300	375

Rajindar Singh
VS1933-1957 / 1876-1900AD
HAMMERED COINAGE

Y# 7 1/3 MOHUR
3.5000 g., Gold **Reverse:** Katar at left

Date	Mintage	Good	VG	F	VF	XF
VS(19)50	—	—	125	185	250	350

Bhupindar Singh
VS1958-1994 / 1900-1937AD
HAMMERED COINAGE

Y# 14 1/6 MOHUR
1.7500 g., Gold **Obverse:** Persian inscription **Obv. Inscription:** "Ahmad Shah Durrani" **Reverse:** Dagger at left

Date	Mintage	VG	F	VF	XF	Unc
VS(19)58	—	—	85.00	100	125	175
VS(19)90	—	—	—	—	—	—

KM# 15 1/3 MOHUR
3.5000 g., Gold **Obverse:** Persian inscription **Obv. Inscription:** "Ahmad Shah Durrani" **Reverse:** Dagger at left

Date	Mintage	VG	F	VF	XF	Unc
VS(19)58	—	—	100	120	140	200

Y# 16 2/3 MOHUR
7.0000 g., Gold **Obverse:** Persian inscription **Obv. Inscription:** "Ahmad Shah Durrani" **Reverse:** Dagger at left

Date	Mintage	VG	F	VF	XF	Unc
VS(19)58	—	—	165	200	250	325

Y# 17 MOHUR
10.5000 g., Gold **Obverse:** Persian inscription **Obv. Inscription:** "Ahmad Shah Durrani" **Reverse:** Dagger at left

Date	Mintage	VG	F	VF	XF	Unc
VS(19)58	—	—	225	265	325	400

Yadvindar Singh
VS1994-2005 / 1937-1948AD
HAMMERED COINAGE

KM# 29 1/6 MOHUR
1.7500 g., Gold **Obverse:** Persian inscription **Obv. Inscription:** "Ahmad Shah Durrani" **Reverse:** Bayoneted rifle at left **Note:** Prev. Y#19.

Date	Mintage	VG	F	VF	XF	Unc
VS(19)94 /(1937)	—	—	75.00	100	125	175

KM# 30 1/3 MOHUR
3.5000 g., Gold **Obverse:** Persian inscription **Obv. Inscription:** "Ahmad Shah Durrani" **Reverse:** Bayoneted rifle at left **Note:** Prev. KM#20.

Date	Mintage	VG	F	VF	XF	Unc
VS(19)94 /(1937AD)	—	—	100	120	140	200

KM# 31 2/3 MOHUR
7.0000 g., Gold **Obverse:** Persian inscription **Obv. Inscription:** "Ahmad Shah Durrani" **Reverse:** Bayoneted rifle at left **Note:** Prev. Y#21.

Date	Mintage	VG	F	VF	XF	Unc
VS(19)94/(1937AD)	—	—	165	200	250	325

RADHANPUR

State located on the Kathiawar peninsula.
The nawabs of Radhanpur were Pathans of the Babi family who rose to high office in the service of Shah Jahan and Murad Bakhsh in Gujarat. Sometime in the late 17th or early 18th centuries, one of the family was appointed faujdar of Radhanpur and the surrounding area. After Aurangzeb's death, Kamal-ud-din Khan Babi seized the governorship of Ahmadabad, but this was relinquished in 1753 to the forces of the Peshwa of Poona and the Gaekwar of Baroda. Radhanpur, however, remained in Babi control as a Maratha Jagir until 1820 when the State came under British protection.
All silver coins of Radhanpur appear to be nazarana issues.

RULERS
Zorawar Khan, AH1241-1291/1825-1874AD

In the name of Queen Victoria

کوین وکٹوریا

And Zorawar Khan

MINT

رادهنپور

Radhanpur

BRITISH PROTECTORATE

Zorawar Khan
AH1241-1291 / 1825-1874AD
HAMMERED COINAGE

KM# 15 MOHUR
Gold, 27 mm. **Obv. Inscription:** "...Zorawar Khan" **Rev. Inscription:** "...Queen Victoria" **Note:** Weight varies: 10.70-11.40 grams.

Date	Mintage	Good	VG	F	VF	XF
AH1277	—	—	—	—	650	1,000

RAJKOT

State located in north central Kathiawar, west India.
The thakurs of Rajkot were Jareja Rajputs and related to the ruling houses of Kutch and Nawanagar. The founder, Jareja Vibhaji was a grandson of Jam Sataji of Nawanagar. After Maratha defeat Rajkot became a tributary to the British and in February 1948 the State was absorbed into Saurashtra.

RULER
Dharmendra Singhji, 1930-1948

Dharmendra Singhji
MEDALLIC COINAGE

X# 1 MOHUR
7.8800 g., Gold **Obverse:** Sunrise **Reverse:** Arms **Note:** Prev. KM#M1.

Date	Mintage	F	VF	XF	Unc
1945	54	—	—	350	550

Note: Mintage figure is from original records.

Date	Mintage	F	VF	XF	Unc
1954 Restrike	—	—	—	200	300

Note: Restrikes have sun slightly higher above the water, as pictured above.

REWA

State located in eastern north-central India.
The rulers of Rewa were Baghela Rajputs of the Solanki clan who probably migrated from Anhilwara Patan in Gujarat about the 11th century. Arriving in Bundelkhand, they carved out for themselves a substantial kingdom, which remained independent until 1597, when they were obliged to become Mughal tributaries under Akbar. With Mughal decline, Rewa began to move once more towards independence, this time under the nominal suzerainty of the Peshwa. In 1812, the raja of Rewa, Jai Singh Deo was coerced into a treaty with the British and, failing to observe its conditions, was forced to yield to British control in 1813-1814. In 1948 Rewa was merged into Vindhya Pradesh.

RULERS
Jai Singh Deo, VS1866-1892/1809-1835AD
Vishvanath Singh, VS1892-1900/1835-1843AD
Raghuraj Singh, VS1900-1937/1843-1880AD
Venkat Raman Singh, VS1937-1975/1880-1918AD
Gulab Singh, VS1975-2003/1918-1946AD

BRITISH PROTECTORATE

Vishvanath Singh
VS1892-1900 / 1835-1843AD
HAMMERED COINAGE

KM# 22 MOHUR
9.7500 g., Gold **Note:** Fr. #1370.

Date	Mintage	Good	VG	F	VF	XF
ND(1835-43)	—	—	—	250	500	800	1,100

INDIA - PRINCELY STATES

REWA

Gulab Singh
VS1975-2003 / 1918-1946AD

MEDALLIC COINAGE

X# M3 1/2 MOHUR
Gold **Subject:** Accession **Obverse:** Arms with small lion supporters **Note:** Weight varies: 4.40-5.40 grams. Prev.KM#33.

Date	Mintage	VG	F	VF	XF	Unc
VS1975(1918)	—	250	375	550	800	—

X# M7 3/4 MOHUR
8.8000 g., Gold **Obverse:** Arms with large lion supporters in sprays **Reverse:** Sprays in inner circle, date at top **Note:** Prev.KM#40.

Date	Mintage	VG	F	VF	XF	Unc
VS1977(1920)	—	250	375	550	800	—

X# M4 MOHUR
Gold **Subject:** Accession **Obverse:** Arms with small lion supporters **Note:** Weight varies: 10.70-11.71 grams. Prev.KM#35.

Date	Mintage	VG	F	VF	XF	Unc
VS1975(1918)	—	250	375	550	800	—

X# M5 MOHUR
Gold **Subject:** Accession **Obverse:** Arms with small lion supporters, large katar below, legend connected **Reverse:** Legend and inscription connected **Note:** Weight varies: 10.70-11.71 grams. Prev.KM#36.

Date	Mintage	VG	F	VF	XF	Unc
VS1975(1918)	—	250	375	550	800	—

X# M6 MOHUR
11.3600 g., Gold **Obverse:** Arms with small lion supporters **Reverse:** Large legend and inscription with two characters/date **Note:** Weight varies: 10.70-11.71 grams. Prev.KM#38.

Date	Mintage	VG	F	VF	XF	Unc
VS1976(1919)	—	275	450	650	900	—

TONK

Tunk

State located partially in Rajputana and in central India. Tonk was founded in 1806 by Amir Khan (d. 1834), the Pathan Pindari leader who received the territory from Holkar. Amir Khan caused great havoc in Central India by his lightning raids into neighboring states. In 1817, he was forced into submission by the East India Company and remained under British control until India's independence. In March 1948, Tonk was incorporated into Rajasthan.

RULERS
Amir Khan, AH1213-1250/1798-1834AD
Wazir Muhammad Khan, AH1250-1281/1834-1864AD
Muhammad Ali Khan, AH1280-1284/1864-1867AD
Muhammad Ibrahim Ali Khan, AH1284-1349/1868-1930AD

MINT MARKS

تونك

Tonk
NOTE: All coins with both AH and AD dates clearly readable command about a 50 per cent premium.

Flower (on all)

Leaf (several forms)

Beginning with the reign of Muhammad Ibrahim Ali Khan, most coins have both AD and AH date. Coins with both dates fully legible are worth about 20% more than listed prices. Coins with one date fully legible are worth prices shown. Coins with both dates off are of little value.

There are many minor and major variations of type, varying with location of date, orientation of leaf, arrangement of legend. Although these fall into easily distinguished patterns, they are strictly for the specialist and are omitted here.

The Tonk rupee was known as the "Chanwarshahi".

BRITISH PROTECTORATE

HAMMERED COINAGE
Regal Series

Y# 22 MOHUR
Gold **Obv. Inscription:** "Muhammad Ibrahim Ali Khan" **Rev. Inscription:** "Victoria, Empress" **Mint:** Tonk **Note:** Weight varies: 10.70-11.40 grams. Fr#1397.

Date	Mintage	Good	VG	F	VF	XF
AH1297	—	—	BV	350	500	850
AH1298	—	—	BV	350	500	850

Y# 23 NAZARANA 2 MOHURS
Gold **Obv. Inscription:** "Muhammad Ibrahim Ali Khan" **Rev. Inscription:** "Victoria, Empress" **Mint:** Tonk **Note:** Weight varies: 21.40-22.80 grams. Fr#1396.

Date	Mintage	Good	VG	F	VF	XF
AH1297	—	—	—	2,250	3,200	—

TRAVANCORE

State located in extreme southwest India. A mint was established in ME965/1789-1790AD.

The region of Travancore had a lengthy history before being annexed by the Vijayanagar kingdom. With Vijayanagar's defeat at the battle of Talikota in 1565, Travancore passed under Muslim control until the late 18th century, when it emerged as a state in its own right under Raja Martanda Varma. At this time, the raja allied himself with British interests as a protection against the Muslim dynasty of Mysore. In 1795 the raja of Travancore officially accepted a subsidiary alliance with the East India Company and remained within the orbit of British influence from then until India's independence.

RULERS
Bala Rama Varma I, ME973-986/1798-1810AD
Rani Parvathi Bai, regent, ME990-1004/1815-1829AD
Rama Varma III, ME1004-1022/1829-1847AD
Martanda Varma II, ME1022-1035/1847-1860AD
Rama Varma IV, ME1035-1055/1860-1880AD
Rama Varma V, ME1057-1062/1880-1885AD
Rama Varma VI, ME1062-1101/1885-1924AD

MONETARY SYSTEM
16 Cash (Kasu) = 1 Chuckram
4 Chuckram = 1 Fanam
2 Fanams = 1 Anantaraya
7 Fanams = 1 Rupee
52-1/2 Fanam = 1 Pagoda

DATING
ME dates are of the Malabar Era. Add 824 or 825 to the ME date for the AD date. (i.e., ME1112 plus 824-825 =1936-1937AD).

KINGDOM

TULABHARAM MEDALLIC COINAGE

These presentation coins were struck prior to the weighing in ceremony of the Maharajah. The balance of his weight in these gold coins were distributed amongst the learned Brahmins and are referred to as Tulabhara Kasu. The legend reads - Sri Patmanabha - , the National Deity.

X# 1 1/4 PAGODA
0.6300 g., Gold, 8.8 mm. **Obverse:** Tamil legend in 3 lines **Note:** Uniface. Prev. KM#M1.

Date	Mintage	F	VF	XF	Unc
ND(1829, 47)	—	—	70.00	100	150

X# 5 1/4 PAGODA
0.6300 g., Gold, 12.7 mm. **Obverse:** Tamil legend in 3 lines **Note:** Uniface. Prev. KM#M5.

Date	Mintage	F	VF	XF	Unc
ND(1850, 55)	—	—	70.00	100	150

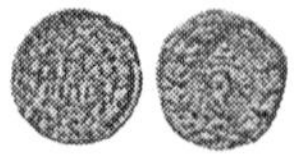

X# 9 1/4 PAGODA
0.6400 g., Gold **Obverse:** Inscription: Tamil in three lines in sprays **Reverse:** Sankha (conch shell) in sprays **Note:** Prev. KM#M9. Size varies: 10.9-12.7mm.

Date	Mintage	F	VF	XF	Unc
ND(1870-1931)	—	45.00	65.00	90.00	135

X# 2 1/2 PAGODA
1.2700 g., Gold, 10.9 mm. **Obverse:** Tamil legend in 3 lines **Note:** Uniface. Prev. KM#M2.

Date	Mintage	F	VF	XF	Unc
ND(1829, 47)	—	50.00	80.00	115	175

X# 6 1/2 PAGODA
1.2700 g., Gold, 14.5 mm. **Obverse:** Tamil legend in 3 lines

Date	Mintage	F	VF	XF	Unc
ND(1850, 55)	—	50.00	80.00	115	175

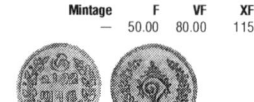

X# 10 1/2 PAGODA
1.2800 g., Gold **Obverse:** Inscription: Tamil in three lines in sprays **Reverse:** Sankha (conch shell) in sprays **Note:** Prev. KM#M10.

Date	Mintage	F	VF	XF	Unc
ND(1870-1931)	—	55.00	85.00	120	175

X# 3 PAGODA
2.5400 g., Gold, 13 mm. **Obverse:** Tamil legend in 3 lines **Note:** Uniface. Prev. KM#M3.

Date	Mintage	F	VF	XF	Unc
ND(1829, 47)	—	80.00	135	185	275

X# 7 PAGODA
2.5400 g., Gold, 17 mm. **Obverse:** Tamil legend in 3 lines **Note:** Uniface. Prev. KM#M7.

Date	Mintage	F	VF	XF	Unc
ND(1850, 55)	—	80.00	135	185	275

X# 11 PAGODA
2.5400 g., Gold **Obverse:** Inscription: Tamil in three lines in sprays **Reverse:** Sankha (conch shell) in sprays **Note:** Prev. KM#M11.

Date	Mintage	F	VF	XF	Unc
ND(1870-1931)	—	85.00	140	200	285

X# 4 2 PAGODA
5.0600 g., Gold, 15.4 mm. **Obverse:** Tamil legend in 3 lines **Note:** Uniface. Prev. KM#M4.

Date	Mintage	F	VF	XF	Unc
ND(1829, 47)	—	120	200	280	400

X# 8 2 PAGODA
5.0600 g., Gold, 20.3 mm. **Obverse:** Tamil legend in 3 lines **Note:** Prev. KM#M8.

Date	Mintage	F	VF	XF	Unc
ND(1850, 55)	—	120	200	280	400

X# 12 2 PAGODA
5.0900 g., Gold **Obverse:** Inscription: Tamil in three lines in sprays **Reverse:** Sankha (conch shell) in sprays **Note:** Prev. KM#M12. Size varies: 20.0-23.9mm.

Date	Mintage	F	VF	XF	Unc
ND(1870-1931)	—	125	210	300	425

Rama Varma IV
ME1035-1055 / 1860-1880AD

HAMMERED COINAGE

KM# 23 ANATARAYA (Fanam)
Gold

Date	Mintage	Good	VG	F	VF	XF
ND(1860-90)	—	—	—	7.50	12.50	18.50

MILLED COINAGE

KM# 25 1/2 PAGODA
1.2800 g., Gold **Obverse:** Large R.V. within sprays **Reverse:** Sankha (conch shell) in sprays

Date	Mintage	VG	F	VF	XF	Unc
1877	—	—	65.00	100	150	250

KM# 26 PAGODA
2.5500 g., Gold **Obverse:** Large R.V. within sprays **Reverse:** Sankha (conch shell) in sprays **Note:** Fr.#1402.

Date	Mintage	VG	F	VF	XF	Unc
1877	—	—	110	175	275	400

KM# 27 2 PAGODA
5.1000 g., Gold **Obverse:** Large R.V. within sprays **Reverse:** Sankha (conch shell) in sprays **Note:** Fr.#1401.

Date	Mintage	VG	F	VF	XF	Unc
1877	—	—	160	265	400	600

Rama Varma V
ME1057-1062 / 1880-1885AD

HAMMERED COINAGE

KM# 30 VIRARAYA FANAM
Gold

Date	Mintage	Good	VG	F	VF	XF
ND(1881)	—	—	7.00	8.00	11.00	15.00

MILLED COINAGE

KM# 31 1/2 SOVEREIGN
3.9940 g., 0.9170 Gold .1177 oz. AGW **Obverse:** Bust of Rama Varma IV 3/4 right **Reverse:** Arms with supporters

Date	Mintage	F	VF	XF	Unc
ME1057//1881	2,000	300	550	900	1,250

KM# 32 SOVEREIGN
7.9881 g., 0.9170 Gold .2354 oz. AGW **Obverse:** Bust of Rama Varma IV 3/4 right **Reverse:** Arms with supporters

Date	Mintage	F	VF	XF	Unc
ME1057//1881	1,000	200	600	1,200	1,600

Rama Varma VI
ME1062-1101 / 1885-1924AD

HAMMERED COINAGE

KM# 39 KALI FANAM
Gold **Note:** Fr.#1405.

Date	Mintage	Good	VG	F	VF	XF
ND(1890-95)	—	—	7.00	8.50	11.00	13.50

Bala Rama Varma II
ME1101-1126 / 1924-1949AD

MILLED COINAGE

KM# 60a CHUCKRAM
Gold **Obverse:** Bust of Bala Rama Barma II right **Reverse:** Sankha (conch shell) in sprays

Date	Mintage	VG	F	VF	XF	Unc
ND(1939-49)	—	—	—	—	—	5,000
Prooflike; restrike						

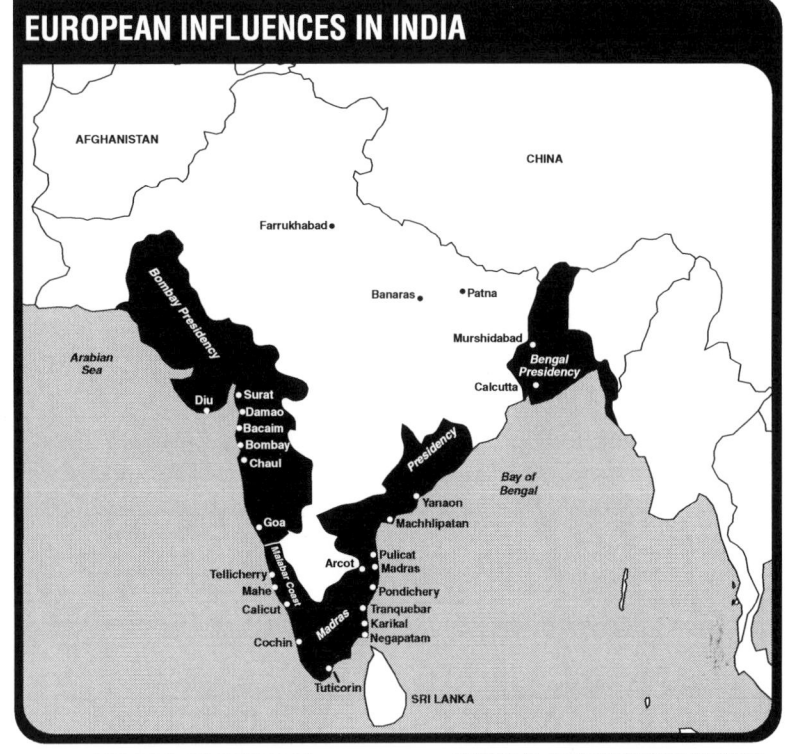

EUROPEAN INFLUENCES IN INDIA

INDIA-FRENCH

It was not until 1664, during the reign of Louis XIV, that the Compagnie des Indes Orientales was formed for the purpose of obtaining holdings on the subcontinent of India. Between 1666 and 1721, French settlements were established at Arcot, Mahe, Surat, Pondichery, Masulipatam, Karikal, Yanam, Murshidabad, Chandernagore, Balasore and Calicut. War with Britain reduced the French holdings to Chandernagore, Pondichery, Karikal, Yanam and Mahe. Chandernagore voted in 1949 to join India and became part of the Republic of India in 1950. Pondichery, Karikal, Yanam and Mahe formed the Pondichery union territory and joined the republic of India in 1954.

RULERS
French, until 1954

MINTS

آرکات

Arcot (Arkat)

Mint mark:

ں

Crescent
A crescent moon mint mark is found to left of the regnal year for those struck at the Pondichery Mint. For listings of similar coins with lotus mint mark refer to India-British-Madras Presidency.

Pondichery
A city south of Madras on the southeast coast which became the site of the French Mint from 1700-1841. Pondichery was settled by the French in 1683. It became their main Indian possession even though it was occupied by the Dutch in 1693-98 and several times by the British from 1761-1816.

PONDICHERY
Dutch Occupation

HAMMERED COINAGE

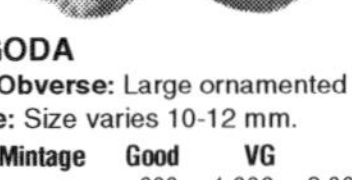

KM# 51 PAGODA
3.4000 g., Gold **Obverse:** Large ornamented crown **Reverse:** 5 fleur-de-lis **Note:** Size varies 10-12 mm.

Date	Mintage	Good	VG	F	VF	XF
ND(1830-48)	—	600	1,000	2,000	3,500	4,200

INDIA-PORTUGUESE

Vasco da Gama, the Portuguese explorer, first visited India in 1498. Portugal seized control of a number of islands and small enclaves on the west coast of India, and for the next hundred years enjoyed a monopoly on trade. With the arrival of powerful Dutch and English fleets in the first half of the 17th century, Portuguese power in the area declined until virtually all of India that remained under Portuguese control were the west coast enclaves of Goa, Damao and Diu. They were forcibly annexed by India in 1962.

RULER
Portuguese, until 1961

DENOMINATION
The denomination of most copper coins appears in numerals on the reverse, though 30 Reis is often given as "1/2 T," and 60 Reis as "T" (T = Tanga). The silver coins have the denomination in words, usually on the obverse until 1850, then on the reverse.

MONETARY SYSTEM
960 Reis = 16 Tanga = 1 Rupia

GOA

Goa was the capitol of Portuguese India and is located 250 miles south of Bombay on the west coast of India. It was taken by Albuquerque in 1510. A mint was established immediately and operated until closed by the British in 1869. Later coins were struck at Calcutta and Bombay. Goa was annexed by India in 1962.

MONETARY SYSTEM
375 Bazarucos = 300 Reis
240 Reis = 1 Pardao
2 Xerafim = 1 Rupia
NOTE: The silver Xerafim was equal to the silver Pardao, but the gold Xerafim varied according to fluctuations in the gold/silver ratio.

COLONY

HAMMERED COINAGE

KM# 241 XERAFIM
Gold **Ruler:** Joao **Obverse:** Arms on crowned globe **Reverse:** Value and date in angles of cross **Note:** Weight varies 0.40-0.41 grams.

Date	Mintage	Good	VG	F	VF	XF
1819	—	450	800	1,350	2,000	—

KM# 223 2 XERAFINS
0.8100 g., Gold **Ruler:** Joao **Obverse:** Crowned round arms **Reverse:** Cross divides value and date

Date	Mintage	Good	VG	F	VF	XF
1815	—	—	—	—	—	—

Note: Reported, not confirmed

INDIA-PORTUGUESE

KM# 242 2 XERAFINS
0.8100 g., Gold **Ruler:** Joao **Obverse:** Crowned round arms **Reverse:** Cross divides value and date

Date	Mintage	Good	VG	F	VF	XF
1819	—	500	950	1,550	2,250	—

KM# 202 4 XERAFINS
1.6300 g., Gold **Ruler:** Maria I **Obverse:** Crowned arms **Reverse:** Cross divides value and date

Date	Mintage	Good	VG	F	VF	XF
1803	—	285	500	850	1,400	—

KM# 243 4 XERAFINS
1.6300 g., Gold **Ruler:** Joao **Obverse:** Crowned round arms **Reverse:** Cross divides value and date

Date	Mintage	Good	VG	F	VF	XF
1819	—	550	1,000	1,650	2,500	—

KM# 192.2 8 XERAFINS
3.2500 g., Gold **Ruler:** Maria I **Obverse:** Crowned round arms **Reverse:** Cross divides value and date

Date	Mintage	Good	VG	F	VF	XF
1804	—	450	800	1,250	1,850	—
1805	—	450	800	1,250	1,850	—

KM# 244 8 XERAFINS
3.2500 g., Gold **Ruler:** Joao **Obverse:** Crowned round arms **Reverse:** Cross divides value and date

Date	Mintage	Good	VG	F	VF	XF
1819	—	500	800	1,500	2,500	—

KM# 245 8 XERAFINS
3.2500 g., Gold **Ruler:** Joao **Obverse:** Crowned round arms **Reverse:** Cross divides value and date **Note:** Similar to 1 Rupia, KM#239

Date	Mintage	Good	VG	F	VF	XF
1819	—	—	—	—	—	—

Note: Reported, not confirmed

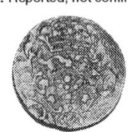

KM# 187 12 XERAFINS
4.8700 g., Gold **Ruler:** Maria I **Obverse:** Crowned arms **Reverse:** Cross divides value and date

Date	Mintage	Good	VG	F	VF	XF
1801	—	275	450	750	1,300	—
1802	—	275	450	750	1,300	—
1803	—	275	400	650	1,150	—
1804	—	275	400	650	1,150	—
1806	—	275	400	650	1,150	—

KM# 222 12 XERAFINS
4.8700 g., Gold **Ruler:** Joao **Obverse:** Crowned round arms **Reverse:** Cross divides value and date

Date	Mintage	Good	VG	F	VF	XF
1808	—	450	650	1,150	1,700	—
1809	—	450	650	1,150	1,700	—
1811	—	450	650	1,150	1,700	—
1812	—	450	650	1,150	1,700	—
1813	—	450	650	1,150	1,700	—
1814	—	450	650	1,150	1,700	—
1815	—	450	650	1,150	1,700	—
1816	—	450	650	1,150	1,700	—

KM# 246 12 XERAFINS
4.8700 g., Gold **Ruler:** Joao **Obverse:** Crowned round arms **Reverse:** Cross divides value and date

Date	Mintage	Good	VG	F	VF	XF
1819	—	500	800	1,400	1,850	—
1820	—	500	800	1,400	1,850	—
1822	—	500	800	1,400	1,850	—
1824	—	500	800	1,400	1,850	—
1825	—	500	800	1,400	1,850	—

KM# 270 12 XERAFINS
4.8700 g., Gold **Ruler:** Maria II **Obverse:** Crowned round arms **Reverse:** Cross divides value and date

Date	Mintage	Good	VG	F	VF	XF
1840	—	550	1,000	1,650	2,350	—
1841	—	550	1,000	1,650	2,350	—

PATTERNS
Including off metal strikes

KM#	Date	Mintage	Identification	Mkt Val
Pn26	1871	—	3 Reis. Gold. . KM#1.	—

INDIA-BRITISH

The civilization of India, which began about 2500 B.C., flourished under a succession of empires - notably those of the Mauryas, the Kushans, the Guptas, the Delhi Sultans and the Mughals – until undermined in the 18th and 19th centuries by European colonial powers.

The Portuguese were the first to arrive, off Calicut in May 1498. It wasn't until 1612, after the Portuguese and Spanish power had begun to wane, that the British East India Company established its initial settlement at Surat. Britain could not have chosen a more propitious time as the central girdle of petty states, and the southern Vijayanagar Empire were crumbling and ripe for foreign exploitation. By the end of the century, English traders were firmly established in Bombay, Madras, Calcutta and lesser places elsewhere, and Britain was implementing its announced policy to create such civil and military institutions as may be the foundation of secure English domination for all time'. By 1757, following the successful conclusion of a war of colonial rivalry with France during which the military victories of Robert Clive, a young officer with the British East India Company, made him a powerful man in India, the British were firmly settled in India not only as traders but as conquerors. During the next 60 years, the British East India Company acquired dominion over most of India by bribery and force, and governed it directly or through puppet princelings.

As a result of the Sepoy Mutiny of 1857-58, a large scale mutiny among Indian soldiers of the Bengal army, control of the government of India was transferred from the East India Company to the British Crown. At this point in world history, India was the brightest jewel in the British imperial diadem, but even then a movement for greater Indian representation in government presaged the Indian Empire's twilight hour less than a century later - it would pass into history on Aug. 15, 1947.

BRITISH

BULLION - TOLA ISSUE - RAM DUE RAI RAGHO SAVAN-TIGER BRAND

X# 85 TOLA
Gold **Obverse:** Tiger walking left, palm tree behind **Obv. Legend:** RAM DUE RAI RAGHO SARAN •CALCUTTA **Reverse:** Crossed rifles **Rev. Legend:** TIGER BRAND

Date	Mintage	F	VF	XF	Unc
ND	—	—	—	200	250

COLONY

MILLED COINAGE

KM# 448a 1/4 RUPEE
Gold **Issuer:** East India Company **Mint:** Calcutta

Date	Mintage	F	VF	XF	Unc
1835.(c)	—	—	—	—	—

KM# 449a 1/2 RUPEE
Gold **Mint:** Calcutta

Date	Mintage	F	VF	XF	Unc
1835.(c)	—	—	—	—	—

KM# 450a RUPEE
Gold **Mint:** Calcutta

Date	Mintage	F	VF	XF	Unc
1835.(c)	—	—	—	—	—

KM# 451.1 MOHUR
11.6600 g., 0.9170 Gold 0.3438 oz. AGW **Mint:** Bombay **Obverse:** Head right, without initials **Obv. Legend:** WILLIAM IIII, KING. **Reverse:** Palm tree, lion walking left **Rev. Legend:** EAST INDIA COMPANY **Edge:** Milled

Date	Mintage	F	VF	XF	Unc
1835(b)	—	450	750	1,200	2,000
1835(b)	—	—	—	—	1,000

Note: Prooflike; Restrike

KM# 451.2 MOHUR
11.6600 g., 0.9170 Gold 0.3438 oz. AGW **Mint:** Calcutta **Obverse:** RS incuse on truncation **Edge:** Milled

Date	Mintage	F	VF	XF	Unc
1835.(c)	29,000	500	900	1,250	2,250
1835.(c) Proof	—	—	—	—	—
1835.(c)	—	—	—	—	1,400

Note: Prooflike; Restrike

KM# 451.3 MOHUR
11.6600 g., 0.9170 Gold 0.3438 oz. AGW **Mint:** Calcutta **Obverse:** F incuse on truncation **Edge:** Milled

Date	Mintage	F	VF	XF	Unc
1835.(c)	111,000	450	750	1,200	2,000
1835.(c) Prooflike; Restrike	—	—	—	—	1,100

KM# 451.4 MOHUR
11.6600 g., 0.9170 Gold 0.3438 oz. AGW **Mint:** Calcutta **Obverse:** RS incuse on truncation **Edge:** Plain

INDIA-BRITISH

Date	Mintage	F	VF	XF	Unc
1835.(c) Proof; Rare	—	—	—	—	—

KM# 451.5 MOHUR
11.6600 g., 0.9170 Gold 0.3438 oz. AGW **Mint:** Calcutta **Obverse:** F incuse on truncation **Edge:** Plain

Date	Mintage	F	VF	XF	Unc
1835.(c) Proof; Rare	—	—	—	—	—

KM# 461.2 MOHUR
11.6600 g., 0.9170 Gold 0.3438 oz. AGW **Mint:** Calcutta **Obverse:** Dot on truncation

Date	Mintage	F	VF	XF	Unc
1841.(c)	601,000	325	400	550	1,000
1841.(c) Proof	—	Value: 4,000			

KM# 461.3 MOHUR
11.6600 g., 0.9170 Gold 0.3438 oz. AGW **Mint:** Madras **Obverse:** S incuse on truncation

Date	Mintage	F	VF	XF	Unc
1841.(m)	32,000	500	625	850	1,500
1841.(m) Proof	—	Value: 4,000			

KM# 462.2 MOHUR
11.6600 g., 0.9170 Gold 0.3438 oz. AGW **Mint:** Calcutta **Obverse:** W.W. incuse, large legend and large date with crosslet 4

Date	Mintage	F	VF	XF	Unc
1841.(c)	—	325	400	550	1,000

KM# A462 MOHUR
11.6600 g., 0.9170 Gold 0.3438 oz. AGW **Mint:** Calcutta **Obverse:** Mule. KM#462 **Reverse:** KM#451

Date	Mintage	F	VF	XF	Unc
1841.(c)	—	—	—	—	1,200

Note: Prooflike; Restrike

KM# 461.1 MOHUR
11.6600 g., 0.9170 Gold 0.3438 oz. AGW **Ruler:** Victoria **Mint:** Bombay **Obverse:** Head left, dot on truncation **Obv. Legend:** VICTORIA QUEEN **Reverse:** Palm tree, lion walking left **Rev. Legend:** EAST INDIA COMPANY **Note:** Type I: Obv. legend continuous.

Date	Mintage	F	VF	XF	Unc
1841.(b)	5,960	—	—	1,250	2,500

KM# 462.1 MOHUR
11.6600 g., 0.9170 Gold 0.3438 oz. AGW **Ruler:** Victoria **Mint:** Calcutta **Obverse:** Head left **Obv. Legend:** VICTORIA QUEEN **Reverse:** Palm tree, lion walking left **Rev. Legend:** EAST INDIA COMPANY **Note:** Type II: Obv. legend divided. Illustration reduced. W.W. incuse, large legend and large date with normal 4.

Date	Mintage	F	VF	XF	Unc
1841.(c)	442,000	325	400	550	1,000
1841.(c) Prooflike; Restrike	—	—	—	—	1,500

Small date

KM# 462.3 MOHUR
11.6600 g., 0.9170 Gold 0.3438 oz. AGW **Ruler:** Victoria **Obverse:** Head left **Obv. Legend:** VICTORIA QUEEN **Reverse:** Palm tree, lion walking left **Rev. Legend:** EAST INDIA COMPANY **Note:** W.W. incuse, small legend and small date with normal 4

Date	Mintage	F	VF	XF	Unc
1841	—	300	475	675	1,450

KM# 452.2 2 MOHURS
23.3200 g., 0.9170 Gold 0.6875 oz. AGW **Mint:** Calcutta **Obverse:** RS incuse on truncation **Edge:** Plain

Date	Mintage	F	VF	XF	Unc
1835.(c) Rare	—	—	—	—	—

KM# 452.1 2 MOHURS
23.3200 g., 0.9170 Gold 0.6875 oz. AGW **Mint:** Calcutta **Obverse:** Head right **Obv. Legend:** WILLIAM IIII, KING. **Reverse:** Palm tree, lion walking left **Rev. Legend:** EAST INDIA COMPANY **Edge:** Milled **Note:** Restrikes have fewer leaves on reverse palm tree. RS incuse on truncation.

Date	Mintage	F	VF	XF	Unc
1835.(c) Rare	1,170	—	—	—	—
1835.(c) Proof; Rare	—	—	—	—	—
1835.(c) Prooflike; Restrike	—	—	—	—	3,000

MILLED COINAGE
Regal Style

KM# 465b 1/12 ANNA (1 Pie)
Gold **Mint:** Calcutta

Date	Mintage	F	VF	XF	Unc
1862(c) Prooflike; Restrike	—	—	—	—	475

KM# 483c 1/12 ANNA (1 Pie)
Gold **Ruler:** Victoria **Mint:** Calcutta **Obverse:** Crowned bust left **Reverse:** Value and date within beaded circle and wreath **Note:** All dates of this type are prooflike restrikes.

Date	Mintage	F	VF	XF	Unc
1891(c)	—	—	—	—	725
1892(c)	—	—	—	—	725
1893(c)	—	—	—	—	725
1895(c)	—	—	—	—	725
1896(c)	—	—	—	—	725
1897(c)	—	—	—	—	725
1898(c)	—	—	—	—	725
1899(c)	—	—	—	—	725
1901(c)	—	—	—	—	725

KM# 466b 1/2 PICE
Gold **Ruler:** Victoria **Mint:** Calcutta **Obverse:** Crowned bust left **Reverse:** Value and date within beaded circle and wreath

Date	Mintage	F	VF	XF	Unc
1862(c) Proof	—	Value: 1,200			

KM# 484c 1/2 PICE
Gold **Ruler:** Victoria **Mint:** Calcutta **Obverse:** Crowned bust left **Reverse:** Value and date within beaded circle and wreath **Note:** All dates of this type are prooflike restrikes.

Date	Mintage	F	VF	XF	Unc
1891(c)	—	—	—	—	950
1892(c)	—	—	—	—	950
1893(c)	—	—	—	—	950
1895(c)	—	—	—	—	950
1896(c)	—	—	—	—	950
1897(c)	—	—	—	—	950
1898(c)	—	—	—	—	950
1899(c)	—	—	—	—	950

KM# 467b 1/4 ANNA
12.8500 g., Gold **Ruler:** Victoria **Mint:** Calcutta **Obverse:** Crowned bust left **Reverse:** Value and date within beaded circle and wreath

Date	Mintage	F	VF	XF	Unc
1862(c) Prooflike; Restrike	—	—	—	—	900

KM# 486c 1/4 ANNA
Gold **Ruler:** Victoria **Mint:** Calcutta **Obverse:** Crowned bust left **Reverse:** Value and date within beaded circle and wreath **Note:** All dates of this type are Prooflike Restrikes.

Date	Mintage	F	VF	XF	Unc
1891(c) P/L; Restrike	—	—	—	—	1,150
1892(c) P/L; Restrike	—	—	—	—	1,150
1893(c) P/L; Restrike	—	—	—	—	1,150
1895(c) P/L; Restrike	—	—	—	—	1,150
1896(c) P/L; Restrike	—	—	—	—	1,150
1897(c) P/L; Restrike	—	—	—	—	1,150
1898(c) P/L; Restrike	—	—	—	—	1,150
1899(c) P/L; Restrike	—	—	—	—	1,150
1900(c) P/L; Restrike	—	—	—	—	1,150
1901(c) P/L; Restrike	—	—	—	—	1,150

KM# 468b 1/2 ANNA
Gold **Ruler:** Victoria **Mint:** Calcutta **Obverse:** Crowned bust left **Reverse:** Value and date within beaded circle and wreath

Date	Mintage	F	VF	XF	Unc
1862 Proof	—	Value: 2,500			

KM# 487c 1/2 ANNA
Gold **Ruler:** Victoria **Obverse:** Crowned bust left **Reverse:** Value and date within beaded circle and wreath **Note:** All dates of this type are Prooflike Restrikes.

Date	Mintage	F	VF	XF	Unc
1877(b)	—	—	—	—	1,100
1890(b)	—	—	—	—	1,100
1890(b)	—	—	—	—	1,100
1892(c)	—	—	—	—	1,100
1893(c)	—	—	—	—	1,100

KM# 534a 1/2 ANNA
Gold **Ruler:** George VI **Mint:** Calcutta **Obverse:** Crowned head left **Reverse:** Denomination and date within decorative outline

Date	Mintage	F	VF	XF	Unc
1940(c)	—	—	—	—	550

Note: Prooflike; Restrike

KM# 469a 2 ANNAS
Gold **Ruler:** Victoria **Obverse:** Crowned bust left **Reverse:** Value and date within wreath

Date	Mintage	F	VF	XF	Unc
1862 Proof	—	Value: 725			

KM# 488c 2 ANNAS
Gold **Ruler:** Victoria **Obverse:** Crowned bust left **Obv. Legend:** VICTORIA EMPRESS **Reverse:** Value and date within wreath **Note:** All dates of this type are Prooflike Restrikes.

Date	Mintage	F	VF	XF	Unc
1891	—	—	—	—	550
1892	—	—	—	—	550
1893	—	—	—	—	550
1896	—	—	—	—	550
1897	—	—	—	—	550
1898	—	—	—	—	550
1900	—	—	—	—	550

KM# 505a 2 ANNAS
Gold **Ruler:** Edward VII **Obverse:** Head right **Obv. Legend:** EDWARD VII KING AND EMPEROR **Reverse:** Crown above denomination, sprays flank **Note:** All dates of this type are prooflike restrikes.

Date	Mintage	F	VF	XF	Unc
1904(c)	—	—	—	—	900
1906(c)	—	—	—	—	900
1910(c)	—	—	—	—	900

KM# 470a 1/4 RUPEE
Gold **Ruler:** Victoria **Obverse:** Crowned bust left, bust A **Obv. Legend:** VICTORIA QUEEN **Reverse:** Value and date within wreath

Date	Mintage	F	VF	XF	Unc
1862(c) Prooflike; Restrike	—	—	—	—	725

KM# 506a 1/4 RUPEE
Gold **Ruler:** Edward VII **Obverse:** Head right **Reverse:** Crown above denomination, sprays flank

Date	Mintage	F	VF	XF	Unc
1910(c)	—	—	—	—	1,000

Note: Prooflike; Restrike

KM# 472a 1/2 RUPEE
Gold **Ruler:** Victoria **Obverse:** Crowned bust left **Reverse:** Value and date within wreath

Date	Mintage	F	VF	XF	Unc
1862(c) Prooflike; Restrike	—	—	—	—	1,200

KM# 491c 1/2 RUPEE
Gold **Ruler:** Victoria **Obverse:** Crowned bust left **Obv. Legend:** VICTORIA EMPRESS **Reverse:** Value and date within wreath **Note:** All dates of this type are Prooflike Restrikes.

Date	Mintage	F	VF	XF	Unc
1891	—	—	—	—	900
1892	—	—	—	—	900
1893	—	—	—	—	900
1896	—	—	—	—	900
1897	—	—	—	—	900
1898	—	—	—	—	900
1899	—	—	—	—	900

KM# 473.1a RUPEE
Gold, 30.78 mm. **Ruler:** Victoria **Obverse:** Crowned bust left **Reverse:** Value and date within wreath **Edge:** Reeded

Date	Mintage	F	VF	XF	Unc
1862(c) Prooflike; Restrike	—	—	—	—	—

KM# 492c RUPEE
Gold **Ruler:** Victoria **Obverse:** Crowned bust left **Obv. Legend:** VICTORIA EMPRESS **Reverse:** Value and date within wreath **Note:** All dates of this type are Prooflike Restrikes.

366 INDIA-BRITISH

Date	Mintage	F	VF	XF	Unc
1891	—	—	—	—	1,000
1892	—	—	—	—	1,000
1893	—	—	—	—	1,000
1898	—	—	—	—	1,000
1900B	—	—	—	—	1,000

KM# 474 5 RUPEES
3.8870 g., 0.9170 Gold 0.1146 oz. AGW **Ruler:** Victoria **Obverse:** Crowned bust left **Obv. Legend:** VICTORIA QUEEN **Reverse:** Value and date within beaded circle and wreath **Edge:** Reeded

Date	Mintage	F	VF	XF	Unc
1870CM	—	450	650	1,000	1,500
1875 Proof	—	Value: 3,000			

KM# 475 5 RUPEES
3.8870 g., 0.9170 Gold 0.1146 oz. AGW **Ruler:** Victoria **Obverse:** Young bust **Obv. Legend:** VICTORIA QUEEN **Edge:** Plain

Date	Mintage	F	VF	XF	Unc
1870 Proof	—	Value: 3,000			

KM# 476 5 RUPEES
3.8870 g., 0.9170 Gold 0.1146 oz. AGW **Ruler:** Victoria **Obverse:** Crowned bust left **Obv. Legend:** VICTORIA QUEEN **Reverse:** Value and date within beaded circle and wreath **Edge:** Reeded

Date	Mintage	F	VF	XF	Unc
1870(c)	13,000	450	650	1,000	1,500
1870(c) Proof	—	Value: 1,650			
1870(c)	—	—	—	—	1,000
Note: Prooflike; Restrike					

KM# 494 5 RUPEES
3.8870 g., 0.9170 Gold 0.1146 oz. AGW **Ruler:** Victoria **Obverse:** Crowned bust left **Obv. Legend:** VICTORIA EMPRESS

Date	Mintage	F	VF	XF	Unc
1879(b) Prooflike; Restrike	—	—	—	—	800

KM# 493.1 5 RUPEES
3.8870 g., 0.9170 Gold 0.1146 oz. AGW **Ruler:** Victoria **Obverse:** Crowned bust left **Obv. Legend:** VICTORIA EMPRESS **Reverse:** Value and date within beaded circle and wreath **Note:** Mule. Obv: 1/4 Rupee, Bust A, KM#490.

Date	Mintage	F	VF	XF	Unc
1879(b) Prooflike; Restrike	—	—	—	—	1,000

KM# 493.2 5 RUPEES
3.8870 g., 0.9170 Gold 0.1146 oz. AGW **Ruler:** Victoria **Reverse:** Value and date within beaded circle and wreath **Note:** Mule. Obv: 1/4 Rupee, Bust B.

Date	Mintage	F	VF	XF	Unc
1879(b) Prooflike; Restrike	—	—	—	—	1,000

KM# 493.3 5 RUPEES
3.8870 g., 0.9170 Gold 0.1146 oz. AGW **Ruler:** Victoria **Reverse:** Value and date within beaded circle and wreath **Note:** Mule. Obv: 1/4 Rupee, Bust C.

Date	Mintage	F	VF	XF	Unc
1879(b) Prooflike; Restrike	—	—	—	—	1,000

KM# 477 10 RUPEES
7.7740 g., 0.9170 Gold 0.2292 oz. AGW **Ruler:** Victoria **Obverse:** Crowned bust left **Obv. Legend:** VICTORIA QUEEN **Reverse:** Value and date within beaded circle and wreath **Edge:** Reeded

Date	Mintage	F	VF	XF	Unc
1870CM Proof	—	Value: 2,000			
1870CM Prooflike; Restrike	—	—	—	—	1,500
1875 Proof	—	Value: 3,750			

KM# 478 10 RUPEES
7.7740 g., 0.9170 Gold 0.2292 oz. AGW **Ruler:** Victoria **Obverse:** Crowned bust left **Obv. Legend:** VICTORIA QUEEN **Edge:** Plain

Date	Mintage	F	VF	XF	Unc
1870 Proof	—	Value: 4,000			

KM# 479 10 RUPEES
7.7740 g., 0.9170 Gold 0.2292 oz. AGW **Ruler:** Victoria **Obverse:** Crowned bust left **Obv. Legend:** VICTORIA QUEEN **Reverse:** Value and date within beaded circle and wreath **Edge:** Reeded

Date	Mintage	F	VF	XF	Unc
1870(c)	7,932	500	700	1,100	1,650
1870(c) Proof	—	Value: 2,000			
1870(c) Prooflike; Restrike	—	—	—	—	1,250

KM# 495 10 RUPEES
7.7740 g., 0.9170 Gold 0.2292 oz. AGW **Ruler:** Victoria **Obverse:** Crowned bust left **Obv. Legend:** VICTORIA EMPRESS **Reverse:** Value and date within beaded circle and wreath **Edge:** Reeded

Date	Mintage	F	VF	XF	Unc
1878(b) Proof	—	Value: 3,500			
1878(b) Prooflike; Restrike	—	—	—	—	1,600
1879(b) Proof	—	Value: 3,500			
1879(b) Prooflike; Restrike	—	—	—	—	1,500

KM# 525 15 RUPEES
7.9881 g., 0.9170 Gold .2354 oz. AGW **Ruler:** George V **Obverse:** Crowned bust left **Obv. Legend:** GEORGE V KING EMPEROR **Reverse:** Denomination and date within circle, wreath surrounds **Note:** This issue is equal in weight and fineness to the British sovereign.

Date	Mintage	F	VF	XF	Unc
1918(b)	2,110,000	275	350	500	750
1918(b) Proof	12	Value: 7,000			
1918(b) P/L; Restrike	—	—	—	—	800

KM# 480 MOHUR
11.6600 g., 0.9170 Gold 0.3438 oz. AGW **Ruler:** Victoria **Obverse:** Crowned bust left **Obv. Legend:** VICTORIA QUEEN **Reverse:** Value and date within beaded circle and wreath

Date	Mintage	F	VF	XF	Unc
1862(c)	153,000	245	350	500	750
1862(c) Proof	Inc. above	Value: 1,250			
1862(c) Prooflike; Restrike	—	—	—	—	850
1862(c)	Inc. above	245	350	500	750
Note: With V on bust					
1862(c)	Inc. above	245	350	500	750
Note: With V on reverse in design below date					
1862(c)	—	245	350	500	750
Note: With V on bust and on reverse					
1862(c)	Inc. above	245	350	500	750
Note: With V on bust and 2 flowers in bottom panel					
1870(c) Proof	—	Value: 1,500			
1870(c) Prooflike; Restrike	—	—	—	—	750
1875(c)	11,000	350	500	800	1,200
Note: With V on bust					
1875(c) Proof	—	Value: 4,500			
1875(c) Prooflike; Restrike	—	—	—	—	800

KM# 481 MOHUR
11.6600 g., 0.9170 Gold 0.3438 oz. AGW **Ruler:** Victoria **Obverse:** Crowned bust left **Obv. Legend:** VICTORIA QUEEN **Reverse:** Value and date within beaded circle and wreath

Date	Mintage	F	VF	XF	Unc
1870(c) Proof	—	Value: 4,000			
1870(c) Prooflike; Restrike	—	—	—	—	850

KM# 482 MOHUR
11.6600 g., 0.9170 Gold 0.3438 oz. AGW **Ruler:** Victoria **Obverse:** Crowned bust left **Reverse:** Value and date within beaded circle and wreath **Note:** Mule.

Date	Mintage	F	VF	XF	Unc
1870(c) Prooflike; Restrike	—	—	—	—	850

KM# 496 MOHUR
11.6600 g., 0.9170 Gold 0.3438 oz. AGW **Ruler:** Victoria **Obverse:** Crowned bust left **Obv. Legend:** VICTORIA EMPRESS **Reverse:** Value and date within beaded circle and wreath

Date	Mintage	F	VF	XF	Unc
1877(c)	10,000	BV	275	350	600
1878(c) Prooflike; Restrike	—	—	—	—	700
1879C	19,000	BV	275	350	600
1879(b) Proof	—	Value: 3,500			
Note: Modified rev.					
1879(b) Prooflike; Restrike	—	—	—	—	650
1881	23,000	BV	275	350	600
1882C	12,000	BV	275	350	600
1882(b) Prooflike; Restrike	—	—	—	—	650
Note: Without C mintmark					
1884(c)	8,643	BV	300	400	700
1885(c)	15,000	BV	275	350	600
1888(c)	15,000	BV	275	350	600
1889(c)	15,000	BV	275	350	600
1889(c) Prooflike; Restrike	—	—	—	—	650
1891(c)	17,000	BV	275	350	600

TRADE COINAGE

The Mansfield Commission of 1868 allowed for the admission of British and Australian sovereigns (see Australian section; sovereigns with shield reverse were struck for export to India) as payment for sums due.

The fifth branch of the Royal Mint was established in a section of the Mumbai (Bombay) Mint as of December 21, 1917. This was a war-time measure, its purpose being to strike into sovereigns the gold blanks supplied by the Mumbai and other Indian mints. The Mumbai sovereigns bear the mint mark 'I' and were struck from August 15, 1918, to April 22, 1919. The branch mint was closed in May 1919.

KM# 525A SOVEREIGN
7.9881 g., 0.9170 Gold .2354 oz. AGW **Ruler:** George V **Obverse:** Head left **Reverse:** St. George slaying the dragon **Note:** Mint mark "I".

Date	Mintage	F	VF	XF	Unc
1918	1,295,000	—	BV	170	200
1918 Proof	—	—	—	—	—
1918 P/L; Restrike	—	—	—	—	850

BULLION COINAGE

Private bullion issues have been recorded in weights of 1/4, 1/2, 1, 5, 10, 20 and 25 Tolas in gold and silver. The actual weight of the Tola is based on the obsolete English Guinea.

KM# A496 TOLA
11.7000 g., 0.9960 Gold .3747 oz. AGW **Ruler:** George V **Obverse:** Crown within wreath **Reverse:** Denomination and weight **Shape:** Scalloped **Note:** Prev. KM#496A.

Date	Mintage	VG	F	VF	XF	Unc
ND(1931)	—	—	—	BV	265	285

INDIA-BRITISH

X# 61 TOLA
11.7000 g., 0.9167 Gold 0.3448 oz. AGW **Issuer:** Habib Bank Ltd. **Mint:** Bombay **Obverse:** Symbol above large "HB" in circle **Obv. Legend:** + HABIB BANK Ltd. + GUINEA GOLD **Reverse:** Lion left in center circle, "Guinea gold" in Gujarati above, in Urdu below value

Date	Mintage	F	VF	XF	Unc
ND	—	BV	245	265	300

KM# B496 5 TOLAS
58.5000 g., 0.9957 Gold 1.8727 oz. AGW **Ruler:** George V **Obverse:** Building **Reverse:** Denomination and weight **Shape:** Square **Note:** Prev. KM#496B.

Date	Mintage	VG	F	VF	XF	Unc
ND(1931)	—	—	—	BV	1,275	1,350

X# 42.2 5 TOLAS
58.3000 g., 0.9950 Gold 1.865 oz. AGW **Obverse:** Modified die, 8-pointed star with jewel in center **Reverse:** Modified die

Date	Mintage	F	VF	XF	Unc
ND	—	—	BV	1,275	1,400

KM# C496 10 TOLAS
117.0000 g., 0.9956 Gold 3.7451 oz. AGW **Ruler:** George V **Obverse:** Legend, crown, weight and denomination **Shape:** Rectangular **Note:** Uniface. Prev. KM#496C.

Date	Mintage	VG	F	VF	XF	Unc
ND(1921)	—	—	—	BV	2,550	2,700

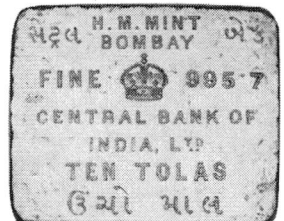

KM# D496 10 TOLAS
0.9957 Gold **Ruler:** George V **Obverse:** Legend, crown, denomination and weight **Shape:** Rectangular **Note:** Prev. KM#496D.

Date	Mintage	VG	F	VF	XF	Unc
ND(1922)	—	—	—	BV	2,550	2,700

BULLION COINAGE
Tola Issue - Central Bank of India

X# 21 TOLA
11.6600 g., 0.9960 Gold 0.3734 oz. AGW **Mint:** Bombay

Date	Mintage	F	VF	XF	Unc
ND	—	—	BV	275	325

X# 22 5 TOLAS
58.3000 g., 0.9957 Gold 1.8663 oz. AGW **Mint:** Bombay

Date	Mintage	F	VF	XF	Unc
ND	—	—	BV	1,300	1,450

X# 23 10 TOLAS
116.6000 g., 0.9956 Gold 3.7323 oz. AGW **Mint:** Bombay **Note:** Uniface.

Date	Mintage	F	VF	XF	Unc
ND	—	—	BV	2,650	3,000

X# 24 10 TOLAS
0.9957 Gold **Mint:** Bombay

Date	Mintage	F	VF	XF	Unc
ND	—	—	BV	2,650	3,000

BULLION COINAGE
Tola Issue - M. S. Manilal Chimanlal & Co. - Bombay

X# 40 1/2 TOLA
5.8800 g., 0.9950 Gold 0.1881 oz. AGW **Mint:** Bombay **Obverse:** 8-pointed badge **Obv. Legend:** M.S. MANICAL CHIMANLAL & CO. - BOMBAY

Date	Mintage	F	VF	XF	Unc
ND(1940s)	—	—	BV	135	175

X# 41 TOLA
11.6600 g., 0.9950 Gold 0.373 oz. AGW **Mint:** Bombay **Obverse:** Outline of India **Rev. Inscription:** GATEWAY OF INDIA / BOMBAY

Date	Mintage	F	VF	XF	Unc
ND	—	—	BV	265	320

X# 42.1 5 TOLAS
58.3000 g., 0.9950 Gold 1.865 oz. AGW **Mint:** Bombay **Obverse:** 8-pointed star with jewel in center

Date	Mintage	F	VF	XF	Unc
ND	—	—	BV	1,275	1,400

X# 43 5 TOLAS
58.3000 g., 0.9950 Gold 1.865 oz. AGW **Mint:** Bombay

Date	Mintage	F	VF	XF	Unc
ND	—	—	BV	1,275	1,400

X# 39 GUINEA
11.6600 g., 0.9166 Gold 0.3436 oz. AGW **Mint:** Bombay

Date	Mintage	F	VF	XF	Unc
ND	—	—	BV	240	300

BULLION COINAGE
Tola Issue - Habib Bank Ltd.

X# 54 1/2 TOLA
5.8500 g., 0.9950 Gold 0.1871 oz. AGW

Date	Mintage	F	VF	XF	Unc
ND	—	—	BV	140	180

X# 55 TOLA
11.6600 g., 0.9950 Gold 0.373 oz. AGW

Date	Mintage	F	VF	XF	Unc
ND	—	—	BV	275	325

INDIA-BRITISH

X# 58 5 TOLAS
58.3000 g., 0.9950 Gold 1.865 oz. AGW

Date	Mintage	F	VF	XF	Unc
ND	—	—	BV	1,300	1,450

BULLION COINAGE
Tola Issue - M/S Rattanchand Rikhabdas Jain - Bombay

X# 80 TOLA
11.6600 g., 0.9950 Gold 0.373 oz. AGW **Mint:** Bombay

Date	Mintage	F	VF	XF	Unc
ND	—	—	BV	275	325

BULLION COINAGE
Tola Issue - Shewpujan Roy Indra San Roy - Star Brand

X# 83 TOLA
11.6600 g., 0.9950 Gold 0.373 oz. AGW **Mint:** Bombay

Date	Mintage	F	VF	XF	Unc
ND	—	—	BV	275	325

TOKEN COINAGE

The British Indian Government introduced a special series of tokens for use by Famine Relief Officials as part of a policy to deal with great famine disasters in Bengal in 1874 and in Southern India in 1876.

KM# Tn2a RUPEE
Gold **Ruler:** Victoria **Subject:** Famine Relief **Obverse:** Value and legend around hole in center **Reverse:** Date and legend around hole in center

Date	Mintage	F	VF	XF	Unc
1874(c) Rare					

MEDALLIC COINAGE
Richard Lobel Issues

X# 91 SOVEREIGN
0.3750 Gold **Subject:** Edward VIII

Date	Mintage	F	VF	XF	Unc
1936 Proof	200	Value: 150			

PATTERNS
Including off metal strikes

P# are in reference to The Coins of the British Commonwealth of Nations Part 4, India, Vol. 1 and 2 by F. Pridmore (Spink and Son Ltd., London 1980).

KM#	Date	Mintage	Identification	Mkt Val
Pn10	(1835)(c)	—	Rupee. Gold. Prid.#177.	—
Pn17	1854	—	5 Rupees. Gold. Plain edge. Prid.#30.	3,500
Pn19	1854	—	10 Rupees. Gold. Plain edge. Prid.#27.	4,750
Pn21	1854	—	Mohur. Gold. Plain edge. Prid.#25.	5,500
Pn23	1854	—	2 Mohurs. Gold. Plain edge. Prid.#6.	9,000
Pn24	1854	—	2 Mohurs. Gold. Plain edge.	—
Pn100	1910(c)	—	Rupee. Gold. Prid.#1050	—
Pn109	1921(c)	—	Anna. Gold. Prid.#1082	—

PROOF SETS

KM#	Date	Mintage	Identification	Issue Price	Mkt Val
PS2	1875 (3)	—	KM#474, 477, 480	—	11,750

BENGAL PRESIDENCY
East India Company
(Until 1835)

In 1633 a group of 8 Englishmen obtained a permit to trade in Bengal from the Nawab of Orissa. Shortly thereafter trading factories were established at Balasore and Hariharpur. Although greater trading privileges were granted to the East India Company by the Emperor Shah Jahan in 1634, by 1642 the 2 original factories were abandoned.

In 1651, through an English surgeon named Broughton, a permit was acquired to trade at Bengal. Hugli was the first location, followed by Kasimbazar, Balasore and Patna (the last 3 in 1653). Calcutta became of increasing importance in this area and on December 20, 1699 Calcutta was declared a presidency and renamed Fort William. During these times there were many conflicts with the Nawab, both diplomatic and military, and the ultimate outcome was the intervention of Clive and the restoration of Calcutta as an important trading center.

During the earlier trading times in Bengal most of the monies used were imported rupees from the Madras factory. These were primarily of the Arcot type. After Clive's victory one of the concessions in the peace treaty was the right to make Mughal type coinage. The Nawab gave specific details as to what form the coinage should take.

In 1765 Emperor Shah Alam gave the East India Company possessions in Bengal, Orissa and Bihar. This made the company nominally responsible only to the Emperor.

In 1777 the "Frozen Year 19" (of Shah Alam) rupees were made at Calcutta and were continued until 1835. The Arcot rupees were discontinued at Calcutta about 1777.

MINTS

علي نگر كلكته

Alinagar Kalkatah (Calcutta)

بنارس

Banaras

NOTE: Coins of similar dates with different legends are listed in Indian Princely States, Awadh under Lucknow Mint, with fixed regnal year 26.

كلكته

Calcutta (Kalkatah)

فرخ اباد

Farrukhabad

مرشد اباد

Murshidabad

ساكر

Sagar

BRITISH COLONY
MILLED COINAGE

KM# 110 1/4 MOHUR
3.3100 g., 0.9170 Gold **Mint:** Murshidabad **Obv. Inscription:** "Shah Alam II Badshah" **Reverse:** Sanat, mint name Murshidabad **Edge:** Vertical milling

Date	Mintage	Good	VG	F	VF	XF
AH1204//19 Frozen	—	—	BV	65.00	90.00	175
AH1204//19 Frozen; Proof	—	Value: 1,250				

KM# 112 MOHUR
13.2600 g., 0.9170 Gold **Mint:** Calcutta **Obverse:** Persian inscription, couplet **Obv. Inscription:** "Shah Alam II Badshah" **Reverse:** Persian-julus (formula), mint name Murshidabad **Edge:** Vertical milling

Date	Mintage	Good	VG	F	VF	XF
AH1202//19	—	—	BV	250	275	450
AH1202//19 Proof	—	Value: 1,650				

KM# 113 MOHUR
12.3600 g., 0.9170 Gold **Mint:** Murshidabad **Obverse:** Persian inscription, couplet, low relief **Obv. Inscription:** "Shah Alam II Badshah" **Reverse:** Persian-julus (formula), mint name Murshidabad, low relief **Edge:** Oblique milling

Date	Mintage	Good	VG	F	VF	XF
AH1202//19	—	—	BV	250	275	375

KM# 114 MOHUR
12.3600 g., 0.9170 Gold **Obverse:** Persian inscription, couplet **Obv. Inscription:** "Shah Alam II Badshah" **Reverse:** Persian-julus (formula), mint name Murshidabad **Note:** Mint mark: crescent.

Date	Mintage	Good	VG	F	VF	XF
AH1202//19	—	—	BV	265	325	475
AH1202//19 Proof	—	Value: 1,750				

PATTERNS
Including off metal strikes

Due to extensive revisions and new information, the following section in part is listed by Pridmore(P#) numbers. These are in reference to The Coins of the Commonwealth of Nations, Part 4, India - Volume I: East India Company Presidency Series ca. 1642-1835, by F. Pridmore (Spink and Son, Ltd.).

KM#	Date	Mintage	Identification	Mkt Val
Pn22c	AH1809	—	1/2 Pie. Gold. . Prid.#392.	—
Pn24e	AH1809	—	Pie. Gold. . Prid.#386.	—

BOMBAY PRESIDENCY

Following a naval victory over the Portuguese on December 24, 1612 negotiations were started that developed into the opening of the first East India Company factory in Surat in 1613. Silver coins for the New World as well as various other foreign coins were used in early trade. Within the decade the Mughal mint at Surat was melting all of these foreign coins and re-minting them as various denominations of Mughal coinage.

Bombay became an English holding as part of the dowry of Catherine of Braganza, Princess of Portugal when she was betrothed to Charles II of England. Also included in the dowry was Tangier and $500,000. With this acquisition the trading center of the Indian West Coast moved from Surat to Bombay.

Possession of Bombay Island took place on February 8, 1665 and by 1672 the East India Company had a mint in Bombay to serve their trading interests. European designed coins were struck here until 1717. Experimental issues of Mughal style rupees with regnal years pertaining to the reigns of James II and William and Mary were made in 1693-94.

From 1717 to 1778 the Mughal style Bombay rupee was the principal coin of the West India trade, although bulk foreign coins were used for striking rupees at Surat.

After the East India Company took over the city of Surat in 1800 they slowed the mint production and finally transferred all activity to Bombay in 1815.

MINTS

منبى

Mumbai (Bombay)

BRITISH COLONY
HAMMERED COINAGE

KM# 236 1/15 MOHUR (Gold Rupee)
0.7700 g., Gold **Mint:** Mumbai **Obverse:** Persian inscription, couplet **Obv. Inscription:** "Shah Alam II Badshah" **Reverse:** Persian-julus (formula), mint name **Note:** Size varies 7-8mm. Privy mark: Crescent.

Date	Mintage	Good	VG	F	VF	XF
AH-//46	—	35.00	60.00	100	250	350

KM# 237.1 1/15 MOHUR (Gold Rupee)
0.7700 g., Gold **Mint:** Mumbai **Obverse:** Persian inscription, couplet **Obv. Inscription:** "Shah Alam II Badshah" **Reverse:** Persian-julus (formula), mint name **Note:** Size varies 7-8mm. Privy mark #4b.

Date	Mintage	Good	VG	F	VF	XF
AH-//46	—	22.50	35.00	75.00	140	250

KM# 237.2 1/15 MOHUR (Gold Rupee)
0.7700 g., Gold **Mint:** Mumbai **Obverse:** Persian inscription, couplet **Obv. Inscription:** "Shah Alam II Badshah" **Reverse:** Persian-julus (formula), mint name **Note:** Size varies 7-8mm. Privy mark #5b.

Date	Mintage	Good	VG	F	VF	XF
AH-//46	—	27.50	45.00	75.00	135	

MADRAS PRESIDENCY

KM# 239 PANCHIA (1/3 Mohur)
3.8600 g., Gold **Mint:** Surat **Obverse:** Persian inscription, couplet **Obv. Inscription:** "Shah Alam II Badshah" **Reverse:** Persian-julus (formula), mint name

Date	Mintage	Good	VG	F	VF	XF
AH-//46	—	85.00	90.00	100	150	250

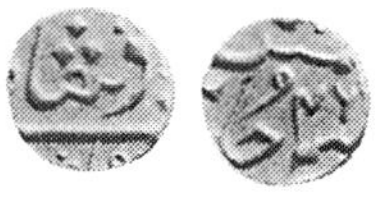

KM# 240 PANCHIA (1/3 Mohur)
3.8600 g., Gold **Mint:** Mumbai **Obverse:** Persian inscription, couplet **Obv. Inscription:** "Shah Alam II Badshah" **Reverse:** Persian-julus (formula), mint name **Note:** Privy mark: crescent.

Date	Mintage	Good	VG	F	VF	XF
AH-//46	—	85.00	90.00	150	250	375

KM# 241 PANCHIA (1/3 Mohur)
3.8600 g., Gold **Mint:** Mumbai **Note:** Privy mark: inverted date.

Date	Mintage	VG	F	VF	XF	Unc
1802//46(1802)	—	120	200	350	500	—

KM# 243 PANCHIA (1/3 Mohur)
3.8600 g., Gold **Mint:** Mumbai **Obverse:** Persian inscription, couplet **Obv. Inscription:** "Shah Alam II Badshah" **Reverse:** Persian-julus (formula), mint name **Note:** Privy mark: normal crown.

Date	Mintage	Good	VG	F	VF	XF
ND-//46	—	85.00	90.00	100	150	250

KM# 245 PANCHIA (1/3 Mohur)
3.8600 g., Gold **Mint:** Mumbai **Obverse:** Persian inscription, couplet **Obv. Inscription:** "Shah Alam II Badshah" **Reverse:** Persian-julus (formula), mint name **Note:** Privy mark: inverted crown.

Date	Mintage	Good	VG	F	VF	XF
ND-//46	—	85.00	90.00	100	150	250

KM# 247 PANCHIA (1/3 Mohur)
3.8800 g., Gold **Mint:** Mumbai **Obverse:** Persian inscription, couplet **Obv. Inscription:** "Shah Alam II Badshah" **Reverse:** Persian-julus (formula), mint name **Note:** Privy mark: Normal crown and 6 petal rosette

Date	Mintage	Good	VG	F	VF	XF
ND-//46	—	85.00	90.00	100	150	250

KM# 249 PANCHIA (1/3 Mohur)
3.8800 g., Gold **Mint:** Mumbai **Obverse:** Persian inscription, couplet **Obv. Inscription:** "Shah Alam II Badshah" **Reverse:** Persian-julus (formula), mint name **Note:** Privy mark: Inverted crown and 6 petal rosette.

Date	Mintage	Good	VG	F	VF	XF
ND-//46	—	85.00	90.00	100	150	250

KM# 242 MOHUR (15 Rupees)
11.5900 g., Gold **Mint:** Mumbai **Obverse:** Persian inscription, couplet **Obv. Inscription:** "Shah Alam II Badshah" **Reverse:** Persian-julus (formula), mint name **Note:** Privy mark: crescent.

Date	Mintage	Good	VG	F	VF	XF
ND-//46	—	225	350	650	1,200	2,000

KM# 214 MOHUR (15 Rupees)
11.5900 g., Gold **Mint:** Surat **Obverse:** Persian inscription, couplet **Obv. Inscription:** "Shah Alam II Badshah" **Reverse:** Persian-julus (formula), mint name **Note:** Size varies 16-19mm.

Date	Mintage	Good	VG	F	VF	XF
ND-//46	—	—	BV	225	275	350

KM# 246 MOHUR (15 Rupees)
11.5900 g., Gold **Mint:** Mumbai **Obverse:** Persian inscription, couplet **Obv. Inscription:** "Shah Alam II Badshah" **Reverse:** Persian-julus (formula), mint name **Note:** Privy mark: inverted crown

Date	Mintage	Good	VG	F	VF	XF
ND-//46	—	—	BV	225	275	350

KM# 244 MOHUR (15 Rupees)
11.5900 g., Gold **Mint:** Mumbai **Obverse:** Persian inscription, couplet **Obv. Inscription:** "Shah Alam II Badshah" **Reverse:** Persian-julus (formula), mint name **Note:** Privy mark: normal crown.

Date	Mintage	Good	VG	F	VF	XF
ND-//46	—	BV	BV	235	300	450

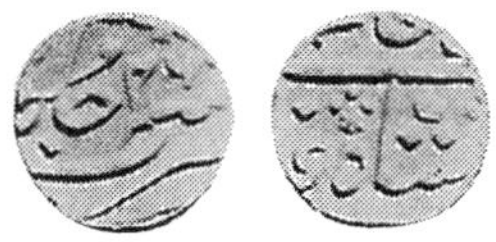

KM# 248 MOHUR (15 Rupees)
11.5900 g., Gold **Mint:** Mumbai **Obverse:** Persian inscription, couplet **Obv. Inscription:** "Shah Alam II Badshah" **Reverse:** Persian-julus (formula), mint name **Note:** Privy marks: normal crown and 6 petal rosette.

Date	Mintage	Good	VG	F	VF	XF
ND-//46	—	BV	BV	225	275	350

KM# 278 PAGODA
3.0000 g., Gold **Mint:** Tellicherry **Obverse:** T-99, Persian Sikkanishini (government coin), date **Reverse:** Persian "Zarb", mint name, julus

Date	Mintage	Good	VG	F	VF	XF
1809	—	65.00	75.00	100	250	400

PATTERNS
Including off metal strikes

KM#	Date	Mintage	Identification	Mkt Val
Pn18	1828	—	Mohur. Copper. Prid.#336.	600
Pn19	1828//46	—	Mohur. Copper. Prid.#337.	—
Pn20	(1828)//46	—	Mohur. Copper. Prid.#338.	700
Pn22	1215//46	—	Mohur. Silver. Prid.#333.	—

MADRAS PRESIDENCY

English trade was begun on the east coast of India in 1611. The first factory was at Mazulipatam and was maintained intermittently until modern times.

Madras was founded in 1639 and Fort St. George was made the chief factory on the east coast in 1641. A mint was established at Fort St. George where coins of the style of Vijayanagar were struck.

The Madras mint began minting copper coins after the renovation. In 1689 silver fanams were authorized to be struck by the new Board of Directors.

In 1692 the Mughal Emperor Aurangzeb gave permission for Mughal type rupees to be struck at Madras. These circulated locally and were also sent to Bengal. The chief competition for the Madras coins were the Arcot rupees. Some of the bulk coins from Madras were sent to the Nawabs mint to be made into Arcot rupees. In 1742 the East India Company applied for and received permission to make their own Arcot rupees. Coining operations ceased in Madras in 1869.

MONETARY SYSTEM
1 Dudu = 10 Cash
8 Dudu = 1 Fanam
36 Fanam = 1 Pagoda (1688-1802)
42 Fanam = 1 Pagoda (1802-1817)
45 Fanam = 1 Pagoda (1817-1835)
3-1/2 Rupees = 1 Pagoda

MINTS

آرکات
Arcot

مچھلي پٽن
Masulipatnam (Machilipatnam)

BRITISH COLONY

This section lists the coins of British India from the reign of William IV (1835) to the reign of George VI (1947). The issues are divided into two main parts:

1. Coins struck under the authority of the East India Company (E.I.C.) from 1835 until the trading monopoly of the E.I.C. was abolished in 1853. From August 2, 1858 the property and powers of the Company were transferred to the British Crown. From November 1, 1858 to November 1, 1862 the coins continued to bear the design and inscription of the Company.

2. Coins struck under the authority of the Crown (Regal issues) from 1862 until 1947.

The first regal issues bear the date 1862 and were struck with the date 1862 unchanged until 1874. From then onward all coins bear the year date.

The copper coins dated 1862 have been tentatively attributed by their size to the mint of issue. The silver coins dated 1862 have been attributed to various years of issue by their characteristic marks according to mint records.

In 1877 Queen Victoria was proclaimed Empress of India and the title of the obverse legend was changed accordingly.

For a detailed account of the work of the various mints and the numerous die varieties the general collector and specialist should refer to "The Coins of the British Commonwealth of Nations to the end of the reign of King George VI - 1952", Part 4, India, Vol. 1 and 2, by F. Pridmore, Spink, 1980.

RULERS
British until 1947

MINT MARKS
The coins of British India were struck at the following mints, indicated in the catalogue by either capital letters after the date when the actual letter appears on the coins or small letters in ( ) designating the mint of issue. Plain dates indicate Royal Mint strikes.

B - Bombay, 1835-1947
C or CM - Calcutta, 1835-1947
H - Ralph Heaton & Sons, Birmingham
¬¬(1857-1858)
I - Bombay, 1918-1919
L - Lahore, 1943-1945
M - Madras, 1869 (closed Sept. 1869)
P - Pretoria, South Africa, 1943-1944
W - J. Watt & Sons, Birmingham (1860)

In 1947 British rule came to an end and India was divided into two self-governing countries, India and Pakistan. In 1971 Bangladesh seceded from Pakistan. All are now independent republics and although they are still members of the British Commonwealth of Nations, their coinages do not belong to the British India series.

MONETARY SYSTEM
3 Pies = 1 Pice (Paisa)
4 Pice = 1 Anna
16 Annas = 1 Rupee
15 Rupees = 1 Mohur

The transition from the coins of the Moslem monetary system began with the silver pattern Rupees of William IV, 1834, issued by the East India Company, with the value on the reverse, given in English, Bengali, Persian and Nagari characters. This coinage was struck for several years, as dated, except for the currency Rupee which was struck from 1835 to 1840, all dated 1835.

The portrait coins issued by the East India Company for Victoria show two different head designs on the obverse, which are called Type I and Type II. The coins with Type I head have a continuous obverse legend and were struck from 1840 to 1851. The coins with the Type II head have a divided obverse legend and were struck from 1850 (Calcutta) until 1862. The date on the coins remained unchanged: the Rupee, 1/2 Rupee and 1/4 Rupee are dated 1840, the 2 Annas and the Mohur are dated 1841. Both issues were struck at the Calcutta, Bombay and Madras Mints. Numerous varieties exist in the rupee series of 1840. Noticable differences in the ribbon designs of the English vs. Indian obverses exist.

Type I coins have on the reverse a dot after the date, those of Type II have no dot, except for some rare ¼ Rupees and 2 Annas. The latter are mules, struck from reverse dies of the preceding issue.

ENGRAVERS' INITIALS
The following initials appear on the obverse on the truncation:
F - William N. Forbes, Calcutta, 1836-1855
R.S. - Robert Saunders, Calcutta, 1826-1836
S Incuse (Type I)
WW raised or incuse (Type II)
WWS or SWW (Type II)
WWB raised (Type II)

The initials WW which appear on all coins of Type II, are those of William Wyon, Chief Engraver of the Royal Mint, London, who prepared this obverse design in 1849.

Proof and Proof-like restrikes
Original proofs are similar to early English Specimen strikes with wire edges and matte finish busts, arms, etc. Restrikes of most of the coins minted from the period 1835 were regularly supplied until this practice was discontinued on July 1, 1970.

INDIA-BRITISH

MADRAS PRESIDENCY

Early proof restrikes are found with slight hairlining from polishing of the old dies. Bust, field, arms etc. are of even smoothness.

Modern proof-like (P/L) restrikes are usually heavily hairlined from excessive polishing of the old dies and have a glassy, varnished or proof-like appearance. Many are common while some are quite scarce including some unusual mulings.

MILLED COINAGE
Pagoda Series

KM# 315c CASH
Gold **Mint:** Soho **Obverse:** E.I. Co. crest, lion rampant left **Reverse:** Value in Persian and English

Date	Mintage	Good	VG	F	VF	XF
1803 Proof	—	—	—	—	—	—

KM# 318c 5 CASH (1 Falus)
Gold **Mint:** Soho **Obverse:** E.I. Co. arms

Date	Mintage	Good	VG	F	VF	XF
1803 Proof	—	—	—	—	—	—

KM# 319c 10 CASH
Gold **Mint:** Soho **Obverse:** E.I. Co. arms **Reverse:** Value in Persian and English

Date	Mintage	Good	VG	F	VF	XF
1808 Proof; Rare	—	—	—	—	—	—

KM# 321c 20 CASH
Gold **Mint:** Soho

Date	Mintage	Good	VG	F	VF	XF
1808 Proof; Rare	—	—	—	—	—	—

KM# 356 PAGODA
2.9700 g., Gold, 17.4 mm. **Obverse:** Value in English and Persian on buckled garter around Gopuram **Obv. Legend:** PAGODA **Reverse:** Value in Tamil and Telugu on ribbon around deity Vishnu **Edge:** Vertical milling

Date	Mintage	Good	VG	F	VF	XF
ND(1808-15)	1,382,000	BV	BV	75.00	125	175

KM# 357 2 PAGODAS
5.9700 g., Gold **Obverse:** Value in English and Persian on buckled garter around Gopuram with 14 stars in field **Obv. Legend:** TWO PAGODAS **Reverse:** Value in Tamil and Telugu on ribbon around deity Vishnu **Edge:** Vertical milling **Note:** Size varies 20.5-22.0mm.

Date	Mintage	Good	VG	F	VF	XF
ND(1808-15)	1,064,000	BV	75.00	125	250	400

KM# 358 2 PAGODAS
5.9700 g., Gold **Obverse:** 18 stars in field, varieties in size of English lettering exist **Obv. Legend:** TWO PAGODAS **Reverse:** Value in Tamil and Telugu on ribbon around deity Vishnu **Edge:** Vertical milling **Note:** Size varies 21.0-22.2mm.

Date	Mintage	Good	VG	F	VF	XF
ND(1808-15)	Inc. above	BV	75.00	125	250	400

MILLED COINAGE
Rupee Series

KM# 416 1/4 MOHUR
2.9100 g., Gold, 17.4 mm. **Mint:** Madras **Obverse:** Inscription, couplet **Obv. Inscription:** "Alamgir II" **Reverse:** Julus (formula), Arkat **Note:** Mint mark: Lotus. Struck at Madras. Prid.#240.

Date	Mintage	Good	VG	F	VF	XF
AH1172//6 Frozen	2,000	175	300	500	850	1,350

KM# 419 1/4 MOHUR
2.9100 g., Gold, 17 mm. **Mint:** Madras **Obverse:** Company crest **Obv. Legend:** BRITISH EAST INDIA COMPANY **Reverse:** Value in Persian **Rev. Inscription:** "of the Honorable English Company" **Edge:** Vertical milling **Note:** Prid.#243.

Date	Mintage	Good	VG	F	VF	XF
ND(1819)	91,834	75.00	125	250	350	600

KM# 422 5 RUPEES
3.8800 g., Gold, 19.5 mm. **Mint:** Madras **Obverse:** Company arms without supporters **Obv. Legend:** BRITISH EAST INDIA COMPANY **Reverse:** Value in Persian **Rev. Inscription:** ...of the Honorable English Company **Edge:** Vertical milling **Note:** Prid.#244.

Date	Mintage	Good	VG	F	VF	XF
ND(1820)	2,179,573	—	—	BV	85.00	135

KM# 417 1/2 MOHUR
5.8300 g., Gold, 21.7 mm. **Obverse:** Inscription, regal title **Obv. Inscription:** "Alamgir II" **Reverse:** Julus (formula), Arkat **Rev. Inscription:** Julus (formula), mint name **Edge:** Indented cord milling **Note:** Mint mark: Lotus. Struck at Madras. Prid.#239.

Date	Mintage	Good	VG	F	VF	XF
AH1172//6 Frozen	7,500	165	275	450	750	1,250

KM# 420 1/2 MOHUR
5.8300 g., Gold, 21.2 mm. **Mint:** Madras **Obverse:** Company crest **Obv. Legend:** ENGLISH EAST INDIA COMPANY **Reverse:** Value in Persian **Rev. Inscription:** "of the Honorable English Company" **Edge:** Vertical milling **Note:** Prid.#242.

Date	Mintage	Good	VG	F	VF	XF
ND(1819)	212,690	125	150	200	350	550

KM# 421.1 MOHUR
11.6600 g., Gold, 28 mm. **Mint:** Madras **Obverse:** Arms with supporters, Small letters **Obv. Legend:** ENGLISH EAST INDIA COMPANY **Reverse:** Value in Persian **Rev. Inscription:** "of the Honorable English Company" **Edge:** Vertical milling **Note:** Prid.#241.

Date	Mintage	Good	VG	F	VF	XF
ND(1819)	117,800	—	—	BV	250	450

KM# 421.2 MOHUR
11.6600 g., Gold, 28 mm. **Mint:** Madras **Obverse:** Arms with supporters, large letters in legend **Obv. Legend:** ENGLISH EAST INDIA COMPANY **Edge:** Vertical milling **Note:** Prid.#241.

Date	Mintage	Good	VG	F	VF	XF
ND(1819)	Inc. above	—	—	BV	250	450

KM# 421.3 MOHUR
11.6600 g., Gold, 28 mm. **Mint:** Madras **Obverse:** Supported helmeted E.I.Co. arms, large letters in legend **Obv. Legend:** ENGLISH EAST INDIA COMPANY **Reverse:** Inscription deviating in style **Rev. Inscription:** "of the Honorable English Company" **Note:** Prid. #241 variety.

Date	Mintage	Good	VG	F	VF	XF
ND(1819)	—	—	—	—	—	—

INDIA-REPUBLIC

The Republic of India, a subcontinent jutting southward from the mainland of Asia, has an area of 1,269,346 sq. mi. (3,287,590 sq. km.) and a population of over 900 million, second only to that of the People's Republic of China. Capital: New Delhi. India's economy is based on agriculture and industrial activity. Engineering goods, cotton apparel and fabrics, handicrafts, tea, iron and steel are exported.

The Republic of India is a member of the Commonwealth of Nations. The president is the Chief of State. The prime minister is the Head of Government.

MONETARY SYSTEM

(Until 1957)

4 Pice = 1 Anna
16 Annas = 1 Rupee

REPUBLIC
MEDALLIC COINAGE

X# 101   GOLD RUPEE
10.0000 g., 0.9999 Gold 0.3215 oz. AGW, 27.1 mm. **Mint:** Pobjoy **Subject:** 50th Anniversary Indian Independence **Obverse:** Chart **Obv. Inscription:** GOLDEN ANNIVERSARY **Reverse:** Bust of Gandhi 3/4 right **Edge:** Reeded

Date	Mintage	F	VF	XF	Unc
1997 Proof	—	Value: 225			

X# 102   GOLD RUPEE
10.0000 g., 0.9999 Gold 0.3215 oz. AGW, 27.1 mm. **Mint:** Pobjoy **Subject:** 50th Anniversary Indian Independence **Obverse:** Asoka column **Reverse:** Goddess Laksmi **Edge:** Reeded

Date	Mintage	F	VF	XF	Unc
1997 Proof	—	Value: 225			

X# 103   GOLD RUPEE
10.0000 g., 0.9999 Gold 0.3215 oz. AGW, 27.1 mm. **Mint:** Pobjoy **Subject:** 50th Anniversary Indian Independence **Obverse:** Asoka column in sprays **Reverse:** Elephant deity Ganesha riding a mouse **Edge:** Reeded

Date	Mintage	F	VF	XF	Unc
1997 Proof	—	Value: 225			

INDONESIA

The Republic of Indonesia, the world's largest archipelago, extends for more than 3,000 miles (4,827 km.) along the equator from the mainland of southeast Asia to Australia. The 17,508 islands comprising the archipelago have a combined area of 788,425 sq. mi. (1,919,440 sq.km.) and a population of 205 million, including East Timor. On August 30, 1999, the Timorese majority voted for independence. The Inter FET (International Forces for East Timor) is now in charge of controlling the chaotic situation. Capitol: Jakarta. Petroleum, timber, rubber, and coffee are exported.

Had Columbus succeeded in reaching the fabled Spice Islands, he would have found advanced civilizations a millennium old, and temples still ranking among the finest examples of ancient art. During the opening centuries of the Christian era, the islands were influenced by Hindu priests and traders who spread their culture and religion. Moslem invasions began in the 13th century, fragmenting the island kingdoms into small states which were unable to resist Western colonial infiltration. Portuguese traders established posts in the 16th century, but they were soon outnumbered by the Dutch who arrived in 1596 and gradually asserted control over the islands comprising present-day Indonesia. Dutch dominance, interrupted by British incursions during the Napoleonic Wars, established the Netherlands East Indies as one of the richest colonial possessions in the world.

The Indonesian independence movement, which began between the two world wars, was encouraged by the Japanese during their 3 1/2-year occupation during World War II. Indonesia proclaimed its independence on Aug. 17, 1945, three days after the surrender of Japan and full sovereignty. On Dec. 27, 1949, after four years of guerilla warfare including two large-scale campaigns by the Dutch in an effort to reassert control, complete independence was established. Rebellions in Bandung and on the Molluccan Islands occurred in 1950. During the reign of President Mohammad Achmad Sukarno (1950-67) the new Republic not only held together but started to develop. West Irian, formerly Netherlands New Guinea, came under the administration of Indonesia on May 1, 1963. In 1965, the army staged an anti-communist coup in which thousands perished.

On November 28, 1975, the Portuguese Province of Timor, an overseas province occupying the eastern half of the East Indian island of Timor, attained independence as the People's Democratic Republic of East Timor. On December 5, 1975, the government of the People's Democratic Republic was seized by a guerrilla faction sympathetic to the Indonesian territorial claim to East Timor which ousted the constitutional government and replaced it with the Provisional Government of East Timor. On July 17, 1976, the Provisional Government enacted a law that dissolved the free republic and made East Timor the 27th province of Indonesia.

The VOC (United East India Company) struck coins and emergency issues for the Indonesian Archipelago and for the islands at various mints in the Netherlands and the islands. In 1798 the VOC was subsumed by the Dutch government, which issued VOC type transitional and regal types during the Batavian Republic and the Kingdom of the Netherlands until independence. The British issued a coinage during the various occupations by the British East Indian Company, 1811-24. Modern coinage issued by the Republic of Indonesia includes separate series for West Irian and for the Riau Archipelago, an area of small islands between Singapore and Sumatra.

MONETARY SYSTEM

100 Sen = 1 Rupiah

REPUBLIC
STANDARD COINAGE

100 Sen = 1 Rupiah

KM# 28   2000 RUPIAH
4.9300 g., 0.9000 Gold .1426 oz. AGW **Subject:** 25th Anniversary of Independence **Obv:** Great Bird of Paradise **Rev:** National emblem

Date	Mintage	F	VF	XF	Unc	BU
1970 Proof	2,970	Value: 125				

KM# 29   5000 RUPIAH
12.3400 g., 0.9000 Gold .3571 oz. AGW **Subject:** 25th Anniversary of Independence **Obv:** Manjusri statue from Temple of Tumpang **Rev:** National emblem

Date	Mintage	F	VF	XF	Unc	BU
1970 Proof	2,150	Value: 260				

KM# 30   10000 RUPIAH
24.6800 g., 0.9000 Gold .7142 oz. AGW **Subject:** 25th Anniversary of Independence **Obv:** Wayang dancer **Rev:** National emblem

Date	Mintage	F	VF	XF	Unc	BU
1970 Proof	1,440	Value: 550				

KM# 31   20000 RUPIAH
49.3700 g., 0.9000 Gold 1.4391 oz. AGW **Subject:** 25th Anniversary of Independence **Obv:** Garuda bird **Rev:** National emblem

Date	Mintage	F	VF	XF	Unc	BU
1970 Proof	1,285	—	—	—	1,150	—

INDONESIA

KM# 32 25000 RUPIAH
61.7100 g., 0.9000 Gold 1.7858 oz. AGW **Subject:** 25th Anniversary of Independence - Gen. Sudirman **Obv:** Bust facing **Rev:** National Emblem

Date	Mintage	F	VF	XF	Unc	BU
1970 Proof	970	Value: 1,350				

KM# 41 100000 RUPIAH
33.4370 g., 0.9000 Gold .9676 oz. AGW **Series:** Conservation **Obv:** National emblem **Rev:** Komodo dragon lizard (varanus komodensis) **Rev. Designer:** Leslie Durbin

Date	Mintage	F	VF	XF	Unc	BU
1974	5,333	—	—	—	675	—
1974 Proof	1,369	Value: 725				

KM# 47 125000 RUPIAH
8.0000 g., 0.9580 Gold .2465 oz. AGW **Subject:** Museum of Struggle '45 **Obv:** National emblem **Rev:** Museum

Date	Mintage	F	VF	XF	Unc	BU
1990 Proof	16,000	Value: 175				

KM# 46 200000 RUPIAH
10.0000 g., 0.9170 Gold .2947 oz. AGW **Subject:** Wildlife **Obv:** National emblem **Rev:** Javan rhinoceros right

Date	Mintage	F	VF	XF	Unc	BU
1987 Proof	5,000	Value: 300				

KM# 51 200000 RUPIAH
10.0000 g., 0.9170 Gold .2947 oz. AGW **Series:** Save the Children **Obv:** National emblem **Rev:** Balinese dancer

Date	Mintage	F	VF	XF	Unc	BU
1990 Proof	3,000	Value: 300				

KM# 48 250000 RUPIAH
17.0000 g., 0.9580 Gold .5238 oz. AGW **Subject:** 45 years - Indonesian Independence **Obv:** National emblem **Rev:** Map, dates and denomination below

Date	Mintage	F	VF	XF	Unc	BU
1990 Proof	16,000	Value: 375				

KM# 57 300000 RUPIAH
17.0000 g., 0.9583 Gold .5238 oz. AGW **Subject:** 50th Anniversary of Independence **Obv:** National emblem **Rev:** Presidential talk show

Date	Mintage	F	VF	XF	Unc	BU
1995 Sets only	3,000	—	—	—	800	—

KM# 65 500,000 RUPIAH
15.0000 g., 0.9990 Gold 0.4818 oz. AGW, 28.2 mm. **Subject:** Centennial of Sukarno's Birth **Obv:** National arms **Rev:** Head left **Edge:** Reeded

Date	Mintage	F	VF	XF	Unc	BU
2001 Proof	500	Value: 375				

KM# 49 750000 RUPIAH
45.0000 g., 0.9580 Gold 1.3866 oz. AGW **Subject:** 45 Years - Arms of Generation 1945 **Obv:** National emblem **Rev:** National emblem within wreath of rice and cotton stalks

Date	Mintage	F	VF	XF	Unc	BU
1990 Proof	16,000	—	—	—	975	—

KM# 58 850000 RUPIAH
50.0000 g., 0.9583 Gold 1.5405 oz. AGW **Subject:** 50th Anniversary of Independence - President Soeharto **Obv:** National emblem **Rev:** Bust facing

Date	Mintage	F	VF	XF	Unc	BU
1995 Sets only	3,000	—	—	—	2,200	—

MEDALLIC COINAGE

X# 1 25 RUPIAH
Gold **Subject:** Prince Diponegoro **Note:** Prev. KM#M1. For earlier issues see Netherlands East Indies listings.

Date	Mintage	F	VF	XF	Unc	BU
ND(1952)(u)	36,000	—	—	225	300	—

PATTERNS
Including off metal strikes

KM#	Date	Mintage	Identification	Mkt Val
Pn10	1990	—	125000 Rupiah. Gold. Gold-plated base metal. KM#47.	—
Pn11	1990	—	250000 Rupiah. Gold. Gold-plated base metal. KM#48.	—
Pn12	1990	—	750000 Rupiah. Gold. Gold-plated base metal. KM#49.	—

PROOF SETS

KM#	Date	Mintage	Identification	Issue Price	Mkt Val
PS1	1970 (10)	970	KM23-32	490	3,400
PS4	1990 (3)	15,750	KM47-49	755	1,525
PS5	1990 (2)	—	KM50-51	—	350
PS6	1995 (2)	3,000	KM57-58	2,975	3,000

IRAN

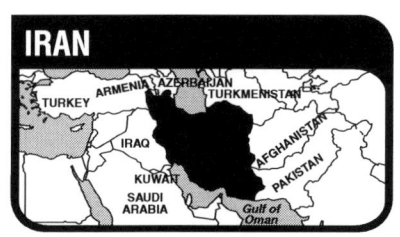

Iran (historically known as Persia until 1931AD) is one of the world's most ancient and resilient nations. Strategically astride the lower land gate to Asia, it has been conqueror and conquered, sovereign nation and vassal state, ever emerging from its periods of glory or travail with its culture and political individuality intact. Iran (Persia) was a powerful empire under Cyrus the Great (600-529 B.C.), its borders extending from the Indus to the Nile. It has also been conquered by the predatory empires of antique and recent times - Assyrian, Medean, Macedonian, Seljuq, Turk, Mongol - and more recently been coveted by Russia, the Third Reich and Great Britain. Revolts against the absolute power of the Persian shahs resulted in the establishment of a constitutional monarchy in 1906.

RULERS

Nadir Mirza, AH1210-1218/1796-1803AD

Qajar Dynasty

فتحعلی

Fath'Ali Shah, AH1212-1250/1797-1834AD

سلطان علی

Sultan Ali Shah, in Tehran
AH1250/1834AD (30 days)

حسین علی

Husayn Ali Shah,
AH1250/1834AD (6 months)
(in outhern Iran only)

شاهنشه انبیا محمد

Muhammad Shah, AH1250-64/1834-48AD
NOTE: Used "Shahansha-I Anbiga Muhammad",
(The Emperor of the Prophets is Muhammad).

ناصر الدین

Nasir al-Din Shah,
AH1264-1313/1848-1896AD

مظفر الدین

Muzaffar al-Din Shah,
AH1313-1324/1896-1907AD

محمد علی

Muhammad Ali Shah, AH1324-1327/1907-1909AD

سلطان احمد

Sultan Ahmad Shah, AH1327-1344/1909-1925AD

Pahlavi Dynasty

رضا

Reza Shah, as prime minister, SH1302-1304/1923-1925AD
as Shah,
SH1304-1320/1925-1941AD

محمد رضا

Mohammad Reza Pahlavi, Shah SH1320-1358/1941-1979AD

جمهوری اسلامی ایران

Islamic Republic, SH1358-/1979-AD

MINT NAMES

Abu Shahr (Bushire)	ابو شهر	Isfahan (Esfahan)	اصفهان
Ardanush		Jelou (Army Mint)	جلو
Ardebil (Ardabil)	اردبیل	Kashan	کاشان
Astarabad (Iran)	استراباد	Kirman (Kerman)	کرمان
Baghdad (Iraq)	بغداد	Kirmanshahan (Kermanshah)	کرمانشاهان
Bandar Abbas	بندر عباس	Khoy (Khoi, Khuy)	خوی
Bandar Abu Shahr	بندر ابو شهر	Lahijan	لاهیجان
Basra (al-Basrah, Iraq)	البصرة	Lahore (Afghanistan)	لاهور
Behbahan (Bihbihan)	بهبهان	Maragheh	مراغه
Bahkar (Bhakhar) (Afghanistan)	بهکر	Mashhad (Meshad Iman Rida)	مشهد
Borujerd Dadiyan	بروجرد	Mazandaran	مازندران
Darband Dawraq Dehdasht	دربند	Nahawand	نهاوند
Dezful	دزفول	Nakhjawan (Azerbaijan)	نخجوان
Eravan (Iravan, Armenia) Farahabad	ایروان	Naseri Nimruz	ناصری
Fouman	فومان	Nukhwi	نخوی
Ganjeh (Ganja, Azerbaijan)	گنجه	Panahabad (Azerbaijan)	پناه آباد
Gilan	گیلان	Peshawar (Afghanistan)	پشاور
Hamadan	همدان	Qandahar (Kandahar, Afghanistan)	قندهار
Herat, (Afghanistan)	هراة	Qazvin	قزوین
Huwayza	حویزه	Qomm (Kumm, Qumm)	قم
Iravan (Yeravan, Armenia)	ایروان	Ra'nash (Ramhurmuz)	رعنش

IRAN

Rasht	رشت
Rekab (Rikab)	ركاب
Reza'iyeh (Army Mint)	رضائیه
Sarakhs	سرخس
Sari	ساری
Sawuj Balagh	ساوج بلاق
Shamakha (Shemakhi, Shimakhi, Azerbaijan)	شماخه
Shiraz	شیراز
Shirwan (Azerbaijan)	شروان
Shushtar	شوشتر
Simnan (Semnan)	سمنان
Sind (Afghanistan)	سند
Sultanabad	صلطان آباذ
Tabaristan (Tabarestan, region N.W. of Iran)	طبرستان
Tabriz	تبریز
Tehran	طهران
Tiflis (Georgia)	تفلیس
Tuyserkan	توی سرکان
Urumi (Reza'iyeh)	ارومی
Yazd	یزد
Zanjan Zegam	زنجان

MINT MARKS
H — Heaton (Birmingham)
L — Leningrad (St. Petersburg)

COIN DATING
Iranian coins were dated according to the Moslem lunar calendar until March 21, 1925 (AD), when dating was switched to a new calendar based on the solar year, indicated by the notation SH. The monarchial calendar system was adopted in 1976 = MS2535 and was abandoned in 1978 = MS2537. The previously used solar year calendar was restored at that time.

MONETARY SYSTEM
1798-1825 (AH 1212-1241)
1250 Dinars = 1 Riyal
8 Riyals = 1 Toman

1825-1931 (AH1241-1344, SH1304-09)
50 Dinars = 1 Shahi
20 Shahis = 1 Kran (Qiran)
10 Krans = 1 Toman

NOTE: From AD1830-34 (AH1245-50) the gold Toman was known as a 'Keshwarsetan.'

1932-Date (SH1310-Date)
5 Dinars = 1 Shahi
20 Shahis = 1 Rial (100 Dinars)
10 Rials = 1 Toman

NOTE: The Toman ceased to be an official unit in 1932, but continues to be applied in popular usage. Thus, 135 Rials' is always expressed as 13 Toman, 5

Hammered Coinage of the Kingdom
Gold and Silver Issues

The precious metal monetary system of Qajar Persia prior to the reforms of 1878 was the direct descendant of the Mongol system introduced by Ghazan Mahmud in 1297AD, and was the last example of a medieval Islamic coinage. It is not a modern system, and cannot be understood as such. It is not possible to list types, dates, and mints as for other countries, both because of the nature of the coinage, and because very little research has been done on the series. The following comments should help elucidate its nature.

STANDARDS: The weight of the primary silver and gold coins was set by law and was expressed in terms of the Mesqal (about 4.61 g) and the Nokhod (24 Nokhod = 1 Mesqal). The primary silver coin was the Rupee from AH1211-1212, the Riyal from AH1212-1241, and the Gheran from AH1241-1344. The standard gold coin was the Toman. Currently the price of gold is quoted in Mesqals.

DENOMINATIONS: In addition to the primary denominations, noted in the last paragraph, fractional pieces were coined, valued at one-eighth, one-fourth, and one-half the primary denomination, usually in much smaller quantities. These were ordinarily struck from the same dies as the larger pieces, sometimes on broad, thin flans, sometimes on thick, dumpy flans. On the smaller pieces the denomination can best be determined only by weighing the coin. The denomination is almost never expressed on the coin!

DEVALUATIONS: From time to time, the standard for silver and gold was reduced, and the old coin recalled and replaced with lighter coin, the difference going to the government coffers. The effect was that of a devaluation of the primary silver and gold coins, or inversely regarded, an increase in the price of silver and gold. The durations of each standard varied from about 2 to 20 years. The standards are given for each ruler, as the denomination can only be determined when the standard is known.

LIGHTWEIGHT AND ALLOYED PIECES: Most of the smaller denomination coins were issued at lighter weights than those prescribed by law, with the difference going to the pockets of the mintmasters. Other mints, notably Hamadan, added excessive amounts of alloy to the coins, and some mintmasters lost their heads as a result. Discrepancies in weight of as much as 15 percent and more are observed, with the result that it is often quite impossible to determine the denomination of a coin!

OVERSIZE COINS: Occasionally multiples of the primary denominations were produced, usually on special occasions, for presentation by the Shah to his favorites. These coins did not circulate (except as bullion), and were usually worn as ornaments. They were the NCLT's' of their day.

MINTS & EPITHETS: Qajar coinage was struck at 34 mints (plus at least a dozen others striking only copper Falus), which are listed previously, with drawings of the mintnames in Persian, as they appear on the coins. However, the Persian script admits of infinite variation and stylistic whimsy, so the forms given are only guides, and not absolute. Only a knowledge of the script will assure correct reading. In addition to the city name, most mintnames were given identifying epithets, which occasionally appear in lieu of the mint name, particularly at Iravan and Mashhad.

TYPES: There were no types in the modern sense, but the arrangement of the legends and the ornamental borders were frequently changed. These changes do not coincide with changes in standards, and cannot be used to determine the mint, which must be found by actually reading the reverse inscriptions.

ARRANGEMENT: The following listings are arranged first by ruler, with various standards explained. Then, the coins are listed by denomination within each reign. For each denomination, one or more pieces, when available, are illustrated, with the mint and date noted beneath each photo. For each type, a date range is given, but this range indicates the years during which the particular type was current, and does not imply that every year of the interval is known on actual coins. Because dates were carelessly engraved, and old dies were used until they wore out or broke, we occasionally find coins of a particular type dated before or after the indicated interval. Such coins command no premium. No attempt has been made to determine which mints actually exist for which types.

KINGDOM

Fath Ali Shah
AH1212-1250 / 1797-1834AD

Fath Ali Khan succeeded his uncle, Agha Muhammad Shah, upon the latter's death on 16 June 1797, striking coins with the nickname Baba Khan. His formal enthronement took place three months later, on 15 or 16 September 1797, at which time he received the name Fath Ali Shah. His coin types are distinguished both by inscription, calligraphy, and weight standard. As the silver and gold weight standards were not altered simultaneously, the type sequences for silver and gold differ.

Note: All coins of this and succeeding reigns for hammered coinage bear the mint & date on the reverse, the mint usually with its distinguishing epithet. Only the obverse is noted in the type descriptions.

Coinage Standards of Fath Ali Shah
NOTE: Prices for silver coins are for average strikes, with some weakness or unevenness. Poorly struck coins are worth less, well-struck and well-centered coins can be worth from 25-100% more, depending on eye appeal and ornateness of design. Gold coins are generally better struck, but really attractive strikes or fancy designs also command a premium.

NOTE: Coins without legible date are worth about half the price of the cheapest date of the mint & type. Coins without legible mint are of little value. This and the previous note apply to coins of the later rulers Muhammad Shah and Nasir al-Din Shah as well as those of Fath Ali Shah.

Gold Types:
R. Same as silver Type CO (Coronation Type). Standard for the toman (=10,000 dinars) is 6.14 g.
S. Inscriptions as Type A (Type S.1) or as Type B (Type S.2) same standard as Type R.
T. Inscriptions as Type B (Type T.1) or as Type C (Type T.2), based on a toman of 5.76 g. (No examples of Type T.2 with mint & date are confirmed at the present time.)
U. Inscriptions as Type C, based on a toman of 5.37 g.
V. Inscriptions as Type C, based on a toman of 4.80 g.
W. Inscriptions as Type C or D, based on a toman of 4.61 g (one mithqal weight).
X. Inscriptions as Type E (*sahebqeran* type), based on a toman of 4.61 g.
Y. Inscriptions as Type F (*keshvarsetan* type), based on a toman of 3.45 g.

HAMMERED COINAGE
Gold Toman Issues

Mint: Borujerd
KM# 751.1   1/4 TOMAN
1.1500 g., Gold **Note:** Type W.

Date	Mintage	F	VF	XF	Unc
AH1236	—	125	160	200	—

Mint: Isfahan
KM# 747   1/4 TOMAN
1.2000 g., Gold **Note:** Type V.

Date	Mintage	F	VF	XF	Unc
AH1228	—	150	200	260	—

Mint: Isfahan
KM# 751.2   1/4 TOMAN
1.1500 g., Gold **Note:** Type W.

Date	Mintage	F	VF	XF	Unc
AH1234	—	150	180	225	—

Mint: Isfahan
KM# 748.1   1/2 TOMAN
2.4000 g., Gold **Note:** Type V.

Date	Mintage	F	VF	XF	Unc
AH1228	—	150	200	250	—

Mint: Tabriz
KM# 744   1/2 TOMAN
2.6800 g., Gold **Note:** Type U.

Date	Mintage	F	VF	XF	Unc
AH1224	—	175	240	300	—

Mint: Tabriz
KM# 748.2   1/2 TOMAN
2.4000 g., Gold **Note:** Type V.

Date	Mintage	F	VF	XF	Unc
AH1228	—	150	200	250	—
AH1231	—	150	200	250	—

Mint: Tabriz
KM# 752.2   1/2 TOMAN
2.3000 g., Gold **Note:** Type W.

Date	Mintage	F	VF	XF	Unc
AH1232	—	120	145	180	—
AH1238	—	120	145	180	—

IRAN

Mint: Tabriz
KM# 756 1/2 TOMAN
2.3000 g., Gold **Note:** Type X.

Date	Mintage	F	VF	XF	Unc
AH1242	—	120	145	180	—

Mint: Tehran
KM# 740 1/2 TOMAN
2.8800 g., Gold **Note:** Type T.

Date	Mintage	F	VF	XF	Unc
AH1220	—	200	275	350	—

Mint: Ardebil
KM# 759.1 TOMAN
3.4500 g., Gold **Obv:** "Keshvarsetan" **Note:** Type Y.

Date	Mintage	F	VF	XF	Unc
AH1246	—	250	300	375	—

Mint: Astarabad
KM# 745.1 TOMAN
5.3700 g., Gold **Note:** Type U.

Date	Mintage	F	VF	XF	Unc
AH1225	—	145	185	250	—

Mint: Borujerd
KM# 753.1 TOMAN
4.6100 g., Gold **Note:** Type W.

Date	Mintage	F	VF	XF	Unc
AH1233	—	125	180	225	—
AH1236	—	125	150	200	—
AH1239	—	125	150	225	—

Mint: Eravan
KM# 753.2 TOMAN
4.6100 g., Gold **Note:** Type W.

Date	Mintage	F	VF	XF	Unc
AH1233	—	140	180	225	—
AH1235	—	140	180	225	—
AH1236	—	150	200	250	—

Mint: Hamadan
KM# 753.3 TOMAN
4.6100 g., Gold **Note:** Type W.

Date	Mintage	F	VF	XF	Unc
AH1240	—	120	140	185	—

Mint: Hamadan
KM# 757.1 TOMAN
4.6100 g., Gold **Obv:** "Sahebqeran" **Note:** Type X.

Date	Mintage	F	VF	XF	Unc
AH1242	—	100	125	175	—

Mint: Hamadan
KM# 759.2 TOMAN
3.4500 g., Gold **Obv:** "Keshvarsetan" **Note:** Type Y.

Date	Mintage	F	VF	XF	Unc
AH1246	—	100	125	175	—
AH1248	—	95.00	115	160	—
AH1249	—	95.00	115	160	—
AH1250	—	100	125	175	—

Mint: Isfahan
KM# 763 TOMAN
3.4500 g., Gold **Obv:** Shah seated on throne, facing right **Rev:** Mint name and date in central circle **Note:** Special type.

Date	Mintage	F	VF	XF	Unc
AH1245	—	650	1,100	1,600	—

Mint: Isfahan
KM# 764 TOMAN
3.4500 g., Gold **Obv:** Shah seated on throne, facing left **Rev:** Mint and date in central square **Note:** Special type.

Date	Mintage	F	VF	XF	Unc
AH1245	—	650	1,100	1,600	—

Mint: Isfahan
KM# 765 TOMAN
3.4500 g., Gold **Obv:** Shah seated on throne, facing left **Rev:** Mint and date in 8-pointed star **Note:** Special type.

Date	Mintage	F	VF	XF	Unc
AH1248//1250	—	600	1,000	1,400	—

Note: All known pieces are dated 1248 on obverse, 1250 on reverse

Mint: Isfahan
KM# 766 TOMAN
3.4500 g., Gold **Obv:** Shah seated on throne, facing left **Rev:** Mint and date in elongated lozenge **Note:** Special type.

Date	Mintage	F	VF	XF	Unc
AH1249	—	600	1,000	1,600	—

Mint: Isfahan
KM# 739.1 TOMAN
6.1400 g., Gold **Note:** Type S.

Date	Mintage	F	VF	XF	Unc
AH1217	—	200	250	325	—

Mint: Isfahan
KM# 745.2 TOMAN
5.3700 g., Gold **Note:** Type U.

Date	Mintage	F	VF	XF	Unc
AH1225	—	135	160	225	—

Mint: Isfahan
KM# 749.1 TOMAN
4.8000 g., Gold **Note:** Type V.

Date	Mintage	F	VF	XF	Unc
AH1228	—	110	120	160	—
AH1229	—	120	140	200	—

Mint: Isfahan
KM# 753.4 TOMAN
4.6100 g., Gold **Note:** Type W.

Date	Mintage	F	VF	XF	Unc
AH1232	—	100	120	160	—
AH1233	—	100	120	160	—
AH1234	—	110	130	170	—
AH1238	—	110	130	170	—
AH1240	—	120	140	185	—

Mint: Isfahan
KM# 757.2 TOMAN
4.6100 g., Gold **Obv:** "Sahebqeran" **Note:** Type X.

Date	Mintage	F	VF	XF	Unc
AH1242	—	120	140	185	—

Mint: Isfahan
KM# 759.3 TOMAN
3.4500 g., Gold **Obv:** "Keshvarsetan" **Note:** Type Y.

Date	Mintage	F	VF	XF	Unc
AH1249	—	100	125	175	—

Mint: Kashan
KM# 741.1 TOMAN
5.7600 g., Gold **Note:** Type T.

Date	Mintage	F	VF	XF	Unc
AH1221	—	200	275	350	—

Mint: Kashan
KM# 749.2 TOMAN
4.8000 g., Gold **Note:** Type V.

Date	Mintage	F	VF	XF	Unc
AH1227	—	110	125	175	—
AH1228	—	110	125	175	—
AH1231	—	120	140	200	—

Mint: Kashan
KM# 753.5 TOMAN
4.6100 g., Gold **Note:** Type W.

Date	Mintage	F	VF	XF	Unc
AH1232	—	110	120	150	—
AH1233	—	110	120	150	—
AH1235	—	115	125	160	—
AH1236	—	115	125	160	—
AH1239	—	120	135	175	—

Mint: Kashan
KM# 759.4 TOMAN
3.4500 g., Gold **Obv:** "Keshvarsetan" **Note:** Type Y.

Date	Mintage	F	VF	XF	Unc
AH1246	—	100	125	175	—

Mint: Khoy
KM# 739.2 TOMAN
6.1400 g., Gold **Note:** Type S.

Date	Mintage	F	VF	XF	Unc
AHxxxx	—	150	185	225	—

Mint: Khoy
KM# 753.6 TOMAN
4.6100 g., Gold **Note:** Type W.

Date	Mintage	F	VF	XF	Unc
AH1232	—	130	175	225	—
AH1233	—	120	160	200	—
AH1234	—	120	160	200	—
AH1235	—	120	160	200	—
AH1236	—	120	160	200	—
AH1238	—	125	165	215	—

Mint: Khoy
KM# 759.5 TOMAN
3.4500 g., Gold **Obv:** "Keshvarsetan" **Note:** Type Y.

Date	Mintage	F	VF	XF	Unc
AH1246	—	100	125	175	—

Mint: Kirman
KM# 759.6 TOMAN
3.4500 g., Gold **Obv:** "Keshvarsetan" **Note:** Type Y.

Date	Mintage	F	VF	XF	Unc
AH1248	—	150	215	275	—
AH1249	—	150	215	275	—

Mint: Kirmanshahan
KM# 753.7 TOMAN
4.6100 g., Gold **Note:** Type W.

Date	Mintage	F	VF	XF	Unc
AH1234	—	100	120	150	—

Mint: Kirmanshahan
KM# 757.3 TOMAN
4.6100 g., Gold **Obv:** "Sahebqeran" **Note:** Type X.

Date	Mintage	F	VF	XF	Unc
AH1241	—	110	135	175	—

Mint: Kirmanshahan
KM# 759.7 TOMAN
3.4500 g., Gold **Obv:** "Keshvarsetan" **Note:** Type Y.

Date	Mintage	F	VF	XF	Unc
AH1246	—	100	125	175	—
AH1248	—	100	125	175	—

IRAN

Mint: Mashhad
KM# 749.3 TOMAN
4.8000 g., Gold **Note:** Type V.

Date	Mintage	F	VF	XF	Unc
AH1232	—	125	150	200	—

Mint: Mazandaran
KM# 749.4 TOMAN
4.8000 g., Gold **Note:** Type V.

Date	Mintage	F	VF	XF	Unc
AH1228	—	110	135	175	—

Mint: Qazvin
KM# 753.8 TOMAN
4.6100 g., Gold **Note:** Type W.

Date	Mintage	F	VF	XF	Unc
AH1231	—	100	120	150	—
AH1232	—	100	120	150	—
AH1234	—	—	120	150	—
AH1235	—	100	120	150	—
AH1236	—	110	120	160	—
AH1240	—	115	135	175	—

Mint: Qazvin
KM# 759.8 TOMAN
3.4500 g., Gold **Obv:** "Keshvarsetan" **Note:** Type Y.

Date	Mintage	F	VF	XF	Unc
AH1246	—	100	125	175	—
AH1248	—	100	125	175	—
AH1249	—	100	125	175	—

Mint: Rasht
KM# 749.5 TOMAN
4.8000 g., Gold **Note:** Type V.

Date	Mintage	F	VF	XF	Unc
AH1231	—	110	140	200	—

Mint: Rasht
KM# 753.9 TOMAN
4.6100 g., Gold **Note:** Type W.

Date	Mintage	F	VF	XF	Unc
AH1230	—	120	140	180	—
AH1231	—	100	120	150	—
AH1232	—	100	120	150	—
AH1235	—	110	125	160	—

Mint: Rasht
KM# 757.4 TOMAN
4.6100 g., Gold **Obv:** "Sahebqeran" **Note:** Type X.

Date	Mintage	F	VF	XF	Unc
AH1243	—	110	130	175	—

Mint: Rasht
KM# 759.9 TOMAN
3.4500 g., Gold **Obv:** "Keshvarsetan" **Note:** Type Y.

Date	Mintage	F	VF	XF	Unc
AH1246	—	95.00	115	160	—
AH1249	—	100	125	175	—
AH1250	—	100	125	175	—

Mint: Shiraz
KM# 749.6 TOMAN
4.8000 g., Gold **Note:** Type V.

Date	Mintage	F	VF	XF	Unc
AH1228	—	110	120	160	—
AH1229	—	120	140	200	—

Mint: Shiraz
KM# 753.10 TOMAN
4.6100 g., Gold **Note:** Type W.

Date	Mintage	F	VF	XF	Unc
AH1232	—	100	120	160	—
AH1233	—	100	120	160	—
AH1234	—	100	120	160	—
AH1239	—	110	130	175	—
AH1240	—	110	130	175	—

Mint: Shiraz
KM# 759.10 TOMAN
3.4500 g., Gold **Obv:** "Keshvarsetan" **Note:** Type Y.

Date	Mintage	F	VF	XF	Unc
AH1248	—	100	125	175	—
AH1249	—	100	125	175	—

Mint: Simnan
KM# 759.11 TOMAN
3.4500 g., Gold **Obv:** "Keshvarsetan" **Note:** Type Y.

Date	Mintage	F	VF	XF	Unc
AH1246	—	250	300	375	—

Mint: Tabriz
KM# 745.3 TOMAN
5.3700 g., Gold **Note:** Type U.

Date	Mintage	F	VF	XF	Unc
AH1224	—	125	160	225	—

Mint: Tabriz
KM# 753.11 TOMAN
4.6100 g., Gold **Note:** Type W.

Date	Mintage	F	VF	XF	Unc
AH1233	—	100	120	150	—
AH1236	—	100	120	150	—
AH1238	—	100	120	150	—

Mint: Tabriz
KM# 757.5 TOMAN
4.6100 g., Gold **Obv:** "Sahebqeran" **Note:** Type X.

Date	Mintage	F	VF	XF	Unc
AH1242	—	110	130	175	—
AH1243	—	110	130	175	—
AH1244	—	110	130	175	—

Mint: Tabriz
KM# 759.12 TOMAN
3.4500 g., Gold **Obv:** "Keshvarsetan" **Note:** Type Y.

Date	Mintage	F	VF	XF	Unc
AH1246	—	90.00	115	160	—

Mint: Tehran
KM# 739.9 TOMAN
6.1400 g., Gold **Note:** Type S.

Date	Mintage	F	VF	XF	Unc
AH1216	—	175	225	275	—

Mint: Tehran
KM# 745.4 TOMAN
5.3700 g., Gold **Note:** Type U.

Date	Mintage	F	VF	XF	Unc
AH1224	—	125	160	225	—

Mint: Tehran
KM# 749.7 TOMAN
4.8000 g., Gold **Note:** Type V.

Date	Mintage	F	VF	XF	Unc
AH1227	—	120	140	185	—
AH1228	—	110	120	150	—
AH1229	—	130	160	200	—
AH1234 (sic)	—	135	175	225	—

Mint: Tehran
KM# 753.12 TOMAN
4.6100 g., Gold **Note:** Type W.

Date	Mintage	F	VF	XF	Unc
AH1232	—	100	120	150	—
AH1234	—	100	120	150	—
AH1235	—	110	130	165	—
AH1239	—	110	130	165	—

Mint: Tehran
KM# 757.6 TOMAN
4.6100 g., Gold **Obv:** "Sahebqeran" **Note:** Type X.

Date	Mintage	F	VF	XF	Unc
AH1242	—	110	130	175	—

Mint: Tehran
KM# 759.13 TOMAN
3.4500 g., Gold **Obv:** "Keshvarsetan" **Note:** Type Y.

Date	Mintage	F	VF	XF	Unc
AH1248	—	100	125	175	—
AH1249	—	100	125	175	—

Mint: Urumi
KM# 757.7 TOMAN
4.6100 g., Gold **Obv:** "Sahebqeran" **Note:** Type X.

Date	Mintage	F	VF	XF	Unc
AH1241	—	125	175	250	—

Mint: Yazd
KM# 739.10 TOMAN
6.1400 g., Gold **Note:** Type S.

Date	Mintage	F	VF	XF	Unc
AH1219	—	200	250	325	—

Mint: Yazd
KM# 741.2 TOMAN
5.7600 g., Gold **Note:** Type T.

Date	Mintage	F	VF	XF	Unc
AH1221	—	200	275	350	—

Mint: Yazd
KM# 745.5 TOMAN
5.3700 g., Gold **Note:** Type U.

Date	Mintage	F	VF	XF	Unc
AH1225	—	135	175	225	—

Mint: Yazd
KM# 749.8 TOMAN
4.8000 g., Gold **Note:** Type V.

Date	Mintage	F	VF	XF	Unc
AH1228	—	110	130	175	—
AH1230	—	120	145	200	—
AH1231	—	120	145	200	—

Mint: Yazd
KM# 753.13 TOMAN
4.6100 g., Gold **Note:** Type W.

Date	Mintage	F	VF	XF	Unc
AH1231	—	100	120	150	—
AH1232	—	100	120	150	—
AH1233	—	—	120	150	—
AH1234	—	100	120	150	—
AH1236	—	110	125	160	—

Mint: Zanjan
KM# 761 TOMAN
4.6100 g., Gold **Obv:** Shah on horseback **Note:** Special type.

Date	Mintage	F	VF	XF	Unc
AH1236	—	750	1,250	2,000	—

Mint: Zanjan
KM# 753.14 TOMAN
4.6100 g., Gold **Note:** Type W.

Date	Mintage	F	VF	XF	Unc
AH1233	—	140	180	225	—

Mint: Kirmanshahan
KM# 754.1 3 TOMAN
13.8200 g., Gold **Note:** Type W.

Date	Mintage	F	VF	XF	Unc
AH1233	—	1,500	2,500	4,000	—

Mint: Zanjan
KM# 762 3 TOMAN
13.8200 g., Gold **Obv:** Shah on horseback **Note:** Special type.

Date	Mintage	F	VF	XF	Unc
AH1239 Rare	—	—	—	—	—

Mint: Tabriz
KM# 746.1 5 TOMAN
26.8500 g., Gold **Note:** Type U.

Date	Mintage	F	VF	XF	Unc
AH1226	—	—	3,000	5,000	—
AH1227	—	—	3,000	5,000	—

Mint: Tehran
KM# 742 5 TOMAN
28.8000 g., Gold **Note:** Type T.

Date	Mintage	F	VF	XF	Unc
AH1221 Rare	—	—	—	—	—

Mint: Tehran
KM# 746.2 5 TOMAN
26.8500 g., Gold **Note:** Type U.

Date	Mintage	F	VF	XF	Unc
AH1227	—	—	3,000	5,000	—

IRAN

Sultan Ali Shah
AH1250 / 1834AD

AH1250/1834AD
Ruled only 30 days
There is only one type for this reign. Obverse: *al-sultan ibn al-sultan Sultan 'Ali Shah Qajar*. Reverse: Mint and date as on the coins of Fath 'Ali Shah.

HAMMERED COINAGE

Mint: Tehran
KM# 772 TOMAN
3.5000 g., Gold **Note:** Pretender issue.

Date	Mintage	F	VF	XF	Unc
AH1250	—	400	650	850	—

Muhammad Shah
AH1250-1264 / 1834-1848AD

Gold Types:
R. Based on a toman of 3.84 g.
S. Based on a toman of 3.45 g.

HAMMERED COINAGE

Mint: Tabriz
KM# 805 1/2 TOMAN
1.9200 g., Gold **Note:** Type R.

Date	Mintage	Good	VG	F	VF	XF
AH1252	—	—	65.00	125	160	200

Mint: Tehran
KM# 811 1/2 TOMAN
1.7200 g., Gold **Note:** Lion and sun type. Similar to 1 Kran, KM#799.

Date	Mintage	Good	VG	F	VF	XF
AH1258	—	—	125	200	250	350

Mint: Hamadan
KM# 806.1 TOMAN
3.8400 g., Gold **Note:** Type R.

Date	Mintage	Good	VG	F	VF	XF
AH1250	—	—	80.00	95.00	110	140

Mint: Isfahan
KM# 806.2 TOMAN
3.8400 g., Gold **Note:** Type R.

Date	Mintage	Good	VG	F	VF	XF
AH1250	—	—	75.00	85.00	95.00	125
AH1252	—	—	75.00	85.00	95.00	125
AH1253	—	—	75.00	85.00	95.00	125

Mint: Isfahan
KM# 809.1 TOMAN
3.8400 g., Gold **Note:** Type S.

Date	Mintage	Good	VG	F	VF	XF
AH1259	—	—	75.00	85.00	95.00	125
AH1260	—	—	—	—	—	—
AH1265 (sic)	—	—	75.00	85.00	95.00	125

Mint: Kirmanshahan
KM# 806.3 TOMAN
3.8400 g., Gold **Note:** Type R.

Date	Mintage	Good	VG	F	VF	XF
AH1250	—	—	85.00	95.00	110	140

Mint: Mashhad
KM# 806.4 TOMAN
3.8400 g., Gold **Note:** Type R.

Date	Mintage	Good	VG	F	VF	XF
AH1254	—	—	95.00	110	125	160

Mint: Mashhad
KM# 809.2 TOMAN
3.8400 g., Gold **Note:** Type S.

Date	Mintage	Good	VG	F	VF	XF
AH1256	—	—	75.00	85.00	95.00	125
AH1257	—	—	75.00	85.00	95.00	125
AH1259	—	—	75.00	85.00	95.00	125
AH1260	—	—	75.00	85.00	95.00	125
AH1261	—	—	75.00	85.00	95.00	125
AH1263	—	—	75.00	85.00	95.00	125
AH1264	—	—	75.00	85.00	95.00	125
AH1265//1265 (sic)	—	—	125	200	275	375

Note: Coins of Mashhad struck in AH1265 (and dated on both sides) are issues of the rebel Hasan Khan Salar after Muhammad Shah's death

Mint: Rasht
KM# 806.5 TOMAN
3.8400 g., Gold **Note:** Type R.

Date	Mintage	Good	VG	F	VF	XF
AH1251	—	—	75.00	85.00	95.00	125
AH1252	—	—	75.00	85.00	95.00	125

Mint: Rasht
KM# 809.3 TOMAN
3.8400 g., Gold **Note:** Type S.

Date	Mintage	Good	VG	F	VF	XF
AH1255	—	—	75.00	85.00	95.00	125
AH1257	—	—	75.00	85.00	95.00	125
AH1258	—	—	75.00	85.00	95.00	125
AH1259	—	—	75.00	85.00	95.00	125
AH1262	—	—	75.00	85.00	95.00	125

Mint: Shiraz
KM# 806.6 TOMAN
3.8400 g., Gold **Note:** Type R.

Date	Mintage	Good	VG	F	VF	XF
AH1252	—	—	75.00	85.00	95.00	125
AH1253	—	—	75.00	85.00	95.00	125

Mint: Shiraz
KM# 809.4 TOMAN
3.8400 g., Gold **Note:** Type S.

Date	Mintage	Good	VG	F	VF	XF
AH1255	—	—	75.00	85.00	95.00	125

Mint: Tabriz
KM# 806.7 TOMAN
3.8400 g., Gold **Note:** Type R.

Date	Mintage	Good	VG	F	VF	XF
AH1250	—	—	75.00	85.00	95.00	125
AH1254	—	—	75.00	85.00	95.00	125

Mint: Tabriz
KM# 809.5 TOMAN
3.8400 g., Gold **Note:** Type S.

Date	Mintage	Good	VG	F	VF	XF
AH1255	—	—	75.00	85.00	95.00	125
AH1256	—	—	75.00	85.00	95.00	125
AH1257	—	—	75.00	85.00	95.00	125
AH1259	—	—	75.00	85.00	95.00	125
AH1261	—	—	75.00	85.00	95.00	125

Mint: Tehran
KM# 812 TOMAN
3.8400 g., Gold **Obv:** Crown above lion and sun within wreath **Rev:** Legend and value within square **Note:** Lion and sun type. Similar to 1 Kran, KM#799.

Date	Mintage	Good	VG	F	VF	XF
AH1258	—	—	125	200	300	400
AH1260	—	—	125	200	300	400
AH1261	—	—	125	200	300	400
AH1262	—	—	125	200	300	400
AH1263	—	—	125	200	300	400

Mint: Tehran
KM# 806.8 TOMAN
3.8400 g., Gold **Note:** Type R.

Date	Mintage	Good	VG	F	VF	XF
AH1251	—	—	75.00	85.00	95.00	125
AH1252	—	—	75.00	85.00	95.00	125

Mint: Tehran
KM# 809.6 TOMAN
3.8400 g., Gold **Note:** Type S.

Date	Mintage	Good	VG	F	VF	XF
AH1255	—	—	75.00	85.00	95.00	125
AH1256	—	—	75.00	85.00	95.00	125
AH1257	—	—	75.00	85.00	95.00	125

Mint: Isfahan
KM# 814 2 TOMAN
6.9000 g., Gold **Obv:** Crowned ruler on throne **Note:** Special type.

Date	Mintage	Good	VG	F	VF	XF
AH1254	—	—	—	—	—	3,000

Mint: Tehran
KM# 807 6 TOMAN
Gold **Obv:** Crowned ruler on throne **Note:** Type R; weight approximately 23 grams.

Date	Mintage	Good	VG	F	VF	XF
AH1251	—	—	—	—	—	5,000

COUNTERMARKED COINAGE

Mint: Tehran
KM# 816 TOMAN
3.4500 g., Gold **Countermark:** Duribe Tehran (12)50 **Note:** Countermark on Fath Ali Shah, KM#759.

CM Date	Host Date	Good	VG	F	VF	XF
AH12(50)	AH1246-49	—	200	300	375	475

Note: Countermarks appear on these coins ranging from AH1246-1249; Anonymous type, could be an issue of either Sultan Ali Shah or Muhammad Shah

Nasir al-Din Shah
AH1264-1313 / 1848-1896AD

The eighth kran was intended largely for ceremonial purposes, and varies considerably in weight. It is the ancestor of the Shahi Sefid of the machine-struck period.

Machine-struck coinage was introduced in AH1293 and became general by AH1296. The latest known hammered coins are dated AH1297. All of the provincial markets were closed when hammered coinage ceased.

All of Nasir al-Din's hammered gold was struck to the 3.45 g toman standard.

All normal hammered silver and gold coinage of this reign bears on the obverse the inscription *al-sultan ibn al-sultan Nasir al-Din Shah Qajar*, occasionally somewhat shortened. The reverse bears the mint & the date, though the date occasionally appears on the obverse or on both sides.

There is great variety of design for both obverse and reverse during this reign, with many attractive and elegant cartouches and calligraphic styles. The more attractive and ornate designs command a significant premium over listed prices, from 25% to at least 200%, depending on attractiveness and rarity.

KRAN STANDARD
AH1293-1344, SH1304-1309,
1876-1931AD

50 Dinars = 1 Shahi
1000 Dinars = 20 Shahis = 1 Kran (Qiron)
10 Krans = 1 Toman

Special Gold Issue
AH1337/1918-1919AD
1 Ashrafi (= 1 Toman)
SH1305-1309/1927-1931AD

Toman replaced by Pahlavi (light standard). Relationship of Pahlavi to Kran not known.

NOTE: Dated reverse dies lacking the ruler's name were not discarded at the end of a reign (especially from Nasir al-Din to Muzaffar al-Din), but remained in use until broken or worn out. Sometimes the old date was scratched out or changed, but often the die was used with the old date unaltered. Some dies with date below wreath retained the old date but had the new date engraved among the lion's legs.

NOTE: Modern imitations exist of many types, particularly the small 1/5, ½ and 1 Toman coins. These are usually underweight (or rarely overweight), and are sold in the bazaars at a small premium over bullion. They are usually crude and probably not intended to deceive collectors, but some are sold for jewelry and some are dated outside the reign of the ruler whose name or portrait they bear.

A few deceptive counterfeits are known of the large 10 Toman pieces.

HAMMERED COINAGE

Mint: Rasht
KM# 851.1 1/5 TOMAN
0.6900 g., Gold

Date	Mintage	Good	VG	F	VF	XF
AH1283	—	—	72.50	120	150	200

Mint: Shiraz
KM# 851.2 1/5 TOMAN
0.6900 g., Gold

Date	Mintage	Good	VG	F	VF	XF
ND	—	—	60.00	120	150	200

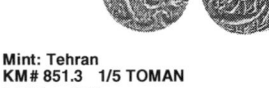

Mint: Tehran
KM# 851.3 1/5 TOMAN
0.6900 g., Gold

Date	Mintage	Good	VG	F	VF	XF
AH1270	—	—	60.00	100	125	160
AH1277	—	—	60.00	100	125	160
AH1294	—	—	60.00	100	125	160

378 IRAN

Mint: Arz-e Aqdas
KM# 862 1/2 TOMAN
1.7200 g., Gold Obv: Inscription in form of toughra

Date	Mintage	Good	VG	F	VF	XF
AH1283	—	—	100	175	215	260

Mint: Herat
KM# 852.1 1/2 TOMAN
1.7200 g., Gold

Date	Mintage	Good	VG	F	VF	XF
AH1276	—	—	175	300	375	475

Mint: Isfahan
KM# 852.2 1/2 TOMAN
1.7200 g., Gold

Date	Mintage	Good	VG	F	VF	XF
AH1271	—	—	55.00	85.00	100	140
AH1273	—	—	55.00	85.00	100	140

Mint: Mashhad
KM# 852.3 1/2 TOMAN
1.7200 g., Gold

Date	Mintage	Good	VG	F	VF	XF
AH1274	—	—	72.50	120	150	200
AH1279	—	—	72.50	120	150	200
AH1280	—	—	72.50	120	150	200
AH1288	—	—	72.50	120	150	200

Mint: Qazvin
KM# 852.4 1/2 TOMAN
1.7200 g., Gold

Date	Mintage	Good	VG	F	VF	XF
AH1271	—	—	60.00	100	125	160

Mint: Sarakhs
KM# 852.5 1/2 TOMAN
1.7200 g., Gold

Date	Mintage	Good	VG	F	VF	XF
AH1276	—	—	200	350	425	525

Mint: Tabriz
KM# 852.6 1/2 TOMAN
1.7200 g., Gold

Date	Mintage	Good	VG	F	VF	XF
AH1275	—	—	55.00	85.00	100	140
AH1282	—	—	55.00	85.00	100	140
AH1294	—	—	90.00	150	185	240

Mint: Tehran
KM# 852.7 1/2 TOMAN
1.7200 g., Gold

Date	Mintage	Good	VG	F	VF	XF
AH1265	—	—	55.00	85.00	100	140
AH1268	—	—	55.00	85.00	100	140
AH1276	—	—	55.00	85.00	100	140
AH1280	—	—	55.00	85.00	100	140
AH1282	—	—	55.00	85.00	100	140
AH1285	—	—	55.00	85.00	100	140

Mint: Tehran
KM# A862 1/2 TOMAN
1.6800 g., Gold

Date	Mintage	Good	VG	F	VF	XF
AH1295 Rare	—	—	—	—	—	—

Mint: Tehran
KM# 860 1/2 TOMAN
1.7200 g., Gold Obv: Profile bust of shah Note: Special types.

Date	Mintage	Good	VG	F	VF	XF
AH1272	—	—	150	250	325	400

Mint: Astarabad
KM# 861.1 TOMAN
3.4500 g., Gold Obv: Crowned profile portrait bust of the shah Rev: Legend and value within star design and beaded circle

Date	Mintage	Good	VG	F	VF	XF
AH1279	—	—	175	300	400	500

Mint: Astarabad
KM# 853.1 TOMAN
3.4500 g., Gold

Date	Mintage	F	VF	XF	Unc
AH1274	—	100	140	175	—
AH1277	—	100	140	175	—
AH1279	—	100	140	175	—

Mint: Hamadan
KM# 853.2 TOMAN
3.4500 g., Gold

Date	Mintage	Good	VG	F	VF	XF
AH1267	—	—	75.00	85.00	95.00	120
AH1268	—	—	75.00	85.00	95.00	120
AH1269	—	—	75.00	85.00	95.00	120
AH1272	—	—	75.00	85.00	95.00	120
AH1272	—	—	75.00	85.00	95.00	120
AH1278	—	—	80.00	90.00	100	130
AH1280	—	—	80.00	90.00	100	130
AH1288	—	—	75.00	85.00	95.00	120

Mint: Isfahan
KM# 853.3 TOMAN
3.4500 g., Gold

Date	Mintage	Good	VG	F	VF	XF
AH1288	—	—	75.00	85.00	95.00	120

Mint: Isfahan
KM# 861.4 TOMAN
3.4500 g., Gold Obv: Profile portrait of the Shah

Date	Mintage	VG	F	VF	XF	Unc
AH1274	—	—	250	275	350	—

Mint: Khoy
KM# 853.4 TOMAN
3.4500 g., Gold

Date	Mintage	Good	VG	F	VF	XF
AH1266	—	—	100	150	200	250
AH1267	—	—	100	150	200	250

Mint: Kirmanshahan
KM# 853.5 TOMAN
3.4500 g., Gold

Date	Mintage	Good	VG	F	VF	XF
AH1273	—	—	85.00	95.00	120	150
AH1274	—	—	85.00	95.00	120	150

Mint: Mashhad
KM# 853.6 TOMAN
3.4500 g., Gold

Date	Mintage	Good	VG	F	VF	XF
AH1266	—	—	75.00	85.00	95.00	120
AH1267	—	—	75.00	85.00	95.00	120
AH1268	—	—	75.00	85.00	95.00	120
AH1273	—	—	75.00	85.00	95.00	120
AH1274	—	—	75.00	85.00	95.00	120
AH1274//1275	—	—	80.00	90.00	100	130
AH1276	—	—	80.00	90.00	100	130
AH1280	—	—	75.00	85.00	95.00	120
AH1286	—	—	80.00	90.00	100	130
AH1287	—	—	80.00	90.00	100	130
AH1288	—	—	80.00	90.00	100	130

Mint: Mashhad
KM# 863 TOMAN
3.4500 g., Gold Obv: Inscription in toughra form Note: Similar to 1 Kran, KM#832.

Date	Mintage	Good	VG	F	VF	XF
AH1286	—	—	125	200	250	325

Mint: Qazvin
KM# 853.7 TOMAN
3.4500 g., Gold

Date	Mintage	Good	VG	F	VF	XF
AH1265	—	—	75.00	85.00	95.00	120
AH1267	—	—	75.00	85.00	95.00	120
AH1268	—	—	75.00	85.00	95.00	120
AH1269	—	—	75.00	85.00	95.00	120
AH1271	—	—	75.00	85.00	95.00	120
AH1273	—	—	75.00	85.00	95.00	120
AH1280	—	—	75.00	85.00	95.00	120
AH1281	—	—	75.00	85.00	95.00	120

Mint: Rasht
KM# 853.8 TOMAN
3.4500 g., Gold

Date	Mintage	Good	VG	F	VF	XF
AH1266	—	—	75.00	85.00	95.00	120
AH1267	—	—	75.00	85.00	95.00	120
AH1268	—	—	75.00	85.00	95.00	120
AH1269	—	—	75.00	85.00	95.00	120
AH1271	—	—	75.00	85.00	95.00	120
AH1272	—	—	75.00	85.00	95.00	120
AH1273	—	—	75.00	85.00	95.00	120
AH1274	—	—	75.00	85.00	95.00	120
AH1275	—	—	75.00	85.00	95.00	120
AH1276	—	—	75.00	85.00	95.00	120
AH1277	—	—	75.00	85.00	95.00	120
AH1278	—	—	75.00	85.00	95.00	120
AH1280	—	—	75.00	85.00	95.00	120

Mint: Rasht
KM# 861.2 TOMAN
3.4500 g., Gold Obv: Profile portrait of the shah

Date	Mintage	Good	VG	F	VF	XF
AH1272	—	—	150	250	325	425

Mint: Sarakhs
KM# 853.9 TOMAN
3.4500 g., Gold

Date	Mintage	Good	VG	F	VF	XF
AH1276	—	—	200	350	450	550

Mint: Tabaristan
KM# 853.10 TOMAN
3.4500 g., Gold

Date	Mintage	Good	VG	F	VF	XF
AH1271	—	—	75.00	85.00	95.00	120
AH1272	—	—	75.00	85.00	95.00	120
AH1273	—	—	75.00	85.00	95.00	120
AH1274	—	—	75.00	85.00	95.00	120
AH1275	—	—	75.00	85.00	95.00	120
AH1276	—	—	75.00	85.00	95.00	120
AH1277	—	—	75.00	85.00	95.00	120
AH1280	—	—	75.00	85.00	95.00	120
AH1288	—	—	80.00	90.00	100	130

Mint: Tabriz
KM# 853.11 TOMAN
3.4500 g., Gold

Date	Mintage	Good	VG	F	VF	XF
AH1265	—	—	75.00	85.00	95.00	120
AH1268	—	—	80.00	90.00	100	130
AH1271	—	—	75.00	85.00	95.00	120
AH1272	—	—	75.00	85.00	95.00	120
AH1274	—	—	75.00	85.00	95.00	120
AH1277	—	—	75.00	85.00	95.00	120
AH1278	—	—	75.00	85.00	95.00	120
AH1280	—	—	75.00	85.00	95.00	120
AH1284	—	—	75.00	85.00	95.00	120

Mint: Tehran
KM# 853.12 TOMAN
3.4500 g., Gold

Date	Mintage	Good	VG	F	VF	XF
AH1265	—	—	75.00	85.00	95.00	120
AH1275	—	—	75.00	85.00	95.00	120
AH1277	—	—	75.00	85.00	95.00	120
AH1281	—	—	75.00	85.00	95.00	120

Mint: Tehran
KM# 861.3 TOMAN
3.4500 g., Gold Obv: Profile portrait of the shah

Date	Mintage	Good	VG	F	VF	XF
AH1273	—	—	135	225	275	350
AH1274	—	—	135	225	275	350
AH1291	—	—	175	300	400	500

Mint: Tehran
KM# 858 TOMAN
3.4500 g., Gold Obv: Facing portrait of the shah Note: Special types.

Date	Mintage	Good	VG	F	VF	XF
AH1271	—	—	300	500	700	900

IRAN 379

Mint: Kirmanshahan
KM# 859 2 TOMAN
6.9000 g., Gold **Obv:** Facing portrait of the shah **Note:** Special types.

Date	Mintage	Good	VG	F	VF	XF
AH1271	—	—	200	350	550	750

Mint: Mashhad
KM# 864 2 TOMAN
6.9000 g., Gold **Obv:** Inscriptions in toughra form

Date	Mintage	Good	VG	F	VF	XF
AH1281	—	—	160	225	350	500

Mint: Tabriz
KM# 854 2 TOMAN
6.9000 g., Gold

Date	Mintage	Good	VG	F	VF	XF
AH1280	—	—	350	600	750	950

Mint: Tabriz
KM# 855 3 TOMAN
10.3500 g., Gold

Date	Mintage	Good	VG	F	VF	XF
AH1280	—	—	—	—	1,250	1,500
AH1292	—	—	—	—	1,250	1,500

Mint: Tehran
KM# 754.3 3 TOMAN
13.8200 g., Gold

Date	Mintage	VG	F	VF	XF	Unc
AH1227	—	—	—	—	—	—

MILLED COINAGE
Gold Toman Standard

Mint: Tehran
KM# 924 2000 DINARS
0.5749 g., 0.9000 Gold .0166 oz. AGW **Obv:** Uniformed bust 1/4 left **Rev:** Legend and value within beaded circle and wreath

Date	Mintage	VG	F	VF	XF	Unc
AH1297	—	—	20.00	40.00	75.00	125
AH1298	—	—	22.50	45.00	100	150
AH1299	—	—	20.00	40.00	75.00	125
AH1300	—	—	20.00	40.00	75.00	135
AH1301	—	—	20.00	40.00	75.00	135

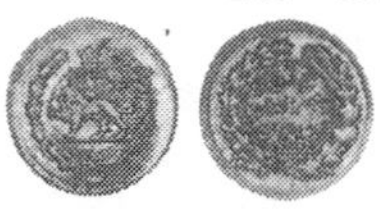

Mint: Tehran
KM# 925 2000 DINARS
0.5749 g., 0.9000 Gold .0166 oz. AGW **Obv:** Crown above lion and sun within wreath **Rev:** Legend and value within beaded circle and wreath

Date	Mintage	VG	F	VF	XF	Unc
AH1309 Rare	—	—	—	—	—	—

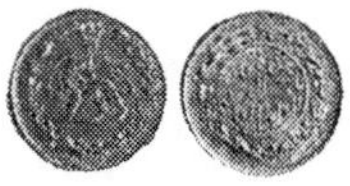

Mint: Tehran
KM# 923 2000 DINARS
0.6520 g., 0.9000 Gold .0188 oz. AGW **Obv:** Crown above lion and sun within wreath **Rev:** Legend and value within beaded circle and wreath

Date	Mintage	F	VF	XF	Unc
AH1295	—	125	175	350	425

Mint: Tehran
KM# 926 5000 DINARS
1.6300 g., 0.9000 Gold .0472 oz. AGW **Obv:** Crown above lion and sun within wreath **Obv. Legend:** "Nasir al-Din Shah" **Rev:** Legend and value within beaded circle and wreath

Date	Mintage	VG	F	VF	XF	Unc
AH1294	—	—	200	400	750	1,250

Mint: Tehran
KM# 921 5000 DINARS
1.4372 g., 0.9000 Gold .0416 oz. AGW

Date	Mintage	VG	F	VF	XF	Unc
AH1296	—	—	100	200	300	400
AH1309	—	—	200	400	750	1,250

Mint: Tehran
KM# 927 5000 DINARS
1.4372 g., 0.9000 Gold .0416 oz. AGW **Obv:** Uniformed bust 1/4 left **Rev:** Legend and value within beaded circle and wreath

Date	Mintage	VG	F	VF	XF	Unc
AH1297	—	—	50.00	70.00	120	200
AH1299	—	—	50.00	70.00	120	200
AH1300	—	—	50.00	70.00	120	200
AH1301	—	—	65.00	120	200	350
AH1303	—	—	65.00	120	200	350
AH1305	—	—	65.00	120	200	350
AH13(0)5	—	—	65.00	120	200	350
AH1307	—	—	125	275	400	600
AH1213	—	—	100	150	275	350
Note: Error for 1312						
AH1313	—	—	150	275	400	600

Mint: Tehran
KM# 928 5000 DINARS
1.4372 g., 0.9000 Gold .0416 oz. AGW **Obv. Legend:** "Nasir Dhu'l Qarnayn"

Date	Mintage	VG	F	VF	XF	Unc
AH1313 Rare	—	—	—	—	—	—

Mint: Tehran
KM# 930 TOMAN
3.4525 g., 0.9000 Gold .0988 oz. AGW **Subject:** 30th Year of Reign **Obv:** Crown above lion and sun within wreath **Rev:** Legend and value within beaded circle and wreath

Date	Mintage	VG	F	VF	XF	Unc
AH1293	—	—	400	500	700	1,000

Mint: Tehran
KM# 932 TOMAN
3.1900 g., 0.9000 Gold .0923 oz. AGW **Obv:** Uniformed bust 1/4 left, without legend **Rev:** First Nasir-type legend and value within beaded circle and wreath

Date	Mintage	VG	F	VF	XF	Unc
ND(1294-95)	—	—	100	185	250	350

Mint: Tehran
KM# 934 TOMAN
3.4525 g., 0.9000 Gold .0988 oz. AGW **Subject:** Shah's Return From Europe **Obv:** Uniformed bust 1/4 left **Rev:** Legend and value within beaded circle and crowned wreath

Date	Mintage	VG	F	VF	XF	Unc
AH1307	—	—	400	750	1,250	1,750

Mint: Tehran
KM# 936 TOMAN
3.4525 g., 0.9000 Gold .0988 oz. AGW **Obv:** Uniformed bust 1/4 left, actual date right **Rev:** First Nasir-type legend within beaded circle and crowned wreath, date added

Date	Mintage	VG	F	VF	XF	Unc
AH1310	—	—	250	400	600	1,000

Mint: Tehran
KM# 937 TOMAN
3.4525 g., 0.9000 Gold .0988 oz. AGW **Obv:** Uniformed bust 1/4 left **Rev:** Second Nasir-type legend within beaded circle and crowned wreath

Date	Mintage	VG	F	VF	XF	Unc
AH1311	—	—	110	165	250	375

Mint: Tehran
KM# 989 TOMAN
2.8744 g., 0.9000 Gold .0832 oz. AGW **Obv:** Crown above lion and sun within wreath **Obv. Legend:** "Nasir al-Din Shah" **Rev:** Legend and value within beaded circle and wreath

Date	Mintage	VG	F	VF	XF	Unc
AH1311	—	—	550	900	1,500	2,500

Note: Although inscribed "Two Tomans", this type is known only on 1 Toman planchets

Mint: Tehran
KM# 933 TOMAN
3.4525 g., 0.9000 Gold .0988 oz. AGW **Obv:** Uniformed bust left **Rev:** First Nasir-type legend within beaded circle and wreath **Note:** Accession date: AH1264. Many of these coins have carelessly engraved dates, especially 1303 onward. Nasir al-Din Shah coins have two dates surrounding the Shah's head. The date to the left is the date of the coin, the date to the right is the accession date.

Date	Mintage	VG	F	VF	XF	Unc
AH1297	—	—	150	300	500	750
Note: Error with accession date AH1294						
AH1297	—	—	65.00	80.00	100	200
AH1298	—	—	100	200	300	500
AH1299	—	—	65.00	80.00	100	175
AH1300	—	—	80.00	165	250	425
AH1301	—	—	65.00	95.00	140	200
AH1303	—	—	65.00	100	150	225
AH1304	—	—	85.00	150	225	400
AH1305	—	—	65.00	90.00	140	200
AH1306	—	—	100	150	250	425
AH1307	—	—	80.00	125	200	325
AH1309	—	—	85.00	125	200	325
AH1311	—	—	100	150	250	375
AH1312	—	—	150	200	275	500

Mint: Tehran
KM# 931 TOMAN
3.4525 g., 0.9000 Gold .0988 oz. AGW **Obv:** Crown above lion and sun within wreath **Rev:** First Nasir-type legend within beaded circle and wreath **Note:** Coins of this type dated AH1296 and of reduced weight, 2.87 grams, .900 gold, have been reported to exist.

Date	Mintage	VG	F	VF	XF	Unc
AH1294	—	—	500	800	1,150	1,750

Mint: Tehran
KM# 938 TOMAN
3.4525 g., 0.9000 Gold .0988 oz. AGW **Obv:** Uniformed bust facing **Rev:** Legend and value within beaded circle and wreath **Note:** Mule.

Date	Mintage	VG	F	VF	XF	Unc
AH1313//1310	—	—	225	350	525	750

380 IRAN

Mint: Tehran
KM# 940 2 TOMAN
6.5150 g., 0.9000 Gold .1885 oz. AGW **Subject:** Discovery of Gold in Khurason **Obv:** Legend within wreath, crown above **Rev:** Legend within wreath

Date	Mintage	VG	F	VF	XF	Unc
AH1295	Rare	—	—	—	—	—

Mint: Tehran
KM# 941 2 TOMAN
6.5150 g., 0.9000 Gold .1885 oz. AGW **Subject:** 8th Emam Commemorative **Obv:** Uniformed bust facing **Rev:** Legend and value within wreath, crown above

Date	Mintage	VG	F	VF	XF	Unc
AH1295	Rare	—	—	—	—	—

Mint: Tehran
KM# 943 2 TOMAN
5.7488 g., 0.9000 Gold .1663 oz. AGW **Subject:** Shah's Return From Europe **Obv:** Uniformed bust 1/4 left **Rev:** Legend and value within beaded circle and wreath, star above

Date	Mintage	VG	F	VF	XF	Unc
AH1299//1307	—	—	525	850	1,400	2,350

Mint: Tehran
KM# 944 2 TOMAN
5.7488 g., 0.9000 Gold .1663 oz. AGW **Subject:** Shah's Visit to Tehran Mint **Obv:** Uniformed bust 1/4 left **Rev:** Legend and value within wreath

Date	Mintage	VG	F	VF	XF	Unc
AH1308	Rare	—	—	—	—	—

Mint: Tehran
KM# 942 2 TOMAN
5.7488 g., 0.9000 Gold .1663 oz. AGW **Obv:** Uniformed bust 1/4 left **Rev:** Legend and value within beaded circle and wreath **Note:** Accession date: AH1264.

Date	Mintage	VG	F	VF	XF	Unc
AH1297	—	—	140	200	275	450
AH1298	—	—	250	400	750	1,250
AH1299	—	—	120	160	200	375

Mint: Tehran
KM# 945 10 TOMAN
28.7440 g., 0.9000 Gold .8317 oz. AGW **Obv:** Uniformed bust 1/4 left **Rev:** Legend within circle and designed border **Rev. Legend:** "Nasir al-Din Shah"

Date	Mintage	VG	F	VF	XF	Unc
AH1297 H	—	—	1,250	1,500	2,250	3,500
AH1311 H	—	—	—	—	7,000	10,000

Mint: Tehran
KM# 946 10 TOMAN
28.7440 g., 0.9000 Gold .8317 oz. AGW **Obv:** Uniformed bust facing with medals on chest

Date	Mintage	VG	F	VF	XF	Unc
AH1311	—	—	2,000	3,000	5,000	7,500

Mint: Tehran
KM# 947 10 TOMAN
28.7440 g., 0.9000 Gold .8317 oz. AGW **Obv:** Lion and sun within wreath **Obv. Legend:** "Nasir al-Din Shah" **Rev:** Legend and value within circle and designed border

Date	Mintage	VG	F	VF	XF	Unc
AH1311	—	—	1,500	2,500	3,500	6,000

Mint: Tehran
KM# 951 25 TOMAN
0.9000 Gold, 50 mm. **Obv:** Uniformed bust 1/4 left **Rev:** Legend and value within circle above lion and sun within wreath **Rev. Legend:** "Nasir al-Din Shah"

Date	Mintage	F	VF	XF	Unc
AH1301 B	—	—	—	15,000	—

Mint: Tehran
KM# 952 25 TOMAN
0.9000 Gold **Subject:** Shah's Return From Europe **Obv:** Uniformed bust 1/4 left within circle and wreath **Rev:** Legend within crowned wreath

Date	Mintage	F	VF	XF	Unc
AH1307	Rare	—	—	—	—

Note: Stack's Hammel sale 9-82 AU realized $17,000

MEDALLIC COINAGE

The following were most likely intended for presentation purposes rather than as a circulation medium

X# M11a 5 TOMAN
28.5500 g., Gold **Note:** Prev. KM#M12.

Date	Mintage	F	VF	XF	Unc
AH1313	—	—	1,000	1,800	2,600

Note: Modern reproductions exist.

IRAN 381

X# M14 10 TOMAN
28.7440 g., 0.9000 Gold 0.8317 oz. AGW **Subject:** 50th Anniversary of Reign of Nasir al-Din **Note:** Prev. KM#M12.

Date	Mintage	F	VF	XF	Unc
AH1313	—	—	4,500	6,500	8,000

X# M6 10 TOMAN
28.7440 g., 0.9000 Gold 0.8317 oz. AGW **Obv:** Legend First Nasir type **Rev:** Lion and sun **Note:** Prev. KM#M8.

Date	Mintage	F	VF	XF	Unc
AH1293 Rare	—	—	—	—	—

X# M8 25 TOMAN
71.7400 g., 0.9000 Gold, 50 mm. **Note:** Prev. KM#M5.

Date	Mintage	F	VF	XF	Unc
AH1301B	—	—	15,000	17,500	22,000

X# M10 25 TOMAN
72.2700 g., 0.9000 Gold **Subject:** Shah's Return From Europe **Note:** Prev. KM#M6.

Date	Mintage	F	VF	XF	Unc
AH1307	—	—	12,500	15,000	20,000

MEDALS OF VALOR

Similar medals have also been reported for AH1325. These are often confused and cataloged as actual coins, and many of the earlier types actually circulated along side regular coinage. Examples with mountings removed sell for 60-80% of the valuations given

X# MV11 NON-DENOMINATED
9.7200 g., Gold **Subject:** Nazir al-Din Shah **Obv:** Sun rising behind lion standing left holding sword in sprays **Rev:** Outer legend in four cartouches around Shah's inscription

Date	Mintage	F	VF	XF	Unc
ND(1848-55)	—	400	600	900	—

X# MV17 NON-DENOMINATED
27.8000 g., Gold **Obv:** Sun rising behind lion lying left in sprays **Rev:** Shah's inscription in sprays

Date	Mintage	F	VF	XF	Unc
AH1209 (error 1290)	—	600	950	1,350	—

X# MV18 NON-DENOMINATED
Gold **Subject:** Nazir al-Din Shah **Obv:** Sun rising above lion standing left on shelf holding sword in sprays **Rev:** Continuous legend around Shah's inscription

Date	Mintage	F	VF	XF	Unc
AH1297	—	500	700	1,000	—

X# MV23 NON-DENOMINATED
14.0500 g., Gold **Obv:** Sun behind lion standing left on shelf holding sword in sprays **Rev:** Continuous legend around Shsh's inscription

Date	Mintage	F	VF	XF	Unc
AH1311	—	400	650	800	1,000

X# MV20 NON-DENOMINATED
13.5700 g., Gold **Obv:** Sun rising behind lion standing left on shelf holding sword in sprays **Rev:** Continuous legend around Shah's inscription **Note:** Weight varies: 13.57 - 14.40 g

Date	Mintage	F	VF	XF	Unc
AH1300	—	400	650	800	1,000

X# MV15 NON-DENOMINATED
13.9800 g., Gold, 34.9 mm. **Obv:** Sun rising above lion standing left on shelf holding sword in sprays **Rev:** Continuous legend around Shah's inscription

Date	Mintage	VG	F	VF	XF	Unc
AH1298	—	—	400	650	800	1,000

Muzaffar al-Din Shah
AH1313-1324 / 1896-1907AD

MILLED COINAGE

KM# 986 2000 DINARS
0.6520 g., 0.9000 Gold .0188 oz. AGW **Obv. Legend:** "Mazaffar-al-Din Shah" **Rev:** Crown above lion and sun within wreath

Date	Mintage	F	VF	XF	Unc
AH9301 Error for 1319	—	200	300	500	750

KM# 991 2000 DINARS
0.5749 g., 0.9000 Gold .0166 oz. AGW **Obv:** Uniformed bust left **Rev:** Legend and value within circle and wreath

Date	Mintage	F	VF	XF	Unc
ND	—	200	300	400	500

KM# 922 2000 DINARS
0.6520 g., 0.9000 Gold .0188 oz. AGW **Rev:** Legend and value within circle and wreath **Note:** Mule. Reverse: KM#923, reverse: KM#991.

Date	Mintage	VG	F	VF	XF	Unc
AH1295 (sic)	—	—	—	—	—	—

KM# 992 2000 DINARS
0.5749 g., 0.9000 Gold .0166 oz. AGW **Obv:** Date and denomination added

Date	Mintage	F	VF	XF	Unc
AH1319 (1901)	—	50.00	100	150	250
AH1322 (1904)	—	50.00	100	150	250
AH1323 (1905)	—	100	200	300	400
AH1324 (1906)	—	100	200	300	400

KM# 994.2 5000 DINARS
1.4372 g., 0.9000 Gold .0416 oz. AGW **Obv:** Bust with headdress 3/4 right divides date **Rev:** Legend within circle and wreath

Date	Mintage	F	VF	XF	Unc
AH1323	—	100	200	300	400

KM# 994.1 5000 DINARS
1.4372 g., 0.9000 Gold .0416 oz. AGW **Obv:** Uniformed bust 3/4 right **Rev:** Legend and value within cirlce and wreath **Note:** Prev. KM#994.

Date	Mintage	F	VF	XF	Unc
AH1316	—	35.00	60.00	80.00	145
AH1318	—	100	200	300	400
AH1319	—	100	200	300	400
AH1320	—	35.00	60.00	100	200
AH1321	—	35.00	60.00	100	200
AH1322	—	35.00	60.00	100	200
AH1324	—	100	200	300	400

Mint: Tehran
KM# 987 5000 DINARS
1.4372 g., 0.9000 Gold .0416 oz. AGW **Obv:** Crown above lion and sun within wreath **Obv. Legend:** "Muzaffar al-Din Shah" **Rev:** Legend and value within circle and wreath

Date	Mintage	F	VF	XF	Unc
AH1314	—	115	225	325	450

Note: AH1314 has 13 left of front legs and 14 between front and back legs

AH1315	—	135	275	450	675

Mint: Tehran
KM# 993 5000 DINARS
1.4372 g., 0.9000 Gold .0416 oz. AGW **Obv:** Uniformed bust left

Date	Mintage	F	VF	XF	Unc
ND	—	175	275	400	550

IRAN

KM# 995 TOMAN
2.8744 g., 0.9000 Gold .0832 oz. AGW, 19 mm. **Obv:** Uniformed bust 3/4 right, accession date, AH1314 above left **Rev:** Legend and value within circle and wreath

Date	Mintage	F	VF	XF	Unc
AH1316	—	65.00	95.00	150	225
AH1318	—	100	200	300	400
AH1319	—	60.00	100	160	250
AH1321	—	100	200	300	400

Mint: Tehran
KM# 988 TOMAN
2.8744 g., 0.9000 Gold .0832 oz. AGW **Obv. Legend:** "Muzaffar al-Din Shah, AH1313-1314" **Rev:** Crown above lion and sun within wreath

Date	Mintage	F	VF	XF	Unc
AH1314	—	150	200	300	550

KM# 996 2 TOMAN
5.7488 g., 0.9000 Gold .1663 oz. AGW, 19 mm. **Obv:** Uniformed bust 3/4 left, date at left **Rev:** Legend within circle and wreath **Rev. Legend:** "Muzaffer al-Din Shah"

Date	Mintage	F	VF	XF	Unc
AH1322 (1904)	—	250	400	750	1,500

KM# 997 2 TOMAN
5.7488 g., 0.9000 Gold .1663 oz. AGW, 19 mm. **Subject:** Royal Birthday **Obv:** Uniformed bust 3/4 left divides legend **Rev:** Legend within circle and wreath **Rev. Legend:** "Muzaffer al-Din Shah"

Date	Mintage	F	VF	XF	Unc
AH1322 (1904)	—	250	500	1,000	1,500

Mint: Tehran
KM# 1000 10 TOMAN
28.7440 g., 0.9000 Gold .8317 oz. AGW **Obv:** Date stamped **Rev:** With denomination

Date	Mintage	F	VF	XF	Unc
AH1314	—	2,500	3,250	5,000	7,000

Mint: Tehran
KM# 998 10 TOMAN
28.7440 g., 0.9000 Gold .8317 oz. AGW **Obv:** Uniformed bust 3/4 left **Rev:** Legend and value within circle and designed border **Rev. Legend:** "Muzaffar al-Din Shah"

Date	Mintage	F	VF	XF	Unc
AH1314	—	2,500	3,500	5,500	8,000

Mint: Tehran
KM# 999 10 TOMAN
28.7440 g., 0.9000 Gold .8317 oz. AGW **Obv:** Uniformed bust 3/4 left **Rev:** Legend and value within circle and designed border

Date	Mintage	F	VF	XF	Unc
AH1314	—	2,500	3,250	5,000	7,000

MEDALLIC COINAGE
The following were most likely intended for presentation purposes rather than as a circulation medium

X# M23 10 TOMAN
Gold **Subject:** Shah's Visit to Brussels Mint **Obv:** Military uniformed bust facing 3/4 right **Note:** Similar to X#M21. Weight varies: 30.97-31.03 grams.

Date	Mintage	F	VF	XF	Unc
AH1318	—	—	1,500	1,700	2,000

Muhammad Ali Shah
AH1324-1327 / 1907-1909AD
MILLED COINAGE

KM# 1024 2000 DINARS
0.5749 g., 0.9000 Gold .0166 oz. AGW **Obv:** Uniformed bust 3/4 left within wreath **Rev:** Legend in wreath

Date	Mintage	F	VF	XF	Unc
AH1326 (1908)	—	75.00	100	150	275
AH1327 (1909)	—	75.00	100	150	275

KM# 1021 5000 DINARS
1.4372 g., 0.9000 Gold .0416 oz. AGW, 17 mm. **Obv:** Legend within circle and wreath **Obv. Legend:** Muhammad Ali Shah **Rev:** Radiant lion holding sword within crowned wreath

Date	Mintage	F	VF	XF	Unc
AH1324 (1906)	—	75.00	100	150	275
AH1325 (1907)	—	75.00	100	150	275

KM# 1025 5000 DINARS
1.4372 g., 0.9000 Gold .0416 oz. AGW, 17 mm. **Obv:** Uniformed bust 3/4 left divides date **Rev:** Legend within circle and wreath **Rev. Legend:** "Muhammad Ali Shah"

Date	Mintage	F	VF	XF	Unc
AH1326 (1908)	—	75.00	100	150	275
AH1362 (1908) Error for 1326	—	75.00	100	150	275
AH1327 (1909)	—	75.00	100	150	275

KM# 1022 TOMAN
2.8744 g., 0.9000 Gold .0832 oz. AGW, 19 mm. **Obv:** Legend within circle and wreath **Obv. Legend:** "Muhammad Ali Shah" **Rev:** Radiant lion holding sword within crowned wreath

Date	Mintage	F	VF	XF	Unc
AH1324 (1906)	—	90.00	150	300	500

KM# 1026 TOMAN
2.8744 g., 0.9000 Gold .0832 oz. AGW **Obv:** Uniformed bust 3/4 left divides date **Rev:** Legend within circle and closed wreath **Rev. Legend:** "Muhammad Ali Shah"

Date	Mintage	F	VF	XF	Unc
AH1327 (1909)	—	90.00	150	300	500

MEDALLIC COINAGE
The following were most likely intended for presentation purposes rather than as a circulation medium

X# M25 5 TOMAN
14.3000 g., 0.9000 Gold 0.4138 oz. AGW **Note:** Prev. KM#M10.

Date	Mintage	F	VF	XF	Unc
AH1326	—	—	—	2,250	3,750

Sultan Ahmad Shah
AH1327-1344 / 1909-1925AD
MILLED COINAGE

KM# 1066 2000 DINARS
0.5749 g., 0.9000 Gold .0166 oz. AGW, 14 mm. **Obv:** Legend within circle and wreath **Obv. Legend:** "Ahmad Shah" **Rev:** Radiant lion holding sword within crowned wreath

Date	Mintage	F	VF	XF	Unc
AH1328 (1910)	—	100	175	250	500
AH1329 (1911)	—	250	550	750	900
AH1330 (1911)	—	100	175	250	500

KM# 1070 2000 DINARS
0.5749 g., 0.9000 Gold .0166 oz. AGW, 14 mm. **Obv:** Uniformed bust 1/4 left divides date **Rev:** Legend within circle and wreath **Rev. Legend:** "Ahmad Shah"

Date	Mintage	F	VF	XF	Unc
AH1332 (1913)	—	22.50	40.00	60.00	130
AH1333 (1914)	—	18.50	35.00	60.00	125
AH1334 (1915)	—	25.00	50.00	100	200
AH1335 (1916)	—	16.50	30.00	40.00	60.00
AH1337 (1918)	—	16.50	30.00	40.00	100
AH1339 (1920)	—	18.50	35.00	50.00	100
AH1340 (1921)	—	18.50	40.00	60.00	120
AH1341 (1922)	—	18.50	35.00	50.00	100
AH1342 (1923)	—	18.50	35.00	50.00	100
AH1343/33 (1924)	—	50.00	100	200	400
AH1343 (1924)	—	25.00	50.00	100	200

KM# 1067 5000 DINARS
1.4372 g., 0.9000 Gold .0416 oz. AGW **Obv:** Legend within circle and wreath **Obv. Legend:** "Ahmad Shah" **Rev:** Radiant lion holding sword within crowned wreath

Date	Mintage	F	VF	XF	Unc
AH1328 (1910)	—	60.00	125	200	275
AH1329 (1911)	—	175	400	600	750
AH1330 (1911)	—	175	400	600	750

IRAN 383

KM# 1071 5000 DINARS
1.4372 g., 0.9000 Gold .0416 oz. AGW, 17 mm. **Obv:** Uniformed bust 1/4 left divides date **Rev:** Legend within circle and wreath **Rev. Legend:** "Ahmad Shah"

Date	Mintage	F	VF	XF	Unc
AH1331 (1912)	—	50.00	100	150	300
AH1332 (1913)	—	40.00	60.00	100	150
AH1333 (1914)	—	50.00	100	200	300
AH1334 (1915)	—	50.00	100	200	300
AH1335 (1916)	—	50.00	100	200	300
AH1336 (1917)	—	35.00	40.00	50.00	90.00
AH1337 (1918)	—	50.00	100	200	300
AH1339 (1920)	—	60.00	125	250	350
AH1340 (1921)	—	35.00	40.00	60.00	110
AH1341 (1922)	—	35.00	40.00	50.00	90.00
AH1342 (1923)	—	35.00	40.00	50.00	90.00
AH1343/33 (1924)	—	100	200	400	600
AH1343 (1924)	—	50.00	100	200	300

KM# 1072 5000 DINARS
1.4372 g., 0.9000 Gold .0416 oz. AGW **Obv:** Bust with headdress 1/4 left within sprigs **Rev. Legend:** "Sahib al-Zaman"

Date	Mintage	F	VF	XF	Unc
AH1339 (1920)	—	100	150	250	600
AH1340 (1921)	—	100	150	250	600

KM# 1068 TOMAN
2.8744 g., 0.9000 Gold .0832 oz. AGW **Obv. Legend:** "Ahmad Shah", AH1328-1332 **Rev:** Lion and sun

Date	Mintage	F	VF	XF	Unc
AH1329 (1911)	—	200	300	500	750

KM# 1074 TOMAN
2.8744 g., 0.9000 Gold .0832 oz. AGW, 19 mm. **Obv:** Uniformed bust 1/4 left divides date **Rev:** Legend within circle and wreath **Rev. Legend:** "Ahmad Shah"

Date	Mintage	F	VF	XF	Unc
AH1332 (1913)	—	75.00	150	250	500
AH1333 (1914)	—	500	750	1,000	1,250
AH1334 (1915)	—	65.00	125	175	300
AH1335 (1916)	—	65.00	125	175	300
AH1337 (1918)	—	BV	60.00	100	175
AH1339 (1920)	—	BV	70.00	100	175
AH1340 (1921)	—	100	200	300	400
AH1341 (1922)	—	BV	60.00	90.00	150
AH1342 (1923)	—	BV	60.00	90.00	150
AH1343 (1924)	—	BV	60.00	90.00	150

KM# 1073 TOMAN
2.8744 g., 0.9000 Gold .0832 oz. AGW, 19 mm. **Obv:** Bust with headdress 1/4 left **Rev:** Ahmad Shah Pattern 2 Toman **Note:** The reverse die used was of an unadopted pattern.

Date	Mintage	F	VF	XF	Unc
AH1332 (1913)	—	300	600	900	1,500
AH1333 (1914)	—	350	650	1,000	1,750

KM# 1075 5 TOMAN
14.3720 g., 0.9000 Gold .4159 oz. AGW, 30 mm. **Obv:** Legend within beaded circle and wreath **Obv. Legend:** "Ahmad Shah" **Rev:** Radiant lion holding sword within wreath

Date	Mintage	F	VF	XF	Unc
AH1332/1 (1913)	—	3,500	4,500	6,000	8,000

Date	Mintage	F	VF	XF	Unc
AH1334/2/1 (1915)	—	1,100	1,600	2,000	2,700

Note: A number of gold medals of 5 Toman weight were struck between 1297 and 1326; These bear a couplet which clearly indicates that they are medals awarded by the Shah for bravery

KM# 1076 10 TOMAN
28.7440 g., 0.9000 Gold .8317 oz. AGW, 37 mm. **Obv:** Uniformed bust 1/4 left within wreath, date below **Obv. Legend:** "Ahmad Shah" **Rev:** Legend within circle and wreath

Date	Mintage	F	VF	XF	Unc
AH1331 (1912)	—	2,400	4,350	6,500	8,500
AH1334 (1915) Rare	—	—	—	—	—
AH1337//1334 (1918)	—	—	—	6,500	8,500

Note: The date on the AH1334 reverse die was not changed for use as the reverse to the 1337 issue

KM# 1077 10 TOMAN
28.7440 g., 0.9000 Gold .8317 oz. AGW **Obv:** Uniformed bust 1/4 left within wreath, date **Rev:** Radiant lion holding sword within wreath

Date	Mintage	F	VF	XF	Unc
AH1337 (1918)	—	1,850	3,000	4,500	5,500

KM# 1080 ASHRAFI
Gold **Obv:** Bust of Ahmad Shah **Rev:** Lion and sun within crowned wreath

Date	Mintage	F	VF	XF	Unc
AH1337 (1918)	—	—	125	250	375

KM# A1081 2 ASHRAFI
Gold **Obv:** Uniformed bust 1/4 left within wreath **Rev:** Crown above lion and sun within wreath

Date	Mintage	F	VF	XF	Unc
AH1337 (1918)	—	—	250	500	750

KM# 1081 5 ASHRAFI
Gold **Obv:** Uniformed bust 1/4 left within wreath **Rev:** Lion and sun within crowned wreath

Date	Mintage	F	VF	XF	Unc
AH1337 (1918)	—	—	500	750	1,000

KM# 1082 10 ASHRAFI
Gold **Obv:** Uniformed bust 1/4 left within wreath **Rev:** Lion and sun within crowned wreath

Date	Mintage	F	VF	XF	Unc
AH1337 (1918)	—	500	1,000	1,500	2,000

Reza Shah
AH1344-1360 / 1925-1941AD
MILLED COINAGE

KM# 1108 TOMAN
2.8744 g., Gold .0832 oz. AGW, 19 mm. **Subject:** Reza's First New Year Celebration **Obv:** Reza type legend **Rev:** Radiant lion holding sword within crowned wreath

Date	Mintage	F	VF	XF	Unc
SH1305 (1926)	—	200	300	500	750

KM# 1111 PAHLAVI
1.9180 g., Gold .0555 oz. AGW **Obv:** Legend within crowned wreath **Rev:** Radiant lion holding sword within crowned wreath

Date	Mintage	F	VF	XF	Unc
SH1305 (1926)	5,000	125	250	400	600

KM# 1114 PAHLAVI
2.8744 g., Gold .0832 oz. AGW **Obv:** Uniformed bust right above sprays **Rev:** Value and legend within beaded circle and crowned wreath

Date	Mintage	F	VF	XF	Unc
SH1306 (1927)	21,000	BV	65.00	85.00	125
SH1307 (1928)	5,000	65.00	90.00	125	185
SH1308 (1929)	989	80.00	100	160	275

KM# 1112 2 PAHLAVI
3.8360 g., Gold .1110 oz. AGW **Obv:** Legend within crowned wreath **Rev:** Radiant lion holding sword within crowned wreath

Date	Mintage	F	VF	XF	Unc
SH1305 (1926)	1,134	250	400	750	1,250

KM# 1115 2 PAHLAVI
3.8360 g., Gold .1110 oz. AGW **Obv:** Uniformed bust right above sprays **Rev:** Value and legend within beaded circle and crowned wreath

Date	Mintage	F	VF	XF	Unc
SH1306 (1927)	2,494	80.00	100	150	250
SH1307 (1928)	7,000	80.00	100	150	230
SH1308 (1929)	789	90.00	115	200	285

KM# 1113 5 PAHLAVI
9.5900 g., Gold .2775 oz. AGW **Obv:** Legend within crowned wreath **Rev:** Radiant lion holding sword within crowned wreath

Date	Mintage	F	VF	XF	Unc
SH1305 (1926)	271	500	700	950	2,000

384 IRAN

KM# 1116 5 PAHLAVI
9.5900 g., Gold .2775 oz. AGW **Obv:** Uniformed bust right above sprays **Rev:** Legend and value within beaded circle and crowned wreath

Date	Mintage	F	VF	XF	Unc
SH1306 (1927)	909	600	1,000	1,500	2,000
SH1307 (1928)	785	600	1,000	1,500	2,000
SH1308 (1929)	121	750	1,250	2,000	2,500

MEDALLIC COINAGE
The following were most likely intended for presentation purposes rather than as a circulation medium

X# M35 TOMAN
2.8700 g., Gold **Subject:** Reza's First New Year Celebration **Note:** Prev. Y#119.

Date	Mintage	F	VF	XF	Unc
SH1305	—	—	—	125	200

REFORM COINAGE

KM# 1132 1/2 PAHLAVI
4.0680 g., 0.9000 Gold .1177 oz. AGW **Obv:** Uniformed bust left **Rev:** Radiant lion holding sword within crowned wreath

Date	Mintage	F	VF	XF	Unc
SH1310 (1931)	696	BV	150	275	375
SH1311 (1932)	286	BV	175	300	400
SH1312 (1933)	892	BV	150	250	350
SH1313 (1934)	531	BV	175	300	400
SH1314 (1935)	—	BV	175	300	400
SH1315 (1936)	1,042	BV	175	275	375

KM# 1133 PAHLAVI
8.1360 g., 0.9000 Gold .2354 oz. AGW **Obv:** Uniformed bust left **Rev:** Radiant lion holding sword within crowned wreath

Date	Mintage	F	VF	XF	Unc
SH1310 (1931)	304	1,500	3,000	4,000	5,000

Muhammad Reza Pahlavi Shah
SH1320-1358 / 1941-1979AD
MEDALLIC COINAGE
The following were most likely intended for presentation purposes rather than as a circulation medium

X# M50 1/2 PAHLAVI
3.9300 g., 0.9000 Gold 0.1137 oz. AGW

Date	Mintage	F	VF	XF	Unc
SH1355	—	—	—	135	225

REFORM COINAGE

KM# 1189 500 RIALS
6.5100 g., 0.9000 Gold .1883 oz. AGW **Subject:** 2500th Anniversary of Persian Empire **Obv:** Small crown over lion and sun above value and dates within circle of crowns **Rev:** Walking griffin with ram antlers

Date	Mintage	F	VF	XF	Unc
SH1350-1971 Proof	11,000	Value: 140			

KM# 1190 750 RIALS
9.7700 g., 0.9000 Gold .2827 oz. AGW **Subject:** 2500th Anniversary of Persian Empire **Obv:** Small crown above lion and sun, value and date below **Rev:** Arms above Stone of Cyrus II and inscription within wreath of crowns

Date	Mintage	F	VF	XF	Unc
SH1350-1971 Proof	10,000	Value: 200			

KM# 1191.1 1000 RIALS
13.0300 g., 0.9000 Gold .3770 oz. AGW **Subject:** 2500th Anniversary of Persian Empire **Obv:** Small crown over lion and sun above value and dates within circle of crowns **Rev:** Polished fields below pillared palace

Date	Mintage	F	VF	XF	Unc
SH1350-1971 Proof	10,000	Value: 275			

KM# 1191.2 1000 RIALS
13.0300 g., 0.9000 Gold .3770 oz. AGW **Subject:** 2500th Anniversary of Persian Empire **Obv:** Small crown over lion and sun above value and dates within circle of crowns **Rev:** Polished fields below pillared palace

Date	Mintage	F	VF	XF	Unc
SH1350-1971 Proof	Inc. above	Value: 275			

KM# 1192 2000 RIALS
26.0600 g., 0.9000 Gold .7541 oz. AGW **Subject:** 2500th Anniversary of Persian Empire **Obv:** Conjoined busts left **Rev:** Small crown over lion and sun above value and dates within circle of crowns

Date	Mintage	F	VF	XF	Unc
SH1350-1971 Proof	9,805	Value: 550			

KM# 1160 1/4 PAHLAVI
2.0340 g., 0.9000 Gold .0589 oz. AGW, 14 mm. **Obv:** Head left, legend above, date below **Rev:** Crown over lion and sun above value within wreath

Date	Mintage	F	VF	XF	Unc
SH1332 (1953)	41,000	BV	50.00	100	125
SH1333 (1954)	7,000	50.00	60.00	125	175
SH1334 (1955)	—	—	BV	45.00	60.00
SH1335 (1956)	41,000	BV	50.00	100	125
SH1336 (1957)	—	BV	50.00	100	175

KM# 1198 1/4 PAHLAVI
2.0340 g., 0.9000 Gold .0589 oz. AGW **Obv:** Head left, legend above, date below, "Aryamehr" added to legend **Rev:** Crown above lion and sun within wreath

Date	Mintage	F	VF	XF	Unc
SH1354 (1975)	106,000	—	—	BV	45.00
SH1355 (1976)	186,000	—	—	BV	45.00
MS2536 (1977)	—	—	—	BV	45.00
MS2537 (1978)	—	—	—	BV	45.00
SH1358 (1979)	—	200	300	400	500

KM# 1160a 1/4 PAHLAVI
2.0340 g., 0.9000 Gold .0589 oz. AGW, 16 mm. **Obv:** Head left, legend above, date below **Rev:** Crown above lion holding sword within wreath **Note:** Thinner and broader.

Date	Mintage	F	VF	XF	Unc
SH1336 (1957)	7,000	—	45.00	75.00	125
SH1337 (1958)	33,000	—	—	BV	50.00
SH1338 (1959)	136,000	—	—	BV	50.00
SH1339 (1960)	156,000	—	—	BV	50.00
SH1340 (1961)	60,000	—	—	BV	50.00
SH1342 (1963)	80,000	—	—	BV	50.00
SH1344 (1965)	30,000	—	60.00	90.00	125
SH1345 (1966)	40,000	—	—	BV	50.00
SH1346 (1967)	30,000	—	—	BV	50.00
SH1347 (1968)	60,000	—	—	BV	50.00
SH1348 (1969)	60,000	—	—	BV	50.00
SH1349 (1970)	80,000	—	—	BV	50.00
SH1350 (1971)	80,000	—	—	BV	50.00
SH1351 (1972)	103,000	—	—	BV	50.00
SH1353 (1974)	—	—	—	BV	50.00

KM# 1147 1/2 PAHLAVI
4.0680 g., 0.9000 Gold .1177 oz. AGW **Obv:** Legend **Obv. Legend:** "Muhammad Reza Shah" **Rev:** Crown above radiant lion holding sword within wreath

Date	Mintage	F	VF	XF	Unc
SH1320 (1941)	—	1,000	2,000	2,500	3,000
SH1321 (1942)	—	—	100	200	300
SH1322 (1943)	—	—	—	BV	85.00
SH1323 (1944)	76,000	—	—	BV	85.00

KM# 1149 1/2 PAHLAVI
4.0680 g., 0.9000 Gold .1177 oz. AGW **Obv:** High relief head left, legend above and date below **Rev:** Crown above radiant lion holding sword within wreath

Date	Mintage	F	VF	XF	Unc
SH1324 (1945)	—	—	—	BV	85.00
SH1325 (1946)	—	—	—	BV	85.00
SH1326 (1947)	36,000	—	BV	85.00	110
SH1327 (1948)	36,000	—	BV	85.00	110
SH1328 (1949)	—	—	—	BV	130
SH1329 (1950)	75	—	275	475	750
SH1330 (1951)	98,000	—	175	300	500

IRAN

KM# 1161 1/2 PAHLAVI
4.0680 g., 0.9000 Gold .1177 oz. AGW **Obv:** Low relief head left, legend above with date below **Rev:** Crown above radiant lion holding sword within wreath

Date	Mintage	F	VF	XF	Unc
SH1330 (1951)	—	—	—	BV	85.00
Note: Mintage included in KM#1149					
SH1332 (1952)	—	—	1,250	2,000	2,500
SH1333 (1954)	—	BV	200	250	300
SH1334 (1955)	—	—	200	250	300
SH1335 (1956)	—	—	—	BV	85.00
SH1336 (1957)	132,000	—	—	BV	85.00
SH1337 (1958)	102,000	—	—	BV	85.00
SH1338 (1959)	140,000	—	—	BV	85.00
SH1339 (1960)	142,000	—	—	BV	85.00
SH1340 (1961)	439,000	—	—	BV	85.00
SH1342 (1963)	40,000	—	—	BV	85.00
SH1344 (1965)	30,000	BV	200	250	300
SH1345 (1966)	40,000	—	—	BV	85.00
SH1346 (1967)	40,000	—	—	BV	85.00
SH1347 (1968)	50,000	—	—	BV	85.00
SH1348 (1969)	40,000	—	—	BV	85.00
SH1349 (1970)	80,000	—	—	BV	85.00
SH1350 (1971)	80,000	—	—	BV	85.00
SH1351 (1972)	103,000	—	—	BV	85.00
SH1352 (1973)	67,000	—	—	BV	85.00
SH1353 (1974)	—	—	—	BV	85.00

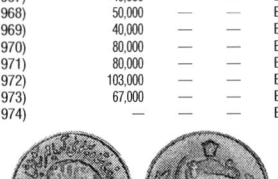

KM# 1199 1/2 PAHLAVI
4.0680 g., 0.9000 Gold .1177 oz. AGW **Obv:** Head left, legend above and date below, "Aryamehr" added to legend **Rev:** Crown above radiant lion holding sword within wreath

Date	Mintage	F	VF	XF	Unc
SH1354 (1975)	37,000	—	—	BV	85.00
SH1355 (1976)	153,000	—	—	BV	85.00
MS2536 (1977)	—	—	—	BV	85.00
MS2537 (1978)	—	—	—	BV	85.00
SH1358 (1979)	—	300	500	1,000	1,500

KM# 1148 PAHLAVI
8.1360 g., 0.9000 Gold .2354 oz. AGW **Obv:** Legend and date **Obv. Legend:** "Muhammad Reza Shah" **Rev:** Crown above radiant lion holding sword within wreath

Date	Mintage	F	VF	XF	Unc
SH1320 (1941)	—	100	2,000	3,000	4,000
Note: Possibly a pattern					
SH1321 (1942)	—	1,000	2,000	3,000	4,000
Note: Possibly a pattern					
SH1322 (1943)	—	—	—	BV	165
SH1323 (1944)	311,000	—	—	BV	165
SH1324 (1945)	—	—	—	BV	165

KM# 1150 PAHLAVI
8.1360 g., 0.9000 Gold .2354 oz. AGW **Obv:** High relief head left, legend above and date below **Rev:** Crown above radiant lion holding sword within wreath

Date	Mintage	F	VF	XF	Unc
SH1324 (1945)	—	—	—	BV	165
SH1325 (1946)	—	—	—	BV	165
SH1326 (1947)	151,000	—	—	BV	165
SH1327 (1948)	20,000	—	—	BV	165
SH1328 (1949)	4,000	—	BV	185	260
SH1329 (1950)	4,000	—	300	500	750
SH1330 (1951)	48,000	—	200	300	400

KM# 1162 PAHLAVI
8.1360 g., 0.9000 Gold .2354 oz. AGW **Obv:** Low relief head left, legend above and date below **Rev:** Crown above radiant lion holding sword within wreath

Date	Mintage	F	VF	XF	Unc
SH1330 (1951)	—	—	—	BV	165
SH1331 (1952)	—	2,000	3,000	3,500	3,750
SH1332 (1953)	—	2,000	3,000	3,500	3,750
SH1333 (1954)	—	BV	200	250	350
SH1334 (1955)	—	BV	200	250	350
SH1335 (1956)	—	—	—	BV	165
SH1336 (1957)	453,000	—	—	BV	165
SH1337 (1958)	665,000	—	—	BV	165
SH1338 (1959)	776,000	—	—	BV	165
SH1339 (1960)	847,000	—	—	BV	165
SH1340 (1961)	528,000	—	—	BV	165
SH1342 (1963)	20,000	—	—	BV	165
SH1344 (1965)	—	BV	200	250	350
SH1345 (1966)	20,000	—	—	BV	165
SH1346 (1967)	30,000	—	—	BV	165
SH1347 (1968)	40,000	—	—	BV	165
SH1348 (1969)	70,000	—	—	BV	165
SH1349 (1970)	70,000	—	—	BV	165
SH1350 (1971)	60,000	—	—	BV	165
SH1351 (1972)	100,000	—	—	BV	165
SH1352 (1973)	320,000	—	—	BV	165
SH1353 (1974)	—	—	—	BV	165

KM# 1200 PAHLAVI
8.1360 g., 0.9000 Gold .2354 oz. AGW **Obv:** Head left, legend above, date below, "Aryamehr" added to legend **Rev:** Crown above radiant lion holding sword within wreath

Date	Mintage	F	VF	XF	Unc
SH1354 (1975)	21,000	—	—	BV	165
SH1355 (1976)	203,000	—	—	BV	165
MS2536 (1977)	—	—	—	BV	165
MS2537 (1978)	—	—	—	BV	165
SH1358 (1979)	—	300	500	1,000	1,500

KM# A1163 2-1/2 PAHLAVI
20.3400 g., 0.9000 Gold .5885 oz. AGW **Obv:** Head left, legend above **Rev:** Inscription and date

Date	Mintage	F	VF	XF	Unc
SH1338 (1959)	—	—	BV	425	450

KM# 1163 2-1/2 PAHLAVI
20.3400 g., 0.9000 Gold .5885 oz. AGW **Obv:** Head left, legend above **Rev:** Crown above lion, sun and value within wreath

Date	Mintage	F	VF	XF	Unc
SH1339 (1960)	1,682	—	—	—	420
SH1340 (1961)	2,788	—	—	BV	420
SH1342 (1963)	30	—	—	—	—
SH1348 (1969)	3,000	—	—	BV	420
SH1350 (1971)	2,000	—	—	BV	420
SH1351 (1972)	2,500	—	—	BV	420
SH1352 (1973)	3,000	—	—	BV	420
SH1353 (1974)	—	—	—	BV	420

KM# 1201 2-1/2 PAHLAVI
20.3400 g., 0.9000 Gold .5885 oz. AGW, 30 mm. **Obv:** Head left, legend above, date below, "Aryamehr" added to legend **Rev:** Crown above radiant lion holding sword within wreath **Edge:** Reeded

Date	Mintage	F	VF	XF	Unc
SH1354 (1975)	18,000	—	—	BV	420
SH1355 (1976)	16,000	—	—	BV	420
MS2536 (1977)	—	—	—	BV	420
MS2537 (1978)	—	—	—	BV	420
SH1358 (1979) Rare	—	—	—	—	750
MS2538 (1979) Rare	—	—	—	—	750

KM# 1164 5 PAHLAVI
40.6799 g., 0.9000 Gold 1.1772 oz. AGW **Obv:** Head left, legend above **Rev:** Crown above lion and sun within wreath

Date	Mintage	F	VF	XF	Unc
SH1339 (1960)	2,225	—	—	BV	825
SH1340 (1961)	2,430	—	—	BV	825
SH1342 (1963)	20	—	—	2,500	4,000
SH1348 (1969)	2,000	—	—	BV	825
SH1350 (1971)	2,000	—	—	BV	825
SH1351 (1972)	2,500	—	—	BV	825
SH1352 (1973)	2,100	—	—	BV	825
SH1353 (1974)	—	—	—	BV	825

KM# 1202 5 PAHLAVI
40.6799 g., 0.9000 Gold 1.1772 oz. AGW **Obv:** Head left, legend above, date below, "Aryamehr" added to legend **Rev:** Crown above radiant lion holding sword within wreath

Date	Mintage	F	VF	XF	Unc
SH1354 (1975)	10,000	—	—	BV	825
SH1355 (1976)	17,000	—	—	BV	825
MS2536 (1977)	—	—	—	BV	825
MS2537 (1978)	—	—	—	BV	825
SH1358 (1979)	—	—	1,250	1,500	1,750

386 IRAN

KM# 1210 10 PAHLAVI
81.3598 g., 0.9000 Gold 2.3544 oz. AGW **Subject:** 50th Anniversary of Pahlavi Rule **Obv:** Conjoined busts left **Rev:** Crown, inscription and date at center circle of circle wreaths

Date	Mintage	F	VF	XF	Unc
MS2535 (1976)	—	—	—	BV	1,650

KM# 1213 10 PAHLAVI
81.3598 g., 0.9000 Gold 2.3544 oz. AGW **Obv:** Head left, legend above, date below, "Aryamehr" added to legend **Rev:** Crown above radiant lion holding sword within wreath

Date	Mintage	F	VF	XF	Unc
MS2537 (1978)	—	—	—	BV	1,650
SH1358 (1979)	—	—	—	4,000	5,000

KM# 1212 10 PAHLAVI
81.3598 g., 0.9000 Gold 2.3544 oz. AGW **Subject:** Centenary of Reza Shah's Birth **Obv:** Conjoined busts left **Rev:** Crown above inscription and date within wreath

Date	Mintage	F	VF	XF	Unc
MS2536 (1977)	—	—	—	BV	1,650

ISLAMIC REPUBLIC
BULLION COINAGE
Issued by the National Bank of Iran

KM# 1238 1/4 AZADI
2.0339 g., 0.9000 Gold .0588 oz. AGW **Obv:** Mosque within circle **Obv. Legend:** "1st Spring of Freedom" **Rev:** Artistic design within hexagon and designed border

Date	Mintage	F	VF	XF	Unc
SH1358 (1979)	—	—	—	—	300

KM# 1265 1/4 AZADI
2.0339 g., 0.9000 Gold 0.0589 oz. AGW **Obv. Legend:** "Spring of Freedom"

Date	Mintage	F	VF	XF	Unc
SH1366 (1987)	—	—	—	—	300
SH1368 (1989)	—	—	—	—	300
SH1369 (1990)	—	—	—	—	300
SH1370 (1991)	—	—	—	—	300

KM# 1239 1/2 AZADI
4.0680 g., 0.9000 Gold .1177 oz. AGW **Obv:** Mosque within circle **Obv. Legend:** "1st Spring of Freedom" **Rev:** Artistic design within hexagon and designed border

Date	Mintage	F	VF	XF	Unc
SH1358 (1979)	—	—	—	—	100

KM# 1250.1 1/2 AZADI
4.0680 g., 0.9000 Gold .1177 oz. AGW **Obv:** Legend shortened **Obv. Legend:** "Spring of Freedom"

Date	Mintage	F	VF	XF	Unc
SH1363 (1984)	—	—	—	—	200

KM# 1250.2 1/2 AZADI
4.0680 g., 0.9000 Gold .1177 oz. AGW **Obv:** Legend larger **Obv. Legend:** "Spring of Freedom"

Date	Mintage	F	VF	XF	Unc
SH1366 (1987)	—	—	—	—	200
SH1368 (1989)	—	—	—	—	200

Date	Mintage	F	VF	XF	Unc
SH1370 (1991)	—	—	—	—	150
SH1381 (2002)	—	—	—	—	95.00

KM# 1240 AZADI
8.1360 g., 0.9000 Gold .2354 oz. AGW **Obv:** Mosque within circle **Obv. Legend:** "1st Spring of Freedom" **Rev:** Artistic design within hexagon and designed border

Date	Mintage	F	VF	XF	Unc
SH1358 (1979)	—	—	—	BV	170

KM# 1264 AZADI
8.1360 g., 0.9000 Gold .2354 oz. AGW **Subject:** Central Bank of Islamic Republic of Iran **Obv:** Bank within circle **Rev:** Head 3/4 right above date

Date	Mintage	F	VF	XF	Unc
SH1370 (1991)	—	—	—	BV	170
SH1373 (1994)	—	—	—	BV	170
SH1374 (1995)	—	—	—	BV	170
SH1375 (1996)	—	—	—	BV	170

KM# 1248.2 AZADI
8.1360 g., 0.9000 Gold .2354 oz. AGW **Obv:** Mosque within circle **Obv. Legend:** "Spring of Freedom" **Rev:** Artistic design within hexagon and designed border **Note:** Larger legend

Date	Mintage	F	VF	XF	Unc
SH1364 (1985)	—	—	—	BV	170
SH1365 (1986)	—	—	—	BV	170
SH1366 (1987)	—	—	—	BV	170
SH1367 (1988)	—	—	—	BV	170
SH1368 (1989)	—	—	—	BV	170
SH1369 (1990)	—	—	—	BV	170
SH1370 (1991)	—	—	—	BV	170

KM# 1248.1 AZADI
8.1360 g., 0.9000 Gold .2354 oz. AGW **Obv:** Mosque within circle **Obv. Legend:** "Spring of Freedom" **Rev:** Artistic design within hexagon and designed border **Note:** Legend shortened

Date	Mintage	F	VF	XF	Unc
SH1363 (1984)	—	—	—	BV	170

Mint: Tehran
KM# A1264 AZADI
8.1360 g., 0.9000 Gold 0.2354 oz. AGW, 23.7 mm. **Obv:** Mosque within circle **Rev:** Head left above date **Edge:** Reeded

Date	Mintage	F	VF	XF	Unc
SH1370 (1991)	—	—	—	BV	170

KM# 1241 2-1/2 AZADI
20.3400 g., 0.9000 Gold .5885 oz. AGW **Obv:** Mosque within circle **Obv. Legend:** "1st Spring of Freedom" **Rev:** Artistic design within hexagon within designed border

Date	Mintage	F	VF	XF	Unc
SH1358 (1979)	6	—	—	—	1,500

Note: A mintage of 6 pieces is reported, but more exist

KM# 1242 5 AZADI
40.6800 g., 0.9000 Gold 1.1770 oz. AGW **Obv:** Mosque within circle **Obv. Legend:** "1st Spring of Freedom" **Rev:** Artistic design within hexagon within designed border

Date	Mintage	F	VF	XF	Unc
SH1358 (1979)	—	—	—	—	3,500

PATTERNS
Including off metal strikes

KM#	Date	Mintage	Identification	Mkt Val
Pn12	SH1281	—	2 Toman. Gold. Crown above lion and sun within wreath. Legend and value within beaded circle and wreath.	1,850
Pn16	SH1294	—	1/2 Toman. Gold. 1.6000 g. Crown above lion and sun within wreath. Legend and value within beaded circle and wreath. KM#926.	550
Pn17	SH1295	—	1/4 Toman. Gold. First Nasir type legend. KM#931.	500
Pn19	SH1297	—	1/4 Toman. Gold. First Nasir type legend. KM#931.	500
Pn20	SH1297	—	1/4 Toman. First bust of Nasir.	500
Pn14	SH1316	—	1/2 Toman. Gilt Bronze. Uniformed bust 1/4 right. Legend and value within beaded circle and wreath. KM#994. Prev. KM#Pn22.	600
Pn23	SH1316	—	Toman. Gilt Bronze. Uniformed bust 1/4 right. Legend and value within beaded circle and wreath. KM#995.	800
Pn32	SH1319	—	1/4 Toman.	300
Pn33	SH1326	—	2000 Dinars. Gold. KM#1024	1,000
Pn33a	SH1326	—	2000 Dinars. Gold. Mule. Obv. KM#1024, Rev. KM#1070.	2,500
Pn34	SH1326	—	5000 Dinars. Gold. Legend in open wreath. KM#1025	1,500
Pn35	SH1326	—	Toman. Gold. Legend in open wreath. KM#1026	375
Pn36	SH1326	—	2 Ashrafi. Legend in open wreath.	2,500
Pn37	SH1331	—	Toman. Gilt Bronze.	1,000
Pn38	SH1331	—	2 Toman. Gilt Bronze. Portrait of Ahmed Shah.	1,000
Pn40	SH1332	—	2000 Dinars. Gold.	—
Pn41	SH1337	—	2 Toman. Gold. KM#1080; "2 Ashrafi"	—
Pn42	SH1337	—	2000 Dinars. Gold. 14.0000 g.	2,000
Pn43	SH1337	—	2000 Dinars. Gold. 14.0000 g.	2,000
Pn44	SH1337	—	5 Toman. Gold. KM#1081; "5 Ashrafi"	3,500
Pn45	SH1337	—	10 Toman. Gold. KM#1082	—

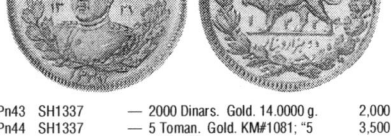

PROOF SETS

KM#	Date	Mintage	Identification	Issue Price	Mkt Val
PS2	SH1350(1971) (9)	9,805	KM#1184-1192	262	825

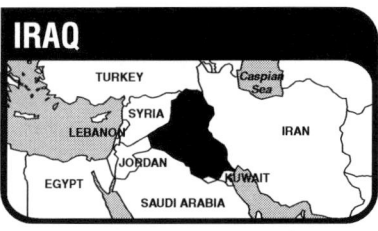

IRAQ

The Republic of Iraq, historically known as Mesopotamia, is located in the Near East and is bordered by Kuwait, Iran, Turkey, Syria, Jordan and Saudi Arabia. It has area of 167,925 sq. mi. (434,920 sq. km.) and a population of 14 million. Capital: Baghdad. The economy of Iraq is based on agriculture and petroleum. Crude oil accounted for 94 percent of the exports before the war with Iran began in 1980.

Mesopotamia was the site of a number of flourishing civilizations of antiquity - Sumeria, Assyria, Babylonia, Parthia, Persia and the Biblical cities of Ur, Ninevehand and Babylon. Desired because of its favored location, which embraced the fertile alluvial plains of the Tigris and Euphrates Rivers, Mesopotamia - 'land between the rivers'- was conquered by Cyrus the Great of Persia, Alexander of Macedonia and by Arabs who made the legendary city of Baghdad the capital of the ruling caliphate. Suleiman the Magnificent conquered Mesopotamia for Turkey in1534, and it formed part of the Ottoman Empire until 1623, and from 1638 to 1917. Great Britain, given a League of Nations mandate over the territory in 1920, recognized Iraq as a kingdom in 1922. Iraq became an independent constitutional monarchy presided over by the Hashemite family, direct descendants of the prophet Mohammed, in 1932. In 1958, the army-led revolution of July 14 overthrew the monarchy and proclaimed a republic.

NOTE: The 'I' mintmark on 1938 and 1943 issues appears on the obverse near the point of the bust. Some of the issues of 1938 have a dot to denote a composition change from nickel to copper-nickel.

RULERS
Ottoman, until 1917
British, 1921-1922
Faisal I, 1921-1933
Ghazi I, 1933-1939
Faisal II, Regency, 1939-1953
 As King, 1953-1958

MINT MARK
I — Bombay

MONETARY SYSTEM

Falus, Fulus   Fals, Fils   Falsan

50 Fils = 1 Dirham
200 Fils = 1 Riyal
1000 Fils = 1 Dinar (Pound)

TITLES

Al-Iraq

SAl-Mamlaka(t) al-Iraqiya(t)

Al-Jumhuriya(t) al-Iraqiya(t)

MESOPOTAMIA
Ottoman Empire

MONETARY SYSTEM
40 Para = 1 Piastre (Kurus)

MINT NAME
Baghdad
al-Basrah (Basra)
al-Hille

HAMMERED COINAGE

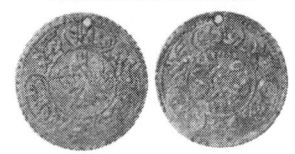

KM# 74 HAYRIYE ALTIN
1.4000 g., Gold **Ruler:** Mahmud II 1808-1839AD **Note:** Size varies: 20-21mm.

388　IRAQ

Date	Mintage	Good	VG	F	VF	XF
AH1223//25 (1831)	—	—	175	350	600	1,000

REPUBLIC
DECIMAL COINAGE

KM# 134 5 DINARS
13.5700 g., 0.9170 Gold .4001 oz. AGW **Subject:** 50th Anniversary of Iraqi Army **Obv:** Value within circle flanked by designs with legend above and below **Rev:** Conjoined armored busts divide dates

Date	Mintage	F	VF	XF	Unc	BU
1971	20,000	—	—	—	BV	285
1971 Proof	—	Value: 325				

KM# 166 50 DINARS
13.7000 g., 0.9170 Gold .4037 oz. AGW **Subject:** International Year of the Child **Obv:** Value within circle flanked designs with legend above and below **Rev:** Child's laureate head right within circle

Date	Mintage	F	VF	XF	Unc	BU
1979 Proof	10,000	Value: 350				
1979 Impaired Proof	Inc. above	BV+10%				

KM# 150 50 DINARS
13.0000 g., 0.9170 Gold .3832 oz. AGW **Subject:** 15th Century of Hegira **Obv:** Value and inscription within center circle of legend **Rev:** Stylized value within Mosque

Date	Mintage	F	VF	XF	Unc	BU
1980 Proof	13,000	Value: 275				
1980 Impaired Proof	Inc. above	BV+10%				

KM# 173 50 DINARS
16.9650 g., 0.9170 Gold .5002 oz. AGW **Subject:** 1st Anniversary of Hussein as President

Date	Mintage	F	VF	XF	Unc	BU
1980 Proof	—	Value: 385				

KM# 157 50 DINARS
13.7000 g., 0.9170 Gold .4040 oz. AGW **Subject:** Nonaligned Nations Baghdad Conference

Date	Mintage	F	VF	XF	Unc	BU
1982 Proof	10,000	Value: 295				

KM# 167 100 DINARS
26.0000 g., 0.9170 Gold .7665 oz. AGW **Subject:** International Year of the Child **Obv:** Value within circle flanked by designs, legend above and below **Rev:** Child's laureate head right within circle

Date	Mintage	F	VF	XF	Unc	BU
1979 Impaired Proof	Inc. above	BV+10%				
1979 Proof	10,000	Value: 575				

KM# 151 100 DINARS
26.0000 g., 0.9170 Gold .7665 oz. AGW **Subject:** 15th Century of Hegira **Obv:** Inscription and value within center circle of legend **Rev:** Styilized value within Mosque

Date	Mintage	F	VF	XF	Unc	BU
1980 Proof	14,000	Value: 525				
1980 Impaired Proof	Inc. above	BV+10%				

KM# 174 100 DINARS
33.9300 g., 0.9170 Gold 1.0003 oz. AGW **Subject:** 1st Anniversary of Hussein as President

Date	Mintage	F	VF	XF	Unc	BU
1980 Proof	—	Value: 765				

KM# 158 100 DINARS
33.9300 g., 0.9170 Gold 1.0003 oz. AGW **Subject:** Nonaligned Nations Baghdad Conference **Obv:** Value within circle with legend above and below **Rev:** Stylized tree divides dates

Date	Mintage	F	VF	XF	Unc	BU
1982 Proof	10,000	Value: 700				

MEDALLIC COINAGE

X# 3 50 DINARS
16.9650 g., 0.9170 Gold .5002 oz. AGW **Subject:** 1st Anniversary of Hussein as President **Obv:** Bust 3/4 left above Legend **Rev:** Arabic legend

Date	Mintage	F	VF	XF	Unc	BU
1980 Proof	10,000	Value: 400				

X# 2 100 DINARS
38.0000 g., 0.9170 Gold 1.1200 oz. AGW **Subject:** Battle of Gadissyiat **Obv:** Bust of Saddam Hussein

Date	Mintage	F	VF	XF	Unc	BU
1980	—	—	—	—	825	—

IRELAND

Ireland, the island located in the Atlantic Ocean west of Great Britain, was settled by a race of tall, red-haired Celts from Gaul about 400 BC. They assimilated the native Erainn and Picts and established a Gaelic civilization. After the arrival of St. Patrick in 432 AD, Ireland evolved into a center of Latin learning, which sent missionaries to Europe and possibly North America. In 1154, Pope Adrian IV gave all of Ireland to English King Henry II to administer as a Papal fief. Because of the enactment of anti-Catholic laws and the awarding of vast tracts of Irish land to Protestant absentee landowners, English control did not become reasonably absolute until 1800 when England and Ireland became the "United Kingdom of Great Britain and Ireland". Religious freedom was restored to the Irish in 1829, but agitation for political autonomy continued until the Irish Free State was established as a Dominion on Dec. 6, 1921 while Northern Ireland remained under the British rule.

RULER
British to 1921

MONETARY SYSTEM
4 Farthings = 1 Penny
12 Pence = 1 Shilling
5 Shillings = 1 Crown
20 Shillings = 1 Pound

KINGDOM
MEDALLIC COINAGE
1900 Reginald Huth Issues

Commemorating the visit of Queen Victoria to Ireland; struck by John Pinches, London, England

X# 2a 3 SHILLING
Gold **Note:** Prev. KM#M2a.

Date	Mintage	F	VF	XF	Unc	BU
MCM (1900) Possibly Unique	—	—	—	—	—	—

X# 3a 3 SHILLING
Gold **Rev:** With III above and Oct: below crown **Note:** Prev. KM#M3a.

Date	Mintage	F	VF	XF	Unc	BU
MCM (1900) Possibly Unique	—	—	—	—	—	—

X# 4a 3 SHILLING
Gold **Rev:** With III above and Sep: below crown **Note:** Prev. KM#M4a.

Date	Mintage	F	VF	XF	Unc	BU
MCM (1900) Possibly Unique	—	—	—	—	—	—

ISLE OF MAN

X# 5a 2 FLORIN
31.8200 g., Gold **Note:** Prev. KM#M5a.

Date	Mintage	F	VF	XF	Unc	BU
1900 Possibly Unique	—	—	—	—	—	—

UNITED KINGDOM

STANDARD COINAGE

KM# 146.2d FARTHING
Gold **Obv:** Laureate bust right **Rev:** Crowned harp **Edge:** Plain
Note: Previously KM#146d

Date	Mintage	F	VF	XF	Unc	BU
1806 Proof, restrike, rare	—	—	—	—	—	—

KM# 147.2d 1/2 PENNY
Gold **Obv:** Laureate bust right **Rev:** Crowned harp **Edge:** Plain
Note: Previously KM#147d

Date	Mintage	F	VF	XF	Unc	BU
1805 Proof, restrike, rare	—	—	—	—	—	—

KM# 148.2d PENNY
Gold **Obv:** Laureate bust right **Rev:** Crowned harp **Edge:** Plain
Note: Prev. KM#148d

Date	Mintage	F	VF	XF	Unc	BU
1805 Proof, restrike, rare	—	—	—	—	—	—

IRELAND REPUBLIC

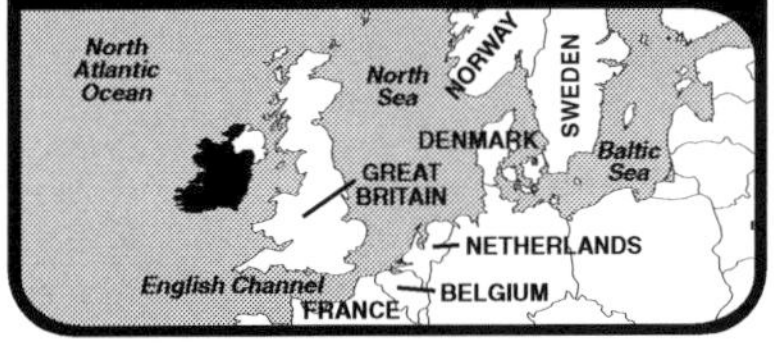

The Republic of Ireland, which occupies five-sixths of the island of Ireland located in the Atlantic Ocean west of Great Britain, has an area of 27,136 sq. mi. (70,280 sq. km.) and a population of 4.3 million. Capital: Dublin. Agriculture and dairy farming are the principal industries. Meat, livestock, dairy products and textiles are exported.

A race of tall, red-haired Celts from Gaul arrived in Ireland about 400 B.C., assimilated the native Erainn and Picts, and established a Gaelic civilization. After the arrival of St. Patrick in 432AD, Ireland evolved into a center of Latin learning, which sent missionaries to Europe and possibly North America. In 1154, Pope Adrian IV gave all of Ireland to English King Henry II to administer as a Papal fief. Because of the enactment of anti-Catholic laws and the awarding of vast tracts of Irish land to Protestant absentee landowners, English control did not become reasonably absolute until 1800 when England and Ireland became the 'United Kingdom of Great Britain and Ireland'. Religious freedom was restored to the Irish in 1829, but agitation for political autonomy continued until the Irish Free State was established as a dominion on Dec. 6, 1921 until 1937 when it became Éire. Ireland proclaimed itself a republic on April 18, 1949. The government, however, does not use the term 'Republic of Ireland', which tacitly acknowledges the partitioning of the island into Ireland and Northern Ireland, but refers to the country simply as 'Ireland'.

RULER
British, until 1921

REPUBLIC

EURO COINAGE
European Economic Community Issues

KM# 46 20 EURO
1.2400 g., 0.9990 Gold 0.0398 oz. AGW, 14 mm. **Subject:** Samuel Beckett 1906-1989 **Obv:** 2006, Erie, Harp **Rev:** Face, value and play **Edge:** Reeded

Date	Mintage	F	VF	XF	Unc	BU
2006 Proof	20,000	Value: 65.00				

MEDALLIC COINAGE
European Currency Unit - ECU

X# 3 50 ECU
15.0000 g., 0.9170 Gold .4421 oz. AGW, 28 mm. **Subject:** EEC Council Meeting in Dublin **Rev. Designer:** Thomas Ryan **Edge:** Reeded

Date	Mintage	F	VF	XF	Unc	BU
1990 Proof	5,000	Value: 475				

PROOF SETS

KM#	Date	Mintage	Identification	Issue Price	Mkt Val
PS5	1990 (3)	—	KMM1-M3	—	500
PS7	2006 (2)	—	KM#45-46	—	110

ISLE OF MAN

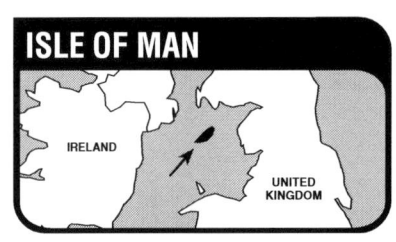

The Isle of Man, a dependency of the British Crown located in the Irish Sea equidistant from Ireland, Scotland and England, has an area of 227 sq. mi. (588 sq. km.) and a population of 68,000. Capital: Douglas. Agriculture, dairy farming, fishing and tourism are the chief industries.

The prevalence of prehistoric artifacts and monuments on the island give evidence that its' mild, almost sub-tropical climate was enjoyed by mankind before the dawn of history. Vikings came to the Isle of Man during the 9th century and remained until ejected by the Scottish in 1266. The island came under the protection of the British Crown in 1288, and in 1406 was granted, in perpetuity, to the earls of Derby, from whom it was inherited, 1736, by the Duke of Atholl. The British Crown purchased the rights and title in 1765; the remaining privileges of the Atholl family were transferred to the crown in 1829. The Isle of Man is ruled by its own legislative council and the House of Keys, the oldest, continuous legislative assembly in the world. Acts of Parliament passed in London do not affect the island unless it is specifically mentioned.

RULERS
James Murray, Duke of Atholl, 1736-1765
British Commencing 1765

MINT MARK
PM - Pobjoy Mint

PRIVY MARKS
(a) - Big Apple – 1988
(at) - Angel Blowing Trumpet – 1997

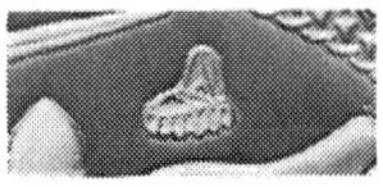

(b) - Baby Crib – 1982
(ba) - Basel Bugle – 1990
(bb) - Big Ben – 1987-1988
(br) - Brooklyn Bridge – 1989
(bs) - Teddy Bear in Stocking – 1996
(c) - Chicago Water Tower CICF – 1990-1991
(cc) - Christmas cracker – 1991
(d) - St. Paul's Cathedral – 1989
(f) - FUN logo – 1988
(fl) - Fleur de Lis – 1990
(fr) - Frauenkirche - Munich Numismata – 1990-1991
(fw) - Fairy w/magic wand – 1999
(h) - Horse - Hong Kong Int. – 1990
(l) - Statue of Liberty – 1987
(lc) - Lion crowned – 1989
(m) - Queen mother's portrait – 1980
(ma) - Maple leaf - CNA – 1990
(mt) - Mistletoe - Christmas – 1987, 1989
(ns) - North Star – 1994
(p) - Carrier Pigeon - Basel – 1988-1989
(pi) - Pine tree – 1986
(pt) - Partridge in a pear tree – 1988
(py) - Poppy – 1995
(s) - Bridge - SINPEX – 1987
(sb) - Soccer ball – 1982
(sc) - Santa Claus – 1995
(sg) - Sleigh - Christmas – 1990
(SL) - St. Louis Arch – 1987
(ss) - Sailing Ship - Sydney – 1988
(t) - Stylized triskelion – 1979
(tb) - Tower Bridge – 1990
(ti) - TICC logo - Tokyo – 1990
(v) - Viking ship – 1990
(vw) - Viking ship in wreath – 1986
(w) - Stylized triskelion – 1985
(x) - Snowman – 1998

PRIVY LETTERS
A - ANA – 1985-1992
C - Coinex, London – 1985-1989
D.M.I.H.E. - Ideal Home Exhibit, London, 1980
D.M.I.H.E.N. - Ideal Home Exhibit, Manchester, 1980
F - FUN – 1987
H - Hong Kong Expo – 1985
L - Long Beach – 1985-1987
T - Torex, Toronto – 1986
U - Uncirculated – 1988, 1990, 1994, 1995
X - Ameripex – 1986

ISLE OF MAN

DECIMAL COINAGE
5 New Pence = 1 Shilling; 25 New Pence = 1 Crown; 100 New Pence = 1 Pound

KM# 19b 1/2 NEW PENNY
4.0000 g., 0.9500 Platinum .1221 oz. APW, 17.4 mm. **Ruler:** Elizabeth II **Obv:** Young bust right **Obv. Designer:** Arnold Machin **Rev:** Flowered weed **Rev. Designer:** Christopher Ironside

Date	Mintage	F	VF	XF	Unc	BU
1975 Proof	600	Value: 175				

KM# 32b 1/2 PENNY
4.0000 g., 0.9500 Platinum .1221 oz. APW, 17.14 mm. **Ruler:** Elizabeth II **Obv:** Young bust right **Obv. Designer:** Arnold Machin **Rev:** Atlantic herring

Date	Mintage	F	VF	XF	Unc	BU
1976 Proof	600	Value: 175				
1978 Proof	600	Value: 175				
1979 (t) Proof	500	Value: 175				

KM# 58c 1/2 PENNY
3.5500 g., 0.9170 Gold .1046 oz. AGW, 17.14 mm. **Ruler:** Elizabeth II **Obv:** Young bust right **Obv. Designer:** Arnold Machin **Rev:** Atlantic herring within net **Rev. Designer:** Leslie Lindsay

Date	Mintage	F	VF	XF	Unc	BU
1980 Proof	—	Value: 80.00				
1982 (b) Proof	500	Value: 80.00				
1983 Proof	—	Value: 80.00				

KM# 58d 1/2 PENNY
4.0000 g., 0.9500 Platinum .1221 oz. APW, 17.14 mm. **Ruler:** Elizabeth II **Obv:** Young bust right **Obv. Designer:** Arnold Machin **Rev:** Atlantic herring within net **Rev. Designer:** Leslie Lindsay

Date	Mintage	F	VF	XF	Unc	BU
1980 Proof	500	Value: 180				
1982 (b) Proof	500	Value: 180				
1983 Proof	—	Value: 180				

KM# 111b 1/2 PENNY
3.5500 g., 0.9170 Gold .1046 oz. AGW, 17.14 mm. **Ruler:** Elizabeth II **Obv:** Young bust right **Obv. Designer:** Arnold Machin **Rev:** Fuchsia blossom on garnished and scrolled shield **Rev. Designer:** Leslie Lindsay

Date	Mintage	F	VF	XF	Unc	BU
1984 Proof	150	Value: 125				

KM# 142b 1/2 PENNY
3.5500 g., 0.9170 Gold .1046 oz. AGW, 17.14 mm. **Ruler:** Elizabeth II **Obv:** Crowned head right **Obv. Designer:** Raphael Maklouf **Rev:** Fuchsia blossom on garnished and scrolled shield **Rev. Designer:** Leslie Lindsay

Date	Mintage	F	VF	XF	Unc	BU
1985 Proof	300	Value: 85.00				

KM# 142c 1/2 PENNY
4.0000 g., 0.9500 Platinum .1221 oz. APW, 17.14 mm. **Ruler:** Elizabeth II **Obv:** Crowned head right **Obv. Designer:** Raphael Maklouf **Rev:** Fuchsia blossom on garnished and scrolled shield **Rev. Designer:** Leslie Lindsay

Date	Mintage	F	VF	XF	Unc	BU
1985 Proof	200	Value: 180				

KM# 20b NEW PENNY
8.0000 g., 0.9500 Platinum .2443 oz. APW, 20.32 mm. **Ruler:** Elizabeth II **Obv:** Young bust right **Obv. Designer:** Arnold Machin **Rev:** Celtic cross **Rev. Designer:** Christopher Ironside

Date	Mintage	F	VF	XF	Unc	BU
1975 Proof	600	Value: 365				

KM# 33b PENNY
8.0000 g., 0.9500 Platinum .2443 oz. APW, 20.32 mm. **Ruler:** Elizabeth II **Obv:** Young bust right **Obv. Designer:** Arnold Machin **Rev:** Loaghtyn sheep

Date	Mintage	F	VF	XF	Unc	BU
1976 Proof	600	Value: 365				
1978 Proof	600	Value: 365				
1979 (t) Proof	500	Value: 365				

KM# 59c PENNY
7.1000 g., 0.9170 Gold .2093 oz. AGW, 20.32 mm. **Ruler:** Elizabeth II **Obv:** Young bust right **Obv. Designer:** Arnold Machin **Rev:** Manx cat **Rev. Designer:** Leslie Lindsay

Date	Mintage	F	VF	XF	Unc	BU
1980 Proof	300	Value: 165				
1982 (b) Proof	500	Value: 165				
1983 Proof	—	Value: 165				

KM# 59d PENNY
8.0000 g., 0.9500 Platinum .2443 oz. APW, 20.32 mm. **Ruler:** Elizabeth II **Obv:** Young bust right **Obv. Designer:** Arnold Machin **Rev:** Manx cat **Rev. Designer:** Leslie Lindsay

Date	Mintage	F	VF	XF	Unc	BU
1980 Proof	500	Value: 365				
1982 (b) Proof	500	Value: 365				
1983 Proof	—	Value: 365				

KM# 112b PENNY
7.1000 g., 0.9170 Gold .2093 oz. AGW, 20.32 mm. **Ruler:** Elizabeth II **Obv:** Young bust right **Obv. Designer:** Arnold Machin **Rev:** Shag bird on tilting shield **Rev. Designer:** Leslie Lindsay

Date	Mintage	F	VF	XF	Unc	BU
1984 Proof	150	Value: 250				

KM# 143b PENNY
7.1000 g., 0.9170 Gold .2093 oz. AGW, 20.32 mm. **Ruler:** Elizabeth II **Obv:** Crowned head right **Obv. Designer:** Raphael Maklouf **Rev:** Shag bird on tilting shield **Rev. Designer:** Leslie Lindsay

Date	Mintage	F	VF	XF	Unc	BU
1985 Proof	300	Value: 175				

KM# 143c PENNY
8.0000 g., 0.9500 Platinum .2443 oz. APW, 20.32 mm. **Ruler:** Elizabeth II **Obv:** Crowned head right **Obv. Designer:** Raphael Maklouf **Rev:** Shag bird on tilting shield **Rev. Designer:** Leslie Lindsay

Date	Mintage	F	VF	XF	Unc	BU
1985 Proof	200	Value: 365				

KM# 21b 2 NEW PENCE
16.0000 g., 0.9500 Platinum .4887 oz. APW, 25.91 mm. **Ruler:** Elizabeth II **Obv:** Young bust right **Obv. Designer:** Arnold Machin **Rev:** Falcons

Date	Mintage	F	VF	XF	Unc	BU
1975 Proof	600	Value: 725				

KM# 34b 2 PENCE
16.0000 g., 0.9500 Platinum .4887 oz. APW, 25.91 mm. **Ruler:** Elizabeth II **Obv:** Young bust right **Obv. Designer:** Arnold Machin **Rev:** Bird in flight over map

Date	Mintage	F	VF	XF	Unc	BU
1976 Proof	600	Value: 725				
1977 Proof	600	Value: 725				
1978 Proof	—	Value: 725				
1979 (t) Proof	500	Value: 725				

KM# 60d 2 PENCE
16.0000 g., 0.9500 Platinum .4887 oz. APW, 25.91 mm. **Ruler:** Elizabeth II **Obv:** Young bust right **Obv. Designer:** Arnold Machin **Rev:** Bird in center of design **Rev. Designer:** Leslie Lindsay

Date	Mintage	F	VF	XF	Unc	BU
1980 Proof	500	Value: 725				
1982 (b) Proof	500	Value: 725				
1983 Proof	—	Value: 725				

KM# 60c 2 PENCE
14.2000 g., 0.9170 Gold .4186 oz. AGW, 25.91 mm. **Ruler:** Elizabeth II **Obv:** Young bust right **Obv. Designer:** Arnold Machin **Rev:** Bird in center of design **Rev. Designer:** Leslie Lindsay

Date	Mintage	F	VF	XF	Unc	BU
1980 Proof	300	Value: 300				
1982 (b) Proof	500	Value: 300				
1983 Proof	—	Value: 300				

KM# 113b 2 PENCE
14.2000 g., 0.9170 Gold .4185 oz. AGW, 25.91 mm. **Ruler:** Elizabeth II **Obv:** Young bust right **Obv. Designer:** Arnold Machin **Rev:** Falcon on ornamented shield **Rev. Designer:** Leslie Lindsay

Date	Mintage	F	VF	XF	Unc	BU
1984 Proof	150	Value: 450				

KM# 144b 2 PENCE
14.2000 g., 0.9170 Gold .4185 oz. AGW, 25.91 mm. **Ruler:** Elizabeth II **Obv:** Crowned head right **Obv. Designer:** Raphael Maklouf **Rev:** Falcon on ornamented shield **Rev. Designer:** Leslie Lindsay

ISLE OF MAN

Date	Mintage	F	VF	XF	Unc	BU
1985 Proof	300				Value: 325	

KM# 144c 2 PENCE
16.0000 g., 0.9500 Platinum .4887 oz. APW, 25.91 mm. **Ruler:** Elizabeth II **Obv:** Crowned head right **Obv. Designer:** Raphael Maklouf **Rev:** Falcon on ornamented shield **Rev. Designer:** Leslie Lindsay

Date	Mintage	F	VF	XF	Unc	BU
1985 Proof	200				Value: 725	

KM# 22b 5 NEW PENCE
12.5000 g., 0.9500 Platinum .3818 oz. APW, 23.59 mm. **Ruler:** Elizabeth II **Obv:** Young bust right **Obv. Designer:** Arnold Machin **Rev:** Towers on hill **Rev. Designer:** Christopher Ironside

Date	Mintage	F	VF	XF	Unc	BU
1975 Proof	600				Value: 550	

KM# 61c 5 PENCE
11.0000 g., 0.9170 Gold .3243 oz. AGW, 23.59 mm. **Ruler:** Elizabeth II **Obv:** Young bust right **Obv. Designer:** Arnold Machin **Rev:** Stylized Loagthyn sheep **Rev. Designer:** Leslie Lindsay

Date	Mintage	F	VF	XF	Unc	BU
1980 Proof	300				Value: 235	
1982 (b) Proof	500				Value: 235	
1983 Proof	—				Value: 235	

KM# 61d 5 PENCE
12.5000 g., 0.9500 Platinum .3818 oz. APW, 23.59 mm. **Ruler:** Elizabeth II **Obv:** Young bust right **Obv. Designer:** Arnold Machin **Rev:** Stylized Loagthyn sheep **Rev. Designer:** Leslie Lindsay

Date	Mintage	F	VF	XF	Unc	BU
1980 Proof	500				Value: 565	
1982 Proof	500				Value: 565	
1983 Proof	—				Value: 565	

KM# 114b 5 PENCE
11.0000 g., 0.9170 Gold .3242 oz. AGW, 23.59 mm. **Ruler:** Elizabeth II **Obv:** Young bust right **Obv. Designer:** Arnold Machin **Rev:** Cushag within design **Rev. Designer:** Leslie Lindsay

Date	Mintage	F	VF	XF	Unc	BU
1984 Proof	150				Value: 400	

KM# 145b 5 PENCE
11.0000 g., 0.9170 Gold .3242 oz. AGW, 23.59 mm. **Ruler:** Elizabeth II **Obv:** Crowned head right **Obv. Designer:** Raphael Maklouf **Rev:** Cushag within design **Rev. Designer:** Leslie Lindsay

Date	Mintage	F	VF	XF	Unc	BU
1985 Proof	300				Value: 235	

KM# 145c 5 PENCE
12.5000 g., 0.9500 Platinum .3818 oz. APW, 23.59 mm. **Ruler:** Elizabeth II **Obv:** Crowned head right **Obv. Designer:** Raphael Maklouf **Rev:** Cushag within design **Rev. Designer:** Leslie Lindsay

Date	Mintage	F	VF	XF	Unc	BU
1985 Proof	200				Value: 565	

KM# 392b 5 PENCE
3.2500 g., 0.9170 Gold .0958 oz. AGW, 18 mm. **Ruler:** Elizabeth II **Obv:** Crowned head right **Obv. Designer:** Raphael Maklouf **Rev:** Golf clubs and ball

Date	Mintage	F	VF	XF	Unc	BU
1994 Proof	10,000				Value: 75.00	

KM# 392c 5 PENCE
3.2500 g., 0.9500 Platinum .0992 oz. APW, 18 mm. **Ruler:** Elizabeth II **Obv:** Crowned head right **Obv. Designer:** Raphael Maklouf **Rev:** Golf clubs and ball

Date	Mintage	F	VF	XF	Unc	BU
1994 Proof	3,500				Value: 150	

KM# 23b 10 NEW PENCE
25.0000 g., 0.9500 Platinum .7636 oz. APW, 28.5 mm. **Ruler:** Elizabeth II **Obv:** Young bust right **Obv. Designer:** Arnold Machin **Rev:** Triskeles **Rev. Designer:** Christopher Ironside

Date	Mintage	F	VF	XF	Unc	BU
1975 Proof	600				Value: 1,000	

KM# 36.1b 10 PENCE
25.0000 g., 0.9500 Platinum .7636 oz. APW, 28.5 mm. **Ruler:** Elizabeth II **Obv:** Young bust right **Obv. Designer:** Arnold Machin **Rev:** Triskeles on map **Rev. Designer:** Christopher Ironside

Date	Mintage	F	VF	XF	Unc	BU
1976 Proof	600				Value: 1,000	
1978 Proof	600				Value: 1,000	
1979 (t) Proof	500				Value: 1,000	

KM# 62c 10 PENCE
22.0000 g., 0.9170 Gold .6486 oz. AGW, 28.5 mm. **Ruler:** Elizabeth II **Obv:** Young bust right **Obv. Designer:** Arnold Machin **Rev:** Falcon within design **Rev. Designer:** Leslie Lindsay

Date	Mintage	F	VF	XF	Unc	BU
1980 Proof	300				Value: 465	
1982 (b) Proof	500				Value: 465	
1983 Proof	—				Value: 465	

KM# 62d 10 PENCE
25.0000 g., 0.9500 Platinum .7636 oz. APW, 28.5 mm. **Ruler:** Elizabeth II **Obv:** Young bust right **Obv. Designer:** Arnold Machin **Rev:** Falcon within design **Rev. Designer:** Leslie Lindsay

Date	Mintage	F	VF	XF	Unc	BU
1980 Proof	500				Value: 1,000	
1982 (b) Proof	500				Value: 1,000	
1983 Proof	—				Value: 1,000	

KM# 115b 10 PENCE
22.0000 g., 0.9170 Gold .6484 oz. AGW, 28.5 mm. **Ruler:** Elizabeth II **Obv:** Young bust right **Obv. Designer:** Arnold Machin **Rev:** Loagthyn ram within shield **Rev. Designer:** Leslie Lindsay

Date	Mintage	F	VF	XF	Unc	BU
1984 Proof	150				Value: 700	

KM# 146b 10 PENCE
22.0000 g., 0.9170 Gold .6484 oz. AGW, 28.5 mm. **Ruler:** Elizabeth II **Obv:** Crowned head right **Obv. Designer:** Raphael Maklouf **Rev:** Loagthyn ram within designed shield **Rev. Designer:** Leslie Lindsay

Date	Mintage	F	VF	XF	Unc	BU
1985 Proof	300				Value: 500	

KM# 146c 10 PENCE
25.0000 g., 0.9500 Platinum .7636 oz. APW, 28.5 mm. **Ruler:** Elizabeth II **Obv:** Crowned head right **Obv. Designer:** Raphael Maklouf **Rev:** Loagthyn ram within designed shield **Rev. Designer:** Leslie Lindsay

Date	Mintage	F	VF	XF	Unc	BU
1985 Proof	200				Value: 1,000	

KM# 337b 10 PENCE
13.6158 g., 0.9170 Gold .4013 oz. AGW, 24.5 mm. **Ruler:** Elizabeth II **Obv:** Crowned head right **Obv. Designer:** Raphael Maklouf **Rev:** Triskeles and value

Date	Mintage	F	VF	XF	Unc	BU
1992 Proof	—				Value: 285	

KM# 337c 10 PENCE
15.4725 g., 0.9500 Platinum .4725 oz. APW, 24.5 mm. **Ruler:** Elizabeth II **Obv:** Crowned head right **Obv. Designer:** Raphael Maklouf **Rev:** Triskeles and value

Date	Mintage	F	VF	XF	Unc	BU
1992 Proof	—				Value: 625	

KM# 90b 20 PENCE
10.0000 g., 0.9170 Gold .2948 oz. AGW, 21.4 mm. **Ruler:** Elizabeth II **Subject:** Medieval Norse History **Obv:** Young bust right **Obv. Designer:** Arnold Machin **Rev:** Ship within small circle of design with Viking helmet above **Rev. Designer:** Leslie Lindsay **Shape:** 7-sided

Date	Mintage	F	VF	XF	Unc	BU
1982 Proof	1,500				Value: 210	
1982 (b) Proof	500				Value: 225	
1983 Proof	—				Value: 225	

KM# 90c 20 PENCE
11.3000 g., 0.9500 Platinum .3452 oz. APW, 21.4 mm. **Ruler:** Elizabeth II **Subject:** Medieval Norse History **Obv:** Young bust right **Obv. Designer:** Arnold Machin **Rev:** Ship within small circle of design with Viking helmet above **Rev. Designer:** Leslie Lindsay **Shape:** 7-sided

Date	Mintage	F	VF	XF	Unc	BU
1982 Proof	250				Value: 500	
1982 (b) Proof	500				Value: 500	
1983 Proof	—				Value: 500	

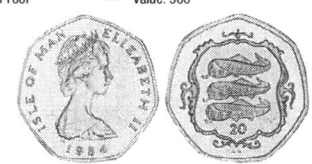

KM# 116b 20 PENCE
5.0000 g., 0.9170 Gold .1474 oz. AGW, 21.4 mm. **Ruler:** Elizabeth II **Subject:** Quincentenary of the College of Arms **Obv:** Young bust right **Obv. Designer:** Arnold Machin **Rev:** Atlantic herring within designed shield **Rev. Designer:** Leslie Lindsay **Shape:** 7-sided

Date	Mintage	F	VF	XF	Unc	BU
1984 Proof	150				Value: 175	

392 ISLE OF MAN

KM# 147b 20 PENCE
5.0000 g., 0.9170 Gold .1474 oz. AGW, 21.4 mm. **Ruler:** Elizabeth II **Obv:** Crowned head right **Obv. Designer:** Raphael Maklouf **Rev:** Atlantic herring within designed shield **Rev. Designer:** Leslie Lindsay **Shape:** 7-sided

Date	Mintage	F	VF	XF	Unc	BU
1985 Proof	300	Value: 120				

KM# 147c 20 PENCE
5.0000 g., 0.9500 Platinum .1527 oz. APW, 21.4 mm. **Ruler:** Elizabeth II **Obv:** Crowned head right **Obv. Designer:** Raphael Maklouf **Rev:** Atlantic herring within designed shield **Rev. Designer:** Leslie Lindsay **Shape:** 7-sided

Date	Mintage	F	VF	XF	Unc	BU
1985 Proof	200	Value: 225				

KM# 24b 50 NEW PENCE
30.4000 g., 0.9500 Platinum .9286 oz. APW, 30 mm. **Ruler:** Elizabeth II **Obv:** Young bust right **Obv. Designer:** Arnold Machin **Rev:** Sailing Viking ship **Rev. Designer:** Christopher Ironside **Shape:** 7-sided

Date	Mintage	F	VF	XF	Unc	BU
1975 Proof	600	Value: 1,225				

KM# 39b 50 PENCE
30.4000 g., 0.9500 Platinum .9286 oz. APW, 30 mm. **Ruler:** Elizabeth II **Obv:** Young bust right **Obv. Designer:** Arnold Machin **Rev:** Sailing Viking ship **Shape:** 7-sided

Date	Mintage	F	VF	XF	Unc	BU
1976 Proof	600	Value: 1,225				
1978 Proof	600	Value: 1,225				
1979 (t) Proof	500	Value: 1,225				

KM# 51b 50 PENCE
30.4000 g., 0.9500 Platinum .9286 oz. APW, 30 mm. **Ruler:** Elizabeth II **Subject:** Manx Millennium of Tynwald **Obv:** Young bust right **Obv. Designer:** Arnold Machin **Rev:** Viking ship **Edge:** H.M.Q.E. II ROYAL VISIT I.O.M. JULY 5, 1979

Date	Mintage	F	VF	XF	Unc	BU
1979 Proof	500	Value: 1,225				

KM# 69b 50 PENCE
26.0000 g., 0.9170 Gold .7666 oz. AGW, 30 mm. **Ruler:** Elizabeth II **Obv:** Young bust right **Obv. Designer:** Arnold Machin **Edge Lettering:** ODINS RAVEN VIKING EXHIBN NEW YORK 1980

Date	Mintage	F	VF	XF	Unc	BU
1980	250	—	—	—	600	650

KM# 69c 50 PENCE
30.4000 g., 0.9500 Platinum .9286 oz. APW, 30 mm. **Ruler:** Elizabeth II **Obv:** Young bust right **Obv. Designer:** Arnold Machin

Date	Mintage	F	VF	XF	Unc	BU
1980 Proof	50	Value: 1,275				

KM# 70c 50 PENCE
26.0000 g., 0.9170 Gold .7666 oz. AGW, 30 mm. **Ruler:** Elizabeth II **Obv:** Young bust right **Obv. Designer:** Arnold Machin **Rev:** Viking longship within design **Shape:** 7-sided

Date	Mintage	F	VF	XF	Unc	BU
1982 (b) Proof	500	Value: 550				
1983 Proof	—	Value: 550				
1980 Proof	300	Value: 550				

KM# 70d 50 PENCE
30.4000 g., 0.9500 Platinum .9286 oz. APW, 30 mm. **Ruler:** Elizabeth II **Obv:** Young bust right **Obv. Designer:** Arnold Machin **Rev:** Viking longship within design **Shape:** 7-sided

Date	Mintage	F	VF	XF	Unc	BU
1982 (b) Proof	500	Value: 1,225				
1983 Proof	—	Value: 1,225				
1980 Proof	500	Value: 1,225				

KM# 71b 50 PENCE
26.0000 g., 0.9170 Gold .7666 oz. AGW, 30 mm. **Ruler:** Elizabeth II **Subject:** Christmas 1980 **Obv:** Young bust right **Obv. Designer:** Arnold Machin **Rev:** Carriage pulled by horses, ship in background **Shape:** 7-sided

Date	Mintage	F	VF	XF	Unc	BU
1980 Proof	250	Value: 600				

KM# 71c 50 PENCE
30.4000 g., 0.9500 Platinum .9286 oz. APW, 30 mm. **Ruler:** Elizabeth II **Obv:** Young bust right **Obv. Designer:** Arnold Machin **Rev:** Carriage pulled by horses, ship in background **Shape:** 7-sided

Date	Mintage	F	VF	XF	Unc	BU
1980 Proof	50	Value: 1,275				

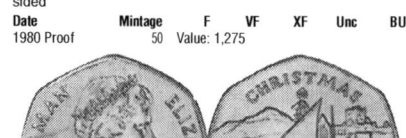

KM# 84 50 PENCE
13.5000 g., Copper-Nickel, 30 mm. **Ruler:** Elizabeth II **Subject:** Christmas 1981 **Obv:** Young bust right **Obv. Designer:** Arnold Machin **Rev:** Boat, standing figures and value **Shape:** 7-sided

Date	Mintage	F	VF	XF	Unc	BU
1981PM BC Proof	Inc. above	Value: 7.50				
1981PM BB Proof	30,000	Value: 7.50				
1981 AA	30,000	—	—	—	3.00	4.00
1981 AB	Inc. above	—	—	—	3.00	4.00
1981 BB Proof	—	Value: 7.50				

KM# 83b 50 PENCE
26.0000 g., 0.9170 Gold .7666 oz. AGW, 30 mm. **Ruler:** Elizabeth II **Subject:** Tourist Trophy Motorcycle Races **Obv:** Young bust right **Obv. Designer:** Arnold Machin **Rev:** Motorcyclist within sprigs **Shape:** 7-sided

Date	Mintage	F	VF	XF	Unc	BU
1981 Proof	250	Value: 600				

KM# 83c 50 PENCE
30.4000 g., 0.9500 Platinum .9286 oz. APW, 30 mm. **Ruler:** Elizabeth II **Subject:** Tourist Trophy Motorcycle Races **Obv:** Young bust right **Obv. Designer:** Arnold Machin **Rev:** Motorcyclist within sprigs **Shape:** 7-sided

Date	Mintage	F	VF	XF	Unc	BU
1981 Proof	50	Value: 1,275				

KM# 84b 50 PENCE
26.0000 g., 0.9170 Gold .7666 oz. AGW, 30 mm. **Ruler:** Elizabeth II **Subject:** Christmas 1981 **Obv:** Young bust right **Obv. Designer:** Arnold Machin **Rev:** Boat, standing figures and value **Shape:** 7-sided

Date	Mintage	F	VF	XF	Unc	BU
1981 Proof	250	Value: 600				

KM# 84c 50 PENCE
30.4000 g., 0.9500 Platinum .9286 oz. APW, 30 mm. **Ruler:** Elizabeth II **Subject:** Christmas 1981 **Obv:** Young bust right **Obv. Designer:** Arnold Machin **Rev:** Boat, standing figures and value **Shape:** 7-sided

Date	Mintage	F	VF	XF	Unc	BU
1981 Proof	—	Value: 1,275				

KM# 101b 50 PENCE
26.0000 g., 0.9170 Gold .7666 oz. AGW, 30 mm. **Ruler:** Elizabeth II **Subject:** Tourist Trophy Motorcycle Races **Obv:** Young bust right **Obv. Designer:** Arnold Machin **Rev:** Motorcyclist within sprigs **Shape:** 7-sided

Date	Mintage	F	VF	XF	Unc	BU
1982 Proof	250	Value: 600				

KM# 101c 50 PENCE
30.4000 g., 0.9500 Platinum .9286 oz. APW, 30 mm. **Ruler:** Elizabeth II **Subject:** Tourist Trophy Motorcycle Races **Obv:** Young bust right **Obv. Designer:** Arnold Machin **Rev:** Motorcyclist within sprigs **Shape:** 7-sided

Date	Mintage	F	VF	XF	Unc	BU
1982 Proof	50	Value: 1,275				

KM# 102b 50 PENCE
26.0000 g., 0.9170 Gold .7666 oz. AGW, 30 mm. **Ruler:** Elizabeth II **Subject:** Christmas 1982 **Obv:** Young bust right **Obv. Designer:** Arnold Machin **Rev:** Carolers around tree **Shape:** 7-sided

Date	Mintage	F	VF	XF	Unc	BU
1982 Proof	250	Value: 600				

KM# 102c 50 PENCE
30.4000 g., 0.9500 Platinum .9286 oz. APW, 30 mm. **Ruler:** Elizabeth II **Subject:** Christmas 1982 **Obv:** Young bust right **Obv. Designer:** Arnold Machin **Rev:** Carolers around tree **Shape:** 7-sided

Date	Mintage	F	VF	XF	Unc	BU
1982 Proof	50	Value: 1,275				

KM# 107b 50 PENCE
26.0000 g., 0.9170 Gold .7666 oz. AGW, 30 mm. **Ruler:** Elizabeth II **Subject:** Christmas 1983 **Obv:** Young bust right **Obv. Designer:** Arnold Machin **Rev:** Ford Model T driving left **Shape:** 7-sided

Date	Mintage	F	VF	XF	Unc	BU
1983 Proof	250	Value: 600				

KM# 107c 50 PENCE
30.4000 g., 0.9500 Platinum .9286 oz. APW, 30 mm. **Ruler:** Elizabeth II **Subject:** Christmas 1983 **Obv:** Young bust right **Obv. Designer:** Arnold Machin **Rev:** Ford Model T driving left **Shape:** 7-sided

Date	Mintage	F	VF	XF	Unc	BU
1983 Proof	50	Value: 1,275				

ISLE OF MAN

KM# 108b 50 PENCE
26.0000 g., 0.9170 Gold .7666 oz. AGW, 30 mm. **Subject:** Tourist Trophy Motorcycle Races **Obv:** Young bust right **Obv. Designer:** Arnold Machin **Rev:** Motorcyclist within sprigs **Rev. Designer:** Leslie Lindsay **Shape:** 7-sided

Date	Mintage	F	VF	XF	Unc	BU
1983 Proof	250	Value: 600				

KM# 108c 50 PENCE
30.4000 g., 0.9500 Platinum .9286 oz. APW, 30 mm. **Ruler:** Elizabeth II **Subject:** Tourist Trophy Motorcycle Races **Obv:** Young bust right **Obv. Designer:** Arnold Machin **Rev:** Motorcyclist within sprigs **Rev. Designer:** Leslie Lindsay **Shape:** 7-sided

Date	Mintage	F	VF	XF	Unc	BU
1983 Proof	50	Value: 1,275				

KM# 125b 50 PENCE
26.0000 g., 0.9170 Gold .7666 oz. AGW, 30 mm. **Ruler:** Elizabeth II **Subject:** Quincentenary of the College of Arms **Obv:** Young bust right **Obv. Designer:** Arnold Machin **Rev:** Viking longship on shield **Shape:** 7-sided

Date	Mintage	F	VF	XF	Unc	BU
1984 Proof	150	Value: 550				

KM# 126b 50 PENCE
26.0000 g., 0.9170 Gold .7666 oz. AGW, 30 mm. **Ruler:** Elizabeth II **Subject:** Tourist Trophy Motorcycle Races **Obv:** Young bust right **Obv. Designer:** Arnold Machin **Rev:** Motorcyclists within sprigs **Shape:** 7-sided

Date	Mintage	F	VF	XF	Unc	BU
1984 Proof	250	Value: 550				

KM# 126c 50 PENCE
30.4000 g., 0.9500 Platinum .9286 oz. APW, 30 mm. **Ruler:** Elizabeth II **Subject:** Tourist Trophy Motorcycle Races **Obv:** Young bust right **Obv. Designer:** Arnold Machin **Rev:** Motorcyclists within sprigs **Shape:** 7-sided

Date	Mintage	F	VF	XF	Unc	BU
1984 Proof	50	Value: 1,275				

KM# 127b 50 PENCE
26.0000 g., 0.9170 Gold .7666 oz. AGW, 30 mm. **Ruler:** Elizabeth II **Subject:** Christmas 1984 **Obv:** Young bust right **Obv. Designer:** Arnold Machin **Rev:** Train and standing figures **Rev. Designer:** Leslie Lindsay **Shape:** 7-sided

Date	Mintage	F	VF	XF	Unc	BU
1984 Proof	250	Value: 550				

KM# 127c 50 PENCE
30.4000 g., 0.9500 Platinum .9286 oz. APW **Ruler:** Elizabeth II **Subject:** Christmas 1984 **Obv:** Young bust right **Obv. Designer:** Arnold Machin **Rev:** Train and standing figures **Rev. Designer:** Leslie Lindsay **Shape:** 7-sided

Date	Mintage	F	VF	XF	Unc	BU
1984 Proof	—	Value: 1,275				

KM# 148b 50 PENCE
26.0000 g., 0.9170 Gold .7666 oz. AGW, 30 mm. **Ruler:** Elizabeth II **Obv:** Crowned head right **Obv. Designer:** Raphael Maklouf **Rev:** Viking longship on shield **Shape:** 7-sided

Date	Mintage	F	VF	XF	Unc	BU
1985 Proof	Est. 300	Value: 550				

KM# 148c 50 PENCE
30.4000 g., 0.9500 Platinum .9286 oz. APW, 30 mm. **Ruler:** Elizabeth II **Obv:** Crowned head right **Obv. Designer:** Raphael Maklouf **Rev:** Viking longship on shield **Shape:** 7-sided

Date	Mintage	F	VF	XF	Unc	BU
1985 Proof	Est. 200	Value: 1,275				

KM# 158b 50 PENCE
26.0000 g., 0.9170 Gold .7666 oz. AGW, 30 mm. **Ruler:** Elizabeth II **Subject:** Christmas 1985 **Obv:** Crowned head right **Obv. Designer:** Raphael Maklouf **Rev:** Airplanes **Rev. Designer:** Leslie Lindsay **Shape:** 7-sided

Date	Mintage	F	VF	XF	Unc	BU
1985 Proof	Est. 250	Value: 550				

KM# 158c 50 PENCE
30.4000 g., 0.9500 Platinum .9286 oz. APW, 30 mm. **Ruler:** Elizabeth II **Subject:** Christmas 1985 **Obv:** Crowned head right **Obv. Designer:** Raphael Maklouf **Rev:** Airplanes **Rev. Designer:** Leslie Lindsay **Shape:** 7-sided

Date	Mintage	F	VF	XF	Unc	BU
1985 Proof	—	Value: 1,275				

KM# 172b 50 PENCE
26.0000 g., 0.9170 Gold .7666 oz. AGW, 30 mm. **Ruler:** Elizabeth II **Subject:** Christmas 1986 **Obv:** Crowned head right **Obv. Designer:** Raphael Maklouf **Rev:** Horse-drawn tram **Shape:** 7-sided

Date	Mintage	F	VF	XF	Unc	BU
1986 Proof	—	Value: 550				

KM# 190b 50 PENCE
26.0000 g., 0.9170 Gold .7666 oz. AGW, 30 mm. **Ruler:** Elizabeth II **Subject:** Christmas 1987 **Obv:** Crowned head right **Obv. Designer:** Raphael Maklouf **Rev:** Bus and standing figures **Shape:** 7-sided

Date	Mintage	F	VF	XF	Unc	BU
1987 Proof	Est. 250	Value: 550				

KM# 190c 50 PENCE
30.4000 g., 0.9500 Platinum .9286 oz. APW, 30 mm. **Ruler:** Elizabeth II **Subject:** Christmas 1987 **Obv:** Crowned head right **Obv. Designer:** Raphael Maklouf **Rev:** Bus and standing figures **Shape:** 7-sided

Date	Mintage	F	VF	XF	Unc	BU
1987 Proof	Est. 50	Value: 1,275				

KM# 244b 50 PENCE
26.0000 g., 0.9170 Gold .7666 oz. AGW, 30 mm. **Ruler:** Elizabeth II **Subject:** Christmas 1988 **Obv:** Crowned head right **Obv. Designer:** Raphael Maklouf **Rev:** Motorbike and sidecar **Shape:** 7-sided

Date	Mintage	F	VF	XF	Unc	BU
1988 Proof	—	Value: 550				

KM# 244c 50 PENCE
30.4000 g., 0.9500 Platinum .9286 oz. APW, 30 mm. **Ruler:** Elizabeth II **Subject:** Christmas 1988 **Obv:** Crowned head right **Obv. Designer:** Raphael Maklouf **Rev:** Motorbike and sidecar **Shape:** 7-sided

Date	Mintage	F	VF	XF	Unc	BU
1988 Proof	—	Value: 1,275				

KM# 259b 50 PENCE
26.0000 g., 0.9170 Gold .7666 oz. AGW, 30 mm. **Ruler:** Elizabeth II **Subject:** Christmas 1989 **Obv:** Crowned head right **Obv. Designer:** Raphael Maklouf **Rev:** Electric trolley car **Shape:** 7-sided

Date	Mintage	F	VF	XF	Unc	BU
1989 Proof	—	Value: 800				

KM# 259c 50 PENCE
30.4000 g., 0.9500 Platinum .9286 oz. APW, 30 mm. **Ruler:** Elizabeth II **Subject:** Christmas 1989 **Obv:** Crowned head right **Obv. Designer:** Raphael Maklouf **Rev:** Electric trolley car **Shape:** 7-sided

Date	Mintage	F	VF	XF	Unc	BU
1989 Proof	—	Value: 1,350				

KM# 282b 50 PENCE
26.0000 g., 0.9170 Gold .7666 oz. AGW, 30 mm. **Ruler:** Elizabeth II **Subject:** Christmas 1990 **Obv:** Crowned head right **Obv. Designer:** Raphael Maklouf **Rev:** Ship and standing figures **Shape:** 7-sided

Date	Mintage	F	VF	XF	Unc	BU
1990 Proof	250	Value: 750				

KM# 282c 50 PENCE
30.4000 g., 0.9500 Platinum .9286 oz. APW, 30 mm. **Ruler:** Elizabeth II **Subject:** Christmas 1990 **Obv:** Crowned head right **Obv. Designer:** Raphael Maklouf **Rev:** TShip and standing figures **Shape:** 7-sided

Date	Mintage	F	VF	XF	Unc	BU
1990 Proof	50	Value: 1,300				

KM# 303b 50 PENCE
26.0000 g., 0.9170 Gold .7666 oz. AGW, 30 mm. **Ruler:** Elizabeth II **Subject:** Christmas 1991 **Obv:** Crowned head right **Obv. Designer:** Raphael Maklouf **Rev:** Nativity scene **Shape:** 7-sided

ISLE OF MAN

Date	Mintage	F	VF	XF	Unc	BU
1991 Proof	250				Value: 685	

KM# 303c 50 PENCE
30.4000 g., 0.9500 Platinum .9286 oz. APW, 30 mm. **Ruler:** Elizabeth II **Subject:** Christmas 1991 **Obv:** Crowned head right **Obv. Designer:** Raphael Maklouf **Rev:** Nativity scene **Shape:** 7-sided

Date	Mintage	F	VF	XF	Unc	BU
1991 Proof	50				Value: 1,300	

KM# 335b 50 PENCE
26.0000 g., 0.9170 Gold 0.7665 oz. AGW, 30 mm. **Ruler:** Elizabeth II **Subject:** Christmas 1992 **Obv:** Crowned head right **Obv. Designer:** Raphael Maklouf **Rev:** Newspaper boy hawking the Manx Mercury **Shape:** 7-sided

Date	Mintage	F	VF	XF	Unc	BU
1992 Proof	250				Value: 685	

KM# 335c 50 PENCE
30.4000 g., 0.9500 Platinum .9286 oz. APW, 30 mm. **Ruler:** Elizabeth II **Subject:** Christmas 1992 **Obv:** Crowned head right **Obv. Designer:** Raphael Maklouf **Rev:** Newspaper boy hawking the Manx Mercury **Shape:** 7-sided

Date	Mintage	F	VF	XF	Unc	BU
1992 Proof	50				Value: 1,300	

KM# 356b 50 PENCE
26.0000 g., 0.9170 Gold .7666 oz. AGW, 30 mm. **Ruler:** Elizabeth II **Subject:** Christmas 1993 **Obv:** Crowned head right **Obv. Designer:** Raphael Maklouf **Rev:** Framed nativity scene **Shape:** 7-sided

Date	Mintage	F	VF	XF	Unc	BU
1993 Proof	Est. 250				Value: 700	

KM# 356c 50 PENCE
30.4000 g., 0.9500 Platinum .9286 oz. APW, 30 mm. **Ruler:** Elizabeth II **Subject:** Christmas 1993 **Obv:** Crowned head right **Obv. Designer:** Raphael Maklouf **Rev:** Framed nativity scene **Shape:** 7-sided

Date	Mintage	F	VF	XF	Unc	BU
1993 Proof	Est. 50				Value: 1,300	

KM# 521b 50 PENCE
26.0000 g., 0.9170 Gold .7666 oz. AGW, 30 mm. **Ruler:** Elizabeth II **Subject:** Christmas 1995 **Obv:** Crowned head right **Obv. Designer:** Raphael Maklouf **Rev:** Sledding scene **Shape:** 7-sided

Date	Mintage	F	VF	XF	Unc	BU
1995 Proof	Est. 250				Value: 675	

KM# 694b 50 PENCE
26.0000 g., 0.9170 Gold .7666 oz. AGW, 30 mm. **Ruler:** Elizabeth II **Subject:** Christmas 1996 **Obv:** Crowned head right **Obv. Designer:** Raphael Maklouf **Rev:** Children throwing snowballs in front of church **Shape:** 7-sided

Date	Mintage	F	VF	XF	Unc	BU
1996 Proof	Est. 250				Value: 675	

KM# 794b 50 PENCE
8.0000 g., 0.9160 Gold .2356 oz. AGW, 27.3 mm. **Ruler:** Elizabeth II **Subject:** Christmas 1997 **Obv:** Crowned head right **Obv. Designer:** Raphael Maklouf **Rev:** Cameo to lower left of figures on book **Shape:** 7-sided

Date	Mintage	F	VF	XF	Unc	BU
1997 Proof	250				Value: 500	

KM# 806b 50 PENCE
8.0000 g., 0.9999 Gold 0.2572 oz. AGW, 27.3 mm. **Ruler:** Elizabeth II **Obv:** Crowned head right **Obv. Designer:** Raphael Maklouf **Rev:** Two motorcycle racers **Edge:** Plain **Shape:** 7-sided

Date	Mintage	F	VF	XF	Unc	BU
1997PM Proof	250				Value: 500	

KM# 905b 50 PENCE
8.0000 g., 0.9999 Gold .2572 oz. AGW, 27.3 mm. **Ruler:** Elizabeth II **Obv:** Head with tiara right **Obv. Designer:** Ian Rank-Broadley **Rev:** Two motorcycle racers **Shape:** 7-sided

Date	Mintage	F	VF	XF	Unc	BU
1998PM Proof	Est. 250				Value: 500	

KM# 908b 50 PENCE
8.0000 g., 0.9167 Gold .2358 oz. AGW, 27.3 mm. **Ruler:** Elizabeth II **Subject:** Christmas 1998 **Obv:** Head with tiara right **Obv. Designer:** Ian Rank-Broadley **Rev:** Kitchen scene **Shape:** 7-sided

Date	Mintage	F	VF	XF	Unc	BU
1998 Proof	250				Value: 500	

KM# 993b 50 PENCE
8.0000 g., 0.9160 Gold .2356 oz. AGW, 27.3 mm. **Ruler:** Elizabeth II **Obv:** Head with tiara right **Obv. Designer:** Rank-Broadley **Rev:** Motorcyclist within sprigs **Shape:** 7-sided

Date	Mintage	F	VF	XF	Unc	BU
1999 Proof	Est. 250				Value: 500	

KM# 1011b 50 PENCE
8.0000 g., 0.9160 Gold .2356 oz. AGW, 27.3 mm. **Ruler:** Elizabeth II **Subject:** Christmas 1999 **Obv:** Head with tiara right **Obv. Designer:** Rank-Broadley. **Rev:** Tree decorating scene **Shape:** 7-sided

Date	Mintage	F	VF	XF	Unc	BU
1999 Proof	Est. 250				Value: 500	

KM# 1050b 50 PENCE
8.0000 g., 0.9160 Gold .2356 oz. AGW, 27.3 mm. **Ruler:** Elizabeth II **Obv:** Head with tiara right **Obv. Designer:** Ian Rank-Broadley **Rev:** Seated figure at desk **Edge:** Plain **Shape:** 7-sided

Date	Mintage	F	VF	XF	Unc	BU
2000 Proof	250				Value: 500	

KM# 1105b 50 PENCE
8.0000 g., 0.9167 Gold .2358 oz. AGW, 27.3 mm. **Ruler:** Elizabeth II **Obv:** Head with tiara right **Rev:** Postman and children **Edge:** Plain **Shape:** 7-sided

Date	Mintage	F	VF	XF	Unc	BU
2001 Proof	250				Value: 500	

KM# 1160b 50 PENCE
8.0000 g., 0.9167 Gold 0.2358 oz. AGW, 27.3 mm. **Ruler:** Elizabeth II **Subject:** Christmas **Obv:** Head with tiara right **Rev:** Scrooge in bed **Edge:** Plain **Shape:** 7-sided

Date	Mintage	F	VF	XF	Unc	BU
2002PM Proof	250				Value: 500	

KM# 1183b 50 PENCE
8.0000 g., 0.9167 Gold 0.2358 oz. AGW, 27.3 mm. **Ruler:** Elizabeth II **Obv:** Head with tiara right **Rev:** "The Snowman and James" **Edge:** Plain **Shape:** 7-sided

Date	Mintage	F	VF	XF	Unc	BU
2003PM Proof	100				Value: 500	

KM# 1262b 50 PENCE
15.4074 g., 0.9167 Gold 0.4541 oz. AGW, 27.3 mm. **Ruler:** Elizabeth II **Subject:** Christmas **Obv:** Head with tiara right **Rev:** Laxey Wheel **Edge:** Plain **Shape:** 7-sided

Date	Mintage	F	VF	XF	Unc	BU
2004PM Proof	250				Value: 625	

ISLE OF MAN

KM# 15 1/2 SOVEREIGN (1/2 Pound)
3.9940 g., 0.9170 Gold .1177 oz. AGW **Ruler:** Elizabeth II
Subject: 200th Anniversary of Acquisition **Obv:** Crowned bust right **Obv. Designer:** T. H. Paget **Rev:** Triskeles on shield within rope wreath **Rev. Designer:** John Nicholson

Date	Mintage	F	VF	XF	Unc	BU
1965	1,500	—	—	—	85.00	95.00

KM# 15a 1/2 SOVEREIGN (1/2 Pound)
4.0000 g., 0.9800 Gold .1260 oz. AGW **Ruler:** Elizabeth II
Subject: 200th Anniversary of Acquisition **Obv:** Crowned bust right **Obv. Designer:** T. H. Paget **Rev:** Triskeles on shield within rope wreath **Rev. Designer:** John Nicholson

Date	Mintage	F	VF	XF	Unc	BU
1965 Proof	1,000	Value: 95.00				

KM# 26 1/2 SOVEREIGN (1/2 Pound)
3.9813 g., 0.9170 Gold .1173 oz. AGW **Ruler:** Elizabeth II **Obv:** Young bust right **Obv. Designer:** Arnold Machin **Rev:** Armored equestrian

Date	Mintage	F	VF	XF	Unc	BU
1973 A	14,000	—	—	—	85.00	95.00
1973 Proof	1,250	Value: 100				
1974 A	6,566	—	—	—	85.00	95.00
1974 B	Inc. above	—	—	—	85.00	95.00
1974 Proof	2,500	Value: 100				
1975 A	1,956	—	—	—	85.00	95.00
1975 B	Inc. above	—	—	—	85.00	95.00
1975 Proof	—	Value: 100				
1976 A	2,558	—	—	—	85.00	95.00
1976 B	Inc. above	—	—	—	85.00	95.00
1976 Proof	—	Value: 100				
1977 A	—	—	—	—	85.00	95.00
1977 B	—	—	—	—	85.00	95.00
1977 Proof	1,250	Value: 100				
1978 Proof	1,250	Value: 100				
1979 (t) A	8,000	—	—	—	85.00	95.00
1979 (t) B	Inc. above	—	—	—	85.00	95.00
1979 (t) Proof	30,000	Value: 100				
1980 A	—	—	—	—	—	—
1980 B	—	—	—	—	—	—
1980 (m) Proof	7,500	Value: 100				
1980 (v) Proof	—	Value: 100				
1982 (b)	40,000	—	—	—	85.00	95.00
1982 (b) Proof	30,000	Value: 100				

KM# 85 1/2 SOVEREIGN (1/2 Pound)
3.9813 g., 0.9170 Gold .1173 oz. AGW **Ruler:** Elizabeth II
Subject: Wedding of Prince Charles and Lady Diana **Obv:** Young bust right **Obv. Designer:** Arnold Machin **Rev:** Portraits of Royal Couple, joined shields

Date	Mintage	F	VF	XF	Unc	BU
1981 Proof	30,000	Value: 100				

KM# 260 1/2 SOVEREIGN (1/2 Pound)
3.9813 g., 0.9170 Gold .1173 oz. AGW **Ruler:** Elizabeth II **Obv:** Young bust right **Obv. Designer:** Arnold Machin **Rev:** Four crowned shields

Date	Mintage	F	VF	XF	Unc	BU
1984	20	—	—	—	200	210
1984 Proof	20	Value: 220				

KM# 264 1/2 SOVEREIGN (1/2 Pound)
3.9813 g., 0.9170 Gold .1173 oz. AGW **Ruler:** Elizabeth II **Obv:** Crowned head right **Obv. Designer:** Raphael Maklouf **Rev:** Four crowned shields

Date	Mintage	F	VF	XF	Unc	BU
1988 Proof	5,879	Value: 90.00				

KM# 16 SOVEREIGN (Pound)
7.9881 g., 0.9170 Gold .2355 oz. AGW **Ruler:** Elizabeth II
Subject: 200th Anniversary of Acquisition **Obv:** Crowned bust right **Obv. Designer:** T. H. Paget **Rev:** Triskeles on shield within rope wreath **Rev. Designer:** John Nicholson

Date	Mintage	F	VF	XF	Unc	BU
1965	2,000	—	—	—	170	180

KM# 16a SOVEREIGN (Pound)
8.0000 g., 0.9800 Gold .2520 oz. AGW **Ruler:** Elizabeth II
Subject: 200th Anniversary of Acquisition **Obv:** Crowned bust right **Obv. Designer:** T. H. Paget **Rev:** Triskeles on shield within rope wreath **Rev. Designer:** John Nicholson

Date	Mintage	F	VF	XF	Unc	BU
1965 Proof	1,000	Value: 185				

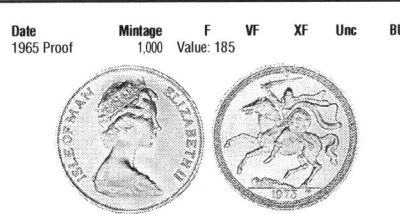

KM# 27 SOVEREIGN (Pound)
7.9627 g., 0.9170 Gold .2347 oz. AGW **Ruler:** Elizabeth II **Obv:** Young bust right **Obv. Designer:** Arnold Machin **Rev:** Armored equestrian

Date	Mintage	F	VF	XF	Unc	BU
1973 A	40,000	—	—	—	165	175
1973 B	Inc. above	—	—	—	165	175
1973 C	Inc. above	—	—	—	165	175
1973 Proof	1,250	Value: 180				
1974 A	8,604	—	—	—	165	175
1974 B	Inc. above	—	—	—	165	175
1974 C	Inc. above	—	—	—	165	175
1974 Proof	2,500	Value: 180				
1975 A	956	—	—	—	165	175
1975 B	Inc. above	—	—	—	165	175
1975 C	Inc. above	—	—	—	165	175
1975 Proof	—	Value: 180				
1976 A	1,238	—	—	—	165	175
1976 B	Inc. above	—	—	—	165	175
1976 C	Inc. above	—	—	—	165	175
1976 Proof	—	Value: 180				
1977 A	—	—	—	—	165	175
1977 B	—	—	—	—	165	175
1977 C	—	—	—	—	165	175
1977 Proof	1,250	Value: 180				
1978 Proof	1,250	Value: 180				
1979 B	—	—	—	—	165	175
1979 C	—	—	—	—	165	175
1979 AA (t)	10,000	—	—	—	165	175
1979 D (t)	—	—	—	—	165	175
1979 (t) Proof	30,000	Value: 180				
1980 D (m) Proof	5,000	Value: 180				
1980 (v) Proof	—	Value: 180				
1982 (b)	30,000	—	—	—	165	175
1982 (b) Proof	40,000	Value: 180				

KM# 44b SOVEREIGN (Pound)
9.0000 g., 0.9500 Platinum .2749 oz. APW **Ruler:** Elizabeth II **Obv:** Young bust right **Obv. Designer:** Arnold Machin **Rev:** Triskeles flanked by designs

Date	Mintage	F	VF	XF	Unc	BU
1978 Proof	1,000	Value: 375				
1979 Proof	—	Value: 375				
1980 Proof	1,000	Value: 375				
1982 (b) Proof	100	Value: 400				

KM# 44c SOVEREIGN (Pound)
7.9627 g., 0.9170 Gold .2347 oz. AGW **Ruler:** Elizabeth II **Obv:** Young bust right **Obv. Designer:** Arnold Machin **Rev:** Triskeles flanked by designs

Date	Mintage	F	VF	XF	Unc	BU
1980 Proof	5,000	Value: 165				
1980 T.T. Proof	300	Value: 225				
1982 (b)	250	—	—	—	225	—
1982 (b) Proof	750	Value: 200				

KM# 86 SOVEREIGN (Pound)
7.9627 g., 0.9170 Gold .2347 oz. AGW **Ruler:** Elizabeth II
Subject: Wedding of Prince Charles and Lady Diana **Obv:** Young bust right **Obv. Designer:** Arnold Machin **Rev:** Portraits of Royal Couple, joined shields

Date	Mintage	F	VF	XF	Unc	BU
1981 Proof	40,000	Value: 165				

KM# 109b SOVEREIGN (Pound)
9.5000 g., 0.3740 Gold .1142 oz. AGW, 22.5 mm. **Ruler:** Elizabeth II **Obv:** Young bust right **Obv. Designer:** Arnold Machin **Rev:** City view with ships within circle **Rev. Designer:** Leslie Lindsay

Date	Mintage	F	VF	XF	Unc	BU
1983 Proof	—	Value: 85.00				

KM# 109c SOVEREIGN (Pound)
7.9627 g., 0.9170 Gold .2347 oz. AGW, 22.5 mm. **Ruler:** Elizabeth II **Obv:** Young bust right **Obv. Designer:** Arnold Machin **Rev:** City view with ships within circle **Rev. Designer:** Leslie Lindsay

Date	Mintage	F	VF	XF	Unc	BU
1983 Proof	—	Value: 170				

KM# 109d SOVEREIGN (Pound)
9.0000 g., 0.9500 Platinum .2749 oz. APW, 22.5 mm. **Ruler:** Elizabeth II **Obv:** Young bust right **Obv. Designer:** Arnold Machin **Rev:** City view with ships within circle **Rev. Designer:** Leslie Lindsay

Date	Mintage	F	VF	XF	Unc	BU
1983 Proof	—	Value: 375				

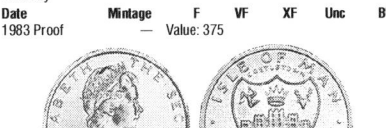

KM# 128b SOVEREIGN (Pound)
9.5000 g., 0.3740 Gold .1142 oz. AGW, 22.5 mm. **Ruler:** Elizabeth II **Obv:** Young bust right **Obv. Designer:** Arnold Machin **Rev:** Crown flanked by designs above city view within shield **Rev. Designer:** Leslie Lindsay

Date	Mintage	F	VF	XF	Unc	BU
1984 Proof	4,950	Value: 85.00				

KM# 128c SOVEREIGN (Pound)
7.9627 g., 0.9170 Gold .2347 oz. AGW, 22.5 mm. **Ruler:** Elizabeth II **Obv:** Young bust right **Obv. Designer:** Arnold Machin **Rev:** Crown flanked by designs above city view within shield **Rev. Designer:** Leslie Lindsay

Date	Mintage	F	VF	XF	Unc	BU
1984 Proof	950	Value: 170				

KM# 128d SOVEREIGN (Pound)
9.0000 g., 0.9500 Platinum .2749 oz. APW, 22.5 mm. **Ruler:** Elizabeth II **Obv:** Young bust right **Obv. Designer:** Arnold Machin **Rev:** Crown flanked by designs above city view within shield **Rev. Designer:** Leslie Lindsay

Date	Mintage	F	VF	XF	Unc	BU
1984 Proof	—	Value: 375				

KM# 261 SOVEREIGN (Pound)
7.9627 g., 0.9170 Gold .2347 oz. AGW, 22.5 mm. **Ruler:** Elizabeth II **Obv:** Young bust right **Obv. Designer:** Arnold Machin **Rev:** Four crowned shields

Date	Mintage	F	VF	XF	Unc	BU
1984	20	—	—	—	350	375
1984 Proof	20	Value: 450				

KM# 135b SOVEREIGN (Pound)
7.9627 g., 0.9170 Gold .2347 oz. AGW, 22.5 mm. **Ruler:** Elizabeth II **Obv:** Young bust right **Obv. Designer:** Arnold Machin **Rev:** Shield **Rev. Designer:** Leslie Lindsay

Date	Mintage	F	VF	XF	Unc	BU
1985 Proof	Est. 150	Value: 185				

KM# 135c SOVEREIGN (Pound)
9.0000 g., 0.9500 Platinum .2749 oz. APW, 22.5 mm. **Ruler:** Elizabeth II **Obv:** Young bust right **Obv. Designer:** Arnold Machin **Rev:** Shield **Rev. Designer:** Leslie Lindsay

Date	Mintage	F	VF	XF	Unc	BU
1985 Proof	Est. 550	Value: 380				

KM# 136b SOVEREIGN (Pound)
7.9627 g., 0.9170 Gold .2347 oz. AGW, 22.5 mm. **Ruler:** Elizabeth II **Obv:** Crowned head right **Obv. Designer:** Raphael Maklouf **Rev:** Shield **Rev. Designer:** Leslie Lindsay

Date	Mintage	F	VF	XF	Unc	BU
1986 Proof	—	Value: 170				

ISLE OF MAN

KM# 136c SOVEREIGN (Pound)
9.0000 g., 0.9500 Platinum .2749 oz. APW, 22.5 mm. **Ruler:** Elizabeth II **Obv:** Crowned head right **Obv. Designer:** Raphael Maklouf **Rev:** Shield **Rev. Designer:** Leslie Lindsay

Date	Mintage	F	VF	XF	Unc	BU
1986 Proof	—	Value: 380				

KM# 265 SOVEREIGN (Pound)
7.9627 g., 0.9170 Gold .2347 oz. AGW, 22.5 mm. **Ruler:** Elizabeth II **Obv:** Crowned head right **Obv. Designer:** Raphael Maklouf **Rev:** Four crowned shields

Date	Mintage	F	VF	XF	Unc	BU
1988 Proof	1,600	Value: 170				
1988	5,876	—	—	—	165	—

KM# 655b SOVEREIGN (Pound)
9.5000 g., 0.9160 Gold .2798 oz. AGW, 22.5 mm. **Ruler:** Elizabeth II **Subject:** Douglas Centenary **Obv:** Crowned head right **Obv. Designer:** Raphael Maklouf **Rev:** City arms **Rev. Designer:** Leslie Lindsay

Date	Mintage	F	VF	XF	Unc	BU
1996 Proof	Est. 10,000	Value: 200				

KM# 28 2 POUNDS
15.9253 g., 0.9170 Gold .4695 oz. AGW **Ruler:** Elizabeth II **Obv:** Young bust right **Obv. Designer:** Arnold Machin **Rev:** Armored equestrian

Date	Mintage	F	VF	XF	Unc	BU
1973 A	3,612	—	—	—	335	345
1973 Proof	1,250	Value: 360				
1974 A	1,257	—	—	—	335	345
1974 B	Inc. above	—	—	—	335	345
1974 Proof	2,500	Value: 360				
1975 A	456	—	—	—	335	345
1975 B	Inc. above	—	—	—	335	345
1975 Proof	—	Value: 360				
1976 A	578	—	—	—	335	345
1976 B	Inc. above	—	—	—	335	345
1976 Proof	—	Value: 360				
1977 A	—	—	—	—	335	345
1977 B	Inc. above	—	—	—	335	345
1977 Proof	1,250	Value: 360				
1978 Proof	1,250	Value: 360				
1979 (t) A	2,000	—	—	—	335	345
1979 (t) B	Inc. above	—	—	—	335	345
1979 (t) Proof	30,000	Value: 360				
1980 (m) Proof	2,000	Value: 360				
1982 (b)	15,000	—	—	—	335	345
1982 (b) Proof	5,000	Value: 360				

KM# 87 2 POUNDS
15.9253 g., 0.9170 Gold .4695 oz. AGW **Ruler:** Elizabeth II **Subject:** Wedding of Prince Charles and Lady Diana **Obv:** Young bust right **Obv. Designer:** Arnold Machin **Rev:** Portraits of Royal Couple, joined shields

Date	Mintage	F	VF	XF	Unc	BU
1981 Proof	5,000	Value: 335				

KM# 257b 2 POUNDS
15.9400 g., 0.9170 Gold .4730 oz. AGW **Ruler:** Elizabeth II **Obv:** Crowned head right **Obv. Designer:** Raphael Maklouf **Rev:** Blimp

Date	Mintage	F	VF	XF	Unc	BU
1989	—	—	—	—	—	—

Note: Reported, not confirmed

KM# 257c 2 POUNDS
18.0000 g., 0.9500 Platinum .5498 oz. APW **Ruler:** Elizabeth II **Obv:** Crowned head right **Obv. Designer:** Raphael Maklouf **Rev:** Blimp **Note:** Reported, not confirmed; most recalled by government; few actually issued

Date	Mintage	F	VF	XF	Unc	BU
1989	—	—	—	—	—	—

Note: Reported, not confirmed

KM# 17 5 POUNDS
39.9403 g., 0.9170 Gold 1.1776 oz. AGW **Ruler:** Elizabeth II **Subject:** 200th Anniversary of Acquisition **Obv:** Crowned bust right **Obv. Designer:** T. H. Paget **Rev:** Triskeles on shield within rope wreath **Rev. Designer:** John Nicholson

Date	Mintage	F	VF	XF	Unc	BU
1965	500	—	—	—	825	845

KM# 17a 5 POUNDS
39.9500 g., 0.9800 Gold 1.2588 oz. AGW **Ruler:** Elizabeth II **Subject:** 200th Anniversary of Acquisition **Obv:** Crowned bust right **Obv. Designer:** T. H. Paget **Rev:** Triskeles on shield within rope wreath **Rev. Designer:** John Nicholson

Date	Mintage	F	VF	XF	Unc	BU
1965 Proof	1,000	Value: 900				

KM# 29 5 POUNDS
39.8134 g., 0.9170 Gold 1.1739 oz. AGW **Ruler:** Elizabeth II **Obv:** Young bust right **Obv. Designer:** Arnold Machin **Rev:** Rearing armored equestrian

Date	Mintage	F	VF	XF	Unc	BU
1973 A	3,035	—	—	—	810	835
1973 B	Inc. above	—	—	—	810	835
1973 C	Inc. above	—	—	—	810	835
1973 D	Inc. above	—	—	—	810	835
1973 E	Inc. above	—	—	—	810	835
1973 Proof	1,250	Value: 850				
1974 A	481	—	—	—	810	835
1974 B	Inc. above	—	—	—	810	835
1974 Proof	2,500	Value: 850				
1975 A	306	—	—	—	810	835
1975 B	Inc. above	—	—	—	810	835
1975 Proof	—	Value: 850				
1976 A	370	—	—	—	810	835
1976 B	Inc. above	—	—	—	810	835
1976 Proof	—	Value: 850				
1977 A	—	—	—	—	810	835
1977 B	Inc. above	—	—	—	810	835
1977 Proof	1,250	Value: 850				
1978 Proof	1,250	Value: 850				
1979 (t) A	1,000	—	—	—	810	835
1979 (t) B	Inc. above	—	—	—	810	835
1979 (t) Proof	1,000	Value: 850				
1980 (m)	250	—	—	—	810	835
1982 (b)	10,000	—	—	—	810	835
1982 (b) Proof	500	Value: 850				

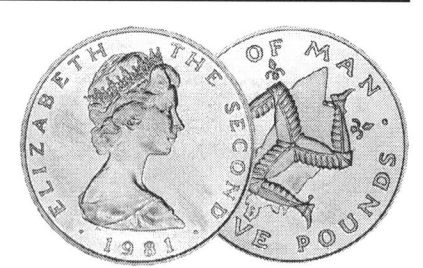

KM# 88b 5 POUNDS
39.9000 g., 0.9170 Gold 1.1764 oz. AGW, 36.5 mm. **Ruler:** Elizabeth II **Obv:** Young bust right **Obv. Designer:** Arnold Machin **Rev:** Triskeles on map **Rev. Designer:** Leslie Lindsay

Date	Mintage	F	VF	XF	Unc	BU
1981 Proof	1,000	Value: 840				
1982 (b) Proof	250	Value: 840				
1982 (b) Proof	750	Value: 840				
1983 Proof	—	Value: 840				

KM# 88c 5 POUNDS
45.5000 g., 0.9500 Platinum 1.3898 oz. APW, 36.5 mm. **Ruler:** Elizabeth II **Obv:** Young bust right **Obv. Designer:** Arnold Machin **Rev:** Triskeles on map **Rev. Designer:** Leslie Lindsay

Date	Mintage	F	VF	XF	Unc	BU
1981 Proof	500	Value: 1,850				
1982 (b) Proof	100	Value: 1,850				
1983 Proof	—	Value: 1,850				

KM# 89 5 POUNDS
39.8134 g., 0.9170 Gold 1.1739 oz. AGW **Ruler:** Elizabeth II **Subject:** Wedding of Prince Charles and Lady Diana **Obv:** Young bust right **Obv. Designer:** Arnold Machin **Rev:** Portraits of Royal Couple, joined shields

Date	Mintage	F	VF	XF	Unc	BU
1981 Proof	1,000	Value: 840				

KM# 134b 5 POUNDS
39.9000 g., 0.9170 Gold 1.1759 oz. AGW, 36.5 mm. **Ruler:** Elizabeth II **Subject:** Quincentenary of the College of Arms **Obv:** Young bust right **Obv. Designer:** Arnold Machin **Rev:** Mounted knight in armor with sword, facing right within circle **Rev. Designer:** Leslie Lindsay

Date	Mintage	F	VF	XF	Unc	BU
1984 Proof	150	Value: 845				

KM# 134c 5 POUNDS
45.5000 g., 0.9500 Platinum 1.3898 oz. APW, 36.5 mm. **Ruler:** Elizabeth II **Subject:** Quincentenary of the College of Arms **Obv:** Young bust right **Obv. Designer:** Arnold Machin **Rev:** Mounted knight in armor with sword facing right within circle **Rev. Designer:** Leslie Lindsay

Date	Mintage	F	VF	XF	Unc	BU
1984 Proof	—	Value: 1,850				

KM# 263 5 POUNDS
39.8300 g., 0.9170 Gold 1.1740 oz. AGW **Ruler:** Elizabeth II **Obv:** Young bust right **Obv. Designer:** Arnold Machin **Rev:** Four crowned shields

Date	Mintage	F	VF	XF	Unc	BU
1984	20	—	—	—	1,250	1,350
1984 Proof	20	Value: 1,650				

KM# 150b 5 POUNDS
39.9000 g., 0.9170 Gold 1.1759 oz. AGW, 36.5 mm. **Ruler:** Elizabeth II **Obv:** Crowned head right **Obv. Designer:** Raphael Maklouf **Rev:** Mounted knight in armor with sword facing right within circle **Rev. Designer:** Leslie Lindsay

Date	Mintage	F	VF	XF	Unc	BU
1985 Proof	Est. 150	Value: 845				

ISLE OF MAN

KM# 150c 5 POUNDS
45.5000 g., 0.9500 Platinum 1.3898 oz. APW, 36.5 mm. **Ruler:** Elizabeth II **Obv:** Crowned head right **Obv. Designer:** Raphael Maklouf **Rev:** Mounted knight in armor with sword facing right within circle **Rev. Designer:** Leslie Lindsay

Date	Mintage	F	VF	XF	Unc	BU
1985 Proof	Est. 100			Value: 1,850		

KM# 466b 5 POUNDS
39.8300 g., 0.9170 Gold 1.1759 oz. AGW, 36.5 mm. **Ruler:** Elizabeth II **Subject:** 50th Anniversary - End of World War II **Obv:** Crowned head right **Obv. Designer:** Raphael Maklouf **Rev:** Bust facing giving peace sign

Date	Mintage	F	VF	XF	Unc	BU
1995 Proof	Est. 850			Value: 850		

KM# 587b 5 POUNDS
39.0830 g., 0.9160 Gold 1.1510 oz. AGW, 36.5 mm. **Ruler:** Elizabeth II **Subject:** European Soccer Championships **Obv:** Crowned head right **Obv. Designer:** Raphael Maklouf **Rev:** Soccer players

Date	Mintage	F	VF	XF	Unc	BU
1996 Proof	Est. 850			Value: 900		

KM# 769b 5 POUNDS
39.8300 g., 0.9167 Gold 1.1740 oz. AGW, 36.5 mm. **Ruler:** Elizabeth II **Subject:** 50th Anniversary - Queen Elizabeth and Prince Philip **Obv:** Crowned head right **Obv. Designer:** Raphael Maklouf **Rev:** Current portrait of Queen Elizabeth and Prince Philip

Date	Mintage	F	VF	XF	Unc	BU
1997 Proof	Est. 850			Value: 900		

KM# 912b 5 POUNDS
39.8300 g., 0.9167 Gold 1.1740 oz. AGW, 36.5 mm. **Ruler:** Elizabeth II **Subject:** 50th Birthday - Prince Charles **Obv:** Head with tiara right **Obv. Designer:** Ian Rank-Broadley **Rev:** Portrait of Prince Charles

Date	Mintage	F	VF	XF	Unc	BU
1998 Proof	Est. 850			Value: 885		

KM# 943b 5 POUNDS
39.8300 g., 0.9167 Gold 1.1739 oz. AGW, 36.5 mm. **Ruler:** Elizabeth II **Subject:** 175th Anniversary of the RNLI **Obv:** Head with tiara right **Obv. Designer:** Ian Rank-Broadley **Rev:** Lifeboat with flag

Date	Mintage	F	VF	XF	Unc	BU
1999 Proof	850			Value: 885		

KM# 347 50 POUNDS
6.2200 g., 0.9990 Gold .2000 oz. AGW **Ruler:** Elizabeth II **Subject:** World Champion - Nigel Mansell **Obv:** Crowned bust right **Obv. Designer:** Raphael Maklouf **Rev:** Two racecars

Date	Mintage	F	VF	XF	Unc	BU
1993 Proof	Est. 5,000			Value: 150		

KM# 401 50 POUNDS
6.2200 g., 0.9990 Gold .2000 oz. AGW **Ruler:** Elizabeth II **Subject:** Indycar World Series Champion - Nigel Mansell **Obv:** Crowned bust right **Obv. Designer:** Raphael Maklouf **Rev:** Two racecars

Date	Mintage	F	VF	XF	Unc	BU
1994 Proof	Est. 5,000			Value: 150		

KM# 1295 1/5 CROWN
6.2200 g., 0.9999 Gold 0.2 oz. AGW, 22 mm. **Ruler:** Elizabeth II **Subject:** Battles that Changed the World **Obv:** Elizabeth II **Rev:** Trojan War scene **Edge:** Reeded

Date	Mintage	F	VF	XF	Unc	BU
2006PM Proof	5,000			Value: 175		

KM# 1297 1/5 CROWN
6.2200 g., 0.9999 Gold 0.2 oz. AGW, 22 mm. **Ruler:** Elizabeth II **Subject:** Battles that Changed the World **Obv:** Elizabeth II **Rev:** Battle of Arbela scene **Edge:** Reeded

Date	Mintage	F	VF	XF	Unc	BU
2006PM Proof	5,000			Value: 175		

KM# 1299 1/5 CROWN
6.2200 g., 0.9999 Gold 0.2 oz. AGW, 22 mm. **Ruler:** Elizabeth II **Subject:** Battles that Changed the World **Obv:** Elizabeth II **Rev:** Battle of Thapsus scene **Edge:** Reeded

Date	Mintage	F	VF	XF	Unc	BU
2006PM Proof	5,000			Value: 175		

KM# 1301 1/5 CROWN
6.2200 g., 0.9999 Gold 0.2 oz. AGW, 22 mm. **Ruler:** Elizabeth II **Subject:** Battles that Changed the World **Obv:** Elizabeth II **Rev:** Battle of Cologne scene **Edge:** Reeded

Date	Mintage	F	VF	XF	Unc	BU
2006PM Proof	5,000			Value: 175		

KM# 1303 1/5 CROWN
6.2200 g., 0.9999 Gold 0.2 oz. AGW, 22 mm. **Ruler:** Elizabeth II **Subject:** Battles that Changed the World **Obv:** Elizabeth II **Rev:** Siege of Valencia scene **Edge:** Reeded

Date	Mintage	F	VF	XF	Unc	BU
2006PM Proof	5,000			Value: 175		

KM# 1305 1/5 CROWN
6.2200 g., 0.9999 Gold 0.2 oz. AGW, 22 mm. **Ruler:** Elizabeth II **Subject:** Battles that Changed the World **Obv:** Elizabeth II **Rev:** Battle of Agincourt scene **Edge:** Reeded

Date	Mintage	F	VF	XF	Unc	BU
2006PM Proof	5,000			Value: 175		

CROWN SERIES
Pobjoy Mint Key
  (M) MATTE - Normal circulation strike
  (U) SPECIAL UNCIRCULATED - Polished or prooflike in appearance, slightly frosted features.
  (P) PROOF - The highest quality obtainable having mirror-like fields and frosted features.

KM# 1129 1/32 CROWN
1.0000 g., 0.9720 Gold 0.0313 oz. AGW, 9.8 mm. **Ruler:** Elizabeth II **Subject:** Queen's Golden Jubilee **Obv:** Head with tiara right **Obv. Designer:** Ian Rank-Broadley **Rev:** Seated crowned Queen holding sceptre at her coronation **Edge:** Plain

Date	Mintage	F	VF	XF	Unc	BU
2002 Prooflike	—	—	—	—	35.00	

KM# 235 1/25 CROWN
1.2441 g., 0.9990 Gold .0400 oz. AGW, 13.9 mm. **Ruler:** Elizabeth II **Obv:** Crowned bust right **Obv. Designer:** Raphael Maklouf **Rev:** Manx cat

Date	Mintage	F	VF	XF	Unc	BU
1988	40,000	—	—	—	30.00	—
1988 Proof	5,000			Value: 35.00		

KM# 252 1/25 CROWN
1.2441 g., 0.9990 Gold .0400 oz. AGW, 13.9 mm. **Ruler:** Elizabeth II **Obv:** Crowned bust right **Obv. Designer:** Raphael Maklouf **Rev:** Persian cat

Date	Mintage	F	VF	XF	Unc	BU
1989	—	—	—	—	40.00	—
1989 Proof	—			Value: 45.00		

KM# 467 1/25 CROWN
1.2441 g., 0.9995 Platinum .0400 oz. APW, 13.9 mm. **Ruler:** Elizabeth II **Obv:** Crowned bust right **Obv. Designer:** Raphael Maklouf **Rev:** Persian cat

Date	Mintage	F	VF	XF	Unc	BU
1989	—	—	—	—	50.00	—
1989 Proof	—			Value: 55.00		

KM# 277 1/25 CROWN
1.2441 g., 0.9990 Gold .0400 oz. AGW, 13.9 mm. **Ruler:** Elizabeth II **Obv:** Crowned bust right **Obv. Designer:** Raphael Maklouf **Rev:** Alley cat

Date	Mintage	F	VF	XF	Unc	BU
1990	—	—	—	—	50.00	—
1990 Proof	—			Value: 55.00		

KM# 294 1/25 CROWN
1.2441 g., 0.9990 Gold .0400 oz. AGW, 13.9 mm. **Ruler:** Elizabeth II **Obv:** Crowned bust right **Obv. Designer:** Raphael Maklouf **Rev:** Norwegian cat

Date	Mintage	F	VF	XF	Unc	BU
1991	—	—	—	—	50.00	—
1991 Proof	—			Value: 55.00		

KM# 322 1/25 CROWN
1.2441 g., 0.9990 Gold .0400 oz. AGW, 13.9 mm. **Ruler:** Elizabeth II **Subject:** America's Cup **Obv:** Crowned bust right **Obv. Designer:** Raphael Maklouf **Rev:** Cameo of "Star of India" above two modern sailboats

Date	Mintage	F	VF	XF	Unc	BU
1992 Prooflike	50,000	—	—	—	50.00	—

KM# 328 1/25 CROWN
1.2441 g., 0.9990 Gold .0400 oz. AGW, 13.9 mm. **Ruler:** Elizabeth II **Obv:** Crowned bust right **Obv. Designer:** Raphael Maklouf **Rev:** Siamese cat

Date	Mintage	F	VF	XF	Unc	BU
1992	—	—	—	—	45.00	—
1992 Proof	—			Value: 47.00		

KM# 338 1/25 CROWN
1.2441 g., 0.9990 Gold .0400 oz. AGW, 13.9 mm. **Ruler:** Elizabeth II **Subject:** Year of the Cockerel **Obv:** Crowned bust right **Obv. Designer:** Raphael Maklouf **Rev:** Cockerel within circle **Rev. Designer:** Barry Stanton

398 ISLE OF MAN

Date	Mintage	F	VF	XF	Unc	BU
1993 Proof	Est. 25,000	Value: 40.00				

KM# 349 1/25 CROWN

1.2441 g., 0.9990 Gold .0400 oz. AGW, 13.9 mm. **Ruler:** Elizabeth II **Obv:** Crowned bust right **Obv. Designer:** Raphael Maklouf **Rev:** Maine Coon cat

Date	Mintage	F	VF	XF	Unc	BU
1993	—	—	—	—	45.00	—
1993 Proof	—	Value: 47.00				

KM# 376 1/25 CROWN

1.2441 g., 0.9990 Gold .0400 oz. AGW, 13.9 mm. **Ruler:** Elizabeth II **Obv:** Crowned bust right **Obv. Designer:** Raphael Maklouf **Rev:** Japanese Bobtail cat

Date	Mintage	F	VF	XF	Unc	BU
1994	—	—	—	—	40.00	—
1994 Proof	—	Value: 42.00				

KM# 402 1/25 CROWN

1.2441 g., 0.9990 Gold .0400 oz. AGW, 13.9 mm. **Ruler:** Elizabeth II **Obv:** Crowned bust right **Obv. Designer:** Raphael Maklouf **Rev:** Pekingese

Date	Mintage	F	VF	XF	Unc	BU
1994 Proof	Est. 25,000	Value: 50.00				

KM# 473 1/25 CROWN

1.2441 g., 0.9995 Platinum .0400 oz. APW, 13.9 mm. **Ruler:** Elizabeth II **Obv:** Crowned bust right **Obv. Designer:** Raphael Maklouf **Rev:** Japanese Bobtail cat

Date	Mintage	F	VF	XF	Unc	BU
1994	—	—	—	—	65.00	—
1994 Proof	—	Value: 70.00				

KM# 442 1/25 CROWN

1.2441 g., 0.9990 Gold .0400 oz. AGW, 13.9 mm. **Ruler:** Elizabeth II **Obv:** Crowned bust right **Obv. Designer:** Raphael Maklouf **Rev:** Turkish cat

Date	Mintage	F	VF	XF	Unc	BU
1995 U	—	—	—	—	40.00	—
1995 Proof	—	Value: 42.00				

KM# 449 1/25 CROWN

1.2441 g., 0.9990 Gold .0400 oz. AGW, 13.9 mm. **Ruler:** Elizabeth II **Subject:** Year of the Pig **Obv:** Crowned bust right **Obv. Designer:** Raphael Maklouf **Rev:** Sow with piglets

Date	Mintage	F	VF	XF	Unc	BU
1995 Proof	Est. 25,000	Value: 45.00				

KM# 478 1/25 CROWN

1.2441 g., 0.9995 Platinum .0400 oz. APW, 13.9 mm. **Ruler:** Elizabeth II **Obv:** Crowned bust right **Obv. Designer:** Raphael Maklouf **Rev:** Turkish cat

Date	Mintage	F	VF	XF	Unc	BU
1995	—	—	—	—	55.00	—
1995 Proof	—	Value: 58.00				

KM# 597 1/25 CROWN

1.2441 g., 0.9990 Gold .0400 oz. AGW, 13.9 mm. **Ruler:** Elizabeth II **Series:** Flower Fairies **Obv:** Crowned bust right **Obv. Designer:** Raphael Maklouf **Rev:** Orchis **Rev. Designer:** Cecily Mary Barker

Date	Mintage	F	VF	XF	Unc	BU
1996 Proof	Est. 25,000	Value: 40.00				

KM# 598 1/25 CROWN

1.2441 g., 0.9990 Gold .0400 oz. AGW, 13.9 mm. **Ruler:** Elizabeth II **Series:** Flower Fairies **Obv:** Crowned bust right **Obv. Designer:** Raphael Maklouf **Rev:** Rose **Rev. Designer:** Cecily Mary Barker

Date	Mintage	F	VF	XF	Unc	BU
1996 Proof	Est. 25,000	Value: 40.00				

KM# 599 1/25 CROWN

1.2441 g., 0.9990 Gold .0400 oz. AGW, 13.9 mm. **Ruler:** Elizabeth II **Series:** Flower Fairies **Obv:** Crowned bust right **Obv. Designer:** Raphael Maklouf **Rev:** Fuchsia **Rev. Designer:** Cecily Mary Barker

Date	Mintage	F	VF	XF	Unc	BU
1996 Proof	Est. 25,000	Value: 40.00				

KM# 600 1/25 CROWN

1.2441 g., 0.9990 Gold .0400 oz. AGW, 13.9 mm. **Ruler:** Elizabeth II **Series:** Flower Fairies **Obv:** Crowned bust right **Obv. Designer:** Raphael Maklouf **Rev:** Pinks **Rev. Designer:** Cecily Mary Barker

Date	Mintage	F	VF	XF	Unc	BU
1996 Proof	Est. 25,000	Value: 40.00				

KM# 613 1/25 CROWN

1.2441 g., 0.9990 Gold .0400 oz. AGW, 13.9 mm. **Ruler:** Elizabeth II **Obv:** Crowned bust right **Obv. Designer:** Raphael Maklouf **Rev:** Burmese cat **Note:** #621a.

Date	Mintage	F	VF	XF	Unc	BU
1996 U	—	—	—	—	40.00	—
1996 Proof	—	Value: 42.00				

KM# 614 1/25 CROWN

1.2441 g., 0.9995 Platinum .0400 oz. APW, 13.9 mm. **Ruler:** Elizabeth II **Obv:** Crowned bust right **Obv. Designer:** Raphael Maklouf **Rev:** Burmese cat

Date	Mintage	F	VF	XF	Unc	BU
1996	—	—	—	—	65.00	—
1996 Proof	—	Value: 70.00				

KM# 728 1/25 CROWN

1.2441 g., 0.9990 Gold .0400 oz. AGW, 13.9 mm. **Ruler:** Elizabeth II **Subject:** Year of the Rat **Obv:** Crowned bust right **Obv. Designer:** Raphael Maklouf **Rev:** Rat

Date	Mintage	F	VF	XF	Unc	BU
1996 Proof	—	—	—	—	—	—

Note: Entire series purchased by one buyer; Mintage, disposition, and market value unknown

KM# 721 1/25 CROWN

1.2441 g., 0.9990 Gold .0400 oz. AGW, 13.9 mm. **Ruler:** Elizabeth II **Subject:** Year of the Ox **Obv:** Crowned bust right **Obv. Designer:** Raphael Maklouf **Rev:** Ox laying down

Date	Mintage	F	VF	XF	Unc	BU
1997 Proof	Est. 20,000	Value: 40.00				

KM# 735 1/25 CROWN

1.2441 g., 0.9990 Gold .0400 oz. AGW, 13.9 mm. **Ruler:** Elizabeth II **Series:** Flower Fairies **Obv:** Crowned bust right **Obv. Designer:** Raphael Maklouf **Rev:** Candytuft **Rev. Designer:** Cecily Mary Barker

Date	Mintage	F	VF	XF	Unc	BU
1997 Proof	Est. 25,000	Value: 40.00				

KM# 735a 1/25 CROWN

1.2504 g., 0.9950 Platinum .0400 oz. APW, 13.9 mm. **Ruler:** Elizabeth II **Series:** Flower Fairies **Obv:** Crowned bust right **Obv. Designer:** Raphael Maklouf **Rev:** Candytuft **Rev. Designer:** Cecily Mary Barker

Date	Mintage	F	VF	XF	Unc	BU
1997 Proof	Est. 7,500	Value: 60.00				

KM# 736 1/25 CROWN

1.2441 g., 0.9999 Gold .0400 oz. AGW, 13.9 mm. **Ruler:** Elizabeth II **Series:** Flower Fairies **Obv:** Crowned bust right **Obv. Designer:** Raphael Maklouf **Rev:** Snowdrop **Rev. Designer:** Cecily Mary Barker

Date	Mintage	F	VF	XF	Unc	BU
1997 Proof	Est. 25,000	Value: 40.00				

KM# 736a 1/25 CROWN

1.2504 g., 0.9950 Platinum .0400 oz. APW, 13.9 mm. **Ruler:** Elizabeth II **Series:** Flower Fairies **Obv:** Crowned bust right **Obv. Designer:** Raphael Maklouf **Rev:** Snowdrop **Rev. Designer:** Cecily Mary Barker

Date	Mintage	F	VF	XF	Unc	BU
1997 Proof	Est. 7,500	Value: 60.00				

KM# 737 1/25 CROWN

1.2441 g., 0.9999 Gold .0400 oz. AGW, 13.9 mm. **Ruler:** Elizabeth II **Series:** Flower Fairies **Obv:** Crowned bust right **Obv. Designer:** Raphael Maklouf **Rev:** Tulip **Rev. Designer:** Cecily Mary Barker

Date	Mintage	F	VF	XF	Unc	BU
1997 Proof	Est. 25,000	Value: 40.00				

KM# 737a 1/25 CROWN

1.2504 g., 0.9950 Platinum .0400 oz. APW, 13.9 mm. **Ruler:** Elizabeth II **Series:** Flower Fairies **Obv:** Crowned bust right **Obv. Designer:** Raphael Maklouf **Rev:** Tulip **Rev. Designer:** Cecily Mary Barker

Date	Mintage	F	VF	XF	Unc	BU
1997 Proof	Est. 7,500	Value: 60.00				

KM# 738 1/25 CROWN

1.2441 g., 0.9999 Gold .0400 oz. AGW, 13.9 mm. **Ruler:** Elizabeth II **Series:** Flower Fairies **Obv:** Crowned bust right **Obv. Designer:** Raphael Maklouf **Rev:** Jasmine **Rev. Designer:** Cecily Mary Barker

Date	Mintage	F	VF	XF	Unc	BU
1997 Proof	Est. 25,000	Value: 40.00				

KM# 738a 1/25 CROWN

1.2504 g., 0.9950 Platinum .0400 oz. APW, 13.9 mm. **Ruler:** Elizabeth II **Series:** Flower Fairies **Obv:** Crowned bust right **Obv. Designer:** Raphael Maklouf **Rev:** Jasmine **Rev. Designer:** Cecily Mary Barker

Date	Mintage	F	VF	XF	Unc	BU
1997 Proof	Est. 7,500	Value: 60.00				

KM# 770 1/25 CROWN

1.2440 g., 0.9999 Gold .0400 oz. AGW, 13.9 mm. **Ruler:** Elizabeth II **Obv:** Crowned bust right **Obv. Designer:** Raphael Maklouf **Rev:** Long-haired Smoke cat

Date	Mintage	F	VF	XF	Unc	BU
1997	—	—	—	—	45.00	—
1997 Proof	—	Value: 50.00				

KM# 770a 1/25 CROWN

1.2440 g., 0.9999 Platinum .0400 oz. APW, 13.9 mm. **Ruler:** Elizabeth II **Obv:** Crowned bust right **Obv. Designer:** Raphael Maklouf **Rev:** Long-haired Smoke cat

Date	Mintage	F	VF	XF	Unc	BU
1997	—	—	—	—	60.00	—
1997 Proof	—	Value: 65.00				

KM# 789 1/25 CROWN

1.2440 g., 0.9999 Gold .0400 oz. AGW, 13.9 mm. **Ruler:** Elizabeth II **Subject:** History of the Cat **Obv:** Crowned bust right **Obv. Designer:** Raphael Maklouf **Rev:** Cat stalking a spider

Date	Mintage	F	VF	XF	Unc	BU
1997 Proof	Est. 25,000	Value: 45.00				

KM# 812 1/25 CROWN

1.2441 g., 0.9999 Gold .0400 oz. AGW, 13.9 mm. **Ruler:** Elizabeth II **Subject:** Year of the Tiger **Obv:** Crowned bust right **Obv. Designer:** Raphael Maklouf **Rev:** Tiger

Date	Mintage	F	VF	XF	Unc	BU
1998 Proof	Est. 20,000	Value: 45.00				

KM# 828 1/25 CROWN

1.2441 g., 0.9999 Gold .0400 oz. AGW, 13.9 mm. **Ruler:** Elizabeth II **Series:** Flower Fairies **Obv:** Crowned bust right **Obv. Designer:** Raphael Maklouf **Rev:** Fairy standing, lavender **Rev. Designer:** Cecily Mary Barker

Date	Mintage	F	VF	XF	Unc	BU
1998 Proof	Est. 25,000	Value: 45.00				

KM# 828a 1/25 CROWN

1.2441 g., 0.9995 Platinum .0400 oz. APW, 13.9 mm. **Ruler:** Elizabeth II **Series:** Flower Fairies **Obv:** Crowned bust right **Obv. Designer:** Raphael Maklouf **Rev:** Fairy standing, lavender **Rev. Designer:** Cecily Mary Barker

Date	Mintage	F	VF	XF	Unc	BU
1998 Proof	Est. 7,500	Value: 60.00				

KM# 829 1/25 CROWN

1.2441 g., 0.9999 Gold .0400 oz. AGW, 13.9 mm. **Ruler:** Elizabeth II **Series:** Flower Fairies **Obv:** Crowned bust right **Obv. Designer:** Raphael Maklouf **Rev:** Two fairies, sweet pea **Rev. Designer:** Cecily Mary Barker

Date	Mintage	F	VF	XF	Unc	BU
1998 Proof	Est. 25,000	Value: 45.00				

KM# 829a 1/25 CROWN

1.2441 g., 0.9995 Platinum .0400 oz. APW, 13.9 mm. **Ruler:** Elizabeth II **Series:** Flower Fairies **Obv:** Crowned bust right **Obv. Designer:** Raphael Maklouf **Rev:** Two fairies, sweet pea **Rev. Designer:** Cecily Mary Barker

Date	Mintage	F	VF	XF	Unc	BU
1998 Proof	Est. 7,500	Value: 60.00				

KM# 830 1/25 CROWN

1.2441 g., 0.9999 Gold .0400 oz. AGW, 13.9 mm. **Ruler:** Elizabeth II **Series:** Flower Fairies **Obv:** Crowned bust right **Obv. Designer:** Raphael Maklouf **Rev:** Two fairies, sweet pea **Rev. Designer:** Cecily Mary Barker

Date	Mintage	F	VF	XF	Unc	BU
1998 Proof	—	Value: 45.00				

KM# 830a 1/25 CROWN

1.2441 g., 0.9995 Platinum .0400 oz. APW, 13.9 mm. **Ruler:** Elizabeth II **Series:** Flower Fairies **Obv:** Crowned bust right **Obv. Designer:** Raphael Maklouf **Rev:** Two fairies, sweet pea **Rev. Designer:** Cecily Mary Barker

Date	Mintage	F	VF	XF	Unc	BU
1998 Proof	Est. 30,000	Value: 60.00				

KM# 831 1/25 CROWN

1.2441 g., 0.9999 Gold .0400 oz. AGW, 13.9 mm. **Ruler:** Elizabeth II **Series:** Flower Fairies **Obv:** Crowned bust right **Obv. Designer:** Raphael Maklouf **Rev:** Fairy standing, daffodil **Rev. Designer:** Cecily Mary Barker

Date	Mintage	F	VF	XF	Unc	BU
1998 Proof	Est. 25,000	Value: 45.00				

KM# 831a 1/25 CROWN

1.2441 g., 0.9995 Platinum .0400 oz. APW, 13.9 mm. **Ruler:** Elizabeth II **Series:** Flower Fairies **Obv:** Crowned bust right **Obv. Designer:** Raphael Maklouf **Rev:** Fairy standing, daffodil **Rev. Designer:** Cecily Mary Barker

Date	Mintage	F	VF	XF	Unc	BU
1998 Proof	Est. 7,500	Value: 60.00				

KM# 853 1/25 CROWN

1.2440 g., 0.9999 Gold .0400 oz. AGW, 13.9 mm. **Ruler:** Elizabeth II **Obv:** Crowned bust right **Obv. Designer:** Raphael Maklouf **Rev:** Birman cat

Date	Mintage	F	VF	XF	Unc	BU
1998	—	—	—	—	40.00	—
1998 Proof	1,000	Value: 42.00				

KM# 853a 1/25 CROWN

1.2440 g., 0.9995 Platinum .0400 oz. APW, 13.9 mm. **Ruler:** Elizabeth II **Obv:** Crowned bust right **Obv. Designer:** Raphael Maklouf **Rev:** Birman cat

Date	Mintage	F	VF	XF	Unc	BU
1998 Proof	—	Value: 60.00				

KM# 859 1/25 CROWN

1.2440 g., 0.9999 Gold .0400 oz. AGW, 13.9 mm. **Ruler:** Elizabeth II **Subject:** History of the Cat **Obv:** Crowned bust right **Obv. Designer:** Raphael Maklouf **Rev:** Egyptian Mau cat with earring

Date	Mintage	F	VF	XF	Unc	BU
1998 Proof	Est. 25,000	Value: 45.00				

KM# 948 1/25 CROWN

1.2440 g., 0.9999 Gold .0400 oz. AGW, 13.9 mm. **Ruler:** Elizabeth II **Subject:** Year of the Rabbit **Obv:** Crowned bust right **Obv. Designer:** Raphael Maklouf **Rev:** Two rabbits

Date	Mintage	F	VF	XF	Unc	BU
1999 Proof	Est. 20,000	Value: 45.00				

KM# 958 1/25 CROWN

1.2440 g., 0.9999 Gold .0400 oz. AGW, 13.9 mm. **Ruler:** Elizabeth II **Obv:** Crowned bust right **Obv. Designer:** Raphael Maklouf **Rev:** British Blue cat

ISLE OF MAN 399

Date	Mintage	F	VF	XF	Unc	BU
1999	—	—	—	—	40.00	—
1999 Proof	—	Value: 42.00				
1999 U Y2K	20,000	—	—	—	40.00	—

KM# 958a 1/25 CROWN
1.2441 g., 0.9995 Platinum .0400 oz. APW, 13.9 mm. **Ruler:** Elizabeth II **Obv:** Crowned bust right **Obv. Designer:** Raphael Maklouf **Rev:** British Blue cat

Date	Mintage	F	VF	XF	Unc	BU
1999 Proof	—	Value: 60.00				

KM# 1052 1/25 CROWN
1.2400 g., 0.9999 Gold .0399 oz. AGW, 13.92 mm. **Ruler:** Elizabeth II **Obv:** Crowned bust right **Obv. Designer:** Raphael Maklouf **Rev:** Scottish fold kitten **Edge:** Reeded

Date	Mintage	F	VF	XF	Unc	BU
2000	—	—	—	—	35.00	—
2000 Proof	—	Value: 45.00				

KM# 1052a 1/25 CROWN
1.2441 g., 0.9995 Platinum .0400 oz. APW, 13.9 mm. **Ruler:** Elizabeth II **Obv:** Crowned bust right **Obv. Designer:** Raphael Maklouf **Rev:** Scottish fold kitten

Date	Mintage	F	VF	XF	Unc	BU
2000	—	—	—	—	42.00	—

KM# 1012 1/25 CROWN
1.2440 g., 0.9999 Gold .0400 oz. AGW, 13.9 mm. **Ruler:** Elizabeth II **Subject:** Year of the Dragon **Obv:** Crowned bust right **Obv. Designer:** Raphael Maklouf **Rev:** Dragon, Chinese characters

Date	Mintage	F	VF	XF	Unc	BU
2000 Proof	Est. 20,000	Value: 45.00				

KM# 1058 1/25 CROWN
1.2440 g., 0.9999 Gold .0400 oz. AGW, 13.92 mm. **Ruler:** Elizabeth II **Subject:** Year of the Snake **Obv:** Bust with tiara right **Obv. Designer:** Ian Rank-Broadley **Rev:** Snake **Edge:** Reeded

Date	Mintage	F	VF	XF	Unc	BU
2001 Proof	20,000	Value: 45.00				

KM# 1067 1/25 CROWN
1.2440 g., 0.9999 Gold .0400 oz. AGW, 13.9 mm. **Ruler:** Elizabeth II **Subject:** Somali Kittens **Obv:** Head with tiara right **Obv. Designer:** Ian Rank-Broadley **Rev:** Two kittens **Edge:** Reeded

Date	Mintage	F	VF	XF	Unc	BU
2001	—	—	—	—	32.00	—
2001 Proof	1,000	Value: 50.00				

KM# 1067a 1/25 CROWN
1.2441 g., 0.9995 Platinum .0400 oz. APW, 13.9 mm. **Ruler:** Elizabeth II **Subject:** Somali Kittens **Obv:** Head with tiara right **Obv. Designer:** Ian Rank-Broadley **Rev:** Two kittens **Edge:** Reeded

Date	Mintage	F	VF	XF	Unc	BU
2001	—	—	—	—	65.00	—

KM# 1086 1/25 CROWN
1.2441 g., 0.9999 Gold .0400 oz. AGW, 13.9 mm. **Ruler:** Elizabeth II **Subject:** Harry Potter **Obv:** Bust with tiara right **Obv. Designer:** Ian Rank-Broadley **Rev:** Boy with magic wand **Edge:** Reeded

Date	Mintage	F	VF	XF	Unc	BU
2001 Proof	10,000	Value: 49.50				

KM# 1088 1/25 CROWN
1.2441 g., 0.9999 Gold .0400 oz. AGW, 13.9 mm. **Ruler:** Elizabeth II **Series:** Harry Potter **Subject:** Journey to Hogwarts School **Obv:** Bust with tiara right **Obv. Designer:** Ian Rank-Broadley **Rev:** Boat full of children going to Hogwarts School **Edge:** Reeded

Date	Mintage	F	VF	XF	Unc	BU
2001 Proof	10,000	Value: 49.50				

KM# 1090 1/25 CROWN
1.2441 g., 0.9999 Gold .0400 oz. AGW, 13.9 mm. **Ruler:** Elizabeth II **Series:** Harry Potter **Subject:** First Quidditch Match **Obv:** Bust with tiara right **Obv. Designer:** Ian Rank-Broadley **Rev:** Harry flying a broom **Edge:** Reeded

Date	Mintage	F	VF	XF	Unc	BU
2001 Proof	10,000	Value: 49.50				

KM# 1092 1/25 CROWN
1.2441 g., 0.9999 Gold .0400 oz. AGW, 13.9 mm. **Ruler:** Elizabeth II **Series:** Harry Potter **Subject:** Birth of Norbert **Obv:** Bust with tiara right **Obv. Designer:** Ian Rank-Broadley **Edge:** Reeded

Date	Mintage	F	VF	XF	Unc	BU
2001 Proof	10,000	Value: 49.50				

KM# 1094 1/25 CROWN
1.2441 g., 0.9999 Gold .0400 oz. AGW, 13.9 mm. **Ruler:** Elizabeth II **Series:** Harry Potter **Subject:** School **Obv:** Bust with tiara right **Obv. Designer:** Ian Rank-Broadley **Rev:** Harry in Potions class **Edge:** Reeded

Date	Mintage	F	VF	XF	Unc	BU
2001 Proof	10,000	Value: 49.50				

KM# 1096 1/25 CROWN
1.2441 g., 0.9999 Gold .0400 oz. AGW, 13.9 mm. **Ruler:** Elizabeth II **Series:** Harry Potter **Subject:** Keys **Obv:** Bust with tiara right **Obv. Designer:** Ian Rank-Broadley **Rev:** Harry chasing a quidditch **Edge:** Reeded

Date	Mintage	F	VF	XF	Unc	BU
2001 Proof	10,000	Value: 49.50				

KM# 1098 1/25 CROWN
1.2441 g., 0.9999 Gold .0400 oz. AGW, 13.9 mm. **Ruler:** Elizabeth II **Subject:** Year of the Horse **Obv:** Bust with tiara right **Obv. Designer:** Ian Rank-Broadley **Rev:** Two horses **Edge:** Reeded

Date	Mintage	F	VF	XF	Unc	BU
2002 Proof	20,000	Value: 49.50				

KM# 1107 1/25 CROWN
1.2440 g., 0.9990 Gold 0.04 oz. AGW, 13.92 mm. **Ruler:** Elizabeth II **Subject:** Bengal Cat **Obv:** Head with tiara right **Obv. Designer:** Ian Rank-Broadley **Rev:** Cat and kitten **Edge:** Reeded

Date	Mintage	F	VF	XF	Unc	BU
2002	—	—	—	—	32.00	—
2002 Proof	1,000	Value: 49.50				

KM# 1107a 1/25 CROWN
1.2440 g., 0.9990 Platinum 0.04 oz. APW, 13.92 mm. **Ruler:** Elizabeth II **Subject:** Bengal Cat **Obv:** Head with tiara right **Obv. Designer:** Ian Rank-Broadley **Rev:** Cat and kitten **Edge:** Reeded

Date	Mintage	F	VF	XF	Unc	BU
2002 Proof	—	Value: 60.00				

KM# 1145 1/25 CROWN
1.2440 g., 0.9999 Gold 0.04 oz. AGW, 13.92 mm. **Ruler:** Elizabeth II **Subject:** Harry Potter Series **Obv:** Bust with tiara right **Obv. Designer:** Ian Rank-Broadley **Rev:** Harry and friends making Polyjuice potion **Edge:** Reeded

Date	Mintage	F	VF	XF	Unc	BU
2002PM Proof	10,000	Value: 55.00				

KM# 1143 1/25 CROWN
1.2440 g., 0.9999 Gold 0.04 oz. AGW, 13.92 mm. **Ruler:** Elizabeth II **Subject:** Harry Potter **Obv:** Bust with tiara right **Obv. Designer:** Ian Rank-Broadley **Rev:** Tom Riddle twirling Harry's magic wand **Edge:** Reeded

Date	Mintage	F	VF	XF	Unc	BU
2002PM Proof	10,000	Value: 55.00				

KM# 1147 1/25 CROWN
1.2440 g., 0.9999 Gold .04 oz. AGW **Ruler:** Elizabeth II **Subject:** Harry Potter **Obv:** Bust with tiara right **Obv. Designer:** Ian Rank-Broadley **Rev:** Harry arrives at the Burrow in a flying car **Edge:** Reeded

Date	Mintage	F	VF	XF	Unc	BU
2002PM Proof	10,000	Value: 55.00				

KM# 1149 1/25 CROWN
1.2440 g., 0.9999 Gold 0.04 oz. AGW, 13.92 mm. **Ruler:** Elizabeth II **Subject:** Harry Potter Series **Obv:** Bust with tiara right **Obv. Designer:** Ian Rank-Broadley **Rev:** Harry retrieves Gryffindor sword from snake **Edge:** Reeded

Date	Mintage	F	VF	XF	Unc	BU
2002PM Proof	10,000	Value: 55.00				

KM# 1151 1/25 CROWN
1.2240 g., 0.9999 Gold 0.0393 oz. AGW, 13.92 mm. **Ruler:** Elizabeth II **Series:** Harry Potter **Obv:** Bust with tiara right **Obv. Designer:** Ian Rank-Broadley **Rev:** Harry and Ron encounter the spider Aragog **Edge:** Reeded

Date	Mintage	F	VF	XF	Unc	BU
2002PM Proof	10,000	Value: 55.00				

KM# 1153 1/25 CROWN
1.2440 g., 0.9999 Gold 0.04 oz. AGW, 13.92 mm. **Ruler:** Elizabeth II **Series:** Harry Potter **Obv:** Bust with tiara right **Obv. Designer:** Ian Rank-Broadley **Rev:** Harry in hospital **Edge:** Reeded

Date	Mintage	F	VF	XF	Unc	BU
2002PM Proof	10,000	Value: 55.00				

KM# 1186 1/25 CROWN
1.2440 g., 0.9999 Gold 0.04 oz. AGW, 13.9 mm. **Ruler:** Elizabeth II **Subject:** Lord of the Rings **Obv:** Bust with tiara right **Obv. Designer:** Ian Rank-Broadley **Rev:** Man with short sword **Edge:** Reeded

Date	Mintage	F	VF	XF	Unc	BU
2003PM Proof	6,000	Value: 50.00				

KM# 1161 1/25 CROWN
1.2440 g., 0.9999 Gold 0.04 oz. AGW, 13.92 mm. **Ruler:** Elizabeth II **Subject:** Cat **Obv:** Head with tiara right **Obv. Designer:** Ian Rank-Broadley **Rev:** Two Balinese kittens **Edge:** Reeded

Date	Mintage	F	VF	XF	Unc	BU
2003PM	—	—	—	—	35.00	—
2003PM Proof	—	Value: 49.50				

KM# 1161a 1/25 CROWN
1.2440 g., 0.9995 Platinum 0.04 oz. APW, 13.92 mm. **Ruler:** Elizabeth II **Subject:** Cat **Obv:** Head with tiara right **Obv. Designer:** Ian Rank-Broadley **Rev:** Two Balinese kittens **Edge:** Reeded

Date	Mintage	F	VF	XF	Unc	BU
2003PM	—	—	—	—	60.00	—

KM# 1167 1/25 CROWN
1.2441 g., 0.9999 Gold 0.04 oz. AGW, 13.9 mm. **Ruler:** Elizabeth II **Subject:** Year of the Goat **Obv:** Head with tiara right **Obv. Designer:** Ian Rank-Broadley **Rev:** Three goats **Edge:** Reeded

Date	Mintage	F	VF	XF	Unc	BU
2003PM Proof	20,000	Value: 49.50				

KM# 1203 1/25 CROWN
1.2440 g., 0.9999 Gold 0.04 oz. AGW, 14 mm. **Ruler:** Elizabeth II **Obv:** Bust with tiara right **Obv. Designer:** Ian Rank-Broadley **Rev:** Harry Potter and patron fighting off a spectre **Edge:** Reeded

Date	Mintage	F	VF	XF	Unc	BU
2004PM Proof	2,500	Value: 50.00				

KM# 1205 1/25 CROWN
1.2440 g., 0.9999 Gold 0.04 oz. AGW, 14 mm. **Ruler:** Elizabeth II **Obv:** Bust with tiara right **Obv. Designer:** Ian Rank-Broadley **Rev:** Harry Potter in the shrieking shack **Edge:** Reeded

Date	Mintage	F	VF	XF	Unc	BU
2004PM Proof	2,500	Value: 50.00				

KM# 1207 1/25 CROWN
1.2440 g., 0.9999 Gold 0.04 oz. AGW, 14 mm. **Ruler:** Elizabeth II **Obv:** Bust with tiara right **Obv. Designer:** Ian Rank-Broadley **Rev:** Harry Potter and Professor Dumbledore **Edge:** Reeded

Date	Mintage	F	VF	XF	Unc	BU
2004PM Proof	2,500	Value: 50.00				

KM# 1209 1/25 CROWN
1.2440 g., 0.9999 Gold 0.04 oz. AGW, 14 mm. **Ruler:** Elizabeth II **Obv:** Bust with tiara right **Obv. Designer:** Ian Rank-Broadley **Rev:** Sirius Black on flying griffin **Edge:** Reeded

Date	Mintage	F	VF	XF	Unc	BU
2004PM Proof	2,500	Value: 50.00				

KM# 1211 1/25 CROWN
1.2440 g., 0.9999 Gold 0.04 oz. AGW, 14 mm. **Ruler:** Elizabeth II **Obv:** Head with tiara right **Obv. Designer:** Ian Rank-Broadley **Rev:** Three Olympic Swimmers **Edge:** Reeded

Date	Mintage	F	VF	XF	Unc	BU
2004PM Proof	5,000	Value: 50.00				

KM# 1213 1/25 CROWN
1.2440 g., 0.9999 Gold 0.04 oz. AGW, 14 mm. **Ruler:** Elizabeth II **Obv:** Head with tiara right **Obv. Designer:** Ian Rank-Broadley **Rev:** Three Olympic Cyclists **Edge:** Reeded

Date	Mintage	F	VF	XF	Unc	BU
2004PM Proof	5,000	Value: 50.00				

KM# 1215 1/25 CROWN
1.2440 g., 0.9999 Gold 0.04 oz. AGW, 14 mm. **Ruler:** Elizabeth II **Obv:** Head with tiara right **Obv. Designer:** Ian Rank-Broadley **Rev:** Three Olympic Runners **Edge:** Reeded

Date	Mintage	F	VF	XF	Unc	BU
2004PM Proof	5,000	Value: 50.00				

KM# 1217 1/25 CROWN
1.2440 g., 0.9999 Gold 0.04 oz. AGW, 14 mm. **Ruler:** Elizabeth II **Obv:** Head with tiara right **Obv. Designer:** Ian Rank-Broadley **Rev:** Three Olympic Sail Boarders **Edge:** Reeded

Date	Mintage	F	VF	XF	Unc	BU
2004PM Proof	5,000	Value: 50.00				

KM# 1240 1/25 CROWN
1.2440 g., 0.9999 Gold 0.04 oz. AGW, 14 mm. **Ruler:** Elizabeth II **Obv:** Head with tiara right **Obv. Designer:** Ian Rank-Broadley **Rev:** Monkey **Edge:** Reeded

Date	Mintage	F	VF	XF	Unc	BU
2004PM Proof	20,000	Value: 50.00				

KM# 1247 1/25 CROWN
1.2440 g., 0.9999 Gold 0.04 oz. AGW, 14 mm. **Ruler:** Elizabeth II **Obv:** Head with tiara right **Obv. Designer:** Ian Rank-Broadley **Rev:** Two Tonkinese cats **Edge:** Reeded

Date	Mintage	F	VF	XF	Unc	BU
2004PM	—	—	—	—	35.00	—
2004PM Proof	1,000	Value: 50.00				

KM# 1269 1/25 CROWN
1.2440 g., 0.9999 Gold 0.04 oz. AGW, 13.92 mm. **Ruler:** Elizabeth II **Obv:** Bust with tiara right **Obv. Designer:** Ian Rank-Broadley **Rev:** Himalayan cat and two kittens **Edge:** Reeded

Date	Mintage	F	VF	XF	Unc	BU
2005PM Proof	—	Value: 50.00				

KM# 1269a 1/25 CROWN
1.2440 g., 0.9950 Platinum 0.0398 oz. APW, 13.92 mm. **Ruler:** Elizabeth II **Obv:** Bust with tiara right **Obv. Designer:** Ian Rank-Broadley **Rev:** Himalayan cat and two kittens **Edge:** Reeded

Date	Mintage	F	VF	XF	Unc	BU
2005PM Proof	—	Value: 90.00				

KM# 236 1/10 CROWN
3.1100 g., 0.9990 Gold .1000 oz. AGW **Ruler:** Elizabeth II **Obv:** Crowned bust right **Obv. Designer:** Raphael Maklouf **Rev:** Manx cat

Date	Mintage	F	VF	XF	Unc	BU
1988	12,000	—	—	—	100	—
1988 Proof	5,000	Value: 102				

KM# 253 1/10 CROWN
3.1100 g., 0.9990 Gold .1000 oz. AGW, 17.95 mm. **Ruler:** Elizabeth II **Obv:** Crowned bust right **Obv. Designer:** Raphael Maklouf **Rev:** Persian cat

Date	Mintage	F	VF	XF	Unc	BU
1989	—	—	—	—	85.00	—
1989 Proof	—	Value: 90.00				

KM# 468 1/10 CROWN
3.1100 g., 0.9995 Platinum .1000 oz. APW, 17.95 mm. **Ruler:** Elizabeth II **Obv:** Crowned bust right **Obv. Designer:** Raphael Maklouf **Rev:** Persian cat

Date	Mintage	F	VF	XF	Unc	BU
1989	—	—	—	—	125	—
1989 Proof	—	Value: 135				

KM# 278 1/10 CROWN
3.1100 g., 0.9990 Gold .1000 oz. AGW, 17.95 mm. **Ruler:** Elizabeth II **Obv:** Crowned bust right **Obv. Designer:** Raphael Maklouf **Rev:** Alley cat

400 ISLE OF MAN

Date	Mintage	F	VF	XF	Unc	BU
1990	—	—	—	—	75.00	—
1990 Proof	—	Value: 80.00				

KM# 295 1/10 CROWN

3.1100 g., 0.9990 Gold .1000 oz. AGW, 17.95 mm. **Ruler:** Elizabeth II **Obv:** Crowned bust right **Obv. Designer:** Raphael Maklouf **Rev:** Norwegian cat

Date	Mintage	F	VF	XF	Unc	BU
1991	—	—	—	—	75.00	—
1991 Proof	—	Value: 80.00				

KM# 323 1/10 CROWN

3.1100 g., 0.9990 Gold .1000 oz. AGW, 17.95 mm. **Ruler:** Elizabeth II **Subject:** America's Cup **Obv:** Crowned bust right **Obv. Designer:** Raphael Maklouf **Rev:** Cameo of "Star of India" above two modern sailboats

Date	Mintage	F	VF	XF	Unc	BU
1992 Prooflike	25,000	—	—	—	125	—

KM# 323a 1/10 CROWN

3.1100 g., 0.9995 Platinum .1000 oz. APW, 17.95 mm. **Ruler:** Elizabeth II **Subject:** America's Cup **Obv:** Crowned bust right **Obv. Designer:** Raphael Maklouf **Rev:** Sailboat

Date	Mintage	F	VF	XF	Unc	BU
1992 Prooflike	5,000	—	—	—	180	—

KM# 329 1/10 CROWN

3.1100 g., 0.9990 Gold .1000 oz. AGW, 17.95 mm. **Ruler:** Elizabeth II **Obv:** Crowned bust right **Obv. Designer:** Raphael Maklouf **Rev:** Siamese cat

Date	Mintage	F	VF	XF	Unc	BU
1992	—	—	—	—	72.00	—
1992 Proof	—	Value: 75.00				

KM# 339 1/10 CROWN

3.1100 g., 0.9990 Gold .1000 oz. AGW, 17.95 mm. **Ruler:** Elizabeth II **Subject:** Year of the Cockerel **Obv:** Crowned bust right **Obv. Designer:** Raphael Maklouf **Rev:** Cockerel in inner circle **Rev. Designer:** Barry Stanton

Date	Mintage	F	VF	XF	Unc	BU
1993 Proof	Est. 20,000	Value: 85.00				

KM# 350 1/10 CROWN

3.1100 g., 0.9990 Gold .1000 oz. AGW, 17.95 mm. **Ruler:** Elizabeth II **Obv:** Crowned bust right **Obv. Designer:** Raphael Maklouf **Rev:** Maine Coon cat

Date	Mintage	F	VF	XF	Unc	BU
1993	—	—	—	—	72.00	—
1993 Proof	—	Value: 75.00				

KM# 377 1/10 CROWN

3.1100 g., 0.9990 Gold .1000 oz. AGW, 17.95 mm. **Ruler:** Elizabeth II **Obv:** Crowned bust right **Obv. Designer:** Raphael Maklouf **Rev:** Japanese Bobtail cat

Date	Mintage	F	VF	XF	Unc	BU
1994	—	—	—	—	72.00	—
1994 Proof	—	Value: 75.00				

KM# 403 1/10 CROWN

3.1100 g., 0.9990 Gold .1000 oz. AGW, 17.95 mm. **Ruler:** Elizabeth II **Obv:** Crowned bust right **Obv. Designer:** Raphael Maklouf **Rev:** Pekingese dog

Date	Mintage	F	VF	XF	Unc	BU
1994 Proof	20,000	Value: 95.00				

KM# 474 1/10 CROWN

3.1100 g., 0.9995 Platinum .1000 oz. APW, 17.95 mm. **Ruler:** Elizabeth II **Obv:** Crowned bust right **Obv. Designer:** Raphael Maklouf **Rev:** Japanese Bobtail cat

Date	Mintage	F	VF	XF	Unc	BU
1994	—	—	—	—	125	—
1994 Proof	—	Value: 135				

KM# 443 1/10 CROWN

3.1100 g., 0.9990 Gold .1000 oz. AGW, 17.95 mm. **Ruler:** Elizabeth II **Obv:** Crowned bust right **Obv. Designer:** Raphael Maklouf **Rev:** Turkish cat

Date	Mintage	F	VF	XF	Unc	BU
1995	—	—	—	—	72.00	—
1995 Proof	—	Value: 75.00				

KM# 450 1/10 CROWN

3.1100 g., 0.9990 Gold .1000 oz. AGW, 17.95 mm. **Ruler:** Elizabeth II **Subject:** Year of the Pig **Obv:** Crowned bust right **Obv. Designer:** Raphael Maklouf **Rev:** Sow with piglets

Date	Mintage	F	VF	XF	Unc	BU
1995 Proof	Est. 20,000	Value: 95.00				

KM# 479 1/10 CROWN

3.1100 g., 0.9995 Platinum .1000 oz. APW, 17.95 mm. **Ruler:** Elizabeth II **Obv:** Crowned bust right **Obv. Designer:** Raphael Maklouf **Rev:** Turkish cat

Date	Mintage	F	VF	XF	Unc	BU
1995	—	—	—	—	125	—
1995 Proof	—	Value: 135				

KM# 601 1/10 CROWN

3.1100 g., 0.9990 Gold .1000 oz. AGW, 17.95 mm. **Ruler:** Elizabeth II **Series:** Flower Fairies **Obv:** Crowned bust right **Obv. Designer:** Raphael Maklouf **Rev:** Orchis **Rev. Designer:** Cecily Mary Barker

Date	Mintage	F	VF	XF	Unc	BU
1996 Proof	Est. 20,000	Value: 90.00				

KM# 602 1/10 CROWN

3.1100 g., 0.9990 Gold .1000 oz. AGW, 17.95 mm. **Ruler:** Elizabeth II **Series:** Flower Fairies **Obv:** Crowned bust right **Obv. Designer:** Raphael Maklouf **Rev:** Rose **Rev. Designer:** Cecily Mary Barker

Date	Mintage	F	VF	XF	Unc	BU
1996 Proof	Est. 20,000	Value: 90.00				

KM# 603 1/10 CROWN

3.1100 g., 0.9990 Gold .1000 oz. AGW, 17.95 mm. **Ruler:** Elizabeth II **Series:** Flower Fairies **Obv:** Crowned bust right **Obv. Designer:** Raphael Maklouf **Rev:** Fuchsia **Rev. Designer:** Cecily Mary Barker

Date	Mintage	F	VF	XF	Unc	BU
1996 Proof	Est. 20,000	Value: 90.00				

KM# 604 1/10 CROWN

3.1100 g., 0.9990 Gold .1000 oz. AGW, 17.95 mm. **Ruler:** Elizabeth II **Obv:** Crowned bust right **Obv. Designer:** Raphael Maklouf **Rev:** Pinks **Rev. Designer:** Cecily Mary Barker

Date	Mintage	F	VF	XF	Unc	BU
1996 Proof	Est. 20,000	Value: 90.00				

KM# 615 1/10 CROWN

3.1100 g., 0.9990 Gold .1000 oz. AGW, 17.95 mm. **Ruler:** Elizabeth II **Obv:** Crowned bust right **Obv. Designer:** Raphael Maklouf **Rev:** Burmese cat

Date	Mintage	F	VF	XF	Unc	BU
1996	—	—	—	—	67.00	—
1996 Proof	—	Value: 70.00				

KM# 616 1/10 CROWN

3.1100 g., 0.9995 Platinum .1000 oz. APW, 17.95 mm. **Ruler:** Elizabeth II **Obv:** Crowned bust right **Obv. Designer:** Raphael Maklouf **Rev:** Burmese cat

Date	Mintage	F	VF	XF	Unc	BU
1996	—	—	—	—	125	—
1996 Proof	—	Value: 135				

KM# 729 1/10 CROWN

3.1100 g., 0.9990 Gold .1000 oz. AGW, 17.95 mm. **Ruler:** Elizabeth II **Subject:** Year of the Rat **Obv:** Crowned bust right **Obv. Designer:** Raphael Maklouf **Rev:** Rat

Date	Mintage	F	VF	XF	Unc	BU
1996 Proof	—	—	—	—	—	—

Note: Entire series purchased by one buyer. Mintage, disposition and market value unknown

KM# 722 1/10 CROWN

3.1100 g., 0.9990 Gold .1000 oz. AGW, 17.95 mm. **Ruler:** Elizabeth II **Subject:** Year of the Ox **Obv:** Crowned bust right **Obv. Designer:** Raphael Maklouf **Rev:** Ox laying down

Date	Mintage	F	VF	XF	Unc	BU
1997 Proof	Est. 15,000	Value: 90.00				

KM# 743 1/10 CROWN

3.1100 g., 0.9990 Gold .1000 oz. AGW, 17.95 mm. **Ruler:** Elizabeth II **Series:** Flower Fairies **Obv:** Crowned bust right **Obv. Designer:** Raphael Maklouf **Rev:** Candytuft **Rev. Designer:** Cecily Mary Barker

Date	Mintage	F	VF	XF	Unc	BU
1997 Proof	Est. 20,000	Value: 80.00				

KM# 743a 1/10 CROWN

3.1259 g., 0.9950 Platinum .1000 oz. APW, 17.95 mm. **Ruler:** Elizabeth II **Series:** Flower Fairies **Obv:** Crowned bust right **Obv. Designer:** Raphael Maklouf **Rev:** Candytuft **Rev. Designer:** Cecily Mary Barker

Date	Mintage	F	VF	XF	Unc	BU
1997 Proof	Est. 5,000	Value: 125				

KM# 744 1/10 CROWN

3.1103 g., 0.9999 Gold .1000 oz. AGW, 17.95 mm. **Ruler:** Elizabeth II **Obv:** Crowned bust right **Obv. Designer:** Raphael Maklouf **Rev:** Snowdrop **Rev. Designer:** Cecily Mary Barker

Date	Mintage	F	VF	XF	Unc	BU
1997 Proof	Est. 20,000	Value: 80.00				

KM# 744a 1/10 CROWN

3.1259 g., 0.9950 Platinum .1000 oz. APW, 17.95 mm. **Ruler:** Elizabeth II **Series:** Flower Fairies **Obv:** Crowned bust right **Obv. Designer:** Raphael Maklouf **Rev:** Snowdrop **Rev. Designer:** Cecily Mary Barker

Date	Mintage	F	VF	XF	Unc	BU
1997 Proof	Est. 5,000	Value: 125				

KM# 745 1/10 CROWN

3.1103 g., 0.9999 Gold .1000 oz. AGW, 17.95 mm. **Ruler:** Elizabeth II **Series:** Flower Fairies **Obv:** Crowned bust right **Obv. Designer:** Raphael Maklouf **Rev:** Tulip **Rev. Designer:** Cecily Mary Barker

Date	Mintage	F	VF	XF	Unc	BU
1997 Proof	Est. 20,000	Value: 80.00				

KM# 745a 1/10 CROWN

3.1259 g., 0.9950 Platinum .1000 oz. APW, 17.95 mm. **Ruler:** Elizabeth II **Series:** Flower Fairies **Obv:** Crowned bust right **Obv. Designer:** Raphael Maklouf **Rev:** Tulip **Rev. Designer:** Cecily Mary Barker

Date	Mintage	F	VF	XF	Unc	BU
1997 Proof	Est. 5,000	Value: 125				

KM# 746 1/10 CROWN

3.1103 g., 0.9999 Gold .1000 oz. AGW, 17.95 mm. **Ruler:** Elizabeth II **Series:** Flower Fairies **Obv:** Crowned bust right **Obv. Designer:** Raphael Maklouf **Rev:** Jasmine **Rev. Designer:** Cecily Mary Barker

Date	Mintage	F	VF	XF	Unc	BU
1997 Proof	Est. 20,000	Value: 80.00				

KM# 746a 1/10 CROWN

3.1259 g., 0.9950 Platinum .1000 oz. APW, 17.95 mm. **Ruler:** Elizabeth II **Series:** Flower Fairies **Obv:** Crowned bust right **Obv. Designer:** Raphael Maklouf **Rev:** Jasmine **Rev. Designer:** Cecily Mary Barker

Date	Mintage	F	VF	XF	Unc	BU
1997 Proof	Est. 5,000	Value: 125				

KM# 771 1/10 CROWN

3.1100 g., 0.9999 Gold .1000 oz. AGW, 17.95 mm. **Ruler:** Elizabeth II **Obv:** Crowned bust right **Obv. Designer:** Raphael Maklouf **Rev:** Long-haired Smoke cat

Date	Mintage	F	VF	XF	Unc	BU
1997	—	—	—	—	67.00	—
1997 Proof	—	Value: 70.00				

KM# 771a 1/10 CROWN

3.1100 g., 0.9995 Platinum .1000 oz. APW, 17.95 mm. **Ruler:** Elizabeth II **Obv:** Crowned bust right **Obv. Designer:** Raphael Maklouf **Rev:** Long-haired Smoke cat

Date	Mintage	F	VF	XF	Unc	BU
1997	—	—	—	—	125	—
1997 Proof	—	Value: 135				

KM# 790 1/10 CROWN

3.1100 g., 0.9999 Gold .1000 oz. AGW, 17.95 mm. **Ruler:** Elizabeth II **Subject:** History of the Cat **Obv:** Crowned bust right **Obv. Designer:** Raphael Maklouf **Rev:** Cat stalking a spider

Date	Mintage	F	VF	XF	Unc	BU
1997 Proof	Est. 20,000	Value: 90.00				

KM# 813 1/10 CROWN

3.1100 g., 0.9999 Gold .1000 oz. AGW, 17.95 mm. **Ruler:** Elizabeth II **Subject:** Year of the Tiger **Obv:** Crowned bust right **Obv. Designer:** Raphael Maklouf **Rev:** Tiger

Date	Mintage	F	VF	XF	Unc	BU
1998 Proof	Est. 15,000	Value: 90.00				

KM# 832 1/10 CROWN

3.1100 g., 0.9999 Gold .1000 oz. AGW, 17.95 mm. **Ruler:** Elizabeth II **Series:** Flower Fairies **Obv:** Crowned bust right **Obv. Designer:** Raphael Maklouf **Rev:** Standing fairy, lavender **Rev. Designer:** Cecily Mary Barker

Date	Mintage	F	VF	XF	Unc	BU
1998 Proof	Est. 20,000	Value: 90.00				

KM# 832a 1/10 CROWN

3.1100 g., 0.9995 Platinum .1000 oz. APW, 17.95 mm. **Ruler:** Elizabeth II **Series:** Flower Fairies **Obv:** Crowned bust right **Obv. Designer:** Raphael Maklouf **Rev:** Standing fairy, lavender **Rev. Designer:** Cecily Mary Barker

Date	Mintage	F	VF	XF	Unc	BU
1998 Proof	Est. 5,000	Value: 125				

KM# 833 1/10 CROWN

3.1100 g., 0.9999 Gold .1000 oz. AGW, 17.95 mm. **Ruler:** Elizabeth II **Series:** Flower Fairies **Obv:** Crowned bust right **Obv. Designer:** Raphael Maklouf **Rev:** Two fairies, sweet pea **Rev. Designer:** Cecily Mary Barker

Date	Mintage	F	VF	XF	Unc	BU
1998 Proof	Est. 20,000	Value: 90.00				

KM# 833a 1/10 CROWN

3.1100 g., 0.9995 Platinum .1000 oz. APW, 17.95 mm. **Ruler:** Elizabeth II **Series:** Flower Fairies **Obv:** Crowned bust right **Obv. Designer:** Raphael Maklouf **Rev:** Two fairies, sweet pea **Rev. Designer:** Cecily Mary Barker

Date	Mintage	F	VF	XF	Unc	BU
1998 Proof	Est. 5,000	Value: 125				

KM# 834 1/10 CROWN

3.1100 g., 0.9999 Gold .1000 oz. AGW, 17.95 mm. **Ruler:** Elizabeth II **Obv:** Crowned bust right **Obv. Designer:** Raphael Maklouf **Rev:** Fairy looking into flower, White Bindweed **Rev. Designer:** Cecily Mary Barker

Date	Mintage	F	VF	XF	Unc	BU
1998 Proof	Est. 20,000	Value: 90.00				

KM# 834a 1/10 CROWN

3.1100 g., 0.9995 Platinum .1000 oz. APW, 17.95 mm. **Ruler:** Elizabeth II **Series:** Flower Fairies **Obv:** Crowned bust right **Obv. Designer:** Raphael Maklouf **Rev:** Fairy looking into flower, White Bindweed **Rev. Designer:** Cecily Mary Barker

Date	Mintage	F	VF	XF	Unc	BU
1998 Proof	Est. 5,000	Value: 125				

KM# 835 1/10 CROWN

3.1100 g., 0.9999 Gold .1000 oz. AGW, 17.95 mm. **Ruler:** Elizabeth II **Series:** Flower Fairies **Obv:** Crowned bust right **Obv. Designer:** Raphael Maklouf **Rev:** Fairy standing with flower, daffodil **Rev. Designer:** Cecily Mary Barker

Date	Mintage	F	VF	XF	Unc	BU
1998 Proof	Est. 20,000	Value: 90.00				

ISLE OF MAN 401

KM# 835a 1/10 CROWN
3.1100 g., 0.9995 Platinum .1000 oz. APW, 17.95 mm. **Ruler:** Elizabeth II **Obv:** Crowned bust right **Obv. Designer:** Raphael Maklouf **Rev:** Fairy standing with flower, daffodil **Rev. Legend:** Flower Fairies **Rev. Designer:** Cecily Mary Barker

Date	Mintage	F	VF	XF	Unc	BU
1998 Proof	Est. 5,000	Value: 125				

KM# 854 1/10 CROWN
3.1100 g., 0.9999 Gold .1000 oz. AGW, 17.95 mm. **Ruler:** Elizabeth II **Obv:** Crowned bust right **Obv. Designer:** Raphael Maklouf **Rev:** Birman cat

Date	Mintage	F	VF	XF	Unc	BU
1998	—	—	—	—	70.00	—
1998 Proof	1,000	Value: 72.00				

KM# 854a 1/10 CROWN
3.1100 g., 0.9995 Platinum .1000 oz. APW, 17.95 mm. **Ruler:** Elizabeth II **Obv:** Crowned bust right **Obv. Designer:** Raphael Maklouf **Rev:** Birman cat

Date	Mintage	F	VF	XF	Unc	BU
1998 Proof	—	Value: 130				

KM# 860 1/10 CROWN
3.1100 g., 0.9999 Gold .1000 oz. AGW, 17.95 mm. **Ruler:** Elizabeth II **Subject:** History of the Cat **Obv:** Crowned bust right **Obv. Designer:** Raphael Maklouf **Rev:** Egyptian Mau cat with earring

Date	Mintage	F	VF	XF	Unc	BU
1998 Proof	Est. 20,000	Value: 90.00				

KM# 949 1/10 CROWN
3.1100 g., 0.9999 Gold .1000 oz. AGW, 17.95 mm. **Ruler:** Elizabeth II **Subject:** Year of the Rabbit **Obv:** Crowned bust right **Obv. Designer:** Raphael Maklouf **Rev:** Two rabbits

Date	Mintage	F	VF	XF	Unc	BU
1999 Proof	—	Value: 90.00				

KM# 960 1/10 CROWN
3.1100 g., 0.9999 Gold .1000 oz. AGW, 17.95 mm. **Ruler:** Elizabeth II **Obv:** Crowned bust right **Obv. Designer:** Raphael Maklouf **Rev:** British Blue cat cleaning its paw

Date	Mintage	F	VF	XF	Unc	BU
1999	—	—	—	—	75.00	—
1999 Proof	—	Value: 90.00				
1999 U Y2K	10,000	—	—	—	75.00	—

KM# 960a 1/10 CROWN
3.1104 g., 0.9995 Platinum .1000 oz. APW, 17.95 mm. **Ruler:** Elizabeth II **Obv:** Crowned bust right **Obv. Designer:** Raphael Maklouf **Rev:** British Blue cat cleaning its paw

Date	Mintage	F	VF	XF	Unc	BU
1999 Proof	—	Value: 125				

KM# 1053 1/10 CROWN
3.1100 g., 0.9999 Gold .1000 oz. AGW, 17.95 mm. **Ruler:** Elizabeth II **Obv:** Crowned bust right **Obv. Designer:** Raphael Maklouf **Rev:** Scottish kitten playing with the world **Edge:** Reeded

Date	Mintage	F	VF	XF	Unc	BU
2000	—	—	—	—	75.00	—
2000 Proof	—	Value: 90.00				

KM# 1053a 1/10 CROWN
3.1104 g., 0.9995 Platinum .1000 oz. APW, 17.95 mm. **Ruler:** Elizabeth II **Obv:** Crowned bust right **Obv. Designer:** Raphael Maklouf **Rev:** Scottish kitten playing with the world

Date	Mintage	F	VF	XF	Unc	BU
2000	—	—	—	—	125	—

KM# 1013 1/10 CROWN
3.1100 g., 0.9999 Gold .1000 oz. AGW, 17.95 mm. **Ruler:** Elizabeth II **Subject:** Year of the Dragon **Obv:** Crowned bust right **Obv. Designer:** Raphael Maklouf **Rev:** Dragon, Chinese characters

Date	Mintage	F	VF	XF	Unc	BU
2000 Proof	Est. 15,000	Value: 90.00				

KM# 1059 1/10 CROWN
3.1100 g., 0.9999 Gold .1000 oz. AGW, 17.95 mm. **Ruler:** Elizabeth II **Subject:** Year of the Snake **Obv:** Bust with tiara right **Obv. Designer:** Ian Rank-Broadley **Rev:** Snake **Edge:** Reeded

Date	Mintage	F	VF	XF	Unc	BU
2001 Proof	15,000	Value: 95.00				

KM# 1068 1/10 CROWN
3.1100 g., 0.9999 Gold .1000 oz. AGW, 18 mm. **Ruler:** Elizabeth II **Obv:** Head with tiara right **Obv. Designer:** Ian Rank-Broadley **Rev:** Somali kittens **Edge:** Reeded

Date	Mintage	F	VF	XF	Unc	BU
2001	—	—	—	—	75.00	—
2001 Proof	1,000	Value: 95.00				

KM# 1068a 1/10 CROWN
3.1100 g., 0.9995 Platinum .1000 oz. APW, 18 mm. **Ruler:** Elizabeth II **Obv:** Head with tiara right **Obv. Designer:** Ian Rank-Broadley **Rev:** Somali kittens **Edge:** Reeded

Date	Mintage	F	VF	XF	Unc	BU
2001	—	—	—	—	135	—

KM# 1099 1/10 CROWN
3.1100 g., 0.9999 Gold .1000 oz. AGW, 17.95 mm. **Ruler:** Elizabeth II **Subject:** Year of the Horse **Obv:** Bust with tiara right **Obv. Designer:** Ian Rank-Broadley **Rev:** Two horses **Edge:** Reeded

Date	Mintage	F	VF	XF	Unc	BU
2002 Proof	15,000	Value: 95.00				

KM# 1108 1/10 CROWN
3.1100 g., 0.9990 Gold 0.0999 oz. AGW, 17.95 mm. **Ruler:** Elizabeth II **Subject:** Bengal Cat **Obv:** Head with tiara right **Obv. Designer:** Ian Rank-Broadley **Rev:** Cat and kitten **Edge:** Reeded

Date	Mintage	VG	F	VF	XF	Unc
2002	—	—	—	—	—	75.00
2002 Proof	—	Value: 95.00				

KM# 1108a 1/10 CROWN
3.1100 g., 0.9990 Platinum 0.0999 oz. APW, 17.95 mm. **Ruler:** Elizabeth II **Subject:** Bengal Cat **Obv:** Head with tiara right **Obv. Designer:** Ian Rank-Broadley **Rev:** Cat and kitten **Edge:** Reeded

Date	Mintage	F	VF	XF	Unc	BU
2002	—	—	—	—	125	—

KM# 1162 1/10 CROWN
3.1100 g., 0.9999 Gold 0.1 oz. AGW, 17.95 mm. **Ruler:** Elizabeth II **Subject:** Cat **Obv:** Head with tiara right **Obv. Designer:** Ian Rank-Broadley **Rev:** Two Balinese kittens **Edge:** Reeded

Date	Mintage	F	VF	XF	Unc	BU
2003PM	—	—	—	—	75.00	—
2003PM Proof	—	Value: 95.00				

KM# 1162a 1/10 CROWN
3.1100 g., 0.9995 Platinum 0.0999 oz. APW, 17.95 mm. **Ruler:** Elizabeth II **Subject:** Cat **Obv:** Head with tiara right **Obv. Designer:** Ian Rank-Broadley **Rev:** Two Balinese kittens **Edge:** Reeded

Date	Mintage	F	VF	XF	Unc	BU
2003PM	—	—	—	—	125	—

KM# 1187 1/10 CROWN
3.1100 g., 0.9999 Gold 0.1 oz. AGW, 18 mm. **Ruler:** Elizabeth II **Subject:** Lord of the Rings **Obv:** Bust with tiara right **Obv. Designer:** Ian Rank-Broadley **Rev:** Aragorn with broad sword **Edge:** Reeded

Date	Mintage	F	VF	XF	Unc	BU
2003PM Proof	4,500	Value: 85.00				

KM# 1241 1/10 CROWN
3.1100 g., 0.9999 Gold 0.1 oz. AGW, 18 mm. **Ruler:** Elizabeth II **Obv:** Head with tiara right **Obv. Designer:** Ian Rank-Broadley **Rev:** Monkey **Edge:** Reeded

Date	Mintage	F	VF	XF	Unc	BU
2004PM Proof	15,000	Value: 95.00				

KM# 1248 1/10 CROWN
3.1100 g., 0.9999 Gold 0.1 oz. AGW, 18 mm. **Ruler:** Elizabeth II **Obv:** Head with tiara right **Obv. Designer:** Ian Rank-Broadley **Rev:** Two Tonkinese cats **Edge:** Reeded

Date	Mintage	F	VF	XF	Unc	BU
2004PM	—	—	—	—	75.00	—
2004PM Proof	1,000	Value: 95.00				

KM# 1270 1/10 CROWN
3.1100 g., 0.9999 Gold 0.1 oz. AGW, 18 mm. **Ruler:** Elizabeth II **Obv:** Bust with tiara right **Obv. Designer:** Ian Rank-Broadley **Rev:** Himalayan cat and two kittens **Edge:** Reeded

Date	Mintage	F	VF	XF	Unc	BU
2005PM Proof	—	Value: 100				

KM# 1270a 1/10 CROWN
3.1100 g., 0.9950 Platinum 0.0995 oz. APW, 18 mm. **Ruler:** Elizabeth II **Obv:** Queen Elizabeth II **Rev:** Himalayan cat and two kittens **Edge:** Reeded

Date	Mintage	F	VF	XF	Unc	BU
2005PM Proof	—	Value: 225				

KM# 1168 1/10 CROWN
3.1100 g., 0.9999 Gold 0.1 oz. AGW, 17.95 mm. **Ruler:** Elizabeth II **Subject:** Year of the Goat **Obv:** Bust with tiara right **Obv. Designer:** Ian Rank-Broadley **Rev:** Three goats **Edge:** Reeded

Date	Mintage	F	VF	XF	Unc	BU
2003PM Proof	—	Value: 95.00				

KM# 237 1/5 CROWN
6.2200 g., 0.9990 Gold .2000 oz. AGW, 22 mm. **Ruler:** Elizabeth II **Obv:** Crowned bust right **Obv. Designer:** Raphael Maklouf **Rev:** Manx cat

Date	Mintage	F	VF	XF	Unc	BU
1988	6,750	—	—	—	175	—
1988 Proof	5,000	Value: 190				

KM# 254 1/5 CROWN
6.2200 g., 0.9990 Gold .2000 oz. AGW, 22 mm. **Ruler:** Elizabeth II **Obv:** Crowned bust right **Obv. Designer:** Raphael Maklouf **Rev:** Persian cat

Date	Mintage	F	VF	XF	Unc	BU
1989	—	—	—	—	150	—
1989 Proof	—	Value: 152				

KM# 274 1/5 CROWN
6.2200 g., 0.9990 Gold .2000 oz. AGW, 22 mm. **Ruler:** Elizabeth II **Obv:** Crowned bust right **Obv. Designer:** Raphael Maklouf **Rev:** Cameo head facing within circle

Date	Mintage	F	VF	XF	Unc	BU
1989 Proof	Est. 5,000	Value: 180				

KM# 469 1/5 CROWN
6.2200 g., 0.9990 Platinum .2000 oz. APW, 22 mm. **Ruler:** Elizabeth II **Obv:** Crowned bust right **Obv. Designer:** Raphael Maklouf **Rev:** Persian cat

Date	Mintage	F	VF	XF	Unc	BU
1989	—	—	—	—	260	—
1989 Proof	—	Value: 265				

KM# 268 1/5 CROWN
6.2200 g., 0.9990 Gold .2000 oz. AGW, 22 mm. **Ruler:** Elizabeth II **Subject:** 150th Anniversary of "Penny Black" Stamp **Obv:** Crowned bust right **Obv. Designer:** Raphael Maklouf **Rev:** Penny Black Stamp

Date	Mintage	F	VF	XF	Unc	BU
1990 Proof	Est. 5,000	Value: 210				

KM# 279.1 1/5 CROWN
6.2200 g., 0.9990 Gold .2000 oz. AGW, 22 mm. **Ruler:** Elizabeth II **Obv:** Crowned bust right **Obv. Designer:** Raphael Maklouf **Rev:** Alley cat

Date	Mintage	F	VF	XF	Unc	BU
1990	—	—	—	—	150	—
1990 Proof	—	Value: 175				

KM# 279.2 1/5 CROWN
6.2200 g., 0.9990 Gold .2000 oz. AGW, 22 mm. **Ruler:** Elizabeth II **Obv:** Crowned bust right **Obv. Designer:** Raphael Maklouf **Rev:** Alley cat **Note:** Error.(Rev) Dies claiming platinum metal content

Date	Mintage	F	VF	XF	Unc	BU
1990	467	—	—	—	400	—

KM# 306 1/5 CROWN
6.2200 g., 0.9990 Gold .2000 oz. AGW, 22 mm. **Ruler:** Elizabeth II **Obv:** Crowned bust right **Obv. Designer:** Raphael Maklouf **Rev:** Queen Mother with two daughters

Date	Mintage	F	VF	XF	Unc	BU
1990 Proof	—	Value: 200				

KM# 306a 1/5 CROWN
6.2200 g., 0.9990 Platinum .2000 oz. APW, 22 mm. **Ruler:** Elizabeth II **Obv:** Crowned bust right **Obv. Designer:** Raphael Maklouf **Rev:** Queen Mother with two daughters

Date	Mintage	F	VF	XF	Unc	BU
1990 Proof	—	Value: 265				

KM# 472 1/5 CROWN
6.2200 g., 0.9990 Platinum .2000 oz. APW, 22 mm. **Ruler:** Elizabeth II **Obv:** Crowned bust right **Obv. Designer:** Raphael Maklouf **Rev:** Alley cat

Date	Mintage	F	VF	XF	Unc	BU
1990	—	—	—	—	265	—
1990 Proof	—	Value: 275				

KM# 819 1/5 CROWN
6.2200 g., 0.9990 Gold .2000 oz. AGW, 22 mm. **Ruler:** Elizabeth II **Subject:** Soccer **Obv:** Crowned bust right **Obv. Designer:** Raphael Maklouf **Rev:** Milano

Date	Mintage	F	VF	XF	Unc	BU
1990 Proof	Est. 500	Value: 135				

KM# 819a 1/5 CROWN
6.2200 g., 0.9990 Platinum .2000 oz. APW, 22 mm. **Ruler:** Elizabeth II **Subject:** Soccer **Obv:** Crowned bust right **Obv. Designer:** Raphael Maklouf **Rev:** Milano

Date	Mintage	F	VF	XF	Unc	BU
1990 Proof	Est. 250	Value: 275				

402 ISLE OF MAN

KM# 820 1/5 CROWN
6.2200 g., 0.9990 Gold .2000 oz. AGW, 22 mm. **Ruler:** Elizabeth II **Subject:** Soccer **Obv:** Crowned bust right **Obv. Designer:** Raphael Maklouf **Rev:** Torino

Date	Mintage	F	VF	XF	Unc	BU
1990 Proof	Est. 500	Value: 135				

KM# 820a 1/5 CROWN
6.2200 g., 0.9990 Platinum .2000 oz. APW, 22 mm. **Ruler:** Elizabeth II **Subject:** Soccer **Obv:** Crowned bust right **Obv. Designer:** Raphael Maklouf **Rev:** Torino

Date	Mintage	F	VF	XF	Unc	BU
1990 Proof	Est. 250	Value: 275				

KM# 821 1/5 CROWN
6.2200 g., 0.9990 Gold .2000 oz. AGW, 22 mm. **Ruler:** Elizabeth II **Subject:** Soccer **Obv:** Crowned bust right **Obv. Designer:** Raphael Maklouf **Rev:** Bologna

Date	Mintage	F	VF	XF	Unc	BU
1990 Proof	Est. 500	Value: 135				

KM# 821a 1/5 CROWN
6.2200 g., 0.9990 Platinum .2000 oz. APW, 22 mm. **Ruler:** Elizabeth II **Subject:** Soccer **Obv:** Crowned bust right **Obv. Designer:** Raphael Maklouf **Rev:** Bologna

Date	Mintage	F	VF	XF	Unc	BU
1990	Est. 250	Value: 275				

KM# 822 1/5 CROWN
6.2200 g., 0.9990 Gold .2000 oz. AGW, 22 mm. **Ruler:** Elizabeth II **Subject:** Soccer **Obv:** Crowned bust right **Obv. Designer:** Raphael Maklouf **Rev:** Palermo

Date	Mintage	F	VF	XF	Unc	BU
1990 Proof	Est. 500	Value: 135				

KM# 822a 1/5 CROWN
6.2200 g., 0.9990 Platinum .2000 oz. APW, 22 mm. **Ruler:** Elizabeth II **Subject:** Soccer **Obv:** Crowned bust right **Obv. Designer:** Raphael Maklouf **Rev:** Palermo

Date	Mintage	F	VF	XF	Unc	BU
1990	Est. 250	Value: 275				

KM# 290 1/5 CROWN
6.2200 g., 0.9990 Gold .2000 oz. AGW, 22 mm. **Ruler:** Elizabeth II **Subject:** 100th Anniversary - American Numismatic Association **Obv:** Crowned bust right **Obv. Designer:** Raphael Maklouf **Rev:** Assorted famous world coins

Date	Mintage	F	VF	XF	Unc	BU
1991 Proof	100	Value: 185				

KM# 296 1/5 CROWN
6.2200 g., 0.9990 Gold .2000 oz. AGW, 22 mm. **Ruler:** Elizabeth II **Obv:** Crowned bust right **Obv. Designer:** Raphael Maklouf **Rev:** Norwegian cat

Date	Mintage	F	VF	XF	Unc	BU
1991	—	—	—	—	145	—
1991 Proof	—	Value: 150				

KM# 302 1/5 CROWN
6.2200 g., 0.9990 Gold .2000 oz. AGW, 22 mm. **Ruler:** Elizabeth II **Subject:** America's Cup **Obv:** Crowned bust right **Obv. Designer:** Raphael Maklouf **Rev:** Cameo above two modern sailboats

Date	Mintage	F	VF	XF	Unc	BU
1991 Proof	Est. 250	Value: 190				

KM# 324 1/5 CROWN
6.2200 g., 0.9990 Gold .2000 oz. AGW, 22 mm. **Ruler:** Elizabeth II **Subject:** America's Cup **Obv:** Crowned bust right **Obv. Designer:** Raphael Maklouf **Rev:** Cameo above two modern sailboats

Date	Mintage	F	VF	XF	Unc	BU
1992 Prooflike	10,000	—	—	—	140	—

KM# 330 1/5 CROWN
6.2200 g., 0.9990 Gold .2000 oz. AGW, 22 mm. **Ruler:** Elizabeth II **Obv:** Crowned bust right **Obv. Designer:** Raphael Maklouf **Rev:** Siamese cat

Date	Mintage	F	VF	XF	Unc	BU
1992	—	—	—	—	145	—
1992 Proof	—	Value: 150				

KM# 340 1/5 CROWN
6.2200 g., 0.9990 Gold .2000 oz. AGW, 22 mm. **Ruler:** Elizabeth II **Subject:** Year of the Cockerel **Obv:** Crowned bust right within circle **Obv. Designer:** Raphael Maklouf **Rev:** Cockerel within circle **Rev. Designer:** Barry Stanton

Date	Mintage	F	VF	XF	Unc	BU
1993 Proof	Est. 10,000	Value: 160				

KM# 351 1/5 CROWN
6.2200 g., 0.9990 Gold .2000 oz. AGW, 22 mm. **Ruler:** Elizabeth II **Obv:** Crowned bust right **Obv. Designer:** Raphael Maklouf **Rev:** Maine Coon cat

Date	Mintage	F	VF	XF	Unc	BU
1993	—	—	—	—	145	—
1993 Proof	—	Value: 160				

KM# 365 1/5 CROWN
6.2200 g., 0.9990 Gold .2000 oz. AGW, 22 mm. **Ruler:** Elizabeth II **Subject:** World Cup Soccer - Type I **Obv:** Crowned bust right **Obv. Designer:** Raphael Maklouf **Rev:** Player in foreground kicking ball

Date	Mintage	F	VF	XF	Unc	BU
1994 Proof	Est. 5,000	Value: 165				

KM# 367 1/5 CROWN
6.2200 g., 0.9990 Gold .2000 oz. AGW, 22 mm. **Ruler:** Elizabeth II **Subject:** World Cup Soccer - Type II **Obv:** Crowned bust right **Obv. Designer:** Raphael Maklouf **Rev:** Three players

Date	Mintage	F	VF	XF	Unc	BU
1994 Proof	Est. 5,000	Value: 165				

KM# 369 1/5 CROWN
6.2200 g., 0.9990 Gold .2000 oz. AGW, 22 mm. **Ruler:** Elizabeth II **Subject:** World Cup Soccer - Type III **Obv:** Crowned bust right **Obv. Designer:** Raphael Maklouf **Rev:** Soccer players

Date	Mintage	F	VF	XF	Unc	BU
1994 Proof	Est. 5,000	Value: 165				

KM# 371 1/5 CROWN
6.2200 g., 0.9990 Gold .2000 oz. AGW, 22 mm. **Ruler:** Elizabeth II **Subject:** World Cup Soccer - Type IV **Obv:** Crowned bust right **Obv. Designer:** Raphael Maklouf **Rev:** Soccer players

Date	Mintage	F	VF	XF	Unc	BU
1994 Proof	Est. 5,000	Value: 165				

KM# 373 1/5 CROWN
6.2200 g., 0.9990 Gold .2000 oz. AGW, 22 mm. **Ruler:** Elizabeth II **Subject:** World Cup Soccer - Type V **Obv:** Crowned bust right **Obv. Designer:** Raphael Maklouf **Rev:** Goalie catching ball in hand

Date	Mintage	F	VF	XF	Unc	BU
1994 Proof	Est. 5,000	Value: 165				

KM# 375 1/5 CROWN
6.2200 g., 0.9990 Gold .2000 oz. AGW, 22 mm. **Ruler:** Elizabeth II **Subject:** World Cup Soccer - Type VI **Obv:** Crowned bust right **Obv. Designer:** Raphael Maklouf **Rev:** Soccer players

Date	Mintage	F	VF	XF	Unc	BU
1994 Proof	Est. 5,000	Value: 165				

KM# 378 1/5 CROWN
6.2200 g., 0.9990 Gold .2000 oz. AGW, 22 mm. **Ruler:** Elizabeth II **Obv:** Crowned bust right **Obv. Designer:** Raphael Maklouf **Rev:** Japanese Bobtail cat

Date	Mintage	F	VF	XF	Unc	BU
1994	—	—	—	—	145	—
1994 Proof	—	Value: 160				

KM# 383 1/5 CROWN
6.2200 g., 0.9990 Gold .2000 oz. AGW, 22 mm. **Ruler:** Elizabeth II **Series:** Preserve Planet Earth **Obv:** Crowned bust right **Obv. Designer:** Raphael Maklouf **Rev:** Woolly mammoth

Date	Mintage	F	VF	XF	Unc	BU
1994 Proof	Est. 5,000	Value: 165				

KM# 388 1/5 CROWN
6.2200 g., 0.9990 Gold .2000 oz. AGW, 22 mm. **Ruler:** Elizabeth II **Series:** Preserve Planet Earth **Obv:** Crowned bust right **Obv. Designer:** Raphael Maklouf **Rev:** Kangaroos

Date	Mintage	F	VF	XF	Unc	BU
1994 Proof	5,000	Value: 165				

KM# 389 1/5 CROWN
6.2200 g., 0.9990 Gold .2000 oz. AGW, 22 mm. **Ruler:** Elizabeth II **Series:** Preserve Planet Earth **Obv:** Crowned bust right **Obv. Designer:** Raphael Maklouf **Rev:** Seals

Date	Mintage	F	VF	XF	Unc	BU
1994 Proof	5,000	Value: 165				

KM# 390 1/5 CROWN
6.2200 g., 0.9990 Gold .2000 oz. AGW, 22 mm. **Ruler:** Elizabeth II **Series:** Preserve Planet Earth **Obv:** Crowned bust right **Obv. Designer:** Raphael Maklouf **Rev:** Deer

Date	Mintage	F	VF	XF	Unc	BU
1994 Proof	5,000	Value: 165				

KM# 404 1/5 CROWN
6.2200 g., 0.9990 Gold .2000 oz. AGW, 22 mm. **Ruler:** Elizabeth II **Obv:** Crowned bust right **Obv. Designer:** Raphael Maklouf **Rev:** Pekingese

Date	Mintage	F	VF	XF	Unc	BU
1994 Proof	10,000	Value: 165				

KM# 409 1/5 CROWN
6.2200 g., 0.9990 Gold .2000 oz. AGW, 22 mm. **Ruler:** Elizabeth II **Series:** Man in Flight **Obv:** Crowned bust right **Obv. Designer:** Raphael Maklouf **Rev:** Manned glider

Date	Mintage	F	VF	XF	Unc	BU
1994 Proof	Est. 5,000	Value: 170				

KM# 410 1/5 CROWN
6.2200 g., 0.9990 Gold .2000 oz. AGW, 22 mm. **Ruler:** Elizabeth II **Series:** Man in Flight **Obv:** Crowned bust right **Obv. Designer:** Raphael Maklouf **Rev:** Dirigible, Ferdinand von Zeppelin

Date	Mintage	F	VF	XF	Unc	BU
1994 Proof	Est. 5,000	Value: 170				

KM# 411 1/5 CROWN
6.2200 g., 0.9990 Gold .2000 oz. AGW, 22 mm. **Ruler:** Elizabeth II **Series:** Man in Flight **Obv:** Crowned bust right **Obv. Designer:** Raphael Maklouf **Rev:** Bust of Louis Bleriot behind plane flying across channel

Date	Mintage	F	VF	XF	Unc	BU
1994 Proof	Est. 5,000	Value: 170				

KM# 412 1/5 CROWN
6.2200 g., 0.9990 Gold .2000 oz. AGW, 22 mm. **Ruler:** Elizabeth II **Series:** Man in Flight **Obv:** Crowned bust right **Obv. Designer:** Raphael Maklouf **Rev:** Plane in flight above ocean

Date	Mintage	F	VF	XF	Unc	BU
1994 Proof	Est. 5,000	Value: 170				

KM# 413 1/5 CROWN
6.2200 g., 0.9990 Gold .2000 oz. AGW, 22 mm. **Ruler:** Elizabeth II **Series:** Man in Flight **Subject:** First England to Australia Flight **Obv:** Crowned bust right **Obv. Designer:** Raphael Maklouf **Rev:** Biplane flying

Date	Mintage	F	VF	XF	Unc	BU
1994 Proof	Est. 5,000	Value: 170				

KM# 414 1/5 CROWN
6.2200 g., 0.9990 Gold .2000 oz. AGW, 22 mm. **Ruler:** Elizabeth II **Series:** Man in Flight **Subject:** 60th Anniversary of Airmail **Obv:** Crowned bust right **Obv. Designer:** Raphael Maklouf **Rev:** Plane flying left above inscription

Date	Mintage	F	VF	XF	Unc	BU
1994 Proof	Est. 5,000	Value: 170				

KM# 415 1/5 CROWN
6.2200 g., 0.9990 Gold .2000 oz. AGW, 22 mm. **Ruler:** Elizabeth II **Series:** Man in Flight **Subject:** 50th Anniversary of International Civil Aviation Organization **Obv:** Crowned bust right **Obv. Designer:** Raphael Maklouf **Rev:** Trademark of ICAO

Date	Mintage	F	VF	XF	Unc	BU
1994 Proof	Est. 5,000	Value: 170				

KM# 416 1/5 CROWN
6.2200 g., 0.9990 Gold .2000 oz. AGW, 22 mm. **Ruler:** Elizabeth II **Series:** Man in Flight **Subject:** First Concorde Flight **Obv:** Crowned bust right **Obv. Designer:** Raphael Maklouf **Rev:** Concorde waiting at airport

Date	Mintage	F	VF	XF	Unc	BU
1994 Proof	Est. 5,000	Value: 170				

KM# 475 1/5 CROWN
6.2200 g., 0.9990 Platinum .2000 oz. APW, 22 mm. **Ruler:** Elizabeth II **Obv:** Crowned bust right **Obv. Designer:** Raphael Maklouf **Rev:** Japanese Bobtail cat

Date	Mintage	F	VF	XF	Unc	BU
1994	—	—	—	—	260	—
1994 Proof	—	Value: 270				

KM# 429 1/5 CROWN
6.2200 g., 0.9990 Gold .2000 oz. AGW, 22 mm. **Ruler:** Elizabeth II **Series:** Man in Flight **Obv:** Crowned bust right **Obv. Designer:** Raphael Maklouf **Rev:** Airplane in flight

Date	Mintage	F	VF	XF	Unc	BU
1995 Proof	Est. 5,000	Value: 170				

KM# 426 1/5 CROWN
6.2200 g., 0.9990 Gold .2000 oz. AGW, 22 mm. **Ruler:** Elizabeth II **Series:** Man in Flight **Obv:** Crowned bust right **Obv. Designer:** Raphael Maklouf **Rev:** Icarus' wings melting

Date	Mintage	F	VF	XF	Unc	BU
1995 Proof	Est. 5,000	Value: 170				

KM# 427 1/5 CROWN
6.2200 g., 0.9990 Gold .2000 oz. AGW, 22 mm. **Ruler:** Elizabeth II **Series:** Man in Flight **Obv:** Crowned bust right **Obv. Designer:** Raphael Maklouf **Rev:** Leonardo Da Vinci and aircraft design

Date	Mintage	F	VF	XF	Unc	BU
1995 Proof	Est. 5,000	Value: 170				

KM# 428 1/5 CROWN

6.2200 g., 0.9990 Gold .2000 oz. AGW, 22 mm. **Ruler:** Elizabeth II **Series:** Man in Flight **Obv:** Crowned bust right **Obv. Designer:** Raphael Maklouf **Rev:** Balloon in flight

Date	Mintage	F	VF	XF	Unc	BU
1995 Proof	Est. 5,000	Value: 170				

KM# 430 1/5 CROWN

6.2200 g., 0.9990 Gold .2000 oz. AGW, 22 mm. **Ruler:** Elizabeth II **Series:** Man in Flight **Subject:** 1st Flight Tokyo to Paris by Abe and Kawachi **Obv:** Crowned bust right **Obv. Designer:** Raphael Maklouf **Rev:** Busts above airplane

Date	Mintage	F	VF	XF	Unc	BU
1995 Proof	Est. 5,000	Value: 170				

KM# 431 1/5 CROWN

6.2200 g., 0.9990 Gold .2000 oz. AGW, 22 mm. **Ruler:** Elizabeth II **Series:** Man in Flight **Subject:** FW109, First Diesel Powered Aircraft **Obv:** Crowned bust right **Obv. Designer:** Raphael Maklouf **Rev:** Grounded airplane

Date	Mintage	F	VF	XF	Unc	BU
1995 Proof	Est. 5,000	Value: 170				

KM# 432 1/5 CROWN

6.2200 g., 0.9990 Gold .2000 oz. AGW, 22 mm. **Ruler:** Elizabeth II **Series:** Man in Flight **Subject:** ME262, First Jet Aircraft **Obv:** Crowned bust right **Obv. Designer:** Raphael Maklouf **Rev:** Jet flying into clouds

Date	Mintage	F	VF	XF	Unc	BU
1995 Proof	Est. 5,000	Value: 170				

KM# 433 1/5 CROWN

6.2200 g., 0.9990 Gold .2000 oz. AGW, 22 mm. **Ruler:** Elizabeth II **Series:** Man in Flight **Subject:** 25th Anniversary of Boeing 747 **Obv:** Crowned bust right **Obv. Designer:** Raphael Maklouf **Rev:** Jumbo jet in flight

Date	Mintage	F	VF	XF	Unc	BU
1995 Proof	Est. 5,000	Value: 170				

KM# 444 1/5 CROWN

6.2200 g., 0.9990 Gold .2000 oz. AGW, 22 mm. **Ruler:** Elizabeth II **Obv:** Crowned bust right **Obv. Designer:** Raphael Maklouf **Rev:** Turkish cat

Date	Mintage	F	VF	XF	Unc	BU
1995	—	—	—	—	150	—
1995 Proof	—	Value: 165				

KM# 451 1/5 CROWN

6.2200 g., 0.9990 Gold .2000 oz. AGW, 22 mm. **Ruler:** Elizabeth II **Subject:** Year of the Pig **Obv:** Crowned bust right **Obv. Designer:** Raphael Maklouf **Rev:** Sow and piglets

Date	Mintage	F	VF	XF	Unc	BU
1995 Proof	Est. 10,000	Value: 165				

KM# 457 1/5 CROWN

6.2200 g., 0.9990 Gold .2000 oz. AGW, 22 mm. **Ruler:** Elizabeth II **Subject:** 95th Birthday of Queen Mother **Obv:** Crowned bust right **Obv. Designer:** Raphael Maklouf **Rev:** Bust of Queen Mother

Date	Mintage	F	VF	XF	Unc	BU
1995 Proof	Est. 5,000	Value: 170				

KM# 459 1/5 CROWN

6.2200 g., 0.9990 Gold .2000 oz. AGW, 22 mm. **Ruler:** Elizabeth II **Series:** Preserve Planet Earth **Obv:** Crowned bust right **Obv. Designer:** Raphael Maklouf **Rev:** Otter

Date	Mintage	F	VF	XF	Unc	BU
1995 Proof	Est. 5,000	Value: 165				

KM# 460 1/5 CROWN

6.2200 g., 0.9990 Gold .2000 oz. AGW, 22 mm. **Ruler:** Elizabeth II **Series:** Preserve Planet Earth **Obv:** Crowned bust right **Obv. Designer:** Raphael Maklouf **Rev:** Egret Birds

Date	Mintage	F	VF	XF	Unc	BU
1995 Proof	Est. 5,000	Value: 165				

KM# 480 1/5 CROWN

6.2200 g., 0.9990 Platinum .2000 oz. APW, 22 mm. **Ruler:** Elizabeth II **Obv:** Crowned bust right **Obv. Designer:** Raphael Maklouf **Rev:** Turkish cat

Date	Mintage	F	VF	XF	Unc	BU
1995	—	—	—	—	255	—
1995 Proof	—	Value: 265				

KM# 483 1/5 CROWN

6.2200 g., 0.9990 Gold .2000 oz. AGW, 22 mm. **Ruler:** Elizabeth II **Series:** Aircraft of World War II **Obv:** Crowned bust right **Obv. Designer:** Raphael Maklouf **Rev:** Hawker Hurricane

Date	Mintage	F	VF	XF	Unc	BU
1995 Proof	Est. 5,000	Value: 185				

KM# 484 1/5 CROWN

6.2200 g., 0.9990 Gold .2000 oz. AGW, 22 mm. **Ruler:** Elizabeth II **Series:** Aircraft of World War II **Obv:** Crowned bust right **Obv. Designer:** Raphael Maklouf **Rev:** P-51 Mustang

Date	Mintage	F	VF	XF	Unc	BU
1995 Proof	Est. 5,000	Value: 185				

KM# 485 1/5 CROWN

6.2200 g., 0.9990 Gold .2000 oz. AGW, 22 mm. **Ruler:** Elizabeth II **Series:** Aircraft of World War II **Obv:** Crowned bust right **Obv. Designer:** Raphael Maklouf **Rev:** Letrov S328

Date	Mintage	F	VF	XF	Unc	BU
1995 Proof	Est. 5,000	Value: 185				

KM# 486 1/5 CROWN

6.2200 g., 0.9990 Gold .2000 oz. AGW, 22 mm. **Ruler:** Elizabeth II **Series:** Aircraft of World War II **Obv:** Crowned bust right **Obv. Designer:** Raphael Maklouf **Rev:** Messerschmitt ME262

Date	Mintage	F	VF	XF	Unc	BU
1995 Proof	Est. 5,000	Value: 185				

KM# 487 1/5 CROWN

6.2200 g., 0.9990 Gold .2000 oz. AGW, 22 mm. **Ruler:** Elizabeth II **Series:** Aircraft of World War II **Obv:** Crowned bust right **Obv. Designer:** Raphael Maklouf **Rev:** JU87 Stuka

Date	Mintage	F	VF	XF	Unc	BU
1995 Proof	Est. 5,000	Value: 185				

KM# 488 1/5 CROWN

6.2200 g., 0.9990 Gold .2000 oz. AGW, 22 mm. **Ruler:** Elizabeth II **Series:** Aircraft of World War II **Obv:** Crowned bust right **Obv. Designer:** Raphael Maklouf **Rev:** MIG 3

Date	Mintage	F	VF	XF	Unc	BU
1995 Proof	Est. 5,000	Value: 185				

KM# 489 1/5 CROWN

6.2200 g., 0.9990 Gold .2000 oz. AGW, 22 mm. **Ruler:** Elizabeth II **Series:** Aircraft of World War II **Obv:** Crowned bust right **Obv. Designer:** Raphael Maklouf **Rev:** Nakajima Ki-49 Donryu

Date	Mintage	F	VF	XF	Unc	BU
1995 Proof	Est. 5,000	Value: 185				

KM# 490 1/5 CROWN

6.2200 g., 0.9990 Gold .2000 oz. AGW, 22 mm. **Ruler:** Elizabeth II **Series:** Aircraft of World War II **Obv:** Crowned bust right **Obv. Designer:** Raphael Maklouf **Rev:** Vickers Wellington

Date	Mintage	F	VF	XF	Unc	BU
1995 Proof	Est. 5,000	Value: 185				

KM# 491 1/5 CROWN

6.2200 g., 0.9990 Gold .2000 oz. AGW, 22 mm. **Ruler:** Elizabeth II **Series:** Aircraft of World War II **Obv:** Crowned bust right **Obv. Designer:** Raphael Maklouf **Rev:** Spitfire

Date	Mintage	F	VF	XF	Unc	BU
1995 Proof	Est. 5,000	Value: 185				

KM# 492 1/5 CROWN

6.2200 g., 0.9990 Gold .2000 oz. AGW, 22 mm. **Ruler:** Elizabeth II **Series:** Aircraft of World War II **Obv:** Crowned bust right **Obv. Designer:** Raphael Maklouf **Rev:** Fokker G. 1a

Date	Mintage	F	VF	XF	Unc	BU
1995 Proof	Est. 5,000	Value: 185				

KM# 493 1/5 CROWN

6.2200 g., 0.9990 Gold .2000 oz. AGW, 22 mm. **Ruler:** Elizabeth II **Series:** Aircraft of World War II **Obv:** Crowned bust right **Obv. Designer:** Raphael Maklouf **Rev:** Commonwealth Boomerang CA-13

Date	Mintage	F	VF	XF	Unc	BU
1995 Proof	Est. 5,000	Value: 185				

KM# 494 1/5 CROWN

6.2200 g., 0.9990 Gold .2000 oz. AGW, 22 mm. **Ruler:** Elizabeth II **Series:** Aircraft of World War II **Obv:** Crowned bust right **Obv. Designer:** Raphael Maklouf **Rev:** Briston Blenheim 142M

Date	Mintage	F	VF	XF	Unc	BU
1995 Proof	Est. 5,000	Value: 185				

KM# 495 1/5 CROWN

6.2200 g., 0.9990 Gold .2000 oz. AGW, 22 mm. **Ruler:** Elizabeth II **Series:** Aircraft of World War II **Obv:** Crowned bust right **Obv. Designer:** Raphael Maklouf **Rev:** Mitsubishi Zero

Date	Mintage	F	VF	XF	Unc	BU
1995 Proof	Est. 5,000	Value: 185				

KM# 496 1/5 CROWN

6.2200 g., 0.9990 Gold .2000 oz. AGW, 22 mm. **Ruler:** Elizabeth II **Series:** Aircraft of World War II **Obv:** Crowned bust right **Obv. Designer:** Raphael Maklouf **Rev:** Heinkel HE111

Date	Mintage	F	VF	XF	Unc	BU
1995 Proof	Est. 5,000	Value: 185				

KM# 497 1/5 CROWN

6.2200 g., 0.9990 Gold .2000 oz. AGW, 22 mm. **Ruler:** Elizabeth II **Series:** Aircraft of World War II **Obv:** Crowned bust right **Obv. Designer:** Raphael Maklouf **Rev:** Boulton Paul P82 Defiant

Date	Mintage	F	VF	XF	Unc	BU
1995 Proof	Est. 5,000	Value: 185				

KM# 498 1/5 CROWN

6.2200 g., 0.9990 Gold .2000 oz. AGW, 22 mm. **Ruler:** Elizabeth II **Series:** Aircraft of World War II **Obv:** Crowned bust right **Obv. Designer:** Raphael Maklouf **Rev:** Boeing B289 - Enola Gay

Date	Mintage	F	VF	XF	Unc	BU
1995 Proof	Est. 5,000	Value: 185				

KM# 499 1/5 CROWN

6.2200 g., 0.9990 Gold .2000 oz. AGW, 22 mm. **Ruler:** Elizabeth II **Series:** Aircraft of World War II **Obv:** Crowned bust right **Obv. Designer:** Raphael Maklouf **Rev:** Douglas DC-3 (C47)

Date	Mintage	F	VF	XF	Unc	BU
1995 Proof	Est. 5,000	Value: 185				

KM# 500 1/5 CROWN

6.2200 g., 0.9990 Gold .2000 oz. AGW, 22 mm. **Ruler:** Elizabeth II **Series:** Aircraft of World War II **Obv:** Crowned bust right **Obv. Designer:** Raphael Maklouf **Rev:** Fairey Swordfish

Date	Mintage	F	VF	XF	Unc	BU
1995 Proof	Est. 5,000	Value: 185				

KM# 501 1/5 CROWN

6.2200 g., 0.9990 Gold .2000 oz. AGW, 22 mm. **Ruler:** Elizabeth II **Series:** Aircraft of World War II **Obv:** Crowned bust right **Obv. Designer:** Raphael Maklouf **Rev:** Curtiss P40

Date	Mintage	F	VF	XF	Unc	BU
1995 Proof	Est. 5,000	Value: 185				

KM# 523 1/5 CROWN

6.2200 g., 0.9990 Gold .2000 oz. AGW, 22 mm. **Ruler:** Elizabeth II **Subject:** America's Cup **Obv:** Crowned bust right **Obv. Designer:** Raphael Maklouf **Rev:** Boats

Date	Mintage	F	VF	XF	Unc	BU
1995 Proof	Est. 5,000	Value: 145				

KM# 525 1/5 CROWN

6.2200 g., 0.9999 Gold .2000 oz. AGW, 22 mm. **Ruler:** Elizabeth II **Series:** Inventions of the Modern World **Obv:** Crowned bust right **Obv. Designer:** Raphael Maklouf **Rev:** Cameo of Tsai Lun, paper and tree

Date	Mintage	F	VF	XF	Unc	BU
1995 Proof	Est. 5,000	Value: 165				

KM# 527 1/5 CROWN

6.2200 g., 0.9999 Gold .2000 oz. AGW, 22 mm. **Ruler:** Elizabeth II **Series:** Inventions of the Modern World **Obv:** Crowned bust right **Obv. Designer:** Raphael Maklouf **Rev:** Cameo of Chang Heng and Seismograph

Date	Mintage	F	VF	XF	Unc	BU
1995 Proof	Est. 5,000	Value: 165				

KM# 529 1/5 CROWN

6.2200 g., 0.9999 Gold .2000 oz. AGW, 22 mm. **Ruler:** Elizabeth II **Series:** Inventions of the Modern World **Obv:** Crowned bust right **Obv. Designer:** Raphael Maklouf **Rev:** Cameo of Tsu Chung Chih and compass cart

Date	Mintage	F	VF	XF	Unc	BU
1995 Proof	Est. 5,000	Value: 165				

KM# 531 1/5 CROWN

6.2200 g., 0.9999 Gold .2000 oz. AGW, 22 mm. **Ruler:** Elizabeth II **Series:** Inventions of the Modern World **Obv:** Crowned bust right **Obv. Designer:** Raphael Maklouf **Rev:** Cameo bust facing and movable type

Date	Mintage	F	VF	XF	Unc	BU
1995 Proof	Est. 5,000	Value: 165				

KM# 533 1/5 CROWN

6.2200 g., 0.9999 Gold .2000 oz. AGW, 22 mm. **Ruler:** Elizabeth II **Series:** Inventions of the Modern World **Obv:** Crowned bust right **Obv. Designer:** Raphael Maklouf **Rev:** Cameo of Charles Babbage and first computer

Date	Mintage	F	VF	XF	Unc	BU
1995 Proof	Est. 5,000	Value: 165				

KM# 535 1/5 CROWN

6.2200 g., 0.9999 Gold .2000 oz. AGW, 22 mm. **Ruler:** Elizabeth II **Series:** Inventions of the Modern World **Obv:** Crowned bust right **Obv. Designer:** Raphael Maklouf **Rev:** Cameo of Fox Talbot, photography

Date	Mintage	F	VF	XF	Unc	BU
1995 Proof	Est. 5,000	Value: 165				

KM# 537 1/5 CROWN

6.2200 g., 0.9999 Gold .2000 oz. AGW, 22 mm. **Ruler:** Elizabeth II **Series:** Inventions of the Modern World **Obv:** Crowned bust right **Obv. Designer:** Raphael Maklouf **Rev:** Cameo of Rudolf Diesel, diesel engine

Date	Mintage	F	VF	XF	Unc	BU
1995 Proof	Est. 5,000	Value: 165				

KM# 539 1/5 CROWN

6.2200 g., 0.9999 Gold .2000 oz. AGW, 22 mm. **Ruler:** Elizabeth II **Series:** Inventions of the Modern World **Obv:** Crowned bust right **Obv. Designer:** Raphael Maklouf **Rev:** Cameo of Wilhelm K. Roentgen and xray of hand

Date	Mintage	F	VF	XF	Unc	BU
1995 Proof	Est. 5,000	Value: 165				

KM# 541 1/5 CROWN

6.2200 g., 0.9999 Gold .2000 oz. AGW, 22 mm. **Ruler:** Elizabeth II **Series:** Inventions of the Modern World **Obv:** Crowned bust right **Obv. Designer:** Raphael Maklouf **Rev:** Cameo bust facing and radio equipment

Date	Mintage	F	VF	XF	Unc	BU
1995 Proof	Est. 5,000	Value: 165				

404 ISLE OF MAN

KM# 543 1/5 CROWN
6.2200 g., 0.9999 Gold .2000 oz. AGW, 22 mm. **Ruler:** Elizabeth II **Series:** Inventions of the Modern World **Obv:** Crowned bust right **Obv. Designer:** Raphael Maklouf **Rev:** Cameo of John L. Baird and television equipment

Date	Mintage	F	VF	XF	Unc	BU
1995 Proof	Est. 5,000	Value: 165				

KM# 545 1/5 CROWN
6.2200 g., 0.9999 Gold .2000 oz. AGW, 22 mm. **Ruler:** Elizabeth II **Series:** Inventions of the Modern World **Obv:** Crowned bust right **Obv. Designer:** Raphael Maklouf **Rev:** Cameo of Alexander Fleming and microscope

Date	Mintage	F	VF	XF	Unc	BU
1995 Proof	Est. 5,000	Value: 165				

KM# 547 1/5 CROWN
6.2200 g., 0.9999 Gold .2000 oz. AGW, 22 mm. **Ruler:** Elizabeth II **Series:** Inventions of the Modern World **Obv:** Crowned bust right **Obv. Designer:** Raphael Maklouf **Rev:** Cameo of Lazlo Biro and ball-point pen

Date	Mintage	F	VF	XF	Unc	BU
1995 Proof	Est. 5,000	Value: 165				

KM# 549 1/5 CROWN
6.2200 g., 0.9999 Gold .2000 oz. AGW, 22 mm. **Series:** Inventions of the Modern World **Obv:** Crowned bust right **Obv. Designer:** Raphael Maklouf **Rev:** Cameo of Wernher von Braun and rocket

Date	Mintage	F	VF	XF	Unc	BU
1996 Proof	Est. 5,000	Value: 165				

KM# 550 1/5 CROWN
6.2200 g., 0.9999 Gold .2000 oz. AGW, 22 mm. **Ruler:** Elizabeth II **Series:** Inventions of the Modern World **Obv:** Crowned bust right **Obv. Designer:** Raphael Maklouf **Rev:** Cameo of Thomas Edison, electricity

Date	Mintage	F	VF	XF	Unc	BU
1996 Proof	Est. 5,000	Value: 165				

KM# 551 1/5 CROWN
6.2200 g., 0.9999 Gold .2000 oz. AGW, 22 mm. **Ruler:** Elizabeth II **Series:** Inventions of the Modern World **Obv:** Crowned bust right **Obv. Designer:** Raphael Maklouf **Rev:** Compass

Date	Mintage	F	VF	XF	Unc	BU
1996 Proof	Est. 5,000	Value: 165				

KM# 552 1/5 CROWN
6.2200 g., 0.9999 Gold .2000 oz. AGW, 22 mm. **Ruler:** Elizabeth II **Series:** Inventions of the Modern World **Obv:** Crowned bust right **Obv. Designer:** Raphael Maklouf **Rev:** Cameo of Michael Faraday, electricity

Date	Mintage	F	VF	XF	Unc	BU
1996 Proof	Est. 5,000	Value: 165				

KM# 553 1/5 CROWN
6.2200 g., 0.9999 Gold .2000 oz. AGW, 22 mm. **Ruler:** Elizabeth II **Series:** Inventions of the Modern World **Obv:** Crowned bust right **Obv. Designer:** Raphael Maklouf **Rev:** Cameo of Emile Berliner and gramophone

Date	Mintage	F	VF	XF	Unc	BU
1996 Proof	Est. 5,000	Value: 165				

KM# 554 1/5 CROWN
6.2200 g., 0.9999 Gold .2000 oz. AGW, 22 mm. **Ruler:** Elizabeth II **Series:** Inventions of the Modern World **Obv:** Crowned bust right **Obv. Designer:** Raphael Maklouf **Rev:** Cameo of Alexander Graham Bell, voice transmission

Date	Mintage	F	VF	XF	Unc	BU
1996 Proof	Est. 5,000	Value: 165				

KM# 561 1/5 CROWN
6.2200 g., 0.9999 Gold .2000 oz. AGW, 22 mm. **Ruler:** Elizabeth II **Series:** 1996 Summer Olympics - Atlanta **Obv:** Crowned bust right **Obv. Designer:** Raphael Maklouf **Rev:** Hurdler

Date	Mintage	F	VF	XF	Unc	BU
1996 Proof	Est. 5,000	Value: 165				

KM# 562 1/5 CROWN
6.2200 g., 0.9999 Gold .2000 oz. AGW, 22 mm. **Ruler:** Elizabeth II **Series:** 1996 Summer Olympics - Atlanta **Obv:** Crowned bust right **Obv. Designer:** Raphael Maklouf **Rev:** Runners

Date	Mintage	F	VF	XF	Unc	BU
1996 Proof	Est. 5,000	Value: 165				

KM# 563 1/5 CROWN
6.2200 g., 0.9999 Gold .2000 oz. AGW, 22 mm. **Ruler:** Elizabeth II **Series:** 1996 Summer Olympics - Atlanta **Obv:** Crowned bust right **Obv. Designer:** Raphael Maklouf **Rev:** Sailing

Date	Mintage	F	VF	XF	Unc	BU
1996 Proof	Est. 5,000	Value: 165				

KM# 564 1/5 CROWN
6.2200 g., 0.9999 Gold .2000 oz. AGW, 22 mm. **Ruler:** Elizabeth II **Series:** 1996 Summer Olympics - Atlanta **Obv:** Crowned bust right **Obv. Designer:** Raphael Maklouf **Rev:** Swimmers

Date	Mintage	F	VF	XF	Unc	BU
1996 Proof	Est. 5,000	Value: 165				

KM# 565 1/5 CROWN
6.2200 g., 0.9999 Gold .2000 oz. AGW, 22 mm. **Ruler:** Elizabeth II **Series:** 1996 Summer Olympics - Atlanta **Obv:** Crowned bust right **Obv. Designer:** Raphael Maklouf **Rev:** Equestrian

Date	Mintage	F	VF	XF	Unc	BU
1996 Proof	Est. 5,000	Value: 165				

KM# 566 1/5 CROWN
6.2200 g., 0.9999 Gold .2000 oz. AGW, 22 mm. **Ruler:** Elizabeth II **Series:** 1996 Summer Olympics - Atlanta **Obv:** Crowned bust right **Obv. Designer:** Raphael Maklouf **Rev:** Cyclists and Nike

Date	Mintage	F	VF	XF	Unc	BU
1996 Proof	Est. 5,000	Value: 165				

KM# 573 1/5 CROWN
6.2200 g., 0.9990 Gold .2000 oz. AGW, 22 mm. **Ruler:** Elizabeth II **Series:** Bicentennial of Robert Burns **Obv:** Crowned bust right **Obv. Designer:** Raphael Maklouf **Rev:** Seated

Date	Mintage	F	VF	XF	Unc	BU
1996 Proof	Est. 5,000	Value: 165				

KM# 574 1/5 CROWN
6.2200 g., 0.9990 Gold .2000 oz. AGW, 22 mm. **Ruler:** Elizabeth II **Series:** Bicentennial of Robert Burns **Obv:** Crowned bust right **Obv. Designer:** Raphael Maklouf **Rev:** Pirate ships

Date	Mintage	F	VF	XF	Unc	BU
1996 Proof	Est. 5,000	Value: 165				

KM# 575 1/5 CROWN
6.2200 g., 0.9990 Gold .2000 oz. AGW, 22 mm. **Ruler:** Elizabeth II **Series:** Bicentennial of Robert Burns **Obv:** Crowned bust right **Obv. Designer:** Raphael Maklouf **Rev:** Auld Lang Syne

Date	Mintage	F	VF	XF	Unc	BU
1996 Proof	Est. 5,000	Value: 165				

KM# 576 1/5 CROWN
6.2200 g., 0.9990 Gold .2000 oz. AGW, 22 mm. **Ruler:** Elizabeth II **Series:** Bicentennial of Robert Burns **Obv:** Crowned bust right **Obv. Designer:** Raphael Maklouf **Rev:** Edinburgh Castle

Date	Mintage	F	VF	XF	Unc	BU
1996 Proof	Est. 5,000	Value: 165				

KM# 581 1/5 CROWN
6.2200 g., 0.9990 Gold .2000 oz. AGW, 22 mm. **Ruler:** Elizabeth II **Subject:** Queen's Birthday **Obv:** Crowned bust right **Obv. Designer:** Raphael Maklouf **Rev:** Flowers

Date	Mintage	F	VF	XF	Unc	BU
1996 Proof	Est. 5,000	Value: 165				

KM# 583 1/5 CROWN
6.2200 g., 0.9990 Gold .2000 oz. AGW, 22 mm. **Ruler:** Elizabeth II **Subject:** Preserve Planet Earth **Obv:** Crowned bust right **Obv. Designer:** Raphael Maklouf **Rev:** Killer whale

Date	Mintage	F	VF	XF	Unc	BU
1996 Proof	Est. 5,000	Value: 165				

KM# 584 1/5 CROWN
6.2200 g., 0.9990 Gold .2000 oz. AGW, 22 mm. **Ruler:** Elizabeth II **Subject:** Preserve Planet Earth **Obv:** Crowned bust right **Obv. Designer:** Raphael Maklouf **Rev:** Razorbill feeding chick

Date	Mintage	F	VF	XF	Unc	BU
1996 Proof	Est. 5,000	Value: 165				

KM# 605 1/5 CROWN
6.2200 g., 0.9990 Gold .2000 oz. AGW, 22 mm. **Ruler:** Elizabeth II **Series:** Flower Fairies **Obv:** Crowned bust right **Obv. Designer:** Raphael Maklouf **Rev:** Orchis **Rev. Designer:** Cecily Mary Barker

Date	Mintage	F	VF	XF	Unc	BU
1996 Proof	Est. 5,000	Value: 170				

KM# 606 1/5 CROWN
6.2200 g., 0.9990 Gold .2000 oz. AGW, 22 mm. **Ruler:** Elizabeth II **Series:** Flower Fairies **Obv:** Crowned bust right **Obv. Designer:** Raphael Maklouf **Rev:** Rose **Rev. Designer:** Cecily Mary Barker

Date	Mintage	F	VF	XF	Unc	BU
1996 Proof	Est. 5,000	Value: 170				

KM# 607 1/5 CROWN
6.2200 g., 0.9990 Gold .2000 oz. AGW, 22 mm. **Ruler:** Elizabeth II **Series:** Flower Fairies **Obv:** Crowned bust right **Obv. Designer:** Raphael Maklouf **Rev:** Fuchsia **Rev. Designer:** Cecily Mary Barker

Date	Mintage	F	VF	XF	Unc	BU
1996 Proof	Est. 5,000	Value: 170				

KM# 608 1/5 CROWN
6.2200 g., 0.9990 Gold .2000 oz. AGW, 22 mm. **Ruler:** Elizabeth II **Series:** Flower Fairies **Obv:** Crowned bust right **Obv. Designer:** Raphael Maklouf **Rev:** Pinks **Rev. Designer:** Cecily Mary Barker

Date	Mintage	F	VF	XF	Unc	BU
1996 Proof	Est. 5,000	Value: 170				

KM# 617 1/5 CROWN
6.2200 g., 0.9990 Gold .2000 oz. AGW, 22 mm. **Ruler:** Elizabeth II **Obv:** Crowned bust right **Obv. Designer:** Raphael Maklouf **Rev:** Burmese cat

Date	Mintage	F	VF	XF	Unc	BU
1996	—	—	—	—	145	—
1996 Proof	—	Value: 160				

KM# 618 1/5 CROWN
6.2200 g., 0.9990 Platinum .2000 oz. APW, 22 mm. **Ruler:** Elizabeth II **Obv:** Crowned bust right **Obv. Designer:** Raphael Maklouf **Rev:** Burmese cat

Date	Mintage	F	VF	XF	Unc	BU
1996	—	—	—	—	260	—
1996 Proof	—	Value: 270				

KM# 625 1/5 CROWN
6.2200 g., 0.9990 Gold .2000 oz. AGW, 22 mm. **Ruler:** Elizabeth II **Obv:** Crowned bust right **Obv. Designer:** Raphael Maklouf **Rev:** Portrait of Ferdinand Magellan, map and ship

Date	Mintage	F	VF	XF	Unc	BU
1996 Proof	Est. 5,000	Value: 165				

KM# 628 1/5 CROWN
6.2200 g., 0.9990 Gold .2000 oz. AGW, 22 mm. **Ruler:** Elizabeth II **Obv:** Crowned bust right **Obv. Designer:** Raphael Maklouf **Rev:** Portrait of Sir Francis Drake, map and ship

Date	Mintage	F	VF	XF	Unc	BU
1996 Proof	Est. 5,000	Value: 165				

KM# 631 1/5 CROWN
6.2200 g., 0.9990 Gold .2000 oz. AGW, 22 mm. **Ruler:** Elizabeth II **Series:** European Football Championship **Obv:** Crowned bust right **Obv. Designer:** Raphael Maklouf **Rev:** Romania vs Bulgaria

Date	Mintage	F	VF	XF	Unc	BU
1996 Proof	Est. 5,000	Value: 165				

KM# 634 1/5 CROWN
6.2200 g., 0.9990 Gold .2000 oz. AGW, 22 mm. **Ruler:** Elizabeth II **Series:** European Football Championship **Obv:** Crowned bust right
Obv. Designer: Raphael Maklouf **Rev:** Czech Republic vs Italy

Date	Mintage	F	VF	XF	Unc	BU
1996 Proof	Est. 5,000	Value: 165				

KM# 637 1/5 CROWN
6.2200 g., 0.9990 Gold .2000 oz. AGW, 22 mm. **Ruler:** Elizabeth II **Series:** European Football Championship **Obv:** Crowned bust right **Obv. Designer:** Raphael Maklouf **Rev:** Germany vs Russia

Date	Mintage	F	VF	XF	Unc	BU
1996 Proof	Est. 5,000	Value: 165				

KM# 640 1/5 CROWN
6.2200 g., 0.9990 Gold .2000 oz. AGW, 22 mm. **Ruler:** Elizabeth II **Series:** European Football Championship **Obv:** Crowned bust right
Obv. Designer: Raphael Maklouf **Rev:** Spain vs France

Date	Mintage	F	VF	XF	Unc	BU
1996 Proof	Est. 5,000	Value: 165				

KM# 643 1/5 CROWN
6.2200 g., 0.9990 Gold .2000 oz. AGW, 22 mm. **Ruler:** Elizabeth II **Series:** European Football Championship **Obv:** Crowned bust right **Obv. Designer:** Raphael Maklouf **Rev:** Turkey vs Croatia

Date	Mintage	F	VF	XF	Unc	BU
1996 Proof	Est. 5,000	Value: 165				

KM# 646 1/5 CROWN
6.2200 g., 0.9990 Gold .2000 oz. AGW, 22 mm. **Ruler:** Elizabeth II **Series:** European Football Championship **Obv:** Crowned bust right **Obv. Designer:** Raphael Maklouf **Rev:** Denmark vs Portugal

Date	Mintage	F	VF	XF	Unc	BU
1996 Proof	Est. 5,000	Value: 165				

KM# 649 1/5 CROWN
6.2200 g., 0.9990 Gold .2000 oz. AGW, 22 mm. **Ruler:** Elizabeth II **Series:** European Football Championship **Obv:** Crowned bust right **Obv. Designer:** Raphael Maklouf **Rev:** Scotland vs England

Date	Mintage	F	VF	XF	Unc	BU
1996 Proof	Est. 5,000	Value: 165				

KM# 652 1/5 CROWN
6.2200 g., 0.9990 Gold .2000 oz. AGW, 22 mm. **Ruler:** Elizabeth II **Series:** European Football Championship **Obv:** Crowned bust right **Obv. Designer:** Raphael Maklouf **Rev:** Holland vs Switzerland

Date	Mintage	F	VF	XF	Unc	BU
1996 Proof	Est. 5,000	Value: 165				

ISLE OF MAN 405

KM# 656 1/5 CROWN
6.2200 g., 0.9990 Gold .2000 oz. AGW, 22 mm. **Ruler:** Elizabeth II **Series:** European Football Championship **Obv:** Crowned bust right **Obv. Designer:** Raphael Maklouf **Rev:** Winner, Germany

Date	Mintage	F	VF	XF	Unc	BU
1996 Proof	Est. 5,000	Value: 165				

KM# 659 1/5 CROWN
6.2200 g., 0.9990 Gold .2000 oz. AGW, 22 mm. **Ruler:** Elizabeth II **Series:** Legend of King Arthur **Obv:** Crowned bust right **Obv. Designer:** Raphael Maklouf **Rev:** King Arthur with sword, orb

Date	Mintage	F	VF	XF	Unc	BU
1996 Proof	Est. 5,000	Value: 165				

KM# 660 1/5 CROWN
6.2200 g., 0.9990 Gold .2000 oz. AGW, 22 mm. **Ruler:** Elizabeth II **Series:** Legend of King Arthur **Obv:** Crowned bust right **Obv. Designer:** Raphael Maklouf **Rev:** 3/4-length figure of Queen Guinevere coming through archway

Date	Mintage	F	VF	XF	Unc	BU
1996 Proof	Est. 5,000	Value: 165				

KM# 661 1/5 CROWN
6.2200 g., 0.9990 Gold .2000 oz. AGW, 22 mm. **Ruler:** Elizabeth II **Series:** Legend of King Arthur **Obv:** Crowned bust right **Obv. Designer:** Raphael Maklouf **Rev:** Sir Lancelot

Date	Mintage	F	VF	XF	Unc	BU
1996 Proof	Est. 5,000	Value: 165				

KM# 662 1/5 CROWN
6.2200 g., 0.9990 Gold .2000 oz. AGW, 22 mm. **Ruler:** Elizabeth II **Series:** Legend of King Arthur **Obv:** Crowned bust right **Obv. Designer:** Raphael Maklouf **Rev:** Merlin

Date	Mintage	F	VF	XF	Unc	BU
1996 Proof	Est. 5,000	Value: 165				

KM# 663 1/5 CROWN
6.2200 g., 0.9990 Gold .2000 oz. AGW, 22 mm. **Ruler:** Elizabeth II **Series:** Legend of King Arthur **Obv:** Crowned bust right **Obv. Designer:** Raphael Maklouf **Rev:** Camelot Castle within circle

Date	Mintage	F	VF	XF	Unc	BU
1996 Proof	Est. 5,000	Value: 165				

KM# 664 1/5 CROWN
6.2200 g., 0.9990 Platinum .2000 oz. APW, 22 mm. **Ruler:** Elizabeth II **Series:** Legend of King Arthur **Obv:** Crowned bust right **Obv. Designer:** Raphael Maklouf **Rev:** King Arthur with sword, orb

Date	Mintage	F	VF	XF	Unc	BU
1996 Proof	Est. 5,000	Value: 255				

KM# 665 1/5 CROWN
6.2200 g., 0.9990 Platinum .2000 oz. APW, 22 mm. **Ruler:** Elizabeth II **Series:** Legend of King Arthur **Obv:** Crowned bust right **Obv. Designer:** Raphael Maklouf **Rev:** Queen Guinevere

Date	Mintage	F	VF	XF	Unc	BU
1996 Proof	Est. 5,000	Value: 255				

KM# 666 1/5 CROWN
6.2200 g., 0.9990 Platinum .2000 oz. APW, 22 mm. **Ruler:** Elizabeth II **Series:** Legend of King Arthur **Obv:** Crowned bust right **Obv. Designer:** Raphael Maklouf **Rev:** Sir Lancelot

Date	Mintage	F	VF	XF	Unc	BU
1996 Proof	Est. 5,000	Value: 255				

KM# 667 1/5 CROWN
6.2200 g., 0.9990 Platinum .2000 oz. APW, 22 mm. **Ruler:** Elizabeth II **Series:** Legend of King Arthur **Obv:** Crowned bust right **Obv. Designer:** Raphael Maklouf **Rev:** Merlin

Date	Mintage	F	VF	XF	Unc	BU
1996 Proof	Est. 5,000	Value: 260				

KM# 668 1/5 CROWN
6.2200 g., 0.9990 Platinum .2000 oz. APW, 22 mm. **Ruler:** Elizabeth II **Series:** Legend of King Arthur **Obv:** Crowned bust right **Obv. Designer:** Raphael Maklouf **Rev:** Camelot Castle

Date	Mintage	F	VF	XF	Unc	BU
1996 Proof	Est. 5,000	Value: 255				

KM# 730 1/5 CROWN
6.2200 g., 0.9990 Gold .2000 oz. AGW, 22 mm. **Ruler:** Elizabeth II **Subject:** Year of the Rat **Obv:** Crowned bust right **Obv. Designer:** Raphael Maklouf **Rev:** Rat

Date	Mintage	F	VF	XF	Unc	BU
1996 Proof	—	—	—	—	—	—

Note: Entire series purchased by one buyer. Mintage, disposition and market value unknown

KM# 766 1/5 CROWN
6.2200 g., 0.9999 Gold .2000 oz. AGW, 22 mm. **Ruler:** Elizabeth II **Subject:** Fridtjof Nansen 1861-1930 **Obv:** Crowned bust right **Obv. Designer:** Raphael Maklouf **Rev:** Portrait, map and ship "The Fram"

Date	Mintage	F	VF	XF	Unc	BU
1997 Proof	Est. 5,000	Value: 175				

KM# 723 1/5 CROWN
6.2200 g., 0.9990 Gold .2000 oz. AGW, 22 mm. **Ruler:** Elizabeth II **Subject:** Year of the Ox **Obv:** Crowned bust right **Obv. Designer:** Raphael Maklouf **Rev:** Ox laying down

Date	Mintage	F	VF	XF	Unc	BU
1997 Proof	Est. 12,000	Value: 170				

KM# 751 1/5 CROWN
6.2200 g., 0.9990 Gold .2000 oz. AGW, 22 mm. **Ruler:** Elizabeth II **Series:** Flower Fairies **Obv:** Crowned bust right **Obv. Designer:** Raphael Maklouf **Rev:** Candytuft **Rev. Designer:** Cecily Mary Barker

Date	Mintage	F	VF	XF	Unc	BU
1997 Proof	Est. 5,000	Value: 165				

KM# 751a 1/5 CROWN
6.2518 g., 0.9950 Platinum .2000 oz. APW, 22 mm. **Ruler:** Elizabeth II **Series:** Flower Fairies **Obv:** Crowned bust right **Obv. Designer:** Raphael Maklouf **Rev:** Candytuft **Rev. Designer:** Cecily Mary Barker

Date	Mintage	F	VF	XF	Unc	BU
1997 Proof	Est. 2,500	Value: 260				

KM# 752 1/5 CROWN
6.2200 g., 0.9999 Gold .2000 oz. AGW, 22 mm. **Ruler:** Elizabeth II **Series:** Flower Fairies **Obv:** Crowned bust right **Obv. Designer:** Raphael Maklouf **Rev:** Snowdrop **Rev. Designer:** Cecily Mary Barker

Date	Mintage	F	VF	XF	Unc	BU
1997 Proof	Est. 5,000	Value: 165				

KM# 752a 1/5 CROWN
6.2518 g., 0.9950 Platinum .2000 oz. APW, 22 mm. **Ruler:** Elizabeth II **Series:** Flower Fairies **Obv:** Crowned bust right **Obv. Designer:** Raphael Maklouf **Rev:** Snowdrop **Rev. Designer:** Cecily Mary Barker

Date	Mintage	F	VF	XF	Unc	BU
1997 Proof	Est. 2,500	Value: 260				

KM# 753 1/5 CROWN
6.2200 g., 0.9999 Gold .2000 oz. AGW, 22 mm. **Ruler:** Elizabeth II **Series:** Flower Fairies **Obv:** Crowned bust right **Obv. Designer:** Raphael Maklouf **Rev:** Tulip **Rev. Designer:** Cecily Mary Barker

Date	Mintage	F	VF	XF	Unc	BU
1997 Proof	Est. 5,000	Value: 165				

KM# 753a 1/5 CROWN
6.2518 g., 0.9950 Platinum .2000 oz. APW, 22 mm. **Ruler:** Elizabeth II **Series:** Flower Fairies **Obv:** Crowned bust right **Obv. Designer:** Raphael Maklouf **Rev:** Tulip **Rev. Designer:** Cecily Mary Barker

Date	Mintage	F	VF	XF	Unc	BU
1997 Proof	Est. 2,500	Value: 260				

KM# 754 1/5 CROWN
6.2200 g., 0.9999 Gold .2000 oz. AGW, 22 mm. **Ruler:** Elizabeth II **Series:** Flower Fairies **Obv:** Crowned bust right **Obv. Designer:** Raphael Maklouf **Rev:** Jasmine **Rev. Designer:** Cecily Mary Barker

Date	Mintage	F	VF	XF	Unc	BU
1997 Proof	Est. 5,000	Value: 165				

KM# 754a 1/5 CROWN
6.2518 g., 0.9950 Platinum .2000 oz. APW, 22 mm. **Ruler:** Elizabeth II **Series:** Flower Fairies **Obv:** Crowned bust right **Obv. Designer:** Raphael Maklouf **Rev:** Jasmine **Rev. Designer:** Cecily Mary Barker

Date	Mintage	F	VF	XF	Unc	BU
1997 Proof	Est. 2,500	Value: 240				

KM# 763 1/5 CROWN
6.2200 g., 0.9999 Gold .2000 oz. AGW, 22 mm. **Ruler:** Elizabeth II **Subject:** Leif Eriksson 999-1001 **Obv:** Crowned bust right **Obv. Designer:** Raphael Maklouf **Rev:** Portrait and Viking ship with map sail

Date	Mintage	F	VF	XF	Unc	BU
1997 Proof	Est. 5,000	Value: 175				

KM# 772 1/5 CROWN
6.2200 g., 0.9999 Gold .2000 oz. AGW, 22 mm. **Ruler:** Elizabeth II **Obv:** Crowned bust right **Obv. Designer:** Raphael Maklouf **Rev:** Long-haired Smoke cat

Date	Mintage	F	VF	XF	Unc	BU
1997	—	—	—	—	145	—
1997 Proof	—	Value: 160				

KM# 772a 1/5 CROWN
6.2200 g., 0.9999 Platinum .2000 oz. APW, 22 mm. **Ruler:** Elizabeth II **Obv:** Crowned bust right **Obv. Designer:** Raphael Maklouf **Rev:** Long-haired Smoke cat

Date	Mintage	F	VF	XF	Unc	BU
1997	—	—	—	—	255	—
1997 Proof	—	Value: 265				

KM# 776 1/5 CROWN
6.2200 g., 0.9999 Gold .2000 oz. AGW, 22 mm. **Ruler:** Elizabeth II **Subject:** History of the Cat **Obv:** Crowned bust right **Obv. Designer:** Raphael Maklouf **Rev:** Cat stalking a spider

Date	Mintage	F	VF	XF	Unc	BU
1997 Proof	Est. 7,500	Value: 165				

KM# 781 1/5 CROWN
6.2200 g., 0.9999 Gold .2000 oz. AGW, 22 mm. **Ruler:** Elizabeth II **Subject:** 90th Anniversary of the TT - 1907 **Obv:** Crowned bust right **Obv. Designer:** Raphael Maklouf **Rev:** 1907 winner Charlie Collier

Date	Mintage	F	VF	XF	Unc	BU
1997 Proof	Est. 5,000	Value: 165				

KM# 783 1/5 CROWN
6.2200 g., 0.9999 Gold .2000 oz. AGW, 22 mm. **Ruler:** Elizabeth II **Subject:** 90th Anniversary of the TT - 1907 **Obv:** Crowned bust right **Obv. Designer:** Raphael Maklouf **Rev:** 1937 winner Omobono Tenni

Date	Mintage	F	VF	XF	Unc	BU
1997 Proof	Est. 5,000	Value: 165				

KM# 785 1/5 CROWN
6.2200 g., 0.9999 Gold .2000 oz. AGW, 22 mm. **Ruler:** Elizabeth II **Subject:** 90th Anniversary of the TT - 1907 **Obv:** Crowned bust right **Obv. Designer:** Raphael Maklouf **Rev:** 1957 winner Bob McIntyre

Date	Mintage	F	VF	XF	Unc	BU
1997 Proof	Est. 5,000	Value: 165				

KM# 787 1/5 CROWN
6.2200 g., 0.9999 Gold .2000 oz. AGW, 22 mm. **Ruler:** Elizabeth II **Subject:** 90th Anniversary of the TT - 1907 **Obv:** Crowned bust right **Obv. Designer:** Raphael Maklouf **Rev:** 1967 winner Mike Hailwood

Date	Mintage	F	VF	XF	Unc	BU
1997 Proof	Est. 5,000	Value: 165				

KM# 792 1/5 CROWN
6.2200 g., 0.9999 Gold .2000 oz. AGW, 22 mm. **Ruler:** Elizabeth II **Subject:** Golden Wedding Anniversary of Queen Elizabeth II and Prince Philip **Obv:** Crowned bust right **Obv. Designer:** Raphael Maklouf **Rev:** Wedding portrait

Date	Mintage	F	VF	XF	Unc	BU
1997 Proof	Est. 3,500	Value: 165				

KM# 798 1/5 CROWN
6.2200 g., 0.9999 Gold .2000 oz. AGW, 22 mm. **Ruler:** Elizabeth II **Series:** Year 2000 **Subject:** Birth of Christ **Obv:** Crowned bust right **Obv. Designer:** Raphael Maklouf **Rev:** Madonna and child with angels

Date	Mintage	F	VF	XF	Unc	BU
1997 Proof	Est. 2,000	Value: 165				

KM# 800 1/5 CROWN
6.2200 g., 0.9999 Gold .2000 oz. AGW, 22 mm. **Ruler:** Elizabeth II **Series:** Year 2000 **Subject:** Fall of the Roman Empire 476 **Obv:** Crowned bust right **Obv. Designer:** Raphael Maklouf **Rev:** Barbarian defeating Roman soldier

Date	Mintage	F	VF	XF	Unc	BU
1997 Proof	Est. 2,000	Value: 165				

KM# 802 1/5 CROWN
6.2200 g., 0.9999 Gold .2000 oz. AGW, 22 mm. **Ruler:** Elizabeth II **Series:** Year 2000 **Subject:** Flight of Mohammed 622 **Obv:** Crowned bust right **Obv. Designer:** Raphael Maklouf **Rev:** Arabs and camels at an oasis

Date	Mintage	F	VF	XF	Unc	BU
1997 Proof	Est. 2,000	Value: 165				

KM# 804 1/5 CROWN
6.2200 g., 0.9999 Gold .2000 oz. AGW, 22 mm. **Ruler:** Elizabeth II **Series:** Year 2000 **Subject:** Norman Conquest 1066 **Obv:** Crowned bust right **Obv. Designer:** Raphael Maklouf **Rev:** William the Conqueror rallying his troops

Date	Mintage	F	VF	XF	Unc	BU
1997 Proof	Est. 2,000	Value: 165				

KM# 807 1/5 CROWN
6.2200 g., 0.9999 Gold .2000 oz. AGW, 22 mm. **Ruler:** Elizabeth II **Series:** World Cup Soccer **Obv:** Crowned bust right **Obv. Designer:** Raphael Maklouf **Rev:** Standing figures shaking hands within circle

Date	Mintage	F	VF	XF	Unc	BU
1998 Proof	Est. 5,000	Value: 165				

KM# 814 1/5 CROWN
6.2200 g., 0.9999 Gold .2000 oz. AGW, 22 mm. **Ruler:** Elizabeth II **Series:** Year of the Tiger **Obv:** Crowned bust right **Obv. Designer:** Raphael Maklouf **Rev:** Tiger

Date	Mintage	F	VF	XF	Unc	BU
1998 Proof	Est. 12,000	Value: 165				

KM# 824 1/5 CROWN
6.2200 g., 0.9999 Gold .2000 oz. AGW, 22 mm. **Ruler:** Elizabeth II **Obv:** Crowned bust right **Obv. Designer:** Raphael Maklouf **Rev:** Portrait of Marco Polo, caravan and palace

Date	Mintage	F	VF	XF	Unc	BU
1998 Proof	Est. 5,000	Value: 165				

KM# 826 1/5 CROWN
6.2200 g., 0.9999 Gold .2000 oz. AGW, 22 mm. **Ruler:** Elizabeth II **Obv:** Crowned bust right **Obv. Designer:** Raphael Maklouf **Rev:** Bust with headdress facing, ship and African map **Note:** Similar to 1 Crown, KM#827.

Date	Mintage	F	VF	XF	Unc	BU
1998 Proof	Est. 5,000	Value: 165				

406 ISLE OF MAN

KM# 836 1/5 CROWN

6.2200 g., 0.9999 Gold .2000 oz. AGW, 22 mm. **Ruler:** Elizabeth II **Series:** Flower Fairies **Obv:** Crowned bust right **Obv. Designer:** Raphael Maklouf **Rev:** Fairy standing, lavender **Rev. Designer:** Cecily Mary Barker

Date	Mintage	F	VF	XF	Unc	BU
1998 Proof	Est. 5,000	Value: 165				

KM# 836a 1/5 CROWN

6.2200 g., 0.9999 Platinum .2000 oz. APW, 22 mm. **Ruler:** Elizabeth II **Series:** Flower Fairies **Obv:** Crowned bust right **Obv. Designer:** Raphael Maklouf **Rev:** Fairy standing, lavender **Rev. Designer:** Cecily Mary Barker

Date	Mintage	F	VF	XF	Unc	BU
1998 Proof	Est. 2,500	Value: 260				

KM# 837 1/5 CROWN

6.2200 g., 0.9999 Gold .2000 oz. AGW, 22 mm. **Ruler:** Elizabeth II **Series:** Flower Fairies **Obv:** Crowned bust right **Obv. Designer:** Raphael Maklouf **Rev:** Two fairies, sweet pea **Rev. Designer:** Cecily Mary Barker

Date	Mintage	F	VF	XF	Unc	BU
1998 Proof	Est. 5,000	Value: 165				

KM# 837a 1/5 CROWN

6.2200 g., 0.9999 Platinum .2000 oz. APW, 22 mm. **Ruler:** Elizabeth II **Series:** Flower Fairies **Obv:** Crowned bust right **Obv. Designer:** Raphael Maklouf **Rev:** Two fairies, sweet pea **Rev. Designer:** Cecily Mary Barker

Date	Mintage	F	VF	XF	Unc	BU
1998 Proof	Est. 2,500	Value: 260				

KM# 838 1/5 CROWN

6.2200 g., 0.9999 Gold .2000 oz. AGW, 22 mm. **Ruler:** Elizabeth II **Series:** Flower Fairies **Obv:** Crowned bust right **Obv. Designer:** Raphael Maklouf **Rev:** Fairy looking into flower, White Bindweed **Rev. Designer:** Cecily Mary Barker

Date	Mintage	F	VF	XF	Unc	BU
1998 Proof	Est. 5,000	Value: 165				

KM# 838a 1/5 CROWN

6.2200 g., 0.9999 Platinum .2000 oz. APW, 22 mm. **Ruler:** Elizabeth II **Series:** Flower Fairies **Obv:** Crowned bust right **Obv. Designer:** Raphael Maklouf **Rev:** Fairy looking into flower, White Bindweed **Rev. Designer:** Cecily Mary Barker

Date	Mintage	F	VF	XF	Unc	BU
1998 Proof	Est. 2,500	Value: 260				

KM# 839 1/5 CROWN

6.2200 g., 0.9999 Gold .2000 oz. AGW, 22 mm. **Ruler:** Elizabeth II **Series:** Flower Fairies **Obv:** Crowned bust right **Obv. Designer:** Raphael Maklouf **Rev:** Fairy standing, daffodil **Rev. Designer:** Cecily Mary Barker

Date	Mintage	F	VF	XF	Unc	BU
1998 Proof	Est. 5,000	Value: 165				

KM# 839a 1/5 CROWN

6.2200 g., 0.9999 Platinum .2000 oz. APW, 22 mm. **Ruler:** Elizabeth II **Series:** Flower Fairies **Obv:** Crowned bust right **Obv. Designer:** Raphael Maklouf **Rev:** Fairy standing, daffodil **Rev. Designer:** Cecily Mary Barker

Date	Mintage	F	VF	XF	Unc	BU
1998 Proof	Est. 2,500	Value: 265				

KM# 845 1/5 CROWN

6.2200 g., 0.9999 Gold .2000 oz. AGW, 22 mm. **Ruler:** Elizabeth II **Series:** Winter Olympics - Nagano **Obv:** Crowned bust right **Obv. Designer:** Raphael Maklouf **Rev:** Ski jumper

Date	Mintage	F	VF	XF	Unc	BU
1998 Proof	Est. 5,000	Value: 165				

KM# 846 1/5 CROWN

6.2200 g., 0.9999 Gold .2000 oz. AGW, 22 mm. **Ruler:** Elizabeth II **Series:** Winter Olympics - Nagano **Obv:** Crowned bust right **Obv. Designer:** Raphael Maklouf **Rev:** Slalom skier

Date	Mintage	F	VF	XF	Unc	BU
1998 Proof	Est. 5,000	Value: 165				

KM# 847 1/5 CROWN

6.2200 g., 0.9999 Gold .2000 oz. AGW, 22 mm. **Ruler:** Elizabeth II **Series:** Winter Olympics - Nagano **Obv:** Crowned bust right **Obv. Designer:** Raphael Maklouf **Rev:** Figure skaters below flames

Date	Mintage	F	VF	XF	Unc	BU
1998	Est. 5,000	Value: 165				

KM# 848 1/5 CROWN

6.2200 g., 0.9999 Gold .2000 oz. AGW, 22 mm. **Ruler:** Elizabeth II **Series:** Winter Olympics - Nagano **Obv:** Crowned bust right **Obv. Designer:** Raphael Maklouf **Rev:** Figure skater, speed skater and skier

Date	Mintage	F	VF	XF	Unc	BU
1998 Proof	Est. 5,000	Value: 165				

KM# 855 1/5 CROWN

6.2200 g., 0.9999 Gold .2000 oz. AGW, 22 mm. **Ruler:** Elizabeth II **Obv:** Crowned bust right **Obv. Designer:** Raphael Maklouf **Rev:** Birman cat

Date	Mintage	F	VF	XF	Unc	BU
1998 Proof	1,000	Value: 150				

KM# 855a 1/5 CROWN

6.2200 g., 0.9995 Platinum .2000 oz. APW, 22 mm. **Ruler:** Elizabeth II **Obv:** Crowned bust right **Obv. Designer:** Raphael Maklouf **Rev:** Birman cat

Date	Mintage	F	VF	XF	Unc	BU
1998 Proof	—	Value: 260				

KM# 861 1/5 CROWN

6.2200 g., 0.9999 Gold .2000 oz. AGW, 22 mm. **Ruler:** Elizabeth II **Series:** History of the Cat **Obv:** Crowned bust right **Obv. Designer:** Raphael Maklouf **Rev:** Egyptian Mau cat with earring

Date	Mintage	F	VF	XF	Unc	BU
1998 Proof	Est. 7,500	Value: 170				

KM# 871 1/5 CROWN

6.2200 g., 0.9999 Gold .2000 oz. AGW, 22 mm. **Ruler:** Elizabeth II **Subject:** 125th Anniversary of the Steam Railway **Obv:** Crowned bust right **Obv. Designer:** Raphael Maklouf **Rev:** "The General"

Date	Mintage	F	VF	XF	Unc	BU
1998 Proof	Est. 5,000	Value: 170				

KM# 873 1/5 CROWN

6.2200 g., 0.9999 Gold .2000 oz. AGW, 22 mm. **Ruler:** Elizabeth II **Subject:** 125th Anniversary of the Steam Railway **Obv:** Crowned bust right **Obv. Designer:** Raphael Maklouf **Rev:** "The Rocket" and portrait

Date	Mintage	F	VF	XF	Unc	BU
1998 Proof	Est. 5,000	Value: 170				

KM# 875 1/5 CROWN

6.2200 g., 0.9999 Gold .2000 oz. AGW, 22 mm. **Ruler:** Elizabeth II **Subject:** 125th Anniversary of the Steam Railway **Obv:** Crowned bust right **Obv. Designer:** Raphael Maklouf **Rev:** Orient Express parlor car, interior view

Date	Mintage	F	VF	XF	Unc	BU
1998 Proof	Est. 5,000	Value: 170				

KM# 877 1/5 CROWN

6.2200 g., 0.9999 Gold .2000 oz. AGW, 22 mm. **Ruler:** Elizabeth II **Subject:** 125th Anniversary of the Steam Railway **Obv:** Crowned bust right **Obv. Designer:** Raphael Maklouf **Rev:** Mount Pilatus railway

Date	Mintage	F	VF	XF	Unc	BU
1998 Proof	Est. 5,000	Value: 170				

KM# 879 1/5 CROWN

6.2200 g., 0.9999 Gold .2000 oz. AGW, 22 mm. **Ruler:** Elizabeth II **Subject:** 125th Anniversary of the Steam Railway **Obv:** Crowned bust right **Obv. Designer:** Raphael Maklouf **Rev:** No. 1 Sutherland locomotive

Date	Mintage	F	VF	XF	Unc	BU
1998 Proof	Est. 5,000	Value: 170				

KM# 881 1/5 CROWN

6.2200 g., 0.9999 Gold .2000 oz. AGW, 22 mm. **Ruler:** Elizabeth II **Subject:** 125th Anniversary of the Steam Railway **Obv:** Crowned bust right **Obv. Designer:** Raphael Maklouf **Rev:** "Flying Scotsman"

Date	Mintage	F	VF	XF	Unc	BU
1998 Proof	Est. 5,000	Value: 170				

KM# 883 1/5 CROWN

6.2200 g., 0.9999 Gold .2000 oz. AGW, 22 mm. **Ruler:** Elizabeth II **Subject:** 125th Anniversary of the Steam Railway **Obv:** Crowned bust right **Obv. Designer:** Raphael Maklouf **Rev:** Mallard locomotive

Date	Mintage	F	VF	XF	Unc	BU
1998 Proof	Est. 5,000	Value: 170				

KM# 885 1/5 CROWN

6.2200 g., 0.9999 Gold .2000 oz. AGW, 22 mm. **Ruler:** Elizabeth II **Subject:** 125th Anniversary of the Steam Railway **Obv:** Crowned bust right **Obv. Designer:** Raphael Maklouf **Rev:** The Big Boy locomotive

Date	Mintage	F	VF	XF	Unc	BU
1998 Proof	Est. 5,000	Value: 170				

KM# 887 1/5 CROWN

6.2200 g., 0.9999 Gold .2000 oz. AGW, 22 mm. **Ruler:** Elizabeth II **Series:** Year 2000 **Obv:** Crowned bust right **Obv. Designer:** Raphael Maklouf **Rev:** American Independence 1776

Date	Mintage	F	VF	XF	Unc	BU
1998 Proof	Est. 2,000	Value: 170				

KM# 889 1/5 CROWN

6.2200 g., 0.9999 Gold .2000 oz. AGW, 22 mm. **Ruler:** Elizabeth II **Series:** Year 2000 **Obv:** Crowned bust right **Obv. Designer:** Raphael Maklouf **Rev:** French Revolution 1789

Date	Mintage	F	VF	XF	Unc	BU
1998 Proof	Est. 2,000	Value: 170				

KM# 891 1/5 CROWN

6.2200 g., 0.9999 Gold .2000 oz. AGW, 22 mm. **Ruler:** Elizabeth II **Series:** Year 2000 **Obv:** Crowned bust right **Obv. Designer:** Raphael Maklouf **Rev:** Reformation of the Church 1517

Date	Mintage	F	VF	XF	Unc	BU
1998 Proof	Est. 2,000	Value: 170				

KM# 893 1/5 CROWN

6.2200 g., 0.9999 Gold .2000 oz. AGW, 22 mm. **Ruler:** Elizabeth II **Series:** Year 2000 **Obv:** Crowned bust right **Obv. Designer:** Raphael Maklouf **Rev:** 400th Anniversary of the Renaissance

Date	Mintage	F	VF	XF	Unc	BU
1998 Proof	Est. 2,000	Value: 170				

KM# 895 1/5 CROWN

6.2200 g., 0.9999 Gold .2000 oz. AGW, 22 mm. **Ruler:** Elizabeth II **Subject:** 125th Anniversary of the Steam Railway **Obv:** Crowned bust right **Obv. Designer:** Raphael Maklouf **Rev:** Ocean wave and sea gull

Date	Mintage	F	VF	XF	Unc	BU
1998 Proof	Est. 5,000	Value: 170				

KM# 913 1/5 CROWN

6.2200 g., 0.9999 Gold .2000 oz. AGW, 22 mm. **Ruler:** Elizabeth II **Subject:** Battle of Waterloo 1815 **Obv:** Crowned bust right **Obv. Designer:** Raphael Maklouf **Rev:** Wellington on horse

Date	Mintage	F	VF	XF	Unc	BU
1999 Proof	Est. 2,000	Value: 170				

KM# 915 1/5 CROWN

6.2200 g., 0.9999 Gold .2000 oz. AGW, 22 mm. **Ruler:** Elizabeth II **Subject:** U.S. Civil War **Obv:** Crowned bust right **Obv. Designer:** Raphael Maklouf **Rev:** Cameos of Lee and Grant, flags, sword and drum

Date	Mintage	F	VF	XF	Unc	BU
1999 Proof	Est. 2,000	Value: 170				

KM# 917 1/5 CROWN

6.2200 g., 0.9999 Gold .2000 oz. AGW, 22 mm. **Ruler:** Elizabeth II **Subject:** Bolshevik Revolution 1917 **Obv:** Crowned bust right **Obv. Designer:** Raphael Maklouf **Rev:** Lenin above the Aurora

Date	Mintage	F	VF	XF	Unc	BU
1999 Proof	Est. 2,000	Value: 170				

KM# 919 1/5 CROWN

6.2200 g., 0.9999 Gold .2000 oz. AGW, 22 mm. **Ruler:** Elizabeth II **Subject:** Armistice Day 1918 **Obv:** Crowned bust right **Obv. Designer:** Raphael Maklouf **Rev:** Biplane above tank

Date	Mintage	F	VF	XF	Unc	BU
1999 Proof	Est. 2,000	Value: 170				

KM# 921 1/5 CROWN

6.2200 g., 0.9999 Gold .2000 oz. AGW, 22 mm. **Ruler:** Elizabeth II **Series:** Summer Olympics - Sydney **Obv:** Crowned bust right **Obv. Designer:** Raphael Maklouf **Rev:** Three javelin throwers

Date	Mintage	F	VF	XF	Unc	BU
1999 Proof	Est. 5,000	Value: 170				

KM# 923 1/5 CROWN

6.2200 g., 0.9999 Gold .2000 oz. AGW, 22 mm. **Ruler:** Elizabeth II **Series:** Summer Olympics - Sydney **Obv:** Crowned bust right **Obv. Designer:** Raphael Maklouf **Rev:** Female diver

Date	Mintage	F	VF	XF	Unc	BU
1999 Proof	Est. 5,000	Value: 170				

ISLE OF MAN 407

KM# 925 1/5 CROWN
6.2200 g., 0.9999 Gold .2000 oz. AGW, 22 mm. **Ruler:** Elizabeth II **Series:** Summer Olympics - Sydney **Obv:** Crowned bust right **Obv. Designer:** Raphael Maklouf **Rev:** Sailboat

Date	Mintage	F	VF	XF	Unc	BU
1999 Proof	Est. 5,000	Value: 170				

KM# 927 1/5 CROWN
6.2200 g., 0.9999 Gold .2000 oz. AGW, 22 mm. **Ruler:** Elizabeth II **Series:** Summer Olympics - Sydney **Obv:** Crowned bust right **Obv. Designer:** Raphael Maklouf **Rev:** Two runners

Date	Mintage	F	VF	XF	Unc	BU
1999 Proof	Est. 5,000	Value: 170				

KM# 929 1/5 CROWN
6.2200 g., 0.9999 Gold .2000 oz. AGW, 22 mm. **Ruler:** Elizabeth II **Series:** Summer Olympics - Sydney **Obv:** Crowned bust right **Obv. Designer:** Raphael Maklouf **Rev:** Two hurdlers

Date	Mintage	F	VF	XF	Unc	BU
1999 Proof	Est. 5,000	Value: 170				

KM# 931 1/5 CROWN
6.2200 g., 0.9999 Gold .2000 oz. AGW, 22 mm. **Ruler:** Elizabeth II **Series:** World Cup Rugby 1999 **Obv:** Crowned bust right **Obv. Designer:** Raphael Maklouf **Rev:** Bust of William Webb Ellis

Date	Mintage	F	VF	XF	Unc	BU
1999 Proof	Est. 5,000	Value: 170				

KM# 933 1/5 CROWN
6.2200 g., 0.9999 Gold .2000 oz. AGW, 22 mm. **Ruler:** Elizabeth II **Series:** World Cup Rugby 1999 **Obv:** Crowned bust right **Obv. Designer:** Raphael Maklouf **Rev:** Rugby scrum

Date	Mintage	F	VF	XF	Unc	BU
1999 Proof	Est. 5,000	Value: 170				

KM# 935 1/5 CROWN
6.2200 g., 0.9999 Gold .2000 oz. AGW, 22 mm. **Ruler:** Elizabeth II **Series:** World Cup Rugby 1999 **Obv:** Crowned bust right **Obv. Designer:** Raphael Maklouf **Rev:** Player running for catch

Date	Mintage	F	VF	XF	Unc	BU
1999 Proof	Est. 5,000	Value: 170				

KM# 937 1/5 CROWN
6.2200 g., 0.9999 Gold .2000 oz. AGW, 22 mm. **Ruler:** Elizabeth II **Series:** World Cup Rugby 1999 **Obv:** Crowned bust right **Obv. Designer:** Raphael Maklouf **Rev:** Goal kick

Date	Mintage	F	VF	XF	Unc	BU
1999 Proof	Est. 5,000	Value: 170				

KM# 939 1/5 CROWN
6.2200 g., 0.9999 Gold .2000 oz. AGW, 22 mm. **Ruler:** Elizabeth II **Series:** World Cup Rugby 1999 **Obv:** Crowned bust right **Obv. Designer:** Raphael Maklouf **Rev:** Tackled ball carrier

Date	Mintage	F	VF	XF	Unc	BU
1999 Proof	Est. 5,000	Value: 170				

KM# 941 1/5 CROWN
6.2200 g., 0.9999 Gold .2000 oz. AGW, 22 mm. **Ruler:** Elizabeth II **Series:** World Cup Rugby 1999 **Obv:** Crowned bust right **Obv. Designer:** Raphael Maklouf **Rev:** Player leaping for catch

Date	Mintage	F	VF	XF	Unc	BU
1999 Proof	Est. 5,000	Value: 170				

KM# 950 1/5 CROWN
6.2200 g., 0.9999 Gold .2000 oz. AGW, 22 mm. **Ruler:** Elizabeth II **Series:** Year of the Rabbit **Obv:** Crowned bust right **Obv. Designer:** Raphael Maklouf **Rev:** Two rabbits

Date	Mintage	F	VF	XF	Unc	BU
1999 Proof	Est. 12,000	Value: 170				

KM# 954 1/5 CROWN
6.2200 g., 0.9999 Gold .2000 oz. AGW, 22 mm. **Ruler:** Elizabeth II **Obv:** Crowned bust right **Obv. Designer:** Raphael Maklouf **Rev:** Portrait Sir Walter Raleigh, ship and dates

Date	Mintage	F	VF	XF	Unc	BU
1999 Proof	Est. 5,000	Value: 170				

KM# 956 1/5 CROWN
6.2200 g., 0.9999 Gold .2000 oz. AGW, 22 mm. **Ruler:** Elizabeth II **Obv:** Crowned bust right **Obv. Designer:** Raphael Maklouf **Rev:** Portrait Robert Falcon Scott and compass

Date	Mintage	F	VF	XF	Unc	BU
1999 Proof	Est. 5,000	Value: 170				

KM# 962 1/5 CROWN
6.2200 g., 0.9999 Gold .2000 oz. AGW, 22 mm. **Ruler:** Elizabeth II **Subject:** British Blue Cat **Obv:** Crowned bust right **Obv. Designer:** Raphael Maklouf **Rev:** Cat cleaning paw

Date	Mintage	F	VF	XF	Unc	BU
1999	—	—	—	—	140	—
1999 Proof	—	Value: 145				
1999 U Y2K	Est. 5,000	—	—	—	150	—

KM# 962a 1/5 CROWN
6.2200 g., 0.9995 Platinum .2000 oz. APW, 22 mm. **Ruler:** Elizabeth II **Subject:** British Blue Cat **Obv:** Crowned bust right **Obv. Designer:** Raphael Maklouf **Rev:** Cat cleaning paw

Date	Mintage	F	VF	XF	Unc	BU
1999 Proof	—	Value: 260				

KM# 975 1/5 CROWN
6.2200 g., 0.9999 Gold .2000 oz. AGW, 22 mm. **Ruler:** Elizabeth II **Series:** The Life and Times of the Queen Mother **Obv:** Crowned bust right **Obv. Designer:** Raphael Maklouf **Rev:** Child in chair

Date	Mintage	F	VF	XF	Unc	BU
1999 Proof	Est. 5,000	Value: 170				

KM# 977 1/5 CROWN
6.2200 g., 0.9999 Gold .2000 oz. AGW, 22 mm. **Ruler:** Elizabeth II **Series:** The Life and Times of the Queen Mother **Obv:** Crowned bust right **Obv. Designer:** Raphael Maklouf **Rev:** Engagement portrait

Date	Mintage	F	VF	XF	Unc	BU
1999 Proof	Est. 5,000	Value: 170				

KM# 979 1/5 CROWN
6.2200 g., 0.9999 Gold .2000 oz. AGW, 22 mm. **Ruler:** Elizabeth II **Series:** The Life and Times of the Queen Mother **Obv:** Crowned bust right **Obv. Designer:** Raphael Maklouf **Rev:** Honeymoon departure

Date	Mintage	F	VF	XF	Unc	BU
1999 Proof	Est. 5,000	Value: 170				

KM# 994 1/5 CROWN
6.2200 g., 0.9999 Gold .2000 oz. AGW, 22 mm. **Ruler:** Elizabeth II **Subject:** The Wedding of HRH Prince Edward **Obv:** Crowned bust right **Obv. Designer:** Raphael Maklouf **Rev:** Portrait of Prince Edward

Date	Mintage	F	VF	XF	Unc	BU
1999 Proof	Est. 5,000	Value: 170				

KM# 995 1/5 CROWN
6.2200 g., 0.9999 Gold .2000 oz. AGW, 22 mm. **Ruler:** Elizabeth II **Series:** The Life and Times of the Queen Mother **Subject:** The Wedding of HRH The Prince Edward **Obv:** Crowned bust right **Obv. Designer:** Raphael Maklouf **Rev:** Head of Prince Edward

Date	Mintage	F	VF	XF	Unc	BU
1999 Proof	Est. 5,000	Value: 170				

KM# 997 1/5 CROWN
6.2200 g., 0.9999 Gold .2000 oz. AGW, 22 mm. **Ruler:** Elizabeth II **Series:** The Life and Times of the Queen Mother **Subject:** The Wedding of HRH The Prince Edward **Obv:** Crowned bust right **Obv. Designer:** Raphael Maklouf **Rev:** Head of Sophie Rhys-Jones

Date	Mintage	F	VF	XF	Unc	BU
1999 Proof	Est. 5,000	Value: 170				

KM# 999 1/5 CROWN
6.2200 g., 0.9999 Gold .2000 oz. AGW, 22 mm. **Ruler:** Elizabeth II **Subject:** 30th Anniversary of First Man on the Moon **Obv:** Crowned bust right **Obv. Designer:** Raphael Maklouf **Rev:** Apollo XI, two moon walkers, date

Date	Mintage	F	VF	XF	Unc	BU
1999 Proof	Est. 2,000	Value: 170				

KM# 1001 1/5 CROWN
6.2200 g., 0.9999 Gold .2000 oz. AGW, 22 mm. **Ruler:** Elizabeth II **Subject:** 30th Anniversary of First Man on the Moon **Obv:** Crowned bust right **Obv. Designer:** Raphael Maklouf **Rev:** Mariner IX, 1971, space craft orbiting Mars

Date	Mintage	F	VF	XF	Unc	BU
1999 Proof	Est. 2,000	Value: 170				

KM# 1003 1/5 CROWN
6.2200 g., 0.9999 Gold .2000 oz. AGW, 22 mm. **Ruler:** Elizabeth II **Subject:** 30th Anniversary of First Man on the Moon **Obv:** Crowned bust right **Obv. Designer:** Raphael Maklouf **Rev:** Apollo-Soyuz link-up

Date	Mintage	F	VF	XF	Unc	BU
1999 Proof	Est. 2,000	Value: 170				

KM# 1005 1/5 CROWN
6.2200 g., 0.9999 Gold .2000 oz. AGW, 22 mm. **Ruler:** Elizabeth II **Subject:** 30th Anniversary of First Man on the Moon **Obv:** Crowned bust right **Obv. Designer:** Raphael Maklouf **Rev:** Viking Mars Lander, 1978

Date	Mintage	F	VF	XF	Unc	BU
1999 Proof	Est. 2,000	Value: 170				

KM# 1007 1/5 CROWN
6.2200 g., 0.9999 Gold .2000 oz. AGW, 22 mm. **Ruler:** Elizabeth II **Subject:** 30th Anniversary of First Man on the Moon **Obv:** Crowned bust right **Obv. Designer:** Raphael Maklouf **Rev:** Shuttle Columbia, 1981

Date	Mintage	F	VF	XF	Unc	BU
1999 Proof	Est. 2,000	Value: 170				

KM# 1009 1/5 CROWN
6.2200 g., 0.9999 Gold .2000 oz. AGW, 22 mm. **Subject:** 30th Anniversary of First Man on the Moon **Obv:** Crowned bust right **Obv. Designer:** Raphael Maklouf **Rev:** Mars Pathfinder, 1997

Date	Mintage	F	VF	XF	Unc	BU
1999 Proof	Est. 2,000	Value: 170				

KM# 984 1/5 CROWN
6.2200 g., 0.9999 Gold .2000 oz. AGW, 22 mm. **Ruler:** Elizabeth II **Subject:** Founding of the UN - Millennium **Obv:** Crowned bust right **Obv. Designer:** Raphael Maklouf **Rev:** UN Building, logo

Date	Mintage	F	VF	XF	Unc	BU
2000 Proof	Est. 2,000	Value: 170				

KM# 985 1/5 CROWN
6.2200 g., 0.9999 Gold .2000 oz. AGW, 22 mm. **Ruler:** Elizabeth II **Subject:** First Man on the Moon - Millennium **Obv:** Crowned bust right **Obv. Designer:** Raphael Maklouf **Rev:** Landing scene, date

Date	Mintage	F	VF	XF	Unc	BU
2000 Proof	Est. 2,000	Value: 170				

KM# 987 1/5 CROWN
6.2200 g., 0.9999 Gold .2000 oz. AGW, 22 mm. **Ruler:** Elizabeth II **Subject:** Fall of the Berlin Wall - Millennium **Obv:** Crowned bust right **Obv. Designer:** Raphael Maklouf **Rev:** Crowds surrounding wall

Date	Mintage	F	VF	XF	Unc	BU
2000 Proof	Est. 2,000	Value: 170				

KM# 989 1/5 CROWN
6.2200 g., 0.9999 Gold .2000 oz. AGW, 22 mm. **Ruler:** Elizabeth II **Subject:** Millennium 2000 - The Future **Obv:** Crowned bust right **Obv. Designer:** Raphael Maklouf **Rev:** International space station

Date	Mintage	F	VF	XF	Unc	BU
2000 Proof	Est. 2,000	Value: 170				

KM# 1014 1/5 CROWN
6.2200 g., 0.9999 Gold .2000 oz. AGW, 22 mm. **Ruler:** Elizabeth II **Subject:** Year of the Dragon **Obv:** Crowned bust right **Obv. Designer:** Raphael Maklouf **Rev:** Dragon, Chinese characters

Date	Mintage	F	VF	XF	Unc	BU
2000 Proof	Est. 12,000	Value: 170				

KM# 1054 1/5 CROWN
6.2200 g., 0.9999 Gold .2000 oz. AGW, 22 mm. **Ruler:** Elizabeth II **Obv:** Crowned bust right **Obv. Designer:** Raphael Maklouf **Rev:** Scottish kitten **Edge:** Reeded

Date	Mintage	F	VF	XF	Unc	BU
2000 Proof	—	Value: 175				
2000	—	—	—	—	145	—

KM# 1020 1/5 CROWN
6.2200 g., 0.9999 Gold .2000 oz. AGW, 22 mm. **Ruler:** Elizabeth II **Obv:** Crowned bust right **Obv. Designer:** Raphael Maklouf **Rev:** Armored portrait of Francisco Pizarro, map and ship **Edge:** Reeded

Date	Mintage	F	VF	XF	Unc	BU
2000 Proof	5,000	Value: 175				

KM# 1022 1/5 CROWN
6.2200 g., 0.9999 Gold .2000 oz. AGW, 22 mm. **Ruler:** Elizabeth II **Obv:** Crowned bust right **Obv. Designer:** Raphael Maklouf **Rev:** Portrait, ship on ice and map, Willem Barents

Date	Mintage	F	VF	XF	Unc	BU
2000 Proof	5,000	Value: 175				

KM# 1024 1/5 CROWN
6.2200 g., 0.9999 Gold .2000 oz. AGW, 22 mm. **Series:** Queen Mother **Obv:** Crowned bust right **Obv. Designer:** Raphael Maklouf **Rev:** 1931 family scene **Edge:** Reeded

Date	Mintage	F	VF	XF	Unc	BU
2000 Proof	5,000	Value: 175				

KM# 1026 1/5 CROWN
6.2200 g., 0.9999 Gold .2000 oz. AGW, 22 mm. **Ruler:** Elizabeth II **Series:** Queen Mother **Obv:** Crowned bust right **Obv. Designer:** Raphael Maklouf **Rev:** 1937 Coronation scene

Date	Mintage	F	VF	XF	Unc	BU
2000 Proof	5,000	Value: 175				

KM# 1028 1/5 CROWN
6.2200 g., 0.9999 Gold .2000 oz. AGW, 22 mm. **Ruler:** Elizabeth II **Series:** Queen Mother **Obv:** Crowned bust right **Obv. Designer:** Raphael Maklouf **Rev:** 1945 Victory Visit scene

Date	Mintage	F	VF	XF	Unc	BU
2000 Proof	5,000	Value: 175				

KM# 1030 1/5 CROWN
6.2200 g., 0.9999 Gold .2000 oz. AGW, 22 mm. **Ruler:** Elizabeth II **Series:** Queen Mother **Obv:** Crowned bust right **Obv. Designer:** Raphael Maklouf **Rev:** 1963 Royal Visit scene

Date	Mintage	F	VF	XF	Unc	BU
2000 Proof	175	Value: 175				

KM# 1032 1/5 CROWN
6.2200 g., 0.9990 Gold .2000 oz. AGW, 22 mm. **Ruler:** Elizabeth II **Subject:** Battle of Britain **Obv:** Crowned bust right **Obv. Designer:** Raphael Maklouf **Rev:** Aerial battle scene **Edge:** Reeded

Date	Mintage	F	VF	XF	Unc	BU
2000 Proof	5,000	Value: 175				

KM# 1034 1/5 CROWN
6.2200 g., 0.9990 Gold .2000 oz. AGW, 22 mm. **Ruler:** Elizabeth II **Subject:** Global Challenge Yacht Race **Obv:** Crowned bust right **Obv. Designer:** Raphael Maklouf **Rev:** Partial view of ship and map

Date	Mintage	F	VF	XF	Unc	BU
2000 Proof	5,000	Value: 175				

KM# 1046 1/5 CROWN
6.2200 g., 0.9999 Gold .2000 oz. AGW, 22 mm. **Ruler:** Elizabeth II **Obv:** Crowned bust right **Obv. Designer:** Raphael Maklouf **Rev:** Prince William's portrait **Edge:** Reeded

Date	Mintage	F	VF	XF	Unc	BU
2000 Proof	5,000	Value: 175				

KM# 1048 1/5 CROWN
6.2200 g., 0.9999 Gold .2000 oz. AGW, 22 mm. **Ruler:** Elizabeth II **Obv:** Crowned bust right **Obv. Designer:** Raphael Maklouf **Rev:** Bust with hat facing

Date	Mintage	F	VF	XF	Unc	BU
2000 Proof	2,000	Value: 175				

KM# 1054a 1/5 CROWN
6.2200 g., 0.9995 Platinum .2000 oz. APW, 22 mm. **Ruler:** Elizabeth II **Obv:** Crowned bust right **Obv. Designer:** Raphael Maklouf **Rev:** Scottish kitten

Date	Mintage	F	VF	XF	Unc	BU
2000	—	—	—	—	255	—

KM# 1060 1/5 CROWN
6.2200 g., 0.9999 Gold .2000 oz. AGW, 22 mm. **Ruler:** Elizabeth II **Subject:** Year of the Snake **Obv:** Bust with tiara right **Obv. Designer:** Ian Rank-Broadley **Rev:** Snake **Edge:** Reeded

Date	Mintage	F	VF	XF	Unc	BU
2001 Proof	12,000	Value: 175				

KM# 1069 1/5 CROWN
6.2200 g., 0.9999 Gold .2000 oz. AGW, 22 mm. **Ruler:** Elizabeth II **Obv:** Head with tiara right **Obv. Designer:** Ian Rank-Broadley **Rev:** Two Somali kittens **Edge:** Reeded

Date	Mintage	F	VF	XF	Unc	BU
2001	—	—	—	—	145	—
2001 Proof	1,000	Value: 175				

KM# 1069a 1/5 CROWN
6.2200 g., 0.9995 Platinum .2000 oz. APW, 22 mm. **Ruler:** Elizabeth II **Obv:** Head with tiara right **Obv. Designer:** Ian Rank-Broadley **Rev:** Somali kittens **Edge:** Reeded

Date	Mintage	F	VF	XF	Unc	BU
2001	—	—	—	—	260	—

KM# 1074 1/5 CROWN
6.2200 g., 0.9999 Gold .2000 oz. AGW, 22 mm. **Ruler:** Elizabeth II **Subject:** Queen Mother **Obv:** Head with tiara right **Obv. Designer:** Ian Rank-Broadley **Rev:** 1948 Silver wedding anniversary **Edge:** Reeded

Date	Mintage	F	VF	XF	Unc	BU
2001 Proof	5,000	Value: 175				

KM# 1075 1/5 CROWN
6.2200 g., 0.9999 Gold .2000 oz. AGW, 22 mm. **Ruler:** Elizabeth II **Subject:** Queen Mother **Obv:** Head with tiara right **Obv. Designer:** Ian Rank-Broadley **Rev:** 1948 holding baby Prince Charles **Edge:** Reeded

Date	Mintage	F	VF	XF	Unc	BU
2001 Proof	5,000	Value: 175				

KM# 1078 1/5 CROWN
6.2200 g., 0.9999 Gold .2000 oz. AGW, 22 mm. **Ruler:** Elizabeth II **Subject:** Martin Frobisher **Obv:** Head with tiara right **Obv. Designer:** Ian Rank-Broadley **Rev:** Portrait, ship and map **Edge:** Reeded

Date	Mintage	F	VF	XF	Unc	BU
2001 Proof	5,000	Value: 175				

KM# 1079 1/5 CROWN
6.2200 g., 0.9999 Gold .2000 oz. AGW, 22 mm. **Ruler:** Elizabeth II **Subject:** Ronald Amundsen **Obv:** Head with tiara right **Obv. Designer:** Ian Rank-Broadley **Rev:** Portrait, ship and dirigible **Edge:** Reeded

Date	Mintage	F	VF	XF	Unc	BU
2001 Proof	5,000	Value: 175				

KM# 1082 1/5 CROWN
6.2200 g., 0.9999 Gold .2000 oz. AGW, 22 mm. **Ruler:** Elizabeth II **Subject:** Queen's 75th Birthday **Obv:** Head with tiara right **Obv. Designer:** Ian Rank-Broadley **Rev:** Flower bouquet with a tiny diamond mounted on the bow of the ribbon **Edge:** Reeded

Date	Mintage	F	VF	XF	Unc	BU
2001 Proof	2,000	Value: 300				

KM# 1117 1/5 CROWN
6.2200 g., 0.9990 Gold 0.1998 oz. AGW, 22 mm. **Ruler:** Elizabeth II **Subject:** Queen Mother's Love of Horses **Obv:** Bust with tiara right **Obv. Designer:** Ian Rank-Broadley **Rev:** Queen Mother and horse **Edge:** Reeded

Date	Mintage	F	VF	XF	Unc	BU
2002 Proof	5,000	Value: 175				

KM# 1109 1/5 CROWN
6.2200 g., 0.9990 Gold 0.1998 oz. AGW, 22 mm. **Ruler:** Elizabeth II **Subject:** Bengal Cat **Obv:** Head with tiara right **Obv. Designer:** Ian Rank-Broadley **Rev:** Cat and kitten **Edge:** Reeded

Date	Mintage	VG	F	VF	XF	Unc
2002	—	—	—	—	—	145
2002 Proof	1,000	Value: 175				

KM# 1109a 1/5 CROWN
6.2200 g., 0.9990 Platinum 0.1998 oz. APW, 22 mm. **Ruler:** Elizabeth II **Subject:** Bengal Cat **Obv:** Head with tiara right **Obv. Designer:** Ian Rank-Broadley **Rev:** Cat and kitten **Edge:** Reeded

Date	Mintage	F	VF	XF	Unc	BU
2002	—	—	—	—	260	—

KM# 1100 1/5 CROWN
6.2200 g., 0.9999 Gold .2000 oz. AGW, 22 mm. **Ruler:** Elizabeth II **Subject:** Year of the Horse **Obv:** Bust with tiara right **Obv. Designer:** Ian Rank-Broadley **Rev:** Two horses **Edge:** Reeded

Date	Mintage	F	VF	XF	Unc	BU
2002 Proof	12,000	Value: 175				

KM# 1113 1/5 CROWN
6.2200 g., 0.9990 Gold 0.1998 oz. AGW, 22 mm. **Ruler:** Elizabeth II **Subject:** Olympics - Salt Lake City **Obv:** Bust with tiara right **Obv. Designer:** Ian Rank-Broadley **Rev:** Skier, torch and flag **Edge:** Reeded

Date	Mintage	F	VF	XF	Unc	BU
2002 Proof	5,000	Value: 175				

KM# 1114 1/5 CROWN
6.2200 g., 0.9990 Gold 0.1998 oz. AGW **Ruler:** Elizabeth II **Subject:** Olympics - Salt Lake City **Obv:** Bust with tiara right **Obv. Designer:** Ian Rank-Broadley **Rev:** Bobsled, torch and stadium **Edge:** Reeded

Date	Mintage	F	VF	XF	Unc	BU
2002 Proof	5,000	Value: 175				

KM# 1120 1/5 CROWN
6.2200 g., 0.9990 Gold 0.1998 oz. AGW, 22 mm. **Ruler:** Elizabeth II **Subject:** World Cup 2002 Japan - Korea **Obv:** Bust with tiara right **Obv. Designer:** Ian Rank-Broadley **Rev:** Player running right **Edge:** Reeded

Date	Mintage	F	VF	XF	Unc	BU
2002 Proof	5,000	Value: 175				

KM# 1122 1/5 CROWN
6.2200 g., 0.9990 Gold 0.1998 oz. AGW, 22 mm. **Ruler:** Elizabeth II **Subject:** World Cup 2002 Japan - Korea **Obv:** Bust with tiara right **Obv. Designer:** Ian Rank-Broadley **Rev:** Player kicking to right **Edge:** Reeded

Date	Mintage	F	VF	XF	Unc	BU
2002 Proof	5,000	Value: 175				

KM# 1124 1/5 CROWN
6.2200 g., 0.9990 Gold 0.1998 oz. AGW, 22 mm. **Ruler:** Elizabeth II **Subject:** World Cup 2002 Japan - Korea **Obv:** Head with tiara right **Obv. Designer:** Ian Rank-Broadley **Rev:** Player kicking to left **Edge:** Reeded

Date	Mintage	F	VF	XF	Unc	BU
2002 Proof	5,000	Value: 175				

KM# 1126 1/5 CROWN
6.2200 g., 0.9990 Gold 0.1998 oz. AGW, 22 mm. **Ruler:** Elizabeth II **Subject:** World Cup 2002 Japan - Korea **Obv:** Head with tiara right **Obv. Designer:** Ian Rank-Broadley **Rev:** Player running to left **Edge:** Reeded

Date	Mintage	F	VF	XF	Unc	BU
2002 Proof	5,000	Value: 175				

KM# 1130 1/5 CROWN
6.2200 g., 0.3750 Gold 0.075 oz. AGW, 22 mm. **Ruler:** Elizabeth II **Subject:** Queen Elizabeth II's Golden Jubilee **Obv:** Bust with tiara right **Obv. Designer:** Ian Rank-Broadley **Rev:** Seated crowned Queen holding scepter at her coronation **Edge:** Reeded

Date	Mintage	F	VF	XF	Unc	BU
2002 Proof	2,002	Value: 62.00				

KM# 1132 1/5 CROWN
6.2200 g., 0.3750 Gold 0.075 oz. AGW, 22 mm. **Ruler:** Elizabeth II **Subject:** Queen Elizabeth II's Golden Jubilee **Obv:** Bust with tiara right **Obv. Designer:** Ian Rank-Broadley **Rev:** Queen on horse **Edge:** Reeded

Date	Mintage	F	VF	XF	Unc	BU
2002 Proof	2,002	Value: 62.00				

KM# 1134 1/5 CROWN
6.2200 g., 0.3750 Gold 0.075 oz. AGW, 22 mm. **Ruler:** Elizabeth II **Subject:** Queen Elizabeth II's Golden Jubilee **Obv:** Head with tiara right **Obv. Designer:** Ian Rank-Broadley **Rev:** Queen with dog **Edge:** Reeded

Date	Mintage	F	VF	XF	Unc	BU
2002 Proof	2,002	Value: 62.00				

KM# 1136 1/5 CROWN
6.2200 g., 0.3750 Gold 0.075 oz. AGW, 22 mm. **Ruler:** Elizabeth II **Subject:** Queen Elizabeth II's Golden Jubilee **Obv:** Bust with tiara right **Obv. Designer:** Ian Rank-Broadley **Rev:** Queen at war memorial **Edge:** Reeded

Date	Mintage	F	VF	XF	Unc	BU
2002 Proof	2,002	Value: 62.00				

KM# 1138 1/5 CROWN
6.2200 g., 0.9990 Gold 0.1998 oz. AGW, 22 mm. **Ruler:** Elizabeth II **Subject:** Queen Mother **Obv:** Bust with tiara right **Obv. Designer:** Ian Rank-Broadley **Rev:** Queen Mother and Castle May **Edge:** Reeded

Date	Mintage	F	VF	XF	Unc	BU
2002 Proof	5,000	Value: 175				

KM# 1140 1/5 CROWN
6.2200 g., 0.9999 Gold 0.2 oz. AGW, 22 mm. **Ruler:** Elizabeth II **Subject:** Princess Diana **Obv:** Bust with tiara right **Obv. Designer:** Ian Rank-Broadley **Rev:** Diana's portrait **Edge:** Reeded

Date	Mintage	F	VF	XF	Unc	BU
2002 Proof	5,000	Value: 175				

KM# 1163 1/5 CROWN
6.2200 g., 0.9999 Gold 0.2 oz. AGW, 22 mm. **Ruler:** Elizabeth II **Subject:** Cat **Obv:** Head with tiara right **Obv. Designer:** Ian Rank-Broadley **Rev:** Two Balinese kittens **Edge:** Reeded

Date	Mintage	F	VF	XF	Unc	BU
2003PM	—	—	—	—	145	—
2003PM Proof	—	Value: 175				

KM# 1163a 1/5 CROWN
6.2200 g., 0.9995 Platinum 0.1999 oz. APW, 22 mm. **Ruler:** Elizabeth II **Subject:** Cat **Obv:** Head with tiara right **Obv. Designer:** Ian Rank-Broadley **Rev:** Two Balinese kittens **Edge:** Reeded

Date	Mintage	F	VF	XF	Unc	BU
2003PM	—	—	—	—	255	—

KM# 1169 1/5 CROWN
6.2200 g., 0.9999 Gold 0.2 oz. AGW, 22 mm. **Ruler:** Elizabeth II **Subject:** Year of the Goat **Obv:** Bust with tiara right **Obv. Designer:** Ian Rank-Broadley **Rev:** Three goats **Edge:** Reeded

Date	Mintage	F	VF	XF	Unc	BU
2003PM Proof	—	Value: 175				

KM# 1175 1/5 CROWN
6.2200 g., 0.9999 Gold 0.2 oz. AGW, 22 mm. **Ruler:** Elizabeth II **Subject:** Olympics **Obv:** Bust with tiara right **Obv. Designer:** Ian Rank-Broadley **Rev:** Swimmers **Edge:** Reeded

Date	Mintage	F	VF	XF	Unc	BU
2003PM Proof	5,000	Value: 175				

KM# 1177 1/5 CROWN
6.2200 g., 0.9999 Gold 0.2 oz. AGW, 22 mm. **Ruler:** Elizabeth II **Subject:** Olympics **Obv:** Bust with tiara right **Obv. Designer:** Ian Rank-Broadley **Rev:** Runners **Edge:** Reeded

Date	Mintage	F	VF	XF	Unc	BU
2003PM Proof	5,000	Value: 175				

KM# 1179 1/5 CROWN
6.2200 g., 0.9999 Gold 0.2 oz. AGW, 22 mm. **Ruler:** Elizabeth II **Subject:** Olympics **Obv:** Bust with tiara right **Obv. Designer:** Ian Rank-Broadley **Rev:** Bicyclists **Edge:** Reeded

Date	Mintage	F	VF	XF	Unc	BU
2003PM Proof	5,000	Value: 175				

KM# 1181 1/5 CROWN
6.2200 g., 0.9999 Gold 0.2 oz. AGW, 22 mm. **Ruler:** Elizabeth II **Subject:** Olympics **Obv:** Head with tiara right **Obv. Designer:** Ian Rank-Broadley **Rev:** Sail Boarders **Edge:** Reeded

Date	Mintage	F	VF	XF	Unc	BU
2003PM Proof	—	Value: 175				

KM# 1188 1/5 CROWN
6.2200 g., 0.9999 Gold 0.2 oz. AGW, 22 mm. **Ruler:** Elizabeth II **Subject:** Lord of the Rings **Obv:** Bust with tiara right **Obv. Designer:** Ian Rank-Broadley **Rev:** Legolas **Edge:** Reeded

Date	Mintage	F	VF	XF	Unc	BU
2003PM Proof	3,500	Value: 175				

KM# 1223 1/5 CROWN
6.2200 g., 0.9999 Gold 0.2 oz. AGW, 22 mm. **Ruler:** Elizabeth II **Obv:** Bust with tiara right **Obv. Designer:** Ian Rank-Broadley **Rev:** D-Day Invasion Plan Map **Edge:** Reeded

Date	Mintage	F	VF	XF	Unc	BU
2004PM Proof	5,000	Value: 175				

KM# 1225 1/5 CROWN
6.2200 g., 0.9999 Gold 0.2 oz. AGW, 22 mm. **Ruler:** Elizabeth II **Obv:** Bust with tiara right **Obv. Designer:** Ian Rank-Broadley **Rev:** Victoria Cross and battle scene **Edge:** Reeded

Date	Mintage	F	VF	XF	Unc	BU
2004PM Proof	5,000	Value: 175				

KM# 1227 1/5 CROWN
6.2200 g., 0.9999 Gold 0.2 oz. AGW, 22 mm. **Ruler:** Elizabeth II **Obv:** Bust with tiara right **Obv. Designer:** Ian Rank-Broadley **Rev:** Silver Star and battle scene **Edge:** Reeded

Date	Mintage	F	VF	XF	Unc	BU
2004PM Proof	5,000	Value: 175				

KM# 1229 1/5 CROWN
6.2200 g., 0.9999 Gold 0.2 oz. AGW, 22 mm. **Ruler:** Elizabeth II **Obv:** Bust with tiara right **Obv. Designer:** Ian Rank-Broadley **Rev:** George Cross and rescue scene **Edge:** Reeded

Date	Mintage	F	VF	XF	Unc	BU
2004PM Proof	5,000	Value: 175				

KM# 1231 1/5 CROWN
6.2200 g., 0.9999 Gold 0.2 oz. AGW, 22 mm. **Ruler:** Elizabeth II **Obv:** Bust with tiara right **Obv. Designer:** Ian Rank-Broadley **Rev:** White Rose of Finland Medal and battle scene **Edge:** Reeded

Date	Mintage	F	VF	XF	Unc	BU
2004PM Proof	5,000	Value: 175				

KM# 1233 1/5 CROWN
6.2200 g., 0.9999 Gold 0.2 oz. AGW, 22 mm. **Ruler:** Elizabeth II **Obv:** Bust with tiara right **Obv. Designer:** Ian Rank-Broadley **Rev:** The Norwegian War Medal and naval battle scene **Edge:** Reeded

Date	Mintage	F	VF	XF	Unc	BU
2004PM Proof	5,000	Value: 175				

KM# 1235 1/5 CROWN
6.2200 g., 0.9999 Gold 0.2 oz. AGW, 22 mm. **Ruler:** Elizabeth II **Obv:** Bust with tiara right **Obv. Designer:** Ian Rank-Broadley **Rev:** French Croix de Guerre and Partisan battle scene **Edge:** Reeded

ISLE OF MAN 409

Date	Mintage	F	VF	XF	Unc	BU
2004PM Proof	5,000				Value: 175	

KM# 1249.1 1/5 CROWN
6.2200 g., 0.9999 Gold 0.2 oz. AGW, 22 mm. **Ruler:** Elizabeth II **Obv:** Head with tiara right **Obv. Designer:** Ian Rank-Broadley **Rev:** Two Tonkinese cats **Edge:** Reeded

Date	Mintage	F	VF	XF	Unc	BU
2004PM	—	—	—	—	145	—
2004PM Proof	1,000				Value: 175	

KM# 1249.2 1/5 CROWN
6.2200 g., 0.9999 Gold 0.2 oz. AGW, 22 mm. **Ruler:** Elizabeth II **Obv:** Head with tiara right **Obv. Designer:** Ian Rank-Broadley **Rev:** Two multicolor Tonkinese cats **Edge:** Reeded

Date	Mintage	F	VF	XF	Unc	BU
2004PM Proof	—				Value: 180	

KM# 1198 1/5 CROWN
6.2200 g., 0.9990 Palladium 0.1998 oz., 22 mm. **Ruler:** Elizabeth II **Subject:** Palladium Bicentennial **Obv:** Head with tiara right **Obv. Designer:** Ian Rank-Broadley **Rev:** Athena **Edge:** Reeded

Date	Mintage	F	VF	XF	Unc	BU
2004PM Proof	999				Value: 300	

KM# 1271 1/5 CROWN
6.2200 g., 0.9999 Gold 0.2 oz. AGW, 22 mm. **Ruler:** Elizabeth II **Obv:** Bust with tiara right **Obv. Designer:** Ian Rank-Broadley **Rev:** Himalayan cat and two kittens **Edge:** Reeded

Date	Mintage	F	VF	XF	Unc	BU
2005PM Proof	—				Value: 225	

KM# 1271a 1/5 CROWN
6.2200 g., 0.9950 Platinum 0.199 oz. APW, 22 mm. **Ruler:** Elizabeth II **Obv:** Bust with tiara right **Obv. Designer:** Ian Rank-Broadley **Rev:** Himalayan cat and two kittens **Edge:** Reeded

Date	Mintage	F	VF	XF	Unc	BU
2005PM Proof	—				Value: 350	

KM# 669 1/4 CROWN
0.9990 Bi-Metallic Gold center in Platinum ring .1249 oz. **Ruler:** Elizabeth II **Series:** Legend of King Arthur **Obv:** Crowned bust right **Obv. Designer:** Raphael Maklouf **Rev:** King Arthur with sword and orb

Date	Mintage	F	VF	XF	Unc	BU
1996 Proof	Est. 5,000				Value: 250	

KM# 670 1/4 CROWN
0.9990 Bi-Metallic .1249 oz. **Ruler:** Elizabeth II **Series:** Legend of King Arthur **Obv:** Crowned bust right **Obv. Designer:** Raphael Maklouf **Rev:** Queen Guinevere

Date	Mintage	F	VF	XF	Unc	BU
1996 Proof	Est. 5,000				Value: 250	

KM# 671 1/4 CROWN
0.9990 Bi-Metallic Gold center in Platinum ring .1249 oz. **Ruler:** Elizabeth II **Series:** Legend of King Arthur **Obv:** Crowned bust right **Obv. Designer:** Raphael Maklouf **Rev:** Sir Lancelot

Date	Mintage	F	VF	XF	Unc	BU
1996 Proof	Est. 5,000				Value: 250	

KM# 672 1/4 CROWN
0.9990 Bi-Metallic Gold center in Platinum ring .1249 oz. **Ruler:** Elizabeth II **Series:** Legend of King Arthur **Obv:** Crowned bust right **Obv. Designer:** Raphael Maklouf **Rev:** Merlin

Date	Mintage	F	VF	XF	Unc	BU
1996 Proof	Est. 5,000				Value: 250	

KM# 673 1/4 CROWN
0.9990 Bi-Metallic Gold center in Platinum ring .1249 oz. **Ruler:** Elizabeth II **Series:** Legend of King Arthur **Obv:** Crowned bust right **Obv. Designer:** Raphael Maklouf **Rev:** Camelot Castle

Date	Mintage	F	VF	XF	Unc	BU
1996 Proof	Est. 5,000				Value: 250	

KM# 674 1/4 CROWN
3.8880 g., 0.9950 Platinum .1244 oz. APW **Ruler:** Elizabeth II **Series:** Legend of King Arthur **Obv:** Crowned bust right **Obv. Designer:** Raphael Maklouf **Rev:** King Arthur with sword and orb

Date	Mintage	F	VF	XF	Unc	BU
1996 Proof	Est. 5,000				Value: 275	

KM# 675 1/4 CROWN
3.8880 g., 0.9950 Platinum .1244 oz. APW **Ruler:** Elizabeth II **Series:** Legend of King Arthur **Obv:** Crowned bust right **Obv. Designer:** Raphael Maklouf **Rev:** Queen Guinevere

Date	Mintage	F	VF	XF	Unc	BU
1996 Proof	Est. 5,000				Value: 275	

KM# 676 1/4 CROWN
3.8880 g., 0.9950 Platinum .1244 oz. APW **Ruler:** Elizabeth II **Series:** Legend of King Arthur **Obv:** Crowned bust right **Obv. Designer:** Raphael Maklouf **Rev:** Sir Lancelot

Date	Mintage	F	VF	XF	Unc	BU
1996 Proof	Est. 5,000				Value: 275	

KM# 677 1/4 CROWN
3.8880 g., 0.9950 Platinum .1244 oz. APW **Ruler:** Elizabeth II **Series:** Legend of King Arthur **Obv:** Crowned bust right **Obv. Designer:** Raphael Maklouf **Rev:** Merlin

Date	Mintage	F	VF	XF	Unc	BU
1996 Proof	Est. 5,000				Value: 275	

KM# 678 1/4 CROWN
3.8880 g., 0.9950 Platinum .1244 oz. APW **Ruler:** Elizabeth II **Series:** Legend of King Arthur **Obv:** Crowned bust right within circle **Obv. Designer:** Raphael Maklouf **Rev:** Castle within circle

Date	Mintage	F	VF	XF	Unc	BU
1996 Proof	Est. 5,000				Value: 275	

KM# 187 1/2 CROWN
15.5500 g., 0.9990 Gold .5000 oz. AGW **Ruler:** Elizabeth II **Subject:** U.S. Constitution **Obv:** Crowned bust right within circle **Obv. Designer:** Raphael Maklouf **Rev:** Statue of Liberty at center of Presidential busts within circle

Date	Mintage	F	VF	XF	Unc	BU
1987 Proof	12,000				Value: 350	

KM# 187a 1/2 CROWN
15.5500 g., 0.9990 Platinum .5000 oz. APW **Ruler:** Elizabeth II **Subject:** U.S. Constitution **Obv:** Crowned bust right within circle **Obv. Designer:** Raphael Maklouf **Rev:** Busts of American presidents, Statue of Liberty at center

Date	Mintage	F	VF	XF	Unc	BU
1987 Proof	250				Value: 650	

KM# 238 1/2 CROWN
15.5500 g., 0.9990 Gold .5000 oz. AGW **Ruler:** Elizabeth II **Obv:** Crowned bust right **Obv. Designer:** Raphael Maklouf **Rev:** Manx cat

Date	Mintage	F	VF	XF	Unc	BU
1988	6,375	—	—	—	345	—
1988 Proof	5,000				Value: 365	

KM# 286 1/2 CROWN
16.4000 g., 0.9480 Gold .5000 oz. AGW **Ruler:** Elizabeth II **Subject:** Australian Bicentennial **Obv:** Crowned bust right within circle **Obv. Designer:** Raphael Maklouf **Rev:** Cockatoo on branch within circle

Date	Mintage	F	VF	XF	Unc	BU
1988 Proof	Est. 7,500				Value: 360	

KM# 287 1/2 CROWN
16.4000 g., 0.9480 Gold .5000 oz. AGW **Ruler:** Elizabeth II **Subject:** Australian Bicentennial **Obv:** Crowned bust right **Obv. Designer:** Raphael Maklouf **Rev:** Koala bear

Date	Mintage	F	VF	XF	Unc	BU
1988 Proof	Est. 7,500				Value: 360	

KM# 288 1/2 CROWN
16.4000 g., 0.9480 Gold .5000 oz. AGW **Ruler:** Elizabeth II **Subject:** Australian Bicentennial **Obv:** Crowned bust right **Obv. Designer:** Raphael Maklouf **Rev:** Duckbill platypus

Date	Mintage	F	VF	XF	Unc	BU
1988 Proof	Est. 7,500				Value: 360	

KM# 289 1/2 CROWN
16.4000 g., 0.9480 Gold .5000 oz. AGW **Ruler:** Elizabeth II **Subject:** Australian Bicentennial **Obv:** Crowned bust right within circle **Obv. Designer:** Raphael Maklouf **Rev:** Kangaroo within circle

Date	Mintage	F	VF	XF	Unc	BU
1988 Proof	Est. 7,500				Value: 360	

KM# 359 1/2 CROWN
15.5500 g., 0.9990 Platinum .5000 oz. APW **Ruler:** Elizabeth II **Subject:** Australian Bicentennial **Obv:** Crowned bust right **Obv. Designer:** Raphael Maklouf **Rev:** Cockatoo

Date	Mintage	F	VF	XF	Unc	BU
1988 Proof	—				Value: 650	

KM# 360 1/2 CROWN
15.5500 g., 0.9990 Platinum .5000 oz. APW **Ruler:** Elizabeth II **Subject:** Australian Bicentennial **Obv:** Crowned bust right **Obv. Designer:** Raphael Maklouf **Rev:** Koala bear

Date	Mintage	F	VF	XF	Unc	BU
1988 Proof	—				Value: 650	

KM# 361 1/2 CROWN
15.5500 g., 0.9990 Platinum .5000 oz. APW **Ruler:** Elizabeth II **Subject:** Australian Bicentennial **Obv:** Crowned bust right **Obv. Designer:** Raphael Maklouf **Rev:** Duckbill platypus

Date	Mintage	F	VF	XF	Unc	BU
1988 Proof	—				Value: 650	

KM# 362 1/2 CROWN
15.5500 g., 0.9990 Platinum .5000 oz. APW **Ruler:** Elizabeth II **Subject:** Australian Bicentennial **Obv:** Crowned bust right **Obv. Designer:** Raphael Maklouf **Rev:** Kangaroo

Date	Mintage	F	VF	XF	Unc	BU
1988 Proof	—				Value: 650	

KM# 363 1/2 CROWN
15.5500 g., 0.9990 Platinum .5000 oz. APW **Ruler:** Elizabeth II **Subject:** Australian Bicentennial **Obv:** Crowned bust right **Obv. Designer:** Raphael Maklouf **Rev:** Dingo Dog

Date	Mintage	F	VF	XF	Unc	BU
1988 Proof	—				Value: 650	

KM# 255 1/2 CROWN
16.4000 g., 0.9480 Gold .5000 oz. AGW **Ruler:** Elizabeth II **Obv:** Crowned bust right **Obv. Designer:** Raphael Maklouf **Rev:** Persian cat

Date	Mintage	F	VF	XF	Unc	BU
1989	—	—	—	—	345	—
1989 Proof	—				Value: 375	

KM# 470 1/2 CROWN
15.5500 g., 0.9990 Platinum .5000 oz. APW **Ruler:** Elizabeth II **Obv:** Crowned bust right **Obv. Designer:** Raphael Maklouf **Rev:** Persian cat

Date	Mintage	F	VF	XF	Unc	BU
1989	—	—	—	—	BV+20%	—
1989 Proof	—	BV+25%				

410 ISLE OF MAN

KM# 1265 1/2 CROWN
15.5500 g., 0.9990 Gold 0.4994 oz. AGW, 30 mm. **Ruler:** Elizabeth II **Obv:** Crowned bust right **Obv. Designer:** Raphael Maklouf **Rev:** Stamp design in black center **Edge:** Reeded

Date	Mintage	F	VF	XF	Unc	BU
1990PM	—	—	—	—	350	—

KM# 280 1/2 CROWN
16.4000 g., 0.9480 Gold .5000 oz. AGW **Ruler:** Elizabeth II **Obv:** Crowned bust right **Obv. Designer:** Raphael Maklouf **Rev:** Alley cat

Date	Mintage	F	VF	XF	Unc	BU
1990	—	—	—	—	365	—
1990 Proof	— Value: 400					

KM# 297 1/2 CROWN
15.5500 g., 0.9990 Gold .5000 oz. AGW **Ruler:** Elizabeth II **Obv:** Crowned bust right **Obv. Designer:** Raphael Maklouf **Rev:** Norwegian cat

Date	Mintage	F	VF	XF	Unc	BU
1991	—	—	—	—	365	—
1991 Proof	— Value: 400					

KM# 325 1/2 CROWN
15.5500 g., 0.9990 Gold .5000 oz. AGW **Ruler:** Elizabeth II **Subject:** America's Cup **Obv:** Crowned bust right **Obv. Designer:** Raphael Maklouf **Rev:** Cameo of "Star of India" above two modern sailboats

Date	Mintage	F	VF	XF	Unc	BU
1992 Prooflike	2,000	—	—	—	360	—

KM# 331 1/2 CROWN
15.5500 g., 0.9990 Gold .5000 oz. AGW **Ruler:** Elizabeth II **Obv:** Crowned bust right **Obv. Designer:** Raphael Maklouf **Rev:** Siamese cat

Date	Mintage	F	VF	XF	Unc	BU
1992	—	—	—	—	365	—
1992 Proof	— Value: 400					

KM# 341 1/2 CROWN
15.5500 g., 0.9990 Gold .5000 oz. AGW **Ruler:** Elizabeth II **Subject:** Year of the Rooster **Obv:** Crowned bust right **Obv. Designer:** Raphael Maklouf **Rev:** Cockerel within circle **Rev. Designer:** Barry Stanton

Date	Mintage	F	VF	XF	Unc	BU
1993 Proof	Est. 5,000 Value: 375					

KM# 352 1/2 CROWN
15.5500 g., 0.9990 Gold .5000 oz. AGW **Ruler:** Elizabeth II **Obv:** Crowned bust right **Obv. Designer:** Raphael Maklouf **Rev:** Maine coon cat

Date	Mintage	F	VF	XF	Unc	BU
1993	—	—	—	—	365	—
1993 Proof	— Value: 400					

KM# 379 1/2 CROWN
15.5500 g., 0.9990 Gold .5000 oz. AGW **Ruler:** Elizabeth II **Obv:** Crowned bust right **Obv. Designer:** Raphael Maklouf **Rev:** Japanese bobtail cat

Date	Mintage	F	VF	XF	Unc	BU
1994	—	—	—	—	365	—
1994 Proof	— Value: 400					

KM# 405 1/2 CROWN
15.5500 g., 0.9990 Gold .5000 oz. AGW **Ruler:** Elizabeth II **Obv:** Crowned bust right **Obv. Designer:** Raphael Maklouf **Rev:** Pekingese dog

Date	Mintage	F	VF	XF	Unc	BU
1994 Proof	5,000 Value: 375					

KM# 476 1/2 CROWN
15.5500 g., 0.9990 Platinum .5000 oz. APW **Ruler:** Elizabeth II **Obv:** Crowned bust right **Obv. Designer:** Raphael Maklouf **Rev:** Japanese bobtail cat

Date	Mintage	F	VF	XF	Unc	BU
1994	—	—	—	—BV+20%	—	—
1994 Proof	— BV+20%					

KM# 445 1/2 CROWN
15.5500 g., 0.9990 Gold .5000 oz. AGW **Ruler:** Elizabeth II **Obv:** Crowned bust right **Obv. Designer:** Raphael Maklouf **Rev:** Turkish cat looking back

Date	Mintage	F	VF	XF	Unc	BU
1995 U	—	—	—	—	365	—
1995 Proof	— Value: 400					

KM# 452 1/2 CROWN
15.5500 g., 0.9990 Gold .5000 oz. AGW **Ruler:** Elizabeth II **Subject:** Year of the Pig **Obv:** Crowned bust right **Obv. Designer:** Raphael Maklouf **Rev:** Sow with piglets

Date	Mintage	F	VF	XF	Unc	BU
1995 Proof	Est. 5,000 Value: 365					

KM# 481 1/2 CROWN
15.5500 g., 0.9990 Platinum .5000 oz. APW **Ruler:** Elizabeth II **Obv:** Crowned bust right **Obv. Designer:** Raphael Maklouf **Rev:** Turkish cat

Date	Mintage	F	VF	XF	Unc	BU
1995	—	—	—	—BV+20%	—	—
1995 Proof	— BV+20%					

KM# 731 1/2 CROWN
15.5517 g., 0.9999 Gold .5000 oz. AGW **Ruler:** Elizabeth II **Subject:** Year of the Rat **Obv:** Crowned bust right **Obv. Designer:** Raphael Maklouf **Rev:** Rat

Date	Mintage	F	VF	XF	Unc	BU
1996 Proof	— Value: 365					

KM# 619 1/2 CROWN
15.5500 g., 0.9990 Gold .5000 oz. AGW **Ruler:** Elizabeth II **Obv:** Crowned bust right **Obv. Designer:** Raphael Maklouf **Rev:** Burmese cat

Date	Mintage	F	VF	XF	Unc	BU
1996 U	—	—	—	—	345	—
1996 Proof	— Value: 375					

KM# 620 1/2 CROWN
15.5500 g., 0.9990 Platinum .5000 oz. APW **Ruler:** Elizabeth II **Obv:** Crowned bust right **Obv. Designer:** Raphael Maklouf **Rev:** Burmese cat

Date	Mintage	F	VF	XF	Unc	BU
1996 U	—	—	—	—BV+20%	—	—
1996 Proof	— Value: 650					

KM# 724 1/2 CROWN
15.5517 g., 0.9999 Gold .5000 oz. AGW **Ruler:** Elizabeth II **Subject:** Year of the Ox **Obv:** Crowned bust right **Obv. Designer:** Raphael Maklouf **Rev:** Ox laying down

Date	Mintage	F	VF	XF	Unc	BU
1996 Proof	Est. 6,000 Value: 350					

KM# 764 1/2 CROWN
15.5517 g., 0.9999 Gold .5000 oz. AGW **Ruler:** Elizabeth II **Obv:** Crowned bust right **Obv. Designer:** Raphael Maklouf **Rev:** Portrait of Leif Eriksson and Viking ship with map sail

Date	Mintage	F	VF	XF	Unc	BU
1997 Proof	Est. 2,500 Value: 365					

KM# 767 1/2 CROWN
15.5517 g., 0.9999 Gold .5000 oz. AGW **Ruler:** Elizabeth II **Obv:** Crowned bust right **Obv. Designer:** Raphael Maklouf **Rev:** Portrait of Fridtjof Nansen, map and ship "The Fram"

Date	Mintage	F	VF	XF	Unc	BU
1997 Proof	Est. 2,500 Value: 345					

KM# 773 1/2 CROWN
15.5517 g., 0.9999 Gold .5000 oz. AGW **Ruler:** Elizabeth II **Obv:** Crowned bust right **Obv. Designer:** Raphael Maklouf **Rev:** Long-haired Smoke cat

Date	Mintage	F	VF	XF	Unc	BU
1997	—	—	—	—	365	—
1997 Proof	— Value: 400					

KM# 791 1/2 CROWN
15.5517 g., 0.9999 Gold .5000 oz. AGW **Ruler:** Elizabeth II **Subject:** History of the Cat **Obv:** Crowned bust right **Obv. Designer:** Raphael Maklouf **Rev:** Cat stalking a spider

Date	Mintage	F	VF	XF	Unc	BU
1997 Proof	Est. 2,500 Value: 375					

KM# 815 1/2 CROWN
15.5000 g., 0.9999 Gold .5000 oz. AGW **Subject:** Year of the Tiger **Obv:** Crowned bust right **Obv. Designer:** Raphael Maklouf **Rev:** Tiger

Date	Mintage	F	VF	XF	Unc	BU
1998 Proof	Est. 6,000 Value: 365					

KM# 856 1/2 CROWN
15.5517 g., 0.9999 Gold .5000 oz. AGW **Ruler:** Elizabeth II **Obv:** Crowned bust right **Obv. Designer:** Raphael Maklouf **Rev:** Birman cat

Date	Mintage	F	VF	XF	Unc	BU
1998	—	—	—	—	365	—
1998 Proof	1,000 Value: 400					

KM# 856a 1/2 CROWN
15.5517 g., 0.9995 Platinum .5000 oz. APW **Ruler:** Elizabeth II **Obv:** Crowned bust right **Obv. Designer:** Raphael Maklouf **Rev:** Birman cat

Date	Mintage	F	VF	XF	Unc	BU
1998						

Note: Reported, not confirmed

KM# 862 1/2 CROWN
15.5517 g., 0.9999 Gold .5000 oz. AGW **Ruler:** Elizabeth II **Subject:** History of the Cat **Obv:** Crowned bust right **Obv. Designer:** Raphael Maklouf **Rev:** Egyptian Mau cat with earring

Date	Mintage	F	VF	XF	Unc	BU
1998 Proof	Est. 250 Value: 400					

KM# 951 1/2 CROWN
15.5517 g., 0.9999 Gold .5000 oz. AGW **Ruler:** Elizabeth II **Subject:** Year of the Rabbit **Obv:** Crowned bust right **Obv. Designer:** Raphael Maklouf **Rev:** Two rabbits

Date	Mintage	F	VF	XF	Unc	BU
1999 Proof	Est. 6,000 Value: 365					

KM# 964 1/2 CROWN
15.5517 g., 0.9999 Gold .5000 oz. AGW **Ruler:** Elizabeth II **Subject:** British Blue cat **Obv:** Crowned bust right **Obv. Designer:** Raphael Maklouf **Rev:** Cat cleaning paw

Date	Mintage	F	VF	XF	Unc	BU
1999	—	—	—	—	360	—
1999 Proof	— Value: 385					

KM# 964a 1/2 CROWN
15.5518 g., 0.9995 Platinum .5000 oz. APW **Ruler:** Elizabeth II **Subject:** British Blue cat **Obv:** Crowned bust right **Obv. Designer:** Raphael Maklouf **Rev:** Cat cleaning paw

Date	Mintage	F	VF	XF	Unc	BU
1999						

Note: Reported, not confirmed

KM# 1055 1/2 CROWN
15.5517 g., 0.9999 Gold .5000 oz. AGW, 30 mm. **Ruler:** Elizabeth II **Subject:** Scottish Fold Kitten **Obv:** Crowned bust right **Obv. Designer:** Raphael Maklouf **Rev:** Kitten playing with world **Edge:** Reeded

Date	Mintage	F	VF	XF	Unc	BU
2000	—	—	—	—	345	—
2000 Proof	— Value: 365					

KM# 1055a 1/2 CROWN
6.2200 g., 0.9995 Platinum .2000 oz. APW **Ruler:** Elizabeth II **Subject:** Scottish Fold Kitten **Obv:** Crowned bust right **Obv. Designer:** Raphael Maklouf **Rev:** Kitten playing with world

Date	Mintage	F	VF	XF	Unc	BU
2000	—	—	—	—	350	—

KM# 1015 1/2 CROWN
15.5517 g., 0.9999 Gold .5000 oz. AGW **Ruler:** Elizabeth II **Subject:** Year of the Dragon **Obv:** Head with tiara right **Obv. Designer:** Ian Rank-Broadley **Rev:** Dragon, Chinese characters

Date	Mintage	F	VF	XF	Unc	BU
2000 Proof	Est. 6,000 Value: 350					

KM# 1061 1/2 CROWN
15.5517 g., 0.9999 Gold .5000 oz. AGW, 30 mm. **Ruler:** Elizabeth II **Subject:** Year of the Snake **Obv:** Bust with tiara right **Obv. Designer:** Ian Rank-Broadley **Rev:** Snake **Edge:** Reeded

Date	Mintage	F	VF	XF	Unc	BU
2001 Proof	6,000 Value: 365					

KM# 1070 1/2 CROWN
15.5517 g., 0.9999 Gold .5000 oz. AGW, 30 mm. **Ruler:** Elizabeth II **Obv:** Head with tiara right **Obv. Designer:** Ian Rank-Broadley **Rev:** Two Somali kittens **Edge:** Reeded

Date	Mintage	F	VF	XF	Unc	BU
2001	—	—	—	—	345	—
2001 Proof	1,000 Value: 365					

KM# 1071 1/2 CROWN
15.5517 g., 0.9995 Platinum .5000 oz. APW, 27 mm. **Ruler:** Elizabeth II **Obv:** Head with tiara right **Obv. Designer:** Ian Rank-Broadley **Rev:** Two Somali kittens **Edge:** Reeded

Date	Mintage	F	VF	XF	Unc	BU
2001	—	—	—	—	645	—

KM# 1110 1/2 CROWN
15.5510 g., 0.9990 Gold 0.4995 oz. AGW, 30 mm. **Ruler:** Elizabeth II **Subject:** Bengal Cat **Obv:** Head with tiara right **Obv. Designer:** Ian Rank-Broadley **Rev:** Cat and kitten **Edge:** Reeded

Date	Mintage	VG	F	VF	XF	Unc
2002	—	—	—	—	—	345
2002 Proof	1,000 Value: 365					

ISLE OF MAN

KM# 1101 1/2 CROWN
15.5500 g., 0.9999 Gold .4999 oz. AGW, 30 mm. **Ruler:** Elizabeth II **Subject:** Year of the Horse **Obv:** Bust with tiara right **Obv. Designer:** Ian Rank-Broadley **Rev:** Two horses **Edge:** Reeded

Date	Mintage	F	VF	XF	Unc	BU
2002 Proof	6,000	Value: 350				

KM# 1110a 1/2 CROWN
6.2200 g., 0.9990 Platinum 0.1998 oz. APW, 30 mm. **Ruler:** Elizabeth II **Subject:** Bengal Cat **Obv:** Head with tiara right **Obv. Designer:** Ian Rank-Broadley **Rev:** Cat and kitten **Edge:** Reeded

Date	Mintage	F	VF	XF	Unc	BU
2002	—	—	—	—	375	—

KM# 1164 1/2 CROWN
15.5510 g., 0.9999 Gold 0.4999 oz. AGW, 30 mm. **Ruler:** Elizabeth II **Subject:** Cat **Obv:** Head with tiara right **Obv. Designer:** Ian Rank-Broadley **Rev:** Two Balinese kittens **Edge:** Reeded

Date	Mintage	F	VF	XF	Unc	BU
2003PM	—	—	—	—	345	—
2003PM Proof	—	Value: 365				

KM# 1164a 1/2 CROWN
15.5510 g., 0.9995 Platinum 0.4997 oz. APW, 30 mm. **Ruler:** Elizabeth II **Subject:** Cat **Obv:** Head with tiara right **Obv. Designer:** Ian Rank-Broadley **Rev:** Two Balinese kittens **Edge:** Reeded

Date	Mintage	F	VF	XF	Unc	BU
2003PM	—	—	—	—	645	—

KM# 1170 1/2 CROWN
15.5510 g., 0.9999 Gold 0.4999 oz. AGW, 30 mm. **Ruler:** Elizabeth II **Subject:** Year of the Goat **Obv:** Bust with tiara right **Obv. Designer:** Ian Rank-Broadley **Rev:** Three goats **Edge:** Reeded

Date	Mintage	F	VF	XF	Unc	BU
2003PM Proof	—	Value: 365				

KM# 1189 1/2 CROWN
15.5510 g., 0.9999 Gold 0.4999 oz. AGW, 30 mm. **Ruler:** Elizabeth II **Subject:** Lord of the Rings **Obv:** Bust with tiara right **Obv. Designer:** Ian Rank-Broadley **Rev:** Gimli with two battle axes **Edge:** Reeded

Date	Mintage	F	VF	XF	Unc	BU
2003PM Proof	1,000	Value: 365				

KM# 1243 1/2 CROWN
15.5520 g., 0.9999 Gold 0.5 oz. AGW, 30 mm. **Ruler:** Elizabeth II **Obv:** Head with tiara right **Obv. Designer:** Ian Rank-Broadley **Rev:** Monkey **Edge:** Reeded

Date	Mintage	F	VF	XF	Unc	BU
2004PM Proof	6,000	Value: 365				

KM# 1250 1/2 CROWN
15.5520 g., 0.9999 Gold 0.5 oz. AGW, 30 mm. **Ruler:** Elizabeth II **Obv:** Head with tiara right **Obv. Designer:** Ian Rank-Broadley **Rev:** Two Tonkinese cats **Edge:** Reeded

Date	Mintage	F	VF	XF	Unc	BU
2004PM	—	—	—	—	345	—
2004PM Proof	1,000	Value: 365				

KM# 1199 1/2 CROWN
15.5500 g., 0.9990 Bi-Metallic .999 Palladium 6.3g center in .9999 Gold 9.25 g ring 0.4994 oz., 30 mm. **Ruler:** Elizabeth II **Subject:** Palladium Bicentennial **Obv:** Bust with tiara right **Obv. Designer:** Ian Rank-Broadley **Rev:** Athena **Edge:** Reeded

Date	Mintage	F	VF	XF	Unc	BU
2004PM Proof	500	Value: 650				

KM# 1272 1/2 CROWN
15.5510 g., 0.9999 Gold 0.4999 oz. AGW, 27 mm. **Ruler:** Elizabeth II **Obv:** Bust with tiara right **Obv. Designer:** Ian Rank-Broadley **Rev:** Himalayan cat and two kittens **Edge:** Reeded

Date	Mintage	F	VF	XF	Unc	BU
2005PM Proof	—	Value: 500				

KM# 1272a 1/2 CROWN
15.5510 g., 0.9950 Platinum 0.4975 oz. APW, 27 mm. **Ruler:** Elizabeth II **Obv:** Bust with tiara right **Obv. Designer:** Ian Rank-Broadley **Rev:** Himalayan cat and two kittens **Edge:** Reeded

Date	Mintage	F	VF	XF	Unc	BU
2005PM Proof	—	Value: 950				
2005PM Proof	—	Value: 950				

KM# 46b CROWN
43.0000 g., 0.9170 Gold 1.2678 oz. AGW, 38.5 mm. **Ruler:** Elizabeth II **Subject:** Millennium of Tynwald **Obv:** Young bust right **Obv. Designer:** Arnold Machin **Rev:** Viking longship **Rev. Designer:** Leslie Lindsay

Date	Mintage	F	VF	XF	Unc	BU
1979 Proof	300	Value: 925				

KM# 46c CROWN
52.0000 g., 0.9500 Platinum 1.5884 oz. APW, 38.5 mm. **Ruler:** Elizabeth II **Subject:** Millennium of Tynwald **Obv:** Young bust right **Obv. Designer:** Arnold Machin **Rev:** Viking longship **Rev. Designer:** Leslie Lindsay

Date	Mintage	F	VF	XF	Unc	BU
1979 Proof	100	Value: 2,150				

KM# 47b CROWN
43.0000 g., 0.9170 Gold 1.2678 oz. AGW, 38.5 mm. **Ruler:** Elizabeth II **Subject:** Millennium of Tynwald **Obv:** Young bust right **Obv. Designer:** Arnold Machin **Rev:** English cog, Castle Rushen **Rev. Designer:** Leslie Lindsay

Date	Mintage	F	VF	XF	Unc	BU
1979 Proof	300	Value: 925				

KM# 47c CROWN
52.0000 g., 0.9500 Platinum 1.5884 oz. APW, 38.5 mm. **Ruler:** Elizabeth II **Subject:** Millennium of Tynwald **Obv:** Young bust right **Obv. Designer:** Arnold Machin **Rev:** English cog, Castle Rushen **Rev. Designer:** Leslie Lindsay

Date	Mintage	F	VF	XF	Unc	BU
1979 Proof	100	Value: 2,150				

KM# 48b CROWN
43.0000 g., 0.9170 Gold 1.2678 oz. AGW, 38.5 mm. **Ruler:** Elizabeth II **Subject:** Millennium of Tynwald **Obv:** Young bust right **Obv. Designer:** Arnold Machin **Rev:** Ship **Rev. Designer:** Leslie Lindsay

Date	Mintage	F	VF	XF	Unc	BU
1979 Proof	300	Value: 925				

KM# 48c CROWN
52.0000 g., 0.9500 Platinum 1.5884 oz. APW, 38.5 mm. **Ruler:** Elizabeth II **Subject:** Millennium of Tynwald **Obv:** Young bust right **Obv. Designer:** Arnold Machin **Rev:** Ship **Rev. Designer:** Leslie Lindsay

Date	Mintage	F	VF	XF	Unc	BU
1979 Proof	100	Value: 2,150				

KM# 49b CROWN
43.0000 g., 0.9170 Gold 1.2678 oz. AGW, 38.5 mm. **Ruler:** Elizabeth II **Subject:** Millennium of Tynwald **Obv:** Young bust right **Obv. Designer:** Arnold Machin **Rev:** Standing figure and ship **Rev. Designer:** Leslie Lindsay

Date	Mintage	F	VF	XF	Unc	BU
1979 Proof	300	Value: 925				

KM# 49c CROWN
52.0000 g., 0.9500 Platinum 1.5884 oz. APW, 38.5 mm. **Ruler:** Elizabeth II **Subject:** Millennium of Tynwald **Obv:** Young bust right **Obv. Designer:** Arnold Machin **Rev:** Standing figure and ship **Rev. Designer:** Leslie Lindsay

Date	Mintage	F	VF	XF	Unc	BU
1979 Proof	100	Value: 2,150				

KM# 50b CROWN
43.0000 g., 0.9170 Gold 1.2678 oz. AGW, 38.5 mm. **Ruler:** Elizabeth II **Subject:** Millennium of Tynwald **Obv:** Young bust right **Obv. Designer:** Arnold Machin **Rev:** Lifeboat and Sir William Hillory portrait **Rev. Designer:** Leslie Lindsay

Date	Mintage	F	VF	XF	Unc	BU
1979 Proof	300	Value: 925				

KM# 50c CROWN
52.0000 g., 0.9500 Platinum 1.5884 oz. APW, 38.5 mm. **Ruler:** Elizabeth II **Subject:** Millennium of Tynwald **Obv:** Young bust right **Obv. Designer:** Arnold Machin **Rev:** Lifeboat and Sir William Hillory portrait **Rev. Designer:** Leslie Lindsay

Date	Mintage	F	VF	XF	Unc	BU
1979 Proof	100	Value: 2,150				

KM# 63b CROWN
52.0000 g., 0.9500 Platinum 1.5884 oz. APW, 38.5 mm. **Ruler:** Elizabeth II **Subject:** Derby Bicentennial **Obv:** Young bust right **Obv. Designer:** Arnold Machin **Rev:** Men racing horses

ISLE OF MAN

Date	Mintage	F	VF	XF	Unc	BU
1980 Proof	500	Value: 2,150				

KM# 63c CROWN
43.0000 g., 0.9170 Gold 1.2678 oz. AGW, 38.5 mm. **Ruler:** Elizabeth II **Subject:** Derby Bicentennial **Obv:** Young bust right **Obv. Designer:** Arnold Machin **Rev:** Men racing horses

Date	Mintage	F	VF	XF	Unc	BU
1980 Proof	—	Value: 925				

KM# 64b CROWN
39.8000 g., 0.9170 Gold 1.1735 oz. AGW, 38.5 mm. **Ruler:** Elizabeth II **Subject:** 1980 Winter Olympics - Lake Placid **Obv:** Young bust right **Obv. Designer:** Arnold Machin **Rev:** Triskeles at center of assorted olympic figures

Date	Mintage	F	VF	XF	Unc	BU
1980	1,500	—	—	—	850	860

Note: With dot between Olympics and Lake

| 1980 Proof | 500 | Value: 870 | | | | |

KM# 64c CROWN
52.0000 g., 0.9500 Platinum 1.5884 oz. APW, 38.5 mm. **Ruler:** Elizabeth II **Subject:** 1980 Winter Olympics - Lake Placid **Obv:** Young bust right **Obv. Designer:** Arnold Machin **Rev:** Triskeles at center of assorted olympic figures

Date	Mintage	F	VF	XF	Unc	BU
1980 Proof	100	Value: 2,150				

Note: With dot between Olympics and Lake

KM# 65b CROWN
39.8000 g., 0.9170 Gold 1.1735 oz. AGW, 38.5 mm. **Ruler:** Elizabeth II **Subject:** 1980 Summer Olympics - Moscow **Obv:** Young bust right **Obv. Designer:** Arnold Machin **Rev:** Triskeles at center of assorted olympic figures

Date	Mintage	F	VF	XF	Unc	BU
1980	1,500	—	—	—	850	860

Note: With dot between Olympiad and Moscow; with dots to right and lft of One Crown

KM# 65c CROWN
52.0000 g., 0.9500 Platinum 1.5884 oz. APW, 38.5 mm. **Ruler:** Elizabeth II **Subject:** 1980 Summer Olympics - Moscow **Obv:** Young bust right **Obv. Designer:** Arnold Machin **Rev:** Triskeles at center of assorted olympic figures

Date	Mintage	F	VF	XF	Unc	BU
1980 Proof	100	Value: 2,150				

Note: With dot between Olympiad and Moscow; with dots to right and left of One Crown

KM# 66b CROWN
39.8000 g., 0.9170 Gold 1.1735 oz. AGW, 38.5 mm. **Ruler:** Elizabeth II **Subject:** 1980 Summer Olympics - Moscow **Obv:** Young bust right **Obv. Designer:** Arnold Machin **Rev:** Triskeles at center of assorted olympic figures

Date	Mintage	F	VF	XF	Unc	BU
1980	1,500	—	—	—	850	860

KM# 66c CROWN
52.0000 g., 0.9500 Platinum 1.5884 oz. APW, 38.5 mm. **Ruler:** Elizabeth II **Subject:** 1980 Summer Olympics - Moscow **Obv:** Young bust right **Obv. Designer:** Arnold Machin **Rev:** Triskeles at center of assorted olympic figures

Date	Mintage	F	VF	XF	Unc	BU
1980 Proof	100	Value: 2,150				

KM# 67b CROWN
39.8000 g., 0.9170 Gold 1.1735 oz. AGW, 38.5 mm. **Ruler:** Elizabeth II **Subject:** 1980 Summer Olympics - Moscow **Obv:** Young bust right **Obv. Designer:** Arnold Machin **Rev:** Triskeles at center of assorted olympic figures

Date	Mintage	F	VF	XF	Unc	BU
1980	1,500	—	—	—	850	860

KM# 67c CROWN
52.0000 g., 0.9500 Platinum 1.5884 oz. APW, 38.5 mm. **Ruler:** Elizabeth II **Subject:** 1980 Summer Olympics - Moscow **Obv:** Young bust right **Obv. Designer:** Arnold Machin **Rev:** Triskeles at center of assorted olympic figures

Date	Mintage	F	VF	XF	Unc	BU
1980 Proof	100	Value: 2,150				

KM# 68c CROWN
5.0000 g., 0.3740 Gold .0601 oz. AGW **Ruler:** Elizabeth II **Subject:** 80th Birthday of Queen Mother, facing **Obv:** Young bust right **Obv. Designer:** Arnold Machin **Rev:** Crowned head facing divides dates

Date	Mintage	F	VF	XF	Unc	BU
1980	50,000	—	—	—	60.00	65.00

KM# 68d CROWN
7.9600 g., 0.9170 Gold .2347 oz. AGW, 38.5 mm. **Ruler:** Elizabeth II **Subject:** 80th Birthday of Queen Mother **Obv:** Young bust right **Obv. Designer:** Arnold Machin **Rev:** Crowned head facing divides dates

Date	Mintage	F	VF	XF	Unc	BU
1980	1,000	—	—	—	165	175

KM# 73b CROWN
5.1000 g., 0.3740 Gold 0.0613 oz. AGW **Ruler:** Elizabeth II **Subject:** Duke of Edinburgh Award Scheme **Obv:** Young bust right **Obv. Designer:** Arnold Machin **Rev:** Bust facing

Date	Mintage	F	VF	XF	Unc	BU
1981 Proof	10,000	Value: 85.00				

KM# 73c CROWN
7.9600 g., 0.9170 Gold .2347 oz. AGW **Ruler:** Elizabeth II **Subject:** Duke of Edinburgh Award Scheme **Obv:** Young bust right **Obv. Designer:** Arnold Machin **Rev:** Bust facing

Date	Mintage	F	VF	XF	Unc	BU
1981 Proof	1,000	Value: 175				

KM# 73d CROWN
52.0000 g., 0.9500 Platinum 1.5884 oz. APW, 38.5 mm. **Ruler:** Elizabeth II **Subject:** Duke of Edinburgh Award Scheme **Obv:** Young bust right **Obv. Designer:** Arnold Machin **Rev:** Bust facing

Date	Mintage	F	VF	XF	Unc	BU
1981 Proof	100	Value: 2,150				

KM# 74b CROWN
5.1000 g., 0.3740 Gold .0613 oz. AGW **Ruler:** Elizabeth II **Subject:** Duke of Edinburgh Award Scheme **Obv:** Young bust right **Obv. Designer:** Arnold Machin **Rev:** Monogram within crowned belt within sprigs

Date	Mintage	F	VF	XF	Unc	BU
1981 Proof	10,000	Value: 65.00				

KM# 74c CROWN
7.9600 g., 0.9170 Gold .2347 oz. AGW **Ruler:** Elizabeth II **Subject:** Duke of Edinburgh Award Scheme **Obv:** Young bust right **Obv. Designer:** Arnold Machin **Rev:** Monogram within crowned belt within sprigs

Date	Mintage	F	VF	XF	Unc	BU
1981 Proof	1,000	Value: 175				

KM# 74d CROWN
52.0000 g., 0.9500 Platinum 1.5884 oz. APW, 38.5 mm. **Ruler:** Elizabeth II **Subject:** Duke of Edinburgh Award Scheme **Obv:** Young bust right **Obv. Designer:** Arnold Machin **Rev:** Monogram within crowned belt within sprigs

Date	Mintage	F	VF	XF	Unc	BU
1981 Proof	100	Value: 2,150				

KM# 75b CROWN
5.1000 g., 0.3740 Gold .0613 oz. AGW **Ruler:** Elizabeth II **Subject:** Duke of Edinburgh Award Scheme **Obv:** Young bust right **Obv. Designer:** Arnold Machin **Rev:** Nursing, hiking, swimming

Date	Mintage	F	VF	XF	Unc	BU
1981 Proof	10,000	Value: 65.00				

KM# 75c CROWN
7.9600 g., 0.9170 Gold .2347 oz. AGW **Ruler:** Elizabeth II **Subject:** Duke of Edinburgh Award Scheme **Obv:** Young bust right **Obv. Designer:** Arnold Machin **Rev:** Nursing, hiking, swimming

Date	Mintage	F	VF	XF	Unc	BU
1981 Proof	1,000	Value: 175				

KM# 75d CROWN
52.0000 g., 0.9500 Platinum 1.5884 oz. APW, 38.5 mm. **Ruler:** Elizabeth II **Subject:** Duke of Edinburgh Award Scheme **Obv:** Young bust right **Obv. Designer:** Arnold Machin **Rev:** Nursing, hiking, swimming

Date	Mintage	F	VF	XF	Unc	BU
1981 Proof	100	Value: 2,150				

ISLE OF MAN 413

KM# 76b CROWN
5.1000 g., 0.3740 Gold .0613 oz. AGW **Ruler:** Elizabeth II
Subject: Duke of Edinburgh Award Scheme **Obv:** Young bust right **Obv. Designer:** Arnold Machin **Rev:** Rock climbing, sailing, motorcycling

Date	Mintage	F	VF	XF	Unc	BU
1981 Proof	10,000	Value: 65.00				

KM# 76c CROWN
7.9600 g., 0.9170 Gold .2347 oz. AGW **Ruler:** Elizabeth II
Subject: Duke of Edinburgh Award Scheme **Obv:** Young bust right **Obv. Designer:** Arnold Machin **Rev:** Rock climbing, sailing, motorcycling

Date	Mintage	F	VF	XF	Unc	BU
1981 Proof	1,000	Value: 175				

KM# 76d CROWN
52.0000 g., 0.9500 Platinum 1.5884 oz. APW, 38.5 mm. **Ruler:** Elizabeth II **Subject:** Duke of Edinburgh Award Scheme **Obv:** Young bust right **Obv. Designer:** Arnold Machin **Rev:** Rock climbing, sailing, motorcycling

Date	Mintage	F	VF	XF	Unc	BU
1981 Proof	100	Value: 2,150				

KM# 77b CROWN
5.1000 g., 0.3740 Gold .0613 oz. AGW **Ruler:** Elizabeth II
Subject: International Year of Disabled **Obv:** Young bust right **Obv. Designer:** Arnold Machin **Rev:** Braille and bust 1/4 left

Date	Mintage	F	VF	XF	Unc	BU
1981 Proof	10,000	Value: 75.00				

KM# 77c CROWN
7.9600 g., 3917.0000 Gold .2347 oz. AGW **Ruler:** Elizabeth II
Subject: International Year of Disabled **Obv:** Young bust right **Obv. Designer:** Arnold Machin **Rev:** Braille and bust 1/4 left

Date	Mintage	F	VF	XF	Unc	BU
1981 Proof	1,000	Value: 180				

KM# 77d CROWN
52.0000 g., 0.9500 Platinum 1.5884 oz. APW, 38.5 mm. **Ruler:** Elizabeth II **Subject:** International Year of Disabled **Obv:** Young bust right **Obv. Designer:** Arnold Machin **Rev:** Braille and bust 1/4 left

Date	Mintage	F	VF	XF	Unc	BU
1981 Proof	100	Value: 2,150				

KM# 78b CROWN
5.1000 g., 0.3740 Gold .0613 oz. AGW **Ruler:** Elizabeth II
Subject: International Year of Disabled **Obv:** Young bust right **Obv. Designer:** Arnold Machin **Rev:** Beethoven, violin and music score

Date	Mintage	F	VF	XF	Unc	BU
1981 Proof	10,000	Value: 75.00				

KM# 78c CROWN
7.9600 g., 0.9170 Gold .2347 oz. AGW **Ruler:** Elizabeth II
Subject: International Year of Disabled **Obv:** Young bust right **Obv. Designer:** Arnold Machin **Rev:** Beethoven, violin and music score

Date	Mintage	F	VF	XF	Unc	BU
1981 Proof	1,000	Value: 180				

KM# 78d CROWN
52.0000 g., 0.9500 Platinum 1.5884 oz. APW, 38.5 mm. **Ruler:** Elizabeth II **Subject:** International Year of Disabled **Obv:** Young bust right **Obv. Designer:** Arnold Machin **Rev:** Beethoven, violin and music score

Date	Mintage	F	VF	XF	Unc	BU
1981 Proof	100	Value: 2,150				

KM# 79b CROWN
5.1000 g., 0.3740 Gold 0.613 oz. AGW **Ruler:** Elizabeth II
Subject: International Year of Disabled **Obv:** Young bust right **Obv. Designer:** Arnold Machin **Rev:** Bust facing

Date	Mintage	F	VF	XF	Unc	BU
1981 Proof	10,000	Value: 75.00				

KM# 79c CROWN
7.9600 g., 0.9170 Gold .2347 oz. AGW **Ruler:** Elizabeth II
Subject: International Year of Disabled **Obv:** Young bust right **Obv. Designer:** Arnold Machin **Rev:** Bust facing

Date	Mintage	F	VF	XF	Unc	BU
1981 Proof	1,000	Value: 180				

KM# 79d CROWN
52.0000 g., 0.9500 Platinum 1.5884 oz. APW, 38.5 mm. **Ruler:** Elizabeth II **Subject:** International Year of Disabled **Obv:** Young bust right **Obv. Designer:** Arnold Machin **Rev:** Bust facing

Date	Mintage	F	VF	XF	Unc	BU
1981 Proof	100	Value: 2,150				

KM# 80b CROWN
5.1000 g., 0.3740 Gold .0613 oz. AGW **Ruler:** Elizabeth II
Subject: International Year of Disabled **Obv:** Young bust right **Obv. Designer:** Arnold Machin **Rev:** Uniformed bust 1/4 left and sailboat

Date	Mintage	F	VF	XF	Unc	BU
1981 Proof	10,000	Value: 75.00				

KM# 80c CROWN
7.9600 g., 0.9170 Gold .2347 oz. AGW **Ruler:** Elizabeth II
Subject: International Year of Disabled **Obv:** Young bust right **Obv. Designer:** Arnold Machin **Rev:** Uniformed bust 1/4 left and sailboat

Date	Mintage	F	VF	XF	Unc	BU
1981 Proof	1,000	Value: 180				

KM# 80d CROWN
52.0000 g., 0.9500 Platinum 1.5884 oz. APW, 38.5 mm. **Ruler:** Elizabeth II **Subject:** International Year of Disabled **Obv:** Young bust right **Obv. Designer:** Arnold Machin **Rev:** Uniformed bust 1/4 left and sailboat

Date	Mintage	F	VF	XF	Unc	BU
1981 Proof	100	Value: 2,150				

KM# 81b CROWN
5.1000 g., 0.3740 Gold .0613 oz. AGW **Ruler:** Elizabeth II
Subject: Wedding of Prince Charles and Lady Diana **Obv:** Young bust right **Obv. Designer:** Arnold Machin **Rev:** Crown above shields **Edge:** Reeded

Date	Mintage	F	VF	XF	Unc	BU
1981 Proof	10,000	Value: 75.00				

KM# 81c CROWN
7.9600 g., 0.9170 Gold .2347 oz. AGW **Ruler:** Elizabeth II **Subject:** Wedding of Prince Charles and Lady Diana **Obv:** Young bust right **Obv. Designer:** Arnold Machin **Rev:** Crown above shields

Date	Mintage	F	VF	XF	Unc	BU
1981 Proof	1,000	Value: 175				

KM# 81d CROWN
52.0000 g., 0.9500 Platinum 1.5884 oz. APW, 38.5 mm. **Ruler:** Elizabeth II **Subject:** Wedding of Prince Charles and Lady Diana **Obv:** Young bust right **Obv. Designer:** Arnold Machin **Rev:** Crown above shields

Date	Mintage	F	VF	XF	Unc	BU
1981 Proof	100	Value: 2,150				

KM# 82b CROWN
5.1000 g., 0.3740 Gold .0613 oz. AGW **Ruler:** Elizabeth II **Subject:** Wedding of Prince Charles and Lady Diana **Obv:** Young bust right **Obv. Designer:** Arnold Machin **Rev:** Conjoined heads right

Date	Mintage	F	VF	XF	Unc	BU
1981 Proof	10,000	Value: 75.00				

KM# 82c CROWN
7.9600 g., 0.9170 Gold .2347 oz. AGW **Ruler:** Elizabeth II **Subject:** Wedding of Prince Charles and Lady Diana **Obv:** Young bust right **Obv. Designer:** Arnold Machin **Rev:** Conjoined heads right

Date	Mintage	F	VF	XF	Unc	BU
1981 Proof	1,000	Value: 175				

KM# 82d CROWN
52.0000 g., 0.9500 Platinum 1.5884 oz. APW, 38.5 mm. **Ruler:** Elizabeth II **Subject:** Wedding of Prince Charles and Lady Diana **Obv:** Young bust right **Obv. Designer:** Arnold Machin **Rev:** Conjoined heads right

Date	Mintage	F	VF	XF	Unc	BU
1981 Proof	—	Value: 2,150				

KM# 91b CROWN
5.1000 g., 0.3740 Gold .0613 oz. AGW **Ruler:** Elizabeth II
Series: XII World Cup - Spain **Obv:** Young bust right **Obv. Designer:** Arnold Machin **Rev:** Half figure holding World Cup trophy within map

Date	Mintage	F	VF	XF	Unc	BU
1982 Proof	40,000	Value: 65.00				

KM# 91c CROWN
7.9600 g., 0.9170 Gold .2347 oz. AGW **Ruler:** Elizabeth II
Series: XII World Cup - Spain **Obv:** Young bust right **Obv. Designer:** Arnold Machin **Rev:** Half figure holding World Cup trophy within map

Date	Mintage	F	VF	XF	Unc	BU
1982 Proof	4,000	Value: 175				

KM# 91d CROWN
52.0000 g., 0.9500 Platinum 1.5884 oz. APW, 38.5 mm. **Ruler:** Elizabeth II **Series:** XII World Cup - Spain **Obv:** Young bust right **Obv. Designer:** Arnold Machin **Rev:** Half figure holding World Cup trophy within map

Date	Mintage	F	VF	XF	Unc	BU
1982 Proof	100	Value: 2,150				

KM# 92b CROWN
5.1000 g., 0.3740 Gold .0613 oz. AGW **Ruler:** Elizabeth II **Series:** XII World Cup - Spain **Obv:** Young bust right **Obv. Designer:** Arnold Machin **Rev:** Triskeles at center of assorted shields

Date	Mintage	F	VF	XF	Unc	BU
1982 Proof	40,000	Value: 65.00				

KM# 92c CROWN
7.9600 g., 0.9170 Gold .2347 oz. AGW **Ruler:** Elizabeth II **Series:** XII World Cup - Spain **Obv:** Young bust right **Rev:** Triskeles at center of assorted shields

Date	Mintage	F	VF	XF	Unc	BU
1982 Proof	4,000	Value: 175				

KM# 92d CROWN
52.0000 g., 0.9500 Platinum 1.5884 oz. APW, 38.5 mm. **Ruler:** Elizabeth II **Series:** XII World Cup - Spain **Obv:** Young bust right **Obv. Designer:** Arnold Machin **Rev:** Triskeles at center of assorted shields

Date	Mintage	F	VF	XF	Unc	BU
1982 Proof	100	Value: 2,150				

KM# 93b CROWN
5.1000 g., 0.3740 Gold .0613 oz. AGW **Ruler:** Elizabeth II
Series: XII World Cup - Spain **Obv:** Young bust right **Obv. Designer:** Arnold Machin **Rev:** Soccer scenes

Date	Mintage	F	VF	XF	Unc	BU
1982 Proof	40,000	Value: 65.00				

KM# 93c CROWN
7.9600 g., 0.9170 Gold .2347 oz. AGW **Ruler:** Elizabeth II
Series: XII World Cup - Spain **Obv:** Young bust right **Obv. Designer:** Arnold Machin **Rev:** Soccer scenes

Date	Mintage	F	VF	XF	Unc	BU
1982 Proof	4,000	Value: 175				

KM# 93d CROWN
52.0000 g., 0.9500 Platinum 1.5884 oz. APW, 38.5 mm. **Ruler:** Elizabeth II **Series:** XII World Cup - Spain **Obv:** Young bust right **Obv. Designer:** Arnold Machin **Rev:** Soccer scenes

414 ISLE OF MAN

Date	Mintage	F	VF	XF	Unc	BU
1982 Proof	100	Value: 2,150				

KM# 94b CROWN
5.1000 g., 0.3740 Gold .0613 oz. AGW **Ruler:** Elizabeth II **Series:** XII World Cup - Spain **Obv:** Young bust right **Obv. Designer:** Arnold Machin **Rev:** Soccer scenes

Date	Mintage	F	VF	XF	Unc	BU
1982 Proof	40,000	Value: 65.00				

KM# 94c CROWN
7.9600 g., 0.9170 Gold .2347 oz. AGW **Ruler:** Elizabeth II **Series:** XII World Cup - Spain **Obv:** Young bust right **Obv. Designer:** Arnold Machin **Rev:** Soccer scenes

Date	Mintage	F	VF	XF	Unc	BU
1982 Proof	4,000	Value: 175				

KM# 94d CROWN
52.0000 g., 0.9500 Platinum 1.5884 oz. APW, 38.5 mm. **Ruler:** Elizabeth II **Series:** XII World Cup - Spain **Obv:** Young bust right **Obv. Designer:** Arnold Machin **Rev:** Soccer scenes

Date	Mintage	F	VF	XF	Unc	BU
1982 Proof	100	Value: 2,150				

KM# 95b CROWN
5.1000 g., 0.3740 Gold .0613 oz. AGW **Ruler:** Elizabeth II **Series:** XII World Cup - Spain **Obv:** Young bust right **Obv. Designer:** Arnold Machin **Rev:** Assorted shields

Date	Mintage	F	VF	XF	Unc	BU
1982 Proof	3,000	Value: 75.00				

KM# 95c CROWN
7.9600 g., 0.9170 Gold .2347 oz. AGW **Ruler:** Elizabeth II **Series:** XII World Cup - Spain **Obv:** Young bust right **Obv. Designer:** Arnold Machin **Rev:** Assorted shields

Date	Mintage	F	VF	XF	Unc	BU
1982 Proof	—	Value: 180				

KM# 95d CROWN
52.0000 g., 0.9500 Platinum 1.5884 oz. APW, 38.5 mm. **Ruler:** Elizabeth II **Series:** XII World Cup - Spain **Obv:** Young bust right **Obv. Designer:** Arnold Machin **Rev:** Assorted shields

Date	Mintage	F	VF	XF	Unc	BU
1982 Proof	—	Value: 2,150				

KM# 96b CROWN
5.1000 g., 0.3740 Gold .0613 oz. AGW **Ruler:** Elizabeth II **Series:** Maritime Heritage **Obv:** Crowned bust right **Rev:** Ship and cameo

Date	Mintage	F	VF	XF	Unc	BU
1982 Proof	22,000	Value: 65.00				

KM# 96c CROWN
7.9600 g., 0.9170 Gold .2347 oz. AGW **Ruler:** Elizabeth II **Series:** Maritime Heritage **Obv:** Young bust right **Obv. Designer:** Arnold Machin **Rev:** Ship and cameo

Date	Mintage	F	VF	XF	Unc	BU
1982 Proof	2,000	Value: 175				

KM# 96d CROWN
52.0000 g., 0.9500 Platinum 1.5884 oz. APW, 38.5 mm. **Ruler:** Elizabeth II **Series:** Maritime Heritage **Obv:** Young bust right **Obv. Designer:** Arnold Machin **Rev:** Ship and cameo

Date	Mintage	F	VF	XF	Unc	BU
1982 Proof	50	Value: 2,150				

KM# 97b CROWN
5.1000 g., 0.3740 Gold .0613 oz. AGW **Ruler:** Elizabeth II **Series:** Maritime Heritage **Obv:** Young bust right **Obv. Designer:** Arnold Machin **Rev:** Ship and cameo

Date	Mintage	F	VF	XF	Unc	BU
1982 Proof	22,000	Value: 65.00				

KM# 97c CROWN
7.9600 g., 0.9170 Gold .2347 oz. AGW **Ruler:** Elizabeth II **Series:** Maritime Heritage **Obv:** Young bust right **Obv. Designer:** Arnold Machin **Rev:** Ship and cameo

Date	Mintage	F	VF	XF	Unc	BU
1982 Proof	2,000	Value: 175				

KM# 97d CROWN
52.0000 g., 0.9500 Platinum 1.5884 oz. APW, 38.5 mm. **Ruler:** Elizabeth II **Series:** Maritime Heritage **Obv:** Young bust right **Obv. Designer:** Arnold Machin **Rev:** Ship and cameo

Date	Mintage	F	VF	XF	Unc	BU
1982 Proof	50	Value: 2,150				

KM# 98b CROWN
5.1000 g., 0.3740 Gold .0613 oz. AGW **Ruler:** Elizabeth II **Series:** Maritime Heritage **Obv:** Young bust right **Obv. Designer:** Arnold Machin **Rev:** Ship and cameo

Date	Mintage	F	VF	XF	Unc	BU
1982 Proof	22,000	Value: 65.00				

KM# 98c CROWN
7.9600 g., 0.9170 Gold .2347 oz. AGW **Ruler:** Elizabeth II **Series:** Maritime Heritage **Obv:** Young bust right **Obv. Designer:** Arnold Machin **Rev:** Ship and cameo

Date	Mintage	F	VF	XF	Unc	BU
1982 Proof	2,000	Value: 175				

KM# 98d CROWN
52.0000 g., 0.9500 Platinum 1.5884 oz. APW, 38.5 mm. **Ruler:** Elizabeth II **Series:** Maritime Heritage **Obv:** Young bust right **Obv. Designer:** Arnold Machin **Rev:** Ship and cameo

Date	Mintage	F	VF	XF	Unc	BU
1982 Proof	50	Value: 2,150				

KM# 99b CROWN
5.1000 g., 0.3740 Gold .0613 oz. AGW **Ruler:** Elizabeth II **Series:** Maritime Heritage **Obv:** Young bust right **Obv. Designer:** Arnold Machin **Rev:** Ship and cameo

Date	Mintage	F	VF	XF	Unc	BU
1982 Proof	22,000	Value: 65.00				

KM# 99c CROWN
7.9600 g., 0.9170 Gold .2347 oz. AGW **Ruler:** Elizabeth II **Series:** Maritime Heritage **Obv:** Young bust right **Obv. Designer:** Arnold Machin **Rev:** Ship and cameo

Date	Mintage	F	VF	XF	Unc	BU
1982 Proof	2,000	Value: 175				

KM# 99d CROWN
52.0000 g., 0.9500 Platinum 1.5884 oz. APW, 38.5 mm. **Ruler:** Elizabeth II **Series:** Maritime Heritage **Obv:** Young bust right **Obv. Designer:** Arnold Machin **Rev:** Ship and cameo

Date	Mintage	F	VF	XF	Unc	BU
1982 Proof	50	Value: 2,150				

KM# 103b CROWN
5.1000 g., 0.3740 Gold .0613 oz. AGW **Ruler:** Elizabeth II **Series:** Manned Flight **Obv:** Young bust right **Obv. Designer:** Arnold Machin **Rev:** Hot air balloon

Date	Mintage	F	VF	XF	Unc	BU
1983 Proof	5,500	Value: 80.00				

KM# 103c CROWN
7.9600 g., 0.9170 Gold .2347 oz. AGW **Ruler:** Elizabeth II **Series:** Manned Flight **Obv:** Young bust right **Obv. Designer:** Arnold Machin **Rev:** Hot air balloon

Date	Mintage	F	VF	XF	Unc	BU
1983 Proof	500	Value: 185				

KM# 103d CROWN
52.0000 g., 0.9500 Platinum 1.5884 oz. APW, 38.5 mm. **Ruler:** Elizabeth II **Series:** Manned Flight **Obv:** Young bust right **Obv. Designer:** Arnold Machin **Rev:** Hot air balloon

Date	Mintage	F	VF	XF	Unc	BU
1983 Proof	50	Value: 2,150				

KM# 104b CROWN
5.1000 g., 0.3740 Gold .0613 oz. AGW **Ruler:** Elizabeth II **Series:** Manned Flight **Obv:** Young bust right **Obv. Designer:** Arnold Machin **Rev:** Biplane

Date	Mintage	F	VF	XF	Unc	BU
1983 Proof	5,500	Value: 80.00				

KM# 104c CROWN
7.9600 g., 0.9170 Gold .2347 oz. AGW **Ruler:** Elizabeth II **Series:** Manned Flight **Obv:** Young bust right **Obv. Designer:** Arnold Machin **Rev:** Biplane

Date	Mintage	F	VF	XF	Unc	BU
1983 Proof	500	Value: 185				

KM# 104d CROWN
52.0000 g., 0.9500 Platinum 1.5884 oz. APW, 38.5 mm. **Ruler:** Elizabeth II **Series:** Manned Flight **Obv:** Young bust right **Obv. Designer:** Arnold Machin **Rev:** Biplane

Date	Mintage	F	VF	XF	Unc	BU
1983 Proof	50	Value: 2,150				

KM# 105b CROWN
5.1000 g., 0.3740 Gold .0613 oz. AGW **Ruler:** Elizabeth II **Series:** Manned Flight **Obv:** Young bust right **Obv. Designer:** Arnold Machin **Rev:** Jet

Date	Mintage	F	VF	XF	Unc	BU
1983 Proof	5,500	Value: 80.00				

KM# 105c CROWN
7.9600 g., 0.9170 Gold .2347 oz. AGW **Ruler:** Elizabeth II **Series:** Manned Flight **Obv:** Young bust right **Obv. Designer:** Arnold Machin **Rev:** Jet

Date	Mintage	F	VF	XF	Unc	BU
1983 Proof	500	Value: 185				

KM# 105d CROWN
52.0000 g., 0.9500 Platinum 1.5884 oz. APW, 38.5 mm. **Ruler:** Elizabeth II **Series:** Manned Flight **Obv:** Young bust right **Obv. Designer:** Arnold Machin **Rev:** Jet

Date	Mintage	F	VF	XF	Unc	BU
1983 Proof	50	Value: 2,150				

KM# 106b CROWN
5.1000 g., 0.3740 Gold .0613 oz. AGW **Ruler:** Elizabeth II **Series:** Manned Flight **Obv:** Young bust right **Obv. Designer:** Arnold Machin **Rev:** Space shuttle

Date	Mintage	F	VF	XF	Unc	BU
1983 Proof	5,500	Value: 80.00				

KM# 106c CROWN
7.9600 g., 0.9170 Gold .2347 oz. AGW **Ruler:** Elizabeth II **Series:** Manned Flight **Obv:** Young bust right **Obv. Designer:** Arnold Machin **Rev:** Space shuttle

Date	Mintage	F	VF	XF	Unc	BU
1983 Proof	500	Value: 185				

KM# 106d CROWN
52.0000 g., 0.9500 Platinum 1.5884 oz. APW, 38.5 mm. **Ruler:** Elizabeth II **Series:** Manned Flight **Obv:** Young bust right **Obv. Designer:** Arnold Machin **Rev:** Space Shuttle

Date	Mintage	F	VF	XF	Unc	BU
1983 Proof	50	Value: 2,150				

KM# 117b CROWN
5.1000 g., 0.3740 Gold .0613 oz. AGW **Ruler:** Elizabeth II **Series:** 1984 Winter Olympics - Sarajevo **Obv:** Young bust right **Obv. Designer:** Arnold Machin **Rev:** Figure skaters **Rev. Designer:** Leslie Lindsay

Date	Mintage	F	VF	XF	Unc	BU
1984 Proof	10,000	Value: 60.00				

ISLE OF MAN

KM# 117c CROWN
7.9600 g., 0.9170 Gold .2347 oz. AGW **Ruler:** Elizabeth II **Series:** 1984 Winter Olympics - Sarajevo **Obv:** Young bust right **Obv. Designer:** Arnold Machin **Rev:** Figure skaters **Rev. Designer:** Leslie Lindsay

Date	Mintage	F	VF	XF	Unc	BU
1984 Proof	1,000	Value: 175				

KM# 117d CROWN
52.0000 g., 0.9500 Platinum 1.5884 oz. APW, 38.5 mm. **Ruler:** Elizabeth II **Series:** 1984 Winter Olympics - Sarajevo **Obv:** Young bust right **Obv. Designer:** Arnold Machin **Rev:** Figure skaters **Rev. Designer:** Leslie Lindsay

Date	Mintage	F	VF	XF	Unc	BU
1984 Proof	100	Value: 2,150				

KM# 118b CROWN
5.1000 g., 0.3740 Gold .0613 oz. AGW **Ruler:** Elizabeth II **Series:** 1984 Olympics - Los Angeles **Obv:** Young bust right **Obv. Designer:** Arnold Machin **Rev:** Runners **Rev. Designer:** Leslie Lindsay

Date	Mintage	F	VF	XF	Unc	BU
1984 Proof	10,000	Value: 65.00				

KM# 118c CROWN
7.9600 g., 0.9170 Gold .2347 oz. AGW **Ruler:** Elizabeth II **Series:** 1984 Olympics - Los Angeles **Obv:** Young bust right **Obv. Designer:** Arnold Machin **Rev:** Runners **Rev. Designer:** Leslie Lindsay

Date	Mintage	F	VF	XF	Unc	BU
1984 Proof	1,000	Value: 175				

KM# 118d CROWN
52.0000 g., 0.9500 Platinum 1.5884 oz. APW, 38.5 mm. **Ruler:** Elizabeth II **Series:** 1984 Olympics - Los Angeles **Obv:** Young bust right **Obv. Designer:** Arnold Machin **Rev:** Runners **Rev. Designer:** Leslie Lindsay

Date	Mintage	F	VF	XF	Unc	BU
1984 Proof	100	Value: 2,100				

KM# 119b CROWN
5.1000 g., 0.3740 Gold .0613 oz. AGW **Ruler:** Elizabeth II **Series:** 1984 Olympics - Los Angeles **Obv:** Young bust right **Obv. Designer:** Arnold Machin **Rev:** Gymnastics **Rev. Designer:** Leslie Lindsay

Date	Mintage	F	VF	XF	Unc	BU
1984 Proof	10,000	Value: 65.00				

KM# 119c CROWN
7.9600 g., 0.9170 Gold .2347 oz. AGW **Ruler:** Elizabeth II **Series:** 1984 Olympics - Los Angeles **Obv:** Young bust right **Obv. Designer:** Arnold Machin **Rev:** Gymnastics **Rev. Designer:** Leslie Lindsay

Date	Mintage	F	VF	XF	Unc	BU
1984 Proof	1,000	Value: 175				

KM# 119d CROWN
52.0000 g., 0.9500 Platinum 1.5884 oz. APW, 38.5 mm. **Ruler:** Elizabeth II **Series:** 1984 Olympics - Los Angeles **Obv:** Young bust right **Obv. Designer:** Arnold Machin **Rev:** Gymnastics **Rev. Designer:** Leslie Lindsay

Date	Mintage	F	VF	XF	Unc	BU
1984 Proof	100	Value: 2,150				

KM# 120b CROWN
5.1000 g., 0.3740 Gold .0613 oz. AGW **Ruler:** Elizabeth II **Series:** 1984 Olympics - Los Angeles **Obv:** Young bust right **Obv. Designer:** Arnold Machin **Rev:** Equestrian **Rev. Designer:** Leslie Lindsay

Date	Mintage	F	VF	XF	Unc	BU
1984 Proof	10,000	Value: 65.00				

KM# 120c CROWN
7.9600 g., 0.9170 Gold .2347 oz. AGW **Ruler:** Elizabeth II **Series:** 1984 Olympics - Los Angeles **Obv:** Young bust right **Obv. Designer:** Arnold Machin **Rev:** Equestrian **Rev. Designer:** Leslie Lindsay

Date	Mintage	F	VF	XF	Unc	BU
1984 Proof	1,000	Value: 175				

KM# 120d CROWN
52.0000 g., 0.9500 Platinum 1.5884 oz. APW, 38.5 mm. **Ruler:** Elizabeth II **Series:** 1984 Olympics - Los Angeles **Obv:** Young bust right **Obv. Designer:** Arnold Machin **Rev:** Equestrian **Rev. Designer:** Leslie Lindsay

Date	Mintage	F	VF	XF	Unc	BU
1984 Proof	100	Value: 2,150				

KM# 121b CROWN
5.1000 g., 0.3740 Gold .0613 oz. AGW **Ruler:** Elizabeth II **Subject:** Quincentenary **Obv:** Young bust right **Obv. Designer:** Arnold Machin **Rev:** Arms with supporters

Date	Mintage	F	VF	XF	Unc	BU
1984 Proof	10,000	Value: 65.00				

KM# 121c CROWN
7.9600 g., 0.9170 Gold .2347 oz. AGW **Ruler:** Elizabeth II **Subject:** Quincentenary **Obv:** Young bust right **Obv. Designer:** Arnold Machin **Rev:** Arms with supporters

Date	Mintage	F	VF	XF	Unc	BU
1984 Proof	1,000	Value: 175				

KM# 121d CROWN
52.0000 g., 0.9500 Platinum 1.5884 oz. APW, 38.5 mm. **Ruler:** Elizabeth II **Subject:** Quincentenary **Obv:** Young bust right **Obv. Designer:** Arnold Machin **Rev:** Arms with supporters

Date	Mintage	F	VF	XF	Unc	BU
1984 Proof	—	Value: 2,150				

KM# 122b CROWN
5.1000 g., 0.3740 Gold .0613 oz. AGW **Ruler:** Elizabeth II **Subject:** Quincentenary **Obv:** Young bust right **Obv. Designer:** Arnold Machin **Rev:** Lion above shields

Date	Mintage	F	VF	XF	Unc	BU
1984 Proof	10,000	Value: 65.00				

KM# 122c CROWN
7.9600 g., 0.9170 Gold .2347 oz. AGW **Ruler:** Elizabeth II **Subject:** Quincentenary **Obv:** Young bust right **Obv. Designer:** Arnold Machin **Rev:** Lion above shields

Date	Mintage	F	VF	XF	Unc	BU
1984 Proof	1,000	Value: 175				

KM# 122d CROWN
52.0000 g., 0.9500 Platinum 1.5884 oz. APW, 38.5 mm. **Ruler:** Elizabeth II **Subject:** Quincentenary **Obv:** Young bust right **Obv. Designer:** Arnold Machin **Rev:** Lion above shields

Date	Mintage	F	VF	XF	Unc	BU
1984 Proof	—	Value: 2,150				

KM# 123b CROWN
5.1000 g., 0.3740 Gold .0613 oz. AGW **Ruler:** Elizabeth II **Subject:** Quincentenary **Obv:** Young bust right **Obv. Designer:** Arnold Machin **Rev:** Bird above shields

Date	Mintage	F	VF	XF	Unc	BU
1984 Proof	10,000	Value: 65.00				

KM# 123c CROWN
7.9600 g., 0.9170 Gold .2347 oz. AGW **Ruler:** Elizabeth II **Subject:** Quincentenary **Obv:** Young bust right **Obv. Designer:** Arnold Machin **Rev:** Bird above shields

Date	Mintage	F	VF	XF	Unc	BU
1984 Proof	1,000	Value: 175				

KM# 123d CROWN
52.0000 g., 0.9500 Platinum 1.5884 oz. APW, 38.5 mm. **Ruler:** Elizabeth II **Subject:** Quincentenary **Obv:** Young bust right **Obv. Designer:** Arnold Machin **Rev:** Bird above shields

Date	Mintage	F	VF	XF	Unc	BU
1984 Proof	—	Value: 2,150				

KM# 124b CROWN
5.1000 g., 0.3740 Gold .0613 oz. AGW **Ruler:** Elizabeth II **Subject:** Quincentenary **Obv:** Crowned bust right **Rev:** Arms with supporters

Date	Mintage	F	VF	XF	Unc	BU
1984 Proof	10,000	Value: 65.00				

KM# 124c CROWN
7.9600 g., 0.9170 Gold .2347 oz. AGW **Ruler:** Elizabeth II **Subject:** Quincentenary **Obv:** Young bust right **Obv. Designer:** Arnold Machin **Rev:** Arms with supporters

Date	Mintage	F	VF	XF	Unc	BU
1984 Proof	1,000	Value: 175				

KM# 124d CROWN
52.0000 g., 0.9500 Platinum 1.5884 oz. APW, 38.5 mm. **Ruler:** Elizabeth II **Subject:** Quincentenary **Obv:** Young bust right **Obv. Designer:** Arnold Machin **Rev:** Arms with supporters

Date	Mintage	F	VF	XF	Unc	BU
1984 Proof	—	Value: 2,150				

KM# 130b CROWN
5.1000 g., 0.3740 Gold .0613 oz. AGW **Ruler:** Elizabeth II **Subject:** 30th Commonwealth Parliamentary Conference **Obv:** Young bust right **Obv. Designer:** Arnold Machin **Rev:** Conjoined heads right within circle **Rev. Legend:** Celtic uncial script

Date	Mintage	F	VF	XF	Unc	BU
1984 Proof	10,000	Value: 65.00				

KM# 130c CROWN
7.9600 g., 0.9170 Gold .2347 oz. AGW **Ruler:** Elizabeth II **Subject:** 30th Commonwealth Parliamentary Conference **Obv:** Young bust right **Obv. Designer:** Arnold Machin **Rev:** Conjoined heads right within circle **Rev. Legend:** Celtic uncial script

Date	Mintage	F	VF	XF	Unc	BU
1984 Proof	1,000	Value: 175				

KM# 130d CROWN
52.0000 g., 0.9500 Platinum 1.5884 oz. APW, 38.5 mm. **Ruler:** Elizabeth II **Subject:** 30th Commonwealth Parliamentary Conference **Obv:** Young bust right **Obv. Designer:** Arnold Machin **Rev:** Conjoined heads right within circle **Rev. Legend:** Celtic uncial script

Date	Mintage	F	VF	XF	Unc	BU
1984 Proof	—	Value: 2,150				

KM# 131b CROWN
5.1000 g., 0.3740 Gold .0613 oz. AGW **Ruler:** Elizabeth II **Subject:** 30th Commonwealth Parliamentary Conference **Obv:** Young bust right **Obv. Designer:** Arnold Machin **Rev:** Throne, sword and shield **Rev. Legend:** Celtic uncial script

Date	Mintage	F	VF	XF	Unc	BU
1984 Proof	10,000	Value: 65.00				

KM# 131c CROWN
7.9600 g., 0.9170 Gold .2347 oz. AGW **Ruler:** Elizabeth II **Subject:** 30th Commonwealth Parliamentary Conference **Obv:** Young bust right **Obv. Designer:** Arnold Machin **Rev:** Throne, sword and shield **Rev. Legend:** Celtic uncial script

Date	Mintage	F	VF	XF	Unc	BU
1984 Proof	1,000	Value: 175				

KM# 131d CROWN
52.0000 g., 0.9500 Platinum 1.5884 oz. APW, 38.5 mm. **Ruler:** Elizabeth II **Subject:** 30th Commonwealth Parliamentary Conference **Obv:** Young bust right **Obv. Designer:** Arnold Machin **Rev:** Throne, shield and sword **Rev. Legend:** Celtic uncial script

Date	Mintage	F	VF	XF	Unc	BU
1984 Proof	—	Value: 2,150				

KM# 132b CROWN
5.1000 g., 0.3740 Gold .0613 oz. AGW **Ruler:** Elizabeth II **Subject:** 30th Commonwealth Parliamentary Conference **Obv:** Young bust right **Obv. Designer:** Arnold Machin **Rev:** crowned head facing within circle **Rev. Legend:** Celtic uncial script

Date	Mintage	F	VF	XF	Unc	BU
1984 Proof	10,000	Value: 65.00				

416 ISLE OF MAN

KM# 132c CROWN
7.9600 g., 0.9170 Gold .2347 oz. AGW **Ruler:** Elizabeth II
Subject: 30th Commonwealth Parliamentary Conference **Obv:** Young bust right **Obv. Designer:** Arnold Machin **Rev:** Crowned head facing within circle **Rev. Legend:** Celtic uncial script

Date	Mintage	F	VF	XF	Unc	BU
1984 Proof	1,000				Value: 175	

KM# 132d CROWN
52.0000 g., 0.9500 Platinum 1.5884 oz. APW, 38.5 mm. **Ruler:** Elizabeth II **Subject:** 30th Commonwealth Parliamentary Conference **Obv:** Young bust right **Obv. Designer:** Arnold Machin **Rev:** Crowned head facing within circle **Rev. Legend:** Celtic uncial script

Date	Mintage	F	VF	XF	Unc	BU
1984 Proof	—				Value: 2,150	

KM# 133b CROWN
5.1000 g., 0.3740 Gold .0613 oz. AGW **Ruler:** Elizabeth II **Subject:** 30th Commonwealth Parliamentary Conference **Obv:** Young bust right **Obv. Designer:** Arnold Machin **Rev:** Conference tent within circle **Rev. Legend:** Celtic uncial script

Date	Mintage	F	VF	XF	Unc	BU
1984 Proof	10,000				Value: 65.00	

KM# 133c CROWN
7.9600 g., 0.9170 Gold .2347 oz. AGW **Ruler:** Elizabeth II **Subject:** 30th Commonwealth Parliamentary Conference **Obv:** Young bust right **Obv. Designer:** Arnold Machin **Rev:** Conference tent **Rev. Legend:** Celtic uncial script

Date	Mintage	F	VF	XF	Unc	BU
1984 Proof	1,000				Value: 175	

KM# 133d CROWN
52.0000 g., 0.9500 Platinum 1.5884 oz. APW, 38.5 mm. **Ruler:** Elizabeth II **Subject:** 30th Commonwealth Parliamentary Conference **Obv:** Young bust right **Obv. Designer:** Arnold Machin **Rev:** Conference tent **Rev. Legend:** Celtic uncial script

Date	Mintage	F	VF	XF	Unc	BU
1984 Proof	—				Value: 2,150	

KM# 216c CROWN
5.1000 g., 0.3740 Gold .0613 oz. AGW **Ruler:** Elizabeth II **Obv:** Crowned bust right **Obv. Designer:** Raphael Maklouf **Rev:** Child half figure facing

Date	Mintage	F	VF	XF	Unc	BU
1985 Proof	Est. 10,000				Value: 65.00	

KM# 216d CROWN
7.9600 g., 0.9170 Gold .2347 oz. AGW **Ruler:** Elizabeth II **Obv:** Crowned bust right **Obv. Designer:** Raphael Maklouf **Rev:** Child half figure facing

Date	Mintage	F	VF	XF	Unc	BU
1985 Proof	Est. 1,000,000				Value: 175	

KM# 216e CROWN
52.0000 g., 0.9500 Platinum 1.5884 oz. APW, 38.5 mm. **Ruler:** Elizabeth II **Obv:** Crowned bust right **Obv. Designer:** Raphael Maklouf **Rev:** Child half figure facing

Date	Mintage	F	VF	XF	Unc	BU
1985 Proof	Est. 100				Value: 2,150	

KM# 217c CROWN
5.1000 g., 0.3740 Gold .0613 oz. AGW **Ruler:** Elizabeth II **Obv:** Crowned bust right **Obv. Designer:** Raphael Maklouf **Rev:** Conjoined busts facing

Date	Mintage	F	VF	XF	Unc	BU
1985 Proof	Est. 10,000				Value: 65.00	

KM# 217d CROWN
7.9600 g., 0.9170 Gold .2347 oz. AGW **Ruler:** Elizabeth II **Obv:** Crowned bust right **Obv. Designer:** Raphael Maklouf **Rev:** Conjoined busts facing

Date	Mintage	F	VF	XF	Unc	BU
1985 Proof	Est. 1,000				Value: 175	

KM# 217e CROWN
52.0000 g., 0.9500 Platinum 1.5884 oz. APW, 38.5 mm. **Ruler:** Elizabeth II **Obv:** Crowned bust right **Obv. Designer:** Raphael Maklouf **Rev:** Conjoined busts facing

Date	Mintage	F	VF	XF	Unc	BU
1985 Proof	Est. 100				Value: 2,150	

KM# 218c CROWN
5.1000 g., 0.3740 Gold .0613 oz. AGW **Ruler:** Elizabeth II **Obv:** Crowned bust right **Obv. Designer:** Raphael Maklouf **Rev:** Conjoined busts facing

Date	Mintage	F	VF	XF	Unc	BU
1985 Proof	Est. 10,000				Value: 65.00	

KM# 218d CROWN
7.9600 g., 0.9170 Gold .2347 oz. AGW **Ruler:** Elizabeth II **Obv:** Crowned bust right **Obv. Designer:** Raphael Maklouf **Rev:** Conjoined busts facing

Date	Mintage	F	VF	XF	Unc	BU
1985 Proof	Est. 1,000				Value: 175	

KM# 218e CROWN
52.0000 g., 0.9500 Platinum 1.5884 oz. APW, 38.5 mm. **Ruler:** Elizabeth II **Obv:** Crowned bust right **Obv. Designer:** Raphael Maklouf **Rev:** Conjoined busts facing

Date	Mintage	F	VF	XF	Unc	BU
1985 Proof	Est. 100				Value: 2,150	

KM# 219c CROWN
5.1000 g., 0.3740 Gold .0613 oz. AGW **Ruler:** Elizabeth II **Obv:** Crowned bust right **Obv. Designer:** Raphael Maklouf **Rev:** Queen Mother and Princess Elizabeth

Date	Mintage	F	VF	XF	Unc	BU
1985 Proof	Est. 10,000				Value: 65.00	

KM# 219d CROWN
7.9600 g., 0.9170 Gold .2347 oz. AGW **Ruler:** Elizabeth II **Obv:** Crowned bust right **Obv. Designer:** Raphael Maklouf **Rev:** Queen Mother and Princess Elizabeth

Date	Mintage	F	VF	XF	Unc	BU
1985 Proof	Est. 1,000				Value: 175	

KM# 219e CROWN
52.0000 g., 0.9500 Platinum 1.5884 oz. APW, 38.5 mm. **Ruler:** Elizabeth II **Obv:** Crowned bust right **Obv. Designer:** Raphael Maklouf **Rev:** Queen Mother and Princess Elizabeth

Date	Mintage	F	VF	XF	Unc	BU
1985 Proof	Est. 100				Value: 2,150	

KM# 220c CROWN
5.1000 g., 0.3740 Gold .0613 oz. AGW **Ruler:** Elizabeth II **Obv:** Crowned bust right **Obv. Designer:** Raphael Maklouf **Rev:** Adult and two children facing

Date	Mintage	F	VF	XF	Unc	BU
1985 Proof	Est. 10,000				Value: 65.00	

KM# 220d CROWN
7.9600 g., 0.9170 Gold .2347 oz. AGW **Ruler:** Elizabeth II **Obv:** Crowned bust right **Obv. Designer:** Raphael Maklouf **Rev:** Adult and two children facing

Date	Mintage	F	VF	XF	Unc	BU
1985 Proof	Est. 1,000				Value: 175	

KM# 220e CROWN
52.0000 g., 0.9500 Platinum 1.5884 oz. APW, 38.5 mm. **Ruler:** Elizabeth II **Obv:** Crowned bust right **Obv. Designer:** Raphael Maklouf **Rev:** Adult and two children facing

Date	Mintage	F	VF	XF	Unc	BU
1985 Proof	Est. 100				Value: 2,150	

KM# 221c CROWN
5.1000 g., 0.3740 Gold .0613 oz. AGW **Ruler:** Elizabeth II **Subject:** 85th Birthday of Queen Mother **Obv:** Crowned bust right **Obv. Designer:** Raphael Maklouf **Rev:** Queen Mother

Date	Mintage	F	VF	XF	Unc	BU
1985 Proof	Est. 10,000				Value: 65.00	

KM# 221d CROWN
7.9600 g., 0.9170 Gold .2347 oz. AGW **Ruler:** Elizabeth II **Subject:** 85th Birthday of Queen Mother **Obv:** Crowned bust right **Obv. Designer:** Raphael Maklouf **Rev:** Queen Mother

Date	Mintage	F	VF	XF	Unc	BU
1985 Proof	Est. 1,000,000				Value: 175	

ISLE OF MAN

KM# 221e CROWN
52.0000 g., 0.9500 Platinum 1.5884 oz. APW, 38.5 mm. **Ruler:** Elizabeth II **Subject:** 85th Birthday of Queen Mother **Obv:** Crowned bust right **Obv. Designer:** Raphael Maklouf **Rev:** Queen Mother

Date	Mintage	F	VF	XF	Unc	BU
1985 Proof	Est. 100	Value: 2,150				

KM# 160c CROWN
5.1000 g., 0.3740 Gold .0613 oz. AGW **Ruler:** Elizabeth II **Series:** World Cup Soccer - Mexico **Obv:** Crowned bust right **Obv. Designer:** Raphael Maklouf **Rev:** Map and soccer players within circle

Date	Mintage	F	VF	XF	Unc	BU
1986 Proof	Est. 10,000	Value: 65.00				

KM# 160d CROWN
7.9600 g., 0.9170 Gold .2347 oz. AGW **Ruler:** Elizabeth II **Series:** World Cup Soccer - Mexico **Obv:** Crowned bust right **Obv. Designer:** Raphael Maklouf **Rev:** Map and soccer players within circle

Date	Mintage	F	VF	XF	Unc	BU
1986 Proof	Est. 1,000	Value: 175				

KM# 160e CROWN
52.0000 g., 0.9500 Platinum 1.5884 oz. APW, 38.5 mm. **Ruler:** Elizabeth II **Series:** World Cup Soccer - Mexico **Obv:** Crowned bust right **Obv. Designer:** Raphael Maklouf **Rev:** Map and soccer players within circle

Date	Mintage	F	VF	XF	Unc	BU
1986 Proof	Est. 200	Value: 2,150				

KM# 161c CROWN
5.1000 g., 0.3740 Gold .0613 oz. AGW **Ruler:** Elizabeth II **Series:** World Cup Soccer - Mexico **Obv:** Raphael Maklouf **Rev:** Soccer players within circle

Date	Mintage	F	VF	XF	Unc	BU
1986 Proof	Est. 10,000	Value: 65.00				

KM# 161d CROWN
7.9600 g., 0.9170 Gold .2347 oz. AGW **Ruler:** Elizabeth II **Series:** World Cup Soccer - Mexico **Obv:** Crowned bust right **Obv. Designer:** Raphael Maklouf **Rev:** Soccer players within circle

Date	Mintage	F	VF	XF	Unc	BU
1986 Proof	Est. 1,000	Value: 175				

KM# 161e CROWN
52.0000 g., 0.9500 Platinum 1.5884 oz. APW, 38.5 mm. **Ruler:** Elizabeth II **Series:** World Cup Soccer - Mexico **Obv:** Crowned bust right **Obv. Designer:** Raphael Maklouf **Rev:** Soccer players within circle

Date	Mintage	F	VF	XF	Unc	BU
1986 Proof	Est. 200	Value: 2,150				

KM# 162c CROWN
5.1000 g., 0.3740 Gold .0613 oz. AGW **Ruler:** Elizabeth II **Series:** World Cup Soccer - Mexico **Obv:** Crowned bust right **Obv. Designer:** Raphael Maklouf **Rev:** Soccer players within circle

Date	Mintage	F	VF	XF	Unc	BU
1986 Proof	Est. 10,000	Value: 65.00				

KM# 162d CROWN
7.9600 g., 0.9170 Gold .2347 oz. AGW **Ruler:** Elizabeth II **Series:** World Cup Soccer - Mexico **Obv:** Crowned bust right **Obv. Designer:** Raphael Maklouf **Rev:** Soccer players within circle

Date	Mintage	F	VF	XF	Unc	BU
1986 Proof	Est. 1,000	Value: 175				

KM# 162e CROWN
52.0000 g., 0.9500 Platinum 1.5884 oz. APW, 38.5 mm. **Ruler:** Elizabeth II **Series:** World Cup Soccer - Mexico **Obv:** Crowned bust right **Obv. Designer:** Raphael Maklouf **Rev:** Soccer players within circle

Date	Mintage	F	VF	XF	Unc	BU
1986 Proof	Est. 200	Value: 2,150				

KM# 163c CROWN
5.1000 g., 0.3740 Gold .0613 oz. AGW **Ruler:** Elizabeth II **Series:** World Cup Soccer - Mexico **Obv:** Crowned bust right **Obv. Designer:** Raphael Maklouf **Rev:** Net and soccer players within circle

Date	Mintage	F	VF	XF	Unc	BU
1986 Proof	Est. 10,000	Value: 65.00				

KM# 163d CROWN
7.9600 g., 0.9170 Gold .2347 oz. AGW **Ruler:** Elizabeth II **Series:** World Cup Soccer - Mexico **Obv:** Crowned bust right **Obv. Designer:** Raphael Maklouf **Rev:** Net and soccer players within circle

Date	Mintage	F	VF	XF	Unc	BU
1986 Proof	Est. 1,000	Value: 175				

KM# 163e CROWN
52.0000 g., 0.9500 Platinum 1.5884 oz. APW, 38.5 mm. **Ruler:** Elizabeth II **Series:** World Cup Soccer - Mexico **Obv:** Crowned bust right **Obv. Designer:** Raphael Maklouf **Rev:** Net and soccer players within circle

Date	Mintage	F	VF	XF	Unc	BU
1986 Proof	Est. 200	Value: 2,150				

KM# 164c CROWN
5.1000 g., 0.3740 Gold .0613 oz. AGW **Ruler:** Elizabeth II **Series:** World Cup Soccer - Mexico **Obv:** Crowned bust right **Obv. Designer:** Raphael Maklouf **Rev:** Globe

Date	Mintage	F	VF	XF	Unc	BU
1986 Proof	Est. 10,000	Value: 65.00				

KM# 164d CROWN
7.9600 g., 0.9170 Gold .2347 oz. AGW **Ruler:** Elizabeth II **Series:** World Cup Soccer - Mexico **Obv:** Crowned bust right **Obv. Designer:** Raphael Maklouf **Rev:** Globe

Date	Mintage	F	VF	XF	Unc	BU
1986 Proof	Est. 1,000	Value: 175				

KM# 164e CROWN
52.0000 g., 0.9500 Platinum 1.5884 oz. APW, 38.5 mm. **Ruler:** Elizabeth II **Series:** World Cup Soccer - Mexico **Obv:** Crowned bust right **Obv. Designer:** Raphael Maklouf **Rev:** Globe

Date	Mintage	F	VF	XF	Unc	BU
1986 Proof	Est. 200	Value: 2,150				

KM# 165c CROWN
5.1000 g., 0.3740 Gold .0613 oz. AGW **Ruler:** Elizabeth II **Series:** World Cup Soccer - Mexico **Obv:** Crowned bust right **Obv. Designer:** Raphael Maklouf **Rev:** Flags within circle

Date	Mintage	F	VF	XF	Unc	BU
1986 Proof	Est. 10,000	Value: 65.00				

KM# 165d CROWN
7.9600 g., 0.9170 Gold .2347 oz. AGW **Ruler:** Elizabeth II **Series:** World Cup Soccer - Mexico **Obv:** Crowned bust right **Obv. Designer:** Raphael Maklouf **Rev:** Flags within circle

Date	Mintage	F	VF	XF	Unc	BU
1986 Proof	Est. 1,000	Value: 175				

KM# 165e CROWN
52.0000 g., 0.9500 Platinum 1.5884 oz. APW, 38.5 mm. **Ruler:** Elizabeth II **Series:** World Cup Soccer - Mexico **Obv:** Crowned bust right **Obv. Designer:** Raphael Maklouf **Rev:** Flags within circle

Date	Mintage	F	VF	XF	Unc	BU
1986 Proof	Est. 200	Value: 2,150				

KM# 173c CROWN
5.1000 g., 0.3740 Gold .0613 oz. AGW **Ruler:** Elizabeth II **Subject:** Prince Andrew's Wedding **Obv:** Crowned bust right **Obv. Designer:** Raphael Maklouf **Rev:** Conjoined heads left

Date	Mintage	F	VF	XF	Unc	BU
1986 Proof	Est. 10,000	Value: 65.00				

KM# 173d CROWN
7.9600 g., 0.9170 Gold .2347 oz. AGW **Ruler:** Elizabeth II **Subject:** Prince Andrew's Wedding **Obv:** Crowned bust right **Obv. Designer:** Raphael Maklouf **Rev:** Conjoined heads left

Date	Mintage	F	VF	XF	Unc	BU
1986 Proof	Est. 1,000	Value: 175				

KM# 173e CROWN
52.0000 g., 0.9500 Platinum 1.5884 oz. APW, 38.5 mm. **Ruler:** Elizabeth II **Subject:** Prince Andrew's Wedding **Obv:** Crowned bust right **Obv. Designer:** Raphael Maklouf **Rev:** Conjoined heads left

Date	Mintage	F	VF	XF	Unc	BU
1986 Proof	Est. 100	Value: 2,150				

KM# 174c CROWN
5.1000 g., 0.3740 Gold .0613 oz. AGW **Ruler:** Elizabeth II **Subject:** Prince Andrew's Wedding **Obv:** Crowned bust right **Obv. Designer:** Raphael Maklouf **Rev:** Two sets of arms

Date	Mintage	F	VF	XF	Unc	BU
1986 Proof	Est. 10,000	Value: 65.00				

KM# 174d CROWN
7.9600 g., 0.9170 Gold .2347 oz. AGW **Ruler:** Elizabeth II **Subject:** Prince Andrew's Wedding **Obv:** Crowned bust right **Obv. Designer:** Raphael Maklouf **Rev:** Two sets of arms

Date	Mintage	F	VF	XF	Unc	BU
1986 Proof	Est. 1,000	Value: 175				

KM# 174e CROWN
52.0000 g., 0.9500 Platinum 1.5884 oz. APW, 38.5 mm. **Ruler:** Elizabeth II **Subject:** Prince Andrew's Wedding **Obv:** Crowned bust right **Obv. Designer:** Raphael Maklouf **Rev:** Two sets of arms

Date	Mintage	F	VF	XF	Unc	BU
1986 Proof	Est. 100	Value: 2,150				

KM# 176a CROWN
31.1000 g., 0.9990 Palladium 1.0000 oz., 38.5 mm. **Ruler:** Elizabeth II **Subject:** United States Constitution Bicentennial **Obv:** Crowned bust right **Obv. Designer:** Raphael Maklouf **Rev:** Statue of Liberty divides dates within circle of Presidential busts

Date	Mintage	F	VF	XF	Unc	BU
1987 Proof	Est. 25,000	Value: 400				

KM# 176b CROWN
31.1000 g., 0.9950 Platinum 1.0000 oz. APW, 38.5 mm. **Ruler:** Elizabeth II **Subject:** United States Constitution Bicentennial **Obv:** Crowned bust right **Obv. Designer:** Raphael Maklouf **Rev:** Statue of Liberty divides dates within circle of Presidential busts

Date	Mintage	F	VF	XF	Unc	BU
1987 Proof	Est. 1,000	Value: 1,325				

KM# 179c CROWN
31.1030 g., 0.9990 Palladium 1.0000 oz. **Ruler:** Elizabeth II **Series:** America's Cup **Obv:** Crowned bust right within circle **Obv. Designer:** Raphael Maklouf **Rev:** Sailboats and map within circle

418 ISLE OF MAN

Date	Mintage	F	VF	XF	Unc	BU
1987 Proof	1,000	Value: 400				

KM# 183c CROWN
31.1030 g., 0.9990 Palladium 1.0000 oz. **Ruler:** Elizabeth II **Series:** America's Cup **Obv:** Crowned bust right **Obv. Designer:** Raphael Maklouf **Rev:** Sailboats and cup

Date	Mintage	F	VF	XF	Unc	BU
1987 Proof	1,000	Value: 400				

KM# 184c CROWN
31.1030 g., 0.9990 Palladium 1.0000 oz. **Ruler:** Elizabeth II **Series:** America's Cup **Obv:** Crowned bust right **Obv. Designer:** Raphael Maklouf **Rev:** Statue of Liberty and sailboats

Date	Mintage	F	VF	XF	Unc	BU
1987 Proof	1,000	Value: 400				

KM# 185c CROWN
31.1030 g., 0.9990 Palladium 1.0000 oz. **Ruler:** Elizabeth II **Series:** America's Cup **Obv:** Crowned bust right **Obv. Designer:** Raphael Maklouf **Rev:** Bust of George Steers and sailboat

Date	Mintage	F	VF	XF	Unc	BU
1987 Proof	1,000	Value: 400				

KM# 186c CROWN
31.1030 g., 0.9990 Palladium 1.0000 oz. **Ruler:** Elizabeth II **Series:** America's Cup **Obv:** Crowned bust right **Obv. Designer:** Raphael Maklouf **Rev:** Bust of Sir Thomas Lipton and sailboat

Date	Mintage	F	VF	XF	Unc	BU
1987 Proof	1,000	Value: 400				

KM# 239 CROWN
31.1000 g., 0.9990 Gold 1.0000 oz. AGW **Ruler:** Elizabeth II **Obv:** Crowned bust right **Obv. Designer:** Raphael Maklouf **Rev:** Manx cat

Date	Mintage	F	VF	XF	Unc	BU
1988 U	4,300	—	—	—	675	700
1988 Proof	5,000	Value: 725				

KM# 256 CROWN
31.1000 g., 0.9990 Gold 1.0000 oz. AGW **Ruler:** Elizabeth II **Obv:** Crowned bust right **Obv. Designer:** Raphael Maklouf **Rev:** Persian cat

Date	Mintage	F	VF	XF	Unc	BU
1989	—	—	—	—	675	700
1989 Proof	—	Value: 725				

KM# 273b CROWN
31.1000 g., 0.9990 Gold 1.0000 oz. AGW **Ruler:** Elizabeth II **Subject:** Royal Visit **Obv:** Crowned bust right **Obv. Designer:** Raphael Maklouf **Rev:** Three scenes from ship

Date	Mintage	F	VF	XF	Unc	BU
1989 Proof	Est. 7,500	Value: 750				

KM# 471 CROWN
31.1035 g., 0.9995 Platinum .9995 oz. APW **Ruler:** Elizabeth II **Obv:** Crowned bust right **Obv. Designer:** Raphael Maklouf **Rev:** Persian cat

Date	Mintage	F	VF	XF	Unc	BU
1989	—	—	—	—BV+20%	—
1989 Proof	—	BV+25%				

KM# 267b CROWN
31.1000 g., 0.9990 Gold 1.0000 oz. AGW **Ruler:** Elizabeth II **Subject:** 150th Anniversary of "Penny Black" Stamp **Obv:** Crowned bust right **Obv. Designer:** Raphael Maklouf **Rev:** Crowned head left within stamp

Date	Mintage	F	VF	XF	Unc	BU
1990 Proof	Est. 1,000	Value: 750				

KM# 267c CROWN
52.0000 g., 0.9500 Platinum 1.5884 oz. APW, 38.5 mm. **Ruler:** Elizabeth II **Subject:** 150th Anniversary of "Penny Black" Stamp **Obv:** Crowned bust right **Obv. Designer:** Raphael Maklouf **Rev:** Crowned head left within stamp

Date	Mintage	F	VF	XF	Unc	BU
1990 Proof	Est. 50	Value: 2,150				

KM# 269b CROWN
6.2200 g., 0.9990 Gold .2000 oz. AGW **Ruler:** Elizabeth II **Series:** World Cup - Italy **Obv:** Crowned bust right **Obv. Designer:** Raphael Maklouf **Rev:** Soccer players and shield

Date	Mintage	F	VF	XF	Unc	BU
1990 Proof	Est. 500	Value: 200				

KM# 269c CROWN
6.2230 g., 0.9990 Platinum .2000 oz. APW **Ruler:** Elizabeth II **Series:** World Cup - Italy **Obv:** Crowned bust right **Obv. Designer:** Raphael Maklouf **Rev:** Soccer players and shield

Date	Mintage	F	VF	XF	Unc	BU
1990 Proof	Est. 100	Value: 275				

KM# 270b CROWN
6.2200 g., 0.9990 Gold .2000 oz. AGW **Ruler:** Elizabeth II **Series:** World Cup - Italy **Obv:** Crowned bust right **Obv. Designer:** Raphael Maklouf **Rev:** Soccer player in center of three shields

Date	Mintage	F	VF	XF	Unc	BU
1990 Proof	Est. 500	Value: 175				

KM# 270c CROWN
6.2230 g., 0.9990 Platinum .2000 oz. APW **Ruler:** Elizabeth II **Series:** World Cup - Italy **Obv:** Crowned bust right **Obv. Designer:** Raphael Maklouf **Rev:** Soccer player in center of three shields

Date	Mintage	F	VF	XF	Unc	BU
1990 Proof	Est. 100	Value: 285				

KM# 271b CROWN
6.2200 g., 0.9990 Gold .2000 oz. AGW **Ruler:** Elizabeth II **Series:** World Cup - Italy **Obv:** Crowned bust right **Obv. Designer:** Raphael Maklouf **Rev:** Three shields flanked by emblems with soccer ball below

Date	Mintage	F	VF	XF	Unc	BU
1990 Proof	Est. 500	Value: 200				

KM# 271c CROWN
6.2230 g., 0.9990 Platinum .2000 oz. APW **Ruler:** Elizabeth II **Series:** World Cup - Italy **Obv:** Crowned bust right **Obv. Designer:** Raphael Maklouf **Rev:** Three shields flanked by emblems with soccer ball below

Date	Mintage	F	VF	XF	Unc	BU
1990 Proof	Est. 100	Value: 285				

ISLE OF MAN 419

KM# 272b CROWN
6.2200 g., 0.9990 Gold .2000 oz. AGW **Ruler:** Elizabeth II
Series: World Cup - Italy **Obv:** Crowned bust right **Obv.**
Designer: Raphael Maklouf **Rev:** Three shields flanked by soccer players

Date	Mintage	F	VF	XF	Unc	BU
1990 Proof	Est. 500	Value: 200				

KM# 272c CROWN
6.2230 g., 0.9990 Platinum .2000 oz. APW **Ruler:** Elizabeth II
Series: World Cup - Italy **Obv:** Crowned bust right **Obv.**
Designer: Raphael Maklouf **Rev:** Three shields flanked by soccer players

Date	Mintage	F	VF	XF	Unc	BU
1990 Proof	Est. 100	Value: 285				

KM# 281 CROWN
31.1000 g., 0.9990 Gold 1.000 oz. AGW **Ruler:** Elizabeth II
Obv: Crowned bust right **Obv. Designer:** Raphael Maklouf **Rev:** Alley cat

Date	Mintage	F	VF	XF	Unc	BU
1990	—	—	—	—	675	700
1990 Proof	—	Value: 725				

KM# 283b CROWN
6.2230 g., 0.9990 Gold .2000 oz. AGW **Ruler:** Elizabeth II **Obv:** Crowned bust right **Obv. Designer:** Raphael Maklouf **Rev:** Bust right with hat and cigar

Date	Mintage	F	VF	XF	Unc	BU
1990 Proof	Est. 500	Value: 200				

KM# 283c CROWN
6.2230 g., 0.9990 Platinum .2000 oz. APW **Ruler:** Elizabeth II
Obv: Crowned bust right **Obv. Designer:** Raphael Maklouf **Rev:** Bust right with hat and cigar

Date	Mintage	F	VF	XF	Unc	BU
1990 Proof	Est. 100	Value: 285				

KM# 284b CROWN
6.2230 g., 0.9990 Gold .2000 oz. AGW **Ruler:** Elizabeth II **Obv:** Crowned bust right **Obv. Designer:** Raphael Maklouf **Rev:** Bust left

Date	Mintage	F	VF	XF	Unc	BU
1990 Proof	Est. 500	Value: 200				

KM# 284c CROWN
6.2230 g., 0.9990 Platinum .2000 oz. APW **Ruler:** Elizabeth II
Obv: Crowned bust right **Obv. Designer:** Raphael Maklouf **Rev:** Bust left

Date	Mintage	F	VF	XF	Unc	BU
1990 Proof	Est. 100	Value: 285				

KM# 298 CROWN
31.1000 g., 0.9990 Gold 1.0000 oz. AGW **Ruler:** Elizabeth II
Obv: Crowned bust right **Obv. Designer:** Raphael Maklouf **Rev:** Norwegian cat

Date	Mintage	F	VF	XF	Unc	BU
1991	—	—	—	—	675	700
1991 Proof	—	Value: 725				

KM# 304b CROWN
6.2200 g., 0.9990 Gold .2000 oz. AGW **Ruler:** Elizabeth II
Subject: 10th Wedding Anniversary **Obv:** Crowned bust right **Obv. Designer:** Raphael Maklouf **Rev:** Head of Prince Charles

Date	Mintage	F	VF	XF	Unc	BU
1991 Proof	—	Value: 165				

KM# 305b CROWN
6.2200 g., 0.9990 Gold .2000 oz. AGW **Ruler:** Elizabeth II
Subject: 10th Wedding Anniversary **Obv:** Crowned bust right **Obv. Designer:** Raphael Maklouf **Rev:** Head of Princess Diana

Date	Mintage	F	VF	XF	Unc	BU
1991 Proof	—	Value: 165				

KM# 334 CROWN
31.1000 g., 0.9990 Gold 1.0000 oz. AGW **Ruler:** Elizabeth II
Obv: Crowned bust right **Obv. Designer:** Raphael Maklouf **Rev:** Seated Siamese cat

Date	Mintage	F	VF	XF	Unc	BU
1992 Proof	—	Value: 725				
1992	—	—	—	—	675	700

KM# 326b CROWN
31.0300 g., 0.9990 Gold 1.0000 oz. AGW **Ruler:** Elizabeth II
Subject: America's Cup - San Diego **Obv:** Crowned bust right **Obv. Designer:** Raphael Maklouf **Rev:** Cameo above sailboats

Date	Mintage	F	VF	XF	Unc	BU
1992 Proof	—	—	—	—	800	850

KM# 342 CROWN
31.1000 g., 0.9990 Gold 1.0000 oz. AGW **Ruler:** Elizabeth II
Subject: Year of the Cockerel **Obv:** Crowned bust right **Obv. Designer:** Raphael Maklouf **Rev:** Cockerel within circle **Rev. Designer:** Barry Stanton

Date	Mintage	F	VF	XF	Unc	BU
1993 Proof	Est. 2,500	Value: 750				

KM# 355 CROWN
31.1000 g., 0.9990 Gold 1.0000 oz. AGW **Ruler:** Elizabeth II
Obv: Crowned bust right **Obv. Designer:** Raphael Maklouf **Rev:** Maine coon cat

Date	Mintage	F	VF	XF	Unc	BU
1993	—	—	—	—	675	700
1993 Proof	—	Value: 725				

KM# 382 CROWN
31.1000 g., 0.9990 Gold 1.0000 oz. AGW **Ruler:** Elizabeth II
Obv: Crowned bust right **Obv. Designer:** Raphael Maklouf **Rev:** Japanese bobtail cat

Date	Mintage	F	VF	XF	Unc	BU
1994	—	—	—	—	675	700
1994 Proof	—	Value: 725				

KM# 408 CROWN
31.1000 g., 0.9990 Gold 1.000 oz. AGW **Ruler:** Elizabeth II
Subject: Year of the Dog **Obv:** Crowned bust right **Obv. Designer:** Raphael Maklouf **Rev:** Pekingese within circle

Date	Mintage	F	VF	XF	Unc	BU
1994 Proof	Est. 5,000	Value: 725				

KM# 477 CROWN
31.1035 g., 0.9995 Platinum .9995 oz. APW **Ruler:** Elizabeth II
Obv: Crowned bust right **Obv. Designer:** Raphael Maklouf **Rev:** Japanese bobtail cat

Date	Mintage	F	VF	XF	Unc	BU
1994	—	—	—	—BV+20%	—
1994 Proof	—	BV_25%				

KM# 703 CROWN
6.2200 g., 0.9999 Gold .2000 oz. AGW **Ruler:** Elizabeth II
Series: Normandy Invasion **Obv:** Crowned bust right **Obv. Designer:** Raphael Maklouf **Rev:** Troop ship and landing craft

Date	Mintage	F	VF	XF	Unc	BU
1994 Proof	Est. 5,000	Value: 165				

KM# 704 CROWN
6.2200 g., 0.9999 Gold .2000 oz. AGW **Ruler:** Elizabeth II
Series: Normandy Invasion **Obv:** Crowned bust right **Obv. Designer:** Raphael Maklouf **Rev:** American troops landing

Date	Mintage	F	VF	XF	Unc	BU
1994 Proof	Est. 5,000	Value: 165				

KM# 705 CROWN
6.2200 g., 0.9999 Gold .2000 oz. AGW **Ruler:** Elizabeth II
Series: Normandy Invasion **Obv:** Crowned bust right **Obv. Designer:** Raphael Maklouf **Rev:** American soldier behind rock

Date	Mintage	F	VF	XF	Unc	BU
1994 Proof	Est. 5,000	Value: 165				

KM# 706 CROWN
6.2200 g., 0.9999 Gold .2000 oz. AGW **Ruler:** Elizabeth II
Series: Normandy Invasion **Obv:** Crowned bust right **Obv. Designer:** Raphael Maklouf **Rev:** German machine gun nest

Date	Mintage	F	VF	XF	Unc	BU
1994 Proof	Est. 5,000	Value: 165				

420 ISLE OF MAN

KM# 707 CROWN
6.2200 g., 0.9999 Gold .2000 oz. AGW **Ruler:** Elizabeth II **Series:** Normandy Invasion **Obv:** Crowned bust right **Obv. Designer:** Raphael Maklouf **Rev:** British troops landing

Date	Mintage	F	VF	XF	Unc	BU
1994 Proof	Est. 5,000	Value: 165				

KM# 708 CROWN
6.2200 g., 0.9999 Gold .2000 oz. AGW **Ruler:** Elizabeth II **Series:** Normandy Invasion **Obv:** Crowned bust right **Obv. Designer:** Raphael Maklouf **Rev:** General Eisenhower left

Date	Mintage	F	VF	XF	Unc	BU
1994 Proof	Est. 5,000	Value: 165				

KM# 709 CROWN
6.2200 g., 0.9999 Gold .2000 oz. AGW **Ruler:** Elizabeth II **Series:** Normandy Invasion **Obv:** Crowned bust right **Obv. Designer:** Raphael Maklouf **Rev:** General Omar Bradley right

Date	Mintage	F	VF	XF	Unc	BU
1994 Proof	Est. 5,000	Value: 165				

KM# 710 CROWN
6.2200 g., 0.9999 Gold .2000 oz. AGW **Ruler:** Elizabeth II **Series:** Normandy Invasion **Obv:** Crowned bust right **Obv. Designer:** Raphael Maklouf **Rev:** General Montgomery left

Date	Mintage	F	VF	XF	Unc	BU
1994 Proof	Est. 5,000	Value: 165				

KM# 482 CROWN
31.1035 g., 0.9995 Platinum .9995 oz. APW **Ruler:** Elizabeth II **Obv:** Crowned bust right **Obv. Designer:** Raphael Maklouf **Rev:** Turkish cat

Date	Mintage	F	VF	XF	Unc	BU
1995	—	—	—	—	BV+20%	—
1995 Proof	—	BV_25%				

KM# 624 CROWN
31.1035 g., 0.9995 Platinum .9995 oz. APW **Ruler:** Elizabeth II **Obv:** Crowned bust right **Obv. Designer:** Raphael Maklouf **Rev:** Burmese cat

Date	Mintage	F	VF	XF	Unc	BU
1996	—	—	—	—	BV+20%	—
1996 Proof	—	BV+25%				

KM# 733 CROWN
31.1035 g., 0.9999 Gold 1.0000 oz. AGW **Ruler:** Elizabeth II **Subject:** Year of the Rat **Obv:** Crowned bust right **Obv. Designer:** Raphael Maklouf **Rev:** Rat

Date	Mintage	F	VF	XF	Unc	BU
1996 Proof						

Note: Entire gold issue purchased by one buyer. Mintage, disposition and market value unknown

KM# 726 CROWN
31.1035 g., 0.9999 Gold 1.0000 oz. AGW **Ruler:** Elizabeth II **Subject:** Year of the Ox **Obv:** Crowned bust right **Obv. Designer:** Raphael Maklouf **Rev:** Ox laying down

Date	Mintage	F	VF	XF	Unc	BU
1997 Proof	Est. 2,000	Value: 725				

KM# 774b CROWN
31.1035 g., 0.9999 Gold 1.0000 oz. AGW **Ruler:** Elizabeth II **Obv:** Crowned bust right **Obv. Designer:** Raphael Maklouf **Rev:** Long-haired Smoke cat

Date	Mintage	F	VF	XF	Unc	BU
1997	—	—	—	—	675	700
1997 Proof	—	Value: 725				

KM# 793a CROWN
28.2800 g., 0.9250 Gold Clad Silver .8411 oz., 38.5 mm. **Ruler:** Elizabeth II **Subject:** 50th Wedding Anniversary of Queen Elizabeth II and Prince Philip **Obv:** Crowned bust right **Obv. Designer:** Raphael Maklouf **Rev:** Conjoined 3/4 length figures facing

Date	Mintage	F	VF	XF	Unc	BU
1997 Proof	Est. 10,000	Value: 40.00				

KM# 817 CROWN
31.1035 g., 0.9999 Gold 1.0000 oz. AGW **Ruler:** Elizabeth II **Subject:** Year of the Tiger **Obv:** Crowned bust right **Obv. Designer:** Raphael Maklouf **Rev:** Tiger

Date	Mintage	F	VF	XF	Unc	BU
1998 Proof	Est. 2,000	Value: 725				

KM# 857b CROWN
31.1035 g., 0.9999 Gold 1.0000 oz. AGW **Ruler:** Elizabeth II **Obv:** Crowned bust right **Obv. Designer:** Raphael Maklouf **Rev:** Birman cat

Date	Mintage	F	VF	XF	Unc	BU
1998	—	—	—	—	675	700
1998 Proof	1,000	Value: 725				

KM# 952b CROWN
31.1035 g., 0.9999 Gold .9999 oz. AGW **Ruler:** Elizabeth II **Subject:** Year of the Rabbit **Obv:** Crowned bust right **Obv. Designer:** Raphael Maklouf **Rev:** Rabbits

Date	Mintage	F	VF	XF	Unc	BU
1999 Proof	Est. 2,000	Value: 725				

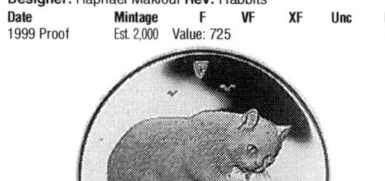

KM# 968 CROWN
31.1035 g., 0.9990 Gold 1.0000 oz. AGW **Ruler:** Elizabeth II **Obv:** Crowned bust right **Obv. Designer:** Raphael Maklouf **Rev:** British Blue cat cleaning its paws

Date	Mintage	F	VF	XF	Unc	BU
1999	—	—	—	—	675	700
1999 Proof	—	Value: 725				

KM# 1057 CROWN
31.1035 g., 0.9999 Gold 1.0000 oz. AGW, 32.7 mm. **Ruler:** Elizabeth II **Subject:** Scottish Fold Kitten **Obv:** Crowned bust right **Obv. Designer:** Raphael Maklouf **Rev:** Kitten playing with world **Edge:** Reeded

Date	Mintage	F	VF	XF	Unc	BU
2000 Proof	—	Value: 725				
2000	—	—	—	—	675	700

KM# 1017 CROWN
31.1035 g., 0.9999 Gold 1.0000 oz. AGW, 32.7 mm. **Ruler:** Elizabeth II **Subject:** Year of the Dragon **Obv:** Crowned bust right **Obv. Designer:** Raphael Maklouf **Rev:** Dragon

Date	Mintage	F	VF	XF	Unc	BU
2000 Proof	Est. 2,000	Value: 725				

KM# 1063 CROWN
31.1035 g., 0.9999 Gold 1.0000 oz. AGW, 32.7 mm. **Ruler:** Elizabeth II **Subject:** Year of the Snake **Obv:** Bust with tiara right **Obv. Designer:** Ian Rank-Broadley **Rev:** Snake **Edge:** Reeded

Date	Mintage	F	VF	XF	Unc	BU
2001 Proof	2,000	Value: 725				

KM# 1073 CROWN
31.1035 g., 0.9999 Gold 1.0000 oz. AGW, 32.7 mm. **Ruler:** Elizabeth II **Subject:** Somali Kittens **Obv:** Bust with tiara right **Obv. Designer:** Ian Rank-Broadley **Rev:** Two kittens **Edge:** Reeded

Date	Mintage	F	VF	XF	Unc	BU
2001	—	—	—	—	675	700
2001 Proof	1,000	Value: 725				

KM# 1103 CROWN
31.1000 g., 0.9999 Gold .9998 oz. AGW **Ruler:** Elizabeth II **Subject:** Year of the Horse **Obv:** Bust with tiara right **Obv. Designer:** Ian Rank-Broadley

Date	Mintage	F	VF	XF	Unc	BU
2002 Proof	2,000	Value: 725				

KM# 1112 CROWN
31.1035 g., 0.9990 Gold 0.999 oz. AGW **Ruler:** Elizabeth II **Subject:** Bengal Cat **Obv:** Bust with tiara right **Obv. Designer:** Ian Rank-Broadley **Rev:** Cat and kitten **Edge:** Reeded

Date	Mintage	F	VF	XF	Unc	BU
2002	—	—	—	—	675	700
2002 Proof	1,000	Value: 725				

KM# 1119 CROWN
35.0000 g., 0.7500 Gold 0.844 oz. AGW, 38.6 mm. **Ruler:** Elizabeth II **Subject:** Golden Jubilee **Obv:** Bust with tiara right **Obv. Designer:** Ian Rank-Broadley **Rev:** Queen Elizabeth II's young laureate bust right **Rev. Designer:** Mary Gillick **Edge:** Reeded **Note:** Red Gold center in a White Gold inner ring within a Yellow Gold outer ring.

Date	Mintage	F	VF	XF	Unc	BU
2002 Proof	999	Value: 625				

KM# 1135b CROWN
28.2800 g., 0.9250 Gold Clad Silver 0.841 oz., 38.6 mm. **Ruler:** Elizabeth II **Subject:** Queen Elizabeth II's Golden Jubilee **Obv:** Bust with tiara right **Obv. Designer:** Ian Rank-Broadley **Rev:** Queen with her pet Corgi **Edge:** Reeded

Date	Mintage	F	VF	XF	Unc	BU
2002 Proof	10,000	Value: 47.50				

KM# 1190 CROWN
31.1035 g., 0.9999 Gold 0.9999 oz. AGW, 32.7 mm. **Ruler:** Elizabeth II **Subject:** Lord of the Rings **Obv:** Bust with tiara right **Obv. Designer:** Ian Rank-Broadley **Rev:** Man on horse **Edge:** Reeded

Date	Mintage	F	VF	XF	Unc	BU
2003PM Proof	1,000	Value: 725				

KM# 1166 CROWN
31.1035 g., 0.9999 Gold 0.9999 oz. AGW, 32.7 mm. **Ruler:** Elizabeth II **Subject:** Cat **Obv:** Head with tiara right **Obv. Designer:** Ian Rank-Broadley **Rev:** Two Balinese kittens **Edge:** Reeded

ISLE OF MAN

Date	Mintage	F	VF	XF	Unc	BU
2003PM	—	—	—	—	675	700
2003PM Proof	—	Value: 725				

KM# 1172 CROWN
31.1035 g., 0.9999 Gold 0.9999 oz. AGW, 32.7 mm. **Ruler:** Elizabeth II **Subject:** Year of the Goat **Obv:** Bust with tiara right **Obv. Designer:** Ian Rank-Broadley **Rev:** Three goats **Edge:** Reeded

Date	Mintage	F	VF	XF	Unc	BU
2003PM Proof	2,000	Value: 725				

Date	Mintage	F	VF	XF	Unc	BU
2004PM Proof	7,500	Value: 50.00				

KM# 1239 CROWN
31.1035 g., 0.9999 Gold 0.9999 oz. AGW, 32.7 mm. **Ruler:** Elizabeth II **Obv:** Bust with tiara right **Obv. Designer:** Ian Rank-Broadley **Rev:** Monkey **Edge:** Reeded

Date	Mintage	F	VF	XF	Unc	BU
2004PM Proof	2,000	Value: 725				

KM# 1242 CROWN
6.2200 g., 0.9999 Gold 0.2 oz. AGW, 22 mm. **Ruler:** Elizabeth II **Obv:** Bust with tiara right **Obv. Designer:** Ian Rank-Broadley **Rev:** Monkey **Edge:** Reeded

Date	Mintage	F	VF	XF	Unc	BU
2004PM Proof	12,000	Value: 175				

KM# 1251 CROWN
31.1035 g., 0.9999 Gold 0.9999 oz. AGW, 32.7 mm. **Ruler:** Elizabeth II **Obv:** Head with tiara right **Obv. Designer:** Ian Rank-Broadley **Rev:** Two Tonkinese cats **Edge:** Reeded

Date	Mintage	F	VF	XF	Unc	BU
2004PM	—	—	—	—	675	700
2004PM Proof	1,000	Value: 750				

KM# 1268 CROWN
31.1030 g., 0.9999 Gold 0.9999 oz. AGW, 32.7 mm. **Ruler:** Elizabeth II **Obv:** Bust with tiara right **Obv. Designer:** Ian Rank-Broadley **Rev:** Himalayan cat and two kittens **Edge:** Reeded

Date	Mintage	F	VF	XF	Unc	BU
2005PM Proof	—	Value: 950				

KM# 1200 2 CROWNS
62.2000 g., 0.9990 Palladium 1.9978 oz., 40 mm. **Ruler:** Elizabeth II **Subject:** Discovery of Palladium Bicentennial **Obv:** Bust with tiara right **Obv. Designer:** Ian Rank-Broadley **Rev:** Pallas Athena left **Edge:** Reeded

Date	Mintage	F	VF	XF	Unc	BU
2004PM Proof	300	Value: 800				

KM# 734 5 CROWN
155.5175 g., 0.9999 Gold 5.0000 oz. AGW **Ruler:** Elizabeth II **Subject:** Year of the Rat **Obv:** Crowned bust right **Obv. Designer:** Raphael Maklouf **Rev:** Rat

Date	Mintage	F	VF	XF	Unc	BU
1996 Proof	—	—	—	—	—	—

Note: Entire series purchased by one buyer. Mintage, disposition, and market value unknown

KM# 727 5 CROWN
155.5175 g., 0.9999 Gold 5.0000 oz. AGW **Ruler:** Elizabeth II **Subject:** Year of the Ox **Obv:** Crowned bust right **Obv. Designer:** Raphael Maklouf **Rev:** Ox laying down

Date	Mintage	F	VF	XF	Unc	BU
1997 Proof	Est. 250	Value: 3,500				

KM# 818 5 CROWN
155.5175 g., 0.9999 Gold 5.0000 oz. AGW **Ruler:** Elizabeth II **Subject:** Year of the Tiger **Obv:** Crowned bust right **Obv. Designer:** Raphael Maklouf **Rev:** Tiger

Date	Mintage	F	VF	XF	Unc	BU
1998 Proof	Est. 250	Value: 3,500				

KM# 953 5 CROWN
155.5175 g., 0.9999 Gold 5.0000 oz. AGW **Ruler:** Elizabeth II **Subject:** Year of the Rabbit **Obv:** Crowned bust right **Obv. Designer:** Raphael Maklouf **Rev:** Two rabbits

Date	Mintage	F	VF	XF	Unc	BU
1999 Proof	Est. 250	Value: 3,500				

KM# 1018 5 CROWN
155.5175 g., 0.9999 Gold 5.0000 oz. AGW **Ruler:** Elizabeth II **Subject:** Year of the Dragon **Obv:** Crowned bust right **Obv. Designer:** Raphael Maklouf **Rev:** Dragon

Date	Mintage	F	VF	XF	Unc	BU
2000 Proof	Est. 250	Value: 3,500				

KM# 1064 5 CROWN
155.5175 g., 0.9999 Gold 5.0000 oz. AGW, 65 mm. **Ruler:** Elizabeth II **Subject:** Year of the Snake **Obv:** Bust with tiara right **Obv. Designer:** Ian Rank-Broadley **Rev:** Snake **Edge:** Reeded

Date	Mintage	F	VF	XF	Unc	BU
2001 Proof	250	Value: 3,750				

KM# 1104 5 CROWN
155.5100 g., 0.9999 Gold 4.9993 oz. AGW, 65 mm. **Ruler:** Elizabeth II **Subject:** Year of the Horse **Obv:** Bust with tiara right **Obv. Designer:** Ian Rank-Broadley **Rev:** Two horses **Edge:** Reeded

Date	Mintage	F	VF	XF	Unc	BU
2002 Proof	250	Value: 3,750				

KM# 1173 5 CROWN
155.5100 g., 0.9999 Gold 4.9993 oz. AGW, 65 mm. **Ruler:** Elizabeth II **Subject:** Year of the Goat **Obv:** Bust with tiara right **Obv. Designer:** Ian Rank-Broadley **Rev:** Three goats **Edge:** Reeded

Date	Mintage	F	VF	XF	Unc	BU
2003PM Proof	250	Value: 3,750				

KM# 1244 5 CROWN
155.5175 g., 0.9999 Gold 4.9995 oz. AGW, 65 mm. **Ruler:** Elizabeth II **Obv:** Bust with tiara right **Obv. Designer:** Ian Rank-Broadley **Rev:** Monkey **Edge:** Reeded

Date	Mintage	F	VF	XF	Unc	BU
2004PM Proof	250	Value: 3,750				

GOLD BULLION COINAGE
Angel Issues

KM# 166 1/20 ANGEL
1.6970 g., 0.9170 Gold .0500 oz. AGW **Ruler:** Elizabeth II **Obv:** Crowned bust right **Obv. Designer:** Raphael Maklouf **Rev:** Archangel Michael slaying dragon

Date	Mintage	F	VF	XF	Unc	BU
1986	—	—	—	—	37.50	—
1986 (pi) Proof	5,000	Value: 45.00				
1987	—	—	—	—	37.50	—
1987 Proof	—	Value: 45.00				

KM# 193 1/20 ANGEL
1.6970 g., 0.9170 Gold .0500 oz. AGW **Obv:** Crowned bust right **Obv. Designer:** Raphael Maklouf **Rev:** Archangel Michael slaying dragon **Rev. Designer:** Leslie Lindsay

Date	Mintage	F	VF	XF	Unc	BU
1988	—	—	—	—	37.50	—
1988 (pi)	—	—	—	—	50.00	—
1989 (h) Proof	Est. 5,000	Value: 50.00				
1989 (mt) Proof	3,000	Value: 50.00				
1990 (sg) Proof	Est. 3,000	Value: 50.00				
1991 (cc) Proof	1,000	Value: 50.00				
1992 (cb) Proof	1,000	Value: 50.00				
1993 Proof	Est. 1,000	Value: 50.00				

KM# 393 1/20 ANGEL
1.5551 g., 0.9999 Gold .0500 oz. AGW **Ruler:** Elizabeth II **Obv:** Crowned bust right **Obv. Designer:** Raphael Maklouf **Rev:** Archangel Michael slaying dragon right

Date	Mintage	F	VF	XF	Unc	BU
1994 (ns) Proof	—	Value: 45.00				
1995 (sc) Proof	—	Value: 50.00				
1996 (bs) Proof	Est. 1,000	Value: 50.00				
1997 (at) Proof	Est. 1,000	Value: 50.00				
1998 (x) Proof	Est. 1,000	Value: 50.00				
1999 (fw) Proof	Est. 1,000	Value: 50.00				
2000 (ch) Proof	Est. 1,000	Value: 50.00				
2000 Proof	—	Value: 45.00				

Note: Christmas candle privy mark

KM# 1106 1/20 ANGEL
1.5552 g., 0.9999 Gold .0500 oz. AGW, 15 mm. **Ruler:** Elizabeth II **Obv:** Bust with tiara right **Obv. Designer:** Ian Rank-Broadley **Rev:** St. Michael slaying dragon, three crown privy mark at right **Edge:** Reeded

Date	Mintage	F	VF	XF	Unc	BU
2001 (3c) Proof	1,000	Value: 50.00				
2002 Proof	—	Value: 50.00				

Note: With candy cane privy mark

KM# 1252 1/20 ANGEL
1.5550 g., 0.9999 Gold 0.05 oz. AGW, 15 mm. **Ruler:** Elizabeth II **Obv:** Bust with tiara right **Obv. Designer:** Ian Rank-Broadley **Rev:** St. Michael and Christmas privy mark **Edge:** Reeded

Date	Mintage	F	VF	XF	Unc	BU
2004PM Proof	1,000	Value: 60.00				

KM# 138 1/10 ANGEL
3.3900 g., 0.9170 Gold .1000 oz. AGW **Ruler:** Elizabeth II **Obv:** Crowned bust right **Obv. Designer:** Raphael Maklouf **Rev:** Archangel Michael slaying dragon

Date	Mintage	F	VF	XF	Unc	BU
1984 Proof	5,000	Value: 75.00				

KM# 140 1/10 ANGEL
3.3900 g., 0.9170 Gold .1000 oz. AGW **Ruler:** Elizabeth II **Obv:** Crowned bust right **Obv. Designer:** Raphael Maklouf **Rev:** Archangel Michael slaying dragon left **Rev. Designer:** Leslie Lindsay

Date	Mintage	F	VF	XF	Unc	BU
1985 Proof	3,000	Value: 80.00				
1985	8,000	—	—	—	70.00	—
1986	—	—	—	—	70.00	—
1986 Proof	—	Value: 80.00				
1987	—	—	—	—	70.00	—
1987 Proof	—	Value: 80.00				

KM# 159 1/10 ANGEL
3.3900 g., 0.9170 Gold .1000 oz. AGW **Ruler:** Elizabeth II **Obv:** Crowned bust right **Obv. Designer:** Raphael Maklouf **Rev:** Archangel Michael slaying dragon left **Rev. Designer:** Leslie Lindsay

Date	Mintage	F	VF	XF	Unc	BU
1985 A	1,000	—	—	—	85.00	—
1985 C	1,000	—	—	—	85.00	—
1985 H	1,000	—	—	—	85.00	—
1985 L	1,000	—	—	—	85.00	—
1985	5,000	—	—	—	70.00	—
1986 A	1,000	—	—	—	85.00	—
1986 T	1,000	—	—	—	85.00	—
1986 X	1,000	—	—	—	85.00	—
1987 A	1,000	—	—	—	85.00	—
1987 F Proof	1,000	Value: 85.00				
1987 L	1,000	—	—	—	85.00	—
1987 (mt) Proof	3,000	Value: 85.00				
1988 A Proof	1,000	Value: 85.00				

KM# 194 1/10 ANGEL
3.3900 g., 0.9170 Gold .1000 oz. AGW **Ruler:** Elizabeth II **Obv:** Crowned bust right **Obv. Designer:** Raphael Maklouf **Rev:** Archangel Michael slaying dragon

Date	Mintage	F	VF	XF	Unc	BU
1988	—	—	—	—	70.00	—
1989 A Proof	250	Value: 100				
1990 A Proof	1,000	Value: 85.00				
1991 A Proof	400	Value: 95.00				

Note: 299 pieces have been melted

| 1992 A | 100 | — | — | — | 110 | — |

KM# 394 1/10 ANGEL
3.1103 g., 0.9999 Gold .1000 oz. AGW **Obv:** Crowned bust right **Obv. Designer:** Raphael Maklouf **Rev:** Archangel Michael

Date	Mintage	F	VF	XF	Unc	BU
1994 Proof	—	Value: 75.00				

KM# 152.1 1/4 ANGEL
8.4830 g., 0.9170 Gold .2500 oz. AGW **Ruler:** Elizabeth II **Obv:** Crowned bust right **Obv. Designer:** Raphael Maklouf **Rev:** Archangel Michael slaying dragon left **Rev. Designer:** Leslie Lindsay

Date	Mintage	F	VF	XF	Unc	BU
1985	2,117	—	—	—	175	—
1985 Proof	51	Value: 200				
1986 L	1,000	—	—	—	175	—
1986 Proof	—	Value: 185				

KM# 152.2 1/4 ANGEL
8.4830 g., 0.9170 Gold .2500 oz. AGW **Ruler:** Elizabeth II **Obv:** Crowned bust right **Obv. Designer:** Raphael Maklouf **Rev:** Archangel Michael slaying dragon **Rev. Designer:** Leslie Lindsay

Date	Mintage	F	VF	XF	Unc	BU
1987	—	—	—	—	175	—
1987 Proof	—	Value: 185				
1987 (s) Proof	1,000	Value: 185				
1987 (SL) Proof	568	Value: 185				
1987 (bb) Proof	1,000	Value: 185				

ISLE OF MAN

KM# 195 1/4 ANGEL
8.4830 g., 0.9170 Gold .2500 oz. AGW **Ruler:** Elizabeth II **Obv:** Crowned bust right **Obv. Designer:** Raphael Maklouf **Rev:** Archangel Michael slaying dragon left **Rev. Designer:** Leslie Lindsay

Date	Mintage	F	VF	XF	Unc	BU
1988	—	—	—	—	175	—
1988 (f) Proof	1,000	Value: 200				
1988 (p) Proof	1,000	Value: 200				
1988 (ss) Proof	1,000	Value: 200				
1989 C (d) Proof	1,000	Value: 200				
1989 (p) Proof	500	Value: 200				
1989 (hk) Proof	1,000	Value: 200				
1989 (y)	—	—	—	—	175	—
1990 (ba) Proof	1,000	Value: 200				

Note: 513 pieces melted

| 1990 (c) Proof | 250 | Value: 220 | | | | |
| 1990 (fl) | 1,000 | — | — | — | 175 | — |

Note: 9 pieces melted

| 1990 (h) Proof | 1,000 | Value: 180 | | | | |
| 1990 (ma) Proof | 200 | Value: 250 | | | | |

Note: 40 pieces melted

| 1990 (tb) | 1,000 | — | — | — | 175 | — |

Note: 10 pieces melted

| 1991 (c) Proof | 200 | Value: 250 | | | | |

Note: 57 pieces melted

| 1991 (fr) Proof | 500 | Value: 200 | | | | |
| 1993 Proof | — | Value: 175 | | | | |

KM# 395 1/4 ANGEL
7.7758 g., 0.9999 Gold .2500 oz. AGW **Ruler:** Elizabeth II **Obv:** Crowned bust right **Obv. Designer:** Raphael Maklouf **Rev:** Archangel Michael slaying dragon

Date	Mintage	F	VF	XF	Unc	BU
1994 Proof	750	Value: 190				

KM# 155 1/2 ANGEL
16.9380 g., 0.9170 Gold .5000 oz. AGW **Ruler:** Elizabeth II **Obv:** Crowned bust right **Obv. Designer:** Raphael Maklouf **Rev:** Archangel Michael slaying dragon left **Rev. Designer:** Leslie Lindsay

Date	Mintage	F	VF	XF	Unc	BU
1985	1,776	—	—	—	350	—
1985 Proof	51	Value: 375				
1986	—	—	—	—	350	—
1986 Proof	3,000	Value: 365				
1987	—	—	—	—	350	—
1987 Proof	—	Value: 365				

KM# 196 1/2 ANGEL
16.9380 g., 0.9170 Gold .5000 oz. AGW **Ruler:** Elizabeth II **Obv:** Crowned bust right **Obv. Designer:** Raphael Maklouf **Rev:** Archangel Michael slaying dragon

Date	Mintage	F	VF	XF	Unc	BU
1988	—	—	—	—	350	—

KM# 396 1/2 ANGEL
15.5517 g., 0.9999 Gold .5000 oz. AGW **Ruler:** Elizabeth II **Obv:** Crowned bust right **Obv. Designer:** Raphael Maklouf **Rev:** Archangel Michael slaying dragon

Date	Mintage	F	VF	XF	Unc	BU
1994 Proof	—	Value: 350				

KM# 139 ANGEL
33.9300 g., 0.9170 Gold 1.0000 oz. AGW **Ruler:** Elizabeth II **Obv:** Young bust right **Obv. Designer:** Arnold Machin **Rev:** Archangel Michael slaying dragon left **Rev. Designer:** Leslie Lindsay

Date	Mintage	F	VF	XF	Unc	BU
1984 Proof	3,000	Value: 725				

KM# 141 ANGEL
33.9300 g., 0.9170 Gold 1.0000 oz. AGW **Ruler:** Elizabeth II **Obv:** Crowned bust right **Obv. Designer:** Raphael Maklouf **Rev:** Archangel Michael slaying dragon left **Rev. Designer:** Leslie Lindsay

Date	Mintage	F	VF	XF	Unc	BU
1985	28,000	—	—	—	700	—
1985 Prooflike	—	—	—	—	—	—
1985 Proof	3,000	Value: 725				
1986	—	—	—	—	700	—
1986 Proof	—	Value: 725				
1987	—	—	—	—	700	—
1987 Proof	—	Value: 725				

KM# 191 ANGEL
33.9300 g., 0.9170 Gold 1.0000 oz. AGW **Ruler:** Elizabeth II **Subject:** Hong Kong Coin Show **Obv:** Crowned bust right **Rev:** Archangel Michael slaying dragon left **Rev. Designer:** Leslie Lindsay

Date	Mintage	F	VF	XF	Unc	BU
1987 Proof	1,000	Value: 725				

KM# 197 ANGEL
33.9300 g., 0.9170 Gold 1.0000 oz. AGW **Ruler:** Elizabeth II **Obv:** Crowned bust right **Obv. Designer:** Raphael Maklouf **Rev:** Archangel Michael slaying dragon left **Rev. Designer:** Leslie Lindsay

Date	Mintage	F	VF	XF	Unc	BU
1988	—	—	—	—	700	—
1988 (ss) Proof	1,000	Value: 725				

KM# 397 ANGEL
31.1035 g., 0.9999 Gold 1.0000 oz. AGW **Ruler:** Elizabeth II **Obv:** Crowned bust right **Obv. Designer:** Raphael Maklouf **Rev:** Archangel Michael slaying dragon right

Date	Mintage	F	VF	XF	Unc	BU
1994 Proof	—	Value: 725				

KM# 156 5 ANGEL
169.6680 g., 0.9170 Gold 5.0000 oz. AGW **Ruler:** Elizabeth II **Obv:** Crowned bust right **Obv. Designer:** Raphael Maklouf **Rev:** Archangel Michael slaying dragon left **Rev. Designer:** Leslie Lindsay

Date	Mintage	F	VF	XF	Unc	BU
1985	104	—	—	—	3,500	—
1985 Proof	90	Value: 3,500				
1986	89	—	—	—	3,500	—
1986 Proof	250	Value: 3,500				
1987	150	—	—	—	3,500	—
1987 Proof	27	Value: 3,500				

KM# 198 5 ANGEL
169.6680 g., 0.9170 Gold 5.0000 oz. AGW **Ruler:** Elizabeth II **Obv:** Crowned bust right **Obv. Designer:** Raphael Maklouf **Rev:** Archangel Michael slaying dragon

Date	Mintage	F	VF	XF	Unc	BU
1988	250	—	—	—	3,500	—

KM# 157 10 ANGEL
339.3350 g., 0.9170 Gold 10.0000 oz. AGW **Ruler:** Elizabeth II **Obv:** Crowned bust right **Obv. Designer:** Raphael Maklouf **Rev:** Archangel Michael slaying dragon left **Rev. Designer:** Leslie Lindsay

Date	Mintage	F	VF	XF	Unc	BU
1985	79	—	—	—	7,000	—
1985 Proof	68	Value: 7,000				
1986	47	—	—	—	7,000	—
1986 Proof	250	Value: 7,000				
1987	150	—	—	—	7,000	—
1987 Proof	30	Value: 7,000				

KM# 199 10 ANGEL
339.3350 g., 0.9170 Gold 10.0000 oz. AGW **Ruler:** Elizabeth II **Obv:** Crowned bust right **Obv. Designer:** Raphael Maklouf **Rev:** Archangel Michael slaying dragon

Date	Mintage	F	VF	XF	Unc	BU
1988 Proof	250	Value: 7,000				

KM# 189 15 ANGEL
508.9575 g., 0.9170 Gold 15.0000 oz. AGW **Ruler:** Elizabeth II **Obv:** Crowned bust right **Obv. Designer:** Raphael Maklouf **Rev:** Archangel Michael slaying dragon

Date	Mintage	F	VF	XF	Unc	BU
1987	150	—	—	—	10,500	—
1987 Proof	18	Value: 11,000				

ISLE OF MAN 423

KM# 200 15 ANGEL
508.9575 g., 0.9170 Gold 15.0000 oz. AGW **Ruler:** Elizabeth II **Obv:** Crowned bust right **Obv. Designer:** Raphael Maklouf **Rev:** Archangel Michael slaying dragon left **Rev. Designer:** Leslie Lindsay

Date	Mintage	F	VF	XF	Unc	BU
1988 Proof	—	Value: 10,500				

KM# 201 20 ANGEL
678.6720 g., 0.9170 Gold 20.0000 oz. AGW, 75.2 mm. **Ruler:** Elizabeth II **Obv:** Crowned bust right **Obv. Designer:** Raphael Maklouf **Rev:** Archangel Michael slaying dragon left **Rev. Designer:** Leslie Lindsay **Note:** Illustration reduced.

Date	Mintage	F	VF	XF	Unc	BU
1988	250	—	—	—	10,500	—
1988 Proof	100	Value: 11,000				

KM# 301 25 ANGEL
848.2750 g., 0.9170 Gold 25.0000 oz. AGW **Ruler:** Elizabeth II **Obv:** Crowned bust right **Obv. Designer:** Raphael Maklouf **Rev:** Archangel Michael slaying dragon

Date	Mintage	F	VF	XF	Unc	BU
1989	—	—	—	—	17,500	—

GOLD BULLION COINAGE
Sovereign Issues

KM# 969 1/5 SOVEREIGN
1.0000 g., 0.9999 Gold .0321 oz. AGW **Ruler:** Elizabeth II **Obv:** Head with tiara right **Obv. Designer:** Ian Rank-Broadley **Rev:** Triskeles **Shape:** Rectangular

Date	Mintage	F	VF	XF	Unc	BU
1999	—	—	—	—	BV+40%	—

KM# 970 1/2 SOVEREIGN
2.5000 g., 0.9999 Gold .0804 oz. AGW **Ruler:** Elizabeth II **Obv:** Head with tiara right **Obv. Designer:** Ian Rank-Broadley **Rev:** Triskeles **Shape:** Rectangular

Date	Mintage	F	VF	XF	Unc	BU
1999	—	—	—	—	BV+30%	—

KM# 971 3/4 SOVEREIGN
3.5000 g., 0.9999 Gold .1125 oz. AGW **Ruler:** Elizabeth II **Obv:** Head with tiara right **Obv. Designer:** Ian Rank-Broadley **Rev:** Triskeles **Shape:** Rectangular

Date	Mintage	F	VF	XF	Unc	BU
1999	—	—	—	—	BV+25%	—

KM# 972 SOVEREIGN
5.0000 g., 0.9999 Gold .1607 oz. AGW **Ruler:** Elizabeth II **Obv:** Head with tiara right **Obv. Designer:** Ian Rank-Broadley **Rev:** Triskeles **Shape:** Rectangular

Date	Mintage	F	VF	XF	Unc	BU
1999	—	—	—	—	BV+20%	—

KM# 973 2 SOVEREIGNS
10.0000 g., 0.9999 Gold .3215 oz. AGW **Ruler:** Elizabeth II **Obv:** Head with tiara right **Obv. Designer:** Ian Rank-Broadley **Rev:** Triskeles **Shape:** Rectangular

Date	Mintage	F	VF	XF	Unc	BU
1999	—	—	—	—	—	—

KM# 974 5 SOVEREIGNS
31.1035 g., 0.9999 Gold .9999 oz. AGW **Ruler:** Elizabeth II **Obv:** Head with tiara right **Obv. Designer:** Ian Rank-Broadley **Rev:** Triskeles **Shape:** Rectangular

Date	Mintage	F	VF	XF	Unc	BU
1999	—	—	—	—	BV+5%	—

GOLD BULLION COINAGE
Platina Issues

KM# 944 1/25 PLATINA
1.2447 g., 0.7500 White Gold .0300 oz. AGW **Ruler:** Elizabeth II **Obv:** Crowned bust right **Obv. Designer:** Raphael Maklouf **Rev:** Crowned arms

Date	Mintage	F	VF	XF	Unc	BU
1999 Proof	Est. 10,000	Value: 40.00				

KM# 945 1/10 PLATINA
3.1103 g., 0.7500 White Gold .0750 oz. AGW **Ruler:** Elizabeth II **Obv:** Crowned bust right **Obv. Designer:** Raphael Maklouf **Rev:** Crowned arms

Date	Mintage	F	VF	XF	Unc	BU
1999 Proof	Est. 7,500	Value: 75.00				

KM# 946 1/5 PLATINA
6.2200 g., 0.7500 White Gold .1500 oz. AGW **Ruler:** Elizabeth II **Obv:** Crowned bust right **Obv. Designer:** Raphael Maklouf **Rev:** Crowned arms flanked by falcons

Date	Mintage	F	VF	XF	Unc	BU
1999 Proof	Est. 5,000	Value: 135				

KM# 947 1/2 PLATINA
15.5517 g., 0.7500 White Gold .3750 oz. AGW **Ruler:** Elizabeth II **Obv:** Crowned bust right **Obv. Designer:** Raphael Maklouf **Rev:** Crowned arms

Date	Mintage	F	VF	XF	Unc	BU
1999 Proof	Est. 3,500	Value: 275				

GOLD & PLATINUM BIMETALLIC BULLION COINAGE

KM# 1065 1/4 ANGEL
Ring Weight: 3.8880 g. **Ring Composition:** 0.9995 Platinum .1244 oz. APW **Center Weight:** 3.8880 g. **Center Composition:** 0.9999 Gold .1249 oz. AGW, 22 mm. **Ruler:** Elizabeth II **Obv:** Crowned bust right **Obv. Designer:** Raphael Maklouf **Rev:** Archangel Michael slaying dragon **Edge:** Reeded

Date	Mintage	F	VF	XF	Unc	BU
1995 Proof	—	Value: 265				

KM# 1066 1/4 NOBLE
Bi-Metallic Platinum center in Gold ring, 22 mm. **Ruler:** Elizabeth II **Obv:** Crowned bust right **Obv. Designer:** Raphael Maklouf **Rev:** Viking ship **Edge:** Reeded

Date	Mintage	F	VF	XF	Unc	BU
1995 Proof	—	Value: 265				

PLATINUM BULLION COINAGE
Noble Series

KM# 266 1/20 NOBLE
1.5551 g., 0.9995 Platinum .0500 oz. APW **Ruler:** Elizabeth II **Obv:** Crowned bust right **Obv. Designer:** Raphael Maklouf **Rev:** Viking ship

Date	Mintage	F	VF	XF	Unc	BU
1989	10,000	Value: 70.00				
1992	—	—	—	—	65.00	—

KM# 137 1/10 NOBLE
3.1100 g., 0.9995 Platinum .1000 oz. APW **Ruler:** Elizabeth II **Obv:** Young bust right **Obv. Designer:** Arnold Machin **Rev:** Viking ship

Date	Mintage	F	VF	XF	Unc	BU
1984	—	—	—	—	130	—
1984 Proof	5,000	Value: 135				

KM# 153 1/10 NOBLE
3.1100 g., 0.9995 Platinum .1000 oz. APW **Ruler:** Elizabeth II **Obv:** Crowned head right **Obv. Designer:** Raphael Maklouf **Rev:** Viking ship

Date	Mintage	F	VF	XF	Unc	BU
1985	99,000	—	—	—	130	—
1985 Proof	5,000	Value: 135				
1986	—	—	—	—	130	—
1986 Proof	5,000	Value: 135				
1987	—	—	—	—	130	—
1987 Proof	5,000	Value: 135				

KM# 202 1/10 NOBLE
3.1100 g., 0.9995 Platinum .1000 oz. APW **Ruler:** Elizabeth II **Obv:** Crowned bust right **Obv. Designer:** Raphael Maklouf **Rev:** Viking ship with hologram sail

Date	Mintage	F	VF	XF	Unc	BU
1988	5,000	—	—	—	130	—
1989	5,000	—	—	—	130	—

ISLE OF MAN

KM# 168 1/4 NOBLE
7.7757 g., 0.9995 Platinum .2500 oz. APW **Ruler:** Elizabeth II **Obv:** Crowned bust right **Obv. Designer:** Raphael Maklouf **Rev:** Viking ship

Date	Mintage	F	VF	XF	Unc	BU
1986 Proof	2,015	Value: 325				
1987 Proof	3,250	Value: 325				
1987PM Proof	750	Value: 325				

KM# 203 1/4 NOBLE
7.7757 g., 0.9995 Platinum .2500 oz. APW **Ruler:** Elizabeth II **Obv:** Crowned bust right **Obv. Designer:** Raphael Maklouf **Rev:** Viking ship

Date	Mintage	F	VF	XF	Unc	BU
1988	—	—	—	—	325	—
1988 (a)	100	—	—	—	325	—
1988 (p) Proof	1,000	Value: 325				
1988 (bb) Proof	1,000	Value: 325				
1989 (br) Proof	250	Value: 325				
1989 (p) Proof	500	Value: 325				
1990 (ba) Proof	1,000	Value: 325				
1990 (ti) Proof	Est. 1,000	Value: 325				

KM# 717 1/4 NOBLE
7.7757 g., 0.9995 Platinum .2500 oz. APW **Ruler:** Elizabeth II **Obv:** Crowned bust right **Obv. Designer:** Raphael Maklouf **Rev:** Ship with hologram sail

Date	Mintage	F	VF	XF	Unc	BU
1996 Proof	Est. 10,000	Value: 325				

KM# 169 1/2 NOBLE
15.5514 g., 0.9995 Platinum .5000 oz. APW **Ruler:** Elizabeth II **Obv:** Crowned bust right **Obv. Designer:** Raphael Maklouf **Rev:** Ship with hologram sail

Date	Mintage	F	VF	XF	Unc	BU
1986 Proof	15	Value: 750				
1987 Proof	3,000	Value: 650				

KM# 204 1/2 NOBLE
15.5514 g., 0.9995 Platinum .5000 oz. APW **Ruler:** Elizabeth II, The 1994 date was issued as part of a two piece set with a rhodium plated silver medal marking the 10th anniversary of the modern platinum noble coin series **Obv:** Crowned bust right **Obv. Designer:** Raphael Maklouf **Rev:** Viking ship

Date	Mintage	F	VF	XF	Unc	BU
1988	3,000	Value: 650				
1989 Proof	3,000	Value: 650				
1994PM Proof	250	Value: 750				

KM# 110 NOBLE
31.1030 g., 0.9995 Platinum .9991 oz. APW **Ruler:** Elizabeth II **Obv:** Young bust right **Obv. Designer:** Arnold Machin **Rev:** Viking ship

Date	Mintage	F	VF	XF	Unc	BU
1983	1,700	—	—	—	1,250	—
1983 Proof	94	Value: 1,275				
1984	—	—	—	—	1,250	—
1984 Proof	2,000	Value: 1,275				

KM# 154 NOBLE
31.1030 g., 0.9995 Platinum .9991 oz. APW **Ruler:** Elizabeth II **Obv:** Crowned bust right **Obv. Designer:** Raphael Maklouf **Rev:** Viking ship

Date	Mintage	F	VF	XF	Unc	BU
1985	—	—	—	—	1,250	—
1985 Proof	3,000	Value: 1,275				
1986	—	—	—	—	1,250	—
1986 Proof	3,000	Value: 1,275				
1987	—	—	—	—	1,250	—
1987 Proof	3,000	Value: 1,275				

KM# 205 NOBLE
31.1030 g., 0.9995 Platinum .9991 oz. APW **Ruler:** Elizabeth II **Obv:** Crowned bust right **Obv. Designer:** Raphael Maklouf **Rev:** Viking ship

Date	Mintage	F	VF	XF	Unc	BU
1988 Proof	3,000	Value: 1,250				
1989 Proof	3,000	Value: 1,250				

KM# 170 5 NOBLE
155.5140 g., 0.9995 Platinum 5.0000 oz. APW **Ruler:** Elizabeth II **Obv:** Crowned bust right **Obv. Designer:** Raphael Maklouf **Rev:** Viking ship

Date	Mintage	F	VF	XF	Unc	BU
1986 Proof	15	Value: 6,500				
1987 Proof	11	Value: 6,500				
1988 Proof	—	Value: 7,000				

KM# 171 10 NOBLE
311.0280 g., 0.9995 Platinum 10.0000 oz. APW, 63 mm. **Ruler:** Elizabeth II **Obv:** Crowned bust right **Obv. Designer:** Raphael Maklouf **Rev:** Viking ship **Note:** Illustration reduced.

Date	Mintage	F	VF	XF	Unc	BU
1986 Proof	15	Value: 12,500				
1987 Proof	11	Value: 12,500				
1988 Proof	—	Value: 13,000				

TRADE COINAGE
Ecu Series

KM# 713 75 ECUS
6.2200 g., 0.9990 Gold .2000 oz. AGW **Ruler:** Elizabeth II **Obv:** Crowned bust right **Obv. Designer:** Raphael Maklouf **Rev:** Triskeles on crowned shield

Date	Mintage	F	VF	XF	Unc	BU
1994	Est. 2,000	—	—	—	190	200

KM# 716 75 ECUS
6.2200 g., 0.9990 Gold .2000 oz. AGW **Ruler:** Elizabeth II **Obv:** Crowned bust right **Obv. Designer:** Raphael Maklouf **Rev:** Falcons on shield

Date	Mintage	F	VF	XF	Unc	BU
1995 Proof	Est. 2,000	Value: 200				

TRADE COINAGE
Sterling Euro Series

KM# 720 50 EURO
6.2200 g., 0.9999 Gold .1999 oz. AGW **Ruler:** Elizabeth II **Subject:** 125th Anniversary of Aida-Verdi **Obv:** Crowned bust right **Obv. Designer:** Raphael Maklouf **Rev:** Head below standing figures

Date	Mintage	F	VF	XF	Unc	BU
1996 Proof	Est. 2,000	Value: 165				

ISLE OF MAN

KM# 797 50 EURO
6.2200 g., 0.9999 Gold .1999 oz. AGW **Ruler:** Elizabeth II **Obv:** Crowned bust right **Obv. Designer:** Raphael Maklouf **Rev:** Head below harp player

Date	Mintage	F	VF	XF	Unc	BU
1997 Proof	Est. 2,000	Value: 165				

KM# 911 50 EURO
6.2200 g., 0.9999 Gold .1999 oz. AGW **Ruler:** Elizabeth II **Subject:** St. George **Obv:** Crowned bust right **Obv. Designer:** Raphael Maklouf **Rev:** Rider spearing dragon as captive damsel watches

Date	Mintage	F	VF	XF	Unc	BU
1998 Proof	Est. 2,000	Value: 175				

MEDALLIC COINAGE
INA Retro Issues

X# 11c.1 4 SHILLING
33.1000 g., 0.9167 Gold 0.9755 oz. AGW **Obv:** Veiled bust left **Obv. Legend:** VICTORIA • DEI GRATIA • IND • IMP **Rev:** Triskelion **Rev. Legend:** IECERIS STABIT QVOCVNQVE **Edge:** Reeded

Date	Mintage	F	VF	XF	Unc	BU
1901 Proof	1	—	—	—	—	—
Note: Medal alignment						
1901 Proof	1	—	—	—	—	—
Note: Coin alignment						

X# 11c.2 4 SHILLING
32.1000 g., 0.9167 Gold 0.9461 oz. AGW **Obv:** Veiled bust left **Obv. Legend:** VICTORIA • DEI GRATIA • IND • IMP **Rev:** Triskelion **Rev. Legend:** IECERIS STABIT QVOCVNQVE **Edge:** Plain **Note:** Medal alignment.

Date	Mintage	F	VF	XF	Unc	BU
1901 Matte Proof						

X# 12.1 4 SHILLING
33.4000 g., 0.9167 Gold 0.9844 oz. AGW **Obv:** Veiled bust left **Obv. Legend:** VICTORIA • DEI • GRA BRITT • REGINA • FID • DEF IND • IMP • **Rev:** Triskelion **Rev. Legend:** IECERIS STABIT QVOCVNQVE **Edge:** Reeded **Note:** Medal alignment.

Date	Mintage	F	VF	XF	Unc	BU
1901 Proof	1	—	—	—	—	—

X# 12.2 4 SHILLING
0.9167 Gold **Obv:** Veiled bust left **Obv. Legend:** VICTORIA • DEI • GRA BRITT • REGINA • FID • DEF IND • IMP • **Rev:** Triskelion **Rev. Legend:** IECERIS STABIT QVOCVNQVE **Edge:** Plain **Note:** Medal alignment.

Date	Mintage	F	VF	XF	Unc	BU
1901 Proof	1	—	—	—	—	—

X# 13c.1 4 SHILLING
0.9167 Gold **Obv:** Crowned bust right **Obv. Legend:** EDWARDVS VII D: G: BRITT: OMN: REX F: D: IND: IMP. **Rev:** Triskelion **Rev. Legend:** IECERIS STABIT QVOCVNQVE **Edge:** Reeded **Note:** Weight varies: 32.2-33.4 grams.

Date	Mintage	F	VF	XF	Unc	BU
1901 Proof	1	—	—	—	—	—
Note: Medal alignment						
1901 Proof	1	—	—	—	—	—
Note: Coin alignment						

X# 13c.2 4 SHILLING
32.2000 g., 0.9167 Gold 0.949 oz. AGW **Obv:** Crowned bust right **Obv. Legend:** EDWARDVS VII D: G: BRITT: OMN: REX F: D: IND: IMP. **Rev:** Triskelion **Rev. Legend:** IECERIS STABIT QVOCVNQVE **Edge:** Plain **Note:** Medal alignment.

Date	Mintage	F	VF	XF	Unc	BU
1901 Proof	1	—	—	—	—	—

X# 14 4 SHILLING
33.2000 g., 0.9167 Gold 0.9785 oz. AGW **Obv:** Head right within pellet circle **Obv. Legend:** EDWARDVS VII DEI GRATIA INDIAE IMPERATOR **Rev:** Trisklion **Rev. Legend:** IECERIS STABIT QVOCVNQVE **Edge:** Plain **Note:** Medal alignment.

Date	Mintage	F	VF	XF	Unc	BU
1901 Proof	1	—	—	—	—	—

MEDALLIC COINAGE
Richard Lobel Issues

X# 2 SOVEREIGN
0.3750 Gold **Subject:** Edward VIII

Date	Mintage	F	VF	XF	Unc	BU
1936 Proof	165	Value: 125				

X# 1c CROWN
Gold **Subject:** Edward VIII **Obv:** Bust of Edward VIII facing left **Obv. Legend:** EDWARD • VIII • KING • & • EMPEROR **Rev:** Peel Castle

Date	Mintage	F	VF	XF	Unc	BU
1936 Proof	—	Value: 500				

PATTERNS
Including off metal strikes

KM#	Date	Mintage	Identification	Mkt Val
Pn20	1987	30	1/2 Crown. Silver.	325
Pn21	1989	—	Crown. Copper-Nickel. Black finish, first penny postage stamp.	—
Pn23	1992	—	5 Pounds. Virenium. Nigell Mansell, KM336.	—

PIEFORTS

KM#	Date	Mintage	Identification	Mkt Val
P4	1983	4,950	Pound. Silver. KM109.	37.50
P5	1983	4,950	Pound. Silver. KM127	37.50
P6	1983	4,950	Pound. Silver. KM130	42.50
P7	1983	4,950	Pound. Silver. KM131	42.50
P8	1984	1,000	Pound. 0.3740 Gold.	150
P9	1984	250	Pound. 0.9170 Gold.	375
P10	1985	4,950	Pound. Silver.	42.50
P11	1985	950	Pound. 0.3740 Gold.	150
P12	1985	250	Pound. 0.9170 Gold.	375
P13	1985	50	Pound. Platinum.	500

TRIAL STRIKES

KM#	Date	Mintage	Identification	Mkt Val
TS1	1813	—	Penny. Tin. Uniface. KM11.	125

MINT SETS

KM#	Date	Mintage	Identification	Issue Price	Mkt Val
MS1	1965 (3)	1,500	KM15-17	—	1,100
MS3	1973 (4)	2,500	KM26-29	760	820
MS4	1974 (4)	250	KM26-29	—	1,400
MS7	1975 (4)	200	KM26-29	—	1,400
MS10	1976 (4)	—	KM26-29	—	1,400
MS12	1977 (4)	180	KM26-29	—	1,400
MS16	1979 (4)	—	KM26-29	—	1,400
MS28	1997 (5)	5,000	KM770-773, 774b	—	1,300

PROOF SETS

KM#	Date	Mintage	Identification	Issue Price	Mkt Val
PS55	2001 (5)	1,000	KM#1067-1070, 1073	—	1,410
PS1	1965 (3)	1,000	KM15a-17a	—	1,180
PS3	1973 (4)	1,250	KM26-29	950	1,500
PS4	1974 (4)	2,500	KM26-29	900	1,500
PS5	1975 (6)	600	KM19b-24b	1,175	4,050
PS6	1975 (4)	—	KM26-29	—	1,500
PS7	1976 (6)	600	KM32b-34b, 35.1b-36.1b, 39b	—	4,050
PS8	1976 (4)	—	KM26-29	—	1,500
PS10	1977 (4)	1,250	KM26-29	—	1,500
PS12	1978 (7)	600	KM32b-34b, 35.1b-36.1b, 39b, 44b	—	4,425
PS14	1979 (7)	500	KM32b-34b, 35.1b, 36.1b, 39b, 44b	2,765	4,425
PS15	1979 (4)	1,000	KM26-29	—	1,500
PS20	1982 (9)	250	KM44c, 58b-62b, 88b, 90b	—	1,295
PS21	1982 (9)	100	KM44b, 58c-62c, 88c, 90c	—	4,000
PS24	1982 (7)	250	KM58c-62c, 70c, 90b	—	2,000
PS25	1982 (7)	400	KM58d-62d, 70d, 90c	—	4,550
PS26	1983 (7)	—	KM58b-62b, 90a, 109a	—	2,550
PS27	1983 (7)	—	KM58b-62b, 90b, 109b	—	345
PS28	1983 (7)	—	KM58c-62c, 90c, 109c	—	1,925
PS17	1980 (7)	—	KM44c, 58c-62c, 70c	—	1,960
PS18	1980 (7)	300	KM44b, 58d-62d, 70d	—	4,425
PS37	1985 (6)	51	KM140-141, 152.1, 155-157	—	11,850
PS31	1985 (9)	150	KM135b, 142b-148b, 150b	3,240	3,000
PS35	1985 (7)	150	KM142b-148b	2,160	2,000
PS32	1985 (9)	100	KM135c, 142c-148c, 150c	3,600	6,550
PS36	1985 (7)	100	KM142c-148c	2,400	4,350
PS38	1986 (7)	17	KM140-141, 152.1, 155-157, 166	—	12,000
PS39	1986 (6)	15	KM153-154, 168-171	—	21,500
PS40	1986 (4)	2,000	KM153-154, 168-169	1,950	2,500
PS41	1986 (5)	2,500	KM140-141, 152.1, 155, 166	—	1,400
PS43	1987 (6)	30	KM140-141, 152.2, 155-157	—	11,850
PS44	1987 (5)	—	KM140-141, 152.2, 155, 166	—	1,400
PS45	1987 (4)	3,000	KM140-141, 152.2, 155	—	1,350
PS46	1987 (6)	11	KM153-154, 168-169, 170-171	—	21,400
PS47	1987 (4)	2,500	KM153-154, 168-169	—	2,400
PS42	1987 (4)	—	KM176a, 177, 187-188	—	1,000
PS48	1988 (5)	611	KM235-239	—	1,425
PS50	1988 (4)	7,500	KM286-289 Medal	—	1,450
PSA51	1994 (2)	250	KM#204 plus Rhodium-plated Silver 31 g medal 10th Anniversary of the Platinum Noble Coin Series	—	1,150
PS51	1996 (5)	500	KM613, 615, 617, 619, 621b	—	1,375
PS52	1998 (5)	1,000	KM853-856, 857b	—	1,385
PS53	1999 (5)	1,000	KM958, 960, 962, 964, 968	1,300	1,385
PS54	2000 (5)	1,000	KM1052-1055, 1057	1,300	1,400
PS60	2003 (3)	—	KM#1186, 1187, 1188	—	320
PS61	2003 (5)	—	KM#1186, 1187, 1188, 1189, 1190 w/gold ring	—	1,400
PS63	2004 (5)	1,000	KM#1247, 1248, 1249.1, 1250, 1251	—	1,425

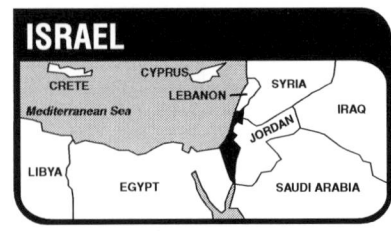

ISRAEL

The state of Israel, a Middle Eastern republic at the eastern end of the Mediterranean Sea, bounded by Lebanon on the north, Syria on the northeast, Jordan on the east, and Egypt on the southwest, has an area of 9,000 sq. mi. (20,770 sq. km.) and a population of 6 million. Capital: Jerusalem. Finished diamonds, chemicals, citrus, textiles, minerals, electronic and transportation equipment are exported.

HEBREW COIN DATING

Modern Israel's coins carry Hebrew dating formed from a combination of the 22 consonant letters of the Hebrew alphabet and read from right to left. The Jewish calendar dates back more than 5700 years; but five millenniums are assumed in the dating of coins (until 1981). Thus, the year 5735 (1975AD) appears as 735, with the first two characters from the right indicating the number of years in hundreds; tav (400), plus shin (300). The next is lamedh (30), followed by a separation mark which has the appearance of double quotation marks, then heh (5).

The separation mark - generally similar to a single quotation mark through 5718 (1958AD), and like a double quotation mark thereafter - serves the purpose of indicating that the letters form a number, not a word, and on some issues can be confused with the character yodh (10), which in a stylized rendering can appear similar, although slightly larger and thicker. The separation mark does not appear in either form on a few commemorative issues.

The Jewish New Year falls in September or October by Christian calendar reckoning. Where dual dating is encountered, with but a few exceptions the Hebrew dating on the coins of modern Israel is 3760 years greater than the Christian dating; 5735 is equivalent to 1975AD, with the 5000 assumed until 1981, when full dates appear on the coins. These exceptions are most of the Hanukka coins, (Feast of Lights), the Bank of Israel gold 50 Pound commemorative of 5725 (1964AD) and others. In such special instances the differential from Christian dating is 3761 years, except in the instance of the 5720 Chanuka Pound, which is dated 1960AD, as is the issue of 5721, an arrangement reflecting the fact that the events fall early in the Jewish year and late in the Christian.

The Star of David is not a mintmark. It appears only on some coins sold by the Israel Government Coins and Medals Corporation Ltd., which is owned by the Israel government, and is a division of the Prime Minister's office and sole distributor to collectors. The Star of David was first used in 1971 on the science coin to signify that it was minted in Jerusalem, but was later used by different mint facilities.

AD Date		Jewish Era
1948	תש״ח	5708
1949	תש״ט	5709
1952	תשי״ב	5712
1954	תשי״ד	5714
1955	תשט״ו	5715
1957	תשי״ז	5717
1958	תשי״ח	5718
1959	תשי״ט	5719
1960	תש״ך	5720
1960	תשך	5720
1961	תשכ״א	5721
1962	תשכ״ב	5722
1963	תשכ״ג	5723
1964	תשכ״ד	5724
1965	תשכ״ה	5725
1966	תשכ״ו	5726
1967	תשכ״ז	5727
1968	תשכ״ח	5728
1969	תשכ״ט	5729
1970	תש״ל	5730
1971	תשל״א	5731
1972	תשל״ב	5732
1973	תשל״ג	5733
1974	תשל״ד	5734
1975	תשל״ה	5735
1976	תשל״ו	5736
1977	תשל״ז	5737
1978	תשל״ח	5738
1979	תשל״ט	5739
1980	תש״ם	5740
1981	תשמ״א	5741
1981	התשמ״א	5741
1982	התשמ״ב	5742
1983	התשמ״ג	5743
1984	התשמ״ד	5744
1985	התשמ״ה	5745
1986	התשמ״ו	5746
1987	התשמ״ז	5747
1988	התשמ״ח	5748
1989	התשמ״ט	5749
1990	התש״ן	5750
1991	התשנ״א	5751
1992	התשנ״ב	5752
1993	התשנ״ג	5753
1994	התשנ״ד	5754
1995	התשנ״ה	5755
1996	התשנ״ו	5756
1997	התשנ״ז	5757
1998	התשנ״ח	5758
1999	התשנ״ט	5759
2000	התש״ס	5760
2001	התשס״א	5761
2002	התשס״ב	5762
2003	התשס״ג	5763
2004	התשס״ד	5764
2005	התשס״ה	5765

MINT MARKS
(o) - Ottawa
(s) - San Francisco
None – Jerusalem

(M) MATTE - Normal circulation strike or a dull finish produced by sandblasting special uncirculated (polish finish) or proof quality dies.

(U) SPECIAL UNCIRCULATED - Polished or prooflike in appearance without any frosted features.

(P) PROOF - The highest quality obtainable having mirror-like fields and frosted features.

MONETARY SYSTEM
1000 Mils = 1 Pound

REPUBLIC

REFORM COINAGE
100 Agorot = 1 Lira

Commencing January 1, 1960-1980

KM# 30 20 LIROT
7.9880 g., 0.9170 Gold .2355 oz. AGW, 22 mm. **Subject:** 100th Anniversary - Birth of Dr. Theodor Herzl **Obv:** Menorah flanked by sprigs within beaded circle **Obv. Designer:** Andre Lasserre **Rev:** Head left within rectangle **Rev. Designer:** Miriam Karoli

Date	Mintage	F	VF	XF	Unc	BU
JE5720-1960(b)	10,460	—	—	—	200	220

KM# 40 50 LIROT
13.3400 g., 0.9170 Gold .3933 oz. AGW, 27 mm. **Subject:** 10th Anniversary - Death of Weizmann **Obv:** Menorah flanked by sprigs within circle **Rev:** Bust left within rectangle

Date	Mintage	F	VF	XF	Unc	BU
JE5723-1962(b) Proof	6,195	Value: 350				
JE5723-1962(b) Proof	10	Value: 1,200				

Note: With "mem"

Note: Without "mem"

KM# 44 50 LIROT
13.3400 g., 0.9170 Gold .3933 oz. AGW, 27 mm. **Subject:** 10th Anniversary - Bank of Israel **Obv:** Menorah flanked by sprigs **Rev:** Artistic design to upper right of text

Date	Mintage	F	VF	XF	Unc	BU
JE5725-1964(b)	5,975	—	—	—	300	—
JE5725-1964(b) Proof	1,502	Value: 3,250				

Note: Includes 702 used officially by the Bank of Israel

KM# 72 50 LIROT
7.0000 g., 0.9000 Gold .2025 oz. AGW **Subject:** 25th Anniversary of Independence **Obv:** Menorah flanked by sprigs above text **Rev:** Text on scroll

Date	Mintage	F	VF	XF	Unc	BU
JE5733-1973(b) Proof	27,724	Value: 180				

ISRAEL 427

KM# 41 100 LIROT
26.6800 g., 0.9170 Gold .7866 oz. AGW, 33 mm. **Subject:** 10th Anniversary - Death of Weizmann **Obv:** Menorah flanked by sprigs within circle **Rev:** Head left within rectangle

Date	Mintage	F	VF	XF	Unc	BU
JE5723-1962(b) Proof	6,196	Value: 575				
Note: With "mem"						
JE5723-1962(b) Proof	10	Value: 1,500				
Note: Without "mem"						

KM# 50 100 LIROT
26.6800 g., 0.9170 Gold .7866 oz. AGW, 33 mm. **Subject:** Victory Commemorative **Obv:** Leafy sprig around sword within artistic star-like design **Rev:** Wailing Wall

Date	Mintage	F	VF	XF	Unc	BU
JE5727-1967(b) Proof	9,004	Value: 595				

KM# 52 100 LIROT
25.0000 g., 0.8000 Gold .6430 oz. AGW, 33 mm. **Subject:** 20th Anniversary - Jerusalem Reunification **Obv:** Building pillars, text and value **Rev:** Menorah flanked by sprigs to upper left of city view

Date	Mintage	F	VF	XF	Unc	BU
JE5728-1968(b) Proof	12,490	Value: 450				

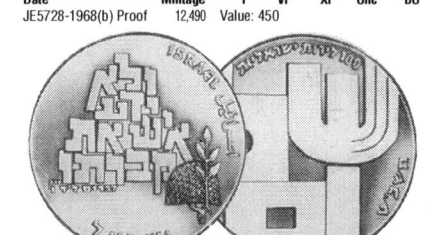

KM# 54 100 LIROT
25.0000 g., 0.8000 Gold .6430 oz. AGW, 33 mm. **Subject:** 21st Anniversary of Independence **Obv:** Block-like letters within triangular design **Rev:** Shalom

Date	Mintage	F	VF	XF	Unc	BU
JE5729-1969(u) Proof	12,500	Value: 475				

KM# 60 100 LIROT
22.0000 g., 0.9000 Gold .6366 oz. AGW, 30 mm. **Subject:** Let My People Go **Obv:** Menorah flanked by sprigs to upper left of text **Rev:** Text within rectangle to right of moon within lines

Date	Mintage	F	VF	XF	Unc	BU
JE5731-1971(b) Proof	9,956	Value: 485				

KM# 73 100 LIROT
13.5000 g., 0.9000 Gold .3906 oz. AGW **Subject:** 25th Anniversary of Independence **Obv:** Text on scroll **Rev:** Menorah flanked by sprigs above text

Date	Mintage	F	VF	XF	Unc	BU
JE5733-1973(b) Proof	27,472	Value: 325				

KM# 74 200 LIROT
27.0000 g., 0.9000 Gold .7813 oz. AGW **Subject:** 25th Anniversary of Independence **Obv:** Menorah flanked by sprigs above text **Rev:** Text on scroll

Date	Mintage	F	VF	XF	Unc	BU
JE5733-1973(b) Proof	17,889	Value: 650				

KM# 82 500 LIROT
28.0000 g., 0.9000 Gold .8102 oz. AGW **Subject:** 1st Anniversary - Death of David Ben Gurion **Obv:** Menorah flanked by sprigs **Rev:** Head left within rectangle

Date	Mintage	F	VF	XF	Unc	BU
JE5735-1974(b) Proof	47,528	Value: 595				

KM# 83 500 LIROT
20.0000 g., 0.9000 Gold .5787 oz. AGW **Subject:** 25th Anniversary of Israel Bond Program **Obv:** Large value above menorah flanked by sprigs **Rev:** Artistic design

Date	Mintage	F	VF	XF	Unc	BU
JE5735-1975(u) Proof	31,693	Value: 425				

KM# 93 1000 LIROT
12.0000 g., 0.9000 Gold .3473 oz. AGW **Subject:** 30th Anniversary of Independence **Obv:** Text and value above menorah flanked by sprigs **Rev:** Text within tree

Date	Mintage	F	VF	XF	Unc	BU
JE5738-1978(b) Proof	12,043	Value: 295				

KM# 105 5000 LIROT
17.2800 g., 0.9000 Gold .5000 oz. AGW **Subject:** 32nd Anniversary of Independence **Obv:** Menorah flanked by sprigs above text and value **Rev:** Sprig divides text

Date	Mintage	F	VF	XF	Unc	BU
JE5740-1980(o) Proof	6,382	Value: 400				

REFORM COINAGE
10 (old) Agorot = 1 New Agora; 100 New Agorot = 1 Sheqel

Commencing February 24, 1980-1985

KM# 125 5 SHEQALIM
8.6300 g., 0.9000 Gold .2497 oz. AGW **Series:** Holyland Sites **Rev:** Qumran Caves **Shape:** 12-sided

Date	Mintage	F	VF	XF	Unc	BU
JE5743-1982(d) Proof	4,927	Value: 200				

KM# 132 5 SHEQALIM
0.8630 g., 0.9000 Gold .2497 oz. AGW **Series:** Holyland Sites **Obv:** Value **Obv. Designer:** Zeev Lipman **Rev:** Herodion Ruins **Rev. Designer:** Dan Gelbart **Shape:** 12-sided

Date	Mintage	F	VF	XF	Unc	BU
JE5744-1983(d) Proof	4,346	Value: 200				

KM# 142 5 SHEQALIM
8.6300 g., 0.9000 Gold .2497 oz. AGW **Series:** Holyland Sites **Obv:** Value **Obv. Designer:** Zeev Lipman **Rev:** Kidron Valley **Rev. Designer:** Dan Gelbart **Shape:** 12-sided

Date	Mintage	F	VF	XF	Unc	BU
JE5745 -1984(b) Proof	2,601	Value: 350				

KM# 154 5 SHEQALIM
8.6300 g., 0.9000 Gold .2497 oz. AGW **Series:** Holyland Sites **Obv:** Value **Rev:** Capernaum **Shape:** 12-sided

Date	Mintage	F	VF	XF	Unc	BU
JE5746-1985(b) Proof	2,633	Value: 250				

KM# 113 10 SHEQALIM
17.2800 g., 0.9000 Gold .5000 oz. AGW **Subject:** 33rd Anniversary of Independence **Obv:** Large stylized value **Rev:** Stylized design within book

Date	Mintage	F	VF	XF	Unc	BU
JE5741-1981(o) Proof	5,634	Value: 400				

428   ISRAEL

KM# 120 10 SHEQALIM
17.2800 g., 0.9000 Gold .5000 oz. AGW **Subject:** 34th Anniversary of Independence **Obv:** Menorah flanked by sprigs above text **Rev:** Head facing
Date	Mintage	F	VF	XF	Unc	BU
JE5742-1982(o) Proof	4,875	Value: 400				

KM# 133 10 SHEQALIM
17.2800 g., 0.9000 Gold .5000 oz. AGW **Subject:** 35th Anniversary of Independence **Obv:** Menorah flanked by sprigs within stylized value **Rev:** Sprig wrapped around sword within star design **Rev. Designer:** Yaacov Zim
Date	Mintage	F	VF	XF	Unc	BU
JE5743-1983(b) Proof	3,814	Value: 400				

KM# 138 10 SHEQALIM
17.2800 g., 0.9000 Gold .5000 oz. AGW **Subject:** 36th Anniversary of Independence **Obv:** Menorah flanked by sprigs **Rev:** Kinsmen
Date	Mintage	F	VF	XF	Unc	BU
JE5744-1984(o) Proof	3,798	Value: 400				

KM# 150 10 SHEQALIM
17.2800 g., 0.9000 Gold .5000 oz. AGW **Subject:** 37th Anniversary of Independence **Obv:** Menorah, text and value within circular designs **Rev:** Scientific achievement
Date	Mintage	F	VF	XF	Unc	BU
JE5745-1985(o) Proof	3,240	Value: 400				

KM# 115 500 SHEQEL
17.2800 g., 0.9000 Gold .5000 oz. AGW **Subject:** 100th Anniversary - Birth of Zeev Jabotinsky **Obv:** Menorah flanked by sprigs above value **Designer:** Gabi Neuman
Date	Mintage	F	VF	XF	Unc	BU
JE5741-1980(o) Proof	7,471	Value: 400				

REFORM COINAGE
10 Sheqalim = 1 Agora; 1000 Sheqalim = 100 Agorot = 1 New Sheqel

September 4, 1985

KM# 342 NEW SHEQEL
3.4600 g., 0.9000 Gold .1001 oz. AGW **Subject:** Wildlife **Obv:** Cedar trees and value **Rev:** Dove and tree trunk
Date	Mintage	F	VF	XF	Unc	BU
JE5752-1991(o) Proof	2,515	Value: 200				

KM# 343 NEW SHEQEL
3.4600 g., 0.9000 Gold .1001 oz. AGW **Series:** Wildlife **Rev:** Roe and lily
Date	Mintage	F	VF	XF	Unc	BU
JE5753-1992(p) Proof	2,000	Value: 200				

KM# 244 NEW SHEQEL
3.4600 g., 0.9000 Gold .1001 oz. AGW **Series:** Wildlife **Obv:** Value at upper right of apple blossom **Rev:** Buck and young Hart standing in grass
Date	Mintage	F	VF	XF	Unc	BU
JE5754-1993(u) Proof	1,679	Value: 200				

KM# 260 NEW SHEQEL
3.4600 g., 0.9000 Gold .1001 oz. AGW **Subject:** Wildlife **Obv:** Palm tree to right of value and text **Rev:** Leopard
Date	Mintage	F	VF	XF	Unc	BU
JE5755-1994(o) Proof	1,355	Value: 225				

KM# 275 NEW SHEQEL
3.4600 g., 0.9000 Gold .1001 oz. AGW **Subject:** Wildlife **Obv:** Grapes **Rev:** Fox
Date	Mintage	F	VF	XF	Unc	BU
JE5756-1995(o) Proof	837	Value: 325				

KM# 291 NEW SHEQEL
3.4600 g., 0.9000 Gold .1001 oz. AGW **Subject:** Wildlife **Rev:** Nightingale
Date	Mintage	F	VF	XF	Unc	BU
JE5757-1996(v) Proof	912	Value: 350				

KM# 307 NEW SHEQEL
3.4600 g., 0.9000 Gold .1001 oz. AGW **Subject:** Wildlife **Obv:** Pomegranates and value **Rev:** Lion **Edge:** Reeded
Date	Mintage	F	VF	XF	Unc	BU
JE5758-1997(u) Proof	770	Value: 375				

KM# 321 NEW SHEQEL
3.4600 g., 0.9000 Gold .1001 oz. AGW **Subject:** Wildlife **Obv:** Fir trees and value **Rev:** Stork
Date	Mintage	F	VF	XF	Unc	BU
JE5759-1998(u) Proof	553	Value: 375				

KM# 348 NEW SHEQEL
3.4600 g., 0.9000 Gold .1001 oz. AGW, 18 mm. **Subject:** Wildlife **Obv:** Acacia tree **Rev:** Ibex **Edge:** Reeded
Date	Mintage	F	VF	XF	Unc	BU
JE5761-2000(u) Proof	700	Value: 325				

KM# 405 NEW SHEQEL
1.2440 g., 0.9990 Gold 0.04 oz. AGW, 13.92 mm. **Obv:** Value **Rev:** Jacob and Rachel floating in air **Edge:** Reeded
Date	Mintage	F	VF	XF	Unc	BU
JE5764 (2004)(u) Proof	—	Value: 75.00				

KM# 405a NEW SHEQEL
1.2440 g., 0.9990 Gold 0.04 oz. AGW, 13.92 mm. **Obv:** Value **Rev:** Arabic legend Israel is mispelled **Edge:** Reeded
Date	Mintage	F	VF	XF	Unc	BU
JE5764 (2004)(u) Proof	682	Value: 110				

KM# 335 10 SHEQALIM
17.2800 g., 0.9000 Gold 0.5 oz. AGW, 30 mm. **Series:** Biblical **Obv:** Arms above denomination **Rev:** Abraham gazing at the stars **Edge:** Reeded
Date	Mintage	F	VF	XF	Unc	BU
JE5759-1999(u) Proof	687	Value: 700				

KM# 414 10 SHEQALIM
16.9600 g., 0.9170 Gold 0.5 oz. AGW, 30 mm. **Subject:** Naomi Shemer **Obv:** Value **Rev:** Portrait of Naomi Shemer **Edge:** Reeded
Date	Mintage	F	VF	XF	Unc	BU
JE5765-2005(u) Proof	Est. 555	Value: 600				

KM# 170 5 NEW SHEQALIM
8.6300 g., 0.9000 Gold .2497 oz. AGW **Series:** Holyland Sites **Rev:** Akko **Shape:** 12-sided
Date	Mintage	F	VF	XF	Unc	BU
JE5747-1986(b) Proof	2,800	Value: 250				

KM# 182 5 NEW SHEQALIM
8.6300 g., 0.9000 Gold .2497 oz. AGW **Series:** Holyland Sites **Obv:** Value **Rev:** Jericho to left of menorah and palm trees **Shape:** 12-sided
Date	Mintage	F	VF	XF	Unc	BU
JE5748-1987(o) Proof	4,000	Value: 225				

KM# 190 5 NEW SHEQALIM
8.6300 g., 0.9000 Gold .2497 oz. AGW **Series:** Holyland Sites **Obv:** Value **Rev:** Caesarea **Shape:** 12-sided
Date	Mintage	F	VF	XF	Unc	BU
JE5749-1988(o) Proof	3,454	Value: 235				

KM# 204 5 NEW SHEQALIM
8.6300 g., 0.9000 Gold .2497 oz. AGW **Series:** Holyland Sites **Obv:** Value **Rev:** Jaffa Harbor **Shape:** 12-sided
Date	Mintage	F	VF	XF	Unc	BU
JE5750-1989(o) Proof	2,402	Value: 275				

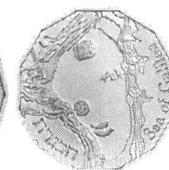

KM# 211 5 NEW SHEQALIM
8.6300 g., 0.9000 Gold .2497 oz. AGW **Series:** Holyland Sites **Obv:** Value **Rev:** Sea of Galilee map
Date	Mintage	F	VF	XF	Unc	BU
JE5751-1990(o) Proof	1,935	Value: 375				

KM# 222 5 NEW SHEQALIM
8.6300 g., 0.9000 Gold .2497 oz. AGW **Subject:** Wildlife **Obv:** Cedar trees and value **Rev:** Dove and tree trunk within legend
Date	Mintage	F	VF	XF	Unc	BU
JE5752-1991(o) Proof	2,000	Value: 300				

KM# 229 5 NEW SHEQALIM
8.6300 g., 0.9000 Gold .2497 oz. AGW **Subject:** IX Paralympic Games **Obv:** Value at center with half horizontal lines at right **Rev:** Shaded star within horizontal lines **Designer:** Abraham Patt
Date	Mintage	F	VF	XF	Unc	BU
JE5752-1992(u) Proof	1,629	Value: 425				

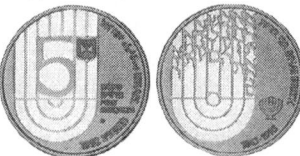

KM# 236 5 NEW SHEQALIM
8.6300 g., 0.9000 Gold .2497 oz. AGW **Subject:** B'nai B'rith **Obv:** Stylized design with value at upper left **Rev:** Stylized design with inscription
Date	Mintage	F	VF	XF	Unc	BU
JE5753-1992(u) Proof	2,305	Value: 325				

ISRAEL 429

KM# 233 5 NEW SHEQALIM
8.6300 g., 0.9000 Gold .2497 oz. AGW **Series:** Wildlife **Obv:** Value at upper right of lily **Rev:** Roe deer facing left
Date	Mintage	F	VF	XF	Unc	BU
JE5753-1992(p) Proof	2,150	Value: 275				

KM# 246 5 NEW SHEQALIM
8.6300 g., 0.9000 Gold .2497 oz. AGW **Series:** Wildlife **Obv:** Value at upper right of apple tree sprig **Rev:** Buck and young hart
Date	Mintage	F	VF	XF	Unc	BU
JE5754-1993(u) Proof	1,782	Value: 275				

KM# 254 5 NEW SHEQALIM
8.6300 g., 0.9000 Gold .2497 oz. AGW **Series:** Independence Day **Subject:** Environment **Obv:** Value **Rev:** World globe within flower
Date	Mintage	F	VF	XF	Unc	BU
JE5754-1994(sa) Proof	1,407	Value: 275				

KM# 262 5 NEW SHEQALIM
8.6300 g., 0.9000 Gold .2497 oz. AGW **Subject:** Wildlife **Obv:** Palm tree and value **Rev:** Leopard
Date	Mintage	F	VF	XF	Unc	BU
JE5755-1994(o) Proof	1,355	Value: 300				

KM# 265 5 NEW SHEQALIM
8.6300 g., 0.9000 Gold .2497 oz. AGW **Series:** Independence Day **Subject:** Anniversary - Medicine **Obv:** Snake on a menorah **Rev:** Value **Designer:** Eliezer Weishoff
Date	Mintage	F	VF	XF	Unc	BU
JE5755-1995(o) Proof	1,147	Value: 325				

KM# 277 5 NEW SHEQALIM
8.6300 g., 0.9000 Gold .2497 oz. AGW **Subject:** Wildlife **Obv:** Value and grape cluster **Rev:** Fox
Date	Mintage	F	VF	XF	Unc	BU
JE5756-1995(u) Proof	872	Value: 350				

KM# 293 5 NEW SHEQALIM
8.6300 g., 0.9000 Gold .2497 oz. AGW **Subject:** Wildlife **Obv:** Fig leaves and value **Rev:** Nightingale
Date	Mintage	F	VF	XF	Unc	BU
JE5757-1996(v) Proof	805	Value: 425				

KM# 309 5 NEW SHEQALIM
8.6300 g., 0.9000 Gold .2497 oz. AGW **Subject:** Wildlife **Obv:** Pomegranates and value **Rev:** Lion walking right
Date	Mintage	F	VF	XF	Unc	BU
JE5758-1997(u) Proof	742	Value: 375				

KM# 323 5 NEW SHEQALIM
8.6300 g., 0.9000 Gold .2497 oz. AGW **Subject:** Wildlife **Obv:** Fir trees and value **Rev:** Stork
Date	Mintage	F	VF	XF	Unc	BU
JE5759-1998(u) Proof	615	Value: 400				

KM# 350 5 NEW SHEQALIM
8.6300 g., 0.9000 Gold .2497 oz. AGW, 22 mm. **Subject:** Wildlife **Obv:** Acacia tree **Rev:** Ibex **Edge:** Reeded
Date	Mintage	F	VF	XF	Unc	BU
JE5761-2000 Proof	600	Value: 425				

KM# 408 5 NEW SHEQALIM
7.7770 g., 0.9990 Gold 0.2498 oz. AGW, 27 mm. **Subject:** FIFA 2006 World Cup **Obv:** Value and soccer ball **Rev:** Map and soccer ball **Edge:** Reeded
Date	Mintage	F	VF	XF	Unc	BU
JE5764-2004 Proof	Est. 777	Value: 350				
Note: Issued in 2006

KM# 166 10 NEW SHEQALIM
17.2800 g., 0.9000 Gold .5000 oz. AGW **Subject:** 38th Anniversary of Independence **Obv:** Value **Rev:** Stylized designs **Designer:** Asaaf Berg and Tidhar Dagan
Date	Mintage	F	VF	XF	Unc	BU
JE5746-1986(d) Proof	2,485	Value: 425				

KM# 179 10 NEW SHEQALIM
17.2800 g., 0.9000 Gold .5000 oz. AGW **Subject:** 39th Anniversary - United Jerusalem
Date	Mintage	F	VF	XF	Unc	BU
JE5747-1987(p) Proof	3,200	Value: 375				

KM# 187 10 NEW SHEQALIM
17.2800 g., 0.9000 Gold .5000 oz. AGW **Subject:** 40th Anniversary of Independence **Obv:** Menorah within stylized value **Obv. Designer:** Asher Kalderon **Rev:** Stylized figures of government within large numeral 40 **Rev. Designer:** Ruben Nutels
Date	Mintage	F	VF	XF	Unc	BU
JE5748-1988(m) Proof	4,575	Value: 400				

KM# 201 10 NEW SHEQALIM
17.2800 g., 0.9000 Gold .5000 oz. AGW **Subject:** 41st Anniversary of Independence **Rev:** Gazelle in forest, legend at left
Date	Mintage	F	VF	XF	Unc	BU
JE5749-1989(o) Proof	2,743	Value: 400				

KM# 214 10 NEW SHEQALIM
17.2800 g., 0.9000 Gold .5000 oz. AGW **Subject:** 42nd Anniversary of Independence **Obv:** Menorah to left of large linear value **Obv. Designer:** Ruben Nutels **Rev:** Archaeology **Rev. Designer:** Ehud Shafrir
Date	Mintage	F	VF	XF	Unc	BU
JE5750-1990(p) Proof	1,815	Value: 650				

KM# 230 10 NEW SHEQALIM
17.2800 g., 0.9000 Gold .5000 oz. AGW **Subject:** 43rd Anniversary of Independence **Obv:** Value within shaded diagonal lines **Rev:** Plane above stylized standing figures
Date	Mintage	F	VF	XF	Unc	BU
JE5751-1991 Proof	2,236	Value: 475				

KM# 227 10 NEW SHEQALIM
17.2800 g., 0.9000 Gold .5000 oz. AGW **Subject:** 44th Anniversary of Independence **Obv:** Value **Rev:** Scales above arched doorway **Note:** Edge varieties exist.
Date	Mintage	F	VF	XF	Unc	BU
JE5752-1992 Proof	1,750	Value: 675				
Note: Struck at the Monnaie de Paris with narrow spaced edge reeding
| JE5752-1992 Proof | 375 | Value: 2,000 | | | | |
Note: Struck at the Utrecht Mint with wide spaced edge reeding

KM# 242 10 NEW SHEQALIM
17.2800 g., 0.9000 Gold .5000 oz. AGW **Series:** Independence Day **Subject:** Tourism **Obv:** Value **Rev:** Tourism objects
Date	Mintage	F	VF	XF	Unc	BU
JE5753-1993(u) Proof	1,944	Value: 450				

KM# 249 10 NEW SHEQALIM
17.2800 g., 0.9000 Gold .5000 oz. AGW **Subject:** Revolt and Heroism **Obv:** Value within beaded diagonal lines **Rev:** Medal with star within beaded diagonal lines to left of flame
Date	Mintage	F	VF	XF	Unc	BU
JE5753-1993(u) Proof	1,583	Value: 450				

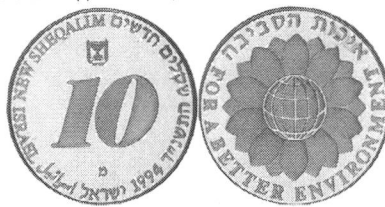

KM# 255 10 NEW SHEQALIM
17.2800 g., 0.9000 Gold .5000 oz. AGW **Series:** Independence Day **Subject:** Environment **Obv:** Slanted value **Rev:** World globe within flower
Date	Mintage	F	VF	XF	Unc	BU
JE5754-1994(sa) Proof	1,482	Value: 550				

KM# 258 10 NEW SHEQALIM
17.2800 g., 0.9000 Gold .5000 oz. AGW **Subject:** Biblical **Rev:** Abraham's willingness to sacrifice Isaac
Date	Mintage	F	VF	XF	Unc	BU
JE5755-1994(o) Proof	1,209	Value: 650				

430 ISRAEL

KM# 266 10 NEW SHEQALIM
17.2800 g., 0.9000 Gold .5000 oz. AGW **Series:** Independence Day **Subject:** Anniversary - Medicine **Obv:** Value **Rev:** Snake on a menorah **Designer:** Eleizer Weishoff

Date	Mintage	F	VF	XF	Unc	BU
JE5755-1995(o) Proof	1,230	Value: 550				

KM# 269 10 NEW SHEQALIM
16.9600 g., 0.9170 Gold .4998 oz. AGW **Subject:** 50th Anniversary - Defeat of Nazi Germany **Obv:** Value above text to right of menorah flanked by sprigs **Rev:** Flag and emblems within v-shaped design

Date	Mintage	F	VF	XF	Unc	BU
JE5755-1995(h) Proof	1,742	Value: 550				

KM# 280 10 NEW SHEQALIM
16.9600 g., 0.9170 Gold .4998 oz. AGW **Subject:** Peace Treaty with Jordan **Designer:** Shimon Keter and David Pesach

Date	Mintage	F	VF	XF	Unc	BU
JE5755-1995(o) Proof	1,451	Value: 495				

KM# 283 10 NEW SHEQALIM
17.2800 g., 0.9000 Gold .5000 oz. AGW **Subject:** Biblical - Solomon's Judgment **Obv:** Value above text **Rev:** Medieval linear design

Date	Mintage	F	VF	XF	Unc	BU
JE5756-1995(o) Proof	961	Value: 650				

KM# 289 10 NEW SHEQALIM
16.9600 g., 0.9170 Gold .4998 oz. AGW **Obv:** Anchor to lower left of value and text **Rev:** Port of Caesarea, ancient ship

Date	Mintage	F	VF	XF	Unc	BU
JE5755-1995(o) Proof	927	Value: 650				

KM# 285 10 NEW SHEQALIM
16.9600 g., 0.9170 Gold .4998 oz. AGW **Subject:** Anniversary - Jerusalem's Third Millennium **Obv:** State arms left of large value **Rev:** Inscription at center

Date	Mintage	F	VF	XF	Unc	BU
JE5756-1996(sa) Proof	1,642	Value: 675				

KM# 296 10 NEW SHEQALIM
17.2800 g., 0.9000 Gold .5000 oz. AGW **Subject:** Biblical **Obv:** Value above text, state arms and star design at left **Rev:** Miriam and the women

Date	Mintage	F	VF	XF	Unc	BU
JE5757-1996(u) Proof	855	Value: 725				

KM# 302 10 NEW SHEQALIM
17.2800 g., 0.9000 Gold .5000 oz. AGW **Subject:** Anniversary - First Zionist Congress Centennial **Obv:** Denomination **Rev:** Portrait of Herzl **Rev. Designer:** Gideon Keitch

Date	Mintage	F	VF	XF	Unc	BU
JE5757-1997(u) Proof	1,326	Value: 495				

KM# 312 10 NEW SHEQALIM
15.5500 g., 0.9990 Gold .4994 oz. AGW **Subject:** 50th Anniversary of Independence **Obv:** Value **Rev:** Flag

Date	Mintage	F	VF	XF	Unc	BU
JE5758-1998(u) Proof	2,406	Value: 495				

KM# 319 10 NEW SHEQALIM
17.2800 g., 0.9000 Gold .5000 oz. AGW **Subject:** Biblical - Noah's Ark **Obv:** Rainbow, dove and value **Rev:** Noah releasing dove from ark

Date	Mintage	F	VF	XF	Unc	BU
JE5758-1998(u) Proof	744	Value: 750				

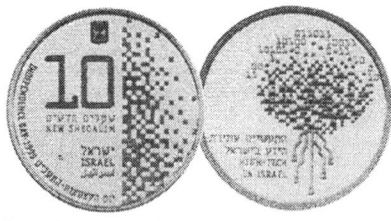

KM# 327 10 NEW SHEQALIM
16.9600 g., 0.9170 Gold .5000 oz. AGW, 30 mm. **Subject:** Anniversary - High-Tech in Israel **Obv:** Value and 01 computer code **Rev:** 01 computer code as bouquet **Designer:** Yigal Gabay

Date	Mintage	F	VF	XF	Unc	BU
JE5759-1999(u) Proof	751	Value: 750				

KM# 330 10 NEW SHEQALIM
16.9600 g., 0.9170 Gold .4998 oz. AGW **Subject:** The Millennium Coin **Obv:** Value and olive branch **Rev:** Year 2000 motif incorporating dove with olive branch

Date	Mintage	F	VF	XF	Unc	BU
JE5759-1999(u) Proof	1,859	Value: 475				

KM# 338 10 NEW SHEQALIM
16.9600 g., 0.9170 Gold .5000 oz. AGW **Subject:** Anniversary - Independence Day **Obv:** Value **Rev:** Arch above inscription **Rev. Inscription:** Love Thy Neighbor, As Thyself **Edge:** Reeded

Date	Mintage	F	VF	XF	Unc	BU
JE5760-2000(u) Proof	794	Value: 725				

KM# 341 10 NEW SHEQALIM
16.9600 g., 0.9170 Gold .5000 oz. AGW, 30 mm. **Series:** Biblical **Obv:** Value **Rev:** Joseph standing before sheaves of wheat into his brothers **Edge:** Reeded

Date	Mintage	F	VF	XF	Unc	BU
JE5760-2000(u) Proof	700	Value: 695				

KM# 346 10 NEW SHEQALIM
16.9600 g., 0.9170 Gold .5000 oz. AGW, 30 mm. **Subject:** Independence Day and Education **Obv:** Value **Rev:** Pomegranate full of symbols - Hebrew for 'ABC - 123', etc. **Edge:** Reeded **Designer:** Asher Kalderon

Date	Mintage	F	VF	XF	Unc	BU
JE5761-2001(u) Proof	660	Value: 650				

KM# 353 10 NEW SHEQALIM
16.9600 g., 0.9170 Gold 0.5 oz. AGW, 30 mm. **Subject:** Music **Obv:** National arms and value **Rev:** Musical instruments **Edge:** Reeded

Date	Mintage	F	VF	XF	Unc	BU
JE5761-2001(u) Proof	766	Value: 700				

KM# 358 10 NEW SHEQALIM
16.9600 g., 0.9166 Gold 0.4998 oz. AGW, 30 mm. **Subject:** Independence - Volunteering **Obv:** Value **Rev:** Heart in hands **Edge:** Reeded

Date	Mintage	F	VF	XF	Unc	BU
JE5762-2002 Proof	617	Value: 650				

KM# 361 10 NEW SHEQALIM
16.9600 g., 0.9170 Gold 0.5 oz. AGW, 30 mm. **Subject:** Tower of Babel **Obv:** National arms in spiral inscription **Rev:** Tower of Hebrew verses **Edge:** Reeded

Date	Mintage	F	VF	XF	Unc	BU
JE5762-2002(o) Proof	750	Value: 700				

KM# 373 10 NEW SHEQALIM
16.9600 g., 0.9170 Gold 0.5 oz. AGW, 30 mm. **Subject:** Space Exploration **Obv:** "Eros" satellite in orbit **Rev:** "Shavit" rocket **Edge:** Reeded

Date	Mintage	F	VF	XF	Unc	BU
JE5763-2003(v) Proof	575	Value: 600				

KM# 376 10 NEW SHEQALIM
16.9600 g., 0.9170 Gold 0.5 oz. AGW, 30 mm. **Obv:** Value **Rev:** Figures floating in air above tree and sheep **Edge:** Reeded

Date	Mintage	F	VF	XF	Unc	BU
JE5763-2003(u) Proof	686	Value: 700				

ISRAEL

KM# 379 10 NEW SHEQALIM
16.9600 g., 0.9170 Gold 0.5 oz. AGW, 30 mm. **Obv:** Value **Rev:** Architectural design **Edge:** Reeded

Date	Mintage	F	VF	XF	Unc	BU
JE5764-2004(u) Proof	555 Value: 700					

KM# 382 10 NEW SHEQALIM
16.9600 g., 0.9170 Gold 0.5 oz. AGW, 30 mm. **Obv:** Value **Rev:** Stylized parent and child **Edge:** Reeded

Date	Mintage	F	VF	XF	Unc	BU
JE5764-2004(u) Proof	555 Value: 700					

KM# 385 10 NEW SHEQALIM
16.9600 g., 0.9170 Gold 0.5 oz. AGW, 30 mm. **Obv:** Four windsurfers, value and national arms **Rev:** Eight windsurfers **Edge:** Reeded

Date	Mintage	F	VF	XF	Unc	BU
JE5764-2004(v) Proof	555 Value: 625					

KM# 388 10 NEW SHEQALIM
16.9600 g., 0.9170 Gold 0.5 oz. AGW, 30 mm. **Subject:** Biblical Burning Bush **Obv:** Burning twig and value **Rev:** Burning Bush **Edge:** Reeded

Date	Mintage	F	VF	XF	Unc	BU
JE5764-2004(v) Proof	555 Value: 700					

KM# 398 10 NEW SHEQALIM
16.9600 g., 0.9166 Gold 0.4998 oz. AGW, 30 mm. **Subject:** Einstein's Relativity Theory **Obv:** Concentric circles above equation **Rev:** Value above signature

Date	Mintage	F	VF	XF	Unc	BU
JE5765-2005(v) Proof	555 Value: 750					

KM# 401 10 NEW SHEQALIM
16.9600 g., 0.9166 Gold 0.4998 oz. AGW, 30 mm. **Series:** Biblical Art **Subject:** Moses and Ten Commandments **Obv:** Ten Commandments and value **Rev:** Moses and Ten Commandments

Date	Mintage	F	VF	XF	Unc	BU
JE5765-2005(u) Proof	555 Value: 700					

KM# 404 10 NEW SHEQALIM
16.9600 g., 0.9166 Gold 0.4998 oz. AGW, 30 mm. **Series:** Independence Day **Subject:** Israel 57th Anniversary **Obv:** Value and olive branch **Rev:** Twisted olive tree **Edge:** Reeded

Date	Mintage	F	VF	XF	Unc	BU
JE5765-2005(u) Proof	555 Value: 600					

KM# 418 10 NEW SHEQALIM
16.9600 g., 0.9170 Gold 0.5 oz. AGW, 30 mm. **Series:** Independence Day **Subject:** Higher Education in Israel **Obv:** Value and design **Rev:** Symbols of Science, Humanities, Technology and Mathamatics **Edge:** Reeded

Date	Mintage	F	VF	XF	Unc	BU
JE5766-2006 Proof	Est. 444 Value: 650					

KM# 411 10 NEW SHEQALIM
16.9600 g., 0.9170 Gold 0.5 oz. AGW, 30 mm. **Subject:** Abraham and the Three Angels **Obv:** Value and stars **Rev:** Abraham and the three angels **Edge:** Reeded

Date	Mintage	F	VF	XF	Unc	BU
JE5766-2006 Proof	Est. 555 Value: 650					

KM# 421 10 NEW SHEQALIM
16.9600 g., 0.9170 Gold 0.5 oz. AGW, 30 mm. **Subject:** UNESCO World Heritage Site, White City Tel Aviv **Obv:** Value and Bauhaus building **Rev:** Face of Bauhaus building and UNESCO symbol **Edge:** Reeded

Date	Mintage	F	VF	XF	Unc	BU
JE5766-2006 Proof	Est. 555 Value: 660					

KM# 299 20 NEW SHEQALIM
31.1035 g., 0.9990 Gold 1.0000 oz. AGW **Obv:** Menorah flanked by sprigs above text, value and date **Rev:** Yitzhak Rabin facing left

Date	Mintage	F	VF	XF	Unc	BU
JE5757-1996(va) Proof	1,949 Value: 975					

KM# 313 20 NEW SHEQALIM
31.1035 g., 0.9990 Gold 1.0000 oz. AGW **Subject:** 50th Anniversary of Independence **Obv:** Value **Rev:** Flag

Date	Mintage	F	VF	XF	Unc	BU
JE5758-1998(u) Proof	2,345 Value: 1,000					

MEDALLIC COINAGE

X# 7 100 SHEKELS
11.9400 g., 0.9167 Gold 0.3519 oz. AGW, 28.9 mm. **Issuer:** Numismatic Center of Mexico **Obv:** Crowned bust of King Solomon right **Rev:** Menorah in sprays with 12 circular symbols **Edge:** Plain

Date	Mintage	F	VF	XF	Unc	BU
JE5722-1962 Proof	— Value: 275					

X# 8 100 SHEKELS
11.8800 g., 0.9167 Gold 0.3501 oz. AGW, 28.9 mm. **Issuer:** Numismatic Center of Mexico **Obv:** Crowned bust of King David right **Rev:** Menorah in sprays with 12 circular symbols **Edge:** Plain

Date	Mintage	F	VF	XF	Unc	BU
JE5722-1962 Proof	— Value: 275					

X# 11a 100 SHEKELS
45.0000 g., 0.9167 Gold 1.3263 oz. AGW, 42 mm. **Issuer:** Numismatic Center of Mexico **Subject:** Year of the Shekel 1964 - 1965 **Obv:** Crowned bust of King David left **Rev:** Menorah in sprays

Date	Mintage	F	VF	XF	Unc	BU
ND(1964)	—	—	—	—	975	—

X# 23 100 EURO
3.5000 g., 0.9167 Gold 0.1032 oz. AGW, 21 mm. **Obv:** Bust of Yitzhak Rabin facing, 3 doves above **Rev:** Israeli and Euro flags

Date	Mintage	F	VF	XF	Unc	BU
1997 Proof	— Value: 200					

PROOF SETS

KM#	Date	Mintage	Identification	Issue Price	Mkt Val
PS1	1927 (14)	34	KM1-7 two each, original case	—	7,500
PS2	1927 (7)	4	KM1-7 original case	—	5,000

432 ITALIAN STATES — EMILIA

a map of the ITALIAN STATES

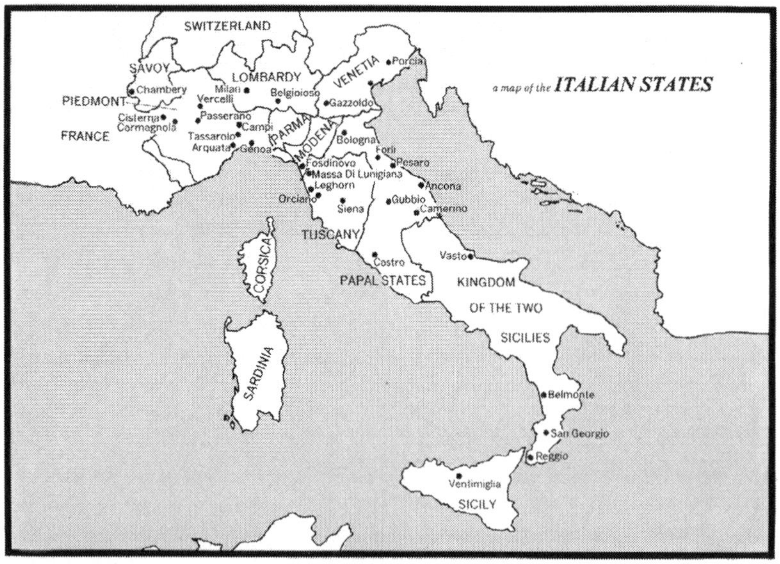

EMILIA
Emilia-Romagna

A northern division of Italy, came under nominal control of the papacy in 755. From 1796-1814 it was incorporated into the Italian Republic and the Kingdom of Napoleon. It returned to the papacy in 1815.

MONETARY SYSTEM
100 Centesimi = 1 Lira

MINT MARKS
B - Bologna
(none) - Birmingham

KINGDOM
STANDARD COINAGE

C# 5 10 LIRE
3.2200 g., 0.9000 Gold .0931 oz. AGW **Obv:** Head left **Obv. Legend:** VITTORIO EMANUELE II **Rev:** Value within wreath **Rev. Legend:** REGIE PROVINGIE DELL . EMILIA B

Date	Mintage	F	VF	XF	Unc	BU
1860B	1,145	600	1,500	3,000	6,000	—

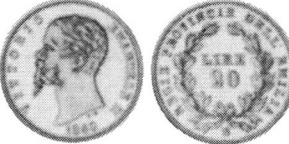

C# 6 20 LIRE
6.4500 g., 0.9000 Gold .1866 oz. AGW **Obv:** Head left **Obv. Legend:** VITTORIO EMANUELE II **Rev:** Value within wreath **Rev. Legend:** REGIE PROVINGIE DELL . EMILIA B

Date	Mintage	F	VF	XF	Unc	BU
1860B Rare	159	—	—	—	—	—

Note: Stack's Hammel sale 9-82 XF realized $24,000; Stack's International sale 3-88 Gem BU realized $16,500

GENOA

A seaport in Liguria, Genoa was a dominant republic and colonial power in the Middle Ages. In 1798 Napoleon remodeled it into the Ligurian Republic, and in 1805 it was incorporated into the Kingdom of Napoleon. Following a brief restoration of the republic, it was absorbed by the Kingdom of Sardinia in 1815.

MINT MARKS
During the occupation by the French forces regular French coins, 1/2, 1, 2, 5, 20 and 40 Francs were struck between 1813 and 1814 with the mint mark C.L.

After Sardinia absorbed Genoa in 1815, regular Sardinian coins were struck until 1860 with a fouled anchor mint mark.

MONETARY SYSTEM
12 Denari = 1 Soldo
20 Soldi = 10 Parpagliola =
5 Cavallotti = 1 Lira (Madonnina)

LIGURIAN REPUBLIC
1798-1805
STANDARD COINAGE

KM# 276 3 DENARI
Copper **Obv:** R. L. A. V 1802 around D. 3, **Rev:** Cross

Date	Mintage	VG	F	VF	XF	Unc
ND(1802)/V(1802)	—	10.00	20.00	35.00	70.00	—

KM# 269 48 LIRE
12.6070 g., 0.9090 Gold .3684 oz. AGW **Obv:** Seated crowned female left, with shield and spear, value below **Obv. Legend:** REPUBLICA LIGURE • AN • VII • **Rev:** Fasces with liberty cap within wreath, date below **Rev. Legend:** NELL'UNIONE LA • FORZA

Date	Mintage	F	VF	XF	Unc	BU
1801//IV	—	400	575	1,000	2,500	—
1804//VII	—	400	575	1,000	2,500	—

KM# 270 96 LIRE
25.2140 g., 0.9170 Gold .7435 oz. AGW **Obv:** Seated crowned female left, with shield and spear, value below **Obv. Legend:** REPUBLICA • LIGURE • AN • IV **Rev:** Fasces with liberty cap within wreath, date below **Rev. Legend:** NELL 'UNIONE LA FORZA

Date	Mintage	F	VF	XF	Unc	BU
1801//IV	—	500	800	1,450	3,500	—
1803//VI	—	500	800	1,450	3,500	—
1804//VII	—	500	800	1,450	3,500	—
1805//VIII	—	500	800	1,450	3,500	—

ITALIAN REPUBLIC
Repubblica Italiana

Created in 1802 out of the Cisalpine Republic (q.v.) with some additions. Converted into the Kingdom of Italy in 1805. Capital: Milan. Years 1-4 of the republic = 1802-1805.

RULER
Napoleon, 1802-1805

MONETARY SYSTEM
(1803)
10 Denari = 1 Soldo
20 Soldi = 1 Lira

PATTERNS
Including off metal strikes

KM#	Date	Mintage	Identification	Mkt Val
Pn9	A.II (1803)M	—	Mezzo (1/2) Doppia. 0.9000 Gold.	—
Pn10	A.II (1803)M	—	Mezzo (1/2) Doppia. 0.9000 Gold. In wreath.	40,000
Pn11	A.II (1803)M	—	Doppia. 0.9000 Gold.	—
Pn12	A.II (1803)M	—	Doppia. 0.9000 Gold. In wreath.	50,000
Pn23	1804M	—	(Venti-20 Lire) Denari 8. 0.9000 Gold. Crossed palm sprig and sword behind scales, bow above. Head right.	32,000
Pn24	1804M	—	(Venti-20 Lire) Denari 8. Copper.	1,350

KINGDOM OF NAPOLEON

Came into being shortly after the first French empire was proclaimed on May 18, 1804; Napoleon's Italian coronation took place at Naples on May 26, 1805.
French rule

RULER
Napoleon I, 1804-1814

MINT MARKS
B - Bologna
M - Milan
V - Venice

MONETARY SYSTEM
100 Centesimi = 20 Soldi
20 Soldi = 1 Lira

KINGDOM
STANDARD COINAGE

KM# 11 20 LIRE
6.4510 g., 0.9000 Gold .1866 oz. AGW **Ruler:** Napoleon I **Obv:** Head left **Obv. Legend:** NAPOLEONE... **Rev:** Shield on eagle within crowned mantle **Rev. Legend:** REGNO D'ITALIA

Date	Mintage	F	VF	XF	Unc	BU
1808M	87,000	175	275	475	1,200	—
1809M	53,000	175	275	475	1,200	—
1810M	114,000	175	275	475	1,200	—
1811M	55,000	175	275	475	1,200	—
1812M	45,000	175	275	475	1,200	—
1813M	39,000	175	300	500	1,250	—
1814M	57,000	175	275	475	1,200	—

KM# 12 40 LIRE
12.9030 g., 0.9000 Gold .3733 oz. AGW **Ruler:** Napoleon I **Obv:** Head left **Obv. Legend:** NAPOLEONE... **Rev:** Shield on eagle within crowned mantle **Rev. Legend:** REGNO D'ITALIA **Note:** Varieties exist.

Date	Mintage	F	VF	XF	Unc	BU
1807M	3,430	500	800	1,750	2,800	—
1808	352,000	275	400	800	1,350	—
	Note: Without mint mark					
1808M	Inc. above	260	275	500	1,200	—
	Note: Edge lettering raised					
1808M	213,000	260	275	500	1,200	—
	Note: Edge lettering incuse					
1809M	38,000	260	300	650	1,275	—
1810M	158,000	260	275	500	1,200	—
1811M	106,000	260	275	500	12,100	—
1812M	56,000	260	300	600	1,250	—
1813M	41,000	260	300	650	1,275	—
1814M	264,000	260	275	500	1,200	—

LOMBARDY-VENETIA

PATTERNS
Including off metal strikes

KM#	Date	Mintage	Identification	Mkt Val
Pn11	1806M	—	20 Lire. Gold.	—
Pn12	1806M	—	40 Lire. Gold.	—

LOMBARDY-VENETIA

Comprised the northern Italian duchies of Milan and Mantua and the Venetian Republic; all these were absorbed into the Kingdom of Napoleon in 1805. After Napoleon's fall they were awarded to Austria and incorporated into the Hapsburg monarchy as the Kingdom of Lombardy-Venetia.

The Lombard campaign of 1859 restored rule under the Kingdom of Italy for Lombard in 1859 and Venetia in 1866.

RULERS
French, until 1814
Austrian, until 1814-48, 1849-59
Italian, until 1946

MINT MARKS
A, W - Vienna
B - Kremnitz
M - Milan
S - Schmollnitz
V - Venice

MONETARY SYSTEM
(Until 1857)
100 Centesimi = 20 Soldi = 1 Lira
6 Lire = 1 Scudo
14 Lire = 1 Ducato
40 Lire = 1 Sovrano

KINGDOM

TRADE COINAGE

C# 9 ZECCHINO
3.5000 g., 0.9000 Gold .1012 oz. AGW **Obv:** Doge kneeling before St. Mark **Obv. Legend:** FRANC. I... **Rev:** Christ standing
Note: Varieties exist.

Date	Mintage	F	VF	XF	Unc	BU
ND(1815)	—	750	1,500	2,000	2,500	—

C# 10.1 1/2 SOVRANO
5.6700 g., 0.9000 Gold .1640 oz. AGW **Obv:** Head laureate right **Rev:** Shield within crowned double-headed eagle

Date	Mintage	F	VF	XF	Unc	BU
1820M	—	400	900	2,000	3,500	—
1822M	—	350	700	1,250	2,000	—
1831M	—	175	300	500	1,000	—

C# 10.2 1/2 SOVRANO
5.6700 g., 0.9000 Gold .1640 oz. AGW

Date	Mintage	F	VF	XF	Unc	BU
1822A	—	200	400	1,250	2,400	—
1823A	—	225	500	1,500	3,000	—
1831A	—	200	400	1,250	2,400	—

C# 10.3 1/2 SOVRANO
5.6700 g., 0.9000 Gold .1640 oz. AGW **Obv:** Head laureate right above V and sprig **Obv. Legend:** FRANCISCVS I.D.G..... **Rev:** Shield within crowned double-headed eagle **Rev. Legend:** GAL.LOD.LL REX....

Date	Mintage	F	VF	XF	Unc	BU
1822V	—	300	800	1,500	3,300	—
1823V	—	150	250	550	1,200	—

C# 10a.1 1/2 SOVRANO
5.6700 g., 0.9000 Gold .1640 oz. AGW

Date	Mintage	F	VF	XF	Unc	BU
1835A	—	—	—	—	—	—

Note: Reported, not confirmed

C# 10a.2 1/2 SOVRANO
5.6700 g., 0.9000 Gold .1640 oz. AGW **Obv:** Head laureate right above M **Rev:** Shield within crowned double-headed eagle
Note: Varieties exist.

Date	Mintage	F	VF	XF	Unc	BU
1835M	—	150	225	550	1,100	—
1835M	—	—	—	—	—	—

Note: Error: AVSIRIAE

C# 20.1 1/2 SOVRANO
5.6700 g., 0.9000 Gold .1640 oz. AGW

Date	Mintage	F	VF	XF	Unc	BU
1837A	—	—	—	—	—	—

Note: Reported, not confirmed

Date	Mintage	F	VF	XF	Unc	BU
1839A	—	200	400	900	1,800	—

C# 20.2 1/2 SOVRANO
5.6700 g., 0.9000 Gold .1640 oz. AGW **Obv:** Head laureate right above M **Obv. Legend:** FERD.I.D.G.AVSTR.... **Rev:** Shield within crowned double-headed eagle **Rev. Legend:** GAL.LOD.ILL....

Date	Mintage	F	VF	XF	Unc	BU
1837M	—	750	1,600	3,250	5,000	—
1838M	—	300	600	1,400	2,250	—
1839M	—	300	600	1,400	2,250	—
1841M	—	300	600	1,400	2,250	—
1842M	—	350	700	1,600	2,500	—
1843M	—	600	1,250	3,250	5,000	—
1844M	—	350	700	1,600	2,500	—
1845M	—	350	700	1,600	2,500	—
1846M	—	350	700	1,600	2,500	—
1847M	—	350	700	1,600	2,500	—
1848M	—	300	700	1,600	2,500	—

C# 20.3 1/2 SOVRANO
5.6700 g., 0.9000 Gold .1640 oz. AGW

Date	Mintage	F	VF	XF	Unc	BU
1837V	—	300	650	1,500	2,400	—
1838V	—	300	650	1,500	2,400	—
1839V	—	300	650	1,500	2,400	—
1840V	—	300	650	1,500	2,400	—
1841V	—	300	650	1,500	2,400	—
1842V	—	650	1,100	1,800	3,000	—
1843V	—	350	700	1,500	2,750	—
1844V	—	350	700	1,500	2,750	—
1845V	—	350	700	1,500	2,750	—
1846V	—	600	1,250	2,000	3,500	—
1847V	—	750	2,000	4,000	6,500	—

C# 20a 1/2 SOVRANO
5.6700 g., 0.9000 Gold .1640 oz. AGW **Obv:** Head laureate right above M **Rev:** Shield within crowned double-headed eagle

Date	Mintage	F	VF	XF	Unc	BU
1849M	—	250	400	800	1,650	—

C# 40.1 1/2 SOVRANO
5.6700 g., 0.9000 Gold .1640 oz. AGW **Obv:** Head laureate right above M **Obv. Legend:** FRANC.10S..... **Rev:** Shield within crowned double-headed eagle

Date	Mintage	F	VF	XF	Unc	BU
1854M	—	600	1,750	3,500	6,500	—
1855M	—	600	1,750	3,500	6,500	—
1856M	—	600	1,750	3,500	6,500	—

C# 40.2 1/2 SOVRANO
5.6700 g., 0.9000 Gold .1640 oz. AGW

Date	Mintage	F	VF	XF	Unc	BU
1854V	—	600	1,750	3,500	6,500	—
1855V	—	600	1,750	3,500	6,500	—
1856V	—	600	1,750	3,500	6,500	—

C# 11.1 SOVRANO
11.3300 g., 0.9000 Gold .3278 oz. AGW **Obv:** Head laureate right above M and sprig **Obv. Legend:** FRANCIS I.D.G..... **Rev:** Shield within crowned double-headed eagle **Rev. Legend:** GAL.LOD.IL.....

Date	Mintage	F	VF	XF	Unc	BU
1820M	—	700	1,500	3,750	7,500	—
1822M	—	350	700	1,400	3,000	—
1823M	—	350	700	1,400	3,000	—
1824M	—	350	1,500	3,750	7,500	—
1826M	—	500	1,000	2,500	5,000	—
1827M	—	500	1,000	2,500	5,000	—
1828M	—	500	1,000	2,500	5,000	—
1829M	—	350	700	1,400	3,000	—
1830/20M	—	—	—	—	—	—
1830M	—	350	700	1,400	3,000	—
1831/21M	—	350	700	1,400	3,000	—
1831M	—	325	650	1,250	2,200	—

C# 11.2 SOVRANO
11.3300 g., 0.9000 Gold .3278 oz. AGW **Obv:** Head laureate right above sprig **Obv. Legend:** FRANCISCVE.... **Rev:** Shield within crowned double-headed eagle **Rev. Legend:** GAL.LOD.IL....

Date	Mintage	F	VF	XF	Unc	BU
1822A	—	625	1,250	2,500	5,000	—
1823A	—	625	1,250	2,500	5,000	—
1831A	—	350	700	1,400	2,800	—

C# 11.3 SOVRANO
11.3300 g., 0.9000 Gold .3278 oz. AGW

Date	Mintage	F	VF	XF	Unc	BU
1822V	—	550	1,000	2,000	3,500	—

C# 11a.1 SOVRANO
11.3300 g., 0.9000 Gold .3278 oz. AGW

Date	Mintage	F	VF	XF	Unc	BU
1835A	—	—	—	—	—	—

Note: Reported, not confirmed

C# 11a.2 SOVRANO
11.3300 g., 0.9000 Gold .3278 oz. AGW **Obv:** Head laureate right above M **Obv. Legend:** FRANCISCVS.... **Rev:** Shield within crowned double-headed eagle **Rev. Legend:** GAL.LOD.ILL....

Date	Mintage	F	VF	XF	Unc	BU
1835M	—	600	1,250	2,500	5,500	—

C# 21.1 SOVRANO
11.3300 g., 0.9000 Gold .3278 oz. AGW **Obv:** Head laureate right **Obv. Legend:** FERD.I.D.AVSTR.... **Rev:** Shield within crowned double-headed eagle **Rev. Legend:** GAL.LOD.ILL....

Date	Mintage	F	VF	XF	Unc	BU
1837A	—	500	800	1,600	3,000	—
1838A Rare	—	—	—	—	—	—
1839A	—	500	800	1,600	3,000	—
1840A Rare	—	—	—	—	—	—
1841A	—	550	900	1,750	3,250	—
1842A Rare	—	—	—	—	—	—
1843A Rare	—	—	—	—	—	—
1845A Rare	—	—	—	—	—	—
1847A	—	850	2,000	4,000	8,500	—

C# 21.2 SOVRANO
11.3300 g., 0.9000 Gold .3278 oz. AGW

Date	Mintage	F	VF	XF	Unc	BU
1837M	—	800	2,000	4,000	8,500	—
1838M	—	400	800	1,600	3,000	—
1840M	—	400	800	1,600	3,000	—
1841M	—	850	2,000	4,000	8,500	—
1848M	—	850	2,000	4,000	8,500	—

C# 21.3 SOVRANO
11.3300 g., 0.9000 Gold .3278 oz. AGW

Date	Mintage	F	VF	XF	Unc	BU
1837V	—	350	750	1,500	3,000	—
1838V	—	350	750	1,500	3,000	—
1840V	—	400	800	1,600	3,200	—
1841V	—	350	750	1,500	3,000	—
1842V	—	350	750	1,500	3,000	—
1843V	—	400	800	1,600	3,200	—

434 ITALIAN STATES — LOMBARDY-VENETIA

Date	Mintage	F	VF	XF	Unc	BU
1844V	—	400	800	1,600	3,200	—
1845V	—	400	800	1,600	3,200	—
1846V	—	350	750	1,500	3,000	—
1847V	—	350	750	1,500	3,000	—

C# 41.1 SOVRANO
11.3300 g., 0.9000 Gold .3278 oz. AGW **Obv:** Head laureate right above M **Obv. Legend:** FRANC 10S.... **Rev:** Shield within crowned double-headed eagle **Rev. Legend:** GAL..LOD.ILL....

Date	Mintage	F	VF	XF	Unc	BU
1853M	—	850	2,000	4,500	8,000	—
1855M	—	850	2,000	4,500	8,000	—
1856M	—	850	2,000	4,500	8,000	—

C# 41.2 SOVRANO
11.3300 g., 0.9000 Gold .3278 oz. AGW

Date	Mintage	F	VF	XF	Unc	BU
1854V	—	1,250	2,500	5,000	9,000	—
1855V	—	1,000	2,000	4,750	8,000	—
1856V	—	1,000	2,000	4,500	8,000	—

REVOLUTIONARY PROVISIONAL GOVERNMENT

PROVISIONAL COINAGE

C# 23 20 LIRE
6.4500 g., 0.9000 Gold .1866 oz. AGW **Obv:** Written and numeral value within wreath above date **Obv. Legend:** GEVERNO PROVVISORIO DI LOMBARDIA **Rev:** Standing crowned figure, star above, M below **Rev. Legend:** ITALIA LIBERA DIO LO VUOLE

Date	Mintage	F	VF	XF	Unc	BU
1848M	4,593	400	700	1,000	2,200	—

C# 24 40 LIRE
12.9000 g., 0.9000 Gold .3733 oz. AGW **Obv:** Written and numeral value within wreath above date **Obv. Legend:** GEVERNO PROVVISORIO DI LOMBARDIA **Rev:** Standing crowned figure, star above, M below **Rev. Legend:** ITALIA LIBERA DIO LO VUOLE

Date	Mintage	F	VF	XF	Unc	BU
1848M	5,875	500	800	1,450	3,000	—

NAPLES & SICILY

Two Sicilies

Consisting of Sicily and the south of Italy, Naples & Sicily came into being in 1130. It passed under Spanish control in 1502; Naples was conquered by Austria in 1707. In 1733 Don Carlos of Spain was recognized as king. From then until becoming part of the United Kingdom of Italy, Naples and Sicily, together and separately, were contested for by Spain, Austria, France, and the republican and monarchial factions of Italy.

RULERS
Bourbon
Ferdinando IV, 1799-1805 (2nd reign)
1815-1816 (restored in Naples)
1816-1825 (as King of the Two Sicilies)
Neapolitan Republic, 1799

Two Sicilies
Francesco I, 1825-1830
Ferdinand II, 1830-1859
Francesco II, 1859-1869

ASSAYERS' INITIALS

A	1676, 78-83	F. Antonio Ariani
A	1730-47	Francesco Antonio Ariani
C	1621-30	Constantino Di Costanzo
C	1631-35	Antonio Di Costanzo
C	1635	G. Antonio Consolo
C	1776	G. Batt Cangiano
N	1642-47, 48	Germano De Novellis
P	1647	Geronimo Pontecorvo
R	1744	Giovanni Russo

ENGRAVERS' INITIALS
Usually found on the obverse below the portrait.

AH	1674	Arina Amerani
BP	1769-98	Bernhard Perger
FA	1766	Ferdinando Aveta
GG	1730-34, 1736-55, 1763	Giovanni de Gennard
IA, IA monogram	1754	Ingnazio Aveta
IM	1688	Giovanni Montemein
MM	1751	Domenico Maria Mazzara
NG	1621	Nicola Galoti at the Torre Annunziata Mint

MONETARY SYSTEM
(Until 1813)
6 Cavalli = 1 Tornese
240 Tornese = 120 Grana = 12 Carlini = 6 Tari = 1 Piastra
5 Grana = 1 Cinquina
100 Grana = 1 Ducato (Tallero)

KINGDOM OF NAPLES
Bourbon Rule
REFORM COINAGE
100 Centesimi = 1 Franco = 1 Lira

C# 112 20 LIRE
6.4500 g., 0.9000 Gold .1866 oz. AGW **Obv:** Head left **Obv. Legend:** GIOACCHINO NAPOLEONE **Rev:** Value within wreath **Rev. Legend:** REGNO DELLE DUE SICILIE.

Date	Mintage	F	VF	XF	Unc	BU
1813	42,000	225	350	550	1,300	—
1813 N	—	1,000	2,500	3,500	6,000	—

C# 104 40 FRANCHI
12.9000 g., 0.9000 Gold .3732 oz. AGW **Obv:** Head left **Obv. Legend:** GIOACCHINO NAPOLEONE.... **Rev:** Value within wreath above date **Rev. Legend:** PRINCE GRAND.....

Date	Mintage	F	VF	XF	Unc	BU
1810 Rare	18	—	—	—	—	—

Note: Bowers and Merena Guia sale 3-88 VF realized $19,800; Superior Pipito sale 12-87 about XF realized $30,250

C# 113 40 LIRE
12.9000 g., 0.9000 Gold .3732 oz. AGW **Obv:** Head left **Obv. Legend:** GIOACCHINO NAPOLEONE **Rev:** Value within wreath **Rev. Legend:** REGNO DELLE DUE SICILIE

Date	Mintage	F	VF	XF	Unc	BU
1813	24,000	325	500	1,000	2,200	—

TWO SICILIES

NOTE: Coins bearing legends FERDINANDO IV were issued for circulation in Naples while those with FERDINANDO I were struck for Two Sicilies.

MONETARY SYSTEM
100 Grana = 1 Ducato (Tallero)

REFORM COINAGE
100 Centesimi = 1 Franco = 1 Lira

C# 127 3 DUCATI
3.7900 g., 0.9960 Gold .1213 oz. AGW **Ruler:** Ferdinando IV as King of the Two Sicilies **Obv:** Crowned head left **Rev:** Genius, without wings, flanked by shield and small crowned pillar

Date	Mintage	VG	F	VF	XF	Unc
1818	—	150	225	350	700	—

C# 138 3 DUCATI
3.7900 g., 0.9960 Gold .1213 oz. AGW **Ruler:** Francesco I **Obv:** Head right, with beard **Obv. Legend:** FRANCISCVS I.... **Rev:** Winged genius flanked by shield and small crowned pillar **Rev. Legend:** REGNI VTR....

Date	Mintage	VG	F	VF	XF	Unc
1826	—	300	450	1,200	2,500	—

C# 154 3 DUCATI
3.7900 g., 0.9960 Gold .1213 oz. AGW **Ruler:** Ferdinand II **Obv:** Head right, without beard **Obv. Legend:** FERDINANDVS II.... **Rev:** Winged genius flanked by shield and small crowned pillar **Rev. Legend:** REGNI VTR....

Date	Mintage	F	VF	XF	Unc	BU
1831	—	200	250	350	800	—
1832	—	200	250	350	800	—
1835	—	200	250	350	800	—

C# 154a 3 DUCATI
3.7900 g., 0.9960 Gold .1213 oz. AGW **Ruler:** Ferdinand II **Obv:** Head right **Rev:** Winged genius flanked by shield and small crowned pillar

Date	Mintage	F	VF	XF	Unc	BU
1837	—	200	250	450	1,000	—

C# 154b 3 DUCATI
3.7900 g., 0.9960 Gold .1213 oz. AGW **Ruler:** Ferdinand II **Obv:** Head right, with beard **Rev:** Winged genius flanked by shield and small crowned pillar

Date	Mintage	F	VF	XF	Unc	BU
1839	—	200	250	325	700	—
1840	—	200	250	350	750	—

C# 154c 3 DUCATI
3.7900 g., 0.9960 Gold .1213 oz. AGW **Ruler:** Ferdinand II **Obv:** Head right, with beard **Obv. Legend:** FERDINANDVS II... **Rev:** Winged genius flanked by shield and small crowned pillar **Rev. Legend:** REGNI VTR....

Date	Mintage	F	VF	XF	Unc	BU
1842	—	200	250	325	700	—
1845	—	200	250	325	700	—
1846	—	200	250	350	750	—
1848	—	200	250	325	700	—

C# 154d 3 DUCATI
3.7900 g., 0.9960 Gold .1213 oz. AGW **Ruler:** Ferdinand II **Obv:** Head right, with beard **Obv. Legend:** FERDINANDVS II... **Rev:** Winged genius flanked by shield and small crowned pillar **Rev. Legend:** REGNI VTR....

Date	Mintage	F	VF	XF	Unc	BU
1850	—	175	225	300	500	—
1851	—	175	225	300	500	—
1852	—	175	225	300	500	—
1854	—	125	175	250	450	—
1856	—	175	225	300	500	—

NAPLES & SICILY — ITALIAN STATES

C# 139 6 DUCATI
7.5700 g., 0.9960 Gold .2424 oz. AGW **Ruler:** Francesco I **Obv:** Head right, with beard **Obv. Legend:** FRANCISCVS I.... **Rev:** Winged genius flanked by shield and small crowned pillar **Rev. Legend:** REGNI VTR....

Date	Mintage	VG	F	VF	XF	Unc
1826	—	225	400	1,500	3,850	—

C# 155 6 DUCATI
7.5700 g., 0.9960 Gold .2424 oz. AGW **Ruler:** Ferdinand II **Obv:** Head right, without beard **Obv. Legend:** FERDINANDVS II.... **Rev:** Winged genius flanked by shield and small crowned pillar **Rev. Legend:** REGNI VTR....

Date	Mintage	F	VF	XF	Unc	BU
1831	—	225	350	525	1,300	—
1833	—	225	350	525	1,300	—
1835	—	250	450	600	1,650	—

C# 155b 6 DUCATI
7.5700 g., 0.9960 Gold .2424 oz. AGW **Ruler:** Ferdinand II **Obv:** Head right, with beard **Obv. Legend:** FERDINANDVS II..... **Rev:** Winged genius flanked by shield and small crowned pillar **Rev. Legend:** REGNI VTR...

Date	Mintage	F	VF	XF	Unc	BU
1840	—	225	350	525	1,300	—

C# 155c 6 DUCATI
7.5700 g., 0.9960 Gold .2424 oz. AGW **Ruler:** Ferdinand II **Obv:** Head right, with beard **Obv. Legend:** FERDINANDVS II... **Rev:** Winged genius flanked by shield and small crowned pillar **Rev. Legend:** REGNI VTR...

Date	Mintage	F	VF	XF	Unc	BU
1842	—	225	350	525	1,300	—
1845	—	225	350	525	1,300	—
1847	—	225	350	525	1,300	—
1848	—	225	350	525	1,300	—
1850	—	225	350	525	1,300	—
1851	—	225	350	525	1,300	—
1852	—	225	350	600	1,300	—
1854	—	225	350	600	1,300	—
1856	—	225	350	600	1,300	—

C# 128 15 DUCATI
18.9300 g., 0.9960 Gold .6062 oz. AGW **Ruler:** Ferdinando IV as King of the Two Sicilies **Obv:** Crowned head left **Obv. Legend:** FERDINANDVS I.D.G.REGNI.... **Rev:** Genius, without wings, flanked by shield and small crowned pillar **Rev. Legend:** HISPANIARVN....

Date	Mintage	VG	F	VF	XF	Unc
1818	—	300	550	850	1,750	—

C# 140 15 DUCATI
18.9300 g., 0.9960 Gold .6062 oz. AGW **Ruler:** Francesco I **Obv:** Head right, with beard **Obv. Legend:** FRANCISVS I... **Rev:** Genius, without wings, flanked by shield and small crowned pillar **Rev. Legend:** REGNI VTR...

Date	Mintage	F	VF	XF	Unc	BU
1825 Rare	—	—	—	—	—	—

Note: Bowers and Merena Guia sale 3-88 XF realized $26,400

C# 156 15 DUCATI
18.9300 g., 0.9960 Gold .6062 oz. AGW **Ruler:** Ferdinand II **Obv:** Head right **Obv. Legend:** FERDINANDVS II.... **Rev:** Genius, without wings, flanked by shield and small crowned pillar **Rev. Legend:** REGNI VTR...

Date	Mintage	F	VF	XF	Unc	BU
1831	—	500	800	1,250	2,750	—

C# 156c 15 DUCATI
18.9300 g., 0.9960 Gold .6062 oz. AGW **Ruler:** Ferdinand II **Obv:** Head right, with beard **Obv. Legend:** FERDINANDVS II.... **Rev:** Winged genius flanked by shield and small crowned pillar **Rev. Legend:** REGNI VTR...

Date	Mintage	F	VF	XF	Unc	BU
1842	—	500	800	1,250	2,750	—
1844	—	475	700	1,000	2,000	—
1845	—	475	700	1,000	2,000	—
1847	—	475	700	1,000	2,000	—

C# 156d 15 DUCATI
18.9300 g., 0.9960 Gold .6062 oz. AGW **Ruler:** Ferdinand II **Obv:** Head right, with beard **Obv. Legend:** FERDINANDVS II... **Rev:** Winged genius flanked by shield and small crowned pillar **Rev. Legend:** REGNI VTR...

Date	Mintage	F	VF	XF	Unc	BU
1848	—	500	800	1,250	2,750	—
1850	—	450	675	800	1,750	—
1851	—	450	675	800	1,750	—
1852	—	450	675	800	1,750	—
1854	—	450	675	800	1,750	—
1856	—	450	675	800	1,750	—

C# 129 30 DUCATI
37.8700 g., 0.9960 Gold 1.2128 oz. AGW **Ruler:** Ferdinando IV as King of the Two Sicilies **Obv:** Crowned head left **Obv. Legend:** FERDINANDVS I.D.G. REGNI.... **Rev:** Genius, without wings, flanked by shield and small crowned pillar

Date	Mintage	VG	F	VF	XF	Unc
1818	—	850	1,200	2,000	3,000	—

C# 141 30 DUCATI
37.8700 g., 0.9960 Gold 1.2128 oz. AGW **Ruler:** Francesco I **Obv:** Head right, with beard **Obv. Legend:** FRANCISVS I.... **Rev:** Genius, without wings, flanked by shield and small crowned pillar **Rev. Legend:** REGNI VTR...

Date	Mintage	VG	F	VF	XF	Unc
1825	—	850	1,200	2,250	4,000	—
1826	—	850	1,200	2,250	4,000	—

C# 157 30 DUCATI
37.8700 g., 0.9960 Gold 1.2128 oz. AGW **Ruler:** Ferdinand II **Obv:** Head right **Obv. Legend:** FERDINANDVS II... **Rev:** Genius, without wings, flanked by shield and small crowned pillar **Rev. Legend:** REGNI VTR...

Date	Mintage	F	VF	XF	Unc	BU
1831	—	850	1,200	2,000	3,600	—
1833	—	850	1,200	2,150	3,750	—
1835	—	850	1,200	2,150	3,750	—

C# 157b 30 DUCATI
37.8700 g., 0.9960 Gold 1.2128 oz. AGW **Ruler:** Ferdinand II **Obv:** Head right, with beard **Obv. Legend:** FERDINANDVS II.... **Rev:** Genius, without wings, flanked by shield and small crowned pillar **Rev. Legend:** REGNI VTR...

Date	Mintage	F	VF	XF	Unc	BU
1839	—	850	1,200	2,150	3,750	—
1840	—	850	1,200	2,150	3,750	—

436 ITALIAN STATES

NAPLES & SICILY

C# 157c 30 DUCATI
37.8700 g., 0.9960 Gold 1.2128 oz. AGW **Ruler:** Ferdinand II **Obv:** Head right, with beard **Obv. Legend:** FERDINANDVS II.... **Rev:** Winged genius flanked by shield and small crowned pillar **Rev. Legend:** REGNI VTR...

Date	Mintage	F	VF	XF	Unc	BU
1842 Rare	—	—	—	—	—	—
1844	—	850	1,200	2,150	3,750	—
1845	—	850	1,200	2,150	3,750	—
1847	—	850	1,200	2,150	3,750	—
1848	—	850	1,200	2,150	3,750	—
1851	—	850	1,200	2,150	3,750	—
1854	—	850	1,200	2,150	3,750	—

C# 157e 30 DUCATI
37.8700 g., 0.9960 Gold 1.2128 oz. AGW **Ruler:** Ferdinand II **Obv:** Head right, with beard **Obv. Legend:** FERDINANDVS II.... **Rev:** Winged genius flanked by shield and small crowned pillar **Rev. Legend:** REGNI VTR....

Date	Mintage	F	VF	XF	Unc	BU
1850	—	850	1,200	2,000	3,000	—
1851	—	850	1,200	2,150	3,750	—
1852	—	850	1,200	2,150	3,750	—

C# 157d 30 DUCATI
37.8700 g., 0.9960 Gold 1.2128 oz. AGW **Ruler:** Ferdinand II **Obv:** Head right, with beard **Obv. Legend:** FERDINANDVS II.... **Rev:** Winged genius flanked by shield and small crowned pillar **Rev. Legend:** REGNI VTR...

Date	Mintage	F	VF	XF	Unc	BU
1854	—	850	1,200	2,150	3,750	—
1856	—	850	1,200	2,150	3,750	—

PATTERNS
Including off metal strikes

KM#	Date	Mintage	Identification	Mkt Val
Pn1	1856	—	60 Grana. Gold. C#152.	4,400

PAPAL STATES

During many centuries prior to the formation of the unified Kingdom of Italy, when Italy was divided into numerous independent papal and ducal states, the Popes held temporal sovereignty over an area in central Italy comprising some 17,000 sq. mi. (44,030 sq. km.) including the city of Rome. At the time of the general unification of Italy under the Kingdom of Sardinia, 1861, the papal dominions beyond Rome were acquired by that kingdom diminishing the Pope's sovereignty to Rome and its environs. In 1870, while France's opposition to papal dispossession was neutralized by its war with Prussia, the Italian army seized weakly defended Rome and made it the capital of Italy, thereby abrogating the last vestige of papal temporal power. In 1871, the Italian Parliament enacted the Law of Guarantees, which guaranteed a special status for the Vatican area, and spiritual freedom and a generous income for the Pope. Pope Pius IX and his successors adamantly refused to acknowledge the validity of these laws and voluntarily "imprisoned" themselves in the Vatican. The impasse between State and Church lasted until the signing of the Lateran Treaty, Feb. 11, 1929, by which Italy recognized the sovereignty and independence of the new Vatican City state.

PONTIFFS
Pius VII, 1800-1823
Sede Vacante, Aug. 20-Sept. 28, 1823
Leo XII, 1823-1829
Sede Vacante, Feb. 10-Mar. 31, 1829
Pius VIII, 1829-1830
Sede Vacante, Nov. 30, 1830-Feb. 2, 1831
Gregory XVI, 1831-1846
Sede Vacante, June 1-16, 1846
Pius IX, 1846-1878
Leo XIII, 1878-1903
St. Pius X, 1903-1914
Benedict XV, 1914-1922

MINT MARKS
B - Bologna
R – Rome

MONETARY SYSTEM
(Until 1860)
5 Quattrini = 1 Baiocco
5 Baiocchi = 1 Grosso
6 Grossi = 4 Carlini = 3 Giulio =
3 Paoli = 1 Testone.
14 Carlini = 1 Piastre
100 Baiocchi = 1 Scudo
10 Testone = Doppia

PAPACY
STANDARD COINAGE

KM# 1358 SCUDO
1.7330 g., 0.9000 Gold .0501 oz. AGW, 14.4 mm. **Ruler:** Pius IX **Obv:** Bust left **Obv. Legend:** PIVS.IX.PON.... **Rev:** Value and date within wreath

Date	Mintage	F	VF	XF	Unc	BU
1853-VIIIB	3,306	70.00	150	200	500	—
1853-VIIIR	209,000	50.00	120	150	200	—
1854-VIIIB	5,539	65.00	150	200	500	—
1854-VIIIR	97,000	50.00	120	150	200	—
1854-IXR	Inc. above	50.00	120	150	200	—
1857-XIIR	16,000	75.00	150	225	500	—

KM# 1361 SCUDO
1.7330 g., 0.9000 Gold .0501 oz. AGW, 16.3 mm. **Ruler:** Pius IX **Obv:** Bust left **Obv. Legend:** PIVS.IX.PONT.... **Rev:** Value and date within wreath

Date	Mintage	F	VF	XF	Unc	BU
1858-XIIR	359,000	50.00	120	150	200	—
1858-XIIIR	Inc. above	50.00	120	150	200	—
1859-XIIIR	103,000	50.00	120	150	200	—
1861-XVR	84,000	50.00	120	150	200	—
1861-XVIR	Inc. above	50.00	120	150	200	—
1862-XVIR	226,000	50.00	120	150	200	—
1862-XVIIR	Inc. above	50.00	120	150	200	—
1863-XVIIR	149,000	50.00	120	150	200	—
1863-XVIIIR	Inc. above	50.00	120	150	200	—
1864-XIXR	5,735	75.00	150	225	500	—
1865-XIXR	21,000	50.00	110	150	200	—

KM# 1088 2 ZECCHINI
6.9040 g., 0.9980 Gold .2215 oz. AGW **Ruler:** Leo XII **Obv:** Legend around Papal arms **Obv. Legend:** LEO XII P.... **Rev:** Seated female left, cross at right **Rev. Legend:** POPVLIS.....

Date	Mintage	F	VF	XF	Unc	BU
1825-IIIR	—	500	900	1,500	3,000	—

KM# 1089 2 ZECCHINI
6.9040 g., 0.9980 Gold .2215 oz. AGW **Ruler:** Leo XII **Obv:** Bust left **Obv. Legend:** LEO.XII.PON.... **Rev:** Standing female with cross, lamb on top of small pillar at right **Rev. Legend:** SVPRA . FIR....

Date	Mintage	F	VF	XF	Unc	BU
1828-VR	—	500	900	1,500	3,000	—

KM# 1106 2-1/2 SCUDI
4.3340 g., 0.9000 Gold .1254 oz. AGW **Ruler:** Gregory XVI

Date	Mintage	F	VF	XF	Unc	BU
1835-VB	—	175	275	375	550	—
1835-VR	—	175	275	375	550	—
1836-VB	—	175	275	375	550	—
1836-VIB	—	150	250	325	450	—
1836-VIR	—	175	275	375	550	—
1837-VIIR	—	175	275	375	550	—
1839-IXR	—	175	275	375	550	—
1840-XB	—	150	250	325	450	—
1841-XIR	—	175	275	375	550	—
1842-XIIB	—	150	250	325	450	—
1842-XIIR	—	225	325	450	650	—
1843-XIIIB	—	175	275	325	450	—
1844-XIIIB	—	175	275	375	550	—
1845-XVB	—	275	500	750	1,000	—
1845-XVR	—	175	275	375	550	—
1846-XVIB	—	150	250	325	450	—

KM# 1117 2-1/2 SCUDI
4.3340 g., 0.9000 Gold .1254 oz. AGW **Ruler:** Pius IX **Obv:** Bust left **Obv. Legend:** PIVS.IX.PON... **Rev:** Value and date within wreath

Date	Mintage	F	VF	XF	Unc	BU
1848-IIR	3,197	200	300	400	600	—
1853-VIIR	117,000	150	200	300	400	—
1853-VIIIR	Inc. above	150	200	300	400	—
1854-VIIIR	276,000	125	175	275	375	—
1854-IXB	32,000	125	175	275	375	—
1854-IXR	Inc. above	125	175	275	375	—
1855-IXR	59,000	125	175	275	375	—
1855-XR	Inc. above	125	175	275	375	—
1856-XB	8,040	150	200	300	400	—
1856-XR	104,000	125	175	275	375	—
1856-XIR	Inc. above	125	175	275	375	—
1857-XR	—	150	200	300	400	—
1857-XIR	—	200	300	400	600	—
1857-XIIB	6,284	200	300	400	600	—
1857-XIIR	—	135	200	285	385	—
1858-XIIR	—	135	200	285	385	—
1858-XIIIB	2,787	200	300	400	600	—
1858-XIIIR	—	135	200	285	385	—
1859-XIIIB	66,000	150	200	300	400	—
1859-XIIIR	—	125	175	275	375	—
1859-XIVR	—	125	175	275	375	—
1860-XIVR	—	125	175	275	375	—
1860-XVR	—	125	175	275	375	—
1861-XVR	—	125	175	275	375	—
1861-XVIR	—	125	175	275	375	—
1862-XVIR	—	125	175	275	375	—
1862-XVIIR	—	125	175	275	375	—
1863-XVIIR	—	125	175	275	375	—

KM# 1105 5 SCUDI
8.6680 g., 0.9000 Gold .2508 oz. AGW **Ruler:** Gregory XVI **Obv:** Legend around bust left **Obv. Legend:** GREGORIVS.XVI.... **Rev:** Legend around standing figures facing **Rev. Legend:** PRINCEPRS...

Date	Mintage	F	VF	XF	Unc	BU
1834-IVR Rare	—	—	—	—	—	—

Note: Bowers and Merena Guia sale 3-88 XF (cleaned) realized $12,650

KM# 1107 5 SCUDI
8.6680 g., 0.9000 Gold .2508 oz. AGW **Ruler:** Gregory XVI **Obv:** Bust left **Obv. Legend:** GREGORIVS.XVI... **Rev:** Value and date within wreath

Date	Mintage	F	VF	XF	Unc	BU
1835-VB	—	325	525	700	950	—
1835-VR	—	325	525	700	950	—
1836-VIR	—	325	525	700	950	—
1837-VIR	—	450	700	900	1,500	—
1837-VIIR	—	325	525	700	950	—
1838-VIIR	—	325	525	700	950	—
1838-VIIIR	—	325	525	700	950	—
1839-VIIIR	—	400	600	800	1,200	—

PAPAL STATES — ITALIAN STATES

Date	Mintage	F	VF	XF	Unc	BU
1839-IXR	—	400	600	800	1,200	—
1840-IXR	—	450	700	900	1,500	—
1841-XIB	—	450	700	900	1,500	—
1841-XIR	—	325	525	700	950	—
1842-XIIB	—	325	525	700	950	—
1842-XIIR	—	325	525	700	950	—
1843-XIIIB	—	450	700	900	1,500	—
1843-XIIIR	—	325	525	700	950	—
1845-XVR	—	325	525	700	950	—
1846-XVIR	—	325	525	700	950	—

KM# 1116 5 SCUDI
8.6680 g., 0.9000 Gold .2508 oz. AGW **Ruler:** Pius IX **Obv:** Bust left **Obv. Legend:** PIVS.IX.PONT.... **Rev:** Value and date within wreath

Date	Mintage	F	VF	XF	Unc	BU
1846-IB	11,000	325	525	700	950	—
1846-IR	5,755	400	600	800	1,200	—
1847-IIR	1,399	450	700	900	1,350	—
1848-IIIR	1,633	425	600	850	1,200	—
1850-IVR	6,473	400	700	850	1,200	—
1854-IXR	104,000	325	525	700	950	—

KM# 1115 5 SCUDI
8.6680 g., 0.9000 Gold .2508 oz. AGW **Obv:** Cardinal arms **Obv. Legend:** SEDE VACANTE.... **Rev:** Radiant dove above value **Rev. Legend:** PON RELINQVAM.... **Note:** Sede Vacante issue.

Date	Mintage	F	VF	XF	Unc	BU
1846R	—	800	1,300	1,800	2,500	—

KM# 1108 10 SCUDI
17.3360 g., 0.9000 Gold .5016 oz. AGW **Ruler:** Gregory XVI **Obv:** Bust left **Obv. Legend:** GREGORIVS.XVI.... **Rev:** Value and date within wreath

Date	Mintage	F	VF	XF	Unc	BU
1835-VB	—	450	700	950	1,500	—
1835-VR	—	375	625	800	1,150	—
1836-VR	—	375	625	800	1,150	—
1836-VB	—	375	625	800	1,150	—
1836-VIR	—	400	675	950	1,400	—
1837-VIR	—	400	675	950	1,400	—
1837-VIIR	—	375	625	800	1,250	—
1838-VIIR	—	375	625	800	1,250	—
1838-VIIIR	—	375	695	800	1,250	—
1839-VIIIR	—	375	625	800	1,250	—
1839-IXR	—	400	675	950	1,400	—
1840-XB	—	400	675	950	1,400	—
1840-XR	—	375	625	800	1,250	—
1841-XR	—	375	625	800	1,250	—
1841-XIB	—	325	625	800	1,250	—
1841-XIR	—	375	625	800	1,250	—
1842-XIR	—	275	625	800	1,250	—
1842-XIIB	—	375	625	800	1,250	—
1842-XIIR	—	375	625	800	1,250	—
1843-XIIIR	—	400	675	950	1,400	—
1844-XIVR	—	400	675	950	1,400	—
1845-XVB	—	375	625	800	1,250	—
1845-XVR	—	450	700	950	1,500	—

KM# 1125 10 SCUDI
17.3360 g., 0.9000 Gold .5016 oz. AGW **Ruler:** Pius IX **Obv:** Bust left **Obv. Legend:** PIVS.IX.PONT.... **Rev:** Value and date within wreath

Date	Mintage	F	VF	XF	Unc	BU
1850-IVR	5,875	650	1,250	1,750	2,750	—
1850-VR	Inc. above	500	1,100	1,550	2,500	—
1856-XIR	2,483	650	1,250	1,750	2,750	—

KM# 1070 DOPPIA
5.4690 g., 0.9170 Gold .1612 oz. AGW **Ruler:** Pius VII **Obv:** Papal arms **Obv. Legend:** PIVS VII.... **Rev:** Seated Saint in clouds, facing **Rev. Legend:** APOSTOLOR....

Date	Mintage	F	VF	XF	Unc	BU
II (1801)R	—	150	250	350	600	—
III (1802)R	—	150	250	350	600	—
IV (1803)R	—	150	250	350	600	—
V (1804)R	—	150	250	350	600	—
VIII (1807)R	—	150	250	350	600	—
X (1809)R	—	300	400	500	750	—

KM# 1077 DOPPIA
5.4690 g., 0.9170 Gold .1612 oz. AGW **Ruler:** Pius VII **Obv:** Papal arms **Obv. Legend:** PIVS.VII.... **Rev:** Seated Saint in clouds, facing **Rev. Legend:** PRINCEPS....

Date	Mintage	F	VF	XF	Unc	BU
XVI (1815)B	—	300	400	600	1,100	—
XVII (1816)B	—	275	325	500	900	—
XXI (1820)B	—	300	400	600	1,000	—
XXII (1829-30)B	—	275	375	500	900	—

KM# 1076 DOPPIA
5.4690 g., 0.9170 Gold .1612 oz. AGW **Ruler:** Pius VII **Obv:** Papal arms **Obv. Legend:** PIVS VII.... **Rev:** Seated Saint in clouds, facing **Rev. Legend:** APOSTOLQRUM... **Note:** Modified design.

Date	Mintage	F	VF	XF	Unc	BU
XVI (1815)R	—	300	400	525	800	—
XVIII (1817)R	—	300	400	525	800	—
XXIV (1823)R	—	300	400	525	800	—

KM# 1087 DOPPIA
5.4690 g., 0.9170 Gold .1612 oz. AGW **Ruler:** Leo XII **Obv:** Papal arms **Obv. Legend:** LEO XII... **Rev:** Seated Saint in clouds, facing **Rev. Legend:** PRINCRES...

Date	Mintage	F	VF	XF	Unc	BU
I (1823)R	—	300	400	525	800	—
II (1824)B	—	300	400	525	800	—
II (1824)R	—	300	400	525	800	—

KM# 1086 DOPPIA
5.4690 g., 0.9170 Gold .1612 oz. AGW **Obv:** Cardinal arms **Obv. Legend:** SEDE VACANTE.... **Rev:** Seated Saint in clouds, facing **Rev. Legend:** PRINCEPS.... **Note:** Sede Vacante issue.

Date	Mintage	F	VF	XF	Unc	BU
1823B	—	325	450	600	1,250	—
1823R	—	325	450	600	1,250	—

KM# 1090 DOPPIA
5.4690 g., 0.9170 Gold .1612 oz. AGW **Obv:** Cardinal arms **Obv. Legend:** SEDE VACANTE.... **Rev:** Seated Saint in clouds, facing **Rev. Legend:** PRINCEPS.... **Note:** Sede Vacante issue.

Date	Mintage	F	VF	XF	Unc	BU
1829B	—	325	450	750	1,500	—
1829R	—	325	450	750	1,500	—

KM# 1102 DOPPIA
5.4690 g., 0.9170 Gold .1612 oz. AGW **Obv:** Cardinal arms **Obv. Legend:** SEDE VACANTE.... **Rev:** Radiant dove above value **Rev. Legend:** VENI.LVMEN.... **Note:** Sede Vacante issue.

Date	Mintage	F	VF	XF	Unc	BU
1830R	—	425	650	1,000	1,800	—

KM# 1103 DOPPIA
5.4500 g., 0.9170 Gold .1606 oz. AGW **Ruler:** Gregory XVI **Obv:** Legend around bust left **Obv. Legend:** GREGORIVS.XVI.PONT.... **Rev:** Seated Saint facing above value **Rev. Legend:** YV.REM.TVERE...

Date	Mintage	F	VF	XF	Unc	BU
1833-IIIR	—	425	650	1,000	1,800	—
1834-IIIB	—	325	450	750	1,500	—

DECIMAL COINAGE
5 Centesimi = 1 Soldi; 20 Soldi = 1 Lira

KM# 1380 5 LIRE
1.6120 g., 0.9000 Gold .0466 oz. AGW **Ruler:** Pius IX **Obv:** Bust left **Obv. Legend:** PIVSIXPON... **Rev:** Value and date within wreath **Rev. Legend:** STATO * PONTIFICIO *

Date	Mintage	F	VF	XF	Unc	BU
1866-XXIR	3,230	225	375	550	900	—
1867-XXIIR	3,787	250	400	700	1,200	—

KM# 1381.1 10 LIRE
3.2250 g., 0.9000 Gold .0933 oz. AGW **Ruler:** Pius IX **Obv:** Bust left **Obv. Legend:** PIUS IX PONT. MAX. A...

Date	Mintage	F	VF	XF	Unc	BU
1866-XXIR	8,579	300	500	850	1,000	—

KM# 1381.2 10 LIRE
3.2250 g., 0.9000 Gold .0933 oz. AGW **Ruler:** Pius IX **Obv:** Bust left **Obv. Legend:** PIUS IX PON. MAX. A... **Rev:** Value and date within wreath **Rev. Legend:** STATO * PONTIFICIO *

ITALIAN STATES

PAPAL STATES

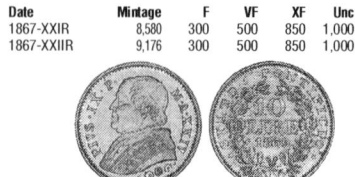

Date	Mintage	F	VF	XF	Unc	BU
1867-XXIR	8,580	300	500	850	1,000	—
1867-XXIIR	9,176	300	500	850	1,000	—

KM# 1381.3 10 LIRE
3.2250 g., 0.9000 Gold .0933 oz. AGW **Ruler:** Pius IX **Obv:** Bust left **Obv. Legend:** PIUS IX P. M. A.... **Rev:** Value and date within wreath **Rev. Legend:** STATO * PONTIFICIO *

Date	Mintage	F	VF	XF	Unc	BU
1869-XXIVR	5,944	350	600	950	1,250	—

KM# 1382.1 20 LIRE
6.4510 g., 0.9000 Gold .1866 oz. AGW **Ruler:** Pius IX **Obv:** Bust left **Obv. Legend:** PIVS IX PON.... **Rev:** Value and date within wreath **Rev. Legend:** STATO * PONTIFICIO * **Edge:** Plain

Date	Mintage	F	VF	XF	Unc	BU
1866-XXR	945	900	1,500	2,500	5,500	—

KM# 1382.2 20 LIRE
6.4510 g., 0.9000 Gold .1866 oz. AGW **Ruler:** Pius IX **Obv:** Bust left **Edge:** Reeded

Date	Mintage	F	VF	XF	Unc	BU
1866-XXR	22,000	450	750	1,000	1,500	—
1866-XXIR	102,000	275	400	600	1,000	—
1867-XXIR	44,000	300	500	850	1,250	—

KM# 1382.3 20 LIRE
6.4510 g., 0.9000 Gold .1866 oz. AGW **Ruler:** Pius IX **Obv:** Bust left **Obv. Legend:** PIVSIXPON.... **Rev:** Value and date within wreath **Rev. Legend:** STATO * PONTIFICIO *

Date	Mintage	F	VF	XF	Unc	BU
1867-XXIIR	57,000	275	400	600	1,000	—
1868-XXIIR	38,000	300	500	850	1,250	—
1868-XXIIIR	Inc. above	450	750	1,000	1,500	—

KM# 1382.4 20 LIRE
6.4510 g., 0.9000 Gold .1866 oz. AGW **Ruler:** Pius IX **Obv:** Bust left **Obv. Legend:** PIVS.IX.PON....

Date	Mintage	F	VF	XF	Unc	BU
1868-XXIIIR	112,000	275	400	600	1,000	—
1869-XXIIIR	54,000	275	400	600	1,000	—
1869-XXIVR	76,000	275	400	600	1,000	—
1870-XXIVR	24,000	350	450	650	1,250	—
1870-XXVR	27,000	300	500	850	1,250	—

KM# 1388 50 LIRE
16.1290 g., 0.9000 Gold .4667 oz. AGW **Ruler:** Pius IX **Obv:** Bust left **Obv. Legend:** PIVS IX PONT.... **Rev:** Value and date within wreath **Rev. Legend:** STATO PONTIFICIO

Date	Mintage	F	VF	XF	Unc	BU
1868-XXIIR	1,172	750	850	2,000	4,000	—
1868-XXIIIR	257	2,300	4,000	6,000	8,000	—
1870-XXIVR	1,460	750	850	2,000	4,000	—

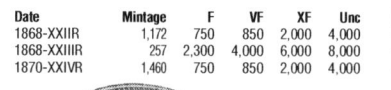

KM# 1383 100 LIRE
32.2580 g., 0.9000 Gold .9335 oz. AGW **Ruler:** Pius IX **Obv:** Bust left **Obv. Legend:** PIVS IX PONT... **Rev:** Value and date within wreath **Rev. Legend:** STATO PONTIFICIO

Date	Mintage	F	VF	XF	Unc	BU
1866-XXIR	1,117	900	1,000	2,500	4,750	—
1868-XXIIIR	545	2,000	2,750	4,500	6,500	—
1869-XXIIIR	625	2,000	2,750	4,500	6,500	—
1869-XXIVR	450	2,500	4,500	7,500	10,000	—

PATTERNS
Including off metal strikes

KM#	Date	Mintage	Identification	Mkt Val
Pn2	1834R	—	5 Scudi. Silver. 17.6000 g. Klippe.	800

PARMA

A town in Emilia, which was a papal possession from 1512 to 1545, was seized by France in 1796, and was attached to the Napoleonic Empire in 1808. In 1814, Parma was assigned to Marie Louise, empress of Napoleon I. It was annexed to Sardinia in 1860.

RULERS
Ferdinando di Borbone, 1765-1802
Maria Luigia, Duchess, 1815-1847
Carlo II di Borbone, 1847-1849
Carlo III di Borbone, 1849-1854
Roberto di Borbone, 1854-1858

MONETARY SYSTEM
Until 1802
12 Denari = 2 Sesini = 1 Soldo
20 Soldi = 1 Lira
7 Lire = 1 Ducato

CITY
REFORM COINAGE
100 Centesimi = 20 Soldi = 1 Lira

C# 31 20 LIRE
6.4500 g., 0.9000 Gold .1866 oz. AGW **Ruler:** Maria Luigia

Date	Mintage	F	VF	XF	Unc	BU
1815	12,000	400	700	1,200	2,000	—
1832	1,000	1,800	3,000	4,500	7,000	—

C# 32 40 LIRE
12.9000 g., 0.9000 Gold .3733 oz. AGW **Ruler:** Maria Luigia **Obv:** Crowned head left **Obv. Legend:** MARIA LUIGIA.... **Rev:** Crowned mantled shield above value **Rev. Legend:** PER. LA GR...

Date	Mintage	F	VF	XF	Unc	BU
1815	220,000	245	300	375	700	—
1821	37,000	265	400	600	1,400	—

PIEDMONT REPUBLIC

Established by Napoleon in 1798 in the Piedmont area of northwest Italy. It was the mainland possession of the kingdom of Sardinia. The republic was overthrown by Austro-Russian forces in 1799.

REPUBLIC
STANDARD COINAGE

C# 5 20 FRANCS
6.4500 g., 0.9000 Gold .1866 oz. AGW **Obv:** Laureate bust left **Obv. Legend:** L'ITALIE DELIVREE.... **Rev:** Value within wreath **Rev. Legend:** LIBERTE' EGALITE...

Date	Mintage	Good	VG	F	VF	XF
L'AN 10 (1801)	1,492	—	300	550	1,000	1,500

SARDINIA

Sardinia is an island located in the Mediterranean Sea, west of the southern Italian peninsula, 9,301 sq. mi.; population 1,645,192. Along with some minor islands, it constitutes an autonomous region of Italy separated on the north from Corsica, France by the Strait of Bonifacio.

Settled by Phoenicians and Greeks before it came under control of Carthage during 600 BC; taken by the Romans in 238 BC; in the Vandal Kingdom during the 5th century; re-conquered by the Byzantine Empire in 533 AD. From the 8th century it was frequently raided by Muslims whose threat was eliminated by Pisa in 1016 as an object of a competitor's bet. The Genoese and Pisans were driven out by the Aragonese during the 14th-15th centuries, remaining under Spanish rule until 1708; held by Austria 1708-17, regained by the Spanish in 1717 until it was finally ceded to Savoy in 1720 in exchange for Sicily, after which the ruler of Savoy and Piedmont took the title as King of Sardinia.

RULERS
Carlo Emanuele IV 1796-1802
Vittorio Emanuele I 1802-1821
Carlo Felice 1821-1831
Carlo Alberto 1831-1849
Vittorio Emanuele II 1849-1878

MINT MARKS
None Before 1802 = Turin (Torino)
Firenze = Florence
B = Bologna
(g) Anchor = Genoa
M = Milan
(t) after 1802 - Eagles head = Turin (Torino)

MINTMASTER'S INITIALS
P – Pietro Perrinet, 1640-42

MINTMASTERS' MARKS
P in oval = Andrea O Luca Podesta
L in diamond = Felippo Lavy
P in shield = Giovanni Parodi
B in shield = Tommaso Battilana

MONETARY SYSTEM
12 Denari = 6 Cagliarese = 1 Soldo
50 Soldi = 10 Reales = 2 1/2 Lire = 1 Scudo Sardo
20 Soldi = 1 Lira
6 Lire = 1 Scudo
2 Scudi Sardi = 1 Doppietta
Commencing 1816
100 Centesimi = 1 Lira

KINGDOM
MAINLAND COINAGE

C# 94 DOPPIA
9.1160 g., 0.9050 Gold .2652 oz. AGW **Ruler:** Vittorio Emanuele I **Obv:** Head left **Obv. Legend:** VICTORIVS EMANVEL. **Rev:** Crowned displayed eagle with shield on breast **Rev. Legend:** D. G. REX. SAR...

Date	Mintage	VG	F	VF	XF	Unc
1814	—	2,000	4,000	8,500	12,000	—

SARDINIA ITALIAN STATES

C# 94a DOPPIA
9.1160 g., 0.9050 Gold .2652 oz. AGW. **Ruler:** Vittorio Emanuele I **Obv:** Head left **Obv. Legend:** VIC. EM. D. G. REX. SAR... **Rev:** Crowned displayed eagle with shield on breast **Rev. Legend:** MONTISF. PR. PED. & ...

Date	Mintage	VG	F	VF	XF	Unc
1815	—	—	—	13,000	15,000	—

Note: Superior Pipito sale 12-87 choice VF realized $13,750;Stack's International sale 3-88 XF realized $11,550

MAINLAND REFORM COINAGE

C# 114.1 10 LIRE
3.2200 g., 0.9000 Gold .0931 oz. AGW. **Ruler:** Carlo Alberto **Obv:** Head left **Obv. Legend:** CAR.ALBERTVS.... **Rev:** Crowned shield within wreath **Rev. Legend:** DVX SAB.... **Note:** Mint mark: Eagle head.

Date	Mintage	F	VF	XF	Unc	BU
1832 P Rare	—	—	—	—	—	—
1833 P	5,004	125	300	450	1,000	—
1835 P	5,118	225	375	550	1,200	—
1838 P	2,826	250	400	575	1,250	—
1839 P	2,237	175	350	500	1,100	—
1841 P	1,583	175	350	500	1,100	—
1842 P	759	250	475	650	1,800	—
1843 P	950	250	475	650	1,800	—
1845 P	3,009	225	450	600	1,500	—
1846 P	970	250	475	650	1,800	—
1847 P	405	250	500	750	2,100	—

C# 114.2 10 LIRE
3.2200 g., 0.9000 Gold .0931 oz. AGW. **Ruler:** Carlo Alberto **Note:** Mint mark: Anchor.

Date	Mintage	F	VF	XF	Unc	BU
1833 P	1,550	225	425	850	1,350	—
1835 P Rare	—	—	—	—	—	—
1841 P	2,809	225	425	850	1,250	—
1843 P	4,566	225	425	850	1,250	—
1844 P	11,000	175	325	450	1,000	—
1845 P	1,535	225	425	850	1,250	—
1846 P	3,373	225	425	850	1,250	—
1847 P Rare	—	—	—	—	—	—

C# 125.1 10 LIRE
3.2200 g., 0.9000 Gold .0931 oz. AGW. **Ruler:** Vittorio Emanuele II

Date	Mintage	F	VF	XF	Unc	BU
1850 P	4,141	300	750	1,250	1,800	—
1853 P	600	—	—	—	—	—

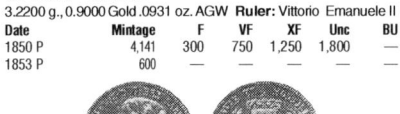

C# 125.2 10 LIRE
3.2200 g., 0.9000 Gold .0931 oz. AGW. **Ruler:** Vittorio Emanuele II **Obv:** Head left **Obv. Legend:** VICTORIVS.... **Rev:** Crowned shield within wreath **Rev. Legend:** DVX SAB.... **Note:** Mint mark: Eagle head.

Date	Mintage	F	VF	XF	Unc	BU
1850 B	2,326	225	400	600	1,000	—
1852 B	—	500	1,000	1,500	2,200	—
1853 B	—	225	400	600	1,000	—
1854 B	1,833	225	400	600	1,000	—
1855 B	2,566	225	400	600	1,000	—
1856 B	2,526	225	400	600	1,000	—
1857 B	7,193	225	400	600	1,000	—
1858 B	2,931	225	400	600	1,000	—
1859 B 1 known	—	—	—	7,040	—	—
1860 B	6,036	225	400	600	1,000	—

C# 95 20 LIRE
6.4500 g., 0.9000 Gold .1866 oz. AGW. **Ruler:** Vittorio Emanuele I **Obv:** Head left **Obv. Legend:** VIC.EM.D.G.REX...
Rev: Crowned shield divides circle and wreath **Rev. Legend:** DVXSAB.... **Note:** Mint mark: Eagle head.

Date	Mintage	F	VF	XF	Unc	BU
1816	19,000	225	350	450	750	—
1817	40,000	150	225	350	600	—
1818	35,000	150	225	350	600	—
1819	22,000	150	225	350	600	—
1820	33,000	150	225	350	600	—

C# 96 20 LIRE
6.4500 g., 0.9000 Gold .1866 oz. AGW. **Ruler:** Vittorio Emanuele I **Obv:** Head left **Obv. Legend:** VIC.EM.D.G.REX.... **Rev:** Crowned pointed shield flanked by sprigs **Rev. Legend:** DVXSAB....

Date	Mintage	F	VF	XF	Unc	BU
1821	—	1,500	2,500	3,750	6,000	—

C# 106.1 20 LIRE
6.4500 g., 0.9000 Gold .1866 oz. AGW. **Ruler:** Carlo Felice **Obv:** Head left **Obv. Legend:** CAR.FELIX D.G.REX... **Rev:** Crowned pointed shield within wreath **Rev. Legend:** DVX SAB GENVAE...

Date	Mintage	F	VF	XF	Unc	BU
1821 L	18,000	145	200	275	475	—
1822 L	7,460	145	200	325	500	—
1823 L	22,000	145	200	275	475	—
1824 L	2,381	200	275	375	650	—
1825 L	28,000	145	200	275	475	—
1826 L	144,000	145	185	250	475	—
1827 L	150,000	145	185	250	475	—
1828 L	95,000	145	185	250	475	—
1828 P	—	225	300	400	650	—
1829 L	61,000	225	300	400	650	—
1829 P	—	225	300	400	650	—
1830 L	—	225	300	400	650	—
1830 P	35,000	200	275	375	600	—
1831 P	42,000	145	200	275	475	—

C# 106.2 20 LIRE
6.4500 g., 0.9000 Gold .1866 oz. AGW. **Ruler:** Carlo Felice **Note:** Mint mark: Anchor.

Date	Mintage	F	VF	XF	Unc	BU
1824 P	2,394	375	500	600	850	—
1825 P	313	375	500	1,000	2,200	—
1827 P	1,766	225	300	400	500	—
1828 P Rare	—	—	—	—	—	—
1829 P	—	225	300	400	500	—
1830 P	3,270	375	500	600	800	—
1831 P Rare	16,189	—	—	—	—	—

C# 115.1 20 LIRE
6.4500 g., 0.9000 Gold .1866 oz. AGW. **Ruler:** Carlo Alberto **Obv:** Head left **Obv. Legend:** CAR.ALBERTVS D.G. REX... **Rev:** Crowned shield within wreath **Rev. Legend:** DVX SAB.GENVAE...

Date	Mintage	F	VF	XF	Unc	BU
1831 P	—	BV	125	140	265	—
1832 P	74,000	BV	125	140	265	—
1833 P Rare	80,000	—	—	—	—	—
1834 P	133,000	BV	125	140	265	—
1835 P	52,000	BV	125	140	265	—
1836 P	90,000	BV	125	140	265	—
1837 P Rare	56,000	—	—	—	—	—
1838 P	120,000	BV	125	140	265	—
1839 P Rare	74,000	—	—	—	—	—
1840 P	176,000	BV	125	140	265	—
1841 P	206,000	145	175	250	375	—
1842 P	66,000	BV	125	140	265	—
1843 P Rare	45,000	—	—	—	—	—
1844 P Rare	34,000	—	—	—	—	—
1845 P	43,000	BV	125	140	265	—
1846 P Rare	43,000	—	—	—	—	—
1847 P	52,000	BV	125	140	265	—
1848 P	59,000	125	150	175	300	—
1849 P	111,000	BV	125	140	250	—

C# 115.2 20 LIRE
6.4500 g., 0.9000 Gold .1866 oz. AGW. **Ruler:** Carlo Alberto **Note:** Mint mark: Eagle head.

Date	Mintage	F	VF	XF	Unc	BU
1831 P	—	BV	125	140	265	—
1832 P	53,000	BV	125	140	265	—
1833 P	16,000	BV	125	140	265	—
1834 P	261,000	BV	125	140	265	—
1836 P Rare	14,000	—	—	—	—	—
1837 P Rare	15,000	—	—	—	—	—
1838 P	31,000	BV	125	140	265	—
1839 P	70,000	BV	125	140	265	—
1840/30 P	28,000	BV	200	300	550	—
1840 P	Inc. above	BV	125	140	265	—
1841 P Rare	31,000	—	—	—	—	—
1842 P	26,000	BV	125	140	265	—
1843 P Rare	24,000	—	—	—	—	—
1844 P	30,000	BV	125	140	265	—
1845 P	35,000	BV	125	140	265	—
1846 P	30,000	BV	125	140	265	—
1847 P	33,000	BV	125	140	265	—
1848 P Rare	59,000	—	—	—	—	—
1849 P	58,000	BV	125	140	265	—

C# 115.3 20 LIRE
6.4500 g., 0.9000 Gold .1866 oz. AGW. **Ruler:** Carlo Alberto **Note:** Turin or Genoa.

Date	Mintage	F	VF	XF	Unc	BU
1834	—	BV	125	140	265	—
1847	—	BV	125	140	265	—

C# 126.1 20 LIRE
6.4500 g., 0.9000 Gold .1866 oz. AGW. **Ruler:** Vittorio Emanuele II **Obv:** Head left, with beard **Obv. Legend:** VICTORIVS... **Rev:** Crowned shield within wreath **Rev. Legend:** DVX SAB... **Note:** Mint mark: Anchor.

Date	Mintage	F	VF	XF	Unc	BU
1850 P	139,000	BV	125	140	245	—
1851 P	296,000	BV	125	140	245	—
1852 P	103,000	BV	125	140	245	—
1853 P	137,000	BV	125	140	245	—
1854 P	142,000	BV	125	140	245	—
1855 P	148,000	BV	125	140	245	—
1856 P	113,000	BV	125	140	245	—
1857 P	59,000	BV	125	140	245	—
1858 P	176,000	BV	125	140	245	—
1859 P	436,000	BV	125	140	245	—
1860 P	163,000	BV	125	140	245	—

C# 126.2 20 LIRE
6.4500 g., 0.9000 Gold .1866 oz. AGW. **Ruler:** Vittorio Emanuele II **Note:** Mint mark: Eagle head.

Date	Mintage	F	VF	XF	Unc	BU
1850 B	66,000	BV	125	140	245	—
1851 B	163,000	BV	125	140	245	—
1852 B	46,000	BV	125	140	245	—
1853 B	41,000	—	—	—	—	—
1855 B	41,000	BV	—	—	245	—
1855 B	—	—	BV	125	140	245

Note: Error: EMMANVEL H for II

1856 B	61,000	375	500	750	1,200	—
1857 B	67,000	BV	125	140	245	—
1858 B	103,000	150	250	400	600	—
1859 B	187,000	BV	125	140	245	—
1860 B	111,000	BV	150	175	375	—
1861 B	156,000	BV	150	175	375	—

C# 126.3 20 LIRE
6.4500 g., 0.9000 Gold .1866 oz. AGW. **Ruler:** Vittorio Emanuele II

Date	Mintage	F	VF	XF	Unc	BU
1860M	23,000	140	200	300	500	—

C# 107.1 40 LIRE
12.9000 g., 0.9000 Gold .3733 oz. AGW. **Ruler:** Carlo Felice **Obv:** Head left **Obv. Legend:** CAR.FELIX D.G.REX... **Rev:** Crowned shield within wreath **Rev. Legend:** DVX SAB.GENVAE... **Note:** Mint mark: Eagle head.

Date	Mintage	F	VF	XF	Unc	BU
1822 L	5,011	300	400	600	1,350	—
1823 L Rare	—	—	—	—	—	—
1825 L	39,000	245	275	325	750	—
1831 L	—	300	400	500	1,150	—
1831 P	7,711	300	400	500	1,150	—

C# 107.2 40 LIRE
12.9000 g., 0.9000 Gold .3733 oz. AGW. **Ruler:** Carlo Felice **Note:** Mint mark: Anchor.

Date	Mintage	F	VF	XF	Unc	BU
1825 P	3,994	300	400	600	1,400	—
1826 P	2,844	300	400	750	1,500	—

ITALIAN STATES

SARDINIA

C# 116.1 50 LIRE
16.1200 g., 0.9000 Gold .4664 oz. AGW **Ruler:** Carlo Alberto
Obv: Head left **Obv. Legend:** CAR.ALBERTVS D.G.REX... **Rev:** Crowned shield within wreath **Rev. Legend:** DVX SAB.GENVAE... **Note:** Mint mark: Eagle head.

Date	Mintage	F	VF	XF	Unc	BU
1832 P Rare	93	—	—	—	—	—
1833 P	1,773	750	1,000	1,500	2,500	—
1834 P Rare	657	—	—	—	—	—
1835 P Rare	1,296	—	—	—	—	—
1836 P	385	900	1,250	1,750	2,750	—
1838 P Rare	992	—	—	—	—	—
1839 P Rare	553	—	—	—	—	—
1840 P Rare	1,402	—	—	—	—	—
1841 P Rare	2,753	—	—	—	—	—
1843 P Rare	586	—	—	—	—	—

C# 116.2 50 LIRE
16.1200 g., 0.9000 Gold .4664 oz. AGW **Ruler:** Carlo Alberto
Note: Mint mark: Anchor.

Date	Mintage	F	VF	XF	Unc	BU
1833 P	92	4,000	5,000	6,500	9,000	—
1835 P Rare	—	—	—	—	—	—
1841 P Rare	562	—	—	—	—	—

C# 97 80 LIRE
25.8000 g., 0.9000 Gold .7466 oz. AGW **Ruler:** Vittorio Emanuele I **Obv:** Head left **Obv. Legend:** VIC.EM.D.G.REX... **Rev:** Crowned pointed shield within wreath **Rev. Legend:** DVX SAB.GENVAE... **Note:** Mint mark: Eagle head.

Date	Mintage	F	VF	XF	Unc	BU
1821	965	4,000	7,000	10,000	20,000	—

C# 108.1 80 LIRE
25.8000 g., 0.9000 Gold .7466 oz. AGW **Ruler:** Carlo Felice **Obv:** Head left **Obv. Legend:** CAR.FELIX D.G.REX... **Rev:** Crowned pointed shield within wreath **Rev. Legend:** DVX SAB.GENVAE... **Note:** Mint mark: Eagle head.

Date	Mintage	F	VF	XF	Unc	BU
1823 L Rare	—	—	—	—	—	—
1824 L	5,919	500	550	650	1,000	—
1825 L	14,000	485	525	600	900	—
1826 L	76,000	485	525	600	900	—
1827 L	38,000	485	525	600	900	—
1828 L	23,000	485	525	600	900	—
1828 P	Inc. above	600	750	1,000	1,500	—
1829 P	8,181	485	525	600	900	—
1830 P	5,972	485	525	600	900	—
1831 P	740	800	1,000	1,250	2,000	—

C# 108.2 80 LIRE
25.8000 g., 0.9000 Gold .7466 oz. AGW **Ruler:** Carlo Felice **Obv:** Head left **Obv. Legend:** CAR.FELIX D.G.REX... **Rev:** Crowned pointed shield within wreath **Rev. Legend:** DVX SAB.GENVAE ET... **Note:** Mint mark: Anchor.

Date	Mintage	F	VF	XF	Unc	BU
1824 P	3,904	525	700	900	1,500	—
1825 P	8,465	500	550	725	1,200	—
1826 P	2,305	700	900	1,100	1,750	—
1827 P	15,000	485	525	600	1,100	—
1828 P	8,961	485	525	600	1,100	—
1829 P	7,436	485	500	600	1,100	—
1830 P	26,000	500	550	725	1,200	—
1831 P	21,000	600	800	1,250	2,000	—

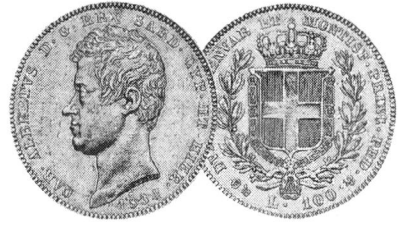

C# 117.1 100 LIRE
32.2500 g., 0.9000 Gold .9332 oz. AGW **Ruler:** Carlo Alberto **Obv:** Head left **Obv. Legend:** CAR.ALBERTVS.... **Rev:** Crowned shield within wreath **Rev. Legend:** DVX SAB.GENVAE ET.... **Note:** Mint mark: Anchor.

Date	Mintage	F	VF	XF	Unc	BU
1832 P	—	600	650	850	1,800	—
1833 P	2,587	625	700	800	1,750	—
1834 P	12,000	600	625	700	1,400	—
1835 P	8,513	600	650	850	1,500	—
1836 P	703	700	900	1,100	2,250	—
1837 P	250	800	1,100	1,350	2,750	—
1838 P Rare	4,774	—	—	—	—	—
1839 P Rare	2,922	—	—	—	—	—
1840 P	1,003	700	900	1,100	2,250	—
1841 P	8,889	600	650	850	1,750	—
1842 P	3,606	700	900	1,100	2,250	—
1843 P	424	1,500	2,000	2,500	4,000	—
1844 P	2,213	1,000	1,500	2,000	3,500	—
1845 P	646	1,000	1,500	2,000	3,500	—

C# 117.2 100 LIRE
32.2500 g., 0.9000 Gold .9332 oz. AGW **Ruler:** Carlo Alberto **Obv:** Head left **Obv. Legend:** CAR.ALBERTVS D.G. REX... **Rev:** Crowned shield within wreath **Rev. Legend:** DVX SAB.GENVAE ET... **Note:** Mint mark: Eagle head.

Date	Mintage	F	VF	XF	Unc	BU
1832 P	—	600	635	750	1,600	—
1833 P	6,769	600	635	750	1,600	—
1834 P	37,000	600	625	700	1,400	—
1835 P	26,000	600	625	700	1,400	—
1836 P	6,236	600	625	700	1,400	—
1837 P	3,885	600	635	750	1,600	—
1838 P Rare	3,916	—	—	—	—	—
1840 P	2,898	600	635	750	1,600	—
1841 P	1,207	700	1,000	1,300	2,000	—
1842 P	864	700	1,000	1,300	2,000	—
1843 P	827	700	900	1,150	2,250	—
1844 P Rare	91	—	—	—	—	—

TUSCANY

Etruria

An Italian territorial division on the west-central peninsula, belonged to the Medici from 1530 to 1737, when it was given to Francis, duke of Lorraine. In 1800 the French established it as part of the Spanish dominions; from 1807 to 1809 it was a French department. After the fall of Napoleon it reverted to its pre-Napoleonic owner, Ferdinand III.

RULERS
Ferdinando III, 1791-1801
Louis I, 1801-1803
Charles Louis, under regency of his
  mother Maria Louisa, 1803-1807
Annexed To France, 1807-1814
Ferdinando III, Restored, 1814-1824
Leopold II, 1824-1848, 1849-1859
Provisional Government, 1859
United to Italian Provisional Government, 1859-1861

MINT MARKS
FIRENZE - Florence
LEGHORN - Livorno
PISIS – Pisa

MONETARY SYSTEM
Until 1826
12 Denari = 3 Quattrini = 1 Soldo
20 Soldi = 1 Lira
10 Lire = 1 Dena
40 Quattrini = 1 Paolo
1-1/2 Paoli = 1 Lira
10 Paoli = 1 Francescone, Scudo, Tallero
3 Zecchini = 1 Ruspone = 40 Lire
1826-1859
100 Quattrini = 1 Fiorino
4 Fiorini = 10 Paoli
1859
100 Centesimi = 1 Lira

DUCHY

STANDARD COINAGE

C# 51 ZECCHINO
3.4900 g., 0.9980 Gold .1119 oz. AGW **Ruler:** Charles Louis under regency of his mother Maria Louisa **Obv:** St. Zenobio kneeling before Christ **Rev:** St. John **Note:** For Levant Trade.

Date	Mintage	F	VF	XF	Unc
ND(1805)	—	4,000	7,500	12,000	20,000

C# 60 ZECCHINO
3.4900 g., 0.9980 Gold .1119 oz. AGW **Ruler:** Ferdinando III, restored **Obv:** Fleur-de-lis **Obv. Legend:** FERDINANDVS III... **Rev:** Seated Saint, face left **Rev. Legend:** S. IOANNES...

Date	Mintage	VG	F	VF	XF	Unc
1816	—	200	300	500	1,100	—
1821	—	200	300	500	1,100	—

C# 76 ZECCHINO
3.4520 g., 0.9980 Gold .1107 oz. AGW **Ruler:** Leopold II **Obv:** Fleur-de-lis **Obv. Legend:** LEOPOLDVS II... **Rev:** Seated Saint, face left **Rev. Legend:** IOANNES...

Date	Mintage	VG	F	VF	XF	Unc
1824	—	150	250	400	850	—
1826	—	150	250	400	850	—
1829	—	150	250	400	850	—
1832	—	150	250	400	850	—
1853	—	150	250	400	850	—

C# 39 RUSPONE (3 Zecchini)
10.4610 g., 0.9990 Gold .3360 oz. AGW **Ruler:** Ferdinando III **Obv:** Fleur-de-lis **Obv. Legend:** FERDINANDVS • III •... **Rev:** St. John the Baptist, seated **Rev. Legend:** S • IOANNES BAPTISTA

Date	Mintage	VG	F	VF	XF	Unc
1801	—	400	800	1,250	2,000	—

C# 43 RUSPONE (3 Zecchini)
10.4110 g., 0.9980 Gold .3340 oz. AGW **Ruler:** Louis I **Obv:** Fleur-de-lis **Obv. Legend:** LUD. D. G... **Rev:** Seated Saint, face right

Date	Mintage	VG	F	VF	XF	Unc
1801	—	500	800	1,600	3,000	—
1803	—	400	650	1,200	2,000	—

ITALY 441

C# 52 RUSPONE (3 Zecchini)
10.4110 g., 0.9980 Gold .3340 oz. AGW **Ruler:** Charles Louis under regency of his mother Maria Louisa **Obv:** Fleur-de-lis **Obv. Legend:** CAROLUS.L.D.C.... **Rev:** Seated Saint, face right **Rev. Legend:** S. IOANNES...

Date	Mintage	VG	F	VF	XF	Unc
1803	—	375	600	800	1,250	—
1804	—	375	600	800	1,250	—
1805	—	300	400	650	1,000	—
1806	—	300	400	650	1,000	—
1807	—	300	400	650	1,000	—

C# 61 RUSPONE (3 Zecchini)
10.4110 g., 0.9980 Gold .3340 oz. AGW **Ruler:** Ferdinando III, restored **Obv:** Fleur-de-lis **Obv. Legend:** FERDINANDVS III... **Rev:** Seated Saint, face right **Rev. Legend:** S. IOANNES...

Date	Mintage	VG	F	VF	XF	Unc
1815	—	350	550	800	1,250	—
1816	—	350	550	800	1,250	—
1818	—	350	550	800	1,250	—
1820	—	350	550	800	1,250	—
1823	—	350	550	800	1,250	—

C# 77 RUSPONE (3 Zecchini)
10.4110 g., 0.9980 Gold .3340 oz. AGW **Ruler:** Leopold II **Obv:** Fleur-de-lis **Obv. Legend:** LEOPOLDVS II... **Rev:** Seated Saint, face right **Rev. Legend:** S. IOANNES...

Date	Mintage	VG	F	VF	XF	Unc
1824	—	275	400	650	1,000	—
1825	—	275	400	650	1,000	—
1829	—	275	400	650	1,000	—
1834	—	275	400	650	1,000	—
1836	—	275	400	650	1,000	—

C# 78 OTTANTA (80) FIORINI
32.6500 g., 0.9990 Gold 1.0487 oz. AGW **Ruler:** Leopold II **Obv:** Fleur-de-lis **Obv. Legend:** LEOPOLDVS II.D.G.P.I... **Rev:** Crowned pointed ornate shield with spikes **Rev. Legend:** SVSCEPTOR...

Date	Mintage	VG	F	VF	XF	Unc
1827	—	700	800	1,200	2,500	—
1828	—	700	800	1,200	2,500	—

1ST PROVISIONAL GOVERNMENT
1859
STANDARD COINAGE

C# 80 RUSPONE (3 Zecchini)
10.4700 g., 0.9980 Gold .3359 oz. AGW **Ruler:** Provisional Government **Obv:** Fleur-de-lis **Obv. Legend:** GOVERNO DELLA... **Rev:** Seated Saint, face right **Rev. Legend:** S. IOANNES...

Date	Mintage	F	VF	XF	Unc	BU
1859	—	3,000	4,000	6,000	10,000	—

ITALY

The Italian Republic, a 700-mile-long peninsula extending into the heart of the Mediterranean Sea, has an area of 116,304 sq. mi. (301,230 sq. km.) and a population of 60 million. Capital: Rome. The economy centers around agriculture, manufacturing, forestry and fishing. Machinery, textiles, clothing and motor vehicles are exported.

From the fall of Rome until modern times, 'Italy' was little more than a geographical expression. Although nominally included in the Empire of Charlemagne and the Holy Roman Empire, it was in reality divided into a number of independent states and kingdoms presided over by wealthy families, soldiers of fortune or hereditary rulers. The 19th century unification movement fostered by Mazzini, Garibaldi and Cavour attained fruition in 1860-70 with the creation of the Kingdom of Italy and the installation of Victor Emmanuel, king of Sardinia, as king of Italy. Benito Mussolini came to power during the post-World War I period of economic and political unrest, and installed a Fascist dictatorship with a figurehead king as titular Head of State. Mussolini entered Italy into the German-Japanese anti-comitern pact (Tri-Partite Pact) and withdrew from the League of Nations. The war did not go well for Italy and Germany was forced to assist Italy in its failed invasion of Greece. The Allied invasion of Sicily on July 10, 1943 and bombings of Rome brought the Fascist council to a no vote of confidence on July 23, 1943. Mussolini was arrested but soon escaped and set up a government in Salo. Rome fell to the Allied forces in June, 1944 and the country was allowed the status of cobelligerent against Germany. The Germans held northern Italy for another year. Mussolini was eventually captured and executed by partisans.

Following the defeat of the Axis powers, the Italian monarchy was dissolved by plebiscite, and the Italian Republic proclaimed.

RULERS
Vittorio Emanuele III, 1900-1946
Umberto II, 1946
Republic, 1946-

MONETARY SYSTEM
100 Centesimi = 1 Lira

KINGDOM
DECIMAL COINAGE

KM# 17 5 LIRE
1.6129 g., 0.9000 Gold .0466 oz. AGW **Ruler:** Vittorio Emanuele II **Obv:** Head left **Obv. Legend:** VITTORIO EMANUELE II **Rev:** Crowned shield within wreath **Rev. Legend:** REGNO D'ITALIA

Date	Mintage	F	VF	XF	Unc	BU
1863T BN	197,000	75.00	100	175	275	—
1865T BN	408,000	100	175	250	400	—

KM# 9.1 10 LIRE
3.2258 g., 0.9000 Gold .0933 oz. AGW, 18 mm. **Ruler:** Vittorio Emanuele II **Obv:** Head left **Obv. Legend:** VITTORIO EMANUELE II **Rev:** Crowned shield within wreath **Rev. Legend:** REGNO D'ITALIA...

Date	Mintage	F	VF	XF	Unc	BU
1861T B in shield	1,916	1,500	3,000	4,500	7,500	—

442 ITALY

KM# 9.2 10 LIRE
3.2258 g., 0.9000 Gold .0933 oz. AGW, 18.5 mm. **Ruler:** Vittorio Emanuele II

Date	Mintage	F	VF	XF	Unc	BU
1863T BN	543,000	75.00	100	150	250	—
1865T BN	444,000	100	175	225	350	—

KM# 9.3 10 LIRE
3.2258 g., 0.9000 Gold .0933 oz. AGW **Ruler:** Vittorio Emanuele II

Date	Mintage	F	VF	XF	Unc	BU
1863T BN	Inc. above	70.00	95.00	125	185	—

KM# 9.4 10 LIRE
3.2258 g., 0.9000 Gold .0933 oz. AGW, 19.5 mm. **Ruler:** Vittorio Emanuele II

Date	Mintage	F	VF	XF	Unc	BU
1863T BN	Inc. above	75.00	100	135	220	—

KM# 47 10 LIRE
3.2258 g., 0.9000 Gold .0933 oz. AGW, 18 mm. **Ruler:** Vittorio Emanuele III **Rev. Designer:** Egidio Boninsegna

Date	Mintage	F	VF	XF	Unc	BU
1910R Rare	—	—	—	—	—	—
Note: All but one piece melted						
1912R	6,796	1,000	1,875	3,750	8,500	—
1926R	40	—	—	12,000	20,000	—
1927R	30	—	—	10,500	17,500	—

KM# 10.1 20 LIRE
6.4516 g., 0.9000 Gold .1867 oz. AGW **Ruler:** Vittorio Emanuele II **Obv:** Head left **Obv. Legend:** VITTORIO EMANUELE II **Rev:** Crowned shield within wreath **Rev. Legend:** REGNO D'ITALIA..

Date	Mintage	F	VF	XF	Unc	BU
1861T B in shield	3,267	135	200	300	500	—
1861T T/F	Inc. above	—	BV	125	165	—
1862T BN	1,955,000	—	—	BV	135	—
1863T BN	2,981,000	—	—	BV	135	—
1864T BN	609,000	—	—	BV	135	—
1865T BN	3,109,000	—	—	BV	135	—
1866T BN	196,000	135	150	200	425	—
1867T BN	276,000	—	BV	125	160	—
1868T BN	340,000	—	BV	125	160	—
1869T BN	185,000	—	BV	125	160	—
1870T bn	55,000	135	200	400	850	—

KM# 10.2 20 LIRE
6.4516 g., 0.9000 Gold .1867 oz. AGW **Ruler:** Vittorio Emanuele II

Date	Mintage	F	VF	XF	Unc	BU
1870R	—	150	300	600	1,450	—
1871R	—	BV	125	200	450	—
1873R	2,174	400	800	1,600	3,500	—
1874R	41,000	—	BV	125	170	—
1875R	51,000	—	BV	125	170	—
1876R	108,000	—	—	BV	135	—
1877R	247,000	—	—	BV	135	—
1878R	316,000	—	—	BV	125	—

KM# 10.3 20 LIRE
6.4516 g., 0.9000 Gold .1867 oz. AGW **Ruler:** Vittorio Emanuele II **Obv:** Head left **Obv. Legend:** VITTORIO EMANUELE II **Rev:** Crowned shield within wreath **Rev. Legend:** REGNO D'ITALIA..

Date	Mintage	F	VF	XF	Unc	BU
1872M BN	—	BV	150	250	500	—
1873M BN	1,018,000	—	—	BV	145	—
1874M BN	255,000	—	BV	125	155	—

KM# 21 20 LIRE
6.4516 g., 0.9000 Gold .1867 oz. AGW **Ruler:** Umberto I **Obv:** Head left **Obv. Legend:** UMBERTO I... **Rev:** Crowned shield within wreath divides value, star above

Date	Mintage	F	VF	XF	Unc	BU
1880R	129,000	—	—	BV	130	—
1881R	843,000	—	—	BV	130	—
1882R	6,970,000	—	—	BV	130	—
1/1882	—	—	BV	125	150	—
1883/2	183,000	—	BV	125	150	—
1883R	182,000	—	—	BV	130	—
1884R	9,775	175	300	500	1,200	—
1885R	165,000	—	—	BV	130	—
1886R	59,000	—	—	BV	130	—
1888R	111,000	—	—	BV	130	—
1889R	—	150	250	400	600	—
1890R	68,000	—	—	BV	130	—
1891R	32,000	—	BV	125	160	—
1893R	41,000	—	—	BV	145	—
1897R	38,000	—	—	BV	155	—

KM# 21a 20 LIRE
Red Gold **Ruler:** Umberto I **Obv:** Head left **Rev:** Crowned shield within wreath divides value, star above

Date	Mintage	F	VF	XF	Unc	BU
1882R	Inc. above	—	—	135	185	—

KM# 37.1 20 LIRE
6.4516 g., 0.9000 Gold .1867 oz. AGW **Ruler:** Vittorio Emanuele III **Obv:** Head left **Rev:** Crowned eagle with Savoy shield on chest

Date	Mintage	F	VF	XF	Unc	BU
1902R	181	—	15,000	25,000	35,000	—
1903R	1,800	650	1,350	2,500	4,500	—
1905R	8,715	450	800	1,350	2,500	—
1908R Rare	—	—	—	—	—	—

KM# 37.2 20 LIRE
6.4516 g., 0.9000 Gold .1867 oz. AGW **Ruler:** Vittorio Emanuele III **Obv:** Head left **Rev:** Crowned eagle with Savoy shield on chest **Note:** A small anchor below the neck indicates that the gold in the coin is from Eritrea.

Date	Mintage	F	VF	XF	Unc	BU
1902R	115	6,500	14,500	30,000	50,000	—

KM# 48 20 LIRE
6.4516 g., 0.9000 Gold .1867 oz. AGW **Ruler:** Vittorio Emanuele III **Obv:** Uniformed bust left **Rev:** Female standing on prow **Designer:** Egidio Boninsegna

Date	Mintage	F	VF	XF	Unc	BU
1910R	Est. 33,000	—	—	—	70,000	—
Note: Six pieces currently known to exist						
1912R	59,000	325	550	1,350	2,200	—
1926R	40	—	—	10,500	17,500	—
1927R	30	—	—	12,000	20,000	—

KM# 64 20 LIRE
6.4516 g., 0.9000 Gold .1867 oz. AGW, 21 mm. **Ruler:** Vittorio Emanuele III **Subject:** 1st Anniversary of Fascist Government **Obv:** Head left **Rev:** Axe head within fasces with value at left **Designer:** Attilio Motti

Date	Mintage	F	VF	XF	Unc	BU
1923R	20,000	310	620	1,300	2,100	2,500

KM# 18 50 LIRE
16.1290 g., 0.9000 Gold .4667 oz. AGW **Ruler:** Vittorio Emanuele II

Date	Mintage	F	VF	XF	Unc	BU
1864T BN	103	10,000	15,000	27,500	35,000	—

KM# 25 50 LIRE
16.1290 g., 0.9000 Gold .4667 oz. AGW **Ruler:** Umberto I **Obv:** Head left **Obv. Legend:** UMBERTO I... **Rev:** Crowned shield within wreath divides value, star above

Date	Mintage	F	VF	XF	Unc	BU
1884R	2,532	900	1,500	2,000	3,250	—
1888R	2,125	1,000	2,000	2,750	3,750	—
1891R	414	1,500	2,500	4,000	7,500	—

KM# 49 50 LIRE
16.1290 g., 0.9000 Gold .4667 oz. AGW **Ruler:** Vittorio Emanuele III **Obv:** Bust left **Rev:** Female with plow **Designer:** Egidio Boninsegna

Date	Mintage	F	VF	XF	Unc	BU
1910R Rare	2,096	—	—	—	—	—
1912R	11,000	550	1,200	2,000	3,000	4,500
1926R	40	—	—	—	30,000	—
1927R	30	—	—	—	25,000	—

KM# 54 50 LIRE
16.1290 g., 0.9000 Gold .4667 oz. AGW, 28 mm. **Ruler:** Vittorio Emanuele III **Subject:** 50th Anniversary of the Kingdom **Obv:** Head left **Rev:** Standing classical couple **Designer:** Domenico Trentacoste

Date	Mintage	F	VF	XF	Unc	BU
ND(1911)R	20,000	450	700	1,350	2,250	3,000

KM# 71 50 LIRE
4.3995 g., 0.9000 Gold .1273 oz. AGW **Ruler:** Vittorio Emanuele III **Obv:** Head left **Rev:** Man striding right

Date	Mintage	F	VF	XF	Unc	BU
1931R Yr. IX	32,000	95.00	130	325	500	—
1931R Yr. X	Inc. above	150	280	475	800	—
1932R Yr. X	12,000	200	325	500	900	—
1933R Yr. XI	6,463	300	425	775	1,500	—

KM# 82 50 LIRE
4.3995 g., 0.9000 Gold .1273 oz. AGW **Ruler:** Vittorio Emanuele III **Obv:** Head left **Rev:** Eagle with wings spread above Savoy shield

Date	Mintage	F	VF	XF	Unc	BU
1936R	790	1,250	2,200	5,000	9,000	15,000

KM# 19.1 100 LIRE
32.2580 g., 0.9000 Gold .9334 oz. AGW **Ruler:** Vittorio Emanuele II **Obv. Legend:** VITTORIO EMANUELE II. **Rev:** Crowned shield within wreath **Rev. Legend:** REGNO D'ITALIA..

Date	Mintage	F	VF	XF	Unc	BU
1864T BN	579	2,000	4,500	8,500	16,000	—

ITALY 443

KM# 19.2 100 LIRE
32.2580 g., 0.9000 Gold .9334 oz. AGW **Ruler:** Vittorio Emanuele II

Date	Mintage	F	VF	XF	Unc	BU
1872R	661	2,000	4,500	8,000	14,000	—
1878R	294	3,500	7,000	12,000	20,000	—

KM# 22 100 LIRE
32.2580 g., 0.9000 Gold .9334 oz. AGW **Ruler:** Umberto I **Obv:** Head left **Obv. Legend:** UMBERTO I... **Rev:** Crowned shield within wreath divides value, star above

Date	Mintage	F	VF	XF	Unc	BU
1880R	145	6,000	12,000	16,000	25,000	—
1882R	1,229	900	1,500	2,500	3,750	—
1883R	4,219	800	1,250	2,250	3,500	—
1888R	1,169	900	1,500	3,000	4,500	—
1891R	209	2,000	4,000	9,000	18,000	—

KM# 39 100 LIRE
32.2580 g., 0.9000 Gold .9334 oz. AGW **Ruler:** Vittorio Emanuele III **Obv:** Head left **Rev:** Crowned eagle with Savoy shield on chest

Date	Mintage	F	VF	XF	Unc	BU
1903R	966	2,000	3,750	8,250	17,250	—
1905R	1,012	1,750	3,000	7,150	14,375	—

KM# 50 100 LIRE
32.2580 g., 0.9000 Gold .9334 oz. AGW **Ruler:** Vittorio Emanuele III **Obv:** Bust left **Rev:** Female with plow **Designer:** Egidio Boninsegna

Date	Mintage	F	VF	XF	Unc	BU
1910R Rare	2,013	—	—	—	—	—
1912R	4,946	—	2,500	4,000	8,000	—
1926R	40	—	13,500	19,500	38,000	—
1927R	30	—	15,750	25,000	40,000	—

KM# 65 100 LIRE
32.2580 g., 0.9000 Gold .9334 oz. AGW, 32 mm. **Ruler:** Vittorio Emanuele III **Subject:** 1st Anniversary of Fascist Government **Obv:** Head left **Rev:** Axe within fasces with value at left **Designer:** Attilio Motti

Date	Mintage	F	VF	XF	Unc	BU
1923R Matte finish	20,000	760	1,150	2,200	5,200	—
1923R Bright finish, rare	—	—	—	—	—	—

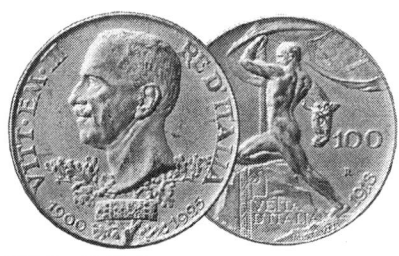

KM# 66 100 LIRE
32.2580 g., 0.9000 Gold .9334 oz. AGW, 35 mm. **Ruler:** Vittorio Emanuele III **Subject:** 25th year of reign, 10th Anniversary - World War I Entry **Obv:** Head left above oak sprigs **Rev:** Heroic male figure kneeling on large rock holding flag and small Victory **Designer:** Aurelio Mistruzzi

Date	Mintage	F	VF	XF	Unc	BU
1925R Matte finish	5,000	1,500	2,250	4,500	8,750	12,000
1925R Bright finish, rare	—	—	—	—	—	—

KM# 72 100 LIRE
8.7990 g., 0.9000 Gold .2546 oz. AGW **Ruler:** Vittorio Emanuele III **Obv:** Head left **Rev:** Female on prow **Designer:** Giuseppe Romagnoli

Date	Mintage	F	VF	XF	Unc	BU
1931R Yr. IX	34,000	BV	275	425	800	—
1931R Yr. X	Inc. above	200	300	500	1,200	—
1932R Yr. X	9,081	185	350	500	1,200	—
1933R Yr. XI	6,464	250	400	750	1,250	—

KM# 83 100 LIRE
8.7990 g., 0.9000 Gold .2546 oz. AGW, 25 mm. **Ruler:** Vittorio Emanuele III **Obv:** Head right **Rev:** Male figure striding left **Designer:** Giuseppe Romagnoli

Date	Mintage	F	VF	XF	Unc	BU
1936R	812	1,350	2,500	5,000	15,000	18,500

KM# 84 100 LIRE
5.1900 g., 0.9000 Gold .1502 oz. AGW, 20 mm. **Ruler:** Vittorio Emanuele III **Obv:** Head right **Rev:** Male figure striding left **Designer:** Giuseppe Romagnoli

Date	Mintage	F	VF	XF	Unc	BU
1937R Yr. XVI	249	—	7,500	13,500	27,000	42,500
1940R Yr. XVIII, rare	2	—	—	—	—	—

FANTASY COINAGE
Vittorio Emanuel III
The following are all considered fantasy types

X# 1 100 LIRE
30.0000 g., Gold **Obv:** Fascist **Rev:** Bust of Vittorio Emmanuel III left wearing helmet

Date	Mintage	F	VF	XF	Unc	BU
1928	—	—	—	—	650	—

FANTASY COINAGE
Benito Mussolini
The following are all considered fantasy types struck ca. 1970

X# 2c 20 LIRE
31.0000 g., Gold

Date	Mintage	F	VF	XF	Unc	BU
(1943) Prooflike	—	—	—	—	—	450

X# 3 20 LIRE
0.5000 Gold, 20 mm.

Date	Mintage	F	VF	XF	Unc	BU
(1943) Prooflike	—	—	—	—	—	145

X# 4 20 LIRE
0.5000 Gold, 17 mm.

Date	Mintage	F	VF	XF	Unc	BU
(1943) Prooflike	—	—	—	—	—	120

X# 5 50 LIRE
Gold **Obv:** Fascist **Rev:** Bust of Mussolini left wearing helmet **Rev. Legend:** MVSSOLINI MCMXLIII

Date	Mintage	F	VF	XF	Unc	BU
(1943)	—	—	—	—	—	275

X# 6 100 LIRE
Gold **Rev:** Bust of Mussolini left wearing helmet **Rev. Legend:** MVSSOLINI MCMXLIII **Note:** Type I.

Date	Mintage	F	VF	XF	Unc	BU
(1943) Prooflike	—	—	—	—	—	500

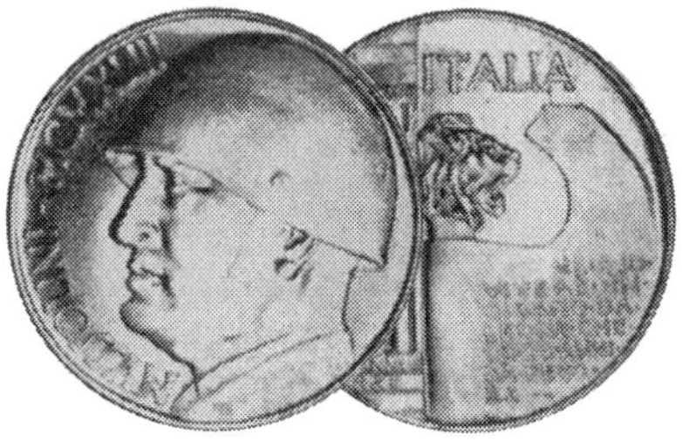

X# 7 100 LIRE

Gold **Rev:** Bust of Mussolini left wearing helmut **Rev. Legend:** MVSSOLINI MCMXLIII **Note:** Type II.

Date	Mintage	F	VF	XF	Unc	BU
(1943) Prooflike	—	—	—	—	—	500

MEDALLIC COINAGE

Umberto II

The following are all considered fantasy types struck ca. 1970

X# M3 100 LIRE

Platinum APW, 37.15 mm. **Ruler:** Umberto II **Obv:** Head left **Rev:** Helmeted arms divide fe - rt **Note:** Weight varies: 31.71-32.09 grams. Presumed to have been struck in the 1960's.

Date	Mintage	F	VF	XF	Unc	BU
1946	5	—	—	—	—	1,850

Note: All five know pieces were sold in the Superior Galleries - Edwards Metcalf and Buddy Ebsen Collection auction of June 1987.

X# M2 100 LIRE

Gold, 37.15 mm. **Ruler:** Umberto II **Obv:** Head left **Rev:** Helmeted arms divide fe - rt **Note:** Weight varies: 31.72-32.12 grams. Presumed to have been struck in the 1960's.

Date	Mintage	F	VF	XF	Unc	BU
1946	—	—	—	—	850	1,250

REPUBLIC

DECIMAL COINAGE

KM# 87a LIRA

8.0000 g., 0.9000 Gold 0.2315 oz. AGW, 21.6 mm. **Obv:** Ceres **Rev:** Orange on branch **Edge:** Plain **Note:** Official Restrike

Date	Mintage	F	VF	XF	Unc	BU
1946 (2006)R Proof	1,999	Value: 400				

KM# 91a LIRA

4.0000 g., 0.9000 Gold 0.1157 oz. AGW, 17.2 mm. **Obv:** Balance scale **Rev:** Cornucopia, date and value **Edge:** Plain **Note:** Official Restrike

Date	Mintage	F	VF	XF	Unc	BU
1951 (2006)R Proof	1,999	Value: 250				

KM# 88a 2 LIRE

11.0000 g., 0.9000 Gold 0.3183 oz. AGW, 24.1 mm. **Obv:** Farmer plowing field **Rev:** Wheat ear **Edge:** Plain **Note:** Official Restrike

Date	Mintage	F	VF	XF	Unc	BU
1946 (2006)R Proof	1,999	Value: 700				

KM# 94a 2 LIRE

5.0000 g., 0.9000 Gold 0.1447 oz. AGW, 18.3 mm. **Obv:** Honey bee **Rev:** Olive branch **Edge:** Reeded **Note:** Official Restrike

Date	Mintage	F	VF	XF	Unc	BU
1953 (2006)R Proof	1,999	Value: 300				

KM# 89a 5 LIRE

16.0000 g., 0.9000 Gold 0.463 oz. AGW, 26.7 mm. **Obv:** Italia with torch **Rev:** Bunch of grapes **Edge:** Reeded **Note:** Official Restrike

Date	Mintage	F	VF	XF	Unc	BU
1946 (2006)R Proof	1,999	Value: 1,000				

KM# 92a 5 LIRE

6.0000 g., 0.9000 Gold 0.1736 oz. AGW, 20.2 mm. **Obv:** Rudder **Rev:** Dolphin and value **Edge:** Plain **Note:** Official Restrike

Date	Mintage	F	VF	XF	Unc	BU
1951 (2006)R Proof	1,999	Value: 400				

KM# 90a 10 LIRE

19.0000 g., 0.9000 Gold 0.5498 oz. AGW, 29 mm. **Obv:** Pegasus **Rev:** Olive branch **Edge:** Lettered **Edge Lettering:** REPVBBLICA ITALIANA **Note:** Official Restrike

Date	Mintage	F	VF	XF	Unc	BU
1946 (2006)R Proof	1,999	Value: 1,000				

KM# 93a 10 LIRE

10.0000 g., 0.9000 Gold 0.2894 oz. AGW, 23.3 mm. **Obv:** Plow **Rev:** Value within wheat ears **Edge:** Plain **Note:** Official Restrike

Date	Mintage	F	VF	XF	Unc	BU
1951 (2006)R Proof	1,999	Value: 600				

KM# 97.1a 20 LIRE

8.0000 g., 0.9000 Gold 0.2315 oz. AGW, 21.3 mm. **Obv:** Head laureate left **Rev:** Oak leaves divides date and value **Edge:** Reeded **Note:** Official Restrike

Date	Mintage	F	VF	XF	Unc	BU
1957 (2006)R Proof	1,999	Value: 500				

KM# 95.1a 50 LIRE

14.0000 g., 0.9000 Gold, 24.8 mm. **Obv:** Italia **Rev:** Vulcan **Edge:** Reeded **Note:** Official Restrike

Date	Mintage	F	VF	XF	Unc	BU
1954 (2006)R Proof	1,999	Value: 500				

KM# 183a 50 LIRE

9.0000 g., 0.9000 Gold 0.2604 oz. AGW, 19.2 mm. **Obv:** Roma **Rev:** Value within wreath **Edge:** Plain **Note:** Official Restrike

Date	Mintage	F	VF	XF	Unc	BU
1996 (2006)R Proof	1,999	Value: 500				

KM# 96.1a 100 LIRE

18.0000 g., 0.9000 Gold 0.5208 oz. AGW, 27.8 mm. **Obv:** Ancient athlete **Rev:** Minerva standing **Edge:** Reeded **Note:** Official Restrike

Date	Mintage	F	VF	XF	Unc	BU
1955 (2006)R Proof	1,999	Value: 1,000				

KM# 159a 100 LIRE

9.0000 g., 0.9000 Gold 0.2604 oz. AGW, 22 mm. **Obv:** Turreted head left **Rev:** Large value within circle flanked by sprigs **Edge:** Segmented reeding **Note:** Official Restrike

Date	Mintage	F	VF	XF	Unc	BU
1993 (2006)R Proof	1,999	Value: 500				

KM# 105a 200 LIRE

11.0000 g., 0.9000 Gold 0.3183 oz. AGW, 24 mm. **Obv:** Head right **Rev:** Value within gear **Edge:** Reeded **Note:** Official Restrike

Date	Mintage	F	VF	XF	Unc	BU
1977 (2006)R Proof	1,999	Value: 700				

KM# 98a 500 LIRE

18.0000 g., 0.9000 Gold 0.5208 oz. AGW, 29 mm. **Obv:** Columbus' ships **Rev:** Bust left within wreath **Edge:** Lettered **Edge Lettering:** REPVBBLICA ITALIANA *** 1958*** **Note:** Official Restrike

Date	Mintage	F	VF	XF	Unc	BU
1958 (2006)R Proof	1,999	Value: 1,000				

KM# 99a 500 LIRE

18.0000 g., 0.9000 Gold 0.5208 oz. AGW, 29 mm. **Obv:** Seated Italia **Rev:** Lady **Edge:** Lettered **Edge Lettering:** "1 CENTENARIO VNITA'D'ITALIA * 1861-1961* " **Note:** Official Restrike

Date	Mintage	F	VF	XF	Unc	BU
1961 (2006)R Proof	1,999	Value: 1,000				

KM# 100a 500 LIRE

18.0000 g., 0.9000 Gold 0.5208 oz. AGW, 29 mm. **Obv:** Dante **Rev:** Hell **Edge:** Lettered **Edge Lettering:** "7 CENTENARIO DELLA NASCITA DI DANTE" **Note:** Official Restrike

Date	Mintage	F	VF	XF	Unc	BU
1965 (2006)R Proof	1,999	Value: 1,000				

KM# 111a 500 LIRE

14.0000 g., Bi-Metallic .750 Gold center in .900 Gold ring, 25.8 mm. **Obv:** Head left within circle **Rev:** Plaza within circle flanked by sprigs **Edge:** Segmented reeding **Note:** Official Restrike

Date	Mintage	F	VF	XF	Unc	BU
1982 (2006)R Proof	1,999	Value: 270				

KM# 101a 1000 LIRE

24.0000 g., 0.9000 Gold 0.6945 oz. AGW, 31.4 mm. **Obv:** Concordia **Rev:** Geometric shape above value **Edge:** Lettered **Edge Lettering:** "REPVBBLICA ITALIANA"

Date	Mintage	F	VF	XF	Unc	BU
1970 (2006)R Proof	1,999	Value: 1,200				

KM# 190a 1000 LIRE

17.0000 g., Bi-Metallic .750 Gold center in .900 Gold ring, 27 mm. **Obv:** Roma **Rev:** European map **Edge:** Segmented reeding **Note:** Official Restrike

Date	Mintage	F	VF	XF	Unc	BU
1997 (2006)R Proof	1,999	Value: 310				

KM# 176 50000 LIRE

7.5000 g., 0.9000 Gold .217 oz. AGW **Subject:** Bank of Italy **Obv:** Bust left **Rev:** Building and value

Date	Mintage	F	VF	XF	Unc	BU
1993R Proof	22,560	Value: 300				

KM# 223 50000 LIRE

7.5000 g., 0.9000 Gold 0.217 oz. AGW, 20 mm. **Subject:** 800th Anniversary - Birth of Saint Anthony of Padova **Obv:** Corner view of Basilica **Rev:** Interior view - Chapel, date and value

Date	Mintage	F	VF	XF	Unc	BU
1995R Proof	9,221	Value: 300				

KM# 225 50000 LIRE

7.5000 g., 0.9000 Gold 0.217 oz. AGW, 20 mm. **Subject:** 800th Anniversary - Battistero in Parma **Obv:** Battistero **Rev:** Decorations from the Battistero, date and value

Date	Mintage	F	VF	XF	Unc	BU
1996R Proof	7,010	Value: 500				

KM# 191 50000 LIRE

7.5000 g., 0.9000 Gold .217 oz. AGW **Subject:** 1600th Anniversary - Death of St. Ambrose **Obv:** St. Ambrose Church in Milan **Rev:** Investiture of St. Ambrose

Date	Mintage	F	VF	XF	Unc	BU
ND(1997)R Proof	5,750	Value: 300				

KM# 228 50000 LIRE

7.5000 g., 0.9000 Gold 0.217 oz. AGW, 20 mm. **Subject:** 850th Anniversary - Church of San Giovanni of the Hermits in Palermo **Obv:** Church of San Giovanni **Rev:** Curved arches

Date	Mintage	F	VF	XF	Unc	BU
1998R Proof	4,900	Value: 325				

KM# 230 50000 LIRE

7.5000 g., 0.9000 Gold 0.217 oz. AGW, 20 mm. **Subject:** 900th Anniversary - Foundation of the Cathedral in Modena **Obv:** Front of Cathedral **Rev:** Arch with lion, date and denomination

Date	Mintage	F	VF	XF	Unc	BU
1999R Proof	5,500	Value: 325				

KM# 232 50000 LIRE

7.5000 g., 0.9000 Gold 0.217 oz. AGW, 20 mm. **Subject:** 500th Anniversary - Birth of Benvenuto Cellini **Obv:** Bust of Cellini **Rev:** Figure, date and denomination

Date	Mintage	F	VF	XF	Unc	BU
2000R Proof	—	Value: 325				

KM# 234 50000 LIRE

7.5000 g., 0.9000 Gold 0.217 oz. AGW, 20 mm. **Subject:** 250th Anniversary - Palace of Caserta **Obv:** Front view of palace **Rev:** Fountain, date and denomination

Date	Mintage	F	VF	XF	Unc	BU
2001R Proof	6,200	Value: 450				

KM# 177 100000 LIRE

15.0000 g., 0.9000 Gold .434 oz. AGW **Subject:** Centennial of the Bank of Italy **Obv:** Bust facing **Rev:** Value and building **Note:** 1996 strikes do not exist.

Date	Mintage	F	VF	XF	Unc	BU
1993 Proof	21,196	Value: 500				

KM# 222 100000 LIRE

15.0000 g., 0.9000 Gold 0.434 oz. AGW, 25 mm. **Subject:** 700th Anniversary - Basilica of Santa Croce in Florence **Obv:** Front of the Basilica of Santa Croce **Rev:** Interior view, date and denomination

Date	Mintage	F	VF	XF	Unc	BU
1995R Proof	8,584	Value: 650				

KM# 224 100000 LIRE

15.0000 g., 0.9000 Gold 0.434 oz. AGW, 25 mm. **Subject:** 600th Anniversary - Foundation of Certosa Di Pavia **Obv:** Exterior angled view **Rev:** Interior view

Date	Mintage	F	VF	XF	Unc	BU
1996R Proof	5,550	Value: 750				

KM# 226 100000 LIRE

15.0000 g., 0.9000 Gold 0.434 oz. AGW, 25 mm. **Subject:** 800th Anniversary - Dedication of the Basilica Superiore of San Nicola of Bari **Obv:** Exterior view of the Basilica **Rev:** Interior view

Date	Mintage	F	VF	XF	Unc	BU
1997R Proof	5,400	Value: 650				

KM# 227 100000 LIRE

15.0000 g., 0.9000 Gold 0.434 oz. AGW, 25 mm. **Subject:** 650th Anniversary - Completion of the Tower - Palace of Siena **Obv:** Tower **Rev:** Anniversary dates and denomination

Date	Mintage	F	VF	XF	Unc	BU
1998R Proof	4,800	Value: 650				

KM# 229 100000 LIRE

15.0000 g., 0.9000 Gold 0.434 oz. AGW, 25 mm. **Subject:** Repair of the Basilica of St. Francis of Assisi **Obv:** Front of Basilica **Rev:** Round seal, date and denomination

Date	Mintage	F	VF	XF	Unc	BU
1999R Proof	5,047	Value: 650				

KM# 231 100000 LIRE

15.0000 g., 0.9000 Gold 0.434 oz. AGW, 20 mm. **Subject:** 700th Anniversary - First Jubilee of 1300 **Obv:** The Quadrangle **Rev:** Detail of the fresco of Giotto

Date	Mintage	F	VF	XF	Unc	BU
2000R Proof	—	Value: 600				

KM# 233 100000 LIRE

15.0000 g., 0.9000 Gold 0.434 oz. AGW, 25 mm. **Subject:** 700th Anniversary - Pulpit at the Church of St. Andrea a Pistoia **Obv:** Full pulpit **Rev:** Enlarged detail of the pulpit

Date	Mintage	F	VF	XF	Unc	BU
2001R Proof	4,500	Value: 800				

ASIAGO ITALY 445

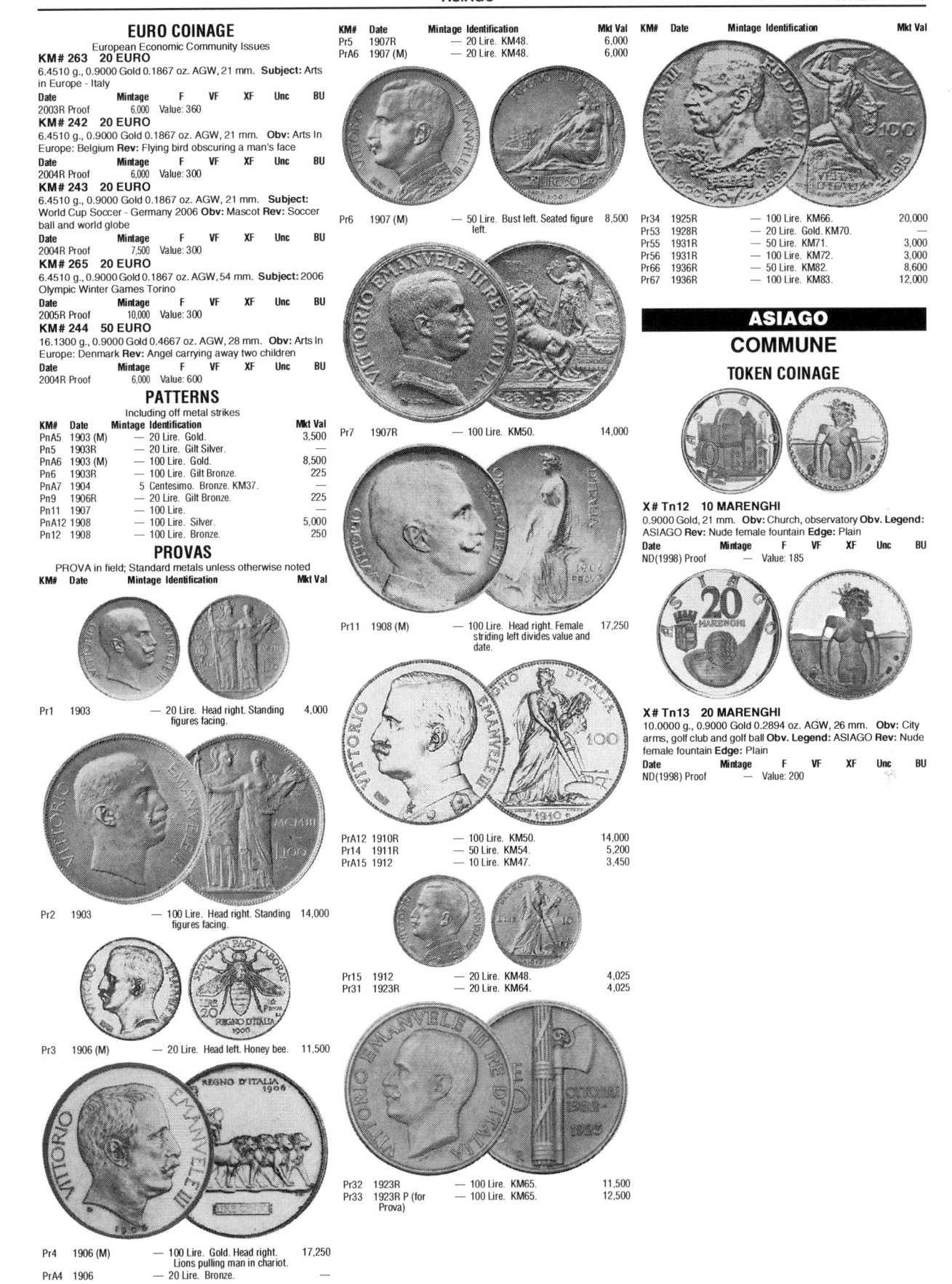

EURO COINAGE
European Economic Community Issues
KM# 263 20 EURO
6.4510 g., 0.9000 Gold 0.1867 oz. AGW, 21 mm. **Subject:** Arts in Europe - Italy

Date	Mintage	F	VF	XF	Unc	BU
2003R Proof	6,000	Value: 360				

KM# 242 20 EURO
6.4510 g., 0.9000 Gold 0.1867 oz. AGW, 21 mm. **Obv:** Arts In Europe: Belgium **Rev:** Flying bird obscuring a man's face

Date	Mintage	F	VF	XF	Unc	BU
2004R Proof	6,000	Value: 300				

KM# 243 20 EURO
6.4510 g., 0.9000 Gold 0.1867 oz. AGW, 21 mm. **Subject:** World Cup Soccer - Germany 2006 **Obv:** Mascot **Rev:** Soccer ball and world globe

Date	Mintage	F	VF	XF	Unc	BU
2004R Proof	7,500	Value: 300				

KM# 265 20 EURO
6.4510 g., 0.9000 Gold 0.1867 oz. AGW, 54 mm. **Subject:** 2006 Olympic Winter Games Torino

Date	Mintage	F	VF	XF	Unc	BU
2005R Proof	10,000	Value: 300				

KM# 244 50 EURO
16.1300 g., 0.9000 Gold 0.4667 oz. AGW, 28 mm. **Obv:** Arts In Europe: Denmark **Rev:** Angel carrying away two children

Date	Mintage	F	VF	XF	Unc	BU
2004R Proof	6,000	Value: 600				

PATTERNS
Including off metal strikes

KM#	Date	Mintage	Identification	Mkt Val
PnA5	1903 (M)	—	20 Lire. Gold.	3,500
Pn5	1903R	—	20 Lire. Gilt Silver.	—
PnA6	1903 (M)	—	100 Lire. Gold.	8,500
Pn6	1903R	—	100 Lire. Gilt Bronze.	225
PnA7	1904	5	Centesimo. Bronze. KM37.	—
Pn9	1906R	—	20 Lire. Gilt Bronze.	225
Pn11	1907	—	100 Lire.	—
PnA12	1908	—	100 Lire. Silver.	5,000
Pn12	1908	—	100 Lire. Bronze.	250

PROVAS
PROVA in field; Standard metals unless otherwise noted

KM#	Date	Mintage	Identification	Mkt Val
Pr1	1903	—	20 Lire. Head right. Standing figures facing.	4,000
Pr2	1903	—	100 Lire. Head right. Standing figures facing.	14,000
Pr3	1906 (M)	—	20 Lire. Head left. Honey bee.	11,500
Pr4	1906 (M)	—	100 Lire. Gold. Head right. Lions pulling man in chariot.	17,250
PrA4	1906	—	20 Lire. Bronze.	—
Pr5	1907R	—	20 Lire. KM48.	6,000
PrA6	1907 (M)	—	20 Lire. KM48.	6,000
Pr6	1907 (M)	—	50 Lire. Bust left. Seated figure left.	8,500
Pr7	1907R	—	100 Lire. KM50.	14,000
Pr11	1908 (M)	—	100 Lire. Head right. Female striding left divides value and date.	17,250
PrA12	1910R	—	100 Lire. KM50.	14,000
Pr14	1911R	—	50 Lire. KM54.	5,200
PrA15	1912	—	10 Lire. KM47.	3,450
Pr15	1912	—	20 Lire. KM48.	4,025
Pr31	1923R	—	20 Lire. KM64.	4,025
Pr32	1923R	—	100 Lire. KM65.	11,500
Pr33	1923R P (for Prova)	—	100 Lire. KM65.	12,500
Pr34	1925R	—	100 Lire. KM66.	20,000
Pr53	1928R	—	20 Lire. Gold. KM70.	—
Pr55	1931R	—	50 Lire. KM71.	3,000
Pr56	1931R	—	100 Lire. KM72.	3,000
Pr66	1936R	—	50 Lire. KM82.	8,600
Pr67	1936R	—	100 Lire. KM83.	12,000

ASIAGO
COMMUNE
TOKEN COINAGE

X# Tn12 10 MARENGHI
0.9000 Gold, 21 mm. **Obv:** Church, observatory **Obv. Legend:** ASIAGO **Rev:** Nude female fountain **Edge:** Plain

Date	Mintage	F	VF	XF	Unc	BU
ND(1998) Proof	—	Value: 185				

X# Tn13 20 MARENGHI
10.0000 g., 0.9000 Gold 0.2894 oz. AGW, 26 mm. **Obv:** City arms, golf club and golf ball **Obv. Legend:** ASIAGO **Rev:** Nude female fountain **Edge:** Plain

Date	Mintage	F	VF	XF	Unc	BU
ND(1998) Proof	—	Value: 200				

IVORY COAST

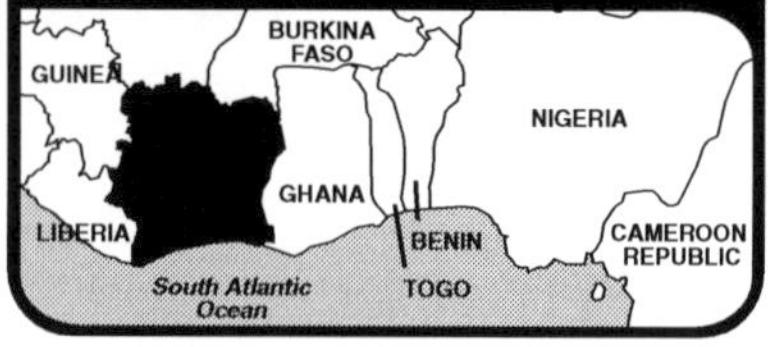

The Republic of the Ivory Coast, (Cote d'Ivoire), a former French Overseas territory located on the south side of the African bulge between Liberia and Ghana, has an area of 124,504 sq. mi. (322,463 sq. km.) and a population of 11.8 million. Capital: Yamoussoukro. The predominantly agricultural economy is one of Africa's most prosperous. Coffee, tropical woods, cocoa, and bananas are exported.

French and Portuguese navigators visited the Ivory Coast in the 15th century. French traders set up establishments in the 19th century, and gradually extended their influence along the coast and inland. The area was organized as a territory in 1893, and from 1904 to 1958 was a constituent unit of the Federation of French West Africa - as a Colony under the Third Republic and an Overseas Territory under the Fourth. In 1958 Ivory Coast became an autonomous republic within the French Community. Independence was attained on Aug. 7, 1960.

REPUBLIC

DECIMAL COINAGE

KM# 2 10 FRANCS
3.2000 g., 0.9000 Gold .0926 oz. AGW

Date	Mintage	F	VF	XF	Unc	BU
1966 Proof	2,000	Value: 85.00				

KM# 3 25 FRANCS
8.0000 g., 0.9000 Gold .2315 oz. AGW **Obv:** Head right **Rev:** Elephant and value within wreath

Date	Mintage	F	VF	XF	Unc	BU
1966 Proof	2,000	Value: 200				

KM# 4 50 FRANCS
16.0000 g., 0.9000 Gold .4630 oz. AGW **Obv:** Head right **Rev:** Elephant and value within wreath

Date	Mintage	F	VF	XF	Unc	BU
1966 Proof	2,000	Value: 345				

KM# 5 100 FRANCS
32.0000 g., 0.9000 Gold .9260 oz. AGW **Obv:** Head right **Rev:** Elephant within wreath

Date	Mintage	F	VF	XF	Unc	BU
1966 Proof	2,000	Value: 675				

PROOF SETS

KM#	Date	Mintage	Identification	Issue Price	Mkt Val
PS1	1966 (4)	2,000	KM#2-5	—	1,300

JAMAICA

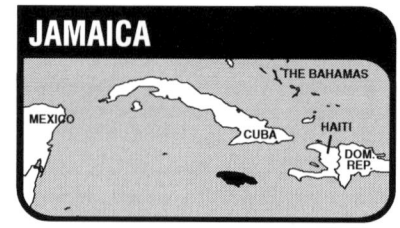

Jamaica, a member of the British Commonwealth is situated in the Caribbean Sea 90 miles south of Cuba, has an area of 4,244 sq. mi. (10,990 sq. km.) and a population of 2.1 million. Capital: Kingston. The economy is founded chiefly on mining, tourism and agriculture. Aluminum, bauxite, sugar, rum and molasses are exported.

Jamaica was discovered by Columbus on May 3, 1494, and settled by Spain in 1509. The island was captured in 1655 by a British naval force under the command of Admiral William Penn, sent by Oliver Cromwell and ceded to Britain by the Treaty of Madrid, 1670. For more than 150 years, the Jamaican economy of sugar, slaves and piracy was one of the most prosperous in the new world. Dissension between the property-oriented island legislature and the home government prompted parliament to establish a crown colony government for Jamaica in 1866. From 1958 to 1961 Jamaica was a member of the West Indies Federation, withdrawing when Jamaican voters rejected the association. The colony attained independence on Aug. 6, 1962. Jamaica is a member of the Commonwealth of Nations. Elizabeth II is the Head of State, as Queen of Jamaica.

In 1758, the Jamaican Assembly authorized stamping a certain amount of Spanish milled coinage. Token coinage by merchants aided the island's monetary supply in the early 19th century. Sterling coinage was introduced in Jamaica in 1825, with the additional silver three halfpence under William IV and Victoria. Certain issues of three pence of William IV and Victoria were intended for colonial use, including Jamaica, as were the last dates of three pence for George VI.

There was an extensive token and work tally coinage for Jamaica in the late 19th and early 20th centuries.

A decimal standard currency system was adopted on Sept. 8, 1969.

RULERS
British, until 1962

MINT MARKS
C - Royal Canadian Mint, Ottawa
H - Heaton
FM - Franklin Mint, U.S.A.**
(fm) - Franklin Mint, U.S.A.*
no mint mark - Royal Mint, London

*NOTE: During 1970 the Franklin Mint produced matte and proof coins (1 cent-1 dollar) using dies similar to/or Royal Mint without the FM mint mark.

NOTE: From 1975-1985 the Franklin Mint produced coinage in up to 3 different qualities. Qualities of issue are designated in ( ) after each date and are defined as follows:

(M) MATTE - Normal circulation strike or a dull finish produced by sandblasting special uncirculated (polish finish) or proof quality dies.

(U) SPECIAL UNCIRCULATED - Polished or proof-like in appearance without any frosted features.

(P) PROOF - The highest quality obtainable having mirror-like fields and frosted features.

MONETARY SYSTEM
4 Farthings = 1 Penny
12 Pence = 1 Shilling
8 Reales = 6 Shillings, 8 Pence
(Commencing 1969)
100 Cents = 1 Dollar

BRITISH COLONY

DECIMAL COINAGE

The Franklin Mint and Royal Mint have both been striking the 1 Cent through 1 Dollar coinage. The 1970 issues were all struck with dies similar to/or Royal Mint without the FM mint mark. The Royal Mint issues have the name JAMAICA extending beyond the native headdress feathers. Those struck after 1970 by the Franklin Mint have the name JAMAICA within the headdress feathers.

KM# 61 20 DOLLARS
15.7484 g., 0.5000 Gold .2531 oz. AGW **Ruler:** Elizabeth II **Subject:** 10th Anniversary of Independence **Obv:** Arms with supporters and dates within rope wreath **Rev:** Map of Jamaica above ships

Date	Mintage	F	VF	XF	Unc	BU
ND(1972)	30,000	—	—	—	175	185
ND(1972) Proof	20,000	Value: 190				

KM# 175 50 DOLLARS
7.7760 g., 0.5833 Gold .1458 oz. AGW **Ruler:** Elizabeth II **Obv:** Arms with supporters **Rev:** Queen Mother's wedding portrait

Date	Mintage	F	VF	XF	Unc	BU
1995 Proof	Est. 5,000	Value: 115				

KM# 67 100 DOLLARS
7.8300 g., 0.9000 Gold .2265 oz. AGW **Ruler:** Elizabeth II **Subject:** Christopher Columbus **Obv:** Arms with supporters **Rev:** Bust with hat 3/4 left

Date	Mintage	F	VF	XF	Unc	BU
1975FM (M)	100	—	—	—	185	200
1975FM (U)	10,000	—	—	—	170	180
1975FM (P)	21,000	Value: 160				

KM# 72 100 DOLLARS
7.8300 g., 0.9000 Gold .2265 oz. AGW **Ruler:** Elizabeth II **Subject:** Admiral Horatio Nelson **Obv:** Arms with supporters **Rev:** Uniformed bust looking left, ship and map at left

Date	Mintage	F	VF	XF	Unc	BU
1976FM (M)	100	—	—	—	200	215
1976FM (P)	8,952	Value: 170				

KM# 77 100 DOLLARS
11.3400 g., 0.9000 Gold .3281 oz. AGW **Ruler:** Elizabeth II **Subject:** 25th Anniversary of Coronation of Elizabeth II **Obv:** Arms with supporters **Rev:** Queen on throne with crown, sceptre and orb

Date	Mintage	F	VF	XF	Unc	BU
ND(1978)	—	—	—	—	225	235
ND(1978) Proof	5,835	Value: 230				

KM# 82 100 DOLLARS
11.3400 g., 0.9000 Gold .3281 oz. AGW **Ruler:** Elizabeth II **Subject:** 10th Anniversary - Investiture of Prince Charles **Obv:** Arms with supporters **Rev:** Crowned half figure left in regal dress

Date	Mintage	F	VF	XF	Unc	BU
ND(1979) Proof	2,891	Value: 235				

JAMAICA

KM# 110 100 DOLLARS
7.1300 g., 0.9000 Gold .2063 oz. AGW **Ruler:** Elizabeth II
Subject: 21st Anniversary of Independence **Obv:** Arms with supporters **Rev:** Number 21 divides heads facing above dates and braided rope

Date	Mintage	F	VF	XF	Unc	BU
ND(1983)FM (P)	638	Value: 220				

KM# 117 100 DOLLARS
7.1300 g., 0.9000 Gold .2063 oz. AGW **Ruler:** Elizabeth II
Subject: 100th Anniversary - Birth of Bustamante **Obv:** Arms with supporters **Rev:** Bust 1/4 left

Date	Mintage	F	VF	XF	Unc	BU
1984FM (P)	531	Value: 220				

KM# 129 100 DOLLARS
11.3400 g., 0.9000 Gold .3281 oz. AGW **Ruler:** Elizabeth II
Subject: 100th Anniversary - Birth of Marcus Garvey **Obv:** Arms with supporters **Rev:** Portrait of Garvey facing

Date	Mintage	F	VF	XF	Unc	BU
1987 Proof	500	Value: 250				

KM# 158 100 DOLLARS
11.3400 g., 0.9000 Gold .3281 oz. AGW **Ruler:** Elizabeth II
Subject: Centennial - Birth of Norman Manley **Obv:** Arms with supporters **Rev:** Head left

Date	Mintage	F	VF	XF	Unc	BU
1993 Proof	500	Value: 280				

KM# 172 100 DOLLARS
15.9800 g., 0.9990 Gold .5132 oz. AGW **Ruler:** Elizabeth II
Subject: Robert Marley **Obv:** Arms with supporters **Rev:** Head left

Date	Mintage	F	VF	XF	Unc	BU
1995 Proof	2,000	Value: 375				

KM# 178 100 DOLLARS
15.9800 g., 0.9990 Gold .5132 oz. AGW **Ruler:** Elizabeth II
Subject: World Cup Soccer **Obv:** Arms with supporters **Rev:** Soccer player

Date	Mintage	F	VF	XF	Unc	BU
1998 Proof	Est. 500	Value: 400				

KM# 180 100 DOLLARS
15.9700 g., 0.9167 Gold .4706 oz. AGW **Ruler:** Elizabeth II
Subject: 50th Anniversary - University of the West Indies **Obv:** Arms with supporters **Rev:** University arms

Date	Mintage	F	VF	XF	Unc	BU
1998 Proof	1,000	Value: 345				

KM# 78 250 DOLLARS
43.2200 g., 0.9000 Gold 1.2507 oz. AGW **Ruler:** Elizabeth II
Subject: 25th Anniversary of Coronation **Obv:** Arms with supporters **Rev:** Queen seated on throne with crown, sceptre and orb

Date	Mintage	F	VF	XF	Unc	BU
ND(1978) Proof	3,005	Value: 875				

KM# 83 250 DOLLARS
43.2200 g., 0.9000 Gold 1.2507 oz. AGW **Ruler:** Elizabeth II
Subject: 10th Anniversary - Investiture of Prince Charles **Obv:** Arms with supporters **Rev:** Crowned half figure left in regal dress

Date	Mintage	F	VF	XF	Unc	BU
ND(1979) Proof	1,650	Value: 900				

KM# 89 250 DOLLARS
11.3400 g., 0.9000 Gold .3281 oz. AGW **Ruler:** Elizabeth II
Subject: 1980 Olympics **Obv:** Arms with supporters **Rev:** Heads around outer circle of previous Gold Medal winners

Date	Mintage	F	VF	XF	Unc	BU
1980 Proof	902	Value: 255				

KM# 95 250 DOLLARS
11.3400 g., 0.9000 Gold .3281 oz. AGW **Ruler:** Elizabeth II
Subject: Wedding of Prince Charles and Lady Diana **Obv:** Crowned bust right

Date	Mintage	F	VF	XF	Unc	BU
1981 Proof	1,491	Value: 245				

KM# 100 250 DOLLARS
11.3400 g., 0.9000 Gold .3281 oz. AGW **Ruler:** Elizabeth II
Subject: World Championship of Football **Obv:** Arms with supporters **Rev:** Goalie catching attempted score

Date	Mintage	F	VF	XF	Unc	BU
1982 Proof	694	Value: 280				

KM# 124 250 DOLLARS
11.3200 g., 0.9000 Gold .3275 oz. AGW **Ruler:** Elizabeth II
Subject: Royal Visit **Obv:** Arms with supporters **Rev:** Conjoined heads of royal couple left

Date	Mintage	F	VF	XF	Unc	BU
1983 Proof	5,000	Value: 235				

KM# 118 250 DOLLARS
11.3400 g., 0.9000 Gold .3281 oz. AGW **Ruler:** Elizabeth II
Subject: Decade for Women **Obv:** Arms with supporters **Rev:** Woman with basket on head facing, map in background

Date	Mintage	F	VF	XF	Unc	BU
1984 Proof	559	Value: 275				

KM# 131 250 DOLLARS
16.0000 g., 0.9000 Gold .4630 oz. AGW **Ruler:** Elizabeth II
Subject: 25th Anniversary of Independence **Obv:** Crowned bust right **Rev:** Arms with supporters

Date	Mintage	F	VF	XF	Unc	BU
1987 Proof	250	Value: 400				

KM# 156 250 DOLLARS
11.3400 g., 0.9000 Gold .3281 oz. AGW **Ruler:** Elizabeth II
Subject: 40th Anniversary - Coronation of Queen Elizabeth **Obv:** Crowned bust right **Rev:** Arms with supporters

Date	Mintage	F	VF	XF	Unc	BU
1993 Proof	Est. 500	Value: 450				

KM# 153 500 DOLLARS
11.3400 g., 0.9000 Gold .3281 oz. AGW **Ruler:** Elizabeth II
Subject: Columbus Quincentennial **Obv:** Arms with supporters **Rev:** "500" on ship's sail

Date	Mintage	F	VF	XF	Unc	BU
1992 Proof	500	Value: 450				

KM# 162 500 DOLLARS
47.5400 g., 0.9170 Gold 1.4017 oz. AGW **Ruler:** Elizabeth II
Subject: Royal Visit **Obv:** Arms with supporters **Rev:** Drummer on island map with yacht at right

Date	Mintage	F	VF	XF	Unc	BU
1994 Proof	100	Value: 1,150				

PIEFORTS

KM#	Date	Mintage	Identification	Mkt Val
P2	1983	32	250 Dollars. 0.9000 Gold. Design like 10 Dollars, KM#80	1,250

JAPAN

Japan, a constitutional monarchy situated off the east coast of Asia, has an area of 145,809 sq. mi. (377,835 sq. km.) and a population of 123.2 million. Capital: Tokyo. Japan, one of the major industrial nations of the world, exports machinery, motor vehicles, electronics and chemicals.

Japan, founded (so legend holds) in 660 B.C. by a direct descendant of the Sun Goddess, was first brought into contact with the west by a storm-blown Portuguese ship in 1542. European traders and missionaries proceeded to enlarge the contact until the Shogunate, sensing a military threat in the foreign presence, expelled all foreigners and restricted relations with the outside world in the 17th century. After Commodore Perry's U.S. flotilla visited in 1854, Japan rapidly industrialized, abolished the Shogunate and established a parliamentary form of government, and by the end of the 19th century achieved the status of a modern economic and military power. A series of wars with China and Russia, and participation with the allies in World War I, enlarged Japan territorially but brought its interests into conflict with the Far Eastern interests of the United States, Britain and the Netherlands, causing it to align with the Axis Powers for the pursuit of World War II. After its defeat in World War II, General Douglas MacArthur forced Japan to renounce military aggression as a political instrument, and he instituted constitutional democratic self-government. Japan quickly gained a position as an economic world power.

Japanese coinage of concern to this catalog includes those issued for the Ryukyu Islands (also called Liuchu), a chain of islands extending southwest from Japan toward Taiwan (Formosa), before the Japanese government converted the islands into a prefecture under the name Okinawa. Many of the provinces of Japan issued their own definitive coinage under the Shogunate.

RULERS

Emperors
Mutsuhito (Meiji), 1867-1912
Years 1-45 明治 or 治明

Yoshihito (Taisho), 1912-1926
Years 1-15 大正 or 正大

Hirohito (Showa), 1926-1989
Years 1-64 昭和 or 和昭

Akihito (Heisei), 1989-
Years 1- 平成

NOTE: The personal name of the emperor is followed by the name that he chose for his regnal era.

MONETARY SYSTEM
Commencing 1870
10 Rin = 1 Sen
100 Sen = 1 Yen

MONETARY UNITS
Rin 厘
Sen 銭
Yen 円 or 圓 or 圓

DATING
Reading right to left, 3x10+2 = 32 year
Dai Nippon Great Japan
Meiji

SHOGUNATE
HAMMERED COINAGE

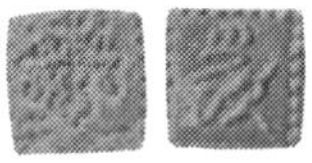

C# 17 SHU (Isshu Gin)
1.3900 g., Gold And Silver .123 gold and .877 silver **Note:** Bunsei era.

Date	Mintage	VG	F	VF	XF	Unc
ND(1824-32)	46,723,000	200	350	450	600	—

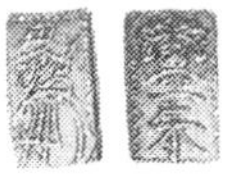

C# 18 2 SHU (Nishu Gin)
1.6200 g., Gold And Silver .298 gold and .702 silver **Note:** Tempo era.

Date	Mintage	VG	F	VF	XF	Unc
ND(1832-58)	103,070,000	20.00	25.00	30.00	40.00	—

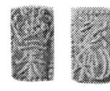

C# 18a 2 SHU (Nishu Gin)
0.7500 g., Gold And Silver .229 gold and .771 silver **Note:** Manen.

Date	Mintage	VG	F	VF	XF	Unc
ND(1860-69)	25,120,000	25.00	35.00	45.00	60.00	—

C# 20 BU (Ichibu)
3.2700 g., Gold And Silver .560 gold and .440 silver **Rev:** Type B mint mark **Note:** Bunsei era.

Date	Mintage	VG	F	VF	XF	Unc
ND(1819-29)	—	125	175	225	275	—

C# 20a BU (Ichibu)
2.8000 g., Gold And Silver .568 gold and .432 silver **Note:** Tempo era.

Date	Mintage	VG	F	VF	XF	Unc
ND(1837-58)	—	150	200	250	350	—

C# 20b BU (Ichibu)
2.2400 g., Gold And Silver .570 gold and .430 silver **Note:** Ansei era.

Date	Mintage	VG	F	VF	XF	Unc
ND(1859)	—	1,250	1,750	2,250	3,250	—

C# 20c BU (Ichibu)
0.8200 g., Gold And Silver .574 gold and .426 silver **Rev:** Without dating mark **Note:** Manen era.

Date	Mintage	VG	F	VF	XF	Unc
ND(1860-67)	—	500	650	800	1,000	—

Note: Similar pieces without dating mark but weighing about 4 grams were made during the Kyoho era, 1716-34

C# 21 2 BU (Ni Bu)
6.5200 g., Gold And Silver .563 gold and .437 silver **Rev:** Type A mark **Note:** Bunsei era.

Date	Mintage	VG	F	VF	XF	Unc
ND(1818-28)	5,972,000	300	400	600	850	—

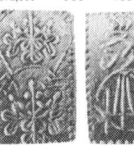

C# 21a 2 BU (Ni Bu)
6.5600 g., Gold And Silver .490 gold and .510 silver **Rev:** Type B mark **Note:** Bunsei era.

Date	Mintage	VG	F	VF	XF	Unc
ND(1828-32)	4,066,000	250	375	500	750	—

C# 21b 2 BU (Ni Bu)
5.6200 g., Gold And Silver .209 gold and .791 silver **Rev:** Without mint mark **Note:** Ansei era.

Date	Mintage	VG	F	VF	XF	Unc
ND(1856-60)	7,103,000	75.00	100	150	200	—

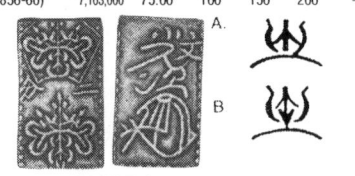

C# 21c.1 2 BU (Ni Bu)
3.0000 g., Gold And Silver .229 gold and .771 silver **Obv:** Paulownia leaf type A **Rev:** Without mint mark **Note:** Manen era.

Date	Mintage	VG	F	VF	XF	Unc
ND(1860)	100,201,000	350	550	750	1,100	—

C# 21c.2 2 BU (Ni Bu)
3.0000 g., Gold And Silver .229 gold and .771 silver **Obv:** Paulownia leaf type B **Note:** Manen era.

Date	Mintage	VG	F	VF	XF	Unc
ND(1860)	Inc. above	250	450	600	850	—

C# 21d 2 BU (Ni Bu)
3.0000 g., Gold And Silver .223 gold and .777 silver **Ruler:** Mutsuhito (Meiji)

Date	Mintage	VG	F	VF	XF	Unc
ND(1868-69)	—	40.00	50.00	65.00	90.00	—

JAPAN 449

C# 22a KOBAN (1 Ryo)
13.1300 g., Gold And Silver .559 gold and .441 silver **Rev:** Mark B **Note:** Brunsei era.

Date	Mintage	VG	F	VF	XF	Unc
ND(1819-28)	Est. 11,043,000	750	1,100	1,600	2,250	—

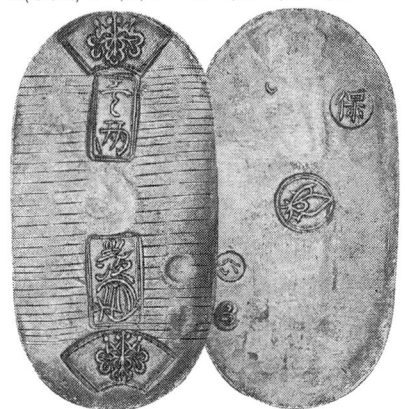

C# 22b KOBAN (1 Ryo)
11.2500 g., Gold And Silver .568 gold and .432 silver **Note:** Tempo era.

Date	Mintage	VG	F	VF	XF	Unc
ND(1837-58)	Est. 8,120,000	750	1,000	1,250	2,000	—

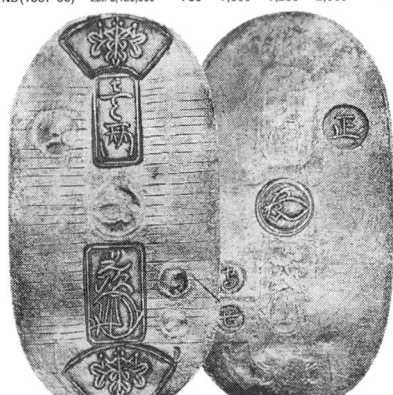

C# 22c KOBAN (1 Ryo)
8.9700 g., Gold And Silver .570 gold and .430 silver **Note:** Ansei era.

Date	Mintage	VG	F	VF	XF	Unc
ND(1859)	351,000	3,000	3,500	5,500	7,500	—

C# 22d KOBAN (1 Ryo)
3.3000 g., Gold And Silver .574 gold and .426 silver **Rev:** Without mint mark **Note:** Manen era.

Date	Mintage	VG	F	VF	XF	Unc
ND(1860-67)	625,000	500	750	950	1,350	—

Note: Koban mintage figures are in Ryo and also include Ichibu Kin

C# 23 GORYOBAN (5 Ryo)
33.7500 g., Gold And Silver .842 gold and .158 silver, 51x89 mm. **Note:** Tempo era.

Date	Mintage	VG	F	VF	XF	Unc
ND(1837-43)	34,000	7,500	12,000	14,000	16,500	—

C# 24.2 OBAN
165.3800 g., Gold And Silver .674 gold and .326 silver, 95x157 mm. **Note:** Tempo era.

Date	Mintage	VG	F	VF	XF	Unc
ND(1838-60)	1,887	—	—	50,000	60,000	—

C# 24a.1 OBAN
112.4000 g., Gold And Silver .344 gold and .639 silver **Note:** Handmade horizontal crenulations. Manen era.

Date	Mintage	VG	F	VF	XF	Unc
ND(1860-62)	17,000		—	18,000	25,000	—

C# 24a.2 OBAN
112.4000 g., Gold And Silver .344 gold and .639 silver **Note:** Machine-made horizontal crenulations. Manen era.

Date	Mintage	VG	F	VF	XF	Unc
ND(1860-62)	Inc. above	—	—	16,000	20,000	—

EMPIRE

DECIMAL COINAGE

Y# 9 YEN
1.6700 g., 0.9000 Gold .0482 oz. AGW, 13.5 mm. **Ruler:** Mutsuhito (Meiji) **Obv:** Value in center of 2 legends, date and authority, dot below **Rev:** Sunburst crest superimposed on sacred mirror, flanked by Military banners, chrysanthemum above with paulownia crest below

Date	Mintage	F	VF	XF	Unc	BU
Yr.4(1871) Low dot	1,841,288	550	850	1,400	2,350	—
Yr.4(1871) Proof	—	Value: 6,500				
Yr.4(1871) High dot	Inc. above	225	350	525	775	—

Y# 9a YEN
1.6700 g., 0.9000 Gold .0482 oz. AGW, 12 mm. **Ruler:** Mutsuhito (Meiji) **Obv:** Value in center of 2 legends, date and authority, dot below **Rev:** Sunburst crest superimposed on sacred mirror, flanked by Military banners, chrysanthemum above with paulownia crest below **Note:** Reduced size.

Date	Mintage	F	VF	XF	Unc	BU
Yr.7(1874)	116,341	2,300	2,800	3,250	4,500	—
Yr.9(1876)	138	6,700	8,500	12,000	16,000	—
Yr.10(1877)	7,246	16,000	24,000	30,000	45,000	—
Yr.13(1880)	112	22,000	27,000	35,000	50,000	—
Yr.25(1892)	—	—	—	—	—	—

Note: None struck for circulation

JAPAN

Y# 10 2 YEN
3.3333 g., 0.9000 Gold .0964 oz. AGW, 16.96 mm. **Ruler:** Mutsuhito (Meiji) **Obv:** Dragon within beaded circle, legends around border **Rev:** Sunburst crest superimposed on sacred mirror, flanked by Military banners, chrysanthemum above with paulownia crest below

Date	Mintage	F	VF	XF	Unc	BU
Yr.3(1870)	883,000	700	900	1,150	1,650	—
Yr.3(1870) Proof	—	Value: 9,500				

Y# 10a 2 YEN
3.3333 g., 0.9000 Gold .0964 oz. AGW, 16.96 mm. **Ruler:** Mutsuhito (Meiji) **Obv:** Dragon within beaded circle, legends around border **Rev:** Sunburst crest superimposed on sacred mirror, flanked by Military banners, chrysanthemum above with paulownia crest below **Note:** Reduced size, same weight.

Date	Mintage	F	VF	XF	Unc	BU
Yr.7(1874)	—	—	—	—	—	—
Note: Reported, not confirmed						
Yr.9(1876)	178	45,000	55,000	70,000	—	—
Yr.10(1877)	39	45,000	60,000	75,000	—	—
Yr.13(1880)	87	45,000	60,000	75,000	—	—
Yr.25(1892)	—	—	—	—	—	—
Note: None struck for circulation						

Y# 11 5 YEN
8.3333 g., 0.9000 Gold .2411 oz. AGW, 23.8 mm. **Ruler:** Mutsuhito (Meiji) **Obv:** Dragon within beaded circle, legends around border **Rev:** Sunburst crest superimposed on sacred mirror, flanked by Military banners, chrysanthemum above with paulownia crest below

Date	Mintage	F	VF	XF	Unc	BU
Yr.3(1870)	273,000	1,400	1,950	2,600	3,500	—
Yr.4(1871)	Inc. above	1,150	1,700	2,400	3,400	—
Yr.4(1871) Proof	—	Value: 10,000				

Y# 11a 5 YEN
8.3333 g., 0.9000 Gold .2411 oz. AGW, 21.8 mm. **Ruler:** Mutsuhito (Meiji) **Obv:** Dragon within beaded circle, legends around border **Rev:** Sunburst crest superimposed on sacred mirror, flanked by Military banners, chrysanthemum above with paulownia crest below **Note:** Reduced size, same weight.

Date	Mintage	F	VF	XF	Unc	BU
Yr.5(1872)	1,057,000	900	1,400	1,900	2,500	—
Yr.6(1873)	3,148,000	900	1,400	1,900	2,500	—
Yr.7(1874)	728,000	1,300	1,800	2,500	3,500	—
Yr.8(1875)	181,000	1,400	1,900	2,500	3,500	—
Yr.9(1876)	146,000	1,850	2,300	2,850	4,200	—
Yr.10(1877)	136,000	3,000	4,000	5,000	7,000	—
Yr.11(1878)	101,000	3,200	4,200	5,000	7,500	—
Yr.13(1880)	78,000	3,200	4,500	5,500	7,500	—
Yr.14(1881)	149,000	3,200	4,300	5,500	7,500	—
Yr.15(1882)	113,000	3,000	4,000	5,500	7,500	—
Yr.16(1883)	108,000	3,000	4,000	5,500	7,500	—
Yr.17(1884)	113,000	3,000	4,000	5,500	7,500	—
Yr.18(1885)	200,000	3,000	4,000	5,500	7,500	—
Yr.19(1886)	179,000	3,000	4,000	5,500	7,500	—
Yr.20(1887)	179,000	3,000	4,000	5,500	7,500	—
Yr.21(1888)	165,000	3,000	4,000	5,500	7,500	—
Yr.22(1889)	353,000	3,000	4,000	5,500	7,500	—
Yr.23(1890)	238,000	3,000	4,000	5,500	7,500	—
Yr.24(1891)	216,000	3,000	4,000	5,500	7,500	—
Yr.25(1892)	263,000	3,000	4,000	5,500	7,500	—
Yr.26(1893)	260,000	4,000	5,400	6,500	11,500	—
Yr.27(1894)	314,000	3,000	4,000	5,500	7,500	—
Yr.28(1895)	320,000	3,000	4,000	5,500	7,500	—
Yr.29(1896)	224,000	3,000	5,400	6,500	11,500	—
Yr.30(1897)	107,000	3,000	5,400	6,500	11,500	—

Y# 32 5 YEN
4.1666 g., 0.9000 Gold .1205 oz. AGW **Ruler:** Mutsuhito (Meiji) **Obv:** Sunburst superimposed on sacred mirror, legends around border, value separated by paulownia crests **Rev:** Value within wreath, chrysanthemum above

Date	Mintage	F	VF	XF	Unc	BU
Yr.30(1897)	111,776	800	1,050	1,400	1,900	—
Yr.31(1898)	55,888	800	1,100	1,450	1,950	—
Yr.36(1903)	21,956	800	950	1,250	2,250	2,750
Yr.44(1911)	59,880	750	900	1,200	2,150	2,500
Yr.45(1912)	59,880	600	750	1,000	1,750	2,000

Y# 39 5 YEN
4.1666 g., 0.9000 Gold .1205 oz. AGW **Ruler:** Yoshihito (Taisho) **Obv:** Sunburst within mirror, 3 legends around border, value on bottom **Rev:** Value and denomination within flowered wreath, chrysanthemum on top

Date	Mintage	F	VF	XF	Unc	BU
Yr.2(1913)	89,820	700	900	1,150	1,850	2,250
Yr.13(1924)	76,037	600	750	950	1,650	2,000

Y# 51 5 YEN
4.1666 g., 0.9000 Gold .1205 oz. AGW **Ruler:** Hirohito (Showa)

Date	Mintage	F	VF	XF	Unc	BU
Yr.5(1930)	852,563	20,000	35,000	50,000	65,000	75,000

Y# 12 10 YEN
16.6666 g., 0.9000 Gold .4823 oz. AGW **Ruler:** Mutsuhito (Meiji) **Obv:** Dragon within beaded circle, legends around border **Rev:** Sunburst crest superimposed on sacred mirror, flanked by Military banners, chrysanthemum above with paulownia crest below

Date	Mintage	F	VF	XF	Unc	BU
Yr.4(1871)	1,867,000	2,800	3,750	4,500	6,000	—
Yr.4(1871) Proof	—	Value: 35,000				

Y# 12a 10 YEN
16.6666 g., 0.9000 Gold .4823 oz. AGW **Ruler:** Mutsuhito (Meiji) **Obv:** Dragon within beaded circle, legends around border **Rev:** Sunburst crest superimposed on sacred mirror, flanked by Military banners, chrysanthemum above with paulownia crest below **Note:** Modified design.

Date	Mintage	F	VF	XF	Unc	BU
Yr.9(1876)	1,925	35,000	45,000	55,000	70,000	—
Yr.10(1877)	36	45,000	55,000	70,000	85,000	—
Yr.13(1880)	136	45,000	55,000	70,000	85,000	—
Yr.25(1892)	—	—	—	—	—	—
Note: None struck for circulation						

Y# 33 10 YEN
8.3333 g., 0.9000 Gold .2411 oz. AGW **Ruler:** Mutsuhito (Meiji) **Obv:** Sunburst superimposed on sacred mirror, legends around border, value separated by paulownia crests **Rev:** Value within wreath, chrysanthemum above

Date	Mintage	VG	F	VF	XF	BU
Yr.30(1897)	2,422,146	—	350	550	750	1,250
Yr.31(1898)	3,176,134	—	350	550	750	1,250
Yr.32(1899)	1,743,006	—	350	550	750	1,250
Yr.33(1900)	1,114,776	—	550	800	1,200	1,700
Yr.34(1901)	1,654,682	—	400	550	750	1,250
Yr.35(1902)	3,023,940	—	400	550	750	1,350
Yr.36(1903)	2,902,184	—	400	550	750	1,350
Yr.37(1904)	724,548	—	750	1,500	2,000	4,000
Yr.40(1907)	157,684	—	450	700	1,250	2,350
Yr.41(1908)	1,160,674	—	400	550	750	1,250
Yr.42(1909)	2,165,660	—	350	550	750	1,200
Yr.43(1910)	8,982	—	7,500	10,000	15,000	25,000

Y# 13 20 YEN
33.3332 g., 0.9000 Gold .9646 oz. AGW **Ruler:** Mutsuhito (Meiji) **Obv:** Dragon within beaded circle, legends around border **Rev:** Sunburst crest superimposed on sacred mirror, flanked by Military banners, chrysanthemum above with paulownia crest below

Date	Mintage	F	VF	XF	Unc	BU
Yr.3(1870)	46,000	20,000	26,000	30,000	37,500	—
Yr.3(1870) Proof	—	Value: 57,500				
Yr.9(1876)	954	35,000	50,000	65,000	100,000	—
Yr.10(1877)	29	45,000	70,000	85,000	110,000	—
Yr.13(1880)	103	40,000	60,000	75,000	100,000	—
Yr.25(1892)	—	—	—	—	—	—
Note: None struck for circulation						

Y# 34 20 YEN
16.6666 g., 0.9000 Gold .4823 oz. AGW **Ruler:** Mutsuhito (Meiji) **Obv:** Sunburst superimposed on sacred mirror, legends around border, authority above, date below **Rev:** Value within wreath, chrysanthemum above

Date	Mintage	VG	F	VF	XF	BU
Yr.30(1897)	1,861,000	—	1,100	1,500	1,750	2,400
Yr.36(1903) Rare	—	—	—	—	—	—
Yr.37(1904)	2,759,470	—	550	1,250	1,750	2,400
Yr.38(1905)	1,045,904	—	550	1,250	1,750	2,400
Yr.39(1906)	1,331,332	—	550	1,250	1,750	2,400
Yr.40(1907)	817,363	—	1,000	2,000	2,500	4,500
Yr.41(1908)	458,082	—	1,250	2,500	3,500	5,500
Yr.42(1909)	557,882	—	1,500	3,000	4,000	6,500
Yr.43(1910)	2,163,644	—	500	1,000	1,600	2,200
Yr.44(1911)	1,470,057	—	500	1,000	1,600	2,200
Yr.45(1912)	1,272,450	—	525	1,100	1,700	2,300

Y# 40.1 20 YEN
16.6666 g., 0.9000 Gold .4823 oz. AGW **Ruler:** Yoshihito (Taisho) **Obv:** Japanese character "first" used in date **Rev:** Value and denomination within wreath, chrysanthemum on top

Date	Mintage	VG	F	VF	XF	BU
Yr.1(1912)	177,644	—	700	1,400	2,200	3,000

Y# 40.2 20 YEN
16.6666 g., 0.9000 Gold .4823 oz. AGW **Ruler:** Yoshihito (Taisho) **Obv:** Sunburst within mirror, 3 legends separated by cherry blossoms, date on bottom **Rev:** Value and denomination within wreath, chrysanthemum on top

Date	Mintage	VG	F	VF	XF	BU
Yr.2(1913)	869,248	—	500	1,000	1,700	2,300
Yr.3(1914)	1,042,890	—	500	1,000	1,700	2,300
Yr.4(1915)	1,509,960	—	500	1,000	1,700	2,300
Yr.5(1916)	2,376,641	—	450	900	1,600	2,200
Yr.6(1917)	6,208,885	—	425	850	1,550	2,150
Yr.7(1918)	3,118,647	—	450	900	1,600	2,200
Yr.8(1919)	1,531,217	—	450	900	1,600	2,200
Yr.9(1920)	370,366	—	550	1,150	1,800	2,650

JAPAN 451

Y# 52 20 YEN
16.6666 g., 0.9000 Gold .4823 oz. AGW **Ruler:** Hirohito (Showa)
Obv: Sunburst within mirror, legends separated by cherry blossoms around border **Rev:** Value and denomination within wreath, chrysanthemum on top

Date	Mintage	VG	F	VF	XF	BU
Yr.5(1930)	11,055,500	—	15,000	25,000	35,000	45,000
Yr.6(1931)	7,526,476	—	17,500	27,500	37,500	47,500
Yr.7(1932) Rare						

REFORM COINAGE

Y# 116 10000 YEN
15.6000 g., 1.0000 Gold .5022 oz. AGW **Ruler:** Akihito (Heisei)
Series: 1998 Nagano Winter Olympics **Obv:** Ski jumper **Rev:** Value, dates, and gentian plant

Date	Mintage	F	VF	XF	Unc	BU
Yr.9(1997) Proof	55,000	Value: 675				

Y# 121 10000 YEN
15.6000 g., 1.0000 Gold .5022 oz. AGW **Ruler:** Akihito (Heisei)
Series: 1998 Nagano Winter Olympics **Obv:** Figure skater **Rev:** Value, dates, and gentian plant

Date	Mintage	F	VF	XF	Unc	BU
Yr.9(1997) Proof	55,000	Value: 675				

Y# 122 10000 YEN
15.6000 g., 1.0000 Gold .5022 oz. AGW **Ruler:** Akihito (Heisei)
Series: 1998 Nagano Winter Olympics **Obv:** Speed skater **Rev:** Value, dates, and gentian plant

Date	Mintage	F	VF	XF	Unc	BU
Yr.10(1998) Proof	55,000	Value: 675				

Y# 124 10000 YEN
20.0000 g., 1.0000 Gold .6430 oz. AGW **Ruler:** Akihito (Heisei)
Subject: 15th Anniversary of Enthronement **Obv:** Chrysanthemum within wreath **Rev:** Stylized Green Phoenix

Date	Mintage	F	VF	XF	Unc	BU
Yr.11(1999) Proof	200,000	Value: 1,200				

Y# 130 10000 YEN
15.6000 g., 0.9990 Gold 0.501 oz. AGW, 26 mm. **Ruler:** Akihito (Heisei) **Subject:** World Cup Soccer **Obv:** Two soccer players **Rev:** Games logo **Edge:** Reeded

Date	Mintage	F	VF	XF	Unc	BU
Yr.14(2002) Proof	100,000	Value: 450				

Y# 136 10000 YEN
15.6000 g., 0.9990 Gold 0.501 oz. AGW, 26 mm. **Ruler:** Akihito (Heisei) **Subject:** Expo 2005 **Obv:** Two owls on globe **Rev:** Expo logo

Date	Mintage	F	VF	XF	Unc	BU
Yr.16(2004) Proof	70,000	Value: 700				

Y# 109 50000 YEN
18.0000 g., 1.0000 Gold .5788 oz. AGW **Ruler:** Akihito (Heisei) **Subject:** Royal wedding of Crown Prince **Obv:** Chrysanthemum flanked by cherry blossom sprigs **Rev:** Pair of herons

Date	Mintage	VG	F	VF	XF	BU
Yr.5(1993)	1,900,000	—	—	—	—	650
Yr.5(1993) Proof	100,000	Value: 850				

Y# 92 100000 YEN
20.0000 g., 1.0000 Gold .6430 oz. AGW **Ruler:** Hirohito (Showa) **Subject:** 60 Years - Reign of Hirohito **Obv:** Large chrysanthemum with legends around border **Rev:** Pair of birds within artistic design **Designer:** Ikuo Hirayama

Date	Mintage	VG	F	VF	XF	BU
Yr.61(1986)	10,000,000	—	—	—	—	1,250
Yr.62(1987)	876,000	—	—	—	—	1,250
Yr.62(1987) Proof	124,000	Value: 1,350				

Y# 105 100000 YEN
30.0000 g., 1.0000 Gold .9646 oz. AGW **Ruler:** Akihito (Heisei) **Subject:** Enthronement of Emperor Akihito **Obv:** Chrysanthemum within wreath **Rev:** Stylized Green Phoenix

Date	Mintage	VG	F	VF	XF	BU
Yr.2(1990)	1,900,000	—	—	—	—	1,250
Yr.2(1990) Proof	100,000	Value: 1,350				

PLATINUM BULLION COINAGE

KM# 20 10 MOMME
Platinum 37.4 oz. APW **Ruler:** Hirohito (Showa)

Date	Mintage	VG	F	VF	XF	BU
1937	1,500	—	—	—	—	1,750

PATTERNS
Including off metal strikes

KM#	Date	Mintage	Identification	Mkt Val
Pn17	Yr.3 (1870)	—	2-1/2 Yen. Gold.	—
Pn18	Yr.3 (1870)	—	5 Yen. Gold.	—
Pn19	Yr.3 (1870)	—	10 Yen. Gold. 32 mm. Dragon within beaded circle, legends around border. Sunburst crest superimposed on sacred mirror, flanked by Military banners, chrysanthemum above with paulownia crest below.	
Pn20	Yr.3 (1870)	—	10 Yen. Gold. Y#12.	
Pn26	Yr.7 (1874)	—	5 Yen. Gold. Dragon, legends around border. Sunburst crest superimposed on sacred mirror within wreath, chrysanthemum above.	

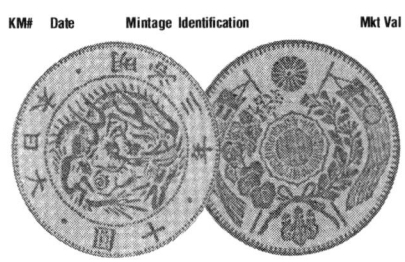

PROOF SETS

KM#	Date	Mintage	Identification	Issue Price	Mkt Val
PS8	1993 (3)	100,000	Y#107-109	100	900
PS15	1997 (3)	33,000	Y#114-116	413	810
PS16	1997 (2)	100,000	Y#114-115	99.00	160
PS17	1997 (3)	33,000	Y#117, 119, 121	406	810
PS22	1998 (3)	33,000	Y#118, 120, 122	375	800
PS29	1999 (2)	100,000	Y#123, 124	370	400
PS38	2002 (2)	50,000	Y#129, 130 World Cup	385	550

452 JERSEY

JERSEY

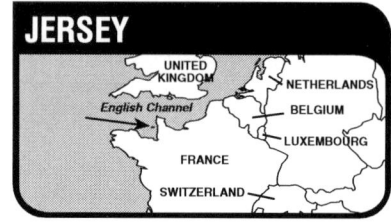

The Bailiwick of Jersey, a British Crown dependency located in the English Channel 12 miles (19 km.) west of Normandy, France, has an area of 45 sq. mi. (117 sq. km.) and a population of 74,000. Capital: St. Helier. The economy is based on agriculture and cattle breeding – the importation of cattle is prohibited to protect the purity of the island's world-famous strain of milch cows.

Jersey was occupied by Neanderthal man by 100,000 B.C., and by Iberians of 2000 B.C. who left their chamber tombs in the island's granite cliffs. Roman legions almost certainly visited the island although they left no evidence of settlement. The country folk of Jersey still speak an archaic form of Norman-French, lingering evidence of the Norman annexation of the island in 933 A.D. Jersey was annexed to England in 1206, 140 years after the Norman Conquest. The dependency is administered by its own laws and customs; laws enacted by the British Parliament do not apply to Jersey unless it is specifically mentioned. During World War II, German troops occupied the island from July 1, 1940 until May 9, 1945.

Coins of pre-Roman Gaul and of Rome have been found in abundance on Jersey.

RULER
British

MINT MARK
H - Heaton, Birmingham

MONETARY SYSTEM
Commencing 1877
12 Pence = 1 Shilling
5 Shillings = 1 Crown
20 Shillings = 1 Pound
100 New Pence = 1 Pound

BRITISH DEPENDENCY

DECIMAL COINAGE
100 New Pence = 1 Pound

Many of the following coins are also struck in silver, gold, and platinum for collectors

KM# 51b POUND
17.5500 g., 0.9170 Gold .5174 oz. AGW **Ruler:** Elizabeth II **Subject:** Bicentennial - Battle of Jersey **Obv:** Young bust right **Rev:** Crowned shaded pointed shield within X design divides dates **Shape:** Square

Date	Mintage	F	VF	XF	Unc	BU
ND(1981) Proof	5,000	Value: 380				

KM# 59b POUND
19.6500 g., 0.9170 Gold .5794 oz. AGW, 22.5 mm. **Ruler:** Elizabeth II **Obv:** Young bust right **Rev:** Shield above written value

Date	Mintage	F	VF	XF	Unc	BU
1983 Proof	250	Value: 425				

Note: 497 pieces were remelted

KM# 60b POUND
19.6500 g., 0.9170 Gold .5794 oz. AGW, 22.5 mm. **Ruler:** Elizabeth II **Obv:** Young bust right **Rev:** Shield above written value

Date	Mintage	F	VF	XF	Unc	BU
1984 Proof	250	Value: 425				

KM# 61b POUND
19.6500 g., 0.9170 Gold .5794 oz. AGW, 22.5 mm. **Ruler:** Elizabeth II **Obv:** Young bust right **Rev:** Shield above written value

Date	Mintage	F	VF	XF	Unc	BU
1984 Proof	250	Value: 425				

KM# 62b POUND
19.6500 g., 0.9170 Gold .5794 oz. AGW, 22.5 mm. **Ruler:** Elizabeth II **Obv:** Young bust right **Rev:** Shield above written value

Date	Mintage	F	VF	XF	Unc	BU
1985 Proof	124	Value: 450				

KM# 65b POUND
19.6500 g., 0.9170 Gold .5794 oz. AGW, 22.5 mm. **Ruler:** Elizabeth II **Obv:** Young bust right **Rev:** Shield above written value

Date	Mintage	F	VF	XF	Unc	BU
1985 Proof	108	Value: 475				

KM# 68b POUND
19.6500 g., 0.9170 Gold .5794 oz. AGW, 22.5 mm. **Ruler:** Elizabeth II **Obv:** Young bust right **Rev:** Shield above written value

Date	Mintage	F	VF	XF	Unc	BU
1986 Proof	250	Value: 425				

KM# 69b POUND
19.6500 g., 0.9170 Gold .5794 oz. AGW, 22.5 mm. **Ruler:** Elizabeth II **Obv:** Young bust right **Rev:** Shield above written value

Date	Mintage	F	VF	XF	Unc	BU
1986 Proof	250	Value: 425				

KM# 71b POUND
19.6500 g., 0.9170 Gold .5794 oz. AGW, 22.5 mm. **Ruler:** Elizabeth II **Obv:** Young bust right **Rev:** Shield above written value

Date	Mintage	F	VF	XF	Unc	BU
1987 Proof	250	Value: 425				

KM# 72b POUND
19.6500 g., 0.9170 Gold .5794 oz. AGW, 22.5 mm. **Ruler:** Elizabeth II **Obv:** Young bust right **Rev:** Shield above written value

Date	Mintage	F	VF	XF	Unc	BU
1987 Proof	250	Value: 425				

KM# 73b POUND
19.6500 g., 0.9170 Gold .5794 oz. AGW, 22.5 mm. **Ruler:** Elizabeth II **Obv:** Young bust right **Rev:** Shield above written value

Date	Mintage	F	VF	XF	Unc	BU
1988 Proof	250	Value: 425				

KM# 74b POUND
19.6500 g., 0.9170 Gold .5794 oz. AGW, 22.5 mm. **Ruler:** Elizabeth II **Obv:** Young bust right **Rev:** Shield above written value

Date	Mintage	F	VF	XF	Unc	BU
1988 Proof	250	Value: 425				

KM# 75b POUND
19.6500 g., 0.9170 Gold .5794 oz. AGW, 22.5 mm. **Ruler:** Elizabeth II **Obv:** Young bust right **Rev:** Shield above written value

Date	Mintage	F	VF	XF	Unc	BU
1989 Proof	250	Value: 425				

KM# 84b POUND
19.6500 g., 0.9170 Gold .5794 oz. AGW, 22.5 mm. **Ruler:** Elizabeth II **Obv:** Young bust right **Rev:** Schooner, The Tickler **Rev. Designer:** Robert Evans

Date	Mintage	F	VF	XF	Unc	BU
1991 Proof	Est. 250	Value: 450				

KM# 85b POUND
19.6500 g., 0.9170 Gold .5794 oz. AGW, 22.5 mm. **Ruler:** Elizabeth II **Obv:** Young bust right **Rev:** Sailing ship, Percy Douglas **Rev. Designer:** Robert Evans

Date	Mintage	F	VF	XF	Unc	BU
1991 Proof	250	Value: 450				

KM# 86b POUND
19.6500 g., 0.9170 Gold .5794 oz. AGW, 22.5 mm. **Ruler:** Elizabeth II **Obv:** Young bust right **Rev:** Sailing ship, Hebe **Rev. Designer:** Robert Evans

Date	Mintage	F	VF	XF	Unc	BU
1992 Proof	Est. 250	Value: 450				

KM# 87b POUND
19.6500 g., 0.9170 Gold .5794 oz. AGW, 22.5 mm. **Ruler:** Elizabeth II **Obv:** Young bust right **Rev:** Ornamented shield **Rev. Designer:** Robert Evans

Date	Mintage	F	VF	XF	Unc	BU
1992 Proof	250	Value: 425				

KM# 88b POUND
19.6500 g., 0.9170 Gold .5794 oz. AGW, 22.5 mm. **Ruler:** Elizabeth II **Obv:** Young bust right **Rev:** Sailing ship, Gemini **Rev. Designer:** Robert Evans

Date	Mintage	F	VF	XF	Unc	BU
1993 Proof	250	Value: 475				

KM# 90b POUND
19.6500 g., 0.9170 Gold .5794 oz. AGW, 22.5 mm. **Ruler:** Elizabeth II **Obv:** Young bust right **Rev:** Sailing ship, Century **Rev. Designer:** Robert Evans

Date	Mintage	F	VF	XF	Unc	BU
1993 Proof	Est. 250	Value: 450				

KM# 91b POUND
19.6500 g., 0.9170 Gold .5794 oz. AGW, 22.5 mm. **Ruler:** Elizabeth II **Obv:** Young bust right **Rev:** Schooner, Resolute **Rev. Designer:** Robert Evans

Date	Mintage	F	VF	XF	Unc	BU
1994 Proof	250	Value: 450				

KM# 110 SOVEREIGN
7.9800 g., 0.9167 Gold .2352 oz. AGW, 22.5 mm. **Ruler:** Elizabeth II **Subject:** William I - Duke of Normandy **Obv:** Crowned bust right **Rev:** William seated on throne **Rev. Designer:** Robert Elderton

Date	Mintage	F	VF	XF	Unc	BU
2000	Est. 2,000	—	—	—	175	—
2000 Proof	Est. 2,000	Value: 225				

KM# 52b 2 POUNDS
15.9800 g., 0.9170 Gold .4712 oz. AGW, 38.5 mm. **Ruler:** Elizabeth II **Subject:** Wedding of Prince Charles and Lady Diana **Obv:** Crowned bust right **Rev:** Conjoined busts right

Date	Mintage	F	VF	XF	Unc	BU
ND(1981) Proof	1,500	Value: 345				

JERSEY 453

KM# 64b 2 POUNDS
47.5400 g., 0.9170 Gold 1.4011 oz. AGW, 38.5 mm. **Ruler:** Elizabeth II **Subject:** 40th Anniversary of Liberation of 1945 **Obv:** Crowned bust right **Rev:** H.M.S. Beagle, destroyer

Date	Mintage	F	VF	XF	Unc	BU
1985 Proof	40	Value: 2,000				

KM# 83b 2 POUNDS
15.9800 g., 0.9170 Gold .4708 oz. AGW **Ruler:** Elizabeth II **Subject:** 90th Birthday of Queen Mother **Obv:** Crowned bust right **Rev:** Crowned double "E" monogram

Date	Mintage	F	VF	XF	Unc	BU
ND(1990) Proof	90	Value: 750				

KM# 89b 2 POUNDS
15.9800 g., 0.9167 Gold .4709 oz. AGW **Ruler:** Elizabeth II **Subject:** 40th Anniversary - Coronation of Queen Elizabeth II **Obv:** Crowned bust right **Rev:** Crown, royal mace and shield

Date	Mintage	F	VF	XF	Unc	BU
ND(1993) Proof	Est. 500	Value: 500				

KM# 39 5 POUNDS
2.6200 g., 0.9170 Gold .0772 oz. AGW **Ruler:** Elizabeth II **Subject:** 25th Wedding Anniversary **Obv:** Young bust right **Rev:** Garden shrew **Rev. Designer:** Norman Sillman

Date	Mintage	F	VF	XF	Unc	BU
1972	8,500	—	—	—	60.00	—
1972 Proof	1,500	Value: 75.00				

KM# 111b 5 POUNDS
39.9400 g., 0.9167 Gold 1.1771 oz. AGW, 38.6 mm. **Ruler:** Elizabeth II **Subject:** Princess Diana **Obv:** Crowned head right **Rev:** Diana's cameo above people **Edge:** Reeded

Date	Mintage	F	VF	XF	Unc	BU
2002 Proof	100	Value: 875				

KM# 113b 5 POUNDS
39.9400 g., 0.9166 Gold 1.177 oz. AGW, 38.6 mm. **Ruler:** Elizabeth II **Subject:** Queen Mother **Obv:** Crowned head right **Rev:** Queen Mother's portrait circa 1918 **Edge:** Reeded

Date	Mintage	F	VF	XF	Unc	BU
2002 Proof	250	Value: 850				

KM# 115b 5 POUNDS
39.9400 g., 0.9166 Gold 1.177 oz. AGW, 38.6 mm. **Ruler:** Elizabeth II **Subject:** Golden Jubilee **Obv:** Crowned head right **Rev:** Abbey procession scene **Edge:** Reeded

Date	Mintage	F	VF	XF	Unc	BU
2002 Proof	100	Value: 860				

KM# 117b 5 POUNDS
39.9400 g., 0.9166 Gold 1.177 oz. AGW, 38.6 mm. **Ruler:** Elizabeth II **Subject:** Duke of Wellington **Obv:** Crowned head right **Rev:** Wellington's portrait with multicolor infantry scene **Edge:** Reeded

Date	Mintage	F	VF	XF	Unc	BU
2002 Proof	200	Value: 850				

KM# 119b 5 POUNDS
39.9400 g., 0.9166 Gold 1.177 oz. AGW, 38.6 mm. **Ruler:** Elizabeth II **Subject:** Golden Jubilee **Obv:** Crowned head right **Rev:** Honor guard and monument **Edge:** Reeded

Date	Mintage	F	VF	XF	Unc	BU
2003 Proof	250	Value: 850				

KM# 121b 5 POUNDS
39.9400 g., 0.9166 Gold 1.177 oz. AGW, 38.6 mm. **Ruler:** Elizabeth II **Obv:** Crowned head right **Rev:** Bust facing and crowned arms with supporters **Edge:** Reeded

Date	Mintage	F	VF	XF	Unc	BU
2003 Proof	200	Value: 875				

KM# 124b 5 POUNDS
39.9400 g., 0.9167 Gold 1.1771 oz. AGW, 38.6 mm. **Ruler:** Elizabeth II **Obv:** Crowned head right **Rev:** British Horsa gliders in flight

Date	Mintage	F	VF	XF	Unc	BU
2004 Proof	500	Value: 1,000				

KM# 126b 5 POUNDS
39.9400 g., 0.9166 Gold 1.177 oz. AGW, 38.6 mm. **Ruler:** Elizabeth II **Obv:** Crowned head right **Rev:** Charge of the Light Brigade scene with one blue uniform behind the Earl of Cardigan **Edge:** Reeded

Date	Mintage	F	VF	XF	Unc	BU
2004 Proof	500	Value: 1,000				

KM# 128b 5 POUNDS
39.9400 g., 0.9167 Gold 1.1771 oz. AGW, 38.6 mm. **Ruler:** Elizabeth II **Subject:** WWII Liberation **Obv:** Crowned head right **Rev:** Big Ben Tower **Edge:** Reeded

Date	Mintage	F	VF	XF	Unc	BU
2005 Proof	150	Value: 1,000				

KM# 129a 5 POUNDS
39.9400 g., 0.9167 Gold 1.1771 oz. AGW, 38.6 mm. **Ruler:** Elizabeth II **Subject:** WWII Liberation **Obv:** Crowned head right **Rev:** Returning evacuees **Edge:** Reeded

Date	Mintage	F	VF	XF	Unc	BU
2005 Proof	150	Value: 1,000				

KM# 40 10 POUNDS
4.6400 g., 0.9170 Gold .1368 oz. AGW **Ruler:** Elizabeth II **Subject:** 25th Wedding Anniversary **Obv:** Young bust right **Rev:** Gold torque, excavated 1899 in St. Helier, Jersey. **Rev. Designer:** Norman Sillman

Date	Mintage	F	VF	XF	Unc	BU
1972	8,500	—	—	—	100	—
1972 Proof	1,500	Value: 110				

KM# 79 10 POUNDS
3.1300 g., 0.9990 Gold .1005 oz. AGW **Ruler:** Elizabeth II **Subject:** 50th Anniversary - The Battle of Britain **Obv:** Crowned bust right **Obv. Designer:** Ian Rank-Broadley **Rev:** Crowned air force badge divides dates

Date	Mintage	F	VF	XF	Unc	BU
ND Proof	Est. 500	Value: 125				

KM# 93 10 POUNDS
3.1300 g., 0.9990 Gold .1005 oz. AGW **Ruler:** Elizabeth II **Subject:** 50th Anniversary of Liberation **Obv:** Crowned bust right **Rev:** Red Cross bringing supplies to Jersey immediately following liberation **Rev. Designer:** Robert Elderton

Date	Mintage	F	VF	XF	Unc	BU
1995 Proof sets only	500	—	—	—	85.00	—

KM# 41 20 POUNDS
9.2600 g., 0.9170 Gold .2729 oz. AGW **Ruler:** Elizabeth II **Subject:** 25th Wedding Anniversary **Obv:** Young bust right **Rev:** Ormer shell **Rev. Designer:** Norman Sillman

Date	Mintage	F	VF	XF	Unc	BU
1972	8,500	—	—	—	200	—
1972 Proof	1,500	Value: 220				

KM# 42 25 POUNDS
11.9000 g., 0.9170 Gold .3507 oz. AGW **Ruler:** Elizabeth II **Subject:** 25th Wedding Anniversary **Obv:** Young bust right **Rev:** Arms of Queen Elizabeth I

Date	Mintage	F	VF	XF	Unc	BU
1972	8,500	—	—	—	250	—
1972 Proof	1,500	Value: 270				

KM# 80 25 POUNDS
7.8100 g., 0.9990 Gold .2509 oz. AGW **Ruler:** Elizabeth II **Subject:** 50th Anniversary - The Battle of Britain **Obv:** Crowned bust right **Rev:** Spitfire **Rev. Designer:** Ian Rank-Broadley

Date	Mintage	F	VF	XF	Unc	BU
1990 Proof	Est. 500	Value: 250				

KM# 94 25 POUNDS
7.8100 g., 0.9990 Gold .2509 oz. AGW **Ruler:** Elizabeth II **Subject:** 50th Anniversary of Liberation **Obv:** Crowned bust right **Rev:** Family encircled around flags with written value below **Rev. Designer:** Robert Elderton

JERSEY

Date	Mintage	F	VF	XF	Unc	BU
1995 Proof sets only	500	—	—	—	215	—

KM# 112 25 POUNDS
7.9800 g., 0.9167 Gold 0.2352 oz. AGW, 22.05 mm. **Ruler:** Elizabeth II **Subject:** Princess Diana **Obv:** Crowned head right **Rev:** Diana's portrait **Edge:** Reeded

Date	Mintage	F	VF	XF	Unc	BU
2002 Proof	2,500	Value: 290				

KM# 114 25 POUNDS
7.9800 g., 0.9166 Gold 0.2352 oz. AGW, 22 mm. **Ruler:** Elizabeth II **Subject:** Queen Mother **Obv:** Crowned head right **Rev:** Queen Mother's portrait circa 1918 **Edge:** Reeded

Date	Mintage	F	VF	XF	Unc	BU
2002 Proof	2,500	Value: 300				

KM# 116 25 POUNDS
7.9800 g., 0.9166 Gold 0.2352 oz. AGW, 22 mm. **Ruler:** Elizabeth II **Subject:** Battle of Britain **Obv:** Crowned head right **Rev:** Abbey procession scene **Edge:** Reeded

Date	Mintage	F	VF	XF	Unc	BU
2002 Proof	2,500	Value: 300				

KM# 118 25 POUNDS
7.9800 g., 0.9166 Gold 0.2352 oz. AGW, 22 mm. **Ruler:** Elizabeth II **Subject:** Duke of Wellington **Obv:** Crowned head right **Rev:** Wellington's portrait with infantry scene **Edge:** Reeded

Date	Mintage	F	VF	XF	Unc	BU
2002 Proof	2,500	Value: 300				

KM# 120 25 POUNDS
7.9800 g., 0.9166 Gold 0.2352 oz. AGW, 22 mm. **Ruler:** Elizabeth II **Subject:** Golden Jubilee **Obv:** Crowned head right **Rev:** Honor guard and monument **Edge:** Reeded

Date	Mintage	F	VF	XF	Unc	BU
2003 Proof	5,000	Value: 300				

KM# 125 25 POUNDS
7.9800 g., 0.9167 Gold 0.2352 oz. AGW, 22 mm. **Ruler:** Elizabeth II **Obv:** Crowned head right **Rev:** British Horsa gliders in flight **Edge:** Reeded **Note:** D-Day

Date	Mintage	F	VF	XF	Unc	BU
2004 Proof	500	Value: 325				

KM# 43 50 POUNDS
22.6300 g., 0.9170 Gold .6670 oz. AGW **Ruler:** Elizabeth II **Subject:** 25th Wedding Anniversary **Obv:** Young bust right **Rev:** Shield above written value **Rev. Designer:** Norman Sillman

Date	Mintage	F	VF	XF	Unc	BU
1972	8,500	—	—	—	475	—
1972 Proof	1,500	Value: 500				

KM# 81 50 POUNDS
15.6100 g., 0.9990 Gold .5014 oz. AGW **Ruler:** Elizabeth II **Subject:** 50th Anniversary - Battle of Britain **Obv:** Crowned bust right **Rev:** Crowned air force badge divides dates **Rev. Designer:** Ian Rank-Broadley

Date	Mintage	F	VF	XF	Unc	BU
ND Proof	Est. 500	Value: 480				

KM# 95 50 POUNDS
15.6100 g., 0.9990 Gold .5014 oz. AGW **Ruler:** Elizabeth II **Subject:** 50th Anniversary of Liberation **Obv:** Crowned bust right **Rev:** Letter V divides dates above figures facing each other with flags

Date	Mintage	F	VF	XF	Unc	BU
1995 Proof sets only	500	—	—	—	435	—

KM# 82 100 POUNDS
31.2100 g., 0.9990 Gold 1.0025 oz. AGW **Ruler:** Elizabeth II **Subject:** 50th Anniversary - The Battle of Britain **Obv:** Crowned bust right **Rev:** Spitfire **Rev. Designer:** Ian Rank-Broadley

Date	Mintage	F	VF	XF	Unc	BU
ND Proof	Est. 500	Value: 900				

KM# 96 100 POUNDS
31.2100 g., 0.9990 Gold 1.0025 oz. AGW **Ruler:** Elizabeth II **Subject:** 50th Anniversary of Liberation **Obv:** Crowned bust right **Rev:** Small shield within map with bird above within diagonal lines into map **Rev. Designer:** Robert Elderton

Date	Mintage	F	VF	XF	Unc	BU
1995 Proof sets only	500	—	—	—	865	—

PIEFORTS

KM#	Date	Mintage	Identification	Mkt Val
P3	2002	100	5 Pounds. 0.9166 Gold. 56.5600 g. 38.6 mm. Queen's portrait. Abbey procession scene. Reeded edge. Underweight piefort	1,400

MINT SETS

KM#	Date	Mintage	Identification	Issue Price	Mkt Val
MS1	1972 (9)	8,500	KM35-43	348	715

PROOF SETS

KM#	Date	Mintage	Identification	Issue Price	Mkt Val
PS6	1972 (9)	1,500	KM35-43	648	975
PS10	1990 (4)	500	KM79-82	1,595	1,750
PS11	1995 (4)	500	KM93-96	1,600	1,600

JORDAN

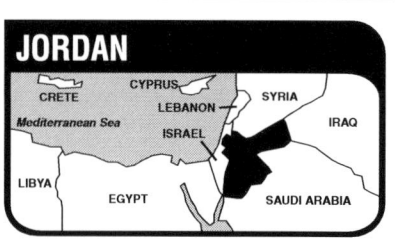

The Hashemite Kingdom of Jordan, a constitutional monarchy in southwest Asia, has an area of 37,738 sq. mi.(91,880 sq. km.) and a population of 3.5 million. Capital: Amman. Agriculture and tourism comprise Jordan's economic base. Chief exports are phosphates, tomatoe sand oranges.

Jordan is the Edom and Moab of the time of Moses. It became part of the Roman province of Arabia in 106 A.D., was conquered by the Arabs in 633-36, and was part of the Ottoman Empire from the 16th century until World War I. At that time, the regions presently known as Jordan and Israel were mandated to Great Britain by the League of Nations as Transjordan and Palestine. In 1922 Transjordan was established as the semi-autonomous Emirate of Transjordan, ruled by the Hashemite Prince Abdullah but still nominally a part of the British mandate. The mandate over Transjordan was terminated in 1946, the country becoming the independent Hashemite Kingdom of Transjordan. The kingdom was renamed the Hashemite Kingdom of Jordan in 1950.

Several 1964 and 1965 issues were limited to respective quantities of 3,000 and 5,000 examples struck to make up sets for sale to collectors.

TITLE

المملكة الاردنية الهاشمية

el-Mamlaka(t)el-Urduniya(t)el-Hashemiya(t)

RULERS
Abdullah Ibn Al-Hussein, 1946-1951
Talal Ibn Abdullah, 1951-1952
Hussein Ibn Talal, 1952-1999
Abdullah Ibn Al-Hussein, 1999-

MONETARY SYSTEM
100 Fils = 1 Dirham
1000 Fils = 10 Dirhams = 1 Dinar
  Commencing 1992
100 Piastres = 1 Dinar

KINGDOM

DECIMAL COINAGE

KM# 29a 1/4 DINAR
33.1900 g., 0.9170 Gold .9785 oz. AGW, 34 mm. **Ruler:** Hussein Ibn Talal **Subject:** 10th Anniversary - Central Bank of Jordan **Obv:** Head right **Rev:** Tree within circlular wreath with dates and value around wreath **Edge:** Milled

Date	Mintage	F	VF	XF	Unc	BU
AH1394-1974 Proof	100	Value: 715				

KM# 52 DINAR
8.5000 g., 0.9170 Gold .2505 oz. AGW, 21 mm. **Ruler:** Hussein Ibn Talal **Subject:** 40th Year of Reign **Obv:** Uniformed bust facing **Rev:** Tughra **Edge:** Milled

Date	Mintage	F	VF	XF	Unc	BU
AH1413-1992 Proof	3,000	Value: 200				

KM# 24 2 DINARS
5.5200 g., 0.9000 Gold .1597 oz. AGW, 21 mm. **Ruler:** Hussein Ibn Talal **Subject:** Forum in Jerash **Edge:** Milled

Date	Mintage	F	VF	XF	Unc	BU
AH1389//1969 Proof	2,425	Value: 125				

JORDAN 455

KM# 25 5 DINARS
13.8200 g., 0.9000 Gold .3999 oz. AGW, 31 mm. **Ruler:** Hussein Ibn Talal **Obv:** Bust left **Rev:** Treasury in Petra **Edge:** Milled

Date	Mintage	F	VF	XF	Unc	BU
AH1389//1969 Proof	1,950	Value: 285				

KM# 26 10 DINARS
27.6400 g., 0.9000 Gold .7998 oz. AGW, 40 mm. **Ruler:** Hussein Ibn Talal **Subject:** Visit of Pope Paul VI **Obv:** Bust left **Rev:** Pope and church within circle above value

Date	Mintage	F	VF	XF	Unc	BU
AH1389//1969 Proof	1,870	Value: 575				

KM# 27 25 DINARS
69.1100 g., 0.9000 Gold 1.9999 oz. AGW, 48 mm. **Ruler:** Hussein Ibn Talal **Obv:** Head right with crowned mantled arms above **Rev:** Dome of the Rock, Jerusalem, above value **Edge:** Milled

Date	Mintage	F	VF	XF	Unc	BU
AH1389//1969 Proof	1,000	Value: 1,400				

KM# 33 25 DINARS
15.0000 g., 0.9170 Gold .4422 oz. AGW, 29.01 mm. **Ruler:** Hussein Ibn Talal **Subject:** 25th Anniversary of Reign **Obv:** Bust right **Rev:** Crowned mantled arms above dates **Edge:** Milled

Date	Mintage	F	VF	XF	Unc	BU
AH1397-1977 FM Proof	4,724	Value: 325				

KM# 45 40 DINARS
14.3100 g., 0.9170 Gold .4216 oz. AGW, 27 mm. **Ruler:** Hussein Ibn Talal **Subject:** 15th century Hijrah calendar **Obv:** Bust facing 1/4 right **Rev:** Sun rays, cloud, domed building and box within flower design and circle **Edge:** Milled

Date	Mintage	F	VF	XF	Unc	BU
AH1400-1980 Proof	9,500	Value: 325				

KM# 50 50 DINARS
15.9800 g., 0.9170 Gold .4710 oz. AGW, 28.40 mm. **Ruler:** Hussein Ibn Talal **Subject:** Five-Year Plan **Obv:** Head right with crowned mantled arms above **Rev:** Fruit flanked by sprigs within circled gear with writing within chain wreath **Edge:** Milled

Date	Mintage	F	VF	XF	Unc	BU
AH1396-1976	250	—	—	350	375	
AH1396-1976 Proof	Inc. above	Value: 425				

KM# 34 50 DINARS
33.4370 g., 0.9000 Gold .9676 oz. AGW, 34 mm. **Ruler:** Hussein Ibn Talal **Subject:** Conservation **Obv:** Head right **Rev:** Bird facing left **Edge:** Milled

Date	Mintage	F	VF	XF	Unc	BU
AH1397-1976	829	—	—	—	675	725
AH1397-1976 Proof	287	Value: 800				

KM# 49 50 DINARS
17.0000 g., 0.9170 Gold .5013 oz. AGW, 29 mm. **Ruler:** Hussein Ibn Talal **Subject:** King Hussein's 50th Birthday **Obv:** Head right within beaded circle **Rev:** Crown above rising sun within wreath **Edge:** Milled

Date	Mintage	F	VF	XF	Unc	BU
AH1406 Proof	2,000	Value: 325				
AH1406-1985 Proof	2,029	Value: 350				

KM# 69 50 DINARS
16.9600 g., 0.9166 Gold .4998 oz. AGW, 30 mm. **Ruler:** Hussein Ibn Talal **Subject:** 50 Years - Jordanian Independence **Obv:** Bust facing **Rev:** Portrait of King Abdullah

Date	Mintage	F	VF	XF	Unc	BU
ND(1996) Proof	Est. 1,000	Value: 400				

KM# 81 50 DINARS
16.9600 g., 0.9166 Gold 0.4998 oz. AGW, 30 mm. **Ruler:** Abdullah Ibn Al-Hussein **Subject:** Abdullah II's Accession to the Throne **Obv:** Abdullah II **Rev:** Crowned and mantled arms **Edge:** Milled

Date	Mintage	F	VF	XF	Unc	BU
AH1420-1999 Proof	1,750	Value: 365				

KM# 67 50 DINARS
6.2200 g., 0.9990 Gold .1998 oz. AGW, 22 mm. **Ruler:** Hussein Ibn Talal **Subject:** UNICEF: For the Children of the World **Obv:** Conjoined busts right **Rev:** Boy, girl and UNICEF logo

Date	Mintage	F	VF	XF	Unc	BU
AH1419-1999 Proof	10,000	Value: 175				

KM# 82 50 DINARS
16.9600 g., 0.9166 Gold 0.4998 oz. AGW, 30 mm. **Ruler:** Abdullah Ibn Al-Hussein **Subject:** Millennium and Baptism of Jesus **Obv:** Abdullah II **Rev:** River baptism scene **Edge:** Milled

Date	Mintage	F	VF	XF	Unc	BU
AH1420-2000 Proof	3,500	Value: 365				

KM# 46 60 DINARS
17.1700 g., 0.9170 Gold .5062 oz. AGW, 27 mm. **Ruler:** Hussein Ibn Talal **Subject:** International Year of the Child **Obv:** Head right **Rev:** Palace of Culture in Amman and two children within circle **Edge:** Milled

Date	Mintage	F	VF	XF	Unc	BU
AH1401-1981 Proof	20,000	Value: 350				

PATTERNS
Including off metal strikes

KM#	Date	Mintage	Identification	Mkt Val
Pn1	AH1387	50	Fils. Gold. 5.6600 g. KM14.	250
Pn2	AH1387	50	5 Fils. Gold. 11.4000 g. KM15.	350
Pn3	AH1387	50	10 Fils. Gold. 18.8000 g. KM16.	400
Pn4	AH1387	50	25 Fils. Gold. 8.8100 g. KM17.	300
Pn5	AH1387	50	50 Fils. Gold. 13.7500 g. KM18.	1,000
Pn6	AH1387	50	Dirham. Gold. 22.8000 g. KM19.	1,200
Pn7	AH1395	170	Fils. Gold. 5.6600 g. As KM14.	300
Pn8	AH1395	170	5 Fils. Gold. 11.4000 g. As KM15.	500
Pn9	AH1395	170	10 Fils. Gold. 18.8000 g. As KM16.	550
Pn10	AH1395	170	25 Fils. Gold. 8.8100 g. As KM17.	350
Pn11	AH1395	170	50 Fils. Gold. 13.7500 g. As KM18.	550
Pn12	AH1395	170	Dirham. Gold. 22.8000 g. As KM19.	750
Pn13	AH1395	110	1/4 Dinar. Gold. 31.4500 g. As KM28.	950

PIEFORTS

KM#	Date	Mintage	Identification	Mkt Val
P2	1981	61	60 Dinars. Gold. 34.3400 g. KM46.	950
P3	1985	700	50 Dinars. Gold. 34.3400 g. KM49.	700
P4	AH1413-1992	500	Dinar. 0.9167 Gold. 17.0000 g. 28.4 mm. Broad piefort of KM-52	400
P5	ND(1996)	400	50 Dinars. 0.9166 Gold. 33.9200 g. 40 mm. Milled edge. Similar to KM#69, with 40mm diameter.	800

PROOF SETS

KM#	Date	Mintage	Identification	Issue Price	Mkt Val
PS3	1969 (7)	—	KM21-27	396	2,000
PS4	1969 (6)	—	KM21-26	—	925
PS5	1969 (7)	—	KM24-27	—	1,900
PS7	1977 (3)	1,000	KM31-32, 34	780	825
PS10	1980 (2)	—	KM44-45	365	525

SPECIMEN SETS (SS)

KM#	Date	Mintage	Identification	Issue Price	Mkt Val
SS4	1968 (6)	50	KMPn1-6	—	4,000
SS5	1975 (7)	110	KMPn7-13	—	2,000

KATANGA

Katanga, the southern province of the former Belgian Congo, had an area of 191,873 sq. mi. (496,951 sq. km.) and was noted for its mineral wealth.

MONETARY SYSTEM
100 Centimes = 1 Franc

PROVINCE
DECIMAL COINAGE

KM# 2a   5 FRANCS
13.3300 g., 0.9000 Gold .3857 oz. AGW **Obv:** Bananas within circle **Rev:** Cross, value and date within circle

Date	Mintage	F	VF	XF	Unc	BU
1961	20,000	—	—	—	285	500

KAZAKHSTAN

The Republic of Kazakhstan (formerly Kazakhstan S.S.R.) is bordered to the west by the Caspian Sea and Russia, to the north by Russia, in the east by the Peoples Republic of China and in the south by Uzbekistan and Kirghizia. It has an area of 1,049,155 sq. mi. (2,717,300 sq. km.) and a population of 16.7 million. Capital: Astana. Rich in mineral resources including coal, tungsten, copper, lead, zinc and manganese with huge oil and natural gas reserves. Agriculture is very important, (it previously represented 20 percent of the total arable acreage of the combined U.S.S.R.) Non-ferrous metallurgy, heavy engineering and chemical industries are leaders in its economy.

The Kazakhs are a branch of the Turkic peoples which led the nomadic life of herdsmen until WW I. In the 13th century they came under Genghis Khan's eldest son Jujiand. Later they became a part of the Golden Horde, a western Mongol empire. Around the beginning of the 16th century they were divided into 3 confederacies, known as *zhuz* or hordes, in the steppes of Turkestan. At the end of the 17th century an incursion by the Kalmucks, a remnant of the Oirat Mongol confederacy, resulted in heavy losses on both sides which facilitated Russian penetration. Resistance to Russian settlements varied throughout the 1800's, but by 1900 over 100 million acres were declared Czarist state property and used for a planned peasant colonization. After a revolution in 1905 Kazakh deputies were elected. In 1916 the tsarist government ordered mobilization of all males, between 19 and 43, for auxiliary service. The Kazakhs rose in defiance which led the governor general of Turkestan to send troops against the rebels. Shortly after the Russian revolution, Kazakh Nationalists asked for full autonomy. The Communist *coup d'etat* of Nov. 1917 led to civil war. In 1919-20 the Red army defeated the "White" Russian forces and occupied Kazakhstan and fought against the Nationalist government formed on Nov. 17, 1917 by Ali Khan Bukey Khan. The Kazakh Autonomous Soviet Socialist Republic was proclaimed on Aug. 26, 1920 within the R.S.F.S.R. Russian and Ukrainian colonization continued while 2 purges in 1927 and 1935 quelled any Kazakh feelings of priority in the matters of their country. On Dec. 5, 1936 Kazakhstan qualified for full status as an S.S.R. and held its first congress in 1937. Independence was declared on Dec. 16, 1991 and Kazakhstan joined the C.I.S.

MONETARY SYSTEM
100 Tyin = 1 Tenge

REPUBLIC
DECIMAL COINAGE

KM# 68   1000 TENGE
7.7800 g., 0.9990 Gold 0.2499 oz. AGW, 20 mm. **Obv:** Two winged ibexes **Rev:** Ancient warrior **Edge:** Reeded

Date	Mintage	F	VF	XF	Unc	BU
2001 Proof	—	Value: 350				

KM# 45   2500 TENGE
7.7800 g., 0.9999 Gold 0.2501 oz. AGW, 20 mm. **Subject:** The Silk Road **Obv:** Value in ornamental frame **Rev:** Caravan of camels around lined cross within circle **Edge:** Reeded

Date	Mintage	F	VF	XF	Unc	BU
1995	—	—	—	—	220	245

KM# 46   5000 TENGE
15.5500 g., 0.9999 Gold 0.4999 oz. AGW, 25 mm. **Subject:** The Silk Road **Obv:** Value in ornamental frame **Rev:** Caravan of camels around lined cross within circle **Edge:** Reeded

Date	Mintage	F	VF	XF	Unc	BU
1995	—	—	—	—	350	375

KM# 47   10000 TENGE
31.1000 g., 0.9999 Gold 0.9998 oz. AGW, 32 mm. **Subject:** The Silk Road **Obv:** Value in ornamental frame **Rev:** Caravan of camels around lined cross within circle **Edge:** Reeded

Date	Mintage	F	VF	XF	Unc	BU
1995	—	—	—	—	700	750

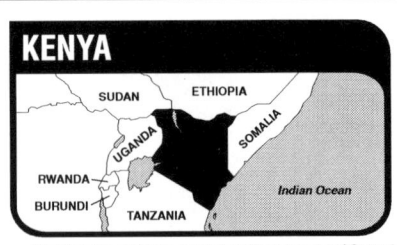

KENYA

The Republic of Kenya, located on the east coast of Central Africa, has an area of 224,961 sq. mi. (582,650 sq. km.) and a population of 20.1 million. Capital: Nairobi. The predominantly agricultural country exports coffee, tea and petroleum products.

The Arabs came to the coast of Kenya in the 8th century and established posts to conduct an ivory and slave trade. The Portuguese followed in the 16th century. After a lengthy and bitter struggle with the sultans of Zanzibar who controlled much of the southeastern coast of Africa, the Portuguese were driven away (late 17th century) and for many years Kenya was simply a port of call on the route to India. German and British interests in the 19th century produced agreements defining their respective spheres of influence. The British sphere was administrated by the Imperial East Africa Co. until 1895, when the British government purchased the company's rights in the East Africa Protectorate which, in 1920, was designated as Kenya Colony and protectorate - the latter being a 10-mile-wide coastal strip together with Mombasa, Lamuand other small islands nominally retained by the Sultan of Zanzibar. Kenya achieved self-government in June of 1963 as a consequence of the 1952-60 Mau Mau terrorist campaign to secure land reforms and political rights for Africans. Independence was attained on Dec. 12, 1963. Kenya became a republic in 1964. It is a member of the Commonwealth of Nations. The president is Chief of State and Head of Government.

RULER
British, until 1964

MONETARY SYSTEM
100 Cents = 1 Shilling

REPUBLIC
STANDARD COINAGE

KM# 7   100 SHILLINGS
7.6000 g., 0.9170 Gold .224 oz. AGW **Subject:** 75th Anniversary - Birth of President Jomo Kenyatta **Obv:** Fly whisk above value and date **Rev:** Bust left **Designer:** Norman Sillman

Date	Mintage	F	VF	XF	Unc	BU
1966	—	—	—	—	160	170
1966 Proof	7,500	Value: 185				

KM# 8   250 SHILLINGS
19.0000 g., 0.9170 Gold .5602 oz. AGW **Subject:** 75th Anniversary - Birth of President Jomo Kenyatta **Obv:** Rooster with axe above value and date **Rev:** Bust left **Designer:** Norman Sillman

Date	Mintage	F	VF	XF	Unc	BU
1966	—	—	—	—	400	420
1966 Proof	1,000	Value: 445				

KM# 9   500 SHILLINGS
38.0000 g., 0.9170 Gold 1.1204 oz. AGW **Subject:** 75th Anniversary - Birth of President Jomo Kenyatta **Obv:** Mountain above value and date **Rev:** Bust left **Designer:** Norman Sillman

KIRIBATI

Date	Mintage	F	VF	XF	Unc	BU
1966	—	—	—	—	775	800
1966 Proof	500	Value: 825				

KM# 22 3000 SHILLING
40.0000 g., 0.9170 Gold 1.1787 oz. AGW **Obv:** President Moi **Rev:** Arms with supporters above value

Date	Mintage	F	VF	XF	Unc	BU
ND (1979) Proof	2,000	Value: 875				

MINT SETS

KM#	Date	Mintage Identification	Issue Price	Mkt Val
MS1	1966 (3)	— KM7-9	—	1,350

PROOF SETS

KM#	Date	Mintage Identification	Issue Price	Mkt Val
PS2	1966 (3)	500 KM7-9	153	1,450

KIRIBATI

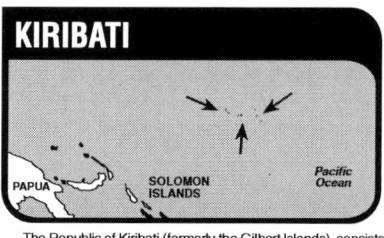

The Republic of Kiribati (formerly the Gilbert Islands), consists of 30 coral atolls and islands spread over more than one million sq. mi. (2,590,000 sq. km.) of the southwest Pacific Ocean, has an area of 332 sq. mi. (717 sq. km.) and a population of 64,200. Capital: Bairiki, on Tarawa. In addition to the Gilbert Islands proper, Kiribati includes Ocean Island, the Central and Southern Line Islands, and the Phoenix Islands, though possession of Canton and Enderbury of the Phoenix Islands is disputed with the United States. Most families engage in subsistence fishing. Copra and phosphates are exported, mostly to Australia and New Zealand.

The Gilbert Islands and the group formerly called the Ellice Islands (now Tuvalu) comprised a single British crown colony, the Gilbert and Ellice Islands.

Spanish mutineers first sighted the islands in 1537, succeeding visits were made by the English navigators John Byron (1764), James Cook (1777), and Thomas Gilbert and John Marshall (1788). An American, Edward Fanning, arrived in 1798. Britain declared a protectorate over the Gilbert and Ellice Islands, and in 1915 began the formation of a colony which was completed when the Phoenix Islands were added to the group in 1937. The Central and Southern Line Islands were administratively attached to the Gilbert and Ellice Islands colony in 1972, and remained attached to the Gilberts when Tuvalu was created in 1975. The colony became self-governing in 1971. Kiribati attained independence on July 12, 1979.

RULER
British, until 1979

MONETARY SYSTEM
100 Cents = 1 Dollar

REPUBLIC

DECIMAL COINAGE

KM# 13a 10 DOLLARS
47.5200 g., 0.9170 Gold 1.4012 oz. AGW **Subject:** 5th Anniversary of Independence **Obv:** Value above national arms **Rev:** Geographical map

Date	Mintage	F	VF	XF	Unc	BU
ND(1984) Proof	50	Value: 1,250				

KM# 27 10 DOLLARS
1.2441 g., 0.9990 Gold .04 oz. AGW **Subject:** Titanic **Obv:** National arms **Rev:** Sinking ships and lifeboats

Date	Mintage	F	VF	XF	Unc	BU
1998 Proof	—	Value: 50.00				

KM# 33 20 DOLLARS
3.1103 g., 0.9990 Gold 0.0999 oz. AGW, 18 mm. **Subject:** Christmas Island Holy Year 2000 **Obv:** National arms above name and date **Rev:** Angel in flight **Edge:** Reeded

Date	Mintage	F	VF	XF	Unc	BU
1999 Proof	—	Value: 85.00				

KM# 26 50 DOLLARS
3.8875 g., 0.9990 Gold .25 oz. AGW **Subject:** Tempora Mutantur **Obv:** National arms **Rev:** Solar system **Shape:** Jagged half of coin **Note:** Similar to KM#24. Half of two-part coin, combined with Western Samoa KM#119, issued in sets only. Value is determined by combining the two parts.

Date	Mintage	F	VF	XF	Unc	BU
ND(1997) Proof	Est. 2,500	Value: 185				

KM# 34 50 DOLLARS
7.7759 g., 0.9990 Gold 0.2498 oz. AGW, 22 mm. **Subject:** Christmas Island Holy Year 2000 **Obv:** National arms above name and date **Rev:** The three "Wise Men" on camels **Edge:** Reeded

Date	Mintage	F	VF	XF	Unc	BU
1999 Proof	—	Value: 185				

KM# 35 100 DOLLARS
15.5518 g., 0.9990 Gold 0.4995 oz. AGW, 30 mm. **Subject:** Christmas Island Holy Year 2000 **Obv:** National arms above name and date **Rev:** Mother and child **Edge:** Reeded

Date	Mintage	F	VF	XF	Unc	BU
1999 Proof	—	Value: 375				

KM# 9 150 DOLLARS
15.9800 g., 0.9170 Gold .4711 oz. AGW **Subject:** Independence - Maneaba - a traditional meeting house **Obv:** National arms **Rev:** Maneaba - a traditional meeting house **Designer:** Mike Hibbert

Date	Mintage	F	VF	XF	Unc	BU
1979	422	—	—	—	335	—
1979 Proof	386	Value: 350				

KM# 11 150 DOLLARS
15.9800 g., 0.9170 Gold .4711 oz. AGW **Subject:** 2nd Anniversary of Independence, and wedding of Prince Charles and Lady Diana **Obv:** National arms

Date	Mintage	F	VF	XF	Unc	BU
1981	750	—	—	—	325	—
1981 Proof	1,500	Value: 340				

KM# 29 200 DOLLARS
31.3000 g., 0.9990 Gold 1.0053 oz. AGW, 35 mm. **Subject:** 10th Anniversary of Emperor Akihito's Reign **Obv:** National arms **Rev:** Conjoined busts left **Edge:** Reeded

Date	Mintage	F	VF	XF	Unc	BU
2000 Proof	500	Value: 700				

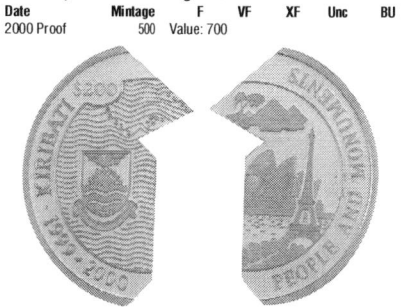

KM# 32 200 DOLLARS
16.5800 g., 0.9990 Gold 0.4003 oz. AGW, 37.8x26.2 mm. **Subject:** People and Monuments **Obv:** National arms within wave-like designs **Rev:** Eiffel Tower **Edge:** Plain **Note:** Irregular shape

Date	Mintage	F	VF	XF	Unc	BU
1999-2000 Proof	—	Value: 300				

KM# 36 500 DOLLARS
85.4700 g., 0.9990 Gold 2.7452 oz. AGW, 42.5 mm. **Obv:** National arms **Rev:** Doves, children, sword point and treaty **Edge:** Plain **Note:** Jagged coin half matching with Samoa KM-136

Date	Mintage	F	VF	XF	Unc	BU
2000 Proof	99	Value: 1,950				

PROOF SETS

KM#	Date	Mintage Identification	Issue Price	Mkt Val
PS2	1981 (2)	— KM10a, 11	—	360
PS3	1999 (3)	— KM#33-35	—	645

458 KOREA

KOREA

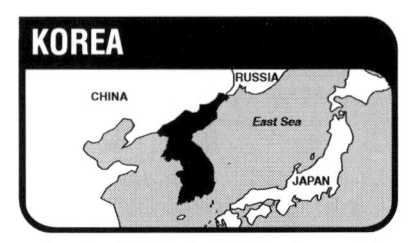

Korea, 'Land of the Morning Calm', occupies a mountainous peninsula in northeast Asia bounded by Manchuria, the Yellow Sea and the Sea of Japan.

According to legend, the first Korean dynasty, that of the House of Tangun, ruled from 2333 B.C. to 1122 B.C. It was followed by the dynasty of Kija, a Chinese scholar, which continued until 193 B.C. and brought a high civilization to Korea. The first recorded period in the history of Korea, the period of the Three Kingdoms, lasted from 57 B.C. to 935 A.D. and achieved the first political unification of the peninsula. The Kingdom of Koryo, from which Korea derived its name, was founded in 935 and continued until 1392, when it was superseded by the Yi Dynasty of King Yi. Sung Kye was to last until the Japanese annexation in 1910.

At the end of the 16th century Korea was invaded and occupied for 7 years by Japan, and from 1627 until the late 19th century it was a semi-independent tributary of China. Japan replaced China as the predominant foreign influence at the end of the Sino-Japanese War (1894-95), only to find her position threatened by Russian influence from 1896 to 1904. The Russian threat was eliminated by the Russo-Japanese War (1904-05) and in 1905 Japan established a direct protectorate over Korea. On Aug. 22, 1910, the last Korean ruler signed the treaty that annexed Korea to Japan as a government generalcy in the Japanese Empire. Japanese suzerainty was maintained until the end of World War II.

From 1633 to 1891 the monetary system of Korea employed cast coins with a square center hole. Fifty-two agencies were authorized to procure these coins from a lesser number of coin foundries. They exist in thousands of varieties. Seed, or mother coins, were used to make the impressions in the molds in which the regular cash coins were cast. Czarist-Russian Korea experimented with Korean coins when Alexiev of Russia, Korea's Financial Advisor, founded the First Asian Branch of the Russo-Korean Bank on March 1, 1898, and authorized the issuing of a set of new Korean coins with a crowned Russian-style quasi-eagle. British-Japanese opposition and the Russo-Japanese War operated to end the Russian coinage experiment in 1904.

RULERS
Yi Sun (Chongjo Changhyo), 1777-1801
Yi Kwang (Sunjo Songhyo), 1801-1835
Yi Whan (Honjong Cholhyo), 1835-1850
Yi Chung (Choljong Yonghyo), 1850-1864
Yi Hyong (Kojong), 1864-1897
as Emperor Kuang Mu, 1897-1907
Japanese Puppet
Yung Hi (Sunjong), 1907-1910

DATING

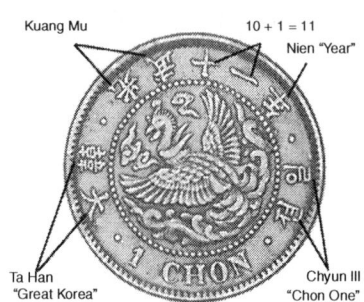

Kuang Mu 10 + 1 = 11
Nien "Year"
Ta Han "Great Korea"
Chyun Il "Chon One"

MONETARY UNITS

文 Mun	兩 Yang, Niang
分 Fun	圜 Hwan, Warn
錢 Chon	圓 Won Whan, Hwan

IDENTIFICATION CHART

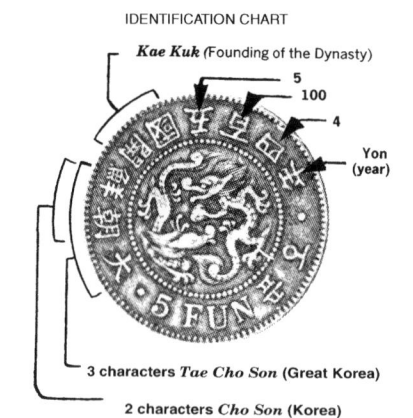

Kae Kuk (Founding of the Dynasty)
5
100
4
Yon (year)
3 characters *Tae Cho Son* (Great Korea)
2 characters *Cho Son* (Korea)

JAPANESE PROTECTORATE

MILLED COINAGE
Coinage Reform of 1892

KM# 1142 5 WON
4.1666 g., 0.9000 Gold .1206 oz. AGW **Ruler:** Yung Hi (Sunjong) **Obv:** Dragon within beaded circle **Rev:** Value within wreath below flower

Date	Mintage	F	VF	XF	Unc	BU
2 (1908)	10,000	14,000	30,000	45,000	65,000	

Note: Heritage Piedmont sale 6-2000 Gem BU realized $86,250

| 3 (1909) 2 known | — | — | — | — | — | — |

KM# 1130 10 WON
8.3333 g., 0.9000 Gold .2412 oz. AGW **Ruler:** Kuang Mu **Obv:** Dragon within beaded circle **Rev:** Value within wreath below flower

Date	Mintage	F	VF	XF	Unc	BU
10 (1906)	5,012	—	13,000	20,000	35,000	—

KM# A1130 10 WON
8.3333 g., 0.9000 Gold .2412 oz. AGW **Ruler:** Yung Hi (Sunjong) **Obv:** Dragon within beaded circle **Rev:** Value within wreath below flower

Date	Mintage	F	VF	XF	Unc	BU
3 (1909) 2 known	—	—	—	—	—	—

KM# 1131 20 WON
16.6666 g., 0.9000 Gold .4823 oz. AGW **Ruler:** Kuang Mu **Obv:** Dragon within beaded circle **Rev:** Value within wreath below flower

Date	Mintage	F	VF	XF	Unc	BU
10 (1906)	2,506	—	25,000	40,000	70,000	—

KM# 1144 20 WON
16.6666 g., 0.9000 Gold .4823 oz. AGW **Ruler:** Yung Hi (Sunjong) **Obv:** Dragon within beaded circle **Rev:** Value within wreath

Date	Mintage	F	VF	XF	Unc	BU
2 (1908) Rare	—	—	—	—	—	—
3 (1909) 2 known	—	—	—	—	—	—

Note: Reported mintages for Year 2 (1908) of 40,000 and Year 3 (1909) of 25,000 exist, but few are known today

KOREA-NORTH

The Democratic Peoples Republic of Korea, situated in northeastern Asia on the northern half of the Korean peninsula between the Peoples Republic of China and the Republic of Korea, has an area of 46,540 sq. mi. (120,540 sq. km.) and a population of 20 million. Capital: Pyongyang. The economy is based on heavy industry and agriculture. Metals, minerals and farm produce are exported.

Japan replaced China as the predominant foreign influence in Korea in 1895 and annexed the peninsular country in 1910. Defeat in World War II brought an end to Japanese rule. U.S. troops entered Korea from the south and Soviet forces entered from the north. The Cairo conference (1943) had established that Korea should be *free and independent*. The Potsdam conference (1945) set the 38th parallel as the line dividing the occupation forces of the United States and Russia. When Russia refused to permit a U.N. commission designated to supervise reunification elections to enter North Korea, an election was held in South Korea which established the Republic of Korea on Aug. 15, 1948. North Korea held an unsupervised election on Aug. 25, 1948, and on Sept. 9, 1948, proclaimed the establishment of the Democratic Peoples Republic of Korea.

NOTE: For earlier coinage see Korea.

MONETARY SYSTEM
100 Chon = 1 Won

CIRCULATION RESTRICTIONS
W/o star: KM#1-4 - General circulation
1 star: KM#5-8 - Issued to visitors from Communist countries.
2 stars: KM#9-12 - Issued to visitors from hard currency countries.

PEOPLES REPUBLIC
DECIMAL COINAGE

KM# 28 100 WON
3.1300 g., 0.9990 Gold .1 oz. AGW **Subject:** 40th Anniversary of People's Republic **Obv:** National arms **Rev:** Leaping equestrian

Date	Mintage	F	VF	XF	Unc	BU
1988 Proof	—	Value: 85.00				

KM# 95.1 200 WON
8.0000 g., 0.9990 Gold **Subject:** 50th Anniversary of Liberation **Obv:** National arms **Rev:** Turtle ship **Note:** Prev. KM#95.

Date	Mintage	F	VF	XF	Unc	BU
1995 In proof sets only	300	Value: 420				

KM# 95.2 200 WON
8.0000 g., 0.9990 Gold 0.2569 oz. AGW, 25 mm. **Subject:** 50th Anniversary of Liberation **Obv:** National arms with fineness closer to arms **Rev:** Turtle ship

Date	Mintage	F	VF	XF	Unc	BU
1995 Proof	—	Value: 420				

KOREA-NORTH

KM# 29 250 WON
7.7800 g., 0.9990 Gold .25 oz. AGW **Subject:** 40th Anniversary of People's Republic **Obv:** National arms **Rev:** Leaping equestrian
Date	Mintage	F	VF	XF	Unc	BU
1988 Proof	—	Value: 185				

KM# 21 250 WON
7.7700 g., 0.9990 Gold .25 oz. AGW **Subject:** World Festival of Youth and Students **Obv:** National arms above D.P.R. of Korea, value and date **Rev:** Flower design
Date	Mintage	F	VF	XF	Unc	BU
1989 Proof	—	Value: 285				

KM# 96 400 WON
16.0000 g., Gold .5138 oz. AGW **Subject:** 50th Anniversary of Liberation **Obv:** National arms **Rev:** Lake on Mount Baektu
Date	Mintage	F	VF	XF	Unc	BU
1995 In proof sets only	100	Value: 700				

KM# 30 500 WON
15.5700 g., 0.9990 Gold .5 oz. AGW **Subject:** 40th Anniversary of People's Republic **Obv:** National arms **Rev:** Leaping equestrian
Date	Mintage	F	VF	XF	Unc	BU
1988 Proof	—	Value: 365				

KM# 147 700 WON
31.1035 g., 0.9990 Gold 1.0000 oz. AGW, 35 mm. **Subject:** Korean Workers' Party **Obv:** National arms **Rev:** Flag and radiant setting sun **Edge:** Plain
Date	Mintage	F	VF	XF	Unc	BU
1996	100	—	—	—	775	—

KM# 165 700 WON
31.1000 g., 0.9990 Gold 0.9989 oz. AGW, 35 mm. **Subject:** 50th Anniversary of People's Republic **Obv:** National arms **Rev:** Flag **Edge:** Plain
Date	Mintage	F	VF	XF	Unc	BU
1998 Proof	500	Value: 725				

KM# 31 1000 WON
31.1300 g., 0.9990 Gold 1 oz. AGW **Subject:** 40th Anniversary of People's Republic **Obv:** National arms **Rev:** Leaping equestrian
Date	Mintage	F	VF	XF	Unc	BU
1988 Proof	—	Value: 700				

KM# 148 1000 WON
15.5500 g., 0.9990 Gold .4999 oz. AGW, 27 mm. **Subject:** Death of Kim Il Sung **Obv:** National arms **Rev:** Bust facing **Edge:** Plain
Date	Mintage	F	VF	XF	Unc	BU
ND(1994)	—	—	—	—	400	—

KM# 149 1000 WON
31.1035 g., 0.9990 Gold 1.0000 oz. AGW, 35 mm. **Subject:** 50th Anniversary - Korean Workers' Party **Obv:** National arms **Rev:** Monument **Edge:** Plain
Date	Mintage	F	VF	XF	Unc	BU
1995	—	—	—	—	725	—

KM# 58 1500 WON
8.0000 g., 0.9990 Gold .2572 oz. AGW **Series:** Olympics **Obv:** National arms **Rev:** Gymnast
Date	Mintage	F	VF	XF	Unc	BU
1990 Proof	Est. 3,000	Value: 215				

KM# 42 1500 WON
15.5500 g., 0.9990 Gold .5 oz. AGW **Subject:** Inter-parliamentary Conference **Obv:** National arms **Rev:** Buildings
Date	Mintage	F	VF	XF	Unc	BU
1991 Proof	1,000	Value: 400				

KM# 43 1500 WON
15.5500 g., 0.9990 Gold .5 oz. AGW **Subject:** Inter-parliamentary Conference **Obv:** National arms **Rev:** Building
Date	Mintage	F	VF	XF	Unc	BU
1991 Proof	800	Value: 400				

KM# 51 1500 WON
8.0000 g., 0.9990 Gold .2572 oz. AGW **Subject:** Soccer **Obv:** National arms **Rev:** Soccer player in mid-kick
Date	Mintage	F	VF	XF	Unc	BU
1991 Proof	1,000	Value: 250				

KM# 150 1500 WON
8.0000 g., 0.9990 Gold .2569 oz. AGW, 22 mm. **Series:** Olympics **Obv:** National arms **Rev:** Cyclists racing **Edge:** Plain
Date	Mintage	F	VF	XF	Unc	BU
1993	—	—	—	—	300	—

KM# 53 2000 WON
31.1000 g., 0.9990 Gold 1 oz. AGW **Subject:** 80th Birthday of Kim Il Sung **Obv:** National arms **Rev:** Kim Il Sung birthplace
Date	Mintage	F	VF	XF	Unc	BU
ND(1992) Proof	500	Value: 745				

KM# 55 2000 WON
31.1000 g., 0.9990 Gold 1 oz. AGW **Subject:** 80th Birthday of Kim Il Sung **Obv:** National arms **Rev:** Bust facing
Date	Mintage	F	VF	XF	Unc	BU
1992 Proof	500	Value: 745				

460 KOREA-NORTH

KM# 57 2000 WON
31.1000 g., 0.9990 Gold 1 oz. AGW **Subject:** 50th Birthday of Kim Jong Il **Rev:** National arms

Date	Mintage	F	VF	XF	Unc	BU
1992 Proof	500			Value: 745		

KM# 151 2000 WON
31.1035 g., 0.9990 Gold 1.0000 oz. AGW, 40 mm. **Subject:** Death of Kim Il Sung **Obv:** National arms **Rev:** Bust facing **Edge:** Plain

Date	Mintage	F	VF	XF	Unc	BU
ND(1994)	—	—	—	—	725	—

KM# 35 2500 WON
15.5500 g., 0.9990 Gold .5 oz. AGW **Subject:** 30th Anniversary of Gorch Fock **Obv:** National arms **Rev:** Sailing ship

Date	Mintage	F	VF	XF	Unc	BU
1988 Proof	Est. 500			Value: 365		

PROOF SETS

KM#	Date	Mintage	Identification	Issue Price	Mkt Val
PS1	1995 (5)	300	KM92-96	—	1,350

KOREA-SOUTH

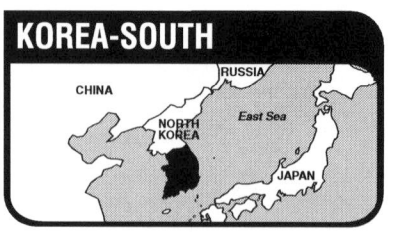

The Republic of Korea, situated in northeastern Asia on the southern half of the Korean peninsula between North Korea and the Korean Strait, has an area of 38,025 sq. mi. (98,480 sq. km.) and a population of 42.5 million. Capital: Seoul. The economy is based on agriculture and light and medium industry. Some of the world's largest oil tankers are built here. Automobiles, plywood, electronics, and textile products are exported.

Japan replaced China as the predominant foreign influence in Korea in 1895 and annexed the peninsular country in 1910. Defeat in World War II brought an end to Japanese rule. U.S. troops entered Korea from the south and Soviet forces entered from the north. The Cairo conference (1943) had established that Korea should be *free and independent*. The Potsdam conference (1945) set the 38th parallel as the line dividing the occupation forces of the United States and Russia. When Russia refused to permit a U.N. commission designated to supervise reunification elections to enter North Korea, an election was held in South Korea on May 10, 1948. By its determination, the Republic of Korea was inaugurated on Aug. 15, 1948.

NOTE: For earlier coinage see Korea.

MINT MARK
(a) – Paris, privy marks only

MONETARY SYSTEM
100 Chon = 1 Hwan

REPUBLIC

REFORM COINAGE
10 Hwan = 1 Won

KM# 14.1 1000 WON
3.8700 g., 0.9000 Gold .1119 oz. AGW, 16 mm. **Obv:** Arms within floral spray **Rev:** Great South Gate in Seoul

Date	Mintage	F	VF	XF	Unc	BU
KE4303-1970 Proof	1,500			Value: 350		

KM# 14.2 1000 WON
3.8700 g., 0.9000 Gold .1119 oz. AGW, 16 mm. **Obv:** Arms within floral spray **Rev:** Great South Gate in Seoul

Date	Mintage	F	VF	XF	Unc	BU
KE4303-1970(a) Proof	100			Value: 1,250		

KM# 15.1 2500 WON
9.6800 g., 0.9000 Gold .2801 oz. AGW, 26 mm. **Obv:** Arms within floral spray **Rev:** Crowned head and temple within circle

Date	Mintage	F	VF	XF	Unc	BU
KE4303-1970 Proof	1,750			Value: 500		

KM# 15.2 2500 WON
9.6800 g., 0.9000 Gold .2801 oz. AGW **Obv:** Arms within floral spray **Rev:** Crowned head and temple within circle

Date	Mintage	F	VF	XF	Unc	BU
KE4303-1970(a) Proof	100			Value: 1,500		

KM# 16.1 5000 WON
19.3600 g., 0.9000 Gold .5602 oz. AGW, 32 mm. **Obv:** Arms within floral spray **Rev:** Iron-clad turtle boats

Date	Mintage	F	VF	XF	Unc	BU
KE4303-1970 Proof	670			Value: 1,850		

KM# 16.2 5000 WON
19.3600 g., 0.9000 Gold .5602 oz. AGW **Obv:** Arms within floral spray **Rev:** Iron-clad turtle boats

Date	Mintage	F	VF	XF	Unc	BU
KE4303-1970(a) Proof	70			Value: 2,500		

KM# 17.1 10000 WON
38.7200 g., 0.9000 Gold 1.1205 oz. AGW **Obv:** Arms above floral spray flanked by phoenix **Rev:** Bust facing

Date	Mintage	F	VF	XF	Unc	BU
KE4303-1970 Proof	435			Value: 5,000		

KM# 17.2 10000 WON
38.7200 g., 0.9000 Gold 1.1205 oz. AGW **Obv:** Arms above floral spray flanked by phoenix **Rev:** Bust facing

Date	Mintage	F	VF	XF	Unc	BU
KE4303-1970(a) Proof	55			Value: 6,000		

KM# 18.1 20000 WON
77.4000 g., 0.9000 Gold 2.2398 oz. AGW, 55 mm. **Obv:** Arms within floral spray **Rev:** Gold crown - Silla Dynasty

Date	Mintage	F	VF	XF	Unc	BU
KE4303-1970 Proof	382			Value: 8,750		

KM# 18.2 20000 WON
77.4000 g., 0.9000 Gold 2.2398 oz. AGW **Obv:** Arms within floral spray **Rev:** Gold Crown - Silla Dynasty

Date	Mintage	F	VF	XF	Unc	BU
KE4303-1970(a) Proof	52			Value: 10,000		

KM# 94 20000 WON
15.5518 g., 0.9990 Gold .5000 oz. AGW, 28 mm. **Series:** World Cup Soccer **Obv:** Soccer logo **Rev:** World Cup soccer trophy **Edge:** Reeded

Date	Mintage	F	VF	XF	Unc	BU
2001 Proof	20,000			Value: 375		

KOREA-SOUTH 461

KM# 19.1 25000 WON
96.8000 g., 0.9000 Gold 2.8012 oz. AGW, 60 mm. **Subject:** King Sejong The Great **Obv:** Arms within floral spray **Rev:** Seated figure facing reading from a book within circle

Date	Mintage	F	VF	XF	Unc	BU
KE4303-1970 Proof	325	Value: 14,000				

KM# 19.2 25000 WON
96.8000 g., 0.9000 Gold 2.8012 oz. AGW, 60 mm. **Subject:** King Sejong The Great **Obv:** Arms within floral spray **Rev:** Seated figure facing reading from a book

Date	Mintage	F	VF	XF	Unc	BU
KE4303-1970(a) Proof	25	Value: 17,000				

KM# 58 25000 WON
16.8100 g., 0.9250 Gold .5000 oz. AGW, 27 mm. **Series:** 1988 Olympics **Obv:** Arms above floral spray **Rev:** Folk dancing

Date	Mintage	F	VF	XF	Unc	BU
1986	42,500	—	—	—	340	350
1986 Proof	117,500	Value: 360				

KM# 64 25000 WON
16.8100 g., 0.9250 Gold .5000 oz. AGW, 27 mm. **Series:** 1988 Olympics **Obv:** Arms above floral spray **Rev:** Fan dancing

Date	Mintage	F	VF	XF	Unc	BU
1987	42,500	—	—	—	340	350
1987 Proof	117,500	Value: 360				

KM# 68 25000 WON
16.8100 g., 0.9250 Gold .5000 oz. AGW, 27 mm. **Series:** 1988 Olympics **Obv:** Arms above floral spray **Rev:** Kite flying

Date	Mintage	F	VF	XF	Unc	BU
1987	47,500	—	—	—	340	350
1987 Proof	47,500	Value: 360				
1988	—	—	—	—	340	350
1988 Proof	—	Value: 360				

KM# 72 25000 WON
16.8100 g., 0.9250 Gold .5000 oz. AGW, 27 mm. **Series:** 1988 Olympics **Obv:** Arms above floral spray **Rev:** Korean Seesaw

Date	Mintage	F	VF	XF	Unc	BU
1988	42,500	—	—	—	340	350
1988 Proof	117,500	Value: 360				

KM# 82 25000 WON
16.8100 g., 0.9250 Gold .5000 oz. AGW **Subject:** Taejon International Exposition **Obv:** Stylized yin-yang within multiple circles **Rev:** Celestial globe

Date	Mintage	F	VF	XF	Unc	BU
1993	40,000	—	—	—	—	375

KM# 95 30000 WON
31.1035 g., 0.9990 Gold 1.0000 oz. AGW, 35 mm. **Series:** World Cup Soccer **Obv:** Soccer logo **Rev:** Nude soccer player flanked by other players **Edge:** Reeded

Date	Mintage	F	VF	XF	Unc	BU
2001 Proof	12,000	Value: 750				

KM# 59 50000 WON
33.6200 g., 0.9250 Gold 1.0000 oz. AGW, 33 mm. **Series:** 1988 Olympics **Obv:** Arms above floral spray **Rev:** Turtle boat

Date	Mintage	F	VF	XF	Unc	BU
1986 Proof	30,000	Value: 725				

KM# 65 50000 WON
33.6200 g., 0.9250 Gold 1.0000 oz. AGW, 33 mm. **Series:** 1988 Olympics **Obv:** Arms above floral spray **Rev:** Great South Gate

Date	Mintage	F	VF	XF	Unc	BU
1987 Proof	30,000	Value: 725				

KM# 69 50000 WON
33.6200 g., 0.9250 Gold 1.0000 oz. AGW, 33 mm. **Series:** 1988 Olympics **Obv:** Arms above floral spray **Rev:** Stylized horse and rider

Date	Mintage	F	VF	XF	Unc	BU
1987 Proof	30,000	Value: 725				

KM# 73 50000 WON
33.6200 g., 0.9250 Gold 1.0000 oz. AGW, 33 mm. **Series:** 1988 Olympics **Obv:** Arms above floral spray **Rev:** Pul Guk Temple

Date	Mintage	F	VF	XF	Unc	BU
1988 Proof	30,000	Value: 725				

KM# 83 50000 WON
33.6200 g., 0.9250 Gold 1.0000 oz. AGW **Subject:** Taejon International Exposition **Obv:** Arms above floral spray **Rev:** Tower of Great Light

Date	Mintage	F	VF	XF	Unc	BU
1993	10,000	—	—	—	775	—

MINT SETS

KM#	Date	Mintage	Identification	Issue Price	Mkt Val
MS5	1993 (6)	10,000	KM78-83	1,180	1,200
MS6	1993 (5)	30,000	KM78-82	443	450

PROOF SETS

KM#	Date	Mintage	Identification	Issue Price	Mkt Val
PS1	1970 (12)	—	KM7-8, 10-13, 14.1-19.1	752	31,500
PS2	1970 (11)	—	KM7-8, 10-13, 14.2-18.2	—	22,350
PS4	1970 (6)	300	KM14.1-19.1	698	32,000
PS5	1970 (6)	25	KM14.2-19.2	—	38,250
PS7	1986 (6)	350,000	KM#41, 50, 54-56, 58	275	465
PSA9	1986 (6)	160,000	KM#46, 50, 54-56, 58	275	475
PS10	2001 (6)	2,002	KM#90-95	—	1,280

KURDISTAN

Kurdistan is a mountainous region with indefinite boundaries forming a nonpolitical region in southeast Turkey in Asia, and in adjoining areas of northwest Iran, northeast Iraq, and northeast Syria. Kurdistan lies chiefly in Turkey south of Armenia and north of the Tigris, extending from the Euphrates on west to the mountains of Iran, west of Hamadan and including Lake Van. It has an area of about 74,000 sq. mi. (191,660 sq. km.) and is inhabited by the Kurds. Chief towns of Kurdistan: Diyarbakir, Bitlis, and Van in Turkey, Mosul and Kirkuk in Iraq, and Kermanshah in Iran. There are also many Kurds in Armenia. A Kurdish autonomous state was provided for in the Treaty of Sèvres, 1920 but the terms were never carried out.

After the second Gulf War, hopes of independence arose once again after the defeat of Iraq, but nothing has become of this motion.

GOVERNMENT IN EXILE

MILLED COINAGE

X# 4   1000 DINARS
0.4990 g., 0.9170 Gold 0.0147 oz. AGW, 27 mm. **Obv:** Sun over mountains **Rev:** Saladin on horseback holding the modern Kurdish flag **Edge:** Plain

Date	Mintage	F	VF	XF	Unc	BU
AH1424 (2003) Proof	100	Value: 425				

X# 6   100000 DINAR
8.4900 g., 0.9166 Gold **Obv:** Mountains **Rev:** Saladin bust facing

Date	Mintage	F	VF	XF	Unc	BU
2006/AH Proof	150	Value: 325				

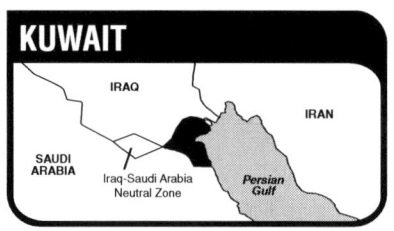

KUWAIT

The State of Kuwait, a constitutional monarchy located on the Arabian Peninsula at the northwestern corner of the Persian Gulf, has an area of 6,880 sq. mi. (17,820 sq. km.) and a population of 1.7 million. Capital: Kuwait. Petroleum, the basis of the economy, provides 95 percent of the exports.

The modern history of Kuwait began with the founding of the city of Kuwait, 1740, by tribesmen who wandered northward from the region of the Qatar Peninsula of eastern Arabia. Fearing that the Turks would take over the sheikhdom, Sheikh Mubarak entered into an agreement with Great Britain, 1899, placing Kuwait under the protection of Britain and empowering Britain to conduct its foreign affairs. Britain terminated the protectorate on June19, 1961, giving Kuwait its independence (by a simple exchange of notes) but agreeing to furnish military aid on request.

Kuwait was invaded and occupied by an army from neighboring Iraq Aug. 2, 1990. Soon thereafter Iraq declared that the country would become a province of Iraq. An international coalition of military forces primarily based in Saudi Arabia led by the United States under terms set by the United Nations, attacked Iraqi military installations to liberate Kuwait. This occurred Jan. 17, 1991. Kuwait City was liberated Feb.27, and a cease-fire was declared Feb. 28. New paper currency was introduced March 24, 1991 to replace earlier notes.

TITLE

الكويت

al-Kuwait

RULER
British Protectorate, until 1961

LOCAL
Al Sabah Dynasty
Abdallah Ibn Sabah, 1762-1812
Jabir Ibn Abdallah, 1812-1859
Sabah Ibn Jabir, 1859-1866
Abdullah Ibn Sabah, 1866-1892
Muhammad Ibn Sabah, 1892-1896
Mubarak Ibn Sabah, 1896-1915
Jabir Ibn Mubarak, 1915-1917
Salim Ibn Mubarak, 1917-1921
Ahmad Ibn Jabir, 1921-1950
Abdullah Ibn Salim, 1950-1965
Sabah Ibn Salim, 1965-1977
Jabir Ibn Ahmad, 1977-

MONETARY SYSTEM
1000 Fils = 1 Dinar

STATE OF KUWAIT

MODERN COINAGE

KM# 9b   FILS
4.0400 g., 0.9170 Gold .1191 oz. AGW, 17 mm. **Ruler:** Jabir Ibn Ahmad **Obv:** Value within circle **Rev:** Ship with sails

Date	Mintage	F	VF	XF	Unc	BU
AH1407-1987 Proof	—	Value: 120				

KM# 10b   5 FILS
5.0500 g., 0.9170 Gold .1488 oz. AGW, 19.5 mm. **Ruler:** Jabir Ibn Ahmad **Obv:** Value within circle **Rev:** Ship with sails

Date	Mintage	F	VF	XF	Unc	BU
AH1407-1987 Proof	—	Value: 145				

KM# 11b   10 FILS
7.6300 g., 0.9170 Gold .2250 oz. AGW, 21 mm. **Ruler:** Jabir Ibn Ahmad **Obv:** Value within circle **Rev:** Ship with sails

Date	Mintage	F	VF	XF	Unc	BU
AH1407-1987 Proof	—	Value: 225				

KM# 12b   20 FILS
5.6700 g., 0.9170 Gold .1672 oz. AGW, 20 mm. **Ruler:** Jabir Ibn Ahmad **Obv:** Value within circle **Rev:** Ship with sails

Date	Mintage	F	VF	XF	Unc	BU
AH1407-1987 Proof	—	Value: 165				

KM# 13b   50 FILS
8.5200 g., 0.9170 Gold .2512 oz. AGW, 23 mm. **Ruler:** Jabir Ibn Ahmad **Obv:** Value within circle **Rev:** Ship with sails

Date	Mintage	F	VF	XF	Unc	BU
AH1407-1987 Proof	—	Value: 250				

KM# 14b   100 FILS
12.3300 g., 0.9170 Gold .3635 oz. AGW, 26 mm. **Ruler:** Jabir Ibn Ahmad **Obv:** Value within circle **Rev:** Ship with sails

Date	Mintage	F	VF	XF	Unc	BU
AH1407-1987 Proof	—	Value: 365				

KM# 8   5 DINARS
13.5720 g., 0.9170 Gold .4001 oz. AGW **Ruler:** Abdullah Ibn Salim **Obv:** Value in Arabic in center circle **Rev:** Dhow sailing left

Date	Mintage	F	VF	XF	Unc	BU
AH1380-1961 Rare Est. 1,000						

KM# 21   50 DINARS
16.9660 g., 0.9170 Gold .5000 oz. AGW **Ruler:** Jabir Ibn Ahmad **Subject:** 25th Anniversary of Kuwait Independence **Obv:** Arabic legend, arched design, falcon, tent, dhow and pearl in a shell **Rev:** Radiant sun, mosque and assembly building with English and Arabic legend

Date	Mintage	F	VF	XF	Unc	BU
AH1406-1986 Proof	—	Value: 400				

KM# 17   100 DINARS
15.9800 g., 0.9170 Gold .4711 oz. AGW **Ruler:** Jabir Ibn Ahmad **Subject:** 15th Century of the Hijira **Obv:** Building, crescent and captain's wheel within circle **Rev:** Dates, building, towers and satellite dish within chained circle

Date	Mintage	F	VF	XF	Unc	BU
AH1401-1981 Proof	10,000	Value: 400				

KM# 19   100 DINARS
15.9800 g., 0.9170 Gold .4711 oz. AGW **Ruler:** Jabir Ibn Ahmad **Subject:** 20th Anniversary of Independence **Obv:** Capital building within circle **Rev:** Courtyard within circle

Date	Mintage	F	VF	XF	Unc	BU
AH1401-1981 Proof	10,000	Value: 400				

MEDALLIC COINAGE

X# 12   50 DINARS
16.9660 g., 0.9170 Gold .5000 oz. AGW **Subject:** 5th Liberation Day **Obv:** State seal **Rev:** Finger print

Date	Mintage	F	VF	XF	Unc	BU
ND (1985) Proof	—	Value: 450				

X# 7   50 DINARS
16.9660 g., 0.9170 Gold .5000 oz. AGW **Subject:** 5th Islamic Summit Conference **Obv:** Arabic, English and French legend, crescent and minaret **Rev:** Dhow

Date	Mintage	F	VF	XF	Unc	BU
ND (1987) Proof	—	Value: 475				

LAOS 463

X# 16 50 DINARS
16.9660 g., 0.9170 Gold .5000 oz. AGW **Subject:** 1st Anniversary
- Liberation Day **Obv:** Concentric legends **Rev:** Building

Date	Mintage	F	VF	XF	Unc	BU
ND (1991) Proof	—	Value: 450				

X# 10 50 DINARS
16.9660 g., 0.9170 Gold .5000 oz. AGW **Subject:** 35th Anniversary
of the National Day **Obv:** Palace **Rev:** Flag on builiding

Date	Mintage	F	VF	XF	Unc	BU
ND (1996)	—	—	—	—	—	425

X# 14 50 DINARS
16.9660 g., 0.9170 Gold .5000 oz. AGW **Subject:** 50th
Anniversary of Exporting 1st Oil Shipment **Obv:** State seal, pump
and tankers **Rev:** Well and tanks

Date	Mintage	F	VF	XF	Unc	BU
ND (1996)	—	—	—	—	—	425

PROOF SETS

KM#	Date	Mintage	Identification	Issue Price	Mkt Val
PS4	1987 (6)	—	KM9b-14b	—	1,275

KYRGYZSTAN

The Republic of Kyrgyzstan, (formerly Kirghiz S.S.R., a Union Republic of the U.S.S.R.), is an independent state since Aug. 31, 1991, a member of the United Nations and of the C.I.S. It was the last state of the Union Republics to declare its sovereignty. Capital: Bishkek (formerly Frunze).

Originally part of the autonomous Turkestan S.S.R. founded on May 1, 1918, the Kyrgyz ethnic area was established on October 14, 1924, as the Kara-Kirghiz Autonomous Region within the R.S.F.S.R. Then on May 25, 1925, the name Kara (black) was dropped. It became an A.S.S.R. on Feb. 1, 1926, and a Union Republic of the U.S.S.R. in 1936. On Dec. 12, 1990, the name was then changed to the Republic of Kyrgyzstan.

REPUBLIC
STANDARD COINAGE

KM# 2 100 SOM
6.2200 g., 0.9990 Gold .2000 oz. AGW **Subject:** Millennium of Manas **Obv:** Arms within circle above date flanked by sprigs **Rev:** Armored equestrian above mountains, value and flying bird

Date	Mintage	F	VF	XF	Unc	BU
1995 Proof	Est. 5,000	Value: 225				

LAOS

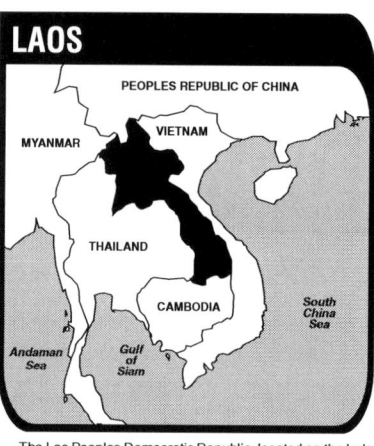

The Lao Peoples Democratic Republic, located on the Indo-Chinese Peninsula between the Socialist Republic of Vietnam and the Kingdom of Thailand, has an area of 91,428 sq. mi. (236,800 km.) and a population of 3.6 million. Capital: Vientiane. Agriculture employs 95 percent of the people. Tin, lumber and coffee are exported.

The first United Kingdom of Lan Xang (Million Elephants) was established in the mid-14th century by King Fa Ngum who ruled an area including present Laos, northeastern Thailand, and the southern part of China's Yunnan province from his capital at Luang Prabang. Thailand and Vietnam obtained control over much of the present Lao territory in the 18th century and remained dominant until France established a protectorate over the area in 1893 and incorporated it into the Union of Indo-China. The Independence of Laos was proclaimed in March of 1945, during the last days of the Japanese occupation of World War II. France reoccupied Laos in 1946, and established it as a constitutional monarchy within the French Union in 1949. In 1953 war erupted between the government and the Pathet Lao, a Communist movement supported by the Vietnamese Communist forces. Peace was declared in 1954 with Laos becoming fully independent in 1955 and the Pathet Lao being permitted to occupy two northern provinces. Civil war broke out again in 1960 with the United States supporting the government of the Kingdom of Laos and the North Vietnamese helping the Communist Pathet Lao, and continued, with intervals of truce and political compromise, until the formation of the Lao Peoples Democratic Republic on Dec. 2, 1975.

NOTE: For earlier coinage, see French Indo-China.

RULERS
Sisavang Vong, 1904-1959
Savang Vatthana, 1959-1975

MONETARY SYSTEM
100 Cents = 1 Piastre
Commencing 1955
100 Att = 1 Kip

MINT MARKS
(a) - Paris, privy marks only
Key - Havana
None - Berlin

NOTE: Private bullion issues previously listed here are now listed in *Unusual World Coins*, 4th Edition, Krause Publications, Inc., 2005.

KINGDOM
STANDARD COINAGE

KM# 9 4000 KIP
4.0000 g., 0.9000 Gold .1157 oz. AGW **Ruler:** Savang Vatthana
Subject: King Savang Vatthana Coronation **Obv:** Head right within circle **Rev:** Radiant sun above statue dividing elephant heads with lamps flanking, all within circle

Date	Mintage	F	VF	XF	Unc	BU
1971 Proof	10,000	Value: 125				

KM# 11 8000 KIP
8.0000 g., 0.9000 Gold .2315 oz. AGW **Ruler:** Savang Vatthana
Subject: King Savang Vatthana Coronation **Obv:** Head right within circle **Rev:** Radiant statue divides elephant heads with lamps flanking, all within circle

LAOS

Date	Mintage	F	VF	XF	Unc	BU
1971 Proof	10,000				Value: 210	

KM# 13 20000 KIP
20.0000 g., 0.9000 Gold .5787 oz. AGW **Ruler:** Savang Vatthana **Subject:** King Savang Vatthana Coronation **Obv:** Head right **Rev:** Elephant statue flanked by lamps

Date	Mintage	F	VF	XF	Unc	BU
1971 Proof	Est. 10,000				Value: 425	

KM# 14 40000 KIP
40.0000 g., 0.9000 Gold 1.1575 oz. AGW **Ruler:** Savang Vatthana **Subject:** King Savang Vatthana Coronation **Rev:** Elephant statue flanked by lamps

Date	Mintage	F	VF	XF	Unc	BU
1971 Proof	Est. 10,000				Value: 825	

KM# 19 50000 KIP
3.6000 g., 0.9000 Gold .1041 oz. AGW **Ruler:** Savang Vatthana **Obv:** Bust of King Savang Vatthana **Rev:** That Luang Temple

Date	Mintage	F	VF	XF	Unc	BU
1975 Proof	175				Value: 260	

KM# 20 50000 KIP
3.6000 g., 0.9000 Gold .1041 oz. AGW **Ruler:** Savang Vatthana **Obv:** Bust of King Savana Vatthana **Rev:** Bust of Laotion maiden 3/4 right

Date	Mintage	F	VF	XF	Unc	BU
1975	100				200	
1975 Proof	175				Value: 260	

KM# 15 80000 KIP
80.0000 g., 0.9000 Gold 2.3151 oz. AGW **Ruler:** Savang Vatthana **Subject:** King Savang Vatthana Coronation **Obv:** Similar to 20000 Kip, KM#13, head right

Date	Mintage	F	VF	XF	Unc	BU
1971 Proof	—			Value: 1,600		

KM# 21 100000 KIP
7.3200 g., 0.9000 Gold .2118 oz. AGW **Ruler:** Savang Vatthana **Obv:** Bust of King Savang Vatthana **Rev:** Statue of Buddha

Date	Mintage	F	VF	XF	Unc	BU
1975	100				375	
1975 Proof	100			Value: 450		

PEOPLES DEMOCRATIC REPUBLIC

STANDARD COINAGE
100 Att = 1 Kip

KM# 42 100 KIP
3.1500 g., 0.9990 Gold .1012 oz. AGW **Obv:** National arms and legend above value **Rev:** 5-masted sailship "Prussia"

Date	Mintage	F	VF	XF	Unc	BU
1988	500				155	200

KM# 43 100 KIP
3.1500 g., 0.9990 Gold .1012 oz. AGW **Subject:** 10th Anniversary of People's Democratic Republic **Obv:** National arms **Rev:** Radiant sun and temple

Date	Mintage	F	VF	XF	Unc	BU
1990	—	—	—	—	160	210

KM# 68 2000 KIP
1.2441 g., 0.9990 Gold .04 oz. AGW **Subject:** That Luang **Obv:** National arms **Rev:** Temple

Date	Mintage	F	VF	XF	Unc	BU
1998 Proof	—			Value: 60.00		

KM# 60 5000 KIP
7.7600 g., 0.5833 Gold .1458 oz. AGW **Series:** Olympics **Obv:** National arms **Rev:** Two boxers

Date	Mintage	F	VF	XF	Unc	BU
1996	Est. 3,000	—	—	—	110	—

KM# 77 10000 KIP
1.2441 g., 0.9999 Gold .0400 oz. AGW, 14 mm. **Subject:** Golden Dragon Fish **Obv:** National arms **Rev:** Jumping fish **Edge:** Reeded **Note:** Date as a latent image.

Date	Mintage	F	VF	XF	Unc	BU
2000-2001	—	—	—	—	50.00	—

KM# 83 50000 KIP
7.7750 g., 0.9990 Gold 0.2497 oz. AGW, 32.2 mm. **Obv:** National arms **Rev:** Red Dragon Fish **Edge:** Reeded

Date	Mintage	F	VF	XF	Unc	BU
2000-2001 Proof	3,000			Value: 185		

KM# 78 100000 KIP
15.5518 g., 0.9999 Gold .4999 oz. AGW, 27 mm. **Subject:** Golden Dragon Fish **Obv:** National arms **Rev:** Multicolored holographic jumping fish **Edge:** Reeded

Date	Mintage	F	VF	XF	Unc	BU
2000-2001 Proof	3,000			Value: 400		

Note: Latent image date

KM# 89 100000 KIP
15.5518 g., 0.9999 Gold 0.5 oz. AGW, 27 mm. **Subject:** Year of the Horse **Obv:** State emblem **Rev:** Horse **Edge:** Reeded

Date	Mintage	F	VF	XF	Unc	BU
2002	2,000			Value: 375		

KM# 95 100000 KIP
15.5518 g., 0.9990 Gold 0.4995 oz. AGW, 27 mm. **Obv:** State emblem **Rev:** Black Gibbon on holographic background **Edge:** Reeded

Date	Mintage	F	VF	XF	Unc	BU
2004 Proof	888			Value: 385		

KM# 90 1000000 KIP
155.5175 g., 0.9999 Gold 4.9995 oz. AGW, 55 mm. **Subject:** Year of the Horse **Obv:** State emblem **Rev:** Horse with multicolor holographic background **Edge:** Reeded

Date	Mintage	F	VF	XF	Unc	BU
2002 Proof	500			Value: 3,500		

MINT SETS

KM#	Date	Mintage	Identification	Issue Price	Mkt Val
MS1	1971 (4)	—	KM7, 8, 10, 12	—	300
MS2	1975 (6)	100	KM16-21	—	1,300
MS3	1975 (3)	300	KM16-18	—	420

PROOF SETS

KM#	Date	Mintage	Identification	Issue Price	Mkt Val
PS1	1971 (5)	10,000	KM9, 11, 13-15	467	3,000
PS2	1971 (4)	20,000	KM7, 8, 10, 12	163	450
PS3	1975 (6)	—	KM16-21	—	1,450
PS4	1975 (3)	650	KM16-18	—	450
PS5	1975 (3)	—	KM19-21	349	960
PS6	1985 (4)	2,000	KM25-28	—	180
PS7	2000-2001 (3)	3,500	KM#74-76	138	200
PS8	2000-2001 (3)	500	KM#74-76	214	300
PS9	2000-2001 (2)	800	KM#78, 83	—	575

LATVIA

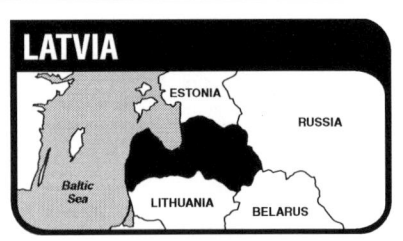

The Republic of Latvia, the central Baltic state in east Europe, has an area of 24,749 sq. mi. (43,601 sq. km.) and a population of 2.6 million. Capital: Riga. Livestock raising and manufacturing are the chief industries. Butter, bacon, fertilizers and telephone equipment are exported.

The Latvians, of Aryan descent primarily from the German Order of Livonian Knights, were nomadic tribesmen who settled along the Baltic prior to the 13th century. Ideally situated as a trade route and lacking a central government, conquered in 1561 by Poland and Sweden. Following the third partition of Poland by Austria, Prussia and Russia in 1795, Latvia came under Russian domination and did not experience autonomy until the Russian Revolution of 1917 provided an opportunity for freedom. The Latvian Republic was established on Nov. 18, 1918. The republic was occupied by Soviet troops and annexed to the Soviet Union in 1940. Following the German occupation of 1941-44, it was retaken by Russia and reestablished as a member republic of the Soviet Union. Western countries, including the United States, did not recognize Latvia's incorporation into the Soviet Union.

The coinage issued during the early 20th Century Republic is now obsolete.

Latvia declared their independence from the U.S.S.R. on August 22, 1991.

MONETARY SYSTEM
100 Santimu = 1 Lats

MODERN REPUBLIC
1991-present
STANDARD COINAGE
100 Santimu = 1 Lats

KM# 59 5 LATI
1.2442 g., 0.9990 Gold 0.04 oz. AGW, 13.92 mm. **Obv:** Bust right **Rev:** Arms with supporters above value **Edge:** Reeded **Note:** Remake of the popular KM-9 design

Date	Mintage	F	VF	XF	Unc	BU
2003 Proof	Est. 20,000			Value: 120		

KM# 42 10 LATU
1.2442 g., 0.9990 Gold .0400 oz. AGW, 13.92 mm. **Obv:** Arms with supporters **Rev:** Sailing ship "Julia Maria" **Edge:** Reeded

Date	Mintage	F	VF	XF	Unc	BU
1997 Proof	—			Value: 55.00		

KM# 29 10 LATU
1.2441 g., 0.9999 Gold .0400 oz. AGW **Subject:** 800th Anniversary - Riga **Obv:** City arms on old coin design **Rev:** City arms and ship on old coin design

Date	Mintage	F	VF	XF	Unc	BU
1998 Proof	—			Value: 55.00		

KM# 43 10 LATU
3.1100 g., 0.5830 Gold .0583 oz. AGW, 18.5 mm. **Series:** Olympics **Obv:** Arms with supporters **Rev:** Javelin thrower **Edge:** Reeded

Date	Mintage	F	VF	XF	Unc	BU
1999 Proof	—			Value: 60.00		

LESOTHO

KM# 41 20 LATU
7.7760 g., 0.5830 Gold .1458 oz. AGW, 25 mm. **Obv:** Arms with supporters **Rev:** Sailing ship "Gekronte Ehlendt" **Edge:** Reeded

Date	Mintage	F	VF	XF	Unc	BU
1997 Proof	—	Value: 110				

KM# 20 100 LATU
13.3380 g., 0.8330 Gold .2501 oz. AGW **Subject:** 75th Anniversary - Declaration of Independence **Obv:** Arms with supporters **Rev:** Artistic lined design above value and dates

Date	Mintage	F	VF	XF	Unc	BU
ND(1993) Proof	5,000	Value: 250				

KM# 40 100 LATU
16.2000 g., 0.9990 Gold .5203 oz. AGW, 24 mm. **Subject:** Development **Obv:** Arms with supporters **Rev:** Partial circle within value **Edge:** Reeded and plain sections

Date	Mintage	F	VF	XF	Unc	BU
1998 Proof	—	Value: 500				

ECU COINAGE

X# 12 150 ECU
31.1030 g., 0.8150 Gold 0.815 oz. AGW, 38 mm. **Issuer:** Numex S.A., Madrid **Obv:** Supported arms **Rev:** Lynx standing right, facing **Rev. Legend:** LATVIJAS REPUBLIKA

Date	Mintage	F	VF	XF	Unc	BU
1993 Proof	600	Value: 625				

PROOF SETS

KM#	Date	Mintage	Identification	Issue Price	Mkt Val
PS1	ND (1993) (3)	1,800	KM18-20	—	325

LEBANON

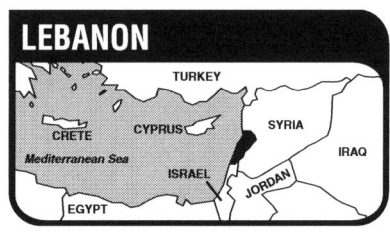

The Republic of Lebanon, situated on the eastern shore of the Mediterranean Sea between Syria and Israel, has an area of 4,015 sq. mi. (10,400 sq. km.) and a population of 3.5 million. Capital: Beirut. The economy is based on agriculture, trade and tourism. Fruit, other foodstuffs and textiles are exported.

Almost at the beginning of recorded history, Lebanon appeared as the well-wooded hinterland of the Phoenicians who exploited its famous forests of cedar. The mountains were a Christian refuge and a Crusader stronghold. Lebanon, the history of which is essentially the same as that of Syria, came under control of the Ottoman Turks early in the 16th century. Following the collapse of the Ottoman Empire after World War I, Lebanon, along with Syria, became a French mandate. The French drew a border around the predominantly Christian Lebanon *Sanjak* or administrative subdivision and on Sept. 1, 1920 proclaimed the area the State of Grand Lebanon (*Etat du Grand Liban*) a republic under French control. France announced the independence of Lebanon on Nov. 26, 1941, but the last British and French troops didn't leave until the end of August 1946.

TITLE

الجمهورية اللبنانية

al-Jomhuriya(t) al-Lubnaniya(t)

MINT MARKS
(a) - Paris, privy marks only
(u) - Utrecht, privy marks only

MONETARY SYSTEM
100 Piastres = 1 Livre (Pound)

REPUBLIC
STANDARD COINAGE

KM# 34 400 LIVRES
8.0000 g., 0.9000 Gold .2315 oz. AGW **Series:** 1980 Winter Olympics **Subject:** Lake Placid **Obv:** Olympic rings on top of design **Rev:** Stylized flame

Date	Mintage	F	VF	XF	Unc	BU
1980 Proof	1,000	Value: 600				

PIEFORTS

KM#	Date	Mintage	Identification	Mkt Val
P3	1980	750	400 Livres. Gold. KM34.	1,400

LESOTHO

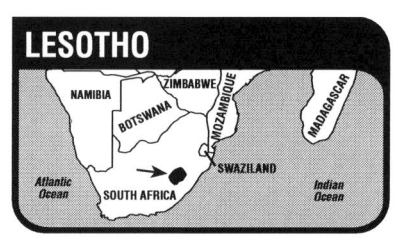

The Kingdom of Lesotho, a constitutional monarchy located within the east-central part of the Republic of South Africa, has an area of 11,720 sq. mi. (30,350 sq. km.) and a population of 1.5 million. Capital: Maseru. The economy is based on subsistence agriculture and livestock raising. Wool, mohair, and cattle are exported.

Lesotho (formerly Basutoland) was sparsely populated until the end of the 16th century. Between the 16th and 19th centuries an influx of refugees from tribal wars led to the development of a distinct Basotho group. During the reign of tribal chief Mashoeshoe I (1823-70), a series of wars with the Orange Free State resulted in the loss of large areas of territory to South Africa. Mashoeshoe appealed to the British for help, and Basutoland was constituted a native state under British protection. In 1871 it was annexed to Cape Colony, but was restored to direct control by the Crown in 1884. From 1884 to 1959 legislative and executive authority was vested in a British High Commissioner. The constitution of 1959 recognized the expressed wish of the people for independence, which was attained on Oct.4, 1966.

Lesotho is a member of the Commonwealth of Nations. The king is Head of State.

RULERS
Moshoeshoe II, 1966-1990
Letsie III, 1990-1995
Moshoeshoe II, 1995-

MONETARY SYSTEM
100 Licente/Lisente = 1 Maloti/Loti

KINGDOM
STANDARD COINAGE
100 Licente/Lisente = 1 Maloti/Loti

KM# 5 LOTI
3.9940 g., 0.9170 Gold .1177 oz. AGW **Ruler:** Moshoeshoe II **Subject:** Independence Attained **Obv:** Native bust right **Rev:** Arms with supporters above value flanked by stars

Date	Mintage	F	VF	XF	Unc	BU
1966 Proof	3,500	Value: 85.00				

KM# 8 LOTI
3.9940 g., 0.9170 Gold .1177 oz. AGW **Ruler:** Moshoeshoe II **Series:** F.A.O. **Obv:** Native bust right **Rev:** Equestrian

Date	Mintage	F	VF	XF	Unc	BU
1969 Proof	3,000	Value: 85.00				

KM# 46a LOTI
18.9800 g., 0.9170 Gold .5626 oz. AGW **Ruler:** Moshoeshoe II **Subject:** Silver Jubilee of King Moshoeshoe II **Obv:** Uniformed bust 1/4 left **Rev:** Crown above arms with supporters flanked by dates

Date	Mintage	F	VF	XF	Unc	BU
1985 Proof	500	Value: 400				

KM# 6 2 MALOTI
7.9880 g., 0.9170 Gold .2355 oz. AGW **Ruler:** Moshoeshoe II **Obv:** Native bust right **Rev:** Arms with supporters above value flanked by stars

Date	Mintage	F	VF	XF	Unc	BU
1966 Proof	—	Value: 175				

KM# 9 2 MALOTI
7.9880 g., 0.9170 Gold .2355 oz. AGW **Ruler:** Moshoeshoe II **Series:** F.A.O. **Obv:** Native bust right **Rev:** Figure on horseback left

Date	Mintage	F	VF	XF	Unc	BU
1969 Proof	3,000	Value: 175				

LESOTHO

KM# 7 4 MALOTI
15.9760 g., 0.9170 Gold .471 oz. AGW **Ruler:** Moshoeshoe II
Obv: Native bust right **Rev:** Arms with supporters above value flanked by stars

Date	Mintage	F	VF	XF	Unc	BU
1966 Proof	3,500	Value: 345				

KM# 10 4 MALOTI
15.9760 g., 0.9170 Gold .471 oz. AGW **Ruler:** Moshoeshoe II
Series: F.A.O. **Obv:** Native bust right **Rev:** Figure on horseback left

Date	Mintage	F	VF	XF	Unc	BU
1969 Proof	3,000	Value: 345				

KM# 11 10 MALOTI
39.9400 g., 0.9170 Gold 1.1776 oz. AGW **Ruler:** Moshoeshoe II
Series: F.A.O. **Obv:** Arms with supporters **Rev:** Farmer leading two oxen

Date	Mintage	F	VF	XF	Unc	BU
1969 Proof	3,000	Value: 825				

KM# 12 20 MALOTI
79.8810 g., 0.9170 Gold 2.3553 oz. AGW **Ruler:** Moshoeshoe II
Series: F.A.O. **Obv:** Arms with supporters **Rev:** Grazing ewe and lamb

Date	Mintage	F	VF	XF	Unc	BU
1969 Proof	3,000	Value: 1,650				

KM# 14 50 MALOTI
4.5000 g., 0.9000 Gold .1302 oz. AGW **Ruler:** Moshoeshoe II
Subject: 10th Anniversary of Independence **Obv:** Arms with supporters within circle **Rev:** Young bust right divides dates

Date	Mintage	F	VF	XF	Unc	BU
ND(1976)	700	—	—	—	125	130
ND(1976) Proof	1,910	Value: 130				

KM# 15 100 MALOTI
9.0000 g., 0.9000 Gold .2604 oz. AGW **Ruler:** Moshoeshoe II
Subject: 10th Anniversary of Independence **Obv:** Uniformed bust 1/4 left divides dates **Rev:** Equestrian and value within circle

Date	Mintage	F	VF	XF	Unc	BU
ND(1976)	450	—	—	—	190	200
ND(1976) Proof	1,410	Value: 180				

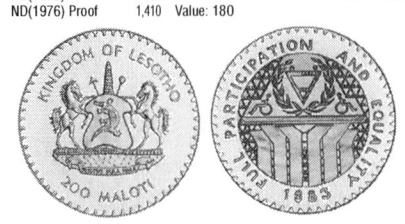

KM# 45 200 MALOTI
15.9800 g., 0.9000 Gold .4624 oz. AGW **Ruler:** Moshoeshoe II
Series: International Year of Disabled Persons **Obv:** Arms with supporters **Rev:** Disabled persons design within circle

Date	Mintage	F	VF	XF	Unc	BU
1983	500	—	—	—	400	420
1983 Proof	500	Value: 450				

KM# 26 250 MALOTI
33.9300 g., 0.9170 Gold 1 oz. AGW **Ruler:** Moshoeshoe II
Series: International Year of the Child **Obv:** Native bust right **Rev:** Busts of 3 children facing with logo below

Date	Mintage	F	VF	XF	Unc	BU
1979	2,500	—	—	—	700	720
1979 Proof	2,000	Value: 750				

KM# 28 250 MALOTI
31.1000 g., 0.9170 Gold .917 oz. AGW **Ruler:** Moshoeshoe II
Subject: 110th Anniversary - Death of King Moshoeshoe I **Obv:** Native bust right **Rev:** Hat within diamond at center, corn ear at left, alligator at right

Date	Mintage	F	VF	XF	Unc	BU
1980	1,500	—	—	—	650	660
1980 Proof	3,000	Value: 675				

KM# 31 250 MALOTI
15.9000 g., 0.9170 Gold .4688 oz. AGW **Ruler:** Moshoeshoe II
Subject: Wedding of Prince Charles and Lady Diana **Obv:** **Designer:** Arms with supporters **Rev:** Conjoined busts left

Date	Mintage	F	VF	XF	Unc	BU
1981	1,000	—	—	—	385	400
1981 Proof	1,500	Value: 345				

KM# 31a 250 MALOTI
15.7500 g., 0.9950 Platinum .5039 oz. APW **Ruler:** Moshoeshoe II **Subject:** Wedding of Prince Charles and Lady Diana **Obv:** Arms with supporters **Rev:** Conjoined busts left

Date	Mintage	F	VF	XF	Unc	BU
1981 Proof	200	Value: 700				

KM# 36 250 MALOTI
16.9600 g., 0.9170 Gold .5001 oz. AGW **Ruler:** Moshoeshoe II
Subject: Duke of Edinburgh Youth Awards **Obv:** Arms with supporters **Rev:** Bust left

Date	Mintage	F	VF	XF	Unc	BU
1981 Proof	1,500	Value: 350				

KM# 36a 250 MALOTI
15.7500 g., 0.9950 Platinum .5039 oz. APW **Ruler:** Moshoeshoe II
Subject: Duke of Edinburgh Youth Awards **Obv:** Arms with supporters **Rev:** Bust left

Date	Mintage	F	VF	XF	Unc	BU
1981 Proof	200	Value: 700				

KM# 33 250 MALOTI
7.1300 g., 0.9000 Gold .2063 oz. AGW **Ruler:** Moshoeshoe II
Subject: Soccer Games **Obv:** Arms with supporters **Rev:** Goalie

Date	Mintage	F	VF	XF	Unc	BU
1982 Proof	551	Value: 250				

KM# 51 250 MALOTI
15.9800 g., 0.9170 Gold .4708 oz. AGW **Ruler:** Moshoeshoe II
Subject: Papal Visit **Obv:** Bust left **Rev:** Arms with supporters

Date	Mintage	F	VF	XF	Unc	BU
1988 Proof	Est. 750	Value: 500				

KM# 29 500 MALOTI
33.9300 g., 0.9170 Gold 1 oz. AGW **Ruler:** Moshoeshoe II
Subject: 110th Anniversary - Death of King Moshoeshoe I **Obv:** Native bust right **Rev:** Hat within diamond at center, corn ear at left, alligator at right

Date	Mintage	F	VF	XF	Unc	BU
1980	1,500	—	—	—	700	720
1980 Proof	3,000	Value: 725				

KM# 39 500 MALOTI
33.9300 g., 0.9170 Gold 1 oz. AGW **Ruler:** Moshoeshoe II
Subject: 15th Anniversary of Commonwealth Membership **Obv:** Arms with supporters **Rev:** Crowned bust right

Date	Mintage	F	VF	XF	Unc	BU
1981 Proof	500	Value: 700				

KM# 39a 500 MALOTI
31.5000 g., 0.9950 Platinum 1.0078 oz. APW **Ruler:** Moshoeshoe II **Subject:** 15th Anniversary of Commonwealth Membership **Obv:** Arms with supporters **Rev:** Crowned bust right

Date	Mintage	F	VF	XF	Unc	BU
1981 Proof	200	Value: 1,350				

KM# 57 500 MALOTI
33.9300 g., 0.9166 Gold 1 oz. AGW **Ruler:** Moshoeshoe II **Subject:** Royal Wedding of Prince Charles and Lady Diana **Obv:** Arms with supporters **Rev:** Conjoined busts left

Date	Mintage	F	VF	XF	Unc	BU
ND(1981) Proof, rare	—	—	—	—	—	—

KM# 57a 500 MALOTI
33.4800 g., 0.9995 Platinum 1 oz. APW **Ruler:** Moshoeshoe II **Subject:** Royal Wedding **Obv:** Arms with supporters **Rev:** Conjoined bust left

Date	Mintage	F	VF	XF	Unc	BU
ND(1981) Proof, rare	—	—	—	—	—	—

PATTERNS
Including off metal strikes

KM#	Date	Mintage	Identification	Mkt Val
Pn6	1966	7	2 Maloti. 0.9160 Gold.	500
Pn7	1966	7	4 Maloti. 0.9160 Gold.	700
Pn8	1966	7	10 Maloti. 0.9160 Gold. Head right. Arms with supporters above value and date.	950
Pn9	1966	7	20 Maloti. 0.9160 Gold.	1,250
Pn19	1980	10	500 Maloti. Brass. KM29. Coin alignment.	110
Pn20	1980	10	500 Maloti. Copper-Nickel. KM29. Medallic alignment.	110

PIEFORTS

KM#	Date	Mintage	Identification	Mkt Val
P2	1981	—	250 Maloti. Gold. KM31.	550
P4	1983	100	200 Maloti. Gold. KM45.	800

MINT SETS

KM#	Date	Mintage	Identification	Issue Price	Mkt Val
MS1	1976 (3)	450	KM13-15	194	315

PROOF SETS

KM#	Date	Mintage	Identification	Issue Price	Mkt Val
PS2	1966 (4)	7	KMPn6-9	—	3,400
PS6	1969 (5)	3,000	KM8-12	450	3,100
PS7	1976 (3)	1,410	KM13-15	285	300
PS8	1976 (2)	—	KM14-15	270	270
PS9	1976 (2)	—	KM13-14	—	135

LIBERIA

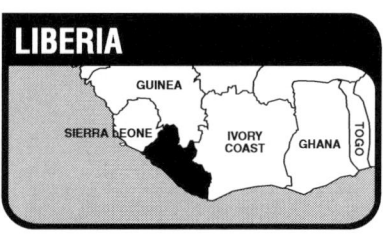

The Republic of Liberia, located on the southern side of the West African bulge between Sierra Leone and Ivory Coast, has an area of 38,250 sq. mi. (111,370 sq. km) and a population of 2.2 million. Capital: Monrovia. The major industries are agriculture, mining and lumbering. Iron ore, diamonds, rubber, coffee and coca are exported.

The Liberian coast was explored and charted by Portuguese navigator Pedro de Cintra in 1461. For the three centuries following Portuguese traders visited the area regularly to trade for gold, slaves and pepper. The modern country of Liberia, Africa's first republic, was settled in 1822 by the American Colonization Society as a homeland for American freed slaves, with the U.S. government furnishing funds and assisting in negotiations for procurement of land from the native chiefs. The various settlements united in 1839 to form the Commonwealth of Liberia, and in 1847 established the country as a republic with a constitution modeled after that of the United States.

U.S. money was declared legal tender in Liberia in 1943, replacing British West African currency.

Most of the Liberian pattern series, particularly of the 1888-90 period, are acknowledged to have been "unofficial" privately sponsored issues, but many collectors of Liberian coins nonetheless, avidly collect them. The "K" number designations on these pieces refer to a listing of Liberian patterns compiled and published by Ernst Kraus.

MINT MARKS
B - Bern, Switzerland
H - Heaton, Birmingham
(l) - London
(s) - San Francisco, U.S.
FM - Franklin Mint, U.S.A.*
PM - Pobjoy Mint

*NOTE: From 1975-1985 the Franklin Mint produced coinage in up to 3 different qualities. Qualities of issue are designated in ( ) after each date and are defined as follows:

(M) MATTE - Normal circulation strike or a dull finish produced by sandblasting special uncirculated (polish finish) or proof quality dies.

(U) SPECIAL UNCIRCULATED - Polished or prooflike in appearance without any frosted features.

(P) PROOF - The highest quality obtainable having mirror-like fields and frosted features.

MONETARY SYSTEM
100 Cents = 1 Dollar

REPUBLIC
STANDARD COINAGE
100 Cents = 1 Dollar

KM# 47b 2 DOLLARS
47.5400 g., Gold **Series:** F.A.O. **Subject:** World Fisheries Conference **Obv:** National arms **Rev:** Longneck croaker fish **Rev. Designer:** Stuart Devlin

Date	Mintage	F	VF	XF	Unc	BU
1983 Proof	600	Value: 950				

KM# 24 2-1/2 DOLLARS
4.1796 g., 0.9000 Gold .1209 oz. AGW **Subject:** Inauguration of President Tolbert **Rev:** Capitol building

Date	Mintage	F	VF	XF	Unc	BU
1972 Proof	—	Value: 95.00				

KM# 62 5 DOLLARS
5.0000 g., 0.9000 Gold .1447 oz. AGW **Subject:** 25th Anniversary of Inter-Continental Hotels **Obv:** Value below hotel flanked by sprigs **Rev:** Letter I within football flanked by dates

Date	Mintage	F	VF	XF	Unc	BU
ND(1971) Proof	—	Value: 110				

KM# 25 5 DOLLARS
8.3592 g., 0.9000 Gold .2419 oz. AGW **Subject:** Inauguration of President Tolbert **Rev:** Full masted ship at sea

Date	Mintage	F	VF	XF	Unc	BU
1972 Proof	—	Value: 175				

KM# 63 10 DOLLARS
11.7200 g., 0.9000 Gold .3391 oz. AGW **Subject:** 25th Anniversary of Inter-Continental Hotels **Obv:** Value below hotel building **Rev:** Letter I within football flanked by dates

Date	Mintage	F	VF	XF	Unc	BU
1971 Proof	—	Value: 245				

KM# 26 10 DOLLARS
16.7185 g., 0.9000 Gold .4838 oz. AGW **Subject:** Inauguration of President Tolbert **Rev:** Head left

Date	Mintage	F	VF	XF	Unc	BU
1972 Proof	—	Value: 350				

KM# 709 10 DOLLARS
0.5100 g., Gold, 11.1 mm. **Subject:** American Civil War **Obv:** National arms **Rev:** Battle of Gettysburg Generals Meade and Lee **Edge:** Reeded

Date	Mintage	F	VF	XF	Unc	BU
2000 Proof	—	Value: 25.00				

KM# 492 10 DOLLARS
3.3930 g., 0.9167 Gold .1000 oz. AGW, 16.5 mm. **Subject:** US Gold Indian Design Copy **Obv:** Incuse Indian design **Rev:** Incuse eagle design **Edge:** Reeded

Date	Mintage	F	VF	XF	Unc	BU
2000	—	—	—	—	125	—

KM# 20 12 DOLLARS
6.0000 g., 0.9000 Gold .1736 oz. AGW **Subject:** 70th Birthday of President Tubman **Obv:** National arms **Rev:** Bust left

Date	Mintage	F	VF	XF	Unc	BU
1965 Proof	400	Value: 130				

KM# 108 15 DOLLARS
1.0000 g., 0.9999 Gold .0321 oz. AGW **Series:** Preserve Planet Earth **Obv:** National arms **Rev:** Compsognathus

Date	Mintage	F	VF	XF	Unc	BU
1993 Proof	—	Value: 32.50				

468 LIBERIA

KM# 19 20 DOLLARS
18.6500 g., 0.9000 Gold .5397 oz. AGW **Subject:** William Vacanarat Shadrach Tubman **Obv:** National arms **Rev:** Head 1/4 left above date flanked by stars

Date	Mintage	F	VF	XF	Unc	BU
1964B	10,000	—	—	—	375	—

KM# 19a 20 DOLLARS
0.9990 Gold **Obv:** National arms **Rev:** Head 1/4 left above date flanked by stars

Date	Mintage	F	VF	XF	Unc	BU
1964B L Proof	100	Value: 425				

Note: Of the total issue, 10,200 were struck of .900 fine gold and bear the "B" mint mark of the Bern Mint below the date, while 100 were struck as proofs of .999 fine gold and are designated by the presence of a small "L" above the date

KM# 64 20 DOLLARS
15.8100 g., 0.9000 Gold .8768 oz. AGW **Subject:** 25th Anniversary of Inter-Continental Hotels **Obv:** Value below hotel building **Rev:** Letter I within football flanked by dates

Date	Mintage	F	VF	XF	Unc	BU
1971 Proof	—	Value: 645				

KM# 27 20 DOLLARS
33.4370 g., 0.9000 Gold .9675 oz. AGW **Subject:** Inauguration of President Tolbert **Obv:** National arms **Rev:** Head left

Date	Mintage	F	VF	XF	Unc	BU
1972 Proof	—	Value: 700				

KM# 283 20 DOLLARS
1.2700 g., 0.9990 Gold .0408 oz. AGW **Subject:** Formula One **Obv:** National arms divide date **Rev:** Damon Hill

Date	Mintage	F	VF	XF	Unc	BU
1994 Proof	25,000	Value: 65.00				

KM# 230 20 DOLLARS
1.2700 g., 0.9990 Gold .0408 oz. AGW **Subject:** Formula One **Obv:** National arms **Rev:** Ayrton Senna **Note:** Similar to 10 Dollars, KM#229.

Date	Mintage	F	VF	XF	Unc	BU
1996 Proof	15,000	Value: 65.00				

KM# 250 20 DOLLARS
1.2700 g., 0.9990 Gold .0408 oz. AGW **Subject:** Dalai Lama **Obv:** National arms **Rev:** Bust with praying hands facing 1/4 left **Note:** Similar to 100 Dollars, KM#252.

Date	Mintage	F	VF	XF	Unc	BU
1996 Proof	15,000	Value: 65.00				

KM# 315 20 DOLLARS
1.2400 g., 0.9990 Gold .0400 oz. AGW **Subject:** Return of Hong Kong to China **Obv:** National arms **Rev:** Dragon **Note:** Similar to 10 Dollars, KM#314.

Date	Mintage	F	VF	XF	Unc	BU
1997 Proof	—	Value: 65.00				

KM# 418 20 DOLLARS
1.2441 g., 0.9999 Gold .0400 oz. AGW **Subject:** Return of Macao to China **Obv:** National arms **Rev:** Dragon and phoenix **Note:** Similar to 10 Dollars, KM#408.

Date	Mintage	F	VF	XF	Unc	BU
1999 Proof	25,000	Value: 55.00				

KM# 616 20 DOLLARS
31.2000 g., 0.9990 Gold Plated Silver 1.0021 oz. ASW AGW, 38.7 mm. **Obv:** National arms **Rev:** Diamond studded scorpion (scorpio) **Edge:** Reeded

Date	Mintage	F	VF	XF	Unc	BU
2002 Proof	—	Value: 60.00				

KM# 617 20 DOLLARS
31.2000 g., 0.9990 Gold Plated Silver 1.0021 oz. ASW AGW, 38.7 mm. **Obv:** National arms **Rev:** Diamond studded archer (sagittarius) **Edge:** Reeded

Date	Mintage	F	VF	XF	Unc	BU
2002 Proof	—	Value: 60.00				

KM# 21 25 DOLLARS
23.3120 g., 0.9000 Gold .6746 oz. AGW **Subject:** 70th Birthday of President Tubman **Obv:** Head 3/4 left above date flanked by stars **Rev:** Trees and sun above value flanked by stars

Date	Mintage	F	VF	XF	Unc	BU
1965	3,000	—	—	—	475	—

KM# 21a 25 DOLLARS
23.3120 g., 0.9990 Gold 0.7487 oz. AGW **Obv:** Head 3/4 left above date flanked by stars **Rev:** Tree and sun above value flanked by stars

Date	Mintage	F	VF	XF	Unc	BU
1965B L Proof	100	Value: 525				

KM# 23 25 DOLLARS
0.9990 Gold **Subject:** 75th Birthday of President Tubman **Obv:** Birthplace of President **Rev:** Head facing above dates

Date	Mintage	F	VF	XF	Unc	BU
ND(1970)B Proof	—	Value: 520				

KM# 28 25 DOLLARS
0.9990 Gold **Subject:** Sesquicentennial - Founding of Liberia **Obv:** Bust 1/4 left **Rev:** Man in canoe below tower and trees with value above

Date	Mintage	F	VF	XF	Unc	BU
ND(1972)B Proof	3,000	Value: 520				

KM# 512 25 DOLLARS
0.7300 g., 0.9990 Gold 0.0234 oz. AGW, 11.1 mm. **Obv:** National arms **Rev:** Bust right **Rev. Legend:** NOFRETETE **Edge:** Reeded **Note:** The American Mint is not an actual mint.

Date	Mintage	F	VF	XF	Unc	BU
2000 Proof	—	Value: 30.00				

KM# 631 25 DOLLARS
0.7300 g., 0.9990 Gold 0.0234 oz. AGW, 11.1 mm. **Obv:** National arms **Rev:** Julius Caesar **Edge:** Reeded

Date	Mintage	F	VF	XF	Unc	BU
2000 Proof	—	Value: 30.00				

KM# 632 25 DOLLARS
0.7300 g., 0.9990 Gold 0.0234 oz. AGW, 11.1 mm. **Obv:** National arms **Rev:** George Washington **Edge:** Reeded

Date	Mintage	F	VF	XF	Unc	BU
2000 Proof	—	Value: 30.00				

KM# 633 25 DOLLARS
0.7300 g., 0.9990 Gold 0.0234 oz. AGW, 11.1 mm. **Obv:** National arms **Rev:** Mahatma Gandhi **Edge:** Reeded

Date	Mintage	F	VF	XF	Unc	BU
2000 Proof	—	Value: 30.00				

KM# 634 25 DOLLARS
0.7300 g., 0.9990 Gold 0.0234 oz. AGW, 11.1 mm. **Obv:** National arms **Rev:** Joan of Arc **Edge:** Reeded

Date	Mintage	F	VF	XF	Unc	BU
2000 Proof	—	Value: 30.00				

KM# 623 25 DOLLARS
0.7300 g., 0.9990 Gold 0.0234 oz. AGW, 11.1 mm. **Obv:** National arms **Rev:** Martin Luther **Edge:** Reeded

Date	Mintage	F	VF	XF	Unc	BU
2000 Proof	—	Value: 30.00				

KM# 624 25 DOLLARS
0.7300 g., 0.9990 Gold 0.0234 oz. AGW, 11.1 mm. **Obv:** National arms **Rev:** Queen Elizabeth II **Edge:** Reeded

Date	Mintage	F	VF	XF	Unc	BU
2000 Proof	—	Value: 30.00				

KM# 625 25 DOLLARS
0.7300 g., 0.9990 Gold 0.0234 oz. AGW, 11.1 mm. **Obv:** National arms **Rev:** Mozart **Edge:** Reeded

Date	Mintage	F	VF	XF	Unc	BU
2000 Proof	—	Value: 30.00				

KM# 626 25 DOLLARS
0.7300 g., 0.9990 Gold 0.0234 oz. AGW, 11.1 mm. **Obv:** National arms **Rev:** Christopher Columbus **Edge:** Reeded

Date	Mintage	F	VF	XF	Unc	BU
2000 Proof	—	Value: 30.00				

KM# 627 25 DOLLARS
0.7300 g., 0.9990 Gold 0.0234 oz. AGW, 11.1 mm. **Obv:** National arms **Rev:** Tutankhamen **Edge:** Reeded

Date	Mintage	F	VF	XF	Unc	BU
2000 Proof	—	Value: 30.00				

KM# 628 25 DOLLARS
0.7300 g., 0.9990 Gold 0.0234 oz. AGW, 11.1 mm. **Obv:** National arms **Rev:** Charlemagne **Edge:** Reeded

Date	Mintage	F	VF	XF	Unc	BU
2000 Proof	—	Value: 30.00				

LIBERIA

KM# 629 25 DOLLARS
0.7300 g., 0.9990 Gold 0.0234 oz. AGW, 11.1 mm. **Obv:** National arms **Rev:** Peter the Great **Edge:** Reeded

Date	Mintage	F	VF	XF	Unc	BU
2000 Proof	—	Value: 30.00				

KM# 630 25 DOLLARS
0.7300 g., 0.9990 Gold 0.0234 oz. AGW, 11.1 mm. **Obv:** National arms **Rev:** Mikhail Gorbachev **Edge:** Reeded

Date	Mintage	F	VF	XF	Unc	BU
2000 Proof	—	Value: 30.00				

KM# 22 30 DOLLARS
15.0000 g., 0.9000 Gold .4340 oz. AGW **Subject:** 70th Birthday of President Tubman **Obv:** National arms **Rev:** Bust left

Date	Mintage	F	VF	XF	Unc	BU
1965 Proof	400	Value: 300				

KM# 231 50 DOLLARS
3.1103 g., 0.9990 Gold .1000 oz. AGW **Subject:** Formula One **Obv:** National arms **Rev:** Ayrton Senna **Note:** Similar to 10 Dollars, KM#229.

Date	Mintage	F	VF	XF	Unc	BU
1996 Proof	10,000	Value: 110				

KM# 251 50 DOLLARS
3.1103 g., 0.9990 Gold .1000 oz. AGW **Subject:** Dalai Lama **Obv:** National arms **Rev:** Bust with praying hands 1/4 left **Note:** Similar to 100 Dollars, KM#252.

Date	Mintage	F	VF	XF	Unc	BU
1996 Proof	10,000	Value: 110				

KM# 316 50 DOLLARS
3.1103 g., 0.9990 Gold .1000 oz. AGW **Subject:** Return of Hong Kong to China **Obv:** National arms **Rev:** Dragon **Note:** Similar to 10 Dollars, KM#314.

Date	Mintage	F	VF	XF	Unc	BU
1997 Proof	—	Value: 100				

KM# 366 50 DOLLARS
3.1103 g., 0.9990 Gold .1000 oz. AGW **Subject:** RMS Titanic **Obv:** National arms **Rev:** Ship sinking **Note:** Similar to 20 Dollars, KM#364.

Date	Mintage	F	VF	XF	Unc	BU
1998 Proof	Est. 2,000	Value: 115				

KM# 419 50 DOLLARS
3.1103 g., 0.9990 Gold .1000 oz. AGW **Subject:** Return of Macao to China **Obv:** National arms **Rev:** Dragon and phoenix **Note:** Similar to 10 Dollars, KM#408.

Date	Mintage	F	VF	XF	Unc	BU
1999 Proof	10,000	Value: 100				

KM# 33 100 DOLLARS
6.0000 g., 0.9000 Gold .1736 oz. AGW **Subject:** Inauguration of President Tolbert **Obv:** Bust facing **Rev:** Joined figures form a tower

Date	Mintage	F	VF	XF	Unc	BU
1976 Proof	175	Value: 225				

KM# 36 100 DOLLARS
10.9300 g., 0.9000 Gold .3163 oz. AGW **Subject:** 130th Anniversary of the Republic **Obv:** Bust 3/4 left **Rev:** National arms

Date	Mintage	F	VF	XF	Unc	BU
1977FM (U)	787	—	—	—	235	—
1977FM (P)	4,250	Value: 220				

KM# 37 100 DOLLARS
10.9300 g., 0.9000 Gold .3163 oz. AGW **Subject:** Organization of African Unity **Obv:** National arms above value flanked by stars **Rev:** Bust facing flanked by stars

Date	Mintage	F	VF	XF	Unc	BU
1979FM (P)	1,656	Value: 220				

KM# 38 100 DOLLARS
11.2000 g., 0.9000 Gold .3241 oz. AGW **Subject:** Organization of African Unity **Obv:** National arms **Rev:** Elephant

Date	Mintage	F	VF	XF	Unc	BU
1979FM (P)	—	Value: 225				

KM# 50 100 DOLLARS
10.9300 g., 0.9000 Gold .3163 oz. AGW **Subject:** 5th Anniversary of Government **Obv:** National arms **Rev:** Leopard

Date	Mintage	F	VF	XF	Unc	BU
1985FM (P)	409	Value: 450				

KM# 61 100 DOLLARS
7.1300 g., 0.9000 Gold .2063 oz. AGW **Series:** Decade For Women **Obv:** National arms **Rev:** Woman mashing grain

Date	Mintage	F	VF	XF	Unc	BU
1985 Proof	318	Value: 200				

KM# 100 100 DOLLARS
6.2200 g., 0.9990 Gold .2000 oz. AGW **Series:** Preserve Planet Earth **Obv:** National arms **Rev:** Protoceratops

Date	Mintage	F	VF	XF	Unc	BU
1993 Proof	Est. 7,500	Value: 165				

KM# 111 100 DOLLARS
6.2200 g., 0.9990 Gold .2000 oz. AGW **Series:** Preserve Planet Earth **Obv:** National arms **Rev:** Corythosaurus

Date	Mintage	F	VF	XF	Unc	BU
1993 Proof	7,500	Value: 165				

KM# 114 100 DOLLARS
6.2200 g., 0.9990 Gold .2000 oz. AGW **Series:** Preserve Planet Earth **Obv:** National arms **Rev:** Atchaeopteryx **Note:** Incorrect spelling.

Date	Mintage	F	VF	XF	Unc	BU
1993 Proof	Est. 7,500	Value: 165				

KM# 117 100 DOLLARS
6.2200 g., 0.9990 Gold .2000 oz. AGW **Series:** Preserve Planet Earth **Obv:** National arms **Rev:** Archaeopteryx **Note:** Correct spelling.

Date	Mintage	F	VF	XF	Unc	BU
1994 Proof	7,500	Value: 165				

KM# 120 100 DOLLARS
6.2200 g., 0.9990 Gold .2000 oz. AGW **Series:** Preserve Planet Earth **Obv:** National arms **Rev:** Gorillas **Note:** Similar to 10 Dollars, KM#120.

Date	Mintage	F	VF	XF	Unc	BU
1994 Proof	Est. 7,500	Value: 165				

KM# 123 100 DOLLARS
6.2200 g., 0.9990 Gold .2000 oz. AGW **Series:** Preserve Planet Earth **Obv:** National arms **Rev:** Pygmy Hippopotami **Note:** Similar to 10 Dollars, KM#122.

Date	Mintage	F	VF	XF	Unc	BU
1994 Proof	Est. 7,500	Value: 165				

KM# 126 100 DOLLARS
6.2200 g., 0.9990 Gold .2000 oz. AGW **Series:** Preserve Planet Earth **Obv:** National arms **Rev:** Trionyx Turtle **Note:** Similar to 10 Dollars, KM#125.

Date	Mintage	F	VF	XF	Unc	BU
1994 Proof	Est. 7,500	Value: 165				

KM# 130 100 DOLLARS
6.2200 g., 0.9990 Gold .2000 oz. AGW **Subject:** Star Trek **Obv:** National arms **Rev:** Captains Kirk and Picard **Note:** Similar to 10 Dollars, KM#129.

Date	Mintage	F	VF	XF	Unc	BU
1995 Proof	—	Value: 175				

KM# 135 100 DOLLARS
6.2200 g., 0.9990 Gold .2000 oz. AGW **Series:** Preserve Planet Earth **Obv:** National arms **Rev:** Leopard

Date	Mintage	F	VF	XF	Unc	BU
1995 Proof	Est. 7,500	Value: 165				

KM# 138 100 DOLLARS
6.2200 g., 0.9990 Gold .2000 oz. AGW **Series:** Preserve Planet Earth **Obv:** National arms **Rev:** Storks

Date	Mintage	F	VF	XF	Unc	BU
1995 Proof	Est. 7,500	Value: 165				

KM# 150 100 DOLLARS
6.2200 g., 0.9990 Gold .2000 oz. AGW **Subject:** Sir Winston Churchill **Obv:** National arms **Rev:** Uniformed bust right, planes, army tanks and ship

Date	Mintage	F	VF	XF	Unc	BU
1995 Proof	Est. 7,500	Value: 145				

KM# 151 100 DOLLARS
6.2200 g., 0.9990 Gold .2000 oz. AGW **Subject:** President Franklin D. Roosevelt **Obv:** National arms **Rev:** President Roosevelt riding in jeep

Date	Mintage	F	VF	XF	Unc	BU
1995 Proof	Est. 7,500	Value: 145				

KM# 152 100 DOLLARS
6.2200 g., 0.9990 Gold .2000 oz. AGW **Subject:** General George Patton **Obv:** National arms **Rev:** General Patton in front of map

Date	Mintage	F	VF	XF	Unc	BU
1995 Proof	Est. 7,500	Value: 145				

KM# 153 100 DOLLARS
6.2200 g., 0.9990 Gold .2000 oz. AGW **Subject:** President Harry S. Truman **Obv:** National arms **Rev:** President Truman facing

Date	Mintage	F	VF	XF	Unc	BU
1995 Proof	Est. 7,500	Value: 145				

KM# 154 100 DOLLARS
6.2200 g., 0.9990 Gold .2000 oz. AGW **Subject:** President Charles de Gaulle **Obv:** National arms **Rev:** President de Gaulle on Champs Elysees

Date	Mintage	F	VF	XF	Unc	BU
1995 Proof	Est. 7,500	Value: 145				

KM# 160 100 DOLLARS
6.2200 g., 0.9990 Gold .2000 oz. AGW **Subject:** Dr. Sun Yat-Sen **Obv:** National arms **Rev:** Uniformed bust facing

Date	Mintage	F	VF	XF	Unc	BU
1995 Proof	Est. 7,500	Value: 145				

KM# 163 100 DOLLARS
6.2200 g., 0.9990 Gold .2000 oz. AGW **Subject:** General Chiang Kai-shek **Obv:** National arms **Rev:** General Chiang Kai-shek

Date	Mintage	F	VF	XF	Unc	BU
1995 Proof	Est. 7,500	Value: 145				

KM# 166 100 DOLLARS
6.2200 g., 0.9990 Gold .2000 oz. AGW **Subject:** Cairo Conference **Obv:** National arms **Rev:** Chiang Kai-shek, Roosevelt and Churchill

470 LIBERIA

Date	Mintage	F	VF	XF	Unc	BU
1995 Proof	Est. 7,500	Value: 145				

KM# 175 100 DOLLARS

6.2200 g., 0.9990 Gold .2000 oz. AGW **Subject:** 375th Anniversary - Pilgrim Fathers **Obv:** National arms **Rev:** Mayflower

Date	Mintage	F	VF	XF	Unc	BU
1995 Proof	7,500	Value: 145				

KM# 176 100 DOLLARS

6.2200 g., 0.9990 Gold .2000 oz. AGW **Subject:** 375th Anniversary - Pilgrim Fathers **Obv:** National arms **Rev:** Cape Cod and Pilgrims in skiff

Date	Mintage	F	VF	XF	Unc	BU
1995 Proof	7,500	Value: 145				

KM# 177 100 DOLLARS

6.2200 g., 0.9990 Gold .2000 oz. AGW **Subject:** 375th Anniversary - Pilgrim Fathers **Obv:** National arms **Rev:** Pilgrim landing party

Date	Mintage	F	VF	XF	Unc	BU
1995 Proof	7,500	Value: 145				

KM# 178 100 DOLLARS

6.2200 g., 0.9990 Gold .2000 oz. AGW **Subject:** 375th Anniversary - Pilgrim Fathers **Obv:** National arms **Rev:** First Thanksgiving scene

Date	Mintage	F	VF	XF	Unc	BU
1995 Proof	7,500	Value: 145				

KM# 209 100 DOLLARS

6.2200 g., 0.9990 Gold .2000 oz. AGW **Subject:** Star Trek **Obv:** National arms **Rev:** Star ships NCC-1701 and NCC-1701D

Date	Mintage	F	VF	XF	Unc	BU
1996 Proof	Est. 7,500	Value: 160				

KM# 252 100 DOLLARS

6.2200 g., 0.9990 Gold .2000 oz. AGW **Subject:** Dalai Lama **Obv:** National arms **Rev:** Bust with praying hands facing 1/4 left

Date	Mintage	F	VF	XF	Unc	BU
1996 Proof	Est. 7,500	Value: 140				

KM# 212 100 DOLLARS

6.2200 g., 0.9990 Gold .2000 oz. AGW **Subject:** Star Trek **Obv:** National arms **Rev:** Scott and McCoy

Date	Mintage	F	VF	XF	Unc	BU
1996 Proof	7,500	Value: 150				

KM# 215 100 DOLLARS

6.2200 g., 0.9990 Gold .2000 oz. AGW **Subject:** Star Trek **Obv:** National arms **Rev:** LaForge and Data

Date	Mintage	F	VF	XF	Unc	BU
1996 Proof	25,000	Value: 150				

KM# 218 100 DOLLARS

6.2200 g., 0.9990 Gold .2000 oz. AGW **Subject:** Star Trek **Obv:** National arms **Rev:** Spock and Uhura **Note:** Similar to 10 Dollars, KM#217.

Date	Mintage	F	VF	XF	Unc	BU
1996 Proof	25,000	Value: 150				

KM# 221 100 DOLLARS

6.2200 g., 0.9990 Gold .2000 oz. AGW **Subject:** Star Trek **Obv:** National arms **Rev:** Worf and Dr. Crusher **Note:** Similar to 10 Dollars, KM#220.

Date	Mintage	F	VF	XF	Unc	BU
1996 Proof	25,000	Value: 150				

KM# 224 100 DOLLARS

6.2200 g., 0.9990 Gold .2000 oz. AGW **Subject:** Preserve Planet Earth **Obv:** National arms **Rev:** Grey Parrot **Note:** Similar to 10 Dollars, KM#223.

Date	Mintage	F	VF	XF	Unc	BU
1996 Proof	25,000	Value: 150				

KM# 227 100 DOLLARS

6.2200 g., 0.9990 Gold .2000 oz. AGW **Subject:** Preserve Planet Earth **Obv:** National arms **Rev:** Love Birds **Note:** Similar to 10 Dollars, KM#226.

Date	Mintage	F	VF	XF	Unc	BU
1996 Proof	25,000	Value: 150				

KM# 232 100 DOLLARS

6.2200 g., 0.9990 Gold .2000 oz. AGW **Subject:** Formula One **Obv:** National arms **Rev:** Ayrton Senna **Note:** Similar to 10 Dollars, KM#229.

Date	Mintage	F	VF	XF	Unc	BU
1996 Proof	20,000	Value: 150				

KM# 237 100 DOLLARS

6.2200 g., 0.9990 Gold .2000 oz. AGW **Subject:** Dr. Sun Yat-Sen

Date	Mintage	F	VF	XF	Unc	BU
1996 Proof	Est. 7,500	Value: 145				

KM# 240 100 DOLLARS

6.2200 g., 0.9990 Gold .2000 oz. AGW **Subject:** General Chiang Kai-shek **Obv:** National arms **Rev:** General Chiang kai-shek **Note:** Similar to 10 Dollars, KM#162.

Date	Mintage	F	VF	XF	Unc	BU
1996 Proof	Est. 7,500	Value: 145				

KM# 243 100 DOLLARS

6.2200 g., 0.9990 Gold .2000 oz. AGW **Subject:** President Chiang Ching-kuo **Obv:** National arms **Rev:** Bust facing **Note:** Similar to 10 Dollars, KM#242.

Date	Mintage	F	VF	XF	Unc	BU
1996 Proof	Est. 7,500	Value: 145				

KM# 246 100 DOLLARS

6.2200 g., 0.9990 Gold .2000 oz. AGW **Subject:** President Lee Teng-hui **Obv:** National arms **Rev:** President Lee Ten-hui **Note:** Similar to 10 Dollars, KM#245.

Date	Mintage	F	VF	XF	Unc	BU
1996 Proof	Est. 7,500	Value: 145				

KM# 253 100 DOLLARS

6.2200 g., 0.9990 Gold .2000 oz. AGW **Subject:** King Rama IX of Thailand **Obv:** National arms **Rev:** King seated on radiant throne

Date	Mintage	F	VF	XF	Unc	BU
1996 Proof	Est. 7,500	Value: 145				

KM# 259 100 DOLLARS

6.2200 g., 0.9990 Gold .2000 oz. AGW **Subject:** Mao Zedong Proclaiming People's Republic **Obv:** National arms **Rev:** Chairman Mao Zedong proclaiming People's Republic **Note:** Similar to 10 Dollars, KM#258.

Date	Mintage	F	VF	XF	Unc	BU
1996 Proof	1,996	Value: 160				

KM# 312 100 DOLLARS

6.2200 g., 0.9990 Gold .2000 oz. AGW **Subject:** Mahatma Gandhi **Obv:** National arms **Rev:** Seated figure facing left in front of Taj Mahal **Note:** Similar to 10 Dollars, KM#311.

Date	Mintage	F	VF	XF	Unc	BU
1997 Proof	Est. 5,000	Value: 150				

KM# 317 100 DOLLARS

6.2200 g., 0.9990 Gold .2000 oz. AGW **Subject:** Return of Hong Kong to China **Obv:** National arms **Rev:** Dragon **Note:** Similar to 10 Dollars, KM#314.

Date	Mintage	F	VF	XF	Unc	BU
1997 Proof	Est. 5,000	Value: 150				

KM# 322 100 DOLLARS

6.2200 g., 0.9990 Gold .2000 oz. AGW **Subject:** Fiftieth Anniversary of the Kon-Tiki Expedition **Obv:** National arms **Rev:** Sailing ship within circle **Note:** Similar to 1 Dollar, KM#320.

Date	Mintage	F	VF	XF	Unc	BU
1997 Proof	Est. 7,500	Value: 150				

KM# 326 100 DOLLARS

6.2200 g., 0.9990 Gold .2000 oz. AGW **Subject:** Jurassic Park **Obv:** National arms **Rev:** Stegosaurus **Note:** Similar to 10 Dollars, KM#325.

Date	Mintage	F	VF	XF	Unc	BU
1997 Proof	Est. 2,500	Value: 160				

KM# 329 100 DOLLARS

6.2200 g., 0.9990 Gold .2000 oz. AGW **Subject:** Golden Wedding Anniversary **Obv:** National arms **Rev:** E & P initials above 2 shields **Note:** Similar to 10 Dollars, KM#328.

Date	Mintage	F	VF	XF	Unc	BU
1997 Proof	Est. 3,500	Value: 160				

KM# 332 100 DOLLARS

6.2200 g., 0.9990 Gold .2000 oz. AGW **Subject:** Golden Wedding Anniversary **Obv:** National arms **Rev:** Royal couple with horse **Note:** Similar to 10 Dollars, KM#331.

Date	Mintage	F	VF	XF	Unc	BU
1997 Proof	Est. 3,500	Value: 160				

KM# 335 100 DOLLARS

6.2200 g., 0.9990 Gold .2000 oz. AGW **Subject:** Golden Wedding Anniversary **Obv:** National arms **Rev:** Royal couple with dogs **Note:** Similar to 10 Dollars, KM#334.

Date	Mintage	F	VF	XF	Unc	BU
1997 Proof	Est. 3,500	Value: 160				

KM# 338 100 DOLLARS

6.2200 g., 0.9990 Gold .2000 oz. AGW **Subject:** Golden Wedding Anniversary **Obv:** National arms **Rev:** Royal couple with children **Note:** Similar to 10 Dollars, KM#337.

Date	Mintage	F	VF	XF	Unc	BU
1997 Proof	Est. 3,500	Value: 160				

KM# 370 100 DOLLARS

6.2200 g., 0.9990 Gold .2000 oz. AGW **Subject:** Star Trek - The Next Generation **Obv:** National arms **Rev:** Romulan Warbird **Note:** Similar to 10 Dollars, KM#369.

Date	Mintage	F	VF	XF	Unc	BU
1997 Proof	Est. 7,500	Value: 150				

KM# 373 100 DOLLARS

6.2200 g., 0.9990 Gold .2000 oz. AGW **Subject:** Star Trek - The Next Generation **Obv:** National arms **Rev:** Klingon Attack Cruiser **Note:** Similar to 10 Dollars, KM#372.

Date	Mintage	F	VF	XF	Unc	BU
1997 Proof	Est. 7,500	Value: 150				

KM# 376 100 DOLLARS

6.2200 g., 0.9990 Gold .2000 oz. AGW **Subject:** Star Trek - The Next Generation **Obv:** National arms **Rev:** U.S.S. Enterprise NCC-1701-D **Note:** Similar to 10 Dollars, KM#375.

Date	Mintage	F	VF	XF	Unc	BU
1997 Proof	Est. 7,500	Value: 150				

KM# 379 100 DOLLARS

6.2200 g., 0.9990 Gold .2000 oz. AGW **Subject:** Star Trek - The Next Generation **Obv:** National arms **Rev:** Klingon Bird of Prey **Note:** Similar to 10 Dollars, KM#378.

Date	Mintage	F	VF	XF	Unc	BU
1997 Proof	Est. 7,500	Value: 150				

KM# 382 100 DOLLARS

6.2200 g., 0.9990 Gold .2000 oz. AGW **Subject:** Star Trek - The Next Generation **Obv:** National arms **Rev:** Borg Cube **Note:** Similar to 10 Dollars, KM#381.

Date	Mintage	F	VF	XF	Unc	BU
1997 Proof	Est. 7,500	Value: 150				

KM# 385 100 DOLLARS

6.2200 g., 0.9990 Gold .2000 oz. AGW **Subject:** Star Trek - The Next Generation **Obv:** National arms **Rev:** Ferengi Marauder **Note:** Similar to 10 Dollars, KM#384.

Date	Mintage	F	VF	XF	Unc	BU
1997 Proof	Est. 7,500	Value: 150				

KM# 473 100 DOLLARS

6.2200 g., 0.9990 Gold .2000 oz. AGW **Subject:** Princess Diana in Memoriam **Obv:** National arms

Date	Mintage	F	VF	XF	Unc	BU
1997 Proof	—	Value: 165				

KM# 365 100 DOLLARS

6.2200 g., 0.9990 Gold .2000 oz. AGW **Subject:** RMS Titanic **Obv:** National arms **Rev:** Ship sinking **Note:** Similar to 20 Dollars, KM#364.

Date	Mintage	F	VF	XF	Unc	BU
1998 Proof	Est. 5,000	Value: 175				

KM# 388 100 DOLLARS

6.2200 g., 0.9990 Gold .2000 oz. AGW **Subject:** President Ronald Reagan **Obv:** National arms **Rev:** Lincoln Memorial below head right **Note:** Similar to 10 Dollars, KM#387.

Date	Mintage	F	VF	XF	Unc	BU
1998 Proof	Est. 7,500	Value: 165				

KM# 392 100 DOLLARS

6.2200 g., 0.9990 Gold .2000 oz. AGW **Subject:** Year of the Rabbit **Obv:** National arms **Rev:** Rabbit running left **Note:** Similar to 20 Dollars, KM#389.

Date	Mintage	F	VF	XF	Unc	BU
1999 Proof	5,000	Value: 165				

KM# 393 100 DOLLARS

6.2200 g., 0.9990 Gold .2000 oz. AGW **Subject:** Year of the Rabbit **Obv:** National arms **Rev:** Rabbit sitting **Note:** Similar to 20 Dollars, KM#390.

Date	Mintage	F	VF	XF	Unc	BU
1999 Proof	5,000	Value: 165				

KM# 394 100 DOLLARS

6.2200 g., 0.9990 Gold .2000 oz. AGW **Subject:** Year of the Rabbit **Obv:** National arms **Rev:** Rabbit running right **Note:** Similar to 20 Dollars, KM#391.

Date	Mintage	F	VF	XF	Unc	BU
1999 Proof	5,000	Value: 165				

KM# 403 100 DOLLARS

6.2200 g., 0.9990 Gold .2000 oz. AGW **Subject:** Christopher Columbus **Obv:** National arms **Rev:** Portrait, ship **Note:** Similar to 10 Dollars, KM#402.

Date	Mintage	F	VF	XF	Unc	BU
1999 Proof	10,000	Value: 175				

KM# 406 100 DOLLARS

6.2200 g., 0.9990 Gold .2000 oz. AGW **Subject:** Captain James Cook **Obv:** National arms **Rev:** Portrait, ship, map **Note:** Similar to 10 Dollars, KM#405.

Date	Mintage	F	VF	XF	Unc	BU
1999 Proof	10,000	Value: 175				

KM# 409 100 DOLLARS

6.2200 g., 0.9990 Gold .2000 oz. AGW **Subject:** Return of Macao to China **Obv:** National arms **Rev:** Dragon and phoenix **Note:** Similar to 10 Dollars, KM#408.

Date	Mintage	F	VF	XF	Unc	BU
1999 Proof	10,000	Value: 175				

LIBERIA

KM# 415 100 DOLLARS
6.2200 g., 0.9990 Gold .2000 oz. AGW **Subject:** The Wedding of Prince Edward and Miss Sophie Rhys-Jones **Obv:** National arms **Rev:** Couple in carriage **Note:** Similar to 10 Dollars, KM#414.

Date	Mintage	F	VF	XF	Unc	BU
1999 Proof	Est. 5,000	Value: 175				

KM# 34 200 DOLLARS
12.0000 g., 0.9000 Gold .3472 oz. AGW **Subject:** Inauguration of President Tolbert **Obv:** Bust facing flanked by stars **Rev:** Man holding horn within circle

Date	Mintage	F	VF	XF	Unc	BU
1976 Proof	100	Value: 350				

KM# 46 200 DOLLARS
15.9800 g., 0.9170 Gold .4712 oz. AGW **Subject:** Year of the Scout **Obv:** National arms **Rev:** Saluting scout divides flags above dates

Date	Mintage	F	VF	XF	Unc	BU
ND(1983)	—	—	—	—	345	—
ND(1983) Proof	—	Value: 375				

KM# 49 200 DOLLARS
15.9800 g., 0.9000 Gold .4624 oz. AGW **Series:** International Year of Disabled Persons **Obv:** National arms **Rev:** Standing elderly figures above disability emblem

Date	Mintage	F	VF	XF	Unc	BU
1983	500	—	—	—	365	—
1983 Proof	500	Value: 475				

KM# 395 200 DOLLARS
12.4444 g., 0.9999 Gold .4000 oz. AGW **Subject:** Year of the Rabbit **Obv:** National arms **Rev:** Rabbit running left **Note:** Similar to 20 Dollars, KM#389.

Date	Mintage	F	VF	XF	Unc	BU
1999 Proof	1,500	Value: 285				

KM# 396 200 DOLLARS
12.4444 g., 0.9999 Gold .4000 oz. AGW **Subject:** Year of the Rabbit **Obv:** National arms **Rev:** Rabbit sitting **Note:** Similar to 20 Dollars, KM#390.

Date	Mintage	F	VF	XF	Unc	BU
1999 Proof	1,500	Value: 285				

KM# 397 200 DOLLARS
12.4444 g., 0.9999 Gold .4000 oz. AGW **Subject:** Year of the Rabbit **Obv:** National arms **Rev:** Rabbit running right **Note:** Similar to 20 Dollars, KM#391.

Date	Mintage	F	VF	XF	Unc	BU
1999 Proof	1,500	Value: 285				

KM# 52 250 DOLLARS
15.5000 g., 0.9990 Gold .5000 oz. AGW **Subject:** President John F. Kennedy **Obv:** National arms divides date **Rev:** Head left

Date	Mintage	F	VF	XF	Unc	BU
1988 Proof	5,000	Value: 365				

KM# 56 250 DOLLARS
15.5000 g., 0.9990 Gold .5000 oz. AGW **Subject:** President Samuel Kanyon Doe **Obv:** National arms **Rev:** Head 3/4 facing

Date	Mintage	F	VF	XF	Unc	BU
1988 Proof	Est. 5,000	Value: 375				

KM# 58 250 DOLLARS
15.5000 g., 0.9990 Gold .5000 oz. AGW **Subject:** President George H. W. Bush **Obv:** National arms **Rev:** Head left

Date	Mintage	F	VF	XF	Unc	BU
1989 Proof	600	Value: 400				

KM# 60 250 DOLLARS
15.5000 g., 0.9990 Gold .5000 oz. AGW **Subject:** Emperor Hirohito **Obv:** National arms **Rev:** Head facing divides dates

Date	Mintage	F	VF	XF	Unc	BU
1989 Proof	600	Value: 400				

KM# 89 250 DOLLARS
15.5000 g., 0.9990 Gold .5000 oz. AGW **Subject:** Formula One **Obv:** National arms **Rev:** Nigel Mansell **Note:** Similar to 10 Dollars, KM#75.

Date	Mintage	F	VF	XF	Unc	BU
1992 Proof	Est. 5,000	Value: 375				

KM# 90 250 DOLLARS
15.5000 g., 0.9990 Gold .5000 oz. AGW **Subject:** Formula One **Obv:** National arms **Rev:** Gerhard Berger **Note:** Similar to 10 Dollars, KM#83.

Date	Mintage	F	VF	XF	Unc	BU
1992 Proof	Est. 5,000	Value: 375				

KM# 91 250 DOLLARS
15.5000 g., 0.9990 Gold .5000 oz. AGW **Subject:** Formula One **Obv:** National arms **Rev:** Aguri Suzuki **Note:** Similar to 10 Dollars, KM#84.

Date	Mintage	F	VF	XF	Unc	BU
1992 Proof	Est. 5,000	Value: 375				

KM# 92 250 DOLLARS
15.5000 g., 0.9990 Gold .5000 oz. AGW **Subject:** Formula One **Obv:** National arms **Rev:** Ayrton Senna **Note:** Similar to 10 Dollars, KM#85.

Date	Mintage	F	VF	XF	Unc	BU
1992 Proof	Est. 5,000	Value: 375				

KM# 93 250 DOLLARS
15.5000 g., 0.9990 Gold .5000 oz. AGW **Subject:** Formula One **Obv:** National arms **Rev:** Ricardo Patrese **Note:** Similar to 10 Dollars, KM#74.

Date	Mintage	F	VF	XF	Unc	BU
1992 Proof	Est. 5,000	Value: 375				

KM# 94 250 DOLLARS
15.5000 g., 0.9990 Gold .5000 oz. AGW **Subject:** Formula One **Obv:** National arms **Rev:** Michael Schumacher **Note:** Similar to 10 Dollars, KM#86.

Date	Mintage	F	VF	XF	Unc	BU
1992 Proof	Est. 5,000	Value: 375				

KM# 95 250 DOLLARS
15.5000 g., 0.9990 Gold .5000 oz. AGW **Subject:** Formula One **Obv:** National arms **Rev:** Alain Prost **Note:** Similar to 10 Dollars, KM#87.

Date	Mintage	F	VF	XF	Unc	BU
1992 Proof	Est. 5,000	Value: 375				

KM# 96 250 DOLLARS
15.5000 g., 0.9990 Gold .5000 oz. AGW **Subject:** Formula One **Obv:** National arms **Rev:** Ukyo Katayama **Note:** Similar to 10 Dollars, KM#88.

Date	Mintage	F	VF	XF	Unc	BU
1992 Proof	Est. 5,000	Value: 375				

KM# 71 250 DOLLARS
15.5000 g., 0.9990 Gold .5000 oz. AGW **Subject:** President Bill Clinton **Obv:** National arms **Rev:** Head right **Note:** Similar to 10 Dollars, KM#68.

Date	Mintage	F	VF	XF	Unc	BU
1993 Proof	Est. 5,000	Value: 375				

KM# 105 250 DOLLARS
15.5000 g., 0.9990 Gold .5000 oz. AGW **Subject:** President John F. Kennedy **Obv:** National arms **Rev:** Head left, funeral caisson below **Note:** Similar to 10 Dollars, KM#104.

Date	Mintage	F	VF	XF	Unc	BU
1993 Proof	Est. 5,000	Value: 375				

KM# 181 250 DOLLARS
15.5000 g., 0.9990 Gold .5000 oz. AGW **Subject:** Formula One **Obv:** National arms **Rev:** Mika Hakkinen

Date	Mintage	F	VF	XF	Unc	BU
1995 Proof	Est. 5,000	Value: 375				

KM# 184 250 DOLLARS
15.5000 g., 0.9990 Gold .5000 oz. AGW **Subject:** Formula One **Obv:** National arms **Rev:** Martin Brundle

Date	Mintage	F	VF	XF	Unc	BU
1995 Proof	Est. 5,000	Value: 375				

KM# 187 250 DOLLARS
15.5000 g., 0.9990 Gold .5000 oz. AGW **Subject:** Formula One **Obv:** National arms **Rev:** Rubens Barrichello

Date	Mintage	F	VF	XF	Unc	BU
1995 Proof	Est. 5,000	Value: 375				

KM# 190 250 DOLLARS
15.5000 g., 0.9990 Gold .5000 oz. AGW **Subject:** Formula One **Obv:** National arms **Rev:** David Coulthard

Date	Mintage	F	VF	XF	Unc	BU
1995 Proof	Est. 5,000	Value: 375				

KM# 193 250 DOLLARS
15.5000 g., 0.9990 Gold .5000 oz. AGW **Subject:** Formula One **Obv:** National arms **Rev:** Jean Alesi

Date	Mintage	F	VF	XF	Unc	BU
1995 Proof	Est. 5,000	Value: 375				

KM# 565 250 DOLLARS
15.5000 g., 0.9990 Gold 0.4978 oz. AGW, 33 mm. **Obv:** National arms **Rev:** Bugatti Royale

Date	Mintage	F	VF	XF	Unc	BU
1995B	—	—	—	—	345	—

KM# 203 250 DOLLARS
15.5000 g., 0.9990 Gold .5000 oz. AGW **Subject:** Formula One **Obv:** National arms **Rev:** Mark Blundell

Date	Mintage	F	VF	XF	Unc	BU
1996 Proof	Est. 5,000	Value: 350				

KM# 204 250 DOLLARS
15.5000 g., 0.9990 Gold .5000 oz. AGW **Subject:** Formula One **Obv:** National arms **Rev:** Johnny Herbert **Note:** Similar to 10 Dollars, KM#200.

Date	Mintage	F	VF	XF	Unc	BU
1996 Proof	Est. 5,000	Value: 350				

KM# 205 250 DOLLARS
15.5000 g., 0.9990 Gold .5000 oz. AGW **Subject:** Formula One **Obv:** National arms **Rev:** Eddie Irvine **Note:** Similar to 10 Dollars, KM#201.

Date	Mintage	F	VF	XF	Unc	BU
1996 Proof	Est. 5,000	Value: 350				

KM# 206 250 DOLLARS
15.5000 g., 0.9990 Gold .5000 oz. AGW **Subject:** Formula One **Obv:** National arms **Rev:** Heinz Frentzen **Note:** Similar to 10 Dollars, KM#202.

Date	Mintage	F	VF	XF	Unc	BU
1996 Proof	Est. 5,000	Value: 350				

KM# 233 250 DOLLARS
15.5000 g., 0.9990 Gold .5000 oz. AGW **Subject:** Formula One **Obv:** National arms **Rev:** Ayrton Senna **Note:** Similar to 10 Dollars, KM#229.

Date	Mintage	F	VF	XF	Unc	BU
1996 Proof	Est. 5,000	Value: 350				

KM# 318 250 DOLLARS
15.5000 g., 0.9990 Gold .5000 oz. AGW **Subject:** Return of Hong Kong **Obv:** National arms **Rev:** Dragon **Note:** Similar to 10 Dollars, KM#314.

Date	Mintage	F	VF	XF	Unc	BU
1997 Proof	—	Value: 350				

KM# 420 250 DOLLARS
15.5000 g., 0.9990 Gold .5000 oz. AGW **Subject:** Return of Macao to China **Obv:** National arms **Rev:** Dragon and phoenix **Note:** Similar to 10 Dollars, KM#408.

Date	Mintage	F	VF	XF	Unc	BU
1999 Proof	Est. 5,000	Value: 350				

KM# 425 250 DOLLARS
15.5000 g., 0.9990 Gold .5000 oz. AGW **Subject:** Liberty **Obv:** National arms **Rev:** Conjoined heads left **Note:** Similar to 10 Dollars, KM#424.

Date	Mintage	F	VF	XF	Unc	BU
1999 Proof	375	Value: 400				

472 LIBERIA

KM# 439 250 DOLLARS
15.5517 g., 0.9999 Gold .5000 oz. AGW, 27 mm. **Subject:** Taipai, Taiwan Rapid Transit System **Obv:** National arms above hole* and dragon **Rev:** Subway train, logo and tunnel hole* **Note:** Struck at Singapore Mint. *As first done on Albanian coins of 1988.

Date	Mintage	F	VF	XF	Unc	BU
1999 Proof	2,000	Value: 365				

KM# 35 400 DOLLARS
24.0000 g., 0.9000 Gold .6945 oz. AGW **Subject:** Inauguration of President Tolbert **Obv:** Bust facing **Rev:** Liberia written within circle

Date	Mintage	F	VF	XF	Unc	BU
1976 Proof	25	Value: 1,250				

KM# 234 500 DOLLARS
31.1035 g., 0.9990 Gold 1.0000 oz. AGW **Subject:** Formula One **Obv:** National arms **Rev:** Ayrton Senna **Note:** Similar to 10 Dollars, KM#229.

Date	Mintage	F	VF	XF	Unc	BU
1996 Proof	Est. 2,500	Value: 725				

KM# 421 500 DOLLARS
31.1035 g., 0.9990 Gold 1.0000 oz. AGW **Subject:** Return of Macao to China **Obv:** National arms **Rev:** Dragon and phoenix **Note:** Similar to 10 Dollars, KM#408.

Date	Mintage	F	VF	XF	Unc	BU
1999 Proof	Est. 1,000	Value: 775				

KM# 247 2500 DOLLARS
155.5175 g., 0.9990 Gold 5.0000 oz. AGW **Subject:** President Lee Teng-hui **Obv:** National arms **Rev:** President Lee Teng-hui **Note:** Similar to 10 Dollars, KM#245.

Date	Mintage	F	VF	XF	Unc	BU
1996 Proof	Est. 250	Value: 3,500				

KM# 235 2500 DOLLARS
155.5175 g., 0.9990 Gold 5.0000 oz. AGW **Subject:** Formula One **Obv:** National arms **Rev:** Ayrton Senna **Note:** Similar to 10 Dollars, KM#229.

Date	Mintage	F	VF	XF	Unc	BU
1996 Proof	Est. 250	Value: 3,500				

KM# 238 2500 DOLLARS
155.5175 g., 0.9990 Gold 5.0000 oz. AGW **Subject:** Dr. Sun Yat-Sen

Date	Mintage	F	VF	XF	Unc	BU
1996 Proof	Est. 250	Value: 3,500				

KM# 241 2500 DOLLARS
155.5175 g., 0.9990 Gold 5.0000 oz. AGW **Subject:** General Chiang Kai-shek **Obv:** National arms **Rev:** General Chiang kai-shek **Note:** Similar to 10 Dollars, KM#162.

Date	Mintage	F	VF	XF	Unc	BU
1996 Proof	Est. 250	Value: 3,500				

KM# 244 2500 DOLLARS
155.5175 g., 0.9990 Gold 5.0000 oz. AGW **Subject:** President Chiang Ching-kuo **Obv:** National arms **Rev:** Bust facing **Note:** Similar to 10 Dollars, KM#242.

Date	Mintage	F	VF	XF	Unc	BU
1996 Proof	Est. 250	Value: 3,500				

KM# 319 2500 DOLLARS
155.5175 g., 0.9990 Gold 5.0000 oz. AGW **Subject:** Return of Hong Kong **Obv:** National arms **Rev:** Dragon **Note:** Similar to 10 Dollars, KM#314.

Date	Mintage	F	VF	XF	Unc	BU
1997 Proof	—	Value: 3,500				

KM# 588 2500 DOLLARS
155.5175 g., 0.9990 Gold 4.995 oz. AGW, 60 mm. **Subject:** Year of the Tiger **Obv:** National arms **Rev:** Tiger above pineapple and flowers within beaded circle **Edge:** Reeded **Note:** Illustration reduced.

Date	Mintage	F	VF	XF	Unc	BU
1998 Proof	—	Value: 3,750				

KM# 398 2500 DOLLARS
155.5175 g., 0.9990 Gold 5.0000 oz. AGW **Subject:** Year of the Rabbit **Obv:** National arms **Rev:** Rabbit running left **Note:** Similar to 20 Dollars, KM#389.

Date	Mintage	F	VF	XF	Unc	BU
1999 Proof	88	Value: 4,000				

KM# 399 2500 DOLLARS
155.5175 g., 0.9990 Gold 5.0000 oz. AGW **Subject:** Year of the Rabbit **Obv:** National arms **Rev:** Rabbit sitting **Note:** Similar to 20 Dollars, KM#390.

Date	Mintage	F	VF	XF	Unc	BU
1999 Proof	88	Value: 4,000				

KM# 400 2500 DOLLARS
155.5175 g., 0.9990 Gold 5.0000 oz. AGW **Subject:** Year of the Rabbit **Obv:** National arms **Rev:** Rabbit running right **Note:** Similar to 20 Dollars, KM#391.

Date	Mintage	F	VF	XF	Unc	BU
1999 Proof	88	Value: 4,000				

KM# 422 2500 DOLLARS
155.5175 g., 0.9990 Gold 5.0000 oz. AGW **Subject:** Return of Macao to China **Obv:** National arms **Rev:** Dragon and phoenix **Note:** Similar to 10 Dollars, KM#408.

Date	Mintage	F	VF	XF	Unc	BU
1999 Proof	Est. 250	Value: 4,000				

KM# 440 2500 DOLLARS
155.5175 g., 0.9999 Gold 5.0000 oz. AGW, 55 mm. **Subject:** Taipai, Taiwan Rapid Transit System **Obv:** National arms above dragon **Rev:** Dragon around subway train viewing sun with diamond inserts **Note:** Struck at Singapore Mint.

Date	Mintage	F	VF	XF	Unc	BU
ND(1999) Proof	50	Value: 3,500				

PATTERNS
Including off metal strikes

KM#	Date	Mintage	Identification	Mkt Val
Pn55	1976	—	100 Dollars. Bronze. KM#33.	150
Pn56	1976	—	200 Dollars. Bronze. KM#34.	175
Pn57	1976	—	400 Dollars. Bronze. KM#35.	200
Pn60	2001	—	100 Dollars. Gold-Plated Base Metal. 3.4200 g. 16 mm. National arms. "9-11" Flag raising scene. Plain edge.	40.00

PIEFORTS

KM#	Date	Mintage	Identification	Mkt Val
P3	1983	100	200 Dollars. Gold. KM#49.	750

PROOF SETS

KM#	Date	Mintage	Identification	Issue Price	Mkt Val
PS16	1997 (3)	—	KM#417, 445, 473	—	250
PS17	1999 (2)	375	KM#424-425	345	400

LIBYA

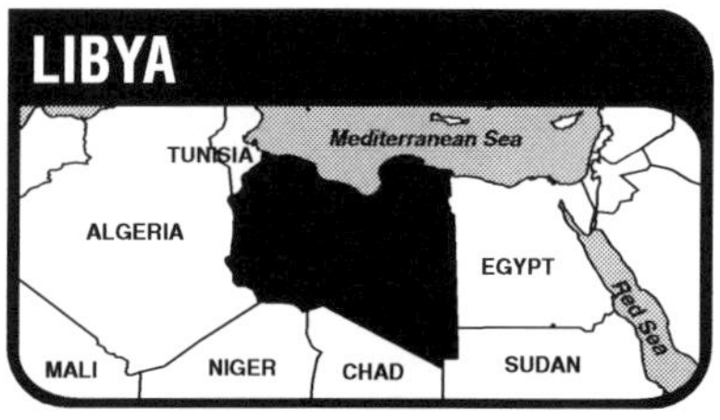

The Socialist People's Libyan Arab Jamahariya, located on the north-central coast of Africa between Tunisia and Egypt, has an area of 679,358 sq. mi. (1,759,540 sq. km.) and a population of 3.9 million. Capital: Tripoli. Crude oil, which accounts for 90 per cent of the export earnings, is the mainstay of the economy.

Libya has been subjected to foreign rule throughout most of its history, various parts of it having been ruled by the Phoenicians, Carthaginians, Vandals, Byzantines, Greeks, Romans, Egyptians, and in the following centuries the Arabs' language, culture and religion were adopted by the indigenous population. Libya was conquered by the Ottoman Turks in 1553, and remained under Turkish domination, becoming a Turkish vilayet in 1835, until it was conquered by Italy and made into a colony in 1911. The name 'Libya', the ancient Greek name for North Africa exclusive of Egypt, was given to the colony by Italy in 1934. Libya came under Allied administration after the fall of Tripoli on Jan. 23, 1943, divided into zones of British and French control. On Dec. 24, 1951, in accordance with a United Nations resolution, Libya proclaimed its independence as a constitutional monarchy, thereby becoming the first country to achieve independence through the United Nations. The monarchy was overthrown by a *coup d'etat* on Sept. 1, 1969, and Libya was established as a republic.

TITLES

المملكة الليبية

al-Mamlaka(t) al-Libiya(t)

الجمهورية الليبية

al-Jomhuriya(t) al-Arabiya(t) al-Libiya(t)

RULERS
Idris I, 1951-1969

MONETARY SYSTEM
10 Milliemes = 1 Piastre
100 Piastres = 1 Pound

SOCIALIST PEOPLE'S REPUBLIC

STANDARD COINAGE
1000 Dirhams = 1 Dinar

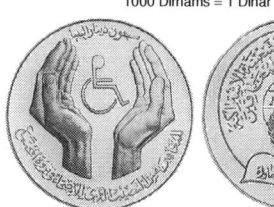

KM# 25 70 DINARS
15.9800 g., 0.9170 Gold .4712 oz. AGW **Subject:** International Year of Disabled Persons **Obv:** Handicap symbol within helping hands **Rev:** Date and emblem within globe with legend above and below

Date	Mintage	F	VF	XF	Unc	BU
1981	4,000	—	—	—	450	—
1981 Proof	4,000	Value: 550				

MEDALLIC COINAGE

X# 5 NON-DENOMINATED
15.9600 g., Gold, 27 mm. **Subject:** Qaddafi - 10th Anniversary as President **Obv:** Bust of Colonel Qaddafi 3/4 right **Rev:** Ancient Fortress

Date	Mintage	F	VF	XF	Unc	BU
ND(1979)	—	—	—	350	500	—

PIEFORTS

KM#	Date	Mintage	Identification	Mkt Val
P2	1981	500	70 Dinars. Gold. KM25.	1,100

PROOF SETS

KM#	Date	Mintage	Identification	Issue Price	Mkt Val
PS1	1952 (5)	32	KM1-5	—	450

TRIPOLI

Tripoli (formerly Ottoman Empire Area of antique Tripolitania, 700-146 B.C.), the capital city and chief port of the Libyan Arab Jamahiriya, is situated on the North African coast on a promontory stretching out into the Mediterranean Sea. It was probably founded by Phoenicians from Sicily, but was under Roman control from 146 B.C. until 450 A.D. Invasion by Vandals and conquest by the Byzantines preceded the Arab invasions of the 11th century which, by destroying the commercial centers of Sabratha and Leptis, greatly enhanced the importance of Tripoli, an importance maintained through periods of Norman and Spanish control. Tripoli fell to the Turks, who made it the capital of the vilayet of Tripoli in 1551 and it remained in their hands until 1911, when it was occupied by the Italians who made it the capital of the Italian province of Tripolitania. British forces entered the city on January 23, 1943, and administered it until establishment of the independent Kingdom of Libya on December 24, 1951.

RULERS
Ottoman, until 1911
 refer to Turkey

LOCAL PASHAS
Ahmad Pasha Qaramanli I,
 AH1123-1158/1711-1745AD
Muhammad Pasha Qaramanli,
 AH1158-1167/1745-1754AD
Ali Pasha Qaramanli I,
 AH1167-1208/1754-1793AD
Ali Burghul Pasha, (rebel)
 AH1208-1209/1793-1795AD
Ahmad Pasha Qaramanli II,
 AH1209-1210/1795-1796AD
Yusuf Pasha Qaramanli,
 AH1210-1248/1796-1833AD (resigned)
Ali Pasha Qaramanli II,
 AH1248-1250/1833-1835AD

MINT NAME
Tarabalus
Tarabalus Gharb = (Tripoli West)
 The appellation *west* serving to distinguish it from Tripoli in Lebanon, which had been an Ottoman Mint in the 16th century. On some of the copper coins, *Gharb* is omitted; several types come both with and without *Gharb*. The mint closed between the 28th and 29th year of the reign of Mahmud II.

MONETARY SYSTEM
The monetary system of Tripoli was confusing and is poorly understood. Theoretically, 40 Para were equal to one Piastre, but due to the debasement of the silver coinage, later issues are virtually pure copper, though the percentage of alloy varies radically even within a given year. The 10 Para and 20 Para pieces were a little heavier than the copper Paras, with which they could easily be confounded, except that the copper Paras were generally thicker, and bear simpler inscriptions. It is not known how many of the coppers were tariffed to the debased Piastre and its fractions. Some authorities consider the copper pieces to be Beshliks (5 Para coins).
 The gold coinage came in two denominations, the Zeri Mahbub (2.4-2.5 g), and the Sultani Altin (3.3-3.4 g). The ratio of the billon Piastres to the gold coins fluctuated from day to day.

BARBARY STATE

OTTOMAN COINAGE

KM# 65 ZERI MAHBUB
2.0000 g., Gold, 27 mm. **Ruler:** Selim III

Date	Mintage	VG	F	VF	XF	Unc
AH1203//14	—	200	400	700	1,500	—

KM# 72 ZERI MAHBUB
2.4500 g., Gold, 21 mm. **Ruler:** Mustafa IV **Note:** Similar to Zeri Mahbub, KM#56.

Date	Mintage	VG	F	VF	XF	Unc
AH1222 Rare	—	—	—	—	—	—

KM# 62 SULTANI
3.5000 g., Gold **Ruler:** Selim III **Obv:** 4-Lined inscription within circle **Rev:** 4-Lined inscription and date within circle **Note:** Size varies 23-27mm.

Date	Mintage	VG	F	VF	XF	Unc
AH1203//14	—	200	400	700	1,500	—
AH1203//15	—	200	400	700	1,500	—
AH1203//17	—	200	400	700	1,500	—
AH1203//19	—	200	400	700	1,500	—

KM# 73 SULTANI
3.3300 g., Gold, 25 mm. **Ruler:** Mustafa IV **Obv:** 4-Lined inscription within circle **Rev:** Inscription and date

Date	Mintage	VG	F	VF	XF	Unc
AH1222 Rare	—	—	—	—	—	—

STANDARD COINAGE
Fifth Standard - Year 28 only; Uncertain metrology

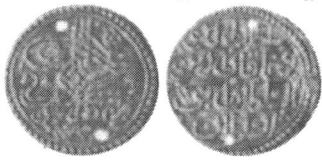

KM# 222 ZERI MAHBUB
Gold **Ruler:** Mahmud II **Obv:** Toughra above text, date **Rev:** 4-lined inscription **Note:** Weight varies 2.30-2.50 grams. Size varies 21-24 mm. Type B.

Date	Mintage	VG	F	VF	XF	Unc
AH1223//12	—	150	200	400	800	—
AH1223//13	—	150	200	400	800	—
AH1223//14	—	150	200	400	800	—

KM# 224 ZERI MAHBUB
Gold **Ruler:** Mahmud II **Obv:** 4-lined inscription within beaded circle **Rev:** Mintname above date within beaded circle **Note:** Type E.

Date	Mintage	VG	F	VF	XF	Unc
AH1223//18	—	150	200	400	800	—

KM# 226 ZERI MAHBUB
Gold **Ruler:** Mahmud II **Obv:** Toughra within beaded circle **Rev:** Text, date within beaded circle

Date	Mintage	VG	F	VF	XF	Unc
AH1223//20	—	200	250	400	800	—

KM# 232 SULTANI
Gold **Ruler:** Mahmud II **Obv:** 4-lined inscription **Rev:** Without lines dividing legend

Date	Mintage	VG	F	VF	XF	Unc
AH1223	—	200	250	400	800	—

KM# 228 SULTANI
Gold **Ruler:** Mahmud II **Obv:** 4-lined inscription **Rev:** Text, date **Note:** Weight varies 3.20-3.40 grams. Size varies 24-26 mm. Type C (variant).

LIBYA / TRIPOLI

Date	Mintage	VG	F	VF	XF	Unc
AH1223 Ornament	—	175	225	400	800	—
AH1223//6	—	175	225	400	800	—
AH1223//19	—	175	225	400	800	—

KM# 227 SULTANI
5.5800 g., Gold, 33 mm. **Ruler:** Mahmud II **Obv:** Toughra

Date	Mintage	VG	F	VF	XF	Unc
AH1223//5	—	300	350	500	1,000	—

KM# 230 SULTANI
Gold **Ruler:** Mahmud II **Obv:** 4-lined inscription **Rev:** 3-lined inscription **Note:** Similar, but broader and thinner.

Date	Mintage	VG	F	VF	XF	Unc
AH1223//14 Rare	—	—	—	—	—	—

LIECHTENSTEIN

The Principality of Liechtenstein, located in central Europe on the east bank of the Rhine between Austria and Switzerland, has an area of 62 sq. mi. (160 sq. km.) and a population of 27,200. Capital: Vaduz. The economy is based on agriculture and light manufacturing. Canned goods, textiles, ceramics and precision instruments are exported.

The lordships of Schellenburg and Vaduz were merged into the principality of Liechtenstein. It was a member of the Rhine Confederation from 1806 to 1815, and of the German Confederation from 1815 to 1866 when it became independent. Liechtenstein's long and close association with Austria was terminated by World War I. In 1921 it adopted the coinage of Switzerland, and two years later entered into a customs union with the Swiss, who also operated its postal and telegraph systems and represented it in international affairs. The tiny principality abolished its army in 1868 and has avoided involvement in all European wars since that time.

RULERS
Prince John II, 1858-1929
Prince Franz I, 1929-1938
Prince Franz Josef II, 1938-1990
Prince Hans Adam II, 1990-

MINT MARKS
A - Vienna
B - Bern

PRINCIPALITY
STANDARD COINAGE
1-1/2 Florins = 1 Vereinsthaler

Y# 1a THALER (Ein)
29.5000 g., 0.9000 Gold 0.8536 oz. AGW **Ruler:** Prince John II **Obv:** Head right **Obv. Legend:** JOHANN II. FURST... **Rev:** Crowned mantled arms **Rev. Legend:** ...XXX EIN PFUND FEIN..

Date	Mintage	F	VF	XF	Unc	BU
1862A M Proof, restrike	50,000	Value: 650				

Y# 1b THALER (Ein)
33.3400 g., Platinum APW **Ruler:** Prince John II **Obv:** Head right **Rev:** Crowned mantled arms

Date	Mintage	F	VF	XF	Unc	BU
1862A M Proof, restrike	—	Value: 1,350				

REFORM COINAGE
100 Heller = 1 Krone

Y# 5 10 KRONEN
3.3875 g., 0.9000 Gold 0.098 oz. AGW **Ruler:** Prince John II **Obv:** Head left **Obv. Legend:** JOHANN II. FURST... **Rev:** Crowned shield within wreath divides value above date

Date	Mintage	F	VF	XF	Unc	BU
1900	1,500	—	—	2,250	4,250	—

Y# 6 20 KRONEN
6.7750 g., 0.9000 Gold 0.196 oz. AGW **Ruler:** Prince John II **Obv:** Head left **Obv. Legend:** JOHANN II. FURST... **Rev:** Crowned shield within wreath divides value above date

Date	Mintage	F	VF	XF	Unc	BU
1898	—	—	—	2,150	3,750	—

REFORM COINAGE
100 Rappen = 1 Frank

Y# 11 10 FRANKEN
3.2258 g., 0.9000 Gold .0933 oz. AGW **Ruler:** Prince Franz I **Obv:** Bust right **Rev:** Crowned shield within wreath flanked by value and letters

Date	Mintage	F	VF	XF	Unc	BU
1930	2,500	—	500	750	1,050	—

Y# 13 10 FRANKEN
3.2258 g., 0.9000 Gold .0933 oz. AGW **Ruler:** Prince Franz Josef II **Obv:** Head left **Rev:** Crowned shield within stars

Date	Mintage	F	VF	XF	Unc	BU
1946B	10,000	—	150	200	285	—

Y# 12 20 FRANKEN
6.4516 g., 0.9000 Gold .1867 oz. AGW **Ruler:** Prince Franz I **Obv:** Bust right within circle **Rev:** Crowned shield within wreath divides value and letters

Date	Mintage	F	VF	XF	Unc	BU
1930	2,500	—	550	800	1,250	—

Y# 14 20 FRANKEN
6.4516 g., 0.9000 Gold .1867 oz. AGW **Ruler:** Prince Franz Josef II **Obv:** Head left **Rev:** Crowned shield within stars

Date	Mintage	F	VF	XF	Unc	BU
1946B	10,000	—	150	225	350	—

Y# 15 25 FRANKEN
5.6450 g., 0.9000 Gold .1633 oz. AGW, 22 mm. **Ruler:** Prince Franz Josef II **Subject:** Franz Josef II and Princess Gina **Obv:** Conjoined busts left **Rev:** Crowned shield **Designer:** Grienauer

Date	Mintage	F	VF	XF	Unc	BU
1956	17,000	—	—	200	275	—

Y# 18 25 FRANKEN
5.6450 g., 0.9000 Gold .1633 oz. AGW **Ruler:** Prince Franz Josef II **Subject:** 100th Anniversary - National Bank **Obv:** Head right **Rev:** Crowned mantled shield

Date	Mintage	F	VF	XF	Unc	BU
1961	20,000	—	—	—	210	—

LITHUANIA 475

Y# 16 50 FRANKEN
11.2900 g., 0.9000 Gold .3267 oz. AGW, 26 mm. **Ruler:** Prince Franz Josef II **Subject:** Franz Josef II and Princess Gina **Obv:** Conjoined busts left **Rev:** Crowned shield **Designer:** Grienauer

Date	Mintage	F	VF	XF	Unc	BU
1956	17,000	—	—	300	380	—

Y# 19 50 FRANKEN
11.2900 g., 0.9000 Gold .3267 oz. AGW **Ruler:** Prince Franz Josef II **Subject:** 100th Anniversary - National Bank **Obv:** Head right **Rev:** Crowned mantled shield

Date	Mintage	F	VF	XF	Unc	BU
1961	20,000	—	—	—	350	—

Y# 21 50 FRANKEN
10.0000 g., 0.9000 Gold .2894 oz. AGW **Ruler:** Prince Franz Josef II **Subject:** 50th Anniversary of Reign **Obv:** Head right **Rev:** Crowned shield divides value and letters

Date	Mintage	F	VF	XF	Unc	BU
1988 Proof	35,000	Value: 235				

Y# 23 50 FRANKEN
10.0000 g., 0.9000 Gold .2894 oz. AGW **Ruler:** Prince Hans Adam II **Subject:** Succession of Hans Adam II **Obv:** Head left divides date **Rev:** Crowned mantled shield divides value and letters

Date	Mintage	F	VF	XF	Unc	BU
1990 Proof	25,000	Value: 225				

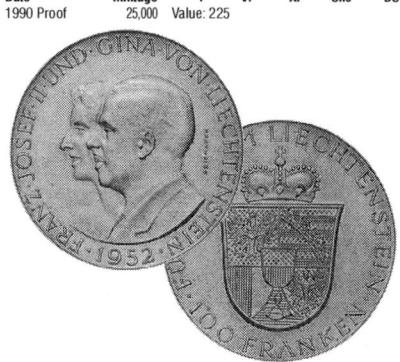

Y# 17 100 FRANKEN
32.2580 g., 0.9000 Gold .9335 oz. AGW, 36 mm. **Ruler:** Prince Franz Josef II **Subject:** Franz Josef II and Princess Gina **Obv:** Conjoined busts left **Rev:** Crowned shield **Designer:** Grienauer

Date	Mintage	F	VF	XF	Unc	BU
1952	4,000	—	1,850	2,550	3,325	—

MEDALLIC COINAGE

X# 7a 5 FRANKEN
Gold, 35.2 mm. **Subject:** Marriage of Crown Prince Johann Adam and Maria **Obv:** Crowned and mantled arms **Obv. Legend:** FELICITER CONJUNCTI + VADUZ 30.JULI.1967 **Rev:** Crown above facing heads **Rev. Legend:** JOHANN • ADAM • PRINC • HEPED • DE LIECHTENSTEIN + MARIA COMT • KINSKY +

Date	Mintage	F	VF	XF	Unc	BU
1967 Proof	—	Value: 400				

X# 5 20 FRANKEN
7.0000 g., Gold **Ruler:** Prince Franz Josef II **Subject:** 60th birthday of Franz Joseph II **Note:** Prev. KM#M5.

Date	Mintage	F	VF	XF	Unc	BU
ND(1966) Proof	—	Value: 165				

X# 6 20 FRANKEN
6.9600 g., Gold **Ruler:** Prince Franz Josef II **Subject:** Marriage of Crown Prince Johann Adam and Maria **Note:** Prev. KM#M6.

Date	Mintage	F	VF	XF	Unc	BU
1967 Proof	—	Value: 165				

ESSAIS

KM#	Date	Mintage	Identification	Mkt Val
E3	1898	35	10 Kronen. Gold. Y5	7,500
E4	1898	35	20 Kronen. Gold. Y6	7,000

MINT SETS

KM#	Date	Mintage	Identification	Issue Price	Mkt Val
MS1	1930 (2)	2,500	Y11-12	—	2,250
MS2	1946 (2)	10,000	Y13-14	—	580
MS3	1956 (2)	15,000	Y15-16	—	650
MS4	1961 (2)	20,000	Y18-19	—	550

PROOF SETS

KM#	Date	Mintage	Identification	Issue Price	Mkt Val
PS1	1988 (2)	35,000	Y20-21	—	280
PS2	1990 (2)	25,000	Y22-23	—	265

LITHUANIA

The Republic of Lithuania, southernmost of the Baltic states in east Europe, has an area of 25,174 sq. mi.(65,201 sq. km.) and a population of *3.6 million. Capital: Vilnius. The economy is based on livestock raising and manufacturing. Hogs, cattle, hides and electric motors are exported.

Lithuania emerged as a grand duchy in the 14th century. In the 15th century it was a major power of central Europe, stretching from the Baltic to the Black Sea. It was joined with Poland in 1569, but lost Smolensk, Chernihiv, and the right bank of the river Dnepr Ukraina in 1667, while the left bank remained under Polish – Lithuania rule until 1793. Following the third partition of Poland by Austria, Prussia and Russia, 1795, Lithuania came under Russian domination and did not regain its independence until shortly before the end of World War I when it declared itself a sovereign republic on Feb. 16, 1918. In fall of 1920, Poland captured Vilna (Vilnius). The republic was occupied by Soviet troops and annexed to the U.S.S.R. in 1940. Following the German occupation of 1941-44, it was retaken by Russia and reestablished as a member republic of the Soviet Union. Western countries, including the United States, did not recognize Lithuania's incorporation into the Soviet Union.

Lithuania declared its independence March 11, 1990 and it was recognized by the United States on Sept. 2, 1991, followed by the Soviet government in Moscow on Sept. 6. They were seated in the UN General Assembly on Sept. 17, 1991.

MODERN REPUBLIC
1991-present

REFORM COINAGE
100 Centas = 1 Litas

KM# 109a LITAS
7.7759 g., 0.9990 Gold .25 oz. AGW, 22.3 mm. **Subject:** 75th Anniversary - Bank of Lithuania **Obv:** National arms above value **Rev:** Bust 1/4 right

Date	Mintage	F	VF	XF	Unc	BU
1997 Proof	1,500	Value: 725				

KM# 120 10 LITU
1.2440 g., 0.9999 Gold .04 oz. AGW, 28.70 mm. **Subject:** Lithuanian gold coinage **Obv:** National arms **Rev:** Medieval minter

Date	Mintage	F	VF	XF	Unc	BU
1999 Proof	5,500	Value: 65.00				

KM# 126 100 LITU
7.7800 g., 0.9999 Gold .2501 oz. AGW, 22.3 mm. **Subject:** Grand Duke Vytautas **Obv:** National arms above value **Rev:** Crowned armored bust right holding sword **Edge Lettering:** IS PRAEITIES TAVO SUNUS TE STIPRYBE SEMIA

Date	Mintage	F	VF	XF	Unc	BU
2000 Proof	2,000	Value: 600				

KM# 136 200 LITU
15.0000 g., Bi-Metallic .900 Gold 7.9g. center in a .925 Silver 7.1g. ring, 27 mm. **Subject:** 750th Anniversary - King Mindaugas **Obv:** Knight on horse **Rev:** Seated King **Edge Lettering:** LIETUVOS KARALYSTE 1253

Date	Mintage	F	VF	XF	Unc	BU
2003 Proof	2,000	Value: 1,200				

KM# 146 500 LITU
31.1000 g., 0.9999 Gold .9998 oz. AGW, 32.5 mm. **Obv:** Knight on horse **Rev:** Palace **Edge:** Plain

Date	Mintage	F	VF	XF	Unc	BU
2005 Proof	1,000	Value: 1,400				

PATTERNS
Including off metal strikes

KM#	Date	Mintage	Identification	Mkt Val
Pn14	1938	2	10 Litu. Gold. Lettered edge. Medal-struck presentation pieces.	—

476 LUXEMBOURG

LUXEMBOURG

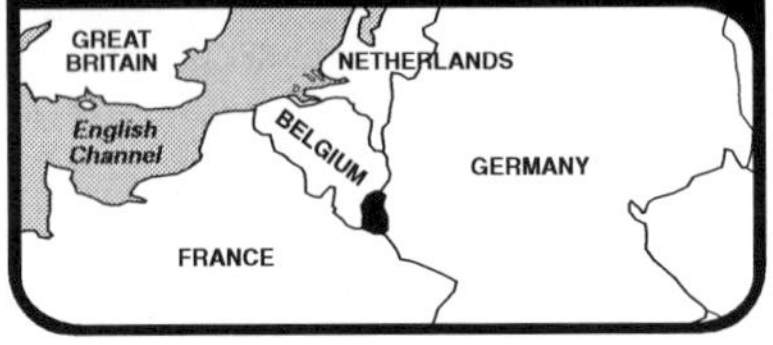

The Grand Duchy of Luxembourg is located in western Europe between Belgium, Germany and France, has an area of 1,103 sq. mi. (2,586 sq. km.) and a population of 377,100. Capital: Luxembourg. The economy is based on steel.

Founded about 963, Luxembourg was a prominent country of the Holy Roman Empire; one of its sovereigns became Holy Roman Emperor as Henry VII, 1308. After being made a duchy by Emperor Charles IV, 1354, Luxembourg passed under the domination of Burgundy, Spain, Austria and France, 1443-1815, regaining autonomy under the Treaty of Vienna, 1815, as a grand duchy in union with the Netherlands, though ostensibly a member of the German Confederation. When Belgium seceded from the Kingdom of the Netherlands, 1830, Luxembourg was forced to cede its greater western section to Belgium. The tiny duchy left the German Confederation in 1867 when the Treaty of London recognized it as an independent state and guaranteed its perpetual neutrality. Luxembourg was occupied by Germany and liberated by American troops in both World Wars.

RULERS
Adolphe, 1890-1905
William IV, 1905-1912
Marie Adelaide, 1912-1919
Charlotte, 1919-1964
Jean, 1964-2000
Henri, 2000-

MINT MARKS
A - Paris
(b) - Brussels, privy marks only
H - Gunzburg
(n) – lion - Namur
(u) - Utrecht, privy marks only

PRIVY MARKS
Angel's head, two headed eagle - Brussels
Sword, Caduceus - Utrecht (1846-74 although struck at Brussels until 1909)
NOTE: Beginning in 1994 the letters "qp" for quality proof appear on Proof coins.

MONETARY SYSTEM
100 Centimes = 1 Franc

GRAND DUCHY
STANDARD COINAGE RESUMED
100 Centimes = 1 Franc

KM# 64 20 FRANCS
6.2200 g., 0.9990 Gold .2 oz. AGW **Ruler:** Jean **Subject:** 150th Anniversary of the Grand Duchy **Obv:** Head left **Rev:** Crowned national arms

Date	Mintage	F	VF	XF	Unc	BU
ND(1989) Proof	50,000	Value: 145				

EURO COINAGE
European Economic Community Issues

KM# 84 5 EURO
6.2200 g., 0.9990 Gold 0.1998 oz. AGW, 20 mm. **Ruler:** Henri **Subject:** European Central Bank **Obv:** Grand Duke Henri **Rev:** Building

Date	Mintage	F	VF	XF	Unc	BU
2003 Proof	20,000	Value: 225				

MEDALLIC COINAGE

X# MA1b 5 FRANCS
41.9000 g., Gold **Issuer:** Banque du Bruxelles. **Subject:** Princess Ermesinde **Note:** Prev. KM#M14b. With ESSAI.

Date	Mintage	F	VF	XF	Unc	BU
ND(1963)(b)	—	—	—	—	—	875

X# M1 20 FRANCS
6.4516 g., 0.9000 Gold .1867 oz. AGW **Subject:** Marriage Commemorative - Prince Jean and Princess Josephine Charlotte **Note:** Prev. KM#M1.

Date	Mintage	F	VF	XF	Unc	BU
1953(b)	25,573	—	—	125	150	200

X# M2b 20 FRANCS
6.4516 g., 0.9000 Gold .1867 oz. AGW **Subject:** 100th Anniversary of Luxembourg **Note:** Prev. KM#M2b. With ESSAI.

Date	Mintage	F	VF	XF	Unc	BU
1963(b)	25,263	—	—	125	135	175

X# M4b 20 FRANCS
6.4516 g., 0.9000 Gold .1867 oz. AGW **Subject:** Coronation **Note:** Prev. KM#M4b. With ESSAI.

Date	Mintage	F	VF	XF	Unc	BU
1964(b)	200	—	—	—	150	200

X# M4c 20 FRANCS
6.4516 g., 0.9000 Gold .1867 oz. AGW **Subject:** Coronation

Date	Mintage	F	VF	XF	Unc	BU
1964(b)	25,050	—	—	125	135	175

X# M31 20 FRANCS
6.4516 g., 0.9000 Gold .1867 oz. AGW **Subject:** 100th Anniversary - Death of Poet Michel Lentz

Date	Mintage	F	VF	XF	Unc	BU
1993 Proof	500	Value: 250				

X# M3c 40 FRANCS
12.9032 g., 0.9000 Gold .3734 oz. AGW **Issuer:** Banque de Bruxelles **Subject:** Princess Ermesinde **Note:** Prev. KM#M3c. With ESSAI.

Date	Mintage	F	VF	XF	Unc	BU
ND(1963)(b)	5,000	—	—	250	270	300

X# M5 40 FRANCS
12.9032 g., 0.9000 Gold .3734 oz. AGW **Obv:** Grand Duchess Charlotte head facing left **Note:** Prev. KM#M5.

Date	Mintage	F	VF	XF	Unc	BU
1964(b)	3,000	—	—	260	280	320

X# M6 40 FRANCS
12.9032 g., 0.9000 Gold .3734 oz. AGW **Obv:** Prince Felix head facing left **Note:** Prev. KM#M6.

Date	Mintage	F	VF	XF	Unc	BU
1964(b)	3,000	—	—	260	280	320

X# M7 40 FRANCS
12.9032 g., 0.9000 Gold .3734 oz. AGW **Obv:** Grand Duke Jean head facing left **Note:** Prev. KM#M7.

Date	Mintage	F	VF	XF	Unc	BU
1964(b)	3,000	—	—	260	280	320

X# M8 40 FRANCS
12.9032 g., 0.9000 Gold .3734 oz. AGW **Obv:** Grand Duchess Josephine Charlotte head facing left **Note:** Prev. KM#M8.

Date	Mintage	F	VF	XF	Unc	BU
1964(b)	3,000	—	—	260	280	320

X# M9b 40 FRANCS
12.9032 g., 0.9000 Gold .3734 oz. AGW **Subject:** 300th Anniversary of Patron Saint (Virgin Mary) **Note:** Prev. KM#M9b. With ESSAI.

Date	Mintage	F	VF	XF	Unc	BU
1966	5,000	—	—	260	280	320

X# M10c 40 FRANCS
12.9032 g., 0.9000 Gold .3734 oz. AGW **Subject:** 100th Anniversary of London Treaty **Obv:** Henry and Amalia conjoined heads facing left **Note:** Prev. KM#M10c. With ESSAI.

Date	Mintage	F	VF	XF	Unc	BU
1967	5,000	—	—	260	280	320

X# M11 40 FRANCS
12.9032 g., 0.9000 Gold .3734 oz. AGW **Subject:** Grand Duke Henry VII **Rev:** Prince Henri charging on horseback **Note:** Prev. KM#M11.

Date	Mintage	F	VF	XF	Unc	BU
1973 (a) Proof	5,000	Value: 285				

X# M12 40 FRANCS
12.9032 g., 0.9000 Gold .3734 oz. AGW **Subject:** 80th Birthday of Princess Josephine Charlotte **Rev:** Fischbach Castle **Note:** Prev. KM#M12.

Date	Mintage	F	VF	XF	Unc	BU
1976 (a) Proof	6,500	Value: 285				

X# M13 40 FRANCS
12.9032 g., 0.9000 Gold .3734 oz. AGW **Subject:** Silver Wedding, 1953-1978 **Note:** Prev. KM#M13.

Date	Mintage	F	VF	XF	Unc	BU
ND(1978) Proof	3,000	Value: 300				

X# M18 40 FRANCS
12.9032 g., 0.9000 Gold .3734 oz. AGW **Subject:** Grand Duke Adolph

Date	Mintage	F	VF	XF	Unc	BU
1982 Proof	1,000	Value: 325				

X# M19 40 FRANCS
12.9032 g., 0.9000 Gold .3734 oz. AGW **Subject:** Grand Duke Guillaume

Date	Mintage	F	VF	XF	Unc	BU
1982 Proof	1,000	Value: 325				

X# M20 40 FRANCS
12.9032 g., 0.9000 Gold .3734 oz. AGW **Subject:** Grand Duchess Marie - Adelaide

Date	Mintage	F	VF	XF	Unc	BU
1982 Proof	1,000	Value: 325				

X# M21 40 FRANCS
12.9032 g., 0.9000 Gold .3734 oz. AGW **Subject:** Grand Duchess Charlotte

Date	Mintage	F	VF	XF	Unc	BU
1982 Proof	1,000	Value: 325				

X# M22 40 FRANCS
12.9032 g., 0.9000 Gold .3734 oz. AGW **Subject:** Grand Duke Jean

Date	Mintage	F	VF	XF	Unc	BU
1982 Proof	1,000	Value: 325				

X# M23 40 FRANCS
12.9032 g., 0.9000 Gold .3734 oz. AGW **Subject:** Grand Duchess Josephine - Charlotte

Date	Mintage	F	VF	XF	Unc	BU
1982 Proof	1,000	Value: 325				

X# M24 40 FRANCS
12.9032 g., 0.9000 Gold .3734 oz. AGW **Subject:** Prince Henri

Date	Mintage	F	VF	XF	Unc	BU
1982 Proof	1,000	Value: 325				

X# M25 40 FRANCS
12.9032 g., 0.9000 Gold .3734 oz. AGW **Subject:** Princess Maria Theresa

Date	Mintage	F	VF	XF	Unc	BU
1982 Proof	1,000	Value: 325				

X# M26 40 FRANCS
12.9032 g., 0.9000 Gold .3734 oz. AGW **Subject:** Count Henry VII

Date	Mintage	F	VF	XF	Unc	BU
1984 Proof	2,000	Value: 350				

MACAO

X# M27 40 FRANCS
12.9032 g., 0.9000 Gold .3734 oz. AGW **Subject:** Visit of Pope John Paul II

Date	Mintage	F	VF	XF	Unc	BU
1985 Proof	1,575	Value: 400				

X# M28 40 FRANCS
12.9032 g., 0.9000 Gold .3734 oz. AGW **Subject:** Rebuilding of the souvenir monument

Date	Mintage	F	VF	XF	Unc	BU
1985 Proof	200	Value: 500				

X# M29 40 FRANCS
12.9032 g., 0.9000 Gold .3734 oz. AGW **Subject:** Death of Grand Duchess Charlotte

Date	Mintage	F	VF	XF	Unc	BU
1985 Proof	470	Value: 450				

X# M30 40 FRANCS
12.9032 g., 0.9000 Gold .3734 oz. AGW **Subject:** 25th Anniversary - London Treaty

Date	Mintage	F	VF	XF	Unc	BU
1992 Proof	1,200	Value: 300				

X# M32 40 FRANCS
12.9032 g., 0.9000 Gold .3734 oz. AGW **Subject:** 40th Wedding Anniversary, 1953-1993

Date	Mintage	F	VF	XF	Unc	BU
ND(1993) Proof	700	Value: 400				

X# M33 40 FRANCS
12.9032 g., 0.9000 Gold .3734 oz. AGW **Subject:** 30th Anniversary of Reign, 1964-1994

Date	Mintage	F	VF	XF	Unc	BU
ND(1994) Proof	700	Value: 400				

X# M34 40 FRANCS
12.9032 g., 0.9000 Gold .3734 oz. AGW **Subject:** 100th Anniversary - Birth of Grand Duchess Charlotte, 1896-1985 **Rev:** Berg Castle

Date	Mintage	F	VF	XF	Unc	BU
ND(1996) Proof	600	Value: 425				

X# M35 40 FRANCS
12.9032 g., 0.9000 Gold .3734 oz. AGW **Subject:** 550th Anniversary - Henri V as Count, 1247-1281

Date	Mintage	F	VF	XF	Unc	BU
ND(1997) Proof	600	Value: 425				

(Xm36) 40 FRANCS
12.9032 g., 0.9000 Gold 0.3734 oz. AGW **Subject:** Grand Duke Henri **Obv:** Portrait **Rev:** Arms

Date	Mintage	F	VF	XF	Unc	BU
ND(2000) Proof	—	Value: 425				

X# M36 40 FRANCS
12.9032 g., 0.9000 Gold .3734 oz. AGW **Subject:** Grand Duke Henri **Obv:** Portrait **Rev:** Arms

Date	Mintage	F	VF	XF	Unc	BU
ND(2000) Proof	—	Value: 425				

ESSAIS

KM#	Date	Mintage	Identification	Mkt Val
E21	1889	—	5 Francs. Gold.	5,000
E22	1901	20	5 Centimes. Gold. Adolph.	1,000
E23	1901	—	10 Centimes. Gold. Adolph.	1,000
E24	1908	—	10 Centimes. Gold. Wilhelm.	1,000
E34	1929	—	5 Francs. Gold.	2,000
E38	1929	—	10 Francs. Gold.	2,000
E39	1939	—	Franc. Gold.	1,500
E52	1946	25	20 Francs. Gold.	1,200
E55	1946	25	50 Francs. Gold.	2,000
E58	1946	25	100 Francs. Gold.	3,000
E63	1962	50	5 Francs. Gold.	1,000
E64	1963	250	20 Francs. Gold.	200
E67	1963	50	100 Francs. Gold.	1,250
E71	ND(1963)	200	250 Francs. Gold.	1,450
E72	1964	200	20 Francs. Gold.	200
E76	1964	200	100 Francs. Gold.	750
EA80	1966	100	40 Francs. Gold.	400
EB81	1967	100	40 Francs. Gold.	400
E84	1971	250	5 Francs. Gold. KM56.	315
E87	1971	250	10 Francs. Gold.	325
E90	1980	500	20 Francs. Gold.	285

PATTERNS
Including off metal strikes

KM#	Date	Mintage	Identification	Mkt Val
Pn12	1901	20	5 Centimes. Gold. Without denomination.	1,000
Pn18	1901	20	10 Centimes. Gold. Without denomination.	1,000
Pn43	1939	—	Franc. Gold.	350

MACAO

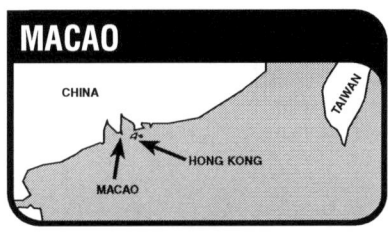

The Province of Macao, a Portuguese overseas province located in the South China Sea 40 miles southwest of Hong Kong, consists of the peninsula of Macao and the islands of Taipa and Coloane. It has an area of 6.2 sq. mi.(16 sq. km.) and a population of 500,000. Capital: Macao. Macao's economy is based on light industry, commerce, tourism, fishing, and gold trading - Macao is one of the entirely free markets for gold in the world. Cement, textiles, fireworks, vegetable oils, and metal products are exported.

Established by the Portuguese in 1557, Macao is the oldest European settlement in the Far East. The Chinese, while agreeing to Portuguese settlement, did not recognize Portuguese sovereign rights and the Portuguese remained largely under control of the Chinese until 1849, when the Portuguese abolished the Chinese customhouse and declared the independence of the port. The Manchu government formally recognized the Portuguese right to *perpetual occupation* of Macao in 1887.

In 1987, Portugal and China agreed that Macao would become a Chinese Territory in 1999. In December of 1999, Macao became a special administrative zone of China.

RULER
Portuguese 1887-1999

MINT MARKS
(p) - Pobjoy Mint
(s) - Singapore Mint

Pobjoy Mint 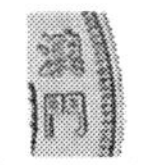   Singapore Mint

MONETARY SYSTEM
100 Avos = 1 Pataca

PORTUGUESE COLONY

STANDARD COINAGE
100 Avos = 1 Pataca

KM# 20b 10 AVOS
4.0000 g., 0.9170 Gold .1179 oz. AGW **Obv:** Portuguese shield flanked by stars below (low star) **Rev:** Value above building

Date	Mintage	F	VF	XF	Unc	BU
1982 Proof	150	Value: 125				

KM# 20c 10 AVOS
4.5000 g., 0.9500 Platinum .1374 oz. APW **Obv:** Portuguese shield flanked by stars below (low star) **Rev:** Value above building

Date	Mintage	F	VF	XF	Unc	BU
1982 Proof	375	Value: 200				

KM# 21b 20 AVOS
5.5000 g., 0.9170 Gold .1621 oz. AGW, 21.1 mm. **Obv:** Portuguese shield flanked by stars, date below (low star) **Rev:** Value above block letter design within vertical rectangle

Date	Mintage	F	VF	XF	Unc	BU
1982 Proof	150	Value: 175				

KM# 21c 20 AVOS
6.2000 g., 0.9500 Platinum .1893 oz. APW, 21.1 mm. **Obv:** Portuguese shield flanked by stars, date below (low star) **Rev:** Value above block letter design within vertical rectangle

Date	Mintage	F	VF	XF	Unc	BU
1982 Proof	375	Value: 285				

KM# 22b 50 AVOS
7.4000 g., 0.9170 Gold .2181 oz. AGW, 23 mm. **Obv:** Portuguese shield flanked by stars below (low star) **Rev:** Value above fallen block letters within vertical rectangle

Date	Mintage	F	VF	XF	Unc	BU
1982 Proof	150	Value: 200				

KM# 22c 50 AVOS
8.4000 g., 0.9500 Platinum .2565 oz. APW, 23 mm. **Obv:** Portuguese shield flanked by stars below above date (low star) **Rev:** Value above fallen block letters within vertical rectangle

Date	Mintage	F	VF	XF	Unc	BU
1982 Proof	375	Value: 385				

KM# 23.1b PATACA
11.6000 g., 0.9170 Gold .342 oz. AGW, 26 mm. **Obv:** Portuguese shield flanked by stars below above date (high stars) **Rev:** Artistic design flanked by upright fish

Date	Mintage	F	VF	XF	Unc	BU
1982(s) Proof	150	Value: 285				

KM# 23.1c PATACA
13.2000 g., 0.9500 Platinum .4032 oz. APW, 26 mm. **Obv:** Portuguese shield flanked by stars below above date (high stars) **Rev:** Artistic design flanked by upright fish

Date	Mintage	F	VF	XF	Unc	BU
1982(s) Proof	375	Value: 600				

KM# 24.1b 5 PATACAS
16.3000 g., 0.9170 Gold .4808 oz. AGW, 29 mm. **Obv:** Portuguese shield flanked by stars below above date (high stars) **Rev:** Large stylized dragon above value

Date	Mintage	F	VF	XF	Unc	BU
1982(s) Proof	150	Value: 400				

KM# 24.1c 5 PATACAS
18.4000 g., 0.9500 Platinum .562 oz. APW, 29 mm. **Obv:** Portuguese shield flanked by stars below above date (high stars) **Rev:** Large stylized dragon above value

Date	Mintage	F	VF	XF	Unc	BU
1982(s) Proof	375	Value: 845				

KM# 40a 100 PATACAS
Platinum APW **Subject:** 35th Anniversary of Grand Prix **Obv:** Sailing ship within circle **Rev:** Race car within circle above dates

Date	Mintage	F	VF	XF	Unc	BU
ND(1988) Proof	10	Value: 2,750				

KM# 49 250 PATACAS
3.9900 g., 0.9170 Gold .1176 oz. AGW **Subject:** Year of the Goat **Obv:** Crowned arms with supporters **Rev:** Goat **Note:** Similar to 1,000 Patacas, KM#51.

Date	Mintage	F	VF	XF	Unc	BU
1991 Proof	Est. 2,500	Value: 110				

KM# 53 250 PATACAS
3.9900 g., 0.9170 Gold .1176 oz. AGW **Subject:** Year of the Monkey **Obv:** Crowned arms with supporters **Rev:** Monkey **Designer:** Robert Lowe **Note:** Similar to 1,000 Patacas, KM#51.

Date	Mintage	F	VF	XF	Unc	BU
1992 Proof	Est. 2,500	Value: 110				

KM# 59 250 PATACAS
3.9900 g., 0.9170 Gold .1176 oz. AGW **Subject:** Year of the Rooster **Obv:** Crowned arms with supporters **Rev:** Rooster **Note:** Similar to 1,000 Patacas, KM#58.

Date	Mintage	F	VF	XF	Unc	BU
1993 Proof	Est. 2,500	Value: 110				

KM# 67 250 PATACAS
3.9900 g., 0.9170 Gold .1176 oz. AGW **Subject:** Year of the Dog **Obv:** Church facade flanked by stars above date **Rev:** Dog **Note:** Similar to 1,000 Patacas, KM#69.

MACAO

Date	Mintage	F	VF	XF	Unc	BU
1994 Proof	Est. 2,500	Value: 110				

KM# 74 250 PATACAS
3.9900 g., 0.9170 Gold .1176 oz. AGW **Subject:** Year of the Pig **Obv:** Church facade flanked by stars above date **Rev:** Pig

Date	Mintage	F	VF	XF	Unc	BU
1995 Proof	—	Value: 110				

KM# 80 250 PATACAS
3.9900 g., 0.9170 Gold .1176 oz. AGW **Subject:** Year of the Rat **Obv:** Church facade flanked by stars above date **Rev:** Rat

Date	Mintage	F	VF	XF	Unc	BU
1996 Proof	—	Value: 120				

KM# 85 250 PATACAS
3.9900 g., 0.9170 Gold .1176 oz. AGW **Subject:** Year of the Ox **Obv:** Church facade flanked by stars above date **Rev:** Ox **Note:** Similar to 100 Patacas, KM#84.

Date	Mintage	F	VF	XF	Unc	BU
1997 Proof	Est. 2,500	Value: 115				

KM# 89 250 PATACAS
3.9900 g., 0.9170 Gold .1176 oz. AGW **Subject:** Year of the Tiger **Obv:** Church facade flanked by stars above date **Rev:** Tiger **Note:** Similar to 100 Patacas, KM#88.

Date	Mintage	F	VF	XF	Unc	BU
1998 Proof	Est. 2,500	Value: 115				

KM# 93 250 PATACAS
3.9900 g., 0.9170 Gold .1176 oz. AGW **Subject:** Year of the Rabbit **Obv:** Church facade flanked by stars above value **Rev:** Rabbit

Date	Mintage	F	VF	XF	Unc	BU
1999 Proof	Est. 2,500	Value: 115				

KM# 99 250 PATACAS
3.9900 g., 0.9167 Gold .1176 oz. AGW, 19.3 mm. **Subject:** Year of the Dragon **Obv:** Church facade flanked by stars above date **Rev:** Dragon **Edge:** Reeded

Date	Mintage	F	VF	XF	Unc	BU
2000 Proof	2,500	Value: 125				

KM# 12 500 PATACAS
7.9600 g., 0.9170 Gold .2347 oz. AGW **Subject:** 25th Anniversary of Grand Prix **Obv:** Church facade flanked by stars above date **Rev:** Race car

Date	Mintage	F	VF	XF	Unc	BU
1978 Proof	550	Value: 300				

KM# 13 500 PATACAS
7.9600 g., 0.9170 Gold .2347 oz. AGW **Obv:** Church facade flanked by stars above date **Rev:** Race car without advertising

Date	Mintage	F	VF	XF	Unc	BU
1978 Proof	5,500	Value: 185				

KM# 15 500 PATACAS
7.9600 g., 0.9170 Gold .2347 oz. AGW **Subject:** Year of the Goat **Obv:** Crowned arms with supporters **Rev:** Goat

Date	Mintage	F	VF	XF	Unc	BU
1979 Proof	5,500	Value: 175				

KM# 42 500 PATACAS
7.9881 g., 0.9170 Gold .2354 oz. AGW **Subject:** 35th Anniversary of Grand Prix **Obv:** Sailing ship within circle **Rev:** Race car within circle

Date	Mintage	F	VF	XF	Unc	BU
ND(1988) Proof	4,500	Value: 185				

KM# 50 500 PATACAS
7.9881 g., 0.9170 Gold .2354 oz. AGW **Subject:** Year of the Goat **Obv:** Crowned arms with supporters **Rev:** Goat **Note:** Similar to 1,000 Patacas, KM#51.

Date	Mintage	F	VF	XF	Unc	BU
1991 Proof	Est. 2,500	Value: 185				

KM# 54 500 PATACAS
7.9900 g., 0.9170 Gold .2352 oz. AGW **Subject:** Year of the Monkey **Obv:** Crowned arms with supporters **Rev:** Monkey **Rev. Designer:** Robert Lowe **Note:** Similar to 1,000 Patacas, KM#51.

Date	Mintage	F	VF	XF	Unc	BU
1992 Proof	Est. 2,500	Value: 200				

KM# 60 500 PATACAS
7.9900 g., 0.9170 Gold .2352 oz. AGW **Subject:** Year of the Rooster **Obv:** Church facade flanked by stars above date **Rev:** Rooster **Note:** Similar to 100 Patacas, KM#58.

Date	Mintage	F	VF	XF	Unc	BU
1993 Proof	Est. 2,500	Value: 200				

KM# 64 500 PATACAS
7.9900 g., 0.9170 Gold .2352 oz. AGW **Subject:** Macao Grand Prix **Obv:** Map above dates **Rev:** Checkered design divides race car and racing bike

Date	Mintage	F	VF	XF	Unc	BU
ND(1993) Proof	4,500	Value: 185				

KM# 68 500 PATACAS
7.9900 g., 0.9170 Gold .2352 oz. AGW **Subject:** Year of the Dog **Obv:** Church facade flanked by stars above date **Rev:** Dog **Note:** Similar to 1,000 Patacas, KM#69.

Date	Mintage	F	VF	XF	Unc	BU
1994 Proof	Est. 2,500	Value: 210				

KM# 75 500 PATACAS
7.9900 g., 0.9170 Gold .2352 oz. AGW **Subject:** Year of the Pig **Obv:** Church facade flanked by stars above date **Rev:** Pig

Date	Mintage	F	VF	XF	Unc	BU
1995 Proof	Est. 2,000	Value: 210				

KM# 81 500 PATACAS
7.9900 g., 0.9170 Gold .2352 oz. AGW **Subject:** Year of the Rat **Obv:** Church facade flanked by stars above date **Rev:** Rat

Date	Mintage	F	VF	XF	Unc	BU
1996 Proof	—	Value: 210				

KM# 86 500 PATACAS
7.9900 g., 0.9170 Gold .2352 oz. AGW **Subject:** Year of the Ox **Obv:** Church facade flanked by stars above date **Rev:** Ox **Note:** Similar to 100 Patacas, KM#84.

Date	Mintage	F	VF	XF	Unc	BU
1997 Proof	2,000	Value: 225				

KM# 90 500 PATACAS
7.9900 g., 0.9170 Gold .2352 oz. AGW **Subject:** Year of the Tiger **Obv:** Church facade flanked by stars above date **Rev:** Tiger **Note:** Similar to 100 Patacas, KM#88.

Date	Mintage	F	VF	XF	Unc	BU
1998 Proof	2,500	Value: 225				

KM# 94 500 PATACAS
7.9900 g., 0.9170 Gold .2352 oz. AGW **Subject:** Year of the Rabbit **Obv:** Church facade flanked by stars above date **Rev:** Rabbit

Date	Mintage	F	VF	XF	Unc	BU
1999 Proof	Est. 2,500	Value: 225				

KM# 100 500 PATACAS
7.9900 g., 0.9167 Gold .2355 oz. AGW, 22.05 mm. **Subject:** Year of the Dragon **Obv:** Church facade flanked by stars above date **Rev:** Dragon **Edge:** Reeded

Date	Mintage	F	VF	XF	Unc	BU
2000 Proof	2,500	Value: 250				

KM# 17 1000 PATACAS
15.9760 g., 0.9170 Gold .4711 oz. AGW **Subject:** Year of the Monkey **Obv:** Crowned arms with supporters **Rev:** Monkey

Date	Mintage	F	VF	XF	Unc	BU
1980 Proof	5,500	Value: 385				

KM# 19 1000 PATACAS
15.9760 g., 0.9170 Gold .4711 oz. AGW **Subject:** Year of the Rooster **Obv:** Crowned arms with supporters **Rev:** Rooster

Date	Mintage	F	VF	XF	Unc	BU
1981	3,500	—	—	345	—	
1981 Proof	Inc. above	Value: 375				

KM# 26 1000 PATACAS
15.9760 g., 0.9170 Gold .4711 oz. AGW **Subject:** Year of the Dog **Obv:** Crowned arms with supporters **Rev:** Dog

Date	Mintage	F	VF	XF	Unc	BU
1982	256	—	—	375	—	
1982 Proof	255	Value: 475				

KM# 28 1000 PATACAS
15.9760 g., 0.9170 Gold .4711 oz. AGW **Subject:** Year of the Pig **Obv:** Crowned arms with supporters **Rev:** Pig

Date	Mintage	F	VF	XF	Unc	BU
1983	400	—	—	375	—	
1983 Proof	500	Value: 450				

KM# 30 1000 PATACAS
15.9760 g., 0.9170 Gold .4711 oz. AGW **Subject:** Year of the Rat **Obv:** Crowned arms with supporters **Rev:** Rat

Date	Mintage	F	VF	XF	Unc	BU
1984	2,000	—	—	345	—	
1984 Proof	3,000	Value: 375				

KM# 32 1000 PATACAS
15.9760 g., 0.9170 Gold .4711 oz. AGW **Subject:** Year of the Ox **Obv:** Crowned arms with supporters **Rev:** Ox

Date	Mintage	F	VF	XF	Unc	BU
1985	10,000	—	—	335	—	
1985 Proof	5,000	Value: 360				

MACAO 479

KM# 35 1000 PATACAS
15.9760 g., 0.9170 Gold .4711 oz. AGW **Subject:** Year of the Tiger **Obv:** Crowned arms with supporters **Rev:** Tiger

Date	Mintage	F	VF	XF	Unc	BU
1986(p)	2,000	—	—	—	335	—
1986(p) Proof	3,000	Value: 360				

KM# 37 1000 PATACAS
15.9760 g., 0.9170 Gold .4711 oz. AGW **Subject:** Year of the Rabbit **Obv:** Crowned arms with supporters **Rev:** Rabbit

Date	Mintage	F	VF	XF	Unc	BU
1987(p)	—	—	—	—	335	—
1987(p) Proof	5,000	Value: 360				

KM# 39 1000 PATACAS
15.9760 g., 0.9170 Gold .4711 oz. AGW **Subject:** Year of the Dragon **Obv:** Crowned arms with supporters **Rev:** Dragon

Date	Mintage	F	VF	XF	Unc	BU
1988 Proof	5,000	Value: 350				

KM# 45 1000 PATACAS
15.9760 g., 0.9170 Gold .4711 oz. AGW **Subject:** Year of the Snake **Obv:** Crowned arms with supporters **Rev:** Snake

Date	Mintage	F	VF	XF	Unc	BU
1989	2,000	—	—	—	335	—
1989 Proof	3,000	Value: 360				

KM# 47 1000 PATACAS
15.9760 g., 0.9170 Gold .4711 oz. AGW **Subject:** Year of the Horse **Obv:** Crowned arms with supporters **Rev:** Horse

Date	Mintage	F	VF	XF	Unc	BU
1990	2,000	—	—	—	335	—
1990 Proof	3,000	Value: 360				

KM# 51 1000 PATACAS
15.9760 g., 0.9170 Gold .4711 oz. AGW **Subject:** Year of the Goat **Obv:** Crowned arms with supporters **Rev:** Goat

Date	Mintage	F	VF	XF	Unc	BU
1991	Est. 500	—	—	—	345	—
1991 Proof	Est. 4,500	Value: 375				

KM# 55 1000 PATACAS
15.9760 g., 0.9170 Gold .4711 oz. AGW **Subject:** Year of the Monkey **Obv:** Crowned arms with supporters **Rev:** Monkey **Rev. Designer:** Robert Lowe

Date	Mintage	F	VF	XF	Unc	BU
1992	Est. 500	—	—	—	345	—
1992 Proof	Est. 4,500	Value: 375				

KM# 61 1000 PATACAS
15.9760 g., 0.9170 Gold .4711 oz. AGW **Subject:** Year of the Rooster **Obv:** Church facade flanked by stars above date **Rev:** Rooster

Date	Mintage	F	VF	XF	Unc	BU
1993	Est. 500	—	—	—	345	—
1993 Proof	Est. 4,500	Value: 375				

KM# 69 1000 PATACAS
15.9760 g., 0.9170 Gold .4711 oz. AGW **Subject:** Year of the Dog **Obv:** Church facade flanked by stars above date **Rev:** Dog

Date	Mintage	F	VF	XF	Unc	BU
1994	Est. 500	—	—	—	345	—
1994 Proof	Est. 4,500	Value: 375				

KM# 76 1000 PATACAS
15.9760 g., 0.9170 Gold .4711 oz. AGW **Subject:** Year of the Pig **Obv:** Church facade flanked by stars above date **Rev:** Pig

Date	Mintage	F	VF	XF	Unc	BU
1995	Est. 500	—	—	—	345	—
1995 Proof	Est. 4,500	Value: 375				

KM# 78 1000 PATACAS
15.9760 g., 0.9170 Gold .4711 oz. AGW **Subject:** Airport **Obv:** Stylized form **Rev:** City aerial view

Date	Mintage	F	VF	XF	Unc	BU
1995 Proof	5,000	Value: 375				

KM# 87 1000 PATACAS
15.9760 g., 0.9170 Gold .4711 oz. AGW **Subject:** Year of the Ox **Obv:** Church facade flanked by stars above date **Rev:** Ox

Date	Mintage	F	VF	XF	Unc	BU
1997 Proof	5,000	Value: 450				

KM# 91 1000 PATACAS
15.9760 g., 0.9170 Gold .4711 oz. AGW **Subject:** Year of the Tiger **Obv:** Church facade flanked by stars above date **Rev:** Tiger

Date	Mintage	F	VF	XF	Unc	BU
1998 Proof	5,000	Value: 450				

KM# 95 1000 PATACAS
15.9760 g., 0.9170 Gold .4711 oz. AGW **Subject:** Year of the Rabbit **Obv:** Church facade flanked by stars above date **Rev:** Rabbit

Date	Mintage	F	VF	XF	Unc	BU
1999 Proof	4,000	Value: 450				

KM# 101 1000 PATACAS
15.9760 g., 0.9167 Gold .4709 oz. AGW, 28.4 mm. **Subject:** Year of the Dragon **Obv:** Church facade flanked by stars above date **Rev:** Dragon **Edge:** Reeded

Date	Mintage	F	VF	XF	Unc	BU
2000	500	—	—	—	400	—
2000 Proof	4,000	Value: 450				

KM# 43 10000 PATACAS
155.5150 g., 0.9990 Gold 5 oz. AGW **Subject:** 35th Anniversary of Grand Prix **Obv:** Sailing ship within circle **Rev:** Race car above dates within circle **Note:** Similar to 500 Patacas, KM#42.

Date	Mintage	F	VF	XF	Unc	BU
1988 Proof	500	Value: 3,500				

KM# 65 10000 PATACAS
155.5150 g., 0.9990 Gold 5 oz. AGW **Subject:** Macao Grand Prix **Obv:** Map above dates **Rev:** Checkered design divides race car and racing bike **Note:** Similar to 500 Patacas, KM#64.

Date	Mintage	F	VF	XF	Unc	BU
1993 Proof	500	Value: 3,500				

BULLION COINAGE
On Wing (Wing-on) Bank

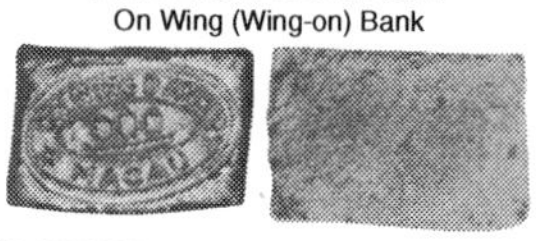

X# 4 1/2 OUNCE
15.5000 g., 0.9990 Gold 0.4978 oz. AGW

Date	Mintage	F	VF	XF	Unc	BU
ND(c.1950)	—	—	BV	375	425	—

X# 5 OUNCE
31.1000 g., 0.9990 Gold 0.9989 oz. AGW

Date	Mintage	F	VF	XF	Unc	BU
ND(c.1950)	—	—	BV	750	800	—

SILGOLD COINAGE

X# 11 400 SILGOLD
0.9990 Bi-Metallic 373.242 Silver/6.2207 Gold, 85 mm. **Issuer:** Money Co., California **Subject:** 35th Macao Grand Prix **Obv:** Fireball between facing dragons **Rev:** Two coin images, colony outline **Rev. Legend:** • MACAU GRANDE PRÉMIO 1988 • XXXV ANIVERSÁRIO **Note:** Illustration reduced.

Date	Mintage	F	VF	XF	Unc	BU
1988 Proof	250	Value: 750				

SPECIAL ADMINISTRATIVE REGION (S.A.R.)

STANDARD COINAGE
100 Avos = 1 Pataca

KM# 103 250 PATACAS
3.9900 g., 0.9167 Gold .1176 oz. AGW **Subject:** Year of the Snake **Obv:** Church facade **Rev:** Snake

Date	Mintage	F	VF	XF	Unc	BU
2001 Proof	2,500	Value: 125				

KM# 108 250 PATACAS
3.9900 g., 0.9167 Gold 0.1176 oz. AGW, 19.3 mm. **Subject:** Year of the Horse **Obv:** Church of St. Paul facade **Rev:** Horse above value **Edge:** Reeded

Date	Mintage	F	VF	XF	Unc	BU
2002 Proof	2,500	Value: 125				

KM# 119 250 PATACAS
3.9900 g., 0.9167 Gold 0.1176 oz. AGW, 19.3 mm. **Subject:** Year of the Goat **Obv:** Church facade **Rev:** Goat above value **Edge:** Reeded

MACAU

Date	Mintage	F	VF	XF	Unc	BU
2003 Proof	2,500	Value: 125				

KM# 104 500 PATACAS
7.9900 g., 0.9167 Gold .2355 oz. AGW **Subject:** Year of the Snake **Obv:** Church facade **Rev:** Snake

Date	Mintage	F	VF	XF	Unc	BU
2001 Proof	2,500	Value: 250				

KM# 109 500 PATACAS
7.9800 g., 0.9167 Gold 0.2352 oz. AGW, 22.05 mm. **Subject:** Year of the Horse **Obv:** Church facade **Rev:** Horse above value **Edge:** Reeded

Date	Mintage	F	VF	XF	Unc	BU
2002 Proof	2,500	Value: 250				

KM# 120 500 PATACAS
7.9800 g., 0.9167 Gold 0.2352 oz. AGW, 22 mm. **Subject:** Year of the Goat **Obv:** Church facade **Rev:** Goat above value **Edge:** Reeded

Date	Mintage	F	VF	XF	Unc	BU
2003 Proof	2,500	Value: 250				

KM# 105 1000 PATACAS
16.9760 g., 0.9167 Gold .4709 oz. AGW **Subject:** Year of the Snake **Obv:** Church facade flanked by stars **Rev:** Snake

Date	Mintage	F	VF	XF	Unc	BU
2001 Proof	4,000	Value: 450				

KM# 110 1000 PATACAS
15.9700 g., 0.9167 Gold 0.4707 oz. AGW, 28.4 mm. **Subject:** Year of the Horse **Obv:** Church facade **Rev:** Horse above value **Edge:** Reeded

Date	Mintage	F	VF	XF	Unc	BU
2002 Proof	4,000	Value: 450				

KM# 121 1000 PATACAS
15.9760 g., 0.9170 Gold .4711 oz. AGW **Subject:** Year of the Goat **Obv:** Church facade flanked by stars **Rev:** Goat above value **Edge:** Reeded

Date	Mintage	F	VF	XF	Unc	BU
2003 Proof	4,000	Value: 450				

PROOF SETS

KM#	Date	Mintage	Identification	Issue Price	Mkt Val
PS1b	1982 (5)	150	KM#20b-24b	—	1,185
PS1c	1982 (5)	375	KM#20c-24c	—	2,320
PS5	1987 (2)	—	KM#36-37	—	410
PS6	1988 (2)	—	KM#38-39	—	415
PS7	1991 (3)	2,500	KM#49-51	775	670
PS8	1992 (3)	2,500	KM#53-55	825	700
PS9	1993 (3)	2,500	KM#59-61	830	700
PS10	1994 (3)	2,500	KM#67-69	825	735
PS11	1995 (3)	2,500	KM#74-76	825	735
PS12	1997 (3)	2,500	KM#85-87	849	840
PS13	1998 (3)	2,500	KM#89-91	855	840
PS14	1999 (3)	2,500	KM#93-95	850	840
PS15	2000 (3)	2,500	KM#99-101	849	825
PS16	2001 (3)	2,500	KM#103-105	849	825
PS17	2002 (3)	4,000	KM#108-110	849	825
PS18	2003 (3)	2,500	KM#119-121	849	825

MACEDONIA

The Republic of Macedonia is land-locked, and is bordered in the north by Yugoslavia, to the east by Bulgaria, in the south by Greece and to the west by Albania and has an area of 9,781 sq. mi. (25,713 sq. km.) and a population at the 1991 census was 2,038,847, of which the predominating ethnic groups were Macedonians. The capital is Skopje.

The Slavs settled in Macedonia since the 6th century, who had been Christianized by Byzantium, were conquered by the non-Slav Bulgars in the 7th century and in the 9th century formed a Macedo-Bulgarian empire, the western part of which survived until Byzantine conquest in 1014. In the 14th century, it fell to Serbia, and in 1355 to the Ottomans. After the Balkan Wars of 1912-13 Turkey was ousted, and Serbia received the greater part of the territory, the balance going to Bulgaria and Greece. In 1918, Yugoslav Macedonia was incorporated into Serbia as "South Serbia", becoming a republic in the S.F.R. of Yugoslavia. Claims to the historical Macedonian territory have long been a source of contention between Bulgaria and Greece.

On Nov. 20, 1991, parliament promulgated a new constitution, and declared its independence on Nov.20, 1992, but failed to secure EC and US recognition owing to Greek objections to the use of the name *Macedonia*. On Dec. 11, 1992, the UN Security Council authorized the expedition of a small peacekeeping force to prevent hostilities spreading into Macedonia.

There is a 120-member single-chamber National Assembly.

REPUBLIC
STANDARD COINAGE

KM# 8 DENAR
15.9800 g., 0.9167 Gold .4709 oz. AGW **Subject:** 5th Anniversary - UN Membership **Obv:** National emblem within circle **Rev:** Storks within circle

Date	Mintage	F	VF	XF	Unc	BU
ND(1996) Proof	1,100	Value: 360				

KM# 10 DENAR
8.0000 g., 0.9160 Gold 0.2356 oz. AGW, 23.3 mm. **Subject:** Macedonian Orthodox Church **Obv:** Half length figure of Saint facing **Rev:** Orthodox cathedral

Date	Mintage	F	VF	XF	Unc	BU
1997	5,000	—	—	—	—	170

KM# 9b DENAR
8.0000 g., 0.9160 Gold 0.2356 oz. AGW, 23.8 mm. **Obv:** Byzantine copper folis coin **Rev:** Ornamented cross

Date	Mintage	F	VF	XF	Unc	BU
2000	2,000	—	—	—	—	210

KM# 12 2 DENARI
7.0000 g., 0.9160 Gold 0.2062 oz. AGW, 23 mm. **Subject:** 50th Anniversary - Faculty of Economics **Obv:** Economics building **Rev:** Economics faculty logo

Date	Mintage	F	VF	XF	Unc	BU
2000	1,000	—	—	—	—	210

KM# 20 5 DENARI
7.9000 g., 0.9160 Gold 0.2327 oz. AGW, 23.8 mm. **Subject:** 60th Anniversary - First session of Parliament **Obv:** Logo of Association of Refugees from Aegean part of Macedonia **Rev:** Refugee mother with three children

Date	Mintage	F	VF	XF	Unc	BU
2000	1,500	—	—	—	—	200

KM# 11 10 DENARI
7.0000 g., 0.9160 Gold 0.2062 oz. AGW, 23 mm. **Subject:** Sts. Cyril and Methodus University **Obv:** Statue divides dates **Rev:** Macedonian Cyrillic alphabet

Date	Mintage	F	VF	XF	Unc	BU
1999	2,000	—	—	—	—	185

KM# 13 10 DENARI
10.0000 g., 0.9160 Gold 0.2945 oz. AGW, 27 mm. **Subject:** 10th Anniversary of Independence **Obv:** Value in circle within radiant map **Rev:** Grape vine

Date	Mintage	F	VF	XF	Unc	BU
2001	1,000	—	—	—	250	280

KM# 22 60 DENARI
6.0000 g., 0.9160 Gold 0.1767 oz. AGW, 23.8 mm. **Subject:** 100th Anniversary - Statehood **Obv:** Monument above value within circle **Rev:** Djorce Petrov

Date	Mintage	F	VF	XF	Unc	BU
2003	500	—	—	—	150	180

KM# 23 60 DENARI
6.0000 g., 0.9160 Gold 0.1767 oz. AGW, 23.8 mm. **Subject:** 100th Anniversary - Statehood **Obv:** Monument above value within circle **Rev:** Krste Petkov-Misirkov

Date	Mintage	F	VF	XF	Unc	BU
2003	500	—	—	—	150	180

KM# 24 60 DENARI
6.0000 g., 0.9160 Gold 0.1767 oz. AGW, 23.8 mm. **Subject:** 100th Anniversary - Statehood **Obv:** Monument above value within circle **Rev:** Metodije Andonov

Date	Mintage	F	VF	XF	Unc	BU
2003	500	—	—	—	150	180

KM# 25 60 DENARI
6.0000 g., 0.9160 Gold 0.1767 oz. AGW, 23.8 mm. **Subject:** 100th Anniversary - Statehood **Obv:** Monument above value within circle **Rev:** Mihailo Apostolski

Date	Mintage	F	VF	XF	Unc	BU
2003	500	—	—	—	150	180

KM# 26 60 DENARI
6.0000 g., 0.9160 Gold 0.1767 oz. AGW, 23.8 mm. **Subject:** 100th Anniversary - Statehood **Obv:** Monument above value within circle **Rev:** Blaze Koneski

Date	Mintage	F	VF	XF	Unc	BU
2003	500	—	—	—	150	180

KM# 21 60 DENARI
8.0000 g., 0.9160 Gold 0.2356 oz. AGW, 23.8 mm. **Subject:** 50th Anniversary of separation from Greece **Obv:** The Monifest **Rev:** Monastery

Date	Mintage	F	VF	XF	Unc	BU
2004	500	—	—	—	165	210

KM# 14a 100 DENARI
18.0000 g., 0.9160 Gold 0.5301 oz. AGW, 32 mm. **Subject:** 100th Anniversary of Statehood **Obv:** Monument above value within circle **Rev:** Cherry tree canon divides circle

Date	Mintage	F	VF	XF	Unc	BU
2003	500	—	—	—	410	480

KM# 15 100 DENARI
6.0000 g., 0.9160 Gold 0.1767 oz. AGW, 23.8 mm. **Subject:** 100th Anniversary of Statehood **Obv:** Monument above value within circle **Rev:** Bust facing within circle

Date	Mintage	F	VF	XF	Unc	BU
2003	500	—	—	—	150	180

KM# 16 100 DENARI
6.0000 g., 0.9160 Gold 0.1767 oz. AGW, 23.8 mm. **Subject:** 100th Anniversary of Statehood **Obv:** Monument above value within circle **Rev:** Head with hat facing within circle

Date	Mintage	F	VF	XF	Unc	BU
2003	500	—	—	—	150	180

KM# 17 100 DENARI
6.0000 g., 0.9160 Gold 0.1767 oz. AGW, 23.8 mm. **Subject:** 100th Anniversary of Statehood **Obv:** Monument above value within circle **Rev:** Head facing within circle

Date	Mintage	F	VF	XF	Unc	BU
2003	500	—	—	—	150	180

KM# 18 100 DENARI
6.0000 g., 0.9160 Gold 0.1767 oz. AGW, 23.8 mm. **Subject:** 100th Anniversary of Statehood **Obv:** Monument above value within circle **Rev:** Bust left within circle

Date	Mintage	F	VF	XF	Unc	BU
2003	500	—	—	—	150	180

KM# 19 100 DENARI
6.0000 g., 0.9160 Gold 0.1767 oz. AGW, 23.8 mm. **Subject:** 100th Anniversary of Statehood **Obv:** Monument above value within circle **Rev:** Bust right within circle

Date	Mintage	F	VF	XF	Unc	BU
2003	500	—	—	—	150	180

MADAGASCAR

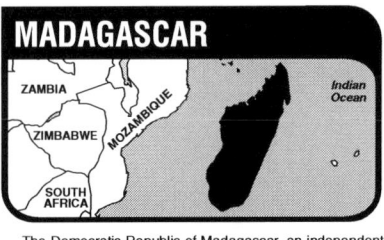

The Democratic Republic of Madagascar, an independent member of the French Community, located in the Indian Ocean 250 miles (402 km.) off the southeast coast of Africa, has an area of 226,656 sq. mi. (587,040 sq. km.) and a population of 10 million. Capital: Antananarivo. The economy is primarily agricultural; large bauxite deposits are being developed. Coffee, vanilla, graphite, and rice are exported.

Successive waves of immigrants from southeast Asia, Africa, Arabia and India populated Madagascar beginning about 2,000 years ago. Diago Diaz, a Portuguese navigator, sighted the island of Madagascar on Aug. 10, 1500, when his ship became separated from an India-bound fleet. Attempts at settlement by the British during the reign of Charles I and by the French during the 17th and 18th centuries were of no avail, and the island became a refuge and supply base for Indian Ocean pirates. Despite considerable influence on the island, the British accepted the imposition of a French protectorate in 1886 in return for French recognition of Britain's sphere of influence in Zanzibar. Madagascar was made a French colony in 1896 after absolute control had been established by military force. Britain occupied the island after the fall of France, 1942, to prevent its seizure by the Japanese, returning it to the Free French in 1943. On Oct. 14, 1958, following a decade of intermittent but bitter warfare, Madagascar, as the Malagasy Republic, became an autonomous state within the French Community. On June 27, 1960, it became a sovereign, independent nation, though remaining nominally within the French Community. The Malagasy Republic was renamed the Democratic Republic of Madagascar in 1975.

MONETARY SYSTEM
100 Centimes = 1 Franc

MINT MARKS
(a) - Paris, privy marks only
SA - Pretoria

DEMOCRATIC REPUBLIC

NOTE: Reverse legends found on Malagasy Democratic Republic coinages.
 A. - *Tanindrazana – Tolom – Piavotana – Fahafahana*; Fatherland – Revolution – Liberty
 B. - *Tanindrazana – Fahafahana – Fahamarinana*; Fatherland – Liberty – Justice
 C. - *Tanindrazana – Fahafahana – Fandrosoana*; Fatherland – Liberty - Progress

MONETARY SYSTEM
5 Francs = 1 Ariary
1 Ariary = 100 Iraimbilanja

STANDARD COINAGE

KM# 16 10 ARIARY
10.0000 g., 0.9170 Gold .2947 oz. AGW **Subject:** World Wildlife Fund **Obv:** Star above value within 3/4 wreath **Rev:** Ibis

Date	Mintage	F	VF	XF	Unc	BU
1988 Proof	Est. 5,000	Value: 215				

MADEIRA ISLANDS

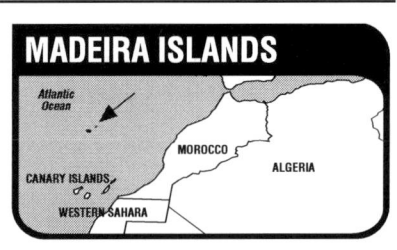

The Madeira Islands, which belong to Portugal, are located 360 miles (492 km.) off the northwest coast of Africa. They have an area of 307 sq. mi. (795 sq. km.). The group consists of two inhabited islands named Madeira and Porto Santo and two groups of uninhabited rocks named Desertas and Selvagens. Capital: Funchal. The two staple products are wine and sugar. Bananas and pineapples are also produced for export.

Although the evidence is insufficient, it is thought that the Phoenicians visited Madeira at an early period. It is also probable that the entire archipelago was explored by Genoese adventurers; an Italian map dated 1351 shows the Madeira Islands quite clearly. The Portuguese navigator Goncalvez Zarco first sighted Porto Santo in 1418, having been driven there by a storm while he was exploring the coast of West Africa. Madeira itself was discovered in 1420. The islands were uninhabited when visited by Zarco, but soon after 1418 Madeira was quickly colonized by Prince Henry the Navigator, aided by the knights of the Order of Christ. British troops occupied the islands in 1801, and again in 1807-14.

RULER
Portuguese

PATTERNS

KM#	Date	Mintage	Identification	Mkt Val
Pn2	1842	—	10 Reis. Gold. KM2.	—

MALAWI

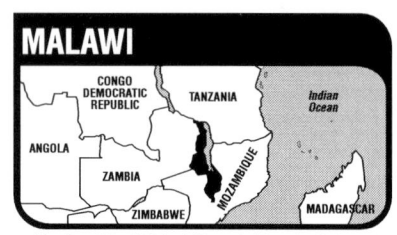

The Republic of Malawi (formerly Nyasaland), located in southeastern Africa to the west of Lake Malawi (Nyasa), has an area of 45,745 sq. mi. (118,480 sq. km.) and a population of 7 million. Capital: Lilongwe. The economy is predominantly agricultural. Tobacco, tea, peanuts and cotton are exported.

Although the Portuguese were the first Europeans to reach the Malawi area, the first meaningful contact was made by missionary-explorer Dr. David Livingstone. He arrived at Lake Malawi on Sept. 16, 1859, and remained to make extensive explorations in the 1860's. Subsequent clashes between settlements of Scottish missionaries and Arab slave traders, and the procurement of development rights by Cecil Rhodes, 1884, stimulated British interest and brought about the establishment of the Nyasaland protectorate in 1891. In 1953 Nyasaland reluctantly joined the Federation of Rhodesia and Nyasaland and, after prolonged protest, was granted self-government within the federation. Nyasaland became the independent nation of Malawi on July 6, 1964, and became a republic two years later. Malawi is a member of the Commonwealth of Nations. The president is the Chief of State and Head of Government.

NOTE: For earlier coinage see Rhodesia and Nyasaland.

MONETARY SYSTEM
12 Pence = 1 Shilling
2 Shillings = 1 Florin
5 Shillings = 1 Crown
20 Shillings = 1 Pound

REPUBLIC

DECIMAL COINAGE
100 Tambala = 1 Kwacha

KM# 14a   10 KWACHA
0.9000 Gold   **Subject:** 10th Anniversary of the Reserve Bank **Obv:** Head right **Rev:** Eagle with wings spread above lined design and value

Date	Mintage	F	VF	XF	Unc	BU
ND(1975)	—	—	—	—	1,250	—

KM# 18a   10 KWACHA
47.5400 g., 0.9170 Gold 1.4011 oz. AGW   **Subject:** 20th Anniversary - Reserve Bank **Obv:** Head right **Rev:** Eagle with wings spread above lined design and value

Date	Mintage	F	VF	XF	Unc	BU
ND(1985) Proof	50	Value: 1,600				

KM# 22   20 KWACHA
10.0000 g., 0.9170 Gold .2948 oz. AGW   **Series:** Save the Children **Subject:** Mother and children **Obv:** Head right **Rev:** Mother and child facing left, buildings and athletic players in background **Rev. Designer:** Willem Vis

Date	Mintage	F	VF	XF	Unc	BU
1992 Proof	Est. 3,000	Value: 230				

KM# 43   50 KWACHA
141.21g., Bronze with gold plated center and silver plated ring. 65 mm.   **Subject:** Republic of China **Obv:** Large building above value within circle **Rev:** Conjoined busts facing within circle **Edge:** Reeded **Note:** Illustration reduced.

Date	Mintage	F	VF	XF	Unc	BU
2004 Proof	—	Value: 85.00				

KM# 17   250 KWACHA
33.4370 g., 0.9000 Gold .9676 oz. AGW   **Series:** Conservation **Subject:** Nyala **Obv:** Head right **Rev:** Nyala (deer)

Date	Mintage	F	VF	XF	Unc	BU
1978 Proof	208	Value: 925				

MALAYSIA

Malaysia came into being on Sept. 16, 1963, as a federation of Malaya (Johore, Kelantan, Kedah, Perlis, Trengganu, Negri-Sembilan, Pahang, Perak, Selangor, Penang, Malacca), Singapore, Sabah (British North Borneo) and Sarawak. Following two serious racial riots involving Malays and Chinese, Singapore withdrew from the federation on Aug. 9, 1965. Malaysia is a member of the Commonwealth of Nations.

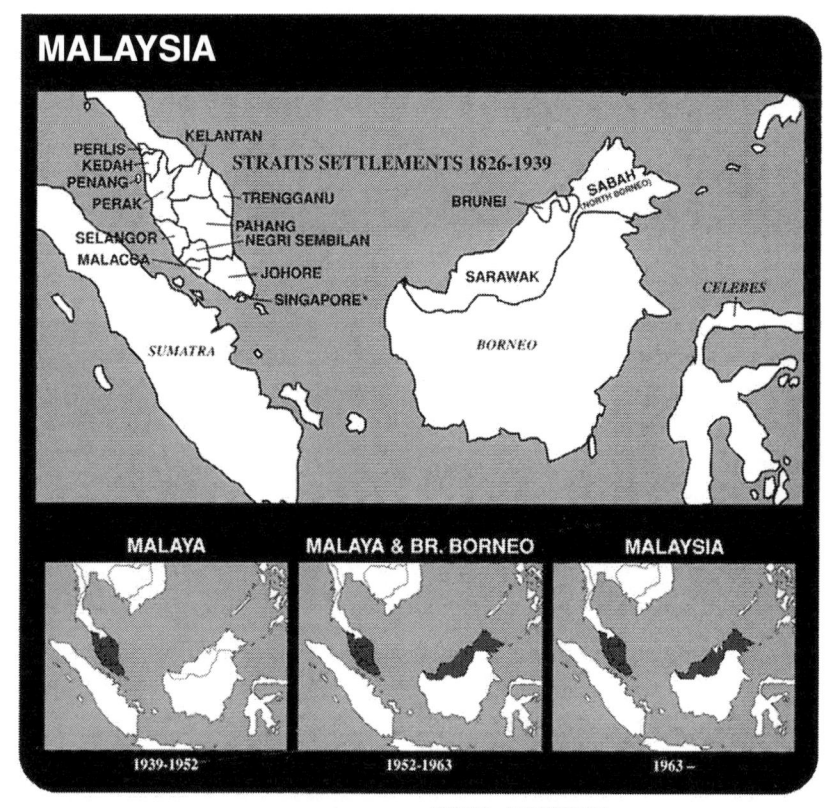

The independent limited constitutional monarchy of Malaysia, which occupies the southern part of the Malay Peninsula in Southeast Asia and the northern part of the island of Borneo, has an area of 127,316 sq. mi. (329,750 sq. km.) and a population of 15.4 million. Capital: Kuala Lumpur. The economy is based on agriculture, mining and forestry. Rubber, tin, timber and palm oil are exported.

MINT MARK
FM - Franklin Mint, U.S.A.
   *NOTE: From 1975-1985 the Franklin Mint produced coinage in up to 3 different qualities. Qualities of issue are designated in ( ) after each date and are defined as follows:
   (M) MATTE - Normal circulation strike or a dull finish produced by sandblasting special uncirculated (polish finish) or proof quality dies.
   (U) SPECIAL UNCIRCULATED - Polished or prooflike in appearance without any frosted features.
   (P) PROOF - The highest quality obtainable having mirror-like fields and frosted features.

MONETARY SYSTEM
100 Sen = 1 Ringgit (Dollar)

CONSTITUTIONAL MONARCHY

STANDARD COINAGE
100 Sen = 1 Ringgit (Dollar)

KM# 11 100 RINGGIT
18.6600 g., 0.9170 Gold .5502 oz. AGW **Subject:** Prime Minister Abdul Rahman Putra Al-haj **Obv:** Bust 3/4 facing **Rev:** Multi-storied building left of full sun

Date	Mintage	F	VF	XF	Unc	BU
1971	100,000	—	—	—	450	475
1971 Proof	500	Value: 1,400				

KM# 73 100 RINGGIT
8.6000 g., 0.9160 Gold 0.2533 oz. AGW, 22 mm. **Subject:** XXI SEA Games **Obv:** Games logo **Rev:** Cartoon mascot **Edge:** Reeded

Date	Mintage	F	VF	XF	Unc	BU
2001 Proof	500	Value: 350				

KM# 76 100 RINGGIT
8.6000 g., 0.9160 Gold 0.2533 oz. AGW, 22 mm. **Subject:** Coronation of Agong XII **Obv:** Head with headdress facing **Rev:** Arms with supporters within sprigs **Edge:** Reeded

Date	Mintage	F	VF	XF	Unc	BU
ND(2002) Proof	300	Value: 350				

KM# 18 200 RINGGIT
7.3000 g., 0.9000 Gold .2212 oz. AGW **Subject:** 3rd Malaysian 5-Year Plan **Shape:** 14-sided

Date	Mintage	F	VF	XF	Unc	BU
1976FM (U)	50,000	—	—	—	150	170
1976FM (P)	887	Value: 230				

KM# 24 200 RINGGIT
7.2200 g., 0.9000 Gold .2089 oz. AGW **Subject:** 9th Southeast Asian Games **Obv:** Arms with supporters **Rev:** Man on horse right

Date	Mintage	F	VF	XF	Unc	BU
1977FM (U)	12,000	—	—	—	150	170
1977FM (P)	417	Value: 410				

KM# 15 250 RINGGIT
10.1100 g., 0.9000 Gold .2925 oz. AGW **Subject:** 25th Anniversary - Employee Provident Fund **Obv:** Value **Rev:** Inscription within circle and design

Date	Mintage	F	VF	XF	Unc	BU
1976FM (U)	30,000	—	—	—	220	235
1976FM (P)	7,706	Value: 280				

KM# 42 250 RINGGIT
8.1000 g., 0.9000 Gold .2344 oz. AGW **Series:** Womens' Decade **Obv:** Date below design **Rev:** World globe

Date	Mintage	F	VF	XF	Unc	BU
1985 Proof	1,500	Value: 260				

KM# 45 250 RINGGIT
7.4300 g., 0.9000 Gold .2144 oz. AGW **Subject:** 30th Anniversary of Independence **Obv:** Arms with supporters above value **Rev:** Numeral 30 divides dates below crossed encased swords, sun and building

Date	Mintage	F	VF	XF	Unc	BU
1987	5,000	—	—	—	160	170
1987 Proof	1,000	Value: 210				

KM# 58 250 RINGGIT
7.1300 g., 0.9000 Gold .2063 oz. AGW **Subject:** 15th Southeast Asian Games **Obv:** Value below full sun on lined background **Rev:** Games logo and stylized swimmer

Date	Mintage	F	VF	XF	Unc	BU
1989 Proof	2,500	Value: 240				

KM# 63 250 RINGGIT
8.6000 g., 0.9000 Gold .2489 oz. AGW **Series:** World Wildlife Fund **Obv:** Panda above World Wildlife Fund **Rev:** Clouded Leopard

Date	Mintage	F	VF	XF	Unc	BU
1992 Proof	3,000	Value: 210				

KM# 21 500 RINGGIT
33.4370 g., 0.9000 Gold .9676 oz. AGW **Series:** Conservation **Obv:** Arms with supporters **Rev:** Malayan Tapir

Date	Mintage	F	VF	XF	Unc	BU
1976	2,894	—	—	—	700	725
1976 Proof	508	Value: 1,700				

KM# 31 500 RINGGIT
10.2600 g., 0.9000 Gold .2969 oz. AGW **Subject:** 4th Malaysian 5-Year Plan **Obv:** Arms with supporters **Rev:** Bust 3/4 facing

Date	Mintage	F	VF	XF	Unc	BU
ND(1981)FM (U)	20,000	—	—	—	240	260
ND(1981)FM (P)	1,000	Value: 430				

MALAYSIA

KM# 34 500 RINGGIT
10.2600 g., 0.9000 Gold .2969 oz. AGW **Subject:** 25th Anniversary of Independence **Obv:** Arms with supporters **Rev:** Bust upholding dagger facing right **Note:** Similar to 1 Ringgit, KM#32.

Date	Mintage	F	VF	XF	Unc	BU
1982	20,000	—	—	—	275	290
1982 Proof	1,000	Value: 410				

KM# 38 500 RINGGIT
10.2600 g., 0.9000 Gold .2969 oz. AGW **Subject:** 5th Malaysian 5-Year Plan **Obv:** Arms with supporters **Rev:** Sun, moon and gear-like designs within circle

Date	Mintage	F	VF	XF	Unc	BU
ND(1986)	10,000	—	—	—	225	250
ND(1986) Proof	1,000	Value: 410				

KM# 70 500 RINGGIT
25.0000 g., 0.9990 Gold 0.803 oz. AGW, 35.25 mm. **Subject:** Millennium **Obv:** Arms with supporters above value **Rev:** Flags within globe **Edge:** Reeded

Date	Mintage	F	VF	XF	Unc	BU
1999 Proof	10,000	Value: 810				

PROOF SETS

KM#	Date	Mintage	Identification	Issue Price	Mkt Val
PS2	1976 (3)	508	KM#19-21	808	1,800
PS4	1976 (3)	2,641	KM#16-18	—	245
PS5	1976 (3)	1,000	KM#13-15	—	400
PS6	1977 (3)	975	KM#22-24	164	550
PS9	1981 (3)	3,000	KM#29-31	—	440
PS10	1982 (3)	4,000	KM#32-34	—	400
PS11	1986	2,000	KM#36-38	—	400
PS13	1987 (3)	1,000	KM#43-45	—	220
PS18	1992 (3)	3,000	KM#61-63	—	250

MALDIVE ISLANDS

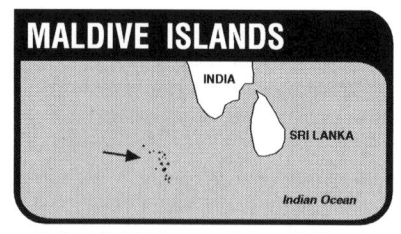

The Republic of Maldives, an archipelago of 2,000 coral islets in the northern Indian Ocean 417 miles (671 km.) west of Ceylon, has an area of 116 sq. mi. (298 sq. km.) and a population of 189,000. Capital: Male. Fishing employs 95 % of the male work force. Dried fish, copra and coir yarn are exported.

The Maldive Islands were visited by Arab traders and converted to Islam in 1153. After being harassed in the 16th and 17th centuries by Mopla pirates of the Malabar coast and Portuguese raiders, the Maldivians voluntarily placed themselves under the suzerainty of Ceylon. In 1887 the islands became an internally self-governing British protectorate and a nominal dependency of Ceylon. Traditionally a sultanate, the Maldives became a republic in 1953 but restored the sultanate in 1954. The Sultanate of the Maldive Islands attained complete internal and external autonomy on July 26, 1965, and on Nov. 11, 1968, again became a republic. The Maldives is a member of the Commonwealth of Nations.

RULERS
Muhammad Imad al-Din V, AH1318-1322/1900-1904AD
Muhammad Shams al-Din III, AH1322-1353/1904-1935AD
Hasan Nur al-Din II, AH1353-1364/1935-1945AD
Abdul-Majid Didi, AH1364-1371/1945-1953AD
First Republic, AH1371-1372/1953-1954AD
Muhammad Farid Didi, AH1372-1388/1954-1968AD
Second Republic, AH1388 to date/1968AD to date*

MINT NAME

محلي

Mahle (Male)

MONETARY SYSTEM
100 Lari = 1 Rupee (Rufiyaa)

2ND REPUBLIC

STANDARD COINAGE
100 Laari = 1 Rufiyaa

KM# 57b 5 RUFIYAA
18.9500 g., 0.9170 Gold .5585 oz. AGW **Series:** F.A.O. **Obv:** National emblem divides dates above **Rev:** Spiny lobster divides circle

Date	Mintage	F	VF	XF	Unc	BU
AH1398-1978 (1978) Proof	200	Value: 575				

KM# 58b 25 RUFIYAA
28.2500 g., 0.9170 Gold .8326 oz. AGW **Series:** F.A.O. **Obv:** National emblem divides dates above **Rev:** Sailing ship

Date	Mintage	F	VF	XF	Unc	BU
AH1398-1978 (1978) Proof	200	Value: 825				

KM# 89 50 RUFIYAA
1.2442 g., 0.9999 Gold .04 oz. AGW **Obv:** National emblem divides dates above **Rev:** Skylab space station

Date	Mintage	F	VF	XF	Unc	BU
AH1415-1995 (1995)	Est. 25,000	—	—	—	60.00	—

KM# 75 100 RUFIYAA
15.9800 g., 0.9170 Gold .4712 oz. AGW **Subject:** Opening of Grand Mosque and Islamic Centre **Obv:** National emblem divides dates above

Date	Mintage	F	VF	XF	Unc	BU
AH1405-1985 (1984) Proof	100	Value: 600				

KM# 67 100 RUFIYAA
15.9800 g., 0.9170 Gold .4712 oz. AGW **Obv:** National emblem divides dates above **Rev:** Disabled figures within lower circle under 1/2 world globe

Date	Mintage	F	VF	XF	Unc	BU
AH1404-1984 (1984)	500	—	—	—	700	—
AH1404-1984 (1984) Proof	500	Value: 800				

KM# 93 1000 RUFIYAA
15.9800 g., 0.9170 Gold .4712 oz. AGW, 28.4 mm. **Subject:** 25 Years of Independence

Date	Mintage	F	VF	XF	Unc	BU
AH1410-1990 (1990) Proof	1,000	Value: 500				

KM# 94 1000 RUFIYAA
15.9800 g., 0.9170 Gold .4712 oz. AGW, 28.4 mm. **Subject:** 25 Years of Republic

Date	Mintage	F	VF	XF	Unc	BU
AH1413-1993 (1993) Proof	500	Value: 550				

PIEFORTS

KM#	Date	Mintage	Identification	Mkt Val
P3	1984	100	100 Rufiyaa. Gold. National emblem - crescent moon, star and palm tree flanked by 2 flags. Disabled persons under an umbrella. KM67.	800

MALI

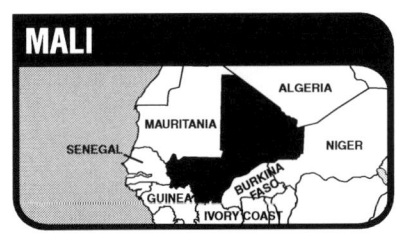

The Republic of Mali, a landlocked country in the interior of West Africa southwest of Algeria, has an area of 482,077 sq. mi. (1,240,000 sq. km.) and a population of 8.1 million. Capital: Bamako. Livestock, fish, cotton and peanuts are exported.

Malians are descendants of the ancient Malinke Kingdom of Mali that controlled the middle Niger from the 11th to the 17th centuries. The French penetrated the Sudan (now Mali) about 1880, and established their rule in 1898 after subduing fierce native resistance. In 1904 the area became the colony of Upper Senegal-Niger (changed to French Sudan in 1920), and became part of the French Union in 1946. In 1958 French Sudan became the Sudanese Republic with complete internal autonomy. Senegal joined with the Sudanese Republic in 1959 to form the Mali Federation which, in 1960, became a fully independent member of the French Community. Upon Senegal's subsequent withdrawal from the Federation, the Sudanese, on Sept. 22, 1960, proclaimed their nation the fully independent Republic of Mali and severed all ties with France.

MINT MARK
(a) - Paris, privy marks only

REPUBLIC
STANDARD COINAGE

KM# 5 10 FRANCS
3.2000 g., 0.9000 Gold .0926 oz. AGW **Subject:** President Modibo Keita **Obv:** Arms of Mali **Rev:** Bust facing **Note:** Similar to 25 Francs, KM#6.

Date	Mintage	F	VF	XF	Unc	BU
1967 Proof	—	Value: 90.00				

KM# 13 10 FRANCS
3.2000 g., 0.9000 Gold .0926 oz. AGW, 23.5 mm. **Subject:** Anniversary of Independence **Obv:** Designs within circle **Rev:** Bust with hat, facing **Note:** Similar to 50 Francs, KM#15.

Date	Mintage	F	VF	XF	Unc	BU
ND Proof	—	—	—	—	—	—

Note: Reported not confirmed

KM# 6 25 FRANCS
8.0000 g., 0.9000 Gold .2315 oz. AGW **Subject:** President Modibo Keita **Obv:** Arms of Mali **Rev:** Bust with hat, facing

Date	Mintage	F	VF	XF	Unc	BU
1967 Proof	—	Value: 165				

KM# 14 25 FRANCS
8.0000 g., 0.9000 Gold .2315 oz. AGW **Subject:** Anniversary of Independence **Obv:** Arms of Mali **Rev:** Bust with hat, facing

Date	Mintage	F	VF	XF	Unc	BU
ND Proof	—	Value: 325				

KM# 7 50 FRANCS
16.0000 g., 0.9000 Gold .4630 oz. AGW **Subject:** President Modibo Keita **Obv:** Arms of Mali **Rev:** Bust with hat, facing

Date	Mintage	F	VF	XF	Unc	BU
1967 Proof	—	Value: 325				

KM# 15 50 FRANCS
16.0000 g., 0.9000 Gold .463 oz. AGW **Subject:** Anniversary of Independence **Obv:** Arms of Mali **Rev:** Bust with hat, facing

Date	Mintage	F	VF	XF	Unc	BU
ND Proof	—	Value: 575				

KM# 8 100 FRANCS
32.0000 g., 0.9000 Gold .926 oz. AGW **Subject:** President Modibo Keita **Obv:** Arms of Mali **Rev:** Bust with hat, facing

Date	Mintage	F	VF	XF	Unc	BU
1967 Proof	—	Value: 645				

KM# 16 100 FRANCS
32.0000 g., 0.9000 Gold .926 oz. AGW **Subject:** Anniversary of Independence **Obv:** Arms of Mali **Rev:** Bust with hat, facing

Date	Mintage	F	VF	XF	Unc	BU
ND Proof	—	Value: 900				

PROOF SETS

KM#	Date	Mintage	Identification	Issue Price	Mkt Val
PS1	1967 (4)	—	KM5-8	—	1,225

MALTA

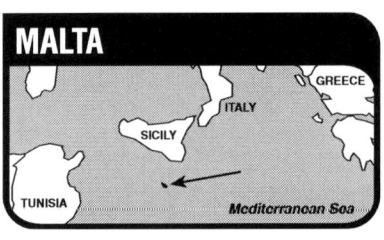

The Republic of Malta, an independent parliamentary democracy, is situated in the Mediterranean Sea between Sicily and North Africa. With the islands of Gozo and Comino, Malta has an area of 124 sq. mi. (320 sq. km.) and a population of 386,000. Capital: Valletta. Malta has no proven mineral resources, an agriculture insufficient to its needs, and a small, but expanding, manufacturing facility. Clothing, textile yarns and fabrics, and knitted wear are exported.

For more than 3,500 years Malta was ruled, in succession by Phoenicians, Carthaginians, Romans, Arabs, Normans, the Knights of Malta, France and Britain. Napoleon seized Malta by treachery in 1798. The French were ousted by a Maltese insurrection assisted by Britain, and in 1814 Malta, of its own free will, became a part of the British Empire. Malta obtained full independence in Sept., 1964; electing to remain within the Commonwealth with the British monarch as the nominal head of state.

Malta became a republic on Dec. 13, 1974, but remained a member of the Commonwealth of Nations. The president is Chief of State. The prime minister is the Head of Government.

RULER
British, until 1964

MONETARY SYSTEM
10 Mils = 1 Cent
100 Cents = 1 Pound

REPUBLIC
DECIMAL COINAGE

10 Mils = 1 Cent; 100 Cents = 1 Pound

KM# 15 5 POUNDS
3.0000 g., 0.9160 Gold .0883 oz. AGW **Obv:** Crowned arms with supporters **Rev:** Hand holding torch within map of Malta

Date	Mintage	F	VF	XF	Unc	BU
1972	18,000	—	—	—	—	70.00

Note: Appears to be proof, but officially issued as "BU"

KM# 16 10 POUNDS
6.0000 g., 0.9170 Gold .1767 oz. AGW **Obv:** Crowned arms with supporters **Rev:** Kenur, a Maltese stone charcoal stove

Date	Mintage	F	VF	XF	Unc	BU
1972	16,000	—	—	—	—	130

Note: Appears to be proof, but officially issued as "BU"

KM# 21 10 POUNDS
3.0000 g., 0.9170 Gold .0883 oz. AGW **Obv:** Crowned arms with supporters **Rev:** Watchtower

Date	Mintage	F	VF	XF	Unc	BU
1973	9,078	—	—	—	65.00	70.00

KM# 26 10 POUNDS
3.0000 g., 0.9170 Gold .0883 oz. AGW **Obv:** Crowned arms with supporters **Rev:** Zerafa flower flanked by date and value

Date	Mintage	F	VF	XF	Unc	BU
1974	9,124	—	—	—	65.00	70.00

MALTA

KM# 34 10 POUNDS
3.0000 g., 0.9170 Gold .0883 oz. AGW **Obv:** Crowned arms with supporters **Rev:** Falcon

Date	Mintage	F	VF	XF	Unc	BU
1975	2,000	—	—	—	80.00	90.00

KM# 35 10 POUNDS
3.0000 g., 0.9170 Gold .0883 oz. AGW **Obv:** Republic emblem within circle **Rev:** Maltese falcon

Date	Mintage	F	VF	XF	Unc	BU
1975	6,448	—	—	—	90.00	95.00

KM# 42 10 POUNDS
3.0000 g., 0.9170 Gold .0883 oz. AGW **Obv:** Republic emblem within circle **Rev:** Swallowtail butterfly above value

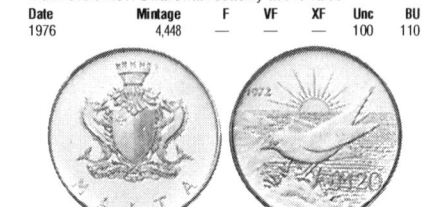

Date	Mintage	F	VF	XF	Unc	BU
1976	4,448	—	—	—	100	110

KM# 17 20 POUNDS
12.0000 g., 0.9170 Gold .3534 oz. AGW **Obv:** Crowned arms with supporters **Rev:** Merill bird

Date	Mintage	F	VF	XF	Unc	BU
1972	16,000	—	—	—	—	245

Note: Appears to be proof, but officially issued as "BU"

KM# 22 20 POUNDS
6.0000 g., 0.9170 Gold .1767 oz. AGW **Obv:** Crowned arms with supporters **Rev:** Dolphins Fountain at Floriana

Date	Mintage	F	VF	XF	Unc	BU
1973	9,075	—	—	—	125	130

KM# 27 20 POUNDS
6.0000 g., 0.9170 Gold .1767 oz. AGW **Obv:** Crowned arms with supporters **Rev:** Gozo boat with lateen sails

Date	Mintage	F	VF	XF	Unc	BU
1974	8,700	—	—	—	125	130

KM# 36 20 POUNDS
6.0000 g., 0.9170 Gold .1767 oz. AGW **Obv:** Crowned arms with supporters **Rev:** Freshwater crab

Date	Mintage	F	VF	XF	Unc	BU
1975	2,000	—	—	—	150	165

KM# 37 20 POUNDS
6.0000 g., 0.9170 Gold .1767 oz. AGW **Obv:** Republic emblem within circle **Rev:** Fresh water crab

Date	Mintage	F	VF	XF	Unc	BU
1975	5,698	—	—	—	130	135

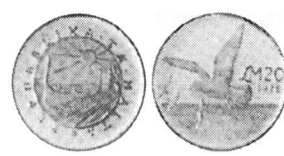

KM# 43 20 POUNDS
6.0000 g., 0.9170 Gold .1767 oz. AGW **Obv:** Republic emblem within circle **Rev:** Storm petrel bird

Date	Mintage	F	VF	XF	Unc	BU
1976	4,098	—	—	—	135	145

KM# 48 25 POUNDS
7.9900 g., 0.9170 Gold .2353 oz. AGW **Subject:** First Gozo coin **Obv:** Republic emblem within circle **Rev:** Figure holding lance facing right within circle

Date	Mintage	F	VF	XF	Unc	BU
1977	4,000	—	—	—	165	170
1977 Proof	3,249	Value: 180				

KM# 18 50 POUNDS
30.0000 g., 0.9170 Gold .8836 oz. AGW **Obv:** Crowned arms with supporters **Rev:** Neptune divides date and value

Date	Mintage	F	VF	XF	Unc	BU
1972	16,000	—	—	—	—	615

Note: Appears to be proof, but officially issued as "BU"

KM# 23 50 POUNDS
15.0000 g., 0.9170 Gold .4418 oz. AGW **Subject:** Auberge de Castille at Valletta **Obv:** Crowned arms with supporters **Rev:** Building with small flag on top above date and value

Date	Mintage	F	VF	XF	Unc	BU
1973	9,075	—	—	—	310	320

KM# 28 50 POUNDS
15.0000 g., 0.9170 Gold .4418 oz. AGW **Subject:** First Maltese coin **Obv:** Crowned arms with supporters **Rev:** Design within wreath

Date	Mintage	F	VF	XF	Unc	BU
1974	8,667	—	—	—	310	320

KM# 38 50 POUNDS
15.0000 g., 0.9170 Gold .4418 oz. AGW **Obv:** Crowned arms with supporters **Rev:** Ornamental stone balcony

Date	Mintage	F	VF	XF	Unc	BU
1975	2,000	—	—	—	325	345

KM# 39 50 POUNDS
15.0000 g., 0.9170 Gold .4418 oz. AGW **Obv:** Republic emblem within circle **Rev:** Ornamental stone balcony

Date	Mintage	F	VF	XF	Unc	BU
1975	5,500	—	—	—	310	320

KM# 44 50 POUNDS
15.0000 g., 0.9170 Gold .4418 oz. AGW **Obv:** Republic emblem **Rev:** Ornamental door knocker

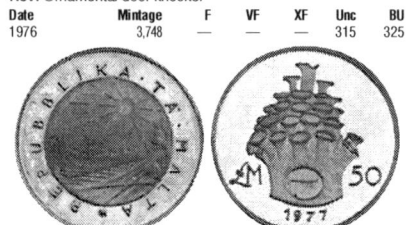

Date	Mintage	F	VF	XF	Unc	BU
1976	3,748	—	—	—	315	325

KM# 49 50 POUNDS
15.9800 g., 0.9170 Gold .4707 oz. AGW **Subject:** Mnara **Obv:** Republic emblem within circle **Rev:** Mnara design flanked by value above date

Date	Mintage	F	VF	XF	Unc	BU
1977	4,000	—	—	—	330	345
1977 Proof	846	Value: 375				

KM# 50 100 POUNDS
31.9600 g., 0.9170 Gold .9413 oz. AGW **Rev:** Father and two children sculpture above value

Date	Mintage	F	VF	XF	Unc	BU
1977	4,000	—	—	—	650	675
1977 Proof	846	Value: 725				

REFORM COINAGE
1982 - Present
100 Cents = 1 Lira

KM# 119 10 LIRI
1.2400 g., 0.9990 Gold 0.0398 oz. AGW, 13.92 mm. **Obv:** Crowned shield within sprigs **Rev:** Xprunara sailboat **Edge:** Reeded

Date	Mintage	F	VF	XF	Unc	BU
2002 Prooflike	Est. 25,000	—	—	—	—	110

MALTA, ORDER OF

KM# 101 25 LIRI
7.9900 g., 0.9170 Gold .2353 oz. AGW **Subject:** 50th Anniversary of George Cross Award **Obv:** Crowned shield within wreath **Obv. Designer:** Galea Bason **Rev:** George cross award

Date	Mintage	F	VF	XF	Unc	BU
1992 Proof	Est. 500			Value: 450		

KM# 122 25 LIRI
3.9940 g., 0.9167 Gold 0.1177 oz. AGW, 19.3 mm. **Subject:** Accession to the European Union **Obv:** Crowned shield within sprigs **Rev:** Maltese flag under European Union star circle **Edge:** Reeded

Date	Mintage	F	VF	XF	Unc	BU
2004 Proof	6,000			Value: 195		

KM# 66 100 LIRI
15.9800 g., 0.9170 Gold .4709 oz. AGW **Series:** International Year of Disabled Persons **Obv:** Republic emblem within circle **Rev:** Puzzle head right with missing pieces on top

Date	Mintage	F	VF	XF	Unc	BU
1983	700	—	—	—	600	650
1983 Proof	600			Value: 1,100		

KM# 89 100 LIRI
17.0000 g., 0.9170 Gold .5007 oz. AGW **Subject:** 25th Anniversary of Independence **Obv:** Crowned shield within sprigs **Rev:** Bust 1/4 right flanked by dates and value

Date	Mintage	F	VF	XF	Unc	BU
1989	5,000				400	425
1989 Proof	2,500			Value: 500		

PIEFORTS

KM#	Date	Mintage	Identification	Issue Price	Mkt Val
P3	1983	—	100 Pounds. 0.9170 Gold. KM66.	—	1,250

MINT SETS

KM#	Date	Mintage	Identification	Issue Price	Mkt Val
MS2	1972 (4)	8,000	KM15-18	210	1,050
MS4	1973 (3)	9,078	KM21-23	—	525
MS6	1974 (3)	—	KM26-28	256	525
MS8	1975 (5)	2,000	KM30, 32, 34, 36, 38	276	700
MS9	1975 (3)	—	KM34, 36, 38	256	650
MS11	1975 (3)	—	KM35, 37, 39	—	550
MS12	1976 (3)	—	KM42-44	—	575
MS15	1977 (3)	4,000	KM48-50	610	1,300

PROOF SETS

KM#	Date	Mintage	Identification	Issue Price	Mkt Val
PS4	1977 (3)	750	KM48-50	909	1,650

ORDER OF MALTA

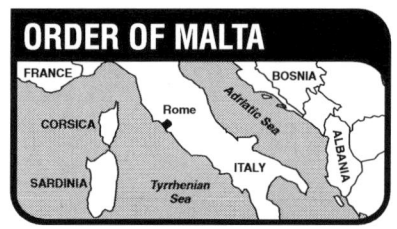

The Order of Malta, modern successor to the Sovereign Military Hospitaller Order of St. John of Jerusalem (the crusading Knights Hospitallers), derives its sovereignty from grants of extraterritoriality by Italy (1928) and the Vatican City (1953), and from its supranational character as a religious military order owing suzerainty to the Holy See. Its territory is confined to Palazzo Malta on Via Condotti, Villa Malta and the crest of the Aventine Hill, all in the city of Rome. The Order maintains diplomatic relations with about 35 governments, including Italy, Spain, Austria, State of Malta, Portugal, Brazil, Guatemala, Panama, Peru, Iran, Lebanon, Philippines, Liberia, Ethiopia, etc.

The Knights Hospitallers were founded in 1099 just before the crusaders' capture of Jerusalem. Father Gerard (died 1120) was the founder and first rector of the Jerusalem hospital. The headquarters of the Order were successively at Jerusalem 1099-1187; Acre 1187-1291; Cyprus 1291-1310; Rhodes 1310-1522; Malta 1530-1798; Trieste 1798-1799; St. Petersburg 1799-1803; Catania 1803-1825; Ferrara 1826-1834; Rome 1834-Present.

The symbolic coins issued by the Order since 1961 are intended to continue the last independent coinage of the Order on Malta in 1798. In traditional tari and scudi denominations, they are issued only in proof condition. They have a theoretical fixed exchange value with the Italian lira, but are not used in commerce.

These medallic issues are perhaps the world's last major symbolic coinage, just as their issuer is the world's last sovereign order of knighthood. Proceeds from the sale of this coinage maintain the Order's hospitals, clinics and leprosariums around the world.

RULERS
French, 1798-1800
Ernesto Paterno-Castello di Carcaci,
 Lieutenant Grand Master, 1955-1962
Fr. Angelo de Mojana di Cologna, 1962-1988
Fr. Giancarlo Pallavicini, Temporary Grand Master, 1988
Fr. Andreas Bertie, 1988-

MONETARY SYSTEM
(Until ca. 1800)
20 Grani = 1 Tari
12 Tari = 1 Scudo

SOVEREIGN ORDER
MEDALLIC COINAGE

X# 3 5 SCUDI
4.0000 g., 0.9160 Gold .1179 oz. AGW **Ruler:** Ernesto Paterno-Castello di Carcaci **Obv:** Large Maltese cross **Obv. Legend:** SUB • HOC • MILITAMVS **Rev:** St. John the Baptist standing with banner, Paschal Lamb at his feet **Note:** Prev. KM#M3.

Date	Mintage	F	VF	XF	Unc	BU
1961 Proof	1,200			Value: 120		

X# 7 5 SCUDI
4.0000 g., 0.9200 Gold .1183 oz. AGW **Ruler:** Angelo de Mojana di Cologna **Obv:** Crowned ornate arms **Rev:** St. John the Baptist standing with banner, Paschal Lamb lying at his feet **Note:** Prev. KM#M7.

Date	Mintage	F	VF	XF	Unc	BU
1962 Proof	200			Value: 400		
1963 Proof	600			Value: 200		

X# 11 5 SCUDI
4.0000 g., 0.9000 Gold .1157 oz. AGW **Ruler:** Angelo de Mojana di Cologna **Obv:** Bust 3/4 left **Rev:** St. John the Baptist standing with banner, Paschal Lamb lying at his feet **Note:** Prev. KM#M11.

Date	Mintage	F	VF	XF	Unc	BU
1964 Proof	1,000			Value: 125		

X# 15 5 SCUDI
4.0000 g., 0.9000 Gold .1157 oz. AGW **Ruler:** Angelo de Mojana di Cologna **Obv:** Bust 3/4 left **Rev:** St. John the Baptist giving banner to kneeling Grand Master **Note:** Prev. KM#M15.

Date	Mintage	F	VF	XF	Unc	BU
1965 Proof	1,000			Value: 125		
1966 Proof	600			Value: 200		

X# 21 5 SCUDI
4.0000 g., 0.9000 Gold .1157 oz. AGW **Ruler:** Angelo de Mojana di Cologna **Obv:** Bust left **Rev:** St. John the Baptist giving banner to kneeling Grand Master **Note:** Prev. KM#M21.

Date	Mintage	F	VF	XF	Unc	BU
1967 Proof	1,000			Value: 125		

X# 27 5 SCUDI
4.0000 g., 0.9000 Gold .1157 oz. AGW **Ruler:** Angelo de Mojana di Cologna **Obv:** Bust right **Rev:** St. John the Baptist giving banner to kneeling Grand Master **Note:** Prev. KM#M27.

Date	Mintage	F	VF	XF	Unc	BU
1968 Proof	1,000			Value: 125		

X# 33.1 5 SCUDI
4.0000 g., 0.9000 Gold .1157 oz. AGW **Ruler:** Angelo de Mojana di Cologna **Obv:** Bust left **Rev:** Crowned Maltese cross **Note:** Prev. KM#M33.1.

Date	Mintage	F	VF	XF	Unc	BU
1969 Proof	1,000			Value: 125		

X# 33.2 5 SCUDI
4.0000 g., 0.9000 Gold .1157 oz. AGW **Ruler:** Angelo de Mojana di Cologna **Obv:** Bust left **Rev:** Crowned Maltese cross **Note:** Prev. KM#M33.2.

Date	Mintage	F	VF	XF	Unc	BU
MCMLXX Proof	1,000			Value: 125		

X# 44 5 SCUDI
4.0000 g., 0.9000 Gold .1157 oz. AGW **Ruler:** Angelo de Mojana di Cologna **Obv:** Bust left **Rev:** St. John standing giving a banner to kneeling Grand Master **Rev. Legend:** SVB • HOC • SI - GNO • MILITAMVS **Note:** Prev. KM#M44.

Date	Mintage	F	VF	XF	Unc	BU
1971 Proof	1,000			Value: 125		
1972 Proof	1,000			Value: 125		
1973 Proof	1,000			Value: 125		
1974 Proof	1,000			Value: 125		
1975 Proof	1,000			Value: 125		

X# 66 5 SCUDI
4.0000 g., 0.9000 Gold .1157 oz. AGW **Ruler:** Angelo de Mojana di Cologna **Obv:** Bust left **Rev:** St. John the Baptist giving banner to kneeling Grand Master **Note:** Prev. KM#M66.

Date	Mintage	F	VF	XF	Unc	BU
1976 Proof	1,000			Value: 125		
1977 Proof	1,000			Value: 125		
1978 Proof	1,000			Value: 125		

X# 78 5 SCUDI
4.0000 g., 0.9000 Gold .1157 oz. AGW **Ruler:** Angelo de Mojana di Cologna **Obv:** Bust right **Rev:** St. John the Baptist giving banner to kneeling Grand Master **Note:** Prev. KM#M78.

Date	Mintage	F	VF	XF	Unc	BU
1979 Proof	1,000			Value: 125		
1980 Proof	600			Value: 185		
1981 Proof	1,000			Value: 135		

X# 94 5 SCUDI
4.0000 g., 0.9000 Gold .1157 oz. AGW, 20 mm. **Ruler:** Angelo de Mojana di Cologna **Subject:** 20th Anniversary of Fr. A. de Mojana **Obv:** Bust left **Rev:** Crowned ornate arms in Order chain **Note:** Prev. KM#M94.

Date	Mintage	F	VF	XF	Unc	BU
ND(1982) Proof	600			Value: 200		

X# 100 5 SCUDI
4.0000 g., 0.9000 Gold .1157 oz. AGW **Ruler:** Angelo de Mojana di Cologna **Obv:** Bust left **Rev:** St. John the Baptist giving banner to kneeling Grand Master **Note:** Prev. KM#M100.

488 MALTA, ORDER OF

Date	Mintage	F	VF	XF	Unc	BU
1983 Proof	600				Value: 175	

X# 107 5 SCUDI
4.0000 g., 0.9000 Gold .1157 oz. AGW **Ruler:** Angelo de Mojana di Cologna **Obv:** Bust left **Rev:** St. John the Baptist giving banner to kneeling Grand Master **Note:** Prev. KM#M106.

Date	Mintage	F	VF	XF	Unc	BU
ND(1984-86) Proof	600				Value: 175	

X# 122 5 SCUDI
4.0000 g., 0.9000 Gold .1157 oz. AGW **Ruler:** Angelo de Mojana di Cologna **Subject:** 25th Anniversary of Fr. A. de Mojana **Obv:** Bust left **Rev:** Crowned ornate arms **Note:** Prev. KM#M122.

Date	Mintage	F	VF	XF	Unc	BU
1987 Proof	600				Value: 175	

X# 128 5 SCUDI
4.0000 g., 0.9000 Gold .1157 oz. AGW **Ruler:** Angelo de Mojana di Cologna **Obv:** Bust left **Rev:** St. John the Baptist giving banner to kneeling Grand Master **Note:** Prev. KM#M128.

Date	Mintage	F	VF	XF	Unc	BU
1988 Proof	600				Value: 185	

X# 134 5 SCUDI
4.0000 g., 0.9000 Gold .1157 oz. AGW **Ruler:** Giancarlo Pallavicini **Subject:** Interregnum **Obv:** Maltese cross with legend SVB. HOC ... **Rev:** St. John the Baptist **Note:** Prev. KM#M134.

Date	Mintage	F	VF	XF	Unc	BU
1988 Proof	Inc. above				Value: 185	

X# 140 5 SCUDI
4.0000 g., 0.9000 Gold .1157 oz. AGW **Ruler:** Andreas Bertie **Obv:** Bust left **Rev:** Crowned and mantled arms **Note:** Prev. KM#M140.

Date	Mintage	F	VF	XF	Unc	BU
1988 Proof	500				Value: 200	

X# 146 5 SCUDI
4.0000 g., 0.9000 Gold .1157 oz. AGW, 20 mm. **Ruler:** Andreas Bertie **Obv:** Bust left **Rev:** St. John the Baptist giving banner to kneeling Grand Master **Note:** Prev. KM#M146.

Date	Mintage	F	VF	XF	Unc	BU
1989 Proof	600				Value: 125	
1990 Proof	600				Value: 125	
1991 Proof	600				Value: 125	

X# 162 5 SCUDI
4.0000 g., 0.9000 Gold .1157 oz. AGW **Ruler:** Andreas Bertie **Note:** Prev. KM#M162.

Date	Mintage	F	VF	XF	Unc	BU
1992 Proof	600				Value: 125	

X# 168 5 SCUDI
4.0000 g., 0.9000 Gold .1157 oz. AGW **Ruler:** Andreas Bertie **Note:** Prev. KM#M168.

Date	Mintage	F	VF	XF	Unc	BU
1993 Proof	600				Value: 125	

X# 175 5 SCUDI
4.0000 g., 0.9000 Gold 0.1157 oz. AGW, 20 mm. **Ruler:** Andreas Bertie **Obv:** Bust left **Obv. Designer:** F. Pioli **Rev:** St. John the Baptist presenting standard of the order to the Grand Master kneeling **Rev. Legend:** SUB HOC SIGNO MILITAMUS

Date	Mintage	F	VF	XF	Unc	BU
1994 Proof	600				Value: 125	
1995 Proof	600				Value: 125	
1996 Proof	—				Value: 125	
1997 Proof	—				Value: 125	
2001 Proof	—				Value: 125	
2002 Proof	—				Value: 125	
2003 Proof	—				Value: 125	
2004 Proof	—				Value: 125	

X# 195 5 SCUDI
4.0000 g., 0.9000 Gold 0.1157 oz. AGW, 20 mm. **Ruler:** Andreas Bertie **Obv:** Bust left **Rev:** Crowned and mantled arms **Rev. Legend:** ELECTIONIS DECENNIUM SUAE IN DOMINO CELEBRANS

Date	Mintage	F	VF	XF	Unc	BU
1998 Proof	—				Value: 125	

X# 201 5 SCUDI
4.0000 g., 0.9000 Gold 0.1157 oz. AGW, 20 mm. **Ruler:** Andreas Bertie **Subject:** 900th Anniversary of Founding of the Order **Obv:** Bust left **Rev. Legend:** NOVE SECOLI DI VITA DEL SOVRANO MILITARE ORDINE DI MALTA **Edge:** Reeded

Date	Mintage	F	VF	XF	Unc	BU
1999 Proof	—				Value: 125	

X# 207 5 SCUDI
4.0000 g., 0.9000 Gold 0.1157 oz. AGW, 20 mm. **Ruler:** Andreas Bertie **Obv:** Bust left **Rev:** Grand Master receiving standard from St. John the Baptist **Rev. Legend:** SUB HOC SIGNO MILITAMUS

Date	Mintage	F	VF	XF	Unc	BU
2000 Proof	—				Value: 125	

X# 4 10 SCUDI
8.0000 g., 0.9160 Gold .2358 oz. AGW **Ruler:** Ernesto Paterno-Castello di Carcaci **Obv:** Large Maltese cross **Rev:** St. John the Baptist standing facing with banner, Paschal Lamb at his feet **Note:** Prev. KM#M4.

Date	Mintage	F	VF	XF	Unc	BU
1961 Proof	1,200				Value: 230	

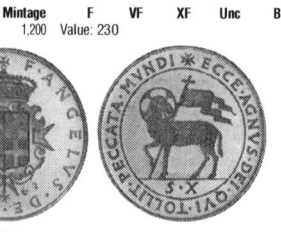

X# 8 10 SCUDI
8.0000 g., 0.9200 Gold .2366 oz. AGW **Ruler:** Angelo de Mojana di Cologna **Obv:** Crowned ornate arms **Rev:** Paschal Lamb standing left with banner **Note:** Prev. KM#M8.

Date	Mintage	F	VF	XF	Unc	BU
1962 Proof	200				Value: 500	
1963 Proof	600				Value: 235	

X# 12 10 SCUDI
8.0000 g., 0.9000 Gold .2314 oz. AGW **Ruler:** Angelo de Mojana di Cologna **Obv:** Bust 3/4 left **Rev:** Paschal Lamb standing left with banner **Rev. Legend:** ✠ ECCE • AGNVS • DEI • QVI • TOLLIT • PECCATA • MVNOI **Note:** Prev. KM#M12.

Date	Mintage	F	VF	XF	Unc	BU
1964 Proof	1,000				Value: 220	

X# 16 10 SCUDI
8.0000 g., 0.9000 Gold .2314 oz. AGW **Ruler:** Angelo de Mojana di Cologna **Note:** Prev. KM#M16.

Date	Mintage	F	VF	XF	Unc	BU
1965 Proof	1,000				Value: 220	
1966 Proof	600				Value: 235	

X# 22 10 SCUDI
8.0000 g., 0.9000 Gold .2314 oz. AGW **Ruler:** Angelo de Mojana di Cologna **Obv:** Bust left **Rev:** Crowned ornate arms **Note:** Prev. KM#M22.

Date	Mintage	F	VF	XF	Unc	BU
1967 Proof	1,000				Value: 220	

X# 28 10 SCUDI
8.0000 g., 0.9000 Gold .2314 oz. AGW **Ruler:** Angelo de Mojana di Cologna **Obv:** Bust right **Rev:** Crowned ornate shields **Note:** Prev. KM#M28.

Date	Mintage	F	VF	XF	Unc	BU
1968 Proof	1,000				Value: 220	

X# 34 10 SCUDI
8.0000 g., 0.9000 Gold .2314 oz. AGW **Ruler:** Angelo de Mojana di Cologna **Obv:** Bust left **Rev:** St. John the Baptist giving banner to kneeling Grand Master **Rev. Legend:** SVB • HOC • SIGNO • MILITAMVS **Note:** Prev. KM#M34.

Date	Mintage	F	VF	XF	Unc	BU
1969 Proof	1,000				Value: 200	
1970 Proof	1,000				Value: 200	

X# 45 10 SCUDI
8.0000 g., 0.9000 Gold .2314 oz. AGW **Ruler:** Angelo de Mojana di Cologna **Obv:** Bust of Fr. A. de Mojana left **Rev:** Paschal Lamb with banner **Note:** Prev. KM#M45.

Date	Mintage	F	VF	XF	Unc	BU
1971 Proof	1,000				Value: 200	

X# 52 10 SCUDI
8.0000 g., 0.9000 Gold .2314 oz. AGW **Ruler:** Angelo de Mojana di Cologna **Obv:** Bust left **Rev:** St. John standing with banner, sheep lying at his feet **Rev. Legend:** NON • SVRREXIT • MAIOR

Date	Mintage	F	VF	XF	Unc	BU
1972 Proof	1,000				Value: 200	

X# 55 10 SCUDI
8.0000 g., 0.9000 Gold .2314 oz. AGW **Ruler:** Angelo de Mojana di Cologna **Obv:** Bust left **Rev:** Paschal Lamb standing left with banner on globe **Rev. Legend:** ECCA • AGNVS • DEI • QVI • TOLLIT • PECCATA • MVNDI **Note:** Prev. KM#M55.

Date	Mintage	F	VF	XF	Unc	BU
1973 Proof	1,000				Value: 220	

X# 61 10 SCUDI
8.0000 g., 0.9000 Gold .2314 oz. AGW **Ruler:** Angelo de Mojana di Cologna **Obv:** Bust left **Rev:** Crowned ornate arms **Note:** Prev. KM#M61.

Date	Mintage	F	VF	XF	Unc	BU
1975 Proof	1,000				Value: 220	
1976 Proof	1,000				Value: 220	

X# 69 10 SCUDI
8.0000 g., 0.9000 Gold .2314 oz. AGW, 25 mm. **Ruler:** Angelo de Mojana di Cologna **Obv:** Bust left **Rev:** St. John the Baptist baptising a person **Note:** Prev. KM#M69.

Date	Mintage	F	VF	XF	Unc	BU
1977 Proof	1,000				Value: 220	
1978 Proof	1,000				Value: 220	

X# 79 10 SCUDI
8.0000 g., 0.9000 Gold .2314 oz. AGW, 25 mm. **Ruler:** Angelo de Mojana di Cologna **Obv:** Bust right **Rev:** Palace **Note:** Prev. KM#M79.

Date	Mintage	F	VF	XF	Unc	BU
1979 Proof	1,000				Value: 220	

X# 84 10 SCUDI
8.0000 g., 0.9000 Gold .2314 oz. AGW, 25 mm. **Ruler:** Angelo de Mojana di Cologna **Obv:** Bust right **Rev:** Maltese cross above clasped hands **Note:** Prev. KM#M84.

Date	Mintage	F	VF	XF	Unc	BU
1980 Proof	600				Value: 300	

X# 89 10 SCUDI
8.0000 g., 0.9000 Gold .2314 oz. AGW, 25 mm. **Ruler:** Angelo de Mojana di Cologna **Series:** World Food Day **Obv:** Bust left **Rev:** Basket of corn ears **Note:** Prev. KM#M89.

Date	Mintage	F	VF	XF	Unc	BU
1981 Proof	1,000				Value: 275	

X# 95 10 SCUDI
8.0000 g., 0.9000 Gold .2314 oz. AGW, 25 mm. **Ruler:** Angelo de Mojana di Cologna **Subject:** 20th Anniversary of Fr. A. de Mojana **Obv:** Bust left **Rev:** Crowned ornate arms in Order chain **Note:** Prev. KM#M95.

Date	Mintage	F	VF	XF	Unc	BU
ND(1982) Proof	600				Value: 300	

MALTA, ORDER OF

X# 101 10 SCUDI
8.0000 g., 0.9000 Gold .2314 oz. AGW, 25 mm. **Ruler:** Angelo de Mojana di Cologna **Obv:** Bust left **Note:** Prev. KM#M101.
Date	Mintage	F	VF	XF	Unc	BU
1983 Proof	600	Value: 300				

X# A107 10 SCUDI
8.0000 g., 0.9000 Gold .2314 oz. AGW, 25 mm. **Ruler:** Angelo de Mojana di Cologna **Obv:** Bust left **Rev:** Altar of Chiesa di Santa Maria al Aventino **Note:** Prev. KM#M107.
Date	Mintage	F	VF	XF	Unc	BU
1984 Proof	600	Value: 300				

X# 112 10 SCUDI
8.0000 g., 0.9000 Gold .2314 oz. AGW, 25 mm. **Ruler:** Angelo de Mojana di Cologna **Obv:** Bust left **Rev:** Maltese cross above clasped hands **Note:** Prev. KM#M112.
Date	Mintage	F	VF	XF	Unc	BU
1985 Proof	600	Value: 300				

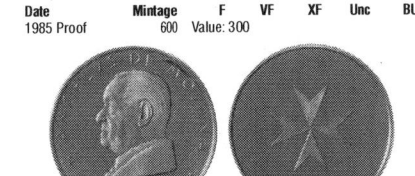

X# 117 10 SCUDI
8.0000 g., 0.9000 Gold .2314 oz. AGW **Ruler:** Angelo de Mojana di Cologna **Obv:** Bust left **Rev:** Large Maltese cross **Note:** Prev. KM#M117.
Date	Mintage	F	VF	XF	Unc	BU
1986 Proof	600	Value: 300				

X# 123 10 SCUDI
8.0000 g., 0.9000 Gold .2314 oz. AGW **Ruler:** Angelo de Mojana di Cologna **Subject:** 25th Anniversary of Fr. A. de Mojana **Obv:** Bust left **Rev:** Crowned ornate arms **Note:** Prev. KM#M123.
Date	Mintage	F	VF	XF	Unc	BU
1987 Proof	600	Value: 300				

X# 129 10 SCUDI
8.0000 g., 0.9000 Gold .2314 oz. AGW **Ruler:** Angelo de Mojana di Cologna **Obv:** Shoulder-length portrait of Fr. A. Mojana left **Rev:** Similar to KM#M112 **Note:** Prev. KM#M129.
Date	Mintage	F	VF	XF	Unc	BU
1988 Proof	600	Value: 300				

X# 135 10 SCUDI
8.0000 g., 0.9000 Gold .2314 oz. AGW **Ruler:** Giancarlo Pallavicini **Subject:** Interregnum **Obv:** Maltese cross with legend SVB. HOC ... **Rev:** St. John the Baptist **Note:** Prev. KM#M135.
Date	Mintage	F	VF	XF	Unc	BU
1988 Proof	Inc. above	Value: 300				

X# 141 10 SCUDI
8.0000 g., 0.9000 Gold .2314 oz. AGW **Ruler:** Giancarlo Pallavicini **Obv:** Fr. Andreas Bertie bust facing left **Rev:** Crowned and mantled arms **Note:** Prev. KM#M141.
Date	Mintage	F	VF	XF	Unc	BU
1988 Proof	500	Value: 300				

X# 147 10 SCUDI
8.0000 g., 0.9000 Gold .2314 oz. AGW, 25 mm. **Ruler:** Andreas Bertie **Obv:** Bust left **Rev:** Head of St. John the Baptist on a platter **Note:** Prev. KM#M147.
Date	Mintage	F	VF	XF	Unc	BU
1989 Proof	600	Value: 270				

X# 152 10 SCUDI
8.0000 g., 0.9000 Gold .2314 oz. AGW, 25 mm. **Ruler:** Andreas Bertie **Obv:** Bust left **Rev:** Crowned and mantled arms **Note:** Prev. KM#M152.
Date	Mintage	F	VF	XF	Unc	BU
1990 Proof	600	Value: 270				

X# 157 10 SCUDI
8.0000 g., 0.9000 Gold .2314 oz. AGW, 25 mm. **Ruler:** Andreas Bertie **Obv:** Bust left **Rev:** St. John the Baptist tending the sick **Note:** Prev. KM#M157.
Date	Mintage	F	VF	XF	Unc	BU
1991 Proof	600	Value: 270				

X# 163 10 SCUDI
8.0000 g., 0.9000 Gold .2314 oz. AGW **Ruler:** Andreas Bertie **Note:** Prev. KM#M163.
Date	Mintage	F	VF	XF	Unc	BU
1992 Proof	600	Value: 270				

X# 169 10 SCUDI
8.0000 g., 0.9000 Gold .2314 oz. AGW **Ruler:** Andreas Bertie **Note:** Prev. KM#M169.
Date	Mintage	F	VF	XF	Unc	BU
1993 Proof	600	Value: 270				

X# 174 10 SCUDI
8.0000 g., 0.9000 Gold .2314 oz. AGW, 25 mm. **Ruler:** Andreas Bertie **Obv:** Bust left **Rev:** Maltese cross above clasped hands **Note:** Prev. KM#M174.
Date	Mintage	F	VF	XF	Unc	BU
1994 Proof	600	Value: 270				

X# 180 10 SCUDI
8.0000 g., 0.9000 Gold .2314 oz. AGW, 25 mm. **Ruler:** Andreas Bertie **Obv:** Bust left **Rev:** Scene of providing medical assistance **Rev. Legend:** INFIRMIS SERVIRE **Note:** Prev. KM#M180.
Date	Mintage	F	VF	XF	Unc	BU
1995 Proof	600	Value: 270				
2002 Proof	—	Value: 270				

X# 185 10 SCUDI
8.0000 g., 0.9000 Gold 0.2315 oz. AGW, 25 mm. **Ruler:** Andreas Bertie **Obv:** Bust left **Rev:** St. John the Baptist aiding an ill man **Rev. Legend:** INFIRMIS SERVIRE FIRMISSIMUM REGNAR
Date	Mintage	F	VF	XF	Unc	BU
1996 Proof	—	Value: 270				
2003 Proof	—	Value: 270				

X# 190 10 SCUDI
8.0000 g., 0.9000 Gold 0.2315 oz. AGW, 25 mm. **Ruler:** Andreas Bertie **Obv:** Bust left **Rev:** Galley of Grand Master Emmanuel Pinto de Fonseca, 1741-1773
Date	Mintage	F	VF	XF	Unc	BU
1997 Proof	—	Value: 270				

X# 196 10 SCUDI
8.0000 g., 0.9000 Gold 0.2315 oz. AGW, 25 mm. **Ruler:** Andreas Bertie **Obv:** Bust left **Rev:** Crowned and mantled arms **Rev. Legend:** ELECTIONIS DECENNIUM SUAE IN DOMINO CELBRANS
Date	Mintage	F	VF	XF	Unc	BU
1998 Proof	—	Value: 270				

X# 202 10 SCUDI
8.0000 g., 0.9000 Gold 0.2315 oz. AGW, 25 mm. **Ruler:** Andreas Bertie **Subject:** 900th Anniversary of Founding of the Order **Obv:** Bust left **Rev. Legend:** NOVE SECOLI DI VITA DEL SOVRANO MILITARE ORDINE DI MALTA **Edge:** Reeded
Date	Mintage	F	VF	XF	Unc	BU
1999 Proof	—	Value: 270				

X# 208 10 SCUDI
8.0000 g., 0.9000 Gold 0.2315 oz. AGW, 25 mm. **Ruler:** Andreas Bertie **Obv:** Bust left **Rev:** Maltese cross
Date	Mintage	F	VF	XF	Unc	BU
2000 Proof	—	Value: 270				

X# 214 10 SCUDI
4.0000 g., 0.9000 Gold 0.1157 oz. AGW, 25 mm. **Ruler:** Andreas Bertie **Obv:** Bust left **Rev:** Maltese cross above clasped hands
Date	Mintage	F	VF	XF	Unc	BU
2001 Proof	—	Value: 250				

X# 224 10 SCUDI
8.0000 g., 0.9000 Gold 0.2315 oz. AGW **Ruler:** Andreas Bertie **Obv:** Bust left **Rev:** Altar in St. Marys Church
Date	Mintage	F	VF	XF	Unc	BU
2004 Proof	—	Value: 270				

X# 39 SOVRANO
8.0500 g., 0.9000 Gold .2329 oz. AGW **Ruler:** Angelo de Mojana di Cologna **Obv:** Bust left **Rev:** Crowned and mantled arms **Rev. Legend:** SOVRANO • MILITARE • ORDINE • DI • MALTA **Note:** Prev. KM#M39.
Date	Mintage	F	VF	XF	Unc	BU
1970	15,000	Value: 245				

HOSPITALLIER ORDER

FANTASY COINAGE

X# 306 2500 LIRAS
13.0000 g., 0.9990 Gold 0.4175 oz. AGW, 36.6 mm. **Subject:** 100th Birthday of Emperor Hirohito **Obv:** Crowned arms **Obv. Legend:** SOVRANO OSPEDALIERO ORDINE DI MALTA **Rev:** Hirohito's portrait **Edge:** Reeded **Note:** Mint: B. H. Mayer.
Date	Mintage	F	VF	XF	Unc	BU
2001 Proof	2,001	Value: 225				

PROOF SETS

KM#	Date	Mintage	Identification	Issue Price	Mkt Val
XPS1	1961 (4)	1,200	X#1-4	—	400
PS2	1961 (4)	—	KMPr1-4	—	535
XPS3	1962 (4)	200	X#5-8	—	1,250
XPS4	1963 (4)	600	X#5-8	—	575
XPS5	1963 (2)	1,000	X#5-6	—	800
XPS6	1964 (4)	1,000	X#9-12	—	400
XPS7	1965 (4)	1,000	X#13-16	—	400
XPS9	1966 (4)	600	X#13-16	—	500
XPS11	1967 (4)	1,000	X#19-22	62.50	400
XPS14	1968 (4)	1,000	X#24, 25, 27, 28	62.50	375
XPS20	1970 (4)	1,000	X#33.2, 34, 37, 38	75.00	375
XPS23	1971 (6)	1,000	X#40-45	78.00	420
XPS27	1972 (4)	1,000	X#44, 50-52	82.00	375
XPS30	1973 (6)	1,000	X#42-44, 48, 53, 55	110	420
XPS33	1974 (6)	1,000	X#44, 52, 56-59	170	420
XPS36	1975 (4)	1,000	X#44, 58, 60, 61	170	375
XPS39	1976 (4)	1,000	X#61, 64-66	180	375
XPS42	1977 (4)	1,000	X#66-69	—	375
XPS45	1978 (4)	1,000	X#66, 69, 72, 73	—	375
XPS48	1979 (3)	1,000	X#76-79	—	375
XPS51	1980 (4)	600	X#78, 82-84	—	575
XPS54	1981 (4)	1,000	X#78, 87-89	—	500
XPS57	1982 (4)	600	X#92-95	—	585
XPS60	1983 (4)	600	X#98-101	—	560
XPS63	1984 (4)	600	X#104, 106, 107, A107	—	550
XPS66	1985 (4)	600	X#107, 110-112	—	550
XPS69	1986 (4)	600	X#107, 115-117	200	550
XPS72	1987 (2)	600	X#122-123	—	475
XPS75	1988 (2)	600	X#128-129	—	485
XPS78	1988 (2)	—	X#134-135	—	485
XPS80	1988 (2)	—	X#130-131	—	47.50
XPS81	1988 (2)	500	X#140-141	—	500
XPS84	1989 (6)	—	X#142-147	—	500
XPS85	1989 (2)	—	X#146-147	—	375
XPS88	1990 (4)	—	X#146, 150-152	—	450
XPS91	1991 (4)	—	X#146, 155-157	—	450
XPS94	1992 (4)	—	X#160-163	—	450
XPS97	1993 (4)	—	X#166-169	—	450
XPS100	1994 (4)	—	X#172, 173, A174, 175	—	450
XPS103	1995 (4)	—	X#175, 178-180	—	450
XPS106	1996 (4)	—	X#175, 183-185	—	450
XPS109	1997 (4)	—	X#175, M188-M190	—	460
XPS112	1998 (4)	—	X#193-196	—	460
XPS115	1999 (4)	—	X#199-202	—	460
XPS118	2000 (4)	—	X#205-208	—	460
XPS121	2000 (4)	—	X#M205-M208	—	325
XPS124	2001 (4)	—	X#175, 212-214	—	460
XPS127	2002 (4)	—	X#175, 180, 183, 187	—	435
XPS130	2003 (4)	—	X#175, 185, 194, 220	—	460
XPS133	2004 (4)	—	X#175, 205, 223, 224	—	460
XPS136	2004 (6)	1,000	X#315-319 Including bronze medal	—	—
XPS137	2005 (6)	2,000	X#315-319 Including bronze medal	—	—

MARSHALL ISLANDS

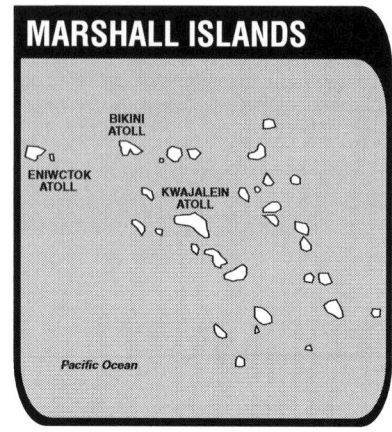

The Republic of the Marshall Islands, an archipelago which is one of the four island groups that make up what is commonly known as Micronesia, consists of 33 coral atolls comprised of over 1,150 islands or islets. It is located east of the Caroline Islands and west-northwest of the Gilbert Islands halfway between Hawaii and Australia. The Ratak chain to the east and the Ralik chain to the west comprise a total land area of 70 sq. mi. (181 sq. km.) with a population of 25,000 of which about 10 % includes Americans who work at the Kwajalein Missile Range. Majuro Atoll is the government and commercial center of the Republic.

Very little is known of the history of the islands before the 16th century. It is believed that many country's vessels visited the islands while searching for new trade routes to the East. In 1788, John Marshall, a British sea captain for whom the islands were named, explored them. The Islands have undergone successive domination by the Spanish, Germans, Japanese and Americans. It was the site of some of the fiercest fighting of the entire Pacific theater during World War II. At the conclusion of the war, the United States, under the direction of the United Nations administered the affairs of the Marshall Islands.

A constitutional government was formed on May 1, 1979 with Amata Kabua being elected as the head of the government. On October 1, 1986, the United States notified the United Nations that the Marshall Islands were to be recognized as a separate nation.

The USA dollar is the current monetary system. Recently, the coinage has had limited redemption policies enforced.

MINT MARKS
M - Medallic Art Co.
R - Roger Williams Mint, Rhode Island
S - Sunshine Mining Co. Mint, Idaho

REPUBLIC

NON-CIRCULATING COLLECTOR COINAGE

The USA dollar is the current monetary system. Recently, the coinage has had limited redemption policies enforced.

KM# 293 DOLLAR
1.5552 g., 0.9990 Gold .0499 oz. AGW **Obv:** Lion **Note:** Similar to 5 Dollars, KM#295.

Date	Mintage	F	VF	XF	Unc	BU
1996	—	—	—	—	45.00	—

KM# 294 2-1/2 DOLLARS
3.1103 g., 0.9990 Gold .0999 oz. AGW **Obv:** Lion **Note:** Similar to 5 Dollars, KM#295.

Date	Mintage	F	VF	XF	Unc	BU
1996	—	—	—	—	85.00	—

KM# 295 5 DOLLARS
7.7759 g., 0.9990 Gold .2497 oz. AGW **Obv:** State seal **Rev:** Lion

Date	Mintage	F	VF	XF	Unc	BU
1996	—	—	—	—	200	—

KM# 3 20 DOLLARS
3.1100 g., 0.9990 Gold .1000 oz. AGW **Rev:** Sun

Date	Mintage	F	VF	XF	Unc	BU
1986 Proof	Est. 5,000	Value: 60.00				

KM# 4 50 DOLLARS
7.7750 g., 0.9990 Gold .2500 oz. AGW **Rev:** Coconut

Date	Mintage	F	VF	XF	Unc	BU
1986 Proof	Est. 5,000	Value: 150				

KM# 17 100 DOLLARS
13.3300 g., 0.5830 Gold .2499 oz. AGW **Subject:** Greg Louganis - World's Greatest Diver **Obv:** State seal and legend **Rev:** Diver

Date	Mintage	F	VF	XF	Unc	BU
1988	Est. 280,000	—	—	—	285	—
1988 Proof	Est. 350,000	Value: 325				

KM# 5 200 DOLLARS
31.1030 g., 0.9990 Gold 1.0000 oz. AGW **Rev:** Stick chart

Date	Mintage	F	VF	XF	Unc	BU
1986 Proof	Est. 5,000	Value: 600				

PROOF SETS

KM#	Date	Mintage Identification	Issue Price	Mkt Val
PS1	1986 (3)	5,000 KM#3-5	1,095	665
PS4	1988 (4)	— KM#17, 20-22	—	700

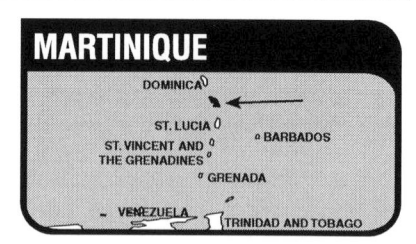

MARTINIQUE

The French Overseas Department of Martinique, located in the Lesser Antilles of the West Indies between Dominica and Saint Lucia, has an area of 425 sq. mi.(1,100 sq. km.) and a population of 290,000. Capital: Fort-de-France. Agriculture and tourism are the major sources of income. Bananas, sugar, and rum are exported.

Christopher Columbus discovered Martinique, probably on June 15, 1502. France took possession on June 25, 1635, and has maintained possession since that time except for three short periods of British occupation during the Napoleonic Wars. A French department since 1946, Martinique voted a reaffirmation of that status in 1958, remaining within the new French Community. Martinique was the birthplace of Napoleon's Empress Josephine, and the site of the eruption of Mt. Pelee in 1902 that claimed 40,000 lives.

The official currency of Martinique is the French franc. The 1897-1922 coinage of the Colony of Martinique is now obsolete.

RULERS
British, 1793-1801
French, 1802-1809

MONETARY SYSTEM
15 Sols = 1 Escalin
20 Sols = 1 Livre
66 Livres = 4 Escudos = 6400 Reis

FRENCH TERRITORY

ESSAIS

KM# E7 20 EURO
7.8000 g., 0.9990 Gold 0.2505 oz. AGW, 27 mm. **Obv:** Shield to left of inscription and date **Rev:** Egret and value **Edge:** Reeded

Date	Mintage	F	VF	XF	Unc	BU
2004 Proof	300	Value: 350				

FRENCH COLONY

COUNTERMARKED COINAGE
1802-1809

6400 Reis = 22 Livres

KM# 31 20 LIVRES
Gold **Countermark:** 20 above eagle **Obv:** Conjoined busts right **Rev:** Crowned ornate shield **Note:** Countermark on false Brazil 6400 Reis, type of KM#199.

CM Date	Host Date	Good	VG	F	VF	XF
ND(c. 1802)	ND(1777-86)	—	850	1,250	2,000	3,500

KM# 32 20 LIVRES
Gold **Countermark:** 20 above eagle **Obv:** Bust right **Rev:** Crowned ornate shield **Note:** Countermark on false or lightweight Brazil 6400 Reis, KM#172.2.

CM Date	Host Date	Good	VG	F	VF	XF
ND(c. 1802)	ND(1751-77)	—	1,000	1,500	2,250	4,500
ND(c. 1802)	ND(1778-79)	—	750	1,150	1,750	4,000

KM# 33 22 LIVRES
Gold **Countermark:** 22 above eagle **Obv:** Conjoined busts right **Rev:** Crowned ornate shield **Note:** Countermark on Brazil 6400 Reis, KM#199.1.

CM Date	Host Date	Good	VG	F	VF	XF
ND(c. 1802)	ND(1777-86)	—	1,000	1,500	2,000	3,500

KM# 34 22 LIVRES
Gold **Countermark:** 22 above eagle **Note:** Countermark on Brazil 6400 Reis, KM#218.2.

CM Date	Host Date	Good	VG	F	VF	XF
ND(c. 1802)	ND(1786-90)	—	1,000	1,500	2,000	3,500

KM# 35 22 LIVRES
Gold **Countermark:** 22 above eagle **Obv:** Bust right **Rev:** Crowned ornate shield **Note:** Countermark on Brazil 6400 Reis, KM#226.1.

CM Date	Host Date	Good	VG	F	VF	XF
ND(c. 1802)	ND(1789-1805)	—	950	1,400	1,850	3,250

KM# 36 22 LIVRES
Gold **Countermark:** 22 above eagle **Obv:** Head right **Rev:** Crowned ornate shield **Note:** Countermark on Portugal 4 Escudos, KM#240.

CM Date	Host Date	Good	VG	F	VF	XF
ND(c. 1802)	ND(1750-76)	—	1,250	2,000	3,000	5,000

KM# 37 22 LIVRES
Gold **Countermark:** 22 above eagle **Obv:** Head right **Rev:** Crowned ornate shield **Note:** Countermark on false Brazil 6400 Reis, type of KM#172.1.

CM Date	Host Date	Good	VG	F	VF	XF
ND(c. 1802)	ND(1751-77)	—	1,500	2,500	3,500	5,500

KM# 38 22 LIVRES
Gold **Countermark:** 22 above eagle **Note:** Countermark on Portuguese 4000 Reis, KM#184.

CM Date	Host Date	Good	VG	F	VF	XF
ND(c. 1802)	ND(1707-22)	—	2,500	4,500	6,500	9,500

KM# 39 22 LIVRES
Gold **Countermark:** 22 above eagle **Obv:** Head right **Rev:** Crowned ornate shield **Note:** Countermark on Brazil 6400 Reis, KM#151.

CM Date	Host Date	Good	VG	F	VF	XF
ND(c. 1802)	ND(1735-50)	—	2,000	3,500	5,500	8,500

ESSAIS

X# E15 20 EURO
8.5300 g., 0.9167 Gold 0.2514 oz. AGW, 27.1 mm. **Series:** Euro **Obv:** Arms **Obv. Inscription:** MARTINIQUE **Rev:** Great Egret **Rev. Legend:** Protection de la Faune **Edge:** Plain

Date	Mintage	F	VF	XF	Unc	BU
2004 Proof	300	Value: 280				

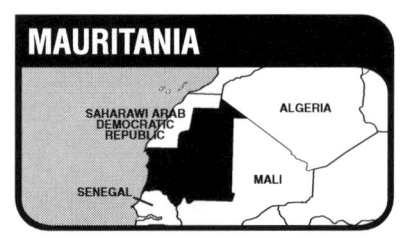

MAURITANIA

The Islamic Republic of Mauritania, located in northwest Africa bounded by Western Sahara, Mali, Algeria, Senegal and the Atlantic Ocean, has an area of 397,955 sq. mi.(1,030,700 sq. km.) and a population of 1.9 million. Capital: Nouakchott. The economy centers on herding, agriculture, fishing and mining. Iron ore, copper concentrates and fish products are exported.

The indigenous Negroid inhabitants were driven out of Mauritania by Berber invaders of the Islamic faith in the 11th century. The Berbers in turn were conquered by Arab invaders, the Beni Hassan, in the 16th century. Arab traders carried on a gainful trade in gum arabic, gold and slaves with Portuguese, Dutch, English and French traders until late in the 19th century when France took control of the area and made it a part of French West Africa, in 1920. Mauritania became a part of the French Union in 1946 and was made an autonomous republic within the new French Community in 1958, when the Islamic Republic of Mauritania was proclaimed. The republic became independent on November 28, 1960, and withdrew from the French Community in 1966.

On June 28, 1973, in a move designed to emphasize its non-alignment with France, Mauritania converted its currency from the old French-supported C.F.A. franc unit to a new unit called the Ouguiya.

MONETARY SYSTEM
5 Khoums = 1 Ouguiya

REPUBLIC

STANDARD COINAGE

KM# 7 500 OUGUIYA
26.0800 g., 0.9200 Gold .7714 oz. AGW **Subject:** 15th Anniversary of Independence **Obv:** Star and crescent flanked by palm trees below dates **Rev:** Value in square flanked by a camel head and fish with design above

Date	Mintage	F	VF	XF	Unc	BU
1975 (a)	1,800	—	—	—	575	625

MAURITIUS

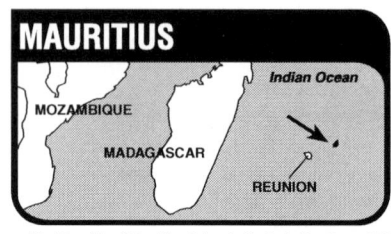

The Republic of Mauritius, is located in the Indian Ocean 500 miles (805 km.) east of Madagascar, has an area of 790 sq. mi. (1,860 sq. km.) and a population of 1 million. Capital: Port Louis. Sugar provides 90 percent of the export revenue.

Cartographic evidence indicates that Arabs and Malays arrived at Mauritius during the Middle Ages. Domingo Fernandez, a Portuguese navigator, visited the island in the early 16th century, but Portugal made no attempt at settlement. The Dutch took possession, and named the island, in 1598. Their colony failed to prosper and was abandoned in 1710. France claimed Mauritius in 1715 and developed a strong and prosperous colony that endured until the island was captured by the British, 1810, during the Napoleonic Wars. British possession was confirmed by the 1814 Treaty of Paris. Mauritius became independent on March 12, 1968. It is a member of the Commonwealth of Nations.

The first coins struck under British auspices for Mauritius were undated (1822) and bore French legends.

RULER
British, until 1968

MINT MARKS
H - Heaton, Birmingham
SA - Pretoria Mint

MONETARY SYSTEM
100 Cents = 1 Rupee

COMMONWEALTH
STANDARD COINAGE
100 Cents = 1 Rupee

KM# 39 200 RUPEES
15.5600 g., 0.9170 Gold .4587 oz. AGW **Subject:** Independence **Obv:** Crowned head right **Rev:** Couple in the forest

Date	Mintage	F	VF	XF	Unc	BU
1971	2,500	—	—	—	325	—
1971 Proof	750	Value: 400				

KM# 42 1000 RUPEES
33.4370 g., 0.9000 Gold .9676 oz. AGW **Series:** Conservation **Subject:** Mauritius flycatcher **Obv:** Young bust right **Rev:** Bird on nest in branch **Rev. Designer:** Christopher Ironside

Date	Mintage	F	VF	XF	Unc	BU
1975	1,966	—	—	—	675	—
1975 Proof	716	Value: 750				

KM# 45 1000 RUPEES
15.9800 g., 0.9170 Gold .4711 oz. AGW **Subject:** 10th Anniversary of Independence **Obv:** Bust right **Rev:** Building

Date	Mintage	F	VF	XF	Unc	BU
1978	1,000	—	—	—	335	—
1978 Proof	1,016	Value: 365				

KM# 47 1000 RUPEES
15.9800 g., 0.9170 Gold .4711 oz. AGW **Subject:** Wedding of Prince Charles and Lady Diana **Obv:** Young bust right **Rev:** Crowned monogram

Date	Mintage	F	VF	XF	Unc	BU
ND(1981)	28	—	—	—	600	—
ND(1981) Proof	22	Value: 950				

KM# 50 1000 RUPEES
15.9800 g., 0.9170 Gold .4711 oz. AGW **Series:** International Year of Disabled Persons **Obv:** Young bust right **Rev:** Disabled emblem within design

Date	Mintage	F	VF	XF	Unc	BU
1982	45	—	—	—	550	—
1982 Proof	48	Value: 925				

GOLD BULLION COINAGE

KM# 57 100 RUPEES
3.4120 g., 0.9170 Gold .1006 oz. AGW **Obv:** Bust 1/4 left **Rev:** Dodo bird

Date	Mintage	F	VF	XF	Unc	BU
1988	—	—	—	—	85.00	—

KM# 58 250 RUPEES
8.5130 g., 0.9170 Gold .25 oz. AGW **Obv:** Bust 1/4 left **Rev:** Dodo bird

Date	Mintage	F	VF	XF	Unc	BU
1988	—	—	—	—	165	—

KM# 59 500 RUPEES
17.0250 g., 0.9170 Gold .5 oz. AGW **Obv:** Bust 1/4 left **Rev:** Dodo bird

Date	Mintage	F	VF	XF	Unc	BU
1988	—	—	—	—	300	—

KM# 60 1000 RUPEES
34.0500 g., 0.9170 Gold 1 oz. AGW **Obv:** Bust 1/4 left **Rev:** Dodo bird

Date	Mintage	F	VF	XF	Unc	BU
1988	—	—	—	—	600	—

PIEFORTS

KM#	Date	Mintage	Identification	Issue Price	Mkt Val
P2	1981	—	1000 Rupees. Gold. KM47.	—	825
P4	1982	—	1000 Rupees. Gold. KM50.	—	1,850

MINT SETS

KM#	Date	Mintage	Identification	Issue Price	Mkt Val
MS2	1988 (4)	—	KM57-60	1,250	1,150

PROOF SETS

KM#	Date	Mintage	Identification	Issue Price	Mkt Val
PS2	1971 (9)	750	KM31-37, 38a, 39	200	645
PS5	1981 (2)	—	KM46a, 47	—	975

MAYOTTE
FRENCH TERRITORY
ESSAIS
Euro Coinage

X# E15 20 EURO
8.5300 g., 0.9167 Gold 0.2514 oz. AGW, 27.1 mm. **Obv:** Arms **Obv. Inscription:** Liberté/égalité/fraternité **Rev:** Two brown lemurs on branches **Rev. Legend:** PROTECTION DE LA FAUNE **Edge:** Plain

Date	Mintage	F	VF	XF	Unc	BU
2004 Proof	300	Value: 280				

MEXICO

The United States of Mexico, located immediately south of the United States has an area of 759,529 sq. mi. (1,967,183 sq. km.) and an estimated population of 100 million. Capital: Mexico City. The economy is based on agriculture, manufacturing and mining. Oil, cotton, silver, coffee, and shrimp are exported.

Mexico was the site of highly advanced Indian civilizations 1,500 years before conquistador Hernando Cortes conquered the wealthy Aztec empire of Montezuma, 1519-21, and founded a Spanish colony, which lasted for nearly 300 years. During the Spanish period, Mexico, then called New Spain, stretched from Guatemala to the present states of Wyoming and California, its present northern boundary having been established by the secession of Texas during 1836 and the war of 1846-48 with the United States.

Independence from Spain was declared by Father Miguel Hidalgo on Sept. 16, 1810, (Mexican Independence Day) and was achieved by General Agustin de Iturbide in 1821. Iturbide became emperor in 1822 but was deposed when a republic was established a year later. For more than fifty years following the birth of the republic, the political scene of Mexico was characterized by turmoil, which saw two emperors (including the unfortunate Maximilian), several dictators and an average of one new government every nine months passing swiftly from obscurity to oblivion. The land, social, economic and labor reforms promulgated by the Reform Constitution of Feb. 5, 1917 established the basis for sustained economic development and participative democracy that have made Mexico one of the most politically stable countries of modern Latin America.

SPANISH COLONY
MILLED COINAGE

100 Centavos = 1 Peso

KM# 112 1/2 ESCUDO
1.6917 g., 0.8750 Gold .0476 oz. AGW **Ruler:** Ferdinand VII **Obv:** Laureate head right **Obv. Legend:** FERD. VII. D. G. HISP. ET IND **Rev:** Crowned oval shield **Note:** Mint mark Mo.

Date	Mintage	VG	F	VF	XF	Unc
1814 JJ	—	100	150	225	375	525
1815/4 JJ	—	150	200	250	400	875
1815 JJ	—	150	200	250	400	—
1816 JJ	—	100	150	225	375	—
1817 JJ	—	150	200	250	400	—
1818 JJ	—	150	200	250	400	—
1819 JJ	—	150	200	250	400	—
1820 JJ	—	200	300	400	550	—

KM# 120 ESCUDO
3.3834 g., 0.8750 Gold .0952 oz. AGW **Obv:** Armored bust right **Obv. Legend:** CAROL • IIII • D • G • ... **Rev:** Crowned shield in order chain, initial letters and mint mark upright **Rev. Legend:** FELIX • A • D • ... **Note:** Mint mark Mo.

Date	Mintage	VG	F	VF	XF	Unc
1801 FM	—	125	165	235	345	—
1801 FT	—	125	165	235	345	650
1802 FT	—	125	165	235	345	—
1803 FT	—	125	165	235	345	—
1804/3 TH	—	125	165	235	345	750
1804 TH	—	125	165	235	345	—
1805 TH	—	125	165	235	345	—
1806/5 TH	—	125	165	235	345	—
1806 TH	—	125	165	235	345	—
1807 TH	—	125	165	235	345	—
1808 TH	—	125	165	235	345	—

KM# 121 ESCUDO
3.3834 g., 0.8750 Gold .0952 oz. AGW **Ruler:** Ferdinand VII **Obv:** Armored bust right **Obv. Legend:** FERDIN.VII... **Rev:** Crowned shield divides designed wreath **Rev. Legend:** FELIX. A. D, initial letters and mint mark upright **Note:** Mint mark Mo.

Date	Mintage	VG	F	VF	XF	Unc
1809 HJ/TH	—	125	165	235	400	—
1809 HJ	—	125	165	235	400	1,150
1811/0 HJ	—	125	165	235	400	—
1812 HJ	—	150	250	300	500	—

KM# 122 ESCUDO
3.3834 g., 0.8750 Gold .0952 oz. AGW **Ruler:** Ferdinand VII **Obv:** Laureate head right **Obv. Legend:** FERDIN. VII. D. G... **Rev:** Crowned shield divides designed wreath **Rev. Legend:** FELIX. A. D, initial letters and mint mark upright **Note:** Mint mark Mo.

Date	Mintage	VG	F	VF	XF	Unc
1814 HJ	—	150	250	300	500	—
1815 HJ	—	150	250	300	500	—
1815 JJ	—	150	250	300	500	—
1816 JJ	—	175	275	325	550	—
1817 JJ	—	150	250	300	500	—
1818 JJ	—	150	250	300	500	—
1819 JJ	—	150	250	300	500	—
1820 JJ	—	150	250	300	500	—

KM# 132 2 ESCUDOS
6.7668 g., 0.8750 Gold .1904 oz. AGW **Obv:** Armored bust of Charles IIII, right **Obv. Legend:** CAROL • IIII • D • G • ... **Rev:** Crowned shield flanked by 2 S in order chain **Rev. Legend:** IN • UTROQ • FELIX • AUSPICE • DEO; initials and mint mark upright **Note:** Mint mark Mo.

Date	Mintage	VG	F	VF	XF	Unc
1801 FT	—	125	225	350	575	—
1802 FT	—	125	225	350	575	—
1803 FT	—	125	225	350	575	—
1804 TH	—	125	225	350	575	—
1805 TH	—	125	225	350	575	—
1806/5 TH	—	125	225	350	575	—
1807 TH	—	125	225	350	575	—
1808 TH	—	125	225	350	575	1,500

KM# 134 2 ESCUDOS
6.7668 g., 0.8750 Gold .1904 oz. AGW **Ruler:** Ferdinand VII **Obv:** Laureate head right **Obv. Legend:** FERDIN. VII. D. G... **Rev:** Crowned shield divides designed wreath **Rev. Legend:** IN. UTROQ. FELIX. AUSPICE. DEO; initials and mint mark upright **Note:** Mint mark Mo.

Date	Mintage	VG	F	VF	XF	Unc
1814Mo HJ	—	250	425	700	1,150	—
1815 JJ	—	250	425	700	1,150	—
1816 JJ	—	250	425	700	1,150	—
1817 JJ	—	250	425	700	1,150	—
1818 JJ	—	250	425	700	1,150	3,750
1819 JJ	—	250	425	700	1,150	—
1820 JJ	—	250	425	700	1,150	—
1821 JJ	—	250	425	700	1,150	—

KM# 144 4 ESCUDOS
13.5337 g., 0.8750 Gold .3807 oz. AGW **Obv:** Armored bust of Charles IIII, right **Obv. Legend:** CAROL • IIII • D • G • ... **Rev:** Crowned shield flanked by 4 S in order chain **Rev. Legend:** IN • UTROQ • FELIX • AUSPICE • DEO; initials and mint mark upright **Note:** Mint mark Mo.

Date	Mintage	VG	F	VF	XF	Unc
1801 FM	—	300	500	750	1,500	—
1801 FT	—	300	500	750	1,500	—
1802 FT	—	350	600	850	1,650	—
1803 FT	—	300	500	750	1,500	—
1804/3 TH	—	300	500	750	1,500	—
1804 TH	—	300	500	750	1,500	—
1805 TH	—	300	500	750	1,500	—
1806/5 TH	—	300	500	750	1,500	—

494   MEXICO

Date	Mintage	VG	F	VF	XF	Unc
1807 TH	—	350	600	850	1,650	—
1808/0 TH	—	300	500	750	1,500	—
1808 TH	—	300	500	750	1,500	—

KM# 145 4 ESCUDOS
13.5337 g., 0.8750 Gold .3807 oz. AGW **Ruler:** Ferdinand VII **Obv:** Armored bust right **Obv. Legend:** FERDIN. VII D. G... **Rev:** Crowned shield divides designed wreath **Rev. Legend:** IN. UTROQ. FELIX. AUSPICE. DEO; initials and mint mark upright **Note:** Mint mark Mo.

Date	Mintage	VG	F	VF	XF	Unc
1810 HJ	—	350	500	900	1,850	—
1811 HJ	—	350	500	900	1,850	—
1812 HJ	—	350	500	900	1,850	—

KM# 146 4 ESCUDOS
13.5337 g., 0.8750 Gold .3807 oz. AGW **Ruler:** Ferdinand VII **Obv:** Laureate head right **Obv. Legend:** FERDIN. VII D. G... **Rev:** Crowned shield divides designed wreath **Rev. Legend:** IN. UTROQ. FELIX. AUSPICE. DEO; initials and mint mark upright **Note:** Mint mark Mo.

Date	Mintage	VG	F	VF	XF	Unc
1814 HJ	—	400	700	1,150	2,500	—
1815 HJ	—	400	700	1,150	2,500	—
1815 JJ	—	400	700	1,150	2,500	—
1816 JJ	—	400	700	1,150	2,500	—
1817 JJ	—	400	700	1,150	2,500	—
1818 JJ	—	400	700	1,150	2,500	—
1819 JJ	—	400	700	1,150	2,500	—
1820 JJ	—	400	700	1,150	2,500	—

KM# 159 8 ESCUDOS
27.0674 g., 0.8750 Gold .7615 oz. AGW **Obv:** Armored bust right **Obv. Legend:** CAROL • IIII • D • G • ... **Rev:** Crowned shield flanked by 8 S in order chain **Rev. Legend:** IN • UTROQ • ... **Note:** Mint mark Mo.

Date	Mintage	VG	F	VF	XF	Unc
1801/0 FT	—	475	550	750	1,150	—
1801 FM	—	450	500	650	1,000	—
1801 FT	—	450	500	650	1,000	—
1802 FT	—	450	500	650	1,000	—
1803 FT	—	450	550	650	1,000	—
1804/3 TH	—	475	550	750	1,150	—
1804 TH	—	450	500	650	1,000	3,500
1805 TH	—	450	500	650	1,000	—
1806 TH	—	450	500	650	1,000	3,500
1807/6 TH	—	475	550	750	1,150	—
1807 TH Mo over inverted Mo	—	475	550	750	1,150	—
1808/7 TH	—	450	500	650	1,250	—
1807 TH	—	500	650	850	1,000	—
1808 TH	—	500	650	850	1,250	—

KM# 160 8 ESCUDOS
27.0674 g., 0.8750 Gold .7615 oz. AGW **Ruler:** Ferdinand VII **Obv:** Armored bust right **Obv. Legend:** FERDIN. VII. D. G... **Rev:** Crowned shield divides designed wreath **Rev. Legend:** IN UTROQ. FELIX **Note:** Mint mark Mo.

Date	Mintage	VG	F	VF	XF	Unc
1808 TH	—	475	550	775	1,250	—
1809 HJ	—	475	550	775	1,350	—
1810 HJ	—	450	500	700	1,350	—
1811/0 HJ	—	475	500	800	1,350	—
1811 HJ H/T	—	475	500	800	1,350	—
1811 HJ	—	475	500	800	1,350	—
1811 JJ	—	450	500	700	1,200	—
1812 JJ	—	450	500	700	1,200	—

KM# 161 8 ESCUDOS
27.0674 g., 0.8750 Gold .7615 oz. AGW **Ruler:** Ferdinand VII **Obv:** Laureate head right **Obv. Legend:** FERDIN. VII. D. G... **Rev:** Crowned shield divides designed wreath **Rev. Legend:** IN UTROQ. FELIX **Note:** Mint mark Mo.

Date	Mintage	VG	F	VF	XF	Unc
1814 JJ	—	450	500	650	1,000	—
1815/4 JJ	—	475	550	750	1,150	—
1815/4 HJ	—	475	550	750	1,150	—
1815 JJ	—	450	500	650	1,000	—
1815 HJ	—	450	500	650	1,000	—
1816 JJ	—	450	500	650	1,000	—
1817 JJ	—	475	550	700	1,150	—
1818/7 JJ	—	450	500	675	1,100	—
1818 JJ	—	450	500	675	1,100	—
1819 JJ	—	450	500	675	1,100	—
1820 JJ	—	450	500	675	1,100	—
1821 JJ	—	475	550	750	1,300	—

EMPIRE OF ITURBIDE

RULER
Augustin I Iturbide, 1822-1823

MINT MARK
Mo - Mexico City

ASSAYERS' INITIALS
JA - Jose Garcia Ansaldo, 1812-1833
JM - Joaquin Davila Madrid, 1809-1833

MILLED COINAGE

100 Centavos = 1 Peso

KM# 312 4 SCUDOS
13.5334 g., 0.8750 Gold **Ruler:** Augustin I Iturbide **Obv:** Head right **Obv. Legend:** AUGUSTINUS DEI... **Rev:** Crowned eagle within ornate shield **Rev. Legend:** CONSTITUT.4.S.I.M...

Date	Mintage	F	VF	XF	Unc	BU
1823Mo JM	—	1,000	1,850	3,750	7,000	—

KM# 313.1 8 SCUDOS
27.0674 g., 0.8750 Gold **Ruler:** Augustin I Iturbide **Obv:** Head right **Obv. Legend:** AUGUSTINUS . DEI... **Rev:** Crowned eagle **Rev. Legend:** CONSTITUT.8.S.I.M...

Date	Mintage	F	VF	XF	Unc	BU
1822Mo JM	—	1,200	2,000	4,000	—	—

Note: American Numismatic Rarities Eliasberg sale 4-05, MS-62 realized $20,700. Superior Casterline sale 5-89 choice AU realized $11,000

KM# 313.2 8 SCUDOS
0.8750 Gold **Ruler:** Augustin I Iturbide **Obv:** Head right, error in legend **Obv. Legend:** AUGSTINUS . DEI... **Rev:** Crowned eagle **Rev. Legend:** CONSTITUT.8.S.I.M...

Date	Mintage	F	VF	XF	Unc	BU
1822Mo JM	—	1,250	2,250	4,500	—	—

KM# 314 8 SCUDOS
0.8750 Gold **Ruler:** Augustin I Iturbide **Obv:** Head right **Obv. Legend:** AUGUSTINUS DEI... **Rev:** Crowned eagle within ornate shield **Rev. Legend:** CONSTITUT.8.S.I.M...

Date	Mintage	F	VF	XF	Unc	BU
1823Mo JM	—	1,000	1,800	3,500	6,500	—

MEXICO

REPUBLIC
First

MINT MARKS
A, AS - Alamos
CE - Real de Catorce
CA, CH - Chihuahua
C, Cn, Gn(error) - Culiacan
D, Do - Durango
EoMo - Estado de Mexico
Ga - Guadalajara
GC - Guadalupe y Calvo
G, Go - Guanajuato
H, Ho - Hermosillo
M, Mo - Mexico City
O, OA - Oaxaca
SLP, PI, P, I/P - San Luis Potosi
Z, Zs – Zacatecas

ASSAYERS' INITIALS

ALAMOS MINT

PG	1862-68	Pascual Gaxiola
DL, L	1866-79	Domingo Larraguibel
AM	1872-74	Antonio Moreno
ML, L	1878-95	Manuel Larraguibel

REAL DE CATORCE MINT

ML	1863	Mariano Cristobal Ramirez

CHIHUAHUA MINT

MR	1831-34	Mariano Cristobal Ramirez
AM	1833-39	Jose Antonio Mucharraz
MJ	1832	Jose Mariano Jimenez
RG	1839-56	Rodrigo Garcia
JC	1856-65	Joaquin Campa
BA	1858	Bruno Arriada
FP	1866	Francisco Potts
JC	1866-1868	Jose Maria Gomez del Campo
MM, M	1868-95	Manuel Merino
AV	1873-80	Antonio Valero
EA	1877	Eduardo Avila
JM	1877	Jacobo Mucharraz
GR	1877	Guadalupe Rocha
MG	1880-82	Manuel Gameros

CULIACAN MINT

CE	1846-70	Clemente Espinosa de los Monteros
C	1870	???
PV	1860-61	Pablo Viruega
MP, P	1871-76	Manuel Onofre Parodi
GP	1876	Celso Gaxiola & Manuel Onofre Parodi
CG, G	1876-78	Celso Gaxiola
JD, D	1878-82	Juan Dominguez
AM, M	1882-1899	Antonio Moreno
F	1870	Fernando Ferrari
JQ, Q	1899-1903	Jesus S. Quiroz

DURANGO MINT

RL	1825-1832	???
RM	1830-48	Ramon Mascarenas
OMC	1840	Octavio Martinez de Castro
CM	1848-76	Clemente Moron
JMR	1849-52	Jose Maria Ramirez
CP, P	1853-64, 1867-73	Carlos Leon de la Pena
LT	1864-65	???
JMP, P	1877	Carlos Miguel de la Palma
PE, E	1878	Pedro Espejo
TB, B	1878-80	Trinidad Barrera
JP	1880-94	J. Miguel Palma
MC, C,	1882-90	Manuel M. Canseco or Melchor Calderon
JB	1885	Jocobo Blanco
ND, D	1892-95	Norberto Dominguez

ESTADO DE MEXICO MINT

L	1828-30	Luis Valazquez de la Cadena
F	1828-30	Francisco Parodi

GUADALAJARA MINT

FS	1818-35	Francisco Suarez
JM	1830-32	???
JG	1836-39, 1842-67	Juan de Dios Guzman
MC	1839-46	Manuel Cueras
JM	1867-69	Jesus P. Manzano
IC, C	1869-77	Ignacio Canizo y Soto
MC	1874-75	Manuel Contreras
JA, A	1877-81	Julio Arancivia
FS, S	1880-82	Fernando Sayago
TB, B	1883-84	Trinidad Barrera
AH, H	1884-85	Antonio Hernandez y Prado
JS, S	1885-95	Jose S. Schiafino

GUADALUPE Y CALVO MINT

MP	1844-52	Manuel Onofre Parodi

GUANAJUATO MINT

JJ	1825-26	Jose Mariano Jimenez
MJ, MR, JM, PG, PJ, PF		???
PM	1841-48, 1853-61	Patrick Murphy
YF	1862-68	Yldefonso Flores
YE	1862-63	Ynocencio Espinoza
FR	1870-78	Faustino Ramirez
SB, RR		???
RS	1891-1900	Rosendo Sandoval

HERMOSILLO MINT

PP	1835-36	Pedro Peimbert
FM	1871-76	Florencio Monteverde
MP	1866	Manuel Onofre Parodi
PR	1866-75	Pablo Rubio
R	1874-75	Pablo Rubio
GR	1877	Guadalupe Rocha
AF, F	1876-77	Alejandro Fourcade
JA, A	1877-83	Jesus Acosta
FM, M	1883-86	Fernando Mendez
FG, G	1886-95	Fausto Gaxiola

MEXICO CITY MINT

Because of the great number of assayers for this mint (Mexico City is a much larger mint than any of the others) there is much confusion as to which initial stands for which assayer at any one time. Therefore we feel that it would be of no value to list the assayers.

OAXACA MINT

AE	1859-91	Agustin Endner
E	1889-90	Agustin Endner
FR	1861-64	Francisco de la Rosa
EN	1890	Eduardo Navarro Luna
N	1890	Eduardo Navarro Luna

POTOSI MINT

JS	1827-42	Juan Sanabria
AM	1838, 1843-49	Jose Antonio Mucharraz
PS	1842-43, 1848-49, 1857-61, 1867-70	Pompaso Sanabria
S	1869-70	Pomposo Sanabria
MC	1849-59	Mariano Catano
RO	1859-65	Romualdo Obregon
MH, H	1870-85	Manuel Herrera Razo
O	1870-73	Juan R. Ochoa
CA, G	1867-70	Carlos Aguirre Gomez
BE, E	1879-81	Blas Escontria
LC, C	1885-86	Luis Cuevas
MR, R	1886-93	Mariano Reyes

ZACATECAS MINT

A	1825-29	Adalco
Z	1825-26	Mariano Zaldivar
V	1824-31	Jose Mariano Vela
O	1829-67	Manuel Ochoa
M	1831-67	Manuel Miner
VL	1860-66	Vicente Larranaga
JS	1867-68, 1876-86	J.S. de Santa Ana
YH	1868-74	Ygnacio Hierro
JA	1874-76	Juan H. Acuna
FZ	18861905	Francisco de P. Zarate

DIE VARIETIES

Similar basic designs were utilized by all the Mexican mints, but many variations are noticeable, particularly in the eagle, cactus and sprays.

1835 Durango, 8 Escudos
Illustration enlarged.
A large winged eagle was portrayed on the earlier coinage of the new republic.

1849 Mexico City, 8 Escudos
Illustration enlarged.
The later eagle featured undersized wings.

1844 Durango, 8 Escudos
Illustration enlarged.
The early renditions of the hand held Liberty cap over open book were massive in the gold escudo series.

1864 Durango, 8 Escudos
Illustration enlarged.
A finer, more petite style was adopted later on in the gold escudo series.

PROFILE EAGLE COINAGE

The first coins of the Republic were of the distinctive Profile Eagle style, sometimes called the "Hooked Neck Eagle". They were struck first in Mexico City in 1823 in denominations of eight reales and eight escudos. In 1824, they were produced at the Durango and Guanajuato mints in addition to Mexico City. Denominations included the one half, one, two and eight reales. No gold escudos of this design were struck in 1824. In 1825, only the eight reales were struck briefly at the Guanajuato mint.

NOTE: For a more extensive examination of Profile Eagle Coinage, please refer to Hookneck - El Aguila de Perfil by Clyde Hubbard and David O Harrow.

496 MEXICO

Type I Obverse/Reverse

NOTE: The cap on the reverse of the curved tall Type I points to the "A" of LIBERTAD.

KM# 382.1 8 ESCUDOS
27.0700 g., 0.8750 Gold .7616 oz. AGW **Obv:** Profile eagle, snake's tail curved **Obv. Legend:** REPUBLICA MEXICANA **Rev:** Open book, hand holding stick with cap, cap points to "A" of LIBERTAD **Rev. Legend:** LIBERTAD EN...

Date	Mintage	F	VF	XF	Unc	BU
1823Mo JM	—	7,000	10,000	20,000	—	—

Note: American Numismatic Rarities Eliasberg sale 4-05, MS-61 realized $55,200.

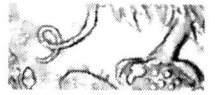

Type II Obverse/Reverse

NOTE: The cap on the reverse of the curved tall Type II points to the "T" of LIBERTAD.

KM# 382.2 8 ESCUDOS
27.0700 g., 0.8750 Gold .7616 oz. AGW **Obv:** Profile eagle, snake's tail looped **Obv. Legend:** REPUBLICA MEXICANA **Rev:** Open book, hand holding stick with cap, cap points to "T" of LIBERTAD **Rev. Legend:** LIBERTAD EN...

Date	Mintage	F	VF	XF	Unc	BU
1823Mo JM	—	6,000	9,000	18,000	—	—

Note: The quality of the strikes of Type I coins is almost always superior to that of the Type II; Details of the eagle feathers, cactus and lettering on the open book are better on most Type I coins but the Type II coins are scarcer; Type I coins outnumber Type II coins by about two to one

FEDERAL COINAGE

KM# 378 1/2 ESCUDO
1.6900 g., 0.8750 Gold .0475 oz. AGW **Obv:** Facing eagle, snake in beak **Obv. Legend:** REPUBLICA MEXICANA **Rev:** Hand holding cap on stick, open book **Rev. Legend:** LIBERTAD...

Date	Mintage	VG	F	VF	XF	Unc
1848C CE	—	40.00	50.00	75.00	150	300
1853C CE	—	40.00	50.00	75.00	150	—
1854C CE	—	40.00	50.00	75.00	150	—
Revised eagle						

Note: Dates 1854-1870 of this type display the revised eagle

1856C CE	—	50.00	100	150	250	—
1857C CE	—	40.00	50.00	75.00	150	—
1859C CE	—	40.00	50.00	75.00	150	—
1860C CE	—	40.00	50.00	75.00	150	—
1862C CE	—	40.00	50.00	75.00	125	—
1863C CE	—	40.00	50.00	75.00	125	300
1866C CE	—	40.00	50.00	75.00	125	—
1867C CE	—	40.00	50.00	75.00	125	250
1870C CE	—	75.00	150	275	450	—

KM# 378.1 1/2 ESCUDO
1.6900 g., 0.8750 Gold .0475 oz. AGW **Obv:** Facing eagle, snake in beak **Rev:** Hand holding cap on stick, open book

Date	Mintage	VG	F	VF	XF	Unc
1833Do RM/RL	—	40.00	50.00	75.00	150	—
1834/1Do RM	—	40.00	50.00	75.00	150	—
1834/3Do RM	—	40.00	50.00	75.00	150	—
1835/2Do RM	—	40.00	50.00	75.00	150	—
1835/3Do RM	—	40.00	50.00	75.00	150	—
1835/4Do RM	—	40.00	50.00	75.00	150	—
1836/5/4Do RM/L	—	45.00	60.00	100	175	450
1836/4Do RM	—	40.00	50.00	75.00	150	—
1837Do RM	—	40.00	50.00	75.00	150	—
1838Do RM	—	45.00	60.00	100	175	—
1843Do RM	—	45.00	60.00	100	175	—
1844/33Do RM	—	45.00	60.00	100	175	—
1844/33Do R./RL	—	65.00	125	275	450	—
1845Do CM	—	45.00	60.00	100	175	—
1846Do RM	—	45.00	60.00	100	175	—
1848Do RM	—	45.00	60.00	100	175	—
1850/33Do JMR	—	45.00	60.00	100	175	475
1851Do JMR	—	45.00	60.00	100	200	—
1852Do JMR	—	45.00	60.00	100	175	—
1853/33Do CP	—	75.00	150	300	500	—
1853Do CP	—	50.00	70.00	150	250	550
1854Do CP	—	40.00	50.00	75.00	150	—
1855Do CP	—	40.00	50.00	75.00	150	—
1859Do CP	—	40.00	50.00	75.00	150	—
1861Do CP	—	40.00	50.00	75.00	150	—
1862Do CP	—	40.00	50.00	75.00	150	—
1864Do LT	—	75.00	125	250	400	—

KM# 378.2 1/2 ESCUDO
1.6900 g., 0.8750 Gold .0475 oz. AGW **Obv:** Facing eagle, snake in beak **Obv. Legend:** REPUBLICA MEXICANA **Rev:** Hand holding cap on stick, open book **Rev. Legend:** LIBERTAD...

Date	Mintage	VG	F	VF	XF	Unc
1825Ga FS	—	45.00	60.00	100	175	—
1829Ga FS	—	45.00	60.00	100	175	—
1831Ga FS	—	45.00	60.00	100	175	—
1834Ga FS	—	45.00	60.00	100	175	—
1835Ga FS	—	45.00	60.00	100	175	—
1837Ga JG	—	45.00	60.00	100	175	—
1838Ga JG	—	45.00	60.00	100	175	—
1839Ga JG	—	—	—	—	—	—
1840Ga MC Unique						
1842Ga JG	—	—	—	—	—	—
1847Ga JG	—	45.00	60.00	100	175	—
1850Ga JG	—	45.00	65.00	125	225	—
1852Ga JG	—	40.00	65.00	75.00	150	—
1859Ga JG	—	45.00	60.00	100	175	—
1861Ga JG	—	40.00	55.00	75.00	150	—

KM# 378.3 1/2 ESCUDO
1.6900 g., 0.8750 Gold .0475 oz. AGW **Obv:** Facing eagle, snake in beak **Obv. Legend:** REPUBLICA MEXICANA **Rev:** Hand holding cap on stick, open book **Rev. Legend:** LIBERTAD...

Date	Mintage	VG	F	VF	XF	Unc
1846GC MP	—	50.00	75.00	100	175	—
1847GC MP	—	50.00	75.00	100	175	450
1848/7GC MP	—	50.00	75.00	100	200	650
1850GC MP	—	50.00	75.00	100	175	—
1851GC MP	—	50.00	75.00	100	175	—
Revised eagle						

KM# 378.4 1/2 ESCUDO
1.6900 g., 0.8750 Gold .0475 oz. AGW **Obv:** Facing eagle, snake in beak **Rev:** Hand holding cap on stick, open book

Date	Mintage	VG	F	VF	XF	Unc
1845Go PM	—	35.00	45.00	65.00	125	—
1849Go PF	—	35.00	50.00	90.00	175	750
1851/41Go PF	—	35.00	45.00	65.00	125	—
1851Go PF	—	35.00	45.00	65.00	125	—
1852Go PF	—	35.00	45.00	65.00	125	—
1852Go PF/FF	—	—	—	—	—	—
1853Go PF	—	35.00	45.00	65.00	125	—
1855Go PF	—	35.00	50.00	80.00	150	—
1857Go PF	—	35.00	45.00	65.00	125	—
1858/7Go PF	—	35.00	45.00	65.00	125	—
1859Go PF	—	35.00	45.00	65.00	125	—
1860Go PF	—	35.00	45.00	65.00	125	—
1861Go PF	—	35.00	45.00	65.00	125	—
1862/1Go YE	—	35.00	45.00	65.00	125	—
1863Go PF	—	35.00	50.00	80.00	150	—
1863Go YF	—	35.00	45.00	65.00	125	—

KM# 378.5 1/2 ESCUDO
1.6900 g., 0.8750 Gold .0475 oz. AGW **Obv:** Facing eagle, snake in beak **Obv. Legend:** REPUBLICA MEXICANA. **Rev:** Hand holding cap on stick, open book **Rev. Legend:** LIBERTAD...

Date	Mintage	VG	F	VF	XF	Unc
1825/1Mo JM	—	50.00	75.00	125	200	—
1825/4Mo JM	—	50.00	75.00	125	200	—
1825Mo JM	—	35.00	50.00	80.00	150	350
1827/6Mo JM	—	35.00	50.00	80.00	150	—
1827Mo JM	—	35.00	50.00	80.00	150	350
1829Mo JM	—	35.00	50.00	80.00	150	—
1831/0Mo JM	—	35.00	50.00	80.00	150	—
1831Mo JM	—	35.00	45.00	65.00	125	—
1832Mo	—	35.00	50.00	90.00	175	450
1833Mo MJ	—	35.00	50.00	90.00	175	450

Note: Olive and oak branches reversed

1834Mo ML	—	35.00	45.00	75.00	150	400
1835Mo ML	—	35.00	45.00	80.00	150	—
1838Mo ML	—	35.00	50.00	90.00	175	—
1839Mo ML	—	35.00	50.00	90.00	175	—
1840Mo ML	—	35.00	45.00	65.00	125	—
1841Mo ML	—	35.00	45.00	65.00	125	—
1842Mo ML	—	35.00	45.00	80.00	150	—
1842Mo MM	—	35.00	45.00	80.00	150	—
1843Mo MM	—	35.00	45.00	65.00	125	—
1844Mo MF	—	35.00	45.00	65.00	125	250
1845Mo MF	—	35.00	45.00	65.00	125	—
1846/5Mo MF	—	35.00	45.00	65.00	125	—
1846Mo MF	—	35.00	45.00	65.00	125	—
1848Mo GC	—	35.00	50.00	90.00	175	450
1850Mo GC	—	35.00	45.00	65.00	125	—
1851Mo GC	—	35.00	45.00	65.00	125	—
1852Mo GC	—	35.00	45.00	65.00	125	—
1853Mo GC	—	40.00	60.00	100	200	650
1854Mo GC	—	35.00	45.00	65.00	125	—
1855Mo GF	—	35.00	45.00	75.00	150	350
1856/4Mo GF	—	35.00	45.00	65.00	125	—
1857Mo GF	—	35.00	45.00	65.00	125	—
1858/7Mo FH/GF	—	35.00	50.00	75.00	150	—
1858Mo FH	—	35.00	45.00	65.00	125	—
1859Mo FH	—	35.00	45.00	65.00	125	—
1860/59Mo FH	—	35.00	45.00	65.00	125	250
1861Mo CH/FH	—	35.00	45.00	80.00	150	—
1862Mo CH	—	35.00	45.00	65.00	125	200
1863/57Mo CH/GF	—	35.00	45.00	65.00	125	250
1868/58Mo PH	—	35.00	45.00	80.00	150	—
1869/59Mo CH	—	35.00	45.00	80.00	150	—

KM# 378.6 1/2 ESCUDO
1.6900 g., 0.8750 Gold .0475 oz. AGW **Obv:** Facing eagle, snake in beak **Obv. Legend:** REPUBLICA MEXICANA. **Rev:** Hand holding cap on stick, open book **Rev. Legend:** LIBERTAD...

Date	Mintage	VG	F	VF	XF	Unc
1860Zs VL	—	40.00	50.00	75.00	150	—
1862/1Zs VL	—	40.00	50.00	75.00	150	—
1862Zs VL	—	35.00	45.00	65.00	125	—

KM# 379 ESCUDO
3.3800 g., 0.8750 Gold .0950 oz. AGW **Obv:** Facing eagle, snake in beak **Rev:** Hand holding cap on stick, open book

Date	Mintage	VG	F	VF	XF	Unc
1846C CE	—	75.00	100	200	350	—
1847C CE	—	60.00	75.00	125	175	—
1848C CE	—	60.00	75.00	125	175	700
1849/8C CE	—	65.00	100	150	225	—

MEXICO

Date	Mintage	VG	F	VF	XF	Unc
1850C CE	—	60.00	75.00	125	175	—
1851C CE	—	65.00	100	150	225	—
1853/1C CE	—	65.00	100	150	225	—
1854C CE	—	60.00	75.00	125	175	—
1856/5/4C CE	—	65.00	100	150	225	—
1856C CE	—	60.00	75.00	125	175	—
1857/1C CE	—	65.00	100	150	225	—
1857C CE	—	60.00	75.00	125	175	—
1861C PV	—	60.00	75.00	125	175	—
1862C CE	—	60.00	75.00	125	175	—
1863C CE	—	60.00	75.00	125	175	—
1866C CE	—	60.00	75.00	125	175	—
1870C CE	—	60.00	75.00	125	175	—

KM# 379.1 ESCUDO
3.3800 g., 0.8750 Gold .0950 oz. AGW **Obv:** Facing eagle, snake in beak **Obv. Legend:** REPUBLICA MEXICANA. **Rev:** Hand holding cap on stick, open book **Rev. Legend:** LIBERTAD...

Date	Mintage	VG	F	VF	XF	Unc
1832Do R.L.	—	—	—	—	—	—
1833/2Do RM/R.L.	—	75.00	125	200	300	—
1834Do RM	—	65.00	100	150	250	—
1835Do RM	—	—	—	—	—	—
1836Do RM/RL	—	65.00	100	150	250	—
1838Do RM	—	65.00	100	150	250	—
1846/38Do RM	—	75.00	125	200	300	—
1850Do RM	—	75.00	125	175	275	—
1851Do JMR	—	75.00	125	175	275	—
1851/31Do JMR	—	75.00	125	200	300	—
1851Do JMR	—	75.00	125	175	275	—
1853Do CP	—	75.00	125	175	275	—
1854/34Do CP	—	75.00	125	175	275	—
1854/44Do CP/RP	—	75.00	125	175	275	—
1855Do CP	—	75.00	125	175	275	—
1859Do CP	—	75.00	125	175	275	—
1861Do CP	—	75.00	125	175	275	—
1864Do LT/CP Rare	—	—	—	—	—	—

KM# 379.2 ESCUDO
3.3800 g., 0.8750 Gold .0950 oz. AGW **Obv:** Facing eagle, snake in beak **Obv. Legend:** REPUBLICA MEXICANA. **Rev:** Hand holding cap on stick, open book

Date	Mintage	VG	F	VF	XF	Unc
1825Ga FS	—	65.00	90.00	125	200	—
1826Ga FS	—	65.00	90.00	125	200	—
1829Ga FS	—	—	—	—	—	—
1831Ga FS	—	65.00	90.00	125	200	—
1834Ga FS	—	65.00	90.00	125	200	—
1835Ga JG	—	65.00	90.00	125	200	—
1842Ga JG/MC	—	65.00	90.00	125	200	—
1843Ga MC	—	65.00	90.00	125	200	—
1847Ga JG	—	65.00	90.00	125	200	—
1848/7Ga JG	—	65.00	90.00	125	200	—
1849Ga JG	—	65.00	90.00	125	200	—
1850/40Ga JG	—	70.00	125	225	325	—
1850Ga JG	—	65.00	90.00	125	200	—
1852/1Ga JG	—	65.00	90.00	125	200	900
1856Ga JG	—	65.00	90.00	125	200	—
1857Ga JG	—	65.00	90.00	125	200	—
1859/7Ga JG	—	65.00	90.00	125	200	—
1860/59Ga JG	—	70.00	100	175	275	—
1860Ga	—	65.00	90.00	125	200	—

KM# 379.3 ESCUDO
3.3800 g., 0.8750 Gold .0950 oz. AGW **Obv:** Facing eagle, snake in beak **Obv. Legend:** REPUBLICA MEXICANA. **Rev:** Hand holding cap on stick, open book

Date	Mintage	VG	F	VF	XF	Unc
1844GC MP	—	75.00	100	175	250	—
1845GC MP	—	75.00	100	175	250	—
1846GC MP	—	75.00	100	175	250	—
1847GC MP	—	75.00	100	175	250	—
1848GC MP	—	75.00	100	175	250	—
1849GC MP	—	75.00	100	175	250	—
1850GC MP	—	100	150	250	500	2,000
1851GC MP Revised eagle	—	75.00	100	175	250	—

KM# 379.4 ESCUDO
3.3800 g., 0.8750 Gold .0950 oz. AGW **Obv:** Facing eagle, snake in beak **Rev:** Hand holding cap on stick, open book

Date	Mintage	VG	F	VF	XF	Unc
1845Go PM	—	65.00	80.00	125	200	—
1849Go PF	—	65.00	80.00	125	200	—
1851Go PF	—	65.00	80.00	125	200	—
1853Go PF	—	65.00	80.00	125	200	—
1860Go PF	—	75.00	125	200	300	—
1862Go YE	—	65.00	80.00	125	200	600

KM# 379.5 ESCUDO
3.3800 g., 0.8750 Gold .0950 oz. AGW **Obv:** Facing eagle, snake in beak **Obv. Legend:** REPUBLICA MEXICANA. **Rev:** Hand holding cap on stick, open book

Date	Mintage	VG	F	VF	XF	Unc
1825Mo JM/FM	—	60.00	70.00	100	150	350
1825Mo JM	—	60.00	70.00	100	150	—
1827/6Mo JM	—	60.00	70.00	100	150	—
1827Mo JM	—	60.00	70.00	100	150	—
1830/29Mo JM	—	60.00	70.00	100	150	—
1831Mo JM	—	60.00	75.00	125	175	550
1832Mo JM	—	60.00	70.00	100	150	—
1833Mo MJ	—	60.00	70.00	100	150	—
1834Mo ML	—	60.00	75.00	125	175	—
1841Mo ML	—	60.00	75.00	125	175	—
1843Mo MM	—	60.00	75.00	125	175	875
1845Mo MF	—	60.00	70.00	100	150	—
1846/5Mo MF	—	60.00	70.00	100	150	—
1848Mo GC	—	60.00	75.00	125	175	—
1850Mo GC	—	60.00	70.00	100	150	—
1856/4Mo GF	—	60.00	70.00	100	150	—
1856/5Mo GF	—	60.00	70.00	100	150	—
1856Mo GF	—	60.00	70.00	100	150	—
1858Mo FH	—	60.00	75.00	125	175	—
1859Mo FH	—	60.00	75.00	125	175	750
1860Mo TH	—	60.00	75.00	125	175	—
1861Mo CH	—	60.00	75.00	125	175	1,000
1862Mo CH	—	60.00	75.00	125	175	—
1863Mo TH	—	60.00	70.00	100	150	—
1869Mo CH	—	60.00	75.00	125	175	650

KM# 379.6 ESCUDO
3.3800 g., 0.8750 Gold .0950 oz. AGW **Obv:** Facing eagle, snake in beak **Rev:** Hand holding cap on stick, open book **Note:** Struck at Zacatecas Mint, mint mark Zs.

Date	Mintage	VG	F	VF	XF	Unc
1853Zs OM	—	100	125	200	300	—
1860/59Zs VL V is inverted A	—	75.00	100	200	350	—
1860Zs VL	—	75.00	100	150	200	—
1862Zs VL	—	75.00	100	150	200	—

KM# 380 2 ESCUDOS
6.7700 g., 0.8750 Gold .1904 oz. AGW **Obv:** Facing eagle, snake in beak **Obv. Legend:** REPUBLICA MEXICANA. **Rev:** Hand holding cap on stick, open book

Date	Mintage	VG	F	VF	XF	Unc
1846C CE	—	125	160	225	325	—
1847C CE	—	125	160	225	325	—
1848C CE	—	125	160	225	325	—
1852C CE	—	125	160	225	325	—
1854C CE	—	125	175	250	375	—
1856/4C CE	—	125	175	250	375	—
1857C CE	—	125	160	225	325	—

KM# 380.1 2 ESCUDOS
6.7700 g., 0.8750 Gold .1904 oz. AGW **Obv:** Facing eagle, snake in beak **Obv. Legend:** REPUBLICA MEXICANA. **Rev:** Hand holding cap on stick, open book **Rev. Legend:** LIBERTAD...

Date	Mintage	VG	F	VF	XF	Unc
1833Do RM	—	300	450	700	1,200	—
1837/4Do RM	—	—	—	—	—	—
1837Do RM	—	—	—	—	—	—
1844Do RM	—	275	400	600	1,000	—

KM# 380.2 2 ESCUDOS
6.7700 g., 0.8750 Gold .1904 oz. AGW **Obv:** Facing eagle, snake in beak **Obv. Legend:** REPUBLICA MEXICANA. **Rev:** Hand holding cap on stick, open book **Rev. Legend:** LIBERTAD...

Date	Mintage	VG	F	VF	XF	Unc
1828EoMo LF	—	700	1,000	1,750	3,000	—

KM# 380.3 2 ESCUDOS
6.7700 g., 0.8750 Gold .1904 oz. AGW **Obv:** Facing eagle, snake in beak **Obv. Legend:** REPUBLICA MEXICANA. **Rev:** Hand holding cap on stick, open book **Rev. Legend:** LIBERTAD...

Date	Mintage	VG	F	VF	XF	Unc
1835Ga FS	—	125	160	225	325	—
1836/5Ga JG	—	145	200	400	500	—
1839/5Ga JG	—	—	—	—	—	—
1839Ga JG	—	125	150	200	285	—
1840Ga MC	—	125	150	200	285	—
1841Ga MC	—	125	165	250	400	—
1847/6Ga JG	—	125	160	225	300	—
1848/7Ga JG	—	125	160	225	300	—
1850/40Ga JG	—	125	150	200	285	—
1851Ga JG	—	125	150	200	285	—
1852Ga JG	—	125	160	225	325	—
1853Ga JG	—	125	150	200	285	—
1854/2Ga JG	—	—	—	—	—	—
1858Ga JG	—	125	150	200	285	—
1859/8Ga JG	—	125	160	225	300	—
1859Ga JG	—	125	160	225	300	—
1860/50Ga JG	—	125	160	225	300	—
1860Ga JG	—	125	160	225	300	750
1861/59Ga JG	—	125	150	200	285	—
1861/0Ga JG	—	125	150	200	285	—
1863/2Ga JG	—	125	160	225	300	800
1863/1Ga JG	—	125	150	200	285	—
1870Ga IC	—	125	150	200	285	—

KM# 380.4 2 ESCUDOS
6.7700 g., 0.8750 Gold .1904 oz. AGW **Obv:** Facing eagle, snake in beak **Rev:** Hand holding cap on stick, open book

Date	Mintage	VG	F	VF	XF	Unc
1844GC MP	—	250	450	1,000	2,000	—
1845GC MP	—	750	1,250	2,000	3,000	—
1846GC MP	—	750	1,250	2,000	3,000	—
1847GC MP	—	500	1,000	2,000	3,000	—
1848GC MP	—	150	200	400	600	—
1849GC MP	—	750	1,250	—	—	—
1850GC MP	—	250	450	1,000	2,000	—

KM# 380.5 2 ESCUDOS
6.7700 g., 0.8750 Gold .1904 oz. AGW **Obv:** Facing eagle, snake in beak **Rev:** Hand holding cap on stick, open book

Date	Mintage	VG	F	VF	XF	Unc
1845Go PM	—	125	160	250	400	—
1849Go PF	—	125	160	250	400	—
1853Go PF	—	150	300	650	1,000	—
1856Go PF	—	—	—	—	—	—
1859Go PF	—	150	300	650	1,000	—
1860/59Go PF	—	—	—	—	—	—
1860Go PF	—	125	160	250	400	—
1862Go YE	—	125	160	250	400	—

KM# 380.6 2 ESCUDOS
6.7700 g., 0.8750 Gold .1904 oz. AGW **Obv:** Facing eagle, snake in beak **Rev:** Hand holding cap on stick, open book

Date	Mintage	VG	F	VF	XF	Unc
1861Ho FM	—	500	1,000	1,500	2,200	—

498 MEXICO

KM# 380.7 2 ESCUDOS
6.7700 g., 0.8750 Gold .1904 oz. AGW **Obv:** Facing eagle, snake in beak **Obv. Legend:** REPUBLICA MEXICANA **Rev:** Hand holding cap on stick, open book **Rev. Legend:** LIBERTAD...

Date	Mintage	VG	F	VF	XF	Unc
1825Mo JM	—	125	150	200	285	—
1827/6Mo JM	—	125	150	200	285	—
1827Mo JM	—	125	150	200	285	—
1830/29Mo JM	—	125	150	200	285	—
1831Mo JM	—	125	150	200	285	—
1833Mo ML	—	125	150	200	285	—
1841Mo ML	—	125	150	200	285	—
1844Mo MF	—	125	150	200	285	—
1845Mo MF	—	125	150	200	285	—
1846Mo MF	—	140	200	400	600	—
1848Mo GC	—	125	150	200	285	—
1850Mo GC	—	125	150	200	285	—
1856/5Mo GF	—	125	150	200	285	—
1856Mo GF	—	125	150	200	285	—
1858Mo FH	—	125	150	200	285	—
1859Mo FH	—	125	150	200	285	—
1861Mo TH	—	125	150	200	285	—
1861Mo CH	—	125	150	200	300	—
1862Mo CH	—	125	150	200	300	—
1863Mo TH	—	125	150	200	300	750
1868Mo PH	—	125	150	200	300	—
1869Mo CH	—	125	150	200	300	—

KM# 380.8 2 ESCUDOS
6.7700 g., 0.8750 Gold .1904 oz. AGW **Obv:** Facing eagle, snake in beak **Obv. Legend:** REPUBLICA MEXICANA. **Rev:** Hand holding cap on stick, open book **Rev. Legend:** LA LIBERTAD...

Date	Mintage	VG	F	VF	XF	Unc
1860Zs VL	—	150	300	600	1,200	—
1862Zs VL	—	250	500	800	1,200	—
1864Zs MO	—	150	300	600	1,200	—

KM# 381 4 ESCUDOS
13.5400 g., 0.8750 Gold .3809 oz. AGW **Obv:** Facing eagle, snake in beak **Obv. Legend:** REPUBLICA MEXICANA. **Rev:** Hand holding cap on stick, open book **Rev. Legend:** LA LIBERTAD...

Date	Mintage	VG	F	VF	XF	Unc
1846C CE	—	1,200	1,700	—	—	—
1847C CE	—	400	650	850	1,500	—
1848C CE	—	600	900	1,250	2,000	—

KM# 381.1 4 ESCUDOS
13.5400 g., 0.8750 Gold .3809 oz. AGW **Obv:** Facing eagle, snake in beak **Obv. Legend:** REPUBLICA MEXICANA. **Rev:** Hand holding cap on stick, open book **Rev. Legend:** LA LIBERTAD....

Date	Mintage	VG	F	VF	XF	Unc
1832Do RM/LR Rare	—	—	—	—	—	—
1832Do RM	—	600	900	1,250	2,000	—
1833Do RM/RL Rare	—	—	—	—	—	—
1852Do JMR Rare	—	—	—	—	—	—

KM# 381.2 4 ESCUDOS
13.5400 g., 0.8750 Gold .3809 oz. AGW **Obv:** Facing eagle, snake in beak **Obv. Legend:** REPUBLICA MEXICANA. **Rev:** Hand holding cap on stick, open book **Rev. Legend:** LA LIBERTAD...

Date	Mintage	VG	F	VF	XF	Unc
1844Ga MC	—	500	750	1,000	1,600	—
1844Ga JG	—	400	650	850	1,350	—

KM# 381.3 4 ESCUDOS
13.5400 g., 0.8750 Gold .3809 oz. AGW **Obv:** Facing eagle, snake in beak **Obv. Legend:** REPUBLICA MEXICANA **Rev:** Hand holding cap on stick, open book **Rev. Legend:** LA LIBERTAD...

Date	Mintage	VG	F	VF	XF	Unc
1844GC MP	—	400	650	850	1,350	—
1845GC MP	—	350	500	700	1,000	—
1846GC MP	—	400	650	850	1,350	—
1848GC MP	—	400	650	850	1,350	—
1850GC MP	—	500	750	1,000	1,600	—

KM# 381.4 4 ESCUDOS
13.5400 g., 0.8750 Gold .3809 oz. AGW **Obv:** Facing eagle, snake in beak **Obv. Legend:** REPUBLICA MEXICANA. **Rev:** Hand holding cap on stick, open book **Rev. Legend:** LA LIBERTAD...

Date	Mintage	VG	F	VF	XF	Unc
1829/8Go MJ	—	250	300	450	850	—
1829Go JM	—	250	300	450	850	—
1829Go MJ	—	250	300	450	850	—
1831Go MJ	—	250	300	450	850	—
1832Go MJ	—	250	300	450	850	—
1833Go MJ	—	250	325	500	900	—
1834Go PJ	—	265	450	650	1,000	—
1835Go PJ	—	265	450	650	1,000	—
1836Go PJ	—	250	325	500	900	—
1837Go PJ	—	250	325	500	900	2,750
1838Go PJ	—	250	325	500	900	—
1839Go PJ	—	265	450	650	1,000	—
1840Go PJ	—	250	325	550	1,000	—
1841Go PJ	—	265	450	650	1,000	—
1845Go PM	—	250	325	500	900	—
1847/5Go YE	—	265	450	650	1,000	—
1847Go PM	—	265	450	650	1,000	—
1849Go PF	—	265	450	650	1,000	—
1851Go PF	—	265	450	650	1,000	—
1852Go PF	—	250	325	500	900	—
1855Go PF	—	250	325	500	900	—
1857/5Go PF	—	250	325	500	900	—
1858/7Go PF	—	250	325	500	900	—
1858Go PF	—	250	325	500	900	—
1859/7Go PF	—	265	450	650	1,000	—
1860Go PF	—	275	475	750	1,200	—
1862Go YE	—	250	325	500	900	—
1863Go YF	—	250	325	500	900	—

KM# 381.6 4 ESCUDOS
13.5400 g., 0.8750 Gold .3809 oz. AGW **Obv:** Facing eagle, snake in beak **Obv. Legend:** REPUBLICA MEXICANA. **Rev:** Hand holding cap on stick, open book **Rev. Legend:** LA LIBERTAD...

Date	Mintage	VG	F	VF	XF	Unc
1825Mo JM	—	250	325	525	950	—
1827/6Mo JM	—	250	325	500	900	—
1829Mo JM	—	250	350	650	1,000	—
1831Mo JM	—	250	350	650	1,000	—
1832Mo JM	—	275	475	750	1,200	—
1844Mo MF	—	250	350	650	1,000	—
1850Mo GC	—	250	350	650	1,000	—
1856Mo GF	—	250	325	500	900	—
1857/6Mo GF	—	250	325	500	900	—
1857Mo GF	—	250	325	500	900	—
1858Mo FH	—	250	350	650	1,000	—
1859/8Mo FH	—	250	350	650	1,000	—
1861Mo CH	—	400	800	1,200	1,750	—
1863Mo CH	—	250	350	650	1,000	2,000
1868Mo PH	—	250	325	500	900	—
1869Mo CH	—	250	325	500	900	1,500

KM# 381.5 4 ESCUDOS
13.5400 g., 0.8750 Gold .3809 oz. AGW **Obv:** Facing eagle, snake in beak **Obv. Legend:** REPUBLICA MEXICANA **Rev:** Hand holding cap on stick, open book

Date	Mintage	VG	F	VF	XF	Unc
1861Ho FM	—	1,000	1,500	2,500	4,000	—

KM# 381.7 4 ESCUDOS
13.5400 g., 0.8750 Gold .3809 oz. AGW **Obv:** Facing eagle, snake in beak **Obv. Legend:** REPUBLICA MEXICANA. **Rev:** Hand holding cap on stick, open book **Rev. Legend:** LA LIBERTAD EN LA LEY... **Note:** Mint mark O, Oa.

Date	Mintage	VG	F	VF	XF	Unc
1861O FR	—	1,500	2,500	4,000	7,000	—

KM# 381.8 4 ESCUDOS
13.5400 g., 0.8750 Gold .3809 oz. AGW **Obv:** Facing eagle, snake in beak **Obv. Legend:** REPUBLICA MEXICANA. **Rev:** Hand holding cap on stick, open book **Rev. Legend:** LA LIBERTAD...

Date	Mintage	VG	F	VF	XF	Unc
1860Zs VL Rare	—	—	—	—	—	—
1862Zs VL	—	750	1,250	2,250	3,750	—

Note: American Numismatic Rarities Eliasberg sale 4-05, MS-64 realized $18,400.

KM# 383 8 ESCUDOS
27.0700 g., 0.8750 Gold .7616 oz. AGW **Obv:** Facing eagle, snake in beak **Obv. Legend:** REPUBLICA MEXICANA **Rev:** Hand holding cap on stick, open book **Rev. Legend:** LA LIBERTAD...

MEXICO

Date	Mintage	F	VF	XF	Unc	BU
1864A PG	—	700	1,250	2,500	—	—
1866A DL	—	—	—	7,500	—	—
1868/7A DL	—	2,000	3,500	5,500	—	—
1869A DL	—	—	4,000	6,000	—	—
1870A DL	—	—	2,500	5,000	—	—
1872A AM Rare	—	—	—	—	—	—

KM# 383.1 8 ESCUDOS
27.0700 g., 0.8750 Gold .7616 oz. AGW **Obv:** Facing eagle, snake in beak **Obv. Legend:** REPUBLICA MEXICANA **Rev:** Hand holding cap on stick, open book **Rev. Legend:** LA LIBERTAD....

Date	Mintage	F	VF	XF	Unc	BU
1841Ca RG	—	550	750	1,250	1,750	—
1842Ca RG	—	500	600	1,000	1,500	—
1843Ca RG	—	500	600	1,000	1,500	—
1844Ca RG	—	500	600	1,000	1,500	—
1845Ca RG	—	500	600	1,000	1,500	—
1846Ca RG	—	650	1,250	1,500	2,000	—
1847Ca RG	—	1,000	2,500	—	—	—
1848Ca RG	—	500	600	1,000	1,500	—
1849Ca RG	—	500	600	1,000	1,500	—
1850/40Ca RG	—	500	600	1,000	1,500	—
1851/41Ca RG	—	500	600	1,000	1,500	—
1852/42Ca RG	—	500	600	1,000	1,500	—
1853/43Ca RG	—	500	600	1,000	1,500	—
1854/44Ca RG	—	500	600	1,000	1,500	—
1855/43Ca RG	—	500	600	1,000	1,500	—
1856/46Ca RG	—	525	650	1,250	1,750	—
1857Ca JC/RG	—	500	550	800	1,250	—
1858Ca JC	—	500	550	800	1,250	—
1858Ca BA/RG	—	500	550	800	1,250	—
1859Ca JC/RG	—	500	550	800	1,250	—
1860Ca JC/RG	—	500	600	1,000	1,500	—
1861Ca JC	—	500	550	800	1,250	—
1862Ca JC	—	500	550	800	1,250	—
1863Ca JC	—	600	1,000	1,750	2,250	—
1864Ca JC	—	550	750	1,250	1,750	—
1865Ca JC	—	750	1,500	2,500	3,500	—
1866Ca JC	—	500	500	1,000	1,500	—
1866Ca FP	—	650	1,250	2,000	2,500	—
1866Ca JG	—	500	600	1,000	1,500	—
1867Ca JG	—	500	550	800	1,250	—
1868Ca JG Concave wings	—	500	550	800	1,250	—
1869Ca MM Regular eagle	—	500	550	800	1,250	—
1870/60Ca MM	—	500	550	750	1,250	—
1871/61Ca MM	—	500	550	750	1,250	—

KM# 383.2 8 ESCUDOS
27.0700 g., 0.8750 Gold .7616 oz. AGW **Obv:** Facing eagle, snake in beak **Obv. Legend:** REPUBLICA MEXICANA. **Rev:** Hand holding cap on stick, open book **Rev. Legend:** LA LIBERTAD...

Date	Mintage	F	VF	XF	Unc	BU
1846C CE	—	500	600	1,000	1,750	—
1847C CE	—	500	550	800	1,250	—
1848C CE	—	500	600	1,000	1,750	—
1849C CE	—	500	550	750	1,250	—
1850C CE	—	500	550	750	1,250	—
1851C CE	—	500	550	800	1,250	—
1852C CE	—	500	550	800	1,250	—
1853/1C CE	—	500	550	750	1,200	—
1854C CE	—	500	550	750	1,200	—
1855/4C CE	—	500	500	1,000	1,750	—
1855C CE	—	500	550	800	1,250	—
1856C CE	—	500	550	750	1,200	—
1857C CE	—	500	550	750	1,200	—
1857C CE	—	—	—	—	—	—
Note: Without periods after C's
1858C CE	—	500	550	750	1,200	—
1859C CE	—	500	550	750	1,200	—
1860/58C CE	—	500	550	800	1,250	—
1860C CE	—	500	550	800	1,250	—
1860C PV	—	500	550	750	1,200	—
1861C PV	—	500	550	800	1,250	—
1861C CE	—	500	550	800	1,250	—
1862C CE	—	500	550	800	1,250	—
1863C CE	—	500	550	800	1,250	—
1864C CE	—	500	550	750	1,200	—
1865C CE	—	500	550	750	1,200	—
1866/5C CE	—	500	550	750	1,200	—
1866C CE	—	500	550	750	1,200	—
1867C CB Error	—	500	550	750	1,200	—
1867C CE/CB	—	500	550	750	1,200	—
1868C CB Error	—	500	550	750	1,200	—
1869C CE	—	500	550	750	1,200	—
1870C CE	—	500	550	800	1,250	—

KM# 383.3 8 ESCUDOS
27.0700 g., 0.8750 Gold .7616 oz. AGW **Obv:** Facing eagle, snake in beak **Obv. Legend:** REPUBLICA MEXICANA **Rev:** Hand holding cap on stick, open book **Rev. Legend:** LA LIBERTAD....

Date	Mintage	F	VF	XF	Unc	BU
1832Do RM	—	500	1,750	2,000	3,000	—
1833Do RM/RL	—	500	550	800	1,250	—
1834Do RM	—	500	550	800	1,250	—
1835Do RM	—	500	550	800	1,250	—
1836Do RM/RL	—	500	550	800	1,250	—
1836Do RM	—	500	550	800	1,250	—
Note: M on snake
1837Do RM	—	500	550	800	1,250	—
1838/6Do RM	—	500	550	800	1,250	—
1838Do RM	—	500	550	800	1,250	—
1839Do RM	—	500	550	750	1,250	2,000
1840/30Do RM/RL	—	500	650	1,000	1,750	—
1841/30Do RM	—	550	750	1,250	2,000	—
1841/0Do RM	—	500	550	750	1,250	—
1841Do RM	—	500	550	800	1,250	—
1841/31Do RM	—	500	550	800	1,250	—
1841/34Do RM	—	500	550	800	1,250	—
1841Do RM/RL	—	500	550	800	1,250	—
1842/32Do RM	—	500	550	800	1,250	—
1843/33Do RM	—	550	750	1,250	2,000	—
1843/1Do RM	—	500	550	800	1,250	—
1843Do RM	—	500	550	800	1,250	—
1844/34Do RM/RL	—	600	1,000	1,500	2,500	—
1844Do RM	—	550	800	1,250	2,000	—
1845/36Do RM	—	500	650	1,000	1,750	—
1845Do RM	—	500	650	1,000	1,750	—
1846Do RM	—	500	550	800	1,250	—
1847/37Do RM	—	500	550	800	1,250	—
1848/37Do RM	—	—	—	—	—	—
1848/38Do CM	—	500	550	800	1,250	—
1849/39Do CM	—	500	550	800	1,250	—
1849Do J.M.R. Rare	—	—	—	—	—	—
1850Do .JMR.	—	500	750	1,250	2,000	—
1851Do JMR	—	500	750	1,250	2,000	—
1852/1Do JMR	—	500	800	1,250	2,000	—
1852Do CP	—	500	800	1,250	2,000	—
1853Do CP	—	500	800	1,250	2,000	—
1854Do CP	—	500	650	1,000	1,750	—
1855/4Do CP	—	500	550	800	1,250	—
1855Do CP	—	500	550	800	1,250	—
1856Do CP	—	500	600	900	1,650	—
1857Do CP	—	500	550	800	1,250	—
Note: French style eagle, 1832-57
1857Do CP	—	500	550	800	1,250	—
Note: Mexican style eagle
1858Do CP	—	500	600	900	1,650	—
1859Do CP	—	500	550	800	1,250	—
1860/59Do CP	—	500	750	1,250	2,000	—
1861/0Do CP	—	500	650	1,000	1,750	—
1862/52Do CP	—	500	550	800	1,250	—
1862/1Do CP	—	500	550	800	1,250	—
1862Do CP	—	500	550	800	1,250	—
1863/53Do CP	—	500	550	800	1,250	—
1864Do LT	—	500	550	800	1,250	2,000
1865/4Do LT	—	600	1,000	1,650	2,750	—
1866/4Do CM	—	1,250	2,000	2,500	—	—
1866Do CM	—	500	650	1,000	1,750	—
1867/56Do CP	—	500	650	1,000	1,750	—
1867/4Do CP	—	500	550	800	1,250	—
1868/4Do CP/LT	—	—	—	—	—	—
1869Do CP	—	650	1,250	1,750	2,750	—
1870Do CP	—	500	650	1,000	1,750	—

KM# 383.4 8 ESCUDOS
27.0700 g., 0.8750 Gold .7616 oz. AGW **Obv:** Facing eagle, snake in beak **Obv. Legend:** REPUBLICA MEXICANA **Rev:** Hand holding cap on stick, open book **Rev. Legend:** LA LIBERTAD...

Date	Mintage	F	VF	XF	Unc	BU
1828EoMo LF Rare	—	—	—	—	—	—
1829EoMo LF	—	3,500	5,500	8,500	—	—

KM# 383.5 8 ESCUDOS
27.0700 g., 0.8750 Gold .7616 oz. AGW **Obv:** Facing eagle, snake in beak **Obv. Legend:** REPUBLICA MEXICANA **Rev:** Hand holding cap on stick, open book **Rev. Legend:** LA LIBERTAD...

Date	Mintage	F	VF	XF	Unc	BU
1825Ga FS	—	600	1,000	1,250	1,750	—
1826Ga FS	—	600	1,000	1,250	1,750	—
1830Ga FS	—	600	1,000	1,250	1,750	—
1836Ga FS	—	750	1,500	2,000	3,000	—
1836Ga JG	—	1,000	2,500	3,500	—	—
1837Ga JG	—	1,000	2,500	3,500	—	—
1840Ga MC Rare	—	—	—	—	—	—
1841/31Ga MC	—	1,000	2,500	—	—	—
1841Ga MC	—	850	1,650	2,250	—	—
1842Ga JG Rare	—	—	3,000	5,000	—	—
1843Ga MC	—	—	2,500	6,500	—	—
1845Ga MC Rare	—	—	—	—	—	—
1847Ga JG	—	2,250	—	—	—	—
1849Ga JG	—	600	1,000	1,250	1,750	—
1850Ga JG	—	550	850	1,100	1,650	—
1851Ga JG	—	1,000	2,500	3,500	—	—
1852/1Ga JG	—	600	1,000	1,250	1,750	—
1855Ga JG	—	1,000	2,500	3,500	—	—
1856Ga JG	—	550	850	1,100	1,650	—
1857Ga JG	—	550	850	1,100	1,650	—
1861/0Ga JG	—	600	1,000	1,250	1,750	—
1861Ga JG	—	500	700	1,200	1,750	—
1863/1Ga JG	—	600	1,000	1,250	1,750	—
1866Ga JG	—	550	850	1,100	1,650	—

KM# 383.6 8 ESCUDOS
27.0700 g., 0.8750 Gold .7616 oz. AGW **Obv:** Facing eagle, snake in beak **Obv. Legend:** REPUBLICA MEXICANA **Rev:** Hand holding cap on stick, open book **Rev. Legend:** LA LIBERTAD...

Date	Mintage	F	VF	XF	Unc	BU
1844GC MP	—	550	750	1,250	2,000	—
1845GC MP	—	550	750	1,250	2,000	—
Note: Eagle's tail square
1845GC MP	—	550	750	1,250	2,000	—
Note: Eagle's tail round
1846GC MP	—	500	650	1,000	1,750	—
Note: Eagle's tail square
1846GC MP	—	500	650	1,000	1,750	—
Note: Eagle's tail round
1847GC MP	—	500	650	1,000	1,750	—
1848GC MP	—	550	750	1,250	2,000	—
1849GC MP	—	550	750	1,250	2,000	—
1850GC MP	—	500	650	1,000	1,750	—

MEXICO

Date	Mintage	F	VF	XF	Unc	BU
1851GC MP	—	500	650	1,000	1,750	—
1852GC MP	—	550	750	1,250	2,000	—

KM# 383.7 8 ESCUDOS
27.0700 g., 0.8750 Gold .7616 oz. AGW **Obv:** Facing eagle, snake in beak **Obv. Legend:** REPUBLICA MEXICANA **Rev:** Hand holding cap on stick, open book **Rev. Legend:** LA LIBERTAD...

Date	Mintage	F	VF	XF	Unc	BU
1828Go MJ	—	750	1,750	2,250	3,000	—
1829Go MJ	—	650	1,500	2,000	2,750	—
1830Go MJ	—	500	550	750	1,000	—
1831Go MJ	—	650	1,500	2,000	2,750	—
1832Go MJ	—	550	1,000	1,500	2,500	—
1833Go MJ	—	500	550	700	1,000	—
1834Go PJ	—	500	550	700	1,000	—
1835Go PJ	—	500	550	700	1,000	—
1836Go PJ	—	500	650	900	1,250	—
1837Go PJ	—	500	650	900	1,250	—
1838/7Go PJ	—	500	550	700	1,000	—
1838Go PJ	—	500	550	800	1,200	—
1839/8Go PJ	—	500	550	700	1,000	—
1839Go PJ	—	500	550	800	1,200	—

Note: Regular eagle

| 1840Go PJ | — | 500 | 550 | 700 | 1,000 | — |

Note: Concave wings

1841Go PJ	—	500	550	700	1,000	—
1842Go PJ	—	500	550	600	900	—
1842Go PM	—	500	550	700	1,000	—
1843Go PM	—	500	550	700	1,000	—

Note: Small eagle

1844/3Go PM	—	500	650	900	1,250	—
1844Go PM	—	500	550	650	1,000	—
1845Go PM	—	500	550	700	1,000	—
1846/5Go PM	—	500	550	800	1,200	—
1846Go PM	—	500	550	700	1,000	—
1847Go PM	—	500	650	900	1,250	—
1848/7Go PM	—	500	550	700	1,000	—
1848Go PM	—	500	550	700	1,000	—
1848Go PF	—	500	550	700	1,000	—
1849Go PF	—	500	550	600	950	—
1850Go PF	—	500	550	600	950	—
1851Go PF	—	500	550	700	1,000	—
1852Go PF	—	500	550	650	1,000	—
1853Go PF	—	500	550	650	1,000	—
1854Go PF	—	500	550	700	1,000	—

Note: Eagle of 1853

| 1854Go PF | — | 500 | 550 | 700 | 1,000 | — |

Note: Eagle of 1855

1855/4Go PF	—	500	550	700	1,000	—
1855Go PF	—	500	550	700	1,000	—
1856Go PF	—	500	550	700	1,000	—
1857Go PF	—	500	550	700	1,000	—
1858Go PF	—	500	550	700	1,000	—
1859Go PF	—	500	550	600	900	—
1860/50Go PF	—	500	550	600	900	—
1860/59Go PF	—	500	550	700	1,100	—
1860Go PF	—	500	550	700	1,100	—
1861/0Go PF	—	500	550	600	850	—
1861Go PF	—	500	550	600	850	—
1862/1Go YE	—	500	550	700	1,000	—
1862Go YE	—	500	550	650	950	—
1862Go YF	—	—	—	—	—	—
1863/53Go YF	—	500	550	700	1,000	2,500
1863Go PF	—	500	550	700	1,000	—
1867/57Go YF/PF	—	500	550	700	1,000	—
1867Go YF	—	500	550	650	950	—
1868/58Go YF	—	500	550	700	1,000	1,750
1870Go FR	—	500	550	600	900	—

KM# 383.8 8 ESCUDOS
27.0700 g., 0.8750 Gold .7616 oz. AGW **Obv:** Facing eagle, snake in beak **Obv. Legend:** REPUBLICA MEXICANA. **Rev:** Hand holding cap on stick, open book **Rev. Legend:** LA LIBERTAD...

Date	Mintage	F	VF	XF	Unc	BU
1863Ho FM	—	550	700	1,000	2,000	—
1864Ho FM	—	650	1,250	1,750	2,750	—
1864Ho PR/FM	—	550	700	1,000	2,000	—
1865Ho FM/PR	—	600	800	1,250	2,500	—
1867/57Ho PR	—	550	700	1,000	2,000	—
1868Ho PR	—	600	800	1,250	2,500	—
1868Ho PR/FM	—	600	800	1,250	2,500	—
1869Ho PR/FM	—	550	700	1,000	2,000	—
1869Ho PR	—	550	700	1,000	2,000	—
1870Ho PR	—	600	800	1,250	2,750	5,500
1871/0Ho PR	—	600	800	1,250	2,500	—
1871Ho PR	—	600	800	1,250	2,500	—
1872/1Ho PR	—	650	1,250	1,750	2,750	—
1873Ho PR	—	550	700	1,000	2,000	—

KM# 383.10 8 ESCUDOS
27.0700 g., 0.8750 Gold .7616 oz. AGW **Obv:** Facing eagle, snake in beak **Obv. Legend:** REPUBLICA MEXICANA **Rev:** Hand holding cap on stick, open book **Rev. Legend:** LA LIBERTAD...

Date	Mintage	F	VF	XF	Unc	BU
1858oa AE	—	2,000	3,000	4,000	6,000	—
1859O AE	—	1,000	2,500	3,750	5,500	—
1860O AE	—	1,000	2,500	3,750	5,500	—
1861O FR	—	600	850	1,250	2,750	—
1862O FR	—	600	850	1,250	2,750	—
1863O FR	—	600	850	1,250	2,750	—
1864O FR	—	600	850	1,250	2,750	—
1867O AE	—	600	850	1,250	2,750	—
1868O AE	—	600	850	1,250	2,750	—
1869O AE	—	600	850	1,250	2,750	—

KM# 383.11 8 ESCUDOS
27.0700 g., 0.8750 Gold .7616 oz. AGW **Obv:** Facing eagle, snake in beak **Obv. Legend:** REPUBLICA MEXICANA **Rev:** Hand holding cap on stick, open book **Rev. Legend:** LA LIBERTAD...

Date	Mintage	F	VF	XF	Unc	BU
1858Zs MO	—	550	750	1,000	2,000	—
1859Zs MO	—	500	550	600	1,000	—
1860/59Zs VL/MO	—	2,000	3,000	4,000	—	—
1860/9Zs MO	—	550	750	1,000	2,000	—
1860Zs MO	—	500	550	700	1,100	—
1861/0Zs VL	—	500	550	700	1,100	—
1861Zs VL	—	500	550	700	1,100	3,000
1862Zs VL	—	500	550	700	1,150	—
1863Zs VL	—	500	550	750	1,200	—
1863Zs MO	—	500	550	700	1,100	—
1864Zs MO	—	750	1,000	1,500	3,500	—
1865Zs MO	—	750	1,000	1,600	3,750	—
1868Zs JS	—	500	600	800	1,250	—
1868Zs YH	—	500	600	800	1,250	—
1869Zs YH	—	500	600	800	1,250	—
1870Zs YH	—	500	600	800	1,250	—
1871Zs YH	—	500	600	800	1,250	—

KM# 383.9 8 ESCUDOS
27.0700 g., 0.8750 Gold .7616 oz. AGW **Obv:** Facing eagle, snake in beak **Obv. Legend:** REPUBLICA MEXICANA **Rev:** Hand holding cap on stick, open book **Rev. Legend:** LA LIBERTAD... **Note:** Formerly reported 1825/3 JM is merely a reworked 5.

Date	Mintage	F	VF	XF	Unc	BU
1824Mo JM	—	600	1,000	1,250	2,000	—

Note: Large book reverse

| 1825Mo JM | — | 500 | 550 | 700 | 1,000 | 2,000 |

Note: Small book reverse

1826/5Mo JM	—	750	1,750	2,250	3,000	—
1827/6Mo JM	—	500	550	700	1,000	—
1827Mo JM	—	500	550	700	1,000	—
1828Mo JM	—	500	550	700	1,000	—
1829Mo JM	—	500	550	700	1,000	—
1830Mo JM	—	500	550	700	1,000	—
1831Mo JM	—	500	550	700	1,000	—
1832/1Mo JM	—	500	550	700	1,000	—
1832Mo JM	—	500	550	700	1,000	—
1833Mo MJ	—	550	750	1,000	1,500	—
1833Mo ML	—	500	550	650	1,000	—
1834Mo ML	—	550	750	1,000	1,500	—
1835/4Mo ML	—	600	1,000	1,250	2,000	—
1836Mo ML	—	500	550	650	1,000	—
1836Mo MF	—	550	750	1,200	2,000	—
1837/6Mo ML	—	500	550	650	1,000	—
1838Mo ML	—	500	550	650	1,000	—
1839Mo ML	—	500	550	650	1,000	—
1840Mo ML	—	500	550	650	1,000	—
1841Mo ML	—	500	550	650	1,000	—
1842/1Mo ML	—	—	—	—	—	—
1842Mo ML	—	500	550	650	1,000	—
1842Mo MM	—	—	—	—	—	—
1843Mo MM	—	500	550	650	1,000	—
1844Mo MF	—	500	550	650	1,000	—
1845Mo MF	—	500	550	650	1,000	—
1846Mo MF	—	600	1,000	1,250	2,000	—
1847Mo MF	—	1,000	2,250	—	—	—
1847Mo RC	—	500	600	800	1,250	—
1848Mo GC	—	500	550	650	1,000	—
1849Mo GC	—	500	550	650	1,000	—
1850Mo GC	—	500	550	650	1,000	2,000
1851Mo GC	—	500	550	650	1,000	—
1852Mo GC	—	500	550	650	1,000	—
1853Mo GC	—	500	550	650	1,000	—
1854/44Mo GC	—	500	550	650	1,000	—
1854/3Mo GC	—	500	550	650	1,000	—
1855Mo GF	—	500	550	650	1,000	—
1856/5Mo GF	—	500	550	600	950	—
1856Mo GF	—	500	550	600	950	—
1857Mo GF	—	500	550	600	950	—
1858Mo FH	—	500	550	600	950	—
1859Mo FH	—	550	750	1,000	1,500	—
1860Mo FH	—	500	550	600	950	—
1860Mo TH	—	500	550	600	950	—
1861/51Mo CH	—	500	550	600	950	—
1862Mo CH	—	500	550	600	950	—
1863/53Mo CH	—	500	550	600	950	4,750
1863/53Mo TH	—	500	550	600	950	—
1867Mo CH	—	500	550	600	950	—
1868Mo CH	—	500	550	600	950	—
1868Mo PH	—	500	550	600	950	—
1869Mo CH	—	500	550	600	950	—

EMPIRE OF MAXIMILIAN

RULER
Maximilian, Emperor, 1864-1867

MINT MARKS
Refer To Republic Coinage

MONETARY SYSTEM
100 Centavos = 1 Peso (8 Reales)

MILLED COINAGE
100 Centavos = 1 Peso

KM# 389 20 PESOS
33.8400 g., 0.8750 Gold .9520 oz. AGW **Ruler:** Maximilian **Obv:** Head right, with beard **Obv. Legend:** MAXIMILIANO EMPERADOR **Rev:** Crowned arms with supporters

Date	Mintage	F	VF	XF	Unc	BU
1866Mo	8,274	500	950	1,450	3,000	—

MEXICO

REPUBLIC
Second
DECIMAL COINAGE
100 Centavos = 1 Peso

KM# 410 PESO
1.6920 g., 0.8750 Gold .0476 oz. AGW **Obv:** Facing eagle, snake in beak **Obv. Legend:** REPUBLICA MEXICANA **Rev:** Value within 1/2 wreath

Date	Mintage	F	VF	XF	Unc	BU
1888AsL/MoM Rare	—	—	—	—	—	—
1888As L Rare	—	—	—	—	—	—

KM# 410.1 PESO
1.6920 g., 0.8750 Gold .0476 oz. AGW **Obv:** Facing eagle, snake in beak **Obv. Legend:** REPUBLICA MEXICANA **Rev:** Value within 1/2 wreath

Date	Mintage	F	VF	XF	Unc	BU
1888Ca/MoM Rare	104	—	—	—	—	—

KM# 410.2 PESO
1.6920 g., 0.8750 Gold .0476 oz. AGW **Obv:** Facing eagle, snake in beak **Obv. Legend:** REPUBLICA MEXICANA **Rev:** Value within 1/2 wreath

Date	Mintage	F	VF	XF	Unc	BU
1873Cn P	1,221	75.00	100	150	250	—
1875Cn P	—	85.00	125	150	250	—
1878Cn G	248	100	175	225	500	—
1879Cn D	—	100	150	200	475	—
1881/0Cn D	338	100	150	200	475	—
1882Cn D	340	100	150	200	475	—
1883Cn D	—	100	150	200	475	—
1884Cn M	—	100	150	200	475	—
1886/4Cn M	277	100	150	225	500	—
1888/7Cn M	2,586	100	175	225	450	—
1888Cn M	Inc. above	65.00	100	150	265	—
1889Cn M Rare	—	—	—	—	—	—
1891/89Cn M	969	75.00	100	150	275	—
1892Cn M	780	75.00	100	150	275	—
1893Cn M	498	85.00	125	150	275	—
1894Cn M	493	80.00	125	150	275	—
1895Cn M	1,143	65.00	100	150	250	300
1896/5Cn M	1,028	65.00	100	150	250	—
1897Cn M	785	65.00	100	150	250	325
1898Cn M	3,521	65.00	100	150	225	—
1898Cn/MoM	Inc. above	65.00	100	150	250	—
1899Cn Q	2,000	65.00	100	150	225	—
1901Cn Q	Inc. above	65.00	100	150	225	—
1901/0Cn Q	2,350	65.00	100	150	225	—
1902Cn Q	2,480	65.00	100	150	225	—
1902Cn/MoQ/C	Inc. above	65.00	100	150	225	—
1904Cn H	3,614	65.00	100	150	225	—
1904Cn/Mo/ H	Inc. above	65.00	100	150	250	—
1905Cn P	1,000	—	—	—	—	—

Note: Reported, not confirmed

KM# 410.3 PESO
1.6920 g., 0.8750 Gold .0476 oz. AGW **Obv:** Facing eagle, snake in beak **Obv. Legend:** REPUBLICA MEXICANA **Rev:** Value within 1/2 wreath

Date	Mintage	F	VF	XF	Unc	BU
1870Go S	—	100	125	150	265	—
1871Go S	500	100	175	225	475	—
1888Go R	210	125	200	250	550	—
1890Go R	1,916	75.00	100	150	265	—
1892Go R	533	100	150	175	350	—
1894Go R	180	150	200	250	550	—
1895Go R	676	100	150	175	325	—
1896/5Go R	4,671	65.00	100	150	250	—
1897/6Go R	4,280	65.00	100	150	250	—
1897Go R	Inc. above	65.00	100	150	250	—
1898Go R	5,193	65.00	100	150	250	750

Note: Regular obverse

Date	Mintage	F	VF	XF	Unc	BU
1898Go R	Inc. above	75.00	100	150	250	750

Note: Mule, 5 Centavos obverse, normal reverse

Date	Mintage	F	VF	XF	Unc	BU
1899Go R	2,748	65.00	100	150	250	—
1900/800Go R	864	75.00	125	150	285	—

KM# 410.4 PESO
1.6920 g., 0.8750 Gold .0476 oz. AGW **Obv:** Facing eagle, snake in beak **Obv. Legend:** REPUBLICA MEXICANA **Rev:** Value within 1/2 wreath

Date	Mintage	F	VF	XF	Unc	BU
1875Ho R Rare	310	—	—	—	—	—
1876Ho F Rare	—	—	—	—	—	—
1888Ho G/MoM Rare	—	—	—	—	—	—

KM# 410.5 PESO
1.6920 g., 0.8750 Gold .0476 oz. AGW **Obv:** Facing eagle, snake in beak **Obv. Legend:** REPUBLICA MEXICANA **Rev:** Value within 1/2 wreath

Date	Mintage	F	VF	XF	Unc	BU
1870Mo C	2,540	45.00	65.00	95.00	185	—
1871Mo M/C	1,000	55.00	100	150	250	—
1872Mo M/C	3,000	45.00	65.00	95.00	185	—
1873/1Mo M	2,900	45.00	65.00	100	200	—
1873Mo M	Inc. above	45.00	65.00	95.00	185	—
1874Mo M	—	45.00	65.00	95.00	185	—
1875Mo B/M	—	45.00	65.00	95.00	185	250
1876/5Mo B/M	—	45.00	65.00	95.00	185	—
1877Mo M	—	45.00	65.00	95.00	185	—
1878Mo M	2,000	45.00	65.00	95.00	185	—
1879Mo M	—	45.00	65.00	95.00	185	—
1880/70Mo M	—	45.00	65.00	95.00	185	—
1881/71Mo M	1,000	45.00	65.00	95.00	185	—
1882/72Mo M	—	45.00	65.00	95.00	185	—
1883/72Mo M	1,000	45.00	65.00	95.00	185	—
1884Mo M	—	45.00	65.00	95.00	185	—
1885/71Mo M	—	45.00	65.00	95.00	185	—
1885Mo M	—	45.00	65.00	95.00	185	—
1886Mo M	1,700	45.00	65.00	95.00	185	—
1887Mo M	2,200	45.00	65.00	95.00	185	—
1888Mo M	1,000	45.00	65.00	95.00	185	—
1889Mo M	500	100	150	200	285	—
1890Mo M	570	100	150	200	285	—
1891Mo M	746	100	150	200	285	—
1892/0Mo M	2,895	45.00	65.00	95.00	185	—
1893Mo M	5,917	45.00	65.00	95.00	185	—
1894/3MMo	—	45.00	65.00	95.00	185	—
1894Mo M	6,244	45.00	65.00	95.00	185	—
1895Mo M	8,994	45.00	65.00	95.00	185	—
1895Mo B	Inc. above	45.00	65.00	95.00	185	—
1896Mo B	7,166	45.00	65.00	95.00	185	—
1896Mo M	Inc. above	45.00	65.00	95.00	185	—
1897Mo M	5,131	45.00	65.00	95.00	185	—
1898/7Mo M	5,368	45.00	65.00	95.00	185	—
1899Mo M	9,515	45.00	65.00	95.00	185	—
1900/800Mo M	9,301	45.00	65.00	95.00	185	—
1900/880Mo M	Inc. above	45.00	65.00	95.00	185	—
1900/890Mo M	Inc. above	45.00	65.00	95.00	185	—
1900Mo M	Inc. above	45.00	65.00	95.00	185	—
1901Mo M Small date	Inc. above	45.00	65.00	95.00	185	—
1901/801Mo M Large date	8,293	45.00	65.00	95.00	185	—
1902Mo M Large date	11,000	45.00	65.00	95.00	185	—
1902Mo M Small date	Inc. above	45.00	65.00	95.00	185	—
1903Mo M Large date	10,000	45.00	65.00	95.00	185	—
1903Mo M Small date	Inc. above	55.00	85.00	125	200	—
1904Mo M	9,845	45.00	65.00	95.00	185	—
1905Mo M	3,429	45.00	65.00	95.00	185	—

KM# 410.6 PESO
1.6920 g., 0.8750 Gold .0476 oz. AGW **Obv:** Facing eagle, snake in beak **Obv. Legend:** REPUBLICA MEXICANA **Rev:** Value within 1/2 wreath

Date	Mintage	F	VF	XF	Unc	BU
1872Zs H	2,024	125	150	175	275	—
1875/3Zs A	—	125	150	200	325	—
1878Zs S	—	125	150	175	275	—
1888Zs Z	280	175	225	325	700	—
1889Zs Z	492	150	175	225	450	—
1890Zs Z	738	150	175	225	450	—

KM# 411 2-1/2 PESOS
4.2300 g., 0.8750 Gold .1190 oz. AGW **Obv:** Facing eagle, snake in beak **Obv. Legend:** REPUBLICA MEXICANA **Rev:** Value within 1/2 wreath

Date	Mintage	F	VF	XF	Unc	BU
1888As/MoL Rare	—	—	—	—	—	—

KM# 411.2 2-1/2 PESOS
4.2300 g., 0.8750 Gold .1190 oz. AGW **Obv:** Facing eagle, snake in beak **Rev:** Value within 1/2 wreath

Date	Mintage	F	VF	XF	Unc	BU
1888Do C Rare	—	—	—	—	—	—

KM# 411.3 2-1/2 PESOS
4.2300 g., 0.8750 Gold .1190 oz. AGW **Obv:** Facing eagle, snake in beak **Obv. Legend:** REPUBLICA MEXICANA **Rev:** Value within 1/2 wreath

Date	Mintage	F	VF	XF	Unc	BU
1871Go S	600	1,250	2,000	2,500	3,250	—
1888Go/MoR	110	1,750	2,250	2,750	3,500	—

KM# 411.4 2-1/2 PESOS
4.2300 g., 0.8750 Gold .1190 oz. AGW **Obv:** Facing eagle, snake in beak **Obv. Legend:** REPUBLICA MEXICANA **Rev:** Value within 1/2 wreath

Date	Mintage	F	VF	XF	Unc	BU
1874Ho R Rare	—	—	—	—	—	—
1888Ho G Rare	—	—	—	—	—	—

KM# 411.5 2-1/2 PESOS
4.2300 g., 0.8750 Gold .1190 oz. AGW **Obv:** Facing eagle, snake in beak **Rev:** Value within 1/2 wreath

Date	Mintage	F	VF	XF	Unc	BU
1870Mo C	820	150	250	350	750	—
1872Mo M/C	800	150	250	350	750	—
1873/2Mo M	—	200	350	750	1,350	—
1874Mo M	—	200	350	750	1,350	—
1874Mo B/M	—	200	350	750	1,350	—
1875Mo B	—	200	350	750	1,350	—
1876Mo B	—	250	500	1,000	1,850	—
1877Mo M	—	200	350	750	1,350	—
1878Mo M	400	200	350	750	1,350	—
1879Mo M	—	200	350	750	1,350	—
1880/79Mo M	—	200	350	750	1,350	—
1881Mo M	400	200	350	750	1,350	—
1882Mo M	—	225	400	850	1,500	2,000
1883/73Mo M	400	200	350	750	1,350	—
1884Mo M	—	250	500	1,000	1,600	—
1885Mo M	—	400	850	1,750	3,000	—
1886Mo M	400	200	350	750	1,350	—
1887Mo M	400	200	350	750	1,350	—
1888Mo M	540	200	350	750	1,350	—
1889Mo M	240	150	300	525	950	—
1890Mo M	420	200	350	750	1,350	—
1891Mo M	188	200	350	750	1,350	—
1892Mo M	240	200	350	750	1,350	—

KM# 411.6 2-1/2 PESOS
4.2300 g., 0.8750 Gold .1190 oz. AGW **Obv:** Facing eagle, snake in beak **Obv. Legend:** REPUBLICA MEXICANA **Rev:** Value within 1/2 wreath

Date	Mintage	F	VF	XF	Unc	BU
1872Zs H	1,300	200	350	500	1,200	—
1873Zs H	—	175	325	475	900	—
1875/3Zs A	—	200	350	750	1,350	—
1877Zs S	—	200	350	750	1,350	—

502 MEXICO

Date	Mintage	F	VF	XF	Unc	BU
1878Zs S	300	200	350	750	1,350	—
1888Zs/MoS	80	300	500	1,000	1,800	—
1889Zs/Mo Z	184	250	450	950	1,600	—
1890Zs Z	326	200	350	750	1,350	—

KM# 412 5 PESOS
8.4600 g., 0.8750 Gold .2380 oz. AGW **Obv:** Facing eagle, snake in beak **Obv. Legend:** REPUBLICA MEXICANA **Rev:** Radiant cap above scales

Date	Mintage	F	VF	XF	Unc	BU
1875As L	—	—	—	—	—	—
1878As L	383	900	1,700	3,000	4,500	—

KM# 412.1 5 PESOS
8.4600 g., 0.8750 Gold .2380 oz. AGW **Obv:** Facing eagle, snake in beak **Obv. Legend:** REPUBLICA MEXICANA **Rev:** Radiant cap above scales

Date	Mintage	F	VF	XF	Unc	BU
1888Ca M Rare	120	—	—	—	—	—

KM# 412.2 5 PESOS
8.4600 g., 0.8750 Gold .2380 oz. AGW **Obv:** Facing eagle, snake in beak **Obv. Legend:** REPUBLICA MEXICANA **Rev:** Radiant cap above scales

Date	Mintage	F	VF	XF	Unc	BU
1873Cn P	—	300	600	1,000	2,000	—
1874Cn P	—	—	—	—	—	—
1875Cn P	—	300	500	800	1,750	—
1876Cn P	—	300	500	800	1,750	—
1877Cn G	—	300	500	800	1,750	—
1882Cn Rare	174	—	—	—	—	—
1888Cn M	—	500	1,000	1,350	2,000	—
1890Cn M	435	250	500	750	1,600	—
1891Cn M	1,390	250	400	500	1,000	—
1894Cn M	484	250	500	750	1,600	—
1895Cn M	142	500	750	1,500	2,500	—
1900Cn Q	1,536	175	300	400	900	—
1903Cn Q	1,000	175	300	400	750	—

KM# 412.3 5 PESOS
8.4600 g., 0.8750 Gold .2380 oz. AGW **Obv:** Facing eagle, snake in beak **Obv. Legend:** REPUBLICA MEXICANA **Rev:** Radiant cap above scales

Date	Mintage	F	VF	XF	Unc	BU
1873/2Do P	—	700	1,250	1,800	3,000	—
1877Do P	—	700	1,250	1,800	3,000	—
1878Do E	—	700	1,250	1,800	3,000	—
1879/7Do B	—	700	1,250	1,800	3,000	—
1879Do B	—	700	1,250	1,800	3,000	—

KM# 412.4 5 PESOS
8.4600 g., 0.8750 Gold .2380 oz. AGW **Obv:** Facing eagle, snake in beak **Obv. Legend:** REPUBLICA MEXICANA **Rev:** Radiant cap above scales

Date	Mintage	F	VF	XF	Unc	BU
1871Go S	1,600	400	800	1,250	2,250	—
1887Go R	140	600	1,200	1,600	3,000	—
1888Go R Rare	65	—	—	—	—	—
1893Go R Rare	16	—	—	—	—	—

KM# 412.5 5 PESOS
8.4600 g., 0.8750 Gold .2380 oz. AGW **Obv:** Facing eagle, snake in beak **Obv. Legend:** REPUBLICA MEXICANA **Rev:** Radiant cap above scales

Date	Mintage	F	VF	XF	Unc	BU
1874Ho R	—	1,750	2,500	3,000	4,500	—
1877Ho R	990	750	1,250	2,000	3,000	—
1877Ho A	Inc. above	650	1,100	1,750	2,750	—
1888Ho G Rare	—	—	—	—	—	—

KM# 412.6 5 PESOS
8.4600 g., 0.8750 Gold .2380 oz. AGW **Obv:** Facing eagle, snake in beak **Obv. Legend:** REPUBLICA MEXICANA **Rev:** Radiant cap above scales

Date	Mintage	F	VF	XF	Unc	BU
1870Mo C	550	200	400	600	1,500	—
1871/69Mo M	1,600	175	300	400	650	—
1871Mo M	Inc. above	175	300	400	650	—
1872Mo M	1,600	175	300	400	650	—
1873/2Mo M	—	200	400	550	850	—
1874Mo M	—	200	400	550	850	—
1875/3Mo B/M	—	200	400	550	950	—
1875Mo B	—	200	400	550	950	—
1876/5Mo B/M	—	200	400	550	1,000	—
1877Mo M	—	250	450	750	1,250	—
1878/7Mo M	400	200	400	550	1,250	—
1878Mo M	Inc. above	200	400	550	1,250	—
1879/8Mo M	—	200	400	550	1,250	—
1880Mo M	—	200	400	550	1,250	—
1881Mo M	—	200	400	550	1,250	—
1882Mo M	200	250	450	750	1,650	—
1883Mo M	200	250	450	750	1,650	—
1884Mo M	—	250	450	750	1,650	—
1886Mo M	200	250	450	750	1,650	—
1887Mo M	200	250	450	750	1,650	—
1888Mo M	250	200	400	550	1,650	—
1889Mo M	190	250	450	750	1,650	—
1890Mo M	149	250	450	750	1,650	—
1891Mo M	156	250	450	750	1,650	—
1892Mo M	214	250	450	750	1,650	—
1893Mo M	1,058	200	400	500	800	—
1897Mo M	370	200	400	550	1,000	—
1898Mo M	376	200	400	550	1,000	—
1900Mo M	1,014	175	300	400	650	1,000
1901Mo M	1,071	175	300	400	650	—
1902Mo M	1,478	175	300	400	650	—
1903Mo M	1,162	175	300	400	650	—
1904Mo M	1,415	175	300	400	650	—
1905Mo M	563	200	400	550	1,500	—

KM# 412.7 5 PESOS
8.4600 g., 0.8750 Gold .2380 oz. AGW **Obv:** Facing eagle, snake in beak **Obv. Legend:** REPUBLICA MEXICANA **Rev:** Radiant cap above scales

Date	Mintage	F	VF	XF	Unc	BU
1874Zs A	—	250	500	750	1,500	—
1875Zs A	—	200	400	500	1,000	—
1877Zs S/A	—	200	400	550	1,000	—
1878/7Zs S/A	—	200	400	550	1,000	—
1883Zs S	—	175	300	450	700	—
1888Zs Z	70	1,000	1,500	2,000	3,000	—
1889Zs Z	373	200	300	500	850	—
1892Zs Z	1,229	175	300	450	700	—

KM# 413 10 PESOS
16.9200 g., 0.8750 Gold .4760 oz. AGW **Obv:** Facing eagle, snake in beak **Obv. Legend:** REPUBLICA MEXICANA **Rev:** Radiant cap above scales

Date	Mintage	F	VF	XF	Unc	BU
1874As DL Rare	—	—	—	—	—	—
1875As L	642	600	1,250	2,500	3,500	—
1878As L	977	500	1,000	2,000	3,000	—
1879As L	1,078	500	1,000	2,000	3,000	—
1880As L	2,629	500	1,000	2,000	3,000	—
1881As L	2,574	500	1,000	2,000	3,000	—
1882As L	3,403	500	1,000	2,000	3,000	—
1883As L	3,597	500	1,000	2,000	3,000	—
1884As L Rare	—	—	—	—	—	—
1885As L	4,562	500	1,000	2,000	3,000	—
1886As L	4,643	500	1,000	2,000	3,000	—
1887As L	3,667	500	1,000	2,000	3,000	—
1888As L	4,521	500	1,000	2,000	3,000	—
1889As L	5,615	500	1,000	2,000	3,000	—
1890As L	4,920	500	1,000	2,000	3,000	—
1891As L	568	500	1,000	2,000	3,000	—
1892As L	—	—	—	—	—	—
1893As L	817	500	1,000	2,000	3,000	—
1894/3As L	1,658	—	—	—	—	—
1894As L	Inc. above	500	1,000	2,000	3,000	—
1895As L	1,237	500	1,000	2,000	3,000	—

KM# 413.1 10 PESOS
16.9200 g., 0.8750 Gold .4760 oz. AGW **Obv:** Facing eagle, snake in beak **Obv. Legend:** REPUBLICA MEXICANA **Rev:** Radiant cap above scales

Date	Mintage	F	VF	XF	Unc	BU
1888Ca M	175	—	—	7,500	—	—

KM# 413.2 10 PESOS
16.9200 g., 0.8750 Gold .4760 oz. AGW **Obv:** Facing eagle, snake in beak **Obv. Legend:** REPUBLICA MEXICANA **Rev:** Radiant cap above scales

Date	Mintage	F	VF	XF	Unc	BU
1881Cn D	—	400	600	1,000	1,750	—
1882Cn D	874	400	600	1,000	1,750	—
1882Cn E	Inc. above	400	600	1,000	1,750	—
1883Cn D	221	—	—	—	—	—
1883Cn M	Inc. above	400	600	1,000	1,750	—
1884Cn M	—	400	600	1,000	1,750	—
1885Cn M	1,235	400	600	1,000	1,750	—
1886Cn M	981	400	600	1,000	1,750	—
1887Cn M	2,289	400	600	1,000	1,750	—
1888Cn M	767	400	600	1,000	1,750	—
1889Cn M	859	400	600	1,000	1,750	—
1890Cn M	1,427	400	600	1,000	1,750	—
1891Cn M	670	400	600	1,000	1,750	—
1892Cn M	379	400	600	1,000	1,750	—
1893Cn M	1,806	400	600	1,000	1,750	—
1895Cn M	179	500	1,000	1,500	2,500	—
1903Cn Q	774	400	600	1,000	1,750	—

MEXICO 503

KM# 413.3 10 PESOS
16.9200 g., 0.8750 Gold .4760 oz. AGW **Obv:** Facing eagle, snake in beak **Obv. Legend:** REPUBLICA MEXICANA **Rev:** Radiant cap above scales

Date	Mintage	F	VF	XF	Unc	BU
1872Do P	1,755	350	500	800	1,250	—
1873/2Do P	1,091	350	500	850	1,350	—
1873/2Do M/P	Inc. above	350	550	900	1,450	—
1874Do M	—	350	550	900	1,450	—
1875Do M	—	350	550	900	1,450	—
1876Do M	—	450	750	1,250	2,000	—
1877Do P	—	350	550	900	1,450	—
1878Do E	582	350	550	900	1,450	—
1879/8Do B	—	350	550	900	1,450	—
1879Do B	—	350	550	900	1,450	—
1880Do P	2,030	350	550	900	1,450	3,750
1881/79Do P	2,617	350	550	900	1,450	—
1882Do P Rare	1,528					
1882Do C	Inc. above	350	550	900	1,450	—
1883Do C	793	450	750	1,250	2,000	—
1884Do C	108	450	750	1,250	2,000	—

KM# 413.4 10 PESOS
16.9200 g., 0.8750 Gold .4760 oz. AGW **Obv:** Facing eagle, snake in beak **Obv. Legend:** REPUBLICA MEXICANA **Rev:** Radiant cap above scales

Date	Mintage	F	VF	XF	Unc	BU
1870Ga C	490	500	800	1,000	1,750	—
1871Ga C	1,910	400	800	1,250	2,250	—
1872Ga C	780	500	1,000	2,000	2,500	—
1873Ga C	422	500	1,000	2,000	3,000	—
1874/3Ga C	477	500	1,000	2,000	3,000	—
1875Ga C	710	500	1,000	2,000	3,000	—
1878Ga A	183	600	1,200	2,500	3,500	—
1879Ga A	200	600	1,200	2,500	3,500	—
1880Ga S	404	500	1,000	2,000	3,000	—
1881Ga S	239	600	1,200	2,500	3,500	—
1891Ga S	196	600	1,200	2,500	3,500	—

KM# 413.5 10 PESOS
16.9200 g., 0.8750 Gold .4760 oz. AGW **Obv:** Facing eagle, snake in beak **Obv. Legend:** REPUBLICA MEXICANA **Rev:** Radiant cap above scales

Date	Mintage	F	VF	XF	Unc	BU
1872Go S	1,400	2,000	4,000	6,500	10,000	—
1887Go R Rare	80					

Note: Stack's Rio Grande Sale 6-93, P/L AU realized, $12,650

| 1888Go R Rare | 68 | — | — | — | — | — |

KM# 413.6 10 PESOS
16.9200 g., 0.8750 Gold .4760 oz. AGW **Obv:** Facing eagle, snake in beak **Obv. Legend:** REPUBLICA MEXICANA **Rev:** Radiant cap above scales

Date	Mintage	F	VF	XF	Unc	BU
1874Ho R Rare	—	—	—	—	—	—
1876Ho F Rare	357	—	—	—	—	—
1878Ho A	814	1,750	3,000	3,500	5,500	—
1879Ho A	—	1,000	2,000	2,500	4,000	—
1880Ho A	—	1,000	2,000	2,500	4,000	—
1881Ho A Rare						

Note: American Numismatic Rarities Eliasberg sale 4-05, MS-62 realized $34,500.

KM# 413.7 10 PESOS
16.9200 g., 0.8750 Gold .4760 oz. AGW **Obv:** Facing eagle, snake in beak **Obv. Legend:** REPUBLICA MEXICANA **Rev:** Radiant cap above scales

Date	Mintage	F	VF	XF	Unc	BU
1870Mo C	480	500	900	1,200	2,000	—
1872/1Mo M/C	2,100	350	550	900	1,350	—
1873Mo M	—	400	600	950	1,450	—
1874/3Mo M	—	400	600	950	1,450	—
1875Mo B/M	—	400	600	950	1,450	—
1876Mo B Rare	—	—	—	—	—	—
1878Mo M	300	400	600	950	1,450	—
1879Mo M	—	—	—	—	—	—
1881Mo M	100	500	1,000	1,600	2,500	—
1882Mo M	—	400	600	950	1,450	—
1883Mo M	100	600	1,000	1,600	2,500	—
1884Mo M	—	600	1,000	1,600	2,500	—
1885Mo M	—	400	600	950	1,450	—
1886Mo M	100	600	1,000	1,600	2,500	—
1887Mo M	100	600	1,000	1,625	2,750	—
1888Mo M	144	450	750	1,200	2,000	—
1889Mo M	88	600	1,000	1,600	2,500	—
1890Mo M	137	600	1,000	1,600	2,500	—
1891Mo M	133	600	1,000	1,600	2,500	—
1892Mo M	45	600	1,000	1,600	2,500	—
1893Mo M	1,361	350	550	900	1,350	—
1897Mo M	239	400	600	950	1,450	—
1898/7Mo M	244	425	625	1,000	1,750	—
1900Mo M	733	400	600	950	1,450	—
1901Mo M	562	350	500	800	1,250	—
1902Mo M	719	350	500	800	1,250	—
1903Mo M	713	350	500	800	1,250	—
1904Mo M	694	350	500	800	1,250	—
1905Mo M	401	400	600	950	1,500	—

KM# 413.8 10 PESOS
16.9200 g., 0.8750 Gold .4760 oz. AGW **Obv:** Facing eagle, snake in beak **Obv. Legend:** REPUBLICA MEXICANA **Rev:** Radiant cap above scales

Date	Mintage	F	VF	XF	Unc	BU
1870oa E	4,614	400	600	900	1,600	—
1871oa E	2,705	400	600	950	1,650	—
1872oa E	5,897	400	600	850	1,500	—
1873oa E	3,537	400	600	850	1,500	—
1874oa E	2,205	400	600	1,200	1,850	—
1875oa E	312	450	750	1,400	2,250	—
1876oa E	766	450	750	1,400	2,250	—
1877oa E	463	450	750	1,400	2,250	—
1878oa E	229	450	750	1,400	2,250	—
1879oa E	210	450	750	1,400	2,250	—
1880oa E	238	450	750	1,400	2,250	—
1881oa E	961	400	600	1,200	2,000	—
1882oa E	170	600	1,000	1,500	2,500	—
1883oa E	111	600	1,000	1,500	2,500	—
1884oa E	325	450	750	1,400	2,250	—
1885oa E	370	450	750	1,400	2,250	—
1886oa E	400	450	750	1,400	2,250	—
1887oa E	—	700	1,250	2,250	4,000	—
1888oa E	—	—	—	—	—	—

KM# 413.9 10 PESOS
16.9200 g., 0.8750 Gold .4760 oz. AGW **Obv:** Facing eagle, snake in beak **Obv. Legend:** REPUBLICA MEXICANA **Rev:** Radiant cap above scales

Date	Mintage	F	VF	XF	Unc	BU
1871Zs H	2,000	350	500	800	1,250	—
1872Zs H	3,092	325	500	750	1,150	—
1873Zs H	936	400	600	950	1,450	—
1874Zs H	—	400	600	950	1,450	—
1875/3Zs A	—	400	600	1,000	1,750	—
1876/5Zs S	—	400	600	1,000	1,750	—
1877Zs S/H	506	400	600	1,000	1,750	—
1878Zs S	711	400	600	1,000	1,750	—
1879/8Zs S	—	450	750	1,400	2,250	—
1879Zs S	—	450	750	1,400	2,250	—
1880Zs S	2,089	350	550	950	1,450	—
1881Zs S	736	400	600	1,000	1,750	—
1882/1Zs Z	—	400	600	1,000	1,750	2,500
1882Zs S	1,599	350	550	950	1,450	—
1883/2Zs S	256	400	600	1,000	1,750	—
1884/3Zs S	—	350	550	950	1,600	—
1884Zs S	—	350	550	950	1,600	—
1885Zs S	1,588	350	550	950	1,450	—
1886Zs S	5,364	350	550	950	1,450	—
1887Zs Z	2,330	350	550	950	1,450	—
1888Zs Z	4,810	350	550	950	1,450	—
1889Zs Z	6,154	300	500	750	1,250	—
1890Zs Z	1,321	350	550	950	1,450	—
1891Zs Z	1,930	350	550	950	1,450	—
1892Zs Z	1,882	350	550	950	1,450	—
1893Zs Z	2,899	350	550	950	1,450	—
1894Zs Z	2,501	350	550	950	1,450	—
1895Zs Z	1,217	350	550	950	1,450	—

KM# 414 20 PESOS
33.8400 g., 0.8750 Gold .9520 oz. AGW **Obv:** Facing eagle, snake in beak **Rev:** Radiant cap above scales

Date	Mintage	F	VF	XF	Unc	BU
1876As L Rare	276	—	—	—	—	—
1877As L Rare	166	—	—	—	—	—
1878As L	—	—	—	—	—	—
1888As L Rare	—	—	—	—	—	—

KM# 414.2 20 PESOS
33.8400 g., 0.8750 Gold .9520 oz. AGW **Obv:** Facing eagle, snake in beak **Obv. Legend:** REPUBLICA MEXICANA **Rev:** Radiant cap above scales

Date	Mintage	F	VF	XF	Unc	BU
1870Cn E	3,749	BV	685	950	2,000	—
1871Cn P	3,046	BV	685	950	2,000	—
1872Cn P	972	BV	685	950	2,000	—
1873Cn P	1,317	BV	685	950	2,000	—
1874Cn P	—	BV	685	950	2,000	—
1875Cn P	—	600	1,200	1,800	2,500	—
1876Cn P	—	BV	685	950	2,000	—
1876Cn G	—	BV	685	950	2,000	—
1877Cn G	167	600	1,000	1,500	3,000	—
1878Cn Rare	842					
1881/0Cn D	2,039	—	—	—	—	—
1881Cn D	Inc. above	BV	685	950	2,000	—
1882/1Cn D	736	BV	685	950	2,000	—
1883Cn M	1,836	BV	685	950	2,000	—
1884Cn M	—	BV	685	950	2,000	—
1885Cn M	544	BV	685	950	2,000	—
1886Cn M	882	BV	685	950	2,000	—
1887Cn M	837	BV	685	950	2,000	—
1888Cn M	473	BV	685	950	2,000	—
1889Cn M	1,376	BV	685	950	2,000	—
1890Cn M	—	800	1,750	3,500	8,750	—
1891Cn M	237	BV	900	1,200	2,250	—
1892Cn M	526	BV	685	950	2,000	—
1893Cn M	2,062	BV	685	950	2,000	—
1894Cn M	4,516	BV	685	950	2,000	—
1895Cn M	3,193	BV	685	950	2,000	—
1896Cn M	4,072	BV	685	950	2,000	—
1897/6Cn M	959	BV	685	950	2,000	—
1897Cn M	Inc. above	BV	685	950	2,000	—
1898Cn M	1,660	BV	685	950	2,000	—
1899Cn M	1,243	BV	685	950	2,000	—
1899Cn Q	Inc. above	BV	900	1,200	2,250	—
1900Cn Q	1,558	BV	685	950	2,000	—
1901Cn Q	Inc. above	BV	685	950	2,000	—
1901/0Cn Q	1,496					
1902Cn Q	1,059	BV	685	950	2,000	—
1903Cn Q	1,121	BV	685	950	2,000	—
1904Cn H	4,646	BV	685	950	2,000	—
1905Cn P	1,738	BV	900	1,200	2,250	—

504 MEXICO

KM# 414.3 20 PESOS
33.8400 g., 0.8750 Gold .9520 oz. AGW **Obv:** Facing eagle, snake in beak **Obv. Legend:** REPUBLICA MEXICANA **Rev:** Radiant cap above scales

Date	Mintage	F	VF	XF	Unc	BU
1870Do P	416	1,000	1,500	2,000	2,500	—
1871/0Do P	1,073	1,000	1,750	2,250	2,750	—
1871Do P	Inc. above	1,000	1,500	2,000	2,500	—
1872/1Do PT	—	1,500	3,000	4,500	7,000	—
1876Do M	—	1,000	1,500	2,000	2,500	—
1877Do P	94	1,500	2,250	2,750	3,250	—
1878Do Rare	258	—	—	—	—	—

KM# 414.4 20 PESOS
33.8400 g., 0.8750 Gold .9520 oz. AGW **Obv:** Facing eagle, snake in beak **Obv. Legend:** REPUBLICA MEXICANA **Rev:** Radiant cap above scales

Date	Mintage	F	VF	XF	Unc	BU
1870Go S	3,250	BV	665	900	1,500	—
1871Go S	20,000	BV	665	900	1,500	2,200
1872Go S	18,000	BV	665	900	1,500	—
1873Go S	7,000	BV	665	900	1,500	—
1874Go S	—	BV	665	900	1,500	—
1875Go S	—	BV	665	900	1,500	—
1876Go S	—	BV	665	900	1,500	—
1876Go M/S	—	—	—	—	—	—
1877Go M/S Rare	15,000	—	—	—	—	—
1877Go R	Inc. above	BV	665	900	1,500	—
1877Go S Rare	1,852	—	—	—	—	—
1878/7Go M/S	13,000	675	1,250	2,000	2,800	—
1878Go M	Inc. above	675	1,250	2,000	2,800	—
1878Go S	Inc. above	BV	665	900	1,500	—
1879Go S	8,202	BV	800	1,200	2,300	—
1880Go S	7,375	BV	665	900	1,500	—
1881Go S	4,909	BV	665	900	1,500	—
1882Go S	4,020	BV	665	900	1,500	—
1883/2Go B	3,705	BV	750	1,150	2,250	—
1883Go B	Inc. above	BV	665	900	1,500	—
1884Go B	1,798	BV	665	900	1,500	—
1885Go R	2,660	BV	665	900	1,500	—
1886Go R	1,090	625	800	1,250	2,500	—
1887Go R	1,009	625	800	1,250	2,500	—
1888Go R	1,011	625	800	1,250	2,500	—
1889Go R	956	625	800	1,250	2,500	—
1890Go R	879	625	800	1,250	2,500	—
1891Go R	818	625	800	1,250	2,500	—
1892Go R	730	625	800	1,250	2,500	—
1893Go R	3,343	BV	665	1,000	2,000	—
1894/3Go R	6,734	BV	665	900	1,500	—
1894Go R	Inc. above	BV	665	900	1,500	—
1895/3Go R	7,118	BV	665	900	1,500	—
1895Go R	Inc. above	BV	665	900	1,500	—
1896Go R	9,219	BV	665	900	1,500	5,750
1897/6Go R	6,781	BV	665	900	1,500	—
1897Go R	Inc. above	BV	665	900	1,500	—
1898Go R	7,710	BV	665	900	1,500	—
1899Go R	8,527	BV	665	900	1,500	—
1900Go R	4,512	550	800	1,250	2,350	—

KM# 414.5 20 PESOS
33.8400 g., 0.8750 Gold .9520 oz. AGW **Obv:** Facing eagle, snake in beak **Obv. Legend:** REPUBLICA MEXICANA **Rev:** Radiant cap above scales

Date	Mintage	F	VF	XF	Unc	BU
1874Ho R Rare	—	—	—	—	—	—
1875Ho R Rare	—	—	—	—	—	—
1876Ho F Rare	—	—	—	—	—	—
1888Ho g Rare	—	—	—	—	—	—

KM# 414.6 20 PESOS
33.8400 g., 0.8750 Gold .9520 oz. AGW **Obv:** Facing eagle, snake in beak **Obv. Legend:** REPUBLICA MEXICANA **Rev:** Radiant cap above scales

Date	Mintage	F	VF	XF	Unc	BU
1870Mo C	14,000	BV	665	850	1,500	—
1871Mo M	21,000	BV	665	850	1,500	—
1872/1Mo M	11,000	BV	665	850	1,650	—
1872Mo M	Inc. above	BV	665	850	1,500	—
1873Mo M	5,600	BV	665	850	1,500	—
1874/2Mo M	—	BV	665	850	1,500	—
1874/2Mo B	—	BV	700	1,000	1,650	—
1875Mo B	—	BV	650	900	1,600	—
1876Mo B	—	BV	650	900	1,600	—
1876Mo M	—	—	—	—	—	—

Note: Reported, not confirmed

Date	Mintage	F	VF	XF	Unc	BU
1877Mo M	2,000	BV	700	1,100	2,000	—
1878Mo M	7,000	BV	650	900	1,600	—
1879Mo M	—	BV	650	900	1,750	—
1880Mo M	—	BV	650	900	1,750	—
1881/0Mo M	—	BV	665	850	1,500	—
1881Mo M	11,000	BV	665	850	1,500	—
1881Mo M	Inc. above	BV	665	850	1,500	—
1882/1Mo M	5,800	BV	665	850	1,500	—
1882Mo M	Inc. above	BV	665	850	1,500	—
1883/1Mo M	4,000	BV	665	850	1,500	—
1883Mo M	Inc. above	BV	665	850	1,500	—
1884/3Mo M	—	BV	650	900	1,600	—
1884Mo M	—	BV	650	900	1,600	—
1885Mo M	6,000	BV	650	900	1,750	—
1886Mo M	10,000	BV	665	850	1,500	—
1887Mo M	12,000	625	800	1,500	2,500	—
1888Mo M	7,300	BV	665	850	1,450	—
1889Mo M	6,477	650	850	1,650	3,750	—
1890Mo M	7,852	BV	665	850	1,550	—
1891/0Mo M	8,725	BV	665	850	1,550	—
1891Mo M	Inc. above	BV	665	850	1,550	—
1892Mo M	11,000	BV	665	850	1,500	—
1893Mo M	15,000	BV	665	850	1,500	—
1894Mo M	14,000	BV	665	850	1,500	—
1895Mo M	13,000	BV	665	850	1,500	—
1896Mo B	14,000	BV	665	850	1,500	—
1897/6Mo M	12,000	BV	665	850	1,500	—
1897Mo M	Inc. above	BV	665	850	1,500	—
1898Mo M	20,000	BV	665	850	1,500	—
1899Mo M	23,000	BV	665	850	1,500	—
1900Mo M	21,000	BV	665	850	1,500	—
1901Mo M	29,000	BV	665	850	1,500	—
1902Mo M	38,000	BV	665	850	1,500	—
1903/2Mo M	31,000	BV	665	850	1,500	—
1903Mo M	Inc. above	BV	665	850	1,500	—
1904Mo M	52,000	BV	665	850	1,500	—
1905Mo M	9,757	BV	665	850	1,500	—

KM# 414.7 20 PESOS
33.8400 g., 0.8750 Gold .9520 oz. AGW **Obv:** Facing eagle, snake in beak **Obv. Legend:** REPUBLICA MEXICANA **Rev:** Radiant cap above scales

Date	Mintage	F	VF	XF	Unc	BU
1870oa E	1,131	750	1,500	2,500	5,000	—
1871oa E	1,591	750	1,500	2,500	5,000	—
1872oa E	255	1,000	1,750	3,000	7,000	—
1888oa E	170	2,000	3,000	5,000	—	—

KM# 414.8 20 PESOS
33.8400 g., 0.8750 Gold .9520 oz. AGW **Obv:** Facing eagle, snake in beak **Rev:** Radiant cap above scales

Date	Mintage	F	VF	XF	Unc	BU
1871Zs H	1,000	3,500	6,500	7,000	9,000	—
1875Zs A	—	4,000	6,000	7,500	9,500	—
1878Zs S	441	4,000	6,000	7,500	9,500	—
1888Zs Z Rare	50	—	—	—	—	—
1889Zs Z	640	3,500	5,500	7,000	9,000	—

KM# 414.1 20 PESOS
33.8400 g., 0.8750 Gold .9520 oz. AGW **Obv:** Facing eagle, snake in beak **Rev:** Radiant cap above scales **Note:** Mint mark CH, Ca.

Date	Mintage	F	VF	XF	Unc	BU
1872CH M	995	BV	700	1,000	2,500	—
1873CH M	950	BV	700	1,000	2,500	—
1874CH M	1,116	BV	685	950	2,500	—
1875CH M	750	BV	700	1,000	2,500	—
1876CH M	600	BV	800	1,250	2,750	—
1877CH Rare	55	—	—	—	—	—
1882CH M	1,758	BV	685	950	2,500	—
1883CH M	161	700	1,000	1,500	3,000	—
1884CH M	496	BV	700	1,000	2,500	—
1885CH M	122	700	1,000	1,500	3,000	—
1887Ca M	550	BV	700	1,000	2,500	—
1888Ca M	351	BV	700	1,000	2,500	—
1889Ca M	464	BV	700	1,000	2,500	—
1890Ca M	1,209	BV	685	950	2,500	—
1891Ca M	2,004	BV	665	900	2,250	—
1893Ca M	418	BV	700	950	2,500	—
1895Ca M	133	700	1,000	1,500	3,000	—

UNITED STATES

DECIMAL COINAGE
100 Centavos = 1 Peso

KM# 461 2 PESOS
1.6666 g., 0.9000 Gold .0482 oz. AGW, 13 mm. **Obv:** National arms **Rev:** Date above value within wreath **Note:** Mint mark Mo.

Date	Mintage	F	VF	XF	Unc	BU
1919	1,670,000	—	BV	35.00	65.00	—
1920/10		BV	35.00	55.00	100	—
1920	4,282,000	—	BV	35.00	50.00	—
1944	10,000	BV	35.00	50.00	70.00	—
1945	Est. 140,000	—	—	—	BV+20%	—
1946	168,000	BV	35.00	50.00	100	—
1947	25,000	BV	35.00	50.00	75.00	—
1948 No specimens known	45,000					

Note: During 1951-1972 a total of 4,590,493 pieces were restruck, most likely dated 1945. In 1996 matte re-strikes were produced

KM# 463 2-1/2 PESOS
2.0833 g., 0.9000 Gold .0602 oz. AGW, 15.5 mm. **Obv:** National arms **Rev:** Miguel Hidalgo y Costilla **Note:** Mint mark Mo.

Date	Mintage	F	VF	XF	Unc	BU
1918	1,704,000	—	BV	45.00	80.00	—
1919	984,000	—	BV	45.00	80.00	—
1920/10	607,000	—	BV	55.00	130	—
1920	Inc. above	—	BV	45.00	65.00	—
1944	20,000	—	BV	45.00	60.00	—
1945	Est. 180,000	—	—	—	BV+18%	—
1946	163,000	—	BV	45.00	60.00	—
1947	24,000	200	265	325	500	—

MEXICO 505

Date	Mintage	F	VF	XF	Unc	BU
1948	63,000	—	BV	45.00	70.00	—

Note: During 1951-1972 a total of 5,025,087 pieces were restruck, most likely dated 1945. In 1996 matte restrikes were produced

KM# 464 5 PESOS
4.1666 g., 0.9000 Gold .1205 oz. AGW, 19 mm. **Obv:** National arms **Rev:** Miguel Hidalgo y Costilla **Note:** Mint mark Mo.

Date	Mintage	F	VF	XF	Unc	BU
1905	18,000	120	175	245	600	—
1906	4,638,000	—	—	BV	90.00	—
1907/6	—	—	—	—	—	—
1907	1,088,000	—	—	BV	95.00	—
1910	100,000	—	—	BV	150	—
1918/7	609,000	—	—	BV	200	—
1918	Inc. above	—	—	BV	100	—
1919	506,000	—	—	BV	100	—
1920	2,385,000	—	—	BV	100	—
1955	Est. 48,000	—	—	—	BV+12%	—

Note: During 1955-1972 a total of 1,767,645 pieces were restruck, most likely dated 1955. In 1996 matte restrikes were produced

KM# 473 10 PESOS
8.3333 g., 0.9000 Gold .2411 oz. AGW, 22.5 mm. **Obv:** National arms **Rev:** Miguel Hidalgo y Costilla **Note:** Mint mark Mo.

Date	Mintage	F	VF	XF	Unc	BU
1905	39,000	—	BV	170	225	—
1906	2,949,000	—	BV	165	185	—
1907	1,589,000	—	BV	165	185	—
1908	890,000	—	BV	165	185	—
1910	451,000	—	BV	165	185	—
1916	26,000	—	BV	175	350	—
1917	1,967,000	—	BV	165	185	—
1919	266,000	—	BV	165	200	—
1920	12,000	—	BV	425	700	—
1959	Est. 50,000	—	—	—	BV+7%	—

Note: *During 1961-1972 a total of 954,983 pieces were restruck, most likely dated 1959. In 1996 matte restrikes were produced

KM# 478 20 PESOS
16.6666 g., 0.9000 Gold .4823 oz. AGW, 27.5 mm. **Obv:** National arms, eagle left **Rev:** Gear-like design within upper circle above value **Note:** Mint mark Mo.

Date	Mintage	F	VF	XF	Unc	BU
1917	852,000	—	—	BV	345	—
1918	2,831,000	—	—	BV	345	—
1919	1,094,000	—	—	BV	345	—
1920/10	462,000	—	—	BV	345	—
1920	Inc. above	—	—	BV	345	—
1921/11	922,000	—	—	BV	345	—
1921/10	—	—	—	—	—	—
1921	Inc. above	—	—	BV	345	—
1959	Est. 13,000	—	—	—	—	—

Note: During 1960-1971 a total of 1,158,414 pieces were restruck, most likely dated 1959. In 1996 matte restrikes were produced

KM# 481 50 PESOS
41.6666 g., 0.9000 Gold 1.2057 oz. AGW, 37 mm. **Subject:** Centennial of Independence **Obv:** National arms **Rev:** Winged Victory **Edge:** Reeded **Designer:** Emilio del Moral **Note:** During 1949-1972 a total of 3,975,654 pieces were restruck, most likely dated 1947. In 1996 matte restrikes were produced. Mint mark Mo.

Date	Mintage	F	VF	XF	Unc	BU
1921	180,000	—	BV	875	950	1,000
1922	463,000	—	—	BV	825	875
1923	432,000	—	—	BV	825	875
1924	439,000	—	—	BV	825	875
1925	716,000	—	—	BV	825	875
1926	600,000	—	—	BV	825	875
1927	606,000	—	—	BV	825	875
1928	538,000	—	—	BV	825	875
1929	458,000	—	—	BV	825	875
1930	372,000	—	—	BV	825	875
1931	137,000	—	—	BV	845	900
1944	593,000	—	—	BV	820	850
1945	1,012,000	—	—	BV	820	850
1946	1,588,000	—	—	BV	820	850
1947	309,000	—	—	—	BV+3%	—
1947 Specimen	—	—	—	—	—	—

Note: Value, $6,500

KM# 482 50 PESOS
41.6666 g., 0.9000 Gold 1.2057 oz. AGW, 39 mm. **Obv:** National arms **Rev:** Winged Victory

Date	Mintage	F	VF	XF	Unc	BU
1943	89,000	—	—	—	BV	845

KM# 506.2 250 PESOS
8.6400 g., 0.9000 Gold .2500 oz. AGW **Subject:** 1986 World Cup Soccer Games **Obv:** National arms, eagle left **Rev:** Without fineness statement

Date	Mintage	F	VF	XF	Unc	BU
1985 Proof	Est. 80,000	Value: 175				

KM# 500.1 250 PESOS
8.6400 g., 0.9000 Gold .2500 oz. AGW **Subject:** 1986 World Cup Soccer Games **Obv:** National arms, eagle left **Rev:** Soccer ball within top 1/2 of design with value, date, and state below

Date	Mintage	F	VF	XF	Unc	BU
1985	100,000	—	—	—	—	175
1986	—	—	—	—	—	175

KM# 500.2 250 PESOS
8.6400 g., 0.9000 Gold .2500 oz. AGW **Subject:** 1986 World Cup Soccer Games **Obv:** National arms, eagle left **Rev:** Without fineness statement

Date	Mintage	F	VF	XF	Unc	BU
1985 Proof	4,506	Value: 175				
1986 Proof	—	Value: 180				

KM# 506.1 250 PESOS
8.6400 g., 0.9000 Gold .2500 oz. AGW **Subject:** 1986 World Cup Soccer Games **Obv:** National arms, eagle left **Rev:** Equestrian left within circle

Date	Mintage	F	VF	XF	Unc	BU
1985	88,000	—	—	—	—	175

KM# 501.1 500 PESOS
17.2800 g., 0.9000 Gold .5000 oz. AGW **Subject:** 1986 World Cup Soccer Games **Obv:** National arms, eagle left **Rev:** Soccer player to right within emblem

Date	Mintage	F	VF	XF	Unc	BU
1985	102,000	—	—	—	—	350
1986	—	—	—	—	—	350

KM# 501.2 500 PESOS
17.2800 g., 0.9000 Gold .5000 oz. AGW **Subject:** 1986 World Cup Soccer Games **Obv:** National arms, eagle left **Rev:** Without fineness statement

Date	Mintage	F	VF	XF	Unc	BU
1985 Proof	5,506	Value: 350				
1986 Proof	—	Value: 350				

KM# 507.1 500 PESOS
17.2800 g., 0.9000 Gold .5000 oz. AGW **Subject:** 1986 World Cup Soccer Games **Obv:** National arms, eagle left **Rev:** Soccer ball within emblem flanked by value and date

Date	Mintage	F	VF	XF	Unc	BU
1985	—	—	—	—	—	350

KM# 507.2 500 PESOS
17.2800 g., 0.9000 Gold .5000 oz. AGW **Subject:** 1986 World Cup Soccer Games **Obv:** National arms, eagle left **Rev:** Without fineness statement

Date	Mintage	F	VF	XF	Unc	BU
1985 Proof	—	Value: 350				

KM# 534 500 PESOS
17.2800 g., 0.9000 Gold .5000 oz. AGW **Subject:** 50th Anniversary - Nationalization of Oil Industry **Obv:** National arms, eagle left **Rev:** Monument **Note:** Similar to 5000 Pesos, KM#531.

Date	Mintage	F	VF	XF	Unc	BU
1988	—	—	—	—	—	350

KM# 513 1000 PESOS
17.2800 g., 0.9000 Gold .5000 oz. AGW **Subject:** 175th Anniversary of Independence **Obv:** National arms, eagle left **Rev:** Conjoined heads left below value

Date	Mintage	F	VF	XF	Unc	BU
1985 Proof	—	Value: 375				

506 MEXICO

KM# 527 1000 PESOS
31.1030 g., 0.9990 Gold 1.0000 oz. AGW. **Subject:** 1986 World Cup Soccer Games **Obv:** National arms, eagle left **Rev:** Value above 3 soccer balls

Date	Mintage	F	VF	XF	Unc	BU
1986	—	—	—	—	—	700

KM# 535 1000 PESOS
34.5590 g., 0.9000 Gold 1.0000 oz. AGW. **Subject:** 50th Anniversary - Nationalization of Oil Industry **Obv:** National arms, eagle left **Rev:** Portrait of Cardenas **Note:** Similar to 5000 Pesos, KM#531.

Date	Mintage	F	VF	XF	Unc	BU
1988 Proof	—	Value: 700				

KM# 528 2000 PESOS
62.2000 g., 0.9990 Gold 2.0000 oz. AGW. **Subject:** 1986 World Cup Soccer Games **Obv:** National arms, eagle left **Rev:** Value above soccer balls

Date	Mintage	F	VF	XF	Unc	BU
1986	—	—	—	—	—	1,400

REFORM COINAGE
1 New Peso = 1000 Old Pesos

KM# 641 20 PESOS
6.2210 g., 0.9990 Gold .1998 oz. AGW, 21.9 mm. **Subject:** UNICEF **Obv:** National arms, eagle left **Rev:** Child playing with lasso **Edge:** Reeded

Date	Mintage	F	VF	XF	Unc	BU
1999 Proof	—	Value: 275				

KM# 696 100 PESOS
29.1690 g., Bi-Metallic .999 Gold 17.154g center in .999 Silver 12.015g ring, 34.5 mm. **Obv:** National arms **Rev:** Zacatecas arms **Edge:** Segmented reeding

Date	Mintage	F	VF	XF	Unc	BU
2003Mo Proof	244,900	Value: 445				

KM# 697 100 PESOS
29.1690 g., Bi-Metallic .999 Gold 17.154g center in .999 Silver 12.015g ring, 34.5 mm. **Obv:** National arms **Rev:** Yucatan arms **Edge:** Segmented reeding

Date	Mintage	F	VF	XF	Unc	BU
2003Mo Proof	235,763	Value: 445				

KM# 698 100 PESOS
29.1690 g., Bi-Metallic .999 Gold 17.154g center in .999 Silver 12.015g ring, 34.5 mm. **Obv:** National arms **Rev:** Veracruz-Llave arms **Edge:** Segmented reeding

Date	Mintage	F	VF	XF	Unc	BU
2003Mo Proof	248,810	Value: 445				

KM# 699 100 PESOS
29.1690 g., Bi-Metallic .999 Gold 17.154g center in .999 Silver 12.015g ring, 34.5 mm. **Obv:** National arms **Rev:** Tlaxcala arms **Edge:** Segmented reeding

Date	Mintage	F	VF	XF	Unc	BU
2003Mo Proof	248,976	Value: 445				

KM# 700 100 PESOS
29.1690 g., Bi-Metallic .999 Gold 17.154g center in .999 Silver 12.015g ring, 34.5 mm. **Obv:** National arms **Rev:** Tamaulipas arms **Edge:** Segmented reeding

Date	Mintage	F	VF	XF	Unc	BU
2004Mo Proof	1,000	Value: 445				

KM# 701 100 PESOS
29.1690 g., Bi-Metallic .999 Gold 17.154g center in .999 Silver 12.015g ring, 34.5 mm. **Obv:** National arms **Rev:** Tabasco arms **Edge:** Segmented reeding

Date	Mintage	F	VF	XF	Unc	BU
2004Mo Proof	1,000	Value: 445				

KM# 702 100 PESOS
29.1690 g., Bi-Metallic .999 Gold 17.154g center in .999 Silver 12.015g ring, 34.5 mm. **Obv:** National arms **Rev:** Sonora arms **Edge:** Segmented reeding

Date	Mintage	F	VF	XF	Unc	BU
2004Mo Proof	1,000	Value: 445				

KM# 703 100 PESOS
29.1690 g., Bi-Metallic .999 Gold 17.154g center in .999 Silver 12.015g ring, 34.5 mm. **Obv:** National arms **Rev:** Sinaloa arms **Edge:** Segmented reeding

Date	Mintage	F	VF	XF	Unc	BU
2004Mo Proof	1,000	Value: 445				

KM# 771 50000 PESOS
0.9990 Gold, 23 mm. **Subject:** World Cup Soccer **Obv:** Mexican Eagle and Snake **Rev:** Kneeling Mayan Pelota player and soccer ball

Date	Mintage	F	VF	XF	Unc	BU
2006Mo Proof	—	Value: 600				

GOLD BULLION COINAGE

KM# 530 1/20 ONZA (1/20 Ounce of Pure Gold)
1.7500 g., 0.9000 Gold .0500 oz. AGW **Obv:** Winged Victory **Rev:** Calendar stone

Date	Mintage	F	VF	XF	Unc	BU
1987	—	—	—	—	—	275
1988	—	—	—	—	—	—

KM# 589 1/20 ONZA (1/20 Ounce of Pure Gold)
1.5551 g., 0.9990 Gold .05 oz. AGW **Obv:** Winged Victory **Rev:** National arms, eagle left

Date	Mintage	F	VF	XF	Unc	BU
1991	10,000	—	—	—	—	BV+30%
1992	65,225	—	—	—	—	BV+30%
1993	10,000	—	—	—	—	BV+30%
1994	10,000	—	—	—	—	BV+30%

KM# 642 1/20 ONZA (1/20 Ounce of Pure Gold)
1.5551 g., 0.9990 Gold .05 oz. AGW **Obv:** National arms, eagle left **Rev:** Native working

Date	Mintage	F	VF	XF	Unc	BU
2000 Proof	—	Value: 50.00				

KM# 671 1/20 ONZA (1/20 Ounce of Pure Gold)
1.5551 g., 0.9990 Gold .05 oz. AGW, 16 mm. **Obv:** National arms, eagle left **Rev:** Winged Victory **Edge:** Reeded **Note:** Design similar to KM#609. Value estimates do not include the high taxes and surcharges added to the issue prices by the Mexican Government.

Date	Mintage	F	VF	XF	Unc	BU
2000	5,300	—	—	—	BV+30%	—
2002Mo	5,000	—	—	—	BV+30%	—
2004Mo	—	—	—	—	BV+30%	—
2005Mo	—	—	—	—	BV+30%	—
2006Mo	—	—	—	—	BV+30%	—

KM# 628 1/15 ONZA (1/15 Ounce of Pure Gold)
0.9990 Gold .0755 oz. AGW **Obv:** Winged Victory above legend **Rev:** National arms, eagle left within circle

Date	Mintage	F	VF	XF	Unc	BU
1987	—	—	—	—	—	275

KM# 541 1/10 ONZA (1/10 Ounce of Pure Gold)
3.1103 g., 0.9990 Gold .1000 oz. AGW **Obv:** National arms, eagle left **Rev:** Winged Victory

Date	Mintage	F	VF	XF	Unc	BU
1991	10,000	—	—	—	—	BV+20%
1992	50,777	—	—	—	—	BV+20%
1993	10,000	—	—	—	—	BV+20%
1994	10,000	—	—	—	—	BV+20%

KM# 672 1/10 ONZA (1/10 Ounce of Pure Gold)
3.1103 g., 0.9990 Gold 0.0999 oz. AGW, 20 mm. **Obv:** National arms, eagle left **Rev:** Winged Victory **Edge:** Reeded **Note:** Design similar to KM#610. Value estimates do not include the high taxes and surcharges added to the issue prices by the Mexican Government.

Date	Mintage	F	VF	XF	Unc	BU
2000	3,500	—	—	—	BV+20%	—
2002Mo	5,000	—	—	—	BV+20%	—
2004Mo	—	—	—	—	BV+20%	—
2005Mo	—	—	—	—	BV+20%	—
2006Mo	—	—	—	—	BV+20%	—
2006Mo Proof	—	BV+22%				

KM# 487 1/4 ONZA (1/4 Ounce of Pure Gold)
8.6396 g., 0.9000 Gold .2500 oz. AGW **Obv:** National arms, eagle left **Rev:** Winged Victory **Note:** Similar to KM#488.

Date	Mintage	F	VF	XF	Unc	BU
1981	313,000	—	—	—	—	BV+11%
1982	—	—	—	—	—	BV+11%

KM# 590 1/4 ONZA (1/4 Ounce of Pure Gold)
7.7758 g., 0.9990 Gold .2500 oz. AGW **Obv:** Winged Victory above legend **Rev:** National arms, eagle left

Date	Mintage	F	VF	XF	Unc	BU
1991	10,000	—	—	—	—	BV+11%
1992	28,106	—	—	—	—	BV+11%
1993	2,500	—	—	—	—	BV+11%
1994	2,500	—	—	—	—	BV+11%

KM# 673 1/4 ONZA (1/4 Ounce of Pure Gold)
7.7758 g., 0.9990 Gold .25 oz. AGW, 26.9 mm. **Obv:** National arms, eagle left **Rev:** Winged Victory **Edge:** Reeded **Note:** Design similar to KM#611. Value estimates do not include the high taxes and surcharges added to the issue prices by the Mexican Government.

Date	Mintage	F	VF	XF	Unc	BU
2000	2,500	—	—	—	BV+12%	—
2002Mo	—	—	—	—	BV+12%	—
2004Mo	—	—	—	—	BV+12%	—
2004Mo Proof	—	BV+15%	—	—	—	—
2005Mo	—	—	—	—	BV+12%	—
2005Mo Proof	—	BV+15%	—	—	—	—
2006Mo	—	—	—	—	BV+15%	—
2006Mo Proof	—	BV+12%	—	—	—	—

KM# 488 1/2 ONZA (1/2 Ounce of Pure Gold)
17.2792 g., 0.9000 Gold .5000 oz. AGW **Obv:** National arms, eagle left **Rev:** Winged Victory

Date	Mintage	F	VF	XF	Unc	BU
1981	193,000	—	—	—	—	BV+8%
1982	—	—	—	—	—	BV+8%
1989 Proof	704	Value: 500				

KM# 591 1/2 ONZA (1/2 Ounce of Pure Gold)
15.5517 g., 0.9990 Gold .5000 oz. AGW **Obv:** Winged Victory above legend **Rev:** National arms, eagle left

Date	Mintage	F	VF	XF	Unc	BU
1991	10,000	—	—	—	—	BV+8%
1992	25,220	—	—	—	—	BV+8%
1993	2,500	—	—	—	—	BV+8%
1994	2,500	—	—	—	—	BV+8%

KM# 674 1/2 ONZA (1/2 Ounce of Pure Gold)
15.5517 g., 0.9990 Gold 0.4995 oz. AGW, 32.9 mm. **Obv:** National arms, eagle left **Rev:** Winged Victory **Edge:** Reeded **Note:** Design similar to KM#612. Value estimates do not include the high taxes and surcharges added to the issue prices by the Mexican Government.

Date	Mintage	F	VF	XF	Unc	BU
2000	1,500	—	—	—	BV+8%	—
2002Mo	—	—	—	—	BV+8%	—
2004Mo	—	—	—	—	BV+8%	—
2005Mo	—	—	—	—	BV+8%	—
2005Mo Proof	—	BV+12%	—	—	—	—
2006Mo	—	—	—	—	BV+8%	—
2006Mo Proof	—	BV+12%	—	—	—	—

KM# 489 ONZA (Ounce of Pure Gold)
34.5585 g., 0.9000 Gold 1.0000 oz. AGW **Obv:** National arms, eagle left **Rev:** Winged Victory **Note:** Similar to KM#488.

Date	Mintage	F	VF	XF	Unc	BU
1981	596,000	—	—	—	—	BV+3%
1985	—	—	—	—	—	BV+3%
1988	—	—	—	—	—	BV+3%

KM# 592 ONZA (Ounce of Pure Gold)
31.1035 g., 0.9990 Gold 1.0000 oz. AGW **Obv:** Winged Victory above legend **Rev:** National arms, eagle left

Date	Mintage	F	VF	XF	Unc	BU
1991	109,193	—	—	—	—	BV+3%
1992	46,281	—	—	—	—	BV+3%
1993	10,000	—	—	—	—	BV+3%
1994	1,000	—	—	—	—	BV+3%

KM# 675 ONZA (Ounce of Pure Gold)
31.1035 g., 0.9990 Gold .999 oz. AGW, 40 mm. **Obv:** National arms, eagle left **Rev:** Winged Victory **Edge:** Reeded **Note:** Design similar to KM#639. Value estimates do not include the high taxes and surcharges added to the issue prices by the Mexican Government.

MEXICO 507

Date	Mintage	F	VF	XF	Unc	BU
2000	2,730	—	—	—	BV+3%	—
2002Mo	—	—	—	—	BV+3%	—
2004Mo	—	—	—	—	BV+3%	—
2005Mo	—	—	—	—	BV+3%	—
2005Mo Proof	—	BV+5%	—	—	—	—
2006Mo	—	—	—	—	BV+3%	—
2006Mo Proof	—	BV+5%	—	—	—	—

PLATINUM BULLION COINAGE

KM# 538 1/4 ONZA (1/4 Ounce)
7.7775 g., 0.9990 Platinum .2500 oz. APW **Obv:** National arms, eagle left **Rev:** Winged Victory

Date	Mintage	F	VF	XF	Unc	BU
1989	704	Value: 400				

BULLION COINAGE
Pre-Columbian • Azteca Series

KM# 558 250 PESOS
7.7758 g., 0.9990 Gold .2500 oz. AGW **Subject:** Native Culture **Obv:** National arms, eagle left within D-shaped circle and designed border **Rev:** Sculpture of Jaguar head within D-shaped circle and designed border

Date	Mintage	F	VF	XF	Unc	BU
1992	10,000	—	—	—	185	—
1992 Proof	2,000	Value: 285				

KM# 559 500 PESOS
15.5517 g., 0.9990 Gold .5000 oz. AGW **Subject:** Native Culture **Obv:** National arms, eagle left within D-shaped circle and designed border **Rev:** Sculpture of Jaguar head within D-shaped circle and designed border

Date	Mintage	F	VF	XF	Unc	BU
1992	10,000	—	—	—	370	—
1992 Proof	2,000	Value: 485				

KM# 560 1000 PESOS
31.1035 g., 0.9990 Gold 1.0000 oz. AGW **Subject:** Native Culture **Obv:** National arms, eagle left within D-shaped circle and designed border **Rev:** Sculpture of Jaguar head within D-shaped circle and designed border

Date	Mintage	F	VF	XF	Unc	BU
1992	17,850	—	—	—	700	—
1992 Proof	2,000	Value: 750				

BULLION COINAGE
Pre-Columbian • Central Veracruz Series

KM# 585 25 NUEVOS PESOS
7.7758 g., 0.9990 Gold .2500 oz. AGW **Subject:** Hacha Ceremonial **Obv:** National arms, eagle left **Rev:** Mask left **Note:** Similar to 100 New Pesos, KM#587.

Date	Mintage	F	VF	XF	Unc	BU
1993	15,500	—	—	—	185	—
1993 Proof	800	Value: 285				

KM# 586 50 NUEVOS PESOS
15.5517 g., 0.9990 Gold .5000 oz. AGW **Subject:** Hacha Ceremonial **Obv:** National arms, eagle left **Rev:** Mask left **Note:** Similar to 100 New Pesos, KM#587.

Date	Mintage	F	VF	XF	Unc	BU
1993	15,500	—	—	—	375	—
1993 Proof	500	Value: 485				

KM# 587 100 NUEVOS PESOS
31.1035 g., 0.9990 Gold 1.0000 oz. AGW **Subject:** Hacha Ceremonial **Obv:** National arms, eagle left **Rev:** Mask left

Date	Mintage	F	VF	XF	Unc	BU
1993	7,150	—	—	—	700	—
1993 Proof	500	Value: 750				

BULLION COINAGE
Pre-Columbian • Mayan Series

KM# 579 25 NUEVOS PESOS
7.7758 g., 0.9990 Gold .2500 oz. AGW **Subject:** Personaje de Jaina **Rev:** Seated figure

Date	Mintage	F	VF	XF	Unc	BU
1994	2,000	—	—	—	185	—
1994 Proof	500	Value: 285				

KM# 580 50 NUEVOS PESOS
15.5517 g., 0.9990 Gold .5000 oz. AGW **Subject:** Personaje de Jaina **Rev:** Seated figure

Date	Mintage	F	VF	XF	Unc	BU
1994	1,000	—	—	—	375	—
1994 Proof	500	Value: 485				

KM# 581 100 NUEVOS PESOS
31.1035 g., 0.9990 Gold 1.0000 oz. AGW **Subject:** Personaje de Jaina **Obv:** National arms, eagle left within six sided shield and designed border **Rev:** Seated figure within six sided shield and designed border

Date	Mintage	F	VF	XF	Unc	BU
1994	1,000	—	—	—	700	—
1994 Proof	500	Value: 750				

BULLION COINAGE
Pre-Columbian • Olmec Series

KM# 600 25 PESOS
7.7758 g., 0.9990 Gold .2500 oz. AGW **Subject:** Sacerdote **Obv:** National arms, eagle left **Rev:** Sculpture **Note:** Similar to 100 Pesos, KM#602.

Date	Mintage	F	VF	XF	Unc	BU
1996	500	—	—	—	185	—
1996 Proof	750	Value: 285				

KM# 601 50 PESOS
15.5517 g., 0.9990 Gold .5000 oz. AGW **Subject:** Sacerdote **Obv:** National arms, eagle left **Rev:** Sculpture **Note:** Similar to 100 Pesos, KM#602.

Date	Mintage	F	VF	XF	Unc	BU
1996	500	—	—	—	375	—
1996 Proof	500	Value: 485				

KM# 602 100 PESOS
31.1035 g., 0.9990 Gold 1.0000 oz. AGW **Subject:** Sacerdote **Obv:** National arms, eagle left within square and designed border **Rev:** Sculpture within square and designed border

Date	Mintage	F	VF	XF	Unc	BU
1996	500	—	—	—	700	—
1996 Proof	500	Value: 750				

BULLION COINAGE
Pre-Columbian • Teotihuacan Series

KM# 624 25 PESOS
7.7758 g., 0.9990 Gold .2500 oz. AGW **Subject:** Serpiente Emplumada **Obv:** National arms, eagle left **Note:** Similar to 100 Pesos, KM#626.

Date	Mintage	F	VF	XF	Unc	BU
1997	500	—	—	—	185	—
1997 Proof	200	Value: 300				

KM# 625 50 PESOS
15.5517 g., 0.9990 Gold .5000 oz. AGW **Subject:** Serpiente Emplumada **Obv:** National arms, eagle left **Note:** Similar to 100 Pesos, KM#626.

Date	Mintage	F	VF	XF	Unc	BU
1997	500	—	—	—	375	—
1997 Proof	200	Value: 500				

KM# 626 100 PESOS
31.1035 g., 0.9990 Gold 1.0000 oz. AGW **Subject:** Teotihuacan - Serpiente Emplumada **Obv:** National arms, eagle left

Date	Mintage	F	VF	XF	Unc	BU
1997	500	—	—	—	700	—
1997 Proof	Est. 200	Value: 775				

BULLION COINAGE
Pre-Columbian • Tolteca Series

KM# 667 25 PESOS
7.7759 g., 0.9990 Gold 0.2498 oz. AGW, 23 mm. **Subject:** Aguila **Obv:** National arms, eagle left **Rev:** Eagle sculpture **Edge:** Reeded

Date	Mintage	F	VF	XF	Unc	BU
1998	300	—	—	—	200	—
1998 Proof	300	Value: 300				

KM# 668 50 PESOS
15.5517 g., 0.9990 Gold 0.4995 oz. AGW, 29 mm. **Subject:** Aguila **Obv:** National arms, eagle left **Rev:** Eagle sculpture **Edge:** Reeded

Date	Mintage	F	VF	XF	Unc	BU
1998	300	—	—	—	385	—
1998 Proof	300	Value: 500				

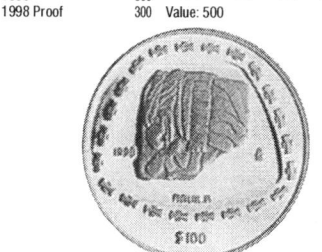

KM# 669 100 PESOS
31.1035 g., 0.9990 Gold 0.999 oz. AGW, 34.5 mm. **Subject:** Aguila **Obv:** National arms, eagle left within designed shield **Rev:** Eagle sculpture within designed shield **Edge:** Reeded

Date	Mintage	F	VF	XF	Unc	BU
1998	300	—	—	—	725	—
1998 Proof	300	Value: 775				

MEDALLIC GOLD COINAGE

KM# M91a 10 PESOS
8.3333 g., 0.9000 Gold .2411 oz. AGW **Subject:** 200th Anniversary - Birth of Hidalgo

Date	Mintage	F	VF	XF	Unc	BU
1953	—	—	—	—	BV	175

KM# M123a 10 PESOS
8.3333 g., 0.9000 Gold .2411 oz. AGW **Subject:** Centennial of Constitution

Date	Mintage	F	VF	XF	Unc	BU
1957	Est. 73,000	—	—	—	BV	175

Note: Mintage includes #M122a

KM# M92a 20 PESOS
16.6666 g., 0.9000 Gold .4823 oz. AGW **Subject:** 200th Anniversary - Birth of Hidalgo

Date	Mintage	F	VF	XF	Unc	BU
1953	—	—	—	—	BV	345

508 MEXICO

KM# M122a 50 PESOS
41.6666 g., 0.9000 Gold 1.2057 oz. AGW **Subject:** Centennial of Constitution

Date	Mintage	F	VF	XF	Unc	BU
1957 Inc. M123a	—	—	—	—	BV	850

MEDALLIC GOLD BULLION COINAGE

X# MB26 1/10 ONZA
0.9990 Gold **Subject:** 5th Birthday of North American born Panda - Tohui **Obv:** Old screw type coining press **Obv. Legend:** CASA DE MONEDA DE MEXICO **Rev:** Mother seated with cub **Rev. Legend:** 5° aniversario del panda

Date	Mintage	F	VF	XF	Unc	BU
1987Mo Proof	—	—	—	—	—	—

Note: Reported, not confirmed

X# MB40 1/4 ONZA
0.9990 Gold **Subject:** 200th Anniversary U.S.A. Constitution **Obv:** Old screw coining press **Obv. Legend:** CASA DE MONEDA DE MEXICO **Rev:** Franklin, Washington and Jefferson seated at table

Date	Mintage	F	VF	XF	Unc	BU
1987Mo Proof	5,000	Value: 250				

X# MB27 1/4 ONZA
0.9990 Gold **Subject:** 5th Birthday of North American born Panda - Tohui **Obv:** Old screw type coining press **Obv. Legend:** CASA DE MONEDA DE MEXICO **Rev:** Mother seated with cub **Rev. Legend:** 5° aniversario del panda

Date	Mintage	F	VF	XF	Unc	BU
1987Mo Proof	—	—	—	—	—	—

Note: Reported, not confirmed

X# MB28 1/2 ONZA
0.9990 Gold **Subject:** 5th Birthday of North American born Panda - Tohui **Obv:** Old screw type coining press **Obv. Legend:** CASA DE MONEDA DE MEXICO **Rev:** Mother seated with cub **Rev. Legend:** 5° aniversario del panda

Date	Mintage	F	VF	XF	Unc	BU
1987Mo Proof	—	—	—	—	—	—

Note: Reported, not confirmed

X# MB29 ONZA
Gold **Subject:** 5th Birthday of North American born Panda - Tohui **Obv:** Old screw type coining press **Obv. Legend:** CASA DE MONEDA DE MEXICO **Rev:** Mother seated with cub **Rev. Legend:** 5° aniversario del panda

Date	Mintage	F	VF	XF	Unc	BU
1987Mo Proof	—	—	—	—	—	—

Note: Reported, not confirmed

X# MB53 2 ONZAS
0.9990 Gold **Subject:** 1988 Seoul Summer Games **Obv:** Old screw coining press **Obv. Legend:** CASA DE MONEDA DE MEXICO **Rev:** Ancient coin surrounded by 12 modern events

Date	Mintage	F	VF	XF	Unc	BU
1988Mo	—	—	—	—	—	—

X# MB30 5 ONZAS
0.9990 Gold **Subject:** 5th Birthday of North American born Panda - Tohui **Obv:** Old screw type coining press **Obv. Legend:** CASA DE MONEDA DE MEXICO **Rev:** Mother seated with cub **Rev. Legend:** 5° aniversario del panda

Date	Mintage	F	VF	XF	Unc	BU
1987Mo Proof	—	—	—	—	—	—

Note: Reported, not confirmed

X# MB31 12 ONZAS
373.2360 g., 0.9990 Gold 11.9878 oz. AGW **Subject:** 5th Birthday of North American born Panda - Tohui **Obv:** Old screw type coining press **Obv. Legend:** CASA DE MONEDA DE MEXICO **Rev:** Mother seated with cub **Rev. Legend:** 5° aniversario del panda

Date	Mintage	F	VF	XF	Unc	BU
1987Mo Proof	100	—	—	—	—	—

X# MB41 12 ONZAS
0.9990 Gold **Subject:** 200th Anniversary of U.S.A. Constitution **Obv:** Old screw coining press **Obv. Legend:** CASA DE MONEDA DE MEXICO **Rev:** Franklin, Washington and Jefferson seated at table

Date	Mintage	F	VF	XF	Unc	BU
1987Mo Proof	5,000	Value: 6,000				

PATTERNS
Including off metal strikes

KM#	Date	Mintage	Identification	Mkt Val
Pn11	1826Go WW	—	8 Escudos. Gold.	—
Pn14	1828	—	1/8 Real. Gold.	—
Pn157	1892Mo AM	—	10 Pesos. Gold.	30,000
Pn158	1892Mo AM	—	20 Pesos. Gold.	30,000

PROOF SETS

KM#	Date	Mintage	Identification	Issue Price	Mkt Val
PS11	1985 (2)	—	KM511, 513	—	350
PS8	1985 (4)	—	KM500.2-501.2, 506.2, 507.2	—	700
PS12	1989 (3)	704	KM488, 494.1, 538, Rainbow	730	850

GUADALAJARA

The Guadalajara Mint made its first coins in 1812 and the mint operated until April 30, 1815. It was to reopen in 1818 and continue operations until 1822. It was the only Royalist mint to strike gold coins, both 4 and 8 Escudos. In addition to these it struck the standard 5 denominations in silver.
Mint mark: GA.

WAR OF INDEPENDENCE

ROYALIST COINAGE

KM# 147 4 ESCUDOS
13.5400 g., 0.8750 Gold .3809 oz. AGW **Ruler:** Ferdinand VII **Obv:** Uniformed bust right **Rev:** Crowned shield divides designed wreath

Date	Mintage	VG	F	VF	XF	Unc
1812GA MR Rare	—	—	—	—	—	—

KM# 162 8 ESCUDOS
27.0700 g., 0.8750 Gold .7616 oz. AGW **Ruler:** Ferdinand VII **Obv:** Large uniformed bust right **Obv. Legend:** FERDIN.VII.D.G... **Rev:** Crowned shield divides designed wreath **Rev. Legend:** UTROQ.FELIX...

Date	Mintage	VG	F	VF	XF	Unc
1812GA MR Rare	—	—	—	—	—	—
1813GA MR	—	600	900	15,000	25,000	—

Note: American Numismatic Rarities Eliasberg sale 4-05, VF-30 realized $23,000.

KM# 163 8 ESCUDOS
27.0700 g., 0.8750 Gold .7616 oz. AGW **Ruler:** Ferdinand VII **Obv:** Small uniformed bust right **Obv. Legend:** FERDIN.VII... **Rev:** Crowned shield divides designed wreath **Rev. Legend:** UTROQ.FELIX...

Date	Mintage	VG	F	VF	XF	Unc
1813GA MR	—	10,000	16,000	30,000	45,000	—

Note: Spink America Gerber sale 6-96 VF or better realized $46,200

KM# 161.1 8 ESCUDOS
27.0700 g., 0.8750 Gold .7616 oz. AGW **Ruler:** Ferdinand VII **Obv:** Laureate head right **Obv. Legend:** FERDIN.VII.D.G... **Rev:** Crowned shield divides designed wreath **Rev. Legend:** UTROQ.FELIX...

Date	Mintage	VG	F	VF	XF	Unc
1821GA FS	—	1,500	2,500	5,000	8,500	—

Note: American Numismatic Rarities Eliasberg sale 4-05, AU-55 realized $20,700.

KM# 164 8 ESCUDOS
27.0700 g., 0.8750 Gold .7616 oz. AGW **Ruler:** Ferdinand VII **Obv:** Draped laureate bust right **Rev:** Crowned shield flanked by pillars

Date	Mintage	VG	F	VF	XF	Unc
1821GA FS	—	5,500	8,000	14,500	23,500	—

MEXICO-REVOLUTIONARY

DURANGO

A state in north central Mexico. Another area of operation for Pancho Villa. The *Muera Huerta* peso originates in this state. The coins were made in Cuencame under the orders of Generals Cemceros and Contreras.

CONSTITUTIONAL ARMY
Cuencame

FANTASY COINAGE

X# 1 20 PESOS
0.5833 Gold **Obv:** National arms **Obv. Legend:** MUERA HUERTA (Death to Huerta) **Rev:** Radiant Liberty cap

Date	Mintage	F	VF	XF	Unc	BU
1914	—	—	—	—	—	—

X# 2 20 PESOS
27.8000 g., 0.9000 Gold 0.8044 oz. AGW

Date	Mintage	F	VF	XF	Unc	BU
1914	—	—	—	—	—	—

GUERRERO

Guerrero is a state on the southwestern coast of Mexico. It was one of the areas of operation of Zapata and his forces in the south of Mexico. The Zapata forces operated seven different mints in this state. The date ranges were from 1914 to 1917 and denominations from 2 Centavos to 2 Pesos. Some were cast but most were struck and the rarest coin of the group is the Suriana 1915 2 Pesos.

EMILIANO ZAPATA
(General Salgado)

REVOLUTIONARY COINAGE

KM# 641 PESO (UN)
Gold-Silver, 29-31 mm. **Obv:** National arms **Rev:** Liberty cap within sprigs **Rev. Inscription:** Oro:0,300 **Note:** Many die varieties exist. Size varies. Weight varies 10.28-14.84g. Coin is 0.30g fine Gold.

Date	Mintage	VG	F	VF	XF	Unc
1914	—	15.00	25.00	35.00	65.00	—

KM# 642 PESO (UN)
Gold-Silver, 30.5-31 mm. **Obv:** National arms **Rev:** Liberty cap within sprigs **Rev. Inscription:** Oro:0,300 **Note:** Weight varies 12.93-14.66g. Coin is 0.300g fine Gold.

Date	Mintage	VG	F	VF	XF	Unc
1914	—	50.00	75.00	100	150	—
1915	—	600	1,000	1,500	1,800	—

KM# 643 2 PESOS (Dos)
Gold-Silver, 38.25-39.6 mm. **Obv:** National arms **Rev:** Radiant sun face above mountains **Rev. Inscription:** Oro:0,595 **Note:** Many varieties exist. Coin is 0.595g fine Gold.

Date	Mintage	VG	F	VF	XF	Unc
1914GRO	—	12.00	20.00	32.00	60.00	—

KM# 644 2 PESOS (Dos)
Gold-Silver, 39-40 mm. **Obv:** National arms **Rev:** Radiant sun and mountains **Rev. Inscription:** Oro:0,595 **Note:** Weight varies 21.71-26.54g. Coin is 0.595g fine Gold.

Date	Mintage	VG	F	VF	XF	Unc
1915GRO	—	65.00	85.00	160	200	—

CAMPO MORADO
REVOLUTIONARY COINAGE

KM# 659 PESO (UN)
Gold-Silver, 30-31 mm. **Obv:** National arms **Rev:** Liberty cap within sprigs **Rev. Inscription:** Oro:0,300 **Note:** Weight varies 12.26-15.81g. Coin is 0.300g fine Gold.

Date	Mintage	VG	F	VF	XF	Unc
1914 CAMPO Mo	—	15.00	30.00	45.00	60.00	—

KM# 658 PESO (UN)
Gold-Silver, 32-32.5 mm. **Obv:** National arms **Rev:** Liberty cap **Rev. Inscription:** Oro:0,300 **Note:** Weight varies 12.42-16.5g. Coin is 0.300g fine Gold.

Date	Mintage	VG	F	VF	XF	Unc
1914 Co Mo Gro	—	500	600	1,000	1,200	—

KM# 661 2 PESOS (Dos)
29.4400 g., Gold-Silver, 39 mm. **Obv:** National arms **Rev:** Sun and mountains **Rev. Inscription:** Oro:0,595 **Note:** Coin is 0.595g fine Gold.

Date	Mintage	VG	F	VF	XF	Unc
1915 Co. Mo.	—	1,600	3,000	7,000	9,000	—

KM# 662 2 PESOS (Dos)
0.5950 g., 1.0000 Gold-Silver, 34.5-35 mm. **Obv:** National arms **Rev:** Liberty cap **Note:** Size varies. Weight varies 18.27-20.08g.

Date	Mintage	VG	F	VF	XF	Unc
1915 C. M. GRO	—	20.00	30.00	45.00	85.00	—

KM# 660 2 PESOS (Dos)
Gold-Silver, 38.9-39 mm. **Obv:** National arms **Rev:** Sun over mountains **Rev. Inscription:** Oro:0,595 **Note:** Weight varies 20.6-26.02g. Coin is 0.595g fine Gold.

Date	Mintage	VG	F	VF	XF	Unc
1915 Co. Mo.	—	12.00	20.00	30.00	50.00	—

SURIANA
REVOLUTIONARY COINAGE

KM# 665 2 PESOS (Dos)
22.9300 g., Gold-Silver, 39 mm. **Obv:** National arms **Rev:** Sun over mountains **Rev. Inscription:** Oro:0,595 **Note:** Coin is 0.595g fine Gold.

Date	Mintage	VG	F	VF	XF	Unc
1915 Rare	—	—	—	18,000	25,000	—

Note: Spink America Gerber sale part 2, 6-96 VF realized $16,500

TAXCO
REVOLUTIONARY COINAGE

KM# 673 PESO (UN)
11.6000 g., Gold-Silver, 30 mm. **Obv:** National arms **Rev:** Liberty cap within sprigs **Rev. Inscription:** Oro:0,300 **Note:** Coin is 0.300g fine Gold.

Date	Mintage	VG	F	VF	XF	Unc
1915	—	250	400	500	800	—

KM# 674 PESO (UN)
Gold-Silver, 30 mm. **Obv:** National arms **Rev:** Liberty cap within sprigs **Rev. Inscription:** Oro:0,300 **Note:** Weight varies 10.51-12.79g. Coin is 0.300g fine Gold.

Date	Mintage	VG	F	VF	XF	Unc
1915	—	100	200	300	500	—

510   MEXICO-REVOLUTIONARY   GUERRERO

KM# 672 PESO (UN)
Gold-Silver, 30-31 mm. **Obv:** National arms **Rev:** Liberty cap within sprigs **Rev. Inscription:** Oro:0,300 **Note:** Weight varies 30-31g. Coin is 0.300g fine Gold.

Date	Mintage	VG	F	VF	XF	Unc
1915	—	12.00	20.00	30.00	45.00	—

PATTERNS
Including off metal strikes

KM#	Date	Mintage	Identification	Mkt Val
Pn647	1914	—	2 Pesos. Gold-Silver. 0.3000 g. Atlixtac.	—

OAXACA

Oaxaca is one of the southern states in Mexico. The coins issued in this state represent the most prolific series of the Revolution. Most of the coins bear the portrait of Benito Juarez, have corded or plain edges and were issued by a provisional government in the state. The exceptions are the rectangular 1 and 3 Centavos pieces that begin the series.

PROVISIONAL GOVERNMENT
REVOLUTIONARY COINAGE

KM# 745 2 PESOS (Dos)
Gold-Silver, 22 mm. **Obv:** Low relief bust left with date flanked by stars below **Rev:** Value above sprigs **Note:** 0.9020 Silver, 0.0100 Gold. Fifth bust, curved bottom 2 over pesos

Date	Mintage	VG	F	VF	XF	Unc
1915	—	12.00	20.00	40.00	60.00	—

KM# 750 5 PESOS
0.1750 Gold, 19 mm. **Obv:** Bust left **Rev:** Value above sprigs **Note:** Third bust, heavy, with short unfinished lapels

Date	Mintage	VG	F	VF	XF	Unc
1915	—	150	200	300	450	—

KM# A752 10 PESOS
0.1500 Gold **Obv:** Bust left with date flanked by stars below **Rev:** Value above sprigs

Date	Mintage	VG	F	VF	XF	Unc
1915 Rare	—	—	—	—	—	—

KM# 752 10 PESOS
0.1750 Gold, 23 mm. **Obv:** Bust left with date flanked by stars below **Rev:** Value above sprigs

Date	Mintage	VG	F	VF	XF	Unc
1915	—	200	300	400	600	—

KM# 753 20 PESOS
0.1750 Gold **Obv:** Bust left with date flanked by stars below **Rev:** Value above sprigs

Date	Mintage	VG	F	VF	XF	Unc
1915	—	400	500	800	1,000	—

KM# 754 20 PESOS
0.1750 Gold, 27 mm. **Obv:** Bust left with date flanked by stars below **Rev:** Value above sprigs

Date	Mintage	VG	F	VF	XF	Unc
1915	—	200	300	500	800	—

KM# A753 20 PESOS
0.1500 Gold **Obv:** Bust left with date flanked by stars below **Rev:** Value above sprigs **Note:** Fourth bust

Date	Mintage	VG	F	VF	XF	Unc
1915 Unique	—	—	—	—	—	—

KM# 755 60 PESOS
50.0000 g., 0.8590 Gold **Obv:** Head left within 3/4 wreath **Rev:** Balance scale below liberty cap **Edge:** Reeded

Date	Mintage	F	VF	XF	Unc	BU
1916 Rare	—	—	8,000	15,000	22,000	—

MOMBASA

Mombasa was a thriving Arabic commercial center when first visited by Portuguese navigator Vasco da Gama in 1498. During the following two centuries Portugal made repeated efforts to capture the island stronghold but was unable to hold it against the assaults of the Muscat Arabs. In 1823 the ruling Mazuri family placed the city under British protection. Britain repudiated the protectorate and it was then seized by Seyyid Said of Oman, 1837, and annexed to Zanzibar. In 1887 the sultan of Zanzibar relinquished the port of Mombasa to British administration. It was occupied by the Imperial British East Africa Company and for the following two decades was the capital of British East Africa.

TITLES
Mombasa

MINT MARKS
H – Birmingham
C/M – Calcutta

MONETARY SYSTEM
4 Pice = 1 Anna
16 Annas = 1 Rupee

PATTERNS
Including off metal strikes

KM#	Date	Mintage	Identification	Mkt Val
Pn2	1888//AH 1306H	—	Pice. Gold. KM#1.4. Rare	—

MONACO

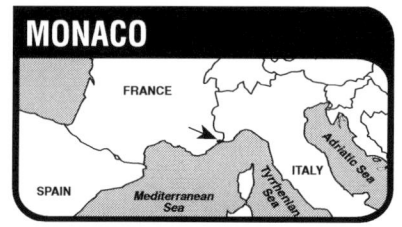

The Principality of Monaco, located on the Mediterranean coast nine miles from Nice, has an area of 0.58 sq. mi. (1.9 sq. km).

Monaco derives its name from Monoikos', the Greek surname for Hercules, the mythological strong man who, according to legend, formed the Monacan headland during one of his twelve labors. Monaco has been ruled by the Grimaldi dynasty since 1297 - Prince Albert II, the present and 32nd monarch of Monaco, is still of that line - except for a period during the French Revolution until Napoleon's downfall when the Principality was annexed to France. Since 1865, Monaco has maintained a customs union with France which guarantees its privileged position as long as the royal line remains intact. Under the new constitution proclaimed on December 17, 1962, the Prince shares his power with an 18-member unicameral National Council.

RULERS
Honore IV, 1795-1819
Honore V, 1819-1841
Florestan I, 1841-1856
Charles III, 1856-1889
Albert I, 1889-1922
Louis II, 1922-1949
Rainier III, 1949-

MINT MARKS
A - Paris

MINT PRIVY MARKS
(a) - Paris (privy marks only)
(C and clasped hands - Francois Cabinas, mint director, 1837-1838

MONETARY SYSTEM
3 Deniers = 1 Liard
4 Liards = 1 Sol
3 Sols = 1 Pezetta
20 Pezettas = 1 Scudo (Ecu)
4 Scudos = 1 Doppia (1 Louis D'or)

PRINCIPALITY

DECIMAL COINAGE
10 Centimes = 1 Decime; 10 Decimes = 1 Franc

KM# 98   20 FRANCS (Vingt)
6.4516 g., 0.9000 Gold .1867 oz. AGW **Ruler:** Charles III **Obv:** Head right **Obv. Legend:** CHARLES III PRINCE... **Rev:** Crowned mantled arms with supporters

Date	Mintage	F	VF	XF	Unc	BU
1878A	25,000	BV	200	300	600	—
1879A	50,000	BV	150	200	500	—

KM# 99   100 FRANCS (Cent)
32.2580 g., 0.9000 Gold .9335 oz. AGW **Ruler:** Charles III **Obv:** Large head right **Obv. Legend:** CHARLES III PRINCE DE MONACO **Rev:** Crowned mantled arms with supporters

Date	Mintage	F	VF	XF	Unc	BU
1882A	5,000	BV	650	850	1,250	—
1884A	15,000	—	BV	625	800	—
1886A	15,000	—	BV	625	800	—

KM# 105   100 FRANCS (Cent)
32.2580 g., 0.9000 Gold .9335 oz. AGW **Ruler:** Albert I **Obv:** Head left **Obv. Legend:** ALBERT I PRINCE.... **Rev:** Crowned oval arms within wreath with ribbon above

Date	Mintage	F	VF	XF	Unc	BU
1891A	20,000	—	BV	650	800	950
1895A	20,000	—	BV	650	800	950
1896A	20,000	—	BV	650	800	950
1901A	15,000	—	BV	650	800	950
1904A	10,000	—	BV	650	800	950

EURO COINAGE

KM# 177   20 EURO
18.0000 g., 0.9250 Gold 0.5353 oz. AGW, 32 mm. **Ruler:** Rainier III **Obv:** Bust right **Rev:** Arms

Date	Mintage	F	VF	XF	Unc	BU
2002 Proof	10,000	Value: 1,100				

KM# 179   100 EURO
29.0000 g., 0.9000 Gold 0.8391 oz. AGW **Ruler:** Rainier III **Obv:** Bust right **Rev:** Knight on horse

Date	Mintage	F	VF	XF	Unc	BU
2003 Proof	1,000	Value: 3,250				

MEDALLIC COINAGE
1966 Spink Issues
Struck by the Paris Mint for Spink and Sons, Ltd. of London

X# M2   200 FRANCS
32.0000 g., 0.9200 Gold .9466 oz. AGW **Subject:** 10th Wedding Anniversary **Note:** Prev. KM#M2.

Date	Mintage	F	VF	XF	Unc	BU
1966 (a)	5,000	—	—	—	675	—
1966 (a) Proof	1,000	Value: 850				

MEDALLIC COINAGE
1974 Paris Issues

X# M4   1000 FRANCS
0.9970 Platinum APW **Subject:** 25th Anniversary of Reign **Note:** Prev. KM#M4.

Date	Mintage	F	VF	XF	Unc	BU
1974 (a) Proof	10,000	Value: 475				

X# M5   2000 FRANCS
0.9970 Platinum APW **Subject:** 25th Anniversary of Reign **Note:** Prev. KM#M5.

Date	Mintage	F	VF	XF	Unc	BU
1974 (a) Proof	10,000	Value: 950				

X# M6   3000 FRANCS
0.9990 Gold **Subject:** 25th Anniversary of Reign **Note:** Prev. KM#M6.

Date	Mintage	F	VF	XF	Unc	BU
1974 (a) Proof	5,000	Value: 575				

PATTERNS
Including off metal strikes

KM#	Date	Mintage	Identification	Mkt Val
Pn12	1838	—	20 Francs. Gold. Head left. Crowned mantled arms above date and value.	—
Pn13	1838	—	40 Francs. Gold.	—
Pn14	1892A	—	20 Francs. 0.9000 Gold.	3,500
Pn15	1934A	15	500 Francs. 0.9000 Gold.	3,220

ESSAIS
Standard metals unless otherwise noted

KM#	Date	Mintage	Identification	Issue Price	Mkt Val
E1	1924	—	50 Centimes. Gold. KM#110	—	2,000
E3	1924	—	Franc. Gold. KM111	—	3,000
E5	1924	—	2 Francs. Gold. Hercules shooting bow to right. Shield below value within circle. KM112	—	4,000
E6	ND(1943) (a)	250	Franc. 0.9000 Gold.	—	625
E10	ND(1943) (a)	250	2 Francs. 0.9000 Gold.	—	725

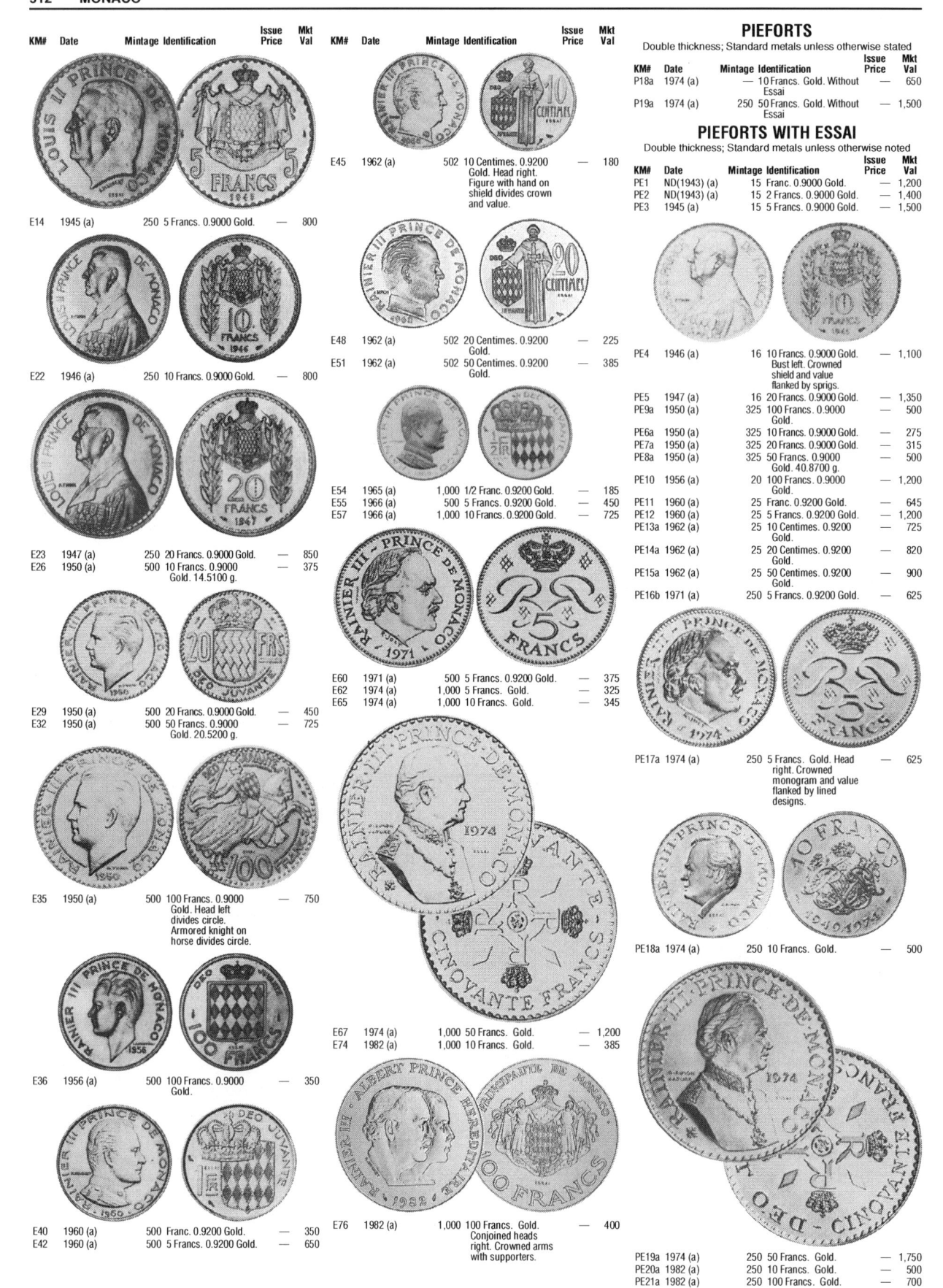

MONACO

KM#	Date	Mintage	Identification	Issue Price	Mkt Val
E14	1945 (a)	250	5 Francs. 0.9000 Gold.	—	800
E22	1946 (a)	250	10 Francs. 0.9000 Gold.	—	800
E23	1947 (a)	250	20 Francs. 0.9000 Gold.	—	850
E26	1950 (a)	500	10 Francs. 0.9000 Gold. 14.5100 g.	—	375
E29	1950 (a)	500	20 Francs. 0.9000 Gold.	—	450
E32	1950 (a)	500	50 Francs. 0.9000 Gold. 20.5200 g.	—	725
E35	1950 (a)	500	100 Francs. 0.9000 Gold. Head left divides circle. Armored knight on horse divides circle.	—	750
E36	1956 (a)	500	100 Francs. 0.9000 Gold.	—	350
E40	1960 (a)	500	Franc. 0.9200 Gold.	—	350
E42	1960 (a)	500	5 Francs. 0.9200 Gold.	—	650
E45	1962 (a)	502	10 Centimes. 0.9200 Gold. Head right. Figure with hand on shield divides crown and value.	—	180
E48	1962 (a)	502	20 Centimes. 0.9200 Gold.	—	225
E51	1962 (a)	502	50 Centimes. 0.9200 Gold.	—	385
E54	1965 (a)	1,000	1/2 Franc. 0.9200 Gold.	—	185
E55	1966 (a)	500	5 Francs. 0.9200 Gold.	—	450
E57	1966 (a)	1,000	10 Francs. 0.9200 Gold.	—	725
E60	1971 (a)	500	5 Francs. 0.9200 Gold.	—	375
E62	1974 (a)	1,000	5 Francs. Gold.	—	325
E65	1974 (a)	1,000	10 Francs. Gold.	—	345
E67	1974 (a)	1,000	50 Francs. Gold.	—	1,200
E74	1982 (a)	1,000	10 Francs. Gold.	—	385
E76	1982 (a)	1,000	100 Francs. Gold. Conjoined heads right. Crowned arms with supporters.	—	400

PIEFORTS
Double thickness; Standard metals unless otherwise stated

KM#	Date	Mintage	Identification	Issue Price	Mkt Val
P18a	1974 (a)	—	10 Francs. Gold. Without Essai	—	650
P19a	1974 (a)	250	50 Francs. Gold. Without Essai	—	1,500

PIEFORTS WITH ESSAI
Double thickness; Standard metals unless otherwise noted

KM#	Date	Mintage	Identification	Issue Price	Mkt Val
PE1	ND(1943) (a)	15	Franc. 0.9000 Gold.	—	1,200
PE2	ND(1943) (a)	15	2 Francs. 0.9000 Gold.	—	1,400
PE3	1945 (a)	15	5 Francs. 0.9000 Gold.	—	1,500
PE4	1946 (a)	16	10 Francs. 0.9000 Gold. Bust left. Crowned shield and value flanked by sprigs.	—	1,100
PE5	1947 (a)	16	20 Francs. 0.9000 Gold.	—	1,350
PE9a	1950 (a)	325	100 Francs. 0.9000 Gold.	—	500
PE6a	1950 (a)	325	10 Francs. 0.9000 Gold.	—	275
PE7a	1950 (a)	325	20 Francs. 0.9000 Gold.	—	315
PE8a	1950 (a)	325	50 Francs. 0.9000 Gold. 40.8700 g.	—	500
PE10	1956 (a)	20	100 Francs. 0.9000 Gold.	—	1,200
PE11	1960 (a)	25	Franc. 0.9200 Gold.	—	645
PE12	1960 (a)	25	5 Francs. 0.9200 Gold.	—	1,200
PE13a	1962 (a)	25	10 Centimes. 0.9200 Gold.	—	725
PE14a	1962 (a)	25	20 Centimes. 0.9200 Gold.	—	820
PE15a	1962 (a)	25	50 Centimes. 0.9200 Gold.	—	900
PE16b	1971 (a)	250	5 Francs. 0.9200 Gold.	—	625
PE17a	1974 (a)	250	5 Francs. Gold. Head right. Crowned monogram and value flanked by lined designs.	—	625
PE18a	1974 (a)	250	10 Francs. Gold.	—	500
PE19a	1974 (a)	250	50 Francs. Gold.	—	1,750
PE20a	1982 (a)	250	10 Francs. Gold.	—	500
PE21a	1982 (a)	250	100 Francs. Gold.	—	700

MONGOLIA

TRIAL STRIKES

KM#	Date	Mintage	Identification	Mkt Val
TS19	1838	—	20 Francs. Gold. Pn10 obverse.	—
TS20	1838	—	20 Francs. Gold. Pn10 reverse.	—
TS21	1838	—	40 Francs. Gold. Pn11 obverse.	5,500
TS22	1838	—	40 Francs. Gold. Pn11 reverse.	5,500

PROOF SETS

KM#	Date	Mintage	Identification	Issue Price	Mkt Val
XPS1	1974 (4)	—	X#M3-XM6	—	1,575

The State of Mongolia, (formerly the Mongolian People's Republic) a landlocked country in central Asia between Russia and the People's Republic of China, has an area of 604,250 sq. mi. (1,565,000 sq. km.) and a population of 2.26 million. Capital: Ulaan Baator. Animal herds and flocks are the chief economic asset. Wool, cattle, butter, meat and hides are exported.

Mongolia (often referred to as Outer Mongolia), one of the world's oldest countries, attained its greatest power in the 13th century when Genghis Khan and his successors conquered all of China and extended their influence westward as far as Hungary and Poland. The empire dissolved in later centuries and in 1691 was brought under suzerainty of the Manchus, who had conquered China in 1644. Afterward the Chinese republican movement led by Sun Yat-sen overthrew the Manchus and set up the Chinese Republic in 1911. Mongolia, with the support of Russia, proclaimed their independence from China and, on March 13, 1921 a Provisional People's Government was established and later, on Nov. 26, 1924 the government proclaimed the Mongolian People's Republic.

Although nominally a dependency of China, Outer Mongolia voted at a plebiscite Oct. 20, 1945 to sever all ties with China and become an independent nation. Opposition to the communist party developed in late 1989 and after demonstrations and hunger strikes, the Politburo resigned on March 12, 1990 and the new State of Mongolia was organized.

On Feb. 12, 1992 it became the first to discard communism as the national political system by adopting a new constitution.

For earlier issues see Russia - Tannu Tuva.

MONETARY SYSTEM
100 Mongo = 1 Tugrik

PEOPLE'S REPUBLIC

DECIMAL COINAGE

KM# 34c TUGRIK
30.0000 g., Gold, 32 mm. **Subject:** 50th Anniversary of the Revolution **Obv:** National arms **Rev:** Man on horse left within beaded circle **Note:** Mintage: 5-10.

Date	Mintage	F	VF	XF	Unc	BU
(1971) Proof	—	Value: 2,500				

KM# 58 100 TUGRIK
1.5600 g., 0.9990 Gold .0500 oz. AGW **Subject:** Discovery of America - Columbus **Obv:** National arms **Rev:** Portrait of Columbus and ship within circle and legend

Date	Mintage	F	VF	XF	Unc	BU
1992 Proof	Est. 10,000	Value: 50.00				

KM# 59 200 TUGRIK
3.1100 g., 0.9990 Gold .1000 oz. AGW **Subject:** Discovery of America - Columbus **Obv:** National arms **Rev:** Portrait of Columbus and ship within circle and legend

Date	Mintage	F	VF	XF	Unc	BU
1992 Proof	Est. 10,000	Value: 75.00				

KM# 45 250 TUGRIK
7.1300 g., 0.9000 Gold .2026 oz. AGW **Series:** Decade for Women **Obv:** National arms **Rev:** Figure on horseback left, value

Date	Mintage	F	VF	XF	Unc	BU
1984 Proof	510	Value: 165				

KM# 72 300 TUGRIK
7.7700 g., 0.9990 Gold .25 oz. AGW **Subject:** Japanese royal wedding **Obv:** National arms above value **Rev:** Royal couple facing each other

Date	Mintage	F	VF	XF	Unc	BU
1993 Proof	Est. 500	Value: 235				

KM# 38 750 TUGRIK
33.4370 g., 0.9000 Gold .9676 oz. AGW **Subject:** Conservation **Rev:** Przewalski horses

Date	Mintage	F	VF	XF	Unc	BU
1976	929	—	—	—	625	—
1976 Proof	374	Value: 825				

KM# 40 750 TUGRIK
18.7900 g., 0.9000 Gold .5437 oz. AGW **Series:** International Year of the Child **Obv:** National arms **Rev:** Children dancing

Date	Mintage	F	VF	XF	Unc	BU
1980 Proof	32,000	Value: 385				

KM# 56 1000 TUGRIK
20.7000 g., 0.9000 Gold .5990 oz. AGW **Subject:** Secret history of the Mongols **Obv:** State emblem above denomination within English legend **Rev:** Portrait of Genghis Khan in heavy clothing

Date	Mintage	F	VF	XF	Unc	BU
1990	Est. 4,000	—	—	—	425	—

KM# 60 1000 TUGRIK
31.1000 g., 0.9990 Gold 1.0000 oz. AGW **Subject:** Discovery of America **Obv:** National arms divide date above value **Rev:** Portrait of Columbus and ship within circle and legend

Date	Mintage	F	VF	XF	Unc	BU
1992 Proof	2,000	Value: 700				

KM# 171 1000 TUGRIK
Gold **Subject:** Year of the Monkey **Obv:** National arms **Rev:** Monkey

Date	Mintage	F	VF	XF	Unc	BU
1992	Est. 2,000	—	—	—	750	—

STATE

DECIMAL COINAGE

KM# 87 100 TUGRIK
1.5600 g., 0.9990 Gold .0500 oz. AGW **Subject:** Year of the Monkey **Obv:** National emblem **Rev:** Monkey **Note:** Similar to 50 Tugrik, KM#86.

Date	Mintage	F	VF	XF	Unc	BU
1992 Proof	10,000	Value: 75.00				

KM# 167 100 TUGRIK
1.5600 g., 0.9990 Gold .0500 oz. AGW **Subject:** Discovery of America - Columbus **Obv:** National emblem **Rev:** Portrait of Columbus and ship within circle and legend

Date	Mintage	F	VF	XF	Unc	BU
1992 Proof	—	Value: 45.00				

KM# 62.1 100 TUGRIK
1.5600 g., 0.9990 Gold .0500 oz. AGW **Subject:** Year of the Rooster **Obv:** National emblem **Rev:** Rooster **Note:** Similar to 50 Tugrik, KM#61.

Date	Mintage	F	VF	XF	Unc	BU
1993 Proof	30,000	Value: 50.00				

KM# 62.2 100 TUGRIK
1.5600 g., 0.9990 Gold .0500 oz. AGW **Obv:** National arms above value **Rev:** Rooster left **Note:** Handstruck.

Date	Mintage	F	VF	XF	Unc	BU
1993 Proof	500	Value: 250				

Note: Strikes tend to be crude and do not have ".999" on them.

KM# 70 100 TUGRIK
1.5600 g., 0.9990 Gold .0500 oz. AGW **Subject:** Japanese Royal Wedding **Obv:** State emblem above value **Rev:** Busts facing each other **Note:** Similar to 50 Tugrik, KM#69.

Date	Mintage	F	VF	XF	Unc	BU
1993 Proof	Est. 3,000	Value: 75.00				

KM# 88 200 TUGRIK
3.1100 g., 0.9990 Gold .1000 oz. AGW **Subject:** Year of the Monkey **Obv:** National emblem **Rev:** Seated monkey **Note:** Similar to 50 Tugrik, KM#86.

Date	Mintage	F	VF	XF	Unc	BU
1992 Proof	—	Value: 100				

MONGOLIA

KM# 168 200 TUGRIK
3.1100 g., 0.9990 Gold .1000 oz. AGW **Subject:** Discovery of America - Columbus **Obv:** State emblem above value **Rev:** Portrait of Columbus and ship within circle and legend
Date	Mintage	F	VF	XF	Unc	BU
1992 Proof	—				Value: 75.00	

KM# 63 200 TUGRIK
3.1100 g., 0.9990 Gold .1000 oz. AGW **Subject:** Year of the Rooster **Obv:** National emblem above value at left, country name at right **Rev:** Rooster **Note:** Similar to 50 Tugrik, KM#61.
Date	Mintage	F	VF	XF	Unc	BU
1993 Proof	500				Value: 200	

KM# 71 200 TUGRIK
3.1100 g., 0.9990 Gold .1000 oz. AGW **Subject:** Japanese Royal Wedding **Obv:** National arms above value **Rev:** Busts facing each other **Note:** Similar to 50 Tugrik, KM#69.
Date	Mintage	F	VF	XF	Unc	BU
1993 Proof	100				Value: 300	

KM# 76 200 TUGRIK
3.1100 g., 0.9990 Gold .1000 oz. AGW **Subject:** Year of the Dog. **Obv:** National emblem **Rev:** Dogs
Date	Mintage	F	VF	XF	Unc	BU
1994 Proof	500				Value: 175	

KM# 73 500 TUGRIK
15.5500 g., 0.9990 Gold .5000 oz. AGW **Subject:** Japanese Royal Wedding **Obv:** State emblem above value **Rev:** Busts facing each other
Date	Mintage	F	VF	XF	Unc	BU
1993 Proof	160				Value: 375	

KM# 197 500 TUGRIK
Gold **Obv:** National emblem **Rev:** Sumo wrestling
Date	Mintage	F	VF	XF	Unc	BU
1998 Proof	—				Value: 50.00	

KM# 158 500 TUGRIK
1.2241 g., 0.9990 Gold .0400 oz. AGW **Subject:** Buddhist Diety Maitreya **Obv:** National emblem **Rev:** Statue
Date	Mintage	F	VF	XF	Unc	BU
1998 Proof	—				Value: 50.00	

KM# 174 500 TUGRIK
1.2441 g., 0.9990 Gold .0400 oz. AGW **Subject:** Year of the Tiger **Obv:** National emblem **Rev:** Tiger
Date	Mintage	F	VF	XF	Unc	BU
1998	—	—	—	—	45.00	

KM# 161 500 TUGRIK
1.2441 g., 0.9990 Gold .0400 oz. AGW **Subject:** Year of the Rabbit **Obv:** Soembo arms within circle **Rev:** Rabbit running left
Date	Mintage	F	VF	XF	Unc	BU
1999	5,000	—	—	—	55.00	—

KM# 206 500 TUGRIK
1.2440 g., 0.9999 Gold 0.04 oz. AGW, 13.92 mm. **Obv:** National emblem above value **Rev:** Five masted sailing junk **Edge:** Reeded
Date	Mintage	F	VF	XF	Unc	BU
2003 Proof	25,000				Value: 50.00	

KM# 207 500 TUGRIK
1.2440 g., 0.9999 Gold .04 oz. AGW, 13.92 mm. **Obv:** National emblem above value **Rev:** Medallion divides busts **Edge:** Reeded
Date	Mintage	F	VF	XF	Unc	BU
2003 Proof	25,000				Value: 50.00	

KM# 210a 500 TUGRIK
31.1035 g., 0.9990 Silver 0.999 oz. ASW, 35x35 mm. **Obv:** Gold plated horse and rider with national emblem and value **Rev:** Gold plated horse and rider above date **Edge:** Reeded
Date	Mintage	F	VF	XF	Unc	BU
2005 Proof	2,500				Value: 65.00	

KM# 91 1000 TUGRIK
31.1000 g., 0.9990 Gold 1.0000 oz. AGW **Subject:** Year of the Monkey **Obv:** National emblem **Rev:** Monkey **Note:** Similar to 50 Tugrik, KM#86.
Date	Mintage	F	VF	XF	Unc	BU
1992 Proof	2,000				Value: 700	

KM# 85 1000 TUGRIK
20.0000 g., 0.9000 Gold .5788 oz. AGW **Obv:** National arms above value **Rev:** Ugedei Khan, Son of Genghis
Date	Mintage	F	VF	XF	Unc	BU
1992 Proof	500				Value: 415	

KM# 169 1000 TUGRIK
20.0000 g., 0.9000 Gold .5788 oz. AGW **Subject:** Discovery of America - Columbus **Obv:** State emblem above value **Rev:** Portrait of Columbus and ship within circle and legend
Date	Mintage	F	VF	XF	Unc	BU
1992 Proof	Est. 2,000				Value: 450	

KM# 66 1000 TUGRIK
31.1000 g., 0.9990 Gold 1.0000 oz. AGW **Subject:** Year of the Rooster **Obv:** National emblem above value at left, country name at right **Rev:** Rooster **Note:** Similar to 50 Tugrik, KM#61.
Date	Mintage	F	VF	XF	Unc	BU
1993 Proof	1,000				Value: 750	

KM# 74 1000 TUGRIK
20.0000 g., 0.9000 Gold .5788 oz. AGW **Subject:** Japanese Royal Wedding **Obv:** State emblem above value **Rev:** Busts of couple facing each other
Date	Mintage	F	VF	XF	Unc	BU
1993 Proof	145				Value: 800	

KM# 78 1000 TUGRIK
31.1035 g., 0.9990 Gold 1.0000 oz. AGW **Subject:** Year of the Dog **Obv:** National emblem **Rev:** Pekingese
Date	Mintage	F	VF	XF	Unc	BU
1994 Proof	500				Value: 725	

KM# 96 1000 TUGRIK
3.1100 g., 0.9990 Gold .1000 oz. AGW **Subject:** Year of the Pig **Obv:** National emblem **Rev:** Wild boar **Note:** Similar to 500 Tugrik, KM#95.
Date	Mintage	F	VF	XF	Unc	BU
1995 Proof	500				Value: 200	

KM# 148 1000 TUGRIK
4.4100 g., 0.9000 Gold .1276 oz. AGW **Subject:** Moscow - Ulaan Blaatar - Bejing Railroad **Obv:** Soembo arms within circle **Rev:** Steam locomotive
Date	Mintage	F	VF	XF	Unc	BU
1995 Proof	—				Value: 125	

KM# 106 1000 TUGRIK
3.1100 g., 0.9990 Gold .1000 oz. AGW **Subject:** Year of the Rat **Obv:** National emblem **Rev:** Rat **Note:** Similar to 50 Tugrik, KM#104.
Date	Mintage	F	VF	XF	Unc	BU
1996 Proof	500				Value: 150	

KM# 128 1000 TUGRIK
3.1100 g., 0.9990 Gold .1000 oz. AGW **Subject:** Year of the Ox **Obv:** National emblem **Rev:** Ox **Note:** Similar to 50 Tugrik, KM#126.
Date	Mintage	F	VF	XF	Unc	BU
1997 Proof	500				Value: 100	

KM# 201 1000 TUGRIK
7.7200 g., Gold, 24.8 mm. **Obv:** Soembo arms **Rev:** Tiger head with diamond inset eyes **Edge:** Reeded
Date	Mintage	F	VF	XF	Unc	BU
1999 Proof	—				Value: 350	

KM# 185 1000 TUGRIK
1.2441 g., 0.9999 Gold .0400 oz. AGW **Subject:** Genius of the Millennium - Da Vinci **Obv:** National arms **Rev:** Male figure study **Note:** Similar to 500 Tugrik, KM#181.
Date	Mintage	F	VF	XF	Unc	BU
1999 Proof	25,000				Value: 45.00	

KM# 113 2000 TUGRIK
7.7760 g., 0.5830 Gold .1458 oz. AGW **Series:** Endangered Wildlife **Obv:** Soembo arms within wreath **Rev:** Snow leopard
Date	Mintage	F	VF	XF	Unc	BU
1994 Proof	Est. 5,000				Value: 150	

MONGOLIA

KM# 114 2000 TUGRIK
7.7760 g., 0.5830 Gold .1458 oz. AGW. **Series:** Olympics **Obv:** Soembo arms within wreath **Rev:** Boxer

Date	Mintage	F	VF	XF	Unc	BU
1994 Proof	Est. 5,000			Value: 150		

KM# 175 2000 TUGRIK
7.7760 g., 0.5830 Gold .1458 oz. AGW. **Subject:** Year of the Tiger **Obv:** National emblem **Rev:** Tiger

Date	Mintage	F	VF	XF	Unc	BU
1998	—	—	—	—	110	120

KM# 163 2500 TUGRIK
7.7759 g., 0.9990 Gold 0.2498 oz. AGW, 22.5 mm. **Subject:** Year of the Rabbit **Obv:** National emblem **Rev:** Rabbit **Edge:** Plain **Note:** Struck at B.H. Mayer's.

Date	Mintage	F	VF	XF	Unc	BU
1999 Proof	1,500			Value: 200		

KM# 81 4000 TUGRIK
15.5940 g., 0.9999 Gold .5009 oz. AGW **Obv:** Soembo arms above value **Rev:** Horse and rider left

Date	Mintage	F	VF	XF	Unc	BU
1992 Proof	Est. 9,000			Value: 650		

KM# 67 5000 TUGRIK
155.5000 g., 0.9990 Gold 5.0000 oz. AGW. **Subject:** Year of the Rooster **Obv:** National emblem above denomination at left, country name at right **Rev:** Rooster **Note:** Similar to 50 Tugrik, KM#51.

Date	Mintage	F	VF	XF	Unc	BU
1993 Proof	50			Value: 3,750		

KM# 79 5000 TUGRIK
155.5000 g., 0.9990 Gold 5.0000 oz. AGW. **Subject:** Year of the Dog **Obv:** National emblem **Rev:** Dog

Date	Mintage	F	VF	XF	Unc	BU
1994 Proof	25			Value: 5,000		

KM# 82 8000 TUGRIK
31.1620 g., 0.9999 Gold 1.0000 oz. AGW **Obv:** Soembo arms above value **Rev:** Chinggis Khan standing

Date	Mintage	F	VF	XF	Unc	BU
1992 Proof	Est. 3,000			Value: 1,200		

KM# 98 10000 TUGRIK
31.1035 g., 0.9990 Gold 1.0000 oz. AGW. **Subject:** Year of the Pig **Obv:** National emblem **Rev:** Wild boar **Note:** Similar to 500 Tugrik, KM#95.

Date	Mintage	F	VF	XF	Unc	BU
1995 Proof	300			Value: 745		

KM# 108 10000 TUGRIK
31.1035 g., 0.9990 Gold 1.0000 oz. AGW. **Subject:** Year of the Rat **Obv:** National emblem **Rev:** Rat **Note:** Similar to 50 Tugrik, KM#104.

Date	Mintage	F	VF	XF	Unc	BU
1996 Proof	300			Value: 745		

KM# 176 10000 TUGRIK
31.1035 g., 0.9990 Gold 1.0000 oz. AGW. **Subject:** Year of the Tiger **Obv:** National emblem **Rev:** Tiger

Date	Mintage	F	VF	XF	Unc	BU
1998	250	—	—	—	—	745

KM# 68 12000 TUGRIK
373.2000 g., 0.9990 Gold 12.0000 oz. AGW **Subject:** Year of the Rooster **Obv:** National emblem above denomination at left, country name at right **Rev:** Rooster **Note:** Similar to 50 Tugrik, KM#61.

Date	Mintage	F	VF	XF	Unc	BU
1993 Proof	25			Value: 8,500		

KM# 119 12000 TUGRIK
7.7700 g., 0.9999 Gold .2498 oz. AGW. **Subject:** Chinggis Khan **Obv:** National emblem and value **Rev:** Bust 3/4 facing **Note:** Similar to 50,000 Tugrik, KM#121.

Date	Mintage	F	VF	XF	Unc	BU
1996 Rare	10	—	—	—	—	—
1996 Proof, rare	10	—	—	—	—	—

KM# 119a 12000 TUGRIK
7.7700 g., 0.9990 Gold .2495 oz. AGW. **Subject:** Chinggis Khan **Obv:** National emblem and value **Rev:** Bust 3/4 facing

Date	Mintage	F	VF	XF	Unc	BU
1996	Est. 10,000	—	—	—	175	180
1996 Proof	Est. 10,000			Value: 195		

KM# 152 12000 TUGRIK
7.7750 g., 0.9990 Gold .2500 oz. AGW **Obv:** Soembo arms above value **Rev:** Ugedei Khan with hat, facing

Date	Mintage	F	VF	XF	Unc	BU
1997 Proof	Est. 10,000			Value: 300		

KM# 120a 25000 TUGRIK
15.5500 g., 0.9990 Gold .4994 oz. AGW. **Subject:** Chinggis Khan **Obv:** National emblem and value **Rev:** Bust 3/4 facing

Date	Mintage	F	VF	XF	Unc	BU
1996	Est. 10,000	—	—	—	350	360
1996 Proof	Est. 10,000			Value: 375		

KM# 144 25000 TUGRIK
15.5940 g., 0.9999 Gold .5000 oz. AGW. **Subject:** Aquila Rapaz **Obv:** National emblem and value **Rev:** Bird standing on rock **Note:** Similar to 500 Tugrik, KM#132.

Date	Mintage	F	VF	XF	Unc	BU
1996 Proof	300			Value: 420		

KM# 145 25000 TUGRIK
15.5940 g., 0.9999 Gold .5000 oz. AGW. **Subject:** Equus Ferus **Obv:** National emblem and value **Rev:** Horse running left **Note:** Similar to 500 Tugrik, KM#133.

Date	Mintage	F	VF	XF	Unc	BU
1996 Proof	300			Value: 420		

KM# 146 25000 TUGRIK
15.5940 g., 0.9999 Gold .5000 oz. AGW. **Subject:** Cameleus Ferus **Obv:** National emblem and value **Rev:** Camel right **Note:** Similar to 500 Tugrik, KM#134.

Date	Mintage	F	VF	XF	Unc	BU
1996 Proof	300			Value: 420		

KM# 147 25000 TUGRIK
15.5940 g., 0.9999 Gold .5000 oz. AGW. **Subject:** Panthera Tigris Altaica **Obv:** National emblem and value **Rev:** Tiger lying on rock **Note:** Similar to 500 Tugrik, KM#135.

Date	Mintage	F	VF	XF	Unc	BU
1996 Proof	300			Value: 420		

KM# 99 50000 TUGRIK
155.5150 g., 0.9990 Gold 5.0000 oz. AGW. **Subject:** Year of the Pig **Obv:** National emblem **Rev:** Pigs in field **Note:** Similar to 2500 Tugrik, KM#97

Date	Mintage	F	VF	XF	Unc	BU
1995 Proof	25			Value: 5,000		

KM# 109 50000 TUGRIK
155.5150 g., 0.9990 Gold 5.0000 oz. AGW. **Subject:** Year of the Rat **Obv:** National emblem **Rev:** Rat **Note:** Similar to 50 Tugrik, KM#104.

Date	Mintage	F	VF	XF	Unc	BU
1996 Proof	25			Value: 4,250		

KM# 121 50000 TUGRIK
31.1000 g., 0.9999 Gold .9998 oz. AGW **Obv:** Soembo arms above value **Rev:** Chinggis Khan bust 3/4 facing

Date	Mintage	F	VF	XF	Unc	BU
1996 Rare	10	—	—	—	—	—
1996 Proof, rare	10	—	—	—	—	—

KM# 121a 50000 TUGRIK
31.1000 g., 0.9990 Gold .9998 oz. AGW. **Subject:** Chinggis Khan **Obv:** Soembo arms above value **Rev:** Bust 3/4 facing

Date	Mintage	F	VF	XF	Unc	BU
1996	Est. 10,000	—	—	—	700	725
1996 Proof	Est. 10,000			Value: 800		

KM# 131 50000 TUGRIK
155.5150 g., 0.9999 Gold 5.0000 oz. AGW. **Subject:** Year of the Ox **Obv:** National emblem **Rev:** Ox **Note:** Similar to 2,500 Tugrik, KM#129.

Date	Mintage	F	VF	XF	Unc	BU
1997 Proof	25			Value: 4,000		

KM# 154 50000 TUGRIK
31.1035 g., 0.9990 Gold 1.0000 oz. AGW **Obv:** Soembo arms above value **Rev:** Ugedei Khan bust 3/4 facing

Date	Mintage	F	VF	XF	Unc	BU
1997 Proof	Est. 10,000			Value: 1,200		

KM# 177 50000 TUGRIK
155.5150 g., 0.9999 Gold 5.0000 oz. AGW. **Subject:** Year of the Tiger **Obv:** National emblem **Rev:** Tiger

Date	Mintage	F	VF	XF	Unc	BU
1998	99	—	—	—	3,750	—

KM# 165 50000 TUGRIK
155.5150 g., 0.9999 Gold 5.0000 oz. AGW. **Subject:** Year of the Rabbit **Obv:** National emblem **Rev:** Rabbit

Date	Mintage	F	VF	XF	Unc	BU
1999	99	—	—	—	3,750	—

KM# 83 250000 TUGRIK
1000.1000 g., 0.9999 Gold 32.1575 oz. AGW, 85 mm. **Subject:** Chinggis Khan **Obv:** Soemba arms **Rev:** Head facing

516 MONGOLIA

Date	Mintage	F	VF	XF	Unc	BU
1992 Proof	Est. 300	Value: 25,000				

PIEFORTS

KM#	Date	Mintage	Identification	Mkt Val
P2	1980	550	750 Tugrik. Gold. KM40.	775

MINT SETS

KM#	Date	Mintage	Identification	Issue Price	Mkt Val
MS3	1996 (3)	10	KM119-121	—	—
MS4	1996 (3)	10,000	KM119a-121a	—	1,100

PROOF SETS

KM#	Date	Mintage	Identification	Issue Price	Mkt Val
PS1	1996 (3)	—	KM105, 106, 108	—	700
PS3	1996 (3)	10	KM119-121	—	—
PS5	1996 (4)	10	KM116-118, 121	—	—
PS6	1996 (4)	10,000	KM116-118, 121a. The *10,000 mintage limit is per denomination including proof and BU single coins as well as coins included in sets.	—	1,000
PS7	1996 (4)	10	KM118, 119-121	—	—
PS8	1996 (4)	10,000	KM118, 119a-121a. The *10,000 mintage limit is per denomination including proof and BU single coins as well as coins included in sets.	—	1,750
PS4	1996	10,000	KM119a-121a. The *10,000 mintage limit is per denomination including proof and BU single coins as well as coins included in sets.	—	1,700
PS10	1997 (3)	10,000	KM152-154	—	2,150

MONTENEGRO

The former independent kingdom of Montenegro, now one of the nominally autonomous federated units of Yugoslavia, was located in southeastern Europe north of Albania. As a kingdom, it had an area of 5,333 sq. mi. (13,812 sq. km.).

Montenegro became an independent state in 1355 following the break-up of the Serb empire. During the Turkish invasion of Albania and Herzegovina in the 15th century, the Montenegrins moved their capital to the remote mountain village of Cetinje where they maintained their independence through two centuries of intermittent attack, emerging as the only one of the Balkan states not subjugated by the Turks.

The coinage, issued under the autocratic rule of Prince Nicholas, is obsolete.

RULER
Nicholas I as Prince 1860-1910
...as King 1910-1918

MINT MARK
- Paris, privy marks only

MONETARY SYSTEM
100 Para = 1 Perper

KINGDOM
STANDARD COINAGE

KM# 8   10 PERPERA
3.3875 g., 0.9000 Gold .0980 oz. AGW **Ruler:** Nicholas I **Obv:** Head right **Rev:** Crowned mantled arms within sprigs above date and value

Date	Mintage	F	VF	XF	Unc	BU
1910	40,000	120	220	310	530	—

KM# 9   10 PERPERA
3.3875 g., 0.9000 Gold .0980 oz. AGW **Ruler:** Nicholas I **Subject:** 50th Year of Reign **Obv:** Head laureate left **Rev:** Crowned mantled arms within sprigs above date and value

Date	Mintage	F	VF	XF	Unc	BU
1910	35,003	130	250	330	560	—

KM# 10   20 PERPERA
6.7751 g., 0.9000 Gold .1960 oz. AGW **Ruler:** Nicholas I **Obv:** Head right **Rev:** Crowned mantled arms within sprigs above date and value

Date	Mintage	F	VF	XF	Unc	BU
1910	30,000	150	275	460	720	—

KM# 11   20 PERPERA
6.7751 g., 0.9000 Gold .1960 oz. AGW **Ruler:** Nicholas I **Subject:** 50th Year of Reign **Obv:** Laureate head left **Rev:** Crowned mantled arms within sprigs above date and value

Date	Mintage	F	VF	XF	Unc	BU
1910	30,003	150	275	460	720	—

KM# 12   100 PERPERA
33.8753 g., 0.9000 Gold .9802 oz. AGW **Ruler:** Nicholas I **Obv:** Head right **Rev:** Crowned and mantled arms

Date	Mintage	F	VF	XF	Unc	BU
1910	301	—	4,500	7,000	12,000	—
1910 Proof	25	Value: 14,000				

KM# 13   100 PERPERA
33.8753 g., 0.9000 Gold .9802 oz. AGW **Ruler:** Nicholas I **Subject:** 50th Year of Reign **Obv:** Laureate head left **Rev:** Crowned mantled arms within sprigs above date and value

Date	Mintage	F	VF	XF	Unc	BU
1910	501	—	4,500	6,500	11,000	—
1910 Proof	Inc. above	Value: 15,000				

TRIAL STRIKES

KM#	Date	Mintage	Identification	Mkt Val
TS1	ND(1910)	—	100 Perpera. Hallmarked edge. Uniface.	6,000
TS2	ND(1910)	—	100 Perpera. TITRE ZZK ESSAI.	5,000

MOROCCO

MOROCCO

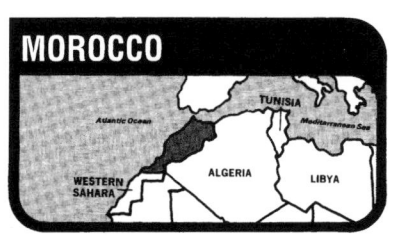

The Kingdom of Morocco, situated on the northwest corner of Africa, has an area of 275,117 sq. mi. (446,550 sq. km.) and a population of 28.5 million. Capital: Rabat. The economy is essentially agricultural. Phosphates, fresh and preserved vegetables, canned fish, and raw materials are exported.

Morocco's strategic position at the gateway to Western Europe has been the principal determinant of its violent, frequently unfortunate history. Time and again the fertile plain between the rugged Atlas Mountains and the sea has echoed the battle's trumpet as Phoenicians, Romans, Vandals, Visigoths, Byzantine Greeks and Islamic Arabs successively conquered and occupied the land. Modern Morocco is a remnant of an early empire formed by the Arabs at the close of the 7th century, which encompassed all of northwest Africa, and most of the Iberian Peninsula. During the 17th and 18th centuries, while under the control of native dynasties, it was the headquarters of the famous Sale pirates. Morocco's strategic position involved it in the competition of 19th century European powers for political influence in Africa, and resulted in the division of Morocco into French and Spanish spheres of interest, which were established as protectorates in 1912. Morocco became independent on March 2, 1956, after France agreed to end its protectorate. Spain signed similar agreements on April 7 of the same year.

TITLES

المغربية

Al-Maghribiya(t)

المملكة المغربية

Al-Mamlaka(t) al-Maghribiya(t)

المحمدية الشريفة

Al-Mohammediya(t) esh-Sherifiya(t)

RULERS
Abd al-Aziz, AH1311-1326/1894-1908AD
Abd al-Hafiz, AH1326-1330/1908-1912AD

French Protectorate, AH1330/1912AD
Yusuf, AH1330-1346/1912-1927AD
Mohammed V, AH1346-1375/1927-1955AD

Kingdom
Mohammed V, AH1376-1381/1956-1962AD
Al-Hasan II, AH1381-1420/1962-1999AD
Mohammed VI, AH1420- /1999- AD

MINTS

(a) - Paris privy marks only

Silver Coins — Bronze Coins
Bi - England (Birmingham)

بانكلند

Ln = bi-England (London)

ببارىز

Pa = bi-Bariz (Paris)

فاس

Fs = Fes (Fas, Fez)

Py - Poissy Inscribed "Paris" but with thunderbolt privy mark.

NOTE: Some of the above forms of the mint names are shown as they appear on the coins, not in regular Arabic script.
NOTES: On the silver coins the denominations are written in words and each series has its own characteristic names:
Y#9-13 (1313-1319) Denomination in 'Preferred" Dirhams.
Y#18-22 (1320-1323) Denomination in fractions of a Rial, but on the 3 larger sizes, the equivalent is given in "Urti parts", 1 Rial 20 = Urti parts.

Y#23-25 (1329) Denomination in Dirhams and in fraction of a Rial.
Y#30-33 (1331-1336) Denomination in Yusuti or "Treasury" Dirhams.

On most of the larger denominations, the denomination is given in the form of a rhymed couplet.
NOTE: Various copper and silver coins dated AH1297-1311 are believed to be patterns. Copper coins similar to Y#14-17, but without denomination on reverse, are patterns.
NOTE: 1, 2, 5 and 10 Mazunas of AH1320 Fes exist in medal alignment and coin alignment (rare). AH1321-1323 Fes strikes are medal alignment only.

KINGDOM
Filali Sharifs - Alawi Dynasty

Sulayman II
AH1207-38/1793-1822AD

HAMMERED COINAGE

Mint: Fes
C# 114   1/2 BENDUQI
1.7000 g., Gold

Date	Mintage	VG	F	VF	XF	Unc
AH1232	—	100	200	350	600	—
AH1236	—	100	200	350	600	—
AH1237	—	100	200	350	600	—

Mint: Fes Hazrat
C# 115   BENDUQI
3.5200 g., Gold

Date	Mintage	VG	F	VF	XF	Unc
AH1216	—	90.00	125	250	375	—
AH1217	—	90.00	125	250	375	—
AH1218	—	90.00	125	250	375	—
AH1219	—	100	150	300	500	—
AH1220	—	100	150	300	500	—
AH1224	—	100	150	300	500	—
AH1234	—	100	150	300	500	—
AH1235	—	100	150	300	500	—
AH1238	—	100	150	300	500	—

Moulay 'Abd al-Rahman
AH1238-76/1822-59AD

HAMMERED COINAGE

Mint: Fes Hazrat
C# 145   1/2 BENDUQI
1.7600 g., Gold

Date	Mintage	VG	F	VF	XF	Unc
AH1240	—	100	200	350	600	—
AH1247 Rare	—	—	—	—	—	—
AH1248	—	90.00	150	250	375	—
AH1250	—	100	200	350	600	—
AH1252 Rare	—	—	—	—	—	—

Mint: Fes
C# 150.1   BENDUQI
3.5200 g., Gold

Date	Mintage	VG	F	VF	XF	Unc
AH1270	—	75.00	100	150	200	—

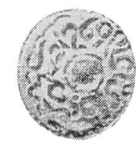

Mint: Fes Hazrat
C# 150.2   BENDUQI
3.5200 g., Gold

Date	Mintage	VG	F	VF	XF	Unc
AH1241	—	80.00	110	175	300	—
AH1242	—	80.00	110	175	300	—
AH1243	—	75.00	100	150	200	—
AH1244	—	75.00	100	150	200	—
AH1245	—	75.00	100	150	200	—
AH1246	—	80.00	110	175	300	—
AH1247	—	75.00	100	150	200	—
AH1248	—	75.00	100	150	200	—
AH1249	—	75.00	100	150	200	—
AH1250	—	75.00	100	150	200	—

Date	Mintage	VG	F	VF	XF	Unc
AH1251	—	80.00	110	175	300	—
AH1252	—	100	150	300	500	—
AH1253	—	80.00	110	175	300	—
AH1254	—	80.00	110	175	300	—
AH1255	—	80.00	110	175	300	—
AH1256	—	80.00	110	175	300	—
AH1257	—	75.00	100	150	200	—
AH1258	—	100	150	300	500	—
AH1259	—	75.00	100	150	200	—
AH1261	—	100	150	300	500	—
AH1266 Rare	—	—	—	—	—	—
AH1267	—	80.00	110	175	300	—
AH1268 Rare	—	—	—	—	—	—
AH1269	—	80.00	110	175	300	—

Mint: Meknes
C# 150.3   BENDUQI
3.5200 g., Gold

Date	Mintage	VG	F	VF	XF	Unc
AH1247 Rare	—	—	—	—	—	—

Sidi Mohammed IV
AH1276-90/1859-73

HAMMERED COINAGE

Mint: Fes
C# 178   BENDUQI
3.5200 g., Gold

Date	Mintage	VG	F	VF	XF	Unc
AH1277 Rare	—	—	—	—	—	—
AH1284 Rare	—	—	—	—	—	—
AH1286 Rare	—	—	—	—	—	—

Mohammed V
AH1346-1381 / 1927-1962AD

STANDARD COINAGE
100 Centimes = 1 Franc

Mint: Paris
Y# 51a   50 FRANCS
Gold **Obv:** Date in inner circle of doubled tri-lobe star, all within circle **Rev:** Value within doubled square within circle

Date	Mintage	F	VF	XF	Unc
AH1371(a) Rare	—	—	—	—	—

BULLION COINAGE

X# 12   500 DIRHAMS
31.1031 g., 0.9170 Gold 1.0000 oz. AGW **Issuer:** First Banking Corporation, Tangier **Obv:** Hercules standing, facing 3/4 right, holding club and hide **Obv. Legend:** FIRST • BANKING • CO - PORATION• TANGIER **Note:** Refiners: N. M. Rothschild & Sons; previous Y#250.

Date	Mintage	F	VF	XF	Unc
ND(1954)	—	—	—	475	650

MOROCCO

KINGDOM
Resumed

al-Hassan II
AH1381-1420 / 1962-1999AD

REFORM COINAGE
100 Santimat = 1 Dirham

Y# 58a SANTIM
0.9170 Gold, 17 mm. **Obv:** Crowned arms with supporters **Rev:** Value flanked by designs

Date	Mintage	F	VF	XF	Unc
AH1394-1974 Proof	30	Value: 425			

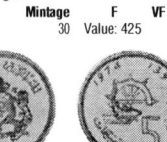

Y# 59a 5 SANTIMAT
0.9170 Gold, 17.5 mm. **Series:** F.A.O. **Obv:** Crowned arms with supporters **Rev:** Value at lower right of captain's wheel

Date	Mintage	F	VF	XF	Unc
AH1394-1974 Proof	30	Value: 485			

Y# 60a 10 SANTIMAT
0.9170 Gold, 20 mm. **Series:** F.A.O. **Obv:** Crowned arms with supporters **Rev:** Value at lower left of designs

Date	Mintage	F	VF	XF	Unc
AH1394-1974 Proof	30	Value: 575			

Y# 61a 20 SANTIMAT
0.9170 Gold, 23 mm. **Obv:** Head left **Rev:** Crowned arms with supporters

Date	Mintage	F	VF	XF	Unc
AH1394-1974 Proof	30	Value: 585			

Y# 62a 50 SANTIMAT
0.9170 Gold, 21 mm. **Obv:** Head left **Rev:** Crowned arms with supporters

Date	Mintage	F	VF	XF	Unc
AH1394-1974 Proof	30	Value: 585			

Y# 63a DIRHAM
0.9170 Gold, 24 mm. **Obv:** Head left **Rev:** Crowned arms with supporters

Date	Mintage	F	VF	XF	Unc
AH1394-1974 Proof	30	Value: 685			

Y# 64b 5 DIRHAMS
23.6500 g., 0.9000 Gold .6844 oz. AGW **Series:** World Food Conference **Obv:** Head left **Rev:** Small value within center of designs

Date	Mintage	F	VF	XF	Unc
AH1395-1975 Proof	20	Value: 1,000			

Y# 65a 50 DIRHAMS
60.1400 g., 0.9000 Gold 1.7404 oz. AGW **Subject:** 20th Anniversary of Independence **Obv:** Head left **Rev:** Crowned arms with supporters

Date	Mintage	F	VF	XF	Unc
AH1395-1975 Proof	40	Value: 1,250			

Y# 67a 50 DIRHAMS
60.1400 g., 0.9000 Gold 1.7404 oz. AGW **Series:** International Women's Year **Obv:** Head left **Rev:** Hand within circled design

Date	Mintage	F	VF	XF	Unc
AH1395-1975 Proof	20	Value: 1,500			

Y# 76a 50 DIRHAMS
60.1400 g., 0.9000 Gold 1.7404 oz. AGW **Subject:** 50th Birthday - King Hassan **Obv:** Head left **Rev:** Crowned arms with supporters flanked by oat sprig, curvy line and dates with value below

Date	Mintage	F	VF	XF	Unc
AH1399-1979 Proof	70	Value: 1,400			

Y# 70a 50 DIRHAMS
60.1400 g., 0.9000 Gold 1.7404 oz. AGW **Series:** International Year of the Child **Obv:** Head left **Rev:** Designs divide globe flanked by dates

Date	Mintage	F	VF	XF	Unc
AH1399-1979 Proof	70	Value: 1,275			

Y# 68a 50 DIRHAMS
60.1400 g., 0.9000 Gold 1.7404 oz. AGW **Subject:** Anniversary - Green March **Obv:** Head left **Obv. Designer:** David Wynne **Rev:** Pointed artistic design with stars on points flanked by dates **Note:** Reverse inscriptions vary slightly for each date.

Date	Mintage	F	VF	XF	Unc
AH1396-1976 Proof	20	Value: 1,750			
AH1397-1977 Proof	20	Value: 1,700			
AH1398-1978 Proof	70	Value: 1,275			
AH1399-1979 Proof	70	Value: 1,275			
AH1400-1980 Proof	30	Value: 1,450			

Y# 74a 150 DIRHAMS
60.1400 g., 0.9000 Gold 1.7404 oz. AGW **Subject:** 15th Hejira Calendar Century **Obv:** Crowned arms with supporters flanked by dates **Rev:** Artistic design within circle flanked by dates

Date	Mintage	F	VF	XF	Unc
AH1401-1980 Proof	30	Value: 1,800			

Y# 73a 150 DIRHAMS
60.1400 g., 0.9000 Gold 1.7404 oz. AGW **Subject:** 20th Anniversary - King Hassan's Coronation **Obv:** Head left **Obv. Designer:** David Wynne **Rev:** Crowned arms with supporters flanked by dates

Date	Mintage	F	VF	XF	Unc
AH1401-1981 Proof	30	Value: 1,700			

Y# 100a 200 DIRHAMS
21.5000 g., 0.9000 Gold 0.6221 oz. AGW, 31.3 mm. **Subject:** GATT Agreement **Obv:** Head left **Rev:** Tower within world globe **Edge:** Reeded

Date	Mintage	F	VF	XF	Unc
AH1416-1995 Proof	—	—	—	—	

Y# 66 250 DIRHAMS
6.4500 g., 0.9000 Gold .1867 oz. AGW **Subject:** Birthday of King Hassan **Obv:** Head left **Obv. Designer:** David Wynne **Rev:** Crowned arms with supporters flanked by dates

MOZAMBIQUE 519

Date	Mintage	F	VF	XF	Unc
AH1395-1975	5,000	—	—	—	130
AH1395-1975 Proof	1,270	Value: 160			
AH1396-1976	3,200	—	—	—	130
AH1396-1976 Proof	450	Value: 175			
AH1397-1977	3,000	—	—	—	130
AH1397-1977 Proof	800	Value: 150			
AH1398-1978	2,000	—	—	—	130
AH1398-1978 Proof	150	Value: 200			

Y# 71 500 DIRHAMS
12.9000 g., 0.9000 Gold .3733 oz. AGW **Subject:** Birthday of King Hassan **Obv:** Head left **Obv. Designer:** David Wynne **Rev:** Crowned arms with supporters flanked by oat sprig, curvy line and dates

Date	Mintage	F	VF	XF	Unc
AH1399-1979	3,000	—	—	—	265
AH1399-1979 Proof	300	Value: 300			
AH1400-1980	100	—	—	—	400
AH1400-1980 Proof	100	Value: 500			
AH1401-1981	100	—	—	—	400
AH1401-1981 Proof	100	Value: 500			
AH1402-1982	100	—	—	—	400
AH1402-1982 Proof	100	Value: 500			
AH1403-1983	2,500	—	—	—	265
AH1403-1983 Proof	Inc. above	Value: 285			
AH1404-1984	100	—	—	—	400
AH1404-1984 Proof	100	Value: 500			
AH1405-1985	275	—	—	—	285
AH1405-1985 Proof	125	Value: 475			
AH1406-1986 Proof	—	Value: 450			
AH1407-1987 Proof	—	Value: 450			
AH1408-1988 Proof	—	Value: 450			
AH1409-1989 Proof	—	Value: 450			
AH1410-1990 Proof	—	Value: 450			
AH1411-1991 Proof	—	Value: 450			
AH1412-1992 Proof	—	Value: 450			
AH1413-1993 Proof	—	Value: 450			

Mohammed VI
AH1420 / 1999AD
REFORM COINAGE
100 Santimat = 1 Dirham

Mint: B.H. Mayer
Y# 95a 250 DIRHAMS
25.0000 g., 0.9999 Gold .8037 oz. AGW, 37 mm. **Subject:** World Children's Day **Obv:** Head 3/4 left **Rev:** Two children standing on an open book within globe **Edge:** Reeded **Note:** Previous Y#95.

Date	Mintage	F	VF	XF	Unc
AH1422-2001 Proof	2,800	Value: 575			

PATTERNS
Including off metal strikes

KM#	Date	Mintage	Identification	Mkt Val
Pn6	AH1297	—	4 Ryals. Gold. .	5,500

PIEFORTS
Double thickness

KM#	Date	Mintage	Identification	Mkt Val
P1	AH1395	10	5 Dirhams. Gold. . Y64b	1,100
P3	AH1395	10	50 Dirhams. Gold. . Y65a.	2,500
P5	AH1395	10	250 Dirhams. Gold. . Y66	400
P6	AH1395	10	50 Dirhams. Gold. . Y68a.	2,100
P8	AH1396	10	50 Dirhams. Gold. . Y68a.	2,500
P9	AH1397	15	250 Dirhams. Gold. . Y66.	375
P10	AH1397	10	50 Dirhams. Gold. . Y68a.	2,500
P11	AH1398	20	250 Dirhams. Gold. . Y66.	350
P12	AH1399	20	50 Dirhams. Gold. . Y68a.	2,000
P15	AH1399	20	50 Dirhams. Gold. . Y76a.	2,000
P16	AH1399	20	500 Dirhams. Gold. . Y71.	800
P17	AH1400	10	50 Dirhams. Gold. . Y68a.	2,500
P19	AH1401	10	150 Dirhams. 0.9000 Gold. . Y73a.	2,500
P18	AH1401	10	150 Dirhams. 0.9000 Gold. . Y74a.	2,500

PIEFORTS WITH ESSAI

KM#	Date	Mintage	Identification	Mkt Val
PE11	AH1372(a)	—	200 Francs. Gold. . Y53.	1,000

PROOF SETS

KM#	Date	Mintage	Identification	Issue Price	Mkt Val
PS1	1974 (6)	30	Y#58a-63a	—	3,650

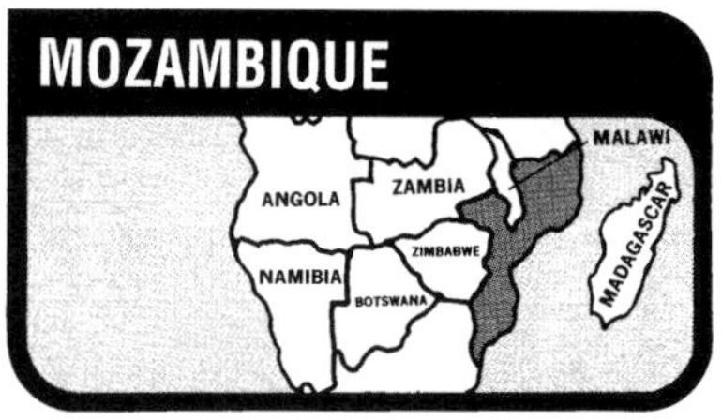

MOZAMBIQUE

The Republic of Mozambique, a former overseas province of Portugal, stretches for 1,430 miles (2,301km.) along the southeast coast of Africa, has an area of 302,330 sq. mi. (801,590 sq. km.) and a population of 14.1 million, 99 % of whom are native Africans of the Bantu tribes. Capital: Maputo. Agriculture is the chief industry. Cashew nuts, cotton, sugar, copra and tea are exported.

Vasco de Gama explored all the coast of Mozambique in 1498 and found Arab trading posts already established along the coast. Portuguese settlement dates from the establishment of the trading post of Mozambique in 1505. Within five years Portugal absorbed all the former Arab sultanates along the east African coast. The area was organized as a colony in 1907 and became an overseas province in 1952. In Sept. of 1974, after more than a decade of guerrilla warfare with the forces of the Mozambique Liberation Front, Portugal agreed to the independence of Mozambique, effective June 25, 1975. The Socialist party, led by President Joaquim Chissano was in power until the 2nd of November, 1990 when they became a republic.

Mozambique became a member of the Commonwealth of Nations in November 1995. The President is Head of State; the Prime Minister is Head of Government.

RULER
Portuguese, until 1975

MONETARY SYSTEM
2880 Reis = 6 Cruzados = 1 Onca

PORTUGUESE COLONY
COLONIAL COINAGE

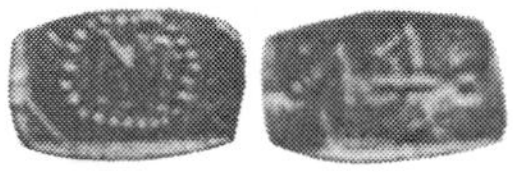

KM# 31 1-1/4 MATICAES
7.2000 g., Gold, 11x17 mm. **Shape:** Rectangular

Date	Mintage	VG	F	VF	XF	Unc
ND	—	750	1,600	3,500	—	—

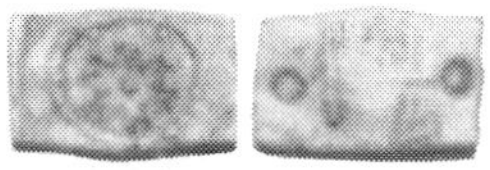

KM# 32 1-1/4 MATICAES
7.2000 g., Gold **Countermark:** Rosette **Obv:** Rosette within circle **Rev:** Value **Note:** Countermark on KM#31

Date	Mintage	VG	F	VF	XF	Unc
ND	—	500	1,500	2,500	—	—

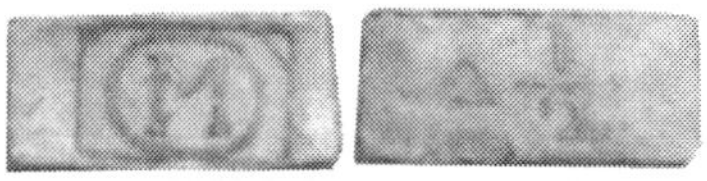

KM# 33 2-1/2 MATICAES
14.5000 g., Gold **Obv:** Letter M within circle **Rev:** Value

Date	Mintage	VG	F	VF	XF	Unc
ND	—	750	2,000	3,000	—	—

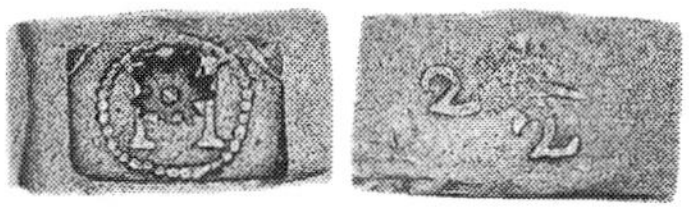

KM# 34 2-1/2 MATICAES
14.5000 g., Gold **Countermark:** Rosette **Obv:** Rosette within letter M within beaded circle **Rev:** Value **Note:** Countermark on KM#33

Date	Mintage	VG	F	VF	XF	Unc
ND	—	250	450	750	—	—

MOZAMBIQUE

PEOPLE'S REPUBLIC
REFORM COINAGE
100 Centavos = 1 Metical; 1980

KM# 106b 50 METICAIS
22.0000 g., 0.9000 Gold .6366 oz. AGW **Subject:** World Fisheries Conference **Obv:** Emblem above value and date **Rev:** Traditional fishing raft

Date	Mintage	F	VF	XF	Unc	BU
1983 Proof	135	Value: 1,000				

KM# 108 2000 METICAIS
17.5000 g., 0.9170 Gold .5158 oz. AGW **Subject:** 10th Anniversary of Independence **Obv:** Emblem above value **Rev:** Star and map divides circle, value at right

Date	Mintage	F	VF	XF	Unc	BU
1985 Proof	100	Value: 675				

KM# 105 5000 METICAIS
17.2790 g., 0.9000 Gold .5000 oz. AGW **Subject:** 5th Anniversary of Independence **Obv:** Emblem above value **Rev:** Figure at left, corn plants in background with tractor above

Date	Mintage	F	VF	XF	Unc	BU
1980 Proof	2,000	Value: 350				

MUSCAT & OMAN

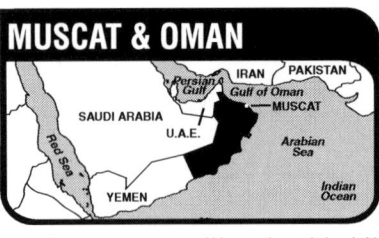

The Portuguese who captured Muscat, the capital and chief port, in 1508, made the first European contact with Muscat and Oman. They occupied the city, utilizing it as a naval base and factory and holding it against land and sea attacks by Arabs and Persians until finally ejected by local Arabs in 1650. It was next occupied by the Persians who maintained control until 1741, when it was taken by Ahmed ibn Sa'id of the present ruling family. Muscat and Oman was the most powerful state in Arabia during the first half of the 19th century, until weakened by the persistent attack of interior nomadic tribes. British influence, initiated by the signing of a treaty of friendship with the Sultanate in 1798, remains a dominant fact of the civil and military phases of the government, although Britain recognizes the Sultanate as a sovereign state.

RULERS
al-Bu Sa'id Dynasty
Sultan bin Ahmad, AH1207-1219/1792-1804AD
Sultan bin Sultan, AH1219-1273/1804-1856AD
Thuwaini bin Sa'id, AH1273-1283/1856-1866AD
Salim bin Thuwaini, AH1283-1285/1866-1868AD
Azzan bin Quais, AH1285-1288/1868-1871AD
Turkee bin Sa'id, AH1288-1306/1871-1888AD
Faisal bin Turkee, AH1306-1332/1888-1913AD
Taimur bin Faisal, AH1332-1351/1913-1932AD
Sa'id bin Taimur, AH1351-1390/1932-1970AD
Qabus bin Sa'id, AH1390-/1970-AD

MONETARY SYSTEM
Until 1970
4 Baiza = 1 Anna
64 Baiza = 1 Rupee
200 Baiza = 1 Saidi (Dasin Dog)/Dhofari Rial
1970-1972
1000 (new) Baisa = 1 Saidi Rial
Commencing 1972
1000 Baisa = 1 Omani Rial

SULTANATE
REFORM COINAGE
1000 (new) Baisa = 1 Saidi Rial

KM# 22a 10 BAISA
Gold **Ruler:** Sa'id bin Taimur **Obv:** Arms **Rev:** Inscription

Date	Mintage	F	VF	XF	Unc	BU
AH1359 Proof	—	Value: 1,850				

KM# 23a 20 BAISA (Baiza)
Gold **Ruler:** Sa'id bin Taimur **Obv:** Arms **Rev:** Inscription

Date	Mintage	F	VF	XF	Unc	BU
AH1359 Proof	—	Value: 1,650				

KM# 39a 25 BAISA
6.0100 g., 0.9160 Gold .1771 oz. AGW **Ruler:** Sa'id bin Taimur **Obv:** Arms **Rev:** Value flanked by marks

Date	Mintage	F	VF	XF	Unc	BU
AH1390 Proof	350	Value: 145				

KM# 24a 50 BAISA
Gold **Ruler:** Sa'id bin Taimur **Obv:** Arms **Rev:** Inscription

Date	Mintage	F	VF	XF	Unc	BU
AH1359 Proof	—	Value: 1,750				

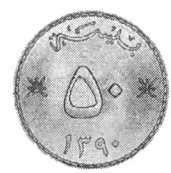

KM# 40a 50 BAISA
12.8100 g., 0.9160 Gold .3775 oz. AGW **Ruler:** Sa'id bin Taimur **Obv:** Arms **Rev:** Value flanked by marks

Date	Mintage	F	VF	XF	Unc	BU
AH1390 Proof	350	Value: 300				

KM# 41a 100 BAISA
22.6300 g., 0.9160 Gold .6670 oz. AGW **Ruler:** Sa'id bin Taimur **Obv:** Arms **Rev:** Value flanked by marks

Date	Mintage	F	VF	XF	Unc	BU
AH1390 Proof	350	Value: 525				

KM# 29a 1/2 DHOFARI RIAL
24.0300 g., 0.9170 Gold .6780 oz. AGW **Ruler:** Sa'id bin Taimur **Obv:** Arms above sprig **Rev:** Inscription within circle and wreath

Date	Mintage	F	VF	XF	Unc	BU
AH1367 Proof	2	Value: 5,500				

Note: Struck for presentation purposes

KM# 34a 1/2 SAIDI RIAL
25.6000 g., 0.9160 Gold .7540 oz. AGW **Ruler:** Sa'id bin Taimur **Obv:** Arms **Rev:** Value

Date	Mintage	F	VF	XF	Unc	BU
AH1381 Proof	150	Value: 650				
AH1382 Proof	100	Value: 700				
AH1390 Proof	350	Value: 600				

Note: Struck for presentation purposes

KM# 31b SAIDI RIAL
46.6500 g., 0.9160 Gold 1.3740 oz. AGW, 33.7 mm. **Ruler:** Sa'id bin Taimur **Obv:** Arms within circle, designs around border **Rev:** Value and date

Date	Mintage	F	VF	XF	Unc	BU
AH1378 Proof	100	Value: 1,250				
AH1390 Proof	350	Value: 1,000				

Note: Struck for presentation purposes

KM# 35 15 SAIDI RIALS
7.9900 g., 0.9160 Gold .2353 oz. AGW **Ruler:** Sa'id bin Taimur

Date	Mintage	F	VF	XF	Unc	BU
AH1381	2,000	—	—	—	180	200
AH1381 Proof	100	Value: 575				

Note: Struck for presentation purposes

PROOF SETS

KM#	Date	Mintage	Identification	Issue Price	Mkt Val
PS4	AH1390 (1970) (3)	350	KM#39a-41a	—	975

MYANMAR

MYANMAR

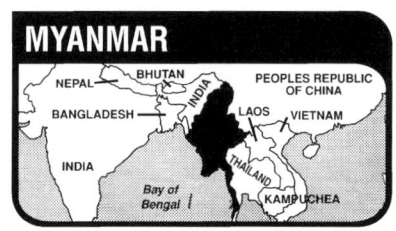

The Union of Myanmar, formerly Burma, a country of Southeast Asia fronting on the Bay of Bengal and the Andaman Sea, has an area of 261,218 sq. mi. (678,500 sq. km.) and a population of 38.8 million. Capital: Yangon (Rangoon). Myanmar is an agricultural country heavily dependent on its leading product (rice) which occupies two-thirds of the cultivated area and accounts for 40% of the value of exports. Mineral resources are extensive, but production is low. Petroleum, lead, tin, silver, zinc, nickel cobalt, and precious stones are exported.

The first European to reach Burma, in about 1435, was Nicolo Di Conti, a Venetian merchant. During the beginning of the reign of Bodawpaya (1781-1819AD) the kingdom comprised most of the same area as it does today including Arakan which was taken over in 1784-85. The British East India Company, while unsuccessful in its 1612 effort to establish posts along the Bay of Bengal, was enabled by the Anglo-Burmese Wars of 1824-86 to expand to the whole of Burma and to secure its annexation to British India. In 1937, Burma was separated from India, becoming a separate British colony with limited self-government. Burma became an independent nation outside the British Commonwealth on Jan. 4, 1948, the constitution of 1948 providing for a parliamentary democracy and the nationalization of certain industries. However, political and economic problems persisted, and on March 2, 1962, Gen. Ne Win took over the government, suspended the constitution, installed himself as chief of state, and pursued a socialistic program with nationalization of nearly all industry and trade. On Jan. 4, 1974, a new constitution adopted by referendum established Burma as a socialist republic under one-party rule. The country name was changed to Myanmar in 1989.

The coins issued by kings Mindon and Thibaw between 1852 and 1885 circulated in Upper Burma. Indian coins were current in Lower Burma, which was annexed in 1852. Burmese coins are frequently known by the equivalent Indian denominations, although their values are inscribed in Burmese units. Upper Burma was annexed in 1885 and the Burmese coinage remained in circulation until 1889, when Indian coins became current throughout Burma. Coins were again issued in the old Burmese denominations after independence in 1948, but these were replaced by decimal issues in 1952. The Chula-Sakarat (CS) dating is sometimes referred to as BE-Burmese Era and began in 638AD.

RULERS
Burmese
Bodawpaya, CS1143-1181/1782-1819AD
Bagyidaw, CS1181-1198/1819-1837AD
Tharawaddy, CS1198-1207/1837-46AD
Pagan, CS1207-1214/1846-53AD
Mindon, CS1214-1240/1853-78AD
Thibaw, CS1240-1248/1880-85AD
British, 1886-1948

MONETARY SYSTEM
(Until 1952)
4 Pyas = 1 Pe
2 Pe = 1 Mu
2 Mu = 1 Mat
5 Mat = 1 Kyat
  NOTE: Originally 10 light Mu = 1 Kyat, eventually 8 heavy Mu = 1 Kyat.
Indian Equivalents
1 Silver Kyat = 1 Rupee = 16 Annas
1 Gold Kyat = 1 Mohur = 16 Rupees

BURMA

STANDARD COINAGE

KM# 13 PE
0.9000 Gold **Obv:** Facing peacock **Rev:** Value in sprays

Date	Mintage	Good	VG	F	VF	XF
CS1214 (1852)	—	40.00	65.00	100	175	—

KM# 19 PE
0.6700 g., Gold **Obv:** Chinze left **Rev:** Denomination within wreath

Date	Mintage	Good	VG	F	VF	XF
CS1228 (1866)	—	45.00	70.00	125	200	—

KM# 14 MU
0.9000 Gold **Obv:** Peacock left, full display **Rev:** Denomination within wreath

Date	Mintage	Good	VG	F	VF	XF
CS1214 (1852)	—	60.00	100	150	250	—

KM# A20 MU
1.2600 g., Gold **Obv:** Chinz left **Rev:** Denomination within wreath

Date	Mintage	VG	F	VF	XF	Unc
CS1228 (1866)	—	1,000	1,500	2,000	—	—

KM# 20 2 MU 1 PE
2.7500 g., Gold **Obv:** Chinze left **Rev:** Denomination within wreath

Date	Mintage	VG	F	VF	XF	Unc
CS1228 (1866)	—	125	175	275	475	—

KM# 26 5 MU (1/2 Mohur)
5.8500 g., Gold **Obv:** Chinze left **Rev:** Denomination within wreath

Date	Mintage	VG	F	VF	XF	Unc
CS1240 (1878)	—	—	—	—	—	—

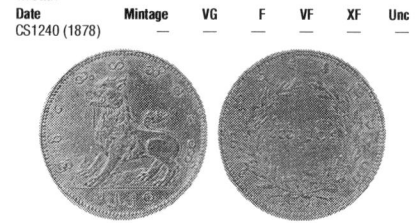

KM# 21 KYAT (Mohur)
11.9400 g., Gold **Obv:** Chinze left **Rev:** Denomination within wreath

Date	Mintage	VG	F	VF	XF	Unc
CS1228 (1866)	—	—	—	—	—	—

UNION OF BURMA

REVOLUTIONARY COINAGE
Patriotic Liberation Army

KM# 43 MU
2.0000 g., 1.0000 Gold .0643 oz. AGW **Obv:** Peacock **Rev:** Legend within star

Date	Mintage	F	VF	XF	Unc	BU
1970-71	—	—	—	—	125	160

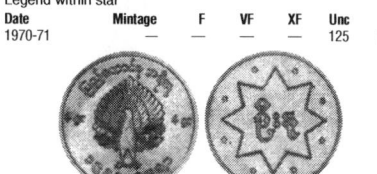

KM# 44 2 MU
4.0000 g., 1.0000 Gold .1286 oz. AGW **Obv:** Peacock **Rev:** Legend within star flanked by stars at points

Date	Mintage	F	VF	XF	Unc	BU
1970-71	—	—	—	—	245	280

KM# 45 4 MU
8.0000 g., 1.0000 Gold .2572 oz. AGW **Obv:** Peacock **Rev:** Legend within star

Date	Mintage	F	VF	XF	Unc	BU
1970-71	—	—	—	—	470	500

UNION OF MYANMAR

DECIMAL COINAGE
100 Pyas = 1 Kyat

KM# A51 300 KYAT
1.2441 g., 0.9990 Gold .04 oz. AGW **Subject:** Year of the Tiger **Obv:** Lotus flower **Rev:** Tiger

Date	Mintage	F	VF	XF	Unc	BU
1998	—	—	—	—	40.00	45.00

KM# 55 2000 KYAT
7.7759 g., 0.9999 Gold .2500 oz. AGW **Subject:** Year of the Tiger **Obv:** Lotus flower **Rev:** Stalking tiger

Date	Mintage	F	VF	XF	Unc	BU
1998 Proof	1,998	Value: 250				

Note: In sets only

KM# 56 5000 KYAT
15.5518 g., 0.9999 Gold .5000 oz. AGW **Subject:** Year of the Tiger **Obv:** Lotus flower **Rev:** Tiger

Date	Mintage	F	VF	XF	Unc	BU
1998 Proof	5,798	Value: 425				

PATTERNS
Including off metal strikes

KM#	Date	Mintage	Identification		Mkt Val
Pn7	CS1214	—	Kyat. Gold. KM10, restrike		—

PROOF SETS

KM#	Date	Mintage	Identification	Issue Price	Mkt Val
PS6	1998 (2)	1,998	KM#55-56	—	675

NAGORNO-KARABAKH

Nagorno-Karabakh, an ethnically Armenian enclave inside Azerbaijan (pop., 1991 est.: 193,000), SW region. It occupies an area of 1,700 sq mi (4,400 square km) on the NE flank of the Karabakh Mountain Range, with the capital city of Stepanakert.

Russia annexed the area from Persia in 1813, and in 1923 it was established as an autonomous province of the Azerbaijan S.S.R. In 1988 the region's ethnic Armenian majority demonstrated against Azerbaijani rule, and in 1991, after the breakup of the U.S.S.R. brought independence to Armenia and Azerbaijan, war broke out between the two ethnic groups. On January 8, 1992 the leaders of Nagorno-Karabakh declared independence as the Republic of Mountainous Karabakh (RMK). Since 1994, following a cease-fire, ethnic Armenians have held Karabakh, though officially it remains part of Azerbaijan. Karabakh remains sovereign, but the political and military condition is volatile and tensions frequently flare into skirmishes.

Its marvelous nature and geographic situation, have all facilitated Karabakh to be a center of science, poetry and, especially, of the musical culture of Azerbaijan.

REPUBLIC

STANDARD COINAGE

KM# 3 50000 DRAMS
7.8000 g., 0.9000 Gold .2257 oz. AGW, 22 mm. **Obv:** National arms **Rev:** Head left above two fists **Edge:** Plain **Note:** Struck at Lialoosin Inc., Los Angeles, CA.

Date	Mintage	F	VF	XF	Unc	BU
1998 Proof	—	Value: 300				

NAMIBIA

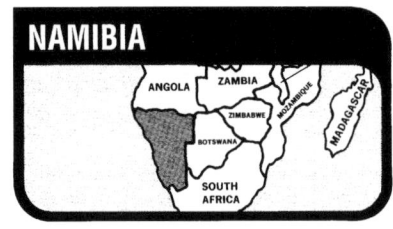

The Republic of Namibia, once the German colonial territory of German Southwest Africa, and later Southwest Africa, is situated on the Atlantic coast of southern Africa, bounded on the north by Angola, on the east by Botswana, and on the south by South Africa. It has an area of 318,261 sq. mi. (824,290 sq. km.) and a population of *1.4 million. Capital: Windhoek. Diamonds, copper, lead, zinc, and cattle are exported.

South Africa undertook the administration of Southwest Africa under the terms of a League of Nations mandate on Dec. 17, 1920. When the League of Nations was dissolved in 1946, its supervisory authority for Southwest Africa was inherited by the United Nations. In 1946 the UN denied South Africa's request to annex Southwest Africa. South Africa responded by refusing to place the territory under a UN trusteeship. In 1950 the International Court of Justice ruled that South Africa could not unilaterally modify the international status of Southwest Africa. A 1966 UN resolution declaring the mandate terminated was rejected by South Africa, and the status of the area remained in dispute. In June 1968 the UN General Assembly voted to rename the territory Namibia. In 1971 the International Court of Justice ruled that South Africa's presence in Namibia was illegal. In Dec. 1973 the UN appointed a UN Commissioner and a multi-racial Advisory Council was appointed. An interim government was formed in 1977 and independence was to be declared by Dec. 31, 1978. This resolution was rejected by major UN powers. In April 1978 South Africa accepted a plan for UN-supervised elections, which led to a political abstention by the Southwest Africa People's Organization (SWAPO) party leading to dissolving of the Minister's Council and National Assembly in Jan. 1983. A Multi-Party Conference (MPC) was formed in May 1984, which held talks with SWAPO. The MPC petitioned South Africa for self-government and on June 17, 1985 the Transitional Government of National Unity was installed. Negotiations were held in 1988 between Angola, Cuba, and South Africa reaching a peaceful settlement on Aug. 5, 1988. By April 1989 Cuban troops were to withdraw from Angola and South African troops from Namibia. The Transitional Government resigned on Feb. 28, 1988 for the upcoming elections of the constituent assembly in Nov. 1989. Independence was finally achieved on March 12, 1990 within the Commonwealth of Nations. The President is the Head of State; the Prime Minister is Head of Government.

MONETARY SYSTEM
100 Cents = 1 Namibia Dollar
1 Namibia Dollar = 1 South African Rand

REPUBLIC
1920 - present

DECIMAL COINAGE

KM# 17 100 DOLLARS
31.1035 g., 0.9999 Gold 1.0000 oz. AGW **Series:** Olympic Games 1996 **Obv:** Arms with supporters **Rev:** Runner and cheetah **Note:** Similar to 10-Dollar, KM#11.

Date	Mintage	F	VF	XF	Unc	BU
1996 Proof	400	Value: 775				

KM# 15 100 DOLLARS
31.1035 g., 0.9999 Gold 1.0000 oz. AGW **Subject:** Marine Life Protection **Obv:** Arms with supporters **Rev:** Multicolor whale and calf **Note:** Similar to 1 Dollar, KM#12.

Date	Mintage	F	VF	XF	Unc	BU
1998 Proof	125	Value: 835				

MEDALLIC BULLION COINAGE

X# MB4 OUNCE
0.9167 Gold **Issuer:** Namibian Miuters (Pty.) Ltd. **Subject:** Independence **Obv:** Supported arms **Rev:** Bust of President Sam Nujoma facing

Date	Mintage	F	VF	XF	Unc	BU
1990 Proof	5,000	Value: 675				

GERMAN ADMINISTRATION

MEDALLIC BULLION COINAGE

X# MB2 5 UNZEN
155.5150 g., 0.9990 Gold 4.9949 oz. AGW, 65 mm. **Subject:** 75th Anniversary Reiter Monument Horseman "Bushriders" of the German Colonial Army **Rev:** Tree, elephants walking left

Date	Mintage	F	VF	XF	Unc	BU
ND(1987)BP Proof	10	Value: 3,750				

ESSAIS
Rand Coinage

X# E1 100 RAND
6.4500 g., 0.9000 Gold 0.1866 oz. AGW **Subject:** 75th Anniversary Reiter Monument Horseman "Bushriders" of the German Colonial Army

Date	Mintage	F	VF	XF	Unc	BU
ND(1987)BP Proof	15	Value: 1,000				

ESSAIS

KM#	Date	Mintage	Identification	Mkt Val
E2	1996	30	100 Dollars. Copper-Nickel. Multicolor, KM#17.	220

NAURU ISLAND

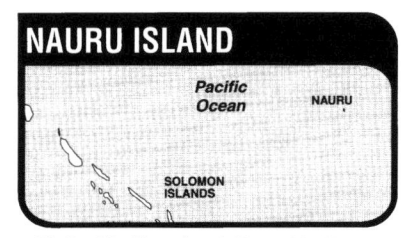

The Republic of Nauru, formerly Pleasant Island, is an island republic in the western Pacific Ocean west of the Gilbert Islands. It has an area of 8-1/2 sq. mi. and a population of 7,254. It is known for its phosphate deposits.

The island was discovered in 1798. It was annexed by Germany in 1888 and made a part of the Marshall Island protectorate. In 1914 the island was occupied by Australia and placed under mandate in 1919. During World War II it was seized by the Japanese in August, 1942. It became a joint Australian, British and New Zealand trust territory in 1947 and remained as such until it became an independent republic in 1968. Nauru has a unique relationship with the Commonwealth of Nations.

RULER
British, until 1968

MONETARY SYSTEM
100 Cents = 1 (Australian) Dollar

REPUBLIC
DECIMAL COINAGE

KM# 4 50 DOLLARS
8.0500 g., 0.9000 Gold .2329 oz. AGW **Series:** 1996 Olympics **Obv:** National arms **Rev:** Javelin throwing

Date	Mintage	F	VF	XF	Unc	BU
1994 Proof	3,000			Value: 185		

KM# 10 50 DOLLARS
7.7760 g., 0.5833 Gold .1458 oz. AGW **Obv:** National arms **Rev:** Crowned emblem above steamship

Date	Mintage	F	VF	XF	Unc	BU
1994 Proof	Est. 3,000			Value: 150		

KM# 11 50 DOLLARS
7.7760 g., 0.5833 Gold .1458 oz. AGW **Subject:** Endangered Wildlife **Obv:** National arms **Rev:** Sea otter

Date	Mintage	F	VF	XF	Unc	BU
1995 Proof	Est. 2,000			Value: 165		

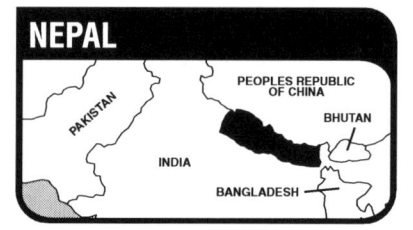

NEPAL

The Kingdom of Nepal, the world's only surviving Hindu kingdom, is a landlocked country occupying the southern slopes of the Himalayas. It has an area of 56,136 sq. mi. (140,800 sq. km.) and a population of 18 million. Capital: Kathmandu. Nepal has deposits of coal, copper, iron and cobalt, but they are largely unexploited. Agriculture is the principal economic activity. Rice, timber and jute are exported, with tourism being the other major foreign exchange earner.

Apart from a brief Muslim invasion in the 14th century, Nepal was able to avoid the mainstream of Northern Indian politics, due to its impregnable position in the mountains. It is therefore a unique survivor of the medieval Hindu and Buddhist culture of Northern India which was largely destroyed by the successive waves of Muslim invasions.

Prior to the late 18th century, Nepal, as we know it today, was divided among a number of small states. Unless otherwise stated, the term *Nepal* applies to the small fertile valley, about 4,500 ft. above sea level, in which the three main cities of Kathmandu, Patan and Bhatgaon are situated.

During the reign of King Yaksha Malla (1428-1482AD), the Nepalese kingdom, with capital at Bhatgaon, was extended northwards into Tibet, and also controlled a considerable area to the south of the hills. After Yaksha Malla's death, the Kingdom was divided among his sons, so four kingdoms were established with capitals at Bhatgaon, Patan, Kathmandu and Banepa, all situated within the small valley, less than 20 miles square. Banepa was quickly absorbed within the territory of Bhatgaon, but the other three kingdoms remained until 1769. The internecine strife between the three kings effectively stopped Nepal from becoming a major military force during this period, although with its fertile land and strategic position, it was by far the wealthiest and most powerful of the Himalayan states.

Apart from agriculture, Nepal owed its prosperity to its position on one of the easiest trade routes between the great monasteries of central Tibet, and India. Nepal made full use of this, and a trading community was set up in Lhasa during the 16th century, and Nepalese coins became the accepted currency medium in Tibet.

The seeds of discord between Nepal and Tibet were sown during the first half of the 18th century, when the Nepalese debased the coinage, and the fate of the Malla kings of Nepal was sealed when Prithvi Narayan Shah, King of the small state of Gorkha, to the west of Kathmandu, was able to gain control of the trans-himalayan trade routes during the years after 1750.

Prithvi Narayan spent several years consolidating his position in hill areas before he finally succeeded in conquering the Kathmandu Valley in 1768, where he established the Shah dynasty, and moved his capital to Kathmandu.

After Prithvi Narayan's death a period of political instability ensued which lasted until the 1840's when the Rana family reduced the monarch to a figurehead and established the post of hereditary Prime Minister. A popular revolution in 1950 toppled the Rana family and reconstituted power in the throne. In 1959 King Mahendra declared Nepal a constitutional monarchy, and in 1962 a new constitution set up a system of *panchayat* (village council) democracy. In 1990, following political unrest, the king's powers were reduced. The country then adopted a system of parliamentary democracy.

DATING

Nepal Samvat Era (NS)
All coins of the Malla kings of Nepal are dated in the Nepal Samvat era (NS). Year 1 NS began in 881, so to arrive at the AD date add 880 to the NS date. This era was exclusive to Nepal, except for one gold coin of Prana Narayan of Cooch Behar.

Saka Era (SE)
Up until 1888AD all coins of the Gorkha Dynasty were dated in the Saka era (SE). To convert from Saka to AD take Saka date and add 78 to arrive at the AD date. Coins dated with this era have SE before the date in the following listing.

Vikrama Samvat Era (VS)
From 1888AD most copper coins were dated in the Vikram Samvat (VS) era. To convert take VS date - 57 =AD date. Coins with this era have VS before the year in the listing. With the exception of a few gold coins struck in 1890 & 1892, silver and gold coins only changed to the VS era in 1911AD, but now this era is used for all coins struck in Nepal.

RULERS

Shah Dynasty

Girvan Yuddha Vikrama

गीर्वाण युद्ध विक्रम सा

SE1720-1738/1799-1816AD
Queens of Girvan Yuddha Vikrama:
Siddhi Lakshmi

सिद्धि लद्मी

Goraksha Rajya Lakshmi

गोरच्त राज्य लद्मी

Rajendra Vikrama

राजेन्द्र विक्रम

SE1738-1769/1816-1847AD
Queens of Rajendra Vikrama:
Samrajya Lakshmi

साम्राज्य लद्मी

Rajya Lakshmi

राज्य लद्मी

Surendra Vikrama

सुरेन्द्र विक्रम सा

SE1769-1803/1847-1881AD
Queens of Surendra Vikrama:
Trailokya Raja Lakshmi

त्रैलोक्य राज लद्मी

Sura Raja Lakshmi

सुर राज लद्मी

Deva Raja Lakshmi

देवराज लद्मी

Punyakumari Raja Lakshmi

पुरायकुमारी राज लद्मी

Prithvi Vira Vikrama

पृथ्वी वीर विक्रम

SE1803-1833/1881-1911AD, VS1938-1968
Queen of Prithvi Vira Vikrama: Lakshmi Divyeswari
Queen of Prithvi Bir Bikram: Lakshmi Divyeswari

लद्मी दिव्येश्वरी

Tribhuvana Bir Bikram

त्रिभुवनवीर विक्रम

VS1968-2007, 2007-2011/1911-1950, 1951-1955AD
(first reign)
VS2058- / 2001- AD (second reign)

Gyanendra Bir Bikram

ज्ञानेन्द्रवीर विक्रम

VS2007/1950-1951AD

NEPAL — SHAH DYNASTY

Mahendra Bir Bikram

महेन्द्रवीर विक्रम

VS2012-2028/1955-1971AD
Queen of Mahendra Bir Bikram:
Ratna Rajya Lakshmi

रन्न राज लदमी

Birendra Bir Bikram

वीरेन्द्र वीर विक्रम

VS2028-2058 /1971-2001AD
Queen of Birendra Bir Bikram:
Aishvarya Rajya Lakshmi

ऐश्वर्य राज्य लद्ग्यो द्वी

VS2028-2058 /1971-2001AD

Dipendra Bir Bikram

VS2058 / 2001AD (reign of 48 hours)

Gyanendra Bir Bikram

VS2058-/2001-AD

MONETARY SYSTEM

Mohar Series

The coinage was almost entirely of silver, with the tiny Jawa being easily the smallest coin in the world. Gold coins were struck on only one or two occasions during the Madra period, from the same dies as the silver coins, but these were probably only used for ceremonial purposes. Gold after 1777AD was struck in greater quantity.

GOLD COINAGE

Nepalese gold coinage until recently did not carry any denominations and was traded for silver, etc. at the local bullion exchange rate. The three basic weight standards used in the following listing are distinguished for convenience, although all were known as Asarphi (gold coin) locally as follows:

GOLD MOHAR
5.60 g multiples and fractions

TOLA
12.48 g multiples and fractions

GOLD RUPEE or ASARPHI
11.66 g multiples and fractions
(Reduced to 10.00 g in 1966)

NOTE: In some instances the gold and silver issues were struck from the same dies.

NUMERALS

Nepal has used more variations of numerals on their coins than any other nation. The most common are illustrated in the numeral chart in the introduction. The chart below illustrates some variations encompassing the last four centuries.

1	2	3	4	5	6	7	8	9	0

NUMERICS

Half	आधा
One	एक
Two	दुइ
Four	चार
Five	पाच
Ten	दसा
Twenty	विसा
Twenty-five	पचीसा
Fifty	पचासा
Hundred	सय

DENOMINATIONS

Paisa	पैसा
Dam	दाम
Mohar	मोरु
Rupee	रुपैयाँ
Ashrapi	असार्फी
Asarfi	अभ्रफो

DIE VARIETIES

Although the same dies were usually used both for silver and gold minor denominations, the gold Mohar is easily recognized being less ornate. The following illustrations are of a silver Mohar, KM#602 and a gold Mohar KM#615 issued by Surendra Vikrama Saha Deva in the period SE1769-1803/1847-1881AD. Note the similar reverse legend. The obverse usually will start with the character for the word Shri either in single or multiples, the latter as Shri Shri Shri or Shri 3.

OBVERSE

SILVER SE1791 — GOLD SE1793

LEGEND

श्री श्री श्री सुरेन्द्र विक्रम साहदेव

Shri Shri Shri Surendra Vikrama Saha Deva (date)

REVERSE

SILVER — GOLD

LEGEND (in center)

श्री ३ भवानी
Shri 3 Bhavani
(around outer circle)

श्री श्री श्री गोरखनाथ
Shri Shri Shri Gorakhanatha

SHAH DYNASTY
KINGDOM
Shah Dynasty

Rana Bahadur
SE1699-1720 / 1777-1799AD

GOLD COINAGE

KM# 509 1/4 MOHAR
1.4000 g., Gold Note: In the name of Queen Raja Rajesvari.

Date	Mintage	Good	VG	F	VF	XF
SE1723 (1801)	—	45.00	55.00	70.00	90.00	—
SE1724 (1802)	—	45.00	55.00	70.00	90.00	—

KM# 511.1 1/4 MOHAR
1.4000 g., Gold Note: In the name of Queen Suvarna Prabha.

Date	Mintage	Good	VG	F	VF	XF
SE1723 (1801)	—	45.00	55.00	70.00	90.00	—

KM# 511.2 3/8 MOHAR
1.4000 g., Gold Note: In the name of Queen Mahamahesvari.

Date	Mintage	Good	VG	F	VF	XF
SE1725 (1803)	—	150	250	350	500	—

KM# 510 1/4 MOHAR
1.4000 g., Gold Note: In the name of Queen Amara Rajesvari.

Date	Mintage	Good	VG	F	VF	XF
SE1724 (1802)	—	85.00	100	125	150	—

KM# 512 3/8 MOHAR
1.4000 g., Gold Note: In the name of Queen Lalita Tripura Sundari.

Date	Mintage	VG	F	VF	XF	Unc
SE1728 (1806)	—	45.00	50.00	65.00	85.00	—
SE1729 (1807)	—	45.00	50.00	65.00	85.00	—
SE1741 (1819)	—	45.00	50.00	65.00	85.00	—

Girvan Yuddha Vikrama
SE1720-1738 / 1799-1816AD

GOLD COINAGE

KM# 535 DAM
0.0044 g., Gold Note: Uniface.

Date	Mintage	VG	F	VF	XF	Unc
ND (1799-1816)	—	10.00	14.00	20.00	30.00	—

KM# 537 1/16 MOHAR
0.3500 g., Gold Note: Three varieties exist.

Date	Mintage	VG	F	VF	XF	Unc
ND (1799-1816)	—	15.00	20.00	25.00	40.00	—

KM# 538 1/8 MOHAR
0.7000 g., Gold

Date	Mintage	VG	F	VF	XF	Unc
ND (1799-1816)	—	22.50	27.50	40.00	60.00	—

KM# 539 1/8 MOHAR
0.7000 g., Gold

Date	Mintage	VG	F	VF	XF	Unc
ND (1799-1816)	—	22.50	27.50	40.00	60.00	—

KM# 540.1 1/4 MOHAR
1.4000 g., Gold Note: In the name of Queen Siddhi Lakshmi.

Date	Mintage	VG	F	VF	XF	Unc
SE1730 (1808)	—	45.00	50.00	65.00	85.00	—

SHAH DYNASTY

NEPAL

KM# 540.3 1/4 MOHAR
1.4000 g., Gold **Note:** In the name of Queen Siddhi Lakshmi.

Date	Mintage	VG	F	VF	XF	Unc
SE1732 (1810)	—	45.00	50.00	65.00	85.00	—
SE1733 (1811)	—	45.00	50.00	65.00	85.00	—

KM# 540.4 1/4 MOHAR
1.4000 g., Gold **Note:** In the name of Queen Siddhi Lakshmi.

Date	Mintage	VG	F	VF	XF	Unc
SE1736 (1814)	—	45.00	50.00	65.00	85.00	—

KM# 540.2 1/4 MOHAR
1.4000 g., Gold **Note:** In the name of Queen Goraksha Rajyalakshmi.

Date	Mintage	VG	F	VF	XF	Unc
SE1738 (1816)	—	120	150	170	200	—

KM# 541 1/2 MOHAR
2.8000 g., Gold

Date	Mintage	VG	F	VF	XF	Unc
SE1728 (1806)	—	75.00	85.00	100	130	—
SE1729 (1807)	—	75.00	85.00	100	130	—
SE1730 (1808)	—	75.00	85.00	100	130	—

KM# 542 1/2 MOHAR
2.8000 g., Gold

Date	Mintage	VG	F	VF	XF	Unc
SE1732 (1810)	—	150	200	250	325	—
SE1733 (1811)	—	150	200	250	325	—

KM# 543 1/2 MOHAR
2.8000 g., Gold

Date	Mintage	VG	F	VF	XF	Unc
SE1736 (1814)	—	150	200	250	325	—

KM# 544 MOHAR
5.6000 g., Gold **Note:** Similar to 1 Mohar, KM#529.

Date	Mintage	VG	F	VF	XF	Unc
SE1723 (1801)	—	130	150	175	225	—
SE1723 (1801)	—	130	150	175	225	—
SE1724 (1802)	—	130	150	175	225	—
SE1728 (1806)	—	130	150	175	225	—

KM# 546 MOHAR
5.6000 g., Gold **Obv:** Square in center

Date	Mintage	VG	F	VF	XF	Unc
SE1733 (1811)	—	150	175	225	265	—

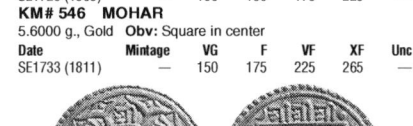

KM# 547 1-1/2 MOHARS
8.4000 g., Gold

Date	Mintage	VG	F	VF	XF	Unc
SE1726 (1804)	—	190	225	275	350	—
SE1728 (1806)	—	190	225	275	350	—
SE1729 (1807)	—	190	225	275	350	—

KM# 548 1-1/2 MOHARS
8.4000 g., Gold **Rev:** Hexagon

Date	Mintage	VG	F	VF	XF	Unc
SE1736 (1814)	—	190	225	275	350	—

KM# 550 2 MOHARS
11.2000 g., Gold **Obv:** Square in center

Date	Mintage	VG	F	VF	XF	Unc
SE1733 (1811)	—	255	275	325	385	—

PRESENTATION COINAGE

KM# 551 2 MOHARS
11.6600 g., Gold **Obv:** Square in center **Note:** In the name of Queen Goraksha Rajya Lakshmi.

Date	Mintage	VG	F	VF	XF	Unc
SE1735 (1813)	—	400	500	550	670	—

Rajendra Vikrama
SE1738-1769/ 1816-1847AD

GOLD COINAGE

KM# 569 DAM
0.0400 g., Gold **Note:** Uniface.

Date	Mintage	VG	F	VF	XF	Unc
ND(1816-47)	—	10.00	14.00	20.00	30.00	—

KM# 570 1/32 MOHAR
0.1800 g., Gold **Note:** Uniface.

Date	Mintage	VG	F	VF	XF	Unc
ND(1816-47)	—	14.00	20.00	25.00	40.00	—

KM# 571 1/16 MOHAR
0.3500 g., Gold

Date	Mintage	VG	F	VF	XF	Unc
ND(1816-47)	—	14.00	20.00	25.00	40.00	—

KM# 572 1/8 MOHAR
0.7000 g., Gold

Date	Mintage	VG	F	VF	XF	Unc
ND(1816-47)	—	22.50	27.50	35.00	50.00	—

KM# 573.1 1/4 MOHAR
0.7000 g., Gold **Note:** In the name of Queen Samrajya Lakshmi. Varieties exist.

Date	Mintage	VG	F	VF	XF	Unc
SE1746 (1824)	—	40.00	50.00	65.00	85.00	—
SE1757 (1835)	—	40.00	50.00	65.00	85.00	—
SE1758 (1836)	—	40.00	50.00	65.00	85.00	—
SE1759 (1837)	—	40.00	50.00	65.00	85.00	—

KM# 573.2 1/4 MOHAR
0.7000 g., Gold **Note:** In the name of Queen Samrajya Lakshmi.

Date	Mintage	VG	F	VF	XF	Unc
SE1757 (1835)	—	40.00	50.00	65.00	85.00	—

KM# 574 1/4 MOHAR
0.7000 g., Gold **Note:** In the name of Queen Rajya Lakshmi.

Date	Mintage	VG	F	VF	XF	Unc
SE1764 (1842)	—	40.00	50.00	65.00	85.00	—

KM# 575 1/2 MOHAR
2.8000 g., Gold

Date	Mintage	VG	F	VF	XF	Unc
SE1741 (1819)	—	150	200	250	325	—

KM# 576 1/2 MOHAR
2.8000 g., Gold

Date	Mintage	VG	F	VF	XF	Unc
SE1744 (1822)	—	65.00	75.00	85.00	100	—
SE1746 (1824)	—	65.00	75.00	85.00	100	—
SE1753 (1831)	—	65.00	75.00	85.00	100	—

KM# 577 1/2 MOHAR
2.8000 g., Gold

Date	Mintage	VG	F	VF	XF	Unc
SE1757 (1835)	—	65.00	75.00	85.00	100	—

KM# 578 1/2 MOHAR
2.8000 g., Gold

Date	Mintage	VG	F	VF	XF	Unc
SE1757 (1835)	—	65.00	75.00	85.00	100	—
SE1758 (1836)	—	65.00	75.00	85.00	100	—
SE1762 (1840)	—	65.00	75.00	85.00	100	—
SE1764 (1842)	—	65.00	75.00	85.00	100	—
SE1766 (1844)	—	65.00	75.00	85.00	100	—

KM# 579 MOHAR
5.6000 g., Gold, 24 mm. **Obv:** Square in center

Date	Mintage	VG	F	VF	XF	Unc
SE1738 (1816)	—	130	150	175	225	—

KM# 580 MOHAR
5.6000 g., Gold, 27 mm. **Obv:** Circle in center

Date	Mintage	VG	F	VF	XF	Unc
SE1741 (1819)	—	130	150	175	225	—
SE1758 (1836)	—	130	150	175	225	—
SE1760 (1838)	—	130	150	175	225	—
SE1764 (1842)	—	130	150	175	225	—

NEPAL — SHAH DYNASTY

Date	Mintage	VG	F	VF	XF	Unc
SE1766 (1844)	—	130	150	175	225	—
SE1768 (1846)	—	130	150	175	225	—

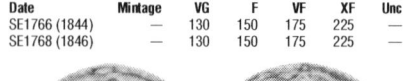

KM# 581 MOHAR
5.6000 g., Gold **Obv:** Square in center

Date	Mintage	VG	F	VF	XF	Unc
SE1746 (1824)	—	135	160	200	265	—
SE1757 (1835)	—	135	160	200	265	—

KM# 582 2 MOHARS
11.2000 g., Gold

Date	Mintage	VG	F	VF	XF	Unc
SE1738 (1816)	—	255	275	325	385	—
SE1741 (1819)	—	255	275	325	385	—
SE1766 (1844)	—	255	275	325	385	—
SE1768 (1846)	—	255	275	325	385	—

KM# 583 2 MOHARS
11.2000 g., Gold **Obv:** Square in center

Date	Mintage	VG	F	VF	XF	Unc
SE1746 (1824)	—	255	275	325	385	—
SE1757 (1835)	—	255	275	325	385	—

PRESENTATION COINAGE

KM# 584 RUPEE
11.6600 g., Gold **Note:** In the name of Queen Rajendra Vikrama.

Date	Mintage	VG	F	VF	XF	Unc
SE1759 (1837)	—	400	500	550	650	—

KM# 585 2 RUPEES
23.3200 g., Gold **Note:** In the name of Queen Rajendra Vikrama.

Date	Mintage	VG	F	VF	XF	Unc
SE1762 (1840)	—	750	1,000	1,250	1,500	—

Surendra Vikrama
SE1769-1803 / 1847-1881AD

GOLD COINAGE

KM# 604 DAM
0.0400 g., Gold **Note:** Uniface. Legend in two lines.

Date	Mintage	VG	F	VF	XF	Unc
ND(1847-81)	—	7.50	10.00	12.50	16.00	—

KM# A604 DAM
0.0400 g., Gold **Note:** Legend in three lines.

Date	Mintage	VG	F	VF	XF	Unc
ND(1847-81)	—	15.00	20.00	25.00	32.00	—

KM# 605 1/32 MOHAR
0.1800 g., Gold **Note:** Uniface.

Date	Mintage	VG	F	VF	XF	Unc
ND(1847-81)	—	14.00	20.00	25.00	35.00	—

KM# 606 1/16 MOHAR
0.3500 g., Gold

Date	Mintage	VG	F	VF	XF	Unc
ND(1847-81)	—	15.00	20.00	25.00	35.00	—

KM# 607 1/8 MOHAR
0.7000 g., Gold

Date	Mintage	VG	F	VF	XF	Unc
ND(1847-81)	—	22.50	27.50	35.00	50.00	—

KM# 608 1/4 MOHAR
1.4000 g., Gold **Note:** In the name of Queen Sura Raja Lakshmi.

Date	Mintage	VG	F	VF	XF	Unc
SE1769 (1847)	—	40.00	50.00	65.00	85.00	—
SE1787 (1865)	—	40.00	50.00	65.00	85.00	—
SE1790 (1868)	—	40.00	50.00	65.00	85.00	—

KM# A608 1/4 MOHAR
1.4000 g., Gold **Note:** In the name of Queen Trailokya Raja Lakshmi.

Date	Mintage	VG	F	VF	XF	Unc
SE1769 (1847)	—	40.00	50.00	65.00	85.00	—
SE1770 (1848)	—	40.00	50.00	65.00	85.00	—

KM# 609 1/4 MOHAR
1.4000 g., Gold **Note:** In the name of Queen Deva Raja Lakshmi.

Date	Mintage	VG	F	VF	XF	Unc
SE1770 (1848)	—	40.00	50.00	65.00	85.00	—

KM# 610 1/4 MOHAR
1.4000 g., Gold **Note:** In the name of Queen Punyakumari Raja Lakshmi.

Date	Mintage	VG	F	VF	XF	Unc
SE1802 (1880)	—	55.00	75.00	100	135	—

KM# 611 1/2 MOHAR
2.8000 g., Gold

Date	Mintage	VG	F	VF	XF	Unc
SE1769 (1847)	—	70.00	80.00	90.00	110	—
SE1770 (1848)	—	70.00	80.00	90.00	110	—
SE1802 (1880)	—	70.00	80.00	90.00	110	—

KM# 612 1/2 MOHAR
2.8000 g., Gold **Rev:** Without horizontal lines

Date	Mintage	VG	F	VF	XF	Unc
SE1790 (1868)	—	70.00	80.00	90.00	110	—

KM# 613 MOHAR
2.8000 g., Gold **Note:** In the name of Queen Deva Raja Lakshmi.

Date	Mintage	VG	F	VF	XF	Unc
SE1769 (1847)	—	115	125	145	175	—
SE1791 (1869)	—	115	125	145	175	—
SE1794 (1872)	—	115	125	145	175	—
SE1802 (1880)	—	115	125	145	175	—

KM# 616 2 RUPEES
Gold **Note:** Similar to 1 Tola, KM#615.

Date	Mintage	VG	F	VF	XF	Unc
SE1794 (1872)	—	450	525	650	800	—

KM# 614.1 1/2 TOLA
6.2400 g., Gold, 21.5 mm.

Date	Mintage	VG	F	VF	XF	Unc
SE1773 (1851)	—	135	145	170	200	—

KM# 614.2 1/2 TOLA
6.2400 g., Gold, 26.5 mm. **Note:** Larger size.

Date	Mintage	VG	F	VF	XF	Unc
SE1786 (1864)	—	135	145	170	200	—
SE1787 (1865)	—	135	145	170	200	—

KM# 615 TOLA
12.4800 g., Gold

Date	Mintage	VG	F	VF	XF	Unc
SE1769 (1847)	—	275	290	315	350	—
SE1773 (1851)	—	275	290	315	350	—
SE1774 (1852)	—	275	290	315	350	—
SE1778 (1856)	—	275	290	315	350	—
SE1780 (1858)	—	275	290	315	350	—
SE1786 (1864)	—	275	290	315	350	—
SE1787 (1865)	—	275	290	315	350	—
SE1791 (1869)	—	275	290	315	350	—
SE1793 (1871)	—	275	290	315	350	—
SE1794 (1872)	—	275	290	315	350	—
SE1802 (1880)	—	275	290	315	350	—

PRESENTATION COINAGE

KM# 617.1 RUPEE
11.6600 g., Gold **Note:** In the name of Queen Trailokyaraja Lakshmi.

Date	Mintage	VG	F	VF	XF	Unc
SE1769 (1847)	—	400	500	550	650	—

KM# 617.2 RUPEE
11.6600 g., Gold **Note:** In the name of Queen Trailokyaraja Lakshmi.

Date	Mintage	VG	F	VF	XF	Unc
SE1771 (1849)	—	285	350	425	525	—

Prithvi Bir Bikram
VS1938-1968 / 1881-1911AD

GOLD COINAGE

KM# 659 DAM
0.0400 g., Gold **Note:** Uniface. Five characters around sword. Similar to 1/64 Mohar, KM#664.

Date	Mintage	VG	F	VF	XF	Unc
ND(1881-1911)	—	—	10.00	14.00	20.00	27.50

KM# 660 DAM
0.0400 g., Gold **Note:** Uniface. Four characters around sword. Similar to 1/64 Mohar, KM#663.

Date	Mintage	VG	F	VF	XF	Unc
ND(1881-1911)	—	—	10.00	14.00	20.00	27.50

Actual Size   2 x Actual Size

KM# 661 DAM
0.0400 g., Gold **Note:** Uniface. Circle around characters.

Date	Mintage	VG	F	VF	XF	Unc
ND(1881-1911)	—	—	10.00	14.00	20.00	27.50

SHAH DYNASTY

NEPAL

KM# 662 DAM
0.0400 g., Gold **Note:** Uniface. Two characters below sword. Varieties exist.

Date	Mintage	VG	F	VF	XF	Unc
ND(1881-1911)	—	—	10.00	14.00	20.00	27.50

KM# 663 1/64 MOHAR
0.0900 g., Gold **Note:** Uniface. Four characters around sword.

Date	Mintage	VG	F	VF	XF	Unc
ND(1881-1911)	—	—	12.50	17.50	22.50	30.00

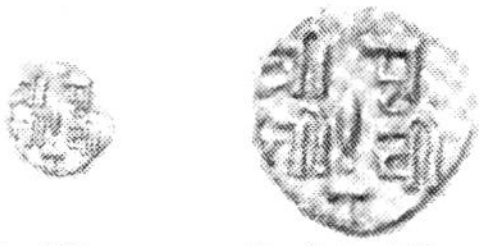

KM# 664 1/64 MOHAR
0.0900 g., Gold **Note:** Uniface. Five characters around sword.

Date	Mintage	VG	F	VF	XF	Unc
ND(1881-1911)	—	—	12.50	17.50	22.50	30.00

KM# 665 1/32 MOHAR
0.1800 g., Gold **Note:** Uniface. Five characters around sword.

Date	Mintage	VG	F	VF	XF	Unc
ND(1881-1911)	—	—	20.00	40.00	75.00	100

KM# 666 1/32 MOHAR
0.1800 g., Gold **Note:** Uniface. Four characters around sword.

Date	Mintage	VG	F	VF	XF	Unc
ND(1881-1911)	—	—	15.00	30.00	75.00	100

KM# 667 1/16 MOHAR
0.3500 g., Gold

Date	Mintage	VG	F	VF	XF	Unc
ND(1881-1911)	—	—	15.00	40.00	75.00	100

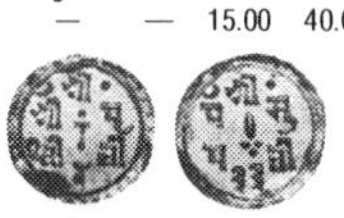

KM# 668 1/16 MOHAR
0.3500 g., Gold

Date	Mintage	F	VF	XF	Unc
SE(18)33 (1911) Proof	—	—	—	—	—
SE(18)33 (1911)	—	15.00	30.00	75.00	100

KM# 669.1 1/8 MOHAR
0.7000 g., Gold **Obv:** Six characters

Date	Mintage	F	VF	XF	Unc
ND (1881)	—	22.50	40.00	75.00	100

KM# 669.2 1/8 MOHAR
0.7000 g., Gold **Obv:** Five characters **Note:** Varieties exist.

Date	Mintage	F	VF	XF	Unc
ND (1881)	—	22.50	40.00	75.00	100

KM# 670 1/8 MOHAR
0.7000 g., Gold

Date	Mintage	F	VF	XF	Unc
SE(18)33 (1911)	—	22.50	40.00	75.00	100

KM# 671.1 1/4 MOHAR
1.4000 g., Gold

Date	Mintage	F	VF	XF	Unc
SE1808 (1886)	—	45.00	60.00	80.00	100
SE1811 (1889)	—	45.00	60.00	80.00	100
SE1817 (1895)	—	40.00	50.00	60.00	80.00
SE1823 (1901)	—	45.00	60.00	80.00	100
SE1829 (1907)	—	40.00	50.00	60.00	80.00

KM# 671.2 1/4 MOHAR
1.4000 g., Gold

Date	Mintage	F	VF	XF	Unc
SE1833 (1911) Proof	—	—	—	—	—
SE1833 (1911)	—	40.00	50.00	60.00	80.00

KM# 672.1 1/2 MOHAR
2.8000 g., Gold

Date	Mintage	F	VF	XF	Unc
SE1805 (1883)	—	70.00	80.00	90.00	110

KM# 672.2 1/2 MOHAR
2.8000 g., Gold

Date	Mintage	F	VF	XF	Unc
SE1817 (1895)	—	70.00	80.00	90.00	110

KM# 672.3 1/2 MOHAR
2.8000 g., Gold

Date	Mintage	F	VF	XF	Unc
SE1823 (1901)	—	70.00	80.00	100	125

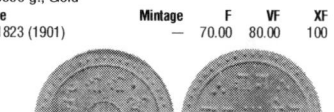

KM# 672.4 1/2 MOHAR
2.8000 g., Gold

Date	Mintage	F	VF	XF	Unc
SE1829 (1907)	—	65.00	75.00	85.00	100

KM# 672.5 1/2 MOHAR
2.8000 g., Gold

Date	Mintage	F	VF	XF	Unc
SE1833 (1911) Proof	—	—	—	—	—
SE1833 (1911)	—	65.00	75.00	85.00	100

KM# 673.1 MOHAR
5.6000 g., Gold

Date	Mintage	F	VF	XF	Unc
SE1804 (1882)	—	128	140	165	200
SE1805 (1883)	—	128	140	165	200
SE1809 (1887)	—	128	140	165	200
SE1817 (1895)	—	128	140	165	200
SE1820 (1898)	—	128	140	165	200
SE1823 (1901)	—	128	140	165	200
SE1825 (1903)	—	128	140	165	200
SE1826 (1904)	—	128	140	165	200
SE1827 (1905)	—	128	140	165	200

KM# 673.2 MOHAR
5.6000 g., Gold **Edge:** Milled

Date	Mintage	F	VF	XF	Unc
SE1828 (1906)	—	125	135	160	200
SE1829 (1907)	—	125	135	160	200
SE1831 (1909)	—	125	135	160	200
SE1833 (1911) Proof	—	—	—	—	—
SE1833 (1911)	—	125	135	160	200

KM# 673.3 MOHAR
5.6000 g., Gold

Date	Mintage	F	VF	XF	Unc
VS1949 (1892)	—	125	135	150	185

KM# 674.1 TOLA
12.4800 g., Gold **Note:** Oblique edge milling.

Date	Mintage	F	VF	XF	Unc
SE1803 (1881)	—	265	275	295	345
SE1805 (1883)	—	265	275	295	345
SE1810 (1888)	—	265	275	295	345
SE1811 (1889)	—	265	275	295	345

KM# 674.2 TOLA
12.4800 g., Gold **Note:** Vertical edge milling.

Date	Mintage	F	VF	XF	Unc
SE1803 (1881)	—	265	275	295	345
SE1804 (1882)	—	265	275	295	345

KM# 674.3 TOLA
12.4800 g., Gold **Edge:** Plain

Date	Mintage	F	VF	XF	Unc
SE1807 (1885)	—	275	280	300	350
SE1817 (1895)	—	275	280	300	350
SE1820 (1898)	—	275	280	300	350
SE1823 (1901)	—	275	280	300	325
SE1824 (1902)	—	275	280	300	325
SE1825 (1903)	—	275	280	300	325
SE1826 (1904)	—	275	280	300	325

KM# 675.1 TOLA
12.4800 g., Gold **Edge:** Vertical milling

Date	Mintage	F	VF	XF	Unc
SE1828 (1906)	—	275	280	300	325
SE1829 (1907)	—	275	280	300	325
SE1831 (1909)	—	275	280	300	325

NEPAL

SHAH DYNASTY

Date	Mintage	F	VF	XF	Unc
SE1832 (1910)	—	275	280	300	325
SE1833 (1911)	—	275	280	300	325
SE1833 (1911) Proof	—	—	—	—	—

KM# 675.2 TOLA
12.4800 g., Gold Edge: Plain

Date	Mintage	F	VF	XF	Unc
VS1947 (1890)	—	265	275	295	335

KM# 675.3 TOLA
12.4800 g., Gold Note: Oblique edge milling.

Date	Mintage	F	VF	XF	Unc
VS1949 (1892)	—	265	275	295	335

KM# 676 DUITOLA ASARPHI
23.3200 g., Gold

Date	Mintage	F	VF	XF	Unc
SE1811 (1889)	—	625	725	825	1,000

KM# 677 DUITOLA ASARPHI
23.3200 g., Gold Rev: Die of 4 Mohars, KM#657

Date	Mintage	F	VF	XF	Unc
SE1817 (1895)	—	625	725	825	1,000

KM# 678 DUITOLA ASARPHI
23.3200 g., Gold Edge: Plain

Date	Mintage	F	VF	XF	Unc
SE1825 (1902)	—	600	700	800	1,000

KM# 679 DUITOLA ASARPHI
23.3200 g., Gold Edge: Milled

Date	Mintage	F	VF	XF	Unc
SE1829 (1907)	—	550	600	700	800

KM# 680 DUITOLA ASARPHI
23.3200 g., Gold Edge: Milled

Date	Mintage	F	VF	XF	Unc
SE1833 (1911) Proof	—	—	—	—	—
SE1833 (1911)	—	550	600	700	800

Tribhuvana Bir Bikram
VS1968-2007 / 1911-1950AD

GOLD COINAGE

KM# 697 DAM
0.0400 g., Gold Note: Uniface.

Date	Mintage	F	VF	XF	Unc
ND (1911)	—	28.00	40.00	75.00	100

KM# 697a DAM
0.0400 g., Gold Note: Uniface, machine struck.

Date	Mintage	F	VF	XF	Unc
ND (1911)	—	28.00	40.00	70.00	100

KM# 698 1/32 MOHAR
0.1800 g., Gold Note: Uniface.

Date	Mintage	F	VF	XF	Unc
ND (1911)	—	38.00	60.00	90.00	125

KM# 699 1/16 MOHAR
0.3500 g., Gold

Date	Mintage	F	VF	XF	Unc
VS(19)77 (1920)	—	50.00	90.00	120	150

KM# 700 1/8 MOHAR
0.7000 g., Gold

Date	Mintage	F	VF	XF	Unc
VS(19)76 (1919)	—	75.00	120	150	200

KM# 701 1/2 MOHAR
2.8000 g., Gold

Date	Mintage	F	VF	XF	Unc
VS1969 (1912)	—	—	—	—	—

KM# 717 1/2 MOHAR
2.8000 g., Gold

Date	Mintage	F	VF	XF	Unc
VS1995 (1938)	—	—	—	—	—

KM# 702 MOHAR
5.6000 g., Gold

Date	Mintage	F	VF	XF	Unc
VS1969 (1912)	—	120	130	150	200
VS1975 (1918)	—	120	130	150	200
VS1978 (1921)	—	120	130	150	200
VS1979 (1922)	—	120	130	150	200
VS1981 (1924)	—	120	130	150	200
VS1983 (1926)	—	120	130	150	200
VS1985 (1928)	—	120	130	150	200
VS1986 (1929)	—	120	130	150	200
VS1987 (1930)	—	120	130	150	200
VS1989 (1932)	—	120	130	150	200
VS1990 (1933)	—	120	130	150	200
VS1991 (1934)	—	120	130	150	200
VS1998 (1941)	—	120	130	150	200
VS1999 (1942)	—	120	130	150	200
VS2000 (1943)	—	120	130	150	200
VS2003 (1946)	—	120	130	150	200
VS2005 (1948)	—	120	130	150	200

KM# 683 MOHAR
5.6000 g., Gold Note: In the name of "Queen Lakshmi Divyeswari" - Regent for Tribhuvana Bir Bikram.

Date	Mintage	F	VF	XF	Unc
VS1971 (1914)	—	120	130	145	185

KM# 722 MOHAR
5.6000 g., Gold

Date	Mintage	F	VF	XF	Unc
VS1993 (1936)	376,000	—	—	—	—
VS1994 (1937)	283,000	—	—	—	—

KM# 727 ASHRAPHI (Tola)
Gold Obv: Trident between moon and sun above crossed Khukris in center

Date	Mintage	F	VF	XF	Unc
VS1992 (1935)	—	275	280	300	350

KM# 703.2 ASHRAPHI (Tola)
Gold

Date	Mintage	F	VF	XF	Unc
VS2005 (1948)	—	265	270	285	315

KM# 703.1 ASHRAPHI (Tola)
Gold Rev: Moon and sun in center Rev. Legend: SRI 3 BHAVANI

Date	Mintage	F	VF	XF	Unc
VS1969 (1912)	—	265	270	285	315
VS1974 (1917)	—	265	270	285	315
VS1975 (1918)	—	265	270	285	315
VS1976 (1919)	—	265	270	285	315
VS1977 (1920)	—	265	270	285	315
VS1978 (1921)	—	265	270	285	315
VS1979 (1922)	—	265	270	285	315
VS1980 (1923)	—	265	270	285	315
VS1981 (1924)	—	265	270	285	315
VS1982 (1925)	—	265	270	285	315
VS1983 (1926)	—	265	270	285	315
VS1984 (1927)	—	265	270	285	315
VS1985 (1928)	—	265	270	285	315
VS1986 (1929)	—	265	270	285	315
VS1987 (1930)	—	265	270	285	315
VS1988 (1931)	—	265	270	285	315
VS1989 (1932)	—	265	270	285	315
VS1990 (1933)	—	265	270	285	315
VS1991 (1934)	—	265	270	285	315
VS1998 (1941)	—	265	270	285	315
VS1999 (1942)	—	265	270	285	315
VS2000 (1943)	—	265	270	285	315
VS2003 (1946)	—	265	270	285	315

KM# 728 DUITOLA ASARPHI
Gold Note: Similar to 1 Tola, KM#703.

Date	Mintage	F	VF	XF	Unc
VS2005 (1948)	—	475	525	575	650

ANONYMOUS HAMMERED COINAGE

KM# 768 1/5 ASARPHI
2.3300 g., Gold

Date	Mintage	F	VF	XF	Unc
VS2010 (1953)	—	60.00	70.00	100
Note: Coins dated VS2010 are normally found as restrikes ca. 1968
VS2012 (1955)	—	—	—	—	—

KM# 774 1/4 ASARPHI
2.9000 g., Gold

Date	Mintage	F	VF	XF	Unc
VS2010 (1953)	—	70.00	80.00	90.00	120
Note: Coins dated VS2010 are normally found as restrikes ca. 1968
VS2012 (1955)	—	—	—	—	—

ASARFI GOLD COINAGE
(Asarphi)

Fractional designations are approximate for this series. Actual Gold Weight (AGW) is used to identify each type.

KM# 741 1/2 ASARPHI
5.8000 g., Gold Obv: Head of Tribhuvan Bir Bikram right on 5-pointed star Note: Portrait type.

Date	Mintage	F	VF	XF	Unc
VS2010 (1953)	—	—	125	145	175

Note: KM#741 is normally found as a restrike ca. 1968

Gyanendra Bir Bikram
VS2007 / 1950-51AD (first reign)

DECIMAL COINAGE
100 Paisa = 1 Rupee

KM# 731 MOHAR
Gold

Date	Mintage	F	VF	XF	Unc
VS2007 (1950) Rare	—	—	—	—	—

KM# 732 TOLA
Gold

Date	Mintage	F	VF	XF	Unc
VS2007 (1950) Rare	—	—	—	—	—

Trivhuvan Bir Bikram
VS2007-2011 / 1951-1955AD (second reign)

ASARFI GOLD COINAGE
(Asarphi)

Fractional designations are approximate for this series. Actual Gold Weight (AGW) is used to identify each type.

KM# 744 ASARPHI
11.6600 g., Gold Obv: Head of Tribhuvan Bir Bikram right on 5-pointed star

Date	Mintage	F	VF	XF	Unc
VS2010 (1953)	—	225	245	285

Note: KM#744 normally found as a restrike ca. 1968

Mahendra Bir Bikram
VS2012-2028 / 1955-1971AD

ASARFI GOLD COINAGE
(Asarphi)

Fractional designations are approximate for this series. Actual Gold Weight (AGW) is used to identify each type.

KM# 767 1/6 ASARPHI
1.9000 g., Gold Subject: Mahendra Coronation

Date	Mintage	F	VF	XF	Unc
VS2013 (1956)	—	—	50.00	60.00	100

KM# 775 1/4 ASARPHI
2.5000 g., Gold Obv: Trident within small circle at center Rev: Dagger flanked by garlands from above Note: Reduced weight.

Date	Mintage	F	VF	XF	Unc
VS2026 (1969)	—	—	—	75.00	110

KM# 796 1/2 ASARPHI
Gold Note: In the name of "Queen Ratna Rajya Lakshmi".

Date	Mintage	F	VF	XF	Unc
VS2012 (1955)	—	—	—	—	—

SHAH DYNASTY
NEPAL

KM# 782 1/2 ASARPHI
5.8000 g., Gold **Obv:** Trident within small circle at center **Rev:** Dagger flanked by garlands from above

Date	Mintage	F	VF	XF	Unc
VS2012 (1955)	—	—	125	140	170
VS2019 (1962)	—	—	125	140	170

KM# 781 1/2 ASARPHI
5.8000 g., Gold **Subject:** Mahendra Coronation

Date	Mintage	F	VF	XF	Unc
VS2013 (1956)	—	—	125	140	170

KM# 783 1/2 ASARPHI
5.0000 g., Gold **Subject:** Birendra Marriage

Date	Mintage	F	VF	XF	Unc
VS2026 (1969)	—	—	—	150	180

KM# 789 ASARPHI
Gold **Obv:** Trident within small center circle **Rev:** Dagger flanked by garlands from above

Date	Mintage	F	VF	XF	Unc
VS2012 (1955)	—	—	230	250	300
VS2019 (1962)	—	—	230	250	300

KM# 798 ASARPHI
11.6600 g., Gold **Note:** In the name of "Queen Ratna Rajya Lakshmi".

Date	Mintage	F	VF	XF	Unc
VS2012 (1955)	—	—	230	250	300
VS2018 (1960)	—	—	230	250	300

KM# 791 ASARPHI
Gold **Subject:** Mahendra Coronation

Date	Mintage	F	VF	XF	Unc
VS2013 (1956)	—	—	230	250	300

KM# 792 ASARPHI
10.0000 g., Gold **Obv:** Trident within small center circle **Rev:** Dagger flanked by garlands from above

Date	Mintage	F	VF	XF	Unc
VS2026 (1969)	—	—	225	245	300

KM# 793 2 ASARFI
Gold

Date	Mintage	F	VF	XF	Unc
VS2012 (1955)	—	—	500	550	625

Birendra Bir Bikram
VS2028-2058 / 1971-2001 AD
DECIMAL COINAGE
100 Paisa = 1 Rupee

KM# 844 1000 RUPEE
33.4370 g., 0.9000 Gold .9676 oz. AGW **Series:** Conservation **Obv:** Crowned bust right **Rev:** Great Indian Rhinoceros **Rev. Designer:** Norman Sillman **Note:** Very small quantity restruck in 1979.

Date	Mintage	F	VF	XF	Unc
VS2031 (1974)	2,176	—	—	—	715
VS2031 (1974) Proof	671	Value: 800			

KM# 1000 1000 RUPEE
33.4370 g., 0.9000 Gold .9676 oz. AGW **Subject:** Rural Women's Advancement

Date	Mintage	F	VF	XF	Unc
VS2038 (1981) Proof	500	Value: 725			

ASARFI GOLD COINAGE
(Asarphi)

Fractional designations are approximate for this series. Actual Gold Weight (AGW) is used to identify each type.

KM# 1167 1/3 ASARFI
11.6500 g., 0.9000 Gold 0.3371 oz. AGW, 28.5 mm. **Obv:** Traditional design **Rev:** Ceremonial Vase **Note:** The Prince's Coming of Age

Date	Mintage	F	VF	XF	Unc
VS2046(1989)	1,000	—	—	—	275

KM# 1050a 0.3G ASARPHI
0.2500 g., 0.9990 Gold .0080 oz. AGW

Date	Mintage	F	VF	XF	Unc
VS2051 (1994)	—	—	—	—	40.00
VS2052 (1995)	—	—	—	—	40.00
VS2053 (1996)	—	—	—	—	35.00
VS2054 (1997)	—	—	—	—	35.00
VS2055 (1998)	—	—	—	—	35.00
VS2056 (1999)	—	—	—	—	35.00
VS2057 (2000)	—	—	—	—	35.00

KM# 1129 0.3G ASARPHI
0.3000 g., 0.9999 Gold .0096 oz. AGW, 7 mm. **Subject:** Buddha **Obv:** Traditional square design **Rev:** Buddha with halo **Edge:** Reeded

Date	Mintage	F	VF	XF	Unc
VS2057 (2000)	25,000	—	—	—	12.00

KM# 825 5.0G ASARPHI
5.0000 g., 0.9990 Gold .1607 oz. AGW

Date	Mintage	F	VF	XF	Unc
VS2028 (1971)	4	—	—	—	—
VS2030 (1973)	—	—	—	—	160
VS2031 (1974)	—	—	—	—	160
VS2036 (1979)	36	—	—	—	160
VS2037 (1980)	45	—	—	—	160

Note: Reports indicate a mintage of 44 pieces struck in .960 gold in 1980

| VS2038 (1981) | — | — | — | — | 160 |

KM# 822a 5.0G ASARPHI
5.0000 g., 0.9990 Gold .1607 oz. AGW **Subject:** Birendra Coronation **Obv:** Crown at center **Rev:** Dagger flanked by garlands from above

Date	Mintage	F	VF	XF	Unc
VS2031 (1974)	500	—	—	—	150

KM# 1021 5.0G ASARPHI
5.0000 g., 0.9000 Gold .1447 oz. AGW **Obv:** Traditional design **Rev:** Dagger flanked by garlands from above

Date	Mintage	F	VF	XF	Unc
VS2039 (1982)	23	—	—	—	—

KM# 1144 5.0G ASARPHI
5.0000 g., 0.9990 Gold .1606 oz. AGW **Subject:** New Parliament Session

Date	Mintage	F	VF	XF	Unc
VS2048 (1991)	—	—	—	—	120

KM# 827 10.0G ASARPHI
10.0000 g., 0.9990 Gold .3215 oz. AGW **Obv:** Traditional design **Rev:** Dagger flanked by garlands from above

Date	Mintage	F	VF	XF	Unc
VS2028 (1971)	Est. 4	—	—	—	—
VS2030 (1973)	50	—	—	—	350
VS2031 (1974)	—	—	—	—	350
VS2033 (1976)	—	—	—	—	350
VS2035 (1978)	—	—	—	—	350
VS2036 (1979)	52	—	—	—	350
VS2037 (1980)	30	—	—	—	350

Note: Reports indicate a mintage of 44 pieces struck in .960 gold in 1980

| VS2038 (1981) | — | — | — | — | 350 |

KM# 829a 10.0G ASARPHI
10.0000 g., 0.9990 Gold .3215 oz. AGW **Subject:** Birendra Coronation **Obv:** Crown **Rev:** Dagger flanked by garlands from above

Date	Mintage	F	VF	XF	Unc
VS2031 (1974) Proof	Est. 500	Value: 285			

KM# 829b 10.0G ASARPHI
10.0000 g., 0.5000 White Gold .1608 oz. AGW

Date	Mintage	F	VF	XF	Unc
VS2031 (1974) Proof	Est. 250	Value: 350			

Note: Sometimes referred to as 1000 Rupees

KM# 852 10.0G ASARPHI
11.6600 g., 0.9000 Gold .3374 oz. AGW **Series:** International Year of the Child **Obv:** Crowned bust right **Rev:** Child reading, emblems flank

Date	Mintage	F	VF	XF	Unc
VS2038 (1974) Proof	4,055	Value: 240			

Note: Struck in 1981

KM# 1022 10.0G ASARPHI
10.0000 g., 0.9000 Gold .2894 oz. AGW **Obv:** Traditional design **Rev:** Dagger flanked by garlands from above

Date	Mintage	F	VF	XF	Unc
VS2039 (1982)	25	—	—	—	—

KM# 1006 10.0G ASARPHI
10.0000 g., 0.5000 Gold .1608 oz. AGW **Subject:** 30th Anniversary Ascent of Mt. Everest **Obv:** Trident within small circle at center **Rev:** Mount Everest

Date	Mintage	F	VF	XF	Unc
VS2040 (1983) Proof	350	Value: 225			

KM# 1022a 10.0G ASARPHI
10.0000 g., 0.9990 Gold .3212 oz. AGW

Date	Mintage	F	VF	XF	Unc
VS2042 (1985)	—	—	—	—	250
VS2046 (1989)	—	—	—	—	235
VS2048 (1991)	—	—	—	—	235
VS2049 (1992)	—	—	—	—	235
VS2050 (1993)	—	—	—	—	225
VS2052 (1995)	—	—	—	—	225
VS2054 (1997)	—	—	—	—	225
VS2056 (1999)	—	—	—	—	225

NEPAL

SHAH DYNASTY

KM# 1034 10.0G ASARPHI
10.0000 g., Gold **Subject:** Crown Prince, Sacred Thread Ceremony **Obv:** Traditional design

Date	Mintage	F	VF	XF	Unc
VS2044 (1987)	1,962	—	—	—	250

KM# 1054 10.0G ASARPHI
10.0000 g., 0.9990 Gold .3215 oz. AGW **Subject:** The New Constitution **Obv:** Traditional design **Rev:** Flags above open book

Date	Mintage	F	VF	XF	Unc
VS2047 (1990)	—	—	—	—	250

KM# 1145 10.0G ASARPHI
10.0000 g., 0.9990 Gold .3212 oz. AGW **Subject:** 50th Anniversary International Monetary Fund

Date	Mintage	F	VF	XF	Unc
VS2051 (1994)	—	—	—	—	225

KM# 1146 10.0G ASARPHI
10.0000 g., 0.9990 Gold .3212 oz. AGW **Subject:** 50th Anniversary World Bank

Date	Mintage	F	VF	XF	Unc
VS2051 (1994)	—	—	—	—	225

KM# 1147 10.0G ASARPHI
10.0000 g., 0.9990 Gold .3212 oz. AGW **Subject:** Queen Aishwariya Golden Anniversary

Date	Mintage	F	VF	XF	Unc
VS2056 (1999)	—	—	—	—	225

KM# 1122 1/25-OZ. ASARFI
1.2441 g., 0.9999 Gold .0400 oz. AGW **Obv:** Traditional square in circle design **Rev:** Buddha's portrait and Ashoka pillar **Note:** Lord Buddha; Similar to Asarfi KM#1124.

Date	Mintage	F	VF	XF	Unc
VS2055 (1998) Proof	30,000	Value: 35.00			

KM# 1130 1/25-OZ. ASARFI
1.2441 g., 0.9999 Gold .0400 oz. AGW, 18 mm. **Subject:** Buddha **Obv:** Traditional square design **Rev:** Buddha with halo **Edge:** Reeded

Date	Mintage	F	VF	XF	Unc
VS2057 (2000)	30,000	—	—	—	35.00

KM# 1033 1/20-OZ. ASARFI
5.8300 g., 0.9600 Gold .1800 oz. AGW **Subject:** Crown Prince, Sacred Thread Ceremony **Obv:** Traditional design

Date	Mintage	F	VF	XF	Unc
VS2044 (1987)	2,774	—	—	—	125

KM# 1079 1/20-OZ. ASARFI
1.5532 g., 0.9990 Gold .0500 oz. AGW **Obv:** Traditional design **Rev:** Buddha **Note:** Similar to 1-oz. Asarfi, KM#1082.

Date	Mintage	F	VF	XF	Unc
VS2052 (1995)	15,000	—	—	—	37.50

KM# 1096 1/20-OZ. ASARFI
1.5532 g., 0.9990 Gold .0500 oz. AGW **Subject:** Buddha's Birth **Obv:** Traditional design **Rev:** Standing figure at center, cameo at right, small figure at left **Note:** Similar to 1500 Rupee, KM#1095.

Date	Mintage	F	VF	XF	Unc
VS2054 (1997)	15,000	—	—	—	40.00

KM# 1108 1/20-OZ. ASARFI
1.5552 g., 0.9990 Gold .0500 oz. AGW **Series:** Nepal Wildlife **Obv:** Traditional design **Rev:** Multicolor tiger **Note:** Similar to 100 Rupees, KM#1102.

Date	Mintage	F	VF	XF	Unc
VS2054 (1998) Proof	15,000	Value: 75.00			

KM# 1107 1/20-OZ. ASARFI
1.5552 g., 0.9990 Gold .0500 oz. AGW **Series:** Nepal Wildlife **Obv:** Traditional design **Rev:** Multicolor leopard **Note:** Similar to 2000 Rupees, KM#1104.

Date	Mintage	F	VF	XF	Unc
VS2054 (1998) Proof	15,000	Value: 75.00			

KM# 1050 1/10-OZ. ASARFI
2.5000 g., 0.9000 Gold .0724 oz. AGW

Date	Mintage	F	VF	XF	Unc
VS2039 (1982)	11	—	—	—	—

KM# 1037 1/10-OZ. ASARFI
3.1100 g., 0.9990 Gold .1000 oz. AGW **Obv:** Traditional design **Rev:** Snow leopard **Note:** Similar to 1-oz. Asarphi, KM#1040.

Date	Mintage	F	VF	XF	Unc
VS2045 (1988)	Est. 10,000	—	—	—	70.00
VS2045 (1988) Proof	2,000	Value: 80.00			

KM# 1080 1/10-OZ. ASARFI
3.1100 g., 0.9990 Gold .1000 oz. AGW **Obv:** Traditional design **Rev:** Buddha **Note:** Similar to 1-oz. Asarphi, KM#1082.

Date	Mintage	F	VF	XF	Unc
VS2052 (1995)	15,000	—	—	—	70.00

KM# 1097 1/10-OZ. ASARFI
3.1100 g., 0.9990 Gold .1000 oz. AGW **Subject:** Buddha's Birth **Obv:** Traditional design **Rev:** Standing figure at center, cameo at right, small figure at left **Note:** Similar to 1500 Rupee, KM#1095.

Date	Mintage	F	VF	XF	Unc
VS2054 (1997)	15,000	—	—	—	70.00

KM# 1109 1/10-OZ. ASARFI
3.1104 g., 0.9999 Gold .1000 oz. AGW **Series:** Nepal Wildlife **Obv:** Traditional design **Rev:** Multicolor leopard **Note:** Similar to 2000 Rupees, KM#1104.

Date	Mintage	F	VF	XF	Unc
VS2054 (1998) Proof	10,000	Value: 100			

KM# 1123 1/10-OZ. ASARFI
3.1104 g., 0.9999 Gold .1000 oz. AGW **Obv:** Traditional square in circle design **Rev:** Buddha's portrait and Ashoka pillar **Note:** Lord Buddha; Similar to Asarfi KM#1124.

Date	Mintage	F	VF	XF	Unc
VS2055 (1998) Proof	15,000	Value: 70.00			

KM# 1131 1/10-OZ. ASARFI
3.1100 g., 0.9990 Gold .1000 oz. AGW, 18 mm. **Subject:** Buddha **Obv:** Traditional square design **Rev:** Buddha with halo **Edge:** Reeded

Date	Mintage	F	VF	XF	Unc
VS2057 (2000)	30,000	—	—	—	70.00

KM# 819 1/4-OZ. ASARFI
2.5000 g., 0.9990 Gold .0803 oz. AGW **Obv:** Traditional design **Rev:** Dagger flanked by garlands from above

Date	Mintage	F	VF	XF	Unc
VS2028 (1971)	4	—	—	—	—
VS2030 (1973)	—	—	—	—	110
VS2031 (1974)	—	—	—	—	110
VS2036 (1979)	—	—	—	—	110
VS2037 (1980)	48	—	—	—	110

KM# 816a 1/4-OZ. ASARFI
7.7700 g., 0.9990 Gold .250 oz. AGW **Subject:** Birendra Coronation **Obv:** Crown **Rev:** Dagger flanked by garlands from above

Date	Mintage	F	VF	XF	Unc
VS2031 (1974)	500	—	—	—	175

KM# 1038 1/4-OZ. ASARFI
7.7700 g., 0.9990 Gold .2500 oz. AGW **Obv:** Traditional design **Rev:** Snow leopard **Note:** Similar to 1-oz. Asarphi, KM#1040, Bullion Series.

Date	Mintage	F	VF	XF	Unc
VS2045 (1988)	8,000	—	—	—	175
VS2045 (1988) Proof	2,000	Value: 185			

KM# 1059 1/4-OZ. ASARFI
7.7700 g., 0.9990 Gold .25 oz. AGW **Obv:** Traditional design **Rev:** Flags above open book **Note:** Similar to 1-oz. Asarphi, KM#1054.

Date	Mintage	F	VF	XF	Unc
VS2047 (1990)	—	—	—	—	175

KM# 1056 1/4-OZ. ASARFI
11.6600 g., 0.9000 Gold .3374 oz. AGW **Series:** Save the Children **Obv:** Traditional design **Rev:** Older and younger children

Date	Mintage	F	VF	XF	Unc
VS2047 (1990) Proof	3,000	Value: 245			

KM# 1093 1/4-OZ. ASARFI
7.7760 g., 0.9990 Gold .25 oz. AGW **Series:** Olympics **Obv:** Traditional design **Rev:** Runner and temple

Date	Mintage	F	VF	XF	Unc
VS2052 (1995)	Est. 3,000	—	—	—	175

KM# 1081 1/4-OZ. ASARFI
7.7759 g., 0.9990 Gold .2500 oz. AGW **Obv:** Traditional design **Rev:** Buddha **Note:** Similar to 1-oz. Asarphi, KM#1082.

Date	Mintage	F	VF	XF	Unc
VS2052 (1995)	15,000	—	—	—	175

KM# 1098 1/4-OZ. ASARFI
7.7759 g., 0.9990 Gold .2500 oz. AGW **Subject:** Buddha's Birth **Obv:** Traditional design **Rev:** Standing figure at center, cameo at right, small figure at left **Note:** Similar to 1500 Rupees, KM#1095.

Date	Mintage	F	VF	XF	Unc
VS2054 (1997)	15,000	—	—	—	175

KM# 1110 1/4-OZ. ASARFI
7.7759 g., 0.9990 Gold .2500 oz. AGW **Series:** Nepal Wildlife **Obv:** Traditional design **Rev:** Multicolor elephants **Note:** Similar to 2000 Rupees, KM#1105.

Date	Mintage	F	VF	XF	Unc
VS2054 (1998) Proof	2,000	Value: 185			

KM# 1112 1/4-OZ. ASARFI
7.7759 g., 0.9990 Gold .2500 oz. AGW **Series:** Nepal Wildlife **Obv:** Traditional design **Rev:** Multicolor rhinoceros **Note:** Similar to 100 Rupees, KM#1103.

Date	Mintage	F	VF	XF	Unc
VS2054 (1998) Proof	2,000	Value: 185			

KM# 1113 1/4-OZ. ASARFI
7.7759 g., 0.9990 Gold .2500 oz. AGW **Series:** Nepal Wildlife **Obv:** Traditional design **Rev:** Multicolor leopard **Note:** Similar to 100 Rupees, KM#1104.

Date	Mintage	F	VF	XF	Unc
VS2054 (1998) Proof	2,000	Value: 185			

KM# 1111 1/4-OZ. ASARFI
7.7759 g., 0.9990 Gold .2500 oz. AGW **Series:** Nepal Wildlife **Obv:** Traditional design **Rev:** Multicolor tiger **Note:** Similar to 100 Rupees, KM#1102.

Date	Mintage	F	VF	XF	Unc
VS2054 (1998) Proof	2,000	Value: 185			

KM# 1008 1/2-OZ. ASARFI
15.9800 g., 0.9000 Gold .4624 oz. AGW **Subject:** 10th Anniversary of Reign **Rev:** Dagger flanked by garlands from above

Date	Mintage	F	VF	XF	Unc
VS2038 (1981)	27	—	—	—	450
VS2038 (1981) Proof	5,092	Value: 325			

KM# 1011 1/2-OZ. ASARFI
15.9800 g., 0.9170 Gold .4712 oz. AGW **Series:** Year of the Scout **Obv:** Traditional design **Rev:** Girl scout filling water jug

SHAH DYNASTY   NEPAL   531

Date	Mintage	F	VF	XF	Unc
VS2039 (1982)	2,000	—	—	—	400

KM# 1045 1/2-OZ. ASARFI
15.0000 g., 0.9000 Gold .4340 oz. AGW **Subject:** 3rd SAARC Summit **Obv:** Traditional design **Rev:** Summit emblem **Note:** Similar to 300 Rupees, KM#1044.

Date	Mintage	F	VF	XF	Unc
VS2044 (1987)	1,000	—	—	—	350

KM# 1039 1/2-OZ. ASARFI
15.5500 g., 0.9990 Gold .5000 oz. AGW **Obv:** Traditional design **Rev:** Snow leopard **Note:** Similar to 1-oz. Asarphi, KM#1040.

Date	Mintage	F	VF	XF	Unc
VS2045 (1988)	Est. 8,000	—	—	—	350
VS2045 (1988) Proof	2,000	Value: 375			

KM# 1124 1/2-OZ. ASARFI
15.5518 g., 0.9999 Gold .5000 oz. AGW **Obv:** Traditional square in circle design **Rev:** Lord Buddha, Ashoka pillar

Date	Mintage	F	VF	XF	Unc
VS2055 (1998) Proof	2,500	Value: 365			

KM# 1132 1/2-OZ. ASARFI
15.5518 g., 0.9999 Gold .5000 oz. AGW, 27 mm. **Subject:** Buddha **Obv:** Traditional square design **Rev:** Buddha with halo **Edge:** Reeded

Date	Mintage	F	VF	XF	Unc
VS2057 (2000) Proof	2,500	Value: 365			

KM# 1027 1-OZ. ASARFI
31.1000 g., 0.9990 Gold 1. oz. AGW **Series:** Wildlife Protection **Obv:** Traditional design **Rev:** Ganges River Dolphins

Date	Mintage	F	VF	XF	Unc
VS2043 (1986) Proof	5,000	Value: 700			

KM# 1040 1-OZ. ASARFI
31.1000 g., 0.9999 Gold 1.0000 oz. AGW **Obv:** Traditional design **Rev:** Snow leopard

Date	Mintage	F	VF	XF	Unc
VS2045 (1988)	Est. 10,000	—	—	—	725
VS2045 (1988) Proof	2,000	Value: 750			

KM# 1082 1-OZ. ASARFI
31.1035 g., 0.9999 Gold 1.0000 oz. AGW **Obv:** Traditional design **Rev:** Buddha

Date	Mintage	F	VF	XF	Unc
VS2052 (1995) Proof	2,500	Value: 700			

KM# 1099 1-OZ. ASARFI
31.1035 g., 0.9999 Gold 1.0000 oz. AGW **Subject:** Buddha's Birth **Obv:** Traditional square in circle design **Rev:** Standing figure at center, cameo at right, small figure at left

Date	Mintage	F	VF	XF	Unc
VS2054 (1997) Proof	2,500	Value: 700			

KM# 1086 1-1/2 OZ. ASARFI
44.6400 g., 0.9167 Gold 1.5 oz. AGW **Subject:** Conquest of Mt. Everest **Obv:** Traditional design **Rev:** Mount Everest

Date	Mintage	F	VF	XF	Unc
VS2050 (1993) Proof	Est. 100	Value: 1,100			

Gyanendra Bir Bikram
VS2058- / 2001- AD

ASARFI GOLD COINAGE
(Asarphi)

Fractional designations are approximate for this series. Actual Gold Weight (AGW) is used to identify each type.

KM# 1153 0.3G ASARPHI
0.3000 g., 0.9999 Gold 0.0096 oz. AGW, 7 mm. **Subject:** Buddha **Obv:** Traditional design **Rev:** Seated Buddha **Edge:** Plain

KM# 1154 1/25-OZ. ASARFI
1.2441 g., 0.9999 Gold 0.04 oz. AGW, 13.92 mm. **Subject:** Buddha **Obv:** Traditional design **Rev:** Seated Buddha **Edge:** Reeded

KM# 1155 1/10-OZ. ASARFI
3.1104 g., 0.9999 Gold 0.1 oz. AGW, 17.95 mm. **Subject:** Buddha **Obv:** Traditional design **Rev:** Seated Buddha **Edge:** Reeded

KM# 1156 1/2-OZ. ASARFI
15.5518 g., 0.9999 Gold 0.5 oz. AGW, 27 mm. **Subject:** Buddha **Obv:** Traditional design **Rev:** Seated Buddha **Edge:** Reeded

PIEFORTS

KM#	Date	Mintage	Identification	Mkt Val
P2	VS2039	48	Asarphi.	1,250

MINT SETS

KM#	Date	Mintage	Identification	Issue Price	Mkt Val
MS19	1997 (3)	—	KM#1096-1098	—	285

PROOF SETS

KM#	Date	Mintage	Identification	Issue Price	Mkt Val
PS2	1911 (6)	—	KM668, 671.2, 672.5, 673.2, 675.1, 680, Gold	—	—
PS10	1988 (4)	2,000	KM#1037-1040	—	1,400
PS11	1995-97 (2)	—	KM#1077, 1099	—	740

NETHERLANDS

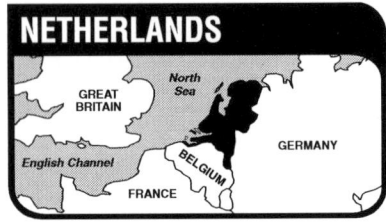

The Kingdom of the Netherlands, a country of western Europe fronting on the North Sea and bordered by Belgium and Germany, has an area of 15,770 sq. mi. (41,500 sq. km.) and a population of 15.7 million. Capital: Amsterdam, but the seat of government is at The Hague. The economy is based on dairy farming and a variety of industrial activities. Chemicals, yarns and fabrics, and meat products are exported.

After being a part of Charlemagne's empire in the 8th and 9th centuries, the Netherlands came under control of Burgundy and the Austrian Hapsburgs, and finally was subjected to Spanish dominion in the 16th century. Led by William of Orange, the Dutch revolted against Spain in 1568. The seven northern provinces formed the Union of Utrecht and declared their independence in 1581, becoming the Republic of the United Netherlands. In the following century, the *Golden Age* of Dutch history, the Netherlands became a great sea and colonial power, a patron of the arts and a refuge for the persecuted. The United Dutch Republic ended in 1795 when the French formed the Batavian Republic. Napoleon made his brother Louis, the King of Holland in 1806, however he abdicated in 1810 when Napoleon annexed Holland. The French were expelled in 1813, and all the provinces of Holland and Belgium were merged into the Kingdom of the United Netherlands under William I, in 1814. The Belgians withdrew in 1830 to form their own kingdom, the last substantial change in the configuration of European Netherlands. German forces invaded in 1940 as the royal family fled to England where a government-in-exile was formed. A German High Commissioner, Arthur Seyss-Inquart, was placed in command until 1945 when the arrival of Allied military forces ended the occupation.

WORLD WAR II COINAGE

U.S. mints in the name of the government in exile and its remaining Curacao and Surinam Colonies during the years 1941-45 minted coinage of the Netherlands Homeland Types -KM #152, 153, 163, 164, 161.1 and 161.2 -. The Curacao and Surinam strikes, distinguished by the presence of a palm tree in combination with a mint mark (P-Philadelphia; D-Denver; S-San Francisco) flanking the date, are incorporated under those titles in this volume. Pieces of this period struck in the name of the homeland bear an acorn and mint mark and are incorporated in the following tabulation.

NOTE: Excepting the World War II issues struck at U.S. mints, all of the modern coins were struck at the Utrecht Mint and bear the caduceus mint mark of that facility. They also bear the mint master's marks.

RULERS

BATAVIAN REPUBLIC
French domination, 1795-1806
KINGDOM OF HOLLAND
French Protectorate
Louis Napoleon, 1806-1810
FRENCH ANNEXATION

From 1810 to 1814, the Netherlands were a part of France. During this period, homeland type coins were not minted. Regular French coins were struck at the Utrecht Mint at this time, and are identified by the fish and mast privy marks. These coins are listed under France.
Napoleon I, 1810-1814
KINGDOM OF THE NETHERLANDS
William I, 1815-1840
William II, 1840-1849
William III, 1849-1890
Wilhelmina I, 1890-1948
Juliana, 1948-1980
Beatrix, 1980—

MINT MARKS
B - Brussels (Belgium), 1821-1830
D - Denver, 1943-1945
P - Philadelphia, 1941-1945
S - San Francisco, 1944-1945

MINT PRIVY MARKS

Harderwijk (Gelderland)

Date	Privy Mark
1730-45	Horse on mountain
1750-52	Falconer
1753-57	Crane
1758-76	Tree
1782-1806	Ear of corn

Dordrecht (Holland)

Date	Privy Mark
1600-1806	Rosette
1795-1806	None

Enkhuizen (West Friesland)

Date	Privy Mark
1761-71	Ship
1791-96	Rosette
1796-1803	Star

Hoorn (West Friesland)

Date	Privy Mark
1751-61	Rooster
1781-91	Rosette
1803-1809	Star

Kampen (Overyssel)

Date	Privy Mark
1763	Half eagle
1763-64, 1795-1807	Eagle
1764-65, 1795	3 dots

Medemblik (West Friesland)

Date	Privy Mark
1771-81	Ship

Middelburg (Zeeland)

Date	Privy Mark
1601-1799	Castle

Utrecht (Utrecht)

Date	Privy Mark
1738-1805	Shield
1806-present	Caduceus

MINT OFFICIALS' PRIVY MARKS

Brussels Mint

Date	Privy Mark
1821-1830	Palm branch

Utrecht Mint

Date	Privy Mark
1806-1810	Bee
1810-1813	Mast
1815-1816	Cloverleaf
1817	Child in swaddling clothes
1818-1840	Torch
1839-1846	Fleur de lis
1846-1874	Sword
1874	Sword in scabbard
1875-87	Broadaxe
1887	Broadaxe and star
1888-1909	Halberd
1909	Halberd and star
1909-1933	Seahorse
1933-42	Grapes
1943-1945	No privy mark
1945-69	Fish
1969-79	Cock
1980	Cock and star (temporal)
1980-88	Anvil with hammer
1989-99	Bow and arrow
2000-	Bow, arrow and star
2001	Wine tendril w/grapes
2002	Wine tendril w/grapes and star
2003	Sails of a clipper

NOTE: A star adjoining the privy mark indicates that the piece was struck at the beginning of the term of office of a successor. (The star was used only if the successor had not chosen his own mark yet.)

NOTE: Since October, 1999, the Dutch Mint has taken the title of Royal Dutch Mint.

MONETARY SYSTEM
1 Penning = 1/2 Duit
2 Duits = 1 Oord
8 Duits = 1 Stuiver (Stiver)
6 Stuiver = 1 Schelling
20 Stuiver = 1 Gulden (Guilder or Florin)
50 Stuiver = 1 Rijksdaalder (Silver Ducat)
60 Stuiver = 1 Ducaton (Silver Rider)
14 Gulden = 1 Golden Rider
Commencing 1815
100 Cents = 1 Gulden
2-1/2 Gulden = 1 Rijksdaalder
Until January 29, 2002
100 Cents = 1 Gulden
Since January 1, 2002
100 Cents = 1 Euro

BATAVIAN REPUBLIC

From 1796 to 1806, the Netherlands was a confederation of seven provinces, each producing coins similar in design but differing in the coat of arms or inscription. Generally the coins of each province contained an abbreviation of the name of the province somewhere in the inscription. Under the Batavian Republic, the following abbreviations were used.

PROVINCE ABBREVIATIONS
G, GEL - Gelderland
HOL, HOLL - Holland
TRANSI - Overijsel
TRA, TRAI, TRAIECTUM - Utrecht
WESTF, WESTRI - Westfriesland
ZEL, ZEELANDIA - Zeeland

TRADE COINAGE

KM# 11.1 DUCAT
3.5000 g., 0.9860 Gold .1109 oz. AGW **Obv:** Standing armored knight divides date **Obv. Legend:** ends:...G or GEL. **Rev:** Inscription within ornamented square

Date	Mintage	F	VF	XF	Unc	BU
1801	Inc. above	80.00	150	300	400	500
1802	Inc. above	150	250	450	600	700
1803	—	650	1,300	2,000	3,250	3,500

KM# 11.2 DUCAT
3.5000 g., 0.9860 Gold .1109 oz. AGW **Obv:** Standing armored knight divides date **Obv. Legend:** ends:...Hol **Rev:** Inscription within ornamented square **Note:** Coins with the star were struck at the Enkhuizen Mint with a total mintage of 630,455. Coins without the star were struck at the Dordrecht Mint with a total mintage of 2,861,825.

Date	Mintage	F	VF	XF	Unc	BU
1801 without star	—	90.00	150	225	300	375
1801 star	—	200	400	600	800	1,000
1802 without star	—	150	250	400	600	800
1802 star	—	150	300	400	550	650
1803 without star	—	80.00	120	165	250	350
1804 without star	—	80.00	120	165	250	350
1805 without star	—	150	300	400	600	850

KM# 11.3 DUCAT
3.5000 g., 0.9860 Gold .1109 oz. AGW **Obv:** Standing armored knight divides date **Obv. Legend:** PAR:CRES:TRA... **Rev:** Inscription within ornamented square **Note:** 1788, 1795, 1800 and 1802 has also been struck at the Stuttgarter Munzstatte in Germany, quanity unknown. Struck in 1812 as payment for soliders value unknown (recently discovered).

Date	Mintage	F	VF	XF	Unc	BU
1801	960,000	70.00	130	200	325	450
1802	1,705,000	70.00	130	200	275	400
1803	2,089,000	70.00	130	200	275	400
1804/3	870,000	100	250	400	750	1,000
1804	Inc. above	70.00	130	200	275	400
1805	1,300,000	70.00	130	200	275	400

KM# 12.1 2 DUCAT
7.0000 g., 0.9860 Gold .2219 oz. AGW **Obv:** Standing armored knight divides date **Obv. Inscription:** ends:...HOL or HOLL **Rev:** Inscription within ornamented square **Note:** Similar to 1 Ducat KM#11.2.

Date	Mintage	F	VF	XF	Unc	BU
1802	—	750	1,350	2,250	3,500	5,000

KM# 12.2 2 DUCAT
7.0000 g., 0.9860 Gold .2219 oz. AGW **Obv:** Standing armored knight divides date **Obv. Legend:** PAR : CRES : TRA ... **Rev:** Inscription within ornamented square **Rev. Inscription:** MO : ORD : PROVIN : FOEDER : BELG • AD LEG • IMP **Note:** Similar to 1 Ducat KM#11.3

Date	Mintage	F	VF	XF	Unc	BU
1801	215,000	325	650	1,000	1,350	1,750
1802	115,000	400	850	1,250	1,750	2,250
1803	365,000	325	650	1,000	1,350	1,750
1804	250,000	325	650	1,000	1,350	1,750
1805	301,000	325	650	1,000	1,350	1,750

KINGDOM OF HOLLAND

STANDARD COINAGE

KM# 33 10 GULDEN
6.8250 g., 0.9170 Gold .2012 oz. AGW **Obv:** Head left **Obv. Legend:** LODEW. NAP. KON... **Rev:** Crowned 4-fold arms divides value, date below **Rev. Legend:** KORIRGRIJK HOLLAND. **Edge Lettering:** DE NAAM DES HEEKEN ZY GELOOFD

NETHERLANDS

Date	Mintage	F	VF	XF	Unc	BU
1808	—	1,200	2,500	4,000	6,000	8,000
1810	—	1,200	2,500	4,000	6,000	8,000

KM# 34 20 GULDEN
13.6500 g., 0.9170 Gold .4024 oz. AGW **Obv:** Head left **Obv. Legend:** LODEW. NAP. KON... **Rev:** Crowned 4-fold arms divides value, date below **Edge Lettering:** DE NAAM DES HEEREN ZY GELOOFD

Date	Mintage	F	VF	XF	Unc	BU
1808	—	1,700	3,500	7,000	10,000	13,000
1810	—	1,700	3,500	7,000	10,000	13,000

TRADE COINAGE

KM# 26.1 DUCAT
3.4940 g., 0.9860 Gold .1108 oz. AGW **Obv:** Standing armored knight divides date **Obv. Legend:** ...HOL **Rev:** Inscription within ornamented square

Date	Mintage	F	VF	XF	Unc	BU
1806	526	600	900	1,300	1,800	2,300

KM# 26.2 DUCAT
3.4940 g., 0.9860 Gold .1108 oz. AGW **Obv:** Standing armored knight divides date **Obv. Legend:** ...TRAIECTUM, TRA or TRAI **Rev:** Inscription within ornamented square

Date	Mintage	F	VF	XF	Unc	BU
1806 small date	794,000	110	190	260	450	525
1807 small date, straight 7	622,000	110	190	260	350	425
1808/7	37,310	175	300	400	650	900
1808	Inc. above	140	250	325	500	750

KM# 26.3 DUCAT
3.4940 g., 0.9860 Gold .1108 oz. AGW **Obv:** Standing armored knight divides date **Obv. Legend:** ...TRAIECTUM, TRA or TRAI **Rev:** Inscription within ornamented square

Date	Mintage	F	VF	XF	Unc	BU
1806 large date	1,300,000	110	190	260	350	425
1807 larage date, curved 7	1,940,000	110	190	260	350	425

KM# 35 DUCAT
3.4300 g., 0.9830 Gold .1084 oz. AGW **Obv:** Head left **Obv. Legend:** LODEW. NAP. KON... **Rev:** Standing armored knight divides date **Rev. Legend:** EENDRAGT....

Date	Mintage	F	VF	XF	Unc	BU
1808	282,870	200	375	525	1,100	—
1809	Inc. above	200	375	525	1,100	—

KM# 38 DUCAT
3.4300 g., 0.9830 Gold .1084 oz. AGW **Obv:** Head left **Obv. Legend:** LODEW. NAP. KON... **Rev:** Crowned 4-fold arms, date below **Rev. Legend:** KONINGRIJK HOLLAND.

Date	Mintage	F	VF	XF	Unc	BU
1809	2,370,620	200	375	525	900	1,000
1810	Inc. above	200	375	525	900	1,000

KM# 27 2 DUCAT
6.9880 g., 0.9830 Gold .2208 oz. AGW **Obv:** Standing armored knight divides date **Obv. Legend:** ...TRA **Rev. Legend:** PAR:CRES:TRA..... **Edge:** Slant-reeded

Date	Mintage	F	VF	XF	Unc	BU
1806	199,000	500	800	1,200	1,500	2,000
1807	156,000	500	800	1,200	1,500	2,000
1808	—	500	800	1,200	1,500	2,000

KINGDOM OF THE NETHERLANDS

STANDARD COINAGE

KM# 60 5 GULDEN
3.3645 g., 0.9000 Gold .0973 oz. AGW, 18.5 mm. **Ruler:** William I **Obv:** Head left **Obv. Legend:** WILLEM KONING... **Rev:** Crowned arms divides value **Rev. Legend:** DER NEDERLANDEN... **Edge:** Reeded **Designer:** J. P. Braemt

Date	Mintage	F	VF	XF	Unc	BU
1826B	842,694	120	300	400	600	800
1827	517,826	175	275	375	850	1,000
1827B	1,628,218	70.00	175	300	500	700

KM# 72 5 GULDEN
3.3645 g., 0.9000 Gold .0973 oz. AGW, 18.5 mm. **Ruler:** William II **Obv:** Head right **Obv. Legend:** WILLEM II KONING... **Rev:** Crowned arms divides value **Rev. Legend:** DER NEDERLANDEN... **Edge:** Reeded **Designer:** J. P. Schouberg

Date	Mintage	F	VF	XF	Unc	BU
1843	1,595	300	900	1,900	2,500	3,000

KM# 77 5 GULDEN
3.3645 g., 0.9000 Gold .0973 oz. AGW, 18.5 mm. **Ruler:** William II **Obv:** Head right **Rev:** Crowned arms within 3/4 wreath **Edge:** Reeded **Designer:** J. P. Schouberg

Date	Mintage	F	VF	XF	Unc	BU
1848 Proof	84	Value: 7,000				

KM# 94 5 GULDEN
3.3645 g., 0.9000 Gold .0973 oz. AGW, 18.5 mm. **Ruler:** William III **Obv:** Head left **Obv. Legend:** WILLEM III KONING... **Rev:** Crowned arms within 3/4 wreath **Edge:** Reeded **Designer:** D. van der Kellen, Jr.

Date	Mintage	F	VF	XF	Unc	BU
1850 Proof	—	Value: 5,000				
1851	10,000	400	1,200	2,000	2,600	3,000

KM# 56 10 GULDEN
6.7290 g., 0.9000 Gold .1947 oz. AGW, 22.5 mm. **Ruler:** William I **Obv:** Head left **Obv. Legend:** WILLEM KONING... **Rev:** Crowned arms divides value **Rev. Legend:** DER NEDERLANDEN... **Edge:** Reeded **Edge Lettering:** GOD ZY MET ONS **Designer:** A. F. Michaut

Date	Mintage	F	VF	XF	Unc	BU
1818	—	1,500	4,000	5,500	7,000	9,500
1819	107,413	650	1,750	3,000	4,500	5,000
1820	33,187	750	2,000	3,200	5,000	6,000
1822	47,560	650	1,750	3,000	4,000	5,000
1823	266,248	250	500	9,000	1,200	1,750
1824	336,333	150	275	450	850	1,200
1824B	3,735,006	125	200	400	550	650
1825	228,365	250	500	900	1,200	1,750
1825B	3,821,017	135	225	450	600	700
1826	—	1,000	4,000	5,000	7,000	9,000
1826B	78,552	650	2,000	3,000	5,000	6,000
1827B	133,736	400	850	1,600	2,500	3,250
1828	14,640	1,000	4,000	5,000	7,000	9,000
1828B/27B	—	175	300	500	1,000	1,250
1828B	561,849	150	275	350	800	1,150
1829	9,484	1,500	4,500	6,500	8,000	10,000
1829B	83,943	650	1,400	2,000	3,000	4,000
1830/20	Inc. above	250	500	1,000	2,000	2,750
1830/28	568,434	1,000	1,200	1,500	3,000	4,000
1830	Inc. above	150	375	650	1,000	1,250
1831/0	98,959	500	950	1,600	2,500	3,250
1831	Inc. above	500	950	1,500	2,000	2,500
1832/1	1,372,000	500	950	1,500	2,000	2,500
1832	Inc. above	150	375	750	1,000	1,150
1833	721,362	175	475	750	900	1,000
1837	457,686	175	475	800	1,000	1,250
1839	326,404	150	375	650	1,000	1,250
1840/37	—	650	1,400	2,000	3,000	4,000
1840	2,760,356	150	275	350	600	900

KM# 71 10 GULDEN
6.7290 g., 0.9000 Gold .1947 oz. AGW, 22.5 mm. **Ruler:** William II **Obv:** Head right **Obv. Legend:** WILLEM II KONING... **Rev:** Crowned arms divides value **Rev. Legend:** DER NEDERLANDEN... **Edge Lettering:** GOD ZY MET ONS **Designer:** J. P. Schouberg

Date	Mintage	F	VF	XF	Unc	BU
1842	860	1,100	2,000	3,500	6,000	7,500

KM# 78 10 GULDEN
6.7290 g., 0.9000 Gold .1947 oz. AGW, 22.5 mm. **Ruler:** William II **Obv:** Head right **Obv. Legend:** WILLEM II KONING... **Rev:** Crowned arms within 3/4 wreath **Edge Lettering:** GOD ZY MET ONS **Designer:** J. P. Schouberg

Date	Mintage	F	VF	XF	Unc	BU
1848 Proof	100	Value: 8,000				

KM# 95 10 GULDEN
6.7290 g., 0.9000 Gold .1947 oz. AGW, 22.5 mm. **Ruler:** William III **Obv:** Head left **Obv. Legend:** WILLEM III KONING... **Rev:** Crowned arms within 3/4 wreath **Edge Lettering:** GOD ZY MET ONS **Designer:** D. van der Kellen, Jr.

Date	Mintage	F	VF	XF	Unc	BU
1850 Proof	—	Value: 6,500				
1851	10,000	500	1,000	1,750	2,500	3,000

KM# 79 20 GULDEN
13.4580 g., 0.9000 Gold .3894 oz. AGW, 27 mm. **Ruler:** William II **Obv:** Head right **Obv. Legend:** WILLEM II KONING... **Rev:** Crowned arms within 3/4 wreath **Edge Lettering:** GOD ZY MET ONS **Designer:** D. van der Kellen, Jr.

Date	Mintage	F	VF	XF	Unc	BU
1848 Proof	95	Value: 15,000				

534 NETHERLANDS

KM# 96 20 GULDEN
13.4580 g., 0.9000 Gold .3894 oz. AGW **Ruler:** William III **Obv:** Head left **Obv. Legend:** WILLEM III KONING... **Rev:** Crowned arms within 3/4 wreath **Edge Lettering:** GOD ZY MET ONS **Designer:** D. van der Kellen, Jr.

Date	Mintage	F	VF	XF	Unc	BU
1850 Proof	—	Value: 8,000				
1851	2,500	600	2,000	3,000	4,000	5,000
1853	136	2,000	4,000	5,000	6,500	7,500

DECIMAL COINAGE

KM# 200b GULDEN
Gold, 25 mm. **Ruler:** Beatrix **Subject:** Investiture of New Queen **Obv:** Conjoined heads left **Rev:** Crowned arms divide date **Designer:** C. E. Bruijn-van Rood **Note:** G added (for gold).

Date	Mintage	F	VF	XF	Unc	BU
1980 Rare	7	—	—	—	—	—

KM# 230 GULDEN
11.0000 g., 0.7500 Gold .2652 oz. AGW **Ruler:** Beatrix **Rev:** Small tulip, "750" added **Edge Lettering:** GOD ZIJ MET ONS **Designer:** B. Ninaber van Eyben **Note:** Similar to KM#205.

Date	Mintage	F	VF	XF	Unc	BU
1999 Proof	1,000	Value: 800				

Note: Approximately 480 of the mintage were melted down

KM# 233b GULDEN
13.2000 g., 0.9990 Gold .4240 oz. AGW, 25 mm. **Ruler:** Beatrix **Obv:** Head left with inscription **Obv. Designer:** G. Verheus and M. Raedecker **Rev:** Child art design **Rev. Designer:** T. van Malis **Note:** 98 of 100 pieces melted down, with 2 known in museum collections.

Date	Mintage	F	VF	XF	Unc	BU
2001 Prooflike; Rare	100	—	—	—	—	—

KM# 205c GULDEN
13.2000 g., 0.9990 Gold 0.424 oz. AGW **Ruler:** Beatrix **Obv:** Head left with vertical inscription **Rev:** Value within vertical and horizontal lines **Edge:** Plain, missing lettering

Date	Mintage	F	VF	XF	Unc	BU
2001 Prooflike	Est. 500	—	—	—	—	550

KM# 123a 2-1/2 GULDEN
88.5000 g., Gold, 38 mm. **Ruler:** Wilhelmina I **Obv:** Crowned head left **Obv. Legend:** WILHELMINA... **Rev:** Crowned arms divides value **Rev. Legend:** DER NEDERLANDEN... **Edge Lettering:** GOD ZIJ MET ONS **Designer:** P. Pander

Date	Mintage	F	VF	XF	Unc	BU
1898 Rare	2	—	—	—	—	—

KM# 201b 2-1/2 GULDEN
Gold **Ruler:** Beatrix **Subject:** Investiture of New Queen **Obv:** Conjoined heads left **Rev:** Crowned arms divide date **Edge Lettering:** GOD * ZIJ * MET * ONS * **Designer:** C. E. Bruijn-van Rood **Note:** G added (for gold).

Date	Mintage	F	VF	XF	Unc	BU
1980 Rare	7	—	—	—	—	—

KM# 151 5 GULDEN
3.3600 g., 0.9000 Gold .0973 oz. AGW, 18 mm. **Ruler:** Wilhelmina I **Obv:** Bust right **Rev:** Crowned arms divide value **Edge:** Reeded **Designer:** J. C. Wienecke **Note:** Counterfeits are prevalent.

Date	Mintage	F	VF	XF	Unc	BU
1912	1,000,000	70.00	80.00	100	160	185
1912 Matte Proof	120	Value: 800				

KM# 105 10 GULDEN
6.7290 g., 0.9000 Gold .1947 oz. AGW, 22.5 mm. **Ruler:** William III **Obv:** Head right **Obv. Legend:** KONING WILLEM DE... **Rev:** Crowned arms divides value, date above **Rev. Legend:** KONINGRI...NEDERLANDEN. **Edge:** Reeded **Designer:** J. P. M. Menger

Date	Mintage	F	VF	XF	Unc	BU
1875	4,110,000	—	—	BV	125	145

KM# 106 10 GULDEN
6.7290 g., 0.9000 Gold .1947 oz. AGW, 22.5 mm. **Ruler:** William III **Obv:** Head right **Obv. Legend:** KONING WILLEM DE... **Rev:** Crowned arms divides value, date below **Rev. Legend:** KONINGRI...NEDERLANDEN. **Edge:** Reeded **Designer:** J. P. M. Menger

Date	Mintage	F	VF	XF	Unc	BU
1876	1,581,106	—	—	—	BV	130
1877	1,108,149	—	—	—	BV	135
1879/7	581,036	130	175	250	350	450
1879	Inc. above	—	—	—	BV	140
1880	50,100	—	BV	145	165	185
1885	67,095	—	BV	135	165	175
1886	51,141	—	BV	145	175	200
1887	40,754	BV	135	175	200	300
1888	35,585	140	200	300	400	500
1889	204,691	—	—	—	BV	135

KM# 118 10 GULDEN
6.7290 g., 0.9000 Gold .1947 oz. AGW, 22.5 mm. **Ruler:** Wilhelmina I **Obv:** Young head left **Obv. Legend:** KONIGGIN WILHELMINA... **Rev:** Crowned arms divides value, date below **Rev. Legend:** ...NEDERLANDEN. **Edge:** Reeded **Designer:** W. J. Schammer

Date	Mintage	F	VF	XF	Unc	BU
1892	61	2,500	4,500	8,000	12,000	15,000
1892 Proof	—	Value: 16,000				
1895/1	149	1,400	2,500	4,500	6,000	8,000
1895/1 Proof	—	Value: 9,500				
1895	Inc. above	900	2,000	3,500	5,500	7,000
1897	453,696	—	—	BV	135	160

KM# 124 10 GULDEN
6.7290 g., 0.9000 Gold .1947 oz. AGW, 22.5 mm. **Ruler:** Wilhelmina I **Obv:** Crowned head right **Obv. Legend:** KONINGIN WILHELMINA... **Rev:** Crowned arms divides value, date below **Rev. Legend:** KONINGRIJK DER NEDERLANDEN **Edge:** Reeded **Designer:** P. Pander

Date	Mintage	F	VF	XF	Unc	BU
1898	99,239	BV	150	200	350	450

KM# 149 10 GULDEN
6.7290 g., 0.9000 Gold .1947 oz. AGW, 22.5 mm. **Ruler:** Wilhelmina I **Obv:** Head right **Rev:** Crowned arms divide value **Edge:** Reeded **Designer:** J. C. Wienecke

Date	Mintage	F	VF	XF	Unc	BU
1911	774,544	—	—	—	BV	135
1911 Proof	8	Value: 1,750				
1912	3,000,000	—	—	—	BV	135
1912 Proof	20	Value: 1,500				
1913	1,133,476	—	—	—	BV	135
1917	4,000,000	—	—	—	BV	135

KM# 162 10 GULDEN
6.7290 g., 0.9000 Gold .1947 oz. AGW, 22.5 mm. **Ruler:** Wilhelmina I **Obv:** Head right **Rev:** Crowned arms divide value **Edge:** Reeded **Designer:** J. C. Wienecke

Date	Mintage	F	VF	XF	Unc	BU
1925	2,000,000	—	—	—	BV	135
1925 Proof	12	Value: 1,500				
1926	2,500,000	—	—	—	BV	135
1926 Proof	—	Value: 1,300				
1927	1,000,000	—	—	—	BV	135
1932	4,323,954	—	—	—	BV	135
1933	2,462,101	—	—	—	BV	135

KM# 207a 50 GULDEN
Gold **Ruler:** Beatrix **Subject:** Dutch-American Friendship **Obv:** Head left **Rev:** Value within lion and eagle **Edge Lettering:** GOT ZIJ MET ONS **Designer:** E. Claus

Date	Mintage	F	VF	XF	Unc	BU
ND(1982) Rare	2	—	—	—	—	—

KM# 212a 50 GULDEN
Gold **Ruler:** Beatrix **Subject:** 300th Anniversary of William and Mary **Obv:** Patterned head left **Rev:** Conjoined heads right **Edge Lettering:** GOD ZIJ MET ONS **Designer:** K. Martens

Date	Mintage	F	VF	XF	Unc	BU
1988 Rare	4	—	—	—	—	—

EURO COINAGE
European Economic Community Issues

KM# 244 10 EURO
6.7200 g., 0.9000 Gold 0.1944 oz. AGW, 22.5 mm. **Ruler:** Beatrix **Subject:** Crown Prince's Wedding **Obv:** Head left **Rev:** Two facing silhouettes **Edge:** Reeded **Designer:** J. van Houwelingen

Date	Mintage	F	VF	XF	Unc	BU
2002 Prooflike	33,000	—	—	—	—	160

KM# 246 10 EURO
6.7200 g., 0.9000 Gold 0.1944 oz. AGW, 22.5 mm. **Ruler:** Beatrix **Subject:** Vincent Van Gogh **Obv:** Head facing **Rev:** Tilted head facing **Edge:** Reeded **Designer:** K. Martens

Date	Mintage	F	VF	XF	Unc	BU
ND(2003) Prooflike	20,000	—	—	—	—	160

KM# 247 10 EURO
6.7200 g., 0.9000 Gold 0.1944 oz. AGW, 22.5 mm. **Ruler:** Beatrix **Subject:** New EEC members **Obv:** Head left **Rev:** Value and legend **Edge:** Reeded **Designer:** M. Mieras and H. Mieras

Date	Mintage	F	VF	XF	Unc	BU
2004 Proof	6,000	Value: 400				

KM# 251 10 EURO
Gold **Ruler:** Beatrix **Subject:** 50 Years of Domestic Autonomy, 1954-2004 (for Netherlands Antilles) **Obv:** Small head left **Rev:** Fruit and date within beaded circle **Edge:** Reeded **Designer:** R. L. Luijters

Date	Mintage	F	VF	XF	Unc	BU
2004 Proof	3,800	Value: 185				

KM# 264 10 EURO
6.7200 g., 0.9000 Gold 0.1944 oz. AGW, 22.5 mm. **Ruler:** Beatrix **Subject:** 60th Anniversary of Liberation **Obv:** Queen and dots **Rev:** Value and dots **Edge:** Reeded **Designer:** Suzan Drummen

Date	Mintage	F	VF	XF	Unc	BU
2005 Proof	6,000	Value: 210				

KM# 249 20 EURO
8.5000 g., 0.9000 Gold 0.2460 oz. AGW, 25 mm. **Ruler:** Beatrix **Subject:** Birth of Crown-Princess - Catharina-Amalia - July 12, 2003 **Obv:** Bust left **Rev:** Holographic images: left, Princess Maxima; front, Princess Catharina-Amalia; right, Prince Willem-Alexander **Edge:** Reeded

Date	Mintage	F	VF	XF	Unc	BU
2004 Proof	5,300	Value: 300				

KM# 262 20 EURO
8.5000 g., 0.9000 Gold 0.246 oz. AGW, 25 mm. **Ruler:** Beatrix **Subject:** Silver Jubilee of Reign **Obv:** Queen's photo **Rev:** Queen taking oath photo **Edge:** Reeded **Designer:** Germaine Kuip

Date	Mintage	F	VF	XF	Unc	BU
2005 Proof	5,001	Value: 345				

KM# 250 50 EURO
13.4400 g., 0.9000 Gold 0.3889 oz. AGW, 27 mm. **Ruler:** Beatrix **Subject:** Birth of Crown-Princess - Catharina-Amalia - July 12, 2003 **Obv:** Bust left **Rev:** Holographic images: left, Princess Maxima; front, Princess Catharina-Amalia; right, Prince Willem-Alexander **Edge:** Reeded

Date	Mintage	F	VF	XF	Unc	BU
2004 Proof	3,500	Value: 500				

KM# 263 50 EURO
13.4400 g., 0.9000 Gold 0.3889 oz. AGW, 27 mm. **Ruler:** Beatrix **Subject:** Silver Jubilee of Reign **Obv:** Queen's photo **Rev:** Queen taking oath photo **Edge:** Reeded **Designer:** Germaine Kuip

Date	Mintage	F	VF	XF	Unc	BU
2005 Proof	3,500	Value: 575				

TRADE COINAGE

KM# 45 DUCAT
3.5000 g., 0.9830 Gold .1106 oz. AGW

Date	Mintage	F	VF	XF	Unc	BU
1814	2,930,270	100	175	275	400	500
1815	672,910	100	175	300	450	550

NETHERLANDS

Date	Mintage	F	VF	XF	Unc	BU
1815 Clover leaf	613,620	100	250	400	600	750
1816	220,570	110	250	400	600	750

KM# 50.1 DUCAT
3.5000 g., 0.9830 Gold .1106 oz. AGW **Ruler:** William I **Obv:** Standing armored knight divides date **Rev:** Inscription within ornamented square **Edge:** Slant-reeded **Note:** Size varies: 20.5-21.5 mm.

Date	Mintage	F	VF	XF	Unc	BU
1817	498,013	200	350	600	750	1,000
1818	1,561,407	75.00	125	200	300	400
1819	111,301	100	200	350	500	650
1820	10,419	175	300	500	700	950
1821	15,073	175	300	500	700	950
1822	11,971	200	450	900	1,200	1,500
1824B	Est. 8,000	600	2,000	4,000	5,000	6,000
1825	119,276	100	200	375	550	600
1825B	48,003	200	425	700	1,000	1,300
1827	138,110	110	225	325	450	600
1827B	27,032	200	550	1,000	1,500	1,800
1828/7	631,800	200	550	1,000	1,500	1,800
1828	Inc. above	100	175	275	400	500
1828B	454,114	200	425	700	1,000	1,300
1829/28	Inc. below	200	550	1,000	1,500	1,800
1829	1,153,100	75.00	125	175	250	300
1829B	247,000	200	550	1,000	1,500	1,800
1830B	11,186	1,000	1,750	2,500	3,000	3,500
1831/30	Inc. below	200	425	700	1,000	1,300
1831	410,915	75.00	125	175	250	300
1833	247,303	100	175	275	400	500
1836/5	235,801	250	725	1,000	1,500	2,000
1836	Inc. above	100	255	400	600	700
1839	118,604	100	200	300	450	550
1840	—	100	200	300	450	550
1840	103,321	150	300	700	850	950

Note: Fleur de lis privy mark

KM# 50.2 DUCAT
3.5000 g., 0.9830 Gold .1106 oz. AGW **Ruler:** William I **Obv:** Standing armored knight divides date **Rev:** Inscription within ornamented square **Edge:** Slant-reeded **Note:** Struck in Russia

Date	Mintage	F	VF	XF	Unc	BU
1818	1,350,000	85.00	135	175	250	350
1827	350,000	130	250	325	450	600
1828	1,300,000	120	225	275	375	500
1829	150,000	85.00	135	175	200	300
1830	2,000,000	85.00	135	175	200	275
1831	1,000,000	85.00	135	175	200	300
1832	1,000,000	100	200	275	350	500
1833	350,000	100	200	275	350	500
1834	150,000	200	350	500	700	1,000
1835	650,000	110	225	325	425	600
1836	300,000	110	225	325	450	650
1837	1,400,000	85.00	170	250	350	550
1838	1,200,000	85.00	170	250	350	550
1839	1,350,000	85.00	170	250	350	550
1840	—	85.00	175	250	350	550

Note: Torch privy mark

KM# 70.1 DUCAT
3.5000 g., 0.9830 Gold .1106 oz. AGW **Ruler:** William II **Obv:** Standing armored knight divides date **Rev:** Inscription within ornamented square **Edge:** Slant-reeded **Note:** Struck in Russia

Date	Mintage	F	VF	XF	Unc	BU
1841	3,904,240	100	300	400	600	800

Note: Torch privy mark

KM# 70.2 DUCAT
3.5000 g., 0.9830 Gold .1106 oz. AGW **Ruler:** William II **Obv:** Standing armored knight divides date **Rev:** Inscription within ornamented square **Edge:** Slant-reeded

Date	Mintage	F	VF	XF	Unc	BU
1841 Fleur de lis privy mark	95,760	100	200	350	450	550

KM# 83.1 DUCAT
3.4940 g., 0.9830 Gold .1106 oz. AGW, 21 mm. **Obv:** Standing knight divides date **Rev:** Inscription within ornamented square **Edge:** Slant-reeded

Date	Mintage	F	VF	XF	Unc	BU
1849	14,344	90.00	175	250	350	450
1872	30,095	300	1,250	2,750	4,000	7,000
1873	40,041	300	1,250	2,500	3,750	6,500
1874	44,005	300	1,250	2,500	3,750	6,500
1876	44,409	300	1,250	2,500	3,750	6,500
1877	14,875	300	1,250	2,750	4,000	7,000
1878	87,310	300	800	1,300	1,900	3,000
1879	20,103	300	1,250	2,500	3,750	6,500
1880	25,372	300	1,250	2,000	3,250	5,000
1885	81,205	200	450	1,000	2,000	3,000
1894	30,407	175	350	750	1,000	2,000
1895/55	58,444	175	500	850	1,200	2,000
1895/59	Inc. above	175	500	850	1,200	2,000
1895	Inc. above	150	300	600	850	1,500
1899	60,686	150	350	700	950	1,200
1901	29,284	400	1,000	1,500	2,400	2,700
1903/1	91,000	400	1,000	1,850	2,400	2,700
1903	Inc. above	250	700	1,000	1,600	2,000
1905	87,995	175	450	700	1,000	1,400
1906	29,379	400	1,000	1,500	2,400	2,700
1908	91,006	150	350	600	900	1,300
1909	106,021	300	600	1,000	1,600	2,000

Note: Halberd with star privy mark

| 1909 | 30,182 | 400 | 1,000 | 2,000 | 2,700 | 3,600 |

Note: Sea horse privy mark

1910	421,447	125	375	525	900	1,100
1910 Proof	—	Value: 1,200				
1912	147,860	125	375	525	900	1,100
1912 Proof	—	Value: 1,200				
1913	205,464	125	375	525	900	1,100
1914	246,560	125	375	525	900	1,100
1916	116,997	125	375	525	900	1,100
1916 Proof	—	Value: 1,250				
1917	216,892	—	BV	90.00	125	150
1920	293,389	—	BV	90.00	125	150
1920 Proof	—	Value: 800				
1921	409,001	—	BV	80.00	95.00	110
1922	49,837	100	350	500	900	1,100
1923	106,674	BV	80.00	250	350	450
1924	84,206	BV	80.00	250	350	450
1925	573,071	—	BV	80.00	95.00	110
1925 Proof	Inc. above	Value: 450				
1926	191,311	—	BV	85.00	110	150
1927	654,424	—	—	—	BV	60.00
1928	571,801	—	—	—	BV	60.00
1932	88,268	200	500	900	1,700	2,100
1937	116,660	BV	80.00	95.00	110	125

KM# 83.2 DUCAT
3.5000 g., 0.9830 Gold .1106 oz. AGW, 21 mm. **Obv:** Standing armored knight divides date **Rev:** Inscription within ornamented square **Edge:** Slant-reeded

Date	Mintage	F	VF	XF	Unc	BU
1849	4,750,000	80.00	140	200	300	350

KM# 190.1 DUCAT
3.4940 g., 0.9830 Gold .1106 oz. AGW, 21 mm. **Ruler:** Beatrix **Obv:** Knight with right leg bent divides date **Rev:** Inscription within decorated square

Date	Mintage	F	VF	XF	Unc	BU
1960	3,605	BV	100	300	400	450
1972 Prooflike	29,205	—	—	—	—	80.00
1974 Prooflike	86,558	—	—	—	—	80.00
1974	Est. 2,000	—	—	300	600	700

Note: Medal struck

| 1975 Prooflike | 204,788 | — | — | — | — | 75.00 |
| 1976 Prooflike | 37,844 | — | — | 85.00 | 150 | 250 |

Note: Of 37,844 pieces struck, 32,000 were melted

| 1978 Prooflike | 29,305 | — | — | — | 85.00 | 100 |
| 1985 Prooflike | 103,863 | — | — | — | — | 80.00 |

KM# 190.2 DUCAT
3.4940 g., 0.9830 Gold .1106 oz. AGW **Ruler:** Beatrix **Obv:** Knight divides date with larger letters in legend **Rev:** Inscription within decorated square

Date	Mintage	F	VF	XF	Unc	BU
1986 Prooflike	95,091	—	—	—	—	85.00
1989 Proof	24,478	Value: 85.00				
1990 Proof	17,500	Value: 85.00				
1991 Proof	11,500	Value: 85.00				
1992 Proof	14,400	Value: 85.00				
1993 Proof	11,100	Value: 90.00				
1994 Proof	11,500	Value: 90.00				
1995 Proof	11,000	Value: 90.00				
1996 Proof	12,000	Value: 90.00				
1997 Proof	11,500	Value: 90.00				
1998 Proof	8,500	Value: 95.00				
1999 Proof	7,550	Value: 95.00				
2000 Proof	8,000	Value: 95.00				
2001 Proof	7,500	Value: 95.00				
2002 Proof	3,400	Value: 110				
2003 Proof	3,800	Value: 110				
2004 Proof	2,400	Value: 175				
2005 Proof	2,243	Value: 145				
2006 Proof	2,500	Value: 145				
2007 Proof	2,500	Value: 130				

KM# 97 2 DUCAT
6.9880 g., 0.9830 Gold .2209 oz. AGW, 27 mm. **Obv:** Standing armored knight divides date **Rev:** Inscription within ornamented square

Date	Mintage	F	VF	XF	Unc	BU
1854 Proof	—	Value: 9,000				
1867 Proof; 6 known	—	Value: 25,000				

KM# 211 2 DUCAT
6.9880 g., 0.9830 Gold .2209 oz. AGW, 26 mm. **Ruler:** Beatrix **Obv:** Knight divides date within beaded circle **Rev:** Inscription within decorated square

Date	Mintage	F	VF	XF	Unc	BU
1988 Prooflike	23,759	—	—	—	—	155
1989 Proof	17,862	Value: 155				
1991 Proof	10,000	Value: 160				
1992 Proof	11,800	Value: 160				
1996 Proof	10,500	Value: 160				
1999 Proof	6,250	Value: 165				
2000 Proof	7,000	Value: 160				
2002 Proof	6,650	Value: 155				
2003 Proof	4,500	Value: 175				
2004 Proof	2,000	Value: 185				
2005 Proof	3,500	Value: 180				
2006 Proof	2,000	Value: 180				
2007 Proof	2,500	Value: 180				

PATTERNS
Including off metal strikes

KM#	Date	Mintage	Identification	Mkt Val
Pn21	1810	—	10 Gulden. Tin. KM33.	350
Pn20	1810	—	10 Gulden. Silver. KM33.	
Pn25	1818	—	5 Cents. Gold. Crowned W divides date. Crowned arms divides value. KM52.	3,500
Pn31	1819	—	1/2 Cent. Gold. KM51.	9,000
Pn36	1820	—	Gulden. Gold. KM55.	
Pn39	1821	—	Gulden. Gold. KM55.	
Pn42	1822	—	5 Cents. Gold. 1.8600 g. KM52.	7,500
Pn43	1822	—	10 Cents. Gold. 2.5000 g. KM53.	7,000
Pn41	1822	—	1/2 Cent. Gold. KM51.	
Pn47	1823	—	3 Gulden. Gold. KM49.	
Pn46	1823	—	Cent. Gold. 5.3900 g. KM47.	6,000
Pn48	1824	—	1/2 Cent. Gold. KM51.	
Pn49	1826	—	Cent. Gold. 3.6600 g. KN47.	6,000
Pn51	1827	—	Cent. Gold. 3.3000 g. KM47.	8,000
Pn52	1840	—	2 2-1/2 Gulden. Gold. KM46.	—
Pn53	1843	—	10 Cents. Gold.	2,500
Pn56	1848	—	5 Cents. Gold. KM74.	—
Pn57	1848	—	10 Cents. Gold. KM74.	—
Pn58	1849	—	25 Cents. Gold. KM81.	—
Pn60	1850	—	5 Gulden. 0.9000 Gold. Head left. Crowned arms within 3/4 wreath. KM94.	3,000
Pn61	1850	—	10 Gulden. 0.9000 Gold. KM95.	5,000
Pn62	1850	—	20 Gulden. 0.9000 Gold. Head left. Crowned arms within 3/4 wreath. KM96.	7,000
Pn69	1867	—	Gulden. Gold. KM93.	—

536 NETHERLANDS

KM#	Date	Mintage	Identification	Mkt Val
Pn70	1868/58	—	1/2 Gulden. Gold. 9.3500 g. KM92.	10,000
Pn72	1872	—	1/2 Cent. Gold. 3.6300 g. KM90.	4,000
Pn73	1873	—	1/2 Cent. Gold. KM90.	—
Pn74	1874	—	2-1/2 Gulden. Gold. Sword in scabbard privy mark, KM82.	—
Pn75	1875	—	Cent. Gold. KM100.	—
Pn77	1876	—	Cent. Gold. KM100.	—
Pn79	1877	—	Cent. Gold. 7.6700 g. KM100.	8,000
Pn80	1879	—	5 Cents. Gold. KM91.	—
Pn81	1884	—	1/2 Cent. Gold. KM109.	—
Pn83	1884	—	2-1/2 Cent. Gold. KM108.	—
Pn84	1884	—	10 Cents. Gold. KM80.	—
Pn82	1884	—	Cent. Gold. KM107.	—
Pn85	1885	—	10 Cents. Gold. KM80.	—
Pn86	1887	—	5 Cents. Gold. KM91.	—
Pn88	1891	—	10 Gulden. Gold. KM118.	—
Pn93	1898	2	Gulden. Gold. KM122.1	—
Pn94	1898	—	2-1/2 Gulden. Gold. KM123.	—
Pn92	1898	—	1/2 Gulden. Gold. 9.3400 g. KM121.1	10,000
Pn96	1902	—	Cent. Gold. KM132.	—
Pn97	1903	—	1/2 Cent. Gold. KM133.	—
Pn98	1903	—	2-1/2 Cent. Gold. KM134.	—
Pn99	1903	—	10 Cents. Gold. KM135.	—
Pn100	1903	—	25 Cents. Gold. KM120.2	—
Pn110	1905	—	1/2 Gulden. Gold. KM121.2	—
Pn120	1910	—	10 Cents. Gold. KM145.	—
PnA124	1928	—	Gulden. Gold. 19 mm.	550
PnA123	1928	—	Gulden. Gold. 28 mm.	700
Pn126	1934	—	10 Cents. Bronze. KM163.	—
Pn140	1980	—	2-1/2 Gulden. Gold. KM201b.	—
Pn138	1980	—	Gulden. Gold. KM200b.	—
Pn158	1988	—	50 Gulden. Gold. KM212.	—

PIEFORTS

KM#	Date	Mintage	Identification	Mkt Val
P2	1808	—	50 Stuivers. Gold.	—
P5	1822	—	3 Gulden. Gold.	5,000
P9	1823	—	Cent. Gold. KM47.	—

PROOF SETS

KM#	Date	Mintage	Identification	Issue Price	Mkt Val
PS39	1992 (3)	6,300	KM190.2, 211, 213	270	235
PS45	1996 (2)	6,500	KM190.2, 211	248	225
PS49	1999 (3)	2,500	KM190.2, 211, 229	—	280
PS50	1999 (2)	1,800	KM190.2, 211	—	240
PS52	2000 (2)	500	KM#190.2, 211 Golden ducats	—	230
PS53	2000 (3)	1,000	KM#190.2, 211, 232 Golden Ducats and Silver Ducat	—	270
PS55	2001 (2)	500	KM#190.2, 242 Gold and Silver Ducat	50.00	60.00
PS56	2002 (2)	—	KM#190.2, 211 Golden Ducats	—	230
PS57	2002 (3)	—	KM#190.2, 211, 232 Golden Ducats and Silver Ducat	—	270
PS58	2003 (2)	—	KM#190.2, 211 Golden ducats in wooden box	230	230

SELECT SETS (FLEUR DE COIN)

KM#	Date	Mintage	Identification	Issue Price	Mkt Val
SS1	1819 (9)	—	KM47-49, 51-56 1 set	—	60,000
SS15	1980 (2)	7	KM200b-201b. Gold.	—	—

NETHERLANDS ANTILLES

The Netherlands Antilles, comprises two groups of islands in the West Indies: Aruba (until 1986), Bonaire and Curacao and their dependencies near the Venezuelan coast and St. Eustatius, Saba, and the southern part of St. Martin (*St. Maarten*) southeast of Puerto Rico. The island group has an area of 371 sq. mi. (960 sq. km.) and a population of 225,000. Capital: Willemstad. Chief industries are the refining of crude oil and tourism. Petroleum products and phosphates are exported.

On Dec. 15, 1954, the Netherlands Antilles were given complete domestic autonomy and granted equality within the Kingdom with Surinam and the Netherlands. On Jan. I, 1986, Aruba achieved *status aparte* as the fourth part of the Dutch realm that was a step towards total independence.

RULERS
Juliana, 1948-1980
Beatrix, 1980-

MINT MARKS
Y – York Mint

Utrecht Mint
(privy marks only)

Date	Privy Mark
1945-1969	Fish
1969	Fish with star
1970-1979	Cock
1980	Cock with star
1982-1988	Anvil with hammer
1988-1999	Bow and arrow
2000	Bow and arrow with star
2001	Wine tendril with grapes
2002	Wine tendril with grapes and star
2003	Sails of a clipper

FM - Franklin Mint, U.S.A.
NOTE: See Kingdom of the Netherlands for more details.
NOTE: From 1975-1985 the Franklin Mint produced coinage in up to 3 different qualities. Qualities of issue are designated in ( ) after each date and are defined as follows:
(M) MATTE - Normal circulation strike or a dull finish produced by sandblasting special uncirculated (polish finish) or proof quality dies.
(U) SPECIAL UNCIRCULATED - Polished or prooflike in appearance without any frosted features.
(P) PROOF - The highest quality obtainable having mirrorlike fields and frosted features.

MONETARY SYSTEM
100 Cents = 1 Gulden

KINGDOM
DECIMAL COINAGE

KM# 26 5 GULDEN
3.3600 g., 0.9000 Gold .0972 oz. AGW, 18 mm. **Ruler:** Beatrix **Obv:** Head left **Rev:** Crown above joined arms of the Antilles and Netherlands **Edge:** Reeded

Date	Mintage	F	VF	XF	Unc	BU
1980 Anvil & hammer Proof	16,000	Value: 70.00				

KM# 27 10 GULDEN
6.7200 g., 0.9000 Gold .1945 oz. AGW, 22.5 mm. **Ruler:** Beatrix **Obv:** Head left **Rev:** Crown above two shields dividing value **Edge:** Reeded

Date	Mintage	F	VF	XF	Unc	BU
1980 Proof, anvil with hammer	6,000	Value: 135				

KM# 75 10 GULDEN
6.7200 g., 0.9000 Gold 0.1944 oz. AGW. **Ruler:** Beatrix **Subject:** 50th Anniversary - End to Dutch Colonial Rule **Obv:** Head left **Rev:** Triangular signatures around value **Edge:** Reeded **Designer:** Ans Mezas-Hummelink

Date	Mintage	F	VF	XF	Unc	BU
2004 Proof	1,000	Value: 180				

KM# 77 10 GULDEN
6.7200 g., 0.9000 Gold 0.1944 oz. AGW, 22.5 mm. **Ruler:** Beatrix **Subject:** Queen's Silver Jubilee **Obv:** Head left **Rev:** Child art and value **Edge:** Reeded

Date	Mintage	F	VF	XF	Unc	BU
2005 Proof	1,500	Value: 175				

KM# 23 50 GULDEN
3.3600 g., 0.9000 Gold .0972 oz. AGW, 18 mm. **Ruler:** Juliana **Subject:** 75th Anniversary of the Royal Convenant **Obv:** Head right **Rev:** Crown above joined arms of the Antilles and Netherlands **Edge:** Reeded

Date	Mintage	F	VF	XF	Unc	BU
1979	11,000	—	—	—	65.00	70.00
1979 Proof	64,000	Value: 65.00				

KM# 21 100 GULDEN
6.7200 g., 0.9000 Gold .1944 oz. AGW **Ruler:** Juliana **Subject:** 150th Anniversary of Bank **Obv:** Head right **Rev:** Head right **Edge:** Reeded

Date	Mintage	F	VF	XF	Unc	BU
1978	26,500	—	—	—	135	140
1978 Proof	23,500	Value: 135				

KM# 46 100 GULDEN
7.7700 g., 0.9990 Gold .2500 oz. AGW, 22 mm. **Ruler:** Beatrix **Obv:** Crowned shield divides date within circle **Obv. Legend:** YEGADA DI SPAŃÓNAN **Rev:** The Santa Maria **Edge:** Plain **Designer:** Dutch Mint

Date	Mintage	F	VF	XF	Unc	BU
1999 Proof	850	Value: 250				

KM# 16 200 GULDEN
7.9500 g., 0.9000 Gold .2300 oz. AGW **Ruler:** Juliana **Subject:** U.S. Bicentennial **Obv:** Head right **Rev:** The Andrew Doria **Edge:** IN GOD WE TRUST ST EUSTATIUS SALUTES FIRST AMERICAN FLAG **Shape:** Octagon

Date	Mintage	F	VF	XF	Unc	BU
1976 FM(M)	100	—	—	—	350	400
1976 FM(U)	5,726	—	—	—	155	165
1976 FM(P)	15,442	Value: 165				

KM# 18 200 GULDEN
7.9500 g., 0.9000 Gold .2300 oz. AGW **Ruler:** Juliana **Obv:** Head right **Rev:** Standing statue left **Edge:** Plain **Shape:** Octagon

Date	Mintage	F	VF	XF	Unc	BU
1977 FM(M)	1,000	—	—	—	165	190
1977 FM(U)	654	—	—	—	250	265
1977 FM(P)	6,878	Value: 160				

KM# 29.1 300 GULDEN
5.0400 g., 0.9000 Gold .1458 oz. AGW **Ruler:** Juliana **Subject:** Abdication of Queen Juliana **Obv:** Head right **Rev:** Crown above joined arms of the Antilles and Netherlands **Edge:** Plain **Shape:** Square

Date	Mintage	F	VF	XF	Unc	BU
1980 (u) Proof, cock and star	29,300	Value: 100				

KM# 29.2 300 GULDEN
5.0400 g., 0.9000 Gold .1458 oz. AGW **Ruler:** Juliana **Subject:** Head right **Obv:** Queen Juliana **Rev:** Crown above joined arms of the Antilles and Netherlands **Edge:** Plain **Note:** Without mint mark or mintmaster's symbol

Date	Mintage	F	VF	XF	Unc	BU
1980 Proof	Inc. above	Value: 320				

PATTERNS
Including off metal strikes

KM#	Date	Mintage	Identification	Mkt Val
Pn7	1981 Y	—	125 Gulden. Gilt Bronze.	750
Pn8	1981 Y	—	125 Gulden. Gold.	3,000
Pn9	1981 Y	—	250 Gulden. Gilt Bronze.	850
Pn10	1981 Y	—	250 Gulden. Gold.	4,000
Pn11	1981 Y	—	500 Gulden. Gilt Bronze.	950
Pn12	1981 Y	—	500 Gulden. Gold.	5,000

PIEFORTS

KM#	Date	Mintage	Identification	Mkt Val
P1	1998	200	5 Gulden. Brass Plated Steel. KM43.	500

PROOF SETS

KM#	Date	Mintage	Identification	Issue Price	Mkt Val
PS18	1976 (2)	13,000	KM15-16	188	325
PS20	1999 (5)	—	KM45-47, with Aruba KM18-19	—	850

NETHERLANDS EAST INDIES

The Netherlands East Indies of the 19th century, ruled by the Dutch with brief sojourns under the British would now be provinces of Sumatra, a part of the Republic of Indonesia. The islands of Indonesia are made up partly of the Malay Archipelago, which encompasses 3,000 islands, which is the largest in the world.

Had Columbus succeeded in reaching the fabled Spice Islands, he would have found advanced civilizations a millennium old, and temples still ranked among the finest examples of ancient art. During the opening centuries of the Christian era, the islands were influenced by Hindu priests and traders who spread their culture and religion. Moslem invasions began in the 13th century, fragmenting the island kingdoms into small states which were unable to resist Western colonial infiltration. Portuguese traders established posts in the 16th century, but they were soon outnumbered by the Dutch who arrived in 1596 and gradually asserted control over the islands comprising present-day Indonesia. Dutch dominance, interrupted by British incursions during the Napoleonic Wars, established the Netherlands East Indies as one of the richest colonial possessions in the world.

The VOC (United East India Company) struck coins and emergency issues for the Indonesian Archipelago and for the islands at various mints in the Netherlands and the islands. In 1798 the VOC was subsumed by the Dutch government, which issued VOC type transitional and regal types during the Batavian Republic and the Kingdom of the Netherlands until independence. The British issued a coinage during the various occupations by the British East Indian Company, 1811-24. Modern coinage issued by the Republic of Indonesia includes separate series for West Irian and for the Riau Archipelago, an area of small islands between Singapore and Sumatra.

RULERS
Batavian Republic, 1799-1806
Louis Napoleon, King of Holland, 1806-1811
Dutch, 1816-1942

MINT MARKS
H - Amsterdam (H)
Hk - Harderwijk (star, rosette, cock, cross, Z)
Hn - Hoorn (star)
E - Enkhuizen (star)
Dt - Dordrecht (rosette)
K - Kampen (eagle)
S - Utrecht
Sa - Soerabaja (Za)

MONETARY SYSTEM
120 Duits = 120 Cents
1 Gulden = 1 Java Rupee
16 Silver Rupees = 1 Gold Mohur

PATTERNS
Including off metal strikes

KM#	Date	Mintage	Identification	Mkt Val
Pn1	1826(u)	—	1/2 Gulden. Gold. KM#302.	—
Pn2	1834(u)	—	1/2 Gulden. Gold. KM#302	—
Pn3	1854(u)	—	1/10 Gulden. Gold. KM#304	—
Pn4	1855(u)	—	1/20 Gulden. Gold. KM#303	—
Pn5	1858(u)	—	2-1/2 Cents. Gold. KM#308	—
Pn6	1860(u)	—	1/2 Cent. Gold. KM#306	—
Pn7	1860(u)	—	Cent. Gold. KM#307	—
Pn8	1885(u)	—	1/10 Gulden. Gold. KM#304	—
Pn9	1885(u)	—	1/4 Gulden. Gold. KM#305	—
Pn12	1902(u)	—	1/2 Cent. Gold. KM#306	—
Pn14	1902(u)	—	Cent. Gold. KM#307	—
Pn16	1902(u)	—	2-1/2 Cents. Gold. KM#308	—
Pn18	1903(u)	—	1/4 Gulden. Gold. KM#310	—
Pn17	1908(u)	—	1/10 Gulden. Gold. KM#309	—
Pn20	1908	—	1/2 Cent. Gold.	—
Pn23	1908	—	Cent. Gold.	—
Pn25	1908	—	2-1/2 Cents. Gold. 22.1220 g. KM#308	—
Pn29	1914	—	5 Cents. Gold.	—
Pn33	1945	—	1/4 Gulden. Gold. KM#319	—

JAVA

LOCAL COINAGE
A mountainous island, 661 miles long by 124 miles at widest part, in greater Sunda island group. Early cultural influence from India. Islam introduced in late 1400's. Java was mainly a Dutch possession from 1619 to 1947 with the exception of a few periods of British occupation, principally 1811-1816.

MONETARY SYSTEM
4 Duit = 1 Stiver
30 Stivers = 1 Rupee (Silver)
66 Stivers = 1 Dollar

DATING SYSTEM
The coins listed are found with AD (Christian) dates, AD and AH (Hejira) dates, and with AD, AH and AS (Aji Saka = Javanese) dates which are explained in the introduction in this catalog.

BATAVIAN REPUBLIC
1799-1806

MINTMASTER'S INITIALS
Z – J.A. Zwekkert

MILLED COINAGE

KM# 209 1/2 RUPEE
8.0060 g., 0.7500 Gold .1929 oz. AGW **Obv:** Arabic script, AD date **Rev:** Arabic script

Date	Mintage	VG	F	VF	XF	Unc
1801	—	300	500	800	1,350	—
1802	—	300	500	800	1,350	—
1803 Unique	—	—	—	—	—	—
1807	—	600	1,100	1,650	2,500	—

BRITISH UNITED EAST INDIA COMPANY

MILLED COINAGE

KM# 248 1/2 MOHUR
8.0060 g., 0.7500 Gold 0.193 oz. AGW **Obv:** Javanese script, dates **Rev:** Arabic script, date

Date	Mintage	VG	F	VF	XF	Unc
AH1668//AS1740 (1813) Rare	—	—	—	—	—	—
Note: (error = AH1228)						
AH1229//AS1743 (1814)	—	—	1,750	2,250	3,500	—

KM# 248a 1/2 MOHUR
8.0060 g., 0.8330 Gold 0.2144 oz. AGW **Obv:** Javanese script, date **Rev:** Arabic script, date **Note:** Varieties exist.

Date	Mintage	VG	F	VF	XF	Unc
AH1230//AS1743 (1815) OZ	—	1,750	2,250	2,500	3,500	—
AH1230//AS1743 (1815)	—	1,750	2,250	2,500	3,500	—
AH1230//AS1743 (1816)	—	1,250	1,750	2,000	2,850	—
Note: (error = AH1231)						
AH1231//AS174 3 (1816)	—	1,250	1,750	2,000	2,850	—
AH1231//AS1743 (1816)	—	1,250	1,750	2,000	2,850	—

KM# 249 1/2 MOHUR
8.0060 g., 0.8330 Gold 0.2144 oz. AGW **Obv:** Javanese script, numerals in date reversed **Rev:** Arabic script, date, M added

Date	Mintage	VG	F	VF	XF	Unc
AH1231//AS1743 (1816) Rare	—	—	—	—	—	—

NEW CALEDONIA

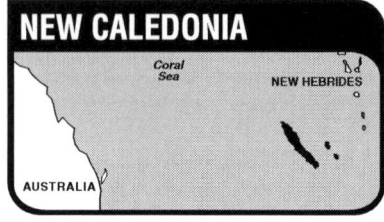

The French Overseas Territory of New Caledonia, is a group of about 25 islands in the South Pacific. They are situated about 750 miles (1,207 km.) east of Australia. The territory, which includes the dependencies of Isle des Pins, Loyalty Islands, Isle Huon, Isles Belep, Isles Chesterfield, Isle Walpole, Wallis and Futuna Islands and has a total land area of 7,358 sq. mi.(19,060 sq. km.) and a population of *156,000. Capital: Noumea. The islands are rich in minerals; New Caledonia has some of the world's largest known deposit of nickel. Nickel, nickel castings, coffee and copra are exported.

The first European to sight New Caledonia was the British navigator Capt. James Cook in 1774. The French took possession in 1853, and established a penal colony on the island in 1864. The European population of the colony remained disproportionately convict until 1897. New Caledonia became an overseas territory within the French Community in 1946, and in 1958 and 1972 chose to remain affiliated with France.

MINT MARK
Paris, privy marks only

MONETARY SYSTEM
100 Centimes = 1 Franc

PIEFORTS

An unknown quantity of gold pieforts were melted in 1983.

KM#	Date	Mintage	Identification	Issue Price	Mkt Val
P1b	1967(a)	20	10 Francs. 0.9200 Gold. KM5.	—	950
P2b	1967(a)	20	20 Francs. 0.9200 Gold. KM6.	—	1,000
P3b	1967(a)	20	50 Francs. 0.9200 Gold. KM7.	—	1,350
P5b	1979(a)	96	2 Francs. 0.9200 Gold. Similar to KM14.	—	925
P6b	1979(a)	94	5 Francs. 0.9200 Gold. Similar to KM4.	—	1,300
P7b	1979(a)	93	10 Francs. 0.9200 Gold. Similar to KM11.	—	850
P8b	1979(a)	95	20 Francs. 0.9200 Gold. Liberty head left. Three ox heads, value at lower left. Similar to KM12.	—	1,200
P10b	1979(a)	96	100 Francs. 0.9200 Gold. Similar to KM15.	—	1,150

NEW HEBRIDES

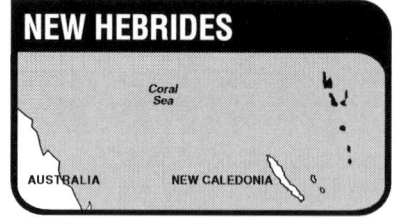

The New Hebrides were discovered by Portuguese navigator Pedro de Quiros in 1606, visited by French explorer Bougainville in 1768, and named by British navigator Capt. James Cook in 1774. Ships of all nations converged on the islands to trade for sandalwood, prompting France and Britain to relinquish their individual claims and declare the islands a neutral zone in 1878. The New Hebrides were placed under the control of a mixed Anglo-French commission of naval officers during the native uprisings of 1887, until achieving independence as Vanuatu, within the Commonwealth of nations on September 30, 1980.

MINT MARK
(a) - Paris, privy marks only

MONETARY SYSTEM
100 Centimes = 1 Franc

PATTERNS
Including off metal strikes

KM#	Date	Mintage	Identification	Mkt Val
Pn3	1979	3	500 Francs. 0.9990 Gold. 62.2000 g.	6,000
Pn4	1979	1	500 Francs. 0.9990 Platinum. 62.2000 g.	9,000

PIEFORTS WITH ESSAI
Double thickness

KM#	Date	Mintage	Identification	Issue Price	Mkt Val
PE2	1966(a)	50	100 Francs. 0.9200 Gold.	—	3,750
PE5	1967(a)	20	10 Francs. 0.9200 Gold.	—	500
PE8	1967(a)	20	20 Francs. 0.9200 Gold.	—	1,000
PE11	1974(a)	119	100 Francs. 0.9200 Gold.	—	3,500
PE14	1979(a)	123	Franc. 0.9200 Gold.	—	200
PE17	1979(a)	115	2 Francs. 0.9200 Gold.	—	250
PE20	1979(a)	116	5 Francs. 0.9200 Gold.	—	350
PE23	1979(a)	116	10 Francs. 0.9200 Gold.	—	500
PE26	1979(a)	115	20 Francs. 0.9200 Gold.	—	625
PE29	1979(a)	116	50 Francs. 0.9200 Gold.	—	1,250

NEW ZEALAND

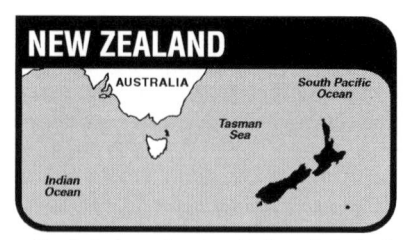

New Zealand, a parliamentary state located in the Southwest Pacific 1,250 miles (2,011 km.) east of Australia, has an area of 103,883 sq. mi. (268,680 sq. km.) and a population of *3.4 million. Capital: Wellington. Wool, meat, dairy products and some manufactured items are exported.

The first European to sight New Zealand was the Dutch navigator Abel Tasman in 1642. The islands were explored by British navigator Capt. James Cook who surveyed it in 1769 and annexed the land to Great Britain. The British government disavowed the annexation and for the next 70 years the only white settlers to arrive were adventurers attracted by the prospects of lumbering, sealing and whaling. Great Britain annexed the land in 1840 by treaty with the native chiefs and made it a dependency of New South Wales. The colony was granted self-government in 1852, a ministerial form of government in 1856, and full dominion status on Sept. 26, 1907. Full internal and external autonomy, which New Zealand had in effect possessed for many years, was formally extended in 1947. New Zealand is a member of the Commonwealth of Nations. Elizabeth II is Head of State as Queen of New Zealand.

Prior to 1933 British coins were the official legal tender but Australian coins were accepted in small transactions. Currency fluctuations caused a distinctive New Zealand coinage to be introduced in 1933. The 1935 Waitangi crown and proof set were originally intended to mark the introduction but delays caused their date to be changed to 1935. The 1940 half crown marked the centennial of British rule, the 1949 and 1953 crowns commemorated Royal visits and the 1953 proof set marked the coronation of Queen Elizabeth.

Decimal Currency was introduced in 1967 with special sets commemorating the last issued of pound sterling (1965) and the first of the decimal issues. Since then dollars and set of coins have been issued nearly every year.

RULER
British

MINTS
(L) – British Royal Mint (Llantrisant)
(C) – Royal Australian Mint (Canberra)
(O) – Royal Canadian Mint
(N) – Norwegian Mint
(P) – South African Mint (Pretoria)

MONETARY SYSTEM
4 Farthings = 1 Penny
12 Pence = 1 Shilling
20 Shillings = 1 Pound

STATE
1907 - present
DECIMAL COINAGE
100 Cents = 1 Dollar

(c) Royal Australian Mint, Canberra

(l) Royal Mint, Llantrisant

(o) Royal Canadian Mint, Ottawa

(n) Norwegian Mint, Kongsberg

(p) South African Mint, Pretoria

(v) Valcambi SA, Switzerland

KM# 90b 50 CENTS
Ring Composition: 0.3750 Gold **Center Composition:** 0.9160 Gold, 32 mm. **Ruler:** Elizabeth II **Subject:** H.M.S. Endeavour **Obv:** Crowned head right within circle **Rev:** Sailing ship within circle

Date	Mintage	F	VF	XF	Unc	BU
1994 Proof	500	Value: 400				

KM# 163 DOLLAR
31.3500 g., 0.9990 Gold 1.0069 oz. AGW, 40.6 mm. **Ruler:** Elizabeth II **Subject:** King Kong **Obv:** Crowned head right **Edge:** Reeded

Date	Mintage	F	VF	XF	Unc	BU
2005 Proof	50,000	—	—	—	—	—

NICARAGUA 539

KM# 88b 5 DOLLARS
47.5250 g., 0.9170 Gold 1.4010 oz. AGW **Ruler:** Elizabeth II
Subject: 40th Anniversary of Coronation **Obv:** Crowned head right **Obv. Designer:** R.D. Maklouf **Rev:** Coronation emblem within squares, all within artistic designed circle

Date	Mintage	F	VF	XF	Unc	BU
1993 Proof	210	Value: 1,200				

KM# 94a 10 DOLLARS
0.9990 Gold .5000 oz. AGW **Ruler:** Elizabeth II **Obv:** Crowned head right **Obv. Designer:** R.D. Maklouf **Rev:** Gold Prospector

Date	Mintage	F	VF	XF	Unc	BU
1995(I) Proof	600	Value: 325				

KM# 98a 10 DOLLARS
0.9990 Gold .5000 oz. AGW **Ruler:** Elizabeth II **Subject:** Sinking of The General Grant **Obv:** Crowned head right **Obv. Designer:** R.D. Maklouf **Rev:** Sinking ship above value

Date	Mintage	F	VF	XF	Unc	BU
1996(I) Proof	650	Value: 350				

KM# 104a 10 DOLLARS
0.9990 Gold .5000 oz. AGW **Ruler:** Elizabeth II **Subject:** Gabriel's Gully **Obv:** Crowned head right **Obv. Designer:** R.D. Maklouf **Rev:** Prospector climbing hill with shovel in hand

Date	Mintage	F	VF	XF	Unc	BU
1997(I) Proof	650	Value: 325				

KM# 129 10 DOLLARS
3.8879 g., 0.9990 Gold .1250 oz. AGW, 18 mm. **Ruler:** Elizabeth II **Obv:** Head with tiara right **Obv. Designer:** Ian Rank-Broadley **Rev:** Salvage ship above value **Edge:** Reeded

Date	Mintage	F	VF	XF	Unc	BU
2001 Proof	600	Value: 125				

KM# 130 10 DOLLARS
7.7759 g., 0.9990 Gold .2500 oz. AGW, 22 mm. **Ruler:** Elizabeth II **Obv:** Head with tiara right **Obv. Designer:** Ian Rank-Broadley **Rev:** Ship above value **Edge:** Reeded

Date	Mintage	F	VF	XF	Unc	BU
2001 Proof	600	Value: 225				

KM# 144 10 DOLLARS
39.9400 g., 0.9166 Gold 1.177 oz. AGW, 38.61 mm. **Ruler:** Elizabeth II **Subject:** Lord of the Rings **Obv:** Head with tiara right **Obv. Designer:** Ian Rank-Broadley **Rev:** Inscribed ring around value **Rev. Designer:** Matthew Bonaccorsi **Edge:** Reeded

Date	Mintage	F	VF	XF	Unc	BU
2003 Proof	—	Value: 1,000				

KM# 157 10 DOLLARS
Gold, 20.1 mm. **Ruler:** Elizabeth II **Subject:** ANZAC **Obv:** Crowned head right **Rev:** Soldiers from Chunuk Bair battle with rifles and bayonets **Edge:** Reeded

Date	Mintage	F	VF	XF	Unc	BU
2005 Proof	1,000	—	—	—	—	—

KM# 165 10 DOLLARS
7.9880 g., 0.9160 Gold 0.2352 oz. AGW, 22.05 mm. **Ruler:** Elizabeth II **Subject:** Lions Rugby Tour **Obv:** Crowned head right **Edge:** Reeded

Date	Mintage	F	VF	XF	Unc	BU
2005 Proof	1,000	—	—	—	—	—

KM# 77 150 DOLLARS
16.9500 g., 0.9170 Gold .4996 oz. AGW **Ruler:** Elizabeth II **Obv:** Crowned head right **Rev:** Kiwi

Date	Mintage	F	VF	XF	Unc	BU
1990 Proof	10,000	Value: 300				

PROOF SETS

KM#	Date	Mintage	Identification	Issue Price	Mkt Val
PS46	2001 (2)	600	KM#129-130	400	450

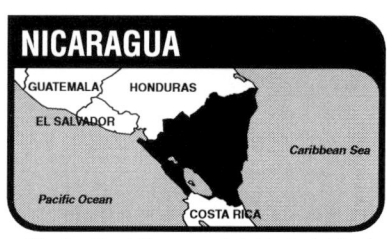

NICARAGUA

The Republic of Nicaragua, situated in Central America between Honduras and Costa Rica, has an area of 50,193 sq. mi. (129,494 sq. km.).

Columbus sighted the coast of Nicaragua on Sept. 12, 1502 during the course of his last voyage of discovery. It was first visited in 1522 by conquistadors from Panama, under the command of Gil Gonzalez. Francisco Hernandez de Cordoba established the first settlements in 1524 at Granada and Leon. Nicaragua was incorporated, for administrative purpose, in the Captaincy General of Guatemala, which included every Central American state but Panama. On September 15, 1821 the Captaincy General of Guatemala declared itself and all the Central American provinces independent of Spain. The next year Nicaragua united with the Mexican Empire of Augustin de Iturbide, only to join in 1823 the federation of the Central American Republic. Within Nicaragua rival cities or juntas such as Leon, Granada and El Viejo vied for power, wealth and influence, often attacking each other at will. To further prove their legitimacy as well as provide an acceptable circulating coinage in those turbulent times (1821-1825), provisional mints functioned intermittently at Granada, Leon and El Viejo. The early coinage reflected traditional but crude Spanish colonial cob-style designs. Nicaragua's first governor was Pedro Arias Davila, appointed on June 1, 1827. When the federation was dissolved, Nicaragua declared itself an independent republic on April 30, 1838.

Dissension between the Liberals and Conservatives of the contending cities kept Nicaragua in turmoil, which made it possible for William Walker to make himself President in 1855. The two major political parties finally united to drive him out and in 1857 he was expelled. A relative peace followed, but by 1912, Nicaragua had requested the U.S. Marines to restore order, which began a U.S. involvement that lasted until the Good Neighbor Policy was adopted in 1933.

MINT MARKS
H - Heaton, Birmingham
HF - Huguenin Freres, Le Locle, Switzerland
Mo - Mexico City

MONETARY SYSTEM
100 Centavos = 1 Peso
NOTE: Former listing for 1823 IL 1/2 Real of Leon has been identified by recognized authorities as a Honduras issue 1823 TL 1/2 Real cataloged there as KM#9.

REPUBLIC
DECIMAL COINAGE

KM# 25 50 CORDOBAS
35.6000 g., 0.9000 Gold 1.0300 oz. AGW **Subject:** 100th Anniversary - Birth of Ruben Dario **Obv:** National emblem within circle **Rev:** Bust 3/4 facing within circle

Date	Mintage	F	VF	XF	Unc	BU
1967HF Prooflike	16,000	—	—	—	—	750

Note: 500 pieces were issued in blue boxes with certificates; Boxed examples command a premium

KM# 37 200 CORDOBAS
2.1000 g., 0.9000 Gold .0608 oz. AGW **Subject:** Pieta by Michelangelo **Obv:** National emblem **Rev:** Sitting figure holding lying figure on lap within circle

Date	Mintage	F	VF	XF	Unc	BU
1975	1,200	—	—	—	60.00	75.00
1975 Proof	1,650	Value: 85.00				

NICARAGUA

KM# 38 500 CORDOBAS
5.4000 g., 0.9000 Gold .1563 oz. AGW **Subject:** Colonial Church, La Merced **Obv:** National emblem **Rev:** Colonial church within circle

Date	Mintage	F	VF	XF	Unc	BU
1975	200	—	—	—	325	350
1975 Proof	100	Value: 650				

KM# 39 500 CORDOBAS
5.4000 g., 0.9000 Gold .1563 oz. AGW **Subject:** Earthquake Relief Issue **Obv:** National emblem **Rev:** "The Bud" by Annigoni

Date	Mintage	F	VF	XF	Unc	BU
1975	1,750	—	—	—	150	175
1975 Proof	1,120	Value: 220				

KM# 40 1000 CORDOBAS
9.5000 g., 0.9000 Gold .2749 oz. AGW **Subject:** U.S. Bicentennial **Obv:** National emblem **Rev:** Liberty bell divides dates

Date	Mintage	F	VF	XF	Unc	BU
1975	3,380	—	—	—	200	225
1975 Proof	2,270	Value: 250				

KM# 48 1000 CORDOBAS
20.0000 g., 0.9000 Gold .5788 oz. AGW **Subject:** 1st Anniversary of Revolution **Obv:** Three 1/2 figures with guns raised **Rev:** Busts of Sandino and Fonseca

Date	Mintage	F	VF	XF	Unc	BU
1980Mo Proof	6,000	Value: 465				

KM# 52 1000 CORDOBAS
20.0000 g., 0.9170 Gold .5896 oz. AGW **Subject:** 50th Anniversary - The Murder of General Augusto Cesar Sandino **Obv:** National emblem **Rev:** Bust with hat facing

Date	Mintage	F	VF	XF	Unc	BU
1984 Proof	1,000	Value: 550				

KM# 53 1000 CORDOBAS
20.0000 g., 0.9170 Gold .5896 oz. AGW **Obv:** National emblem **Rev:** Birthplace of Augusto Cesar Sandino

Date	Mintage	F	VF	XF	Unc	BU
1984 Proof	1,000	Value: 550				

KM# 54 1000 CORDOBAS
20.0000 g., 0.9170 Gold .5896 oz. AGW **Obv:** National emblem **Rev:** Facing busts of Generals Sandino, Estrada and Umanzor

Date	Mintage	F	VF	XF	Unc	BU
1984 Proof	1,000	Value: 550				

KM# 41 2000 CORDOBAS
19.2000 g., 0.9000 Gold .5556 oz. AGW **Subject:** U.S. Bicentennial **Obv:** National emblem **Rev:** Betsy Ross sewing flag on left, astronaut placing flag on moon on right

Date	Mintage	F	VF	XF	Unc	BU
1975	320	—	—	—	525	550
1975 Proof	100	Value: 850				

PATTERNS
Including off metal strikes.

KM#	Date	Mintage	Identification	Mkt Val
Pn11	1912H	1	1/2 Centavo. Gold. KM10; unique.	—
Pn13	1912H	1	Centavo. Gold. KM#11.	—
Pn15	1912H	1	5 Centavos. Gold. KM12.	—
Pn16	1912H	1	10 Centavos. Gold. KM13.	—
Pn17	1912H	1	25 Centavos. Gold. KM14.	—
Pn18	1912H	1	50 Centavos. Gold. KM#15.	—
Pn19	1912H	1	Cordoba. Gold. KM16.	—

MINT SETS

KM#	Date	Mintage	Identification	Issue Price	Mkt Val
MS1	1975 (5)	—	KM37-41	—	1,150

PROOF SETS

KM#	Date	Mintage	Identification	Issue Price	Mkt Val
PS1	1912 (7)	10	KM10-16	—	4,500
PS2	1912 (3)	2	Pn10, Pn12, Pn14	—	4,500
PS3	1912 (7)	1	Pn11, Pn13, Pn15-19	—	—
PS4	1972 (5)	20,000	KM17.3-19.3, 24.3, 26	8.00	15.00
PS5	1975 (7)	—	KM32, 33, 35, 37, 38, 40, 41	—	1,750
PS7	1975 (3)	—	KM32, 33, 35	115	90.00
PS8	1975 (3)	—	KM34, 36, 39	—	255
PS9	1975 (2)	—	KM37, 39	—	255

NIGER

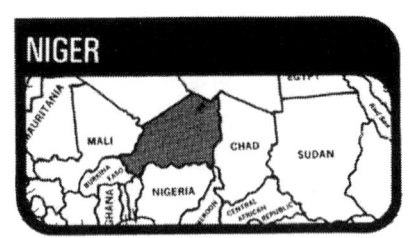

The Republic of Niger, located in West Africa's Sahara region 1,000 miles (1,609 km.) from the Mediterranean shore, has an area of 489,191 sq. mi. (1,267,000 sq. km.) and a population of *7.4 million. Capital: Niamey. The economy is based on subsistence agriculture and raising livestock. Peanuts, peanut oil, and livestock are exported.

Although four-fifths of Niger is arid desert, it was, some 6,000 years ago inhabited and an important economic crossroads. Its modern history began in the 19th century with the beginning of contacts with British and German explorers searching for the mouth of the Niger River. Niger was incorporated into French West Africa in 1896, but it was 1922 before all native resistance was quelled and Niger became a French colony. In 1958 the voters approved the new French Constitution and elected to become an autonomous republic within the French Community. On Aug. 3, 1960, Niger withdrew from the Community and proclaimed its independence.

REPUBLIC
DECIMAL COINAGE

KM# 1 10 FRANCS
4.2000 g., 0.9000 Gold .1215 oz. AGW **Subject:** Independence Commemorataive **Obv:** President Diori Hamani left **Rev:** Flagged arms

Date	Mintage	F	VF	XF	Unc	BU
ND(1960) Proof	1,000	Value: 90.00				

KM# 7 10 FRANCS
3.2000 g., 0.9000 Gold .0926 oz. AGW **Obv:** Ostriches **Rev:** Flagged arms

Date	Mintage	F	VF	XF	Unc	BU
1968 Proof	1,000	Value: 125				

KM# 2 25 FRANCS
8.0000 g., 0.9000 Gold .2315 oz. AGW **Subject:** Independence Commemorative **Obv:** President Diori Hamani left **Rev:** Flagged arms

Date	Mintage	F	VF	XF	Unc	BU
ND(1960) Proof	1,000	Value: 165				

KM# 9 25 FRANCS
8.0000 g., 0.9000 Gold .2315 oz. AGW **Obv:** Barbary sheep **Rev:** Flagged arms

Date	Mintage	F	VF	XF	Unc	BU
1968 Proof	1,000	Value: 185				

KM# 3 50 FRANCS
16.0000 g., 0.9000 Gold .4630 oz. AGW **Subject:**
Independence Commemorative **Obv:** President Diori Hamani left
Rev: Flagged arms

Date	Mintage	F	VF	XF	Unc	BU
ND(1960) Proof	1,000	Value: 325				

KM# 10 50 FRANCS
16.0000 g., 0.9000 Gold .4630 oz. AGW **Subject:**
Independence Commemorative **Obv:** Lion **Rev:** Flagged arms

Date	Mintage	F	VF	XF	Unc	BU
1968 Proof	1,000	Value: 400				

KM# 4 100 FRANCS
32.0000 g., 0.9000 Gold .9260 oz. AGW **Subject:**
Independence Commemorative **Obv:** President Diori Hamani left
Rev: Flagged arms

Date	Mintage	F	VF	XF	Unc	BU
ND(1960) Proof	1,000	Value: 800				

KM# 11 100 FRANCS
32.0000 g., 0.9000 Gold .9260 oz. AGW **Subject:**
Independence Commemorative **Obv:** President Diori Hamani left
Rev: Flagged arms

Date	Mintage	F	VF	XF	Unc	BU
1968 Proof	1,000	Value: 800				

KM# 16a 6000 CFA FRANCS - 4 AFRICA
11.0000 g., 0.9990 Bi-Metallic .999 Silver center in .999 Gold ring
0.3533 oz., 28.3 mm. **Obv:** Mosquito and "STOP MALARIA"
within circle **Rev:** Elephant head within map **Edge:** Plain

Date	Mintage	F	VF	XF	Unc	BU
2005	10	—	—	—	450	—

KM# 15a 150000 CFA FRANCS - 100 AFRICA
13.2000 g., 0.9990 Gold Plated Silver 0.424 oz. ASW AGW,
28.4 mm. **Obv:** President Tandja, map and lion cub **Rev:**
Elephant head within map **Edge:** Plain

Date	Mintage	F	VF	XF	Unc	BU
2005	25	—	—	—	275	—

ESSAIS

KM#	Date	Mintage	Identification	Issue Price	Mkt Val
E1	1960	—	10 Francs. Silver. 39.4000 g. Lion facing. Arms. Thick planchet.	—	125
E2	1960	—	25 Francs.	—	200
E3	1960	—	50 Francs.	—	325
E4	1960	—	100 Francs.	—	650
E7	1968	—	10 Francs. Gold. 31.7800 g. KM8.	—	1,750
E8	1968	—	10 Francs. Silver.	—	35.00
E9	1968	—	25 Francs. Silver.	—	40.00
E10	1968	—	50 Francs. Silver.	—	45.00
E11	1968	—	100 Francs. Silver.	—	50.00

PROOF SETS

KM#	Date	Mintage	Identification	Issue Price	Mkt Val
PS1	1960 (4)	1,000	KM1-4	—	1,380
PS2	1968 (4)	—	KM7, 9-11	—	1,500

NIGERIA

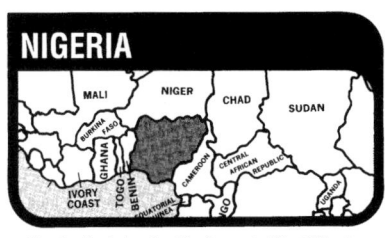

Nigeria, situated on the Atlantic coast of West Africa has an area of 356,669 sq. mi. (923,770 sq. km.).

Following the Napoleonic Wars, the British expanded their trade with the interior of Nigeria. The Berlin Conference of 1885 recognized British claims to a sphere of influence in that area, and in the following year the Royal Niger Company was chartered. Direct British control of the territory was initiated in 1900, and in 1914 the amalgamation of Northern and Southern Nigeria into the Colony and Protectorate of Nigeria was effected. In 1960, following a number of territorial and constitutional changes, Nigeria was granted independence within the British Commonwealth as a federation of the Northern, Western and Eastern regions. Nigeria altered its political relationship with Great Britain on Oct. 1, 1963, by proclaiming itself a republic. It did, however, elect to remain a member of the Commonwealth of Nations.

On May 30, 1967, the Eastern Region of the republic an area occupied principally by the proud and resourceful Ibo tribe – seceded from Nigeria and proclaimed itself the independent Republic of Biafra with Odumegwu Ojukwu as Chief of State. Civil war erupted and raged for 31 months. Casualties, including civilian, were about two million, the majority succumbing to malnutrition and disease. Biafra surrendered to the federal government on January 15, 1970.

For earlier coinage refer to British West Africa.

Arms Mottos
Short: Unity and faith
Long: Unity and Faith, Peace and Progress

BRITISH COLONY

DECIMAL COINAGE

KM# 16 1000 NAIRA
47.5400 g., 0.9166 Gold 1.4010 oz. AGW **Ruler:** Elizabeth II
Subject: 100 Years - Banking in Nigeria **Obv:** Arms with
supporters **Rev:** Bank building **Edge:** Reeded

Date	Mintage	F	VF	XF	Unc	BU
1994 Proof	100	Value: 2,250				

NIUE

Niue, or Savage Island, a dependent state of New Zealand is located in the Pacific Ocean east of Tonga and southeast of Samoa. The size is 100 sq. mi. (260 sq. km.) with a population of *2,000. Chief village and port is Alofi. Bananas and copra are exported.

Discovered by Captain Cook in 1774, it was originally part of the Cook Islands administration but has been separate since 1922.

MINT MARK
PM - Pobjoy Mint

NEW ZEALAND DEPENDENT STATE

DECIMAL COINAGE

KM# 81 10 DOLLARS
1.2440 g., 0.9990 Gold .0400 oz. AGW **Subject:** Liberty Gold Bullion **Obv:** Crowned head right **Rev:** Statue of Liberty

Date	Mintage	F	VF	XF	Unc	BU
1997	—	—	—	—	30.00	—

KM# 93 20 DOLLARS
1.2440 g., 0.9990 Gold .0400 oz. AGW **Obv:** Crowned arms within sprigs **Rev:** Bust facing **Rev. Legend:** …The People's Princess

Date	Mintage	F	VF	XF	Unc	BU
1997 Proof	Est. 10,000	Value: 30.00

KM# 94 20 DOLLARS
1.2440 g., 0.9990 Gold .0400 oz. AGW **Obv:** Crowned arms within sprigs **Rev:** Bust facing **Rev. Legend:** …Princess of Wales

Date	Mintage	F	VF	XF	Unc	BU
1997 Proof	Est. 10,000	Value: 30.00

KM# 95 20 DOLLARS
1.2440 g., 0.9990 Gold .0400 oz. AGW **Obv:** Crowned arms within sprigs **Rev:** Head left above sprigs **Rev. Legend:** …Princess of Wales

Date	Mintage	F	VF	XF	Unc	BU
1997 Proof	Est. 10,000	Value: 30.00

KM# 106 20 DOLLARS
1.2440 g., 0.9990 Gold .0400 oz. AGW **Obv:** Crowned head right **Rev:** Bust facing **Rev. Legend:** …In Memoriam

Date	Mintage	F	VF	XF	Unc	BU
1998 Proof	Est. 10,000	Value: 30.00

KM# 107 20 DOLLARS
1.2440 g., 0.9990 Gold .0400 oz. AGW **Obv:** Crowned head right **Rev:** Bust facing **Rev. Legend:** …Princess of Wales

Date	Mintage	F	VF	XF	Unc	BU
1998 Proof	Est. 10,000	Value: 30.00

KM# 117 20 DOLLARS
1.2400 g., 0.9990 Gold .0395 oz. AGW **Subject:** 50th Anniversary of Peanuts **Obv:** Crowned head right **Rev:** Snoopy and Woodstock

Date	Mintage	F	VF	XF	Unc	BU
2000 Proof	Est. 10,000	Value: 32.00

KM# 125 20 DOLLARS
1.2400 g., 0.9999 Gold .0399 oz. AGW, 13.9 mm. **Subject:** Snoopy as an Ace **Obv:** Crowned head right **Rev:** Snoopy flying his dog house **Edge:** Reeded

Date	Mintage	F	VF	XF	Unc	BU
2001 Proof	10,000	Value: 32.00

KM# 148 20 DOLLARS
1.2400 g., 0.9999 Gold 0.0399 oz. AGW, 13.92 mm. **Subject:** Pokémon Series **Obv:** Crowned shield within sprigs **Rev:** Pikachu **Edge:** Reeded

Date	Mintage	F	VF	XF	Unc	BU
2002PM Proof	10,000	Value: 30.00

KM# 153 20 DOLLARS
1.2400 g., 0.9999 Gold 0.0399 oz. AGW, 13.9 mm. **Subject:** Pokémon Series **Obv:** Crowned shield within sprigs **Rev:** Pichu **Edge:** Reeded

Date	Mintage	F	VF	XF	Unc	BU
2002PM Proof	10,000	Value: 30.00

KM# 158 20 DOLLARS
1.2400 g., 0.9999 Gold 0.0399 oz. AGW, 13.92 mm. **Subject:** Pokémon Series **Obv:** Crowned shield within sprigs **Rev:** Mewtwo **Edge:** Reeded

Date	Mintage	F	VF	XF	Unc	BU
2002PM Proof	10,000	Value: 30.00

KM# 163 20 DOLLARS
, 13.9 mm. **Subject:** Pokémon Series **Obv:** Crowned shield within sprigs **Rev:** Entei **Edge:** Reeded

Date	Mintage	F	VF	XF	Unc	BU
2002PM Proof	10,000	Value: 30.00

KM# 168 20 DOLLARS
1.2400 g., 0.9999 Gold 0.0399 oz. AGW, 13.9 mm. **Subject:** Pokémon Series **Obv:** Crowned shield within sprigs **Rev:** Celebi **Edge:** Reeded

Date	Mintage	F	VF	XF	Unc	BU
2002PM Proof	10,000	Value: 30.00

KM# 79 25 DOLLARS
1.2441 g., 0.9990 Gold .0400 oz. AGW **Obv:** Crowned arms within sprigs **Rev:** Half length bust left

Date	Mintage	F	VF	XF	Unc	BU
1994 Proof	Est. 25,000	Value: 30.00

KM# 82 25 DOLLARS
3.1000 g., 0.9990 Gold .1000 oz. AGW **Series:** Liberty Gold Bullion **Obv:** Crowned head right **Rev:** Statue of Liberty

Date	Mintage	F	VF	XF	Unc	BU
1997	—	—	—	—	—	70.00

KM# 96 25 DOLLARS
3.1000 g., 0.9990 Gold .1000 oz. AGW **Obv:** Crowned arms within sprigs **Rev:** Bust facing **Rev. Legend:** …The People's Princess

Date	Mintage	F	VF	XF	Unc	BU
1997 Proof	Est. 7,500	Value: 70.00

KM# 97 25 DOLLARS
3.1000 g., 0.9990 Gold .1000 oz. AGW **Obv:** Crowned arms within sprigs **Rev:** Bust facing **Rev. Legend:** …Princess of Wales

Date	Mintage	F	VF	XF	Unc	BU
1997 Proof	Est. 7,500	Value: 70.00

KM# 98 25 DOLLARS
3.1000 g., 0.9990 Gold .1000 oz. AGW **Obv:** Crowned arms within sprigs **Rev:** Head left above sprigs **Rev. Legend:** …Princess of Wales

Date	Mintage	F	VF	XF	Unc	BU
1997 Proof	Est. 7,500	Value: 70.00

KM# 71 50 DOLLARS
7.7000 g., 0.5830 Gold .1444 oz. AGW **Series:** Olympics **Obv:** Crowned arms within sprigs **Rev:** Discus thrower

Date	Mintage	F	VF	XF	Unc	BU
1992 Proof	6,000	Value: 120

KM# 66 50 DOLLARS
7.7760 g., 0.5830 Gold .1458 oz. AGW **Obv:** Crowned arms within sprigs **Rev:** Bust left and rocket launch

Date	Mintage	F	VF	XF	Unc	BU
1993 Proof	—	Value: 100

KM# 83 50 DOLLARS
6.2200 g., 0.9990 Gold .2000 oz. AGW **Series:** Liberty Gold Bullion **Obv:** Crowned head right **Rev:** Statue of Liberty

Date	Mintage	F	VF	XF	Unc	BU
1997	—	—	—	—	—	140

KM# 108 50 DOLLARS
3.1100 g., 0.9999 Gold .1000 oz. AGW **Obv:** Crowned head right **Rev:** Bust facing **Rev. Legend:** …In Memoriam

Date	Mintage	F	VF	XF	Unc	BU
1998 Proof	Est. 7,500	Value: 70.00

KM# 109 50 DOLLARS
3.1100 g., 0.9999 Gold .1000 oz. AGW **Obv:** Crowned head right **Rev:** Bust facing **Rev. Legend:** …Princess of Wales

Date	Mintage	F	VF	XF	Unc	BU
1998 Proof	Est. 7,500	Value: 70.00

KM# 118 50 DOLLARS
3.1103 g., 0.9999 Gold .1000 oz. AGW **Subject:** 50th Anniversary of Peanuts **Obv:** Crowned head right **Rev:** Snoopy and Woodstock

Date	Mintage	F	VF	XF	Unc	BU
2000 Proof	Est. 7,500	Value: 70.00

KM# 126 50 DOLLARS
3.1100 g., 0.9999 Gold .1000 oz. AGW, 17.9 mm. **Subject:** Snoopy as an Ace **Obv:** Crowned head right **Rev:** Snoopy flying his dog house **Edge:** Reeded

Date	Mintage	F	VF	XF	Unc	BU
2001 Proof	7,500	Value: 70.00

KM# 149 50 DOLLARS
3.1100 g., 0.9999 Gold 0.1 oz. AGW, 17.9 mm. **Subject:** Pokémon Series **Obv:** Crowned shield within sprigs **Rev:** Pikachu **Edge:** Reeded

Date	Mintage	F	VF	XF	Unc	BU
2002PM Proof	7,500	Value: 70.00

KM# 154 50 DOLLARS
3.1100 g., 0.9999 Gold 0.1 oz. AGW, 17.9 mm. **Subject:** Pokémon Series **Obv:** Crowned shield within sprigs **Rev:** Pichu **Edge:** Reeded

Date	Mintage	F	VF	XF	Unc	BU
2002PM Proof	7,500	Value: 70.00

KM# 159 50 DOLLARS
3.1100 g., 0.9999 Gold 0.1 oz. AGW, 17.9 mm. **Subject:** Pokémon Series **Obv:** Crowned shield within sprigs **Rev:** Mewtwo **Edge:** Reeded

Date	Mintage	F	VF	XF	Unc	BU
2002PM Proof	7,500	Value: 70.00

KM# 164 50 DOLLARS
3.1100 g., 0.9999 Gold 0.1 oz. AGW, 17.9 mm. **Subject:** Pokémon Series **Obv:** Crowned shield within sprigs **Rev:** Entei **Edge:** Reeded

Date	Mintage	F	VF	XF	Unc	BU
2002PM Proof	7,500	Value: 70.00

KM# 169 50 DOLLARS
3.1100 g., 0.9999 Gold 0.1 oz. AGW, 17.9 mm. **Subject:** Pokémon Series **Obv:** Crowned shield within sprigs **Rev:** Celebi **Edge:** Reeded

Date	Mintage	F	VF	XF	Unc	BU
2002PM Proof	7,500	Value: 70.00

KM# 84 100 DOLLARS
15.5517 g., 0.9990 Gold .5000 oz. AGW **Series:** Liberty Gold Bullion **Obv:** Crowned head right **Rev:** Statue of Liberty

Date	Mintage	F	VF	XF	Unc	BU
1997 Proof	—	Value: 350

KM# 99 100 DOLLARS
6.2200 g., 0.9990 Gold .2000 oz. AGW **Obv:** Crowned arms within sprigs **Rev:** Bust facing **Rev. Legend:** …The People's Princess

Date	Mintage	F	VF	XF	Unc	BU
1997 Proof	Est. 5,000	Value: 140

KM# 100 100 DOLLARS
6.2200 g., 0.9990 Gold .2000 oz. AGW **Obv:** Crowned arms within sprigs **Rev:** Bust facing **Rev. Legend:** …Princess of Wales

Date	Mintage	F	VF	XF	Unc	BU
1997 Proof	Est. 5,000	Value: 140

KM# 101 100 DOLLARS
6.2200 g., 0.9990 Gold .2000 oz. AGW **Obv:** Crowned arms within sprigs **Rev:** Head left above sprigs **Rev. Legend:** …Princess of Wales

Date	Mintage	F	VF	XF	Unc	BU
1997 Proof	Est. 5,000	Value: 140

KM# 110 100 DOLLARS
6.2200 g., 0.9990 Gold .2000 oz. AGW **Obv:** Crowned head right **Rev:** Bust facing **Rev. Legend:** …In Memoriam

Date	Mintage	F	VF	XF	Unc	BU
1998 Proof	Est. 5,000	Value: 140

KM# 111 100 DOLLARS
6.2200 g., 0.9990 Gold .2000 oz. AGW **Obv:** Crowned head right **Rev:** Bust facing **Rev. Legend:** …Princess of Wales

Date	Mintage	F	VF	XF	Unc	BU
1998 Proof	Est. 5,000	Value: 140

KM# 119 100 DOLLARS
6.2200 g., 0.9990 Gold .2000 oz. AGW **Subject:** 50th Anniversary of Peanuts **Obv:** Crowned head right **Rev:** Snoopy and Woodstock

Date	Mintage	F	VF	XF	Unc	BU
2000 Proof	Est. 5,000	Value: 140

KM# 127 100 DOLLARS
6.2200 g., 0.9990 Gold .2000 oz. AGW, 22 mm. **Subject:** Snoopy as an Ace **Obv:** Crowned head right **Rev:** Snoopy flying his dog house **Edge:** Reeded

Date	Mintage	F	VF	XF	Unc	BU
2001 Proof	5,000	Value: 140

KM# 150 100 DOLLARS
6.2200 g., 0.9999 Gold 0.2 oz. AGW, 22 mm. **Subject:** Pokémon Series **Obv:** Crowned shield within sprigs **Rev:** Pikachu **Edge:** Reeded

Date	Mintage	F	VF	XF	Unc	BU
2002PM Proof	5,000	Value: 140

KM# 155 100 DOLLARS
6.2200 g., 0.9999 Gold 0.2 oz. AGW, 22 mm. **Subject:** Pokémon Series **Obv:** Crowned shield within sprigs **Rev:** Pichu **Edge:** Reeded

Date	Mintage	F	VF	XF	Unc	BU
2002PM Proof	5,000	Value: 140				

KM# 160 100 DOLLARS
6.2200 g., 0.9999 Gold 0.2 oz. AGW, 22 mm. **Subject:** Pokémon Series **Obv:** Crowned shield within sprigs **Rev:** Mewtwo **Edge:** Reeded

Date	Mintage	F	VF	XF	Unc	BU
2002PM Proof	5,000	Value: 140				

KM# 165 100 DOLLARS
6.2200 g., 0.9999 Gold 0.2 oz. AGW, 22 mm. **Subject:** Pokémon Series **Obv:** Crowned shield within sprigs **Rev:** Entei **Edge:** Reeded

Date	Mintage	F	VF	XF	Unc	BU
2002PM Proof	5,000	Value: 140				

KM# 170 100 DOLLARS
6.2200 g., 0.9999 Gold 0.2 oz. AGW, 22 mm. **Subject:** Pokémon Series **Obv:** Crowned shield within sprigs **Rev:** Celebi **Edge:** reeded

Date	Mintage	F	VF	XF	Unc	BU
2002PM Proof	5,000	Value: 140				

KM# 42 200 DOLLARS
6.9117 g., 0.9000 Gold .2000 oz. AGW **Obv:** Crowned arms within sprigs **Rev:** General Douglas MacArthur 1/4 left

Date	Mintage	F	VF	XF	Unc	BU
1989 Proof	Est. 2,500	Value: 140				

KM# 50 200 DOLLARS
6.9117 g., 0.9000 Gold .2000 oz. AGW **Obv:** Crowned arms within sprigs **Rev:** General George S. Patton

Date	Mintage	F	VF	XF	Unc	BU
1989 Proof	—	Value: 140				

KM# 45 200 DOLLARS
6.9117 g., 0.9000 Gold .2000 oz. AGW **Obv:** Crowned arms within sprigs **Rev:** General Dwight David Eisenhower in front of flags

Date	Mintage	F	VF	XF	Unc	BU
1990 Proof	2,500	Value: 140				

KM# 51 200 DOLLARS
6.9117 g., 0.9000 Gold .2000 oz. AGW **Obv:** Crowned arms within sprigs **Rev:** Admiral William Halsey

Date	Mintage	F	VF	XF	Unc	BU
1990 Proof	—	Value: 140				

KM# 52 200 DOLLARS
6.9117 g., 0.9000 Gold .2000 oz. AGW **Obv:** Crowned arms within sprigs **Rev:** President Franklin D. Roosevelt

Date	Mintage	F	VF	XF	Unc	BU
1990 Proof	—	Value: 140				

KM# 53 200 DOLLARS
6.9117 g., 0.9000 Gold .2000 oz. AGW **Obv:** Crowned arms within sprigs **Rev:** Sir Winston Churchill

Date	Mintage	F	VF	XF	Unc	BU
1990 Proof	—	Value: 140				

KM# 9 250 DOLLARS
8.4830 g., 0.9170 Gold .2500 oz. AGW **Series:** Olympics **Subject:** Tennis **Obv:** Crowned arms within sprigs **Rev:** Boris Becker

Date	Mintage	F	VF	XF	Unc	BU
1987 Proof	1,000	Value: 170				

KM# 10 250 DOLLARS
8.4830 g., 0.9170 Gold .2500 oz. AGW **Subject:** 24th Olympiad Tennis Games, Seoul 1988 **Obv:** Crowned arms within sprigs **Rev:** Steffi Graf

Date	Mintage	F	VF	XF	Unc	BU
1987 Proof	1,000	Value: 175				

KM# 20 250 DOLLARS
10.0000 g., 0.9170 Gold .2948 oz. AGW **Obv:** Crowned arms within sprigs **Rev:** John F. Kennedy left

Date	Mintage	F	VF	XF	Unc	BU
1988 Proof	5,000	Value: 200				

KM# 39 250 DOLLARS
10.0000 g., 0.9170 Gold .2948 oz. AGW **Subject:** Soccer **Obv:** Crowned arms within sprigs **Rev:** Soccer player to left of cameo

Date	Mintage	F	VF	XF	Unc	BU
1988 Proof	Est. 5,000	Value: 200				

KM# 41 250 DOLLARS
10.0000 g., 0.9170 Gold .2948 oz. AGW **Subject:** 24th Olympic Games, Seoul 1988 **Obv:** Crowned arms within sprigs **Rev:** Cameos of Navratilova, Graf and Evert, tennis champions

Date	Mintage	F	VF	XF	Unc	BU
1988 Proof	Est. 5,000	Value: 215				

KM# 48 250 DOLLARS
10.0000 g., 0.9170 Gold .2948 oz. AGW **Subject:** 24th Olympic Games, Seoul 1988 **Obv:** Crowned arms within sprigs **Rev:** Steffi Graf with cup

Date	Mintage	F	VF	XF	Unc	BU
1988 Proof	5,000	Value: 210				

KM# 26 250 DOLLARS
10.0000 g., 0.9170 Gold .2948 oz. AGW **Series:** Davis Cup Tennis **Obv:** Crowned arms within sprigs **Rev:** Davis cup

Date	Mintage	F	VF	XF	Unc	BU
1989 Proof	500	Value: 275				

KM# 49 250 DOLLARS
10.0000 g., 0.9170 Gold .2948 oz. AGW **Subject:** 24th Olympic Games, Seoul 1988 **Obv:** Crowned arms within sprigs **Rev:** Steffi Graf

Date	Mintage	F	VF	XF	Unc	BU
1989 Proof	3,000	Value: 210				

KM# 54 250 DOLLARS
10.0000 g., 0.9170 Gold .2948 oz. AGW **Subject:** Soccer - Italian **Obv:** Crowned arms within sprigs

Date	Mintage	F	VF	XF	Unc	BU
1990 Proof	Est. 2,500	Value: 210				

KM# 112 250 DOLLARS
15.5500 g., 0.9999 Gold .5000 oz. AGW **Obv:** Crowned head right **Rev:** Bust facing **Rev. Legend:** ...In Memoriam

Date	Mintage	F	VF	XF	Unc	BU
1998 Proof	Est. 3,000	Value: 345				

NORTHERN MARIANA ISLANDS

COMMONWEALTH
US Administration

MEDALLIC COINAGE

X# 2 5 DOLLARS
1.2440 g., 0.9999 Gold 0.04 oz. AGW, 13.92 mm. **Subject:** Discovered by Ferdinand Magellen **Obv:** Emblem above eagle **Rev:** Spanish galleon **Edge:** Reeded

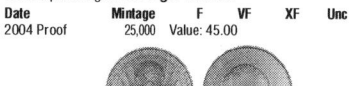

Date	Mintage	F	VF	XF	Unc	BU
2004 Proof	25,000	Value: 45.00				

X# 4 5 DOLLARS
1.2440 g., 0.9999 Gold 0.04 oz. AGW, 13.92 mm. **Obv:** Emblem above eagle **Rev:** Bust of Pope John Paul II facing **Edge:** Reeded

Date	Mintage	F	VF	XF	Unc	BU
2004 Proof	15,000	Value: 50.00				

X# 6 5 DOLLARS
1.2440 g., 0.9999 Gold 0.04 oz. AGW, 13.92 mm. **Obv:** Emblem above eagle **Rev:** Einstein sticking his tongue out **Edge:** Reeded

Date	Mintage	F	VF	XF	Unc	BU
2004 Proof	25,000	Value: 50.00				

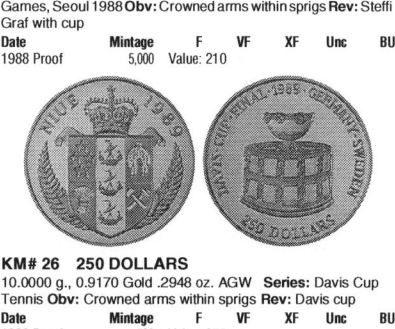

544 NORWAY

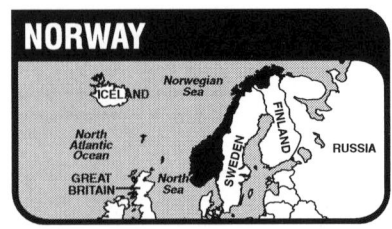

NORWAY

The Kingdom of Norway (*Norge, Noreg*), a constitutional monarchy located in northwestern Europe, has an area of 150,000 sq. mi. (324,220 sq. km.), including the island territories of Spitzbergen (Svalbard) and Jan Mayen, and a population of *4.2 million. Capital: Oslo (Christiana). The diversified economic base of Norway includes shipping, fishing, forestry, agriculture, and manufacturing. Nonferrous metals, paper and paperboard, paper pulp, iron, steel and oil are exported.

A united Norwegian kingdom was established in the 9th century, the era of the indomitable Norse Vikings who ranged far and wide, visiting the coasts of northwestern Europe, the Mediterranean, Greenland and North America. In the 13th century the Norse kingdom was united briefly with Sweden, then passed through inheritance in 1380 to the rule of Denmark which was maintained until 1814. In 1814 Norway fell again under the rule of Sweden. The union lasted until 1905 when the Norwegian Parliament arranged a peaceful separation and invited a Danish prince (King Haakon VII) to ascend the throne of an independent Kingdom of Norway.

RULERS
Danish, until 1814
Swedish, 1814-1905
Haakon VII, 1905-1957
Olav V, 1957-1991
Harald V, 1991-

MINT MARKS
(h) - Crossed hammers – Kongsberg

MINT OFFICIALS' INITIALS
Kongsberg

AB, B	1961-1980	Arne Jon Bakken
AB*	1980	Ole R. Kolberg
B	1861	Brynjulf Bergslien
CHL, star(s)	1836-88	Caspar Herman Langberg in Kongsberg
I, IT	1880-1918	Ivar Trondsen, engraver
IAR		Angrid Austlid Rise, engraver
IGM	1797-1806	Johan Georg Madelung in Altona
IGP	1807-24	Johan Georg Prahm in Kongsberg
JMK	1825-36	Johan Michael Kruse in Kongsberg
K	1981	Ole R. Kolberg
M	1815-30	Gregorius Middelthun
OH	1959	Oivind Hansen, engraver

Lettered Edges for Kongsberg Mint

Number	Edges
1	HAEC BOREAS CYMBRO FERT ORNAMENTO LABORUM
2	DET KLIPPERNE YDER VOR BERGMAND UDBRYDER HVA HYTTEN DA GYDER AF MYNTEN VI NYDER
3	DANNER KONGIS NORDSKE FIELDE SLIGE FRUGTER HAR I VAELDE
4	I DETTE ANSIGT DANNEMARK OG NORGE SKUER SIN MONARK
5	NICHT AUS SILBER-SUCHT DIESE NORDENS-FRUCHT WIRD ZU GOTTES EHR GESUCHT
6	STORE KONGE NORDENS AERE LAD DE FRUGTER YNDIG VAERE SOM DIG NORSKE KLIPPER BAERE
7	VAERE SOM DIG NORSKE SAADAN NORDENS SKAT GUD GIEMTE TIL KONG CHRISTIAN DEND FEMTE

MONETARY SYSTEM
1794-1873
120 Skilling = 1 Speciedaler
1873-
100 Ore = 1 Krone (30 Skilling)

KINGDOM
DECIMAL COINAGE

KM# 347 10 KRONER
4.4803 g., 0.9000 Gold .1296 oz. AGW **Obv:** Head right **Obv. Legend:** OSCAR II NORGES... **Rev:** Crowned arms divides value

Date	Mintage	VG	F	VF	XF	Unc
1874	24,000	—	200	450	700	1,000

KM# 358 10 KRONER
4.4803 g., 0.9000 Gold .1296 oz. AGW **Obv:** Head right **Obv. Legend:** OSCAR II NORGES... **Rev:** Crowned arms within wreath

Date	Mintage	VG	F	VF	XF	Unc
1877	20,000	—	250	450	650	950
1902	24,100	BV	100	200	375	600

KM# 375 10 KRONER
4.4803 g., 0.9000 Gold .1296 oz. AGW **Ruler:** Haakon VII **Obv:** Crowned head right **Rev:** King Olaf Haraldson, the Saint

Date	Mintage	F	VF	XF	Unc	BU
1910	52,600	BV	165	275	450	—

KM# 348 20 KRONER
8.9606 g., 0.9000 Gold .2593 oz. AGW **Obv:** Head right **Obv. Legend:** OSCAR II NORGES... **Rev:** Crowned arms divides value

Date	Mintage	VG	F	VF	XF	Unc
1874	198,000	—	100	150	300	500
1875	105,000	—	100	150	300	450

KM# 355 20 KRONER
8.9600 g., 0.9000 Gold .2593 oz. AGW **Obv:** Head right **Obv. Legend:** OSCAR II NORGES... **Rev:** Crowned arms within wreath

Date	Mintage	VG	F	VF	XF	Unc
1876	109,000	—	BV	150	250	400
1877	38,000	—	150	250	450	700
1878	139,000	—	BV	150	225	375
1879	46,000	—	BV	150	225	375
1883	36,000	—	3,000	6,000	9,000	12,500
1886	101,000	—	BV	150	225	400
1902	50,400	—	—	BV	200	350

KM# 376 20 KRONER
8.9600 g., 0.9000 Gold .2593 oz. AGW **Ruler:** Haakon VII **Obv:** Crowned head right **Rev:** King Olaf II, the Saint

Date	Mintage	F	VF	XF	Unc	BU
1910	250,000	BV	185	275	450	—

KM# 435 1500 KRONER
17.0000 g., 0.9170 Gold .5 oz. AGW **Ruler:** Olav V **Subject:** 1994 Olympics **Obv:** Head left **Rev:** Ancient Norwegian skier

Date	Mintage	VG	F	VF	XF	BU
1991 Proof	30,000	Value: 375				

KM# 442 1500 KRONER
17.0000 g., 0.9170 Gold .5 oz. AGW **Ruler:** Harald V **Subject:** 1994 Olympics **Obv:** Head right **Rev:** Birkebeiners **Designer:** Ingrid Austlid Rise

Date	Mintage	VG	F	VF	XF	BU
1992 Proof	30,000	Value: 375				

KM# 445 1500 KRONER
17.0000 g., 0.9170 Gold .5 oz. AGW **Ruler:** Harald V **Subject:** World Cycling Championships **Obv:** Arms **Rev:** Two 19th century cyclists

Date	Mintage	VG	F	VF	XF	BU
1993 Proof	6,390	Value: 500				

KM# 446 1500 KRONER
17.0000 g., 0.9170 Gold .5 oz. AGW **Ruler:** Harald V **Subject:** Edvard Grieg **Obv:** Crowned shield **Rev:** Figure playing piano

Date	Mintage	VG	F	VF	XF	BU
1993 Proof	5,139	Value: 550				

KM# 451 1500 KRONER
17.0000 g., 0.9170 Gold .5 oz. AGW **Ruler:** Harald V **Subject:** 1994 Olympics **Obv:** Head right **Rev:** Telemark skier **Designer:** Ingrid Austlid Rise

Date	Mintage	VG	F	VF	XF	BU
1993 Proof	30,000	Value: 385				

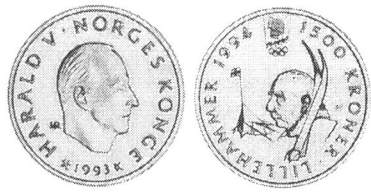

KM# 452 1500 KRONER
17.0000 g., 0.9170 Gold .5 oz. AGW **Ruler:** Harald V **Subject:** Roald Amundsen **Obv:** Head right **Rev:** Bust left with skis on shoulder **Designer:** Ingrid Austlid Rise

Date	Mintage	VG	F	VF	XF	BU
1993 Proof	22,000	Value: 450				

OMAN 545

KM# 467 1500 KRONER
16.9600 g., 0.9170 Gold .4994 oz. AGW **Ruler:** Olav V **Subject:** Year 2000 **Obv:** Head right **Rev:** Tree and roots

Date	Mintage	VG	F	VF	XF	BU
2000 Proof	7,500	Value: 425				

KM# 470 1500 KRONER
16.9600 g., 0.9170 Gold .5000 oz. AGW, 27 mm. **Ruler:** Harald V **Subject:** Nobel Peace Prize Centennial **Obv:** Head right **Rev:** Reverse design of the prize medal **Edge:** Plain

Date	Mintage	VG	F	VF	XF	BU
ND(2001) Matte Proof	7,500	Value: 385				

KM# 473 1500 KRONER
16.9600 g., 0.9170 Gold 0.5 oz. AGW, 27 mm. **Ruler:** Harald V **Subject:** 1905 Liberation **Obv:** Three kings **Rev:** Various leaf types **Edge:** Plain

Date	Mintage	F	VF	XF	Unc	BU
2003 Proof	10,000	Value: 525				

KM# 475 1500 KRONER
16.9600 g., 0.9170 Gold 0.5 oz. AGW, 27 mm. **Ruler:** Harald V **Subject:** 1905 Liberation **Obv:** Three kings **Rev:** Liquid drops on hard surface **Edge:** Plain

Date	Mintage	F	VF	XF	Unc	BU
2004 Proof	10,000	Value: 525				

KM# 477 1500 KRONER
16.9600 g., 0.9170 Gold 0.5 oz. AGW, 27 mm. **Ruler:** Harald V **Obv:** Three kings **Rev:** Binary language **Edge:** Plain

Date	Mintage	F	VF	XF	Unc	BU
2005 Proof	—	Value: 525				

OCCUSSI - AMBENO
SULTANATE
MEDALLIC COINAGE

X# 9 15 DOLLARS
3.1300 g., 0.9999 Gold 0.1006 oz. AGW, 18 mm. **Issuer:** State Bank **Subject:** Year of the Ox **Obv:** Crown **Rev:** Ox drinking water **Edge:** Reeded

Date	Mintage	F	VF	XF	Unc	BU
1997 Proof	3,000	Value: 295				

X# 10 25 DOLLARS
7.7400 g., 0.9999 Gold 0.2488 oz. AGW, 22.9 mm. **Issuer:** State Bank **Subject:** First directly elected President and Vice-president of Taiwan **Obv:** Crown **Rev:** Busts of President and Vice-president facing **Edge:** Reeded

Date	Mintage	F	VF	XF	Unc	BU
1996 Proof	3,100	Value: 325				

X# 11 50 DOLLARS
15.5100 g., 0.9999 Gold 0.4986 oz. AGW, 30 mm. **Issuer:** State Bank **Subject:** First directly elected President and Vice-president of Taiwan **Obv:** Crown **Rev:** Busts of President and Vice-president facing **Edge:** Reeded

Date	Mintage	F	VF	XF	Unc	BU
1996 Proof	5,100	Value: 525				

X# 12 50 DOLLARS
15.5100 g., 0.9999 Gold 0.4986 oz. AGW, 30 mm. **Issuer:** State Bank **Subject:** Year of the Ox **Obv:** Crown **Rev:** Water buffalo cow lying with calf **Edge:** Reeded

Date	Mintage	F	VF	XF	Unc	BU
1997 Proof	3,000	Value: 525				

OMAN

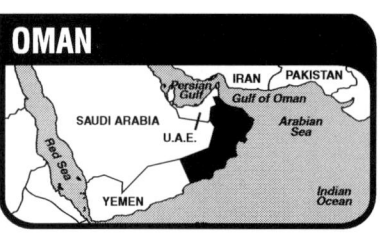

The Sultanate of Oman (formerly Muscat and Oman), an independent monarchy located in the southeastern part of the Arabian Peninsula, has an area of 82,030 sq. mi. (212,460 sq. km.) and a population of *1.3 million. Capital: Muscat. The economy is based on agriculture, herding and petroleum. Petroleum products, dates, fish and hides are exported.

The Portuguese who captured Muscat, the capital and chief port, in 1508, made the first European contact with Muscat and Oman. They occupied the city, utilizing it as a naval base and factory and holding it against land and sea attacks by Arabs and Persians until finally ejected by local Arabs in 1650. It was next occupied by the Persians who maintained control until 1741, when it was taken by Ahmed ibn Sa'id of the present ruling family. Muscat and Oman was the most powerful state in Arabia during the first half of the 19th century, until weakened by the persistent attack of interior nomadic tribes. British influence, initiated by the signing of a treaty of friendship with the Sultanate in 1798, remains a dominant fact of the civil and military phases of the government, although Britain recognizes the Sultanate as a sovereign state.

Sultan Sa'id bin Taimur was overthrown by his son, Qabus bin Sa'id, on July 23, 1970. The new sultan changed the nation's name to Sultanate of Oman.

TITLES
Muscat
Oman

SULTANATE
DECIMAL COINAGE

1000 (new) Baisa = 1 Saidi Rial

KM# 42 1/2 SAIDI RIAL
25.6000 g., 0.9170 Gold .7548 oz. AGW **Obv:** National arms within circle **Rev:** Value and date

Date	Mintage	F	VF	XF	Unc	BU
AH1391 (1971) Proof	100	Value: 700				

Note: Struck for presentation purposes

KM# 44 SAIDI RIAL
46.6500 g., 0.9170 Gold 1.3755 oz. AGW **Obv:** National arms within circle with star and moon border **Rev:** Value and date

Date	Mintage	F	VF	XF	Unc	BU
AH1391 (1971) Proof	100	Value: 1,000				
AH1394 (1974) Proof	250	Value: 1,000				

Note: Struck for presentation purposes

KM# 43 15 SAIDI RIALS
5.8100 g., 0.9170 Gold .1713 oz. AGW **Obv:** National arms **Rev:** Value

Date	Mintage	F	VF	XF	Unc	BU
AH1391 (1971) Proof	112	Value: 650				

Note: Struck for presentation purposes

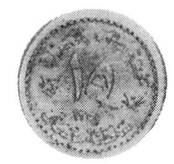

OMAN

KM# 53 15 SAIDI RIALS
7.9800 g., 0.9170 Gold .2353 oz. AGW **Obv:** National arms **Rev:** Value and date

Date	Mintage	F	VF	XF	Unc	BU
AH1391 (1971) Proof	224	Value: 550				

Note: Struck for presentation purposes

REFORM COINAGE

1000 Baisa = 1 Omani Rial

KM# 45 25 BAISA
5.9600 g., 0.9170 Gold .1757 oz. AGW, 18 mm. **Obv:** National arms **Rev:** Value and date

Date	Mintage	F	VF	XF	Unc	BU
AH1392 (1972)	100	—	—	—	150	—
AH1392 (1972) Proof	50	Value: 200				
AH1394 (1974) Proof	250	Value: 150				
AH1395 (1975) Proof	250	Value: 150				

Note: Struck for presentation purposes

KM# 46 50 BAISA
12.8900 g., 0.9170 Gold .3801 oz. AGW **Obv:** National arms **Rev:** Value and date

Date	Mintage	F	VF	XF	Unc	BU
AH1392 (1972)	200	—	—	—	285	—
AH1392 (1972) Proof	50	Value: 325				
AH1394 (1974) Proof	250	Value: 285				
AH1395 (1975) Proof	250	Value: 285				

Note: Struck for presentation purposes

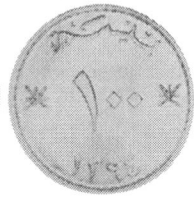

KM# 47 100 BAISA
22.7400 g., 0.9170 Gold .6705 oz. AGW **Obv:** National arms **Rev:** Value and date

Date	Mintage	F	VF	XF	Unc	BU
AH1392 (1972)	200	—	—	—	500	—
AH1392 (1972) Proof	50	Value: 550				
AH1394 (1974) Proof	250	Value: 500				
AH1395 (1975) Proof	250	Value: 500				

Note: Struck for presentation purposes

KM# 57 1/4 OMANI RIAL
12.8900 g., 0.9170 Gold .3799 oz. AGW **Subject:** Fort al Hazam **Obv:** National arms **Rev:** Fort

Date	Mintage	F	VF	XF	Unc	BU
AH1397 (1976) Proof	1,000	Value: 285				
AH1408 (1987) Proof	250	Value: 425				

KM# 48 1/2 OMANI RIAL
25.6000 g., 0.9170 Gold .7548 oz. AGW **Obv:** National arms **Rev:** Value and date

Date	Mintage	F	VF	XF	Unc	BU
AH1392 (1972) Proof	124	Value: 675				
AH1394 (1974)	250	—	—	—	675	—
AH1395 (1975)	250	—	—	—	675	—

Note: Struck for presentation purposes

KM# 58 1/2 OMANI RIAL
19.6700 g., 0.9170 Gold .5797 oz. AGW **Subject:** Fort Mirbat **Obv:** National arms **Rev:** Fort

Date	Mintage	F	VF	XF	Unc	BU
AH1397 (1976) Proof	1,000	Value: 425				
AH1408 (1987) Proof	250	Value: 550				

KM# 69 1/2 OMANI RIAL
19.6700 g., 0.9170 Gold .5800 oz. AGW **Subject:** 10th National Day **Obv:** Crowned arms **Rev:** Value

Date	Mintage	VG	F	VF	XF	Unc
AH1400-1979 Proof	600	Value: 485				

Note: Struck for presentation purposes

KM# 87 1/2 OMANI RIAL
10.0000 g., 0.9170 Gold .2947 oz. AGW **Subject:** Youth Year **Obv:** National arms, date and value **Rev:** Youth with banner within sprigs

Date	Mintage	VG	F	VF	XF	Unc
AH1403-1982 Proof	1,000	Value: 285				

KM# 54 OMANI RIAL
46.6500 g., 0.9170 Gold 1.3755 oz. AGW **Obv:** National arms **Rev:** Value and date **Note:** Similar to KM#44.

Date	Mintage	F	VF	XF	Unc	BU
AH1392 (1972) Proof	124	Value: 1,000				
AH1394 (1974) Proof	250	Value: 1,000				
AH1395 (1975) Proof	250	Value: 1,000				

Note: Struck for presentation purposes

KM# 59 OMANI RIAL
25.6000 g., 0.9170 Gold .7545 oz. AGW **Subject:** Fort Buraimi **Obv:** National arms and value **Rev:** Fort

Date	Mintage	F	VF	XF	Unc	BU
AH1397 (1976) Proof	1,000	Value: 550				
AH1408 (1987) Proof	250	Value: 675				

KM# 70 OMANI RIAL
25.6000 g., 0.9170 Gold .7548 oz. AGW **Subject:** 10th National Day

Date	Mintage	F	VF	XF	Unc	BU
AH1400 (1979) Proof	300	Value: 650				

Note: Struck for presentation purposes

KM# 84a OMANI RIAL
20.0000 g., 0.9170 Gold .5894 oz. AGW, 30 mm. **Subject:** Youth Year **Obv:** National arms above value **Rev:** Youth with banner

Date	Mintage	F	VF	XF	Unc	BU
AH1403 (1982) Proof	900	Value: 435				

KM# 112 OMANI RIAL
20.0000 g., 0.9170 Gold .5894 oz. AGW **Subject:** Youth Year **Obv:** National arms **Rev:** Radiant design **Note:** Similar to 1/2 Omani Rial, KM#91.

Date	Mintage	F	VF	XF	Unc	BU
AH1413 (1992) Proof	900	Value: 450				

KM# 135 OMANI RIAL
20.0000 g., 0.9170 Gold .5894 oz. AGW **Subject:** Youth Year **Obv:** Crowned arms **Rev:** Radiant design **Note:** Similar to 1/2 Omani Rial, KM#91.

Date	Mintage	F	VF	XF	Unc	BU
AH1413 (1992) Proof; Rare	110	—	—	—	—	—

KM# 93 OMANI RIAL
39.9400 g., 0.9167 Gold 1.1771 oz. AGW **Subject:** Heritage Year **Obv:** National arms **Rev:** Radiant design **Note:** Similar to 1/2 Omani Rial, KM#92.

Date	Mintage	F	VF	XF	Unc	BU
AH1414 (1993) Proof	1,000	Value: 900				

KM# 146 OMANI RIAL
39.9400 g., 0.9167 Gold 1.1771 oz. AGW **Subject:** 250th Anniversary - Al Bu Sa'id Dynasty **Obv:** Portrait **Rev:** National arms and value **Note:** Similar to 1/2 Omani Rial, KM#111.

Date	Mintage	F	VF	XF	Unc	BU
AH1414 (1994) Proof	500	Value: 975				

KM# 140a OMANI RIAL
22.8000 g., 0.9160 Gold .6715 oz. AGW **Subject:** 25th National Day Anniversary - Burj Al Nahda **Obv:** National arms **Rev:** Burj Al Nahda

Date	Mintage	F	VF	XF	Unc	BU
1995 Proof	—	Value: 500				

KM# 102 OMANI RIAL
37.8000 g., 0.9160 Gold 1.1132 oz. AGW **Subject:** 26th National Day Anniversary - Sultanah **Obv:** National arms **Rev:** Sailing ship - Sultanah within circle

Date	Mintage	F	VF	XF	Unc	BU
1996 Proof	—	Value: 825				

KM# 136a OMANI RIAL
37.8000 g., 0.9167 Gold 1.1141 oz. AGW, 38.6 mm. **Subject:** 27th National Day Anniversary - Al Nahdha **Rev:** Al Nahdha Tower, coconut tree and Frankincense tree from the Dhofar Region

Date	Mintage	F	VF	XF	Unc	BU
AH1418-1997 Proof	—	Value: 825				

KM# 139a OMANI RIAL
37.8000 g., 0.9167 Gold 1.1141 oz. AGW, 38.6 mm. **Subject:** 28th National Day Anniversary - Private Sector Year **Obv:** National arms **Rev:** Radiant design

Date	Mintage	F	VF	XF	Unc	BU
AH1418 (1997)	—	—	—	—	825	—

KM# 149a OMANI RIAL
37.8000 g., 0.9167 Gold 1.1141 oz. AGW, 38.61 mm. **Subject:** 29th National Day Anniversary - 1420/1999 **Obv:** National arms **Rev:** Palm tree (Khalas) and camels caravan

Date	Mintage	F	VF	XF	Unc	BU
ND(1999)	—	—	—	—	825	—

KM# 147a OMANI RIAL
37.8000 g., 0.9160 Gold 1.1141 oz. AGW, 38.61 mm. **Subject:** 30th National Day **Obv:** National arms **Rev:** Factory and symbols of commerce, value in center circle **Edge:** Reeded

Date	Mintage	F	VF	XF	Unc	BU
2000	—	—	—	—	825	—

KM# 154a OMANI RIAL
37.8000 g., 0.9160 Gold 1.1132 oz. AGW, 38.6 mm. **Subject:** 31st National Day and Environment Year **Obv:** National arms **Rev:** Multicolor map design **Edge:** Reeded

Date	Mintage	F	VF	XF	Unc	BU
2001	350	—	—	—	850	—
2001 Proof	105	Value: 950				

OMAN 547

KM# 62 5 OMANI RIALS
45.6500 g., 0.9170 Gold 1.3454 oz. AGW **Subject:** 7th Anniversary - Reign of Sultan Qabus bin Sa'id **Obv:** National arms **Rev:** Bust 3/4 left

Date	Mintage	F	VF	XF	Unc	BU
AH1397 (1976) Proof	1,000	Value: 1,000				
AH1408 (1987) Proof	250	Value: 1,100				

KM# 89 5 OMANI RIALS
20.0000 g., 0.9170 Gold .5894 oz. AGW **Subject:** Agricultural Year **Obv:** National arms **Rev:** Farm fields above dates within center circle **Note:** Similar to 1/2 Omani Rial, KM#85.

Date	Mintage	F	VF	XF	Unc	BU
AH1409 (1988) Proof	200	Value: 435				

KM# 90 5 OMANI RIALS
20.0000 g., 0.9170 Gold .5894 oz. AGW **Subject:** Industry Year **Obv:** National arms **Rev:** Gears **Note:** Similar to 1/2 Omani Rial, KM#86.

Date	Mintage	F	VF	XF	Unc	BU
AH1411-1991 (1990) Proof	410	Value: 435				

KM# 141a 5 OMANI RIALS
31.0000 g., 0.9160 Gold .9130 oz. AGW **Obv:** National arms and value within circle **Rev:** Monument

Date	Mintage	F	VF	XF	Unc	BU
1995 Proof	—	Value: 675				

KM# 142a 10 OMANI RIALS
36.4000 g., 0.9160 Gold 1.0720 oz. AGW **Subject:** 25th National Day Anniversary - Central Bank **Obv:** National arms and value **Rev:** Central Bank of Oman

Date	Mintage	F	VF	XF	Unc	BU
1995 Proof	—	Value: 800				

KM# 49 15 OMANI RIALS
7.9900 g., 0.9170 Gold .2355 oz. AGW **Obv:** National arms **Rev:** Value

Date	Mintage	F	VF	XF	Unc	BU
AH1392 (1972) Proof	124	Value: 350				
AH1394 (1974)	300	—	—	—	250	—

Note: Struck for presentation purposes

KM# 55 15 OMANI RIALS
7.9900 g., 0.9170 Gold .2355 oz. AGW **Subject:** 10th National Day **Obv:** Crowned arms **Rev:** Value

Date	Mintage	F	VF	XF	Unc	BU
AH1400 (1979) Proof	1,000	Value: 400				

Note: Struck for presentation purposes

KM# 56 15 OMANI RIALS
20.0000 g., 0.9170 Gold .5897 oz. AGW **Subject:** 15th Anniversary - Reign of Sultan **Obv:** Head 1/4 left within 3/4 wreath and designed border **Rev:** Crowned arms over country map within circle

Date	Mintage	F	VF	XF	Unc	BU
AH1406 (1985) Proof	2,000	Value: 435				

KM# 56a 15 OMANI RIALS
31.0100 g., 0.9170 Gold .9144 oz. AGW **Subject:** 15th Anniversary - Reign of Sultan **Obv:** Head 1/4 left within 3/4 wreath and designed border **Rev:** Crowned arms over country map within circle

Date	Mintage	F	VF	XF	Unc	BU
AH1406 (1985) Proof	200	Value: 800				

KM# 98 20 OMANI RIALS
20.0000 g., 0.9170 Gold .5897 oz. AGW **Subject:** 20th National Day - Sultan Sa'id **Obv:** National arms **Rev:** Bust 1/4 left within circle and designs around border **Note:** Similar to 2 Omani Rials, KM#81.

Date	Mintage	F	VF	XF	Unc	BU
AH1411 (1990) Proof	1,200	Value: 450				

KM# 137.1 20 OMANI RIALS
48.6500 g., 0.9167 Gold 1.4338 oz. AGW **Subject:** 20th Anniversary of Sultan's Reign **Obv:** Crowned arms within designed circle, legend above and below **Rev:** Value within designed circle with dates below flanked by leaves

Date	Mintage	F	VF	XF	Unc	BU
AH1411 (1990)	500	—	—	—	1,100	—

KM# 137.2 20 OMANI RIALS
65.3700 g., 0.9170 Gold 1.9273 oz. AGW **Subject:** 20th Anniversary of Sultan's Reign **Obv:** Crowned arms within designed circle with legend above and below **Rev:** Value within designed circle above dates flanked by leaves **Note:** Prev. KM#137.

Date	Mintage	VG	F	VF	XF	Unc
AH1411-1990 Proof	—	Value: 1,450				

KM# 143a 20 OMANI RIALS
41.2000 g., 0.9160 Gold 1.2133 oz. AGW **Subject:** 25th National Day Anniversary **Obv:** National arms and value **Rev:** Radiant value within circle

Date	Mintage	F	VF	XF	Unc	BU
1995 Proof	—	Value: 900				

KM# 74 25 OMANI RIALS
10.0000 g., 0.9170 Gold .2947 oz. AGW **Series:** World Wildlife Fund **Obv:** National arms within circle **Rev:** Masked Booby

Date	Mintage	VG	F	VF	XF	Unc
AH1407-1987 Proof	5,000	Value: 225				

KM# 99 25 OMANI RIALS
10.0000 g., 0.9170 Gold .2947 oz. AGW **Series:** World Wildlife Fund **Obv:** Crown above arms with legends above and below **Rev:** Masked Booby

Date	Mintage	F	VF	XF	Unc	BU
AH1407-1987 Proof; Rare						

Note: Struck for presentation purposes

KM# 88 25 OMANI RIALS
10.0000 g., 0.9170 Gold .2947 oz. AGW **Series:** Save the Children **Obv:** National arms within circle **Rev:** School Master with pupils

Date	Mintage	VG	F	VF	XF	Unc
AH1411-1991 Proof	Est. 3,000	Value: 240				

KM# 100 25 OMANI RIALS
10.0000 g., 0.9170 Gold .2947 oz. AGW **Series:** Save the Children **Obv:** Crown above arms with legends above and below **Rev:** School Master with pupils

Date	Mintage	F	VF	XF	Unc	BU
AH1411-1991 Proof; Rare	—	—	—	—	—	—

Note: Struck for presentation purposes

KM# 144a 25 OMANI RIALS
50.2000 g., 0.9160 Gold 1.4784 oz. AGW **Subject:** 25th National Day Anniversary - Sultan Qaboos bin Said **Obv:** National arms and value **Rev:** Multicolor bust facing

Date	Mintage	F	VF	XF	Unc	BU
1995 Proof	—	Value: 1,100				

KM# 63 75 OMANI RIALS
33.4370 g., 0.9000 Gold .9676 oz. AGW **Subject:** Conservation **Obv:** National arms above date **Rev:** Arabian Tahr

Date	Mintage	F	VF	XF	Unc	BU
AH1397 (1976)	825	—	—	—	675	725
AH1397 (1976) Proof	325	Value: 925				

MEDALLIC COINAGE

A series of 3 silver and 4 gold medallic coins were produced in AH1391/1971AD and are inscribed STATE OF OMAN (Dawlat Uman). These were issued by the exile government of Imam Ghalib Ibn Ali in Dammam, Saudi Arabia, and distributed from a post box in Amman, Jordan. The Imamate had enjoyed effective autonomy in the interior of Oman from 1920-54, at which time the Sultan resumed direct control. Imamist forces in Oman were finally driven out in 1959. The Imam has been in exile since 1955.

X# M4 50 RYALS
4.0000 g., 0.9170 Gold .1179 oz. AGW **Obv:** Star and crescent above crossed flags and 2 swords **Rev:** Sailboat and rocky coast **Note:** Prev. KM#M4.

Date	Mintage	F	VF	XF	Unc	BU
AH1391	4,000	—	—	—	185	—

X# M5 100 RYALS
8.0000 g., 0.9170 Gold .2359 oz. AGW **Obv:** Star and crescent above crossed flags and 2 swords **Rev:** Flower **Note:** Prev. KM#M5.

Date	Mintage	F	VF	XF	Unc	BU
AH1391	4,000	—	—	—	250	—

X# M6 200 RYALS
16.0000 g., 0.9170 Gold .4718 oz. AGW **Obv:** Star and crescent above crossed flags and 2 swords **Rev:** Secretary bird **Note:** Prev. KM#M6.

Date	Mintage	F	VF	XF	Unc	BU
AH1391	4,000	—	—	—	400	—

X# M7 500 RYALS
40.0000 g., 0.9170 Gold 1.1794 oz. AGW **Obv:** Star and crescent above crossed flags and 2 swords **Rev:** Mosque **Note:** Prev. KM#M7.

Date	Mintage	F	VF	XF	Unc	BU
AH1391	4,000	—	—	—	900	—

PROOF SETS

KM#	Date	Mintage	Identification	Issue Price	Mkt Val
PS1	AH1394 (3)	250	KM#45-47	—	935
PS2	AH1395 (3)	250	KM#45-47	—	935
PS3	AH1397 (3)	—	KM#60, 61, 63	780	985
PSA6	1996 (2)	—	KM#101-102	640	875

PAKISTAN

The Islamic Republic of Pakistan, located on the Indian subcontinent between India and Afghanistan, has an area of 310,404 sq. mi. (803,940 sq. km.) and a population of 130 million. Capital: Islamabad. Pakistan is mainly an agricultural land although the industrial base is expanding rapidly. Yarn, textiles, cotton, rice, medical instruments, sports equipment and leather are exported.

Afghan and Turkish intrusions into northern India between the 11th and 18th centuries resulted in large numbers of Indians being converted to Islam. The idea of a separate Moslem state independent of Hindu India developed in the 1930's and was agreed to by Britain in 1946. The Islamic majority areas of India, consisting of the separate geographic entities known as East and West Pakistan, achieved self-government as Pakistan, with dominion status in the British Commonwealth, when the British withdrew from India on Aug. 14, 1947. Pakistan became a republic in 1956. When a basic constitutional crisis initiated by the election of Dec. 1, 1970 - the first direct general election in Pakistani history - could not be resolved by the leaders of East and West Pakistan, the East Pakistanis seceded from the Islamic Republic of Pakistan (March 26, 1971) and formed the independent People's Republic of Bangladesh. After many years of vacillation between civilian and military regimes, the people of Pakistan held a free national election in November, 1988 and installed the first of a series of democratic governments under a parliamentary system. Pakistan was a member of the Commonwealth of Nations, but was suspended from membership October 1999. In 2004, Pakistan was re-admitted.

TITLE
Pakistan

MONETARY SYSTEM
100 Paisa = 1 Rupee

ISLAMIC REPUBLIC

DECIMAL COINAGE

100 Paisa = 1 Rupee

KM# 43 500 RUPEES
4.5000 g., 0.9170 Gold .1325 oz. AGW, 19 mm. **Subject:** 100th Anniversary - Birth of Mohammad Ali Jinnah **Obv:** Crescent and star **Rev:** Bust facing flanked by dates

Date	Mintage	F	VF	XF	Unc	BU
ND(1976)	500	—	—	—	125	135
ND(1976) Proof	500	Value: 150				

KM# 49 500 RUPEES
3.6400 g., 0.9170 Gold .1073 oz. AGW, 19 mm. **Subject:** 100th Anniversary - Birth of Allama Mohammad Iqbal **Obv:** Value and date above sprigs **Rev:** Head leaning on hand flanked by dates

Date	Mintage	F	VF	XF	Unc	BU
1977	500	—	—	—	120	130
1977 Proof	200	Value: 150				

KM# 50 1000 RUPEES
9.0000 g., 0.9170 Gold .2650 oz. AGW, 25 mm. **Subject:** Islamic Summit Conference **Obv:** Islamic summit minar **Rev:** Design within center circle

Date	Mintage	F	VF	XF	Unc	BU
1977	400	—	—	—	220	250
Z1977 Proof	400	Value: 300				

KM# 44 3000 RUPEES
33.4370 g., 0.9000 Gold .9676 oz. AGW, 39 mm. **Obv:** Crescent within monument with star at upper left **Rev:** Astor Markhor and value

Date	Mintage	F	VF	XF	Unc	BU
1976	902	—	—	—	750	800
1976 Proof	273	Value: 900				

MINT SETS

KM#	Date	Mintage	Identification	Issue Price	Mkt Val
MS8	1976 (2)	—	KM41, 43	63.00	155
MS10	1977 (2)	—	KM47, 50	—	225

PROOF SETS

KM#	Date	Mintage	Identification	Issue Price	Mkt Val
PS6	1976 (2)	—	KM41, 43	90.50	185
PS8	1977 (2)	—	KM47, 50	—	300

PALAU

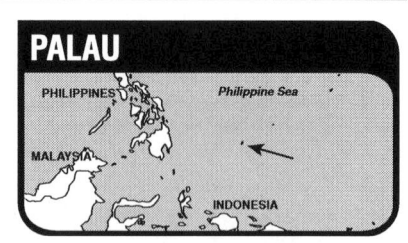

The Republic of Palau, a group of about 100 islands and islets, is generally considered a part of the Caroline Islands. It is located about 1,000 miles southeast of Manila and about the same distance southwest of Saipan and has an area of 179 sq. mi. and a population of 12,116. Capital: Koror.

The islands were administered as part of the Caroline Islands under the Spanish regime until they were sold to Germany in 1899. Seized by Japan in 1914, it was mandated to them in 1919 and Koror was made the administrative headquarters of all the Japanese mandated islands in 1921. During World War II the islands were taken by the Allies, in 1944, with the heaviest fighting taking place on Peleliu. They became part of the U.S. Trust Territory of the Pacific Islands in 1947. In 1980 they became internally self-governing and independent. Control over foreign policy, except defense, was approved in 1986. Palau became an independent nation in 1995.

REPUBLIC

COLLECTOR COINAGE

KM# 26 DOLLAR
1.2441 g., 0.9999 Gold .0400 oz. AGW, 13.94 mm. **Series:** Marine Life Protection **Obv:** Two mermaids **Rev:** Jumping dolphin

Date	Mintage	F	VF	XF	Unc	BU
1998 Proof	10,000	Value: 35.00				

KM# 31 DOLLAR
1.2441 g., 0.9999 Gold .0400 oz. AGW, 13.94 mm. **Series:** Marine Life Protection **Obv:** Mermaid holding cockatoo **Rev:** Sea turtle

Date	Mintage	F	VF	XF	Unc	BU
1998 Proof	—	Value: 40.00				

KM# 82 DOLLAR
1.2441 g., 0.9999 Gold 0.04 oz. AGW, 13.94 mm. **Obv:** Seated Mermaid and sailboat **Rev:** Multicolor shark **Edge:** Reeded

Date	Mintage	F	VF	XF	Unc	BU
1999 Proof	—	Value: 35.00				

KM# 36 DOLLAR
1.2441 g., 0.9999 Gold .0400 oz. AGW, 13.94 mm. **Series:** Marine Life Protection **Obv:** Mermaid and dolphin **Rev:** Manta ray

Date	Mintage	F	VF	XF	Unc	BU
1999 Proof	—	Value: 37.50				

KM# 83 DOLLAR
1.2441 g., 0.9999 Gold 0.04 oz. AGW, 13.94 mm. **Obv:** Diving Mermaid **Rev:** Multicolor jumping Swordfish **Edge:** Reeded

Date	Mintage	F	VF	XF	Unc	BU
2000 Proof	—	Value: 35.00				

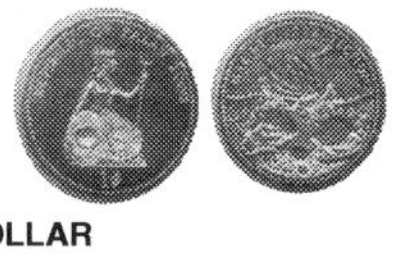

KM# 84 DOLLAR
1.2441 g., 0.9999 Gold 0.04 oz. AGW, 13.94 mm. **Obv:** Seated Mermaid **Rev:** Multicolor fish and wreck **Edge:** Reeded

PALAU

KM# 85 DOLLAR
1.2441 g., 0.9999 Gold 0.04 oz. AGW, 13.94 mm. **Obv:** Seated Mermaid and ship **Rev:** Multicolor fish and coral **Edge:** Reeded
Date	Mintage	F	VF	XF	Unc	BU
2000 Proof	—	Value: 35.00				

KM# 86 DOLLAR
1.2441 g., 0.9999 Gold 0.04 oz. AGW, 13.94 mm. **Subject:** Marine Life Protection **Obv:** Prone Mermaid **Rev:** Two fish
Date	Mintage	F	VF	XF	Unc	BU
2001 Proof	—	Value: 35.00				

KM# 87 DOLLAR
1.2441 g., 0.9999 Gold 0.04 oz. AGW, 13.94 mm. **Subject:** Marine Life Protection **Obv:** Seated Mermaid with raised arm above value **Rev:** Two glittering fish
Date	Mintage	F	VF	XF	Unc	BU
2001 Proof	—	Value: 35.00				

KM# 88 DOLLAR
1.2441 g., 0.9999 Gold 0.04 oz. AGW, 13.94 mm. **Subject:** Marine Life Protection **Obv:** Figurehead Mermaid and value **Rev:** Black and white striped fish
Date	Mintage	F	VF	XF	Unc	BU
2001 Proof	—	Value: 35.00				

KM# 89 DOLLAR
1.2441 g., 0.9999 Gold 0.04 oz. AGW, 13.94 mm. **Subject:** Marine Life Protection **Obv:** Figurehead Mermaid and value **Rev:** Black and white striped fish
Date	Mintage	F	VF	XF	Unc	BU
2001 Proof	—	Value: 35.00				

KM# 90 DOLLAR
1.2441 g., 0.9999 Gold 0.04 oz. AGW, 13.94 mm. **Subject:** Marine Life Protection **Obv:** Figurehead Mermaid and value **Rev:** Multicolor whales
Date	Mintage	F	VF	XF	Unc	BU
2002 Proof	—	Value: 35.00				

KM# 91 DOLLAR
1.2441 g., 0.9999 Gold 0.04 oz. AGW, 13.94 mm. **Subject:** Marine Life Protection **Obv:** Figurehead Mermaid and value **Rev:** Pufferfish
Date	Mintage	F	VF	XF	Unc	BU
2002 Proof	—	Value: 35.00				

KM# 92 DOLLAR
1.2441 g., 0.9999 Gold 0.04 oz. AGW, 13.94 mm. **Subject:** Marine Life Protection **Obv:** Seated Mermaid with both arms raised and value **Rev:** Jellyfish
Date	Mintage	F	VF	XF	Unc	BU
2002 Proof	—	Value: 35.00				

KM# 93 DOLLAR
1.2441 g., 0.9999 Gold 0.04 oz. AGW, 13.94 mm. **Subject:** Marine Life Protection **Obv:** Figurehead Mermaid and value **Rev:** Fish
Date	Mintage	F	VF	XF	Unc	BU
2002 Proof	—	Value: 35.00				

KM# 94 DOLLAR
1.2441 g., 0.9999 Gold 0.04 oz. AGW, 13.94 mm. **Subject:** Marine Life Protection **Obv:** Figurehead mermaid and value **Rev:** Lionfish
Date	Mintage	F	VF	XF	Unc	BU
2002 Proof	—	Value: 35.00				

KM# 95 DOLLAR
1.2441 g., 0.9999 Gold 0.04 oz. AGW, 13.94 mm. **Subject:** Marine Life Protection **Obv:** Mermaid riding dolphin and value **Rev:** Starfish
Date	Mintage	F	VF	XF	Unc	BU
2003 Proof	—	Value: 35.00				

KM# 96 DOLLAR
1.2441 g., 0.9999 Gold 0.04 oz. AGW, 13.94 mm. **Subject:** Marine Life Protection **Obv:** Seated Mermaid on shell and value **Rev:** Multicolor Orca **Edge:** Reeded Proof
Date	Mintage	F	VF	XF	Unc	BU
2003 Proof	—	Value: 35.00				

KM# 97 DOLLAR
1.2441 g., 0.9999 Gold 0.04 oz. AGW, 13.94 mm. **Subject:** Marine Life Protection **Obv:** Mermaid under radiant sun and value **Rev:** Crab
Date	Mintage	F	VF	XF	Unc	BU
2003 Proof	—	Value: 35.00				

KM# 98 DOLLAR
1.2441 g., 0.9999 Gold 0.04 oz. AGW, 13.94 mm. **Subject:** Marine Life Protection **Obv:** Mermaid riding turtle and value **Rev:** Two glittering fish
Date	Mintage	F	VF	XF	Unc	BU
2003 Proof	—	Value: 35.00				

KM# 99 DOLLAR
1.2441 g., 0.9999 Gold 0.04 oz. AGW, 13.94 mm. **Subject:** Marine Life Protection **Obv:** Mermaid under radiant sun and value **Rev:** Clownfish
Date	Mintage	F	VF	XF	Unc	BU
2004 Proof	—	Value: 35.00				

KM# 100 DOLLAR
1.2441 g., 0.9999 Gold 0.04 oz. AGW, 13.94 mm. **Subject:** Marine Life Protection **Obv:** Mermaid flanked by dolphins **Rev:** Multicolor dolphin head
Date	Mintage	F	VF	XF	Unc	BU
2004 Proof	—	Value: 35.00				

KM# 101 DOLLAR
1.2441 g., 0.9999 Gold 0.04 oz. AGW, 13.94 mm. **Subject:** Marine Life Protection **Obv:** Mermaid sitting in a shell listening to a conch shell **Rev:** Sea Horse
Date	Mintage	F	VF	XF	Unc	BU
2005 Proof	—	Value: 35.00				

KM# 112 10 DOLLARS
1.4900 g., 0.9990 Gold 0.0479 oz. AGW, 11 x 19 mm. **Obv:** Value, date and inscription **Rev:** Mermaid **Edge:** Plain **Shape:** Rectangle
Date	Mintage	F	VF	XF	Unc	BU
1995 Proof	—	Value: 50.00				

KM# 10 200 DOLLARS
31.1035 g., 0.9990 Gold 1.0000 oz. AGW **Subject:** Independence **Obv:** Mermaid and Neptune **Rev:** Nautilus and seascape
Date	Mintage	F	VF	XF	Unc	BU
1994 Proof	—	Value: 720				

KM# 29 200 DOLLARS
31.1035 g., 0.9990 Gold 1.0000 oz. AGW **Subject:** Marine - Life Protection **Obv:** Two mermaids **Rev:** Multicolor high-relief dolphin **Note:** Similar to Dollar, KM#25.
Date	Mintage	F	VF	XF	Unc	BU
1998 Proof	200	Value: 720				

KM# 34 200 DOLLARS
31.1035 g., 0.9990 Gold 1.0000 oz. AGW **Subject:** Marine - Life Protection **Obv:** Mermaid with cockatoo **Rev:** Multicolor high-relief turtle **Note:** Similar to Dollar, KM#30.
Date	Mintage	F	VF	XF	Unc	BU
1998 Proof	—	Value: 720				

KM# 39 200 DOLLARS
31.1035 g., 0.9990 Gold 1.0000 oz. AGW **Subject:** Marine - Life Protection **Obv:** Mermaid with dolphin **Rev:** Multicolor high-relief manta ray **Note:** Similar to Dollar, KM#35.
Date	Mintage	F	VF	XF	Unc	BU
1999 Proof	—	Value: 720				

ESSAIS
Standard metals unless otherwise noted

KM#	Date	Mintage Identification	Issue Price	Mkt Val
E1	1992	— Dollar. 0.9990 Gold. 25.9600 g. Seated mermaid and sailboat. Multicolor sea life. KM1.	—	1,500
E2	1992	— 5 Dollars. 0.9990 Gold. 25.9700 g. Seated Neptune and ship. Multicolor sea life. Reeded edge. KM2.	—	1,500

PROOF SETS

KM#	Date	Mintage Identification	Issue Price	Mkt Val
PS1	1992	— KME1, E2	—	3,000

PALESTINE

Palestine, which corresponds to Canaan of the Bible, was settled by the Philistines about the 12th century B.C. and shortly thereafter was settled by the Jews who established the kingdoms of Israel and Judah. Because of its position as part of the land bridge connecting Asia and Africa, Palestine was invaded and conquered by nearly all of the historic empires of ancient Europe and Asia. In the 16th century it became a part of the Ottoman Empire. After falling to the British in World War I, it, together with Transjordan, was mandated to Great Britain by the League of Nations, 1922.

For more than half a century prior to the termination of the British mandate over Palestine, 1948, Zionist leaders had sought to create a Jewish homeland for Jews who were dispersed throughout the world. For almost as long, Jews fleeing persecution had immigrated to Palestine. The Nazi persecutions of the 1930s and 1940s increased the Jewish movement to Palestine and generated international support for the creation of a Jewish state, first promulgated by the Balfour Declaration of 1917, which asserted British support for the endeavor. The state of Israel was proclaimed as the Jewish state in the territory that was Palestine. The remainder of that territory was occupied by Jordanian and Egyptian armies. Israel demonetized the coins of Palestine on Sept. 15, 1948, the Jordan government declared Palestine currency no longer legal tender on June 30, 1951, and Egypt declared it no longer legal tender in Gaza on June 9, 1951.

TITLES
Filastin
Paleshtina (E.I.)

MONETARY SYSTEM
1000 Mils = 1 Pound

BRITISH ADMINISTRATION
MEDALLIC COINAGE
Richard Lobel Issue

X# M2 SOVEREIGN
0.3750 Gold **Subject:** Edward VIII

Date	Mintage	F	VF	XF	Unc	BU
1936 Proof	250	Value: 175				

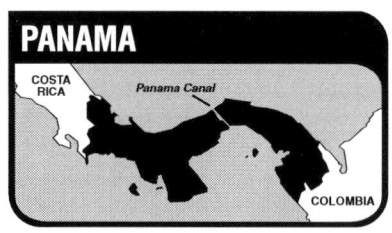

PANAMA

The Republic of Panama, a Central American Country situated between Costa Rica and Colombia, has an area of 29,762 sq. mi. (78,200 sq. km.) and a population of *2.4 million. Capital: Panama City. The Panama Canal is the country's biggest asset; servicing world related transit trade and international commerce. Bananas, refined petroleum, sugar and shrimp are exported.

Discovered in 1501 by the Spanish conquistador Rodrigo Galvan de Bastidas, the land of Panama was soon explored and after a few attempts at settlement was successfully colonized by the Spanish. It was in Panama in 1513 that Vasco Nunez de Balboa became the first European to see the Pacific Ocean. The first Pacific-coast settlement, founded in 1519 on the site of a village the natives called Panama, was named *Nuestra Senora de la Asuncion de Panama* (Our Lady of the Assumption of Panama). The settlement soon became a city and eventually, albeit briefly, an Audiencia (judicial tribunal).

In 1578 the city of Panama, being a primary transshipment center for treasure and supplies to and from Spain's South Pacific-coast colonies, was chosen for a new mint, and minting had begun there by 1580. By late 1582 or 1583 production was halted, possibly due to the fact that there were no nearby silver mines to sustain it. In it's brief operation, the Panama Mint must not have made many coins, as the corpus of surviving specimens known today from this colonial mint is less than 40.

The city of Panama, known today as the Old City of Panama, was sacked and burned in 1671 by the famous Henry Morgan in one of the greatest pirate victories against the Spanish Main.

Panama declared its independence in 1821 and joined the Confederation of Greater Colombia. In 1903, after Colombia rejected a treaty enabling the United States to build a canal across the Isthmus, Panama with the support of the United States proclaimed its independence from Colombia and became a sovereign republic.

The 1904 2-1/2 centesimos known as the 'Panama Pill' or 'Panama Pearl' is one of the world's smaller silver coins and a favorite with collectors.

MINT MARKS
FM - Franklin Mint, U.S.A.*
CHI in circle - Valcambi Mint, Balerna, Switzerland
RCM – Royal Canadian Mint

*NOTE: From 1975-1985 the Franklin Mint produced coinage in up to 3 different qualities. Qualities of issue are designated in ( ) after each date and are defined as follows:

(M) MATTE - Normal circulation strike or a dull finish produced by sandblasting special uncirculated (polish finish) or proof quality dies.

(U) SPECIAL UNCIRCULATED - Polished or proof-like in appearance without any frosted features.

(P) PROOF - The highest quality obtainable having mirror-like fields and frosted features.

MONETARY SYSTEM
100 Centesimos = 1 Balboa

REPUBLIC
DECIMAL COINAGE

KM# 72 20 BALBOAS
2.1400 g., 0.5000 Gold .0344 oz. AGW **Obv:** National coat of arms **Rev:** Figure of Eight Butterfly **Rev. Designer:** Gilroy Roberts

Date	Mintage	F	VF	XF	Unc	BU
1981FM (U)	205	—	—	—	225	—
1981FM (P)	4,445	Value: 80.00				
1981FM (P) FDC	Inc. above	Value: 90.00				

KM# 81 20 BALBOAS
2.1400 g., 0.5000 Gold .0344 oz. AGW **Obv:** National coat of arms **Rev:** Hummingbird

Date	Mintage	F	VF	XF	Unc	BU
1982FM (U)	140	—	—	—	275	—
1982FM (P)	3,445	Value: 85.00				
1982FM (P) FDC	Inc. above	Value: 95.00				

KM# 92 20 BALBOAS
2.1400 g., 0.5000 Gold .0344 oz. AGW **Obv:** National coat of arms **Rev:** Banded Butterfly fish

Date	Mintage	F	VF	XF	Unc	BU
1983FM (U)	—	—	—	—	200	—
1983FM (P)	1,671	Value: 85.00				
1983FM (P) FDC	Inc. above	Value: 110				

KM# 97 20 BALBOAS
2.1400 g., 0.5000 Gold .0344 oz. AGW **Obv:** National coat of arms **Rev:** Puma

Date	Mintage	F	VF	XF	Unc	BU
1984FM (U)	100	—	—	—	600	—
1984FM (P)	357	Value: 350				
1984FM (P) FDC	Inc. above	Value: 400				

KM# 102 20 BALBOAS
2.1400 g., 0.5000 Gold .0344 oz. AGW **Obv:** National coat of arms **Rev:** Harpy Eagle

Date	Mintage	F	VF	XF	Unc	BU
1985FM (P)	817	Value: 250				
1985FM (P) FDC	Inc. above	Value: 325				

KM# 73 50 BALBOAS
5.3700 g., 0.5000 Gold .0861 oz. AGW **Subject:** Christmas 1981 **Obv:** National coat of arms **Rev:** Stylized dove flanked by flowers

Date	Mintage	F	VF	XF	Unc	BU
1981FM (U)	154	—	—	—	225	—
1981FM (P)	1,940	Value: 85.00				
1981FM (P) FDC	Inc. above	Value: 100				

KM# 82 50 BALBOAS
5.3700 g., 0.5000 Gold .0861 oz. AGW **Subject:** Christmas 1982 **Obv:** National coat of arms **Rev:** Star of Bethlehem flanked by flowers

Date	Mintage	F	VF	XF	Unc	BU
1982FM (U)	60	—	—	—	450	—
1982FM (P)	1,361	Value: 95.00				
1982FM (P) FDC	Inc. above	Value: 100				

KM# 94 50 BALBOAS
5.3700 g., 0.5000 Gold .0861 oz. AGW **Subject:** Christmas 1983 **Obv:** National coat of arms **Rev:** Poinsettia

Date	Mintage	F	VF	XF	Unc	BU
1983FM (U)	—	—	—	—	225	—
1983FM (P)	1,283	Value: 110				
1983FM (P) FDC	Inc. above	Value: 130				

KM# 99 50 BALBOAS
5.3700 g., 0.5000 Gold .0861 oz. AGW **Subject:** Peace at Christmas **Obv:** National coat of arms **Rev:** Lion and lamb

Date	Mintage	F	VF	XF	Unc	BU
1984FM (P)	—	Value: 550				
1984FM (P) FDC	—	Value: 700				

PANAMA 551

KM# 55 75 BALBOAS
10.6000 g., 0.5000 Gold .1704 oz. AGW **Subject:** 75th Anniversary of Independence **Obv:** National coat of arms **Rev:** Flag flanked by dates, flowers and stars

Date	Mintage	F	VF	XF	Unc	BU
ND1978FM (U)	410	—	—	—	180	—
ND1978FM (P)	9,161	Value: 130				
1978FM (P) FDC	Inc. above	Value: 140				

KM# 41 100 BALBOAS
8.1600 g., 0.9000 Gold .2361 oz. AGW **Subject:** 500th Anniversary - Birth of Balboa **Obv:** National coat of arms **Rev:** Armored head 1/4 left

Date	Mintage	F	VF	XF	Unc	BU
1975FM (U)	44,000	—	—	—	165	—
1975FM (P)	75,000	Value: 165				
1975FM (P) FDC	Inc. above	Value: 170				
1976FM (M)	50	—	—	—	600	—
1976FM (U)	3,013	—	—	—	165	—
1976FM (P)	11,000	Value: 165				
1976FM (P) FDC	Inc. above	Value: 170				
1977FM (M)	50	—	—	—	550	—
1977FM (U)	324	—	—	—	225	—
1977FM (P)	5,092	Value: 175				
1977FM (P) FDC	Inc. above	Value: 180				

KM# 56 100 BALBOAS
8.1600 g., 0.9000 Gold .2361 oz. AGW **Subject:** Peace and Progress **Obv:** National coat of arms **Rev:** Dove orchid within circle

Date	Mintage	F	VF	XF	Unc	BU
1978FM (M)	50	—	—	—	500	—
1978FM (U)	300	—	—	—	250	—
1978FM (P)	6,086	Value: 165				
1978FM (P) FDC	Inc. above	Value: 175				

KM# 60 100 BALBOAS
8.1600 g., 0.9000 Gold .2361 oz. AGW **Subject:** Pre-Columbian Art - Golden Turtle **Obv:** National coat of arms **Rev:** Stylized turtle

Date	Mintage	F	VF	XF	Unc	BU
1979FM (M)	50	—	—	—	350	—
1979FM (U)	240	—	—	—	300	—
1979FM (P)	4,829	Value: 165				
1979FM (P) FDC	Inc. above	Value: 175				

KM# 66 100 BALBOAS
8.1600 g., 0.9000 Gold .2361 oz. AGW **Subject:** Pre-Columbian Art - Golden Condor **Obv:** National coat of arms **Rev:** Styilized condor within circle

Date	Mintage	F	VF	XF	Unc	BU
1980FM (U)	209	—	—	—	400	—
1980FM (P)	2,411	Value: 200				
1980FM (P) FDC	Inc. above	Value: 250				

KM# 67 100 BALBOAS
7.1300 g., 0.5000 Gold .1146 oz. AGW **Subject:** Panama Canal Centennial **Obv:** National coat of arms **Rev:** Bust 1/4 left

Date	Mintage	F	VF	XF	Unc	BU
ND (1980)FM (U)	77	—	—	—	700	—
ND (1980)FM (P)	2,468	Value: 135				
ND(1980)FM (P) FDC	Inc. above	Value: 150				

KM# 74 100 BALBOAS
7.1300 g., 0.5000 Gold .1146 oz. AGW **Subject:** Pre-Columbian Art **Obv:** National coat of arms **Rev:** Cocie Peoples' Ceremonial Mask

Date	Mintage	F	VF	XF	Unc	BU
1981FM (U)	174	—	—	—	325	—
1981FM (P)	1,841	Value: 150				
1981FM (P) FDC	Inc. above	Value: 160				

KM# 83 100 BALBOAS
7.1300 g., 0.5000 Gold .1146 oz. AGW **Subject:** Pre-Columbian Art **Obv:** National coat of arms **Rev:** Native design within quartered circle

Date	Mintage	F	VF	XF	Unc	BU
1982FM (U)	26	—	—	—	850	—
1982FM (P)	578	Value: 200				
FM (P) FDC	Inc. above	Value: 300				

KM# 95 100 BALBOAS
7.1300 g., 0.5000 Gold .1146 oz. AGW **Subject:** Pre-Columbian Art **Obv:** National coat of arms **Rev:** Cocie style birds

Date	Mintage	F	VF	XF	Unc	BU
1983FM (U)	—	—	—	—	350	—
1983FM (P)	1,308	Value: 150				
1983FM (P) FDC	Inc. above	Value: 160				

KM# 100 100 BALBOAS
7.1300 g., 0.5000 Gold .1146 oz. AGW **Subject:** Pre-Columbian Art **Obv:** National coat of arms **Rev:** Native art

Date	Mintage	F	VF	XF	Unc	BU
1984FM (U)	—	—	—	—	400	—
1984FM (P)	—	Value: 165				
1984FM (P) FDC	—	Value: 180				

KM# 131 100 BALBOAS
8.3000 g., 0.9000 Gold .2402 oz. AGW **Subject:** Panama Canal Transfer **Obv:** Bust left **Rev:** Ship in canal under Panamanian flag

Date	Mintage	F	VF	XF	Unc	BU
1999 Proof	1,000	Value: 300				

KM# 43 150 BALBOAS
9.3000 g., 0.9990 Platinum .2987 oz. APW **Subject:** 150th Anniversary - Panamanian Congress **Obv:** National coat of arms **Rev:** Bust left divides dates

Date	Mintage	F	VF	XF	Unc	BU
ND (1976)FM (M)	30	—	—	—	850	—
ND (1976)FM (U)	510	—	—	—	425	—
ND (1976)FM (P)	13,000	Value: 375				
ND(1976)FM (P) FDC	Inc. above	Value: 425				

KM# 68 150 BALBOAS
7.6700 g., 0.5000 Gold .1233 oz. AGW **Subject:** Sesquicentenarium - Death of Simon Bolivar **Obv:** National coat of arms **Rev:** Armored bust 1/4 left

Date	Mintage	F	VF	XF	Unc	BU
ND (1980)FM (U)	169	—	—	—	550	—
ND (1980)FM (P)	1,837	Value: 225				
ND(1980)FM (P) FDC	Inc. above	Value: 250				

KM# 61 200 BALBOAS
9.5000 g., 0.9800 Platinum .2994 oz. APW **Subject:** Panama Canal Treaty Implementation **Obv:** National coat of arms **Rev:** Flag above map

Date	Mintage	F	VF	XF	Unc	BU
1979FM (P)	2,178	Value: 340				
1979FM (P) FDC	Inc. above	Value: 375				

KM# 69 200 BALBOAS
9.9300 g., 0.9800 Platinum .2940 oz. APW **Subject:** Champions of Boxing **Obv:** National coat of arms **Rev:** Boxer and flag

Date	Mintage	F	VF	XF	Unc	BU
1980 Proof	219	Value: 600				
1980 Proof FDC	Inc. above	Value: 625				

552   PANAMA

KM# 42 500 BALBOAS
41.7000 g., 0.9000 Gold 1.2067 oz. AGW **Subject:** 500th Anniversary - Birth of Balboa **Obv:** National coat of arms **Rev:** Kneeling armored figure, sword in left hand, flag in right

Date	Mintage	F	VF	XF	Unc	BU
1975FM (M)	10	—	—	—	3,000	—
1975FM (U)	1,496	—	—	—	820	—
1975FM (P)	9,824	Value: 820				
1975FM (P) FDC	Inc. above	Value: 835				
1976FM (M)	10	—	—	—	3,000	—
1976FM (U)	160	—	—	—	875	—
1976FM (P)	2,669	Value: 825				
1976FM (P) FDC	Inc. above	Value: 845				
1977FM (P)	1,980	Value: 835				
1977FM (M)	10	—	—	—	3,000	—
1977FM (U)	59	—	—	—	1,250	—
1977FM (P) FDC	Inc. above	Value: 855				

KM# 62 500 BALBOAS
41.7000 g., 0.9000 Gold 1.2067 oz. AGW **Obv:** National coat of arms **Rev:** Jaguar

Date	Mintage	F	VF	XF	Unc	BU
1979FM (U)	130	—	—	—	965	—
1979FM (P)	1,657	Value: 835				
1979FM (P) FDC	Inc. above	Value: 900				

KM# 75 500 BALBOAS
37.1800 g., 0.5000 Gold .5977 oz. AGW **Obv:** National coat of arms **Rev:** Sailfish

Date	Mintage	F	VF	XF	Unc	BU
1981FM (U)	41	—	—	—	1,850	—
1981FM (P)	487	Value: 675				
1981FM (P) FDC	Inc. above	Value: 725				

KM# 57 500 BALBOAS
41.7000 g., 0.9000 Gold 1.2067 oz. AGW **Subject:** 30th Anniversary - Organization of American States **Obv:** National coat of arms **Rev:** Globe showing North and South America

Date	Mintage	F	VF	XF	Unc	BU
ND(1978)FM (M)	10	—	—	—	2,250	—
ND(1978)FM (U)	106	—	—	—	975	—
ND(1978)FM (P)	2,009	Value: 835				
ND(1978)FM (P) FDC	Inc. above	Value: 860				

KM# 70 500 BALBOAS
37.1800 g., 0.5000 Gold .5977 oz. AGW **Obv:** National coat of arms **Rev:** Great egrets

Date	Mintage	F	VF	XF	Unc	BU
1980FM (U)	54	—	—	—	1,500	—
1980FM (P)	612	Value: 650				
1980FM (P) FDC	Inc. above	Value: 750				

KM# 84 500 BALBOAS
37.1800 g., 0.5000 Gold .5977 oz. AGW **Subject:** Death of General Omar Torrijos **Obv:** National coat of arms **Rev:** Uniformed bust right

Date	Mintage	F	VF	XF	Unc	BU
1982FM (U)	97	—	—	—	1,200	—
1982FM (P)	398	Value: 700				
1982FM (P) FDC	Inc. above	Value: 750				

PAPUA NEW GUINEA 553

KM# 96 500 BALBOAS
37.1800 g., 0.5000 Gold .5977 oz. AGW **Obv:** National coat of arms **Rev:** Owl Butterfly **Shape:** Scalloped

Date	Mintage	F	VF	XF	Unc	BU
1983FM (U)	—	—	—	—	1,100	—
1983FM (P)	469	Value: 675				
1983FM (P) FDC	Inc. above	Value: 725				

KM# 101 500 BALBOAS
37.1200 g., 0.5000 Gold .5968 oz. AGW **Subject:** Golden Eagle **Obv:** National coat of arms **Rev:** National eagle holding a ribbon, stars above

Date	Mintage	F	VF	XF	Unc	BU
1984FM (U)	10	—	—	—	4,750	—
1984FM (P)	156	Value: 1,750				
1984FM (P) FDC	Inc. above	Value: 1,800				

KM# 103 500 BALBOAS
37.1800 g., 0.5000 Gold .5977 oz. AGW **Subject:** National Eagle **Obv:** National coat of arms **Rev:** National eagle holding an ribbon, stars above **Shape:** Scalloped

Date	Mintage	F	VF	XF	Unc	BU
1985FM (P)	184	Value: 1,600				
1985FM (P) FDC	Inc. above	Value: 1,650				

PATTERNS
Including off metal strikes.

KM#	Date	Mintage	Identification	Mkt Val
PnC4	1953	—	Centesimo. 0.9000 Gold. 17b	—
PnE4	1953	—	1/10 Balboa. 0.9000 Gold. 18a	—
PnG4	1953	—	1/4 Balboa. 0.9000 Gold. 19a	—
PnI4	1953	—	1/2 Balboa. 0.9000 Gold. 20a	—

PIEFORTS

KM#	Date	Mintage	Identification	Mkt Val
P1	1982	—	Centesimo. 0.4000 Gold. The 1982 series of 1-50 Centesimos were struck as pieforts in .400 Gold outside the normal minting facility without consent from the National Bank of Panama.	550
P2	1982	—	5 Centesimos. 0.4000 Gold.	650
P3	1982	—	1/10 Balboa. 0.4000 Gold.	750
P4	1982	20	1/4 Balboa. 0.4000 Gold.	950
P5	1982	—	50 Centesimos. 0.4000 Gold.	1,000

TRIAL STRIKES

KM#	Date	Mintage	Identification	Mkt Val
TS1	1982	—	Centesimo. 0.4000 Gold. The 1982 series 1-50 Centesimos were struck as uniface trial strikes in .400 Gold outside the normal minting facility without consent from the National Bank or authorization from the Government of Panama. Reverse piefort.	250
TS2	1982	—	Centesimo. 0.4000 Gold. Obverse piefort.	250
TS3	1982	—	5 Centesimos. 0.4000 Gold. Reverse piefort	300
TS4	1982	—	5 Centesimos. 0.4000 Gold. Obverse piefort	30,000
TS5	1982	—	1/10 Balboa. 0.4000 Gold. Reverse piefort	375
TS6	1982	—	1/10 Balboa. 0.4000 Gold. Obverse piefort	375
TS7	1982	—	1/4 Balboa. 0.4000 Gold. Reverse piefort	500
TS8	1982	—	1/4 Balboa. 0.4000 Gold. Obverse piefort	500
TS9	1982	—	50 Centesimos. 0.4000 Gold. Reverse piefort	500
TS10	1982	—	50 Centesimos. 0.4000 Gold. Obverse piefort	500

PAPUA NEW GUINEA

Papua New Guinea occupies the eastern half of the island of New Guinea. It lies north of Australia near the equator and borders on West Irian. The country, which includes nearby Bismark archipelago, Buka and Bougainville, has an area of 178,260 sq. mi. (461,690 sq. km.) and a population of 3.7 million that is divided into more than 1,000 separate tribes speaking more than 700 mutually unintelligible languages. Capital: Port Moresby. The economy is agricultural, and exports copra, rubber, cocoa, coffee, tea, gold and copper

In 1884 Germany annexed the area known as German New Guinea (also Neu Guinea or Kaiser Wilhelmsland) comprising the northern section of eastern New Guinea, and granted its administration and development to the Neu-Guinea Compagnie. Administration reverted to Germany in 1889 following the failure of the company to exercise adequate administration. While a German protectorate, German New Guinea had an area of 92,159 sq. mi. (238,692 sq. km.) and a population of about 250,000. Capital: Herbertshohe, 1 of 4 capitals of German New Guinea. The seat of government was transferred to Rabaul in 1910. Copra was the chief crop.

Australian troops occupied German New Guinea in Aug. 1914, shortly after Great Britain declared war on Germany. It was mandated to Australia by the League of Nations in 1920, known as the Territory of New Guinea. The territory was invaded and most of it was occupied by Japan in 1942. Following the Japanese surrender, it came under U.N. trusteeship, Dec. 13, 1946, with Australia as the administering power.

The Papua and New Guinea act, 1949, provided for the government of Papua and New Guinea as one administrative unit. On Dec. 1, 1973, Papua New Guinea became self-governing with Australia retaining responsibility for defense and foreign affairs. Full independence was achieved on Sept. 16, 1975. Papua New Guinea is a member of the Commonwealth of Nations. Elizabeth II is Head of State.

MINT MARK

FM - Franklin Mint, U.S.A.
NOTE: From 1975-1985 the Franklin Mint produced coinage in up to 3 different qualities. Qualities of issue are designated in ( ) after each date and are defined as follows:

(M) MATTE - Normal circulation strike or a dull finish produced by sandblasting special uncirculated (polish finish) or proof quality dies.

(U) SPECIAL UNCIRCULATED - Polished or prooflike in appearance without any frosted features.

(P) PROOF - The highest quality obtainable having mirror-like fields and frosted features.

MONETARY SYSTEM
100 Toea = 1 Kina

COMMONWEALTH

STANDARD COINAGE
100 Toea = 1 Kina

KM# 33 10 KINA
1.5710 g., 0.9990 Gold .0504 oz. AGW **Obv:** National emblem **Rev:** Butterfly

Date	Mintage	F	VF	XF	Unc	BU
1992 Proof	—	Value: 45.00				

KM# 33a 10 KINA
1.5710 g., 0.9950 Platinum .0502 oz. APW **Obv:** National emblem **Rev:** Butterfly

Date	Mintage	F	VF	XF	Unc	BU
1992 Proof	—	Value: 75.00				

KM# 42 50 KINA
6.2200 g., 0.9000 Gold .18 oz. AGW, 21.9 mm. **Obv:** Crowned head right **Rev:** Golden butterfly and value **Edge:** Reeded

Date	Mintage	F	VF	XF	Unc	BU
1993 Proof	—	Value: 130				

KM# 38 50 KINA
7.9700 g., 0.9000 Gold .2306 oz. AGW **Subject:** Centennial of First Coinage **Obv:** National emblem within wreath **Rev:** Bird of Paradise **Note:** Similar to 5 Kina, KM#37.

Date	Mintage	F	VF	XF	Unc	BU
1994 Proof	1,500	Value: 175				

PAPUA NEW GUINEA

KM# 9 100 KINA
9.5700 g., 0.9000 Gold .2769 oz. AGW **Subject:** Independence **Obv:** Head 3/4 left **Rev:** Bird of paradise

Date	Mintage	F	VF	XF	Unc	BU
1975FM (M)	100	—	—	—	225	—
1975FM (U)	8,081	—	—	—	190	—
1975FM (P)	18,000	Value: 195				

KM# 10 100 KINA
9.5700 g., 0.9000 Gold .2769 oz. AGW **Subject:** 1st Anniversary of Independence **Obv:** Symbolic design around center hole **Rev:** National emblem above circular designs around center hole

Date	Mintage	F	VF	XF	Unc	BU
1976FM (M)	100	—	—	—	225	—
1976FM (U)	250	—	—	—	195	—
1976FM (P)	8,020	Value: 200				

KM# 12 100 KINA
9.5700 g., 0.9000 Gold .2769 oz. AGW **Obv:** National emblem **Rev:** Papuan hornbill

Date	Mintage	F	VF	XF	Unc	BU
1977FM (M)	100	—	—	—	225	—
1977FM (U)	362	—	—	—	200	—
1977FM (P)	3,460	Value: 210				

KM# 13 100 KINA
9.5700 g., 0.9000 Gold .2769 oz. AGW **Obv:** National emblem **Rev:** Bird-wing butterfly **Shape:** 7-sided

Date	Mintage	F	VF	XF	Unc	BU
1978FM (U)	400	—	—	—	245	—
1978FM (P)	4,751	Value: 200				

KM# 14 100 KINA
9.5700 g., 0.9000 Gold .2769 oz. AGW **Obv:** National emblem **Rev:** Four Faces of the Nation

Date	Mintage	F	VF	XF	Unc	BU
1979FM (M)	102	—	—	—	215	—
1979FM (U)	286	—	—	—	200	—
1979FM (P)	3,492	Value: 190				

KM# 16 100 KINA
7.8300 g., 0.5000 Gold .1258 oz. AGW **Subject:** South Pacific Festival of Arts **Obv:** National emblem **Rev:** Design divides circle

Date	Mintage	F	VF	XF	Unc	BU
1980 Proof	7,500	Value: 95.00				

KM# 17 100 KINA
9.5700 g., 0.9000 Gold .2769 oz. AGW **Subject:** 5th Anniversary of Independence **Obv:** National emblem **Rev:** Map and flag

Date	Mintage	F	VF	XF	Unc	BU
1980FM (M)	30	—	—	—	345	—
1980FM (P)	1,118	Value: 200				

KM# 19 100 KINA
9.5700 g., 0.9000 Gold .2769 oz. AGW **Obv:** Head 1/4 left **Rev:** Bird of paradise and stars

Date	Mintage	F	VF	XF	Unc	BU
1981FM (P)	685	Value: 210				

KM# 22 100 KINA
9.5700 g., 0.9000 Gold .2769 oz. AGW **Subject:** Royal Visit **Obv:** National emblem **Rev:** Conjoined heads right

Date	Mintage	F	VF	XF	Unc	BU
1982FM (P)	484	Value: 220				

KM# 24 100 KINA
9.5700 g., 0.9000 Gold .2769 oz. AGW **Subject:** 10th Anniversary - Bank of Papua New Guinea **Obv:** Symbol around center hole **Rev:** National emblem above center hole

Date	Mintage	F	VF	XF	Unc	BU
1983FM (P)	378	Value: 235				

KM# 27 100 KINA
9.5700 g., 0.9000 Gold .2769 oz. AGW **Subject:** 100th Anniversary - Founding of British and German Protectorates **Obv:** National emblem **Rev:** Value above flags

Date	Mintage	F	VF	XF	Unc	BU
1984FM (P)	274	Value: 250				

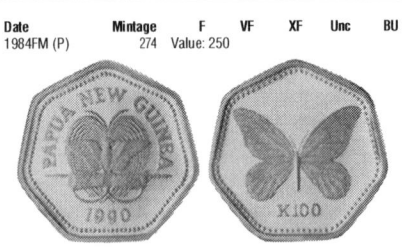

KM# 29 100 KINA
9.5700 g., 0.9000 Gold .2769 oz. AGW **Obv:** National emblem **Rev:** Queen Alexandra Butterfly **Shape:** 7-sided

Date	Mintage	F	VF	XF	Unc	BU
1990	500	—	—	—	225	—
1990 Proof	Est. 5,000	Value: 200				
1992 Proof	Est. 5,000	Value: 200				

KM# 29a 100 KINA
9.5700 g., 0.9950 Platinum .3061 oz. APW **Obv:** National emblem **Rev:** Queen Alexandra butterfly

Date	Mintage	F	VF	XF	Unc	BU
1992	500	—	—	—	375	—
1992 Proof	Est. 5,000	Value: 360				

KM# 35 100 KINA
9.5700 g., 0.9000 Gold .2769 oz. AGW **Subject:** 9th South Pacific Games **Obv:** National emblem **Rev:** Artistic design **Shape:** 7-sided

Date	Mintage	F	VF	XF	Unc	BU
1991 Proof	5,000	Value: 195				

PROOF SETS

KM#	Date	Mintage	Identification	Issue Price	Mkt Val
PS11	1992 (4)	250	KM29a, 33, 33a, 34	—	800

PARAGUAY

The Republic of Paraguay, a landlocked country in the heart of South America surrounded by Argentina, Bolivia and Brazil, has an area of 157,048 sq. mi. (406,750 sq. km.).

Paraguay was first visited by Alejo Garcia, a shipwrecked Spaniard, in 1524. The interior was explored by Sebastian Cabot in 1527 and 1528, when he sailed up the Parana and Paraguay rivers. Asuncion, which would become the center of a Spanish colonial province embracing much of southern South America, was established by the Spanish explorer Juan de Salazar on Aug. 15, 1537. For 150 years the history of Paraguay was largely the history of the agricultural colonies established by the Jesuits in the south and east to Christianize the Indians. In 1811, following the outbreak of the South American wars of independence, Paraguayan patriots overthrew the local Spanish authorities and proclaimed their country's independence.

During the Triple Alliance War (1864-1870) in which Paraguay faced Argentina, Brazil and Uruguay, Asuncion's ladies gathered in an Assembly on Feb. 24, 1867 and decided to give up their jewelry in order to help the national defense. The President of the Republic, Francisco Solano Lopez accepted the offering and ordered one twentieth of it be used to mint the first Paraguayan gold coins according to the Decree of the 11th of Sept., 1867.

Two dies were made, one by Bouvet, and another by an American, Leonard Charles, while only the die made by Bouvet was eventually used.

MINT MARK
HF – Hugillen Ferres, LeLocle, Switzerland

CONTRACTORS
(Chas. J.) SHAW - for Ralph Heaton, Birmingham Mint

MONETARY SYSTEM
100 Centesimos = 1 Peso

REPUBLIC

REAL COINAGE

KM# A2   4 PESOS FUERTES
6.5700 g., 0.9000 Gold .1901 oz. AGW Note: First Paraguayan gold coin.

Date	Mintage	F	VF	XF	Unc	BU
1867 Rare	—	—	—	—	—	—

Note: American Numismatic Rarities Eliasberg sale 4-05, EF-40 realized $41,400

CUT AND COUNTERMARKED COINAGE
War of the Triple Alliance

In 1864 Brazil sent troops into Uruguay to help quell a civil war. Paraguay, which had harbored border disputes with both Brazil and Argentina, took this occasion to declare war on Brazil. In 1865, the Paraguayan military attempted to cross Argentina with hopes of attacking southern Brazil. This armed aggression pushed Argentina, Brazil and Uruguay to form a triple alliance against Paraguay with the intent to overthrow their government and settle all boundary disputes on the terms of the allies.

The resulting War of the Triple Alliance lasted until March of 1870, decimating the Paraguayan population and leaving them at the mercy of their neighbors. New borders were established with Brazil in 1872 and Argentina in 1876, at which time all occupation troops were withdrawn.

During the war both Brazil and Paraguay used some cut and countermarked coins as emergency currency. Spanish and Spanish colonial coins were already in circulation and cut fractions were often being used in local trade. These pieces became the hosts for Brazilian countermarks in denominations of 100 Reis, 200 Reis and 400 Reis, as well as Paraguayan countermarks in denominations of 1 Real, 2 Reales and 4 Pesos Fuertes. Many examples have crenulated, curved or wavy edge cuts.

All cut coins, including these emergency countermarked issues, were outlawed in Paraguay by decree of February 24, 1872.

KM# E2   4 PESOS FUERTES
6.2470 g., Gold Countermark: Incuse 4 Edge: Oblique edge reeding Note: Countermark applied to 1/4 cut of Spanish or Spanish Colonial 8 Escudos. Of the two known examples of this type, one has a weight of 6.247g, while the other weighs 6.70g.

CM Date	Host Date	Good	VG	F	VF	XF
ND(1865-72)	17xx 2 Known	—	—	—	—	—

REFORM COINAGE
100 Centimos = 1 Guarani

KM# 151a   GUARANI
Gold, 18 mm.

Date	Mintage	F	VF	XF	Unc	BU
1976 Proof	—	—	—	—	—	—

KM# 165a   GUARANI
Gold, 18 mm.

Date	Mintage	F	VF	XF	Unc	BU
1978 Proof	—	—	—	—	—	—
1980 Proof	—	—	—	—	—	—

KM# 166b   5 GUARANIES
Gold, 20 mm.

Date	Mintage	F	VF	XF	Unc	BU
1978 Proof	—	—	—	—	—	—
1980 Proof	—	—	—	—	—	—

KM# 153a   10 GUARANIES
Gold, 22 mm.

Date	Mintage	F	VF	XF	Unc	BU
1976 Proof	—	—	—	—	—	—

KM# 167a   10 GUARANIES
Gold, 22 mm.

Date	Mintage	F	VF	XF	Unc	BU
1978 Proof	—	—	—	—	—	—
1980 Proof	—	—	—	—	—	—

KM# 169a   50 GUARANIES
Gold, 25 mm.

Date	Mintage	F	VF	XF	Unc	BU
1980 Proof	—	—	—	—	—	—

KM# 38   1500 GUARANIES
10.7000 g., 0.9000 Gold .3096 oz. AGW Obv: National arms Rev: Uniformed bust of General A. Stroessner facing

Date	Mintage	F	VF	XF	Unc	BU
1972 Proof	Est. 1,500	Value: 325				

KM# 39   1500 GUARANIES
10.7000 g., 0.9000 Gold .3096 oz. AGW Subject: Munich Olympics Obv: National arms Rev: Runner

Date	Mintage	F	VF	XF	Unc	BU
1972 Proof	Est. 1,500	Value: 750				

KM# 40   1500 GUARANIES
10.7000 g., 0.9000 Gold .3096 oz. AGW Subject: Munich Olympics Obv: National arms Rev: Broad jumper

Date	Mintage	F	VF	XF	Unc	BU
1972 Proof	Est. 1,500	Value: 750				

KM# 41   1500 GUARANIES
10.7000 g., 0.9000 Gold .3096 oz. AGW Subject: Munich Olympics Obv: National arms Rev: Soccer

Date	Mintage	F	VF	XF	Unc	BU
1972 Proof	Est. 1,500	Value: 750				

KM# 42   1500 GUARANIES
10.7000 g., 0.9000 Gold .3096 oz. AGW Subject: Munich Olympics Obv: National arms Rev: Hurdler

Date	Mintage	F	VF	XF	Unc	BU
1972 Proof	Est. 1,500	Value: 750				

KM# 43   1500 GUARANIES
10.7000 g., 0.9000 Gold .3096 oz. AGW Subject: Munich Olympics Obv: National arms Rev: High Jumper

Date	Mintage	F	VF	XF	Unc	BU
1973 Proof	1,500	Value: 750				

KM# 44   1500 GUARANIES
10.7000 g., 0.9000 Gold .3096 oz. AGW Subject: Munich Olympics Obv: National arms Rev: Boxer

Date	Mintage	F	VF	XF	Unc	BU
1973 Proof	Est. 1,500	Value: 750				

KM# 70   1500 GUARANIES
10.7000 g., 0.9000 Gold .3096 oz. AGW Obv: National arms Rev: Mariscal Jose F. Estigarriba

Date	Mintage	F	VF	XF	Unc	BU
1973 Proof	Est. 1,500	Value: 400				

KM# 71   1500 GUARANIES
10.7000 g., 0.9000 Gold .3096 oz. AGW Obv: National arms Rev: Head of Mariscal Francisco Solano Lopez facing

Date	Mintage	F	VF	XF	Unc	BU
1973 Proof	Est. 1,500	Value: 400				

KM# 72   1500 GUARANIES
10.7000 g., 0.9000 Gold .3096 oz. AGW Obv: National arms Rev: Bust of General Jose E. Diaz facing

Date	Mintage	F	VF	XF	Unc	BU
1973 Proof	Est. 1,500	Value: 400				

KM# 73   1500 GUARANIES
10.7000 g., 0.9000 Gold .3096 oz. AGW Obv: National arms Rev: Head of General Bernardino Caballero facing

Date	Mintage	F	VF	XF	Unc	BU
1973 Proof	Est. 1,500	Value: 400				

KM# 74   1500 GUARANIES
10.7000 g., 0.9000 Gold .3096 oz. AGW Obv: National arms Rev: Teotihucana Culture sculpture facing

Date	Mintage	F	VF	XF	Unc	BU
1973 Proof	Est. 1,500	Value: 400				

KM# 75   1500 GUARANIES
10.7000 g., 0.9000 Gold .3096 oz. AGW Obv: National arms Rev: Huasteca Culture sculpture

Date	Mintage	F	VF	XF	Unc	BU
1973 Proof	Est. 1,500	Value: 400				

KM# 76   1500 GUARANIES
10.7000 g., 0.9000 Gold .3096 oz. AGW Obv: National arms Rev: Mixteca Culture sculpture

PARAGUAY

Date	Mintage	F	VF	XF	Unc	BU
1973 Proof	Est. 1,500				Value: 400	

KM# 77 1500 GUARANIES
10.7000 g., 0.9000 Gold .3096 oz. AGW **Obv:** National arms
Rev: Veracruz Ceramica vase

Date	Mintage	F	VF	XF	Unc	BU
1973 Proof	Est. 1,500				Value: 400	

KM# 78 1500 GUARANIES
10.7000 g., 0.9000 Gold .3096 oz. AGW **Obv:** National arms
Rev: Veracruz Culture sculpture

Date	Mintage	F	VF	XF	Unc	BU
1973 Proof	Est. 1,500				Value: 400	

KM# 79 1500 GUARANIES
10.7000 g., 0.9000 Gold .3096 oz. AGW **Obv:** National arms
Rev: Bust of Albrecht Durer facing

Date	Mintage	F	VF	XF	Unc	BU
1973 Proof	Est. 1,500				Value: 400	

KM# 80 1500 GUARANIES
10.7000 g., 0.9000 Gold .3096 oz. AGW **Obv:** National arms
Rev: Bust of Johann Wolfgang Goethe facing

Date	Mintage	F	VF	XF	Unc	BU
1973 Proof	Est. 1,500				Value: 400	

KM# 119 1500 GUARANIES
10.7000 g., 0.9000 Gold .3096 oz. AGW **Obv:** National arms
Rev: Bust of President Abraham Lincoln left

Date	Mintage	F	VF	XF	Unc	BU
1974 Proof	Est. 1,500				Value: 400	

KM# 120 1500 GUARANIES
10.7000 g., 0.9000 Gold .3096 oz. AGW **Obv:** National arms
Rev: Bust of Ludwig van Beethoven left

Date	Mintage	F	VF	XF	Unc	BU
1974 Proof	Est. 1,500				Value: 750	

KM# 121 1500 GUARANIES
10.7000 g., 0.9000 Gold .3096 oz. AGW **Obv:** National arms
Rev: Head of Otto von Bismarck right

Date	Mintage	F	VF	XF	Unc	BU
1974 Proof	Est. 1,500				Value: 400	

KM# 122 1500 GUARANIES
10.7000 g., 0.9000 Gold .3096 oz. AGW **Obv:** National arms
Rev: Head of Albert Einstein left

Date	Mintage	F	VF	XF	Unc	BU
1974 Proof	Est. 1,500				Value: 400	

KM# 123 1500 GUARANIES
10.7000 g., 0.9000 Gold .3096 oz. AGW **Obv:** National arms
Rev: Giuseppe Garibaldi facing

Date	Mintage	F	VF	XF	Unc	BU
1974 Proof	Est. 1,500				Value: 400	

KM# 124 1500 GUARANIES
10.7000 g., 0.9000 Gold .3096 oz. AGW **Obv:** National arms
Rev: Alessandro Manzoni facing

Date	Mintage	F	VF	XF	Unc	BU
1974 Proof	Est. 1,500				Value: 400	

KM# 125 1500 GUARANIES
10.7000 g., 0.9000 Gold .3096 oz. AGW **Obv:** National arms
Rev: William Tell and son facing

Date	Mintage	F	VF	XF	Unc	BU
1974 Proof	Est. 1,500				Value: 400	

KM# 126 1500 GUARANIES
10.7000 g., 0.9000 Gold .3096 oz. AGW **Obv:** National arms
Rev: Head of John F. Kennedy left

Date	Mintage	F	VF	XF	Unc	BU
1974 Proof	Est. 1,500				Value: 400	

KM# 127 1500 GUARANIES
10.7000 g., 0.9000 Gold .3096 oz. AGW **Obv:** National arms
Rev: Head of Konrad Adenauer left

Date	Mintage	F	VF	XF	Unc	BU
1974 Proof	Est. 1,500				Value: 400	

KM# 128 1500 GUARANIES
10.7000 g., 0.9000 Gold .3096 oz. AGW **Obv:** National arms
Rev: Head of Winston Churchill left

Date	Mintage	F	VF	XF	Unc	BU
1974 Proof	Est. 1,500				Value: 400	

KM# 129 1500 GUARANIES
10.7000 g., 0.9000 Gold .3096 oz. AGW **Obv:** National arms
Rev: Head of Pope John XXIII left

Date	Mintage	F	VF	XF	Unc	BU
1974 Proof	Est. 1,500				Value: 400	

KM# 130 1500 GUARANIES
10.7000 g., 0.9000 Gold .3096 oz. AGW **Obv:** National arms
Rev: Head of Pope Paul VI left

Date	Mintage	F	VF	XF	Unc	BU
1974 Proof	Est. 1,500				Value: 400	

KM# 179 1500 GUARANIES
10.7000 g., 0.9000 Gold .3096 oz. AGW **Obv:** National arms
Rev: Parliament building

Date	Mintage	F	VF	XF	Unc	BU
1975 Proof	1,500				Value: 400	

KM# 180 1500 GUARANIES
10.7000 g., 0.9000 Gold **Subject:** Apollo 11 Mission **Obv:** National arms **Rev:** Eagle landing on moon with earth at left

Date	Mintage	F	VF	XF	Unc	BU
1975 Proof	1,500				Value: 500	

KM# 181 1500 GUARANIES
10.7000 g., 0.9000 Gold **Subject:** Apollo 15 Mission **Obv:** National arms **Rev:** Apollo mission design within circle

Date	Mintage	F	VF	XF	Unc	BU
1975 Proof	1,500				Value: 500	

KM# 182 1500 GUARANIES
10.7000 g., 0.9000 Gold **Obv:** National arms **Rev:** Friendship Bridge

Date	Mintage	F	VF	XF	Unc	BU
1975 Proof	1,500				Value: 400	

KM# 183 1500 GUARANIES
10.7000 g., 0.9000 Gold **Obv:** National arms **Rev:** Holy Trinity Chruch

Date	Mintage	F	VF	XF	Unc	BU
1975 Proof	1,500				Value: 400	

KM# 184 1500 GUARANIES
10.7000 g., 0.9000 Gold **Obv:** National arms **Rev:** Ruins of Humaita

Date	Mintage	F	VF	XF	Unc	BU
1975 Proof	Est. 1,500				Value: 400	

KM# 45 3000 GUARANIES
21.3000 g., 0.9000 Gold .6164 oz. AGW **Obv:** National arms
Rev: Uniformed bust of General A. Stroessner facing

Date	Mintage	F	VF	XF	Unc	BU
1972 Proof	Est. 1,500				Value: 500	

KM# 46 3000 GUARANIES
21.3000 g., 0.9000 Gold .6164 oz. AGW **Subject:** Munich Olympics **Obv:** National arms **Rev:** Runner

Date	Mintage	F	VF	XF	Unc	BU
1972 Proof	Est. 1,500				Value: 1,500	

KM# 47 3000 GUARANIES
21.3000 g., 0.9000 Gold .6164 oz. AGW **Subject:** Munich Olympics **Obv:** Radiant star within wreath **Rev:** Broad jumper

Date	Mintage	F	VF	XF	Unc	BU
1972 Proof	Est. 1,500				Value: 1,500	

KM# 48 3000 GUARANIES
21.3000 g., 0.9000 Gold .6164 oz. AGW **Subject:** Munich Olympics **Obv:** National arms **Rev:** Soccer

Date	Mintage	F	VF	XF	Unc	BU
1972 Proof	Est. 1,500				Value: 1,500	

KM# 49 3000 GUARANIES
21.3000 g., 0.9000 Gold .6164 oz. AGW **Subject:** Munich Olympics **Obv:** National arms **Rev:** Hurdler

Date	Mintage	F	VF	XF	Unc	BU
1972 Proof	Est. 1,500				Value: 1,500	

PARAGUAY 557

KM# 50 3000 GUARANIES
21.3000 g., 0.9000 Gold .6164 oz. AGW **Subject:** Munich Olympics **Obv:** National arms **Rev:** High jumper

Date	Mintage	F	VF	XF	Unc	BU
1972 Proof	Est. 1,500	Value: 1,500				

KM# 84 3000 GUARANIES
21.3000 g., 0.9000 Gold .6164 oz. AGW **Obv:** National arms **Rev:** Bust of General Bernardino Caballero facing

Date	Mintage	F	VF	XF	Unc	BU
1973 Proof	Est. 1,500	Value: 750				

KM# 89 3000 GUARANIES
21.3000 g., 0.9000 Gold .6164 oz. AGW **Obv:** National arms **Rev:** Veracruz Culture sculpture facing

Date	Mintage	F	VF	XF	Unc	BU
1973 Proof	Est. 1,500	Value: 750				

KM# 51 3000 GUARANIES
21.3000 g., 0.9000 Gold .6164 oz. AGW **Subject:** Munich Olympics **Obv:** National arms **Rev:** Boxer

Date	Mintage	F	VF	XF	Unc	BU
1973 Proof	Est. 1,500	Value: 1,500				

KM# 85 3000 GUARANIES
21.3000 g., 0.9000 Gold .6164 oz. AGW **Obv:** National arms **Rev:** Teotihucana Culture sculpture facing

Date	Mintage	F	VF	XF	Unc	BU
1973 Proof	Est. 1,500	Value: 750				

KM# 90 3000 GUARANIES
21.3000 g., 0.9000 Gold .6164 oz. AGW **Obv:** National arms **Rev:** Bust of Albrecht Durer facing

Date	Mintage	F	VF	XF	Unc	BU
1973 Proof	Est. 1,500	Value: 750				

KM# 81 3000 GUARANIES
21.3000 g., 0.9000 Gold .6164 oz. AGW **Obv:** National arms **Rev:** Head of Mariscal Jose F. Estigarribia facing

Date	Mintage	F	VF	XF	Unc	BU
1973 Proof	Est. 1,500	Value: 750				

KM# 86 3000 GUARANIES
21.3000 g., 0.9000 Gold .6164 oz. AGW **Obv:** National arms **Rev:** Huasteca Culture sculpture

Date	Mintage	F	VF	XF	Unc	BU
1973 Proof	Est. 1,500	Value: 750				

KM# 91 3000 GUARANIES
21.3000 g., 0.9000 Gold .6164 oz. AGW **Obv:** National arms **Rev:** Bust of Johann Wolfgang von Goethe facing

Date	Mintage	F	VF	XF	Unc	BU
1973 Proof	Est. 1,500	Value: 750				

KM# 82 3000 GUARANIES
21.3000 g., 0.9000 Gold .6164 oz. AGW **Obv:** National arms **Rev:** Bust of Mariscal Francisco Solano Lopez facing

Date	Mintage	F	VF	XF	Unc	BU
1973 Proof	Est. 1,500	Value: 750				

KM# 87 3000 GUARANIES
21.3000 g., 0.9000 Gold .6164 oz. AGW **Obv:** National arms **Rev:** Mixteca Culture sculpture

Date	Mintage	F	VF	XF	Unc	BU
1973 Proof	Est. 1,500	Value: 750				

KM# 131 3000 GUARANIES
21.3000 g., 0.9000 Gold .6164 oz. AGW **Obv:** National arms **Rev:** Bust of President Abraham Lincoln left

Date	Mintage	F	VF	XF	Unc	BU
1974 Proof	Est. 1,500	Value: 750				

KM# 83 3000 GUARANIES
21.3000 g., 0.9000 Gold .6164 oz. AGW **Obv:** National arms **Rev:** Bust of General Jose E. Diaz facing

Date	Mintage	F	VF	XF	Unc	BU
1973 Proof	Est. 1,500	Value: 750				

KM# 88 3000 GUARANIES
21.3000 g., 0.9000 Gold .6164 oz. AGW **Obv:** National arms **Rev:** Veracruz Ceramica vase

Date	Mintage	F	VF	XF	Unc	BU
1973 Proof	Est. 1,500	Value: 750				

KM# 132 3000 GUARANIES
21.3000 g., 0.9000 Gold .6164 oz. AGW **Obv:** National arms **Rev:** Bust of Ludwig van Beethoven left

Date	Mintage	F	VF	XF	Unc	BU
1974 Proof	Est. 1,500	Value: 1,350				

PARAGUAY

KM# 133 3000 GUARANIES
21.3000 g., 0.9000 Gold .6164 oz. AGW **Obv:** National arms
Rev: Bust of Otto von Bismarck right
Date	Mintage	F	VF	XF	Unc	BU
1974 Proof	Est. 1,500	Value: 750				

KM# 138 3000 GUARANIES
21.3000 g., 0.9000 Gold .6164 oz. AGW **Obv:** National arms
Rev: Head of President John F. Kennedy left
Date	Mintage	F	VF	XF	Unc	BU
1974 Proof	Est. 1,500	Value: 750				

KM# 161 3000 GUARANIES
21.3000 g., 0.9000 Gold .6164 oz. AGW **Obv:** National arms
Rev: Holy Trinity Chruch
Date	Mintage	F	VF	XF	Unc	BU
1975 Proof	—	Value: 700				

KM# 134 3000 GUARANIES
21.3000 g., 0.9000 Gold .6164 oz. AGW **Obv:** National arms
Rev: Head of Albert Einstein left
Date	Mintage	F	VF	XF	Unc	BU
1974 Proof	Est. 1,500	Value: 750				

KM# 139 3000 GUARANIES
21.3000 g., 0.9000 Gold .6164 oz. AGW **Obv:** National arms
Rev: Head of Konrad Adenauer left
Date	Mintage	F	VF	XF	Unc	BU
1974 Proof	Est. 1,500	Value: 750				

KM# 162 3000 GUARANIES
21.3000 g., 0.9000 Gold .6164 oz. AGW **Obv:** National arms
Rev: Parliament building
Date	Mintage	F	VF	XF	Unc	BU
1975 Proof	—	Value: 700				

KM# 135 3000 GUARANIES
21.3000 g., 0.9000 Gold .6164 oz. AGW **Obv:** National arms
Rev: Head of Giuseppe Garibaldi facing
Date	Mintage	F	VF	XF	Unc	BU
1974 Proof	Est. 1,500	Value: 750				

KM# 140 3000 GUARANIES
21.3000 g., 0.9000 Gold .6164 oz. AGW **Obv:** National arms
Rev: Head of Sir Winston Churchill left
Date	Mintage	F	VF	XF	Unc	BU
1974 Proof	Est. 1,500	Value: 750				

KM# 163 3000 GUARANIES
21.3000 g., 0.9000 Gold .6164 oz. AGW **Obv:** National arms
Rev: Friendship bridge
Date	Mintage	F	VF	XF	Unc	BU
1975 Proof	—	Value: 700				

KM# 136 3000 GUARANIES
21.3000 g., 0.9000 Gold .6164 oz. AGW **Obv:** National arms
Rev: Bust of Alessandro Manzoni facing
Date	Mintage	F	VF	XF	Unc	BU
1974 Proof	Est. 1,500	Value: 750				

KM# 141 3000 GUARANIES
21.3000 g., 0.9000 Gold .6164 oz. AGW **Obv:** National arms
Rev: Head of Pope John XXIII left
Date	Mintage	F	VF	XF	Unc	BU
1974 Proof	Est. 1,500	Value: 750				

KM# 164 3000 GUARANIES
21.3000 g., 0.9000 Gold .6164 oz. AGW **Obv:** National arms
Rev: Humaita ruins
Date	Mintage	F	VF	XF	Unc	BU
1975 Proof	—	Value: 700				

KM# 137 3000 GUARANIES
21.3000 g., 0.9000 Gold .6164 oz. AGW **Obv:** National arms
Rev: William Tell and son facing
Date	Mintage	F	VF	XF	Unc	BU
1974 Proof	Est. 1,500	Value: 750				

KM# 142 3000 GUARANIES
21.3000 g., 0.9000 Gold .6164 oz. AGW **Obv:** National arms
Rev: Head of Pope Paul VI left
Date	Mintage	F	VF	XF	Unc	BU
1974 Proof	Est. 1,500	Value: 750				

KM# 175 3000 GUARANIES
21.3000 g., 0.9000 Gold .6164 oz. AGW **Subject:** Apollo 11 Mission **Obv:** National arms **Rev:** Eagle landing on moon with earth at upper left
Date	Mintage	F	VF	XF	Unc	BU
1975 Proof	—	Value: 1,000				

PARAGUAY 559

KM# 176 3000 GUARANIES
21.3000 g., 0.9000 Gold .6164 oz. AGW **Subject:** Apollo 15 Mission within circle **Obv:** National arms **Rev:** Apollo mission design within circle

Date	Mintage	F	VF	XF	Unc	BU
1975 Proof	—				Value: 1,000	

KM# 52 4500 GUARANIES
31.9000 g., 0.9000 Gold .9231 oz. AGW **Obv:** National arms **Rev:** General A. Stroessner

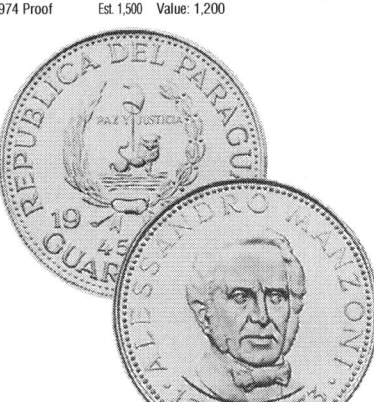

Date	Mintage	F	VF	XF	Unc	BU
1972 Proof	Est. 1,500				Value: 950	

KM# 53 4500 GUARANIES
31.9000 g., 0.9000 Gold .9231 oz. AGW **Subject:** Munich Olympics **Obv:** National arms **Rev:** Runner

Date	Mintage	F	VF	XF	Unc	BU
1972 Proof	Est. 1,500				Value: 2,700	

KM# 54 4500 GUARANIES
31.9000 g., 0.9000 Gold .9231 oz. AGW **Subject:** Munich Olympics **Obv:** National arms **Rev:** Broad jumper

Date	Mintage	F	VF	XF	Unc	BU
1972 Proof	Est. 1,500				Value: 2,700	

KM# 55 4500 GUARANIES
31.9000 g., 0.9000 Gold .9231 oz. AGW **Subject:** Munich Olympics **Obv:** National arms **Rev:** Soccer

Date	Mintage	F	VF	XF	Unc	BU
1972 Proof	Est. 1,500				Value: 2,700	

KM# 56 4500 GUARANIES
31.9000 g., 0.9000 Gold .9231 oz. AGW **Subject:** Munich Olympics **Obv:** National arms **Rev:** Hurdler

Date	Mintage	F	VF	XF	Unc	BU
1972 Proof	Est. 1,500				Value: 2,700	

KM# 57 4500 GUARANIES
31.9000 g., 0.9000 Gold .9231 oz. AGW **Subject:** Munich Olympics **Obv:** National arms **Rev:** High jumper

Date	Mintage	F	VF	XF	Unc	BU
1972 Proof	Est. 1,500				Value: 2,700	

KM# 58 4500 GUARANIES
31.9000 g., 0.9000 Gold .9231 oz. AGW **Subject:** Munich Olympics **Obv:** National arms **Rev:** Boxer

Date	Mintage	F	VF	XF	Unc	BU
1973 Proof	Est. 1,500				Value: 2,700	

KM# 92 4500 GUARANIES
31.9000 g., 0.9000 Gold .9231 oz. AGW **Obv:** National arms **Rev:** Bust of Mariscal Jose F. Estigarribia facing

Date	Mintage	F	VF	XF	Unc	BU
1973 Proof	Est. 1,500				Value: 1,200	

KM# 93 4500 GUARANIES
31.9000 g., 0.9000 Gold .9231 oz. AGW **Obv:** National arms **Rev:** Bust of Mariscal Francisco Solano Lopez facing

Date	Mintage	F	VF	XF	Unc	BU
1973 Proof	Est. 1,500				Value: 1,200	

KM# 94 4500 GUARANIES
31.9000 g., 0.9000 Gold .9231 oz. AGW **Obv:** National arms **Rev:** Head of General Jose E. Diaz facing

Date	Mintage	F	VF	XF	Unc	BU
1973 Proof	Est. 1,500				Value: 1,200	

KM# 95 4500 GUARANIES
31.9000 g., 0.9000 Gold .9231 oz. AGW **Obv:** National arms **Rev:** Head of General Bernardino Caballero facing

Date	Mintage	F	VF	XF	Unc	BU
1973 Proof	Est. 1,500				Value: 1,200	

KM# 96 4500 GUARANIES
31.9000 g., 0.9000 Gold .9231 oz. AGW **Obv:** National arms **Rev:** Teotihucana Culture sculpture

Date	Mintage	F	VF	XF	Unc	BU
1973 Proof	Est. 1,500				Value: 1,200	

KM# 97 4500 GUARANIES
31.9000 g., 0.9000 Gold .9231 oz. AGW **Obv:** National arms **Rev:** Huasteca Culture sculpture

Date	Mintage	F	VF	XF	Unc	BU
1973 Proof	Est. 1,500				Value: 1,200	

KM# 98 4500 GUARANIES
31.9000 g., 0.9000 Gold .9231 oz. AGW **Obv:** National arms **Rev:** Mixteca Culture sculpture

Date	Mintage	F	VF	XF	Unc	BU
1973 Proof	Est. 1,500				Value: 1,200	

KM# 99 4500 GUARANIES
31.9000 g., 0.9000 Gold .9231 oz. AGW **Obv:** National arms **Rev:** Veracruz Ceramica sculpture

Date	Mintage	F	VF	XF	Unc	BU
1973 Proof	Est. 1,500				Value: 1,200	

KM# 100 4500 GUARANIES
31.9000 g., 0.9000 Gold .9231 oz. AGW **Obv:** National arms **Rev:** Veracruz Culture bust

Date	Mintage	F	VF	XF	Unc	BU
1973 Proof	Est. 1,500				Value: 1,200	

KM# 101 4500 GUARANIES
31.9000 g., 0.9000 Gold .9231 oz. AGW **Obv:** National arms **Rev:** Bust of Albrecht Durer facing

Date	Mintage	F	VF	XF	Unc	BU
1973 Proof	Est. 1,500				Value: 1,200	

KM# 102 4500 GUARANIES
31.9000 g., 0.9000 Gold .9231 oz. AGW **Obv:** National arms **Rev:** Johann Wolfgang Goethe facing

Date	Mintage	F	VF	XF	Unc	BU
1973 Proof	Est. 1,500				Value: 1,200	

KM# 103 4500 GUARANIES
31.9000 g., 0.9000 Gold .9231 oz. AGW **Obv:** National arms **Rev:** Ludwig van Beethoven left

Date	Mintage	F	VF	XF	Unc	BU
1974 Proof	Est. 1,500				Value: 2,100	

KM# 104 4500 GUARANIES
31.9000 g., 0.9000 Gold .9231 oz. AGW **Obv:** National arms **Rev:** Head of Otto von Biscarck right

Date	Mintage	F	VF	XF	Unc	BU
1974 Proof	Est. 1,500				Value: 1,200	

KM# 105 4500 GUARANIES
31.9000 g., 0.9000 Gold .9231 oz. AGW **Obv:** National arms **Rev:** Giuseppe Garibaldi facing

Date	Mintage	F	VF	XF	Unc	BU
1974 Proof	Est. 1,500				Value: 1,200	

KM# 106 4500 GUARANIES
31.9000 g., 0.9000 Gold .9231 oz. AGW **Obv:** National arms **Rev:** Alessandro Manzoni facing

Date	Mintage	F	VF	XF	Unc	BU
1974 Proof	Est. 1,500				Value: 1,200	

KM# 143 4500 GUARANIES
31.9000 g., 0.9000 Gold .9231 oz. AGW **Obv:** National arms **Rev:** President Abraham Lincoln left

Date	Mintage	F	VF	XF	Unc	BU
1974 Proof	Est. 1,500				Value: 1,200	

KM# 144 4500 GUARANIES
31.9000 g., 0.9000 Gold .9231 oz. AGW **Obv:** National arms **Rev:** Albert Einstein left

Date	Mintage	F	VF	XF	Unc	BU
1974 Proof	Est. 1,500				Value: 1,200	

KM# 145 4500 GUARANIES
31.9000 g., 0.9000 Gold .9231 oz. AGW **Obv:** National arms **Rev:** William Tell and son facing

Date	Mintage	F	VF	XF	Unc	BU
1974 Proof	Est. 1,500				Value: 1,200	

KM# 146 4500 GUARANIES
31.9000 g., 0.9000 Gold .9231 oz. AGW **Obv:** National arms **Rev:** President John F. Kennedy left

Date	Mintage	F	VF	XF	Unc	BU
1974 Proof	Est. 1,500				Value: 1,200	

KM# 147 4500 GUARANIES
31.9000 g., 0.9000 Gold .9231 oz. AGW **Obv:** National arms **Rev:** Konrad Adenauer left

Date	Mintage	F	VF	XF	Unc	BU
1974 Proof	Est. 1,500				Value: 1,200	

KM# 148 4500 GUARANIES
31.9000 g., 0.9000 Gold .9231 oz. AGW **Obv:** National arms **Rev:** Sir Winston Churchill left

Date	Mintage	F	VF	XF	Unc	BU
1974 Proof	Est. 1,500				Value: 1,200	

KM# 149 4500 GUARANIES
31.9000 g., 0.9000 Gold .9231 oz. AGW **Obv:** National arms **Rev:** Pope JOhn XXIII left

Date	Mintage	F	VF	XF	Unc	BU
1974 Proof	Est. 1,500				Value: 1,200	

KM# 150 4500 GUARANIES
31.9000 g., 0.9000 Gold .9231 oz. AGW **Obv:** National arms **Rev:** Pope Paul VI left

Date	Mintage	F	VF	XF	Unc	BU
1974 Proof	Est. 1,500				Value: 1,200	

KM# 185 4500 GUARANIES
31.9000 g., 0.9000 Gold .9231 oz. AGW **Obv:** National arms **Rev:** Parliament building

Date	Mintage	F	VF	XF	Unc	BU
1975 Proof	Est. 1,500				Value: 1,200	

KM# 186 4500 GUARANIES
31.9000 g., 0.9000 Gold .9231 oz. AGW **Subject:** Apollo 11 Mission **Obv:** National arms **Rev:** Eagle landing on moon with earth at upper left

Date	Mintage	F	VF	XF	Unc	BU
1975 Proof	Est. 1,500				Value: 1,200	

KM# 187 4500 GUARANIES
31.9000 g., 0.9000 Gold .9231 oz. AGW **Subject:** Apollo 15 Mission **Obv:** National arms **Rev:** Apollo mission designs within circle

Date	Mintage	F	VF	XF	Unc	BU
1975 Proof	Est. 1,500				Value: 1,200	

KM# 188 4500 GUARANIES
31.9000 g., 0.9000 Gold .9231 oz. AGW **Obv:** National arms **Rev:** Friendship bridge

Date	Mintage	F	VF	XF	Unc	BU
1975 Proof	Est. 1,500				Value: 1,200	

KM# 189 4500 GUARANIES
31.9000 g., 0.9000 Gold .9231 oz. AGW **Obv:** National arms **Rev:** Holy Trinity Church

Date	Mintage	F	VF	XF	Unc	BU
1975 Proof	Est. 1,500				Value: 1,200	

KM# 190 4500 GUARANIES
31.9000 g., 0.9000 Gold .9231 oz. AGW **Obv:** National arms **Rev:** Ruins of Humaita

Date	Mintage	F	VF	XF	Unc	BU
1975 Proof	Est. 1,500				Value: 1,200	

KM# 30 10000 GUARANIES
46.0100 g., 0.9000 Gold 1.3315 oz. AGW **Subject:** 4th Term of President Stroessner **Obv:** Seated lion with liberty cap on pole within circle **Rev:** Head of President Stroessner left **Note:** Similar to 300 Guaranies KM#29. KM#30 struck for presentation.

Date	Mintage	F	VF	XF	Unc	BU
ND(1968) Proof	Est. 50				Value: 4,500	

KM# 168 70000 GUARANIES
46.0000 g., 0.9000 Gold 1.3310 oz. AGW **Subject:** 6th Term of President A. Stroessner **Obv:** Seated lion with Liberty cap on pole within circle **Rev:** Bust of President A. Stroessner left

Date	Mintage	F	VF	XF	Unc	BU
ND(1978) Proof	300				Value: 1,100	

560 PARAGUAY

KM# 170 100000 GUARANIES
46.0000 g., 0.9000 Gold 1.3310 oz. AGW **Subject:** 7th Term of President A. Stroessner **Obv:** Seated lion with Liberty cap on pole within circle **Rev:** Bust of President A. Stroessner left

Date	Mintage	F	VF	XF	Unc	BU
ND(1983) Proof	300	Value: 1,100				

KM# 172 250000 GUARANIES
46.0000 g., 0.9170 Gold 1.3561 oz. AGW **Obv:** Bank building within circle **Rev:** Conjoined busts of Caballero and Stroessner left

Date	Mintage	F	VF	XF	Unc	BU
ND(1987) Proof	Est. 500	Value: 1,100				

Note: 250 pieces remelted

KM# 174 300000 GUARANIES
46.0000 g., 0.9170 Gold 1.3561 oz. AGW **Subject:** 8th Term of President A. Stroessner **Obv:** Seated lion with Liberty cap on pole within circle **Rev:** Bust of President A. Stroessner left

Date	Mintage	F	VF	XF	Unc	BU
ND(1988) Proof	Est. 500	Value: 1,100				

Note: 250 pieces remelted

PATTERNS
Including off metal strikes

KM#	Date	Mintage	Identification	Mkt Val
Pn3	1855	—	4 Pesos. Gold. Seated lion with radiant liberty cap on pole. Seated Justice within wreath, date below.	—
Pn4	1855	—	4 Pesos. Silver.	—
Pn5	1855	—	4 Pesos. Gilt Silver.	—
Pn6	1855	—	4 Pesos. Copper.	—
Pn18	1867	—	4 Pesos. Gold. Seated lion with radiant liberty cap on pole. Seated Justice within wreath, date below.	—
PnA19	1867	—	4 Pesos. Silver.	—
Pn19	1867	—	4 Pesos. Copper.	—
Pn20	1867	—	1/4 Real. Gold. Seated lion with radiant liberty cap on pole. Star above shield within sprays.	—
Pn36	1873	—	5 Pesos. Silver.	—
PnE37	18xx	—	Peso. Gold. Struck over Peru 8 Escudos.	—

Note: UBS Sale #63, 9-05, set of PnA37-E37, MS-63-65 realized $25,200

PnC37	18xx	—	20 Centimos. Gold. Struck over Argentina Argentino.	—
PnD37	18xx	—	50 Centavos. Gold. Struck over Chile 10 Pesos.	—
Pn44	1976	—	10 Guarani. Gold.	450
Pn45	1976	—	10 10 Guaranies. Gold.	750
Pn46	1978	—	10 Guarani. Gold.	450
Pn47	1978	—	10 5 Guaranies. Gold.	550
Pn48	1978	—	10 10 Guaranies. Gold.	750
Pn49	1980	—	10 Guarani. Gold.	450
Pn50	1980	—	10 5 Guaranies. Gold.	550
Pn51	1980	—	10 10 Guaranies. Gold.	750
Pn52	1980	—	10 50 Guaranies. Gold.	1,100

PROOF SETS

KM#	Date	Mintage	Identification	Issue Price	Mkt Val
PS2	1972 (24)	150	KM31-36, 38-43, 45-50, 52-57	—	—
PS3	1973 (48)	150	KM37, 44, 51, 58-102	—	—
PS4	1974 (48)	150	KM103-150	—	—
PS5	1975 (24)	150	KM155-164, 175-176, 179-190	—	—

PERU

The Republic of Peru, located on the Pacific coast of South America, has an area of 496,225 sq. mi. (1,285,220sq. km.) and a population of *21.4 million. Capital: Lima. The diversified economy includes mining, fishing and agriculture. Fish meal, copper, sugar, zinc and iron ore are exported.

Once part of the great Inca Empire that reached from northern Ecuador to central Chile, the conquest of Peru by Francisco Pizarro began in 1531. Desirable as the richest of the Spanish viceroyalties, it was torn by warfare between avaricious Spaniards until the arrival in 1569 of Francisco de Toledo, who initiated 2-1/2 centuries of efficient colonial rule, which made Lima the most aristocratic colonial capital and the stronghold of Spain's American possessions. Jose de San Martin of Argentina proclaimed Peru's independence on July 28, 1821; Simon Bolivar of Venezuela secured it in December, 1824 when he defeated the last Spanish army in South America. After several futile attempts to re-establish its South American empire, Spain recognized Peru's independence in 1879.

Andres de Santa Cruz, whose mother was a high-ranking Inca, was the best of Bolivia's early presidents, and temporarily united Peru and Bolivia 1836-39, thus realizing his dream of a Peruvian/Bolivian confederation. This prompted the separate coinages of North and South Peru. Peruvian resistance and Chilean intervention finally broke up the confederation, sending Santa Cruz into exile. A succession of military strongman presidents ruled Peru until Marshall Castilla revitalized Peruvian politics in the mid-19th century and repulsed Spain's attempt to reclaim its one-time colony. Subsequent loss of southern territory to Chile in the War of the Pacific, 1879-81, and gradually increasing rejection of foreign economic domination, combined with recent serious inflation, affected the country numismatically.

As a result of the discovery of silver at Potosi in 1545, a mint was eventually authorized in 1565 with the first minting of coinage taking place in 1568. The mint had an uneven life span during the Spanish Colonial period from 1568-72. It was closed from 1573-76, reopened from 1577-88. It remained closed until 1659-1660 when an unauthorized coinage in both silver and gold were struck. After being closed in 1660, it remained closed until 1684 when it struck cob style coins until 1752.

RULER
Spanish until 1822

MINT MARKS
AREQUIPA, AREQ = Arequipa
AYACUCHO = Ayacucho
(B) = Brussels
CUZCO (monogram), Cuzco, Co. Cuzco
L, LIMAE (monogram), Lima
(monogram), LIMA = Lima
L*M = Lima
LI*M = Lima
(L) = London
PASCO (monogram), Pasco, Paz, Po= Pasco
P, (P) = Philadelphia
P = Peru (Lima)
P* = Peru (Lima)
S = San Francisco
(W) = Waterbury, CT, USA
0500 scan in 19th century

NOTE: The LIMAE monogram appears in three forms. The early LM monogram form looks like a dotted L with M. The later LIMAE monogram has all the letters of LIMAE more readily distinguishable. The third form appears as an M monogram during early Republican issues.

MONETARY SYSTEM
16 Reales = 2 Pesos = 1 Escudo

SPANISH COLONY
MILLED COINAGE

KM# 125 1/2 ESCUDO
1.6875 g., 0.8730 Gold .0475 oz. AGW **Obv:** Laureate head right **Obv. Legend:** FERDND • VII... **Rev:** Crowned arms in order chain

Date	Mintage	VG	F	VF	XF	Unc
1814L JP	—	200	400	700	1,250	—
1815L JP	—	200	400	700	1,250	—
1816L JP	—	200	400	700	1,250	—
1817L JP	—	200	400	700	1,250	—
1818L JP	—	200	400	700	1,250	1,750
1819L JP	—	200	400	700	1,250	—

PERU

Date	Mintage	VG	F	VF	XF	Unc
1820L JP	—	200	400	700	1,250	—
1821L JP	—	200	400	700	1,250	—

KM# 89 ESCUDO
3.3834 g., 0.8750 Gold .0952 oz. AGW **Obv:** Bust of Charles IV, right **Obv. Legend:** CAROL • IIII... **Rev:** Crowned arms in order chain **Note:** Mint mark in monogram.

Date	Mintage	VG	F	VF	XF	Unc
1801LIMAE IJ	—	100	175	265	450	—
1802LIMAE IJ	—	100	175	265	450	—
1803LIMAE IJ	—	100	175	265	450	—
1803LIMAE JP	—	100	175	265	450	—
1804LIMAE JP	—	100	175	265	450	—
1805LIMAE JP	—	100	175	265	450	—
1806LIMAE JP	—	100	175	265	450	—
1807LIMAE JP	—	100	175	265	450	—
1808LIMAE JP	—	125	200	300	500	—

KM# 110 ESCUDO
3.3834 g., 0.8750 Gold .0952 oz. AGW **Obv:** Uniformed Lima (imaginary) bust right **Obv. Legend:** FERDIN • VII... **Rev:** Crowned arms divides value in order chain **Note:** Mint mark in monogram.

Date	Mintage	VG	F	VF	XF	Unc
1809LIMAE JP Rare	—	—	—	—	—	—
1810LIMAE JP	—	250	450	950	1,650	—
1811LIMAE JP	—	350	650	1,150	2,000	—

KM# 119 ESCUDO
3.3834 g., 0.8750 Gold .0952 oz. AGW **Obv:** Draped laureate bust right **Obv. Legend:** FERDIN • VII... **Rev:** Crowned arms in order chain **Note:** Mint mark in monogram.

Date	Mintage	VG	F	VF	XF	Unc
1812LIMAE JP	—	175	300	500	850	—
1813LIMAE JP	—	150	250	400	750	—
1814LIMAE JP	—	150	300	500	850	—

KM# 126 ESCUDO
3.3834 g., 0.8750 Gold .0952 oz. AGW **Obv:** Laureate head right **Obv. Legend:** FERDIN • VII... **Rev:** Crowned arms in order chain **Note:** Mint mark in monogram.

Date	Mintage	VG	F	VF	XF	Unc
1814LIMAE JP	—	125	200	300	500	—
1815LIMAE JP	—	125	200	300	500	—
1816LIMAE JP	—	125	200	300	500	—
1817LIMAE JP	—	125	200	300	500	—
1818LIMAE JP	—	150	225	350	600	—
1819LIMAE JP	—	150	225	350	600	—
1820LIMAE JP	—	125	200	300	500	—
1821LIMAE JP	—	125	200	300	500	—

KM# 100 2 ESCUDOS
6.7668 g., 0.8750 Gold .1904 oz. AGW **Obv:** Bust of Charles IIII, right **Obv. Legend:** CAROL • IIII • ... **Rev:** Crowned arms in order chain **Note:** Mint mark in monogram.

Date	Mintage	VG	F	VF	XF	Unc
1802LIMAE IJ	—	175	375	675	900	—
1804LIMAE JP	—	150	300	575	775	—
1805LIMAE JP	—	150	300	575	775	—
1806LIMAE JP	—	175	375	675	900	—
1807LIMAE JP	—	175	375	675	900	—
1808LIMAE JP	—	150	300	575	775	—

KM# 111 2 ESCUDOS
6.7668 g., 0.8750 Gold .1904 oz. AGW **Obv:** Uniformed Lima (imaginary) bust right **Obv. Legend:** FERDIN • VII... **Rev:** Crowned arms in order chain **Note:** Mint mark in monogram.

Date	Mintage	VG	F	VF	XF	Unc
1809LIMAE JP	—	350	650	1,200	2,000	—
1810LIMAE JP	—	350	650	1,200	2,000	—
1811LIMAE JP Smaller bust	—	350	650	1,200	2,000	—

KM# 120 2 ESCUDOS
6.7668 g., 0.8750 Gold .1904 oz. AGW **Obv:** Draped laureate bust right **Obv. Legend:** FERDIN • VII... **Rev:** Crowned arms in order chain **Note:** Mint mark in monogram.

Date	Mintage	VG	F	VF	XF	Unc
1812LIMAE JP	—	225	450	750	1,250	—
1813LIMAE JP	—	225	450	750	1,250	—

KM# 127 2 ESCUDOS
6.7668 g., 0.8750 Gold .1904 oz. AGW **Obv:** Laureate head right **Obv. Legend:** FERDIN • VII... **Rev:** Crowned arms in order chain **Note:** Mint mark in monogram.

Date	Mintage	VG	F	VF	XF	Unc
1814LIMAE JP	—	175	375	675	950	—
1815LIMAE JP	—	175	325	600	900	—
1816LIMAE JP	—	175	400	700	1,100	—
1817LIMAE JP	—	200	400	700	1,000	—
1818LIMAE JP	—	150	300	575	850	—
1819LIMAE JP	—	150	300	575	850	—
1820LIMAE JP	—	200	400	700	1,100	—
1821LIMAE JP	—	175	325	600	900	—

KM# 98 4 ESCUDOS
13.5337 g., 0.8750 Gold .3807 oz. AGW **Obv:** Bust of Charles IIII, right **Obv. Legend:** CAROL • IIII... **Rev:** Crowned arms in order chain **Note:** Mint mark in monogram.

Date	Mintage	VG	F	VF	XF	Unc
1801LIMAE IJ	—	475	650	900	1,250	—
1804LIMAE JP	—	475	650	900	1,250	—
1805LIMAE JP	—	475	650	900	1,250	—
1806LIMAE JP	—	475	650	900	1,250	—
1807LIMAE JP	—	475	650	900	1,250	—
1808LIMAE JP Rare	—	—	—	—	—	—

KM# 112 4 ESCUDOS
13.5337 g., 0.8750 Gold .3807 oz. AGW **Obv:** Uniformed Lima (imaginary) bust right **Obv. Legend:** FERDIN • VII... **Rev:** Crowned arms in order chain **Note:** Mint mark in monogram.

Date	Mintage	VG	F	VF	XF	Unc
1809LIMAE JP	—	1,500	2,000	3,250	6,000	—
1810LIMAE JP	—	1,250	1,850	3,000	5,500	—

Note: American Numismatic Rarities Eliasberg sale 4-05, AU-50 realized $13,800

KM# 121 4 ESCUDOS
13.5337 g., 0.8750 Gold .3807 oz. AGW **Obv:** Large laureate draped bust right **Obv. Legend:** FERDIN • VII... **Rev:** Crowned arms in order chains **Note:** Mint mark in monogram.

Date	Mintage	VG	F	VF	XF	Unc
1812LIMAE JP	—	1,500	2,000	3,250	5,750	—

KM# 122 4 ESCUDOS
13.5337 g., 0.8750 Gold .3807 oz. AGW **Obv:** Small laureate draped bust right **Obv. Legend:** FERDIN • VII... **Rev:** Crowned arms in order chain **Note:** Mint mark in monogram.

Date	Mintage	VG	F	VF	XF	Unc
1812LIMAE JP	—	1,200	2,000	3,750	6,500	—

Note: American Numismatic Rarities Eliasberg sale 4-05, MS-61 realized $14,950

1813LIMAE JP	—	1,200	2,000	3,750	6,500	—

Note: American Numismatic Rarities Eliasberg sale 4-05, AU-58 realized $9,200

KM# 128 4 ESCUDOS
13.5337 g., 0.8750 Gold .3807 oz. AGW **Obv:** Laureate head right **Obv. Legend:** FERDIN • VII... **Rev:** Crowned arms in order chain **Note:** Mint mark in monogram.

Date	Mintage	VG	F	VF	XF	Unc
1814LIMAE JP	—	575	750	1,200	1,800	—
1815LIMAE JP	—	450	600	900	1,500	—
1816LIMAE JP	—	450	600	900	1,500	—
1817LIMAE JP	—	600	900	1,500	2,000	—
1818LIMAE JP	—	450	600	900	1,450	—
1819LIMAE JP	—	475	650	1,000	1,500	—
1820LIMAE JP	—	500	700	1,100	1,750	—
1821LIMAE JP	—	575	750	1,200	1,800	—

KM# 101 8 ESCUDOS
27.0674 g., 0.8750 Gold .7615 oz. AGW **Obv:** Bust of Charles IIII, right **Obv. Legend:** CAROL • IIII... **Rev:** Crowned arms in order chain **Rev. Legend:** VTROQ • FELIX • AUSPICE • DEO **Note:** Mint mark in monogram.

Date	Mintage	VG	F	VF	XF	Unc
1801LIMAE IJ	—	500	550	700	1,100	—
1802LIMAE IJ	—	500	550	700	1,100	—
1803LIMAE IJ	—	500	550	700	1,100	—
1803LIMAE JP	—	500	550	800	1,350	—
1804LIMAE IJ	—	600	900	1,800	3,000	—
1804LIMAE JP	—	500	550	800	1,350	—
1805LIMAE JP	—	500	550	700	1,100	—
1806/5LIMAE JP	—	500	550	700	1,100	—
1806LIMAE JP	—	500	550	700	1,100	—
1807LIMAE JP	—	500	550	700	1,100	—
1808LIMAE JP	—	500	550	700	1,100	3,750

562   PERU

Date	Mintage	VG	F	VF	XF	Unc
1814LIMAE JP	—	500	550	700	1,100	—
1815LIMAE JP	—	500	550	700	1,100	—
1816LIMAE JP	—	500	550	800	1,350	—
1817LIMAE JP	—	500	550	700	1,100	—
1818LIMAE JP	—	500	550	700	1,100	—
1819LIMAE JP	—	500	550	700	1,250	—
1820LIMAE JP	—	500	550	700	1,250	—
1821LIMAE JP	—	500	550	750	1,150	—

KM# 107 8 ESCUDOS
27.0000 g., 0.8750 Gold .7596 oz. AGW **Obv:** Uniformed Lima (imaginary) bust right **Obv. Legend:** FERDIN • VII... **Rev:** Crowned arms in order chain **Rev. Legend:** VTROQ • FELIX • AUSPICE • DEO **Note:** Mint mark in monogram.

Date	Mintage	VG	F	VF	XF	Unc
1808LIMAE JP	—	550	1,350	2,500	4,000	—
1809LIMAE JP	—	550	800	1,500	2,250	—
1810LIMAE JP	—	550	800	1,500	2,250	4,000
1811LIMAE JP	—	550	800	1,500	2,250	3,750

KM# 118 8 ESCUDOS
27.0674 g., 0.8750 Gold .7615 oz. AGW **Obv:** Large laureate draped bust right **Obv. Legend:** FERDIN • VII... **Rev:** Crowned arms in order chain **Rev. Legend:** VTROQ • FELIX • AUSPICE • DEO **Note:** Mint mark in monogram.

Date	Mintage	VG	F	VF	XF	Unc
1811LIMAE JP Rare	—	—	—	—	—	—
1812LIMAE JP	—	550	900	1,500	2,500	—

KM# 124 8 ESCUDOS
27.0674 g., 0.8750 Gold .7615 oz. AGW **Obv:** Small laureate draped bust right **Obv. Legend:** FERDIN • VII... **Rev:** Crowned arms in order chain **Rev. Legend:** VTROQ • FELIX • AUSPICE • DEO **Note:** Mint mark in monogram.

Date	Mintage	VG	F	VF	XF	Unc
1812LIMAE JP	—	500	700	950	1,450	—
1813LIMAE JP	—	500	700	950	1,450	—

KM# 129.1 8 ESCUDOS
27.0674 g., 0.8750 Gold .7615 oz. AGW **Obv:** Small laureate head right **Obv. Legend:** FERDIN • VII... **Rev:** Crowned arms in order chain **Rev. Legend:** VTROQ • FELIX • AUSPICE • DEO **Note:** Mint mark in monogram.

KM# 129.2 8 ESCUDOS
27.0674 g., 0.8750 Gold .7615 oz. AGW **Obv:** Large laureate head right **Obv. Legend:** FERDIN • VII... **Rev:** Crowned arms in order chain **Rev. Legend:** VTROQ • FELIX • AUSPICE • DEO

Date	Mintage	VG	F	VF	XF	Unc
1824Co G	—	750	1,250	1,850	2,750	—

REPUBLIC
REAL - ESCUDO COINAGE

KM# 146.2 1/2 ESCUDO
1.6873 g., 0.8750 Gold .0475 oz. AGW **Obv:** Wreath above date **Obv. Legend:** .CUZCO G.M. **Rev:** Arms without shield

Date	Mintage	VG	F	VF	XF	Unc
1826CUZCO GM	—	35.00	75.00	120	210	—

KM# 146.1 1/2 ESCUDO
1.6873 g., 0.8750 Gold .0475 oz. AGW **Obv:** Wreath above date **Obv. Legend:** .LIMA.I.M. **Rev:** Arms without shield **Note:** Mint mark in monogram.

Date	Mintage	VG	F	VF	XF	Unc
1826LIMAE JM	—	45.00	90.00	150	275	—
1827LIMAE JM	—	60.00	125	225	425	—
1828LIMAE JM	—	35.00	70.00	115	200	—
1829LIMAE JM	—	30.00	50.00	80.00	150	—
1833LIMAE MM	—	35.00	70.00	115	200	300
1836LIMAE TM	—	35.00	70.00	115	200	—
1836LIMAE MM	—	—	—	—	—	—
1839LIMAE MB	—	60.00	125	225	425	—
1840LIMAE MB	—	30.00	50.00	80.00	150	—
1841LIMAE MB	—	35.00	70.00	115	200	—
1842LIMAE MB	—	45.00	75.00	125	250	—
1850LIMAE MB	—	35.00	70.00	115	200	—
1851LIMAE MB	—	75.00	125	250	550	1,500
1856LIMAE MB	—	45.00	90.00	150	275	500

Note: For coins of this type dated 1838 M, see North Peru

KM# 147.2 ESCUDO
3.3750 g., 0.8750 Gold .0949 oz. AGW **Obv. Legend:** REPUBLICA PERUANA

Date	Mintage	VG	F	VF	XF	Unc
1826CUZCO GM	—	100	160	285	550	—
1830CUZCO G	—	100	160	285	550	—

KM# 147.1 ESCUDO
3.3750 g., 0.8750 Gold .0949 oz. AGW **Obv. Legend:** REPUBLICA PERUANA **Note:** Mint mark in monogram.

Date	Mintage	VG	F	VF	XF	Unc
1826LIMAE JM	—	70.00	120	240	425	—
1827LIMAE JM	—	95.00	165	300	500	—
1828/7LIMAE JM	—	70.00	120	240	425	—
1828LIMAE JM	—	70.00	120	240	425	—
1829LIMAE JM	—	55.00	85.00	165	285	—
1833LIMAE MM	—	—	—	—	—	2,550

KM# 147.3 ESCUDO
3.3750 g., 0.8750 Gold .0949 oz. AGW **Obv:** Small wreath above flagged arms, date below **Obv. Legend:** REPUBLICA PERUANA... **Rev:** Standing Liberty **Rev. Legend:** FIRME Y FELIZ... **Note:** Mint mark in monogram.

Date	Mintage	VG	F	VF	XF	Unc
1840CUZco A	—	60.00	85.00	165	285	700
1845CUZco A	—	60.00	75.00	120	250	650
1846CUZco A	—	60.00	85.00	165	285	700

KM# 147.4 ESCUDO
3.3750 g., 0.8750 Gold .0949 oz. AGW **Obv. Legend:** REPUB PERUANA **Note:** Mint mark in monogram.

Date	Mintage	VG	F	VF	XF	Unc
1850LIMAE MB	—	—	—	—	—	—
1855LIMAE MB	—	70.00	120	240	425	—

KM# 149.1 2 ESCUDOS
6.8500 g., 0.8750 Gold .1899 oz. AGW **Obv:** Small wreath above flagged arms, date below **Obv. Legend:** REPUBLICA PERUANA... **Rev:** Standing Liberty **Rev. Legend:** FIRME Y FELIZ... **Note:** Mint mark in monogram.

Date	Mintage	VG	F	VF	XF	Unc
1828/7LIMAE JM	—	150	200	325	700	—
1828LIMAE JM	—	150	200	325	700	—
1829LIMAE JM	—	120	150	200	350	550
1833LIMAE MM	—	—	—	—	—	3,750

KM# 149.2 2 ESCUDOS
6.8500 g., 0.8750 Gold .1899 oz. AGW **Obv:** Small wreath above flagged arms, date below **Obv. Legend:** REPUB. PERUANA... **Rev:** Standing Liberty **Rev. Legend:** FIRME Y FELIZ... **Note:** Mint mark in monogram.

Date	Mintage	VG	F	VF	XF	Unc
1850LIMAE MB	—	120	150	245	450	650
1851LIMAE MB	—	120	150	240	425	650
1853LIMAE MB	—	120	130	150	275	450
1854LIMAE MB	—	135	175	300	550	750
1855LIMAE MB	—	135	175	300	550	750

KM# 150.1 4 ESCUDOS
13.5000 g., 0.8750 Gold .3798 oz. AGW **Obv. Legend:** REPUB. PERUANA

Date	Mintage	VG	F	VF	XF	Unc
1828LIMA JM Rare	—	—	—	—	—	—

KM# 150.2 4 ESCUDOS
13.5000 g., 0.8750 Gold .3798 oz. AGW **Obv:** Medium wreath above flagged arms, date below **Obv. Legend:** REPUBLICA PERUANA... **Rev:** Standing Liberty **Rev. Legend:** FIRME Y FELIZ... **Note:** Mint mark in monogram.

Date	Mintage	VG	F	VF	XF	Unc
1850LIMAE MB	—	250	350	600	1,000	3,200
1853LIMAE MB	—	300	475	750	1,500	—

KM# 150.3 4 ESCUDOS
13.5000 g., 0.8750 Gold .3798 oz. AGW **Obv:** Medium wreath above flagged arms, date below **Obv. Legend:** REPUBLICA PERUANA... **Rev:** Standing Liberty **Rev. Legend:** FIRME Y FELIZ... **Note:** Mint mark in monogram.

Date	Mintage	VG	F	VF	XF	Unc
1854LIMAE MB	—	250	325	550	900	—

PERU 563

KM# 150.4 4 ESCUDOS
13.5000 g., 0.8750 Gold .3798 oz. AGW **Obv:** Medium wreath above flagged arms, date below **Obv. Legend:** REPUBLICA PERUANA... **Rev:** Standing Liberty **Rev. Legend:** FIRME Y FELIZ... **Note:** Mint mark in monogram.

Date	Mintage	VG	F	VF	XF	Unc
1855LIMAE MB	—	245	275	375	650	—

KM# 148.2 8 ESCUDOS
27.0000 g., 0.8750 Gold .7596 oz. AGW **Obv:** Medium wreath above flagged arms, date below **Obv. Legend:** REPUBLICA PERUANA • CUZCO • B. A. **Rev:** Standing Liberty **Rev. Legend:** FIRME Y FELIZ POR LA UNION

Date	Mintage	VG	F	VF	XF	Unc
1826CUZCO GM	—	475	550	750	1,400	3,500
1827CUZCO G	—	475	550	750	1,400	—
1828/7CUZCO G	—	475	500	650	1,100	—
1828CUZCO G	—	475	500	650	1,100	—
1829CUZCO G	—	475	550	750	1,400	—
1830CUZCO G	—	475	500	650	1,100	2,750
1831CUZCO G	—	475	500	600	850	—
1832CUZCO VOARSH	—	475	500	650	900	1,850
1833CUZCO BoAr	—	475	500	600	850	1,650
1834CUZCO BoAr	—	475	500	650	1,000	2,750

KM# 148.1 8 ESCUDOS
27.0000 g., 0.8750 Gold .7596 oz. AGW **Obv:** Medium wreath above flagged arms, date below **Obv. Legend:** REPUBLICA PERUANA... **Rev:** Standing Liberty **Rev. Legend:** FIRME Y FELIZ... **Note:** Mint mark in monogram.

Date	Mintage	VG	F	VF	XF	Unc
1826LIMAE JM	—	475	500	600	850	—
1827LIMAE JM	—	475	500	650	950	—
1828LIMAE JM	—	475	550	800	1,500	—
1829/8LIMAE JM	—	475	500	650	950	—
1829LIMAE JM	—	475	500	650	950	2,250
1830LIMAE JM	—	475	500	650	950	—
1833LIMAE MM	—	475	500	600	850	—
1840LIMAE MB	—	475	550	800	1,500	—

KM# 148.3 8 ESCUDOS
27.0000 g., 0.8750 Gold .7596 oz. AGW **Obv:** Medium wreath above flagged arms, date below **Obv. Legend:** REPUBLICA PERUANA.... **Rev:** Standing Liberty **Rev. Legend:** FIRME Y FELIZ... **Note:** Mint mark in monogram.

Date	Mintage	VG	F	VF	XF	Unc
1835CUZco B	—	475	500	650	1,200	3,500
1836CUZco B	—	475	550	800	1,500	3,000
1839CUZco A	—	475	550	800	1,500	3,000
1840CUZco A	—	475	500	600	1,000	—
1843CUZco A	—	475	500	650	1,200	3,500
1844CUZco A	—	475	550	750	1,350	—
1845CUZco A	—	475	500	600	900	—

KM# 148.6 8 ESCUDOS
27.0000 g., 0.8750 Gold .7596 oz. AGW **Obv:** Medium wreath above flagged arms, date below **Obv. Legend:** REPUBLICA PERUANA... **Rev:** Standing Liberty **Rev. Legend:** FIRME Y FELIZ... **Note:** Mint mark in monogram.

Date	Mintage	VG	F	VF	XF	Unc
1850LIMA MB	—	475	500	600	950	—

KM# 148.4 8 ESCUDOS
27.0000 g., 0.8750 Gold .7596 oz. AGW **Obv:** Medium wreath above flagged arms, date below **Obv. Legend:** REPUBLICA PERUANA... **Rev:** Standing Liberty **Rev. Legend:** FIRME Y FELIZ... **Note:** Mint mark: LIMA

Date	Mintage	VG	F	VF	XF	Unc
1853LIMA MB	—	475	575	900	1,500	—
1854LIMA MB	—	475	500	550	800	—
1855LIMA MB	—	475	500	550	850	—

KM# 148.5 8 ESCUDOS
27.0000 g., 0.8750 Gold .7596 oz. AGW **Obv:** Medium wreath above flagged arms, date below **Obv. Legend:** REPUB. PERUANA... **Rev:** Standing Liberty **Rev. Legend:** FIRME Y FELIZ... **Note:** Mint mark in monogram.

Date	Mintage	VG	F	VF	XF	Unc
1855LIMA MB	—	475	500	550	800	—

REPUBLIC
Republic of Peru

TRANSITIONAL COINAGE
Issued during the changeover to the decimal system

KM# 184 4 ESCUDOS
13.5000 g., 0.8750 Gold .3798 oz. AGW **Obv:** Small wreath above flagged arms within sprigs, date below **Obv. Legend:** REBUBLICA PERUANA... **Rev:** Seated Liberty **Rev. Legend:** FIRME Y FELIZ...

Date	Mintage	F	VF	XF	Unc	BU
1863 YB Rare	—	—	—	—	—	—

Note: American Numismatic Rarities Eliasberg sale 4-05, MS-61 realized $32,200

KM# 183 8 ESCUDOS
27.0000 g., 0.8750 Gold .7596 oz. AGW **Obv:** Small wreath above flagged arms within sprigs, date below **Obv. Legend:** REPUBLICA PERUANA... **Rev:** Seated Liberty **Rev. Legend:** FIRME Y FELIZ...

Date	Mintage	F	VF	XF	Unc	BU
1862 YB	—	375	475	650	1,250	—
1863/2 YB	—	350	450	600	950	—
1863 YB	—	350	450	600	950	1,850

DECIMAL COINAGE
100 Centavos (10 Dineros) = 1 Sol; 10 Soles = 1 Libra

KM# 192 5 SOLES
8.0645 g., 0.9000 Gold .2334 oz. AGW **Obv:** Small wreath above flagged arms within sprigs, date below **Obv. Legend:** REPUBLICA PERUANA... **Rev:** Seated Liberty **Rev. Legend:** FIRME Y FELIZ... **Note:** Mint mark: LIMA

Date	Mintage	F	VF	XF	Unc	BU
1863LIMA YB	—	BV	165	250	475	—

PERU

KM# 193 10 SOLES
16.1290 g., 0.9000 Gold .4667 oz. AGW **Obv:** Small wreath above flagged arms within sprigs, date below **Obv. Legend:** REPUBLICA PERUANA... **Rev:** Seated Liberty **Rev. Legend:** FIRME Y FELIZ... **Note:** Mint mark: LIMA

Date	Mintage	F	VF	XF	Unc	BU
1863LIMA YB	—	—	BV	350	600	1,150

KM# 194 20 SOLES
32.2581 g., 0.9000 Gold .9334 oz. AGW **Obv:** Small wreath above flagged arms within sprigs, date below **Obv. Legend:** REPUBLICA PERUANA... **Rev:** Seated Liberty **Rev. Legend:** FIRME Y FELIZ... **Note:** Mint mark: LIMA

Date	Mintage	F	VF	XF	Unc	BU
1863LIMA YB	—	BV	620	650	950	—

DECIMAL COINAGE

100 Centavos (10 Dineros) = 1 Sol; 10 Soles = 1 Libra

KM# 268 1/2 SOL
9.3500 g., 0.9000 Gold .2706 oz. AGW **Subject:** 150th Anniversary - Battle of Ayacucho **Obv:** National arms **Rev:** Monument and value

Date	Mintage	F	VF	XF	Unc	BU
1976	10,000	—	—	—	200	—

KM# 269 SOL
23.4000 g., 0.9000 Gold .6772 oz. AGW **Subject:** 150th Anniversary - Battle of Ayacucho **Obv:** National arms within circle **Rev:** Monument divides value within circle **Note:** Mint mark in monogram.

Date	Mintage	F	VF	XF	Unc	BU
1976LIMA	10,000	—	—	—	475	—

KM# 235 5 SOLES
2.3404 g., 0.9000 Gold .0677 oz. AGW **Obv:** National arms above date **Rev:** Seated Liberty flanked by shield and column

Date	Mintage	F	VF	XF	Unc	BU
1956	4,510	—	—	BV	55.00	—
1957	2,146	—	—	BV	55.00	—
1959	1,536	—	—	BV	65.00	—
1960	8,133	—	—	BV	55.00	—
1961	1,154	—	—	BV	65.00	—
1962	1,550	—	—	BV	55.00	—
1963	3,945	—	—	BV	55.00	—
1964	2,063	—	—	BV	60.00	—
1965	14,000	—	—	BV	55.00	—
1966	4,738	—	—	BV	55.00	—
1967	3,651	—	—	BV	55.00	—
1969	127	—	—	BV	175	—

KM# 236 10 SOLES
4.6070 g., 0.9000 Gold .1354 oz. AGW **Obv:** National arms above date **Rev:** Seated Liberty flanked by shield and column

Date	Mintage	F	VF	XF	Unc	BU
1956	5,410	—	—	BV	95.00	—
1957	1,300	—	—	BV	100	—
1959	1,103	—	—	BV	100	—
1960	7,178	—	—	BV	95.00	—
1961	1,634	—	—	BV	100	—
1962	1,676	—	—	BV	100	—
1963	3,372	—	—	BV	95.00	—
1964	1,554	—	—	BV	100	—
1965	14,000	—	—	BV	95.00	—
1966	2,601	—	—	BV	95.00	—
1967	3,002	—	—	BV	95.00	—
1968	100	—	BV	110	220	—
1969	100	—	BV	110	220	—

KM# 229 20 SOLES
9.3614 g., 0.9000 Gold .2709 oz. AGW, 22 mm. **Obv:** National arms **Rev:** Seated Liberty flanked by shield and column

Date	Mintage	F	VF	XF	Unc	BU
1950	1,800	—	—	BV	210	—
1951	9,264	—	—	BV	190	225
1952	424	—	—	BV	225	—
1953	1,435	—	—	BV	210	—
1954	1,732	—	—	BV	210	—
1955	1,971	—	—	BV	210	—
1956	1,201	—	—	BV	210	—
1957	11,000	—	—	BV	190	200
1958	11,000	—	—	BV	190	200
1959	12,000	—	—	BV	190	200
1960	7,753	—	—	BV	190	200
1961	1,825	—	—	BV	210	—
1962	2,282	—	—	BV	200	—
1963	3,892	—	—	BV	190	—
1964	1,302	—	—	BV	210	—
1965	12,000	—	—	BV	190	200
1966	4,001	—	—	BV	190	200
1967	5,003	—	—	BV	190	200
1968	640	—	—	BV	210	—
1969	640	—	—	BV	210	—

KM# 219 50 SOLES
33.4363 g., 0.9000 Gold .9675 oz. AGW **Obv:** Head with headdress left **Rev:** Sculpture

Date	Mintage	F	VF	XF	Unc	BU
1930	5,584	BV	675	950	1,600	—
1931	5,538	BV	675	950	1,500	—
1967	10,000	—	—	—	665	—
1968	300	—	—	—	700	—
1969	403	—	—	—	700	—

KM# 230 50 SOLES
23.4056 g., 0.9000 Gold .6772 oz. AGW **Obv:** National arms **Rev:** Seated Liberty flanked by shield and column **Note:** Similar to KM#229.

Date	Mintage	F	VF	XF	Unc	BU
1950	1,927	—	—	BV	470	—
1951	5,292	—	—	BV	470	525
1952	1,201	—	—	BV	525	—
1953	1,464	—	—	BV	470	—
1954	1,839	—	—	BV	470	—
1955	1,898	—	—	BV	470	—
1956	11,000	—	—	BV	470	500
1957	11,000	—	—	BV	470	500
1958	11,000	—	—	BV	470	500
1959	5,734	—	—	BV	470	500
1960	2,139	—	—	BV	470	—
1961	1,110	—	—	BV	525	—
1962	3,319	—	—	BV	470	—
1963	3,089	—	—	BV	470	—
1964/3	2,425	—	—	BV	470	—
1964	Inc. above	—	—	BV	470	—
1965	23,000	—	—	BV	470	500
1966	3,409	—	—	BV	470	525
1967	5,805	—	—	BV	470	525
1968	443	—	—	BV	550	—
1969	443	—	—	BV	550	—
1970	553	—	—	BV	550	—

KM# 242 50 SOLES
23.4056 g., 0.9000 Gold .6772 oz. AGW **Subject:** 400th Anniversary of Lima Mint **Obv:** National arms above value **Obv. Designer:** Armando Pareja **Rev:** Pillars of Hercules within inner circle **Rev. Designer:** Alonso de Rincon

Date	Mintage	F	VF	XF	Unc	BU
ND(1965)	17,000	—	—	—	470	525

KM# 250 50 SOLES
23.4056 g., 0.9000 Gold .6772 oz. AGW **Subject:** 100th Anniversary of Peru-Spain Naval Battle **Obv:** National arms above value **Rev:** Victory standing on globe divides dates **Designer:** Armando Pareja

Date	Mintage	F	VF	XF	Unc	BU
ND(1966)	6,409	—	—	—	550	600

KM# 231 100 SOLES
46.8071 g., 0.9000 Gold 1.3544 oz. AGW **Obv:** National arms **Rev:** Seated Liberty flanked by shield and column

Date	Mintage	F	VF	XF	Unc	BU
1950	1,176	—	—	BV	940	965
1951	8,241	—	—	BV	940	965
1952	126	—	—	2,000	3,000	3,500
1953	498	—	—	BV	940	975
1954	1,808	—	—	BV	940	965
1955	901	—	—	BV	940	965
1956	1,159	—	—	BV	940	965
1957	550	—	—	BV	940	975
1958	101	—	—	3,000	4,000	4,500
1959	4,710	—	—	BV	940	965
1960	2,207	—	—	BV	940	965
1961	6,982	—	—	BV	940	965
1962	9,678	—	—	BV	940	965
1963	7,342	—	—	BV	940	965
1964	11,000	—	—	BV	940	965
1965	23,000	—	—	BV	940	965
1966	3,409	—	—	BV	940	965
1967	6,431	—	—	BV	940	965
1968	540	—	—	BV	940	975
1969	540	—	—	BV	940	975
1970	425	—	—	BV	940	975

PERU 565

KM# 243 100 SOLES
46.8071 g., 0.9000 Gold 1.3544 oz. AGW **Subject:** 400th Anniversary of Lima Mint **Obv:** National arms **Obv. Designer:** Armando Pareja **Rev:** Pillars of Hercules within inner circle **Rev. Designer:** Alonso de Rincon

Date	Mintage	F	VF	XF	Unc	BU
ND(1965)	27,000	—	—	—	935	960

KM# 251 100 SOLES
46.8071 g., 0.9000 Gold 1.3544 oz. AGW **Subject:** 100th Anniversary of Peru-Spain Naval Battle **Obv:** National arms **Rev:** Victory standing on globe divides dates **Designer:** Armando Pareja

Date	Mintage	F	VF	XF	Unc	BU
ND(1966)	6,253	—	—	—	950	1,000

KM# 277 50000 SOLES
16.8600 g., 0.9170 Gold .5004 oz. AGW **Subject:** Alfonso Ugarte **Obv:** National arms within circle **Rev:** Head left **Note:** Mint mark in monogram.

Date	Mintage	F	VF	XF	Unc	BU
1979LIMA	10,000	—	—	—	360	385

KM# 278 50000 SOLES
16.8600 g., 0.9170 Gold .5004 oz. AGW **Subject:** Elias Aguirre **Obv:** National arms within circle **Rev:** Head left **Note:** Mint mark in monogram.

Date	Mintage	F	VF	XF	Unc	BU
1979LIMA	10,000	—	—	—	360	385

KM# 279 50000 SOLES
16.8600 g., 0.9170 Gold .5004 oz. AGW **Subject:** F. Garcia Calderon **Obv:** National arms within circle **Rev:** Bust left **Note:** Mint mark in monogram.

Date	Mintage	F	VF	XF	Unc	BU
1979LIMA	10,000	—	—	—	360	385

KM# 280 100000 SOLES
33.9000 g., 0.9170 Gold .9995 oz. AGW **Subject:** Francisco Bolognese **Obv:** National arms within circle **Rev:** Bust left **Note:** Mint mark in monogram.

Date	Mintage	F	VF	XF	Unc	BU
1979LIMA	10,000	—	—	—	700	750

KM# 281 100000 SOLES
33.9000 g., 0.9170 Gold .9995 oz. AGW **Subject:** Andres A. Caceres **Obv:** National arms within circle **Rev:** Head left **Note:** Mint mark in monogram.

Date	Mintage	F	VF	XF	Unc	BU
1979LIMA	10,000	—	—	—	700	750

KM# 282 100000 SOLES
33.9000 g., 0.9170 Gold .9995 oz. AGW **Subject:** Miguel Grau **Obv:** National arms within circle **Rev:** Bust left **Note:** Mint mark in monogram.

Date	Mintage	F	VF	XF	Unc	BU
1979LIMA	10,000	—	—	—	700	750

REFORM COINAGE
1/M Intis = 1 Nuevo Sol; 100 (New) Centimos = 1 Nuevo Sol

KM# 312 NUEVO SOL
33.6250 g., 0.9170 Gold 1.0000 oz. AGW **Obv:** National arms **Rev:** Cultural artifacts within circle **Note:** Similar to KM#311.

Date	Mintage	F	VF	XF	Unc	BU
1994	899					
1994 Proof	100	Value: 750				

TRADE COINAGE

KM# 210 1/5 LIBRA (Pound)
1.5976 g., 0.9170 Gold .0471 oz. AGW **Obv:** Shield within sprigs with small radiant sun above **Rev:** Head with headband right **Note:** Struck at Lima.

Date	Mintage	F	VF	XF	Unc	BU
1906 GOZF	106,000	—	BV	35.00	45.00	—
1907 GOZF	31,000	—	BV	35.00	45.00	—
1907 GOZG	—	—	BV	35.00	45.00	—
1909 GOZG	—	—	BV	35.00	45.00	—
1910 GOZG	—	—	BV	35.00	45.00	—
1911 GOZF	62,000	—	BV	35.00	45.00	—
1911 GOZG	—	—	BV	35.00	45.00	—
1912 GOZG	—	—	BV	35.00	45.00	—
1912 POZG	—	—	BV	35.00	45.00	—
1913 POZG	60,000	—	BV	35.00	45.00	—
1914 POZG	25,000	—	BV	35.00	45.00	—
1914 PBLG	Inc. above					
Note: Reported, not confirmed						
1915	10,000	—	BV	30.00	45.00	—
1916	13,000	—	—	—	—	—
Note: Reported, not confirmed						
1917	3,896	—	BV	35.00	45.00	—
1918	16,000	—	BV	35.00	45.00	—
1919	10,000	—	BV	35.00	45.00	—
1920	72,000	—	BV	35.00	45.00	—
1922	8,110	—	BV	35.00	45.00	—
1923	27,000	—	BV	35.00	45.00	—
1924	—	—	BV	35.00	45.00	—
1925	20,000	—	BV	35.00	45.00	—
1926	11,000	—	BV	35.00	45.00	—
1927	14,000	—	BV	35.00	45.00	—
1928	9,322	—	BV	35.00	45.00	—
1929	8,971	—	BV	35.00	45.00	—
1930	9,991	—	BV	40.00	55.00	—
1953 BBR	9,821	—	—	BV	50.00	—
1955 ZBR	10,000	—	—	BV	50.00	—
1958 ZBR	5,098	—	—	BV	40.00	—
1959 ZBR	6,308	—	—	BV	40.00	—
1960 ZBR	6,083	—	—	BV	40.00	—
1961 ZBR	12,000	—	—	BV	40.00	—
1962 ZBR	5,431	—	—	BV	40.00	—
1963 ZBR	11,000	—	—	BV	40.00	—
1964 ZBR	25,000	—	—	BV	40.00	—
1965 ZBR	19,000	—	—	BV	40.00	—
1966 ZBR	60,000	—	—	BV	40.00	—
1967 BBR	9,914	—	—	BV	40.00	—
1968 BBR	—	—	—	BV	40.00	—
1968 BBB	4,781	—	—	BV	40.00	—
1969 BBB	15,000	—	—	BV	40.00	—

KM# 209 1/2 LIBRA (Pound)
3.9940 g., 0.9170 Gold .1177 oz. AGW **Obv:** Shield within sprigs with radiant sun above **Rev:** Head with headband right

Date	Mintage	F	VF	XF	Unc	BU
1902 ROZF	7,800	—	BV	85.00	100	—
1903 ROZF	7,245	—	BV	85.00	100	—
1904 ROZF	8,360	—	BV	85.00	100	—
1905 ROZF	8,010	—	BV	85.00	100	—
1905 GOZF	Inc. above	—	BV	85.00	100	—
1906 GOZF	9,176	—	BV	85.00	100	—
1907 GOZG	—	—	BV	85.00	100	—
1908 GOZG	8,180	—	BV	85.00	100	—
1953 BBR	9,210	—	BV	85.00	100	—
1955 ZBR	14,000	—	—	BV	90.00	—
1961 ZBR	752	—	—	BV	110	—
1962 ZBR	4,286	—	—	BV	95.00	—
1963 ZBR	908	—	—	BV	110	—
1964 ZBR	10,000	—	—	BV	90.00	—
1965 ZBR	5,490	—	—	BV	95.00	—
1966 ZBR	44,000	—	—	BV	90.00	—
1967 BBR	—	—	—	BV	90.00	—
1968 BBB	Inc. above	—	—	BV	90.00	—
1969 BBB	4,400	—	—	BV	95.00	—

KM# 207 LIBRA (Pound)
7.9881 g., 0.9170 Gold .2354 oz. AGW **Obv:** Shield within sprigs with radiant sun above **Rev:** Head with headband right

Date	Mintage	VG	F	VF	XF	Unc
1898 ROZF	—	—	—	—	BV	175
1899 ROZF	—	—	—	—	BV	175
1900 ROZF	64,000	—	—	—	BV	175
1901 ROZF	81,000	—	—	—	BV	165
1902 ROZF	89,000	—	—	—	BV	165
1903 ROZF	100,000	—	—	—	BV	165
1904 ROZF	33,000	—	—	—	BV	165
1905 ROZF	141,000	—	—	—	BV	175
1905 GOZF	—	—	—	—	BV	165
1906 GOZF	201,000	—	—	—	BV	165
1907 GOZG	Inc. above	—	—	—	BV	165
1908 GOZG	36,000	—	—	—	BV	175
1909 GOZG	52,000	—	—	—	BV	175
1910 GOZG	47,000	—	—	—	BV	175
1911 GOZG	42,000	—	—	—	BV	175
1912 GOZG	54,000	—	—	—	BV	185
1912 POZG	Inc. above	—	—	—	BV	185
1913 POZG	—	—	—	—	BV	175
1914 POZG	—	—	—	—	BV	185
1914 PBLG	119,000	—	—	—	BV	175
1915 PVG	91,000	—	—	—	BV	180
1915 PMGG	Inc. above	—	—	—	BV	200
1915	Inc. above	—	—	—	BV	170
1916	582,000	—	—	—	BV	165
1917	1,928,000	—	—	—	BV	165

566 PERU

Date	Mintage	VG	F	VF	XF	Unc
1918	600,000	—	—	—	BV	165
1919	Inc. above	—	—	—	BV	165
1920	152,000	—	—	—	BV	175
1921	Inc. above	—	—	—	BV	180
1922	13,000	—	—	—	BV	185
1923	15,000	—	—	—	BV	185
1924	8,113	—	—	—	BV	185
1925	9,068	—	—	—	BV	180
1926	4,596	—	—	—	BV	180
1927	8,360	—	—	—	BV	180
1928	2,184	—	—	—	BV	180
1929	3,119	—	—	—	BV	180
1930	1,050	—	—	—	BV	180
1959 ZBR	605	—	—	—	BV	250
1961 ZBR	402	—	—	—	BV	250
1962 ZBR	6,203	—	—	—	BV	180
1963 ZBR	302	—	—	—	BV	260
1964 ZBR	13,000	—	—	—	BV	180
1965 ZBR	9,917	—	—	—	BV	180
1966 ZBR	39,000	—	—	—	BV	180
1967 BBR	2,002	—	—	—	BV	180
1968 BBR	7,307	—	—	—	BV	185
1969 BBR	7,307	—	—	—	BV	185

TOKEN COINAGE

KM# Tn2 5 SOLES
2.3404 g., 0.9000 Gold .0677 oz. AGW

Date	Mintage	F	VF	XF	Unc	BU
1910	—	60.00	80.00	110	150	200

NORTH PERU
STATE
Estado Nor-Peruano
STATE COINAGE

KM# 159 1/2 ESCUDO
1.6875 g., 0.8750 Gold .0475 oz. AGW **Obv:** Wreath above date **Obv. Legend:** .LIMA. **Rev:** Arms without shield

Date	Mintage	VG	F	VF	XF	Unc
1838 M	—	100	200	350	550	1,000

Note: This coin is identical to the Republic type, KM#146.1 and can only be identified by the date

KM# 160 ESCUDO
3.3750 g., 0.8750 Gold .0949 oz. AGW **Obv:** Small wreath above flagged arms, date below **Obv. Legend:** EST.NOR-PERUANO... **Rev:** Standing Liberty **Rev. Legend:** FIRME Y FELIZ...

Date	Mintage	VG	F	VF	XF	Unc
1838 M	—	500	1,000	1,500	2,500	5,500

KM# 161 2 ESCUDOS
6.7500 g., 0.8750 Gold .1899 oz. AGW **Obv:** Small wreath above flagged arms, date below **Obv. Legend:** EST.NOR-PERUANO... **Rev:** Standing Liberty **Rev. Legend:** FIRME Y FELIZ...

Date	Mintage	VG	F	VF	XF	Unc
1838 M	—	1,500	2,000	2,500	3,500	—

KM# 162 4 ESCUDOS
13.5000 g., 0.8750 Gold .3798 oz. AGW **Obv:** Medium wreath above flagged arms, date below **Obv. Legend:** ESTADO NOR-PERUANO... **Rev:** Standing Liberty **Rev. Legend:** FIRME Y FELIZ...

Date	Mintage	VG	F	VF	XF	Unc
1838 M	—	2,000	3,500	6,000	11,500	—

KM# 156 8 ESCUDOS
27.0000 g., 0.8750 Gold .7596 oz. AGW **Obv:** Medium wreath above flagged arms, date below **Obv. Legend:** ESTADO NOR-PERUANO... **Rev:** Standing Liberty **Rev. Legend:** FIRME Y FELIZ...

Date	Mintage	VG	F	VF	XF	Unc
1836 TM Rare	—	—	—	—	—	—
1838 TM	—	1,500	2,500	4,000	7,000	—

SOUTH PERU

The Republic of Peru, located on the Pacific coast of South America, has an area of 496,225 sq. mi. (1,285,220sq. km.) and a population of *21.4 million. Capital: Lima. The diversified economy includes mining, fishing and agriculture. Fishmeal, copper, sugar, zinc and iron ore are exported.

Once part of the great Inca Empire that reached from northern Ecuador to central Chile, the conquest of Peru by Francisco Pizarro began in 1531. Desirable as the richest of the Spanish viceroyalties, it was torn by warfare between avaricious Spaniards until the arrival in 1569 of Francisco de Toledo, who initiated 2-1/2 centuries of efficient colonial rule, which made Lima the most aristocratic colonial capital and the stronghold of Spain's American possessions. Jose de San Martin of Argentina proclaimed Peru's independence on July 28, 1821; Simon Bolivar of Venezuela secured it in December, 1824 when he defeated the last Spanish army in South America. After several futile attempts to re-establish its South American Empire, Spain recognized Peru's independence in 1879.

Andres de Santa Cruz, whose mother was a high-ranking Inca, was the best of Bolivia's early presidents, and temporarily united Peru and Bolivia 1836-39, thus realizing his dream of a Peruvian/Bolivian confederation. This prompted the separate coinages of North and South Peru. Peruvian resistance and Chilean intervention finally broke up the confederation, sending Santa Cruz into exile. A succession of military strongman presidents ruled Peru until Marshall Castilla revitalized Peruvian politics in the mid-19th century and repulsed Spain's attempt to reclaim its one-time colony. Subsequent loss of southern territory to Chile in the War of the Pacific, 1879-81, and gradually increasing rejection of foreign economic domination, combined with recent serious inflation, affected the country numismatically.

As a result of the discovery of silver at Potosi in 1545, a mint was eventually authorized in 1565 with the first coinage taking place in 1568. The mint had an uneven life span during the Spanish Colonial period from 1568-72. It was closed from 1573-76, reopened from 1577-88. It remained closed until 1659-1660 when an unauthorized coinage in both silver and gold were struck. After being closed in 1660, it remained closed until 1684 when it struck cob style coins until 1752.

MINT MARKS
AREQUIPA, AREQ = Arequipa
AYACUCHO = Ayacucho
(B) = Brussels
CUZCO (monogram), Cuzco, Co. Cuzco
L, LM, LIMAE (monogram), Lima (monogram), LIMA = Lima
(L) = London
PASCO (monogram), Pasco, Paz, Po= Pasco
P, (P) = Philadelphia
S = San Francisco
(W) = Waterbury, CT, USA

NOTE: The LIMAE monogram appears in three forms. The early LM monogram form looks like a dotted L with M. The later LIMAE monogram has all the letters of LIMAE more readily distinguishable. The third form appears as an M monogram during early Republican issues.

MINT ASSAYERS' INITIALS
The letter(s) following the dates of Peruvian coins are the assayer's initials appearing on the coins. They generally appear at the 11 o'clock position on the Colonial coinage and at the 5 o'clock position along the rim on the obverse or reverse on the Republican coinage.

DATING
Peruvian 5, 10 and 20 centavos, issued from 1918-1944, bear the dates written in Spanish. The following table translates those written dates into numerals:
1918 - UN MIL NOVECIENTOS DIECIOCHO
1919 - UN MIL NOVECIENTOS DIECINUEVE
1920 - UN MIL NOVECIENTOS VEINTE
1921 - UN MIL NOVECIENTOS VEINTIUNO
1923 - UN MIL NOVECIENTOS VEINTITRES
1926 - UN MIL NOVECIENTOS VEINTISEIS
1934 - UN MIL NOVECIENTOS TREINTICUATRO
1935 - UN MIL NOVECIENTOS TREINTICINCO
1937 - UN MIL NOVECIENTOS TREINTISIETE
1939 - UN MIL NOVECIENTOS TREINTINUEVE
1940 - UN MIL NOVECIENTOS CUARENTA
1941 - UN MIL NOVECIENTOS CUARENTIUNO
U.S. Mints
1942 - MIL NOVECIENTOS CUARENTA Y DOS
Lima Mint
1942 - UN MIL NOVECIENTOS CUARENTIDOS
U.S. Mints
1943 - MIL NOVECIENTOS CUARENTA Y TRES
1944 - MIL NOVECIENTOS CUARENTA Y CUATRO
Lima Mint
1944 - MIL NOVECIENTOS CUARENTICUATRO

MONETARY SYSTEM
100 Centavos (10 Dineros) = 1 Sol
10 Soles = 1 Libra

STATE
Estado Sud Peruano
STATE COINAGE

KM# 167 8 ESCUDOS
27.0000 g., 0.8750 Gold .7596 oz. AGW **Obv:** Flagged radiant sun face, stars above **Obv. Legend:** ESTADO SUD PERUANO... **Rev:** Volcano, castle and ship within wreath **Rev. Legend:** FEDERACION.B.A...

Date	Mintage	VG	F	VF	XF	Unc
1837 BA	—	550	750	1,000	1,850	—

REPUBLIC
Republic Sud Peruano
REPUBLIC COINAGE

KM# 173 1/2 ESCUDO
1.6875 g., 0.8750 Gold .0475 oz. AGW **Obv:** Radiant sun face, stars above **Obv. Legend:** REPUB. SUD PERUANA... **Rev:** Value within wreath **Note:** Mint mark in monogram.

Date	Mintage	VG	F	VF	XF	Unc
1838CUZCO MS	—	75.00	140	220	450	900

KM# 174 ESCUDO
3.3750 g., 0.8750 Gold .0949 oz. AGW **Obv:** Radiant sun face, stars above **Obv. Legend:** REPUB. SUD PERUANA... **Rev:** Value within wreath

Date	Mintage	VG	F	VF	XF	Unc
1838 MS	—	90.00	160	280	525	1,250

KM# 171 8 ESCUDOS
27.0000 g., 0.8750 Gold .7596 oz. AGW **Obv:** Flagged radiant sun face, stars above **Obv. Legend:** REPUB. SUD PERUANA... **Rev:** Volcano, castle and ship within wreath **Rev. Legend:** Q.CONFEDERACION.M.S...

Date	Mintage	VG	F	VF	XF	Unc
1837 BA	—	550	700	950	2,000	5,500
1838 MS	—	550	700	900	1,850	5,000

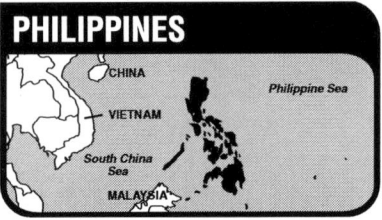

PHILIPPINES

The Republic of the Philippines, an archipelago in the western Pacific 500 miles (805 km.) from the southeast coast of Asia, has an area of 115,830 sq. mi. (300,000 sq. km.) and a population of *64.9 million. Capital: Manila. The economy of the 7,000-island group is based on agriculture, forestry and fishing. Timber, coconut products, sugar and hemp are exported.

Migration to the Philippines began about 30,000 years ago when land bridges connected the islands with Borneo and Sumatra. Ferdinand Magellan claimed the islands for Spain in 1521. The first permanent settlement was established by Miguel de Legazpi at Cebu April 1565. Manila was established in 1572. A British expedition captured Manila and occupied the Spanish colony in October 1762, but returned it to Spain by the treaty of Paris, 1763. Spain held the Philippines despite growing Filipino nationalism until 1898 when they were ceded to the United States at the end of the Spanish-American War. The Philippines became a self-governing commonwealth under the United States in 1935, and attained independence as the Republic of the Philippines on July 4, 1946.

RULER
Spanish, until 1898

MINT MARKS
(b) Brussels, privy marks only
BSP - Bangko Sentral Pilipinas
D - Denver, 1944-1945
(Lt) - Llantrisant
M, MA - Manila
PM - Pobjoy Mint
S - San Francisco, 1903-1947
SGV - Madrid
(Sh) - Sherritt
(US) - United States
FM - Franklin Mint, U.S.A.*
(VDM) - Vereinigte Deutsche Metall Werks; Altona, Germany
Star - Manila (Spanish) = Manila

*NOTE: From 1975-1977 the Franklin Mint produced coinage in up to 3 different qualities. Beginning in 1978 only (U) and (P) were struck. Qualities of issue are designated in ( ) after each date and are defined as follows:

(M) MATTE - Normal circulation strike or a dull finish produced by sandblasting special uncirculated (polish-finish) or proof quality dies.

(U) SPECIAL UNCIRCULATED - Polished or prooflike in appearance without any frosted features.

(P) PROOF - The highest quality obtainable having mirror-like fields and frosted features.

MONETARY SYSTEM
8 Octavos = 4 Quartos = 1 Real
8 Reales = 1 Peso

SPANISH COLONY

COUNTERSTAMPED COINAGE
MANILA/1828 Type III

Reverse: Crowned Spanish royal arms.
KM# 34 8 ESCUDOS
Gold **Counterstamp:** Type III **Note:** Counterstamp on Mexico City 8 Escudos, KM#383.

CS Date	Host Date	Good	VG	F	VF	XF
1828	1825 JM Rare	—	—	—	—	—

Note: The above is in the collection of Fabrica Nacional de Moneda y Timbre de Madrid (Spain)

COUNTERMARKED COINAGE
Ferdinand VII

Silver
Oval Type V and Round Type V
Round Type V
Actual size 9-10mm

These countermarks were introduced by decree of October 27, 1832 due to the problems encountered with the larger countermarks of 1828-1830. Pierced or holed coins were declared not valid but later were countermarked directly over the hole with Type V or Type VI countermarks and circulated freely. The latter types exist countermarked on both sides directly over the hole and are very scarce. These countermarks were retired in 1834 after the death of Ferdinand VII and replaced with a similar design showing - Y II - for Isabel II, Type VI. Coins dated 1835 and later with either Type V countermark should be considered counterfeit.

KM# 85 8 ESCUDOS
Gold **Countermark:** Crowned F. 7. o **Note:** Countermark on Chile 8 Escudos, KM#84.

CM Date	Host Date	Good	VG	F	VF	XF
ND(1832-34)	1822 FD	3,000	4,000	6,000	8,500	—
ND(1832-34)	1825 I Unique	—	—	—	—	—
ND(1832-34)	1826 I Unique	—	—	—	—	—

KM# A86 8 ESCUDOS
Gold **Countermark:** Crowned F. 7. o **Note:** Countermark on Colombia 8 Escudos, KM#82.2.

CM Date	Host Date	Good	VG	F	VF	XF
ND(1832-34)	1825 Rare	—	—	—	—	—

Note: Superior Ebsen sale 6-87 VF realized $13,750.

KM# 86 8 ESCUDOS
Gold **Countermark:** Crowned F. 7. o **Note:** Countermark on Mexico - Estado 8 Escudos, KM#383.4.

CM Date	Host Date	Good	VG	F	VF	XF
ND(1832-34)	1829 LF Unique	—	—	—	—	—

Note: Other coin types may exist with this particular countermark

COUNTERMARKED COINAGE
Isabel II

Silver
Type VI

This countermark was introduced after the death of Ferdinand VII on December 20, 1834. It exists with several varieties of crowns. Countermarking of foreign coins was halted in Manila by the edict of March 31, 1837 after Spain had recognized the independence of Mexico, Peru, Colombia, Bolivia, Chile and other former colonies in Central and South America. Coins bearing the Type VI countermark dated 1838 or later should be considered counterfeit.

KM# 141.5 8 ESCUDOS
Gold **Countermark:** Y • II • **Note:** Countermark on Argentina-Provincias Del Rio De La Plata 8 Escudos, KM#21.

CM Date	Host Date	Good	VG	F	VF	XF
ND(1834-37)	1828 P	6,000	7,000	9,000	13,500	—

Note: The above countermarks have been reported on other coins, (i.e. U.S. 1/2 Dollar, Dollar, and Spanish 20 Reales).

KM# 141.1 8 ESCUDOS
Gold **Countermark:** Y • II • **Note:** Countermark on Colombia 8 Escudos, KM#82.1.

CM Date	Host Date	Good	VG	F	VF	XF
ND(1834-37)	1826 JF	3,000	4,000	6,000	8,500	—
ND(1834-37)	1831 RS	4,000	5,000	7,000	10,000	—
ND(1834-37)	1832 RS	—	—	—	12,800	25,000

568 PHILIPPINES

CM Date	Host Date	Good	VG	F	VF	XF
ND(1834-37)	1835 RS	—	—	—	16,500	—

Note: Glendining's John J. Ford, Jr. sale 10-89.

KM# 141.2 8 ESCUDOS
Gold **Countermark:** Y • II • **Note:** Countermark on Colombia 8 Escudos, KM#82.2.

CM Date	Host Date	Good	VG	F	VF	XF
ND(1834-37)	1833 UR	3,000	4,000	6,000	8,500	—

KM# 141.4 8 ESCUDOS
Gold **Countermark:** Y • II • **Note:** Countermark on Mexico City 8 Escudos, KM#383.9.

CM Date	Host Date	Good	VG	F	VF	XF
ND(1834-37)	1825 JM	—	—	—	15,000	—
ND(1834-37)	1834 ML	—	—	—	20,000	—

Note: Sotheby's Geneva gold coins of the Hispanic world sale 5-90 realized $13,200.

KM# 141.3 8 ESCUDOS
Gold **Countermark:** Y • II • **Note:** Countermark on Mexico City Iturbide 8 Scudos, KM#313.1.

CM Date	Host Date	Good	VG	F	VF	XF
ND(1834-37)	1822	—	—	—	20,500	—

Note: Glendining's John J. Ford, Jr. sale 10-89 realized $16,500.

KM# 140 ESCUDO
Gold **Countermark:** Y • II • **Note:** Countermark on Colombia 1 Escudo, KM#81.2.

CM Date	Host Date	Good	VG	F	VF	XF
ND(1834-37)	1827FM Unique	—	—	—	—	—

DECIMAL COINAGE
100 Centavos = 1 Peso

KM# 142 PESO
1.6915 g., 0.8750 Gold .0476 oz. AGW

Date	Mintage	F	VF	XF	Unc	BU
1861/0	237,000	45.00	80.00	125	350	—
1861	Inc. above	45.00	80.00	110	350	—
1862/1	143,000	50.00	80.00	135	350	—
1862	Inc. above	45.00	80.00	135	375	—
1863/2	236,000	45.00	80.00	125	375	—
1863	Inc. above	45.00	75.00	125	350	—
1864/0	274,000	45.00	80.00	135	350	—
1864	Inc. above	45.00	75.00	120	350	—
1865/0	189,000	50.00	100	145	400	—
1865/3	Inc. above	75.00	100	200	450	—
1865	Inc. above	45.00	85.00	150	400	—
1866/5	77,000	150	250	400	1,200	—
1866	Inc. above	150	250	400	1,200	—
1867	12,000	350	700	1,250	3,500	—
1868/6	28,000	45.00	75.00	125	300	—

Note: An additional 372,724 pieces were struck between 1869-74, all dated 1868

| 1868/7 | Inc. above | 45.00 | 75.00 | 125 | 300 | — |
| 1868 | Inc. above | 40.00 | 60.00 | 85.00 | 275 | — |

KM# 143 2 PESOS
3.3830 g., 0.8750 Gold .0952 oz. AGW **Obv:** Head laureate left **Rev:** Crowned arms, pillars divides value

Date	Mintage	F	VF	XF	Unc	BU
1861/0	265,000	75.00	165	175	500	—
1861	Inc. above	75.00	150	150	500	—
1862/1	237,000	75.00	125	175	500	—
1862	Inc. above	75.00	110	175	500	—
1863/2	176,000	75.00	125	200	500	—
1863	Inc. above	75.00	110	175	500	—
1864/0	181,000	75.00	135	200	500	—
1864/3	Inc. above	75.00	135	200	500	—
1864	Inc. above	75.00	135	200	500	—
1865	34,000	135	175	300	800	—
1866/5	16,000	400	600	1,250	3,000	—
1866	Inc. above	400	600	1,250	3,000	—
1868/6	48,000	75.00	130	180	375	—

Note: An additional 304,691 pieces were struck between 1869-73, all dated 1868.

| 1868 | Inc. above | 65.00 | 100 | 160 | 350 | — |

KM# 144 4 PESOS
6.7661 g., 0.8750 Gold .1903 oz. AGW **Obv:** Head laureate left **Rev:** Crowned arms, pillars divides value

Date	Mintage	F	VF	XF	Unc	BU
1861	183,000	140	175	245	475	—
1862/0	—	—	165	225	—	—
1862/1	507,000	135	165	225	450	—
1862	Inc. above	125	145	200	450	—
1863	475,000	125	145	200	450	—
1864	461,000	125	145	200	500	—
1865	241,000	145	200	300	700	—
1866/65	44,000	400	600	1,500	3,000	—
1866	Inc. above	400	600	1,500	3,000	—
1867	1,530	1,200	1,800	3,000	8,000	—
1868	36,000	125	145	175	375	—

Note: 51,521,505 were struck between 1869-73, all dated 1868.

KM# 151 4 PESOS
6.7661 g., 0.8750 Gold .1903 oz. AGW **Obv:** Head left **Rev:** Crowned arms, pillars divides value

Date	Mintage	F	VF	XF	Unc	BU
1880 Rare	—	—	—	—	25,000	—
1881	—	—	—	—	40,000	—
1882	—	800	1,200	1,500	2,250	—
1885	—	—	—	—	20,000	—

COMMONWEALTH
MEDALLIC COINAGE

X# 11b DOLLAR
Gold, 38 mm. **Subject:** Opening of the Manila Mint **Obv:** Bust of President Wilson left **Obv. Legend:** PRESIDENT OF THE UNITED STATES **Obv. Designer:** Clifford Hewitt **Rev:** Justice kneeling left, cherub in front **Rev. Legend:** TO COMMEMORATE THE OPENING OF THE MINT **Edge:** Plain

Date	Mintage	F	VF	XF	Unc	BU
1920	8	—	8,000	10,000	18,000	25,000

REPUBLIC
REFORM COINAGE
100 Sentimos = 1 Piso

KM# 202b PISO
19.3000 g., 0.9170 Gold .5691 oz. AGW **Subject:** Pope Paul VI Visit **Obv:** Bust of Ferdinand Marcos left **Rev:** Bust of Pope Paul VI right **Designer:** Frank Gasparro

Date	Mintage	F	VF	XF	Unc	BU
1970	1,000	—	—	—	—	575

KM# 213 1000 PISO
9.9500 g., 0.9000 Gold .2879 oz. AGW **Subject:** 3rd Anniversary of the New Society **Obv:** Shield **Rev:** Head left

Date	Mintage	F	VF	XF	Unc	BU
1975	23,000	—	—	—	200	215
1975 Proof	13,000	Value: 230				

KM# 216 1500 PISO
20.5500 g., 0.9000 Gold .5947 oz. AGW **Subject:** I.M.F. Meeting **Obv:** Map **Rev:** Stylized star in center of world globe emblems

Date	Mintage	F	VF	XF	Unc	BU
1976	5,500	—	—	—	420	435
1976 Proof	6,500	Value: 445				

KM# 219 1500 PISO
20.5500 g., 0.9000 Gold .5947 oz. AGW **Subject:** 5th Anniversary of the New Society **Obv:** Head facing **Rev:** Redesigned bank seal within circle

Date	Mintage	F	VF	XF	Unc	BU
ND(1977)	4,000	—	—	—	420	435
ND(1977) Proof	6,000	Value: 445				

KM# 223 1500 PISO
20.5500 g., 0.9000 Gold .5947 oz. AGW **Subject:** Inauguration of New Mint Facilities **Obv:** Flowers **Rev:** Bank, gold bars, paper money and coins

Date	Mintage	F	VF	XF	Unc	BU
1978	3,000	—	—	—	420	435
1978 Proof	3,000	Value: 445				

KM# 234 1500 PISO
9.9500 g., 0.9000 Gold .2879 oz. AGW **Subject:** Pope John Paul II Visit **Obv:** Standing figure in prayer, crowd in background **Rev:** Bust 3/4 left

Date	Mintage	F	VF	XF	Unc	BU
1981 Proof	1,000	Value: 525				
1982 Proof	—	—				

KM# 237 1500 PISO
9.7800 g., 0.9000 Gold .2830 oz. AGW **Subject:** 40th Anniversary of Bataan-Corregidor **Obv:** Shield of arms **Rev:** Conjoined military heads left

Date	Mintage	F	VF	XF	Unc	BU
ND(1982)FM (U)	1,000	—	—	—	300	325
ND(1982)FM (P)	445	Value: 400				

KM# 282 2000 PISO
10.0000 g., 0.5000 Gold 0.1608 oz. AGW, 27 mm. **Subject:** Asia Pacific Economic Cooperation **Obv:** Head of Fidel Ramos 3/4 right **Rev:** World globe logo and value **Edge:** Reeded

Date	Mintage	F	VF	XF	Unc	BU
1996 Proof	3,000	Value: 225				

KM# 231 2500 PISO
14.5700 g., 0.5000 Gold .2342 oz. AGW **Subject:** 100th Anniversary - Birth of General Douglas MacArthur **Obv:** Military standing figures **Rev:** Uniformed bust with pipe facing 1/4 left

Date	Mintage	F	VF	XF	Unc	BU
ND(1980)FM (P)	3,073	Value: 275				

KM# 247 2500 PISO
15.0000 g., 0.5000 Gold .2414 oz. AGW **Subject:** President Aquino's Visit in Washington **Obv:** Bust of President Aquino left **Rev:** Bust of President Reagan right

Date	Mintage	F	VF	XF	Unc	BU
1986 Proof	Est. 250	Value: 475				

KM# 266 2500 PISO
7.9800 g., 0.9167 Gold .2352 oz. AGW **Subject:** Papal Visit 1995 **Obv:** Shield of arms **Rev:** Pope John Paul II left **Note:** Similar to 100 Piso, KM#264.

Date	Mintage	F	VF	XF	Unc	BU
ND(1994) Proof	—	Value: 325				

KM# 220 5000 PISO
68.7400 g., 0.9000 Gold 1.9893 oz. AGW **Subject:** 5th Anniversary of the New Society **Obv:** Design within beaded circle **Rev:** Conjoined busts of Ferdinand and Imelda Marcos right

Date	Mintage	F	VF	XF	Unc	BU
ND(1977)FM (U)	100	—	—	—	1,650	—
ND(1977)FM (P)	3,832	Value: 1,400				

KM# 267 5000 PISO
16.8100 g., 0.9250 Gold .4999 oz. AGW **Subject:** Papal Visit 1995 **Obv:** Shield of arms **Rev:** Bust of Pope John Paul II left **Note:** Similar to 100 Piso, KM#264.

Date	Mintage	F	VF	XF	Unc	BU
ND(1994) Proof	—	Value: 500				

KM# 283 5000 PISO
Gold **Subject:** 50th Anniversary - Central Bank in the Philippines

Date	Mintage	F	VF	XF	Unc	BU
1999 Proof	2,000	Value: 475				

KM# 255 10000 PESOS
33.5500 g., 0.9250 Gold 1 oz. AGW **Subject:** People Power 1992 **Obv:** Bust of Aquino facing 3/4 right **Rev:** Map, scroll, dates and dove

Date	Mintage	F	VF	XF	Unc	BU
ND(1992) Proof	1,600	Value: 950				

TRIAL STRIKES

KM#	Date	Mintage	Identification	Mkt Val
TS2	1859	—	4 Pesos. Gold-Plated Bronze.	—
	1859	—	4 Pesos. Gold-Plated Bronze.	1,000
TS6	1861	—	2 Pesos. Gold-Plated Bronze.	—
TS3	1861	—	Peso. Gold-Plated Bronze.	—
TS4	1861	—	Peso. Gold-Plated Bronze.	—
TS5	1861	—	2 Pesos. Gold-Plated Bronze.	—

PROOF SETS

KM#	Date	Mintage	Identification	Issue Price	Mkt Val
PS21	1986 (2)	—	KM#246-247	—	610
PS22	ND(1994) (3)	—	KM264-265, 267 Papal Visit 1995	—	800

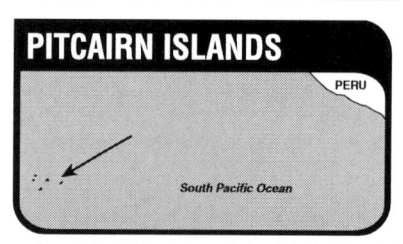

PITCAIRN ISLANDS

A small volcanic island, along with the uninhabited islands of Oeno, Henderson, and Ducie, constitute the British Colony of Pitcairn Islands. The main island has an area of about 2 sq. mi. (5 sq. km.) and a population of *68. It is located 1350 miles southeast of Tahiti. The islanders subsist on fishing, garden produce and crops. The sale of postage stamps and carved curios to passing ships brings cash income.

Discovered in 1767 by a British naval officer, Pitcairn was not occupied until 1790 when Fletcher Christian and nine mutineers from the British ship, *HMS Bounty*, along with some Tahitian men and women went ashore, and survived in obscurity until discovered by American whalers in 1808.

Adamstown is the chief settlement, located on the north coast, one of the few places that island-made longboats can land. The primary religion is Seventh-day Adventist and a public school provides basic education. In 1898 the settlement was placed under the jurisdiction of the Commissioner for the Western Pacific. Since 1970 this British settlement has been governed through a locally elected council under a governor.

New Zealand currency has been used since July 10, 1967.

BRITISH COLONY
REGULAR COINAGE

KM# 2 250 DOLLARS
15.9800 g., 0.9170 Gold .4708 oz. AGW **Subject:** Drafting of Constitution, 1838-1988 **Obv:** Crowned bust right **Rev:** Sailing ship

Date	Mintage	F	VF	XF	Unc	BU
ND(1988) Proof	2,500	Value: 345				

KM# 6 250 DOLLARS
15.9800 g., 0.9170 Gold .4708 oz. AGW **Subject:** HMAV Bounty, 1789-1989 **Obv:** Crowned bust right **Rev:** Ship

Date	Mintage	F	VF	XF	Unc	BU
ND(1989) Proof	2,500	Value: 345				

KM# 9 250 DOLLARS
15.9800 g., 0.9170 Gold .4708 oz. AGW **Subject:** Establishment of Settlement, 1790-1990 **Obv:** Crowned bust right **Rev:** Ship in flames within circle **Rev. Designer:** Robert Elderton

Date	Mintage	F	VF	XF	Unc	BU
ND(1990) Proof	500	Value: 365				

POLAND

The Republic of Poland, located in central Europe, has an area of 120,725 sq. mi. (312,680 sq. km.) and a population of *38.2 million. Capital: Warszawa (Warsaw). The economy is essentially agricultural, but industrial activity provides the products for foreign trade. Machinery, coal, coke, iron, steel and transport equipment are exported.

Poland, which began as a Slavic duchy in the 10th century and reached its peak of power between the 14th and 16th centuries, has had a turbulent history of invasion, occupation or partition by Mongols, Turkey, Transylvania, Sweden, Austria, Prussia and Russia.

The first partition took place in 1772. Prussia took Polish Pomerania, Russia took part of the eastern provinces, and Austria occupied Galicia and its capital city Lwów. The second partition occurred in 1793 when Russia took another slice of the eastern provinces and Prussia took what remained of western Poland. The third partition, 1795, literally removed Poland from the map. Russia took what was left of the eastern provinces. Prussia seized most of central Poland, including Warsaw. Austria took what was left of the south. Napoleon restored to Poland much of the territory lost to Prussia and Austria, but after his defeat another partition returned the Duchy of Warsaw to Prussia, made Kraków into a tiny republic, and declared what remained to be the Kingdom of Poland under the czar and in permanent union with Russia.

Poland re-emerged as an independent state recognized by the Treaty of Versailles on June 28, 1919, and maintained its independence until 1939 when it was invaded by, and partitioned between, Germany and Russia. Poland's present boundaries were determined by the U.S.-British-Russian agreement of Aug. 16, 1945. The Government of National Unity was replaced when the Polish Communist-Socialist faction claimed victory at the polls in 1947 and established a Peoples Democratic Republic' of the Soviet type in 1952. On December 29, 1989 Poland was proclaimed as the Republic of Poland.

RULERS
Friedrich August I, King of Saxony,
   as Duke, 1807-1814
Alexander I, Czar of Russia,
   as King, 1815-1825
Nicholas I, Czar of Russia,
   as King, 1825-1855

MINT MARKS
MV, MW, MW-monogram - Warsaw Mint, 1965-
MW - Moneta Wschovensis, 1650-1655
FF - Stuttgart Germany 1916-1917
(w) - Warsaw 1923-39 (opened officially in 1924)
   arrow mintmark
CHI - Valcambi, Switzerland
   Other letters appearing with date denote the Mintmaster at the time the coin was struck.

MINT OFFICIALS' INITIALS
Mint officials' initials usually appear flanking the shield or by the date.

MONETARY SYSTEM
Until 1815
1 Solidus = 1 Schilling
3 Solidi = 2 Poltura = 1 Grosz
3 Poltura = 1-1/2 Grosze = 1 Polturak
6 Groszy = 1 Szostak
18 Groszy = 1 Tympf = 1 Ort
30 Groszy = 4 Silbergroschen = 1 Zloty
1 Talar = 1 Zloty
6 Zlotych = 1 Reichsthaler
8 Zlotych = 1 Speciesthaler
5 Speciesthaler = 1 August D'or
3 Ducats = 1 Stanislaus D'or

GRAND DUCHY OF WARSZAWA
TRADE COINAGE

C# 88 DUKAT
3.5000 g., 0.9860 Gold .1109 oz. AGW **Ruler:** Friedrich August I **Obv:** Head right **Obv. Legend:** FRID.AVG.REX... **Rev:** Crowned oval arms within sprays divides date above **Rev. Legend:** AUREUS NUMMUS...

Date	Mintage	VG	F	VF	XF	Unc
1812 IB	8,546	250	450	750	1,500	—
1813 IB	3,000	450	800	2,000	3,000	—

CONGRESS - KINGDOM OF POLAND
STANDARD COINAGE

C# 136.1 20 ZLOTYCH - 3 RUBLES
3.8900 g., 0.9170 Gold .1147 oz. AGW **Ruler:** Nicholas I **Obv:** Shield within wreath on breast, 3 shields in wings **Rev:** Value, date

Date	Mintage	F	VF	XF	Unc	BU
1834MW	243	850	2,450	4,250	7,500	—
1835MW	350	850	2,450	4,250	7,500	—
1836MW	307	850	2,450	4,250	7,500	—
1837MW	423	850	2,450	4,250	7,500	—
1838MW	66	1,750	3,500	7,000	12,000	—
1839MW	57	1,750	3,500	7,000	12,000	—
1840MW	—	2,750	5,000	8,500	14,500	—

C# 136.2 20 ZLOTYCH - 3 RUBLES
3.8900 g., 0.9170 Gold .1147 oz. AGW **Ruler:** Nicholas I **Obv:** Shield within wreath on breast, 3 shields in wings **Rev:** Value, date **Note:** Mint mark: St. Petersburg "USB".

Date	Mintage	F	VF	XF	Unc	BU
1834 ПД	77,000	200	300	600	1,000	—
1835 ПД	52,000	200	300	600	1,000	—
1836 ПД	10,000	225	350	600	1,000	—
1837 ПД	30,000	200	300	600	1,000	—
1838 ПД	17,000	225	350	600	1,000	—
1839 ПД	11,000	225	350	600	1,000	—

C# 136.3 20 ZLOTYCH - 3 RUBLES
3.8900 g., 0.9170 Gold .1147 oz. AGW **Ruler:** Nicholas I **Obv:** Shield within wreath on breast, 3 shields in wings **Rev:** Value, date

Date	Mintage	F	VF	XF	Unc	BU
1840	5,473,000	275	475	600	1,250	—
1841 ПД Proof, unique						

Note: Superior Pipito sale 12-87 Proof realized $12,100

C# 102 25 ZLOTYCH
4.8900 g., 0.9170 Gold .1442 oz. AGW **Ruler:** Alexander I **Obv:** Head right **Obv. Legend:** SA.W.ROS.KROL POLSKI... **Rev:** Crowned and mantled oval shield on breast

Date	Mintage	F	VF	XF	Unc	BU
1817 IB	96,000	225	650	850	2,350	—
1818 IB	55,000	225	650	850	2,650	—
1819 IB	1,124	225	650	850	2,650	—

C# 102a 25 ZLOTYCH
4.8900 g., 0.9170 Gold .1442 oz. AGW **Ruler:** Alexander I **Obv:** Head right **Obv. Legend:** SA.W.ROS.KROL POLSKI... **Rev:** Crowned and mantled oval shield on breast **Note:** Struck in collar.

Date	Mintage	F	VF	XF	Unc	BU
1818 IB Rare	86,000					
1822 IB	479	650	1,150	2,600	4,750	—
1823 IB	612	900	1,650	3,250	5,250	—
1824 IB	636	650	1,150	2,600	4,750	—
1825 IB	134	650	1,150	2,600	4,750	—
1828 IB	385	650	1,150	2,600	4,750	—

C# 118 25 ZLOTYCH
4.8900 g., 0.9170 Gold .1442 oz. AGW **Ruler:** Nicholas I **Obv:** Laureate head right **Obv. Legend:** WSKRZESICIEL KROL... **Rev:** Value and date within wreath **Note:** Struck in collar.

Date	Mintage	F	VF	XF	Unc	BU
1828 FH	241	900	1,650	4,000	6,000	—
1829 FH	66	1,100	1,850	4,500	6,500	—
1830	618	900	1,650	4,000	6,000	—
1832 KG	152	900	1,650	4,000	6,000	—
1833 KG	424	900	1,650	4,000	6,000	—

C# 103 50 ZLOTYCH
9.7800 g., 0.9170 Gold .2884 oz. AGW **Ruler:** Alexander I **Obv:** Head right **Obv. Legend:** SA.W.ROS.KROL POLSKI... **Rev:** Crowned and mantled oval shield on breast

Date	Mintage	F	VF	XF	Unc	BU
1817 IB	17,000	450	700	1,250	3,250	—
1818 IB	50,000	450	900	1,450	3,500	—
1819 IB	20,000	450	900	1,550	4,000	—

C# 103.1 50 ZLOTYCH
9.7367 g., 0.9170 Gold .2871 oz. AGW **Ruler:** Alexander I

Date	Mintage	F	VF	XF	Unc	BU
1817 IB Proof, rare	—	—	—	—	—	—

C# 103a 50 ZLOTYCH
9.7800 g., 0.9170 Gold .2884 oz. AGW **Ruler:** Alexander I **Obv:** Head right **Obv. Legend:** SA.W.ROS.KROL POLSKI... **Rev:** Crowned and mantled oval shield on breast

Date	Mintage	F	VF	XF	Unc	BU
1819 IB	Inc. above	475	775	1,250	3,250	—
1820 IB	7,098	475	775	1,350	3,350	—
1821 IB	2,638	475	975	1,850	4,000	—
1822 IB	1,610	475	975	1,850	4,250	—
1823 IB	251	900	1,850	3,000	6,000	—
1827 IB	62	1,250	2,250	3,250	6,500	—

C# 119 50 ZLOTYCH
9.7800 g., 0.9170 Gold .2884 oz. AGW **Ruler:** Nicholas I **Obv:** Laureate head right **Obv. Legend:** WSKRZESICIEL KROL... **Rev:** Value and date within wreath

Date	Mintage	F	VF	XF	Unc	BU
1827 FH	62	1,250	2,250	3,250	6,500	—
1829 FH	238	900	2,000	3,000	6,000	—

C# 119.1 50 ZLOTYCH
9.7367 g., 0.9170 Gold .2871 oz. AGW **Ruler:** Nicholas I

Date	Mintage	F	VF	XF	Unc	BU
1829 FH Proof	237	—	—	—	—	—

TRADE COINAGE

C# 125 DUKAT
3.5000 g., 0.9860 Gold .1109 oz. AGW **Ruler:** Nicholas I **Obv:** Armored figure divides date **Rev:** Inscription within ornamented square

Date	Mintage	F	VF	XF	Unc	BU
1831	163,000	200	300	400	750	—

POLAND 571

REPUBLIC
STANDARD COINAGE
100 Groszy = 1 Zloty

Y# 17.1a 5 ZLOTYCH
Gold **Obv:** Crowned eagle with wings open **Rev:** Adoption of the Constitution

Date	Mintage	F	VF	XF	Unc	BU
1925(w) Rare	2	—	—	—	—	—

Y# 17.2c 5 ZLOTYCH
Gold **Obv:** Without monogram by date **Rev:** Adoption of the Constitution

Date	Mintage	F	VF	XF	Unc	BU
1925(w) Rare	1	—	—	—	—	—

Y# 17.3a 5 ZLOTYCH
43.3300 g., 0.9000 Gold 1.3407 oz. AGW **Obv:** Crowned eagle with wings open, mint mark to right of date **Rev:** Adoption of the Constitution **Edge Lettering:** SALUS REIPUBLICAE SUPREMA LEX

Date	Mintage	F	VF	XF	Unc	BU
1925(w) Rare	1	—	—	—	—	—

Y# 17.4 5 ZLOTYCH
43.3300 g., 0.9000 Gold 1.3407 oz. AGW **Obv:** Without monogram by date, with mint mark **Rev:** Adoption of the Constitution **Designer:** Stanislaw Lewandowski

Date	Mintage	F	VF	XF	Unc	BU
1925(w)	1,000	—	—	1,000	1,200	

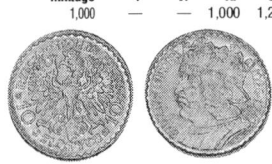

Y# 32 10 ZLOTYCH
3.2258 g., 0.9000 Gold .0933 oz. AGW **Obv:** Crowned eagle with wings open **Rev:** Crowned head left **Note:** Never released into circulation; similar design to Y#33.

Date	Mintage	F	VF	XF	Unc	BU
ND(1925)(w)	50,000	—	BV	85.00	165	225

Y# 33 20 ZLOTYCH
6.4516 g., 0.9000 Gold .1867 oz. AGW **Obv:** Crowned eagle with wings open **Rev:** Crowned head of Boleslaw I left **Note:** Never released into circulation.

Date	Mintage	F	VF	XF	Unc	BU
ND(1925)(w)	27,000	—	BV	145	215	325

MEDALLIC COINAGE

X# M14a 5 ZLOTYCH
Gold

Date	Mintage	F	VF	XF	Unc	BU
1925 Rare	2	—	—	—	—	—

PEOPLES REPUBLIC
STANDARD COINAGE

Y# 83 500 ZLOTYCH
30.0000 g., 0.9000 Gold .8681 oz. AGW **Obv:** Imperial eagle above value **Rev:** Head of Tadeusz Kosciuszko right

Date	Mintage	F	VF	XF	Unc	BU
1976MW	2,318	—	—	—	900	

Y# 85 500 ZLOTYCH
30.0000 g., 0.9000 Gold .8681 oz. AGW **Obv:** Imperial eagle above value **Rev:** Kazimierz Pulaski left

Date	Mintage	F	VF	XF	Unc	BU
1976MW	2,315	—	—	—	900	

Y# 138 1000 ZLOTYCH
3.4000 g., 0.9000 Gold .0984 oz. AGW **Subject:** Visit of Pope John Paul II **Obv:** Eagle with wings open divides date **Rev:** 1/2 Figure of Pope 1/4 left

Date	Mintage	F	VF	XF	Unc	BU
1982CHI	900	—	—	—	450	
1982CHI Proof	1,700	Value: 500				
1985CHI Rare	1	—	—	—	—	—
1985CHI Proof, rare	2	—	—	—	—	—
1986CHI	83	—	—	—	700	
1986CHI Proof	53	Value: 850				

Y# 168 1000 ZLOTYCH
3.1100 g., 0.9990 Gold .1000 oz. AGW **Subject:** Papal Visit in America **Obv:** Imperial eagle above value **Rev:** Half figure of Pope 3/4 left **Note:** Similar to KM#163.

Date	Mintage	F	VF	XF	Unc	BU
1987MW Proof	201	Value: 400				

Y# 174 1000 ZLOTYCH
3.1100 g., 0.9990 Gold .1000 oz. AGW **Subject:** 10th Anniversary of Pope John Paul II **Obv:** Imperial eagle above value **Rev:** Bust left **Note:** Similar to KM#177.

Date	Mintage	F	VF	XF	Unc	BU
1988MW Proof	1,000	Value: 225				

Y# 186 1000 ZLOTYCH
3.1100 g., 0.9990 Gold .1000 oz. AGW **Subject:** Pope John Paul II **Obv:** Imperial eagle above value **Rev:** Bust left on patterned background

Date	Mintage	F	VF	XF	Unc	BU
1989MW In sets only	Est. 1,000	—	—	—	200	—

Y# 90 2000 ZLOTYCH
8.0000 g., 0.9000 Gold .2315 oz. AGW **Obv:** Eagle with wings open divides date **Rev:** Head of Fryderyk Chopin left

Date	Mintage	F	VF	XF	Unc	BU
1977MW Proof	4,000	Value: 375				

Y# 102 2000 ZLOTYCH
8.0000 g., 0.9000 Gold .2315 oz. AGW **Obv:** Eagle with wings open divides date **Rev:** Duke Mieszko I

Date	Mintage	F	VF	XF	Unc	BU
1979MW Proof	3,000	Value: 375				

Y# 106 2000 ZLOTYCH
8.0000 g., 0.9000 Gold .2315 oz. AGW **Obv:** Eagle with wings open divides date **Rev:** Head of Mikolaj Kopernik 1/4 right

Date	Mintage	F	VF	XF	Unc	BU
1979MW Proof	5,000	Value: 350				

Y# 107 2000 ZLOTYCH
8.0000 g., 0.9000 Gold .2315 oz. AGW **Obv:** Eagle with wings open divides date **Rev:** Profile of Maria Skiodowska Curie left, symbol at right

Date	Mintage	F	VF	XF	Unc	BU
1979MW Proof	5,000	Value: 350				

Y# 111 2000 ZLOTYCH
8.0000 g., 0.9000 Gold .2315 oz. AGW **Series:** Winter Olympics **Obv:** Imperial eagle above value **Rev:** Ski jumper

Date	Mintage	F	VF	XF	Unc	BU
1980MW Proof	5,250	Value: 350				

Y# 116 2000 ZLOTYCH
8.0000 g., 0.9000 Gold .2315 oz. AGW **Obv:** Imperial eagle above value **Rev:** King Boleslaw I Chrobry

Date	Mintage	F	VF	XF	Unc	BU
1980MW Proof	2,500	Value: 375				

Y# 119 2000 ZLOTYCH
8.0000 g., 0.9000 Gold .2315 oz. AGW **Obv:** Imperial eagle above value **Rev:** Kazimierz I

Date	Mintage	F	VF	XF	Unc	BU
1980MW Proof	2,500	Value: 375				

Y# 131 2000 ZLOTYCH
8.0000 g., 0.9000 Gold .2315 oz. AGW **Obv:** Imperial eagle above value **Rev:** Wladyslaw I Herman **Note:** Similar to 200 Zlotych, Y#129.

Date	Mintage	F	VF	XF	Unc	BU
1981MW Proof	3,113	Value: 375				

Y# 135 2000 ZLOTYCH
8.0000 g., 0.9000 Gold .2315 oz. AGW **Obv:** Imperial eagle above value **Rev:** Boleslaw II

Date	Mintage	F	VF	XF	Unc	BU
1981MW Proof	—	Value: 375				

Y# 139 2000 ZLOTYCH
6.8000 g., 0.9000 Gold .1968 oz. AGW **Subject:** Visit of Pope John Paul II **Obv:** Imperial eagle above value **Rev:** Half-figure of Pope 1/4 left

Date	Mintage	F	VF	XF	Unc	BU
1982CHI	500	—	—	—	800	—
1982CHI Proof	1,250	Value: 900				
1985CHI Rare	1	—	—	—	—	—
1985CHI Proof, rare	Est. 2	—	—	—	—	—
1986CHI	Est. 54	—	—	—	1,250	
1986CHI Proof	Est. 79	Value: 1,300				

Y# 169 2000 ZLOTYCH
7.7700 g., 0.9990 Gold .2500 oz. AGW **Subject:** Papal Visit in America **Obv:** Imperial eagle above value **Rev:** Half-figure of Pope with staff left **Note:** Similar to KM#163.

Date	Mintage	F	VF	XF	Unc	BU
1987MW Proof	201	Value: 500				

Y# 175 2000 ZLOTYCH
7.7700 g., 0.9990 Gold .2500 oz. AGW **Subject:** 10th Anniversary of Pope John Paul II **Obv:** Imperial eagle above value **Rev:** Bust left **Note:** Similar to KM#177.

Date	Mintage	F	VF	XF	Unc	BU
1988 Proof	1,000	Value: 275				

Y# 187 2000 ZLOTYCH
7.7700 g., 0.9990 Gold .2500 oz. AGW **Obv:** Imperial eagle above value **Rev:** Bust left on patterned background **Note:** Pope John Paul II.

POLAND

Date	Mintage	F	VF	XF	Unc	BU
1989MW In sets only	Est. 1,000	—	—	—	250	—

Y# 170 5000 ZLOTYCH
15.5500 g., 0.9990 Gold .5000 oz. AGW **Subject:** Papal Visit in America **Obv:** Imperial eagle above value **Rev:** Half-figure of Pope with staff left **Note:** Similar to KM#163.

Date	Mintage	F	VF	XF	Unc	BU
1987MW Proof	201	Value: 700				

Y# 176 5000 ZLOTYCH
15.5500 g., 0.9990 Gold .5000 oz. AGW **Subject:** 10th Anniversary of Pope John Paul II **Obv:** Imperial eagle above value **Rev:** Bust left **Note:** Similar to Y#177.

Date	Mintage	F	VF	XF	Unc	BU
1988MW Proof	1,000	Value: 500				

Y# 188 5000 ZLOTYCH
15.5500 g., 0.9990 Gold .5000 oz. AGW **Obv:** Imperial eagle above value **Rev:** Bust left on patterned background **Note:** Pope John Paul II.

Date	Mintage	F	VF	XF	Unc	BU
1989MW In sets only	Est. 1,000,000	—	—	—	475	—

Y# 140 10000 ZLOTYCH
34.5000 g., 0.9000 Gold .9984 oz. AGW **Subject:** Visit of Pope John Paul II **Obv:** Imperial eagle above value **Rev:** Half-figure of Pope 1/4 left

Date	Mintage	F	VF	XF	Unc	BU
1982CHI	200	—	—	—	1,850	—
1982CHI Proof	700	Value: 1,950				
1985CHI Proof, rare	1	—	—	—	—	—
1986CHI Rare	Est. 6	—	—	—	—	—
1986CHI Proof, rare	Est. 13	—	—	—	—	—

Y# 171 10000 ZLOTYCH
31.1030 g., 0.9990 Gold 1.0000 oz. AGW **Subject:** Papal Visit in America **Obv:** Imperial eagle above value **Rev:** Half-figure of Pope left **Note:** Similar to KM#163.

Date	Mintage	F	VF	XF	Unc	BU
1987MW Proof	201	Value: 1,350				

Y# 177 10000 ZLOTYCH
31.1030 g., 0.9990 Gold 1.0000 oz. AGW **Subject:** 10th Anniversary of Pope John Paul II **Obv:** Imperial eagle above value **Rev:** Bust left

Date	Mintage	F	VF	XF	Unc	BU
1988MW	1,000	—	—	—	975	—
1988MW Proof	1,000	Value: 1,000				

Y# 189 10000 ZLOTYCH
31.1030 g., 0.9990 Gold 1.0000 oz. AGW **Subject:** Pope John Paul II **Obv:** Imperial eagle above value **Rev:** Bust left on patterned background

Date	Mintage	F	VF	XF	Unc	BU
1989MW Proof	Est. 2,000	Value: 850				

Y# 163 200000 ZLOTYCH
373.2420 g., 0.9990 Gold 12.0000 oz. AGW, 70 mm. **Subject:** Papal Visit in America **Obv:** Imperial eagle above value **Rev:** Half-figure with staff left **Note:** Illustration reduced.

Date	Mintage	F	VF	XF	Unc	BU
1987 Proof	101	Value: 9,500				

Y# 178 200000 ZLOTYCH
373.2420 g., 0.9990 Gold 12.0000 oz. AGW, 70 mm. **Subject:** 10th Anniversary of Pope John Paul II **Obv:** Imperial eagle above value **Rev:** Bust with chin resting on thumbs left **Note:** Illustration reduced.

Date	Mintage	F	VF	XF	Unc	BU
1988MW Proof	300	Value: 9,250				

Y# 190 200000 ZLOTYCH
373.2420 g., 0.9990 Gold 12.0000 oz. AGW **Obv:** Imperial eagle above value **Rev:** Pope John Paul II **Note:** Similar to KM#189.

Date	Mintage	F	VF	XF	Unc	BU
1989MW Proof	Est. 200	Value: 9,250				

REPUBLIC
Democratic

STANDARD COINAGE

Y# 219 20000 ZLOTYCH
3.1100 g., 0.9990 Gold .1 oz. AGW **Subject:** 10th Anniversary of Solidarity **Obv:** Crowned eagle **Rev:** Solidarity monument with city view background **Note:** Similar to 10000 Zlotych, Y#195.

Date	Mintage	F	VF	XF	Unc	BU
1990 Proof	1,004	Value: 145				

Y# 220 50000 ZLOTYCH
13.1000 g., 0.9990 Gold .4212 oz. AGW **Subject:** 10th Anniversary of Solidarity **Obv:** Imperial eagle above value **Rev:** Solidarity monument with city view background **Note:** Similar to 10000 Zlotych, Y#195.

Date	Mintage	F	VF	XF	Unc	BU
1990 Proof	1,001	Value: 400				

Y# 221 100000 ZLOTYCH
15.5500 g., 0.9990 Gold .5000 oz. AGW **Subject:** 10th Anniversary of Solidarity **Obv:** Imperial eagle above value **Rev:** Buildiings, symbols **Note:** Similar to 10000 Zlotych, Y#195.

Date	Mintage	F	VF	XF	Unc	BU
1990 Proof	Est. 1,000	Value: 450				

Y# 205 200000 ZLOTYCH
31.1000 g., 0.9990 Gold 1.0000 oz. AGW **Obv:** Imperial eagle above value **Rev:** Fryderyk Chopin

Date	Mintage	F	VF	XF	Unc	BU
1990 Proof	10,000	Value: 735				

Y# 206 200000 ZLOTYCH
31.1000 g., 0.9990 Gold 1.0000 oz. AGW **Obv:** Imperial eagle above value **Rev:** Tadeusz Kosciuszko

Date	Mintage	F	VF	XF	Unc	BU
1990 Proof	10,000	Value: 735				

Y# 207 200000 ZLOTYCH
31.1000 g., 0.9990 Gold 1.0000 oz. AGW **Obv:** Imperial eagle above value **Rev:** Marszalck Pilsudski

Date	Mintage	F	VF	XF	Unc	BU
1990 Proof	10,000	Value: 735				

Y# 222 200000 ZLOTYCH
31.1000 g., 0.9990 Gold 1.0000 oz. AGW **Subject:** Solidarity **Obv:** Solidarity monument with city view background **Rev:** Solidarity monument with city view background

Date	Mintage	F	VF	XF	Unc	BU
1990 Proof	Est. 1,000	Value: 800				

Y# 208 500000 ZLOTYCH
62.2000 g., 0.9990 Gold 2.0000 oz. AGW **Obv:** Imperial eagle above value **Rev:** Fryderyk Chopin **Note:** Similar to 100,000 Zlotych, Y#199.

Date	Mintage	F	VF	XF	Unc	BU
1990 Proof	2,000	Value: 1,475				

Y# 209 500000 ZLOTYCH
62.2000 g., 0.9990 Gold 2.0000 oz. AGW **Obv:** Imperial eagle above value **Rev:** Uniformed figure on horse **Note:** Similar to 100,000 Zlotych, Y#200.

Date	Mintage	F	VF	XF	Unc	BU
1990 Proof	2,000	Value: 1,475				

Y# 210 500000 ZLOTYCH
62.2000 g., 0.9990 Gold 2.0000 oz. AGW **Obv:** Imperial eagle above value **Rev:** Bust of Marszalek Pilsudski 1/4 left **Note:** Similar to 100,000 Zlotych, Y#201.

Date	Mintage	F	VF	XF	Unc	BU
1990 Proof	2,000	Value: 1,475				

Y# 211 1000000 ZLOTYCH
373.2000 g., 0.9990 Gold 12.0000 oz. AGW **Obv:** Imperial eagle above value **Rev:** Fryderyk Chopin **Note:** Similar to 100,000 Zlotych, Y#199.

Date	Mintage	F	VF	XF	Unc	BU
1990 Proof	250	Value: 8,450				

Y# 212 1000000 ZLOTYCH
373.2000 g., 0.9990 Gold 12.0000 oz. AGW **Obv:** Imperial eagle above value **Rev:** Uniformed figure on horse **Note:** Similar to 100,000 Zlotych, Y#200.

Date	Mintage	F	VF	XF	Unc	BU
1990 Proof	250	Value: 8,450				

Y# 213 1000000 ZLOTYCH
373.2000 g., 0.9990 Gold 12.0000 oz. AGW **Obv:** Imperial eagle above value **Rev:** Bust of Marszalek Pilsudski 1/4 left **Note:** Similar to 100,000 Zlotych, Y#201.

Date	Mintage	F	VF	XF	Unc	BU
1990 Proof	250	Value: 8,450				

REFORM COINAGE
100 Old Zlotych = 1 Grosz; 10,000 Old Zlotych = 1 Zloty

As far back as 1990, production was initiated for the new 1 Grosz - 1 Zlotych coins for a forthcoming monetary reform. It wasn't announced until the Act of July 7, 1994 and was enacted on January 1, 1995.

Y# 292 50 ZLOTYCH
3.1000 g., 0.9999 Gold .1000 oz. AGW **Obv:** Crowned eagle with wings open, all within circle **Rev:** Golden eagle

Date	Mintage	F	VF	XF	Unc	BU
1995	2,000	—	—	—	150	—

Y# 293 100 ZLOTYCH
7.7800 g., 0.9999 Gold .2500 oz. AGW **Obv:** Crowned eagle with wings open, all within circle **Rev:** Golden eagle

Date	Mintage	F	VF	XF	Unc	BU
1995	1,500	—	—	—	250	—

Y# 328 100 ZLOTYCH
8.0000 g., 0.9000 Gold .2315 oz. AGW **Obv:** Crowned eagle with wings open divides date **Rev:** Bust of Stefan Batory 1/4 right

Date	Mintage	F	VF	XF	Unc	BU
1997 Proof	2,000	Value: 275				

Y# 339 100 ZLOTYCH
8.0000 g., 0.9000 Gold .2315 oz. AGW **Obv:** Crowned eagle with wings open divides date **Rev:** Sigismund III 1/4 left

Date	Mintage	F	VF	XF	Unc	BU
1998 Proof	2,500	Value: 275				

Y# 361 100 ZLOTYCH
8.0000 g., 0.9000 Gold .2315 oz. AGW **Obv:** Crowned eagle in inner circle **Rev:** Pope John Paul II left

Date	Mintage	F	VF	XF	Unc	BU
1999 Proof	7,000	Value: 250				

POLAND 573

Y# 371 100 ZLOTYCH
8.0000 g., 0.9000 Gold .2315 oz. AGW **Obv:** Crowned eagle with wings open divides date **Rev:** Władysław IV in frame

Date	Mintage	F	VF	XF	Unc	BU
1999 Proof	2,300	Value: 275				

Y# 383 100 ZLOTYCH
8.0000 g., 0.9000 Gold .2315 oz. AGW **Obv:** Crowned eagle with wings open divides date **Rev:** Bust of Zygmunt II left

Date	Mintage	F	VF	XF	Unc	BU
1999 Proof	2,000	Value: 245				

Y# 384 100 ZLOTYCH
8.0000 g., 0.9000 Gold .2315 oz. AGW **Subject:** 100th Anniversary - Gniezno Convention **Obv:** Old coin designs **Rev:** Seated figures of Bolesław Chrobry and Otto III

Date	Mintage	F	VF	XF	Unc	BU
2000 Proof	2,200	Value: 245				

Y# 396 100 ZLOTYCH
8.0000 g., 0.9000 Gold .2315 oz. AGW **Obv:** Crowned eagle with wings open divides date **Rev:** Queen Jadwiga facing **Edge:** Plain

Date	Mintage	F	VF	XF	Unc	BU
2000 Proof	2,000	Value: 275				

Y# 402 100 ZLOTYCH
8.0000 g., 0.9000 Gold .2315 oz. AGW, 21 mm. **Subject:** Jan Kazimierz II (1648-68) **Obv:** Crowned eagle with wings open **Rev:** Armored bust 1/4 left with names and dates on shoulder **Edge:** Plain

Date	Mintage	F	VF	XF	Unc	BU
2000 Proof	2,000	Value: 275				

Y# 416 100 ZLOTYCH
8.0000 g., 0.9000 Gold .2315 oz. AGW, 21 mm. **Subject:** Władysław I (1320-33) **Obv:** Crowned eagle with wings open **Rev:** Crowned bust facing **Edge:** Plain

Date	Mintage	F	VF	XF	Unc	BU
2001 Proof	2,000	Value: 275				

Y# 417 100 ZLOTYCH
8.0000 g., 0.9000 Gold .2315 oz. AGW, 21 mm. **Subject:** Bolesław III (1102-1138) **Obv:** Crowned eagle with wings open **Rev:** Pointed crowned bust facing **Edge:** Plain

Date	Mintage	F	VF	XF	Unc	BU
2001 Proof	2,000	Value: 275				

Y# 462 100 ZLOTYCH
8.0000 g., 0.9000 Gold 0.2315 oz. AGW, 21 mm. **Obv:** Crowned eagle with wings open **Rev:** Jan Sobieski III **Edge:** Plain

Date	Mintage	F	VF	XF	Unc	BU
2001MV Proof	2,200	Value: 275				

Y# 436 100 ZLOTYCH
8.0000 g., 0.9000 Gold 0.2315 oz. AGW, 21 mm. **Subject:** World Cup Soccer **Obv:** Crowned eagle with wings open and world background **Rev:** Soccer player **Edge:** Plain

Date	Mintage	F	VF	XF	Unc	BU
2002 Proof	4,500	Value: 275				

Y# 429 100 ZLOTYCH
8.0000 g., 0.9000 Gold 0.2315 oz. AGW, 21 mm. **Obv:** Crowned eagle with wings open **Rev:** Crowned bust facing **Edge:** Plain

Date	Mintage	F	VF	XF	Unc	BU
2002 Proof	2,400	Value: 275				

Y# 430 100 ZLOTYCH
8.0000 g., 0.9000 Gold 0.2315 oz. AGW, 21 mm. **Obv:** Crowned eagle with wings open **Rev:** Crowned bust 1/4 left **Edge:** Plain

Date	Mintage	F	VF	XF	Unc	BU
2002 Proof	2,200	Value: 275				

Y# 454 100 ZLOTYCH
8.0000 g., 0.9000 Gold 0.2315 oz. AGW, 21 mm. **Obv:** Crowned eagle with wings open **Rev:** Uniformed bust 1/4 left **Edge:** Plain

Date	Mintage	F	VF	XF	Unc	BU
2003MW Proof	2,000	Value: 275				

Y# 466 100 ZLOTYCH
8.0000 g., 0.9000 Gold 0.2315 oz. AGW, 21 mm. **Subject:** 750th Anniversary - City Charter **Obv:** Door knocker and church **Rev:** Clock face and tower **Edge:** Plain

Date	Mintage	F	VF	XF	Unc	BU
2003MW Proof	2,100	Value: 275				

Y# 467 100 ZLOTYCH
8.0000 g., 0.9000 Gold 0.2315 oz. AGW, 21 mm. **Obv:** Crowned eagle with wings open **Rev:** Kazimierz IV (1447-1492) **Edge:** Plain

Date	Mintage	F	VF	XF	Unc	BU
2003MW Proof	2,300	Value: 275				

Y# 476 100 ZLOTYCH
8.0000 g., 0.9000 Gold 0.2315 oz. AGW, 21 mm. **Obv:** Crowned eagle with wings open **Rev:** Stanislaus I and eagle **Edge:** Plain

Date	Mintage	F	VF	XF	Unc	BU
2003MW Proof	2,500	Value: 275				

Y# 494 100 ZLOTYCH
8.0000 g., 0.9000 Gold 0.2315 oz. AGW, 21 mm. **Obv:** Crowned eagle with wings open **Rev:** King Przemysł II (1295-1296) **Edge:** Plain

Date	Mintage	F	VF	XF	Unc	BU
2004MW Proof	3,400	Value: 260				

Y# 495 100 ZLOTYCH
8.0000 g., 0.9000 Gold 0.2315 oz. AGW, 21 mm. **Obv:** Crowned eagle with wings open **Rev:** King Zygmunt I (1506-1548) **Edge:** Plain

Date	Mintage	F	VF	XF	Unc	BU
2004MW Proof	3,400	Value: 260				

Y# 540 100 ZLOTYCH
8.0000 g., 0.9000 Gold 0.2315 oz. AGW, 21 mm. **Obv:** St. Peters Basilica dome **Rev:** Pope John Paul II and baptismal font **Edge:** Plain

Date	Mintage	F	VF	XF	Unc	BU
2005MW Proof	18,700	Value: 375				

Y# 581 100 ZLOTYCH
8.0000 g., 0.9000 Gold 0.2315 oz. AGW, 21 mm. **Obv:** Line of soccer players on soccer ball surface with Polish eagle in one of the sections **Rev:** Two soccer players **Edge:** Plain

Date	Mintage	F	VF	XF	Unc	BU
2006MW Proof	—	Value: 300				

Y# 294 200 ZLOTYCH
15.5000 g., 0.9000 Gold .4485 oz. AGW **Obv:** Crowned eagle with wings open within beaded circle **Rev:** Golden eagle

Date	Mintage	F	VF	XF	Unc	BU
1995	1,000	—	—	—	500	—

Y# 299 200 ZLOTYCH
15.5000 g., 0.9000 Gold .4485 oz. AGW **Subject:** XII Chopin Piano Competition **Obv:** Crowned eagle with wings open divides date **Rev:** Bust of Chopin 1/4 right below tree **Edge:** Lettered

Date	Mintage	F	VF	XF	Unc	BU
1995 Proof	500	Value: 925				

Y# 316 200 ZLOTYCH
15.5000 g., 0.9000 Gold .4485 oz. AGW **Obv:** Stylized design to right of eagle **Rev:** Henryk Sienkiewicz

Date	Mintage	F	VF	XF	Unc	BU
1996 Proof	Est. 1,000	Value: 425				

Y# 320 200 ZLOTYCH
15.5000 g., 0.9000 Gold .4485 oz. AGW **Subject:** Millennium of Gdansk (Danzig) **Obv:** Crowned eagle with wings open within shield **Rev:** City arms in old coin style

Date	Mintage	F	VF	XF	Unc	BU
1996	2,000	—	—	—	—	375

574 POLAND

Y# 323 200 ZLOTYCH
15.5000 g., 0.9000 Gold .4485 oz. AGW **Subject:** St. Adalbert's Martyrdom **Obv:** Crowned eagle with wings open within circle **Rev:** Figure standing within center design flanked by other figures

Date	Mintage	F	VF	XF	Unc	BU
1997 Proof	2,000	Value: 375				

Y# 346 200 ZLOTYCH
15.5000 g., 0.9000 Gold .4485 oz. AGW **Obv:** Imperial eagle above value **Rev:** Standing Pope with arms wide open

Date	Mintage	F	VF	XF	Unc	BU
1998 Proof	5,000	Value: 375				

Y# 353 200 ZLOTYCH
15.5000 g., 0.9000 Gold .4485 oz. AGW **Subject:** 200th Birthday - Adam Mickiewicz **Obv:** Small crowned eagle at lower right, quote written above **Rev:** Portrait with silhouette

Date	Mintage	F	VF	XF	Unc	BU
1998 Proof	3,000	Value: 375				

Y# 367 200 ZLOTYCH
15.5000 g., 0.9000 Gold .4485 oz. AGW **Obv:** Crowned eagle on sash, music design **Rev:** Head of Fryderyk Chopin 1/4 left with music background

Date	Mintage	F	VF	XF	Unc	BU
1999 Proof	2,000	Value: 375				

Y# 385 200 ZLOTYCH
15.5000 g., 0.9000 Gold .4485 oz. AGW **Obv:** Crowned eagle with wings open, feather at right **Rev:** Head of Juliusz Slowacki left

Date	Mintage	F	VF	XF	Unc	BU
1999 Proof	1,900	Value: 375				

Y# 386 200 ZLOTYCH
15.5000 g., 0.9000 Gold .4485 oz. AGW **Subject:** 1000th Anniversary - Gniezno Convention **Obv:** Old coin designs **Rev:** Seated figures of Boleslaw Chrobry and Otto III

Date	Mintage	F	VF	XF	Unc	BU
2000 Proof	1,250	Value: 385				

Y# 393 200 ZLOTYCH
15.5000 g., 0.9000 Gold .4485 oz. AGW, 27 mm. **Subject:** 1000 Years - Wroclzaw (Breslau) **Obv:** Crowned eagle with wings open within beaded circle **Rev:** Bust of Jesus facing, holding city arms **Edge:** Plain

Date	Mintage	F	VF	XF	Unc	BU
2000 Proof	2,000	Value: 375				

Y# 397 200 ZLOTYCH
23.3200 g., 0.9000 Gold .6748 oz. AGW **Subject:** Solidarity **Obv:** Crowned eagle with wings open **Rev:** Multicolor Soldiarity logo, map and two children **Edge:** Plain

Date	Mintage	F	VF	XF	Unc	BU
2000 Proof	2,500	Value: 550				

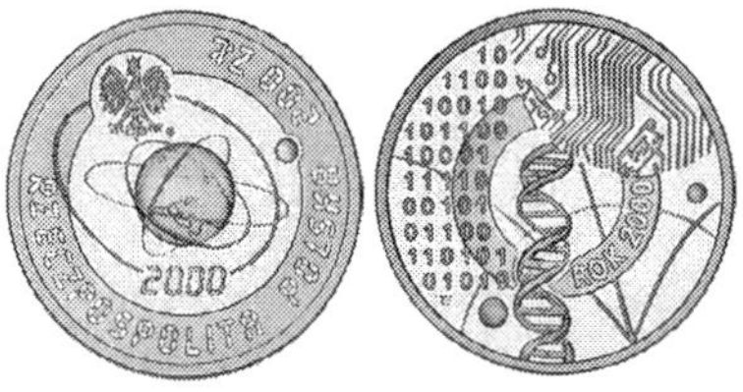

Y# 375 200 ZLOTYCH
13.6000 g., Gold And Silver **Subject:** Millennium **Obv:** Crowned eagle and world globe **Rev:** Various computer, DNA and atomic symbols **Note:** .900 Gold center in .925 Silver inner ring in a .900 Gold outer ring.

Date	Mintage	F	VF	XF	Unc	BU
2000 Proof	6,000	Value: 250				

Y# 463 200 ZLOTYCH
15.5000 g., 0.9000 Gold 0.4485 oz. AGW, 27 mm. **Obv:** Standing violinist **Rev:** Henry Wieniawski **Edge:** Lettered **Edge Lettering:** "XII MIEDZYNARODOWY KONKURS SKRZYPCOWY IM HENRYKA WIENIAWSKIEGO"

Date	Mintage	F	VF	XF	Unc	BU
2001MW Proof	2,000	Value: 375				

Y# 407 200 ZLOTYCH
Tri-Metallic Gold with Palladium center, Gold with Silver ring, Gold with Copper outer limit, 27 mm. **Subject:** Year 2001 **Obv:** Crowned eagle with wings open within a swirl **Rev:** Couple looking into the future **Edge:** Plain

Date	Mintage	F	VF	XF	Unc	BU
2001 Proof	4,000	Value: 275				

Y# 420 200 ZLOTYCH
15.5000 g., 0.9000 Gold .4485 oz. AGW, 27 mm. **Subject:** Cardinal Stefan Wyszynski **Obv:** Pillar divides arms and eagle **Rev:** Bust left within arch **Edge Lettering:** "100 ROCZNIA URODZIN"

Date	Mintage	F	VF	XF	Unc	BU
2001 Proof	4,500	Value: 375				

Y# 438 200 ZLOTYCH
15.5000 g., 0.9000 Gold 0.4485 oz. AGW, 27 mm. **Subject:** Pope John Paul II **Obv:** Bust left and small eagle with wings open **Rev:** Pope facing radiant Holy Door **Edge:** Plain

Date	Mintage	F	VF	XF	Unc	BU
2002 Proof	5,000	Value: 385				

Y# 470 200 ZLOTYCH
15.5000 g., 0.9000 Gold 0.4485 oz. AGW, 27 mm. **Subject:** Gas and Oil Industry **Obv:** Crowned eagle, oil wells and refinery **Rev:** Scientist at work **Edge:** Plain

Date	Mintage	F	VF	XF	Unc	BU
2003MW Proof	2,100	Value: 385				

Y# 472 200 ZLOTYCH
15.5000 g., 0.9000 Gold 0.4485 oz. AGW, 27 mm. **Obv:** Standing Pope John Paul II **Rev:** Seated Pope **Edge:** Plain

Date	Mintage	F	VF	XF	Unc	BU
2003MW Proof	4,900	Value: 385				

Y# 483 200 ZLOTYCH
15.5000 g., 0.9000 Gold 0.4485 oz. AGW, 27 mm. **Subject:** Poland Joining the European Union **Obv:** Polish euro coin design elements **Rev:** Polish euro coin design elements **Edge:** Plain

Date	Mintage	F	VF	XF	Unc	BU
2004MW Proof	4,400	Value: 375				

Y# 511 200 ZLOTYCH
15.5000 g., 0.9000 Gold 0.4485 oz. AGW, 27 mm. **Subject:** Warsaw Fine Arts Academy Centennial **Obv:** Campus view **Rev:** Statue and building **Edge:** Plain

Date	Mintage	F	VF	XF	Unc	BU
2004MW Proof	5,000	Value: 365				

Y# 519 200 ZLOTYCH
15.5000 g., 0.9000 Gold 0.4485 oz. AGW, 27 mm. **Subject:** Olympics **Obv:** Woman and crowned eagle **Rev:** Ancient runners painted on pottery **Edge:** Plain

Date	Mintage	F	VF	XF	Unc	BU
2004MW Proof	6,000	Value: 365				

Y# 538 200 ZLOTYCH
15.5000 g., 0.9000 Gold 0.4485 oz. AGW, 27 mm. **Obv:** Horse drawn carriage **Rev:** Konstanty Ildefons Galczynski in top hat **Edge:** Plain

Date	Mintage	F	VF	XF	Unc	BU
2005MW Proof	3,500	Value: 375				

Y# 536 200 ZLOTYCH
15.5000 g., 0.9000 Gold 0.4485 oz. AGW, 27 mm. **Obv:** Chopin **Rev:** Nagoya Castle roof tops and Mt. Fuji **Edge:** Plain **Note:** Aichi Expo Japan

Date	Mintage	F	VF	XF	Unc	BU
2005MW Proof	4,200	Value: 375				

Y# 295 500 ZLOTYCH
31.1035 g., 0.9999 Gold 1.0000 oz. AGW **Obv:** Crowned eagle with wings open within beaded circle **Rev:** Golden eagle

Date	Mintage	F	VF	XF	Unc	BU
1995	500	—	—	—	800	—

PATTERNS
Including off metal strikes

KM#	Date	Mintage	Identification	Mkt Val
Pn123	1813 IB	—	Dukat. Copper.	—
Pn141	1818 IB	—	25 Zlotych. Gold.	—
Pn215	1840MW	—	20 Zlotych - 3 Rubles. Gold.	—
Pn227	1840 АЧ	—	20 Zlotych - 3 Rubles. Gold.	—
Pn239	1922	3	100 Marek. Gold.	—
Pn242	1923	1	50 Marek. Gold.	—
Pn245	1923	—	2 Grosze. Gold.	—
Pn264	1924	10	20 Zlotych. Gold.	—
Pn268	1924	1	50 Zlotych. Gold.	—

POLAND 575

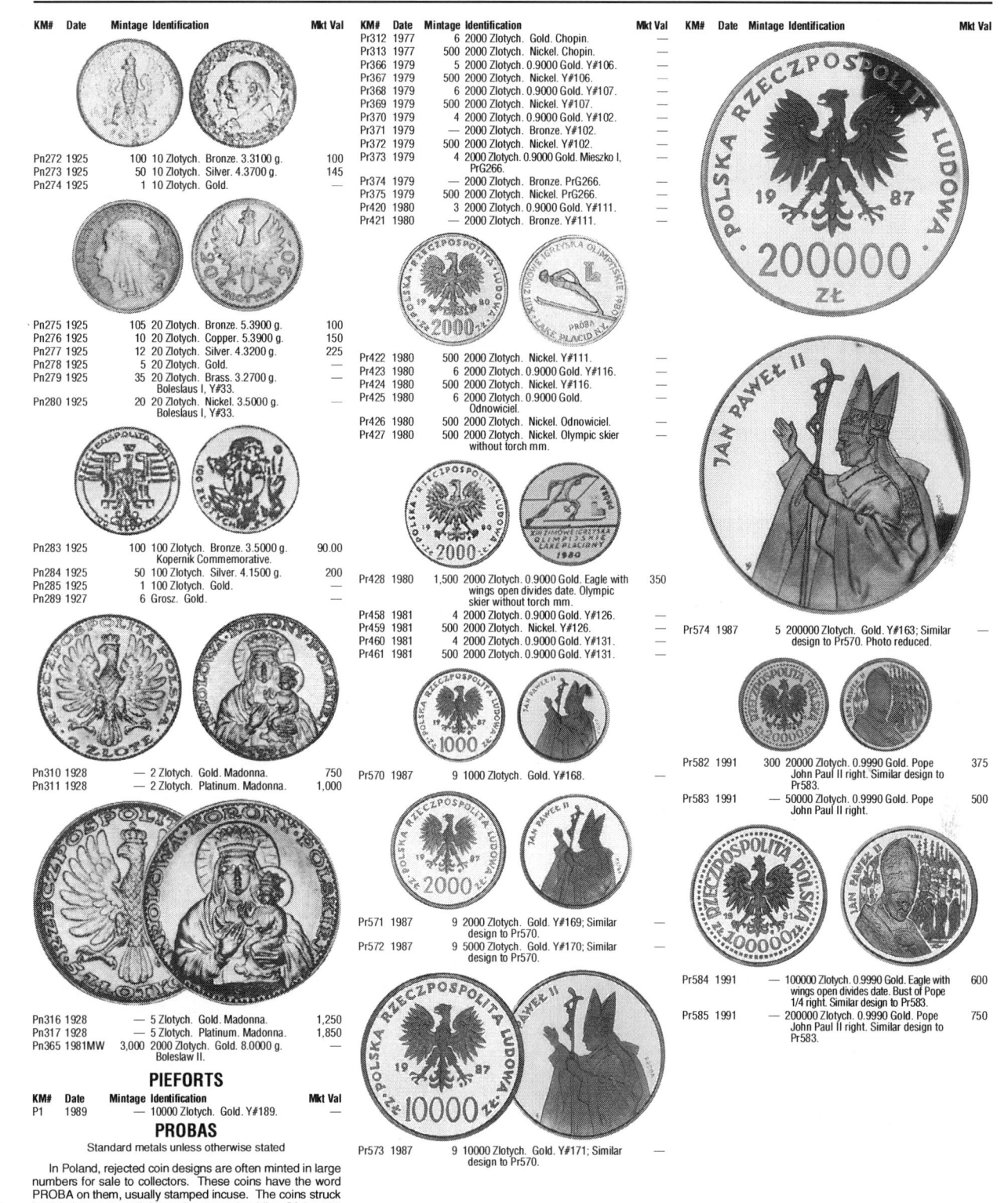

KM#	Date	Mintage	Identification	Mkt Val
Pn272	1925	100	10 Zlotych. Bronze. 3.3100 g.	100
Pn273	1925	50	10 Zlotych. Silver. 4.3700 g.	145
Pn274	1925	1	10 Zlotych. Gold.	—
Pn275	1925	105	20 Zlotych. Bronze. 5.3900 g.	100
Pn276	1925	10	20 Zlotych. Copper. 5.3900 g.	150
Pn277	1925	12	20 Zlotych. Silver. 4.3200 g.	225
Pn278	1925	5	20 Zlotych. Gold.	—
Pn279	1925	35	20 Zlotych. Brass. 3.2700 g. Boleslaus I, Y#33.	—
Pn280	1925	20	20 Zlotych. Nickel. 3.5000 g. Boleslaus I, Y#33.	—
Pn283	1925	100	100 Zlotych. Bronze. 3.5000 g. Kopernik Commemorative.	90.00
Pn284	1925	50	100 Zlotych. Silver. 4.1500 g.	200
Pn285	1925	1	100 Zlotych. Gold.	—
Pn289	1927	6	Grosz. Gold.	—
Pn310	1928	—	2 Zlotych. Gold. Madonna.	750
Pn311	1928	—	2 Zlotych. Platinum. Madonna.	1,000
Pn316	1928	—	5 Zlotych. Gold. Madonna.	1,250
Pn317	1928	—	5 Zlotych. Platinum. Madonna.	1,850
Pn365	1981MW	3,000	2000 Zlotych. Gold. 8.0000 g. Bolesław II.	—

PIEFORTS

KM#	Date	Mintage	Identification	Mkt Val
P1	1989	—	10000 Zlotych. Gold. Y#189.	—

PROBAS

Standard metals unless otherwise stated

In Poland, rejected coin designs are often minted in large numbers for sale to collectors. These coins have the word PROBA on them, usually stamped incuse. The coins struck in nickel are not available to the general public. Of the 500 pieces struck, 250 pieces are distributed among the members of the Polish Numismatic Society and the other 250 pieces are distributed between various banks and museums.

KM#	Date	Mintage	Identification	Mkt Val
Pr168	1969	5	10 Zlotych. Gold. PROBA at lower right.	—
Pr288	1976	500	500 Zlotych. Nickel. Y#83.	20.00
Pr289	1976	300	500 Zlotych. 0.9000 Gold. Y#83.	700
Pr290	1976	500	500 Zlotych. Nickel. Kosciuszko.	20.00
Pr291	1976	500	500 Zlotych. Nickel. Y#85.	20.00
Pr292	1976	300	500 Zlotych. 0.9000 Gold. Y#85.	700
Pr293	1976	500	500 Zlotych. Nickel. Pulaski facing.	20.00
Pr312	1977	6	2000 Zlotych. Gold. Chopin.	—
Pr313	1977	500	2000 Zlotych. Nickel. Chopin.	—
Pr366	1979	5	2000 Zlotych. 0.9000 Gold. Y#106.	—
Pr367	1979	500	2000 Zlotych. Nickel. Y#106.	—
Pr368	1979	6	2000 Zlotych. 0.9000 Gold. Y#107.	—
Pr369	1979	500	2000 Zlotych. Nickel. Y#107.	—
Pr370	1979	4	2000 Zlotych. 0.9000 Gold. Y#102.	—
Pr371	1979	—	2000 Zlotych. Bronze. Y#102.	—
Pr372	1979	500	2000 Zlotych. Nickel. Y#102.	—
Pr373	1979	4	2000 Zlotych. 0.9000 Gold. Mieszko I, PrG266.	—
Pr374	1979	—	2000 Zlotych. Bronze. PrG266.	—
Pr375	1979	500	2000 Zlotych. Nickel. PrG266.	—
Pr420	1980	3	2000 Zlotych. 0.9000 Gold. Y#111.	—
Pr421	1980	—	2000 Zlotych. Bronze. Y#111.	—
Pr422	1980	500	2000 Zlotych. Nickel. Y#111.	—
Pr423	1980	6	2000 Zlotych. 0.9000 Gold. Y#116.	—
Pr424	1980	500	2000 Zlotych. Nickel. Y#116.	—
Pr425	1980	6	2000 Zlotych. 0.9000 Gold. Odnowiciel.	—
Pr426	1980	500	2000 Zlotych. Nickel. Odnowiciel.	—
Pr427	1980	500	2000 Zlotych. Nickel. Olympic skier without torch mm.	—
Pr428	1980	1,500	2000 Zlotych. 0.9000 Gold. Eagle with wings open divides date. Olympic skier without torch mm.	350
Pr458	1981	4	2000 Zlotych. 0.9000 Gold. Y#126.	—
Pr459	1981	500	2000 Zlotych. Nickel. Y#126.	—
Pr460	1981	4	2000 Zlotych. 0.9000 Gold. Y#131.	—
Pr461	1981	500	2000 Zlotych. Nickel. Y#131.	—
Pr570	1987	9	1000 Zlotych. Gold. Y#168.	—
Pr571	1987	9	2000 Zlotych. Gold. Y#169; Similar design to Pr570.	—
Pr572	1987	9	5000 Zlotych. Gold. Y#170; Similar design to Pr570.	—
Pr573	1987	9	10000 Zlotych. Gold. Y#171; Similar design to Pr570.	—
Pr574	1987	5	200000 Zlotych. Gold. Y#163; Similar design to Pr570. Photo reduced.	—
Pr582	1991	300	20000 Zlotych. 0.9990 Gold. Pope John Paul II right. Similar design to Pr583.	375
Pr583	1991	—	50000 Zlotych. 0.9990 Gold. Pope John Paul II right.	500
Pr584	1991	—	100000 Zlotych. 0.9990 Gold. Eagle with wings open divides date. Bust of Pope 1/4 right. Similar design to Pr583.	600
Pr585	1991	—	200000 Zlotych. 0.9990 Gold. Pope John Paul II right. Similar design to Pr583.	750

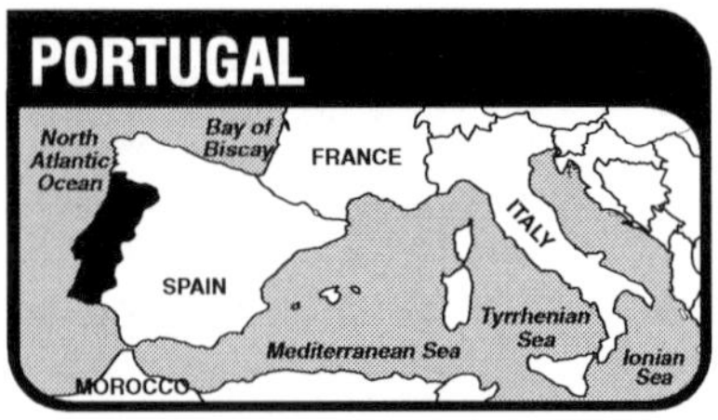

PORTUGAL

The Portuguese Republic, located in the western part of the Iberian Peninsula in southwestern Europe, has an area of 35,553 sq. mi. (92,080 sq. km.) and a population of *10.5 million. Capital: Lisbon. Portugal's economy is based on agriculture, tourism, minerals, fisheries and a rapidly expanding industrial sector. Textiles account for 33% of the exports and Portuguese wine is world famous. Portugal has become Europe's number one producer of copper and the world's largest producer of cork.

After centuries of domination by Romans, Visigoths and Moors, Portugal emerged in the 12th century as an independent kingdom financially and philosophically prepared for the great period of exploration that would soon follow. Attuned to the inspiration of Prince Henry the Navigator (1394-1460), Portugal's daring explorers of the 15th and 16th centuries roamed the world's oceans from Brazil to Japan in an unprecedented burst of energy and endeavor that culminated in 1494 with Portugal laying claim to half the transoceanic world. Unfortunately for the fortunes of the tiny kingdom, the Portuguese population was too small to colonize this vast territory. Less than a century after Portugal laid claim to half the world, English, French and Dutch trading companies had seized the lion's share of the world's colonies and commerce, and Portugal's place as an imperial power was lost forever. The monarchy was overthrown in 1910 and a republic was established.

On April 25, 1974, the government of Portugal was seized by a military junta which reached agreements providing for independence for the Portuguese overseas provinces of Portuguese Guinea (*Guinea-Bissau*), Mozambique, Cape Verde Islands, Angola, and St. Thomas and Prince Islands (*Sao Tome and Principe*).

On January 1, 1986, Portugal became the eleventh member of the European Economic Community and in the first half of 1992 held its first EEC Presidency.

RULERS
Joao, As Prince Regent, 1799-1816
Joao, As King (Joao VI), 1816-1826
Pedro IV, 1826-1828
Miguel, 1828-1834
Maria II, 1834-1853
Pedro V, 1853-1861
Luiz I, 1861-1889
Carlos I, 1889-1908
Manuel II, 1908-1910
Republic, 1910 to date

NOTE: The coins of Philip II and Philip III are so similar that it is not possible to give an absolute attribution. Portuguese authorities rely on legend variants and many times these are lacking in certainty. The "Philippvs" name is attributed to both rulers but it is likely that "Philipvs" is only Philip III.

MINT MARKS
E - Evora
L - Lisbon
P - Porto
No Mint mark – Lisbon

MONETARY SYSTEM
Until 1825
20 Reis = 1 Vintem
100 Reis = 1 Tostao
480 Reis = 24 Vintens = 1 Cruzado
1600 Reis = 1 Escudo
6400 Reis = 4 Escudos = 1 Peca

NOTE: The primary denomination was the Peca, weighing 14.34 g, tariffed at 6400 Reis until 1825, and at 7500 Reis after 1826. The weight was not changed.

1826-1836
7500 Reis = 1 Peca
Beginning in 1836 all coins were expressed in terms of Reis and arranged in a decimal sequence (until 1910).

Commencing 1910
100 Centavos = 1 Escudo

KINGDOM
MILLED COINAGE

KM# 341 400 REIS (Pinto, 480 Reis)
1.0720 g., 0.9170 Gold .0316 oz. AGW **Ruler:** Joao, as Prince Regent **Obv:** Legend in crowned wreath **Obv. Legend:** JOANNES P R...

Date	Mintage	VG	F	VF	XF	Unc
1807	8,857	240	525	700	1,000	—

KM# 359 400 REIS (Pinto, 480 Reis)
1.0720 g., 0.9170 Gold .0316 oz. AGW **Ruler:** Joao VI **Obv:** Legend in crowned wreath **Obv. Legend:** JOAN VI...

Date	Mintage	VG	F	VF	XF	Unc
1818	4,401	350	700	1,100	1,700	—
1819	1,387	900	1,800	2,750	3,750	—
1820 Rare	200	—	—	—	—	—
1821	266	1,300	2,750	3,700	4,600	—

KM# 337 1/2 ESCUDO (800 Reis)
1.7920 g., 0.9170 Gold .0528 oz. AGW **Ruler:** Joao, as Prince Regent **Obv:** Laureate bust right **Obv. Legend:** JOANNES D. G. PORT. ET ALG. P. REGENS **Rev:** Crowned ornate oval arms

Date	Mintage	VG	F	VF	XF	Unc
1805	3,278	200	450	650	1,000	1,650
1806	—	650	1,450	2,000	3,000	—
1807	5,253	150	360	550	900	—

KM# 361 1/2 ESCUDO (800 Reis)
1.7920 g., 0.9170 Gold .0528 oz. AGW **Ruler:** Joao VI **Obv:** Laureate bust right **Obv. Legend:** JOANNES VI D. G. PORT... **Rev:** Crowned arms on globe within wreath

Date	Mintage	VG	F	VF	XF	Unc
1818	270	300	750	1,500	3,200	—
1819	5,536	250	700	1,400	2,250	—
1820 Rare	82	—	—	—	—	—
1821	286	300	750	1,500	3,200	—

KM# 360 1000 REIS (Quartinho, 1200 Reis)
2.6800 g., 0.9170 Gold .0790 oz. AGW **Ruler:** Joao VI **Obv:** Crowned arms on globe divides value above **Obv. Legend:** JOANNES VI D G PORT... **Rev:** Maltese cross, rosettes in angles **Rev. Legend:** IN HOC...

Date	Mintage	VG	F	VF	XF	Unc
1818	3,144	400	850	1,450	2,350	—
1819	1,247	850	1,200	1,800	2,750	—
1820	270	800	1,700	2,750	4,750	—
1821	275	800	1,700	2,750	4,750	—

KM# 338 ESCUDO (1600 Reis)
3.5800 g., 0.9170 Gold .1057 oz. AGW **Ruler:** Joao, as Prince Regent **Obv:** Laureate bust right **Obv. Legend:** JOANNES D. G. PORT ET ALG P. REGENS **Rev:** Crowned ornate oval arms

Date	Mintage	VG	F	VF	XF	Unc
1805 Rare	143	—	—	—	—	—
1807	800	280	700	1,100	1,650	—

KM# 362 ESCUDO (1600 Reis)
3.5850 g., 0.9170 Gold .1057 oz. AGW **Ruler:** Joao VI **Obv:** Laureate bust right **Obv. Legend:** JOANNES VI D. G. PORT...REX **Rev:** Crowned ornate oval arms

Date	Mintage	VG	F	VF	XF	Unc
1818	1,804	350	800	1,400	2,600	3,200
1819	1,523	375	900	1,700	3,200	—
1821 Rare	270	—	—	—	—	—

KM# 339 1/2 PECA (3200 Reis)
7.1500 g., 0.9170 Gold .2107 oz. AGW **Ruler:** Joao, as Prince Regent **Obv:** Laureate bust right **Obv. Legend:** JOANNES D. G. PORT ET ALG. P. REGENS **Rev:** Crowned ornate oval arms **Note:** Revalued to 3750 Reis in 1826.

Date	Mintage	VG	F	VF	XF	Unc
1805 Rare	74	—	—	—	—	—

KM# 342 1/2 PECA (3200 Reis)
7.1500 g., 0.9170 Gold .2107 oz. AGW **Ruler:** Joao, as Prince Regent **Obv:** Laureate bust right **Obv. Legend:** JOANNES D. G. PORT ET ALG. P. REGENS **Rev:** Crowned ornate oval arms **Note:** Revalued to 3750 Reis in 1826.

Date	Mintage	VG	F	VF	XF	Unc
1807	483	250	520	850	1,500	—

KM# 363 1/2 PECA (3200 Reis)
7.1500 g., 0.9170 Gold .2107 oz. AGW **Ruler:** Joao VI **Obv:** Laureate bust right **Obv. Legend:** JOANNES VI D G... **Rev:** Crowned arms on globe within wreath **Note:** Revalued to 3750 Reis in 1826.

Date	Mintage	VG	F	VF	XF	Unc
1818	100	—	300	600	1,100	1,850
1819 Rare	1,700	—	—	—	—	—
1820	242	—	900	2,000	3,500	6,500
1821	196	—	900	2,000	3,500	8,500
1822	14,000	—	150	200	350	650
1823 Rare	—	—	—	—	—	—

KM# 379 1/2 PECA (3200 Reis)
7.1500 g., 0.9170 Gold .2107 oz. AGW **Ruler:** Pedro IV **Obv:** Laureate head right **Obv. Legend:** PETRUS IV D G... **Rev:** Crowned oval arms within wreath **Note:** Revalued to 3750 Reis in 1826.

Date	Mintage	VG	F	VF	XF	Unc
1827	1,713	—	300	500	800	1,450

KM# 387 1/2 PECA (3200 Reis)
7.1500 g., 0.9170 Gold .2107 oz. AGW **Ruler:** Miguel **Obv:** Laureate bust right **Obv. Legend:** MICHAEL I... **Rev:** Crowned arms within palm wreath **Note:** Revalued to 3750 Reis in 1826.

Date	Mintage	VG	F	VF	XF	Unc
1828	242	—	750	1,450	2,200	3,500

KM# 396 1/2 PECA (3200 Reis)
7.1500 g., 0.9170 Gold .2107 oz. AGW **Ruler:** Miguel **Obv:** Armored laureate bust right **Obv. Legend:** MICHAEL I... **Rev:** Crowned arms within crossed palms **Note:** Revalued to 3750 Reis in 1826.

Date	Mintage	VG	F	VF	XF	Unc
1830	525	—	500	800	1,350	2,750
1831	225	—	600	900	1,650	3,200

PORTUGAL 577

KM# 332 PECA (6400 Reis)
14.3420 g., 0.9170 Gold .4228 oz. AGW **Ruler:** Joao, as Prince Regent **Obv:** Laureate bust right **Obv. Legend:** IOANNES D. G. PORT ET ALG. P. REGENS **Rev:** Crowned oval arms in frame **Note:** Revalued to 7500 Reis in 1826.

Date	Mintage	VG	F	VF	XF	Unc
1802	30,000	800	1,600	3,250	5,500	—

KM# 336 PECA (6400 Reis)
14.3420 g., 0.9170 Gold .4228 oz. AGW **Ruler:** Joao, as Prince Regent **Obv:** Laureate bust right **Obv. Legend:** JOANNES D. G. PORT ET ALG. P. REGENS **Rev:** Crowned ornate oval arms **Note:** Revalued to 7500 Reis in 1826. Similar pieces with "R" after date were struck in Rio de Janeiro and are found listed under Brazil.

Date	Mintage	VG	F	VF	XF	Unc
1804 Rare	476	—	—	—	—	—
1805	27,000	275	550	1,000	1,250	—
1806	41,000	225	500	850	1,150	—
1807	36,000	400	850	1,400	1,650	—
1808	27,000	275	550	1,000	1,250	—
1809	13,000	275	500	850	1,150	—
1812	25,000	275	500	850	1,150	—
1813	5,590	600	1,200	2,100	3,500	—
1814 Rare	21	—	—	—	—	—
1815	305	650	1,300	2,400	4,500	—
1816 Rare	—	—	—	—	—	—

KM# 364 PECA (6400 Reis)
14.3420 g., 0.9170 Gold .4228 oz. AGW **Ruler:** Joao VI **Obv:** Laureate bust right **Obv. Legend:** JOANNES.VID.G.PORT... **Rev:** Crowned arms on globe within wreath **Note:** Revalued to 7500 Reis in 1826. Similar pieces with "R" after date were struck in Rio de Janeiro and are listed under Brazil.

Date	Mintage	VG	F	VF	XF	Unc
1818 Rare	291	—	—	—	—	—
1819	1,727	—	2,900	5,200	8,500	14,000
1820	1,687	—	2,900	5,200	8,500	14,000
1821	391	—	9,500	12,500	16,000	18,500
1822	30,000	—	275	400	600	900
1823	27,000	—	350	525	700	1,150
1824	1,553	—	350	525	750	1,250

KM# 378 PECA (6400 Reis)
14.3420 g., 0.9170 Gold .4228 oz. AGW **Ruler:** Pedro IV **Obv:** Laureate head right **Obv. Legend:** PETRUS.IV.D.G... **Rev:** Crowned oval arms within wreath **Note:** Revalued to 7500 Reis in 1826. Similar pieces dated 1825 with square shield on reverse are patterns.

Date	Mintage	VG	F	VF	XF	Unc
1826	10,883	—	450	850	1,650	4,000
1828	1,255	—	600	1,200	2,700	5,000

KM# 388 PECA (6400 Reis)
14.3420 g., 0.9170 Gold .4228 oz. AGW **Ruler:** Miguel **Obv:** Laureate bust right **Obv. Legend:** MICHAEL I... **Rev:** Crowned arms within palm wreath with floral garland

Date	Mintage	VG	F	VF	XF	Unc
1828	—	—	650	1,350	2,200	3,500

KM# 397 PECA (6400 Reis)
14.3420 g., 0.9170 Gold .4228 oz. AGW, 31 mm. **Ruler:** Miguel **Obv:** Laureate bust right **Obv. Legend:** MICHAEL.I.D.G... **Rev:** Crowned arms within crossed palms with flower garland **Note:** Modified design.

Date	Mintage	VG	F	VF	XF	Unc
1830	2,274	—	350	650	1,150	2,200
1831	1,618	—	475	950	1,650	2,650

KM# 404 PECA (6400 Reis)
14.3420 g., 0.9170 Gold .4228 oz. AGW **Ruler:** Maria II **Obv:** Head left **Obv. Legend:** MARIA.II.D.G.PORTUG... **Rev:** Crowned arms within wreath **Note:** Modified design.

Date	Mintage	VG	F	VF	XF	Unc
1833	1,265	—	1,000	2,000	4,000	6,500

KM# 405 PECA (6400 Reis)
14.3420 g., 0.9170 Gold .4228 oz. AGW **Ruler:** Maria II **Obv:** Crowned bust left **Obv. Legend:** MARIA.II.D.G.PORTUG... **Rev:** Crowned arms within wreath

Date	Mintage	VG	F	VF	XF	Unc
1833	—	—	850	1,650	3,000	5,000
1834	32,000	—	300	500	950	1,650

KM# 407 PECA (6400 Reis)
14.3420 g., 0.9170 Gold .4228 oz. AGW **Ruler:** Maria II **Obv:** Crowned bust left, continuous legend **Obv. Legend:** MARIA.II.D.G.PORTUG... **Rev:** Crowned arms within wreath

Date	Mintage	VG	F	VF	XF	Unc
1835	2,989	—	375	750	1,500	2,150

DECIMAL COINAGE

New denominations, all expressed in terms of Reis were introduced by Maria II in 1836, to bring Portugal's currency into decimal form. Some of the coins retained old names, as follows:

1000 Reis Silver - Coroa

100 Reis Silver - Tostao

The diameter of the new copper coins, first minted by Maria II in 1837, was smaller than the earlier coinage, but the weight was unaltered. However, in 1882, Luis I reduced the size and weight of the copper currency.

The Real and 2 Reis pieces dated 1853 were issued for circulation in Mozambique and will be found in those listings.

KM# 486 1000 REIS
1.7900 g., 0.9170 Gold .0528 oz. AGW **Ruler:** Maria II **Obv:** Crowned head left **Obv. Legend:** MARIA II... **Rev:** Crowned mantled arms

Date	Mintage	VG	F	VF	XF	Unc
1851	12,000	60.00	80.00	100	165	—

KM# 495 1000 REIS
1.7735 g., 0.9170 Gold .0523 oz. AGW **Ruler:** Pedro V **Obv:** Head right **Obv. Legend:** PETRVS V... **Rev:** Crowned mantled arms

Date	Mintage	VG	F	VF	XF	Unc
1855	68,000	60.00	80.00	100	150	—

KM# 496 2000 REIS
3.5470 g., 0.9170 Gold .1045 oz. AGW **Ruler:** Pedro V **Obv:** Child head right **Obv. Legend:** PETRVS V... **Rev:** Crowned mantled arms

Date	Mintage	F	VF	XF	Unc	BU
1856	38,000	115	175	225	325	—
1857	44,000	115	175	225	300	—

KM# 500 2000 REIS
3.5470 g., 0.9170 Gold .1045 oz. AGW **Ruler:** Pedro V **Obv:** Young head right **Obv. Legend:** PETRVS V... **Rev:** Crowned mantled arms

Date	Mintage	F	VF	XF	Unc	BU
1858	13,000	115	175	225	375	—
1859	16,000	115	175	225	375	—
1860	53,000	115	175	225	375	—

KM# 511 2000 REIS
3.5470 g., 0.9170 Gold .1045 oz. AGW **Ruler:** Luiz I **Obv:** Head left **Obv. Legend:** LUDOVICUS I... **Rev:** Crowned arms within wreath

Date	Mintage	F	VF	XF	Unc	BU
1864	101,000	85.00	135	200	350	—
1865	95,000	85.00	135	200	350	—
1866	86,000	85.00	135	200	350	—

KM# 518 2000 REIS
3.5470 g., 0.9170 Gold .1045 oz. AGW **Ruler:** Luiz I **Obv:** Head left **Obv. Legend:** LUDOVICUS I... **Rev:** Crowned mantled arms

578 PORTUGAL

Date	Mintage	F	VF	XF	Unc	BU
1868	24,000	85.00	135	200	350	—
1869	11,000	95.00	150	240	425	—
1870	500	850	1,650	—	—	—
1871	500	380	750	1,100	1,500	—
1872	1,000	150	280	550	875	—
1874	5,000	95.00	150	225	425	—
1875	2,000	130	260	375	650	—
1876	5,000	130	260	375	650	—
1877	2,250	100	175	275	475	—
1878	22,000	95.00	150	350	450	—
1881	1,000	230	460	700	1,100	—
1888	500	900	1,850	2,800	4,400	—

KM# 475 2500 REIS
4.7800 g., 0.9170 Gold .1410 oz. AGW **Ruler:** Maria II **Obv:** Crowned head left **Obv. Legend:** MARIA II... **Rev:** Crowned mantled arms

Date	Mintage	F	VF	XF	Unc	BU
1838	1,114	400	700	1,200	2,250	—

KM# 487 2500 REIS
4.4800 g., 0.9170 Gold .1321 oz. AGW **Ruler:** Maria II **Obv:** Crowned head left **Obv. Legend:** MARIA II... **Rev:** Crowned mantled arms

Date	Mintage	F	VF	XF	Unc	BU
1851	58,000	120	210	300	500	—

KM# 489 2500 REIS
4.4800 g., 0.9170 Gold .1321 oz. AGW **Ruler:** Maria II **Obv:** Crowned head left **Obv. Legend:** MARIA II... **Rev:** Crowned mantled arms

Date	Mintage	F	VF	XF	Unc	BU
1853	1,010	400	700	1,200	2,250	—

KM# 476.1 5000 REIS
9.5600 g., 0.9170 Gold .2819 oz. AGW **Ruler:** Maria II **Obv:** Crowned head left **Obv. Legend:** MARIA II... **Rev:** Crowned mantled arms

Date	Mintage	F	VF	XF	Unc	BU
1838	2,410	550	750	1,250	2,250	—
1845 Rare	401	—	—	—	—	—

KM# 476.2 5000 REIS
8.9600 g., 0.9170 Gold .2642 oz. AGW **Ruler:** Maria II **Obv:** Crowned head left **Obv. Legend:** MARIA.II.PORTUG: .... **Rev:** Crowned mantled arms

Date	Mintage	F	VF	XF	Unc	BU
1851	57,000	200	250	400	700	—

KM# 505 5000 REIS
8.8675 g., 0.9170 Gold .2613 oz. AGW **Ruler:** Pedro V **Obv:** Head right **Obv. Legend:** PETRUS V... **Rev:** Crowned mantled arms

Date	Mintage	F	VF	XF	Unc	BU
1860	52,000	185	225	300	575	—
1861	81,000	185	225	300	575	—

KM# 508 5000 REIS
8.8675 g., 0.9170 Gold .2613 oz. AGW **Ruler:** Luiz I **Obv:** Head left **Obv. Legend:** LUDOVICUS I... **Rev:** Crowned arms within wreath

Date	Mintage	F	VF	XF	Unc	BU
1862	166,000	175	200	275	500	—
1863	38,000	175	200	275	525	—

KM# 516 5000 REIS
8.8675 g., 0.9170 Gold .2613 oz. AGW **Ruler:** Luiz I **Obv:** Head left **Obv. Legend:** LUDOVICUS I... **Rev:** Crowned mantled arms

Date	Mintage	F	VF	XF	Unc	BU
1867	45,000	175	200	275	500	—
1868	64,000	175	200	275	500	—
1869	77,000	175	200	275	500	—
1870	61,000	175	200	275	500	—
1871	47,000	175	200	275	500	—
1872	28,000	175	200	275	500	—
1874	6,800	175	200	275	500	—
1875	10,000	175	200	275	500	—
1876	15,000	175	200	275	500	—
1877	9,400	300	350	575	1,000	—
1878	8,400	175	200	350	500	—
1880	7,000	375	575	925	1,400	—
1883	23,000	175	200	350	500	—
1886	27,000	175	200	350	500	—
1887	44,000	175	200	275	500	—
1888	4,800	175	200	275	500	—
1889	9,000	175	200	275	500	—

KM# 520 10000 REIS
17.7350 g., 0.9170 Gold .5227 oz. AGW **Ruler:** Luiz I **Obv:** Head left **Obv. Legend:** LUDOVICUS I... **Rev:** Crowned mantled arms

Date	Mintage	F	VF	XF	Unc	BU
1878	23,000	350	400	550	950	1,250
1879	36,000	350	400	550	950	1,250
1880	30,000	350	400	550	950	1,250
1881	19,000	350	400	550	950	1,250
1882	15,000	350	400	550	950	1,250
1883	8,500	375	450	550	950	1,250
1884	13,000	360	425	550	950	1,250
1885	21,000	360	425	550	950	1,250
1886	1,800	400	525	650	1,100	—
1888	7,000	425	575	850	1,500	—
1889	4,400	425	575	800	1,400	—

REPUBLIC
DECIMAL COINAGE

New denominations, all expressed in terms of Reis were introduced by Maria II in 1836, to bring Portugal's currency into decimal form. Some of the coins retained old names, as follows:

1000 Reis Silver - Coroa

100 Reis Silver - Tostao

The diameter of the new copper coins, first minted by Maria II in 1837, was smaller than the earlier coinage, but the weight was unaltered. However, in 1882, Luis I reduced the size and weight of the copper currency.

The Real and 2 Reis pieces dated 1853 were issued for circulation in Mozambique and will be found in those listings.

KM# 631a ESCUDO
4.6000 g., 0.9167 Gold 0.1356 oz. AGW, 16 mm. **Subject:** Last Escudo **Obv:** Design above shield with "Au" above top left corner of shield **Rev:** Flower design above value **Edge:** Plain

Date	Mintage	F	VF	XF	Unc	BU
2001INCM	50,000	—	—	—	115	—

KM# 639b 100 ESCUDOS
24.0000 g., 0.9170 Gold .7075 oz. AGW, 34 mm. **Subject:** Golden Age of Portuguese Discoveries - Gil Eanes **Obv:** Shield within circle **Rev:** Ship with flag on top of sails

Date	Mintage	F	VF	XF	Unc	BU
1987	5,772	—	—	—	540	—

KM# 640b 100 ESCUDOS
24.0000 g., 0.9170 Gold .7075 oz. AGW, 34 mm. **Subject:** Golden Age of Portuguese Discoveries - Nuno Tristao **Obv:** Shield flanked by crowns within circle **Rev:** Ship

Date	Mintage	F	VF	XF	Unc	BU
1987	5,497	—	—	—	540	—

KM# 640c 100 ESCUDOS
31.1190 g., 0.9990 Palladium 1.0000 oz. **Subject:** Golden Age of Portuguese Discoveries - Nuno Tristao **Obv:** Shield flanked by crowns within circle **Rev:** Ship

Date	Mintage	F	VF	XF	Unc	BU
1987	323	—	—	—	475	—
1987 Proof	2,000	Value: 450				

KM# 641b 100 ESCUDOS
24.0000 g., 0.9170 Gold .7075 oz. AGW, 34 mm. **Subject:** Golden Age of Portuguese Discoveries - Diogo Cao **Obv:** Shield to upper right of center design with value below **Rev:** Compass within center of sailboat and map

Date	Mintage	F	VF	XF	Unc	BU
1987	5,256	—	—	—	520	—
1987 Proof	5,387	Value: 540				

KM# 642b 100 ESCUDOS
24.0000 g., 0.9170 Gold .7077 oz. AGW, 34 mm. **Subject:** Golden Age of Portuguese Discoveries - Bartolomeu Dias **Obv:** Shield within circle **Rev:** Stylized boat and map

Date	Mintage	F	VF	XF	Unc	BU
ND(1988)	5,503	—	—	—	520	—

KM# 642c 100 ESCUDOS
31.1190 g., 0.9990 Platinum 1.0000 oz. APW **Subject:** Golden

PORTUGAL 579

Age of Portuguese Discoveries - Bartolomeu Dias **Obv:** Shield within circle **Rev:** Stylized boat and map

Date	Mintage	F	VF	XF	Unc	BU
ND(1988)	907	—	—	—	1,350	—
ND(1988) Proof	2,000	Value: 1,450				

KM# 646b 100 ESCUDOS
24.0000 g., 0.9170 Gold .7077 oz. AGW **Subject:** Discovery of the Canary Islands **Obv:** Shield with supporters above value **Rev:** Ship

Date	Mintage	F	VF	XF	Unc	BU
1989 Proof	2,981	Value: 560				

KM# 647b 100 ESCUDOS
24.0000 g., 0.9170 Gold .7077 oz. AGW, 34 mm. **Subject:** Discovery of Madeira **Obv:** Cross and shield **Rev:** Ship

Date	Mintage	F	VF	XF	Unc	BU
1989 Proof	2,996	Value: 560				

KM# 647c 100 ESCUDOS
31.1190 g., 0.9990 Palladium 1.0000 oz. **Subject:** Discovery of Madeira **Obv:** Cross and shield **Rev:** Ship

Date	Mintage	F	VF	XF	Unc	BU
1989 Proof	2,500	Value: 450				

KM# 648b 100 ESCUDOS
24.0000 g., 0.9170 Gold .7077 oz. AGW **Subject:** Discovery of the Avores **Obv:** Shield to right within design **Rev:** Ship and stars within design

Date	Mintage	F	VF	XF	Unc	BU
ND(1989) Proof	5,495	Value: 540				

KM# 649b 100 ESCUDOS
24.0000 g., 0.9170 Gold .7077 oz. AGW, 34 mm. **Subject:** Celestial Navigation **Obv:** Value in center flanked by shield and circled star designs **Rev:** Artistic designs

Date	Mintage	F	VF	XF	Unc	BU
1990 Proof	2,958	Value: 560				

KM# 649c 100 ESCUDOS
31.1190 g., 0.9990 Platinum 1.0000 oz. APW **Subject:** Celestial Navigation **Obv:** Value in center flanked by shield and circled star designs **Rev:** Artistic designs

Date	Mintage	F	VF	XF	Unc	BU
1990 Proof	2,500	Value: 1,500				

KM# 658b 200 ESCUDOS
27.2000 g., 0.9170 Gold .8000 oz. AGW **Subject:** Columbus and Portugal **Obv:** Shield, value and date to left of design **Rev:** Head left, map, cross, dates and 1/2 star design

Date	Mintage	F	VF	XF	Unc	BU
1991 Proof	3,500	Value: 585				

KM# 658c 200 ESCUDOS
31.1190 g., 0.9990 Platinum 1.000 oz. APW **Subject:** Columbus and Portugal **Obv:** Shield, value and date to left of design **Rev:** Head left, map, cross, dates and 1/2 star design

Date	Mintage	F	VF	XF	Unc	BU
1991 Proof	2,500	Value: 1,350				

KM# 658d 200 ESCUDOS
31.1190 g., 0.9990 Palladium 1.0000 oz. **Subject:** Columbus and Portugal **Obv:** Shield, value and date to left of design **Rev:** Head left, map, cross, dates and 1/2 star design

Date	Mintage	F	VF	XF	Unc	BU
1991 Proof	2,500	Value: 450				

KM# 659b 200 ESCUDOS
27.2000 g., 0.9170 Gold .8000 oz. AGW **Subject:** Westward Navigation **Obv:** Shield and value within design **Rev:** Stylized ship

Date	Mintage	F	VF	XF	Unc	BU
1991 Proof	3,500	Value: 585				

KM# 659c 200 ESCUDOS
31.1190 g., 0.9990 Platinum 1.0000 oz. APW **Subject:** Westward Navigation **Obv:** Shield and value within design **Rev:** Stylized ship

Date	Mintage	F	VF	XF	Unc	BU
1991 Proof	2,500	Value: 1,350				

KM# 659d 200 ESCUDOS
31.1190 g., 0.9990 Palladium 1.0000 oz. **Subject:** Westward Navigation **Obv:** Shield and value within design **Rev:** Stylized ship

Date	Mintage	F	VF	XF	Unc	BU
1991 Proof	2,500	Value: 450				

KM# 660b 200 ESCUDOS
27.2000 g., 0.9170 Gold .8000 oz. AGW **Subject:** New World - America **Obv:** Shield within design **Rev:** Head 1/4 left and ships

Date	Mintage	F	VF	XF	Unc	BU
ND(1992) Proof	6,000	Value: 585				

KM# 660c 200 ESCUDOS
31.1190 g., 0.9990 Platinum 1.0000 oz. APW **Subject:** New World - America **Obv:** Shield within design **Rev:** Head 1/4 left and ships

Date	Mintage	F	VF	XF	Unc	BU
ND(1992) Proof	2,500	Value: 1,350				

KM# 660d 200 ESCUDOS
31.1190 g., 0.9990 Palladium 1.0000 oz. **Subject:** New World - America **Obv:** Shield within design **Rev:** Head 1/4 left and ships

Date	Mintage	F	VF	XF	Unc	BU
ND(1992) Proof	2,500	Value: 450				

KM# 661b 200 ESCUDOS
27.2000 g., 0.9170 Gold .8000 oz. AGW **Obv:** Shield and value within thin lined cross **Rev:** Standing figure and map

Date	Mintage	F	VF	XF	Unc	BU
ND(1992) Proof	3,500	Value: 585				

KM# 661c 200 ESCUDOS
31.1190 g., 0.9990 Platinum 1.0000 oz. APW **Obv:** Shield and value within thin lined cross **Rev:** Standing figure and map

Date	Mintage	F	VF	XF	Unc	BU
ND(1992) Proof	2,500	Value: 1,350				

KM# 661d 200 ESCUDOS
31.1190 g., 0.9990 Palladium 1.0000 oz. **Obv:** Shield and value within thin lined cross **Rev:** Standing figure and map

Date	Mintage	F	VF	XF	Unc	BU
ND(1992) Proof	2,500	Value: 450				

KM# 665b 200 ESCUDOS
27.2000 g., 0.9170 Gold .8020 oz. AGW **Subject:** Tanegashima - 1st Portuguese Ship to Japan **Obv:** Shield **Rev:** Ship

Date	Mintage	F	VF	XF	Unc	BU
ND(1993) Proof	7,000	Value: 600				

KM# 666b 200 ESCUDOS
27.2000 g., 0.9170 Gold .8020 oz. AGW **Subject:** Espingarda **Obv:** Inscription divides globe and shield **Rev:** Mounted cavalryman shooting rifle

Date	Mintage	F	VF	XF	Unc	BU
1993 Proof	7,000	Value: 600				

KM# 666c 200 ESCUDOS
31.1190 g., 0.9990 Palladium 1.0000 oz. **Subject:** Espingarda **Obv:** Inscription divides globe and shield **Rev:** Mounted cavalryman shooting rifle

Date	Mintage	F	VF	XF	Unc	BU
1993 Proof	2,000	Value: 450				

KM# 667b 200 ESCUDOS
27.2000 g., 0.9170 Gold .8020 oz. AGW **Obv:** Ship at right of shield **Rev:** Armored busts and date to right of column

Date	Mintage	F	VF	XF	Unc	BU
1993 Proof	7,000	Value: 600				

KM# 668b 200 ESCUDOS
27.2000 g., 0.9170 Gold .8020 oz. AGW **Rev:** Arte Namban

Date	Mintage	F	VF	XF	Unc	BU
1993 Proof	7,000	Value: 600				

580 PORTUGAL

KM# 668c 200 ESCUDOS
31.1190 g., 0.9990 Platinum 1.0000 oz. APW **Rev:** Arte Namban
Date	Mintage	F	VF	XF	Unc	BU
1993 Proof	2,000	Value: 1,350				

KM# 670b 200 ESCUDOS
27.2000 g., 0.9170 Gold .8020 oz. AGW **Obv:** Shield to upper left of ships **Rev:** Bust 1/4 right flanked by dates and symbol
Date	Mintage	F	VF	XF	Unc	BU
ND(1994) Proof	2,000	Value: 600				

KM# 671b 200 ESCUDOS
27.2000 g., 0.9170 Gold .8020 oz. AGW **Subject:** Treaty of Tordesilhas **Obv:** Ship flanked by map, shield, designs and value **Rev:** Left 1/2 of coin is conjoined crowned heads right, arms above, right 1/2 of coin is crown head left, arms on bottom
Date	Mintage	F	VF	XF	Unc	BU
ND(1994) Proof	2,000	Value: 600				

KM# 671c 200 ESCUDOS
31.1190 g., 0.9990 Palladium 1.0000 oz. **Subject:** Treaty of Tordesilhas **Obv:** Ship flanked by map, shield, designs and value **Rev:** Left 1/2 of coin is conjoined crowned heads right, arms above, right 1/2 of coin is crown head left, arms on bottom
Date	Mintage	F	VF	XF	Unc	BU
ND(1994) Proof	1,000	Value: 450				

KM# 672b 200 ESCUDOS
27.2000 g., 0.9170 Gold .8020 oz. AGW **Subject:** Dividing Up The World **Obv:** Shield, map, value and date **Rev:** Ship, map and divided arms
Date	Mintage	F	VF	XF	Unc	BU
1994 Proof	3,000	Value: 600				

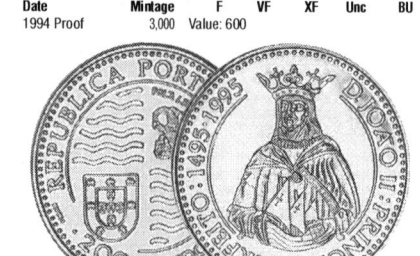

KM# 673b 200 ESCUDOS
27.2000 g., 0.9170 Gold .8020 oz. AGW **Obv:** Water divides shield and design **Rev:** Crowned 1/2 length figure facing
Date	Mintage	F	VF	XF	Unc	BU
ND(1994) Proof	2,000	Value: 600				

KM# 673c 200 ESCUDOS
31.1190 g., 0.9990 Platinum 1.0000 oz. APW **Obv:** Water divides shield and design **Rev:** Crowned 1/2 length figure facing
Date	Mintage	F	VF	XF	Unc	BU
ND(1994) Proof	1,000	Value: 1,350				

KM# 681b 200 ESCUDOS
27.2000 g., 0.9170 Gold .8016 oz. AGW **Obv:** Shield and globe above date and value **Rev:** Armored standing figure
Date	Mintage	F	VF	XF	Unc	BU
1995 Proof	4,000	Value: 565				

KM# 682b 200 ESCUDOS
27.2000 g., 0.9170 Gold .8016 oz. AGW **Obv:** Shield, value, fruit sprig and flower sprig **Rev:** Moluca Islands and ship
Date	Mintage	F	VF	XF	Unc	BU
1995 Proof	4,000	Value: 565				

KM# 682c 200 ESCUDOS
31.1190 g., 0.9995 Palladium 1.0000 oz. **Obv:** Shield, value, fruit sprig and flower sprig **Rev:** Moluca Islands and ship
Date	Mintage	F	VF	XF	Unc	BU
1995	1,000	Value: 450				

Note: In proof sets only

KM# 683b 200 ESCUDOS
27.2000 g., 0.9170 Gold .8016 oz. AGW **Obv:** Ship, tree and shield **Rev:** Solar and Timor Islands
Date	Mintage	F	VF	XF	Unc	BU
1995 Proof	4,000	Value: 565				

KM# 684b 200 ESCUDOS
27.2000 g., 0.9170 Gold .8016 oz. AGW **Obv:** Shield, dates, globe and value **Rev:** Map and ships
Date	Mintage	F	VF	XF	Unc	BU
1995 Proof	4,000	Value: 565				

KM# 684c 200 ESCUDOS
31.1190 g., 0.9995 Platinum 1.0000 oz. APW **Obv:** Shield, dates, globe and value **Rev:** Map and ships
Date	Mintage	F	VF	XF	Unc	BU
1995	1,000	Value: 1,350				

Note: In proof sets only

KM# 689b 200 ESCUDOS
27.0000 g., 0.9166 Gold .8015 oz. AGW **Subject:** 1512 Portugal - Siam Alliance **Obv:** Ship, shield, dates and value **Rev:** Portuguese and Siamese arms
Date	Mintage	F	VF	XF	Unc	BU
1996 Proof	3,000	Value: 565				

KM# 690b 200 ESCUDOS
27.2000 g., 0.9166 Gold .8015 oz. AGW **Subject:** 1513 Portuguese Arrival in China **Obv:** Shield within globe flanked by leafy sprigs **Rev:** Ship, map and building
Date	Mintage	F	VF	XF	Unc	BU
1996 Proof	3,000	Value: 565				

KM# 690c 200 ESCUDOS
31.1190 g., 0.9995 Palladium 1.0000 oz. **Subject:** 1513 Portuguese Arrival in China **Obv:** Shield within globe flanked by leafy sprigs **Rev:** Ship, map and building
Date	Mintage	F	VF	XF	Unc	BU
1996 Proof	1,000	Value: 450				

KM# 691b 200 ESCUDOS
27.2000 g., 0.9166 Gold .8015 oz. AGW **Subject:** 1557 Portuguese Establishment in Macau **Obv:** Shield at upper left above building **Rev:** Building at upper left of ship
Date	Mintage	F	VF	XF	Unc	BU
1996 Proof	4,000	Value: 565				

KM# 692b 200 ESCUDOS
27.2000 g., 0.9166 Gold .8015 oz. AGW **Subject:** 1582 Portuguese Discovery of Taiwan **Obv:** Flower sprig to left of shield **Rev:** Ship
Date	Mintage	F	VF	XF	Unc	BU
1996 Proof	3,000	Value: 585				

KM# 692c 200 ESCUDOS
31.1190 g., 0.9995 Platinum 1.0000 oz. APW **Subject:** 1582 Portuguese Discovery of Taiwan **Obv:** Flower sprig to left of shield **Rev:** Ship
Date	Mintage	F	VF	XF	Unc	BU
1996 Proof	1,000	Value: 1,350				

PORTUGAL 581

KM# 697b 200 ESCUDOS
27.2000 g., 0.9167 Gold .8017 oz. AGW **Obv:** National arms
Rev: S. Francisco Xavier
Date	Mintage	F	VF	XF	Unc	BU
1997 Proof	4,000	Value: 565				

KM# 698b 200 ESCUDOS
27.2000 g., 0.9167 Gold .8017 oz. AGW **Obv:** Shield to left of designs and value **Rev:** Two seated figures talking
Date	Mintage	F	VF	XF	Unc	BU
1997 Proof	5,000	Value: 565				

KM# 699b 200 ESCUDOS
27.2000 g., 0.9167 Gold .8017 oz. AGW **Obv:** Shield and map of South America **Rev:** Bto. Jose de Anchieta
Date	Mintage	F	VF	XF	Unc	BU
1997 Proof	4,000	Value: 565				

KM# 699c 200 ESCUDOS
31.1190 g., 0.9995 Palladium 1.0000 oz. **Obv:** Shield and map of South America **Rev:** Bto. Jose de Anchieta
Date	Mintage	F	VF	XF	Unc	BU
1997 Proof	1,000	Value: 450				

KM# 700b 200 ESCUDOS
27.2000 g., 0.9160 Gold .8017 oz. AGW **Obv:** National cross and shield **Rev:** Irmao Bento de Gois, map of China's coast
Date	Mintage	F	VF	XF	Unc	BU
1997 Proof	4,000	Value: 565				

KM# 700c 200 ESCUDOS
31.1190 g., 0.9995 Platinum 1.0000 oz. APW **Obv:** National cross and shield **Rev:** Irmao Bento de Gois, map of China's coast
Date	Mintage	F	VF	XF	Unc	BU
1997 Proof	1,000	Value: 1,350				

KM# 709b 200 ESCUDOS
27.2000 g., 0.9167 Gold .8017 oz. AGW **Obv:** Three ships, shield, and value **Rev:** Bust of Vasco Da Gama left, dates
Date	Mintage	F	VF	XF	Unc	BU
1998 Proof	5,000	Value: 565				

KM# 709c 200 ESCUDOS
31.1190 g., 0.9995 Platinum 1.0000 oz. APW **Obv:** Three ships, shield, and value **Rev:** Bust of Vasco da Gama, dates
Date	Mintage	F	VF	XF	Unc	BU
1998 Proof	1,000	Value: 1,350				

KM# 710b 200 ESCUDOS
27.2000 g., 0.9167 Gold .8017 oz. AGW **Subject:** Discovery of Africa **Obv:** Shield, ship, and palm tree **Rev:** Ship, map, and hunter
Date	Mintage	F	VF	XF	Unc	BU
1998 Proof	5,000	Value: 565				

KM# 711b 200 ESCUDOS
27.2000 g., 0.9167 Gold .8017 oz. AGW **Subject:** Mozambique **Obv:** Shield above mermaid **Rev:** Two ships and island map
Date	Mintage	F	VF	XF	Unc	BU
1998 Proof	6,000	Value: 565				

KM# 712b 200 ESCUDOS
27.2000 g., 0.9167 Gold .8017 oz. AGW **Subject:** India 1498 **Obv:** Shield and sailing ship **Rev:** Ship and coastal map of India
Date	Mintage	F	VF	XF	Unc	BU
1998 Proof	5,000	Value: 565				

KM# 712c 200 ESCUDOS
31.1190 g., 0.9995 Palladium 1.0000 oz. **Subject:** India 1498 **Obv:** Shield and sailing ship **Rev:** Ship and coastal map of India
Date	Mintage	F	VF	XF	Unc	BU
1998 Proof	1,000	Value: 450				

KM# 716b 200 ESCUDOS
27.2000 g., 0.9167 Gold .8017 oz. AGW, 36 mm. **Subject:** Death on the Sea **Obv:** Shield, globe and ropes **Rev:** Stylized sinking ship **Edge:** Reeded
Date	Mintage	F	VF	XF	Unc	BU
1999INCM Proof	1,000	Value: 600				

KM# 717b 200 ESCUDOS
27.2000 g., 0.9167 Gold .8017 oz. AGW **Subject:** Brasil 1500 **Obv:** Fleet of sailing ships **Rev:** Head right
Date	Mintage	F	VF	XF	Unc	BU
1999INCM Proof	1,000	Value: 600				

KM# 718b 200 ESCUDOS
27.2000 g., 0.9167 Gold .8017 oz. AGW **Subject:** Brasil **Obv:** Natives and palm trees **Rev:** Ship, native, and map
Date	Mintage	F	VF	XF	Unc	BU
1999 Proof	1,000	Value: 600				

KM# 719b 200 ESCUDOS
27.2000 g., 0.9167 Gold .8017 oz. AGW **Subject:** Duarte Pacheco Pereira **Rev:** Armored half-length bust facing
Date	Mintage	F	VF	XF	Unc	BU
1999INCM Proof	1,000	Value: 600				

PORTUGAL

KM# 728b 200 ESCUDOS
27.2000 g., 0.9166 Gold .8016 oz. AGW, 36 mm. **Subject:** Terra Do Lavrado **Obv:** Shield and compass **Rev:** Labrador coast and ship **Edge:** Reeded

Date	Mintage	F	VF	XF	Unc	BU
2000 Proof	Est. 1,375	Value: 585				

KM# 729b 200 ESCUDOS
27.2000 g., 0.9166 Gold .8016 oz. AGW **Subject:** Terra Dos Corte-Real **Obv:** Cross above shield **Rev:** Ship above 1501-1502 **Designer:** Reeded

Date	Mintage	F	VF	XF	Unc	BU
2000 Proof	Est. 1,375	Value: 585				

KM# 729c 200 ESCUDOS
31.1190 g., 0.9995 Palladium 1.0000 oz. **Subject:** Terra Dos Corte-Real **Obv:** Cross above shield **Rev:** Ship above 1501-1502 **Edge:** Reeded

Date	Mintage	F	VF	XF	Unc	BU
2000 Proof	Est. 250	Value: 600				

KM# 730b 200 ESCUDOS
27.2000 g., 0.9166 Gold .8016 oz. AGW **Obv:** Maltese crosses above compass **Rev:** Ship below maltese cross within map **Edge:** Reeded **Edge Lettering:** Terra Florida

Date	Mintage	F	VF	XF	Unc	BU
2000 Proof	Est. 1,375	Value: 585				

KM# 731b 200 ESCUDOS
27.2000 g., 0.9166 Gold .8016 oz. AGW **Subject:** Fernao de Magalhaes **Obv:** Shield, ship, and value **Rev:** Bearded portrait **Edge:** Reeded

Date	Mintage	F	VF	XF	Unc	BU
2000 Proof	Est. 1,375	Value: 585				

KM# 731c 200 ESCUDOS
31.1190 g., 0.9995 Platinum 1.0000 oz. APW **Subject:** Fernao de Magalhaes **Obv:** Shield, ship, and value **Rev:** Bearded portrait **Edge:** Reeded

Date	Mintage	F	VF	XF	Unc	BU
2000 Proof	Est. 250	Value: 1,350				

KM# 686c 500 ESCUDOS
17.5000 g., 0.9177 Gold .5159 oz. AGW **Subject:** 800th Anniversary - Birth of Saint Anthony **Obv:** Church to left of shield, date and value **Rev:** Seated figure holding cross and book within arch

Date	Mintage	F	VF	XF	Unc	BU
1995 Proof	5,000	Value: 380				

EURO COINAGE
European Economic Community Issues

KM# 749b 5 EURO
17.5000 g., 0.9166 Gold 0.5157 oz. AGW, 30 mm. **Obv:** National arms and value within partial stamp design **Rev:** Partial postal stamp design

Date	Mintage	F	VF	XF	Unc	BU
2003INCM Proof	—	Value: 400				

KM# 750b 8 EURO
31.1000 g., 0.9166 Gold 0.9165 oz. AGW, 36 mm. **Obv:** National arms, value and flag-covered globe **Rev:** Flag-covered globe and "Euro 2004" soccer games logo

Date	Mintage	F	VF	XF	Unc	BU
2003INCM Proof	—	Value: 650				

KM# 751b 8 EURO
31.1000 g., 0.9166 Gold 0.9165 oz. AGW, 36 mm. **Obv:** National arms and value below many bubbles **Rev:** "Euro 2004" soccer games logo below many hearts

Date	Mintage	F	VF	XF	Unc	BU
2003INCM Proof	—	Value: 650				

KM# 752b 8 EURO
31.1000 g., 0.9166 Gold 0.9165 oz. AGW, 36 mm. **Obv:** National arms and value **Rev:** "Euro 2004" soccer games logo in center with partial text background

Date	Mintage	F	VF	XF	Unc	BU
2003INCM Proof	—	Value: 650				

KM# 756b 8 EURO
31.1000 g., 0.9166 Gold 0.9165 oz. AGW, 36 mm. **Subject:** Euro 2004 Soccer **Obv:** National arms **Rev:** Stylized goal keeper **Edge:** Reeded

Date	Mintage	F	VF	XF	Unc	BU
2004INCM Proof	10,000	Value: 650				

KM# 757b 8 EURO
31.1000 g., 0.9166 Gold 0.9165 oz. AGW, 36 mm. **Subject:** Euro 2004 Soccer **Obv:** National arms **Rev:** Face of player making a shot **Edge:** Reeded

Date	Mintage	F	VF	XF	Unc	BU
2004INCM Proof	10,000	Value: 650				

KM# 758b 8 EURO
31.1000 g., 0.9166 Gold 0.9165 oz. AGW, 36 mm. **Subject:** Euro 2004 Soccer **Obv:** National arms **Rev:** Symbolic explosion of a goal **Edge:** Reeded

Date	Mintage	F	VF	XF	Unc	BU
2004INCM Proof	10,000	Value: 650				

PATTERNS
Including off metal strikes

KM#	Date	Mintage	Identification	Mkt Val
Pn29	1803	—	Peca. Copper. Circular wreath.	1,000
Pn30	1803	—	Peca. Copper Gilt. Circular wreath.	1,200
Pn31	1803	—	Peca. Copper Gilt.	1,200
Pn32	1803	—	Peca. Copper Gilt. Wreath connected to shield.	1,200
Pn33	ND	—	Peca. Lead. Royal bust.	350
Pn34	ND	—	Peca. Lead. Bust and legend.	350
Pn35	ND	—	Peca. Lead Gilt. Bust and legend.	650
Pn36	1804	—	Peca. Lead. Date incuse.	400
Pn37	1804	—	Peca. Lead. Date in relief.	450
Pn56	1822	—	Peca. Silver. Shield over wreath.	2,000
Pn57	1826	—	Peca. Copper Gilt. Square arms.	—
Pn58	1826	—	Peca. Copper. Square arms.	—
Pn59	1826	—	Peca. Copper. Oval arms, KM378	—
Pn61	1828	—	1/2 Peca. Copper Gilt. KM387.	1,000
Pn62	1828	—	Peca. Lead. Laureate bust right. Crowned arms within wreath. KM388.	800
Pn63	1828	—	Peca. Nickel-Silver. KM388.	1,000
Pn64	1828	—	Peca. Copper Gilt. For royal approval, KM388.	1,250
Pn69	1829	—	Peca. Copper. Engraved by Dubois.	600
Pn70	1830	—	Peca. Copper. KM397.	950
Pn71	1830	—	Peca. Copper. Inward palms.	950
Pn72	1831	—	Peca. Copper. Inward palms.	—
Pn82	1833	—	Peca. Silver. High neck.	—
Pn80	1833	—	1/2 Peca. Tin. Head left. Crowned mantled arms. Maria II.	2,000
Pn81	1833	—	Peca. Tin. Maria II.	2,250
Pn96	1836	—	2500 Reis. 0.9170 Gold. Crowned head left. Crowned mantled arms. W. Wyon. Rare.	—

PORTUGAL 583

KM#	Date	Mintage	Identification	Mkt Val
Pn97	1836	—	5000 Reis. Copper. Crowned head left. Crowned mantled arms. W. Wyon.	750
Pn98	1836	—	5000 Reis. Gold. 0.9170 Gold. W. Wyon. Rare.	

Note: American Numismatic Rarities Eliasberg sale 4-05, PR-64 realized $21,850.

KM#	Date	Mintage	Identification	Mkt Val
Pn103	1842	—	500 Reis. Gold. Reeded edge.	
Pn105	1842	—	1000 Reis. Gold. Crowned head left. Crowned mantled arms. Reeded edge.	—
Pn111	1856	—	5000 Reis. Gold. Maria II.	—
Pn114	ND	—	10000 Reis. Porcelain.	—
Pn115	1858	—	10000 Reis. Copper Gilt.	1,200
Pn117	1859	—	10000 Reis. Copper Gilt. Mantled arms.	1,200
Pn123	1861	—	10000 Reis. Copper. Mantled arms.	1,250
Pn122	1861	—	10000 Reis. Gold. Mantled arms.	—
Pn142	ND	—	5000 Reis. Copper. Crowned head left. Crowned mantled arms. Queen Victoria.	1,650
Pn143	1863	—	5000 Reis. Copper. Head left. Crowned mantled arms. Charles Wiener engraver.	1,650
Pn146	1865	—	5000 Reis. Copper. Charles Wiener engraver.	500
Pn147	1865	—	5000 Reis. Silver.	1,000
Pn148	1866	—	5000 Reis. Gold. Charles Wiener engraver.	—
Pn149	1866	—	5000 Reis. Silver. Charles Wiener engraver.	500
Pn150	1866	—	5000 Reis. Copper. Head left. Crowned mantled arms. Charles Wiener engraver.	200
Pn151	1866	—	5000 Reis. Copper Gilt. Charles Wiener engraver.	300
Pn152	1866	—	5000 Reis. Tin. Charles Wiener engraver.	200
Pn153	1866	—	5000 Reis. Lead.	200
Pn159	1878	—	10000 Reis. Copper. Shield over royal mantle.	300
Pn169	1879	—	5000 Reis. Copper. Shield over royal mantle.	450
Pn170	1879	—	5000 Reis. Gold.	—
Pn162	1879	—	500 Reis. Gold. Head left. Crowned arms within wreath. Plain edge. Rotated 90 degrees.	—
Pn164	1879	—	1000 Reis. Gold. Value between palms.	—
Pn165	1879	—	1000 Reis. Gold. Crowned date.	—
Pn168	1879	—	1000 Reis. Gold. Shield over royal mantle.	—
Pn172	1880	—	2200 Reis. Copper.	175
Pn173	1880	—	5000 Reis. Copper.	185
Pn174	1880	—	5000 Reis. Copper. 'ENS' incuse.	150
Pn176	1883	—	1000 Reis. Gold. Value inside wreath.	—
Pn180	1888	—	5000 Reis. Nickel. Small type, old monarch.	175
Pn181	1888	—	5000 Reis. Copper. Small type, old monarch.	175
Pn191	1895	—	5000 Reis. Silver Gilt. Head right. Crowned mantled arms.	15,000
Pn192	1895	—	5000 Reis. Gold.	—
Pn199	1900	—	10000 Reis. Gold.	—
Pn210	1912	—	Escudo. Gold. 'October 5, 1910'.	600
Pn211	1912	—	Escudo. Gold. Obverse variety.	600
Pn212	1912	—	Escudo. Gold.	600
Pn221	1920	—	5 Escudos. Gold. 'Abundance Through Labor'	—
Pn234	1953	—	20 Escudos. Gold. 'National Revival'.	—

PROVAS
Stamped

KM#	Date	Mintage	Identification	Mkt Val
Pr20	1966	—	20 Escudos. Gold. Salazar Bridge, KM592.	2,500

TRIAL STRIKES

KM#	Date	Mintage	Identification	Mkt Val
TS1	1802	—	6400 Reis. Lead. Obverse.	850
TS2	1803	—	6400 Reis. Lead. Obverse type of 1805.	350
TS3	ND	—	6400 Reis. Lead. Reverse.	350
TS8	1805	—	3200 Reis. Lead. Obverse.	350
TS9	ND	—	3200 Reis. Lead. Obverse.	350
TS10	ND	—	3200 Reis. Lead. Reverse.	350
TS12	ND	—	7500 Reis. Lead.	—
TS13	ND	—	7500 Reis. Copper. Obverse.	—
TS14	1829	—	7500 Reis. Lead. Obverse, Dubois.	250
TS15	1829	—	7500 Reis. Lead. Reverse, Dubois.	250
TS16	1829	—	7500 Reis. Lead. Obverse, radiant field.	—
TS17	1829	—	7500 Reis. Lead. Obverse, ray variety.	250
TS18	1866	—	5000 Reis. Silver. Obverse, Charles Wiener.	150
TS19	1866	—	5000 Reis. Silver. Reverse, Charles Wiener.	150
TS20	1866	—	5000 Reis. Copper. Obverse, Charles Wiener.	60.00
TS21	1866	—	5000 Reis. Copper. Reverse, Charles Wiener.	60.00
TS22	1866	—	5000 Reis. Lead. Obverse, Charles Wiener.	60.00
TS23	1866	—	5000 Reis. Lead. Reverse, Charles Wiener.	60.00
TS32	ND	—	10000 Reis. Tin. Reverse.	—

MINT SETS

KM#	Date	Mintage	Identification	Issue Price	Mkt Val
MS9	1987/8 (4)	5,000	KM639b-642b	2,080	2,200

PROOF SETS

KM#	Date	Mintage	Identification	Issue Price	Mkt Val
PS8	1987/88 (4)	2,000	KM639a, 640c, 641b, 642c; Prestige	2,200	2,750
PS10	1989/90 (4)	5,000	KM646b-649b	2,425	2,450
PS11	1989/90 (4)	2,500	KM646a, 647c, 648b, 649c; Prestige	2,650	2,800
PS13	1991/92 (4)	3,500	KM658b-661b	2,350	2,350
PS14	1991/92 (4)	2,500	KM658c-661c; Prestige	2,400	3,000
PS17	1993 (4)	5,000	KM665b-668b	1,980	2,500
PS18	1993 (4)	2,000	KM665a, 666c, 667b, 668c; Prestige	2,300	2,150
PS21	1994 (4)	—	KM670b-673b	—	2,400
PS22	1994 (4)	1,000	KM670a, 671c, 672b, 673c; Prestige	—	2,175
PS25	1995 (4)	2,000	KM681b-684b	1,980	2,000
PS26	1995 (4)	1,000	KM681a, 682c, 683b, 684c	1,800	2,100
PS30	1996 (4)	2,000	KM689b, 690b, 691b, 692b	—	2,000
PS31	1996 (4)	1,000	KM689a, 690c, 691b, 692c	—	2,100
PS34	1997 (4)	4,000	KM697b-700b	1,980	2,000
PS35	1997 (4)	1,000	KM697a, 698b, 699c, 700c	2,000	2,250
PS38	1998 (4)	5,000	KM709b-712b	1,980	1,980
PS39	1998 (4)	1,000	KM709c, 710a, 711b, 712c	2,000	2,250
PS41	1999 (4)	1,000	KM716b-719b	1,800	1,800
PS43	2000 (4)	1,000	KM#728b-731b	1,405	1,850
PS44	2000 (4)	250	KM#728a, 729c, 730b, 731c	2,988	3,000

QATAR

The State of Qatar, an emirate in the Persian Gulf between Bahrain and Trucial Oman, has an area of 4,247sq. mi. (11,000 sq. km.) and a population of *469,000. Capital: Doha. Oil is the chief industry and export.

Qatar was under Turkish control from 1872 until the beginning of World War I when the Ottoman Turks evacuated the Qatar Peninsula. In 1916 Sheikh Abdullah placed Qatar under the protection of Great Britain and gave Britain responsibility for its defense and foreign relations. Qatar joined with Dubai in a Monetary Union and issued coins and paper money in 1966 and 1969. When Britain announced in 1968 that it would end treaty relationships with the Persian Gulf sheikhdoms in 1971, this union was dissolved; Qatar joined Bahrain and the seven trucial sheikhdoms (called the United Arab Emirates) in an effort to form a union of Arab Emirates. However the nine sheikhdoms were unable to agree on terms of union, and Qatar declared its independence as the State of Qatar on Sept. 3, 1971.

TITLE

دولة قطر

Daulat Qatar

RULERS
Al-Thani Dynasty
Qasim Bin Muhammad, 1876-1913
Abdullah Bin Qasim, 1913-1948
Ali Bin Abdullah, 1948-1960
Ahmad Bin Ali, 1960-1972
Khalifah bin Hamad, 1972-1995
Hamad bin Khalifah, 1995-

MONETARY SYSTEM
100 Dirhem = 1 Riyal

EMIRATE

STANDARD COINAGE

KM# 17 100 RIYALS
Gold **Ruler:** Hamad bin Khalifah **Subject:** 15th Asian Games **Obv:** Arms above value **Rev:** Games mascot Fox on Bicycle cartoon character

Date	Mintage	F	VF	XF	Unc	BU
2006 Proof	Est. 10,000	Value: 525				

KM# 18 100 RIYALS
17.0000 g., 0.9200 Gold 0.5028 oz. AGW, 31 mm. **Ruler:** Hamad bin Khalifah **Obv:** Arms **Rev:** Central Bank building **Edge:** Reeded

Date	Mintage	F	VF	XF	Unc	BU
2006 Proof	300	Value: 1,200				

KM# 19 100 RIYALS
10.0000 g., 0.9999 Gold 0.3215 oz. AGW, 24.5 mm. **Ruler:** Hamad bin Khalifah **Subject:** 15th Asian Games **Obv:** Arms **Rev:** Khalifa Stadium **Edge:** Reeded

Date	Mintage	F	VF	XF	Unc	BU
2006 Proof	—	Value: 465				

KM# 20 100 RIYALS
10.0000 g., 0.9999 Gold 0.3215 oz. AGW, 24.5 mm. **Ruler:** Hamad bin Khalifah **Subject:** 15th Asian Games **Obv:** Arms **Rev:** Two fighting oryxes **Edge:** Reeded

Date	Mintage	F	VF	XF	Unc	BU
2006 Proof	—	Value: 465				

KM# 21 100 RIYALS
10.0000 g., 0.9999 Gold 0.3215 oz. AGW, 24.5 mm. **Ruler:** Hamad bin Khalifah **Subject:** 15th Asian Games **Obv:** Arms **Rev:** Falcon bust **Edge:** Reeded

Date	Mintage	F	VF	XF	Unc	BU
2006 Proof	—	Value: 465				

KM# 22 100 RIYALS
10.0000 g., 0.9999 Gold 0.3215 oz. AGW, 24.5 mm. **Ruler:** Hamad bin Khalifah **Subject:** 15th Asian Games **Obv:** Arms **Rev:** Coffee pot **Edge:** Reeded

Date	Mintage	F	VF	XF	Unc	BU
2006 Proof	—	Value: 465				

KM# 23 100 RIYALS
10.0000 g., 0.9999 Gold 0.3215 oz. AGW, 24.5 mm. **Ruler:** Hamad bin Khalifah **Subject:** 15th Asian Games **Obv:** Arms **Rev:** Radiant sun **Edge:** Reeded

Date	Mintage	F	VF	XF	Unc	BU
2006 Proof	—	Value: 465				

KM# 7 500 RIYALS
17.0000 g., 0.9170 Gold .5012 oz. AGW, 31 mm. **Ruler:** Hamad bin Khalifah **Subject:** Central Bank **Obv:** National arms **Rev:** Bank building **Edge:** Plain

Date	Mintage	F	VF	XF	Unc	BU
ND(1998) Proof	100	Value: 700				

KM# 24 10000 RIYALS
1000.0000 g., 0.9999 Gold 32.1475 oz. AGW, 75.3 mm. **Ruler:** Hamad bin Khalifah **Subject:** 15th Asian Games **Obv:** Arms **Rev:** Radiant sun **Edge:** Reeded

Date	Mintage	F	VF	XF	Unc	BU
2006 Proof	—	Value: 35,000				

RAS AL-KHAIMAH

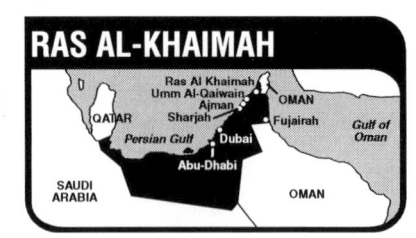

Ras al-Khaimah is only one of the coin issuing emirates that was not one of the original members of the United Arab Emirates. It was a part of Sharjah. It has an estimated area of 650 sq. mi. (1700 sq. km.) and a population of 30,000. Ras al Khaimah is the only member of the United Arab Emirates that has agriculture as its principal industry.

TITLE

رأس الخيمة

Ras al-Khaimah(t)

RULERS
Sultan bin Salim al-Qasimi,/1921-1948
Saqr Bin Muhammad al-Qasimi,/1948—

MONETARY SYSTEM
100 Dirhams = 1 Rial

UNITED ARAB EMIRATE

NON-CIRCULATING LEGAL TENDER COINAGE

KM# 21 50 RIYALS
10.3500 g., 0.9000 Gold .2995 oz. AGW **Ruler:** Saqr bin Muhammad al Qasimi **Subject:** Centennial of Italian Unification **Obv:** Value within circle **Rev:** Head left

Date	Mintage	F	VF	XF	Unc	BU
1970 Proof	Est. 2,000	Value: 375				

KM# 10 50 RIYALS
10.3500 g., 0.9000 Gold .2995 oz. AGW **Ruler:** Saqr bin Muhammad al Qasimi **Subject:** Gigi Riva **Obv:** Value within circle **Rev:** Head left

Date	Mintage	F	VF	XF	Unc	BU
ND (1970) Proof	Est. 2,000	Value: 400				

KM# 22 75 RIYALS
15.5300 g., 0.9000 Gold .4494 oz. AGW **Ruler:** Saqr bin Muhammad al Qasimi **Subject:** Centennial of Italian Unification, Rome as the Capital **Obv:** Value within circle **Rev:** Figure with gun walking left

Date	Mintage	F	VF	XF	Unc	BU
1970 Proof	Est. 2,000	Value: 500				

KM# 11 75 RIYALS
15.5300 g., 0.9000 Gold .4494 oz. AGW **Ruler:** Saqr bin Muhammad al Qasimi **Subject:** Gianni Rivera **Obv:** Value within circle **Rev:** Head left

Date	Mintage	F	VF	XF	Unc	BU
ND (1970) Proof	Est. 2,000	Value: 475				

KM# 12 100 RIYALS
20.7000 g., 0.9000 Gold .5990 oz. AGW **Ruler:** Saqr bin Muhammad al Qasimi **Subject:** World Chmapionship Football - Jules Rimet Cup **Obv:** Value within circle **Rev:** Jules Rimet Cup in front of soccer ball

Date	Mintage	F	VF	XF	Unc	BU
1970 Proof	Est. 2,000	Value: 675				

KM# 23 100 RIYALS
20.7000 g., 0.9000 Gold .5990 oz. AGW **Ruler:** Saqr bin Muhammad al Qasimi **Subject:** Centennial of Italian Unification - WWI Victory

Date	Mintage	F	VF	XF	Unc	BU
1970 Proof	Est. 2,000	Value: 600				

KM# 24 100 RIYALS
31.0500 g., 0.9000 Gold .8985 oz. AGW **Ruler:** Saqr bin Muhammad al Qasimi **Subject:** Centennial of Italian Unification **Rev:** Standing Italia

Date	Mintage	F	VF	XF	Unc	BU
1970 Proof	Est. 2,000	Value: 1,000				

KM# 13 150 RIYALS
31.0500 g., 0.9000 Gold .8985 oz. AGW **Ruler:** Saqr bin Muhammad al Qasimi **Series:** 1972 Munich Olympics **Obv:** Value within circle **Rev:** Figures within olympic circles and flaming torch

Date	Mintage	F	VF	XF	Unc	BU
ND (1970) Proof	3,060	Value: 1,850				

KM# 25 200 RIYALS
41.4000 g., 0.9000 Gold 1.1980 oz. AGW **Ruler:** Saqr bin Muhammad al Qasimi **Subject:** Centennial of Italian Unification - Romulus and Remus **Obv:** Value within circle **Rev:** Wolf within designed circle

Date	Mintage	F	VF	XF	Unc	BU
1970 Proof	Est. 2,000	Value: 1,250				

KM# 14 200 RIYALS
41.4000 g., 0.9000 Gold 1.1980 oz. AGW **Ruler:** Saqr bin Muhammad al Qasimi **Subject:** Champions of Sport **Note:** Similar to KM#8.

Date	Mintage	F	VF	XF	Unc	BU
ND (1970) Proof	Est. 2,000	Value: 1,450				

PROOF SETS

KM#	Date	Mintage	Identification	Issue Price	Mkt Val
PS2	(1970) (9)	—	KM#5-8, 10-14	—	6,700
PS3	1970 (8)	—	KM#17-19, 21-25	—	4,250
PS4	(1970) (5)	—	KM#10-14	—	4,850
PS5	1970 (5)	—	KM#21-25	—	3,750
PS8	1970 (4)	—	KM#6, 10-12	—	1,900

REUNION

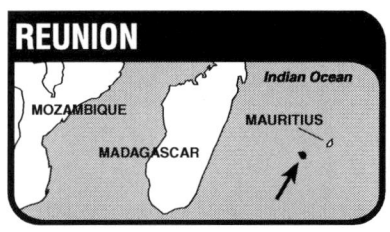

The Department of Reunion, an overseas department of France located in the Indian Ocean 400 miles (640 km.) east of Madagascar, has an area of 969 sq. mi. (2,510 sq. km.) and a population of *566,000. Capital: Saint-Denis. The island's volcanic soil is extremely fertile. Sugar, vanilla, coffee and rum are exported.

Although first visited by Portuguese navigators in the 16th century, Reunion was uninhabited when claimed for France by Capt. Goubert in 1638. The French first colonized the Isle de Bourbon in 1662 as a layover station for ships rounding the Cape of Good Hope to India. It was renamed Reunion in 1793. The island remained in French possession except for the period of 1810-15, when the British occupied it. Reunion became an overseas department of France in 1946, and in 1958 voted to continue that status within the new French Union.

During the first half of the 19th century, Reunion was officially known as Isle de Bonaparte (1801-14) and Isle de Bourbon (1814-48). Reunion coinage of those periods is so designated.

The world debut of the Euro was here on January 1, 2002.

MINT MARK
(a) – Paris, privy marks only

MONETARY SYSTEM
100 Centimes = 1 Franc

FRENCH DEPARTMENT

ESSAIS

Standard metals unless otherwise noted
X# E15 20 EURO
8.5300 g., 0.9167 Gold 0.2514 oz. AGW, 27.1 mm. **Series:** Euro **Obv:** Arms **Rev:** Yellow-nosed Albatros **Rev. Legend:** Protecton de la Faune **Edge:** Plain

Date	Mintage	F	VF	XF	Unc	BU
2004 Proof	300	Value: 325				

RHODESIA

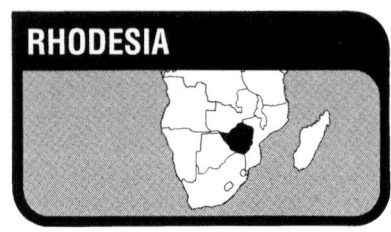

The Republic of Rhodesia or Southern Rhodesia (now known as the Republic of Zimbabwe), located in the east-central part of southern Africa, has an area of 150,804 sq. mi. (390,580sq. km.) and a population of *10.1 million. Capital: Harare (formerly Salisbury). The economy is based on agriculture and mining. Tobacco, sugar, asbestos, copper, chrome, ore and coal are exported.

The Rhodesian area contains extensive evidence of the habitat of paleolithic man and earlier civilizations, notably the world-famous ruins of Zimbabwe, a gold-trading center that flourished about the 14th or 15th century A.D. The Portuguese of the 16th century were the first Europeans to attempt to develop south-central Africa, but it remained for Cecil Rhodes and the British South Africa Co. to open the hinterlands. Rhodes obtained a concession for mineral rights from local chiefs in 1888 and administered his African empire (named Southern Rhodesia in 1895) through the British South Africa Co. until 1923, when the British government annexed the area after the white settlers voted for existence as a separate entity, rather than for incorporation with the Union of South Africa. From Sept. of 1953 through 1963 Southern Rhodesia was joined with the British Protectorates of Northern Rhodesia and Nyasaland into a multiracial federation, known as the Federation of Rhodesia and Nyasaland. When the federation was dissolved at the end of 1963, Northern Rhodesia and Nyasaland became the independent states of Zambia and Malawi.

Britain was prepared to grant independence to Southern Rhodesia but declined to do so when the politically dominant white Rhodesians refused to give assurances of representative government. On Nov. 11, 1965, following two years of unsuccessful negotiation with the British government, Prime Minister Ian Smith issued an unilateral declaration of independence. Britain responded with economic sanctions supported by the United Nations. After further futile attempts to effect an accommodation, the Rhodesian Parliament severed all ties with Britain and on March 2, 1970, established the Republic of Rhodesia.

On March 3, 1978, Prime Minister Ian Smith and three moderate black nationalist leaders signed an agreement providing for black majority rule. The name of the country was changed to Zimbabwe Rhodesia. Following a conference in London in December 1979, the opposition government conceded and it was agreed that the British Government should resume control. A British Governor soon returned to Southern Rhodesia. One of his first acts was to affirm the nullification of the purported declaration of independence. On April 18, 1980 pursuant to an act of the British Parliament, the colony of Southern Rhodesia became independent as the Republic of Zimbabwe, which remains a member of the British Commonwealth of Nations.

RULER
British, until 1966

MONETARY SYSTEM
12 Pence = 1 Shilling = 10 Cents
10 Shillings = 1 Dollar
20 Shillings = 1 Pound

BRITISH COLONY
Self-Governing

POUND COINAGE

KM# 5 10 SHILLINGS
3.9940 g., 0.9160 Gold .1177 oz. AGW **Obv:** Crowned bust right **Rev:** Sable antelope **Rev. Designer:** Thomas Sasseen

Date	Mintage	F	VF	XF	Unc	BU
1966 Proof	6,000	Value: 100				

KM# 6 POUND
7.9881 g., 0.9160 Gold .2354 oz. AGW **Obv:** Crowned bust right **Rev:** Lion **Rev. Designer:** Thomas Sasseen

Date	Mintage	F	VF	XF	Unc	BU
1966 Proof	5,000	Value: 200				

KM# 7 5 POUNDS
39.9403 g., 0.9160 Gold 1.1772 oz. AGW **Obv:** Crowned bust of Queen Elizabeth II right **Obv. Designer:** Arnold Machin **Rev:** Arms with supporters divides date **Rev. Designer:** Thomas Sasseen

Date	Mintage	F	VF	XF	Unc	BU
1966 Proof	3,000	Value: 875				

PROOF SETS

KM#	Date	Mintage	Identification	Issue Price	Mkt Val
PS3	1966 (3)	2,000	KM#5-7	280	1,000

ROMANIA

Romania (formerly the Socialist Republic of Romania), a country in southeast Europe, has an area of 91,699 sq. mi. (237,500 sq. km.) and a population of 23.2 million. Capital: Bucharest. Machinery, foodstuffs, raw minerals and petroleum products are exported. Heavy industry and oil have become increasingly important to the economy since 1959.

In 1526, Hungary came under Turkish rule. With defeat in 1526, Hungary came under Turkish rule. Transylvania became a separate principality under the protection of the Sultan (1541).

In 1881, Carol I became king. In 1888, Romania became a constitutional monarchy with a bicameral legislature. Neutral during the First Balkan War (1912), Romania joined Serbia and Greece in the Second Balkan War (1913) against Bulgaria The intervention and deployment of Romanian troops into Bulgaria resulted in the acquisition of southern Dobruja.

When WW I began, the kingdom was neutral until 1916, when the Romanian army invaded Transylvania, but Austro-German, Turkish and Bulgarian forces occupied the south of the country. The Romanians, with the triumph of the Allies, persisted in keeping Moldavia. In March 1918, the Bessarabian legislature voted in favor of reunification with Romania. With the triumph of the Allies, the Romanian army liberated their southern region and reoccupied Transylvania. Bukovina (Oct. 28, 1918) and Transylvania (Dec. 1) proclaimed their reunification with Romania. In 1919, the Romanian army shattered the Bolshevik forces, which were installed in Hungary.

A new constitution was adopted in 1923. During this period in history, the Romanian government struggled with domestic problems, agrarian reform and economic reconstruction.

In the background of WW II, in 1940, after the defeat of France, following the Soviet-Nazi agreement of August 1939, the Red army occupied Bessarabia and northern Bukovina (June). Later, northern Transylvania was annexed by Hungary (August) and southern Dobruja was returned to Bulgaria (September). In this context, King Carol II abdicated in favor of his son Mihai.

The government was reorganized along Fascist lines between September 14, 1940 & January 23, 1941. A military dictatorship followed when the German's Antonescu installed himself as chief of state. When the Germans invaded the Soviet Union, Romania also became involved in recovering the regions of Bessarabia and northern Bukovina annexed by Stalin in 1940.

On August 23, 1944, King Mihai I proclaimed an armistice with the Allied Forces. The Romanian army drove out the Germans and Hungarians in northern Transylvania, but the country was subsequently occupied by the Soviet army. That monarchy was abolished on December 30, 1947, and Romania became a "People's Republic" based on the Soviet regime. The process of sovietization included Soviet regime. The anti-Communist combative resistance movement developed frequent purges of dissidents: mainly political but also clerical, cultural and peasants. Romanian elite disappeared into the concentration camps. The anti-Communist combative resistance movement developed in spite of the Soviet army presence until 1956. The partisans remained in the mountains until 1964. With the accession of N. Ceausescu to power, Romania began to exercise a considerable degree of independence, refusing to participate in the invasion of Czechoslovakia (August 1968). In 1965, it was proclaimed a "Socialist Republic". After 1977, an oppressed and impoverished domestic scene worsened.

On December 17, 1989, an anti-Communist revolt in Timisoara. On December 22, 1989 the Communist government was overthrown. Ceausescu and his wife were arrested and later executed. The new government established a republic, the constitutional name being Romania.

RULERS
Carol I (as Prince), 1866-81 (as King), 1881-1914
Ferdinand I, 1914-1927
Mihai I, 1927-1930
Carol II, 1930-1940
Mihai I, 1940-1947

MINT MARKS
(a) - Paris, privy marks only
(b) - Brussels, privy marks only
angel head (1872-1876),
no marks (1894-1924)
B - Bucharest (1870-1900)
B - Hamburg, Germany
C - Candescu, chief engineer of the Bucharest Mint (1870-)
FM - Franklin Mint, USA
H - Heaton, Birmingham, England
HF - Huguenin Freres & Co., Le Locle, Switzerland
J - Hamburg
KN - Kings Norton, Birmingham, England
(p) - Thunderbolt - Poissy, France
zig zag (1924)
V - Vienna, Austria
W - Watt (James Watt & Co.)
Huguenin - Le Locle, Switzerland
( ) - no marks, 1930 (10, 20 Lei),
1932 (100 Lei), Royal Mint – London

ROMANIA 587

MINT OFFICIALS' INITIALS

Initials	Date	Name
BASSARAB		Costache Bassarab
C	1870	Candescu
IOANA BASSARAB	1941-45	Ioana Bassarab Starostescu
E.W. BECKER (wing)	1939-40	E.W. Becker Lucien Bazor
P.M. DAMMANN	1922	P.M. Dammann
C.D.	1990	C. Dumitrescu
V.G.	1990	Vasile Gabor
H.I.; H.IONESCU	1939-52	Haralamb Ionescu
I. Jalea	1935-41	Ion Jalea
KULLRICH, C	1879-1901	Wilhelm Kullrich
LAVRILLIER	1930-32	A. Larrillier
A.M.; A. MICHAUX	1906	Alfons Michaux
A. MURNU (torch)	1940	A. Murnu Henry Auguste Jules Patey
A. ROMANESCU	1946	A.Rromanescu
A. SCHARFF	1894-1901	Anton Scharff
STERN	1872	
TASSET	1910-14	Ernst Paulini Tasset
LEOP. WIENER	1879	Wiener Leopold Wyon

MONETARY SYSTEM
100 Bani = 1 Leu

KINGDOM
STANDARD COINAGE

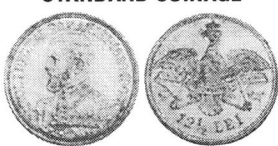

KM# 36 12-1/2 LEI
4.0325 g., 0.9000 Gold .1167 oz. AGW, 19 mm. **Ruler:** Carol I **Subject:** 40th Anniversary - Reign of Carol I **Obv:** Bearded bust left **Rev:** Crowned eagle and banner **Designer:** A. Michaux

Date	Mintage	F	VF	XF	Unc	BU
1906	32,000	110	180	320	450	—

KM# 5 20 LEI
6.4516 g., 0.9000 Gold .1867 oz. AGW **Ruler:** Carol I **Obv:** Head left **Obv. Legend:** CAROL I DOMNULU (Prince) **Rev:** Value, date within wreath **Edge:** Reeded

Date	Mintage	F	VF	XF	Unc	BU
1868(b)	200	—	4,300	8,500	12,000	—
1868 Proof	—	Value: 40,000				

KM# 7 20 LEI
6.4516 g., 0.9000 Gold .1867 oz. AGW **Ruler:** Carol I **Obv:** Head left **Obv. Legend:** CAROL I DOMNUL (Prince) **Rev:** Value, date within wreath

Date	Mintage	F	VF	XF	Unc	BU
1870C	5,000	800	1,200	2,000	3,500	—

KM# 20 20 LEI
6.4516 g., 0.9000 Gold .1867 oz. AGW **Ruler:** Carol I **Obv:** Head left **Obv. Legend:** CAROL I REGE (King) **Rev:** Crowned arms with supporters within crowned mantle, divided date **Note:** Varieties exist.

Date	Mintage	F	VF	XF	Unc	BU
1883B	185,290	125	160	220	340	—
1890B	196,000	130	175	240	360	—

KM# 37 20 LEI
6.4516 g., 0.9000 Gold .1867 oz. AGW, 20 mm. **Ruler:** Carol I **Subject:** 40th Anniversary - Reign of Carol I **Obv:** Bearded head left **Rev:** Head left **Edge:** Reeded **Designer:** A. Michaux

Date	Mintage	F	VF	XF	Unc	BU
ND(1906)(b)	15,000	135	185	260	425	—

KM# 38 25 LEI
8.0650 g., 0.9000 Gold .2333 oz. AGW, 30 mm. **Ruler:** Carol I **Subject:** 40th Anniversary - Reign of Carol I **Obv:** Uniformed bust left **Rev:** Crowned eagle and banner **Designer:** A. Michaux

Date	Mintage	F	VF	XF	Unc	BU
ND(1906)(b)	24,000	210	320	540	800	—

KM# 39 50 LEI
16.1300 g., 0.9000 Gold .4667 oz. AGW, 35 mm. **Ruler:** Carol I **Subject:** 40th Anniversary - Reign of Carol I **Obv:** Uniformed bust left **Rev:** Equestrian **Designer:** A. Michaux

Date	Mintage	F	VF	XF	Unc	BU
ND(1906)(b)	28,000	325	500	800	1,500	—

KM# 40 100 LEI
32.2600 g., 0.9000 Gold .9335 oz. AGW, 36 mm. **Ruler:** Carol I **Subject:** 40th Anniversary - Reign of Carol I **Designer:** Alfons Michaux **Note:** Similar to KM#35.

Date	Mintage	F	VF	XF	Unc	BU
ND(1906)(b)	3,000	650	900	1,900	3,200	—

MEDALLIC COINAGE

X# M1 20 LEI
6.4516 g., 0.9000 Gold .1867 oz. AGW **Ruler:** Ferdinand I **Subject:** Ferdinand I Coronation **Designer:** P. M. Dammann **Note:** Prev. KM#M1.

Date	Mintage	F	VF	XF	Unc	BU
1922(a)	300,000	150	250	450	650	—

X# M5 20 LEI
6.4516 g., 0.9000 Gold .1867 oz. AGW **Ruler:** Carol II **Subject:** Centennial - Birth of Carol I **Designer:** E. W. Becker **Note:** Prev. KM#M2.

Date	Mintage	F	VF	XF	Unc	BU
1939C	—	150	250	550	800	—

X# M6 20 LEI
6.4516 g., 0.9000 Gold .1867 oz. AGW **Ruler:** Carol II **Designer:** E. W. Becker **Note:** Prev. KM#M3.

Date	Mintage	F	VF	XF	Unc	BU
1939C	—	150	250	550	800	—

X# M9 20 LEI
6.4516 g., 0.9000 Gold .1867 oz. AGW **Ruler:** Carol II **Subject:** Carol II 10th Anniversary **Designer:** E. W. Becker **Note:** Prev. KM#M4.

Date	Mintage	F	VF	XF	Unc	BU
1940C	—	150	250	550	800	—

X# M10 20 LEI
6.4516 g., 0.9000 Gold .1867 oz. AGW **Ruler:** Carol II **Designer:** E. W. Becker **Note:** Prev. KM#M5.

Date	Mintage	F	VF	XF	Unc	BU
1940C	—	150	250	550	800	—

X# M13 20 LEI
6.5500 g., 0.9000 Gold .1895 oz. AGW **Ruler:** Mihai I **Subject:** Romanian Kings **Note:** Prev. KM#M6.

Date	Mintage	F	VF	XF	Unc	BU
1944	1,000,000	—	BV	135	175	225

X# M2 25 LEI
8.0645 g., 0.9000 Gold .2333 oz. AGW **Ruler:** Ferdinand I **Subject:** Ferdinand I Coronation **Designer:** P. M. Dammann **Note:** Prev. KM#M7.

Date	Mintage	F	VF	XF	Unc	BU
1922	150,000	250	400	600	900	—

ROMANIA

X# M3 50 LEI
16.1290 g., 0.9000 Gold .4667 oz. AGW **Ruler:** Ferdinand I
Subject: Ferdinand I Coronation **Designer:** P. M. Dammann
Note: Prev. KM#M8.

Date	Mintage	F	VF	XF	Unc	BU
1922	105,000	400	600	950	1,450	—

X# M4 100 LEI
32.2580 g., 0.9000 Gold .9335 oz. AGW **Ruler:** Ferdinand I
Subject: Ferdinand I Coronation **Designer:** P. M. Dammann
Note: Prev. KM#M9.

Date	Mintage	F	VF	XF	Unc	BU
1922	30,000	750	1,250	2,000	3,500	5,000

X# M7 100 LEI
32.5000 g., 0.9000 Gold .9404 oz. AGW **Ruler:** Carol II **Subject:** Centennial - Birth of Carol I **Designer:** E. W. Becker **Note:** Prev. KM#M10.

Date	Mintage	F	VF	XF	Unc	BU
1939C	—	1,500	2,500	3,750	6,000	—

X# M8 100 LEI
32.5000 g., 0.9000 Gold .9404 oz. AGW **Ruler:** Carol II
Designer: E. W. Becker **Note:** Prev. KM#M11.

Date	Mintage	F	VF	XF	Unc	BU
1939C	—	1,500	2,500	3,750	6,000	—

X# M11 100 LEI
32.5000 g., 0.9000 Gold .9404 oz. AGW **Ruler:** Carol II **Subject:** Carol II 10th Anniversary **Designer:** E. W. Becker **Note:** Prev. KM#M12.

Date	Mintage	F	VF	XF	Unc	BU
1940C	—	1,250	2,000	3,250	5,000	—

X# M12 100 LEI
32.5000 g., 0.9000 Gold .9404 oz. AGW **Ruler:** Carol II **Note:** Prev. KM#M14.

Date	Mintage	F	VF	XF	Unc	BU
1940C	—	1,250	2,000	3,250	5,000	—

MEDALLIC COINAGE
Galbeni Issues

The medals listed below were issued with the commemorative gold coins listed earlier in this section. These are referred to as Galbeni.

X# MG1 100 LEI
42.0000 g., 0.9000 Gold 1.2153 oz. AGW **Ruler:** Carol II
Designer: E. W. Becker **Note:** Prev. KM#M15.

Date	Mintage	F	VF	XF	Unc	BU
1939	—	—	—	1,150	1,800	—

X# MG2 100 LEI
42.0000 g., 0.9000 Gold 1.2153 oz. AGW **Ruler:** Carol II
Designer: E. W. Becker **Note:** Prev. KM#M16.

Date	Mintage	F	VF	XF	Unc	BU
1939	—	—	—	1,150	1,800	—

X# MG3 100 LEI
42.0000 g., 0.9000 Gold 1.2153 oz. AGW **Ruler:** Carol II
Subject: Carol II 10th Anniversary **Note:** Similar to KM#M16. Prev. KM#M17.

Date	Mintage	F	VF	XF	Unc	BU
1940	—	—	—	1,750	3,000	—

X# MG4 100 LEI
42.0000 g., 0.9000 Gold 1.2153 oz. AGW **Ruler:** Carol II **Rev:** Mounted horse facing right **Note:** Prev. KM#M18.

Date	Mintage	F	VF	XF	Unc	BU
1940	—	—	—	3,250	5,000	—

ROMANIA

SOCIALIST REPUBLIC
STANDARD COINAGE

KM# 99 500 LEI
8.0000 g., 0.9000 Gold .2038 oz. AGW **Subject:** 2,050th Anniversary of First Independent State **Obv:** National emblem divides date **Rev:** Fighting figures within circle

Date	Mintage	F	VF	XF	Unc	BU
1982FM	508	—	—	—	900	—
1983FM	346	—	—	—	1,000	—

Note: Edge numbered

KM# 101 1000 LEI
16.0000 g., 0.9000 Gold .4167 oz. AGW **Subject:** 2,050th Anniversary of First Independent State **Obv:** National emblem divides date **Rev:** Head with headdress left flanked by diamonds

Date	Mintage	F	VF	XF	Unc	BU
1983FM	342	—	—	—	2,250	—

Note: Edge numbered

REPUBLIC
STANDARD COINAGE

KM# 203 10 LEI
1.2240 g., 0.9990 Gold 0.0393 oz. AGW **Subject:** Cucuteni Romania **Obv:** Romania's Coat of Arms with denomination **Rev:** Cheekpiece of the gold helmet in the Cucuteni-Baiceni hoard **Edge:** Milled **Designer:** Cristian Ciornei

Date	Mintage	F	VF	XF	Unc	BU
2006 Proof	500	Value: 200				

KM# 136 500 LEI
8.6400 g., 0.9000 Gold .25 oz. AGW, 24 mm. **Subject:** Revolution of 1848 **Obv:** Upper and lower shield divides value **Rev:** Half length figure with head facing right flanked by dates

Date	Mintage	F	VF	XF	Unc	BU
1998 Proof	Est. 2,000	Value: 300				

KM# 170 500 LEI
6.2200 g., 0.9990 Gold, 12 mm. **Subject:** History of Gold **Rev:** "Big clip" of Pietroasa

Date	Mintage	F	VF	XF	Unc	BU
2001	250	—	—	—	—	165

KM# 171 500 LEI
6.2200 g., 0.9990 Gold 0.1998 oz. AGW **Subject:** History of Gold **Rev:** "Medium Clip" of Pietroasa

Date	Mintage	F	VF	XF	Unc	BU
2001	250	—	—	—	—	165

KM# 172 500 LEI
6.2200 g., 0.9990 Gold 0.1998 oz. AGW **Subject:** History of Gold **Rev:** 12-sided golden bowl

Date	Mintage	F	VF	XF	Unc	BU
2001	250	—	—	—	—	165

KM# 173 500 LEI
6.2200 g., 0.9990 Gold 0.1998 oz. AGW **Subject:** History of Gold **Rev:** Pitcher

Date	Mintage	F	VF	XF	Unc	BU
2001	250	—	—	—	—	165

KM# 176 500 LEI
6.2200 g., 0.9990 Gold 0.1998 oz. AGW, 23 mm. **Subject:** Christian Monuments **Rev:** Mogosoaia Palace **Shape:** Square

Date	Mintage	F	VF	XF	Unc	BU
2001	250	—	—	—	—	165

KM# 174 500 LEI
6.2200 g., 0.9990 Gold 0.1998 oz. AGW **Subject:** Christian Monuments **Rev:** Bistritz Monastery

Date	Mintage	F	VF	XF	Unc	BU
2002	250	—	—	—	—	165

KM# 175 500 LEI
6.2200 g., 0.9990 Gold 0.1998 oz. AGW **Subject:** Christian Monuments **Rev:** Coltea Church

Date	Mintage	F	VF	XF	Unc	BU
2002	250	—	—	—	—	165

KM# 204 500 LEI
31.1035 g., 0.9990 Gold 0.999 oz. AGW **Subject:** Romania's Accession to European Union, January 1 2007 **Obv:** Romania's Coat of Arms surrounded by 12 stars of European Union **Rev:** Map of the European Union including Romania **Edge:** Plain **Designer:** Cristian Ciornei

Date	Mintage	F	VF	XF	Unc	BU
2007 Proof	250	Value: 1,000				

KM# 205 500 LEI
31.1035 g., 0.9990 Gold 0.999 oz. AGW **Subject:** Nicolae Balcescu (1819-1852) **Obv:** Romania's Coat of Arms and **Obv. Inscription:** Justice and Brotherhood **Rev:** Portrait of Nicolae Balcescu **Edge:** Plain

Date	Mintage	F	VF	XF	Unc	BU
2007 Proof	250	Value: 1,000				

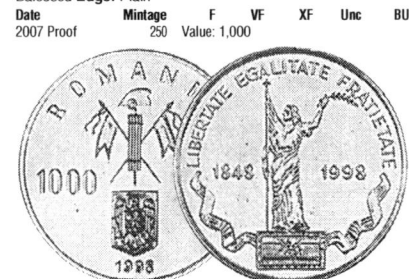

KM# 137 1000 LEI
31.1035 g., 0.9990 Gold 1 oz. AGW, 35 mm. **Subject:** Revolution of 1848 **Obv:** Crossed flags and shield flanked by value **Rev:** Victory flanked by dates **Edge:** Plain

Date	Mintage	F	VF	XF	Unc	BU
1998 Proof	Est. 1,000	Value: 775				

KM# 144 1000 LEI
31.1035 g., 0.9990 Gold 1 oz. AGW, 35 mm. **Subject:** 80th Anniversary - Union of Transylvania **Obv:** Shield to right of value **Rev:** Large building and the arms of Wallachia, Moldova and Transylvania **Edge:** Plain

Date	Mintage	F	VF	XF	Unc	BU
1998 Proof	2,000	Value: 750				

KM# 151 1000 LEI
31.1035 g., 0.9990 Gold 1 oz. AGW, 35 mm. **Subject:** Visit of Pope John Paul II **Obv:** Shield **Rev:** Portraits of Pope and Patriarch Theoctist **Edge:** Plain

Date	Mintage	F	VF	XF	Unc	BU
1999 Proof	1,000	Value: 800				

KM# 156 1000 LEI
15.5510 g., 0.9990 Gold .4995 oz. AGW, 27 mm. **Subject:** 1900th Anniversary of the First Roman-Dacian War **Obv:** Traian's column and shield **Rev:** Monument divides cameos **Edge:** Plain

Date	Mintage	VG	F	VF	XF	Unc
2001 Proof	500	Value: 450				

KM# 157 2000 LEI
31.1030 g., 0.9990 Gold .9990 oz. AGW, 35 mm. **Obv:** Shield and quill within circle **Rev:** Bust 3/4 left **Edge:** Plain

Date	Mintage	VG	F	VF	XF	Unc
2000 Proof	1,500	Value: 775				

KM# 181 2000 LEI
25.0000 g., Bi-Metallic .999 Silver, 10g center in .999 Gold, 15g ring, 35 mm. **Subject:** Ion Heliade Radulescu (1802-1872) **Obv:** Lyre at left, national arms at right in divided circle design **Rev:** Ion Heliade Radulescu above signature **Edge:** Reeded

Date	Mintage	F	VF	XF	Unc	BU
2002 Proof	500	Value: 575				

KM# 155 5000 LEI
31.1030 g., 0.9990 Gold .9990 oz. AGW, 35 mm. **Subject:** Michael the Brave's Unification of Romania in 1600 **Obv:** Shield and old seal within circle **Rev:** Bust with headdress and church **Edge:** Plain

Date	Mintage	F	VF	XF	Unc	BU
2000 Proof	Est. 1,500	Value: 825				

KM# 182 5000 LEI
31.1030 g., 0.9990 Gold 0.999 oz. AGW, 35 mm. **Subject:** 2000 Years of Christianity **Rev:** Jesus Christ

Date	Mintage	F	VF	XF	Unc	BU
2000 Proof	—	Value: 775				

KM# 162 5000 LEI
31.1035 g., 0.9990 Gold 0.999 oz. AGW, 35 mm. **Subject:** Constantin Brancusi 125th Anniversary of Birth **Obv:** National arms, value and sculpture **Rev:** Bearded portrait and signature **Edge:** Plain

Date	Mintage	F	VF	XF	Unc	BU
2001 Proof	500	Value: 850				

KM# 183 5000 LEI
31.1030 g., 0.9990 Gold 0.999 oz. AGW, 35 mm. **Subject:** Ion Luca Caragiale, playright (1852-1912) **Obv:** National arms, value and masks of Comedy and Tragedy **Rev:** Portrait **Edge:** Plain

Date	Mintage	F	VF	XF	Unc	BU
2002 Proof	250	Value: 850				

KM# 184 5000 LEI
31.1030 g., 0.9990 Gold 0.999 oz. AGW, 35 mm. **Subject:** Bran Castle (1378-2003) **Obv:** Two coats of arms on shield above value **Rev:** Castle view **Edge:** Plain

Date	Mintage	F	VF	XF	Unc	BU
2003 Proof	250	Value: 850				

KM# 185 5000 LEI
31.1030 g., 0.9990 Gold 0.999 oz. AGW, 35 mm. **Subject:** Stephen the Great **Obv:** National arms, value above coin design in wall **Rev:** Portrait of Stephen and Putna Monastery

Date	Mintage	F	VF	XF	Unc	BU
2004 Proof	250	Value: 850				

PATTERNS
Including off metal strikes

KM#	Date	Mintage	Identification	Mkt Val
Pn11	1867	—	20 Lei. Gold. Berlin Mint. KM#5.	14,000
Pn12	1868	—	20 Lei. Gold. Plain edge.	10,000
Pn28	1870B	—	Leu. 0.8350 Silver. Medal rotation.	800
Pn29	1870	—	20 Lei. Gold.	3,000
Pn46	1890	—	20 Lei. Gold.	2,000
Pn64	1905	—	5 Bani. Gold. Without center hole.	1,500
Pn65	1905	—	5 Bani. Gold. Without center hole.	1,200
Pn78	1905	—	10 Bani. Gold. Without branches. KM29. Without center hole.	1,650
Pn79	1905	—	10 Bani. Gold. KM29. With center hole.	1,400
Pn84	1905	—	10 Bani. Gold. KM32. Without center hole.	1,250
Pn94	1905	—	20 Bani. Gold. Without center hole.	1,750
Pn95	1905	—	20 Bani. Gold. With center hole.	1,500
Pn109	1906	—	Leu. Gold.	—
Pn111	1906	—	12-1/2 Lei. Lead.	250
Pn112	1906	—	12-1/2 Lei. White Metal.	250
Pn113	1906	—	12-1/2 Lei. Brass.	250
Pn114	1906	—	12-1/2 Lei. Pewter.	—
Pn115	1906	—	12-1/2 Lei. Gilt Bronze.	250
PnA116	1906	—	12-1/2 Lei. Bronze. Plain edge.	250
Pn116	1906	—	12-1/2 Lei. Aluminum.	250
Pn117	1906	—	12-1/2 Lei. Aluminum. Gilt.	250
Pn118	1906	—	12-1/2 Lei. Copper.	350
Pn119	1906	—	12-1/2 Lei. Copper-Nickel.	—
Pn120	1906	—	12-1/2 Lei. Silver.	550
Pn121	1906	—	12-1/2 Lei. Gold.	1,200
Pn122	1906	—	12-1/2 Lei. Gold. Pale.	2,150
Pn123	1906	—	20 Lei. Copper.	350
Pn124	1906	—	20 Lei. Bronze.	200
Pn125	1906	—	20 Lei. White Metal.	—
Pn126	1906	—	20 Lei. White Metal. Gilt.	—
Pn127	1906	—	20 Lei. Gold.	1,200
Pn128	1906	—	20 Lei. Gold. Pale.	2,150
Pn129	1906	—	25 Lei. Pewter.	250
Pn130	1906	—	25 Lei. Zinc.	400
Pn131	1906	—	25 Lei. Lead.	200
Pn132	1906	—	25 Lei. Copper.	175
Pn133	1906	—	25 Lei. Gilt Copper.	—
Pn134	1906	—	25 Lei. Aluminum.	175
Pn135	1906	—	25 Lei. Brass.	175
Pn136	1906	—	25 Lei. Bronze. Antique.	175
Pn137	1906	—	25 Lei. Gilt Bronze.	175

ROMANIA

KM#	Date	Mintage	Identification	Mkt Val
Pn138	1906	—	25 Lei. Silver.	800
Pn139	1906	—	25 Lei. Gold.	2,400
Pn140	1906	—	25 Lei. Gold. Pale.	4,000
Pn141	1906	—	50 Lei. Aluminum.	350
Pn142	1906	—	50 Lei. Bronze.	400
Pn143	1906	—	50 Lei. White Metal.	—
Pn144	1906	—	50 Lei. Pewter.	425
Pn145	1906	—	50 Lei. Brass.	400
Pn146	1906	—	50 Lei. Silver.	850
Pn147	1906	12	50 Lei. Gold.	12,500
Pn148	1906	—	100 Lei. Copper.	650
Pn149	1906	—	100 Lei. Bronze.	650
Pn150	1906	—	100 Lei. Silver.	—
Pn151	1906	—	100 Lei. Gold.	5,000
Pn197	1922	—	20 Lei. Gold.	2,000
Pn198	1922	—	25 Lei. Gold.	2,500
Pn199	1922	—	50 Lei. Gold.	4,000
Pn200	1922	—	100 Lei. Gold.	5,500
Pn219	1930	—	20 Lei. Gold. Plain.	—
Pn220	1930	—	20 Lei. Gold. Ornamented.	—
Pn221	1930	—	100 Lei. Gold. Plain.	—
Pn222	1930	—	100 Lei. Gold. Ornamented.	—
Pn223	1931	—	20 Lei. Gold. Plain.	—
Pn224	1931	—	20 Lei. Gold. Ornamented.	—
Pn225	1931	—	100 Lei. Gold. Plain.	—
Pn226	1931	—	100 Lei. Gold. Ornamented.	—
Pn227	1932	—	20 Lei. Gold. Plain.	—
Pn228	1932	—	20 Lei. Gold. Ornamented.	—
Pn230	1932	—	100 Lei. Gold. Plain.	—
Pn231	1932	—	100 Lei. Gold. Ornamented.	—
Pn232	1933	—	20 Lei. Gold. Plain.	—
Pn233	1933	—	20 Lei. Gold. Ornamented.	—
Pn234	1933	—	100 Lei. Gold. Plain.	—
Pn235	1933	—	100 Lei. Gold. Ornamented.	—
Pn236	1934	—	20 Lei. Gold. Plain.	—
Pn237	1934	—	20 Lei. Gold. Ornamented.	—
Pn238	1934	—	100 Lei. Gold. Plain.	—
Pn239	1934	—	100 Lei. Gold. Ornamented.	—
Pn240	1935	—	20 Lei. Gold. Plain.	—
Pn241	1935	—	20 Lei. Gold. Ornamented.	—
Pn243	1935	—	100 Lei. Gold. Plain.	—
Pn244	1935	—	100 Lei. Gold. Ornamented.	—
Pn246	1936	—	20 Lei. Gold. Plain.	—
Pn247	1936	—	20 Lei. Gold. Ornamented.	—
Pn249	1936	—	100 Lei. Gold. Plain.	—
Pn250	1936	—	100 Lei. Gold. Ornamented.	—
Pn254	1937	—	20 Lei. Gold. Plain.	—
Pn255	1937	—	20 Lei. Gold. Ornamented.	—
Pn257	1937	—	100 Lei. Gold. Plain.	—
Pn258	1937	—	100 Lei. Gold. Ornamented.	—
Pn259	1938	—	Leu. Copper-Nickel-Zinc.	400
Pn260	1938	—	20 Lei. Gold. Plain.	—
Pn261	1938	—	20 Lei. Gold. Ornamented.	—
Pn262	1938	—	100 Lei. Gold. Plain.	—
Pn263	1938	—	100 Lei. Gold. Ornamented.	—
Pn264	1939	—	20 Lei. Gold. Plain.	—
Pn265	1939	—	20 Lei. Gold. Ornamented.	—
Pn266	1939	—	20 Lei. Gold. Arms.	—
Pn267	1939	—	20 Lei. Gold. Eagle.	—
Pn268	1939	—	100 Lei. Gold. Plain.	—
Pn269	1939	—	100 Lei. Gold. Ornamented.	—
Pn270	1939	—	100 Lei. Gold. Bust.	—
Pn271	1940	—	20 Lei. Gold. Plain.	3,000
Pn272	1940	—	20 Lei. Gold. Ornamented.	3,000
Pn273	1940	—	100 Lei. Gold. Plain.	—
Pn274	1940	—	100 Lei. Gold. Ornamented.	—

PIEFORTS

KM#	Date	Mintage	Identification	Mkt Val
P5	1906	—	12-1/2 Lei. Gold.	—
P6	1906	—	25 Lei. Gold.	—
P7	1906	—	50 Lei. Lead.	325
P8	1906	—	50 Lei. Copper.	325
P9	1906	—	50 Lei. Silver.	1,200
P10	1906	—	50 Lei. Gold.	—

MINT SETS

KM#	Date	Mintage	Identification	Issue Price	Mkt Val
MS1	1982FM	—	KM#98-99	429	1,600
MS2	1983FM (4)	—	KM#98-101	850	4,300

RUSSIA (U.S.S.R.)

Russia, formerly the central power of the Union of Soviet Socialist Republics and now of the Commonwealth of Independent States occupies the northern part of Asia and the eastern part of Europe, has an area of 17,075,400 sq. km. Capital: Moscow.

The first Russian dynasty was founded in Novgorod by the Viking Rurik in 862 A.D. under Yaroslav the Wise (1019-54). The subsequent Kievan state became one of the great commercial and cultural centers of Europe before falling to the Mongols of the Batu Khan, 13th century, who were suzerains of Russia until late in the 15th century when Ivan III threw off the Mongol yoke. The Russian Empire was enlarged, solidified and Westernized during the reigns of Ivan the Terrible, Peter the Great and Catherine the Great, and by 1881 extended to the Pacific and into Central Asia. Contemporary Russian history began in March of 1917 when Tsar Nicholas II abdicated under pressure and was replaced by a provisional government composed of both radical and conservative elements. This government rapidly lost ground to the Bolshevik wing of the Socialist Democratic Labor Party which attained power following the Bolshevik Revolution which began on Nov. 7, 1917. After the Russian Civil War, the regional governments, national states and armies became federal republics of the Russian Socialist Federal Soviet Republic. These autonomous republics united to form the Union of Soviet Socialist Republics that was established as a federation under the premiership of Lenin on Dec. 30, 1922.

KINGDOM
TRADE COINAGE

X# 2   4 DUCAT
14.0000 g., Gold **Obv:** Laureate bust of Franz Joseph I of Austria right **Obv. Legend:** ALEXANDER • II • D • G • RUSSIAE IMPERATOR **Rev:** Imperial eagle

Date	Mintage	F	VF	XF	Unc	BU
1905	—	—	—	—	—	—

EMPIRE
RULERS
Paul I, 1796-1801
Alexander I, 1801-1825
Nicholas I, 1825-1855
Alexander II, 1855-1881
Alexander III, 1881-1894
Nicholas II, 1894-1917

MINT MARKS

(sp) (l) - LMD (ЛМД) monogram in oval, (Leningrad), (St. Petersburg) 1977-1997

(m) - MMD (ММД) monogram in oval, Moscow, 1977-

(sp) - LMD (ЛМД) monogram in oval, St. Petersburg, 1998-

MINT OFFICIALS' INITIALS

Ekaterinburg Mint

Initials	Years	Mintmaster
НМ	1810-21	Nicholai Mundt
ИФ	1811	Ivan Felkner
ФГ	1811-23	Franz German
ПГ	1823-25	Peter Gramatchikov
ИШ	1825	Ivan Shevkunov
ИК	1825-30	Ivan Kolobov
ФХ	1830-37	Fedor Khvochinski
КТ	1837	Konstantin Tomson
НА	1837-39	Nicholai Alexeev

Izhora (Kolpino) Mint

МК	1810-11	Mikhail Kleiner
ПС	1811-14	Paul Stupitzyn
ЯБ	1820-21	Yakov Wilson

Kolyvan and Souzan Mints

ПБ	1810-11	Peter Berezowski
АМ	1812-17	Alexei Maleev
ДБ	1817-18	Dmitri Bikhtov
АД	1818-21	Alexander Deichmann
АМ	1821-30	Andrei Mevius

Leningrad Mints

| АГ | 1921-1922 | A.F. Hartman |
| ПЛ | 1922-1927 | P.V. Latishev |

London Mints

| Т.Р. | 1924 | Thomas Ross |
| ФР | 1924 | Thomas Ross |

St. Petersburg Mint

ФЦ	1797-1801	Fedor Tsetreus
МБ	1798-99	M. Bobrovshchikov
ОМ	1798-1801	Ossip Medzher
АИ	1799-1800	Alexei Ivanov
АИ	1801-03	Alexie Ivanov
ФГ	1803-17	Fedor Gelman
ХЛ	1804-05	Christopher Leo
МК	1808-09	Mikhail Kleiner
МФ	1812-22	Mikhail Fedorov
ПС	1811-25	Paul Stupitzyn
ПД	1820-38	Paul Danilov
НГ	1825-42	Nikolai Grachev
АЧ	1839-43	Alexei Chadov
КБ	1844-46	Constantine Butenev
АГ	1846-57	Alexander Gertov
ПА	1847-52	Paul Alexiev
НI	1848-77	Nicholai Iossa
ФБ	1856-61	Fedor Blum
ПФ	1858-62	Paul Follendorf
МИ	1861-63	Mikhail Ivanov
АБ	1863	Alexander Belozerov
АС	1864-65	Aggei Svechin
НФ	1864-82	Nikolai Follendorf
СШ	1865-66	Sergei Shostak
ДС	1882-83	Dmitri Sabaneev
АГ	1883-99	Appolon Grasgov
ЭБ	1899-1913	Elikum Babayantz
ФЗ	1899-1901	Felix Zaleman
АР	1901-05	Alexander Redko
ЭБ	1906-1913	Elikum Babayantz
ВС	1913-17	Victor Smirnov

NOTE: St. Petersburg Mint became Petrograd in 1914 and Leningrad in 1924. It was renamed St. Petersburg in 1991.

MONETARY SYSTEM
100 Kopeks = Rouble, Ruble РУБЛЪ
10 Roubles = Imperial ИМПЕРIАЛЪ
10 Roubles = Chervonetz ЧЕРВОНЕЦ
NOTE: Mintage figures for years after 1885 are for fiscal years and may or may not reflect actual rarity, the commemorative and 1917 silver figures being exceptions.
NOTE: For silver coins with Zlotych and Kopek or Ruble denominations see Poland.
NOTE: For gold coins with Zlotych and Ruble denominations see Poland.
NOTE: Gold coins of 1 Ducat or Chervonetz denomination with both multiples and fractions are known before Peter I. Most Russian authorities agree that these pieces were not meant to be coins but were only made as awards for the military. The higher the rank of the individual the larger the gold piece. Thus the range was from a gold denga for a common soldier to a "Portugal" or 10 Ducat size for a high ranking officer.

STANDARD COINAGE

C# 177   3 ROUBLES
10.3500 g., Platinum .3327 oz. APW **Ruler:** Nicholas I **Note:** The low mintage figures incorporated in the following listings of Russian platinum issues are not necessarily reflective of relative scarcity as many of the issues were restruck at later dates using original dies in unrecorded quantities.

Date	Mintage	F	VF	XF	Unc	BU
1828СПБ	20,000	600	1,200	1,850	3,500	—
1828СПБ Proof	—	Value: 4,000				
1829СПБ	43,000	450	650	1,200	3,000	—
1830СПБ	106,000	450	650	1,200	3,000	—
1831СПБ	87,000	450	650	1,200	3,000	—
1832СПБ	66,000	450	650	1,200	3,000	—
1833СПБ	85,000	450	675	1,250	3,250	—
1834СПБ	91,000	450	625	1,200	3,000	—
1835СПБ	139,000	450	675	1,250	3,250	—
1836СПБ	44,000	450	650	1,200	3,000	—
1837СПБ	46,000	450	650	1,200	3,000	—
1838СПБ	49,000	450	650	1,200	3,000	—
1839СПБ Proof; Rare	6	—	—	—	—	—
1840СПБ Proof; Rare	3	—	—	—	—	—
1841СПБ	17,000	450	675	1,250	3,250	—
1842СПБ	146,000	450	650	1,200	3,000	—
1843СПБ	172,000	450	650	1,200	3,000	—

RUSSIA

Date	Mintage	F	VF	XF	Unc	BU
1844СПБ	215,000	450	675	1,250	3,250	—
1845СПБ	50,000	600	1,200	1,850	3,500	—
Common date Proof	—	Value: 3,500				

Y# 26 3 ROUBLES
3.9260 g., 0.9170 Gold .1157 oz. AGW

Date	Mintage	F	VF	XF	Unc	BU
1869СПБ НІ	143,000	175	225	400	1,500	2,000
1870СПБ НІ	200,000	175	225	400	1,500	2,000
1871СПБ НІ	200,000	175	225	400	1,500	2,000
1872СПБ НІ	100,000	175	225	400	1,600	2,200
1873СПБ НІ	77,000	175	225	400	1,600	2,200
1874СПБ НІ	270,000	175	225	400	1,500	2,000
1875СПБ НІ	100,000	175	225	400	1,600	2,200
1876СПБ НІ	63,000	175	225	400	1,600	2,200
1877СПБ НІ	50,000	175	225	400	1,650	2,250
1877СПБ НФ	Inc. above	175	225	400	1,600	2,200
1878СПБ НФ	194,000	175	225	400	1,500	2,000
1879СПБ НФ	—	—	—	—	6,000	—
1880СПБ НФ	100,000	175	225	400	1,600	2,200
1881СПБ НФ	48,000	175	225	400	1,650	2,250
1882СПБ НФ	—	—	2,200	3,500	7,500	—
1883СПБ ДС	9,007	175	225	350	1,650	2,250
1883СПБ АГ Rare	Inc. above					
1884СПБ АГ	47,000	175	225	350	1,650	2,250
1885СПБ АГ	29,000	175	250	375	1,750	2,500
Common date Proof	—	Value: 4,500				

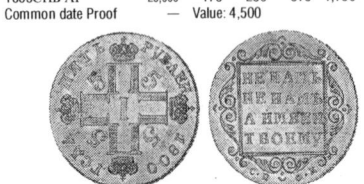

C# 104.1 5 ROUBLES
6.0800 g., 0.9860 Gold .1928 oz. AGW **Ruler:** Paul I **Obv:** Monograms of Paul I in cruciform with 4 crowns, value in angles **Rev:** Inscription within ornamented square

Date	Mintage	F	VF	XF	Unc	BU
1801СМ АИ	180,000	500	1,000	3,000	5,500	—
1801СМ АИ	180,000	500	1,000	3,000	5,500	—

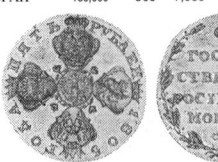

C# 131 5 ROUBLES
6.0800 g., 0.9860 Gold .1928 oz. AGW **Ruler:** Alexander I **Obv:** Designed cross with 4 crowns **Rev:** Crown above inscription within wreath

Date	Mintage	F	VF	XF	Unc	BU
1802СПБ Rare	15	—	—	—	—	—
1803СПБ ХЛ Rare	6	—	—	—	—	—
1804СПБ ХЛ	37,000	600	1,200	7,500	12,000	—
1805СПБ ХЛ	8,109	600	1,200	7,500	12,000	—

C# 132 5 ROUBLES
6.5440 g., 0.9170 Gold .1929 oz. AGW **Ruler:** Alexander I **Obv:** Crowned double imperial eagle **Rev:** Crown above inscription within wreath

Date	Mintage	F	VF	XF	Unc	BU
1817СПБ ФГ	710,000	150	200	650	1,750	—
1818СПБ МФ	1,520,000	150	200	650	1,750	—
1819СПБ МФ	963,000	150	200	650	1,750	—
1822СПБ МФ	—	150	200	650	1,750	—
1823СПБ ПС	440,000	150	200	650	1,750	—
1824СПБ ПС	276,000	150	200	650	1,750	—
1825СПБ ПС	101,000	400	750	2,000	3,000	—
1825СПБ ПС Proof	—	Value: 5,000				
1825СПБ ПД	Inc. above	350	600	1,250	2,000	—
Common date Proof	—	Value: 3,500				

C# 174 5 ROUBLES
6.5440 g., 0.9170 Gold .1929 oz. AGW **Ruler:** Nicholas I **Obv:** Crowned double imperial eagle **Rev:** Crown above inscription within wreath

Date	Mintage	F	VF	XF	Unc	BU
1826СПБ ПД	212,000	150	200	650	1,750	—
1827СПБ ПД	—	300	500	2,000	3,500	—
1828СПБ ПД	604,000	150	200	650	1,750	3,000
1829СПБ ПД	733,000	150	200	650	1,750	3,000
1830СПБ ПД	490,000	150	200	650	1,750	3,000
1831СПБ ПД	846,000	150	200	650	1,750	3,000

C# 176 5 ROUBLES
6.5440 g., 0.9170 Gold .1929 oz. AGW **Ruler:** Nicholas I **Subject:** Discovery of Gold at Kolyvan Mines **Obv:** Crowned double imperial eagle **Rev:** Value, text and date within circle

Date	Mintage	F	VF	XF	Unc	BU
1832СПБ ПД	1,000	1,200	2,500	5,000	7,500	—
1832СПБ ПД Proof	—	Value: 10,000				

C# 175.1 5 ROUBLES
6.5440 g., 0.9170 Gold .1929 oz. AGW **Ruler:** Nicholas I **Obv:** Crowned double imperial eagle **Rev:** Value, text and date within circle

Date	Mintage	F	VF	XF	Unc	BU
1832СПБ ПД	481,000	175	250	325	600	1,200
1833СПБ ПД	829,000	175	250	325	600	1,200
1834СПБ ПД	1,346,000	150	200	275	500	1,000
1835СПБ ПД	1,440,000	150	200	275	500	1,000
1835СПБ Inc. above	Inc. above	—	—	—	—	—
1835 ПД Rare	Inc. above	—	—	—	—	—

Note: Without mintmark

1836СПБ ПД	953,000	175	250	325	600	1,200
1837СПБ ПД	48,000	250	450	950	1,750	3,000
1838СПБ ПД	302,000	175	250	325	650	1,250
1839СПБ АЧ	1,609,000	150	200	275	475	850
1840СПБ АЧ	1,277,000	150	200	275	475	850
1841СПБ АЧ	1,668,000	150	180	225	450	650
1842СПБ АЧ	2,180,000	150	200	275	475	850
1843СПБ АЧ	1,852,000	150	200	275	475	850
1844СПБ КБ	2,365,000	150	200	275	475	850
1845СПБ КБ	2,842,000	150	200	275	475	850
1846СПБ КБ	3,442,000	150	200	275	475	850
Common date Proof	—	Value: 5,000				

C# 175.2 5 ROUBLES
6.5440 g., 0.9170 Gold .1929 oz. AGW **Ruler:** Nicholas I **Obv:** Crowned double imperial eagle **Rev:** Value, text and date within circle

Date	Mintage	F	VF	XF	Unc	BU
1842MW	695	1,500	2,000	5,000	10,000	—
1846MW	62	2,000	3,000	6,000	14,000	—
1848MW	485	1,500	2,000	5,000	10,000	—
1849MW	133	1,500	2,000	5,000	10,000	—
Common date Proof	—	Value: 10,000				

C# 175.3 5 ROUBLES
6.5440 g., 0.9170 Gold .1929 oz. AGW **Ruler:** Nicholas I **Obv:** Crowned double imperial eagle **Rev:** Value, text and date within circle **Note:** Different eagle.

Date	Mintage	F	VF	XF	Unc	BU
1846	—	—	—	—	—	—
1846СПБ АГ	—	150	200	275	475	850

Note: Mintage included in C#175.1

1847СПБ АГ	3,900,000	150	200	300	550	950
1848СПБ АГ	2,900,000	145	185	275	475	850
1849СПБ АГ	3,100,000	145	185	275	475	850
1850СПБ АГ	3,900,000	145	185	275	475	850
1851СПБ АГ	3,400,000	145	185	275	475	850
1852СПБ АГ	3,900,000	145	185	275	475	850
1853СПБ АГ	3,900,000	145	185	275	475	850
1854СПБ АГ	3,900,000	145	185	275	475	850
Common date Proof	—	Value: 5,000				

Y# A26 5 ROUBLES
6.5440 g., 0.9170 Gold .1929 oz. AGW **Ruler:** Alexander II **Obv:** Crowned double imperial eagle **Rev:** Value, text and date in circle

Date	Mintage	F	VF	XF	Unc	BU
1855СПБ АГ	3,400,000	150	200	300	525	900
1856СПБ АГ	3,800,000	150	200	300	525	900
1857СПБ АГ	4,500,000	150	200	300	525	900
1858СПБ АГ	3,500,000	150	200	300	525	900
1858СПБ ПУ	—	150	200	300	525	900
Common date Proof	—	Value: 4,500				

Y# B26 5 ROUBLES
6.5440 g., 0.9170 Gold .1929 oz. AGW **Obv:** Crowned double imperial eagle, ribbons on crown **Rev:** Value, text and date within circle

Date	Mintage	F	VF	XF	Unc	BU
1859СПБ ПФ	3,900,000	145	185	275	475	850
1860СПБ ПФ	3,600,000	145	185	275	475	850
1861СПБ ПФ	3,500,000	145	185	275	475	850
1862СПБ ПФ	6,354,000	145	185	275	475	850
1863СПБ МИ	7,200,000	145	185	275	475	850
1864СПБ АС	3,900,000	145	185	275	475	850
1865СПБ АС	3,902,000	145	185	275	475	850
1865СПБ СШ	Inc. above	145	185	275	475	850
1866СПБ СШ	3,900,000	145	185	275	475	850
1866СПБ НІ	Inc. above	145	185	275	475	850
1867СПБ НІ	3,494,000	145	185	275	475	850
1868СПБ НІ	3,400,000	145	185	275	475	850
1869СПБ НІ	3,900,000	145	185	275	475	850
1870СПБ НІ	5,000,000	145	185	275	475	850
1871СПБ НІ	800,000	145	185	275	475	850
1872СПБ НІ	2,400,000	145	185	275	475	850
1873СПБ НІ	3,000,000	145	185	275	475	850
1874СПБ НІ	4,800,000	145	185	275	475	850
1875СПБ НІ	4,000,000	145	185	275	475	850
1876СПБ НІ	6,000,000	145	185	275	475	850
1877СПБ НІ	6,600,000	145	185	275	475	850
1877СПБ НФ	Inc. above	150	200	300	500	900
1878СПБ НФ	6,800,000	145	185	275	475	850
1879СПБ НФ	7,225,000	145	185	275	475	850
1880СПБ НФ	6,200,000	145	185	275	475	850
1881СПБ НФ	5,500,000	145	185	275	475	850
1882СПБ НФ	4,547,000	145	185	275	475	850
1883СПБ ДС	5,632,000	145	185	275	475	850
1883СПБ АГ	Inc. above	145	185	275	475	850
1884СПБ АГ	4,801,000	145	185	275	475	850
1885СПБ АГ	5,433,000	145	185	275	475	850
Common date Proof	—	Value: 4,500				

Y# 42 5 ROUBLES
6.4516 g., 0.9000 Gold .1867 oz. AGW **Ruler:** Alexander III **Obv:** Head right **Rev:** Crowned double imperial eagle, ribbons on crown **Note:** Without mint mark, moneyer's initials on edge. Edge varieties exist.

Date	Mintage	F	VF	XF	Unc	BU
1886 АГ	351,000	165	225	325	550	950
1887 АГ	3,261,000	150	200	300	475	850
1888 АГ	5,257,000	150	200	300	475	850
1889 АГ	4,200,000	150	200	300	475	850
1890 АГ	5,600,000	150	200	300	475	850
1891 АГ	541,000	150	200	300	475	850
1892 АГ	128,000	175	250	350	600	1,000
1893 АГ	598,000	150	200	300	475	850
1894 АГ	598,000	150	200	300	475	850
Common date Proof	—	Value: 3,250				

RUSSIA 593

Y# A61 5 ROUBLES
6.4516 g., 0.9000 Gold .1867 oz. AGW **Ruler:** Nicholas II **Obv:** Head left **Rev:** Crowned double imperial eagle, ribbons on crown, within circle flanked by stars **Note:** Without mint mark, moneyer's initials on edge.

Date	Mintage	F	VF	XF	Unc	BU
1895 АГ	36	—	9,000	20,000	35,000	—
1896 АГ	33	—	9,000	20,000	35,000	—

Y# 62 5 ROUBLES
4.3013 g., 0.9000 Gold .1244 oz. AGW **Ruler:** Nicholas II **Obv:** Head left **Rev:** Crowned double-headed imperial eagle, ribbons on crown **Note:** Struck at St. Petersburg without mint mark.

Date	Mintage	F	VF	XF	Unc	BU
1897 АГ	5,372,000	—	BV	90.00	110	220
1897 АГ Proof	—	Value: 3,500				
1898 АГ	52,378,000	—	BV	90.00	110	220
1899 ЭБ	20,400,000	—	BV	90.00	110	220
1899 ФЗ	Inc. above	—	BV	90.00	100	120	250
1900 ФЗ	31,000	—	BV	90.00	110	220
1901 ФЗ	7,500,000	—	—	BV	95.00	200
1901 АР	Inc. above	—	BV	90.00	110	220
1902 АР	6,240,000	—	—	BV	95.00	200
1903 АР	5,148,000	—	—	BV	95.00	200
1904 АР	2,016,000	—	—	BV	95.00	200
1906 ЭБ	10	—	—	7,000	10,000	—
1907 ЭБ	109	—	—	4,000	7,500	—
1909 ЭБ	—	—	BV	90.00	110	220
1910 ЭБ	200,000	—	BV	90.00	110	220
1911 ЭБ	100,000	BV	100	200	400	650
1901-11 Common date proof	—	Value: 2,500				

C# 178 6 ROUBLES
20.7100 g., Platinum .6655 oz. APW **Ruler:** Nicholas I **Obv:** Crowned double imperial eagle **Rev:** Value, text and date within circle

Date	Mintage	F	VF	XF	Unc	BU
1829СПБ	828	1,250	2,500	3,500	5,500	—
1830СПБ	8,610	1,750	3,500	5,000	8,500	—
1830СПБ Proof	—	Value: 20,000				
1831СПБ	2,784	2,000	4,000	6,000	9,000	—
1832СПБ	1,502	2,000	4,000	6,500	10,000	—
1833СПБ	302	2,500	4,500	7,000	11,500	—
1834СПБ Rare	11	—	—	—	—	—
1835СПБ Rare	107	—	—	—	—	—
1836СПБ Proof; Rare	11	—	—	—	—	—
1837СПБ	253	2,500	4,500	7,000	11,500	—
1838СПБ Rare	12	—	—	—	—	—
1839СПБ Rare	2	—	—	—	—	—
1840СПБ Rare	—	—	—	—	—	—
1841СПБ	170	2,500	5,000	7,500	12,500	—
1842СПБ	121	2,500	5,000	7,500	12,500	—
1843СПБ	127	2,500	5,000	7,500	12,500	—
1844СПБ Rare	4	—	—	—	—	—
1845СПБ Rare	2	—	—	—	—	—
Common date Proof	—	Value: 10,000				

Y# 63 7 ROUBLES 50 KOPEKS
6.4516 g., 0.9000 Gold .1867 oz. AGW **Ruler:** Nicholas II **Obv:** Head left **Rev:** Crowned double imperial eagle, ribbons on crown **Note:** Without mint mark, moneyer's initials on edge.

Date	Mintage	F	VF	XF	Unc	BU
1897 АГ	16,829,000	140	170	250	450	—

C# 133 10 ROUBLES
12.1700 g., 0.9860 Gold .3858 oz. AGW **Ruler:** Alexander I **Obv:** Designed cross with 4 crowns **Rev:** Crown above inscription within wreath

Date	Mintage	F	VF	XF	Unc	BU
1802СПБ	74,000	3,750	4,500	6,000	10,000	—
1802СПБ АИ	Inc. above	3,750	4,500	6,000	10,000	—
1804СПБ ХЛ	72,000	3,750	4,500	6,000	10,000	—
1805СПБ ХЛ	55,000	3,000	4,000	5,000	9,500	—

Y# A42 10 ROUBLES
12.9039 g., 0.9000 Gold .3734 oz. AGW **Ruler:** Alexander III **Obv:** Head right **Rev:** Crowned double imperial eagle, ribbons on crown **Note:** Without mint mark, moneyer's initials on edge.

Date	Mintage	F	VF	XF	Unc	BU
1886 АГ	57,000	400	750	1,350	3,000	—
1887 АГ	475,000	400	750	1,250	2,850	—
1888 АГ	23,000	400	750	1,350	3,000	—
1889 АГ	343,000	400	650	1,250	2,850	—
1890 АГ	15,000	400	750	1,350	3,500	—
1891 АГ	3,010	450	950	1,500	3,750	—
1892 АГ	8,006	450	950	1,500	4,500	—
1893 АГ Rare	1,008	—	—	—	—	—

Note: UBS Sale #67 9-06, XF realized $13,280

| 1894 АГ | 1,007 | 600 | 1,000 | 2,250 | 5,500 | — |
| Common date Proof | — | Value: 4,500 | | | | |

Y# A63 10 ROUBLES
12.9039 g., 0.9000 Gold .3734 oz. AGW **Ruler:** Nicholas II **Obv:** Head left **Rev:** Crowned double imperial eagle, ribbons on crown, within circle flanked by stars **Rev. Legend:** ИМПЕРIАЛЪ (IMPERIAL) **Note:** Moneyer's initials on edge.

Date	Mintage	F	VF	XF	Unc	BU
1895 АГ	125	—	15,000	25,000	45,000	—
1895 АГ	125	—	15,000	25,000	45,000	—
1895 АГ	125	—	15,000	25,000	45,000	—
1896 АГ	125	—	15,000	25,000	45,000	—
1897 АГ	125	—	15,000	25,000	45,000	—

Y# 64 10 ROUBLES
8.6026 g., 0.9000 Gold .2489 oz. AGW **Ruler:** Nicholas II **Obv:** Head left **Rev:** Crowned double-headed imperial eagle, ribbons on crown **Note:** Without mint mark. Moneyer's initials on edge.

Date	Mintage	F	VF	XF	Unc	BU
1898 АГ	200,000	—	—	BV	190	375
1899 АГ	27,600,000	—	—	BV	175	360
1899 ФЗ	Inc. above	—	—	BV	175	360
1899 ЭБ	Inc. above	—	—	BV	190	375
1900 ФЗ	6,021,000	—	—	BV	175	360
1901 ФЗ	2,377,000	—	—	BV	190	360
1901 АР	Inc. above	—	—	BV	200	365
1902 АР	2,019,000	—	—	BV	190	360
1903 АР	2,817,000	—	—	BV	190	360
1904 АР	1,025,000	—	—	BV	190	360
1906 ЭБ Proof	10	Value: 15,000				
1909 ЭБ	50,000	—	—	BV	175	250	450
1910 ЭБ	100,000	—	—	BV	175	250	450
1911 ЭБ	50,000	—	—	BV	175	250	450
1901-11 Common date proof	—	Value: 4,500				

C# 179 12 ROUBLES
41.4100 g., Platinum 1.3311 oz. APW **Ruler:** Nicholas I **Obv:** Crowned double imperial eagle **Rev:** Value, text and date within circle **Note:** Varieties exist.

Date	Mintage	F	VF	XF	Unc	BU
1830СПБ	119	3,500	7,000	12,000	20,000	—
1831СПБ	1,463	3,000	5,000	8,000	17,500	—
1832СПБ	1,102	3,000	5,000	8,000	18,000	—
1833СПБ	255	5,000	9,000	15,000	24,000	—
1834СПБ Proof	11	Value: 25,000				
1835СПБ	127	5,000	9,500	15,000	25,000	—
1836СПБ Proof	11	Value: 25,000				
1837СПБ	53	6,500	10,000	15,000	25,000	—
1838СПБ Rare	12	7,000	15,000	20,000	50,000	—
1839СПБ Rare	2	—	—	—	75,000	—
1840СПБ Rare	—	—	—	—	75,000	—
1841СПБ	75	7,500	15,000	20,000	40,000	—
1842СПБ	115	6,000	12,500	20,000	35,000	—
1843СПБ	122	6,000	12,500	20,000	35,000	—
1844СПБ Proof; Rare	4	15,000	20,000	40,000	60,000	—
1845СПБ Rare	2	—	—	—	75,000	—
Common date Proof	—	Value: 20,000				

Y# 65.1 15 ROUBLES
12.9039 g., 0.9000 Gold .3734 oz. AGW **Ruler:** Nicholas II **Obv:** Head left **Rev:** Crowned double imperial eagle, ribbons on crown **Note:** Without mint mark. Moneyer's initials on edge. Wide rim, legend ends at back of neck.

Date	Mintage	F	VF	XF	Unc	BU
1897 АГ	11,900,000	BV	275	375	575	—

Y# 65.2 15 ROUBLES
12.9039 g., 0.9000 Gold .3734 oz. AGW **Ruler:** Nicholas II **Obv:** Head left **Rev:** Crowned double imperial eagle, ribbons on crown **Note:** Narrow rim, 4 letters of legend under neck. Moneyer's initials on edge.

Date	Mintage	F	VF	XF	Unc	BU
1897 АГ	Inc. above	BV	275	375	500	—

Y# 27 25 ROUBLES
32.7200 g., 0.9170 Gold .9640 oz. AGW **Ruler:** Alexander II **Obv:** Crowned double imperial eagle, ribbons on crown **Rev:** Value, text and date within circle

Date	Mintage	F	VF	XF	Unc	BU
1876СПБ Proof	100	Value: 100,000				

Note: Impaired Proofs are valued at approximately $70,000

594 RUSSIA

Y# A65 25 ROUBLES
32.2500 g., 0.9000 Gold .9332 oz. AGW **Ruler:** Nicholas II **Obv:** Head left **Rev:** Crowned double imperial eagle, ribbons on crown, within circle flanked by rosettes **Rev. Legend:** 2-1/2 ИМПЕРIАЛЬА (IMPERIALS) **Note:** Struck at St. Petersburg without mint mark.

Date	Mintage	F	VF	XF	Unc	BU
1896	300	—	—	50,000	65,000	—
Note: UBS Sale #67 9-06, XF realized $51,565
1908	150	—	—	70,000	90,000	—
1908 Proof	25	Value: 95,000

Y# B65 37 ROUBLES 50 KOPEKS
32.2500 g., 0.9000 Gold .9335 oz. AGW **Ruler:** Nicholas II **Obv:** Head left **Rev:** Crowned double-headed imperial eagle within beaded circle **Rev. Legend:** 100 ФРАНКОВЪ **Note:** Without mint mark.

Date	Mintage	F	VF	XF	Unc	BU
1902	225	—	—	—	75,000	—
Note: UBS sale #67 9-06, near Unc realized $68,750.
1902 Proof	—	Value: 75,000
Note: Impaired Proofs are valued at approximately $60,000.

РСФСР (R.S.F.S.R.)
(Russian Soviet Federated Socialist Republic)
TRADE COINAGE

Y# 85 CHERVONETZ (10 Roubles)
8.6026 g., 0.9000 Gold .2489 oz. AGW **Obv:** National arms, PCФCP below arms **Rev:** Standing figure with head right **Edge Lettering:** Mintmaster's initials

Date	Mintage	F	VF	XF	Unc	BU
1923 ПЛ	2,751,000	275	400	600	750	1,250
1923 ПЛ Proof	—	Value: 8,000
1975	250,000	—	—	—	BV+10%	—
1976 ЛМД	1,000,000	—	—	—	BV+10%	—
1976 Rare	—	—	—	—	—	—
1977 ММД	1,000,000	—	—	—	BV+10%	—
1977 ЛМД	1,000,000	—	—	—	BV+10%	—
1978 ММД	350,000	—	—	—	BV+10%	—
1979 ММД	1,000,000	—	—	—	BV+10%	—
1980 ЛМД	900,000	—	—	—	BV+10%	—
1980 ММД	—	—	—	—	—	—
1980 ММД Proof	100,000	Value: 195
1981 ММД	1,000,000	—	—	—	BV+10%	—
1981 ЛМД Rare	—	—	—	—	—	—
1982 ММД	65,000	—	—	—	BV+10%	—
1982 ЛМД Rare	—	—	—	—	—	—

Y# A86 CHERVONETZ (10 Roubles)
8.6026 g., 0.9000 Gold .2489 oz. AGW **Obv:** National arms with CCCP below **Rev:** Standing figure with head right

Date	Mintage	F	VF	XF	Unc	BU
1925 Unique	600,000	—	—	—	—	—

Note: Chervonetz were first struck in 1923 under the R.S.F.S.R. government; in 1925 the U.S.S.R. government attempted a new issue of these coins, of which only one remaining coin is known; from 1975 to 1982 the U.S.S.R. government continued striking the original type with new dates

CCCP (U.S.S.R.)
(Union of Soviet Socialist Republics)
STANDARD COINAGE

Y# 268 5 ROUBLES
7.7758 g., 0.9990 Palladium .2500 oz. **Series:** Ballet **Obv:** National arms with CCCP and value below **Rev:** Ballerina

Date	Mintage	F	VF	XF	Unc	BU
1991(l)	9,000	—	—	—	150	—

Y# 238 10 ROUBLES
15.5500 g., 0.9990 Palladium .5000 oz. **Series:** Ballet **Obv:** National arms with CCCP and value below **Rev:** Ballerina

Date	Mintage	F	VF	XF	Unc	BU
1990(l)	Est. 15,000	—	—	—	265	—

Y# 269 10 ROUBLES
15.5500 g., 0.9990 Palladium .5000 oz. **Series:** Ballet **Obv:** National arms with CCCP and value below **Rev:** Ballerina

Date	Mintage	F	VF	XF	Unc	BU
1991(l)	15,000	—	—	—	265	—

Y# 285 10 ROUBLES
2.6600 g., 0.5850 Gold .0500 oz. AGW **Series:** Ballet **Obv:** National arms with CCCP and value below **Rev:** Ballerina

Date	Mintage	F	VF	XF	Unc	BU
1991(l)	6,000	—	—	—	55.00	—

Y# 212 25 ROUBLES
31.1000 g., 0.9990 Palladium 1.0000 oz. **Subject:** Monument to Vladimir, Grand Duke of Kiev and Millennium of Christianity in Russia **Obv:** National arms with CCCP and value below **Rev:** Monument

Date	Mintage	F	VF	XF	Unc	BU
1988(l)	7,000	—	—	—	500	—

Y# 231 25 ROUBLES
31.1000 g., 0.9990 Palladium 1.0000 oz. **Series:** Ballet **Obv:** National arms with CCCP and value below **Rev:** Ballerina

Date	Mintage	F	VF	XF	Unc	BU
1989(l) Matte proof	—	Value: 525
1989(l) Proof	3,000	Value: 525
1989(l)	27,000	—	—	—	500	—

Y# 224 25 ROUBLES
31.1000 g., 0.9990 Palladium 1.0000 oz. **Subject:** 500th Anniversary of Russian State **Obv:** National arms with CCCP and value below **Rev:** Ivan III on throne

Date	Mintage	F	VF	XF	Unc	BU
1989(l) Proof	Est. 12,000	Value: 500

Y# 239 25 ROUBLES
31.1000 g., 0.9990 Palladium 1.0000 oz. **Series:** Ballet **Obv:** National arms with CCCP and value below **Rev:** Ballerina

Date	Mintage	F	VF	XF	Unc	BU
1990(l) Proof	3,000	Value: 525
1990(l)	27,000	—	—	—	500	—

Y# 243 25 ROUBLES
31.1000 g., 0.9990 Palladium 1.0000 oz. **Subject:** 250th Anniversary - Discovery of Russian America **Obv:** National arms with CCCP and value below **Rev:** Ship, St. Peter

Date	Mintage	F	VF	XF	Unc	BU
1990(l) Proof	6,500	Value: 500

Y# 244 25 ROUBLES
31.1000 g., 0.9990 Palladium 1.0000 oz. **Subject:** 250th Anniversary - Discovery of Russian America **Obv:** National arms with CCCP and value below **Rev:** Ship, St. Paul

Date	Mintage	F	VF	XF	Unc	BU
1990(l) Proof	6,500	Value: 500

RUSSIA 595

Y# 250 25 ROUBLES
31.1000 g., 0.9990 Palladium 1.0000 oz. **Subject:** 500th Anniversary of Russian State **Obv:** National arms with CCCP and value below **Rev:** Peter the Great

Date	Mintage	F	VF	XF	Unc	BU
1990(l) Proof	12,000	Value: 500				

Y# 270 25 ROUBLES
31.1000 g., 0.9990 Palladium 1.0000 oz. **Series:** Ballet **Obv:** National arms with CCCP and value below **Rev:** Ballerina

Date	Mintage	F	VF	XF	Unc	BU
1991(l) Proof	30,000	Value: 500				
1991(l)	30,000	—	—	—	500	—

Y# 265 25 ROUBLES
31.1000 g., 0.9990 Palladium 1.0000 oz. **Note:** Three Saints Harbor - Russian settlement in America.

Date	Mintage	F	VF	XF	Unc	BU
1991 Proof	Est. 6,500	Value: 500				

Y# 266 25 ROUBLES
31.1000 g., 0.9990 Palladium 1.0000 oz. **Note:** Novo Archangelsk 1799 - three-masted ship

Date	Mintage	F	VF	XF	Unc	BU
1991(l) Proof	Est. 6,500	Value: 500				

Y# 276 25 ROUBLES
31.1000 g., 0.9990 Palladium 1.0000 oz. **Subject:** 500th Anniversary of Russian State **Obv:** National arms with CCCP and value below **Rev:** Abolition of Serfdom in Russia **Rev. Designer:** Nikolay Nosov

Date	Mintage	F	VF	XF	Unc	BU
1991(l) Proof	Est. 12,000	Value: 500				

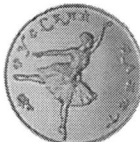

Y# 286 25 ROUBLES
5.3200 g., 0.5850 Gold .1 oz. AGW **Series:** Ballet **Obv:** National arms with CCCP and value below **Rev:** Ballerina

Date	Mintage	F	VF	XF	Unc	BU
1991(l)	5,000	—	—	—	110	—

Y# 286a 25 ROUBLES
3.1100 g., 0.9990 Gold .1 oz. AGW **Series:** Ballet **Obv:** National arms with CCCP and value below **Rev:** Ballerina

Date	Mintage	F	VF	XF	Unc	BU
1991(l) Proof	1,500	Value: 250				

Y# 213 50 ROUBLES
8.6397 g., 0.9000 Gold .2500 oz. AGW **Subject:** 1000th Anniversary of Russian Architecture **Obv:** National arms divide CCCP with value below **Rev:** Cathedral of st. Sophia in Novgorod

Date	Mintage	F	VF	XF	Unc	BU
1988(m)	25,000	—	—	—	185	—

Y# 225 50 ROUBLES
8.6397 g., 0.9000 Gold .2500 oz. AGW **Subject:** 500th Anniversary of Russian State **Obv:** National arms with CCCP and value below **Rev:** Cathedral of the Ascension

Date	Mintage	F	VF	XF	Unc	BU
1989(m) Proof	Est. 25,000	Value: 185				

Y# 251 50 ROUBLES
8.6397 g., 0.9000 Gold .2500 oz. AGW **Subject:** 500th Anniversary of Russian State **Obv:** National arms with CCCP and value below **Rev:** Moscow Church of the Archangel

Date	Mintage	F	VF	XF	Unc	BU
1990(m) Proof	25,000	Value: 185				

Y# 277 50 ROUBLES
8.6440 g., 0.9000 Gold .2500 oz. AGW **Subject:** 500th Anniversary of Russian State **Obv:** National arms with CCCP and value below **Rev:** St. Isaac Cathedral in St. Petersburg

Date	Mintage	F	VF	XF	Unc	BU
1991(m) Proof	25,000	Value: 185				

Y# 287 50 ROUBLES
13.3000 g., 0.5850 Gold .2500 oz. AGW **Subject:** Bolshoi Ballet **Obv:** National arms with CCCP and value below **Rev:** Ballerina

Date	Mintage	F	VF	XF	Unc	BU
1991(l)	2,400	—	—	—	250	—

Y# 287a 50 ROUBLES
7.7800 g., 0.9990 Gold .2500 oz. AGW **Subject:** Bolshoi Ballet **Obv:** National arms with CCCP and value below **Rev:** Ballerina

Date	Mintage	F	VF	XF	Unc	BU
1991(l) Proof	1,500	Value: 450				

Y# A163 100 ROUBLES
17.2800 g., 0.9000 Gold .5000 oz. AGW **Series:** 1980 Olympics **Obv:** National arms divide CCCP with value below **Rev:** Upright design with star on top and sprig within world globe, olympic rings below

Date	Mintage	F	VF	XF	Unc	BU
1977(l) Proof	38,000	Value: 375				
1977(m)	Inc. above	—	—	—	350	—
1977(m) Proof	Inc. above	Value: 375				
1977(l)	44,000	—	—	—	350	—

Y# 151 100 ROUBLES
17.2800 g., 0.9000 Gold .5000 oz. AGW **Series:** 1980 Olympics **Obv:** National arms divide CCCP with value below **Rev:** Lenin Stadium

Date	Mintage	F	VF	XF	Unc	BU
1978(l)	62,000	—	—	—	350	—
1978(l) Proof	45,000	Value: 375				
1978(m)	Inc. above	—	—	—	350	—
1978(m) Proof	Inc. above	Value: 375				

Y# 162 100 ROUBLES
17.2800 g., 0.9000 Gold .5000 oz. AGW **Series:** 1980 Olympics **Obv:** National arms divide CCCP with value below **Rev:** Waterside Grandstand **Rev. Designer:** Nikolay Nosov

Date	Mintage	F	VF	XF	Unc	BU
1978 Rare	—	—	—	—	—	—
1978 Proof, rare	—	—	—	—	—	—
1978(l)	57,000	—	—	—	350	—
1978(l) Proof	43,000	Value: 375				
1978(m) Rare	Inc. above	—	—	—	—	—
1978(m) Proof, rare	Inc. above	—	—	—	—	—

Y# 173 100 ROUBLES
17.2800 g., 0.9000 Gold .5000 oz. AGW **Series:** 1980 Olympics **Obv:** National arms divide CCCP with value below **Rev:** Velodrome Building

Date	Mintage	F	VF	XF	Unc	BU
1979(l)	55,000	—	—	—	350	—
1979(l) Proof	42,000	Value: 375				
1979(m) Rare	Inc. above	—	—	—	—	—
1979(m) Proof	Inc. above	Value: 375				

Y# 174 100 ROUBLES
17.2800 g., 0.9000 Gold .5000 oz. AGW **Series:** 1980 Olympics **Obv:** National arms divide CCCP with value below **Rev:** Druzhba Sports Hall

Date	Mintage	F	VF	XF	Unc	BU
1979(m)	54,000	—	—	—	350	—
1979(l) Proof	38,000	Value: 375				

RUSSIA

Y# 186 100 ROUBLES
17.2800 g., 0.9000 Gold .5000 oz. AGW **Series:** 1980 Olympics
Obv: National arms divide CCCP with value below **Rev:** Torch

Date	Mintage	F	VF	XF	Unc	BU
1980(m)	25,000	—	—	—	350	—
1980(l) Proof	28,000	Value: 375				

Y# 214 100 ROUBLES
17.2800 g., 0.9000 Gold .5000 oz. AGW **Series:** 1980 Olympics
Subject: 1000th Anniversary of Minting in Russia - Coin design of St. Vladimir (977-1015) **Obv:** National arms divide CCCP with value below **Rev:** Ancient coin design

Date	Mintage	F	VF	XF	Unc	BU
1988(m)	14,000	—	—	—	385	—

Y# 226 100 ROUBLES
17.2800 g., 0.9000 Gold .5000 oz. AGW **Series:** 1980 Olympics
Subject: 500th Anniversary of Russian State **Obv:** National arms with CCCP and value below **Rev:** Seal of Ivan III

Date	Mintage	F	VF	XF	Unc	BU
1989(m) Proof	Est. 14,000	Value: 450				

Y# 252 100 ROUBLES
17.2800 g., 0.9000 Gold .5000 oz. AGW **Series:** 1980 Olympics
Subject: 500th Anniversary of Russian State **Obv:** National arms divide CCCP with value below **Rev:** Peter the Great Monument

Date	Mintage	F	VF	XF	Unc	BU
1990(m) Proof	14,000	Value: 450				

Y# 278 100 ROUBLES
17.2800 g., 0.9000 Gold .5000 oz. AGW **Series:** 1980 Olympics
Subject: 500th Anniversary of Russian State **Obv:** National arms with CCCP and value below **Rev:** Tolstoi Monument

Date	Mintage	F	VF	XF	Unc	BU
1991(m) Proof	14,000	Value: 385				

Y# 288 100 ROUBLES
26.5900 g., 0.5850 Gold .5000 oz. AGW **Subject:** Bolshoi Ballet
Obv: CCCP and value below building **Rev:** Ballerina

Date	Mintage	F	VF	XF	Unc	BU
1991(l)	1,200	—	—	—	500	—

Y# 288a 100 ROUBLES
15.5500 g., 0.9990 Gold .5000 oz. AGW **Subject:** Bolshoi Ballet
Obv: National arms with CCCP and value below **Rev:** Ballerina

Date	Mintage	F	VF	XF	Unc	BU
1991(l) Proof	1,500	Value: 750				

Y# 152 150 ROUBLES
15.5400 g., 0.9990 Platinum .4991 oz. APW **Series:** 1980 Olympics **Obv:** National arms divide CCCP with value below **Rev:** Upright design with star on top within wreath, Olympic rings below

Date	Mintage	F	VF	XF	Unc	BU
1977(l)	9,910	—	—	—	650	—
1977(m) Proof	24,000	Value: 675				

Y# 163 150 ROUBLES
15.5400 g., 0.9990 Platinum .4991 oz. APW **Series:** 1980 Olympics **Obv:** National arms divide CCCP with value below **Rev:** Throwing discus

Date	Mintage	F	VF	XF	Unc	BU
1978(l)	13,000	—	—	—	650	—
1978(l) Proof	20,000	Value: 675				

Y# 175 150 ROUBLES
15.5400 g., 0.9990 Platinum .4991 oz. APW **Series:** 1980 Olympics **Obv:** National arms divide CCCP with value below **Rev:** Greek wrestlers **Rev. Designer:** Nikolay Nosov

Date	Mintage	F	VF	XF	Unc	BU
1979(l)	14,000	—	—	—	650	—
1979(l)	19,000	—	—	—	650	—

Y# 176 150 ROUBLES
15.5400 g., 0.9990 Platinum .4991 oz. APW **Series:** 1980 Olympics **Obv:** National arms divide CCCP with value below **Rev:** Roman chariot racers

Date	Mintage	F	VF	XF	Unc	BU
1979(l)	9,728	—	—	—	650	—
1979(l) Proof	17,000	Value: 675				

Y# 187 150 ROUBLES
15.5400 g., 0.9990 Platinum .4991 oz. APW **Series:** 1980 Olympics **Obv:** National arms divide CCCP with value below **Rev:** Ancient Greek runners

Date	Mintage	F	VF	XF	Unc	BU
1980(l)	7,820	—	—	—	650	—
1980(l) Proof	13,000	Value: 675				

Y# 215 150 ROUBLES
15.5500 g., 0.9990 Platinum .5000 oz. APW **Subject:** 1000th Anniversary of Russian Literature **Obv:** National arms with CCCP and value below **Rev:** Chronicler writing epic about Grand Duke Igor

Date	Mintage	F	VF	XF	Unc	BU
1988(l)	16,000	—	—	—	650	—

Y# 227 150 ROUBLES
15.5500 g., 0.9990 Platinum .5000 oz. APW **Subject:** 500th Anniversary of Russian State **Obv:** National arms with CCCP and value below **Rev:** Ugra River Encounter

Date	Mintage	F	VF	XF	Unc	BU
1989(l) Proof	Est. 16,000	Value: 650				

Y# 245 150 ROUBLES
15.5500 g., 0.9990 Platinum .5000 oz. APW **Subject:** 250th Anniversary - Discovery of Russian America **Obv:** National arms with CCCP and value below **Rev:** Ship - St. Gavriil **Rev. Designer:** Nikolay Nosov

Date	Mintage	F	VF	XF	Unc	BU
1990(l) Proof	6,500	Value: 675				

Y# 253 150 ROUBLES
15.5500 g., 0.9990 Platinum .5000 oz. APW **Subject:** 500th Anniversary of Russian State **Obv:** National arms with CCCP and value below **Rev:** Battle of Poltava River **Rev. Designer:** Nikolay Nosov

Date	Mintage	F	VF	XF	Unc	BU
1990(l) Proof	16,000	Value: 650				

RUSSIA

Y# 267   150 ROUBLES
15.5500 g., 0.9990 Platinum .5000 oz. APW **Subject:** 250th Anniversary - Discovery of Russian America **Obv:** National arms with CCCP and value below **Rev:** Bishop Veniaminov with ship in background

Date	Mintage	F	VF	XF	Unc	BU
1991(l) Proof	Est. 6,500	Value: 675				

Y# 279   150 ROUBLES
17.5000 g., 0.9990 Platinum .5000 oz. APW **Subject:** 500th Anniversary of Russian State - War of Liberation Against Napoleon **Obv:** National arms with CCCP and value below **Rev:** Monument divides heads

Date	Mintage	F	VF	XF	Unc	BU
1991(l) Proof	16,000	Value: 650				

RUSSIAN FEDERATION
Issued by БАНК РОССИИ
(Bank Russia)

STANDARD COINAGE

Y# 420   5 ROUBLES
7.7758 g., 0.9990 Palladium .2500 oz. **Subject:** Ballet **Obv:** Double-headed eagle **Rev:** Ballerina

Date	Mintage	F	VF	XF	Unc	BU
1993	6,000	—	—	—	150	—
1993 Proof	2,000	Value: 160				

Y# 431   5 ROUBLES
7.7758 g., 0.9990 Palladium .2500 oz. **Subject:** Ballet - Sleeping Beauty **Obv:** Double-headed eagle **Rev:** Ballerina

Date	Mintage	F	VF	XF	Unc	BU
1994	4,000	—	—	—	150	—
1994 Proof	5,000	Value: 160				

Y# 435   5 ROUBLES
7.7758 g., 0.9990 Palladium .2500 oz. **Obv:** Double-headed eagle **Rev:** Ballerina

Date	Mintage	F	VF	XF	Unc	BU
1995 Proof	4,000	Value: 160				

Y# 352   10 ROUBLES
15.5517 g., 0.9990 Palladium .5000 oz. **Series:** Olympics **Obv:** Double-headed eagle **Rev:** Cubertin and Butovsky and torch

Date	Mintage	F	VF	XF	Unc	BU
1993 Proof	7,500	Value: 250				

Y# 416   10 ROUBLES
1.5552 g., 0.9990 Gold .0500 oz. AGW **Subject:** Ballet **Obv:** Double-headed eagle **Rev:** Ballerina

Date	Mintage	F	VF	XF	Unc	BU
1993	57,000	—	—	—	50.00	—
1993 Proof	11,500	Value: 60.00				

Y# 421   10 ROUBLES
15.5500 g., 0.9990 Palladium .5000 oz. **Subject:** Russian Ballet **Obv:** Double-headed eagle **Rev:** Ballerina **Designer:** A. Baklanov

Date	Mintage	F	VF	XF	Unc	BU
1993(l)	4,000	—	—	—	250	—
1993(l) Proof	2,000	Value: 265				

Y# 424   10 ROUBLES
1.5552 g., 0.9990 Gold .0500 oz. AGW **Subject:** Russian Ballet **Obv:** Double-headed eagle **Rev:** Ballerina **Designer:** A. Baklanov

Date	Mintage	F	VF	XF	Unc	BU
1994(m) Proof	7,000	Value: 60.00				

Y# 432   10 ROUBLES
15.5500 g., 0.9990 Palladium .5000 oz. **Subject:** Russian Ballet **Obv:** Double-headed eagle **Rev:** Ballerina **Designer:** A. Baklanov

Date	Mintage	F	VF	XF	Unc	BU
1994(l)	3,000	—	—	—	250	—
1994(l) Proof	1,500	Value: 275				

Y# 436   10 ROUBLES
15.5500 g., 0.9990 Palladium .5000 oz. **Subject:** Ballet - Sleeping Beauty **Obv:** Double-headed eagle **Rev:** Ballerina **Designer:** A. Baklanov

Date	Mintage	F	VF	XF	Unc	BU
1995(sp) Proof	1,500	Value: 275				

Y# 438   10 ROUBLES
1.5552 g., 0.9990 Gold .0500 oz. AGW **Subject:** Ballet - Sleeping Beauty **Obv:** Double-headed eagle **Rev:** Ballerina **Designer:** A. Baklanov

Date	Mintage	F	VF	XF	Unc	BU
1995(m) Proof	7,000	Value: 60.00				

Y# 484   10 ROUBLES
1.5552 g., 0.9990 Gold .0500 oz. AGW **Subject:** Ballet - Nutcracker **Obv:** Double-headed eagle **Rev:** Nutcracker doll **Designer:** A. Baklanov

Date	Mintage	F	VF	XF	Unc	BU
1996(m) Proof	7,500	Value: 60.00				

Y# 569   10 ROUBLES
1.5500 g., 0.9990 Gold .0498 oz. AGW **Subject:** Ballet - Swan Lake **Obv:** Double-headed eagle **Rev:** Ballerina **Designer:** A. Baklanov

Date	Mintage	F	VF	XF	Unc	BU
1997(sp) Proof	2,500	Value: 65.00				

Y# 353   25 ROUBLES
31.1035 g., 0.9990 Palladium 1.0000 oz. **Subject:** Age of enlightenment 17th century. **Obv:** Double-headed eagle **Rev:** Catherine the Great **Designer:** A. Baklanov

Date	Mintage	F	VF	XF	Unc	BU
1992(l) Proof	5,500	Value: 500				

Y# 395   25 ROUBLES
3.1104 g., 0.9990 Platinum .1000 oz. APW **Subject:** Russian Ballet **Obv:** Double-headed eagle **Rev:** Ballerina **Designer:** A. Baklanov

Date	Mintage	F	VF	XF	Unc	BU
1993(l) Proof	750	—	—	—	185	—

Y# 410   25 ROUBLES
3.1100 g., 0.9990 Gold .1000 oz. AGW **Series:** Wildlife **Obv:** Double-headed eagle **Rev:** Bear **Designer:** A. Baklanov

Date	Mintage	F	VF	XF	Unc	BU
1993(m) Proof	2,000	Value: 125				

Y# 417   25 ROUBLES
3.1100 g., 0.9990 Gold .1000 oz. AGW **Subject:** Russian Ballet **Obv:** Double-headed eagle **Rev:** Ballerina **Designer:** A. Baklanov

Date	Mintage	F	VF	XF	Unc	BU
1993(m)	12,500	—	—	—	110	—
1993(m) Proof	6,000	Value: 125				

RUSSIA

Y# 422 25 ROUBLES
31.1035 g., 0.9990 Palladium 1.0000 oz. **Subject:** Russian Ballet
Obv: Double-headed eagle **Rev:** Ballerina **Designer:** A. Baklanov
Date	Mintage	F	VF	XF	Unc	BU
1993(l)	3,000	—	—	—	500	—
1993(l) Proof	2,000	Value: 525				

Y# 452 25 ROUBLES
31.1035 g., 0.9990 Palladium 1.0000 oz. **Subject:** Russian and World Culture **Obv:** Double-headed eagle **Rev:** M.P. Musorgsky **Designer:** A. Baklanov
Date	Mintage	F	VF	XF	Unc	BU
1993(m) Proof	5,500	Value: 500				

Y# 517 25 ROUBLES
31.1035 g., 0.9990 Palladium 1.0000 oz., 37 mm. **Subject:** First Russian Global Circumnavigation **Obv:** Double-headed eagle **Rev:** Sloop Nadyezhda **Designer:** A. Baklanov
Date	Mintage	F	VF	XF	Unc	BU
1993(l) Proof	2,500	Value: 500				

Y# 518 25 ROUBLES
31.1035 g., 0.9990 Palladium 1.0000 oz., 37 mm. **Series:** First Russian Global Circumnavigation **Obv:** Double-headed eagle **Rev:** Sloop Neva **Designer:** A. Baklanov
Date	Mintage	F	VF	XF	Unc	BU
1993(l) Proof	25,000	Value: 500				

Y# 425 25 ROUBLES
3.1100 g., 0.9990 Gold .1000 oz. AGW **Subject:** Russian Ballet
Obv: Double-headed eagle **Rev:** Ballerina **Designer:** A. Baklanov
Date	Mintage	F	VF	XF	Unc	BU
1994(m) Proof	5,000	Value: 115				

Y# 428 25 ROUBLES
3.1104 g., 0.9990 Platinum .1000 oz. APW **Subject:** Russian Ballet
Obv: Double-headed eagle **Rev:** Ballerina **Designer:** A. Baklanov
Date	Mintage	F	VF	XF	Unc	BU
1994(l) Proof	900	Value: 185				

Y# 433 25 ROUBLES
31.1035 g., 0.9990 Palladium 1.0000 oz. **Subject:** Russian Ballet
Obv: Double-headed eagle **Rev:** Ballerina **Designer:** A. Baklanov
Date	Mintage	F	VF	XF	Unc	BU
1994(l)	2,000	—	—	—	525	—
1994(l) Proof	1,500	Value: 525				

Y# 521 25 ROUBLES
31.1035 g., 0.9990 Palladium 1.0000 oz. **Subject:** First Russian Antarctic Expedition, 1819-21 **Obv:** Double-headed eagle **Rev:** Sloop Mirny **Designer:** A. Baklanov
Date	Mintage	F	VF	XF	Unc	BU
1994 Proof	4,000	Value: 500				

Y# 522 25 ROUBLES
31.1035 g., 0.9990 Palladium 1.0000 oz. **Obv:** Double-headed eagle **Rev:** Sloop Vostok
Date	Mintage	F	VF	XF	Unc	BU
1994 Proof	4,000	Value: 500				

Y# 524 25 ROUBLES
3.1103 g., 0.9990 Gold .1000 oz. AGW **Series:** Wildlife **Obv:** Double-headed eagle **Rev:** Sable's head
Date	Mintage	F	VF	XF	Unc	BU
1994 Proof	4,000	Value: 110				

Y# 530 25 ROUBLES
31.1035 g., 0.9990 Palladium 1.0000 oz. **Obv:** Double-headed eagle **Rev:** Andre Ruble
Date	Mintage	F	VF	XF	Unc	BU
1994 Proof	6,000	Value: 500				

Y# 534 25 ROUBLES
4.3198 g., 0.9000 Gold .1245 oz. AGW **Obv:** Double-headed eagle **Rev:** Baikal railroad tunnel
Date	Mintage	F	VF	XF	Unc	BU
1994 Proof	3,000	Value: 140				

Y# 437 25 ROUBLES
31.1035 g., 0.9990 Palladium 1.0000 oz. **Obv:** Double-headed eagle **Rev:** Ballerina
Date	Mintage	F	VF	XF	Unc	BU
1995 Proof	1,500	Value: 525				

Y# 439 25 ROUBLES
3.1100 g., 0.9990 Gold .1000 oz. AGW **Obv:** Double-headed eagle **Rev:** Ballerina
Date	Mintage	F	VF	XF	Unc	BU
1995 Proof	5,000	Value: 120				

Y# 442 25 ROUBLES
3.1104 g., 0.9990 Platinum .1000 oz. APW **Obv:** Double-headed eagle **Rev:** Ballerina
Date	Mintage	F	VF	XF	Unc	BU
1995 Proof	900	Value: 185				

Y# 475 25 ROUBLES
31.1035 g., 0.9990 Palladium 1.0000 oz. **Obv:** Double-headed eagle **Rev:** Alexander Nevski

1995 Proof   6,000   Value: 500

Y# 486   25 ROUBLES
3.1103 g., 0.9990 Gold .1000 oz. AGW **Subject:** Ballet - Nutcracker **Obv:** Double headed eagle **Rev:** Figure with nutcracker doll

Date	Mintage	F	VF	XF	Unc	BU
1996 Proof	7,500				Value: 125	

Y# 571   25 ROUBLES
3.1103 g., 0.9990 Gold .1000 oz. AGW **Subject:** Ballet - Swan Lake **Obv:** Double-headed eagle **Rev:** Winged figure of Rothbart and Swan

Date	Mintage	F	VF	XF	Unc	BU
1997 Proof	2,000				Value: 175	

Y# 354   50 ROUBLES
8.6397 g., 0.9990 Gold .2500 oz. AGW **Obv:** Double-headed eagle **Rev:** Moscow's Pashkov Palace

Date	Mintage	F	VF	XF	Unc	BU
1992 Proof	7,500				Value: 215	

Y# 516   50 ROUBLES
8.6397 g., 0.9000 Gold .2500 oz. AGW **Obv:** Double-headed eagle **Rev:** Chubuku (snow) ram on map **Note:** Yakutia.

Date	Mintage	F	VF	XF	Unc	BU
1992 Proof	25,000				Value: 225	

Y# 355   50 ROUBLES
8.6397 g., 0.9000 Gold .2500 oz. AGW **Series:** Olympics **Obv:** Double-headed eagle **Rev:** Figure skater

Date	Mintage	F	VF	XF	Unc	BU
1993 Proof	7,500				Value: 215	

Y# 356   50 ROUBLES
7.7758 g., 0.9990 Platinum .2498 oz. APW **Series:** Olympics **Obv:** Double-headed eagle **Rev:** Formal riding

Date	Mintage	F	VF	XF	Unc	BU
1993 Proof	7,500				Value: 375	

Y# 396   50 ROUBLES
7.7758 g., 0.9990 Platinum .2498 oz. APW **Subject:** Bolshoi Ballet **Obv:** Double-headed eagle **Rev:** Ballerina

Date	Mintage	F	VF	XF	Unc	BU
1993 Proof	750	—	—	—	400	—

Y# 411   50 ROUBLES
7.7800 g., 0.9990 Gold .2500 oz. AGW **Series:** Wildlife **Obv:** Double-headed eagle **Rev:** Bear between trees and sprigs

Date	Mintage	F	VF	XF	Unc	BU
1993 Proof	1,480				Value: 245	

Y# 418   50 ROUBLES
7.7800 g., 0.9990 Gold .2500 oz. AGW **Subject:** Bolshoi Ballet **Obv:** Double-headed eagle **Rev:** Ballerina

Date	Mintage	F	VF	XF	Unc	BU
1993	4,700	—	—	—	300	
1993 Proof	1,500				Value: 350	

Y# 453   50 ROUBLES
7.7800 g., 0.9990 Gold .2500 oz. AGW **Subject:** Sergei Rachmaninov **Obv:** Double-headed eagle **Rev:** Head right

Date	Mintage	F	VF	XF	Unc	BU
1993 Proof	7,500				Value: 215	

Y# 426   50 ROUBLES
7.7759 g., 0.9990 Gold .2500 oz. AGW **Subject:** Bolshoi Ballet **Obv:** Double-headed eagle **Rev:** Ballerina

Date	Mintage	F	VF	XF	Unc	BU
1994 Proof	2,500				Value: 250	

Y# 429   50 ROUBLES
7.7759 g., 0.9990 Platinum .2500 oz. APW **Subject:** Bolshoi Ballet **Obv:** Double-headed eagle **Rev:** Ballerina

Date	Mintage	F	VF	XF	Unc	BU
1994 Proof	900				Value: 475	

Y# 525   50 ROUBLES
7.7759 g., 0.9990 Gold .2500 oz. AGW **Series:** Wildlife **Obv:** Double-headed eagle **Rev:** Sable in tree

Date	Mintage	F	VF	XF	Unc	BU
1994 Proof	2,500				Value: 220	

Y# 531   50 ROUBLES
7.7759 g., 0.9990 Gold .2500 oz. AGW **Rev:** Dmitri Grigorievich Levitsky

Date	Mintage	F	VF	XF	Unc	BU
1994 Proof	8,000				Value: 240	

Y# A475   50 ROUBLES
7.7800 g., 0.9990 Gold .2499 oz. AGW **Series:** Wildlife **Obv:** Double-headed eagle **Rev:** Lynx

Date	Mintage	F	VF	XF	Unc	BU
1995 Proof	10,000				Value: 215	

Y# 408   50 ROUBLES
7.7800 g., 0.9990 Gold .2499 oz. AGW **Subject:** 50th Anniversary - United Nations **Obv:** Double-headed eagle **Rev:** Blacksmith with anvil at feet, UN logo at top, building at left **Note:** Similar to 3 Roubles, Y#407.

Date	Mintage	F	VF	XF	Unc	BU
1995 Proof	5,000				Value: 220	

Y# 440   50 ROUBLES
7.7800 g., 0.9990 Gold .2499 oz. AGW **Subject:** Bolshoi Ballet - Sleeping Beauty **Obv:** Double-headed eagle **Rev:** Ballerina

Date	Mintage	F	VF	XF	Unc	BU
1995 Proof	2,500				Value: 350	

Y# 443   50 ROUBLES
7.7759 g., 0.9990 Platinum .2500 oz. APW **Subject:** Bolshoi Ballet - Sleeping Beauty **Obv:** Double-headed eagle **Rev:** Male dancer

Date	Mintage	F	VF	XF	Unc	BU
1995 Proof	900				Value: 475	

Y# 496   50 ROUBLES
8.6397 g., 0.9000 Gold .2500 oz. AGW **Subject:** F. Nansen and the "Fram" **Obv:** Double-headed eagle **Rev:** F. Nansen and the "Fram"

Date	Mintage	F	VF	XF	Unc	BU
1995 Proof	5,000				Value: 210	

Y# 480   50 ROUBLES
7.7800 g., 0.9990 Gold .2499 oz. AGW **Obv:** Double-headed eagle **Rev:** Dmitri Donskoy Monument

Date	Mintage	F	VF	XF	Unc	BU
1996 Proof	10,000				Value: 210	

Y# 487   50 ROUBLES
7.7800 g., 0.9990 Gold .2499 oz. AGW **Subject:** Ballet - Nutcracker **Obv:** Double-headed eagle **Rev:** Marsha and Drosselmeyer with broken doll

Date	Mintage	F	VF	XF	Unc	BU
1996 Proof	2,500				Value: 250	

RUSSIA

Y# 501 50 ROUBLES
8.6397 g., 0.9000 Gold .2500 oz. AGW **Obv:** Double-headed eagle **Rev:** Church of the Savior on the Nereditza River

Date	Mintage	F	VF	XF	Unc	BU
1996 Proof	10,000	Value: 200				

Y# 537 50 ROUBLES
7.7759 g., 0.9990 Gold .2500 oz. AGW **Series:** Wildlife **Obv:** Double-headed eagle **Rev:** Tiger head

Date	Mintage	F	VF	XF	Unc	BU
1996 Proof	1,500	Value: 225				

Y# 546 50 ROUBLES
8.6397 g., 0.9000 Gold .2500 oz. AGW **Obv:** Double-headed eagle **Rev:** Cruiser Varyag 1904

Date	Mintage	F	VF	XF	Unc	BU
1996 Proof	1,500	Value: 250				

Y# 555 50 ROUBLES
8.6397 g., 0.9000 Gold .2500 oz. AGW **Subject:** 850th Anniversary - Moscow **Obv:** Double-headed eagle **Rev:** Shield flanked by designs

Date	Mintage	F	VF	XF	Unc	BU
1997 Proof	10,000	Value: 210				

Y# 572 50 ROUBLES
7.7759 g., 0.9990 Gold .2500 oz. AGW **Subject:** Ballet - Swan Lake **Obv:** Double-headed eagle **Rev:** Prince Siegfried with crossbow and swan

Date	Mintage	F	VF	XF	Unc	BU
1997 Proof	1,500	Value: 225				

Y# 595 50 ROUBLES
7.7759 g., 0.9990 Gold .2500 oz. AGW **Series:** Wildlife **Obv:** Double-headed eagle **Rev:** Polar bear

Date	Mintage	F	VF	XF	Unc	BU
1997 Proof	1,500	Value: 220				

Y# 357 100 ROUBLES
17.5000 g., 0.9000 Gold .5000 oz. AGW **Obv:** Double-headed eagle **Rev:** Michael Lomonossov

Date	Mintage	F	VF	XF	Unc	BU
1992 Proof	5,700	Value: 375				

Y# 375 100 ROUBLES
17.5000 g., 0.9000 Gold .5000 oz. AGW **Obv:** Double-headed eagle **Rev:** Wooly Mammoth within radiant map **Note:** Yakutia

Date	Mintage	F	VF	XF	Unc	BU
1992	14,000	—	—	—	385	—

Y# 412 100 ROUBLES
15.5500 g., 0.9990 Gold .5000 oz. AGW **Series:** Wildlife **Obv:** Double-headed eagle **Rev:** Black bear

Date	Mintage	F	VF	XF	Unc	BU
1993 Proof	1,400	Value: 365				

Y# 419 100 ROUBLES
15.5500 g., 0.9990 Gold .5000 oz. AGW **Subject:** Bolshoi Ballet **Obv:** Double-headed eagle **Rev:** Ballerina

Date	Mintage	F	VF	XF	Unc	BU
1993	2,700	—	—	—	500	—
1993 Proof	1,500	Value: 575				

Y# 454 100 ROUBLES
17.5000 g., 0.9000 Gold .5000 oz. AGW **Obv:** Double-headed eagle **Rev:** Peter Tchaikovsky

Date	Mintage	F	VF	XF	Unc	BU
1993 Proof	5,700	Value: 500				

Y# 427 100 ROUBLES
15.5500 g., 0.9990 Gold .5000 oz. AGW **Subject:** Bolshoi Ballet **Obv:** Double-headed eagle **Rev:** Ballerina

Date	Mintage	F	VF	XF	Unc	BU
1994 Proof	2,500	Value: 550				

Y# 526 100 ROUBLES
15.5500 g., 0.9990 Gold .5000 oz. AGW **Series:** Wildlife **Obv:** Double-headed eagle **Rev:** Sable in tree

Date	Mintage	F	VF	XF	Unc	BU
1994 Proof	2,500	Value: 400				

Y# 532 100 ROUBLES
15.5500 g., 0.9990 Gold .5000 oz. AGW **Obv:** Double-headed eagle **Rev:** Vassili Vassilievich Kandinsky - The Blue Horse

Date	Mintage	F	VF	XF	Unc	BU
1994 Proof	6,000	Value: 400				

Y# 502 100 ROUBLES
17.5000 g., 0.9000 Gold .5000 oz. AGW **Obv:** Double-headed eagle **Rev:** Order of Alexander Nevsky

Date	Mintage	F	VF	XF	Unc	BU
1995 Proof	5,000	Value: 500				

Y# 441 100 ROUBLES
15.5500 g., 0.9990 Gold .5000 oz. AGW **Subject:** Ballet - Sleeping Beauty **Obv:** Double-headed eagle **Rev:** Ballerina

Date	Mintage	F	VF	XF	Unc	BU
1995 Proof	2,500	Value: 695				

Y# 497 100 ROUBLES
17.5000 g., 0.9000 Gold .5000 oz. AGW **Obv:** Double-headed eagle **Rev:** Icebreaker "Krassin"

Date	Mintage	F	VF	XF	Unc	BU
1995 Proof	2,500	Value: 500				

RUSSIA 601

Y# 499 100 ROUBLES
17.5000 g., 0.9000 Gold .5000 oz. AGW **Series:** Wildlife **Obv:** Double-headed eagle **Rev:** Lynx

Date	Mintage	F	VF	XF	Unc	BU
1995 Proof	3,500			Value: 500		

Y# 481 100 ROUBLES
17.5000 g., 0.9000 Gold .5000 oz. AGW **Obv:** Double-headed eagle **Rev:** All Saints Church in Kulishki

Date	Mintage	F	VF	XF	Unc	BU
1996 Proof	5,000			Value: 365		

Y# 489 100 ROUBLES
15.5517 g., 0.9990 Gold .5000 oz. AGW **Subject:** Ballet - Nutcracker **Obv:** Double-headed eagle **Rev:** Dancing Prince

Date	Mintage	F	VF	XF	Unc	BU
1996 Proof	2,500			Value: 400		

Y# 539 100 ROUBLES
15.5517 g., 0.9990 Gold .5000 oz. AGW **Series:** Wildlife **Obv:** Double-headed eagle **Rev:** Amur tiger

Date	Mintage	F	VF	XF	Unc	BU
1996 Proof	1,000			Value: 420		

Y# 548 100 ROUBLES
17.5000 g., 0.9000 Gold .5000 oz. AGW **Subject:** Battleships of WWII **Obv:** Double-headed eagle **Rev:** Destroyers, "Gremysiy and Soobrazitelny"

Date	Mintage	F	VF	XF	Unc	BU
1996 Proof	1,000			Value: 500		

Y# 557 100 ROUBLES
17.2890 g., 0.9000 Gold .5000 oz. AGW **Subject:** 850th Anniversary - Moscow **Obv:** Double-headed eagle **Rev:** Yuri Dolgoruky Monument

Date	Mintage	F	VF	XF	Unc	BU
1997 Proof	5,000			Value: 500		

Y# 574 100 ROUBLES
15.5517 g., 0.9990 Gold .5000 oz. AGW **Subject:** Ballet - Swan Lake **Obv:** Double-headed eagle **Rev:** Prince Siegfried and Odette'd Duet

Date	Mintage	F	VF	XF	Unc	BU
1997 Proof	1,500			Value: 400		

Y# 596 100 ROUBLES
15.5517 g., 0.9990 Gold .5000 oz. AGW **Series:** Wildlife **Obv:** Double-headed eagle **Rev:** Polar bear on ice floe

Date	Mintage	F	VF	XF	Unc	BU
1997 Proof	1,000			Value: 425		

Note: Notice the face on the bear's hind quarter

Y# 623 100 ROUBLES
15.7200 g., 0.9990 Gold .5049 oz. AGW **Obv:** Double-headed eagle **Rev:** Serge Julievech Witte

Date	Mintage	F	VF	XF	Unc	BU
1997 Proof	1,000			Value: 400		

Y# 358 150 ROUBLES
15.5517 g., 0.9990 Platinum .5000 oz. APW **Subject:** Naval Battle of Chesme **Obv:** Double-headed eagle **Rev:** Two battle ships

Date	Mintage	F	VF	XF	Unc	BU
1992 Proof	3,000			Value: 675		

Y# 397 150 ROUBLES
15.5517 g., 0.9990 Platinum .5000 oz. APW **Subject:** Ballet **Obv:** Double-headed eagle **Rev:** Ballerina

Date	Mintage	F	VF	XF	Unc	BU
1993 Proof	750	—	—	—	700	—

Y# 455 150 ROUBLES
15.5517 g., 0.9990 Platinum .5000 oz. APW **Obv:** Double-headed eagle **Rev:** Igor Stravinsky

Date	Mintage	F	VF	XF	Unc	BU
1993 Proof	3,000			Value: 675		

Y# 519 150 ROUBLES
15.5517 g., 0.9990 Platinum .5000 oz. APW **Subject:** First Global Circumnavigation **Obv:** Double-headed eagle **Rev:** Sloops - Nadyezdha and Neva

Date	Mintage	F	VF	XF	Unc	BU
1993 Proof	2,500			Value: 675		

Y# 430 150 ROUBLES
15.5517 g., 0.9990 Platinum .5000 oz. APW **Subject:** Bolshoi Ballet **Obv:** Double-headed eagle **Rev:** Ballerina

Date	Mintage	F	VF	XF	Unc	BU
1994 Proof	900			Value: 950		

Y# 523 150 ROUBLES
15.5517 g., 0.9990 Platinum .5000 oz. APW **Subject:** First Global Circumnavigation **Obv:** Double-headed eagle **Rev:** Sloops - "Mirny" and "Vostok"

Date	Mintage	F	VF	XF	Unc	BU
1994 Proof	4,000			Value: 675		

Y# 533 150 ROUBLES
15.5517 g., 0.9990 Platinum .5000 oz. APW **Subject:** Michail Alexandrowich Vrubel - The Demon **Obv:** Double-headed eagle **Rev:** Michail Alexandrowich Vrubel - The Demon

Date	Mintage	F	VF	XF	Unc	BU
1994 Proof	3,000			Value: 675		

602 RUSSIA

Y# 444 150 ROUBLES
15.5517 g., 0.9990 Platinum .5000 oz. APW **Subject:** Ballet - Sleeping Beauty **Obv:** Double-headed eagle **Rev:** Male dancer
Date	Mintage	F	VF	XF	Unc	BU
1995 Proof	900	Value: 900				

Y# 503 150 ROUBLES
15.5517 g., 0.9990 Platinum .5000 oz. APW **Subject:** Battle of the Neva River in 1240 **Obv:** Double-headed eagle **Rev:** Armored equestrians fighting
Date	Mintage	F	VF	XF	Unc	BU
1995 Proof	3,000	Value: 675				

Y# 413 200 ROUBLES
31.1035 g., 0.9990 Gold 1.0000 oz. AGW **Series:** Wildlife **Obv:** Double-headed eagle **Rev:** Bear with cub
Date	Mintage	F	VF	XF	Unc	BU
1993 Proof	1,000	Value: 1,200				

Y# 527 200 ROUBLES
31.1035 g., 0.9990 Gold 1.0000 oz. AGW **Series:** Wildlife **Obv:** Double-headed eagle **Rev:** Two sables
Date	Mintage	F	VF	XF	Unc	BU
1994 Proof	2,000	Value: 1,200				

Y# 500 200 ROUBLES
31.1035 g., 0.9990 Gold 1.0000 oz. AGW **Series:** Wildlife **Obv:** Double-headed eagle **Rev:** Seated lynx
Date	Mintage	F	VF	XF	Unc	BU
1995 Proof	1,750	Value: 1,250				

Y# 540 200 ROUBLES
31.1035 g., 0.9990 Gold 1.0000 oz. AGW **Series:** Wildlife **Obv:** Double-headed eagle **Rev:** Amur tiger
Date	Mintage	F	VF	XF	Unc	BU
1996 Proof	1,000	Value: 1,200				

Y# 598 200 ROUBLES
31.1035 g., 0.9990 Gold 1.0000 oz. AGW **Series:** Wildlife **Obv:** Double-headed eagle **Rev:** Seated polar bear
Date	Mintage	F	VF	XF	Unc	BU
1997 Proof	1,000	Value: 1,100				

Y# 589 1000 ROUBLES
155.5000 g., 0.9990 Gold 4.9944 oz. AGW **Obv:** Double-headed eagle **Rev:** The Bark "Krusenstern" - 4-masted ship **Note:** Photo reduced.
Date	Mintage	F	VF	XF	Unc	BU
1997 Proof	250	Value: 5,000				

Y# 541 10000 ROUBLES
1111.0861 g., 0.9990 Gold 35.6865 oz. AGW, 100 mm. **Series:** Wildlife **Obv:** Double-headed eagle **Rev:** Amur tiger with two cubs **Note:** Illustration reduced.
Date	Mintage	F	VF	XF	Unc	BU
1996 Prooflike	100	—	—	—	—	25,000

Y# 599 10000 ROUBLES
1111.0861 g., 0.9990 Gold 35.6865 oz. AGW, 100 mm. **Series:** Wildlife **Obv:** Double-headed eagle **Rev:** Seated polar bear with two cubs **Note:** Illustration reduced.
Date	Mintage	F	VF	XF	Unc	BU
1997 Proof	100	Value: 25,000				

REFORM COINAGE
January 1, 1998

1,000 Old Roubles = 1 New Rouble

Y# 829 5 ROUBLES
47.2400 g., 0.9000 Bi-Metallic Gold And Silver .900 Silver 21.34g center in .900 Gold 25.9g ring 1.3669 oz., 39.5 mm. **Obv:** Double-headed eagle **Rev:** Uglich city view **Edge:** Reeded
Date	Mintage	F	VF	XF	Unc	BU
2004(SP) Proof	5,000	Value: 850				

Y# 695 10 ROUBLES
1.5500 g., 0.9990 Gold .0499 oz. AGW, 12 mm. **Subject:** Russian Ballet **Obv:** Double-headed eagle **Rev:** Standing knight within flower wreath **Edge:** Reeded
Date	Mintage	F	VF	XF	Unc	BU
1999(m) Proof	2,500	Value: 70.00				

Y# 686 10 ROUBLES
1.6100 g., 0.9990 Gold .0517 oz. AGW, 12 mm. **Subject:** Bolshoi Theater 225 Years **Obv:** Double-headed eagle within circle **Rev:** Building above number 225 **Edge:** Reeded
Date	Mintage	F	VF	XF	Unc	BU
2001 Proof	3,000	Value: 60.00				

Y# 697 25 ROUBLES
3.2000 g., 0.9990 Gold .1028 oz. AGW, 16 mm. **Subject:** Russian Ballet **Obv:** Double-headed eagle **Rev:** Dancing Saracen **Edge:** Reeded
Date	Mintage	F	VF	XF	Unc	BU
1999(sp) Proof	2,000	Value: 175				

Y# 687 25 ROUBLES
3.2000 g., 0.9990 Gold .1028 oz. AGW, 16 mm. **Subject:** Bolshoi Theater **Obv:** Double-headed eagle **Rev:** Ballerina **Edge:** Reeded
Date	Mintage	F	VF	XF	Unc	BU
2001 Proof	2,500	Value: 145				

Y# 743 25 ROUBLES
3.2000 g., 0.9990 Gold 0.1028 oz. AGW, 16 mm. **Subject:** Zodiac Signs: **Obv:** Double-headed eagle within beaded circle **Rev:** Leo **Edge:** Reeded
Date	Mintage	F	VF	XF	Unc	BU
2002 Proof	10,000	Value: 125				

RUSSIA

Y# 763 25 ROUBLES
3.2000 g., 0.9990 Gold 0.1028 oz. AGW, 16 mm. **Subject:** Zodiac Signs **Obv:** Double-headed eagle within beaded circle **Rev:** Capricorn **Edge:** Reeded

Date	Mintage	F	VF	XF	Unc	BU
2002(m)	10,000	—	—	—	—	125

Y# 764 25 ROUBLES
3.2000 g., 0.9990 Gold 0.1028 oz. AGW, 16 mm. **Subject:** Zodiac Signs **Obv:** Double-headed eagle within beaded circle **Rev:** Virgo **Edge:** Reeded

Date	Mintage	F	VF	XF	Unc	BU
2002(SP)	10,000	—	—	—	—	125

Y# 765 25 ROUBLES
3.2000 g., 0.9990 Gold 0.1028 oz. AGW, 16 mm. **Subject:** Zodiac Signs **Obv:** Double-headed eagle within beaded circle **Rev:** Sagittarius **Edge:** Reeded

Date	Mintage	F	VF	XF	Unc	BU
2002(SP)	10,000	—	—	—	—	125

Y# 767 25 ROUBLES
3.2000 g., 0.9990 Gold 0.1028 oz. AGW, 16 mm. **Subject:** Zodiac signs **Obv:** Double-headed eagle within beaded circle **Rev:** Scorpio **Edge:** Reeded

Date	Mintage	F	VF	XF	Unc	BU
2002(m)	10,000	—	—	—	—	125

Y# 769 25 ROUBLES
3.2000 g., 0.9990 Gold .1028 oz. AGW **Subject:** Zodiac Signs **Obv:** Double-headed eagle within beaded circle **Rev:** Libra **Edge:** Reeded

Date	Mintage	F	VF	XF	Unc	BU
2002(SP)	10,000	—	—	—	—	125

Y# 821 25 ROUBLES
3.2000 g., 0.9990 Gold 0.1028 oz. AGW, 16 mm. **Subject:** Zodiac signs **Obv:** Double-headed eagle within beaded circle **Rev:** Cancer **Edge:** Reeded

Date	Mintage	F	VF	XF	Unc	BU
2003(SP)	50,000	—	—	—	—	125

Y# 830 25 ROUBLES
177.9600 g., 0.9000 Bi-Metallic Gold And Silver .900 Silver 172.78g planchet with .900 Gold 5.18g insert 5.1494 oz., 60 mm. **Subject:** Monetary reform of Peter the Great **Obv:** Double-headed eagle **Rev:** Gold insert replicating the obverse and reverse designs of a 1704 one rouble coin **Edge:** Reeded **Note:** Illustration reduced.

Date	Mintage	F	VF	XF	Unc	BU
2004(SP) Proof	1,000	Value: 335				

Y# 935 25 ROUBLES
3.2000 g., 0.9990 Gold 0.1028 oz. AGW, 16 mm. **Obv:** Double-headed eagle **Rev:** Taurus bull **Edge:** Reeded

Date	Mintage	F	VF	XF	Unc	BU
2005	10,000	—	—	—	—	125

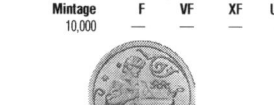

Y# 937 25 ROUBLES
3.2000 g., 0.9990 Gold 0.1028 oz. AGW, 16 mm. **Obv:** Double-headed eagle **Rev:** Aquarius water carrier **Edge:** Reeded

Date	Mintage	F	VF	XF	Unc	BU
2005	10,000	—	—	—	—	125

Y# 927 25 ROUBLES
3.2000 g., 0.9990 Gold 0.1028 oz. AGW, 16 mm. **Obv:** Double-headed eagle **Rev:** Sagittarius the archer **Edge:** Reeded

Date	Mintage	F	VF	XF	Unc	BU
2005	10,000	—	—	—	—	125

Y# 929 25 ROUBLES
3.2000 g., 0.9990 Gold 0.1028 oz. AGW, 16 mm. **Obv:** Double-headed eagle **Rev:** Capricorn as half goat and fish **Edge:** Reeded

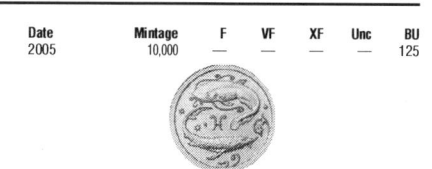

Date	Mintage	F	VF	XF	Unc	BU
2005	10,000	—	—	—	—	125

Y# 931 25 ROUBLES
3.2000 g., 0.9990 Gold 0.1028 oz. AGW, 16 mm. **Obv:** Double-headed eagle **Rev:** Pisces as catfish and sturgeon **Edge:** Reeded

Date	Mintage	F	VF	XF	Unc	BU
2005	10,000	—	—	—	—	125

Y# 933 25 ROUBLES
3.2000 g., 0.9990 Gold 0.1028 oz. AGW, 16 mm. **Obv:** Double-headed eagle **Rev:** Aries ram **Edge:** Reeded

Date	Mintage	F	VF	XF	Unc	BU
2005	10,000	—	—	—	—	125

Y# 898 25 ROUBLES
3.2000 g., 0.9990 Gold 0.1028 oz. AGW, 16 mm. **Obv:** Double-headed eagle **Rev:** Gemini twins **Edge:** Reeded

Date	Mintage	F	VF	XF	Unc	BU
2005	10,000	—	—	—	—	125

Y# 900 25 ROUBLES
3.2000 g., 0.9990 Gold 0.1028 oz. AGW, 16 mm. **Obv:** Double-headed eagle **Rev:** Cancer crawfish **Edge:** Reeded

Date	Mintage	F	VF	XF	Unc	BU
2005 Proof	10,000	Value: 125				

Y# 902 25 ROUBLES
3.2000 g., 0.9990 Gold 0.1028 oz. AGW, 16 mm. **Obv:** Double-headed eagle **Rev:** Leo lion **Edge:** Reeded

Date	Mintage	F	VF	XF	Unc	BU
2005	10,000	—	—	—	—	125

Y# 915 25 ROUBLES
3.2000 g., 0.9990 Gold 0.1028 oz. AGW, 16 mm. **Obv:** Double-headed eagle **Rev:** Virgos standing lady **Edge:** Reeded

Date	Mintage	F	VF	XF	Unc	BU
2005 Proof	10,000	Value: 125				

Y# 920 25 ROUBLES
3.2000 g., 0.9990 Gold 0.1028 oz. AGW, 16 mm. **Obv:** Double-headed eagle **Rev:** Two stylized birds forming balance scale **Edge:** Reeded

Date	Mintage	F	VF	XF	Unc	BU
2005	10,000	—	—	—	—	125

Y# 922 25 ROUBLES
3.2000 g., 0.9990 Gold 0.1028 oz. AGW, 16 mm. **Obv:** Double-headed eagle **Rev:** Scorpio scorpion **Edge:** Reeded

Date	Mintage	F	VF	XF	Unc	BU
2005	10,000	—	—	—	—	125

RUSSIA

Y# 648 50 ROUBLES
8.7500 g., 0.9000 Gold .2532 oz. AGW **Subject:** 50th Anniversary - Diplomacy with China **Obv:** Double-headed eagle **Rev:** Moscow Kremlin and Tiananmen Gate

Date	Mintage	F	VF	XF	Unc	BU
1999 Proof	1,000	Value: 400				

Y# 692 50 ROUBLES
8.7500 g., 0.9000 Gold .2532 oz. AGW, 22.6 mm. **Obv:** Double-headed eagle **Rev:** Alexander Pushkin **Edge:** Reeded

Date	Mintage	F	VF	XF	Unc	BU
1999(m) Proof	1,500	Value: 245				

Y# 698 50 ROUBLES
8.7500 g., 0.9990 Gold .2534 oz. AGW, 22.6 mm. **Subject:** Russian Ballet **Obv:** Double-headed eagle **Rev:** Dancing figures **Edge:** Reeded

Date	Mintage	F	VF	XF	Unc	BU
1999(m) Proof	1,500	Value: 245				

Y# 702 50 ROUBLES
8.7500 g., 0.9000 Gold .2532 oz. AGW, 22.6 mm. **Subject:** Russian Explorer N.M. Przhevalsky **Obv:** Double-headed eagle **Rev:** Armored bust 1/4 right **Edge:** Reeded

Date	Mintage	F	VF	XF	Unc	BU
1999(sp) Proof	1,500	Value: 245				

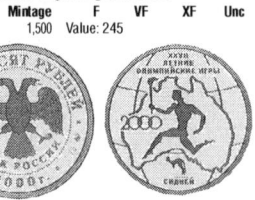

Y# 672 50 ROUBLES
8.7100 g., 0.9000 Gold .2520 oz. AGW **Series:** Olympics **Obv:** Double-headed eagle **Rev:** Torch runner on map

Date	Mintage	F	VF	XF	Unc	BU
2000 Proof	1,000	Value: 275				

Y# 718 50 ROUBLES
8.7500 g., 0.9000 Gold .2532 oz. AGW, 22.6 mm. **Subject:** Field Marshal Suvorov **Obv:** Double-headed eagle **Rev:** Cameo above cannons **Edge:** Reeded

Date	Mintage	F	VF	XF	Unc	BU
2000(sp) Proof	500	Value: 285				

Y# 725 50 ROUBLES
7.8900 g., 0.9990 Gold .2534 oz. AGW, 22.6 mm. **Obv:** Double-headed eagle **Rev:** Snow leopard head **Edge:** Reeded

Date	Mintage	F	VF	XF	Unc	BU
2000(sp) Proof	1,000	Value: 250				

Y# 679 50 ROUBLES
8.7500 g., 0.9990 Gold .2532 oz. AGW, 22.6 mm. **Subject:** Bolshoi Theater **Obv:** Double-headed eagle within beaded circle **Rev:** Dueling figures **Edge:** Reeded

Date	Mintage	F	VF	XF	Unc	BU
2001 Proof	2,000	Value: 225				

Y# 684 50 ROUBLES
8.7500 g., 0.9000 Gold .2532 oz. AGW, 22.6 mm. **Subject:** Siberian Exploration **Obv:** Double-headed eagle within beaded circle **Rev:** Head with hat 1/4 right and boat **Edge:** Reeded

Date	Mintage	F	VF	XF	Unc	BU
2001 Proof	1,500	Value: 225				

Y# 757 50 ROUBLES
8.6444 g., 0.9000 Gold 0.2501 oz. AGW, 22.6 mm. **Subject:** Olympics **Obv:** Double-headed eagle within beaded circle **Rev:** Figure skater and flying eagle **Edge:** Reeded

Date	Mintage	F	VF	XF	Unc	BU
2002 Proof	3,000	Value: 250				

Y# 782 50 ROUBLES
7.8900 g., 0.9990 Gold 0.2534 oz. AGW, 22.6 mm. **Subject:** Works of Dionissy **Obv:** Double-headed eagle within beaded circle **Rev:** Half-length figure holding child flanked by double headed eagle and church **Edge:** Reeded

Date	Mintage	F	VF	XF	Unc	BU
2002(m) Proof	1,500	Value: 245				

Y# 786 50 ROUBLES
8.7500 g., 0.9000 Gold 0.2532 oz. AGW, 22.6 mm. **Subject:** Admiral Nakhimov **Obv:** Double-headed eagle within beaded circle **Rev:** Bust facing within circle above flags and anchor **Edge:** Reeded

Date	Mintage	F	VF	XF	Unc	BU
2002(SP) Proof	1,500	Value: 245				

Y# 788 50 ROUBLES
8.7500 g., 0.9000 Gold 0.2532 oz. AGW, 22.6 mm. **Subject:** World Cup Soccer **Obv:** Double-headed eagle within beaded circle **Rev:** Stylized player kicking soccer ball **Edge:** Reeded

Date	Mintage	F	VF	XF	Unc	BU
2002(m) Proof	3,000	Value: 225				

Y# 822 50 ROUBLES
7.8900 g., 0.9990 Gold 0.2534 oz. AGW, 22.6 mm. **Subject:** Zodiac Signs **Obv:** Double-headed eagle within beaded circle **Rev:** Virgo **Edge:** Reeded

Date	Mintage	F	VF	XF	Unc	BU
2003(sp)	30,000	—	—	—	—	210

Y# 823 50 ROUBLES
7.8900 g., 0.9990 Gold 0.2534 oz. AGW, 22.6 mm. **Subject:** Zodiac signs **Obv:** Double-headed eagle within beaded circle **Rev:** Libra **Edge:** Reeded

Date	Mintage	F	VF	XF	Unc	BU
2003(m)	30,000	—	—	—	—	210

Y# 868 50 ROUBLES
8.6400 g., 0.9000 Gold 0.25 oz. AGW, 23 mm. **Rev:** Peter I monetary reform

Date	Mintage	F	VF	XF	Unc	BU
2003(m) Proof	1,500	Value: 225				

Y# 869 50 ROUBLES
8.6400 g., 0.9000 Gold 0.25 oz. AGW, 23 mm. **Rev:** Ski race

Date	Mintage	F	VF	XF	Unc	BU
2003(m) Proof	1,500	Value: 225				

Y# 870 50 ROUBLES
8.6400 g., 0.9000 Gold .2500 oz. AGW, 23 mm. **Rev:** Soccer player

Date	Mintage	F	VF	XF	Unc	BU
2004(sp) Proof	1,000	Value: 225				

Y# 871 50 ROUBLES
8.6400 g., 0.9000 Gold 0.25 oz. AGW, 23 mm. **Rev:** Olympic athletes

Date	Mintage	F	VF	XF	Unc	BU
2004(m) Proof	2,000	Value: 225				

Y# 872 50 ROUBLES
8.6400 g., 0.9000 Gold 0.25 oz. AGW, 23 mm. **Rev:** Virgin of the Son Icon

Date	Mintage	F	VF	XF	Unc	BU
2004(m)	1,500	Value: 225				

Y# 911 50 ROUBLES
7.8900 g., 0.9990 Gold 0.2534 oz. AGW, 22.6 mm. **Obv:** Double-headed eagle **Rev:** Kazan University Building **Edge:** Reeded

Date	Mintage	F	VF	XF	Unc	BU
2005 Proof	1,500	Value: 225				

Y# 894 50 ROUBLES
7.8900 g., 0.9990 Gold 0.2534 oz. AGW, 22.6 mm. **Subject:** 60th Anniversary - Victory Over Germany **Obv:** Double-headed eagle **Rev:** 60th Anniversary - Victory Over Germany medal **Edge:** Reeded

Date	Mintage	F	VF	XF	Unc	BU
2005 Proof	7,000	Value: 210				

Date	Mintage	F	VF	XF	Unc	BU
2002(m) Proof	3,000	Value: 225				

RUSSIA

Y# 907 50 ROUBLES
7.8900 g., 0.9990 Gold 0.2534 oz. AGW, 22.6 mm. **Subject:** Helsinki Games **Obv:** Double-headed eagle **Rev:** Stylized track and field athletes **Edge:** Reeded

Date	Mintage	F	VF	XF	Unc	BU
2005 Proof	1,500	Value: 220				

Y# 694 100 ROUBLES
17.4500 g., 0.9000 Gold .5049 oz. AGW, 30 mm. **Subject:** Alexander Pushkin **Obv:** Double-headed eagle **Rev:** Head 1/4 right, tree and scenes **Edge:** Reeded

Date	Mintage	F	VF	XF	Unc	BU
1999 Proof	1,000	Value: 425				

Y# 700 100 ROUBLES
15.7200 g., 0.9990 Gold .5049 oz. AGW, 30 mm. **Subject:** Russian Ballet **Obv:** Double-headed eagle **Rev:** Ballerina **Edge:** Reeded

Date	Mintage	F	VF	XF	Unc	BU
1999(sp) Proof	1,500	Value: 425				

Y# 703 100 ROUBLES
17.4500 g., 0.9000 Gold .5049 oz. AGW, 30 mm. **Subject:** Russian Explorer N.M. Przhevalsky **Obv:** Double-headed eagle **Rev:** Two men viewing lake **Edge:** Reeded

Date	Mintage	F	VF	XF	Unc	BU
1999(sp) Proof	1,000	Value: 425				

Y# 713 100 ROUBLES
17.4500 g., 0.9000 Gold .5049 oz. AGW, 30 mm. **Subject:** Department of Mining 300 Years **Obv:** Double-headed eagle **Rev:** Miner and equipment **Edge:** Reeded

Date	Mintage	F	VF	XF	Unc	BU
2000(m) Proof	1,000	Value: 425				

Y# 726 100 ROUBLES
15.7200 g., 0.9990 Gold .5049 oz. AGW, 30 mm. **Obv:** Double-headed eagle **Rev:** Snow leopard on branch **Edge:** Reeded

Date	Mintage	F	VF	XF	Unc	BU
2000(sp) Proof	1,000	Value: 425				

Y# 685 100 ROUBLES
17.4500 g., 0.9000 Gold .5049 oz. AGW, 30 mm. **Subject:** Siberian Exploration **Obv:** Double-headed eagle within beaded circle **Rev:** Head and silhouette left, sailboat and other designs **Edge:** Reeded

Date	Mintage	F	VF	XF	Unc	BU
2001 Proof	1,000	Value: 425				

Y# 688 100 ROUBLES
15.7200 g., 0.9990 Gold .5049 oz. AGW, 30 mm. **Subject:** Bolshoi Theater 225 Years **Obv:** Double-headed eagle within beaded circle **Rev:** Three dancers with swords **Edge:** Reeded

Date	Mintage	F	VF	XF	Unc	BU
2001 Proof	1,500	Value: 425				

Y# 792 100 ROUBLES
17.4500 g., 0.9000 Gold 0.5049 oz. AGW, 30 mm. **Subject:** Hermitage **Obv:** Double-headed eagle within beaded circle **Rev:** Ancient battle scene sculpted on comb **Edge:** Reeded

Date	Mintage	F	VF	XF	Unc	BU
2002(SP) Proof	1,000	Value: 425				

Y# 874 100 ROUBLES
17.4500 g., 0.9000 Gold 0.5049 oz. AGW, 30 mm. **Rev:** Petrozavodsk

Date	Mintage	F	VF	XF	Unc	BU
2003(m) Proof	1,000	Value: 425				

Y# 875 100 ROUBLES
17.4500 g., 0.9000 Gold .5049 oz. AGW, 30 mm. **Rev:** Kamchatka

Date	Mintage	F	VF	XF	Unc	BU
2003(sp) Proof	1,500	Value: 425				

Y# 832 100 ROUBLES
17.2800 g., 0.9000 Gold 0.5 oz. AGW, 30 mm. **Subject:** 2nd Kamchatka Expedition **Obv:** Double-headed eagle **Rev:** Shaman and two seated men **Edge:** Reeded

Date	Mintage	F	VF	XF	Unc	BU
2004(SP) Proof	1,500	Value: 425				

Y# 727 200 ROUBLES
31.3700 g., 0.9990 Gold 1.0076 oz. AGW, 33 mm. **Obv:** Double-headed eagle **Rev:** Snow leopard on branch **Edge:** Reeded

Date	Mintage	F	VF	XF	Unc	BU
2000(sp) Proof	500	Value: 1,000				

Y# 796 1000 ROUBLES
0.9990 Gold, 50 mm. **Subject:** The Bark Sedov **Obv:** Double-headed eagle **Rev:** Four-masted sailing ship **Edge:** Reeded

Date	Mintage	F	VF	XF	Unc	BU
2001(m) Proof	250	—	—	—	—	

Y# 878 1000 ROUBLES
156.4000 g., 0.9990 Gold 5.0233 oz. AGW, 50 mm. **Rev:** Cronstadt

Date	Mintage	F	VF	XF	Unc	BU
2003(m) Proof	250	Value: 4,000				

Y# 728 10000 ROUBLES
822.8449 g., 0.9990 Gold 26.4551 oz. AGW, 100 mm. **Obv:** Double-headed eagle **Rev:** Snow leopard with two cubs **Edge:** Reeded **Note:** Illustration reduced.

Date	Mintage	F	VF	XF	Unc	BU
2000(m) Proof	100	Value: 18,500				

Y# 784 10000 ROUBLES
1001.1000 g., 0.9990 Gold 32.1539 oz. AGW, 100 mm. **Subject:** Works of Dionissy **Obv:** Double-headed eagle **Rev:** Interior view of the carved portal of the Virgin of the Nativity Church **Edge:** Reeded **Note:** Illustration reduced.

Date	Mintage	F	VF	XF	Unc	BU
2002(SP) Prooflike	100	—	—	—	—	23,000

Y# 879 10000 ROUBLES
1001.1000 g., 0.9990 Gold 32.1539 oz. AGW, 100 mm. **Rev:** St. Petersburg area map

Date	Mintage	F	VF	XF	Unc	BU
2003 Proof	200	Value: 25,000				

606 RUSSIA

Y# 880 10000 ROUBLES
1001.1000 g., 0.9990 Gold 32.1539 oz. AGW, 100 mm. **Rev:** Church of the Transfiguration of the Savior, Novgorod

Date	Mintage	F	VF	XF	Unc	BU
2004 Proof	100	Value: 25,000				

Y# 896 10000 ROUBLES
1001.1000 g., 0.9990 Gold 32.1539 oz. AGW, 100 mm. **Subject:** 60th Anniversary - Victory Over Germany **Obv:** Double-headed eagle **Rev:** Soldiers dishonoring captured Nazi flags and standards **Edge:** Reeded

Date	Mintage	F	VF	XF	Unc	BU
2005 Proof	250	Value: 24,000				

Y# 913 10000 ROUBLES
1001.1000 g., 0.9990 Gold 32.1539 oz. AGW, 100 mm. **Obv:** Two headed eagle **Rev:** Kazan Kremlin view **Edge:** Reeded

Date	Mintage	F	VF	XF	Unc	BU
2005	150	—	—	—	—	—

NOVODELS

KM#	Date	Mintage	Identification	Mkt Val
N386	1802СПБ ХЛ	—	10 Roubles. Gold. Oblique milling edge.	10,000
N387	1802СПБ АИ	—	10 Roubles. Gold. Oblique milling edge. Double weight.	65,000
N398	1803СПБ ХЛ	—	5 Roubles. Gold. Oblique milling edge.	35,000
N399	1803СПБ ХЛ	—	10 Roubles. Gold. Oblique milling edge.	35,000
N434	1809СПБ ХЛ	—	10 Roubles. Gold. Oblique milling edge.	70,000

PATTERNS
Including off metal strikes

KM#	Date	Mintage	Identification	Mkt Val
Pn64	ND(1804)	—	1/2 Rouble. Gold.	—
Pn100	1836	—	10 Roubles. Gold. Conjoined busts left. Value, date within beaded circle.	70,000
Pn124	1849MW	—	5 Roubles. Gold. Crowned double imperial eagle. Value, date within circle.	—
Pn141	1886	—	5 Roubles. Gold. Head right. Crowned double imperial eagle, value and date below. Plain edge.	—
Pn142	1895	36	5 Roubles. Gold. Head left. Crowned double imperial eagle, ribbons on crown, within circle. C#A61.	35,000
Pn143	1895	125	10 Roubles. Gold. Head left. Crowned double imperial eagle within circle. C#A63.	35,000
Pn144	1895	5	1/3 Imperial. Gold. Head left. Crowned double imperial eagle, ribbons on crown, within circle. 1/3 Imperial (5 Russ).	30,000
Pn145	1895	5	2/3 Imperial. Gold. Head left. Crowned double imperial eagle, ribbons on crown, within circle. 2/3 Imperial (10 Russ).	45,000
Pn146	1895	5	Imperial. Gold. Head left. Crowned double imperial eagle, ribbons on crown, within circle. Imperial (15 Russ).	45,000
Pn147	1896	5	5 Roubles. Gold. C#A61.	40,000
Pn148	1896	125	10 Roubles. Gold. Head left. Crowned double imperial eagle, ribbons on crown, within circle. C#A63.	35,000
Pn396	ND	—	100 Roubles. 0.9000 Gold. Y#162	—

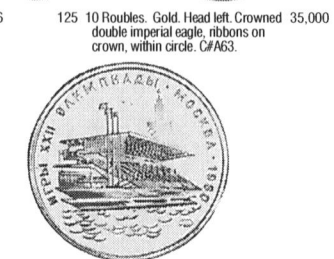

Note: Pn390-Pn396 minor varieties exist

MINT SETS

KM#	Date	Mintage	Identification	Issue Price	Mkt Val
MS33	1991 (3)	—	Y#268-270	245	1,950
MS35	1993 (3)	2,700	Y#416-419	—	960
MS36	1993 (3)	3,000	Y#420-422	—	1,950
MS37	1994 (3)	2,000	Y#431-433	—	1,950

PROOF SETS

KM#	Date	Mintage	Identification	Issue Price	Mkt Val
PS1	Mixed dates (5)	—	Y#152, 163, 175-176, 187	—	1,500
PS5	1991 (3)	1,500	Y#286a-288a	—	1,450
PS6	1993 (4)	1,500	Y#416-419	—	1,230
PS7	1993 (3)	750	Y#395-397	—	725
PS8	1993 (3)	2,000	Y#420-422	—	2,050
PS10	1994 (4)	2,500	Y#424-427	—	1,255
PS11	1994 (3)	900	Y#428-430	—	1,360
PS12	1994 (3)	1,500	Y#431-433	—	2,050
PS14	1995 (4)	2,500	Y#438-441	1,250	1,250
PS15	1995 (3)	1,500	Y#435-437	875	875
PS16	1995 (3)	900	Y#442-444	1,350	1,350

RUSSIA (KALININGRAD) ENCLAVE (OBLAST)

MEDALLIC COINAGE

X# 3 20 MAROK
12.1000 g., 0.5850 Gold 0.2276 oz. AGW, 28 mm. **Series:** Glory of Russian Arms **Obv:** Value in sprays **Obv. Legend:** ЗАПАДНЫЙ АНКЛАВ РОССИИ - КАЛИНИНГРАД **Rev:** Kalachnikov AK-47 Assault Rifle **Rev. Legend:** ★★★ РУССОГО ОРУЖИЯ ★★★ **Rev. Inscription:** СЛАВА **Edge:** Plain

Date	Mintage	F	VF	XF	Unc	BU
2002 Proof	8	Value: 1,250				

X# 6 20 MAROK
11.6000 g., 0.5850 Gold 0.2182 oz. AGW, 28 mm. **Series:** Glory of Russian Arms **Obv:** Value in sprays **Obv. Legend:** ЗАПАДНЫЙ АНКЛАВ РОССИИ - КАЛИНИНГРАД **Rev:** K-50 Helicopter **Rev. Legend:** ★★★ РУССОГО ОРУЖИЯ ★★★ **Rev. Inscription:** СЛАВА **Edge:** Reeded

Date	Mintage	F	VF	XF	Unc	BU
2003 Proof	8	Value: 1,250				

X# 9 20 MAROK
11.6000 g., 0.5850 Gold 0.2182 oz. AGW, 28 mm. **Series:** Glory of Russian Arms **Obv:** Value in sprays **Obv. Legend:** ЗАПАДНЫЙ АНКЛАВ РОССИИ - КАЛИНИНГРАД **Rev:** T-34 Tank **Rev. Legend:** ★★★ РУССОГО ОРУЖИЯ ★★★ **Rev. Inscription:** СЛАВА

Date	Mintage	F	VF	XF	Unc	BU
2003 Proof	8	Value: 1,250				

X# 12 20 MAROK
11.6000 g., 0.5850 Gold 0.2182 oz. AGW, 28 mm. **Series:** Glory of Russian Arms **Obv:** Value in sprays **Obv. Legend:** ЗАПАДНЫЙ АНКЛАВ РОССИИ - КАЛИНИНГРАД **Rev:** MiG-29 Jet Fighter **Rev. Legend:** ★★★ РУССОГО ОРУЖИЯ ★★★ **Rev. Inscription:** СЛАВА **Edge:** Reeded

Date	Mintage	F	VF	XF	Unc	BU
2003 Proof	8	Value: 1,250				

X# 18 20 MAROK
11.6000 g., 0.5850 Gold 0.2182 oz. AGW, 28 mm. **Series:** Glory of Russian Arms **Obv:** Value in sprays **Obv. Legend:** ЗАПАДНЫЙ АНКЛАВ РОССИИ - КАЛИНИНГРАД **Rev:** S-13 Submarine **Rev. Legend:** ★★★ РУССОГО ОРУЖИЯ ★★★ **Rev. Inscription:** СЛАВА **Edge:** Reeded

Date	Mintage	F	VF	XF	Unc	BU
2003 Proof	8	Value: 1,250				

X# 21 20 MAROK
11.6000 g., 0.5850 Gold 0.2182 oz. AGW, 28 mm. **Series:** Glory of Russian Arms **Obv:** Value in sprays **Obv. Legend:** ЗАПАДНЫЙ АНКЛАВ РОССИИ - КАЛИНИНГРАД **Rev:** BTR Armored Personel Carrier **Rev. Legend:** ★★★ РУССОГО ОРУЖИЯ ★★★ **Rev. Inscription:** СЛАВА **Edge:** Reeded

Date	Mintage	F	VF	XF	Unc	BU
2003 Proof	8	Value: 1,250				

X# 27 20 MAROK
11.6000 g., 0.5850 Gold 0.2182 oz. AGW, 28 mm. **Series:** Glory of Russian Arms **Obv:** Value in sprays **Obv. Legend:** ЗАПАДНЫЙ АНКЛАВ РОССИИ - КАЛИНИНГРАД **Rev:** 45mm Field Cannon **Rev. Legend:** ★★★ РУССОГО ОРУЖИЯ ★★★ **Rev. Inscription:** СЛАВА **Edge:** Reeded

Date	Mintage	F	VF	XF	Unc	BU
2003 Proof	8	Value: 1,250				

RWANDA

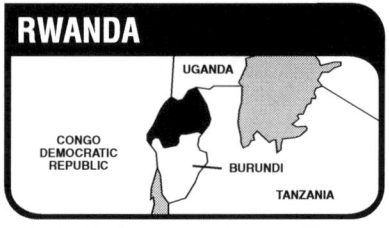

The Republic of Rwanda, located in central Africa between the Republic of the Congo and Tanzania, has an area of 10,169 sq. mi. (26,340 sq. km.) and a population of 7.3 million. Capital: Kigali. The economy is based on agriculture and mining. Coffee and tin are exported.

German Lieutenant Count von Goetzen was the first European to visit Rwanda, 1894. Four years later the court of the Mwami (the Tutsi king of Rwanda) willingly permitted the kingdom to become a protectorate of Germany. In 1916, during the African campaigns of World War I, Belgian troops from Congo occupied Rwanda. After the war it, together with Burundi, became a Belgian League of Nations mandate under the name of the Territory of Ruanda-Urundi. Following World War II, Ruanda-Urundi became a Belgian administered U.N. trust territory. The Tutsi monarchy was deposed by the U.N. supervised election of 1961, after which Belgium granted Rwanda internal autonomy. On July 1, 1962, the U.N. terminated the Belgian trusteeship and granted full independence to both Rwanda and Burundi.

For earlier coinage see Belgian Congo, and Rwanda and Burundi.

MINT MARKS
(a) - Paris, privy marks only
(b) - Brussels, privy marks only

MONETARY SYSTEM
100 Centimes = 1 Franc

REPUBLIC

STANDARD COINAGE

KM# 1 10 FRANCS
3.0000 g., 0.9000 Gold .1085 oz. AGW **Obv:** Value above flag draped arms **Rev:** Head 3/4 right

Date	Mintage	VG	F	VF	XF	Unc
1965	10,000	—	—	—	—	85.00
1965 Proof	—	Value: 90.00				

KM# 2 25 FRANCS
7.5000 g., 0.9000 Gold .2170 oz. AGW **Obv:** Value above flag draped arms **Rev:** Head 3/4 right **Note:** Similar to 10 Francs, KM#1.

Date	Mintage	F	VF	XF	Unc	BU
1965 Proof	4,000	Value: 180				

KM# 3 50 FRANCS
15.0000 g., 0.9000 Gold .4340 oz. AGW **Obv:** Value above flag draped arms **Rev:** Head 3/4 right **Note:** Similar to 10 Francs, KM#1.

Date	Mintage	F	VF	XF	Unc	BU
1965 Proof	3,000	Value: 325				

KM# 4 100 FRANCS
30.0000 g., 0.9000 Gold .8681 oz. AGW **Obv:** Value above flag draped arms **Rev:** Head 3/4 right

Date	Mintage	F	VF	XF	Unc	BU
1965 Proof	3,000	Value: 625				

KM# 19 2000 FRANCS
7.8000 g., 0.9990 Gold .25 oz. AGW **Subject:** Nelson Mandela **Obv:** Flag draped arms above value **Rev:** Head facing **Note:** Similar to 5,000 Francs, KM#20.

Date	Mintage	F	VF	XF	Unc	BU
1990 Proof	Est. 50,000	Value: 225				

KM# 20 5000 FRANCS
15.5300 g., 0.9990 Gold .5 oz. AGW **Subject:** Nelson Mandela **Obv:** Value below flag draped arms **Rev:** Head facing

Date	Mintage	F	VF	XF	Unc	BU
1990 Proof	3,000	Value: 450				

PROOF SETS

KM#	Date	Mintage	Identification	Issue Price	Mkt Val
PS1	1965(a) (4)	3,000	KM1-4	—	1,225

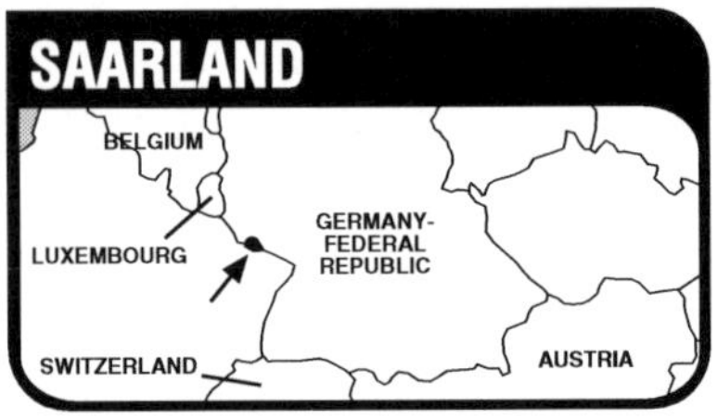

SAARLAND

The Saar, the 10th state of the German Federal Republic, is located in the coal-rich Saar basin on the Franco-German frontier, and has an area of 991 sq. mi. and a population of 1.2 million. Capital: Saarbrucken. It is an important center of mining and heavy industry.

From the late 14th century until the fall of Napoleon, the city of Saarbrucken was ruled by the counts of Nassau-Saarbrucken, but the surrounding territory was subject to the political and cultural domination of France. At the close of the Napoleonic era, the Saarland came under the control of Prussia. France was awarded the Saar coal mines following World War I, and the Saarland was made an autonomous territory of the League of Nations, its future political affiliation to be determined by referendum. The plebiscite, 1935, chose re-incorporation into Germany. France reoccupied the Saarland, 1945, establishing strong economic ties and assuming the obligation of defense and foreign affairs. After sustained agitation by West Germany, France agreed, 1955, to there turn of the Saar to Germany by Jan. 1957.

MINT MARK
(a) - Paris - privy marks only

ESSAIS
Standard metals unless otherwise noted

KM#	Date	Mintage	Identification	Issue Price	Mkt Val
E2	1954(a)	—	10 Franken. Gold. KM1. Reported, not confirmed.	—	—
E4	1954(a)	50	20 Franken. Gold. KM2.	—	2,000
E6	1954(a)	—	50 Franken. Gold. KM3. Reported, not confirmed.	—	—
E7	1955(a)	50	100 Franken. Gold. Arms within circular design. Value. KM4.	—	2,500

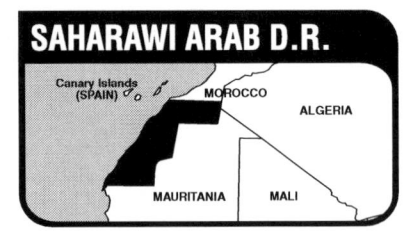

SAHARAWI ARAB D.R.

The Saharawi Arab Democratic Republic, located in northwest Africa has an area of 102,703 sq. mi. and a population (census taken 1974) of 76,425. Formerly known as Spanish Sahara, the area is bounded on the north by Morocco, on the east and southeast by Mauritania, on the northeast by Algeria, and on the west by the Atlantic Ocean. Capital: El Aaium. Agriculture, fishing and mining are the three main industries. Exports are barley, livestock and phosphates.

A Spanish trading post was established in 1476 but was abandoned in 1524. A Spanish protectorate for the region was proclaimed in 1884. The status of the Spanish Sahara changed from a colony to an overseas province in 1958. Spain relinquished its holdings in 1975 and it was divided between Mauritania, which gave up its claim in August 1979 and Morocco, which subsequently occupied the entire territory. The official languages are Spanish and an Arab dialect: The Hassaniya.

DEMOCRATIC REPUBLIC

NON-CIRCULATING COLLECTOR COINAGE

KM# 51a   500 PESETAS
Bi-Metallic .999Silver center in .999 Gold plated .999 Silver ring, 26 mm. **Obv:** National arms within circle **Rev:** Two Fennec foxes within circle **Edge:** Segmented reeded

Date	Mintage	F	VF	XF	Unc	BU
2004	25	—	—	—	235	250

KM# 52a   500 PESETAS
Bi-Metallic .999 Silver center in .999 Gold plated .999 Silver ring, 26 mm. **Obv:** National arms within circle **Rev:** Independence map divides circle **Edge:** Segmented reeding

Date	Mintage	F	VF	XF	Unc	BU
2004	25	—	—	—	235	250

KM# 6   1000 PESETAS
3.1000 g., 0.9990 Gold .1000 oz. AGW **Series:** Transportation **Obv:** National arms **Rev:** Arab walking with camel **Note:** Similar to 500 Pesetas, KM#2.

Date	Mintage	F	VF	XF	Unc	BU
1991	508	—	—	—	145	165

KM# 38   40000 PESETAS
15.5200 g., 0.9000 Gold .4491 oz. AGW **Subject:** 20th Anniversary - Diplomacy between Venezuela and Saharawi Arab Democratic Republic **Obv:** Arms of Venezuela and Saharawi Arab Democratic Republic **Rev:** Bolivar and El Uali

Date	Mintage	F	VF	XF	Unc	BU
1997 Proof	90	Value: 1,000				

KM# 38a   40000 PESETAS
15.5000 g., 0.9990 Gold .4978 oz. AGW **Subject:** 20th Anniversary - Diplomacy between Venezuela and Saharawi Arab Democratic Republic **Obv:** Arms of Venezuela and Saharawi Arab Democratic Republic **Rev:** Bolivar and El Uali

Date	Mintage	F	VF	XF	Unc	BU
1997 Proof, Rare	10	—	—	—	—	—

PATTERNS

KM#	Date	Mintage	Identification	Mkt Val
Pn2	1997	8	40000 Pesetas. Copper. KM#38.	3,000
Pn3	1997	8	40000 Pesetas. Silver. KM#38.	3,000

PIEFORTS

KM#	Date	Mintage	Identification	Mkt Val
P2	1997	8	40000 Pesetas. Gold. KM#38.	6,000

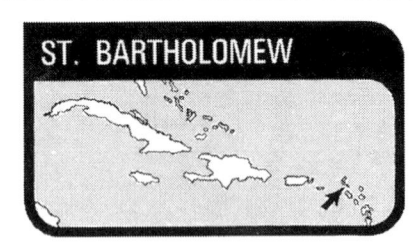

ST. BARTHOLOMEW

FRENCH COLONY

ESSAIS

X# E15   20 EURO
8.5300 g., 0.9167 Gold 0.2514 oz. AGW, 27.1 mm. **Series:** Euro **Obv:** Arms **Rev:** Pied-billed Grebe **Rev. Legend:** Protection de la Faune **Edge:** Plain

Date	Mintage	F	VF	XF	Unc	BU
2004 Proof	300	Value: 300				

SAINT HELENA

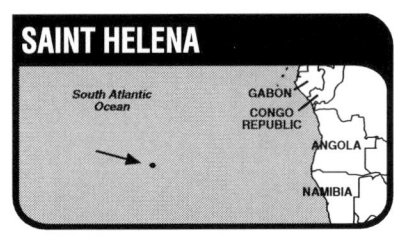

Saint Helena, a British colony located about 1,150 miles (1,850 km.) from the west coast of Africa, has an area of 47 sq. mi. (410 sq. km.) and a population of *7,000. Capital: Jamestown. Flax, lace, and rope are produced for export. Ascension and Tristan da Cunha are dependencies of Saint Helena.

The island was discovered and named by the Portuguese navigator Joao de Nova Castella in 1502. The Portuguese imported livestock, fruit trees, and vegetables but established no permanent settlement. The Dutch occupied the island temporarily, 1645-51. The original European settlement was founded by representatives of the British East India Company sent to annex the island after the departure of the Dutch. The Dutch returned and captured Saint Helena from the British on New Year's Day, 1673, but were in turn ejected by a British force under Sir Richard Munden. Thereafter Saint Helena was the undisputed possession of Great Britain. The island served as the place of exile for Napoleon, several Zulu chiefs, and an ex-sultan of Zanzibar.

RULER
British

MINT MARK
PM - Pobjoy Mint

MONETARY SYSTEM
12 Pence = 1 Shilling
100 Pence = 1 Pound

BRITISH COLONY

STANDARD COINAGE

KM# 12b 50 PENCE
47.5400 g., 0.9170 Gold 1.4017 oz. AGW, 38.5 mm. **Ruler:** Elizabeth II **Subject:** 150th Anniversary - Saint Helena Colony **Obv:** Young bust right **Rev:** Half figure above crowned shield flanked by designs

Date	Mintage	VG	F	VF	XF	Unc
ND(1984) Proof	150	Value: 985				

KM# 14b 50 PENCE
47.5400 g., 0.9160 Gold 1.4011 oz. AGW, 38.5 mm. **Ruler:** Elizabeth II **Subject:** Queen Mother **Obv:** Crowned bust right **Rev:** Queen Mother and equestrian within circle

Date	Mintage	VG	F	VF	XF	Unc
1995 Proof	150	Value: 1,000				

KM# 22b 50 PENCE
47.5400 g., 0.9166 Gold 1.401 oz. AGW, 38.6 mm. **Ruler:** Elizabeth II **Obv:** Crowned bust right **Rev:** Crowned bust of the Queen Mother right **Edge:** Reeded

Date	Mintage	F	VF	XF	Unc	BU
ND(2000) Proof	100	Value: 1,050				

KM# 19b 50 PENCE
47.5400 g., 0.9166 Gold 1.401 oz. AGW, 38.6 mm. **Ruler:** Elizabeth II **Subject:** 75th Birthday of Queen Elizabeth II **Obv:** Crowned bust right **Rev:** Bust facing within circle and rose sprigs **Edge:** Reeded

Date	Mintage	F	VF	XF	Unc	BU
2001 Proof	75	Value: 1,100				

KM# 20b 50 PENCE
47.5400 g., 0.9166 Gold 1.401 oz. AGW, 38.6 mm. **Ruler:** Elizabeth II **Subject:** Centennial - Death of Queen Victoria **Obv:** Crowned bust right **Rev:** Half-length figure facing and ship within circle **Edge:** Reeded

Date	Mintage	F	VF	XF	Unc	BU
2001 Proof	100	Value: 1,050				

KM# 30b 50 PENCE
39.9400 g., 0.9166 Gold 1.177 oz. AGW, 38.6 mm. **Ruler:** Elizabeth II **Subject:** 50th Anniversary of Queen's Coronation **Obv:** Crowned bust right **Rev:** Crowned Queen facing with scepter and orb **Edge:** Reeded

Date	Mintage	F	VF	XF	Unc	BU
ND(2003) Proof	50	Value: 975				

KM# 31b 50 PENCE
39.9400 g., 0.9166 Gold 1.177 oz. AGW, 38.6 mm. **Ruler:** Elizabeth II **Subject:** 50th Anniversary of Coronation **Obv:** Crowned bust right **Rev:** Coronation implements **Edge:** Reeded

Date	Mintage	F	VF	XF	Unc	BU
ND(2003) Proof	50	Value: 975				

KM# 11 2 POUNDS
15.9800 g., 0.9170 Gold .4712 oz. AGW **Ruler:** Elizabeth II **Series:** International Year of the Scout **Obv:** Young bust right **Rev:** Scouts and tent

Date	Mintage	VG	F	VF	XF	Unc
ND(1983)	2,000	—	—	—	—	450
ND(1983) Proof	2,000	Value: 500				

SAINT HELENA & ASCENSION

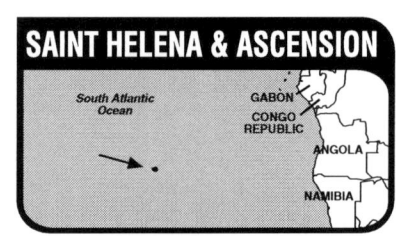

STANDARD COINAGE

100 Pence = 1 Pound

KM# 7b 50 PENCE
47.5400 g., 0.9170 Gold 1.4017 oz. AGW, 38.5 mm. **Ruler:** Queen Elizabeth II **Subject:** Wedding of Prince Andrew and Sarah Ferguson **Obv:** Crowned bust right **Rev:** Conjoined busts of couple right within circle

Date	Mintage	F	VF	XF	Unc	BU
ND(1986) Proof	50	Value: 1,150				

KM# 10 50 POUNDS
32.2600 g., 0.9990 Platinum 1.0051 oz. APW **Ruler:** Queen Elizabeth II **Subject:** 165th Anniversary of Napoleon's Death **Obv:** Crowned bust right **Rev:** Sailing ship at right and 1/2 figure at left looking right **Note:** Similar to KM#9.

Date	Mintage	F	VF	XF	Unc	BU
1986 Proof	5,000	Value: 1,350				

610 SAINT KITTS & NEVIS

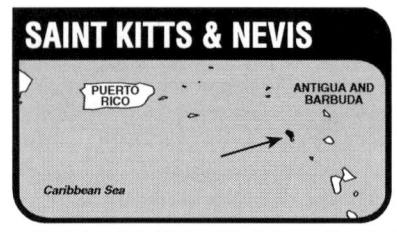

SAINT KITTS & NEVIS

This independent state, located in the Leeward Islands of the West Indies, south of Puerto Rico, comprises the islands of St. Kitts, Nevis and Anguilla. The country has an area of 101 sq. mi. (261 sq. km.) and a population of 41,000. Capital: Basseterre, on St. Kitts (as it may be called in abbreviated form). The islands export sugar, cotton, lobsters, beverages and electrical equipment.

St. Kitts was discovered by Columbus in 1493 and was settled by Thomas Warner, an Englishman, in 1623. The Treaty of Utrecht, 1713, ceded the island to the British. France protested British occupancy, and on three occasions between 1616 and 1782 seized the island and held it for short periods. St. Kitts used the coins and currency of the British Caribbean Territories (Eastern Group).

In early 1967 the Colony was, together with the islands of Nevis and Anguilla, united politically as a self-governing British Associated State. However, in June 1967 Anguilla declared its independence, severing ties with Britain and established a so-called "Republic of Anguilla". Britain refused to accept this and established a Commissioner to govern Anguilla; this arrangement continues to the present time.

St. Kitts and Nevis became a member of the Commonwealth of Nations on Sept. 19, 1983. Queen Elizabeth II is Head of State.

From approximately 1750-1830, billon 2 sous of the French colony of Cayenne were countermarked SK' and used on St. Kitts. They were valued at 1-1/2 Pence Sterling. (St. Kitts and Nevis now use East Caribbean Currency.)

RULER
British

MONETARY SYSTEM
100 Cents = 1 East Caribbean Dollar

BRITISH ASSOCIATED STATE
STANDARD COINAGE

100 Cents = 1 Dollar

KM# 3b   10 DOLLARS
47.5400 g., 0.9170 Gold 1.4013 oz. AGW, 38.8 mm. **Subject:** Royal Visit **Obv:** Crowned bust right **Obv. Designer:** Raphael Maklouf **Rev:** Crowned arms with supporters

Date	Mintage	F	VF	XF	Unc	BU
1985 Proof	250			Value: 1,150		

KM# 5   100 DOLLARS
7.9900 g., 0.9170 Gold .2356 oz. AGW **Subject:** 200th Anniversary - Siege of Brimstone Hill **Rev:** Brimstone hill

Date	Mintage	F	VF	XF	Unc	BU
ND(1982)	250	—	—	—	200	220
ND(1982) Proof	15	Value: 675				

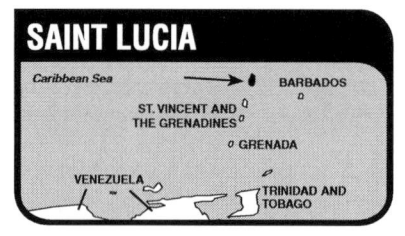

SAINT LUCIA

Saint Lucia, an independent island nation located in the Windward Islands of the West Indies between Saint Vincent and Martinique, has an area of 238 sq. mi. (620 sq. km.) and a population of *150,000. Capital: Castries. The economy is agricultural. Bananas, copra, cocoa, sugar and logwood are exported.

Columbus discovered Saint Lucia in 1502. The first attempts at settlement undertaken by the British in 1605 and 1638 were frustrated by sickness and the determined hostility of the fierce Carib inhabitants. The French settled it in 1650 and made a treaty with the natives. Until 1814, when the island became a definite British possession, it was the scene of a continuous conflict between the British and French, which saw the island change, hands on at least 14 occasions. In 1967, under the West Indies Act, Saint Lucia was established as a British associated state, self-governing in internal affairs. Complete independence was attained on February 22, 1979. Saint Lucia is a member of the Commonwealth of Nations. Elizabeth II is Head of State as Queen of Saint Lucia.

Prior to 1950, the island used sterling, which was superseded by the currency of the British Caribbean Territories (Eastern Group) and the East Caribbean State.

RULER
British

MONETARY SYSTEM
100 Cents = 1 Dollar

BRITISH ASSOCIATED STATE
MODERN COINAGE

100 Cents = 1 Dollar

KM# 13b   10 DOLLARS
47.5400 g., 0.9170 Gold 1.4013 oz. AGW, 38.8 mm. **Subject:** Royal Visit - Queen Elizabeth II **Obv:** Crowned bust right **Obv. Designer:** Raphael Maklouf **Rev:** Crowned arms with supporters **Rev. Legend:** • ROYAL VISIT 1985 • TEN DOLLARS below

Date	Mintage	F	VF	XF	Unc	BU
1985 Proof	250			Value: 1,150		

KM# 15   500 DOLLARS
15.9800 g., 0.9170 Gold .4709 oz. AGW **Subject:** Papal Visit - John Paul II **Obv:** Crowned arms with supporters within circle **Rev:** Bust left **Rev. Legend:** • PAPAL VISIT JULY 1986 •

Date	Mintage	F	VF	XF	Unc	BU
1986 Proof	100			Value: 850		

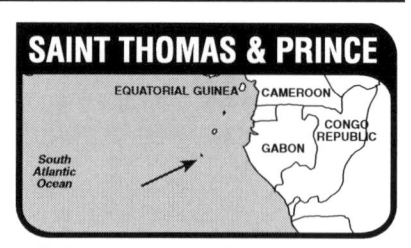

SAINT THOMAS & PRINCE

The Democratic Republic of St. Thomas & Prince (São Tomé e Príncipe) is located in the Gulf of Guinea 150 miles (241 km.) off the western coast of Africa. It has an area of 372 sq. mi. (960 sq. km.) and a population of *121,000. Capital: São Tomé. The economy of the islands is based on cocoa, copra and coffee.

Saint Thomas and Saint Prince were uninhabited when discovered by Portuguese navigators Joao de Santarem and Pedro de Escobar in 1470. After the failure of their initial settlement of 1485, the Portuguese successfully colonized St. Thomas with a colony of prisoners and exiled Jews in 1493. An initial prosperity based on the sugar trade gave way to a time of misfortune, 1567-1709, that saw the colony attacked and occupied or plundered by the French and Dutch, ravaged by the slave revolt of 1595; and finally rendered destitute by the transfer of the world sugar trade to Brazil. In the late 1800s, the colony turned from the production of sugar to cocoa, the basis of its present economy

The islands were designated a Portuguese overseas province in 1951. On April 25, 1974, the government of Portugal was seized by a military junta, which reached agreements providing for independence for the Portuguese overseas provinces of Portuguese Guinea (Guinea-Bissau), Mozambique, Cape Verde Islands, Angola, and Saint Thomas and Prince Islands. The Democratic Republic of São Tomé and Principe was declared on July 12, 1975.

RULERS
Portuguese, until 1975

MINT MARKS
R – Rio

MONETARY SYSTEM
100 Centavos = 1 Escudo

DEMOCRATIC REPUBLIC
STANDARD COINAGE

100 Centimos = 1 Dobra

KM# 41b   100 DOBRAS
47.5400 g., 0.9170 Gold 1.4017 oz. AGW **Subject:** World Fisheries Conference **Obv:** Arms with supporters **Rev:** Figure standing in boat with fish net

Date	Mintage	F	VF	XF	Unc	BU
ND(1984) Proof	100			Value: 1,250		

KM# 42b   100 DOBRAS
47.5400 g., 0.9170 Gold 1.4017 oz. AGW **Subject:** 10th Anniversary of Independence **Obv:** Arms with supporters **Rev:** Value, stars and map

Date	Mintage	F	VF	XF	Unc	BU
ND(1985) Proof	50			Value: 1,400		

KM# 102 1000 DOBRAS
1.2500 g., 0.9990 Gold .0402 oz. AGW **Subject:** Diana - Queen of the Hearts **Obv:** Arms with supporters **Rev:** Bust with hat left **Note:** Prev. KM#85.2.

Date	Mintage	F	VF	XF	Unc	BU
1997 Proof	3,000	Value: 60.00				

KM# 36 2500 DOBRAS
6.4800 g., 0.9000 Gold .1875 oz. AGW **Subject:** Independence **Obv:** Arms with supporters **Rev:** World friendship

Date	Mintage	F	VF	XF	Unc	BU
1977	100	—	—	—	225	250
1977 Proof	170	Value: 200				

KM# 37 2500 DOBRAS
6.4800 g., 0.9000 Gold .1875 oz. AGW **Subject:** Independence - World Population **Obv:** Arms with supporters **Rev:** World population

Date	Mintage	F	VF	XF	Unc	BU
1977	100	—	—	—	225	250
1977 Proof	170	Value: 200				

KM# 38 2500 DOBRAS
6.4800 g., 0.9000 Gold .1875 oz. AGW **Subject:** Independence **Obv:** Arms with supporters **Rev:** Folklore monument

Date	Mintage	F	VF	XF	Unc	BU
1977	100	—	—	—	225	250
1977 Proof	170	Value: 200				

KM# 39 2500 DOBRAS
6.4800 g., 0.9000 Gold .1875 oz. AGW **Subject:** Independence **Obv:** Arms with supporters **Rev:** World unity

Date	Mintage	F	VF	XF	Unc	BU
1977	100	—	—	—	225	250
1977 Proof	170	Value: 200				

KM# 40 2500 DOBRAS
6.4800 g., 0.9000 Gold .1875 oz. AGW **Subject:** Independence **Obv:** Arms with supporters **Rev:** Mother and child

Date	Mintage	F	VF	XF	Unc	BU
1977	100	—	—	—	225	250
1977 Proof	170	Value: 200				

KM# 83 2500 DOBRAS
6.2207 g., 0.9999 Gold .2000 oz. AGW **Obv:** Arms with supporters **Rev:** Hummingbird hologram **Note:** Similar to 1,000 Dobras, KM#80.

Date	Mintage	F	VF	XF	Unc	BU
1998(1997) Proof	2,500	Value: 250				

KM# 84 2500 DOBRAS
6.2207 g., 0.9999 Gold .2000 oz. AGW **Obv:** Arms with supporters **Rev:** Butterfly hologram **Note:** Similar to 1,000 Dobras, KM#82.

Date	Mintage	F	VF	XF	Unc	BU
1998(1997) Proof	2,500	Value: 250				

KM# 51 10000 DOBRAS
7.7750 g., 0.9000 Gold .2250 oz. AGW **Obv:** Arms with supporters **Rev:** Sea turtle

Date	Mintage	F	VF	XF	Unc	BU
1992 Proof	500	Value: 325				

KM# 72 25000 DOBRAS
15.5500 g., 0.9990 Gold .5 oz. AGW **Obv:** Arms with supporters **Rev:** Elvis Presley

Date	Mintage	F	VF	XF	Unc	BU
1993 Proof	—	Value: 550				

DUAL DENOMINATED COINAGE

KM# 69 25000 DOBRAS - 50 ECU
6.7200 g., 0.9000 Gold .1944 oz. AGW **Subject:** 15th Anniversary of Association With European Common Market **Obv:** Arms with supporters **Rev:** Old harbor scene **Note:** Similar to 2500 Dobras, 5 Ecu, KM#68.

Date	Mintage	F	VF	XF	Unc	BU
1993 Proof	1,000	Value: 220				

MINT SETS

KM#	Date	Mintage	Identification	Issue Price	Mkt Val
MS2	1977 (5)	100	KM36-40	655	1,250

PROOF SETS

KM#	Date	Mintage	Identification	Issue Price	Mkt Val
PS2	1977 (5)	170	KM36-40	805	1,000

SAINT VINCENT

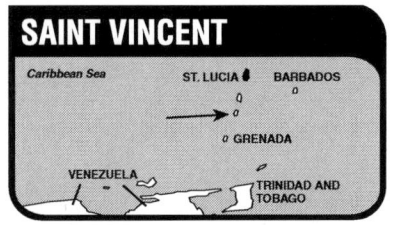

Saint Vincent and the Grenadines, consisting of the island of Saint Vincent and the northern Grenadines (a string of islets stretching southward from Saint Vincent), is located in the Windward Islands of the West Indies, West of Barbados and south of Saint Lucia. The tiny nation has an area of 150sq. mi. (340 sq. km.) and a population of *105,000. Capital: Kingstown. Arrowroot, cotton, sugar, molasses, rum and cocoa are exported. Tourism is a principal industry.

Saint Vincent was discovered by Columbus on Jan. 22, 1498, but was left undisturbed for more than a century. The British began colonization early in the 18th century against bitter and prolonged Carib resistance. The island was taken by the French in 1779, but was restored to the British in 1783, at the end of the American Revolution. Saint Vincent and the northern Grenadines became a British associated state in Oct. 1969. Independence under the name of Saint Vincent and the Grenadines was attained at midnight of Oct. 26, 1979. The new nation chose to become a member of the Commonwealth of Nations with Elizabeth II as Head of State and Queen of Saint Vincent.

A local coinage was introduced in 1797, with the gold withdrawn in 1818 and the silver in 1823. This was replaced by sterling. From the mid-1950's, Saint Vincent used the currency of the British Caribbean Territories (Eastern Group), than that of the East Caribbean States.

RULER
British

MONETARY SYSTEM
6 Black Dogs = 4 Stampees = 1 Bit = 9 Pence
1797-1811
8 Shillings, 3 Pence = 11 Bits = 1 Dollar

BRITISH COLONY
MODERN COINAGE

KM# 14b 10 DOLLARS
47.5400 g., 0.9170 Gold 1.4013 oz. AGW **Subject:** Royal Visit **Obv:** Crowned bust right **Rev:** Flower above shield within circle

Date	Mintage	F	VF	XF	Unc	BU
1985 Proof	250	Value: 1,050				

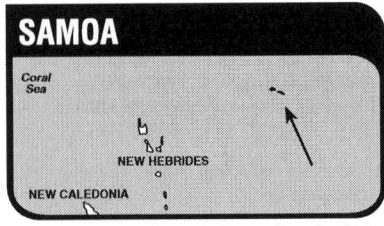

SAMOA

The Independent State of Samoa (formerly Western Samoa), located in the Pacific Ocean 1,600 miles (2,574 km.) northeast of New Zealand, has an area of 1,097 sq. mi. (2,860 sq. km.) and a population of *182,000. Capital: Apia. The economy is based on agriculture, fishing and tourism. Copra, cocoa and bananas are exported.

The first European to sight the Samoan group of islands was the Dutch navigator Jacob Roggeveen in 1722. Great Britain, the United States and Germany established consular representation at Apia in 1847, 1853 and 1861 respectively. The conflicting interests of the three powers produced the Berlin agreement of 1889, which declared Samoa neutral and had the effect of establishing a tripartite protectorate over the islands. A further agreement, 1899, recognized the rights of the United States in those islands east of 171 deg. west longitude (American Samoa) and of Germany in the other islands (Western Samoa). New Zealand occupied Western Samoa at the start of World War I and administered it as a League of Nations mandate and U. N. trusteeship until Jan. 1, 1962, when it became an independent state.

Samoa is a member of the Commonwealth of Nations. The Chief Executive is Chief of State. The prime minister is the Head of Government. The present Head of State, Malietoa Tanumafili II, holds his position for life. The Legislative Assembly will elect future Heads of State for 5-year terms.

Samoa, which had used New Zealand coinage, converted to a decimal coinage in 1967.

RULERS
British, until 1962
Malietoa Tanumafili II, 1962—

MONETARY SYSTEM
100 Sene = 1 Tala

INDEPENDENT STATE

STANDARD COINAGE

KM# 113   10 TALA
1.2442 g., 0.9999 Gold .04 oz. AGW **Series:** Olympics **Obv:** National arms **Rev:** Discus thrower

Date	Mintage	F	VF	XF	Unc	BU
1995	Est. 25,000	—	—	—	45.00	—

KM# 76   50 TALA
31.1030 g., 0.9990 Palladium 1 oz. **Subject:** Kon-Tiki **Obv:** National arms **Rev:** Raft and bamboo poles

Date	Mintage	F	VF	XF	Unc	BU
1988 Proof	6,500	Value: 450				

KM# 78   50 TALA
7.7700 g., 0.9990 Gold .25 oz. AGW **Subject:** Trans-Antarctica Expedition **Obv:** Sled dogs and musher and single dog head facing left **Rev:** Six doves above snake on rock, value at upper left

Date	Mintage	F	VF	XF	Unc	BU
1988 Proof	30,000	Value: 175				

KM# 90   50 TALA
7.7760 g., 0.5833 Gold .1458 oz. AGW **Series:** 1996 Olympics **Obv:** National arms **Rev:** Discus thrower

Date	Mintage	F	VF	XF	Unc	BU
1993 Proof	7,500	Value: 115				

KM# 92   50 TALA
7.7760 g., 0.5833 Gold .1458 oz. AGW **Subject:** World Cup Soccer **Obv:** National arms **Rev:** Soccer players

Date	Mintage	F	VF	XF	Unc	BU
1993 Proof	Est. 3,000	Value: 115				

KM# 106   50 TALA
7.7760 g., 0.5833 Gold .1458 oz. AGW **Obv:** National arms **Rev:** Portrait

Date	Mintage	F	VF	XF	Unc	BU
1993 Proof	Est. 3,000	Value: 115				

KM# 107   50 TALA
7.7760 g., 0.5833 Gold .1458 oz. AGW **Subject:** The Endeavor **Obv:** National arms **Rev:** Sailing ship within radiant sun

Date	Mintage	F	VF	XF	Unc	BU
1994 Proof	Est. 2,500	Value: 115				

KM# 108   50 TALA
7.7760 g., 0.5833 Gold .1458 oz. AGW **Series:** Endangered Wildlife **Obv:** National arms **Rev:** Dolphins

Date	Mintage	F	VF	XF	Unc	BU
1995 Proof	Est. 2,500	Value: 125				

KM# 119   50 TALA
3.8875 g., 0.9990 Gold .25 oz. AGW **Subject:** Tempora Mutantur **Obv:** National arms **Rev:** Man with torch **Note:** 1/2 of 2-part coin, combined with Kiribati KM#26, issued in sets only; Value is determined by combining the 2 parts.

Date	Mintage	F	VF	XF	Unc	BU
ND(1997) Proof	Est. 2,500	Value: 175				

KM# 21   100 TALA
15.5500 g., 0.9170 Gold .4583 oz. AGW **Subject:** U.S. Bicentennial **Obv:** National arms **Rev:** Equestrian and USA map **Rev. Designer:** James Berry

Date	Mintage	F	VF	XF	Unc	BU
1976 Proof	2,000	Value: 320				

KM# 23   100 TALA
15.5500 g., 0.9170 Gold .4583 oz. AGW **Series:** Montreal Olympics **Obv:** National arms **Rev:** Weight lifter

Date	Mintage	F	VF	XF	Unc	BU
1976 Proof	2,500	Value: 320				

KM# 25   100 TALA
15.5500 g., 0.9170 Gold .4583 oz. AGW **Subject:** Queen's Silver Jubilee **Rev. Designer:** James Berry

Date	Mintage	F	VF	XF	Unc	BU
1977 Proof	2,500	Value: 320				

KM# 27   100 TALA
15.5500 g., 0.9170 Gold .4583 oz. AGW **Subject:** Lindbergh's New York to Paris flight **Obv:** National arms **Rev:** Bust 1/4 right, plane, statue of Liberty, Eiffel tower and dates

Date	Mintage	F	VF	XF	Unc	BU
1977 Proof	660	Value: 335				

KM# 29   100 TALA
15.5500 g., 0.9170 Gold .4583 oz. AGW **Subject:** 50th Anniversary - Transpacific Flight **Obv:** National arms **Rev:** Globe with plane flying across Pacific Ocean, portrait of Lindbergh facing left

Date	Mintage	F	VF	XF	Unc	BU
1978 Proof	1,500	Value: 325				

KM# 31   100 TALA
15.5500 g., 0.9170 Gold .4583 oz. AGW **Subject:** XI Commonwealth Games **Obv:** National arms **Rev:** Runners

Date	Mintage	F	VF	XF	Unc	BU
1978 Proof	1,000	Value: 325				

KM# 34   100 TALA
12.5000 g., 0.9170 Gold .3686 oz. AGW **Subject:** Bicentenary - death of Capt. James Cook **Obv:** National arms **Rev:** Portrait of Cook at left of sailing ship

Date	Mintage	F	VF	XF	Unc	BU
1979 Proof	1,000	Value: 255				

KM# 37   100 TALA
7.5000 g., 0.9170 Gold .2211 oz. AGW **Series:** 1980 Olympics **Obv:** National arms **Rev:** Hurdles event **Rev. Designer:** E.W. Roberts

Date	Mintage	F	VF	XF	Unc	BU
1980	250	—	—	—	175	—
1980 Proof	1,000	Value: 155				

KM# 42   100 TALA
7.5000 g., 0.9170 Gold .2211 oz. AGW **Subject:** Gov. Wilhelm Solf **Obv:** National arms **Rev:** Uniformed bust left flanked by huts and palm trees

Date	Mintage	F	VF	XF	Unc	BU
1980	250	—	—	—	165	—
1980 Proof	1,000	Value: 155				

KM# 45   100 TALA
7.5000 g., 0.9170 Gold .2211 oz. AGW **Subject:** Wedding of Prince Charles and Lady Diana **Obv:** National arms **Rev:** Conjoined busts left **Rev. Designer:** E.W. Roberts

Date	Mintage	F	VF	XF	Unc	BU
1981	250	—	—	—	160	—
1981 Proof	1,500	Value: 155				

KM# 49   100 TALA
7.5000 g., 0.9170 Gold .2211 oz. AGW **Subject:** IYDP - President Franklin Roosevelt **Obv:** National arms **Rev:** Seated figure in wheelchair facing

Date	Mintage	F	VF	XF	Unc	BU
1981	250	—	—	—	160	—
1981 Proof	1,500	Value: 155				

SAN MARINO 613

KM# 52 100 TALA
7.5000 g., 0.9170 Gold .2211 oz. AGW **Subject:** Commonwealth Games **Obv:** National arms **Rev:** Javelin thrower **Rev. Designer:** E.W. Roberts

Date	Mintage	F	VF	XF	Unc	BU
1982	250	—	—	—	160	—
1982 Proof	1,000	Value: 155				

KM# 55 100 TALA
7.5000 g., 0.9170 Gold .2211 oz. AGW **Subject:** South Pacific Games **Obv:** National arms **Rev:** Runner **Rev. Designer:** E.W. Roberts

Date	Mintage	F	VF	XF	Unc	BU
1983	—	—	—	—	160	—
1983 Proof	1,000	Value: 155				

KM# 60 100 TALA
7.5000 g., 0.9170 Gold .2211 oz. AGW **Series:** Summer Olympics **Obv:** National arms **Rev:** Boxing match

Date	Mintage	F	VF	XF	Unc	BU
1984	200	—	—	—	185	200
1984 Proof	500	Value: 175				

KM# 68 100 TALA
7.5000 g., 0.9000 Gold .217 oz. AGW **Subject:** America's Cup Race **Obv:** National arms **Rev:** Ship

Date	Mintage	F	VF	XF	Unc	BU
1987 Proof	5,000	Value: 160				

KM# 77 100 TALA
7.5000 g., 0.9000 Gold .217 oz. AGW **Subject:** Kon-Tiki **Obv:** National arms **Rev:** Boat and inscription

Date	Mintage	F	VF	XF	Unc	BU
1988 Proof	1,500	Value: 165				

KM# 81 100 TALA
7.5000 g., 0.9170 Gold .2211 oz. AGW **Series:** Save the Children **Obv:** National arms **Rev:** Children playing

Date	Mintage	F	VF	XF	Unc	BU
1990 Proof	3,000	Value: 155				

KM# 84 100 TALA
7.5000 g., 0.9170 Gold .2211 oz. AGW **Subject:** RA expeditions **Obv:** National arms **Rev:** Ship (RA II)

Date	Mintage	F	VF	XF	Unc	BU
1991 Proof	5,000	Value: 155				

KM# 87 100 TALA
7.5000 g., 0.9000 Gold .217 oz. AGW **Series:** Olympics **Obv:** National arms **Rev:** Torch runner

Date	Mintage	F	VF	XF	Unc	BU
1991 Proof	6,000	Value: 150				

KM# 96 100 TALA
7.5000 g., 0.9170 Gold .2211 oz. AGW **Subject:** Tigris Expedition **Obv:** National arms **Rev:** Tigris sailing

Date	Mintage	F	VF	XF	Unc	BU
1994 Proof	2,000	Value: 185				

KM# 126 100 TALA
7.5000 g., 0.9160 Gold 0.2209 oz. AGW, 28.5 mm. **Subject:** Robert Louis Stevenson **Obv:** National arms **Rev:** Ship and portrait **Edge:** Reeded

Date	Mintage	F	VF	XF	Unc	BU
ND(1994) Proof	2,000	Value: 165				

KM# 130 200 TALA
14.7000 g., 0.9990 Gold .3561 oz. AGW, 38.7x22.85 mm. **Subject:** People and Buildings **Obv:** National arms, value and dates **Rev:** Statue of Liberty **Edge:** Plain **Shape:** Coin halved, with jagged inside edge

Date	Mintage	F	VF	XF	Unc	BU
1999-2000 Proof	—	Value: 250				

KM# 136 500 TALA
69.8200 g., 0.9990 Gold 2.2425 oz. AGW, 36.4 mm. **Obv:** National arms **Rev:** Dove and sword handle above two soldiers **Edge:** Plain **Note:** Jagged coin half matching with Kiribati KM-36

Date	Mintage	F	VF	XF	Unc	BU
2000 Proof	99	Value: 1,600				

KM# 56 1000 TALA
31.1000 g., 0.9170 Gold .917 oz. AGW **Subject:** South Pacific Games **Obv:** National arms **Rev:** Runner

Date	Mintage	F	VF	XF	Unc	BU
1983 Proof	100	Value: 645				

KM# 61 1000 TALA
31.1000 g., 0.9170 Gold .917 oz. AGW **Series:** 1984 Olympics **Obv:** National arms **Rev:** Boxing match **Rev. Designer:** E.W. Roberts

Date	Mintage	F	VF	XF	Unc	BU
1984 Proof	100	Value: 635				

KM# 65 1000 TALA
33.9500 g., 0.9170 Gold 1.001 oz. AGW **Subject:** Prince Andrew and Sarah Fereguson's Marriage **Obv:** National arms **Rev:** Conjoined busts left

Date	Mintage	F	VF	XF	Unc	BU
1986 Proof	50	Value: 750				

KM# 110 1000 TALA
33.9500 g., 0.9170 Gold 1.001 oz. AGW **Subject:** 40th Anniversary - Reign of Queen Elizabeth II **Obv:** National arms **Rev:** Royal carriage and guard around Order of the Garter

Date	Mintage	F	VF	XF	Unc	BU
1992 Proof	Est. 150	Value: 685				

PROOF SETS

KM#	Date	Mintage	Identification	Issue Price	Mkt Val
PS3	1988 (3)	—	KM75-77	—	650
PS4	1991 (2)	1,000	KM83-84	—	175
PS5	1994 (3)	500	KM94-96	—	245

SAN MARINO

The Republic of San Marino, the oldest and smallest republic in the world is located in north central Italy entirely surrounded by the Province of Emilia-Romagna. It has an area of 24 sq. mi. (60 sq. km.) and a population of *23,000. Capital: San Marino. The principal economic activities are farming, livestock raising, cheese making, tourism and light manufacturing. Building stone, lime, wheat, hides and baked goods are exported. The government derives most of its revenue from the sale of postage stamps for philatelic purposes.

According to tradition, San Marino was founded about 350AD by a Christian stonecutter as a refuge against religious persecution. While gradually acquiring the institutions of an independent state, it avoided the factional fights of the Middle Ages and, except for a brief period in fief to Cesare Borgia, retained its freedom despite attacks on its sovereignty by the Papacy, the Lords of Rimini, Napoleon and Mussolini. In 1862 San Marino established a customs union with, and put itself under the protection of, Italy. A Communist-Socialist coalition controlled the Government for 12 years after World War II. The Christian Democratic Party has been the core of government since 1957. In 1978 a Communist-Socialist coalition again came into power and remained in control until 1991.

San Marino has its own coinage, but Italian and Vatican City coins and currency are also in circulation.

MINT MARKS
M - Milan
R - Rome

MONETARY SYSTEM
100 Centesimi = 1 Lira

REPUBLIC

STANDARD COINAGE

KM# 7 10 LIRE
3.2258 g., 0.9000 Gold .0933 oz. AGW **Obv:** Smoking towers within circle **Rev:** Standing Saint facing divides value **Note:** 16,000 coins melted at the mint.

Date	Mintage	F	VF	XF	Unc	BU
1925R	20,000	175	500	800	1,250	—

KM# 8 20 LIRE
6.4516 g., 0.9000 Gold .1867 oz. AGW **Obv:** Smoking towers **Rev:** Standing Saint figure divides value **Note:** 7,334 coins were melted at the mint.

Date	Mintage	F	VF	XF	Unc	BU
1925R	9,334	400	700	1,200	2,300	—

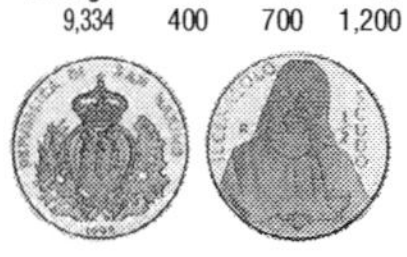

KM# 416 1/2 SCUDO
1.6100 g., 0.9000 Gold .0466 oz. AGW, 14 mm. **Subject:** Ilcenacolo **Obv:** Crowned pointed shield within sprigs **Rev:** Bearded bust facing **Edge:** Reeded **Note:** 1,915 coins melted at the mint.

Date	Mintage	F	VF	XF	Unc	BU
1998	8,000	—	—	—	40.00	—

KM# 413 1/2 SCUDO
1.6100 g., 0.9000 Gold .0466 oz. AGW **Subject:** Ritratto di Agnolo Doni **Obv:** Crowned pointed shield within sprigs **Rev:** Head 3/4 right

SAN MARINO

Date	Mintage	F	VF	XF	Unc	BU
1999 Proof	8,000		Value: 37.50			

KM# 407 1/2 SCUDO
1.6100 g., 0.9000 Gold .0466 oz. AGW **Subject:** Ritratto di Giovane Donna **Obv:** Crowned pointed shield within sprigs **Rev:** Head left

Date	Mintage	F	VF	XF	Unc	BU
2000 Proof	6,000	—	—	—	37.50	—

KM# 433 1/2 SCUDO
1.6100 g., 0.9000 Gold .0466 oz. AGW, 13.8 mm. **Subject:** Cavaliere **Obv:** Crowned arms within sprigs **Rev:** Horse and rider **Edge:** Reeded

Date	Mintage	F	VF	XF	Unc	BU
2001 Proof	4,500		Value: 37.50			

KM# 38 SCUDO
3.0000 g., 0.9170 Gold .0883 oz. AGW **Obv:** Crowned pointed shield within sprigs **Rev:** Standing Saint facing **Note:** 2,491 coins melted at the mint.

Date	Mintage	F	VF	XF	Unc	BU
1974	87,000	—	—	—	65.00	—

KM# 49 SCUDO
3.0000 g., 0.9170 Gold .0883 oz. AGW **Obv:** Crowned pointed shield within sprigs **Rev:** Value and date within wreath **Note:** 37,668 coins melted at the mint.

Date	Mintage	F	VF	XF	Unc	BU
1975	90,000	—	—	—	70.00	—

KM# 60 SCUDO
3.0000 g., 0.9170 Gold .0883 oz. AGW **Obv:** Smoking towers **Rev:** Laureate head right **Note:** 30,026 coins melted at the mint.

Date	Mintage	F	VF	XF	Unc	BU
1976	65,000	—	—	—	65.00	—

KM# 73 SCUDO
3.0000 g., 0.9170 Gold .0883 oz. AGW **Obv:** Smoking towers **Rev:** Democrazia **Note:** 1,839 coins melted at the mint.

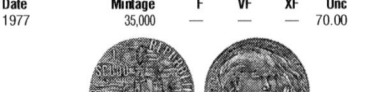

Date	Mintage	F	VF	XF	Unc	BU
1977	35,000	—	—	—	70.00	—

KM# 86 SCUDO
3.0000 g., 0.9170 Gold .0883 oz. AGW **Obv:** Smoking towers **Rev:** Miss Liberta **Note:** 9,021 coins melted at the mint.

Date	Mintage	F	VF	XF	Unc	BU
1978	38,000	—	—	—	70.00	—

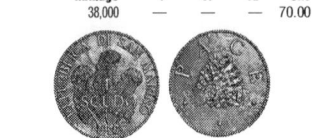

KM# 99 SCUDO
3.0000 g., 0.9170 Gold .0883 oz. AGW **Obv:** Value within upright feathers **Rev:** Peace **Note:** 4,152 coins melted at the mint.

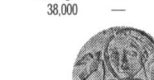

Date	Mintage	F	VF	XF	Unc	BU
1979	38,000	—	—	—	70.00	—

KM# 113 SCUDO
3.0000 g., 0.9170 Gold .0883 oz. AGW **Rev:** Head on hands facing, dove at left **Note:** 10,309 coins melted at the mint.

Date	Mintage	F	VF	XF	Unc	BU
1980	38,000	—	—	—	70.00	—

KM# 128 SCUDO
3.0000 g., 0.9170 Gold .0883 oz. AGW **Subject:** World Food Day **Obv:** Crowned pointed shield within sprigs above inscription **Rev:** Seated figure reading **Note:** 196 coins melted at the mint.

Date	Mintage	F	VF	XF	Unc	BU
1981	31,000	—	—	—	70.00	—

KM# 142 SCUDO
3.0000 g., 0.9170 Gold .0883 oz. AGW **Obv:** Crowned shield **Rev:** Head left **Note:** 1,192 coins melted at the mint.

Date	Mintage	F	VF	XF	Unc	BU
1982R	17,000	—	—	—	70.00	—

KM# 156 SCUDO
2.0000 g., 0.9170 Gold .059 oz. AGW **Rev:** Perpetual Liberty **Designer:** Guido Veroi **Note:** 917 coins melted at the mint.

Date	Mintage	F	VF	XF	Unc	BU
1983R	14,000	—	—	—	65.00	—

KM# 170 SCUDO
2.0000 g., 0.9170 Gold .059 oz. AGW **Subject:** Peace **Obv:** Crowned shield in front of city scene **Rev:** Half-figure holding laurel branch left **Note:** 979 coins melted at the mint.

Date	Mintage	F	VF	XF	Unc	BU
1984R	11,000	—	—	—	65.00	—

KM# 184 SCUDO
2.0000 g., 0.9170 Gold .059 oz. AGW **Subject:** International Year for Youth **Rev:** Head left **Note:** 1,162 coins melted at the mint.

Date	Mintage	F	VF	XF	Unc	BU
1985R	10,000	—	—	—	90.00	—

KM# 198 SCUDO
3.3920 g., 0.9170 Gold .1 oz. AGW **Subject:** Insects at Work **Rev:** Large ant **Note:** 1,308 coins melted at the mint.

Date	Mintage	F	VF	XF	Unc	BU
1986R	9,000	—	—	—	80.00	—

KM# 211 SCUDO
3.3920 g., 0.9170 Gold .1 oz. AGW **Subject:** European Year for Environment **Obv:** Robe-like design with seagull at right **Rev:** Nude children under sprig **Note:** 962 coins melted at the mint.

Date	Mintage	F	VF	XF	Unc	BU
1987R	8,000	—	—	—	80.00	—

KM# 228 SCUDO
3.3920 g., 0.9170 Gold .1 oz. AGW **Subject:** Disarmament **Obv:** Smoking towers **Rev:** Design within globe **Note:** 873 coins melted at the mint.

Date	Mintage	F	VF	XF	Unc	BU
1988R	7,000	—	—	—	80.00	—

KM# 241 SCUDO
3.2258 g., 0.9000 Gold .0933 oz. AGW **Subject:** French Revolution **Rev:** Standing figure holding flag **Note:** 731 coins melted at the mint.

Date	Mintage	F	VF	XF	Unc	BU
1989R	7,500	—	—	—	75.00	—

KM# 258 SCUDO
3.2258 g., 0.9000 Gold .0933 oz. AGW **Subject:** San Marino's Presidency of the European Council **Obv:** Crowned pointed shield within sprigs **Rev:** Bust facing

Date	Mintage	F	VF	XF	Unc	BU
1990R	7,300	—	—	—	75.00	—

KM# 273 SCUDO
3.2258 g., 0.9000 Gold .0933 oz. AGW **Subject:** Peace **Obv:** Crowned pointed shield within sprigs **Rev:** Child fleeing

Date	Mintage	F	VF	XF	Unc	BU
1991R Proof	Est. 7,500		Value: 75.00			

KM# 288 SCUDO
3.2258 g., 0.9000 Gold .0933 oz. AGW **Subject:** San Marino's Entry Into the United Nations **Obv:** Crowned shield within sprigs **Rev:** UN logo

Date	Mintage	F	VF	XF	Unc	BU
1992R	8,500		Value: 75.00			

KM# 303 SCUDO
3.2258 g., 0.9000 Gold .0933 oz. AGW **Series:** International Monetary Fund **Rev:** Three standing figures within pointed oblong design **Designer:** Laura Cretara **Note:** 455 coins melted at the mint.

Date	Mintage	F	VF	XF	Unc	BU
1993R	7,500	—	—	—	70.00	—
1993R Proof	—		Value: 75.00			

KM# 319 SCUDO
3.2258 g., 0.9000 Gold .0933 oz. AGW **Series:** International Year of the Family **Obv:** Crowned shield within sprigs **Rev:** Couple facing each other **Note:** Sets only. 648 coins melted at the mint.

Date	Mintage	F	VF	XF	Unc	BU
1994R Proof	7,500		Value: 80.00			

SAN MARINO

KM# 335 SCUDO
3.2258 g., 0.9000 Gold .0933 oz. AGW **Series:** 50th Anniversary - United Nations **Obv:** Crowned shield within sprigs **Rev:** Vertical dolphin and nude figure on triangle sides **Note:** Sets only. 494 coins melted at the mint.

Date	Mintage	F	VF	XF	Unc	BU
1995R Proof	6,500	Value: 75.00				

KM# 338 SCUDO
3.2258 g., 0.9000 Gold .0933 oz. AGW **Series:** 1996 Olympics **Rev:** Boxers **Note:** 664 coins melted at the mint.

Date	Mintage	F	VF	XF	Unc	BU
1996 Proof	7,000	Value: 75.00				

KM# 373 SCUDO
3.2258 g., 0.9000 Gold .0933 oz. AGW **Rev:** Michelangelo's "Kneeling Angel" **Note:** 412 coins melted at the mint.

Date	Mintage	F	VF	XF	Unc	BU
1997 Proof	6,500	Value: 75.00				

KM# 417 SCUDO
3.2258 g., 0.9000 Gold .0933 oz. AGW, 15.9 mm. **Subject:** Canone Delle Proporzioni **Obv:** Crowned pointed shield within sprigs **Rev:** Anatomical drawing **Edge:** Reeded **Note:** 312 coins melted at the mint.

Date	Mintage	F	VF	XF	Unc	BU
1998 Proof	6,000	Value: 75.00				

KM# 414 SCUDO
3.2258 g., 0.9000 Gold .0933 oz. AGW **Subject:** La Velata **Obv:** Crowned shield **Rev:** Head facing 1/4 left

Date	Mintage	F	VF	XF	Unc	BU
1999 Proof	8,000	Value: 75.00				

KM# 408 SCUDO
3.2258 g., 0.9000 Gold .0933 oz. AGW **Obv:** Crowned shield **Rev:** La Primavera

Date	Mintage	F	VF	XF	Unc	BU
2000 Proof	—	Value: 75.00				

KM# 434 SCUDO
3.2200 g., 0.9000 Gold .0932 oz. AGW, 16 mm. **Subject:** Tiziano **Obv:** Crowned arms within sprigs **Rev:** Bearded bust left **Edge:** Reeded

Date	Mintage	F	VF	XF	Unc	BU
2001 Proof	4,500	Value: 75.00				

KM# 39 2 SCUDI
6.0000 g., 0.9170 Gold .1769 oz. AGW **Obv:** Crowned pointed shield within wreath **Rev:** Standing figure facing **Note:** 1,637 coins melted at the mint.

Date	Mintage	F	VF	XF	Unc	BU
1974	77,000	—	—	—	125	—

KM# 50 2 SCUDI
6.0000 g., 0.9170 Gold .1769 oz. AGW **Obv:** Crowned pointed shield within wreath **Rev:** Value and date within wreath **Note:** 3,373 coins melted at the mint.

Date	Mintage	F	VF	XF	Unc	BU
1975	80,000	—	—	—	125	—

KM# 61 2 SCUDI
6.0000 g., 0.9170 Gold .1769 oz. AGW **Obv:** Smoking towers **Rev:** Head 3/4 right **Note:** 20,246 coins melted at the mint.

Date	Mintage	F	VF	XF	Unc	BU
1976	55,000	—	—	—	125	—

KM# 74 2 SCUDI
6.0000 g., 0.9170 Gold .1769 oz. AGW **Obv:** Date at right of smoking towers **Rev:** Democrazia **Note:** 912 coins melted at the mint.

Date	Mintage	F	VF	XF	Unc	BU
1977	34,000	—	—	—	130	—

KM# 87 2 SCUDI
6.0000 g., 0.9170 Gold .1769 oz. AGW **Obv:** Value at upper left of smoking towers **Rev:** Libertas **Note:** 8,120 coins melted at the mint.

Date	Mintage	F	VF	XF	Unc	BU
1978	37,000	—	—	—	130	—

KM# 100 2 SCUDI
6.0000 g., 0.9170 Gold .1769 oz. AGW **Subject:** Peace **Obv:** Three upright feathers **Rev:** Clasped hands **Note:** 3,238 coins melted at the mint.

Date	Mintage	F	VF	XF	Unc	BU
1979	37,000	—	—	—	130	—

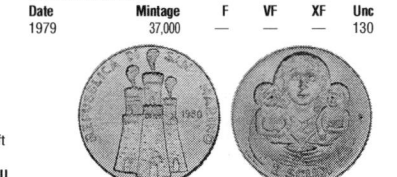

KM# 114 2 SCUDI
6.0000 g., 0.9170 Gold .1769 oz. AGW **Subject:** Justice **Obv:** Smoking towers **Rev:** Mother holding 2 children **Note:** 9,340 coins melted at the mint.

Date	Mintage	F	VF	XF	Unc	BU
1980	37,000	—	—	—	130	—

KM# 129 2 SCUDI
6.0000 g., 0.9170 Gold .1769 oz. AGW **Series:** World Food Day **Obv:** Crowned pointed arms within wreath above sprigs **Rev:** Seated nude figure with knees bent upright **Note:** 196 coins melted at the mint.

Date	Mintage	F	VF	XF	Unc	BU
1981	30,000	—	—	—	130	—

KM# 143 2 SCUDI
6.0000 g., 0.9170 Gold .1769 oz. AGW **Obv:** Crown above smoking towers flanked by sprig and design **Rev:** Stylized seated nude right **Note:** 244 coins melted at the mint.

Date	Mintage	F	VF	XF	Unc	BU
1982R	16,000	—	—	—	135	—

KM# 157 2 SCUDI
4.0000 g., 0.9170 Gold .1179 oz. AGW **Subject:** Perpetual Liberty **Obv:** Inscription above crowned shield and sprig **Rev:** Smoking towers on top of head left **Designer:** Guido Veroi **Note:** 17 coins melted at the mint.

Date	Mintage	F	VF	XF	Unc	BU
1983R	13,000	—	—	—	110	—

KM# 171 2 SCUDI
4.0000 g., 0.9170 Gold .1179 oz. AGW **Subject:** Liberty **Obv:** Crowned shield in front of city scene **Rev:** Standing figure with arms outstretched left **Note:** 12 coins melted at the mint.

Date	Mintage	F	VF	XF	Unc	BU
1984R	10,000	—	—	—	110	—

KM# 185 2 SCUDI
4.0000 g., 0.9170 Gold .1179 oz. AGW **Series:** International Year for Youth **Obv:** Crown above smoking towers on rock flanked by sprigs **Rev:** Head right divides flower and date **Note:** 200 coins melted at the mint.

Date	Mintage	F	VF	XF	Unc	BU
1985R	9,000	—	—	—	110	—

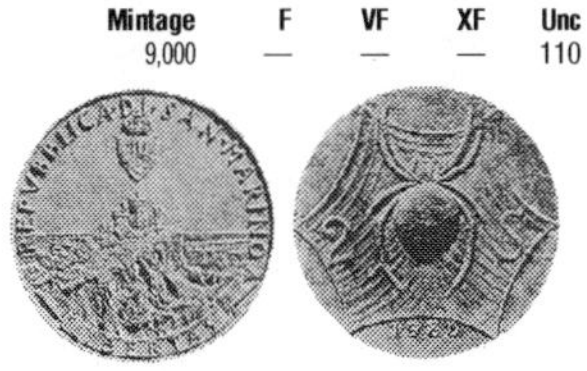

KM# 199 2 SCUDI
6.7840 g., 0.9170 Gold .2 oz. AGW **Obv:** Crowned shield above view **Rev:** Spider within web divides 2S **Note:** 329 coins melted at the mint.

Date	Mintage	F	VF	XF	Unc	BU
1986R	8,000	—	—	—	150	—

SAN MARINO

KM# 212 2 SCUDI
6.7840 g., 0.9170 Gold .2 oz. AGW **Subject:** European Year for Envrionment **Rev:** Sprig divides dancing figures **Note:** 14 coins melted at the mint.

Date	Mintage	F	VF	XF	Unc	BU
1987R	7,000	—	—	—	150	—

KM# 229 2 SCUDI
6.7840 g., 0.9170 Gold .2 oz. AGW **Subject:** Disarmament **Rev:** Value above sprig within clasped hands, all within world globe design **Note:** 7 coins melted at the mint.

Date	Mintage	F	VF	XF	Unc	BU
1988R	6,000	—	—	—	150	—

KM# 242 2 SCUDI
6.4516 g., 0.9000 Gold .1867 oz. AGW **Subject:** French Revolution **Rev:** Dates above building

Date	Mintage	F	VF	XF	Unc	BU
1989R	6,500	—	—	—	130	—

KM# 259 2 SCUDI
6.4516 g., 0.9000 Gold .1867 oz. AGW **Subject:** San Marino's Presidency of the European Council **Obv:** Crowned shield within wreath **Rev:** World globe **Designer:** Carmela Colaneri

Date	Mintage	F	VF	XF	Unc	BU
1990R	6,800	—	—	—	130	—

KM# 274 2 SCUDI
6.4516 g., 0.9000 Gold .1867 oz. AGW **Subject:** Peace **Obv:** Crowned shield within wreath **Rev:** New shoots growing from stump

Date	Mintage	F	VF	XF	Unc	BU
1991R Proof	Est. 6,500	Value: 130				

KM# 289 2 SCUDI
6.4516 g., 0.9000 Gold .1867 oz. AGW **Subject:** San Marino's Entry Into the United Nations **Obv:** Crowned shield within wreath **Rev:** UN logo above inscription

Date	Mintage	F	VF	XF	Unc	BU
1992R Proof	7,500	Value: 130				

KM# 304 2 SCUDI
6.4516 g., 0.9000 Gold .1867 oz. AGW **Series:** International Monetary Fund **Obv:** Crowned shield within wreath **Rev:** Two stylized figures within globe design **Designer:** Laura Cretara **Note:** 106 coins melted at the mint.

Date	Mintage	F	VF	XF	Unc	BU
1993R	6,500	—	—	—	130	—
1993R Proof	—	Value: 140				

KM# 320 2 SCUDI
6.4516 g., 0.9000 Gold .1867 oz. AGW **Series:** International Year of the Family **Obv:** Crowned shield within wreath **Rev:** Family divides value **Note:** Sets only. 252 coins melted at the mint.

Date	Mintage	F	VF	XF	Unc	BU
1994R Proof	6,500	Value: 140				

KM# 336 2 SCUDI
6.4516 g., 0.9000 Gold .1867 oz. AGW **Series:** 50th Anniversary - United Nations **Obv:** Crowned shield within wreath **Rev:** Seated figure with arms outstretched below value within triangular design **Note:** Sets only.

Date	Mintage	F	VF	XF	Unc	BU
1995R Proof	Est. 7,000	Value: 140				

KM# 339 2 SCUDI
6.4516 g., 0.9000 Gold .1867 oz. AGW **Series:** 1996 Olympics **Subject:** Track and Field **Obv:** Crowned shield within wreath **Rev:** Three athletes standing left **Note:** 1 coin melted at the mint.

Date	Mintage	F	VF	XF	Unc	BU
1996 Proof	6,000	Value: 140				

KM# 374 2 SCUDI
6.4516 g., 0.9000 Gold .1867 oz. AGW **Rev:** Michelangelo's "David" **Note:** 124 coins melted at the mint.

Date	Mintage	F	VF	XF	Unc	BU
1997 Proof	5,800	Value: 140				

KM# 418 2 SCUDI
6.4516 g., 0.9000 Gold .1867 oz. AGW, 21 mm. **Subject:** Vergine Delle Rocce **Obv:** Crowned shield within wreath **Rev:** Female Saint facing **Edge:** Reeded **Note:** Struck at Rome. 334 coins melted at the mint.

Date	Mintage	F	VF	XF	Unc	BU
1998 Proof	5,500	Value: 140				

KM# 415 2 SCUDI
6.4516 g., 0.9000 Gold .1867 oz. AGW **Subject:** Sposalizio Della Vergine **Obv:** Crowned shield within wreath **Rev:** Three seated figures

Date	Mintage	F	VF	XF	Unc	BU
1999 Proof	8,000	Value: 135				

KM# 409 2 SCUDI
6.4516 g., 0.9000 Gold .1867 oz. AGW **Subject:** Madonna Della Melagrna **Obv:** Crowned shield within wreath **Rev:** Madonna and child

Date	Mintage	F	VF	XF	Unc	BU
2000 Proof	6,000	Value: 135				

KM# 435 2 SCUDI
6.4400 g., 0.9000 Gold .1863 oz. AGW, 21 mm. **Subject:** Flora **Obv:** Crowned arms within sprigs **Rev:** Bust 1/4 left and value **Edge:** Reeded

Date	Mintage	F	VF	XF	Unc	BU
2001 Proof	4,500	Value: 135				

KM# 457 2 SCUDI
6.4516 g., 0.9000 Gold .1867 oz. AGW, 21 mm. **Obv:** Crowned arms within sprigs **Rev:** Madonna and Child **Edge:** Reeded

Date	Mintage	F	VF	XF	Unc	BU
2002R Proof	3,000	Value: 145				

KM# 459 2 SCUDI
6.4516 g., 0.9000 Gold .1867 oz. AGW, 21 mm. **Obv:** Crowned arms within sprigs **Rev:** Nostradamus above value **Edge:** Reeded

Date	Mintage	F	VF	XF	Unc	BU
2003R Proof	7,500	Value: 145				

KM# 464 2 SCUDI
6.4516 g., 0.9000 Gold .1867 oz. AGW, 21 mm. **Subject:** The Domagnano Treasure **Obv:** Crowned arms within sprigs **Rev:** Gothic Eagle Brooch, 5 Mark coin of 1952 **Edge:** Reeded

Date	Mintage	F	VF	XF	Unc	BU
2004R Proof	6,500	Value: 155				

KM# 62 5 SCUDI
15.0000 g., 0.9170 Gold .4422 oz. AGW **Obv:** Value below smoking towers **Rev:** Head left **Note:** 25 coins melted at mint.

Date	Mintage	F	VF	XF	Unc	BU
1976	8,000	—	—	—	625	—

KM# 75 5 SCUDI
15.0000 g., 0.9170 Gold .4422 oz. AGW **Subject:** Democrazia **Obv:** Value below smoking towers **Rev:** Stylized head left **Note:** 29 coins melted at mint.

Date	Mintage	F	VF	XF	Unc	BU
1977	16,000	—	—	—	315	—

KM# 101 5 SCUDI
15.0000 g., 0.9170 Gold .4422 oz. AGW **Subject:** Peace **Obv:** Value within upright feathers **Rev:** Stylized hands and arms **Note:** 161 coins melted at mint.

Date	Mintage	F	VF	XF	Unc	BU
1979	24,000	—	—	—	315	—

SAN MARINO 617

KM# 115 5 SCUDI
15.0000 g., 0.9170 Gold .4422 oz. AGW **Subject:** Justice **Obv:** Smoking towers **Rev:** Head at upper right of birds **Note:** 1,428 coins melted at mint.

Date	Mintage	F	VF	XF	Unc	BU
1980	24,000	—	—	—	315	—

KM# 130 5 SCUDI
15.0000 g., 0.9170 Gold .4422 oz. AGW **Series:** World Food Day **Obv:** Crowned shield on sprigs above inscription **Rev:** Seated nude figure with knees bent upright **Note:** 33 coins melted at mint.

Date	Mintage	F	VF	XF	Unc	BU
1981	24,000	—	—	—	315	—

KM# 144 5 SCUDI
15.0000 g., 0.9170 Gold .4422 oz. AGW **Subject:** Defense of Liberty **Obv:** Crown above smoking towers flanked by sprig and design **Rev:** Value above stylized hands **Note:** 19 coins melted at mint.

Date	Mintage	F	VF	XF	Unc	BU
1982R	15,000	—	—	—	315	—

KM# 158 5 SCUDI
10.0000 g., 0.9170 Gold .2949 oz. AGW **Subject:** Perpetual Liberty **Obv:** Inscription above crowned shield and sprig **Rev:** Standing figure and child walking right **Designer:** Guido Veroi **Note:** 25 coins melted at mint.

Date	Mintage	F	VF	XF	Unc	BU
1983R	11,000	—	—	—	250	—

KM# 172 5 SCUDI
10.0000 g., 0.9170 Gold .2949 oz. AGW **Subject:** Justice **Obv:** Crowned shield in front of castle view **Rev:** Liberty walking on parapet of castle **Designer:** Pietro Giampaoli **Note:** 28 coins melted at mint.

Date	Mintage	F	VF	XF	Unc	BU
1984R	9,000	—	—	—	300	—

KM# 186 5 SCUDI
10.0000 g., 0.9170 Gold .2949 oz. AGW **Subject:** Libertas **Obv:** Crown above smoking towers on rock flanked by sprigs **Rev:** Three nude dancing figures **Note:** 13 coins melted at mint.

Date	Mintage	F	VF	XF	Unc	BU
1985R	7,400	—	—	—	400	—

KM# 200 5 SCUDI
16.9500 g., 0.9170 Gold .5 oz. AGW **Subject:** Work **Obv:** Crowned shield above view **Rev:** Bee within honey comb design divides value **Note:** 14 coins melted at mint.

Date	Mintage	F	VF	XF	Unc	BU
1986R	7,000	—	—	—	350	—

KM# 215 5 SCUDI
16.9500 g., 0.9170 Gold .5 oz. AGW **Subject:** United Nations **Obv:** Crowned shield within wreath **Rev:** Value to left of building and tower **Note:** 49 coins melted at mint.

Date	Mintage	F	VF	XF	Unc	BU
1987R	6,000	—	—	—	350	—

KM# 230 5 SCUDI
16.9500 g., 0.9170 Gold .5 oz. AGW **Subject:** Human Rights **Obv:** Crowned shield within wreath **Obv. Designer:** Valentini **Rev:** Stylized flame within wreath, value at upper left **Rev. Designer:** Sergio Giandomenico **Note:** 11 coins melted at mint.

Date	Mintage	F	VF	XF	Unc	BU
1988R	5,000	—	—	—	350	—

KM# 245 5 SCUDI
16.9500 g., 0.9170 Gold .5 oz. AGW **Subject:** Entrance of San Marino in Common Market

Date	Mintage	F	VF	XF	Unc	BU
1989R	6,000	—	—	—	350	—

KM# 260 5 SCUDI
16.9500 g., 0.9170 Gold .5 oz. AGW **Subject:** Founding of the Republic **Obv:** Doves in front of smoking towers **Rev:** Three kneeling figures to right of standing figure **Designer:** Bino Bini

Date	Mintage	F	VF	XF	Unc	BU
1990R Proof	6,500	Value: 350

KM# 275 5 SCUDI
16.9500 g., 0.9170 Gold .5 oz. AGW **Subject:** Peace and Freedom **Obv:** Crowned shield within wreath **Rev:** Tree divides family **Designer:** Bino Bini

Date	Mintage	F	VF	XF	Unc	BU
1991R Proof	7,000	Value: 350

KM# 290 5 SCUDI
16.9500 g., 0.9170 Gold .5 oz. AGW **Subject:** Customer Agreement with European Economic Community **Obv:** Crowned shield within wreath **Rev:** Value and oat sprig within center of circle of stars

Date	Mintage	F	VF	XF	Unc	BU
1992R Proof	Est. 6,500	Value: 350

KM# 305 5 SCUDI
16.9500 g., 0.9170 Gold .5 oz. AGW **Series:** International Monetary Fund **Obv:** Crowned shield within wreath **Rev:** Stylized figure holding scale above shield **Designer:** Laura Cretara **Note:** 68 coins melted at the mint.

Date	Mintage	F	VF	XF	Unc	BU
1993R Proof	5,500	Value: 350

KM# 321 5 SCUDI
16.9500 g., 0.9170 Gold .5 oz. AGW **Series:** International Year of the Family **Obv:** Crowned shield within wreath **Rev:** Family divides value **Note:** 207 coins melted at the mint.

Date	Mintage	F	VF	XF	Unc	BU
1994R Proof	5,500	Value: 350

KM# 337 5 SCUDI
16.9500 g., 0.9170 Gold .5 oz. AGW **Series:** 50th Anniversary - United Nations **Obv:** Crowned shield within wreath **Rev:** Seated nude figure and squirrel flanked by dates above value **Note:** 65 coins melted at the mint.

Date	Mintage	F	VF	XF	Unc	BU
1995R Proof	5,000	Value: 350

SAN MARINO

KM# 343 5 SCUDI
16.9500 g., 0.9170 Gold .5 oz. AGW. **Subject:** Pieta **Obv:** Crowned shield within wreath **Rev:** Mary receives Jesus' body **Note:** 19 coins melted at the mint.
Date	Mintage	F	VF	XF	Unc	BU
1996 Proof	5,840	Value: 350				

KM# 375 5 SCUDI
16.9500 g., 0.9170 Gold .5 oz. AGW **Subject:** The Annunciation **Obv:** Crowned shield within wreath **Rev:** Angel **Note:** 469 coins melted at the mint.
Date	Mintage	F	VF	XF	Unc	BU
1997 Proof	5,500	Value: 350				

KM# 412 5 SCUDI
16.9590 g., 0.9170 Gold .5 oz. AGW **Subject:** Madonna Della Seggiola **Obv:** Crowned shield within wreath **Rev:** Woman with 2 children **Note:** 1,151 coins melted at the mint.
Date	Mintage	F	VF	XF	Unc	BU
1998 Proof	5,000	Value: 350				

KM# 388 5 SCUDI
16.9590 g., 0.9170 Gold .5 oz. AGW **Subject:** Birth of Venus **Obv:** Crowned shield within wreath **Rev:** Venus standing in shell
Date	Mintage	F	VF	XF	Unc	BU
1999 Proof	Est. 5,500	Value: 350				

KM# 420 5 SCUDI
16.9590 g., 0.9170 Gold .5 oz. AGW **Subject:** Tiziano's painting "Rape of Europa" **Obv:** Crowned shield within wreath **Rev:** Europa on a bull's (Zeus) back
Date	Mintage	F	VF	XF	Unc	BU
2000 Proof	4,500	—	—	—	350	—

KM# 439 5 SCUDI
16.9655 g., 0.9166 Gold .5000 oz. AGW, 28 mm. **Subject:** San Marino's World Bank Membership **Obv:** Crowned arms within sprigs **Rev:** Orchid and bee within globe **Edge:** Reeded
Date	Mintage	F	VF	XF	Unc	BU
2001 Proof	4,000	Value: 350				

KM# 88 10 SCUDI
30.0000 g., 0.9170 Gold .8844 oz. AGW **Obv:** Smoking towers within circle **Rev:** Head left **Note:** 54 coins melted at the mint.
Date	Mintage	F	VF	XF	Unc	BU
1978	20,000	—	—	—	625	—

EURO COINAGE

KM# 460 20 EURO
6.4510 g., 0.9000 Gold 0.1867 oz. AGW, 21 mm. **Subject:** 1600th Anniversary of Ravenna **Obv:** National arms **Rev:** Bas-relief wall design **Edge:** Reeded
Date	Mintage	F	VF	XF	Unc	BU
2002R Proof	4,550	Value: 375				

KM# 455 20 EURO
6.4516 g., 0.9000 Gold 0.1867 oz. AGW, 21 mm. **Obv:** Three plumes **Rev:** Giotto's "Presentation of Jesus at the Temple" **Edge:** Reeded
Date	Mintage	F	VF	XF	Unc	BU
2003R Proof	7,300	Value: 245				

KM# 465 20 EURO
6.4510 g., 0.9000 Gold 0.1867 oz. AGW, 21 mm. **Obv:** Three plumes **Rev:** Marco Polo meeting Kublai Khan **Edge:** Reeded
Date	Mintage	F	VF	XF	Unc	BU
2004R Proof	7,300	Value: 255				

KM# 470 20 EURO
6.4510 g., 0.9000 Gold 0.1867 oz. AGW, 21 mm. **Subject:** International Day of Peace **Obv:** Stylized faces and leaves
Date	Mintage	F	VF	XF	Unc	BU
2005R Proof	5,300	Value: 300				

KM# 461 50 EURO
16.1290 g., 0.9000 Gold 0.4667 oz. AGW, 28 mm. **Subject:** 1600th Anniversary of Ravenna **Obv:** National arms **Rev:** Wall painting **Edge:** Reeded
Date	Mintage	F	VF	XF	Unc	BU
2002R Proof	4,550	Value: 775				

KM# 456 50 EURO
16.1290 g., 0.9000 Gold 0.4667 oz. AGW, 28 mm. **Obv:** Three plumes **Rev:** Giotto's "The Pentecost" **Edge:** Reeded
Date	Mintage	F	VF	XF	Unc	BU
2003R Proof	7,300	Value: 500				

KM# 466 50 EURO
16.1290 g., 0.9000 Gold 0.4667 oz. AGW, 28 mm. **Obv:** Three plumes **Rev:** Marco Polo **Edge:** Reeded
Date	Mintage	F	VF	XF	Unc	BU
2004R Proof	7,300	Value: 525				

KM# 471 50 EURO
16.1290 g., 0.9000 Gold 0.4667 oz. AGW, 28 mm. **Subject:** International Day of Peace **Obv:** Group of people gathering
Date	Mintage	F	VF	XF	Unc	BU
2005R Proof	5,300	Value: 500				

PROVAS

KM#	Date	Mintage	Identification	Mkt Val
Pr1	1925R	75	20 Lire. Gold. KM8.	3,300

MINT SETS

KM#	Date	Mintage	Identification	Issue Price	Mkt Val
MS4	1974 (2)	60,000	KM38-39	—	185
MS7	1975 (2)	90,000	KM49-50	—	185
MS9	1976 (2)	40,000	KM60-61	—	185
MS11	1977 (2)	30,000	KM73-74	—	185
MS13	1978 (2)	—	KM86-87	—	160
MS15	1979 (2)	—	KM99-100	—	160
MS17	1980 (2)	—	KM113-114	—	160
MS20	1981 (2)	—	KM128-129	—	160
MS23	1982 (2)	—	KM142-143	—	170
MS26	1983 (2)	—	KM156-157	—	175
MS29	1984 (2)	—	KM170-171	—	175
MS32	1985 (2)	—	KM184-185	—	200
MS35	1986 (2)	—	KM198-199	—	190
MS38	1987 (2)	—	KM211-212	—	190
MS41	1988 (2)	—	KM228-229	—	190
MS44	1989 (2)	6,500	KM241-242	—	170
MS47	1990 (2)	6,800	KM258-259	—	175

PROOF SETS

KM#	Date	Mintage	Identification	Issue Price	Mkt Val
PS4	1991 (2)	6,800	KM273-274	—	175
PS5	1993 (2)	—	KM303-304	158	160
PS6	1994 (2)	7,500	KM319-320	—	200
PS8	1995 (2)	7,000	KM335-336	161	175
PS12	1999 (3)	8,000	KM413-415	179	180
PS13	2000 (3)	6,000	KM407-409	179	180
PS14	2001 (3)	4,500	KM433-435	179	180
PS15	2002 (2)	37,000	KM448-449	—	175
PS17	2003 (2)	7,300	KM#455-456	—	750
PS18	2004 (2)	7,300	KM#465-466	—	780
PS19	2005 (2)	5,300	KM#470-471	—	800

SAUDI ARABIA

The Kingdom of Saudi Arabia, an independent and absolute hereditary monarchy comprising the former sultanate of Nejd, the old kingdom of Hejaz, Asir and Al Hasa, occupies four-fifths of the Arabian peninsula. The kingdom has an area of 830,000 sq. mi. (2,149,690 sq. km.) and a population of *16.1 million. Capital: Riyadh. The economy is based on oil, which provides 85 percent of Saudi Arabia's revenue.

Mohammed united the Arabs in the 7th century and his followers founded a great empire with its capital at Medina. The Turks established nominal rule over much of Arabia in the 16th and 17th centuries, and in the 18th century divided it into principalities.

The Kingdom of Saudi Arabia was created by King Abd Al-Aziz Bin Saud (1882-1953), a descendant of earlier Wahhabi rulers of the Arabian peninsula. In 1901 he seized Riyadh, capital of the Sultanate of Nejd, and in 1905 established himself as Sultan. In 1913 he captured the Turkish province of Al Hasa; took the Hejaz in 1925 and by 1926 most of Asir. In 1932 he combined Nejd and Hejaz into the single kingdom of Saudi Arabia. Asir was incorporated into the kingdom a year later.

TITLES

العربية السعودية

Al-Arabiya(t) as-Sa'udiya(t)

المملكة العربية السعودية

Al-Mamlaka(t) al-'Arabiya(t) as-Sa'udiya(t)

RULERS

al Sa'ud Dynasty
Abd Al-Aziz Bin Sa'ud, (Ibn Sa'ud), AH1344-1373/1926-1953AD
Sa'ud Bin Abd Al-Aziz, AH1373-1383/1953-1964AD
Faisal Bin Abd Al-Aziz, AH1383-1395/1964-1975AD
Khalid Bin Abd Al-Aziz, AH1395-1403/1975-1982AD
Fahad Bin Abd Al-Aziz, AH1403-/1982-AD

MONETARY SYSTEM

Until 1960
20-22 Ghirsh = 1 Riyal
40 Riyals = 1 Guinea
NOTE: Copper-nickel, reeded-edge coins dated AH1356 and silver coins dated AH1354 were struck at the U. S. Mint in Philadelphia between 1944-1949.

KINGDOM

TRADE COINAGE

KM# 36 GUINEA
7.9881 g., 0.9170 Gold .2354 oz. AGW **Obv:** Inscription within beaded circle, legend above, crossed swords below within design flanked by palm trees **Rev:** Inscription within beaded circle, legend above, value below within design flanked by palm trees

Date	Mintage	F	VF	XF	Unc	BU
AH1370 (1950)	2,000,000	—	—	BV	175	200

X# 21 GUINEA
8.0000 g., Gold, 21.8 mm. **Obv. Inscription:** "R22", "22" or no notation on obverse **Rev. Inscription:** "MDM22" at left **Note:** Commercial copy of 1 Guinea, KM#36.

Date	Mintage	F	VF	XF	Unc	BU
AH1370 (1950)	—	—	—	—	—BV+10%	

KM# 43 GUINEA
7.9881 g., 0.9170 Gold .2354 oz. AGW

Date	Mintage	F	VF	XF	Unc	BU
AH1377 (1957)	1,579,000	—	—	BV	200	250

BULLION COINAGE
Post WWII Issues

KM# 35 SOVEREIGN (Pound)
7.9881 g., 0.9170 Gold .2354 oz. AGW **Obv:** Eagle with wings open **Rev:** Three lined inscription within horizontal bars **Note:** KM#35 and KM#34 were struck at the Philadelphia Mint for a concession payment for oil to the Saudi Government. Most were melted into bullion.

Date	Mintage	F	VF	XF	Unc	BU
ND(1947)	123,000	—	300	500	750	

KM# 34 4 POUNDS
31.9500 g., 0.9170 Gold .9420 oz. AGW **Obv:** Eagle with wings open **Rev:** Three lined inscription within horizontal bars **Note:** KM#34 and KM#35 were struck at the Philadelphia Mint for a concession payment for oil to the Saudi Government. Most were melted into bullion.

Date	Mintage	F	VF	XF	Unc	BU
ND(1945-46)	91,000	—	650	800	1,200	

FANTASY COINAGE

X# 12 5 DIRHAM
15.0000 g., 0.9990 Silver 0.4818 oz. ASW, 27 mm. **Issuer:** Umar Ibrahim Vadillo **Obv:** Legend around Kalima **Rev:** Kaaba

Date	Mintage	F	VF	XF	Unc	BU
ND(1999) Proof	—	Value: 15.00				

X# 13 DINAR
4.3000 g., 0.9170 Gold 0.1268 oz. AGW, 23 mm. **Issuer:** Umar Ibrahim Vadillo **Obv:** Legend around Kalima **Rev:** Domed tomb, mineret

Date	Mintage	F	VF	XF	Unc	BU
ND(1999) Proof	—	Value: 200				

X# 14 HEAVY DINAR
8.6000 g., 0.9170 Gold 0.2535 oz. AGW, 26 mm. **Issuer:** Umar Ibrahim Vadillo **Obv:** Legend around Kalima **Rev:** Domed tomb, mineret

Date	Mintage	F	VF	XF	Unc	BU
ND(1999) Proof	—	Value: 300				

PATTERNS
Including off metal strikes

KM#	Date	Mintage	Identification	Mkt Val
Pn4	AH1370	—	Guinea. Aluminum. KM#36.	1,500
Pn5	AH1370	—	Guinea. Bronze. KM#36, reeded edge, with Paris privy marks.	3,500
Pn6	AH1370	—	Guinea. Gold. KM#36, reeded edge, with Paris privy marks, Rare.	

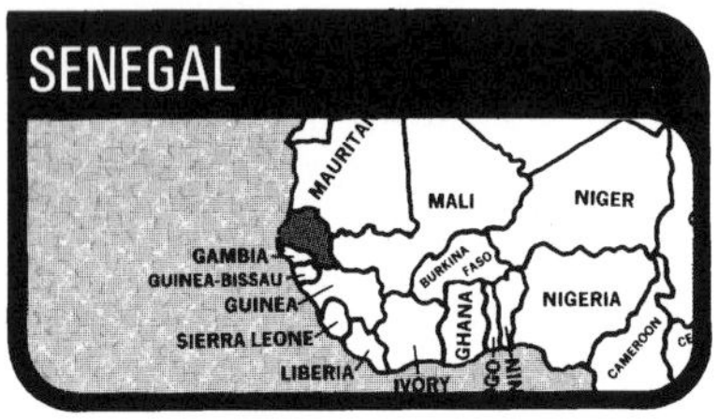

620 SENEGAL

The Republic of Senegal, located on the bulge of West Africa between Mauritania and Guinea-Bissau, has an area of 75,750 sq. mi. (196,190 sq. km.) and a population of *7.5 million. Capital: Dakar. The economy is primarily agricultural. Peanuts and products, phosphates, and canned fish are exported.

An abundance of megalithic remains indicates that Senegal was inhabited in prehistoric times. The Portuguese had some trading stations on the banks of the Senegal River in the 15th century. French commercial establishments date from the 17th century. The French gradually acquired control over the interior regions, which were administered as a protectorate until 1920, and as a colony thereafter. After the 1958 French constitutional referendum, Senegal became a member of the French Community with virtual autonomy. In 1959 Senegal and the French Soudan merged to form the Mali Federation, which became fully independent on June 20, 1960. (April 4, the date the transfer of power agreement was signed with France, is celebrated as Senegal's independence day). The Federation broke up on Aug. 20, 1960, when Senegal seceded and proclaimed the Republic of Senegal. Soudan became the Republic of Mali a month later.

Senegal is a member of a monetary union of autonomous republics called the Monetary Union of West African States (*Union Monetaire Ouest-Africaine*). The other members are Ivory Coast, Benin, Burkina Faso (Upper Volta), Niger, Mauritania and Togo. Mali was a member, but seceded in 1962. Some of the member countries have issued coinage in addition to the common currency issued by the Monetary Union of West African States.

REPUBLIC
STANDARD COINAGE

KM# 1 10 FRANCS
3.2000 g., 0.9000 Gold .0926 oz. AGW **Subject:** 8th Anniversary of Independence **Obv:** Star above shield within wreath **Rev:** Stars above value and date

Date	Mintage	F	VF	XF	Unc	BU
1968 Proof	—	Value: 85.00				

KM# 2 25 FRANCS
8.0000 g., 0.9000 Gold .2315 oz. AGW **Subject:** 8th Anniversary of Independence **Obv:** Star above shield within wreath **Rev:** Stars above value and date

Date	Mintage	F	VF	XF	Unc	BU
1968 Proof	—	Value: 175				

KM# 3 50 FRANCS
16.0000 g., 0.9000 Gold .463 oz. AGW **Subject:** 8th Anniversary of Independence **Obv:** Star above shield within wreath **Rev:** Stars above value and date

Date	Mintage	F	VF	XF	Unc	BU
1968 Proof	—	Value: 325				

KM# 4 100 FRANCS
32.0000 g., 0.9000 Gold .926 oz. AGW **Subject:** 8th Anniversary of Independence **Obv:** Star above shield within wreath **Rev:** Stars above value and date

Date	Mintage	F	VF	XF	Unc	BU
1968 Proof	—	Value: 650				

KM# 7 250 FRANCS
3.9800 g., 0.9170 Gold .1172 oz. AGW **Subject:** 25th Anniversary of Eurafrique Program **Obv:** Star above shield within wreath **Rev:** Bust facing

Date	Mintage	F	VF	XF	Unc	BU
1975	1,000	—	—	—	90.00	—
1975 Proof	1,250	Value: 90.00				

KM# 8 500 FRANCS
7.9600 g., 0.9170 Gold .2344 oz. AGW **Subject:** 25th Anniversary of Eurafrique Program **Obv:** Star above shield within wreath **Rev:** Bust facing

Date	Mintage	F	VF	XF	Unc	BU
1975	500	—	—	—	200	—
1975 Proof	1,250	Value: 165				

KM# 9 1000 FRANCS
15.9500 g., 0.9160 Gold .4697 oz. AGW **Subject:** 25th Anniversary of Eurafrique Program **Obv:** Star above shield within wreath **Rev:** Bust facing

Date	Mintage	F	VF	XF	Unc	BU
1975	217	—	—	—	375	—
1975 Proof	1,250	Value: 325				

KM# 10 2500 FRANCS
39.9300 g., 0.9160 Gold 1.176 oz. AGW **Subject:** 25th Anniversary of Eurafrique Program **Obv:** Star above shield within wreath **Rev:** Bust facing

Date	Mintage	F	VF	XF	Unc	BU
1975	195	—	—	—	875	—
1975 Proof	1,250	Value: 825				

MINT SETS

KM#	Date	Mintage	Identification	Issue Price	Mkt Val
MS1	1975 (4)	195	KM#7-10	—	1,550

PROOF SETS

KM#	Date	Mintage	Identification	Issue Price	Mkt Val
PS1	1968 (4)	—	KM#1-4	—	1,225

SERBIA

Serbia, a former inland Balkan kingdom has an area of 34,116 sq. mi. (88,361 sq. km.). Capital: Belgrade.

Serbia emerged as a separate kingdom in the 12th century and attained its greatest expansion and political influence in the mid-14th century. After the Battle of Kosovo, 1389, Serbia became a vassal principality of Turkey and remained under Turkish suzerainty until it was re-established as an independent kingdom by the 1878 Treaty of Berlin. Following World War I, which had its immediate cause in the assassination of Austrian Archduke Francis Ferdinand by a Serbian nationalist, Serbia joined with the Croats and Slovenes to form the new Kingdom of the South Slavs with Peter I of Serbia as King. The name of the kingdom was later changed to Yugoslavia. Invaded by Germany during World War II, Serbia emerged as a constituent republic of the Socialist Federal Republic of Yugoslavia.

RULERS
Michael, Obrenovich III
...as Prince, 1839-1842, 1860-1868
Milan, Obrenovich IV,
...as Prince, 1868-1882
...as King, 1882-1889
Alexander I, 1889-1902
Peter I, 1903-1918

MINT MARKS
A - Paris
(a) - Paris, privy mark only
(g) - Gorham Mfg. Co., Providence, R.I.
H - Birmingham
V - Vienna
БП - (BP) Budapest

MONETARY SYSTEM
100 Para = 1 Dinara

DENOMINATIONS
ПАРА = Para
ПАРЕ = Pare
ДИНАР = Dinar
ДИНАРА = Dinara

KINGDOM
STANDARD COINAGE

KM# 16 10 DINARA
3.2258 g., 0.9000 Gold .0933 oz. AGW **Ruler:** Milan I as King **Obv:** Head right **Obv. Legend:** Short title like KM#17 **Rev:** Value, date within crowned wreath

Date	Mintage	F	VF	XF	Unc	BU
1882	300,000	80.00	140	190	340	—

KM# 14 20 DINARA
6.4516 g., 0.9000 Gold .1867 oz. AGW **Ruler:** Milan I as Prince **Obv:** Head right **Obv. Legend:** Full title **Rev:** Value, date within crowned wreath

Date	Mintage	F	VF	XF	Unc	BU
1879A	50,000	135	175	320	600	—
1879A Proof	—	Value: 5,000				

KM# 17.2 20 DINARA
6.4516 g., 0.9000 Gold .1867 oz. AGW, 0.1867 mm. **Ruler:** Milan I as King **Obv:** Head right **Obv. Legend:** Short title **Rev:** Value, date within crowned wreath **Edge:** Type II **Edge Lettering:** БОГ*ЧУВА*СРБИJУ***

Date	Mintage	F	VF	XF	Unc	BU
1882V	—	—	—	—	—	—

KM# 17.1 20 DINARA
6.4516 g., 0.9000 Gold .1867 oz. AGW **Ruler:** Milan I as King **Obv:** Head right **Obv. Legend:** Short title **Rev:** Value, date within crowned wreath **Edge:** Type I **Edge Lettering:** БОГ*ЧУВА*СРБИJУ***

Date	Mintage	F	VF	XF	Unc	BU
1882V	300,000	120	150	200	340	—

REPUBLIC
STANDARD COINAGE

KM# 44 5000 DINARA
3.4550 g., 0.9000 Gold 0.1 oz. AGW, 20 mm. **Obv:** Crowned and mantled Serbian royal arms **Rev:** Nikola Tesla

Date	Mintage	F	VF	XF	Unc	BU
2006 Proof	2,000	Value: 125				

KM# 45 10000 DINARA
8.6400 g., 0.9000 Gold 0.25 oz. AGW, 25 mm. **Obv:** Crowned and mantled Serbian royal arms **Rev:** Nikola Tesla

Date	Mintage	F	VF	XF	Unc	BU
2006 Proof	1,000	Value: 275				

PATTERNS
Including off metal strikes

KM#	Date	Mintage	Identification	Mkt Val
Pn1	1882V	—	20 Dinara. Copper.	1,250
PnD6	1904	4	5 Dinara. Gold. 44.5000 g.	—
Pn6	1917	—	5 Para. Gold.	—
Pn7	1917	—	10 Para. Gold.	—
Pn8	1917	—	20 Para. Gold.	—
Pn9	1917	—	20 Dinara. Gold.	—

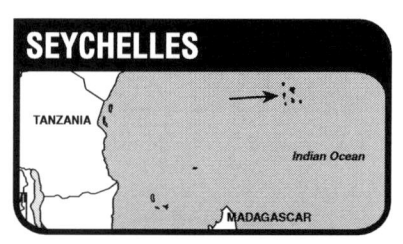

SEYCHELLES

The Republic of Seychelles, an archipelago of 85 granite and coral islands situated in the Indian Ocean 600 miles (965 km.) northeast of Madagascar, has an area of 156 sq. mi. (455 sq. km.) and a population of *70,000. Among these islands are the Aldabra Islands, the Farquhar Group, and Ile Desroches, which the United Kingdom ceded to the Seychelles upon its independence. Capital: Victoria, on Mahe. The economy is based on fishing, a plantation system of agriculture, and tourism. Copra, cinnamon and vanilla are exported.

Although the Seychelles is marked on Portuguese charts of the early 16th century, the first recorded visit to the islands, by an English ship, occurred in 1609. The Seychelles were annexed to France by Captain Lazare Picault in 1743 and permanently settled in 1768, with the intention of establishing spice plantations to compete with the Dutch monopoly of the spice trade. British troops seized the islands in 1810, during the Napoleonic Wars; the Treaty of Paris, 1814, formally ceded them to Britain. The Seychelles was a dependency of Mauritius until Aug. 31, 1903, when they became a separate British Crown Colony. The colony was granted limited internal self-government in 1970, and attained independence on June 28, 1976, becoming Britain's last African possession to do so. Seychelles is a member of the Commonwealth of Nations. The president is the Head of State and of Government.

RULER
British, until 1976

MINT MARKS
M – South African Mint Co.
M in oval – South African Mint Co.
 On coins dated 2000 and up in
 Place of PM
PM - Pobjoy Mint
None - British Royal Mint

MONETARY SYSTEM
100 Cents = 1 Rupee

REPUBLIC
STANDARD COINAGE

KM# 52b 20 RUPEES
33.9000 g., 0.9170 Gold .9994 oz. AGW **Subject:** 5th Anniversary of Central Bank **Obv:** Arms with supporters **Rev:** Turtle at center of symbols of commerce

Date	Mintage	F	VF	XF	Unc	BU
1983 Proof	50	Value: 1,000				

KM# 53b 25 RUPEES
47.5400 g., 0.9170 Gold 1.4015 oz. AGW **Series:** F.A.O. **Subject:** World Fisheries Conference **Obv:** Arms with supporters **Rev:** Fish trap **Rev. Designer:** Stuart Devlin

Date	Mintage	F	VF	XF	Unc	BU
1983 Proof	100	Value: 1,100				

SEYCHELLES

KM# 96 25 RUPEES
1.2400 g., 0.9990 Gold .0398 oz. AGW **Subject:** Diana - The People's Princess **Obv:** Arms with supporters **Rev:** Diana holding baby Prince William

Date	Mintage	F	VF	XF	Unc	BU
1997 Proof	Est. 10,000	Value: 55.00				

KM# 100 25 RUPEES
1.2400 g., 0.9990 Gold .0398 oz. AGW **Subject:** Diana - The People's Princess **Obv:** Arms with supporters **Rev:** Diana holding young cancer patient

Date	Mintage	F	VF	XF	Unc	BU
1997 Proof	Est. 10,000	Value: 55.00				

KM# 92 25 RUPEES
1.2400 g., 0.9990 Gold .0398 oz. AGW **Subject:** Diana - The People's Princess **Obv:** Arms with supporters **Rev:** Head 1/4 right **Note:** Similar to KM#91.

Date	Mintage	F	VF	XF	Unc	BU
1997 Proof	Est. 10,000	Value: 50.00				

KM# 104 25 RUPEES
1.2441 g., 0.9999 Gold .0400 oz. AGW **Subject:** Diana - The People's Princess **Obv:** Arms with supporters **Rev:** Diana in summer clothes

Date	Mintage	F	VF	XF	Unc	BU
1998 Proof	Est. 10,000	Value: 60.00				

KM# 75 50 RUPEES
1.2440 g., 0.9999 Gold .0497 oz. AGW **Series:** Endangered Wildlife **Obv:** Arms with supporters **Rev:** Milkweed Butterfly **Note:** Similar to 25 Rupees, KM#74.

Date	Mintage	F	VF	XF	Unc	BU
1994 PM Prooflike	—	—	—	—	—	45.00

KM# 107 50 RUPEES
3.1100 g., 0.5833 Gold .0583 oz. AGW **Series:** Olympics Games 2000 **Obv:** Arms with supporters **Rev:** Two divers

Date	Mintage	F	VF	XF	Unc	BU
1997 Proof	5,000	Value: 65.00				

KM# 76 100 RUPEES
3.1103 g., 0.9999 Gold .1000 oz. AGW **Series:** Endangered Wildlife **Obv:** Arms with supporters **Rev:** Milkweed Butterfly

Date	Mintage	F	VF	XF	Unc	BU
1994 PM Prooflike	—	—	—	—	—	100

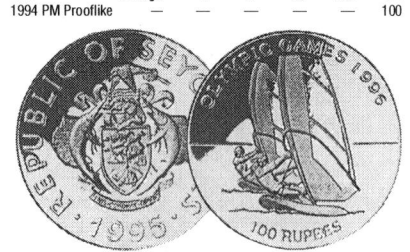

KM# 82 100 RUPEES
7.7760 g., 0.5830 Gold .1458 oz. AGW **Series:** Olympics **Obv:** Arms with supporters **Rev:** Sailboats

Date	Mintage	F	VF	XF	Unc	BU
1995 Proof	Est. 3,000	Value: 125				

KM# 86 100 RUPEES
7.7760 g., 0.5830 Gold .1458 oz. AGW **Subject:** British Queen Mother **Obv:** Arms with supporters **Rev:** Wedding portrait

Date	Mintage	F	VF	XF	Unc	BU
1995	Est. 5,000	—	—	—	135	150

KM# 93 100 RUPEES
7.7760 g., 0.5830 Gold .1458 oz. AGW **Subject:** Diana - The People's Princess **Obv:** Arms with supporters **Rev:** Bust facing

Date	Mintage	F	VF	XF	Unc	BU
1997 Proof	Est. 7,500	Value: 120				

KM# A97 100 RUPEES
7.7760 g., 0.5830 Gold .1458 oz. AGW **Subject:** Diana - The People's Princess **Obv:** Arms with supporters **Rev:** Diana holding newborn Prince William

Date	Mintage	F	VF	XF	Unc	BU
1997	7,500	Value: 120				

KM# 101 100 RUPEES
7.7760 g., 0.5830 Gold .1458 oz. AGW **Subject:** Diana - The People's Princess **Obv:** Arms with supporters **Rev:** Diana holding young cancer patient

Date	Mintage	F	VF	XF	Unc	BU
1997 Proof	Est. 7,500	Value: 115				

KM# 105 100 RUPEES
7.7760 g., 0.5830 Gold .1458 oz. AGW **Subject:** Diana - The People's Princess **Obv:** Arms with supporters **Rev:** Diana in summer clothes

Date	Mintage	F	VF	XF	Unc	BU
1998 Proof	Est. 7,500	Value: 115				

KM# 111 100 RUPEES
6.2200 g., 0.9999 Gold .2000 oz. AGW **Subject:** Marriage of Prince Edward **Obv:** Arms with supporters **Rev:** Tied monograms and birds

Date	Mintage	F	VF	XF	Unc	BU
1999 Proof	Est. 2,000	Value: 185				

KM# 116 100 RUPEES
6.2200 g., 0.9999 Gold .2000 oz. AGW, 22 mm. **Subject:** 100th Birthday Queen Mother **Obv:** Arms with supporters **Rev:** Queen Mother's portrait **Edge:** Reeded

Date	Mintage	F	VF	XF	Unc	BU
2000 Proof	2,000	Value: 175				

KM# 66 250 RUPEES
6.2200 g., 0.9990 Gold .2000 oz. AGW **Series:** Endangered Wildlife **Obv:** Arms with supporters **Rev:** Magpie Robin

Date	Mintage	F	VF	XF	Unc	BU
1993 Proof	—	Value: 165				

KM# 77 250 RUPEES
6.2200 g., 0.9990 Gold .2000 oz. AGW **Series:** Endangered Wildlife **Obv:** Arms with supporters **Rev:** Milkweed Butterfly

Date	Mintage	F	VF	XF	Unc	BU
1993 Proof	—	Value: 200				
1994 PM Prooflike	—	—	—	—	150	—
1996 PM Proof	5,000	Value: 185				

KM# 84 250 RUPEES
6.2200 g., 0.9990 Gold .2000 oz. AGW **Series:** Endangered Wildlife **Obv:** Arms with supporters **Rev:** Paradise Flycatcher Bird

Date	Mintage	F	VF	XF	Unc	BU
1996 Proof	Est. 5,000	Value: 185				

KM# 98 250 RUPEES
6.2200 g., 0.9990 Gold .2000 oz. AGW **Subject:** Diana - The People's Princess **Obv:** Arms with supporters **Rev:** Diana holding newborn Prince William

Date	Mintage	F	VF	XF	Unc	BU
1997 Proof	Est. 5,000	Value: 185				

KM# 102 250 RUPEES
6.2200 g., 0.9990 Gold .2000 oz. AGW **Subject:** Diana - The People's Princess **Obv:** Arms with supporters **Rev:** Diana holding young cancer patient

Date	Mintage	F	VF	XF	Unc	BU
1997 Proof	Est. 5,000	Value: 185				

KM# 94 250 RUPEES
6.2200 g., 0.9990 Gold .2000 oz. AGW **Subject:** Diana - The People's Princess **Obv:** Arms with supporters **Rev:** Bust facing **Note:** Similar to 25 Rupees, KM#91.

Date	Mintage	F	VF	XF	Unc	BU
1997 Proof	Est. 5,000	Value: 185				

KM# 106 250 RUPEES
6.2200 g., 0.9990 Gold .2000 oz. AGW **Subject:** Diana - The People's Princess **Obv:** Arms with supporters **Rev:** Diana in summer dress

Date	Mintage	F	VF	XF	Unc	BU
1998 Proof	Est. 5,000	Value: 185				

KM# 123 250 RUPEES
6.2200 g., 0.9999 Gold 0.2 oz. AGW, 22 mm. **Obv:** National arms **Rev:** Benedict XVI blessing crowd at St. Peter's Square **Edge:** Reeded

Date	Mintage	F	VF	XF	Unc	BU
2005 Proof	—	Value: 200				

KM# 122 250 RUPEES
6.2200 g., 0.9999 Gold 0.2 oz. AGW, 22 mm. **Obv:** National arms **Rev:** Description John Paul II in mitre waving **Edge:** Reeded

Date	Mintage	F	VF	XF	Unc	BU
2005 Proof	—	Value: 200				

KM# 62 500 RUPEES
7.1300 g., 0.9000 Gold .2036 oz. AGW **Series:** Decade for Women **Obv:** Arms with supporters **Rev:** Value below standing figures

Date	Mintage	F	VF	XF	Unc	BU
1985 Proof	500	Value: 175				

KM# 29 1000 RUPEES
15.9800 g., 0.9170 Gold .4707 oz. AGW **Subject:** Declaration of Independence **Obv:** President Mancham **Rev:** Tortoise, date, value

Date	Mintage	F	VF	XF	Unc	BU
1976	5,000	—	—	—	335	—
1976 Proof	1,000	Value: 375				

KM# 56 1000 RUPEES
15.9800 g., 0.9170 Gold .4707 oz. AGW **Subject:** 10th Anniversary of Independence **Obv:** Arms with supporters **Rev:** Design above shark tail design dividing dates

Date	Mintage	F	VF	XF	Unc	BU
ND(1986) Proof	100	Value: 415				

KM# 58 1000 RUPEES
15.9800 g., 0.9170 Gold .4707 oz. AGW **Subject:** 10th Anniversary of Liberation **Obv:** Arms with supporters **Rev:** Standing figure divides dates

Date	Mintage	F	VF	XF	Unc	BU
ND(1987) PM Proof	100	Value: 400				

KM# 61 1000 RUPEES
15.9400 g., 0.9170 Gold .4698 oz. AGW **Subject:** 100th Anniversary of Central Bank **Obv:** Arms with supporters **Rev:** Sea turtle

Date	Mintage	F	VF	XF	Unc	BU
ND(1988) PM Proof	Est. 5,000	Value: 345				

KM# 73 1000 RUPEES
15.9800 g., 0.9170 Gold .4710 oz. AGW **Subject:** Central Banking

Date	Mintage	F	VF	XF	Unc	BU
1993 Proof	Est. 200	Value: 375				

KM# 41 1500 RUPEES
33.4370 g., 0.9000 Gold .9676 oz. AGW **Subject:** Conservation **Obv:** Arms with supporters **Rev:** Flycatcher birds

Date	Mintage	F	VF	XF	Unc	BU
1978	683	—	—	—	675	—
1978 Proof	201	Value: 975				

PIEFORTS

KM#	Date	Mintage	Identification	Mkt Val
P4	1984	100	50 Rupees. 0.9000 Gold.	1,500

PROOF SETS

KM#	Date	Mintage	Identification	Issue Price	Mkt Val
PS4	1976 (9)	1,000	KM#21-26, 27a, 28a, 29	375	375

SHARJAH

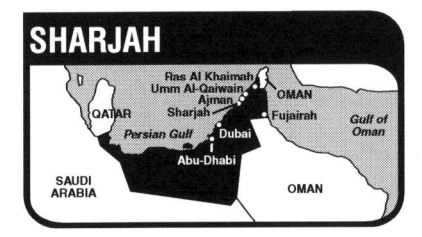

Sharjah is the only one of the emirates that shares boundaries with all of the others plus Oman. It has an area of 1,000 sq. mi. (2,600 sq. km.) and a population of 40,000. Sharjah was an important pirate base in the 18th and early 19th centuries. Most of the treaties and diplomatic relations were with Great Britain.

TITLE
Ash-Sharqa(t)

RULERS
Saqr Bin Khalid al-Qasimi, 1883-1914
Khalid Bin Ahmad al-Qasimi, 1914-1924
Sultan Bin Saqr al-Qasimi, 1924-1951
Saqr Bin Sultan al-Qasimi, 1951-1965
Khalid Bin Muhammad al-Qasimi, 1965-1972
Sultan Bin Muhammad al-Qasimi, 1972-

EMIRATE

NON-CIRCULATING LEGAL TENDER COINAGE

KM# 7 25 RIYALS
5.1800 g., 0.9000 Gold .1499 oz. AGW **Ruler:** Khalid bin Muhammad al-Qasimi **Subject:** Mona Lisa **Obv:** National arms **Rev:** Bust facing

Date	Mintage	F	VF	XF	Unc	BU
AH1389-1970 Proof	6,775	Value: 165				

KM# 8 50 RIYALS
10.3600 g., 0.9000 Gold .2998 oz. AGW **Ruler:** Khalid bin Muhammad al-Qasimi **Subject:** Mexico World Soccer Cup **Obv:** National arms **Rev:** World soccer cup within globe design

Date	Mintage	F	VF	XF	Unc	BU
AH1389-1970 Proof	1,815	Value: 275				

KM# 9 100 RIYALS
20.7300 g., 0.9000 Gold .5999 oz. AGW **Ruler:** Khalid bin Muhammad al-Qasimi **Subject:** Bicentennial - Napoleon **Obv:** National arms **Rev:** Uniformed bust facing 1/4 left divides logo and dated

Date	Mintage	F	VF	XF	Unc	BU
AH1389-1970 Proof	—	Value: 465				

KM# 10 100 RIYALS
20.7300 g., 0.9000 Gold .5999 oz. AGW **Ruler:** Khalid bin Muhammad al-Qasimi **Subject:** Bolivar **Obv:** National arms **Rev:** Head right

Date	Mintage	F	VF	XF	Unc	BU
AH1389-1970 Proof	—	Value: 450				

KM# 11 200 RIYALS
41.4600 g., 0.9000 Gold 1.1998 oz. AGW **Ruler:** Khalid bin Muhammad al-Qasimi **Subject:** Khalid III **Obv:** National arms **Rev:** Head facing

Date	Mintage	F	VF	XF	Unc	BU
AH1389-1970 Proof	435	Value: 900				

PROOF SETS

KM#	Date	Mintage	Identification	Issue Price	Mkt Val
PS1	1970 (9)	—	KM#2-5, 7-11	—	2,400
PS2	1970 (5)	—	KM#7-11	—	2,250

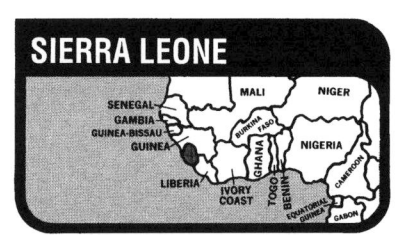

SIERRA LEONE

The Republic of Sierra Leone, a British Commonwealth nation located in western Africa between Guinea and Liberia, has an area of 27,699 sq. mi. (71,740 sq. km.) and a population of *4.1 million. Capital: Freetown. The economy is predominantly agricultural but mining contributes significantly to export revenues. Diamonds, iron ore, palm kernels, cocoa, and coffee are exported.

The coast of Sierra Leone was first visited by Portuguese and British slavers in the 15th and 16th centuries. The first settlement, at Freetown, 1787, was established as a refuge for freed slaves within the British Empire, runaway slaves from the United States and Negroes discharged from the British armed forces. The first settlers were virtually wiped out by tribal attacks and disease. The colony was re-established under the auspices of the Sierra Leone Company and transferred to the British Crown in 1807. The interior region was secured and established as a protectorate in 1896. Sierra Leone became independent within the Commonwealth on April 27, 1961, and adopted a republican constitution ten years later. It is a member of the Commonwealth of Nations. The president is Chief of State and Head of Government.

For similar coinage refer to British West Africa.

RULER
British, until 1971

MONETARY SYSTEM
Until 1906
100 Cents = 50 Pence = 1 Dollar
Commencing 1964
100 Cents = 1 Leone = 1 Dollar
NOTE: Sierra Leone's official currency is the Leone.

BRITISH COLONY
Sierra Leone Company

MEDALLIC COINAGE
Richard Lobel Issues

X# M2 SOVEREIGN
0.3750 Gold **Subject:** Edward VIII

Date	Mintage	F	VF	XF	Unc	BU
1936 Proof	150	Value: 125				

REPUBLIC

STANDARD COINAGE

KM# 21b LEONE
0.9170 Gold **Obv:** Value above arms **Rev:** Head of right Sir Milton Margai

Date	Mintage	F	VF	XF	Unc	BU
1964 Proof	10	Value: 2,500				

624 SIERRA LEONE

KM# 26b LEONE
Gold **Subject:** 10 Anniversary of Bank **Obv:** Head of Dr. Siaka Stevens right **Rev:** Lion right within circle

Date	Mintage	F	VF	XF	Unc	BU
1974	100	—	—	—	1,250	—

KM# 40a LEONE
16.0000 g., 0.9170 Gold .4716 oz. AGW **Subject:** Freetown Bicentennial **Obv:** Numeral 200 within design **Rev:** Bust of Dr. Joseph Saidu Momoh left **Shape:** Octagon

Date	Mintage	F	VF	XF	Unc	BU
1987 Proof	1,250	Value: 375				

KM# 39 100 LEONES
15.9800 g., 0.9170 Gold .4711 oz. AGW **Series:** Year of the Scout **Obv:** Lion within shield **Rev:** Head of Dr. Siaka Stevens right

Date	Mintage	F	VF	XF	Unc	BU
ND(1983)	2,000	—	—	—	345	—
ND(1983) Proof	2,000	Value: 400				

KM# 22 1/4 GOLDE
13.6360 g., 0.9000 Gold .3946 oz. AGW, 24 mm. **Subject:** 5th Anniversary of Independence **Obv:** Value within map **Rev:** Lion head facing

Date	Mintage	F	VF	XF	Unc	BU
ND(1966)	5,000	—	—	—	275	320

KM# 22a 1/4 GOLDE
15.0000 g., 0.9160 Gold .4418 oz. AGW **Subject:** 5th Anniversary of Independence **Obv:** Value within map **Rev:** Lion head facing

Date	Mintage	F	VF	XF	Unc	BU
ND(1966) Proof	600	Value: 350				

KM# 22b 1/4 GOLDE
10.3150 g., Palladium **Subject:** 5th Anniversary of Independence **Obv:** Value within map **Rev:** Lion head facing

Date	Mintage	F	VF	XF	Unc	BU
ND(1966) Proof	100	Value: 325				

KM# 23 1/2 GOLDE
27.2730 g., 0.9000 Gold .7891 oz. AGW, 32 mm. **Subject:** 5th Anniversary of Independence **Obv:** Value within map **Rev:** Lion head facing

Date	Mintage	F	VF	XF	Unc	BU
ND(1966)	2,500	—	—	—	550	575

KM# 23a 1/2 GOLDE
30.0000 g., 0.9160 Gold .8836 oz. AGW **Subject:** 5th Anniversary of Independence **Obv:** Value within map **Rev:** Lion head facing

Date	Mintage	F	VF	XF	Unc	BU
ND(1966) Proof	600	Value: 650				

KM# 23b 1/2 GOLDE
20.6290 g., Palladium **Subject:** 5th Anniversary of Independence **Obv:** Value within map **Rev:** Lion head facing

Date	Mintage	F	VF	XF	Unc	BU
ND(1966) Proof	100	Value: 600				

KM# 24 GOLDE
54.5450 g., 0.9000 Gold 1.5783 oz. AGW, 48 mm. **Subject:** 5th Anniversary of Independence **Obv:** Value within map **Rev:** Lion head facing

Date	Mintage	F	VF	XF	Unc	BU
ND(1966)	1,500	—	—	—	800	900
ND(1966)	1,500	—	—	—	1,150	1,200

KM# 24a GOLDE
60.0000 g., 0.9160 Gold 1.7672 oz. AGW **Subject:** 5th Anniversary of Independence **Obv:** Value within map **Rev:** Lion head facing

Date	Mintage	F	VF	XF	Unc	BU
ND(1966) Proof	400	Value: 1,300				

KM# 24b GOLDE
41.2590 g., Palladium **Subject:** 5th Anniversary of Independence **Obv:** Value within map **Rev:** Lion head facing

Date	Mintage	F	VF	XF	Unc	BU
ND(1966) Proof	100	Value: 1,150				

KM# 24c GOLDE
41.2590 g., Platinum APW **Subject:** 5th Anniversary of Independence **Obv:** Value within map **Rev:** Lion head facing

Date	Mintage	F	VF	XF	Unc	BU
ND(1966) Proof	—	Value: 1,750				

KM# 37 5 GOLDE
15.9800 g., 0.9170 Gold .4711 oz. AGW **Subject:** O.A.U. Summit Conference **Obv:** Head of Dr. Siaka Stevens right **Rev:** Map within circle

Date	Mintage	F	VF	XF	Unc	BU
1980	457	—	—	—	345	—
1980 Proof	325	Value: 375				

KM# 42 5 GOLDE
15.9980 g., 0.9170 Gold .4711 oz. AGW **Series:** World Wildlife Fund **Obv:** Bust of Dr. Joseph Saidu Momoh left **Rev:** Duiker Zebra

Date	Mintage	F	VF	XF	Unc	BU
1987 Proof	5,000	Value: 335				

KM# 28 10 GOLDE
57.6000 g., 0.9160 Gold 1.6965 oz. AGW **Subject:** 70th Birthday - Dr. Siaka Stevens **Obv:** Lion facing right **Rev:** Head right

Date	Mintage	F	VF	XF	Unc	BU
ND(1975)	727	—	—	—	1,200	—
ND(1975) Proof	307	Value: 1,350				

DOLLAR DENOMINATED COINAGE

KM# 270 10 DOLLARS
28.2800 g., 0.9250 Gold Clad Silver 0.841 oz., 38.6 mm. **Subject:** Queen's Golden Jubilee **Obv:** National arms **Rev:** Queen Elizabeth II and Prince Philip visiting blacksmiths in Sierra Leone **Edge:** Reeded

Date	Mintage	F	VF	XF	Unc	BU
2002 Proof	10,000	Value: 50.00				

KM# 271 10 DOLLARS
28.2800 g., 0.9250 Gold Clad Silver 0.841 oz., 38.6 mm. **Subject:** Queen's Golden Jubilee **Obv:** National arms **Rev:** Queen Elizabeth II, Prince Charles and Princess Anne **Edge:** Reeded

Date	Mintage	F	VF	XF	Unc	BU
2002 Proof	10,000	Value: 50.00				

SIERRA LEONE 625

KM# 283 10 DOLLARS
28.2800 g., 0.9250 Gold Clad Silver 0.841 oz., 38.6 mm.
Subject: Queen Elizabeth's Golden Jubilee **Obv:** National arms **Rev:** Queen and young Prince Charles **Edge:** Reeded

Date	Mintage	F	VF	XF	Unc	BU
2002 Proof	10,000	Value: 47.50				

KM# 286 10 DOLLARS
28.2800 g., 0.9250 Gold Clad Silver 0.841 oz., 38.6 mm.
Subject: Queen Elizabeth's Golden Jubilee **Obv:** National arms **Rev:** Queen and Prince Philip **Edge:** Reeded

Date	Mintage	F	VF	XF	Unc	BU
2002 Proof	10,000	Value: 47.50				

KM# 277 10 DOLLARS
28.2800 g., 0.9250 Gold Clad Silver 0.841 oz., 38.6 mm.
Subject: British Queen Mother **Obv:** National arms **Rev:** Bust facing in garden with dog within sprigs **Edge:** Reeded

Date	Mintage	F	VF	XF	Unc	BU
2002 Proof	10,000	Value: 47.50				

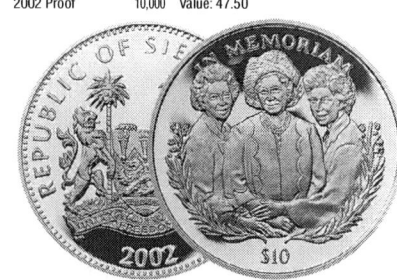

KM# 280 10 DOLLARS
28.2800 g., 0.9250 Gold Clad Silver 0.841 oz., 38.6 mm.
Subject: British Queen Mother **Obv:** National arms **Rev:** Conjoined busts facing within sprigs **Edge:** Reeded

Date	Mintage	F	VF	XF	Unc	BU
2002 Proof	10,000	Value: 47.50				

KM# 73 20 DOLLARS
1.2441 g., 0.9990 Gold .0400 oz. AGW **Subject:** Diana - The Peoples' Princess **Obv:** Arms **Rev:** Head facing

Date	Mintage	F	VF	XF	Unc	BU
1997 Proof	Est. 101,000	Value: 47.50				

KM# 79 20 DOLLARS
1.2441 g., 0.9990 Gold .0400 oz. AGW **Subject:** Diana - The Peoples' Princess **Obv:** Arms **Rev:** Lady Diana and Mother Theresa

Date	Mintage	F	VF	XF	Unc	BU
1997 Proof	Est. 101,000	Value: 55.00				

KM# 85 20 DOLLARS
1.2441 g., 0.9990 Gold .0400 oz. AGW **Subject:** Diana - The Peoples' Princess **Obv:** Arms **Rev:** Lady Diana and AIDS patient

Date	Mintage	F	VF	XF	Unc	BU
1997 Proof	Est. 101,000	Value: 42.50				

KM# 91 20 DOLLARS
1.2441 g., 0.9990 Gold .0400 oz. AGW **Subject:** Diana - The Peoples' Princess **Obv:** Arms **Rev:** With sons William and Harry

Date	Mintage	F	VF	XF	Unc	BU
1997 Proof	Est. 101,000	Value: 45.00				

KM# 105 20 DOLLARS
1.2441 g., 0.9990 Gold .0400 oz. AGW **Subject:** In Memorium **Obv:** Arms **Rev:** Lady Diana

Date	Mintage	F	VF	XF	Unc	BU
1998 Proof	Est. 10,000	Value: 50.00				

KM# 144 20 DOLLARS
1.2441 g., 0.9990 Gold .0400 oz. AGW **Subject:** Year of the Dragon **Obv:** Arms **Rev:** Dragon

Date	Mintage	F	VF	XF	Unc	BU
2000 Proof	Est. 15,000	Value: 55.00				

KM# 180 20 DOLLARS
1.2400 g., 0.9990 Gold .0399 oz. AGW **Subject:** Buddha **Obv:** Arms **Rev:** Seated Buddha **Edge:** Reeded **Note:** Struck at Pobjoy Mint.

Date	Mintage	F	VF	XF	Unc	BU
2000 Proof	Est. 5,000	Value: 55.00				

KM# 181 20 DOLLARS
1.2400 g., 0.9990 Gold .0399 oz. AGW **Obv:** Arms **Rev:** Goddess of Mercy

Date	Mintage	F	VF	XF	Unc	BU
2000 Proof	Est. 5,000	Value: 55.00				

KM# 182 20 DOLLARS
1.2400 g., 0.9990 Gold .0399 oz. AGW **Obv:** Arms **Rev:** Tzai-yen holding scroll

Date	Mintage	F	VF	XF	Unc	BU
2000 Proof	Est. 5,000	Value: 55.00				

KM# 216 20 DOLLARS
1.2441 g., 0.9990 Gold .0400 oz. AGW **Subject:** P'an Ku **Obv:** National arms **Rev:** Dragon and three animals

Date	Mintage	F	VF	XF	Unc	BU
2001 Proof	Est. 5,000	Value: 60.00				

KM# 200 20 DOLLARS
1.2441 g., 0.9990 Gold .0400 oz. AGW, 13.9 mm. **Subject:** Year of the Snake **Obv:** National arms **Rev:** Snake **Edge:** Reeded

Date	Mintage	F	VF	XF	Unc	BU
2001 Proof	Est. 50,000	Value: 60.00				

KM# 208 20 DOLLARS
1.2441 g., 0.9990 Gold .0400 oz. AGW **Subject:** P'an Ku **Obv:** National arms **Rev:** Dragon

Date	Mintage	F	VF	XF	Unc	BU
2001 Proof	Est. 5,000	Value: 60.00				

KM# 258 20 DOLLARS
1.2400 g., 0.9990 Gold .0398 oz. AGW, 13.92 mm. **Subject:** Year of the Horse **Obv:** National arms **Rev:** Horse **Edge:** Reeded

Date	Mintage	F	VF	XF	Unc	BU
2002 Proof	5,000	Value: 55.00				

KM# 272 30 DOLLARS
6.2200 g., 0.3750 Gold 0.075 oz. AGW, 22 mm. **Subject:** Queen's Golden Jubilee **Obv:** National arms **Rev:** Queen Elizabeth II and Prince Philip **Edge:** Reeded

Date	Mintage	F	VF	XF	Unc	BU
2002 Proof	5,000	Value: 95.00				

KM# 273 30 DOLLARS
6.2200 g., 0.3750 Gold 0.075 oz. AGW, 22 mm. **Subject:** Queen's Golden Jubilee **Obv:** National arms **Rev:** Queen Elizabeth II, Prince Charles and Princess Anne **Edge:** Reeded

Date	Mintage	F	VF	XF	Unc	BU
2002 Proof	5,000	Value: 95.00				

KM# 74 50 DOLLARS
3.1100 g., 0.9990 Gold .1000 oz. AGW **Subject:** Diana - The Peoples' Princess **Obv:** Arms **Rev:** Portrait of Lady Diana

Date	Mintage	F	VF	XF	Unc	BU
1997 Proof	Est. 7,500	Value: 85.00				

KM# 80 50 DOLLARS
3.1100 g., 0.9990 Gold .1000 oz. AGW **Subject:** Diana - The Peoples' Princess **Obv:** Arms **Rev:** Lady Diana and Mother Theresa

Date	Mintage	F	VF	XF	Unc	BU
1997 Proof	Est. 7,500	Value: 90.00				

KM# 86 50 DOLLARS
3.1100 g., 0.9990 Gold .1000 oz. AGW **Subject:** Diana - The Peoples' Princess **Obv:** Arms **Rev:** Lady Diana and AIDS patient

Date	Mintage	F	VF	XF	Unc	BU
1997 Proof	Est. 7,500	Value: 80.00				

KM# 92 50 DOLLARS
3.1100 g., 0.9990 Gold .1000 oz. AGW **Subject:** Diana - The Peoples' Princess **Obv:** Arms **Rev:** With sons William and Harry

Date	Mintage	F	VF	XF	Unc	BU
1997 Proof	Est. 7,500	Value: 85.00				

KM# 106 50 DOLLARS
3.1100 g., 0.9990 Gold .1000 oz. AGW **Subject:** Diana - The Peoples' Princess **Obv:** Arms **Rev:** Portrait of Lady Diana

Date	Mintage	F	VF	XF	Unc	BU
1998 Proof	Est. 7,500	Value: 90.00				

KM# 184 50 DOLLARS
3.1100 g., 0.9990 Gold .1000 oz. AGW **Obv:** Arms **Rev:** Goddess of Mercy

Date	Mintage	F	VF	XF	Unc	BU
2000 Proof	Est. 5,000	Value: 95.00				

KM# 145 50 DOLLARS
3.1100 g., 0.9990 Gold .1000 oz. AGW **Subject:** Year of the Dragon **Obv:** Arms **Rev:** Dragon

Date	Mintage	F	VF	XF	Unc	BU
2000 Proof	Est. 20,000	Value: 90.00				

KM# 183 50 DOLLARS
3.1100 g., 0.9990 Gold .1000 oz. AGW **Obv:** Arms **Rev:** Seated Buddha **Edge:** Reeded

Date	Mintage	F	VF	XF	Unc	BU
2000 Proof	Est. 5,000	Value: 95.00				

KM# 185 50 DOLLARS
3.1100 g., 0.9990 Gold .1000 oz. AGW **Obv:** Arms **Rev:** Tzai-yen holding scroll

Date	Mintage	F	VF	XF	Unc	BU
2000 Proof	Est. 5,000	Value: 95.00				

KM# 217 50 DOLLARS
3.1103 g., 0.9990 Gold .1000 oz. AGW **Subject:** P'an Ku **Obv:** National arms **Rev:** Dragon and three animals

Date	Mintage	F	VF	XF	Unc	BU
2001 Proof	Est. 5,000	Value: 95.00				

KM# 201 50 DOLLARS
3.1103 g., 0.9990 Gold .1000 oz. AGW, 18 mm. **Subject:** Year of the Snake **Obv:** National arms **Rev:** Snake **Edge:** Reeded

Date	Mintage	F	VF	XF	Unc	BU
2001 Proof	Est. 10,000	Value: 95.00				

KM# 209 50 DOLLARS
3.1103 g., 0.9990 Gold .1000 oz. AGW **Subject:** P'an Ku **Obv:** National arms **Rev:** Dragon

Date	Mintage	F	VF	XF	Unc	BU
2001 Proof	Est. 5,000	Value: 95.00				

KM# 259 50 DOLLARS
3.1100 g., 0.9990 Gold .0999 oz. AGW, 17.95 mm. **Subject:** Year of the Horse **Obv:** National arms **Rev:** Horse **Edge:** Reeded

Date	Mintage	F	VF	XF	Unc	BU
2002 Proof	5,000	Value: 95.00				

KM# 51 100 DOLLARS
6.2200 g., 0.9999 Gold .2000 oz. AGW **Subject:** Shanghai Coin and Stamp Exposition **Obv:** Arms **Rev:** Crowned lion

Date	Mintage	F	VF	XF	Unc	BU
1997 Proof	Est. 5,000	Value: 175				

KM# 52 100 DOLLARS
6.2200 g., 0.9999 Gold .2000 oz. AGW **Subject:** Shanghai Coin and Stamp Exposition **Obv:** Arms **Rev:** Crowned lion

Date	Mintage	F	VF	XF	Unc	BU
1997 Proof	Est. 5,000	Value: 175				

KM# 55 100 DOLLARS
6.2200 g., 0.9999 Gold .2000 oz. AGW **Subject:** Golden Wedding Anniversary **Obv:** Arms **Rev:** E and P monogram

Date	Mintage	F	VF	XF	Unc	BU
1997 Proof	Est. 3,500	Value: 175				

KM# 58 100 DOLLARS
6.2200 g., 0.9999 Gold .2000 oz. AGW **Subject:** Golden Wedding Anniversary **Obv:** Arms **Rev:** Yacht

Date	Mintage	F	VF	XF	Unc	BU
1997 Proof	Est. 3,500	Value: 175				

KM# 61 100 DOLLARS
6.2200 g., 0.9999 Gold .2000 oz. AGW **Subject:** Golden Wedding Anniversary **Obv:** Arms **Rev:** Royal couple

Date	Mintage	F	VF	XF	Unc	BU
1997 Proof	Est. 10,000	Value: 175				

KM# 64 100 DOLLARS
6.2200 g., 0.9999 Gold .2000 oz. AGW **Subject:** Golden Wedding Anniversary **Obv:** Arms **Rev:** Fireworks above palace

Date	Mintage	F	VF	XF	Unc	BU
1997 Proof	Est. 3,500	Value: 175				

KM# 67 100 DOLLARS
6.2200 g., 0.9999 Gold .2000 oz. AGW **Subject:** Golden Wedding Anniversary **Obv:** Arms **Rev:** Queen with two children

Date	Mintage	F	VF	XF	Unc	BU
1997 Proof	Est. 3,500	Value: 175				

KM# 70 100 DOLLARS
6.2200 g., 0.9999 Gold .2000 oz. AGW **Subject:** Golden Wedding Anniversary **Obv:** Arms **Rev:** Royal couple with two children

Date	Mintage	F	VF	XF	Unc	BU
1997 Proof	Est. 3,500	Value: 175				

KM# 75 100 DOLLARS
6.2200 g., 0.9999 Gold .2000 oz. AGW **Subject:** Diana - The Peoples' Princess **Obv:** Arms **Rev:** Portrait of Lady Diana

Date	Mintage	F	VF	XF	Unc	BU
1997 Proof	Est. 5,000	Value: 165				

KM# 81 100 DOLLARS
6.2200 g., 0.9999 Gold .2000 oz. AGW **Subject:** Diana - The Peoples' Princess **Obv:** Arms with supporters **Rev:** Diana with Mother Theresa

Date	Mintage	F	VF	XF	Unc	BU
1997 Proof	Est. 5,000	Value: 175				

KM# 87 100 DOLLARS
6.2200 g., 0.9999 Gold .2000 oz. AGW **Subject:** Diana - The Peoples' Princess **Obv:** Arms **Rev:** Lady Diana and AIDS patient

Date	Mintage	F	VF	XF	Unc	BU
1997 Proof	Est. 5,000	Value: 155				

KM# 93 100 DOLLARS
6.2200 g., 0.9999 Gold .2000 oz. AGW **Subject:** Diana - The Peoples' Princess **Obv:** Arms **Rev:** With sons William and Harry

Date	Mintage	F	VF	XF	Unc	BU
1997 Proof	Est. 5,000	Value: 160				

KM# 97 100 DOLLARS
6.2200 g., 0.9999 Gold .2000 oz. AGW **Subject:** Jurassic Park **Obv:** Arms **Rev:** Velociraptor

Date	Mintage	F	VF	XF	Unc	BU
1997 Proof	Est. 5,000	Value: 175				

KM# 100 100 DOLLARS
6.2200 g., 0.9999 Gold .2000 oz. AGW **Subject:** Queen Victoria's Diamond Jubilee Centennial **Obv:** Arms **Rev:** Crowned bust with diamond necklace facing

Date	Mintage	F	VF	XF	Unc	BU
1997 Proof	Est. 3,500	Value: 200				

KM# 107 100 DOLLARS
6.2200 g., 0.9999 Gold .2000 oz. AGW **Subject:** Diana - The People's Princess **Obv:** Arms **Rev:** Head half left

Date	Mintage	F	VF	XF	Unc	BU
1998 Proof	Est. 5,000	Value: 165				

KM# 111 100 DOLLARS
6.2200 g., 0.9999 Gold .2000 oz. AGW **Subject:** Dr. Livingstone **Obv:** Arms **Rev:** Dr. Livingstone above figures in boat

Date	Mintage	F	VF	XF	Unc	BU
1998 Proof	Est. 5,000	Value: 170				

KM# 114 100 DOLLARS
6.2200 g., 0.9999 Gold .2000 oz. AGW **Subject:** Amerigo Vespucci **Obv:** Arms **Rev:** Ship and mountainous portrait

Date	Mintage	F	VF	XF	Unc	BU
1999 Proof	Est. 5,000	Value: 175				

KM# 117 100 DOLLARS
6.2200 g., 0.9999 Gold .2000 oz. AGW **Subject:** Charles Darwin **Obv:** Arms **Rev:** Ship and portrait

Date	Mintage	F	VF	XF	Unc	BU
1999 Proof	Est. 5,000	Value: 175				

KM# 120 100 DOLLARS
6.2200 g., 0.9999 Gold .2000 oz. AGW **Subject:** China 2000 Series **Obv:** Arms **Rev:** Kneeling terra cotta warrior

Date	Mintage	F	VF	XF	Unc	BU
1999 Proof	Est. 5,000	Value: 165				

KM# 123 100 DOLLARS
6.2200 g., 0.9999 Gold .2000 oz. AGW **Subject:** China 2000 Series - Ming Dynasty **Obv:** Arms **Rev:** Temple of Heaven

Date	Mintage	F	VF	XF	Unc	BU
1999 Proof	Est. 5,000	Value: 165				

KM# 126 100 DOLLARS
6.2200 g., 0.9999 Gold .2000 oz. AGW **Subject:** China 2000 Series **Obv:** Arms **Rev:** Portion of the Great Wall

Date	Mintage	F	VF	XF	Unc	BU
1999 Proof	Est. 5,000	Value: 165				

KM# 129 100 DOLLARS
6.2200 g., 0.9999 Gold .2000 oz. AGW **Series:** China 2000 **Obv:** Arms **Rev:** Bronze chariot

Date	Mintage	F	VF	XF	Unc	BU
1999 Proof	Est. 5,000	Value: 165				

KM# 132 100 DOLLARS
6.2200 g., 0.9999 Gold .2000 oz. AGW **Series:** China 2000 **Obv:** Arms **Rev:** First century armillary sphere

Date	Mintage	F	VF	XF	Unc	BU
1999 Proof	Est. 5,000	Value: 165				

KM# 135 100 DOLLARS
6.2200 g., 0.9999 Gold .2000 oz. AGW **Series:** China 2000 **Obv:** Arms **Rev:** Tang Dynasty royal horse

Date	Mintage	F	VF	XF	Unc	BU
1999 Proof	Est. 5,000	Value: 165				

KM# 138 100 DOLLARS
6.2200 g., 0.9999 Gold .2000 oz. AGW **Subject:** Macau Return to China **Obv:** Arms **Rev:** Church, car, roulette wheel, and hands shaking

Date	Mintage	F	VF	XF	Unc	BU
1999 Proof	Est. 5,000	Value: 175				

KM# 141 100 DOLLARS
6.2200 g., 0.9999 Gold .2000 oz. AGW **Subject:** Prince Edward's Wedding **Obv:** Arms **Rev:** Symbolic wedding design

Date	Mintage	F	VF	XF	Unc	BU
1999 Proof	Est. 5,000	Value: 175				

KM# 146 100 DOLLARS
6.2200 g., 0.9999 Gold .2000 oz. AGW **Subject:** Year of the Dragon **Obv:** Arms **Rev:** Dragon

Date	Mintage	F	VF	XF	Unc	BU
2000 Proof	Est. 20,000	Value: 165				

KM# 186 100 DOLLARS
6.2200 g., 0.9999 Gold .2000 oz. AGW **Obv:** Arms **Rev:** Seated Buddha **Edge:** Reeded

Date	Mintage	F	VF	XF	Unc	BU
2000	Est. 5,000	Value: 175				

KM# 187 100 DOLLARS
6.2200 g., 0.9999 Gold .2000 oz. AGW **Obv:** Arms **Rev:** Goddess of Mercy

Date	Mintage	F	VF	XF	Unc	BU
2000 Proof	Est. 5,000	Value: 175				

KM# 188 100 DOLLARS
6.2200 g., 0.9999 Gold .2000 oz. AGW **Obv:** Arms **Rev:** Tzai-yen holding scroll

Date	Mintage	F	VF	XF	Unc	BU
2000 Proof	Est. 5,000	Value: 175				

KM# 251 100 DOLLARS
6.2200 g., 0.9990 Gold .1998 oz. AGW, 22 mm. **Series:** Big Cats **Obv:** National arms **Rev:** Male and female lions **Edge:** Reeded

Date	Mintage	F	VF	XF	Unc	BU
2001 Proof	5,000	Value: 175				

KM# 252 100 DOLLARS
6.2200 g., 0.9990 Gold .1998 oz. AGW, 22 mm. **Series:** Big Cats **Rev:** Tiger **Edge:** Reeded

Date	Mintage	F	VF	XF	Unc	BU
2001 Proof	5,000	Value: 175				

KM# 253 100 DOLLARS
6.2200 g., 0.9990 Gold .1998 oz. AGW, 22 mm. **Series:** Big Cats **Rev:** Cheetah **Edge:** Reeded

Date	Mintage	F	VF	XF	Unc	BU
2001 Proof	5,000	Value: 175				

KM# 254 100 DOLLARS
6.2200 g., 0.9990 Gold .1998 oz. AGW, 22 mm. **Series:** Big Cats **Rev:** Cougar **Edge:** Reeded

Date	Mintage	F	VF	XF	Unc	BU
2001 Proof	5,000	Value: 175				

KM# 255 100 DOLLARS
6.2200 g., 0.9990 Gold .1998 oz. AGW, 22 mm. **Series:** Big Cats **Rev:** Black panther **Edge:** Reeded

Date	Mintage	F	VF	XF	Unc	BU
2001 Proof	5,000	Value: 175				

KM# 202 100 DOLLARS
6.2200 g., 0.9990 Gold .2000 oz. AGW, 22 mm. **Subject:** Year of the Snake **Obv:** National arms **Rev:** Snake **Edge:** Reeded

Date	Mintage	F	VF	XF	Unc	BU
2001 Proof	—	Value: 175				

KM# 210 100 DOLLARS
6.2200 g., 0.9990 Gold .2000 oz. AGW **Subject:** P'an Ku **Obv:** National arms **Rev:** Dragon

Date	Mintage	F	VF	XF	Unc	BU
2001 Proof	Est. 10,000	Value: 175				

KM# 218 100 DOLLARS
6.2200 g., 0.9990 Gold .2000 oz. AGW **Subject:** P'an Ku **Obv:** National arms **Rev:** Dragon and three animals

Date	Mintage	F	VF	XF	Unc	BU
2001 Proof	Est. 10,000	Value: 175				

KM# 224 100 DOLLARS
6.2200 g., 0.9990 Gold .2000 oz. AGW, 22 mm. **Series:** The Big Five **Obv:** National arms **Rev:** Rhino **Edge:** Reeded

Date	Mintage	F	VF	XF	Unc	BU
2001 Proof	Est. 5,000	Value: 175				

KM# 227 100 DOLLARS
6.2200 g., 0.9990 Gold .2000 oz. AGW **Series:** The Big Five **Obv:** National arms **Rev:** Lion

Date	Mintage	F	VF	XF	Unc	BU
2001 Proof	Est. 5,000	Value: 175				

KM# 230 100 DOLLARS
6.2200 g., 0.9990 Gold .2000 oz. AGW **Series:** The Big Five **Obv:** National arms **Rev:** Leopard

Date	Mintage	F	VF	XF	Unc	BU
2001 Proof	Est. 5,000	Value: 175				

KM# 233 100 DOLLARS
6.2200 g., 0.9990 Gold .2000 oz. AGW **Series:** The Big Five **Obv:** National arms **Rev:** Elephants

Date	Mintage	F	VF	XF	Unc	BU
2001 Proof	Est. 5,000	Value: 175				

KM# 236 100 DOLLARS
6.2200 g., 0.9990 Gold .2000 oz. AGW **Series:** The Big Five **Obv:** National arms **Rev:** Buffalo

Date	Mintage	F	VF	XF	Unc	BU
2001 Proof	Est. 5,000	Value: 175				

KM# 239 100 DOLLARS
6.2200 g., 0.9990 Gold .2000 oz. AGW **Series:** The Big Five **Obv:** National arms **Rev:** All five animals

Date	Mintage	F	VF	XF	Unc	BU
2001 Proof	Est. 5,000	Value: 175				

KM# 274 100 DOLLARS
6.2200 g., 0.9999 Gold 0.2 oz. AGW, 22 mm. **Subject:** Queen's Golden Jubilee **Obv:** National arms **Rev:** Queen Elizabeth II and Prince Philip **Edge:** Reeded

Date	Mintage	F	VF	XF	Unc	BU
2002 Proof	2,002	Value: 175				

KM# 275 100 DOLLARS
6.2200 g., 0.9999 Gold 0.2 oz. AGW, 22 mm. **Subject:** Queen's Golden Jubilee **Obv:** National arms **Rev:** Queen Elizabeth II, Prince Charles and Princess Anne **Edge:** Reeded

Date	Mintage	F	VF	XF	Unc	BU
2002 Proof	5,000	Value: 175				

KM# 284 100 DOLLARS
6.2200 g., 0.9999 Gold 0.2 oz. AGW, 22 mm. **Subject:** Queen Elizabeth's Golden Jubilee **Obv:** National arms **Rev:** Queen and young Prince Charles **Edge:** Reeded

Date	Mintage	F	VF	XF	Unc	BU
2002 Proof	2,002	Value: 175				

KM# 287 100 DOLLARS
6.2200 g., 0.9999 Gold 0.2 oz. AGW, 22 mm. **Subject:** Queen Elizabeth's Golden Jubilee **Obv:** National arms **Rev:** Queen and Prince Philip **Edge:** Reeded

Date	Mintage	F	VF	XF	Unc	BU
2002 Proof	2,002	Value: 175				

KM# 278 100 DOLLARS
6.2200 g., 0.9999 Gold 0.2 oz. AGW, 22 mm. **Subject:** British Queen Mother **Obv:** National arms **Rev:** Queen Mother in garden with dog **Edge:** Reeded

Date	Mintage	F	VF	XF	Unc	BU
2002 Proof	2,000	Value: 175				

KM# 281 100 DOLLARS
6.2200 g., 0.9999 Gold 0.2 oz. AGW, 22 mm. **Subject:** British Queen Mother **Obv:** National arms **Rev:** Queen Mother with daughters **Edge:** Reeded

Date	Mintage	F	VF	XF	Unc	BU
2002 Proof	2,000	Value: 175				

KM# 260 100 DOLLARS
6.2200 g., 0.9990 Gold .1998 oz. AGW, 22 mm. **Subject:** Year of the Horse **Obv:** National arms **Rev:** Horse **Edge:** Reeded

Date	Mintage	F	VF	XF	Unc	BU
2002 Proof	2,000	Value: 175				

KM# 290 100 DOLLARS
6.2200 g., 0.9999 Gold 0.2 oz. AGW, 22 mm. **Subject:** Olympics **Obv:** National arms **Rev:** Victory goddess Nike **Edge:** Reeded **Note:** The leone is the official currency of Sierra Leone

Date	Mintage	F	VF	XF	Unc	BU
2003 Proof	5,000	Value: 175				
2004 Proof	5,000	Value: 175				

KM# 293 100 DOLLARS
6.2200 g., 0.9999 Gold 0.2 oz. AGW, 22 mm. **Subject:** Olympics **Obv:** National arms **Rev:** Ancient archer **Edge:** Reeded

Date	Mintage	F	VF	XF	Unc	BU
2003 Proof	5,000	Value: 175				
2004 Proof	5,000	Value: 175				

KM# 240 250 DOLLARS
15.5500 g., 0.9999 Gold .4999 oz. AGW, 29.9 mm. **Subject:** Centennial of Queen Victoria's Diamond Jubilee **Obv:** Arms **Rev:** Crowned bust with diamond necklace facing **Edge:** Reeded **Note:** This denomination was never offered to the public. The entire issue is reported to have been commissioned by and sold to a single purchaser.

Date	Mintage	F	VF	XF	Unc	BU
1997 Proof	Est. 1,000	Value: 375				

KM# 76 250 DOLLARS
15.5000 g., 0.9990 Gold .5000 oz. AGW **Subject:** Diana - The Peoples' Princess **Obv:** Arms **Rev:** Portrait of Lady Diana

Date	Mintage	F	VF	XF	Unc	BU
1997 Proof	Est. 3,000	Value: 370				

KM# 82 250 DOLLARS
15.5000 g., 0.9990 Gold .5000 oz. AGW **Subject:** Diana - The Peoples' Princess **Obv:** Arms **Rev:** Mother Theresa and Lady Diana

Date	Mintage	F	VF	XF	Unc	BU
1997 Proof	Est. 3,000	Value: 385				

KM# 88 250 DOLLARS
15.5000 g., 0.9990 Gold .5000 oz. AGW **Subject:** Diana - The Peoples' Princess **Obv:** Arms **Rev:** Lady Diana with AIDS patient

Date	Mintage	F	VF	XF	Unc	BU
1997 Proof	Est. 3,000	Value: 360				

KM# 94 250 DOLLARS
15.5000 g., 0.9990 Gold .5000 oz. AGW **Subject:** Diana - The Peoples' Princess **Obv:** Arms **Rev:** Lady Diana with sons William and Harry

Date	Mintage	F	VF	XF	Unc	BU
1997 Proof	Est. 3,000	Value: 365				

KM# 108 250 DOLLARS
15.5000 g., 0.9990 Gold .5000 oz. AGW **Subject:** Diana - The Peoples' Princess **Obv:** Arms **Rev:** Head half left

Date	Mintage	F	VF	XF	Unc	BU
1998 Proof	Est. 3,000	Value: 370				

KM# 147 250 DOLLARS
15.5000 g., 0.9990 Gold .5000 oz. AGW **Subject:** Year of the Dragon **Obv:** Arms **Rev:** Dragon

Date	Mintage	F	VF	XF	Unc	BU
2000 Proof	Est. 5,000	Value: 370				

KM# 189 250 DOLLARS
15.5000 g., 0.9990 Gold .5000 oz. AGW **Obv:** Arms **Rev:** Seated Buddha

SINGAPORE

Date	Mintage	F	VF	XF	Unc	BU
2000 Proof	Est. 5,000			Value: 385		

KM# 190 250 DOLLARS
15.5500 g., 0.9990 Gold .5000 oz. AGW **Obv:** Arms **Rev:** Goddess of Mercy

Date	Mintage	F	VF	XF	Unc	BU
2000 Proof	Est. 5,000			Value: 385		

KM# 191 250 DOLLARS
15.5500 g., 0.9990 Gold .5000 oz. AGW **Obv:** Arms **Rev:** Tzai-yen holding scroll

Date	Mintage	F	VF	XF	Unc	BU
2000 Proof	Est. 5,000			Value: 385		

KM# 219 250 DOLLARS
15.5518 g., 0.9990 Gold .5000 oz. AGW **Subject:** P'an Ku **Obv:** National arms **Rev:** Dragon and three animals

Date	Mintage	F	VF	XF	Unc	BU
2001 Proof	Est. 2,000			Value: 385		

KM# 203 250 DOLLARS
15.5118 g., 0.9990 Gold .5000 oz. AGW, 30 mm. **Subject:** Year of the Snake **Obv:** National arms **Rev:** Snake **Edge:** Reeded

Date	Mintage	F	VF	XF	Unc	BU
2001 Proof	Est. 5,000			Value: 375		

KM# 211 250 DOLLARS
15.5518 g., 0.9990 Gold .5000 oz. AGW **Subject:** P'an Ku **Obv:** National arms **Rev:** Dragon

Date	Mintage	F	VF	XF	Unc	BU
2001 Proof	Est. 2,000			Value: 385		

KM# 261 250 DOLLARS
15.5500 g., 0.9990 Gold .4994 oz. AGW, 30 mm. **Subject:** Year of the Horse **Obv:** National arms **Rev:** Horse **Edge:** Reeded

Date	Mintage	F	VF	XF	Unc	BU
2002 Proof	2,000			Value: 385		

KM# 148 500 DOLLARS
31.1035 g., 0.9990 Gold 1.0000 oz. AGW **Subject:** Year of the Dragon **Obv:** Arms **Rev:** Dragon **Note:** Similar to 10 Dollars, KM#143.

Date	Mintage	F	VF	XF	Unc	BU
2000 Proof	Est. 1,000			Value: 765		

KM# 192 500 DOLLARS
31.1035 g., 0.9990 Gold 1.0000 oz. AGW **Obv:** Arms **Rev:** Seated Buddha **Edge:** Reeded **Note:** Struck at Pobjoy Mint.

Date	Mintage	F	VF	XF	Unc	BU
2000 Proof	Est. 5,000			Value: 740		

KM# 193 500 DOLLARS
31.1035 g., 0.9990 Gold 1.0000 oz. AGW **Obv:** Arms **Rev:** Goddess of Mercy

Date	Mintage	F	VF	XF	Unc	BU
2000 Proof	Est. 5,000			Value: 740		

KM# 194 500 DOLLARS
31.1035 g., 0.9990 Gold 1.0000 oz. AGW **Obv:** Arms **Rev:** Tzai-yen holding scroll

Date	Mintage	F	VF	XF	Unc	BU
2000 Proof	Est. 5,000			Value: 740		

KM# 204 500 DOLLARS
31.1035 g., 0.9990 Gold 1.000 oz. AGW, 32.7 mm. **Subject:** Year of the Snake **Obv:** National arms **Rev:** Snake **Edge:** Reeded

Date	Mintage	F	VF	XF	Unc	BU
2001 Proof	Est. 1,000			Value: 765		

KM# 212 500 DOLLARS
31.1035 g., 0.9990 Gold 1.0000 oz. AGW **Subject:** P'an Ku **Obv:** National arms **Rev:** Dragon

Date	Mintage	F	VF	XF	Unc	BU
2001 Proof	Est. 1,000			Value: 765		

KM# 220 500 DOLLARS
31.1035 g., 0.9990 Gold 1.0000 oz. AGW **Subject:** P'an Ku **Obv:** National arms **Rev:** Dragon and three animals

Date	Mintage	F	VF	XF	Unc	BU
2001 Proof	Est. 1,000			Value: 765		

KM# 262 500 DOLLARS
31.1000 g., 0.9990 Gold .9989 oz. AGW, 32.7 mm. **Subject:** Year of the Horse **Obv:** National arms **Rev:** Horse **Edge:** Reeded

Date	Mintage	F	VF	XF	Unc	BU
2002 Proof	1,000			Value: 765		

KM# 294 500 DOLLARS
31.1000 g., 0.9999 Gold 0.9998 oz. AGW, 32.7 mm. **Obv:** National arms **Rev:** Multicolor Astro Boy cartoon **Edge:** Reeded **Note:** The leone is Sierra Leone's official currency

Date	Mintage	F	VF	XF	Unc	BU
2003 Proof	2,003			Value: 750		

KM# 299 500 DOLLARS
31.1035 g., 0.9999 Gold 0.9999 oz. AGW, 32.7 mm. **Obv:** National arms **Rev:** Nelson Mandela **Edge:** Reeded

Date	Mintage	F	VF	XF	Unc	BU
2004 Proof	—			Value: 750		

KM# 149 2500 DOLLARS
155.5175 g., 0.9990 Gold 5.0000 oz. AGW **Subject:** Year of the Dragon **Obv:** Arms **Rev:** Dragon

Date	Mintage	F	VF	XF	Unc	BU
2000 Proof	250			Value: 3,500		

KM# 195 2500 DOLLARS
155.5175 g., 0.9990 Gold 5.0000 oz. AGW **Obv:** Arms **Rev:** Seated Buddha **Edge:** Reeded

Date	Mintage	F	VF	XF	Unc	BU
2000 Proof	Est. 250			Value: 3,500		

KM# 196 2500 DOLLARS
155.5175 g., 0.9990 Gold 5.0000 oz. AGW **Obv:** Arms **Rev:** Goddess of Mercy

Date	Mintage	F	VF	XF	Unc	BU
2000 Proof	Est. 250			Value: 3,500		

KM# 197 2500 DOLLARS
155.5175 g., 0.9990 Gold 5.0000 oz. AGW **Obv:** Arms **Rev:** Tzai-yen holding scroll

Date	Mintage	F	VF	XF	Unc	BU
2000 Proof	Est. 250			Value: 3,500		

KM# 205 2500 DOLLARS
155.5175 g., 0.9990 Gold 5.0000 oz. AGW, 50 mm. **Subject:** Year of the Snake **Obv:** National arms **Rev:** Snake **Edge:** Reeded

Date	Mintage	F	VF	XF	Unc	BU
2001 Proof	Est. 250			Value: 3,550		

KM# 213 2500 DOLLARS
155.5175 g., 0.9990 Gold 5.0000 oz. AGW **Subject:** P'an Ku **Obv:** National arms **Rev:** Dragon

Date	Mintage	F	VF	XF	Unc	BU
2001 Proof	Est. 250			Value: 3,550		

KM# 263 2500 DOLLARS
155.5100 g., 0.9990 Gold 4.9948 oz. AGW, 50 mm. **Subject:** Year of the Horse **Obv:** National arms **Rev:** Horse **Edge:** Reeded

Date	Mintage	F	VF	XF	Unc	BU
2002 Proof	250			Value: 3,550		

MINT SETS

KM#	Date	Mintage	Identification	Issue Price	Mkt Val
MS1	1966 (3)	—	KM#22-24	—	1,650

PROOF SETS

KM#	Date	Mintage	Identification	Issue Price	Mkt Val
PS2	1964 (6)	12	KM#16a-20a, 21b	—	5,750
PS4	1966 (3)	400	KM#22a-24a	—	1,950

SINGAPORE

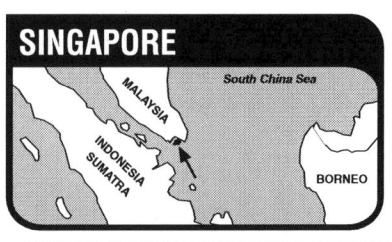

The Republic of Singapore, a member of the Commonwealth of Nations situated off the southern tip of the Malay peninsula, has an area of 224 sq. mi. (633 sq. km.) and a population of *2.7 million. Capital: Singapore. The economy is based on entrepôt trade, manufacturing and oil. Rubber, petroleum products, machinery and spices are exported.

Singapore's modern history - it was an important shipping center in the 14th century before the rise of Malacca and Penang - began in 1819 when Sir Thomas Stamford Raffles, an agent for the British East India Company, founded the town of Singapore. By 1825 its trade exceeded that of Malacca and Penang combined. The opening of the Suez Canal (1869) and the demand for rubber and tin created by the automobile and packaging industries combined to make Singapore one of the major ports of the world. In 1826 Singapore, Penang and Malacca were combined to form the Straits Settlements, which was made a Crown Colony in 1867. Singapore became a separate Crown Colony in 1946 when the Straits Settlements was dissolved. It joined in the formation of Malaysia in 1963, but broke away on Aug. 9, 1965, to become an independent republic. The President is Chief of State. The prime minister is Head of Government.

For earlier coinage see Straits Settlements, Malaya, Malaya and British Borneo.

MINT MARK
sm = "*sm*" - Singapore Mint monogram

MONETARY SYSTEM
100 Cents = 1 Dollar

REPUBLIC

STANDARD COINAGE
100 Cents = 1 Dollar

KM# 28 DOLLAR
3.1100 g., 0.9990 Gold .1000 oz. AGW **Obv:** Arms with supporters **Rev:** Carp and lotus flower

Date	Mintage	F	VF	XF	Unc	BU
1983	20,000	—	—	—	BV+15%	—
1984	10,000	—	—	—	BV+15%	—

KM# 144 DOLLAR
1.5552 g., 0.9990 Gold .0400 oz. AGW **Subject:** Year of the Rat **Obv:** Arms with supporters **Rev:** Lion head right

Date	Mintage	F	VF	XF	Unc	BU
1996 Proof	2,688	—	—	—	BV+25%	—

KM# 158 DOLLAR
1.5552 g., 0.9990 Gold .0400 oz. AGW **Subject:** Year of the Ox **Obv:** Arms with supporters **Rev:** Lion head **Note:** Similar to 20 Dollars, KM#161.

Date	Mintage	F	VF	XF	Unc	BU
1997 Proof	Est. 2,200	—	—	—	BV+25%	—

KM# 186 DOLLAR
0.3000 g., 0.9999 Gold 0.0096 oz. AGW, 7 mm. **Subject:** Year of the Monkey **Obv:** Arms with supporters **Rev:** Seated monkey **Edge:** Plain

Date	Mintage	F	VF	XF	Unc	BU
2004	8,000	—	—	—	32.00	—

KM# 29 2 DOLLARS
7.7750 g., 0.9990 Gold .2500 oz. AGW **Obv:** Arms with supporters **Rev:** Qilin **Designer:** Henry Steiner

Date	Mintage	F	VF	XF	Unc	BU
1983	20,000	—	—	—	BV+12%	—
1984	10,000	—	—	—	BV+12%	—

SINGAPORE

KM# 30 5 DOLLARS
15.5500 g., 0.9990 Gold .5000 oz. AGW **Obv:** Arms with supporters **Rev:** Phoenix **Designer:** Henry Steiner

Date	Mintage	F	VF	XF	Unc	BU
1983	10,000	—	—	—	BV+9%	—
1984	10,000	—	—	—	BV+9%	—

KM# 79 5 DOLLARS
1.5550 g., 0.9990 Gold .0500 oz. AGW **Obv:** Arms with supporters **Rev:** Lion head

Date	Mintage	F	VF	XF	Unc	BU
1990	8,000	—	—	—	BV+20%	—
1990 Proof	Est. 2,000	—	—	—	BV+25%	—

KM# 87 5 DOLLARS
1.5550 g., 0.9990 Gold .0500 oz. AGW **Subject:** Year of the Goat **Obv:** Arms with supporters **Rev:** Lion head

Date	Mintage	F	VF	XF	Unc	BU
1991	8,000	—	—	—	BV+20%	—
1991 Proof	2,500	—	—	—	BV+25%	—

KM# 108 5 DOLLARS
1.5550 g., 0.9990 Gold .0500 oz. AGW **Subject:** Year of the Monkey **Obv:** Arms with supporters

Date	Mintage	F	VF	XF	Unc	BU
1992	6,500	—	—	—	BV+20%	—
1992 Proof	2,000	—	—	—	BV+25%	—

KM# 117 5 DOLLARS
1.5550 g., 0.9990 Gold .0500 oz. AGW **Subject:** Year of the Rooster **Obv:** Arms with supporters **Rev:** Lion head

Date	Mintage	F	VF	XF	Unc	BU
1993	3,400	—	—	—	BV+20%	—
1993 Proof	Est. 1,500	—	—	—	BV+25%	—

Note: In proof sets only

KM# 128 5 DOLLARS
1.5550 g., 0.9990 Gold .0500 oz. AGW **Subject:** Year of the Dog **Obv:** Arms with supporters **Rev:** Lion head

Date	Mintage	F	VF	XF	Unc	BU
1994	—	—	—	—	BV+20%	—
1994 Proof	Est. 1,500	—	—	—	BV+25%	—

Note: In proof sets only

KM# 133 5 DOLLARS
1.5550 g., 0.9990 Gold .0500 oz. AGW **Subject:** Year of the Pig **Obv:** Arms with supporters

Date	Mintage	F	VF	XF	Unc	BU
1995	—	—	—	—	BV+20%	—
1995 Proof	1,500	—	—	—	BV+25%	—

KM# 145 5 DOLLARS
3.1103 g., 0.9990 Gold .1000 oz. AGW **Subject:** Year of the Rat **Obv:** Arms with supporters **Rev:** Lion head

Date	Mintage	F	VF	XF	Unc	BU
1996 Proof	1,600	—	—	—	BV+20%	—

KM# 157 5 DOLLARS
7.7760 g., 0.9999 Gold .2500 oz. AGW **Series:** UNICEF **Obv:** Arms with supporters **Rev:** Children using computer

Date	Mintage	F	VF	XF	Unc	BU
1997 Proof	10,000 Value: 350					

KM# 159 5 DOLLARS
3.1103 g., 0.9999 Gold .1000 oz. AGW **Subject:** Year of the Ox **Obv:** Arms with supporters **Rev:** Lion head

Date	Mintage	F	VF	XF	Unc	BU
1997 Proof	Est. 1,000	—	—	—	BV+20%	—

KM# 172 5 DOLLARS
31.1030 g., 0.9990 Gold 1.0000 oz. AGW **Subject:** Millennium **Obv:** Arms with supporters above latent date within beaded circle **Rev:** Millennium design **Edge:** Scalloped

Date	Mintage	F	VF	XF	Unc	BU
2000 Proof	3,000 Value: 1,000					

KM# 31 10 DOLLARS
31.1000 g., 0.9990 Gold 1.0000 oz. AGW **Subject:** Year of the Dragon **Obv:** Arms with supporters **Rev:** Dragon **Designer:** Henry Steiner

Date	Mintage	F	VF	XF	Unc	BU
1983	10,000	—	—	—	BV+10%	—
1984 Proof	10,000	—	—	—	BV+10%	—

KM# 80 10 DOLLARS
3.1103 g., 0.9990 Gold .1000 oz. AGW **Obv:** Arms with supporters **Rev:** Lion head

Date	Mintage	F	VF	XF	Unc	BU
1990	Est. 5,000	—	—	—	BV+15%	—
1990 Proof	Est. 2,000	—	—	—	BV+20%	—

KM# 88 10 DOLLARS
3.1103 g., 0.9990 Gold .1000 oz. AGW **Subject:** Year of the Goat **Obv:** Arms with supporters **Rev:** Lion head with goat privy mark at lower left

Date	Mintage	F	VF	XF	Unc	BU
1991	5,500	—	—	—	BV+15%	—
1991 Proof	2,500	—	—	—	BV+20%	—

KM# 109 10 DOLLARS
3.1103 g., 0.9990 Gold .1000 oz. AGW **Obv:** Arms with supporters **Rev:** Lion head **Note:** Year of the Monkey privy mark.

Date	Mintage	F	VF	XF	Unc	BU
1992	4,000	—	—	—	BV+15%	—
1992 Proof	2,000	—	—	—	BV+20%	—

KM# 118 10 DOLLARS
3.1103 g., 0.9990 Gold .1000 oz. AGW **Obv:** Arms with supporters **Rev:** Lion head with rooster privy mark at lower left **Note:** Lion/Year of the Rooster privy mark.

Date	Mintage	F	VF	XF	Unc	BU
1993	Est. 1,500	—	—	—	BV+20%	—

Note: In proof sets only

| 1993 | 3,100 | — | — | — | BV+15% | — |

KM# 129 10 DOLLARS
3.1103 g., 0.9990 Gold .1000 oz. AGW **Obv:** Arms with supporters **Rev:** Lion head with dog privy mark at lower left **Note:** Lion/Year of the Dog privy mark.

Date	Mintage	F	VF	XF	Unc	BU
1994 Proof	Est. 1,500	—	—	—	BV+20%	—

Note: In proof sets only

| 1994 | — | — | — | — | BV+15% | — |

KM# 134 10 DOLLARS
3.1103 g., 0.9990 Gold .1000 oz. AGW **Obv:** Arms with supporters **Rev:** Lion head with pig privy mark at lower left **Note:** Lion/Year of the Pig privy mark.

Date	Mintage	F	VF	XF	Unc	BU
1995	—	—	—	—	BV+15%	—
1995 Proof	—	BV+20%	—	—	—	—

KM# 146 10 DOLLARS
7.7759 g., 0.9990 Gold .2500 oz. AGW **Obv:** Arms with supporters **Note:** Year of the Rat privy mark.

Date	Mintage	F	VF	XF	Unc	BU
1996 Proof	2,688	—	—	—	BV+10%	—

KM# 160 10 DOLLARS
7.7759 g., 0.9990 Gold .2500 oz. AGW **Obv:** Arms with supporters **Rev:** Lion head with ox privy marks at lower left **Note:** Lion/Year of the Ox privy mark. Similar to KM#154.

Date	Mintage	F	VF	XF	Unc	BU
1997 Proof	Est. 2,200	—	—	—	BV+10%	—

KM# 185 10 DOLLARS
31.1040 g., 0.9999 Gold 0.9999 oz. AGW, 32.12 mm. **Subject:** Suzhou Industrial Park **Obv:** Arms with supporters **Rev:** "Harmony" Sculpture **Edge:** Lettered edge

Date	Mintage	F	VF	XF	Unc	BU
2004 Proof	500 Value: 800					

KM# 187 10 DOLLARS
62.2060 g., 0.9990 Silver 1.998 oz. ASW, 40.7 mm. **Subject:** Year of the Monkey **Obv:** Arms with supporters **Rev:** Seated monkey **Edge:** Reeded

Date	Mintage	F	VF	XF	Unc	BU
2004 Proof	35,000 Value: 85.00					

KM# 147 20 DOLLARS
15.5517 g., 0.9990 Gold .5000 oz. AGW **Obv:** Arms with supporters **Rev:** Lion head with rat privy mark at lower left **Note:** Lion/Year of the Rat privy mark.

Date	Mintage	F	VF	XF	Unc	BU
1996 Proof	2,688	—	—	—	BV+15%	—

KM# 161 20 DOLLARS
15.5517 g., 0.9990 Gold .5000 oz. AGW **Obv:** Arms with supporters **Rev:** Lion head with ox privy mark at lower left **Note:** Lion/Year of the Ox privy mark.

Date	Mintage	F	VF	XF	Unc	BU
1997 Proof	Est. 2,200	—	—	—	BV+15%	—

KM# 81 25 DOLLARS
7.7757 g., 0.9990 Gold .2500 oz. AGW **Obv:** Arms with supporters **Rev:** Lion head

Date	Mintage	F	VF	XF	Unc	BU
1990	Est. 5,000	—	—	—	BV+12%	—
1990 Proof	Est. 2,000	—	—	—	BV+15%	—

SINGAPORE

KM# 89 25 DOLLARS
7.7757 g., 0.9990 Gold .2500 oz. AGW **Obv:** Arms with supporters **Rev:** Lion head with goat privy mark at lower left **Note:** Year of the Goat privy mark.

Date	Mintage	F	VF	XF	Unc	BU
1991	5,500	—	—	—	BV+12%	—
1991 Proof	2,500	—	—	—	BV+15%	—

KM# 110 25 DOLLARS
7.7757 g., 0.9990 Gold .2500 oz. AGW **Obv:** Arms with supporters **Rev:** Lion head with monkey privy mark at lower left **Note:** Year of the Monkey privy mark.

Date	Mintage	F	VF	XF	Unc	BU
1992	4,000	—	—	—	BV+12%	—
1992 Proof	2,000	—	—	—	BV+15%	—

KM# 119 25 DOLLARS
7.7757 g., 0.9990 Gold .2500 oz. AGW **Obv:** Arms with supporters **Rev:** Lion head with rooster privy mark at lower left **Note:** Year of the Rooster privy mark.

Date	Mintage	F	VF	XF	Unc	BU
1993	3,000	—	—	—	BV+12%	—
1993	Est. 1,500	—	—	—	BV+15%	—

Note: In proof sets only

KM# 130 25 DOLLARS
7.7757 g., 0.9990 Gold .2500 oz. AGW **Obv:** Arms with supporters **Rev:** Lion head with dog privy mark at lower left **Note:** Year of the Dog privy mark.

Date	Mintage	F	VF	XF	Unc	BU
1994	—	—	—	—	BV+12%	—
1994	Est. 1,500	—	—	—	BV+15%	—

Note: In proof sets only

KM# 135 25 DOLLARS
7.7757 g., 0.9990 Gold .2500 oz. AGW **Obv:** Arms with supporters **Rev:** Lion head with pig privy mark at lower left **Note:** Year of the Pig privy mark.

Date	Mintage	F	VF	XF	Unc	BU
1995	—	—	—	—	BV+12%	—
1995 Proof	1,500	—	—	—	BV+15%	—

KM# 78 50 DOLLARS
10.0000 g., 0.9160 Gold .2945 oz. AGW **Series:** Save the Children Fund **Obv:** Arms with supporters **Rev:** Children, kayak, palm tree and value

Date	Mintage	F	VF	XF	Unc	BU
1989 Proof	3,000	Value: 420				

KM# 82 50 DOLLARS
15.5500 g., 0.9990 Gold .5000 oz. AGW **Obv:** Arms with supporters **Rev:** Lion head

Date	Mintage	F	VF	XF	Unc	BU
1990	Est. 5,000	—	—	—	BV+10%	—
1990 Proof	Est. 2,000	—	—	—	BV+12%	—

KM# 90 50 DOLLARS
15.5500 g., 0.9990 Gold .5000 oz. AGW **Obv:** Arms with supporters **Rev:** Lion head with goat privy mark at lower left **Note:** Year of the Goat privy mark.

Date	Mintage	F	VF	XF	Unc	BU
1991	5,500	—	—	—	BV+10%	—
1991 Proof	2,500	—	—	—	BV+12%	—

KM# 111 50 DOLLARS
15.5500 g., 0.9990 Gold .5000 oz. AGW **Obv:** Arms with supporters **Rev:** Lion head with monkey privy mark at lower left **Note:** Year of the Monkey privy mark.

Date	Mintage	F	VF	XF	Unc	BU
1992	4,000	—	—	—	BV+10%	—
1992 Proof	2,000	—	—	—	BV+12%	—

KM# 120 50 DOLLARS
15.5500 g., 0.9990 Gold .5000 oz. AGW **Obv:** Arms with supporters **Rev:** Lion head with rooster privy mark at lower left **Note:** Year of the Rooster privy mark.

Date	Mintage	F	VF	XF	Unc	BU
1993	2,600	—	—	—	BV+10%	—
1993	Est. 1,500	—	—	—	BV+12%	—

Note: In proof sets only

KM# 131 50 DOLLARS
15.5500 g., 0.9990 Gold .5000 oz. AGW **Obv:** Arms with supporters **Rev:** Lion head with dog privy mark at lower left **Note:** Year of the Dog privy mark.

Date	Mintage	F	VF	XF	Unc	BU
1994	—	—	—	—	BV+10%	—
1994	Est. 1,500	—	—	—	BV+12%	—

Note: In proof sets only

KM# 140 50 DOLLARS
31.1035 g., 0.9999 Gold 1.0000 oz. AGW **Series:** 50th Anniversary - United Nations **Obv:** Arms with supporters **Rev:** UN logo within design

Date	Mintage	F	VF	XF	Unc	BU
1995 Proof	1,000	Value: 950				

KM# 136 50 DOLLARS
15.5500 g., 0.9990 Gold .5000 oz. AGW **Obv:** Arms with supporters **Rev:** Lion head with pig privy marks at lower left **Note:** Year of the Pig privy mark.

Date	Mintage	F	VF	XF	Unc	BU
1995	—	—	—	—	BV+10%	—
1995 Proof	1,500	—	—	—	BV+12%	—

KM# 148 50 DOLLARS
31.1035 g., 0.9999 Gold 1.0000 oz. AGW **Obv:** Arms with supporters **Rev:** Lion head with rat privy mark at lower left **Note:** Lion/Year of the Rat privy mark.

Date	Mintage	F	VF	XF	Unc	BU
1996 Proof	2,688	—	—	—	BV+9%	—

KM# 152 50 DOLLARS
31.1035 g., 0.9999 Gold 1.0000 oz. AGW **Subject:** 50th Anniversary - Singapore Airlines **Obv:** Arms with supporters **Rev:** Airplane in front of numeral 50

Date	Mintage	F	VF	XF	Unc	BU
1997 Proof	1,800	Value: 1,100				

KM# 162 50 DOLLARS
31.1035 g., 0.9999 Gold 1.0000 oz. AGW **Obv:** Arms with supporters **Rev:** Lion head with ox privy mark at lower left **Note:** Lion/Year of the Ox privy mark.

Date	Mintage	F	VF	XF	Unc	BU
1997 Proof	Est. 2,200	—	—	—	BV+9%	—

KM# 170 50 DOLLARS
31.1035 g., 0.9999 Gold 1.0000 oz. AGW **Subject:** Parliament **Obv:** Arms with supporters **Rev:** Parliament buildings

Date	Mintage	F	VF	XF	Unc	BU
1999 Proof	1,000	Value: 1,480				

KM# 12 100 DOLLARS
6.9119 g., 0.9000 Gold .2000 oz. AGW **Subject:** 10th Anniversary of Independence **Obv:** Arms with supporters **Rev:** Building **Designer:** Ng Ah Kuan

Date	Mintage	F	VF	XF	Unc	BU
1975	100,000	—	—	—	120	130
1975 Proof	3,000	Value: 330				

KM# 83 100 DOLLARS
31.1000 g., 0.9990 Gold 1.0000 oz. AGW **Obv:** Arms with supporters **Rev:** Lion head

Date	Mintage	F	VF	XF	Unc	BU
1990	Est. 5,000	—	—	—	BV+7%	—
1990 Proof	Est. 2,000	—	—	—	BV+9%	—

SINGAPORE

KM# 91 100 DOLLARS
31.1000 g., 0.9990 Gold 1.0000 oz. AGW **Obv:** Arms with supporters **Rev:** Lion head with goat privy marks at lower left **Note:** Year of the Goat privy mark.

Date	Mintage	F	VF	XF	Unc	BU
1991	13,000	—	—	—	BV+7%	—
1991 Proof	2,500	—	—	—	BV+9%	—

KM# 112 100 DOLLARS
31.1000 g., 0.9990 Gold 1.0000 oz. AGW **Obv:** Arms with supporters **Rev:** Lion head with monkey privy marks at lower left **Note:** Year of the Monkey privy mark.

Date	Mintage	F	VF	XF	Unc	BU
1992	4,000	—	—	—	BV+7%	—
1992 Proof	2,000	—	—	—	BV+9%	—

KM# 106 100 DOLLARS
31.1000 g., 0.9990 Gold 1.0000 oz. AGW **Subject:** 25th Anniversary - Board of Commissioners of Currency **Obv:** Arms with supporters **Rev:** Stylized dollar sign and value within circle

Date	Mintage	F	VF	XF	Unc	BU
1992 Proof	800	Value: 860				

KM# 121 100 DOLLARS
31.1000 g., 0.9990 Gold 1.0000 oz. AGW **Obv:** Arms with supporters **Rev:** Lion head with rooster privy mark at lower left **Note:** Year of the Rooster privy mark.

Date	Mintage	F	VF	XF	Unc	BU
1993	3,100	—	—	—	BV+7%	—
1993 Proof	Est. 1,500	—	—	—	BV+9%	—

Note: In proof sets only

KM# 132 100 DOLLARS
31.1000 g., 0.9990 Gold 1.0000 oz. AGW **Obv:** Arms with supporters **Rev:** Lion head with dog privy mark at lower left **Note:** Year of the Dog privy mark.

Date	Mintage	F	VF	XF	Unc	BU
1994	—	—	—	—	BV+7%	—
1994 Proof	Est. 1,500	—	—	—	BV+9%	—

Note: In proof sets only

KM# 137 100 DOLLARS
31.1000 g., 0.9990 Gold 1.0000 oz. AGW **Obv:** Arms with supporters **Rev:** Lion head with pig privy marks at lower left **Note:** Year of the Pig privy mark.

Date	Mintage	F	VF	XF	Unc	BU
1995	—	—	—	—	BV+7%	—
1995 Proof	1,500	—	—	—	BV+9%	—

KM# 7 150 DOLLARS
24.8830 g., 0.9160 Gold .7360 oz. AGW **Subject:** 150th Anniversary - Founding of Singapore **Obv:** Arms with supporters **Rev:** Lighthouse and value

Date	Mintage	F	VF	XF	Unc	BU
ND(1969)	198,000	—	—	—	700	750
ND(1969) Proof	500	Value: 2,400				

KM# 107 200 DOLLARS
31.1035 g., 0.9990 Platinum 1.0000 oz. APW **Subject:** 25th Anniversary - Board of Commissioners of Currency **Obv:** Arms with supporters **Rev:** Stylized dollar sign and value within circle **Note:** Similar to KM#106.

Date	Mintage	F	VF	XF	Unc	BU
1992 Proof	300	Value: 1,380				

KM# 13 250 DOLLARS
17.2797 g., 0.9000 Gold .5000 oz. AGW **Subject:** 10th Anniversary of Independence **Obv:** Arms with supporters **Rev:** Four grasped hands below value **Designer:** Tan Huay Peng

Date	Mintage	F	VF	XF	Unc	BU
ND(1975)	30,000	—	—	—	370	390
ND(1975) Proof	2,000	Value: 750				

KM# 96 250 DOLLARS
31.1040 g., 0.9990 Gold 1.0000 oz. AGW **Subject:** 25th Anniversary of Independence **Obv:** Arms with supporters **Rev:** Stylized numeral 25 above city view with value at lower right

Date	Mintage	F	VF	XF	Unc	BU
1990 Proof	6,000	Value: 900				

KM# 114 250 DOLLARS
31.1035 g., 0.9990 Gold 1.0000 oz. AGW **Subject:** Year of the Rooster **Obv:** Arms with supporters **Rev:** Stylized rooster

Date	Mintage	F	VF	XF	Unc	BU
1993 Proof	10,000	Value: 1,000				

KM# 123 250 DOLLARS
31.1035 g., 0.9990 Gold 1.0000 oz. AGW **Subject:** Year of the Dog **Obv:** Arms with supporters **Rev:** Stylized dog within designs

Date	Mintage	F	VF	XF	Unc	BU
1994 Proof	7,500	Value: 900				

KM# 127 250 DOLLARS
31.1035 g., 0.9990 Gold 1.0000 oz. AGW **Subject:** Year of the Pig **Obv:** Arms with supporters **Rev:** Stylized pig within design

Date	Mintage	F	VF	XF	Unc	BU
1995 Proof	7,500	Value: 900				

KM# 143 250 DOLLARS
31.1035 g., 0.9990 Gold 1.0000 oz. AGW **Subject:** Year of the Rat **Obv:** Arms with supporters **Rev:** Stylized rat within designs

Date	Mintage	F	VF	XF	Unc	BU
1996 Proof	7,500	Value: 900				

KM# 155 250 DOLLARS
31.1035 g., 0.9990 Gold 1.0000 oz. AGW **Subject:** Year of the Ox **Obv:** Arms with supporters **Rev:** Stylized ox within designs

Date	Mintage	F	VF	XF	Unc	BU
1997 Proof	7,800	Value: 800				

KM# 166 250 DOLLARS
31.1035 g., 0.9990 Gold 1.0000 oz. AGW **Subject:** Year of the Tiger **Obv:** Arms with supporters **Rev:** Stylized tiger

Date	Mintage	F	VF	XF	Unc	BU
1998 Proof	7,600	Value: 900				

KM# 169 250 DOLLARS
31.1035 g., 0.9990 Gold 1.0000 oz. AGW **Obv:** Arms with supporters **Rev:** Stylized rabbit within designs **Edge:** Reeded

Date	Mintage	F	VF	XF	Unc	BU
1999 Proof	7,600	Value: 900				

SINGAPORE

KM# 176 250 DOLLARS
31.1035 g., 0.9990 Gold 1.0000 oz. AGW, 32.12 mm. **Subject:** Year of the Dragon **Obv:** Arms with supporters **Rev:** Stylized dragon **Edge:** Reeded

Date	Mintage	F	VF	XF	Unc	BU
2000 Proof	7,600	Value: 1,000				

KM# 178 250 DOLLARS
31.1035 g., 0.9990 Gold 0.999 oz. AGW, 32.1 mm. **Subject:** Year of the Snake **Obv:** Arms with supporters **Rev:** Stylized snake **Edge:** Reeded

Date	Mintage	F	VF	XF	Unc	BU
2001 Proof	7,000	Value: 900				

KM# 183 250 DOLLARS
31.1035 g., 0.9999 Gold 0.9999 oz. AGW, 32.12 mm. **Subject:** Year of the Horse **Obv:** Arms with supporters **Rev:** Horse **Edge:** Reeded

Date	Mintage	F	VF	XF	Unc	BU
2002 Proof	7,600	Value: 850				

KM# 188 250 DOLLARS
31.1030 g., 0.9999 Gold 0.9999 oz. AGW, 32.12 mm. **Subject:** Year of the Monkey **Obv:** Arms with supporters **Rev:** Seated monkey **Edge:** Reeded

Date	Mintage	F	VF	XF	Unc	BU
2004 Proof	7,000	Value: 800				

KM# 14 500 DOLLARS
34.5594 g., 0.9000 Gold 1.0000 oz. AGW **Subject:** 10th Anniversary of Independence **Obv:** Arms with supporters **Rev:** Lion head **Designer:** Tan Huay Peng

Date	Mintage	F	VF	XF	Unc	BU
ND(1975)	30,000	—	—	—	900	950
ND(1975) Proof	2,000	Value: 2,000				

KM# 21 500 DOLLARS
16.9650 g., 0.9160 Gold .5000 oz. AGW **Subject:** Year of the Rooster **Obv:** Arms with supporters **Rev:** Rooster

Date	Mintage	F	VF	XF	Unc	BU
1981sm Proof	12,000	Value: 900				

KM# 24 500 DOLLARS
16.9650 g., 0.9160 Gold .5000 oz. AGW **Subject:** Year of the Dog **Obv:** Arms with supporters **Rev:** Dog

Date	Mintage	F	VF	XF	Unc	BU
1982sm Proof	5,500	Value: 850				

KM# 27 500 DOLLARS
16.9650 g., 0.9160 Gold .5000 oz. AGW **Subject:** Year of the Pig **Obv:** Arms with supporters **Rev:** Pig

Date	Mintage	F	VF	XF	Unc	BU
1983sm Proof	5,000	Value: 850				

KM# 34 500 DOLLARS
16.9650 g., 0.9160 Gold .5000 oz. AGW **Subject:** Year of the Rat **Obv:** Arms with supporters **Rev:** Rat

Date	Mintage	F	VF	XF	Unc	BU
1984sm Proof	4,000	Value: 800				

KM# 45 500 DOLLARS
16.9650 g., 0.9160 Gold .5000 oz. AGW **Subject:** Year of the Ox **Obv:** Arms with supporters **Rev:** Ox

Date	Mintage	F	VF	XF	Unc	BU
1985sm Proof	4,000	Value: 700				

KM# 60 500 DOLLARS
16.9650 g., 0.9160 Gold .5000 oz. AGW **Subject:** Year of the Tiger **Obv:** Arms with supporters **Rev:** Tiger

Date	Mintage	F	VF	XF	Unc	BU
1986sm Proof	3,000	Value: 1,200				

KM# 64 500 DOLLARS
16.9650 g., 0.9160 Gold .5000 oz. AGW **Subject:** Year of the Rabbit **Obv:** Arms with supporters **Rev:** Rabbit

Date	Mintage	F	VF	XF	Unc	BU
1987sm Proof	2,400	Value: 1,950				

KM# 73 500 DOLLARS
16.9650 g., 0.9160 Gold .5000 oz. AGW **Subject:** Year of the Dragon **Obv:** Arms with supporters **Rev:** Dragon

Date	Mintage	F	VF	XF	Unc	BU
1988sm Proof	4,000	Value: 970				

KM# 72 500 DOLLARS
16.9650 g., 0.9160 Gold .5000 oz. AGW **Subject:** Year of the Snake **Obv:** Arms with supporters **Rev:** Snake

Date	Mintage	F	VF	XF	Unc	BU
1989sm Proof	2,500	Value: 1,500				

KM# 76 500 DOLLARS
16.9650 g., 0.9160 Gold .5000 oz. AGW **Subject:** Year of the Horse **Obv:** Arms with supporters **Rev:** Horse

Date	Mintage	F	VF	XF	Unc	BU
1990sm Proof	5,000	Value: 750				

KM# 97 500 DOLLARS
31.1040 g., 0.9990 Platinum 1.0000 oz. APW **Subject:** 25th Anniversary of Independence **Obv:** Arms with supporters **Rev:** Numeral 25 and value above city view

Date	Mintage	F	VF	XF	Unc	BU
1990 Proof	2,000	Value: 1,150				

KM# 85 500 DOLLARS
16.9650 g., 0.9160 Gold .5000 oz. AGW **Subject:** Year of the Goat **Obv:** Arms with supporters **Rev:** Goat

Date	Mintage	F	VF	XF	Unc	BU
1991sm Proof	5,000	Value: 700				

SINGAPORE

KM# 93 500 DOLLARS
16.9650 g., 0.9160 Gold .5000 oz. AGW **Subject:** Year of the Monkey **Obv:** Arms with supporters **Rev:** Monkey

Date	Mintage	F	VF	XF	Unc	BU
1992sm Proof	5,000	Value: 700				

MEDALLIC GOLD BULLION COINAGE

X# MB90 1/2 OUNCE
15.5670 g., 0.9999 Gold 0.5004 oz. AGW, 27 mm. **Subject:** Singapore International Coin Convention **Obv:** Four Chinese characters - "Good wishes to one and all" **Obv. Legend:** REPUBLIC OF SINGAPORE **Obv. Inscription:** "Good wishes to one and all" **Rev. Legend:** "Lord Maitreya" **Edge:** Reeded

Date	Mintage	F	VF	XF	Unc	BU
1992sm Proof	500	BV+20%				

X# MB100 1/2 OUNCE
15.5500 g., 0.9999 Gold 0.4999 oz. AGW, 27 mm. **Subject:** Singapore International Coin Convention **Obv:** Archaic Chinese Liu Hai seated, one of the immortals of Taoism, within four Chinese characters **Obv. Inscription:** "Wealth entering from all directions" **Rev:** Archaic Chinese Bi Gan, God of Literature and Wealth standing between two children **Edge:** Reeded

Date	Mintage	F	VF	XF	Unc	BU
1993sm Proof	500	BV+20%				

X# MB111 1/2 OUNCE
15.5500 g., 0.9999 Gold 0.4999 oz. AGW, 28.5 mm. **Subject:** Singapore-Taisei International Coin Convention **Obv:** Facing dragons **Rev:** Archaic Chinese hero Kwan Yu horseback 3/4 right **Edge:** Reeded

Date	Mintage	F	VF	XF	Unc	BU
1994sm Proof	288	BV+25%				

X# MB47 OUNCE
31.1106 g., 0.9999 Gold 1.0001 oz. AGW, 32.1 mm. **Subject:** National Coin Fair **Obv:** Archaic Chinese character -"Dragon" **Obv. Legend:** REPUBLIC OF SINGAPORE **Rev:** Pearl between two facing dragons **Edge:** Reeded

Date	Mintage	F	VF	XF	Unc	BU
1988sm Proof	500	BV+15%				

X# MBB55 OUNCE
31.1100 g., 0.9999 Gold 1.0001 oz. AGW, 32.05 mm. **Subject:** Singapore International Coin Convention **Obv:** Peaches of Immortality **Obv. Legend:** REPUBLIC OF SINGAPORE **Rev:** Gods of Prosperity, Luck and Longevity **Edge:** Reeded

Date	Mintage	F	VF	XF	Unc	BU
1989sm Proof	250	BV+20%				

X# MB27 5 SINGOLD
1.5553 g., 0.9999 Gold 0.05 oz. AGW, 13.92 mm. **Series:** Chinese Lunar Year **Subject:** Year of the Rabbit **Obv:** Four Chinese characters - "Amiable countenance" **Obv. Legend:** REPUBLIC OF SINGAPORE **Rev:** Rabbit hopping 3/4 right **Edge:** Reeded

Date	Mintage	F	VF	XF	Unc	BU
1987sm	8,000	—	—	—	—BV+25%	
1987sm Proof	1,000	BV+30%				

X# MB37 5 SINGOLD
1.5553 g., 0.9999 Gold 0.05 oz. AGW, 13.92 mm. **Series:** Chinese Lunar Year **Subject:** Year of the Dragon **Obv:** Four Chinese characters - "Goodwill, success and prosperity" **Obv. Legend:** REPUBLIC OF SINGAPORE **Rev:** Flying dragon facing left **Edge:** Reeded

Date	Mintage	F	VF	XF	Unc	BU
1988sm	10,000	—	—	—	—BV+25%	
1988sm Proof	500	BV+30%				

X# MB28 10 SINGOLD
3.1106 g., 0.9999 Gold 0.1 oz. AGW, 17.92 mm. **Series:** Chinese Lunar Year **Subject:** Year of the Rabbit **Obv:** Four Chinese characters - "Amiable countenance" **Obv. Legend:** REPUBLIC OF SINGAPORE **Rev:** Rabbit hopping 3/4 right **Edge:** Reeded

Date	Mintage	F	VF	XF	Unc	BU
1987sm	8,000	—	—	—	—BV+20%	
1987sm Proof	1,000	BV+25%				

X# MB38 10 SINGOLD
3.1106 g., 0.9999 Gold 0.1 oz. AGW, 17.95 mm. **Series:** Chinese Lunar Year **Subject:** Year of the Dragon **Obv:** Four Chinese characters - "Goodwill, success and prosperity" **Obv. Legend:** REPUBLIC OF SINGAPORE **Rev:** Flying dragon facing left **Edge:** Reeded

Date	Mintage	F	VF	XF	Unc	BU
1988sm	10,000	—	—	—	—BV+20%	
1988sm Proof	500	BV+25%				

X# MB29 25 SINGOLD
7.7765 g., 0.9999 Gold 0.25 oz. AGW, 21.95 mm. **Series:** Chinese Lunar Year **Subject:** Year of the Rabbit **Obv:** Four Chinese characters - "Amiable countenance" **Obv. Legend:** REPUBLIC OF SINGAPORE **Rev:** Rabbit hopping 3/4 right **Edge:** Reeded

Date	Mintage	F	VF	XF	Unc	BU
1987sm	8,000	—	—	—	—BV+20%	
1987sm Proof	1,000	BV+25%				

X# MB39 25 SINGOLD
7.7765 g., 0.9990 Gold 0.2498 oz. AGW, 21.95 mm. **Series:** Chinese Lunar Year **Subject:** Year of the Dragon **Obv:** Four Chinese characters - "Goodwill, success and prosperity" **Obv. Legend:** REPUBLIC OF SINGAPORE **Rev:** Flying dragon facing left **Edge:** Reeded

Date	Mintage	F	VF	XF	Unc	BU
1988sm	10,000	—	—	—	—BV+20%	
1988sm Proof	500	BV+25%				

X# MB30 50 SINGOLD
15.5530 g., 0.9999 Gold 0.5 oz. AGW, 27 mm. **Series:** Chinese Lunar Year **Subject:** Year of the Rabbit **Obv:** Four Chinese characters - "Amiable countenance" **Obv. Legend:** REPUBLIC OF SINGAPORE **Rev:** Rabbit hopping 3/4 right **Edge:** Reeded

Date	Mintage	F	VF	XF	Unc	BU
1987sm	8,000	—	—	—	—BV+15%	
1987sm Proof	1,000	BV+20%				

X# MB40 50 SINGOLD
15.5530 g., 0.9999 Gold 0.5 oz. AGW, 27 mm. **Series:** Chinese Lunar Year **Subject:** Year of the Dragon **Obv:** Four Chinese characters - "Goodwill, success and prosperity" **Obv. Legend:** REPUBLIC OF SINGAPORE **Rev:** Flying dragon facing left **Edge:** Reeded

Date	Mintage	F	VF	XF	Unc	BU
1988sm	10,000	—	—	—	—BV+15%	
1988sm Proof	500	BV+20%				

X# MB31 100 SINGOLD
31.1061 g., 0.9999 Gold 1 oz. AGW, 32.1 mm. **Series:** Chinese Lunar Year **Subject:** Year of the Rabbit **Obv:** Four Chinese characters - "Amiable countenance" **Obv. Legend:** REPUBLIC OF SINGAPORE **Rev:** Rabbit hopping 3/4 right **Edge:** Reeded

Date	Mintage	F	VF	XF	Unc	BU
1987sm	10,000	—	—	—	—BV+15%	
1987sm Proof	1,000	BV+20%				

X# MB41 100 SINGOLD
31.1061 g., 0.9990 Gold 0.9991 oz. AGW, 32.1 mm. **Series:** Chinese Lunar Year **Subject:** Year of the Dragon **Obv:** Four Chinese characters - "Goodwill, success and prosperity" **Obv. Legend:** REPUBLIC OF SINGAPORE **Rev:** Flying dragon facing left **Edge:** Reeded

Date	Mintage	F	VF	XF	Unc	BU
1988sm	15,000	—	—	—	—BV+15%	
1988sm Proof	1,000	BV+20%				

X# MB42 (500) SINGOLD/5 OUNCES
155.5306 g., 0.9999 Gold 4.9999 oz. AGW **Series:** Chinese Lunar Year **Subject:** Year of the Dragon **Obv:** Four Chinese characters - "Goodwill, success and prosperity" **Obv. Legend:** REPUBLIC OF SINGAPORE **Rev:** Pearl between two facing dragons **Edge:** Reeded

Date	Mintage	F	VF	XF	Unc	BU
1988sm Proof	500	BV+20%				

SINGAPORE 633

X# MB20 (1200) SINGOLD/12 OUNCES
373.2733 g., 0.9999 Gold 11.9998 oz. AGW, 65 mm. **Series:** Chinese Lunar Year **Subject:** Year of the Tiger **Obv:** Four Chinese characters - "Awe-inspiring power and might" **Obv. Legend:** REPUBLIC OF SINGAPORE **Rev:** Tiger prowling **Edge:** Reeded

Date	Mintage	F	VF	XF	Unc	BU
1986sm Proof	250					BV+20%

X# MB32 (1200) SINGOLD/12 OUNCES
373.2733 g., 0.9999 Gold 11.9998 oz. AGW, 76 mm. **Series:** Chinese Lunar Year **Subject:** Year of the Rabbit **Obv:** Four Chinese characters - "Amiable countenance" **Obv. Legend:** REPUBLIC OF SINGAPORE **Rev:** Rabbit hopping 3/4 right **Edge:** Reeded **Note:** Illustration reduced.

Date	Mintage	F	VF	XF	Unc	BU
1987sm Proof	250					BV+20%

X# MB43 (1200) SINGOLD/12 OUNCES
373.2733 g., 0.9999 Gold 11.9998 oz. AGW, 65 mm. **Series:** Chinese Lunar Year **Subject:** Year of the Dragon **Obv:** Four Chinese characters - "Goodwill, success and prosperity" **Obv. Legend:** REPUBLIC OF SINGAPORE **Rev:** Pearl between five facing dragons **Edge:** Reeded **Note:** Illustration reduced.

Date	Mintage	F	VF	XF	Unc	BU
1988sm Proof	200					BV+20%

X# MB54 (1200) SINGOLD/12 OUNCES
373.2733 g., 0.9999 Gold 11.9998 oz. AGW, 65 mm. **Series:** Chinese Lunar Year **Subject:** Year of the Snake **Obv:** Four Chinese characters - "Grace, wisdom and sprite" **Obv. Legend:** REPUBLIC OF SINGAPORE **Rev:** Snake wrapped around lady **Edge:** Reeded

Date	Mintage	F	VF	XF	Unc	BU
1989sm Proof	50					BV+30%

X# MB61 (1200) SINGOLD/12 OUNCES
373.2733 g., 0.9999 Gold 11.9998 oz. AGW, 65 mm. **Series:** Chinese Lunar Year **Subject:** Year of the Horse **Obv:** Four Chinese characters - "Reward and success" **Obv. Legend:** REPUBLIC OF SINGAPORE **Rev:** Two horses at water's edge **Edge:** Reeded

Date	Mintage	F	VF	XF	Unc	BU
1990sm Proof	50					BV+30%

X# MB74 (1200) SINGOLD/12 OUNCES
373.2733 g., 0.9999 Gold 11.9998 oz. AGW, 65 mm. **Series:** Chinese Lunar Year **Subject:** Year of the Goat **Obv:** Four Chinese characters - "The sun, it's peace and warmth during spring" **Obv. Legend:** REPUBLIC OF SINGAPORE **Rev:** Goat standing 3/4 right **Edge:** Reeded

Date	Mintage	F	VF	XF	Unc	BU
1991sm Proof	50					BV+30%

X# MB87 (1200) SINGOLD/12 OUNCES
373.2733 g., 0.9999 Gold 11.9998 oz. AGW, 65 mm. **Series:** Chinese Lunar Year **Subject:** Year of the Monkey **Obv:** Four Chinese characters - "Intelligent, enthusiastic and witty" **Obv. Legend:** REPUBLIC OF SINGAPORE **Rev:** Two Golden Hair monkeys perched on branch **Edge:** Reeded

Date	Mintage	F	VF	XF	Unc	BU
1992sm Proof	50					BV+30%

X# MB98 (1200) SINGOLD/12 OUNCES
373.2733 g., 0.9999 Gold 11.9998 oz. AGW **Series:** Chinese Lunar Year **Subject:** Year of the Rooster **Obv:** Four Chinese characters - "Confidence and bravity" **Obv. Legend:** REPUBLIC OF SINGAPORE **Rev:** Rooster right standing on one leg facing left **Edge:** Reeded

Date	Mintage	F	VF	XF	Unc	BU
1993sm Proof	50					BV+30%

X# MB108 (1200) SINGOLD/12 OUNCES
373.2733 g., 0.9999 Gold 11.9998 oz. AGW, 65 mm. **Series:** Chinese Lunar Year **Subject:** Year of the Dog **Obv:** Four Chinese characters - "Loyalty, comradeship, strength and faithfulness" **Obv. Legend:** REPUBLIC OF SINGAPORE **Rev:** Dog left under peach tree **Rev. Designer:** Artist Lang Shihnung **Edge:** Reeded

Date	Mintage	F	VF	XF	Unc	BU
1994sm Proof	50					BV+30%

X# MB119 (1200) SINGOLD/12 OUNCES
373.2733 g., 0.9999 Gold 11.9998 oz. AGW, 65 mm. **Series:** Chinese Lunar Year **Subject:** Year of the Boar **Obv:** Four Chinese characters - "Boundless prosperity and happiness" **Obv. Legend:** REPUBLIC OF SINGAPORE **Edge:** Reeded

Date	Mintage	F	VF	XF	Unc	BU
1995sm Proof	50					BV+30%

X# MB2 5 SINGOLD (1/20 Ounce)
1.5553 g., 0.9990 Gold 0.05 oz. AGW, 13.92 mm. **Series:** Chinese Lunar Year **Subject:** Year of the Rat **Obv:** Chinese character - "Life" **Obv. Legend:** REPUBLIC OF SINGAPORE **Rev:** Rat left **Edge:** Reeded

Date	Mintage	F	VF	XF	Unc	BU
1984sm	5,000	—	—	—	—	BV+20%

X# MB7 5 SINGOLD (1/20 Ounce)
1.5553 g., 0.9999 Gold 0.05 oz. AGW, 13.92 mm. **Series:** Chinese Lunar Year **Subject:** Year of the Ox **Obv:** Four Chinese characters - "Success through industry" **Obv. Legend:** REPUBLIC OF SINGAPORE **Rev:** Child riding ox right **Edge:** Reeded

Date	Mintage	F	VF	XF	Unc	BU
1985sm	5,000	—	—	—	—	BV+20%

X# MB15 5 SINGOLD (1/20 Ounce)
1.5553 g., 0.9999 Gold 0.05 oz. AGW, 13.92 mm. **Series:** Chinese Lunar Year **Subject:** Year of the Tiger **Obv:** Four Chinese characters - "Awe-inspiring power and might **Obv. Legend:** REPUBLIC OF SINGAPORE **Rev:** Tiger prowling **Edge:** Reeded

Date	Mintage	F	VF	XF	Unc	BU
1986sm	20,000	—	—	—	—	BV+20%

X# MB49 5 SINGOLD (1/20 Ounce)
1.5553 g., 0.9999 Gold 0.05 oz. AGW, 13.92 mm. **Series:** Chinese Lunar Year **Subject:** Year of the Snake **Obv:** Four Chinese characters - "Grace, wisdom and sprite" **Obv. Legend:** REPUBLIC OF SINGAPORE **Rev:** Snake poised upright behind lady **Edge:** Reeded

Date	Mintage	F	VF	XF	Unc	BU
1989sm	5,000	—	—	—	—	BV+20%
1989sm Proof	200					BV+30%

X# MB52 5 SINGOLD (1/20 Ounce)
15.5530 g., 0.9999 Gold 0.5 oz. AGW, 27 mm. **Series:** Chinese Lunar Year **Subject:** Year of the Snake **Obv:** Four Chinese characters - "Grace, wisdom and sprite" **Obv. Legend:** REPUBLIC OF SINGAPORE **Rev:** Snake poised upright behind lady **Edge:** Reeded

Date	Mintage	F	VF	XF	Unc	BU
1989sm	2,500	—	—	—	—	BV+20%
1989sm Proof	200					BV+30%

X# MB56 5 SINGOLD (1/20 Ounce)
1.5553 g., 0.9999 Gold 0.05 oz. AGW, 13.92 mm. **Series:** Chinese Lunar Year **Subject:** Year of the Horse **Obv:** Four Chinese characters - "Reward and success" **Obv. Legend:** REPUBLIC OF SINGAPORE **Rev:** Horse rearing left **Edge:** Reeded

Date	Mintage	F	VF	XF	Unc	BU
1990sm	30,000	—	—	—	—	BV+20%
1990sm Proof	200					BV+30%

X# MB59 5 SINGOLD (1/20 Ounce)
15.5530 g., 0.9999 Gold 0.5 oz. AGW, 27 mm. **Series:** Chinese Lunar Year **Subject:** Year of the Horse **Obv:** Four Chinese characters - "Reward and success" **Obv. Legend:** REPUBLIC OF SINGAPORE **Rev:** Horse rearing left **Edge:** Reeded

Date	Mintage	F	VF	XF	Unc	BU
1990sm	5,000	—	—	—	—	BV+20%
1990sm Proof	200					BV+30%

X# MB69 5 SINGOLD (1/20 Ounce)
1.5553 g., 0.9999 Gold 0.05 oz. AGW, 13.92 mm. **Series:** Chinese Lunar Year **Subject:** Year of the Goat **Obv:** Four Chinese characters - "The sun, it's peace and warmth during spring" **Obv. Legend:** REPUBLIC OF SINGAPORE **Rev:** Goat standing 3/4 right **Edge:** Reeded

Date	Mintage	F	VF	XF	Unc	BU
1991sm	30,000	—	—	—	—	BV+20%
1991sm Proof	250					BV+30%

X# MB82 5 SINGOLD (1/20 Ounce)
1.5553 g., 0.9999 Gold 0.05 oz. AGW, 13.92 mm. **Series:** Chinese Lunar Year **Subject:** Year of the Monkey **Obv:** Four Chinese characters - "Intelligent, enthusiastic and witty" **Obv. Legend:** REPUBLIC OF SINGAPORE **Rev:** Golden Hair monkey left perched on branch **Edge:** Reeded

Date	Mintage	F	VF	XF	Unc	BU
1992sm	30,000	—	—	—	—	BV+20%
1992sm Proof	250	BV+30%				

X# MB93 5 SINGOLD (1/20 Ounce)
1.5553 g., 0.9999 Gold 0.05 oz. AGW, 13.92 mm. **Series:** Chinese Lunar Year **Subject:** Year of the Rooster **Obv:** Four Chinese characters - "Confidence and bravity" **Obv. Legend:** REPUBLIC OF SINGAPORE **Rev:** Rooster right standing on one leg facing left **Edge:** Reeded

Date	Mintage	F	VF	XF	Unc	BU
1993sm	15,000	—	—	—	—	BV+20%
1993sm Proof	500	BV+30%				

X# MB103 5 SINGOLD (1/20 Ounce)
1.5553 g., 0.9999 Gold 0.05 oz. AGW, 13.92 mm. **Series:** Chinese Lunar Year **Subject:** Year of the Dog **Obv:** Four Chinese characters - "Loyalty, comradeship, strength and faithfulness" **Obv. Legend:** REPUBLIC OF SINGAPORE **Rev:** Dog left under peach tree **Rev. Designer:** Artist Lang Shihning **Edge:** Reeded

Date	Mintage	F	VF	XF	Unc	BU
1994sm	15,000	—	—	—	—	BV+20%
1994sm Proof	500	BV+30%				

X# MB106 5 SINGOLD (1/20 Ounce)
1.5553 g., 0.9999 Gold 0.05 oz. AGW, 27 mm. **Series:** Chinese Lunar Year **Subject:** Year of the Dog **Obv:** Four Chinese characters - "Loyalty, comradeship, strength and faithfulness" **Obv. Legend:** REPUBLIC OF SINGAPORE **Rev:** Dog left under peach tree **Rev. Designer:** Artist Lang Shihning **Edge:** Reeded

Date	Mintage	F	VF	XF	Unc	BU
1994sm	3,000	—	—	—	—	BV+20%
1994sm Proof	500	BV+30%				

X# MB114 5 SINGOLD (1/20 Ounce)
1.5553 g., 0.9999 Gold 0.05 oz. AGW, 13.92 mm. **Series:** Chinese Lunar Year **Subject:** Year of the Boar **Obv:** Four Chinese characters - "Boundless prosperity and happiness" **Obv. Legend:** REPUBLIC OF SINGAPORE **Rev:** Sow and two piglets **Rev. Designer:** Artist James Koh **Edge:** Reeded

Date	Mintage	F	VF	XF	Unc	BU
1995sm	15,000	—	—	—	—	BV+20%
1995sm Proof	500	BV+30%				

X# MB3 10 SINGOLD (1/10 Ounce)
3.1106 g., 0.9999 Gold 0.1 oz. AGW, 17.95 mm. **Series:** Chinese Lunar Year **Subject:** Year of the Rat **Obv:** Chinese character - "Knowing and being aware" **Obv. Legend:** REPUBLIC OF SINGAPORE **Rev:** Rat left **Edge:** Reeded

Date	Mintage	F	VF	XF	Unc	BU
1984sm	5,000	—	—	—	—	BV+15%

X# MB8 10 SINGOLD (1/10 Ounce)
3.1106 g., 0.9999 Gold 0.1 oz. AGW, 17.95 mm. **Series:** Chinese Lunar Year **Subject:** Year of the Ox **Obv:** Four Chinese characters - "Success through industry" **Obv. Legend:** REPUBLIC OF SINGAPORE **Rev:** Child riding ox right **Edge:** Reeded

Date	Mintage	F	VF	XF	Unc	BU
1985sm	5,000	—	—	—	—	BV+15%

X# MB16 10 SINGOLD (1/10 Ounce)
3.1106 g., 0.9999 Gold 0.1 oz. AGW, 17.95 mm. **Series:** Chinese Lunar Year **Subject:** Year of the Tiger **Obv:** Four Chinese characters - "Awe-inspiring power and might" **Obv. Legend:** REPUBLIC OF SINGAPORE **Rev:** Tiger prowling **Edge:** Reeded

Date	Mintage	F	VF	XF	Unc	BU
1986sm	—	—	—	—	—	BV+15%

X# MB50 10 SINGOLD (1/10 Ounce)
3.1106 g., 0.9999 Gold 0.1 oz. AGW, 17.95 mm. **Series:** Chinese Lunar Year **Subject:** Year of the Snake **Obv:** Four Chinese characters - "Grace, wisdom and sprite" **Obv. Legend:** REPUBLIC OF SINGAPORE **Rev:** Snake poised upright behind lady **Edge:** Reeded

Date	Mintage	F	VF	XF	Unc	BU
1989sm	5,000	—	—	—	—	BV+15%
1989sm Proof	200	BV+25%				

X# MB57 10 SINGOLD (1/10 Ounce)
3.1106 g., 0.9999 Gold 0.1 oz. AGW, 17.95 mm. **Series:** Chinese Lunar Year **Subject:** Year of the Horse **Obv:** Four Chinese characters - "Reward and success" **Obv. Legend:** REPUBLIC OF SINGAPORE **Rev:** Horse rearing left **Edge:** Reeded

Date	Mintage	F	VF	XF	Unc	BU
1990sm	15,000	—	—	—	—	BV+15%
1990sm Proof	200	BV+25%				

X# MB70 10 SINGOLD (1/10 Ounce)
3.1106 g., 0.9999 Gold 0.1 oz. AGW, 17.95 mm. **Series:** Chinese Lunar Year **Subject:** Year of the Goat **Obv:** Four Chinese characters - "The sun, it's peace and warmth during spring" **Obv. Legend:** REPUBLIC OF SINGAPORE **Rev:** Goat standing 3/4 right **Edge:** Reeded

Date	Mintage	F	VF	XF	Unc	BU
1991sm	15,000	—	—	—	—	BV+15%
1991sm Proof	250	BV+25%				

X# MB83 10 SINGOLD (1/10 Ounce)
3.1106 g., 0.9999 Gold 0.1 oz. AGW, 17.95 mm. **Series:** Chinese Lunar Year **Subject:** Year of the Monkey **Obv:** Four Chinese characters - "Intelligent, enthusiastic and witty" **Obv. Legend:** REPUBLIC OF SINGAPORE **Rev:** Golden Hair monkey perched on branch **Edge:** Reeded

Date	Mintage	F	VF	XF	Unc	BU
1992sm	15,000	—	—	—	—	BV+15%
1992sm Proof	250	BV+25%				

X# MB94 10 SINGOLD (1/10 Ounce)
3.1106 g., 0.9999 Gold 0.1 oz. AGW, 17.95 mm. **Series:** Chinese Lunar Year **Subject:** Year of the Rooster **Obv:** Four Chinese characters - "Confidence and bravity" **Obv. Legend:** REPUBLIC OF SINGAPORE **Rev:** Rooster right standing on one leg facing left **Edge:** Reeded

Date	Mintage	F	VF	XF	Unc	BU
1993sm	10,000	—	—	—	—	BV+15%
1993sm Proof	500	BV+25%				

X# MB104 10 SINGOLD (1/10 Ounce)
3.1106 g., 0.9999 Gold 0.1 oz. AGW, 17.95 mm. **Series:** Chinese Lunar Year **Subject:** Year of the Dog **Obv:** Four Chinese characters - "Loyalty, comradeship, strength and faithfulness" **Obv. Legend:** REPUBLIC OF SINGAPORE **Rev:** Dog left under peach tree **Rev. Designer:** Artist Lang Shihning **Edge:** Reeded

Date	Mintage	F	VF	XF	Unc	BU
1994sm	10,000	—	—	—	—	BV+15%
1994sm Proof	500	BV+25%				

X# MB115 10 SINGOLD (1/10 Ounce)
3.1106 g., 0.9999 Gold 0.1 oz. AGW, 17.95 mm. **Series:** Chinese Lunar Year **Subject:** Year of the Boar **Obv:** Four Chinese characters - "Boundless prosperity and happiness" **Obv. Legend:** REPUBLIC OF SINGAPORE **Rev:** Sow and two piglets **Rev. Designer:** Artist James Koh **Edge:** Reeded

Date	Mintage	F	VF	XF	Unc	BU
1995sm	10,000	—	—	—	—	BV+15%
1995sm Proof	500	BV+25%				

X# MB4 25 SINGOLD (1/4 Ounce)
7.7765 g., 0.9999 Gold 0.25 oz. AGW, 21.95 mm. **Series:** Chinese Lunar Year **Subject:** Year of the Rat **Obv:** Chinese character - "Heavens" **Obv. Legend:** REPUBLIC OF SINGAPORE **Rev:** Rat left **Edge:** Reeded

Date	Mintage	F	VF	XF	Unc	BU
1984sm	2,500	—	—	—	—	BV+15%

X# MB9 25 SINGOLD (1/4 Ounce)
7.7765 g., 0.9999 Gold 0.25 oz. AGW, 21.95 mm. **Series:** Chinese Lunar Year **Subject:** Year of the Ox **Obv:** Four Chinese characters - "Success through industry" **Obv. Legend:** REPUBLIC OF SINGAPORE **Rev:** Child riding ox right **Edge:** Reeded

Date	Mintage	F	VF	XF	Unc	BU
1985sm	2,500	—	—	—	—	BV+15%

X# MB17 25 SINGOLD (1/4 Ounce)
7.7765 g., 0.9999 Gold 0.25 oz. AGW, 21.95 mm. **Series:** Chinese Lunar Year **Subject:** Year of the Tiger **Obv:** Four Chinese characters - "Awe-inspiring power and might" **Obv. Legend:** REPUBLIC OF SINGAPORE **Rev:** Tiger prowling **Edge:** Reeded

Date	Mintage	F	VF	XF	Unc	BU
1986sm	10,000	—	—	—	—	BV+15%

X# MB51 25 SINGOLD (1/4 Ounce)
7.7765 g., 0.9999 Gold 0.25 oz. AGW, 21.95 mm. **Series:** Chinese Lunar Year **Subject:** Year of the Snake **Obv:** Four Chinese characters - "Grace, wisdom and sprite" **Obv. Legend:** REPUBLIC OF SINGAPORE **Rev:** Snake poised upright behind lady **Edge:** Reeded

Date	Mintage	F	VF	XF	Unc	BU
1989sm	2,500	—	—	—	—	BV+15%
1989sm Proof	200	BV+25%				

X# MB58 25 SINGOLD (1/4 Ounce)
7.7765 g., 0.9999 Gold 0.25 oz. AGW, 21.95 mm. **Subject:** Year of the Horse **Obv:** Four Chinese characters - "Reward and success" **Obv. Legend:** REPUBLIC OF SINGAPORE **Rev:** Horse rearing left **Edge:** Reeded

Date	Mintage	F	VF	XF	Unc	BU
1990sm	5,000	—	—	—	—	BV+15%
1990sm Proof	200	BV+25%				

X# MB71 25 SINGOLD (1/4 Ounce)
7.7765 g., 0.9999 Gold 0.25 oz. AGW, 21.95 mm. **Series:** Chinese Lunar Year **Subject:** Year of the Goat **Obv:** Four Chinese characters - "The sun, it's peace and warmth during spring" **Obv. Legend:** REPUBLIC OF SINGAPORE **Rev:** Goat standing 3/4 right **Edge:** Reeded

Date	Mintage	F	VF	XF	Unc	BU
1991sm	4,000	—	—	—	—	BV+15%
1991sm Proof	250	BV+25%				

X# MB84 25 SINGOLD (1/4 Ounce)
7.7765 g., 0.9999 Gold 0.25 oz. AGW, 21.95 mm. **Series:** Chinese Lunar Year **Subject:** Year of the Monkey **Obv:** Four Chinese characters - "Intelligent, enthusiastic and witty" **Obv. Legend:** REPUBLIC OF SINGAPORE **Rev:** Golden Hair monkey perched on branch **Edge:** Reeded

Date	Mintage	F	VF	XF	Unc	BU
1992sm	4,000	—	—	—	—	BV+15%
1992sm Proof	250	BV+25%				

X# MB95 25 SINGOLD (1/4 Ounce)
7.7765 g., 0.9999 Gold 0.25 oz. AGW, 21.95 mm. **Series:** Chinese Lunar Year **Subject:** Year of the Rooster **Obv:** Four Chinese characters - "Confidence and bravity" **Obv. Legend:** REPUBLIC OF SINGAPORE **Rev:** Rooster right standing on one leg facing left **Edge:** Reeded

Date	Mintage	F	VF	XF	Unc	BU
1993sm	6,000	—	—	—	—	BV+15%
1993sm Proof	500	BV+25%				

X# MB105 25 SINGOLD (1/4 Ounce)
7.7765 g., 0.9999 Gold 0.25 oz. AGW, 21.95 mm. **Series:** Chinese Lunar Year **Subject:** Year of the Dog **Obv:** Four Chinese characters - "Loyalty, comradeship, strength and faithfulness" **Obv. Legend:** REPUBLIC OF SINGAPORE **Rev:** Dog left under peach tree **Rev. Designer:** Artist Lang Shihning **Edge:** Reeded

Date	Mintage	F	VF	XF	Unc	BU
1994sm	6,000	—	—	—	—	BV+15%
1994sm Proof	500	BV+25%				

X# MB116 25 SINGOLD (1/4 Ounce)
7.7765 g., 0.9999 Gold 0.25 oz. AGW, 21.95 mm. **Series:** Chinese Lunar Year **Subject:** Year of the Boar **Obv:** Four Chinese characters - "Boundless prosperity and happiness" **Obv. Legend:** REPUBLIC OF SINGAPORE **Rev:** Sow and two piglets **Rev. Designer:** Artist James Koh **Edge:** Reeded

Date	Mintage	F	VF	XF	Unc	BU
1995sm	6,000	—	—	—	—	BV+15%
1995sm Proof	500	BV+25%				

X# MB5 50 SINGOLD (1/2 Ounce)
15.5530 g., 0.9999 Gold 0.5 oz. AGW, 27 mm. **Series:** Chinese Lunar Year **Subject:** Year of the Rat **Obv:** Chinese character - "Happiness" **Obv. Legend:** REPUBLIC OF SINGAPORE **Rev:** Rat left **Edge:** Reeded

Date	Mintage	F	VF	XF	Unc	BU
1984sm	2,500	—	—	—	—	BV+10%

X# MB10 50 SINGOLD (1/2 Ounce)
15.5530 g., 0.9999 Gold 0.5 oz. AGW, 27 mm. **Series:** Chinese Lunar Year **Subject:** Year of the Ox **Obv:** Four Chinese characters - "Success through industry" **Obv. Legend:** REPUBLIC OF SINGAPORE **Rev:** Child riding ox right **Edge:** Reeded

Date	Mintage	F	VF	XF	Unc	BU
1985sm	2,500	—	—	—	—	BV+10%

SINGAPORE 635

X# MB18 50 SINGOLD (1/2 Ounce)
15.5530 g., 0.9999 Gold 0.5 oz. AGW, 27 mm. **Series:** Chinese Lunar Year **Subject:** Year of the Tiger **Obv:** Four Chinese characters **Obv. Legend:** REPUBLIC OF SINGAPORE **Rev:** Tiger prowling **Edge:** Reeded

Date	Mintage	F	VF	XF	Unc	BU
1986sm	15,000	—	—	—	—	BV+10%

X# MB72 50 SINGOLD (1/2 Ounce)
15.5530 g., 0.9999 Gold 0.5 oz. AGW **Series:** Chinese Lunar Year **Subject:** Year of the Goat **Obv:** Four Chinese characters - "The sun, it's peace and warmth during spring" **Obv. Legend:** REPUBLIC OF SINGAPORE **Rev:** Goat standing 3/4 right **Edge:** Reeded

Date	Mintage	F	VF	XF	Unc	BU
1991sm	4,000	—	—	—	—	BV+10%
1991sm Proof	250	BV+20%				

X# MB85 50 SINGOLD (1/2 Ounce)
15.5530 g., 0.9999 Gold 0.5 oz. AGW, 27 mm. **Series:** Chinese Lunar Year **Subject:** Year of the Monkey **Obv:** Four Chinese characters - "Intelligent, enthusiastic and witty" **Obv. Legend:** REPUBLIC OF SINGAPORE **Edge:** Reeded

Date	Mintage	F	VF	XF	Unc	BU
1992sm	4,000	—	—	—	—	BV+10%
1992sm Proof	250	BV+20%				

X# MB96 50 SINGOLD (1/2 Ounce)
15.5530 g., 0.9999 Gold 0.5 oz. AGW, 27 mm. **Series:** Chinese Lunar Year **Subject:** Year of the Rooster **Obv:** Four Chinese characters - "Confidence and bravity" **Obv. Legend:** REPUBLIC OF SINGAPORE **Rev:** Rooster right standing on one leg facing left **Edge:** Reeded

Date	Mintage	F	VF	XF	Unc	BU
1993sm	3,000	—	—	—	—	BV+10%
1993sm Proof	500	BV+20%				

X# MB117 50 SINGOLD (1/2 Ounce)
15.5530 g., 0.9999 Gold 0.5 oz. AGW, 27 mm. **Series:** Chinese Lunar Year **Subject:** Year of the Boar **Obv:** Four Chinese characters - "Boundless prosperity and happiness" **Obv. Legend:** REPUBLIC OF SINGAPORE **Rev:** Sow and two piglets **Rev. Designer:** Artist James Koh **Edge:** Reeded

Date	Mintage	F	VF	XF	Unc	BU
1995sm	3,000	—	—	—	—	BV+10%
1995sm Proof	500	BV+20%				

X# MB19 100 SINGOLD (1 Ounce)
31.1061 g., 0.9999 Gold 1 oz. AGW, 32.1 mm. **Series:** Chinese Lunar Year **Subject:** Year of the Tiger **Obv:** Four Chinese characters - "Awe-inspiring power and might **Obv. Legend:** REPUBLIC OF SINGAPORE **Rev:** Tiger prowling **Edge:** Reeded

Date	Mintage	F	VF	XF	Unc	BU
1986sm	15,000	—	—	—	—	BV+10%

X# MB53 100 SINGOLD (1 Ounce)
31.1061 g., 0.9999 Gold 1 oz. AGW, 32.1 mm. **Series:** Chinese Lunar Year **Subject:** Year of the Snake **Obv:** Four Chinese characters - "Grace, wisdom and sprite" **Obv. Legend:** REPUBLIC OF SINGAPORE **Rev:** Snake poised upright behind lady **Edge:** Reeded

Date	Mintage	F	VF	XF	Unc	BU
1989sm	2,500	—	—	—	—	BV+10%
1989sm Proof	200	BV+20%				

X# MB60 100 SINGOLD (1 Ounce)
31.1061 g., 0.9999 Gold 1 oz. AGW, 32.1 mm. **Series:** Chinese Lunar Year **Subject:** Year of the Horse **Obv:** Four Chinese characters - "Reward and success" **Obv. Legend:** REPUBLIC OF SINGAPORE **Rev:** Horse rearing left **Edge:** Reeded

Date	Mintage	F	VF	XF	Unc	BU
1990sm	5,000	—	—	—	—	BV+10%
1990sm Proof	200	BV+20%				

X# MB73 100 SINGOLD (1 Ounce)
31.1061 g., 0.9999 Gold 1 oz. AGW, 32.1 mm. **Series:** Chinese Lunar Year **Subject:** Year of the Goat **Obv:** Four Chinese characters - "The sun, it's peace and warmth during spring" **Obv. Legend:** REPUBLIC OF SINGAPORE **Rev:** Goat standing 3/4 right **Edge:** Reeded

Date	Mintage	F	VF	XF	Unc	BU
1991sm	4,000	—	—	—	—	BV+10%
1991sm Proof	250	BV+20%				

X# MB86 100 SINGOLD (1 Ounce)
31.1061 g., 0.9999 Gold 1 oz. AGW, 32.1 mm. **Series:** Chinese Lunar Year **Subject:** Year of the Monkey **Obv:** Four Chinese characters - "Intelligent, enthusiastic and witty" **Obv. Legend:** REPUBLIC OF SINGAPORE **Rev:** Golden Hair monkey left perched on branch **Edge:** Reeded

Date	Mintage	F	VF	XF	Unc	BU
1992sm	4,000	—	—	—	—	BV+10%
1992sm Proof	250	BV+20%				

X# MB97 100 SINGOLD (1 Ounce)
31.1061 g., 0.9999 Gold 1 oz. AGW, 32.1 mm. **Series:** Chinese Lunar Year **Subject:** Year of the Rooster **Obv:** Four Chinese characters - "Confidence and bravity" **Obv. Legend:** REPUBLIC OF SINGAPORE **Rev:** Rooster right standing on one leg facing left **Edge:** Reeded

Date	Mintage	F	VF	XF	Unc	BU
1993sm	4,000	—	—	—	—	BV+10%
1993sm Proof	500	BV+20%				

X# MB107 100 SINGOLD (1 Ounce)
31.1061 g., 0.9999 Gold 1 oz. AGW, 32.1 mm. **Series:** Chinese Lunar Year **Subject:** Year of the Dog **Obv:** Four Chinese characters - "Loyalty, comradeship, strength and faithfulness" **Obv. Legend:** REPUBLIC OF SINGAPORE **Rev:** Dog left under peach tree **Rev. Designer:** Artist Lang Shihning **Edge:** Reeded

Date	Mintage	F	VF	XF	Unc	BU
1994sm	3,000	—	—	—	—	BV+10%
1994sm Proof	500	BV+20%				

X# MB118 100 SINGOLD (1 Ounce)
31.1061 g., 0.9999 Gold 1 oz. AGW, 32.1 mm. **Series:** Chinese Lunar Year **Subject:** Year of the Boar **Obv:** Four Chinese characters - "Boundless prosperity and happiness" **Obv. Legend:** REPUBLIC OF SINGAPORE **Rev:** Sow and two piglets **Rev. Designer:** Artist James **Edge:** Reeded

Date	Mintage	F	VF	XF	Unc	BU
1995sm	3,000	—	—	—	—	BV+10%
1995sm Proof	500	BV+20%				

X# MB62 5 GRAMS
5.0000 g., 0.9999 Gold 0.1607 oz. AGW, 19.41 mm. **Obv:** Six Chinese characters - "Accomplishment by emulation of the Eight Immortals" **Obv. Legend:** REPUBLIC OF SINGAPORE **Rev:** Tsao Guojn standing **Edge:** Reeded

Date	Mintage	F	VF	XF	Unc	BU
1990sm Proof	500	BV+20%				

X# MB63 5 GRAMS
5.0000 g., 0.9999 Gold 0.1607 oz. AGW, 19.41 mm. **Obv:** Six Chinese characters - "Accomplishment by emulation of the Eight Immortals" **Obv. Legend:** REPUBLIC OF SINGAPORE **Rev:** Han Zhongli standing **Edge:** Reeded

Date	Mintage	F	VF	XF	Unc	BU
1990sm Proof	500	BV+20%				

X# MB64 5 GRAMS
5.0000 g., 0.9999 Gold 0.1607 oz. AGW, 19.41 mm. **Obv:** Six Chinese characters - "Accomplishment by emulation of the Eight Immortals" **Obv. Legend:** REPUBLIC OF SINGAPORE **Rev:** Lu Dongbin standing **Edge:** Reeded

Date	Mintage	F	VF	XF	Unc	BU
1990sm Proof	500	BV+20%				

X# MB65 5 GRAMS
5.0000 g., 0.9999 Gold 0.1607 oz. AGW, 19.41 mm. **Obv:** Six Chinese characters - "Accomplishment by emulation of the Eight Immortals" **Obv. Legend:** REPUBLIC OF SINGAPORE **Rev:** Zhang Guolao **Edge:** Reeded

Date	Mintage	F	VF	XF	Unc	BU
1990sm Proof	500	—	—	—	—	BV+20%

X# MB76 5 GRAMS
5.0000 g., 0.9999 Gold 0.1607 oz. AGW, 19.41 mm. **Subject:** Singapore International Coin Convention **Obv:** Eight Chinese characters - "Accomplishment by emulation of the Eight Immortals" **Obv. Legend:** REPUBLIC OF SINGAPORE **Rev:** Li Tieguai **Edge:** Reeded

Date	Mintage	F	VF	XF	Unc	BU
1991sm Proof	500	BV+20%				

X# MB77 5 GRAMS
5.0000 g., 0.9999 Gold 0.1607 oz. AGW **Subject:** Singapore International Coin Convention **Obv:** Eight Chinese characters - "Accomplishment by emulation of the Eight Immortals" **Obv. Legend:** REPUBLIC OF SINGAPORE **Rev:** Lan Tsaiho **Edge:** Reeded

Date	Mintage	F	VF	XF	Unc	BU
1991sm Proof	500	BV+20%				

X# MB78 5 GRAMS
5.0000 g., 0.9999 Gold 0.1607 oz. AGW, 19.41 mm. **Subject:** Singapore International Coin Convention **Obv:** Eight Chinese characters - "Accomplishment by emulation of the Eight Immortals" **Obv. Legend:** REPUBLIC OF SINGAPORE **Rev:** He Shiangu **Edge:** Reeded

Date	Mintage	F	VF	XF	Unc	BU
1991sm Proof	500	BV+20%				

X# MB79 5 GRAMS
5.0000 g., 0.9999 Gold 0.1607 oz. AGW, 19.41 mm. **Subject:** Singapore International Coin Convention **Obv:** Eight Chinese characters - "Accomplishment by emulation of the Eight Immortals" **Obv. Legend:** REPUBLIC OF SINGAPORE **Rev:** Han Shiangzi **Edge:** Reeded

Date	Mintage	F	VF	XF	Unc	BU
1991sm Proof	500	BV+20%				

MEDALLIC PLATINUM BULLION COINAGE

X# MBA21 OUNCE
31.1186 g., 0.9995 Platinum 1 oz. APW, 32 mm. **Series:** Chinese Lunar Year **Subject:** Year of the Tiger **Obv:** Four Chinese characters - "Awe-inspiring power and might" **Obv. Legend:** REPUBLIC OF SINGAPORE **Rev:** Tiger prowling **Edge:** Reeded

Date	Mintage	F	VF	XF	Unc	BU
1986sm Prooflike	1,000	—	—	—	—	BV+10%

X# MB44 OUNCE
31.1186 g., 0.9995 Platinum 1 oz. APW, 32 mm. **Series:** Chinese Lunar Year **Subject:** Year of the Dragon **Obv:** Four Chinese characters - "Goodwill, success and prosperity" **Obv. Legend:** REPUBLIC OF SINGAPORE **Rev:** Flying dragon, pearl at left **Edge:** Reeded

Date	Mintage	F	VF	XF	Unc	BU
1988sm	1,500	—	—	—	—	BV+10%

MINT SETS

KM#	Date	Mintage	Identification	Issue Price	Mkt Val
MS11	1975 (3)	30,000	KM#12-14	—	1,100
MS28	1990 (5)	5,000	KM#79-83	—	900

PROOF SETS

KM#	Date	Mintage	Identification	Issue Price	Mkt Val
PS8	1975 (3)	2,000	KM#12-14	—	1,600
PS27	1990 (5)	2,000	KM#79-83	—	850
PSA28	1990 (3)	1,000	KM#95-97	—	1,700
PS29	1991 (5)	2,500	KM#87-91	—	850
PS32	1992 (5)	2,000	KM#108-112 Ingot	—	850
PS33	1992 (5)	200	KM#105-107	—	1,600
PS35	1993 (5)	1,500	KM#117-121 Ingot	—	875
PS38	1994 (5)	1,500	KM#128-132 Ingot	—	875
PS41	1995 (5)	1,500	KM#133-137 Ingot	1,718	875
PS42	1995 (3)	2,689	KM#138-140	1,052	750
PS44	1996 (5)	2,688	KM#144-148 Ingot	—	900
PS48	1997 (5)	888	KM#151, 151a, 152 Ingot	—	625
PS49	1997 (5)	2,200	KM#158-162	—	1,000
PS50	1998 (5)	1,998	KM#164-166 Ingot	—	675
PS54	2000 (3)	2,000	KM#174-176 Plus Ingot	—	685
PS56	2001 (3)	2,000	KM#178-180 plus copper-nickel ingot	—	685

636 SLOVAKIA

SLOVAKIA

The Republic of Slovakia has an area of 18,923 sq. mi. (49,035 sq. km.) and a population of 4.9 million. Capital: Bratislava. Textiles, steel, and wood products are exported.

The Slovak lands were united with the Czechs and the Czechoslovak State came into existence on Oct. 28, 1918 upon the dissolution of Austro-Hungarian Empire at the close of World War I. In March 1939, the German-influenced Slovak government proclaimed Slovakia independent and Germany incorporated the Czech lands into the Third Reich as the "Protectorate of Bohemia and Moravia". A Czechoslovak government-in-exile was setup in London in July 1940. The Soviet and USA forces liberated the area by May, 1945. At the close of World War II, Communist influence increased steadily while pressure for liberalization culminated in the overthrow of the Stalinist leader Antonin Novotn'y and his associates in 1968.The Communist Party then introduced far reaching reforms which received warnings from Moscow, followed by occupation by Warsaw Pact forces resulting in stationing of Soviet forces. Mass civilian demonstrations for reform began in Nov.1989 and the Federal Assembly abolished the Communist Party's sole right to govern. New governments followed on Dec. 3 and Dec. 10 and the Czech and Slovak Federal Republic was formed. The Movement for Democratic Slovakia was apparent in the June 1992 elections with the Slovak National Council adopting a declaration of sovereignty. Later, a constitution for an independent Slovakia with the Federal Assembly voting for the dissolution of the Republic came into effect on Dec. 31, 1992, and two new republics came into being on Jan. 1, 1993.

MINT MARK

Kremnica Mint

REPUBLIC

STANDARD COINAGE
100 Halierov = 1 Slovak Koruna (Sk)

KM# 29 5000 KORUN
7.0000 g., 0.9000 Gold .2025 oz. AGW, 24 mm. **Subject:** 1100th Anniversary - Death of Great Moravian King Svatopluk **Obv:** Double cross on shield, value and date **Rev:** Head of Svatopluk and ruin of castle Devin **Edge:** Milled **Designer:** Vojtech Pohanka

Date	Mintage	F	VF	XF	Unc	BU
1994 Proof	5,000	Value: 500				

KM# 36 5000 KORUN
9.5000 g., 0.9000 Gold .2749 oz. AGW, 26 mm. **Subject:** Banska Stiavnica Historical Mines - UNESCO **Obv:** Double cross on shield, value, date and upright design **Rev:** Steepled buildings **Edge:** Milled **Designer:** Milan Vircik

Date	Mintage	F	VF	XF	Unc	BU
1997 Proof	8,000	Value: 325				

KM# 46 5000 KORUN
9.5000 g., 0.9000 Gold .2749 oz. AGW, 26 mm. **Subject:** Spissky Castle - UNESCO **Obv:** Double cross on shield and lion within design above date **Rev:** Scenic design and value **Edge:** Milled **Designer:** Pavel Karoly

Date	Mintage	F	VF	XF	Unc	BU
1998 Proof	6,000	Value: 325				

KM# 54 5000 KORUN
9.5000 g., 0.9000 Gold .2749 oz. AGW, 26 mm. **Subject:** 500th Anniversary - Kremnica Mint **Obv:** Hungarian coin design **Rev:** Hungarian coin design **Edge:** Reeded **Designer:** Jan Cernaj

Date	Mintage	F	VF	XF	Unc	BU
ND(1999) Proof	5,500	Value: 325				

KM# 58 5000 KORUN
Tri-Metallic 31.1035, .999 Silver, 1.00 oz ASW with 6.22, .999 Gold, .20 oz AGW and .31, .999 Platinum, .10 oz. APW, 50 mm. **Series:** Third Millennium **Obv:** "The Universe" **Rev:** Three hands **Edge:** Plain **Shape:** Triangular **Designer:** Patrik Kovacovsky

Date	Mintage	F	VF	XF	Unc	BU
2001 Proof	8,000	Value: 400				

KM# 61 5000 KORUN
9.5000 g., 0.9000 Gold 0.2749 oz. AGW, 26 mm. **Subject:** Vikolinec Village **Obv:** Enclosed communal well **Rev:** Window and fence **Edge:** Reeded

Date	Mintage	F	VF	XF	Unc	BU
2002 Proof	7,200	Value: 325				

KM# 80 5000 KORUN
9.5000 g., 0.9000 Gold 0.2749 oz. AGW, 26 mm. **Subject:** Historic Town of Bardejov **Obv:** National arms and value left of Town Hall **Rev:** Zachariah in window frame left of St. Aegidius Church **Edge:** Reeded

Date	Mintage	F	VF	XF	Unc	BU
2004 Proof	9,000	Value: 300				

KM# 83 5000 KORUN
9.5000 g., 0.9000 Gold 0.2749 oz. AGW, 26 mm. **Subject:** Leopold I Coronation **Obv:** Mounted Herald with Bratislava Castile in background **Rev:** Leopold I and Crown of St. Stephan **Edge:** Reeded

Date	Mintage	F	VF	XF	Unc	BU
2005 Proof	7,500	Value: 350				

KM# 52 10000 KORUN
19.0000 g., 0.9000 Gold .5498 oz. AGW, 34 mm. **Subject:** 2000 Bi-millennium **Obv:** Double cross on shield, value and historical scenes **Rev:** Jesus with churches **Edge:** Milled **Designer:** Stefan Novotny **Note:** Similar to 2000 Korun, KM#51.

Date	Mintage	F	VF	XF	Unc	BU
MM(2000) Proof	Est. 3,500	Value: 600				

KM# 64 10000 KORUN
17.1050 g., Bi-Metallic 1.555g, .999 Palladium round center in a 15.55g, .900 Gold square, 29.5 x 29.5 mm. **Subject:** 10th Anniversary of the Republic **Obv:** Young head left within circular inscription above double cross within shield **Rev:** Bratislava castle above value **Edge:** Segmented reeding **Shape:** Square

Date	Mintage	F	VF	XF	Unc	BU
2003 Proof	6,000	Value: 750				

KM# 79 10000 KORUN
24.8828 g., Bi-Metallic .999 Gold 12.4414g 23mm round center in .999 Palladium 12.4414g 40mm pentagon, 40 mm. **Subject:** Slovakian entry into the European Union **Obv:** National arms above date in center **Rev:** European map with entry date **Edge:** Plain

Date	Mintage	F	VF	XF	Unc	BU
2004 Proof	7,200	Value: 800				

SLOVENIA

The Republic of Slovenia is located northwest of Yugoslavia in the valleys of the Danube River. It has an area of 7,819 sq. mi. and a population of *1.9 million. Capital: Ljubljana. Agriculture is the main industry with large amounts of hops and fodder crops grown as well as many varieties of fruit trees. Sheep raising, timber production and the mining of mercury from one of the country's oldest mines are also very important to the economy.

Slovenia was important as a land route between Europe and the eastern Mediterranean region. The Roman Catholic Austro-Hungarian Empire gained control of the area during the 14th century and retained its dominance until World War I. The United Kingdom of the Serbs, Croats and Slovenes (Yugoslavia) was founded in 1918 and consisted of various groups of South Slavs.

In 1929, King Alexander declared his assumption of power temporarily, however he was assassinated in 1934. His son Peter's regent, Prince Paul tried to settle internal problems, however, the Slovenes denounced the agreement he made. He resigned in 1941 and Peter assumed the throne. Peter was forced to flee when Yugoslavia was occupied. Slovenia was divided between Germany and Italy. Even though Yugoslavia attempted to remain neutral, the Nazis occupied the country and were resisted by guerilla armies, most notably Marshal Josif Broz Tito.

Under Marshal Tito, the Constitution of 1946 established 6 constituent republics which made up Yugoslavia. Each republic was permitted Liberties under supervision of the Communist Party.

In Oct. 1989 the Slovene Assembly voted a constitutional amendment giving it the right to secede from Yugoslavia. A referendum on Dec. 23, 1990 resulted in a majority vote for independence, which was formally declared on Dec. 26.

On June 25 Slovenia declared independence, but agreed to suspend this for 3 months at peace talks sponsored by the EC. Federal troops moved into Slovenia on June 27 to secure Yugoslavia's external borders, but after some fighting withdrew by the end of July. The 3-month moratorium agreed at the EC having expired, Slovenia (and Croatia) declared their complete independence of the Yugoslav federation on Oct.8, 1991.

MINT MARKS
Based on last digit in date.
(K) - Kremnitz (Slovakia): open 4, upturned 5
(BP) - Budapest (Hungary): closed 4, downturned 5

MONETARY SYSTEM
100 Stotinov = 1 Tolar

REPUBLIC

STANDARD COINAGE
100 Stotinow = 1 Tolar

KM# 2.1 5000 TOLARJEV
7.0000 g., 0.9000 Gold .2025 oz. AGW **Subject:** 1st Anniversary of Independence **Obv:** Value within circle at left, date at right **Rev:** Bird's beak at center of spiral
Date	Mintage	F	VF	XF	Unc	BU
1991 Proof	4,000	Value: 235				

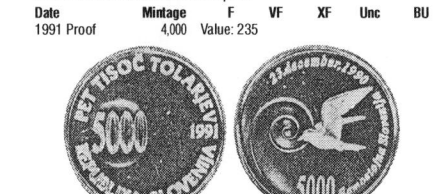

KM# 2.2 5000 TOLARJEV
7.0000 g., 0.9000 Gold .2025 oz. AGW **Obv:** Value within circle at left, date at right **Rev:** Bird's beak lower center of spiral
Date	Mintage	F	VF	XF	Unc	BU
1991 Proof	Inc. above	Value: 200				

KM# 11 5000 TOLARJEV
7.0000 g., 0.9000 Gold .2025 oz. AGW, 24 mm. **Subject:** Battle of Sisek **Obv:** Value below date **Rev:** City view, arms and date
Date	Mintage	F	VF	XF	Unc	BU
1993 Proof	Est. 2,000	Value: 200				

KM# 14 5000 TOLARJEV
7.0000 g., 0.9000 Gold .2025 oz. AGW, 24 mm. **Subject:** 300th Anniversary - Establishment of Operosorum Labacensium Academy **Obv:** Value below date **Rev:** Beehive among bees
Date	Mintage	F	VF	XF	Unc	BU
1993 Proof	2,000	Value: 215				

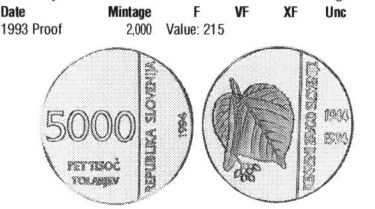

KM# 18 5000 TOLARJEV
7.0000 g., 0.9000 Gold .2025 oz. AGW, 24 mm. **Subject:** 50th Anniversary - Slovenian Bank **Obv:** Value and vertical date **Rev:** Leaf and dates
Date	Mintage	F	VF	XF	Unc	BU
1994 Proof	2,000	Value: 200				

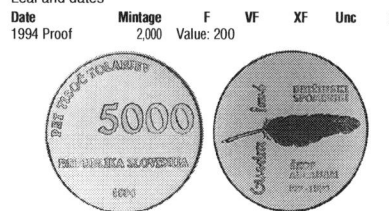

KM# 20 5000 TOLARJEV
7.0000 g., 0.9000 Gold .2025 oz. AGW **Subject:** 1000th Anniversary - Bishop Abraham - Glagolitic Alphabet **Obv:** Value **Rev:** Feather
Date	Mintage	F	VF	XF	Unc	BU
1994 Proof	1,000	Value: 210				

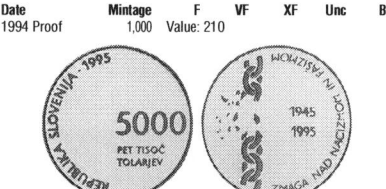

KM# 24 5000 TOLARJEV
7.0000 g., 0.9000 Gold .2025 oz. AGW, 24 mm. **Subject:** 50th Anniversary - Defeat of Fascism **Obv:** Value **Rev:** Vertical chain link design and dates
Date	Mintage	F	VF	XF	Unc	BU
1995 Proof	1,000	Value: 210				

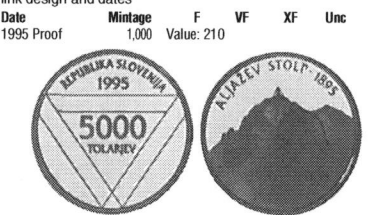

KM# 28 5000 TOLARJEV
7.0000 g., 0.9000 Gold .2025 oz. AGW, 24 mm. **Subject:** Aljazev Stolp and Mountain Summit **Obv:** Value within triangle design **Rev:** Head facing in front of mountains
Date	Mintage	F	VF	XF	Unc	BU
1995 Proof	1,000	Value: 210				

KM# 31 5000 TOLARJEV
7.0000 g., 0.9000 Gold .2025 oz. AGW, 24 mm. **Subject:** 100th Anniversary - First Railway in Slovenia **Obv:** Date within design at upper right, value at left **Rev:** Train below dates
Date	Mintage	F	VF	XF	Unc	BU
1996 Proof	1,000	Value: 215				

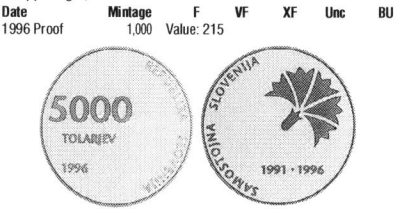

KM# 35 5000 TOLARJEV
7.0000 g., 0.9000 Gold .2025 oz. AGW, 24 mm. **Subject:** 5th Anniversary of Independence **Obv:** Value above date **Rev:** Pink carnation above dates
Date	Mintage	F	VF	XF	Unc	BU
1996 Proof	1,000	Value: 210				

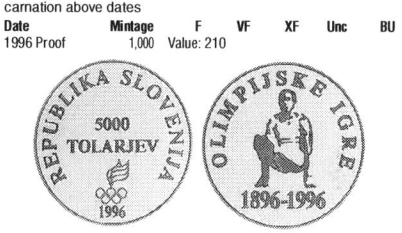

KM# 37 5000 TOLARJEV
7.0000 g., 0.9000 Gold .2025 oz. AGW, 24 mm. **Series:** Olympics **Obv:** Value above olympic rings and flag **Rev:** Gymnast above dates
Date	Mintage	F	VF	XF	Unc	BU
1996 Proof	1,000	Value: 225				

KM# 40 5000 TOLARJEV
7.0000 g., 0.9000 Gold .2025 oz. AGW, 24 mm. **Subject:** Zois Ziga
Date	Mintage	F	VF	XF	Unc	BU
1997 Proof	1,000	Value: 210				

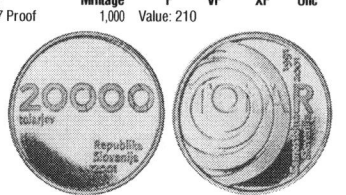

KM# 44 20000 TOLARJEV
7.0000 g., 0.9000 Gold 0.2025 oz. AGW, 24 mm. **Subject:** 10th Anniversary of Slovenia and the Tolar **Obv:** Value **Rev:** Tree rings and inscription **Edge:** Reeded
Date	Mintage	F	VF	XF	Unc	BU
2001 Proof	1,000	Value: 275				

KM# 47 20000 TOLARJEV
7.0000 g., 0.9000 Gold 0.2025 oz. AGW, 24 mm. **Subject:** World Cup Soccer **Obv:** Value **Rev:** Soccer player and rising sun **Edge:** Reeded
Date	Mintage	F	VF	XF	Unc	BU
2002 Proof	1,500	Value: 275				

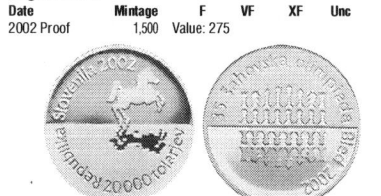

KM# 49 20000 TOLARJEV
7.0000 g., 0.9000 Gold 0.2025 oz. AGW, 24 mm. **Subject:** 35th Chess Olympiad **Obv:** Rearing horse and reflection **Rev:** Chess pieces in starting positions and reflection **Edge:** Reeded

SLOVENIA

Date	Mintage	F	VF	XF	Unc	BU
2002 Proof	500	Value: 300				

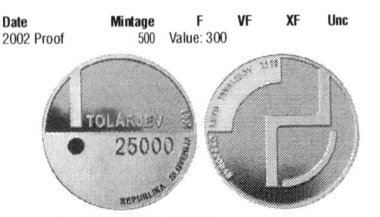

KM# 54 25000 TOLARJEV
7.0000 g., 0.9000 Gold 0.2025 oz. AGW, 24 mm. **Subject:** European Year of the Disabled **Obv:** Value **Rev:** Stylized wheel chair **Edge:** Reeded

Date	Mintage	F	VF	XF	Unc	BU
2003 Proof	300	Value: 300				

KM# 56 25000 TOLARJEV
7.0000 g., 0.9000 Gold 0.2025 oz. AGW, 24 mm. **Subject:** 60th Anniversary of the Slovenian Assembly **Obv:** Value in partial star design **Rev:** Dates in partial star design **Edge:** Reeded

Date	Mintage	F	VF	XF	Unc	BU
2003 Proof	300	Value: 300				

KM# 59 25000 TOLARJEV
7.0000 g., 0.9000 Gold 0.2025 oz. AGW, 24 mm. **Subject:** 250th Anniversary of Jurij Vega's Birth **Obv:** Value **Rev:** Facial profile left looking down within mathematical graph **Edge:** Reeded

Date	Mintage	F	VF	XF	Unc	BU
2004	300	—	—	—	—	300

KM# 61 25000 TOLARJEV
7.0000 g., 0.9000 Gold 0.2025 oz. AGW, 24 mm. **Subject:** 1000th Anniversary Town of Bled **Obv:** Value **Rev:** Castle and towers silhouette **Edge:** Reeded

Date	Mintage	F	VF	XF	Unc	BU
2004	300	—	—	—	—	300

KM# 66 25000 TOLARJEV
7.0000 g., 0.9000 Gold 0.2025 oz. AGW, 24 mm. **Subject:** Centennial of Slovene Sokol Association **Obv:** Perched hawk above value **Rev:** Rising sun and reflection **Edge:** Reeded

Date	Mintage	F	VF	XF	Unc	BU
2005	1,000	—	—	—	—	285

KM# 67 25000 TOLARJEV
7.0000 g., 0.9000 Gold 0.2025 oz. AGW, 24 mm. **Subject:** Centennial of Slovene Film **Obv:** Value above clapboard **Rev:** Film segment **Edge:** Reeded

Date	Mintage	F	VF	XF	Unc	BU
2005	1,000	—	—	—	—	285

PROOF SETS

KM#	Date	Mintage	Identification	Issue Price	Mkt Val
PS1	1991 (2)	—	KM#1, 2.2	—	325

SOLOMON ISLANDS

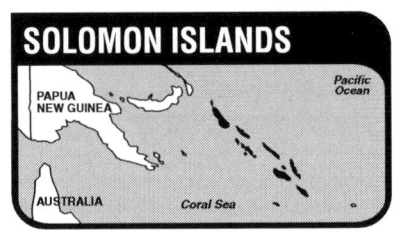

The Solomon Islands are made up of approximately 200 islands. They are located in the southwest Pacific east of Papua New Guinea, have an area of 10,983 sq. mi. (28,450 sq. km.) and a population of *552,000. Capital: Honiara. The most important islands of the Solomon chain are Guadalcanal (scene of some of the fiercest fighting of World War II), Malaitia, New Georgia, Florida, Vella Lavella, Choiseul, Rendova, San Cristobal, the Lord Howe group, the Santa Cruz islands, and the Duff group. Copra is the only important cash crop but it is hoped that timber will become an economic factor.

The Solomon Islands were discovered by Spanish navigator Alvaro de Mendana in 1567, and in 1569 he made an unsuccessful attempt to colonize them. European knowledge of the group would not be completed until the end of the 19th century. Germany declared a protectorate over the northern Solomon's in 1885. The British protectorate over the southern Solomons was established in 1893. In 1899 Germany transferred its claim to all Solomon Islands except Buka and Bougainville to Great Britain in exchange for recognition of German claims in Western Samoa. Australia occupied the two German islands in 1914, and administered them after 1920.

The Japanese invaded the Solomons during 1942-43, but were driven out by an American counteroffensive after a series of bloody clashes.

Following World War II, the islands returned to the status of a British protectorate. In 1976 the protectorate was abolished, and the Solomons became a self-governing dependency. Full independence was achieved on July 7,1978. Solomon Islands is a member of the Commonwealth of Nations. Queen Elizabeth II is Head of State, as Queen of the Solomon Islands.

RULER
British, until 1978

MINT MARK
FM - Franklin Mint, U.S.A.*
   NOTE: From 1977-1985 the Franklin Mint produced coinage in up to 3 different qualities. Qualities of issue are designated in ( ) after each date and are defined as follows:
   (M) MATTE - Normal circulation strike or a dull finish produced by sandblasting special uncirculated (polish finish) or proof quality dies.
   (U) SPECIAL UNCIRCULATED - Polished or proof-like in appearance without any frosted features.
   (P) PROOF - The highest quality obtainable having mirror-like fields and frosted features.

MONETARY SYSTEM
100 Cents = 1 Dollar

COMMONWEALTH NATION
STANDARD COINAGE

KM# 31 10 DOLLARS
3.1300 g., 0.9990 Gold .1006 oz. AGW, 16.5 mm. **Subject:** 50th Anniversary of Pearl Harbor **Obv:** Crowned head right **Rev:** Map of Pearl Harbor **Rev. Designer:** Willem Vis

Date	Mintage	F	VF	XF	Unc	BU
1991 Proof	Est. 500	Value: 70.00				

KM# 36 10 DOLLARS
3.1300 g., 0.9990 Gold .1006 oz. AGW, 16.5 mm. **Subject:** 50th Anniversary - Battle of the Coral Sea **Rev:** Planes dropping bombs within circle **Rev. Designer:** Willem Vis

Date	Mintage	F	VF	XF	Unc	BU
1992 Proof	500	Value: 70.00				

KM# 42 10 DOLLARS
3.1300 g., 0.9990 Gold .1006 oz. AGW, 16.5 mm. **Subject:** 50th Anniversary - Battle of Guadalcanal **Rev:** Battle scene within circle **Rev. Designer:** Willem Vis

Date	Mintage	F	VF	XF	Unc	BU
1992 Proof	500	Value: 70.00				

KM# 55 10 DOLLARS
3.1300 g., 0.9990 Gold .1006 oz. AGW, 16.5 mm. **Rev:** Marine and armored tank within circle **Rev. Designer:** Willem Vis

Date	Mintage	F	VF	XF	Unc	BU
1995 Proof	Est. 500	Value: 75.00				

KM# 32 25 DOLLARS
7.8100 g., 0.9990 Gold .2514 oz. AGW, 22 mm. **Subject:** 50th Anniversary - Pearl Harbor **Obv:** Crowned head right **Rev:** Pearl Harbor battle scene within circle **Rev. Designer:** Willem Vis

Date	Mintage	F	VF	XF	Unc	BU
1991 Proof	Est. 3,000	Value: 170				

KM# 37 25 DOLLARS
7.8100 g., 0.9990 Gold .2514 oz. AGW, 22 mm. **Subject:** 50th Anniversary - Battle of the Coral Sea **Rev:** Pearl Harbor battle scene within circle **Rev. Designer:** Willem Vis

Date	Mintage	F	VF	XF	Unc	BU
1992 Proof	Est. 3,000	Value: 170				

KM# 43 25 DOLLARS
7.8100 g., 0.9990 Gold .2514 oz. AGW, 22 mm. **Subject:** 50th Anniversary - Battle of Guadalcanal **Rev:** Uniformed soldiers and armored tank in woods within circle **Rev. Designer:** Willem Vis

Date	Mintage	F	VF	XF	Unc	BU
1992 Proof	Est. 3,000	Value: 170				

KM# 56 25 DOLLARS
7.8100 g., 0.9990 Gold .2514 oz. AGW, 22 mm. **Subject:** 50th Anniversary - Iwo Jima Flag Raising **Rev:** Uniformed soldiers raising flag within circle **Rev. Designer:** Willem Vis

Date	Mintage	F	VF	XF	Unc	BU
1995 Proof	Est. 2,500	Value: 175				

SOLOMON ISLANDS

KM# 33 50 DOLLARS
15.6000 g., 0.9990 Gold .5016 oz. AGW, 27 mm. **Subject:** 50th Anniversary - Pearl Harbor **Obv:** Crowned head right **Rev:** Pearl Harbor battle scene within circle **Rev. Designer:** Willem Vis

Date	Mintage	F	VF	XF	Unc	BU
1991 Proof	Est. 500	Value: 340				

KM# 38 50 DOLLARS
15.6000 g., 0.9990 Gold .5016 oz. AGW, 27 mm. **Subject:** 50th Anniversary - Battle of the Coral Sea **Rev:** Planes bombing ship within circle **Rev. Designer:** Willem Vis

Date	Mintage	F	VF	XF	Unc	BU
1992 Proof	Est. 500	Value: 340				

KM# 44 50 DOLLARS
15.6000 g., 0.9990 Gold .5016 oz. AGW, 27 mm. **Subject:** 50th Anniversary - Battle of Guadalcanal **Rev:** Uniformed soldiers within circle **Rev. Designer:** Willem Vis

Date	Mintage	F	VF	XF	Unc	BU
1992 Proof	Est. 500	Value: 340				

KM# 60 50 DOLLARS
7.7600 g., 0.5830 Gold .1458 oz. AGW **Series:** Endangered Wildlife **Obv:** Crowned head right **Rev:** Descending eagle

Date	Mintage	F	VF	XF	Unc	BU
1993 Proof	Est. 3,000	Value: 125				

KM# 57 50 DOLLARS
15.6100 g., 0.9990 Gold .5016 oz. AGW, 27 mm. **Rev:** MacArthur accepting Japanese surrender **Rev. Designer:** Willem Vis

Date	Mintage	F	VF	XF	Unc	BU
1995 Proof	500	Value: 345				

Note: In proof sets only

KM# 9 100 DOLLARS
9.3700 g., 0.9000 Gold .2711 oz. AGW **Subject:** Attainment of Sovereignty **Obv:** Young bust right **Rev:** Arms with supporters

Date	Mintage	F	VF	XF	Unc	BU
1978FM (M)	50	—	—	—	245	—
1978FM (U)	213	—	—	—	200	—
1978FM (P)	3,159	Value: 185				

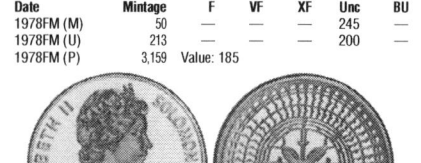

KM# 11 100 DOLLARS
7.6400 g., 0.5000 Gold .1228 oz. AGW **Subject:** Native Art **Obv:** Young bust right **Rev:** Artistic design in center of designed circles

Date	Mintage	F	VF	XF	Unc	BU
1980FM (U)	50	—	—	—	185	—
1980FM (P) Proof	7,500	Value: 90.00				

KM# 12 100 DOLLARS
7.6400 g., 0.5000 Gold .1228 oz. AGW **Obv:** Young bust right **Rev:** Shark

Date	Mintage	F	VF	XF	Unc	BU
1981 Proof	675	Value: 145				

KM# 14 100 DOLLARS
9.3700 g., 0.9000 Gold .2711 oz. AGW **Subject:** Battle of Guadalcanal **Obv:** Young bust right **Rev:** Uniformed soldiers

Date	Mintage	F	VF	XF	Unc	BU
1982FM (P)	311	Value: 220				

KM# 18 100 DOLLARS
9.3700 g., 0.9000 Gold .2711 oz. AGW **Subject:** 5th Anniversary of Independence **Obv:** Young bust right within circle, radiant border **Rev:** Arms with supporters in front of flag within circle, radiant border **Shape:** Pentagon

Date	Mintage	F	VF	XF	Unc	BU
1983FM (P)	268	Value: 225				

KM# 21 100 DOLLARS
7.5000 g., 0.9170 Gold .2211 oz. AGW **Series:** 1984 Olympics **Rev:** Weightlifter **Rev. Designer:** E.W. Roberts

Date	Mintage	F	VF	XF	Unc	BU
1984 Proof	500	Value: 160				

KM# 34 100 DOLLARS
31.2100 g., 0.9990 Gold 1.0035 oz. AGW, 32.69 mm. **Subject:** 50th Anniversary of Pearl Harbor **Obv:** Crowned head right **Rev:** Pearl Harbor battle scene within circle **Rev. Designer:** Willem Vis

Date	Mintage	F	VF	XF	Unc	BU
1991 Proof	Est. 500	Value: 675				

KM# 39 100 DOLLARS
31.2100 g., 0.9990 Gold 1.0035 oz. AGW, 32.69 mm. **Subject:** 50th Anniversary - Battle of Coral Sea **Rev:** Soldiers in lifeboats, burning building and boat, all within circle **Rev. Designer:** Willem Vis

Date	Mintage	F	VF	XF	Unc	BU
1992 Proof	Est. 500	Value: 675				

KM# 45 100 DOLLARS
31.2100 g., 0.9990 Gold 1.0035 oz. AGW, 32.69 mm. **Subject:** 50th Anniversary - Battle of Guadalcanal **Rev:** Planes bombing ship within circle **Rev. Designer:** Willem Vis

Date	Mintage	F	VF	XF	Unc	BU
1992 Proof	Est. 500	Value: 675				

KM# 58 100 DOLLARS
31.2100 g., 0.9990 Gold 1.0035 oz. AGW, 32.69 mm. **Rev:** B-25 bomber and mushroom cloud within circle **Rev. Designer:** Willem Vis

Date	Mintage	F	VF	XF	Unc	BU
1995 Proof	Est. 500	Value: 685				

Note: In proof sets only

PATTERNS
Including off metal strikes

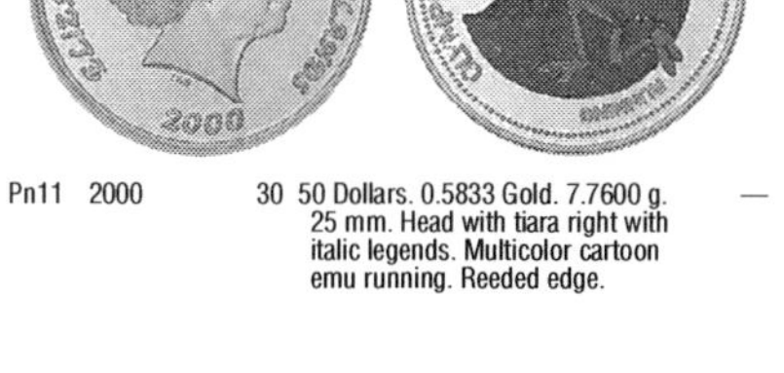

KM#	Date	Mintage	Identification	Mkt Val
Pn11	2000	30	50 Dollars. 0.5833 Gold. 7.7600 g. 25 mm. Head with tiara right with italic legends. Multicolor cartoon emu running. Reeded edge.	—

SOLOMON ISLANDS

PROOF SETS

KM#	Date	Mintage	Identification	Issue Price	Mkt Val
PS8	1991 (4)	500	KM#31-34	1,650	1,250
PS9	1991 (2)	—	KM#30a, 32	—	185
PS10	1992 (4)	500	KM#36-39	1,595	1,250
PS11	1992 (4)	500	KM#42-45	1,595	1,250
PS12	1995 (4)	500	KM#55-58	1,595	1,275

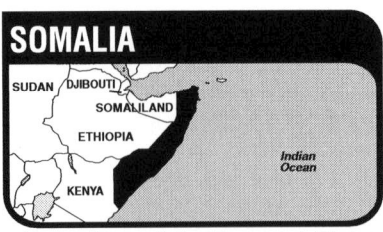

SOMALIA

The Somali Democratic Republic, comprised of the former Italian Somaliland, is located on the coast of the eastern projection of the African continent commonly referred to as the "Horn". It has an area of 178,201 sq. mi. (461,657 sq. km.) and a population of *8.2 million. Capital: Mogadishu. The economy is pastoral and agricultural. Livestock, bananas and hides are exported.

The area of the British Somaliland Protectorate was known to the Egyptians at least 1,500 years B.C., and was occupied by the Arabs and Portuguese before British sea captains obtained trading and anchorage rights in 1827. The land of sandy clay and sporadic rainfall acquired a strategic importance with the opening of the Suez Canal in 1869. After negotiating treaties with the tribes, Britain declared the area a protectorate in 1888. Italy acquired Italian Somaliland in 1895 by purchase from the Sultan of Zanzibar. Britain occupied Italian Somaliland in 1941 and administered it until April 1, 1950, when it was returned to Italy as a U.N. trusteeship. The British Somaliland protectorate became independent on June 26, 1960. Five days later it joined with Italian Somaliland to form the Somali Republic. The country was under a revolutionary military regime installed Oct. 21, 1969. After eleven years of civil war rebel forces fought their way into the capital. A.M. Muhammad became president in Aug. 1991, but inter-factional fighting continued. A UN-sponsored truce was signed in March 1992 and a peace plan and pact was signed Jan. 15, 1993.

The Northern Somali National Movement (SNM) declared a secession of the northwestern Somaliland Republic on May 17, 1991, which is not recognized by the Somali Democratic Republic.

TITLE
Al-Jumhuriya(t)as - Somaliya(t)

RULERS
Italian, until 1941
British, until 1950

MINT MARKS
Az - Arezzo (Italy)
R – Rome

SOMALI REPUBLIC
STANDARD COINAGE

100 Centesimi = 1 Somalo

KM# 10   20 SHILLINGS / SCELLINI
2.8000 g., 0.9000 Gold .0810 oz. AGW **Subject:** 5th Anniversary of Independence **Obv:** Bust facing **Rev:** Crowned arms with supporters

Date	Mintage	F	VF	XF	Unc	BU
1965Az Proof	6,325	Value: 65.00				
1966Az Proof	—	Value: 65.00				

KM# 11   50 SHILLINGS
7.0000 g., 0.9000 Gold .2025 oz. AGW **Subject:** 5th Anniversary of Independence **Obv:** Bust facing **Rev:** Crowned arms with supporters

Date	Mintage	F	VF	XF	Unc	BU
1965Az Proof	6,325	Value: 145				
1966Az Proof	—	Value: 145				

KM# 12   100 SHILLINGS
14.0000 g., 0.9000 Gold .4051 oz. AGW **Subject:** 5th Anniversary of Independence **Obv:** Bust facing **Rev:** Crowned arms with supporters

Date	Mintage	F	VF	XF	Unc	BU
1965Az Proof	6,325	Value: 285				
1966Az Proof	—	Value: 285				

KM# 13   200 SHILLINGS
28.0000 g., 0.9000 Gold .8102 oz. AGW **Subject:** 5th Anniversary of Independence **Obv:** Bust facing **Rev:** Arms with supporters **Note:** Similar to 100 Shillings, KM#12.

Date	Mintage	F	VF	XF	Unc	BU
1965Az Proof	6,325	Value: 575				
1966Az Proof	—	Value: 575				

KM# 14   500 SHILLINGS
70.0000 g., 0.9000 Gold 2.0257 oz. AGW **Subject:** 5th Anniversary of Independence **Obv:** Bust facing **Rev:** Arms with supporters **Note:** Similar to 100 Shillings, KM#12.

Date	Mintage	F	VF	XF	Unc	BU
1965Az Proof	6,325	Value: 1,425				
1966Az Proof	—	Value: 1,425				

SOMALIA

DEMOCRATIC REPUBLIC

STANDARD COINAGE

100 Centesimi = 1 Somalo

KM# 16 20 SHILLINGS
2.8000 g., 0.9000 Gold .0810 oz. AGW **Subject:** 10th Anniversary of Independence **Obv:** Crowned arms with supporters **Rev:** Star-like design within circle

Date	Mintage	F	VF	XF	Unc	BU
ND(1970) Proof	8,000	Value: 90.00				

KM# 17 50 SHILLINGS
7.0000 g., 0.9000 Gold .2025 oz. AGW **Subject:** 10th Anniversary of Independence **Obv:** Crowned arms with supporters **Rev:** Half-figure with bowl right

Date	Mintage	F	VF	XF	Unc	BU
ND(1970) Proof	8,000	Value: 175				

KM# 18 50 SHILLINGS
7.0000 g., 0.9000 Gold .2025 oz. AGW **Subject:** 1st Anniversary of 1969 Revolution **Obv:** Crowned arms with supporters **Rev:** Wheat sprig

Date	Mintage	F	VF	XF	Unc	BU
ND(1970) Proof	—	Value: 175				

KM# 19 100 SHILLINGS
14.0000 g., 0.9000 Gold .4051 oz. AGW **Subject:** 10th Anniversary of Independence **Obv:** Crowned arms with supporters flanked by dates **Rev:** Bust with headscarf and fruit basket on back left

Date	Mintage	F	VF	XF	Unc	BU
ND(1970) Proof	8,000	Value: 320				

KM# 20 100 SHILLINGS
14.0000 g., 0.9000 Gold .4051 oz. AGW **Subject:** 1st Anniversary of the 1969 Revolution **Obv:** Crowned arms with supporters **Rev:** Hand, helmet and gun in front of design

Date	Mintage	F	VF	XF	Unc	BU
ND(1970) Proof	—	Value: 300				

KM# 21 200 SHILLINGS
28.0000 g., 0.9000 Gold .8102 oz. AGW **Subject:** 10th Anniversary of Independence **Obv:** Crowned arms with supporters **Rev:** Supplies on camel

Date	Mintage	F	VF	XF	Unc	BU
ND(1970) Proof	8,000	Value: 675				

KM# 22 200 SHILLINGS
28.0000 g., 0.9000 Gold .8102 oz. AGW **Subject:** 1st Anniversary of 1969 Revolution **Obv:** Crowned arms with supporters **Rev:** Monument

Date	Mintage	F	VF	XF	Unc	BU
ND(1970) Proof	—	Value: 645				

KM# 23 500 SHILLINGS
70.0000 g., 0.9000 Gold 2.0257 oz. AGW **Subject:** 10th Anniversary of Independence **Obv:** Crowned arms with supporters **Rev:** Building within map

Date	Mintage	F	VF	XF	Unc	BU
ND(1970) Proof	8,000	Value: 1,450				

REFORM COINAGE

100 Senti = 1 Shilling

KM# 40b 25 SHILLINGS
47.5400 g., 0.9170 Gold 1.4011 oz. AGW **Subject:** World Fisheries Conference **Obv:** Crowned arms with supporters **Rev:** Green sea turtle

Date	Mintage	F	VF	XF	Unc	BU
ND(1984) Proof	200	Value: 1,100				

KM# 33 1500 SHILLINGS
15.9800 g., 0.9170 Gold .4711 oz. AGW **Subject:** 10th Anniversary of Republic **Obv:** Crowned arms with supporters **Rev:** Workers facing

Date	Mintage	F	VF	XF	Unc	BU
ND(1979)	500	—	—	—	345	350
ND(1979) Proof	500	Value: 360				

KM# 34 1500 SHILLINGS
15.9800 g., 0.9170 Gold .4711 oz. AGW **Subject:** 10th Anniversary of Republic **Obv:** Crowned arms with supporters **Rev:** Seated figures in front of tents

Date	Mintage	F	VF	XF	Unc	BU
ND(1979)	500	—	—	—	345	350
ND(1979) Proof	500	Value: 360				

KM# 35 1500 SHILLINGS
15.9800 g., 0.9170 Gold .4711 oz. AGW **Subject:** 10th Anniversary of Republic **Obv:** Crowned arms with supporters **Rev:** Lab workers

Date	Mintage	F	VF	XF	Unc	BU
ND(1979)	500	—	—	—	345	350
ND(1979) Proof	500	Value: 360				

KM# 36 1500 SHILLINGS
15.9800 g., 0.9170 Gold .4711 oz. AGW **Subject:** 10th Anniversary of Republic **Obv:** Crowned arms with supporters **Rev:** Dancers

Date	Mintage	F	VF	XF	Unc	BU
ND(1979)	500	—	—	—	345	350
ND(1979) Proof	500	Value: 360				

KM# 37 1500 SHILLINGS
15.9800 g., 0.9170 Gold .4711 oz. AGW **Subject:** 10th Anniversary of Republic **Obv:** Crowned arms with supporters **Rev:** Man and woman

Date	Mintage	F	VF	XF	Unc	BU
1979	500	—	—	—	345	350
1979 Proof	500	Value: 360				

KM# 39 1500 SHILLINGS
15.9800 g., 0.9170 Gold .4711 oz. AGW **Series:** International Year of Disabled Persons **Obv:** Crowned arms with supporters **Rev:** Emblem above busts facing

Date	Mintage	F	VF	XF	Unc	BU
1983	—	—	—	—	350	375
1983 Proof	—	Value: 400				

642 SOMALIA

REPUBLIC OF SOMALIA
STANDARD COINAGE

100 Centesimi = 1 Somalo
KM# 142 250 SHILLINGS
22.0000 g., Tri-Metallic Gold Plated Brass center in Silver Plated Brass inner ring within a Gold Plated Brass outer ring, 38 mm. **Subject:** 100th Birthday - British Queen Mother **Obv:** Crowned arms with supporters above value **Rev:** Queen Mother **Edge:** Reeded

Date	Mintage	F	VF	XF	Unc	BU
ND (1999)	—	—	—	—	35.00	40.00

PIEFORTS

KM#	Date	Mintage	Identification	Mkt Val
P2	1983	—	1500 Shillings. Gold. KM39.	875

MINT SETS

KM#	Date	Mintage	Identification	Issue Price	Mkt Val
MS1	1979 (5)	—	KM33-37	2,375	1,750

PROOF SETS

KM#	Date	Mintage	Identification	Issue Price	Mkt Val
PS1	1965 (5)	6,325	KM10-14	—	2,250
PS2	1965 (5)	—	KM10-14. Gilt copper nickel.	—	—
PS3	1970 (5)	8,000	KM16, 17, 19, 21, 23	335	2,700
PS4	1970 (3)	14,500	KM18, 20, 22	—	1,120

SOUTH AFRICA

The Republic of South Africa, located at the southern tip of Africa, has an area of 471,445 sq. mi. (1,221,043 sq. km.) and a population of *30.2 million. Capitals: Administrative, Pretoria; Legislative, Cape Town; Judicial, Bloemfontein. Manufacturing, mining and agriculture are the principal industries. Exports include wool, diamonds, gold, and metallic ores.

Portuguese navigator Bartholomew Diaz became the first European to sight the region of South Africa when he rounded the Cape of Good Hope in 1488, but throughout the 16th century the only white men to come ashore were the survivors of ships wrecked while attempting the stormy Cape passage. Jan van Riebeeck of the Dutch East India Company established the first permanent settlement in 1652. In subsequent decades additional Dutch, German and Huguenot refugees from France settled in the Cape area to form the Afrikaner segment of today's population.

Great Britain captured the Cape colony in 1795, and again in 1806, receiving permanent title in 1814. To escape British political rule and cultural dominance, many Afrikaner farmers (Boers) migrated northward (the Great Trek) beginning in 1836, and established the independent Boer Republics of the Transvaal (the South African Republic, Zuid Afrikaansche Republiek) in 1852, and the Orange Free State in 1854. British political intrigues against the two republics, coupled with the discovery of diamonds and gold in the Boer-settled regions, led to the bitter Boer Wars (1880-81, 1899-1902) and the incorporation of the Boer republics into the British Empire.

On May 31, 1910, the two former Boer Republics (Transvaal and Orange Free State) were joined with the British colonies of Cape of Good Hope and Natal to form the Union of South Africa, a dominion of the British Empire. In 1934 the Union achieved status as a sovereign state within the British Empire.

Political integration of the various colonies did not still the conflict between the Afrikaners and the English-speaking groups, which continued to have a significant impact on political developments. A resurgence of Afrikaner nationalism in the 1940s and 1950s led to a referendum in the white community authorizing the relinquishment of dominion status and the establishment of a republic. The decision took effect on May 31, 1961. The Republic of South Africa withdrew from the British Commonwealth in Oct. 1961.

The apartheid era ended April 27, 1994 with the first democratic election for all people of South Africa. Nelson Mandela was inaugurated President May 10, 1994, and South Africa was readmitted into the Commonwealth of Nations. Walvis Bay, former enclave of Cape Province, transferred to Namibia.

South African coins and currency bear inscriptions in tribal languages, Afrikaans and English.

RULERS
British, until 1934

MONETARY SYSTEM

Until 1961
12 Pence = 1 Shilling
2 Shillings = 1 Florin
20 Shillings = 1 Pound (Pond)

Commencing 1961
100 Cents = 1 Rand

REPUBLIK
Zuid-Afrikaansche Republiek

MONETARY SYSTEM
12 Pence = 1 Shilling
20 Shillings = 1 Pond

Beware of counterfeit double shafts. Aside from there being two shafts on the wagon in the coat of arms (reverse), the two wheels of the wagon must be the same size. On single shaft wagons, the rear wheel is noticeably larger than the front wheel.

STANDARD COINAGE
12 Pence = 1 Shilling; 20 Shillings = 1 Pond

KM# 9.1 1/2 POND
3.9940 g., 0.9160 Gold 0.1176 oz. AGW **Obv:** Bust left **Obv. Legend:** ZUID AFRIKAANSCHE REPUBLIEK **Rev:** Double shaft wagon tongue

Date	Mintage	F	VF	XF	Unc	BU
1892	10,000	100	150	300	550	—
1892 Proof	—	Value: 5,500				

Note: 20-25 pieces

KM# 9.2 1/2 POND
3.9940 g., 0.9160 Gold 0.1176 oz. AGW **Obv:** Bust left **Obv. Legend:** ZUID AFRIKAANSCHE REPUBLIEK **Rev:** Single shaft wagon tongue

Date	Mintage	F	VF	XF	Unc	BU
1892 Unique	—	—	—	—	—	—
1893	—	350	900	1,950	3,000	—
1894	39,000	80.00	100	250	450	—
1895	135,000	85.00	110	375	600	—
1896	104,000	75.00	90.00	200	400	—
1897	75,000	75.00	90.00	200	400	—

KM# 11 1/2 POND
0.9990 Gold **Subject:** Veld-Boer War Siege Issue **Obv:** Monogram and date **Rev:** Inscription

Date	Mintage	F	VF	XF	Unc	BU
1902	986	750	1,350	2,750	5,000	—

KM# 1.1 POND (Een)
7.9880 g., 0.9160 Gold 0.2352 oz. AGW **Obv:** Head left **Obv. Legend:** THOMAS FRANCOIS... **Rev:** Flagged arms above banner, eagle above

Date	Mintage	F	VF	XF	Unc	BU
1874	174	2,000	4,000	7,000	10,000	—

KM# 1.2 POND (Een)
7.9880 g., 0.9160 Gold 0.2352 oz. AGW **Obv:** Head left **Rev:** Flagged arms above banner, eagle above

Date	Mintage	F	VF	XF	Unc	BU
1874	695	1,500	3,500	6,000	8,500	—

KM# 10.1 POND (Een)
7.9880 g., 0.9160 Gold 0.2352 oz. AGW **Obv:** Bust left **Obv. Legend:** ZUID AFRIKAANSCHE REPUBLIEK **Rev:** Double shaft wagon tongue

Date	Mintage	F	VF	XF	Unc	BU
1892	16,000	170	250	400	900	—

SOUTH AFRICA

Date	Mintage	F	VF	XF	Unc	BU
1892 Proof, rare, 12-15 pieces	—	—	—	—	—	—

Note: David Akers John Jay Pittman sale 8-99, choice proof realized $12,650, hairlined proof realized $4,600

KM# 10.2 POND (Een)
7.9880 g., 0.9160 Gold 0.2352 oz. AGW **Obv:** Bust left **Obv. Inscription:** ZUID AFRIKAANSCHE REPUBLIEK **Rev:** Single shaft wagon tongue

Date	Mintage	F	VF	XF	Unc	BU
1892	—	450	800	2,000	4,500	—
1893	62,000	160	185	375	750	—
1894	318,000	160	175	325	700	—
1895	336,000	160	185	450	850	—
1896	235,000	160	175	325	600	—
1897	311,000	160	175	275	450	—
1898	137,000	145	155	175	350	—
1898/99	130	2,500	3,000	5,000	7,500	—
1898/9 Unique	—	—	—	—	—	—
1900	788,000	150	160	175	325	—

PATTERNS
1874 Würden Issues
Struck in Brussels, Belgium.

X# Pn10 3 PENCE
Gold **Note:** Prev. KM#Pn23. Struck especially for mining magnate Sammie Marks.

Date	Mintage	F	VF	XF	Unc	BU
1898	215	—	—	3,000	4,000	—

UNION OF SOUTH AFRICA
Dominion under Great Britain
STANDARD COINAGE
12 Pence = 1 Shilling; 2 Shillings = 1 Florin; 20 Shillings = 1 Pound

KM# 20 1/2 SOVEREIGN
3.9940 g., 0.9170 Gold .1177 oz. AGW **Ruler:** George V **Obv:** Head left **Rev:** Armored figure on rearing horse **Note:** British type with Pretoria mint mark: SA.

Date	Mintage	F	VF	XF	Unc	BU
1923 Proof	655	Value: 525				
1925	947,000	—	BV	90.00	150	—
1926	809,000	—	BV	90.00	150	—

KM# 42 1/2 POUND
3.9940 g., 0.9170 Gold .1177 oz. AGW **Ruler:** George V **Obv:** Head left **Obv. Designer:** T.H. Paget **Rev:** Springbok **Rev. Designer:** Coert L. Steynberg **Note:** Similar to 1 Pound, KM#43.

Date	Mintage	F	VF	XF	Unc	BU
1952	4,002	—	—	—	100	—
1952 Proof	12,000	Value: 110				

KM# 53 1/2 POUND
3.9940 g., 0.9170 Gold .1177 oz. AGW **Ruler:** Elizabeth II **Obv:** Laureate head right **Obv. Designer:** Mary Gillick **Rev. Designer:** Coert L. Steynberg

Date	Mintage	F	VF	XF	Unc	BU
1953 Proof	4,000	Value: 110				
1954 Proof	1,275	Value: 115				
1955 Proof	900	Value: 120				
1956 Proof	508	Value: 210				
1957 Proof	560	Value: 180				
1958 Proof	515	Value: 195				
1959	500	—	—	—	100	—
1959 Proof	630	Value: 165				
1960	1,052	—	—	—	90.00	—
1960 Proof	1,950	Value: 100				

KM# 21 SOVEREIGN
7.9881 g., 0.9170 Gold .2354 oz. AGW **Ruler:** George V **Obv:** Head left **Rev:** Armored figure on rearing horse **Note:** British type with Pretoria mint mark: SA.

Date	Mintage	F	VF	XF	Unc	BU
1923	64	200	300	400	700	—
1923 Proof	655	Value: 650				
1924	3,184	700	1,350	2,250	4,500	—
1925	6,086,000	—	—	BV	170	—
1926	11,108,000	—	—	BV	170	—
1927	16,379,999	—	—	BV	170	—
1928	18,235,000	—	—	BV	170	—

KM# A22 SOVEREIGN
7.9881 g., 0.9170 Gold .2354 oz. AGW **Ruler:** George V **Obv:** Modified effigy, slightly smaller bust

Date	Mintage	F	VF	XF	Unc	BU
1929	12,024,000	—	—	BV	165	—
1930	10,028,000	—	—	BV	165	—
1931	8,512,000	—	—	BV	165	—
1932	1,067,000	—	—	BV	175	—

KM# 43 POUND
7.9881 g., 0.9170 Gold .2354 oz. AGW **Ruler:** George VI **Obv:** Head left **Obv. Designer:** T.H. Paget **Rev:** Springbok **Rev. Designer:** Coert L. Steynberg

Date	Mintage	F	VF	XF	Unc	BU
1952	4,508	—	—	—	180	—
1952 Proof	12,000	Value: 195				

KM# 54 POUND
7.9881 g., 0.9170 Gold .2354 oz. AGW **Ruler:** Elizabeth II **Obv:** Laureate head right **Obv. Designer:** Mary Gillick **Rev:** Springbok **Rev. Designer:** Coert L. Steynberg

Date	Mintage	F	VF	XF	Unc	BU
1953 Proof	4,000	Value: 190				
1954 Proof	1,275	Value: 200				
1955 Proof	900	Value: 210				
1956 Proof	508	Value: 250				
1957 Proof	560	Value: 235				
1958 Proof	515	Value: 240				
1959	502	—	—	—	175	—
1959 Proof	630	Value: 230				
1960	1,161	—	—	—	170	—
1960 Proof	1,950	Value: 170				

REPUBLIC
STANDARD COINAGE
100 Cents = 1 Rand

KM# 63 RAND
3.9940 g., 0.9170 Gold .1177 oz. AGW **Obv:** Springbok **Rev:** Bust of Jan van Riebeeck 1/4 right

Date	Mintage	F	VF	XF	Unc	BU
1961	4,246	—	—	—	BV+15%	—
1961 Proof	4,932	—	—	—	BV+20%	—
1962	3,955	—	—	—	BV+15%	—
1962 Proof	2,344	—	—	—	BV+20%	—
1963	4,023	—	—	—	BV+15%	—
1963 Proof	2,508	—	—	—	BV+20%	—
1964	5,866	—	—	—	BV+15%	—
1964 Proof	4,000	—	—	—	BV+20%	—
1965	10,000	—	—	—	BV+15%	—
1965 Proof	6,024	—	—	—	BV+20%	—
1966	10,000	—	—	—	BV+15%	—
1966 Proof	11,000	—	—	—	BV+20%	—
1967	10,000	—	—	—	BV+15%	—
1967 Proof	11,000	—	—	—	BV+20%	—
1968	10,000	—	—	—	BV+15%	—
1968 Proof	11,000	—	—	—	BV+20%	—
1969	10,000	—	—	—	BV+15%	—
1969 Proof	8,000	—	—	—	BV+20%	—
1970	10,000	—	—	—	BV+15%	—
1970 Proof	7,000	—	—	—	BV+20%	—
1971	10,000	—	—	—	BV+15%	—
1971 Proof	7,650	—	—	—	BV+20%	—
1972	12,000	—	—	—	BV+15%	—
1972 Proof	7,500	—	—	—	BV+20%	—
1973	15,000	—	—	—	BV+15%	—
1973 Proof	12,000	—	—	—	BV+20%	—
1974	23,000	—	—	—	BV+15%	—
1974 Proof	17,000	—	—	—	BV+20%	—
1975	12,000	—	—	—	BV+15%	—
1975 Proof	18,000	—	—	—	BV+20%	—
1976	12,000	—	—	—	BV+15%	—
1976 Proof	21,000	—	—	—	BV+20%	—
1977	27,000	—	—	—	BV+15%	—
1977 Proof	20,000	—	—	—	BV+20%	—
1978	13,000	—	—	—	BV+15%	—
1978 Proof	19,000	—	—	—	BV+20%	—
1979	17,000	—	—	—	BV+15%	—
1979 Proof	17,000	—	—	—	BV+20%	—
1980	14,000	—	—	—	BV+15%	—
1980 Proof	18,000	—	—	—	BV+20%	—
1981	9,274	—	—	—	BV+15%	—
1981 Proof	10,000	—	—	—	BV+20%	—
1982	14,000	—	—	—	BV+15%	—
1982 Proof	14,000	—	—	—	BV+20%	—
1983	15,000	—	—	—	BV+20%	—

KM# 182 RAND
3.1103 g., 0.9999 Gold .1000 oz. AGW **Subject:** 30th Anniversary - First Heart Transplant **Rev:** Doctor working on heart

Date	Mintage	F	VF	XF	Unc	BU
1997 Proof	1,000	Value: 115				

KM# 178 RAND
3.1103 g., 0.9999 Gold .1000 oz. AGW **Subject:** San Tribe **Rev:** Tribesman hunting

Date	Mintage	F	VF	XF	Unc	BU
1998 Proof	—	Value: 115				

KM# 219 RAND
3.1103 g., 0.9999 Gold .1000 oz. AGW, 16.5 mm. **Obv:** National arms **Rev:** Zulu warrior **Edge:** Reeded

Date	Mintage	F	VF	XF	Unc	BU
1999 Proof	1,000	Value: 115				

KM# 239 RAND
3.1103 g., 0.9999 Gold 0.1 oz. AGW, 16.5 mm. **Obv:** National arms **Rev:** Three Xhosa tribe members **Edge:** Reeded

Date	Mintage	F	VF	XF	Unc	BU
2000 Proof	—	Value: 115				

KM# 247 RAND
3.1103 g., 0.9999 Gold 0.1 oz. AGW, 16.5 mm. **Obv:** Crowned arms **Obv. Designer:** A.L. Sutherland **Rev:** Seated figure with headdress **Edge:** Reeded

Date	Mintage	F	VF	XF	Unc	BU
2001 Proof	—	Value: 115				

KM# 183 2 RAND
7.7700 g., 0.9999 Gold .2500 oz. AGW **Subject:** Early Man **Obv:** Arms with supporters **Rev:** Australopithecus Africanus

Date	Mintage	F	VF	XF	Unc	BU
1997 Proof	1,000	Value: 185				

KM# 180 2 RAND
7.7770 g., 0.9999 Gold .2500 oz. AGW **Obv:** Arms with supporters **Rev:** Coelacanth fish and fossil

644 SOUTH AFRICA

Date	Mintage	F	VF	XF	Unc	BU
1998 Proof	—	Value: 195				

KM# 220 2 RAND
7.7759 g., 0.9999 Gold .2500 oz. AGW **Obv:** Arms with supporters **Rev:** Thrinaxodon dinosaur

Date	Mintage	F	VF	XF	Unc	BU
1999 Proof	1,000	Value: 200				

KM# 241 2 RAND
7.7770 g., 0.9999 Gold 0.25 oz. AGW, 22 mm. **Obv:** Arms with supporters **Rev:** "Little Foot" skeleton find **Edge:** Reeded

Date	Mintage	F	VF	XF	Unc	BU
2000 Proof	—	Value: 185				

KM# 249 2 RAND
7.7770 g., 0.9999 Gold 0.25 oz. AGW, 22 mm. **Obv:** Crowned arms **Obv. Designer:** A.L. Sutherland **Rev:** Gondwana theoretical landmass and dinosaur **Edge:** Reeded

Date	Mintage	F	VF	XF	Unc	BU
2001 Proof	—	Value: 195				

KM# 278 5 RAND
3.1104 g., 0.9999 Gold 0.1 oz. AGW, 16.5 mm. **Obv:** Protea flower **Rev:** Soccer player heading the ball **Edge:** Reeded

Date	Mintage	F	VF	XF	Unc	BU
2002	—	—	—	—	115	125

KM# 289 5 RAND
3.1100 g., 0.9999 Gold 0.1 oz. AGW, 16.5 mm. **Subject:** 10th Anniversary of South African Democracy **Obv:** Protea flower **Rev:** Inscription covered flag **Edge:** Reeded

Date	Mintage	F	VF	XF	Unc	BU
2004 Proof	1,000	Value: 115				

KM# 279 25 RAND
31.1035 g., 0.9999 Gold 0.9999 oz. AGW, 32.7 mm. **Obv:** Protea flower **Rev:** Soccer player kicking ball **Edge:** Reeded

Date	Mintage	F	VF	XF	Unc	BU
2002	—	—	—	—	700	—

KM# 290 25 RAND
31.1035 g., 0.9999 Gold 0.9999 oz. AGW, 32.7 mm. **Subject:** 10th Anniversary of South African Democracy **Obv:** Protea flower **Rev:** Two images of Nelson Mandela **Edge:** Reeded

Date	Mintage	F	VF	XF	Unc	BU
2004 Proof	5,000	Value: 700				

BULLION COINAGE

Mint mark: GRC - Gold Reef City

KM# 105 1/10 KRUGERRAND
3.3900 g., 0.9170 Gold .1000 oz. AGW

Date	Mintage	F	VF	XF	Unc	BU
1980	857,000	—	—	—	BV+15%	—
1980 Proof	60	Value: 2,500				
1981	1,321,000	—	—	—	BV+15%	—
1981 Proof	7,500	Value: 90.00				
1982	1,065,000	—	—	—	BV+15%	—
1982 Proof	11,000	Value: 85.00				
1983	508,000	—	—	—	BV+15%	—
1983 Proof	12,000	Value: 85.00				
1984	898,000	—	—	—	BV+15%	—
1984 Proof	13,000	Value: 85.00				
1985	282,000	—	—	—	BV+15%	—
1985 Proof	6,700	Value: 85.00				
1986	87,000	—	—	—	BV+15%	—
1986 Proof	8,001	Value: 85.00				
1987	53,000	—	—	—	BV+15%	—
1987 Proof	6,065	Value: 85.00				
1987 GRC Proof	1,126	Value: 400				
1988	87,000	—	—	—	BV+15%	—
1988 Proof	2,056	Value: 90.00				
1988 GRC Proof	949	Value: 400				
1989	—	—	—	—	BV+15%	—
1989 Proof	3,316	Value: 90.00				
1989 GRC Proof	377	Value: 1,000				
1990	—	—	—	—	BV+15%	—
1990 Proof	3,459	Value: 90.00				
1990 GRC Proof	1,096	Value: 275				
1991 Proof	3,524	Value: 90.00				
1991 GRC Proof	426	Value: 275				
1992 Proof	1,789	Value: 90.00				
1993	54,000	—	—	—	BV+15%	—
1993 Proof	3,811	Value: 90.00				
1994	86,000	—	—	—	BV+15%	—
1994 Proof	—	Value: 90.00				
1995	25,000	—	—	—	BV+15%	—
1995 Proof	750	Value: 120				
1996 Proof	4,000	Value: 90.00				
1997 Proof	3,410	Value: 90.00				
1997 Proof	30	Value: 300				

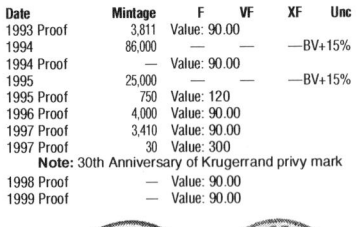

Note: 30th Anniversary of Krugerrand privy mark

| 1998 Proof | — | Value: 90.00 | | | | |
| 1999 Proof | — | Value: 90.00 | | | | |

KM# 106 1/4 KRUGERRAND
8.4800 g., 0.9170 Gold .2500 oz. AGW **Obv:** Bust left **Rev:** Springbok divides date **Rev. Designer:** Coert L. Steynberg

Date	Mintage	F	VF	XF	Unc	BU
1980	534,000	—	—	—	BV+10%	—
1980 Proof	60	Value: 3,000				
1981	726,000	—	—	—	BV+10%	—
1981 Proof	7,500	Value: 195				
1982	1,269,000	—	—	—	BV+10%	—
1982 Proof	11,000	Value: 195				
1983	64,000	—	—	—	BV+10%	—
1983 Proof	12,000	Value: 195				
1984	503,000	—	—	—	BV+10%	—
1984 Proof	13,000	Value: 195				
1985	594,000	—	—	—	BV+10%	—
1985 Proof	6,700	Value: 195				
1986 Proof	8,001	Value: 195				
1987 Proof	6,050	Value: 195				
1987 GRC Proof	1,121	Value: 500				
1988	5,946	—	—	—	BV+10%	—
1988 Proof	2,056	Value: 200				
1988 GRC Proof	835	Value: 500				
1989	5,943	—	—	—	BV+10%	—
1989 Proof	3,316	Value: 200				
1989 GRC Proof	318	Value: 1,400				
1990 Proof	2,750	Value: 200				
1990 GRC Proof	1,066	Value: 400				
1991 Proof	1,626	Value: 200				
1991 GRC Proof	426	Value: 400				
1992 Proof	1,629	Value: 200				
1993 Proof	3,061	Value: 200				
1994	39,000	—	—	—	BV+10%	—
1994 Proof	1,874	Value: 200				
1995	13,000	—	—	—	BV+10%	—
1995 Proof	1,095	Value: 215				
1996 Proof	1,853	Value: 200				
1997 Proof	1,440	Value: 200				
1997 Proof	30	Value: 450				

Note: 30th Anniversary of Krugerrand privy mark

| 1998 Proof | — | Value: 200 | | | | |
| 1999 Proof | — | Value: 200 | | | | |

KM# 107 1/2 KRUGERRAND
16.9700 g., 0.9170 Gold .5000 oz. AGW **Obv:** Bust left **Rev:** Springbok divides date **Rev. Designer:** Coert L. Steynberg

Date	Mintage	F	VF	XF	Unc	BU
1980	374,000	—	—	—	BV+8%	—
1980 Proof	60	Value: 3,500				
1981	178,000	—	—	—	BV+8%	—
1981 Proof	9,000	Value: 375				
1982	429,000	—	—	—	BV+8%	—
1982 Proof	13,000	Value: 375				
1983	60,000	—	—	—	BV+8%	—
1983 Proof	14,000	Value: 375				
1984	187,000	—	—	—	BV+8%	—
1984 Proof	9,900	Value: 375				
1985	104,000	—	—	—	BV+8%	—
1985 Proof	5,945	Value: 375				
1986 Proof	8,002	Value: 375				
1987 Proof	5,389	Value: 375				
1987 GRC Proof	1,186	Value: 800				
1988	5,454	—	—	—	BV+8%	—
1988 Proof	2,282	Value: 400				
1988 GRC Proof	1,026	Value: 800				
1989	4,980	—	—	—	BV+8%	—
1989 Proof	3,727	Value: 400				
1989 GRC Proof	399	Value: 1,500				
1990 Proof	2,850	Value: 400				
1990 GRC Proof	1,066	Value: 500				
1991 Proof	3,459	Value: 400				
1991 GRC Proof	426	Value: 500				
1992 Proof	1,501	Value: 400				
1993	11,000	—	—	—	BV+8%	—
1993 Proof	2,439	Value: 400				
1994	16,000	—	—	—	BV+8%	—
1994 Proof	2,146	Value: 400				
1995	10,000	—	—	—	BV+8%	—
1995 Proof	1,012	Value: 400				
1996 Proof	1,788	Value: 400				
1997 Proof	2,000	Value: 400				
1997 Proof	30	Value: 550				

Note: 30th Anniversary of Krugerrand privy mark

| 1998 Proof | — | Value: 375 | | | | |
| 1999 Proof | — | Value: 400 | | | | |

KM# 73 KRUGERRAND
33.9305 g., 0.9170 Gold 1.0000 oz. AGW **Obv:** Bust left **Rev:** Springbok divides date **Rev. Designer:** Coert L. Steynberg

Date	Mintage	F	VF	XF	Unc	BU
1967	40,000	—	—	—	BV+5%	—
1967 Proof	10,000	Value: 725				
1968	20,000	—	—	—	BV+5%	—
1968 Proof	5,000	Value: 1,000				

Note: Frosted bust and frosted reverse

1968 Proof	8,956	Value: 745				
1969	20,000	—	—	—	BV+5%	—
1969 Proof	10,000	Value: 725				
1970	211,000	—	—	—	BV+5%	—
1970 Proof	10,000	Value: 720				
1971	550,000	—	—	—	BV+5%	—
1971 Proof	6,000	Value: 720				
1972	544,000	—	—	—	BV+5%	—
1972 Proof	6,625	Value: 720				
1973	859,000	—	—	—	BV+5%	—
1973 Proof	10,000	Value: 720				
1974	3,204,000	—	—	—	BV+5%	—
1974 Proof	6,352	Value: 720				
1975	4,804,000	—	—	—	BV+5%	—
1975 Proof	5,600	Value: 720				
1976	3,005,000	—	—	—	BV+5%	—
1976 Proof	6,600	Value: 720				
1977	3,331,000	—	—	—	BV+5%	—

Note: 188 serrations on edge

| 1977 Proof | 8,500 | Value: 720 | | | | |

Note: 188 serrations on edge

| 1977 | Inc. above | — | — | — | BV+5% | — |

Note: 220 serrations on edge

| 1977 Proof | Inc. above | Value: 720 | | | | |

Note: 220 serrations on edge

1978	6,012,000	—	—	—	BV+5%	—
1978 Proof	10,000	Value: 720				
1979	4,941,000	—	—	—	BV+5%	—
1979 Proof	12,000	Value: 720				
1980	3,143,000	—	—	—	BV+5%	—
1980 Proof	12,000	Value: 720				
1981	3,560,000	—	—	—	BV+5%	—
1981 Proof	13,000	Value: 720				
1982	2,566,000	—	—	—	BV+5%	—
1982 Proof	17,000	Value: 720				
1983	3,368,000	—	—	—	BV+5%	—
1983 Proof	19,000	Value: 720				
1984	2,070,000	—	—	—	BV+5%	—
1984 Proof	14,000	Value: 720				
1985	875,000	—	—	—	BV+5%	—
1985 Proof	10,000	Value: 720				
1986 Proof	20,000	Value: 720				
1987	11,000	—	—	—	BV+5%	—
1987 Proof	11,000	Value: 720				
1987 GRC Proof	1,160	Value: 1,200				
1988	615,000	—	—	—	BV+5%	—
1988 Proof	4,268	Value: 725				
1988 GRC Proof	1,220	Value: 1,200				
1989	194,000	—	—	—	BV+5%	—
1989 Proof	5,070	Value: 725				
1989 GRC Proof	987	Value: 1,600				
1990	391,000	—	—	—	BV+5%	—
1990 Proof	3,032	Value: 725				
1990 GRC Proof	1,066	Value: 1,600				
1991	283,000	—	—	—	BV+5%	—
1991 Proof	2,181	Value: 725				
1991 GRC Proof	426	Value: 1,600				
1992	1,803	—	—	—	BV+5%	—
1992 Proof	2,067	Value: 725				
1993	162,000	—	—	—	BV+5%	—
1993 Proof	3,963	Value: 725				
1994	130,000	—	—	—	BV+5%	—
1994 Proof	1,761	Value: 725				
1995	59,000	—	—	—	BV+5%	—

SOUTH AFRICA

Date	Mintage	F	VF	XF	Unc	BU
1995 Proof	1,678	Value: 725				
1996 Proof	2,188	Value: 725				
1997 Proof	1,663	Value: 725				
1997 SS Proof	72	Value: 850				
1997 Proof	30	Value: 1,250				

Note: 30th Anniversary of Krugerrand privy mark

Date	Mintage	F	VF	XF	Unc	BU
1998 Proof	—	Value: 725				
1999 Proof	—	Value: 725				

KM# 118 OUNCE
33.9305 g., 0.9170 Gold 1.0000 oz. AGW Subject: 75th Anniversary of Parliament Obv: Crossed scepters divide lion and shield Rev: Parliament building

Date	Mintage	F	VF	XF	Unc	BU
1985 Proof	3,019	Value: 1,200				

KM# 184 OUNCE
31.1070 g., 0.9999 Gold 1.0000 oz. AGW Subject: Presidential Inauguration

Date	Mintage	F	VF	XF	Unc	BU
1994 Proof	1,742	Value: 750				

KM# 185 OUNCE
31.1070 g., 0.9999 Gold 1.0000 oz. AGW Subject: Rugby

Date	Mintage	F	VF	XF	Unc	BU
1995 Proof	406	Value: 775				

KM# 131 1/10 PROTEA
3.3900 g., 0.9170 Gold .1000 oz. AGW Subject: 100th Anniversary of Johannesburg

Date	Mintage	F	VF	XF	Unc	BU
1986 Proof	5,212	Value: 115				

KM# 123 1/10 PROTEA
3.3900 g., 0.9170 Gold .1000 oz. AGW Subject: Bartolomeu Dias Obv: Protea flower Rev: Crown above point of radiant star, map of Africa at right

Date	Mintage	F	VF	XF	Unc	BU
1988 Proof	2,199	Value: 115				

KM# 126 1/10 PROTEA
3.3900 g., 0.9170 Gold .1000 oz. AGW Subject: Huguenots Obv: Protea flowers Rev: Descending dove and design divide dates below small cross, all within circle

Date	Mintage	F	VF	XF	Unc	BU
1988 Proof	2,060	Value: 115				

KM# 129 1/10 PROTEA
3.3900 g., 0.9170 Gold .1000 oz. AGW Subject: The Great Trek Obv: Protea flower Rev: Stylized wheel and arrow design

Date	Mintage	F	VF	XF	Unc	BU
1988 Proof	2,999	Value: 115				

KM# 171 1/10 PROTEA
3.3900 g., 0.9170 Gold .1000 oz. AGW Subject: South African Nursing Schools Obv: Protea Flower Rev: Aladdin lamp divides dates within cross design Note: Similar to 1 Rand, KM#142.

Date	Mintage	F	VF	XF	Unc	BU
1991 Proof	3,950	Value: 115				

KM# 144 1/10 PROTEA
3.3900 g., 0.9170 Gold .1000 oz. AGW Subject: Coinage Centennial Obv: Protea flower Rev: Assorted coin designs

Date	Mintage	F	VF	XF	Unc	BU
1992 Proof	2,503	Value: 115				

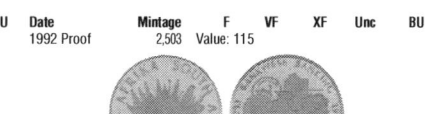

KM# 172 1/10 PROTEA
3.3900 g., 0.9170 Gold .1000 oz. AGW Subject: 200 Years of Banking Obv: Protea flower Rev: Towers divide lion head and coin designs Note: Similar to 1 Rand, KM#168.

Date	Mintage	F	VF	XF	Unc	BU
1993 Proof	5,064	Value: 100				
1993 Proof	5,064	Value: 115				

KM# 187 1/10 PROTEA
3.3900 g., 0.9170 Gold .1000 oz. AGW Subject: Conservation

Date	Mintage	F	VF	XF	Unc	BU
1994 Proof	1,485	Value: 125				

KM# 193 1/10 PROTEA
3.3900 g., 0.9170 Gold .1000 oz. AGW Subject: Railways

Date	Mintage	F	VF	XF	Unc	BU
1995 Proof	1,217	Value: 125				

KM# 199 1/10 PROTEA
3.3900 g., 0.9170 Gold .1000 oz. AGW Subject: Constitution

Date	Mintage	F	VF	XF	Unc	BU
1996 Proof	946	Value: 125				

KM# 205 1/10 PROTEA
3.3900 g., 0.9170 Gold .1000 oz. AGW Subject: Women of South Africa Designer: Natanya van Niekerk

Date	Mintage	F	VF	XF	Unc	BU
1997 Proof	648	Value: 130				

KM# 211 1/10 PROTEA
3.3900 g., 0.9170 Gold .1000 oz. AGW Subject: Year of the Child

Date	Mintage	F	VF	XF	Unc	BU
1998 Proof	—	Value: 130				

KM# 250 1/10 PROTEA
3.1103 g., 0.9999 Gold 0.1 oz. AGW, 16.5 mm. Obv: Protea flower Rev: Mine cart and entrance Edge: Reeded

Date	Mintage	F	VF	XF	Unc	BU
1999 Proof	—	Value: 115				

KM# 256 1/10 PROTEA
3.1103 g., 0.9999 Gold 0.1 oz. AGW, 16.5 mm. Obv: Protea flower Rev: Grape vines and building Edge: Reeded

Date	Mintage	F	VF	XF	Unc	BU
2000 Proof	—	Value: 115				

KM# 262 1/10 PROTEA
3.1103 g., 0.9999 Gold 0.1 oz. AGW, 16.5 mm. Obv: Protea flower Rev: Lion and partial shield Edge: Reeded

Date	Mintage	F	VF	XF	Unc	BU
2001 Proof	—	Value: 115				

KM# 121 PROTEA
33.9300 g., 0.9170 Gold 1.0000 oz. AGW Subject: 100th Anniversary of Johannesburg

Date	Mintage	F	VF	XF	Unc	BU
1986 Proof	4,701	Value: 735				

KM# 124 PROTEA
33.9300 g., 0.9170 Gold 1.0000 oz. AGW Subject: Bartolomeu Dias Obv: Protea flower Rev: Crown above point of radiant star design, map of Africa at right

Date	Mintage	F	VF	XF	Unc	BU
1988 Proof	3,776	Value: 735				

KM# 127 PROTEA
33.9300 g., 0.9170 Gold 1.0000 oz. AGW Subject: Huguenots Obv: Protea flowers Obv. Designer: A.L. Sutherland Rev: Descending dove and design divide dates below small cross, all within circle

Date	Mintage	F	VF	XF	Unc	BU
1988 Proof	3,391	Value: 735				

KM# 130 PROTEA
33.9300 g., 0.9170 Gold 1.0000 oz. AGW Subject: The Great Trek Obv: Protea flower Rev: Wheel and arrow design

Date	Mintage	F	VF	XF	Unc	BU
1988 Proof	2,956	Value: 735				

KM# 186 PROTEA
33.9300 g., 0.9170 Gold 1.0000 oz. AGW Subject: Nursing

Date	Mintage	F	VF	XF	Unc	BU
1991 Proof	3,004	Value: 735				

KM# 146 PROTEA
33.9300 g., 0.9170 Gold 1.0000 oz. AGW Subject: Coinage Centennial Obv: Protea flower Obv. Designer: A.L. Sutherland Rev: Assorted coin designs

Date	Mintage	F	VF	XF	Unc	BU
1992 Proof	1,752	Value: 750				

KM# 173 PROTEA
33.9300 g., 0.9170 Gold 1.0000 oz. AGW Subject: 200 Years of Banking Note: Similar to 1 Rand, KM#168.

Date	Mintage	F	VF	XF	Unc	BU
1993 Proof	2,032	Value: 735				
1993 GRC Proof	500	Value: 800				

KM# 188 PROTEA
33.9300 g., 0.9170 Gold 1.0000 oz. AGW Subject: Conservation

Date	Mintage	F	VF	XF	Unc	BU
1994 Proof	1,187	Value: 735				
1994 Proof	600	Value: 800				

Note: PTA.ZOO

KM# 194 PROTEA
33.9300 g., 0.9170 Gold 1.0000 oz. AGW Subject: Railway

Date	Mintage	F	VF	XF	Unc	BU
1995 Proof	694	Value: 800				

KM# 200 PROTEA
33.9300 g., 0.9170 Gold 1.0000 oz. AGW Subject: Constitution

Date	Mintage	F	VF	XF	Unc	BU
1996 Proof	641	Value: 800				

KM# 206 PROTEA
33.9300 g., 0.9170 Gold 1.0000 oz. AGW Subject: Women of South Africa Designer: Natanya van Niekerk

Date	Mintage	F	VF	XF	Unc	BU
1997 Proof	207	Value: 825				

SOUTH AFRICA

KM# 212 PROTEA
33.9300 g., 0.9170 Gold 1.0000 oz. AGW **Subject:** Year of the Child

Date	Mintage	F	VF	XF	Unc	BU
1998 Proof	—	Value: 825				

KM# 251 PROTEA
31.1035 g., 0.9999 Gold 0.9999 oz. AGW, 32.7 mm. **Obv:** Protea flower **Rev:** Miner **Edge:** Reeded

Date	Mintage	F	VF	XF	Unc	BU
1999 Proof	—	Value: 735				

KM# 257 PROTEA
31.1035 g., 0.9999 Gold 0.9999 oz. AGW, 32.7 mm. **Obv:** Protea flower **Rev:** Worker holding basket **Edge:** Reeded

Date	Mintage	F	VF	XF	Unc	BU
2000 Proof	—	Value: 735				

KM# 263 PROTEA
31.1035 g., 0.9999 Gold 0.9999 oz. AGW, 32.7 mm. **Obv:** Protea flower **Rev:** Child on sandy beach and partial sun **Edge:** Reeded

Date	Mintage	F	VF	XF	Unc	BU
2001 Proof	—	Value: 735				

NATURA GOLD BULLION COINAGE

KM# 189 1/10 OUNCE
3.1104 g., 0.9990 Gold .1000 oz. AGW **Rev:** Lions drinking

Date	Mintage	F	VF	XF	Unc	BU
1994 Proof	6,660	Value: 115				

KM# 195 1/10 OUNCE
3.1104 g., 0.9990 Gold .1000 oz. AGW **Rev:** Rhinocerous drinking

Date	Mintage	F	VF	XF	Unc	BU
1995 Proof	2,703	Value: 115				

KM# 201 1/10 OUNCE
3.1104 g., 0.9990 Gold .1000 oz. AGW **Rev:** Elephant **Rev. Designer:** Natanya van Niekerk

Date	Mintage	F	VF	XF	Unc	BU
1996 Proof	9,014	Value: 115				

KM# 207 1/10 OUNCE
3.1104 g., 0.9990 Gold .1000 oz. AGW **Rev:** Buffalo **Rev. Designer:** Natanya van Niekerk

Date	Mintage	F	VF	XF	Unc	BU
1997 Proof	3,590	Value: 115				

KM# 213 1/10 OUNCE
3.1104 g., 0.9990 Gold .1000 oz. AGW **Rev:** Leopard **Rev. Designer:** Natanya van Niekerk

Date	Mintage	F	VF	XF	Unc	BU
1998 Proof	—	Value: 115				

KM# 252 1/10 OUNCE
3.1103 g., 0.9999 Gold 0.1 oz. AGW, 16.5 mm. **Obv:** Greater Kudu head **Rev:** Koodoo herd drinking **Edge:** Reeded

Date	Mintage	F	VF	XF	Unc	BU
1999 Proof	—	Value: 115				

KM# 258 1/10 OUNCE
3.1103 g., 0.9999 Gold 0.1 oz. AGW, 16.5 mm. **Obv:** Ibex head **Rev:** Ibex drinking **Edge:** Reeded

Date	Mintage	F	VF	XF	Unc	BU
2000 Proof	—	Value: 115				

KM# 264 1/10 OUNCE
3.1103 g., 0.9999 Gold 0.1 oz. AGW, 16.5 mm. **Obv:** Gemsbok head **Rev:** Gemsbok drinking **Edge:** Reeded

Date	Mintage	F	VF	XF	Unc	BU
2001 Proof	—	Value: 115				

KM# 190 1/4 OUNCE
7.7770 g., 0.9999 Gold .2500 oz. AGW **Rev:** Lions

Date	Mintage	F	VF	XF	Unc	BU
1994 Proof	4,159	Value: 200				

KM# 196 1/4 OUNCE
7.7770 g., 0.9999 Gold .2500 oz. AGW **Rev:** Rhinoceros

Date	Mintage	F	VF	XF	Unc	BU
1995 Proof	1,752	Value: 200				

KM# 202 1/4 OUNCE
7.7770 g., 0.9999 Gold .2500 oz. AGW **Rev:** Elephant **Rev. Designer:** Natanya van Niekerk

Date	Mintage	F	VF	XF	Unc	BU
1996 Proof	3,740	Value: 200				

KM# 208 1/4 OUNCE
7.7770 g., 0.9999 Gold .2500 oz. AGW **Rev:** Buffalo **Rev. Designer:** Natanya van Niekerk

Date	Mintage	F	VF	XF	Unc	BU
1997 Proof	2,164	Value: 200				

KM# 214 1/4 OUNCE
7.7770 g., 0.9999 Gold .2500 oz. AGW **Rev:** Leopard **Rev. Designer:** Natanya van Niekerk

Date	Mintage	F	VF	XF	Unc	BU
1998 Proof	—	Value: 200				

KM# 253 1/4 OUNCE
7.7770 g., 0.9999 Gold 0.25 oz. AGW, 22 mm. **Obv:** Kudu heads within circle below value **Rev:** Two Kudu fighting **Edge:** Reeded

Date	Mintage	F	VF	XF	Unc	BU
1999 Proof	—	Value: 200				

KM# 259 1/4 OUNCE
7.7770 g., 0.9999 Gold 0.25 oz. AGW, 22 mm. **Obv:** Ibex head **Rev:** Two Ibexe males facing off **Edge:** Reeded

Date	Mintage	F	VF	XF	Unc	BU
2000 Proof	—	Value: 200				

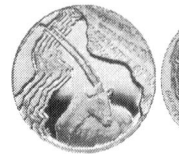

KM# 265 1/4 OUNCE
7.7770 g., 0.9999 Gold 0.25 oz. AGW, 22 mm. **Obv:** Gemsbok head **Rev:** Two Gemsbok males facing off **Edge:** Reeded

Date	Mintage	F	VF	XF	Unc	BU
2001 Proof	—	Value: 200				

KM# 191 1/2 OUNCE
15.5530 g., 0.9999 Gold .5000 oz. AGW **Rev:** Lions

Date	Mintage	F	VF	XF	Unc	BU
1994 Proof	3,999	Value: 365				

KM# 197 1/2 OUNCE
15.5530 g., 0.9999 Gold .5000 oz. AGW **Rev:** Rhinocerous

Date	Mintage	F	VF	XF	Unc	BU
1995 Proof	1,551	Value: 365				

KM# 203 1/2 OUNCE
15.5530 g., 0.9999 Gold .5000 oz. AGW **Rev:** Elephant **Rev. Designer:** Natanya van Niekerk

Date	Mintage	F	VF	XF	Unc	BU
1996 Proof	3,457	Value: 365				

KM# 209 1/2 OUNCE
15.5530 g., 0.9999 Gold .5000 oz. AGW **Rev:** Buffalo **Rev. Designer:** Natanya van Niekerk

Date	Mintage	F	VF	XF	Unc	BU
1997 Proof	1,912	Value: 365				

KM# 215 1/2 OUNCE
15.5530 g., 0.9999 Gold .5000 oz. AGW **Rev:** Leopard **Rev. Designer:** Natanya van Niekerk

Date	Mintage	F	VF	XF	Unc	BU
1998 Proof	—	Value: 365				

KM# 254 1/2 OUNCE
15.5518 g., 0.9990 Gold 0.4995 oz. AGW, 27 mm. **Obv:** Greater Kudu head **Rev:** Kudu attacked by lion **Edge:** Reeded

Date	Mintage	F	VF	XF	Unc	BU
1999 Proof	—	Value: 365				

KM# 260 1/2 OUNCE
15.5518 g., 0.9990 Gold 0.4995 oz. AGW, 27 mm. **Obv:** Ibex head **Rev:** Ibex head **Edge:** Reeded

Date	Mintage	F	VF	XF	Unc	BU
2000 Proof	—	Value: 365				

KM# 266 1/2 OUNCE
15.5518 g., 0.9990 Gold 0.4995 oz. AGW, 27 mm. **Obv:** Gemsbok head **Rev:** Gemsbok grazing **Edge:** Reeded

Date	Mintage	F	VF	XF	Unc	BU
2001 Proof	—	Value: 365				

KM# 192 OUNCE
31.1070 g., 0.9999 Gold 1.0000 oz. AGW **Rev:** Lions

Date	Mintage	F	VF	XF	Unc	BU
1994 Proof	2,902	Value: 700				
1994 Pre.Zoo Proof	775	Value: 750				

KM# 198 OUNCE
31.1070 g., 0.9999 Gold 1.0000 oz. AGW **Rev:** Rhinoceros

Date	Mintage	F	VF	XF	Unc	BU
1995 Proof	1,800	Value: 700				
1995 Hluhuwe Proof	350	Value: 750				

KM# 204 OUNCE
31.1070 g., 0.9999 Gold 1.0000 oz. AGW **Rev:** Elephant **Rev. Designer:** Natanya van Niekerk

Date	Mintage	F	VF	XF	Unc	BU
1996 Proof	4,472	Value: 700				
1996 Mandleve Proof	—	Value: 750				

KM# 210 OUNCE
31.1070 g., 0.9999 Gold 1.0000 oz. AGW **Rev:** Buffalo **Rev. Designer:** Natanya van Niekerk

Date	Mintage	F	VF	XF	Unc	BU
1997 Proof	2,472	Value: 700				
1997 SS Proof	220	Value: 750				

KM# 216 OUNCE
31.1070 g., 0.9999 Gold 1.0000 oz. AGW **Rev:** Leopard **Rev. Designer:** Natanya van Niekerk

Date	Mintage	F	VF	XF	Unc	BU
1998 Proof	—	Value: 700				

KM# 255 OUNCE
31.1035 g., 0.9990 Gold 0.999 oz. AGW, 32.7 mm. **Obv:** Greater Kudu head **Rev:** Kudu eating tree leaves **Edge:** Reeded

Date	Mintage	F	VF	XF	Unc	BU
1999 Proof	—	Value: 700				

KM# 261 OUNCE
31.1035 g., 0.9990 Gold 0.999 oz. AGW, 32.7 mm. **Obv:** Ibex head **Rev:** Ibex head **Edge:** Reeded

Date	Mintage	F	VF	XF	Unc	BU
2000 Proof	—	Value: 700				

KM# 267 OUNCE
31.1035 g., 0.9990 Gold 0.999 oz. AGW, 32.7 mm. **Obv:** Gemsbok head **Rev:** Gemsbok grazing **Edge:** Reeded

Date	Mintage	F	VF	XF	Unc	BU
2001 Proof	—	Value: 700				

PATTERNS
Including off metal strikes

KM#	Date	Mintage	Identification	Mkt Val
PnA23	1898	215	3 Pence. Gold. KM#3.	4,000

Note: Struck for mining magnate Sammie Marks.

PROOF SETS

KM#	Date	Mintage	Identification	Issue Price	Mkt Val
PS1	1923 (10)	655	KM#12.1-17.1, 18, 19.1, 20-21	—	1,500
PS24	1952 (11)	12,000	KM#32.2, 33, 34.2-39.2, 41-43	—	300
PS26	1953 (11)	3,000	KM#44-54	29.40	300
PS28	1953 (2)	1,000	KM#53-54	25.20	270
PS29	1954 (11)	875	KM#44-54	29.40	325
PS31	1954 (2)	350	KM#53-54	25.20	280
PS32	1955 (11)	600	KM#44-54	29.40	350
PS34	1955 (2)	300	KM#53-54	25.20	310
PS35	1956 (11)	350	KM#44-54	29.40	450
PS37	1956 (2)	158	KM#53-54	25.20	400
PS38	1957 (11)	380	KM#44-54	29.40	440
PS40	1957 (2)	180	KM#53-54	25.20	400
PS41	1958 (11)	360	KM#44-54	29.40	450
PS43	1958 (2)	155	KM#53-54	25.20	400
PS44	1959 (11)	390	KM#44-54	29.40	525
PS45	1959 (9)	560	KM#44-52	4.35	275
PS46	1959 (2)	240	KM#53-54	25.20	400
PS47	1960 (11)	1,500	KM#44-51, 53-55	29.40	300
PS49	1960 (2)	450	KM#53-54	25.20	275
PS50	1961 (9)	3,139	KM#56-64	—	200
PS52	1961 (2)	793	KM#63-64 BV + 20%	—	—
PS53	1962 (9)	1,544	KM#56-64	—	210
PS55	1962 (2)	800	KM#63-64 BV+20%	—	—
PS56	1963 (9)	1,500	KM#56-64	—	200
PS58	1963 (2)	1,008	KM#63-64 BV+20%	—	—

S. GEORGIA & THE S. SANDWICH IS.

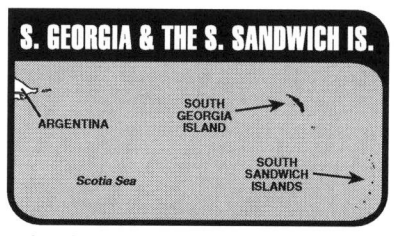

South Georgia and the South Sandwich Islands are a dependency of the Falkland Islands, and located about 800 miles east of them. South Georgia is 1,450 sq. mi. (1,770 sq. km.), and the South Sandwich Islands are 120 sq. mi. (311 sq. km.) Fishing and Antarctic research are the main industries. The islands were claimed for Great Britain in 1775 by Captain James Cook.

RULER
British since 1775

BRITISH ADMINISTRATION

STANDARD COINAGE

KM# 2.1 20 POUNDS
6.2200 g., 0.9999 Gold .2 oz. AGW **Subject:** 100th Birthday - Queen Mother **Obv:** Crowned bust of Queen Elizabeth II right **Obv. Designer:** Ian Rank-Broadley **Rev:** Crowned arms with supporters **Edge:** Reeded

Date	Mintage	F	VF	XF	Unc	BU
2000 Proof	—	Value: 185				

KM# 2.2 20 POUNDS
6.2200 g., 0.9990 Gold 0.1998 oz. AGW, 22 mm. **Obv:** Crowned bust of Queen Elizabeth II right **Obv. Designer:** Ian Rank-Broadley **Rev:** Crowned arms with supporters with a tiny black sapphire mounted below **Edge:** Reeded

Date	Mintage	F	VF	XF	Unc	BU
2000 Proof	1,000	Value: 190				

KM# 5 20 POUNDS
6.2200 g., 0.9999 Gold .2 oz. AGW, 22 mm. **Obv:** Crowned bust of Queen Elizabeth II right **Rev:** Standing figure on the deck of the ship within circle **Edge:** Reeded

Date	Mintage	F	VF	XF	Unc	BU
2000 Proof	—	Value: 175				

KM# 6 20 POUNDS
6.2200 g., 0.9999 Gold .2 oz. AGW **Subject:** 225th Anniversary - Possession by Captain Cook **Obv:** Crowned bust of Queen Elizabeth II right **Rev:** Bust right

Date	Mintage	F	VF	XF	Unc	BU
2000 Proof	—	Value: 175				

KM# 8 20 POUNDS
6.2200 g., 0.9999 Gold .2000 oz. AGW, 22 mm. **Obv:** Crowned bust right **Obv. Designer:** Ian Rank-Broadley **Rev:** Sir Ernest H. Shackleton and ship **Edge:** Reeded

Date	Mintage	F	VF	XF	Unc	BU
2001 Proof	Est. 2,000	Value: 175				

KM# 10 20 POUNDS
6.2200 g., 0.9999 Gold .2000 oz. AGW **Obv:** Crowned bust right **Obv. Designer:** Ian Rank-Broadley **Rev:** Sir Joseph Banks cameo and ship

Date	Mintage	F	VF	XF	Unc	BU
2001 Proof	Est. 2,000	Value: 175				

KM# 16 20 POUNDS
6.2200 g., 0.9999 Gold 0.2 oz. AGW, 22 mm. **Subject:** Princess Diana **Obv:** Crowned bust right **Obv. Designer:** Ian Rank-Broadley **Rev:** Diana's portrait **Edge:** reeded

Date	Mintage	F	VF	XF	Unc	BU
2002PM Proof	—	Value: 175				

KM# 12 20 POUNDS
6.2200 g., 0.9990 Gold 0.1998 oz. AGW, 22 mm. **Subject:** Queen Elizabeth II's Golden Jubilee **Obv:** Crowned bust right **Obv. Designer:** Ian Rank-Broadley **Rev:** Young crowned bust right **Edge:** Reeded

Date	Mintage	F	VF	XF	Unc	BU
2002 Proof	2,002	Value: 175				

KM# 14 20 POUNDS
6.2200 g., 0.9990 Gold 0.1998 oz. AGW, 22 mm. **Subject:** Queen Elizabeth II's Golden Jubilee **Obv:** Crowned bust right **Obv. Designer:** Ian Rank-Broadley **Rev:** National arms **Edge:** Reeded

Date	Mintage	F	VF	XF	Unc	BU
2002 Proof	2,002	Value: 175				

KM#	Date	Mintage	Identification	Issue Price	Mkt Val
PS59	1964 (9)	3,000	KM#56-64	—	190
PS61	1964 (2)	1,000	KM#63-64 BV+20%		
PS62	1965 (9)	5,099	KM#63-64, 65.1, 66.2, 67.1, 68.2, 69.1, 70.2, 71.1	23.50	185
PS63	1965 (9)	85	KM#63-64, 65.1-66.2, 67.1, 68.2, 69.1, 70.2, 71.2 V.I.P.	—	1,200
PS65	1965 (2)	925	KM#63-64 BV+20%	18.15	—
PS66	1966 (9)	10,000	KM#63-64, 65.2, 66.1, 67.2, 68.1, 69.2, 70.1, 71.2	24.10	185
PS68	1966 (2)	1,000	KM#63-64 BV+20%	18.15	—
PS69	1967 (9)	10,000	KM#63-64, 65.2, 66.1, 67.2, 68.1, 69.2, 70.1, 72.2	24.10	185
PS71	1967 (2)	1,000	KM#63-64 BV+20%	18.15	—
PS72	1968 (9)	10,000	KM#63-64, 71.1, 74.1, 75.2, 76.1, 77.2, 78.1, 79.2	35.00	185
PS74	1968 (2)	1,000	KM#63-64 BV+20%	28.00	—
PS75	1969 (9)	7,000	KM#63-64, 65.2, 66.1, 67.2, 68.1, 69.2, 70.1, 80.2	34.85	185
PS77	1969 (2)	1,000	KM#63-64 BV+20%	27.85	—
PS78	1970 (10)	6,000	KM#63-64, 81-88	35.05	185
PS80	1970 (2)	1,000	KM#63-64 BV+20%	28.05	—
PS81	1971 (10)	7,000	KM#63-64, 81-88	35.00	185
PS83	1971 (2)	650	KM#63-64 BV+20%	28.00	—
PS84	1972 (10)	6,000	KM#63-64, 81-88	32.80	185
PS86	1972 (2)	1,500	KM#63-64 BV+20%	26.25	—
PS87	1973 (10)	6,850	KM#63-64, 81-88	32.00	185
PS89	1973 (2)	6,088	KM#63-64 BV+20%	25.60	—
PS90	1974 (10)	11,000	KM#63-64, 81-87, 89	52.50	185
PS92	1974 (2)	5,600	KM#63-64 BV+20%	45.00	—
PS93	1975 (10)	12,500	KM#63-64, 81-87, 88	116	185
PS95	1975 (2)	7,000	KM#63-64 BV+20%	102	—
PS96	1976 (10)	14,000	KM#63-64, 88, 90-96	92.00	185
PS98	1976 (2)	8,000	KM#63-64 BV+20%	80.50	—
PS99	1977 (10)	12,000	KM#63-64, 81-88	92.00	185
PS101	1977 (2)	8,000	KM#63-64 BV+20%	80.50	—
PS102	1978 (10)	10,000	KM#63-64, 81-88	—	185
PS104	1978 (2)	9,000	KM#63-64 BV+20%	—	—
PS105	1979 (10)	10,000	KM#63-64, 97-103, 104a	—	185
PS107	1979 (2)	10,000	KM#63-64 BV+20%	—	—
PS108	1980 (10)	10,000	KM#63-64, 81-88	—	185
PS110	1980 (2)	8,000	KM#63-64 BV+20%	—	—
PS111	1980 (2)	8,000	KM#63-64	—	—
PS112	1980 (3)	60	KM#105-107	—	9,000
PS113	1981 (10)	6,000	KM#63-64, 81-88	—	185
PS115	1981 (2)	6,238	KM#63-64 BV+20%	—	—
PS116	1982 (10)	7,100	KM#63-64, 108-115	—	190
PS118	1982 (2)	6,930	KM#63-64 BV+20%	—	—
PS119	1983 (10)	7,300	KM#63-64, 81-88	—	185
PS121	1983 (2)	7,300	KM#63-64 BV+20%	—	—
PS125	1986 (2)	428	KM#73, 121 Plus large gold plated Silver #1	—	1,400
PS126	1986 (2)	750	KM#121, 131	—	700
PS127	1986 (3)	500	KM#119, 121, 131	—	725
PS129	1987 (4)	750	KM#73, 105-107	—	1,050
PS130	1987 GRC (4)	1,121	KM#73, 105-107	—	2,900
PS132	1988 (4)	806	KM#73, 105-107	—	1,050
PS135	1988 (3)	600	KM#124, 127, 130	—	2,750
PS137	1989 (4)	—	KM#73, 105-107	—	1,050
PS138	1989 GRC (4)	318	KM#73, 105-107	—	5,500
PS140	1990 (4)	—	KM#73, 105-107	—	1,050
PS141	1990 GRC (4)	1,066	KM#73, 105-107	—	2,775
PSA1431991 GRC (4)		426	KM#73, 105-107	—	2,775
PS146	1994 (4)	168	KM#189-192 Wood case	—	1,200
PS147	1994 (4)	1,750	KM#189-192 Velvet case	—	1,175
PS148	1994 (3)	420	KM#167, 187-188	—	750
PS150	1995 (4)	750	KM#73, 105-107	—	1,400
PS151	1995	—	KM#73, 105-107 Wooden box	—	1,425
PS152	1995 (4)	89	KM#195-198 Wood case	—	1,200
PS153	1995 (4)	925	KM#195-198 Velvet case	—	1,175
PS154	1995 (3)	210	KM#152, 193-194	—	755
PS156	1996 (4)	368	KM#201-402 Wood case	—	1,200
PS157	1996 (4)	1,677	KM#201-204 Velvet case	—	1,175
PS158	1996 (3)	346	KM#169, 199-200	—	760
PS159	1997 (4)	500	KM#73, 105-107	—	1,100
PS160	1997 (4)	500	KM#207-210 Wood case	—	1,200
PS161	1997 (4)	1,015	KM#207-210 Velvet case	—	1,175
PS162	1997 (3)	144	KM#181, 205-206	—	780
PS163	1997 (4)	30	KM#73, 105-107, 30 Year Wine set with privy marks	—	2,550
PS164	1997 (9)	3,596	KM#159-166, 170	—	40.00
PS165	1998 (9)	—	KM#159-166, 170	—	40.00
PS166	1998 (4)	—	KM#213-216 Wood case	—	1,200
PS167	1998 (4)	—	KM#213-216 Velvet case	—	1,175
PS168	1998 (3)	—	KM#177, 211-212	—	780

SOUTHERN RHODESIA

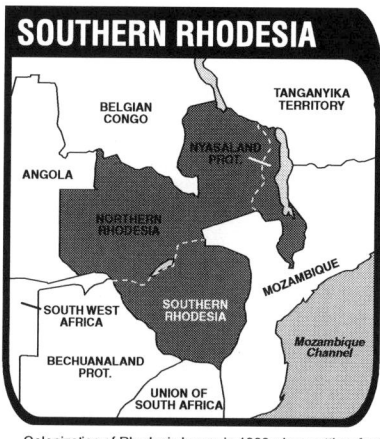

Colonization of Rhodesia began in 1890 when settlers forcibly acquired Shona lands and then Ndebele lands in 1893. It was named as Rhodesia, after Cecil Rhodes who led the build-up of the Colony.

Rhodesia became a self-governing colony under the name of Southern Rhodesia in 1923. Consequent upon later political difficulties and disagreement with the British authorities over common emancipation of the people, a unilateral declaration of independence (UDI) was declared on November 11, 1965.

Following United Nations sanctions against the country, various renamings as Rhodesia and Rhodesia-Zimbabwe, and elections in February 1980, the country became independent on April 18, 1980, as the Republic of Zimbabwe as a member of the Commonwealth of Nations.

RULER
British, until 1966

MONETARY SYSTEM
12 Pence = 1 Shilling
2 Shillings = 1 Florin
5 Shillings = 1 Crown
20 Shillings = 1 Pound

BRITISH COLONY

MEDALLIC COINAGE
Richard Lobel Issues

X# 5 SOVEREIGN
0.3750 Gold **Subject:** Edward VIII

Date	Mintage	F	VF	XF	Unc	BU
1936 Proof	165	Value: 200				

648 SPAIN

The Spanish State, forming the greater part of the Iberian Peninsula of southwest Europe, has an area of 195,988 sq. mi. (504,714 sq. km.) and a population of 39.4 million including the Balearic and the Canary Islands. Capital: Madrid. The economy is based on agriculture, industry and tourism. Machinery, fruit, vegetables and chemicals are exported.

It isn't known when man first came to the Iberian Peninsula - the Altamira caves off the Cantabrian coast approximately 50 miles west of Santander were fashioned in Paleolithic times. Spain was a battleground for centuries before it became a united nation, fought for by Phoenicians, Carthaginians, Greeks, Celts, Romans, Vandals, Visigoths and Moors. Ferdinand and Isabella destroyed the last Moorish stronghold in 1492, freeing the national energy and resources for the era of discovery and colonization that would make Spain the most powerful country in Europe during the 16th century. After the destruction of the Spanish Armada, 1588, Spain never again played a major role in European politics. Forcing Ferdinand to give up his throne and placing him under military guard at Valencay in 1808, Napoleonic France ruled Spain until 1814. When the monarchy was restored in 1814 it continued, only interrupted by the short-lived republic of 1873-74, until the exile of Alfonso XIII in 1931 when the Second Republic was established.

Discontent against the mother country increased after 1808 as colonists faced new imperialist policies from Napoleon or Spanish liberals. The revolutionary movement was established which resulted in the eventual independence of the Vice-royalties of New Spain, New Granada and Rio de la Plata within 2 decades.

The doomed republic was trapped in a tug-of-war between the right and left wing forces inevitably resulting in the Spanish Civil War of 1936-38. The leftist Republicans were supported by the U.S.S.R. and the International Brigade, which consisted of mainly communist volunteers from all over the western world. The right wing Nationalists were supported by the Fascist governments of Italy and Germany. Under the leadership of Gen. Francisco Franco, the Nationalists emerged victorious and immediately embarked on a program of reconstruction and neutrality as dictated by the new "Caudillo"(leader) Franco.

The monarchy was reconstituted in 1947 under the regency of General Francisco Franco; the king designate to be crowned after Franco's death. Franco died on Nov.20, 1975. Two days after his passing, Juan Carlos de Borbon, the grandson of Alfonso XIII, was proclaimed King of Spain.

RULERS
Carlos IV, 1788-1808
Jose Napoleon, 1808-1813
Ferdinand VII, 1808-1833 (in exile until 1814)
Isabel II, 1833-1868
Carlos IV, 1833-1840 (pretender)
Provisional Government, 1868-1871
Amadeo I, 1871-1873
1st Republic, 1873-1874
Carlos VII, 1872-1875 (pretender)
Alfonso XII, 1874-1885
Regency, 1885-1886
Alfonso XIII, 1886-1931
  2nd Republic and Civil War, 1931-1939
Francisco Franco, 1939-1947
  as Caudillo and regent, 1947-1975
Juan Carlos I, 1975-

NOTE: From 1868 to 1982, two dates may be found on most Spanish coinage. The larger date is the year of authorization and the smaller date incused on the two 6-pointed-stars found on most types is the year of issue. The latter appears in parentheses in these listings.

HOMELAND MINT MARKS
Until 1851
(b) Brussels, privy marks only
B - Burgos
B, BA – Barcelona
(c) - Scalloped shell – Coruna
C – Catalonia
C, CA (monogram) – Cuenca
G – Granada
G – Flower over G – Granada
J, JA – Jubia

M, crowned M, ligate MD – Madrid
P, p., P., P,L, PA – Pamplona
S, SL – Seville
Sr – Santander
T, To (monogram), Tole – Toledo
V, VA, VAL – Valencia
VD, VDL, VL, VLL – Valladolid
Crowned C – Cadiz
Crowned M – Madrid
Aqueduct – Segovia until 1864
(f) Flags – Valladolid

NOTE: The Catalonia Mint was located at Reus between February 1-25, 1809 and March 31, 1809 to May 20, 1810 and again from April 14 to August 15, 1810. It was then temporarily located at Tarragonia until May 9, 1811 and finally located at Palma de Mallorca from June 2, 1811 to June 20, 1814.

Until 1980
OM - Oeschger Mesdach & Co.
3-pointed star - Segovia after 1868
4-pointed star - Jubia
6-pointed star - Madrid
7-pointed star - Seville
8-pointed star - Barcelona

NOTE: Letters after date are initials of mint officials.

COLONIAL MINT MARKS
Many Spanish Colonial mints struck coins similar to regular Spanish issues until the 1820's. These issues are easily distinguished from regular Spanish issues by the following mint marks.
C, CH, Ch – Chihuahua, Mexico
Co – Cuzco, Peru
D, DO, Do – Durango, Mexico
Ga – Guadalajara, Mexico
G, GG – Guatemala
G, Go – Guanajuato, Mexico
L, LIMAE, LIMA – Lima, Peru
M, MA – Manila, Philippines
M, Mo – Mexico City, Mexico
NG – Nueva Grenada, Guatemala
NR – Nueva Reino, Colombia
PDV – Valladolid Michoacan, Mexico
P, PN, Pn – Popayan, Colombia
P, POTOSI – Potosi, Bolivia
So – Santiago, Chile
Z, Zs – Zacatecas, Mexico
5-pointed Star – Manila, Philippines

MINT OFFICIALS' INITIALS
BARCELONA MINT

Initial	Date	Name
CC	1842-43	?
PS	1836-41, 1843-48	Francisco Paradaltas and Simeon Sola y Roca
SM	1850	Simeon Sola y Roca and Francisco Miro
SP	1822-23	Pablo Sala and Francisco Paradaltas

MADRID MINT

Initials	Date	Name
AF	1808	Antonio de Goycoechea
AI	1807-08	Antonio de Goycoechea and Ildefonso de Urquiza
AI	1808-12	Antonio Rafael Narvaez and Isidoro Ramos del Manzano
FA	1799-1808	Francisco Herrera and Antonio Goicoechea
FM	1801	Francisco Herrera and Manuel de Lamas
IA	1808	Ildefonso de Urquiza and Antonio Goycoechea
IA	1810	Isidoro Ramos del Manzano and Antonio Rafael Narvaez
IG	1808-10	Ildefonso de Urquiza and Gregorio Lazaro Labrqandero
MF	1788-1802	Manuel de Lamas and Francisco Herrera
RN	1812-13	Antonio Rafael Narvaez
RS	1810-12	Antonio Rafael Narvaez and Jose Sanchez Delgado

SEVILLE MINT

Initials	Date	Name
C	1790-91, 1801-08	Carlos Tiburcio de Roxas
CJ	1815-21	Carlos Tiburcio de Roxas and Joaquin Delgado Diaz
CN	1791-1810, 1812	Carlos Tiburcio de Roxas and Nicolas Lamas
DR	1835-38	Joaquin Delgado Diaz and Benito de Roxas
J	1823	Jose Sanchez Delgado o Joaquin Delgado
JB	1824-33	Joaquin Delgado Diaz and Benito de Roxas
LA	1810, 1812	Leonardo Carrero and Antonio de Larra
RD	1821-23	Carlos Tiburcio de Roxas and Joaquin Delgado Diaz
RD	1835	Benito de Roxas and Joaquin Delgado

VALENCIA MINT

Initials	Date	Name
GS	1811	Gregorio Lazaro Labrandero and Sixto Giber Polo
R	1821	?
SG	1809-14	Sixto Giber Polo

MONETARY SYSTEM
34 Maravedi = 1 Real (of Silver)
16 Reales = 1 Escudo

NOTE: The early coinage of Spain is listed by denomination based on a system of 16 Reales de Plata (silver) = 1 Escudo (gold). However, in the Constitutional periol from 1808-1850, a concurrent system was introduced in which 20 Reales de Vellon (billon) = 8 Reales de Plata. This system does not necessarily refer to the composition of the coin itself. To avoid confusion we have listed the coins using the value as it appears on each coin, ignoring the monetary base.

KINGDOM

EARLY REAL COINAGE

KM# 492 1/2 ESCUDO
1.6900 g., 0.8750 Gold .0475 oz. AGW **Ruler:** Ferdinand VII In exile until 1814 **Obv:** Laureate head right **Obv. Legend:** FERDIN.VII... **Rev:** Crowned arms in order chain **Note:** Mint mark: Crowned M.

Date	Mintage	VG	F	VF	XF	Unc
1817 GJ	—	50.00	70.00	125	150	—

KM# 434 ESCUDO
3.3800 g., 0.8750 Gold .0951 oz. AGW **Ruler:** Carlos IV **Obv:** Bust right **Obv. Legend:** CAROL • IIII • D • G • HISP • ETIND • R • **Rev:** Crowned arms in order chain **Rev. Legend:** FELIX • A • D • ... **Note:** Mint mark: Crowned M.

Date	Mintage	VG	F	VF	XF	Unc
1801 FA	—	80.00	125	185	275	—
1807 FA	—	80.00	125	185	275	—

KM# 493 ESCUDO
3.3800 g., 0.8750 Gold .0951 oz. AGW **Ruler:** Ferdinand VII In exile until 1814 **Obv:** Head right **Rev:** Crowned arms in order chain **Note:** Similar to 1/2 Escudo, KM#492. Mint mark: Crowned M.

Date	Mintage	VG	F	VF	XF	Unc
1817 GJ	—	150	300	500	800	—

KM# 435.1 2 ESCUDOS
6.7700 g., 0.8750 Gold .1905 oz. AGW **Ruler:** Carlos IV **Obv:** Bust right **Obv. Legend:** CAROL • IIII • D • G • HISP • ETIND • R • **Rev:** Crowned arms in order chain **Rev. Legend:** IN • UTROQ • FELIX... **Note:** Mint mark: Crowned M.

Date	Mintage	VG	F	VF	XF	Unc
1801 MF	—	160	200	250	325	500
1801 FM	—	175	250	350	500	800
1801 FA/MF	—	175	225	275	350	500
1801 FA	—	160	200	250	325	500
1802 FA	—	160	200	250	325	500
1803 FA	—	160	200	250	325	500
1804 FA	—	160	200	250	325	500
1805 FA	—	160	200	250	325	500
1806 FA	—	160	200	250	325	500
1807 FA	—	160	200	250	325	500
1807 AI	—	160	200	250	325	500
1808 AI	—	160	200	250	325	500
1808 FA	—	300	600	1,000	1,500	500

KM# 435.2 2 ESCUDOS
6.7700 g., 0.8750 Gold .1905 oz. AGW **Ruler:** Carlos IV **Obv:** Bust right **Obv. Legend:** CAROL • IIII • D • G ... **Rev:** Crowned arms in order chain **Rev. Legend:** IN • UTROQ • FELIX ... **Note:** Mint mark: S, S/L.

SPAIN 649

Date	Mintage	VG	F	VF	XF	Unc
1801 CN	—	160	200	250	325	500
1802 CN	—	160	200	250	325	500
1803 CN	—	160	200	250	325	500
1804 CN	—	160	200	250	325	500
1805 CN	—	200	250	350	500	750
1806 CN	—	160	200	250	325	750
1807 CN	—	160	200	250	325	500
1808 CN	—	160	200	250	325	500

KM# 457 2 ESCUDOS
6.7700 g., 0.8750 Gold .1905 oz. AGW **Ruler:** Ferdinand VII In exile until 1814 **Obv:** Wide armored bust right **Rev:** Crowned arms

Date	Mintage	F	VF	XF	Unc	BU
1808S CN	—	200	250	375	575	—
1809S CN	—	225	300	425	650	—

KM# 455 2 ESCUDOS
6.7700 g., 0.8750 Gold .1905 oz. AGW **Ruler:** Ferdinand VII In exile until 1814 **Obv:** Wide armored bust right **Obv. Legend:** FERDINAN.VII.D.G... **Rev:** Crowned arms in order chain **Rev. Legend:** IN.UTROQ.FELIX...

Date	Mintage	VG	F	VF	XF	Unc
1808S CN	—	160	200	250	375	575
1809S CN	—	175	225	300	425	650

KM# 456.1 2 ESCUDOS
6.7700 g., 0.8750 Gold .1905 oz. AGW **Ruler:** Ferdinand VII In exile until 1814 **Obv:** Draped bust right **Obv. Legend:** FERDIN.VII.D.G... **Rev:** Crowned arms in order chain **Rev. Legend:** IN.UTROQ.FELIX...

Date	Mintage	VG	F	VF	XF	Unc
1809S CN	—	200	300	450	700	1,000

KM# 468 2 ESCUDOS
6.7700 g., 0.8750 Gold .1905 oz. AGW **Ruler:** Ferdinand VII In exile until 1814 **Obv:** Laureate bust right **Obv. Legend:** FERDIN.VII.D.G... **Rev:** Crowned arms in order chain **Rev. Legend:** IN.UTROQ.FELIX... **Note:** Mint mark: Crowned C, large and small varieties exist.

Date	Mintage	VG	F	VF	XF	Unc
1811 CI	—	160	200	275	400	600
1812 CI	—	160	200	275	400	600
1813 CI	—	200	225	325	500	750
1813 CJ	—	160	200	275	400	600
1814 CJ	—	160	200	275	400	600

KM# 469 2 ESCUDOS
6.7700 g., 0.8750 Gold .1905 oz. AGW **Ruler:** Ferdinand VII In exile until 1814 **Obv:** Laureate bust right **Obv. Inscription:** FERDIN.VII.D.G... **Rev:** Crowned arms in order chain **Rev. Legend:** IN.UTROQ.FELIX... **Note:** Varieties in the bust design exist.

Date	Mintage	F	VF	XF	Unc
1811C SF	—	550	1,100	1,850	2,750
1812C SF	—	500	950	1,500	2,250
1813C SF	—	400	800	1,300	1,950

KM# 456.2 2 ESCUDOS
6.7700 g., 0.8750 Gold .1905 oz. AGW **Ruler:** Ferdinand VII In exile until 1814 **Obv:** Draped bust right **Rev:** Crowned arms in order chain **Note:** Mint mark: Crowned C.

Date	Mintage	VG	F	VF	XF	Unc
1811 CI	—	300	500	800	1,350	2,000

KM# 467 2 ESCUDOS
6.7700 g., 0.8750 Gold .1905 oz. AGW **Ruler:** Ferdinand VII In exile until 1814 **Obv:** Laureate armored bust right **Obv. Legend:** FERDIN.VII.D.G... **Rev:** Crowned arms in order chain **Rev. Legend:** IN.UTROQ.FELIX... **Note:** Mint mark: Crowned C.

Date	Mintage	VG	F	VF	XF	Unc
1811 CI	—	160	250	350	550	850

KM# 478 2 ESCUDOS
6.7700 g., 0.8750 Gold .1905 oz. AGW **Ruler:** Ferdinand VII In exile until 1814 **Obv:** Large laureate military bust right **Obv. Legend:** FERDIN.VII.D.G... **Rev:** Crowned arms in order chain **Rev. Legend:** IN.UTROQ.FELIX... **Note:** Mint mark: Crowned M.

Date	Mintage	VG	F	VF	XF	Unc
1812 IJ	—	225	400	650	1,000	1,500

KM# 480 2 ESCUDOS
6.7700 g., 0.8750 Gold .1905 oz. AGW **Ruler:** Ferdinand VII In exile until 1814 **Obv:** Small laureate military bust right **Obv. Legend:** FERDIN.VII.D.G... **Rev:** Crowned arms in order chain **Rev. Legend:** IN.UTROQ.FELIX... **Note:** Mint mark: Crowned M.

Date	Mintage	VG	F	VF	XF	Unc
1813 IG	—	300	550	950	1,500	2,250
1813 IJ	—	200	325	450	650	1,000
1813 GJ	—	160	200	275	400	600
1814 GJ	—	160	275	400	50.00	850

KM# 483.1 2 ESCUDOS
6.7700 g., 0.8750 Gold .1905 oz. AGW **Ruler:** Ferdinand VII In exile until 1814 **Obv:** Laureate head right **Obv. Legend:** FERDIN.VII.D.G... **Rev:** Crowned arms in order chain **Rev. Legend:** IN.UTROQ.FELIX... **Note:** Mint mark: Crowned M.

Date	Mintage	VG	F	VF	XF	Unc
1814 GJ	—	160	225	275	350	525
1815 GJ	—	175	275	400	550	850
1816 GJ	—	200	325	525	650	1,000
1817 GJ	—	200	325	525	650	1,000
1818 GJ	—	160	200	250	350	525
1819 GJ	—	160	200	250	350	525
1820 GJ	—	160	175	225	300	450
1822 AJ	—	200	325	525	650	1,000
1823 AJ	—	200	350	550	800	1,200
1824 AJ	—	160	175	225	300	450
1825 AJ	—	160	175	225	300	450
1826 AJ	—	175	225	300	400	600
1827 AJ	—	175	250	350	500	750
1828 AJ	—	175	275	400	550	850
1829 AJ	—	160	175	225	300	450
1830 AJ	—	160	175	225	300	450
1831 AJ	—	160	175	225	300	450
1832 AJ	—	160	175	225	300	450
1833 AJ	—	160	175	225	300	450

KM# 483.2 2 ESCUDOS
6.7700 g., 0.8750 Gold .1905 oz. AGW **Ruler:** Ferdinand VII In exile until 1814 **Obv:** Laureate head right **Obv. Legend:** FERDIN.VII.D.G.... **Rev:** Crowned arms in order chain **Rev. Legend:** IN.UTROQ.FELIX... **Note:** Mint mark: S, S/L.

Date	Mintage	VG	F	VF	XF	Unc
1815 CJ	—	160	175	225	275	425
1816 CJ	—	160	175	225	275	425
1817 CJ	—	175	225	300	400	600
1818 CJ	—	160	175	225	275	425
1819 CJ	—	160	175	225	275	425
1820 CJ	—	160	175	225	275	425
1821 CJ	—	160	200	250	350	525
1824 J	—	450	750	1,350	1,950	—
1824 JB	—	175	225	325	450	675
1825 JB	—	160	175	225	275	425
1826 JB	—	160	175	225	275	425
1827 JB	—	160	175	225	275	425
1828 JB	—	175	225	325	450	675
1829 JB	—	175	225	325	450	675
1830 JB	—	175	275	400	550	850
1831 JB	—	160	175	225	275	425
1832 JB	—	160	175	225	275	425
1833 JB	—	160	175	225	275	425

KM# 436.1 4 ESCUDOS
13.5400 g., 0.8750 Gold .3809 oz. AGW **Ruler:** Carlos IV **Obv:** Bust right **Obv. Legend:** CAROL • IIII • D • G • HISP • ET IND • R • **Rev:** Crowned arms in order chain **Rev. Legend:** IN • UTROQ • FELIX • AUSPICE • DEO • **Note:** Mint mark: Crowned M.

Date	Mintage	VG	F	VF	XF	Unc
1801 FA	—	300	350	450	575	725
1801 MF	—	400	700	850	1,250	1,600
1803 FA	—	325	400	500	675	800

KM# 436.2 4 ESCUDOS
13.5400 g., 0.8750 Gold .3809 oz. AGW **Ruler:** Carlos IV **Obv:** Bust right **Rev:** Crowned arms in order chain **Note:** Mint mark: S, S/L.

Date	Mintage	VG	F	VF	XF	Unc
1801 C	—	1,000	2,200	3,000	4,500	—
1808 C	—	1,000	2,200	3,000	4,500	—

KM# 484 4 ESCUDOS
13.5400 g., 0.8750 Gold .3809 oz. AGW **Ruler:** Ferdinand VII In exile until 1814 **Obv:** Laureate head right **Obv. Legend:** FERDIN.VII.D.G... **Rev:** Crowned arms in order chain **Rev. Legend:** IN.UTROQ.FELIX... **Note:** Mint mark: Crowned M.

Date	Mintage	VG	F	VF	XF	Unc
1814 GJ	—	325	500	600	800	—
1815 GJ	—	325	450	575	725	—
1816 GJ	—	375	600	800	1,200	—
1818 GJ	—	325	500	650	800	—
1819 GJ	—	325	450	575	725	—
1820 GJ	—	300	350	450	575	—
1824 AI	—	750	1,500	2,100	3,000	—

KM# 437.1 8 ESCUDOS
27.0700 g., 0.8750 Gold .7616 oz. AGW **Ruler:** Carlos IV **Obv:** Armored bust right **Obv. Legend:** CAROL • IIII • D • G • .. **Rev:** Crowned arms in order chain **Rev. Legend:** IN • UTROQ • FELIX • AUSPICE • DEO • **Note:** Mint mark: Crowned M.

Date	Mintage	VG	F	VF	XF	Unc
1802 FA	—	575	750	1,250	1,700	—
1803 FA	—	900	1,700	2,500	4,000	—
1805 FA	—	650	1,100	1,600	2,600	—

650 SPAIN

KM# 470 8 ESCUDOS
27.0700 g., 0.8750 Gold .7616 oz. AGW **Ruler:** Ferdinand VII In exile until 1814 **Obv:** Laureate armored bust right **Obv. Legend:** FERDIN.VII.D.G.. **Rev:** Crowned arms in order chain **Rev. Legend:** IN.UTROQ.FELIX... **Note:** Mint mark: Crowned C.

Date	Mintage	VG	F	VF	XF	Unc
1811 CI	—	700	1,000	2,500	4,250	—

KM# 481 8 ESCUDOS
27.0700 g., 0.8750 Gold .7616 oz. AGW **Ruler:** Ferdinand VII In exile until 1814 **Obv:** Laureate head right **Obv. Legend:** FERDIN.VII.D.G... **Rev:** Crowned arms in order chain **Rev. Legend:** IN.UTROQ.FELIX...

Date	Mintage	VG	F	VF	XF	Unc
1813C SF	—	3,000	7,000	10,000	15,000	—
1814C SF	—	3,500	7,500	11,000	—	—

Note: Stack's CICF sale 4-89, XF realized $16,500

KM# 485 8 ESCUDOS
27.0700 g., 0.8750 Gold .7616 oz. AGW **Ruler:** Ferdinand VII In exile until 1814 **Obv:** Laureate head right **Obv. Legend:** FERDIN.VII.D.G... **Rev:** Crowned arms in order chain **Rev. Legend:** IN.UTROQ.FELIX... **Note:** Mint mark: Crowned M.

Date	Mintage	VG	F	VF	XF	Unc
1814 GJ	—	1,000	2,000	2,800	4,000	—
1816 GJ	—	1,500	3,000	4,200	6,000	—
1817 GJ	—	1,100	2,250	3,100	4,500	—
1819 GJ	—	1,800	3,500	5,000	7,500	—
1820 GJ	—	600	800	1,250	1,800	—

DE VELLON COINAGE
1808-1850

KM# 542 80 REALES
6.7700 g., 0.8750 Gold .1905 oz. AGW **Ruler:** Jose Napolean **Obv:** Head left **Obv. Legend:** IOSEPH.NAP.D.G... **Rev:** Crowned arms divides value in order chain **Note:** Mint mark: Crowned M.

Date	Mintage	VG	F	VF	XF	Unc
1809 AI	—	160	250	350	400	550
1810 AI	—	275	500	1,000	1,500	2,000

KM# 552 80 REALES
6.7700 g., 0.8750 Gold .1905 oz. AGW **Ruler:** Jose Napolean **Obv:** Laureate head left **Obv. Legend:** IOSEPH.NAP.D.G... **Rev:** Crowned arms divides value in order chain **Rev. Legend:** IN.UTROQ.FELIX... **Note:** Mint mark: Crowned M.

Date	Mintage	VG	F	VF	XF	Unc
1811 AI	440,000	160	275	375	450	550
1812/1 AI	—	200	350	550	750	1,000
1812 AI	238,000	200	350	550	750	1,000
1813 RN	161,000	250	375	650	1,200	1,500

KM# 564.2 80 REALES
6.7700 g., 0.8750 Gold .1905 oz. AGW **Ruler:** Ferdinand VII In exile until 1814 **Obv:** Head right **Obv. Legend:** FERN... **Rev:** Crowned arms divides value in order chain **Rev. Legend:** REY DE LAS... **Note:** Mint mark: Crowned M.

Date	Mintage	VG	F	VF	XF	Unc
1822 SR	—	150	185	250	300	—
1823 SR	—	160	225	275	375	—

KM# 564.1 80 REALES
6.7700 g., 0.8750 Gold .1905 oz. AGW **Ruler:** Ferdinand VII In exile until 1814 **Obv:** Head right **Rev:** Crowned arms divides value in order chain **Note:** Mint mark: B, BA.

Date	Mintage	VG	F	VF	XF	Unc
1822 SP	—	175	275	500	800	—
1823 SP	—	160	225	275	350	425

KM# 564.3 80 REALES
6.7700 g., 0.8750 Gold .1905 oz. AGW **Ruler:** Ferdinand VII In exile until 1814 **Obv:** Head right **Rev:** Crowned arms divides value in order chain **Note:** Mint mark: S, S/L.

Date	Mintage	VG	F	VF	XF	Unc
1823 RD	—	200	400	700	1,000	—

KM# 577.2 80 REALES
6.7700 g., 0.8750 Gold .1905 oz. AGW **Ruler:** Isabel II **Obv:** Head right **Obv. Legend:** ISABEL 2... **Rev:** Crowned arms divides value in order chain **Rev. Legend:** REYNA DE ESPANA... **Note:** Mint mark: Crowned M.

Date	Mintage	VG	F	VF	XF	Unc
1834 CR	—	160	200	250	350	450
1835 CR	—	160	200	250	350	450
1836 CR	—	160	200	250	350	450

KM# 577.3 80 REALES
6.7700 g., 0.8750 Gold .1905 oz. AGW **Ruler:** Isabel II **Obv:** Head right **Obv. Legend:** ...DIOS **Rev:** Crowned arms divides value in order chain **Rev. Legend:** Y DE LAS INDIAS **Note:** Mint mark: S, S/L.

Date	Mintage	VG	F	VF	XF	Unc
1835 DR	—	200	250	475	700	—
1836 DR	—	200	250	475	700	—

KM# 577.1 80 REALES
6.7700 g., 0.8750 Gold .1905 oz. AGW **Ruler:** Isabel II **Obv:** Head right **Obv. Legend:** Legend ends: DIOS **Rev:** Crowned arms divides value in order chain **Rev. Legend:** Y DE LAS INDIAS **Note:** Mint mark: B, B/A.

Date	Mintage	VG	F	VF	XF	Unc
1836 PS	—	300	600	1,200	2,000	—

KM# 580 80 REALES
6.7700 g., 0.8750 Gold .1905 oz. AGW **Ruler:** Isabel II **Obv:** Head right **Obv. Legend:** ...CONSTITUCION **Rev:** Crowned arms divides value in order chain **Note:** Mint mark: B, BA.

Date	Mintage	VG	F	VF	XF	Unc
1837 PS	—	200	300	500	750	—
1838 PS	—	175	225	325	450	—

KM# 578.2 80 REALES
6.7700 g., 0.8750 Gold .1905 oz. AGW **Ruler:** Isabel II **Obv:** Large head right **Obv. Legend:** ...CONST **Rev:** Crowned arms divides value in order chain **Note:** Mint mark: Crowned M.

Date	Mintage	VG	F	VF	XF	Unc
1837 CR	—	200	325	500	950	—
1838 CL	—	160	200	400	900	—
1839 CL	—	200	375	650	1,000	—
1840 CL	—	160	200	400	600	—
1841 CL	—	200	250	475	700	—
1842 CL	—	200	275	500	850	—
1843 CL	—	160	200	250	325	—
1844 CL	—	160	200	250	325	—
1845 CL	—	160	200	250	325	—
1846 CL	—	200	250	475	700	—
1847 CL	—	160	200	250	325	—
1848 CL	—	200	350	475	700	—
1849 CL	—	275	500	900	1,600	—

KM# 578.3 80 REALES
6.7700 g., 0.8750 Gold .1905 oz. AGW **Ruler:** Isabel II **Obv:** Large head right **Obv. Legend:** ...CONST **Rev:** Crowned arms divides value in order chain **Note:** Mint mark: S, S/L.

Date	Mintage	VG	F	VF	XF	Unc
1837 DR	—	200	350	575	800	—
1838 DR	—	225	400	600	900	—
1838 RD	—	225	400	800	1,200	—
1839 RD	—	175	250	375	600	—
1840 RD	—	175	225	300	425	—
1841 RD	—	175	250	350	450	—
1842 RD	—	175	225	300	425	—
1843 RD	—	175	250	350	450	—
1844 RD	—	160	225	300	425	—
1845 RD	—	175	225	325	450	—
1846 RD	—	175	225	300	425	—
1847 RD	—	175	250	400	500	—
1848 RD	—	200	500	1,000	1,600	—

KM# 578.1 80 REALES
6.7700 g., 0.8750 Gold .1905 oz. AGW **Ruler:** Isabel II **Obv:** Large head right **Obv. Legend:** ISABEL 2... **Rev:** Crowned arms divides value in order chain **Rev. Legend:** REYNA DE LAS... **Note:** Mint mark: B, BA.

Date	Mintage	VG	F	VF	XF	Unc
1838 PS	—	200	275	400	600	—
1839 PS	—	160	200	250	350	—
1840 PS	—	160	200	250	350	—
1841 PS	—	160	200	250	350	—
1842 CC	—	160	200	250	350	—
1842 PS	—	600	1,250	2,000	3,500	—
1843 CC	—	600	1,250	2,000	3,500	—
1844 PS	—	160	200	250	325	—
1845 PS	—	160	200	250	325	—
1846 PS	—	160	200	250	325	—
1847 PS	—	160	200	275	350	—
1848 PS	—	200	350	500	850	—

KM# A579 80 REALES
6.7700 g., 0.8750 Gold 0.1905 oz. AGW **Ruler:** Isabel II **Obv:** Small head right **Obv. Legend:** ISABEL 2... **Rev:** Crowned arms divides value in order chain **Rev. Legend:** REYNA DE LAS...

Date	Mintage	VG	F	VF	XF	Unc
1841B PS	—	160	200	250	400	—
1844B PS	—	160	200	250	400	—

KM# 565 160 REALES
13.5400 g., 0.8750 Gold .3809 oz. AGW **Ruler:** Ferdinand VII In exile until 1814 **Obv:** Head right **Obv. Legend:** FERN... **Rev:** Crowned arms divides value in order chain **Rev. Legend:** REY DE LAS... **Note:** Mint mark: Crowned M.

Date	Mintage	VG	F	VF	XF	Unc
1822 SR	—	300	400	700	1,150	—

SPAIN 651

KM# 545 320 REALES
27.0700 g., 0.8750 Gold .7616 oz. AGW **Ruler:** Jose Napolean **Obv:** Laureate head left **Obv. Legend:** IOSEPH.NAP.D.G... **Rev:** Crowned arms divides value in order chain **Rev. Legend:** IN UTROQ.FELIX... **Note:** Mint mark: Crowned M.

Date	Mintage	VG	F	VF	XF	Unc
1810 AI	64,000	1,500	3,800	7,500	10,000	—
1810 RS	Inc. above	1,750	4,000	8,000	11,500	—
1812 RS	60,000	1,500	3,600	7,200	9,500	—

KM# 566 320 REALES
27.0700 g., 0.8750 Gold .7616 oz. AGW **Ruler:** Ferdinand VII In exile until 1814 **Obv:** Head right **Obv. Legend:** FERN... **Rev:** Crowned arms divides value in order chain **Rev. Legend:** REY DE LAS... **Note:** Mint mark: Crowned M.

Date	Mintage	VG	F	VF	XF	Unc
1822 SR	—	650	1,300	2,750	4,750	—
1823 SR	—	1,100	2,400	5,000	7,500	—

DECIMAL COINAGE
Real System
100 Centimos = 10 Decimos = 1 Real

KM# 610 20 REALES
1.6674 g., 0.9000 Gold .0482 oz. AGW **Ruler:** Isabel II **Obv:** Draped laureate bust left **Obv. Legend:** ISABEL II... **Rev:** Crowned oval arms above sprigs, value below **Rev. Legend:** REYNA DE LAS... **Note:** Mint mark: 6-pointed star.

Date	Mintage	F	VF	XF	Unc	BU
1861	—	125	180	275	375	—
1862	—	375	850	1,700	2,500	—
1863	—	550	1,300	2,600	3,500	—

KM# 616.2 40 REALES
3.3349 g., 0.9000 Gold .0965 oz. AGW **Ruler:** Isabel II **Obv:** Draped laureate bust left **Obv. Legend:** ISABEL II... **Rev:** Crowned oval arms above sprigs, value below **Rev. Legend:** REYNA DE LAS... **Note:** Mint mark: 6-pointed star.

Date	Mintage	F	VF	XF	Unc	BU
1861	—	200	300	400	550	—
1862	—	100	125	150	200	—
1863	—	100	125	150	200	—

KM# 616.1 40 REALES
3.3349 g., 0.9000 Gold .0965 oz. AGW **Ruler:** Isabel II **Obv:** Draped laureate bust left **Rev:** Crowned oval arms above sprigs, value below **Note:** Mint mark: 8-pointed star.

Date	Mintage	F	VF	XF	Unc	BU
1863	—	100	125	150	200	—
1864	—	450	900	1,600	2,250	—

KM# 618.1 40 REALES
3.3349 g., 0.9000 Gold .0965 oz. AGW **Ruler:** Isabel II **Obv:** Draped laureate bust left **Obv. Legend:** ISABEL 2... **Rev:** Crowned mantled arms **Rev. Legend:** REYNA DE LAS... **Note:** Mint mark: 6-pointed star.

Date	Mintage	F	VF	XF	Unc	BU
1864	—	70.00	80.00	90.00	125	—

KM# 618.2 40 REALES
3.3349 g., 0.9000 Gold .0965 oz. AGW **Ruler:** Isabel II **Obv:** Draped laureate bust left **Rev:** Crowned mantled arms **Rev. Legend:** DOBLÓN DE 100 REALES **Note:** Mint mark: 7-pointed star.

Date	Mintage	F	VF	XF	Unc	BU
1864	—	185	375	650	950	—

KM# 594.2 100 REALES
8.3371 g., 0.9000 Gold .2412 oz. AGW **Ruler:** Isabel II **Obv:** Young head left **Obv. Legend:** ISABEL 2... **Rev:** Crowned oval arms within order chain **Rev. Legend:** DOBLÓN DE 100 REALES **Note:** Mint mark: 6-pointed star.

Date	Mintage	F	VF	XF	Unc	BU
1850 CL	—	200	250	350	450	—
1850 DG	—	1,750	3,500	6,500	9,500	—
1851 CL	—	350	600	1,000	1,500	—

KM# 594.1 100 REALES
8.3371 g., 0.9000 Gold .2412 oz. AGW **Ruler:** Isabel II **Obv:** Young head left **Obv. Legend:** ISABEL 2... **Rev:** Crowned oval arms within order chain **Rev. Legend:** DOBLÓN DE 100 REALES **Note:** Mint mark: 8-pointed star.

Date	Mintage	F	VF	XF	Unc	BU
1850 SM	—	400	850	1,450	2,200	—
1851 SM	—	1,500	3,000	5,000	7,500	—

KM# 594.3 100 REALES
8.3371 g., 0.9000 Gold .2412 oz. AGW **Ruler:** Isabel II **Obv:** Young head left **Rev:** Crowned oval arms within order chain **Note:** Mint mark: 7-pointed star.

Date	Mintage	F	VF	XF	Unc	BU
1850 RD	—	450	900	1,500	2,200	—

KM# 596.2 100 REALES
8.3371 g., 0.9000 Gold .2412 oz. AGW **Ruler:** Isabel II **Obv:** Young head left **Rev:** Crowned oval arms above sprigs, value below **Note:** Mint mark: 6-pointed star.

Date	Mintage	F	VF	XF	Unc	BU
1851	—	900	1,800	2,700	3,500	—
1852	—	900	1,800	2,700	3,500	—
1854	—	190	235	325	400	—
1855	—	190	235	325	400	—

KM# 596.1 100 REALES
8.3371 g., 0.9000 Gold .2412 oz. AGW **Ruler:** Isabel II **Obv:** Young head left **Obv. Legend:** ISABEL 2... **Rev:** Crowned oval arms above sprigs, value below **Rev. Legend:** REYNA DE LAS ESPANAS **Note:** Mint mark: 8-pointed star.

Date	Mintage	F	VF	XF	Unc	BU
1851	—	900	1,800	2,700	3,500	—
1854	—	200	245	350	425	—
1855	—	190	235	325	400	—

KM# 596.3 100 REALES
8.3371 g., 0.9000 Gold .2412 oz. AGW **Ruler:** Isabel II **Obv:** Young head left **Obv. Legend:** ISABEL 2... **Rev:** Crowned oval arms above sprigs, value below **Rev. Legend:** REYNA DE LAS ESPANAS **Note:** Mint mark: 7-pointed star.

Date	Mintage	F	VF	XF	Unc	BU
1852	—	1,000	2,000	3,000	4,000	—
1854	—	190	235	325	400	—
1855	—	190	235	300	375	—

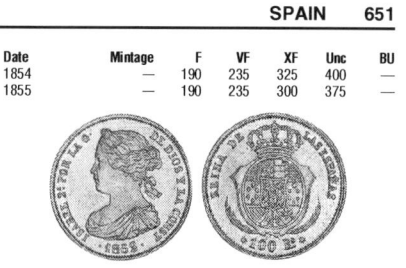

KM# 605.1 100 REALES
8.3371 g., 0.9000 Gold .2412 oz. AGW **Ruler:** Isabel II **Obv:** Draped laureate bust left **Obv. Legend:** ISABEL 2... **Rev:** Crowned oval arms above sprigs, value below **Rev. Legend:** REYNA DE LAS ESPANAS **Note:** Mint mark: 8-pointed star.

Date	Mintage	F	VF	XF	Unc	BU
1856	—	400	600	900	1,500	—
1857	—	180	210	250	280	—
1858	—	200	250	325	400	—
1859	—	180	210	250	280	—
1860	—	180	210	240	270	—
1861	—	375	600	800	1,000	—
1862	—	180	210	250	300	—

KM# 605.2 100 REALES
8.3371 g., 0.9000 Gold .2412 oz. AGW **Ruler:** Isabel II **Obv:** Draped laureate bust left **Obv. Legend:** ISABEL 2... **Rev:** Crowned oval arms above sprigs, value below **Rev. Legend:** REYNA DE LAS ESPANAS **Note:** Mint mark: 6-pointed star.

Date	Mintage	F	VF	XF	Unc	BU
1856	—	180	210	240	270	—
1857	—	350	500	650	800	—
1858	—	200	250	325	400	—
1859	—	180	210	250	280	—
1860	—	180	210	240	270	—
1861	—	180	210	240	270	—
1862	—	180	210	240	270	—

KM# 605.3 100 REALES
8.3371 g., 0.9000 Gold .2412 oz. AGW **Ruler:** Isabel II **Obv:** Draped laureate bust left **Rev:** Crowned oval arms above sprigs, value below **Note:** Mint mark: 7-pointed star.

Date	Mintage	F	VF	XF	Unc	BU
1856	—	400	750	1,250	1,600	—
1857	—	180	210	250	280	—
1858	—	190	240	280	375	—
1859	—	180	210	250	280	—
1860	—	180	210	240	270	—
1861	—	180	210	240	270	—
1862	—	180	210	240	270	—

KM# 617.1 100 REALES
8.3371 g., 0.9000 Gold .2412 oz. AGW **Ruler:** Isabel II **Obv:** Draped laureate bust left **Obv. Legend:** ISABEL 2... **Rev:** Crowned mantled arms **Rev. Legend:** REYNA DE LAS ESPANAS **Note:** Mint mark: 6-pointed star.

Date	Mintage	F	VF	XF	Unc	BU
1863	—	180	210	240	270	—
1864	—	180	210	240	270	—

KM# 617.2 100 REALES
8.3371 g., 0.9000 Gold .2412 oz. AGW **Ruler:** Isabel II **Obv:** Draped laureate bust left **Rev:** Crowned mantled arms **Note:** Mint mark: 7-pointed star.

Date	Mintage	F	VF	XF	Unc	BU
1863	—	250	400	650	950	—
1864	—	300	450	750	1,250	—

Note: For similar coins, with denominations expressed Cs. de Peso, see Philippines

SPAIN

SECOND DECIMAL COINAGE
Escudo System

100 Centimos = 1 Escudo

KM# 630 2 ESCUDOS
1.6774 g., 0.9000 Gold .0485 oz. AGW **Ruler:** Isabel II **Obv:** Draped laureate bust left **Obv. Legend:** ISABEL 2... **Rev:** Crowned mantled arms **Rev. Legend:** REYNA DE LAS ESPANAS **Note:** Mint mark: 6-pointed star.

Date	Mintage	F	VF	XF	Unc	BU
1865	—	125	180	275	375	—
1868 (68)	—	350	800	1,600	2,200	—

KM# 631.1 4 ESCUDOS
3.3548 g., 0.9000 Gold .0971 oz. AGW **Ruler:** Isabel II **Obv:** Draped laureate bust left **Obv. Legend:** ISABEL 2... **Rev:** Crowned mantled arms **Rev. Legend:** REYNA DE LAS ESPANAS **Note:** Mint mark: 6-pointed star.

Date	Mintage	F	VF	XF	Unc	BU
1865	—	90.00	120	150	180	—
1866	—	90.00	120	150	180	—
1867	—	90.00	120	150	180	—
1868 (68)	—	90.00	140	175	210	—

KM# 631.2 4 ESCUDOS
3.3548 g., 0.9000 Gold .0971 oz. AGW **Ruler:** Isabel II **Obv:** Draped laureate bust left **Rev:** Crowned mantled arms **Note:** Mint mark: 7-pointed star.

Date	Mintage	F	VF	XF	Unc	BU
1865	—	275	550	950	1,300	—
1866	—	200	400	700	1,000	—

KM# 636.1 10 ESCUDOS
8.3870 g., 0.9000 Gold .2427 oz. AGW **Ruler:** Isabel II **Obv:** Draped laureate bust left **Obv. Legend:** ISABEL 2... **Rev:** Crowned mantled arms **Rev. Legend:** REYNA DE LAS ESPANAS **Note:** Mint mark: 6-pointed star.

Date	Mintage	F	VF	XF	Unc	BU
1865	—	200	240	300	375	—
1866	—	200	300	450	600	—
1867	—	180	210	250	280	—
1868 (68)	—	180	210	240	270	—

KM# 636.2 10 ESCUDOS
8.3870 g., 0.9000 Gold .2427 oz. AGW **Ruler:** Isabel II **Obv:** Draped laureate bust left **Rev:** Crowned mantled arms **Note:** Mint mark: 7-pointed star.

Date	Mintage	F	VF	XF	Unc	BU
1866	—	1,200	2,500	4,500	6,500	—

KM# 636.3 10 ESCUDOS
8.3870 g., 0.9000 Gold .2427 oz. AGW **Ruler:** Isabel II **Obv:** Draped laureate bust left **Obv. Legend:** ISABEL 2... **Rev:** Crowned mantled arms **Rev. Legend:** REYNA DE LAS ESPANAS **Note:** Mint mark: 6-pointed star.

Date	Mintage	F	VF	XF	Unc	BU
1868 (73)	—	180	210	240	270	—

THIRD DECIMAL COINAGE

10 Milesimas = 1 Centimo

100 Centesimos = 1 Peseta

KM# 677 10 PESETAS
3.2258 g., 0.9000 Gold .0933 oz. AGW **Ruler:** Alfonso XII **Obv:** Young head right **Obv. Legend:** ALFONSO XII... **Rev:** Crowned mantled arms **Rev. Legend:** REY CONST... **Note:** Mint mark: 6-pointed star.

Date	Mintage	F	VF	XF	Unc	BU
1878 (78) EM-M	91,000	150	225	300	400	—
1879 (79) EM-M	33,000	700	1,250	1,800	2,500	—
1878 (61) DE-M	496	—	—	—	1,000	—
1878 (62) DE-M	18,000	—	—	—	150	—

Note: The above 2 coins dated (61) and (62) were restruck by the Spanish Mint from original dies in 1961 and 1962 and are considered official restrike issues

KM# 693 20 PESETAS
6.4516 g., 0.9000 Gold .1867 oz. AGW **Ruler:** Alfonso XIII **Obv:** Toddler's head right **Obv. Legend:** ALFONSO XIII... **Rev:** Crowned mantled arms **Rev. Legend:** REY CONST... **Note:** Mint mark: 6-pointed star.

Date	Mintage	F	VF	XF	Unc	BU
1889 (89) MP-M	875,000	—	235	275	375	—
1890 (90) MP-M	2,344,000	—	195	225	260	—
1887 (61) PG-V	800	—	—	450	750	—
1887 (62) PG-V	11,000	—	—	125	175	—

Note: The above 2 coins dated (61) and (62) were restruck by the Spanish Mint from original dies in 1961 and 1962 and are considered official restrike issues

KM# 701 20 PESETAS
6.4516 g., 0.9000 Gold .1867 oz. AGW **Ruler:** Alfonso XIII **Obv:** Child's head right **Obv. Legend:** ALFONSO XIII... **Rev:** Crowned mantled arms **Rev. Legend:** REY CONST... **Note:** Mint mark: 6-pointed star.

Date	Mintage	F	VF	XF	Unc	BU
1892 (92) PG-M	2,430,000	850	1,250	2,250	3,000	—

KM# 709 20 PESETAS
6.4516 g., 0.9000 Gold .1867 oz. AGW **Ruler:** Alfonso XIII **Obv:** Child's head right **Obv. Legend:** ALFONSO XIII POR... **Rev:** Crowned mantled arms **Rev. Legend:** REY CONST... **Note:** Mint mark: 6-pointed star.

Date	Mintage	F	VF	XF	Unc	BU
1899 (99) SM-V	2,086,000	—	225	300	400	—
1896 (61) PG-V	900	—	—	400	500	—
1896 (62) PG-V	12,000	—	—	135	165	—

Note: The above 2 coins dated (61) and (62) were restruck by the Spanish Mint from original dies in 1961 and 1962 and are considered official restrike issues

KM# 724 20 PESETAS
6.4516 g., 0.9000 Gold .1867 oz. AGW **Obv:** Head right **Rev:** Crowned and mantled shield **Note:** Mint mark: 6-pointed star.

Date	Mintage	F	VF	XF	Unc	BU
1904 (04) SM-V	3,814	850	1,650	2,250	3,000	—

KM# 667 25 PESETAS
8.0645 g., 0.9000 Gold .2333 oz. AGW **Ruler:** Amadeo I **Obv:** Head right **Obv. Legend:** AMADEO I... **Rev:** Crowned mantled arms **Note:** Mint mark: 6-pointed star.

Date	Mintage	F	VF	XF	Unc	BU
1871 (75) SD-M Rare	25	—	—	—	—	—

KM# 673 25 PESETAS
8.0645 g., 0.9000 Gold .2333 oz. AGW **Ruler:** Alfonso XII **Obv:** Young head right **Obv. Legend:** ALFONSO XII... **Rev:** Crowned mantled arms **Rev. Legend:** REY CONST.. **Note:** Mint mark: 6-pointed star.

Date	Mintage	F	VF	XF	Unc	BU
1876 (76) DE-M	1,281,000	—	180	200	225	—
1877 (77) DE-M	10,048,000	—	175	190	220	—
1878 (78) DE-M	5,192,000	—	175	190	220	—
1878 (78) EM-M	3,000,000	—	175	190	220	—
1879 (79) EM-M	3,478,000	—	175	190	220	—
1880 (80) MS-M	6,863,000	—	175	190	220	—
1876 (61) DE-M	300	—	—	1,500	2,000	—
1876 (62) DE-M	6,000	—	—	250	350	—

Note: For above 2 coins dated (61) and (62) see note after 10 Pesetas, KM#677

KM# 687 25 PESETAS
8.0645 g., 0.9000 Gold .2333 oz. AGW **Ruler:** Alfonso XII **Obv:** Head right **Obv. Legend:** ALFONSO XII... **Rev:** Crowned mantled arms **Rev. Legend:** REY CONST... **Note:** Mint mark: 6-pointed star.

Date	Mintage	F	VF	XF	Unc	BU
1881 (81) MS-M	4,366,000	—	175	200	225	—
1882 (82) MS-M	414,000	—	400	600	700	—
1883 (83) MS-M	669,000	—	400	500	600	—
1884 (84) MS-M	1,033,000	—	225	300	400	—
1885 (85) MS-M	503,000	—	1,000	1,500	1,800	—
1885 (86) MS-M	491,000	—	3,400	4,500	10,000	—

KM# 664 100 PESETAS
32.2581 g., 0.9000 Gold .9334 oz. AGW **Ruler:** Provisional Government **Subject:** Provisional Government **Obv:** Standing Liberty, date below **Rev:** Crowned oval mantled arms **Note:** Mint mark: 6-pointed star.

Date	Mintage	F	VF	XF	Unc	BU
1870 (70) SD-M Rare	12	—	—	—	—	—

SPAIN 653

KM# 668a 100 PESETAS
0.9000 Yellow Gold **Ruler:** Amadeao I **Subject:** Provisional Government **Obv:** Head right **Obv. Legend:** AMADEO I... **Rev:** Crowned oval mantled arms **Note:** Mint mark: 6-pointed star.
Date	Mintage	F	VF	XF	Unc	BU
1871 (71) SD-M Rare	25	—	—	—	—	—

KM# 668b 100 PESETAS
0.9000 Red Gold **Ruler:** Amadeao I **Subject:** Provisional Government **Obv:** Head right **Rev:** Crowned oval mantled arms **Note:** Mint mark: 6-pointed star.
Date	Mintage	F	VF	XF	Unc	BU
1871 (71) SD-M Rare	50	—	—	—	—	—

KM# 708 100 PESETAS
0.9000 Red Gold **Ruler:** Alfonso XIII **Subject:** Provisional Government **Obv:** Child's head right **Obv. Legend:** ALFONSO XIII POR... **Rev:** Crowned arms, pillars, value below **Note:** Mint mark: 6-pointed star.
Date	Mintage	F	VF	XF	Unc	BU
1897 (97) SG-V	150,000	600	1,000	1,500	2,000	—
1897 (61) SG-V	810	—	—	1,250	1,500	—
1897 (62) SG-V	6,000	—	—	800	900	—

Note: The above 2 coins were restruck by the Spanish Mint from original dies in 1961 and 1962 and are considered official restrike issues

DECIMAL COINAGE
Peseta System

100 Centimos = 1 Peseta

X# 15a 40 PESETAS
Gold **Ruler:** Isabel II **Note:** Prev. KY#198a.
Date	Mintage	F	VF	XF	Unc	BU
1904 JP-L Unique; Proof	—	—	—	—	—	—

X# 16a 50 PESETAS
Gold **Ruler:** Isabel II **Note:** Prev. KY#197a.
Date	Mintage	F	VF	XF	Unc	BU
1904 JP-L Unique; Proof	—	—	—	—	—	—

X# 8a 100 PESETAS
Gold **Ruler:** Isabel II **Note:** Prev. KY#187a.
Date	Mintage	F	VF	XF	Unc	BU
1894 Proof	2	—	—	—	—	—

X# 11c 100 PESETAS
Gold **Ruler:** Maria Christina **Note:** Piefort.
Date	Mintage	F	VF	XF	Unc	BU
1894 JP-L Proof	—	—	—	—	—	—

X# 17 150 PESETAS
Gold **Ruler:** Isabel II **Note:** Prev. KY#195.
Date	Mintage	F	VF	XF	Unc	BU
1904 Unique	—	—	—	—	—	—

X# 18 200 PESETAS
Gold **Ruler:** Isabel II **Obv:** Similar to 150 Pesetas, X#17 **Rev:** Arms of Castile and Leon **Note:** Prev. KY#194.
Date	Mintage	F	VF	XF	Unc	BU
1904 Unique	—	—	—	—	—	—

PRETENDER COINAGE
Charles VII 1872-1875

A grandson of Charles V who claimed the throne and maintained a court and government in exile. All Charles VII pieces were made at the Brussels Mint.

NOTE: Some pretender issues which circulated are listed in the regular coinage.

KM# PT12 5 PESETAS
1.6129 g., 0.9000 Gold .0467 oz. AGW **Ruler:** Charles VII **Obv:** Laureate head right **Rev:** Crowned arms divide value **Note:** Counterfeits exist.
Date	Mintage	F	VF	XF	Unc	BU
1874 Rare	—	—	—	—	—	—

KINGDOM
1949 - Present

DECIMAL COINAGE
Peseta System

100 Centimos = 1 Peseta

KM# 840 5000 PESETAS
1.6800 g., 0.9990 Gold .0540 oz. AGW **Ruler:** Juan Carlos I **Subject:** Discovery of America **Obv:** Crown within beaded circle **Rev:** Crown above compass face within beaded circle
Date	Mintage	F	VF	XF	Unc	BU
1989	6,000	—	—	—	—	60.00
1989 Proof	8,000	Value: 60.00				

KM# 870 5000 PESETAS
1.6800 g., 0.9990 Gold .0540 oz. AGW **Ruler:** Juan Carlos I **Obv:** Bust of Philip V facing **Rev:** Compass face
Date	Mintage	F	VF	XF	Unc	BU
1990	3,000	—	—	—	—	65.00
1990 Proof	4,000	Value: 65.00				

KM# 894 5000 PESETAS
1.6800 g., 0.9990 Gold .0540 oz. AGW **Ruler:** Juan Carlos I **Obv:** Bust of Fernando VI 1/4 right **Rev:** Crown above compass face within beaded circle
Date	Mintage	F	VF	XF	Unc	BU
1991	1,000	—	—	—	—	90.00
1991 Proof	2,000	Value: 90.00				

KM# 842 10000 PESETAS
3.3700 g., 0.9990 Gold .1084 oz. AGW **Ruler:** Juan Carlos I **Subject:** Discovery of America **Obv:** Crown above monogram within beaded circle **Rev:** Armillary sphere within beaded circle
Date	Mintage	F	VF	XF	Unc	BU
1989	5,000	—	—	—	—	95.00
1989 Proof	7,000	Value: 95.00				

KM# 871 10000 PESETAS
3.3700 g., 0.9990 Gold .1084 oz. AGW **Ruler:** Juan Carlos I **Series:** 1992 Olympics **Obv:** Bust right **Rev:** Stylized field hockey player
Date	Mintage	F	VF	XF	Unc	BU
1990	3,000	—	—	—	—	95.00
1990 Proof	5,000	Value: 95.00				

Note: Uncirculated strikes have medallic die alignment and edges with reeded and plain sections; Proof strikes have coin die alignment and reeded edges

KM# 872 10000 PESETAS
3.3700 g., 0.9990 Gold .1084 oz. AGW **Ruler:** Juan Carlos I **Series:** 1992 Olympics **Obv:** Bust right **Rev:** Stylized gymnast
Date	Mintage	F	VF	XF	Unc	BU
1990	2,000	—	—	—	—	100
1990 Proof	3,000	Value: 100				

Note: Uncirculated strikes have medallic die alignment and edges with reeded and plain sections; Proof strikes have coin die alignment and reeded edges

KM# 874 10000 PESETAS
3.3700 g., 0.9990 Gold .1084 oz. AGW **Ruler:** Juan Carlos I **Obv:** Quauchtemoc within beaded circle **Rev:** Crown above compass face within beaded circle
Date	Mintage	F	VF	XF	Unc	BU
1990	9,000	—	—	—	—	100
1990 Proof	2,000	Value: 100				

KM# 895 10000 PESETAS
3.3700 g., 0.9990 Gold .1084 oz. AGW **Ruler:** Juan Carlos I **Series:** Olympics **Obv:** Bust 3/4 right within circle **Rev:** Tae Kwon Do participant within circle
Date	Mintage	F	VF	XF	Unc	BU
1991	2,000	—	—	—	—	180
1991 Proof	3,000	Value: 180				

Note: Uncirculated strikes have medallic die alignment and edges with reeded and plain sections; Proof strikes have coin die alignment and reeded edges.

KM# 897 10000 PESETAS
3.3700 g., 0.9990 Gold .1084 oz. AGW **Ruler:** Juan Carlos I **Obv:** Tupac Amaru II within beaded circle **Rev:** Armillary sphere within beaded circle
Date	Mintage	F	VF	XF	Unc	BU
1991	1,000	—	—	—	—	150
1991 Proof	2,000	Value: 150				

KM# 915 10000 PESETAS
3.3700 g., 0.9990 Gold .1084 oz. AGW **Ruler:** Juan Carlos I **Series:** Olympics **Obv:** Bust 1/4 right within circle **Rev:** Baseball player within circle
Date	Mintage	F	VF	XF	Unc	BU
1992	1,000	—	—	—	—	180

SPAIN

Date | Mintage | F | VF | XF | Unc | BU
1992 Proof | 6,000 | | | | | Value: 180
Note: Uncirculated strikes have medallic die alignment and edges with reeded and plain sections; Proof strikes have coin die alignment and reeded edges

KM# 843 20000 PESETAS
6.7500 g., 0.9990 Gold .2170 oz. AGW **Ruler:** Juan Carlos I **Subject:** Discovery of America **Obv:** Head facing within beaded circle **Rev:** Pinzon Brother within beaded circle

Date	Mintage	F	VF	XF	Unc	BU
1989	5,000	—	—	—	—	160
1989 Proof	6,500	Value: 160				

KM# 875 20000 PESETAS
6.7500 g., 0.9990 Gold .2170 oz. AGW **Ruler:** Juan Carlos I **Subject:** 1992 Olympics - La Sagrada Familia **Obv:** Bust 1/4 right within beaded circle **Rev:** Cathedral towers within beaded circle

Date	Mintage	F	VF	XF	Unc	BU
1990	4,000	—	—	—	—	180
1990 Proof	10,000	Value: 180				

Note: Uncirculated strikes have medallic die alignment and edges with reeded and plain sections; Proof strikes have coin die alignment and reeded edges

KM# 876 20000 PESETAS
6.7500 g., 0.9990 Gold .2170 oz. AGW **Ruler:** Juan Carlos I **Series:** 1992 Olympics **Obv:** Bust 1/4 right within beaded circle **Rev:** Ruins of Empuries within beaded circle

Date	Mintage	F	VF	XF	Unc	BU
1990	2,000	—	—	—	—	180
1990 Proof	4,000	Value: 180				

Note: Uncirculated strikes have medallic die alignment and edges with reeded and plain sections; Proof strikes have coin die alignment and reeded edges

KM# 877 20000 PESETAS
6.7500 g., 0.9990 Gold .2170 oz. AGW **Ruler:** Juan Carlos I **Subject:** Tupac Amaru I **Obv:** Bust 1/4 right within beaded circle **Rev:** Stylized standing figure with hat and scepter within beaded circle

Date	Mintage	F	VF	XF	Unc	BU
1990	2,000	—	—	—	—	180
1990 Proof	3,000	Value: 180				

KM# 898 20000 PESETAS
6.7500 g., 0.9990 Gold .2170 oz. AGW **Ruler:** Juan Carlos I **Series:** Olympics **Obv:** Bust 1/4 right within circle **Rev:** Montjuic Stadium within circle

Date	Mintage	F	VF	XF	Unc	BU
1991	2,000	—	—	—	—	270
1991 Proof	3,000	Value: 270				

Note: Uncirculated strikes have medallic die alignment and edges with reeded and plain sections; Proof strikes have coin die alignment and reeded edges

KM# 899 20000 PESETAS
6.7500 g., 0.9990 Gold .2170 oz. AGW **Ruler:** Juan Carlos I **Subject:** Huascar **Obv:** Bust facing within beaded circle **Rev:** Armored bust with spear within beaded circle

Date	Mintage	F	VF	XF	Unc	BU
1991	1,000	—	—	—	—	240
1991 Proof	2,000	Value: 240				

KM# 916 20000 PESETAS
6.7500 g., 0.9990 Gold .2170 oz. AGW **Ruler:** Juan Carlos I **Series:** Olympics **Obv:** Bust 1/4 right within circle **Rev:** Dome building within circle

Date	Mintage	F	VF	XF	Unc	BU
1992	1,000	—	—	—	—	270
1992 Proof	3,000	Value: 270				

Note: Uncirculated strikes have medallic die alignment and edges with reeded and plain sections; Proof strikes have coin die alignment and reeded edges

KM# 1003 20000 PESETAS
6.7500 g., 0.9990 Gold .2170 oz. AGW **Ruler:** Juan Carlos I **Obv:** Bust facing within beaded circle **Rev:** Worker feeding screw press

Date	Mintage	F	VF	XF	Unc	BU
1992	1,000	—	—	—	—	270
1992 Proof	—	Value: 270				

KM# 929 20000 PESETAS
6.7500 g., 0.9990 Gold .2170 oz. AGW **Ruler:** Juan Carlos I **Subject:** Holy Jacobean Year **Rev:** Conveyance of Santiago's body

Date	Mintage	F	VF	XF	Unc	BU
1993 Proof	2,000	Value: 240				

KM# 944 20000 PESETAS
6.7500 g., 0.9990 Gold .2170 oz. AGW **Ruler:** Juan Carlos I **Subject:** Paleolithic Cave Painting **Rev:** Stylized animal cave paintings

Date	Mintage	F	VF	XF	Unc	BU
1994 Proof	8,000	Value: 260				

KM# 958 20000 PESETAS
6.7500 g., 0.9990 Gold .2170 oz. AGW **Ruler:** Juan Carlos I **Subject:** Ancient Sculpture - Dama de Elche **Rev:** Hooded bust left

Date	Mintage	F	VF	XF	Unc	BU
1995 Proof	8,000	Value: 220				

KM# 971 20000 PESETAS
6.7500 g., 0.9990 Gold .2170 oz. AGW **Ruler:** Juan Carlos I **Rev:** Pillars and arches

Date	Mintage	F	VF	XF	Unc	BU
1996 Proof	Est. 6,000	Value: 220				

KM# 844 40000 PESETAS
13.5000 g., 0.9990 Gold .4341 oz. AGW **Ruler:** Juan Carlos I **Subject:** Discovery of America **Obv:** Standing figure divides date and beaded circle **Rev:** Sea monster attacking ship within beaded circle

Date	Mintage	F	VF	XF	Unc	BU
1989	4,500	—	—	—	—	325
1989 Proof	6,000	Value: 325				

KM# 878 40000 PESETAS
13.5000 g., 0.9990 Gold .4341 oz. AGW **Ruler:** Juan Carlos I **Subject:** Felipe II **Obv:** Standing figure divides date and beaded circle **Rev:** King seated on throne within beaded circle

Date	Mintage	F	VF	XF	Unc	BU
1990	2,000	—	—	—	—	350
1990 Proof	3,000	Value: 350				

KM# 900 40000 PESETAS
13.5000 g., 0.9990 Gold .4341 oz. AGW **Ruler:** Juan Carlos I **Obv:** Standing figure divides beaded circle and dates **Rev:** Imperial double eagle

Date	Mintage	F	VF	XF	Unc	BU
1991	1,000	—	—	—	—	450
1991 Proof	2,000	Value: 450				

KM# 1004 40000 PESETAS
13.5000 g., 0.9990 Gold .4341 oz. AGW **Ruler:** Juan Carlos I **Obv:** Standing figure divides beaded circle and dates **Rev:** Horse-powered coin press

Date	Mintage	F	VF	XF	Unc	BU
1992	1,000	—	—	—	—	500
1992 Proof	—	Value: 500				

KM# 979 40000 PESETAS
13.5000 g., 0.9990 Gold .4341 oz. AGW **Ruler:** Juan Carlos I **Subject:** Patrimonio de la Humanidad **Obv:** UNESCO logo **Rev:** Statues at Abu Simbel

Date	Mintage	F	VF	XF	Unc	BU
1996 Proof	4,000	Value: 425				

KM# 1023 40000 PESETAS
13.5000 g., 0.9990 Gold .4341 oz. AGW, 30 mm. **Ruler:** Juan Carlos I **Series:** "Patrimonio de la Humanidad - UNESCO" **Obv:** UNESCO logo **Rev:** Horyu-Ji pagoda **Edge:** Reeded

SPAIN 655

Date **Mintage** F VF XF Unc BU
1997 Proof 4,000 Value: 425

KM# 845 80000 PESETAS
27.0000 g., 0.9990 Gold .8682 oz. AGW **Ruler:** Juan Carlos I **Subject:** Discovery of America **Obv:** Crowned busts of Juan Carlos and Sofia facing each other within beaded circle **Rev:** Crowned busts of Ferdinand and Isabella facing each other within beaded circle

Date	Mintage	F	VF	XF	Unc	BU
1989	6,000	—	—	—	—	640
1989 Proof	7,000	Value: 640				

KM# 879 80000 PESETAS
27.0000 g., 0.9990 Gold .8682 oz. AGW **Ruler:** Juan Carlos I **Series:** 1992 Olympics **Obv:** Royal family facing within circle **Rev:** Discus thrower within circle

Date	Mintage	F	VF	XF	Unc	BU
1990	3,000	—	—	—	—	640
1990 Proof	5,000	Value: 640				

Note: Uncirculated strikes have medallic die alignment and edges with reeded and plain sections; Proof strikes have coin die alignment and reeded edges

KM# 880 80000 PESETAS
27.0000 g., 0.9990 Gold .8682 oz. AGW **Ruler:** Juan Carlos I **Series:** 1992 Olympics **Obv:** Royal family facing **Rev:** Prince Balthasar Carlos on horseback

Date	Mintage	F	VF	XF	Unc	BU
1990	1,000	—	—	—	—	675
1990 Proof	4,000	Value: 675				

Note: Uncirculated strikes have medallic die alignment and edges with reeded and plain sections; Proof strikes have coin die alignment and reeded edges

KM# 881 80000 PESETAS
27.0000 g., 0.9990 Gold .8682 oz. AGW **Ruler:** Juan Carlos I **Subject:** Carlos V **Obv:** Crowned heads of Juan Carlos and Sofia facing each other within beaded circle **Rev:** Armored half-figure facing within beaded circle

Date	Mintage	F	VF	XF	Unc	BU
1990	2,000	—	—	—	—	675
1990 Proof	3,000	Value: 675				

KM# 901 80000 PESETAS
27.0000 g., 0.9990 Gold .8682 oz. AGW **Ruler:** Juan Carlos I **Series:** Olympics **Obv:** Royal family facing **Rev:** Women tossing man on blanket within circle

Date	Mintage	F	VF	XF	Unc	BU
1991	1,000	—	—	—	—	1,000
1991 Proof	2,000	Value: 1,000				

Note: Uncirculated strikes have medallic die alignment and edges with reeded and plain sections; Proof strikes have coin die alignment and reeded edges

KM# 902 80000 PESETAS
27.0000 g., 0.9990 Gold .8682 oz. AGW **Ruler:** Juan Carlos I **Subject:** Carlos III **Obv:** Crowned busts of Juan Carlos and Sofia facing each other within beaded circle **Rev:** Armored bust right within beaded circle

Date	Mintage	F	VF	XF	Unc	BU
1991	1,000	—	—	—	—	925
1991 Proof	2,000	Value: 925				

KM# 917 80000 PESETAS
27.0000 g., 0.9990 Gold .8682 oz. AGW **Ruler:** Juan Carlos I **Series:** Olympics **Rev:** Two children playing within circle

Date	Mintage	F	VF	XF	Unc	BU
1992	1,000	—	—	—	—	1,000
1992 Proof	2,000	Value: 1,000				

Note: Uncirculated strikes have medallic die alignment and edges with reeded and plain sections; Proof strikes have coin die alignment and reeded edges

KM# 1005 80000 PESETAS
27.0000 g., 0.9990 Gold .8682 oz. AGW **Ruler:** Juan Carlos I **Obv:** Crowned busts of Juan Carlos and Sofia facing each other within beaded circle **Rev:** Hammer minting scene

Date	Mintage	F	VF	XF	Unc	BU
1992	1,000	—	—	—	—	1,000
1992 Proof	—	Value: 1,000				

KM# 930 80000 PESETAS
27.0000 g., 0.9990 Gold .8682 oz. AGW **Ruler:** Juan Carlos I **Subject:** Holy Jacobean Year **Obv:** Head left **Rev:** French Fraternity of Santiago Medallion within beaded circle

Date	Mintage	F	VF	XF	Unc	BU
1993 Proof	1,500	Value: 850				

KM# 945 80000 PESETAS
27.0000 g., 0.9990 Gold .8682 oz. AGW **Ruler:** Juan Carlos I **Rev:** Iberian Lynx

Date	Mintage	F	VF	XF	Unc	BU
1994 Proof	5,000	Value: 750				

KM# 959 80000 PESETAS
27.0000 g., 0.9990 Gold .8682 oz. AGW **Ruler:** Juan Carlos I **Rev:** Leda and the Swan

Date	Mintage	F	VF	XF	Unc	BU
1995 Proof	5,000	Value: 800				

KM# 972 80000 PESETAS
27.0000 g., 0.9990 Gold .8682 oz. AGW **Ruler:** Juan Carlos I **Rev:** Folk dancers

Date	Mintage	F	VF	XF	Unc	BU
1996 Proof	Est. 3,500	Value: 800				

KM# 1028 80000 PESETAS
27.0000 g., 0.9990 Gold .8672 oz. AGW, 38 mm. **Ruler:** Juan Carlos I **Subject:** House of Borbon **Obv:** Head of Ferdinand VI right within circle and beaded border **Rev:** Crowned shield within circle and beaded border **Edge:** Reeded

Date	Mintage	F	VF	XF	Unc	BU
1997 Proof	4,000	Value: 800				

656 SPAIN

MEDALLIC COINAGE
Ecu Series

X# M25 10 ECU
3.4500 g., 0.9000 Gold .0998 oz. AGW, 16 mm. **Ruler:** Juan Carlos I **Obv:** Large value, 12 stars within small circle **Obv. Legend:** ESPAÑA **Rev:** Crowned pillars of Hercules **Rev. Inscription:** PLV SVL TRA **Edge:** Reeded **Note:** Prev. KM#M3 and Bruce#XM5.

Date	Mintage	F	VF	XF	Unc	BU
1989M Prooflike	28,040	Value: 120				

X# M19 25 ECU
168.7500 g., 0.9250 Silver 5.0185 oz. ASW, 73 mm. **Obv:** Three portraits **Rev:** Large sailing ships **Edge:** Plain **Note:** Illustration reduced.

Date	Mintage	F	VF	XF	Unc	BU
1995 Proof	75,000	Value: 150				

X# M26 50 ECU
17.2700 g., 0.9000 Gold .4997 oz. AGW, 28 mm. **Ruler:** Juan Carlos I **Obv:** Large value, 12 stars within circle **Obv. Legend:** ESPAÑA **Rev:** Bust of Philip II left **Rev. Legend:** : PHILIP • II • D • G • HISPAN • ET • IND • REX : **Edge:** Reeded **Note:** Prev. KM#M4 and Bruce#XM6.

Date	Mintage	F	VF	XF	Unc	BU
1989M Prooflike	15,310	Value: 450				

X# M27 100 ECU
34.5500 g., 0.9000 Gold .9997 oz. AGW **Ruler:** Juan Carlos I **Obv:** Large value, 12 stars within circle below **Obv. Legend:** ESPAÑA **Rev:** Charles V horseback right **Rev. Legend:** • CAES • CAROLVS • V • AVGVSTVS • IMPERATOR • **Edge:** Reeded **Note:** Prev. KM#M5 and Bruce#XM7.

Date	Mintage	F	VF	XF	Unc	BU
1989M Prooflike	10,000	Value: 1,000				

X# M38 100 ECU
34.5500 g., 0.9000 Gold 0.9997 oz. AGW, 40 mm. **Ruler:** Juan Carlos I **Series:** Madrid Culture **Obv:** Large value, 12 stars within small circle, Madrid emblem **Obv. Legend:** ESPAÑA **Rev:** Charles III standing facing **Rev. Legend:** MADRID CAPITAL EUROPEA DE LA CULTURE **Edge:** Reeded

Date	Mintage	F	VF	XF	Unc	BU
1992M Prooflike	10,000	—	—	—	850	—

X# M44 100 ECU
34.5500 g., 0.9000 Gold 0.9997 oz. AGW, 40 mm. **Ruler:** Juan Carlos I **Obv:** Large early sailing ship, 12 stars within small circle **Obv. Legend:** ESPAÑA **Rev:** Don Juan de Borbon seated, facing 3/4 right **Edge:** Reeded

Date	Mintage	F	VF	XF	Unc	BU
1993M Prooflike	2,020	—	—	—	950	—

X# M48 100 ECU
34.5500 g., 0.9000 Gold .9997 oz. AGW **Ruler:** Juan Carlos I **Obv:** Two riders on toy-like horse **Obv. Legend:** ESPAÑA **Obv. Designer:** B. Castellanos **Rev:** Bust of Cervantes facing 3/4 left **Rev. Legend:** MIGUEL DE CERVANTES **Edge:** Reeded

Date	Mintage	F	VF	XF	Unc	BU
1994M Prooflike	3,500	—	—	—	950	—

EURO COINAGE
European Union Issues

KM# 1075 200 EURO
13.5000 g., 0.9990 Gold 0.4336 oz. AGW, 30 mm. **Ruler:** Juan Carlos I **Obv:** Spanish King and Queen left **Rev:** Mythological Europa riding on the back of a bull **Note:** Birth of the Euro

Date	Mintage	F	VF	XF	Unc	BU
2003Crowned M Proof	20,000	Value: 500				

KM# 1062 200 EURO
13.5000 g., 0.9990 Gold 0.4336 oz. AGW, 30 mm. **Ruler:** Juan Carlos I **Obv:** Seated crowned figures on shield flanked by date and value **Rev:** Crowned busts facing each other on coin design **Edge:** Reeded

Date	Mintage	F	VF	XF	Unc	BU
2004Crowned Proof	5,000	Value: 540				

KM# 1066 200 EURO
13.5000 g., 0.9990 Gold 0.4336 oz. AGW, 30 mm. **Ruler:** Juan Carlos I **Subject:** European Peace and Freedom **Obv:** Juan Carlos **Rev:** European map on clasped hands **Edge:** Reeded

Date	Mintage	F	VF	XF	Unc	BU
2005Crowned M Proof	4,000	Value: 650				

KM# 1058 400 EURO
27.0000 g., 0.9990 Gold 0.8672 oz. AGW, 38 mm. **Ruler:** Juan Carlos I **Obv:** Bust facing **Rev:** Dali's painting "Girl at the Window" **Edge:** Reeded

Date	Mintage	F	VF	XF	Unc	BU
2004Crowned M Proof	5,000	Value: 975				

MEDALLIC COINAGE
Juan Carlos I Issue
X# M2 500 PESETAS
27.0000 g., Gold **Ruler:** Juan Carlos I **Subject:** Last Barcelona 5 Peseta of 1808 Commemorative

Date	Mintage	F	VF	XF	Unc	BU
1978	500	—	—	—	550	—

PROOF SETS

KM#	Date	Mintage	Identification	Issue Price	Mkt Val
PS11	1989 (5)	—	KM#M1-M5	—	950
PS12	1989 (5)	—	KM#840, 842-845	3,177	1,775
PS16	1995 (6)	I.A.	KM#938, 953, 956-959	—	1,350
PS17	1995 (4)	25,000	KM#938, 953, 956-959	—	300
PS18	1996 (6)	—	KM#966-967, 969-972	1,675	1,300
PS19	1996 (6)	—	KM#966-967, 969-972	1,650	1,300
PS20	1996 (4)	—	KM#966-967, 969-972	—	240
PS23	1996 (6)	—	KM#973-979	702	600

PROOF-LIKE SETS (PL)

KM#	Date	Mintage	Identification	Issue Price	Mkt Val
XPS1	1989M (5)	—	X23-27	—	1,700
XPS2	1992M (4)	—	X35-38	—	1,000
XPS3	1993M (2)	—	X43, X44	—	950

CATALONIA

Catalonia, a triangular territory forming the northeast corner of the Iberian Peninsula, was formerly a province of Spain and also formerly a principality of Aragon. In 1833 the region was divided into four provinces, Barcelona, Gerona, Lerida and Tarragona.

RULERS
Ferdinand (Fernando) VII, 1808-1833
Isabel II, 1833-1868

MINT MARK
C – Catalonia

MONETARY SYSTEM
12 Ardites (Dineros) = 8 Ochavos =
4 Quartos = 1 Sueldo
6 Sueldos = 1 Peseta
5 Pesetas = 1 Duro

AUTONOMOUS COMMUNITY

MEDALLIC COINAGE
Ecu Series - Sertons International, Barcelona
X# M13 250 ECU
25.4500 g., 0.9167 Gold 0.7501 oz. AGW, 38 mm. **Subject:** 20th Anniversary Death of Composer Pau Casals **Obv:** Eight stylized figures above arms **Obv. Legend:** CATALUNYA **Rev:** Casals playing cello behind music score **Edge:** Reeded

Date	Mintage	F	VF	XF	Unc	BU
1993 Proof	1,000	Value: 750				

X# M16 250 ECU
25.4500 g., 0.9167 Gold 0.7501 oz. AGW, 38 mm. **Obv:** Eight stylized figures above arms **Obv. Legend:** CATALUNYA **Rev:** Bust of Josep Pla i Casadevall, journalist and scriptwriter 3/4 left, open book behind

Date	Mintage	F	VF	XF	Unc	BU
1994 Proof	1,000	Value: 750				

MEDALLIC COINAGE
Ecu Series - Uncertain Issuer
X# M20 100 ECU
34.5500 g., 0.9000 Gold 0.9997 oz. AGW, 40 mm. **Obv:** Arms **Obv. Legend:** VINDICAMUS HEREDITATEM PATRUM NOSTRORUM **Rev:** Ehric Prat de la Riba i Sarrà **Edge:** Reeded

Date	Mintage	F	VF	XF	Unc	BU
1993C Proof	3,100	Value: 950				

X# M21 1000 ECU
337.5000 g., 0.9000 Gold 9.7658 oz. AGW, 73 mm. **Obv:** Arms **Obv. Legend:** VINDICAMUS HEREDITATEM PATRUM NOSTRORUM **Rev:** Francesc Macià i Llusà **Edge:** Reeded

Date	Mintage	F	VF	XF	Unc	BU
1993C Proof	200	Value: 8,000				

PROOF SETS

KM#	Date	Mintage	Identification	Issue Price	Mkt Val
XPS1	1993c (5)	100	X17-21	—	9,000

VALENCIA

Valencia is a maritime province of eastern Spain with a capital city of Valencia. Once a former kingdom, Valencia included the present provinces of Castellon de la Plana and Alicante.

RULERS
Ferdinand (Fernando) VII, 1808-1833

PROVINCE
STANDARD COINAGE
KM# 50 1/2 ESCUDO
1.6917 g., 0.9170 Gold .0499 oz. AGW **Obv:** Crowned diamond shield with vertical stripes, L at each side **Rev:** Helmeted arms

Date	Mintage	VG	F	VF	XF	Unc
ND	—	225	450	900	1,500	—

SRI (SHRI) LANKA

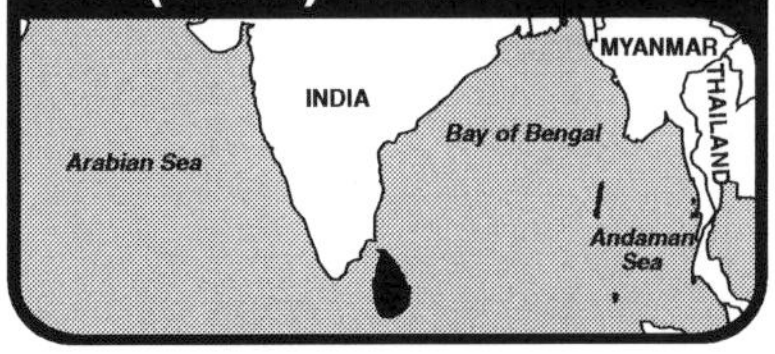

The Democratic Socialist Republic of Sri Lanka (formerly Ceylon) situated in the Indian Ocean 18 miles (29 km.) southeast of India, has an area of 25,332 sq. mi. (65,610 sq. km.) and a population of *16.9 million. Capital: Colombo. The economy is chiefly agricultural. Tea, coconut products and rubber are exported.

Sri Lanka remains a member of the Commonwealth of Nations. The president is Chief of State. The prime minister is Head of Government. The present leaders of the country have reverted the country name back to Sri Lanka.

RULER
British, 1796-1948

DEMOCRATIC SOCIALIST REPUBLIC

DECIMAL COINAGE
100 Cents = 1 Rupee

KM# 144a RUPEE
Gold **Subject:** Inauguration of President Jayawardene **Obv:** Head left **Rev:** Navy emblem

Date	Mintage	F	VF	XF	Unc	BU
1978 Proof	40	—	—	—	—	—

KM# 151b RUPEE
0.9167 Gold **Subject:** 3rd Anniversary of 2nd Executive President Premadusa **Obv:** Lions with swords above rectangular design **Rev:** Bust facing within wreath

Date	Mintage	F	VF	XF	Unc	BU
1992 Proof	100	—	—	—	—	—

KM# 153 500 RUPEES
1.6000 g., 0.5000 Gold .0257 oz. AGW **Subject:** 5th South Asian Federation Games **Obv:** Stylized seated figure **Rev:** Value above logo and inscription

Date	Mintage	F	VF	XF	Unc	BU
1991 Proof	8,000	Value: 50.00				

KM# 160 5000 RUPEES
7.9800 g., 0.9167 Gold .2352 oz. AGW **Subject:** 50 Years of Independence **Obv:** Flag and value within wreath **Rev:** Avalokitheshvara, an aspirant Buddha, seated in a graceful stance within circle

Date	Mintage	F	VF	XF	Unc	BU
1998 Proof	5,000	Value: 245				

REVOLUTION

TAX REFUND TOKEN
Liberation Tigers of Tamil Eelam

X# Tn1 8 GRAMS
8.0000 g., 0.8333 Gold 0.2143 oz. AGW, 22.7 mm. **Obv:** Tiger head facing **Obv. Legend:** "Thamil Eelam Veeduthalai Puligal" **Obv. Inscription:** LIBERATION / TIGERS OF / TAMIL EELAM **Rev. Legend:** "Thamil Eela Meedpunithi - Kadan Meelal" (Tamil Eelam Savings - Fund - Loan Returned) **Rev. Inscription:** "20 Ma / 8 Giram / Aadee 1990" **Edge:** Reeded

Date	Mintage	F	VF	XF	Unc	BU
1990 Rare	—	—	—	—	—	—

Note: A tax was imposed of 2 gold sovereigns and at a later date, some families were refunded with this token. Most were remelted.

STRAITS SETTLEMENTS

Straits Settlements, a former British crown colony situated on the Malay Peninsula of Asia, was formed in 1826 by combining the territories of Singapore, Penang and Malacca. The colony was administered by the East India Company until its abolition in 1858. Straits Settlements was a part of British India from 1858 to 1867 at which time it became a Crown Colony.

The Straits Settlements coinage gradually became acceptable legal tender in the neighboring Federated as well as the Unfederated Malay States. The Straits Settlements were dissolved in 1946, while the coinage continued to circulate until demonetized at the end of 1952.

RULER
British

MINT MARKS
H - Heaton, Birmingham
W - Soho Mint
B - Bombay

MONETARY SYSTEM
100 Cents = 1 Dollar

PATTERNS
Including off metal strikes

KM#	Date	Mintage	Identification	Mkt Val
Pn6	1891	—	1/4 Cent. Gold. KM#14.	20,000
Pn8	1891	—	1/2 Cent. Gold. KM#15.	20,000
Pn10	1891	—	Cent. Gold. KM#16.	18,000

SUDAN

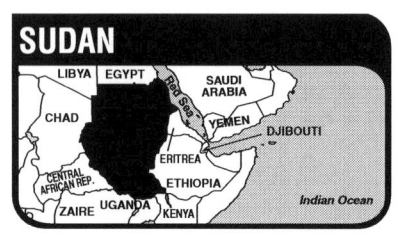

The Democratic Republic of the Sudan, located in northeast Africa on the Red Sea between Egypt and Ethiopia, has an area of 967,500 sq. mi. (2,505,810 sq. km.) and a population of *24.5 million. Capital: Khartoum. Agriculture and livestock raising are the chief occupations. Cotton, gum arabic and peanuts are exported.

The Sudan, site of the powerful Nubian kingdom of Roman times, was a collection of small independent states from the 14th century until 1820-22 when it was conquered and united by Mohammed Ali, Pasha of Egypt. Egyptian forces were driven from the area during the Mahdist revolt, 1881-98, but the Sudan was retaken by Anglo-Egyptian expeditions, 1896-98, and established as an Anglo-Egyptian condominium in 1899. Britain supplied the administrative apparatus and personnel, but the appearance of joint Anglo-Egyptian administration was continued until Jan. 9, 1954, when the first Sudanese self-government parliament was inaugurated. The Sudan achieved independence on Jan. 1, 1956 with the consent of the British and Egyptian government.

TITLES

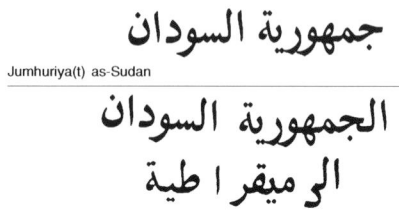

جمهورية السودان

Jumhuriya(t) as-Sudan

الجمهورية السودان الى ميقراطية

Al-Arabiya(t) as-Sa'udiya(t)al-Jumhuriya(t) as-Sudan ad-Dimiqratiya(t)

MINT NAME

مالناپور

Omdurman

EGYPTIAN POSSESSION

Mohammed Ahmed
AH1298-1302/1881-85AD
(the Mahdi)

REVOLUTIONARY COINAGE

Mint: Khartoum
KM# 3 100 PIASTRES
Gold **Note:** Struck by the Mahdi, which is a copy of the Egyptian coin 100 Qirsh, KM#235.1 under the Ottoman sultan. This issue is more crude than the Egyptian type and has crude edge milling. Reverse Arabic legend "Struck in Misr AH1255 Year 2" (Egypt); however they were struck in the Sudan about AH1302.

Date	Mintage	VG	F	VF	XF	Unc
AH1255-2	—	—	2,000	3,500	—	—

REPUBLIC

STANDARD COINAGE

KM# 78 25 POUNDS
8.2500 g., 0.9170 Gold .2432 oz. AGW **Subject:** Khartoum Meeting of O.A.U. **Obv:** Eagle divides value **Rev:** African map within circle

Date	Mintage	F	VF	XF	Unc
AH1398-1978	15	—	—	—	600
AH1398-1978 Proof	467	Value: 225			

Note: Without countermarks
AH1398-1978 Proof 350 Value: 180
Note: With countermarks of B23 in hexagon and bell between dates

KM# 82 25 POUNDS
8.2500 g., 0.9170 Gold .2432 oz. AGW **Subject:** 1,400th Anniversary of Islam **Obv:** Eagle divides value **Rev:** Buildings and upright design

Date	Mintage	F	VF	XF	Unc
AH1400-1980	7,500	—	—	—	170
AH1400-1980 Proof	5,500	Value: 180			

KM# 79 50 POUNDS
17.5000 g., 0.9170 Gold .5160 oz. AGW **Subject:** Khartoum Meeting of O.A.U. **Obv:** Eagle divides value **Rev:** African map within circle

Date	Mintage	F	VF	XF	Unc
AH1398-1978	11	—	—	—	1,500
AH1398-1978 Proof	211	Value: 420			

Note: Without countermarks
AH1398-1978 Proof 350 Value: 380
Note: With countermarks of B23 in hexagon and bell between dates

KM# 83 50 POUNDS
17.5000 g., 0.9170 Gold .5160 oz. AGW **Subject:** 1,400th Anniversary of Islam **Obv:** Eagle divides value **Rev:** Buildings and upright design

Date	Mintage	F	VF	XF	Unc
AH1400-1979	3,000	—	—	—	365
AH1400-1979 Proof	2,000	Value: 400			

KM# 89 50 POUNDS
7.9900 g., 0.9170 Gold .2353 oz. AGW **Subject:** 25th Anniversary of Independence

Date	Mintage	F	VF	XF	Unc
AH1401-1981	5,000	—	—	—	165
AH1401-1981 Proof	5,000	Value: 185			

KM# 72 100 POUNDS
33.4370 g., 0.9000 Gold .9676 oz. AGW **Subject:** Conservation **Obv:** Eagle divides dates **Rev:** Scimitar-horned oryx

Date	Mintage	F	VF	XF	Unc
AH1396-1976	872	—	—	—	700
AH1396-1976 Proof	251	Value: 750			

KM# 90 100 POUNDS
15.9800 g., 0.9170 Gold .4706 oz. AGW **Subject:** 25th Anniversary of Independence

Date	Mintage	F	VF	XF	Unc
AH1401-1981	2,500	—	—	—	325
AH1401-1981 Proof	2,500	Value: 375			

KM# 91 100 POUNDS
15.9800 g., 0.9170 Gold .4706 oz. AGW **Series:** Year of the Disabled Person **Obv:** Eagle divides value **Rev:** Stylized arrowhead within wreath

Date	Mintage	F	VF	XF	Unc
AH1401-1981	2,000	—	—	—	375
AH1401-1981 Proof	2,000	Value: 475			

KM# 93 100 POUNDS
8.1000 g., 0.9170 Gold .2388 oz. AGW **Series:** Decade for Women **Obv:** Eagle divides value **Rev:** Half female figure facing right

Date	Mintage	F	VF	XF	Unc
AH1404-1984 Proof	513	Value: 225			

ESSAIS

KM#	Date	Mintage	Identification	Mkt Val
E5	AH1978	25	25 Pounds. Aluminum. .	40.00
E6	AH1978	21	25 Pounds. Copper. .	75.00
E7	AH1978	25	50 Pounds. Aluminum. .	40.00
E8	AH1978	21	50 Pounds. Copper. .	85.00
E12	AH1979	21	50 Pounds. Copper. . KM83.	85.00
E17	AH1980	25	25 Pounds. Aluminum. .	40.00
E18	AH1980	20	25 Pounds. Copper. .	75.00
E19	AH1980	25	50 Pounds. Aluminum. .	40.00
E20	AH1980	21	50 Pounds. Copper. .	85.00

PIEFORTS

KM#	Date	Mintage	Identification	Mkt Val
P5	AH1978	5	25 Pounds. Copper. .	185
P10	AH1979	—	25 Pounds. Brass. . KM83.	185
P11	AH1979	10	25 Pounds. Silver. 22.5 mm. KM83.	185
P12	AH1979	—	50 Pounds. Copper. KM83. Gold plated.	—
P15	AH1980	5	25 Pounds. Copper.	185
P16	AH1979	—	50 Pounds. Gold. KM83.	—
P19	AH1981	Est. 500	100 Pounds. Gold. KM91.	1,350

PROOF SETS

KM#	Date	Mintage	Identification	Issue Price	Mkt Val
PS7	1978 (4)	Est. 500	KM76-79	—	625
PS9	1980 (4)	Est. 500	KM80-83	—	645

SURINAME

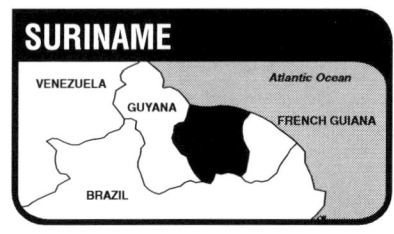

SURINAME

The Republic of Suriname also known as Dutch Guiana, located on the north central coast of South America between Guyana and French Guiana has an area of 63,037 sq. mi. (163,270 sq. km.) and a population of *433,000. Capital: Paramaribo. The country is rich in minerals and forests, and self-sufficient in rice, the staple food crop. The mining, processing and exporting of bauxite is the principal economic activity.

Lieutenants of Amerigo Vespucci sighted the Guiana coast in 1499. Spanish explorers of the 16th century, disappointed at finding no gold, departed leaving the area to be settled by the British in 1652. The colony prospered and the Netherlands acquired it in 1667 in exchange for the Dutch rights in Nieuw Nederland (state of New York). During the European wars of the 18th and 19th centuries, which were fought in part in the new world, Suriname was occupied by the British from 1781-1784 and 1796-1814. Suriname became an autonomous part of the Kingdom of the Netherlands on Dec. 15, 1954. Full independence was achieved on Nov. 25, 1975. In 1980, a coup installed a military government, which has since been dissolved.

RULER
Dutch, until 1975

MINT MARKS
(B) - British Royal Mint, no mint mark
FM - Franklin Mint, U.S.A.**
P - Philadelphia, U.S.A.
S - Sydney
(u) - Utrecht (privy marks only)
**NOTE: From 1975-1985 the Franklin Mint produced coinage in up to 3 different qualities. Qualities of issue are designated in ( ) after each date and are defined as follows:
(M) MATTE - Normal circulation strike or a dull finish produced by sandblasting special uncirculated (polish finish) or proof quality dies.
(U) SPECIAL UNCIRCULATED - Polished or prooflike in appearance without any frosted features.
(P) PROOF - The highest quality obtainable having mirror-like fields and frosted features.

MONETARY SYSTEM
100 Cents = 1 Gulden (Guilders)

After January, 2004
1 Dollar = 100 Cents

REPUBLIC
MODERN COINAGE

KM# 18a 100 GULDEN
6.7200 g., 0.9000 Yellow Gold .1945 oz. AGW **Subject:** 1st Anniversary of Independence **Obv:** Flag, Surinam map, rising sun within circle **Rev:** Arms with supporters divide date
Date	Mintage	F	VF	XF	Unc	BU
1976(u)	19,100	—	—	—	—	135
1976(u) Proof	4,749	Value: 145				

KM# 18b 100 GULDEN
6.7200 g., 0.9000 Red Gold 0.1944 oz. AGW **Subject:** 1st Anniversary of Independence **Obv:** Flag, Surinam map, rising sun within circle **Rev:** Arms with supporters divide date
Date	Mintage	F	VF	XF	Unc	BU
1976(u)	900	—	—	—	175	200

KM# 20 200 GULDEN
7.1200 g., 0.5000 Gold .1144 oz. AGW **Subject:** 1st Anniversary of Revolution **Obv:** Revolution monument **Rev:** Allegorical group of revolutionaries **Edge:** Reeded
Date	Mintage	F	VF	XF	Unc	BU
1981FM (U)	11,000	—	—	—	130	—
1981FM (P) Proof	1,363	Value: 175				

KM# 22 250 GUILDER
6.7200 g., 0.9000 Gold .1945 oz. AGW **Subject:** 5th Anniversary of Revolution **Obv:** Dove and "10" on map-shaped flag **Rev:** Stylized fist on star design **Edge:** Reeded
Date	Mintage	F	VF	XF	Unc	BU
1985(u)	5,000	—	—	—	150	160
1985(u) Proof	200	Value: 225				

KM# 33 250 GUILDER
7.9800 g., 0.9170 Gold .2353 oz. AGW **Subject:** World Cup Soccer **Obv:** Arms with supporters within wreath **Rev:** Soccer player R. Gullit, stadium and half-globe **Rev. Designer:** Willem Vis **Edge:** Reeded
Date	Mintage	F	VF	XF	Unc	BU
1990(B) Proof	1,000	Value: 225				

KM# 37 250 GUILDER
7.9800 g., 0.9170 Gold .2353 oz. AGW **Series:** Save the Children **Obv:** Arms with supporters within wreath **Rev:** Children looking at spider web **Rev. Designer:** Willem Vis **Edge:** Reeded
Date	Mintage	F	VF	XF	Unc	BU
1991 Proof	3,000	Value: 200				
1992	—	—	—	—	165	—

KM# 25 500 GUILDER
7.9800 g., 0.9170 Gold .2353 oz. AGW **Subject:** 43rd General Assembly, Military Sports Organization CISM **Obv:** Arms with supporters **Rev:** Globe, laurel wreath, rings and sword within flower design **Edge:** Reeded
Date	Mintage	F	VF	XF	Unc	BU
ND(1988)(B) Proof	2,500	Value: 200				

KM# 29 500 GUILDER
7.9800 g., 0.9170 Gold .2353 oz. AGW **Series:** Seoul Olympics **Subject:** Anthony Nesty, butterfly gold medalist **Obv:** Arms with supporters within wreath **Rev:** Swimmer within circle **Edge:** Reeded
Date	Mintage	F	VF	XF	Unc	BU
1988(B) Proof	Est. 2,000	Value: 225				

KM# 31 500 GUILDER
7.9800 g., 0.9170 Gold .2353 oz. AGW **Subject:** 125th Anniversary - De Surinaamsche Bank **Obv:** Arms with supporters **Rev:** Abstract design **Edge:** Reeded **Designer:** Robert Elderton
Date	Mintage	F	VF	XF	Unc	BU
1990(B) Proof	Est. 2,000	Value: 250				

KM# 35 500 GUILDER
7.9800 g., 0.9170 Gold .2353 oz. AGW **Subject:** 15th Anniversary of Independence **Obv:** Arms with supporters within wreath **Rev:** Floral design **Edge:** Reeded
Date	Mintage	F	VF	XF	Unc	BU
ND(1990)(B) Proof	Est. 1,250	Value: 275				

KM# 39 500 GUILDER
7.9800 g., 0.9170 Gold .2353 oz. AGW **Subject:** 35th Anniversary of Central Bank **Obv:** Arms with supporters **Rev:** Symetric arrow design and dates within circle and legend **Edge:** Reeded
Date	Mintage	F	VF	XF	Unc	BU
1992(B) Proof	Est. 300	Value: 325				

KM# 26 1000 GUILDER
15.9800 g., 0.9170 Gold .4708 oz. AGW **Subject:** 40th Anniversary - Military Sports Organization CISM **Obv:** Arms with supporters **Rev:** Globe, laurel wreath, rings and sword within flower design **Edge:** Reeded
Date	Mintage	F	VF	XF	Unc	BU
ND(1988)(B) Proof	1,250	Value: 375				

KM# 48 1000 GUILDER
4.8000 g., Gold Plated Brass .4708 oz. **Series:** Olympics **Obv:** Arms with supporters **Rev:** Three cyclists **Edge:** Reeded **Note:** Struck at Capetown.
Date	Mintage	F	VF	XF	Unc	BU
1992	—	—	—	—	—	—

KM# 48a 1000 GUILDER
7.9800 g., 0.9170 Gold .2355 oz. AGW **Series:** Olympics **Obv:** Arms with supporters **Rev:** Three cyclists **Edge:** Reeded **Note:** Struck at Capetown.
Date	Mintage	F	VF	XF	Unc	BU
1992 Proof	400	Value: 250				

KM# 51 50000 GULDEN
7.9800 g., 0.9170 Gold .2353 oz. AGW **Subject:** Hindu Immigration **Obv:** Arms with supporters **Rev:** Hindu couple with ship in background **Edge:** Reeded
Date	Mintage	F	VF	XF	Unc	BU
ND(1998)(B) Proof	Est. 1,000	Value: 350				

KM# 53 75000 GULDEN
7.9800 g., 0.9170 Gold .2353 oz. AGW **Subject:** Coppename Bridge **Edge:** Reeded
Date	Mintage	F	VF	XF	Unc	BU
1999 Proof	1,000	Value: 375				

KM# 54 100000 GULDEN
7.9800 g., 0.9170 Gold .2353 oz. AGW **Subject:** 25th Anniversary of Independence **Obv:** Arms with supporters **Edge:** Reeded
Date	Mintage	F	VF	XF	Unc	BU
2000 Proof	1,000	Value: 400				

KM# 55 100000 GULDEN
7.9800 g., 0.9170 Gold 0.2353 oz. AGW **Subject:** River Bridge **Obv:** Arms with supporters **Rev:** Bridge over Suriam River **Edge:** Reeded
Date	Mintage	F	VF	XF	Unc	BU
2000 Proof	1,000	Value: 400				

KM# 56 100000 GULDEN
7.9800 g., 0.9170 Gold 0.2353 oz. AGW **Subject:** Millennium 2000-2001 **Obv:** Arms with supporters **Rev:** Circles **Edge:** Reeded
Date	Mintage	F	VF	XF	Unc	BU
2000 Proof	1,500	Value: 450				

KM# 57 125,000 GULDEN
15.0000 g., 0.5850 Gold 0.2821 oz. AGW **Subject:** Millennium 2000-2001 **Obv:** Arms with supporters **Rev:** Circles **Edge:** Reeded
Date	Mintage	F	VF	XF	Unc	BU
2000 Proof	2,500	Value: 400				

KM# 64 400 DOLLARS
Gold **Subject:** 30 Years of Independence
Date	Mintage	F	VF	XF	Unc	BU
2006	—	—	—	—	—	500

PROOF SETS

KM#	Date	Mintage	Identification	Issue Price	Mkt Val
PS4	1976 (3)	—	KM16-18	145	160

SWAZILAND

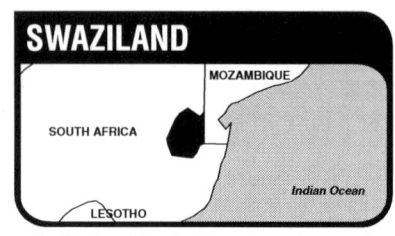

The Kingdom of Swaziland, located in southeastern Africa, has an area of 6,704 sq. mi. (17,360 sq. km.) and a population of *756,000. Capital: Mbabane (administrative); Lobamba (legislative). The diversified economy includes mining, agriculture, and light industry. Asbestos, iron ore, wood pulp, and sugar are exported.

The people of the present Swazi nation established themselves in an area including what is now Swaziland in the early 1800s. The first Swazi contact with the British came early in the reign of the extremely able Swazi leader Mswati when he asked the British for aid against Zulu raids into Swaziland. The British and Transvaal responded by guaranteeing the independence of Swaziland, 1881. South Africa assumed the power of protection and administration in 1894 and Swaziland continued under this administration until the conquest of the Transvaal during the Anglo-Boer War, when administration was transferred to the British government. After World War II, Britain began to prepare Swaziland for independence, which was achieved on Sept. 6, 1968. The Kingdom is a member of the Commonwealth of Nations. King Mswati III is Head of State. The prime minister is Head of Government.

RULERS
Sobhuza II, 1968-1982
Queen Dzeliwe, Regent for
Prince Makhosetive, 1982-1986
King Msawati III, 1986-

MONETARY SYSTEM
100 Cents = 1 Luhlanga
25 Luhlanga = 1 Lilangeni
(plural - Emalangeni)

KINGDOM
STANDARD COINAGE
100 Cents = 1 Luhlanga; 25 Luhlanga = 1 Lilangeni

KM# 6 LILANGENI
33.9305 g., 0.9170 Gold 1 oz. AGW **Ruler:** Sobhuza II **Subject:** Independence Commemorative **Obv:** Head 3/4 left **Rev:** Arms with supporters **Designer:** Tommy Sasseen **Note:** Approximately 1,450 melted.

Date	Mintage	F	VF	XF	Unc	BU
1968 Proof	2,000	Value: 675				

DECIMAL COINAGE
100 Cents = 1 Lilangeni (plural emelangeni)

KM# 29.1 LILANGENI
15.5500 g., 0.9990 Gold .5 oz. AGW **Ruler:** Sobhuza II **Subject:** 80th Anniversary - Birth of King Sobhuza II **Obv:** Head 1/4 right **Rev:** Arms with supporters

Date	Mintage	F	VF	XF	Unc	BU
ND(1979)	1,250	—	—	—	350	—
ND(1979) Proof	Inc. above	Value: 375				

KM# 29.2 LILANGENI
15.5500 g., 0.9990 Gold .5 oz. AGW **Ruler:** Sobhuza II **Subject:** 80th Anniversary - Birth of King Sobhuza II **Obv:** Head 1/4 right **Rev:** Dates 1923-1979 above arms with supporters

Date	Mintage	F	VF	XF	Unc	BU
ND(1979)	—	—	—	—	400	—

KM# 15 5 EMALANGENI
5.5600 g., 0.9000 Gold .1609 oz. AGW **Ruler:** Sobhuza II **Subject:** 75th Anniversary - Birth of King Sobhuza II **Obv:** Head 1/4 right **Rev:** Arms with supporters within circle

Date	Mintage	F	VF	XF	Unc	BU
1974 Proof	60,000	Value: 120				

KM# 17 10 EMALANGENI
11.1200 g., 0.9000 Gold .3218 oz. AGW **Ruler:** Sobhuza II **Subject:** 75th Anniversary - Birth of King Sobhuza II **Obv:** Head 1/4 right **Rev:** Standing figure divides date and value within circle **Shape:** Scalloped

Date	Mintage	F	VF	XF	Unc	BU
1974 Proof	Est. 40,000	Value: 275				

KM# 19 20 EMALANGENI
22.2300 g., 0.9000 Gold .6433 oz. AGW **Ruler:** Sobhuza II **Subject:** 75th Anniversary - Birth of King Sobhuza II **Obv:** Head 1/4 right **Rev:** Child facing and UNICEF emblem **Shape:** 10-sided

Date	Mintage	F	VF	XF	Unc	BU
1974 Proof	Est. 25,000	Value: 450				

KM# 20 25 EMALANGENI
27.7800 g., 0.9000 Gold .8039 oz. AGW **Ruler:** Sobhuza II **Subject:** 75th Anniversary - Birth of King Sobhuza II **Obv:** Head 1/4 right **Rev:** Conjoined busts facing within circle

Date	Mintage	F	VF	XF	Unc	BU
1974	Est. 15,000	—	—	—	—	565

KM# 26 50 EMALANGENI
4.3100 g., 0.9000 Gold .1247 oz. AGW **Ruler:** Sobhuza II **Subject:** 75th Anniversary - Birth of King Sobhuza II **Obv:** Head 1/4 right **Rev:** Antelope

Date	Mintage	F	VF	XF	Unc	BU
1975	3,510	—	—	—	95.00	100
1975 Proof	3,262	Value: 110				

KM# 27 100 EMALANGENI
8.6400 g., 0.9000 Gold .25 oz. AGW **Ruler:** Sobhuza II **Subject:** 75th Anniversary - Birth of King Sobhuza II **Obv:** Head 1/4 right **Rev:** Bust 1/4 left

Date	Mintage	F	VF	XF	Unc	BU
ND(1975)	1,000	—	—	—	185	195
ND(1975) Proof	1,000	Value: 225				

KM# 35 250 EMALANGENI
15.9800 g., 0.9170 Gold .4711 oz. AGW **Ruler:** Sobhuza II **Subject:** Diamond Jubilee of King Sobhuza II **Obv:** Head 1/4 right **Rev:** Elephant

Date	Mintage	F	VF	XF	Unc	BU
1981	2,000	—	—	—	325	345
1981 Proof	2,000	Value: 375				

KM# 38 250 EMALANGENI
15.9800 g., 0.9170 Gold .4711 oz. AGW **Ruler:** King Msawati III **Subject:** Accession of King Makhosetive **Obv:** Bust facing **Rev:** Bust facing

Date	Mintage	F	VF	XF	Unc	BU
ND(1986)	250	—	—	—	345	365
ND(1986) Proof	250	Value: 400				

GOLD BULLION COINAGE

KM# 30 2 EMALANGENI
31.1000 g., 0.9990 Gold 1 oz. AGW **Ruler:** Sobhuza II **Subject:** 80th Anniversary - Birth of King Sobhuza II **Obv:** Head 1/4 right **Rev:** Young bust of Queen Elizabeth II right

Date	Mintage	F	VF	XF	Unc	BU
ND(1979)	1,250	—	—	—	675	700
ND(1979) Proof	Inc. above	Value: 725				

KM# 36 5 EMALANGENI
31.1000 g., 0.9990 Gold 1 oz. AGW **Ruler:** Sobhuza II **Subject:** Queen Elizabeth II's Silver Jubilee **Obv:** Head 1/4 right within circle **Rev:** Crowned bust of Queen Elizabeth II facing divides dates within circle

Date	Mintage	F	VF	XF	Unc	BU
ND(1978) Proof	—	Value: 725				

SWEDEN

MINT SETS

KM#	Date	Mintage	Identification	Issue Price	Mkt Val
MS2	1975 (3)	1,000	KM25-27	—	310

PROOF SETS

KM#	Date	Mintage	Identification	Issue Price	Mkt Val
PS3	1974 (4)	—	KM15, 17, 19, 20	745	1,300
PS4	1974 (3)	—	KM14, 16, 17	70.00	390
PS5	1975 (3)	—	KM25-27	—	395
PS6	1975 (2)	—	KM26-27	252	335
PS8	1979 (2)	—	KM29.1, 30	1,172	1,100

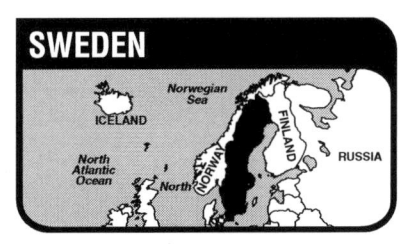

The Kingdom of Sweden, a limited constitutional monarchy located in northern Europe between Norway and Finland, has an area of 173,732 sq. mi. (449,960 sq. km.) and a population of *8.5 million. Capital: Stockholm. Mining, lumbering and a specialized machine industry dominate the economy. Machinery, paper, iron and steel, motor vehicles and wood pulp are exported.

Olaf Skottkonung founded Sweden as a Christian stronghold late in the 10th century. After conquering Finland late in the 13th century, Sweden, together with Norway, came under the rule of Denmark, 1397-1523, in an association known as the Union of Kalmar. Modern Sweden had its beginning in 1523 when Gustaf Vasa drove the Danes out of Sweden and was himself chosen king. Under Gustaf Adolphus II and Charles XII, Sweden was one of the great powers of 17th century Europe – until Charles invaded Russia in 1708, and was defeated at the Battle of Pultowa in June, 1709. Early in the 18th century, a coalition of Russia, Poland and Denmark took away Sweden's Baltic empire and in 1809 Sweden was forced to cede Finland to Russia. The Treaty of Kiel ceded Norway to Sweden in January 1814. The Norwegians resisted for a time but later signed the Act of Union at the Convention of Moss in August 1814, The Union was dissolved in 1905 and Norway became independent. A new constitution that took effect on Jan. 1, 1975, restricts the function of the king largely to a ceremonial role.

RULERS
Gustaf IV Adolf, 1792-1809
Carl XIII, 1809-1818
Carl XIV Johan, 1818-1844
Oscar I, 1844-1859
Carl XV Adolf, 1859-1872
Oscar II, 1872-1907
Gustaf V, 1907-1950
Gustaf VI, 1950-1973
Carl XVI Gustaf, 1973-

MINT OFFICIALS' INITIALS

Initials	Date	Name
AG, G	1838-55	Alexander Grandinson
AL	1898-1916	Adolf Lindberg, engraver
CB	1821-37	Christopher Borg
D	1986-	Bengt Dennis
EB	1876-1908	Emil Brusewitz
EL	1916-1944	Erik Lindberg, engraver
G	1799-1830	Lars Grandel, engraver
G	1830-53	Ludvig Persson Lundgren
G	1927-1945	Alf Grabe
LA	1854-97	Lea Ahlborn, engraver
LB	1819-21	Lars Bergencreutz
LH	1944-1974	Leo Holmberg, engraver
OL	1773-1819	Olof Lidijn
	1723-30	Esaias Zedritz (t.f.)
ST, T	1855-76	Sebastian Tham
TS	1945-1961	Torsten Swensson
U	1961-1986	Benkt Ulvfot
W	1908-1927	Karl-August Wallroth

ENGRAVERS

Stockholm

Date	Name
1799-1830	L. Grandel

Avesta

Date	Name
1790-1808	C. E. Norman

MONETARY SYSTEM

1798-1830
48 Skilling = 1 Riksdaler Species
2 Riksdaler (Speciesdaler) = 1 Ducat

1830-1855
32 Skilling Banco = 1 Riksdaler Riksgalds
12 Riksdaler Riksgalds = 3 Riksdaler Species

1855-1873
100 Ore = 4 Riksdaler Riksmynt
4 Riksdaler Riksmynt = 1 Riksdaler Species
Commencing 1873
100 Ore = 1 Riksdaler Riksmynt = 1 Krona

KINGDOM

REFORM COINAGE
1873 - present

KM# 756 5 KRONOR
2.2402 g., 0.9000 Gold .0648 oz. AGW **Ruler:** Oscar II **Obv:** Head right **Obv. Legend:** OSCAR II SVERIGES... **Rev:** Value, 3 crowns above sprigs

Date	Mintage	F	VF	XF	Unc	BU
1881 EB	65,000	45.00	60.00	120	200	—
1882 EB	30,000	55.00	70.00	200	300	—
1883 EB	28,000	60.00	90.00	200	300	—
1886/3 EB	42,000	BV	55.00	150	275	—
1886 EB	Inc. above	BV	55.00	150	275	—
1894 EB	51,000	BV	55.00	100	200	—
1899 EB	104,000	BV	50.00	80.00	175	—

KM# 766 5 KRONOR
2.2402 g., 0.9000 Gold .0648 oz. AGW **Ruler:** Oscar II **Obv:** Head right **Rev:** Value and crowns within wreath

Date	Mintage	F	VF	XF	Unc	BU
1901 EB	109,186	BV	50.00	70.00	100	—

KM# 797 5 KRONOR
2.2402 g., 0.9000 Gold .0648 oz. AGW **Ruler:** Gustaf V **Obv:** Head right **Rev:** Value and crowns above sprigs

Date	Mintage	F	VF	XF	Unc	BU
1920 W	103,000	BV	50.00	70.00	100	—

KM# 732 10 KRONOR
4.4803 g., 0.9000 Gold .1296 oz. AGW **Ruler:** Oscar II **Obv:** Head right **Obv. Legend:** OSCAR II SVERIGES... **Rev:** Crowned mantled arms

Date	Mintage	F	VF	XF	Unc	BU
1873 ST	200,000	—	90.00	140	250	—
1874/3 ST	461,000	—	BV	100	200	—
1874 ST	Inc. above	—	BV	100	200	—
1874 ST Proof	—	Value: 1,500				
1876 ST	133,000	—	BV	175	300	—

KM# 743 10 KRONOR
4.4803 g., 0.9000 Gold .1296 oz. AGW **Ruler:** Oscar II **Obv:** Head right **Obv. Legend:** "OCH" replaces "O" in royal title **Rev:** Crowned mantled arms

Date	Mintage	F	VF	XF	Unc	BU
1876 EB	37,000	BV	100	215	350	—
1877 EB	55,000	BV	150	375	500	—
1880 EB	27,000	BV	150	400	475	—
1880 EB L. A.	Inc. above	BV	150	450	600	—
1883 EB L. A.	149,000	—	BV	90.00	150	—
1883 LA	Inc. above	—	BV	95.00	160	—
1883 L. A.	Inc. above	—	BV	95.00	160	—
Note: Larger "L. A."						
1894 EB	36,000	—	BV	130	200	—
1895 EB	65,000	—	BV	160	215	—

KM# 767 10 KRONOR
4.4803 g., 0.9000 Gold .1296 oz. AGW **Ruler:** Oscar II **Obv:** Large head right **Rev:** Crowned and mantled arms

SWEDEN

KM# 733 20 KRONOR
8.9606 g., 0.9000 Gold .2593 oz. AGW **Ruler:** Oscar II **Obv:** Head right **Obv. Legend:** OSCAR II SVERIGES... **Rev:** Crowned mantled arms

Date	Mintage	F	VF	XF	Unc	BU
1873 ST	115,000	—	BV	275	525	—
1874 ST	240,000	—	BV	250	500	—
1875 ST	359,000	—	BV	225	450	—
1876/5 ST	240,000	BV	300	850	1,250	—
1876 ST	Inc. above	BV	300	850	1,250	—

KM# 744 20 KRONOR
8.9606 g., 0.9000 Gold .2593 oz. AGW **Ruler:** Oscar II **Obv:** Head right **Obv. Legend:** OSCAR II SVERIGES... **Rev:** Crowned mantled arms

Date	Mintage	F	VF	XF	Unc	BU
1876 EB	Inc. above	—	BV	250	400	—
1877 EB	103,000	—	BV	220	425	—

KM# 748 20 KRONOR
8.9606 g., 0.9000 Gold .2593 oz. AGW **Ruler:** Oscar II **Obv:** Head right **Obv. Legend:** "OCH" replaces "O" in royal title **Rev:** Crowned mantled arms

Date	Mintage	F	VF	XF	Unc	BU
1877 EB	Inc. above	—	BV	275	450	—
1878/7 EB	245,000	—	BV	250	400	—
1878 EB	Inc. above	—	BV	250	400	—
1879 EB	75,000	—	BV	275	450	—
1879 EB Proof, Unique	—	Value: 10,000				
1880 EB	127,000	—	BV	240	450	—
1881 EB	47,000	—	BV	375	750	—
1884 EB	191,000	—	BV	220	350	—
1885 EB	6,250	—	BV	1,600	2,250	—
1886 EB	173,000	—	BV	220	400	—
1887 EB	59,000	—	BV	375	500	—
1889 EB	202,000	—	BV	200	375	—
1890 EB	155,000	—	BV	210	350	—
1895 EB	135,000	—	BV	210	350	—
1898 EB	313,000	—	BV	200	325	—
1899 EB	261,000	—	BV	200	325	—

KM# 765 20 KRONOR
8.9606 g., 0.9000 Gold .2593 oz. AGW **Ruler:** Oscar II **Obv:** Head right **Obv. Legend:** OSCAR II SVERIGES... **Rev:** Crowned and mantled arms

Date	Mintage	F	VF	XF	Unc	BU
1900 EB	104,000	—	BV	215	400	—
1901 EB	226,679	—	BV	180	245	—
1902 EB	113,810	—	BV	190	265	—
1901 EB	213,286	—	BV	90.00	125	—
1901 EB Proof	Inc. above	Value: 525				

KM# 800 20 KRONOR
8.9606 g., 0.9000 Gold .2593 oz. AGW **Ruler:** Gustaf V **Obv:** Head right **Rev:** Crowned arms within order chain divide value

Date	Mintage	F	VF	XF	Unc	BU
1925 W	387,257	185	320	465	765	—

KM# 868 1000 KRONOR
5.8000 g., 0.9000 Gold .1678 oz. AGW **Ruler:** Carl XVI Gustaf **Subject:** 350th Anniversary of Swedish Colony in Delaware **Obv:** Head left **Rev:** Ship at sea

Date	Mintage	F	VF	XF	Unc	BU
ND(1988)	10,000	—	—	—	235	285

KM# 870 1000 KRONOR
5.8000 g., 0.9000 Gold .1678 oz. AGW **Ruler:** Carl XVI Gustaf **Subject:** Ice Hockey **Obv:** Three small crowns within designed circle **Rev:** Hockey goalie within circle **Designer:** Bo Thoren

Date	Mintage	F	VF	XF	Unc	BU
1989	20,000	—	—	—	175	225

KM# 876 1000 KRONOR
5.8000 g., 0.9000 Gold .1678 oz. AGW **Ruler:** Carl XVI Gustaf **Subject:** The Vasa - Arms **Obv:** Head left **Rev:** The Vasa - Arms

Date	Mintage	F	VF	XF	Unc	BU
1990	15,000	—	—	—	185	250

KM# 880 1000 KRONOR
5.8000 g., 0.9000 Gold .1678 oz. AGW **Ruler:** Carl XVI Gustaf **Subject:** 200th Anniversary - Death of Gustaf III **Obv:** Crowned arms within order chain **Rev:** Head right

Date	Mintage	F	VF	XF	Unc	BU
ND(1992)	15,000	—	—	—	185	250

KM# 883 1000 KRONOR
5.8000 g., 0.9000 Gold .1678 oz. AGW **Ruler:** Carl XVI Gustaf **Subject:** 20th Anniversary of Reign **Obv:** Head left **Rev:** Crown

Date	Mintage	F	VF	XF	Unc	BU
1993	15,000	—	—	—	175	225

KM# 884 1000 KRONOR
5.8000 g., 0.9000 Gold .1678 oz. AGW **Ruler:** Carl XVI Gustaf **Subject:** 50th Birthday of Queen Silvia **Obv:** Crowned head right **Rev:** Crowned arms with supporters

Date	Mintage	F	VF	XF	Unc	BU
ND(1993)	14,000	—	—	—	175	225
ND(1993) Prooflike	1,000	—	—	—	—	385

KM# 887 1000 KRONOR
5.8000 g., 0.9000 Gold .1678 oz. AGW **Ruler:** Carl XVI Gustaf **Subject:** 100th Anniversary - Swedish Coinage **Obv:** Head left **Rev:** Coin designs within circle

Date	Mintage	F	VF	XF	Unc	BU
ND(1995)	14,000	—	—	—	175	225
ND(1995) Prooflike	1,000	—	—	—	—	350

KM# 889 1000 KRONOR
5.8000 g., 0.9000 Gold .1678 oz. AGW **Ruler:** Carl XVI Gustaf **Subject:** 50th Birthday - King Carl XVI Gustaf **Obv:** Head left **Rev:** Crowned arms with supporters

Date	Mintage	F	VF	XF	Unc	BU
ND(1996)	14,000	—	—	—	175	225
ND(1996) Prooflike	1,000	—	—	—	—	350

KM# 891 1000 KRONOR
5.8000 g., 0.9000 Gold .1678 oz. AGW **Ruler:** Carl XVI Gustaf **Subject:** Kalmar Union - Queen Margareta **Obv:** Head left **Rev:** Crowned head left and shield

Date	Mintage	F	VF	XF	Unc	BU
1997	Est. 15,000	—	—	—	150	190

KM# 893 1000 KRONOR
5.8000 g., 0.9000 Gold .1678 oz. AGW **Ruler:** Carl XVI Gustaf **Subject:** 25th Anniversary - Reign of King Carl XVI **Obv:** Head 1/4 left **Rev:** Crown above sceptre, crowned monogram and orb

Date	Mintage	F	VF	XF	Unc	BU
1998	15,000	—	—	—	150	190

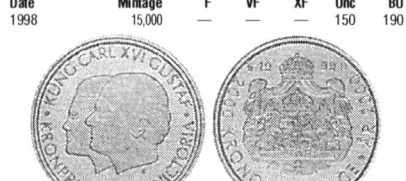

KM# 899 2000 KRONOR
13.0000 g., 0.9000 Gold 0.3762 oz. AGW, 26 mm. **Ruler:** Carl XVI Gustaf **Subject:** Millennium **Obv:** Conjoined heads of King Gustaf and Crown Princess Victoria left **Rev:** Crowned mantled arms **Edge:** Plain

Date	Mintage	F	VF	XF	Unc	BU
1999	30,000	—	—	—	265	—
1999 Prooflike	2,000	—	—	—	—	280

SWEDEN

KM# 909 2000 KRONOR
12.0000 g., 0.9000 Gold 0.3472 oz. AGW, 26 mm. **Ruler:** Carl XVI Gustaf **Subject:** 750th Anniversary of Stockholm **Obv:** City seal with three towers and gate **Rev:** Three towers of city hall **Edge:** Plain

Date	Mintage	F	VF	XF	Unc	BU
ND (2002) Proof	5,000	Value: 350				

KM# 903 2000 KRONOR
12.0000 g., 0.9990 Gold .3472 oz. AGW **Ruler:** Carl XVI Gustaf **Subject:** 30th Anniversary of Reign

Date	Mintage	F	VF	XF	Unc	BU
2003	—	—	—	—	260	—

KM# 905 2000 KRONOR
12.0000 g., 0.9000 Gold .3472 oz. AGW, 26 mm. **Ruler:** Carl XVI Gustaf **Subject:** St. Birgitta's 700th Anniversary of birth **Obv:** Gothic letter B above value **Rev:** St. Birgitta **Edge:** Plain

Date	Mintage	F	VF	XF	Unc	BU
ND (2003)	8,000	—	—	—	260	—

KM# 912 2000 KRONOR
12.0000 g., 0.9000 Gold Royal Palace in Stockholm 250th Anniversary 0.3472 oz. AGW, 26 mm. **Ruler:** Carl XVI Gustaf **Subject:** Two antique keys over map **Rev:** Royal Palace in Stockholm **Edge:** Plain

Date	Mintage	F	VF	XF	Unc	BU
ND (2004) Proof	5,243	Value: 300				

KM# 914 2000 KRONOR
12.0000 g., 0.9000 Gold .3472 oz. AGW, 26 mm. **Ruler:** Carl XVI Gustaf **Obv:** Stylized flames **Rev:** Dag Hammarskjold **Edge:** Plain

Date	Mintage	F	VF	XF	Unc	BU
ND (2005) Proof	5,000	Value: 300				

KM# 907 2000 KRONOR
12.0000 g., 0.9000 Gold .3472 oz. AGW, 26 mm. **Ruler:** Carl XVI Gustaf **Subject:** Centennial of the end of the Union between Norway and Sweden **Obv:** Split disc **Rev:** Flag pole dividing two clouds

Date	Mintage	F	VF	XF	Unc	BU
2005	5,000	—	—	—	260	—

TRADE COINAGE

KM# 716 CAROLIN (10 Francs)
3.2258 g., 0.9000 Gold .0933 oz. AGW **Ruler:** Carl XV Adolf **Obv:** Head right **Obv. Legend:** CARL XV SVERIGES... **Rev:** 3 Crowns within round shield, crown above

Date	Mintage	F	VF	XF	Unc	BU
1868	33,000	70.00	125	225	400	—
1869	31,000	70.00	125	250	450	—
1871	5,153	120	225	350	675	—
1871	Inc. above	250	350	675	950	—
Note: Larger ear						
1872	12,000	100	200	325	600	—
1872	Inc. above	225	400	550	850	—
Note: Larger ear						

KM# 542 DUCAT
3.5000 g., 0.9760 Gold .1098 oz. AGW **Ruler:** Gustaf IV Adolf **Obv:** Armored bust right **Obv. Legend:** GUSTAF • IV • ADOLPH • SV • ... **Rev:** Crowned, round arms within order chain, divided date below **Rev. Legend:** GUD OCH FOLKET •

Date	Mintage	VG	F	VF	XF	Unc
1801 OL	3,100	200	500	1,100	2,000	—
1802 OL	4,827	180	500	1,100	1,450	—
1803 OL	7,300	175	325	725	1,400	—
1804 OL	8,700	180	350	750	1,450	—
1805 OL	13,000	150	300	675	1,250	—
1806 OL	14,000	150	300	675	1,250	—
1807 OL	11,000	125	285	625	1,150	—
1808 OL	33,000	125	285	625	1,150	—
1809 OL	21,000	125	285	625	1,150	—

KM# 562 DUCAT
3.5000 g., 0.9760 Gold .1098 oz. AGW **Ruler:** Gustaf IV Adolf **Obv:** Armored bust right **Obv. Legend:** GUSTAF IV... **Rev:** 3 crowns in crowned round shield, within order chain, divided date

Date	Mintage	VG	F	VF	XF	Unc
1801 OL	900	500	1,100	2,250	4,250	—

KM# 567 DUCAT
3.5000 g., 0.9760 Gold .1098 oz. AGW **Ruler:** Gustaf IV Adolf **Obv:** Armored bust right **Obv. Legend:** GUSTAF IV ADOLPH... **Rev:** 3 crowns in crowned round shield, within order chain, divided date, radiant star above

Date	Mintage	F	VF	XF	Unc
1804 OL	1,254	400	950	1,900	3,750	—

KM# 581 DUCAT
3.5000 g., 0.9760 Gold .1098 oz. AGW **Ruler:** Carl XIII **Obv:** Head right **Obv. Legend:** CARL XIII SVERIGES... **Rev:** Crowned shield within order chain, divided date

Date	Mintage	VG	F	VF	XF	Unc
1810 OL	14,000	150	325	600	1,075	—
1811 OL	9,750	175	400	650	1,175	—
1812 OL	16,000	150	325	600	1,075	—
1813 OL	26,000	150	325	600	1,075	—
1814 OL	22,000	150	325	650	1,075	—

KM# 582 DUCAT
3.5000 g., 0.9760 Gold .1098 oz. AGW **Ruler:** Carl XIII **Subject:** Dalarna Mines Commemorative **Obv:** Head right **Obv. Legend:** CARL XIII SVERIGES... **Rev:** Crowned shield within order chain, radiant star above, divided date below

Date	Mintage	VG	F	VF	XF	Unc
1810 OL	1,322	300	650	1,250	2,450	—

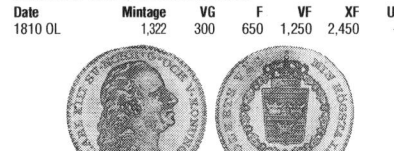

KM# 591 DUCAT
3.5000 g., 0.9760 Gold .1098 oz. AGW **Ruler:** Carl XIII **Obv:** Head right **Obv. Legend:** CARL XIII SV... **Rev:** Crowned shield within order chain, divided date below

Date	Mintage	VG	F	VF	XF	Unc
1815 OL	8,060	150	325	650	1,175	—
1816 OL	6,130	175	375	700	1,300	—
1817 OL	5,673	200	425	800	1,500	—

KM# 594 DUCAT
3.5000 g., 0.9760 Gold .1098 oz. AGW **Ruler:** Carl XIV Johan **Obv:** Head right **Obv. Inscription:** CARL XIV SVERIGES... **Rev:** Crowned shield within order chain, divided date below

Date	Mintage	VG	F	VF	XF	Unc
1818 OL	6,389	100	225	500	900	—
1819 OL	1,828	425	850	1,650	2,350	—
1820 LB	7,248	125	350	750	1,275	—
1821 LB	19,000	100	225	500	900	—
1822 CB	5,222	100	250	550	950	—
1823 AG	3,155	300	650	1,250	2,350	—
1824 CB Rare	3,370	—	—	—	—	—
1825 CB	8,127	100	250	550	975	—
1826 CB	4,126	200	500	1,000	2,150	—
1827/6 CB	4,579	100	250	550	950	—
1828 CB	5,150	100	225	450	850	—
1829 CB	5,642	110	300	650	1,300	—

KM# 628 DUCAT
3.5000 g., 0.9760 Gold .1098 oz. AGW **Ruler:** Carl XIV Johan **Obv:** Head right **Obv. Legend:** CARL XIV SVERIGES... **Rev:** Crowned mantled arms

Date	Mintage	VG	F	VF	XF	Unc
1830 CB	5,269	90.00	200	375	850	—
1831 CB	3,917	100	225	550	1,075	—
1832 CB	2,082	100	275	650	1,300	—
1833 CB	2,310	100	275	650	1,200	—
1834 CB	3,142	90.00	200	400	975	—

KM# 628a DUCAT
3.4856 g., 0.9760 Gold .1094 oz. AGW **Ruler:** Carl XIV Johan **Obv:** Head right **Obv. Legend:** CARL XIV SVERIGES... **Rev:** Crowned mantled arms

Date	Mintage	VG	F	VF	XF	Unc
1835 CB	7,622	90.00	200	375	900	—
1836 CB Rare	1,947	—	—	—	—	—
1837 CB	13,000	80.00	175	350	750	—
1838 AG	15,000	80.00	175	350	750	—
1839 AG	10,000	80.00	175	350	750	—
1840 AG	1,840	125	300	700	1,500	—
1841 AG	13,000	80.00	175	350	800	—
1842 AG	30,000	80.00	175	350	700	—
1843 AG	74,000	75.00	160	325	540	—

KM# 662 DUCAT
3.4856 g., 0.9760 Gold .1094 oz. AGW **Ruler:** Oscar I **Obv:** Head right **Obv. Legend:** OSCAR SVERIGES... **Rev:** Crowned mantled arms

Date	Mintage	VG	F	VF	XF	Unc
1844 AG Rare	946	—	—	—	—	—
1845/4 AG	46,000	125	300	600	650	—

KM# 668 DUCAT
3.4856 g., 0.9760 Gold .1094 oz. AGW **Ruler:** Oscar I **Obv:** Head right **Obv. Legend:** OSCAR SVERIGES... **Rev:** Crowned mantled arms

Date	Mintage	VG	F	VF	XF	Unc
1845/4 AG	Inc. above	80.00	160	350	800	—
1845 AG	Inc. above	75.00	150	275	700	—
1846 AG	22,000	75.00	150	275	475	—
1847/4 AG	18,000	80.00	165	300	450	—
1847 AG	Inc. above	75.00	150	275	475	—
1848 AG	37,000	75.00	150	275	475	—
1849/4 AG	14,000	80.00	165	300	650	—
1849 AG	Inc. above	75.00	150	275	450	—
1850 AG	20,000	75.00	200	375	750	—
1851 AG	16,000	75.00	150	275	700	—
1852 AG	27,000	75.00	150	275	450	—
1853 AG	13,000	75.00	200	375	750	—
1854 AG	20,000	75.00	150	250	450	—
Note: Small AG						
1854 AG	Inc. above	75.00	150	250	450	—
Note: Large AG						
1855 AG	18,000	75.00	150	250	450	—
1856 ST	12,000	75.00	200	350	750	—
1857 ST	27,000	75.00	150	275	450	—
Note: Small ST						
1857 ST	Inc. above	75.00	150	250	420	—
Note: Large ST						
1858 ST	41,000	75.00	150	250	420	—
1859 ST	31,000	75.00	150	275	485	—

SWEDEN

KM# 709 DUCAT
3.4856 g., 0.9760 Gold .1094 oz. AGW **Ruler:** Carl XV Adolf **Obv:** Head right **Obv. Inscription:** CARL XV SVERIGES... **Rev:** Crowned mantled arms

Date	Mintage	VG	F	VF	XF	Unc
1860 ST	58,000	75.00	150	275	425	—
1861/0 ST	38,000	75.00	150	325	425	—
1861 ST	Inc. above	75.00	150	275	425	—
1862 ST	42,000	75.00	150	275	425	—
1863 ST	37,000	75.00	150	250	425	—
1864/3 ST	38,000	75.00	140	325	450	—
1864 ST	Inc. above	75.00	125	275	425	—
Note: Small "L. A."						
1864 ST	Inc. above	75.00	125	275	425	—
Note: Larger "L. A."						
1865 ST	39,000	75.00	125	275	425	—
Note: Large year and "ST"						
1865 ST	Inc. above	75.00	125	275	425	—
Note: Smaller year and "ST"						
1866 ST	32,000	75.00	125	275	425	—
Note: Large "ST"						
1866 ST	Inc. above	75.00	125	275	425	—
Note: Smaller "ST"						
1867 ST	11,000	75.00	125	275	450	—
1867 TS	Inc. above	200	500	750	1,500	—
1868 ST	9,398	75.00	150	300	425	—
Note: Small "ST"						
1868 ST	Inc. above	75.00	150	300	600	—
Note: Larger "ST"						

KM# 629 2 DUCAT
7.0000 g., 0.9860 Gold .2219 oz. AGW **Ruler:** Carl XIV Johan **Obv:** Head right **Obv. Legend:** CARL XIV SVERIGES... **Rev:** Crowned mantled arms

Date	Mintage	VG	F	VF	XF	Unc
1830 CB Rare	2	—	—	—	—	—
1836 CB	1,500	275	700	1,400	2,150	—
1837 CB	1,989	275	700	1,400	2,150	—
1838 AG Rare	1,000	—	—	—	—	—
1839 AG	2,200	350	800	1,550	2,650	—
1842 AG Rare	1,546	—	—	—	—	—
1843 AG	2,159	250	650	1,300	1,950	—

KM# 680 2 DUCAT
7.0000 g., 0.9860 Gold .2219 oz. AGW **Ruler:** Oscar I **Obv:** Head right **Obv. Legend:** OSCAR SVERIGES... **Rev:** Crowned mantled arms

Date	Mintage	VG	F	VF	XF	Unc
1850 AG	819	400	800	1,800	2,600	—
1852 AG Rare	386	—	—	—	—	—
1857 ST	763	375	700	1,375	1,725	—

KM# 645 4 DUCAT
13.9424 g., 0.9760 Gold .4376 oz. AGW **Ruler:** Carl XIV Johan **Obv:** Head right **Obv. Legend:** CARL XIV SVERIGES... **Rev:** Crowned oval mantled arms

Date	Mintage	VG	F	VF	XF	Unc
1837 CB	1,625	550	1,100	2,000	3,000	—
1838 AG	625	600	1,200	2,150	3,500	—
1839 AG	2,000	450	950	2,000	3,500	—
1841 AG Rare	2,084	—	—	—	—	—
1843 AG	4,405	400	850	1,500	2,600	—

KM# 670 4 DUCAT
13.9424 g., 0.9760 Gold .4376 oz. AGW **Ruler:** Oscar I **Obv:** Head right **Obv. Legend:** OSCAR SVERIGES... **Rev:** Crowned mantled arms

Date	Mintage	VG	F	VF	XF	Unc
1846 AG	400	700	1,400	2,500	3,750	—
1850 AG	507	500	1,000	2,000	3,200	—
1852 AG Rare	2	—	—	—	—	—

ECU COINAGE

X# 13 150 ECU
6.7200 g., 0.7500 Gold 0.162 oz. AGW, 23 mm. **Ruler:** Carl XVI Gustaf **Issuer:** CITV, Vaduz **Obv:** Early sailing ship **Rev:** Bust of Gustaf Adolphus 3/4 right **Rev. Legend:** GUSTAVUS ADOLPHUS 1594 • 1632 - ILLE FACIET **Edge:** Reeded

Date	Mintage	F	VF	XF	Unc	BU
1992 Proof	1,000	Value: 250				

X# 19 150 ECU
6.7200 g., 0.7500 Gold 0.162 oz. AGW, 23 mm. **Ruler:** Carl XVI Gustaf **Issuer:** CITV, Vaduz **Subject:** 800th Anniversary Port of Visby **Obv:** Visby arms **Rev:** Early sailing ships leaving port **Rev. Legend:** 800 YEARS HANSA / VISBY **Edge:** Reeded

Date	Mintage	F	VF	XF	Unc	BU
1994 Proof	400	Value: 250				

PATTERNS
Including off metal strikes

KM#	Date	Mintage	Identification	Mkt Val
Pn26	1830	—	Carolin/32 Skillingar. Gold.	—
Pn27	1830	—	Carolin/32 Skillingar. Gold.	—
Pn28	1830	—	2 Carolin/32 Skillingar. Gold. Value changed from 1 to 2.	—
Pn29	ND(1830)	—	1/10 Carolin. Gold.	750
Pn30	ND(1930)	—	1/4 Carolin. Gold.	750
Pn31	ND(1830)	—	1/2 Carolin. Gold.	750
Pn32	ND(1830)	—	Carolin. Gold.	1,200
Pn33	ND(1830)	—	2 Carolin. Gold.	1,500
Pn90	1880	—	5 Kronor. Gold. 15.5000 g. Grams on reverse.	—
Pn91	1880	—	5 Kronor. Gold. 16.0000 g. Grams on reverse.	—
Pn92	1880	—	5 Kronor. Gold. 16.5000 g. Grams on reverse.	—

PROOF-LIKE SETS (PL)

KM#	Date	Mintage	Identification	Issue Price	Mkt Val
PL1	1993 (2)	1,000	KM#882, 884	—	460
PL2	1995 (2)	1,000	KM#886, 887	—	425
PL3	ND(1996) (2)	1,000	KM#888, 889	—	425
PL4	1999 (2)	2,000	KM#898-899	—	300

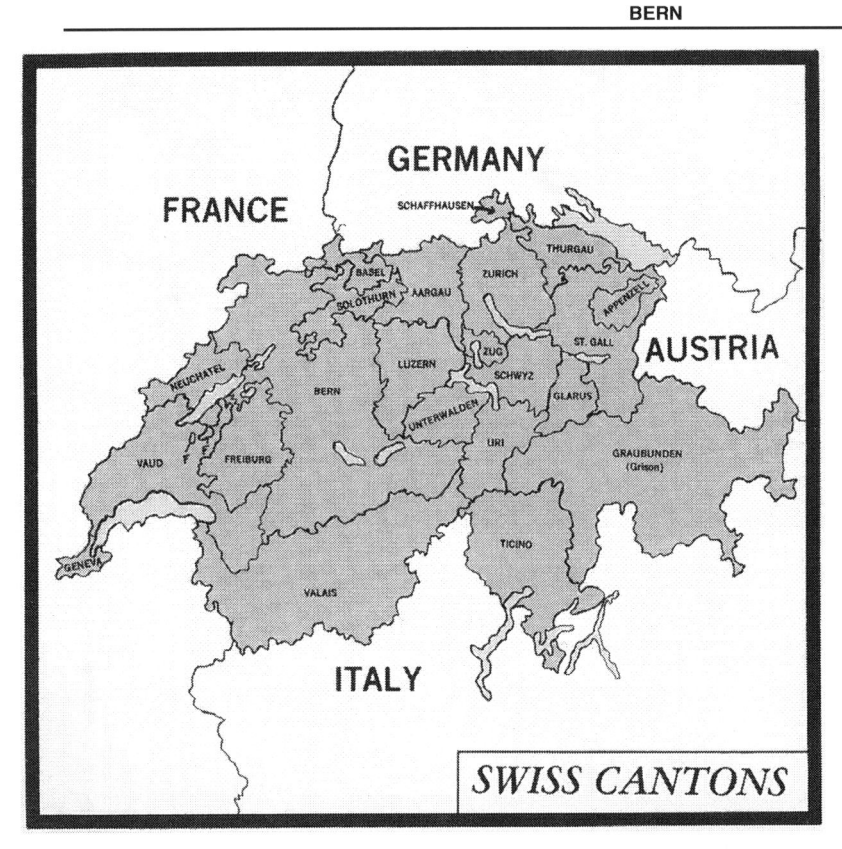

In Switzerland, canton is the name given to each of the 23 states comprising the Swiss Federation. The origin of the cantons is rooted in the liberty-loving instincts of the peasants of Helvetia.

After the Romans departed Switzerland to defend Rome against the barbarians, Switzerland became, in the Middle Ages, a federation of fiefs of the Holy Roman Empire. In 888 it was again united by Rudolf of Burgundy, a minor despot, and for 150 years Switzerland had a king. Upon the death of the last Burgundian king, the kingdom crumbled into a loose collection of feudal fiefs ruled by bishops and ducal families who made their own laws and levied their own taxes. Eventually this division of rule by arbitrary despots became more than the freedom-loving and resourceful peasants could bear. The citizens living in the remote valleys of Uri, Schwyz (from which Switzerland received its name) and Unterwalden decided to liberate themselves from all feudal obligations and become free.

On Aug. 1, 1291, the elders of these three small states met on a tiny heath known as the Rutli on the shores of the Lake of Lucerne and negotiated an eternal pact' which recognized their right to local self-government, and pledged one another assistance against any encroachment upon these rights. The pact was the beginning of the Everlasting League' and the foundation of the Swiss Confederation.

CANTONAL MINT MARKS OF SWITZERLAND

Mint Mark	Canton	Mint
A., B.	Geneva	Geneva 1847, Auguste Bovet
A., B.	Graubunden	Geneva 1842, Antoine Bovy
A-B	Graubunden	Private coiner 1836, antoine Bovy
A-B	Graubunden	Geneva 1842, Antoine Bovy
B	Basel	Basel 1826, Bel-Bessiere
B	Glarus	Unknown site 1806-14
B	Graubunden	Beren 1820
B	Graubunden	Private coiner 1826
B	Luzern	Luzern 1807-14, Bruppacher
B	Schwyz	Schwyz or Aargau 1810
B	Zurich	Zurich 1806-13, Bruckmann
BEL	Basel	Basel 1826, Bel-Bessiere
BEL	Freiburg	Freiburg 1830-46, Bel-Bessiere
BEL	Vaud	Lausanne 1826-34, Bel-Bessiere
D	Zurich	Stuttgart 1842-48
DB	Schwyz	Schwyz 1843-46
F	Glarus	Unknown site 1806-07
G	Geneva	Geneva An 8-13
H	Geneva	Geneva 1817, Hoyer
H	Schwyz	Schwyz or Aargau 1810-11
HB	Graubunden	Private coiner 1836, Bruppacher
K	St. Gall	St. Gall 1807-17, Kukler
M	Aargau	Aargau 1807-08, Meyer
M	Schwyz	Aargau or Schwyz 1844
N	Graubunden	Bern 1825, Nett
SIBEER	Vaud	Lausanne 1845, Siber
Star	Ticino	Luzern 1813

BERN

A city and canton in west central Switzerland. It was founded as a military post in 1191 and became an imperial city with the mint right in 1218. It was admitted to the Swiss Confederation as a canton in 1353.

CANTON
REFORM COINAGE
Commencing 1803

KM# 163 DUPLONE
7.6400 g., 0.9000 Gold .2210 oz. AGW **Obv:** Crowned, spade arms of Bern within sprigs **Obv. Legend:** BERNENSIS RESPUBLICA **Rev:** Standing Swiss with fasces above date **Rev. Legend:** DEUS PROVIDEBIT

Date	Mintage	F	VF	XF	Unc	BU
1819	—	400	750	1,250	2,100	2,800
1829	—	500	900	1,750	2,800	3,500

TRADE COINAGE

KM# 155.1 4 DUCAT
14.0000 g., 0.9860 Gold .4438 oz. AGW **Obv:** Crowned, spade arms of Bern within sprigs **Obv. Legend:** BERNENSIS RESPUBLICA **Rev:** Value, date within wreath **Rev. Legend:** BENEDICTUS SIT IEHOVA DEUS

Date	Mintage	VG	F	VF	XF	Unc
1825	—	1,600	3,200	5,000	8,000	11,000

GENEVA

A canton and city in southwestern Switzerland. The city became a bishopric c.400 AD and was part of the Burgundian Kingdom for 500 years. They became completely independent in 1530. In 1798 they were occupied by France but became independent again in 1813. They joined the Swiss Confederation in 1815.

CANTON
DECIMAL COINAGE
100 Centimes = 1 Franc

KM# 139 10 FRANCS
3.8000 g., 0.7500 Gold 0.0916 oz. AGW **Obv:** Arms within circle **Obv. Legend:** POST.TENE.BRAS.LUX **Rev:** Value, date **Rev. Legend:** REP.ET CANT DE GENEVE

Date	Mintage	F	VF	XF	Unc	BU
1848	336	450	900	1,500	2,300	3,200

KM# 140 20 FRANCS
7.6000 g., 0.7500 Gold .1833 oz. AGW **Obv:** Arms within circle **Obv. Legend:** POST.TENE.BRAS.LUX **Rev:** Value, date **Rev. Legend:** REP. ET CANT DE GENEVE

Date	Mintage	F	VF	XF	Unc	BU
1848	3,421	300	600	1,200	1,600	2,100

GRAUBUNDEN

The largest and most easterly of the Swiss Cantons. The district was set up in the reign of Roman Emperor Augustus and was one of the various factions sparring for power in the 14th and 15th centuries. The name is derived from "Grey League". The first coins were issued in c.1600. They joined the Swiss Confederation in 1803.

MINTMASTERS' INITIALS
A-B - Bouey
H.B. - Bruppacher

MONETARY SYSTEM
15 Rappen = 6 Bluzger = 1 Schweizer Batzen
10 Schweizer Batzen = 1 Frank
16 Franken = 1 Duplone

CANTON
STANDARD COINAGE

KM# 10 16 FRANKEN
7.6400 g., 0.9000 Gold 0.2211 oz. AGW **Obv:** Three shield divided by circular wreath **Obv. Legend:** BUNDEN CANTON... **Rev:** Value and date within wreath

Date	Mintage	F	VF	XF	Unc	BU
1813	100	1,200	2,800	5,500	8,500	10,000

LUZERN

Lucerne
A canton and city in central Switzerland. The city grew around the Benedictine Monastery which was founded in 750. They joined the Swiss Confederation as the 4th member in 1332. Few coins were issued before the 1500s.

MINT OFFICIALS' INITIALS

Initials	Date	Name
B	1794-1807	Bruppacher
HL	?	Hedlinger

SWISS CANTONS-LUZERN

CITY
STANDARD COINAGE

KM# 98 10 FRANKS
Gold **Obv:** Crowned garlanded shield, date in exergue **Obv. Legend:** CANTON LUCERN. **Rev:** Knight leaning on oval shield **Rev. Legend:** SCHWEIZR...

Date	Mintage	F	VF	XF	Unc	BU
1804	—	450	850	1,400	2,000	2,500

KM# 102 20 FRANKS
Gold **Obv:** Crowned garlanded shield, value in exergue **Obv. Legend:** CANTON LUCERN **Rev:** Knight leaning on oval shield **Rev. Legend:** SCHWEIZER...

Date	Mintage	F	VF	XF	Unc	BU
1807 B	—	1,000	2,100	3,500	5,250	7,500

SCHWYZ
Schwytz, Suitensis

A canton in central Switzerland. In 1291 it became one of the three cantons that would ultimately become the Swiss Confederation and were known as the "Everlasting League". The first coinage was issued in 1624.

MINT OFFICIALS' INITIALS

Initials	Date	Name
DB	1843-46	?
H	1810-11	?
M	1844	?

CANTON
TRADE COINAGE

KM# 66 DUCAT
3.5000 g., 0.9860 Gold 0.111 oz. AGW **Obv:** Rampant lion supporting shield **Obv. Legend:** CANTON SCHWYZ **Rev:** Legend and date within wreath **Note:** Given as a winner's prize at a shooting meeting.

Date	Mintage	F	VF	XF	Unc	BU
1844 M	50	3,000	5,000	8,500	12,000	16,000

SOLOTHURN
Solodornensis, Soleure

A canton in northwest Switzerland. Bracteates were struck in the 1300s even though the mint right was not officially granted until 1381. They joined the Swiss Confederation in 1481.

MINT OFFICIAL'S INITIALS

Initials	Date	Name
T		Thiebaud

CANTON
STANDARD COINAGE

KM# 74 8 FRANKEN
3.8200 g., 0.9000 Gold 0.1105 oz. AGW **Obv:** Crowned shield within wreath **Obv. Legend:** CANTON SOLOTH **Rev:** Standing knight, oval shield, value **Rev. Legend:** SCHWEIZER...

Date	Mintage	F	VF	XF	Unc	BU
1813	106	1,500	3,500	6,000	8,500	11,000

KM# 75 16 FRANKEN
7.6400 g., 0.9000 Gold 0.2211 oz. AGW **Obv:** Crowned shield within wreath **Obv. Legend:** CANTON SOLOTH **Rev:** Standing knight, oval shield, value **Rev. Legend:** SCHWEIZER...

Date	Mintage	F	VF	XF	Unc	BU
1813	150	2,000	4,500	7,000	10,000	13,500

REFORM COINAGE
Commencing 1804

10 Rappen = 4 Kreuzer = 1 Batzen; 10 Batzen = 1 Frank

KM# 76 32 FRANKEN
15.2800 g., 0.9000 Gold 0.4421 oz. AGW **Obv:** Crowned shield within wreath **Rev:** Standing knight, oval shield, value

Date	Mintage	F	VF	XF	Unc	BU
1813 Rare	—	—	—	—	—	—

ZURICH
Thicurinae, Thuricensis, Ticurinae, Turicensis

A canton in north central Switzerland. It was the mint for the dukes of Swabia in the 10th and 11th centuries. The mint right was obtained in 1238. The first coinage struck were bracteates and the last coins were struck in 1848. It joined the Swiss Confederation in 1351.

MINT OFFICIALS' INITIALS
B - Bruckmann
AV - A. Vorster

CANTON
TRADE COINAGE

KM# A185 DUCAT
3.5000 g., 0.9860 Gold 0.111 oz. AGW **Obv:** Rampant lion next to oval shield **Obv. Legend:** TURICENSIS * DUCATUS REPUBLICAE **Rev:** Legend, date within ornate wreath **Rev. Legend:** IUSTITUA ET CONCORDIA 1810

Date	Mintage	F	VF	XF	Unc	BU
1810 B	—	550	1,100	1,750	2,250	2,800

MEDALLIC COINAGE

X# M2 DUCAT
3.5000 g., 0.9860 Gold 0.111 oz. AGW **Obv:** Bust r. of Magister Zwingli **Rev:** 9-line legend and date

Date	Mintage	F	VF	XF	Unc	BU
1819	—	—	250	350	500	800

SWITZERLAND

The Swiss Confederation, located in central Europe north of Italy and south of Germany, has an area of 15,941 sq. mi. (41,290 sq. km.).

Switzerland, the habitat of lake dwellers in prehistoric times, was peopled by the Celtic Helvetians when Julius Caesar made it a part of the Roman Empire in 58 B.C. After the decline of Rome, Switzerland was invaded by Teutonic tribes, who established small temporal holdings which in the Middle Ages, became a federation of fiefs of the Holy Roman Empire. As a nation, Switzerland originated in 1291 when the districts of Nidwalden, Schwyz and Uri united to defeat Austria and attain independence as the Swiss Confederation. After acquiring new cantons in the 14th century, Switzerland was made independent from the Holy Roman Empire by the 1648 Treaty of Westphalia. The revolutionary armies of Napoleonic France occupied Switzerland and set up the Helvetian Republic, 1798-1803. After the fall of Napoleon, the Congress of Vienna, 1815, recognized the independence of Switzerland and guaranteed its neutrality. The Swiss Constitutions of 1848 and 1874 established a union modeled upon that of the United States.

MINT MARKS
A - Paris
AB - Strasbourg
B - Bern
B. - Brussels 1874
BA - Basel
BB - Strasbourg
S – Solothurn

NOTE: The coinage of Switzerland has been struck at the Bern Mint since 1853 with but a few exceptions. All coins minted there carry a B' mint mark through 1969, except for the 2-Centime and 2-Franc values where the mintmark was discontinued after 1968. In 1968 and 1969 some issues were struck at both Bern (B) and in London (no mint mark).

MONETARY SYSTEM
10 Rappen = 1 Batzen
10 Batzen = 1 Franc
16 Franken = 1 Duplone

CONFEDERATION
Confoederatio Helvetica

MONETARY SYSTEM
100 Rappen (Centimes) = 1 Franc

DECIMAL COINAGE

KM# A48 5 FRANCS
Gold

Date	Mintage	F	VF	XF	Unc	BU
1948B	Est. 50	—	—	—	15,000	—

KM# 36 10 FRANCS
3.2258 g., 0.9000 Gold .0933 oz. AGW **Obv:** Young bust left **Rev:** Radiant cross above date and sprigs **Designer:** Fritz Ulysse Landry

Date	Mintage	F	VF	XF	Unc	BU
1911B	100,000	75.00	150	250	350	500
1912B	200,000	—	BV	75.00	125	175
1913B	600,000	—	BV	70.00	95.00	150
1914B	200,000	—	BV	75.00	115	160
1915B	400,000	—	BV	70.00	100	125
1916B	130,000	—	BV	75.00	115	160
1922B	1,020,000	—	—	BV	70.00	95.00

KM# 31.1 20 FRANCS
6.4516 g., 0.9000 Gold .1867 oz. AGW **Obv:** Crowned head left **Obv. Legend:** CONFOEDERATIO HELVETICA **Rev:** Shield divides value, star above, date below, all within wreath **Edge:** Reeded

Date	Mintage	F	VF	XF	Unc	BU
1883	250,000	—	BV	125	160	210

SWITZERLAND

KM# 31.2 20 FRANCS
6.4516 g., 0.9000 Gold .1867 oz. AGW **Edge:** DOMINUS XXX /XXXXXXXXXX PROVIDEBIT

Date	Mintage	F	VF	XF	Unc	BU
1896B	Inc. above	—	—	—	—	—

Note: Reported, not confirmed

KM# 31.3 20 FRANCS
6.4516 g., 0.9000 Gold .1867 oz. AGW **Obv:** Crowned head left **Obv. Legend:** CONFOEDERATIO HELVETICA **Rev:** Shield divides value, star above, date below, all within wreath **Edge:** DOMINUS XXX PROVIDEBIT XXXXXXXXXX

Date	Mintage	F	VF	XF	Unc	BU
1886	250,000	—	BV	125	160	210
1887B	176	—	—	18,000	27,500	38,500
1888B	4,224	—	3,000	6,000	9,000	12,500
1889B	100,000	BV	135	170	200	300
1890B	125,000	—	BV	125	160	250
1891B	100,000	BV	125	150	175	250
1892B	100,000	BV	125	150	175	250
1893B	100,000	BV	125	150	175	250
1893B	25	—	—	—	—	30,000

Note: Struck of bright Valaisan gold from Gondo with a small cross punched in the center of the Swiss cross

1894B	121,000	—	BV	135	170	250
1895B	200,000	—	BV	130	165	250
1895B	19	—	—	—	—	30,000

Note: Struck of bright Valaisan gold from Gondo with a small cross punched in the center of the Swiss cross

| 1896B | 400,000 | — | BV | 125 | 160 | 225 |

KM# 35.1 20 FRANCS
6.4516 g., 0.9000 Gold .1867 oz. AGW **Obv:** Young head left **Obv. Legend:** HELVETIA **Rev:** Shield within oak branches divides value **Designer:** Fritz Ulysse Landry

Date	Mintage	F	VF	XF	Unc	BU
1897B	400,000	—	BV	125	150	210
1897B Rare	29					

Note: Struck of bright Valaisan gold from Gondo with a small cross punched in the center of the Swiss cross

1898B	400,000	—	BV	125	150	210
1899B	300,000	—	BV	125	150	210
1900B	400,000	—	BV	125	150	210
1901B	500,000	—	—	BV	140	175
1902B	600,000	—	—	BV	140	175
1903B	200,000	—	—	BV	145	190
1904B	100,000	—	BV	150	200	225
1905B	100,000	—	BV	150	200	225
1906B	100,000	—	BV	150	200	225
1907B	150,000	—	—	BV	140	185
1908B	355,000	—	—	—	135	175
1909B	400,000	—	—	—	135	175
1910B	375,000	—	—	—	135	175
1911B	350,000	—	—	—	135	175
1912B	450,000	—	—	—	135	175
1913B	700,000	—	—	—	135	175
1914B	700,000	—	—	—	135	175
1915B	750,000	—	—	—	135	175
1916B	300,000	—	—	—	135	175
1922B	2,783,678	—	—	—	BV	135
1925B	400,000	—	—	—	135	150
1926B	50,000	BV	125	150	165	210
1927B	5,015,000	—	—	—	BV	150
1930B	3,371,764	—	—	—	BV	150
1935B	175,000	—	—	BV	150	185
1935L-B	20,008,813	—	—	—	BV	135

Note: The 1935L-B issue was struck in 1945, 1946 and 1947

KM# 35.2 20 FRANCS
6.4516 g., 0.9000 Gold .1867 oz. AGW **Obv:** Bust left **Rev:** Shield within oak branches divides value **Edge Lettering:** AD LEGEM ANNI MCMXXXI

Date	Mintage	F	VF	XF	Unc	BU
1947B	9,200,000	—	—	—	BV	145
1949B	10,000,000	—	—	—	BV	145

KM# 49 25 FRANCS
5.6450 g., 0.9000 Gold .1634 oz. AGW **Obv:** Value above small cross **Rev:** William Tell with bow **Note:** Not available in commercial channels.

Date	Mintage	F	VF	XF	Unc	BU
1955B	5,000,000	—	—	—	—	—
1958B	5,000,000	—	—	—	—	—
1959B	5,000,000	—	—	—	—	—

KM# 50 50 FRANCS
11.2900 g., 0.9000 Gold .3267 oz. AGW **Obv:** Value above small cross **Rev:** Three standing figures facing **Note:** Not available in commercial channels.

Date	Mintage	F	VF	XF	Unc	BU
1955B	2,000,000	—	—	—	—	—
1958B	2,000,000	—	—	—	—	—
1959B	2,000,000	—	—	—	—	—

KM# 39 100 FRANCS
32.2581 g., 0.9000 Gold .9334 oz. AGW **Obv:** Young bust left **Rev:** Radiant cross above value, date and sprigs **Designer:** Fritz Ulysse Landry

Date	Mintage	F	VF	XF	Unc	BU
1925B	5,000	—	4,000	6,000	7,500	10,000

COMMEMORATIVE COINAGE

KM# 95 50 FRANCS
11.2900 g., 0.9000 Gold .3267 oz. AGW, 25 mm. **Obv:** Landscape and value **Rev:** Heidi and goat running **Edge:** Lettered **Designer:** Albrecht Schnider

Date	Mintage	F	VF	XF	Unc	BU
2001B Proof	7,000	Value: 325				

KM# 102 50 FRANCS
6.4516 g., 0.9000 Gold .1867 oz. AGW, 25 mm. **Subject:** Expo '02 **Obv:** Value **Rev:** Aerial view of 3 lakes landscape **Edge:** Lettered **Designer:** Max Matter

Date	Mintage	F	VF	XF	Unc	BU
2002B Proof	5,000	Value: 285				

KM# 105 50 FRANCS
11.2900 g., 0.9000 Gold .3267 oz. AGW, 25 mm. **Obv:** Skier and value **Rev:** St. Moritz city view **Edge:** Lettered **Designer:** Andreas His

Date	Mintage	F	VF	XF	Unc	BU
2003B Proof	4,000	Value: 285				

KM# 123 50 FRANCS
11.2900 g., 0.9000 Gold .3267 oz. AGW, 25 mm. **Subject:** FIFA Centennial **Obv:** FIFA depicting Wilhelm Tell **Rev:** Soccer ball on left value on right **Designer:** Joaquin Jimenez

Date	Mintage	F	VF	XF	Unc	BU
2004B Proof	Est. 6,000	Value: 300				

KM# 110 50 FRANCS
11.2900 g., 0.9000 Gold .3267 oz. AGW, 25 mm. **Obv:** Value **Rev:** Mountain **Edge:** Lettered with 13 stars **Edge Lettering:** DOMINUS PROVIDEBIT **Designer:** Stephan Bundi

Date	Mintage	F	VF	XF	Unc	BU
2004B Proof	Est. 7,000	Value: 345				

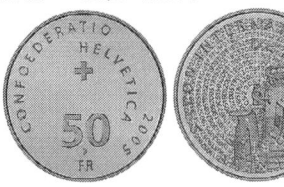

KM# 113 50 FRANCS
11.2900 g., 0.9000 Gold .3267 oz. AGW, 25 mm. **Subject:** Geneva Motor Show **Obv:** Value **Rev:** Partial view of an antique car **Edge:** Lettered **Edge Lettering:** DOMINUS PROVIDEBIT **Designer:** Roger Pfund

Date	Mintage	F	VF	XF	Unc	BU
2005B Proof	Est. 6,000	Value: 285				

KM# 116 50 FRANCS
11.2900 g., 0.9000 Gold .3267 oz. AGW, 25 mm. **Obv:** Value **Rev:** Swiss Guardsman **Edge Lettering:** "Dominus Providebit" **Designer:** Rudolf Mirer

Date	Mintage	F	VF	XF	Unc	BU
2006B Proof	Est. 6,000	Value: 350				

KM# 120 50 FRANCS
11.2900 g., 0.9000 Gold .3267 oz. AGW, 25 mm. **Subject:** National Bank Centennial **Obv:** Value **Rev:** Wood cutter **Edge Lettering:** DOMINUS PROVIDEBIT

Date	Mintage	F	VF	XF	Unc	BU
2007B Proof	6,000	Value: 300				

KM# 81 100 FRANCS
22.5800 g., 0.9000 Gold .6534 oz. AGW **Subject:** 200th Anniversary of Helvetian Republic **Obv:** Value and boxed crosses design **Rev:** 1798 coin design within square flanked by crosses

Date	Mintage	F	VF	XF	Unc	BU
1998B Proof	2,500	Value: 750				

KM# 83 100 FRANCS
22.5800 g., 0.9000 Gold .6534 oz. AGW **Subject:** 150th Anniversary of Swiss Confederation **Obv:** Value and boxed crosses design **Rev:** 1848 coin design within square flanked by crosses

Date	Mintage	F	VF	XF	Unc	BU
1998B Proof	2,500	Value: 750				

KM# 88 100 FRANCS
22.5800 g., 0.9000 Gold .6534 oz. AGW **Subject:** Wine Festival **Obv:** Value and small fox looking up at grapes **Rev:** Small fox eating grapes and cresent

668 SWITZERLAND

Date	Mintage	F	VF	XF	Unc	BU
1999B Proof	3,000	Value: 575				

KM# 96 100 FRANCS
22.5800 g., 0.9000 Gold .6534 oz. AGW, 28 mm. **Subject:** 2000 Years of Christianity **Obv:** Inscription and date divides value **Rev:** Stylized baby **Edge:** Lettered

Date	Mintage	F	VF	XF	Unc	BU
2000B Proof	3,000	Value: 575				

KM# 71.1 250 FRANCS
8.0000 g., 0.9000 Gold .2315 oz. AGW **Subject:** 700 Years of Confederation **Obv:** Diagonal and horizontal inscription to right of value **Rev:** Dates **Edge:** Plus sign (+) between dates

Date	Mintage	F	VF	XF	Unc	BU
1991B	296,741	—	—	—	225	275

Note: 200,000 recalled and melted due to poor quality

KM# 71.2 250 FRANCS
8.0000 g., 0.9000 Gold .2315 oz. AGW **Subject:** 700 Years of Confederation **Edge:** Elongated plus sign between dates

Date	Mintage	F	VF	XF	Unc	BU
1991B	193,259	—	—	—	225	275

COMMEMORATIVE COINAGE
Shooting Festival

The listings which follow have traditionally been categorized in many catalogs as Swiss Shooting Thalers. Technically, all are medallic issues rather than coins, excepting the Solothurn issue of 1855. According to the Swiss Federal Finance Department, the issue was legally equal to the then current-silver 5 Francs issue to which it was identical in design, aside from bearing an edge inscription which read, EIDGEN FREISCHIESSEN SOLOTHURN (National Shooting Fest Solothurn).

For the silver issues of 1855-1885, the presence of the denomination was only intended to indicate these coins were of the same weight and fineness as prescribed for legal tender coins.

Beginning with the issues of 1934, denominations and sizes were no longer the same as regular Swiss legal tender issues. These coins all have legends indicating that they could only be redeemed during and at the shooting fest of issue.

Exceptional quality BU examples for 1934 and 1939 will command a premium over the prices listed.

KM# S19 100 FRANCS
25.9000 g., 0.9000 Gold .7494 oz. AGW **Subject:** Federal Festival in Fribourg

Date	Mintage	F	VF	XF	Unc	BU
1934B	2,000	—	—	1,800	3,000	2,750

X# S21 100 FRANCS
17.5000 g., 0.9000 Gold .5064 oz. AGW **Subject:** Federal Festival in Lucerne **Note:** Prev. KM#S21.

Date	Mintage	F	VF	XF	Unc	BU
1939B	6,000	—	—	400	600	700

KM# S56 200 FRANCS
13.9600 g., 0.9860 Gold .4426 oz. AGW **Subject:** Albisgutli Centennial (Zurich City)

Date	Mintage	F	VF	XF	Unc	BU
1998 Matte Proof	100	Value: 1,200				

KM# S47 500 FRANCS
13.0000 g., 0.9990 Gold .3762 oz. AGW **Subject:** Federal Festival in Thun (Bern)

Date	Mintage	F	VF	XF	Unc	BU
1995 Proof	500	Value: 850				

KM# S49 500 FRANCS
13.0000 g., 0.9900 Gold .3762 oz. AGW **Subject:** Sempach "Battle Shoot" (Lucerne)

Date	Mintage	F	VF	XF	Unc	BU
1996 Proof	96	Value: 1,000				

KM# S51 500 FRANCS
13.0000 g., 0.9990 Gold .3762 oz. AGW **Subject:** Schaffhausen Festival

Date	Mintage	F	VF	XF	Unc	BU
1997 Proof	97	Value: 1,000				

KM# S53 500 FRANCS
13.0000 g., 0.9990 Gold .3762 oz. AGW **Subject:** Schwyz Festival

Date	Mintage	F	VF	XF	Unc	BU
1998 Proof	98	Value: 1,000				

KM# S58 500 FRANCS
13.0000 g., 0.9990 Gold .3762 oz. AGW **Subject:** Wallis Festival in Sion

Date	Mintage	F	VF	XF	Unc	BU
1999 Proof	99	Value: 1,000				

KM# S60 500 FRANCS
13.0000 g., 0.9990 Gold .3762 oz. AGW **Subject:** Federal Festival in Biere (Vaud)

Date	Mintage	F	VF	XF	Unc	BU
2000 Proof	300	Value: 1,000				

KM# S62 500 FRANCS
0.9990 Gold .3762 oz. AGW **Issuer:** Uri Festival **Obv:** Head laureate left within star border **Rev:** Train and tunnel

Date	Mintage	F	VF	XF	Unc	BU
2001 Proof	150	Value: 1,100				

KM# S64 500 FRANCS
13.0000 g., 0.9990 Gold .3762 oz. AGW **Subject:** Zurich Festival

Date	Mintage	F	VF	XF	Unc	BU
2002 Proof	150	Value: 1,200				

KM# S66 500 FRANCS
13.0000 g., 0.9990 Gold .3762 oz. AGW **Issuer:** Basel Festival

Date	Mintage	F	VF	XF	Unc	BU
2003 Proof	150	Value: 1,100				

KM# S68 500 FRANCS
15.5000 g., 0.9990 Gold .4485 oz. AGW **Issuer:** Fribourg Festival

Date	Mintage	F	VF	XF	Unc	BU
2004 Proof	150	Value: 1,000				

KM# S70 500 FRANCS
15.5000 g., 0.9990 Gold .4978 oz. AGW **Subject:** Brusio Festival

Date	Mintage	F	VF	XF	Unc	BU
2005 Proof	150	Value: 900				

KM# S72 500 FRANCS
25.6000 g., 0.5850 Gold 0.4815 oz. AGW **Subject:** Solothurn Festival

Date	Mintage	F	VF	XF	Unc	BU
2006 Proof	200	Value: 750				

KM# S74 500 FRANCS
25.6000 g., 0.5850 Gold .4815 oz. AGW **Subject:** Luzern Festival

Date	Mintage	F	VF	XF	Unc	BU
2007	200	Value: 750				

KM# S23 1000 FRANCS
26.0000 g., 0.9000 Gold .7524 oz. AGW **Subject:** Zurich "Field Shoot" in Oberhasli

Date	Mintage	F	VF	XF	Unc	BU
1984 Proof	300	Value: 1,450				

KM# S25 1000 FRANCS
26.0000 g., 0.9000 Gold .7524 oz. AGW **Subject:** Uri Festival in Altdorf

Date	Mintage	F	VF	XF	Unc	BU
1985 Proof	300	Value: 1,350				

KM# S27 1000 FRANCS
26.0000 g., 0.9000 Gold .7524 oz. AGW **Subject:** Federal Festival in Appenzell

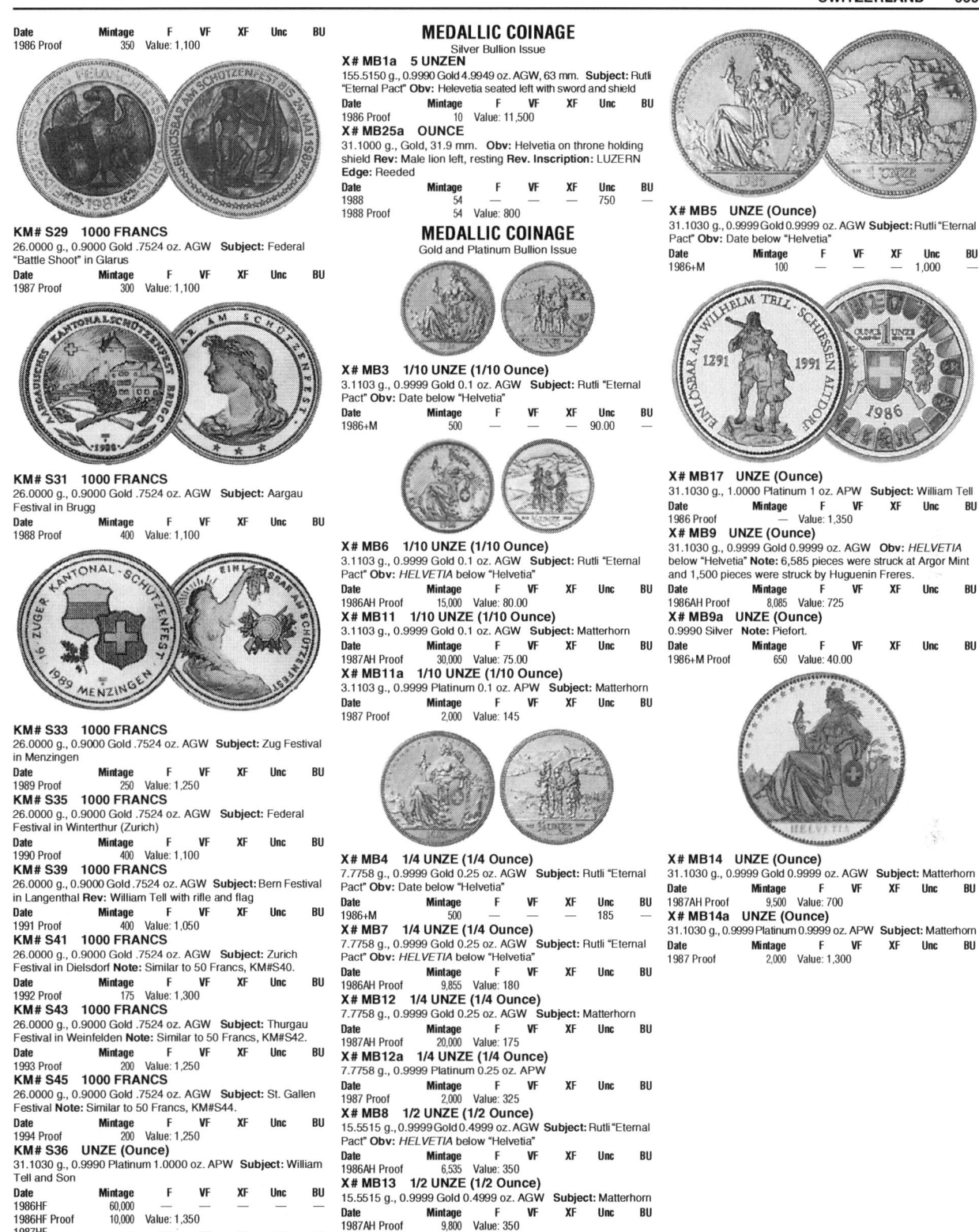

SWITZERLAND 669

KM# S29 1000 FRANCS
26.0000 g., 0.9000 Gold .7524 oz. AGW **Subject:** Federal "Battle Shoot" in Glarus

Date	Mintage	F	VF	XF	Unc	BU
1986 Proof	350			Value: 1,100		

KM# S31 1000 FRANCS
26.0000 g., 0.9000 Gold .7524 oz. AGW **Subject:** Aargau Festival in Brugg

Date	Mintage	F	VF	XF	Unc	BU
1987 Proof	300			Value: 1,100		

KM# S33 1000 FRANCS
26.0000 g., 0.9000 Gold .7524 oz. AGW **Subject:** Zug Festival in Menzingen

Date	Mintage	F	VF	XF	Unc	BU
1988 Proof	400			Value: 1,100		

KM# S35 1000 FRANCS
26.0000 g., 0.9000 Gold .7524 oz. AGW **Subject:** Federal Festival in Winterthur (Zurich)

Date	Mintage	F	VF	XF	Unc	BU
1989 Proof	250			Value: 1,250		

KM# S35 1000 FRANCS
26.0000 g., 0.9000 Gold .7524 oz. AGW **Subject:** Federal Festival in Winterthur (Zurich)

Date	Mintage	F	VF	XF	Unc	BU
1990 Proof	400			Value: 1,100		

KM# S39 1000 FRANCS
26.0000 g., 0.9000 Gold .7524 oz. AGW **Subject:** Bern Festival in Langenthal **Rev:** William Tell with rifle and flag

Date	Mintage	F	VF	XF	Unc	BU
1991 Proof	400			Value: 1,050		

KM# S41 1000 FRANCS
26.0000 g., 0.9000 Gold .7524 oz. AGW **Subject:** Zurich Festival in Dielsdorf **Note:** Similar to 50 Francs, KM#S40.

Date	Mintage	F	VF	XF	Unc	BU
1992 Proof	175			Value: 1,300		

KM# S43 1000 FRANCS
26.0000 g., 0.9000 Gold .7524 oz. AGW **Subject:** Thurgau Festival in Weinfelden **Note:** Similar to 50 Francs, KM#S42.

Date	Mintage	F	VF	XF	Unc	BU
1993 Proof	200			Value: 1,250		

KM# S45 1000 FRANCS
26.0000 g., 0.9000 Gold .7524 oz. AGW **Subject:** St. Gallen Festival **Note:** Similar to 50 Francs, KM#S44.

Date	Mintage	F	VF	XF	Unc	BU
1994 Proof	200			Value: 1,250		

KM# S36 UNZE (Ounce)
31.1030 g., 0.9990 Platinum 1.0000 oz. APW **Subject:** William Tell and Son

Date	Mintage	F	VF	XF	Unc	BU
1986HF	60,000	—	—	—	—	—
1986HF Proof	10,000			Value: 1,350		
1987HF	—	—	—	—	—	—
1987HF Proof	15,000			Value: 1,350		

KM# S37 UNZE (Ounce)
31.1030 g., 0.9990 Platinum 1.0000 oz. APW **Subject:** William Tell

Date	Mintage	F	VF	XF	Unc	BU
1988HF Proof	10,000			Value: 1,350		

KM# S37a UNZE (Ounce)
Brass, 32 mm. **Note:** Specimen Strike.

Date	Mintage	F	VF	XF	Unc	BU
1988HF Proof	1,000			Value: 75.00		

MEDALLIC COINAGE
Silver Bullion Issue

X# MB1a 5 UNZEN
155.5150 g., 0.9990 Gold 4.9949 oz. AGW, 63 mm. **Subject:** Rutli "Eternal Pact" **Obv:** Helvetia seated left with sword and shield

Date	Mintage	F	VF	XF	Unc	BU
1986 Proof	10			Value: 11,500		

X# MB25a OUNCE
31.1000 g., Gold, 31.9 mm. **Obv:** Helvetia on throne holding shield **Rev:** Male lion left, resting **Rev. Inscription:** LUZERN **Edge:** Reeded

Date	Mintage	F	VF	XF	Unc	BU
1988	54	—	—	—	750	—
1988 Proof	54			Value: 800		

MEDALLIC COINAGE
Gold and Platinum Bullion Issue

X# MB3 1/10 UNZE (1/10 Ounce)
3.1103 g., 0.9999 Gold 0.1 oz. AGW **Subject:** Rutli "Eternal Pact" **Obv:** Date below "Helvetia"

Date	Mintage	F	VF	XF	Unc	BU
1986+M	500	—	—	—	90.00	—

X# MB6 1/10 UNZE (1/10 Ounce)
3.1103 g., 0.9999 Gold 0.1 oz. AGW **Subject:** Rutli "Eternal Pact" **Obv:** HELVETIA below "Helvetia"

Date	Mintage	F	VF	XF	Unc	BU
1986AH Proof	15,000			Value: 80.00		

X# MB11 1/10 UNZE (1/10 Ounce)
3.1103 g., 0.9999 Gold 0.1 oz. AGW **Subject:** Matterhorn

Date	Mintage	F	VF	XF	Unc	BU
1987AH Proof	30,000			Value: 75.00		

X# MB11a 1/10 UNZE (1/10 Ounce)
3.1103 g., 0.9999 Platinum 0.1 oz. APW **Subject:** Matterhorn

Date	Mintage	F	VF	XF	Unc	BU
1987 Proof	2,000			Value: 145		

X# MB4 1/4 UNZE (1/4 Ounce)
7.7758 g., 0.9999 Gold 0.25 oz. AGW **Subject:** Rutli "Eternal Pact" **Obv:** Date below "Helvetia"

Date	Mintage	F	VF	XF	Unc	BU
1986+M	500	—	—	—	185	—

X# MB7 1/4 UNZE (1/4 Ounce)
7.7758 g., 0.9999 Gold 0.25 oz. AGW **Subject:** Rutli "Eternal Pact" **Obv:** HELVETIA below "Helvetia"

Date	Mintage	F	VF	XF	Unc	BU
1986AH Proof	9,855			Value: 180		

X# MB12 1/4 UNZE (1/4 Ounce)
7.7758 g., 0.9999 Gold 0.25 oz. AGW **Subject:** Matterhorn

Date	Mintage	F	VF	XF	Unc	BU
1987AH Proof	20,000			Value: 175		

X# MB12a 1/4 UNZE (1/4 Ounce)
7.7758 g., 0.9999 Platinum 0.25 oz. APW

Date	Mintage	F	VF	XF	Unc	BU
1987 Proof	2,000			Value: 325		

X# MB8 1/2 UNZE (1/2 Ounce)
15.5515 g., 0.9999 Gold 0.4999 oz. AGW **Subject:** Rutli "Eternal Pact" **Obv:** HELVETIA below "Helvetia"

Date	Mintage	F	VF	XF	Unc	BU
1986AH Proof	6,535			Value: 350		

X# MB13 1/2 UNZE (1/2 Ounce)
15.5515 g., 0.9999 Gold 0.4999 oz. AGW **Subject:** Matterhorn

Date	Mintage	F	VF	XF	Unc	BU
1987AH Proof	9,800			Value: 350		

X# MB13a 1/2 UNZE (1/2 Ounce)
15.5515 g., 0.9999 Platinum 0.4999 oz. APW **Subject:** Matterhorn

Date	Mintage	F	VF	XF	Unc	BU
1987 Proof	2,000			Value: 650		

X# MB5 UNZE (Ounce)
31.1030 g., 0.9999 Gold 0.9999 oz. AGW **Subject:** Rutli "Eternal Pact" **Obv:** Date below "Helvetia"

Date	Mintage	F	VF	XF	Unc	BU
1986+M	100	—	—	—	1,000	—

X# MB17 UNZE (Ounce)
31.1030 g., 1.0000 Platinum 1 oz. APW **Subject:** William Tell

Date	Mintage	F	VF	XF	Unc	BU
1986 Proof	—			Value: 1,350		

X# MB9 UNZE (Ounce)
31.1030 g., 0.9999 Gold 0.9999 oz. AGW **Obv:** HELVETIA below "Helvetia" **Note:** 6,585 pieces were struck at Argor Mint and 1,500 pieces were struck by Huguenin Freres.

Date	Mintage	F	VF	XF	Unc	BU
1986AH Proof	8,085			Value: 725		

X# MB9a UNZE (Ounce)
0.9990 Silver **Note:** Piefort.

Date	Mintage	F	VF	XF	Unc	BU
1986+M Proof	650			Value: 40.00		

X# MB14 UNZE (Ounce)
31.1030 g., 0.9999 Gold 0.9999 oz. AGW **Subject:** Matterhorn

Date	Mintage	F	VF	XF	Unc	BU
1987AH Proof	9,500			Value: 700		

X# MB14a UNZE (Ounce)
31.1030 g., 0.9999 Platinum 0.9999 oz. APW **Subject:** Matterhorn

Date	Mintage	F	VF	XF	Unc	BU
1987 Proof	2,000			Value: 1,300		

SWITZERLAND

X# MB15 12 UNZEN (One Pound)
373.2360 g., 0.9999 Gold 11.9986 oz. AGW, 78 mm. **Subject:** Matterhorn **Obv:** HELVETIA below "Helvetia" **Note:** Illustration reduced.

Date	Mintage	F	VF	XF	Unc	BU
1987 Proof	250	Value: 8,500				

ESSAIS

KM#	Date	Mintage Identification	Mkt Val
E4	1911	— 10 Francs. Gold.	12,500

PATTERNS
Including off metal strikes

KM#	Date	Mintage Identification	Mkt Val
Pn17	1871B	— 20 Francs. Gold. Shield within sprigs, date below. Value within wreath.	5,500
Pn19	1871	— 20 Francs. Gold. Crowned head left. Shield within sprigs, value below.	15,000
Pn24	1873	1,000 20 Francs. Gold. Seated Helvetia. Value, date within wreath. Obv.: Helvetia. Rev: Head mint mark above sprays.	3,500
Pn26	1873	— 20 Francs. Gold. Obv: Helvetia. Rev: Without head mint mark above sprays.	2,250
Pn34	1883	— 20 Francs. Gold.	15,000
Pn39	1897B	12 20 Francs. Gold.	35,000
Pn40	1910	56 10 Francs. Gold. Reeded edge.	15,000
Pn41	1910	I.A. 10 Francs. Gold. Plain edge.	22,500
Pn81	1947	— 20 Francs. Gold.	—

MINT SETS

KM#	Date	Mintage Identification	Issue Price	Mkt Val
MS24	1991 (2)	110,000 KM#70-71	210	310

CAMPILIONI
ITALIAN ENCLAVE
CASINO COINAGE

X# 1 20 FRANCS
6.4516 g., 0.9000 Gold 0.1867 oz. AGW

Date	Mintage	F	VF	XF	Unc	BU
1950	—	—	—	—	200	—

X# 2 100 FRANCS
32.2581 g., 0.9000 Gold 0.9334 oz. AGW

Date	Mintage	F	VF	XF	Unc	BU
1950	—	—	—	—	775	—

SYRIA

The Syrian Arab Republic, located in the Near East at the eastern end of the Mediterranean Sea, has an area of 71,498 sq. mi. (185,180 sq. km.) and a population of *12 million. Capital: Greater Damascus. Agriculture and animal breeding are the chief industries. Cotton, crude oil and livestock are exported.

Ancient Syria, a land bridge connecting Europe, Africa and Asia, has spent much of its history in thrall to the conqueror's whim. Its subjection by Egypt about 1500 B.C. was followed by successive conquests by the Hebrews, Phoenicians, Babylonians, Assyrians, Persians, Macedonians, Romans, Byzantines and finally, in 636 A.D., by the Moslems. The Arabs made Damascus, one of the oldest continuously inhabited cities of the world, the trade center and capital of an empire stretching from India to Spain. In 1516, following the total destruction of Damascus by the Mongols of Tamerlane, Syria fell to the Ottoman Turks and remained a part of Turkey until the end of World War I. The League of Nations gave France a mandate to the Levant states of Syria and Lebanon in 1920. In 1930, following a series of uprisings, France recognized Syria as an independent republic, but still subject to the mandate. Lebanon became fully independent on Nov. 22, 1943, and Syria on Jan. 1, 1944.

TITLES

الجمهورية السورية

al-Jumhuriya(t) al-Suriya(t)

الجمهورية لعربية السورية

al-Jumhuriya(t) al-Arabiya(t) as-Suriya(t)

RULERS
Ottoman, until 1918
Faysal, 1918-1920

MINT MARK
(a)- Paris, privy marks only

MINT NAMES

دمشق

Damascus (Dimask)

حلب

Haleb (Aleppo)

KINGDOM
STANDARD COINAGE

KM# 67 DINAR
6.7000 g., Gold **Obv:** Crowned shield within sprigs **Rev:** Design within wreath

Date	Mintage	F	VF	XF	Unc	BU
AH1338 (1919)	Est. 12	—	—	—	8,000	—

REPUBLIC
STANDARD COINAGE

KM# 84 1/2 POUND
3.3793 g., 0.9000 Gold .0978 oz. AGW **Obv:** Imperial eagle **Rev:** Inscription within rectangle above sprigs

Date	Mintage	F	VF	XF	Unc	BU
AH1369-1950	100,000	BV	70.00	80.00	125	175

KM# 86 POUND
6.7586 g., 0.9000 Gold .1956 oz. AGW **Obv:** Imperial eagle **Rev:** Inscription and value within rectangle above sprigs

Date	Mintage	F	VF	XF	Unc	BU
AH1369-1950	250,000	—	BV	145	175	225

SYRIAN ARAB REPUBLIC

MEDALLIC COINAGE

X# 1 POUND
8.0000 g., 0.9000 Gold .2315 oz. AGW

Date	Mintage	F	VF	XF	Unc	BU
AH1398/1978	20,000	—	—	—	185	—

X# 2 5 POUNDS
40.0000 g., 0.9000 Gold 1.1574 oz. AGW **Obv:** Eagle arms, ornaments below **Rev:** Bust of Hafez al-Assad **Note:** Similar to M1.

Date	Mintage	F	VF	XF	Unc	BU
AH1398/1978	5,000	—	—	—	975	—

TANZANIA

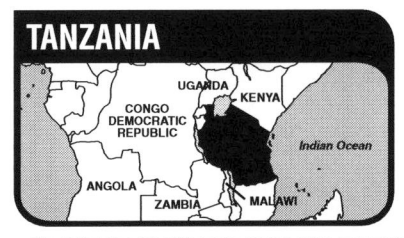

The United Republic of Tanzania, located on the east coast of Africa between Kenya and Mozambique, consists of Tanganyika and the islands of Zanzibar and Pemba. It has an area of 364,900 sq. mi. (945,090 sq. km.) and a population of *25.2 million. Capital: Dar es Salaam (Haven of Peace). The chief exports are cotton, coffee, diamonds, sisal, cloves, petroleum products, and cashew nuts.

Tanzania is a member of the Commonwealth of Nations. The President is Chief of State.

NOTE: For earlier coinage see East Africa.

REPUBLIC

STANDARD COINAGE

100 Senti = 1 Shilingi

KM# 17 1000 SHILINGI
8.1000 g., 0.9000 Gold .2344 oz. AGW **Series:** Decade for Women **Obv:** President J.K. Nyerere left flanked by flowers **Obv. Designer:** Christopher Ironside **Rev:** Half figure separating grain

Date	Mintage	F	VF	XF	Unc	BU
1984 Proof	500	Value: 200				

KM# 60 1000 SHILINGI
1.2440 g., 0.9990 Gold 0.04 oz. AGW, 13.92 mm. **Obv:** National arms **Rev:** Primitive gold refining scene **Edge:** Reeded

Date	Mintage	F	VF	XF	Unc	BU
1998 Proof	—	Value: 60.00				

KM# 9 1500 SHILINGI
33.4370 g., 0.9000 Gold .9676 oz. AGW **Subject:** Conservation **Obv:** President J.K. Nyerere left flanked by flowers **Obv. Designer:** Christopher Ironside **Rev:** Cheetahs

Date	Mintage	F	VF	XF	Unc	BU
1974	2,779	—	—	—	685	725
1974 Proof	866	Value: 775				

KM# 15 2000 SHILINGI
15.9800 g., 0.9170 Gold .4712 oz. AGW **Subject:** 20th Anniversary of Independence **Obv:** President J.K. Nyerere **Obv. Designer:** Philip Nathan **Rev:** National arms

Date	Mintage	F	VF	XF	Unc	BU
ND(1981)	110	—	—	—	375	400
ND(1981) Proof	Inc. above	Value: 425				

KM# 19 2000 SHILINGI
15.9800 g., 0.9170 Gold .4712 oz. AGW **Subject:** Conservation **Obv:** President J.K. Nyerere left flanked by flowers **Obv. Designer:** Christopher Ironside **Rev:** Banded Green Sunbird

Date	Mintage	F	VF	XF	Unc	BU
1986 Proof	5,000	Value: 335				

KM# 25 2000 SHILINGI
10.0000 g., 0.9170 Gold .2948 oz. AGW **Series:** Save the Children Fund **Obv:** President Mwinyi right flanked by small sprigs **Rev:** Child and calf within circle

Date	Mintage	F	VF	XF	Unc	BU
1990 Proof	Est. 3,000	Value: 235				

KM# 31 2500 SHILINGI
46.8500 g., 0.9170 Gold 1.3808 oz. AGW **Subject:** 25 Years of Independence **Obv:** President J.K. Nyerere 1/4 left within circle **Obv. Designer:** Philip Nathan **Rev:** National arms

Date	Mintage	F	VF	XF	Unc	BU
ND(1985) Proof	—	Value: 1,000				

KM# 42 10000 SHILINGI
31.1035 g., 0.9999 Gold 1.0000 oz. AGW, 32.5 mm. **Subject:** Serengeti Wildlife **Obv:** National arms **Rev:** Lion, Cheetah and Zebra **Edge:** Reeded

Date	Mintage	F	VF	XF	Unc	BU
1998 Proof	Est. 1,000	Value: 735				

KM# 58 50000 SHILINGI
155.5100 g., 0.9990 Gold 4.9948 oz. AGW **Subject:** Serengeti Wildlife **Obv:** National arms **Rev:** Lion, Cheetah and Zebra

Date	Mintage	F	VF	XF	Unc	BU
1998 Proof	—	Value: 5,800				

THAILAND

The Kingdom of Thailand (formerly Siam), a constitutional monarchy located in the center of mainland Southeast Asia between Burma and Laos, has an area of 198,457 mi. (514,000 sq. km.) and a population of *55.5 million. Capital: Bangkok. The economy is based on agriculture and mining. Rubber, rice, teakwood, tin and tungsten are exported.

The history of The Kingdom of Siam, the only country in south and Southeast Asia that was never colonized by an European power, dates from the 6th century A.D. when Thai people started to migrate into the area a process that accelerated with the Mongol invasion of China in the 13th century. After 400 years of sporadic warfare with the neighboring Burmese, King Taskin won the last battle in 1767. He founded a new capital, Dhonburi, on the west bank of the Chao Praya River. King Rama I moved the capital to Bangkok in 1782, thus initiating the so-called Bangkok Period of Siamese coinage characterized by Pot Duang money (bullet coins) stamped with regal symbols.

The Portuguese, who were followed by the Dutch, British and French, introduced the Thai to the Western world. Rama III of the present ruling dynasty negotiated a treaty of friendship and commerce with Britain in 1826, and in 1896 the independence of the kingdom was guaranteed by an Anglo-French accord.

In 1909 Siam ceded to Great Britain its suzerain rights over the dependencies of Kedah, Kelantan, Trengganu and Perlis, Malay states situated in southern Siam just north of British Malaya, which eliminated any British jurisdiction in Siam proper.

The absolute monarchy was changed into a constitutional monarchy in 1932.

On Dec. 8, 1941, after five hours of fighting, Thailand agreed to permit Japanese troops passage through the country to invade Northern British Malaysia. This eventually led to increased Japanese intervention and finally occupation of the country. On Jan. 25, 1942, Thailand declared war on Great Britain and the United States. A free Thai guerilla movement was soon organized to counteract the Japanese. In July 1943 Japan transferred the four northern Malay States back to Thailand. These were returned to Great Britain after peace treaties were signed in 1946.

RULERS
Rama V (Phra Maha Chulalongkorn), 1868-1910
Rama VI (Phra Maha Vajiravudh), 1910-1925
Rama VII (Phra Maha Prajadhipok), 1925-1935
Rama VIII (Phra Maha Ananda Mahidol), 1935-1946
Rama IX (Phra Maha Bhumifhol Adulyadej), 1946-

MONETARY SYSTEM
Old currency system
2 Solos = 1 Att
2 Att = 1 Sio (Pai)
2 Sio = 1 Sik
2 Sik = 1 Fuang
2 Fuang = 1 Salung (not Sal'ung)
4 Salung = 1 Baht
4 Baht = 1 Tamlung
20 Tamlung = 1 Chang

UNITS OF OLD THAI CURRENCY

MINT MARKS
H-Heaton Birmingham

DATING

Typical BE Dating

Typical CS Dating

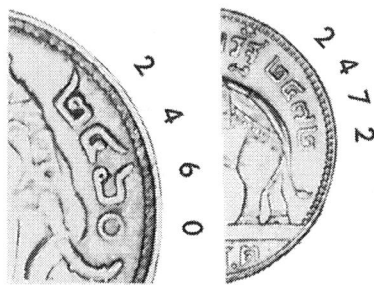

NOTE: Sometimes the era designator BE or CS will actually appear on the coin itself.

Denomination

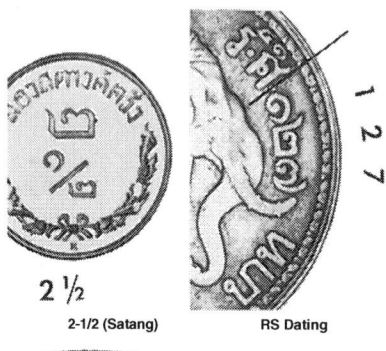

2 ½
2-1/2 (Satang)

RS Dating

DATE CONVERSION TABLES
B.E. date - 543 = A.D. date
Ex: 2516 - 543 = 1973
R.S. date + 1781 = A.D. date
Ex: 127 + 1781 = 1908
C.S. date + 638 = A.D. date
Ex 1238 + 638 = 1876

Primary denominations used were 1 Baht, 1/4 and 1/8 Baht up to the reign of Rama IV. Other denominations are much scarcer.

KINGDOM OF SIAM
until 1939

BULLET COINAGE
Gold Pot Duang

C# 152 1/32 GOLD BAHT
0.4800 g., Gold Ruler: Rama IV

Date	Mintage	VG	F	VF	XF	Unc
ND P'ra Tao	—	250	850	1,500	2,000	—

C# 162 1/32 GOLD BAHT
0.4800 g., Gold Ruler: Rama IV

Date	Mintage	VG	F	VF	XF	Unc
ND Mongkut						

Note: No examples of this type have been confirmed

C# 92 1/16 GOLD BAHT
0.9600 g., Gold Ruler: Rama III

Date	Mintage	VG	F	VF	XF	Unc
ND Prasat	—	75.00	120	350	500	700

C# 153 1/16 GOLD BAHT
0.9600 g., Gold Ruler: Rama IV

Date	Mintage	VG	F	VF	XF	Unc
ND P'ra Tao	—	100	150	375	550	700

C# 163 1/16 GOLD BAHT
0.9600 g., Gold Ruler: Rama IV

Date	Mintage	VG	F	VF	XF	Unc
ND Mongkut	—	70.00	100	325	500	700

C# 93 1/8 GOLD BAHT
1.9600 g., Gold Ruler: Rama III

Date	Mintage	VG	F	VF	XF	Unc
ND Prasat	—	125	200	500	900	1,500

C# 103 1/8 GOLD BAHT
1.9600 g., Gold Ruler: Rama III

Date	Mintage	VG	F	VF	XF	Unc
ND Dok Mai	—	150	200	800	1,000	1,200

C# 113 1/8 GOLD BAHT
1.9600 g., Gold Ruler: Rama III

Date	Mintage	VG	F	VF	XF	Unc
ND Bai Matum	—	150	200	800	1,000	1,200

C# 154 1/8 GOLD BAHT
1.9600 g., Gold Ruler: Rama IV

Date	Mintage	VG	F	VF	XF	Unc
ND P'ra Tao	—	100	175	350	700	900

C# 155 1/4 GOLD BAHT
3.8500 g., Gold Ruler: Rama IV

Date	Mintage	VG	F	VF	XF	Unc
ND P'ra Tao	—	200	400	675	900	1,200

C# 165 1/4 GOLD BAHT
3.8500 g., Gold Ruler: Rama IV

Date	Mintage	VG	F	VF	XF	Unc
ND Mongkut	—	250	425	700	900	1,200

C# 105 1/2 GOLD BAHT
7.7000 g., Gold Ruler: Rama III

Date	Mintage	VG	F	VF	XF	Unc
ND Dok Mai Rare	—	—	—	—	—	—

C# 166 1/2 GOLD BAHT
7.7000 g., Gold Ruler: Rama IV

Date	Mintage	VG	F	VF	XF	Unc
ND Mongkut	—	250	400	900	2,000	2,500

C# 96 GOLD BAHT
15.4000 g., Gold Ruler: Rama III

Date	Mintage	VG	F	VF	XF	Unc
ND Prasat	—	900	1,800	10,000	15,000	20,000

C# 167 GOLD BAHT
15.4000 g., Gold Ruler: Rama IV

Date	Mintage	VG	F	VF	XF	Unc
ND Mongkut	—	800	1,650	3,000	6,000	8,000

C# 167.5 1-1/2 GOLD BAHT (Met Kanoon)
23.1000 g., Gold Ruler: Rama IV

THAILAND 673

Date | **Mintage** | **VG** | **F** | **VF** | **XF** | **Unc**
ND Mongkut — — — — 40,000 —
Note: Unlike other bullet coins this does not have its ends hammered into the normal bullet configuration

C# 168 2 GOLD BAHT
30.8000 g., Gold Ruler: Rama IV

Date | **Mintage** | **VG** | **F** | **VF** | **XF** | **Unc**
ND Mongkut — — — 15,000 20,000 —

C# 169 4 GOLD BAHT
61.6000 g., Gold Ruler: Rama IV

Date | **Mintage** | **VG** | **F** | **VF** | **XF** | **Unc**
ND Mongkut Rare — — — — — —

TRANSITIONAL COINAGE

A series of hammered flat coinage ordered by Rama IV to alleviate a shortage in small bullet coinage while awaiting arrival of the modern coinage presses from England.

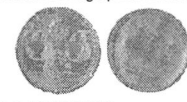

C# 172 GOLD 1/2 FUANG
1.0000 g., Gold Ruler: Rama IV Obv: "Chakra" above royal crown and "P'ra Tao" at left and right Note: Uniface.

Date | **Mintage** | **VG** | **F** | **VF** | **XF** | **Unc**
ND(c.1856) Rare — — — — — —

C# 175 GOLD FUANG
1.8000 g., Gold Ruler: Rama IV Obv: Royal crown Rev. Legend: "Krungthep" (Bangkok)

Date | **Mintage** | **VG** | **F** | **VF** | **XF** | **Unc**
ND(c.1856) Rare — — — — — —
Note: Taisei-Baldwin-Gillio Singapore sale 3-96 AU realized $42,000

C# 176 GOLD SALUNG
3.8000 g., Gold Ruler: Rama IV Obv: Royal crown Rev. Legend: "Krungthep" (Bangkok)

Date | **Mintage** | **VG** | **F** | **VF** | **XF** | **Unc**
ND(c.1856) Rare — — — — — —

STANDARD COINAGE

Y# 8a FUANG (1/8 Baht)
0.9000 g., 1.9400 Gold Ruler: Rama IV Obv: Three crowns within circle Rev: Elephant within chakra in circle Edge: Reeded Note: Thin flan.

Date | **Mintage** | **F** | **VF** | **XF** | **Unc** | **BU**
ND(1864) — 800 1,600 3,000 5,000 —

Y# 32b FUANG (1/8 Baht)
Gold Ruler: Rama V Obv: Uniformed bust left Rev: Crowned shield flanked by crowns

Date | **Mintage** | **F** | **VF** | **XF** | **Unc** | **BU**
ND(1876) — 800 1,600 3,500 6,000 —

Y# 32c FUANG (1/8 Baht)
Gold Ruler: Rama V Obv: Bust left Rev: National arms

Date | **Mintage** | **F** | **VF** | **XF** | **Unc** | **BU**
RS122 (1903) — 500 1,000 1,500 2,500 —
RS123 (1904) — 1,500 3,000 5,000 7,000 —
RS124 (1905) — 1,500 3,000 5,000 7,000 —
RS125 (1906) — 1,500 3,000 5,000 7,000 —
RS126 (1907) — 1,500 3,000 5,000 7,000 —
RS127 (1908) — 1,500 3,000 5,000 7,000 —
RS128 (1909) — 1,500 3,000 5,000 7,000 —
RS129 (1910) — 1,500 3,000 5,000 7,000 —

Y# 7a 1/16 BAHT (1 Sik)
1.0000 g., 0.9000 Gold Ruler: Rama IV Edge: Reeded

Date | **Mintage** | **F** | **VF** | **XF** | **Unc** | **BU**
ND(1864) — — — — — —

Y# 9a SALU'NG (1/4 Baht)
Gold Ruler: Rama IV Obv: Three crowns within circle Rev: Elephant within chakra

Date | **Mintage** | **F** | **VF** | **XF** | **Unc** | **BU**
ND(1864) — — — — — —

Y# 10.2a 2 SALU'NG (1/2 Baht)
7.5500 g., Gold Ruler: Rama IV

Date | **Mintage** | **F** | **VF** | **XF** | **Unc** | **BU**
ND(1864) Rare — — — — — —
Note: Spink-Taisei Auction #15, 9-93 Unc. realized $23,000

Y# 15.5 2 SALU'NG (1/2 Baht)
7.5500 g., Gold Ruler: Rama V Edge: Reeded

Date | **Mintage** | **F** | **VF** | **XF** | **Unc** | **BU**
ND(1894) — — — — — —

Y# 11a BAHT
15.2500 g., Gold Ruler: Rama IV Obv: Three crowns Rev: Elephant within chakra

Date | **Mintage** | **F** | **VF** | **XF** | **Unc** | **BU**
ND(1864) Rare — — — — — —
Note: Spink-Taisei Auction #15, 9-93 Unc. realized $34,000

Y# 12a 2 BAHT
30.3000 g., Gold Ruler: Rama IV Obv: Three crowns Rev: Elephant within chakra

Date | **Mintage** | **F** | **VF** | **XF** | **Unc** | **BU**
ND(1864) Rare — — — — — —
Note: Spink-Taisei Auction #15, 9-93 Unc. realized $44,000

Y# 13 POT DUENG (2-1/2 Baht)
2.2000 g., 0.9970 Gold Ruler: Rama IV Obv: Three crowns Rev: Elephant within chakra

Date | **Mintage** | **F** | **VF** | **XF** | **Unc** | **BU**
ND(1863) — 800 1,500 2,500 4,000 —

Y# 13.5 POT DUENG (2-1/2 Baht)
Gold Ruler: Rama V Obv: Three crowns Rev: Elephant within chakra

Date | **Mintage** | **F** | **VF** | **XF** | **Unc** | **BU**
ND(1894) — 600 1,000 1,800 2,600 —

Y# 13.1 POT DUENG (2-1/2 Baht)
Gold Ruler: Rama V Note: Weight varies: 1.90-2.00 grams.

Date | **Mintage** | **F** | **VF** | **XF** | **Unc** | **BU**
ND(1894) — 650 1,250 2,000 2,800 —

Y# A12a TAMLUNG (4 Baht)
60.7700 g., 0.9970 Gold Ruler: Rama IV Obv: Diamond shape design divides legend, inscription within, all within circle Rev: Three crowns within circle

Date | **Mintage** | **F** | **VF** | **XF** | **Unc** | **BU**
ND(1864) Rare — — — — — —
Note: Spink-Taisei Auction #4, 2-88, XF specimen realized $74,800

Y# 14 PIT (4 Baht)
0.9970 Gold 3.40 oz. AGW Ruler: Rama IV Obv: Three crowns Rev: Elephant within chakra Edge: Reeded

Date | **Mintage** | **F** | **VF** | **XF** | **Unc** | **BU**
ND(1863) — 1,000 1,500 2,300 4,000 —

Y# 14.5 PIT (4 Baht)
0.9970 Gold Ruler: Rama V Obv: Three crowns Rev: Elephant within chakra Note: Weight varies: 3.65-4.00 grams.

Date | **Mintage** | **F** | **VF** | **XF** | **Unc** | **BU**
ND(1894) — 1,000 1,600 2,500 3,500 —

Y# 15 TOT (8 Baht)
6.8000 g., 0.9970 Gold Ruler: Rama IV Obv: Three crowns Rev: Elephant within chakra Edge: Reeded

Date | **Mintage** | **F** | **VF** | **XF** | **Unc** | **BU**
ND(1863) — 1,250 2,500 4,500 10,000 —

Y# 15.1 TOT (8 Baht)
Gold Ruler: Rama V Note: Weight varies: 7.30-8.00 grams.

Date | **Mintage** | **F** | **VF** | **XF** | **Unc** | **BU**
ND(1894) — 1,000 1,750 2,800 6,500 —

Y# 15.6 TOT (8 Baht)
Gold Ruler: Rama V Rev: Elephant within chakra

Date | **Mintage** | **F** | **VF** | **XF** | **Unc** | **BU**
ND(1896) — — — — — —
Note: Reported, not confirmed

PRESENTATION COINAGE
Bannakin (Royal Gift) Coins

KM# A10 POT DUENG (2-1/2 Baht)
2.1500 g., Gold Ruler: Rama IV

Date | **Mintage** | **F** | **VF** | **XF** | **Unc** | **BU**
ND(1857-58) Rare — — — — — —

674   THAILAND

KINGDOM OF THAILAND
1939-
DECIMAL COINAGE

25 Satang = 1 Salung; 100 Satang = 1 Baht

Y# 366   100 BAHT
7.7759 g., 0.9999 Gold .2500 oz. AGW, 22 mm.
Subject: Year of the Dragon **Obv:** Bust 1/4 left **Rev:** Dragon with golden plated pearl **Edge:** Reeded

Date	Mintage	F	VF	XF	Unc	BU
BE2543 (2000) Proof	1,800	Value: 200				

Y# 88   150 BAHT
3.7500 g., 0.9000 Gold .1085 oz. AGW **Ruler:** Rama IX
Subject: Queen Sirikit 36th Birthday **Obv:** Bust right **Rev:** Crowned monogram

Date	Mintage	F	VF	XF	Unc	BU
BE2511 (1968)	202,000	—	—	—	100	—

Y# 89   300 BAHT
7.5000 g., 0.9000 Gold .2170 oz. AGW **Ruler:** Rama IX
Subject: Queen Sirikit 36th Birthday **Obv:** Bust right **Rev:** Crowned monogram

Date	Mintage	F	VF	XF	Unc	BU
BE2511 (1968)	101,000	—	—	—	175	—

Y# 90   600 BAHT
15.0000 g., 0.9000 Gold .4340 oz. AGW **Ruler:** Rama IX
Subject: Queen Sirikit 36th Birthday **Obv:** Crowned bust right **Rev:** Crowned monogram within wreath

Date	Mintage	F	VF	XF	Unc	BU
BE2511 (1968)	46,000	—	—	—	325	380

Y# 94   800 BAHT
20.0000 g., 0.9000 Gold .5787 oz. AGW **Ruler:** Rama IX
Subject: 25th Anniversary - Reign of King Rama IX **Obv:** Head right **Rev:** Radiant crowned monogram flanked by sprigs

Date	Mintage	F	VF	XF	Unc	BU
BE2514 (1971)	22,000	—	—	—	425	485

Y# 200   1500 BAHT
3.7500 g., 0.9000 Gold .1085 oz. AGW **Ruler:** Rama IX
Subject: 60th Birthday - King Rama IX **Obv:** Bust facing **Rev:** Radiant crowned emblem

Date	Mintage	F	VF	XF	Unc	BU
BE2530 (1987)	5,000	—	—	—	95.00	—
BE2530 (1987) Proof	400	Value: 175				

Y# 216   1500 BAHT
3.7500 g., 0.9000 Gold .1085 oz. AGW **Ruler:** Rama IX
Subject: 42nd Anniversary - Reign of King Rama IX **Obv:** Bust facing **Rev:** Crowned monogram

Date	Mintage	F	VF	XF	Unc	BU
BE2531 (1988)	11,000	—	—	—	90.00	—
BE2531 (1988) Proof	995	Value: 160				

Y# 265   1500 BAHT
3.7500 g., 0.9000 Gold .1085 oz. AGW **Ruler:** Rama IX
Subject: Queen's 60th Birthday **Obv:** Crowned bust facing **Rev:** Crowned monogram **Note:** Similar to 10 Baht, Y#261.

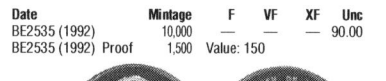

Date	Mintage	F	VF	XF	Unc	BU
BE2535 (1992)	10,000	—	—	—	90.00	—
BE2535 (1992) Proof	1,500	Value: 150				

Y# 380   2000 BAHT
6.2200 g., 0.9990 Gold 0.1998 oz. AGW, 22 mm. **Ruler:** Rama IX **Subject:** UNICEF **Obv:** Bust 3/4 left **Rev:** Girl with Thai desk **Edge:** Reeded

Date	Mintage	F	VF	XF	Unc	BU
BE2540-1997 Proof	1,700	Value: 175				

Y# 119   2500 BAHT
15.0000 g., 0.9000 Gold .4340 oz. AGW **Ruler:** Rama IX
Subject: Crown Prince Vajiralongkorn and Princess Soamsawali Wedding **Obv:** Conjoined busts right **Rev:** Crowned monogram within lightning bolts

Date	Mintage	F	VF	XF	Unc	BU
BE2520 (1977)	20,000	—	—	—	300	325

Y# 126   2500 BAHT
15.0000 g., 0.9000 Gold .4340 oz. AGW **Ruler:** Rama IX
Subject: Investiture of Princess Sirindhorn **Obv:** Bust 1/4 right **Rev:** Crowned monogram

Date	Mintage	F	VF	XF	Unc	BU
BE2520 (1977)	5,000	—	—	—	320	350

Y# 170   2500 BAHT
15.0000 g., 0.9000 Gold .4340 oz. AGW **Ruler:** Rama IX
Series: International Year of Disabled Persons **Obv:** Bust left **Rev:** Emblem within sprigs

Date	Mintage	F	VF	XF	Unc	BU
BE2526 (1983)	92	—	—	—	1,400	—
BE2526 (1983) Proof	793	Value: 1,250				

Y# 207   2500 BAHT
15.9800 g., 0.9000 Gold .4625 oz. AGW **Ruler:** Rama IX
Series: 25th Anniversary of World Wildlife Fund **Obv:** Bust left **Rev:** Elephant left within circle

Date	Mintage	F	VF	XF	Unc	BU
BE2530 (1987) Proof	Est. 5,000	Value: 350				

Y# 325   2500 BAHT
3.7500 g., 0.9000 Gold .1085 oz. AGW **Ruler:** Rama IX
Subject: 50th Anniversary - Reign of King Rama IX **Obv:** Bust facing **Rev:** National arms **Note:** Similar to 20 Baht, Y#321.1.

Date	Mintage	F	VF	XF	Unc	BU
BE2539 (1996)	—	—	—	—	85.00	—
BE2539 (1996) Proof	—	Value: 135				

Y# 369   2500 BAHT
155.5175 g., 0.9999 Gold 5.0000 oz. AGW, 55 mm. **Ruler:** Rama IX **Subject:** Year of the Dragon **Obv:** Bust left **Rev:** Two dragons with pearl hologram **Edge:** Reeded

Date	Mintage	F	VF	XF	Unc	BU
BE2543 (2000) In sets only	500	—	—	—	3,500	—

Y# 129   3000 BAHT
15.0000 g., 0.9000 Gold .4340 oz. AGW **Ruler:** Rama IX
Subject: Graduation of Crown Prince Vijiralongkorn **Obv:** Bust left **Rev:** Crowned elephant head facing within frame

Date	Mintage	F	VF	XF	Unc	BU
BE2521 (1978)	10,000	—	—	—	320	340

Y# 201   3000 BAHT
7.5000 g., 0.9000 Gold .2170 oz. AGW **Ruler:** Rama IX
Subject: 60th Birthday - King Rama IX **Obv:** Uniformed bust facing **Rev:** Radiant crowned emblem

Date	Mintage	F	VF	XF	Unc	BU
BE2530 (1987)	3,000	—	—	—	165	—
BE2530 (1987) Proof	400	Value: 275				

Y# 217   3000 BAHT
7.5000 g., 0.9000 Gold .2170 oz. AGW **Ruler:** Rama IX
Subject: 42nd Anniversary - Reign of King Rama IX **Obv:** Uniformed bust facing **Rev:** Radiant crowned monogram

Date	Mintage	F	VF	XF	Unc	BU
BE2531 (1988)	7,904	—	—	—	175	—
BE2531 (1988) Proof	780	Value: 325				

Y# 266   3000 BAHT
7.5000 g., 0.9000 Gold .2170 oz. AGW **Ruler:** Rama IX
Subject: Queen's 60th Birthday **Obv:** Crowned bust facing **Rev:** Crowned monogram

Date	Mintage	F	VF	XF	Unc	BU
BE2535 (1992)	7,000	—	—	—	175	—
BE2535 (1992) Proof	1,100	Value: 330				

Y# 326   3000 BAHT
7.5000 g., 0.9000 Gold .2170 oz. AGW **Ruler:** Rama IX
Subject: 50th Anniversary - Reign of King Rama IX **Obv:** Uniformed bust facing **Rev:** National arms

Date	Mintage	F	VF	XF	Unc	BU
BE2539 (1996)	—	—	—	—	185	—
BE2539 (1996) Proof	—	Value: 325				

Y# 153   4000 BAHT
17.1700 g., 0.9000 Gold .4969 oz. AGW **Ruler:** Rama IX
Series: International Year of the Child **Obv:** Bust left **Rev:** Two children playing

Date	Mintage	F	VF	XF	Unc	BU
BE2524 (1981) Proof	3,963	Value: 365				

THAILAND

Y# 104 5000 BAHT
33.4370 g., 0.9000 Gold .9676 oz. AGW **Ruler:** Rama IX **Series:** Conservation **Obv:** Bust 1/4 left **Rev:** White-eyed River Martin

Date	Mintage	F	VF	XF	Unc	BU
BE2517 (1974)	2,602	—	—	—	685	725
BE2517 (1974) Proof	623	Value: 1,800				

Y# 122 5000 BAHT
30.0000 g., 0.9000 Gold .8681 oz. AGW **Ruler:** Rama IX **Subject:** 50th Birthday - King Rama IX **Obv:** Bust left **Rev:** Radiant crowned monogram

Date	Mintage	F	VF	XF	Unc	BU
BE2520 (1977)	6,400	—	—	—	620	650

Y# 156 6000 BAHT
15.0000 g., 0.9000 Gold .4341 oz. AGW **Ruler:** Rama IX **Subject:** 50th Birthday - Queen Sirikit **Obv:** Crowned bust 1/4 left **Rev:** Crowned monogram

Date	Mintage	F	VF	XF	Unc	BU
BE2525 (1982)	1,471	—	—	—	450	500
BE2525 (1982) Proof	99	Value: 4,000				

Y# 167 6000 BAHT
15.0000 g., 0.9000 Gold .4341 oz. AGW **Ruler:** Rama IX **Subject:** 700th Anniversary - Thai Alphabet **Obv:** Seated figure left **Rev:** Inscription

Date	Mintage	F	VF	XF	Unc	BU
BE2526 (1983)	700	—	—	—	350	380
BE2526 (1983) Proof	235	Value: 620				

Y# 174 6000 BAHT
15.0000 g., 0.9000 Gold .4341 oz. AGW **Ruler:** Rama IX **Subject:** 84th Birthday - Princess Mother **Obv:** Bust left **Rev:** Crown on stand flanked by others

Date	Mintage	F	VF	XF	Unc	BU
BE2527 (1984)	835	—	—	—	350	380
BE2527 (1984) Proof	246	Value: 650				

Y# 202 6000 BAHT
15.0000 g., 0.9000 Gold .4341 oz. AGW **Ruler:** Rama IX **Subject:** 60th Birthday - King Rama IX **Obv:** Uniformed bust facing **Rev:** Radiant crowned emblem

Date	Mintage	F	VF	XF	Unc	BU
BE2530 (1987)	2,000	—	—	—	325	350
BE2530 (1987) Proof	350	Value: 475				

Y# 247 6000 BAHT
15.0000 g., 0.9000 Gold .4341 oz. AGW **Ruler:** Rama IX **Subject:** Asian Institute of Technology **Obv:** Kneeling and seated figures within circle **Rev:** Emblem

Date	Mintage	F	VF	XF	Unc	BU
BE2530 (1987)	700	—	—	—	350	380
BE2530 (1987) Proof	100	Value: 650				

Y# 218 6000 BAHT
15.0000 g., 0.9000 Gold .4341 oz. AGW **Ruler:** Rama IX **Subject:** 42nd Anniversary - Reign of King Rama IX **Obv:** Uniformed bust facing **Rev:** Radiant crowned monogram

Date	Mintage	F	VF	XF	Unc	BU
BE2531 (1988)	6,067	—	—	—	320	340
BE2531 (1988) Proof	670	Value: 500				

Y# 246 6000 BAHT
15.0000 g., 0.9000 Gold .4341 oz. AGW **Ruler:** Rama IX **Subject:** World Health Organization

Date	Mintage	F	VF	XF	Unc	BU
BE2534 (1991)	5,000	—	—	—	350	380
BE2534 (1991) Proof	591	Value: 600				

Y# 258 6000 BAHT
15.0000 g., 0.9000 Gold .4341 oz. AGW **Ruler:** Rama IX **Subject:** Princess Sirindhorn's Magsaysay Foundation Award **Obv:** Princess seated with children **Rev:** Obverse of medal above larger reverse with inscription

Date	Mintage	F	VF	XF	Unc	BU
BE2535 (1992)	1,600	—	—	—	350	380
BE2535 (1992) Proof	500	Value: 650				

Y# 267 6000 BAHT
15.0000 g., 0.9000 Gold .4341 oz. AGW **Ruler:** Rama IX **Subject:** Queen's 60th Birthday **Obv:** Crowned bust facing **Rev:** Crowned monogram

Date	Mintage	F	VF	XF	Unc	BU
BE2535 (1992)	7,000	—	—	—	320	340
BE2535 (1992) Proof	1,200	Value: 450				

Y# 275 6000 BAHT
15.0000 g., 0.9000 Gold .4341 oz. AGW **Ruler:** Rama IX **Subject:** 64th Birthday - King Rama IX **Obv:** Conjoined busts left **Rev:** Crowned monograms

Date	Mintage	F	VF	XF	Unc	BU
BE2535 (1992)	3,000	—	—	—	330	350
BE2535 (1992) Proof	500	Value: 600				

Y# 291 6000 BAHT
15.0000 g., 0.9000 Gold .4341 oz. AGW **Ruler:** Rama IX **Subject:** 100th Anniversary of Rama VII **Obv:** Bust left **Rev:** Royal crown and accoutrements

Date	Mintage	F	VF	XF	Unc	BU
BE2536 (1993)	2,484	—	—	—	330	350
BE2536 (1993) Proof	300	Value: 600				

Y# 327 6000 BAHT
15.0000 g., 0.9000 Gold .4341 oz. AGW **Ruler:** Rama IX **Subject:** King's 50th Year of Reign **Obv:** Uniformed bust facing **Rev:** National arms

Date	Mintage	F	VF	XF	Unc	BU
BE2539 (1996)	—	—	—	—	320	340
BE2539 (1996) Proof	—	Value: 550				

Y# 337 6000 BAHT
15.0000 g., 0.9000 Gold .4341 oz. AGW **Ruler:** Rama IX **Series:** F.A.O. **Subject:** 50th Anniversary - Reign of King Rama IX and World Food Summit **Obv:** Bust left within circle **Rev:** King planting seedlings before adoring crowd

Date	Mintage	F	VF	XF	Unc	BU
BE2539 (1996)	—	—	—	—	320	340
BE2539 (1996) Proof	—	Value: 550				

Y# 370 6000 BAHT
15.0000 g., 0.9000 Gold .4341 oz. AGW **Ruler:** Rama IX **Subject:** King's 72nd Birthday **Obv:** King's portrait **Rev:** Crowned emblem

Date	Mintage	F	VF	XF	Unc	BU
BE2542 (1999)	20,000	—	—	—	300	320
BE2542 (1999) Proof	10,000	Value: 400				

Y# 378 6000 BAHT
15.0000 g., 0.9000 Gold .4340 oz. AGW, 26 mm. **Ruler:** Rama IX **Subject:** King's 72nd Birthday **Obv:** King and Rama I portraits **Rev:** Two royal symbols **Edge:** Reeded

Date	Mintage	F	VF	XF	Unc	BU
BE2543(2000) Proof	—	Value: 375				

Y# 390 7500 BAHT
15.0000 g., 0.9000 Gold 0.434 oz. AGW, 26 mm. **Ruler:** Rama IX **Subject:** King's 75th Birthday **Obv:** King's portrait **Rev:** Royal crown in radiant oval **Edge:** Reeded

Date	Mintage	F	VF	XF	Unc	BU
BE2545(2002)	—	—	—	—	325	345
BE2545(2002) Proof	—	Value: 450				

Y# 139 9000 BAHT
12.0000 g., 0.9000 Gold .3472 oz. AGW **Ruler:** Rama IX **Series:** F.A.O. Ceres Medal **Subject:** Queen's Anniversary **Obv:** Crowned bust 3/4 facing **Rev:** Medal design

Date	Mintage	F	VF	XF	Unc	BU
BE2523 (1980)	3,900	—	—	—	375	400

Y# A143 9000 BAHT
12.0000 g., 0.9000 Gold .3472 oz. AGW **Ruler:** Rama IX **Subject:** Centennial - Birth of King Rama VI **Obv:** Uniformed bust right **Rev:** Radiant crown on stand flanked by others

Date	Mintage	F	VF	XF	Unc	BU
BE2524 (1981)	2,600	—	—	—	375	400

Y# 148 9000 BAHT
15.0000 g., 0.9000 Gold .4340 oz. AGW **Ruler:** Rama IX **Subject:** King Rama IX Anniversary of Reign

Date	Mintage	F	VF	XF	Unc	BU
BE2524 (1981)	4,000	—	—	—	375	400

Y# 151 9000 BAHT
15.0000 g., 0.9000 Gold .4340 oz. AGW **Ruler:** Rama IX **Subject:** Bicentennial of Bangkok **Obv:** Uniformed conjoined busts left **Rev:** Emblem

Date	Mintage	F	VF	XF	Unc	BU
BE2525 (1982)	3,290	—	—	—	375	400

Y# 395 9000 BAHT
15.0000 g., 0.9000 Gold 0.434 oz. AGW, 26 mm. **Ruler:** Rama IX **Subject:** 80th Birthday of Princess **Obv:** Bust half right **Rev:** Crowned emblem and value **Edge:** Reeded

Date	Mintage	F	VF	XF	Unc	BU
BE2546 (2003)	—	—	—	—	400	425
BE2546 (2003) Proof	—	Value: 700				

BULLION COINAGE

In 1943, the government of Thailand made an internal loan by virtue of the Royal Act of Internal Loan related regulation of the Ministry of Finance, both dated 17th May, 1943.

Eight years later another Regulation of the Ministry of Finance dated 11th June, 1951 related to the actual redemption of the loan above mentioned was proclaimed with the following effect: Bond holders have the choice to be paid either in gold coins or gold bars or in other forms, all of which should bear the Garuda emblem and the specific inscription as to its weight and gold purity.

TIBET

KM# 1 50 BAHT
8.6930 g., 0.9950 Gold .2781 oz. AGW **Ruler:** Rama IX **Obv:** Mythical creature "Garuda" flanked by sprigs **Rev:** Inscription

Date	Mintage	F	VF	XF	Unc	BU
ND(1951)	—	—	225	275	375	—

KM# 2 100 BAHT
17.3870 g., 0.9950 Gold .5562 oz. AGW **Ruler:** Rama IX **Obv:** Mythical creature "Garuda" flanked by sprigs **Rev:** Inscription

Date	Mintage	F	VF	XF	Unc	BU
ND(1951)	—	—	425	500	650	—

KM# 3 1000 BAHT
173.8790 g., 0.9950 Gold 5.5620 oz. AGW **Ruler:** Rama IX **Obv:** Mythical creature "Garuda" flanked by sprigs **Rev:** Inscription

Date	Mintage	F	VF	XF	Unc	BU
ND(1951)	—	—	6,000	9,000	14,000	—

PATTERNS
Including off metal strikes

KM#	Date	Mintage	Identification	Mkt Val
Pn17	ND(1860)	—	4 Baht. Gold. With single outline around Thai legend. Y#A12a.	—
Pn50	RS127	—	Satang. Gold. Y#35a.	10,000
Pn51	RS127	—	5 Satang. Gold. Y#36a.	10,000
Pn52	RS127	—	10 Satang. Gold. Y#37a.	10,000

PIEFORTS

KM#	Date	Mintage	Identification	Mkt Val
P2	BE2524	61	4000 Baht. Gold. I.Y.O.C.	2,200
P4	BE2526	—	2500 Baht. Gold. I.Y.D.P.	6,500

PROOF SETS

KM#	Date	Mintage	Identification	Issue Price	Mkt Val
PS3	2000 (5)	500	Y#363-365, 367, 369	3,480	3,650
PS4	2000 (2)	1,800	Y#366, 368	446	450

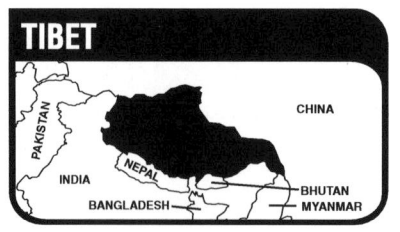

Tibet, an autonomous region of China located in central Asia between the Himalayan and Kunlun Mns. has an area of 471,660 sq. mi. (1,221,599 sq. km.) and a population of *1.9 million. Capital: Lhasa. The economy is based on agriculture and livestock raising. Wool, livestock, salt and hides are exported.

Lamaism, a form of Buddhism, developed in Tibet in the 8th century. From that time until the 1900s, the Tibetan rulers virtually isolated the country from the outside world. The British in India achieved some influence in the early 20th century. British troops were sent with the Young Husband mission to extend trade in the north of India in December 1903; leaving during September 1904. The 13th Dalai Lama had fled to Urga where he remained until 1907. In April 1905 a revolt broke out and spread through southwestern Szechuan and northwestern Yunnan. Chao Erh-feng was appointed to subdue this rebellion and entered Lhasa in January 1910 with 2,000 troops. The Dalai Lama fled to India until he returned in June 1912., The British encouraged Tibet to declare its independence from China in 1913. The Communist revolution in China marked a new era in Tibetan history. Chinese Communist troops invaded Tibet in Oct., 1950. After a token resistance, Tibet signed an agreement with China in which China recognized the spiritual and temporal leadership of the Dalai Lama, and Tibet recognized the suzerainty of China. In 1959, a nationwide revolt triggered by Communist-initiated land reform broke out. The revolt was ruthlessly crushed. The dalai lama fled to India, and on Sept. 1,1965, the Chinese made Tibet an autonomous region of China.

The first coins to circulate in Tibet were those of neighboring Nepal from about 1570. Shortly after 1720, the Nepalese government began striking specific issues for use in Tibet. These coins had a lower silver content than those struck for use in Nepal and were exchanged with the Tibetans for an equal weight in silver bullion. Around 1763 the Tibetans struck their own coins for the first time in history. The number of coins struck at that time must have been very small. Larger quantities of coins were struck by the Tibetan government mint, which opened in 1791 with the permission of the Chinese. Operations of this mint however were suspended two years later. The Chinese opened a second mint in Lhasa in 1792. It produced a coinage until 1836. Shortly thereafter, the Tibetan mint was reopened and the government of Tibet continued to strike coins until 1953.

DATING
Based on the Tibetan calendar, Tibetan coins are dated by the cycle which contains 60 years. To calculate the western date use the following formula: Number of cycles -1, x 60 + number of years + 1026. Example 15th cycle 25th year = 1891 AD. Example: 15th cycle, 25th year 15 - 1 x 60 + 25 + 1026 = 1891AD.

13/30 = 1776	14/30 = 1836	15/30 = 1896
13/40 = 1786	14/40 = 1846	15/40 = 1906
13/50 = 1796	14/50 = 1856	15/50 = 1916
13/60 = 1806	14/60 = 1866	15/60 = 1926
14/10 = 1816	15/10 = 1876	16/10 = 1936
14/20 = 1826	15/20 = 1886	16/20 = 1946

Certain Sino-Tibetan issues are dated in the year of reign of the Emperor of China.

MONETARY SYSTEM
15 Skar = 1-1/2 Sho = 1 Tangka
10 Sho = 1 Srang

TANGKA
CY

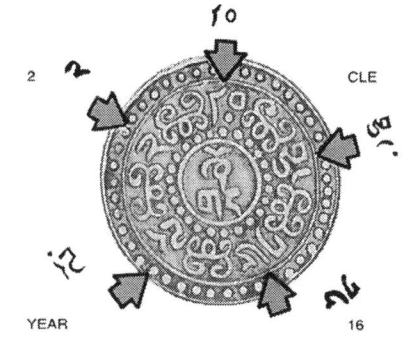

16(th)CYCLE 2(nd)YEAR = 1928AD

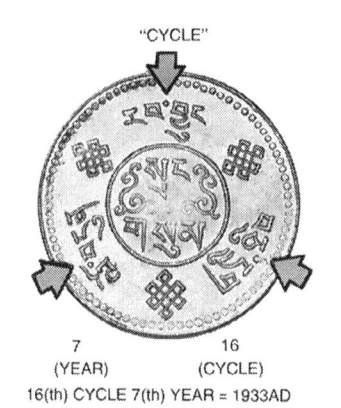

16(th) CYCLE 7(th) YEAR = 1933AD

NUMERALS

25	༢༥ ཉེར་ལྔ
26	༢༦ ཉེར་དྲུག
27	༢༧ ཉེར་བདུན
28	༢༨ ཉེར་བརྒྱད

CHINESE AUTHORITY
SHO-SRANG COINAGE

Y# 22 20 SRANG
Gold **Obv:** Eight Buddhist lucky symbols in outer circle **Edge:** Reeded

Date	Mintage	F	VF	XF	Unc	BU
BE15-52 (1918)	—	425	575	825	1,150	—

Note: With dot in reverse center

| BE15-53 (1919) | — | 425 | 575 | 825 | 1,150 | — |

Note: With large circle in reverse center; Silver strikings for 15-53 exist and are believed to be forgeries

| BE15-53 (1919) | — | 425 | 575 | 825 | 1,150 | — |

Note: With small circle in reverse center

| BE15-54 (1920) | — | 425 | 575 | 825 | 1,150 | — |

Note: With dot in reverse center

| BE15-54 (1920) | — | 425 | 575 | 825 | 1,100 | — |

Note: Silver strikings for 15-54 exist and are believed to be forgeries; Deceptive forgeries struck in high grade gold also exist; without dot in reverse center

| BE15-55 (1921) | — | 700 | 1,000 | 1,500 | 2,000 | — |

TRADE COINAGE
1 Rupee = 3 Tangka

Total mintage of the 1 Rupee between 1902 and 1942 was between 25.5 and 27.5 million according to Chinese sources. In addition to the types illustrated above, large quantities of the following coins also circulated in Tibet: China Dollars, Y#318a, 329, and 345 plus Szechuan issues Y#449 and 459, and Indian Rupees, KM#473, 492, and 508.

Rupees exist with local merchant countermarks in Chinese, Tibetan, and other scripts. Examples of crown-size rupees struck in silver (26.30-27.50 grams) and gold (36.30 grams) are considered fantasies.

Y# 1a 1/4 RUPEE
5.4500 g., Gold

Date	Mintage	F	VF	XF	Unc	BU
ND(1905)	—	1,150	1,900	2,650	3,450	—

Y# 2a 1/2 RUPEE
9.3800 g., Gold

Date	Mintage	F	VF	XF	Unc	BU
ND(1905)	—	1,250	2,000	2,750	3,500	—

Y# 3.2a RUPEE
20.6700 g., Gold **Note:** Prev. Y#3b.

Date	Mintage	F	VF	XF	Unc	BU
ND(ca. 1903-05)	—	900	1,200	1,750	—	—

Note: An example with two obverses exists (20.40 grams)

Y# 3b RUPEE
Gold

Date	Mintage	F	VF	XF	Unc	BU
ND(ca.1930)	—	—	—	—	—	—

MEDALLIC COINAGE
Australian Mint Issues

Authorized by the Dalai Lama in exile and produced by the Royal Australian Mint in May, 1978.

X# 3 5 SHO
13.0400 g., 0.5000 Gold 0.2096 oz. AGW, 29.50 mm. **Obv:** Lion standing left, mountain behind **Edge:** Reeded

Date	Mintage	F	VF	XF	Unc	BU
Yr.16-21 (1947) Proof	250	Value: 200				

X# 6 10 SRANG
0.5000 Gold, 32.20 mm. **Obv:** Lion standing left, mountain behind **Edge:** Reeded

Date	Mintage	F	VF	XF	Unc	BU
Yr. 16-24 (1950) Proof	500	Value: 275				

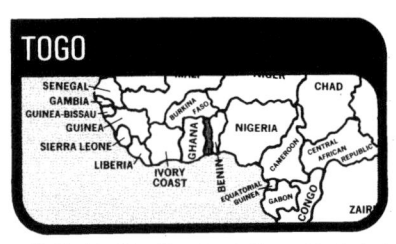

TOGO

The Republic of Togo (formerly part of German Togoland), situated on the Gulf of Guinea in West Africa between Ghana and Dahomey, has an area of 21,622 sq.mi. (56,790 sq. km.) and a population of *3.4 million. Capital: Lome. Agriculture and herding, the production of dyewoods, and the mining of phosphates and iron ore are the chief industries. Copra, phosphates and coffee are exported.

Although Brazilians were the first traders to settle in Togo, Germany achieved possession, in 1884, by inducing coastal chiefs to place their territories under German protection. The German protectorate was extended international recognition at the Berlin conference of 1885 and its ultimate boundaries delimited by treaties with France in 1897 and with Britain in 1904. Anglo-French forces occupied Togoland in 1914, subsequently becoming a League of Nations mandate and a U.N. trusteeship divided, for administrative purpose, between Great Britain and France. The British portion voted in 1957 for incorporation with Ghana. The French portion became the independent Republic of Togo on April 27, 1960.

RULERS
German, 1884-1914
Anglo - French, 1914-1957
French, 1957-1960

MINT MARK
(a) - Paris, privy marks only

MONETARY SYSTEM
100 Centimes = 1 Franc

REPUBLIC
INSTITUT MONETAIRE

KM# 20b 6000 CFA FRANCS - 4 AFRICA
11.0000 g., 0.9990 Bi-Metallic .999 Silver center in .999 Gold ring 0.3533 oz., 28.3 mm. **Obv:** Elephants fighting within circle **Rev:** Elephant head on map within circle **Edge:** Plain

Date	Mintage	F	VF	XF	Unc	BU
2003	5	—	—	—	450	—

KM# 21b 6000 CFA FRANCS - 4 AFRICA
11.0000 g., 0.9990 Bi-Metallic .999 Silver center in .999 Gold ring 0.3533 oz., 28.3 mm. **Obv:** Topless girl within circle **Rev:** Elephant head on map within circle **Edge:** Plain

Date	Mintage	F	VF	XF	Unc	BU
2003	5	—	—	—	450	—

KM# 30a 6000 CFA FRANCS - 4 AFRICA
Bi-Metallic .999 Silver center in .999 Gold plated .999 Silver ring, 28.4 mm. **Obv:** President **Rev:** Elephant head on map within circle

Date	Mintage	F	VF	XF	Unc	BU
2003	5	—	—	—	480	—

KM# 32 6000 CFA FRANCS - 4 AFRICA
0.9990 Silver, 28.4 mm. **Obv:** Fighting elephants within circle **Rev:** Elephant head on map within circle

Date	Mintage	F	VF	XF	Unc	BU
2003	5	—	—	—	480	—

KM# 32a 6000 CFA FRANCS - 4 AFRICA
Bi-Metallic .999 Silver center in .999 Gold plated .999 Silver ring, 28.4 mm. **Obv:** Fighting elephants within circle **Rev:** Elephant head on map within circle

Date	Mintage	F	VF	XF	Unc	BU
2003	5	—	—	—	480	—

KM# 33a 6000 CFA FRANCS - 4 AFRICA
Bi-Metallic .999 Silver center in .999 Gold plated .999 Silver ring, 28.4 mm. **Obv:** Topless girl within circle **Rev:** Elephant head on map within circle

Date	Mintage	F	VF	XF	Unc	BU
2003	5	—	—	—	480	—

KM# 23a 150000 CFA FRANCS - 100 AFRICA
13.2000 g., 0.9990 Gold Plated Silver, 28.4 mm. **Obv:** President and map **Rev:** Elephant head on map

Date	Mintage	F	VF	XF	Unc	BU
ND(2003)	25	—	—	—	265	—

KM# 31a 150000 CFA FRANCS - 100 AFRICA
Bi-Metallic .999 Silver center in .999 Gold plated .999 Silver ring **Obv:** President **Rev:** Elephant head on map within circle

Date	Mintage	F	VF	XF	Unc	BU
2003	5	—	—	—	480	—

STANDARD COINAGE
100 Centimes = 1 Franc

KM# 26 1000 FRANCS
1.2440 g., 0.9999 Gold 0.04 oz. AGW, 13.92 mm. **Obv:** National arms **Rev:** Convex Nike **Edge:** Plain

Date	Mintage	F	VF	XF	Unc	BU
2004 Proof	5,000	Value: 60.00				

TOKELAU

KM# 27 1000 FRANCS
1.2440 g., 0.9999 Gold 0.04 oz. AGW, 13.92 mm. **Obv:** National arms **Rev:** Concave Nike **Edge:** Plain

Date	Mintage	F	VF	XF	Unc	BU
2004 Proof	5,000	Value: 60.00				

KM# 10 15000 FRANCS
4.4800 g., 0.9170 Gold .1320 oz. AGW **Subject:** 10th Year of General Gnassingbe Eyadema as President **Obv:** Arms with supporters **Rev:** Head facing

Date	Mintage	F	VF	XF	Unc	BU
1977 Proof	75	Value: 150				

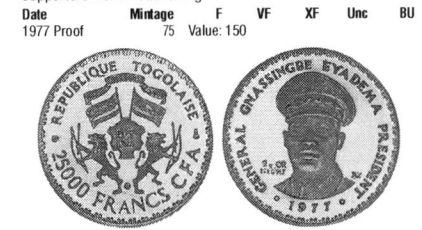

KM# 11 25000 FRANCS
9.0000 g., 0.9170 Gold .2653 oz. AGW **Subject:** 10th Year of General Gnassingbe Eyadema as President **Obv:** Arms with supporters **Rev:** Head facing

Date	Mintage	F	VF	XF	Unc	BU
1977 Proof	75	Value: 275				

KM# 12 50000 FRANCS
18.0000 g., 0.9170 Gold .5306 oz. AGW **Subject:** 10th Year of General Gnassingbe Eyadema as President **Obv:** Arms with supporters **Rev:** Head facing **Note:** Similar to 25,000 Francs, KM#11.

Date	Mintage	F	VF	XF	Unc	BU
1977 Proof	50	Value: 525				

ESSAIS

KM#	Date	Mintage	Identification	Mkt Val
E13	1977	25	15000 Francs. Aluminum. KM#10.	100
E14	1977	20	15000 Francs. Copper. KM#10.	100
E15	1977	25	25000 Francs. Aluminum. KM#11.	150
E16	1977	20	25000 Francs. Copper. KM#11.	150

PIEFORTS

KM#	Date	Mintage	Identification	Mkt Val
P4	1977	5	15000 Francs. Copper. KM#10.	200
P4a	1977	10	15000 Francs. Silver. KM#10.	200
P4b	1977	2	15000 Francs. Gold. KM#10.	800
P5	1977	5	25000 Francs. Copper. KM#11.	300
P5a	1977	10	25000 Francs. Silver. KM#11.	300
P5b	1977	2	25000 Francs. Gold. KM#11.	1,000

TOKELAU ISLANDS

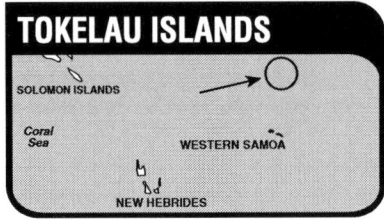

Tokelau or Union Islands, a New Zealand Territory located in the South Pacific 2,100 miles (3,379 km.) northeast of New Zealand and 300 miles (483 km.) north of Samoa, has an area of 4 sq. mi. (10 sq. km.) and a population of *2,000. Geographically, the group consists of four atolls - Atafu, Nukunono, Fakaofo and Swains – but the last belongs to American Samoa (and the United States claims the other three). The people are of Polynesian origin; Samoan is the official language. The New Zealand Minister for Foreign Affairs governs the islands; councils of family elders handle local government at the village level. The chief settlement is Fenuafala, on Fakaofo. It is connected by wireless with the offices of the New Zealand Administrative Center, located at Apia, Western Samoa. Subsistence farming and the production of copra for export are the main occupations. Revenue is also derived from the sale of postage stamps and, since 1978,coins.

Great Britain annexed the group of islands in 1889. They were added to the Gilbert and Ellice Islands colony in 1916. In 1926, they were brought under the jurisdiction of Western Samoa, which was held as a mandate of the League of Nations by New Zealand. They were declared a part of New Zealand in 1948.

Tokelau Islands issued its first coin in 1978, a "$1 TahiTala," Tokelauan for "One Dollar."

RULER
British

MINT MARK
PM - Pobjoy

NEW ZEALAND TERRITORY
STANDARD COINAGE

KM# 31 10 TALA
1.2440 g., 0.9990 Gold 0.04 oz. AGW, 13.92 mm. **Ruler:** Elizabeth II **Obv:** Elizabeth II **Rev:** Ship, the Golden Hind above value **Edge:** Reeded

Date	Mintage	F	VF	XF	Unc	BU
1997 Proof	—	Value: 52.50				

TONGA

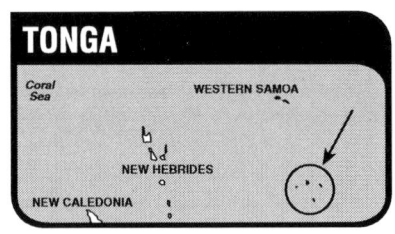

The Kingdom of Tonga (or Friendly Islands) is an archipelago situated in the southern Pacific Ocean south of Western Samoa and east of Fiji comprised of 150 islands. Tonga has an area of 270 sq. mi. (748 sq. km.) and a population of *100,000. Capital: Nuku'alofa. Primarily agricultural, the kingdom exports bananas and copra.

Dutch navigators Willem Schouten and Jacob Lemaire were the first Europeans to visit Tonga in 1616. The noted Dutch explorer Abel Tasman who visited the Tongatapu group in 1643 followed them. No further European contact was made until 1773 when British navigator Capt. James Cook arrived and, impressed by the peaceful deportment of the natives, named the islands the Friendly Islands. Within a few years of Cook's visit, Tonga was embroiled in a civil war that lasted until the great chief Taufa'ahau, who reigned as Siasoi Tupou I (1845-93), was converted to Christianity and brought unity and peace to the islands. Tonga became a self-governing protectorate of Great Britain in 1900 and a fully independent state on June 4, 1970. The monarchy is a member of the Commonwealth of Nations. King Taufa'ahau is Head of State and Government.

RULERS
Queen Salote, 1918-1965
King Taufa'ahau IV, 1967—2006

MONETARY SYSTEM
12 Pence = 1 Shilling
20 Shillings = 1 Pound

KINGDOM
STANDARD COINAGE

16 Pounds = 1 Koula

KM# 1 1/4 KOULA
8.1250 g., 0.9160 Gold .2395 oz. AGW **Ruler:** Queen Salote **Obv:** Head right **Rev:** Crowned arms

Date	Mintage	F	VF	XF	Unc	BU
1962	—	—	—	—	165	—
1962 Proof	6,300	Value: 175				

KM# 1a 1/4 KOULA
Platinum APW **Ruler:** Queen Salote **Obv:** Head right **Rev:** Crowned arms

Date	Mintage	F	VF	XF	Unc	BU
1962 Proof	—	Value: 600				

KM# 2 1/2 KOULA
16.2500 g., 0.9160 Gold .4789 oz. AGW **Ruler:** Queen Salote **Obv:** Crowned arms **Rev:** Standing female half left

Date	Mintage	F	VF	XF	Unc	BU
1962	—	—	—	—	335	—
1962 Proof	3,000	Value: 350				

KM# 2a 1/2 KOULA
Platinum APW **Ruler:** Queen Salote **Obv:** Crowned arms **Rev:** Standing female half left

Date	Mintage	F	VF	XF	Unc	BU
1962 Proof	—	Value: 850				

KM# 3 KOULA
32.5000 g., 0.9160 Gold .9278 oz. AGW **Ruler:** Queen Salote **Obv:** Crowned arms below value **Rev:** Standing figure half left

Date	Mintage	F	VF	XF	Unc	BU
1962	1,500	—	—	—	650	—
1962 Proof	—	Value: 675				

KM# 3a KOULA
Platinum APW **Ruler:** Queen Salote **Obv:** Crowned arms below value **Rev:** Standing figure half left

TONGA

Date	Mintage	F	VF	XF	Unc	BU
1962 Proof	—	Value: 1,350				

DECIMAL COINAGE

100 Senti = 1 Pa'anga; 100 Pa'anga = 1 Hau

KM# 77b PA'ANGA
26.0000 g., 0.9170 Gold .7666 oz. AGW, 30 mm. **Ruler:** King Taufa'ahau IV **Subject:** Christmas **Obv:** Head right **Rev:** Praying hands **Shape:** 7-sided

Date	Mintage	F	VF	XF	Unc	BU
1982 Proof	250	Value: 550				

KM# 77c PA'ANGA
30.4000 g., 0.9500 Platinum .9286 oz. APW, 30 mm. **Ruler:** King Taufa'ahau IV **Subject:** Christmas **Obv:** Head right **Rev:** Praying hands **Shape:** 7-sided

Date	Mintage	F	VF	XF	Unc	BU
1982 Proof	25	Value: 1,200				

KM# 80b PA'ANGA
26.0000 g., 0.9170 Gold .7666 oz. AGW, 30 mm. **Ruler:** King Taufa'ahau IV **Subject:** Christmas **Obv:** Head right **Rev:** Kneeling Joseph and Mary **Shape:** 7-sided

Date	Mintage	F	VF	XF	Unc	BU
1983 Proof	250	Value: 550				

KM# 80c PA'ANGA
30.4000 g., 0.9500 Platinum .9286 oz. APW, 30 mm. **Ruler:** King Taufa'ahau IV **Subject:** Christmas **Obv:** Head right **Rev:** Kneeling Joseph and Mary **Shape:** 7-sided

Date	Mintage	F	VF	XF	Unc	BU
1983 Proof	25	Value: 1,200				

KM# 81b PA'ANGA
26.0000 g., 0.9170 Gold .7666 oz. AGW, 30 mm. **Ruler:** King Taufa'ahau IV **Subject:** Christmas **Obv:** Head right **Rev:** After Bellini's Madonna & Child **Rev. Designer:** Leslie Lindsay **Shape:** 7-sided

Date	Mintage	F	VF	XF	Unc	BU
1984 Proof	250	Value: 550				

KM# 81c PA'ANGA
30.4000 g., 0.9500 Platinum .9286 oz. APW, 30 mm. **Ruler:** King Taufa'ahau IV **Subject:** Christmas **Obv:** Head right **Rev:** After Bellini's Madonna & Child **Rev. Designer:** Leslie Lindsay **Shape:** 7-sided

Date	Mintage	F	VF	XF	Unc	BU
1984 Proof	25	Value: 1,200				

KM# 118b PA'ANGA
26.0000 g., 0.9170 Gold .7666 oz. AGW **Ruler:** King Taufa'ahau IV **Subject:** Christmas **Obv:** Head right **Rev:** Dove with laurel branch **Rev. Designer:** Barry Stanton

Date	Mintage	F	VF	XF	Unc	BU
1985 Proof	250	Value: 550				

KM# 118c PA'ANGA
30.4000 g., 0.9500 Platinum .9286 oz. APW **Ruler:** King Taufa'ahau IV **Subject:** Christmas **Obv:** Head right **Rev:** Dove with laurel branch **Rev. Designer:** Barry Stanton

Date	Mintage	F	VF	XF	Unc	BU
1985 Proof	—	Value: 1,200				

KM# 123b PA'ANGA
26.0000 g., 0.9170 Gold .7666 oz. AGW **Ruler:** King Taufa'ahau IV **Subject:** Christmas **Obv:** Head right **Rev:** Three Wise Men

Date	Mintage	F	VF	XF	Unc	BU
1986 Proof	—	Value: 550				

KM# 123c PA'ANGA
30.4000 g., 0.9500 Platinum .9286 oz. APW **Ruler:** King Taufa'ahau IV **Subject:** Christmas **Obv:** Head right **Rev:** Three Wise Men

Date	Mintage	F	VF	XF	Unc	BU
1986 Proof	—	Value: 1,200				

KM# 127b PA'ANGA
26.0000 g., 0.9170 Gold .7666 oz. AGW **Ruler:** King Taufa'ahau IV **Subject:** Christmas **Obv:** Head right **Rev:** After Albrecht Durer, Madonna and child

Date	Mintage	F	VF	XF	Unc	BU
1988 Proof	—	Value: 550				

KM# 127c PA'ANGA
30.4000 g., 0.9500 Platinum .9286 oz. APW **Ruler:** King Taufa'ahau IV **Subject:** Christmas **Obv:** Head right **Rev:** After Albrecht Durer, Madonna and child

Date	Mintage	F	VF	XF	Unc	BU
1988 Proof	—	Value: 1,200				

KM# 64 10 PA'ANGA
4.0000 g., 0.9170 Gold .0117 oz. AGW **Ruler:** King Taufa'ahau IV **Series:** F.A.O. **Subject:** Rural Women's Advancement **Obv:** Queen Salote **Rev:** Female symbol on dove

Date	Mintage	F	VF	XF	Unc	BU
1980	750	—	—	12.50	16.00	
1980 Proof	2,000	Value: 18.50				

KM# 90 10 PA'ANGA
5.1000 g., 0.3750 Gold .0615 oz. AGW **Ruler:** King Taufa'ahau IV **Subject:** 100th Anniversary of Automobile Industry **Obv:** Head right **Rev:** Rolls Royce and Silver Ghost **Note:** Similar to 50 Seniti, KM#82

Date	Mintage	F	VF	XF	Unc	BU
1985 Proof	1,000	Value: 45.00				

KM# 90a 10 PA'ANGA
7.9600 g., 0.9170 Gold .2347 oz. AGW **Ruler:** King Taufa'ahau IV **Subject:** 100th Anniversary of Automobile Industry **Obv:** Head right **Rev:** Rolls Royce and Silver Ghost

Date	Mintage	F	VF	XF	Unc	BU
1985 Proof	500	Value: 165				

KM# 91 10 PA'ANGA
5.1000 g., 0.3750 Gold .0615 oz. AGW **Ruler:** King Taufa'ahau IV **Subject:** 100th Anniversary of Automobile Industry **Obv:** Head right **Rev:** Range Rover and Land Rover **Note:** Similar to 50 Seniti, KM#83.2

Date	Mintage	F	VF	XF	Unc	BU
1985 Proof	1,000	Value: 45.00				

KM# 91a 10 PA'ANGA
7.9600 g., 0.9170 Gold .2347 oz. AGW **Ruler:** King Taufa'ahau IV **Subject:** 100th Anniversary of Automobile Industry **Obv:** Head right **Rev:** Range Rover and Land Rover

Date	Mintage	F	VF	XF	Unc	BU
1985 Proof	500	Value: 165				

KM# 92 10 PA'ANGA
5.1000 g., 0.3750 Gold .0615 oz. AGW **Ruler:** King Taufa'ahau IV **Subject:** 100th Anniversary of Automobile Industry **Obv:** Head right **Rev:** Mini Morris Cowley and Touring Car **Note:** Similar to 50 Seniti, KM#84.

Date	Mintage	F	VF	XF	Unc	BU
1985 Proof	1,000	Value: 45.00				

KM# 92a 10 PA'ANGA
7.9600 g., 0.9170 Gold .2347 oz. AGW **Ruler:** King Taufa'ahau IV **Subject:** 100th Anniversary of Automobile Industry **Obv:** Head right **Rev:** Mini Morris Cowley and Touring Car

Date	Mintage	F	VF	XF	Unc	BU
1985 Proof	500	Value: 165				

KM# 93 10 PA'ANGA
5.1000 g., 0.3750 Gold .0615 oz. AGW **Ruler:** King Taufa'ahau IV **Subject:** 100th Anniversary of Automobile Industry **Obv:** Head right **Rev:** MGB GT and MG TA **Note:** Similar to 50 Seniti, KM#85.

Date	Mintage	F	VF	XF	Unc	BU
1985 Proof	1,000	Value: 45.00				

KM# 93a 10 PA'ANGA
7.9600 g., 0.9170 Gold .2347 oz. AGW **Ruler:** King Taufa'ahau IV **Subject:** 100th Anniversary of Automobile Industry **Obv:** Head right **Rev:** MGB GT and MG TA

Date	Mintage	F	VF	XF	Unc	BU
1985 Proof	500	Value: 165				

KM# 108 10 PA'ANGA
5.1000 g., 0.3750 Gold .0615 oz. AGW **Ruler:** King Taufa'ahau IV **Subject:** 85th Birthday of Queen Mother **Obv:** Head right **Rev:** Queen Mother as a young girl **Note:** Similar to 50 Seniti, KM#98.

Date	Mintage	F	VF	XF	Unc	BU
1985 Proof	1,000	Value: 45.00				

KM# 108a 10 PA'ANGA
7.9600 g., 0.9170 Gold .2347 oz. AGW **Ruler:** King Taufa'ahau IV **Subject:** 85th Birthday of Queen Mother **Obv:** Head right **Rev:** Queen Mother as a young girl

Date	Mintage	F	VF	XF	Unc	BU
1985 Proof	500	Value: 165				

KM# 109 10 PA'ANGA
5.1000 g., 0.3750 Gold .0615 oz. AGW **Ruler:** King Taufa'ahau IV **Subject:** 85th Birthday of Queen Mother **Obv:** Head right **Rev:** Wedding of King George VI and Elizabeth **Note:** Similar to 50 Seniti, KM#99.

Date	Mintage	F	VF	XF	Unc	BU
1985 Proof	1,000	Value: 45.00				

KM# 109a 10 PA'ANGA
7.9600 g., 0.9170 Gold .2347 oz. AGW **Ruler:** King Taufa'ahau IV **Subject:** 85th Birthday of Queen Mother **Obv:** Head right **Rev:** Wedding of King George VI and Elizabeth

Date	Mintage	F	VF	XF	Unc	BU
1985 Proof	500	Value: 165				

KM# 110 10 PA'ANGA
5.1000 g., 0.3750 Gold .0615 oz. AGW **Ruler:** King Taufa'ahau IV **Subject:** 85th Birthday of Queen Mother **Obv:** Head right **Rev:** King George VI and Elizabeth **Note:** Similar to 50 Seniti, KM#100.

Date	Mintage	F	VF	XF	Unc	BU
1985 Proof	1,000	Value: 45.00				

KM# 110a 10 PA'ANGA
7.9600 g., 0.9170 Gold .2347 oz. AGW **Ruler:** King Taufa'ahau IV **Subject:** 85th Birthday of Queen Mother **Obv:** Head right **Rev:** King George VI and Elizabeth

Date	Mintage	F	VF	XF	Unc	BU
1985 Proof	500	Value: 165				

KM# 111 10 PA'ANGA
5.1000 g., 0.3750 Gold .0615 oz. AGW **Ruler:** King Taufa'ahau IV **Subject:** 85th Birthday of Queen Mother **Obv:** Head right **Rev:** Queen Mother holding Queen Elizabeth II **Note:** Similar to 50 Seniti, KM#101.

Date	Mintage	F	VF	XF	Unc	BU
1985 Proof	1,000	Value: 45.00				

KM# 111a 10 PA'ANGA
7.9600 g., 0.9170 Gold .2347 oz. AGW **Ruler:** King Taufa'ahau IV **Subject:** 85th Birthday of Queen Mother **Obv:** Head right **Rev:** Queen Mother holding Queen Elizabeth II

Date	Mintage	F	VF	XF	Unc	BU
1985 Proof	500	Value: 165				

KM# 112 10 PA'ANGA
5.1000 g., 0.3750 Gold .0615 oz. AGW **Ruler:** King Taufa'ahau IV **Subject:** 85th Birthday of Queen Mother **Obv:** Head right **Rev:** Queen Mother facing **Note:** Similar to 50 Seniti, KM#102.

Date	Mintage	F	VF	XF	Unc	BU
1985 Proof	1,000	Value: 45.00				

KM# 112a 10 PA'ANGA
7.9600 g., 0.9170 Gold .2347 oz. AGW **Ruler:** King Taufa'ahau IV **Subject:** 85th Birthday of Queen Mother **Obv:** Head right **Rev:** Queen Mother facing

Date	Mintage	F	VF	XF	Unc	BU
1985 Proof	500	Value: 165				

KM# 126a 10 PA'ANGA
31.1030 g., 0.9990 Palladium 1.0000 oz. **Ruler:** King Taufa'ahau IV **Subject:** America's Cup **Obv:** Head right **Rev:** National flags and sailboat

Date	Mintage	F	VF	XF	Unc	BU
1987 Proof	25,000	Value: 365				

680 TONGA

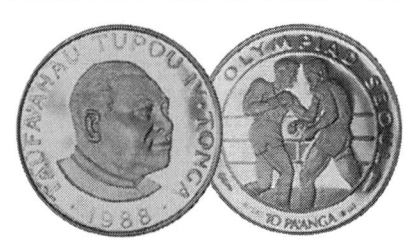

KM# 130 10 PA'ANGA
15.5500 g., 0.9990 Gold .5000 oz. AGW **Ruler:** King Taufa'ahau IV **Subject:** Summer Olympics **Obv:** Head right **Rev:** Boxing match within circle

Date	Mintage	F	VF	XF	Unc	BU
1988 Proof	Est. 2,000	Value: 350				

KM# 131 10 PA'ANGA
31.1000 g., 0.9990 Palladium 1.0000 oz. **Ruler:** King Taufa'ahau IV **Series:** Summer Olympics **Obv:** Head right **Rev:** Shot putter within circle

Date	Mintage	F	VF	XF	Unc	BU
1988 Proof	Est. 2,000	Value: 375				

KM# 132 10 PA'ANGA
15.6300 g., 0.9500 Palladium .5000 oz. **Ruler:** King Taufa'ahau IV **Series:** Summer Olympics **Obv:** Head right **Rev:** Discus thrower within circle

Date	Mintage	F	VF	XF	Unc	BU
1988 Proof	Est. 2,000	Value: 195				

KM# 173 10 PA'ANGA
1.2441 g., 0.9999 Gold .0400 oz. AGW, 13.92 mm. **Ruler:** King Taufa'ahau IV **Subject:** Destruction of the English Privateer "Port-au-Prince" **Obv:** Crowned arms **Rev:** Looted shipwreck and native **Edge:** Reeded

Date	Mintage	F	VF	XF	Unc	BU
1998 Proof	—	Value: 40.00				

KM# 172 10 PA'ANGA
1.2441 g., 0.9999 Gold .0400 oz. AGW, 13.92 mm. **Ruler:** King Taufa'ahau IV **Subject:** King's 80th Birthday July 3, 1998 **Obv:** National arms within circle **Rev:** Bust 3/4 left **Edge:** Reeded **Note:** Struck at Valcambi Mint.

Date	Mintage	F	VF	XF	Unc	BU
1998 Proof	—	Value: 40.00				

KM# 65 20 PA'ANGA
0.8000 g., 0.9170 Gold .0235 oz. AGW **Ruler:** King Taufa'ahau IV **Series:** F.A.O. **Subject:** Rural Women's Advancement **Obv:** Head of Queen Salote right **Rev:** Female symbol on dove

Date	Mintage	F	VF	XF	Unc	BU
1980	750	—	—	BV	20.00	
1980 Proof	2,000	Value: 18.50				

KM# 53 25 PA'ANGA
5.0000 g., 0.9170 Gold .1474 oz. AGW **Ruler:** King Taufa'ahau IV **Subject:** Constitution Centennial **Obv:** Head facing **Rev:** National arms **Designer:** Norman Sillman

Date	Mintage	F	VF	XF	Unc	BU
1975	405	—	—	—	110	—
1975 Proof	105	Value: 120				

KM# 54 50 PA'ANGA
10.0000 g., 0.9170 Gold .2948 oz. AGW **Ruler:** King Taufa'ahau IV **Subject:** Constitution Centennial **Obv:** Head facing **Rev:** National arms **Designer:** Norman Sillman

Date	Mintage	F	VF	XF	Unc	BU
1975	205	—	—	—	220	—
1975 Proof	105	Value: 230				

KM# 55 75 PA'ANGA
15.0000 g., 0.9170 Gold .4423 oz. AGW **Ruler:** King Taufa'ahau IV **Subject:** Constitution Centennial **Obv:** Queen Salote Tupou III **Rev:** National arms **Designer:** Norman Sillman

Date	Mintage	F	VF	XF	Unc	BU
1975	204	—	—	—	325	—
1975 Proof	105	Value: 335				

KM# 56 100 PA'ANGA
20.0000 g., 0.9170 Gold .5897 oz. AGW **Ruler:** King Taufa'ahau IV **Subject:** Constitution Centennial **Obv:** Uniformed bust left **Rev:** National arms **Designer:** Norman Sillman

Date	Mintage	F	VF	XF	Unc	BU
ND(1975)	205	—	—	—	425	—
ND(1975) Proof	105	Value: 435				

KM# 167 100 PA'ANGA
17.7000 g., 0.5833 Gold .3319 oz. AGW **Ruler:** King Taufa'ahau IV **Subject:** 25th Jubilee of Accession **Obv:** Head left at center of circle with dove, crown and stars **Rev:** National arms within circle

Date	Mintage	F	VF	XF	Unc	BU
ND(1990) Proof	Est. 5,000	Value: 235				

KM# 155 100 PA'ANGA
17.7000 g., 0.5833 Gold .3319 oz. AGW **Ruler:** King Taufa'ahau IV **Series:** Olympics **Obv:** Crowned arms within circle **Rev:** Gymnast on rings

Date	Mintage	F	VF	XF	Unc	BU
1993 Proof	3,000	Value: 235				

KM# 163 100 PA'ANGA
17.7000 g., 0.5833 Gold .3319 oz. AGW **Ruler:** King Taufa'ahau IV **Subject:** World Cup Soccer **Obv:** Crowned arms within circle **Rev:** Goalie

Date	Mintage	F	VF	XF	Unc	BU
1994 Proof	Est. 3,000	Value: 235				

KM# 164 100 PA'ANGA
17.7000 g., 0.5833 Gold .3319 oz. AGW **Ruler:** King Taufa'ahau IV **Series:** 1996 Olympic Games **Obv:** Crowned arms within circle **Rev:** High jumper

Date	Mintage	F	VF	XF	Unc	BU
1994 Proof	Est. 3,000	Value: 235				

KM# 165 100 PA'ANGA
17.7000 g., 0.5833 Gold .3319 oz. AGW **Ruler:** King Taufa'ahau IV **Series:** Endangered Wildlife **Obv:** Crowned arms within circle **Rev:** Leguan Lizard

Date	Mintage	F	VF	XF	Unc	BU
1994 Proof	Est. 2,000	Value: 235				

KM# 21 1/4 HAU
16.0000 g., 0.9800 Palladium .5041 oz. **Ruler:** King Taufa'ahau IV **Subject:** Coronation of Taufa'ahau Tupou IV **Obv:** Head right, small crowns around border **Obv. Designer:** Maurice Meers **Rev:** Crowned arms **Rev. Designer:** Ernest Hyde **Edge Lettering:** HISTORICALLY THE FIRST PALLADIUM COINAGE

Date	Mintage	F	VF	XF	Unc	BU
1967	1,700	—	—	—	200	—

KM# 23 1/2 HAU
32.0000 g., 0.9800 Palladium 1.0082 oz. **Ruler:** King Taufa'ahau IV **Subject:** Coronation of Taufa'ahau Tupou IV **Obv. Designer:** Maurice Meers **Rev:** National arms **Rev. Designer:** Ernest Hyde **Edge Lettering:** HISTORICALLY THE FIRST PALLADIUM COINAGE

Date	Mintage	F	VF	XF	Unc	BU
1967	1,650	—	—	—	385	—

KM# 122 1/2 HAU
10.0000 g., 0.9170 Gold .2948 oz. AGW **Ruler:** King Taufa'ahau IV **Subject:** Wildlife **Obv:** Head right **Rev:** Ground dwelling birds

Date	Mintage	F	VF	XF	Unc	BU
1986 Proof	5,000	Value: 210				

KM# 25 HAU
64.0000 g., 0.9800 Palladium 2.0164 oz. **Ruler:** King Taufa'ahau IV **Subject:** Coronation of Taufa'ahau Tupou IV **Obv:** Head right, small crowns around border **Obv. Designer:** Maurice Meers **Rev:** National arms **Rev. Designer:** Ernest Hyde **Edge Lettering:** HISTORICALLY THE FIRST PALLADIUM COINAGE

Date	Mintage	F	VF	XF	Unc	BU
1967	1,500	—	—	—	775	—

KM# 75 HAU
7.9900 g., 0.9170 Gold .2356 oz. AGW **Ruler:** King Taufa'ahau IV **Subject:** Wedding and Treaty of Friendship **Obv:** Head right **Rev:** Wedding of Prince Charles and Lady Diana

Date	Mintage	F	VF	XF	Unc	BU
1981	500	—	—	—	175	—
1981 Proof	2,500	Value: 165				

KM# 79 HAU
7.9900 g., 0.9170 Gold .2356 oz. AGW **Ruler:** King Taufa'ahau IV **Subject:** Commonwealth Games **Obv:** Head right **Rev:** Runners and emblem **Designer:** Philip Nathan

Date	Mintage	F	VF	XF	Unc	BU
1982	500	—	—	—	175	—
1982 Proof	500	Value: 175				

KM# 94 HAU
52.0000 g., 0.9500 Platinum 1.5884 oz. APW **Ruler:** King Taufa'ahau IV **Subject:** 100th Anniversary of Automobile Industry **Obv:** Head right **Rev:** Rolls Royce and Silver Ghost **Note:** Similar to 50 Seniti, KM#82.

Date	Mintage	F	VF	XF	Unc	BU
1985 Proof	—	Value: 2,150				

KM# 95 HAU
52.0000 g., 0.9500 Platinum 1.5884 oz. APW **Ruler:** King Taufa'ahau IV **Subject:** 100th Anniversary of Automobile Industry **Obv:** Head right **Rev:** Range Rover and Land Rover **Note:** Similar to 50 Seniti, KM#83.

Date	Mintage	F	VF	XF	Unc	BU
1985 Proof	—	Value: 2,150				

KM# 96 HAU
52.0000 g., 0.9500 Platinum 1.5884 oz. APW **Ruler:** King Taufa'ahau IV **Subject:** 100th Anniversary of Automobile Industry **Obv:** Head right **Rev:** Mini Morris Cowley and Touring Car **Note:** Similar to 50 Seniti, KM#84.

Date	Mintage	F	VF	XF	Unc	BU
1985 Proof	—	Value: 2,150				

KM# 97 HAU
52.0000 g., 0.9500 Platinum 1.5884 oz. APW **Ruler:** King Taufa'ahau IV **Subject:** 100th Anniversary of Automobile Industry **Obv:** Head right **Rev:** MGB GT and MG TA **Note:** Similar to 50 Seniti, KM#85.

Date	Mintage	F	VF	XF	Unc	BU
1985 Proof	—	Value: 2,150				

KM# 113 HAU
52.0000 g., 0.9500 Platinum 1.5884 oz. APW **Ruler:** King Taufa'ahau IV **Subject:** 85th Birthday of Queen Mother **Obv:** Head right **Rev:** Queen Mother as a young girl **Note:** Similar to 50 Seniti, KM#98.

Date	Mintage	F	VF	XF	Unc	BU
1985 Proof	—	Value: 2,150				

KM# 114 HAU
52.0000 g., 0.9500 Platinum 1.5884 oz. APW **Ruler:** King Taufa'ahau IV **Subject:** 85th Birthday of Queen Mother **Obv:** Head right **Rev:** Wedding of King George VI and Elizabeth **Note:** Similar to 50 Seniti, KM#99.

Date	Mintage	F	VF	XF	Unc	BU
1985 Proof	—	Value: 2,150				

KM# 115 HAU
52.0000 g., 0.9500 Platinum 1.5884 oz. APW **Ruler:** King Taufa'ahau IV **Subject:** 85th Birthday of Queen Mother **Obv:** Head right **Rev:** King George VI and Elizabeth **Note:** Similar to 50 Seniti, KM#100.

Date	Mintage	F	VF	XF	Unc	BU
1985 Proof	—	Value: 2,150				

KM# 116 HAU
52.0000 g., 0.9500 Platinum 1.5884 oz. APW **Ruler:** King Taufa'ahau IV **Subject:** 85th Birthday of Queen Mother **Obv:** Head right **Rev:** Queen Mother holding Queen Elizabeth II **Note:** Similar to 50 Seniti, KM#101.

Date	Mintage	F	VF	XF	Unc	BU
1985 Proof	—	Value: 2,150				

KM# 117 HAU
52.0000 g., 0.9500 Platinum 1.5884 oz. APW **Ruler:** King Taufa'ahau IV **Subject:** 85th Birthday of Queen Mother **Obv:** Head right **Rev:** Queen Mother facing **Note:** Similar to 50 Seniti, KM#102.

Date	Mintage	F	VF	XF	Unc	BU
1985 Proof	—	Value: 2,150				

KM# 76 5 HAU
15.9800 g., 0.9170 Gold .4711 oz. AGW **Ruler:** King Taufa'ahau IV **Subject:** Wedding and Treaty of Friendship **Obv:** Head right **Rev:** Wedding of Prince Charles and Lady Diana

Date	Mintage	F	VF	XF	Unc	BU
1981	250	—	—	—	350	—
1981 Proof	1,000	Value: 335				

COUNTERMARKED COMMEMORATIVE COINAGE

Commemorative coins which contain a countermark creating a new commemorative representation. The Date listed refers to the original date the coin was struck.

KM# 22 1/4 HAU
16.0000 g., 0.9800 Palladium .5040 oz. **Ruler:** King Taufa'ahau IV **Countermark:** 1918/TTIV/1968 **Edge Lettering:** HISTORICALLY THE FIRST PALLADIUM COINAGE **Note:** Countermark on KM#21.

Date	Mintage	F	VF	XF	Unc	BU
1967	400	—	—	—	225	—

KM# 24 1/2 HAU
32.0000 g., 0.9800 Palladium 1.0082 oz. **Ruler:** King Taufa'ahau IV **Countermark:** 1918/TTIV/1968 **Obv:** Head right, small crowns around border **Rev:** Crowned arms **Edge Lettering:** HISTORICALLY THE FIRST PALLADIUM COINAGE **Note:** Countermark on KM#23.

Date	Mintage	F	VF	XF	Unc	BU
ND(1967)	513	—	—	—	450	—

KM# 26 HAU
64.0000 g., 0.9800 Palladium 2.0164 oz. **Ruler:** King Taufa'ahau IV **Countermark:** 1918/TTIV/1968 **Edge Lettering:** HISTORICALLY THE FIRST PALLADIUM COINAGE **Note:** Countermark on KM#25.

Date	Mintage	F	VF	XF	Unc	BU
ND(1967)	400	—	—	—	875	—

MINT SETS

KM#	Date	Mintage	Identification	Issue Price	Mkt Val
MS1	1962 (3)	—	KM#1-3	—	1,000
MS2	1967 (3)	1,500	KM#21, 23, 25	207	1,275
MS3	1968 (3)	400	KM#22, 24, 26	—	1,550
MS10	1975 (4)	—	KM#53-56	385	885
MS18	1980 (2)	750	KM#64-65, Gold	30.00	45.00

PROOF SETS

KM#	Date	Mintage	Identification	Issue Price	Mkt Val
PS1	1962 (3)	250	KM#1-3	—	1,070
PS2	1962 (3)	25	KM#1a-3a. Platinum.	—	2,400
PS10	1975 (4)	105	KM#53-56	538	950
PS14	1980 (2)	200	KM#64-65	60.00	45.00
PSA15	1981 (3)	—	KM#74-76	—	450
PS19	1985 (5)	1,000	KM#108-112, .374 Gold	315	200
PS20	1985 (5)	500	KM#108a-112a, .917 Gold	775	725
PS21	1985 (5)	50	KM#113-117, .950 Platinum. BV+15%.	5,850	—
PS24	1985 (4)	1,000	KM#90-93, .374 Gold	252	170
PS25	1985 (4)	500	KM#90a-93a, .917 Gold	620	580
PS26	1985 (4)	50	KM#94-97, .950 Platinum. BV+15%.	4,680	—
PS28	1988 (4)	2,000	KM#129-132	—	950

TRINIDAD & TOBAGO

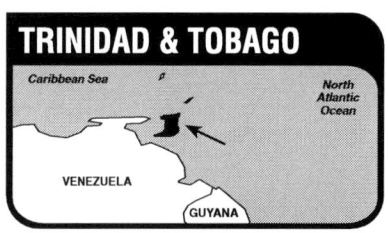

The Republic of Trinidad and Tobago is situated 7 miles (11 km.) off the coast of Venezuela, has an area of 1,981 sq. mi. (5,130 sq. km.) and a population of *1.2 million. Capital: Port-of-Spain. The island of Trinidad contains the world's largest natural asphalt bog. Birds of Paradise live on little Tobago, the only place outside of their native New Guinea where they can be found in a wild state. Petroleum and petroleum products are the mainstay of the economy. Petroleum products, crude oil and sugar are exported.

Columbus discovered Trinidad and Tobago in 1498. Trinidad remained under Spanish rule from the time of its settlement in 1592 until its capture by the British in 1797. It was ceded to the British in 1802. Tobago was occupied at various times by the French, Dutch and English before being ceded to Britain in 1814. Trinidad and Tobago were merged into a single colony in 1888. The colony was part of the Federation of the West Indies until Aug. 31, 1962, when it became independent. A new constitution establishing a republican form of government was adopted on Aug. 1, 1976. Trinidad and Tobago is a member of the Commonwealth of Nations. The President is Chief of State. The Prime Minister is Head of Government.

RULER
British, until 1976

MINT MARKS
FM - Franklin Mint, U.S.A.*
*NOTE: From 1975-1985 the Franklin Mint produced coinage in up to 3 different qualities. Qualities of issue are designated in ( ) after each date and are defined as follows:
(M) MATTE - Normal circulation strike or a dull finish produced by sandblasting special uncirculated (polish finish) or proof quality dies.
(U) SPECIAL UNCIRCULATED - Polished or proof-like in appearance without any frosted features.
(P) PROOF - The highest quality obtainable having mirror-like fields and frosted features.

MONETARY SYSTEM
100 Cents = 1 Dollar

REPUBLIC

STANDARD COINAGE

KM# 37 100 DOLLARS
6.2100 g., 0.5000 Gold .0998 oz. AGW **Obv:** National arms **Rev:** Flying birds and value

Date	Mintage	F	VF	XF	Unc	BU
1976FM (M)	200	—	—	—	110	120
1976FM (P)	29,000	Value: 70.00				

KM# 41 100 DOLLARS
6.2100 g., 0.5000 Gold .0998 oz. AGW **Subject:** 5th Anniversary of the Republic **Obv:** National arms **Rev:** Hummingbird and flower

Date	Mintage	F	VF	XF	Unc	BU
1981FM (U)	100	—	—	—	175	195
1981FM (P)	400	Value: 150				

TRINIDAD & TOBAGO

KM# 50 100 DOLLARS
6.2100 g., 0.5000 Gold .0998 oz. AGW **Subject:** 20th Anniversary of Independence **Obv:** National arms **Rev:** Building within circle

Date	Mintage	F	VF	XF	Unc	BU
1982FM (P)	1,380	Value: 100				

KM# 56 200 DOLLARS
11.1700 g., 0.5000 Gold .1796 oz. AGW **Subject:** 20th Anniversary of Central Bank **Obv:** National arms **Rev:** Building below value

Date	Mintage	F	VF	XF	Unc	BU
1984FM (P)	1,200	Value: 145				

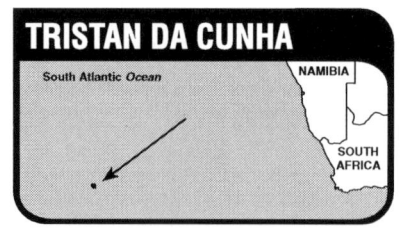

TRISTAN DA CUNHA

Tristan da Cunha is the principal island and group name of a small cluster of volcanic islands located in the South Atlantic midway between the Cape of Good Hope and South America, and 1,500 miles (2,414 km.) south-southwest of the British colony of St. Helena. The other islands are Inaccessible, Gough, and the three Nightingale Islands. The group, which comprises a dependency of St. Helena, has a total area of 40 sq. mi. (104 sq. km.) and a population of less than 300. There is a village of 60 houses called Edinburgh. Potatoes are the staple subsistence crop.

Portuguese admiral Tristao da Cunha discovered Tristan da Cunha in 1506. Unsuccessful attempts to colonize the islands were made by the Dutch in 1656, but the first permanent inhabitant didn't arrive until 1810. During the exile of Napoleon on St. Helena, Britain placed a temporary garrison on Tristan da Cunha to prevent any attempt to rescue Napoleon from his island prison. The islands were formally annexed to Britain in 1816 and became a dependency of St. Helena in 1938.

RULER
British

MINT MARK
PM - Pobjoy Mint

MONETARY SYSTEM
Sterling until 1961
1961 – South African Rand
1963 – Reverted to Sterling
25 Pence = 1 Crown
4 Crowns = 1 Pound

ST. HELENA DEPENDENCY

STANDARD COINAGE

KM# 7a 50 PENCE
47.5400 g., 0.9170 Gold 1.4001 oz. AGW, 38.5 mm. **Ruler:** Elizabeth II **Subject:** 40th Wedding Anniversary of Queen Elizabeth and Prince Philip **Obv:** Crowned head right **Rev:** Crowned initials at center of flower design **Rev. Designer:** Ronald Dutton

Date	Mintage	F	VF	XF	Unc	BU
ND(1987) Proof	75	Value: 985				

KM# 9b 50 PENCE
47.5400 g., 0.9170 Gold 1.4001 oz. AGW, 38.6 mm. **Ruler:** Elizabeth II **Subject:** Winston Churchill **Obv:** Crowned bust right **Rev:** Uniformed bust 1/4 left and two fighter planes

Date	Mintage	F	VF	XF	Unc	BU
1999	Est. 125	Value: 985				

KM# 10b 50 PENCE
47.5400 g., 0.9166 Gold 1.401 oz. AGW, 38.6 mm. **Ruler:** Elizabeth II **Subject:** Queen Mother's 100th Birthday **Obv:** Crowned bust right **Obv. Designer:** Raphael Maklouf **Rev:** Bust of Queen Mother right **Edge:** Reeded

Date	Mintage	F	VF	XF	Unc	BU
ND(2000) Proof	100	Value: 985				

KM# 11b 50 PENCE
47.5400 g., 0.9166 Gold 1.401 oz. AGW, 38.6 mm. **Ruler:** Elizabeth II **Subject:** Princess Anne's 50th Birthday **Obv:** Crowned bust right **Obv. Designer:** Raphael Maklouf **Rev:** Bust of Princess Anne facing **Edge:** Reeded

Date	Mintage	F	VF	XF	Unc	BU
ND(2000) Proof	50	Value: 1,000				

KM# 13b 50 PENCE
47.5400 g., 0.9166 Gold 1.401 oz. AGW, 38.6 mm. **Subject:** Centennial of Queen Victoria's Death **Obv:** Crowned bust right **Rev:** Crown and veil on half length female facing left within oval circle **Edge:** Reeded

Date	Mintage	F	VF	XF	Unc	BU
2001 Proof	100	Value: 985				

KM# 12b 50 PENCE
47.5400 g., 0.9166 Gold 1.401 oz. AGW, 38.6 mm. **Obv:** Crowned bust right **Rev:** Crowned bust facing

Date	Mintage	F	VF	XF	Unc	BU
2001 Proof	75	Value: 1,000				

KM# 6 2 POUNDS
15.9800 g., 0.9170 Gold .4712 oz. AGW **Ruler:** Elizabeth II **Series:** International Year of the Scout **Obv:** Young bust right **Rev:** Sailboat

Date	Mintage	F	VF	XF	Unc	BU
1983	2,000	—	—	—	350	375
1983 Proof	2,000	Value: 500				

TUNISIA

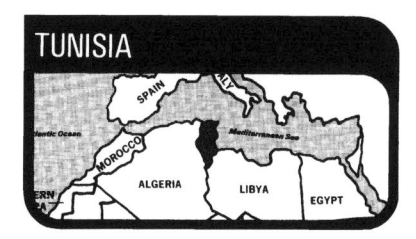

The Republic of Tunisia, located on the northern coast of Africa between Algeria and Libya, has an area of 63,170sq. mi. (163,610 sq. km.) and a population of *7.9 million. Capital: Tunis. Agriculture is the backbone of the economy. Crude oil, phosphates, olive oil, and wine are exported.

Tunisia, settled by the Phoenicians in the 12th century B.C., was the center of the seafaring Carthaginian Empire. After the total destruction of Carthage, Tunisia became part of Rome's African province. It remained a part of the Roman Empire (except for the 439-533 interval of Vandal conquest) until taken by the Arabs, 648, who administered it until the Turkish invasion of 1570. Under Turkish control, the public revenue was heavily dependent upon the piracy of Mediterranean shipping, an endeavor that wasn't abandoned until 1819 when a coalition of powers threatened appropriate reprisal. Deprived of its major source of income, Tunisia underwent a financial regression that ended in bankruptcy, enabling France to establish a protectorate over the country in 1881. National agitation and guerrilla fighting forced France to grant Tunisia internal autonomy in 1955 and to recognize Tunisian independence on March 20, 1956. Tunisia abolished the monarchy and established a republic on July 25, 1957.

TITLES

المملكة التونسية

al-Mamlaka al-Tunisiya

الجمهورية العراقية

al-Jumhuriya al-Tunisiya

al-Amala al-Tunisiya
(Tunisian Protectorate)

MINT MARKS
A - Paris, AH1308/1891-AH1348/1928
(a) - Paris, privy marks,
  AH1349/1929-AH1376/1957
FM - Franklin Mint, Franklin Center, PA
  Numismatic Italiana, Arezzo, Italy

FRENCH PROTECTORATE

HAMMERED COINAGE

KM# 200 25 PIASTRES
4.9200 g., 0.9000 Gold .1424 oz. AGW, 20 mm. **Ruler:** Muhammad al-Sadiq Bey **Obv:** Legend within wreath **Rev:** Text above date within wreath

Date	Mintage	F	VF	XF	Unc	BU
AH1298	—	120	250	500	750	—
AH1300	—	150	300	600	950	—

KM# 209 25 PIASTRES
4.9200 g., 0.9000 Gold .1424 oz. AGW **Ruler:** Ali Bey "Struck in his name" **Obv:** Legend within wreath **Rev:** Text above date within wreath

Date	Mintage	F	VF	XF	Unc	BU
AH1300	—	100	120	150	250	—
AH1302	—	100	120	150	250	—

KM# 214 25 PIASTRES (15 Francs)
4.9200 g., 0.9000 Gold .1424 oz. AGW **Ruler:** Ali Bey "Struck in his name" **Obv:** Legend divides value within wreath **Rev:** Text above date within wreath

Date	Mintage	F	VF	XF	Unc	BU
AH1307A	52,000	100	140	200	350	—
AH1308A	120,000	100	140	200	350	—
AH1308A Proof	—	Value: 2,000				

KM# 212 25 PIASTRES (15 Francs)
4.9200 g., 0.9000 Gold .1424 oz. AGW **Ruler:** Ali Bey "Struck in his name" **Obv:** Arabic legend divides value within wreath **Rev:** Text above date within wreath

Date	Mintage	F	VF	XF	Unc	BU
AH1308	Inc. above	100	140	200	350	—

KM# 204 50 PIASTRES
9.8400 g., 0.9000 Gold .2847 oz. AGW, 26 mm. **Ruler:** Muhammad al-Sadiq Bey

Date	Mintage	F	VF	XF	Unc	BU
AH1299	—	300	400	650	1,000	—

KM# 213 50 PIASTRES
9.8400 g., 0.9000 Gold .2847 oz. AGW **Ruler:** Ali Bey "Struck in his name"

Date	Mintage	F	VF	XF	Unc	BU
AH1304	—	200	350	500	750	—

KM# 211 100 PIASTRES
19.6800 g., 0.9000 Gold .5695 oz. AGW **Ruler:** Ali Bey "Struck in his name"

Date	Mintage	F	VF	XF	Unc	BU
AH1303	—	400	650	1,000	1,500	—

DECIMAL COINAGE
100 Centimes = 1 Franc

The following coins all bear French inscriptions on one side, Arabic on the other, and usually have both AH and AD dates. Except for KM#246-48, they are struck in the name of the Tunisian Bey.

KM# 226 10 FRANCS
3.2258 g., 0.9000 Gold .0933 oz. AGW **Ruler:** Ali Bey "Struck in his name" **Obv:** Legend flanked by sprigs **Obv. Legend:** ALI **Rev:** Value, date in center circle of ornate design

Date	Mintage	F	VF	XF	Unc	BU
AH1308/1891A	400,000	—	65.00	85.00	120	—
AH1308/1891A Proof	—	Value: 1,250				
AH1309/1892A	83	—	—	450	850	—
AH1310/1893A	83	—	—	450	850	—
AH1311/1894A	83	—	—	450	850	—
AH1313/1895A	83	—	—	450	850	—
AH1314/1896A	83	—	—	450	850	—
AH1315/1897A	83	—	—	450	850	—
AH1316/1898A	83	—	—	450	850	—
AH1317/1899A	83	—	—	450	850	—
AH1318/1900A	83	—	—	450	850	—
AH1319/1901A	80	—	—	450	850	—
AH1319/1901A	80	—	—	450	850	—
AH1320/1902A	83	—	—	450	850	—

KM# 233 10 FRANCS
3.2258 g., 0.9000 Gold .0933 oz. AGW **Ruler:** Muhammad al-Hadi Bey "Struck in his name" **Obv. Legend:** MUHAMMAD AL-HADI

Date	Mintage	F	VF	XF	Unc	BU
AH1321/1903A	83	—	—	450	900	—
AH1322/1904A	83	—	—	450	900	—
AH1323/1905A	83	—	—	450	900	—
AH1324/1906A	83	—	—	450	900	—

KM# 240 10 FRANCS
3.2258 g., 0.9000 Gold .0933 oz. AGW **Ruler:** Muhammad al-Nasir Bey "Struck in his name" **Obv. Legend:** MUHAMMAD AL-NASIR

Date	Mintage	F	VF	XF	Unc	BU
AH1325/1907A	36	—	—	500	900	—
AH1326/1908A	166	—	—	300	500	—
AH1327/1909A	83	—	—	450	850	—
AH1328/1910A	83	—	—	450	850	—
AH1329/1911A	83	—	—	450	850	—
AH1330/1912A	83	—	—	450	850	—
AH1331/1913A	83	—	—	450	850	—
AH1332/1914A	83	—	—	450	850	—
AH1334/1915A	83	—	—	450	850	—
AH1334/1916A	83	—	—	450	850	—
AH1336/1917A	83	—	—	450	850	—
AH1337/1918A	83	—	—	450	850	—
AH1338/1919A	83	—	—	450	850	—
AH1339/1920A	83	—	—	450	850	—
AH1340/1921A	83	—	—	450	850	—

KM# 252 10 FRANCS
3.2258 g., 0.9000 Gold .0933 oz. AGW **Ruler:** Muhammad al-Habib Bey "Struck in his name" **Obv. Legend:** MUHAMMAD AL-HABIB BEY

Date	Mintage	F	VF	XF	Unc	BU
AH1341/1922A	83	—	—	450	850	—
AH1342/1923A	169	—	—	300	500	—
AH1343/1924A	83	—	—	450	850	—
AH1344/1925A	83	—	—	450	850	—
AH1345/1926A	83	—	—	450	850	—
AH1346/1927A	83	—	—	450	850	—
AH1347/1928A	83	—	—	450	850	—

KM# 227 20 FRANCS
6.4516 g., 0.9000 Gold .1867 oz. AGW **Ruler:** Ali Bey "Struck in his name" **Obv:** Legend flanked by sprigs **Obv. Legend:** ALI **Rev:** Value, date in center circle of ornate design

Date	Mintage	F	VF	XF	Unc	BU
AH1308/1891A	400,000	—	—	BV	135	—
AH1308/1891 Proof	—	Value: 1,500				
AH1309/1892	937,000	—	—	BV	135	—
AH1310/1892A	Inc. above	—	—	BV	135	—
AH1310/1893A	35,000	—	—	BV	135	—
AH1311/1894A	20	—	—	550	1,000	—
AH1313/1895A	20	—	—	550	1,000	—
AH1314/1896A	20	—	—	550	1,000	—
AH1315/1897A	164,000	—	—	BV	135	—
AH1316/1898A	150,000	—	—	BV	135	—
AH1316/1899A	150,000	—	—	BV	135	—
AH1318/1900A	150,000	—	—	BV	135	—
AH1319/1901A	150,000	—	—	BV	145	—
AH1319/1901A	150,000	—	—	BV	145	—
AH1320/1902A	20	—	—	550	1,000	—

KM# 234 20 FRANCS
6.4516 g., 0.9000 Gold .1867 oz. AGW **Ruler:** Muhammad al-Hadi Bey "Struck in his name" **Obv:** Inscription within sprigs **Obv. Legend:** MUHAMMAD AL-HADI **Rev:** Value and date within center circle

Date	Mintage	F	VF	XF	Unc	BU
AH1321/1903A	300,000	—	—	BV	135	—
AH1321/1904A	600,000	—	—	BV	135	—
AH1322/1904A	Inc. above	—	—	BV	135	—
AH1323/1905A	23	—	—	550	1,000	—
AH1324/1906A	23	—	—	550	1,000	—

KM# 241 20 FRANCS
6.4516 g., 0.9000 Gold .1867 oz. AGW **Ruler:** Muhammad al-Nasir Bey "Struck in his name" **Obv. Legend:** MUHAMMAD AL-NASIR

Date	Mintage	F	VF	XF	Unc	BU
AH1325/1907A	26	—	—	550	1,000	—
AH1326/1908A	46	—	—	450	850	—
AH1327/1909A	23	—	—	550	1,000	—
AH1328/1910A	23	—	—	550	1,000	—
AH1329/1911A	23	—	—	550	1,000	—
AH1330/1912A	23	—	—	550	1,000	—
AH1331/1913A	23	—	—	550	1,000	—
AH1332/1914A	23	—	—	550	1,000	—
AH1334/1915A	23	—	—	550	1,000	—
AH1334/1916A	23	—	—	550	1,000	—
AH1336/1917A	23	—	—	550	1,000	—
AH1337/1918A	23	—	—	550	1,000	—
AH1338/1919A	23	—	—	550	1,000	—
AH1339/1920A	23	—	—	550	1,000	—
AH1340/1921A	23	—	—	550	1,000	—

KM# 253 20 FRANCS
6.4516 g., 0.9000 Gold .1867 oz. AGW **Ruler:** Muhammad al-Habib Bey "Struck in his name" **Obv. Legend:** MUHAMMAD AL-HABIB

Date	Mintage	F	VF	XF	Unc	BU
AH1341/1922A	23	—	—	650	1,100	—
AH1342/1923A	49	—	—	450	850	—
AH1343/1924A	23	—	—	550	1,000	—
AH1344/1925A	23	—	—	550	1,000	—
AH1345/1926A	23	—	—	550	1,000	—
AH1346/1927A	23	—	—	550	1,000	—
AH1347/1928A	23	—	—	550	1,000	—

KM# 257 100 FRANCS
6.5500 g., 0.9000 Gold .1895 oz. AGW **Ruler:** Ahmad Pasha Bey "Struck in his name" **Obv:** Inscription within oblong design

684 TUNISIA

flanked by sprigs **Obv. Legend:** AHMAD **Rev:** Value and date within center circle of design

Date	Mintage	F	VF	XF	Unc	BU
AH1349/1930(a)	3,000	—	—	BV	145	—
AH1350/1931(a)	33	—	—	500	900	—
AH1351/1932(a)	3,000	—	—	BV	145	—
AH1352/1933(a)	33	—	—	500	900	—
AH1353/1934(a)	133	—	—	300	400	—
AH1354/1935(a)	3,000	—	—	BV	145	—
AH1355/1936(a)	33	—	—	500	900	—
AH1356/1937(a)	33	—	—	500	900	—

MEDALLIC COINAGE

X# 3 100 FRANCS
6.5500 g., 0.9000 Gold .1895 oz. AGW **Ruler:** Ahmad Pasha Bey "Struck in his name" **Obv. Legend:** AHMED BEY **Edge:** Lettered **Note:** Previous KM#M1.1.

Date	Mintage	F	VF	XF	Unc	BU
AH1357//1938(a)	66	—	—	475	650	—
AH1358//1939(a)	33	—	—	575	750	—
AH1359//1940(a)	33	—	—	575	750	—

X# 4 100 FRANCS
6.5500 g., 0.9000 Gold .1895 oz. AGW **Ruler:** Ahmad Pasha Bey "Struck in his name" **Obv. Legend:** AHMED BEY **Edge:** Milled **Note:** Previous KM#M1.2.

Date	Mintage	F	VF	XF	Unc	BU
AH1360//1941(a)	33	—	—	575	750	—
AH1361//1942(a)	33	—	—	575	750	—

X# 5 100 FRANCS
6.5500 g., 0.9000 Gold .1895 oz. AGW **Ruler:** Muhammad al-Munsif Bey "Struck in his name" **Obv. Legend:** MUHAMMAD AL-MUNSIF BEY **Note:** Previous KM#M2.

Date	Mintage	F	VF	XF	Unc	BU
AH1362//1943(a)	33	—	—	750	1,100	—

X# 6 100 FRANCS
6.5500 g., 0.9000 Gold .1895 oz. AGW **Ruler:** Muhammad al-Amin Bey "Struck in his name" **Obv. Legend:** MUHAMMAD AL-AMIN BEY **Note:** Previous KM#M3.

Date	Mintage	F	VF	XF	Unc	BU
AH1363//1943(a)	66	—	—	425	600	—
AH1364//1944(a)	68	—	—	475	650	—
AH1365//1945(a)	33	—	—	575	750	—
AH1366//1946(a)	33	—	—	575	750	—
AH1367//1947(a)	33	—	—	575	750	—
AH1368//1948(a)	33	—	—	575	750	—
AH1369//1949(a)	33	—	—	575	750	—
AH1370//1950(a)	33	—	—	575	750	—
AH1371//1951(a)	63	—	—	475	650	—
AH1372//1952(a)	63	—	—	475	650	—
AH1373//1953(a)	63	—	—	475	650	—
AH1374//1954(a)	63	—	—	475	650	—
AH1375//1955(a)	63	—	—	475	650	—

KINGDOM
Muhammad al-Amin Bey as Premier

MEDALLIC COINAGE

X# 9 100 FRANCS
6.5500 g., 0.9000 Gold .1895 oz. AGW **Obv. Legend:** MUHAMMAD AL-AMIN, PREMIER **Note:** Previous KM#M8.

Date	Mintage	F	VF	XF	Unc	BU
AH1376/1956(a)	63	—	—	600	1,000	—

REPUBLIC
DECIMAL COINAGE
1000 Millim = 1 Dinar

KM# 286 2 DINARS
3.8000 g., 0.9000 Gold .1099 oz. AGW **Subject:** 10th Anniversary of Republic **Obv:** Head of Habib Bourguiba left **Rev:** Towered building flanked by dates

Date	Mintage	F	VF	XF	Unc	BU
ND(1967) NI Proof	7,259	Value: 85.00				

KM# 283 5 DINARS
11.7900 g., 0.9000 Gold .3412 oz. AGW **Obv:** Head of Habib Bourguiba left, French legend **Rev:** Shield above sprigs, value and banner, French legend

Date	Mintage	F	VF	XF	Unc	BU
1962 Proof	—	Value: 550				

KM# 320 5 DINARS
11.7900 g., 0.9000 Gold .3412 oz. AGW **Obv:** Arabic legends **Rev:** Arabic legends

Date	Mintage	F	VF	XF	Unc	BU
1962 Proof	—	Value: 550				

KM# 284 5 DINARS
11.7900 g., 0.9000 Gold .3412 oz. AGW **Obv:** Head of Habib Bourguiba left, French legends **Rev:** Shield above value, French legends

Date	Mintage	F	VF	XF	Unc	BU
1963 Proof	—	Value: 550				

KM# 321 5 DINARS
9.3600 g., 0.9000 Gold .2708 oz. AGW **Obv:** Arabic legends **Rev:** Arabic legends

Date	Mintage	F	VF	XF	Unc	BU
1963 Proof	—	Value: 550				

KM# 287 5 DINARS
9.5000 g., 0.9000 Gold .2749 oz. AGW **Subject:** 10th Anniversary of Republic **Obv:** Head of Habib Bourguiba left **Rev:** Minaret

Date	Mintage	F	VF	XF	Unc	BU
ND(1967) NI Proof	7,259	Value: 200				

KM# 284a 5 DINARS
9.3600 g., 0.9000 Gold .2708 oz. AGW **Obv:** Head of Habib Bourguiba left **Rev:** Shield above value

Date	Mintage	F	VF	XF	Unc	BU
1976 Proof	—	Value: 500				

KM# 310 5 DINARS
9.4120 g., 0.9000 Gold .2723 oz. AGW **Obv:** Head of Habib Bourguiba left **Rev:** President's return

Date	Mintage	F	VF	XF	Unc	BU
1981 Proof	1,450	Value: 215				

KM# 326 5 DINARS
9.4120 g., 0.9000 Gold .2723 oz. AGW **Rev:** Arabic legends

Date	Mintage	F	VF	XF	Unc	BU
AH1402 Proof	725	Value: 225				

KM# 325 5 DINARS
9.4120 g., 0.9000 Gold .2723 oz. AGW **Obv:** President **Rev:** Coat of arms **Note:** French legends.

Date	Mintage	F	VF	XF	Unc	BU
1982 Proof	725	Value: 225				

KM# 327 5 DINARS
9.4120 g., 0.9000 Gold .2723 oz. AGW **Subject:** 25th Anniversary of Republic **Note:** French legends.

Date	Mintage	F	VF	XF	Unc	BU
1983-85 Proof	—	Value: 225				

KM# 328 5 DINARS
9.4120 g., 0.9000 Gold .2723 oz. AGW **Note:** Arabic legends.

Date	Mintage	F	VF	XF	Unc	BU
AH1403-05 Proof	—	Value: 225				

KM# 330 5 DINARS
9.4120 g., 0.9000 Gold .2723 oz. AGW **Note:** Arabic legends.

Date	Mintage	F	VF	XF	Unc	BU
AH1408	375	—	—	—	275	—
AH1409	Inc. above	—	—	—	275	—

KM# 329 5 DINARS
9.4120 g., 0.9000 Gold .2723 oz. AGW **Obv:** Map **Rev:** Allegorical design **Note:** French legends.

Date	Mintage	F	VF	XF	Unc	BU
1988	375	—	—	—	275	—
1989	Inc. above	—	—	—	275	—

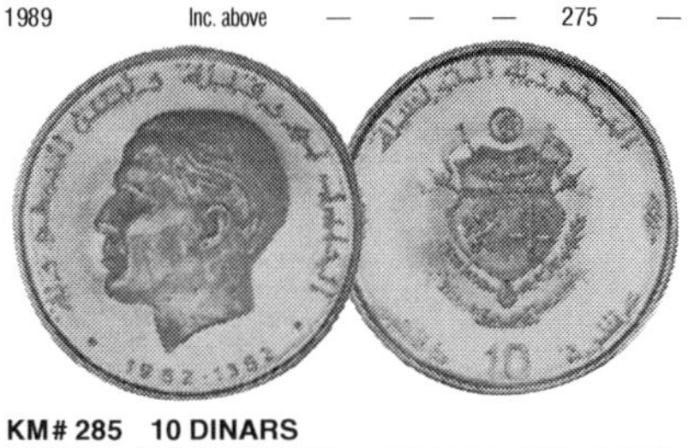

KM# 285 10 DINARS
23.4800 g., 0.9000 Gold .6795 oz. AGW **Obv:** Head of Habib Bourguiba left, Arabic legends **Rev:** Shield above value, Arabic legends

Date	Mintage	F	VF	XF	Unc	BU
AH1382-1962 Proof	—	Value: 850				
AH1384-1964 Proof	—	Value: 850				

KM# 322 10 DINARS
23.4800 g., 0.9000 Gold .6795 oz. AGW **Obv:** French legends **Rev:** French legends

Date	Mintage	F	VF	XF	Unc	BU
1962 Proof	—	Value: 850				

KM# 288 10 DINARS
19.0000 g., 0.9000 Gold .5498 oz. AGW **Subject:** 10th Anniversary of Republic **Obv:** Head of Habib Bourguiba left **Rev:** Towered building flanked by dates

Date	Mintage	F	VF	XF	Unc	BU
ND(1967) NI Proof	6,480	Value: 400				

KM# 324 10 DINARS
0.9000 Gold **Subject:** 20th Anniversary of Independence **Obv:** Head of Habib Bourguiba left **Rev:** Shield

Date	Mintage	F	VF	XF	Unc	BU
1976	Est. 2,000	—	—	—	750	—

KM# 345 10 DINARS
18.8080 g., 0.9000 Gold .5442 oz. AGW **Subject:** 20th Anniversary - Central Bank

Date	Mintage	F	VF	XF	Unc	BU
1978	2,000	—	—	—	700	—

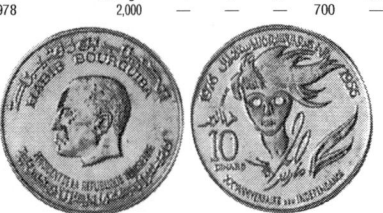

KM# 342 10 DINARS
18.7700 g., 0.9000 Gold .5431 oz. AGW **Obv:** Head of Habib Bourguiba left, French legends **Rev:** Stylized head facing, French legends

Date	Mintage	F	VF	XF	Unc	BU
1979	—	—	—	—	900	—

TUNIS / TUNISIA

KM# 343 10 DINARS
18.7700 g., 0.9000 Gold .5431 oz. AGW **Obv:** Head of Habib Bourguiba left, Arabic legends **Rev:** Shield, Arabic legends
Date	Mintage	F	VF	XF	Unc	BU
AH1399 (1979)	—	—	—	—	900	—

KM# 311 10 DINARS
18.8240 g., 0.9000 Gold .5447 oz. AGW **Obv:** Habib Bourguiba **Rev:** President's return
Date	Mintage	F	VF	XF	Unc	BU
1981 Proof	2,000	Value: 550

KM# 312 10 DINARS
18.8080 g., 0.9000 Gold .5442 oz. AGW **Subject:** 25th Anniversary of Independence **Obv:** Head of Habib Bourguiba left **Rev:** Silhouette of girl
Date	Mintage	F	VF	XF	Unc	BU
1981 Proof	2,000	Value: 550

KM# 323 10 DINARS
18.8080 g., 0.9000 Gold .5442 oz. AGW **Obv:** Head left **Rev:** Statue of Burgiba
Date	Mintage	F	VF	XF	Unc	BU
AH1405 (1985) Proof	2,000	Value: 550

KM# 337 10 DINARS
18.8080 g., 0.9000 Gold .5442 oz. AGW **Subject:** 30th Anniversary of Independence
Date	Mintage	F	VF	XF	Unc	BU
1986 Proof	—	Value: 550

KM# 338 10 DINARS
18.8080 g., 0.9000 Gold .5442 oz. AGW **Subject:** 30th Anniversary of Republic
Date	Mintage	F	VF	XF	Unc	BU
1987 Proof	2,000	Value: 550

KM# 341 10 DINARS
18.8080 g., 0.9000 Gold .5442 oz. AGW **Note:** Arabic legends.
Date	Mintage	F	VF	XF	Unc	BU
AH1408	375	—	—	—	650	—
AH1409	Inc. above	—	—	—	650	—

KM# 340 10 DINARS
18.8080 g., 0.9000 Gold .5442 oz. AGW **Obv:** Map **Rev:** Allegorical design **Note:** French legends.
Date	Mintage	F	VF	XF	Unc	BU
1988	375	—	—	—	650	—
1989	Inc. above	—	—	—	650	—

KM# 289 20 DINARS
38.0000 g., 0.9000 Gold 1.0996 oz. AGW **Subject:** 10th Anniversary of Republic **Rev:** Minaret
Date	Mintage	F	VF	XF	Unc	BU
ND(1967) NI	3,536	—	—	—	775	—

KM# 290 40 DINARS
76.0000 g., 0.9000 Gold 2.1991 oz. AGW **Subject:** 10th Anniversary of Republic **Obv:** Head left **Rev:** Minaret **Note:** Similar to 20 Dinars, KM#289.
Date	Mintage	F	VF	XF	Unc	BU
ND(1967) NI Proof	3,031	Value: 1,550

KM# 353 50 DINARS
0.9000 Gold, 34 mm. **Subject:** 13th Anniversary of the Bloodless November 7, 1987 Coup **Obv:** National arms **Rev:** Two interlocked currycombs, each with the number 21
Date	Mintage	F	VF	XF	Unc	BU
2000-1421 Proof	—	Value: 750

KM# 317 75 DINARS
15.5500 g., 0.9000 Gold .4500 oz. AGW **Series:** International Year of the Child **Obv:** Head of Habib Bourguiba left **Rev:** Standing figures facing left
Date	Mintage	F	VF	XF	Unc	BU
1982 Proof	4,518	Value: 325

KM# 352 100 DINARS
38.0000 g., 0.9000 Gold 1.0996 oz. AGW, 40 mm. **Subject:** United Nations **Obv:** National arms above value **Rev:** UN logo on stylized hand **Edge:** Reeded
Date	Mintage	F	VF	XF	Unc	BU
AH1424-2003 Proof	—	Value: 800

PATTERNS
Including off metal strikes

KM#	Date	Mintage	Identification	Mkt Val
Pn13	AH1305	—	25 Piastres. Gold. Legend divides value within wreath. Text within wreath. KM#212.	950

ESSAIS
Standard metals unless otherwise noted

KM#	Date	Mintage	Identification	Mkt Val
E12	1930(a)	—	100 Francs. Gold. KM#257, uniface.	375
E-A19	AH1354(a)	—	100 Francs. Gilt Bronze. KM#257.	—
E19	1938(a)	—	100 Francs. Gilt Bronze. KM-M1.	110
E20	1938(a)	—	100 Francs. Gold. KM-M1.	950
E33	1968(a)	—	70 1/2 Dinar. Gold.	550

PIEFORTS
Double thickness; standard metals unless otherwise noted

KM#	Date	Mintage	Identification	Issue Price	Mkt Val
P3	1982	55	75 Dinars. Gold. KM#317.	—	1,250

PROOF SETS

KM#	Date	Mintage	Identification	Issue Price	Mkt Val
PS2	1967 (5)	3,031	KM#286-290	—	2,000

TUNIS

Tunis, the capital and major seaport of Tunisia, existed in the Carthaginian era, but its importance dates only from the Moslem conquest, following which it became a major center of Arab power and prosperity. Spain seized it in 1535, lost it in 1564, retook it in 1573 and ceded it to the Turks in 1574. Thereafter the history of Tunis merged with that of Tunisia.

Local Rulers
Ali Bey, AH1299-1320/1882-1902AD
Muhammad Al-Hadi Bey, AH1320-1324/1902-1906AD
Muhammad Al-Nasir Bey, AH1324-1340/1906-1922AD
Muhammad Al-Habib Bey, AH1340-1348/1922-1929AD
Ahmad Pasha Bey, AH1348-1361/1929-1942AD
Muhammad Al-Munsif Bey, AH1361-1362/1942-1943AD
Muhammad Al-Amin Bey, AH1362-1376/1943-1957AD

NOTE: All coins struck until AH1298/1881AD bear the name of the Ottoman Sultan; the name of the Bey of Tunis was added in AH1272/1855AD. After AH1298, when the French established their protectorate, only the Bey's name appears on the coin until AH1376/1956AD.

OTTOMAN EMPIRE

HAMMERED COINAGE

KM# 122 5 PIASTRES
0.9800 g., 0.9000 Gold .0284 oz. AGW, 12 mm. **Ruler:** Sultan Abdul Mejid with Muhammad Bey AH1272-76/1856-59AD **Obv:** Legend within wreath **Rev:** Text, date within wreath
Date	Mintage	VG	F	VF	XF	Unc
AH1272	—	22.50	30.00	70.00	125	—
AH1273	—	22.50	30.00	70.00	125	—
AH1274	—	22.50	30.00	70.00	125	—
AH1275	—	22.50	30.00	70.00	125	—

KM# 162 5 PIASTRES
0.9800 g., 0.9000 Gold .0284 oz. AGW **Ruler:** Sultan Abdul Aziz with Muhammad al-Sadiq Bey AH1276-93/1860-76AD **Obv:** Legend **Rev:** Text, date
Date	Mintage	VG	F	VF	XF	Unc
AH1281	—	22.50	32.50	55.00	100	—
AH1281 Proof	—	Value: 150

KM# 169 5 PIASTRES
0.9800 g., 0.9000 Gold .0284 oz. AGW **Ruler:** Sultan Abdul Aziz with Muhammad al-Sadiq Bey AH1276-93/1860-76AD **Obv:** Legend **Rev:** Text, date
Date	Mintage	VG	F	VF	XF	Unc
AH1288	—	22.50	32.50	50.00	90.00	—
AH1289	—	22.50	32.50	50.00	90.00	—
AH1290	—	22.50	32.50	50.00	90.00	—

Note: Varieties exist
| AH1291 | — | 22.50 | 32.50 | 50.00 | 90.00 | — |

Note: Varieties exist
| AH1292 | — | 25.00 | 40.00 | 60.00 | 100 | — |

KM# 195 5 PIASTRES
0.9800 g., 0.9000 Gold .0284 oz. AGW, 12.5 mm. **Ruler:** Sultan Abdul Hamid II with Muhammad al-Sadiq Bey AH1293/1876-82AD **Obv:** Legend within wreath **Rev:** Text, date within wreath
Date	Mintage	VG	F	VF	XF	Unc
AH1294	—	40.00	75.00	150	250	—

KM# 123 10 PIASTRES
1.7700 g., 1.0000 Gold .0569 oz. AGW **Ruler:** Sultan Abdul Mejid with Muhammad Bey AH1272-76/1856-59AD **Obv:** Legend within wreath **Rev:** Text, date within wreath
Date	Mintage	VG	F	VF	XF	Unc
AH1272	—	40.00	60.00	95.00	150	—

KM# 124 10 PIASTRES
1.9700 g., 0.9000 Gold .0570 oz. AGW **Ruler:** Sultan Abdul Mejid with Muhammad Bey AH1272-76/1856-59AD **Obv:** Legend within wreath **Rev:** Text, date within wreath
Date	Mintage	VG	F	VF	XF	Unc
AH1272	—	40.00	60.00	95.00	150	—
AH1274	—	40.00	60.00	95.00	150	—

KM# 150 10 PIASTRES
1.9700 g., 0.9000 Gold .0570 oz. AGW **Ruler:** Sultan Abdul Aziz with Muhammad al-Sadiq Bey AH1276-93/1860-76AD **Obv:** Legend within wreath **Rev:** Text, date within wreath
Date	Mintage	VG	F	VF	XF	Unc
AH1280	—	42.50	65.00	90.00	185	—
AH1281	—	42.50	65.00	90.00	185	—
AH1281 Proof	—	Value: 300
AH1284	—	42.50	65.00	90.00	185	—
AH1287	—	42.50	65.00	90.00	185	—
AH1288	—	42.50	65.00	90.00	185	—

KM# 199 10 PIASTRES
1.9700 g., 0.9000 Gold .0570 oz. AGW **Ruler:** Sultan Abdul

TUNISIA / TUNIS

Hamid II with Muhammad al-Sadiq Bey AH1293-99/1876-82AD
Obv: Legend within wreath **Rev:** Text, date within wreath

Date	Mintage	VG	F	VF	XF	Unc
AH1295	—	—	—	—	—	—

KM# 125 20 PIASTRES
3.5500 g., 1.0000 Gold .1141 oz. AGW, 21 mm. **Ruler:** Sultan Abdul Mejid with Muhammad Bey AH1272-76/1856-59AD **Obv:** Legend within wreath **Rev:** Text, date within wreath

Date	Mintage	VG	F	VF	XF	Unc
AH1272	—	100	150	225	400	—

KM# 133 25 PIASTRES
4.9200 g., 0.9000 Gold .1424 oz. AGW, 20 mm. **Ruler:** Sultan Abdul Mejid with Muhammad Bey AH1272-76/1856-59AD **Obv:** Legend within wreath **Rev:** Text, date within wreath

Date	Mintage	VG	F	VF	XF	Unc
AH1273	—	125	165	250	420	—
AH1274	—	125	165	250	420	—
AH1275	—	125	165	250	420	—

KM# 139 25 PIASTRES
4.9000 g., Gold, 20 mm. **Ruler:** Sultan Abdul Mejid with Muhammad al-Sadiq Bey AH1276-77/1859-1860AD

Date	Mintage	VG	F	VF	XF	Unc
AH1276	—	0.20	225	350	700	—

KM# 148 25 PIASTRES
4.9200 g., 0.9000 Gold .1424 oz. AGW **Ruler:** Sultan Abdul Aziz with Muhammad al-Sadiq Bey AH1276-93/1860-76AD **Obv:** Legend within wreath **Rev:** Text, date within wreath

Date	Mintage	VG	F	VF	XF	Unc
AH1278	—	120	160	225	300	—
AH1279	—	120	160	225	300	—
AH1280	—	120	160	225	300	—
AH1281	—	120	160	225	300	—
AH1281 Proof	—	Value: 400				
AH1282 Rare	—	—	—	—	—	—
AH1283	—	120	160	225	300	—
AH1284 Rare	—	—	—	—	—	—
AH1285	—	120	160	225	300	—
AH1286 Rare	—	—	—	—	—	—
AH1287	—	120	160	225	300	—
AH1288	—	120	160	225	300	—
AH1289	—	120	135	175	250	—
AH1290	—	120	135	175	250	—
AH1291	—	120	135	175	250	—

KM# 177 25 PIASTRES
4.9200 g., 0.9000 Gold .1424 oz. AGW, 20 mm. **Ruler:** Sultan Murad V with Muhammad al-Sadiq Bey AH1293/1876AD

Date	Mintage	VG	F	VF	XF	Unc
AH1293	—	300	500	850	1,500	—

KM# 196 25 PIASTRES
4.9200 g., 0.9000 Gold .1424 oz. AGW **Ruler:** Sultan Abdul Hamid II with Muhammad al-Sadiq Bey AH1293-99/1876-82AD **Obv:** Legend within wreath **Rev:** Text, date within wreath

Date	Mintage	VG	F	VF	XF	Unc
AH1294	—	100	120	175	250	—
AH1295	—	100	120	175	250	—
AH1296	—	100	120	175	250	—
AH1297	—	100	120	175	250	—
AH1298 Rare	—	—	—	—	—	—

KM# 126 40 PIASTRES
7.1000 g., 1.0000 Gold .2283 oz. AGW, 26 mm. **Ruler:** Sultan Abdul Mejid with Muhammad Bey AH1272-76/1856-59AD **Obv:** Legend within wreath **Rev:** Text, date within wreath

Date	Mintage	VG	F	VF	XF	Unc
AH1272	—	150	200	325	550	—

KM# 127 50 PIASTRES
9.8400 g., 0.9000 Gold .2847 oz. AGW **Ruler:** Sultan Abdul Mejid with Muhammad Bey AH1272-76/1856-59AD **Obv:** Legend within wreath **Rev:** Text, date within wreath

Date	Mintage	VG	F	VF	XF	Unc
AH1272	—	200	250	325	525	—
AH1273	—	200	250	325	525	—
AH1274	—	200	250	325	525	—
AH1275	—	200	250	325	525	—

KM# 140 50 PIASTRES
9.8000 g., Gold, 26 mm. **Ruler:** Sultan Abdul Mejid with Muhammad al-Sadiq Bey AH1276-77/1859-1860AD

Date	Mintage	VG	F	VF	XF	Unc
AH1276	—	225	325	500	800	—

KM# 152 50 PIASTRES
9.8400 g., 0.9000 Gold .2847 oz. AGW **Ruler:** Sultan Abdul Aziz with Muhammad al-Sadiq Bey AH1276-93/1860-76AD **Obv:** Legend within wreath **Rev:** Text, date within wreath

Date	Mintage	VG	F	VF	XF	Unc
AH1280	—	200	235	300	500	—
AH1281	—	200	235	285	350	—
AH1281 Proof	—	Value: 550				
AH1286	—	200	235	285	350	—
AH1288	—	200	235	285	350	—
AH1293	—	250	285	350	550	—

KM# 197 50 PIASTRES
9.8400 g., 0.9000 Gold .2847 oz. AGW, 26 mm. **Ruler:** Sultan Abdul Hamid II with Muhammad al-Sadiq Bey AH1293-99/1876-82AD **Obv:** Legend within wreath, without "al-Ghazi" **Rev:** Text, date within wreath

Date	Mintage	VG	F	VF	XF	Unc
AH1294 Rare	—	—	—	—	—	—

KM# 198 50 PIASTRES
9.8400 g., 0.9000 Gold .2847 oz. AGW, 26 mm. **Ruler:** Sultan Abdul Hamid II with Muhammad al-Sadiq Bey AH1293-99/1876-82AD **Obv:** Legend within wreath, "al-Ghazi" added **Rev:** Text, date within wreath

Date	Mintage	VG	F	VF	XF	Unc
AH1295 Rare	—	—	—	—	—	—
AH1297	—	200	250	300	500	—

KM# 128 80 PIASTRES
14.2100 g., 1.0000 Gold .4569 oz. AGW, 31 mm. **Ruler:** Sultan Abdul Mejid with Muhammad Bey AH1272-76/1856-59AD **Obv:** Legend within wreath **Rev:** Text, date within wreath

Date	Mintage	VG	F	VF	XF	Unc
AH1272	—	350	475	950	1,250	—

KM# 129 100 PIASTRES
17.7100 g., 1.0000 Gold .5694 oz. AGW, 33 mm. **Ruler:** Sultan Abdul Mejid with Muhammad Bey AH1272-76/1856-59AD **Obv:** Legend within wreath **Rev:** Text, date within wreath

Date	Mintage	VG	F	VF	XF	Unc
AH1272	—	425	625	975	1,450	—

KM# 130 100 PIASTRES
19.6800 g., 0.9000 Gold .5695 oz. AGW **Ruler:** Sultan Abdul Mejid with Muhammad Bey AH1272-76/1856-59AD **Obv:** Legend within wreath **Rev:** Text, date within wreath

Date	Mintage	VG	F	VF	XF	Unc
AH1272	—	400	525	750	1,200	—
AH1273	—	400	525	750	1,200	—
AH1274	—	400	525	750	1,200	—

KM# 141 100 PIASTRES
19.7000 g., Gold, 33 mm. **Ruler:** Sultan Abdul Mejid with Muhammad al-Sadiq Bey AH1276-77/1859-1860AD **Obv:** Legend within wreath **Rev:** Text, date within wreath

Date	Mintage	VG	F	VF	XF	Unc
AH1276	—	1,000	1,250	1,600	2,200	—

KM# 149 100 PIASTRES
19.6800 g., 0.9000 Gold .5695 oz. AGW **Ruler:** Sultan Abdul Aziz with Muhammad al-Sadiq Bey AH1276-93/1860-76AD **Obv:** Legend within wreath **Rev:** Text, date within wreath **Note:** KM#148-150,152,161,164 and 166, dated AH1281, were all struck at Tunis, from dies produced at the Heaton Mint in Birmingham, hence their obvious superiority.

Date	Mintage	VG	F	VF	XF	Unc
AH1279	—	400	575	975	2,000	—
AH1280	—	400	575	975	2,000	—
AH1281	—	400	575	975	2,000	—
AH1281 Proof	—	Value: 3,200				
AH1283	—	400	575	975	2,000	—
AH1285	—	400	575	975	2,000	—
AH1286	—	400	575	975	2,000	—

Note: KM#148-150, 152, 161, 162, 164 and 166, dated AH1281, were all struck at Tunis, from dies produced at the Heaton Mint in Birmingham, hence their obvious superiority.

KM# A199 100 PIASTRES
19.6800 g., 0.9000 Gold .5695 oz. AGW, 33 mm. **Ruler:** Sultan Abdul Hamid II with Muhammad al-Sadiq Bey AH1293-99 / 1876-82AD

Date	Mintage	VG	F	VF	XF	Unc
AH1295	—	—	—	—	—	—

Note: Reported, not confirmed

KM# 87 SULTANI
0.9860 Gold, 20 mm. **Ruler:** Mahmud II AH1223-25/1808-39AD **Note:** Weight varies: 2.50-3.20 grams.

Date	Mintage	VF	XF	Unc	BU
AH1236	—	200	300	425	600

COUNTERMARKED COINAGE
AH1295/1878AD

KM# 163 5 PIASTRES
0.9800 g., 0.9000 Gold .0284 oz. AGW **Ruler:** Sultan Abdul Hamid II with Muhammad al-Sadiq Bey AH1293-99/1876-82AD **Countermark:** Star **Note:** Countermark on KM#162.

CM Date	Host Date	Good	VG	F	VF	XF
ND	AH1295	—	22.50	35.00	60.00	120

KM# 170 5 PIASTRES
0.9800 g., 0.9000 Gold .0284 oz. AGW **Ruler:** Sultan Abdul Hamid II with Muhammad al-Sadiq Bey AH1293-99/1876-82AD **Countermark:** Star **Note:** Countermark on KM#169.

CM Date	Host Date	Good	VG	F	VF	XF
ND	AH1288	—	22.50	35.00	60.00	120
ND	AH1289	—	22.50	35.00	60.00	120
ND	AH1290	—	22.50	35.00	60.00	120
ND	AH1291	—	22.50	35.00	60.00	120

KM# 151 10 PIASTRES
1.9700 g., 0.9000 Gold .0570 oz. AGW **Ruler:** Sultan Abdul Hamid II with Muhammad al-Sadiq Bey AH1293-99/1876-82AD **Countermark:** Star **Note:** Countermark on KM#150.

CM Date	Host Date	Good	VG	F	VF	XF
ND	AH1281	—	45.00	70.00	85.00	160
ND	AH1288	—	45.00	70.00	85.00	160

TURKEY

PATTERNS
Including off metal strikes

KM#	Date	Mintage	Identification	Mkt Val
Pn8	AH1281	—	5 Piastres. Copper. Legend. Text, date. KM#162.	250
Pn9	AH1281	—	10 Piastres. Copper. Legend within wreath. Text, date within wreath. KM#150	250
Pn10	AH1281	—	25 Piastres. Copper. Legend within wreath. Text, date within wreath. KM#148.	250
Pn11	AH1281	—	50 Piastres. Copper. KM#152.	325
Pn12	AH1281	—	100 Piastres. Copper. Legend within wreath. Text, date within wreath. KM#149.	375

PROOF SETS

KM#	Date	Mintage	Identification	Issue Price	Mkt Val
PS1	1864 (AH1281)	(5)	KM#148-150, 152, 162	—	4,750

Turkey, located partially in Europe and partially in Asia between the Black and the Mediterranean Seas, has an area of 301,382 sq. mi. (780,580 sq. km).

The Ottoman Turks, a tribe from Central Asia, first appeared in the early 13th century, and by the 17th century had established the Ottoman Empire which stretched from the Persian Gulf to the southern frontier of Poland, and from the Caspian Sea to the Algerian plateau. The defeat of the Turkish navy by the Holy League in 1571, and of the Turkish forces besieging Vienna in 1683, began the steady decline of the Ottoman Empire which, accelerated by the rise of nationalism, contracted its European border, and by the end of World War I deprived it of its Arab lands. The present Turkish boundaries were largely fixed by the Treaty of Lausanne in 1923. The sultanate and caliphate, the political and spiritual ruling institutions of the old empire, were separated and the sultanate abolished in 1922. On Oct. 29, 1923, Turkey formally became a republic.

RULERS
Selim III, AH1203-1222/1789-1807AD
Mustafa IV, AH1222-1223/1807-1808AD
Mahmud II, AH1223-1255/1808-1839AD
Abdul Mejid, AH1255-12771839-1861AD
Abdul Aziz, AH1277-1293/1861-1876AD
Murad V, AH1293/1876AD
Abdul Hamid II, AH1293-1327/1876-1909AD
Muhammad V, AH1327-1336/1909-1918AD
Muhammad VI, AH1336-1341/1918-1923AD
Republic, AH1341/AD1923-

MINT NAMES

اماسیاه
Amasiah

آمد
Amid
  Diarbakar
  Kara Amid

آنکارا (ایاسوَلیک)
Ankara
  (Anguriyah)

انگوریه
Ayasulik

آزاک
Azak

بغداد
Baghdad
  See Iraq-Mesopotamia

بلگراد
Belgrad

Bitlis
  (Bidlis)

بوسنه سرای
Bosnasaray
  Saray

بروسة
Bursa
  (Brusah)

کنسا
Canca or Chaniche
  Gurnushhane

قسطنتنیه
Constantine
  (Constaniyah, Qusantinah) See Algeria-Algiers

قسطنطنیة
Constantinople
  (Qustantiniyah)

دمشق
Damascus
  (Damask) See Syria

دیاربکر
Diarbakar
  (See Amid)

ادرنة
Edirne
  (Adrianople)

تفلیس
Erevan
  (Erewan, Revan, Yerevan) See Armenia

ارزروم
Erzerum

فیلیپ
Filibe
  (Philipopolis - Plovdiv)

جلیبولو
Gelibolu
  (Gallipoli)

کنجه
Genje
  (Azerbaijan)

کنسا
Gumushhane
  (Canca)

حلب
Halab
  (Aleppo) See Syria

TURKEY

MINT NAMES

Islambul (Istanbul)	اسلامبول or اسلامول
Izmir (Smyrna)	ازمير
Jaza'lr (See Algeria-Algiers)	لجزاير
Kara Amid (Amid)	كارآمد
Kars	
Kastamonu	كستامونو
Kibris (Cyprus)	قبريس (قبرس)
Konya (Khanja)	كنيا
Kosova	قوصوه
Makkah (Mecca) See Saudi Arabia	
Manistir	مناستر
Mardin	ماردين
Al-Mascara See Algeria-Algiers	المعسكر
Medea	مديه
Misr See Egypt	مصر
Nackhchawan See Azerbaijan	نخجوان
Nigbolu	نكبولي or نگبولو
Novabirda Novar	نوابرده
Ohri	خري
Ordu-yu Humayun	
Qaratova	
Sakiz (Scio)	سكيز
Salonika (Selanik, Saloniki)	سلانيك
Saray Bosnasarzy	سراي
Serez (Siroz)	سرز (سيروز)
Shamakhi See Azerbaijan	شماخ
Shirvan See Azerbaijan	شيروان
Sidrekapsi	سدره قپسي
Sivas	سيواس
Sofia	صوفيه
Tire	تيره
Tokat	توكت
Trebizond Trabzon	طرابوزان
Tunis See Tunisia-Tunis	تونس
Uskub	اسكوب
Yenishehir	يني شهر
Zabid See Yemen	زبيد

MONETARY SYSTEM
Gold Coinage
100 Kurush (Piastres) = 1 Turkish Pound (Lira)

MINT VISIT ISSUES
From time to time, certain cities of the Ottoman Empire, such as Bursa, Edirne, Kosova, Manistir and Salonika were honored by having special coins struck at Istanbul, but with inscriptions stating that they were struck in the city of honor. These were produced on the occasion of the Sultan's visit to that city. The coins were struck in limited, but not small quantities, and were probably intended for distribution to the notables of the city and the Sultan's own followers. Because they were of the same size and type as the regular circulation issues struck at Istanbul, many specimens found their way into circulation and worn or mounted specimens are found today, although some have been preserved in XF or better condition. Mintage statistics are not known.

MONNAIE DE LUXE
In the 23rd year of the reign of Abdul Hamid II, two parallel series of gold coins were produced, regular mint issues and monnaies de luxe', which were intended primarily for presentation and jewelry purposes. The Monnaie de Luxe' were struck to a slightly less weight and the same fineness as regular issues, but were broader and thinner, and from more ornate dies.

Coins are listed by type, followed by a list of reported years. Most of the reported years have never been confirmed and other years may also exist. Mintage figures are known for the AH1293 and 1327 series, but are unreliable and of little utility.

Although some years are undoubtedly much rarer than others, there is at present no date collecting of Ottoman gold and therefore little justification for higher prices for rare dates.

There is no change in design in the regular series. Only the toughra, accessional date and regnal year vary. The deluxe series show ornamental changes. The standard coins generally do not bear the denomination.

INITIAL LETTERS

Letters, symbols and numerals were placed on coins during the reigns of Mustafa II (1695) until Selim III (1789). They have been observed in various positions but the most common position being over *bin* in the third row of the obverse.

HONORIFIC TITLES

El Ghazi   Reshat

The first coinage of Abdul Hamid II has a flower right of the toughra while the second coinage has *el Ghazi* (The Victorious). The first coinage of Mohammad Reshat V has *Reshat* right of the toughra while his second coinage has *el Ghazi*.

OTTOMAN EMPIRE

Selim III
AH1203-22/1789-1807AD
First Toughra Series
Heavy coinage based on a Piastre weighing approximately 19.20 g with first toughra.
First Toughra inscribed: *Han Sellim bin Mustafa al-Muzaffer Dai'ma*.

Second Toughra Series
Heavy coinage based on a Piastre weighing approximately 19.20 g with second toughra.
Second Toughra inscribed: *Selim Han bin Mustafa al-Muzaffer Dai'ma*.

MILLED COINAGE
Gold Issues

KM# 510 1/4 ZERI MAHBUB
Gold **Obverse:** Toughra **Reverse:** Text, date **Rev. Inscription:** "Azza Nasara" **Mint:** Islambul **Note:** Weight varies 0.5-0.6 grams. Dav. #334.

Date	Mintage	VG	F	VF	XF	Unc
AH1203//14	—	25.00	35.00	50.00	75.00	—
AH1203//15	—	25.00	35.00	50.00	75.00	—
AH1203//16	—	25.00	35.00	50.00	75.00	—
AH1203//17	—	25.00	35.00	50.00	75.00	—

Note: With "Azza Nasara."

KM# 517 1/2 ZERI MAHBUB
Gold **Mint:** Islambul **Note:** Weight varies 1.10-1.20 grams. Second toughra.

Date	Mintage	VG	F	VF	XF	Unc
AH1203//14	—	40.00	65.00	80.00	100	—
AH1203//15	—	40.00	65.00	80.00	100	—
AH1203//16	—	40.00	65.00	80.00	100	—
AH1203//17	—	40.00	65.00	80.00	100	—
AH1203//18	—	50.00	80.00	120	180	—
AH1203//19	—	100	200	300	400	—

TURKEY

KM# 523 ZERI MAHBUB
2.4000 g., Gold, 21 mm. **Obverse:** Toughra above text within circle **Reverse:** Text, value **Mint:** Islambul **Note:** Reduced size.

Date	Mintage	VG	F	VF	XF	Unc
AH1203//14	—	60.00	75.00	90.00	120	—
AH1203//15	—	60.00	75.00	90.00	120	—
AH1203//16	—	60.00	75.00	90.00	120	—
AH1203//17	—	60.00	75.00	90.00	120	—
AH1203//18	—	60.00	75.00	90.00	120	—
AH1203//19	—	60.00	75.00	90.00	120	—

KM# 514 1/4 ALTIN (Findik)
0.9000 g., Gold **Obverse:** Toughra **Reverse:** Text, value and date **Mint:** Islambul **Note:** Plain borders.

Date	Mintage	VG	F	VF	XF	Unc
AH1203//14	—	25.00	35.00	50.00	70.00	—
AH1203//15	—	25.00	35.00	50.00	70.00	—
AH1203//16	—	25.00	35.00	50.00	70.00	—
AH1203//17	—	25.00	35.00	50.00	70.00	—
AH1203//18	—	25.00	35.00	50.00	70.00	—
AH1203//19	—	30.00	50.00	75.00	125	—

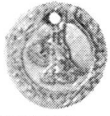

KM# 520 1/2 ALTIN
Gold **Obverse:** Toughra within circle **Reverse:** Text, value and date within circle **Mint:** Islambul **Note:** Weight varies 0.75-0.8 grams.

Date	Mintage	VG	F	VF	XF	Unc
AH1203//18	—	70.00	90.00	130	185	—

KM# 527 ALTIN
3.4500 g., Gold **Obverse:** Toughra within circle **Reverse:** Text, value and date within circle **Mint:** Islambul

Date	Mintage	VG	F	VF	XF	Unc
AH1203//17	—	75.00	95.00	135	185	—
AH1203//18	—	75.00	95.00	135	185	—
AH1203//19	—	75.00	95.00	135	185	—

Mustafa IV
AH1222-23/1807-08AD

MILLED COINAGE
Gold Issues

KM# 544 1/2 ZERI MAHBUB
1.2000 g., Gold **Obverse:** Toughra above text and date **Reverse:** Text, value **Mint:** Qustantiniyah

Date	Mintage	VG	F	VF	XF	Unc
AH1222//1	—	60.00	100	175	250	—
AH1222//2	—	60.00	100	200	300	—

KM# 545 ZERI MAHBUB
2.3500 g., Gold **Obverse:** Toughra above text and date **Reverse:** Text, value **Mint:** Qustantiniyah

Date	Mintage	VG	F	VF	XF	Unc
AH1222//1	—	90.00	200	300	400	—
AH1222//2	—	125	300	400	500	—

KM# 543 1/4 ALTIN
0.7700 g., Gold **Obverse:** Toughra within circle **Reverse:** Text, value and date within circle **Mint:** Qustantiniyah

Date	Mintage	VG	F	VF	XF	Unc
AH1222//1	—	40.00	60.00	100	150	—
AH1222//2	—	45.00	65.00	120	175	—

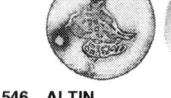

KM# 546 ALTIN
3.2000 g., Gold **Obverse:** Toughra **Reverse:** Text, value and date **Mint:** Qustantiniyah

Date	Mintage	VG	F	VF	XF	Unc
AH1222//1	—	75.00	100	125	170	—
AH1222//2	—	90.00	120	145	200	—

Mahmud II
AH1223-55/1808-39AD

Gold emissions of Mahmud II are characterized by several simultaneous series, each with its characteristic name. They are distinguished by weight and by special symbols, such as the ornament right of the toughra, the border, and variations in design. These are indicated for each series, along with the weights and diameters of each denomination. Each series comprises several denominations, with the basic unit known as the Altin (Gold Coin) or Tak (Single); other denominations include the Double (Clifte), Half (Yarim, or Nisfiye), and Quarter (Ceyrek or Rubiye). Not all denominations were struck in every series. Some series can be divided into several sub varieties, which are listed separately. Finally a few coins were struck that do not fit into any of the series.

MILLED COINAGE
Gold Zeri Mahbub Issues

Zeri Mahbub - Beloved Gold Series

The obverse of all denominations consists of a toughra, with mintname and date below on the 1 and 1/2 Zeri Mahbub only. The reverse of the 1 and 1/2 bears a four-line inscription; the reverse of the 1/4, the mint and date.

FIRST TYPE:

Lily on 1 and 1/2 Zeri Mahbub, branch with one rose on the 1/4 Zeri Mahbub.

SECOND TYPE:

Rose replaces lily on 1 and 1/2 Zeri Mahbub, branch with 2 roses replaces branch with one rose on the 1/4 Zeri Mahbub.

KM# 605 1/4 ZERI MAHBUB
Gold **Obverse:** Toughra **Reverse:** Text, value and date **Mint:** Qustantiniyah **Note:** First type; Weight varies: 0.70-0.80 grams.

Date	Mintage	VG	F	VF	XF	Unc
AH1223//1	—	16.50	20.00	30.00	40.00	—
AH1223//2	—	16.50	20.00	30.00	40.00	—
AH1223//3	—	16.50	25.00	40.00	60.00	—
AH1223//4	—	16.50	20.00	30.00	40.00	—
AH1223//5	—	16.50	20.00	30.00	40.00	—

KM# 608 1/4 ZERI MAHBUB
Gold **Obverse:** Toughra **Reverse:** Text, value and date **Mint:** Qustantiniyah **Note:** Second type; Weight varies: 0.75-0.79 grams.

Date	Mintage	VG	F	VF	XF	Unc
AH1223//6	—	16.50	20.00	30.00	45.00	—
AH1223//7	—	16.50	20.00	30.00	45.00	—
AH1223//8	—	16.50	20.00	30.00	45.00	—
AH1223//9	—	16.50	20.00	30.00	45.00	—
AH1223//10	—	16.50	20.00	30.00	45.00	—
AH1223//11	—	16.50	20.00	35.00	50.00	—
AH1223//12	—	16.50	20.00	35.00	50.00	—
AH1223//13	—	16.50	20.00	35.00	50.00	—
AH1223//14	—	16.50	20.00	35.00	50.00	—

KM# 606 1/2 ZERI MAHBUB
Gold **Obverse:** Toughra above text and date **Reverse:** Text, value **Mint:** Qustantiniyah **Note:** First type; Weight varies: 1.10-1.20 grams.

Date	Mintage	VG	F	VF	XF	Unc
AH1223//1	—	35.00	50.00	70.00	90.00	—
AH1223//2	—	35.00	50.00	70.00	90.00	—
AH1223//3	—	35.00	50.00	70.00	90.00	—
AH1223//4	—	35.00	50.00	70.00	90.00	—
AH1223//5	—	35.00	50.00	70.00	90.00	—

KM# 609 1/2 ZERI MAHBUB
Gold, 18 mm. **Mint:** Qustantiniyah **Note:** Second type; Weight varies: 1.10-1.20 grams.

Date	Mintage	VG	F	VF	XF	Unc
AH1223//8	—	40.00	60.00	100	140	—
AH1223//12	—	40.00	60.00	100	140	—

KM# 607 ZERI MAHBUB
Gold **Obverse:** Toughra above text and date **Reverse:** Text, value **Mint:** Qustantiniyah **Note:** First type; Weight varies: 2.30-2.40 grams.

Date	Mintage	VG	F	VF	XF	Unc
AH1223//1	—	60.00	80.00	125	180	—
AH1223//2	—	60.00	80.00	125	180	—
AH1223//5	—	150	275	400	750	—

KM# 610 ZERI MAHBUB
Gold **Obverse:** Toughra above text and date **Reverse:** Text, value **Mint:** Qustantiniyah **Note:** Second type; Weight varies: 2.30-2.40 grams.

Date	Mintage	VG	F	VF	XF	Unc
AH1223//6	—	50.00	75.00	85.00	125	—
AH1223//7	—	50.00	75.00	85.00	125	—
AH1223//8	—	50.00	75.00	85.00	125	—
AH1223//9	—	50.00	75.00	85.00	125	—
AH1223//10	—	50.00	75.00	85.00	125	—
AH1223//11	—	50.00	75.00	85.00	125	—
AH1223//12	—	50.00	75.00	85.00	125	—
AH1223//14	—	50.00	75.00	85.00	125	—
AH1223//15	—	50.00	75.00	85.00	125	—

MILLED COINAGE
Gold Rumi Issue

Characterized by a flower right of toughra and an ornamental border, consisting of a wavy line hexagon, on both sides.

KM# 612 1/2 RUMI ALTIN
1.2000 g., Gold **Obverse:** Toughra within beaded circle of ornate border **Reverse:** Text, value and date within beaded circle of ornate border **Mint:** Qustantiniyah

Date	Mintage	VG	F	VF	XF	Unc
AH1223//10	—	75.00	100	125	175	—
AH1223//11	—	75.00	100	125	175	—
AH1223//12	—	75.00	100	125	175	—
AH1223//13	—	75.00	100	125	175	—

KM# 613 RUMI ALTIN
2.4000 g., Gold **Mint:** Qustantiniyah

Date	Mintage	VG	F	VF	XF	Unc
AH1223//10	—	200	250	300	350	—

TURKEY

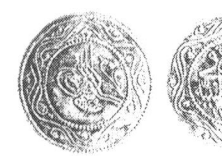

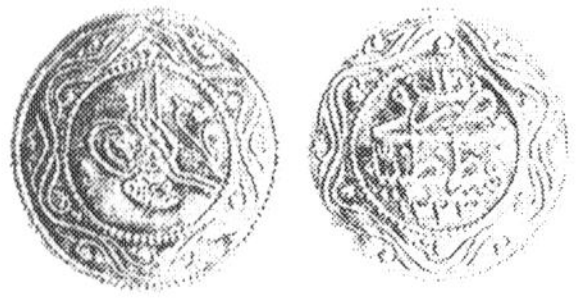

KM# 614 2 RUMI ALTIN
Gold **Obverse:** Toughra within beaded circle of ornate border **Reverse:** Text, value and date within beaded circle of ornate border **Mint:** Qustantiniyah **Note:** Weight varies: 4.70-4.80 grams.

Date	Mintage	VG	F	VF	XF	Unc
AH1223//8	—	100	120	140	200	—
AH1223//9	—	100	120	140	200	—
AH1223//10	—	100	120	140	200	—
AH1223//11	—	100	120	140	200	—
AH1223//12	—	100	120	140	200	—
AH1223//13	—	100	120	140	200	—
AH1223//14	—	100	130	160	225	—

MILLED COINAGE
New Gold Rumi Issues

Similar to the Rumi series, except the wavy borders are replaced by an inscription containing the name and titles of Mahmud II

KM# 616 RUMI ALTIN
2.4000 g., Gold, 23 mm. **Obverse:** Toughra within beaded circle **Reverse:** Text, value and date within beaded circle **Mint:** Qustantiniyah

Date	Mintage	VG	F	VF	XF	Unc
AH1223//9	—	—	—	—	—	—
Note: Reported, not confirmed
AH1223//10	—	50.00	60.00	90.00	125	—
AH1223//11	—	50.00	60.00	90.00	125	—
AH1223//12	—	50.00	60.00	90.00	125	—
AH1223//13	—	50.00	60.00	90.00	125	—
AH1223//14	—	50.00	60.00	90.00	125	—
AH1223//15	—	50.00	60.00	90.00	125	—

KM# 617 2 RUMI ALTIN
Gold **Obverse:** Toughra within beaded circle **Reverse:** Text, value and date within beaded circle **Mint:** Qustantiniyah **Note:** Weight varies: 4.70-4.80 grams.

Date	Mintage	VG	F	VF	XF	Unc
AH1223//9	—	110	130	160	200	—
AH1223//10	—	110	130	160	200	—
AH1223//11	—	110	130	160	200	—
AH1223//12	—	110	130	160	200	—

MILLED COINAGE
Gold El-Aliye Surre Issues

Surre refers to a purse, the amount sent by the sultan annually to the Hejaz for the holy cities. Pilgrims to Mecca used them. They bear the mint name Darulhilafe in place of Constantinople, with either of 2 epithets, El-Aliye (the Lofty) or Es-Seniye (the Sublime), and are therefore known as Elaliye and Esseniye Altins, respectively.

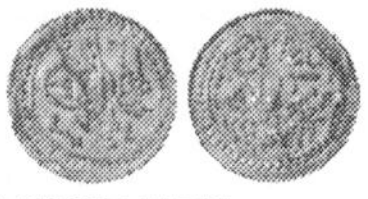

KM# 619 1/4 SURRE ALTIN
0.4800 g., Gold **Obverse:** Toughra, flowers within circle **Reverse:** Value, text and date within circle **Mint:** Darulhilafe

Date	Mintage	VG	F	VF	XF	Unc
AH1223//15 (1822)	—	30.00	50.00	100	150	—
AH1223//16 (1823)	—	30.00	50.00	100	150	—

KM# 620 1/2 SURRE ALTIN
0.7800 g., Gold, 15-16 mm. **Obverse:** Toughra, flowers within circle **Reverse:** Text, value and date within circle **Mint:** Darulhilafe

Date	Mintage	VG	F	VF	XF	Unc
AH1223//15	—	40.00	60.00	150	250	—
AH1223//16	—	40.00	60.00	150	250	—

KM# 621 SURRE ALTIN
1.5600 g., Gold **Obverse:** Toughra, flowers within circle **Reverse:** Text, value and date within circle **Mint:** Darulhilafe

Date	Mintage	VG	F	VF	XF	Unc
AH1223//15	—	60.00	85.00	110	150	—
AH1223//16	—	60.00	85.00	110	150	—

MILLED COINAGE
Gold Esseniye Surre Issues

KM# 623 1/4 SURRE ALTIN
0.4800 g., Gold **Obverse:** Toughra, flowers within circle **Reverse:** Text, value and date within circle **Mint:** Darulhilafe

Date	Mintage	VG	F	VF	XF	Unc
AH1223//15	—	30.00	45.00	100	150	—

KM# 624 1/4 SURRE ALTIN
0.7800 g., Gold **Obverse:** Toughra, flowers within circle **Reverse:** Text, value and date within circle **Mint:** Darulhilafe

Date	Mintage	VG	F	VF	XF	Unc
AH1223//15	—	50.00	75.00	200	300	—

KM# 625 SURRE ALTIN
1.5000 g., Gold **Obverse:** Toughra, flowers within beaded circle **Reverse:** Text, value and date within beaded circle **Mint:** Darulhilafe

Date	Mintage	VG	F	VF	XF	Unc
AH1223//15	—	60.00	90.00	150	225	—

MILLED COINAGE
Unnamed Gold Issues

The following type does not fit into any of the recognized series

KM# 627 1/4 ALTIN
0.5800 g., Gold **Obverse:** Toughra **Reverse:** Text, value and date **Mint:** Qustantiniyah **Note:** Considered a 1/4 Zeri Mahbub. "Azze Nasaru" above mint name.

Date	Mintage	VG	F	VF	XF	Unc
AH1223//13	—	16.00	20.00	40.00	60.00	—
AH1223//14	—	16.00	20.00	40.00	60.00	—
AH1223//15	—	16.00	20.00	40.00	60.00	—

MILLED COINAGE
Gold Adli Issues

These types are similar to the Zeri Mahbub series, except the word Adli replaces the flower right of the toughra.

KM# 629 1/4 ADLI ALTIN
Gold **Obverse:** Toughra above text and date **Reverse:** Text, value **Mint:** Qustantiniyah **Note:** Weight varies: 0.40-0.45 grams.

Date	Mintage	VG	F	VF	XF	Unc
AH1223//16	—	20.00	30.00	75.00	125	—
AH1223//17	—	20.00	30.00	75.00	125	—

KM# 630 1/2 ADLI ALTIN
Gold **Obverse:** Toughra above text and date **Reverse:** Text, value **Mint:** Qustantiniyah **Note:** Weight varies: 0.75-0.85 grams.

Date	Mintage	VG	F	VF	XF	Unc
AH1223//15	—	45.00	60.00	75.00	90.00	—
AH1223//16						
Note: Reported, not confirmed
AH1223//17	—	45.00	60.00	75.00	90.00	—
AH1223//18	—	45.00	60.00	75.00	90.00	—
AH1223//19	—	45.00	60.00	75.00	90.00	—
AH1223//20	—	45.00	60.00	75.00	90.00	—
AH1223//21	—	45.00	60.00	75.00	90.00	—
AH1223//22	—	45.00	60.00	75.00	90.00	—
AH1223//23	—	45.00	60.00	75.00	90.00	—
AH1223//24						
Note: Reported, not confirmed
AH1223//25	—	45.00	60.00	75.00	90.00	—
AH1223//26						
Note: Reported, not confirmed
AH1223//27	—	45.00	60.00	75.00	90.00	—
AH1223//28						
Note: Reported, not confirmed
AH1223//29	—	45.00	60.00	75.00	90.00	—
AH1223//30	—	45.00	60.00	75.00	90.00	—
AH1223//31	—	45.00	60.00	75.00	90.00	—
AH1223//32	—	45.00	60.00	75.00	90.00	—

KM# 631 ADLI ALTIN
Gold **Obverse:** Toughra above text and date **Reverse:** Text, value **Mint:** Qustantiniyah **Note:** Weight varies: 1.50-1.60 grams.

Date	Mintage	VG	F	VF	XF	Unc
AH1223//15	—	35.00	45.00	90.00	135	—
AH1223//17	—	35.00	45.00	90.00	135	—
AH1223//18	—	35.00	45.00	90.00	135	—
AH1223//19	—	35.00	45.00	90.00	135	—
AH1223//20	—	35.00	45.00	90.00	135	—

MILLED COINAGE
New Gold Adli Issues

The toughra appears on the obverse, with the mint name and date on the reverse, additional legends around and the mint name Qustantinyah has epithet Al-Mahrusa added.

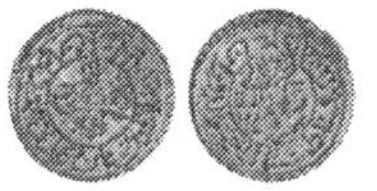

KM# 633 1/4 NEW ADLI ALTIN
Gold **Obverse:** Toughra within circle **Reverse:** Text, value and date within circle **Mint:** Qustantiniyah **Note:** Weight varies: 0.38-0.43 grams.

Date	Mintage	VG	F	VF	XF	Unc
AH1223//15	—	12.00	20.00	30.00	45.00	—
AH1223//17	—	12.00	20.00	30.00	45.00	—
AH1223//18	—	12.00	20.00	30.00	45.00	—
AH1223//19	—	12.00	20.00	30.00	45.00	—
AH1223//20	—	12.00	20.00	30.00	45.00	—
AH1223//21	—	12.00	20.00	30.00	45.00	—
AH1223//22	—	12.00	20.00	30.00	45.00	—
AH1223//23	—	12.00	20.00	30.00	45.00	—
AH1223//24	—	12.00	20.00	40.00	55.00	—

KM# 634 1/2 NEW ADLI ALTIN
0.7800 g., Gold **Obverse:** Toughra within circle **Reverse:** Text, value and date within circle **Mint:** Qustantiniyah

TURKEY 691

Date	Mintage	VG	F	VF	XF	Unc
AH1223//16	—	30.00	40.00	50.00	75.00	—
AH1223//17	—	30.00	40.00	50.00	75.00	—
AH1223//18	—	30.00	40.00	50.00	75.00	—
AH1223//19	—	30.00	40.00	50.00	75.00	—
AH1223//20	—	30.00	40.00	50.00	75.00	—
AH1223//21	—	—	—	—	—	—

Note: Reported, not confirmed

KM# 635 NEW ADLI ALTIN
1.5800 g., Gold Obverse: Toughra within circle Reverse: Text, value and date within circle Mint: Qustantiniyah

Date	Mintage	VG	F	VF	XF	Unc
AH1223//16	—	35.00	40.00	65.00	90.00	—
AH1223//17	—	35.00	40.00	65.00	90.00	—
AH1223//18	—	35.00	40.00	65.00	90.00	—
AH1223//19	—	35.00	40.00	65.00	90.00	—
AH1223//20	—	35.00	40.00	65.00	90.00	—
AH1223//21	—	—	—	—	—	—

Note: Reported, not confirmed

| AH1223//22 | — | — | — | — | — | — |

Note: Reported, not confirmed

MILLED COINAGE
Gold Hayriye Issues

This type is similar to the New Adli series, but in place of the legend around the edge, there are alternating ovals of inscription and branches

KM# 637 1/2 HAYRIYE ALTIN
0.8600 g., Gold Obverse: Toughra within center circle of flowers and ovals Reverse: Value and date within center circle of flowers and ovals Mint: Qustantiniyah

Date	Mintage	VG	F	VF	XF	Unc
AH1223//21	—	25.00	35.00	45.00	65.00	—
AH1223//22	—	25.00	35.00	45.00	65.00	—
AH1223//23	—	25.00	35.00	45.00	65.00	—
AH1223//24	—	25.00	35.00	45.00	65.00	—
AH1223//25	—	25.00	35.00	45.00	65.00	—
AH1223//26	—	25.00	35.00	45.00	65.00	—

KM# 638 HAYRIYE ALTIN
1.7300 g., Gold Obverse: Toughra within center circle of flowers and ovals Reverse: value and date within center circle of flowers and ovals Mint: Qustantiniyah

Date	Mintage	VG	F	VF	XF	Unc
AH1223//21	—	35.00	40.00	50.00	90.00	—
AH1223//22	—	35.00	40.00	50.00	90.00	—
AH1223//23	—	35.00	40.00	50.00	90.00	—
AH1223//24	—	35.00	40.00	50.00	90.00	—
AH1223//25	—	35.00	40.00	50.00	90.00	—
AH1223//26	—	—	—	—	—	—

Note: Reported, not confirmed

KM# 639 2 HAYRIYE ALTIN
3.5500 g., Gold Obverse: Toughra within center circle of flowers and ovals Reverse: Value and date within center circle of flowers and ovals Mint: Qustantiniyah

Date	Mintage	VG	F	VF	XF	Unc
AH1223//21	—	100	125	150	200	—

MILLED COINAGE
New Gold Yeni Issues

The New Yeni series is found in one denomination, distinguished by a star-like wavy pattern around the edge

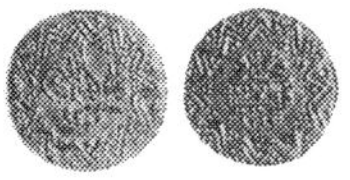

KM# 641 1/4 NEW ALTIN (Yeni Rubiye)
Gold, 12 mm. Obverse: Toughra within center of star design Reverse: Value and date within center of star design Mint: Qustantiniyah Note: Weight varies: 0.26-0.31 grams.

Date	Mintage	VG	F	VF	XF	Unc
AH1223//24	—	15.00	25.00	40.00	55.00	—
AH1223//25	—	15.00	25.00	40.00	55.00	—
AH1223//26	—	15.00	25.00	40.00	55.00	—
AH1223//27	—	15.00	25.00	40.00	55.00	—
AH1223//28	—	15.00	25.00	40.00	55.00	—
AH1223//29	—	—	—	—	—	—

Note: Reported, not confirmed

| AH1223//30 | — | 17.50 | 22.50 | 25.00 | 30.00 | — |

MILLED COINAGE
Gold Cedid Mahmudiye Issues

This type is similar to the Hayriye, but with ovals of inscriptions and branches replaced by a wreath design

KM# 643 1/4 CEDID MAHMUDIYE
Gold Obverse: Toughra within designed wreath Reverse: Value, text and date within designed wreath Mint: Qustantiniyah Note: Weight varies: 0.38-0.40 grams.

Date	Mintage	VG	F	VF	XF	Unc
AH1223//26	—	15.00	25.00	35.00	45.00	—
AH1223//27	—	15.00	25.00	35.00	45.00	—
AH1223//28	—	15.00	25.00	35.00	45.00	—
AH1223//29	—	15.00	25.00	35.00	45.00	—
AH1223//30	—	15.00	25.00	35.00	45.00	—
AH1223//31	—	15.00	25.00	35.00	45.00	—
AH1223//32	—	15.00	25.00	35.00	45.00	—

KM# 644 1/2 CEDID MAHMUDIYE
Gold Obverse: Toughra, flowers within designed wreath Reverse: Value, text and date within designed wreath Mint: Qustantiniyah Note: Weight varies: 0.70-0.80 grams.

Date	Mintage	VG	F	VF	XF	Unc
AH1223//26	—	22.00	35.00	50.00	70.00	—
AH1223//27	—	22.00	35.00	50.00	70.00	—
AH1223//28	—	22.00	35.00	50.00	70.00	—
AH1223//29	—	22.00	35.00	50.00	70.00	—
AH1223//30	—	22.00	35.00	50.00	70.00	—
AH1223//31	—	22.00	35.00	50.00	70.00	—
AH1223//32	—	22.00	35.00	50.00	70.00	—

KM# 645 CEDID MAHMUDIYE
Gold Obverse: Toughra, flowers within designed wreath Reverse: Text, value, date and flowers within designed wreath Mint: Qustantiniyah Note: Weight varies: 1.58-1.60 grams.

Date	Mintage	VG	F	VF	XF	Unc
AH1223//26	—	35.00	45.00	60.00	80.00	—
AH1223//27	—	35.00	45.00	60.00	80.00	—
AH1223//28	—	35.00	45.00	60.00	80.00	—
AH1223//29	—	35.00	45.00	60.00	80.00	—
AH1223//30	—	35.00	45.00	60.00	80.00	—
AH1223//31	—	35.00	45.00	60.00	80.00	—
AH1223//32	—	35.00	45.00	60.00	80.00	—

MILLED COINAGE
Gold Mint Visit Issues

The gold coins continued to be struck to the weights and finenesses of the old Ottoman system, but were tariffed at the going price of gold. The same continues to hold true today. Both regular and the Monnaie de Luxe series were produced.

KM# 647 1/2 HAYRIYE ALTIN
0.8800 g., Gold Obverse: Toughra within center circle of stars and ovals Reverse: Text, value and date within center circle of stars and ovals Mint: Edirne

Date	Mintage	VG	F	VF	XF	Unc
AH1223//24	—	60.00	100	150	250	—

KM# 648 HAYRIYE ALTIN
1.8000 g., Gold Obverse: Toughra within center circle of stars and ovals Reverse: Text, value and date within center circle of stars and ovals Mint: Edirne

Date	Mintage	VG	F	VF	XF	Unc
AH1223//24	—	100	120	150	200	—

KM# 649 2 HAYRIYE ALTIN
3.5500 g., Gold Obverse: Toughra within center circle of stars and ovals Reverse: Text, value and date within center circle of stars and ovals Mint: Edirne

Date	Mintage	VG	F	VF	XF	Unc
AH1223//24	—	175	225	275	350	—

Abdul Mejid
AH1255-77/1839-61AD

MILLED COINAGE
Gold Issues

KM# 677 25 KURUSH
1.8040 g., 0.9170 Gold .0532 oz. AGW Obverse: Toughra within sprays, stars above Reverse: Text, value and date within wreath, star above Mint: Qustantiniyah

Date	Mintage	VG	F	VF	XF	Unc
AH1255//17	—	BV	40.00	70.00	150	—
AH1255//18	—	BV	40.00	70.00	150	—
AH1255//19	—	BV	40.00	70.00	150	—
AH1255//20	—	BV	40.00	70.00	150	—
AH1255//21	—	BV	40.00	70.00	150	—
AH1255//22	—	BV	40.00	70.00	150	—
AH1255//23	—	BV	40.00	70.00	150	—

KM# 678 50 KURUSH
3.6080 g., 0.9170 Gold .1064 oz. AGW Obverse: Toughra within sprays, stars above Reverse: Text, value and date within wreath, star above Mint: Qustantiniyah

Date	Mintage	VG	F	VF	XF	Unc
AH1255//6	—	BV	70.00	90.00	150	—
AH1255//7	—	BV	70.00	90.00	150	—
AH1255//8	—	BV	70.00	90.00	150	—
AH1255//9	—	BV	70.00	90.00	150	—
AH1255//10	—	BV	70.00	90.00	150	—
AH1255//11	—	BV	70.00	90.00	150	—
AH1255//12	—	BV	70.00	90.00	150	—
AH1255//13	—	BV	70.00	90.00	150	—
AH1255//15	—	BV	70.00	90.00	150	—
AH1255//16	—	BV	70.00	90.00	150	—
AH1255//17	—	BV	70.00	90.00	150	—
AH1255//20	—	1,750	2,500	3,500	5,000	—
AH1255//22	—	1,750	2,500	3,500	5,000	—

692 TURKEY

KM# 679 100 KURUSH
7.2160 g., 0.9170 Gold .2128 oz. AGW **Obverse:** Toughra within sprays, stars above **Reverse:** Text, value and date within wreath, star above **Mint:** Qustantiniyah

Date	Mintage	VG	F	VF	XF	Unc
AH1255//5	—	—	—	BV	150	—
AH1255//6	—	—	—	BV	150	—
AH1255//7	—	—	—	BV	150	—
AH1255//8	—	—	—	BV	150	—
AH1255//9	—	—	—	BV	150	—
AH1255//10	—	—	—	BV	150	—
AH1255//11	—	—	—	BV	150	—
AH1255//12	—	—	—	BV	150	—
AH1255//13	—	—	—	BV	150	—
AH1255//14	—	—	—	BV	150	—
AH1255//15	—	—	—	BV	150	—
AH1255//16	—	—	—	BV	150	—
AH1255//17	—	—	—	BV	150	—
AH1255//18	—	—	—	BV	150	—
AH1255//19	—	—	—	BV	150	—
AH1255//20	—	—	—	BV	150	—
AH1255//21	—	—	—	BV	150	—
AH1255//22	—	—	—	BV	150	—
AH1255//23	—	—	—	BV	150	—

KM# 680 250 KURUSH
18.0400 g., 0.9170 Gold .5319 oz. AGW **Obverse:** Toughra within sprays, stars above **Reverse:** Text, value and date within wreath, star above **Mint:** Qustantiniyah **Note:** This is the first Ottoman coin to bear a numeral denomination, the 250 is the 6 o'clock on the obverse

Date	Mintage	VG	F	VF	XF	Unc
AH1255//7	—	BV	350	600	900	—
AH1255//18	—	BV	350	600	900	—
AH1255//22	—	2,000	3,000	4,000	6,000	—

Note: This is the first Ottoman coin to bear a numeral denomination, the 250 is at 6 o'clock on the obverse

KM# 681 500 KURUSH
36.0800 g., 0.9170 Gold 1.0638 oz. AGW **Mint:** Qustantiniyah

Date	Mintage	VG	F	VF	XF	Unc
AH1255//18	9,140	BV	700	900	1,200	—
AH1255//20	—	2,000	3,000	4,000	6,000	—
AH1255//22	—	2,000	3,000	4,000	6,000	—

MILLED COINAGE
Gold Mint Visit Issues

The gold coins continued to be struck to the weights and finenesses of the old Ottoman system, but were tariffed at the going price of gold. The same continues to hold true today. Both regular and the Monnaie de Luxe series were produced.

KM# 682 50 KURUSH
3.6080 g., 0.9170 Gold .1064 oz. AGW **Subject:** Mint Visit Coinage **Obverse:** Toughra within sprays, stars above **Reverse:** Text, value and date within wreath, star above **Mint:** Edirne

Date	Mintage	VG	F	VF	XF	Unc
AH1255//8	10,000	—	250	450	650	1,150

KM# 683 100 KURUSH
7.2160 g., 0.9170 Gold .2128 oz. AGW **Subject:** Mint Visit Coinage **Obverse:** Toughra within sprays, stars above **Reverse:** Text, value and date within wreath, star above **Mint:** Edirne

Date	Mintage	VG	F	VF	XF	Unc
Z1255//8	10,000	—	300	525	700	1,400

MILLED COINAGE
Pre-Reform

These issues are of standard, fineness and denominations of silver coinage similar to the ninth (1, 10 and 20 Para) and the tenth (1 1/2, 3 and 6 Kurush) series of Mahmud II (KM#594-596, 601-603)

KM# 660 1/2 ZERI MAHBUB
0.8000 g., Gold **Obverse:** Toughra above text and date **Reverse:** Text, value **Mint:** Qustantiniyah

Date	Mintage	VG	F	VF	XF	Unc
AH1255//1	—	45.00	60.00	95.00	130	—
AH1255//2	—	45.00	60.00	95.00	130	—
AH1255//3	—	45.00	60.00	95.00	130	—
AH1255//4	—	45.00	60.00	95.00	130	—
AH1255//5	—	45.00	60.00	95.00	130	—
AH1255//6	—	75.00	100	120	200	—

KM# 657 1/4 MEMDUHIYE ALTIN
Gold **Obverse:** Toughra, flower sprig **Reverse:** Text, value and date **Mint:** Qustantiniyah **Note:** Weight varies: 0.38-0.40 grams.

Date	Mintage	VG	F	VF	XF	Unc
AH1255//1	—	17.50	25.00	45.00	75.00	—
AH1255//2	—	17.50	25.00	45.00	75.00	—
AH1255//3	—	17.50	25.00	45.00	75.00	—
AH1255//4	—	17.50	25.00	45.00	75.00	—
AH1255//5	—	17.50	25.00	45.00	75.00	—

KM# 658 1/2 MEMDUHIYE ALTIN
Gold **Obverse:** Toughra, flower sprig **Reverse:** Text, value and date **Mint:** Qustantiniyah **Note:** Weight varies: 0.78-0.80 grams.

Date	Mintage	VG	F	VF	XF	Unc
AH1255//1	—	40.00	50.00	80.00	100	—
AH1255//2	—	40.00	50.00	80.00	100	—
AH1255//3	—	40.00	50.00	80.00	100	—
AH1255//4	—	40.00	50.00	80.00	100	—
AH1255//5	—	40.00	50.00	80.00	100	—

KM# 659 MEMDUHIYE ALTIN
Gold **Obverse:** Toughra, flower sprig **Reverse:** Text, value and date **Mint:** Qustantiniyah **Note:** Weight varies: 1.58-1.60 grams.

Date	Mintage	VG	F	VF	XF	Unc
AH1255//1	—	45.00	55.00	95.00	180	—
AH1255//2	—	45.00	55.00	95.00	180	—
AH1255//3	—	45.00	55.00	95.00	180	—
AH1255//4	—	45.00	55.00	95.00	180	—
AH1255//5	—	45.00	55.00	95.00	180	—

Note: The Memduhiye issue of Abdul Mejid was of the same fineness, weight and diameter as the Mahmudiye issue of Mahmud II; Although officially valued at 20 Piastres, the actual value of the Memduhiye Altin varied with the relative prices of gold and silver

Abdul Aziz
AH1277-93/1861-76AD

MILLED COINAGE
Gold Issues

KM# 694 25 KURUSH
1.8040 g., 0.9170 Gold .0532 oz. AGW **Obverse:** Toughra within sprays and stars **Reverse:** Text, value and date within wreath, star above **Mint:** Qustantiniyah

Date	Mintage	VG	F	VF	XF	Unc
AH1277//1	52,000	BV	40.00	60.00	80.00	—
AH1277//2	86,000	BV	40.00	60.00	80.00	—
AH1277//3	89,000	BV	40.00	60.00	80.00	—
AH1277//4	69,000	BV	40.00	60.00	80.00	—
AH1277//5	67,000	BV	40.00	60.00	80.00	—
AH1277//6	73,000	BV	40.00	60.00	80.00	—
AH1277//7	116,000	BV	40.00	60.00	80.00	—
AH1277//9	177,000	BV	40.00	60.00	80.00	—
AH1277//11	65,000	BV	40.00	60.00	80.00	—
AH1277//12	122,000	BV	40.00	60.00	80.00	—
AH1277//13	152,000	BV	40.00	60.00	80.00	—
AH1277//15	17,000	BV	60.00	80.00	120	—

KM# 695 50 KURUSH
3.6080 g., 0.9170 Gold .1064 oz. AGW **Obverse:** Toughra within sprays and stars **Reverse:** Text, date and value within wreath, star above **Mint:** Qustantiniyah

Date	Mintage	VG	F	VF	XF	Unc
AH1277//1	5,800	75.00	150	250	400	—
AH1277//2	—	75.00	150	250	400	—
AH1277//3	—	1,750	2,500	3,500	5,000	—
AH1277//7	2,000	70.00	100	180	300	—
AH1277//8	2,000					

Note: Reported, not confirmed

| AH1277//9 | 25,000 | 70.00 | 100 | 180 | 300 | — |

KM# 696 100 KURUSH
7.2160 g., 0.9170 Gold .2128 oz. AGW **Obverse:** Toughra within sprays and stars **Reverse:** Text, value and date within wreath, star above **Mint:** Qustantiniyah

Date	Mintage	VG	F	VF	XF	Unc
AH1277//1	2,347,000	—	—	BV	145	—
AH1277//2	3,129,000	—	—	BV	145	—
AH1277//3	478,000	—	—	BV	145	—
AH1277//4	628,000	—	—	BV	145	—
AH1277//5	561,000	—	—	BV	145	—
AH1277//6	330,000	—	—	BV	145	—
AH1277//7	1,491,000	—	—	BV	145	—
AH1277//8	495,000	—	—	BV	145	—
AH1277//9	1,570,000	—	—	BV	145	—
AH1277//10	304,000	—	—	BV	145	—
AH1277//11	866,000	—	—	BV	145	—
AH1277//12	372,000	—	—	BV	145	—
AH1277//13	246,000	—	—	BV	145	—
AH1277//14	286,000	—	—	BV	145	—
AH1277//15	3,600	140	160	200	300	—

KM# 697 250 KURUSH
18.0400 g., 0.9170 Gold .5319 oz. AGW **Obverse:** Toughra within sprays and stars **Reverse:** Text, value and date within wreath, star above **Mint:** Qustantiniyah

Date	Mintage	VG	F	VF	XF	Unc
AH1277//1	3,880	375	450	800	1,250	—
AH1277//3	—	375	525	900	1,550	—
AH1277//7	2,800	345	425	600	1,000	—
AH1277//8	30,000	345	375	475	700	—
AH1277//9	8,000	345	375	500	750	—

KM# 698 500 KURUSH
36.0800 g., 0.9170 Gold 1.0638 oz. AGW **Obverse:** Toughra within sprays and stars **Reverse:** Text, value and date within wreath, star above **Mint:** Qustantiniyah

Date	Mintage	VG	F	VF	XF	Unc
AH1277//1	3,180	BV	700	1,000	1,400	—
AH1277//3	1,580	700	850	1,250	1,750	—
AH1277//5	—	800	1,000	1,750	2,500	—
AH1277//7	21,000	BV	700	850	1,100	—
AH1277//8	71,000	BV	700	850	1,100	—
AH1277//9	74,000	BV	700	850	1,100	—
AH1277//10	30,000	BV	700	850	1,100	—
AH1277//11	36,000	BV	700	850	1,100	—
AH1277//13	59,000	BV	700	850	1,100	—

TURKEY 693

MILLED COINAGE
Gold Mint Visit Issues

The gold coins continued to be struck to the weights and finenesses of the old Ottoman system, but were tariffed at the going price of gold. The same continues to hold true today. Both regular and the Monnaie de Luxe series were produced.

KM# 706 25 KURUSH
1.8040 g., 0.9170 Gold .0532 oz. AGW **Subject:** Mint Visit Coinage **Obverse:** Toughra within sprays and stars **Reverse:** Text, value and date within wreath, star above **Mint:** Bursa

Date	Mintage	VG	F	VF	XF	Unc
AH1277//1	4,800	—	150	300	450	650

KM# 707 50 KURUSH
3.6080 g., 0.9170 Gold .1064 oz. AGW **Subject:** Mint Visit Coinage **Obverse:** Toughra within sprays and stars **Reverse:** Text, value and date within wreath, star above **Mint:** Bursa

Date	Mintage	VG	F	VF	XF	Unc
AH1277//1	2,476	—	200	400	650	1,000

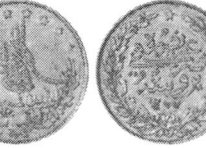

KM# 708 100 KURUSH
7.2160 g., 0.9170 Gold .2128 oz. AGW **Subject:** Mint Visit Coinage **Obverse:** Toughra within sprays and stars **Reverse:** Text, value and date within wreath, star above **Mint:** Bursa

Date	Mintage	VG	F	VF	XF	Unc
AH1277//1	9,737	—	400	650	1,000	1,600

Murad V
AH1293/1876AD

MILLED COINAGE
Gold Issues

KM# 713 25 KURUSH
1.8040 g., 0.9170 Gold .0532 oz. AGW **Obverse:** Toughra within sprays and stars **Reverse:** Text, value and date within wreath, star above **Mint:** Qustantiniyah

Date	Mintage	VG	F	VF	XF	Unc
AH1293//1	14,000	100	200	350	500	—

KM# 714 50 KURUSH
3.6080 g., 0.9170 Gold .1064 oz. AGW **Obverse:** Toughra within sprays and stars **Reverse:** Text, value and date within wreath, star above **Mint:** Qustantiniyah

Date	Mintage	VG	F	VF	XF	Unc
AH1293//1	4,500	300	500	750	1,250	—

KM# 715 100 KURUSH
7.2160 g., 0.9170 Gold .2128 oz. AGW **Obverse:** Toughra within sprays and stars **Reverse:** Text, value and date within wreath, star above **Mint:** Qustantiniyah

Date	Mintage	VG	F	VF	XF	Unc
AH1293//1	7,700	—	BV	200	300	—

SULTANATE

Abdul Hamid II
AH1293-1327/1876-1909AD

MILLED COINAGE
Gold Issues

KM# 745 12-1/2 KURUSH
0.8770 g., 0.9170 Gold .0258 oz. AGW **Series:** Monnaie de Luxe **Obverse:** Toughra **Mint:** Qustantiniyah

Date	Mintage	VG	F	VF	XF	Unc
AH1293//25	720	40.00	90.00	200	350	—
AH1293//26	720	—	—	—	—	—
AH1293//27	720	—	—	—	—	—
AH1293//28	800	40.00	120	200	300	—
AH1293//29	11,696	30.00	70.00	150	220	—
AH1293//30	13,208	30.00	70.00	150	220	—
AH1293//31	24,504	30.00	70.00	150	220	—
AH1293//32	14,392	30.00	70.00	150	220	—
AH1293//33	13,032	30.00	70.00	150	220	—
AH1293//34	—	40.00	120	200	300	—

KM# 723 25 KURUSH
1.8040 g., 0.9170 Gold .0532 oz. AGW **Obverse:** Toughra within sprays and stars **Reverse:** Text, value and date within wreath, star above **Mint:** Qustantiniyah

Date	Mintage	VG	F	VF	XF	Unc
AH1293//1 Rare	—	—	—	—	—	—
AH1293//2 Rare	3,600	—	—	—	—	—
AH1293//3	5,400	50.00	100	150	200	—
AH1293//4	3,600	50.00	100	150	200	—
AH1293//5	—	50.00	100	125	175	—
AH1293//6	9,340	50.00	100	125	175	—

KM# 729 25 KURUSH
1.8040 g., 0.9170 Gold .0532 oz. AGW **Obverse:** Toughra; "el-Ghazi" to right **Reverse:** Text, value and date within wreath, star above **Mint:** Qustantiniyah

Date	Mintage	VG	F	VF	XF	Unc
AH1293//6 Rare	560	—	—	—	—	—
AH1293//7	49,000	—	BV	40.00	50.00	—
AH1293//8	4,600	—	BV	45.00	60.00	—
AH1293//9	6,000	—	BV	45.00	60.00	—
AH1293//10	6,800	—	BV	45.00	60.00	—
AH1293//11	36,000	—	BV	40.00	50.00	—
AH1293//12	36,000	—	BV	40.00	50.00	—
AH1293//13	40,000	—	BV	40.00	50.00	—
AH1293//14	52,000	—	BV	40.00	50.00	—
AH1293//15	12,000	—	BV	40.00	50.00	—
AH1293//16	2,000	—	BV	50.00	65.00	—
AH1293//17	40,000	—	BV	40.00	50.00	—
AH1293//18	14,000	—	BV	40.00	50.00	—
AH1293//19	59,000	—	BV	40.00	50.00	—
AH1293//20	43,000	—	BV	40.00	50.00	—
AH1293//21	38,000	—	BV	40.00	50.00	—
AH1293//22	36,000	—	BV	40.00	50.00	—
AH1293//23	52,000	—	BV	40.00	50.00	—
AH1293//24	43,000	—	BV	40.00	50.00	—
AH1293//25	57,000	—	BV	40.00	50.00	—
AH1293//26	47,800	—	BV	45.00	70.00	—
AH1293//27	99,500	—	BV	45.00	70.00	—
AH1293//28	77,300	—	BV	45.00	70.00	—
AH1293//29	101,548	—	BV	45.00	70.00	—
AH1293//30	156,280	—	BV	45.00	70.00	—
AH1293//31	58,404	—	BV	45.00	70.00	—
AH1293//32	112,000	—	BV	45.00	70.00	—
AH1293//33	15,535	—	BV	45.00	70.00	—
AH1293//34	115,484	—	BV	45.00	70.00	—

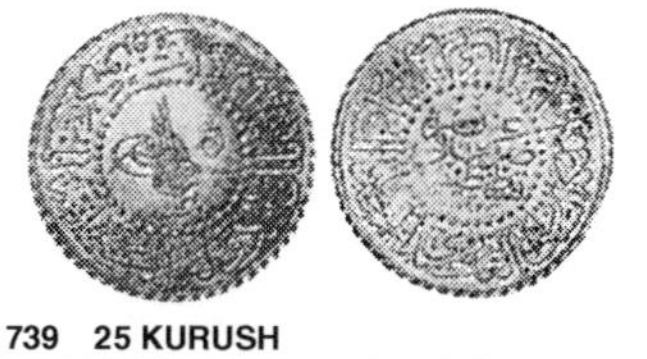

KM# 739 25 KURUSH
1.7540 g., 0.9170 Gold .0517 oz. AGW **Series:** Monnaie de Luxe **Obverse:** Toughra; "el-Ghazi" to right **Reverse:** Text, value and date in beaded circle within circular text **Mint:** Qustantiniyah

Date	Mintage	VG	F	VF	XF	Unc
AH1293//18 Rare	—	—	—	—	—	—
AH1293//23	26,000	50.00	65.00	95.00	150	—
AH1293//24	17,000	50.00	65.00	95.00	150	—
AH1293//25	—	50.00	65.00	95.00	150	—
AH1293//26	7,620	50.00	65.00	95.00	150	—
AH1293//27	7,620	50.00	70.00	120	180	—
AH1293//28	9,268	50.00	70.00	120	180	—
AH1293//29	29,056	50.00	70.00	120	180	—
AH1293//30	27,964	50.00	70.00	120	180	—
AH1293//31	39,192	50.00	70.00	120	180	—
AH1293//32	41,696	50.00	70.00	120	180	—
AH1293//33	17,728	50.00	70.00	120	180	—
AH1293//34	—	50.00	95.00	150	200	—

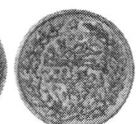

KM# 724 50 KURUSH
3.6080 g., 0.9170 Gold .1064 oz. AGW **Obverse:** Toughra within sprays and stars **Reverse:** Text, value and date within wreath, star above **Mint:** Qustantiniyah

Date	Mintage	VG	F	VF	XF	Unc
AH1293//1	5,700	80.00	100	150	300	—
AH1293//3	200	120	250	425	850	—
AH1293//6	8,200	100	200	350	750	—

KM# 731 50 KURUSH
3.6080 g., 0.9170 Gold .1064 oz. AGW **Obverse:** Toughra; "el-Ghazi" to right **Reverse:** Text, value and date within wreath, star above **Mint:** Qustantiniyah

Date	Mintage	VG	F	VF	XF	Unc
AH1293//7	6,500	—	BV	75.00	95.00	—
AH1293//8	2,000	—	BV	80.00	100	—
AH1293//9	3,000	—	BV	80.00	100	—
AH1293//10	6,000	—	BV	75.00	95.00	—
AH1293//11	14,000	—	BV	75.00	90.00	—
AH1293//12	3,600	—	BV	80.00	100	—
AH1293//13	5,000	—	BV	75.00	95.00	—
AH1293//14	8,000	—	BV	75.00	95.00	—
AH1293//15	6,000	—	BV	75.00	95.00	—
AH1293//16	2,000	—	BV	80.00	100	—
AH1293//17	13,000	—	BV	75.00	90.00	—
AH1293//18	6,000	—	BV	75.00	90.00	—
AH1293//19	11,000	—	BV	75.00	90.00	—
AH1293//20	18,000	—	BV	75.00	90.00	—
AH1293//21	12,000	—	BV	75.00	90.00	—
AH1293//22	13,000	—	BV	75.00	90.00	—
AH1293//23	18,000	—	BV	75.00	90.00	—
AH1293//24	10,000	—	BV	75.00	90.00	—
AH1293//25	15,000	—	BV	75.00	90.00	—
AH1293//26	13,956	—	BV	75.00	90.00	—
AH1293//27	14,200	—	BV	75.00	95.00	—
AH1293//28	33,450	—	BV	75.00	92.00	—
AH1293//29	24,244	—	BV	75.00	92.00	—
AH1293//30	66,000	—	BV	75.00	92.00	—
AH1293//31	58,612	—	BV	75.00	92.00	—
AH1293//32	48,000	—	BV	75.00	92.00	—
AH1293//33	16,145	—	BV	75.00	92.00	—
AH1293//34	6,276	—	BV	90.00	150	—

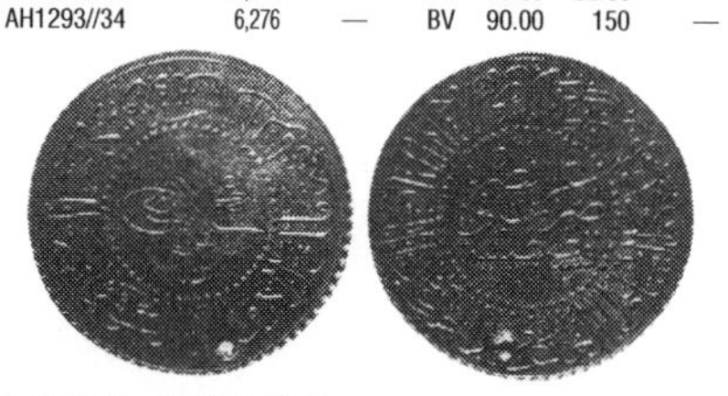

KM# 740 50 KURUSH
3.5080 g., 0.9170 Gold .1034 oz. AGW **Series:** Monnaie de Luxe **Obverse:** Toughra; "el-Ghazi" to right **Reverse:** Text, value and date in beaded circle within circular text **Mint:** Qustantiniyah

Date	Mintage	VG	F	VF	XF	Unc
AH1293//18 Rare	—	—	—	—	—	—
AH1293//23	14,000	BV	75.00	110	160	—
AH1293//24	8,980	BV	75.00	110	160	—
AH1293//25	—	BV	75.00	110	160	—
AH1293//26	5,436	BV	75.00	110	160	—
AH1293//27	6,630	BV	75.00	140	200	—
AH1293//28	8,660	BV	75.00	140	200	—
AH1293//29	14,924	BV	75.00	140	200	—
AH1293//30	18,812	BV	75.00	140	200	—
AH1293//31	22,460	BV	75.00	140	200	—
AH1293//32	27,542	BV	75.00	140	200	—
AH1293//33	12,886	BV	75.00	140	200	—
AH1293//34	—	BV	75.00	180	250	—

694 TURKEY

KM# 725 100 KURUSH
7.2160 g., 0.9170 Gold .2128 oz. AGW **Obverse:** Toughra within sprays and stars **Reverse:** Text, value and date within wreath, star above **Mint:** Qustantiniyah

Date	Mintage	VG	F	VF	XF	Unc
AH1293//1	77,000	BV	150	200	275	—
AH1293//2	415,000	BV	150	200	275	—
AH1293//3	97,000	BV	150	200	275	—
AH1293//4	1,530	150	200	300	400	—
AH1293//6	220,000	BV	150	200	275	—

KM# 730 100 KURUSH
7.2160 g., 0.9170 Gold .2128 oz. AGW **Obverse:** Toughra; "el-Ghazi" to right **Reverse:** Text, value and date within wreath, star above **Mint:** Qustantiniyah

Date	Mintage	VG	F	VF	XF	Unc
AH1293//6	1,220	—	—	BV	145	—
AH1293//7	415,000	—	—	BV	145	—
AH1293//8	18,000	—	—	BV	145	—
AH1293//9	23,000	—	—	BV	145	—
AH1293//10	572,000	—	—	BV	145	—
AH1293//11	255,000	—	—	BV	145	—
AH1293//12	2,000	—	—	BV	145	—
AH1293//13	2,000	—	—	BV	145	—
AH1293//14	18,000	—	—	BV	145	—
AH1293//15	2,000	—	—	BV	145	—
AH1293//16	722,000	—	—	BV	145	—
AH1293//17	3,350	—	—	BV	145	—
AH1293//18	165,000	—	—	BV	145	—
AH1293//19	3,000	—	—	BV	145	—
AH1293//20	728,000	—	—	BV	145	—
AH1293//21	4,400	—	—	BV	145	—
AH1293//22	186,000	—	—	BV	145	—
AH1293//23	225,000	—	—	BV	145	—
AH1293//24	2,850	—	—	BV	145	—
AH1293//25	3,000	—	—	BV	145	—
AH1293//26	2,000	—	—	150	180	—
AH1293//27	48,200	—	—	BV	160	—
AH1293//28	865,011	—	—	BV	150	—
AH1293//29	1,026,275	—	—	BV	150	—
AH1293//30	1,643,795	—	—	BV	150	—
AH1293//31	2,748,448	—	—	BV	150	—
AH1293//32	1,951,611	—	—	BV	150	—
AH1293//33	962,672	—	—	BV	150	—
AH1293//34	1,715,274	—	BV	200	250	—

KM# 741 100 KURUSH
7.0160 g., 0.9170 Gold .2068 oz. AGW **Series:** Monnaie de Luxe **Obverse:** Toughra; "el-Ghazi" to right **Reverse:** Text, value and date in beaded circle within circular text **Mint:** Qustantiniyah

Date	Mintage	VG	F	VF	XF	Unc
AH1293//18 Rare	—	—	—	—	—	—
AH1293//23	10,000	—	BV	145	190	—
AH1293//24	9,600	—	BV	145	190	—
AH1293//25	3,635	—	BV	145	190	—
AH1293//26	5,590	—	BV	145	190	—
AH1293//27	9,580	—	BV	150	220	—
AH1293//28	13,638	—	BV	150	220	—
AH1293//29	18,129	—	BV	150	220	—
AH1293//30	22,796	—	BV	150	220	—
AH1293//31	31,126	—	BV	150	220	—
AH1293//32	42,662	—	BV	150	220	—
AH1293//33	18,716	—	BV	150	220	—
AH1293//34	—	—	BV	180	250	—

KM# 726 250 KURUSH
18.0400 g., 0.9170 Gold .5319 oz. AGW **Obverse:** Toughra within sprays and stars **Reverse:** Text, value and date within wreath, star above **Mint:** Qustantiniyah

Date	Mintage	VG	F	VF	XF	Unc
AH1293//1	120	600	1,000	1,600	2,000	—

KM# 732 250 KURUSH
18.0400 g., 0.9170 Gold .5319 oz. AGW **Obverse:** Toughra; "el-Ghazi" to right **Reverse:** Text, value and date within wreath, star above **Mint:** Qustantiniyah

Date	Mintage	VG	F	VF	XF	Unc
AH1293//11	—	—	BV	350	450	—
AH1293//12	—	—	BV	350	450	—
AH1293//13	—	—	BV	350	450	—
AH1293//14	—	—	BV	350	450	—
AH1293//15	—	—	BV	350	450	—
AH1293//16	—	—	BV	350	450	—
AH1293//17	—	—	BV	350	450	—
AH1293//18	—	—	BV	350	450	—
AH1293//19	—	—	BV	350	450	—
AH1293//20	—	—	BV	350	450	—
AH1293//21	—	—	BV	350	450	—
AH1293//22	—	—	BV	350	450	—
AH1293//23	—	—	BV	350	450	—
AH1293//24	—	—	BV	350	450	—
AH1293//25	—	—	BV	350	450	—
AH1293//26	1,428	—	BV	350	450	—
AH1293//27	1,450	—	BV	375	450	—
AH1293//28	7,027	—	BV	375	450	—
AH1293//29	7,522	—	BV	375	450	—
AH1293//30	4,900	—	BV	375	450	—
AH1293//31	8,552	—	BV	375	450	—
AH1293//32	8,729	—	BV	375	450	—
AH1293//33	2,669	—	BV	375	450	—
AH1293//34	6,478	—	BV	400	600	—

KM# 742 250 KURUSH
17.5400 g., 0.9170 Gold .5169 oz. AGW **Series:** Monnaie de Luxe **Obverse:** Toughra; "el-Ghazi" to right **Reverse:** Text, value and date within beaded circle, designed wreath **Mint:** Qustantiniyah

Date	Mintage	VG	F	VF	XF	Unc
AH1293//24	—	BV	360	475	750	—
AH1293//25	—	BV	360	500	750	—
AH1293//26	1,538	BV	360	500	750	—
AH1293//27	1,770	BV	360	500	750	—
AH1293//28	1,520	BV	360	500	750	—
AH1293//29	1,631	BV	360	500	750	—
AH1293//30	1,922	BV	360	500	750	—
AH1293//31	1,778	BV	360	500	750	—
AH1293//32	2,650	BV	360	500	750	—
AH1293//33	931	BV	450	800	1,000	—
AH1293//34 Rare	—	—	—	—	—	—

KM# 727 500 KURUSH
36.0800 g., 0.9170 Gold 1.0638 oz. AGW **Obverse:** Toughra within sprays and stars **Reverse:** Text, value and date within wreath, star above **Mint:** Qustantiniyah

Date	Mintage	VG	F	VF	XF	Unc
AH1293//1	220	BV	725	775	950	—
AH1293//2	5,580	BV	—	700	750	900	—
AH1293//3	54,000	—	BV	700	850	—
AH1293//4	60	BV	750	800	1,000	—
AH1293//6	2,600	BV	700	750	900	—

KM# 733 500 KURUSH
36.0800 g., 0.9170 Gold 1.0638 oz. AGW **Obverse:** Toughra; "el-Ghazi" to right **Reverse:** Text, value and date within wreath, star above **Mint:** Qustantiniyah

Date	Mintage	VG	F	VF	XF	Unc
AH1293//11	200	—	BV	700	800	—
AH1293//12	200	—	BV	700	800	—
AH1293//13	200	—	BV	700	800	—
AH1293//14	200	—	BV	700	800	—
AH1293//15	200	—	BV	700	800	—
AH1293//16	15,000	—	BV	700	750	—
AH1293//17	200	—	BV	700	800	—
AH1293//18	200	—	BV	700	800	—
AH1293//19	200	—	BV	700	800	—
AH1293//20	200	—	BV	700	800	—
AH1293//21	200	—	BV	700	800	—
AH1293//22	200	—	BV	700	800	—
AH1293//23	15,000	—	BV	700	750	—
AH1293//24	8,048	—	BV	700	775	—
AH1293//25	11,000	—	BV	700	775	—
AH1293//26	8,735	—	BV	650	800	—
AH1293//27	22,450	—	BV	745	850	—
AH1293//28	35,918	—	BV	745	850	—
AH1293//29	16,621	—	BV	745	850	—
AH1293//30	33,129	—	BV	745	850	—
AH1293//31	40,953	—	BV	745	850	—
AH1293//32	32,516	—	BV	745	850	—
AH1293//33	16,403	—	BV	745	850	—
AH1293//34	39,028	—	BV	745	850	—

KM# 746 500 KURUSH
35.0800 g., 0.9170 Gold 1.0338 oz. AGW **Series:** Monnaie de Luxe **Obverse:** Radiant Toughra above crossed flags, ornamental base **Reverse:** Inscription and date within star and designed border **Mint:** Qustantiniyah

Date	Mintage	VG	F	VF	XF	Unc
AH1293//26	550	725	800	900	1,200	—
AH1293//27	1,428	725	800	900	1,200	—
AH1293//28	858	725	800	900	1,200	—
AH1293//29	804	725	800	900	1,200	—
AH1293//30	1,204	725	800	900	1,200	—
AH1293//31	1,021	725	800	900	1,200	—
AH1293//32	1,334	725	800	900	1,200	—
AH1293//33	812	725	800	900	1,200	—
AH1293//34	—	725	800	900	1,200	—

TURKEY 695

Muhammad V
AH1327-36/1909-18AD
MILLED COINAGE
Gold Issues

KM# 762 12-1/2 KURUSH
0.9020 g., 0.9170 Gold .0266 oz. AGW **Series:** Monnaie de Luxe **Obverse:** Toughra; "Reshat" to right **Reverse:** Value and date within designed wreath **Mint:** Qustantiniyah

Date	Mintage	VG	F	VF	XF	Unc
AH1327//2	43,568	30.00	50.00	90.00	130	—
AH1327//3	50,368	30.00	50.00	90.00	130	—
AH1327//4	19,344	30.00	50.00	90.00	130	—
AH1327//5	9,160	30.00	50.00	90.00	130	—
AH1327//6	11,880	30.00	50.00	90.00	130	—

KM# 752 25 KURUSH
1.8040 g., 0.9170 Gold .0532 oz. AGW **Obverse:** Toughra; "Reshat" to right **Reverse:** Inscription and date within wreath, star on top **Mint:** Qustantiniyah

Date	Mintage	VG	F	VF	XF	Unc
AH1327//1	115,484	—	BV	40.00	50.00	—
AH1327//2	194,740	—	BV	40.00	50.00	—
AH1327//3	249,416	—	BV	40.00	50.00	—
AH1327//4	338,172	—	BV	40.00	50.00	—
AH1327//5	167,592	—	BV	40.00	50.00	—
AH1327//6	72,872	—	BV	40.00	50.00	—

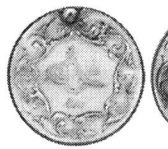

KM# 763 25 KURUSH
1.7540 g., 0.9170 Gold .0517 oz. AGW **Series:** Monnaie de Luxe **Obverse:** Toughra within designed wreath **Reverse:** Inscription and date within designed wreath **Mint:** Qustantiniyah

Date	Mintage	VG	F	VF	XF	Unc
AH1327//2	47,788	BV	60.00	90.00	120	—
AH1327//3	70,775	BV	60.00	90.00	120	—
AH1327//4	47,088	BV	60.00	90.00	120	—
AH1327//5	25,964	50.00	80.00	110	140	—
AH1327//6	23,348	50.00	80.00	110	140	—

KM# 773 25 KURUSH
1.8040 g., 0.9170 Gold .0532 oz. AGW **Obverse:** Toughra; "el-Ghazi" to right **Reverse:** Inscription and date within wreath, star on top **Mint:** Qustantiniyah

Date	Mintage	VG	F	VF	XF	Unc
AH1327//7	22,420	—	BV	45.00	75.00	—
AH1327//8	5,926	—	BV	45.00	75.00	—
AH1327//9	4,060	—	BV	45.00	75.00	—
AH1327//10	53,524	1,000	1,500	2,000	—	—

KM# 774 25 KURUSH
1.7540 g., 0.9170 Gold .0517 oz. AGW **Series:** Monnaie de Luxe **Obverse:** Toughra **Mint:** Qustantiniyah

Date	Mintage	VG	F	VF	XF	Unc
AH1327//8	10,612	1,750	2,500	3,500	5,000	—

KM# 753 50 KURUSH
3.6080 g., 0.9170 Gold .1064 oz. AGW **Obverse:** Toughra; "Reshat" to right **Reverse:** Inscription and date within wreath, star on top **Mint:** Qustantiniyah

Date	Mintage	VG	F	VF	XF	Unc
AH1327//1	6,276	1,000	1,500	2,000	3,000	—
AH1327//2	89,712	—	BV	75.00	95.00	—
AH1327//3	75,442	—	BV	75.00	95.00	—
AH1327//4	96,030	—	BV	75.00	95.00	—
AH1327//5	40,618	—	BV	75.00	95.00	—
AH1327//6	26,408	—	BV	80.00	110	—

KM# 764 50 KURUSH
3.5080 g., 0.9170 Gold .1034 oz. AGW **Series:** Monnaie de Luxe **Obverse:** Toughra within designed wreath **Reverse:** Inscription and date within designed wreath **Mint:** Qustantiniyah

Date	Mintage	VG	F	VF	XF	Unc
AH1327//2	25,224	BV	75.00	140	180	—
AH1327//3	23,971	BV	75.00	140	180	—
AH1327//4	15,716	BV	75.00	140	180	—
AH1327//5	17,118	BV	75.00	140	180	—
AH1327//6	8,706	BV	75.00	180	250	—

KM# 775 50 KURUSH
3.6080 g., 0.9170 Gold .1064 oz. AGW **Obverse:** Toughra; "el-Ghazi" to right **Mint:** Qustantiniyah

Date	Mintage	VG	F	VF	XF	Unc
AH1327//7	9,175	BV	75.00	150	250	—
AH1327//8	7,330	BV	75.00	150	250	—
AH1327//9	2,000	BV	75.00	150	250	—
AH1327//10	53,524	1,000	1,500	2,000	3,000	—

KM# 781 50 KURUSH
3.5080 g., 0.9170 Gold .1034 oz. AGW **Series:** Monnaie de Luxe **Obverse:** Toughra **Mint:** Qustantiniyah

Date	Mintage	VG	F	VF	XF	Unc
AH1327//8	3,291	250	500	800	1,200	—

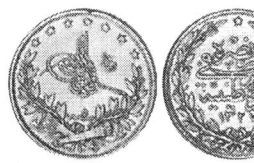

KM# 754 100 KURUSH
7.2160 g., 0.9170 Gold .2125 oz. AGW **Obverse:** Toughra; "Reshat" to right **Reverse:** Inscription and date within wreath, star on top **Mint:** Qustantiniyah

Date	Mintage	VG	F	VF	XF	Unc
AH1327//1	1,715,274	—	BV	150	165	—
AH1327//2	3,376,679	—	BV	150	165	—
AH1327//3	4,627,115	—	BV	150	165	—
AH1327//4	3,591,676	—	BV	150	165	—
AH1327//5	881,895	—	BV	150	165	—
AH1327//6	3,769,100	—	BV	150	165	—
AH1327//7	2,989,609	—	BV	150	165	—

KM# 755 100 KURUSH
7.0160 g., 0.9170 Gold .2068 oz. AGW **Series:** Monnaie de Luxe **Obverse:** Toughra within designed wreath **Reverse:** Inscription and date within designed wreath

Date	Mintage	VG	F	VF	XF	Unc
AH1327//1	—	—	BV	180	250	—
AH1327//2	37,110	—	BV	180	250	—
AH1327//3	53,738	—	BV	180	250	—
AH1327//4	41,507	—	BV	180	250	—
AH1327//5	58,819	—	BV	180	250	—
AH1327//6	19,768	—	BV	180	250	—

KM# 776 100 KURUSH
7.2160 g., 0.9170 Gold .2128 oz. AGW **Obverse:** Toughra; "el-Ghazi" to right **Reverse:** Inscription and date within wreath, star on top **Mint:** Qustantiniyah

Date	Mintage	VG	F	VF	XF	Unc
AH1327//7	1,232,090	—	BV	150	170	—
AH1327//8	Inc. above	—	BV	150	170	—
AH1327//9	3,582,005	—	BV	150	170	—
AH1327//10	—	—	BV	160	200	—

KM# 782 100 KURUSH
7.0160 g., 0.9170 Gold .2068 oz. AGW **Series:** Monnaie de Luxe **Obverse:** Toughra **Mint:** Qustantiniyah

Date	Mintage	Good	VG	F	VF	XF
AH1327//8 (1916)	13,250	—	250	400	600	1,000

KM# 756 250 KURUSH
18.0400 g., 0.9170 Gold .5319 oz. AGW **Obverse:** Toughra; "Reshat" to right **Reverse:** Inscription and date within wreath, star on top **Mint:** Qustantiniyah

Date	Mintage	VG	F	VF	XF	Unc
AH1327//1	6,878	—	BV	400	500	—
AH1327//2	9,207	—	BV	400	500	—
AH1327//3	9,990	—	BV	400	500	—
AH1327//4	13,400	—	BV	400	500	—
AH1327//5	18,143	—	BV	400	500	—
AH1327//6	6,155	—	BV	400	500	—

KM# 757 250 KURUSH
17.5400 g., 0.9170 Gold .5619 oz. AGW **Series:** Monnaie de Luxe **Obverse:** Toughra within designed wreath **Reverse:** Inscription and date within designed wreath **Mint:** Qustantiniyah

Date	Mintage	VG	F	VF	XF	Unc
AH1327//1	—	BV	400	600	800	—
AH1327//2	6,995	BV	400	600	800	—
AH1327//3	12,084	BV	400	600	800	—
AH1327//4	10,250	BV	400	600	800	—
AH1327//5	16,879	BV	400	600	800	—
AH1327//6	9,039	BV	400	600	800	—

KM# 777 250 KURUSH
18.0400 g., 0.9170 Gold .5319 oz. AGW **Obverse:** Toughra; "el-Ghazi" to right **Reverse:** Inscription and date within wreath, star on top **Mint:** Qustantiniyah

Date	Mintage	VG	F	VF	XF	Unc
AH1327//7	30	1,250	1,750	2,800	4,000	—
AH1327//8	21	1,750	2,500	3,500	5,000	—
AH1327//9	28	1,750	2,500	3,500	5,000	—

696 TURKEY

KM# 783 250 KURUSH
17.5400 g., 0.9170 Gold .5619 oz. AGW **Series:** Monnaie de Luxe **Obverse:** Toughra within designed wreath **Reverse:** Inscription and date within designed wreath **Mint:** Qustantiniyah

Date	Mintage	VG	F	VF	XF	Unc
AH1327//8	3,107	1,250	1,750	2,500	3,500	—

KM# 758 500 KURUSH
17.5400 g., 0.9170 Gold .5619 oz. AGW **Obverse:** Toughra; "Reshat" to right **Reverse:** Inscription and date within wreath, star on top **Mint:** Qustantiniyah

Date	Mintage	VG	F	VF	XF	Unc
AH1327//1	39,028	—	BV	525	650	—
AH1327//2	37,474	—	BV	525	650	—
AH1327//3	53,900	—	BV	525	650	—
AH1327//4	41,863	—	BV	525	650	—
AH1327//5	36,996	—	BV	525	650	—
AH1327//6	17,792	—	BV	525	650	—

KM# 765 500 KURUSH
35.0800 g., 0.9170 Gold 1.0338 oz. AGW **Series:** Monnaie de Luxe **Obverse:** Radiant Toughra above crossed flags, ornamental base **Reverse:** Inscription and date within designed wreath **Mint:** Qustantiniyah

Date	Mintage	VG	F	VF	XF	Unc
AH1327//2	1,718	BV	750	900	1,350	—
AH1327//3	4,631	BV	750	900	1,350	—
AH1327//4	3,887	BV	750	900	1,350	—
AH1327//5	5,145	BV	750	900	1,350	—
AH1327//6	2,401	BV	750	900	1,350	—

KM# 784 500 KURUSH
36.0800 g., 0.9170 Gold 1.0638 oz. AGW **Obverse:** Toughra; "el-Ghazi" to right **Reverse:** Inscription and date within wreath, star on top **Mint:** Qustantiniyah

Date	Mintage	VG	F	VF	XF	Unc
AH1327//7	484	1,750	2,500	3,500	5,000	—
AH1327//8	19	1,750	2,750	4,250	6,000	—
AH1327//9	22	1,750	2,750	4,250	6,000	—
AH1327//10	—	1,750	2,500	3,500	5,000	—

KM# 778 500 KURUSH
35.0800 g., 0.9170 Gold 1.0338 oz. AGW **Series:** Monnaie de Luxe **Obverse:** Radiant Toughra above crossed flags, ornamental base **Reverse:** Inscription and date within designed wreath **Mint:** Qustantiniyah **Note:** Struck at Qustantiniyah

Date	Mintage	VG	F	VF	XF	Unc
AH1327//7	295	1,200	1,750	2,500	3,500	—
AH1327//8	1,618	1,000	1,500	2,200	3,000	—

MILLED COINAGE
Gold Mint Visit Issues
Muhammad V's visit to Bursa

KM# 787 25 KURUSH
1.8040 g., 0.9170 Gold .0532 oz. AGW **Obverse:** Toughra in center of sprigs and stars **Reverse:** Inscription and date within wreath, star on top **Mint:** Bursa

Date	Mintage	F	VF	XF	Unc
AH1327//1	—	185	275	400	800

KM# 788 50 KURUSH
3.6080 g., 0.9170 Gold .1064 oz. AGW **Obverse:** Toughra in center of sprigs and stars **Reverse:** Inscription and date within wreath, star on top **Mint:** Bursa

Date	Mintage	F	VF	XF	Unc
AH1327//1	—	165	275	350	650

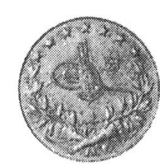

KM# 789 100 KURUSH
7.2160 g., 0.9170 Gold .2128 oz. AGW **Obverse:** Toughra in center of sprigs and stars **Reverse:** Inscription and date within wreath, star on top **Mint:** Bursa

Date	Mintage	F	VF	XF	Unc
AH1327//1	—	215	325	400	700

MILLED COINAGE
Gold Mint Visit Issues
Muhammad V visit to Edirne

KM# 793 50 KURUSH
3.6080 g., 0.9170 Gold .1064 oz. AGW **Obverse:** Toughra in center of sprigs and stars **Reverse:** Inscription and date within wreath, star on top **Mint:** Edirne

Date	Mintage	F	VF	XF	Unc
AH1327//2	—	200	275	350	600

KM# 794 100 KURUSH
7.2160 g., 0.9170 Gold .2128 oz. AGW **Obverse:** Toughra in center of sprigs and stars **Reverse:** Inscription and date within wreath, star on top **Mint:** Edirne

Date	Mintage	F	VF	XF	Unc
AH1327//2	—	250	350	475	700

KM# 795 500 KURUSH
36.0800 g., 0.9170 Gold 1.0638 oz. AGW **Obverse:** Toughra in center of sprigs and stars **Reverse:** Inscription and date within wreath, star on top **Mint:** Edirne

Date	Mintage	F	VF	XF	Unc
AH1327//2	—	1,500	2,500	3,500	4,000

MILLED COINAGE
Gold Mint Visit Issues
Muhammad Vs visit to Kosova

KM# 799 50 KURUSH
3.6080 g., 0.9170 Gold .1064 oz. AGW **Obverse:** Toughra in center of sprigs and stars **Reverse:** Inscription and date within wreath, star on top **Mint:** Kosova

Date	Mintage	F	VF	XF	Unc
AH1327//3	1,200	225	275	400	700

KM# 800 100 KURUSH
7.2160 g., 0.9170 Gold .2128 oz. AGW **Obverse:** Toughra in center of stars and sprigs **Reverse:** Inscription and date within wreath, star on top **Mint:** Kosova

TURKEY 697

Date	Mintage	F	VF	XF	Unc
AH1327//3	750	250	300	450	750

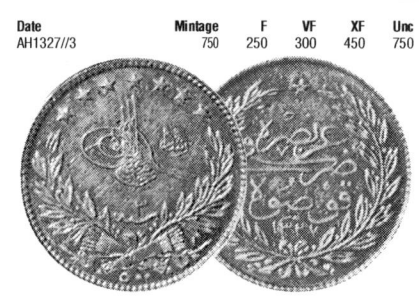

KM# 801 500 KURUSH
36.0800 g., 0.9170 Gold 1.0638 oz. AGW **Obverse:** Toughra in center of stars and sprigs **Reverse:** Inscription and date within wreath, star on top **Mint:** Kosova

Date	Mintage	F	VF	XF	Unc
AH1327//3	20	3,000	4,000	5,000	6,000

MILLED COINAGE
Gold Mint Visit Issues
Muhammad V's visit to Manastir

KM# 805 50 KURUSH
3.6080 g., 0.9170 Gold .1064 oz. AGW **Obverse:** Toughra in center of sprigs and stars **Reverse:** Inscription and date within wreath, star on top **Mint:** Manastir

Date	Mintage	F	VF	XF	Unc
AH1327//3	1,200	200	325	450	700

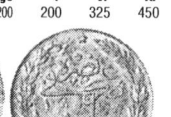

KM# 806 100 KURUSH
7.2160 g., 0.9170 Gold .2128 oz. AGW **Obverse:** Toughra in center of sprigs and stars **Reverse:** Inscription and date within wreath, star on top **Mint:** Manastir

Date	Mintage	F	VF	XF	Unc
AH1327//3	750	225	350	450	750

KM# 807 500 KURUSH
36.0800 g., 0.9170 Gold 1.0638 oz. AGW **Obverse:** Toughra in center of sprigs and stars **Reverse:** Inscription and date within wreath, star on top **Mint:** Manastir

Date	Mintage	F	VF	XF	Unc
AH1327//3	20	2,500	4,000	5,000	6,250

MILLED COINAGE
Gold Mint Visit Issues
Muhammad V's visit to Salonika

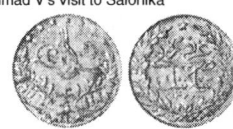

KM# 811 50 KURUSH
3.6080 g., 0.9170 Gold .1064 oz. AGW **Obverse:** Toughra in center of sprigs and stars **Reverse:** Inscription and date within wreath, star on top **Mint:** Salonika

Date	Mintage	F	VF	XF	Unc
AH1327//3	1,200	200	325	400	700

KM# 812 100 KURUSH
7.2160 g., 0.9170 Gold .2128 oz. AGW **Obverse:** Toughra in center of sprigs and stars **Reverse:** Inscription and date within wreath, star on top **Mint:** Salonika

Date	Mintage	F	VF	XF	Unc
AH1327//3	750	225	350	450	750

KM# 813 500 KURUSH
36.0800 g., 0.9170 Gold 1.0638 oz. AGW **Obverse:** Toughra in center of sprigs and stars **Reverse:** Inscription and date within wreath, star on top **Mint:** Salonika

Date	Mintage	F	VF	XF	Unc
AH1327//3	20	2,500	4,000	5,250	6,750

Muhammad VI
AH1336-41/1918-23AD
MILLED COINAGE
Gold Issues

KM# 819 25 KURUSH
1.8040 g., 0.9170 Gold .0532 oz. AGW **Obverse:** Toughra in center of sprigs and stars **Reverse:** Inscription and date within wreath, star on top **Mint:** Qustantiniyah

Date	Mintage	VG	F	VF	XF	Unc
AH1336//1	53,524	37.50	45.00	60.00	100	—
AH1336//2	62,253	37.50	45.00	60.00	100	—
AH1336//3	52,421	40.00	75.00	150	200	—
AH1336//4	400	50.00	90.00	200	300	—
AH1336//5	819	80.00	140	240	375	—

KM# 825 25 KURUSH
1.7540 g., 0.9170 Gold .0517 oz. AGW **Series:** Monnaie de Luxe **Obverse:** Toughra **Mint:** Qustantiniyah

Date	Mintage	VG	F	VF	XF	Unc
AH1336//2	8,400	60.00	80.00	100	150	—
AH1336//3	11,179	60.00	80.00	100	150	—

KM# 820 50 KURUSH
3.6080 g., 0.9170 Gold .1064 oz. AGW **Obverse:** Toughra in center of sprigs and stars **Reverse:** Inscription and date within wreath, star on top **Mint:** Qustantiniyah

Date	Mintage	VG	F	VF	XF	Unc
AH1336//1	162,363	100	125	150	300	—
AH1336//2	346	100	125	150	300	—
AH1336//3	447	150	200	250	500	—
AH1336//4	200	250	450	750	1,500	—
AH1336//5	204	200	300	450	1,000	—

KM# 821 100 KURUSH
7.2160 g., 0.9170 Gold .2128 oz. AGW **Obverse:** Toughra in center of sprigs and stars **Reverse:** Inscription and date within wreath, star on top **Mint:** Qustantiniyah

Date	Mintage	VG	F	VF	XF	Unc
AH1336//1	5,036,830	BV	150	165	185	—
AH1336//2	37,634	BV	150	165	185	—
AH1336//3	30,313	160	185	225	450	—
AH1336//4	200	400	600	800	1,000	—
AH1336//5	—	400	600	800	1,000	—

KM# 826 100 KURUSH
7.0160 g., 0.9170 Gold .2068 oz. AGW **Series:** Monnaie de Luxe **Obverse:** Toughra in center of legend **Reverse:** Inscription and date in center of legend **Mint:** Qustantiniyah

Date	Mintage	VG	F	VF	XF	Unc
AH1336//2	33,077	250	300	325	375	—
AH1336//3	20,248	250	300	325	375	—

KM# 822 250 KURUSH
18.0400 g., 0.9170 Gold .5319 oz. AGW **Obverse:** Toughra in center of sprigs and stars **Reverse:** Inscription and date within wreath, star on top **Mint:** Qustantiniyah

Date	Mintage	VG	F	VF	XF	Unc
AH1336//1	39	1,750	3,000	4,500	6,500	—
AH1336//2	26	1,750	3,000	4,500	6,500	—
AH1336//3	31	1,750	3,000	4,500	6,500	—
AH1336//4	20	1,750	3,000	4,500	6,500	—
AH1336//5	21	1,750	3,000	4,500	6,500	—

KM# 827 250 KURUSH
17.5400 g., 0.9170 Gold .5169 oz. AGW **Series:** Monnaie de Luxe **Obverse:** Toughra within beaded circle **Reverse:** Inscription and date within beaded circle **Mint:** Qustantiniyah

Date	Mintage	VG	F	VF	XF	Unc
AH1336//2	5,995	BV	500	700	900	—
AH1336//3	12,739	BV	425	600	800	—

698 TURKEY

KM# 823 500 KURUSH
36.0800 g., 0.9170 Gold 1.0638 oz. AGW **Obverse:** Toughra in center of sprigs and stars **Reverse:** Inscription and date within wreath, star on top **Mint:** Qustantiniyah

Date	Mintage	VG	F	VF	XF	Unc
AH1336//1	26,984	1,000	1,200	1,450	1,800	—
AH1336//2	22,192	1,000	1,200	1,450	1,800	—
AH1336//3	16,424	1,000	1,200	1,450	1,800	—
AH1336//4	23	2,000	4,000	6,000	8,000	—
AH1336//5	22	2,000	4,000	6,000	8,000	—

KM# 824 500 KURUSH
35.0800 g., 0.9170 Gold 1.0338 oz. AGW **Series:** Monnaie de Luxe **Obverse:** Radiant Toughra above crossed flags, ornamental base **Reverse:** Inscription and date within designed wreath **Mint:** Qustantiniyah

Date	Mintage	VG	F	VF	XF	Unc
AH1336//1	—	1,000	1,250	1,750	2,400	—
AH1336//2	—	BV	750	950	1,300	—
AH1336//3	5,207	BV	750	950	1,300	—
AH1336//4	88	1,500	2,000	2,500	3,200	—

REPUBLIC
STANDARD COINAGE
Old Monetary System

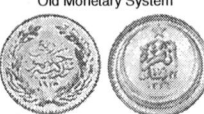

KM# 840 25 KURUSH
1.8040 g., 0.9170 Gold .0532 oz. AGW **Obverse:** Inscription and date within wreath **Reverse:** Star divides inner circle above inscription and date

Date	Mintage	F	VF	XF	Unc
1926	4,539	40.00	75.00	140	175
1927	14,000	40.00	75.00	120	150
1928	8,424	40.00	75.00	130	165
1929	—	40.00	75.00	120	150

KM# 844 25 KURUSH
1.7540 g., 0.9170 Gold .0517 oz. AGW, 23 mm. **Series:** Monnaie de Luxe **Obverse:** Radiant star and crescent above inscription within sprigs **Reverse:** Value and date within designed wreath

Date	Mintage	F	VF	XF	Unc
1927	4,103	50.00	80.00	150	200
1928	4,549	50.00	80.00	150	200

KM# 841 50 KURUSH
3.6080 g., 0.9170 Gold .1064 oz. AGW **Obverse:** Inscription and date within wreath **Reverse:** Star divides circle above inscription and date

Date	Mintage	F	VF	XF	Unc
1926	2,168	100	150	200	275
1927	2,116	100	150	200	275
1928	2,431	100	150	200	275
1929	—	100	150	200	275

KM# 845 50 KURUSH
3.5080 g., 0.9170 Gold .1034 oz. AGW, 28 mm. **Series:** Monnaie de Luxe **Obverse:** Radiant star and crescent above inscription within sprigs **Reverse:** Inscription and date within designed wreath

Date	Mintage	F	VF	XF	Unc
1927	3,903	75.00	150	250	375
1928	3,620	75.00	150	250	375

KM# 842 100 KURUSH
7.2160 g., 0.9170 Gold .2128 oz. AGW **Obverse:** Inscription and date within wreath **Reverse:** Star divides circle above inscription and date

Date	Mintage	F	VF	XF	Unc
1926	1,073	BV	175	250	350
1927	—	BV	175	250	350
1928	920	BV	175	250	350
1929	—	BV	175	250	350

KM# 846 100 KURUSH
7.0160 g., 0.9170 Gold .2069 oz. AGW, 35 mm. **Series:** Monnaie de Luxe

Date	Mintage	F	VF	XF	Unc
1927	8,676	BV	150	250	350
1928	6,092	BV	150	250	350

KM# 843 250 KURUSH
18.0400 g., 0.9170 Gold .5319 oz. AGW **Obverse:** Inscription and date within wreath **Reverse:** Star divides circle above inscription and date

Date	Mintage	F	VF	XF	Unc
1926	604	375	450	600	750
1927	886	375	450	600	750
1928	110	375	450	600	750
1929	—	375	450	600	750

KM# 847 250 KURUSH
17.5400 g., 0.9170 Gold .5169 oz. AGW, 45 mm. **Series:** Monnaie de Luxe **Obverse:** Radiant star and crescent above inscription within sprigs **Reverse:** Inscription and date within designed wreath

Date	Mintage	F	VF	XF	Unc
1927	7,411	—	BV	450	650
1928	5,045	—	BV	450	650

KM# 839 500 KURUSH
36.0800 g., 0.9170 Gold 1.0638 oz. AGW **Obverse:** Inscription and date within wreath **Reverse:** Star divides circle above inscription and date

Date	Mintage	F	VF	XF	Unc
1925	226	BV	750	1,000	1,500
1926	2,268	—	BV	725	875
1927	4,011	—	BV	725	875
1928	375	BV	750	1,000	1,500
1929	—	BV	750	1,000	1,500

KM# 848 500 KURUSH
35.0800 g., 0.9170 Gold 1.0344 oz. AGW, 49 mm. **Series:** Monnaie de Luxe **Obverse:** Radiant star and crescent above inscription within sprigs **Reverse:** Inscription and date within designed wreath

TURKEY 699

Date	Mintage	F	VF	XF	Unc
1927	5,097	—	BV	725	875
1928	2,242	—	BV	725	875

DECIMAL COINAGE
Western numerals and Latin alphabet

40 Para = 1 Kurus; 100 Kurus = 1 Lira

Mintage figures of the 1930s and early 1940s may not be exact. It is suspected that in some cases, figures for a particular year may include quantities struck with the previous year's date.

KM# 884a 1/2 KURUS (20 Para)
3.9000 g., 0.9160 Gold .1149 oz. AGW, 16 mm. **Series:** Nostalgia **Obverse:** Center hole and date **Reverse:** Center hole divides value and sprig **Edge:** Plain **Mint:** Istanbul

Date	Mintage	F	VF	XF	Unc
1948	441	—	—	—	85.00

KM# 881a KURUS
4.9000 g., 0.9160 Gold .1443 oz. AGW, 18 mm. **Series:** Nostalgia **Obverse:** Date below hole in center **Reverse:** Hole in center flanked by oat sprig and value **Edge:** Plain **Mint:** Istanbul

Date	Mintage	F	VF	XF	Unc
1949	441	—	—	—	110

KM# 885a 2-1/2 KURUS
6.9000 g., 0.9160 Gold .2032 oz. AGW, 21 mm. **Series:** Nostalgia **Obverse:** Date below center hole **Reverse:** Hole in center divides oat sprig and value **Edge:** Plain **Mint:** Istanbul

Date	Mintage	F	VF	XF	Unc
1950	441	—	—	—	150

KM# 886a 25 KURUS
10.0000 g., 0.9160 Gold .2945 oz. AGW, 22.6 mm. **Series:** Nostalgia **Obverse:** Crescent and star **Reverse:** Value within wreath **Edge:** Plain **Mint:** Istanbul

Date	Mintage	F	VF	XF	Unc
1951	441	—	—	—	215

KM# 941a 1/2 LIRA
8.0000 g., 0.9170 Gold .2358 oz. AGW **Subject:** 100th Anniversary of Atatürk's Birth **Obverse:** Crescent and star at top of mountain, signature above globe below **Reverse:** Head of Kemal Atatürk right

Date	Mintage	F	VF	XF	Unc
ND(1981)	25,000				165

KM# 942a LIRA
16.0000 g., 0.9170 Gold .4716 oz. AGW **Subject:** 100th Anniversary of Atatürk's Birth **Obverse:** Crescent and star at top of mountain, signature above globe below **Reverse:** Head of Kemal Atatürk right

Date	Mintage	F	VF	XF	Unc
ND(1981)	25,000	—	—	—	335

KM# 904 500 LIRA
6.0000 g., 0.9170 Gold .1769 oz. AGW **Subject:** 50th Anniversary of Republic **Obverse:** Bust facing **Reverse:** Cascading star within flower to upper right of inscription

Date	Mintage	F	VF	XF	Unc
1973	30,000	—	—	—	135

KM# 920 500 LIRA
8.0000 g., 0.9170 Gold .2358 oz. AGW **Series:** F.A.O. **Obverse:** Mother breastfeeding infant **Reverse:** Value and date within wreath

Date	Mintage	F	VF	XF	Unc
1978 Proof	650	Value: 210			

KM# 921 500 LIRA
8.0000 g., 0.9170 Gold .2358 oz. AGW **Subject:** 705th Anniversary - Death o6.75f Jalaladdin Rumi, Poet

Date	Mintage	F	VF	XF	Unc
1978 Proof	900	Value: 475			

KM# 930 500 LIRA
8.0000 g., 0.9170 Gold .2358 oz. AGW **Series:** F.A.O.

Date	Mintage	F	VF	XF	Unc
1979 Proof	783	Value: 210			

KM# 968b 500 LIRA
47.5400 g., 0.9170 Gold 1.4009 oz. AGW **Subject:** World Fisheries Conference **Obverse:** Value **Reverse:** Turbot fish **Rev. Designer:** Stuart Devlin

Date	Mintage	F	VF	XF	Unc
ND(1984) Proof	74	Value: 1,250			

KM# 922 1000 LIRA
16.0000 g., 0.9170 Gold .4717 oz. AGW **Series:** F.A.O. **Obverse:** Anatolic bride's head left **Reverse:** Value and date within wreath

Date	Mintage	F	VF	XF	Unc
1978 Proof	650	Value: 500			

KM# 923 1000 LIRA
16.0000 g., 0.9170 Gold .4717 oz. AGW **Subject:** 705th Anniversary - Death of Jalaladdin Rumi, Poet

Date	Mintage	F	VF	XF	Unc
1978 Proof	450	Value: 1,000			

KM# 932 1000 LIRA
16.0000 g., 0.9170 Gold .4717 oz. AGW **Series:** F.A.O.

Date	Mintage	F	VF	XF	Unc
1979 Proof	900	Value: 400			

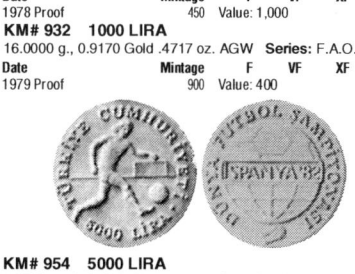

KM# 954 5000 LIRA
7.1300 g., 0.5000 Gold .1146 oz. AGW **Subject:** World Championship Soccer - Madrid **Obverse:** Soccer player kicking the ball **Reverse:** Soccer ball as world globe with SPANYA'82 across middle

Date	Mintage	F	VF	XF	Unc
ND(1982) Proof	2,400	Value: 145			

KM# 933 10000 LIRA (10 Bin Lira)
17.1700 g., 0.9000 Gold .4900 oz. AGW **Subject:** UNICEF and I.Y.C. **Obverse:** Value within wreath **Reverse:** Multiracial children dancing, city view above, logos and date below **Note:** Similar to 500 Lira, KM#931

Date	Mintage	F	VF	XF	Unc
1979(1981) Proof	4,450	Value: 350			

KM# 955 30000 LIRA
15.9800 g., 0.9170 Gold .4712 oz. AGW **Series:** International Year of Disabled Persons **Obverse:** Value within wreath **Reverse:** Stylized seated figure missing legs and globe design

Date	Mintage	F	VF	XF	Unc
1981	140				420
1981 Proof	3,000	Value: 460			

KM# 961 30000 LIRA
15.9800 g., 0.9170 Gold .4712 oz. AGW **Series:** International Year of the Scout **Obverse:** Value within wreath **Reverse:** Emblems within circle

Date	Mintage	F	VF	XF	Unc
ND(1983)	2,000	—	—	—	450
ND(1983) Proof	2,000	Value: 500			

KM# 973 50000 LIRA (50 Bin Lira)
7.1300 g., 0.9000 Gold .2063 oz. AGW **Series:** Decade for Women **Obverse:** Value and date within wreath **Reverse:** Half-figure of female facing **Rev. Designer:** Suat Ozyonum

Date	Mintage	F	VF	XF	Unc
1984 Proof	800	Value: 160			

KM# 956 100000 LIRA (100 Bin Lira)
33.8200 g., 0.9170 Gold .9972 oz. AGW **Subject:** Islamic World 15th Century **Reverse:** City view above value within circle

Date	Mintage	F	VF	XF	Unc
1982 Proof	12,000	Value: 675			

KM# 974 200000 LIRA
33.8200 g., 0.9170 Gold .9972 oz. AGW **Subject:** 50th Anniversary of Women's Suffrage

Date	Mintage	F	VF	XF	Unc
ND(1984) Proof	62	Value: 1,850			

KM# 1002 200000 LIRA
7.2160 g., 0.9170 Gold .2126 oz. AGW **Subject:** 400th Anniversary - Death of Architect Sinan **Obverse:** Value within wreath **Reverse:** Arched city view

Date	Mintage	F	VF	XF	Unc
ND(1988) Proof	244	Value: 325			

KM# 1004 200000 LIRA
7.2160 g., 0.9170 Gold .2126 oz. AGW **Subject:** Teacher's Day **Obverse:** Value within wreath **Reverse:** Stylized design divides date

Date	Mintage	F	VF	XF	Unc
1989 Proof	197	Value: 350			

KM# 994 200000 LIRA
7.2160 g., 0.9170 Gold .2126 oz. AGW **Subject:** 75th Anniversary - Battle of Gallipoli

Date	Mintage	F	VF	XF	Unc
ND(1990) Proof	Est. 494	Value: 325			

KM# 1008 500000 LIRA
7.1300 g., 0.9000 Gold .2063 oz. AGW **Subject:** Yunus Emre **Obverse:** Value within wreath **Reverse:** Inscription and arched brick facade

Date	Mintage	F	VF	XF	Unc
1991 Proof	288	Value: 320			

KM# 1017 500000 LIRA
7.1400 g., 0.9000 Gold .2066 oz. AGW **Subject:** 100 Years of Peace and Harmony - Turkish Jews **Obverse:** Value within wreath **Reverse:** Standing figures next to ship

Date	Mintage	F	VF	XF	Unc
ND(1992) Proof	485	Value: 320			

KM# 1032 500000 LIRA
7.2160 g., 0.9166 Gold .2126 oz. AGW **Subject:** Southeast Anatolian Project **Obverse:** Value within wreath **Reverse:** Design within wreath

Date	Mintage	F	VF	XF	Unc
ND(1994) Proof	950	Value: 300			

700 TURKEY

KM# 1034 500000 LIRA
7.2160 g., 0.9166 Gold .2126 oz. AGW **Subject:** 75th Anniversary - Turkish National Assembly **Obverse:** Value and date within wreath **Reverse:** Building in front of upright designs

Date	Mintage	F	VF	XF	Unc
1995 Proof	255	Value: 300			

KM# 1036 500000 LIRA
7.2160 g., 0.9166 Gold .2126 oz. AGW **Subject:** Istanbul Gold Exchange **Obverse:** Value and date within wreath **Reverse:** AR above inscription and date

Date	Mintage	F	VF	XF	Unc
1995 Proof	271	Value: 300			

KM# 1039 500000 LIRA
7.2160 g., 0.9166 Gold .2126 oz. AGW **Obverse:** Value and date within wreath **Reverse:** Sailing ship - "Piri Reis"

Date	Mintage	F	VF	XF	Unc
1995 Proof	1,904	Value: 300			

KM# 1066 1000000 LIRA
1.2441 g., 0.9990 Gold .0400 oz. AGW **Obverse:** Value in wreath **Reverse:** Head of King Croesus of Lydia right **Edge:** Reeded **Mint:** Istanbul

Date	Mintage	F	VF	XF	Unc
1997 Proof	10,465	Value: 45.00			

KM# 1067 1000000 LIRA
1.2441 g., 0.9990 Gold **Obverse:** Value and date within wreath **Reverse:** Ancient Lydian coin portraying lion

Date	Mintage	F	VF	XF	Unc
1997 Proof	3,848	Value: 45.00			

KM# 1097 60000000 LIRA
15.0000 g., 0.9167 Gold .4921 oz. AGW **Subject:** 700th Anniversary - The Ottoman Empire **Obverse:** Value within wreath **Reverse:** Ottoman coat of arms **Edge:** Reeded **Mint:** Istanbul

Date	Mintage	F	VF	XF	Unc
1999 Proof	1,904	Value: 400			

GOLD BULLION COINAGE

Since 1943, the Turkish government has issued regular and deluxe gold coins in five denominations corresponding to the old traditional 25, 50, 100, 250, and 500 Kurus of the Ottoman period. The regular coins are all dated 1923, plus the year of the republic (e.g. 1923/40 = 1963), de Luxe coins bear actual AD dates. For a few years, 1944-1950, the bust of Ismet Inonu replaced that of Kemal Ataturk.

KM# 850 25 KURUSH
1.8041 g., 0.9170 Gold .0532 oz. AGW, 15 mm. **Obverse:** Head of Ismet Inonu

Date	Mintage	F	VF	XF	Unc
1923/20	—	BV	50.00	65.00	90.00
1923/22	3,228	BV	50.00	75.00	120
1923/23	2,757	BV	50.00	75.00	120
1923/24	46,000	BV	50.00	65.00	90.00
1923/25	20,000	BV	50.00	70.00	110
1923/26	11,000	BV	50.00	70.00	110

KM# 851 25 KURUSH
1.8041 g., 0.9170 Gold .0532 oz. AGW **Obverse:** Head of Ataturk left **Reverse:** Legend and date within wreath

Date	Mintage	F	VF	XF	Unc
1923/20	14,000	—	BV	40.00	55.00
1923/27	18,000	—	BV	40.00	55.00
1923/28	15,000	—	BV	40.00	55.00
1923/29	15,000	—	BV	40.00	55.00
1923/30	17,000	—	BV	40.00	55.00
1923/31	19,000	—	BV	40.00	55.00
1923/32	5,455	—	BV	40.00	55.00
1923/33	11,000	—	BV	40.00	55.00
1923/34	20,000	—	BV	40.00	55.00
1923/35	25,000	—	BV	40.00	55.00
1923/36	34,000	—	BV	40.00	55.00
1923/37	31,000	—	BV	40.00	55.00
1923/38	35,000	—	BV	40.00	55.00
1923/39	46,000	—	BV	40.00	55.00
1923/40	49,000	—	BV	40.00	55.00
1923/41	59,000	—	BV	40.00	55.00
1923/42	74,000	—	BV	40.00	55.00
1923/43	90,000	—	BV	40.00	55.00
1923/44	85,000	—	BV	40.00	55.00
1923/45	73,000	—	BV	40.00	55.00
1923/46	89,000	—	BV	40.00	55.00
1923/47	119,000	—	BV	40.00	55.00
1923/48	112,000	—	BV	40.00	55.00
1923/49	112,000	—	BV	40.00	55.00
1923/50	67,000	—	BV	40.00	55.00
1923/51	40,000	—	BV	40.00	55.00
1923/52	71,000	—	BV	40.00	55.00
1923/53	124,000	—	BV	40.00	55.00
1923/54	196	—	BV	40.00	55.00
1923/55	112,000	—	BV	40.00	55.00
1923/56	—	—	BV	40.00	55.00
1923/57	—	—	BV	40.00	55.00
1923/60	—	—	BV	40.00	55.00
1923/64	—	—	BV	40.00	55.00
1923/65	—	—	BV	40.00	55.00
1923/66	—	—	BV	40.00	55.00

KM# 870 25 KURUSH
1.7540 g., 0.9170 Gold .0517 oz. AGW **Series:** Monnaie de Luxe **Obverse:** Head of Atatürk left **Reverse:** Country name and date in ornate monogram within circle of stars, floral border surrounds

Date	Mintage	F	VF	XF	Unc
1942	138	—	50.00	75.00	150
1943	386	—	50.00	75.00	125
1944	811	—	50.00	75.00	125
1946	235	—	50.00	75.00	150
1950	2,053	—	BV	45.00	60.00
1951	2,035	—	BV	45.00	60.00
1952	3,374	—	BV	45.00	60.00
1953	1,944	—	BV	45.00	60.00
1954	2,244	—	BV	45.00	60.00
1955	2,573	—	BV	45.00	60.00
1956	4,004	—	BV	45.00	60.00
1957	8,842	—	BV	45.00	60.00
1958	9,546	—	BV	45.00	60.00
1959	17,000	—	BV	40.00	55.00
1960	19,000	—	BV	40.00	55.00
1961	35,000	—	BV	40.00	55.00
1962	31,000	—	BV	40.00	55.00
1963	47,000	—	BV	40.00	55.00
1964	57,000	—	BV	40.00	55.00
1965	78,000	—	BV	40.00	55.00
1966	106,000	—	BV	40.00	55.00
1967	114,000	—	BV	40.00	55.00
1968	152,000	—	BV	40.00	55.00
1969	163,000	—	BV	40.00	55.00
1970	224,000	—	BV	40.00	55.00
1971	306,000	—	BV	40.00	55.00
1972	271,000	—	BV	40.00	55.00
1973	162,000	—	BV	40.00	55.00
1974	141,000	—	BV	40.00	55.00
1975	202,000	—	BV	40.00	55.00
1976	583,000	—	BV	40.00	55.00
1977	1,089,000	—	BV	40.00	55.00
1978	238,000	—	BV	40.00	55.00
1980	—	—	BV	40.00	55.00

KM# 875 25 KURUSH
1.7540 g., 0.9170 Gold .0517 oz. AGW **Series:** Monnaie de Luxe **Obverse:** Head of Ismet Inonu left

Date	Mintage	F	VF	XF	Unc
1943	—	70.00	90.00	140	200
Note: Mintage included in KM#870					
1944	—	70.00	90.00	140	200
Note: Mintage included in KM#870					
1945	592	70.00	90.00	140	200
1946	—	70.00	90.00	140	200
Note: Mintage included in KM#870					
1947	3,443	70.00	90.00	125	185
1948	714	70.00	90.00	140	200
1949	552	70.00	90.00	140	200

KM# 852 50 KURUSH
3.6083 g., 0.9170 Gold .1063 oz. AGW, 18 mm. **Obverse:** Head of Ismet Inonu left

Date	Mintage	F	VF	XF	Unc
1923/20	—	BV	95.00	125	175
1923/22	1,093	BV	95.00	125	175
1923/23	897	BV	120	140	200
1923/24	11,000	BV	95.00	125	175
1923/25	3,004	BV	95.00	125	175
1923/26	817	BV	120	140	200
1923/27	5,228	BV	95.00	125	175

KM# 853 50 KURUSH
3.6083 g., 0.9170 Gold .1063 oz. AGW **Obverse:** Head of Atatürk left **Reverse:** Legend and date within wreath

Date	Mintage	F	VF	XF	Unc
1923/20	12,000	—	BV	75.00	90.00
1923/27	Inc. above	—	BV	75.00	90.00
1923/28	3,300	—	BV	75.00	90.00
1923/29	6,384	—	BV	75.00	90.00
1923/30	4,590	—	BV	75.00	90.00
1923/31	9,068	—	BV	75.00	90.00
1923/32	4,344	—	BV	75.00	90.00
1923/33	3,958	—	BV	75.00	90.00
1923/34	9,499	—	BV	75.00	90.00
1923/35	9,307	—	BV	75.00	90.00
1923/36	12,000	—	BV	75.00	90.00
1923/37	9,049	—	BV	75.00	90.00
1923/38	9,854	—	BV	75.00	90.00
1923/39	11,000	—	BV	75.00	90.00
1923/40	13,000	—	BV	75.00	90.00
1923/41	13,000	—	BV	75.00	90.00
1923/42	18,000	—	BV	75.00	90.00
1923/43	26,000	—	BV	75.00	90.00
1923/44	26,000	—	BV	75.00	90.00
1923/45	25,000	—	BV	75.00	90.00
1923/46	28,000	—	BV	75.00	90.00
1923/47	38,000	—	BV	75.00	90.00
1923/48	35,000	—	BV	75.00	90.00
1923/49	28,000	—	BV	75.00	90.00
1923/50	16,000	—	BV	75.00	90.00
1923/51	8,000	—	BV	75.00	90.00
1923/52	14,000	—	BV	75.00	90.00
1923/53	28,000	—	BV	75.00	90.00
1923/54	54,000	—	BV	75.00	90.00
1923/55	16,000	—	BV	75.00	90.00
1923/57	—	—	BV	75.00	90.00
1923/65	—	—	BV	75.00	90.00
1923/66	—	—	BV	75.00	90.00

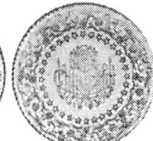

KM# 871 50 KURUSH
3.5080 g., 0.9170 Gold .1034 oz. AGW **Series:** Monnaie de Luxe **Obverse:** Head of Kemal Atatürk left within circle of stars, wreath surrounds **Reverse:** Country name and date in ornate monogram within circle of stars, floral border surrounds

Date	Mintage	F	VF	XF	Unc
1942	115	100	150	200	250
1943	91	100	150	200	250
1944	950	80.00	120	140	175
1946	565	80.00	120	140	175
1950	1,971	—	BV	80.00	140
1951	1,780	—	BV	80.00	140
1952	2,557	—	BV	80.00	140
1953	2,392	—	BV	80.00	140
1954	1,714	—	BV	80.00	140
1955	4,143	—	BV	75.00	115
1956	2,956	—	BV	75.00	115
1957	6,855	—	BV	75.00	115
1958	6,381	—	BV	75.00	115
1959	12,000	—	—	BV	75.00
1960	12,000	—	—	BV	75.00
1961	15,000	—	—	BV	75.00
1962	22,000	—	—	BV	75.00
1963	29,000	—	—	BV	75.00
1964	34,000	—	—	BV	75.00
1965	44,000	—	—	BV	75.00
1966	58,000	—	—	BV	75.00
1967	64,000	—	—	BV	75.00
1968	82,000	—	—	BV	75.00
1969	79,000	—	—	BV	75.00
1970	109,000	—	—	BV	75.00
1971	154,000	—	—	BV	75.00
1972	110,000	—	—	BV	75.00
1973	73,000	—	—	BV	75.00
1974	45,000	—	—	BV	75.00
1975	72,000	—	—	BV	75.00

TURKEY

Date	Mintage	F	VF	XF	Unc
1976	196,000	—	—	BV	75.00
1977	361,000	—	—	BV	75.00
1978	161,000	—	—	BV	75.00
1980	—	—	—	BV	75.00

KM# 876 50 KURUSH
3.5080 g., 0.9170 Gold .1034 oz. AGW **Series:** Monnaie de Luxe **Obverse:** Head of Ismet Inonu left

Date	Mintage	F	VF	XF	Unc
1943	—	—	150	200	250

Note: Mintage included in KM#871

| 1944 | — | — | 120 | 170 | 220 |

Note: Mintage included in KM#871

| 1946 | — | — | 90.00 | 140 | 190 |

Note: Mintage included in KM#871

1947	3,481	—	90.00	140	190
1948	773	—	90.00	140	190
1949	582	—	90.00	140	190

KM# 872 100 KURUSH
7.0160 g., 0.9170 Gold .2069 oz. AGW **Series:** Monnaie de Luxe **Obverse:** Head of Atatürk left within circle of stars, wreath surrounds **Reverse:** Country name and date in ornate monogram within circle of stars, floral border surrounds

Date	Mintage	F	VF	XF	Unc
1942	8,659	—	145	160	225
1943	6,594	—	145	160	225
1944	7,160	—	145	160	225
1948	14,000	—	145	160	200
1950	25,000	—	145	160	200
1951	35,000	—	145	160	185
1952	41,000	—	145	160	185
1953	32,000	—	145	160	185
1954	24,000	—	145	160	185
1955	4,881	—	145	160	200
1956	11,000	—	BV	145	160
1957	49,000	—	BV	145	160
1958	67,000	—	BV	145	160
1959	89,000	—	BV	145	160
1960	57,000	—	BV	145	160
1961	77,000	—	BV	145	160
1962	108,000	—	BV	145	160
1963	146,000	—	BV	145	160
1964	128,000	—	BV	145	160
1965	157,000	—	BV	145	160
1966	190,000	—	BV	145	160
1967	177,000	—	BV	145	160
1968	143,000	—	BV	145	160
1969	206,000	—	BV	145	160
1970	253,000	—	BV	145	160
1971	293,000	—	BV	145	160
1972	222,000	—	BV	145	160
1973	140,000	—	BV	145	160
1974	82,000	—	BV	145	160
1975	142,000	—	BV	145	160
1976	265,000	—	BV	145	160
1977	277,000	—	BV	145	160
1978	86,000	—	BV	145	160
1980	—	—	BV	145	160

KM# 877 100 KURUSH
7.0160 g., 0.9170 Gold .2069 oz. AGW, 22 mm. **Series:** Monnaie de Luxe **Obverse:** Head of Ismet Inonu left

Date	Mintage	F	VF	XF	Unc
1943	—	150	190	265	325

Note: Mintage included in KM#872

| 1944 | — | 150 | 190 | 265 | 375 |

Note: Mintage included in KM#872

1945	2,202	150	190	265	400
1946	8,863	150	190	265	325
1947	28,000	150	190	265	325
1948	—	150	190	265	325

Note: Mintage included in KM#872

| 1949 | 6,578 | 150 | 190 | 265 | 325 |
| 1950 | — | 150 | 190 | 265 | 325 |

Note: Mintage included in KM#872

KM# 854 100 KURUSH
7.2160 g., 0.9170 Gold .2126 oz. AGW **Obverse:** Head of Ismet Inonu left **Reverse:** legend and date within wreath

Date	Mintage	F	VF	XF	Unc
1923/20	—	—	BV	150	165
1923/22 Rare	3	—	—	—	—
1923/23	381,000	—	BV	150	165
1923/24	2,274	—	BV	155	175
1923/25	28,000	—	BV	150	165
1923/26	2,097	—	BV	155	175
1923/27	17,000	—	BV	150	165

KM# 855 100 KURUSH
7.2160 g., 0.9170 Gold .2126 oz. AGW **Obverse:** Head of Atatürk left **Reverse:** Legend and date within wreath

Date	Mintage	F	VF	XF	Unc
1923/20	29,000	—	—	BV	150
1923/27	Inc. above	—	—	BV	150
1923/28 Rare	3	—	—	—	—
1923/29	2,111	—	—	BV	150
1923/30	13,000	—	—	BV	150
1923/31	109,000	—	—	BV	150
1923/32	134,000	—	—	BV	150
1923/33	216,000	—	—	BV	150
1923/34	463,000	—	—	BV	150
1923/35	405,000	—	—	BV	150
1923/36	25,000	—	—	BV	150
1923/37	131,000	—	—	BV	150
1923/38	159,000	—	—	BV	150
1923/39	85,000	—	—	BV	150
1923/40	10,000	—	—	BV	150
1923/41	164,000	—	—	BV	150
1923/42	63,000	—	—	BV	150
1923/43	56,000	—	—	BV	150
1923/44	198,000	—	—	BV	150
1923/45	176,000	—	—	BV	150
1923/46	1,290,000	—	—	BV	150
1923/47	513,000	—	—	BV	150
1923/48	600	—	—	BV	165
1923/49	1,300	—	—	BV	150
1923/50	47,000	—	—	BV	150
1923/51	240,000	—	—	BV	150
1923/52	1,046,999	—	—	BV	150
1923/53	550,000	—	—	BV	150
1923/54	18,000	—	—	BV	150
1923/55	309,000	—	—	BV	150
1923/57	—	—	—	BV	150
1923/58	—	—	—	BV	150
1923/59	—	—	—	BV	150
1923/60	—	—	—	BV	150
1923/61	—	—	—	BV	150
1923/62	—	—	—	BV	150
1923/63	—	—	—	BV	150
1923/64	—	—	—	BV	150
1923/65	—	—	—	BV	150

KM# 873 250 KURUSH
17.5400 g., 0.9170 Gold .5169 oz. AGW **Series:** Monnaie de Luxe **Obverse:** Head of Atatürk left within circle of stars, wreath surrounds **Reverse:** Country name and date in ornate monogram within circle of stars, floral border surrounds

Date	Mintage	F	VF	XF	Unc
1942	10,000	—	385	425	600
1943	11,000	—	385	425	600
1944	15,000	—	385	650	900
1946	16,000	—	385	650	900
1947	42,000	—	385	425	600
1950	13,000	—	385	425	600
1950	45,000	—	385	425	600
1951	41,000	—	—	BV	375
1952	59,000	—	—	BV	375
1953	45,000	—	—	BV	375
1954	40,000	—	—	BV	375
1955	7,067	—	—	BV	375
1956	14,000	—	—	BV	375
1957	47,000	—	—	BV	375
1958	75,000	—	—	BV	375
1959	93,000	—	—	BV	375
1960	50,000	—	—	BV	375
1961	65,000	—	—	BV	375
1962	99,000	—	—	BV	375
1963	137,000	—	—	BV	375
1964	152,000	—	—	BV	375
1965	194,000	—	—	BV	375
1966	218,000	—	—	BV	375
1967	201,000	—	—	BV	375
1968	150,000	—	—	BV	375
1969	262,000	—	—	BV	375
1970	301,000	—	—	BV	375
1971	356,000	—	—	BV	375
1972	305,000	—	—	BV	375
1973	198,000	—	—	BV	375
1974	142,000	—	—	BV	375
1975	223,000	—	—	BV	375
1976	345,000	—	—	BV	375
1977	227,000	—	—	BV	375
1978	311,000	—	—	BV	375
1980	—	—	—	BV	375

KM# 878 250 KURUSH
17.5400 g., 0.9170 Gold .5169 oz. AGW, 27 mm. **Series:** Monnaie de Luxe **Obverse:** Head of Ismet Inonu left

Date	Mintage	F	VF	XF	Unc
1943	—	—	—	BV	375

Note: Mintage included in KM#873

| 1944 | — | — | — | BV | 375 |

Note: Mintage included in KM#873

| 1945 | 4,135 | — | — | 385 | 550 |
| 1946 | — | — | — | BV | 375 |

Note: Mintage included in KM#873

| 1947 | — | — | — | BV | 375 |

Note: Mintage included in KM#873

| 1948 | — | — | — | BV | 375 |

Note: Mintage included in KM#873

| 1949 | 11,000 | — | — | BV | 375 |
| 1950 | — | — | — | BV | 375 |

Note: Mintage included in KM#873

KM# 856 250 KURUSH
18.0400 g., 0.9170 Gold .5319 oz. AGW **Obverse:** Head of Ismet Inonu left

Date	Mintage	F	VF	XF	Unc
1923/20	—	—	BV	395	425
1923/23	14,000	—	BV	395	425
1923/24	60	—	BV	425	525

KM# 857 250 KURUSH
18.0400 g., 0.9170 Gold .5319 oz. AGW **Obverse:** Head of Atatürk left

Date	Mintage	F	VF	XF	Unc
1923/20	10,000	—	—	BV	400
1923/29 Rare	3	—	—	—	—
1923/30	130	—	450	700	900
1923/31	—	—	450	700	900
1923/38	245	—	395	425	600
1923/39	389	—	395	425	600
1923/40	435	—	395	425	600
1923/41	349	—	395	425	600
1923/42	460	—	395	425	600
1923/43	1,008	—	BV	395	425
1923/44	712	—	BV	395	425
1923/45	1,034	—	BV	395	425
1923/46	1,035	—	BV	395	425
1923/47	1,408	—	BV	395	425
1923/48	904	—	BV	395	425
1923/49	1,066	—	BV	395	425
1923/50	975	—	BV	395	425
1923/51	298	—	BV	395	425
1923/52	610	—	BV	395	425
1923/53	586	—	BV	395	425
1923/54	289	—	BV	395	425
1923/55	267	—	BV	395	425
1923/57	—	—	BV	395	425
1923/70	—	—	BV	395	425

KM# 858 500 KURUSH
36.0800 g., 0.9170 Gold 1.0638 oz. AGW, 35 mm. **Obverse:** Head of Ismet Inonu left **Reverse:** Legend and date within wreath

TURKEY

Date	Mintage	F	VF	XF	Unc
1923/20	—	—	BV	750	850
1923/23	9,006	—	BV	750	850
1923/24	7,923	—	750	850	1,000
1923/25	272	—	800	950	1,100

KM# 859 500 KURUSH
36.0800 g., 0.9170 Gold 1.0638 oz. AGW **Obverse:** Head of Atatürk left **Reverse:** Legend and date within wreath

Date	Mintage	F	VF	XF	Unc
1923/20	12,000	—	BV	750	800
1923/27	615	—	BV	850	1,000
1923/28	34	—	BV	850	1,000
1923/29	137	—	BV	800	950
1923/30	45	—	BV	800	950
1923/31	100	—	BV	800	950
1923/32	74	—	BV	800	950
1923/33	268	—	BV	750	850
1923/34	758	—	BV	750	850
1923/35	1,586	—	—	BV	750
1923/36	765	—	—	BV	750
1923/37	983	—	—	BV	750
1923/38	1,738	—	—	BV	750
1923/39	2,629	—	—	BV	750
1923/40	2,763	—	—	BV	750
1923/41	3,440	—	—	BV	750
1923/42	3,335	—	—	BV	750
1923/43	4,914	—	—	BV	750
1923/44	4,308	—	—	BV	750
1923/45	3,488	—	—	BV	750
1923/46	5,636	—	—	BV	750
1923/47	7,588	—	—	BV	750
1923/48	6,060	—	—	BV	750
1923/49	4,235	—	—	BV	750
1923/50	4,733	—	—	BV	750
1923/51	2,757	—	—	BV	750
1923/52	2,041	—	—	BV	750
1923/53	4,819	—	—	BV	750
1923/54	1,401	—	—	BV	750
1923/55	1,484	—	—	BV	750
1923/57	—	—	—	BV	750
1923/69	—	—	—	BV	750

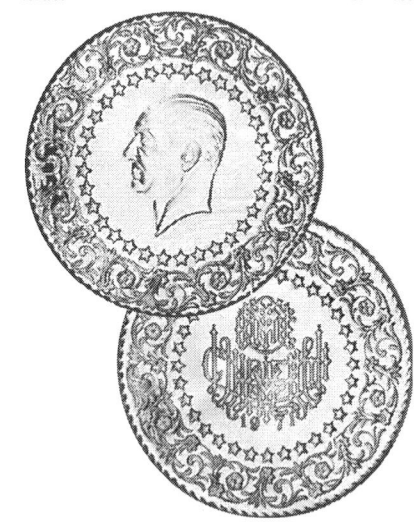

KM# 874 500 KURUSH
35.0800 g., 0.9170 Gold 1.0338 oz. AGW **Series:** Monnaie de Luxe **Obverse:** Head of Atatürk left within circle of stars, wreath surrounds **Reverse:** Country name and date in ornate monogram within circle of stars, floral border surrounds

Date	Mintage	F	VF	XF	Unc
1942	2,949	—	—	BV	745
1943	1,210	—	—	BV	745
1944	1,254	—	—	BV	745
1947	3,699	—	—	BV	745
1950	59	—	—	BV	760
1951	21	—	—	BV	760
1952	26	—	—	BV	760
1953	35	—	—	BV	760
1954	182	—	—	BV	760
1955	14	—	—	BV	760
1956	13	—	—	BV	760
1957	68	—	—	BV	760
1958	121	—	—	BV	760
1959	294	—	—	BV	760
1960	208	—	—	BV	760
1961	619	—	—	BV	745
1962	1,228	—	—	BV	745
1963	1,985	—	—	BV	745
1964	2,787	—	—	BV	745
1965	4,631	—	—	BV	745
1966	5,572	—	—	BV	745
1967	6,637	—	—	BV	745
1968	5,983	—	—	BV	745
1969	7,152	—	—	BV	745
1970	11,000	—	—	BV	745
1971	15,000	—	—	BV	745
1972	15,000	—	—	BV	745
1973	7,939	—	—	BV	745
1974	5,412	—	—	BV	745
1975	6,205	—	—	BV	745
1976	11,000	—	—	BV	745
1977	6,931	—	—	BV	745
1978	5,740	—	—	BV	745
1980	—	—	—	BV	745

KM# 879 500 KURUSH
35.0800 g., 0.9170 Gold 1.0338 oz. AGW **Series:** Monnaie de Luxe **Obverse:** Head of Ismet Inonu left within circle of stars **Reverse:** Country name and date in ornate monogram within circle of stars, floral border surrounds

Date	Mintage	F	VF	XF	Unc
1943	—	—	—	BV	745

Note: Mintage included in KM#874

| 1944 | — | — | — | BV | 745 |

Note: Mintage included in KM#874

1945	115	—	—	BV	745
1946	298	—	—	BV	745
1947	—	—	—	BV	745

Note: Mintage included in KM#874

| 1948 | 40 | — | — | BV | 745 |

PIEFORTS

KM#	Date	Mintage	Identification	Mkt Val
P3	1981	—	30000 Lira. Gold. . KM#955	1,350

MINT SETS

KM#	Date	Mintage	Identification	Issue Price	Mkt Val
MS34	2000 (4)	25,000	KM#881a, 884a, 885a, 886a Mixed dates; Gold Coin Nostalgia Set	325	325
MS35	2000 (7)	10,000	KM#860.1a, 881a, 884a, 885a, 886a, 893.1a, 905a Mixed dates; Silver and Gold Nostalgia Set	350	350

TURKS & CAICOS ISLANDS

The Colony of the Turks and Caicos Islands, a British colony situated in the West Indies at the eastern end of the Bahama Islands, has an area of 166 sq. mi. (430 sq.km.) and a population of *10,000. Capital: Cockburn Town, on Grand Turk. The principal industry of the colony is the production of salt, which is gathered by raking. Salt, crayfish, and conch shells are exported.

The Turks and Caicos Islands were discovered by Juan Ponce de Leon in 1512, but were not settled until 1678 when Bermudians arrived to rake salt from the salt ponds. The Spanish drove the British settlers from the island in 1710, during the long War of the Spanish Succession. They returned and throughout the remaining years of the war repulsed repeated attacks by France and Spain. In 1799 the islands were granted representation in the Bahamian assembly, but in 1848, on petition of the inhabitants, they were made a separate colony under Jamaica. They were annexed by Jamaica in 1873 and remained a dependency until 1959 when they became a unit territory of the Federation of the West Indies. When the Federation was dissolved in 1962, the Turks and Caicos Islands became a separate Crown Colony.

RULER
British

MONETARY SYSTEM
100 Cents = 1 East Caribbean Dollar
1 Crown = 1 Dollar U.S.A.

CROWN COLONY

STANDARD COINAGE

KM# 234 5 CROWNS
3.1104 g., 0.9995 Platinum 0.1 oz. APW, 16.5 mm. **Ruler:** Elizabeth II **Subject:** ANA Salute to Coin Collecting **Obv:** Crowned head right **Rev:** Astronaut on the moon **Edge:** Reeded

Date	Mintage	F	VF	XF	Unc	BU
1994 Proof	200	Value: 145				

KM# 238 5 CROWNS
1.5600 g., 0.9999 Gold 0.0502 oz. AGW, 13.7 mm. **Ruler:** Elizabeth II **Obv:** Crowned head right **Rev:** Two Bottle-nosed Dolphins **Edge:** Reeded

Date	Mintage	F	VF	XF	Unc	BU
1998 Proof	—	Value: 50.00				

KM# 9.1 25 CROWNS
4.5000 g., 0.5000 Gold .0723 oz. AGW **Ruler:** Elizabeth II **Obv:** Young bust right **Obv. Designer:** Arnold Machin **Rev:** National arms

Date	Mintage	F	VF	XF	Unc	BU
1975	1,272	—	—	—	50.00	60.00
1975 Proof	2,096	Value: 60.00				

KM# 9.2 25 CROWNS
4.5000 g., 0.5000 Gold .0723 oz. AGW, 19 mm. **Ruler:** Elizabeth II **Obv:** Young bust right **Obv. Designer:** Arnold Machin **Rev:** National arms

Date	Mintage	F	VF	XF	Unc	BU
1976	—	—	—	—	50.00	60.00
1976 Proof	2,185	Value: 60.00				
1977 Proof	2,125	Value: 60.00				

KM# 3 50 CROWNS
9.0000 g., 0.5000 Gold .1447 oz. AGW **Ruler:** Elizabeth II **Subject:** Centenary - Birth of Churchill **Obv:** National arms **Rev:** Bust 1/4 left

TURKS & CAICOS ISLANDS

Rev. Designer: Michael Rizzello **Edge Lettering:** REDEEMABLE AT TURKS AND CAICOS FOR U.S. CURRENCY

Date	Mintage	F	VF	XF	Unc	BU
1974 Matte	30,000	—	—	—	100	110
1974 Proof	4,000	Value: 120				

KM# 10 50 CROWNS
6.2200 g., 0.5000 Gold .1 oz. AGW **Ruler:** Elizabeth II **Subject:** Age of Exploration **Obv:** Young bust right **Obv. Designer:** Arnold Machin **Rev:** Head od Christopher Columbus right and 3 ships

Date	Mintage	F	VF	XF	Unc	BU
1975	2,863	—	—	—	80.00	90.00
1975 Proof	1,577	Value: 100				

KM# 15 50 CROWNS
6.2200 g., 0.5000 Gold .1 oz. AGW **Ruler:** Elizabeth II **Subject:** U.S. Bicentennial **Obv:** Young bust right **Obv. Designer:** Arnold Machin **Rev:** Cameos facing each other below flags and crossed scepter and sword

Date	Mintage	F	VF	XF	Unc	BU
1976	905	—	—	—	100	110
1976 Proof	2,421	Value: 90.00				

KM# 20 50 CROWNS
9.0000 g., 0.5000 Gold .1447 oz. AGW **Ruler:** Elizabeth II **Subject:** Queen's Silver Jubilee **Obv:** Young bust right **Obv. Designer:** Arnold Machin **Rev:** Crown and date within sprigs above banner

Date	Mintage	F	VF	XF	Unc	BU
1977	—	—	—	—	100	110
1977 Proof	2,903	Value: 120				

KM# 34 50 CROWNS
9.0000 g., 0.5000 Gold .1447 oz. AGW **Ruler:** Elizabeth II **Subject:** 25th Anniversary of Coronation **Obv:** Young bust right **Rev:** Lion of England right

Date	Mintage	F	VF	XF	Unc	BU
1978 Proof	261	Value: 175				

KM# 35 50 CROWNS
9.0000 g., 0.5000 Gold .1447 oz. AGW **Ruler:** Elizabeth II **Obv:** Young bust right **Rev:** Griffin of Edward III left

Date	Mintage	F	VF	XF	Unc	BU
1978 Proof	266	Value: 175				

KM# 36 50 CROWNS
9.0000 g., 0.5000 Gold .1447 oz. AGW **Ruler:** Elizabeth II **Obv:** Young bust right **Rev:** Red Dragon of Wales left

Date	Mintage	F	VF	XF	Unc	BU
1978 Proof	266	Value: 175				

KM# 37 50 CROWNS
9.0000 g., 0.5000 Gold .1447 oz. AGW **Ruler:** Elizabeth II **Obv:** Young bust right **Rev:** White Greyhound of Richmond

Date	Mintage	F	VF	XF	Unc	BU
1978 Proof	270	Value: 175				

KM# 38 50 CROWNS
9.0000 g., 0.5000 Gold .1447 oz. AGW **Ruler:** Elizabeth II **Obv:** Young bust right **Rev:** The Unicorn of Scotland right

Date	Mintage	F	VF	XF	Unc	BU
1978 Proof	268	Value: 175				

KM# 39 50 CROWNS
9.0000 g., 0.5000 Gold .1447 oz. AGW **Ruler:** Elizabeth II **Obv:** Young bust right **Rev:** White Horse of Hannover left

Date	Mintage	F	VF	XF	Unc	BU
1978 Proof	266	Value: 175				

KM# 40 50 CROWNS
9.0000 g., 0.5000 Gold .1447 oz. AGW **Ruler:** Elizabeth II **Obv:** Young bust right **Rev:** Black Bull of Clarence Left

Date	Mintage	F	VF	XF	Unc	BU
1978 Proof	269	Value: 175				

KM# 41 50 CROWNS
9.0000 g., 0.5000 Gold .1447 oz. AGW **Ruler:** Elizabeth II **Obv:** Young bust right **Rev:** Yale of Beaufort left

Date	Mintage	F	VF	XF	Unc	BU
1978 Proof	254	Value: 175				

KM# 42 50 CROWNS
9.0000 g., 0.5000 Gold .1447 oz. AGW **Ruler:** Elizabeth II **Obv:** Young bust right **Obv. Designer:** Arnold Machin **Rev:** Falcon of the Plantagenets right

Date	Mintage	F	VF	XF	Unc	BU
1978 Proof	265	Value: 175				

KM# 43 50 CROWNS
9.0000 g., 0.5000 Gold .1447 oz. AGW **Ruler:** Elizabeth II **Obv:** Young bust right **Obv. Designer:** Arnold Machin **Rev:** White Lion of Mortimer left

Date	Mintage	F	VF	XF	Unc	BU
1978 Proof	265	Value: 175				

KM# 4 100 CROWNS
18.0150 g., 0.5000 Gold .2896 oz. AGW **Ruler:** Elizabeth II **Subject:** Birth of Churchill Centenary **Obv:** National arms **Rev:** Bust 1/4 left

Date	Mintage	F	VF	XF	Unc	BU
1974	4,500	—	—	—	200	210
1974 Proof	5,100	Value: 210				

KM# 11 100 CROWNS
12.4400 g., 0.5000 Gold .2000 oz. AGW **Ruler:** Elizabeth II **Subject:** Age of Exploration **Obv:** Young bust right **Obv. Designer:** Arnold Machin **Rev:** Spacecraft flying around globe

Date	Mintage	F	VF	XF	Unc	BU
1975	756	—	—	—	145	150
1975 Proof	1,508	Value: 135				

KM# 17 100 CROWNS
18.0150 g., 0.5000 Gold .2896 oz. AGW **Ruler:** Elizabeth II **Obv:** Young bust right **Obv. Designer:** Arnold Machin **Rev:** 4 Vicoria cameos left

Date	Mintage	F	VF	XF	Unc	BU
1976	250	—	—	—	215	220
1976 Proof	350	Value: 225				
1977	1,655	—	—	—	210	215
1977 Proof	2,648	Value: 220				

KM# 22 100 CROWNS
18.0150 g., 0.5000 Gold .2896 oz. AGW **Ruler:** Elizabeth II **Obv:** Young bust right **Obv. Designer:** Arnold Machin **Rev:** 4 George III cameos right

Date	Mintage	F	VF	XF	Unc	BU
1977	—	—	—	—	215	220
1977 Proof	844	Value: 225				

KM# 44 100 CROWNS
18.0150 g., 0.5000 Gold .2896 oz. AGW **Ruler:** Elizabeth II **Subject:** XI Commonwealth Games

Date	Mintage	F	VF	XF	Unc	BU
1978 Proof	540	Value: 250				

KM# 46 100 CROWNS
18.0150 g., 0.5000 Gold .2896 oz. AGW **Ruler:** Elizabeth II **Subject:** 10th Anniversary - Prince Charles' Investiture **Obv:** Young bust right **Obv. Designer:** Arnold Machin **Rev:** Head of Prince Charles facing left at right with crown, crossed sword and sceptre at left

Date	Mintage	F	VF	XF	Unc	BU
1979	10,000	—	—	—	210	215

KM# 50 100 CROWNS
12.9600 g., 0.5000 Gold .2083 oz. AGW **Ruler:** Elizabeth II **Subject:** Lord Mountbatten **Obv:** Crowned bust right **Rev:** Bust 1/4 right flanked by dates

Date	Mintage	F	VF	XF	Unc	BU
1980 Proof	—	Value: 155				

TURKS & CAICOS ISLANDS

KM# 54 100 CROWNS
6.4800 g., 0.9000 Gold .1875 oz. AGW **Ruler:** Elizabeth II **Subject:** Wedding of Princes Charles and Lady Diana **Rev:** Conjoined busts left

Date	Mintage	F	VF	XF	Unc	BU
1981 Proof	1,205	Value: 135				

KM# 59 100 CROWNS
6.4800 g., 0.9000 Gold .1875 oz. AGW **Ruler:** Elizabeth II **Subject:** World Football Championship **Obv:** Young bust right **Obv. Designer:** Arnold Machin **Rev:** Football players

Date	Mintage	F	VF	XF	Unc	BU
1982 Proof	565	Value: 225				

KM# 62 100 CROWNS
7.1300 g., 0.9000 Gold .2063 oz. AGW **Ruler:** Elizabeth II **Series:** Decade for Women **Rev:** Half-length figure right

Date	Mintage	F	VF	XF	Unc	BU
1985 Proof	313	Value: 275				

KM# 65 100 CROWNS
10.0000 g., 0.9170 Gold .2949 oz. AGW **Ruler:** Elizabeth II **Series:** World Wildlife Fund **Obv:** Crowned bust right **Rev:** Spiny lobster

Date	Mintage	F	VF	XF	Unc	BU
1988 Proof	Est. 5,000	Value: 220				

KM# 237 100 CROWNS
155.5175 g., 0.9990 Gold Plated Silver 4.995 oz. ASW AGW, 63.7 mm. **Ruler:** Elizabeth II **Subject:** Queen's Golden Wedding Anniversary **Obv:** National arms **Rev:** Wedding portrait of Queen and Prince Philip **Edge:** Reeded and numbered **Note:** Photo reduced.

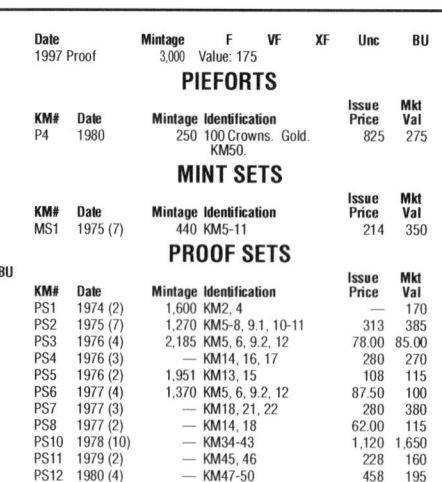

Date	Mintage	F	VF	XF	Unc	BU
1997 Proof	3,000	Value: 175				

PIEFORTS

KM#	Date	Mintage	Identification	Issue Price	Mkt Val
P4	1980	250	100 Crowns. Gold. KM50.	825	275

MINT SETS

KM#	Date	Mintage	Identification	Issue Price	Mkt Val
MS1	1975 (7)	440	KM5-11	214	350

PROOF SETS

KM#	Date	Mintage	Identification	Issue Price	Mkt Val
PS1	1974 (2)	1,600	KM2, 4	—	170
PS2	1975 (7)	1,270	KM5-8, 9.1, 10-11	313	385
PS3	1976 (4)	2,185	KM5, 6, 9.2, 12	78.00	85.00
PS4	1976 (3)	—	KM14, 16, 17	280	270
PS5	1976 (2)	1,951	KM13, 15	108	115
PS6	1977 (4)	1,370	KM5, 6, 9.2, 12	87.50	100
PS7	1977 (3)	—	KM18, 21, 22	280	380
PS8	1977 (2)	—	KM14, 18	62.00	115
PS10	1978 (10)	—	KM34-43	1,120	1,650
PS11	1979 (2)	—	KM45, 46	228	160
PS12	1980 (4)	—	KM47-50	458	195

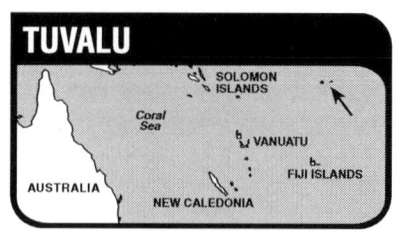

TUVALU

Tuvalu (formerly the Ellice or Lagoon Islands of the Gilbert and Ellice Islands), located in the South Pacific north of the Fiji Islands, has an area of 10 sq. mi. (26 sq.km.) and a population of *9,000. Capital: Funafuti. The independent state includes the islands of Nanumanga, Nanumea, Nui, Niutao, Viatupa, Funafuti, Nukufetau, Nukulailai and Nurakita. The latter four islands were claimed by the United States until relinquished by the Feb. 7, 1979, Treaty of Friendship signed by the United States and Tuvalu. The principal industries are copra production and phosphate mining.

The islands were discovered in 1764 by John Byron, a British navigator, and annexed by Britain in 1892. In 1915 they became part of the crown colony of the Gilbert and Ellice Islands. In 1974 the islanders voted to separate from the Gilberts, becoming on Jan. 1, 1976, the separate constitutional dependency of Tuvalu. Full independence was attained on Oct. 1, 1978. Tuvalu is a member of the Commonwealth of Nations. Elizabeth II is Head of State as Queen of Tuvalu.

RULER
British, until 1978

MONETARY SYSTEM
100 Cents = 1 Dollar

PARLIMENTARY DEMOCRACY
STANDARD COINAGE

KM# 9 50 DOLLARS
15.9800 g., 0.9170 Gold .4710 oz. AGW **Obv:** Young bust right **Rev:** Native meeting hut

Date	Mintage	F	VF	XF	Unc	BU
1976 Proof	2,074	Value: 345				

KM# 14 50 DOLLARS
15.9800 g., 0.9170 Gold .4710 oz. AGW **Subject:** Wedding of Prince Charles and Lady Diana **Obv:** Young bust right **Rev:** Three plumes within crown, value at right

Date	Mintage	F	VF	XF	Unc	BU
1981 Proof	5,000	Value: 335				

KM# 29 100 DOLLARS
7.7760 g., 0.5833 Gold .1458 oz. AGW **Subject:** 40th Anniversary of Coronation **Obv:** Crowned head right **Rev:** Coronation scene

Date	Mintage	F	VF	XF	Unc	BU
1993 Proof	—	Value: 110				

KM# 21 100 DOLLARS
7.7760 g., 0.5833 Gold .1458 oz. AGW **Subject:** Todos Los Santos

Date	Mintage	F	VF	XF	Unc	BU
1994 Proof	3,000	Value: 115				

KM# 23 100 DOLLARS
7.7760 g., 0.5833 Gold .1458 oz. AGW **Subject:** 1994 World Cup Soccer **Obv:** Crowned head right **Rev:** Soccer ball to upper left of eagle head and wing

Date	Mintage	F	VF	XF	Unc	BU
1994 Proof	3,000	Value: 120				

UGANDA

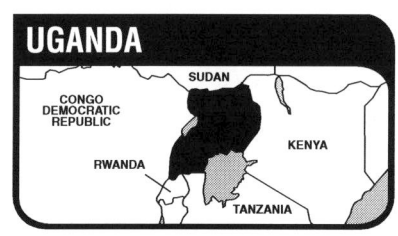

The Republic of Uganda, a former British protectorate located astride the equator in east-central Africa, has an area of 91,134 sq. mi. (236,040 sq. km.) and a population of *17 million. Capital: Kampala. Agriculture, including livestock, is the basis of the economy; there is some mining of copper, tin, gold and lead. Coffee, cotton, copper and tea are exported.

Uganda was first visited by Arab slavers in the 1830s. They were followed in the 1860s by British explorers searching for the headwaters of the Nile. The explorers, and the missionaries who followed them into the Lake Victoria region of south central Africa in 1877-79, found well-developed African kingdoms dating back several centuries. In 1894 the local native Kingdom of Buganda was established as a British protectorate that was extended in 1896 to encompass an area substantially the same as the present Republic of Uganda. The protectorate was given a ministerial form of government in 1955, full internal self-government on March 1, 1962, and complete independence on Oct. 9, 1962. Uganda is a member of the Commonwealth of Nations. The president is Chief of State and Head of Government.

For earlier coinage refer to East Africa.

RULER
British, until 1962

MONETARY SYSTEM
100 Cents = 1 Shilling

REPUBLIC

MEDALLIC

KM# M1 POUND
7.9800 g., 0.9170 Gold 0.2353 oz. AGW, 22 mm. **Subject:** OAU **Obv:** Idi Amin right **Rev:** Ugandan arms **Edge:** Reeded

Date	Mintage	F	VF	XF	Unc	BU
1975	2,000	—	—	—	350	—
1975 Proof	200	Value: 750				

STANDARD COINAGE

KM# 14 50 SHILLINGS
6.9100 g., 0.9000 Gold .1999 oz. AGW **Subject:** Visit of Pope Paul VI **Obv:** National arms **Rev:** Martyrs' shrine within circle

Date	Mintage	F	VF	XF	Unc	BU
1969 Proof	4,390	Value: 145				
1970 Proof	Inc. above	Value: 150				

KM# 15 100 SHILLINGS
13.8200 g., 0.9000 Gold .3999 oz. AGW **Subject:** Visit of Pope Paul VI **Obv:** National arms **Rev:** Bust right within map and circle

Date	Mintage	F	VF	XF	Unc	BU
1969 Proof	4,190	Value: 295				
1970 Proof	Inc. above	Value: 300				

KM# 16 500 SHILLINGS
69.1200 g., 0.9000 Gold 2.0002 oz. AGW **Subject:** Visit of Pope Paul VI **Obv:** National arms **Rev:** Bust with hat facing within world globe

Date	Mintage	F	VF	XF	Unc	BU
1969 Proof	1,680	Value: 1,425				
1970 Proof	Inc. above	Value: 1,450				

KM# 17 1000 SHILLINGS
138.2400 g., 0.9000 Gold 4.0005 oz. AGW **Subject:** Visit of Pope John Paul VI **Obv:** National arms **Rev:** Head right

Date	Mintage	F	VF	XF	Unc	BU
1969 Proof	1,390	Value: 2,825				
1970 Proof	Inc. above	Value: 2,850				

KM# 24 1000 SHILLINGS
10.0000 g., 0.5000 Gold .1607 oz. AGW **Subject:** Wedding of Prince Charles and Lady Diana **Obv:** National arms **Rev:** Conjoined busts right **Rev. Designer:** E.W. Roberts

Date	Mintage	F	VF	XF	Unc	BU
1981 Proof	1,500	Value: 125				

KM# 31 2000 SHILLINGS
15.9800 g., 0.9170 Gold .4710 oz. AGW **Series:** International Year of Disabled Persons **Obv:** National arms **Rev:** Stylized standing figure with cane

Date	Mintage	F	VF	XF	Unc	BU
1981	2,005	—	—	—	550	600
1981 Proof	2,005	Value: 700				

KM# 117 4000 SHILLINGS
1.5300 g., Gold, 16 mm. **Subject:** Famous Places **Obv:** Arms with supporters **Rev:** Matterhorn Mountain within circle **Edge:** Plain

Date	Mintage	F	VF	XF	Unc	BU
ND Proof	—	Value: 75.00				

KM# 25 5000 SHILLINGS
33.9300 g., 0.9170 Gold 1 oz. AGW **Subject:** Wildlife **Obv:** Bust of Dr. Milton Obote facing **Rev:** East African crowned crane

Date	Mintage	F	VF	XF	Unc	BU
1981	100	—	—	—	700	750
1981 Proof	100	Value: 775				

PIEFORTS

KM#	Date	Mintage	Identification	Mkt Val
P2	1981	505	2000 Shillings. 0.9170 Gold. KM31.	750

PROOF SETS

KM#	Date	Mintage	Identification	Issue Price	Mkt Val
PS2	1969 (10)	1,390	KM8-17	790	4,825
PS4	1970 (10)	I.A.	KM8-17, mintage included in KM-PS2	790	4,900

UKRAINE

Ukraine (formerly the Ukrainian Soviet Socialist Republic) is bordered by Russia to the east, Russia and Belarus to the north, Poland, Slovakia and Hungary to the west, Romania and Moldova to the southwest and in the south by the Black Sea and the Sea of Azov. It has an area of 233,088 sq. mi. (603,700 sq. km.) and a population of 51.9 million. Capital: Kyiv (Kiev). Coal, grain, vegetables and heavy industrial machinery are major exports.

The territory of Ukraine has been inhabited for over 30,000 years. As the result of its location, Ukraine has served as the gateway to Europe for millennia and its early history has been recorded by Arabic, Greek, Roman, as well as Ukrainian historians.

Ukraine, which was known as *Rus'* until the sixteenth century (and from which the name Russia was derived in the 17th century) became the major political and cultural center of Eastern Europe in the 9th century. The Rus' Kingdom, under a dynasty of Varangian origin, due to its position on the intersection of the north-south Scandinavia to Byzantium and the east-west Orient to Europe trade routes, became a focal point of world trade. At its apex Rus' stretched from the Baltic to the Black Sea and from the upper Volga River in the east, almost to the Vistula River in the west. It has family ties to many European dynasties. In 988 knyaz (king) Volodymyr adopted Christianity from Byzantium. With it came church books written in the Cyrillic alphabet, which originated in Bulgaria. The Mongol invasion in 1240 brought an end to the might of the Rus' Kingdom.

In the seventeenth century, after almost four hundred years of Mongol, Lithuanian, Polish, and Turkish domination, the Cossack State under Hetman Bohdan Khmelnytsky regained Ukrainian independence. The Hetman State lasted until the mid-eighteenth century and was followed by a period of foreign rule. Eastern Ukraine was controlled by Russia, which enforced russification through introduction of the Russian language and prohibiting the use of the Ukrainian language in schools, books and public life. Western Ukraine came under relatively benign Austro-Hungarian rule.

With the disintegration of the Russian and Austro-Hungarian Empires in 1917 and 1918. Eastern Ukraine declared its full independence on January 22,1918 and Western Ukraine followed suit on November 1 of that year. On January 22, 1919 both parts united into one state that had to defend itself on three fronts: from the "Red Bolsheviks" and their puppet Ukrainian Soviet Republic formed in Kharkiv, from the "White" czarist Russian forces, and from Poland. Ukraine lost the war. In 1920 Eastern Ukraine was occupied by the Bolsheviks and in 1922 was incorporated into the Soviet Union. There followed a brief resurgence of Ukrainian language and culture which Stalin suppressed in 1928. The artificial famine-genocide of 1932-33 killed 7-10 million Ukrainians, and Stalinist purges in the mid-1930s took a heavy toll. Western Ukraine was partitioned between Poland, Romania, Hungary and Czechoslovakia.

On August 24, 1991 Ukraine once again declared its independence. On December 1, 1991 over 90% of Ukraine's electorate approved full independence from the Soviet Union. On December 5, 1991 the Ukrainian Parliament abrogated the 1922 treaty which incorporated Ukraine into the Soviet Union. Later, Leonid Kravchuk was elected president by a 65% majority.

Ukraine is a charter member of the United Nations and has inherited the third largest nuclear arsenal in the world.

RULERS
Russian (Eastern, Northern, Southern,
  Central Ukraine), 1654-1917
Austrian (Western Ukraine),
  1774-1918

MINT
Without mm - Lugansk; Kiev (1997-1998)

MONETARY SYSTEM
(1) Kopiyka
(2) Kopiyky КОПіИКН
(5 and up) Kopiyok КОПИОК
100 Kopiyok = 1 Hrynia ГРИВЕНЬ
100,000 Karbovanetsiv = 1 Hryni or Hryven)

REPUBLIC
REFORM COINAGE
September 2, 1996

100,000 Karbovanets = 1 Hryvnia; 100 Kopiyok = 1 Hryvnia; The Kopiyok has replaced the Karbovanet

KM# 178 2 HRYVNI
1.2400 g., 0.9999 Gold 0.0399 oz. AGW, 13.92 mm. **Obv:** National arms flanked by dates within beaded circle **Rev:** Salamander divides beaded circle **Edge:** Plain

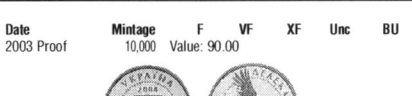

Date	Mintage	F	VF	XF	Unc	BU
2003 Proof	10,000			Value: 90.00		

KM# 227 2 HRYVNI
1.2400 g., 0.9999 Gold 0.0399 oz. AGW, 13.92 mm. **Obv:** National arms divides dates within beaded circle **Rev:** Flying Stork divides beaded circle **Edge:** Plain

Date	Mintage	F	VF	XF	Unc	BU
2004 Proof	10,000			Value: 75.00		

KM# 351 2 HRYVNI
1.2400 g., 0.9999 Gold 0.0399 oz. AGW, 13.9 mm. **Obv:** National arms within beaded circle **Rev:** Scythian horseman depicted on golden plaque **Edge:** Plain

Date	Mintage	F	VF	XF	Unc	BU
2005	15,000	—	—	—	65.00	—

KM# 403 2 HRYVNI
1.2400 g., Gold, 13.92 mm. **Subject:** Ram **Obv:** National arms **Edge:** Plain

Date	Mintage	F	VF	XF	Unc	BU
2006	10,000	—	—	—	65.00	—

KM# 404 2 HRYVNI
1.2400 g., Gold, 13.92 mm. **Subject:** Bull **Obv:** National arms **Edge:** Plain

Date	Mintage	F	VF	XF	Unc	BU
2006	10,000	—	—	—	65.00	—

KM# 406 2 HRYVNI
1.2400 g., Gold, 13.92 mm. **Subject:** The Twins **Obv:** National arms **Edge:** Plain

Date	Mintage	F	VF	XF	Unc	BU
2006	10,000	—	—	—	65.00	—

KM# 408 2 HRYVNI
1.2400 g., Gold, 13.92 mm. **Subject:** Hedgehog **Obv:** National arms **Edge:** Plain

Date	Mintage	F	VF	XF	Unc	BU
2006	10,000	—	—	—	65.00	—

KM# 431 2 HRYVNI
1.2400 g., Gold, 13.92 mm. **Subject:** Steppe Marmot **Obv:** National arms

Date	Mintage	F	VF	XF	Unc	BU
2007	10,000	—	—	—	65.00	—

KM# 143 10 HRYVEN
4.3110 g., 0.9000 Gold 0.1247 oz. AGW, 16 mm. **Subject:** 10 Years Independence **Obv:** National arms **Rev:** Parliament building on map **Edge:** Plain

Date	Mintage	F	VF	XF	Unc	BU
2001 Proof	3,000			Value: 300		

KM# 126 20 HRYVEN
Bi-Metallic Gold center in Silver ring, 31 mm. **Subject:** Paleolithic Age **Obv:** Eagle on captains wheel **Rev:** Pottery and petroglyphs **Edge:** Reeded and plain sections

Date	Mintage	F	VF	XF	Unc	BU
2000 Proof	3,000			Value: 200		

KM# 127 20 HRYVEN
Bi-Metallic Gold center in silver ring **Subject:** Trypolean Culture **Obv:** Eagle on captains wheel **Rev:** Ancient sculptures **Edge:** Reeded and plain alternating

Date	Mintage	F	VF	XF	Unc	BU
2000 Proof	3,000			Value: 200		

KM# 128 20 HRYVEN
Bi-Metallic Gold center in Silver ring **Subject:** The Olbian City State **Obv:** Eagle on captains wheel **Rev:** Ancient coin in center circle of Greek figures

Date	Mintage	F	VF	XF	Unc	BU
2000 Proof	3,000			Value: 225		

KM# 174 20 HRYVEN
14.7000 g., Bi-Metallic .916 Gold 6.22g center in .925 Silver 8.39g ring, 31 mm. **Subject:** "Kyiv Rus" Culture **Obv:** Old arms of Ukraine, Prince and a cathedral model in his hand and princess **Rev:** Old Rus earring **Edge:** Reeded and plain sections

Date	Mintage	F	VF	XF	Unc	BU
2001 Proof	2,000			Value: 300		

KM# 175 20 HRYVEN
14.7000 g., Bi-Metallic .916 Gold 6.22g center in .925 Silver 8.39g ring, 31 mm. **Subject:** Scythian Culture **Obv:** Warrior with a bowl in his hand and to the right, a Queen of Scythia **Rev:** Stylized horse flanked by pagasists **Edge:** Reeded and plain sections

Date	Mintage	F	VF	XF	Unc	BU
2001 Proof	2,000			Value: 250		

KM# 59 50 HRYVEN
3.1104 g., 0.9999 Gold .1 oz. AGW, 16 mm. **Subject:** St. Sophia Cathedral in Kiev **Obv:** Cathedral **Rev:** Mother of God Mossaic **Edge:** Segmented reeding **Note:** Minted in 1996, issued on July 28, 1997.

Date	Mintage	F	VF	XF	Unc	BU
1996	2,000	—	—	—	450	—

KM# 124 50 HRYVEN
17.6300 g., 0.9000 Gold .5101 oz. AGW, 25 mm. **Subject:** Birth of Jesus **Obv:** Two angels, arms and value **Rev:** Nativity scene **Edge:** Plain

Date	Mintage	F	VF	XF	Unc	BU
1999 Proof	3,000			Value: 600		

UKRAINE   707

KM# 125 50 HRYVEN
17.6300 g., 0.9000 Gold .5101 oz. AGW, 25 mm. **Subject:** Conversion of the Russ to Christianity **Obv:** National arms, angels and value **Rev:** Baptism scene **Edge:** Plain

Date	Mintage	F	VF	XF	Unc	BU
2000 Proof	3,000				Value: 600	

KM# 426 50 HRYVEN
15.5500 g., Gold, 25 mm. **Subject:** Nestor - The Chronicler **Obv:** National arms

Date	Mintage	F	VF	XF	Unc	BU
2006	5,000	—	—	—	450	—

KM# 63 100 HRYVEN
17.2797 g., 0.9000 Gold .5 oz. AGW, 25 mm. **Subject:** Kyiv Psalm book **Obv:** Open book divides shield and value **Rev:** Monk writing book **Edge:** Plain **Note:** Minted in 1997, issued in January 1998.

Date	Mintage	F	VF	XF	Unc	BU
1997 Proof	2,000				Value: 600	

KM# 65 100 HRYVEN
17.2797 g., 0.9000 Gold .5 oz. AGW **Subject:** Poem "Eneida" by Ivan P. Kotlyarevsky **Obv:** Helmet and musical instruments divide shield and value **Rev:** Seated helmeted figure playing a bandre

Date	Mintage	F	VF	XF	Unc	BU
1998 Proof	2,000				Value: 600	

KM# 68 100 HRYVEN
17.2797 g., 0.9000 Gold .5 oz. AGW, 25 mm. **Subject:** St. Michael's Cathedral **Obv:** Arms, value and date in center of design **Rev:** Cathedral behind human silhouettes **Edge:** Plain

Date	Mintage	F	VF	XF	Unc	BU
1998 Proof	3,000				Value: 600	

KM# 71 100 HRYVEN
17.2797 g., 0.9000 Gold .5 oz. AGW, 25 mm. **Subject:** Kyiv-Pechersk Assumption Cathedral **Obv:** Arms, value and date within beaded star **Rev:** Cathedral behind carved ruins **Edge:** Plain

Date	Mintage	F	VF	XF	Unc	BU
1998 Proof	3,000				Value: 600	

KM# 345 100 HRYVEN
34.5594 g., 0.9000 Gold 1 oz. AGW, 32 mm. **Obv:** National arms above value between two stylized cranes **Rev:** Riders approaching castle gate **Edge:** Segmented reeding

Date	Mintage	F	VF	XF	Unc	BU
2004 Proof	2,000				Value: 850	

KM# 60 125 HRYVEN
7.7759 g., 0.9999 Gold .25 oz. AGW, 20 mm. **Obv:** St. Sophia Cathedral in Kiev **Rev:** Ornate Mosaic of the Mother of God - "Ozanta" **Edge:** Segmented reeding **Note:** Minted in 1996, issued on July 28, 1997.

Date	Mintage	F	VF	XF	Unc	BU
1996	4,000	—	—	—	400	—

KM# 199 100 HRYVNIAS
31.1000 g., 0.9000 Gold 0.8999 oz. AGW, 32 mm. **Subject:** Ancient Scythian Culture **Obv:** National arms above ornamental design and value within rope wreath **Rev:** Ancient craftsmen and jewelry **Edge:** Reeded

Date	Mintage	F	VF	XF	Unc	BU
2003 Proof	1,500				Value: 900	

KM# 37 200 HRYVEN
17.5000 g., 0.9000 Gold .5 oz. AGW, 25 mm. **Obv:** National arms within beaded circle **Rev:** Bust of Taras G. Shevchenko facing **Edge:** Plain **Note:** Minted in 1996, issued on March 12, 1997.

Date	Mintage	F	VF	XF	Unc	BU
1996 Proof	10,000				Value: 600	

KM# 38 200 HRYVEN
17.5000 g., 0.9000 Gold .5 oz. AGW, 25 mm. **Subject:** Pecherska Lavra **Obv:** Church above date and value within beaded circle **Rev:** Standing angelic figure with radiant dove within cloud-like wings **Edge:** Plain **Note:** Minted in 1996, issued on April 10, 1997.

Date	Mintage	F	VF	XF	Unc	BU
1996 Proof	20,000				Value: 600	

KM# 61 250 HRYVEN
15.5518 g., 0.9999 Gold .5 oz. AGW, 25 mm. **Obv:** St. Sophia Cathedral in Kiev **Rev:** St. Sophia **Edge:** Segmented reeding **Note:** Minted in 1996, issued on July 28, 1997.

Date	Mintage	F	VF	XF	Unc	BU
1996	3,000	—	—	—	650	—

KM# 62 500 HRYVEN
31.1035 g., 0.9999 Gold 1 oz. AGW, 32 mm. **Obv:** St. Sophia Cathedral in Kiev **Rev:** St. Sophia **Edge:** Segmented reeding **Note:** Minted in 1996, issued on July 28, 1997.

Date	Mintage	F	VF	XF	Unc	BU
1996	1,000	—	—	—	3,500	—

PATTERNS
Including off metal strikes

KM#	Date	Mintage Identification	Mkt Val
Pn18	1998	— 100 Hryvnias. Brass.	—
Pn19	ND(1998)	— 100 Hryvnias. Brass.	—
Pn20	1998	— 100 Hryvnias. Brass.	—
Pn21	ND(1998)	— 100 Hryvnias. Brass.	—
Pn22	1998	— 100 Hryvnias. Brass.	—
Pn23	ND(1998)	— 100 Hryvnias. Brass.	—

UMM AL QAIWAIN

UMM AL QAIWAIN - U.A.E.

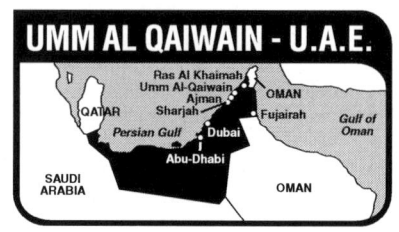

This emirate, one of the original members of the United Arab Emirates, is the second smallest, least developed and lowest in population. The area is 300 sq. mi. (800 sq. km.) and the population is 5,000. The first recognition by the West was in 1820. Most of the emirate is uninhabited desert. Native boat building is an important activity.

TITLE

ام القيوين

Umm al Qaiwain

RULERS
Ahmad Bin Abdullah al-Mualla, 1872-1904
Rashid Bin Ahmad al-Mualla, 1904-1929
Ahmad Bin Rashid al-Mualla, 1929-1981
Rashid Bin Ahmad al-Mualla, 1981-

EMIRATE

NON-CIRCULATING LEGAL TENDER COINAGE

KM# 6 25 RIYALS
5.1800 g., 0.9000 Gold .1499 oz. AGW **Ruler:** Ahmad bin Rashid al-Mualla **Obv:** Dates within crossed flags, sprigs at left and right within circle **Rev:** Old cannon within wreath

Date	Mintage	F	VF	XF	Unc	BU
AH1389 (1969) Proof	500	Value: 175				

KM# 7 50 RIYALS
10.3600 g., 0.9000 Gold .2998 oz. AGW **Ruler:** Ahmad bin Rashid al-Mualla **Obv:** Dates within crossed flags, sprigs at left and right within circle **Rev:** Fort of the 19th Century

Date	Mintage	F	VF	XF	Unc	BU
AH1389 (1969) Proof	420	Value: 285				

KM# 8 100 RIYALS
20.7300 g., 0.9000 Gold .5999 oz. AGW **Ruler:** Ahmad bin Rashid al-Mualla **Obv:** Dates within crossed flags, sprigs at left and right within circle **Rev:** Gazelles

Date	Mintage	F	VF	XF	Unc	BU
AH1389 (1969) Proof	300	Value: 485				

KM# 9 200 RIYALS
41.4600 g., 0.9000 Gold 1.1998 oz. AGW **Ruler:** Ahmad bin Rashid al-Mualla **Obv:** Dates within crossed flags, sprigs at left and right within circle **Rev:** Head of Sheik Ahmed Ben Rashid as Moalia left

Date	Mintage	F	VF	XF	Unc	BU
AH1389 (1969) Proof	230	Value: 900				

PROOF SETS

KM#	Date	Mintage	Identification	Issue Price	Mkt Val
PS2	1970 (4)	230	KM#6-9	—	1,850
PS3	1970 (8)	—	KM#1-4, 6-9	—	2,150

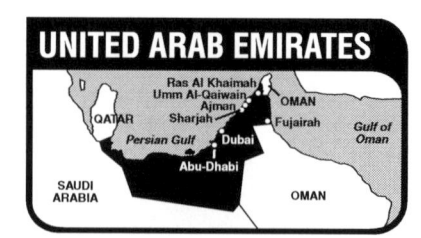

UNITED ARAB EMIRATES

The seven United Arab Emirates (formerly known as the Trucial Sheikhdoms or States), located along the southern shore of the Persian Gulf, are comprised of the Sheikhdoms of Abu Dhabi, Dubai, al-Sharjah, Ajman, Umm al Qaiwain, Ras al-Khaimah and al-Fujairah. They have a combined area of about 32,000 sq. mi. (83,600 sq. km.) and a population of *2.1 million. Capital: Abu Zaby (Abu Dhabi). Since the oil strikes of 1958-60, the economy has centered about petroleum.

The Trucial States came under direct British influence in 1892 when the Maritime Truce Treaty enacted after the supression of pirate activity along the Trucial Coast was enlarged to enjoin the states from disposing of any territory, or entering into any foreign agreements, without British consent in return for British protection from external aggression. In March of 1971 Britain reaffirmed its decision to terminate its treaty relationships with the Trucial Sheikhdoms, whereupon the seven states joined with Bahrain and Qatar in an effort to form a union of Arab Emirates under British protection. When the prospective members failed to agree on terms of union, Bahrain and Qatar declared their respective independence, Aug. and Sept. of 1971. Six of the sheikhdoms united to form the United Arab Emirates on Dec. 2, 1971.Ras al-Khaimah joined a few weeks later.

TITLE

الامارات العربية المتحدة

al-Imara(t) al-Arabiya(t) al-Muttahida(t)

MONETARY SYSTEM

Falus, Fulus   Fals, Fils   Falsan

100 Fils = 1 Dirham

UNITED EMIRATES

STANDARD COINAGE

KM# 12 500 DIRHAMS
19.9700 g., 0.9170 Gold .5886 oz. AGW, 25 mm. **Subject:** 5th Anniversary - United Arab Emirates **Obv:** Head /4 right, inscription above **Rev:** Dates

Date	Mintage	F	VF	XF	Unc	BU
ND(1976) Proof	13,450	Value: 425				

KM# 23 500 DIRHAMS
19.9700 g., 0.9170 Gold .5886 oz. AGW, 25 mm. **Subject:** Commemoration - Death of Sheikh Rashid Bin Saeed Al Maktoum **Obv:** Bust right **Rev:** Dubai International Trade Center **Note:** Similar to 50 Dirhams, KM#17.

Date	Mintage	F	VF	XF	Unc	BU
ND(1992) Proof	2,000	Value: 475				

KM# 24 500 DIRHAMS
19.9700 g., 0.9170 Gold .5886 oz. AGW, 25 mm. **Subject:** 10th Anniversary - U.A.E. Central Bank **Obv:** Bust of Shaikh Zayed Bin Sultan Al-Nahyan right **Rev:** Bank building **Note:** Similar to 50 Dirhams, KM#18.

Date	Mintage	F	VF	XF	Unc	BU
ND(1992) Proof	1,000	Value: 500				

KM# 25 500 DIRHAMS
19.9700 g., 0.9170 Gold .5886 oz. AGW, 25 mm. **Subject:** 20th Anniversary - Women's Union **Obv:** Heraldic eagle **Rev:** Seal in wreath **Note:** Similar to 1000 Dirhams, KM#28.

Date	Mintage	F	VF	XF	Unc	BU
ND(1996) Proof	1,000	Value: 500				

KM# 8 750 DIRHAMS
17.1700 g., 0.9000 Gold .4969 oz. AGW, 25 mm. **Subject:** IYC and UNICEF **Obv:** Value **Rev:** Armored horseman divides emblems

Date	Mintage	F	VF	XF	Unc	BU
AH1400-1980 Proof	3,063	Value: 375				

KM# 13 1000 DIRHAMS
39.9400 g., 0.9170 Gold 1.1771 oz. AGW, 40 mm. **Subject:** 5th Anniversary - United Arab Emirates **Obv:** Head 1/4 right **Rev:** Dates

Date	Mintage	F	VF	XF	Unc	BU
ND(1976) Proof	12,500	Value: 850				

KM# 26 1000 DIRHAMS
39.9400 g., 0.9170 Gold 1.1771 oz. AGW, 40 mm. **Subject:** Death of Shaikh Rashid Bin Saeed Al Maktoum **Obv:** Bust right **Rev:** Dubai International Trade Center **Note:** Similar to 50 Dirhams, KM#17.

Date	Mintage	F	VF	XF	Unc	BU
ND(1992) Proof	2,000	Value: 875				

KM# 27 1000 DIRHAMS
39.9400 g., 0.9170 Gold 1.1771 oz. AGW, 40 mm. **Subject:** 10th Anniversary - U.A.E. Central Bank **Obv:** Bust half right **Rev:** Bank building **Note:** Similar to 50 Dirhams, KM#18.

Date	Mintage	F	VF	XF	Unc	BU
ND(1992) Proof	1,000	Value: 900				

KM# 28 1000 DIRHAMS
39.9400 g., 0.9170 Gold 1.1771 oz. AGW, 40 mm. **Subject:** 20th Anniversary - General Women's Union **Obv:** Bust right **Rev:** Seal in wreath

Date	Mintage	F	VF	XF	Unc	BU
ND(1996) Proof	1,000	Value: 900				

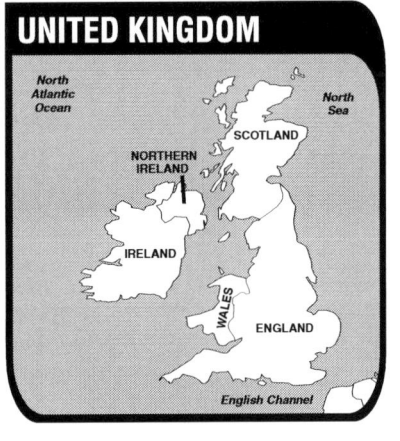

UNITED KINGDOM

KINGDOM

MEDALLIC COINAGE
Ecu Series

X# M21 ECU
4.2800 g., 0.7500 Gold 0.1032 oz. AGW, 19.1 mm. **Ruler:** Elizabeth II **Obv:** Neptune and Europa behind Ecu Nations globe **Rev:** Ship on Thames River approaching Tower Bridg **Edge:** Reeded **Note:** Prev. X#21.

Date	Mintage	F	VF	XF	Unc	BU
1993 Proof	2,500	Value: 125				

X# M22 ECU
5.6400 g., 0.7500 Gold 0.136 oz. AGW, 22.3 mm. **Ruler:** Elizabeth II **Obv:** Neptune and Europa behind Ecu Nations globe **Rev:** Ship on Thames River approaching Tower Bridge **Edge:** Reeded **Note:** Prev. X#22.

Date	Mintage	F	VF	XF	Unc	BU
1993 Proof	—	Value: 145				

UNITED STATES

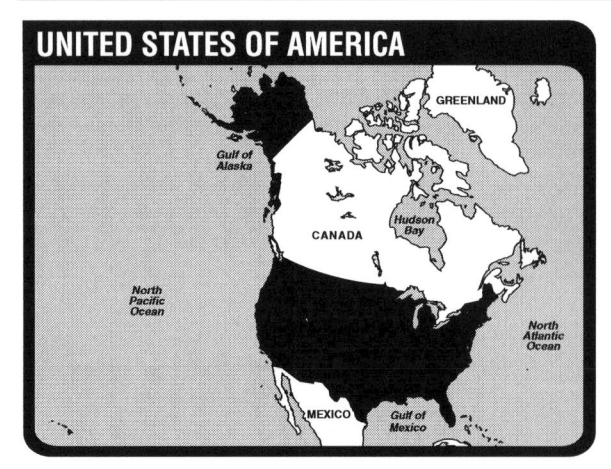

The United States of America as politically organized, under the Articles of Confederation consisted of the 13 original British-American colonies; New Hampshire, Massachusetts, Rhode Island, Connecticut, New York, New Jersey, Pennsylvania, Delaware, Virginia, North Carolina, South Carolina, Georgia and Maryland. Clustered along the eastern seaboard of North American between the forests of Maine and the marshes of Georgia. Under the Article of Confederation, the United States had no national capital: Philadelphia, where the "United States in Congress Assembled", was the "seat of government". The population during this political phase of America's history (1781-1789) was about 3 million, most of whom lived on self-sufficient family farms. Fishing, lumbering and the production of grains for export were major economic endeavors. Rapid strides were also being made in industry and manufacturing by 1775, the (then) colonies were accounting for one-seventh of the world's production of raw iron.

On the basis of the voyage of John Cabot to the North American mainland in 1497, England claimed the entire continent. The first permanent English settlement was established at Jamestown, Virginia, in 1607. France and Spain also claimed extensive territory in North America. At the end of the French and Indian Wars (1763), England acquired all of the territory east of the Mississippi River, including East and West Florida. From 1776 to 1781, the States were governed by the Continental Congress. From 1781 to 1789, they were organized under the Articles of Confederation, during which period the individual States had the right to issue money. Independence from Great Britain was attained with the American Revolution in 1776. The Constitution organized and governs the present United States. It was ratified on Nov. 21, 1788.

MINT MARKS
C – Charlotte, N.C., 1838-61
CC – Carson City, NV, 1870-93
D – Dahlonega, GA, 1838-61
D – Denver, CO, 1906-present
O – New Orleans, LA, 1838-1909
P – Philadelphia, PA, 1793-present
S – San Francisco, CA, 1854-present
W – West Point, NY, 1984-present

MONETARY SYSTEM
Trime = 3 Cents
Nickel = 5 Cents
Dime = 10 Cents
Quarter = 25 Cents
Half Dollar = 50 Cents
Dollar = 100 Cents
Quarter Eagle = $2.50 Gold
Stella = $4.00 Gold
Half Eagle = $5.00 Gold
Eagle = $10.00 Gold
Double Eagle = $20.00 Gold

BULLION COINS
Silver Eagle = $1.00
Gold 1/10 Ounce = $5.00
Gold ¼ Ounce = $10.00
Gold ½ Ounce = $25.00
Gold Ounce = $50.00
Platinum 1/10 Ounce = $10.00
Platinum ¼ Ounce = $25.00
Platinum ½ Ounce = $50.00
Platinum Ounce = $100.00

CIRCULATION COINAGE

DOLLAR

GOLD

Liberty Head - Type 1
Liberty head left, within circle of stars
Value, date within 3/4 wreath

KM# 73   0.9000 GOLD   0.0484 oz. AGW.   13 mm.   1.6720 g.   Designer: James B. Longacre   Notes: On the "closed wreath" varieties of 1849, the wreath on the reverse extends closer to the numeral 1.

Date	Mintage	F-12	VF-20	XF-40	AU-50	MS-60
1849 open wreath	688,567	110	140	200	235	425
1849 closed wreath	Inc. above	110	135	190	220	365
1849C closed wreath	11,634	800	950	1,250	1,900	8,000
1849C open wreath	Inc. above	—	—	—	—	—
1849D open wreath	21,588	950	1,300	1,800	2,350	7,000
1849O open wreath	215,000	125	175	240	325	1,000
1850	481,953	110	145	200	215	360
1850C	6,966	900	1,150	1,600	2,300	9,000
1850D	8,382	975	1,250	1,650	2,800	10,000
1850O	14,000	185	275	375	850	3,600
1851	3,317,671	110	145	190	215	315
1851C	41,267	840	1,150	1,500	1,950	4,900
1851D	9,882	950	1,200	1,600	2,500	5,650
1851O	290,000	135	175	225	265	750
1852	2,045,351	110	145	200	215	330
1852C	9,434	800	1,150	1,400	1,700	5,100
1852D	6,360	950	1,250	1,600	2,300	10,000
1852O	140,000	125	165	230	385	1,500
1853	4,076,051	110	135	190	200	245
1853C	11,515	900	1,100	1,400	1,750	6,200
1853D	6,583	975	1,150	1,600	2,400	9,700
1853O	290,000	135	160	235	270	665
1854	736,709	110	145	200	230	335
1854D	2,935	990	1,400	2,350	6,000	13,000
1854S	14,632	245	360	525	840	2,450

Indian Head - Type 2
Indian head with headdress, left   Value, date within wreath

KM# 83   0.9000 GOLD   0.0484 oz. AGW.   15 mm.   1.6720 g.   Designer: James B. Longacre

Date	Mintage	F-12	VF-20	XF-40	AU-50	MS-60
1854	902,736	210	315	440	650	3,600
1855	758,269	210	315	440	650	3,600
1855C	9,803	975	1,450	3,500	11,000	33,000
1855D	1,811	3,000	4,750	9,800	22,000	48,000
1855O	55,000	345	475	700	1,400	7,800
1856S	24,600	575	900	1,400	2,300	8,500

Indian Head - Type 3
Indian head with headdress, left   Value, date within wreath

KM# 86   0.9000 GOLD   0.0484 oz. AGW.   15 mm.   1.6720 g.   Designer: James B. Longacre   Notes: The 1856 varieties are distinguished by whether the 5 in the date is slanted or upright. The 1873 varieties are distinguished by the amount of space between the upper left and lower left serifs in the 3.

Date	Mintage	F-12	VF-20	XF-40	AU-50	MS-60	Prf-65
1856 upright 5	1,762,936	135	170	210	275	575	—
1856 slanted 5	Inc. above	140	160	195	250	400	50,000
1856D	1,460	2,950	3,800	5,800	8,000	32,000	—
1857	774,789	130	166	200	215	290	31,000
1857C	13,280	900	1,150	1,750	3,750	14,000	—
1857D	3,533	1,000	1,300	2,300	4,400	11,000	—
1857S	10,000	250	500	615	1,300	5,800	—
1858	117,995	135	160	200	220	325	27,500
1858D	3,477	925	1,250	1,600	2,750	10,000	—
1858S	10,000	300	400	575	1,300	5,500	—
1859	168,244	145	170	200	215	260	17,000
1859C	5,235	885	1,050	1,700	4,000	15,000	—
1859D	4,952	1,000	1,400	1,800	3,100	11,000	—
1859S	15,000	185	225	480	1,050	5,000	—
1860	36,668	135	170	190	240	400	14,500
1860D	1,566	2,000	2,800	3,800	7,000	23,000	—
1860S	13,000	280	380	480	750	2,300	—
1861	527,499	140	155	190	215	325	14,000
1861D mintage unrecorded	—	4,600	7,000	10,000	18,000	47,500	—
1862	1,361,390	130	150	200	240	325	15,000
1863	6,250	370	500	925	2,100	3,750	18,000
1864	5,950	270	350	440	750	950	18,000
1865	3,725	270	350	570	750	1,600	18,000
1866	7,130	275	360	470	670	950	18,000
1867	5,250	300	400	515	675	1,100	17,500
1868	10,525	265	290	415	490	950	19,000
1869	5,925	315	335	530	800	1,300	17,000
1870	6,335	245	285	400	480	850	16,000
1870S	3,000	290	475	750	1,150	2,300	—
1871	3,930	250	285	380	470	750	18,000
1872	3,530	245	275	400	480	975	18,000
1873 closed 3	125,125	300	425	800	950	1,600	—
1873 open 3	Inc. above	130	160	200	250	325	—
1874	198,820	130	160	200	245	340	18,000
1875	420	1,600	2,350	3,850	4,700	340	32,500
1876	3,245	220	275	345	475	650	16,750
1877	3,920	145	190	345	450	800	18,000
1878	3,020	180	250	350	465	675	15,500
1879	3,030	170	225	325	350	525	14,000
1880	1,636	150	180	200	240	440	14,000
1881	7,707	150	175	200	250	550	11,500
1882	5,125	160	180	200	265	600	9,500
1883	11,007	150	175	200	275	600	9,400
1884	6,236	140	155	200	260	550	9,400
1885	12,261	140	165	215	265	585	9,400
1886	6,016	150	175	215	285	550	9,400
1887	8,543	145	170	200	260	550	9,400
1888	16,580	145	170	200	250	550	9,400
1889	30,729	150	180	200	240	400	9,000

$2.50 (QUARTER EAGLE)

GOLD

Liberty Cap

Liberty cap on head, right, flanked by stars — Heraldic eagle

KM# 27 0.9160 GOLD 0.1289 oz. AGW. 20 mm. 4.3700 g. **Designer:** Robert Scot
Notes: The 1796 "no stars" variety does not have stars on the obverse. The 1804 varieties are distinguished by the number of stars on the obverse.

Date	Mintage	F-12	VF-20	XF-40	MS-60
1796 no stars	963	30,000	42,000	70,000	165,000
1796 stars	432	28,000	40,000	63,000	140,000
1797	427	17,000	23,000	27,500	120,000
1798	1,094	4,750	10,000	12,500	55,000
1802/1	3,035	4,400	8,000	9,500	32,000
1804 13-star reverse	3,327	23,500	36,500	72,000	200,000
1804 14-star reverse	Inc. above	4,800	7,400	9,000	27,500
1805	1,781	6,000	7,500	9,000	21,000
1806/4	1,616	5,750	8,000	9,500	23,000
1806/5	Inc. above	6,000	8,000	18,000	77,000
1807	6,812	5,500	7,000	9.00	21,000

Turban Head

Turban on head, left, flanked by stars — Banner above eagle

KM# 40 0.9160 GOLD 0.1289 oz. AGW. 20 mm. 4.3700 g. **Designer:** John Reich

Date	Mintage	F-12	VF-20	XF-40	MS-60
1808	2,710	22,500	31,000	45,000	125,000

Turban on head, left, within circle of stars — Banner above eagle

KM# 46 0.9160 GOLD 0.1289 oz. AGW. 18.5 mm. 4.3700 g. **Designer:** John Reich

Date	Mintage	F-12	VF-20	XF-40	MS-60
1821	6,448	5,500	6,250	7,500	23,000
1824/21	2,600	5,500	6,250	7,250	22,000
1825	4,434	5,500	6,500	7,800	21,000
1826/25	760	6,000	7,000	8,500	36,000
1827	2,800	5,500	7,500	9,000	22,500

Turban on head, left, within circle of stars — Banner above eagle

KM# 49 0.9160 GOLD 0.1289 oz. AGW. 18.2 mm. 4.3700 g. **Designer:** John Reich

Date	Mintage	F-12	VF-20	XF-40	MS-60
1829	3,403	4,900	5,850	6,700	12,500
1830	4,540	4,950	5,850	6,700	12,500
1831	4,520	4,950	5,850	6,700	12,500
1832	4,400	4,950	5,850	6,700	12,500
1833	4,160	4,950	5,850	6,800	12,750
1834	4,000	8,800	12,000	16,000	36,000

Classic Head

Classic head, left, within circle of stars — No motto above eagle

KM# 56 0.8990 GOLD 0.1209 oz. AGW. 18.2 mm. 4.1800 g. **Designer:** William Kneass

Date	Mintage	VF-20	XF-40	AU-50	MS-60	MS-65
1834	112,234	475	675	965	3,300	27,000
1835	131,402	475	675	950	3,200	32,000
1836	547,986	475	675	940	3,100	29,000
1837	45,080	500	800	1,500	4,000	35,000
1838	47,030	500	625	1,100	3,200	30,000
1838C	7,880	1,700	3,000	8,000	27,000	55,000
1839	27,021	500	900	1,900	5,500	—
1839C	18,140	1,500	2,650	4,500	26,500	—
1839D	13,674	1,750	3,450	8,000	24,000	—
1839O	17,781	700	1,100	2,500	7,250	—

Coronet Head

Coronet head, left, within circle of stars — No motto above eagle

KM# 72 0.9000 GOLD 0.121 oz. AGW. 18 mm. 4.1800 g. **Designer:** Christian Gobrecht **Notes:** Varieties for 1843 are distinguished by the size of the numerals in the date. One 1848 variety has "Cal." inscribed on the reverse, indicating it was made from California gold. The 1873 "closed-3" and "open-3" varieties are distinguished by the amount of space between the upper left and lower left serifs in the 3 in the date.

1948 "Cal."

Date	Mintage	F-12	VF-20	XF-40	AU-50	MS-60	Prf-65
1840	18,859	160	190	900	2,950	6,000	—
1840C	12,822	975	1,400	1,600	6,000	13,000	—
1840D	3,532	2,000	3,200	8,700	15,500	35,000	—
1840O	33,580	250	400	825	2,100	11,000	—
1841	—	—	48,000	85,000	96,000	—	—
1841C	10,281	750	1,500	2,000	3,500	18,500	—
1841D	4,164	950	2,100	4,750	11,000	25,000	—
1842	2,823	500	900	2,600	6,500	20,000	140,000
1842C	6,729	700	1,700	3,500	8,000	27,000	—
1842D	4,643	900	2,100	4,000	11,750	38,000	—
1842O	19,800	240	370	1,200	2,500	14,000	—
1843	100,546	160	180	450	915	3,000	140,000
1843C small date	26,064	1,500	2,400	5,500	8,000	29,000	—
1843C large date	Inc. above	800	1,600	2,200	3,500	8,800	—
1843D small date	36,209	920	1,800	2,350	3,250	10,500	—
1843O small date	288,002	165	190	250	350	1,700	—
1843O large date	76,000	210	260	465	1,600	8,000	—
1844	6,784	225	365	850	2,000	7,500	140,000
1844C	11,622	700	1,600	2,600	7,000	20,000	—
1844D	17,332	785	1,650	2,200	3,200	7,800	—
1845	91,051	190	250	350	600	1,275	140,000
1845D	19,460	950	1,900	2,600	3,900	15,000	—
1845O	4,000	550	1,050	2,300	9,000	20,000	—
1846	21,598	200	275	500	950	6,000	140,000
1846C	4,808	725	1,575	3,500	9,250	18,750	—
1846D	19,303	800	1,400	2,000	3,000	12,000	—
1846O	66,000	170	280	400	1,150	6,500	—
1847	29,814	140	220	360	825	3,800	—
1847C	23,226	900	1,800	2,300	3,500	7,250	—
1847D	15,784	800	1,650	2,250	3,250	10,500	—
1847O	124,000	160	240	400	1,000	4,000	—
1848	7,497	315	500	850	2,400	7,000	125,000
1848 "Cal."	1,389	8,000	15,000	26,000	36,000	50,000	—
1848C	16,788	800	1,600	2,100	3,800	14,000	—
1848D	13,771	1,000	2,000	2,500	4,500	12,000	—
1849	23,294	180	275	475	1,000	2,600	—
1849C	10,220	800	1,475	2,150	5,150	23,500	—
1849D	10,945	950	2,000	2,500	4,500	18,000	—
1850	252,923	160	180	275	350	1,100	—
1850C	9,148	800	1,500	2,100	3,400	17,500	—
1850D	12,148	950	1,800	2,500	4,000	15,000	—
1850O	84,000	170	225	450	1,200	4,900	—
1851	1,372,748	145	180	200	225	325	—
1851C	14,923	900	1,750	2,300	4,800	13,000	—
1851D	11,264	950	1,700	2,600	4,200	13,000	—
1851O	148,000	160	200	220	1,000	4,650	—
1852	1,159,681	150	175	200	250	325	—
1852C	9,772	675	1,500	2,100	4,250	18,000	—
1852D	4,078	840	1,600	2,800	7,250	17,000	—
1852O	140,000	160	190	300	950	5,000	—
1853	1,404,668	150	180	200	225	350	—
1853D	3,178	950	2,100	3,400	4,900	18,000	—
1854	596,258	150	180	215	240	350	—
1854C	7,295	800	1,500	2,400	5,000	14,750	—
1854D	1,760	1,750	2,900	6,950	12,000	27,500	—
1854O	153,000	150	185	240	425	1,600	—

UNITED STATES

Date	Mintage	F-12	VF-20	XF-40	AU-50	MS-60	Prf-65
1854S	246	32,500	70,000	115,000	215,000	300,000	—
1855	235,480	145	180	225	250	360	—
1855C	3,677	800	1,675	3,300	6,500	25,000	—
1855D	1,123	1,750	3,250	7,500	24,000	46,000	—
1856	384,240	145	175	210	250	390	75,000
1856C	7,913	650	1,150	2,200	4,400	15,500	—
1856D	874	3,500	6,700	12,500	30,000	72,500	—
1856O	21,100	180	240	750	1,500	8,000	—
1856S	71,120	160	250	375	950	4,500	—
1857	214,130	150	190	205	230	380	75,000
1857D	2,364	875	1,750	2,900	3,850	13,000	—
1857O	34,000	155	210	350	1,100	4,600	—
1857S	69,200	160	210	340	900	5,500	—
1858	47,377	150	200	250	360	1,350	59,000
1858C	9,056	825	1,500	2,100	3,350	9,250	—
1859	39,444	150	185	265	400	1,250	61,000
1859D	2,244	1,000	1,900	3,300	4,900	20,000	—
1859S	15,200	200	350	1,000	2,800	7,000	—
1860	22,675	150	200	265	470	1,300	58,000
1860C	7,469	815	1,550	2,200	3,950	21,000	—
1860S	35,600	170	250	675	1,200	4,000	—
1861	1,283,878	150	180	210	230	325	31,500
1861S	24,000	200	400	1,000	3,700	7,400	—
1862	98,543	160	200	300	520	1,375	32,500
1862/1	Inc. above	450	950	2,000	4,000	8,000	—
1862S	8,000	500	1,000	2,100	4,500	17,000	—
1863	30	—	—	—	—	—	95,000
1863S	10,800	250	500	1,500	3,200	13,500	—
1864	2,874	2,500	5,500	8,800	21,500	37,500	27,000
1865	1,545	2,400	6,000	8,000	19,000	38,000	30,000
1865S	23,376	160	225	650	1,650	5,000	—
1866	3,110	650	1,300	3,500	6,000	11,500	25,000
1866S	38,960	180	300	650	1,600	6,250	—
1867	3,250	190	385	900	1,250	4,800	27,000
1867S	28,000	170	250	625	1,750	4,000	—
1868	3,625	170	235	400	675	1,600	27,000
1868S	34,000	150	200	300	1,100	4,000	—
1869	4,345	170	250	450	715	3,000	24,500
1869S	29,500	160	240	440	775	5,000	—
1870	4,555	165	225	425	740	3,800	22,750
1870S	16,000	155	215	400	800	4,900	—
1871	5,350	160	230	325	600	2,200	24,000
1871S	22,000	150	185	280	530	2,200	—
1872	3,030	200	400	750	1,100	4,650	22,000
1872S	18,000	155	225	415	900	4,500	—
1873 closed 3	178,025	155	170	210	260	535	22,500
1873 open 3	Inc. above	155	165	195	250	300	—
1873S	27,000	160	225	425	900	2,800	—
1874	3,940	170	240	380	720	2,100	32,000
1875	420	1,750	3,500	5,000	11,000	21,500	32,500
1875S	11,600	150	200	300	850	4,500	—
1876	4,221	170	275	675	925	3,200	22,000
1876S	5,000	170	225	525	980	3,300	—
1877	1,652	275	400	800	1,100	3,250	22,000
1877S	35,400	150	160	200	230	635	—
1878	286,260	150	160	200	225	275	26,000
1878S	178,000	150	160	200	235	340	—
1879	88,990	150	160	195	235	300	26,000
1879S	43,500	155	200	300	550	2,150	—
1880	2,996	170	210	335	600	1,300	20,250
1881	691	900	2,200	3,400	5,000	10,000	19,000
1882	4,067	160	210	290	400	700	15,000
1883	2,002	175	220	440	1,000	2,600	15,500
1884	2,023	175	225	420	600	1,600	16,000
1885	887	400	715	1,800	2,500	4,400	15,000
1886	4,088	170	190	270	425	1,100	16,500
1887	6,282	175	200	245	325	700	16,500
1888	16,098	160	180	240	285	340	15,000
1889	17,648	155	180	230	250	325	17,000
1890	8,813	170	190	240	280	500	13,750
1891	11,040	165	175	215	230	400	14,000
1892	2,545	170	180	250	325	765	15,000
1893	30,106	165	175	200	240	300	14,000
1894	4,122	170	180	225	325	800	13,500
1895	6,199	150	175	225	275	395	12,500
1896	19,202	150	175	225	235	285	12,500
1897	29,904	150	175	210	235	285	12,500
1898	24,165	150	175	210	235	285	12,500
1899	27,350	150	175	210	235	300	12,500
1900	67,205	150	175	240	320	415	12,500
1901	91,322	150	175	200	235	275	12,500
1902	133,733	150	170	200	235	275	12,500
1903	201,257	150	170	200	235	275	13,000
1904	160,960	150	170	200	240	275	12,500
1905	217,944	150	170	200	240	275	12,500
1906	176,490	150	170	200	240	275	12,500
1907	336,448	150	170	200	240	275	12,500

Indian Head

KM# 128 0.9000 GOLD 0.121 oz. AGW. 18 mm. 4.1800 g. **Designer:** Bela Lyon Pratt

Date	Mintage	VF-20	XF-40	AU-50	MS-60	MS-63	MS-65	Prf-65
1908	565,057	165	220	230	275	1,800	8,500	16,000
1909	441,899	175	220	230	275	2,600	11,000	30,000
1910	492,682	175	220	230	275	2,600	12,500	18,000
1911	704,191	175	220	230	280	1,600	12,500	16,000
1911D	55,680	2,700	3,650	5,000	10,500	24,500	90,000	16,000
1912	616,197	175	220	230	275	2,800	16,000	16,000
1913	722,165	175	220	230	280	1,725	14,000	16,500
1914	240,117	175	235	230	480	8,500	34,000	16,500
1914D	448,000	175	220	230	300	2,650	40,000	23,000
1915	606,100	175	220	230	275	1,650	13,500	15,250
1925D	578,000	175	220	230	275	1,450	7,000	—
1926	446,000	175	220	230	275	1,450	7,000	—
1927	388,000	175	220	230	275	1,450	7,000	—
1928	416,000	175	220	230	275	1,450	7,000	—
1929	532,000	180	230	250	340	1,600	10,000	—

$3

GOLD

Indian head with headdress, left   Value, date within wreath

KM# 84 0.9000 GOLD 0.1452 oz. AGW. 20.5 mm. 5.0150 g. **Designer:** James B. Longacre **Notes:** The 1873 "closed-3" and "open-3" varieties are distinguished by the amount of space between the upper left and lower left serifs of the 3 in the date.

Date	Mintage	VF-20	XF-40	AU-50	MS-60	MS-65	Prf-65
1854	138,618	850	1,100	2,000	3,400	18,000	125,000
1854D	1,120	8,300	15,000	29,000	65,000	—	—
1854O	24,000	1,000	2,000	4,000	20,000	—	—
1855	50,555	900	1,100	2,000	3,300	32,000	120,000
1855S	6,600	1,025	2,150	5,700	25,000	—	—
1856	26,010	880	1,100	2,150	3,500	27,000	—
1856S	34,500	900	1,500	2,350	10,000	—	—
1857	20,891	900	1,100	2,100	3,500	—	62,500
1857S	14,000	950	2,200	5,500	18,000	—	—
1858	2,133	950	1,800	3,000	9,000	—	62,500
1859	15,638	900	1,800	1,800	3,000	—	60,000
1860	7,155	900	1,600	2,000	3,600	21,000	46,000
1860S	7,000	950	2,000	7,000	17,000	—	—
1861	6,072	925	1,500	2,200	3,600	27,000	46,000
1862	5,785	925	1,850	2,200	3,600	28,000	46,500
1863	5,039	900	1,450	2,200	3,600	20,000	43,000
1864	2,680	950	1,500	2,300	3,600	29,000	42,000
1865	1,165	1,350	2,500	6,000	10,000	39,000	40,000
1866	4,030	970	1,100	2,000	3,600	27,500	42,000
1867	2,650	950	1,100	2,400	4,000	28,000	41,500
1868	4,875	740	1,100	2,100	3,000	22,000	42,000
1869	2,525	1,150	2,200	2,600	4,000	—	46,000
1870	3,535	1,000	1,500	2,400	5,000	—	47,000
1870S unique							

Note: H. W. Bass Collection. AU50, cleaned. Est. value, $1,250,000.

1871	1,330	1,000	1,500	2,000	4,000	27,500	47,000
1872	2,030	900	1,800	2,250	3,600	—	33,000
1873 open 3, proof only	25	3,300	5,000	8,700	—	—	—
1873 closed 3, mintage unknown		4,000	6,000	10,000	—	—	42,000
1874	41,820	800	1,300	1,900	3,000	16,000	42,000
1875 proof only	20	20,000	28,000	47,500	—	—	175,000
1876	45	6,000	10,000	16,500	—	—	60,000
1877	1,488	1,200	2,900	5,200	12,000	60,000	43,500
1878	82,324	800	1,300	1,900	3,000	16,000	43,000
1879	3,030	850	1,300	2,000	2,650	19,000	32,000
1880	1,036	850	1,700	3,000	4,000	20,000	29,500
1881	554	1,400	2,750	5,500	8,000	24,000	25,000
1882	1,576	925	1,400	2,000	3,500	22,000	25,000
1883	989	1,000	1,600	3,500	3,600	24,000	25,000
1884	1,106	1,250	1,700	2,200	3,600	24,000	24,000
1885	910	1,300	1,800	2,850	3,900	24,000	25,000
1886	1,142	1,250	1,800	3,000	4,000	20,000	24,000
1887	6,160	900	1,300	2,000	3,000	18,000	21,000
1888	5,291	950	1,500	2,000	3,300	20,000	23,000
1889	2,429	925	1,300	1,700	3,100	18,000	22,000

$5 (HALF EAGLE)

GOLD

Liberty Cap

Liberty cap on head, right, flanked by stars   Heraldic eagle

KM# 19 0.9160 GOLD 0.258 oz. AGW. 25 mm. 8.7500 g. **Designer:** Robert Scot **Notes:** From 1795 through 1798, varieties exist with either a "small eagle" or a "large (heraldic) eagle" on the reverse. After 1798, only the heraldic eagle was used. Two 1797 varieties are distinguished by the size of the 8 in the date. 1806 varieties are distinguished by whether the top of the 6 has a serif.

UNITED STATES 713

Date	Mintage	F-12	VF-20	XF-40	MS-60
1825/24	Inc. above	—	—	250,000	350,000
Note: 1825/4, Bowers & Merena, March 1989, XF, $148,500.					
1826	18,069	4,000	7,500	9,300	32,000
1827	24,913	6,000	10,000	12,250	34,000
1828/7	28,029	15,000	27,500	41,000	125,000
Note: 1828/7, Bowers & Merena, June 1989, XF, $20,900.					
1828	Inc. above	6,000	13,000	21,000	7,000
1829 large planchet	57,442	15,000	27,500	50,000	135,000
Note: 1829 large planchet, Superior, July 1985, MS-65, $104,500.					
1829 small planchet	Inc. above	37,500	50,000	82,500	140,000
Note: 1829 small planchet, private sale, 1992 (XF-45), $89,000.					
1830 small "5D."	126,351	14,500	17,500	21,000	40,000
1830 large "5D."	Inc. above	14,500	17,500	21,000	40,000
1831	140,594	14,500	17,500	21,000	42,500
1832 curved-base 2, 12 stars	157,487	50,000	80,000	135,000	—
1832 square-base 2, 13 stars	Inc. above	14,500	17,500	21,000	40,000
1833	193,630	14,500	17,500	21,000	40,000
1834 plain 4	50,141	14,500	17,500	21,000	40,000
1834 crosslet 4	Inc. above	14,500	17,500	21,000	40,000

Classic Head

Classic head, left, within circle of stars
No motto above eagle

KM# 57   0.8990 **GOLD** 0.2418 oz. AGW. 22.5 mm. 8.3600 g. **Designer:** William Kneass   **Notes:** 1834 varieties are distinguished by whether the 4 has a serif at its far right.

Date	Mintage	VF-20	XF-40	AU-50	MS-60	MS-65
1834 plain 4	658,028	390	550	950	3,000	48,000
1834 crosslet 4	Inc. above	1,650	2,900	6,000	20,000	—
1835	371,534	390	560	1,000	3,150	70,000
1836	553,147	390	550	1,000	2,950	70,000
1837	207,121	390	585	1,200	3,500	75,000
1838	286,588	390	5,500	1,000	3,700	58,000
1838C	17,179	2,200	4,000	13,000	38,500	—
1838D	20,583	2,000	3,850	9,000	25,000	—

Coronet Head

Coronet head, left, within circle of stars
No motto above eagle

KM# 69   0.9000 **GOLD** 0.242 oz. AGW. 21.6 mm. 8.3590 g. **Designer:** Christian Gobrecht   **Notes:** Varieties for the 1842 Philadelphia strikes are distinguished by the size of the letters in the reverse inscriptions. Varieties for the 1842-C and -D strikes are distinguished by the size of the numerals in the date. Varieties for the 1843-O strikes are distinguished by the size of the letters in the reverse inscriptions.

Date	Mintage	F-12	VF-20	XF-40	MS-60	Prf-65
1839	118,143	250	275	480	4,000	—
1839/8 curved date	Inc. above	275	325	700	2,250	—
1839C	17,205	1,250	2,300	2,900	24,000	—
1839D	18,939	1,125	2,200	3,200	22,000	—
1840	137,382	200	230	360	3,700	—
1840C	18,992	1,200	2,200	3,000	26,000	—
1840D	22,896	1,200	2,200	3,000	16,000	—
1840O	40,120	200	365	875	11,000	—
1841	15,833	200	400	875	5,500	—
1841C	21,467	1,200	1,850	2,400	20,000	—
1841D	30,495	1,400	1,800	2,350	15,000	—
1841O 2 known	50	—	—	—	—	—
1842 small letters	27,578	2,000	345	1,100	—	—
1842 large letters	Inc. above	350	750	2,000	11,000	—
1842C small date	28,184	4,500	10,000	23,000	110,000	—
1842C large date	Inc. above	900	1,800	2,200	18,000	—
1842D small date	59,608	1,000	2,000	2,300	15,000	—
1842D large date	Inc. above	1,400	2,350	6,500	48,000	—
1842O	16,400	550	1,000	3,400	22,000	—
1843	611,205	200	230	330	1,850	—
1843C	44,201	1,250	1,850	2,500	14,000	—
1843D	98,452	1,250	1,950	2,600	13,000	—
1843O small letters	19,075	300	660	1,700	26,000	—
1843O large letters	82,000	200	265	1,175	12,000	—
1844	340,330	200	230	330	2,000	—
1844C	23,631	1,300	1,900	3,000	24,000	—
1844D	88,982	1,500	1,950	2,400	12,000	—
1844O	364,600	220	250	375	4,700	—
1845	417,099	200	235	260	2,000	—
1845D	90,629	1,300	1,900	2,400	12,500	—
1845O	41,000	235	415	800	9,900	—
1846	395,942	200	230	330	2,400	—
1846C	12,995	1,350	1,900	3,000	24,000	—

Date	Mintage	F-12	VF-20	XF-40	MS-60
1795 small eagle	8,707	11,500	17,000	19,000	47,000
1795 large eagle	Inc. above	8,800	14,000	20,000	75,000
1796/95 small eagle	6,196	12,000	17,500	24,000	75,000
1797/95 large eagle	3,609	8,600	14,000	22,000	150,000
1797 15 stars, small eagle	Inc. above	14,000	21,000	35,000	150,000
1797 16 stars, small eagle	Inc. above	13,000	17,500	34,000	145,000
1798 small eagle	—	90,000	155,000	275,000	—
1798 large eagle, small 8	24,867	3,300	4,500	6,000	21,000
1798 large eagle, large 8, 13-star reverse	Inc. above	3,000	3,700	4,500	17,500
1798 large eagle, large 8, 14-star reverse	Inc. above	3,000	4,200	7,000	35,000
1799	7,451	3,000	3,800	5,300	16,500
1800	37,628	3,000	3,800	5,000	8,800
1802/1	53,176	3,000	4,000	4,300	8,900
1803/2	33,506	3,000	3,800	4,300	8,700
1804 small 8	30,475	3,000	3,800	4,300	8,700
1804 large 8	Inc. above	3,000	3,800	4,300	9,600
1805	33,183	3,000	3,800	4,300	8,600
1806 pointed 6	64,093	3,200	3,700	4,300	9,000
1806 round 6	Inc. above	3,000	3,700	4,300	8,600
1807	32,488	3,000	3,800	4,300	8,700

Turban Head

Capped draped bust, left, flanked by stars   Healdic eagle

KM# 38   0.9160 **GOLD** 0.258 oz. AGW. 25 mm. 8.7500 g. **Designer:** John Reich
Notes: The 1810 varieties are distinguished by the size of the numerals in the date and the size of the 5 in the "5D." on the reverse. The 1811 varieties are distinguished by the size of the 5 in the "5D." on the reverse.

Date	Mintage	F-12	VF-20	XF-40	MS-60
1807	51,605	2,400	3,000	4,300	8,400
1808	55,578	2,400	3,000	4,300	8,250
1808/7	Inc. above	3,000	3,800	4,500	13,000
1809/8	33,875	2,500	3,000	3,750	8,500
1810 small date, small 5	100,287	9,600	22,500	32,000	95,000
1810 small date, large 5	Inc. above	2,300	3,000	3,800	8,500
1810 large date, small 5	Inc. above	13,500	24,000	32,000	115
1810 large date, large 5	Inc. above	2,600	3,000	3,750	8,500
1811 small 5	99,581	2,600	3,000	3,750	8,500
1811 large 5	Inc. above	2,500	2,900	38,000	9,000
1812	58,087	2,400	2,850	4,000	8,000

Capped head, left, within circle of stars   Healdic eagle

KM# 43   0.9160 **GOLD** 0.258 oz. AGW. 25 mm. 8.7500 g. **Designer:** John Reich
Notes: 1820 varieties are distinguished by whether the 2 in the date has a curved base or square base and by the size of the letters in the reverse inscriptions. 1832 varieties are distinguished by whether the 2 in the date has a curved base or square base and by the number of stars on the reverse. 1834 varieties are distinguished by whether the 4 has a serif at its far right.

Date	Mintage	F-12	VF-20	XF-40	MS-60
1813	95,428	2,400	2,750	3,800	7,800
1814/13	15,454	2,500	2,800	3,500	10,000
1815	635	27,000	33,000	70,000	—
Note: 1815, private sale, Jan. 1994, MS-61, $150,000					
1818	48,588	2,475	3,100	4,000	8,250
1819	51,723	9,600	16,500	275,000	62,000
1820 curved-base 2, small letters	263,806	2,600	3,000	4,500	11,000
1820 curved-base 2, large letters	Inc. above	2,600	3,000	4,150	20,000
1820 square-base 2	Inc. above	2,600	3,000	3,800	14,000
1821	34,641	7,000	15,000	23,000	70,000
1822 3 known	—	—	—	—	1,000,000
Note: 1822, private sale, 1993, VF-30, $1,000,000.					
1823	14,485	2,500	3,400	5,000	16,000
1824	17,340	5,000	10,000	16,000	38,000
1825/21	29,060	5,150	9,500	12,000	38,000

714 UNITED STATES

Date	Mintage	F-12	VF-20	XF-40	MS-60	Prf-65
1846D	80,294	1,250	1,800	2,400	13,000	—
1846O	58,000	215	375	1,000	11,500	—
1847	915,981	200	230	250	1,650	—
1847C	84,151	1,350	1,800	2,400	13,000	—
1847D	64,405	1,400	2,000	2,000	10,000	—
1847O	12,000	550	2,200	6,750	28,000	—
1848	260,775	200	230	275	1,500	—
1848C	64,472	1,400	1,900	2,250	19,250	—
1848D	47,465	1,450	2,000	2,350	14,500	—
1849	133,070	200	230	280	2,800	—
1849C	64,823	1,500	1,900	2,400	14,000	—
1849D	39,036	1,550	2,000	2,600	16,500	—
1850	64,491	200	300	625	4,250	—
1850C	63,591	1,350	1,850	2,300	14,000	—
1850D	43,984	1,450	1,950	2,500	33,000	—
1851	377,505	200	230	250	2,800	—
1851C	49,176	1,300	1,900	2,350	17,500	—
1851D	62,710	1,400	1,950	2,400	15,000	—
1851O	41,000	280	590	1,500	13,000	—
1852	573,901	200	230	260	1,400	—
1852C	72,574	1,350	1,900	2,450	7,750	—
1852D	91,584	1,450	2,000	2,450	13,000	—
1853	305,770	200	230	250	1,400	—
1853C	65,571	1,500	1,950	2,350	8,500	—
1853D	89,678	1,550	2,000	2,500	11,000	—
1854	160,675	200	230	260	2,000	—
1854C	39,283	1,400	1,900	2,300	14,000	—
1854D	56,413	1,400	1,875	2,200	11,500	—
1854O	46,000	225	300	525	8,250	—
1854S	268	—	—	—	—	—

Note: 1854S, Bowers & Merena, Oct. 1982, AU-55, $170,000.

Date	Mintage	F-12	VF-20	XF-40	MS-60	Prf-65
1855	117,098	200	230	250	1,800	—
1855C	39,788	1,400	1,900	2,300	16,000	—
1855D	22,432	1,500	1,950	2,400	19,000	—
1855O	11,100	315	675	2,100	20,000	—
1855S	61,000	200	390	1,000	15,500	—
1856	197,990	200	230	240	2,300	—
1856C	28,457	1,450	1,875	2,400	20,000	—
1856D	19,786	1,475	1,950	2,600	15,000	—
1856O	10,000	370	650	1,600	14,000	—
1856S	105,100	200	300	700	6,750	—
1857	98,188	200	230	260	1,600	123,500
1857C	31,360	1,400	1,900	2,500	9,500	—
1857D	17,046	1,500	2,000	2,650	14,500	—
1857O	13,000	340	640	1,400	15,000	—
1857S	87,000	200	300	700	11,000	—
1858	15,136	200	240	550	3,850	190,000
1858C	38,856	1,400	1,900	2,350	11,000	—
1858D	15,362	1,500	2,000	2,450	12,500	—
1858S	18,600	400	825	2,350	31,000	—
1859	16,814	200	325	625	7,000	—
1859C	31,847	1,400	1,900	2,450	16,000	—
1859D	10,366	1,600	2,150	2,600	16,000	—
1859S	13,220	615	1,800	4,150	30,000	—
1860	19,825	200	280	575	3,500	100,000
1860C	14,813	1,500	2,100	3,000	15,000	—
1860D	14,635	1,500	1,900	2,600	15,000	—
1860S	21,200	500	1,100	2,100	27,000	—
1861	688,150	200	230	245	1,450	100,000
1861C	6,879	1,500	2,400	3,900	25,000	—
1861D	1,597	3,000	4,700	7,000	50,000	—
1861S	18,000	500	1,100	4,500	36,500	—
1862	4,465	400	800	1,850	20,000	96,000
1862S	9,500	1,500	3,000	6,000	62,000	—
1863	2,472	450	1,200	3,750	27,500	90,000
1863S	17,000	600	1,450	4,100	35,500	—
1864	4,220	350	650	1,850	15,000	72,000
1864S	3,888	2,300	4,750	16,000	55,000	—
1865	1,295	500	1,450	4,100	20,000	82,500
1865S	27,612	475	1,400	2,400	20,000	—
1866S	9,000	750	1,750	4,000	40,000	—

Coronet head, left, within circle of stars
"In God We Trust" above eagle

KM# 101 0.9000 GOLD 0.242 oz. AGW. 21.6 mm. 8.3590 g. **Designer:** Christian Gobrecht **Notes:** The 1873 "closed-3" and "open-3" varieties are known and are distinguished by the amount of space between the upper left and lower left serifs of the 3 in the date.

Date	Mintage	VF-20	XF-40	AU-50	MS-60	MS-63	MS-65	Prf-65
1866	6,730	800	1,650	3,500	16,500	—	—	70,000
1866S	34,920	900	2,600	8,800	25,000	—	—	—
1867	6,920	500	1,500	3,300	11,500	—	—	70,000
1867S	29,000	1,400	2,900	8,000	34,500	—	—	—
1868	5,725	650	1,000	3,500	11,500	—	—	70,000
1868S	52,000	400	1,550	4,000	20,000	—	—	—
1869	1,785	925	2,400	3,500	17,500	34,000	—	65,000
1869S	31,000	500	1,750	4,000	26,000	—	—	—
1870	4,035	800	2,000	2,850	18,000	—	—	75,000
1870CC	7,675	5,250	15,000	30,000	110,000	137,500	200,000	—
1870S	17,000	950	2,600	8,250	29,000	—	—	—
1871	3,230	900	1,700	3,300	12,500	—	—	70,000
1871CC	20,770	1,250	3,000	12,000	60,000	—	—	—
1871S	25,000	500	950	2,950	13,000	—	—	—
1872	1,690	850	1,925	3,000	15,000	18,000	—	60,000
1872CC	16,980	1,250	5,000	20,000	60,000	—	—	—
1872S	36,400	460	800	3,400	13,500	—	—	—
1873 closed 3	49,305	215	225	440	1,200	6,500	24,000	70,000
1873 open 3	63,200	215	220	350	850	3,650	—	—
1873CC	7,416	2,600	12,500	27,500	60,000	—	—	—
1873S	31,000	525	1,400	3,250	21,000	—	—	—
1874	3,508	660	1,675	2,500	13,000	26,000	—	66,000
1874CC	21,198	850	1,700	9,500	36,000	—	—	—
1874S	16,000	640	2,100	4,800	22,500	—	—	—
1875	220	34,000	45,000	60,000	190,000	—	—	185,000
1875CC	11,828	1,400	4,500	11,500	52,000	—	—	—
1875S	9,000	715	2,250	5,000	16,500	32,500	—	—
1876	1,477	1,100	2,500	4,125	11,000	14,500	55,000	60,000
1876CC	6,887	1,450	5,000	14,000	46,500	82,500	165,000	—
1876S	4,000	2,000	3,600	9,500	30,000	—	—	—
1877	1,152	900	2,750	4,000	13,750	29,000	—	75,000
1877CC	8,680	1,000	3,300	11,000	52,500	—	—	—
1877S	26,700	400	650	1,400	9,200	—	—	—
1878	131,740	215	220	240	425	2,000	—	50,000
1878CC	9,054	3,100	7,200	20,000	60,000	—	—	—
1878S	144,700	215	220	3,000	675	4,250	—	—
1879	301,950	215	220	225	400	2,000	12,000	55,000
1879CC	17,281	575	1,500	3,150	22,000	—	—	—
1879S	426,200	215	225	240	950	3,300	—	—
1880	3,166,436	215	225	225	235	840	7,500	54,000
1880CC	51,017	425	815	1,375	9,900	—	—	—
1880S	1,348,900	215	220	225	235	800	5,750	—
1881	5,708,802	215	220	225	235	775	4,800	54,000
1881/80	Inc. above	330	600	750	1,500	4,500	—	—
1881CC	13,886	550	1,500	7,000	22,500	60,000	—	—
1881S	969,000	215	220	225	235	775	7,150	—
1882	2,514,568	215	220	225	235	800	6,150	54,000
1882CC	82,817	415	625	900	7,500	40,000	—	—
1882S	969,000	215	220	225	235	800	4,500	—
1883	233,461	215	220	225	260	1,200	—	40,000
1883CC	12,958	460	1,100	3,200	18,000	—	—	—
1883S	83,200	215	240	315	1,000	2,950	—	—
1884	191,078	215	220	225	650	2,250	—	35,000
1884CC	16,402	550	975	3,000	17,000	—	—	—
1884S	177,000	215	220	225	345	2,000	—	—
1885	601,506	215	220	225	260	825	4,800	35,000
1885S	1,211,500	215	220	225	235	790	4,000	—
1886	388,432	215	220	225	235	1,125	5,600	44,000
1886S	3,268,000	215	220	225	235	815	4,500	—
1887	87	—	14,500	20,000	—	—	—	120,000
1887S	1,912,000	215	220	225	235	800	4,800	—
1888	18,296	215	230	300	550	1,500	—	29,000
1888S	293,900	215	220	320	1,200	4,000	—	—
1889	7,565	350	440	515	1,150	2,400	—	30,000
1890	4,328	400	475	550	2,200	6,500	—	27,000
1890CC	53,800	330	460	615	1,600	8,000	55,000	—
1891	61,413	215	220	230	450	1,900	5,400	29,000
1891CC	208,000	315	415	525	750	3,150	31,500	—
1892	753,572	215	220	225	235	880	7,000	30,000
1892CC	82,968	315	400	575	1,500	6,000	33,500	—
1892O	10,000	515	1,000	1,375	3,300	—	—	—
1892S	298,400	215	220	225	525	3,300	—	—
1893	1,528,197	215	220	225	235	800	3,900	34,000
1893CC	60,000	345	465	770	1,400	6,350	—	—
1893O	110,000	225	315	480	950	6,500	—	—
1893S	224,000	215	220	225	245	825	9,000	—
1894	957,955	215	220	225	235	800	2,600	35,000
1894O	16,600	200	360	570	1,300	5,500	—	—
1894S	55,900	240	375	575	2,900	10,000	—	—
1895	1,345,936	215	220	225	235	800	4,500	29,000
1895S	112,000	215	275	400	3,150	6,500	26,000	—
1896	59,063	215	220	225	235	9,750	4,500	30,000
1896S	155,400	215	240	300	1,150	6,000	24,500	—
1897	867,883	215	220	225	235	825	4,500	35,000
1897S	354,000	215	220	235	865	5,150	—	—
1898	633,495	215	220	225	235	885	6,000	30,000
1898S	1,397,400	215	220	225	230	950	—	—
1899	1,710,729	215	220	225	235	730	3,600	30,000
1899S	1,545,000	215	220	225	235	1,000	9,600	—
1900	1,405,730	215	220	225	235	790	3,600	30,000
1900S	329,000	215	220	230	245	900	14,000	—
1901	616,040	215	220	225	235	750	3,650	27,000
1901S	3,648,000	215	220	225	235	730	3,600	—
1902	172,562	215	220	225	235	730	4,400	27,000
1902S	939,000	215	220	225	235	730	3,600	—
1903	227,024	215	220	225	235	730	4,000	27,000
1903S	1,855,000	215	220	225	235	730	3,600	—
1904	392,136	215	220	225	235	730	3,600	27,000
1904S	97,000	215	240	285	900	3,850	9,600	—
1905	302,308	215	220	225	235	740	4,000	27,000
1905S	880,700	215	225	250	235	1,500	9,600	—
1906	348,820	215	220	225	235	745	3,600	26,000
1906D	320,000	215	220	225	235	930	3,200	—
1906S	598,000	215	220	230	240	900	4,400	—
1907	626,192	215	220	225	235	730	3,400	23,000
1907D	888,000	215	220	225	235	730	3,400	—
1908	421,874	215	220	225	235	730	3,400	—

UNITED STATES 715

Indian Head

KM# 129 0.9000 **GOLD** .2420 oz. AGW. 21.6 mm. 8.3590 g. **Designer:** Bela Lyon Pratt

Date	Mintage	VF-20	XF-40	AU-50	MS-60	MS-63	MS-65	Prf-65
1908	578,012	330	355	385	460	4,350	25,000	25,500
1908D	148,000	330	355	385	460	4,350	27,500	—
1908S	82,000	330	415	430	1,275	4,350	24,000	—
1909	627,138	330	355	385	460	4,350	25,000	36,000
1909D	3,423,560	330	355	385	460	4,350	25,000	—
1909O	34,200	2,000	3,400	6,000	21,000	66,000	260,000	—
1909S	297,200	330	355	385	1,400	11,000	45,000	—
1910	604,250	330	355	385	460	4,350	25,000	37,000
1910D	193,600	330	355	385	460	4,350	42,500	—
1910S	770,200	330	355	385	1,000	6,000	44,000	—
1911	915,139	330	355	385	460	4,350	25,000	28,500
1911D	72,500	475	535	515	4,500	37,000	241,500	—
1911S	1,416,000	340	355	385	560	4,350	41,500	—
1912	790,144	330	355	385	460	4,350	25,000	28,500
1912S	392,000	330	365	400	1,700	13,500	93,500	—
1913	916,099	330	355	385	460	4,350	25,000	28,000
1913S	408,000	340	350	385	1,400	11,500	120,000	—
1914	247,125	330	355	385	460	4,350	25,000	28,500
1914D	247,000	335	355	385	460	4,350	26,000	—
1914S	263,000	340	365	400	1,375	13,500	100,000	—
1915	588,075	330	355	385	460	4,350	25,000	39,000
1915S	164,000	340	400	385	2,000	17,000	110,000	—
1916S	240,000	330	355	385	560	4,350	25,000	—
1929	662,000	4,200	9,600	10,500	13,250	17,500	45,000	—

$10 (EAGLE)

GOLD

Liberty Cap
Small eagle

KM# 21 0.9160 **GOLD** 0.5159 oz. AGW. 33mm. 17.5000 g. **Designer:** Robert Scot

Date	Mintage	F-12	VF-20	XF-40	MS-60
1795 13 leaves	5,583	18,000	24,000	33,000	70,000
1795 9 leaves	Inc. above	26,000	40,000	60,000	230,000
1796	4,146	23,000	27,500	38,000	80,000
1797 small eagle	3,615	30,000	38,000	45,000	185,000

Liberty cap on head, right, flanked by stars   Heraldic eagle

KM# 30 0.9160 **GOLD** 0.5159 oz. AGW. 33mm. 17.5000 g. **Designer:** Robert Scot **Notes:** The 1798/97 varieties are distinguished by the positioning of the stars on the obverse.

Date	Mintage	F-12	VF-20	XF-40	MS-60
1797 large eagle	10,940	9,000	11,000	14,000	40,000
1798/97 9 stars left, 4 right	900	11,000	19,000	29,000	100,000
1798/97 7 stars left, 6 right	842	23,000	30,000	65,000	—
1799	37,449	8,000	10,000	12,500	31,000
1800	5,999	8,200	11,000	12,000	33,000
1801	44,344	8,200	11,000	12,000	29,000
1803	15,017	8,200	11,000	12,000	32,000
1804	3,757	9,500	11,500	14,000	38,000

Coronet Head
Old-style head, left, within circle of stars
No motto above eagle

KM# 66.1 0.9000 **GOLD** 0.4839 oz. AGW. 27 mm. 16.7180 g. **Designer:** Christian Gobrecht

Date	Mintage	F-12	VF-20	XF-40	MS-60	Prf-65
1838	7,200	800	1,200	2,900	35,500	—
1839 large letters	38,248	800	1,150	1,950	32,000	—

New-style head, left, within circle of stars
No motto above eagle

KM# 66.2 0.9000 **GOLD** 0.4839 oz. AGW. 27 mm. 16.7180 g. **Designer:** Christian Gobrecht **Notes:** The 1842 varieties are distinguished by the size of the numerals in the date.

Date	Mintage	F-12	VF-20	XF-40	MS-60	Prf-65
1839 small letters	Inc. above	825	1,600	3,500	30,000	—
1840	47,338	410	435	650	10,500	—
1841	63,131	410	435	500	9,500	—
1841O	2,500	1,400	2,400	5,000	30,000	—
1842 small date	81,507	410	435	650	16,500	—
1842 large date	Inc. above	410	435	475	9,500	—
1842O	27,400	410	450	500	22,500	—
1843	75,462	410	435	500	19,000	—
1843O	175,162	410	435	475	12,000	—
1844	6,361	800	1,350	2,900	16,750	—
1844O	118,700	410	435	475	15,000	—
1845	26,153	410	600	775	14,000	—
1845O	47,500	410	435	700	16,500	—
1846	20,095	435	625	900	20,000	—
1846O	81,780	410	435	770	14,750	—
1847	862,258	410	435	380	3,000	—
1847O	571,500	410	435	450	4,850	—
1848	145,484	410	435	450	4,300	—
1848O	38,850	410	525	1,050	14,000	—
1849	653,618	410	435	450	3,400	—
1849O	23,900	425	710	2,100	25,000	—
1850	291,451	410	435	450	3,600	—
1850O	57,500	410	440	880	—	—
1851	176,328	410	435	500	5,150	—
1851O	263,000	410	435	450	5,750	—
1852	263,106	410	435	370	5,000	—
1852O	18,000	425	650	1,100	19,000	—
1853	201,253	410	435	450	3,500	—
1853O	51,000	410	435	500	13,000	—
1854	54,250	410	435	450	6,000	—
1854O small date	52,500	410	435	675	11,000	—
1854O large date	Inc. above	420	475	875		—
1854S	123,826	410	435	450	5,500	—
1855	121,701	410	435	450	4,150	—
1855O	18,000	415	435	1,250	20,000	—
1855S	9,000	800	1,500	2,500	29,500	—
1856	60,490	410	435	450	4,500	—
1856O	14,500	425	725	1,250	10,000	—
1856S	68,000	410	435	515	8,500	—
1857	16,606	410	515	850	12,000	—
1857O	5,500	600	1,000	1,850	20,000	—
1857S	26,000	410	450	1,000	10,000	—
1858	2,521	3,000	5,200	8,200	35,000	—
1858O	20,000	410	460	790	10,000	—
1858S	11,800	900	1,600	3,100	34,000	—
1859	16,093	410	435	800	10,500	—
1859O	2,300	2,000	4,000	8,200	47,500	—
1859S	7,000	1,200	1,800	4,500	40,000	—
1860	15,105	410	475	800	8,000	—
1860O	11,100	425	600	1,300	8,250	—
1860S	5,000	1,400	3,250	6,100	40,500	—
1861	113,233	410	435	450	4,000	—
1861S	15,500	690	1,600	2,950	32,500	—
1862	10,995	410	550	1,200	13,500	—
1862S	12,500	700	2,000	3,000	37,000	—
1863	1,248	2,400	3,650	10,000	42,500	—
1863S	10,000	700	1,600	3,350	24,000	—
1864	3,580	775	1,600	4,500	18,000	—
1864S	2,500	2,600	5,100	13,000	50,000	—
1865	4,005	900	1,950	3,500	32,000	—

UNITED STATES

Date	Mintage	F-12	VF-20	XF-40	MS-60	Prf-65
1865S	16,700	1,700	5,500	12,000	45,000	—
1865S /inverted 186	—	1,300	3,000	6,100	50,000	—
1866S	8,500	1,000	2,800	3,800	44,000	—

New-style head, left, within circle of stars
"In God We Trust" above eagle

KM# 102 0.9000 **GOLD** 0.4839 oz. AGW. 27 mm. 16.7180 g. **Designer:** Christian Gobrecht **Notes:** The 1873 "closed-3" and "open-3" varieties are distinguished by the amount of space between the upper left and lower left serifs of the 3 in the date.

Date	Mintage	VF-20	XF-40	AU-50	MS-60	MS-63	MS-65	Prf-65
1866	3,780	850	1,800	5,000	17,000	—	—	75,000
1866S	11,500	1,550	4,000	8,000	26,000	—	—	—
1867	3,140	1,500	2,600	5,000	26,000	—	—	75,000
1867S	9,000	2,000	6,000	12,000	40,000	—	—	—
1868	10,655	550	800	2,000	18,000	—	—	60,000
1868S	13,500	1,300	2,600	4,000	24,000	—	—	—
1869	1,855	1,600	3,000	6,000	36,000	—	—	—
1869S	6,430	1,600	2,700	6,250	25,000	—	—	—
1870	4,025	850	1,500	2,500	18,000	—	—	60,000
1870CC	5,908	10,000	22,000	42,000	90,000	—	—	—
1870S	8,000	1,300	3,000	7,000	34,000	—	—	—
1871	1,820	1,600	3,000	5,000	25,000	—	—	75,000
1871CC	8,085	2,600	6,000	21,000	60,000	—	—	—
1871S	16,500	1,300	1,700	6,000	30,000	—	—	—
1872	1,650	2,400	3,600	11,000	18,000	33,000	—	60,000
1872CC	4,600	3,150	11,000	24,000	60,000	—	—	—
1872S	17,300	550	950	1,800	22,000	—	—	—
1873 closed 3	825	5,000	1,000	17,500	55,000	—	—	60,000
1873CC	4,543	6,000	12,500	28,000	58,000	—	—	—
1873S	12,000	950	2,350	5,100	25,000	—	—	—
1874	53,160	290	425	450	2,100	8,750	—	60,000
1874CC	16,767	950	3,100	10,500	40,000	—	—	—
1874S	10,000	1,150	3,250	7,250	4,000	—	—	—
1875	120	40,000	59,000	80,000	95,000	—	—	185,000

Note: 1875, Akers, Aug. 1990, Proof, $115,000.

Date	Mintage	VF-20	XF-40	AU-50	MS-60	MS-63	MS-65	Prf-65
1875CC	7,715	4,250	11,000	25,000	65,000	—	—	—
1876	732	3,500	6,250	17,000	55,000	—	—	60,000
1876CC	4,696	2,400	7,950	23,000	50,000	—	—	—
1876S	5,000	1,475	2,000	6,500	40,000	—	—	—
1877	817	2,650	5,750	9,250	—	—	—	—
1877CC	3,332	2,600	6,400	15,000	48,000	—	—	—
1877S	17,000	500	850	2,200	23,000	—	—	—
1878	73,800	420	425	450	1,000	5,000	—	60,000
1878CC	3,244	4,000	10,000	16,000	47,000	—	—	—
1878S	26,100	475	615	2,150	16,000	—	—	—
1879	384,770	420	425	450	665	2,850	—	50,000
1879/78	Inc. above	420	450	800	1,250	2,000	—	—
1879CC	1,762	9,500	15,000	26,000	60,000	—	—	—
1879O	1,500	2,300	3,750	10,000	28,750	—	—	—
1879S	224,000	420	425	450	1,100	7,750	—	—
1880	1,644,876	420	425	450	465	2,250	—	45,000
1880CC	11,190	590	900	1,800	14,500	—	—	—
1880O	9,200	450	800	1,400	13,000	—	—	—
1880S	506,250	420	425	450	465	3,300	—	—
1881	3,877,260	420	425	450	465	1,200	—	45,000
1881CC	24,015	515	800	950	7,000	20,000	—	—
1881O	8,350	550	820	1,600	6,750	—	—	—
1881S	970,000	420	425	450	465	—	—	—
1882	2,324,480	420	425	450	465	1,200	—	42,000
1882CC	6,764	950	1,300	3,000	13,000	35,000	—	—
1882O	10,820	420	575	1,200	7,700	16,750	—	—
1882S	132,000	420	425	450	465	4,200	—	—
1883	208,740	420	425	450	465	2,400	—	42,000
1883CC	12,000	575	915	2,600	14,000	35,000	—	—
1883O	800	3,300	7,200	10,500	33,500	—	—	—
1883S	38,000	420	425	450	1,350	13,000	—	—
1884	76,905	420	425	450	750	4,000	—	46,000
1884CC	9,925	600	1,100	2,250	13,000	35,000	—	—
1884S	124,250	420	425	450	575	6,500	—	—
1885	253,527	420	425	450	465	4,200	—	43,000
1885S	228,000	420	425	450	465	4,300	22,000	—
1886	236,160	420	425	450	465	1,800	—	41,000
1886S	826,000	420	425	450	465	1,500	—	—
1887	53,680	420	425	450	800	4,750	—	37,000
1887S	817,000	420	425	450	465	1,950	—	—
1888	132,996	420	425	450	850	5,700	—	38,500
1888O	21,335	420	425	450	675	4,500	—	—
1888S	648,700	420	425	450	465	2,700	—	—
1889	4,485	600	700	1,100	2,700	7,200	—	43,000
1889S	425,400	420	425	450	465	1,500	22,000	—
1890	58,043	420	425	450	825	5,200	22,000	37,500
1890CC	17,500	420	450	650	2,000	13,500	—	—
1891	91,868	420	425	450	465	1,900	—	32,500
1891CC	103,732	515	575	770	1,350	6,000	—	—
1892	797,552	420	425	450	465	1,300	13,000	38,000
1892CC	40,000	475	600	825	3,800	9,000	22,000	—
1892O	28,688	420	425	450	465	6,000	—	—
1892S	115,500	420	425	450	465	4,500	—	—

Date	Mintage	VF-20	XF-40	AU-50	MS-60	MS-63	MS-65	Prf-65
1893	1,840,895	420	425	450	465	850	—	36,000
1893CC	14,000	550	900	1,800	8,500	18,000	—	—
1893O	17,000	420	425	450	625	5,300	—	—
1893S	141,350	420	425	450	500	4,400	—	—
1894	2,470,778	420	425	450	465	1,400	22,000	35,000
1894O	107,500	420	425	475	1,200	5,250	—	—
1894S	25,000	420	450	900	3,500	8,800	—	—
1895	567,826	420	425	450	465	1,400	22,000	33,000
1895O	98,000	420	425	475	525	4,800	—	—
1895S	49,000	420	425	700	2,250	9,550	—	—
1896	76,348	420	425	450	465	2,100	—	31,500
1896S	123,750	420	425	485	2,500	11,000	—	—
1897	1,000,159	420	425	450	465	1,400	22,000	35,000
1897O	42,500	420	425	450	750	4,200	—	—
1897S	234,750	420	425	450	870	5,000	—	—
1898	812,197	420	425	450	465	1,450	22,000	35,000
1898S	473,600	420	425	450	465	4,250	—	—
1899	1,262,305	420	425	450	465	1,400	22,000	31,000
1899O	37,047	420	425	450	550	4,750	—	—
1899S	841,000	420	425	450	465	3,250	—	—
1900	293,960	420	425	450	465	1,400	22,000	30,500
1900S	81,000	420	425	450	850	5,200	—	—
1901	1,718,825	420	425	450	465	1,400	22,000	30,500
1901O	72,041	420	425	450	465	3,700	—	—
1901S	2,812,750	420	425	450	465	1,400	22,000	—
1902	82,513	420	425	450	465	2,450	—	30,500
1902S	469,500	420	425	450	465	1,400	22,000	—
1903	125,926	420	425	450	465	2,500	—	30,000
1903O	112,771	420	425	450	465	3,250	—	—
1903S	538,000	420	425	450	465	1,400	22,000	—
1904	162,038	420	425	450	465	2,400	—	31,500
1904O	108,950	420	425	450	465	3,700	—	—
1905	201,078	420	425	450	465	1,450	22,000	30,000
1905S	369,250	420	425	450	1,100	4,500	—	—
1906	165,497	420	425	450	465	2,275	22,000	30,000
1906D	981,000	420	425	450	465	1,450	22,000	—
1906O	86,895	420	425	450	470	3,400	—	—
1906S	457,000	420	425	450	515	4,400	22,000	—
1907	1,203,973	420	425	450	465	1,400	—	30,000
1907D	1,030,000	420	425	450	465	1,400	—	—
1907S	210,500	420	425	450	600	4,650	—	—

Indian Head
No motto next to eagle

KM# 125 0.9000 **GOLD** 0.4839 oz. AGW. 27 mm. 16.7180 g. **Designer:** Augustus Saint-Gaudens **Notes:** 1907 varieties are distinguished by whether the edge is rolled or wired, and whether the legend "E Pluribus Unum" has periods between each word.

Date	Mintage	VF-20	XF-40	AU-50	MS-60	MS-63	MS-65	Prf-65
1907 wire edge, periods before and after legend	500	9,500	14,900	16,900	22,000	36,500	65,000	—
1907 same, without stars on edge, unique								
1907 rolled edge, periods	42	26,000	38,500	49,000	66,500	98,500	250,000	—
1907 without periods	239,406	470	480	530	625	2,950	9,800	—
1908 without motto	33,500	470	480	530	735	4,650	14,500	—
1908D without motto	210,000	475	485	535	635	6,250	38,500	—

"In God We Trust" left of eagle

KM# 130 0.9000 **GOLD** 0.4839 oz. AGW. 27 mm. 16.7180 g. **Designer:** Augustus Saint-Gaudens

Date	Mintage	VF-20	XF-40	AU-50	MS-60	MS-63	MS-65	Prf-65
1908	341,486	470	480	530	595	4,450	14,500	52,500
1908D	836,500	475	485	540	625	6,850	29,000	—
1908S	59,850	485	495	620	2,950	8,200	25,500	—
1909	184,863	470	480	530	595	2,450	10,000	54,500
1909D	121,540	475	485	535	675	4,150	34,500	—
1909S	292,350	475	485	535	675	4,350	13,900	—
1910	318,704	470	480	530	595	2,350	8,500	54,500
1910D	2,356,640	465	475	525	595	2,185	8,600	—
1910S	811,000	475	485	535	675	7,250	55,000	—
1911	505,595	465	475	525	590	2,185	8,600	52,500
1911D	30,100	595	675	950	4,200	21,500	120,000	—
1911S	51,000	530	555	645	1,050	7,750	14,500	—
1912	405,083	470	480	530	595	2,350	9,350	52,500
1912S	300,000	475	485	535	675	5,300	48,500	—

UNITED STATES

Date	Mintage	VF-20	XF-40	AU-50	MS-60	MS-63	MS-65	Prf-65
1913	442,071	470	480	530	595	2,350	8,400	52,500
1913S	66,000	525	600	775	3,900	27,500	100,000	—
1914	151,050	470	480	530	595	2,400	9,000	52,500
1914D	343,500	470	480	530	595	2,450	15,500	—
1914S	208,000	480	490	540	715	6,350	32,500	—
1915	351,075	470	480	530	595	2,350	8,500	55,000
1915S	59,000	600	725	775	3,150	14,500	65,000	—
1916S	138,500	495	510	570	675	4,850	18,500	—
1920S	126,500	7,800	11,000	14,500	28,500	69,000	275,000	—
1926	1,014,000	465	475	525	575	1,485	5,500	—
1930S	96,000	5,500	7,000	8,500	14,500	31,500	67,500	—
1932	4,463,000	465	475	525	575	1,485	5,500	—
1933	312,500	110,000	140,000	150,000	185,000	245,000	650,000	—

$20 (DOUBLE EAGLE)

GOLD

Liberty

Coronet head, left, within circle of stars
"Twenty D." below eagle, no motto above eagle

KM# 74.1 0.9000 **GOLD** 0.9677 oz. AGW. 34 mm. 33.4360 g. **Designer:** James B. Longacre

Date	Mintage	VF-20	XF-40	AU-50	MS-60	MS-63	MS-65	Prf-65
1849 unique, in Smithsonian collection	1	—	—	—	—	—	—	—
1850	1,170,261	885	1,325	3,000	8,000	47,500	175,000	—
1850O	141,000	1,000	2,400	7,600	36,000	—	—	—
1851	2,087,155	850	865	970	3,600	23,000	—	—
1851O	315,000	850	1,400	2,600	26,000	—	—	—
1852	2,053,026	850	865	1,000	3,650	14,000	—	—
1852O	190,000	900	1,100	3,800	19,000	—	—	—
1853	1,261,326	850	875	1,000	5,000	24,000	—	—
1853O	71,000	875	2,200	3,600	36,000	—	—	—
1854	757,899	850	865	1,050	6,000	24,000	—	—
1854O	3,250	45,000	70,000	165,000	350,000	—	—	—
1854S	141,468	850	900	1,500	5,000	13,000	44,000	—
1855	364,666	850	900	1,450	10,000	—	—	—
1855O	8,000	3,400	9,500	23,000	88,000	—	—	—
1855S	879,675	850	900	1,500	7,200	17,000	—	—
1856	329,878	850	865	1,200	8,900	30,000	—	—
1856O	2,250	70,000	90,000	200,000	425,000	—	—	—
1856S	1,189,750	850	865	1,300	5,500	14,000	35,000	—
1857	439,375	850	865	975	3,400	30,000	—	—
1857O	30,000	1,300	2,650	4,800	30,000	130,000	—	—
1857S	970,500	850	865	1,200	4,800	8,000	—	—
1858	211,714	875	1,000	1,500	5,800	40,000	—	—
1858O	35,250	1,750	2,600	7,600	29,000	—	—	—
1858S	846,710	850	875	1,700	10,500	—	—	—
1859	43,597	1,100	2,450	4,400	32,000	—	—	—
1859O	9,100	4,700	9,000	22,000	85,000	—	—	—
1859S	636,445	850	865	1,800	5,000	—	—	—
1860	577,670	850	865	1,000	4,400	23,000	—	—
1860O	6,600	4,650	9,000	23,000	89,000	—	—	—
1860S	544,950	850	865	1,000	6,400	23,000	—	—
1861	2,976,453	850	865	1,000	3,000	11,000	40,000	—
1861O	17,741	3,300	6,500	23,000	88,000	—	—	—
1861S	768,000	900	950	2,450	11,000	35,000	—	—

Coronet head, left, within circle of stars
Paquet design, "Twenty D." below eagle

KM# 93 0.9000 **GOLD** 0.9677 oz. AGW. 33.4360 g. **Notes:** In 1861 the reverse was redesigned by Anthony C. Paquet, but it was withdrawn soon after its release. The letters in the inscriptions on the Paquet-reverse variety are taller than on the regular reverse.

Date	Mintage	VF-20	XF-40	AU-50	MS-60	MS-63	MS-65	Prf-65
1861 2 Known	—	—	—	—	—	—	—	—

Note: 1861 Paquet reverse, Bowers & Merena, Nov. 1988, MS-67, $660,000.

| 1861S | — | 17,500 | 38,500 | 80,000 | 245,000 | — | — | — |

Note: Included in mintage of 1861S, KM#74.1

Coronet head, left, within circle of stars
"Twenty D." below eagle. "In God We Trust" above eagle

KM# 74.2 0.9000 **GOLD** 0.9677 oz. AGW. 34 mm. 33.4360 g. **Designer:** James B. Longacre **Notes:** The 1873 "closed-3" and "open-3" varieties are known and are distinguished by the amount of space between the upper left and lower left serif in the 3 in the date.

Date	Mintage	VF-20	XF-40	AU-50	MS-60	MS-63	MS-65	Prf-65
1866	698,775	845	900	2,100	6,000	32,000	—	—
1866S	842,250	845	850	2,000	16,000	—	—	—
1867	251,065	845	850	925	2,400	23,000	—	—
1867S	920,750	845	850	1,600	15,000	—	—	—
1868	98,600	845	950	2,000	10,000	44,000	—	—
1868S	837,500	845	850	1,900	9,500	—	—	—
1869	175,155	845	850	1,250	6,000	24,000	—	—
1869S	686,750	845	850	1,100	5,300	33,000	—	—
1870	155,185	845	1,000	1,750	10,000	—	—	—
1870CC	3,789	100,000	150,000	260,000	700,000	—	—	—
1870S	982,000	845	850	860	5,300	27,000	—	—
1871	80,150	845	850	1,500	4,500	30,000	—	—
1871CC	17,387	6,750	11,000	27,000	45,000	—	—	—
1871S	928,000	845	850	860	4,400	22,000	—	—
1872	251,880	845	850	860	3,000	25,000	—	—
1872CC	26,900	2,200	2,500	7,000	33,000	—	—	—
1872S	780,000	845	850	860	3,000	24,000	—	—
1873 closed 3	Est. 208,925	845	850	1,100	2,600	—	—	—
1873 open 3	Est. 1,500,900	845	850	860	990	12,000	—	—
1873CC	22,410	2,600	4,750	8,000	36,000	100,000	—	—
1873S	1,040,600	845	850	860	1,800	23,000	—	—
1874	366,800	845	850	860	1,400	22,000	—	—
1874CC	115,085	1,500	1,900	2,650	9,200	—	—	—
1874S	1,214,000	845	850	860	1,700	28,000	—	—
1875	295,740	845	850	860	1,000	13,000	—	—
1875CC	111,151	1,300	1,500	1,850	3,000	19,000	—	—
1875S	1,230,000	845	850	860	1,100	18,000	—	—
1876	583,905	775	790	810	975	11,500	78,500	185,000
1876CC	138,441	1,300	1,500	1,900	5,750	37,000	—	—
1876S	1,597,000	845	850	860	990	12,000	—	—

Coronet head, left, within circle of stars
"Twenty Dollars" below eagle

KM# 74.3 0.9000 **GOLD** 0.9677 oz. AGW. 33.4360 g.

Date	Mintage	VF-20	XF-40	AU-50	MS-60	MS-63	MS-65	Prf-65
1877	397,670	825	830	840	850	5,250	—	—
1877CC	42,565	1,500	1,900	2,600	17,500	—	—	—
1877S	1,735,000	825	830	840	875	12,500	—	—
1878	543,645	825	830	840	850	5,600	—	—
1878CC	13,180	2,200	3,000	6,000	26,000	—	—	—
1878S	1,739,000	825	830	840	850	22,000	—	—
1879	207,630	825	830	840	1,000	14,000	—	—
1879CC	10,708	2,000	4,000	7,000	34,000	—	—	—
1879O	2,325	7,000	9,000	24,000	75,000	120,000	—	—
1879S	1,223,800	825	830	840	1,200	—	—	—
1880	51,456	825	830	840	3,000	16,500	—	—
1880S	836,000	825	830	840	950	16,000	—	—
1881	2,260	4,500	6,750	13,750	52,000	—	—	105,000
1881S	727,000	825	830	840	900	17,500	—	—
1882	630	8,000	22,000	35,000	80,000	135,000	—	—
1882CC	39,140	1,200	1,500	2,200	7,000	—	—	—
1882S	1,125,000	825	830	840	850	16,000	—	—
1883 proof only	92	—	—	14,000	—	—	—	—
1883CC	59,962	1,350	1,600	2,000	4,800	21,500	—	—
1883S	1,189,000	825	830	840	850	9,000	—	—
1884 proof only	71	—	—	15,000	—	—	—	150,000
1884CC	81,139	1,250	1,550	1,900	3,100	—	—	—
1884S	916,000	825	830	840	850	7,000	—	—

718 UNITED STATES

Date	Mintage	VF-20	XF-40	AU-50	MS-60	MS-63	MS-65	Prf-65
1885	828	7,000	8,500	12,000	35,000	—	—	—
1885CC	9,450	3,000	4,000	6,000	13,000	—	—	—
1885S	683,500	825	830	840	850	7,000	—	—
1886	1,106	9,800	16,500	33,000	58,000	98,500	—	96,000
1887	121	—	—	16,500	—	—	—	142,500
1887S	283,000	825	830	840	850	14,000	—	—
1888	226,266	825	830	840	850	4,500	32,000	—
1888S	859,600	825	8,300	840	850	5,500	—	—
1889	44,111	680	695	725	900	12,800	—	93,500
1889CC	30,945	1,500	1,600	2,200	4,700	17,500	—	—
1889S	774,700	825	830	840	850	7,250	—	—
1890	75,995	825	860	840	850	6,500	—	27,000
1890CC	91,209	1,250	1,600	2,000	4,750	22,000	—	—
1890S	802,750	825	830	840	850	8,800	—	—
1891	1,442	3,500	5,000	9,500	40,000	—	—	62,500
1891CC	5,000	3,500	7,250	9,500	20,000	45,000	—	—
1891S	1,288,125	825	830	840	850	3,500	—	—
1892	4,523	1,300	2,000	2,600	6,000	20,000	—	55,000
1892CC	27,265	1,300	1,600	2,200	5,000	31,000	—	—
1892S	930,150	825	830	840	850	4,000	—	—
1893	344,339	825	830	840	850	2,600	—	60,000
1893CC	18,402	1,600	1,900	2,500	5,000	18,000	—	—
1893S	996,175	670	680	695	725	3,000	—	—
1894	1,368,990	670	680	695	725	1,700	—	55,000
1894S	1,048,550	670	680	695	725	2,600	—	—
1895	1,114,656	670	680	695	725	1,300	13,000	54,000
1895S	1,143,500	670	680	695	725	2,500	15,000	—
1896	792,663	670	680	695	725	2,000	13,000	49,000
1896S	1,403,925	670	680	695	725	2,400	—	—
1897	1,383,261	670	680	695	725	1,350	—	55,000
1897S	1,470,250	670	680	695	725	1,400	14,000	—
1898	170,470	670	680	695	725	1,325	4,500	96,000
1898S	2,575,175	670	680	695	725	1,300	11,000	—
1899	1,669,384	670	680	695	725	1,050	8,500	49,000
1899S	2,010,300	670	680	695	725	1,900	12,500	—
1900	1,874,584	670	680	695	725	1,000	6,000	49,000
1900S	2,459,500	670	680	695	725	2,300	—	—
1901	111,526	670	680	695	725	1,000	6,500	—
1901S	1,596,000	670	680	695	725	3,850	—	—
1902	31,254	670	680	695	1,175	10,750	—	94,000
1902S	1,753,625	670	680	695	725	4,000	—	—
1903	287,428	670	680	695	725	1,000	6,000	51,500
1903S	954,000	670	680	695	725	1,800	12,000	—
1904	6,256,797	670	680	695	725	1,135	4,650	94,000
1904S	5,134,175	670	680	695	725	1,000	6,600	—
1905	59,011	675	700	735	1,250	15,500	—	110,000
1905S	1,813,000	670	680	695	725	3,850	16,500	—
1906	69,690	675	685	700	825	7,400	22,500	90,000
1906D	620,250	670	680	695	725	2,350	15,000	—
1906S	2,065,750	670	680	695	725	2,300	19,000	—
1907	1,451,864	670	680	695	725	1,000	7,500	—
1907D	842,250	670	680	695	725	2,350	7,000	—
1907S	2,165,800	670	680	695	725	2,400	17,000	—

Saint-Gaudens
Roman numerals in date   No motto below eagle

KM# 126 0.9000 **GOLD** 0.9677 oz. AGW. 34 mm. 33.4360 g. **Designer:** Augustus Saint-Gaudens

Date	Mintage	VF-20	XF-40	AU-50	MS-60	MS-63	MS-65	Prf-65
MCMVII (1907) high relief, unique, AU-55, $150,000	—	—	—	—	—	—	—	—
MCMVII (1907) high relief, wire rim	11,250	7,000	9,750	11,000	13,500	23,500	49,500	—
MCMVII (1907) high relief, flat rim	Inc. above	7,250	10,250	11,500	15,000	27,650	55,000	—

Arabic numerals in date   No motto below eagle

KM# 127 0.9000 **GOLD** 0.9677 oz. AGW. 34 mm. 33.4360 g. **Designer:** Augustus Saint-Gaudens

Date	Mintage	VF-20	XF-40	AU-50	MS-60	MS-63	MS-65	Prf-65
1907 large letters on edge, unique	—	—	—	—	—	—	—	—
1907 small letters on edge	361,667	670	685	730	805	935	3,350	—
1908	4,271,551	660	675	710	765	825	1,400	—
1908D	663,750	670	685	720	790	935	9,000	—

Roman numerals in date   No motto below eagle

KM# Pn1874 0.9000 **GOLD** 0.9677 oz. AGW. 34 mm. 33.4360 g. **Designer:** Augustus Saint-Gaudens **Notes:** The "Roman numerals" varieties for 1907 use Roman numerals for the date instead of Arabic numerals. The lettered-edge varieties have "E Pluribus Unum" on the edge, with stars between the words.

Date	Mintage	VF-20	XF-40	AU-50	MS-60	MS-63	MS-65	Prf-65
1907 extremely high relief, unique	—	—	—	—	—	—	—	—
1907 extremely high relief, lettered edge	—	—	—	—	—	—	—	—

Note: 1907 extremely high relief, lettered edge, Prf-68, private sale, 1990, $1,500,000.

"In God We Trust" below eagle

KM# 131 0.9000 **GOLD** 0.9677 oz. AGW. 34 mm. 33.4360 g. **Designer:** Augustus Saint-Gaudens

Date	Mintage	VF-20	XF-40	AU-50	MS-60	MS-63	MS-65	Prf-65
1908	156,359	665	680	720	815	1,750	21,500	49,500
1908 Roman finish; Prf64 Rare	—	—	—	—	—	—	—	—
1908D	349,500	670	685	730	805	955	5,350	—
1908S	22,000	1,450	2,000	4,350	8,250	20,000	43,000	—
1909/8	161,282	670	685	770	1,375	5,400	32,500	—
1909	Inc. above	680	705	740	865	3,350	42,500	49,000
1909D	52,500	710	725	865	1,950	8,250	37,500	—
1909S	2,774,925	670	685	730	785	910	5,250	—
1910	482,167	665	680	720	815	925	7,350	49,000
1910D	429,000	665	680	720	790	895	2,600	—
1910S	2,128,250	670	685	735	795	960	8,000	—
1911	197,350	670	685	740	805	1,875	15,500	39,500
1911D	846,500	665	680	720	790	895	1,500	—
1911S	775,750	665	680	720	795	895	6,200	—
1912	149,824	670	685	735	830	1,675	19,500	44,000
1913	168,838	670	685	735	835	2,850	33,000	44,000
1913D	393,500	665	680	720	790	935	6,500	—
1913S	34,000	720	735	770	1,450	4,200	42,500	—
1914	95,320	680	695	720	1,275	3,900	25,000	41,500
1914D	453,000	665	680	720	790	905	3,250	—
1914S	1,498,000	665	680	720	790	895	2,000	—
1915	152,050	670	685	730	795	2,150	28,500	47,500
1915S	567,500	665	680	720	790	895	2,000	—
1916S	796,000	670	685	730	830	925	2,450	—
1920	228,250	660	675	710	790	955	62,500	—
1920S	558,000	12,500	14,500	22,500	41,500	88,000	210,000	—
1921	528,500	13,500	24,800	35,000	100,000	240,000	950,000	—
1922	1,375,500	660	675	710	765	845	2,450	—
1922S	2,658,000	835	925	1,250	2,150	4,200	39,500	—
1923	566,000	660	675	710	765	845	4,650	—
1923D	1,702,250	670	685	720	775	845	1,500	—
1924	4,323,500	660	675	710	765	825	1,400	—
1924D	3,049,500	950	1,500	1,800	2,950	8,250	75,000	—
1924S	2,927,500	935	1,550	1,850	3,000	8,000	44,500	—
1925	2,831,750	660	675	710	765	825	1,400	—
1925D	2,938,500	1,550	2,100	2,375	4,450	11,500	96,000	—
1925S	3,776,500	1,350	1,950	3,450	9,000	26,500	90,000	—
1926	816,750	660	675	710	765	825	1,400	—
1926D	481,000	7,500	11,000	13,500	26,500	41,500	115,000	—
1926S	2,041,500	1,050	1,550	1,725	2,600	4,950	35,000	—
1927	2,946,750	660	675	710	765	825	1,400	—
1927D	180,000	155,000	220,000	265,000	340,000	1,500,000	2,100,000	—
1927S	3,107,000	5,000	7,850	12,750	26,500	57,500	130,000	—
1928	8,816,000	660	675	710	765	825	1,400	—
1929	1,779,750	5,750	9,000	12,500	18,500	39,500	105,000	—
1930S	74,000	15,500	26,500	30,000	39,000	125,000	235,000	—
1931	2,938,250	9,800	14,500	18,850	30,000	68,500	110,000	—
1931D	106,500	9,000	11,850	21,500	32,500	95,000	130,000	—

UNITED STATES 719

Date	Mintage	VF-20	XF-40	AU-50	MS-60	MS-63	MS-65	Prf-65
1932	1,101,750	8,000	14,500	16,000	25,000	72,500	110,000	—
1933	445,500	—	—	—	—	—	9,000,000	—

Note: Sotheby/Stack's Sale, July 2002. Eleven known, only one currently available.

COMMEMORATIVE COINAGE
1892-1954

All commemorative half dollars of 1892-1954 have the following specifications: diameter – 30.6 millimeters; weight – 12.5000 grams; composition – 0.9000 silver, 0.3617 ounces actual silver weight. Values for PDS sets contain one example each from the Philadelphia, Denver and San Francisco mints. Type coin prices are the most inexpensive single coin available from the date and mint-mark combinations listed.

DOLLAR

LOUISIANA PURCHASE EXPOSITION. KM# 120 0.9000 Gold 0.0484 oz. AGW. 15 mm. 1.6720 g. **Obverse:** William McKinley **Obv. Designer:** Charles E. Barber

Date	Mintage	AU-50	MS-60	MS-63	MS-64	MS-65
1903	17,500	715	765	1,080	2,150	3,300

LOUISIANA PURCHASE EXPOSITION. KM# 119 0.9000 Gold 0.0484 oz. AGW. 15 mm. 1.6720 g. **Obverse:** Jefferson **Designer:** Charles E. Barber

Date	Mintage	AU-50	MS-60	MS-63	MS-64	MS-65
1903	17,500	700	765	1,160	1,900	3,100

LEWIS AND CLARK EXPOSITION. KM# 121 0.9000 Gold 0.7736 oz. AGW. 15 mm. 1.6720 g. **Obv. Designer:** Charles E. Barber

Date	Mintage	AU-50	MS-60	MS-63	MS-64	MS-65
1904	10,025	1,050	1,350	2,550	5,900	12,250
1905	10,041	1,300	1,625	3,300	7,000	18,500

PANAMA-PACIFIC EXPOSITION. KM# 136 0.9000 Gold 0.0484 oz. AGW. 15 mm. 1.6720 g. **Obv. Designer:** Charles Keck

Date	Mintage	AU-50	MS-60	MS-63	MS-64	MS-65
1915S	15,000	650	750	950	1,500	2,450

MCKINLEY MEMORIAL. KM# 144 0.9000 Gold 0.0484 oz. AGW. 15 mm. 1.6720 g. **Obv. Designer:** Charles E. Barber **Rev. Designer:** George T. Morgan

Date	Mintage	AU-50	MS-60	MS-63	MS-64	MS-65
1916	9,977	625	685	800	1,550	2,350
1917	10,000	785	800	1,325	2,200	3,800

GRANT MEMORIAL. KM# 152.1 0.9000 Gold 0.0484 oz. AGW. 15 mm. 1.6720 g. **Obv. Designer:** Laura G. Fraser **Notes:** Without an incuse "star" above the word GRANT on the obverse.

Date	Mintage	AU-50	MS-60	MS-63	MS-64	MS-65
1922	5,000	1,875	1,900	2,350	3,650	4,900

Star

GRANT MEMORIAL. KM# 152.2 0.9000 Gold 0.0484 oz. AGW. 15 mm. 1.6720 g. **Obv. Designer:** Laura G. Fraser **Notes:** Variety with an incuse "star" above the word GRANT on the obverse.

Date	Mintage	AU-50	MS-60	MS-63	MS-64	MS-65
1922	5,016	1,800	1,950	2,400	3,700	4,400

$2.50 (QUARTER EAGLE)

PANAMA-PACIFIC EXPOSITION. KM# 137 0.9000 Gold 0.121 oz. AGW. 18 mm. 4.1800 g. **Obv. Designer:** Charles E. Barber **Rev. Designer:** George T. Morgan

Date	Mintage	AU-50	MS-60	MS-63	MS-64	MS-65
1915S	6,749	1,750	2,100	4,350	6,300	8,000

PHILADELPHIA SESQUICENTENNIAL. KM# 161 0.9000 Gold 0.121 oz. AGW. 18 mm. 4.1800 g. **Obv. Designer:** John R. Sinnock

Date	Mintage	AU-50	MS-60	MS-63	MS-64	MS-65
1926	46,019	525	565	850	1,700	4,200

$50

PANAMA-PACIFIC EXPOSITION OCTAGONAL. KM# 139 0.9000 Gold 2.419 oz. AGW. 44 mm. 83.5900 g. **Obv. Designer:** Robert Aitken

Date	Mintage	AU-50	MS-60	MS-63	MS-64	MS-65
1915S	645	52,500	55,000	80,000	99,500	148,000

PANAMA-PACIFIC EXPOSITION ROUND. KM# 138 0.9000 Gold 2.419 oz. AGW. 44 mm. 83.5900 g. **Obv. Designer:** Robert Aitken

Date	Mintage	AU-50	MS-60	MS-63	MS-64	MS-65
1915S	483	54,000	60,000	82,500	105,000	145,000

COMMEMORATIVE COINAGE
1982-PRESENT

All commemorative silver dollar coins of 1982-present have the following specifications: diameter -- 38.1 millimeters; weight -- 26.7300 grams; composition -- 0.9000 silver, 0.7736 ounces actual silver weight. All commemorative $5 coins of 1982-present have the following specificiations: diameter -- 21.6 millimeters; weight -- 8.3590 grams; composition: 0.9000 gold, 0.242 ounces actual gold weight.

Note: In 1982, after a hiatus of nearly 20 years, coinage of commemorative half dollars resumed. Those designated with a 'W' were struck at the West Point Mint. Some issues were struck in copper--nickel. Those struck in silver have the same size, weight and composition as the prior commemorative half-dollar series.

$5 (HALF EAGLE)

STATUE OF LIBERTY CENTENNIAL. KM# 215 Designer: Elizabeth Jones.

Date	Mintage	Proof	MS-65	Prf-65
1986W	95,248	—	190	—
1986W	—	(404,013)	—	190

CONSTITUTION BICENTENNIAL. KM# 221 Designer: Marcel Jovine.

Date	Mintage	Proof	MS-65	Prf-65
1987W	214,225	—	190	—
1987W	—	(651,659)	—	190

OLYMPICS. KM# 223 Obv. Designer: Elizabeth Jones **Rev. Designer:** Marcel Jovine

Date	Mintage	Proof	MS-65	Prf-65
1988W	62,913	—	190	—
1988W	—	(281,456)	—	190

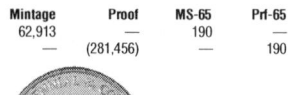

BICENTENNIAL OF THE CONGRESS. KM# 226 Obv. Designer: John Mercanti

Date	Mintage	Proof	MS-65	Prf-65
1989W	46,899	—	190	—
1989W	—	(164,690)	—	190

MOUNT RUSHMORE 50TH ANNIVERSARY. KM# 230 Obv. Designer: John Mercanti **Rev. Designer:** Robert Lamb and William C. Cousins

Date	Mintage	Proof	MS-65	Prf-65
1991W	31,959	—	285	—
1991W	—	(111,991)	—	225

COLUMBUS QUINCENTENARY. KM# 239 Obv. Designer: T. James Ferrell **Rev. Designer:** Thomas D. Rogers, Sr.

Date	Mintage	Proof	MS-65	Prf-65
1992W	—	(79,730)	—	285
1992W	24,329	—	320	—

OLYMPICS. KM# 235 Obv. Designer: James C. Sharpe and T. James Ferrell **Rev. Designer:** James M. Peed

Date	Mintage	Proof	MS-65	Prf-65
1992W	27,732	—	310	—
1992W	—	(77,313)	—	240

JAMES MADISON AND BILL OF RIGHTS. KM# 242 Obv. Designer: Scott R. Blazek **Rev. Designer:** Joseph D. Peña

Date	Mintage	Proof	MS-65	Prf-65
1993W	—	(78,651)	—	265
1993W	22,266	—	325	—

WORLD WAR II 50TH ANNIVERSARY. KM# 245 Obv. Designer: Charles J. Madsen **Rev. Designer:** Edward S. Fisher

Date	Mintage	Proof	MS-65	Prf-65
1993W	—	(65,461)	—	330
1993W	23,089	—	360	—

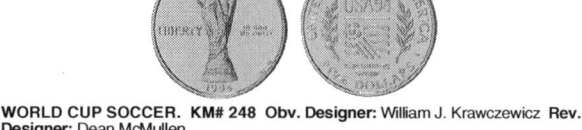

WORLD CUP SOCCER. KM# 248 Obv. Designer: William J. Krawczewicz **Rev. Designer:** Dean McMullen

Date	Mintage	Proof	MS-65	Prf-65
1994W	22,464	—	325	—
1994W	—	(89,619)	—	265

CIVIL WAR. KM# 256 Obv. Designer: Don Troiani **Rev. Designer:** Alfred Maletsky

Date	Mintage	Proof	MS-65	Prf-65
1995W	12,735	—	900	—
1995W	—	(55,246)	—	535

OLYMPICS. KM# 261 Obverse: Torch runner

Date	Mintage	Proof	MS-65	Prf-65
1995W	—	(57,442)	—	410

Date	Mintage	Proof	MS-65	Prf-65
1995W	14,675	—	775	—

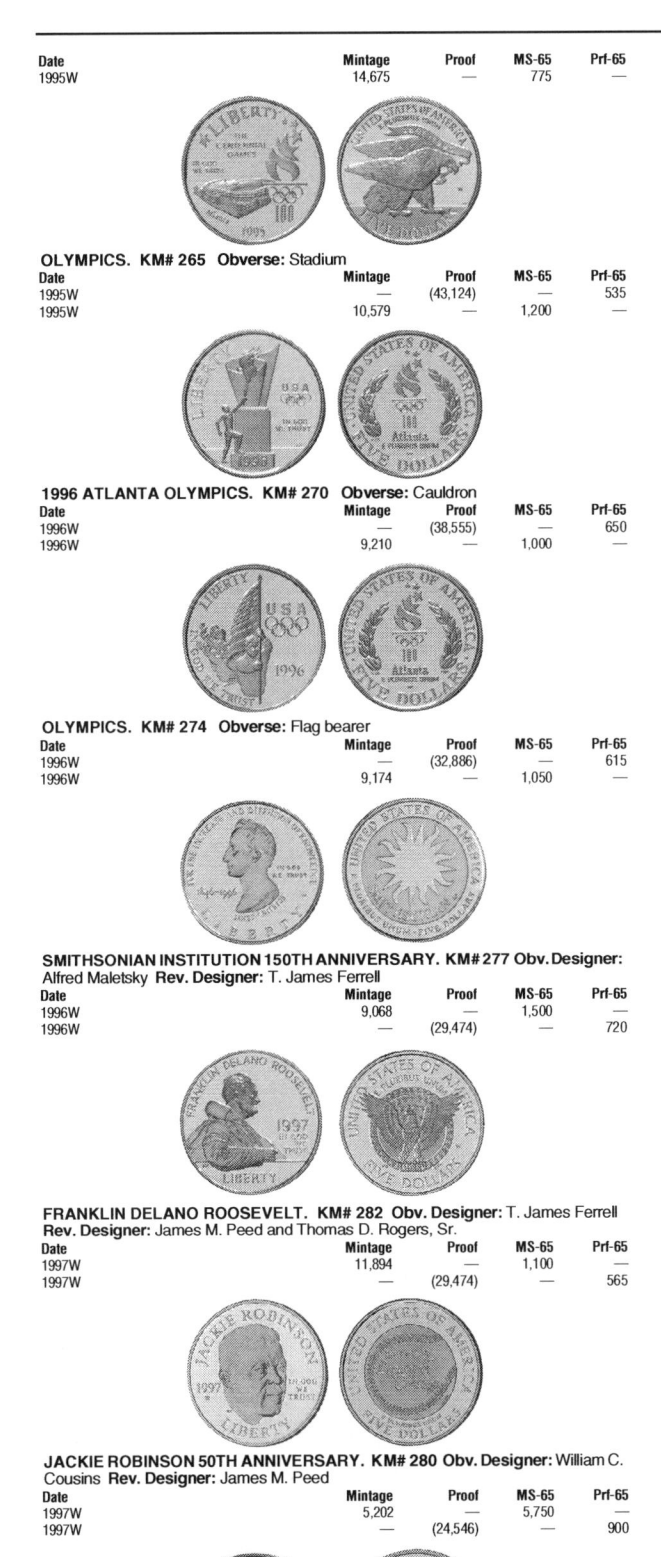

OLYMPICS. KM# 265 Obverse: Stadium

Date	Mintage	Proof	MS-65	Prf-65
1995W	—	(43,124)	—	535
1995W	10,579	—	1,200	—

1996 ATLANTA OLYMPICS. KM# 270 Obverse: Cauldron

Date	Mintage	Proof	MS-65	Prf-65
1996W	—	(38,555)	—	650
1996W	9,210	—	1,000	—

OLYMPICS. KM# 274 Obverse: Flag bearer

Date	Mintage	Proof	MS-65	Prf-65
1996W	—	(32,886)	—	615
1996W	9,174	—	1,050	—

SMITHSONIAN INSTITUTION 150TH ANNIVERSARY. KM# 277 Obv. Designer: Alfred Maletsky **Rev. Designer:** T. James Ferrell

Date	Mintage	Proof	MS-65	Prf-65
1996W	9,068	—	1,500	—
1996W	—	(29,474)	—	720

FRANKLIN DELANO ROOSEVELT. KM# 282 Obv. Designer: T. James Ferrell **Rev. Designer:** James M. Peed and Thomas D. Rogers, Sr.

Date	Mintage	Proof	MS-65	Prf-65
1997W	11,894	—	1,100	—
1997W	—	(29,474)	—	565

JACKIE ROBINSON 50TH ANNIVERSARY. KM# 280 Obv. Designer: William C. Cousins **Rev. Designer:** James M. Peed

Date	Mintage	Proof	MS-65	Prf-65
1997W	5,202	—	5,750	—
1997W	—	(24,546)	—	900

GEORGE WASHINGTON DEATH BICENTENNIAL. KM# 300 Designer: Laura G. Fraser.

Date	Mintage	Proof	MS-65	Prf-65
1999W	22,511	—	475	—
1999W	—	(41,693)	—	475

CAPITOL VISITOR CENTER. KM# 326 Designer: Elizabeth Jones.

Date	Mintage	Proof	MS-65	Prf-65
2001W	6,761	—	2,150	—
2001W	—	(27,652)	—	465

2002 SALT LAKE CITY WINTER OLYMPICS. KM# 337 Designer: Donna Weaver.

Date	Mintage	Proof	MS-65	Prf-65
2002W	10,585	—	555	—
2002W	—	(32,877)	—	510

SAN FRANCISCO MINT MUSEUM. KM# 395 Obverse: Frontal view of entrance **Reverse:** Eagle as on 1860's $5. Gold.

Date	Mintage	Proof	MS-65	Prf-65
2006	—	—	—	—

JAMESTOWN - 400TH ANNIVERSARY. KM# 406 Obverse: Settler and Native American **Reverse:** Jamestown Memorial Church ruins

Date	Mintage	Proof	MS-65	Prf-65
2007W	—	—	—	—
2007W	—	—	—	—

$10 (EAGLE)

LOS ANGELES XXIII OLYMPIAD. KM# 211 0.9000 Gold 0.4839 oz. AGW. 27 mm. 16.7180 g. **Obv. Designer:** James M. Peed and John Mercanti **Rev. Designer:** John Mercanti

Date	Mintage	Proof	MS-65	Prf-65
1984W	75,886	—	365	—
1984P	—	(33,309)	—	365
1984D	—	(34,533)	—	365
1984S	—	(48,551)	—	365
1984W	—	(381,085)	—	355

LIBRARY OF CONGRESS. KM# 312 Platinum-Gold-Alloy 16.2590 g. **Obv. Designer:** John Mercanti **Rev. Designer:** Thomas D. Rogers, Sr. **Notes:** Composition is 48 percent platinum, 48 percent gold, and 4 percent alloy.

Date	Mintage	Proof	MS-65	Prf-65
2000W	6,683	—	3,600	—
2000W	—	(27,167)	—	1,350

UNITED STATES

AMERICAN EAGLE BULLION COINS

GOLD $5

KM# 216 0.9167 GOLD 0.1 oz. 16.5mm. 3.3930 g. **Obv. Designer:** Augustus Saint-Gaudens **Rev. Designer:** Miley Busiek

Date	Mintage	Unc	Prf.
MCMLXXXVI (1986)	912,609	85.00	—
MCMLXXXVII (1987)	580,266	80.00	—
MCMLXXXVIII (1988)	159,500	200	—
MCMLXXXVIII (1988)P	(143,881)	—	80.00
MCMLXXXIX (1989)	264,790	85.00	—
MCMLXXXIX (1989)P	(82,924)	—	80.00
MCMXC (1990)	210,210	90.00	—
MCMXC (1990)P	(99,349)	—	80.00
MCMXCI (1991)	165,200	110	—
MCMXCI (1991)P	(70,344)	—	80.00
1992	209,300	95.00	—
1992P	(64,902)	—	80.00
1993	210,709	90.00	—
1993P	(58,649)	—	80.00
1994	206,380	90.00	—
1994W	(62,100)	—	80.00
1995	223,025	80.00	—
1995W	(62,650)	—	80.00
1996	401,964	80.00	—
1996W	(58,440)	—	80.00
1997	528,515	80.00	—
1997W	(35,000)	—	91.00
1998	1,344,520	70.00	—
1998W	(39,653)	—	80.00
1999	2,750,338	70.00	—
1999W	(48,426)	—	80.00
2000	569,153	85.00	—
2000W	(50,000)	—	90.00
2001	269,147	85.00	—
2001W	(37,547)	—	80.00
2002	230,027	85.00	—
2002W	(40,864)	—	80.00
2003	245,029	85.00	—
2003W	(40,634)	—	85.00
2004	250,016	85.00	—
2004W	(35,481)	—	90.00
2005	300,043	80.00	—
2005W	48,455	—	95.00
2006	285,006	75.00	—
2006W	—	—	80.00

GOLD $10

KM# 217 0.9167 GOLD 0.25 oz. 22mm. 8.4830 g. **Obv. Designer:** Augustus Saint-Gaudens **Rev. Designer:** Miley Busiek

Date	Mintage	Unc	Prf.
MCMLXXXVI (1986)	726,031	175	—
MCMLXXXVII (1987)	269,255	175	—
MCMLXXXVIII (1988)	49,000	175	—
MCMLXXXVIII (1988)P	(98,028)	—	200
MCMLXXXIX (1989)	81,789	175	—
MCMLXXXIX (1989)P	(53,593)	—	200
MCMXC (1990)	41,000	175	—
MCMXC (1990)P	(62,674)	—	200
MCMXCI (1991)	36,100	425	—
MCMXCI (1991)P	(50,839)	—	200
1992	59,546	175	—
1992P	(46,290)	—	200
1993	71,864	175	—
1993P	(46,271)	—	200
1994	72,650	175	—
1994W	(47,600)	—	200
1995	83,752	175	—
1995W	(47,545)	—	200
1996	60,318	175	—
1996W	(39,190)	—	200
1997	108,805	175	—
1997W	(29,800)	—	200
1998	309,829	175	—
1998W	(29,733)	—	200
1999	564,232	175	—
1999W	(34,416)	—	200
2000	128,964	175	—
2000W	(36,000)	—	200
2001	71,280	175	—
2001W	(25,630)	—	200
2002	62,027	175	—
2002W	(29,242)	—	200
2003	74,029	175	—
2003W	(31,000)	—	200
2004	72,014	175	—
2004W	(29,127)	—	200
2005	72,015	175	—
2005W	34,637	—	200
2006	60,004	175	—
2006W	—	—	200

GOLD $25

KM# 218 0.9167 GOLD 0.5 oz. 27mm. 16.9660 g. **Obv. Designer:** Augustus Saint-Gaudens **Rev. Designer:** Miley Busiek

Date	Mintage	Unc	Prf.
MCMLXXXVI (1986)	599,566	500	—
MCMLXXXVII (1987)	131,255	350	—
MCMLXXXVII (1987)P	(143,398)	—	400
MCMLXXXVIII (1988)	45,000	550	—
MCMLXXXVIII (1988)P	(76,528)	—	400
MCMLXXXIX (1989)	44,829	650	—
MCMLXXXIX (1989)P	(44,264)	—	400
MCMXC (1990)	31,000	800	—
MCMXC (1990)P	(51,636)	—	400
MCMXCI (1991)	24,100	1,300	—
MCMXCI (1991)P	(53,125)	—	400
1992	54,404	500	—
1992P	(40,982)	—	400
1993	73,324	350	—
1993P	(43,319)	—	400
1994	62,400	350	—
1994W	(44,100)	—	400
1995	53,474	385	—
1995W	(45,511)	—	400
1996	39,287	525	—
1996W	(35,937)	—	400
1997	79,605	350	—
1997W	(26,350)	—	400
1998	169,029	350	—
1998W	(25,896)	—	400
1999	263,013	350	—
1999W	(30,452)	—	400
2000	79,287	350	—
2000W	(32,000)	—	400
2001	48,047	500	—
2001W	(23,261)	—	400
2002	70,027	350	—
2002W	(26,646)	—	400
2003	79,029	350	—
2003W	(29,000)	—	400
2004	98,040	350	—
2004W	(27,731)	—	400
2005	80,023	350	—
2005W	33,598	—	400
2006	66,005	345	—
2006W	—	—	400

GOLD $50

KM# 219 0.9167 GOLD 1 oz. 32.7mm. 33.9310 g. **Obv. Designer:** Augustus Saint-Gaudens **Rev. Designer:** Miley Busiek

Date	Mintage	Unc	Prf.
MCMLXXXVI (1986)	1,362,650	715	—
MCMLXXXVI (1986)W	(446,290)	—	725

Date	Mintage	Unc	Prf.
MCMLXXXVII (1987)	1,045,500	715	—
MCMLXXXVII (1987)W	(147,498)	—	725
MCMLXXXVIII (1988)	465,000	715	—
MCMLXXXVIII (1988)W	(87,133)	—	725
MCMLXXXIX (1989)	415,790	715	—
MCMLXXXIX (1989)W	(53,960)	—	725
MCMXC (1990)	373,210	715	—
MCMXC (1990)W	(62,401)	—	725
MCMXCI (1991)	243,100	715	—
MCMXCI (1991)W	(50,411)	—	725
1992	275,000	715	—
1992W	(44,835)	—	725
1993	480,192	715	—
1993W	(34,389)	—	725
1994	221,633	715	—
1994W	(36,300)	—	725
1995	200,636	715	—
1995W	(46,553)	—	725
1996	189,148	715	—
1996W	(37,302)	—	725
1997	664,508	715	—
1997W	(28,000)	—	725
1998	1,468,530	710	—
1998W	(26,060)	—	725
1999	1,505,026	710	—
1999W	(31,446)	—	725
2000	433,319	715	—
2000W	(33,000)	—	725
2001	143,605	715	—
2001W	(24,580)	—	725
2002	222,029	715	—
2002W	(24,242)	—	725
2003	416,032	715	—
2003W	(29,000)	—	725
2004	417,019	715	—
2004W	(28,731)	—	725
2005	356,555	715	—
2005W	34,695	—	725
2006	237,510	710	—
2006W	—	—	725
2006W Reverse Proof	(10,000)	—	3,250

PLATINUM $10

KM# 283 0.9995 PLATINUM .1000 oz. 3.1100 g. **Obv. Designer:** John Mercanti **Rev. Designer:** Thomas D. Rogers Sr

Date	Mintage	Unc	Prf.
1997	70,250	150	—
1997W	(36,996)	—	150
1998	39,525	150	—
1999	55,955	145	—
2000	34,027	145	—
2001	52,017	145	—
2002	23,005	145	—
2003	22,007	145	—
2004	15,010	165	—
2005	14,013	170	—
2006	11,001	—	—

KM# 289 0.9995 PLATINUM .1000 oz. 3.1100 g. **Obv. Designer:** John Mercanti

Date	Mintage	Unc	Prf.
1998W	(19,832)	—	150

KM# 301 0.9995 PLATINUM .1000 oz. 3.1100 g. **Obv. Designer:** John Mercanti

Date	Mintage	Unc	Prf.
1999W	(19,123)	—	145

KM# 314 0.9995 PLATINUM .1000 oz. 3.1100 g. **Obv. Designer:** John Mercanti

Date	Mintage	Unc	Prf.
2000W	(15,651)	—	145

KM# 327 0.9995 PLATINUM .1000 oz. 3.1100 g. **Obv. Designer:** John Mercanti

Date	Mintage	Unc	Prf.
2001W	(12,193)	—	145

KM# 339 0.9995 PLATINUM .1000 oz. 3.1100 g. **Obv. Designer:** John Mercanti

Date	Mintage	Unc	Prf.
2002W	(12,365)	—	145

KM# 351 0.9995 PLATINUM .1000 oz. 3.1100 g. **Obv. Designer:** John Mercanti **Rev. Designer:** Al Maletsky

Date	Mintage	Unc	Prf.
2003W	(8,161)	—	175

KM# 364 0.9995 PLATINUM .1000 oz. 3.1100 g. **Obv. Designer:** John Mercanti

Date	Mintage	Unc	Prf.
2004W	(6,846)	—	350

KM# 377 0.9995 PLATINUM 0.0999 oz. 3.1100 g. **Obv. Designer:** John Mercanti **Rev. Designer:** Donna Weaver

Date	Mintage	Unc	Prf.
2005W	8,000	—	210

KM# 389 0.9995 PLATINUM 0.0999 oz. 17mm. 3.1100 g.

Date	Mintage	Unc	Prf.
2006W	—	—	—

PLATINUM $25

KM# 284 0.9995 PLATINUM 0.2500 oz. 7.7857 g. **Obv. Designer:** John Mercanti **Rev. Designer:** Thomas D. Rogers Sr

Date	Mintage	Unc	Prf.
1997	27,100	365	—
1997W	(18,628)	—	365
1998	38,887	350	—
1999	39,734	350	—
2000	20,054	350	—
2001	21,815	365	—
2002	27,405	350	—
2003	25,207	365	—
2004	18,010	365	—
2005	12,013	365	—
2006	12,001	—	—

724 UNITED STATES

KM# 290 0.9995 PLATINUM .2500 oz. 7.7857 g. **Obv. Designer:** John Mercanti

Date	Mintage	Unc	Prf.
1998W	(14,860)	—	350

KM# 302 0.9995 PLATINUM .2500 oz. 7.7857 g. **Obv. Designer:** John Mercanti

Date	Mintage	Unc	Prf.
1999W	(13,514)	—	350

KM# 315 0.9995 PLATINUM .2500 oz. 7.7857 g. **Obv. Designer:** John Mercanti

Date	Mintage	Unc	Prf.
2000W	(11,995)	—	350

KM# 328 0.9995 PLATINUM .2500 oz. 7.7857 g. **Obv. Designer:** John Mercanti

Date	Mintage	Unc	Prf.
2001W	(8,858)	—	320

KM# 340 0.9995 PLATINUM .2500 oz. 7.7857 g. **Obv. Designer:** John Mercanti

Date	Mintage	Unc	Prf.
2002W	(9,282)	—	320

KM# 352 0.9995 PLATINUM .2500 oz. 7.7857 g. **Obv. Designer:** John Mercanti **Rev. Designer:** Al Maletsky

Date	Mintage	Unc	Prf.
2003W	(6,045)	—	385

KM# 365 0.9995 PLATINUM .2500 oz. 7.7857 g. **Obv. Designer:** John Mercanti

Date	Mintage	Unc	Prf.
2004W	(5,035)	—	950

KM# 378 0.9995 PLATINUM 0.2502 oz. 7.7857 g. **Obv. Designer:** John Mercanti **Rev. Designer:** Donna Weaver

Date	Mintage	Unc	Prf.
2005W	6,424	—	410

KM# 390 0.9995 PLATINUM 0.2502 oz. 22mm. 7.7857 g.

Date	Mintage	Unc	Prf.
2006W	—	—	—

PLATINUM $50

KM# 285 0.9995 PLATINUM 0.5000 oz. 15.5520 g. **Obv. Designer:** John Mercanti **Rev. Designer:** Thomas D. Rogers Sr

Date	Mintage	Unc	Prf.
1997	20,500	660	—
1997W	(15,432)	—	660
1998	32,415	660	—
1999	32,309	660	—
2000	18,892	660	—
2001	12,815	660	—
2002	24,005	660	—
2003	17,409	660	—
2004	98,040	660	—
2005	9,013	660	—
2006	9,602	—	—

KM# 291 0.9995 PLATINUM .5000 oz. 15.5520 g. **Obv. Designer:** John Mercanti

Date	Mintage	Unc	Prf.
1998W	(13,821)	—	660

KM# 303 0.9995 PLATINUM .5000 oz. 15.5520 g. **Obv. Designer:** John Mercanti

Date	Mintage	Unc	Prf.
1999W	(11,098)	—	660

KM# 316 0.9995 PLATINUM .5000 oz. 15.5520 g. **Obv. Designer:** John Mercanti

Date	Mintage	Unc	Prf.
2000W	(11,049)	—	660

KM# 329 0.9995 PLATINUM .5000 oz. 15.5520 g. **Obv. Designer:** John Mercanti

Date	Mintage	Unc	Prf.
2001W	(8,268)	—	660

UNITED STATES 725

KM# 341 0.9995 **PLATINUM** .5000 oz. 15.5520 g. **Obv. Designer:** John Mercanti

Date	Mintage	Unc	Prf.
2002W	(8,772)	—	660

KM# 353 0.9995 **PLATINUM** .5000 oz. 15.5520 g. **Obv. Designer:** John Mercanti **Rev. Designer:** Al Maletsky

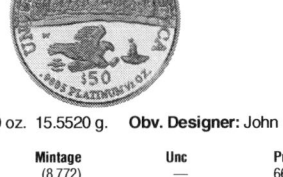

Date	Mintage	Unc	Prf.
2003W	(6,181)	—	660

KM# 366 0.9995 **PLATINUM** .5000 oz. 15.5520 g. **Obv. Designer:** John Mercanti

Date	Mintage	Unc	Prf.
2004W	(4,886)	—	2,600

KM# 379 0.9995 **PLATINUM** .5000 oz. 15.5520 g. **Obv. Designer:** John Mercanti **Rev. Designer:** Donna Weaver

Date	Mintage	Unc	Prf.
2005W Proof	5,720	—	735

KM# 391 0.9995 **PLATINUM** 0.4998 oz. 27mm. 15.5520 g.

Date	Mintage	Unc	Prf.
2006W	—	—	—

PLATINUM $100

KM# 286 0.9995 **PLATINUM** 1.000 oz. 31.1050 g. **Obv. Designer:** John Mercanti **Rev. Designer:** Thomas D. Rogers Sr

Date	Mintage	Unc	Prf.
1997	56,000	1,350	—
1997W	(15,885)	—	1,400
1998	133,002	1,350	—
1999	56,707	1,350	—
2000	18,892	1,350	—
2001	14,070	1,350	—
2002	11,502	1,350	—
2003	8,007	1,350	—
2004	7,009	1,350	—
2005	6,310	1,350	—
2006	6,000	1,350	—

KM# 292 0.9995 **PLATINUM** 1.000 oz. 31.1050 g. **Obv. Designer:** John Mercanti

Date	Mintage	Unc	Prf.
1998W	(14,203)	—	1,275

KM# 304 0.9995 **PLATINUM** 1.000 oz. 31.1050 g. **Obv. Designer:** John Mercanti

Date	Mintage	Unc	Prf.
1999W	—	—	1,275

KM# 317 0.9995 **PLATINUM** 1.000 oz. 31.1050 g. **Obv. Designer:** John Mercanti

Date	Mintage	Unc	Prf.
2000W	—	—	1,275

KM# 330 0.9995 **PLATINUM** 1.000 oz. 31.1050 g. **Obv. Designer:** John Mercanti

Date	Mintage	Unc	Prf.
2001W	(8,990)	—	1,275

KM# 342 0.9995 **PLATINUM** 1.000 oz. 31.1050 g. **Obv. Designer:** John Mercanti

Date	Mintage	Unc	Prf.
2002W	(9,834)	—	1,275

KM# 354 0.9995 **PLATINUM** 1.000 oz. 31.1050 g. **Obv. Designer:** John Mercanti **Rev. Designer:** Al Maletsky

Date	Mintage	Unc	Prf.
2003W	(6,991)	—	1,275

726 UNITED STATES

KM# 367   0.9995 **PLATINUM** 1.000 oz. 31.1050 g.   **Obv. Designer:** John Mercanti **Rev. Designer:** Donna Weaver

Date	Mintage	Unc	Prf.
2004W	(5,833)	—	4,500

KM# 380   0.9995 **PLATINUM** 0.9995 oz. 31.1050 g.   **Obv. Designer:** John Mercanti **Rev. Designer:** Donna Weaver

Date	Mintage	Unc	Prf.
2005W	6,700	—	1,345

KM# 392   0.9995 **PLATINUM** 0.9995 oz. 33mm. 31.1050 g.

Date	Mintage	Unc	Prf.
2006W	—	—	—

UNITED STATES
PATTERNS

The United States pattern section contains Judd cross reference numbers and selected descriptive references from the 6th edition of *United States Pattern, Experimental and Trial Pieces* edited by Abe Kosoff from the original edition by J. Hewitt Judd, M.D. Copyright 1977, 1959 Western Publishing Company, Inc. Used by permission.

Market values established in this section are based on auction results gleened from *Auction Prices Realized*, an annual compilation of U.S. auction firm sales edited by Bob Wilhite and Tom Michael and published by Krause Publications of Iola, Wisconsin. Due to the wide variance in grade amongst U.S. patterns, these values represent only an average example of the type. To determine values for patterns of greater or lesser quality the serious collector may wish to research the market trend of a given type over time by using several volumes of *Auction Prices Realized* as well as original auction catalogs.

NOTE: Photographs are representative of the type group, and not always the particular listing that it appears above.

KM#	Date	Mintage	Identification	Mkt Val
Pn14	1803	—	5 Dollars. Copper. Reeded edge. Restrikes from rusty dies. J27.	—
Pn16	1804	—	5 Dollars. Silver. Reeded edge. Restrike. J29. Rare.	—
Pn17	1804	—	5 Dollars. Silver. Plain edge. Restrike. J30. Unique.	—

Note: Bowers Harry W. Bass Jr. sale 5-99, MS-65 realized $13,800.

KM#	Date	Mintage	Identification	Mkt Val
Pn18	1804	—	5 Dollars. Copper. Reeded edge. Restrike. J31.	—
Pn19	1804	—	5 Dollars. Tin. Restrike. J32.	—
Pn20	1804	—	10 Dollars. Gold. Plain 4 in date. Beaded border. J33.	—
Pn21	1804	—	10 Dollars. Silver. Reeded edge. 4-5 struck. J34.	—
Pn22	1804	—	10 Dollars. Silver. Plain edge. J34a.	—
Pn23	1805	—	2-1/2 Dollars. Copper. Reeded edge. Restrike. J35.	—
Pn24	1805	—	5 Dollars. Silver. Restrike. J36.	—
Pn25	1805	—	5 Dollars. Copper. Restrike. J37.	16,500
Pn26	1805	—	5 Dollars. Tin. Restrike. J38.	16,750
Pn28	1808	—	5 Dollars. Silver. Reeded edge. Restrike. J39.	—
Pn29	1808	—	5 Dollars. Silver. Plain edge. Restrike. J40.	—
Pn30	1810	—	2 Cent. White Metal. Restrike. J41.	—
Pn34	1814	—	50 Cents. Platinum. J44.	50,600
Pn40	1831	—	2-1/2 Dollars. Silver. Reeded edge. J49. Unique.	—
Pn41	1834	—	2-1/2 Dollars. Copper. Reeded edge. J50. Rare.	—
Pn42	1834	—	5 Dollars. Copper. Plain edge. J51.	—
Pn43	1834	—	5 Dollars. Copper. Plain edge. J51a.	—

Note: The authenticity of this piece has been questioned

KM#	Date	Mintage	Identification	Mkt Val
Pn60	1836	5	Gold Dollar. Gold. Plain edge. Coin turn. J67.	—

Note: Heritage Orlando sale #394, 1-06, PR-65 realized $24,725

KM#	Date	Mintage	Identification	Mkt Val
Pn61	1836	—	Gold Dollar. Gold. Plain edge. Medal turn. J68.	15,000
Pn62	1836	—	Gold Dollar. Silver. Plain edge. J69.	9,750
Pn62a	1836	—	Gold Dollar. Gilt Silver. Plain edge. J69a.	9,750
Pn63	1836	—	Gold Dollar. Copper. Plain edge. J70.	7,500
Pn63a	1836	—	Gold Dollar. Copper Gilt. Plain edge. J70a.	7,500
Pn64	1836	—	Gold Dollar. Oroide. Plain edge. J71.	—
Pn106	1846	—	2-1/2 Dollars. Copper. Reeded edge. J110a.	—

KM#	Date	Mintage	Identification	Mkt Val
Pn111	1849	—	Gold Dollar. Gold. 25.8000 g. Plain edge. J115.	10,500
Pn112	1849	3	Gold Dollar. Silver. J116.	17,850
Pn113	1849	—	20 Dollars. Gold. Reeded edge. J117. Unique.	—
Pn114	1849	—	20 Dollars. Gilt Brass. Reeded edge. J118. Unique.	—
Pn131	1852	6	Gold Half Dollar. Gold. 13.0000 g. Reeded edge. J135.	13,750
Pn132	1852	4	Gold Dollar. Gold. 25.8000 g. Reeded edge. J136.	10,000
Pn133	1852	2	Gold Dollar. Gold. Plain edge. J137.	17,500
Pn134	1852	—	Gold Dollar. Silver. Plain edge. Thick planchet. J138.	5,000
Pn134a	1852	—	Gold Dollar. Silver. Plain edge. Thin planchet. J138.	5,200
Pn135	1852	—	Gold Dollar. Copper. Plain edge. J139.	3,500
Pn136	1852	—	Gold Dollar. Copper-Nickel. Plain edge. J140.	4,600
Pn137	1852	—	Gold Dollar. Nickel. Plain edge. J140a.	7,500
Pn138	1852	—	Gold Dollar. Gold. Plain edge. J141. Rare.	—
Pn139	1852	—	Gold Dollar. Silver. Plain edge. J142. Rare.	—
Pn140	1852	—	Gold Dollar. Copper. Plain edge. J143.	12,650
Pn141	1852	—	Gold Dollar. Nickel. Plain edge. J144. Unique.	—
Pn142	1852	—	Gold Dollar. Gold. 25.8000 g. Plain edge. Thick planchet. J145.	18,500
Pn142a	1852	—	Gold Dollar. Gold. Plain edge. Thin planchet. J145.	12,500
Pn143	1852	5	Gold Dollar. Silver. Plain edge. J146.	8,500
Pn144	1852	—	Gold Dollar. Copper. Plain edge. J147.	5,000
Pn145	1852	—	Gold Dollar. Copper-Nickel. Plain edge. J148.	5,000
Pn146	1852	—	Gold Dollar. Nickel. Plain edge. Thin planchet. J148a.	—
Pn147	1852	—	Gold Dollar. Brass. Plain edge. J148b. Restrikes exist from cracked dies. Gilt examples also exist.	7,000
Pn180	1855	—	Gold Dollar. White Metal. Plain edge. J175a. Unique.	—
Pn181	1855	—	10 Dollars. Copper. Reeded edge. Restrike. J176. Rare.	—
Pn195	1857	—	2-1/2 Dollars. Copper. Reeded edge. J189.	4,750
Pn196	ND(1857)	—	20 Dollars. Copper. Plain edge. J190. Unique.	28,750
Pn233	1858	—	Gold Dollar. Gold. Reeded edge. J224. Unique.	—
Pn234	1858	—	Gold Dollar. Copper. Reeded edge. J225.	12,500
Pn266	1859	—	Gold Dollar. Copper. Reeded edge. J256.	5,000

KM#	Date	Mintage	Identification	Mkt Val
Pn267	1859	—	20 Dollars. Copper. Reeded edge. J257.	8,500
Pn267a	1859	—	20 Dollars. Copper Bronzed. Reeded edge. J257.	8,000
Pn267b	1859	—	20 Dollars. Copper Gilt. Reeded edge. J257.	10,500
Pn268	1859	—	20 Dollars. Copper. Reeded edge. J258.	—

Note: Heritage Orlando sale #394, 1-06, PR-64 realized $32,200

KM#	Date	Mintage	Identification	Mkt Val
Pn268a	1859	—	20 Dollars. Copper. Reeded edge. J258.	—
Pn269	1859	—	20 Dollars. Copper. Reeded edge. J259.	—
Pn270	1859	—	20 Dollars. Copper. Reeded edge. J260.	32,000
Pn270a	1859	—	20 Dollars. Copper Gilt. Reeded edge. J260.	—
Pn271	1859	—	20 Dollars. Copper. Reeded edge. J261.	—
Pn271a	1859	—	20 Dollars. Copper Gilt. Reeded edge. J261.	—
Pn272	1859	—	20 Dollars. Copper. Reeded edge. J262.	25,000
Pn272a	1859	—	20 Dollars. Copper Gilt. Reeded edge. J262.	—
Pn273	1859	—	20 Dollars. Copper. Reeded edge. J263.	13,500
Pn278	1860	—	2-1/2 Dollars. Copper-Nickel. J268.	—
Pn280	1857//1860	—	2-1/2 Dollars. Copper. Reeded edge. J270.	6,750
Pn281	1860	—	5 Dollars. Gold. Reeded edge. J271. Rare.	—
Pn282	1860	—	5 Dollars. Copper. Reeded edge. J272.	9,200
Pn282a	1860	—	5 Dollars. Copper Gilt. Reeded edge. J272.	5,750
Pn283	1860	—	20 Dollars. Gold. Reeded edge. J272a. Unique.	—
Pn284	1860	—	20 Dollars. Copper. Reeded edge. J273.	25,000
Pn284a	1860	—	20 Dollars. Copper Gilt. Reeded edge. J273.	25,000
Pn292	1861	—	2-1/2 Dollars. Silver. Reeded edge. J281.	8,500
Pn293	1861	—	2-1/2 Dollars. Copper. Reeded edge. J282.	5,000
Pn294	1861	—	5 Dollars. Copper. Reeded edge. J283.	4,250
Pn294a	1861	—	5 Dollars. Copper Bronzed. Reeded edge. J283.	4,150
Pn294b	1861	—	5 Dollars. Copper Gilt. Reeded edge. J283.	3,000
Pn295	1861	—	10 Dollars. Gold. Reeded edge. J284.	—
Pn296	1861	—	10 Dollars. Copper. Reeded edge. J285.	4,500
Pn297	1861	—	10 Dollars. Copper Bronzed. Reeded edge. J285.	4,250
Pn297a	1861	—	10 Dollars. Copper Gilt. Reeded edge. J285.	3,000
Pn298	1861	—	10 Dollars. Gold. Reeded edge. J286.	—
Pn299	1861	—	10 Dollars. Copper. Reeded edge. J287.	4,250
Pn300	1861	—	10 Dollars. Copper Bronzed. Reeded edge. J287.	4,000
Pn300a	1861	—	10 Dollars. Copper Gilt. Reeded edge. J287.	4,000
Pn301	1861	—	20 Dollars. Copper. J288.	12,500
Pn301a	1861	—	20 Dollars. Copper Gilt. J288.	12,500
Pn302	1861	—	20 Dollars. Copper. Reeded edge. J289. Unique.	30,000

728 UNITED STATES — PATTERNS

KM#	Date	Mintage	Identification	Mkt Val
Pn310	1862	—	10 Dollars. Copper. Reeded edge. J297.	3,500
Pn310a	1862	—	10 Dollars. Copper Bronzed. Reeded edge. J297.	3,250
Pn311	1862	—	10 Dollars. Copper. Reeded edge. J298.	3,500
Pn311a	1862	—	10 Dollars. Copper Bronzed. Reeded edge. J298.	3,450
Pn311b	1862	—	10 Dollars. Copper Gilt. Reeded edge. J298.	2,750
Pn369	1863	—	10 Dollars. Gold. Reeded edge. J349. Rare.	—
Pn370	1863	—	10 Dollars. Copper. Reeded edge. J350.	5,000
Pn371	1863	—	10 Dollars. Gold. Reeded edge. J351. Rare.	—
Pn372	1863	—	10 Dollars. Copper. Reeded edge. J352.	3,000
Pn424	1864	—	3 Dollars. Copper. Reeded edge. J400.	—
Pn425	1864	—	3 Dollars. Copper-Nickel. Reeded edge. J401.	—
Pn426	1864	—	3 Dollars. Nickel. Reeded edge. J402.	—
Pn468	1865	—	Gold Dollar. Copper. Reeded edge. J438.	10,925
Pn469	1865	—	2-1/2 Dollars. Copper. Reeded edge. J439.	8,000
Pn470	1865	2	3 Dollars. Gold. Reeded edge. J440.	14,950
Pn471	1865	—	3 Dollars. Copper. Reeded edge. J441.	4,400
Pn472	1865	—	3 Dollars. Silver. Reeded edge. J441a.	—
Pn473	1865	—	3 Dollars. Copper. Reeded edge. J442.	—
Pn474	1865	—	3 Dollars. Copper-Nickel. Reeded edge. J443.	—
Pn475	1865	—	3 Dollars. Nickel. Reeded edge. J444.	10,000
Pn476	1865	—	3 Dollars. Bronze. Reeded edge. J444a.	—
Pn477	1865	2	5 Dollars. Gold. Reeded edge. J445. Rare.	—
Pn478	1865	—	5 Dollars. Copper. Reeded edge. J446.	5,250
Pn479	1865	—	5 Dollars. Copper. Reeded edge. J447.	—
Pn480	1865	—	5 Dollars. Aluminum. Reeded edge. J448.	—
Pn481	1865	—	10 Dollars. Gold. Reeded edge. J449. Rare.	—
Pn482	1865	—	10 Dollars. Copper. Reeded edge. J450.	6,500
Pn483	1865	—	10 Dollars. Copper. Reeded edge. J451.	—
Pn484	1865	2	20 Dollars. Gold. Reeded edge. J452. Rare.	—
Pn485	1865	—	20 Dollars. Copper. Reeded edge. J453.	10,925
Pn486	1865	—	20 Dollars. Copper Gilt. Reeded edge. J453.	5,500
Pn487	1865	—	20 Dollars. Copper. Reeded edge. J454.	—
Pn576	1866	2	Dollar. Silver. Reeded edge. J540. Rare.	—
Pn578	1866	—	2-1/2 Dollars. Nickel. Reeded edge. J542.	5,200
Pn579	1866	—	3 Dollars. Nickel. Reeded edge. J543.	5,300
Pn580	1866	—	3 Dollars. Aluminum. Reeded edge. J544.	—
Pn581	1866	—	5 Dollars. White Metal. Plain edge. J545.	—
Pn582	1866	—	5 Dollars. Copper. Reeded edge. J546.	14,175
Pn583	1866	—	5 Dollars. White Metal. Plain edge. J547.	—
Pn584	1866	—	10 Dollars. Copper. Reeded edge. J548.	9,750
Pn585	1866	—	20 Dollars. Copper. Reeded edge. J549.	—
Pn585a	1866	—	20 Dollars. Copper Gilt. Reeded edge. J549.	35,650
Pn632	1867	—	Gold Dollar. Copper. Reeded edge. J594.	12,500
Pn633	1867	—	2-1/2 Dollars. Copper. Reeded edge. J595.	6,750
Pn634	1867	—	3 Dollars. Copper. Reeded edge. J596.	8,000
Pn635	1867	—	3 Dollars. Nickel. Reeded edge. J597.	18,400
Pn636	1867	—	3 Dollars. Silver. Reeded edge. J598.	12,500
Pn637	1867	—	5 Dollars. Copper. Reeded edge. J599.	6,500
Pn638	1867	—	5 Dollars. Nickel. Reeded edge. J600.	—
Pn639	1867	2	5 Dollars. Nickel. Plain edge. J601.	—
Pn640	1867	—	10 Dollars. Copper. Reeded edge. J602.	13,250
Pn641	1867	—	10 Dollars. Nickel. Reeded edge. J603.	—
Pn642	1867	—	20 Dollars. Copper. Reeded edge. J604.	10,350
Pn697	1868	—	Gold Dollar. Aluminum. Reeded edge. J653.	8,000
Pn698	1868	—	2-1/2 Dollars. Aluminum. Reeded edge. J654.	8,500
Pn699	1868	—	3 Dollars. Aluminum. Reeded edge. J655.	9,000
Pn700	1868	—	5 Dollars. Copper. Reeded edge. J656.	20,700
Pn700a	1868	—	5 Dollars. Copper Gilt. Reeded edge. J656.	—
Pn701	1868	—	5 Dollars. Copper. Plain edge. J657.	8,000
Pn702	1868	—	5 Dollars. Aluminum. Reeded edge. J658.	6,500
Pn703	1868	—	5 Dollars. Aluminum. Plain edge. J659.	8,000
Pn704	1868	—	5 Dollars. Aluminum. Reeded edge. J660.	7,500
Pn705	1868	4	10 Dollars. Gold. Reeded edge. J661. Rare.	—
Pn706	1868	—	10 Dollars. Copper. Reeded edge. J662.	5,750
Pn706a	1868	—	10 Dollars. Copper Gilt. Reeded edge. J662.	5,600
Pn707	1868	—	10 Dollars. Aluminum. Reeded edge. J663.	7,500
Pn708	1868	—	10 Dollars. Aluminum. Reeded edge. J664.	6,500
Pn709	1868	—	20 Dollars. Aluminum. Reeded edge. J665.	14,500
Pn817	1869	—	Gold Dollar. Copper. Reeded edge. J766.	8,650
Pn818	1869	—	Gold Dollar. Aluminum. Reeded edge. J767.	8,000
Pn819	1869	—	Gold Dollar. Nickel. Reeded edge. J768.	10,000
Pn820	1869	—	2-1/2 Dollars. Copper. Reeded edge. J769.	6,500
Pn821	1869	—	2-1/2 Dollars. Aluminum. Reeded edge. J770.	5,750
Pn822	1869	—	2-1/2 Dollars. Nickel. Reeded edge. J771.	9,000
Pn823	1869	—	3 Dollars. Copper. Reeded edge. J772.	6,500
Pn824	1869	—	3 Dollars. Aluminum. Reeded edge. J773.	6,000
Pn825	1869	—	3 Dollars. Nickel. Reeded edge. J774.	12,500
Pn826	1869	—	5 Dollars. Copper. Reeded edge. J775.	7,000
Pn827	1869	—	5 Dollars. Aluminum. Reeded edge. J776.	7,000
Pn828	1869	—	5 Dollars. Nickel. Reeded edge. J777.	10,000
Pn829	1869	—	5 Dollars. Brass. Reeded edge. J778.	—
Pn830	1869	—	10 Dollars. Copper. Reeded edge. Thick planchet. J779.	12,650
Pn830a	1869	—	10 Dollars. Copper Bronzed. Reeded edge. Thick planchet. J779a.	12,500
Pn830b	1869	—	10 Dollars. Copper. Reeded edge. Thin planchet. J779.	12,500
Pn830c	1869	—	10 Dollars. Copper Bronzed. Reeded edge. Thin planchet. J779.	12,500
Pn831	1869	—	10 Dollars. Aluminum. Reeded edge. J780.	—
Pn832	1869	—	10 Dollars. Copper. Reeded edge. J781.	7,000
Pn833	1869	—	10 Dollars. Aluminum. Reeded edge. J782.	5,750
Pn834	1869	—	10 Dollars. Nickel. Reeded edge. J783.	—
Pn835	1869	—	20 Dollars. Copper. Reeded edge. J784.	8,500
Pn836	1869	—	20 Dollars. Aluminum. Reeded edge. J785.	9,500
Pn837	1869	—	20 Dollars. Nickel. Reeded edge. J786.	—
Pn1078	1870	—	Gold Dollar. Copper. Reeded edge. J1023.	8,500
Pn1079	1870	—	Gold Dollar. Aluminum. Reeded edge. J1024.	—
Pn1080	1870	—	Gold Dollar. Nickel. Reeded edge. J1025.	—
Pn1081	1870	—	2-1/2 Dollars. Copper. Reeded edge. J1026.	4,750
Pn1082	1870	—	2-1/2 Dollars. Aluminum. Reeded edge. J1027.	8,500
Pn1083	1870	—	2-1/2 Dollars. Nickel. Reeded edge. J1028.	9,000
Pn1084	1870	—	3 Dollars. Copper. Reeded edge. J1029.	6,000
Pn1085	1870	—	3 Dollars. Aluminum. Reeded edge. J1030.	8,500
Pn1086	1870	—	3 Dollars. Nickel. Reeded edge. J1031.	9,500
Pn1087	1870	—	5 Dollars. Copper. Reeded edge. J1032.	7,000
Pn1088	1870	—	5 Dollars. Aluminum. Reeded edge. J1033.	—
Pn1089	1870	—	5 Dollars. Nickel. Reeded edge. J1034.	—
Pn1219	1871	—	Gold Dollar. Copper. Reeded edge. J1161.	7,500
Pn1220	1871	—	Gold Dollar. Aluminum. Reeded edge. J1162.	9,500
Pn1221	1871	—	Gold Dollar. Nickel. Reeded edge. J1163.	10,000
Pn1222	1871	—	2-1/2 Dollars. Copper. Reeded edge. J1164.	5,000
Pn1223	1871	—	2-1/2 Dollars. Aluminum. Reeded edge. J1165.	7,500
Pn1224	1871	—	2-1/2 Dollars. Nickel. Reeded edge. J1166.	9,500
Pn1225	1871	—	3 Dollars. Copper. Reeded edge. J1167.	13,500
Pn1226	1871	—	3 Dollars. Aluminum. Reeded edge. J1168.	—
Pn1227	1871	—	3 Dollars. Nickel. Reeded edge. J1169.	—
Pn1228	1871	—	5 Dollars. Copper. Reeded edge. J1170.	4,650
Pn1229	1871	—	5 Dollars. Aluminum. Reeded edge. J1171.	9,500

Note: Heritage CSNS sale #404, 4-06, PR-64 realized $23,000

KM#	Date	Mintage	Identification	Mkt Val
Pn1230	1871	—	5 Dollars. Nickel. Reeded edge. J1172.	4,750
Pn1231	1871	—	10 Dollars. Copper. Reeded edge. J1173.	7,000
Pn1232	1871	—	10 Dollars. Aluminum. Reeded edge. J1174.	12,000
Pn1233	1871	—	10 Dollars. Nickel. Reeded edge. J1175.	10,000
Pn1234	1871	—	20 Dollars. Copper. Reeded edge. J1176.	17,250
Pn1235	1871	—	20 Dollars. Aluminum. Reeded edge. J1177.	—
Pn1236	1871	—	20 Dollars. Copper. Reeded edge. J1178.	—

PATTERNS

UNITED STATES

KM#	Date	Mintage Identification	Mkt Val
Pn1283	1872	— Gold Dollar. Gold. Reeded edge. J1224, Rare.	—
Pn1284	1872	— Gold Dollar. Copper. Reeded edge. J1225.	9,000
Pn1285	1872	— Gold Dollar. Aluminum. Reeded edge. J1226.	19,000
Pn1286	1872	— Gold Dollar. Copper. Reeded edge. J1227.	7,000
Pn1287	1872	— Gold Dollar. Aluminum. Reeded edge. J1228.	7,500
Pn1288	1872	— Gold Dollar. Silver. Reeded edge. J1229.	—
Pn1289	1872	— 2-1/2 Dollars. Gold. Reeded edge. J1230, Rare.	—
Pn1290	1872	— 2-1/2 Dollars. Copper. Reeded edge. J1231.	11,000
Pn1291	1872	— 2-1/2 Dollars. Aluminum. Reeded edge. J1232.	15,000
Pn1292	1872	— 2-1/2 Dollars. Copper. Reeded edge. J1233.	9,500
Pn1293	1872	— 2-1/2 Dollars. Aluminum. Reeded edge. J1234.	8,000
Pn1294	1872	— 3 Dollars. Gold. Reeded edge. J1235, Rare.	—
Pn1295	1872	— 3 Dollars. Copper. Reeded edge. J1236.	12,000
Pn1296	1872	— 3 Dollars. Aluminum. Reeded edge. J1237.	20,125
Pn1297	1872	— 3 Dollars. Copper. Reeded edge. J1238.	7,250
Pn1298	1872	— 3 Dollars. Aluminum. Reeded edge. J1239.	6,500
Pn1299	1872	— 5 Dollars. Gold. Reeded edge. J1240, Rare.	—
Pn1300	1872	— 5 Dollars. Copper. Reeded edge. J1241.	16,000
Pn1301	1872	— 5 Dollars. Aluminum. Reeded edge. J1242.	13,500
Pn1302	1872	— 5 Dollars. Copper. Reeded edge. J1243.	8,000
Pn1303	1872	— 5 Dollars. Aluminum. Reeded edge. J1244.	14,500
Pn1304	1872	— 10 Dollars. Gold. Reeded edge. J1245, Rare.	—
Pn1305	1872	— 10 Dollars. Copper. Reeded edge. J1246.	40,250
Pn1306	1872	— 10 Dollars. Aluminum. Reeded edge. J1247.	16,500
Pn1307	1872	— 10 Dollars. Copper. Reeded edge. J1248.	7,500
Pn1308	1872	— 10 Dollars. Aluminum. Reeded edge. J1249.	9,000

KM#	Date	Mintage Identification	Mkt Val
Pn1309	1872	— 20 Dollars. Gold. Reeded edge. J1250, Rare.	—
Pn1310	1872	— 20 Dollars. Copper. Reeded edge. J1251.	14,500
Pn1311	1872	— 20 Dollars. Aluminum. Reeded edge. J1252.	50,000
Pn1312	1872	— 20 Dollars. Copper. Reeded edge. J1253.	16,500
Pn1312a	1872	— 20 Dollars. Copper Gilt. Reeded edge. J1253.	5,350
Pn1313	1872	— 20 Dollars. Aluminum. Reeded edge. J1254.	—
Pn1393	1873	— Gold Dollar. Copper. Reeded edge. J1331.	5,750
Pn1394	1873	— Gold Dollar. Aluminum. Reeded edge. J1332.	10,350
Pn1395	1873	— 2-1/2 Dollars. Copper. Reeded edge. J1333.	6,000
Pn1396	1873	— 2-1/2 Dollars. Aluminum. Reeded edge. J1334.	—

Note: Heritage CSNS sale #404, 4-06, PR-65 realized $13,800

Pn1397	1873	— 3 Dollars. Copper. Reeded edge. J1335.	6,650
Pn1397a	1873	— 3 Dollars. Copper Gilt. Reeded edge. J1335.	5,350
Pn1398	1873	— 3 Dollars. Aluminum. Reeded edge. J1336.	5,550
Pn1399	1873	2 5 Dollars. Gold. Reeded edge. J1337, Rare.	—
Pn1400	1873	— 5 Dollars. Copper. Reeded edge. J1338.	16,000
Pn1401	1873	— 5 Dollars. Aluminum. Reeded edge. J1339.	—
Pn1402	1873	— 5 Dollars. Copper. Reeded edge. J1340.	7,000
Pn1403	1873	— 5 Dollars. Aluminum. Reeded edge. J1341.	8,000
Pn1404	1873	— 10 Dollars. Copper. Reeded edge. J1342.	7,250
Pn1405	1873	— 10 Dollars. Aluminum. Reeded edge. J1343.	7,250
Pn1406	1873	— 20 Dollars. Copper. Reeded edge. J1344.	13,250
Pn1407	1873	— 20 Dollars. Aluminum. Reeded edge. J1345.	8,650
Pn1427	1874	— Gold Dollar. Copper. Reeded edge. J1365.	7,500
Pn1428	1874	— Gold Dollar. Aluminum. Reeded edge. J1366.	—
Pn1429	1874	— 2-1/2 Dollars. Copper. Reeded edge. J1367.	7,500
Pn1430	1874	— 2-1/2 Dollars. Aluminum. Reeded edge. J1368.	4,750
Pn1431	1874	— 3 Dollars. Copper. Reeded edge. J1369.	7,500
Pn1432	1874	— 3 Dollars. Aluminum. Reeded edge. J1370.	6,350
Pn1433	1874	— 5 Dollars. Copper. Reeded edge. J1371.	7,000
Pn1434	1874	— 5 Dollars. Copper. Reeded edge. J1372.	7,000
Pn1435	1874	2 10 Dollars. Gold. Reeded edge. J1373.	276,000
Pn1436	1874	— 10 Dollars. Copper. Reeded edge. J1374.	—

Note: Heritage Atlanta sale #402, 4-06, PR-65 realized $34,500

Pn1436a	1874	— 10 Dollars. Copper Gilt. Reeded edge. J1374.	—
Pn1437	1874	— 10 Dollars. Copper. Plain edge. J1375.	11,500
Pn1437a	1874	— 10 Dollars. Copper Gilt. Plain edge. J1375.	6,350

KM#	Date	Mintage Identification	Mkt Val
Pn1438	1874	— 10 Dollars. Aluminum. Reeded edge. J1376.	35,000
Pn1439	1874	— 10 Dollars. Nickel. Reeded edge. J1377.	15,000
Pn1440	1874	— 10 Dollars. Nickel. Plain edge. J1378.	—
Pn1441	1874	— 10 Dollars. Copper. Reeded edge. J1379.	7,500
Pn1442	1874	— 10 Dollars. Aluminum. Reeded edge. J1380.	8,500
Pn1443	1874	— 20 Dollars. Copper. Reeded edge. J1381.	9,500
Pn1444	1874	— 20 Dollars. Aluminum. Reeded edge. J1382.	10,500
Pn1494	1875	— Gold Dollar. Copper. Reeded edge. J1432.	7,000
Pn1494a	1875	— Gold Dollar. Copper Gilt. Reeded edge. J1432.	4,500
Pn1495	1875	— Gold Dollar. Aluminum. Reeded edge. J1433.	7,500
Pn1496	1875	— 2-1/2 Dollars. Copper. Reeded edge. J1434.	11,000
Pn1496a	1875	— 2-1/2 Dollars. Copper Gilt. Reeded edge. J1434.	7,500
Pn1497	1875	— 2-1/2 Dollars. Aluminum. Reeded edge. J1435.	10,350
Pn1498	1875	— 3 Dollars. Copper. Reeded edge. J1436.	15,000
Pn1498a	1875	— 3 Dollars. Copper Gilt. Reeded edge. J1436.	12,000
Pn1499	1875	— 3 Dollars. Aluminum. Reeded edge. J1437.	10,500
Pn1500	1875	2 5 Dollars. Gold. Reeded edge. J1438.	—
Pn1501	1875	— 5 Dollars. Copper. Reeded edge. J1439.	27,600
Pn1502	1875	— 5 Dollars. Aluminum. Reeded edge. J1440.	—
Pn1503	1875	— 5 Dollars. White Metal. J1440a.	—
Pn1504	1875	— 5 Dollars. Copper. Reeded edge. J1441.	8,250
Pn1504a	1875	— 5 Dollars. Copper Gilt. Reeded edge. J1441.	6,750
Pn1505	1875	— 5 Dollars. Aluminum. Reeded edge. J1442.	20,700
Pn1505a	1875	— 5 Dollars. Aluminum Gilt. Reeded edge. J1442.	—
Pn1506	1875	2 10 Dollars. Gold. Reeded edge. J1443.	—
Pn1507	1875	— 10 Dollars. Copper. Reeded edge. J1444.	7,500
Pn1507a	1875	— 10 Dollars. Copper Gilt. Reeded edge. J1444.	6,750
Pn1508	1875	— 10 Dollars. Aluminum. Reeded edge. J1445.	20,000
Pn1509	1875	— 10 Dollars. White Metal. J1445a, Rare.	—
Pn1510	1875	— 10 Dollars. Copper. Reeded edge. J1446.	9,200
Pn1510a	1875	— 10 Dollars. Copper Gilt. Reeded edge. J1446.	4,375
Pn1511	1875	— 10 Dollars. Aluminum. Reeded edge. J1447.	18,500
Pn1512	1875	— 20 Dollars. Copper. Reeded edge. J1448.	8,750
Pn1513	1875	— 20 Dollars. Aluminum. Reeded edge. J1449.	15,000
Pn1544	1876	— Gold Dollar. Copper. Reeded edge. J1478.	11,500
Pn1545	1876	— Gold Dollar. Aluminum. Reeded edge. J1479.	—

730 UNITED STATES — PATTERNS

KM#	Date	Mintage	Identification	Mkt Val
Pn1546	1876	—	2-1/2 Dollars. Copper. Reeded edge. J1480.	5,750
Pn1547	1876	—	2-1/2 Dollars. Aluminum. Reeded edge. J1481.	—
Pn1548	1876	—	3 Dollars. Copper. Reeded edge. J1482.	10,000
Pn1549	1876	—	3 Dollars. Aluminum. Reeded edge. J1483.	—
Pn1550	1876	—	5 Dollars. Copper. Reeded edge. J1484. Rare.	—

Note: Heritage Dallas sale #407, PR-64 realized $12,650

KM#	Date	Mintage	Identification	Mkt Val
Pn1551	1876	—	5 Dollars. Aluminum. Reeded edge. J1485.	—
Pn1552	1876	—	10 Dollars. Copper. Reeded edge. J1486.	10,925
Pn1553	1876	—	10 Dollars. Aluminum. Reeded edge. J1487.	—
Pn1554	1876	—	20 Dollars. Gold. Reeded edge. J1488. Rare.	—
Pn1555	1876	—	20 Dollars. Copper. Reeded edge. J1489.	14,950
Pn1555a	1876	—	20 Dollars. Copper Gilt. Reeded edge. J1489.	4,850
Pn1556	1876	—	20 Dollars. Gold. Reeded edge. J1490. Rare.	—
Pn1557	1876	—	20 Dollars. Copper. Reeded edge. J1491.	—
Pn1558	1876	—	20 Dollars. Copper Gilt. Plain edge. J1492.	36,250
Pn1559	1876	—	20 Dollars. Copper. Reeded edge. J1493.	29,000
Pn1560	1876	—	20 Dollars. Aluminum. Reeded edge. J1494.	—
Pn1624	1877	—	10 Dollars. Copper. Reeded edge. J1545.	—

Note: Heritage Long Beach sale #400, 2-06, PR-64 realized $13,800

KM#	Date	Mintage	Identification	Mkt Val
Pn1624a	1877	—	10 Dollars. Copper Gilt. Reeded edge. J1545.	—
Pn1625	1877	—	50 Dollars. Gold. Reeded edge. J1546.	—
Pn1638	1878	13	Goloid Dollar. Goloid. Reeded edge. J1557.	2,450
Pn1639	1878	—	Goloid Dollar. Silver. Reeded edge. J1558.	8,500
Pn1639a	1878	—	Goloid Dollar. Silver. Reeded edge. Lightweight. J1558.	11,000
Pn1640	1878	—	Goloid Dollar. Copper. Reeded edge. J1559.	8,000
Pn1641	1878	4	Goloid Dollar. Goloid. Reeded edge. J1560.	13,800
Pn1642	1878	—	Goloid Dollar. Silver. Reeded edge. J1561.	—
Pn1643	1878	—	Goloid Dollar. Copper. Reeded edge. J1562.	3,450
Pn1644	1878	—	Goloid Metric Dollar. Goloid. Reeded edge. J1563.	2,550
Pn1645	1878	—	Goloid Metric Dollar. Silver. Reeded edge. J1564.	7,350
Pn1645a	1878	—	Goloid Metric Dollar. Silver. Reeded edge. Lightweight restrike. J1564.	2,200
Pn1647	1878	2	2-1/2 Dollars. Gold. Reeded edge. J1566. Rare.	—
Pn1648	1878	—	2-1/2 Dollars. Copper. Reeded edge. J1567.	9,200
Pn1648a	1878	—	2-1/2 Dollars. Copper Gilt. Reeded edge. J1567.	4,375

KM#	Date	Mintage	Identification	Mkt Val
Pn1649	1878	—	5 Dollars. Copper. Reeded edge. J1568.	9,000
Pn1649a	1878	—	5 Dollars. Copper Gilt. Reeded edge. J1568.	5,750
Pn1650	1878	—	5 Dollars. Copper. Without pellets. Reeded edge. J1568a.	4,000
Pn1651	1878	—	5 Dollars. Copper. Reeded edge. J1569.	7,750
Pn1651a	1878	—	5 Dollars. Copper Gilt. Reeded edge. J1569.	5,500
Pn1652	1878	—	5 Dollars. Gold. Reeded edge. J1570. Rare.	—
Pn1653	1878	—	5 Dollars. Copper. Reeded edge. J1571.	5,500
Pn1654	1878	—	5 Dollars. Gold. Reeded edge. J1572. Rare.	—
Pn1655	1878	—	5 Dollars. Copper. Reeded edge. J1573.	5,500
Pn1656	1878	—	5 Dollars. Copper. Reeded edge. J1574.	7,000
Pn1656a	1878	—	5 Dollars. Copper Gilt. Reeded edge. J1574.	—

Note: Heritage Orlando sale #394, 1-06, PR-67 realized $21,850

KM#	Date	Mintage	Identification	Mkt Val
Pn1657	1878	—	5 Dollars. Brass. Reeded edge. J1574a.	—
Pn1658	1878	—	5 Dollars. Gold. Reeded edge. J1575.	299,000
Pn1659	1878	—	5 Dollars. Copper. Reeded edge. J1576.	7,650
Pn1659a	1878	—	5 Dollars. Copper Gilt. Reeded edge. J1576.	9,775
Pn1660	1878	—	5 Dollars. Gold. Reeded edge. J1577. Rare.	—
Pn1661	1878	—	5 Dollars. Copper. Reeded edge. J1578.	8,500
Pn1661a	1878	—	5 Dollars. Copper Gilt. Reeded edge. J1578.	9,000
Pn1662	1878	—	10 Dollars. Gold. Plain edge. J1579.	345,000
Pn1663	1878	—	10 Dollars. Copper. Reeded edge. Thin planchet. J1580.	6,500
Pn1663a	1878	—	10 Dollars. Copper. Reeded edge. Thick planchet. J1580.	4,650
Pn1663b	1878	—	10 Dollars. Copper Gilt. Reeded edge. J1580.	34,500
Pn1664	1878	—	10 Dollars. Gold. Reeded edge. J1581. Rare.	—
Pn1665	1878	—	10 Dollars. Copper. Reeded edge. J1582.	8,750

KM#	Date	Mintage	Identification	Mkt Val
Pn1701	1879	—	Metric Dollar. Silver Alloy. 25.0000 g. Reeded edge. J1617.	3,600
Pn1702	1879	—	Metric Dollar. Silver. Light etching, light restrike. J1618.	7,500
Pn1703	1879	—	Metric Dollar. Copper. Reeded edge. J1619.	7,500
Pn1704	1879	—	Metric Dollar. Aluminum. Reeded edge. J1620.	—
Pn1705	1879	—	Metric Dollar. Lead. Reeded edge. J1621.	—
Pn1706	1879	—	Metric Dollar. Silver Alloy. Reeded edge. J1622.	8,650
Pn1707	1879	—	Metric Dollar. Copper. Reeded edge. J1623.	—

Note: Heritage Orlando sale #394, 1-06, PR-67 realized $23,000

KM#	Date	Mintage	Identification	Mkt Val
Pn1708	1879	—	Metric Dollar. Aluminum. Reeded edge. J1624.	16,100
Pn1709	1879	—	Metric Dollar. White Metal. Reeded edge. J1625.	—
Pn1710	1879	—	Goloid Metric Dollar. Goloid. 14.0000 g. Reeded edge. J1626.	3,500
Pn1711	1879	—	Goloid Metric Dollar. Silver. Reeded edge. J1627.	3,200
Pn1712	1879	—	Goloid Metric Dollar. Copper. Reeded edge. J1628.	—

Note: Heritage Orlando sale #394, 1-06, PR-66 realized $12,650

KM#	Date	Mintage	Identification	Mkt Val
Pn1713	1879	—	Goloid Metric Dollar. Aluminum. Reeded edge. J1629.	8,000
Pn1714	1879	—	Goloid Metric Dollar. Lead. Reeded edge. J1630.	—
Pn1715	1879	—	Goloid Metric Dollar. Goloid. 14.0000 g. Reeded edge. J1631.	10,925
Pn1716	1879	—	Goloid Metric Dollar. Copper. Reeded edge. J1632.	7,200
Pn1717	1879	—	Goloid Metric Dollar. Aluminum. Reeded edge. J1633.	9,200
Pn1718	1879	—	Goloid Metric Dollar. White Metal. Reeded edge. J1634.	30,000
Pn1719	1879	415	$4. Gold. 109.0000 g. Reeded edge. These are patterns rather than coins struck for circulation. Examples in other metals also exist; values listed here are only for those struck in gold. J1719.	—
Pn1720	1879	—	$4. Gold. Restrike. 103-109 grams. Worn obverse die. J1636.	95,000
Pn1721	1879	—	$4. Copper. Reeded edge. J1636.	20,000
Pn1722	1879	—	$4. Aluminum. Reeded edge. J1637.	39,100

CALIFORNIA — UNITED STATES

KM#	Date	Mintage	Identification	Mkt Val
Pn1723	1879	10	$4. Gold. Reeded edge. J1638.	345,000
	1879	10	$4. Gold. Reeded edge. J1638.	345,000
Pn1724	1879	—	$4. Copper. Reeded edge. J1639.	28,750
Pn1725	1879	—	$4. Aluminum. Reeded edge. J1640.	90,000
Pn1726	1879	—	$4. White Metal. Reeded edge. J1641.	—
Pn1727	1879	—	Metric 20 Dollar. Copper. Reeded edge. J1642.	46,000
Pn1728	1879	4	Metric 20 Dollar. Gold. 540.5000 g. Reeded edge. J1643.	258,750
Pn1728a	1879	—	Metric 20 Dollar. Gold. 516.0000 g. Reeded edge. Restrike. J1643.	—
Pn1729	1879	—	Metric 20 Dollar. Copper. Reeded edge. J1644.	—
Pn1730	1880	—	Metric Dollar. Silver Alloy. Reeded edge. J1645.	4,900
Pn1731	1880	—	Metric Dollar. Copper. Reeded edge. J1646.	11,500
Pn1732	1880	—	Metric Dollar. Aluminum. Reeded edge. J1647.	25,000
Pn1733	1880	—	Metric Dollar. Silver Alloy. Reeded edge. J1648.	5,750
Pn1734	1880	—	Metric Dollar. Copper. Reeded edge. J1649.	6,000
Pn1735	1880	—	Metric Dollar. Aluminum. Reeded edge. J1650.	11,000
Pn1736	1880	—	Goloid Metric Dollar. Goloid. Reeded edge. J1651.	8,500
Pn1737	1880	—	Goloid Metric Dollar. Copper. Reeded edge. J1652.	6,350
Pn1738	1880	—	Goloid Metric Dollar. Aluminum. Reeded edge. J1653.	8,750
Pn1739	1880	—	Goloid Metric Dollar. Goloid. Reeded edge. J1654.	8,650
Pn1740	1880	—	Goloid Metric Dollar. Copper. Reeded edge. J1655.	9,200
Pn1741	1880	—	Goloid Metric Dollar. Aluminum. Reeded edge. J1656.	—

Note: Heritage Palm Beach sale #412, 3-06, PR-67 realized $40,250

KM#	Date	Mintage	Identification	Mkt Val
Pn1742	1880	15	$4. Gold. Reeded edge. J1657.	241,500
Pn1743	1880	—	$4. Copper. Reeded edge. J1658.	37,375
Pn1744	1880	—	$4. Aluminum. Reeded edge. J1659.	32,200
Pn1745	1880W	10	$4. Gold. Reeded edge. J1660.	368,000
Pn1746	1880	—	$4. Copper. Reeded edge. J1661.	36,800
Pn1746a	1880	—	$4. Copper Gilt. Reeded edge. J1661.	37,500
Pn1747	1880	—	$4. Aluminum. J1662.	86,350
Pn1748	1880	—	5 Dollars. Copper. Reeded edge. J1663.	6,500
Pn1824	1884	—	Gold Dollar. Copper. Reeded edge. J1733.	—
Pn1825	1884	—	2-1/2 Dollars. Copper. Reeded edge. J1734.	—
Pn1826	1884	—	3 Dollars. Copper. Reeded edge. J1735.	—
Pn1827	1884	—	5 Dollars. Copper. Reeded edge. J1736.	—

Note: Heritage Orlando sale #394, 1-06, PR-64 realized $57,500

KM#	Date	Mintage	Identification	Mkt Val
Pn1828	1884	—	10 Dollars. Copper. Reeded edge. J1737.	—

Note: Heritage Orlando sale #394, 1-06, PR-65 realized $57,500

KM#	Date	Mintage	Identification	Mkt Val
Pn1829	1884	—	20 Dollars. Copper. Reeded edge. J1738.	—
Pn1842	1885	—	Gold Dollar. Aluminum. Reeded edge. J1751.	15,000
Pn1843	1885	—	2-1/2 Dollars. Aluminum. Reeded edge. J1752.	17,500
Pn1844	1885	—	3 Dollars. Aluminum. Reeded edge. J1753.	20,000
Pn1845	1885	—	5 Dollars. Aluminum. Reeded edge. J1754.	17,250
Pn1846	1885	—	10 Dollars. Aluminum. Reeded edge. J1755.	21,850
Pn1847	1885	—	20 Dollars. Aluminum. Reeded edge. J1756.	38,500
Pn1865	1906	—	20 Dollars. Gold. Lettered edge. J1773.	—
Pn1866	1907	500	10 Dollars. Gold. Stars on edge. J1774.	—
Pn1867	1907	50	10 Dollars. Gold. Plain edge. J1774a.	—
Pn1868	1907	40	10 Dollars. Gold. Rolled beveled edge. J1775.	—
Pn1869	(1907) MCMVII	—	20 Dollars. Gold. Lettered edge. J1776.	—
Pn1870	(1907) MCMVII	—	20 Dollars. Lead. Lettered edge. J1777.	—
Pn1871	(1907) MCMVII	20	20 Dollars. Gold. Lettered edge. J1778.	—
Pn1872	(1907) MCMVII	—	20 Dollars. Lead. J1778a.	—
Pn1873	(1907) MCMVII	2	20 Dollars. Lead. J1778b.	—
Pn1875	(1907) MCMVII	—	20 Dollars. Gold. Lettered edge. 2-3 known. J1779.	—
Pn1876	1907	—	20 Dollars. Brass. Lettered edge. Mutilated at mint by being squashed between rollers. J1779a.	—
Pn1891	1915	7	Gold Dollar. Gold. Reeded edge. Without "S" mint mark. J1793.	8,500
Pn1892	1915	2	Gold Dollar. Silver. Plain edge. J1793a.	20,900
Pn1893	1915	2	Gold Dollar. Silver. Plain edge. J1793b.	—
Pn1904	1916	—	Gold Dollar. Nickel. Reeded edge. J1802.	13,800

US TERRITORIAL GOLD CALIFORNIA

Fractional and Small Size California Gold

During the California gold rush a wide variety of U.S. and foreign coins were used for small change, but only limited quantities of these coins were available. Gold dust was in common use, although this offered the miner a relatively low value for his gold.

By 1852 California jewelers had begun to manufacture 25¢, 50¢ and $1 gold pieces in round and octagonal shapes. Makers included M. Deriberpe, Antoine Louis Nouizillet, Isadore Routhier, Robert B. Gray, Pierre Frontier, Eugene Deviercy, Herman J. Brand, and Herman and Jacob Levison. Reuben N. Hershfield and Noah Mitchell made their coins in Leavenworth, Kansas and most of their production was seized in August 1871. Herman Kroll made California gold coins in New York City in the 1890s. Only two or three of these companies were in production at any one time. Many varieties bear the makers initials. Frontier and his partners made most of the large Liberty Head, Eagle reverse, and Washington Head design types. Most of the small Liberty Head types were made first by Nouizillet and later by Gray and then the Levison brothers and lastly by the California Jewelry Co. Coins initialed "G.G." are apparently patterns made by Frontier and Deviercy for the New York based firm of Gaime, Guillemot & Co.

Most of the earlier coins were struck from gold alloys and had an intrinsic value of about 50-60 percent of face value. They were generally struck from partially hubbed dies and with reeded collars. A few issues were struck with a plain collar or a collar with reeding on only 7 of the 8 sides. Many issues are too poorly struck or too thin to have a clear and complete image of the collar. The later coins and some of the earlier coins were struck from laminated or plated gold planchets, or from gold plated silver planchets. Most of the last dates of issue are extremely thin and contain only token amounts of gold.

Circumstantial evidence exists that the coins issued through 1856 circulated as small change. The San Francisco mint was established in 1854, and by 1856 it had ramped up its production enough to satisfy the local need for small change. However, some evidence exists that these small gold coins may have continued to circulate on occasion through to 1871. After 1871, the gold content of the coins dramatically decreases and it is very unlikely that any of these last issues circulated.

Although the Private Coinages Act of 1864 outlawed all private coinage, this law was not enforced in California and production of small denominated gold continued through 1882. In the spring of 1883, Col. Henry Finnegass of the U.S. Secret Service halted production of the denominated private gold pieces. Non-denominated tokens (lacking DOLLARS, CENTS or the equivalent) were also made during this latter period, sometimes by the same manufacturing jeweler using the same obverse die and the same planchets as the small denomination gold coins. Production of these tokens continues to this day, with most issues made after the 1906 earthquake and fire being backdated to 1847-1865 and struck from brass or gold plated brass planchets.

Approximately 25,000 pieces of California small denomination gold coins are estimated to exist, in a total of over 500 varieties. A few varieties are undated, mostly gold rush era pieces; and a few of the issues are backdated, mostly those from the 1880's. This listing groups varieties together in easily identified categories. The prices quoted are for the most common variety in each group. UNC prices reflect the median auction prices realized of MS60 to MS62 graded coins. BU prices reflect the median auction prices realized of MS63 to MS64 graded coins. Pre-1871 true MS-65 coins are rare and sell for substantial premiums over the prices on this list. Post-1871 coins are rarely found with wear and often have a cameo proof appearance. Auction prices realized are highly volatile and it is not uncommon to find recent records of sales at twice or half of the values shown here. Many of the rarity estimates published in the 1980s and earlier have proven to be too high, so caution is advised when paying a premium for a rare variety. In addition, many varieties that have a refined appearance command higher prices than equivalent grade but scarcer varieties that have a more crude appearance.

Several counterfeits of California Fractional Gold coins exist. Beware of 1854 and 1858 dated round 1/2 dollars, and 1871 dated round dollars that have designs that do not match any of the published varieties. Beware of reeded edge Kroll coins being sold as originals (see the listings below).

For further information consult "California Pioneer Fractional Gold" by W. Breen and R.J. Gillio and "The Brasher Bulletin" the official newsletter of The Society of Private and Pioneer Numismatists.

1/4 DOLLAR (OCTAGONAL)

KM# 1.1 Obverse: Large Liberty head, left **Reverse:** Value and date within beaded circle

Date	XF	AU	Unc	BU
1853	100.100.	150	200	300
1854	100.100.	150	250	350
1855	100.100.	150	250	350
1856	100.100.	150	260	375

732 UNITED STATES — CALIFORNIA

KM# 1.10 Obverse: "Oriental" Liberty head, left, above date Reverse: "1/4 CALDOLL" within wreath

Date	XF	AU	Unc	BU
1881	—	—	1,000	3,000

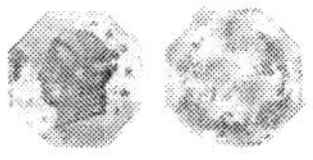

KM# 1.11 Obverse: Large Liberty head, left, above 1872 Reverse: Value and 1871 within wreath

Date	XF	AU	Unc	BU
1872-71	—	—	1,000	3,000

KM# 1.2 Obverse: Liberty head, left Reverse: Value and date within wreath

Date	XF	AU	Unc	BU
1859	65.	110	200	450
1864	75.	125	250	400
1866	75.	125	250	400
1867	65.	110	250	400
1868	70.	125	200	350
1869	70.	125	200	350
1870	65.	110	200	350
1871	65.	110	200	350

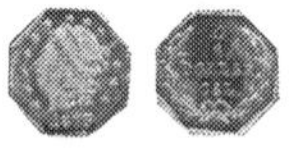

KM# 1.3 Obverse: Large Liberty head, left, above date Reverse: Value and "CAL" within wreath

Date	XF	AU	Unc	BU
1872	65.	110	250	400
1873	50.	85.00	175	300

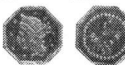

KM# 1.4 Obverse: Small Liberty head, left Reverse: Value and date within beaded circle

Date	XF	AU	Unc	BU
1853	125.	250	325	425

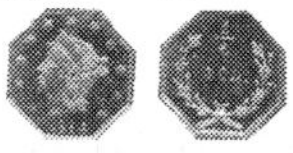

KM# 1.5 Obverse: Small Liberty head, left, above date Reverse: Value within wreath

Date	XF	AU	Unc	BU
1854	125.	250	300	350

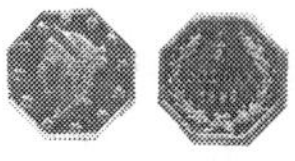

KM# 1.6 Obverse: Small Liberty head, left Reverse: Value and date within wreath

Date	XF	AU	Unc	BU
1855	—	—	—	—
1856	—	—	—	—
1857 Plain edge	—	—	—	—
Note: Kroll type date				
1857 Reeded edge	—	—	—	—
Note: Kroll type date				
1860	—	—	—	—
1870	—	—	—	—

KM# 1.7 Obverse: Liberty head, left Reverse: Value in shield and date within wreath

Date	XF	AU	Unc	BU
1863	150.	350	500	—
1864	65.	110	240	—
1865	85.	145	250	550
1866	85.	145	250	400
1867	75.	125	200	400
1868	75.	125	200	—
1869	75.	125	190	300
1870	75.	125	200	350

KM# 1.8 Obverse: Small Liberty head, left, above date Reverse: Value and "CAL" within wreath

Date	XF	AU	Unc	BU
1870	65.	110	200	300
1871	65.	110	175	250
1871	65.	110	175	250
1873	175.	250	400	—

Date	XF	AU	Unc	BU
1874	65.	110	175	275
1875/3	350.	700	1,000	—
1876	65.	110	200	300

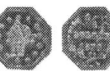

KM# 1.9 Obverse: "Goofy" Liberty head, left Reverse: Value and date within wreath

Date	XF	AU	Unc	BU
1870	85.	145	200	300

KM# 2.1 Obverse: Large indian head, left, above date Reverse: Value within wreath

Date	XF	AU	Unc	BU
1852	100.100.	175	240	450
Note: Back dated issue				
1868	100.100.	175	240	450
Note: Back dated issue				
1874	85.	160	220	400
Note: Back dated issue				
1876	85.	160	220	400
1880	75.	150	200	350
1881	85.	160	220	400

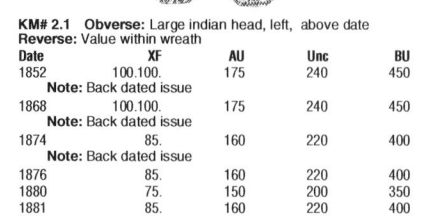

KM# 2.2 Obverse: Large indian head, left, above date Reverse: Value within wreath

Date	XF	AU	Unc	BU
1872	65.	110	210	300
1873/2	200.	350	550	800
1873	90.	160	250	350
1874	65.	110	210	300
1875	90.	160	250	350
1876	90.	160	250	350

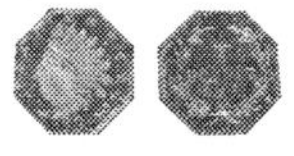

KM# 2.3 Obverse: Small indian head, left, above date Reverse: Vallue and CAL within wreath

Date	XF	AU	Unc	BU
1875	90.	160	250	350
1876	90.	160	250	500
1881	—	—	500	1,100

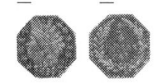

KM# 2.4 Obverse: "Aztec" indian head, left, above date Reverse: Value and CAL within wreath

Date	XF	AU	Unc	BU
1880	65.	110	210	300

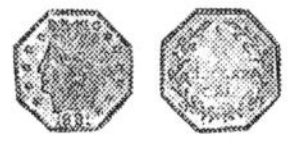

KM# 2.6 Obverse: "Dumb" indian head, left, above date Reverse: Value and CAL within wreath

Date	XF	AU	Unc	BU
1881	—	—	650	—

KM# 2.7 Obverse: "Young" indian head, left, above date Reverse: Value within wreath

Date	XF	AU	Unc	BU
1881	—	—	450	—

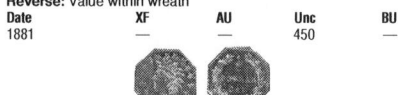

KM# 2.8 Obverse: Indian head, left, above date Reverse: Value and "CAL" within wreath

Date	XF	AU	Unc	BU
1882	—	—	500	750

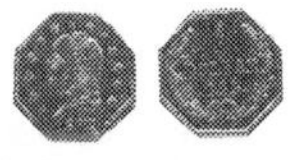

KM# 3 Obverse: Washington head, left, above date Reverse: Value and CAL within wreath

Date	XF	AU	Unc	BU
1872	—	—	400	950

1/4 DOLLAR (ROUND)

KM# 4 Obverse: Defiant eagle above date Reverse: "25¢" within wreath

Date	XF	AU	Unc	BU
1854	11,000.	22,000	33,000	44,000

KM# 5.1 Obverse: Large Liberty head, left Reverse: Value and date within wreath

Date	XF	AU	Unc	BU
1853	400.	700	1,000	1,500
1854	150.	250	400	600
1859	70.	120	225	275
1865	90.	160	250	350
1866	—	—	200	300
1867	—	—	200	300
1868	—	—	200	300
1870	—	—	200	300
1871	—	—	200	300

KM# 5.2 Obverse: Large Liberty head, left, above date Reverse: Value and CAL within wreath

Date	XF	AU	Unc	BU
1871	—	—	200	275
1872	—	—	200	275
1873	—	—	180	260

KM# 5.3 Obverse: Small Liberty head, left Reverse: "25¢" in wreath

Date	XF	AU	Unc	BU
	1,000.	1,650	2,450	3,500

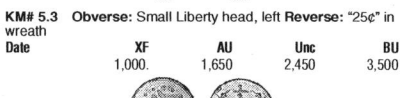

KM# 5.4 Obverse: Small Liberty head, left Reverse: "1/4 DOLL." or "DOLLAR" and date in wreath

Date	XF	AU	Unc	BU
	90.	150	200	350
Note: Rare counterfeit exists				
1853	500.	800	1,200	2,500
1853 10 stars	120.	200	275	365
Note: Kroll type				
1855 11 stars	—	—	50.00	100.00100
Note: Kroll type				
1856	100.100.		175	250	350
1860	65.	110	175	275
1864	75.	125	200	300
1865	90.	135	225	350
1866	125.	210	600	350
1867	65.	110	175	350
1869	65.	100.00100	175	300
1870	125.	210	250	450

KM# 5.5 Obverse: Small Liberty head, left Reverse: Value in shield and date within wreath

Date	XF	AU	Unc	BU
1863	80.	160	200	—

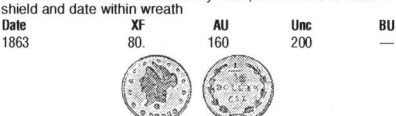

KM# 5.6 Obverse: Small Liberty head, left, above date Reverse: Value and "CAL" within wreath

Date	XF	AU	Unc	BU
	100.100.	175	500	—
1870	80.	160	200	250
1871	80.	160	200	250
1871	—	—	210	350
1873	—	—	300	500
1874	—	—	300	500
1875	—	—	250	475
1876	—	—	225	450

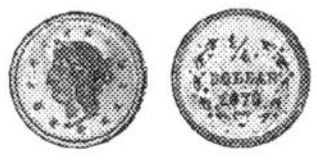

KM# 5.7 Obverse: "Goofy" Liberty head, left Reverse: Value and date within wreath

CALIFORNIA

Date	XF	AU	Unc	BU
1870	110.	160	220	250

KM# 5.8 **Obverse:** Liberty head, left, with "H" and date below **Reverse:** Value and "CAL" in wreath

Date	XF	AU	Unc	BU
1871	80.	125	160	250

KM# 6.1 **Obverse:** Large indian head, left, above date **Reverse:** Value within wreath

Date	XF	AU	Unc	BU
1852	—	—	200	300
Note: Back dated issue				
1868	—	—	250	375
Note: Back dated issue				
1874	—	—	190	275
Note: Back dated issue				
1876	—	—	200	325
1878/6	—	—	200	300
1880	—	—	200	325
1881	—	—	200	325

KM# 6.2 **Obverse:** Large indian head, left, above date **Reverse:** Value and "CAL" within wreath

Date	XF	AU	Unc	BU
1872/1	—	—	200	300
1873	—	—	180	275
1874	—	—	180	275
1875	—	—	200	300
1876	—	—	200	300

KM# 6.3 **Obverse:** Small indian head, left, above date **Reverse:** Value within wreath

Date	XF	AU	Unc	BU
1875	75.	125	250	400
1876	65.	110	200	350
1881 Rare	—	—	—	—

KM# 6.4 **Obverse:** "Young" indian head, left, above date **Reverse:** Value and CAL within wreath

Date	XF	AU	Unc	BU
1882	400.	725	1,225	1,750

KM# 7 **Obverse:** Washington head, left, above date **Reverse:** Value and CAL within wreath

Date	XF	AU	Unc	BU
1872	—	—	600	900

1/2 DOLLAR (OCTAGONAL)

KM# 8.1 **Obverse:** Liberty head, left, above date **Reverse:** "1/2 DOLLAR" in beaded circle, "CALIFORNIA GOLD" around circle

Date	XF	AU	Unc	BU
1853	165.	280	350	450
1854	110.	225	285	350
Note: Rare counterfeit exists				
1854	165.	280	350	450
1856	165.	285	365	450

KM# 8.10 **Obverse:** "Goofy" Liberty head, left **Reverse:** Value and date within wreath

Date	XF	AU	Unc	BU
1870	55.	110	200	300

KM# 8.11 **Obverse:** "Oriental" Liberty head, left, above date **Reverse:** "1/2 CALDOLL" within wreath

Date	XF	AU	Unc	BU
1881	250.	450	750	1,150

KM# 8.2 **Obverse:** Liberty head, left **Reverse:** Small eagle with rays ("peacock")

Date	XF	AU	Unc	BU
1853	400.	600	1,000	1,500

KM# 8.3 **Obverse:** Large Liberty head, left **Reverse:** Large eagle with date

Date	XF	AU	Unc	BU
1853	750.	1,350	2,250	—

KM# 8.4 **Obverse:** Liberty head, left **Reverse:** Value and date within wreath

Date	XF	AU	Unc	BU
1859	—	130	200	275
1866	—	200	300	400
1867	—	130	225	300
1868	—	130	225	300
1869	—	130	250	350
1870	—	130	250	350
1871	—	130	225	300

KM# 8.5 **Obverse:** Large Liberty head, left, above date **Reverse:** Value and "CAL" within wreath

Date	XF	AU	Unc	BU
1872	—	130	250	350
1873	—	130	225	300

KM# 8.6 **Obverse:** Liberty head, left **Reverse:** Date in wreath, "HALF DOL. CALIFORNIA GOLD" around wreath

Date	XF	AU	Unc	BU
1854	100.100	250	350	500
1855	90.	200	300	400
1856	90.	200	265	325
1856	165.	350	1,100	—
Note: Back date issue struck in 1864				
1868	60.	110	185	275
Note: Kroll type date				

KM# 8.7 **Obverse:** Small Liberty head, left **Reverse:** "HALF DOLLAR" and date in wreath

Date	XF	AU	Unc	BU
1864	—	175	275	350
1870	—	175	275	—

KM# 8.8 **Obverse:** Liberty head, left **Reverse:** "CAL. GOLD HALF DOL" and date in wreath

Date	XF	AU	Unc	BU
1869	—	175	200	350
1870	—	175	200	350

KM# 8.9 **Obverse:** Small Liberty head, left, above date **Reverse:** Value and "CAL" in wreath

Date	XF	AU	Unc	BU
1870	55.	110	200	300
1871	55.	110	200	250
1871	55.	100.00100	165	250
1873	85.	200	300	600
1874	85.	200	300	600
1875	250.	475	1,000	—
1876	55.	110	200	250

KM# 9.1 **Obverse:** Large indian head, left above date **Reverse:** Value within wreath

UNITED STATES 733

Date	XF	AU	Unc	BU
1852	—	—	500	900
Note: Back dated issue				
1868	—	—	650	1,000
Note: Back dated issue				
1874	—	175	500	900
Note: Back dated issue				
1876	—	—	300	400
1880	—	—	300	400
1881	—	—	300	400

KM# 9.2 **Obverse:** Large indian head, left, above date **Reverse:** Value and "CAL" within wreath

Date	XF	AU	Unc	BU
1852	—	—	450	700
Note: Back dated issue				
1868	—	—	260	550
Note: Back dated issue				
1872	—	—	200	300
1873/2	—	—	200	400
1873	—	—	200	300
1874/3	—	—	250	350
1874	—	—	200	300
1875	—	—	250	425
1876	—	—	250	400
1878/6	—	—	250	400
1880	—	—	500	1,000
1881	—	—	250	400

KM# 9.3 **Obverse:** Small indian head, left above date **Reverse:** Value and CAL within wreath

Date	XF	AU	Unc	BU
1875	—	175	225	350
1876	—	175	225	350

KM# 9.4 **Obverse:** "Young" indian head, left above date **Reverse:** Value and CAL within wreath

Date	XF	AU	Unc	BU
1881	—	—	550	850
1882 Rare	—	—	—	—

1/2 DOLLAR (ROUND)

KM# 10 **Obverse:** Arms of California and date **Reverse:** Eagle and legends

Date	XF	AU	Unc	BU
1853	1,250.	3,500	4,500	5,500

KM# 11.1 **Obverse:** Liberty head, left **Reverse:** Large eagle and legends

Date	XF	AU	Unc	BU
1854	1,000.	2,700	6,000	—

KM# 11.11 **Obverse:** "Goofy" Liberty head, left **Reverse:** Value and date within wreath

Date	XF	AU	Unc	BU
1870	125.	225	400	700

KM# 11.12 **Obverse:** Liberty head, left, with "H" and date below **Reverse:** Value and "CAL" within wreath

Date	XF	AU	Unc	BU
1871	90.	175	200	275

KM# 11.2 **Obverse:** Liberty head, left, above date **Reverse:** "HALF DOL. CALIFORNIA GOLD" around wreath

Date	XF	AU	Unc	BU
1854	175.	210	300	450

UNITED STATES — CALIFORNIA

KM# 11.3 **Obverse:** Liberty head, left **Reverse:** Date in wreath, value and "CALIFORNIA GOLD" around wreath

Date	XF	AU	Unc	BU
1852	145.	180	275	400
1852	145.	180	275	400
1853	145.	180	275	400
1853	165.	200	300	425
1853	165.	200	300	425
1853 Date on reverse	125.	160	225	300

Note: Kroll type

| 1854 Large head | 300. | 600 | 1,000 | 1,600 |
| 1854 Small head | — | — | 100.00100 | 200 |

Note: Common counterfeits exist

| 1855 Date on reverse | 175. | 210 | 325 | 550 |

Note: Kroll type

| 1856 | 100.100. | 135 | 225 | 325 |
| 1860/56 | 125. | 185 | 250 | 400 |

KM# 11.4 **Obverse:** Liberty head, left **Reverse:** Small eagle and legends

Date	XF	AU	Unc	BU
1853 Rare	—	—	—	—
1853	5,000.	8,000	10,000	15,000

KM# 11.5 **Obverse:** Liberty head, left **Reverse:** Value in wreath; "CALIFORNIA GOLD" and date around wreath

Date	XF	AU	Unc	BU
1853	150.	250	750	1,500

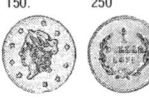

KM# 11.6 **Obverse:** Liberty head, left **Reverse:** Value and date within wreath

Date	XF	AU	Unc	BU
Rare	—	—	—	—
1854	850.	2,000	—	—

Note: Common counterfeit without "FD" beneath truncation

1855	155.	300	450	600
1859	140.	250	350	500
1859	—	150	175	250
1865	—	150	225	350
1866	—	165	250	400
1867	—	150	225	350
1868	—	165	250	400
1869	—	165	250	400
1870	—	132	225	350
1871	—	125	200	300
1873	—	170	250	450

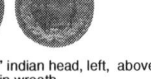

KM# 11.7 **Obverse:** Liberty head, left, above date **Reverse:** Value and "CAL" within wreath

Date	XF	AU	Unc	BU
1870	—	125	250	400
1871	—	125	250	400
1871	—	200	400	—
1872	—	—	250	400
1873	—	200	400	1,000
1874	—	125	250	750
1875	—	125	300	800
1876	—	100.00100	250	—

KM# 11.8 **Obverse:** Liberty head, left **Reverse:** Value and date within wreath, "CALIFORNIA GOLD" outside

Date	XF	AU	Unc	BU
1863	265.	425	675	950

Note: This issue is a rare Kroll type. All 1858 dates of this type are counterfeits

KM# 11.9 **Obverse:** Liberty head, left **Reverse:** "HALF DOLLAR" and date in wreath

Date	XF	AU	Unc	BU
1864	100.100.	165	250	350
1866	200.	330	500	700
1867	100.100.	165	250	350
1868	100.100.	165	250	350
1869	125.	200	300	—
1870	—	200	350	—

KM# 12.1 **Obverse:** Large indian head, left, above date **Reverse:** Value within wreath

Date	XF	AU	Unc	BU
1852	—	—	350	675
1868	—	—	300	600
1874	—	—	300	600
1876	—	—	200	250
1878/6	—	—	300	450
1880	—	—	250	400
1881	—	—	250	400

KM# 12.2 **Obverse:** Large indian head, left, above date **Reverse:** Value and CAL within wreath

Date	XF	AU	Unc	BU
1872	—	—	200	300
1873/2	—	—	350	650
1873	—	—	200	300
1874/3	—	—	300	450
1874	—	—	200	300
1875/3	—	—	200	300
1875	—	—	300	500
1876/5	—	—	200	300
1876	—	—	340	600

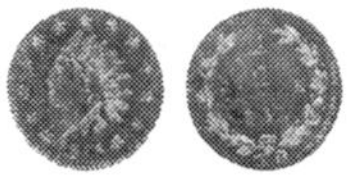

KM# 12.3 **Obverse:** Small indian head, left, above date **Reverse:** Value and CAL within wreath

Date	XF	AU	Unc	BU
1875	100.100.	165	250	450
1876	75.	100.00100	200	300

KM# 12.4 **Obverse:** "Young" indian head, left, above date **Reverse:** Value and CAL within wreath

Date	XF	AU	Unc	BU
1882	—	350	850	—

DOLLAR (OCTAGONAL)

KM# 13.1 **Obverse:** Liberty head, left **Reverse:** Large eagle and legends

Date	XF	AU	Unc	BU
1853	3,000.	3,500	5,500	—
1854	1,000.	1,500	2,000	4,000

KM# 13.2 **Obverse:** Liberty head, left **Reverse:** Value and date in beaded circle; "CALIFORNIA GOLD", initials around circle

Date	XF	AU	Unc	BU
1853	275.	500	750	1,100
1853	450.	800	1,100	—
1853	300.	450	900	—
1853	275.	450	750	1,200
1854	450.	800	1,100	—
1854	300.	500	900	1,600
1855	350.	600	900	—
1856	2,100.	3,300	5,000	—
1863 Reeded edge	150.	225	325	500
1863 Plain edge	—	—	40.00	80.00

Note: Reeded edge 1863 dates are Kroll types, while plain edge examples are Kroll restrikes

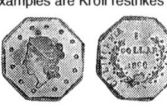

KM# 13.3 **Obverse:** Liberty head, left **Reverse:** Value and date inside wreath; legends outside wreath

Date	XF	AU	Unc	BU
1854 Rare	—	—	—	—

Note: Bowers and Marena sale 5-99, XF $9,775

1854	275.	500	750	1,100
1855	275.	500	750	1,100
1858	150.	250	350	600

Note: 1858 dates are Kroll types

1859	1,900.	—	—	—
1860	—	450	750	100.00100
1868	—	450	750	1,100
1869	—	350	6,600	900
1870	—	350	600	900
1871	—	300	400	850

KM# 13.4 **Obverse:** "Goofy" Liberty head, left **Reverse:** Value and date within wreath

Date	XF	AU	Unc	BU
1870	—	250	1,000	1,500

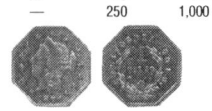

KM# 13.5 **Obverse:** Liberty head, left, above date **Reverse:** Value and date within wreath; "CALIFORNIA GOLD" around wreath

Date	XF	AU	Unc	BU
1871	—	350	600	900
1874	—	3,000	—	—
1875	—	3,000	—	—
1876	—	2,000	—	—

KM# 14.1 **Obverse:** Large indian head, left, above date **Reverse:** "1 DOLLAR" within wreath; "CALIFORNIA GOLD" around wreath

Date	XF	AU	Unc	BU
1872	—	350	600	900
1873/2	—	400	700	1,100
1873	—	600	750	—
1874	—	525	850	1,300
1875	—	475	600	1,000
1876/5	—	700	1,000	1,300

KM# 14.2 **Obverse:** Small indian head, left, above date **Reverse:** "1 DOLLAR CAL" within wreath

Date	XF	AU	Unc	BU
1875	700.	900	1,200	—
1876	—	1,000	1,400	—

KM# 14.3 **Obverse:** Indian head, left, above date **Reverse:** "1 DOLLAR" within wreath; "CALIFORNIA GOLD" around wreath

Date	XF	AU	Unc	BU
1876	—	500	750	—

DOLLAR (ROUND)

KM# 15.1 **Obverse:** Liberty head, left **Reverse:** Large eagle and legends

Date	XF	AU	Unc	BU
1853 Rare	—	—	—	—

Note: Superior sale Sept. 1987 MS-63 $35,200

KM# 15.2 **Obverse:** Liberty head, left **Reverse:** Value and date within wreath; "CALIFORNIA GOLD" around wreath

Date	XF	AU	Unc	BU
1854	3,000.	5,500	—	—
1854	5,000.	7,500	—	—
1854 Rare	—	—	—	—

Note: Superior sale Sept. 1988 Fine $13,200

1857 2 known	—	—	—	—
1870	500.	1,250	2,000	—
1871	850.	1,450	2,500	—

Note: Coutnerfeits reported

KM# 15.3 **Obverse:** Liberty head, left, above date **Reverse:** Value within wreath; "CALIFORNIA GOLD" around wreath

Date	XF	AU	Unc	BU
1870	500.	1,000	1,400	2,000
1871	500.	1,000	1,400	2,000

CALIFORNIA — UNITED STATES

KM# 15.4 Obverse: "Goofy" Liberty head, left Reverse: Value and date within wreath; "CALIFORNIA GOLD" around wreath

Date	XF	AU	Unc	BU
1870	400.	1,000	1,500	—

KM# 16 Obverse: Large indian head, left, above date Reverse: Value within wreath; "CALIFORNIA GOLD" outside wreath

Date	XF	AU	Unc	BU
1872	650.	1,100	1,800	2,400

U.S. TERRITORIAL GOLD COINAGE

CALIFORNIA

Baldwin & Company

5 DOLLARS

KM# 17 Obverse: Liberty head, left, above date Reverse: Eagle

Date	Fine	VF	XF	Unc
1850	4,000	6,500	10,000.	25,000

10 DOLLARS

KM# 18 Obverse: Equestrian, right, swinging rope, above date and value Reverse: Eagle

Date	Fine	VF	XF	Unc
1850	15,000	22,500	48,500.	85,000

Note: Bass Sale May 2000, MS-64 $149,500

KM# 19 Obverse: Coronet head, left, within circle of stars, date below Reverse: Eagle

Date	Fine	VF	XF	Unc
1851	9,000	14,500	28,500.	50,000

20 DOLLARS

KM# 20 Obverse: Coronet head, left, within circle of stars, date below Reverse: Eagle

Date	Fine	VF	XF	Unc
1851	—	—	—	—

Note: Stack's Superior Sale Dec. 1988, XF-40 $52,800; Beware of copies cast in base metals

Blake & Company

20 DOLLARS

KM# 21 Obverse: Value within small center circle, legend around Reverse: Coining screw press above date and value

Date	Fine	VF	XF	Unc
1855 Rare	—	—	—	—

Note: Many modern copies exist

J. H. Bowie

5 DOLLARS

KM# 22 Obverse: Tree above date Reverse: Value

Date	Fine	VF	XF	Unc
1849 Rare	—	—	—	—

Note: Americana Sale Jan. 2001, AU-58 $253,000

Cincinnati Mining and Trading Company

5 DOLLARS

KM# 23 Obverse: Draped bust with headress, left Reverse: Eagle with shield, left, date below

Date	Fine	VF	XF	Unc
1849 Rare	—	—	—	—

10 DOLLARS

KM# 24 Obverse: Draped bust with headdress, left Reverse: Eagle with shield, left, date below

Date	Fine	VF	XF	Unc
1849 Rare	—	—	—	—

Note: Brand Sale 1984, XF $104,500

Dubosq & Company

5 DOLLARS

KM# 26

Date	Fine	VF	XF	Unc
1850	25,000	42,500	—	—

10 DOLLARS

KM# 27 Obverse: Coronet head, left, within circle of stars, date below Reverse: Eagle

Date	Fine	VF	XF	Unc
1850	25,000	45,000	65,000.	—

Dunbar & Company

5 DOLLARS

KM# 28 Obverse: Coronet head, left, within circle of stars, date below Reverse: Eagle

Date	Fine	VF	XF	Unc
1851	22,500	32,500	55,000.	—

Note: Spink & Son Sale 1988, AU $62,000

Augustus Humbert / United States Assayer

10 DOLLARS

KM# 29.1 Obverse: Eagle, ribbon, value Reverse: Inscription, date Note: "AUGUSTUS HUMBERT" imprint.

Date	Fine	VF	XF	Unc
1852/1	2,000	3,500	5,500.	15,000
1852	1,500	2,500	4,750.	11,500

KM# 29.2 Note: Error: IINITED.

Date	Fine	VF	XF	Unc
1852/1 Rare	—	—	—	—
1852 Rare	—	—	—	—

20 DOLLARS

KM# 30 Obverse: Eagle, ribbon, banner and value Reverse: Inscription, date

Date	Fine	VF	XF	Unc
1852/1	4,500	6,000	9,500.	—

Note: Mory Sale June 2000, AU-53 $13,800; Garrett Sale March 1980, Humbert's Proof $325,000; Private Sale May 1989, Humbert's Proof (PCGS Pr-65) $1,350,000; California Sale Oct. 2000, Humbert's Proof (PCGS Pr-65) $552,000

UNITED STATES — CALIFORNIA

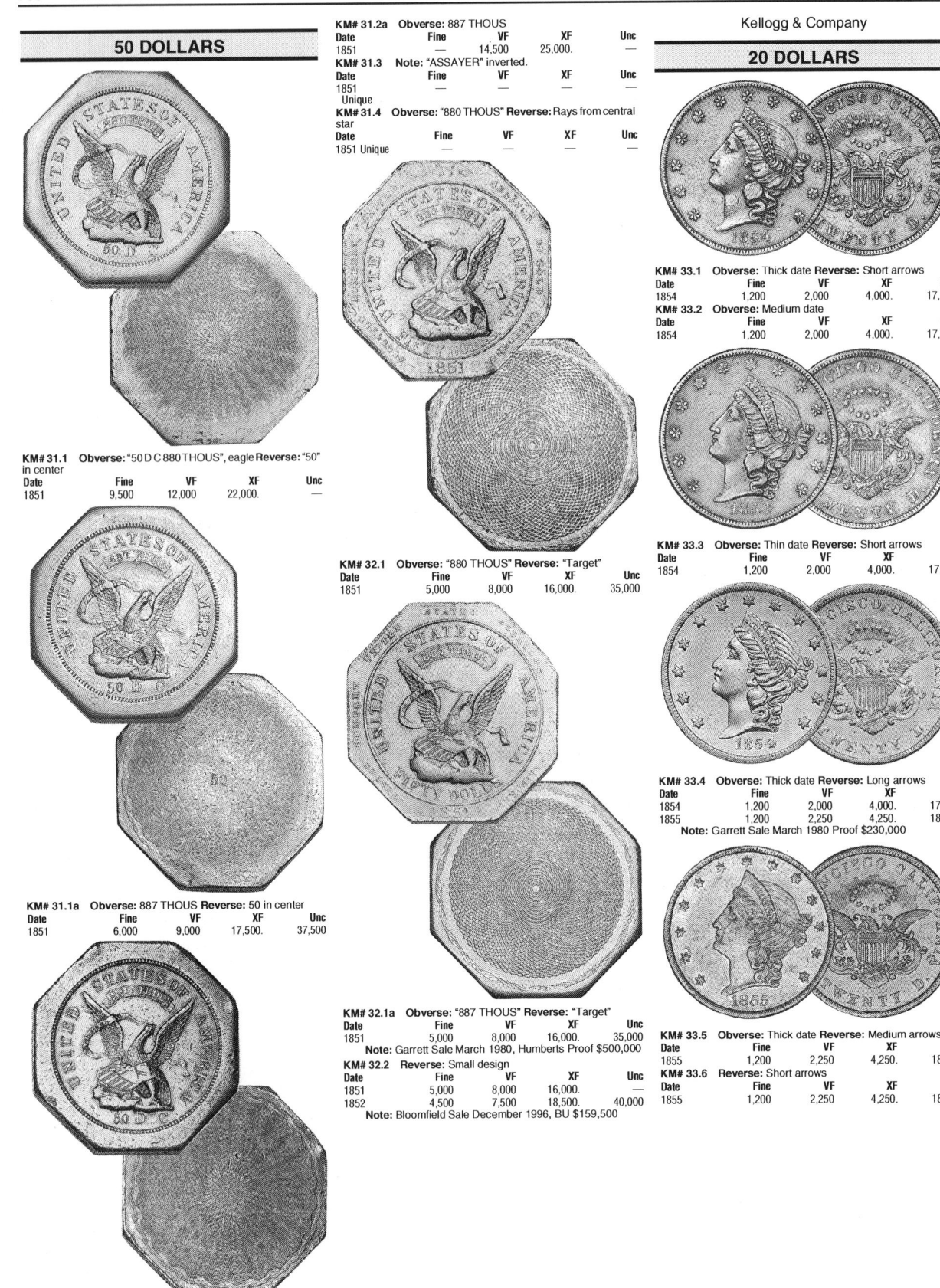

50 DOLLARS

KM# 31.1 Obverse: "50 D C 880 THOUS", eagle Reverse: "50" in center

Date	Fine	VF	XF	Unc
1851	9,500	12,000	22,000.	—

KM# 31.1a Obverse: 887 THOUS Reverse: 50 in center

Date	Fine	VF	XF	Unc
1851	6,000	9,000	17,500.	37,500

KM# 31.2 Obverse: "880 THOUS" Reverse: Without "50"

Date	Fine	VF	XF	Unc
1851	5,000	8,000	16,500.	35,500

KM# 31.2a Obverse: 887 THOUS

Date	Fine	VF	XF	Unc
1851	—	14,500	25,000.	—

KM# 31.3 Note: "ASSAYER" inverted.

Date	Fine	VF	XF	Unc
1851 Unique	—	—	—	—

KM# 31.4 Obverse: "880 THOUS" Reverse: Rays from central star

Date	Fine	VF	XF	Unc
1851 Unique	—	—	—	—

KM# 32.1 Obverse: "880 THOUS" Reverse: "Target"

Date	Fine	VF	XF	Unc
1851	5,000	8,000	16,000.	35,000

KM# 32.1a Obverse: "887 THOUS" Reverse: "Target"

Date	Fine	VF	XF	Unc
1851	5,000	8,000	16,000.	35,000

Note: Garrett Sale March 1980, Humberts Proof $500,000

KM# 32.2 Reverse: Small design

Date	Fine	VF	XF	Unc
1851	5,000	8,000	16,000.	—
1852	4,500	7,500	18,500.	40,000

Note: Bloomfield Sale December 1996, BU $159,500

Kellogg & Company

20 DOLLARS

KM# 33.1 Obverse: Thick date Reverse: Short arrows

Date	Fine	VF	XF	Unc
1854	1,200	2,000	4,000.	17,500

KM# 33.2 Obverse: Medium date

Date	Fine	VF	XF	Unc
1854	1,200	2,000	4,000.	17,500

KM# 33.3 Obverse: Thin date Reverse: Short arrows

Date	Fine	VF	XF	Unc
1854	1,200	2,000	4,000.	17,500

KM# 33.4 Obverse: Thick date Reverse: Long arrows

Date	Fine	VF	XF	Unc
1854	1,200	2,000	4,000.	17,500
1855	1,200	2,250	4,250.	18,500

Note: Garrett Sale March 1980 Proof $230,000

KM# 33.5 Obverse: Thick date Reverse: Medium arrows

Date	Fine	VF	XF	Unc
1855	1,200	2,250	4,250.	18,500

KM# 33.6 Reverse: Short arrows

Date	Fine	VF	XF	Unc
1855	1,200	2,250	4,250.	18,500

CALIFORNIA

50 DOLLARS

KM# 34 **Obverse:** Coronet head, left, within circle of stars **Reverse:** Banner above eagle, written value in legend

Date	Fine	VF	XF	Unc
1855	—	—	—	—

Note: Heritage ANA Sale August 1977, Proof $156,500

Massachusettes and California Company

5 DOLLARS

KM# 35 **Obverse:** Rearing equestrian within shield, flanked by upright bear and deer **Reverse:** Value within wreath, date below

Date	Fine	VF	XF	Unc
1849	40,000	65,000	—	—

Miners Bank

10 DOLLARS

Date	Fine	VF	XF	Unc
(1849)	—	8,500	17,500.	45,000

Note: Garrett Sale March 1980, MS-65 $135,000

Date	Fine	VF	XF	Unc
(1849)	—	—	—	—

Note: Rare, as most specimens have heavy copper alloy

Moffat & Company

5 DOLLARS

KM# 37.1 **Obverse:** Coronet head, left, within circle of stars, date below **Reverse:** Eagle, shield on breast

Date	Fine	VF	XF	Unc
1849	1,000	1,500	3,500.	12,000

KM# 37.2 **Obverse:** Coronet head, left, within circle of stars, date below **Reverse:** Die break at "DOL"

Date	Fine	VF	XF	Unc
1849	1,000	1,500	3,500.	12,000

KM# 37.3 **Obverse:** Coronet head, left, within circle of stars, date below **Reverse:** Die break on shield

Date	Fine	VF	XF	Unc
1849	1,000	1,500	3,500.	12,000

KM# 37.4 **Obverse:** Coronet head, left, within circle of stars, date below **Reverse:** Small letters

Date	Fine	VF	XF	Unc
1850	1,100	1,650	4,200.	14,000

KM# 37.5 **Obverse:** Coronet head, left, within circle of stars, date below **Reverse:** Large letters

Date	Fine	VF	XF	Unc
1850	1,100	1,650	4,200.	14,000

Note: Garrett Sale March 1980, MS-60 $21,000

10 DOLLARS

KM# 38.1 **Obverse:** Coronet head, left, within circle of stars, date below **Reverse:** Value: "TEN DOL.", arrow below period

Date	Fine	VF	XF	Unc
1849	1,650	3,500	6,000.	15,000

KM# 38.2 **Obverse:** Coronet head, left, within circle of stars, date below **Reverse:** Arrow above period

Date	Fine	VF	XF	Unc
1849	1,650	3,500	6,000.	15,000

KM# 38.3 **Obverse:** Coronet head, left, within circle of stars, date below **Reverse:** Value: "TEN D.", large letters

Date	Fine	VF	XF	Unc
1849	2,250	5,000	7,500.	16,500

KM# 38.4 **Obverse:** Coronet head, left, within circle of stars, date below **Reverse:** Small letters

Date	Fine	VF	XF	Unc
1849	—	5,000	7,500.	16,500

KM# 39.1 **Obverse:** Coronet head, left, within circle of stars, date below **Reverse:** Banner above eagle **Note:** "MOFFAT & CO." imprint, wide date

Date	Fine	VF	XF	Unc
1852	2,500	5,500	10,000.	20,000

KM# 39.2 **Obverse:** Coronet head, left, within circle of stars, date below **Reverse:** 880 thous. in banner above eagle **Note:** Close date. Struck by Augustus Humbert.

Date	Fine	VF	XF	Unc
1852	2,000	4,250	9,000.	18,500

20 DOLLARS

KM# 40 **Obverse:** Coronet head, left, within circle of stars, date below **Reverse:** Circle of stars and rays above eagle **Note:** Struck by Curtis, Perry, & Ward.

Date	Fine	VF	XF	Unc
1853	2,150	3,750	6,000.	16,500

Norris, Greig, & Norris

HALF EAGLE

KM# 41.1 **Obverse:** Date in center of circle of stars and legend **Reverse:** Period after "ALLOY"

Date	Fine	VF	XF	Unc
1849	2,250	3,750	7,250.	20,000

KM# 41.2 **Obverse:** Date in center of circle of stars and legend **Reverse:** Period after "ALLOY"

Date	Fine	VF	XF	Unc
1849	2,250	3,750	7,250.	20,000

KM# 41.3 **Obverse:** Date in center of circle of stars and legend **Reverse:** Period after "ALLOY"

Date	Fine	VF	XF	Unc
1849	1,750	3,000	6,750.	20,000

KM# 41.4 **Obverse:** Date in center of circle of stars and legend **Reverse:** Without period after "ALLOY"

Date	Fine	VF	XF	Unc
1849	1,750	3,000	6,750.	20,000

KM# 42 **Obverse:** "STOCKTON" beneath date

Date	Fine	VF	XF	Unc
1850 Unique	—	—	—	—

J. S. Ormsby

5 DOLLARS

KM# 43.1 **Obverse:** "J.S.O." in center **Reverse:** Value within circle of stars

Date	Fine	VF	XF	Unc
(1849) Unique	—	—	—	—

KM# 43.2 **Obverse:** "J.S.O." in center **Reverse:** Value within circle of stars

Date	Fine	VF	XF	Unc
(1849) Unique	—	—	—	—

Note: Superior Auction 1989, VF $137,500

UNITED STATES / CALIFORNIA

10 DOLLARS

KM# 44 **Obverse:** "J.S.O." in center **Reverse:** Value in center circle of stars

Date	Fine	VF	XF	Unc
(1849) Rare	—	—	—	—

Note: Garrett Sale March 1980, F-12 $100,000; Ariagno Sale June 1999, AU-50 $145,000

Pacific Company

5 DOLLARS

KM# 45 **Obverse:** Stars within rays of Liberty cap, value below **Reverse:** Eagle

Date	Fine	VF	XF	Unc
1849 Rare	—	—	—	—

Note: Garrett Sale March 1980, VF-30 $180,000

10 DOLLARS

KM# 46.1 **Obverse:** Stars within rays of Liberty cap, value below **Reverse:** Eagle, date below

Date	Fine	VF	XF	Unc
1849 Rare	—	—	—	—

Note: Waldorf Sale 1964, $24,000

KM# 46.2 **Obverse:** Stars within rays of Liberty cap, value below **Reverse:** Eagle

Date	Fine	VF	XF	Unc
1849 Rare	—	—	—	—

1 DOLLAR

KM# A45 **Obverse:** Stars within rays of Liberty cap, value below **Reverse:** Eagle

Date	Fine	VF	XF	Unc
(1849) Unique	—	—	—	—

Note: Mory Sale June 2000, EF-40 $57,500

Templeton Reid

10 DOLLARS

KM# 47 **Obverse:** Date in center **Reverse:** Value in center

Date	Fine	VF	XF	Unc
1849 Unique	—	—	—	—

20 DOLLARS

KM# 48

Date	Fine	VF	XF	Unc
1849 Unknown	—	—	—	—

Note: The only known specimen was stolen from the U.S. Mint in 1858 and has never been recovered. For additional listings of Templeton Reid, see listings under Georgia

Schultz & Company

5 DOLLARS

KM# 49 **Obverse:** Coronet head, left, within circle of stars, date below **Reverse:** Eagle, shield on breast, value below

Date	Fine	VF	XF	Unc
1851	—	36,800	50,000.	—

United States Assay Office of Gold

10 DOLLARS

KM# 50.1 **Obverse:** TEN DOLS 884 THOUS **Reverse:** "O" of "OFFICE" below "I" of "UNITED"

Date	Fine	VF	XF	Unc
1852	—	—	—	—

Note: Garrett Sale March 1980, MS-60 $18,000

KM# 51.2 **Obverse:** TEN DOLS, 884 THOUS **Reverse:** "O" below "N", strong beads

Date	Fine	VF	XF	Unc
1852	1,750	2,500	3,850.	9,500

KM# 51.3 **Obverse:** TEN DOLS, 884 THOUS **Reverse:** Weak beads

Date	Fine	VF	XF	Unc
1852	1,750	2,500	3,850.	9,500

KM# 52 **Obverse:** TEN D, 884 THOUS **Reverse:** Inscription, date

Date	Fine	VF	XF	Unc
1853	5,000	7,750	14,500.	—

KM# 52a **Obverse:** 900 THOUS **Reverse:** Inscription, date

Date	Fine	VF	XF	Unc
1853	2,700	4,200	6,500.	—

Note: Garrett Sale March 1980, MS-60 $35,000

20 DOLLARS

KM# 53 **Obverse:** 884/880 THOUS **Reverse:** Inscription, date

Date	Fine	VF	XF	Unc
1853	8,500	12,500	17,500.	23,500

KM# 53a **Obverse:** 900/880 THOUS **Reverse:** Inscription, date

Date	Fine	VF	XF	Unc
1853	1,550	2,750	4,250.	10,000

Note: 1853 Liberty Head listed under Moffat & Company

50 DOLLARS

KM# 54 **Obverse:** 887 THOUS **Reverse:** "Target"

Date	Fine	VF	XF	Unc
1852	4,000	6,500	13,500.	26,500

COLORADO   UNITED STATES   739

Date	Fine	VF	XF	Unc
1852	1,500	2,650	5,500.	13,500

KM# 59.1 Obverse: Short neck, small date **Reverse:** Eagle, shield on breast

Date	Fine	VF	XF	Unc
1852 Rare	—	—	—	—

Note: Eliasberg Sale May 1996, EF-45 $36,300; S.S. Central America Sale December 2000, VF-30 realized $12,650

KM# 59.2 Obverse: Plugged date **Reverse:** Eagle, shield on breast

Date	Fine	VF	XF	Unc
1855	6,000	8,000	12,500.	28,500

20 DOLLARS

KM# 60 Obverse: Large head **Reverse:** Eagle, shield on breast, value in banner above

Date	Fine	VF	XF	Unc
1855 Rare	—	—	—	—

KM# 61 Obverse: Small head **Reverse:** Eagle, shield on breast, value in banner above

Date	Fine	VF	XF	Unc
1855	7,000	11,000	20,000.	—

50 DOLLARS

KM# 62 Obverse: Coronet head, left, within circle of stars, date below **Reverse:** Value within wreath

Date	Fine	VF	XF	Unc
1855	—	—	—	—

Note: Bloomfield Sale December 1996, BU $170,500

KM# 54a Obverse: 900 THOUS **Reverse:** "Target"

Date	Fine	VF	XF	Unc
1852	5,000	7,000	14,500.	28,500

Wass, Molitor & Company

5 DOLLARS

KM# 55.1 Obverse: Small head, rounded bust **Reverse:** Eagle, shield on breast

Date	Fine	VF	XF	Unc
1852	2,000	4,000	6,750.	16,500

KM# 55.2 Obverse: Coronet head, left, within circle of stars **Reverse:** Eagle, shield on breast **Note:** Thick planchet.

Date	Fine	VF	XF	Unc
1852 Unique	—	—	—	—

KM# 56 Obverse: Large head, pointed bust **Reverse:** Eagle, shield on breast

Date	Fine	VF	XF	Unc
1852	2,000	4,500	8,500.	17,500

10 DOLLARS

KM# 57 Obverse: Long neck, large date **Reverse:** Eagle, shield on breast

Date	Fine	VF	XF	Unc
1852	2,750	5,000	8,500.	15,500

KM# 58 Obverse: Short neck, wide date **Reverse:** Eagle, shield on breast

COLORADO

Clark, Gruber & Company

2-1/2 DOLLARS

KM# 63 Obverse: Coronet head, left, within circle of stars, date below **Reverse:** Eagle, shield on breast

Date	Fine	VF	XF	Unc
1860	750	1,300	2,500.	8,500

Note: Garrett Sale March 1980, MS-65 $12,000

KM# 64.1 Obverse: Coronet head, left, within circle of stars, date below **Reverse:** Eagle, shield on breast

Date	Fine	VF	XF	Unc
1861	1,500	2,750	—	11,500

KM# 64.2 Obverse: Coronet head, left, within circle of stars, date below **Reverse:** Eagle, shield on breast **Note:** Extra high edge.

Date	Fine	VF	XF	Unc
1861	850	1,750	3,500.	12,500

5 DOLLARS

KM# 65 Obverse: Coronet head, left, within circle of stars, date below **Reverse:** Eagle, shield on breast

Date	Fine	VF	XF	Unc
1860	1,000	1,750	3,000.	9,200

Note: Garrett Sale March 1980, MS-63 $9,000

KM# 66 Obverse: Coronet head, left, within circle of stars, date below **Reverse:** Eagle, shield on breast

Date	Fine	VF	XF	Unc
1861	1,500	2,500	4,500.	13,500

10 DOLLARS

KM# 67 Obverse: Mountain above value **Reverse:** Eagle, shield on breast

Date	Fine	VF	XF	Unc
1860	2,750	3,750	8,000.	21,500

KM# 68 Obverse: Coronet head, left, within circle of stars, date below **Reverse:** Eagle, shield on breast

UNITED STATES

Date	Fine	VF	XF	Unc
1861	1,500	2,500	4,500.	15,500

20 DOLLARS

KM# 69 Obverse: Mountain above value **Reverse:** Eagle, shield on breast

Date	Fine	VF	XF	Unc
1860	25,000	55,000	75,000.	100,000

Note: Eliasberg Sale May 1996, AU $90,200; Schoonmaker Sale June 1997, VCF $62,700

KM# 70 Obverse: Coronet head, left, within circle of stars, date below **Reverse:** Circle of stars and rays above eagle

Date	Fine	VF	XF	Unc
1861	7,000	10,000	21,500.	—

J. J. Conway

2-1/2 DOLLARS

KM# 71 Obverse: & CO. in center **Reverse:** Value in center

Date	Fine	VF	XF	Unc
(1861)	—	45,000	70,000.	—

5 DOLLARS

KM# 72.1 Obverse: & CO. in center **Reverse:** Value in center

Date	Fine	VF	XF	Unc
(1861) Rare	—	—	—	—

Note: Brand Sale June 1984, XF-40 $44,000

KM# 72.2 Obverse: & CO. in center **Reverse:** Numeral 5 omitted

Date	Fine	VF	XF	Unc
(1861) Unique	—	—	—	—

10 DOLLARS

KM# 73 Obverse: & CO. within circle **Reverse:** Numeral value within circle of stars

Date	Fine	VF	XF	Unc
(1861) Rare	—	60,000	—	—

COLORADO

John Parsons

2-1/2 DOLLARS

KM# 74 Obverse: Minting press **Reverse:** Eagle, shield on breast, value below

Date	Fine	VF	XF	Unc
(1861) Rare	—	—	—	—

Note: Garrett Sale March 1980, VF-20 $85,000

5 DOLLARS

KM# 75 Obverse: Minting press **Reverse:** Eagle, shield on breast, value below

Date	Fine	VF	XF	Unc
(1861) Rare	—	—	—	—

Note: Garrett Sale March 1980, VF-20 $100,000

GEORGIA

Christopher Bechtler

2-1/2 DOLLARS

KM# 76.1 Obverse: "2.50" in center **Reverse:** "GEORGIA", "64 G, 22 CARATS"

Date	Fine	VF	XF	Unc
ND	1,650	2,650	5,000.	10,000

KM# 76.2 Obverse: 2.50 in center **Reverse:** "GEORGIA", "64 G, 22 CARATS", even 22

Date	Fine	VF	XF	Unc
ND	1,850	2,850	5,500.	11,500

5 DOLLARS

KM# 77 Obverse: "RUTHERF" **Reverse:** "128 G", "22 CARATS" below

Date	Fine	VF	XF	Unc
ND	2,000	3,500	5,500.	11,500

KM# 78.1 Obverse: "RUTHERFORD" **Reverse:** "128 G", "22 CARATS" below

Date	Fine	VF	XF	Unc
ND	2,000	3,750	6,000.	12,500

KM# 78.2 Obverse: Value in center **Reverse:** Colon after "128 G:"

Date	Fine	VF	XF	Unc
ND	—	20,000	30,000.	—

Note: Akers Pittman Sale October 1997, VF-XF $26,400

Templeton Reid

2-1/2 DOLLARS

KM# 79 Obverse: Date in center **Reverse:** "2.50" in center

Date	Fine	VF	XF	Unc
1830	12,500	32,500	55,000.	—

5 DOLLARS

KM# 80 Obverse: "$ 5" in center above date **Reverse:** "$ 5" in center

Date	Fine	VF	XF	Unc
1830 Rare	—	—	—	—

Note: Garrett Sale November 1979, XF-40 $200,000

10 DOLLARS

KM# 81 Obverse: With date **Reverse:** Written value

Date	Fine	VF	XF	Unc
1830 Rare	—	—	—	—

KM# 82 Obverse: Undated **Reverse:** Written value

Date	Fine	VF	XF	Unc
(1830) Rare	—	—	—	—

Note: Also see listings under California

NORTH CAROLINA

August Bechtler

DOLLAR

KM# 83.1 Obverse: Numeral "1" in center **Reverse:** "CAROLINA, 27 G. 21C."

Date	Fine	VF	XF	Unc
(1842-52)	450	650	1,150.	2,950

KM# 83.2 Obverse: Numeral "1" in center **Reverse:** "CAROLINA, 27 G. 21C."

Date	Fine	VF	XF	Unc
(1842-52)	450	650	1,150.	2,950

NORTH CAROLINA

5 DOLLARS

KM# 84 Obverse: Value in center Reverse: "CAROLINA", "134 G. 21 CARATS"
Date	Fine	VF	XF	Unc
(1842-52)	1,750	3,500	6,000.	12,500

KM# 85 Obverse: Value in center Reverse: "CAROLINA", "128 G. 22 CARATS"
Date	Fine	VF	XF	Unc
(1842-52)	3,000	5,500	8,000.	15,000

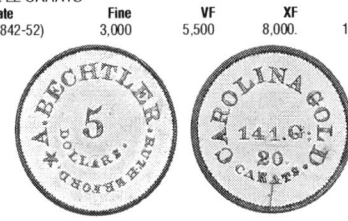

KM# 86 Obverse: Value in center Reverse: "CAROLINA", "141 G: 20 CARATS"
Date	Fine	VF	XF	Unc
(1842-52)	2,750	4,850	7,500.	14,500

Note: Proof restrikes exist from original dies; in the Akers Pittman Sale October 1997, an example sold for $14,300

Christopher Bechtler

DOLLAR

KM# 87 Obverse: 28 G. Reverse: CAROLINA, N reversed
Date	Fine	VF	XF	Unc
(1831-42)	900	1,200	1,700.	3,750

KM# 88.1 Obverse: 28. G. centered without star Reverse: N. CAROLINA
Date	Fine	VF	XF	Unc
(1831-42)	1,500	2,200	3,500.	8,000

KM# 88.2 Obverse: N. CAROLINA Reverse: 28 G high without star
Date	Fine	VF	XF	Unc
(1831-42)	2,500	4,500	6,500.	12,000

KM# 89 Obverse: 30 G. Reverse: N. CAROLINA
Date	Fine	VF	XF	Unc
(1831-42)	850	1,200	2,750.	5,500

2-1/2 DOLLARS

KM# 90.1 Obverse: 250 in center Reverse: CAROLINA, 67 G. 21 CARATS
Date	Fine	VF	XF	Unc
(1831-42)	1,250	2,250	5,500.	11,500

KM# 90.2 Obverse: 250 in center Reverse: 64 G 22 CARATS, uneven 22
Date	Fine	VF	XF	Unc
(1831-42)	1,450	2,850	6,000.	12,000

KM# 90.3 Reverse: Even 22
Date	Fine	VF	XF	Unc
(1831-42)	1,650	3,000	6,500.	12,500

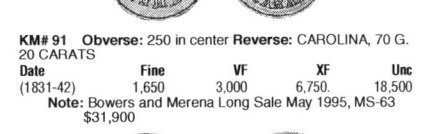

KM# 91 Obverse: 250 in center Reverse: CAROLINA, 70 G. 20 CARATS
Date	Fine	VF	XF	Unc
(1831-42)	1,650	3,000	6,750.	18,500

Note: Bowers and Merena Long Sale May 1995, MS-63 $31,900

KM# 92.1 Obverse: RUTHERFORD in a circle, border of large beads Reverse: NORTH CAROLINA, 250, 20 C. 75 G.
Date	Fine	VF	XF	Unc
(1831-42)	—	7,500	11,500.	25,000

KM# 92.2 Obverse: RUTHERFORD in circle Reverse: NORTH CAROLINA, 250, without 75 G, wide 20 C.
Date	Fine	VF	XF	Unc
(1831-42)	2,800	5,000	7,000.	14,500

KM# 92.3 Obverse: Narrow 20 C
Date	Fine	VF	XF	Unc
(1831-42)	2,800	5,000	7,000.	14,500

KM# 93.1 Obverse: RUTHERFORD in a circle Reverse: NORTH CAROLINA without 75 G, CAROLINA above 250 instead of GOLD
Date	Fine	VF	XF	Unc
(1831-42) Unique	—	—	—	—

KM# 93.2 Obverse: NORTH CAROLINA, 20 C Reverse: 75 G, border finely serrated
Date	Fine	VF	XF	Unc
(1831-42)	4,500	7,500	10,500.	—

5 DOLLARS

KM# 94 Obverse: Numeral value in center Reverse: CAROLINA, 134 G., star, 21 CARATS
Date	Fine	VF	XF	Unc
(1831-42)	1,650	3,250	6,000.	11,000

KM# 95 Obverse: Numeral value in center Reverse: 21 above CARATS, without star
Date	Fine	VF	XF	Unc
(1831-42) Unique	—	—	—	—

KM# 96.1 Obverse: RUTHERFORD Reverse: CAROLINA, 140 G. 20 CARATS
Date	Fine	VF	XF	Unc
1834	1,750	3,750	6,500.	11,500

KM# 96.2 Obverse: Numeral value in center Reverse: 140 .C., 20 CARATS
Date	Fine	VF	XF	Unc
1834	2,000	4,000	7,000.	12,500

KM# 97.1 Obverse: RUTHERF Reverse: CAROLINA. 140 G. 20 CARATS; 20 close to CARATS
Date	Fine	VF	XF	Unc
1834	1,800	3,850	6,750.	12,000

KM# 97.2 Obverse: Written value in center Reverse: 20 away from CARATS
Date	Fine	VF	XF	Unc
1834	2,500	6,500	11,500.	—

KM# 98 Obverse: RUTHERF Reverse: CAROLINA, 141 G, 20 CARATS
Date	Fine	VF	XF	Unc
(1831-42) Proof restrike	—	—	—	15,500

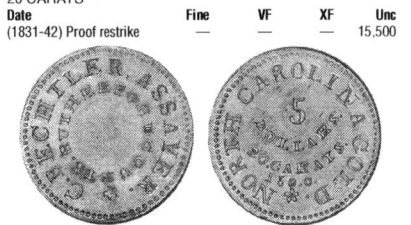

KM# 99.1 Obverse: RUTHEFER in a circle Reverse: NORTH CAROLINA, 150 G, below 20 CARATS
Date	Fine	VF	XF	Unc
(1831-42)	2,800	4,500	8,500.	18,500

UNITED STATES

KM# 99.2 Obverse: RUTHEFER in a circle **Reverse:** Without 150 G

Date	Fine	VF	XF	Unc
(1831-42)	3,200	6,000	10,000.	20,000

OREGON

Oregon Exchange Company

5 DOLLARS

KM# 100 Obverse: Beaver above date and sprigs **Reverse:** Value

Date	Fine	VF	XF	Unc
1849	10,000	18,500	33,350.	—

10 DOLLARS

KM# 101 Obverse: Beaver above date and sprigs **Reverse:** Value

Date	Fine	VF	XF	Unc
1849	20,000	40,000	65,000.	—

UTAH

Mormon Issues

2-1/2 DOLLARS

KM# 102 Obverse: Design above eye **Reverse:** Clasped hands above date

Date	Fine	VF	XF	Unc
1849	4,000	7,000	13,500.	24,500

5 DOLLARS

KM# 103 Obverse: Design above eye **Reverse:** Clasped hands above date

Date	Fine	VF	XF	Unc
1849	4,000	7,000	12,000.	23,500

KM# 104 Obverse: Designs above eye and stars **Reverse:** Clasped hands above date

Date	Fine	VF	XF	Unc
1850	4,500	7,500	15,000.	25,500

NORTH CAROLINA

KM# 105 Obverse: Lion facing left above date **Reverse:** Design on eagle breast

Date	Fine	VF	XF	Unc
1860	6,500	12,000	25,000.	37,500

10 DOLLARS

KM# 106 Obverse: Design above eye **Reverse:** Clasped hands above date

Date	Fine	VF	XF	Unc
1849 Rare	—	—	—	—

Note: Heritage ANA Sale July 1988, AU $93,000

20 DOLLARS

KM# 107 Obverse: Design above eye **Reverse:** Clasped hands above date

Date	Fine	VF	XF	Unc
1849	22,500	47,500	85,000.	—

URUGUAY

The Oriental Republic of Uruguay (so called because of its location on the east bank of the Uruguay River) is situated on the Atlantic coast of South America between Argentina and Brazil. This South American country has an area of 68,536 sq. mi. (176,220 sq. km.) and a population of *3 million. Capital: Montevideo. Uruguay's chief economic assets are its rich, rolling grassy plains. Meat, wool, hides and skins are exported.

Uruguay was discovered in 1516 by Juan Diaz de Solis, a Spaniard, but settled by the Portuguese who founded Colonia in 1680. Spain contested Portuguese possession and, after a long struggle, gained control of the country in 1778. During the general South American struggle for independence, Uruguay's first attempt was led by Gaucho soldier Jose Gervasio Artigas leading the Banda Oriental which was quelled by Spanish and Portuguese forces in 1811. The armistice was soon broken and Argentine force from Buenos Aires cast off the Spanish bond in the Plata region in 1814 only to be reconquered by the Portuguese from Brazil in the struggle of 1816-20. Revolt flared anew in 1825 and independence was reasserted in 1828 with the help of Argentina. The Uruguayan Republic was established in 1830.

MINT MARKS
A - Paris, Berlin, Vienna
(a) Paris, privy marks only
D - Lyon (France)
H - Birmingham
Mx, Mo - Mexico City
(p) - Poissy, France
So - Santiago (Small O above S)
(u) - Utrecht

MONETARY SYSTEM
100 Centesimo = 1 Peso
1975-1993
1000 Old Pesos = 1 Nuevo (New) Peso
Commencing 1994
1000 Nuevos Pesos = 1 Peso Uruguayo

REPUBLIC

DECIMAL COINAGE

KM# 27   5 PESOS
8.4850 g., 0.9170 Gold .2501 oz. AGW, 22 mm. **Subject:** Constitution Centennial **Obv:** Artigas head right, L. BAZOR in left field behind neck **Rev:** Date flanked by sprigs below value

Date	Mintage	F	VF	XF	Unc	BU
1930(a)	Est. 100,000	—	—	170	180	200

Note: Only 14,415 were released; Remainder withheld

KM# 58b   50 PESOS
Gold **Subject:** Centennial - Birth of Rodo **Obv:** Rodo facing **Rev:** Feather, value and date

Date	Mintage	F	VF	XF	Unc	BU
1971So Proof	100	Value: 375				

KM# 55b   1000 PESOS
Gold **Series:** F.A.O. **Obv:** Stylized radiant sun with face **Rev:** Assorted stylized designs within circle

Date	Mintage	F	VF	XF	Unc	BU
1969So	450	—	—	—	800	850

URUGUAY

REFORM COINAGE
1000 Old Pesos = 1 Nuevo (New) Peso

KM# 71b CENTESIMO
6.2600 g., 0.9000 Gold .1811 oz. AGW, 19 mm. **Obv:** Radiant sun with face **Rev:** Value in front of supine wheat stalk
Date	Mintage	F	VF	XF	Unc	BU
1979So Proof	50	Value: 185				

KM# 72b 2 CENTESIMOS
9.2500 g., 0.9000 Gold .2676 oz. AGW, 21 mm. **Obv:** Radiant sun with face **Rev:** Value in front of supine wheat stalk
Date	Mintage	F	VF	XF	Unc	BU
1979So Proof	52	Value: 285				

KM# 73b 5 CENTESIMOS
12.5500 g., 0.9000 Gold .3631 oz. AGW, 23 mm. **Obv:** Steer left **Rev:** Value in front of supine wheat stalk
Date	Mintage	F	VF	XF	Unc	BU
1979So Proof	52	Value: 365				

KM# 66b 10 CENTESIMOS
6.0000 g., 0.9000 Gold .1736 oz. AGW, 19 mm. **Obv:** Horse left **Rev:** Value flanked by sprigs
Date	Mintage	F	VF	XF	Unc	BU
1976So Proof	50	Value: 175				

KM# 67b 20 CENTESIMOS
10.5000 g., 0.9000 Gold .3038 oz. AGW, 22 mm. **Obv:** Small building on top of hill **Rev:** Value flanked by sprigs
Date	Mintage	F	VF	XF	Unc	BU
1976So Proof	50	Value: 350				

KM# 68b 50 CENTESIMOS
15.0000 g., 0.9000 Gold .4340 oz. AGW, 25.5 mm. **Obv:** Scale **Rev:** Value flanked by sprigs
Date	Mintage	F	VF	XF	Unc	BU
1976So Proof	50	Value: 500				

KM# 69b NUEVO PESO
23.0000 g., 0.9000 Gold .6655 oz. AGW, 30 mm. **Obv:** Head of Jose Gervasio Artigas left **Rev:** Value in front of supine wheat stalk
Date	Mintage	F	VF	XF	Unc	BU
1976So Proof	50	Value: 625				

KM# 74b NUEVO PESO
11.6500 g., 0.9000 Gold .3371 oz. AGW, 24 mm. **Obv:** Radiant sun peeking over arms within wreath **Rev:** Flower and value
Date	Mintage	F	VF	XF	Unc	BU
1980So Proof	100	Value: 325				

KM# 77a 2 NUEVO PESOS
14.5300 g., 0.9000 Gold .4204 oz. AGW, 25 mm. **Subject:** World Food Day **Obv:** Wheat stalks divide date country name **Rev:** Value
Date	Mintage	F	VF	XF	Unc	BU
1981 Proof	100	Value: 425				

KM# 65b 5 NUEVO PESOS
Gold **Subject:** 150th Anniversary - Revolutionary Movement **Obv:** Artigas head facing within square above inscription **Rev:** Upright design
Date	Mintage	F	VF	XF	Unc	BU
ND(1975)So Proof	1,000	Value: 550				

Note: 50 pieces each in aluminum, alpaca and copper are reported to have been struck

KM# 70a 5 NUEVO PESOS
30.0000 g., 0.9000 Gold .8681 oz. AGW **Subject:** 250th Anniversary - Founding of Montevideo **Obv:** Head facing to left of value **Rev:** Crowned shield within wreath
Date	Mintage	F	VF	XF	Unc	BU
1976So Proof	100	Value: 675				

KM# 75b 5 NUEVO PESOS
15.6000 g., 0.9000 Gold .4514 oz. AGW, 26.15 mm. **Obv:** National flag **Rev:** Flower and value
Date	Mintage	F	VF	XF	Unc	BU
1980So Proof	100	Value: 450				

KM# 79b 10 NUEVO PESOS
19.4800 g., 0.9000 Gold .5637 oz. AGW, 28 mm. **Obv:** Bust of Jose Gervasio Artigas half left **Rev:** Flower and value
Date	Mintage	F	VF	XF	Unc	BU
1981So Proof	100	Value: 525				

M# 86b 20 NUEVO PESOS
19.6000 g., 0.9170 Gold .5776 oz. AGW, 30 mm. **Subject:** World Fisheries Conference **Obv:** Radiant sun peeking out above arms within wreath **Rev:** Fish
Date	Mintage	F	VF	XF	Unc	BU
1984 Proof	100	Value: 550				

KM# 91a 5000 NUEVO PESOS
42.7600 g., Gold **Obv:** Double wheel design **Rev:** Snowflake design
Date	Mintage	F	VF	XF	Unc	BU
1987	—	—				

KM# 85 20000 NUEVO PESOS
20.0000 g., 0.9000 Gold .5787 oz. AGW **Obv:** Hydroelectric dam **Rev:** Radiant sun peeking out above arms within wreath
Date	Mintage	F	VF	XF	Unc	BU
1983So Proof	2,500	Value: 425				

KM# 89 20000 NUEVO PESOS
19.8700 g., 0.9000 Gold .5750 oz AGW oz. AGW, 33.1 mm. **Subject:** 130th Anniversary of Gold Coinage and 25th Meeting of Inter-American Bank Governors **Obv:** Radiant sun peeking out above arms within wreath of assorted flags **Rev:** Map within U-shaped design below value and inscription **Edge:** Reeded
Date	Mintage	F	VF	XF	Unc	BU
1984 Proof	1,500	Value: 425				

GOLD BULLION COINAGE

KM# 108 1/4 GAUCHO
8.6400 g., 0.9000 Gold .2500 oz. AGW **Obv:** Head of Gaucho right **Rev:** Value within wreath
Date	Mintage	F	VF	XF	Unc	BU
1992 Proof	—	Value: 225				

744 URUGUAY

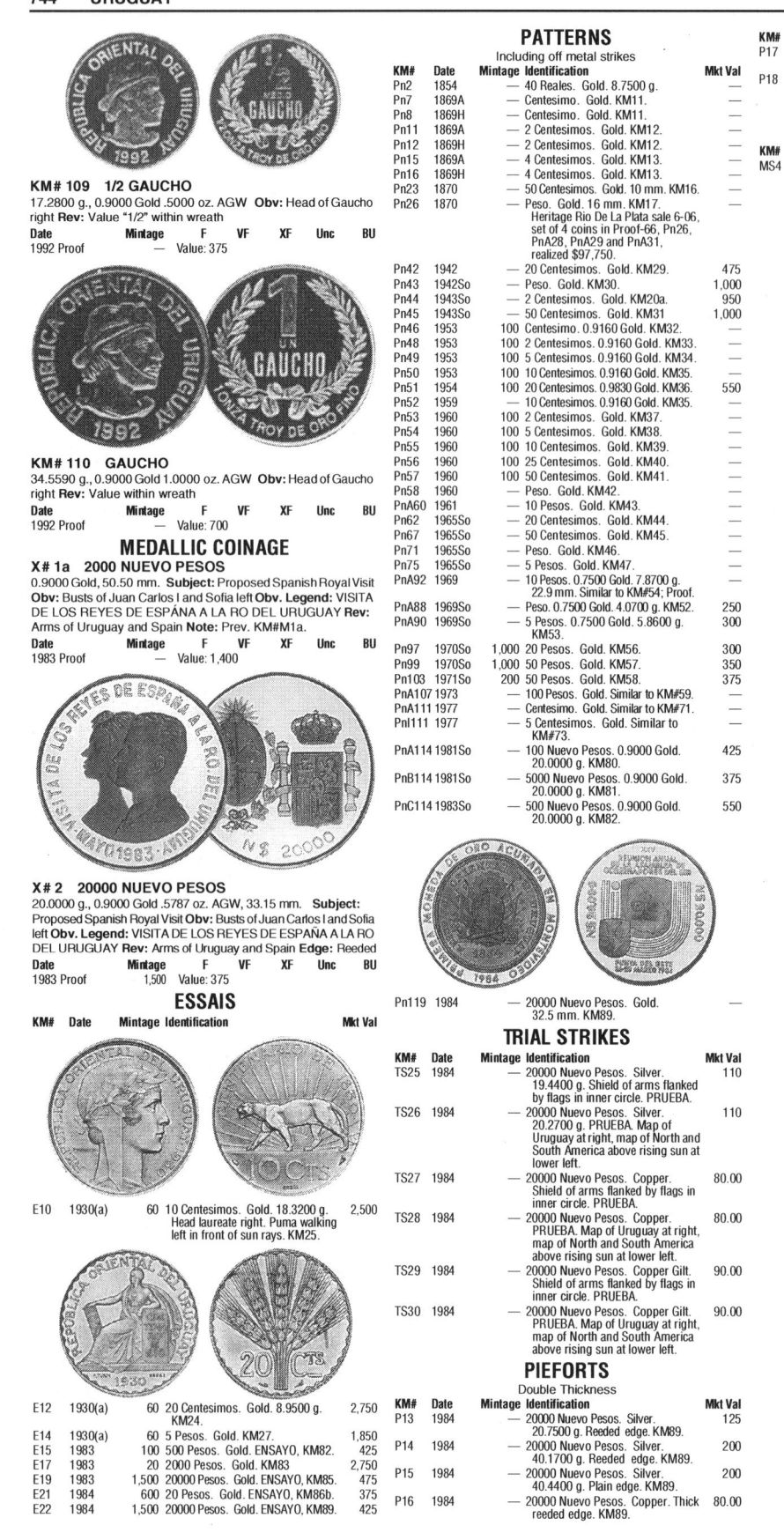

KM# 109 1/2 GAUCHO
17.2800 g., 0.9000 Gold .5000 oz. AGW **Obv:** Head of Gaucho right **Rev:** Value "1/2" within wreath

Date	Mintage	F	VF	XF	Unc	BU
1992 Proof	— Value: 375					

KM# 110 GAUCHO
34.5590 g., 0.9000 Gold 1.0000 oz. AGW **Obv:** Head of Gaucho right **Rev:** Value within wreath

Date	Mintage	F	VF	XF	Unc	BU
1992 Proof	— Value: 700					

MEDALLIC COINAGE

X# 1a 2000 NUEVO PESOS
0.9000 Gold, 50.50 mm. **Subject:** Proposed Spanish Royal Visit **Obv:** Busts of Juan Carlos I and Sofia left **Obv. Legend:** VISITA DE LOS REYES DE ESPÁNA A LA RO DEL URUGUAY **Rev:** Arms of Uruguay and Spain **Note:** Prev. KM#M1a.

Date	Mintage	F	VF	XF	Unc	BU
1983 Proof	— Value: 1,400					

X# 2 20000 NUEVO PESOS
20.0000 g., 0.9000 Gold .5787 oz. AGW, 33.15 mm. **Subject:** Proposed Spanish Royal Visit **Obv:** Busts of Juan Carlos I and Sofia left **Obv. Legend:** VISITA DE LOS REYES DE ESPAÑA A LA RO DEL URUGUAY **Rev:** Arms of Uruguay and Spain **Edge:** Reeded

Date	Mintage	F	VF	XF	Unc	BU
1983 Proof	1,500	Value: 375				

ESSAIS

KM#	Date	Mintage	Identification	Mkt Val
E10	1930(a)	60	10 Centesimos. Gold. 18.3200 g. Head laureate right. Puma walking left in front of sun rays. KM25.	2,500
E12	1930(a)	60	20 Centesimos. Gold. 8.9500 g. KM24.	2,750
E14	1930(a)	60	5 Pesos. Gold. KM27.	1,850
E15	1983	100	500 Pesos. Gold. ENSAYO, KM82.	425
E17	1983	20	2000 Pesos. Gold. KM83	2,750
E19	1983	1,500	20000 Pesos. Gold. ENSAYO, KM85.	475
E21	1984	600	20 Pesos. Gold. ENSAYO, KM86b.	375
E22	1984	1,500	20000 Pesos. Gold. ENSAYO, KM89.	425

PATTERNS
Including off metal strikes

KM#	Date	Mintage	Identification	Mkt Val
Pn2	1854	—	40 Reales. Gold. 8.7500 g.	—
Pn7	1869A	—	Centesimo. Gold. KM11.	—
Pn8	1869H	—	Centesimo. Gold. KM11.	—
Pn11	1869A	—	2 Centesimos. Gold. KM12.	—
Pn12	1869H	—	2 Centesimos. Gold. KM12.	—
Pn15	1869A	—	4 Centesimos. Gold. KM13.	—
Pn16	1869H	—	4 Centesimos. Gold. KM13.	—
Pn23	1870	—	50 Centesimos. Gold. 10 mm. KM16.	—
Pn26	1870	—	Peso. Gold. 16 mm. KM17. Heritage Rio De La Plata sale 6-06, set of 4 coins in Proof-66, Pn26, PnA28, PnA29 and PnA31, realized $97,750.	—
Pn42	1942	—	20 Centesimos. Gold. KM29.	475
Pn43	1942So	—	Peso. Gold. KM30.	1,000
Pn44	1943So	—	2 Centesimos. Gold. KM20a.	950
Pn45	1943So	—	50 Centesimos. Gold. KM31	1,000
Pn46	1953	100	Centesimo. 0.9160 Gold. KM32.	—
Pn48	1953	100	2 Centesimos. 0.9160 Gold. KM33.	—
Pn49	1953	100	5 Centesimos. 0.9160 Gold. KM34.	—
Pn50	1953	100	10 Centesimos. 0.9160 Gold. KM35.	—
Pn51	1954	100	20 Centesimos. 0.9830 Gold. KM36.	550
Pn52	1959	—	10 Centesimos. 0.9160 Gold. KM35.	—
Pn53	1960	100	2 Centesimos. Gold. KM37.	—
Pn54	1960	100	5 Centesimos. Gold. KM38.	—
Pn55	1960	100	10 Centesimos. Gold. KM39.	—
Pn56	1960	100	25 Centesimos. Gold. KM40.	—
Pn57	1960	100	50 Centesimos. Gold. KM41.	—
Pn58	1960	—	Peso. Gold. KM42.	—
PnA60	1961	—	10 Pesos. Gold. KM43.	—
Pn62	1965So	—	20 Centesimos. Gold. KM44.	—
Pn67	1965So	—	50 Centesimos. Gold. KM45.	—
Pn71	1965So	—	Peso. Gold. KM46.	—
Pn75	1965So	—	5 Pesos. Gold. KM47.	—
PnA92	1969	—	10 Pesos. 0.7500 Gold. 7.8700 g. 22.9 mm. Similar to KM#54; Proof.	—
PnA88	1969So	—	Peso. 0.7500 Gold. 4.0700 g. KM52.	250
PnA90	1969So	—	5 Pesos. 0.7500 Gold. 5.8600 g. KM53.	300
Pn97	1970So	1,000	20 Pesos. Gold. KM56.	300
Pn99	1970So	1,000	50 Pesos. Gold. KM57.	350
Pn103	1971So	200	50 Pesos. Gold. KM58.	375
PnA107	1973	—	100 Pesos. Gold. Similar to KM#59.	—
PnA111	1977	—	Centesimo. Gold. Similar to KM#71.	—
PnI111	1977	—	5 Centesimos. Gold. Similar to KM#73.	—
PnA114	1981So	—	100 Nuevo Pesos. 0.9000 Gold. 20.0000 g. KM80.	425
PnB114	1981So	—	5000 Nuevo Pesos. 0.9000 Gold. 20.0000 g. KM81.	375
PnC114	1983So	—	500 Nuevo Pesos. 0.9000 Gold. 20.0000 g. KM82.	550
Pn119	1984	—	20000 Nuevo Pesos. Gold. 32.5 mm. KM89.	—

TRIAL STRIKES

KM#	Date	Mintage	Identification	Mkt Val
TS25	1984	—	20000 Nuevo Pesos. Silver. 19.4400 g. Shield of arms flanked by flags in inner circle. PRUEBA.	110
TS26	1984	—	20000 Nuevo Pesos. Silver. 20.2700 g. PRUEBA. Map of Uruguay at right, map of North and South America above rising sun at lower left.	110
TS27	1984	—	20000 Nuevo Pesos. Copper. Shield of arms flanked by flags in inner circle. PRUEBA.	80.00
TS28	1984	—	20000 Nuevo Pesos. Copper. PRUEBA. Map of Uruguay at right, map of North and South America above rising sun at lower left.	80.00
TS29	1984	—	20000 Nuevo Pesos. Copper Gilt. Shield of arms flanked by flags in inner circle. PRUEBA.	90.00
TS30	1984	—	20000 Nuevo Pesos. Copper Gilt. PRUEBA. Map of Uruguay at right, map of North and South America above rising sun at lower left.	90.00

PIEFORTS
Double Thickness

KM#	Date	Mintage	Identification	Mkt Val
P13	1984	—	20000 Nuevo Pesos. Silver. 20.7500 g. Reeded edge. KM89.	125
P14	1984	—	20000 Nuevo Pesos. Silver. 40.1700 g. Reeded edge. KM89.	200
P15	1984	—	20000 Nuevo Pesos. Silver. 40.4400 g. Plain edge. KM89.	200
P16	1984	—	20000 Nuevo Pesos. Copper. Thick reeded edge. KM89.	80.00
P17	1984	—	20000 Nuevo Pesos. Copper. Reeded edge. KM89.	80.00
P18	1984	—	20000 Nuevo Pesos. Copper Gilt. KM89.	100

MINT SETS

KM#	Date	Mintage Identification	Issue Price	Mkt Val
MS4	1976 (4)	— KM#Pn107-110	—	400

UTOPIA - A WORLD UNITED

UNITED NATIONS ADMINISTRATION

FANTASY COINAGE

Struck by the Medallic Art Co., New York

X# 1b DOLLAR
Gold **Obv:** Dragon and eagle **Rev:** United Nations arms **Note:** Prev. KY#16b.

Date	Mintage	F	VF	XF	Unc	BU
1948	6	—	—	—	—	—

X# 2 1-1/4 OUNCES
0.7500 Gold **Obv:** Dragon and eagle **Rev:** United Nations arms **Rev. Legend:** NVMMVS AVREVS **Note:** Prev. KY#16c.

Date	Mintage	F	VF	XF	Unc	BU
1948	—	—	—	—	550	700

X# 3 2-1/2 OUNCES
0.7500 Gold **Obv:** Dragon and eagle **Rev:** United Nations arms **Note:** Prev. KY#16d.

Date	Mintage	F	VF	XF	Unc	BU
1948	—	—	—	—	1,000	1,250

X# 4 3-3/4 OUNCES
0.7500 Gold **Obv:** Dragon and eagle **Rev:** United Nations arms **Note:** Prev. KY#16e.

Date	Mintage	F	VF	XF	Unc	BU
1948	—	—	—	—	1,400	1,650

UZBEKISTAN

The Republic of Uzbekistan (formerly the Uzbek S.S.R.), is bordered on the north by Kazakhstan, to the east by Kirghizia and Tajikistan, on the south by Afghanistan and on the west by Turkmenistan. The republic is comprised of the regions of Andizhan, Bukhara, Dzhizak, Ferghana, Kashkadar, Khorezm (Khiva), Namangan, Navoi, Samarkand, Surkhan-.Darya, Syr-Darya, Tashkent and the Karakalpak Autonomous Republic. It has an area of 172,741 sq. mi. (447,400 sq. km.) and a population of 20.3 million. Capital: Tashkent.

On June 20, 1990 the Uzbek Supreme Soviet adopted a declaration of sovereignty, and in Aug. 1991, following an unsuccessful coup, declared itself independent as the "Republic of Uzbekistan", which was confirmed by referendum in Dec. That same month Uzbekistan became a member of the CIS.

PATTERNS
Including off metal strikes

KM#	Date	Mintage	Identification	Mkt Val
Pn1	1994	—	Som. Gold-Plated Bronze. 15.1300 g. 31 mm. National arms. Muhammad Taragay Ulugbek (1394-1449). Reeded edge. Proof	100
Pn2	1995	—	Tiyin. 0.8000 Gold Plated Silver. 15.2200 g. 31 mm. National arms. Samarkand building. Reeded edge. Proof	200

VANUATU

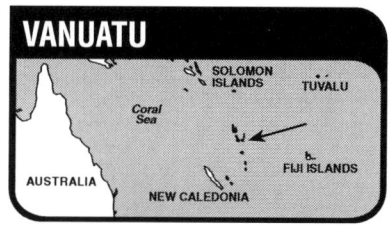

The Republic of Vanuatu, formerly New Hebrides Condominium, a group of islands located in the South Pacific 500 miles (800 km.) west of Fiji, were under the joint sovereignty of Great Britain and France. The islands have an area of 5,700 sq. mi. (14,760 sq. km.) and a population of 165,000, mainly Melanesians of mixed blood. Capital: Port-Vila. The volcanic and coral islands, while malarial land subject to frequent earthquakes, are extremely fertile, and produce copra, coffee, tropical fruits and timber for export.

The New Hebrides were discovered by Portuguese navigator Pedro de Quiros (sailing under orders by the King of Spain) in 1606, visited by French explorer Bougainville in 1768, and named by British navigator Capt. James Cook in 1774. Ships of all nations converged on the islands to trade for sandalwood, prompting France and Britain to relinquish their individual claims and declare the islands a neutral zone in 1878. The New Hebrides were placed under the control of a mixed Anglo-French commission of naval officers during the native uprisings of 1887, and established as a condominium under the joint sovereignty of France and Great Britain in 1906.

Vanuatu became an independent republic within the Commonwealth in July 1980. A president is Head of State and the Prime Minister is Head of Government.

MINT MARK
(a) - Paris, privy marks only

MONETARY SYSTEM
Francs until 1983
Vatu to Present

REPUBLIC

STANDARD COINAGE

KM# 31 50 VATU
1.2441 g., 0.9990 Gold .0400 oz. AGW **Obv:** National arms **Rev:** Spanish 1704 gold coin design

Date	Mintage	F	VF	XF	Unc	BU
1998 Proof	—	Value: 30.00				

KM# 32 50 VATU
1.2441 g., 0.9990 Gold .0400 oz. AGW **Obv:** National arms **Rev:** Boar tusk necklace

Date	Mintage	F	VF	XF	Unc	BU
1998 Proof	—	Value: 30.00				

KM# 23 100 VATU
7.7760 g., 0.5830 Gold .1458 oz. AGW **Series:** Endangered Wildlife **Obv:** National arms **Rev:** Kingfisher

Date	Mintage	F	VF	XF	Unc	BU
1994 Proof	Est. 2,000	Value: 140				

KM# 2 10000 VATU
15.9800 g., 0.9170 Gold .4712 oz. AGW **Subject:** 1st Anniversary of Independence **Obv:** National arms **Rev:** Crab flanked by palm trees

Date	Mintage	F	VF	XF	Unc	BU
1981	538	—	—	—	345	—
1981 Proof	1,054	Value: 325				

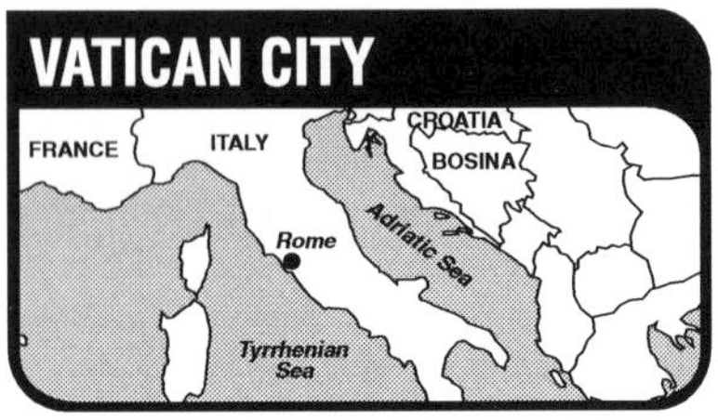

VATICAN CITY

The State of the Vatican City, a papal state on the right bank of the Tiber River within the boundaries of Rome, has an area of 0.17 sq. mi. (0.44 sq. km.) and a population of *775. Capital: Vatican City.

Vatican City State, comprising the Vatican, St. Peter's, extra-territorial right to Castel Gandolfo and 13 buildings throughout Rome, is all that remains of the extensive Papal States over which the Pope exercised temporal power in central Italy. During the struggle for Italian unification, the Papal States, including Rome, were forcibly incorporated into the Kingdom of Italy in 1870. The resultant confrontation of crozier and sword remained unresolved until the signing of the Lateran Treaty, Feb. 11, 1929, between the Vatican and the Kingdom of Italy which recognized the independence and sovereignty of the State of the Vatican City, defined the relationship between the government and the church within Italy, and financially compensated the Holy See for the territorial losses from 1870.

Today the Pope exercises supreme legislative, executive and judicial power within the Vatican City, and the State of the Vatican City is recognized by many nations as an independent sovereign state under the temporal jurisdiction of the Pope, even to the extent of ambassadorial exchange. The Pope, is of course, the head of the Roman Catholic Church.

PONTIFFS
Pius XI, 1922-1939
  Sede Vacante, Feb. 10 - Mar. 2, 1939
Pius XII, 1939-1958
  Sede Vacante, Oct. 9 - 28, 1958
John XXIII, 1958-1963
  Sede Vacante, June 3 - 21,1963
Paul VI, 1963-1978
  Sede Vacante, Aug. 6 - 26, 1978
John Paul I, Aug. 26 - Sept. 28, 1978
  Sede Vacante, Sept. 28 - Oct. 16, 1978
John Paul II, 1978-2005
  Sede Vacante, April 2 - 19, 2005
Benedict XVI, 2005-

MINT MARK
                                    Commencing 1981
R – Rome

MONETARY SYSTEM
100 Centesimi = 1 Lira (thru 2002)
100 Euro Cent = 1 Euro

DATING
Most Vatican coins indicate the regnal year of the pope preceded by the word *Anno* (or an abbreviation), even if the *anno domini* date is omitted.

CITY STATE

Pius XI

STANDARD COINAGE
100 Centesimi = 1 Lira

Y# 9   100 LIRE
8.8000 g., 0.9000 Gold .2546 oz. AGW, 23.5 mm. **Obverse:** Bust right **Reverse:** Standing Jesus facing with child at feet **Designer:** Aurelio Mistruzzi

Date	Mintage	F	VF	XF	Unc
1929/VIII	10,000	—	200	400	500
1930/IX	2,621	—	300	500	800
1931/X	3,343	—	180	325	500
1932/XI	5,073	—	175	250	375
1934/XIII	2,533	—	180	325	500
1935/XIV	2,015	—	180	325	500

Y# 19   100 LIRE
8.8000 g., 0.9000 Gold .2546 oz. AGW, 23.5 mm. **Subject:** Jubilee **Obverse:** Bust right **Reverse:** Standing Jesus facing with child at feet **Designer:** Aurelio Mistruzzi

Date	Mintage	F	VF	XF	Unc
1933-34	23,000	—	180	325	500

Y# 10   100 LIRE
5.1900 g., 0.9000 Gold .1501 oz. AGW, 20.5 mm. **Obverse:** Bust right **Reverse:** Standing Jesus facing with child at feet

Date	Mintage	F	VF	XF	Unc
1936/XV	8,239	—	—	325	500
1937/XVI	2,000	—	—	2,000	3,000
1938 Rare	6	—	—	—	—

Pius XII

STANDARD COINAGE
100 Centesimi = 1 Lira

Y# 30.1   100 LIRE
5.1900 g., 0.9000 Gold .1501 oz. AGW **Obverse:** Head right **Obv. Legend:** AN **Reverse:** Standing Jesus divides value **Designer:** Aurelio Mistruzzi

Date	Mintage	F	VF	XF	Unc
1939/I	2,700	—	—	300	500
1940/II	2,000	—	—	300	500

Y# 30.2   100 LIRE
5.1900 g., 0.9000 Gold .1501 oz. AGW **Obverse:** Head right **Obv. Legend:** A **Reverse:** Standing Jesus divides value

Date	Mintage	F	VF	XF	Unc
1941/III	2,000	—	—	300	550

Y# 39   100 LIRE
5.1900 g., 0.9000 Gold .1501 oz. AGW **Obverse:** Head right **Reverse:** Caritas seated facing flanked by children

Date	Mintage	F	VF	XF	Unc
1942/IV	2,000	—	—	300	550
1943/V	1,000	—	—	350	600
1944/VI	1,000	—	—	350	600
1945/VII	1,000	—	—	350	600
1946/VIII	1,000	—	—	350	600
1947/IX	1,000	—	—	350	600
1948/X	5,000	—	—	300	500
1949/XI	1,000	—	—	350	600

Y# 48   100 LIRE
5.1900 g., 0.9000 Gold .1501 oz. AGW **Subject:** Holy Year **Obverse:** Crowned bust left **Reverse:** Opening of the Holy Year Door

Date	Mintage	F	VF	XF	Unc
MCML (1950)	20,000	—	—	300	500

Y# 53.1   100 LIRE
5.1900 g., 0.9000 Gold .1501 oz. AGW **Obverse:** Bust right **Obv. Legend:** AN **Reverse:** Caritas standing facing holding child with another at feet

Date	Mintage	F	VF	XF	Unc
1951/XIII	1,000	—	—	350	550
1952/XIV	1,000	—	—	350	550
1953/XV	1,000	—	—	350	550
1954/XVI	1,000	—	—	350	550
1955/XVII	1,000	—	—	350	550

Y# 53.2   100 LIRE
5.1900 g., 0.9000 Gold .1501 oz. AGW **Obverse:** Bust right **Obv. Legend:** A **Reverse:** Caritas standing facing holding child with another at feet

Date	Mintage	F	VF	XF	Unc
1956/XVIII	1,000	—	—	350	550

Y# A53   100 LIRE
5.1900 g., 0.9000 Gold .1501 oz. AGW **Obverse:** Bust right **Reverse:** Crowned shield divides value

Date	Mintage	F	VF	XF	Unc
1957/XIX	2,000	—	—	300	450
1958/XX	3,000	—	—	300	450

John XXIII

STANDARD COINAGE
100 Centesimi = 1 Lira

Y# 66   100 LIRE
5.1900 g., 0.9000 Gold .1501 oz. AGW **Obverse:** Bust right **Reverse:** Crowned shield divides value

Date	Mintage	F	VF	XF	Unc
1959/I	3,000	—	1,100	1,500	2,280

John Paul II

STANDARD COINAGE
100 Centesimi = 1 Lira

Y# 356   50000 LIRE
7.5000 g., 0.9170 Gold 0.2211 oz. AGW **Obverse:** Pope and Holy Year Door **Reverse:** John the Baptist and St. John the Evangelist facing each other **Designer:** Giovani Contri

Date	Mintage	F	VF	XF	Unc
1996R Proof	6,000	Value: 300			

Y# 288   50000 LIRE
7.5000 g., 0.9170 Gold .2211 oz. AGW **Obverse:** Pope and Holy Year Door **Reverse:** St. Paul facing **Designer:** Giovani Contri

Date	Mintage	F	VF	XF	Unc
1997/XIX Proof	6,000	Value: 300			

VATICAN CITY

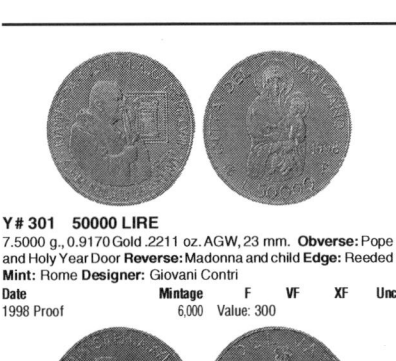

Y# 301 50000 LIRE
7.5000 g., 0.9170 Gold .2211 oz. AGW, 23 mm. **Obverse:** Pope and Holy Year Door **Reverse:** Madonna and child **Edge:** Reeded **Mint:** Rome **Designer:** Giovani Contri

Date	Mintage	F	VF	XF	Unc
1998 Proof	6,000			Value: 300	

Y# 320 50000 LIRE
7.5000 g., 0.9170 Gold .2211 oz. AGW **Obverse:** Pope and Holy Year Door **Reverse:** Statue of St. Peter **Designer:** Giovani Contri

Date	Mintage	F	VF	XF	Unc
1999 Proof	—			Value: 300	

Y# 316 50000 LIRE
7.5000 g., 0.9170 Gold .2211 oz. AGW **Subject:** Prodigal Son **Obverse:** Bust right **Reverse:** Jesus on cross, standing figures at sides **Mint:** Rome **Designer:** Enrico Manfrini

Date	Mintage	F	VF	XF	Unc
2000/XXII Proof	6,000			Value: 300	

Y# 357 100000 LIRE
15.0000 g., 0.9170 Gold 0.4422 oz. AGW **Obverse:** Pope and Holy Year Door **Reverse:** Basilica of St. John Lateran **Designer:** Giovani Contri

Date	Mintage	F	VF	XF	Unc
1996R Proof	6,000			Value: 550	

Y# 289 100000 LIRE
15.0000 g., 0.9170 Gold .4422 oz. AGW **Obverse:** Pope and Holy Year Door **Reverse:** Basilica of St. Paul outside the walls **Designer:** Giovani Contri

Date	Mintage	F	VF	XF	Unc
1997/XIX Proof	6,000			Value: 550	

Y# 302 100000 LIRE
15.0000 g., 0.9170 Gold .4422 oz. AGW, 28 mm. **Obverse:** Pope and Holy Year Door **Reverse:** Basilica of St. Mary Major **Edge:** Reeded **Mint:** Rome **Designer:** Giovani Contri

Date	Mintage	F	VF	XF	Unc
1998 Proof	6,000			Value: 550	

Y# 321 100000 LIRE
15.0000 g., 0.9170 Gold .4422 oz. AGW **Obverse:** Pope and Holy Year Door **Reverse:** St. Peter's Basilica **Designer:** Giovani Contri

Date	Mintage	F	VF	XF	Unc
1999 Proof	—			Value: 550	

Y# 317 100000 LIRE
15.0000 g., 0.9170 Gold .4422 oz. AGW **Obverse:** Bust right **Reverse:** Crucifixion scene **Mint:** Rome **Designer:** Enrico Manfrini

Date	Mintage	F	VF	XF	Unc
2000/XXII Proof	6,000			Value: 550	

EURO COINAGE

Y# 361 20 EURO
6.0000 g., 0.9170 Gold 0.1769 oz. AGW **Subject:** Roots of Faith **Reverse:** Noah's Ark **Mint:** Rome **Designer:** Floriano Bodini

Date	Mintage	F	VF	XF	Unc
2002	2,800			Value: 1,100	

Y# 351 20 EURO
6.0000 g., 0.9166 Gold 0.1768 oz. AGW, 21 mm. **Reverse:** Moses being found in floating basket **Edge:** Reeded **Mint:** Rome **Designer:** Floriano Bodini

Date	Mintage	F	VF	XF	Unc
2003R Proof	2,800			Value: 1,100	

Y# 363 20 EURO
6.0000 g., 0.9170 Gold, 21 mm. **Reverse:** David slaying Goliath **Designer:** Floriano Bodini

Date	Mintage	F	VF	XF	Unc
2004/XXVIIR Proof	3,050			Value: 1,000	

Y# 362 50 EURO
15.0000 g., 0.9170 Gold 0.4422 oz. AGW **Subject:** Roots of Faith **Reverse:** Sacrifice of Abraham **Designer:** Floriano Bodini

Date	Mintage	F	VF	XF	Unc
2002 Proof	2,800			Value: 1,950	

Y# 352 50 EURO
15.0000 g., 0.9166 Gold 0.442 oz. AGW, 28 mm. **Reverse:** Moses receiving the Ten Commandments **Edge:** Reeded **Mint:** Rome **Designer:** Floriano Bodini

Date	Mintage	F	VF	XF	Unc
2003R Proof	2,800			Value: 1,950	

Y# 364 50 EURO
15.0000 g., 0.9170 Gold .4422 oz. AGW **Reverse:** Judgement of Solomon **Designer:** Floriano Bodini

Date	Mintage	F	VF	XF	Unc
2004/XXVIIR Proof	3,050			Value: 1,850	

MINT SETS

KM#	Date	Mintage	Identification	Issue Price	Mkt Val
MS1	1929 (9)	10,000	Y#1-9	—	470
MS3	1930 (9)	2,621	Y#1-9	—	825
MS5	1931 (9)	3,343	Y#1-9	—	575
MS7	1932 (9)	5,073	Y#1-9	—	475
MS9	1933-34 (9)	23,235	Y#11-19	—	500
MS11	1934 (9)	2,533	Y#1-9	—	575
MS13	1935 (9)	2,105	Y#1-9	—	685
MS15	1936 (9)	8,239	Y#1-8, 10	—	350
MS17	1937 (9)	2,000	Y#1-8, 10	—	3,075
MS19	1938 (3)	—	Y#1-2, 10 Rare	—	—
MS20	1939 (9)	2,700	Y#22-30.1	—	435
MS23	1940 (9)	2,000	Y#22, 23, 24a-27a, 28-30.1	—	470
MS25	1941 (9)	2,000	Y#22, 23, 24a-27a, 28-30.2	—	580
MS27	1942 (9)	2,000	Y#31-39	—	630
MS29	1943 (9)	1,000	Y#31-39	—	820
MS31	1944 (9)	1,000	Y#31-39	—	820
MS33	1945 (9)	1,000	Y#31-39	—	820
MS34	1945 (8)	1,000	Y#31-38	—	320
MS35	1946 (9)	1,000	Y#31-39	—	820
MS37	1947 (5)	1,000	Y#39-43	—	530
MS40	1948 (5)	5,000	Y#39-43	—	280
MS42	1949 (5)	1,000	Y#39-43	—	535
MS44	1950 (5)	20,000	Y#44-48	—	265
MS46	1951 (5)	1,000	Y#49.1-53.1	—	500
MS54	1956 (7)	1,000	Y#49.2-55	—	500
MS48	1952 (5)	1,000	Y#49.1-52.1, 53.1	—	500
MS50	1953 (5)	1,000	Y#49.1-52.1, 53.1	—	500
MS52	1955 (7)	1,000	Y#49.1-55	—	550
MS60	1959 (9)	3,000	Y#58.1-64.1, 65-66	—	1,300

PROOF SETS

KM#	Date	Mintage	Identification	Issue Price	Mkt Val
PS4	1997 (2)	6,000	Y#288-289	547	625

PROVA SETS

KM#	Date	Mintage	Identification	Issue Price	Mkt Val
PrS1	1951 (4)	103	Pr1-Pr4	—	300
PrS2	1952 (4)	103	Pr5-Pr8	—	300
PrS3	1953 (4)	103	Pr9-Pr12	—	300
PrS4	1955 (6)	103	Pr13-Pr18	—	425
PrS5	1956 (6)	103	Pr19-Pr24	—	425
PrS6	1957 (7)	103	Pr25-31	—	425
PrS7	1958 (8)	103	Pr32-Pr39	—	600
PrS8	1959 (8)	103	Pr40-Pr47	—	600
PrS9	1960 (8)	103	Pr48-Pr55	—	600
PrS10	1961 (8)	103	Pr56-Pr63	—	600
PrS11	1962 (8)	103	Pr64-Pr71	—	600
PrS12	1962 (8)	103	Pr72-Pr79	—	600
PrS13	1963 (8)	103	Pr80-Pr87	—	600
PrS14	1964 (8)	103	Pr88-Pr95	—	600
PrS15	1965 (8)	103	Pr96-103	—	600
PrS16	1966 (8)	103	Pr104-Pr111	—	600
PrS17	1967 (8)	103	Pr112-Pr119	—	600
PrS18	1968 (8)	103	Pr120-Pr127	—	600
PrS19	1969 (8)	103	Pr128-Pr135	—	600
PrS20	1970 (8)	103	Pr136-Pr143	—	600
PrS21	1971 (8)	103	Pr144-Pr151	—	600
PrS22	1972 (8)	103	Pr152-Pr159	—	600
PrS23	1973 (8)	103	Pr160-Pr167	—	600
PrS24	1974 (8)	103	Pr168-Pr175	—	600
PrS25	1975 (8)	103	Pr176-Pr183	—	600
PrS26	1975 (8)	103	Pr184-Pr191	—	600

748 VENEZUELA

The Republic of Venezuela ("Little Venice"), located on the northern coast of South America between Colombia and Guyana, has an area of 352,145 sq. mi. (912,050 sq. km.) and a population of 20 million. Capital: Caracas. Petroleum and mining provide a significant portion of Venezuela's exports. Coffee, grown on 60,000 plantations, is the chief crop. Metalurgy, refining, oil, iron and steel production are the main employment industries.

Columbus discovered Venezuela on his third voyage in 1498. Initial exploration did not reveal Venezuela to be a land of great wealth. An active pearl trade operated on the offshore islands and slavers raided the interior in search of Indians to be sold into slavery, but no significant mainland settlements were made before 1567 when Caracas was founded. Venezuela, the home of Bolivar, was among the first South American colonies to rebel against Spain in 1810. The declaration of Independence of Venezuela was signed by seven provinces which are represented by the seven stars of the Venezuelan flag. Coinage of Caracas and Margarita use the seven stars in their designs. These original provinces were: Barcelona, Barinas, Caracas, Cumana, Margarita, Merida and Trujillo. The Provinces of Coro, Guyana and Maracaibo were added to Venezuela during the Independence War. Independence was attained in 1821 but not recognized by Spain until 1845. Together with Ecuador, Panama and Colombia, Venezuela was part of "Gran Colombia" until 1830, when it became a sovereign and independent state.

RULER
Republic, 1823-present

MINT MARKS
A - Paris
(a) - Paris, privy marks only
(aa) - Altena
(b) - Berlin
(bb) - Brussels
(cc) – Canada
(c) - Caracas
(d) - Denver
H, Heaton - Heaton, Birmingham
(l) - London
(m) - Madrid
(mm) - Mexico
(o) - Ontario
(p) - Philadelphia
(s) - San Francisco
(sc) - Schwerte - Vereinigte Deutsche Nickelwerke
(w) - Werdohl - Vereinigte Deutsche Metalwerke

ENGRAVER'S INITIALS
W. W. – William Wyon

MONETARY SYSTEM
100 Centimos = 1 Bolivar

REPUBLIC OF VENEZUELA

REFORM COINAGE
1871-1879; 100 Centavos = 1 Venezolano

Y# 17 5 VENEZOLANOS
8.0645 g., 0.9000 Gold .2333 oz. AGW **Obv:** Arms within sprigs above banner, cornucopias above **Obv. Legend:** ESTRADOS UNIDOS DE VENEZUELA. **Rev:** Head right **Rev. Legend:** BOLIVAR LIBERTADOR

Date	Mintage	F	VF	XF	Unc	BU
1875A	69,000	200	250	350	600	800

REFORM COINAGE
1896; 100 Centimos = 1 Bolivar

Y# 31 GR 3.2258 (10 Bolivares)
3.2258 g., 0.9000 Gold .0933 oz. AGW **Obv:** National arms above ribbon, plants flank, cornucopias above **Rev:** Head of Bolivar right **Rev. Designer:** Albert Barre

Date	Mintage	F	VF	XF	Unc	BU
1930(p)	Est. 500,000	—	BV	65.00	80.00	100

Note: Only 10% of the total mintage was released; the balance remaining as part of the nation's gold reserve

Y# 32 GR 6.4516 (20 Bolivares)
6.4516 g., 0.9000 Gold .1867 oz. AGW **Obv:** Arms within sprigs above banner, cornucopias above **Obv. Legend:** ESTRADOS UNIDOS DE VENEZUELA **Rev:** Head of Bolivar right **Rev. Legend:** BOLIVAR LIBERTADOR **Rev. Designer:** Albert Barre

Date	Mintage	F	VF	XF	Unc	BU
1879(bb)	41,000	—	BV	200	500	750
1880(bb) 1 and 8 close	84,000	—	BV	190	450	650
1880(bb) 1 and 8 apart	Inc. above	—	BV	190	450	65.00
1880(bb) Tight 8's	Inc. above	—	BV	190	450	650
1886(c) High 6	23,000	BV	190	250	350	550
1886(c) Low 6	Inc. above	BV	190	250	350	550
1887(c)	132,000	BV	220	400	650	1,100
1888/6(c)	81,000	BV	210	250	500	850
1888(c)	Inc. above	200	220	400	650	1,100
1904(a)	100,000	—	BV	130	140	150
1905(a)	100,000	—	BV	130	140	150
1910(a)	70,000	—	BV	130	145	160

Note: Die varieties exist in the placement of dot between date and Lei, Type 1 is evenly spaced, Type 2 had dot closer to L of Lei

| 1911(a) | 80,000 | — | BV | 130 | 140 | 150 |

Note: Die varieties exist in the placement of dot between date and Lei, Type 1 is evenly spaced, Type 2 had dot closer to L of Lei

| 1912(a) | 150,000 | — | BV | 130 | 140 | 150 |

Note: Die varieties exist in the placement of the torch privy mark in relation to bust truncation; Type 1 is well below truncation, Type 2 is slightly below truncation and Type 3 is in line with the truncation

Y# 67 50 BOLIVARES
15.5500 g., 0.9000 Gold .4500 oz. AGW **Subject:** 50th Anniversary of Central Bank **Obv:** Flag design with initials in circle at right **Rev:** Building facade

Date	Mintage	F	VF	XF	Unc	BU
1990(c) Proof	5,000	Value: 500				

Y# 34 100 BOLIVARES
32.2580 g., 0.9000 Gold .9334 oz. AGW **Obv:** Arms within sprigs above banner, cornucopias above **Obv. Legend:** ESTRADOS UNIDOS DE VENEZUELA **Rev:** Head right **Rev. Legend:** BOLIVAR LIBERTADOR

Date	Mintage	F	VF	XF	Unc	BU
1886(c) Normal date	4,250	BV	700	800	1,100	1,500
1886(c) 8 and 6 close	Inc. above	BV	700	800	1,100	1,500
1886(c) 8 and 6 apart	Inc. above	BV	700	800	1,100	1,500
1887(c)	28,000	BV	700	800	1,100	1,500
1888(c)	32,000	BV	700	800	1,100	1,500
1889(c)	23,000	BV	700	800	1,100	1,500

Y# 54 500 BOLIVARES
18.0000 g., 0.9000 Gold .5209 oz. AGW, 30 mm. **Subject:** Nationalization of Oil Industry **Obv:** Oil derricks within inset at left **Rev:** Head of Bolivar left within inset

Date	Mintage	F	VF	XF	Unc	BU
1975(c) Proof	100	Value: 13,000				

Y# 48.1 1000 BOLIVARES
33.4370 g., 0.9000 Gold .9676 oz. AGW, 34 mm. **Subject:** Conservation Series - Cock of the Rocks **Obv:** National arms above ribbon, plants flank, cornucopias above **Rev:** Bird on branch

Date	Mintage	F	VF	XF	Unc	BU
1975(l)	5,047	—	—	—	675	725
1975(l) Proof	483	Value: 1,250				

Y# 48.2 1000 BOLIVARES
33.4370 g., 0.9000 Gold .9676 oz. AGW, 34 mm. **Subject:** Conservation Series - Cock of the Rocks **Obv:** National arms above ribbon, plants flank, cornucopias above **Rev:** Bird on branch with smooth wings

Date	Mintage	F	VF	XF	Unc	BU
1975(l)	Inc. above	—	—	—	700	800

Y# 59 3000 BOLIVARES
31.1000 g., 0.9000 Gold .9000 oz. AGW **Subject:** 200th Anniversary - Birth of Simon Bolivar **Obv:** Building **Rev:** Bookshelves back of 3/4 figure looking left

Date	Mintage	F	VF	XF	Unc	BU
ND(1983)(w) Proof	10,000	Value: 685				

Y# 62 5000 BOLIVARES
15.5500 g., 0.9000 Gold .4500 oz. AGW, 27 mm. **Obv:** National arms above ribbon, plants flank, cornucopias above **Rev:** Bust of Bolivar 3/4 left, dates below

Date	Mintage	F	VF	XF	Unc	BU
1988(cc) Proof	25,000	Value: 315				

Y# 63 5000 BOLIVARES
15.5500 g., 0.9000 Gold .4500 oz. AGW, 27 mm. **Obv:** National arms above ribbon, plants flank, cornucopias above **Rev:** Bust of Bolivar facing, dates below

Date	Mintage	F	VF	XF	Unc	BU
1988(cc) Proof	25,000	Value: 315				

Y# 65 5000 BOLIVARES
15.5500 g., 0.9000 Gold .4500 oz. AGW, 27 mm. **Obv:** National arms above ribbon, plants flank, cornucopias above **Rev:** Head of Bolivar left, dates below

VENEZUELA 749

Date Mintage F VF XF Unc BU
1990(mm) Proof 10,000 Value: 325

Y# 73 5000 BOLIVARES
15.5500 g., 0.9000 Gold .4500 oz. AGW, 27 mm. **Subject:** 200th Anniversary - Sucre's Birth **Obv:** National arms above ribbon, plants flank, cornucopias above **Rev:** Bust of Bolivar looking left, dates below

Date	Mintage	F	VF	XF	Unc	BU
1995(cc) Proof	10,000	Value: 325				

Y# 61 10000 BOLIVARES
31.1000 g., 0.9000 Gold .9000 oz. AGW, 35 mm. **Obv:** National arms above ribbon, plants flank, cornucopias above **Rev:** Head of Bolivar right **Rev. Designer:** Albert Barre

Date	Mintage	F	VF	XF	Unc	BU
1987(c) Proof	50,000	Value: 635				

MEDALLIC COINAGE
Banco Italo - Venezolana - Personalities of World War II Series

Struck by the Karlsruhe Mint, Baden, Germany

X# MB1 20 BOLIVARES
6.0000 g., 0.9000 Gold 0.1736 oz. AGW **Rev:** Bust of Mackenzie King of Canada

Date	Mintage	F	VF	XF	Unc	BU
1957	—	—	—	120	135	150

X# MB2 20 BOLIVARES
6.0000 g., 0.9000 Gold 0.1736 oz. AGW **Rev:** Bust of Chiang Kai-shek of China

Date	Mintage	F	VF	XF	Unc	BU
1957	—	—	—	120	135	150

X# MB3 20 BOLIVARES
6.0000 g., 0.9000 Gold 0.1736 oz. AGW **Rev:** Bust of Mannerheim of Finland

Date	Mintage	F	VF	XF	Unc	BU
1957	—	—	—	120	135	150

X# MB4 20 BOLIVARES
6.0000 g., 0.9000 Gold 0.1736 oz. AGW **Rev:** Bust of Charles de Gaulle of France

Date	Mintage	F	VF	XF	Unc	BU
1957	—	—	—	120	135	150

X# MB5 20 BOLIVARES
6.0000 g., 0.9000 Gold 0.1736 oz. AGW **Rev:** Bust of Marshal Petain of France

Date	Mintage	F	VF	XF	Unc	BU
1957	—	—	—	120	135	150

X# MB6 20 BOLIVARES
6.0000 g., 0.9000 Gold 0.1736 oz. AGW **Rev:** Bust of Adolf Hitler of Germany

Date	Mintage	F	VF	XF	Unc	BU
1957	—	—	—	120	135	150

X# MB7 20 BOLIVARES
6.0000 g., 0.9000 Gold 0.1736 oz. AGW **Rev:** Bust of Erwin Rommel of Germany

Date	Mintage	F	VF	XF	Unc	BU
1957	—	—	—	120	135	150

X# MB8 20 BOLIVARES
6.0000 g., 0.9000 Gold 0.1736 oz. AGW **Rev:** Bust of Winston Churchill of Great Britain

Date	Mintage	F	VF	XF	Unc	BU
1957	—	—	—	120	135	150

X# MB9 20 BOLIVARES
6.0000 g., 0.9000 Gold 0.1736 oz. AGW **Rev:** Bust of Bernard Montgomery of Great Britain

Date	Mintage	F	VF	XF	Unc	BU
1957	—	—	—	120	135	150

X# MB10 20 BOLIVARES
6.0000 g., 0.9000 Gold 0.1736 oz. AGW **Rev:** Bust of Benito Mussolini of Italy

Date	Mintage	F	VF	XF	Unc	BU
1957	—	—	—	120	135	150

X# MB11 20 BOLIVARES
6.0000 g., 0.9000 Gold 0.1736 oz. AGW **Rev:** Bust of Vittorio Emanuel III of Italy

Date	Mintage	F	VF	XF	Unc	BU
1957	—	—	—	120	135	150

X# MB12 20 BOLIVARES
6.0000 g., 0.9000 Gold 0.1736 oz. AGW **Rev:** Bust of Tojo of Japan

Date	Mintage	F	VF	XF	Unc	BU
1957	—	—	—	120	135	150

X# MB13 20 BOLIVARES
6.0000 g., 0.9000 Gold 0.1736 oz. AGW **Rev:** Bust of Dwight D. Eisenhower of U.S.A.

Date	Mintage	F	VF	XF	Unc	BU
1957	—	—	—	120	135	150

X# MB14 20 BOLIVARES
6.0000 g., 0.9000 Gold 0.1736 oz. AGW **Rev:** Bust of Douglas MacArthur of U.S.A.

Date	Mintage	F	VF	XF	Unc	BU
1957	—	—	—	120	135	150

X# MB15 20 BOLIVARES
6.0000 g., 0.9000 Gold 0.1736 oz. AGW **Rev:** Bust of Franklin D. Roosevelt of U.S.A.

Date	Mintage	F	VF	XF	Unc	BU
1957	—	—	—	50.00	75.00	—

X# MB16 20 BOLIVARES
6.0000 g., 0.9000 Gold 0.1736 oz. AGW **Rev:** Bust of Harry S. Truman of U.S.A.

Date	Mintage	F	VF	XF	Unc	BU
1957	—	—	—	120	135	150

X# MB17 20 BOLIVARES
6.0000 g., 0.9000 Gold 0.1736 oz. AGW **Rev:** Bust of Joseph Stalin of U.S.S.R.

Date	Mintage	F	VF	XF	Unc	BU
1957	—	—	—	120	135	150

VENEZUELA

X# MB18 20 BOLIVARES
6.0000 g., 0.9000 Gold 0.1736 oz. AGW Rev: Bust of Marshall Tito of Yugoslavia

Date	Mintage	F	VF	XF	Unc	BU
1957	—	—	—	120	135	150

X# MB19 60 BOLIVARES
22.2000 g., 0.9000 Gold 0.6424 oz. AGW Rev: Bust of Mackenzie King of Canada

Date	Mintage	F	VF	XF	Unc	BU
1957	—	—	—	435	450	475

X# MB20 60 BOLIVARES
22.2000 g., 0.9000 Gold 0.6424 oz. AGW Rev: Bust of Chiang Kai-shek of China

Date	Mintage	F	VF	XF	Unc	BU
1957	—	—	—	435	450	475

X# MB21 60 BOLIVARES
22.2000 g., 0.9000 Gold 0.6424 oz. AGW Rev: Bust of Mannerheim of Finland

Date	Mintage	F	VF	XF	Unc	BU
1957	—	—	—	435	450	475

X# MB22 60 BOLIVARES
22.2000 g., 0.9000 Gold 0.6424 oz. AGW Rev: Bust of Charles de Gaulle of France

Date	Mintage	F	VF	XF	Unc	BU
1957	—	—	—	435	450	475

X# MB23 60 BOLIVARES
22.2000 g., 0.9000 Gold 0.6424 oz. AGW Rev: Bust of Marshal Petain of France

Date	Mintage	F	VF	XF	Unc	BU
1957	—	—	—	435	450	475

X# MB24 60 BOLIVARES
22.2000 g., 0.9000 Gold 0.6424 oz. AGW Rev: Bust of Adolf Hitler of Germany

Date	Mintage	F	VF	XF	Unc	BU
1957	—	—	—	435	450	475

X# MB25 60 BOLIVARES
22.2000 g., 0.9000 Gold 0.6424 oz. AGW Rev: Bust of Erwin Rommel of Germany

Date	Mintage	F	VF	XF	Unc	BU
1957	—	—	—	435	450	475

X# MB26 60 BOLIVARES
22.2000 g., 0.9000 Gold 0.6424 oz. AGW Rev: Bust of Winston Churchilll of Great Britain

Date	Mintage	F	VF	XF	Unc	BU
1957	—	—	—	435	450	475

X# MB27 60 BOLIVARES
22.2000 g., 0.9000 Gold 0.6424 oz. AGW Rev: Bust of Bernard Montgomery of Great Britain

Date	Mintage	F	VF	XF	Unc	BU
1957	—	—	—	435	450	475

X# MB28 60 BOLIVARES
22.2000 g., 0.9000 Gold 0.6424 oz. AGW Rev: Bust of Benito Mussolini of Italy

Date	Mintage	F	VF	XF	Unc	BU
1957	—	—	—	435	450	475

X# MB29 60 BOLIVARES
22.2000 g., 0.9000 Gold 0.6424 oz. AGW Rev: Bust of Vittorio Emanuel III of Italy

Date	Mintage	F	VF	XF	Unc	BU
1957	—	—	—	435	450	475

X# MB30 60 BOLIVARES
22.2000 g., 0.9000 Gold 0.6424 oz. AGW Rev: Bust of Tojo of Japan

Date	Mintage	F	VF	XF	Unc	BU
1957	—	—	—	435	450	475

X# MB31 60 BOLIVARES
22.2000 g., 0.9000 Gold 0.6424 oz. AGW Rev: Bust of Dwight D. Eisenhower of U.S.A.

Date	Mintage	F	VF	XF	Unc	BU
1957	—	—	—	435	450	475

X# MB32 60 BOLIVARES
22.2000 g., 0.9000 Gold 0.6424 oz. AGW Rev: Bust of Douglas MacArthur of U.S.A.

Date	Mintage	F	VF	XF	Unc	BU
1957	—	—	—	435	450	475

X# MB33 60 BOLIVARES
22.2000 g., 0.9000 Gold 0.6424 oz. AGW Rev: Bust of Franklin D. Roosevelt of U.S.A.

Date	Mintage	F	VF	XF	Unc	BU
1957	—	—	—	435	450	475

X# MB34 60 BOLIVARES
22.2000 g., 0.9000 Gold 0.6424 oz. AGW Rev: Bust of Harry S. Truman of U.S.A.

Date	Mintage	F	VF	XF	Unc	BU
1957	—	—	—	435	450	475

X# MB35 60 BOLIVARES
22.2000 g., 0.9000 Gold 0.6424 oz. AGW Rev: Bust of Joseph Stalin of U.S.S.R.

Date	Mintage	F	VF	XF	Unc	BU
1957	—	—	—	435	450	475

X# MB36 60 BOLIVARES
22.2000 g., 0.9000 Gold 0.6424 oz. AGW Rev: Bust of Marshall Tito of Yugoslavia

Date	Mintage	F	VF	XF	Unc	BU
1957	—	—	—	435	450	475

X# MB60 160 BOLIVARES
50.0000 g., 0.9000 Gold 1.4468 oz. AGW Rev: Bust of Adolf Hitler of Germany

Date	Mintage	F	VF	XF	Unc	BU
1959 Proof	—	Value: 1,150				

PRIVATE PATTERNS
Karl Goetz Issues

Struck at later dates using original or imitation dies. Additional mulings with Goetz German patterns exist, but are most likely modern restrikes or reproductions

X# Pn6 5 BOLIVARES
33.9400 g., Gold Rev: Bust of General Juan Gomez

Date	Mintage	F	VF	XF	Unc	BU
1930	—	—	—	750	1,000	—

X# Pn7 5 BOLIVARES
Platinum APW Rev: Bust of General Juan Gomez Note: Prepared by Karl Goetz. Weight varies: 36.15-40.90 grams.

Date	Mintage	F	VF	XF	Unc	BU
1930	4	—	—	1,250	1,650	—

REPUBLIC

MEDALLIC COINAGE
Inter-Change Bank Suiza - Chiefs Series

X# MB121 5 BOLIVARES
0.9000 Gold, 13.9 mm. **Series:** 16th Century Chiefs **Obv:** Crossed arrows **Obv. Legend:** CACIQUES DE VENEZUELA **Rev:** Head facing slightly left **Rev. Legend:** CACIQUES DE VENEZUELA - GUAICAIPURO **Edge:** Reeded **Note:** Weight varies: 1.43-1.52 grams.

Date	Mintage	F	VF	XF	Unc	BU
ND(1962?)	—	—	—	BV	45.00	—

X# MB122 5 BOLIVARES
0.9000 Gold, 13.9 mm. **Series:** 16th Century Chiefs **Obv:** Crossed arrows **Obv. Legend:** CACIQUES DE VENEZUELA **Rev:** Head facing **Rev. Legend:** CACIQUES DE VENEZUELA - TIUNA **Edge:** Reeded **Note:** Weight varies: 1.43-1.52 grams.

Date	Mintage	F	VF	XF	Unc	BU
ND(1962?)	—	—	—	BV	45.00	—

X# MB123 5 BOLIVARES
0.9000 Gold, 13.9 mm. **Series:** 16th Century Chiefs **Obv:** Crossed arrows **Obv. Legend:** CACIQUES DE VENEZUELA **Rev:** Head facing almost right **Rev. Legend:** CACIQUES DE VENEZUELA - CHACAO **Edge:** Reeded **Note:** Weight varies: 1.43-1.52 grams.

Date	Mintage	F	VF	XF	Unc	BU
ND(1962?)	—	—	—	BV	45.00	—

X# MB124 5 BOLIVARES
0.9000 Gold, 13.9 mm. **Series:** 16th Century Chiefs **Obv:** Crossed arrows **Obv. Legend:** CACIQUES DE VENEZUELA **Rev:** Head facing 3/4 right **Rev. Legend:** CACIQUES DE VENEZUELA - MARA **Edge:** Reeded **Note:** Weight varies: 1.43-1.52 grams.

Date	Mintage	F	VF	XF	Unc	BU
ND(1962?)	—	—	—	BV	45.00	—

X# MB125 5 BOLIVARES
0.9000 Gold, 13.9 mm. **Series:** 16th Century Chiefs **Obv:** Crossed arrows **Obv. Legend:** CACIQUES DE VENEZUELA **Rev:** Head facing slightly right **Rev. Legend:** CACIQUES DE VENEZUELA - NAIGUATÁ **Edge:** Reeded **Note:** Weight varies: 1.43-1.52 grams.

Date	Mintage	F	VF	XF	Unc	BU
ND(1962?)	—	—	—	BV	45.00	—

X# MB126 5 BOLIVARES
0.9000 Gold, 13.9 mm. **Series:** 16th Century Chiefs **Obv:** Crossed arms **Obv. Legend:** CACIQUES DE VENEZUELA **Rev:** Head left **Rev. Legend:** CACIQUES DE VENEZUELA - SOROCAIMA **Edge:** Reeded **Note:** Weight varies: 1.43-1.52 grams.

Date	Mintage	F	VF	XF	Unc	BU
ND(1962?)	—	—	—	BV	45.00	—

X# MB127 5 BOLIVARES
0.9000 Gold, 13.9 mm. **Series:** 16th Century Chiefs **Obv:** Crossed arms **Obv. Legend:** CACIQUES DE VENEZUELA **Rev:** Head facing slightly right **Rev. Legend:** CACIQUES DE VENEZUELA - PARAMACAY **Edge:** Reeded **Note:** Weight varies: 1.43-1.52 grams.

Date	Mintage	F	VF	XF	Unc	BU
ND(1962?)	—	—	—	BV	45.00	—

X# MB128 5 BOLIVARES
0.9000 Gold, 13.9 mm. **Series:** 16th Century Chiefs **Obv:** Crossed arrows **Obv. Legend:** CACIQUES DE VENEZUELA **Rev:** Head facing **Rev. Legend:** CACIQUES DE VENEZUELA - TAMANACO **Edge:** Reeded **Note:** Weight varies: 1.43-1.52 grams.

Date	Mintage	F	VF	XF	Unc	BU
ND(1962?)	—	—	—	BV	45.00	—

X# MB129 5 BOLIVARES
0.9000 Gold, 13.9 mm. **Series:** 16th Century Chiefs **Obv:** Crossed arrows **Obv. Legend:** CACIQUES DE VENEZUELA **Rev:** Head right **Rev. Legend:** CACIQUES DE VENEZUELA - GUAICAMACUTO **Edge:** Reeded **Note:** Weight varies: 1.43-1.52 grams.

Date	Mintage	F	VF	XF	Unc	BU
ND(1962?)	—	—	—	BV	45.00	—

X# MB130 5 BOLIVARES
0.9000 Gold, 13.9 mm. **Series:** 16th Century Chiefs **Obv:** Crossed arrows **Obv. Legend:** CACIQUES DE VENEZUELA **Rev:** Head facing slightly left **Rev. Legend:** CACIQUES DE VENEZUELA - ARICHUNA **Edge:** Reeded **Note:** Weight varies: 1.43-1.52 grams.

Date	Mintage	F	VF	XF	Unc	BU
ND(1962?)	—	—	—	BV	45.00	—

X# MB131 5 BOLIVARES
0.9000 Gold, 13.9 mm. **Series:** 16th Century Chiefs **Obv:** Crossed arms **Obv. Legend:** CACIQUES DE VENEZUELA **Rev:** Head 3/4 left **Rev. Legend:** CACIQUES DE VENEZUELA - MURACHI **Edge:** Reeded **Note:** Weight varies: 1.43-1.52 grams.

Date	Mintage	F	VF	XF	Unc	BU
ND(1962?)	—	—	—	BV	45.00	—

X# MB132 5 BOLIVARES
0.9000 Gold, 13.9 mm. **Series:** 16th Century Chiefs **Obv:** Crossed arrows **Obv. Legend:** CACIQUES DE VENEZUELA **Rev:** Head left **Rev. Legend:** CACIQUES DE VENEZUELA - TEREPAIMA **Edge:** Reeded **Note:** Weight varies: 1.43-1.52 grams.

Date	Mintage	F	VF	XF	Unc	BU
ND(1962?)	—	—	—	BV	45.00	—

X# MB133 5 BOLIVARES
0.9000 Gold, 13.9 mm. **Series:** 16th Century Chiefs **Obv:** Crossed arrows **Obv. Legend:** CACIQUES DE VENEZUELA **Rev:** Head slightly left **Rev. Legend:** CACIQUES DE VENEZUELA - PARAMACONI **Edge:** Reeded **Note:** Weight varies: 1.43-1.52 grams.

Date	Mintage	F	VF	XF	Unc	BU
ND(1962?)	—	—	—	BV	45.00	—

X# MB134 5 BOLIVARES
0.9000 Gold, 13.9 mm. **Series:** 16th Century Chiefs **Obv:** Crossed arrows **Obv. Legend:** CACIQUES DE VENEZUELA **Rev:** Head facing **Rev. Legend:** CACIQUES DE VENEZUELA - MANAURE **Edge:** Reeded **Note:** Weight varies: 1.43-1.52 grams.

Date	Mintage	F	VF	XF	Unc	BU
ND(1962?)	—	—	—	BV	45.00	—

X# MB135 5 BOLIVARES
0.9000 Gold, 13.9 mm. **Series:** 16th Century Chiefs **Obv:** Crossed arrows **Obv. Legend:** CACIQUES DE VENEZUELA **Rev:** Two heads jugate almost right **Rev. Legend:** CACIQUES DE VENEZUELA - CHICURAMAY **Edge:** Reeded **Note:** Weight varies: 1.43-1.52 grams.

Date	Mintage	F	VF	XF	Unc	BU
ND(1962?)	—	—	—	BV	45.00	—

X# MB136 5 BOLIVARES
0.9000 Gold, 13.9 mm. **Series:** 16th Century Chiefs **Obv:** Crossed arrows **Obv. Legend:** CACIQUES DE VENEZUELA **Rev:** Head 3/4 right **Rev. Legend:** CACIQUES DE VENEZUELA - YORACUY **Edge:** Reeded **Note:** Weight varies: 1.43-1.52 grams.

Date	Mintage	F	VF	XF	Unc	BU
ND(1962?)	—	—	—	BV	45.00	—

X# MB137 5 BOLIVARES
0.9000 Gold, 13.9 mm. **Series:** 16th Century Chiefs **Obv:** Crossed arrows **Obv. Legend:** CACIQUES DE VENEZUELA **Rev:** Head

facing **Rev. Legend:** CACIQUES DE VENEZUELA - URIMARE **Edge:** Reeded **Note:** Weight varies: 1.43-1.52 grams.

Date	Mintage	F	VF	XF	Unc	BU
ND(1962?)	—	—	—	BV	45.00	—

X# MB138 5 BOLIVARES

0.9000 Gold, 13.9 mm. **Series:** 16th Century Chiefs **Obv:** Crossed arms **Obv. Legend:** CACIQUES DE VENEZUELA **Rev:** Two heads jugate left **Rev. Legend:** CACIQUES DE VENEZUELA - YORACO **Edge:** Reeded **Note:** Weight varies: 1.43-1.52 grams.

Date	Mintage	F	VF	XF	Unc	BU
ND(1962?)	—	—	—	BV	45.00	—

X# MB139 10 BOLIVARES

0.9000 Gold, 19 mm. **Series:** 16th Century Chiefs **Obv:** Crossed arrows **Obv. Legend:** CACIQUES DE VENEZUELA **Rev:** Head facing slightly left **Rev. Legend:** CACIQUES DE VENEZUELA - GUAICAIPURO **Edge:** Reeded

Date	Mintage	F	VF	XF	Unc	BU
ND(1962?)	—	—	—	BV	75.00	—

X# MB140 10 BOLIVARES

0.9000 Gold, 19 mm. **Series:** 16th Century Chiefs **Obv:** Crossed arrows **Obv. Legend:** CACIQUES DE VENEZUELA **Rev:** Head facing **Rev. Legend:** CACIQUES DE VENEZUELA - TIUNA **Edge:** Reeded

Date	Mintage	F	VF	XF	Unc	BU
ND(1962?)	—	—	—	BV	75.00	—

X# MB141 10 BOLIVARES

0.9000 Gold, 19 mm. **Series:** 16th Century Chiefs **Obv:** Crossed arrows **Obv. Legend:** CACIQUES DE VENEZUELA **Rev:** Head facing almost right **Rev. Legend:** CACIQUES DE VENEZUELA - CHACAO **Edge:** Reeded

Date	Mintage	F	VF	XF	Unc	BU
ND(1962?)	—	—	—	BV	75.00	—

X# MB142 10 BOLIVARES

0.9000 Gold, 19 mm. **Series:** 16th Century Chiefs **Obv:** Crossed arrows **Obv. Legend:** CACIQUES DE VENEZUELA **Rev:** Head facing 3/4 right **Rev. Legend:** CACIQUES DE VENEZUELA - MARA **Edge:** Reeded

Date	Mintage	F	VF	XF	Unc	BU
ND(1962?)	—	—	—	BV	75.00	—

X# MB143 10 BOLIVARES

0.9000 Gold, 19 mm. **Series:** 16th Century Chiefs **Obv:** Crossed arrows **Obv. Legend:** CACIQUES DE VENEZUELA **Rev:** Head facing slightly right **Rev. Legend:** CACIQUES DE VENEZUELA - NAIGUATÁ **Edge:** Reeded

Date	Mintage	F	VF	XF	Unc	BU
ND(1962?)	—	—	—	BV	75.00	—

X# MB144 10 BOLIVARES

0.9000 Gold, 19 mm. **Series:** 16th Century Chiefs **Obv:** Crossed arrows **Obv. Legend:** CACIQUES DE VENEZUELA **Rev:** Head left **Rev. Legend:** CACIQUES DE VENEZUELA - SOROCAIMA **Edge:** Reeded

Date	Mintage	F	VF	XF	Unc	BU
ND(1962?)	—	—	—	BV	75.00	—

X# MB145 10 BOLIVARES

0.9000 Gold, 19 mm. **Series:** 16th Century Chiefs **Obv:** Crossed arrows **Obv. Legend:** CACIQUES DE VENEZUELA **Rev:** Head left **Rev. Legend:** CACIQUES DE VENEZUELA - SOROCAIMA **Edge:** Reeded

Date	Mintage	F	VF	XF	Unc	BU
ND(1962?)	—	—	—	BV	75.00	—

X# MB146 10 BOLIVARES

0.9000 Gold, 19 mm. **Series:** 16th Century Chiefs **Obv:** Crossed arrows **Obv. Legend:** CACIQUES DE VENEZUELA **Rev:** Head facing **Rev. Legend:** CACIQUES DE VENEZUELA - TAMANACO **Edge:** Reeded

Date	Mintage	F	VF	XF	Unc	BU
ND(1962?)	—	—	—	BV	75.00	—

X# MB147 10 BOLIVARES

0.9000 Gold, 19 mm. **Series:** 16th Century Chiefs **Obv:** Crossed arrows **Obv. Legend:** CACIQUES DE VENEZUELA **Rev:** Head right **Rev. Legend:** CACIQUES DE VENEZUELA - GUIACAMACUTO **Edge:** Reeded

Date	Mintage	F	VF	XF	Unc	BU
ND(1962?)	—	—	—	BV	75.00	—

X# MB148 10 BOLIVARES

0.9000 Gold, 19 mm. **Series:** 16th Century Chiefs **Obv:** Crossed arrows **Obv. Legend:** CACIQUES DE VENEZUELA **Rev:** Head facing slightly left **Rev. Legend:** CACIQUES DE VENEZUELA - ARICHUNA **Edge:** Reeded

Date	Mintage	F	VF	XF	Unc	BU
ND(1962?)	—	—	—	BV	75.00	—

X# MB149 10 BOLIVARES

0.9000 Gold, 19 mm. **Series:** 16th Century Chiefs **Obv:** Crossed arrows **Obv. Legend:** CACIQUES DE VENEZUELA **Rev:** Head 3/4 left **Rev. Legend:** CACIQUES DE VENEZUELA - MURACHI **Edge:** Reeded

Date	Mintage	F	VF	XF	Unc	BU
ND(1962?)	—	—	—	BV	75.00	—

X# MB150 10 BOLIVARES

0.9000 Gold, 19 mm. **Series:** 16th Century Chiefs **Obv:** Crossed arrows **Obv. Legend:** CACIQUES DE VENEZUELA **Rev:** Head left **Rev. Legend:** CACIQUES DE VENEZUELA - TEREPAIMA **Edge:** Reeded

Date	Mintage	F	VF	XF	Unc	BU
ND(1962?)	—	—	—	BV	75.00	—

X# MB151 10 BOLIVARES

0.9000 Gold, 19 mm. **Series:** 16th Century Chiefs **Obv:** Crossed arrows **Obv. Legend:** CACIQUES DE VENEZUELA **Rev:** Head slightly left **Rev. Legend:** CACIQUES DE VENEZUELA - PARAMACONI **Edge:** Reeded

Date	Mintage	F	VF	XF	Unc	BU
ND(1962?)	—	—	—	BV	75.00	—

X# MB152 10 BOLIVARES

0.9000 Gold, 19 mm. **Series:** 16th Century Chiefs **Obv:** Crossed arrows **Obv. Legend:** CACIQUES DE VENEZUELA **Rev:** Head facing **Rev. Legend:** CACIQUES DE VENEZUELA - MANAURE **Edge:** Reeded

Date	Mintage	F	VF	XF	Unc	BU
ND(1962?)	—	—	—	BV	75.00	—

X# MB153 10 BOLIVARES

0.9000 Gold, 19 mm. **Series:** 16th Century Chiefs **Obv:** Crossed arrows **Obv. Legend:** CACIQUES DE VENEZUELA **Rev:** Two heads jugate almost right **Rev. Legend:** CACIQUES DE VENEZUELA - CHICURAMAY **Edge:** Reeded

Date	Mintage	F	VF	XF	Unc	BU
ND(1962?)	—	—	—	BV	75.00	—

X# MB154 10 BOLIVARES

0.9000 Gold, 19 mm. **Series:** 16th Century Chiefs **Obv:** Crossed arrows **Obv. Legend:** CACIQUES DE VENEZUELA **Rev:** Head 3/4 right **Rev. Legend:** CACIQUES DE VENEZUELA - YORACUY **Edge:** Reeded

Date	Mintage	F	VF	XF	Unc	BU
ND(1962?)	—	—	—	BV	75.00	—

X# MB155 10 BOLIVARES

0.9000 Gold, 19 mm. **Series:** 16th Century Chiefs **Obv:** Crossed arrows **Obv. Legend:** CACIQUES DE VENEZUELA **Rev:** Head facing **Rev. Legend:** CACIQUES DE VENEZUELA - URIMARE **Edge:** Reeded

Date	Mintage	F	VF	XF	Unc	BU
ND(1962?)	—	—	—	BV	75.00	—

X# MB156 10 BOLIVARES

0.9000 Gold, 19 mm. **Series:** 16th Century Chiefs **Obv:** Crossed arrows **Obv. Legend:** CACIQUES DE VENEZUELA **Rev:** Two heads jugate left **Rev. Legend:** CACIQUES DE VENEZUELA - YORACO **Edge:** Reeded

Date	Mintage	F	VF	XF	Unc	BU
ND(1962?)	—	—	—	BV	75.00	—

X# MB85 20 BOLIVARES

6.6667 g., 0.9000 Gold 0.1929 oz. AGW, 21.2 mm. **Series:** 16th Century Indian Chiefs **Obv:** Hand holding bunch of arrows **Obv. Legend:** CACIQUES DE VENEZUELA **Rev:** Head facing slightly left **Rev. Legend:** CACIQUES DE VENEZUELA - GUAICAIPURO **Edge:** Reeded **Note:** Weight varies: 5.95-6.00 grams.

Date	Mintage	F	VF	XF	Unc	BU
1957	—	—	—	BV	145	—

X# MB86 20 BOLIVARES

6.6667 g., 0.9000 Gold 0.1929 oz. AGW, 21.2 mm. **Series:** 16th Century Indian Chiefs **Obv:** Hand holding bunch of arrows **Obv. Legend:** CACIQUES DE VENEZUELA **Rev:** Head facing **Rev. Legend:** CACIQUES DE VENEZUELA - TIUNA **Edge:** Reeded **Note:** Weight varies: 5.95-6.00 grams.

Date	Mintage	F	VF	XF	Unc	BU
1957	—	—	—	BV	145	—

X# MB87 20 BOLIVARES

6.6667 g., 0.9000 Gold 0.1929 oz. AGW, 21.2 mm. **Series:** 16th Century Indian Chiefs **Obv:** Hand holding bunch of arrows **Obv. Legend:** CACIQUES DE VENEZUELA **Rev:** Head facing almost right **Rev. Legend:** CACIQUES DE VENEZUELA - CHACAO **Edge:** Reeded **Note:** Weight varies: 5.95-6.00 grams.

Date	Mintage	F	VF	XF	Unc	BU
1957	—	—	—	BV	145	—

X# MB88 20 BOLIVARES

6.6667 g., 0.9000 Gold 0.1929 oz. AGW, 21.2 mm. **Series:** 16th Century Indian Chiefs **Obv:** Hand holding bunch of arrows **Obv. Legend:** CACIQUES DE VENEZUELA **Rev:** Head facing 3/4 right **Rev. Legend:** CACIQUES DE VENEZUELA - MARA **Edge:** Reeded **Note:** Weight varies: 5.95-6.00 grams.

Date	Mintage	F	VF	XF	Unc	BU
1957	—	—	—	BV	145	—

X# MB89 20 BOLIVARES

6.6667 g., 0.9000 Gold 0.1929 oz. AGW, 21.2 mm. **Series:** 16th Century Indian Chiefs **Obv:** Hand holding bunch of arrows **Obv. Legend:** CACIQUES DE VENEZUELA **Rev:** Head facing slightly right **Rev. Legend:** CACIQUES DE VENEZUELA - NAIGUATÁ **Edge:** Reeded **Note:** Weight varies: 5.95-6.00 grams.

Date	Mintage	F	VF	XF	Unc	BU
1957	—	—	—	BV	145	—

X# MB90 20 BOLIVARES

6.6667 g., 0.9000 Gold 0.1929 oz. AGW, 21.2 mm. **Series:** 16th Century Indian Chiefs **Obv:** Hand holding bunch of arrows **Obv. Legend:** CACIQUES DE VENEZUELA **Rev:** Head left **Rev. Legend:** CACIQUES DE VENEZUELA - SOROCAIMA **Edge:** Reeded **Note:** Weight varies: 5.95-6.00 grams.

Date	Mintage	F	VF	XF	Unc	BU
1957	—	—	—	BV	145	—

X# MB91 20 BOLIVARES

6.6667 g., 0.9000 Gold 0.1929 oz. AGW, 21.2 mm. **Series:** 16th Century Indian Chiefs **Obv:** Hand holding bunch of arrows **Obv. Legend:** CACIQUES DE VENEZUELA **Rev:** Head facing slightly right **Rev. Legend:** CACIQUES DE VENEZUELA - PARAMACAY **Edge:** Reeded **Note:** Weight varies: 5.95-6.00 grams.

Date	Mintage	F	VF	XF	Unc	BU
1957	—	—	—	BV	145	—

X# MB92 20 BOLIVARES

6.6667 g., 0.9000 Gold 0.1929 oz. AGW, 21.2 mm. **Series:** 16th Century Indian Chiefs **Obv:** Hand holding bunch of arrows **Obv. Legend:** CACIQUES DE VENEZUELA **Rev:** Head facing **Rev. Legend:** CACIQUES DE VENEZUELA - TAMANACO **Edge:** Reeded **Note:** Weight varies: 5.95-6.00 grams.

Date	Mintage	F	VF	XF	Unc	BU
1957	—	—	—	BV	145	—

X# MB93 20 BOLIVARES

6.6667 g., 0.9000 Gold 0.1929 oz. AGW, 21.2 mm. **Series:** 16th Century Indian Chiefs **Obv:** Hand holding bunch of arrows **Obv. Legend:** CACIQUES DE VENEZUELA **Rev:** Head right **Rev. Legend:** CACIQUES DE VENEZUELA - GUAICAMACUTO **Edge:** Reeded **Note:** Weight varies: 5.95-6.00 grams.

Date	Mintage	F	VF	XF	Unc	BU
1957	—	—	—	BV	145	—

X# MB94 20 BOLIVARES

6.6667 g., 0.9000 Gold 0.1929 oz. AGW, 21.2 mm. **Series:** 16th Century Indian Chiefs **Obv:** Hand holding bunch of arrows **Obv. Legend:** CACIQUES DE VENEZUELA **Rev:** Head facing slightly left **Rev. Legend:** CACIQUES DE VENEZUELA - ARICHUNA **Edge:** Reeded **Note:** Weight varies: 5.95-6.00 grams.

Date	Mintage	F	VF	XF	Unc	BU
1957	—	—	—	BV	145	—

X# MB95 20 BOLIVARES

6.6667 g., 0.9000 Gold 0.1929 oz. AGW, 21.2 mm. **Series:** 16th Century Indian Chiefs **Obv:** Hand holding bunch of arrows **Obv. Legend:** CACIQUES DE VENEZUELA **Rev:** Head 3/4 left **Rev. Legend:** CACIQUES DE VENEZUELA - MURACHI **Edge:** Reeded **Note:** Weight varies: 5.95-6.00 grams.

Date	Mintage	F	VF	XF	Unc	BU
1957	—	—	—	BV	145	—

X# MB96 20 BOLIVARES

6.6667 g., 0.9000 Gold 0.1929 oz. AGW **Series:** 16th Century Indian Chiefs **Obv:** Hand holding bunch of arrows **Obv. Legend:** CACIQUES DE VENEZUELA **Rev:** Head left **Rev. Legend:** CACIQUES DE VENEZUELA - TEREPAIMA **Edge:** Reeded **Note:** Weight varies: 5.95-6.00 grams.

Date	Mintage	F	VF	XF	Unc	BU
1957	—	—	—	BV	145	—

X# MB97 20 BOLIVARES

6.6667 g., 0.9000 Gold 0.1929 oz. AGW, 21.2 mm. **Series:** 16th Century Indian Chiefs **Obv:** Hand holding bunch of arrows **Obv. Legend:** CACIQUES DE VENEZUELA **Rev:** Head slightly left **Rev. Legend:** CACIQUES DE VENEZUELA - RARAMACONI **Edge:** Reeded **Note:** Weight varies: 5.95-6.00 grams.

Date	Mintage	F	VF	XF	Unc	BU
1957	—	—	—	BV	145	—

X# MB98 20 BOLIVARES

6.6667 g., 0.9000 Gold 0.1929 oz. AGW **Series:** 16th Century Indian Chiefs **Obv:** Hand holding bunch of arrows **Obv. Legend:** CACIQUES DE VENEZUELA **Rev:** Head facing **Rev. Legend:** CACIQUES DE VENEZUELA - MANAURE **Edge:** Reeded **Note:** Weight varies: 5.95-6.00 grams.

Date	Mintage	F	VF	XF	Unc	BU
1957	—	—	—	BV	145	—

X# MB99 20 BOLIVARES

6.6667 g., 0.9000 Gold 0.1929 oz. AGW **Series:** 16th Century Indian Chiefs **Obv:** Hand holding bunch of arrows **Obv. Legend:** CACIQUES DE VENEZUELA **Rev:** Two heads jugate almost right **Rev. Legend:** CACIQUES DE VENEZUELA - CHICURAMAY **Edge:** Reeded **Note:** Weight varies: 5.95-6.00 grams.

Date	Mintage	F	VF	XF	Unc	BU
1957	—	—	—	BV	145	—

X# MB100 20 BOLIVARES

6.6667 g., 0.9000 Gold 0.1929 oz. AGW, 21.2 mm. **Series:** 16th Century Indian Chiefs **Obv:** Hand holding bunch of arrows **Obv. Legend:** CACIQUES DE VENEZUELA **Rev:** Head 3/4 right **Rev. Legend:** CACIQUES DE VENEZUELA - YORACUY **Edge:** Reeded **Note:** Weight varies: 5.95-6.00 grams.

Date	Mintage	F	VF	XF	Unc	BU
1957	—	—	—	BV	145	—

X# MB101 20 BOLIVARES

6.6667 g., 0.9000 Gold 0.1929 oz. AGW, 21.2 mm. **Series:** 16th Century Indian Chiefs **Obv:** Hand holding bunch of arrows **Obv. Legend:** CACIQUES DE VENEZUELA **Rev:** Head facing **Rev. Legend:** CACIQUES DE VENEZUELA - URIMARE **Edge:** Reeded **Note:** Weight varies: 5.95-6.00 grams.

Date	Mintage	F	VF	XF	Unc	BU
1957	—	—	—	BV	145	—

X# MB102 20 BOLIVARES

6.6667 g., 0.9000 Gold 0.1929 oz. AGW, 21.2 mm. **Series:** 16th Century Indian Chiefs **Obv:** Hand holding bunch of arrows **Obv. Legend:** CACIQUES DE VENEZUELA **Rev:** Two heads jugate left **Rev. Legend:** CACIQUES DE VENEZUELA - YORACO **Edge:** Reeded **Note:** Weight varies: 5.95-6.00 grams.

Date	Mintage	F	VF	XF	Unc	BU
1957	—	—	—	BV	145	—

X# MB67 60 BOLIVARES

22.2000 g., 0.9000 Gold 0.6424 oz. AGW, 30.1 mm. **Series:** 16th Century Indian Chiefs **Obv:** Hand holding bunch of arrows **Obv. Legend:** CACIQUES DE VENEZUELA **Rev:** Head facing slightly left **Rev. Legend:** CACIQUES DE VENEZUELA - GUAICAIPURO **Edge:** Reeded

Date	Mintage	F	VF	XF	Unc	BU
1955	—	—	—	BV	475	—

X# MB68 60 BOLIVARES

22.2000 g., 0.9000 Gold 0.6424 oz. AGW, 30.1 mm. **Series:** 16th Century Indian Chiefs **Subject:** Hand holding bunch of arrows **Obv. Legend:** CACIQUES DE VENEZUELA **Rev:** Head facing **Rev. Legend:** CACIQUES DE VENEZUELA - TIUNA **Edge:** Reeded

Date	Mintage	F	VF	XF	Unc	BU
1955	—	—	—	BV	475	—

X# MB69 60 BOLIVARES

22.2000 g., 0.9000 Gold 0.6424 oz. AGW, 30.1 mm. **Series:** 16th Century Indian chiefs **Obv:** Hand holding bunch of arrows **Obv. Legend:** CACIQUES DE VENEZUELA **Rev:** Head facing almost right **Rev. Legend:** CACIQUES DE VENEZUELA - CHACAO **Edge:** Reeded

Date	Mintage	F	VF	XF	Unc	BU
1955	—	—	—	BV	475	—

X# MB70 60 BOLIVARES

22.2000 g., 0.9000 Gold 0.6424 oz. AGW, 30.1 mm. **Series:** 16th Century Indian Chiefs **Obv:** Hand holding bunch of arrows **Obv. Legend:** CACIQUES DE VENEZUELA **Rev:** Head facing 3/4 right **Rev. Legend:** CACIQUES DE VENEZUELA - MARA **Edge:** Reeded

Date	Mintage	F	VF	XF	Unc	BU
1955	—	—	—	BV	475	—

X# MB71 60 BOLIVARES

22.2000 g., 0.9000 Gold 0.6424 oz. AGW, 30.1 mm. **Series:** 16th Century Indian Chiefs **Obv:** Hand holding bunch of arrows **Obv. Legend:** CACIQUES DE VENEZUELA **Rev:** Head facing slightly right **Rev. Legend:** CACIQUES DE VENEZUELA - NAIGUATÁ **Edge:** Reeded

Date	Mintage	F	VF	XF	Unc	BU
1955	—	—	—	BV	475	—

X# MB72 60 BOLIVARES

22.2000 g., 0.9000 Gold 0.6424 oz. AGW, 30.1 mm. **Series:** 16th Century Indian Chiefs **Obv:** Hand holding bunch of arrows **Obv. Legend:** CACIQUES DE VENEZUELA **Rev:** Head left **Rev. Legend:** CACIQUES DE VENEZUELA - SOROCAIMA **Edge:** Reeded

Date	Mintage	F	VF	XF	Unc	BU
1955	—	—	—	BV	475	—

X# MB73 60 BOLIVARES

22.2000 g., 0.9000 Gold 0.6424 oz. AGW, 30.1 mm. **Series:** 16th Century Indian Chiefs **Obv:** Hand holding bunch of arrows **Obv. Legend:** CACIQUES DE VENEZUELA **Rev:** Head facing slightly right **Rev. Legend:** CACIQUES DE VENEZUELA - PARAMACAY **Edge:** Reeded

Date	Mintage	F	VF	XF	Unc	BU
1955	—	—	—	BV	475	—

X# MB74 60 BOLIVARES

22.2000 g., 0.9000 Gold 0.6424 oz. AGW, 30.1 mm. **Series:** 16th Century Indian Chiefs **Obv:** Hand holding bunch of arrows **Obv. Legend:** CACIQUES DE VENEZUELA **Rev:** Head facing **Rev. Legend:** CACIQUES DE VENEZUELA - TAMANACO **Edge:** Reeded

Date	Mintage	F	VF	XF	Unc	BU
1955	—	—	—	BV	475	—

X# MB75 60 BOLIVARES

22.2000 g., 0.9000 Gold 0.6424 oz. AGW, 30.1 mm. **Series:** 16th Century Indian Chiefs **Obv:** Hand holding bunch of arrows **Obv. Legend:** CACIQUES DE VENEZUELA **Rev:** Head right **Rev. Legend:** CACIQUES DE VENEZUELA - GUAICAMACUTO **Edge:** Reeded

Date	Mintage	F	VF	XF	Unc	BU
1955	—	—	—	BV	475	—

X# MB76 60 BOLIVARES

22.2000 g., 0.9000 Gold 0.6424 oz. AGW, 30.1 mm. **Series:** 16th Century Indian Chiefs **Obv:** Hand holding bunch of arrows **Obv. Legend:** CACIQUES DE VENEZUELA **Rev:** Head facing slightly left **Rev. Legend:** CACIQUES DE VENEZUELA - ARICHUNA **Edge:** Reeded

Date	Mintage	F	VF	XF	Unc	BU
1955	—	—	—	BV	475	—

X# MB77 60 BOLIVARES

22.2000 g., 0.9000 Gold 0.6424 oz. AGW, 30.1 mm. **Series:** 16th Century Indian Chiefs **Obv:** Hand holding bunch of arrows **Obv. Legend:** CACIQUES DE VENEZUELA **Rev:** Head 3/4 left **Rev. Legend:** CACIQUES DE VENEZUELA - MURACHI **Edge:** Reeded

Date	Mintage	F	VF	XF	Unc	BU
1955	—	—	—	BV	475	—

X# MB78 60 BOLIVARES

22.2000 g., 0.9000 Gold 0.6424 oz. AGW, 30.1 mm. **Series:** 16th Century Indian Chiefs **Obv:** Hand holding bunch of arrows **Obv. Legend:** CACIQUES DE VENEZUELA **Rev:** Head left **Rev. Legend:** CACIQUES DE VENEZUELA - TEREPAIMA **Edge:** Reeded

Date	Mintage	F	VF	XF	Unc	BU
1955	—	—	—	BV	475	—

X# MB79 60 BOLIVARES

22.2000 g., 0.9000 Gold 0.6424 oz. AGW, 30.1 mm. **Series:** 16th Century Indian Chiefs **Obv:** Hand holding bunch of arrows **Obv. Legend:** CACIQUES DE VENEZUELA **Rev:** Head slightly left **Rev. Legend:** CACIQUES DE VENEZUELA - PARAMACONI **Edge:** Reeded

Date	Mintage	F	VF	XF	Unc	BU
1955	—	—	—	BV	475	—

X# MB80 60 BOLIVARES

22.2000 g., 0.9000 Gold 0.6424 oz. AGW, 30.1 mm. **Series:** 16th Century Indian Chiefs **Obv:** Hand holding bunch of arrows **Obv. Legend:** CACIQUES DE VENEZUELA **Rev:** Head facing **Rev. Legend:** CACIQUES DE VENEZUELA - MANAURE **Edge:** Reeded

Date	Mintage	F	VF	XF	Unc	BU
1955	—	—	—	BV	475	—

X# MB81 60 BOLIVARES

22.2000 g., 0.9000 Gold 0.6424 oz. AGW, 30.1 mm. **Series:** 16th Century Indian Chiefs **Obv:** Hand holding bunch of arrows **Obv. Legend:** CACIQUES DE VENEZUELA **Rev:** Two heads jugate almost right **Rev. Legend:** CACIQUES DE VENEZUELA - CHICURAMAY **Edge:** Reeded

Date	Mintage	F	VF	XF	Unc	BU
1955	—	—	—	BV	475	—

X# MB82 60 BOLIVARES

22.2000 g., 0.9000 Gold 0.6424 oz. AGW, 30.1 mm. **Series:** 16th Century Indian Chiefs **Obv:** Hand holding bunch of arrows **Obv. Legend:** CACIQUES DE VENEZUELA **Rev:** Head 3/4 right **Rev. Legend:** CACIQUES DE VENEZUELA - YARACUY **Edge:** Reeded

Date	Mintage	F	VF	XF	Unc	BU
1955	—	—	—	BV	475	—

X# MB83 60 BOLIVARES

22.2000 g., 0.9000 Gold 0.6424 oz. AGW, 30.1 mm. **Series:** 16th Century Indian Chiefs **Obv:** Hand holding bunch of arrows **Obv. Legend:** CACIQUES DE VENEZUELA **Rev:** Head facing **Rev. Legend:** CACIQUES DE VENEZUELA - URIMARE **Edge:** Reeded

Date	Mintage	F	VF	XF	Unc	BU
1955	—	—	—	BV	475	—

X# MB84 60 BOLIVARES

22.2000 g., 0.9000 Gold 0.6424 oz. AGW, 30.1 mm. **Series:** 16th Century Indian Chiefs **Obv:** Hand holding bunch of arrows **Obv. Legend:** CACIQUES DE VENEZUELA **Rev:** Two heads jugate left **Rev. Legend:** CACIQUES DE VENEZUELA - YORACO **Edge:** Reeded

Date	Mintage	F	VF	XF	Unc	BU
1955	—	—	—	BV	475	—

X# MB103 60 BOLIVARES

20.0000 g., 0.9000 Gold 0.5787 oz. AGW, 37.10 mm. **Series:** 16th Century Chiefs, 1955-1960 **Obv:** Condor **Obv. Legend:** CACIQUES DE VENEZUELA **Rev:** Head facing slightly left **Rev. Legend:** CACIQUES DE VENEZUELA - GUAICAIPURO **Edge:** Reeded

Date	Mintage	F	VF	XF	Unc	BU
ND(1961)	—	—	—	BV	425	—

X# MB104 60 BOLIVARES

20.0000 g., 0.9000 Gold 0.5787 oz. AGW, 37.10 mm. **Series:** 16th Century Chiefs, 1955-1960 **Obv:** Condor **Obv. Legend:** CACIQUES DE VENEZUELA **Rev:** Head facing **Rev. Legend:** CACIQUES DE VENEZUELA - TIUNA **Edge:** Reeded

Date	Mintage	F	VF	XF	Unc	BU
ND(1961)	—	—	—	BV	425	—

X# MB105 60 BOLIVARES

20.0000 g., 0.9000 Gold 0.5787 oz. AGW, 37.10 mm. **Series:** 16th Century Chiefs, 1955-1960 **Obv:** Condor **Obv. Legend:** CACIQUES DE VENEZUELA **Rev:** Head facing almost righ **Rev. Legend:** CACIQUES DE VENEZUELA - CHACAO **Edge:** Reeded

Date	Mintage	F	VF	XF	Unc	BU
ND(1961)	—	—	—	BV	425	—

X# MB106 60 BOLIVARES

20.0000 g., 0.9000 Gold 0.5787 oz. AGW, 37.10 mm. **Series:** 16th Century Chiefs, 1955-1960 **Obv:** Condor **Obv. Legend:** CACIQUES DE VENEZUELA **Rev:** Head facing 3/4 right **Rev. Legend:** CACIQUES DE VENEZUELA - MARA **Edge:** Reeded

Date	Mintage	F	VF	XF	Unc	BU
ND(1961)	—	—	—	BV	425	—

X# MB107 60 BOLIVARES

20.0000 g., 0.9000 Gold 0.5787 oz. AGW, 37.10 mm. **Series:** 16th Century Chiefs, 1955-1960 **Obv:** Condor **Obv. Legend:** CACIQUES DE VENEZUELA **Rev:** Head facing slightly right **Rev. Legend:** CACIQUES DE VENEZUELA - NAIGUATÁ **Edge:** Reeded

Date	Mintage	F	VF	XF	Unc	BU
ND(1961)	—	—	—	BV	425	—

X# MB109 60 BOLIVARES

20.0000 g., 0.9000 Gold 0.5787 oz. AGW, 37.10 mm. **Series:** 16th Century Chiefs, 1955-1960 **Obv:** Condor **Obv. Legend:** CACIQUES DE VENEZUELA **Rev:** Head left **Rev. Legend:** CACIQUES DE VENEZUELA - SOROCAIMA **Edge:** Reeded

Date	Mintage	F	VF	XF	Unc	BU
ND(1961)	—	—	—	BV	425	—

X# MB110 60 BOLIVARES

20.0000 g., 0.9000 Gold 0.5787 oz. AGW, 37.10 mm. **Series:** 16th Century Chiefs, 1955-1960 **Obv:** Condor **Obv. Legend:** CACIQUES DE VENEZUELA **Rev:** Head facing slightly right **Rev. Legend:** CACIQUES DE VENEZUELA - PARAMACAY **Edge:** Reeded

Date	Mintage	F	VF	XF	Unc	BU
ND(1961)	—	—	—	BV	425	—

X# MB111 60 BOLIVARES

20.0000 g., 0.9000 Gold 0.5787 oz. AGW, 37.10 mm. **Series:** 16th Century Chiefs, 1955-1960 **Obv:** Condor **Obv. Legend:** CACIQUES DE VENEZUELA **Rev:** Head facing **Rev. Legend:** CACIQUES DE VENEZUELA - TAMANACO **Edge:** Reeded

Date	Mintage	F	VF	XF	Unc	BU
ND(1961)	—	—	—	BV	425	—

X# MB112 60 BOLIVARES

20.0000 g., 0.9000 Gold 0.5787 oz. AGW, 37.10 mm. **Series:** 16th Century Chiefs, 1955-1960 **Obv:** Condor **Obv. Legend:** CACIQUES DE VENEZUELA **Rev:** Head right **Rev. Legend:** CACIQUES DE VENEZUELA - GUAICAMACUTO **Edge:** Reeded

Date	Mintage	F	VF	XF	Unc	BU
ND(1961)	—	—	—	BV	425	—

X# MB113 60 BOLIVARES

20.0000 g., 0.9000 Gold 0.5787 oz. AGW, 37.10 mm. **Series:** 16th Century Chiefs, 1955-1960 **Obv:** Condor **Obv. Legend:** CACIQUES DE VENEZUELA **Rev:** Head facing slightly left **Rev. Legend:** CACIQUES DE VENEZUELA - ARICHUNA **Edge:** Reeded **Note:** Prev. XMB74.

Date	Mintage	F	VF	XF	Unc	BU
ND(1961)	—	—	—	BV	425	—

X# MB114 60 BOLIVARES

20.0000 g., 0.9000 Gold 0.5787 oz. AGW, 37.10 mm. **Series:** 16th Century Chiefs, 1955-1960 **Obv:** Condor **Obv. Legend:** CACIQUES DE VENEZUELA **Rev:** Head 3/4 left **Rev. Legend:** CACIQUES DE VENEZUELA - MURACHI **Edge:** Reeded

Date	Mintage	F	VF	XF	Unc	BU
ND(1961)	—	—	—	BV	425	—

X# MB115 60 BOLIVARES

20.0000 g., 0.9000 Gold 0.5787 oz. AGW, 37.10 mm. **Series:** 16th Century Chiefs, 1955-1960 **Obv:** Condor **Obv. Legend:** CACIQUES DE VENEZUELA **Rev:** Head left **Rev. Legend:** CACIQUES DE VENEZUELA - TEREPAIMA **Edge:** Reeded

Date	Mintage	F	VF	XF	Unc	BU
ND(1961)	—	—	—	BV	425	—

X# MB116 60 BOLIVARES

20.0000 g., 0.9000 Gold 0.5787 oz. AGW, 37.10 mm. **Series:** 16th Century Chiefs, 1955-1960 **Obv:** Condor **Obv. Legend:** CACIQUES DE VENEZUELA **Rev:** Head slightly left **Rev. Legend:** CACIQUES DE VENEZUELA - PARAMACONI **Edge:** Reeded

Date	Mintage	F	VF	XF	Unc	BU
ND(1961)	—	—	—	BV	425	—

VIETNAM

X# MB117 60 BOLIVARES
20.0000 g., 0.9000 Gold 0.5787 oz. AGW, 37.10 mm. **Series:** 16th Century Chiefs, 1955-1960 **Obv:** Condor **Obv. Legend:** CACIQUES DE VENEZUELA **Rev:** Head facing **Rev. Legend:** CACIQUES DE VENEZUELA - MANAURE **Edge:** Reeded

Date	Mintage	F	VF	XF	Unc	BU
ND(1961)	—	—	—	BV	425	—

X# MB118 60 BOLIVARES
20.0000 g., 0.9000 Gold 0.5787 oz. AGW, 37.10 mm. **Series:** 16th Century Chiefs, 1955-1960 **Obv:** Condor **Obv. Legend:** CACIQUES DE VENEZUELA **Rev:** Two heads jugate almost right **Rev. Legend:** CACIQUES DE VENEZUELA - CHICURAMAY **Edge:** Reeded

Date	Mintage	F	VF	XF	Unc	BU
ND(1961)	—	—	—	BV	425	—

X# MB119 60 BOLIVARES
20.0000 g., 0.9000 Gold 0.5787 oz. AGW, 37.10 mm. **Series:** 16th Century Chiefs, 1955-1960 **Obv:** Condor **Obv. Legend:** CACIQUES DE VENEZUELA **Rev:** Head 3/4 right **Rev. Legend:** CACIQUES DE VENEZUELA - YARACUY **Edge:** Reeded

Date	Mintage	F	VF	XF	Unc	BU
ND(1961)	—	—	—	BV	425	—

X# MB120 60 BOLIVARES
20.0000 g., 0.9000 Gold 0.5787 oz. AGW, 37.10 mm. **Series:** 16th Century Chiefs, 1955-1960 **Obv:** Condor **Obv. Legend:** CACIQUES DE VENEZUELA **Rev:** Two heads jugate left **Rev. Legend:** CACIQUES DE VENEZUELA - YORACO **Edge:** Reeded

Date	Mintage	F	VF	XF	Unc	BU
ND(1961)	—	—	—	BV	425	—

ESSAIS

KM#	Date	Mintage	Identification	Mkt Val
EA18	1875	—	Venezolano. 0.9000 Gold. 16 mm.	20,000

Note: Akers Pittman sale 8-99, very choice Proof realized $18,400

| E19 | 1875 | — | 5 Venezolanos. Gold-Plated Copper. 22 mm. | 15,000 |

| E20 | 1875 | — | 5 Venezolanos. 0.9000 Gold. Arms within sprigs above banner, cornucopias above. Head right. | 15,000 |

Note: Akers Pittman sale 8-99, very choice Proof realized $20,700

E21	1875	—	10 Venezolanos. Gold-Plated Copper. 28 mm.	25,000
E22	1875	—	10 Venezolanos. 0.9000 Gold.	25,000
E23	1875	—	20 Venezolanos. Gold-Plated Copper.	15,000
E24	1875	—	20 Venezolanos. 0.9000 Gold. 35 mm.	16,000

PATTERNS
Including off metal strikes

KM#	Date	Mintage	Identification	Mkt Val
Pn44	1875	—	10 Venezolanos. 0.9000 Gold.	—

Note: Akers Pittman sale 8-99, choice Proof realized $25,300+

| Pn46 | 1888 | — | 50 Bolivares. 0.9000 Gold. | — |

Note: Baldwin's Auction 12-99, realized $37,500

Pn53	1990(c)	—	50 Bolivares. Gold. Medal rotation	650
Pn54	1990(c)	—	50 Bolivares. Gold. Coin rotation.	650
Pn55	1990(c)	—	50 Bolivares. Gold.	1,100

KM#	Date	Mintage	Identification	Mkt Val
Pn56	1990	—	5000 Bolivares. Copper-Nickel. Y65.	2,000

TRIAL STRIKES

KM#	Date	Mintage	Identification	Mkt Val
TS12	1975(c)	—	500 Bolivares. Gold plated; Uniface reverse.	15,000
TS11	1975(c)	—	500 Bolivares. Gold plated; Uniface obverse.	15,000

MINT SETS

KM#	Date	Mintage	Identification	Issue Price	Mkt Val
MS1	1975 (3)	—	Y46-48	250	725

PROOF SETS

KM#	Date	Mintage	Identification	Issue Price	Mkt Val
PS1	1975 (3)	—	Y46-48	—	1,350

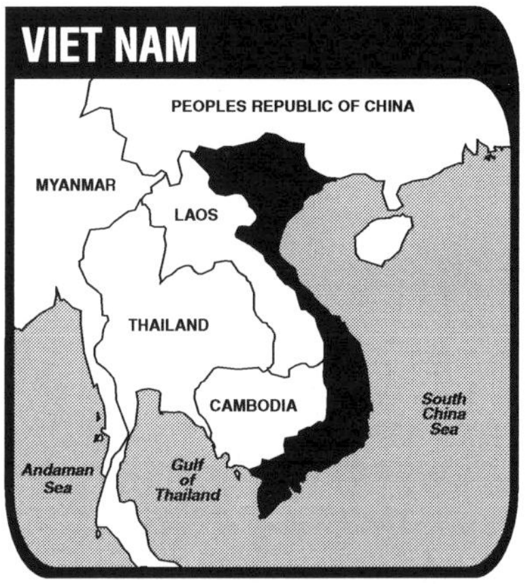

VIET NAM

In 207 B.C. a Chinese general set up the Kingdom of Nam-Viet on the Red River. This kingdom was over-thrown by the Chinese under the Han Dynasty in 111 B.C., where upon the country became a Chinese province under the name of Giao-Chi, which was later changed to Annam or peaceful or pacified South. Chinese rule was maintained until 968, when the Vietnamese became independent until 1407 when China again invaded Viet Nam. The Chinese were driven out in 1428 and the country became independent and named Dai-Viet. Gia Long united the North and South as Dai Nam in 1802.

After the French conquered Dai Nam, they split the country into three parts. The South became the Colony of Cochin china; the North became the Protectorate of Tonkin; and the central became the Protectorate of Annam. The emperors were permitted to have their capital in Hue and to produce small quantities of their coins, presentation pieces, and bullion bars. Annam had an area of 57,840 sq. mi. (141,806 sq. km.) and a population of about 6 million. Chief products of the area are silk, cinnamon and rice. There are important mineral deposits in the mountainous inland.

EMPERORS

Thanh Thai, 1888-1907 — 成泰

Duy Tan, 1907-1916 — 維新

Khai Dinh, 1916-1925 — 啓定

Bao Dai, 1926-1945 — 保大

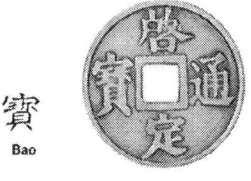

IDENTIFICATION

Khai 啓

Bao 寶

Dinh 定

Thong 通

VIETNAM

CYCLICAL DATES

	庚	辛	壬	癸	甲	乙	丙	丁	戊	己
戌	1850 1910		1862 1922		1874 1934		1886 1946		1838 1898	
亥		1851 1911		1863 1923		1875 1935		1887 1947		1839 1899
子	1840 1900		1852 1912		1864 1924		1876 1936		1888 1948	
丑		1841 1901		1853 1913		1865 1925		1877 1937		1889 1949
寅	1830 1890		1842 1902		1854 1914		1866 1926		1878 1938	
卯		1831 1891		1843 1903		1855 1915		1867 1927		1879 1939
辰	1880 1940		1832 1892		1844 1904		1856 1916		1868 1928	
巳		1881 1941		1833 1893		1845 1905		1857 1917		1869 1929
午	1870 1930		1882 1942		1834 1894		1846 1906		1858 1918	
未		1871 1931		1883 1943		1835 1895		1847 1907		1859 1919
申	1860 1920		1872 1932		1884 1944		1836 1896		1848 1908	
酉		1861 1921		1873 1933		1885 1945		1837 1897		1849 1909

NOTE: This table has been adapted from *Chinese Bank Notes* by Ward Smith and Brian Matravers.

Cyclical dates consist of a pair of characters one of which indicates the animal associated with that year. Every 60 years, this pair of characters is repeated. The first character of a cyclical date corresponds to a character in the first row of the chart above. The second character is taken from the column at left. In this catalog where a cyclical date is used, the abbreviation CD appears before the A.D. date.

Annamese silver and gold coins were sometimes dated according to the year of the emperor's reign. In this case, simply add the year of reign to the year in which the reign would be 1849 (1847 plus 3 = 1850 -1 = 1849 or 1847 = 1; 1848 = 2; 1849 = 3). In this catalog the A.D. date appears in parenthesis followed by the year of reign.

NUMERALS

NUMBER	CONVENTIONAL	FORMAL	COMMERCIAL
1	一 元	壹 弌	一
2	二	弍 貳	〢
3	三	叁 弎	〣
4	四	肆	〤
5	五	伍	〥
6	六	陸	〦
7	七	柒	〧
8	八	捌	〨
9	九	玖	〩
10	十	拾 什	十
20	十二 or 廿	拾貳	〢十
25	五十二 or 五廿	伍拾貳	〢十〥
30	十三 or 卅	拾叁	〣十
100	百 一	佰壹	一百
1,000	千 一	仟壹	一千
10,000	萬 一	萬壹	一万
100,000	萬十 億一	萬拾 億壹	十万
1,000,000	萬百 一	萬佰壹	一百万

NOTE: This table has been adapted from *Chinese Bank Notes* by Ward Smith and Brian Matravers.

MONETARY SYSTEM
10 Dong (zinc) = 1 Dong (copper)
600 Dong (zinc) = 1 Quan (string of ¬¬cash)
Approx. 2600 Dong (zinc) = 1 Piastre
NOTE: Ratios between metals changed frequently, therefore the above is given as an approximate relationship.

SILVER and GOLD
2-1/2 Quan = 1 Lang
10 Tien (Mace) = 1 Lang (Tael)
14 to 17 Piastres (silver) = 1 Piastre (gold)
14 to 17 Lang (silver) = 1 Lang (gold)

The real currency of Dai Nam and An Nam consisted of copper and zinc coins similar to Chinese cash-style coins and were called sapeques and dongs by the French.

The smaller gold pieces saw a limited circulation, mainly among the local merchants and foreign traders. The larger gold pieces were used mainly for hoarding, while most of these were intended as rewards and gifts. Many of these gold pieces appear to have been struck from silver coin dies or vice-versa.

NOTE: Sch# are in reference to Albert Schroeder's *Annam, Etudes Numismatiques* or to the same numbering system used in *Gold and Silver Coins of Annam*", by Bernard Permar and John Novak.

CHARACTER IDENTIFICATION

The Vietnamese used Chinese-style characters for official documents and coins and bars. Some were modified to their liking and will sometimes not match the Chinese character for the same word. The above identification and this table will translate most of the Vietnamese characters (Chinese-style) on their coins and bars described herein.
Chinese/French
Vietnamese/English

安南
An Nam = name of the French protectorate

大南
Dai Nam = name of the country under Gia Long's Nguyen dynasty

越南
Viet Nam = name used briefly during Minh Mang's reign and became the modern name of the country

河內
Ha Noi = city and province in north Dai NamTonkin

內帑
Noi Thang = court treasury in the capital of Hue

年
Nien = year

造
Tao = made

銀
Ngan = silver

金
Kim = gold

錢
Tien = a weight of about 3.78 grams

兩
Lang = a weight of about 37.78 grams

貫
Quan = a string of cash-style coins

分
Phan = a weight of about .38 grams

文
Van = cash-style coins

中平
Trung Binh = a name of weight standard

SOUTH DAI VIET
GOLD MILLED COINAGE

X# 13 7 TIEN
Gold **Ruler:** Tu Duc **Obv:** Large characters **Rev:** Large, thick facing dragons **Note:** Schroeder #402.2. Weight varies: 26.45-27.00 grams. Prev. KM#552.

Date	Mintage	VG	F	VF	XF	Unc
ND(1848-83)	—	1,250	2,500	4,000	6,000	—

Note: A French copy

UNITED DAI NAM
GOLD MILLED COINAGE

KM# 318 1/2 TIEN
1.8000 g., Gold **Ruler:** Thieu Tri **Obv. Inscription:** "Thieu Tri Thong Bao" **Rev:** Blank **Note:** Schroeder #257.

Date	Mintage	VG	F	VF	XF	Unc
ND(1841-47)	—	150	275	425	650	—

KM# 212 TIEN
Gold **Ruler:** Minh Mang **Obv. Inscription:** "Minh Mang Thong Bao" **Rev:** Five planets **Note:** Schroeder #209.1. Weight varies: 3.65-4.00 grams.

Date	Mintage	VG	F	VF	XF	Unc
ND(1820-41)	—	300	550	850	1,350	—

KM# 213 TIEN
Gold **Ruler:** Minh Mang **Rev:** Mirror image **Note:** Schroeder #209.2.

Date	Mintage	VG	F	VF	XF	Unc
ND(1820-41)	—	300	550	850	1,350	—

VIETNAM 755

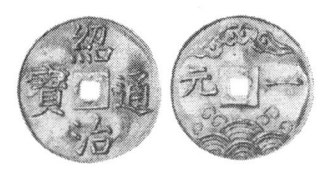

KM# 320 TIEN
Gold Ruler: Thieu Tri Obv. Inscription: "Thieu Tri Thong Bao".
Rev. Inscription: "Nhat Nguyen" Note: Schroeder #250B.

Date	Mintage	VG	F	VF	XF	Unc
ND(1841-47)	—	350	650	1,100	1,750	—

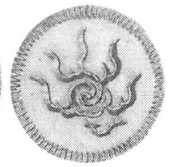

KM# 321 TIEN
Gold Ruler: Thieu Tri Rev: Flaming sun with lower flames right
Note: Schroeder #287.1.

Date	Mintage	VG	F	VF	XF	Unc
ND(1841-47)	—	325	600	950	1,450	—

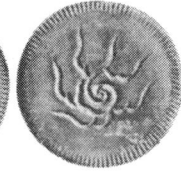

KM# 322 TIEN
Gold Ruler: Thieu Tri Rev: Flaming sun with lower flames left
Note: Schroeder #287.2.

Date	Mintage	VG	F	VF	XF	Unc
ND(1841-47)	—	325	600	950	1,450	—

KM# 323 TIEN
3.8000 g., Gold Ruler: Thieu Tri Rev: Scepter and swastika
Note: Schroeder #288.

Date	Mintage	VG	F	VF	XF	Unc
ND(1841-47)	—	325	600	950	1,450	—

KM# 324 TIEN
4.0000 g., Gold Ruler: Thieu Tri Rev: Guitar Note: Schroeder #289.1.

Date	Mintage	VG	F	VF	XF	Unc
ND(1841-47)	—	325	600	950	1,450	—

KM# 325 TIEN
Gold Ruler: Thieu Tri Rev: Mirror image Note: Schroeder #289.2.

Date	Mintage	VG	F	VF	XF	Unc
ND(1841-47)	—	—	—	—	1,800	—

KM# 326 TIEN
Gold Ruler: Thieu Tri Rev: Horn Note: Schroeder #290.

Date	Mintage	VG	F	VF	XF	Unc
ND(1841-47)	—	325	600	950	1,450	—

KM# 327 TIEN
3.8000 g., Gold Ruler: Thieu Tri Rev: Fan Note: Schroeder #291.

Date	Mintage	VG	F	VF	XF	Unc
ND(1841-47)	—	325	600	950	1,450	—

KM# 329 TIEN
4.2000 g., Gold Ruler: Thieu Tri Rev: Clappers Note: Schroeder #293.

Date	Mintage	VG	F	VF	XF	Unc
ND(1841-47)	—	325	600	950	1,450	—

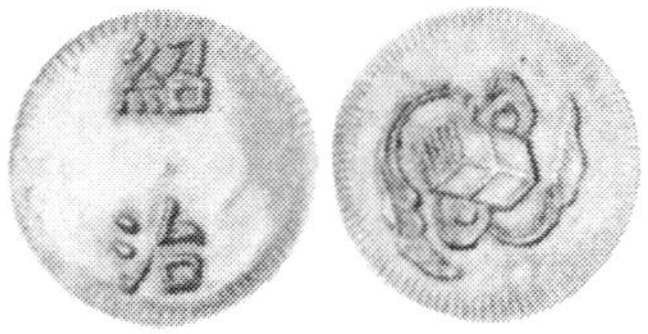

KM# 330 TIEN
4.0000 g., Gold Ruler: Thieu Tri Rev: Books Note: Schroeder #294.

Date	Mintage	VG	F	VF	XF	Unc
ND(1841-47)	—	325	600	950	1,450	—

KM# 331 TIEN
3.8000 g., Gold Ruler: Thieu Tri Rev: "Tam Da" above the Three Plenties Note: Schroeder #295.

Date	Mintage	VG	F	VF	XF	Unc
ND(1841-47)	—	325	600	950	1,450	—

KM# 328 TIEN
4.0000 g., Gold Ruler: Thieu Tri Rev: Calabash Note: Schroeder #292.

Date	Mintage	VG	F	VF	XF	Unc
ND(1841-47)	—	325	600	950	1,450	—

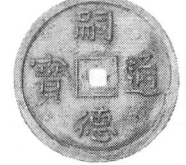

KM# 515 TIEN
3.7000 g., Gold Ruler: Tu Duc Rev. Inscription: "Nhat Nguyen"
Note: Schroeder #353B.

Date	Mintage	VG	F	VF	XF	Unc
ND(1848-83)	—	—	1,350	2,000	3,000	—

KM# 516 TIEN
3.8000 g., Gold Ruler: Tu Duc Rev: Inscription on dragon Rev. Inscription: "Nhat Nguyen Tien Viet Tu" Note: Schroeder #377.

Date	Mintage	VG	F	VF	XF	Unc
ND(1848-83)	—	325	600	950	1,450	—

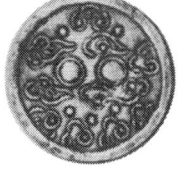

KM# 517 TIEN
Gold Ruler: Tu Duc Rev: Sun, moon, and five planets Note: Schroeder #386A.

Date	Mintage	VG	F	VF	XF	Unc
ND(1848-83)	—	325	600	950	1,450	—

KM# 518 TIEN
Gold Ruler: Tu Duc Rev: Scepter and swastika Note: Schroeder #388B.

Date	Mintage	VG	F	VF	XF	Unc
ND(1848-83)	—	650	1,100	1,800	3,000	—

KM# 215 1-1/2 TIEN
5.7000 g., Gold Ruler: Minh Mang Obv. Inscription: "Minh Mang" Rev: Five Precious symbols Note: Schroeder #211.
Weight varies: 5.40-6.50 grams.

Date	Mintage	VG	F	VF	XF	Unc
ND(1820-41)	—	350	650	1,000	1,600	—

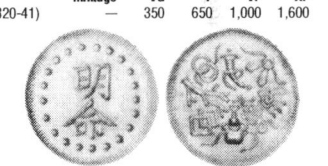

KM# 216 1-1/2 TIEN
5.7000 g., Gold Ruler: Minh Mang Rev: Eight Precious symbols
Note: Schroeder #212.

Date	Mintage	VG	F	VF	XF	Unc
ND(1820-41)	—	350	650	1,000	1,600	—

KM# 217 1-1/2 TIEN
5.7000 g., Gold Ruler: Minh Mang Rev: Mirror image Note: Schroeder #213.

Date	Mintage	VG	F	VF	XF	Unc
ND(1820-41)	—	350	650	1,000	1,600	—

756 VIETNAM

KM# 520 1-1/2 TIEN
5.6000 g., Gold **Ruler:** Tu Duc **Obv. Inscription:** "Tu Duc Thong Bao" **Rev. Inscription:** "Su Dan Phu Tho" **Note:** Schroeder #406.

Date	Mintage	VG	F	VF	XF	Unc
ND(1848-83)	—	350	650	950	1,450	—

KM# 219 2 TIEN
7.8000 g., Gold **Ruler:** Minh Mang **Obv. Inscription:** "Minh Mang" **Rev:** Inscription above the Three Plenties **Rev. Inscription:** "Tam Da" **Note:** Schroeder #210.

Date	Mintage	VG	F	VF	XF	Unc
ND(1820-41)	—	350	650	1,000	1,600	—

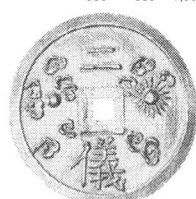

KM# 333 2 TIEN
Gold **Ruler:** Thieu Tri **Obv. Inscription:** "Thieu Tri Thong Bao" **Rev:** Inscription between sun and moon **Rev. Inscription:** "Nhi Nghi" **Note:** Schroeder #281.

Date	Mintage	VG	F	VF	XF	Unc
ND(1841-47)	—	350	650	1,000	1,600	—

KM# 522 2 TIEN
7.3000 g., Gold **Ruler:** Tu Duc **Obv. Inscription:** "Tu Duc Thong Bao" **Rev:** Inscription on dragon **Rev. Inscription:** "Nhi Tien Viet Hien" **Note:** Schroeder #378.

Date	Mintage	VG	F	VF	XF	Unc
ND(1848-83)	—	350	650	1,000	1,600	—

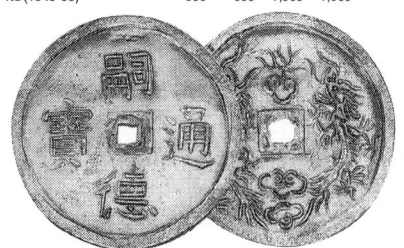

KM# 523 2 TIEN
Gold **Ruler:** Tu Duc **Rev:** Flaming sun between facing dragons **Note:** Schroeder #402B.

Date	Mintage	VG	F	VF	XF	Unc
ND(1848-83)	—	400	750	1,150	1,750	—

KM# 335 2-1/2 TIEN
8.9000 g., Gold **Ruler:** Thieu Tri **Obv. Inscription:** "Thieu Tri Thong Bao" **Rev:** Facing dragon **Note:** Schroeder #280B.

Date	Mintage	VG	F	VF	XF	Unc
ND(1841-47)	—	—	—	—	3,250	—

KM# 525 2-1/2 TIEN
8.9000 g., Gold **Ruler:** Tu Duc **Obv. Inscription:** "Thieu Tri Thong Bao, Trieu Dan Lai Chi" **Rev:** Inscription around facing dragon **Rev. Inscription:** "Long Van Khe Hoi" **Note:** Schroeder #375.

Date	Mintage	VG	F	VF	XF	Unc
ND(1848-83)	—	400	700	1,150	1,700	—

KM# 221 3 TIEN
Gold **Ruler:** Minh Mang **Obv:** Large sun, large inscription **Obv. Inscription:** "Minh Mang Thong Bao" **Note:** Schroeder #207. Weight varies: 11.50-13.30 grams.

Date	Mintage	VG	F	VF	XF	Unc
ND(1820-41)	—	550	1,000	1,700	2,600	—

KM# 226 3 TIEN
Gold **Ruler:** Minh Mang **Obv:** Small sun, large inscription **Note:** Schroeder #208.

Date	Mintage	VG	F	VF	XF	Unc
Yr. 14 (1833)	—	550	1,000	1,700	2,600	—

KM# 227 3 TIEN
Gold **Ruler:** Minh Mang **Obv:** Small sun, medium inscription **Note:** Schroeder #206C.

Date	Mintage	VG	F	VF	XF	Unc
Yr. 15 (1834)	—	550	1,000	1,700	2,600	—

KM# 229 3 TIEN
Gold **Ruler:** Minh Mang **Obv:** Small sun, small inscription **Note:** Schroeder #206D.

Date	Mintage	VG	F	VF	XF	Unc
Yr. 16 (1835)	—	—	—	2,000	—	—

KM# 337 3 TIEN
13.5400 g., Gold **Ruler:** Thieu Tri **Obv. Inscription:** "Thieu Tri Thong Bao" **Rev:** Large dragon **Note:** Schroeder #285.

Date	Mintage	VG	F	VF	XF	Unc
ND(1841-47)	—	550	1,000	1,700	2,600	—

KM# 338 3 TIEN
13.5400 g., Gold **Ruler:** Thieu Tri **Rev:** Small dragon left **Note:** Schroeder #286.

Date	Mintage	VG	F	VF	XF	Unc
ND(1841-47)	—	550	1,000	1,700	2,600	—

KM# 529 3 TIEN
11.2000 g., Gold **Ruler:** Tu Duc **Rev:** Inscription on facing dragon **Rev. Inscription:** "Long Van" **Note:** Schroeder #373B.

Date	Mintage	VG	F	VF	XF	Unc
ND(1848-83)	—	600	1,100	1,900	2,900	—

KM# 530 3 TIEN
11.3000 g., Gold **Ruler:** Tu Duc **Rev:** Inscription on facing dragon **Rev. Inscription:** "Tam Tien Viet Lang" **Note:** Schroeder #379B.

Date	Mintage	VG	F	VF	XF	Unc
ND(1848-83)	—	550	1,000	1,700	2,600	—

KM# 528 3 TIEN
11.0000 g., Gold **Ruler:** Tu Duc **Rev:** Inscription above Three Longevities **Rev. Inscription:** "Tam Thao" **Note:** Schroeder #407.

Date	Mintage	VG	F	VF	XF	Unc
ND(1848-83)	—	600	1,100	1,900	2,900	—

KM# 527 3 TIEN
13.2400 g., Gold **Ruler:** Tu Duc **Obv. Inscription:** "Tu duc Thong Bao" **Note:** Schroeder #413.

Date	Mintage	VG	F	VF	XF	Unc
ND(1848-83)	—	550	1,000	1,700	2,600	—

KM# 535 4 TIEN
15.0000 g., Gold **Ruler:** Tu Duc **Rev:** Inscription on dragon **Rev. Inscription:** "Tu Tien Viet De" **Note:** Schroeder #380.

Date	Mintage	VG	F	VF	XF	Unc
ND(1848-83)	—	650	1,200	2,100	3,200	—

VIETNAM

KM# 536 4 TIEN
13.1600 g., Gold **Ruler:** Tu Duc **Rev:** Flaming sun between facing dragons **Note:** Schroeder #402C.

Date	Mintage	VG	F	VF	XF	Unc
ND(1848-83)	—	—	—	—	7,000	

KM# 532 4 TIEN
14.7000 g., Gold **Ruler:** Tu Duc **Obv. Inscription:** "Tu duc Thong Bao" **Rev. Inscription:** "Su Dan Phu Tho" **Note:** Schroeder #406.

Date	Mintage	VG	F	VF	XF	Unc
ND(1848-83)	—	650	1,200	2,100	3,200	—

KM# 533 4 TIEN
Gold **Ruler:** Tu Duc **Obv:** Large characters **Rev:** Inscription between the Four Perfections **Rev. Inscription:** "Tu My" **Note:** Schroeder #409.1. Weight varies: 14.50-15.20 grams.

Date	Mintage	VG	F	VF	XF	Unc
ND(1848-83)	—	650	1,200	2,100	3,200	—

KM# 534 4 TIEN
Gold **Ruler:** Tu Duc **Obv:** Small characters **Rev:** Finer style **Note:** Schroeder #409.2.

Date	Mintage	VG	F	VF	XF	Unc
ND(1848-83)	—	650	1,200	2,100	3,200	—

KM# 223 5 TIEN
19.2000 g., Gold **Ruler:** Minh Mang **Obv. Inscription:** "Minh Mang Thong Bao" **Rev. Inscription:** "Phu Tho Da Nam" **Note:** Schroeder #205.

Date	Mintage	VG	F	VF	XF	Unc
ND(1820-41)	—	1,000	2,000	—	5,000	

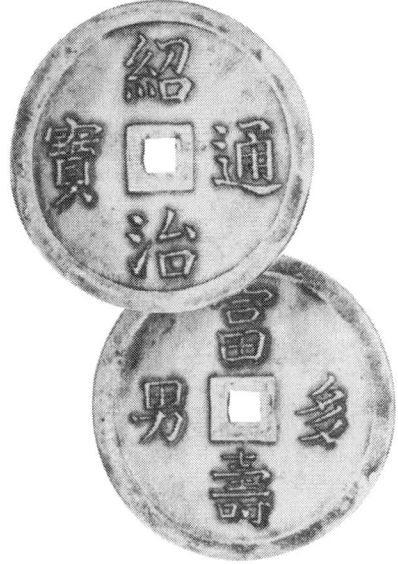

KM# 340 5 TIEN
17.6100 g., Gold **Ruler:** Thieu Tri **Obv. Inscription:** "Thieu Tri Thong Bao" **Rev. Inscription:** "Phu Tho Da Nam" **Note:** Schroeder #253B.

Date	Mintage	VG	F	VF	XF	Unc
ND(1841-47)	—	1,100	2,200	3,500	5,500	—

KM# 341 5 TIEN
19.5000 g., Gold **Ruler:** Thieu Tri **Obv. Inscription:** "Thieu Tri Thong Bao, Van The Vinh Lai" **Note:** Schroeder #279.

Date	Mintage	VG	F	VF	XF	Unc
ND(1841-47)	—	1,100	—	3,500	5,500	

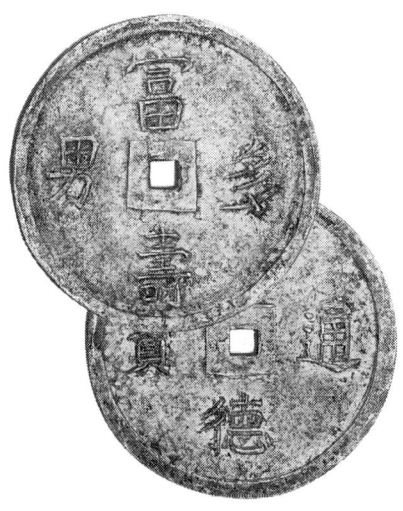

KM# 538 5 TIEN
Gold **Ruler:** Tu Duc **Obv. Inscription:** "Tu Duc Thong Bao" **Rev:** Inscription around dragon **Rev. Inscription:** "Long Van Khe Hoi" **Note:** Schroeder #374B. Weight varies: 18.00-20.00 grams.

Date	Mintage	VG	F	VF	XF	Unc
ND(1848-83)	—	950	1,850	3,100	4,850	

KM# 544 5 TIEN
18.8000 g., Gold **Ruler:** Tu Duc **Rev:** Inscription on dragon **Rev. Inscription:** "Ngu Tien Viet Ngai" **Note:** Schroeder #381.

Date	Mintage	VG	F	VF	XF	Unc
ND(1848-83)	—	1,000	2,000	3,250	5,000	

KM# 542 5 TIEN
19.2200 g., Gold **Ruler:** Tu Duc **Obv. Inscription:** "Tu Duc Thong Bao, Van The Vinh Lai" **Note:** Schroeder #404.

Date	Mintage	VG	F	VF	XF	Unc
ND(1848-83)	—	1,100	2,200	3,500	5,500	—

KM# 541 5 TIEN
19.0000 g., Gold **Ruler:** Tu Duc **Obv. Inscription:** "Tu Duc Thong Bao, Trieu Dan Lai Chi" **Rev:** Facing dragon **Note:** Schroeder #405.

758 VIETNAM

Date	Mintage	VG	F	VF	XF	Unc
ND(1848-83)	—	1,000	2,000	3,250	5,000	—

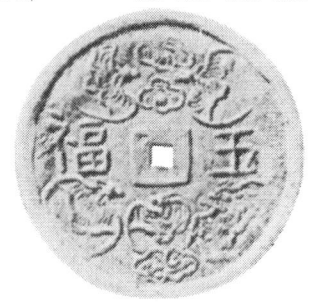

KM# 543 5 TIEN
18.0000 g., Gold **Ruler:** Tu Duc **Obv. Inscription:** "Tu Duc Thong Bao" **Rev:** Inscription and five bats **Rev. Inscription:** "Ngu Phuc" **Note:** Schroeder #410.

Date	Mintage	VG	F	VF	XF	Unc
ND(1848-83)	—	1,000	2,000	3,250	5,000	—

KM# 539 5 TIEN
18.9000 g., Gold **Ruler:** Tu Duc **Obv:** Sun with eight rays at center **Rev:** Inscription on facing dragon **Rev. Inscription:** "Long Van" **Note:** Schroeder #414C.

Date	Mintage	VG	F	VF	XF	Unc
ND(1848-83)	—	950	1,850	3,100	4,850	—

KM# 540 5 TIEN
18.2400 g., Gold **Ruler:** Tu Duc **Obv:** Sun with twelve rays at center **Note:** Schroeder #414D.

Date	Mintage	VG	F	VF	XF	Unc
ND(1848-83)	—	950	1,850	3,100	4,850	—

KM# 546 6 TIEN
23.0000 g., Gold **Ruler:** Tu Duc **Obv. Inscription:** "Tu Duc Thong Bao" **Rev:** Inscription on dragon **Rev. Inscription:** "Luc Tien Viet Thinh" **Note:** Schroeder #382.

Date	Mintage	VG	F	VF	XF	Unc
ND(1848-83)	—	1,100	2,200	3,500	5,500	—

KM# 224 7 TIEN
Gold **Ruler:** Minh Mang **Obv. Inscription:** "Minh Mang Thong Bao" **Rev:** Large dragon left **Note:** Weight varies: 26.50-27.50 grams.

Date	Mintage	VG	F	VF	XF	Unc
ND(1820-40)	—	1,100	2,200	3,500	5,500	—

KM# 225 7 TIEN
Gold **Ruler:** Minh Mang **Obv. Inscription:** "Minh Mang Thong Bao" **Rev:** Large dragon

Date	Mintage	VG	F	VF	XF	Unc
Yr 13//(1832)	—	1,100	2,200	3,500	5,500	—

KM# 228 7 TIEN
Gold **Ruler:** Minh Mang **Obv. Inscription:** "Minh Mang Thong Bao" **Rev:** Large dragon left **Note:** Schroeder #206.

Date	Mintage	VG	F	VF	XF	Unc
Yr 15//(1834)	—	1,100	2,200	3,500	5,500	—

KM# 230 7 TIEN
Gold **Ruler:** Minh Mang **Obv. Inscription:** "Minh Mang Thong Bao" **Rev:** Large dragon **Note:** Schroeder #206B.

Date	Mintage	VG	F	VF	XF	Unc
Yr 16//(1835)	—	1,100	2,200	3,500	5,500	—

KM# 345 7 TIEN
26.7500 g., Gold **Ruler:** Thieu Tri **Rev:** Flaming sun between facing dragons **Note:** Schroeder #278.

Date	Mintage	VG	F	VF	XF	Unc
ND(1841-47)	—	1,100	2,200	3,500	5,500	—

KM# 343 7 TIEN
Gold **Ruler:** Thieu Tri **Obv. Inscription:** "Thieu Tri Thong Bao" **Rev:** Dragon left **Note:** Schroeder #283. Weight varies: 26.60-27.00 grams.

Date	Mintage	VG	F	VF	XF	Unc
ND(1841-47)	—	1,100	2,200	3,500	5,500	—

KM# 344 7 TIEN
Gold **Ruler:** Thieu Tri **Rev:** Dragon right **Note:** Schroeder #284. Weight varies: 28.15-28.20 grams.

Date	Mintage	VG	F	VF	XF	Unc
ND(1841-47)	—	1,150	2,250	3,750	5,750	—

KM# 548 7 TIEN
Gold **Ruler:** Tu Duc **Obv:** Dentilated border **Obv. Inscription:** "Tu Duc Thong Bao" **Rev:** Dentilated border, dragon left **Note:** Schroeder #368B.

Date	Mintage	VG	F	VF	XF	Unc
ND(1848-83)	—	1,150	2,250	3,750	5,750	—

KM# 553 7 TIEN
26.0000 g., Gold **Ruler:** Tu Duc **Rev:** Inscription on dragon **Rev. Inscription:** "That Tien Viet Hue" **Note:** Schroeder #383B.

Date	Mintage	VG	F	VF	XF	Unc
ND(1848-83)	—	1,150	2,250	3,750	5,750	—

KM# 550 7 TIEN
26.2000 g., Gold **Ruler:** Tu Duc **Rev:** Inscription on facing dragon **Rev. Inscription:** "Long Van" **Note:** Schroeder #414B.

Date	Mintage	VG	F	VF	XF	Unc
ND(1848-83)	—	1,100	2,200	3,500	5,500	—

VIETNAM 759

KM# 551 7 TIEN
Gold **Ruler:** Tu Duc **Obv:** Small characters **Rev:** Small, thin, curved facing dragons **Note:** Schroeder #402.1. Weight varies: 26.45-27.00 grams.

Date	Mintage	VG	F	VF	XF	Unc
ND(1848-83)	—	1,150	2,250	3,750	5,750	—

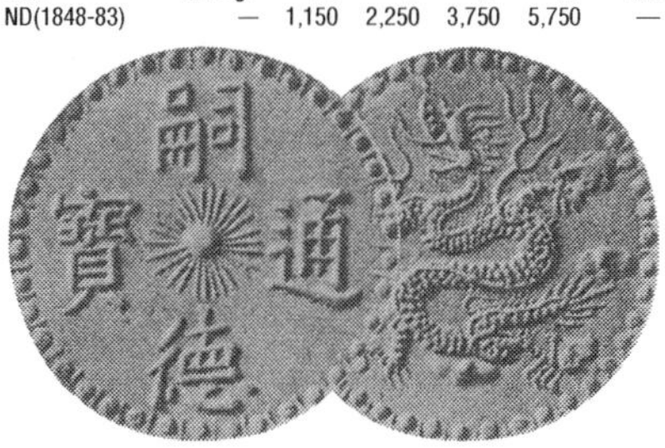

KM# 549 7 TIEN
26.8000 g., Gold **Ruler:** Tu Duc **Obv:** Pearled border **Rev:** Pearled border **Note:** Schroeder #411.

Date	Mintage	VG	F	VF	XF	Unc
ND(1848-83)	—	1,150	—	3,750	5,750	—

KM# 555 8 TIEN
30.5000 g., Gold **Ruler:** Tu Duc **Obv. Inscription:** "Tu Duc Thong Bao" **Rev:** Inscription on dragon **Rev. Inscription:** "Bat Tien Viet Thuan" **Note:** Schroeder #384B.

Date	Mintage	VG	F	VF	XF	Unc
ND(1848-83)	—	1,300	2,500	4,500	6,500	—

KM# 557 9 TIEN
Gold **Ruler:** Tu Duc **Obv. Inscription:** "Tu Duc Thong Bao" **Rev:** Inscription on dragon **Rev. Inscription:** "Cuu Tien Viet Nhan" **Note:** Schroeder #385B. Weight varies: 34.07-34.20 grams.

Date	Mintage	VG	F	VF	XF	Unc
ND(1848-83)	—	1,400	2,800	5,000	7,500	—

KM# 560.1 LANG
Gold **Ruler:** Tu Duc **Obv:** Sun with 10 rays **Obv. Inscription:** "Tu Duc Thong Bao" **Rev:** Inscription on facing dragon, Sun with 11 rays **Rev. Inscription:** "Long Van" **Note:** Schroeder #414. Weight varies: 37.00-37.690 grams.

Date	Mintage	VG	F	VF	XF	Unc
ND(1848-83)	—	2,600	5,200	8,000	12,500	—

KM# 561 LANG
37.4000 g., Gold **Ruler:** Tu Duc **Rev:** Inscription on dragon **Rev. Inscription:** "Nhat Lang Viet Trung" **Note:** Schroeder #376B.

Date	Mintage	VG	F	VF	XF	Unc
ND(1848-83)	—	2,700	5,400	9,000	13,500	—

KM# 559 LANG
Gold **Ruler:** Tu Duc **Obv. Inscription:** "Tu Duc Thong Bao, Van The Vinh Lai" **Note:** Schroeder #403. Weight varies: 37.70-38.00 grams. Illustration reduced.

Date	Mintage	VG	F	VF	XF	Unc
ND(1848-83)	—	2,800	5,600	9,200	14,500	—

KM# 560.2 LANG
Gold **Ruler:** Tu Duc **Obv:** Sun with 16 rays **Obv. Inscription:** "Tu Duc Thong Bao" **Rev:** Inscription on facing dragon, Sun with 16 rays **Note:** Weight varies: 37 - 37.69 grams.

Date	Mintage	VG	F	VF	XF	Unc
ND(1848-83)	—	2,600	5,200	8,000	12,500	—

BULLION GOLD BARS

KM# 232 TIEN
Gold **Ruler:** Minh Mang **Note:** Schroeder #200. Weight unknown.

Date	Mintage	VG	F	VF	XF	Unc
ND(1820-41)	—	300	600	900	1,500	—

KM# 347 TIEN
3.9000 g., 0.8500 Gold **Ruler:** Thieu Tri **Issuer:** Court Treasury **Note:** Schroeder #273. Fineness on edge.

Date	Mintage	VG	F	VF	XF	Unc
ND(1841-47)	—	300	600	900	1,500	—

760 VIETNAM

KM# 563 TIEN
Gold **Ruler:** Tu Duc **Issuer:** Court Treasury **Note:** Schroeder #397. Weight unknown.

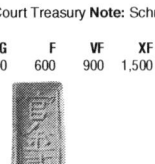

Date	Mintage	VG	F	VF	XF	Unc
ND(1848-83)	—	300	600	900	1,500	—

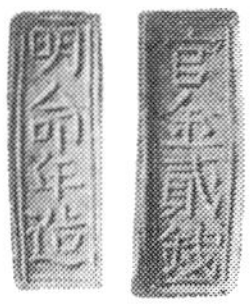

KM# 233 2 TIEN
Gold **Ruler:** Minh Mang **Note:** Schroeder #201. Weight unknown.

Date	Mintage	VG	F	VF	XF	Unc
ND(1820-41)	—	325	650	1,000	1,650	—

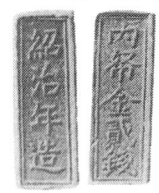

KM# 349 2 TIEN
7.5000 g., 0.8500 Gold **Ruler:** Thieu Tri **Issuer:** Court Treasury **Note:** Schroeder #274. Fineness on edge.

Date	Mintage	VG	F	VF	XF	Unc
ND(1841-47)	—	350	700	1,150	2,000	—

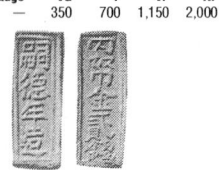

KM# 565 2 TIEN
Gold **Ruler:** Tu Duc **Issuer:** Court Treasury **Note:** Schroeder #398. Weight unknown. Fineness on edge.

Date	Mintage	VG	F	VF	XF	Unc
ND(1848-83)	—	350	700	1,150	2,000	—

KM# 234 3 TIEN
Gold **Ruler:** Minh Mang **Note:** Schroeder #202. Weight unknown.

Date	Mintage	VG	F	VF	XF	Unc
ND(1820-41)	—	500	1,000	1,750	2,700	—

KM# 351 3 TIEN
11.3000 g., Gold **Ruler:** Thieu Tri **Note:** Schroeder #275.

Date	Mintage	VG	F	VF	XF	Unc
ND(1841-47)	—	500	1,000	1,750	2,700	—

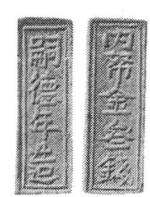

KM# 567 3 TIEN
Gold **Ruler:** Tu Duc **Issuer:** Court Treasury **Note:** Schroeder #399. Weight unknown.

Date	Mintage	VG	F	VF	XF	Unc
ND(1848-83)	—	500	1,000	1,750	2,700	—

KM# 235 4 TIEN
Gold **Ruler:** Minh Mang **Note:** Schroeder #203. Weight unknown.

Date	Mintage	VG	F	VF	XF	Unc
ND(1820-41) Rare	—	—	—	—	—	—

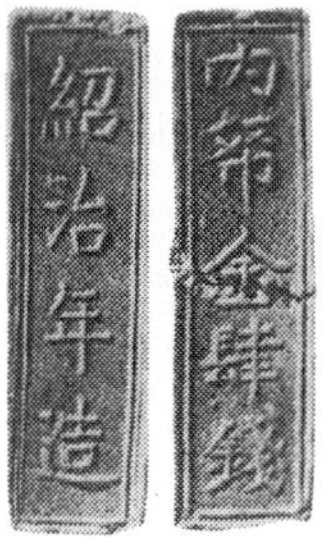

KM# 236 4 TIEN
15.2500 g., 0.8500 Gold **Ruler:** Thieu Tri **Issuer:** Court Treasury **Note:** Schroeder #276.

Date	Mintage	VG	F	VF	XF	Unc
ND(1841-47) Rare	—	—	—	—	—	—

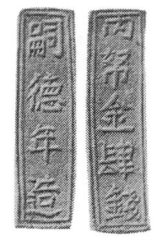

KM# 569 4 TIEN
Gold **Ruler:** Tu Duc **Issuer:** Court Treasury **Note:** Schroeder #400. Weight unknown. Fineness on edge.

Date	Mintage	VG	F	VF	XF	Unc
ND(1848-83) Rare	—	—	—	—	—	—

KM# 237 5 TIEN
Gold **Ruler:** Minh Mang **Note:** Schroeder #204. Weight unknown.

Date	Mintage	VG	F	VF	XF	Unc
ND(1820-41) Rare	—	—	—	—	—	—

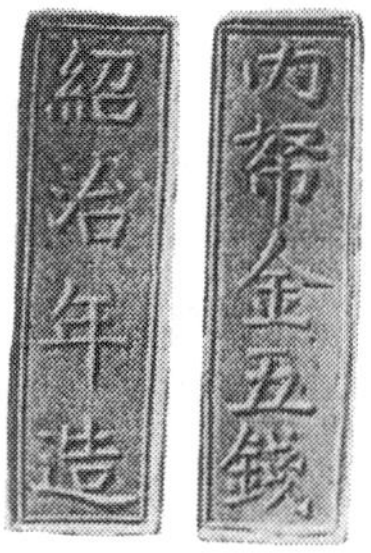

KM# 353 5 TIEN
18.8500 g., 0.8500 Gold **Ruler:** Thieu Tri **Issuer:** Court Treasury **Note:** Schroeder #277. Fineness on edge.

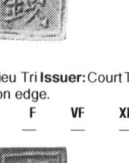

Date	Mintage	VG	F	VF	XF	Unc
ND(1841-47) Rare	—	—	—	—	—	—

KM# 571 5 TIEN
Gold **Ruler:** Tu Duc **Issuer:** Court Treasury **Note:** Schroeder #401. Fineness on edge. Weight unknown.

Date	Mintage	VG	F	VF	XF	Unc
ND(1848-83) Rare	—	—	—	—	—	—

KM# 238 LANG
0.8500 Gold **Ruler:** Minh Mang **Note:** Schroeder #190. Very crude. Weight unknown.

Date	Mintage	VG	F	VF	XF	Unc
ND(1820-41) Rare	—	—	—	—	—	—

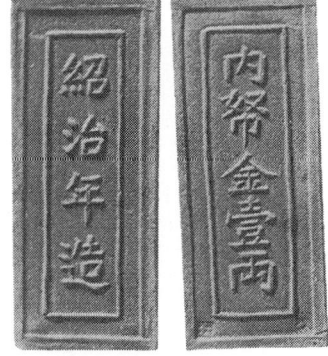

KM# 355 LANG
Gold **Ruler:** Thieu Tri **Issuer:** Court Treasury **Note:** Schroeder #268.

Date	Mintage	VG	F	VF	XF	Unc
ND(1841-47) Rare	—	—	—	—	—	—

VIETNAM 761

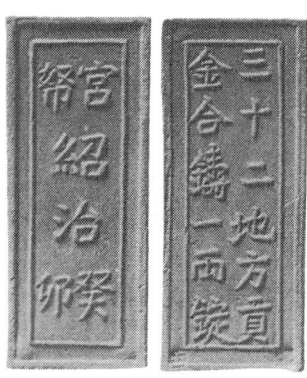

KM# 359 LANG
Gold **Ruler:** Thieu Tri **Issuer:** Court Treasury **Note:** Schroeder #269. Fineness on edge.
Date	Mintage	VG	F	VF	XF	Unc
CD1843 Rare	—	—	—	—	—	—

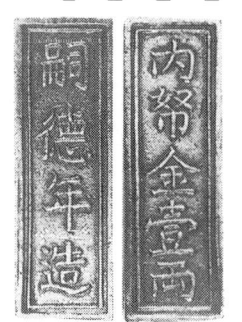

KM# 573 LANG
37.4000 g., 0.9500 Gold **Ruler:** Tu Duc **Issuer:** Court Treasury **Note:** Schroeder #391. Fineness on edge.
Date	Mintage	VG	F	VF	XF	Unc
ND(1848-83) Rare	—	—	—	—	—	—

Note: Stack's NYINC sale 12/89 virtual Uncirculated realized $8,250

KM# 574 LANG
0.8500 Gold **Ruler:** Tu Duc **Issuer:** Court Treasury **Note:** Schroeder #392. Fineness on edge.
Date	Mintage	VG	F	VF	XF	Unc
ND(1848-83) Rare	—	—	—	—	—	—

KM# 239 5 LANG
0.8500 Gold **Ruler:** Minh Mang **Note:** Schroeder #191. Weight unknown. Fineness on edge.
Date	Mintage	VG	F	VF	XF	Unc
ND(1820-41) Rare	—	—	—	—	—	—

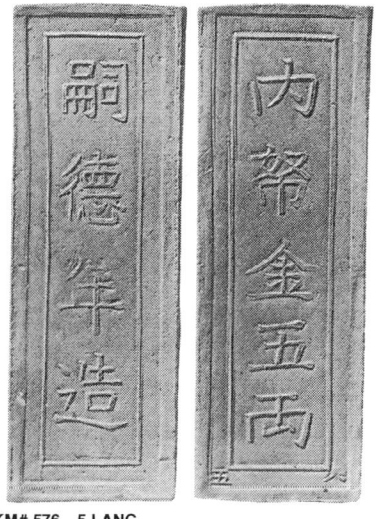

KM# 576 5 LANG
190.2500 g., Gold, 28.5x 82 mm. **Ruler:** Tu Duc **Issuer:** Court Treasury **Note:** Schroeder #394. Fineness on edge; illustration reduced.
Date	Mintage	VG	F	VF	XF	Unc
ND(1848-83) Rare	—	—	—	—	—	—

KM# 240 10 LANG
0.8500 Gold **Ruler:** Minh Mang **Issuer:** Court Treasury **Note:** Schroeder #192. Fineness on edge. Weight unknown. Similar to 10 Lang, Schroeder #173.
Date	Mintage	VG	F	VF	XF	Unc
CD1837 Rare	—	—	—	—	—	—

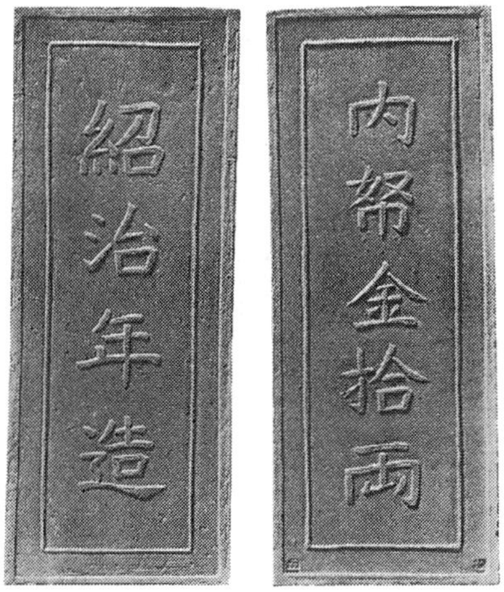

KM# 357 10 LANG
382.4000 g., 0.7500 Gold, 43x108 mm. **Ruler:** Thieu Tri **Issuer:** Court Treasury **Note:** Schroeder #270. Fineness on edge; illustration reduced.
Date	Mintage	VG	F	VF	XF	Unc
ND(1841-47) Rare	—	—	—	—	—	—

KM# 578 10 LANG
0.9000 Gold, 30x100 mm. **Ruler:** Tu Duc **Rev:** Four characters **Note:** Schroeder #396. Fineness on edge. All inscriptions engraved.
Date	Mintage	VG	F	VF	XF	Unc
ND(1848-83) Rare	—	—	—	—	—	—

KM# 582 10 LANG
Gold **Ruler:** Tu Duc **Obv. Legend:** "Bac Ninh" **Rev:** Two characters (engraved) plus hallmark **Note:** Schroeder #395.
Date	Mintage	VG	F	VF	XF	Unc
CB1849 Rare	—	—	—	—	—	—

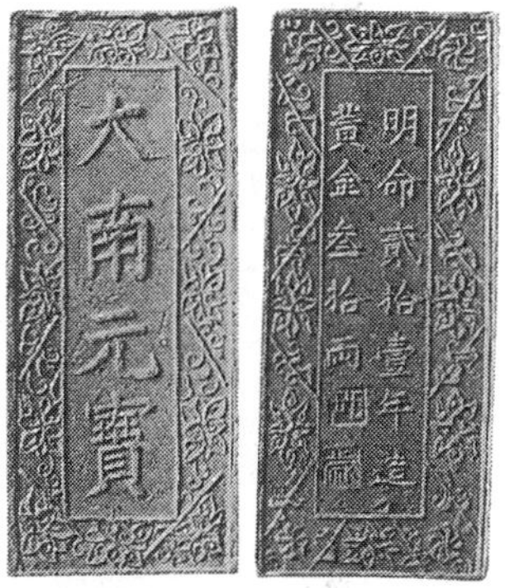

KM# 241 30 LANG
0.7500 Gold, 43x101 mm. **Ruler:** Minh Mang **Obv. Inscription:** "Dai Nam Nguyen Bao" **Note:** Schroeder #193. Weight unknown; illustration reduced. Fineness on edge. Similar to 40 Lang.
Date	Mintage	VG	F	VF	XF	Unc
ND(1840)/21 Rare	—	—	—	—	—	—

KM# 243 40 LANG
0.9000 Gold, 43x112 mm. **Ruler:** Minh Mang **Obv. Inscription:** "Viet Nam Nguyen Bao" **Note:** Schroeder #194. Fineness on edge.
Date	Mintage	VG	F	VF	XF	Unc
ND(1820-41) Rare	—	—	—	—	—	—

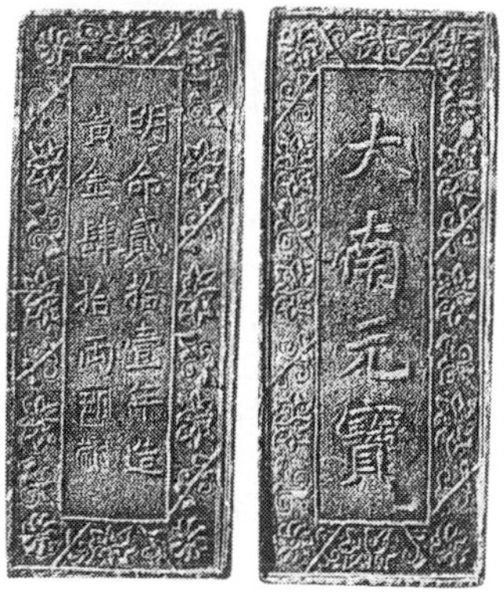

KM# 242 40 LANG
0.7500 Gold, 43x107 mm. **Ruler:** Minh Mang **Obv. Inscription:** "Dai Nam Nguyen Bao" **Note:** Schroeder #195. Weight unknown. Fineness on edge. Illustration reduced.
Date	Mintage	VG	F	VF	XF	Unc
ND(1840)/21 Rare	—	—	—	—	—	—

VIETNAM

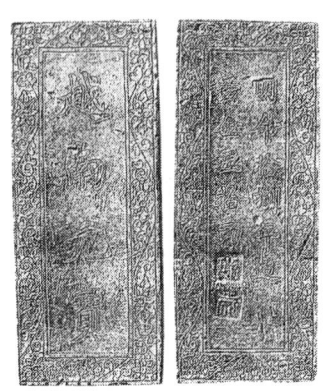

KM# 246 50 LANG
0.7500 Gold, 48x118 mm. **Ruler:** Minh Mang **Obv. Inscription:** "Viet Nam Nguyen Bao" **Note:** Schroeder #196. Weight unknown; illustration reduced. Fineness on edge.

Date	Mintage	VG	F	VF	XF	Unc
ND(1837)/18 Rare	—	—	—	—	—	—

KM# 247 50 LANG
0.8000 Gold, 49x115 mm. **Ruler:** Minh Mang **Obv.** Inscription framed within ornate border **Obv. Inscription:** "Dai Nam Nguyen Bao" **Rev:** Inscription framed within ornate border **Note:** Schroeder #197. Fineness on edge.

Date	Mintage	VG	F	VF	XF	Unc
ND(1838)/19 Rare	—	—	—	—	—	—

KM# 360 50 LANG
1917.3500 g., 0.7000 Gold **Ruler:** Thieu Tri **Issuer:** Court Treasury **Note:** Schroeder #271. Fineness on edge, illustration reduced.

Date	Mintage	VG	F	VF	XF	Unc
CD1843 Rare	—	—	—	—	—	—

KM# 244 100 LANG
0.8500 Gold, 59x138 mm. **Ruler:** Minh Mang **Obv.** Inscription framed within ornate border, small characters **Obv. Inscription:** "Viet Nam Nguyen Bao" **Rev:** Inscription framed within ornate border **Note:** Schroeder #198. Weight unknown. Fineness on edge.

Date	Mintage	VG	F	VF	XF	Unc
ND(1833)/14 Rare	—	—	—	—	—	—

KM# 245 100 LANG
0.8500 Gold **Ruler:** Minh Mang **Note:** Schroeder #199. Similar to KM#244, but large characters on obverse.

Date	Mintage	VG	F	VF	XF	Unc
ND(1833)/14 Rare	—	—	—	—	—	—

KM# 361 100 LANG
3831.0000 g., 0.7000 Gold, 78x146 mm. **Ruler:** Thieu Tri **Issuer:** Court Treasury **Obv:** Inscription framed within ornate border **Rev:** Inscription framed within ornate border **Note:** Schroeder #272. Fineness on edge. Illustration reduced.

Date	Mintage	VG	F	VF	XF	Unc
CD1843 Rare	—	—	—	—	—	—

TRADE COINAGE

KM# 580 7 TIEN 2 PHAN (Dollar)
Silver **Ruler:** Tu Duc **Rev. Inscription:** "That Tien Nhi Phan" **Note:** Originally considered fantasies, it has now been determined these were issued for payment of the war ransom to France in April 1865.

Date	Mintage	VG	F	VF	XF	Unc
ND1865	—	90.00	180	300	500	—

FRENCH PROTECTORATE OF ANNAM

GOLD MILLED COINAGE

KM# 619 1/2 TIEN
1.8000 g., Gold **Ruler:** Dong Khanh **Obv. Inscription:** "Dong Khanh Thong Bao" **Rev:** Blank **Note:** Schroeder #424.

Date	Mintage	VG	F	VF	XF	Unc
ND(1885-88)	—	150	275	425	650	—

KM# 634 TIEN
3.9000 g., Gold **Ruler:** Thanh Thai **Obv. Inscription:** "Thanh Thai Thong Bao" **Rev. Inscription:** "Nhat Nguyen" **Note:** Schroeder #432.

Date	Mintage	VG	F	VF	XF	Unc
ND(1888-1907)	—	350	650	950	1,450	—

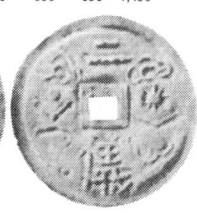

KM# 621 1-1/2 TIEN
Gold **Ruler:** Dong Khanh **Obv. Inscription:** "Dong Kanh Thong Bao" **Rev:** Inscription between moon and sun **Rev. Inscription:** "Nhi Nghi" **Note:** Schroeder #425.1. Weight varies: 6-40-6.90 grams.

Date	Mintage	VG	F	VF	XF	Unc
ND(1885-88)	—	240	450	750	1,150	—

KM# 622 1-1/2 TIEN
Gold **Ruler:** Dong Khanh **Rev:** Inscription between sun and moon **Rev. Inscription:** "Nhi Nghi" **Note:** Schroeder #425.2.

Date	Mintage	VG	F	VF	XF	Unc
ND(1885-88)	—	240	450	750	1,150	—

KM# 636 1-1/2 TIEN
6.6000 g., Gold **Ruler:** Thanh Thai **Obv. Inscription:** "Thanh Thai Thong Bao" **Rev:** Inscription between moon and sun **Rev. Inscription:** "Nhi Nghi" **Note:** Schroeder #435.

Date	Mintage	VG	F	VF	XF	Unc
ND(1888-1907)	—	275	475	750	1,150	—

KM# 638 3 TIEN
Gold **Ruler:** Thanh Thai **Obv. Inscription:** "Thanh Thai Thong Bao" **Rev:** Dragon **Note:** Weight varies: 10.50-12.40 grams. Schroeder #433.

Date	Mintage	VG	F	VF	XF	Unc
ND(1888-1907)	—	1,000	2,000	3,250	5,000	—

KM# 639 3 TIEN
Gold **Ruler:** Thanh Thai **Obv. Inscription:** "Thanh Thai Thong Bao" **Rev:** Dragon above three Longevities **Rev. Inscription:** "Tam Tho" **Note:** Weight varies: 10.00-10.50 grams. Schroeder #436.

Date	Mintage	VG	F	VF	XF	Unc
ND(1888-1907)	—	600	1,000	1,700	2,600	—

KM# 641 4 TIEN
14.5000 g., Gold **Ruler:** Thanh Thai **Obv. Inscription:** "Tu My" **Rev:** Inscription between Four Perfections **Note:** Schroeder #437.

Date	Mintage	VG	F	VF	XF	Unc
ND(1888-1907)	—	700	1,250	2,100	3,200	—

KM# 643 5 TIEN
15.4800 g., Gold **Ruler:** Thanh Thai **Obv. Legend:** "Than Thai Thong Bao" **Rev:** Dragon

Date	Mintage	VG	F	VF	XF	Unc
ND(1888-1907)	—	650	1,200	2,000	3,000	—

KM# 645 6 TIEN
23.0000 g., Gold **Ruler:** Thanh Thai **Obv. Inscription:** "Thanh Thai Thong Bao" **Rev:** Large dragon **Note:** Schroeder #382A.

Date	Mintage	VG	F	VF	XF	Unc
ND(1888-1907)	—	1,100	2,200	3,500	5,500	—

KM# 647 LANG
Gold **Ruler:** Thanh Thai **Obv. Inscription:** "Thanh-thai Thong-bao" at right, "Van The Vinh Lai" at left **Note:** Weight unknown. Schroeder #431.

Date	Mintage	VG	F	VF	XF	Unc
ND(1888-1907)	—	3,000	5,700	9,500	15,000	—

SOCIALIST REPUBLIC — VIETNAM

BULLION GOLD BARS

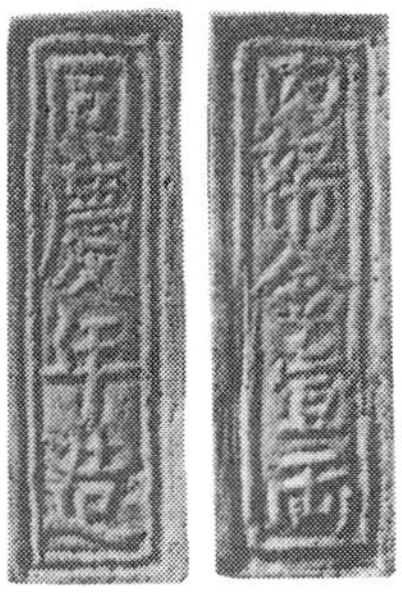

KM# 624 LANG
0.8500 Gold **Ruler:** Dong Khanh **Issuer:** Court Treasury **Note:** Schroeder #423. Crude.

Date	Mintage	VG	F	VF	XF	Unc
ND(1885-88)	Rare	—	—	—	—	—

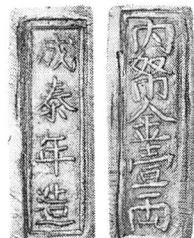

KM# 649 LANG
0.8500 Gold **Ruler:** Thanh Thai **Issuer:** Court Treasury **Obv. Inscription:** "Thanh-thai Nien-tao" **Rev. Inscription:** "Noi Thang Kim Nhat Lang" **Note:** Fineness on edge; weight varies: 36.10-36.70 grams; Schroeder#429.

Date	Mintage	VG	F	VF	XF	Unc
ND(1888-1907)	Rare	—	—	—	—	—

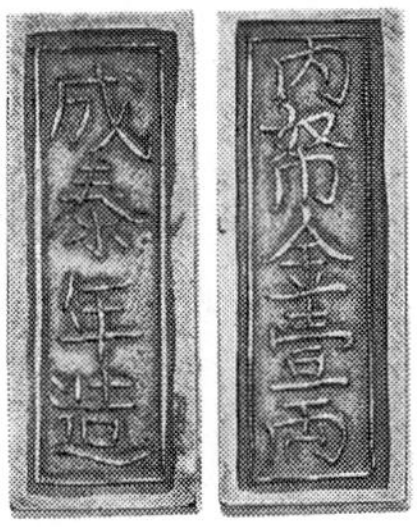

KM# 650 LANG
0.8000 Gold **Ruler:** Thanh Thai **Issuer:** Court Treasury **Obv. Inscription:** "Thanh-thai Nien-tao" **Rev. Inscription:** "Noi Thang Kim Nhat Lang" **Note:** Fineness on edge; Schroeder #430.

Date	Mintage	VG	F	VF	XF	Unc
ND(1888-1907)	Rare	—	—	—	—	—

NORTH VIET NAM
INDEPENDENT COMMUNIST STATE

PRESENTATION COINAGE

KM# A5 10 VIET
4.1625 g., 0.9000 Gold 0.1205 oz. AGW, 17 mm. **Obv:** Head of Ho Chi Minh right **Obv. Legend:** "CHU-TICH HO-CHI-MINH" **Rev:** Denomination above grain sheaves **Rev. Legend:** "VIETNAM DAN-CHU CONG-HOA" **Rev. Inscription:** 10 Viet

Date	Mintage	F	VF	XF	Unc	BU
1948(v)	—	—	—	250	350	400

KM# B5 20 VIET
8.3250 g., 0.9000 Gold 0.2409 oz. AGW, 21 mm. **Obv:** Head of Ho Chi Minh right **Obv. Legend:** "CHU-TICH HO-CHI-MINH" **Rev:** Denomination above grain sheaves **Rev. Legend:** "VIETNAM DAN-CHU CONG-HOA" **Rev. Inscription:** "20 VIET"

Date	Mintage	F	VF	XF	Unc	BU
1948(v)	—	—	—	400	500	550

KM# C5 50 VIET
16.6500 g., 0.9000 Gold 0.4818 oz. AGW, 29 mm. **Obv:** Head of Ho Chi Minh right **Obv. Legend:** "CHU-TICH HO-CHI-MINH" **Rev:** Denomination above grain sheaves **Rev. Legend:** "VIETNAM DAN-CHU CONG-HOA" **Rev. Inscription:** "50 VIET"

Date	Mintage	F	VF	XF	Unc	BU
1948(v)	—	—	—	600	700	750

SOCIALIST REPUBLIC

The Socialist Republic of Viet Nam, located in Southeast Asia west of the South China Sea, has an area of 127,300 sq. mi. (329,560 sq. km.) and a population of *66.8 million. Capital: Hanoi. Agricultural products, coal, and mineral ores are exported.

At the start of World War II, Vietnamese Communists fled to China's Kwangsi provinces where Ho Chi Minh organized the Revolution to free Viet Nam of French rule. The Japanese occupied Viet Nam during World War II. As the end of the war drew near, they ousted the Vichy French administration and granted Viet Nam independence under a puppet government headed by Bao Dai, Emperor of Annam. The Bao Dai government collapsed at the end of the war, and on Sept. 2, 1945, Ho Chi Minh proclaimed the existence of an independent Viet Nam consisting of Cochin-China, Annam, and Tonkin, and set up a Communist government. France recognized the new government as a free state, but reneged and in 1949 reinstalled Bao Dai as Ruler of Viet Nam and extended the regime independence within the French Union. Ho Chi Minh led a guerrilla war, in the first Indochina war, against the French which raged on to the disastrous defeat of the French at Dien Bien Phu on May 7, 1954.

An agreement signed at Geneva on July 21, 1954, provided for a temporary division of Viet Nam at the 17th parallel of latitude, between a Communist-supported North and a U.S.-supported South. In Oct. 1955, South Viet Nam deposed Bao Dai by referendum and authorized the establishment of a republic with Ngo Dinh Diem as president. The Republic of South Viet Nam was proclaimed on Oct. 26, 1955, and was immediately recognized by some Western Powers.

The activities of Communists in South Viet Nam led to the second Indochina war which came to a brief halt in 1973 (when a cease-fire was arranged and U.S. forces withdrew), but it didn't end until April 30, 1975 when South Viet Nam surrendered unconditionally. The two Viet Nams were reunited as the Socialist Republic of Viet Nam on July 2, 1976.

NOTE: For earlier coinage refer to French Indo-China or Tonkin.

MONETARY SYSTEM
10 Xu = 1 Hao
10 Hao = 1 Dong

STANDARD COINAGE

KM# 41 500 DONG
3.1030 g., 0.9990 Gold 0.0997 oz. AGW **Subject:** 100th Anniversary - Birth of Ho Chi Minh **Obv:** Arms **Obv. Legend:** "CONG HOA XA HOI CHU NGHIA VIET NAM" **Note:** KM#41 were minted at the Havana Mint (h) as "Gift Coins" to the Vietnamese people and were delivered encapsulated and in presentation boxes. This piece is cataloged as A24 and illustrated in Gunter Schon's World Coins Catalogue.

Date	Mintage	F	VF	XF	Unc	BU
1989(L)	—	—	—	—	350	500

KM# 54 5000 DONG
1.2441 g., 0.9999 Gold .0400 oz. AGW, 13.92 mm. **Subject:** Year of the Dragon **Obv:** Arms **Obv. Legend:** "CONG HOA XA HOI CHU NGHIA VIET NAM" **Rev:** Dragon with radiant sun **Rev. Legend:** "RONG VIET NAM" **Edge:** Reeded

Date	Mintage	F	VF	XF	Unc	BU
2000(S)	—	Value: 40.00				

KM# 64 5000 DONG
1.2441 g., 0.9999 Gold 0.04 oz. AGW, 13.92 mm. **Subject:** Year of the Snake **Obv:** State emblem **Rev:** Sea snake **Edge:** Reeded

Date	Mintage	F	VF	XF	Unc	BU
2001	—	—	—	—	55.00	75.00

KM# 67 5000 DONG
1.2441 g., 0.9999 Gold 0.04 oz. AGW, 13.9 mm. **Subject:** Year of the Horse **Obv:** State emblem **Rev:** Horse **Edge:** Reeded

Date	Mintage	F	VF	XF	Unc	BU
2002	28,000	—	—	—	35.00	55.00

KM# 55 20000 DONG
7.7749 g., 0.9999 Gold .2500 oz. AGW, 22 mm. **Subject:** Year of the Dragon **Obv:** Arms **Obv. Legend:** "CONG HOA XA HOI CHU NGHIA VIET NAM" **Rev:** Dragon and clouds **Rev. Legend:** "RONG VIET NAM" **Edge:** Reeded

Date	Mintage	F	VF	XF	Unc	BU
2000(S) Proof	1,800	Value: 225				

KM# 65 20000 DONG
7.7759 g., 0.9999 Gold 0.25 oz. AGW, 22 mm. **Subject:** Year of the Snake **Obv:** State emblem **Rev:** Sea snake **Edge:** Reeded

Date	Mintage	F	VF	XF	Unc	BU
2001(S) Proof	—	Value: 225				

Note: Issued in a replica Faberge egg

KM# 68 20000 DONG
7.7759 g., 0.9999 Gold 0.25 oz. AGW, 22 mm. **Subject:** Year of the Horse **Obv:** State emblem **Rev:** Horse **Edge:** Reeded

Date	Mintage	F	VF	XF	Unc	BU
2002 Proof	1,800	Value: 220				

KM# 56 50000 DONG
15.5518 g., 0.9999 Gold .5000 oz. AGW, 27 mm. **Subject:** Year of the Dragon **Obv:** Arms **Obv. Legend:** "CONG HOA XA HOI CHU NGHIA VIET NAM" **Rev:** Dragon before radiant sun **Rev. Legend:** "RONG VIET NAM" **Edge:** Reeded

Date	Mintage	F	VF	XF	Unc	BU
2000(S) Proof	3,800	Value: 375				

KM# 66 50000 DONG
15.5518 g., 0.9999 Gold 0.5 oz. AGW, 27 mm. **Subject:** Year of the Snake **Obv:** State emblem **Rev:** Multicolor holographic King Cobra **Edge:** Reeded

Date	Mintage	F	VF	XF	Unc	BU
2001(S) Proof	3,200	Value: 400				

KM# 69 50000 DONG
15.5518 g., 0.9999 Gold 0.5 oz. AGW, 27 mm. **Subject:** Year of the Horse **Obv:** State emblem **Rev:** Multicolor holographic horse **Edge:** Reeded

Date	Mintage	F	VF	XF	Unc	BU
2002 Proof	3,800	Value: 375				

PROOF SETS

KM#	Date	Mintage	Identification	Issue Price	Mkt Val
PS3	2000(S) (2)	800	KM#55-56	—	570
PS5	2001(S) (2)	—	KM#59, 66	—	440
PS6	2001(S) (2)	—	KM#65-66	—	625

WEST AFRICAN STATES

The West African States, a former federation of eight French colonial territories on the northwest coast of Africa, has an area of 1,831,079 sq. mi. (4,742,495 sq. km.) and a population of about 17 million. Capital: Dakar. The constituent territories were Mauritania, Senegal, Dahomey, French Sudan, Ivory Coast, Upper Volta, Niger and French Guinea.

The members of the federation were overseas territories within the French Union until Sept. of 1958 when all but French Guinea approved the constitution of the Fifth French Republic, thereby electing to become autonomous members of the new French Community. French Guinea voted to become the fully independent Republic of Guinea. The other seven attained independence in 1960. The French West Africa territories were provided with a common currency, a practice which was continued as the monetary union of the West African States which provides a common currency to the autonomous republics of Dahomey (now Benin), Senegal, Upper Volta (now Burkina Faso), Ivory Coast, Mali, Togo and Niger.

For earlier coinage refer to Togo, and French West Africa.

MINT MARK
(a)- Paris, privy marks only

MONETARY SYSTEM
100 Centimes = 1 Franc

FEDERATION
STANDARD COINAGE

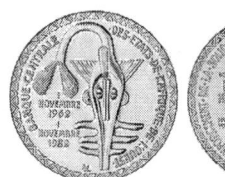

KM# 12 5000 FRANCS
14.4900 g., 0.9000 Gold .4193 oz. AGW **Subject:** 20th Anniversary of Monetary Union **Obv:** Gold weight in the shape of a fish, "Taku", a symbol of prosperity **Rev:** Six interlaced birds symbolizing states **Designer:** R. Joly

Date	Mintage	F	VF	XF	Unc	BU
1982(a)	—	—	—	—	400	485

ESSAIS

KM#	Date	Mintage	Identification	Issue Price	Mkt Val
E4b	1967(a)	21	100 Francs. Gold. KM4.	—	750
E6b	1972(a)	17	50 Francs. Gold. KM6.	—	700
E10	1980(a)	5	25 Francs. Gold.	—	1,800
E14	1982(a)	12	5000 Francs. Gold. KM11.	—	1,500

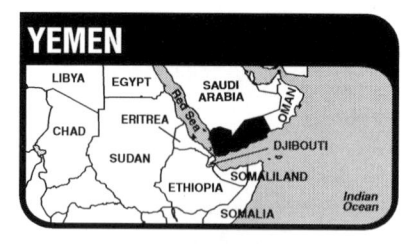

YEMEN

YEMEN MUTAWAKKILITE

One of the oldest centers of civilization in the Middle East, Yemen was once part of the Minaean Kingdom and of the ancient Kingdom of Sheba, after which it was captured successively by Egyptians, Ethiopians and Romans. It was converted to Islam in 628 A.D. and administered as a caliphate until 1538, when it came under Ottoman occupation in 1849. The second Ottoman occupation which began in 1872 was maintained until 1918 when autonomy was achieved through revolution.

TITLE

المملكة المتوكلية اليمنية

al-Mamlaka(t) al-Mutawakkiliya(t) al-Yamaniya(t)

RULER
Ottoman, until 1625

QASIMID IMAMS
al-Mansur Muhammad bin Yahya,
 (Imam Mansur) AH1307-1322/1890-1904AD
al Hadi al-Hasan bin Yahya
 (Counter Imam, in Sa'da) AH1322/1904AD
al-Mutawakkil Yahya bin Muhammad
 (Imam Yahya) AH1322-1367/1904-1948AD
al-Nasir Ahmad bin Yahya,
 (Imam Ahmad) AH1367-1382/
 1948-1962AD
al-Badr Muhammad bin Ahmad,
 (Imam Badr) AH1382-1388/
 1962-1968AD (mostly in exile)

MINT NAME

صنعاء

San'a

MONETARY SYSTEM
After Accession of Iman Yahya
AH1322/1904AD
1 Zalat = 1/160 Riyal
2 Zalat = 1 Halala = 1/80 Riyal
2 Halala = 1 Buqsha = 1/40 Riyal
40 Buqsha = 1 Riyal

NOTE: The Riyal was called an IMADI (RIYAL) during the reign of Imam Yahya "Imadi" honorific name for Yahyawi and an AHMADI (RIYAL) during the reign of Imam Ahmad. The 1 Zalat, Y#2.1, D1, A3, A4 and all Imam Yahya gold strikes except Y#F10, bear no indication of value. Many of the Mutawakkilite coins after AH1322/1904AD bear the denomination expressed as fraction of the Riyal as follows.

BRONZE and ALUMINUM
Thumn ushr = 1/80 Riyal = 1/2 Buqsha = 1 Halala
Rub ushr = 1/40 Riyal = 1 Buqsha
Nisf ushr = 1/20 Riyal = 2 Buqsha = 1/2 Bawlah
Nisf thumn = 1/16 Riyal = 2-1/2 Buqsha
Ushr = 1/10 Riyal = 4 Buqsha = 1 Bawlah
Thumn = 1/8 Riyal = 5 Buqsha
Rub = 1/4 Riyal = 10 Buqsha
Nisf = 1/2 Riyal = 20 Buqsha
1 Riyal (Imadi, Ahmadi) = 40 Buqsha

DATING
All coins of Imam Yahya have accession date AH1322 on obverse and actual date of issue on reverse. All coins of Imam Ahmad bear accession date AH1367 on obverse and actual date on reverse.

If not otherwise noted, all coins of Imam Yahya and Imam Ahad as well as the early issues of the Republic (Y#20 through Y#A25 and Y#32), were struck at the mint in Sana'a. The Sana'a Mint was essentially a medieval mint, using hand-cut dies and crudely machined blanks. There is a large amount of variation from one die to the next in arrangement of legends and ornaments, form of crescents, number of stars, size of the circle, etc., and literally hundreds of subtypes could be identified. Types are divided only when there are changes in the inscriptions, or major variations in the basic type, such as the presence or absence of "Rabb al-Alamin" in the legend or the position of the word *Sana* (= year) in relation to the year.

NOTE: All "ZALAT" coins are without mint name or denomination.

KINGDOM
GOLD PRESENTATION COINAGE

All Imam Yahya gold strikes are considered presentation issues which were based on the gold standard of the Turkish Lira.

Y# A10 1/8 LIRA (1/40 Riyal)
0.9200 g., Gold **Ruler:** al-Mutawakkil Yahya bin Muhammad (Imam Yahya) AH1322-1367 / 1904-1948AD **Note:** Accession date: AH1322.

Date	Mintage	VG	F	VF	XF	Unc
AH(13)44	—	—	—	—	1,350	—

Y# B10 1/4 LIRA (1/20 Riyal)
1.7000 g., Gold **Ruler:** al-Mutawakkil Yahya bin Muhammad (Imam Yahya) AH1322-1367 / 1904-1948AD **Note:** Accession date: AH1322.

Date	Mintage	VG	F	VF	XF	Unc
AH(13)44	—	—	—	—	1,500	—

Y# C10 1/2 LIRA (1/10 Riyal)
3.3100 g., Gold **Ruler:** al-Mutawakkil Yahya bin Muhammad (Imam Yahya) AH1322-1367 / 1904-1948AD **Note:** Accession date: AH1322.

Date	Mintage	VG	F	VF	XF	Unc
AH(13)44	—	—	—	—	1,650	—

Y# D10 LIRA (1/5 Riyal)
6.8000 g., Gold **Ruler:** al-Mutawakkil Yahya bin Muhammad (Imam Yahya) AH1322-1367 / 1904-1948AD **Obv:** Crescent below accession date AH1322

Date	Mintage	VG	F	VF	XF	Unc
AH(13)44	—	—	—	—	2,000	—

Y# E10 2-1/2 LIRA (1/2 Riyal)
17.7000 g., Gold **Ruler:** al-Mutawakkil Yahya bin Muhammad (Imam Yahya) AH1322-1367 / 1904-1948AD **Obv:** Crescent below accession date AH1322

Date	Mintage	VG	F	VF	XF	Unc
AH(13)44	—	—	—	—	3,500	—

Y# K10 2-1/2 LIRA (1/2 Riyal)
Gold **Ruler:** al-Mutawakkil Yahya bin Muhammad (Imam Yahya) AH1322-1367 / 1904-1948AD **Note:** Weight varies: 17.44-17.82 grams. Accession date: AH1322.

Date	Mintage	VG	F	VF	XF	Unc
AH1352	—	—	—	—	2,500	—

Y# F10 5 LIRA (1 Riyal)
35.5000 g., Gold **Ruler:** al-Mutawakkil Yahya bin Muhammad (Imam Yahya) AH1322-1367 / 1904-1948AD **Note:** Similar to 1 Imadi Riyal, Y#7.

Date	Mintage	VG	F	VF	XF	Unc
AH1344 Rare	—	—	—	—	—	—

Note: Dies of AH1344 Riyal silver and gold strikes are not identical

Y# P10 5 LIRA (1 Riyal)
34.2400 g., Gold **Ruler:** al-Mutawakkil Yahya bin Muhammad (Imam Yahya) AH1322-1367/1904-1948AD **Note:** Thin planchet strike of 10 Lira (2 Riyal), Y#N10.

Date	Mintage	VG	F	VF	XF	Unc
AH1358 2 known	—	—	—	—	3,250	—

Y# M10 10 LIRA (2 Riyal)
69.8300 g., Gold **Ruler:** al-Mutawakkil Yahya bin Muhammad (Imam Yahya) AH1322-1367 / 1904-1948AD **Obv:** Similar to Gold 2-1/2 Lira, Y#K10 **Note:** Accession date: AH1322.

Date	Mintage	VG	F	VF	XF	Unc
AH1352	—	—	—	—	6,500	—

YEMEN ARAB REPUBLIC

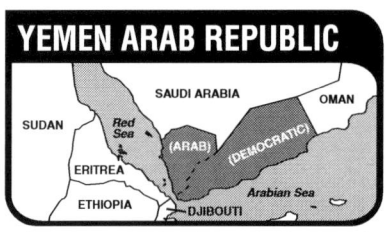

The northwestern region of present day Yemen was dominated by Ottoman Turks until 1918. Formal boundaries were established in 1934 and a Republic was formed in 1962 leading to an eight year civil war between royalist imam and new republican forces.

Y# N10 10 LIRA (2 Riyal)
69.8300 g., Gold **Ruler:** al-Mutawakkil Yahya bin Muhammad (Imam Yahya) AH1322-1367 / 1904-1948AD **Obv:** Crescent below accession date AH1322 **Rev:** Two crossed flags in center **Rev. Legend:** "Duriba bi-dar al-khilafa al-mutawakkiliya bi Sana'a 'asimat al-Yamam sana 1358"

Date	Mintage	VG	F	VF	XF	Unc
AH1358 4 known	—	—	—	—	5,500	—

GOLD COINAGE

Imam Ahmad gold strikes were based on the gold standard of the Turkish Lira (7.2164 g gold). Strikes on the British Gold Standard can have an additional countermark of an Arabic 1, 2, or 4, probably indicating the equivalence to 1, 2, or 4 British Sovereigns.

Y# G15 GOLD 1/4 RIYAL (1 Lira - Sovereign)
Gold **Ruler:** al-Nasir Ahmad bin Yahya (Imam Ahmad) AH1367-1382 / 1948-1962AD **Obv:** Crescent below accession date AH1367 **Note:** Weight varies: 6.30-8.90 grams. Dies of silver 1/4 Ahmadi riyal, (Y#15) were used.

Date	Mintage	F	VF	XF	Unc	BU
AH(13)71	—	—	450	850	1,500	—
AH(13)75/3	—	—	450	850	1,500	—
AH(13)75	—	—	450	850	1,500	—
AH(13)77/5	—	—	450	850	1,500	—

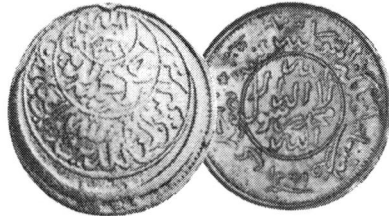

Y# G16.1 GOLD 1/2 RIYAL (2-1/2 Lira - 2 Sovereigns)
Gold **Ruler:** al-Nasir Ahmad bin Yahya (Imam Ahmad) AH1367-1382 / 1948-1962AD **Obv:** Double crescent below accession date AH1367 **Rev:** Full dates; denomination and mint name read inward **Note:** Weight varies: 15.57-17.99 grams.

Date	Mintage	F	VF	XF	Unc	BU
AH1369 Rare	—	—	—	—	—	—
Note: Currently, one known						
AH1370	—	425	650	1,200	2,000	—
AH1371	—	425	650	1,200	2,000	—
AH1375	—	425	650	1,200	2,000	—
AH(13)75	—	425	650	1,200	2,000	—
AH1377	—	425	650	1,200	2,000	—

Y# G16.2 GOLD 1/2 RIYAL (2-1/2 Lira - 2 Sovereigns)
Gold **Ruler:** al-Nasir Ahmad bin Yahya (Imam Ahmad) AH1367-1382 / 1948-1962AD **Obv:** Double crescent below accession date AH1367 **Rev:** Full date; denomination and mint name read outward **Note:** Dies of silver 1/2 Ahmadi Riyal, (Y#16) were used.

Date	Mintage	F	VF	XF	Unc	BU
AH1377	—	425	650	1,200	2,000	—
AH1378	—	425	650	1,200	2,000	—
AH1379	—	425	650	1,200	2,000	—
AH1380	—	425	650	1,200	2,000	—
AH1381	—	425	650	1,200	2,000	—

Y# G17.1 GOLD RIYAL (5 Lira - 4 Sovereigns)
32.4860 g., 0.9000 Gold 0.94 oz. AGW, 40 mm. **Ruler:** al-Nasir Ahmad bin Yahya (Imam Ahmad) AH1367-1382 / 1948-1962AD **Obv:** Double crescent below accession date AH1367 with incuse Arabic number four above sword handles **Rev:** Arabic legend and inscription

Date	Mintage	F	VF	XF	Unc	BU
AH1371 Rare	—	—	—	—	—	—
AH1372 Rare	—	—	—	—	—	—

Y# G17.2 GOLD RIYAL (5 Lira - 4 Sovereigns)
32.4860 g., 0.9000 Gold, 40 mm. **Ruler:** al-Nasir Ahmad bin Yahya (Imam Ahmad) AH1367-1382 / 1948-1962AD **Obv:** Double crescent below accession date AH1367 without incuse Arabic number four above sword handles **Rev:** Arabic legend and inscription **Note:** Weight varies: 30.46-39.06 grams. Dies of silver Ahmadi Riyal (Y#17) were used.

Date	Mintage	F	VF	XF	Unc	BU
AH1373	—	750	1,000	1,800	—	—
AH1374	—	750	1,000	1,800	—	—
AH1375	—	750	1,000	1,800	—	—
AH1377	—	750	1,000	1,800	—	—
AH1378	—	750	1,000	1,800	—	—
AH1381	—	750	1,000	1,800	—	—

REPUBLIC

DECIMAL COINAGE

100 Fils = 1 Riyal/Rial

KM# 1a RIYAL
20.4800 g., 0.9000 Gold .5926 oz. AGW **Subject:** Qadhi Mohammed Mahmud Azzubairi Memorial **Obv:** National arms **Rev:** Figure on camel right

Date	Mintage	F	VF	XF	Unc	BU
1969 Proof	100	Value: 435				

KM# 4a 2 RIYALS
42.2900 g., 0.9000 Gold 1.2238 oz. AGW **Subject:** Qadhi Mohammed Mahmud Azzubairi Memorial **Obv:** National arms **Rev:** Roaring lion's head 3/4 left

Date	Mintage	F	VF	XF	Unc	BU
1969 Proof	100	Value: 1,000				

KM# 6 5 RIYALS/RIALS
4.9000 g., 0.9000 Gold .1418 oz. AGW **Subject:** Qadhi Mohammed Mahmud Azzubairi Memorial **Obv:** Monument **Rev:** Denomination within circle

Date	Mintage	F	VF	XF	Unc	BU
1969 Proof	—	Value: 140				

KM# 7 10 RIYALS/RIALS
9.8000 g., 0.9000 Gold .2836 oz. AGW **Subject:** Qadhi Mohammed Mahmud Azzubairi Memorial **Obv:** National arms **Rev:** Three leaping gazelles right

Date	Mintage	F	VF	XF	Unc	BU
1969 Proof	—	Value: 225				

KM# 8 20 RIYALS/RIALS
19.6000 g., 0.9000 Gold .5672 oz. AGW **Subject:** Apollo II - Moon Landing **Obv:** Eagle with shield on breast and flags on legs **Rev:** Shuttle above astronauts on moons surface

Date	Mintage	F	VF	XF	Unc	BU
1969 Proof	—	Value: 420				

KM# 9 20 RIYALS/RIALS
19.6000 g., 0.9000 Gold .5672 oz. AGW **Subject:** Qadhi Mohammed Mahmud Azzubairi Memorial **Obv:** National arms **Rev:** Camel with rider right

Date	Mintage	F	VF	XF	Unc	BU
1969 Proof	—	Value: 450				

YEMEN ARAB REPUBLIC

KM# 18 20 RIYALS/RIALS
0.9000 Gold **Subject:** Albakiriah Mosque **Rev:** Mosque within oval **Shape:** Octagon

Date	Mintage	F	VF	XF	Unc	BU
AH1395-1975	—	—	—	—	265	—
AH1395-1975 Proof	3,500	Value: 285				

KM# 19 25 RIYALS/RIALS
0.9000 Gold **Subject:** Oil Exploration **Obv:** National arms within rounded square **Rev:** Oil derricks in field, rounded square surrounds

Date	Mintage	F	VF	XF	Unc	BU
AH1395-1975	—	—	—	—	160	—
AH1395-1975 Proof	3,500	Value: 180				

KM# 10 30 RIYALS
29.4000 g., 0.9000 Gold .8508 oz. AGW **Subject:** Qadhi Mohammed Mahmud Azzubairi Memorial **Obv:** National arms **Rev:** Head 3/4 right

Date	Mintage	F	VF	XF	Unc	BU
1969 Proof	—	Value: 635				

KM# 11a 50 RIYALS/RIALS
49.0000 g., 0.9000 Gold 1.4180 oz. AGW **Subject:** Qadhi Mohammed Mahmud Azzubairi Memorial **Obv:** National arms above dates and denomination

Date	Mintage	F	VF	XF	Unc	BU
1969 Proof	—	Value: 1,100				

KM# 20 50 RIYALS/RIALS
9.1000 g., 0.9000 Gold .2633 oz. AGW **Subject:** Mona Lisa **Rev:** Mona Lisa within box, chain with ornaments surrounds

Date	Mintage	F	VF	XF	Unc	BU
AH1395-1975	—	—	—	—	250	—
AH1395-1975 Proof	3,500	Value: 350				

KM# 21 75 RIYALS
13.6500 g., 0.9000 Gold .3950 oz. AGW **Series:** Montreal Olympics **Obv:** Arms **Rev:** XXI Olympiad

Date	Mintage	F	VF	XF	Unc	BU
AH1395-1975	—	—	—	—	300	—
AH1395-1975 Proof	3,500	Value: 375				

KM# 22 100 RIALS
18.2000 g., 0.9000 Gold .5266 oz. AGW **Obv:** National arms **Rev:** Domed buildings

Date	Mintage	F	VF	XF	Unc	BU
AH1395-1975	—	—	—	—	400	—
AH1395-1975 Proof	3,500	Value: 450				

KM# 24 500 RIYALS/RIALS
15.9800 g., 0.9170 Gold .4711 oz. AGW **Series:** International Year of the Disabled Person **Obv:** National arms **Rev:** Head of Bolivar facing, tiny logos flank below

Date	Mintage	F	VF	XF	Unc	BU
AH1401-1981	—	—	—	—	400	—
AH1401-1981 Proof	—	Value: 500				

Y# 48 500 RIYALS/RIALS
15.9000 g., 0.9170 Gold .4686 oz. AGW **Subject:** 20th Anniversary of the Revolution **Rev:** Ship within small center circle, figures above, oil derrick at left, grain sprig at right, circle surrounds all

Date	Mintage	F	VF	XF	Unc	BU
AH1402-1982 Proof	1,000	Value: 385				

PIEFORTS

KM#	Date	Mintage	Identification	Mkt Val
P2	1981	—	500 Riyals/Rials. Gold. I.Y.P.D.; KM#24	1,000

TRIAL STRIKES

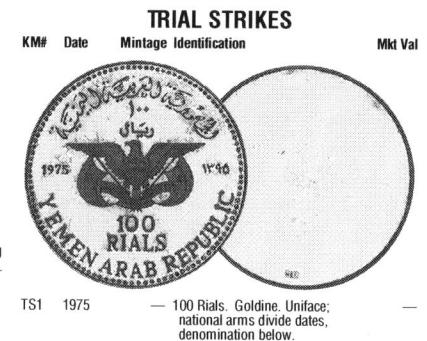

KM#	Date	Mintage	Identification	Mkt Val
TS1	1975	—	100 Rials. Goldine. Uniface; national arms divide dates, denomination below.	—

MINT SETS

KM#	Date	Mintage	Identification	Issue Price	Mkt Val
MS2	1975 (5)	—	KM#18-22	360	1,375

PROOF SETS

KM#	Date	Mintage	Identification	Issue Price	Mkt Val
PS1	1969 (7)	2,000	KM#1, 4, 6, 7, 9-11	375	1,350
PS4	1969 (3)	—	KM#2, 3, 6	78.00	175
PS6	1975 (5)	3,500	KM#18-22	485	1,650

YEMEN EASTERN ADEN PROTECTORATE

Between 1200 B.C. and the 6th century A.D., what is now the Peoples Democratic Republic of Yemen was part of the Minaean kingdom. In subsequent years it was controlled by Persians, Egyptians and Turks. Aden, one of the cities mentioned in the Bible, had been a port for trade between the East and West for 2,000 years. British rule began in 1839 when the British East India Co. seized control to put an end to the piracy threatening trade with India. To protect their foothold in Aden, the British found it necessary to extend their control into the area known historically as the Hadhramaut, and to sign protection treaties with the sheiks of the hinterland.

QUA'ITI STATE
COUNTERMARKED COINAGE

KM# 40 SOVEREIGN
Gold **Countermark:** Arabic **Note:** Countermark on English Sovereign, KM#767.

CM Date	Host Date	Good	VG	F	VF	XF
AH1307	1887-92 Rare	—	—	—	—	—

YEMEN, DEMOCRATIC REPUBLIC OF

The southeast region of present day Yemen was predominately controlled by the British since their occupation of Aden in 1839. Independence was declared November 30, 1967 after the collapse of the Federation of South Arabia and the withdrawal of the British.

TITLES
Al-Jumhuriya(t) al-Yamaniya(t)
ad-Dimiqratiya(t) ash-Sha'biya(t)

MONETARY SYSTEM
1000 Fils = 1 Dinar

PEOPLES DEMOCRATIC REPUBLIC
DECIMAL COINAGE

KM# 13 50 DINARS
15.9800 g., 0.9170 Gold .4712 oz. AGW **Series:** International Year of Disabled Persons **Obv:** National arms **Rev:** Triangular design within wreath divides date

Date	Mintage	F	VF	XF	Unc	BU
1981	2,100	—	—	—	500	550
1981 Proof	1,100	Value: 750				

YUGOSLAVIA

The Federal Republic of Yugoslavia, formerly the Socialist Federal Republic of Yugoslavia, a Balkan country located on the east shore of the Adriatic Sea, has an area of 39,450 sq. mi. (102,173 sq. km.) and a population of 10.5 million. Capital: Belgrade. The chief industries area agriculture, mining, manufacturing and tourism. Machinery, nonferrous metals, meat and fabrics are exported.

Yugoslavia was proclaimed on Dec. 1, 1918, after the union of the Kingdom of Serbia, Montenegro and the South Slav territories of Austria-Hungary; and changed its official name from the Kingdom of the Serbs, Croats and Slovenes to the Kingdom of Yugoslavia on Oct. 3, 1929.The republic was composed of six autonomous republics -Serbia, Croatia, Slovenia, Bosnia-Herzegovina, Macedonia and Montenegro - and two autonomous provinces within Serbia: Kosovo-Mehohija and Vojvodina. The government of Yugoslavia attempted to remain neutral in World War II but, yielding to German pressure, aligned itself with the Axis powers in March of 1941; a few days later it was overthrown by revolutionary forces and its neutrality reasserted. The Nazis occupied the country on April 6, and throughout the remaining war years were resisted by a number of guerrilla armies, notably that of Marshal Josip Broz Tito. After the defeat of the Axis powers, a leftist coalition headed by Tito abolished the monarchy and, on Jan. 31, 1946, established a "People's Republic". The collapse of the Federal Republic during 1991-1992 has resulted in the autonomous republics of Croatia, Slovenia, Bosnia-Herzegovina and Macedonia declaring their respective independence. Bosnia-Herzegovina is under military contest with the Serbian, Croat and Muslim populace opposing each other. Besides the remainder of the older Serbian sectors, a Serbian enclave in Knin located in southern Croatia has emerged called REPUBLIKE SRPSKEKRAJINE or Serbian Republic - Krajina whose capital is Knin and has also declared its independence in1992 when the former Republics of Serbia and Montenegro became the Federal Republic of Yugoslavia.

The name Yugoslavia appears on the coinage in letters of the Cyrillic alphabet alone until formation of the Federated Peoples Republic of Yugoslavia in 1953, after which both the Cyrillic and Latin alphabets are employed. From 1965, the coin denomination appears in the 4 different languages of the federated republics in letters of both the Cyrillic and Latin alphabets.

DENOMINATIONS
Para ПАРА
Dinar, ДИНАР, Dinara ДИНАРА
Dinari ДИНАРИ, Dinarjev

RULERS
Petar I, 1918-1921
Alexander I, 1921-1934
Petar II, 1934-1945

MINT MARKS
(a) - Paris, privy marks only
(b) - Brussels
(k) - КОВНИЦА,...А.Д. = Kovnica, A.D. (Akcionarno Drustvo) Belgrade
(l) - London
(p) - Poissy (thunderbolt)
(v) – Vienna

MONETARY SYSTEM
100 Para = 1 Dinar

KINGDOM OF THE SERBS, CROATS AND SLOVENES
STANDARD COINAGE

KM# 7 20 DINARA
6.4516 g., 0.9000 Gold .1867 oz. AGW, 21 mm. **Ruler:** Alexander I **Obv:** Head left **Rev:** Denomination and date within crowned wreath **Edge:** Milled

768 YUGOSLAVIA

Date	Mintage	F	VF	XF	Unc	BU
1925	1,000,000	135	150	185	250	—
1925 Proof	—	—	—	—	—	—

KINGDOM OF YUGOSLAVIA
TRADE COINAGE

Trade-coinage countermarks were applied by the Yugoslav Control Office for Noble Metals to confirm gold purity. The initial countermark displayed a sword, but part way through the first production year, this was retired and the second countermark, showing an ear of corn, was used.

KM# 12.1 DUKAT
3.4900 g., 0.9860 Gold .1106 oz. AGW **Ruler:** Alexander I **Countermark:** Birds **Obv:** Head left, small legend with КОВНИЦ, А.Д. below head **Obv. Designer:** Richard Plecht **Rev:** Crowned double eagle with shield on breast **Rev. Designer:** Joseph Prinz **Edge:** Milled

Date	Mintage	F	VF	XF	Unc	BU
1931(k)	Est. 50,000	—	100	150	200	—
1932(k) Rare	Inc. below	—	—	—	—	—

Note: The 1932(k) examples with sword countermark are believed to be mint sports

KM# 12.2 DUKAT
3.4900 g., 0.9860 Gold .1106 oz. AGW **Ruler:** Alexander I **Countermark:** Ear of corn **Obv:** Head left **Rev:** Crowned double eagle with shield on breast **Note:** Forgeries bearing no countermark exist for 1932 and possibly other dates. Small legend on both sides

Date	Mintage	F	VF	XF	Unc	BU
1931(k)	Est. 150,000	—	90.00	140	185	—
1932(k)	Est. 70,000	—	95.00	145	195	—
1933(k)	Est. 40,000	—	135	185	300	—
1934(k)	Est. 2,000	—	500	850	1,250	—

KM# 12.3 DUKAT
3.4900 g., 0.9860 Gold .1106 oz. AGW **Ruler:** Alexander I **Countermark:** Sword **Obv:** Head left **Rev:** Crowned double eagle with shield on breast **Note:** Mule.

Date	Mintage	F	VF	XF	Unc	BU
1931(k)	—	—	—	3,000	5,000	—

KM# 13.1 DUKAT
3.4900 g., 0.9860 Gold .1106 oz. AGW **Ruler:** Alexander I **Obv:** Head left **Rev:** Crowned double eagle with shield on breast **Note:** Large legend on both sides.

Date	Mintage	F	VF	XF	Unc	BU
1931(k)	2,869	—	—	3,500	5,500	—

KM# 13.2 DUKAT
3.4900 g., 0.9860 Gold .1106 oz. AGW **Ruler:** Alexander I **Countermark:** Sword **Obv:** Head left **Rev:** Crowned double eagle with shield on breast **Note:** Large-letter varieties bear the Kovnica, A.D. mint mark but were actually struck in Vienna.

Date	Mintage	F	VF	XF	Unc	BU
1931(k)	Inc. above	—	—	4,000	6,500	—

KM# 14.1 4 DUKATA
13.9600 g., 0.9860 Gold .4425 oz. AGW **Ruler:** Alexander I **Countermark:** Sword **Obv:** Jugate busts of royal couple left **Obv. Designer:** Richard Placht **Rev:** Crowned double eagle with shield on breast **Rev. Designer:** Joseph Prinz **Edge:** Milled **Note:** Small legend on both sides. The 1932(k) examples with birds countermark are believed to be mint sports.

Date	Mintage	F	VF	XF	Unc	BU
1931(k)	Est. 10,000	—	450	750	950	—
1932(k) Rare	Inc. below	—	—	—	—	—

KM# 14.2 4 DUKATA
13.9600 g., 0.9860 Gold .4425 oz. AGW **Ruler:** Alexander I **Countermark:** Ear of corn **Obv:** Conjoined busts of royal couple left **Rev:** Crowned double eagle with shield on breast

Date	Mintage	F	VF	XF	Unc	BU
1931(k)	Est. 15,000	—	450	750	950	—
1932(k)	Est. 10,000	—	400	725	1,000	—
1933(k)	Est. 2,000	—	1,000	1,600	2,500	—

KM# 14.3 4 DUKATA
13.9600 g., 0.9860 Gold .4425 oz. AGW **Ruler:** Alexander I **Obv:** Jugate busts of royal couple left **Rev:** Crowned double eagle with shield on breast **Note:** Without countermark on either side. Only one genuine piece has been reported.

Date	Mintage	F	VF	XF	Unc	BU
1931(k) Rare	—	—	—	—	—	—

KM# A15.1 4 DUKATA
13.9600 g., 0.9860 Gold .4425 oz. AGW **Ruler:** Alexander I **Obv:** Conjoined busts of royal couple left **Rev:** Crowned double eagle with shield on breast **Note:** Large legend on both sides. Sword Countermark.

Date	Mintage	F	VF	XF	Unc	BU
1931(k) Rare	51	—	—	—	—	—

KM# A15.2 4 DUKATA
13.9600 g., 0.9860 Gold .4425 oz. AGW **Ruler:** Alexander I **Countermark:** Sword **Obv:** Conjoined busts of royal couple left, large legend **Rev:** Crowned double eagle with shield on breast, large legend **Note:** Large-letter varieties bear the Kovnica, A.D. mint mark but were actually struck in Vienna.

Date	Mintage	F	VF	XF	Unc	BU
1931(k)	Inc. above	—	—	—	—	—

SOCIALIST FEDERAL REPUBLIC
STANDARD COINAGE

KM# 51 100 DINARA
7.8200 g., 0.9000 Gold .2263 oz. AGW **Subject:** 25th Anniversary of Republic **Obv:** State emblem within circle **Rev:** Figures with arms raised, large rock in background

Date	Mintage	F	VF	XF	Unc	BU
ND(1968) Proof	10,000	Value: 165				
ND(1968) NI Proof	Inc. above	Value: 165				

KM# 52 200 DINARA
15.6400 g., 0.9000 Gold .4526 oz. AGW, 30 mm. **Subject:** 25th Anniversary of Republic **Obv:** State emblem within circle **Rev:** Head left

Date	Mintage	F	VF	XF	Unc	BU
ND(1968) Proof	10,000	Value: 325				
ND(1968) NI Proof	Inc. above	Value: 325				

KM# 53 500 DINARA
39.1000 g., 0.9000 Gold 1.1315 oz. AGW, 45 mm. **Subject:** 25th Anniversary of Republic **Obv:** State emblem **Rev:** Figures with arms raised, large rock in background

Date	Mintage	F	VF	XF	Unc	BU
ND(1968) Proof	10,000	Value: 800				
ND(1968) NI Proof	Inc. above	Value: 800				

YUGOSLAVIA

KM# 54 1000 DINARA
78.2000 g., 0.9000 Gold 2.2630 oz. AGW, 55 mm. **Subject:** 25th Anniversary of Republic **Obv:** State emblem **Rev:** Bust of Tito left

Date	Mintage	F	VF	XF	Unc	BU
ND(1968) Proof	10,000	Value: 1,600				
ND(1968) NI Proof	Inc. above	Value: 1,600				

KM# 148 1000 DINARA
3.5000 g., 0.9000 Gold .1013 oz. AGW **Subject:** 1990 Chess Olympiad **Obv:** State emblem above denomination **Rev:** Logo

Date	Mintage	F	VF	XF	Unc	BU
1990 Proof	2,000	Value: 175				

KM# 72 1500 DINARA
8.8000 g., 0.9000 Gold .2546 oz. AGW, 24 mm. **Subject:** 8th Mediterranean Games at Split **Obv:** State emblem above rings **Rev:** Head left **Designer:** Zlatara Majdanpek

Date	Mintage	F	VF	XF	Unc	BU
1978 Proof	35,000	Value: 190				

KM# 73 2000 DINARA
11.8000 g., 0.9000 Gold .3414 oz. AGW, 27 mm. **Subject:** 8th Mediterranean Games at Split **Obv:** State emblem above city view **Rev:** Head left **Designer:** Zlatara Majdanpek

Date	Mintage	F	VF	XF	Unc	BU
1978 Proof	35,000	Value: 250				

KM# 74 2500 DINARA
14.7000 g., 0.9000 Gold .4254 oz. AGW **Subject:** 8th Mediterranean Games at Split **Obv:** State emblem above stadium **Rev:** Bust left

Date	Mintage	F	VF	XF	Unc	BU
1978 Proof	35,000	Value: 300				

KM# 75 5000 DINARA
29.5000 g., 0.9000 Gold .8536 oz. AGW, 38 mm. **Subject:** 8th Mediterranean Games at Split **Obv:** State emblem above palace of Diocletian in Split **Rev:** Bust left **Designer:** Zlatara Majdanpek

Date	Mintage	F	VF	XF	Unc	BU
1978 Proof	12,000	Value: 600				

KM# 95 5000 DINARA
8.0000 g., 0.9000 Gold .2315 oz. AGW, 24 mm. **Series:** 1984 Winter Olympics **Obv:** Emblem and Olympic logo on separate shields within flat bottom circle **Rev:** Olympic emblem within circle

Date	Mintage	F	VF	XF	Unc	BU
1982 Proof	55,000	Value: 165				

KM# 104 5000 DINARA
8.0000 g., 0.9000 Gold .2315 oz. AGW, 24 mm. **Series:** 1984 Winter Olympics **Obv:** Emblem and Olympic logo on separate shields within flat bottom circle **Rev:** Bust 3/4 left within circle

Date	Mintage	F	VF	XF	Unc	BU
1983 Proof	55,000	Value: 165				

KM# 111 5000 DINARA
8.0000 g., 0.9000 Gold .2315 oz. AGW, 24 mm. **Series:** 1984 Winter Olympics **Obv:** Emblem and Olympic logo on separate shields within flat bottom circle **Rev:** Olympic torch within circle

Date	Mintage	F	VF	XF	Unc	BU
1984 Proof	55,000	Value: 165				

KM# 123 10000 DINARA
8.0000 g., 0.9000 Gold .2315 oz. AGW, 24 mm. **Subject:** World Ski Jumping Championship

Date	Mintage	F	VF	XF	Unc	BU
1985 Proof	10,000	Value: 175				

KM# 124 10000 DINARA
5.0000 g., 0.9000 Gold .1447 oz. AGW **Subject:** Sinjska Alka

Date	Mintage	F	VF	XF	Unc	BU
ND(1985) Proof	12,000	Value: 150				

KM# 125 20000 DINARA
8.0000 g., 0.9000 Gold .2315 oz. AGW **Subject:** Sinjska Alka

Date	Mintage	F	VF	XF	Unc	BU
ND(1985) Proof	8,000	Value: 250				

KM# 126 40000 DINARA
14.0000 g., 0.9000 Gold .4083 oz. AGW **Subject:** Sinjska Alka **Obv:** State emblem left of map outline **Rev:** Three figures on horseback

Date	Mintage	F	VF	XF	Unc	BU
ND(1985) Proof	5,000	Value: 475				

KM# 130 50000 DINARA
8.0000 g., 0.9000 Gold .2315 oz. AGW **Subject:** 200th Anniversary - Birth of Karajich **Obv:** State emblem on shield within flat bottom circle **Rev:** Squared head right

Date	Mintage	F	VF	XF	Unc	BU
1987 Proof	Est. 10,000	Value: 185				

KM# 138 2000000 DINARA
8.0000 g., 0.9000 Gold .2315 oz. AGW **Subject:** Non-aligned Summit **Obv:** State emblem above denomination **Rev:** Symbols within circle

Date	Mintage	F	VF	XF	Unc	BU
ND(1989) Proof	5,000	Value: 240				

FEDERAL REPUBLIC

STANDARD COINAGE

KM# 166 150 NOVIH DINARA
7.8000 g., 0.9000 Gold .2257 oz. AGW **Subject:** 110th

770 YUGOSLAVIA

Anniversary - National Bank Obv: National arms, building at left Rev: Peace dove in flight

Date	Mintage	F	VF	XF	Unc	BU
ND(1995) Proof	100,000			Value: 180		

KM# 175 600 NOVIH DINARA
3.4550 g., 0.9000 Gold .1 oz. AGW Subject: Chilander Monastery Obv: Monastery Rev: Portraits of SS Simon and Sava

Date	Mintage	F	VF	XF	Unc	BU
1998(1999)	10,000	—	—	—	—	125

KM# 172 1000 NOVIH DINARA
8.6400 g., 0.9000 Gold .25 oz. AGW Subject: Nikola Tesla Obv: National arms Rev: Head 3/4 left

Date	Mintage	F	VF	XF	Unc	BU
1996 Proof	4,617			Value: 250		

KM# 176 1500 NOVIH DINARA
8.6400 g., 0.9000 Gold .2500 oz. AGW Subject: Chilander Monastery Obv: Monastery Rev: Portraits of SS Simon and Sava

Date	Mintage	F	VF	XF	Unc	BU
1998(1999)	Est. 5,000	—	—	—	—	190

KM# 177 3000 NOVIH DINARA
17.2770 g., 0.9000 Gold .4999 oz. AGW Subject: Chilander Monastery Obv: Monastery Rev: Portraits of SS Simon and Sava

Date	Mintage	F	VF	XF	Unc	BU
1998 Proof	500			Value: 425		
1999 Proof	500			Value: 425		

KM# 178 6000 NOVIH DINARA
34.5550 g., 0.9000 Gold .9999 oz. AGW Subject: Chilander Monastery Obv: Monastery Rev: Portraits of SS Simon and Sava

Date	Mintage	F	VF	XF	Unc	BU
1998 Proof	500			Value: 750		
1999 Proof	500			Value: 750		

PATTERNS
Including off metal strikes

Patterns Pn1-Pn8 previously listed here are now listed under Serbia.

KM#	Date	Mintage	Identification	Mkt Val
Pn14	1925(a)	—	10 Dinara. Gold.	—
Pn15	1926(k)	—	Dukat. Gold.	—
Pn16	1926	—	4 Dukata. Silver. 39.5 mm. River scene.	—
Pn17	1926(k)	—	4 Dukata. Gold. River scene.	—
Pn19	1931	—	4 Dukata. Gold. 15.0000 g. ESSAI.	—
Pn20	ND	—	4 Dukata. Silver.	—

PIEFORTS

KM#	Date	Mintage	Identification	Mkt Val
P1	ND(1931-1934)	—	4 Dukata. Gold. 46.4500 g. Conjoined busts.	—

TRIAL STRIKES

KM#	Date	Mintage	Identification	Mkt Val
TS1	1931(a)	—	Dukat. Gold. Uniface. ESSAI Paris/1931.	—
TS2	1931(a)	—	4 Dukata. Gold. Uniface. ESSAI Paris/1931.	—
TS3	1931	—	4 Dukata. Bronze. Uniface.	—
TS4	ND(1931)(k)	—	4 Dukata. 0.9167 Gold. 46.5000 g. Uniface obverse. KM#14 (hallmarked 22K on edge).	—
TS5	1931(k)	—	4 Dukata. Platinum. Uniface.	—
TS6	1931(k)	—	8 Dukata. Gold. Uniface.	—
TS7	1931	—	8 Dukata. 0.9000 Gold. 30.6180 g. Uniface. ESSAI/PARIS/1931.	—
TS8	1931	2	12 Dukata. 0.9000 Gold. Uniface. ESSAI/PARIS/1931. 45.875-46.45 grams.	—

PROOF SETS

KM#	Date	Mintage	Identification	Issue Price	Mkt Val
PS1	1968 (6)	10,000	KM49-54	—	3,000
PS2	1968 (4)	10,000	KM51-54	—	2,900
PS5	1978 (11)	12,000	KM65-75	—	1,400
PS15	Mixed dates (3)	—	KM95, 104, 111	—	375
PS16	1985 (6)	—	KM119-121, 124-126	—	950
PS17	1985 (4)	—	KM116-118, 123	—	250
PS20	1987 (3)	—	KM128-130	—	250
PS22	1989 (3)	—	KM136-138	—	300
PS24	1990 (3)	—	KM146-148	—	260
PS26	1998(1999) (4)	—	KM#175-178	—	1,400
PS27	1998-1999 (4)	—	KM#175-176 dated 1998; KM#177-178 dated 1999	—	1,400

ZAÏRE

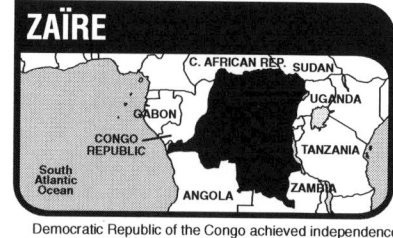

Democratic Republic of the Congo achieved independence on June 30, 1960. It followed the same monetary system as when under the Belgians. Monetary Reform of 1967 introduced new denominations and coins. The name of the country was changed to Zaire in 1971.

Under the command of Laurent Kabila, rebel forces overthrew ruler Sese Seko Mobutu in May of 1997. Self appointed President Kabila has officially renamed the country the Democratic Republic of Congo.

MONETARY SYSTEM
100 Makuta = 1 Zaire

1993 -
3,000,000 old Zaires = 1 Nouveau Zaire

REPUBLIC
DECIMAL COINAGE

KM# 2 10 ZAIRES
9.9600 g., 0.9000 Gold .2882 oz. AGW Obv: Mobutu bust left Rev: Hotel Intercontinental

Date	Mintage	F	VF	XF	Unc	BU
1971 Proof	—			Value: 215		

KM# 3 10 ZAIRES
6.0400 g., 0.9990 Platinum .1940 oz. APW Obv: Mobutu bust left Rev: Hotel Intercontinental

Date	Mintage	F	VF	XF	Unc	BU
1971 Proof	—			Value: 265		

KM# 4 20 ZAIRES
20.9000 g., 0.9000 Gold .6048 oz. AGW Obv: Mobutu bust left Rev: Hotel Intercontinental

Date	Mintage	F	VF	XF	Unc	BU
1971 Proof	—			Value: 445		

KM# 5 20 ZAIRES
3.8900 g., 0.9990 Platinum .1250 oz. APW Obv: Mobutu bust left Rev: Hotel Intercontinental

Date	Mintage	F	VF	XF	Unc	BU
1971 Proof	—			Value: 170		

KM# 6 50 ZAIRES
46.9600 g., 0.9000 Gold 1.3590 oz. AGW Obv: Mobutu bust 3/4 left Rev: Hotel Intercontinental

Date	Mintage	F	VF	XF	Unc	BU
1971 Proof	—			Value: 1,000		

KM# 11 100 ZAIRES
33.4370 g., 0.9000 Gold .9676 oz. AGW **Subject:** Conservation **Obv:** Mobuto bust 1/4 right **Rev:** Leopard right

Date	Mintage	F	VF	XF	Unc	BU
1975	1,415	—	—	—	675	725
1975 Proof	279	Value: 850				

PROOF SETS

KM#	Date	Mintage	Identification	Issue Price	Mkt Val
PS1	1971 (6)	—	KM1-6	—	2,125

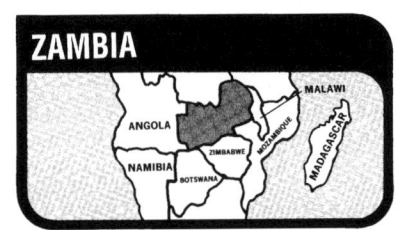

ZAMBIA

The Republic of Zambia (formerly Northern Rhodesia), a landlocked country in south-central Africa, has an area of 290,586 sq. mi. (752,610 sq. km.) and a population of *7.9 million. Capital: Lusaka. The economy of Zambia is based principally on copper, of which Zambia is the world's third largest producer. Copper, zinc, lead, cobalt and tobacco are exported.

The area that is now Zambia was brought within the British sphere of influence in 1888 by empire builder Cecil Rhodes, who obtained mining concessions in south-central Africa from indigenous chiefs. The territory was ruled by the British South Africa Company, which Rhodes established, until 1924 when its administration was transferred to the British government as a protectorate. In 1953, Northern Rhodesia was joined with Nyasaland and the colony of Southern Rhodesia to form the Federation of Rhodesia and Nyasaland. Northern Rhodesia seceded from the Federation on Oct. 24, 1964, and became the independent Republic of Zambia. Zambia is a member of the Commonwealth of Nations. The president is Chief of State.

Zambia converted to a decimal coinage on January 16, 1969.
For earlier coinage refer to Rhodesia and Nyasaland.

RULER
British, until 1964

MONETARY SYSTEM
12 Pence = 1 Shilling
20 Shillings = 1 Pound

REPUBLIC
DECIMAL COINAGE
100 Ngwee = 1 Kwacha

KM# 20 250 KWACHA
33.6300 g., 0.9000 Gold .9371 oz. AGW **Subject:** Conservation **Obv:** Head of K.D. Kaunda right, date below **Rev:** African wild dog right, denomination below

Date	Mintage	F	VF	XF	Unc	BU
1979	455	—	—	—	675	725
1979 Proof	245	Value: 850				

KM# 54 2000 KWACHA
3.1103 g., 0.9999 Gold .1000 oz. AGW **Subject:** Diana - The People's Princess **Obv:** National arms with supporters divide date, denomination below **Rev:** Head facing **Note:** Similar to 200 Kwacha, KM#52.

Date	Mintage	F	VF	XF	Unc	BU
1997 Proof	—	Value: 85.00				

KM# 70 5000 KWACHA
7.7759 g., 0.9990 Gold .2500 oz. AGW **Subject:** Taipai Subway **Obv:** National arms **Rev:** Train with inset diamond headlight **Note:** Struck at Singapore Mint.

Date	Mintage	F	VF	XF	Unc	BU
1998 Proof	999	Value: 350				

KM# 83 5000 KWACHA
27.0000 g., 0.9990 Gold .8672 oz. AGW, 48x30 mm. **Subject:** 100th Birthday - Queen Mother **Obv:** Head with tiara right divides date above arms **Rev:** Black and white photo of an elderly Queen Mother **Shape:** Oval

Date	Mintage	F	VF	XF	Unc	BU
2000 Proof	100	Value: 700				

KM# 81 5000 KWACHA
27.0000 g., 0.9990 Gold .8672 oz. AGW, 48x30 mm. **Subject:** 100th Birthday - Queen Mother **Obv:** Head with tiara right divides date above arms **Rev:** Black and white photo of the Queen Mother as a young lady **Edge:** Reeded **Shape:** Oval

Date	Mintage	F	VF	XF	Unc	BU
2000 Proof	100	Value: 700				

KM# 82 5000 KWACHA
27.0000 g., 0.9990 Gold .8672 oz. AGW, 48x30 mm. **Subject:** 100th Birthday - Queen Mother **Obv:** Head with tiara right divides date above arms **Rev:** Black ad white photo of Queen Mother on throne at 1937 coronation **Shape:** Oval

Date	Mintage	F	VF	XF	Unc	BU
2000 Proof	100	Value: 700				

KM# 71 10000 KWACHA
15.5518 g., 0.9999 Gold .5000 oz. AGW **Subject:** Taipai Subway **Obv:** National arms **Rev:** Train with inset diamond headlight **Note:** Struck at Singapore Mint.

Date	Mintage	F	VF	XF	Unc	BU
1998 Proof	99	Value: 650				

KM# 94 40000 KWACHA
31.1035 g., 0.9999 Gold 1.0000 oz. AGW, 37.9 mm. **Series:** Wildlife Protection **Obv:** Arms with supporters above crowned head right **Rev:** Holographic lion head **Edge:** Reeded

Date	Mintage	F	VF	XF	Unc	BU
2001 Proof	—	Value: 700				

KM# 153.1 40000 KWACHA
47.5400 g., 0.9166 Gold 1.401 oz. AGW, 39 mm. **Subject:** Queen Victoria **Obv:** Crowned head right within ornate frame divides date above arms with supporters **Rev:** Crowned head with veil facing left **Edge:** Reeded

Date	Mintage	F	VF	XF	Unc	BU
2001 Proof	1	—	—	—	—	—

Note: Medallic die alignment

KM# 153.2 40000 KWACHA
47.5400 g., 0.9166 Gold 1.401 oz. AGW, 39 mm. **Subject:** Queen Victoria **Obv:** Crowned head right within ornate frame divides date above arms with supporters **Rev:** Crowned head with veil facing left **Edge:** Reeded

772 ZAMBIA

Date	Mintage	F	VF	XF	Unc	BU
2001 Matte	1	—	—	—	—	—

Note: Coin die alignment

KM# 154.1 40000 KWACHA
47.5400 g., 0.9166 Gold 1.401 oz. AGW, 39 mm. **Subject:** Edward VII **Obv:** Crowned head right within ornate frame divides date above arms with supporters **Rev:** Crowned bust right **Edge:** Reeded

Date	Mintage	F	VF	XF	Unc	BU
2001 Proof	1	—	—	—	—	—

Note: Medallic die rotation

KM# 154.2 40000 KWACHA
47.5400 g., 0.9166 Gold 1.401 oz. AGW, 39 mm. **Subject:** Edward VII **Obv:** Crowned head right within ornate frame divides date above arms with supporters **Rev:** Crowned bust right **Edge:** Reeded

Date	Mintage	F	VF	XF	Unc	BU
2001 Matte	1	—	—	—	—	—

Note: Coin die alignment

KM# 72 500000 KWACHA
155.5175 g., 0.9999 Gold 5.0000 oz. AGW **Subject:** Taipai Subway **Obv:** National arms **Rev:** Train with inset diamond headlight **Note:** Struck at Singapore Mint.

Date	Mintage	F	VF	XF	Unc	BU
1998 Proof	99	Value: 3,500				

PROOF SETS

KM#	Date	Mintage	Identification	Issue Price	Mkt Val
PS10	2000 (4)	100	KM#81-83	—	2,100

ZANZIBAR

The British protectorate of Zanzibar and adjacent small islands, located in the Indian Ocean 22 miles (35 km.) off the coast of Tanganyika, comprised a portion of British East Africa. Zanzibar was also the name of a sultanate which included the Zanzibar and Kenya protectorates. Zanzibar has an area of 637 sq. mi. (1,651 sq. km.). Chief city: Zanzibar. The islands are noted for their cloves, of which Zanzibar is the world's foremost producer.

Zanzibar came under Portuguese control in 1503, was conquered by the Omani Arabs in 1698, became independent of Oman in 1860, and (with Pemba) came under British control in 1890. Britain granted the protectorate self-government in 1961, and independence within the British Commonwealth on Dec. 19, 1963. On April 26, 1964, Tanganyika and Zanzibar (with Pemba) united to form the United Republic of Tanganyika and Zanzibar. The name of the country, which remained within the British Commonwealth was changed to Tanzania on Oct. 29, 1964.

TITLE

زنجبار زنجبارا

Zanjibara

RULER
Sultan Ali Bin Hamud, 1902-1911AD

MONETARY SYSTEM
64 Pysa (Pice) = 1 Rupee
136 Pysa = 1 Ryal (to 1908)
100 Cents = 1 Rupee (to 1909)

SULTANATE
STANDARD COINAGE

KM# 5 2-1/2 RIYALS
Gold

Date	Mintage	F	VF	XF	Unc	BU
AH1299	—	—	—	14,000	25,000	—

KM# 6 5 RIYALS
Gold

Date	Mintage	F	VF	XF	Unc	BU
AH1299	2,000	—	—	8,000	15,000	—

Printed in Great Britain
by Amazon